THE OFFICIAL® 2011 PRICE GUIDE TO FOOTBALL CARDS

DR. JAMES BECKETT

THIRTIETH EDITION

HOUSE OF COLLECTIBLES
Random House Reference • New York

Important Notice: All of the information, including valuations, in this book has been compiled from the most reliable sources, and every effort has been made to eliminate errors and questionable data. Nevertheless, the possibility of error, in a work of such immense scope, always exists. The publisher will not be held responsible for losses that may occur in the purchase, sale, or other transaction of items because of information contained herein. Readers who feel they have discovered errors are invited to *write* and inform us, so they may be corrected in subsequent editions. Those seeking further information on the topics covered in this book are advised to refer to the complete line of *Official Price Guides* published by the House of Collectibles.

 Published in the United States by House of Collectibles, an imprint of The Random House Information Group, a division of Random House Inc., New York, and in Canada by Random House of Canada Limited, Toronto.

House of Collectibles and colophon are trademarks of Random House, Inc.

Random House is a registered trademark of Random House, Inc.

Please address inquiries about electronic licensing of any products for use on a network, in software, or on CD-ROM to the Subsidiary Rights Department, Random House Information Group, fax 212-572-6003
Visit the House of Collectibles Web site: www.houseofcollectibles.com

This book is available for special discounts for bulk purchases for sales promotions or premiums. Special editions, including personalized covers, excerpts of existing books, and corporate imprints, can be created in large quantities for special needs. For more information, write to:

Random House, Inc.,
Special Markets/Premium Sales
1745 Broadway, MD 6-2
New York, NY 10019

or e-mail specialmarket@randomhouse.com

Manufactured in the United States of America

ISSN: 0748-1365

ISBN: 978-0-375-72338-4

10 9 8 7 6 5 4 3 2 1

Thirtieth Edition: August 2010

Table of Contents

Table of Contents

Table of Contents

Table of Contents

Table of Contents

Table of Contents

Table of Contents

Table of Contents

About the Author

Jim Beckett, the leading authority on sportscard values in the United States, maintains a wide range of activities in the world of sports. He possesses one of the finest collections of sportscards and autographs in the world, has made numerous appearances on radio and television, and has been frequently cited in many national publications. He was awarded the first "Special Achievement Award for Contributions to the Hobby" by the National Sports Collectors Convention in 1980, the "Jock-Jaspersen Award for Hobby Dedication" in 1983, and the "Buck Barker, Spirit of the Hobby Award" in 1991.

Dr. Beckett is the author of *Beckett Baseball Card Price Guide, The Official Price Guide to Baseball Cards, Beckett Almanac of Baseball Cards and Collectibles, Beckett Football Card Price Guide, The Official Price Guide to Football Cards, Beckett Hockey Card Price Guide and Alphabetical Checklist, Beckett Basketball Card Price Guide, The Official Price Guide to Basketball Cards,* and *Beckett Baseball Card Alphabetical Checklist.* In addition, he is the founder and publisher of sports collectible magazines: *Beckett Baseball, Beckett Basketball, Beckett Football, Beckett Hockey,* and *Beckett Sports Card Monthly.*

Jim Beckett received his Ph.D. in Statistics from Southern Methodist University in 1975. Prior to starting Beckett Publications in 1984, Dr. Beckett served as an Associate Professor of Statistics at Bowling Green State University and as a Vice President of a consulting firm in Dallas, Texas. He currently resides in Dallas.

How to Use This Book

Isn't it great? Every year this book gets better with all the new sets coming out. But even more exciting is that every year there are more attractive choices and, subsequently, more interest in the cards we love so much. This edition has been enhanced and expanded from the previous edition. The cards you collect —who appears on them, what they look like, where they are from, and (most important to most of you) what their current values are—are enumerated within. Many of the features contained in the other *Beckett Price Guides* have been incorporated into this volume since condition-grading, terminology, and many other aspects of collecting are common to the card hobby in general. We hope you find the book both interesting and useful in your collecting pursuits.

The Beckett Guide has been successful where other attempts have failed because it is complete, current, and valid. This price guide contains not just one but two price columns for all the football cards listed. These account for most of the major releases in existence. The prices were added to the card lists just prior to printing and reflect not the author's opinions or desires but the going retail prices for each card, based on the marketplace (sports memorabilia conventions and shows, sportscard shops, hobby papers, current mail-order catalogs, Internet sales, auction results, and other firsthand reporting of actually realized prices).

What is the best price guide available on the market today? Of course card sellers will prefer the price guide with the highest prices, while card buyers will naturally prefer the one with the lowest prices. Accuracy, however, is the true test. Use the price guide used by more collectors and dealers than all the others combined. Look for the Beckett name. I won't put my name on anything I won't stake my reputation on. Not the lowest and not the highest—but the most accurate, with integrity.

To facilitate your use of this book, read the complete introductory section on the following pages before going to the pricing pages. Every collectible field has its own terminology; we've tried to capture most of these terms and definitions in our glossary. Please read carefully the section on grading and the condition of your cards, as you will not be able to determine which price column is appropriate for a given card without first knowing its condition.

Prices in This Guide

Prices found in this guide reflect current retail rates just prior to the printing of this book. They do not reflect the for-sale prices of the author, the publisher, the distributors, the advertisers, or any card dealers associated with this guide. No one is obligated in any way to buy, sell, or trade his or her cards based on these prices. The price listings were compiled by the author from actual buy/sell transactions at sports conventions, sportscard shops, buy/sell advertisements in the hobby papers, for-sale prices from dealer catalogs and price lists, and discussions with leading hobbyists in the U.S. and Canada. All prices are in U.S. dollars.

Introduction

Welcome to the exciting world of sportscard collecting, one of America's most popular avocations. You have made a good choice in buying this book, since it will open up to you the entire panorama of this field in the simplest, most concise way.

The growth of *Beckett Baseball, Beckett Basketball, Beckett Football, Beckett Hockey,* and *Beckett Sports Card Monthly* is an indication of the unprecedented popularity of sportscards. Founded in 1984 by Dr. James Beckett, *Beckett Baseball* contains the most extensive and accepted monthly price guide, collectible glossy superstar covers, colorful feature articles, "Hot List," Convention Calendar, tips for beginners, "Readers Write" letters to and responses from the editor, information on errors and varieties, autograph collecting tips, and profiles of the sport's hottest stars. Published every month, *Beckett Baseball* is the hobby's largest paid circulation periodical. The other five magazines were built on the success of *Baseball.*

So collecting sportscards—while still pursued as a hobby with youthful exuberance by kids in the neighborhood—has also taken on the trappings of an industry, with thousands of full- and part-time card dealers, as well as vendors of supplies, clubs, and conventions. In fact, each year since 1980 thousands of hobbyists have assembled for a National Sports Collectors Convention, at which hundreds of dealers have displayed their wares, seminars have been conducted, autographs penned by sports notables, and millions of cards changed hands. The Beckett Guide is the best annual guide available to the exciting world of football cards. Read it and use it. May your enjoyment and your card collection increase in the coming months and years.

How to Collect

Each collection is personal and reflects the individuality of its owner. There are no set rules on how to collect cards. Since card collecting is a hobby or leisure pastime, what you collect, how much you collect, and how much time and money you spend collecting are entirely up to you. The funds you have available for collecting and your own personal taste should determine how you collect. The information and ideas presented here are intended to help you get the most enjoyment from this hobby.

It is impossible to collect every card ever produced. Therefore, beginners as well as intermediate and advanced collectors usually specialize in some way. One of the reasons this hobby is popular is that individual collectors can define and tailor their collecting methods to match their own tastes. To give you some ideas of the various approaches to collecting, we will list some of the more popular areas of specialization.

Many collectors select complete sets from particular years. For example, they may concentrate on assembling complete sets from all the years since their birth or since they became avid sports fans. They may try to collect a card for every player during that specified period of time. Many others wish to acquire only certain players. Usually such players are the superstars of the sport, but occasionally collectors will specialize in all the cards of players who attended a particular college or came from a certain town. Some collectors are only interested in the first cards or Rookie Cards of certain players.

Another fun way to collect cards is by team. Most fans have a favorite team, and it is natural for that loyalty to be translated into a desire for cards of the players on that favorite team. For most of the recent years, team sets (all the cards from a given team for that year) are readily available at a reasonable price. See Beckett.com for searchable player checklists.

Preserving Your Cards

Cards are fragile. They must be handled properly in order to retain their value. Careless handling can easily result in creased or bent cards. It is, however, not recommended that tweezers or tongs be used to pick up your cards since such utensils might mar or indent card surfaces and thus reduce those cards' conditions and values. In general, your cards should be handled directly as little as possible. This is sometimes easier to say than to do.

Although there are still many who use custom boxes, storage trays, or even shoe boxes, plastic sheets are the preferred method of many collectors for storing cards. A collection stored in plastic pages in a three-ring album allows you to view your collection at any time without the need to touch the card itself. Cards can also be kept in single holders (of various types and thicknesses) designed for the enjoyment of each card individually. For a large collection, some collectors may use a combination of the above methods. When purchasing plastic sheets for your cards, be sure that you find the pocket size that fits the cards snugly. Don't put your 1951 Bowman in a sheet designed to fit 1981 Topps.

Most hobby and collectibles shops and virtually all collectors' conventions will have these plastic pages available in quantity for the various sizes offered, or you can purchase them directly from the advertisers in this book. Also, remember that pocket size isn't the only factor to consider when looking for plastic sheets. Other factors such as safety, economy, appearance, availability, or personal preference also may indicate which types of sheets a collector may want to buy.

Damp, sunny, and/or hot conditions. No, this is not a weather forecast, but rather three elements to avoid in extremes if you are interested in preserving your collection. Too much (or too little) humidity can cause gradual deterioration of a card. Direct, bright sun (or fluorescent light) over time will bleach out the color of a card. Extreme heat accelerates the decomposition of the card. On the other hand, many cards have lasted more than 50 years without much scientific intervention. So be cautious, even if the above factors typically present a problem only when present in the extreme. It never hurts to be prudent.

Terminology

Each hobby has its own language to describe its area of interest. The following list defines the most important terminology and abbreviations that may appear in this book:

AS - All-Star.

CL - Checklist card. A card that lists in order the cards and players in the set or series. Older checklist cards in mint condition that have not been checked off are very desirable and command large premiums.

COMMON CARD - The typical card of any set; it has no premium value accruing from subject matter, numerical scarcity, popular demand, or anomaly.

COR - Corrected card. A version of an error card that was fixed by the manufacturer.

DIE-CUT - A card with its stock partially cut. In some cases, after removal or appropriate folding, the remaining part of the card can be made to stand up.

DP - Double Print. A card that was printed in approximately double the quantity compared to other cards in the same series, or draft pick card.

ERR - Error card. A card with erroneous information, spelling, or depiction on either side of the card. Most errors are never corrected by the producing card company.

FOIL - A special type of sticker with a metallic-looking surface.

HL - Highlight card, for example from the 1978 Topps subset.

HOF - Hall of Fame, or Hall of Famer (also abbreviated HOFer).

HOR - Horizontal pose on a card as opposed to the standard vertical orientation found on most cards.

IA - In Action card. A special type of card depicting a player in an action photo, such as the 1982 Topps cards.

LL - League leader card. A card depicting the leader or leaders in a specific statistical category from the previous season. Not to be confused with team leader (TL).

LOGO - NFLPA logo on card.

MVP - Most Valuable Player.

NO LOGO - No NFLPA logo on card.

NO TR - No trade reference on card.

NPO - No position.

OFF - Officials cards.

O-ROY - Offensive Rookie of the Year.

PARALLEL - A card that is similar in design to its counterpart from a basic set, but offers a distinguishing quality.

PB - Pro Bowl.

RB - Record Breaker card or running back.

RC - Rookie Card. A player's first appearance on a regular issue card from one of the major card companies. With a few exceptions, each player has only one RC in any given set. A Rookie Card typically cannot be an All-Star, Highlight, In Action, league leader, Super Action, or team leader card. It can, however, be a coach card or draft pick card.

REDEMPTION - A program established by manufacturers that allows collectors to mail in a special card (usually a random insert) in return for special cards, sets, or other prizes not available through conventional channels.

RET - Retired.

REV NEG - Reversed or flopped photo side of the card. This is a major type of error card, but only some are corrected.

ROY - Rookie of the Year.

SB - Super Bowl.

SET - One each of an entire run of cards of the same type, produced by a particular manufacturer during a single season. In other words, if you have a complete set of 1975 Topps football cards, then you have every card from #1 up to and including #528; i.e., all the different cards that were produced.

SP - Single or Short Print. A card which was printed in lesser quantity compared to the other cards in the same series (also see DP). This term can only be used in a relative sense and in reference to one particular set. For instance, the 1989 Pro Set Pete Rozelle SP is less common than the other cards in that set, but it isn't necessarily scarcer than regular cards of any other set.

TC - Team card or team checklist card.

TL - Team leader card or Top Leader.

UER - Uncorrected error card.

XRC - Extended Rookie Card. A player's first appearance on a card, but issued in a set that was not distributed nationally or in packs. In football sets, this term generally refers to the 1984 and 1985 Topps USFL sets.

Understanding Card Values

Determining Value

Why are some cards more valuable than others? Obviously, the economic laws of supply and demand are applicable to card collecting just as they are to any other field where a commodity is bought, sold, or traded in a free, unregulated market.

Supply (the number of cards available on the market) is less than the total number of cards originally produced since attrition diminishes that original quantity. Each year a percentage of cards is typically thrown away, destroyed, or otherwise lost to collectors. This percentage is much, much smaller today than it was in the past because more and more people have become increasingly aware of the value of their cards.

For those who collect only mint condition cards, the supply of older cards can be quite small indeed. Until recently, collectors were not so conscious of the need to preserve the condition of their cards. For this reason, it is difficult to know exactly how many 1962 Topps are currently available, mint or otherwise. It is generally accepted that there are fewer 1962 Topps available than 1972, 1982, or 1992 Topps cards. If demand were equal for each of these sets, the law of supply and demand would increase the price for the least available sets.

Demand, however, is never equal for all sets, so price correlations can be complicated. The demand for a card is influenced by many factors. These include: (1) the age of the card; (2) the number of cards printed; (3) the player(s) portrayed on the card; (4) the attractiveness and popularity of the set; and (5) the physical condition of the card.

In general, (1) the older the card, (2) the fewer the number of the cards printed, (3) the more famous, popular, and talented the player, (4) the more attractive and popular the set, and (5) the better the condition of the card, the higher the value of the card will be. There are exceptions to all but one of these factors: the condition of the card. Given two cards similar in all respects except condition, the one in the better condition will always be valued higher.

While those guidelines help to establish the value of a card, the countless exceptions and peculiarities make any simple, direct mathematical formula to determine card values impossible.

Regional Variation

Since the market varies from region to region, card prices of local players may be higher. This is known as a regional premium. How significant the premium is—and if there is any premium at all—depends on the local popularity of the team and the player.

The largest regional premiums usually do not apply to superstars, who often are so well known nationwide that the prices of their key cards are too high for local dealers to realize a premium.

Lesser stars often command the strongest premiums. Their popularity is concentrated in their home region, creating local demand that greatly exceeds overall demand.

Regional premiums can apply to popular retired players and sometimes can be found in the areas where the players grew up or starred in college.

A regional discount is the converse of a regional premium. Regional discounts occur when a player has been so popular in his region for so long that local collectors and dealers have accumulated quantities of his cards. The abundant supply may make the cards available in that area at the lowest prices anywhere.

Set Prices

A somewhat paradoxical situation exists in the price of a complete set vs. the combined cost of the individual cards in the set. In nearly every case, the sum of the prices for the individual cards is higher than the cost for the complete set. This is prevalent especially in the cards of the past few years. The reasons for this apparent anomaly stem from the habits of collectors and from the carrying costs to dealers. Today, each card in a set normally is produced in the same quantity as all others in its set.

Many collectors pick up only stars, superstars, and particular teams. As a result, the dealer is left with a shortage of certain player cards and an abundance of others. He therefore incurs an expense in simply "carrying" these less desirable cards in stock. On the other hand, if he sells a complete set, he gets rid of large numbers of cards at one time. For this reason, he generally is willing to receive less money for a complete set. By doing this, he recovers all of his costs and also makes a profit.

Set prices do not include rare card varieties, unless specifically stated. Of course, the prices for sets do include one example of each type for the given set, but this is the least expensive variety.

Grading Your Cards

Each hobby has its own grading terminology—stamps, coins, comic books, record collecting, etc. Collectors of sportscards are no exception. The one invariable criterion for determining the value of a card is its condition: the better the condition of the card, the more valuable it is. Condition grading, however, is subjective. Individual card dealers and collectors differ in the strictness of their grading, but the stated condition of a card should be determined without regard to whether it is being bought or sold.

No allowance is made for age. A 1952 card is judged by the same standards as a 1992 card. But there are specific sets and cards that are condition-sensitive because of their border color, consistently poor centering, etc. Such cards and sets sometimes command premiums above the listed percentages in mint condition.

Condition Guide

Grades

Mint (Mt) - A card with no flaws or wear. The card has four perfect corners, 55/45 or better centering from top to bottom and from left to right, original gloss, smooth edges, and original color borders. A mint card does not have print spots, color, or focus imperfections.

Near Mint-Mint (NrMt-Mt) - A card with one minor flaw. Any one of the following would lower a mint card to near mint-mint: one corner with a slight touch of wear, barely noticeable print spots, color or focus imperfections. The card must have 60/40 or better centering in both directions, original gloss, smooth edges, and original color borders.

Near Mint (NrMt) - A card with one minor flaw. Any one of the following would lower a mint card to near mint: one fuzzy corner or two to four corners with slight touches of wear, 70/30 to 60/40 centering, slightly rough edges, minor print spots, color or focus imperfections. The card must have original gloss and original color borders.

Excellent-Mint (ExMt) - A card with two or three fuzzy, but not rounded, corners and centering no worse than 80/20. The card may have no more than two of the following: slightly rough edges, very slightly discolored borders, minor print spots, color or focus imperfections. The card must have original gloss.

Excellent (Ex) - A card with four fuzzy but definitely not rounded corners and centering no worse than 80/20. The card may have a small amount of original gloss lost, rough edges, slightly discolored borders and minor print spots, color or focus imperfections.

Very Good (Vg) - A card that has been handled but not abused: slightly rounded corners with slight layering, slight notching on edges, a significant amount of gloss lost from the surface but no scuffing and moderate discoloration of borders. The card may have a few light creases.

Good (G), Fair (F), Poor (P) - A well-worn, mishandled, or abused card: badly rounded and layered corners, scuffing, most or all original gloss missing, seriously discolored borders, moderate or heavy creases, and one or more serious flaws. The grade of good, fair, or poor depends on the severity of wear and flaws. Good, fair, and poor cards generally are used only as fillers.

Selling Your Cards

Just about every collector sells cards or will sell cards eventually. Someday you may be interested in selling your duplicates or maybe even your whole collection. You may sell to other collectors, friends, or dealers. You may even sell cards you purchased from a certain dealer back to that same dealer. In any event, it helps to know some of the mechanics of the typical transaction between buyer and seller.

Dealers will buy cards in order to resell them to other collectors who are interested in the cards. Dealers will always pay a higher percentage for items that (in their opinion) can be resold quickly, and a much lower percentage for those items that are perceived as having low demand and hence are slow moving. In either case, dealers must buy at a price that allows for the expense of doing business and a margin for profit.

If you have cards for sale, the best advice we can give is that you get several offers for your cards—either from card shops or at a card show—and take the best offer, all things considered. Note, the "best" offer may not be the one for the highest amount. And remember, if a dealer really wants your cards, he won't let you get away without making his best competitive offer. Another alternative is to place your cards in an auction as one or several lots.

Many people think nothing of going into a department store and paying $15 for an item of clothing for which the store paid $5. But if you were selling your $15 card to a dealer and he offered you $5 for it, you might think his markup unreasonable. To complete the analogy, most department stores (and card dealers) that consistently pay $10 for $15 items eventually go out of business. An exception is when the dealer has lined up a willing buyer for the item(s) you are attempting to sell, or if the cards are so hot that it's likely he'll have to hold the cards for only a short period of time.

In those cases, an offer of up to 75% of book value still will allow the dealer to make a reasonable profit considering the short time he will need to hold the merchandise. In general, however, most cards and collections will bring offers in the range of 25% to 50% of retail price. Also consider that most material from the past five to 20 years is plentiful. If that's what you're selling, don't be surprised if your best offer is well below that range.

2001 Absolute Memorabilia

Card	Low	High
❑ COMP.SET w/o SP's (100)	12.50	30.00
❑ 1 David Boston	.30	.75
❑ 2 Jake Plummer	.40	1.00
❑ 3 Thomas Jones	.40	1.00
❑ 4 Jamal Anderson	.40	1.00
❑ 5 Chris Redman	.50	1.25
❑ 6 Jamal Lewis	.50	1.25
❑ 7 Qadry Ismail	.40	1.00
❑ 8 Ray Lewis	.50	1.25
❑ 9 Shannon Sharpe	.50	1.25
❑ 10 Travis Taylor	.30	.75
❑ 11 Trent Dilfer	.40	1.00
❑ 12 Elvis Grbac	.40	1.00
❑ 13 Eric Moulds	.40	1.00
❑ 14 Rob Johnson	.40	1.00
❑ 15 Muhsin Muhammad	.40	1.00
❑ 16 Brian Urlacher	.60	1.50
❑ 17 Cade McNown	.40	1.00
❑ 18 Marcus Robinson	.40	1.00
❑ 19 Akili Smith	.30	.75
❑ 20 Corey Dillon	.40	1.00
❑ 21 Peter Warrick	.40	1.00
❑ 22 Courtney Brown	.30	.75
❑ 23 Tim Couch	.30	.75
❑ 24 Emmitt Smith	1.25	3.00
❑ 25 Troy Aikman	.75	2.00
❑ 26 Brian Griese	.40	1.00
❑ 27 Ed McCaffrey	.40	1.00
❑ 28 John Elway	1.25	3.00
❑ 29 Mike Anderson	.40	1.00
❑ 30 Rod Smith	.40	1.00
❑ 31 Terrell Davis	.50	1.25
❑ 32 Barry Sanders	1.25	3.00
❑ 33 James Stewart	.30	.75
❑ 34 Ahman Green	.50	1.25
❑ 35 Antonio Freeman	.50	1.25
❑ 36 Brett Favre	1.50	4.00
❑ 37 Edgerrin James	.50	1.25
❑ 38 Marvin Harrison	.50	1.25
❑ 39 Peyton Manning	1.25	3.00
❑ 40 Fred Taylor	.50	1.25
❑ 41 Jimmy Smith	.40	1.00
❑ 42 Keenan McCardell	.40	1.00
❑ 43 Mark Brunell	.50	1.25
❑ 44 Sylvester Morris	.30	.75
❑ 45 Tony Gonzalez	.40	1.00
❑ 46 Dan Marino	1.50	4.00
❑ 47 Jay Fiedler	.40	1.00
❑ 48 Lamar Smith	.40	1.00
❑ 49 Cris Carter	.50	1.25
❑ 50 Daunte Culpepper	.50	1.25
❑ 51 Randy Moss	.60	1.50
❑ 52 Drew Bledsoe	.50	1.25
❑ 53 Terry Glenn	.40	1.00
❑ 54 Aaron Brooks	.40	1.00
❑ 55 Joe Horn	.40	1.00
❑ 56 Ricky Williams	.50	1.25
❑ 57 Amani Toomer	.40	1.00
❑ 58 Ike Hilliard	.40	1.00
❑ 59 Kerry Collins	.40	1.00
❑ 60 Ron Dayne	.40	1.00
❑ 61 Tiki Barber	.50	1.25
❑ 62 Chad Pennington	.50	1.25
❑ 63 Curtis Martin	.50	1.25
❑ 64 Laveranues Coles	.50	1.25
❑ 65 Vinny Testaverde	.40	1.00
❑ 66 Wayne Chrebet	.40	1.00
❑ 67 Charles Woodson	.50	1.25
❑ 68 Rich Gannon	.40	1.00
❑ 69 Tim Brown	.50	1.25
❑ 70 Tyrone Wheatley	.40	1.00
❑ 71 Corey Simon	.30	.75
❑ 72 Donovan McNabb	.60	1.50
❑ 73 Duce Staley	.40	1.00
❑ 74 Jerome Bettis	.50	1.25
❑ 75 Plaxico Burress	.40	1.00
❑ 76 Doug Flutie	.50	1.25
❑ 77 Junior Seau	.50	1.25
❑ 78 Charlie Garner	.40	1.00
❑ 79 Jeff Garcia	.40	1.00
❑ 80 Jerry Rice	1.00	2.50
❑ 81 Steve Young	.60	1.50
❑ 82 Terrell Owens	.50	1.25
❑ 83 Darrell Jackson	.40	1.00
❑ 84 Ricky Watters	.40	1.00
❑ 85 Shaun Alexander	.50	1.25
❑ 86 Isaac Bruce	.50	1.25
❑ 87 Kurt Warner	.60	1.50
❑ 88 Marshall Faulk	.50	1.25
❑ 89 Torry Holt	.40	1.00
❑ 90 Brad Johnson	.40	1.00
❑ 91 Keyshawn Johnson	.40	1.00
❑ 92 Mike Alstott	.40	1.00
❑ 93 Shaun King	.30	.75
❑ 94 Warren Sapp	.40	1.00
❑ 95 Warrick Dunn	.50	1.25
❑ 96 Eddie George	.50	1.25
❑ 97 Jevon Kearse	.40	1.00
❑ 98 Steve McNair	.50	1.25
❑ 99 Jeff George	.40	1.00
❑ 100 Stephen Davis	.40	1.00
❑ 101 Jason McKinley RC	1.25	3.00
❑ 102 Bobby Newcombe RC	1.50	4.00
❑ 103 Cedrick Wilson RC	2.00	5.00
❑ 104 Ken-Yon Rambo RC	1.25	3.00
❑ 105 Kevin Kasper RC	1.50	4.00
❑ 106 Jamal Reynolds RC	1.50	4.00
❑ 107 Scotty Anderson RC	1.50	4.00
❑ 108 T.J. Houshmandzadeh RC	3.00	8.00
❑ 109 Chris Taylor RC	1.25	3.00
❑ 110 Vinny Sutherland RC	1.25	3.00
❑ 111 Jabari Holloway RC	1.50	4.00
❑ 112 Shad Meier RC	1.25	3.00
❑ 113 Correll Buckhalter RC	2.00	5.00
❑ 114 Dan Alexander RC	1.50	4.00
❑ 115 David Allen RC	1.25	3.00
❑ 116 LaMont Jordan RC	2.00	5.00
❑ 117 Nate Clements RC	2.00	5.00
❑ 118 Reggie White RC	1.25	3.00
❑ 119 Javon Green RC	1.25	3.00
❑ 120 Shaun Rogers RC	2.00	5.00
❑ 121 Heath Evans RC	1.50	4.00
❑ 122 Moran Norris RC	1.25	3.00
❑ 123 Ben Leard RC	1.25	3.00
❑ 124 David Rivers RC	1.25	3.00
❑ 125 A.J. Feeley RC	1.50	4.00
❑ 126 Boo Williams RC	1.50	4.00
❑ 127 Ronney Daniels RC	1.25	3.00
❑ 128 Alge Crumpler RC	2.00	5.00
❑ 129 Todd Heap RC	2.00	5.00
❑ 130 Tim Hasselbeck RC	1.50	4.00
❑ 131 Josh Booty RC	1.50	4.00
❑ 132 Jamie Winborn RC	1.50	4.00
❑ 133 Brian Allen RC	1.25	3.00
❑ 134 Sedrick Hodge RC	1.25	3.00
❑ 135 Tommy Polley RC	1.50	4.00
❑ 136 Torrance Marshall RC	1.50	4.00
❑ 137 Damione Lewis RC	1.50	4.00
❑ 138 Marcus Stroud RC	1.50	4.00
❑ 139 Aaron Schobel RC	2.00	5.00
❑ 140 DeLawrence Grant RC	1.25	3.00
❑ 141 Fred Smoot RC	2.00	5.00
❑ 142 Jamar Fletcher RC	1.25	3.00
❑ 143 Ken Lucas RC	1.50	4.00
❑ 144 Will Allen RC	2.00	5.00
❑ 145 Adam Archuleta RC	1.50	4.00
❑ 146 Derrick Gibson RC	1.25	3.00
❑ 147 Jarrod Cooper RC	1.50	4.00
❑ 148 Eddie Berlin RC	1.25	3.00
❑ 149 Steve Smith RC	5.00	12.00
❑ 150 Willie Middlebrooks RC	1.50	4.00
❑ 151 Michael Vick RPM RC	10.00	25.00
❑ 152 Drew Brees RPM RC	20.00	50.00
❑ 153 Chris Weinke RPM RC	4.00	10.00
❑ 154 M.Tuiasosopo RPM RC	4.00	10.00
❑ 155 Mike McMahon RPM RC	4.00	10.00
❑ 156 Deuce McAllister RPM RC	6.00	15.00
❑ 157 Leonard Davis RPM RC	4.00	10.00
❑ 158 L.Tomlinson RPM RC	25.00	60.00
❑ 159 A.Thomas RPM RC	5.00	12.00
❑ 160 Travis Henry RPM RC	5.00	12.00
❑ 161 James Jackson RPM RC	4.00	10.00
❑ 162 Michael Bennett RPM RC	5.00	12.00
❑ 163 Kevan Barlow RPM RC	4.00	10.00
❑ 164 Travis Minor RPM RC	4.00	10.00
❑ 165 David Terrell RPM RC	4.00	10.00
❑ 166 Santana Moss RPM RC	8.00	20.00
❑ 167 Rod Gardner RPM RC	4.00	10.00
❑ 168 Quincy Morgan RPM RC	4.00	10.00
❑ 169 Freddie Mitchell RPM RC	3.00	8.00
❑ 170 Reggie Wayne RPM RC	12.00	30.00
❑ 171 Koren Robinson RPM RC	5.00	12.00
❑ 172 Chad Johnson RPM RC	12.00	30.00
❑ 173 Chris Chambers RPM RC	8.00	20.00
❑ 174 Josh Heupel RPM RC	5.00	12.00
❑ 175 Andre Carter RPM RC	5.00	12.00
❑ 176 Justin Smith RPM RC	5.00	12.00
❑ 177 R.Seymour RPM RC	5.00	12.00
❑ 178 Dan Morgan RPM RC	5.00	12.00
❑ 179 Gerard Warren RPM RC	4.00	10.00
❑ 180 R.Ferguson RPM RC	5.00	12.00
❑ 181 Sage Rosenfels RPM RC	5.00	12.00
❑ 182 Rudi Johnson RPM RC	5.00	12.00
❑ 183 Snoop Minnis RPM RC	4.00	10.00
❑ 184 Jesse Palmer RPM RC	5.00	12.00
❑ 185 Quincy Carter RPM RC	4.00	10.00

2002 Absolute Memorabilia

Card	Low	High
❑ COMP.SET w/o SP's (150)	12.50	30.00
❑ 1 Aaron Brooks	.30	.75
❑ 2 Ahman Green	.30	.75
❑ 3 Alge Crumpler	.30	.75
❑ 4 Amani Toomer	.30	.75
❑ 5 Andre Carter	.25	.60
❑ 6 Anthony Thomas	.30	.75
❑ 7 Antonio Freeman	.40	1.00
❑ 8 Antowain Smith	.30	.75
❑ 9 Az-Zahir Hakim	.25	.60
❑ 10 Bill Schroeder	.30	.75
❑ 11 Brad Johnson	.30	.75
❑ 12 Brett Favre	1.00	2.50
❑ 13 Brian Griese	.30	.75
❑ 14 Brian Urlacher	.50	1.25
❑ 15 Chad Johnson	.40	1.00
❑ 16 Chad Pennington	.40	1.00
❑ 17 Champ Bailey	.40	1.00
❑ 18 Charles Woodson	.40	1.00
❑ 19 Charlie Batch	.30	.75
❑ 20 Charlie Garner	.30	.75
❑ 21 Chris Chambers	.40	1.00
❑ 22 Chris Redman	.25	.60
❑ 23 Chris Weinke	.25	.60
❑ 24 Corey Dillon	.30	.75
❑ 25 Correll Buckhalter	.30	.75
❑ 26 Cris Carter	.40	1.00
❑ 27 Curtis Martin	.40	1.00
❑ 28 Darnay Scott	.30	.75
❑ 29 Darrell Jackson	.30	.75
❑ 30 Daunte Culpepper	.30	.75
❑ 31 David Boston	.25	.60
❑ 32 David Terrell	.25	.60
❑ 33 Derrick Alexander	.30	.75
❑ 34 Derrick Mason	.30	.75
❑ 35 Deuce McAllister	.40	1.00
❑ 36 Dominic Rhodes	.30	.75
❑ 37 Donald Hayes	.25	.60
❑ 38 Donovan McNabb	.50	1.25
❑ 39 Doug Flutie	.40	1.00
❑ 40 Drew Bledsoe	.40	1.00
❑ 41 Drew Brees	.60	1.50
❑ 42 Duce Staley	.30	.75
❑ 43 Ed McCaffrey	.30	.75
❑ 44 Eddie George	.30	.75
❑ 45 Edgerrin James	.40	1.00
❑ 46 Elvis Joseph	.25	.60

Card	Low	High
❑ 47 Emmitt Smith	1.00	2.50
❑ 48 Eric Moulds	.30	.75
❑ 49 Frank Sanders	.25	.60
❑ 50 Fred Taylor	.40	1.00
❑ 51 Freddie Mitchell	.25	.60
❑ 52 Garrison Hearst	.30	.75
❑ 53 Gerard Warren	.25	.60
❑ 54 Germane Crowell	.25	.60
❑ 55 Isaac Bruce	.40	1.00
❑ 56 Jake Plummer	.30	.75
❑ 57 Jamal Anderson	.30	.75
❑ 58 Jamal Lewis	.30	.75
❑ 59 James Allen	.25	.60
❑ 60 James Jackson	.25	.60
❑ 61 James Stewart	.25	.60
❑ 62 Jason Brookins	.25	.60
❑ 63 Jay Fiedler	.30	.75
❑ 64 Jeff Garcia	.30	.75
❑ 65 Jerome Bettis	.40	1.00
❑ 66 Jerry Rice	.75	2.00
❑ 67 Jevon Kearse	.30	.75
❑ 68 Jim Miller	.30	.75
❑ 69 Jimmy Smith	.30	.75
❑ 70 Joe Horn	.30	.75
❑ 71 Joey Galloway	.30	.75
❑ 72 Jon Kitna	.30	.75
❑ 73 Junior Seau	.40	1.00
❑ 74 Keenan McCardell	.30	.75
❑ 75 Kendrell Bell	.25	.60
❑ 76 Kerry Collins	.30	.75
❑ 77 Kevan Barlow	.25	.60
❑ 78 Kevin Dyson	.30	.75
❑ 79 Kevin Johnson	.25	.60
❑ 80 Kevin Kasper	.25	.60
❑ 81 Keyshawn Johnson	.30	.75
❑ 82 Kordell Stewart	.30	.75
❑ 83 Koren Robinson	.25	.60
❑ 84 Kurt Warner	.40	1.00
❑ 85 LaDainian Tomlinson	.60	1.50
❑ 86 Lamar Smith	.30	.75
❑ 87 Laveranues Coles	.40	1.00
❑ 88 MarTay Jenkins	.25	.60
❑ 89 Mark Brunell	.30	.75
❑ 90 Marshall Faulk	.40	1.00
❑ 91 Marty Booker	.30	.75
❑ 92 Marvin Harrison	.40	1.00
❑ 93 Snoop Minnis	.25	.60
❑ 94 Michael Bennett	.30	.75
❑ 95 Michael Strahan	.40	1.00
❑ 96 Michael Vick	.40	1.00
❑ 97 Mike Alstott	.30	.75
❑ 98 Mike Anderson	.30	.75
❑ 99 Mike McMahon	.25	.60
❑ 100 Muhsin Muhammad	.30	.75
❑ 101 Nate Clements	.25	.60
❑ 102 Oronde Gadsden	.25	.60
❑ 103 Peter Warrick	.30	.75
❑ 104 Peyton Manning	.75	2.00
❑ 105 Plaxico Burress	.30	.75
❑ 106 Priest Holmes	.40	1.00
❑ 107 Quincy Carter	.25	.60
❑ 108 Quincy Morgan	.25	.60
❑ 109 Rocket Ismail	.30	.75
❑ 111 Ray Lewis	.40	1.00
❑ 112 Reggie Wayne	.40	1.00
❑ 113 Rich Gannon	.30	.75
❑ 114 Rickey Dudley	.25	.60
❑ 115 Ricky Watters	.30	.75
❑ 116 Ricky Williams	.40	1.00
❑ 117 Rod Gardner	.25	.60
❑ 118 Rod Smith	.30	.75
❑ 119 Robert Ferguson	.30	.75
❑ 120 Santana Moss	.30	.75
❑ 121 Shaun Alexander	.40	1.00
❑ 122 Stephen Davis	.30	.75
❑ 123 Steve McNair	.40	1.00
❑ 124 Steve Smith	.40	1.00
❑ 125 Terrell Davis	.40	1.00
❑ 126 Terrell Owens	.40	1.00
❑ 127 Terry Glenn	.30	.75
❑ 128 Thomas Jones	.30	.75
❑ 129 Tiki Barber	.40	1.00
❑ 130 Tim Brown	.40	1.00
❑ 131 Tim Couch	.25	.60
❑ 132 Todd Heap	.30	.75
❑ 133 Todd Pinkston	.25	.60
❑ 134 Tom Brady	1.00	2.50
❑ 135 Tony Boselli	.30	.75
❑ 136 Tony Gonzalez	.30	.75
❑ 137 Torry Holt	.40	1.00
❑ 138 Travis Henry	.30	.75
❑ 139 Travis Taylor	.25	.60
❑ 140 Trent Dilfer	.30	.75
❑ 141 Trent Green	.30	.75
❑ 142 Troy Brown	.30	.75
❑ 143 Troy Hambrick	.25	.60
❑ 144 Trung Canidate	.25	.60
❑ 145 Vinny Testaverde	.30	.75
❑ 146 Warren Sapp	.30	.75
❑ 147 Warrick Dunn	.30	.75
❑ 148 Wayne Chrebet	.30	.75
❑ 149 Wesley Walls	.30	.75
❑ 150 Zach Thomas	.40	1.00
❑ 151 Quentin Jammer RC	2.00	5.00
❑ 152 Randy Fasani RC	1.50	4.00
❑ 153 Kurt Kittner RC	1.25	3.00
❑ 154 Chad Hutchinson RC	1.25	3.00
❑ 155 Major Applewhite RC	2.00	5.00
❑ 156 Wes Pate RC	1.25	3.00
❑ 157 J.T. O'Sullivan RC	2.00	5.00
❑ 158 Ryan Denney RC	1.25	3.00
❑ 159 Ronald Curry RC	2.00	5.00
❑ 160 Lamar Gordon RC	2.00	5.00
❑ 161 Brian Westbrook RC	6.00	15.00
❑ 162 Jonathan Wells RC	2.00	5.00
❑ 163 Ricky Williams RC	1.50	4.00
❑ 164 Verron Haynes RC	1.50	4.00
❑ 165 Josh Scobey RC	1.50	4.00
❑ 166 Larry Ned RC	1.25	3.00
❑ 167 Adrian Peterson RC	2.00	5.00
❑ 168 Chester Taylor RC	3.00	8.00
❑ 169 Luke Staley RC	1.25	3.00
❑ 170 Damien Anderson RC	1.50	4.00
❑ 171 Lee Mays RC	1.25	3.00
❑ 172 Deion Branch RC	2.00	5.00
❑ 173 Terry Charles RC	1.25	3.00
❑ 174 Woody Dantzler RC	1.50	4.00
❑ 175 Jason McAddley RC	1.50	4.00
❑ 176 Kelly Campbell RC	1.50	4.00
❑ 177 Freddie Milons RC	1.25	3.00
❑ 178 Kahlil Hill RC	1.25	3.00
❑ 179 Brian Poli-Dixon RC	1.25	3.00
❑ 180 Mike Echols RC	1.25	3.00
❑ 181 Pete Rebstock RC	1.25	3.00
❑ 182 Dwight Freeney RC	3.00	8.00
❑ 183 Bryan Thomas RC	1.25	3.00
❑ 184 Charles Grant RC	2.00	5.00
❑ 185 Kalimba Edwards RC	1.50	4.00
❑ 186 Ryan Sims RC	2.00	5.00
❑ 187 John Henderson RC	2.00	5.00
❑ 188 Wendell Bryant RC	1.25	3.00
❑ 189 Albert Haynesworth RC	2.00	5.00
❑ 190 Larry Tripplett RC	1.25	3.00
❑ 191 Phillip Buchanon RC	2.00	5.00
❑ 192 Lito Sheppard RC	2.00	5.00
❑ 193 Mike Rumph RC	1.25	3.00
❑ 194 Levar Fisher RC	1.25	3.00
❑ 195 Ed Reed RC	6.00	15.00
❑ 196 Rocky Calmus RC	1.50	4.00
❑ 197 Michael Lewis RC	2.00	5.00
❑ 198 Napoleon Harris RC	1.50	4.00
❑ 199 Robert Thomas RC	1.25	3.00
❑ 200 Anthony Weaver RC	1.25	3.00
❑ 201 Ladell Betts RPM RC	3.00	8.00
❑ 202 Antonio Bryant RPM RC	4.00	10.00
❑ 203 Reche Caldwell RPM RC	3.00	8.00
❑ 204 David Carr RPM RC	3.00	8.00
❑ 205 Tim Carter RPM RC	2.50	6.00
❑ 206 Eric Crouch RPM RC	3.00	8.00
❑ 207 Rohan Davey RPM RC	3.00	8.00
❑ 208 Andre Davis RPM RC	2.50	6.00
❑ 209 T.J. Duckett RPM RC	3.00	8.00
❑ 210 DeShaun Foster RPM RC	3.00	8.00
❑ 211 Jabar Gaffney RPM RC	3.00	8.00
❑ 212 Daniel Graham RPM RC	2.50	6.00
❑ 213 William Green RPM RC	2.50	6.00
❑ 214 Joey Harrington RPM RC	3.00	8.00
❑ 215 David Garrard RPM RC	5.00	12.00
❑ 216 Ron Johnson RPM RC	2.50	6.00
❑ 217 Ashley Lelie RPM RC	3.00	8.00
❑ 218 Josh McCown RPM RC	3.00	8.00
❑ 219 Maurice Morris RPM RC	3.00	8.00
❑ 220 Julius Peppers RPM RC	6.00	15.00
❑ 221 Clinton Portis RPM RC	8.00	20.00
❑ 222 Patrick Ramsey RPM RC	3.00	8.00
❑ 223 Antwaan Randle El RPM RC	3.00	8.00
❑ 224 Josh Reed RPM RC	2.50	6.00
❑ 225 Cliff Russell RPM RC	2.00	5.00
❑ 226 Jeremy Shockey RPM RC	5.00	12.00
❑ 227 Donte Stallworth RPM RC	3.00	8.00
❑ 228 Travis Stephens RPM RC	2.00	5.00
❑ 229 Javon Walker RPM RC	3.00	8.00
❑ 230 Marquise Walker RPM RC	2.00	5.00
❑ 231 Roy Williams RPM RC	4.00	10.00
❑ 232 Mike Williams RPM RC	2.00	5.00

2004 Absolute Memorabilia

❑ COMP.SET w/o SP's (150) 40.00 80.00
❑ 151-233 PRINT RUN 750 SER.#'d SETS
❑ UNPRICED SPECTRUM PLATINUM #'d TO 1

Card	Low	High
❑ 1 Anquan Boldin	1.25	3.00
❑ 2 Emmitt Smith	3.00	8.00
❑ 3 Josh McCown	1.00	2.50
❑ 4 Marcel Shipp	1.25	3.00
❑ 5 Michael Vick	1.25	3.00
❑ 6 Peerless Price	1.00	2.50
❑ 7 T.J. Duckett	1.00	2.50
❑ 8 Warrick Dunn	1.00	2.50
❑ 9 Jamal Lewis	1.00	2.50
❑ 10 Kyle Boller	1.00	2.50
❑ 11 Ray Lewis	1.25	3.00
❑ 12 Terrell Suggs	.75	2.00
❑ 13 Drew Bledsoe	1.25	3.00
❑ 14 Eric Moulds	1.00	2.50
❑ 15 Josh Reed	1.25	3.00
❑ 16 Travis Henry	1.00	2.50
❑ 17 DeShaun Foster	1.00	2.50
❑ 18 Jake Delhomme	1.00	2.50
❑ 19 Julius Peppers	1.00	2.50
❑ 20 Muhsin Muhammad	1.00	2.50
❑ 21 Stephen Davis	1.00	2.50
❑ 22 Steve Smith	1.25	3.00
❑ 23 Anthony Thomas	1.00	2.50
❑ 24 Brian Urlacher	1.25	3.00
❑ 25 Marty Booker	1.00	2.50
❑ 26 Rex Grossman	1.25	3.00
❑ 27 Carson Palmer	1.50	4.00
❑ 28 Chad Johnson	1.00	2.50
❑ 29 Corey Dillon	1.00	2.50
❑ 30 Peter Warrick	1.00	2.50
❑ 31 Rudi Johnson	1.00	2.50
❑ 32 Andre Davis	.75	2.00
❑ 33 Dennis Northcutt	.75	2.00
❑ 34 Lee Suggs	1.25	3.00
❑ 35 Tim Couch	1.00	2.50
❑ 36 Jeff Garcia	1.25	3.00
❑ 37 William Green	.75	2.00
❑ 38 Antonio Bryant	1.25	3.00
❑ 39 Quincy Carter	.75	2.00
❑ 40 Roy Williams S	1.00	2.50
❑ 41 Terence Newman	1.00	2.50
❑ 42 Keyshawn Johnson	1.00	2.50
❑ 43 Garrison Hearst	1.00	2.50
❑ 44 Champ Bailey	1.00	2.50
❑ 45 Ashley Lelie	1.00	2.50
❑ 46 Jake Plummer	1.00	2.50
❑ 47 Rod Smith	1.00	2.50
❑ 48 Shannon Sharpe	1.00	2.50
❑ 49 Charles Rogers	1.00	2.50
❑ 50 Joey Harrington	1.00	2.50
❑ 51 Ahman Green	1.25	3.00
❑ 52 Brett Favre	3.00	8.00
❑ 53 Donald Driver	1.25	3.00
❑ 54 Javon Walker	1.00	2.50
❑ 55 Robert Ferguson	.75	2.00
❑ 56 Andre Johnson	1.25	3.00
❑ 57 David Carr	1.00	2.50
❑ 58 Domanick Davis	1.00	2.50
❑ 59 Edgerrin James	1.25	3.00
❑ 60 Marvin Harrison	1.25	3.00
❑ 61 Peyton Manning	2.50	6.00
❑ 62 Reggie Wayne	1.00	2.50

❑ 63 Byron Leftwich 1.25 3.00
❑ 64 Fred Taylor 1.00 2.50
❑ 65 Jimmy Smith 1.00 2.50
❑ 66 Dante Hall 1.00 2.50
❑ 67 Priest Holmes 1.25 3.00
❑ 68 Tony Gonzalez 1.25 3.00
❑ 69 Trent Green 1.00 2.50
❑ 70 Chris Chambers 1.00 2.50
❑ 71 Jay Fiedler .75 2.00
❑ 72 David Boston .75 2.00
❑ 73 Ricky Williams 1.25 3.00
❑ 74 Zach Thomas 1.25 3.00
❑ 75 Daunte Culpepper 1.25 3.00
❑ 76 Michael Bennett 1.00 2.50
❑ 77 Moe Williams .75 2.00
❑ 78 Randy Moss 1.25 3.00
❑ 79 David Givens 1.00 2.50
❑ 80 Deion Branch 1.00 2.50
❑ 81 Kevin Faulk 1.00 2.50
❑ 82 Richard Seymour .75 2.00
❑ 83 Tom Brady 3.00 8.00
❑ 84 Troy Brown 1.00 2.50
❑ 85 Ty Law 1.00 2.50
❑ 86 Aaron Brooks 1.00 2.50
❑ 87 Deuce McAllister 1.25 3.00
❑ 88 Donte Stallworth 1.00 2.50
❑ 89 Joe Horn 1.00 2.50
❑ 90 Amani Toomer 1.00 2.50
❑ 91 Jeremy Shockey 1.00 2.50
❑ 92 Kerry Collins 1.00 2.50
❑ 93 Michael Strahan 1.00 2.50
❑ 94 Tiki Barber 1.25 3.00
❑ 95 Chad Pennington 1.25 3.00
❑ 96 Curtis Martin 1.25 3.00
❑ 97 Santana Moss 1.00 2.50
❑ 98 Wayne Chrebet 1.00 2.50
❑ 99 Justin McCareins .75 2.00
❑ 100 Charles Woodson 1.25 3.00
❑ 101 Jerry Porter 1.00 2.50
❑ 102 Jerry Rice 2.50 6.00
❑ 103 Rich Gannon 1.00 2.50
❑ 104 Tim Brown 1.25 3.00
❑ 105 Warren Sapp 1.00 2.50
❑ 106 A.J. Feeley 1.00 2.50
❑ 107 Brian Westbrook 1.25 3.00
❑ 108 Correll Buckhalter 1.00 2.50
❑ 109 Donovan McNabb 1.25 3.00
❑ 110 Freddie Mitchell .75 2.00
❑ 111 Terrell Owens 1.25 3.00
❑ 112 Jevon Kearse 1.00 2.50
❑ 113 Todd Pinkston .75 2.00
❑ 114 Antwaan Randle El 1.00 2.50
❑ 115 Hines Ward 1.25 3.00
❑ 116 Jerome Bettis 1.25 3.00
❑ 117 Kendrell Bell .75 2.00
❑ 118 Plaxico Burress 1.00 2.50
❑ 119 Tommy Maddox 1.00 2.50
❑ 120 Duce Staley 1.00 2.50
❑ 121 Drew Brees 1.25 3.00
❑ 122 LaDainian Tomlinson 1.50 4.00
❑ 123 Kevan Barlow 1.00 2.50
❑ 124 Tai Streets .75 2.00
❑ 125 Tim Rattay .75 2.00
❑ 126 Darrell Jackson 1.00 2.50
❑ 127 Koren Robinson 1.25 3.00
❑ 128 Matt Hasselbeck 1.25 3.00
❑ 129 Shaun Alexander 1.25 3.00
❑ 130 Isaac Bruce 1.00 2.50
❑ 131 Kurt Warner 1.25 3.00
❑ 132 Marc Bulger 1.00 2.50
❑ 133 Marshall Faulk 1.25 3.00
❑ 134 Torry Holt 1.25 3.00
❑ 135 Derrick Brooks 1.00 2.50
❑ 136 Keenan McCardell .75 2.00
❑ 137 Mike Alstott 1.00 2.50
❑ 138 Thomas Jones 1.00 2.50
❑ 139 Charlie Garner 1.00 2.50
❑ 140 Derrick Mason 1.00 2.50
❑ 141 Drew Bennett 1.00 2.50
❑ 142 Eddie George 1.00 2.50
❑ 143 Keith Bulluck .75 2.00
❑ 144 Steve McNair 1.25 3.00
❑ 145 LaVar Arrington 1.00 2.50
❑ 146 Laveranues Coles 1.00 2.50
❑ 147 Patrick Ramsey 1.00 2.50
❑ 148 Rod Gardner .75 2.00
❑ 149 Clinton Portis 1.25 3.00
❑ 150 Mark Brunell 1.00 2.50
❑ 151 Craig Krenzel AU RC 7.50 15.00
❑ 152 Andy Hall AU RC 6.00 12.00
❑ 153 Josh Harris RC 1.50 4.00
❑ 154 Jim Sorgi AU RC 7.50 15.00
❑ 155 Jeff Smoker AU RC 7.50 15.00
❑ 156 John Navarre AU RC 7.50 15.00
❑ 157 Jared Lorenzen AU RC 6.00 12.00
❑ 158 Cody Pickett AU RC 7.50 15.00
❑ 159 Casey Bramlet RC 1.50 4.00
❑ 160 Matt Mauck AU RC 7.50 15.00
❑ 161 B.J. Symons AU RC 7.50 15.00
❑ 162 Bradlee Van Pelt RC 2.00 5.00
❑ 163 Ryan Dinwiddie RC 1.50 4.00
❑ 164 Michael Turner RC 6.00 15.00
❑ 165 Drew Henson RC 1.50 4.00
❑ 166 Troy Fleming RC 1.50 4.00
❑ 167 Adimchinobe Echemandu RC 2.00 5.00
❑ 168 Quincy Wilson RC 2.00 5.00
❑ 169 Derrick Ward RC 2.50 6.00
❑ 170 Bruce Perry RC 1.50 4.00
❑ 171 Brandon Miree RC 1.50 4.00
❑ 172 Jarrett Payton AU RC 5.00 12.00
❑ 173 Ran Carthon RC 1.50 4.00
❑ 174 Carlos Francis AU RC 6.00 12.00
❑ 175 Samie Parker RC 2.00 5.00
❑ 176 Jerricho Cotchery RC 2.50 6.00
❑ 177 Ernest Wilford RC 2.00 5.00
❑ 178 Johnnie Morant RC 2.00 5.00
❑ 179 Maurice Mann AU RC 7.50 15.00
❑ 180 D.J. Hackett RC 2.50 6.00
❑ 181 Drew Carter RC 2.50 6.00
❑ 182 P.K. Sam RC 1.50 4.00
❑ 183 Jamaar Taylor RC 1.50 4.00
❑ 184 Ryan Krause RC 1.50 4.00
❑ 185 Triandos Luke RC 1.50 4.00
❑ 186 Jeris McIntyre RC 1.50 4.00
❑ 187 Clarence Moore AU RC 7.50 15.00
❑ 188 Mark Jones RC 1.50 4.00
❑ 189 Sloan Thomas AU RC 6.00 12.00
❑ 190 Sean Taylor RC 2.50 6.00
❑ 191 Derek Abney RC 1.50 4.00
❑ 192 Jonathan Vilma RC 2.50 6.00
❑ 193 Tommie Harris RC 2.50 6.00
❑ 194 D.J. Williams RC 2.50 6.00
❑ 195 Will Smith RC 2.50 6.00
❑ 196 Kenechi Udeze RC 2.50 6.00
❑ 197 Vince Wilfork RC 2.50 6.00
❑ 198 Ahmad Carroll RC 2.50 6.00
❑ 199 Jason Babin RC 2.00 5.00
❑ 200 Chris Gamble RC 2.00 5.00
❑ 201 Larry Fitzgerald RPM RC 10.00 25.00
❑ 202 DeAngelo Hall RPM RC 3.00 8.00
❑ 203 Matt Schaub RPM RC 8.00 20.00
❑ 204 Michael Jenkins RPM AU RC 10.00 25.00
❑ 205 Devard Darling RPM AU RC 10.00 25.00
❑ 206 J.P. Losman RPM RC 3.00 8.00
❑ 207 Lee Evans RPM RC 4.00 10.00
❑ 208 Keary Colbert RPM AU RC 8.00 20.00
❑ 209 Bernard Berrian RPM AU RC 12.50 30.00
❑ 210 Chris Perry RPM RC 3.00 8.00
❑ 211 Kellen Winslow RPM RC 4.00 10.00
❑ 212 Luke McCown RPM RC 3.00 8.00
❑ 213 Julius Jones RPM RC 4.00 10.00
❑ 214 Darius Watts RPM RC 2.50 6.00
❑ 215 Tatum Bell RPM AU RC 10.00 25.00
❑ 216 Kevin Jones RPM RC 3.00 8.00
❑ 217 Roy Williams RPM RC 4.00 10.00
❑ 218 Dunta Robinson RPM RC 2.50 6.00
❑ 219 Greg Jones RPM AU RC 10.00 25.00
❑ 220 Reggie Williams RPM RC 3.00 8.00
❑ 221 Mewelde Moore RPM RC 3.00 8.00
❑ 222 Ben Watson RPM RC 3.00 8.00
❑ 223 Cedric Cobbs RPM RC 2.50 6.00
❑ 224 Dev Henderson RPM AU RC 10.00 25.00
❑ 225 Eli Manning RPM RC 20.00 50.00
❑ 226 Robert Gallery RPM RC 3.00 8.00
❑ 227 Roethlisberger RPM RC 25.00 60.00
❑ 228 Philip Rivers RPM RC 12.00 30.00
❑ 229 Derrick Hamilton RPM RC 2.00 5.00
❑ 230 Rashaun Woods RPM RC 2.00 5.00
❑ 231 Steven Jackson RPM RC 8.00 20.00
❑ 232 Michael Clayton RPM RC 3.00 8.00
❑ 233 Ben Troupe RPM RC 2.50 6.00

2005 Absolute Memorabilia

❑ 151-205 PRINT RUN 999 SER.#'d SETS
❑ 206-234 PRINT RUN 750 SER.#'d SETS
❑ UNPRICED PLATINUM PRINT RUN 1 SET
❑ HOBBY PRINTED ON HOLOFOIL STOCK
❑ 1 Anquan Boldin 1.00 2.50
❑ 2 Kurt Warner 1.25 3.00
❑ 3 Josh McCown 1.00 2.50
❑ 4 Larry Fitzgerald 1.25 3.00
❑ 5 Alge Crumpler 1.00 2.50
❑ 6 Michael Vick 1.25 3.00
❑ 7 Peerless Price .75 2.00
❑ 8 T.J. Duckett .75 2.00
❑ 9 Warrick Dunn 1.00 2.50
❑ 10 Deion Sanders 1.50 4.00
❑ 11 Derrick Mason 1.00 2.50
❑ 12 Ed Reed 1.00 2.50
❑ 13 Jamal Lewis 1.00 2.50
❑ 14 Kyle Boller 1.00 2.50
❑ 15 Ray Lewis 1.25 3.00
❑ 16 Todd Heap 1.00 2.50
❑ 17 Eric Moulds 1.00 2.50
❑ 18 J.P. Losman 1.00 2.50
❑ 19 Lee Evans 1.00 2.50
❑ 20 Travis Henry 1.00 2.50
❑ 21 Willis McGahee 1.25 3.00
❑ 22 DeShaun Foster 1.00 2.50
❑ 23 Jake Delhomme 1.25 3.00
❑ 24 Julius Peppers 1.00 2.50
❑ 25 Keary Colbert .75 2.00
❑ 26 Stephen Davis 1.00 2.50
❑ 27 Steve Smith 1.25 3.00
❑ 28 Brian Urlacher 1.25 3.00
❑ 29 Muhsin Muhammad 1.00 2.50
❑ 30 Thomas Jones 1.00 2.50
❑ 31 Rex Grossman 1.25 3.00
❑ 32 Carson Palmer 1.25 3.00
❑ 33 Chad Johnson 1.00 2.50
❑ 34 Peter Warrick .75 2.00
❑ 35 Rudi Johnson 1.00 2.50
❑ 36 T.J. Houshmandzadeh 1.00 2.50
❑ 37 Antonio Bryant 1.00 2.50
❑ 38 Dennis Northcutt .75 2.00
❑ 39 Trent Dilfer 1.00 2.50
❑ 40 Kellen Winslow 1.25 3.00
❑ 41 Lee Suggs 1.00 2.50
❑ 42 Reuben Droughns .75 2.00
❑ 43 Drew Bledsoe 1.25 3.00
❑ 44 Jason Witten 1.25 3.00
❑ 45 Julius Jones 1.25 3.00
❑ 46 Keyshawn Johnson 1.00 2.50
❑ 47 Terence Newman .75 2.00
❑ 48 Roy Williams S 1.00 2.50
❑ 49 Jake Plummer 1.00 2.50
❑ 50 Rod Smith 1.00 2.50
❑ 51 Ashley Lelie .75 2.00
❑ 52 Tatum Bell 1.00 2.50
❑ 53 Charles Rogers .75 2.00
❑ 54 Joey Harrington 1.25 3.00
❑ 55 Kevin Jones 1.00 2.50
❑ 56 Roy Williams WR 1.25 3.00
❑ 57 Ahman Green 1.25 3.00
❑ 58 Brett Favre 3.00 8.00
❑ 59 Donald Driver 1.25 3.00
❑ 60 Javon Walker 1.00 2.50
❑ 61 Andre Johnson 1.00 2.50
❑ 62 David Carr 1.00 2.50
❑ 63 Domanick Davis .75 2.00
❑ 64 Brandon Stokley .75 2.00
❑ 65 Dallas Clark 1.00 2.50
❑ 66 Edgerrin James 1.00 2.50
❑ 67 Marvin Harrison 1.25 3.00
❑ 68 Peyton Manning 2.00 5.00

Card	Low	High
❑ 69 Reggie Wayne	1.00	2.50
❑ 70 Reggie Williams	1.00	2.50
❑ 71 Byron Leftwich	1.00	2.50
❑ 72 Fred Taylor	1.25	3.00
❑ 73 Jimmy Smith	1.00	2.50
❑ 74 Priest Holmes	1.25	3.00
❑ 75 Tony Gonzalez	1.00	2.50
❑ 76 Dante Hall	1.00	2.50
❑ 77 Trent Green	1.00	2.50
❑ 78 Eddie Kennison	.75	2.00
❑ 79 A.J. Feeley	.75	2.00
❑ 80 Chris Chambers	1.00	2.50
❑ 81 Zach Thomas	1.25	3.00
❑ 82 Junior Seau	1.25	3.00
❑ 83 Marty Booker	.75	2.00
❑ 84 Daunte Culpepper	1.25	3.00
❑ 85 Nate Burleson	1.00	2.50
❑ 86 Michael Bennett	1.00	2.50
❑ 87 Onterrio Smith	.75	2.00
❑ 88 Corey Dillon	1.00	2.50
❑ 89 Deion Branch	1.00	2.50
❑ 90 Tom Brady	2.50	6.00
❑ 91 Troy Brown	.75	2.00
❑ 92 Tedy Bruschi	1.25	3.00
❑ 93 Aaron Brooks	.75	2.00
❑ 94 Donte Stallworth	1.00	2.50
❑ 95 Joe Horn	1.00	2.50
❑ 96 Deuce McAllister	1.25	3.00
❑ 97 Amani Toomer	1.00	2.50
❑ 98 Plaxico Burress	1.00	2.50
❑ 99 Jeremy Shockey	1.25	3.00
❑ 100 Eli Manning	2.50	6.00
❑ 101 Tiki Barber	1.25	3.00
❑ 102 Chad Pennington	1.25	3.00
❑ 103 Laveranues Coles	1.00	2.50
❑ 104 Curtis Martin	1.25	3.00
❑ 105 Justin McCareins	.75	2.00
❑ 106 Wayne Chrebet	1.00	2.50
❑ 107 Jerry Porter	1.00	2.50
❑ 108 LaMont Jordan	1.00	2.50
❑ 109 Randy Moss	1.25	3.00
❑ 110 Kerry Collins	1.00	2.50
❑ 111 Charles Woodson	1.00	2.50
❑ 112 Brian Westbrook	1.25	3.00
❑ 113 Donovan McNabb	1.25	3.00
❑ 114 Jevon Kearse	1.00	2.50
❑ 115 Terrell Owens	1.25	3.00
❑ 116 Ben Roethlisberger	3.00	8.00
❑ 117 Hines Ward	1.25	3.00
❑ 118 Duce Staley	1.00	2.50
❑ 119 Jerome Bettis	1.25	3.00
❑ 120 Antonio Gates	1.25	3.00
❑ 121 Eric Parker	.75	2.00
❑ 122 Keenan McCardell	1.00	2.50
❑ 123 Drew Brees	1.25	3.00
❑ 124 LaDainian Tomlinson	1.50	4.00
❑ 125 Brandon Lloyd	.75	2.00
❑ 126 Kevan Barlow	.75	2.00
❑ 127 Tim Rattay	.75	2.00
❑ 128 Koren Robinson	1.00	2.50
❑ 129 Darrell Jackson	1.00	2.50
❑ 130 Jerry Rice	2.50	6.00
❑ 131 Matt Hasselbeck	1.00	2.50
❑ 132 Shaun Alexander	1.25	3.00
❑ 133 Isaac Bruce	1.00	2.50
❑ 134 Marc Bulger	1.00	2.50
❑ 135 Marshall Faulk	1.25	3.00
❑ 136 Steven Jackson	1.50	4.00
❑ 137 Torry Holt	1.00	2.50
❑ 138 Brian Griese	1.00	2.50
❑ 139 Michael Clayton	1.00	2.50
❑ 140 Michael Pittman	.75	2.00
❑ 141 Mike Alstott	1.00	2.50
❑ 142 Chris Brown	1.00	2.50
❑ 143 Drew Bennett	1.00	2.50
❑ 144 Steve McNair	1.25	3.00
❑ 145 Clinton Portis	1.25	3.00
❑ 146 LaVar Arrington	1.25	3.00
❑ 147 Santana Moss	1.00	2.50
❑ 148 Patrick Ramsey	1.00	2.50
❑ 149 Rod Gardner	.75	2.00
❑ 150 Sean Taylor	1.00	2.50
❑ 151 DeMarcus Ware RC	4.00	10.00
❑ 152 Shawne Merriman RC	2.50	6.00
❑ 153 Thomas Davis RC	2.00	5.00
❑ 154 Derrick Johnson RC	2.50	6.00
❑ 155 Travis Johnson RC	1.50	4.00
❑ 156 David Pollack RC	2.00	5.00
❑ 157 Erasmus James RC	2.00	5.00
❑ 158 Marcus Spears RC	2.50	6.00
❑ 159 Fabian Washington RC	2.50	6.00
❑ 160 Marlin Jackson RC	2.00	5.00
❑ 161 Cedric Benson RC	2.50	6.00
❑ 162 Matt Roth RC	2.50	6.00
❑ 163 Dan Cody RC	2.50	6.00
❑ 164 Bryant McFadden RC	2.00	5.00
❑ 165 Chris Henry RC	2.50	6.00
❑ 166 Brandon Jones RC	2.50	6.00
❑ 167 Marion Barber RC	8.00	20.00
❑ 168 Brandon Jacobs RC	3.00	8.00
❑ 169 Jerome Mathis RC	2.50	6.00
❑ 170 Craphonso Thorpe RC	2.00	5.00
❑ 171 Alvin Pearman RC	1.50	4.00
❑ 172 Darren Sproles RC	3.00	8.00
❑ 173 Fred Gibson RC	2.00	5.00
❑ 174 Roydell Williams RC	2.00	5.00
❑ 175 Airese Currie RC	2.00	5.00
❑ 176 Damien Nash RC	2.00	5.00
❑ 177 Dan Orlovsky RC	2.50	6.00
❑ 178 Adrian McPherson RC	2.00	5.00
❑ 179 Larry Brackins RC	1.50	4.00
❑ 180 Aaron Rodgers RC	8.00	20.00
❑ 181 Cedric Houston RC	2.50	6.00
❑ 182 Mike Williams	2.00	5.00
❑ 183 Heath Miller RC	5.00	12.00
❑ 184 Dante Ridgeway RC	1.50	4.00
❑ 185 Craig Bragg RC	1.50	4.00
❑ 186 Deandra Cobb RC	2.00	5.00
❑ 187 Derek Anderson RC	2.50	6.00
❑ 188 Paris Warren RC	2.00	5.00
❑ 189 David Greene RC	2.00	5.00
❑ 190 Lionel Gates RC	1.50	4.00
❑ 191 Anthony Davis RC	2.00	5.00
❑ 192 Noah Herron RC	2.50	6.00
❑ 193 Ryan Fitzpatrick RC	2.50	6.00
❑ 194 J.R. Russell RC	1.50	4.00
❑ 195 Jason White RC	2.50	6.00
❑ 196 Kay-Jay Harris RC	2.00	5.00
❑ 197 Steve Savoy RC	1.50	4.00
❑ 198 T.A. McLendon RC	1.50	4.00
❑ 199 Taylor Stubblefield RC	1.50	4.00
❑ 200 Josh Davis RC	1.50	4.00
❑ 201 Shaun Cody RC	2.00	5.00
❑ 202 Rasheed Marshall RC	2.00	5.00
❑ 203 Chad Owens RC	2.50	6.00
❑ 204 Tab Perry RC	2.50	6.00
❑ 205 James Kilian RC	1.50	4.00
❑ 206 Adam Jones RPM RC	3.00	8.00
❑ 207 Alex Smith QB RPM RC	12.00	30.00
❑ 208 Antrel Rolle RPM RC	4.00	10.00
❑ 209 Andrew Walter RPM RC	3.00	8.00
❑ 210 Braylon Edwards RPM RC	10.00	25.00
❑ 211 Cadillac Williams RPM RC	10.00	25.00
❑ 212 Carlos Rogers RPM RC	4.00	10.00
❑ 213 Charlie Frye RPM RC	4.00	10.00
❑ 214 Ciatrick Fason RPM RC	3.00	8.00
❑ 215 Courtney Roby RPM RC	3.00	8.00
❑ 216 Eric Shelton RPM RC	3.00	8.00
❑ 217 Frank Gore RPM RC	8.00	20.00
❑ 218 J.J. Arrington RPM RC	4.00	10.00
❑ 219 Kyle Orton RPM RC	6.00	15.00
❑ 220 Jason Campbell RPM RC	6.00	15.00
❑ 221 Mark Bradley RPM RC	3.00	8.00
❑ 222 Mark Clayton RPM RC	4.00	10.00
❑ 223 Matt Jones RPM RC	4.00	10.00
❑ 224 Maurice Clarett RPM	3.00	8.00
❑ 225 Reggie Brown RPM RC	3.00	8.00
❑ 226 Ronnie Brown RPM RC	12.00	30.00
❑ 227 Roddy White RPM RC	5.00	12.00
❑ 228 Ryan Moats RPM RC	3.00	8.00
❑ 229 Roscoe Parrish RPM RC	3.00	8.00
❑ 230 Stefan LeFors RPM RC	3.00	8.00
❑ 231 Terrence Murphy RPM RC	2.50	6.00
❑ 232 Troy Williamson RPM RC	4.00	10.00
❑ 233 Vernand Morency RPM RC	3.00	8.00
❑ 234 Vincent Jackson RPM RC	5.00	12.00

2005 Absolute Memorabilia Retail

Card	Low	High
❑ COMPLETE SET (150)	15.00	30.00

❑ *VETERANS: .1X TO .25X BASIC CARDS
❑ *ROOKIES 151-205: .2X TO .5X BASIC CARDS
❑ RETAIL PRINTED ON WHITE STOCK

2006 Absolute Memorabilia

Card	Low	High
❑ 1 Anquan Boldin	1.00	2.50
❑ 2 J.J. Arrington	.75	2.00
❑ 3 Kurt Warner	1.25	3.00
❑ 4 Larry Fitzgerald	1.25	3.00
❑ 5 Marcel Shipp	.75	2.00
❑ 6 Alge Crumpler	1.00	2.50
❑ 7 Michael Jenkins	1.00	2.50
❑ 8 Michael Vick	1.25	3.00
❑ 9 T.J. Duckett	.75	2.00
❑ 10 Warrick Dunn	1.00	2.50
❑ 11 Derrick Mason	1.00	2.50
❑ 12 Jamal Lewis	1.00	2.50
❑ 13 Kyle Boller	1.00	2.50
❑ 14 Mark Clayton	1.00	2.50
❑ 15 Ray Lewis	1.25	3.00
❑ 16 Todd Heap	1.00	2.50
❑ 17 Eric Moulds	1.00	2.50
❑ 18 J.P. Losman	1.00	2.50
❑ 19 Josh Reed	.75	2.00
❑ 20 Lee Evans	1.00	2.50
❑ 21 Willis McGahee	1.25	3.00
❑ 22 DeShaun Foster	1.00	2.50
❑ 23 Jake Delhomme	1.00	2.50
❑ 24 Julius Peppers	1.00	2.50
❑ 25 Keary Colbert	1.00	2.50
❑ 26 Stephen Davis	1.00	2.50
❑ 27 Steve Smith	1.25	3.00
❑ 28 Brian Urlacher	1.25	3.00
❑ 29 Cedric Benson	1.00	2.50
❑ 30 Rex Grossman	1.25	3.00
❑ 31 Thomas Jones	1.00	2.50
❑ 32 Muhsin Muhammad	1.00	2.50
❑ 33 Carson Palmer	1.25	3.00
❑ 34 Chad Johnson	1.00	2.50
❑ 35 Rudi Johnson	1.00	2.50
❑ 36 T.J. Houshmandzadeh	1.00	2.50
❑ 37 Charlie Frye	1.00	2.50
❑ 38 Dennis Northcutt	.75	2.00
❑ 39 Reuben Droughns	1.00	2.50
❑ 40 Braylon Edwards	1.25	3.00
❑ 41 Drew Bledsoe	1.25	3.00
❑ 42 Jason Witten	1.25	3.00
❑ 43 Julius Jones	1.00	2.50
❑ 44 Keyshawn Johnson	1.00	2.50
❑ 45 Roy Williams S	1.00	2.50
❑ 46 Terry Glenn	1.00	2.50
❑ 47 Ashley Lelie	.75	2.00
❑ 48 Jake Plummer	1.00	2.50
❑ 49 Rod Smith	1.00	2.50
❑ 50 Tatum Bell	.75	2.00

❑ 51 Mike Anderson	1.00	2.50
❑ 52 Joey Harrington	.75	2.00
❑ 53 Kevin Jones	1.00	2.50
❑ 54 Mike Williams	1.00	2.50
❑ 55 Roy Williams WR	1.25	3.00
❑ 56 Marcus Pollard	.75	2.00
❑ 57 Aaron Rodgers	1.25	3.00
❑ 58 Brett Favre	2.50	6.00
❑ 59 Donald Driver	1.25	3.00
❑ 60 Javon Walker	1.00	2.50
❑ 61 Samkon Gado	1.25	3.00
❑ 62 Bubba Franks	.75	2.00
❑ 63 Andre Johnson	1.00	2.50
❑ 64 Corey Bradford	.75	2.00
❑ 65 David Carr	.75	2.00
❑ 66 Domanick Davis	1.00	2.50
❑ 67 Jabar Gaffney	.75	2.00
❑ 68 Edgerrin James	1.00	2.50
❑ 69 Dallas Clark	1.00	2.50
❑ 70 Marvin Harrison	1.25	3.00
❑ 71 Peyton Manning	2.00	5.00
❑ 72 Reggie Wayne	1.00	2.50
❑ 73 Brandon Stokley	1.00	2.50
❑ 74 Byron Leftwich	1.00	2.50
❑ 75 Fred Taylor	1.00	2.50
❑ 76 Jimmy Smith	1.00	2.50
❑ 77 Matt Jones	1.00	2.50
❑ 78 Ernest Wilford	.75	2.00
❑ 79 Larry Johnson	1.00	2.50
❑ 80 Tony Gonzalez	1.00	2.50
❑ 81 Trent Green	1.00	2.50
❑ 82 Eddie Kennison	.75	2.00
❑ 83 Dante Hall	1.00	2.50
❑ 84 Chris Chambers	1.00	2.50
❑ 85 Randy McMichael	.75	2.00
❑ 86 Terrell Owens	1.25	3.00
❑ 87 Ronnie Brown	1.25	3.00
❑ 88 Zach Thomas	1.25	3.00
❑ 89 Marty Booker	.75	2.00
❑ 90 Daunte Culpepper	1.25	3.00
❑ 91 Mewelde Moore	.75	2.00
❑ 92 Nate Burleson	1.00	2.50
❑ 93 Troy Williamson	1.00	2.50
❑ 94 Corey Dillon	1.00	2.50
❑ 95 David Givens	1.00	2.50
❑ 96 Deion Branch	1.00	2.50
❑ 97 Tedy Bruschi	1.25	3.00
❑ 98 Tom Brady	2.00	5.00
❑ 99 Aaron Brooks	1.00	2.50
❑ 100 Deuce McAllister	1.00	2.50
❑ 101 Donte Stallworth	1.00	2.50
❑ 102 Joe Horn	1.00	2.50
❑ 103 Eli Manning	1.50	4.00
❑ 104 Jeremy Shockey	1.25	3.00
❑ 105 Plaxico Burress	1.00	2.50
❑ 106 Tiki Barber	1.25	3.00
❑ 107 Chad Pennington	1.00	2.50
❑ 108 Curtis Martin	1.25	3.00
❑ 109 Laveranues Coles	1.00	2.50
❑ 110 Justin McCareins	.75	2.00
❑ 111 Kerry Collins	1.00	2.50
❑ 112 LaMont Jordan	1.00	2.50
❑ 113 Randy Moss	1.25	3.00
❑ 114 Jerry Porter	1.00	2.50
❑ 115 Brian Westbrook	1.00	2.50
❑ 116 Donovan McNabb	1.25	3.00
❑ 117 Reggie Brown	.75	2.00
❑ 118 Ryan Moats	1.00	2.50
❑ 119 Antwaan Randle El	1.00	2.50
❑ 120 Ben Roethlisberger	2.00	5.00
❑ 121 Willie Parker	1.50	4.00
❑ 122 Hines Ward	1.25	3.00
❑ 123 Antonio Gates	1.25	3.00
❑ 124 Drew Brees	1.25	3.00
❑ 125 Keenan McCardell	1.00	2.50
❑ 126 LaDainian Tomlinson	1.50	4.00
❑ 127 Alex Smith QB	1.00	2.50
❑ 128 Brandon Lloyd	1.00	2.50
❑ 129 Frank Gore	1.25	3.00
❑ 130 Kevan Barlow	1.00	2.50
❑ 131 Darrell Jackson	1.00	2.50
❑ 132 Joe Jurevicius	.75	2.00
❑ 133 Matt Hasselbeck	1.00	2.50
❑ 134 Shaun Alexander	1.00	2.50
❑ 135 Isaac Bruce	1.00	2.50
❑ 136 Marc Bulger	1.00	2.50
❑ 137 Steven Jackson	1.25	3.00
❑ 138 Torry Holt	1.00	2.50
❑ 139 Cadillac Williams	1.25	3.00
❑ 140 Chris Simms	1.00	2.50
❑ 141 Joey Galloway	1.00	2.50
❑ 142 Michael Clayton	1.00	2.50
❑ 143 Chris Brown	1.00	2.50
❑ 144 Drew Bennett	1.00	2.50
❑ 145 Steve McNair	1.00	2.50
❑ 146 Tyrone Calico	.75	2.00
❑ 147 Clinton Portis	1.25	3.00
❑ 148 LaVar Arrington	1.25	3.00
❑ 149 Mark Brunell	1.00	2.50
❑ 150 Santana Moss	1.00	2.50
❑ 151 Greg Jennings RC	4.00	10.00
❑ 152 Joseph Addai RC	3.00	8.00
❑ 153 Erik Meyer RC	2.00	5.00
❑ 154 Drew Olson RC	1.50	4.00
❑ 155 Darrell Hackney RC	2.00	5.00
❑ 156 Paul Pinegar RC	1.50	4.00
❑ 157 Brandon Kirsch RC	2.00	5.00
❑ 158 Andre Hall RC	2.00	5.00
❑ 159 Taurean Henderson RC	2.50	6.00
❑ 160 Derrick Ross RC	2.00	5.00
❑ 161 Mike Bell RC	2.50	6.00
❑ 162 Wendell Mathis RC	2.00	5.00
❑ 163 Gerald Riggs RC	2.00	5.00
❑ 164 John David Washington RC	2.00	5.00
❑ 165 Devin Aromashodu RC	2.50	6.00
❑ 166 Ben Obomanu RC	2.00	5.00
❑ 167 David Anderson RC	2.00	5.00
❑ 168 Marques Colston RC	6.00	15.00
❑ 169 Kevin McMahan RC	2.00	5.00
❑ 170 Miles Austin RC	6.00	15.00
❑ 171 Martin Nance RC	2.00	5.00
❑ 172 Greg Lee RC	1.50	4.00
❑ 173 Hank Baskett RC	2.50	6.00
❑ 174 Anthony Mix RC	2.00	5.00
❑ 175 D'Brickashaw Ferguson RC	2.50	6.00
❑ 176 Kamerion Wimbley RC	2.50	6.00
❑ 177 Tamba Hali RC	2.50	6.00
❑ 178 Mathias Kiwanuka RC	3.00	8.00
❑ 179 Brodrick Bunkley RC	2.00	5.00
❑ 180 John McCargo RC	2.00	5.00
❑ 181 Claude Wroten RC	1.50	4.00
❑ 182 Gabe Watson RC	1.50	4.00
❑ 183 D'Qwell Jackson RC	2.00	5.00
❑ 184 Abdul Hodge RC	2.00	5.00
❑ 185 Ernie Sims RC	2.00	5.00
❑ 186 Chad Greenway RC	2.50	6.00
❑ 187 Bobby Carpenter RC	2.00	5.00
❑ 188 Manny Lawson RC	2.50	6.00
❑ 189 DeMeco Ryans RC	3.00	8.00
❑ 190 Rocky McIntosh RC	2.50	6.00
❑ 191 Thomas Howard RC	2.00	5.00
❑ 192 Jon Alston RC	1.50	4.00
❑ 193 A.J. Nicholson RC	1.50	4.00
❑ 194 Tye Hill RC	2.00	5.00
❑ 195 Antonio Cromartie RC	2.50	6.00
❑ 196 Johnathan Joseph RC	2.00	5.00
❑ 197 Kelly Jennings RC	2.50	6.00
❑ 198 Jimmy Williams RC	2.50	6.00
❑ 199 Ashton Youboty RC	2.00	5.00
❑ 200 Alan Zemaitis RC	2.50	6.00
❑ 201 Anwar Phillips RC	2.00	5.00
❑ 202 Jason Allen RC	2.00	5.00
❑ 203 Cedric Griffin RC	2.00	5.00
❑ 204 Ko Simpson RC	2.00	5.00
❑ 205 Pat Watkins RC	2.50	6.00
❑ 206 Donte Whitner RC	2.50	6.00
❑ 207 Bernard Pollard RC	2.00	5.00
❑ 208 Darnell Bing RC	2.00	5.00
❑ 209 De'Arrius Howard RC	2.50	6.00
❑ 210 Ethan Kilmer RC	2.50	6.00
❑ 211 Bennie Brazell RC	2.00	5.00
❑ 212 Haloti Ngata RC	2.50	6.00
❑ 213 Jeremy Bloom RC	2.00	5.00
❑ 214 Jay Cutler RC	6.00	15.00
❑ 215 Marcus Vick RC	1.50	4.00
❑ 216 Roman Harper RC	2.00	5.00
❑ 217 Anthony Smith RC	2.50	6.00
❑ 218 Daniel Bullocks RC	2.50	6.00
❑ 219 Eric Smith RC	2.00	5.00
❑ 220 Dusty Dvoracek RC	2.50	6.00
❑ 221 Brodie Croyle AU RC	6.00	15.00
❑ 222 Ingle Martin AU RC	5.00	12.00
❑ 223 Reggie McNeal AU RC	5.00	12.00
❑ 224 Bruce Gradkowski AU RC	6.00	15.00
❑ 225 D.J. Shockley AU RC	5.00	12.00
❑ 226 P.J. Daniels AU RC	4.00	10.00
❑ 227 Marques Hagans AU RC	5.00	12.00
❑ 228 Jerome Harrison RC	5.00	12.00
❑ 229 Wali Lundy AU RC	6.00	15.00
❑ 230 Cedric Humes AU RC	5.00	12.00
❑ 231 Quinton Ganther AU RC	4.00	10.00
❑ 232 Garrett Mills AU RC	5.00	12.00
❑ 233 Anthony Fasano AU RC	6.00	15.00
❑ 234 Tony Scheffler AU RC	8.00	20.00
❑ 235 Leonard Pope AU RC	6.00	15.00
❑ 236 David Thomas AU RC	6.00	15.00
❑ 237 Dominique Byrd AU RC	5.00	12.00
❑ 238 Jai Lewis AU/299 RC	5.00	12.00
❑ 239 Devin Hester AU RC	30.00	50.00
❑ 240 Willie Reid AU RC	5.00	12.00
❑ 241 Brad Smith AU RC	6.00	15.00
❑ 242 Cory Rodgers AU RC	6.00	15.00
❑ 243 Skyler Green AU RC	4.00	10.00
❑ 244 Domenik Hixon AU RC	6.00	15.00
❑ 245 Mike Hass AU RC	6.00	15.00
❑ 246 Jonathan Orr AU/299 RC	5.00	12.00
❑ 247 Delanie Walker AU/299 RC	5.00	12.00
❑ 248 Adam Jennings AU/299 RC	5.00	12.00
❑ 249 Jeff Webb AU/299 RC	5.00	12.00
❑ 250 Todd Watkins AU RC	4.00	10.00
❑ 251 Chad Jackson RPM RC	3.00	8.00
❑ 252 Laurence Maroney RPM RC	5.00	12.00
❑ 253 Tarvaris Jackson RPM RC	4.00	10.00
❑ 254 Michael Huff RPM RC	4.00	10.00
❑ 255 Mario Williams RPM RC	5.00	12.00
❑ 256 Marcedes Lewis RPM RC	4.00	10.00
❑ 257 Maurice Drew RPM RC	8.00	20.00
❑ 258 Vince Young RPM RC	10.00	25.00
❑ 259 LenDale White RPM RC	5.00	12.00
❑ 260 Reggie Bush RPM RC	10.00	25.00
❑ 261 Matt Leinart RPM RC	6.00	15.00
❑ 262 Michael Robinson RPM RC	3.00	8.00
❑ 263 Vernon Davis RPM RC	4.00	10.00
❑ 264 Brandon Williams RPM RC	3.00	8.00
❑ 265 Derek Hagan RPM RC	3.00	8.00
❑ 266 Jason Avant RPM RC	4.00	10.00
❑ 267 Brandon Marshall RPM RC	4.00	10.00
❑ 268 Omar Jacobs RPM RC	2.50	6.00
❑ 269 Santonio Holmes RPM RC	10.00	25.00
❑ 270 Jerious Norwood RPM RC	4.00	10.00
❑ 271 Demetrius Williams RPM RC	3.00	8.00
❑ 272 Sinorice Moss RPM RC	4.00	10.00
❑ 273 Leon Washington RPM RC	5.00	12.00
❑ 274 Kellen Clemens RPM RC	4.00	10.00
❑ 275 A.J. Hawk RPM RC	6.00	15.00
❑ 276 Maurice Stovall RPM RC	3.00	8.00
❑ 277 DeAngelo Williams RPM RC	8.00	20.00
❑ 278 Charlie Whitehurst RPM RC	4.00	10.00
❑ 279 Travis Wilson RPM RC	2.50	6.00
❑ 280 Joe Klopfenstein RPM RC	3.00	8.00
❑ 281 Brian Calhoun RPM RC	3.00	8.00

2007 Absolute Memorabilia

❑ 1 Tony Romo	2.00	5.00
❑ 2 Julius Jones	1.00	2.50
❑ 3 Terry Glenn	1.00	2.50
❑ 4 Terrell Owens	1.25	3.00
❑ 5 Marion Barber	1.25	3.00
❑ 6 Reuben Droughns	1.00	2.50
❑ 7 Eli Manning	1.25	3.00
❑ 8 Plaxico Burress	1.00	2.50
❑ 9 Jeremy Shockey	1.00	2.50
❑ 10 Brandon Jacobs	1.00	2.50
❑ 11 Donovan McNabb	1.25	3.00
❑ 12 Brian Westbrook	1.00	2.50
❑ 13 Reggie Brown	.75	2.00
❑ 14 Hank Baskett	1.00	2.50
❑ 15 Jason Campbell	1.00	2.50
❑ 16 Clinton Portis	1.00	2.50
❑ 17 Santana Moss	1.00	2.50
❑ 18 Ladell Betts	.75	2.00
❑ 19 Brandon Lloyd	1.00	2.50

- ❑ 20 Chris Cooley 1.00 2.50
- ❑ 21 Rex Grossman 1.00 2.50
- ❑ 22 Cedric Benson 1.00 2.50
- ❑ 23 Muhsin Muhammad 1.00 2.50
- ❑ 24 Bernard Berrian .75 2.00
- ❑ 25 Devin Hester 1.25 3.00
- ❑ 26 Brian Urlacher 1.25 3.00
- ❑ 27 Jon Kitna .75 2.00
- ❑ 28 Kevin Jones .75 2.00
- ❑ 29 Roy Williams 1.00 2.50
- ❑ 30 Mike Furrey 1.00 2.50
- ❑ 31 Ernie Sims .75 2.00
- ❑ 32 Tatum Bell .75 2.00
- ❑ 33 Brett Favre 2.50 6.00
- ❑ 34 Vernand Morency 1.00 2.50
- ❑ 35 Donald Driver 1.25 3.00
- ❑ 36 Greg Jennings 1.00 2.50
- ❑ 37 AJ Hawk 1.25 3.00
- ❑ 38 Tarvaris Jackson 1.00 2.50
- ❑ 39 Chester Taylor .75 2.00
- ❑ 40 Troy Williamson .75 2.00
- ❑ 41 Mewelde Moore .75 2.00
- ❑ 42 Michael Vick 1.25 3.00
- ❑ 43 Warrick Dunn 1.00 2.50
- ❑ 44 Joe Horn 1.00 2.50
- ❑ 45 Alge Crumpler 1.00 2.50
- ❑ 46 Jerious Norwood 1.00 2.50
- ❑ 47 Jake Delhomme 1.00 2.50
- ❑ 48 DeShaun Foster 1.00 2.50
- ❑ 49 Steve Smith 1.00 2.50
- ❑ 50 DeAngelo Williams 1.25 3.00
- ❑ 51 Drew Brees 1.25 3.00
- ❑ 52 Deuce McAllister 1.00 2.50
- ❑ 53 Marques Colston 1.25 3.00
- ❑ 54 Devery Henderson .75 2.00
- ❑ 55 Reggie Bush 1.50 4.00
- ❑ 56 Jeff Garcia 1.00 2.50
- ❑ 57 Cadillac Williams 1.00 2.50
- ❑ 58 Joey Galloway 1.00 2.50
- ❑ 59 Michael Clayton 1.00 2.50
- ❑ 60 Matt Leinart 1.25 3.00
- ❑ 61 Edgerrin James 1.00 2.50
- ❑ 62 Anquan Boldin 1.00 2.50
- ❑ 63 Larry Fitzgerald 1.25 3.00
- ❑ 64 Marc Bulger 1.00 2.50
- ❑ 65 Steven Jackson 1.25 3.00
- ❑ 66 Torry Holt 1.00 2.50
- ❑ 67 Isaac Bruce 1.00 2.50
- ❑ 68 Randy McMichael .75 2.00
- ❑ 69 Drew Bennett .75 2.00
- ❑ 70 Alex Smith 1.25 3.00
- ❑ 71 Frank Gore 1.25 3.00
- ❑ 72 Darrell Jackson 1.00 2.50
- ❑ 73 Ashley Lelie 1.00 2.50
- ❑ 74 Vernon Davis 1.00 2.50
- ❑ 75 Matt Hasselbeck 1.00 2.50
- ❑ 76 Shaun Alexander 1.00 2.50
- ❑ 77 Deion Branch 1.00 2.50
- ❑ 78 J.P. Losman .75 2.00
- ❑ 79 Lee Evans 1.00 2.50
- ❑ 80 Josh Reed .75 2.00
- ❑ 81 Daunte Culpepper 1.00 2.50
- ❑ 82 Ronnie Brown 1.00 2.50
- ❑ 83 Chris Chambers 1.00 2.50
- ❑ 84 Marty Booker .75 2.00
- ❑ 85 Zach Thomas 1.00 2.50
- ❑ 86 Tom Brady 2.50 6.00
- ❑ 87 Laurence Maroney 1.25 3.00
- ❑ 88 Randy Moss 1.25 3.00
- ❑ 89 Chad Jackson .75 2.00
- ❑ 90 Ben Watson .75 2.00
- ❑ 91 Donte' Stallworth 1.00 2.50
- ❑ 92 Chad Pennington 1.00 2.50
- ❑ 93 Thomas Jones 1.00 2.50
- ❑ 94 Laveranues Coles 1.00 2.50
- ❑ 95 Jerricho Cotchery .75 2.00
- ❑ 96 Leon Washington 1.00 2.50
- ❑ 97 Steve McNair 1.00 2.50
- ❑ 98 Willis McGahee 1.00 2.50
- ❑ 99 Derrick Mason .75 2.00
- ❑ 100 Demetrius Williams .75 2.00
- ❑ 101 Mark Clayton 1.00 2.50
- ❑ 102 Carson Palmer 1.25 3.00
- ❑ 103 Rudi Johnson 1.00 2.50
- ❑ 104 Chad Johnson 1.00 2.50
- ❑ 105 T.J. Houshmandzadeh 1.00 2.50
- ❑ 106 Charlie Frye 1.00 2.50
- ❑ 107 Braylon Edwards 1.00 2.50
- ❑ 108 Travis Wilson .75 2.00
- ❑ 109 Kellen Winslow 1.00 2.50
- ❑ 110 Jamal Lewis 1.00 2.50
- ❑ 111 Ben Roethlisberger 2.00 5.00
- ❑ 112 Willie Parker 1.00 2.50
- ❑ 113 Hines Ward 1.25 3.00
- ❑ 114 Santonio Holmes 1.00 2.50
- ❑ 115 Ahman Green 1.00 2.50
- ❑ 116 Andre Johnson 1.00 2.50
- ❑ 117 Matt Schaub 1.00 2.50
- ❑ 118 DeMeco Ryans 1.00 2.50
- ❑ 119 Owen Daniels .75 2.00
- ❑ 120 Peyton Manning 2.00 5.00
- ❑ 121 Joseph Addai 1.25 3.00
- ❑ 122 Marvin Harrison 1.25 3.00
- ❑ 123 Reggie Wayne 1.00 2.50
- ❑ 124 Dallas Clark .75 2.00
- ❑ 125 Byron Leftwich 1.00 2.50
- ❑ 126 Fred Taylor 1.00 2.50
- ❑ 127 Matt Jones 1.00 2.50
- ❑ 128 Reggie Williams 1.00 2.50
- ❑ 129 Marcedes Lewis .75 2.00
- ❑ 130 Maurice Jones-Drew 1.25 3.00
- ❑ 131 Vince Young 1.25 3.00
- ❑ 132 LenDale White 1.00 2.50
- ❑ 133 Brandon Jones .75 2.00
- ❑ 134 Jay Cutler 1.25 3.00
- ❑ 135 Travis Henry 1.00 2.50
- ❑ 136 Javon Walker 1.00 2.50
- ❑ 137 Rod Smith 1.00 2.50
- ❑ 138 Mike Bell 1.00 2.50
- ❑ 139 Brandon Marshall 1.00 2.50
- ❑ 140 Larry Johnson 1.00 2.50
- ❑ 141 Eddie Kennison .75 2.00
- ❑ 142 Tony Gonzalez 1.00 2.50
- ❑ 143 Brodie Croyle 1.00 2.50
- ❑ 144 LaMont Jordan 1.00 2.50
- ❑ 145 Ronald Curry 1.00 2.50
- ❑ 146 Philip Rivers 1.25 3.00
- ❑ 147 LaDainian Tomlinson 1.50 4.00
- ❑ 148 Vincent Jackson .75 2.00
- ❑ 149 Michael Turner 1.25 3.00
- ❑ 150 Antonio Gates 1.00 2.50
- ❑ 151 A.J. Davis RC 3.00 8.00
- ❑ 152 Aaron Rouse RC 5.00 12.00
- ❑ 153 Ahmad Bradshaw RC 6.00 15.00
- ❑ 154 Alonzo Coleman RC 4.00 10.00
- ❑ 155 Anthony Spencer RC 5.00 12.00
- ❑ 156 Brandon Siler RC 4.00 10.00
- ❑ 157 Buster Davis RC 4.00 10.00
- ❑ 158 Chris Houston RC 4.00 10.00
- ❑ 159 Dallas Baker RC 4.00 10.00
- ❑ 160 Dan Bazuin RC 4.00 10.00
- ❑ 161 Danny Ware RC 5.00 12.00
- ❑ 162 David Ball RC 3.00 8.00
- ❑ 163 David Irons RC 3.00 8.00
- ❑ 164 D'Juan Woods RC 4.00 10.00
- ❑ 165 Earl Everett RC 4.00 10.00
- ❑ 166 Eric Frampton RC 4.00 10.00
- ❑ 167 Eric Weddle RC 4.00 10.00
- ❑ 168 Eric Wright RC 5.00 12.00
- ❑ 169 Fred Bennett RC 3.00 8.00
- ❑ 170 Gary Russell RC 4.00 10.00
- ❑ 171 H.B. Blades RC 4.00 10.00
- ❑ 172 Jarrett Hicks RC 4.00 10.00
- ❑ 173 Jarvis Moss RC 5.00 12.00
- ❑ 174 Jason Snelling RC 4.00 10.00
- ❑ 175 Jerard Rabb RC 4.00 10.00
- ❑ 176 Jemalle Cornelius RC 4.00 10.00
- ❑ 177 Tyler Thigpen RC 5.00 12.00
- ❑ 178 Jon Beason RC 5.00 12.00
- ❑ 179 Jonathan Wade RC 4.00 10.00
- ❑ 180 Jordan Kent RC 4.00 10.00
- ❑ 181 Josh Gattis RC 3.00 8.00
- ❑ 182 Kenneth Darby RC 5.00 12.00
- ❑ 183 DeMarcus Tank Tyler RC 4.00 10.00
- ❑ 184 Levi Brown RC 5.00 12.00
- ❑ 185 Marcus McCauley RC 4.00 10.00
- ❑ 186 Tim Shaw RC 4.00 10.00
- ❑ 187 Michael Okwo RC 4.00 10.00
- ❑ 188 Mike Walker RC 5.00 12.00
- ❑ 189 Nate Ilaoa RC 5.00 12.00
- ❑ 190 Reggie Ball RC 4.00 10.00
- ❑ 191 Rhema McKnight RC 4.00 10.00
- ❑ 192 Zak DeOssie RC 4.00 10.00
- ❑ 193 Rufus Alexander RC 5.00 12.00
- ❑ 194 Ryan McBean RC 5.00 12.00
- ❑ 195 Ryne Robinson RC 4.00 10.00
- ❑ 196 Selvin Young RC 5.00 12.00
- ❑ 197 Steve Breaston RC 5.00 12.00
- ❑ 198 Stewart Bradley RC 5.00 12.00
- ❑ 199 Thomas Clayton RC 4.00 10.00
- ❑ 200 Tim Crowder RC 5.00 12.00
- ❑ 201 Aaron Ross AU RC 6.00 15.00
- ❑ 202 Adam Carriker AU RC 5.00 12.00
- ❑ 203 Alan Branch AU RC EXCH 5.00 12.00
- ❑ 204 Amobi Okoye AU RC 6.00 15.00
- ❑ 205 Aundrae Allison AU RC 5.00 12.00
- ❑ 206 Ben Patrick AU RC 5.00 12.00
- ❑ 207 Brandon Meriweather AU RC 6.00 15.00
- ❑ 208 Chansi Stuckey AU RC 6.00 15.00
- ❑ 209 Charles Johnson AU RC EXCH 4.00 10.00
- ❑ 210 Chris Davis AU RC 5.00 12.00
- ❑ 211 Chris Leak AU RC 5.00 12.00
- ❑ 212 Courtney Taylor AU RC 5.00 12.00
- ❑ 213 Craig Buster Davis AU RC EXCH 6.00 15.00
- ❑ 214 Darius Walker AU RC 5.00 12.00
- ❑ 215 Darrelle Revis AU RC 8.00 20.00
- ❑ 216 David Clowney AU RC 6.00 15.00
- ❑ 217 David Harris AU RC 5.00 12.00
- ❑ 218 Daymeion Hughes AU RC 5.00 12.00
- ❑ 219 DeShawn Wynn AU RC 6.00 15.00
- ❑ 220 Dwayne Wright AU RC 5.00 12.00
- ❑ 221 Ikaika Alama-Francis AU RC 6.00 15.00
- ❑ 222 Isaiah Stanback AU RC 6.00 15.00
- ❑ 223 Jacoby Jones AU RC 6.00 15.00
- ❑ 224 Jamaal Anderson AU RC 5.00 12.00
- ❑ 225 James Jones AU RC 6.00 15.00
- ❑ 226 Jared Zabransky AU RC 6.00 15.00
- ❑ 227 Jeff Rowe AU RC 5.00 12.00
- ❑ 228 Joel Filani AU RC 5.00 12.00
- ❑ 229 Jordan Palmer AU RC 6.00 15.00
- ❑ 230 Josh Wilson AU RC 5.00 12.00
- ❑ 231 Kenny Scott AU RC 4.00 10.00
- ❑ 232 Kolby Smith AU RC 6.00 15.00
- ❑ 233 LaMarr Woodley AU RC 15.00 25.00
- ❑ 234 LaRon Landry AU RC 8.00 20.00
- ❑ 235 Laurent Robinson AU RC 6.00 15.00
- ❑ 236 Lawrence Timmons AU RC 6.00 15.00
- ❑ 237 Leon Hall AU RC 6.00 15.00
- ❑ 238 Matt Spaeth AU RC 6.00 15.00
- ❑ 239 Michael Griffin AU RC 6.00 15.00
- ❑ 240 Paul Posluszny AU RC 8.00 20.00
- ❑ 241 Quentin Moses AU RC 5.00 12.00
- ❑ 242 Ray McDonald AU RC 5.00 12.00
- ❑ 243 Reggie Nelson AU RC 5.00 12.00
- ❑ 244 Ronnie McGill AU RC 5.00 12.00
- ❑ 245 Sabby Piscitelli AU RC 6.00 15.00
- ❑ 246 Scott Chandler AU RC 5.00 12.00
- ❑ 247 Toby Korrodi AU RC 5.00 12.00
- ❑ 248 Tyler Palko AU RC 5.00 12.00
- ❑ 249 Victor Abiamiri AU RC 6.00 15.00
- ❑ 250 Zach Miller AU RC 6.00 15.00
- ❑ 251 JaMarcus Russell RPM RC 5.00 12.00
- ❑ 252 Calvin Johnson RPM RC 10.00 25.00
- ❑ 253 Joe Thomas RPM RC 4.00 10.00
- ❑ 254 Gaines Adams RPM RC 4.00 10.00
- ❑ 255 Greg Olsen RPM RC 5.00 12.00
- ❑ 256 Adrian Peterson RPM RC 25.00 60.00
- ❑ 257 Ted Ginn RPM RC 6.00 15.00
- ❑ 258 Patrick Willis RPM RC 6.00 15.00
- ❑ 259 Marshawn Lynch RPM RC 6.00 15.00
- ❑ 260 Brady Quinn RPM RC 8.00 20.00
- ❑ 261 Dwayne Bowe RPM RC 6.00 15.00
- ❑ 262 Robert Meachem RPM RC 4.00 10.00
- ❑ 263 Anthony Gonzalez RPM RC 5.00 12.00
- ❑ 264 Kevin Kolb RPM RC 6.00 15.00
- ❑ 265 John Beck RPM RC 4.00 10.00
- ❑ 266 Drew Stanton RPM RC 3.00 8.00
- ❑ 267 Sidney Rice RPM RC 8.00 20.00
- ❑ 268 Dwayne Jarrett RPM RC 4.00 10.00
- ❑ 269 Kenny Irons RPM RC 4.00 10.00
- ❑ 270 Chris Henry RPM RC 3.00 8.00
- ❑ 271 Steve Smith RPM RC 6.00 15.00
- ❑ 272 Brian Leonard RPM RC 3.00 8.00
- ❑ 273 Brandon Jackson RPM RC 4.00 10.00
- ❑ 274 Lorenzo Booker RPM RC 4.00 10.00
- ❑ 275 Yamon Figurs RPM RC 2.50 6.00
- ❑ 276 Jason Hill RPM RC 4.00 10.00
- ❑ 277 Paul Williams RPM RC 3.00 8.00
- ❑ 278 Tony Hunt RPM RC 4.00 10.00
- ❑ 279 Trent Edwards RPM RC 6.00 15.00
- ❑ 280 Garrett Wolfe RPM RC 4.00 10.00
- ❑ 281 Johnnie Lee Higgins RPM RC 4.00 10.00
- ❑ 282 Michael Bush RPM RC 4.00 10.00
- ❑ 283 Antonio Pittman RPM RC 4.00 10.00
- ❑ 284 Troy Smith RPM RC 5.00 12.00

2008 Absolute Memorabilia

Card	Low	High
❑ 1 Anquan Boldin	.50	1.25
❑ 2 Edgerrin James	.50	1.25
❑ 3 Kurt Warner	.60	1.50
❑ 4 Larry Fitzgerald	.60	1.50
❑ 5 Matt Leinart	.60	1.50
❑ 6 Jerious Norwood	.50	1.25
❑ 7 Roddy White	.50	1.25
❑ 8 Michael Turner	.60	1.50
❑ 9 Joey Harrington	.50	1.25
❑ 10 Steve McNair	.50	1.25
❑ 11 Willis McGahee	.50	1.25
❑ 12 Derrick Mason	.40	1.00
❑ 13 Yamon Figurs	.40	1.00
❑ 14 Ray Lewis	.60	1.50
❑ 15 Trent Edwards	.60	1.50
❑ 16 Marshawn Lynch	.60	1.50
❑ 17 Fred Jackson RC	.75	2.00
❑ 18 Lee Evans	.50	1.25
❑ 19 Josh Reed	.40	1.00
❑ 20 Jake Delhomme	.50	1.25
❑ 21 DeAngelo Williams	.50	1.25
❑ 22 Steve Smith	.50	1.25
❑ 23 Jon Beason	.40	1.00
❑ 24 Rex Grossman	.50	1.25
❑ 25 Adrian Peterson	.40	1.00
❑ 26 Greg Olsen	.50	1.25
❑ 27 Devin Hester	.60	1.50
❑ 28 Brian Urlacher	.60	1.50
❑ 29 Carson Palmer	.60	1.50
❑ 30 Chad Johnson	.50	1.25
❑ 31 Rudi Johnson	.50	1.25
❑ 32 T.J. Houshmandzadeh	.50	1.25
❑ 33 Kenny Watson	.40	1.00
❑ 34 Derek Anderson	.50	1.25
❑ 35 Jamal Lewis	.50	1.25
❑ 36 Braylon Edwards	.50	1.25
❑ 37 Kellen Winslow	.50	1.25
❑ 38 Josh Cribbs	.60	1.50
❑ 39 Tony Romo	1.00	2.50
❑ 40 Terrell Owens	.60	1.50
❑ 41 Jason Witten	.60	1.50
❑ 42 Marion Barber	.60	1.50
❑ 43 DeMarcus Ware	.50	1.25
❑ 44 Jay Cutler	.60	1.50
❑ 45 Brandon Marshall	.50	1.25
❑ 46 Selvin Young	.40	1.00
❑ 47 Brandon Stokley	.50	1.25
❑ 48 Tony Scheffler	.40	1.00
❑ 49 Jon Kitna	.50	1.25
❑ 50 Tatum Bell	.40	1.00
❑ 51 Roy Williams WR	.50	1.25
❑ 52 Calvin Johnson	.60	1.50
❑ 53 Shaun McDonald	.40	1.00
❑ 54 Aaron Rodgers	.60	1.50
❑ 55 Greg Jennings	.50	1.25
❑ 56 Donald Driver	.50	1.25
❑ 57 James Jones	.40	1.00
❑ 58 Ryan Grant	.60	1.50
❑ 59 Matt Schaub	.50	1.25
❑ 60 Ahman Green	.50	1.25
❑ 61 Andre Johnson	.50	1.25
❑ 62 Kevin Walter	.50	1.25
❑ 63 Owen Daniels	.40	1.00
❑ 64 Peyton Manning	1.00	2.50
❑ 65 Reggie Wayne	.50	1.25
❑ 66 Marvin Harrison	.60	1.50
❑ 67 Joseph Addai	.60	1.50
❑ 68 Anthony Gonzalez	.50	1.25
❑ 69 David Garrard	.50	1.25
❑ 70 Fred Taylor	.50	1.25
❑ 71 Maurice Jones-Drew	.50	1.25
❑ 72 Jerry Porter	.50	1.25
❑ 73 Reggie Williams	.50	1.25
❑ 74 Brodie Croyle	.50	1.25
❑ 75 Tony Gonzalez	.50	1.25
❑ 76 Larry Johnson	.50	1.25
❑ 77 Kolby Smith	.40	1.00
❑ 78 Dwayne Bowe	.50	1.25
❑ 79 John Beck	.40	1.00
❑ 80 Ted Ginn	.50	1.25
❑ 81 Ernest Wilford	.40	1.00
❑ 82 Ronnie Brown	.50	1.25
❑ 83 Tarvaris Jackson	.50	1.25
❑ 84 Adrian Peterson	1.25	3.00
❑ 85 Chester Taylor	.40	1.00
❑ 86 Bernard Berrian	.50	1.25
❑ 87 Tom Brady	1.00	2.50
❑ 88 Laurence Maroney	.50	1.25
❑ 89 Randy Moss	.60	1.50
❑ 90 Wes Welker	.60	1.50
❑ 91 Drew Brees	.60	1.50
❑ 92 Deuce McAllister	.50	1.25
❑ 93 Marques Colston	.50	1.25
❑ 94 Reggie Bush	.60	1.50
❑ 95 Devery Henderson	.40	1.00
❑ 96 Eli Manning	.60	1.50
❑ 97 Brandon Jacobs	.50	1.25
❑ 98 Derrick Ward	.50	1.25
❑ 99 Plaxico Burress	.50	1.25
❑ 100 Steve Smith	.50	1.25
❑ 101 Kellen Clemens	.50	1.25
❑ 102 Thomas Jones	.50	1.25
❑ 103 Laveranues Coles	.50	1.25
❑ 104 Jerricho Cotchery	.40	1.00
❑ 105 JaMarcus Russell	.60	1.50
❑ 106 Justin Fargas	.40	1.00
❑ 107 Michael Bush	.50	1.25
❑ 108 Javon Walker	.50	1.25
❑ 109 Zach Miller	.50	1.25
❑ 110 Donovan McNabb	.60	1.50
❑ 111 Brian Westbrook	.50	1.25
❑ 112 Kevin Curtis	.40	1.00
❑ 113 Reggie Brown	.40	1.00
❑ 114 Ben Roethlisberger	1.00	2.50
❑ 115 Willie Parker	.50	1.25
❑ 116 Santonio Holmes	.50	1.25
❑ 117 Hines Ward	.50	1.25
❑ 118 Philip Rivers	.60	1.50
❑ 119 LaDainian Tomlinson	.75	2.00
❑ 120 Antonio Gates	.50	1.25
❑ 121 Vincent Jackson	.40	1.00
❑ 122 Alex Smith	.50	1.25
❑ 123 Frank Gore	.50	1.25
❑ 124 Vernon Davis	.40	1.00
❑ 125 Isaac Bruce	.50	1.25
❑ 126 Arnaz Battle	.40	1.00
❑ 127 Matt Hasselbeck	.50	1.25
❑ 128 Lofa Tatupu	.50	1.25
❑ 129 Deion Branch	.50	1.25
❑ 130 Nate Burleson	.40	1.00
❑ 131 Julius Jones	.50	1.25
❑ 132 Marc Bulger	.50	1.25
❑ 133 Steven Jackson	.60	1.50
❑ 134 Torry Holt	.50	1.25
❑ 135 Randy McMichael	.40	1.00
❑ 136 Jeff Garcia	.50	1.25
❑ 137 Cadillac Williams	.50	1.25
❑ 138 Warrick Dunn	.50	1.25
❑ 139 Joey Galloway	.50	1.25
❑ 140 Michael Clayton	.50	1.25
❑ 141 Vince Young	.50	1.25
❑ 142 LenDale White	.50	1.25
❑ 143 Alge Crumpler	.50	1.25
❑ 144 Justin Gage	.40	1.00
❑ 145 Roydell Williams	.40	1.00
❑ 146 Jason Campbell	.50	1.25
❑ 147 Clinton Portis	.50	1.25
❑ 148 Chris Cooley	.50	1.25
❑ 149 Santana Moss	.40	1.00
❑ 150 Ladell Betts	.40	1.00
❑ 151 Adrian Arrington AU RC	5.00	12.00
❑ 152 Alex Brink RC	2.50	6.00
❑ 153 Ali Highsmith RC	1.50	4.00
❑ 154 Allen Patrick AU RC	5.00	12.00
❑ 155 Andre Woodson AU RC	6.00	15.00
❑ 156 Anthony Alridge RC	2.00	5.00
❑ 157 Antoine Cason AU RC	6.00	15.00
❑ 158 Aqib Talib AU RC	6.00	15.00
❑ 159 Arman Shields RC	2.00	5.00
❑ 160 Brad Cottam AU RC	6.00	15.00
❑ 161 Brandon Flowers AU RC	6.00	15.00
❑ 162 Calais Campbell RC	2.00	5.00
❑ 163 Caleb Campbell RC	2.50	6.00
❑ 164 Chauncey Washington AU RC	5.00	12.00
❑ 165 Chevis Jackson RC	2.00	5.00
❑ 166 Chris Long AU RC	6.00	15.00
❑ 167 Colt Brennan AU RC	20.00	50.00
❑ 168 Cory Boyd AU RC	5.00	12.00
❑ 169 Craig Steltz RC	2.00	5.00
❑ 170 Curtis Lofton AU RC	6.00	15.00
❑ 171 Dan Connor AU RC	6.00	15.00
❑ 172 Dantrell Savage RC	2.50	6.00
❑ 173 Darius Reynaud RC	2.00	5.00
❑ 174 Darrell Strong RC	2.00	5.00
❑ 175 Davone Bess RC	3.00	8.00
❑ 176 Dennis Dixon AU RC	6.00	15.00
❑ 177 Derrick Harvey AU RC	5.00	12.00
❑ 178 DJ Hall RC	2.00	5.00
❑ 179 D.Rodgers-Cromartie AU RC	6.00	15.00
❑ 180 Erik Ainge AU RC	6.00	15.00
❑ 181 Erin Henderson RC	2.00	5.00
❑ 182 Ernie Wheelwright RC	2.00	5.00
❑ 183 Fred Davis AU RC	6.00	15.00
❑ 184 Joe Jon Finley RC	2.00	5.00
❑ 185 Jacob Hester AU RC	6.00	15.00
❑ 186 Jacob Tamme AU RC	6.00	15.00
❑ 187 Jalen Parmele RC	2.00	5.00
❑ 188 Jamar Adams RC	2.00	5.00
❑ 189 Jason Rivers RC	2.50	6.00
❑ 190 Jaymar Johnson RC	2.00	5.00
❑ 191 Jed Collins RC	2.00	5.00
❑ 192 Jermichael Finley AU RC	10.00	20.00
❑ 193 Jerod Mayo AU RC	8.00	20.00
❑ 194 John Carlson AU RC	6.00	15.00
❑ 195 Jonathan Hefney RC	2.00	5.00
❑ 196 Jordon Dizon AU RC	6.00	15.00
❑ 197 Josh Johnson AU RC	6.00	15.00
❑ 198 Josh Morgan AU RC	6.00	15.00
❑ 199 Justin Forsett AU RC	6.00	15.00
❑ 200 Justin Harper RC	2.00	5.00
❑ 201 Kalvin McRae RC	2.00	5.00
❑ 202 Keenan Burton AU RC	5.00	12.00
❑ 203 Keith Rivers AU RC	6.00	15.00
❑ 204 Kellen Davis RC	1.50	4.00
❑ 205 Kenneth Moore RC	2.00	5.00
❑ 206 Kenny Phillips AU RC	8.00	20.00
❑ 207 Kentwan Balmer AU RC	5.00	12.00
❑ 208 Kevin Robinson AU RC	5.00	12.00
❑ 209 Lavelle Hawkins AU RC	5.00	12.00
❑ 210 Lawrence Jackson AU RC	5.00	12.00
❑ 211 Leodis McKelvin AU RC	6.00	15.00
❑ 212 Marcus Henry RC	2.00	5.00
❑ 213 Marcus Monk RC	2.50	6.00
❑ 214 Marcus Smith AU RC	5.00	12.00
❑ 215 M. Thomas AU RC EXCH	5.00	12.00
❑ 216 Mark Bradford RC	2.00	5.00
❑ 217 Martellus Bennett AU RC	6.00	15.00
❑ 218 Martin Rucker AU RC	5.00	12.00
❑ 219 Matt Flynn AU RC	6.00	15.00
❑ 220 Mike Jenkins AU RC	6.00	15.00
❑ 221 Mike Hart AU RC	6.00	15.00
❑ 222 Owen Schmitt RC	2.50	6.00
❑ 223 Pat Sims RC	2.00	5.00
❑ 224 Paul Hubbard AU/91 RC	5.00	12.00
❑ 225 Paul Smith RC	2.50	6.00
❑ 226 Peyton Hillis RC	2.50	6.00
❑ 227 Phillip Merling RC	2.00	5.00
❑ 228 Pierre Garcon RC	4.00	10.00
❑ 229 Quentin Groves RC	2.00	5.00
❑ 230 Reggie Smith RC	2.00	5.00
❑ 231 Robert Killebrew RC	2.00	5.00
❑ 232 Ryan Grice-Mullen RC	2.50	6.00
❑ 233 Ryan Torain AU RC	8.00	20.00
❑ 234 Adarius Bowman RC	2.00	5.00
❑ 235 Sam Keller RC	2.50	6.00
❑ 236 Sedrick Ellis AU RC	6.00	15.00
❑ 237 Shawn Crable RC	2.50	6.00
❑ 238 Simeon Castille RC	2.00	5.00
❑ 239 Tashard Choice AU RC	10.00	20.00
❑ 240 Terrell Thomas RC	2.00	5.00
❑ 241 Dorien Bryant RC	2.00	5.00
❑ 242 Thomas Brown AU RC	6.00	15.00
❑ 243 Tim Hightower AU RC	12.00	30.00
❑ 244 Tracy Porter RC	3.00	8.00
❑ 245 Vernon Gholston AU RC	6.00	15.00
❑ 246 Bernard Morris RC	2.00	5.00
❑ 247 Will Franklin	5.00	12.00
❑ 248 Xavier Adibi RC	2.00	5.00
❑ 249 Xavier Omon RC	2.50	6.00
❑ 250 Zackary Bowman RC	2.00	5.00

❑ 251 Chad Henne RPM AU RC 20.00 40.00
❑ 252 Dustin Keller RPM AU RC 10.00 20.00
❑ 253 J.Stewart RPM AU RC 25.00 50.00
❑ 254 Steve Slaton RPM AU RC 12.00 30.00
❑ 255 Earl Bennett RPM AU RC 6.00 15.00
❑ 256 Brian Brohm RPM AU RC 10.00 25.00
❑ 257 J. Charles RPM AU RC 10.00 25.00
❑ 258 M.Manningham RPM AU RC 12.50 25.00
❑ 259 Felix Jones RPM AU RC 30.00 60.00
❑ 260 DeS.Jackson RPM AU RC 25.00 50.00
❑ 261 Kevin O'Connell RPM AU RC 6.00 15.00
❑ 262 K.Smith RPM AU RC EXCH 15.00 30.00
❑ 263 Jerome Simpson RPM AU RC 5.00 12.00
❑ 264 D.McFadden RPM AU RC 30.00 60.00
❑ 265 H.Douglas RPM AU RC EXCH 6.00 15.00
❑ 266 J.D.Booty RPM AU RC 6.00 15.00
❑ 267 R.Mendenhall RPM AU RC 25.00 50.00
❑ 268 Malcolm Kelly RPM AU RC 6.00 15.00
❑ 269 Matt Ryan RPM AU RC 50.00 120.00
❑ 270 Joe Flacco RPM AU RC 50.00 100.00
❑ 271 Early Doucet RPM AU RC 6.00 15.00
❑ 272 Andre Caldwell RPM AU RC 6.00 15.00
❑ 273 James Hardy RPM AU RC 5.00 12.00
❑ 274 Jordy Nelson RPM AU RC 12.00 30.00
❑ 275 G.Dorsey RPM AU RC EXCH 10.00 25.00
❑ 276 Chris Johnson RPM AU RC 50.00 80.00
❑ 277 Eddie Royal RPM AU RC 20.00 40.00
❑ 278 Matt Forte RPM AU RC 30.00 60.00
❑ 279 Ray Rice RPM AU RC 15.00 40.00
❑ 280 Devin Thomas RPM AU RC 6.00 15.00
❑ 281 Limas Sweed RPM AU RC 6.00 15.00
❑ 282 Dexter Jackson RPM AU RC 6.00 15.00
❑ 283 Donnie Avery RPM AU RC 12.00 30.00
❑ 284 J.Long RPM AU RC EXCH 6.00 15.00

2009 Absolute Memorabilia

❑ 1 Kurt Warner .50 1.25
❑ 2 Larry Fitzgerald .50 1.25
❑ 3 Tim Hightower .40 1.00
❑ 4 Matt Ryan .50 1.25
❑ 5 Michael Turner .40 1.00
❑ 6 Roddy White .40 1.00
❑ 7 Derrick Mason .30 .75
❑ 8 Joe Flacco .50 1.25
❑ 9 Willis McGahee .40 1.00
❑ 10 Lee Evans .40 1.00
❑ 11 James Hardy .40 1.00
❑ 12 Terrell Owens .50 1.25
❑ 13 DeAngelo Williams .50 1.25
❑ 14 Jake Delhomme .40 1.00
❑ 15 Jonathan Stewart .40 1.00
❑ 16 Steve Smith .40 1.00
❑ 17 Greg Olsen .30 .75
❑ 18 Jay Cutler .50 1.25
❑ 19 Matt Forte .50 1.25
❑ 20 Carson Palmer .50 1.25
❑ 21 Cedric Benson .40 1.00
❑ 22 Chad Ochocinco .40 1.00
❑ 23 Brady Quinn .40 1.00
❑ 24 Braylon Edwards .40 1.00
❑ 25 Jamal Lewis .40 1.00
❑ 26 Marion Barber .50 1.25
❑ 27 Tashard Choice .40 1.00
❑ 28 Tony Romo .75 2.00
❑ 29 Brandon Marshall .40 1.00
❑ 30 Correll Buckhalter .30 .75
❑ 31 Kyle Orton .40 1.00
❑ 32 Calvin Johnson .50 1.25
❑ 33 Daunte Culpepper .40 1.00
❑ 34 Kevin Smith .40 1.00
❑ 35 Aaron Rodgers .50 1.25
❑ 36 Greg Jennings .50 1.25
❑ 37 Ryan Grant .40 1.00
❑ 38 Andre Johnson .40 1.00
❑ 39 Matt Schaub .40 1.00
❑ 40 Steve Slaton .40 1.00
❑ 41 Anthony Gonzalez .40 1.00
❑ 42 Joseph Addai .50 1.25
❑ 43 Peyton Manning .75 2.00
❑ 44 Reggie Wayne .40 1.00
❑ 45 David Garrard .40 1.00
❑ 46 Maurice Jones-Drew .40 1.00
❑ 47 Marcedes Lewis .30 .75
❑ 48 Dwayne Bowe .40 1.00
❑ 49 Jamaal Charles .40 1.00
❑ 50 Matt Cassel .40 1.00
❑ 51 Tony Gonzalez .40 1.00
❑ 52 Chad Pennington .40 1.00
❑ 53 Ted Ginn .40 1.00
❑ 54 Ronnie Brown .40 1.00
❑ 55 Adrian Peterson 1.00 2.50
❑ 56 Bernard Berrian .40 1.00
❑ 57 Visanthe Shiancoe .30 .75
❑ 58 Laurence Maroney .40 1.00
❑ 59 Tom Brady .75 2.00
❑ 60 Wes Welker .50 1.25
❑ 61 Randy Moss .50 1.25
❑ 62 Drew Brees .50 1.25
❑ 63 Jeremy Shockey .30 .75
❑ 64 Reggie Bush .50 1.25
❑ 65 Eli Manning .50 1.25
❑ 66 Brandon Jacobs .40 1.00
❑ 67 Kevin Boss .30 .75
❑ 68 Thomas Jones .40 1.00
❑ 69 Jerricho Cotchery .30 .75
❑ 70 Leon Washington .40 1.00
❑ 71 Darren McFadden .50 1.25
❑ 72 JaMarcus Russell .40 1.00
❑ 73 Justin Fargas .30 .75
❑ 74 Brian Westbrook .40 1.00
❑ 75 Kevin Curtis .30 .75
❑ 76 Donovan McNabb .50 1.25
❑ 77 Ben Roethlisberger .75 2.00
❑ 78 Santonio Holmes .40 1.00
❑ 79 Rashard Mendenhall .40 1.00
❑ 80 Philip Rivers .50 1.25
❑ 81 LaDainian Tomlinson .50 1.25
❑ 82 Darren Sproles .40 1.00
❑ 83 Frank Gore .40 1.00
❑ 84 Josh Morgan .30 .75
❑ 85 Vernon Davis .30 .75
❑ 86 Matt Hasselbeck .40 1.00
❑ 87 T.J. Houshmandzadeh .40 1.00
❑ 88 John Carlson .40 1.00
❑ 89 Marc Bulger .40 1.00
❑ 90 Steven Jackson .40 1.00
❑ 91 Donnie Avery .40 1.00
❑ 92 Antonio Bryant .40 1.00
❑ 93 Derrick Ward .40 1.00
❑ 94 Kellen Winslow Jr. .40 1.00
❑ 95 Chris Johnson .50 1.25
❑ 96 Brandon Jones .30 .75
❑ 97 Justin Gage .30 .75
❑ 98 Chris Cooley .40 1.00
❑ 99 Clinton Portis .40 1.00
❑ 100 Jason Campbell .40 1.00
❑ 101 Aaron Maybin RC 2.00 5.00
❑ 102 Aaron Kelly AU/149 RC 5.00 12.00
❑ 103 Aaron Brown RC 2.00 5.00
❑ 104 Alphonso Smith RC 1.50 4.00
❑ 105 Andre Smith RC 2.00 5.00
❑ 106 Anthony Hill RC 1.25 3.00
❑ 107 Arian Foster RC 2.00 5.00
❑ 108 Asher Allen RC 1.50 4.00
❑ 109 Austin Collie AU/149 RC 15.00 30.00
❑ 110 B.J. Raji AU/99 RC 8.00 20.00
❑ 111 Bernard Scott RC 2.00 5.00
❑ 112 Bradley Fletcher RC 1.50 4.00
❑ 113 Brandon Tate AU/149 RC 5.00 12.00
❑ 114 Brandon Gibson AU/149 RC 6.00 15.00
❑ 115 Brian Orakpo AU/99 RC 8.00 20.00
❑ 116 Brian Cushing AU/99 RC 8.00 20.00
❑ 117 Brian Hartline RC 2.00 5.00
❑ 118 Brooks Foster AU/149 RC 5.00 12.00
❑ 119 Cameron Morrah AU/149 RC 4.0010.00
❑ 120 Cedric Peerman AU/99 RC 5.00 12.00
❑ 121 Chase Coffman AU/149 RC 5.00 12.00
❑ 122 Chris Ogbonnaya RC 2.00 5.00
❑ 123 Chris Owens RC 1.50 4.00
❑ 124 Clay Matthews AU/99 RC 10.00 25.00
❑ 125 Clint Sintim AU/99 RC 6.00 15.00
❑ 126 Cody Brown RC 1.50 4.00
❑ 127 Connor Barwin RC 1.50 4.00
❑ 128 C.Ingram AU/149 RC 4.00 10.00
❑ 129 Curtis Painter RC 2.00 5.00
❑ 130 Darcel McBath RC 2.00 5.00
❑ 131 Darius Butler RC 2.00 5.00
❑ 132 David Johnson RC 1.50 4.00
❑ 133 David Veikune RC 1.50 4.00
❑ 134 DeAndre Levy RC 2.00 5.00
❑ 135 D.Byrd AU/149 RC EXCH 5.00 12.00
❑ 136 Devin Moore AU/99 RC 5.00 12.00
❑ 137 Davon Drew RC 1.50 4.00
❑ 138 D.Edison AU/149 RC 4.00 10.00
❑ 139 Eddie Williams RC 1.50 4.00
❑ 140 Eugene Monroe RC 1.50 4.00
❑ 141 Evander Hood RC 3.00 8.00
❑ 142 Everette Brown AU/149 RC 6.00 15.00
❑ 143 Gartrell Johnson RC 1.50 4.00
❑ 144 Hunter Cantwell AU/149 RC 6.00 15.00
❑ 145 Jairus Byrd RC 2.50 6.00
❑ 146 J.Laurinaitis AU/149 RC 8.00 20.00
❑ 147 James Casey AU/149 RC 5.00 12.00
❑ 148 James Davis RC 2.00 5.00
❑ 149 Jared Cook AU/149 RC 5.00 12.00
❑ 150 Jarett Dillard AU/149 RC 6.00 15.00
❑ 151 Jason Williams RC 2.00 5.00
❑ 152 Javarris Williams RC 1.50 4.00
❑ 153 Jeremy Childs RC 1.50 4.00
❑ 154 Jerraud Powers RC 1.50 4.00
❑ 155 John Phillips RC 2.00 5.00
❑ 156 Johnny Knox AU/149 RC 15.00 30.00
❑ 157 Kaluka Maiava RC 2.00 5.00
❑ 158 Keith Null RC 2.00 5.00
❑ 159 Kenny McKinley AU/149 RC 6.00 15.00
❑ 160 Kevin Ogletree AU/149 RC 8.00 20.00
❑ 161 Kory Sheets RC 1.50 4.00
❑ 162 Lardarius Webb RC 2.00 5.00
❑ 163 Larry English AU/99 RC 6.00 15.00
❑ 164 Louis Murphy AU/149 RC 8.00 20.00
❑ 165 Louis Delmas RC 2.00 5.00
❑ 166 Malcolm Jenkins AU/149 RC 6.0015.00
❑ 167 Manuel Johnson RC 1.50 4.00
❑ 168 Marko Mitchell RC 1.50 4.00
❑ 169 Bear Pascoe RC 2.00 5.00
❑ 170 Michael Mitchell RC 2.00 5.00
❑ 171 Michael Oher RC 3.00 8.00
❑ 172 Mike Teel RC 2.00 5.00
❑ 173 Mike Goodson AU/149 RC 6.00 15.00
❑ 174 Nathan Brown AU/149 RC 5.00 12.00
❑ 175 P.J. Hill AU/149 RC 5.00 12.00
❑ 176 Patrick Chung RC 2.00 5.00
❑ 177 Peria Jerry RC 1.50 4.00
❑ 178 Quan Cosby AU/149 RC 5.00 12.00
❑ 179 Quinn Johnson AU/149 RC 5.00 12.00
❑ 180 Quinten Lawrence RC 1.50 4.00
❑ 181 R.Jennings AU/149 RC 6.00 15.00
❑ 182 Rashad Johnson RC 1.50 4.00
❑ 183 Rey Maualuga AU/99 RC 10.00 25.00
❑ 184 Richard Quinn RC 1.50 4.00
❑ 185 Robert Ayers RC 2.00 5.00
❑ 186 Ron Brace RC 1.50 4.00
❑ 187 Ryan Mouton RC 1.50 4.00
❑ 188 Sammie Stroughter RC 2.00 5.00
❑ 189 Sean Smith RC 2.00 5.00
❑ 190 S.Nelson AU/149 RC EXCH 5.00 12.00
❑ 191 Sherrod Martin RC 1.50 4.00
❑ 192 Tiquan Underwood RC 1.50 4.00
❑ 193 Tom Brandstater RC 2.00 5.00
❑ 194 Tony Fiammetta AU/149 RC 5.00 12.00
❑ 195 Travis Beckum AU/149 RC 5.00 12.00
❑ 196 Tyrell Sutton RC 1.50 4.00
❑ 197 Tyrone McKenzie RC 1.50 4.00
❑ 198 Darius Passmore RC 1.50 4.00
❑ 199 Vontae Davis AU/149 RC 6.00 15.00
❑ 200 William Moore RC 1.50 4.00
❑ 201 M.Stafford RPM AU/299 RC 40.00 80.00
❑ 202 J. Smith RPM AU/199 RC 5.00 12.00
❑ 203 Ty.Jackson RPM AU/149 RC 6.00 15.00
❑ 204 A. Curry RPM AU/299 RC 8.00 20.00
❑ 205 M.Sanchez RPM AU/299 RC 75.00 150.00
❑ 206 Heyward-By RPM AU/199 RC 10.00 25.00
❑ 207 M.Crabtree RPM AU/299 RC 35.00 60.00
❑ 208 K.Moreno RPM AU/249 RC 30.00 60.00
❑ 209 J.Freeman RPM AU/199 RC 15.00 40.00
❑ 210 J.Maclin RPM AU/199 RC 15.00 40.00
❑ 211 Pettigrew RPM AU/299 RC 8.00 20.00
❑ 212 P.Harvin RPM AU/299 RC 40.00 80.00
❑ 213 D.Brown RPM AU/199 RC 20.00 40.00
❑ 214 Nicks RPM AU/199 RC EXCH 12.00 30.00
❑ 215 K.Britt RPM AU/299 RC EXCH 10.00 25.00
❑ 216 Chris Wells RPM AU/249 RC 20.00 50.00
❑ 217 B.Robiskie RPM AU/299 RC 6.00 15.00
❑ 218 Pat White RPM AU/149 RC 20.00 40.00
❑ 219 Massaquoi RPM AU/149 RC EX 6.00 15.00
❑ 220 L.McCoy RPM AU/199 RC 15.00 40.00
❑ 221 S.Greene RPM AU/299 RC 12.00 30.00
❑ 222 G.Coffee RPM AU/299 RC 8.00 20.00
❑ 223 D.Williams RPM AU/199 RC 6.00 15.00
❑ 224 J.Ringer RPM AU/299 RC 6.00 15.00
❑ 225 M.Wallace RPM AU/299 RC 15.00 40.00
❑ 226 R.Barden RPM AU/149 RC 5.00 12.00
❑ 227 P.Turner RPM AU/299 RC 5.00 12.00
❑ 228 Deon Butler RPM AU/299 RC 6.00 15.00
❑ 229 Iglesias RPM AU/149 RC EXCH 6.00 15.00
❑ 230 McGee RPM AU/149 RC EXCH 6.00 15.00

Card	Low	High
231 Mike Thomas RPM AU/149 RC	6.00	15.00
232 Andre Brown RPM AU/249 RC	5.00	12.00
233 Bomar RPM AU/199 RC EXCH	5.00	12.00
234 Nate Davis RPM AU/199 RC	6.00	15.00

2000 Aurora

Card	Low	High
COMPLETE SET (150)	12.50	30.00
1 David Boston	.25	.60
2 Thomas Jones RC	.60	1.50
3 Rob Moore	.15	.40
4 Jake Plummer	.15	.40
5 Frank Sanders	.15	.40
6 Jamal Anderson	.25	.60
7 Chris Chandler	.15	.40
8 Tim Dwight	.25	.60
9 Doug Johnson RC	.40	1.00
10 Tony Banks	.15	.40
11 Qadry Ismail	.15	.40
12 Jamal Lewis RC	1.00	2.50
13 Chris Redman RC	.30	.75
14 Travis Taylor RC	.40	1.00
15 Doug Flutie	.25	.60
16 Rob Johnson	.15	.40
17 Eric Moulds	.25	.60
18 Peerless Price	.15	.40
19 Antowain Smith	.15	.40
20 Steve Beuerlein	.15	.40
21 Tim Biakabutuka	.15	.40
22 Patrick Jeffers	.25	.60
23 Muhsin Muhammad	.15	.40
24 Curtis Enis	.08	.25
25 Cade McNown	.08	.25
26 Marcus Robinson	.25	.60
27 Dez White RC	.40	1.00
28 Corey Dillon	.25	.60
29 Ron Dugans RC	.30	.75
30 Darnay Scott	.15	.40
31 Akili Smith	.08	.25
32 Peter Warrick RC	.40	1.00
33 Tim Couch	.15	.40
34 JaJuan Dawson RC	.30	.75
35 Kevin Johnson	.25	.60
36 Dennis Northcutt RC	.40	1.00
37 Travis Prentice RC	.40	1.00
38 Troy Aikman	.50	1.25
39 Rocket Ismail	.15	.40
40 Emmitt Smith	.50	1.25
41 Jason Tucker	.08	.25
42 Terrell Davis	.25	.60
43 Olandis Gary	.25	.60
44 Brian Griese	.25	.60
45 Ed McCaffrey	.25	.60
46 Rod Smith	.15	.40
47 Charlie Batch	.25	.60
48 Germane Crowell	.08	.25
49 Reuben Droughns RC	.50	1.25
50 Herman Moore	.15	.40
51 Barry Sanders	.60	1.50
52 Brett Favre	.75	2.00
53 Bubba Franks RC	.40	1.00
54 Antonio Freeman	.25	.60
55 Dorsey Levens	.15	.40
56 Bill Schroeder	.15	.40
57 Marvin Harrison	.25	.60
58 Edgerrin James	.40	1.00
59 Peyton Manning	.60	1.50
60 Terrence Wilkins	.08	.25
61 Mark Brunell	.25	.60
62 Keenan McCardell	.15	.40
63 Jimmy Smith	.15	.40
64 R.Jay Soward RC	.30	.75
65 Shyrone Stith RC	.40	1.00
66 Fred Taylor	.25	.60
67 Derrick Alexander	.15	.40
68 Donnell Bennett	.08	.25
69 Tony Gonzalez	.15	.40
70 Elvis Grbac	.15	.40
71 Sylvester Morris RC	.30	.75
72 Damon Huard	.25	.60
73 James Johnson	.08	.25
74 Dan Marino	.75	2.00
75 Tony Martin	.15	.40
76 O.J. McDuffie	.15	.40
77 Quinton Spotwood RC	.30	.75
78 Cris Carter	.25	.60
79 Daunte Culpepper	.30	.75
80 Randy Moss	.50	1.25
81 Robert Smith	.25	.60
82 Troy Walters RC	.40	1.00
83 Drew Bledsoe	.30	.75
84 Tom Brady RC	12.50	25.00
85 Kevin Faulk	.15	.40
86 Terry Glenn	.15	.40
87 J.R. Redmond RC	.30	.75
88 Marc Bulger RC	.75	2.00
89 Sherrod Gideon RC	.30	.75
90 Keith Poole	.08	.25
91 Ricky Williams	.25	.60
92 Kerry Collins	.15	.40
93 Ron Dayne RC	.40	1.00
94 Ike Hilliard	.15	.40
95 Amani Toomer	.08	.25
96 Wayne Chrebet	.15	.40
97 Laveranues Coles RC	.50	1.25
98 Curtis Martin	.25	.60
99 Chad Pennington RC	1.00	2.50
100 Vinny Testaverde	.15	.40
101 Tim Brown	.25	.60
102 Rich Gannon	.25	.60
103 Napoleon Kaufman	.15	.40
104 Jerry Porter RC	.50	1.25
105 Tyrone Wheatley	.15	.40
106 Charles Johnson	.15	.40
107 Donovan McNabb	.40	1.00
108 Todd Pinkston RC	.40	1.00
109 Duce Staley	.25	.60
110 Jerome Bettis	.25	.60
111 Plaxico Burress RC	.75	2.00
112 Troy Edwards	.08	.25
113 Richard Huntley	.08	.25
114 Tee Martin RC	.40	1.00
115 Kordell Stewart	.15	.40
116 Isaac Bruce	.25	.60
117 Trung Canidate RC	.30	.75
118 Marshall Faulk	.30	.75
119 Torry Holt	.25	.60
120 Kurt Warner	.50	1.25
121 Jermaine Fazande	.08	.25
122 Trevor Gaylor RC	.30	.75
123 Jim Harbaugh	.15	.40
124 Junior Seau	.25	.60
125 Giovanni Carmazzi RC	.30	.75
126 Charlie Garner	.15	.40
127 Terrell Owens	.25	.60
128 Jerry Rice	.50	1.25
129 J.J. Stokes	.15	.40
130 Steve Young	.30	.75
131 Shaun Alexander RC	1.25	3.00
132 Christian Fauria	.08	.25
133 Jon Kitna	.25	.60
134 Derrick Mayes	.15	.40
135 Ricky Watters	.15	.40
136 Mike Alstott	.25	.60
137 Warrick Dunn	.25	.60
138 Jacquez Green	.08	.25
139 Joe Hamilton RC	.30	.75
140 Shaun King	.08	.25
141 Eddie George	.25	.60
142 Jevon Kearse	.25	.60
143 Steve McNair	.25	.60
144 Yancey Thigpen	.08	.25
145 Frank Wycheck	.08	.25
146 Albert Connell	.08	.25
147 Stephen Davis	.25	.60
148 Todd Husak RC	.40	1.00
149 Brad Johnson	.25	.60
150 Michael Westbrook	.15	.40
S1 Jon Kitna Sample	.40	1.00

1948 Bowman

Card	Low	High
COMPLETE SET (108)	4500.00	6000.00
COMMON 1/4/7/-/-/-	12.00	20.00
COMMON 2/5/8/-/-/-	15.00	25.00
COMMON SP 3/6/9 /-/-/-	65.00	100.00
WRAPPER (1-CENT)	150.00	250.00
1 Joe Tereshinski RC	80.00	150.00
2 Larry Olsonoski RC	15.00	25.00
3 Johnny Lujack SP RC	250.00	350.00
4 Ray Poole RC	12.00	20.00
5 Bill DeCorrevont RC	15.00	25.00
6 Paul Briggs SP RC	65.00	100.00
7 Steve Van Buren RC	125.00	200.00
8 Kenny Washington RC	40.00	60.00
9 Nolan Luhn SP RC	65.00	100.00
10 Chris Iversen RC	12.00	20.00
11 Jack Wiley RC	15.00	25.00
12 Charley Conerly SP RC	250.00	350.00
13 Hugh Taylor RC	15.00	25.00
14 Frank Seno RC	15.00	25.00
15 Gil Bouley SP RC	65.00	100.00
16 Tommy Thompson RC	20.00	35.00
17 Charley Trippi RC	60.00	100.00
18 Vince Banonis SP RC	65.00	100.00
19 Art Faircloth RC	12.00	20.00
20 Clyde Goodnight RC	15.00	25.00
21 Bill Chipley SP RC	65.00	100.00
22 Sammy Baugh RC	350.00	500.00
23 Don Kindt RC	15.00	25.00
24 John Koniszewski SP RC	65.00	100.00
25 Pat McHugh RC	12.00	20.00
26 Bob Waterfield RC	125.00	200.00
27 Tony Compagno SP RC	65.00	100.00
28 Paul Governali RC	15.00	25.00
29 Pat Harder RC	40.00	60.00
30 Vic Lindskog SP RC	65.00	100.00
31 Salvatore Rosato RC	12.00	20.00
32 John Mastrangelo RC	15.00	25.00
33 Fred Gehrke SP RC	65.00	100.00
34 Bosh Pritchard RC	12.00	20.00
35 Mike Micka RC	15.00	25.00
36 Bulldog Turner SP RC	150.00	250.00
37 Len Younce RC	12.00	20.00
38 Pat West RC	15.00	25.00
39 Russ Thomas SP RC	65.00	100.00
40 James Peebles RC	12.00	20.00
41 Bob Skoglund RC	15.00	25.00
42 Walt Stickle SP RC	65.00	100.00
43 Whitey Wistert RC	15.00	25.00
44 Paul Christman RC	40.00	60.00
45 Jay Rhodemyre SP RC	65.00	100.00
46 Tony Minisi RC	12.00	20.00
47 Bob Mann RC	15.00	25.00
48 Mal Kutner SP RC	70.00	110.00
49 Dick Poillon RC	12.00	20.00
50 Charles Cherundolo RC	15.00	25.00
51 Gerald Cowhig SP RC	65.00	100.00
52 Neill Armstrong RC	15.00	25.00
53 Frank Maznicki RC	15.00	25.00
54 John Sanchez SP RC	65.00	100.00
55 Frank Reagan RC	12.00	20.00
56 Jim Hardy RC	15.00	25.00
57 John Badaczewski SP	65.00	100.00
58 Robert Nussbaumer RC	12.00	20.00
59 Marvin Pregulman RC	15.00	25.00
60 Elbie Nickel SP RC	75.00	125.00
61 Alex Wojciechowicz RC	90.00	150.00
62 Walt Schlinkman RC	15.00	25.00
63 Pete Pihos SP RC	150.00	225.00
64 Joseph Sulaitis RC	12.00	20.00
65 Mike Holovak RC	30.00	50.00
66 Cy Souders SP RC	65.00	100.00
67 Paul McKee RC	12.00	20.00
68 Bill Moore RC	15.00	25.00
69 Frank Minini SP RC	65.00	100.00
70 Jack Ferrante RC	12.00	20.00

❑ 71 Les Horvath RC	35.00	50.00
❑ 72 Ted Fritsch Sr. SP RC	70.00	110.00
❑ 73 Tex Coulter RC	15.00	25.00
❑ 74 Boley Dancewicz RC	15.00	25.00
❑ 75 Dante Mangani SP RC	65.00	100.00
❑ 76 James Hefti RC	12.00	20.00
❑ 77 Paul Sarringhaus RC	15.00	25.00
❑ 78 Joe Scott SP RC	65.00	100.00
❑ 79 Bucko Kilroy RC	15.00	25.00
❑ 80 Bill Dudley RC	75.00	125.00
❑ 81 Mar.Goldberg SP RC	70.00	110.00
❑ 82 John Cannady RC	12.00	20.00
❑ 83 Perry Moss RC	15.00	25.00
❑ 84 Harold Crisler SP RC	70.00	110.00
❑ 85 Bill Gray RC	12.00	20.00
❑ 86 John Clement RC	15.00	25.00
❑ 87 Dan Sandifer SP RC	65.00	100.00
❑ 88 Ben Kish RC	12.00	20.00
❑ 89 Herbert Banta RC	15.00	25.00
❑ 90 Bill Garnaas SP RC	65.00	100.00
❑ 91 Jim White RC	12.00	20.00
❑ 92 Frank Barzilauskas RC	15.00	25.00
❑ 93 Vic Sears SP RC	65.00	100.00
❑ 94 John Adams RC	12.00	20.00
❑ 95 George McAfee RC	90.00	150.00
❑ 96 Ralph Heywood SP RC	65.00	100.00
❑ 97 Joe Muha RC	12.00	20.00
❑ 98 Fred Enke RC	15.00	25.00
❑ 99 Harry Gilmer SP RC	100.00	175.00
❑ 100 Bill Miklich RC	12.00	20.00
❑ 101 Joe Gottlieb RC	15.00	25.00
❑ 102 Bud Angsman SP RC	70.00	110.00
❑ 103 Tom Farmer RC	12.00	20.00
❑ 104 Bruce Smith RC	40.00	75.00
❑ 105 Bob Cifers SP RC	65.00	100.00
❑ 106 Ernie Steele RC	12.00	20.00
❑ 107 Sid Luckman RC	175.00	300.00
❑ 108 Buford Ray SP RC	250.00	400.00

1950 Bowman

❑ COMPLETE SET (144)	3000.00	4000.00
❑ WRAPPER (5-CENT)	100.00	175.00
❑ 1 Doak Walker	150.00	250.00
❑ 2 John Greene RC	18.00	25.00
❑ 3 Bob Nowasky RC	18.00	25.00
❑ 4 Jonathan Jenkins RC	18.00	25.00
❑ 5 Y.A.Tittle RC	175.00	250.00
❑ 6 Lou Groza RC	100.00	175.00
❑ 7 Alex Agase RC	20.00	30.00
❑ 8 Mac Speedie RC	30.00	50.00
❑ 9 Tony Canadeo RC	50.00	90.00
❑ 10 Larry Craig RC	20.00	30.00
❑ 11 Ted Fritsch Sr.	20.00	30.00
❑ 12 Joe Golding RC	18.00	25.00
❑ 13 Martin Ruby RC	18.00	25.00
❑ 14 George Taliaferro	20.00	30.00
❑ 15 Tank Younger RC	30.00	50.00
❑ 16 Glenn Davis RC	75.00	125.00
❑ 17 Bob Waterfield	75.00	125.00
❑ 18 Val Jansante RC	18.00	25.00
❑ 19 Joe Geri RC	18.00	25.00
❑ 20 Jerry Nuzum RC	18.00	25.00
❑ 21 Elmer Bud Angsman	18.00	25.00
❑ 22 Billy Dewell	18.00	25.00
❑ 23 Steve Van Buren	50.00	90.00
❑ 24 Cliff Patton RC	18.00	25.00
❑ 25 Bosh Pritchard	18.00	25.00
❑ 26 Johnny Lujack	50.00	80.00
❑ 27 Sid Luckman	75.00	125.00
❑ 28 Bulldog Turner	35.00	60.00
❑ 29 Bill Dudley	35.00	60.00
❑ 30 Hugh Taylor	20.00	30.00
❑ 31 George Thomas RC	18.00	25.00
❑ 32 Ray Poole	18.00	25.00
❑ 33 Travis Tidwell RC	18.00	25.00
❑ 34 Gail Bruce RC	18.00	25.00
❑ 35 Joe Perry RC	125.00	200.00
❑ 36 Frankie Albert RC	30.00	50.00
❑ 37 Bobby Layne	125.00	200.00
❑ 38 Leon Hart	25.00	40.00
❑ 39 B.Hoernschemeyer RC	20.00	30.00
❑ 40 Dick Barwegan RC	18.00	25.00
❑ 41 Adrian Burk RC	20.00	30.00
❑ 42 Barry French RC	18.00	25.00
❑ 43 Marion Motley RC	150.00	250.00
❑ 44 Jim Martin	20.00	30.00
❑ 45 Otto Graham RC	300.00	450.00
❑ 46 Al Baldwin RC	18.00	25.00
❑ 47 Larry Coutre RC	20.00	30.00
❑ 48 John Rauch	18.00	25.00
❑ 49 Sam Tamburo RC	18.00	25.00
❑ 50 Mike Swistowicz RC	18.00	25.00
❑ 51 Tom Fears RC	90.00	150.00
❑ 52 Elroy Hirsch RC	125.00	225.00
❑ 53 Dick Huffman RC	18.00	25.00
❑ 54 Bob Gage RC	18.00	25.00
❑ 55 Buddy Tinsley RC	18.00	25.00
❑ 56 Bill Blackburn RC	18.00	25.00
❑ 57 John Cochran RC	18.00	25.00
❑ 58 Bill Fischer	18.00	25.00
❑ 59 Whitey Wistert	20.00	30.00
❑ 60 Clyde Scott RC	18.00	25.00
❑ 61 Walter Barnes RC	18.00	25.00
❑ 62 Bob Perina RC	18.00	25.00
❑ 63 Bill Wightkin RC	18.00	25.00
❑ 64 Bob Goode RC	18.00	25.00
❑ 65 Al Demao RC	18.00	25.00
❑ 66 Harry Gilmer	20.00	30.00
❑ 67 Bill Austin RC	18.00	25.00
❑ 68 Joe Scott	18.00	25.00
❑ 69 Tex Coulter	20.00	30.00
❑ 70 Paul Salata RC	18.00	25.00
❑ 71 Emil Sitko RC	20.00	30.00
❑ 72 Bill Johnson C RC	18.00	25.00
❑ 73 Don Doll RC	18.00	25.00
❑ 74 Dan Sandifer RC	18.00	25.00
❑ 75 John Panelli RC	18.00	25.00
❑ 76 Bill Leonard RC	18.00	25.00
❑ 77 Bob Kelly RC	18.00	25.00
❑ 78 Dante Lavelli RC	100.00	175.00
❑ 79 Tony Adamle RC	20.00	30.00
❑ 80 Dick Wildung RC	18.00	25.00
❑ 81 Tobin Rote RC	30.00	50.00
❑ 82 Paul Burris RC	18.00	25.00
❑ 83 Lowell Tew RC	18.00	25.00
❑ 84 Barney Poole RC	18.00	25.00
❑ 85 Fred Naumetz RC	18.00	25.00
❑ 86 Dick Hoerner RC	18.00	25.00
❑ 87 Bob Reinhard RC	18.00	25.00
❑ 88 Howard Hartley RC	18.00	25.00
❑ 89 Darrell Hogan RC	18.00	25.00
❑ 90 Jerry Shipkey RC	18.00	25.00
❑ 91 Frank Tripucka	20.00	30.00
❑ 92 Buster Ramsey RC	18.00	25.00
❑ 93 Pat Harder	20.00	30.00
❑ 94 Vic Sears RC	18.00	25.00
❑ 95 Tommy Thompson QB	20.00	30.00
❑ 96 Bucko Kilroy	20.00	30.00
❑ 97 George Connor	30.00	50.00
❑ 98 Fred Morrison RC	18.00	25.00
❑ 99 Jim Keane RC	18.00	25.00
❑ 100 Sammy Baugh	150.00	250.00
❑ 101 Harry Ulinski RC	18.00	25.00
❑ 102 Frank Spaniel RC	18.00	25.00
❑ 103 Charley Conerly	50.00	90.00
❑ 104 Dick Hensley RC	18.00	25.00
❑ 105 Eddie Price RC	18.00	25.00
❑ 106 Ed Carr RC	18.00	25.00
❑ 107 Leo Nomellini	45.00	75.00
❑ 108 Verl Lillywhite RC	18.00	25.00
❑ 109 Wallace Triplett RC	18.00	25.00
❑ 110 Joe Watson RC	18.00	25.00
❑ 111 Cloyce Box RC	20.00	30.00
❑ 112 Billy Stone RC	18.00	25.00
❑ 113 Earl Murray RC	18.00	25.00
❑ 114 Chet Mutryn RC	20.00	30.00
❑ 115 Ken Carpenter RC	20.00	30.00
❑ 116 Lou Rymkus RC	20.00	30.00
❑ 117 Dub Jones RC	20.00	30.00
❑ 118 Clayton Tonnemaker	18.00	25.00
❑ 119 Walt Schlinkman RC	18.00	25.00
❑ 120 Billy Grimes RC	18.00	25.00
❑ 121 George Ratterman RC	20.00	30.00
❑ 122 Bob Mann	18.00	25.00
❑ 123 Buddy Young RC	30.00	50.00
❑ 124 Jack Zilly RC	18.00	25.00
❑ 125 Tom Kalmanir RC	18.00	25.00
❑ 126 Frank Sinkovitz RC	18.00	25.00
❑ 127 Elbert Nickel	20.00	30.00
❑ 128 Jim Finks RC	40.00	75.00
❑ 129 Charley Trippi	35.00	60.00
❑ 130 Tom Wham RC	18.00	25.00
❑ 131 Ventan Yablonski RC	18.00	25.00
❑ 132 Chuck Bednarik	75.00	125.00
❑ 133 Joe Muha	18.00	25.00
❑ 134 Pete Pihos	45.00	80.00
❑ 135 Washington Serini RC	18.00	25.00
❑ 136 George Gulyanics RC	18.00	25.00
❑ 137 Ken Kavanaugh	20.00	30.00
❑ 138 Howie Livingston RC	18.00	25.00
❑ 139 Joe Tereshinski	18.00	25.00
❑ 140 Jim White	18.00	25.00
❑ 141 Gene Roberts RC	18.00	25.00
❑ 142 Bill Swiacki	20.00	30.00
❑ 143 Norm Standlee RC	18.00	25.00
❑ 144 Knox Ramsey RC	50.00	100.00

1951 Bowman

❑ COMPLETE SET (144)	2500.00	3500.00
❑ WRAPPER (1-CENT)	150.00	250.00
❑ WRAPPER (5-CENT)	175.00	300.00
❑ 1 Weldon Humble RC !	50.00	80.00
❑ 2 Otto Graham	150.00	250.00
❑ 3 Mac Speedie	20.00	35.00
❑ 4 Norm Van Brocklin RC	200.00	300.00
❑ 5 Woodley Lewis RC	15.00	25.00
❑ 6 Tom Fears	30.00	50.00
❑ 7 George Musacco RC	12.00	20.00
❑ 8 George Taliaferro	15.00	25.00
❑ 9 Barney Poole	12.00	20.00
❑ 10 Steve Van Buren	35.00	60.00
❑ 11 Whitey Wistert	15.00	25.00
❑ 12 Chuck Bednarik	50.00	80.00
❑ 13 Bulldog Turner	30.00	50.00
❑ 14 Bob Williams RC	12.00	20.00
❑ 15 Johnny Lujack	35.00	60.00
❑ 16 Roy Rebel Steiner	12.00	20.00
❑ 17 Jug Girard	15.00	25.00
❑ 18 Bill Neal RC	12.00	20.00
❑ 19 Travis Tidwell	12.00	20.00
❑ 20 Tom Landry RC	350.00	500.00
❑ 21 Arnie Weinmeister RC	35.00	60.00
❑ 22 Joe Geri	12.00	20.00
❑ 23 Bill Walsh C RC	15.00	30.00
❑ 24 Fran Rogel	12.00	20.00
❑ 25 Doak Walker	35.00	60.00
❑ 26 Leon Hart	20.00	35.00
❑ 27 Thurman McGraw RC	12.00	20.00
❑ 28 Buster Ramsey	12.00	20.00
❑ 29 Frank Tripucka	20.00	35.00
❑ 30 Don Paul DB RC	12.00	20.00
❑ 31 Alex Loyd RC	12.00	20.00
❑ 32 Y.A.Tittle	75.00	135.00
❑ 33 Verl Lillywhite	12.00	20.00
❑ 34 Sammy Baugh	110.00	175.00
❑ 35 Chuck Drazenovich RC	12.00	20.00
❑ 36 Bob Goode	12.00	20.00
❑ 37 Horace Gillom RC	15.00	25.00
❑ 38 Lou Rymkus	15.00	25.00
❑ 39 Ken Carpenter	12.00	20.00
❑ 40 Bob Waterfield	45.00	75.00
❑ 41 Vitamin Smith RC	15.00	25.00
❑ 42 Glenn Davis	35.00	60.00
❑ 43 Dan Edwards RC	12.00	20.00
❑ 44 John Rauch	12.00	20.00
❑ 45 Zollie Toth RC	12.00	20.00
❑ 46 Pete Pihos	35.00	60.00
❑ 47 Russ Craft RC	12.00	20.00
❑ 48 Walter Barnes	12.00	20.00
❑ 49 Fred Morrison	12.00	20.00
❑ 50 Ray Bray RC	12.00	20.00
❑ 51 Ed Sprinkle RC	15.00	25.00

- ❑ 52 Floyd Reid RC 12.00 20.00
- ❑ 53 Billy Grimes 12.00 20.00
- ❑ 54 Ted Fritsch Sr. 15.00 25.00
- ❑ 55 Al DeRogatis RC 15.00 25.00
- ❑ 56 Charley Conerly 45.00 75.00
- ❑ 57 Jon Baker RC 12.00 20.00
- ❑ 58 Tom McWilliams 12.00 20.00
- ❑ 59 Jerry Shipkey 12.00 20.00
- ❑ 60 Lynn Chandnois RC 15.00 25.00
- ❑ 61 Don Doll 12.00 20.00
- ❑ 62 Lou Creekmur 30.00 50.00
- ❑ 63 Bob Hoernschemeyer 15.00 25.00
- ❑ 64 Tom Wham 12.00 20.00
- ❑ 65 Bill Fischer 12.00 20.00
- ❑ 66 Robert Nussbaumer 12.00 20.00
- ❑ 67 Gordy Soltau RC 12.00 20.00
- ❑ 68 Visco Grgich RC 12.00 20.00
- ❑ 69 John Strzykalski RC 12.00 20.00
- ❑ 70 Pete Stout RC 12.00 20.00
- ❑ 71 Paul Lipscomb RC 12.00 20.00
- ❑ 72 Harry Gilmer 20.00 35.00
- ❑ 73 Dante Lavelli 30.00 50.00
- ❑ 74 Dub Jones 15.00 25.00
- ❑ 75 Lou Groza 45.00 75.00
- ❑ 76 Elroy Hirsch 45.00 75.00
- ❑ 77 Tom Kalmanir 12.00 20.00
- ❑ 78 Jack Zilly 12.00 20.00
- ❑ 79 Bruce Alford RC 12.00 20.00
- ❑ 80 Art Weiner 12.00 20.00
- ❑ 81 Brad Ecklund RC 12.00 20.00
- ❑ 82 Bosh Pritchard 12.00 20.00
- ❑ 83 John Green RC 12.00 20.00
- ❑ 84 Ebert Van Buren RC 12.00 20.00
- ❑ 85 Julie Rykovich RC 12.00 20.00
- ❑ 86 Fred Davis 12.00 20.00
- ❑ 87 John Hoffman RC 12.00 20.00
- ❑ 88 Tobin Rote 15.00 25.00
- ❑ 89 Paul Burris 12.00 20.00
- ❑ 90 Tony Canadeo 30.00 50.00
- ❑ 91 Emlen Tunnell RC 60.00 100.00
- ❑ 92 Otto Schnellbacher RC 12.00 20.00
- ❑ 93 Ray Poole 12.00 20.00
- ❑ 94 Darrell Hogan 12.00 20.00
- ❑ 95 Frank Sinkovitz 12.00 20.00
- ❑ 96 Ernie Stautner 45.00 75.00
- ❑ 97 Elmer Bud Angsman 12.00 20.00
- ❑ 98 Jack Jennings RC 12.00 20.00
- ❑ 99 Jerry Groom RC 12.00 20.00
- ❑ 100 John Prchlik RC 12.00 20.00
- ❑ 101 J. Robert Smith RC 12.00 20.00
- ❑ 102 Bobby Layne 75.00 135.00
- ❑ 103 Frankie Albert 20.00 35.00
- ❑ 104 Gail Bruce 12.00 20.00
- ❑ 105 Joe Perry 45.00 75.00
- ❑ 106 Leon Heath RC 12.00 20.00
- ❑ 107 Ed Quirk RC 12.00 20.00
- ❑ 108 Hugh Taylor 15.00 25.00
- ❑ 109 Marion Motley 60.00 100.00
- ❑ 110 Tony Adamle 12.00 20.00
- ❑ 111 Alex Agase 15.00 25.00
- ❑ 112 Tank Younger 20.00 35.00
- ❑ 113 Bob Boyd RC 12.00 20.00
- ❑ 114 Jerry Williams RC 12.00 20.00
- ❑ 115 Joe Golding 12.00 20.00
- ❑ 116 Sherman Howard RC 12.00 20.00
- ❑ 117 John Wozniak RC 12.00 20.00
- ❑ 118 Frank Reagan 12.00 20.00
- ❑ 119 Vic Sears 12.00 20.00
- ❑ 120 Clyde Scott 12.00 20.00
- ❑ 121 George Gulyanics 12.00 20.00
- ❑ 122 Bill Wightkin 12.00 20.00
- ❑ 123 Chuck Hunsinger RC 12.00 20.00
- ❑ 124 Jack Cloud 12.00 20.00
- ❑ 125 Abner Wimberly RC 12.00 20.00
- ❑ 126 Dick Wildung 12.00 20.00
- ❑ 127 Eddie Price 12.00 20.00
- ❑ 128 Joe Scott 12.00 20.00
- ❑ 129 Jerry Nuzum 12.00 20.00
- ❑ 130 Jim Finks 20.00 35.00
- ❑ 131 Bob Gage 12.00 20.00
- ❑ 132 Bill Swiacki 15.00 25.00
- ❑ 133 Joe Watson 12.00 20.00
- ❑ 134 Ollie Cline RC 12.00 20.00
- ❑ 135 Jack Lininger RC 12.00 20.00
- ❑ 136 Fran Polsfoot RC 12.00 20.00
- ❑ 137 Charley Trippi 30.00 50.00
- ❑ 138 Ventan Yablonski 12.00 20.00
- ❑ 139 Emil Sitko 12.00 20.00
- ❑ 140 Leo Nomellini 30.00 60.00
- ❑ 141 Norm Standlee 12.00 20.00
- ❑ 142 Eddie Saenz RC 12.00 20.00
- ❑ 143 Al Demao 12.00 20.00
- ❑ 144 Bill Dudley ! 75.00 150.00
- ❑ NNO Johnny Lujack Proof 175.00 300.00
- ❑ NNO Bob Gage Proof 75.00 125.00
- ❑ NNO Darrell Hogan Proof 75.00 125.00

1952 Bowman Large

- ❑ COMPLETE SET (144) 9500.00 12500.00
- ❑ COMMON CARD (1-72) 20.00 35.00
- ❑ COMMON CARD (73-144) 25.00 40.00
- ❑ WRAPPER (5-CENT) 30.00 60.00
- ❑ 1 Norm Van Brocklin SP 350.00 500.00
- ❑ 2 Otto Graham 200.00 300.00
- ❑ 3 Doak Walker 60.00 100.00
- ❑ 4 Steve Owen CO RC 50.00 80.00
- ❑ 5 Frankie Albert 30.00 50.00
- ❑ 6 Laurie Niemi RC 20.00 35.00
- ❑ 7 Chuck Hunsinger 20.00 35.00
- ❑ 8 Ed Modzelewski 30.00 50.00
- ❑ 9 Joe Spencer SP RC 40.00 75.00
- ❑ 10 Chuck Bednarik SP 200.00 350.00
- ❑ 11 Barney Poole 20.00 35.00
- ❑ 12 Charley Trippi 40.00 75.00
- ❑ 13 Tom Fears 40.00 75.00
- ❑ 14 Paul Brown CO RC 150.00 250.00
- ❑ 15 Leon Hart 30.00 50.00
- ❑ 16 Frank Gifford RC 350.00 500.00
- ❑ 17 Y.A.Tittle 200.00 300.00
- ❑ 18 Charlie Justice SP 100.00 175.00
- ❑ 19 George Connor SP 100.00 175.00
- ❑ 20 Lynn Chandnois 20.00 35.00
- ❑ 21 Billy Howton RC 30.00 50.00
- ❑ 22 Kenneth Snyder RC 20.00 35.00
- ❑ 23 Gino Marchetti RC 150.00 250.00
- ❑ 24 John Karras 20.00 35.00
- ❑ 25 Tank Younger 30.00 50.00
- ❑ 26 Tommy Thompson LB RC 20.00 35.00
- ❑ 27 Bob Miller SP RC 200.00 300.00
- ❑ 28 Kyle Rote SP RC 100.00 175.00
- ❑ 29 Hugh McElhenny RC 150.00 250.00
- ❑ 30 Sammy Baugh 225.00 350.00
- ❑ 31 Jim Dooley RC 25.00 45.00
- ❑ 32 Ray Mathews 20.00 35.00
- ❑ 33 Fred Cone RC 20.00 35.00
- ❑ 34 Al Pollard RC 20.00 35.00
- ❑ 35 Brad Ecklund 20.00 35.00
- ❑ 36 John Hancock SP RC 250.00 350.00
- ❑ 37 Elroy Hirsch SP 125.00 200.00
- ❑ 38 Keever Jankovich RC 20.00 35.00
- ❑ 39 Emlen Tunnell 75.00 125.00
- ❑ 40 Steve Dowden RC 20.00 35.00
- ❑ 41 Claude Hipps RC 20.00 35.00
- ❑ 42 Norm Standlee 20.00 35.00
- ❑ 43 Dick Todd CO RC 20.00 35.00
- ❑ 44 Babe Parilli 30.00 50.00
- ❑ 45 Steve Van Buren SP 200.00 300.00
- ❑ 46 Art Donovan SP RC 250.00 350.00
- ❑ 47 Bill Fischer 20.00 35.00
- ❑ 48 George Halas CO RC 160.00 275.00
- ❑ 49 Jerrell Price 20.00 35.00
- ❑ 50 John Sandusky RC 20.00 35.00
- ❑ 51 Ray Beck 20.00 35.00
- ❑ 52 Jim Martin 25.00 45.00
- ❑ 53 Joe Bach CO RC 20.00 35.00
- ❑ 54 Glen Christian SP RC 40.00 75.00
- ❑ 55 Andy Davis SP RC 40.00 75.00
- ❑ 56 Tobin Rote 25.00 45.00
- ❑ 57 Wayne Millner RC CO 50.00 90.00
- ❑ 58 Zollie Toth 20.00 35.00
- ❑ 59 Jack Jennings 20.00 35.00
- ❑ 60 Bill McColl RC 20.00 35.00
- ❑ 61 Les Richter RC 25.00 45.00
- ❑ 62 Walt Michaels RC 25.00 45.00
- ❑ 63 Charley Conerly SP 500.00 750.00
- ❑ 64 Howard Hartley SP 40.00 75.00
- ❑ 65 Jerome Smith RC 20.00 35.00
- ❑ 66 James Clark RC 20.00 35.00
- ❑ 67 Dick Logan RC 20.00 35.00
- ❑ 68 Wayne Robinson RC 20.00 35.00
- ❑ 69 James Hammond RC 20.00 35.00
- ❑ 70 Gene Schroeder RC 20.00 35.00
- ❑ 71 Tex Coulter 25.00 45.00
- ❑ 72 John Schweder SP RC 400.00 600.00
- ❑ 73 Vitamin Smith SP 90.00 150.00
- ❑ 74 Joe Campanella RC 25.00 40.00
- ❑ 75 Joe Kuharich CO RC 30.00 50.00
- ❑ 76 Herman Clark RC 25.00 40.00
- ❑ 77 Dan Edwards 25.00 40.00
- ❑ 78 Bobby Layne 175.00 300.00
- ❑ 79 Bob Hoernschemeyer 30.00 50.00
- ❑ 80 John Carr Blount RC 25.00 40.00
- ❑ 81 John Kastan SP RC 90.00 150.00
- ❑ 82 Harry Minarik SP RC 90.00 150.00
- ❑ 83 Joe Perry 75.00 125.00
- ❑ 84 Buddy Parker CO RC 30.00 50.00
- ❑ 85 Andy Robustelli RC 125.00 200.00
- ❑ 86 Dub Jones 30.00 50.00
- ❑ 87 Mal Cook RC 25.00 40.00
- ❑ 88 Billy Stone 25.00 40.00
- ❑ 89 George Taliaferro 30.00 50.00
- ❑ 90 Thomas Johnson SP RC 90.00 150.00
- ❑ 91 Leon Heath SP 60.00 100.00
- ❑ 92 Pete Pihos 60.00 100.00
- ❑ 93 Fred Benners RC 25.00 40.00
- ❑ 94 George Tarasovic RC 25.00 40.00
- ❑ 95 Buck Shaw CO RC 25.00 40.00
- ❑ 96 Bill Wightkin 25.00 40.00
- ❑ 97 John Wozniak 25.00 40.00
- ❑ 98 Bobby Dillon RC 30.00 50.00
- ❑ 99 Joe Stydahar SP RC 450.00 650.00
- ❑ 100 Dick Alban SP RC 90.00 150.00
- ❑ 101 Arnie Weinmeister 35.00 60.00
- ❑ 102 Bobby Cross RC 25.00 40.00
- ❑ 103 Don Paul DB 25.00 40.00
- ❑ 104 Buddy Young 35.00 60.00
- ❑ 105 Lou Groza 75.00 125.00
- ❑ 106 Ray Pelfrey RC 25.00 40.00
- ❑ 107 Maurice Nipp RC 25.00 40.00
- ❑ 108 Hubert Johnston SP RC 450.00 650.00
- ❑ 109 Vol.Quinlan SP RC 60.00 100.00
- ❑ 110 Jack Simmons RC 25.00 40.00
- ❑ 111 George Ratterman 30.00 50.00
- ❑ 112 John Badaczewski RC 25.00 40.00
- ❑ 113 Bill Reichardt 25.00 40.00
- ❑ 114 Art Weiner 25.00 40.00
- ❑ 115 Keith Flowers RC 25.00 40.00
- ❑ 116 Russ Craft 25.00 40.00
- ❑ 117 Jim O'Donahue SP RC 90.00 150.00
- ❑ 118 Darrell Hogan SP 60.00 100.00
- ❑ 119 Frank Ziegler RC 25.00 40.00
- ❑ 120 Dan Towler 35.00 60.00
- ❑ 121 Fred Williams RC 25.00 40.00
- ❑ 122 Jimmy Phelan CO RC 25.00 40.00
- ❑ 123 Eddie Price 25.00 40.00
- ❑ 124 Chet Ostrowski RC 25.00 40.00
- ❑ 125 Leo Nomellini 60.00 100.00
- ❑ 126 S.Romanik RC SP! 200.00 300.00
- ❑ 127 Ollie Matson SP RC 200.00 300.00
- ❑ 128 Dante Lavelli 50.00 90.00
- ❑ 129 Jack Christiansen RC 100.00 175.00
- ❑ 130 Dom Moselle RC 25.00 40.00
- ❑ 131 John Rapacz RC 25.00 40.00
- ❑ 132 Chuck Ortmann UER RC 25.00 40.00
- ❑ 133 Bob Williams 25.00 40.00
- ❑ 134 Chuck Ulrich RC 25.00 40.00
- ❑ 135 Gene Ronzani CO SP RC 450.00 650.00
- ❑ 136 Bert Rechichar SP 60.00 100.00
- ❑ 137 Bob Waterfield 75.00 125.00
- ❑ 138 Bobby Walston RC 30.00 50.00
- ❑ 139 Jerry Shipkey 25.00 40.00
- ❑ 140 Yale Lary RC 125.00 200.00
- ❑ 141 Gordy Soltau 25.00 40.00
- ❑ 142 Tom Landry 450.00 600.00
- ❑ 143 John Papit RC 25.00 40.00
- ❑ 144 Jim Lansford SP RC 1800.00 3000.00

1952 Bowman Small

COMPLETE SET (144)	3500.00	5000.00
COMMON CARD (1-72)	15.00	25.00
COMMON CARD (73-144)	18.00	30.00
WRAPPER (1-CENT)	40.00	60.00
1 Norm Van Brocklin	200.00	350.00
2 Otto Graham	125.00	200.00
3 Doak Walker	35.00	60.00
4 Steve Owen CO RC	35.00	60.00
5 Frankie Albert	20.00	35.00
6 Laurie Niemi RC	15.00	25.00
7 Chuck Hunsinger	15.00	25.00
8 Ed Modzelewski	20.00	35.00
9 Joe Spencer RC	15.00	25.00
10 Chuck Bednarik	45.00	75.00
11 Barney Poole	15.00	25.00
12 Charley Trippi	35.00	60.00
13 Tom Fears	35.00	60.00
14 Paul Brown CO RC	90.00	150.00
15 Leon Hart	20.00	35.00
16 Frank Gifford RC	200.00	400.00
17 Y.A.Tittle	75.00	125.00
18 Charlie Justice	30.00	45.00
19 George Connor	20.00	35.00
20 Lynn Chandnois	15.00	25.00
21 Billy Howton RC	25.00	40.00
22 Kenneth Snyder RC	15.00	25.00
23 Gino Marchetti RC	75.00	125.00
24 John Karras	15.00	25.00
25 Tank Younger	20.00	35.00
26 Tommy Thompson LB RC	15.00	25.00
27 Bob Miller RC	15.00	25.00
28 Kyle Rote RC	30.00	50.00
29 Hugh McElhenny RC	100.00	175.00
30 Sammy Baugh	150.00	250.00
31 Jim Dooley RC	18.00	30.00
32 Ray Mathews	15.00	25.00
33 Fred Cone RC	15.00	25.00
34 Al Pollard RC	15.00	25.00
35 Brad Ecklund	15.00	25.00
36 John Lee Hancock RC	15.00	25.00
37 Elroy Hirsch	35.00	60.00
38 Keever Jankovich	15.00	25.00
39 Emlen Tunnell	30.00	50.00
40 Steve Dowden RC	15.00	25.00
41 Claude Hipps	15.00	25.00
42 Norm Standlee	15.00	25.00
43 Dick Todd CO RC	15.00	25.00
44 Babe Parilli	20.00	35.00
45 Steve Van Buren	40.00	75.00
46 Art Donovan RC	125.00	200.00
47 Bill Fischer	15.00	25.00
48 George Halas CO RC	150.00	250.00
49 Jerrell Price	15.00	25.00
50 John Sandusky RC	15.00	25.00
51 Ray Beck	15.00	25.00
52 Jim Martin	18.00	30.00
53 Joe Bach CO RC	15.00	25.00
54 Glen Christian RC	15.00	25.00
55 Andy Davis RC	15.00	25.00
56 Tobin Rote	18.00	30.00
57 Wayne Millner RC CO	30.00	50.00
58 Zollie Toth	15.00	25.00
59 Jack Jennings	15.00	25.00
60 Bill McColl RC	15.00	25.00
61 Les Richter RC	18.00	30.00
62 Walt Michaels RC	18.00	30.00
63 Charley Conerly	40.00	75.00
64 Howard Hartley	15.00	25.00
65 Jerome Smith RC	15.00	25.00
66 James Clark	15.00	25.00
67 Dick Logan	15.00	25.00
68 Wayne Robinson RC	15.00	25.00
69 James Hammond	15.00	25.00
70 Gene Schroeder RC	15.00	25.00
71 Tex Coulter	18.00	30.00
72 John Schweder	15.00	25.00
73 Vitamin Smith	20.00	35.00
74 Joe Campanella RC	18.00	30.00
75 Joe Kuharich CO RC	20.00	35.00
76 Herman Clark	18.00	30.00
77 Dan Edwards	18.00	30.00
78 Bobby Layne	90.00	150.00
79 Bob Hoernschemeyer	20.00	35.00
80 John Carr Blount RC	18.00	30.00
81 John Kastan RC	18.00	30.00
82 Harry Minarik	18.00	30.00
83 Joe Perry	40.00	75.00
84 Buddy Parker CO RC	20.00	35.00
85 Andy Robustelli RC	75.00	125.00
86 Dub Jones	20.00	35.00
87 Mal Cook	18.00	30.00
88 Billy Stone	18.00	30.00
89 George Taliaferro	20.00	35.00
90 Thomas Johnson RC	18.00	30.00
91 Leon Heath	18.00	30.00
92 Pete Pihos	35.00	50.00
93 Fred Benners	18.00	30.00
94 George Tarasovic RC	18.00	30.00
95 Buck Shaw CO RC	18.00	30.00
96 Bill Wightkin	18.00	30.00
97 John Wozniak	18.00	30.00
98 Bobby Dillon RC	20.00	35.00
99 Joe Stydahar RC CO	30.00	45.00
100 Dick Alban RC	18.00	30.00
101 Arnie Weinmeister	25.00	40.00
102 Bobby Cross RC	18.00	30.00
103 Don Paul DB	18.00	30.00
104 Buddy Young	25.00	40.00
105 Lou Groza	45.00	75.00
106 Ray Pelfrey	18.00	30.00
107 Maurice Nipp RC	18.00	30.00
108 Hubert Johnston RC	18.00	30.00
109 Volney Quinlan RC	18.00	30.00
110 Jack Simmons RC	18.00	30.00
111 George Ratterman	20.00	35.00
112 John Badaczewski	18.00	30.00
113 Bill Reichardt	18.00	30.00
114 Art Weiner	18.00	30.00
115 Keith Flowers RC	18.00	30.00
116 Russ Craft	18.00	30.00
117 Jim O'Donahue RC	18.00	30.00
118 Darrell Hogan	18.00	30.00
119 Frank Ziegler RC	18.00	30.00
120 Dan Towler	25.00	40.00
121 Fred Williams RC	18.00	30.00
122 Jimmy Phelan CO RC	18.00	30.00
123 Eddie Price	18.00	30.00
124 Chet Ostrowski RC	18.00	30.00
125 Leo Nomellini	40.00	75.00
126 Steve Romanik RC	18.00	30.00
127 Ollie Matson RC	75.00	125.00
128 Dante Lavelli	35.00	60.00
129 Jack Christiansen RC	50.00	80.00
130 Dom Moselle RC	18.00	30.00
131 John Rapacz RC	18.00	30.00
132 Chuck Ortmann UER RC	18.00	30.00
133 Bob Williams	18.00	30.00
134 Chuck Ulrich RC	18.00	30.00
135 Gene Ronzani CO RC	18.00	30.00
136 Bert Rechichar	20.00	35.00
137 Bob Waterfield	45.00	75.00
138 Bobby Walston RC	20.00	35.00
139 Jerry Shipkey	18.00	30.00
140 Yale Lary RC	50.00	80.00
141 Gordy Soltau	18.00	30.00
142 Tom Landry	250.00	400.00
143 John Papit RC	18.00	30.00
144 Jim Lansford RC	100.00	175.00

1953 Bowman

COMPLETE SET (96)	2200.00	3400.00
WRAPPER (5-CENT)	90.00	150.00
1 Eddie LeBaron RC	75.00	125.00
2 John Dottley	18.00	30.00
3 Babe Parilli	20.00	35.00
4 Bucko Kilroy	20.00	35.00
5 Joe Tereshinski	18.00	30.00
6 Doak Walker	45.00	75.00
7 Fran Polsfoot	18.00	30.00
8 Sisto Averno RC	18.00	30.00
9 Marion Motley	45.00	75.00
10 Pat Brady RC	18.00	30.00
11 Norm Van Brocklin	75.00	125.00
12 Bill McColl	18.00	30.00
13 Jerry Groom	18.00	30.00
14 Al Pollard	18.00	30.00
15 Dante Lavelli	30.00	50.00
16 Eddie Price	18.00	30.00
17 Charley Trippi	30.00	50.00
18 Elbert Nickel	20.00	35.00
19 George Taliaferro	20.00	35.00
20 Charley Conerly	50.00	80.00
21 Bobby Layne	75.00	125.00
22 Elroy Hirsch	60.00	100.00
23 Jim Finks	25.00	40.00
24 Chuck Bednarik	45.00	75.00
25 Kyle Rote	25.00	40.00
26 Otto Graham	100.00	175.00
27 Harry Gilmer	20.00	35.00
28 Tobin Rote	20.00	35.00
29 Billy Stone	18.00	30.00
30 Buddy Young	25.00	40.00
31 Leon Hart	25.00	40.00
32 Hugh McElhenny	45.00	75.00
33 Dale Samuels	18.00	30.00
34 Lou Creekmur	30.00	50.00
35 Tom Catlin RC	18.00	30.00
36 Tom Fears	35.00	60.00
37 George Connor	25.00	40.00
38 Bill Walsh C	18.00	30.00
39 Leo Sanford SP RC	30.00	45.00
40 Horace Gillom	20.00	35.00
41 John Schweder SP	30.00	45.00
42 Tom O'Connell RC	18.00	30.00
43 Frank Gifford SP	175.00	300.00
44 Frank Continetti SP RC	30.00	45.00
45 John Olszewski SP RC	30.00	45.00
46 Dub Jones	20.00	35.00
47 Don Paul LB SP RC	30.00	45.00
48 Gerald Weatherly RC	18.00	30.00
49 Fred Bruney SP RC	30.00	45.00
50 Jack Scarbath RC	18.00	30.00
51 John Karras	18.00	30.00
52 Al Conway RC	18.00	30.00
53 Emlen Tunnell SP	75.00	125.00
54 Gern Nagler SP RC	30.00	45.00
55 Kenneth Snyder SP	30.00	45.00
56 Y.A.Tittle	90.00	150.00
57 John Rapacz SP	30.00	45.00
58 Harley Sewell SP RC	30.00	45.00
59 Don Bingham RC	18.00	30.00
60 Darrell Hogan	18.00	30.00
61 Tony Curcillo RC	18.00	30.00
62 Ray Renfro SP RC	30.00	50.00
63 Leon Heath	18.00	30.00
64 Tex Coulter SP	30.00	45.00
65 Dewayne Douglas RC	18.00	30.00
66 J. Robert Smith SP	30.00	45.00
67 Bob McChesney SP RC	30.00	45.00
68 Dick Alban SP	30.00	45.00
69 Andy Kozar RC	18.00	30.00
70 Merwin Hodel SP RC	30.00	45.00
71 Thurman McGraw	18.00	30.00
72 Cliff Anderson RC	18.00	30.00
73 Pete Pihos	35.00	60.00
74 Julie Rykovich	18.00	30.00
75 John Kreamcheck SP RC	30.00	45.00
76 Lynn Chandnois	18.00	30.00
77 Cloyce Box SP	30.00	45.00
78 Ray Mathews	18.00	30.00
79 Bobby Walston	20.00	35.00
80 Jim Dooley	18.00	30.00
81 Pat Harder SP	30.00	45.00
82 Jerry Shipkey	18.00	30.00
83 Bobby Thomason RC	18.00	30.00
84 Hugh Taylor	20.00	35.00
85 George Ratterman	20.00	35.00
86 Don Stonesifer RC	18.00	30.00
87 John Williams SP RC	30.00	45.00

- ❑ 88 Leo Nomellini 30.00 50.00
- ❑ 89 Frank Ziegler 18.00 30.00
- ❑ 90 Don Paul DB UER 18.00 30.00
- ❑ 91 Tom Dublinski 18.00 30.00
- ❑ 92 Ken Carpenter 18.00 30.00
- ❑ 93 Ted Marchibroda RC 25.00 40.00
- ❑ 94 Chuck Drazenovich 18.00 30.00
- ❑ 95 Lou Groza SP 75.00 125.00
- ❑ 96 William Cross SP RC 50.00 100.00

1954 Bowman

- ❑ COMPLETE SET (128) 1200.00 1800.00
- ❑ COMMON CARD (1-64) 3.00 5.00
- ❑ COMMON SP (65-96) 15.00 25.00
- ❑ COMMON CARD (97-128) 3.00 5.00
- ❑ WRAPPER (1-CENT) 10.00 15.00
- ❑ WRAPPER (5-CENT) 25.00 30.00
- ❑ 1 Ray Mathews ! 15.00 30.00
- ❑ 2 John Huzvar RC 3.00 5.00
- ❑ 3 Jack Scarbath 3.00 5.00
- ❑ 4 Doug Atkins RC 30.00 50.00
- ❑ 5 Bill Stits RC 3.00 5.00
- ❑ 6 Joe Perry 18.00 30.00
- ❑ 7 Kyle Rote 7.50 15.00
- ❑ 8 Norm Van Brocklin 25.00 50.00
- ❑ 9 Pete Pihos 12.00 20.00
- ❑ 10 Babe Parilli 4.00 8.00
- ❑ 11 Zeke Bratkowski RC 15.00 25.00
- ❑ 12 Ollie Matson 15.00 25.00
- ❑ 13 Pat Brady 3.00 5.00
- ❑ 14 Fred Enke 3.00 5.00
- ❑ 15 Harry Ulinski 3.00 5.00
- ❑ 16 Bob Garrett RC 3.00 5.00
- ❑ 17 Bill Bowman RC 3.00 5.00
- ❑ 18 Leo Rucka RC 3.00 5.00
- ❑ 19 John Cannady 3.00 5.00
- ❑ 20 Tom Fears 15.00 25.00
- ❑ 21 Norm Willey RC 3.00 5.00
- ❑ 22 Floyd Reid 3.00 5.00
- ❑ 23 George Blanda RC 100.00 175.00
- ❑ 24 Don Doheney RC 3.00 5.00
- ❑ 25 John Schweder 3.00 5.00
- ❑ 26 Bert Rechichar 3.00 5.00
- ❑ 27 Harry Dowda RC 3.00 5.00
- ❑ 28 John Sandusky 3.00 5.00
- ❑ 29 Les Bingaman RC 7.50 15.00
- ❑ 30 Joe Arenas RC 3.00 5.00
- ❑ 31 Ray Wietecha RC 3.00 5.00
- ❑ 32 Elroy Hirsch 18.00 30.00
- ❑ 33 Harold Giancanelli RC 3.00 5.00
- ❑ 34 Billy Howton 4.00 8.00
- ❑ 35 Fred Morrison 3.00 5.00
- ❑ 36 Bobby Cavazos RC 3.00 5.00
- ❑ 37 Darrell Hogan 3.00 5.00
- ❑ 38 Buddy Young 4.00 8.00
- ❑ 39 Charlie Justice 12.00 20.00
- ❑ 40 Otto Graham 50.00 80.00
- ❑ 41 Doak Walker 20.00 35.00
- ❑ 42 Y.A.Tittle 35.00 60.00
- ❑ 43 Buford Long RC 3.00 5.00
- ❑ 44 Volney Quinlan 3.00 5.00
- ❑ 45 Bobby Thomason 3.00 5.00
- ❑ 46 Fred Cone 3.00 5.00
- ❑ 47 Gerald Weatherly 3.00 5.00
- ❑ 48 Don Stonesifer 3.00 5.00
- ❑ 49A Lynn Chandnois ERR 3.00 5.00
- ❑ 49B Lynn Chandnois COR 3.00 5.00
- ❑ 50 George Taliaferro 3.00 5.00
- ❑ 51 Dick Alban 3.00 5.00
- ❑ 52 Lou Groza 20.00 35.00
- ❑ 53 Bobby Layne 35.00 60.00
- ❑ 54 Hugh McElhenny 20.00 40.00
- ❑ 55 Frank Gifford 60.00 100.00
- ❑ 56 Leon McLaughlin RC 3.00 5.00
- ❑ 57 Chuck Bednarik 20.00 40.00
- ❑ 58 Art Hunter RC 3.00 5.00
- ❑ 59 Bill McColl 3.00 5.00
- ❑ 60 Charley Trippi 15.00 25.00
- ❑ 61 Jim Finks 7.50 15.00
- ❑ 62 Bill Lange G RC 3.00 5.00
- ❑ 63 Laurie Niemi 3.00 5.00
- ❑ 64 Ray Renfro 4.00 8.00
- ❑ 65 Dick Chapman SP RC 15.00 25.00
- ❑ 66 Bob Hantla SP RC 15.00 25.00
- ❑ 67 Ralph Starkey SP RC 15.00 25.00
- ❑ 68 Don Paul LB 15.00 25.00
- ❑ 69 Kenneth Snyder 15.00 25.00
- ❑ 70 Tobin Rote SP 18.00 30.00
- ❑ 71 Art DeCarlo SP RC 15.00 25.00
- ❑ 72 Tom Keane SP RC 15.00 25.00
- ❑ 73 Hugh Taylor SP 18.00 30.00
- ❑ 74 Warren Lahr SP RC 15.00 25.00
- ❑ 75 Jim Neal SP RC 15.00 25.00
- ❑ 76 Leo Nomellini SP 35.00 60.00
- ❑ 77 Dick Yelvington SP RC 15.00 25.00
- ❑ 78 Les Richter SP 18.00 30.00
- ❑ 79 Bucko Kilroy SP 18.00 30.00
- ❑ 80 John Martinkovic SP RC 15.00 25.00
- ❑ 81 Dale Dodrill SP RC 15.00 25.00
- ❑ 82 Ken Jackson SP RC 15.00 25.00
- ❑ 83 Paul Lipscomb 15.00 25.00
- ❑ 84 John Bauer SP RC 15.00 25.00
- ❑ 85 Lou Creekmur SP 30.00 50.00
- ❑ 86 Eddie Price 15.00 25.00
- ❑ 87 Kenneth Farragut SP RC 15.00 25.00
- ❑ 88 Dave Hanner RC SP 18.00 30.00
- ❑ 89 Don Boll SP RC 15.00 25.00
- ❑ 90 Chet Hanulak SP RC 15.00 25.00
- ❑ 91 Thurman McGraw 15.00 25.00
- ❑ 92 Don Heinrich SP RC 18.00 30.00
- ❑ 93 Dan McKown SP RC 15.00 25.00
- ❑ 94 Bob Fleck SP RC 15.00 25.00
- ❑ 95 Jerry Hilgenberg SP RC 15.00 25.00
- ❑ 96 Bill Walsh C 15.00 25.00
- ❑ 97A Tom Finnin ERR 35.00 60.00
- ❑ 97B Tom Finnan COR RC 4.00 8.00
- ❑ 98 Paul Barry RC 3.00 5.00
- ❑ 99 Chick Jagade 3.00 5.00
- ❑ 100 Jack Christiansen 12.00 20.00
- ❑ 101 Gordy Soltau 3.00 5.00
- ❑ 102A Emlen Tunnel ERR 15.00 25.00
- ❑ 102B Emlen Tunnell COR 12.00 20.00
- ❑ 102C Emlen Tunnell COR 12.00 20.00
- ❑ 103 Stan West RC 3.00 5.00
- ❑ 104 Jerry Williams 3.00 5.00
- ❑ 105 Veryl Switzer RC 3.00 5.00
- ❑ 106 Billy Stone 3.00 5.00
- ❑ 107 Jerry Watford RC 3.00 5.00
- ❑ 108 Elbert Nickel 4.00 8.00
- ❑ 109 Ed Sharkey RC 3.00 5.00
- ❑ 110 Steve Meilinger RC 3.00 5.00
- ❑ 111 Dante Lavelli 12.00 20.00
- ❑ 112 Leon Hart 7.50 15.00
- ❑ 113 Charley Conerly 18.00 30.00
- ❑ 114 Richard Lemmon RC 3.00 5.00
- ❑ 115 Al Carmichael RC 3.00 5.00
- ❑ 116 George Connor 12.00 20.00
- ❑ 117 John Olszewski 3.00 5.00
- ❑ 118 Ernie Stautner 15.00 25.00
- ❑ 119 Ray Smith RC 3.00 5.00
- ❑ 120 Neil Worden RC 3.00 5.00
- ❑ 121 Jim Dooley 3.00 5.00
- ❑ 122 Arnold Galiffa 3.00 5.00
- ❑ 123 Kline Gilbert RC 3.00 5.00
- ❑ 124 Bob Hoernschemeyer 4.00 8.00
- ❑ 125 Wilford White RC 7.50 15.00
- ❑ 126 Art Spinney RC 3.00 5.00
- ❑ 127 Joe Koch RC 3.00 5.00
- ❑ 128 John Lattner RC ! 40.00 80.00

1955 Bowman

- ❑ COMPLETE SET (160) 1000.00 1600.00
- ❑ COMMON CARD (1-64) 3.00 5.00
- ❑ COMMON CARD (65-160) 5.00 8.00
- ❑ WRAPPER (1-CENT) 150.00 225.00
- ❑ WRAPPER (5-CENT) 60.00 120.00
- ❑ 1 Doak Walker ! 40.00 75.00
- ❑ 2 Mike McCormack RC 18.00 30.00
- ❑ 3 John Olszewski 3.00 5.00
- ❑ 4 Dorne Dibble RC 3.00 5.00
- ❑ 5 Lindon Crow RC 3.00 5.00
- ❑ 6 Hugh Taylor UER 4.00 8.00
- ❑ 7 Frank Gifford 45.00 75.00
- ❑ 8 Alan Ameche RC 25.00 40.00
- ❑ 9 Don Stonesifer 3.00 5.00
- ❑ 10 Pete Pihos 7.50 15.00
- ❑ 11 Bill Austin 3.00 5.00
- ❑ 12 Dick Alban 3.00 5.00
- ❑ 13 Bobby Walston 4.00 8.00
- ❑ 14 Len Ford RC 25.00 40.00
- ❑ 15 Jug Girard 3.00 5.00
- ❑ 16 Charley Conerly 15.00 25.00
- ❑ 17 Volney Peters RC 3.00 5.00
- ❑ 18 Max Boydston RC 3.00 5.00
- ❑ 19 Leon Hart 6.00 12.00
- ❑ 20 Bert Rechichar 3.00 5.00
- ❑ 21 Lee Riley RC 3.00 5.00
- ❑ 22 Johnny Carson RC 3.00 5.00
- ❑ 23 Harry Thompson 3.00 5.00
- ❑ 24 Ray Wietecha 3.00 5.00
- ❑ 25 Ollie Matson 15.00 25.00
- ❑ 26 Eddie LeBaron 7.50 15.00
- ❑ 27 Jack Simmons 3.00 5.00
- ❑ 28 Jack Christiansen 7.50 15.00
- ❑ 29 Bucko Kilroy 4.00 8.00
- ❑ 30 Tom Keane 3.00 5.00
- ❑ 31 Dave Leggett RC 3.00 5.00
- ❑ 32 Norm Van Brocklin 25.00 40.00
- ❑ 33 Harlon Hill RC 4.00 8.00
- ❑ 34 Robert Haner RC 3.00 5.00
- ❑ 35 Veryl Switzer 3.00 5.00
- ❑ 36 Dick Stanfel RC 6.00 12.00
- ❑ 37 Lou Groza 15.00 25.00
- ❑ 38 Tank Younger 6.00 12.00
- ❑ 39 Dick Flanagan RC 3.00 5.00
- ❑ 40 Jim Dooley 3.00 5.00
- ❑ 41 Ray Collins RC 3.00 5.00
- ❑ 42 John Henry Johnson RC 25.00 40.00
- ❑ 43 Tom Fears 7.50 15.00
- ❑ 44 Joe Perry 18.00 30.00
- ❑ 45 Gene Brito RC 3.00 5.00
- ❑ 46 Bill Johnson C 3.00 5.00
- ❑ 47 Dan Towler 6.00 12.00
- ❑ 48 Dick Moegle RC 4.00 8.00
- ❑ 49 Kline Gilbert 3.00 5.00
- ❑ 50 Les Gobel RC 3.00 5.00
- ❑ 51 Ray Krouse RC 3.00 5.00
- ❑ 52 Pat Summerall RC 35.00 70.00
- ❑ 53 Ed Brown RC 6.00 12.00
- ❑ 54 Lynn Chandnois 3.00 5.00
- ❑ 55 Joe Heap RC 3.00 5.00
- ❑ 56 John Hoffman 3.00 5.00
- ❑ 57 Howard Ferguson RC 3.00 5.00
- ❑ 58 Bobby Watkins RC 3.00 5.00
- ❑ 59 Charlie Ane RC 3.00 5.00
- ❑ 60 Ken MacAfee E RC 4.00 8.00
- ❑ 61 Ralph Guglielmi RC 4.00 8.00
- ❑ 62 George Blanda 35.00 60.00
- ❑ 63 Kenneth Snyder 3.00 5.00
- ❑ 64 Chet Ostrowski 3.00 5.00
- ❑ 65 Buddy Young 7.50 15.00
- ❑ 66 Gordy Soltau 5.00 8.00
- ❑ 67 Eddie Bell RC 5.00 8.00
- ❑ 68 Ben Agajanian RC 6.00 12.00
- ❑ 69 Tom Dahms RC 5.00 8.00
- ❑ 70 Jim Ringo RC 30.00 50.00
- ❑ 71 Bobby Layne 45.00 75.00
- ❑ 72 Y.A.Tittle 45.00 75.00
- ❑ 73 Bob Gaona RC 5.00 8.00
- ❑ 74 Tobin Rote 6.00 12.00
- ❑ 75 Hugh McElhenny 18.00 30.00
- ❑ 76 John Kreamcheck 5.00 8.00
- ❑ 77 Al Dorow RC 6.00 12.00
- ❑ 78 Bill Wade 7.50 15.00
- ❑ 79 Dale Dodrill 5.00 8.00
- ❑ 80 Chuck Drazenovich 5.00 8.00
- ❑ 81 Billy Wilson RC 6.00 12.00
- ❑ 82 Les Richter 6.00 12.00
- ❑ 83 Pat Brady 5.00 8.00
- ❑ 84 Bob Hoernschemeyer 6.00 12.00

❑ 85 Joe Arenas	5.00	8.00
❑ 86 Len Szafaryn UER RC	5.00	8.00
❑ 87 Rick Casares RC	12.00	20.00
❑ 88 Leon McLaughlin	5.00	8.00
❑ 89 Charley Toogood RC	5.00	8.00
❑ 90 Tom Bettis RC	5.00	8.00
❑ 91 John Sandusky	5.00	8.00
❑ 92 Bill Wightkin	5.00	8.00
❑ 93 Darrel Brewster RC	5.00	8.00
❑ 94 Marion Campbell	7.50	15.00
❑ 95 Floyd Reid	5.00	8.00
❑ 96 Chick Jagade	5.00	8.00
❑ 97 George Taliaferro	5.00	8.00
❑ 98 Carlton Massey RC	5.00	8.00
❑ 99 Fran Rogel	5.00	8.00
❑ 100 Alex Sandusky RC	5.00	8.00
❑ 101 Bob St.Clair RC	25.00	40.00
❑ 102 Al Carmichael	5.00	8.00
❑ 103 Carl Taseff RC	5.00	8.00
❑ 104 Leo Nomellini	15.00	25.00
❑ 105 Tom Scott	5.00	8.00
❑ 106 Ted Marchibroda	7.50	15.00
❑ 107 Art Spinney	5.00	8.00
❑ 108 Wayne Robinson	5.00	8.00
❑ 109 Jim Ricca RC	5.00	8.00
❑ 110 Lou Ferry RC	5.00	8.00
❑ 111 Roger Zatkoff RC	5.00	8.00
❑ 112 Lou Creekmur	7.50	15.00
❑ 113 Kenny Konz RC	5.00	8.00
❑ 114 Doug Eggers RC	5.00	8.00
❑ 115 Bobby Thomason	5.00	8.00
❑ 116 Bill McPeak RC	5.00	8.00
❑ 117 William Brown RC	5.00	8.00
❑ 118 Royce Womble RC	5.00	8.00
❑ 119 Frank Gatski RC	20.00	35.00
❑ 120 Jim Finks	7.50	15.00
❑ 121 Andy Robustelli	15.00	25.00
❑ 122 Bobby Dillon	5.00	8.00
❑ 123 Leo Sanford	5.00	8.00
❑ 124 Elbert Nickel	6.00	12.00
❑ 125 Wayne Hansen RC	5.00	8.00
❑ 126 Buck Lansford RC	5.00	8.00
❑ 127 Gern Nagler	5.00	8.00
❑ 128 Jim Salsbury RC	5.00	8.00
❑ 129 Dale Atkeson RC	5.00	8.00
❑ 130 John Schweder	5.00	8.00
❑ 131 Dave Hanner	6.00	12.00
❑ 132 Eddie Price	5.00	8.00
❑ 133 Vic Janowicz	15.00	30.00
❑ 134 Ernie Stautner	15.00	25.00
❑ 135 James Parmer RC	5.00	8.00
❑ 136 Emlen Tunnell UER	12.00	20.00
❑ 137 Kyle Rote	7.50	15.00
❑ 138 Norm Willey	5.00	8.00
❑ 139 Charley Trippi	12.00	20.00
❑ 140 Billy Howton	6.00	12.00
❑ 141 Bobby Clatterbuck RC	5.00	8.00
❑ 142 Bob Boyd	5.00	8.00
❑ 143 Bob Toneff RC	6.00	12.00
❑ 144 Jerry Helluin RC	5.00	8.00
❑ 145 Adrian Burk	5.00	8.00
❑ 146 Walt Michaels	6.00	12.00
❑ 147 Zollie Toth	5.00	8.00
❑ 148 Frank Varrichione RC	5.00	8.00
❑ 149 Dick Bielski RC	5.00	8.00
❑ 150 George Ratterman	6.00	12.00
❑ 151 Mike Jarmoluk RC	5.00	8.00
❑ 152 Tom Landry	125.00	200.00
❑ 153 Ray Renfro	6.00	12.00
❑ 154 Zeke Bratkowski	6.00	12.00
❑ 155 Jerry Norton RC	5.00	8.00
❑ 156 Maurice Bassett RC	5.00	8.00
❑ 157 Volney Quinlan	5.00	8.00
❑ 158 Chuck Bednarik	18.00	30.00
❑ 159 Don Colo RC	5.00	8.00
❑ 160 L.G. Dupre RC	20.00	40.00

1991 Bowman

❑ COMPLETE SET (561)	5.00	12.00
❑ COMP.FACT.SET (561)	5.00	12.00
❑ 1 Jeff George RS	.08	.25
❑ 2 Richmond Webb RS	.01	.05
❑ 3 Emmitt Smith RS	.50	1.25
❑ 4 Mark Carrier DB RS UER	.01	.05
❑ 5 Steve Christie RS	.01	.05
❑ 6 Keith Sims RS	.01	.05
❑ 7 Rob Moore RS UER	.08	.25
❑ 8 Johnny Johnson RS	.01	.05
❑ 9 Eric Green RS	.01	.05
❑ 10 Ben Smith RS	.01	.05
❑ 11 Tory Epps RS	.01	.05
❑ 12 Andre Rison	.02	.10
❑ 13 Shawn Collins	.01	.05
❑ 14 Chris Hinton	.01	.05
❑ 15 Deion Sanders	.15	.40
❑ 16 Darion Conner	.01	.05
❑ 17 Michael Haynes	.08	.25
❑ 18 Chris Miller	.02	.10
❑ 19 Jessie Tuggle	.01	.05
❑ 20 Scott Fulhage	.01	.05
❑ 21 Bill Fralic	.01	.05
❑ 22 Floyd Dixon	.01	.05
❑ 23 Oliver Barnett	.01	.05
❑ 24 Mike Rozier	.01	.05
❑ 25 Tory Epps	.01	.05
❑ 26 Tim Green	.01	.05
❑ 27 Steve Broussard	.01	.05
❑ 28 Bruce Pickens RC	.01	.05
❑ 29 Mike Pritchard RC	.08	.25
❑ 30 Andre Reed	.02	.10
❑ 31 Darryl Talley	.01	.05
❑ 32 Nate Odomes	.01	.05
❑ 33 Jamie Mueller	.01	.05
❑ 34 Leon Seals	.01	.05
❑ 35 Keith McKeller	.01	.05
❑ 36 Al Edwards	.01	.05
❑ 37 Butch Rolle	.01	.05
❑ 38 Jeff Wright RC	.01	.05
❑ 39 Will Wolford	.01	.05
❑ 40 James Williams	.01	.05
❑ 41 Kent Hull	.01	.05
❑ 42 James Lofton	.02	.10
❑ 43 Frank Reich	.02	.10
❑ 44 Bruce Smith	.08	.25
❑ 45 Thurman Thomas	.08	.25
❑ 46 Leonard Smith	.01	.05
❑ 47 Shane Conlan	.01	.05
❑ 48 Steve Tasker	.02	.10
❑ 49 Ray Bentley	.01	.05
❑ 50 Cornelius Bennett	.02	.10
❑ 51 Stan Thomas	.01	.05
❑ 52 Shaun Gayle	.01	.05
❑ 53 Wendell Davis	.01	.05
❑ 54 James Thornton	.01	.05
❑ 55 Mark Carrier DB	.02	.10
❑ 56 Richard Dent	.02	.10
❑ 57 Ron Morris	.01	.05
❑ 58 Mike Singletary	.02	.10
❑ 59 Jay Hilgenberg	.01	.05
❑ 60 Donnell Woolford	.01	.05
❑ 61 Jim Covert	.01	.05
❑ 62 Jim Harbaugh	.08	.25
❑ 63 Neal Anderson	.02	.10
❑ 64 Brad Muster	.01	.05
❑ 65 Kevin Butler	.01	.05
❑ 66 Trace Armstrong UER	.01	.05
❑ 67 Ron Cox	.01	.05
❑ 68 Peter Tom Willis	.01	.05
❑ 69 Johnny Bailey	.01	.05
❑ 70 Mark Bortz UER	.01	.05
❑ 71 Chris Zorich RC	.08	.25
❑ 72 Lamar Rogers RC	.01	.05
❑ 73 David Grant UER	.01	.05
❑ 74 Lewis Billups	.01	.05
❑ 75 Harold Green	.02	.10
❑ 76 Ickey Woods	.01	.05
❑ 77 Eddie Brown	.01	.05
❑ 78 David Fulcher	.01	.05
❑ 79 Anthony Munoz	.02	.10
❑ 80 Carl Zander	.01	.05
❑ 81 Rodney Holman	.01	.05
❑ 82 James Brooks	.02	.10
❑ 83 Tim McGee	.01	.05
❑ 84 Boomer Esiason	.02	.10
❑ 85 Leon White	.01	.05
❑ 86 James Francis UER	.01	.05
❑ 87 Mitchell Price RC	.01	.05
❑ 88 Ed King RC	.01	.05
❑ 89 Eric Turner RC	.02	.10
❑ 90 Rob Burnett RC	.02	.10
❑ 91 Leroy Hoard	.02	.10
❑ 92 Kevin Mack UER	.01	.05
❑ 93 Thane Gash UER	.01	.05
❑ 94 Gregg Rakoczy	.01	.05
❑ 95 Clay Matthews	.02	.10
❑ 96 Eric Metcalf	.02	.10
❑ 97 Stephen Braggs	.01	.05
❑ 98 Frank Minnifield	.01	.05
❑ 99 Reggie Langhorne	.01	.05
❑ 100 Mike Johnson	.01	.05
❑ 101 Brian Brennan	.01	.05
❑ 102 Anthony Pleasant	.01	.05
❑ 103 Godfrey Myles UER RC	.01	.05
❑ 104 Russell Maryland RC	.08	.25
❑ 105 James Washington RC	.01	.05
❑ 106 Nate Newton	.02	.10
❑ 107 Jimmie Jones	.01	.05
❑ 108 Jay Novacek	.08	.25
❑ 109 Alexander Wright	.01	.05
❑ 110 Jack Del Rio	.02	.10
❑ 111 Jim Jeffcoat	.01	.05
❑ 112 Mike Saxon	.01	.05
❑ 113 Troy Aikman	.30	.75
❑ 114 Issiac Holt	.01	.05
❑ 115 Ken Norton	.02	.10
❑ 116 Kelvin Martin	.01	.05
❑ 117 Emmitt Smith	1.00	2.50
❑ 118 Ken Willis	.01	.05
❑ 119 Daniel Stubbs	.01	.05
❑ 120 Michael Irvin	.08	.25
❑ 121 Danny Noonan	.01	.05
❑ 122 Alvin Harper RC	.08	.25
❑ 123 Reggie Johnson RC	.01	.05
❑ 124 Vance Johnson	.01	.05
❑ 125 Steve Atwater	.01	.05
❑ 126 Greg Kragen	.01	.05
❑ 127 John Elway	.50	1.25
❑ 128 Simon Fletcher	.01	.05
❑ 129 Wymon Henderson	.01	.05
❑ 130 Ricky Nattiel	.01	.05
❑ 131 Shannon Sharpe	.20	.50
❑ 132 Ron Holmes	.01	.05
❑ 133 Karl Mecklenburg	.01	.05
❑ 134 Bobby Humphrey	.01	.05
❑ 135 Clarence Kay	.01	.05
❑ 136 Dennis Smith	.01	.05
❑ 137 Jim Juriga	.01	.05
❑ 138 Melvin Bratton	.01	.05
❑ 139 Mark Jackson UER	.01	.05
❑ 140 Michael Brooks	.01	.05
❑ 141 Alton Montgomery	.01	.05
❑ 142 Mike Croel RC	.01	.05
❑ 143 Mel Gray	.02	.10
❑ 144 Michael Cofer	.01	.05
❑ 145 Jeff Campbell	.01	.05
❑ 146 Dan Owens	.01	.05
❑ 147 Robert Clark UER	.01	.05
❑ 148 Jim Arnold	.01	.05
❑ 149 William White	.01	.05
❑ 150 Rodney Peete	.02	.10
❑ 151 Jerry Ball	.01	.05
❑ 152 Bennie Blades	.01	.05
❑ 153 Barry Sanders UER	.50	1.25
❑ 154 Andre Ware	.02	.10
❑ 155 Lomas Brown	.01	.05
❑ 156 Chris Spielman	.02	.10
❑ 157 Kelvin Pritchett RC	.02	.10
❑ 158 Herman Moore RC	.08	.25
❑ 159 Chris Jacke	.01	.05
❑ 160 Tony Mandarich	.01	.05
❑ 161 Perry Kemp	.01	.05

Card	Low	High
❑ 162 Johnny Holland	.01	.05
❑ 163 Mark Lee	.01	.05
❑ 164 Anthony Dilweg	.01	.05
❑ 165 Scott Stephen RC	.01	.05
❑ 166 Ed West	.01	.05
❑ 167 Mark Murphy	.01	.05
❑ 168 Darrell Thompson	.01	.05
❑ 169 James Campen RC	.01	.05
❑ 170 Jeff Query	.01	.05
❑ 171 Brian Noble	.01	.05
❑ 172 Sterling Sharpe UER	.08	.25
❑ 173 Robert Brown	.01	.05
❑ 174 Tim Harris	.01	.05
❑ 175 LeRoy Butler	.02	.10
❑ 176 Don Majkowski	.01	.05
❑ 177 Vinnie Clark RC	.01	.05
❑ 178 Esera Tuaolo RC	.01	.05
❑ 179 Lorenzo White UER	.01	.05
❑ 180 Warren Moon	.08	.25
❑ 181 Sean Jones	.02	.10
❑ 182 Curtis Duncan	.01	.05
❑ 183 Al Smith	.01	.05
❑ 184 Richard Johnson CB RC	.01	.05
❑ 185 Tony Jones WR	.01	.05
❑ 186 Bubba McDowell	.01	.05
❑ 187 Bruce Matthews	.02	.10
❑ 188 Ray Childress	.01	.05
❑ 189 Haywood Jeffires	.02	.10
❑ 190 Ernest Givins	.02	.10
❑ 191 Mike Munchak	.02	.10
❑ 192 Greg Montgomery	.01	.05
❑ 193 Cody Carlson RC	.01	.05
❑ 194 Johnny Meads	.01	.05
❑ 195 Drew Hill UER	.01	.05
❑ 196 Mike Dumas RC	.01	.05
❑ 197 Darryll Lewis RC	.02	.10
❑ 198 Rohn Stark	.01	.05
❑ 199 Clarence Verdin UER	.01	.05
❑ 200 Mike Prior	.01	.05
❑ 201 Eugene Daniel	.01	.05
❑ 202 Dean Biasucci	.01	.05
❑ 203 Jeff Herrod	.01	.05
❑ 204 Keith Taylor	.01	.05
❑ 205 Jon Hand	.01	.05
❑ 206 Pat Beach	.01	.05
❑ 207 Duane Bickett	.01	.05
❑ 208 Jessie Hester UER	.01	.05
❑ 209 Chip Banks	.01	.05
❑ 210 Ray Donaldson	.01	.05
❑ 211 Bill Brooks	.01	.05
❑ 212 Jeff George	.08	.25
❑ 213 Tony Siragusa RC	.02	.10
❑ 214 Albert Bentley	.01	.05
❑ 215 Joe Valerio	.01	.05
❑ 216 Chris Martin	.01	.05
❑ 217 Christian Okoye	.01	.05
❑ 218 Stephone Paige	.01	.05
❑ 219 Percy Snow	.01	.05
❑ 220 David Szott	.01	.05
❑ 221 Derrick Thomas	.08	.25
❑ 222 Todd McNair	.01	.05
❑ 223 Albert Lewis	.01	.05
❑ 224 Neil Smith	.08	.25
❑ 225 Barry Word	.01	.05
❑ 226 Robb Thomas	.01	.05
❑ 227 John Alt	.01	.05
❑ 228 Jonathan Hayes	.01	.05
❑ 229 Kevin Ross	.01	.05
❑ 230 Nick Lowery	.01	.05
❑ 231 Tim Grunhard	.01	.05
❑ 232 Dan Saleaumua	.01	.05
❑ 233 Steve DeBerg	.01	.05
❑ 234 Harvey Williams RC	.08	.25
❑ 235 Nick Bell RC UER	.01	.05
❑ 236 Mervyn Fernandez UER	.01	.05
❑ 237 Howie Long	.08	.25
❑ 238 Marcus Allen	.08	.25
❑ 239 Eddie Anderson	.01	.05
❑ 240 Ethan Horton	.01	.05
❑ 241 Lionel Washington	.01	.05
❑ 242 Steve Wisniewski UER	.01	.05
❑ 243 Bo Jackson UER	.10	.30
❑ 244 Greg Townsend	.01	.05
❑ 245 Jeff Jaeger	.01	.05
❑ 246 Aaron Wallace	.01	.05
❑ 247 Garry Lewis	.01	.05
❑ 248 Steve Smith	.01	.05
❑ 249 Willie Gault UER	.01	.05
❑ 250 Scott Davis	.01	.05
❑ 251 Jay Schroeder	.01	.05
❑ 252 Don Mosebar	.01	.05
❑ 253 Todd Marinovich RC	.01	.05
❑ 254 Irv Pankey	.01	.05
❑ 255 Flipper Anderson	.01	.05
❑ 256 Tom Newberry	.01	.05
❑ 257 Kevin Greene	.02	.10
❑ 258 Mike Wilcher	.01	.05
❑ 259 Bern Brostek	.01	.05
❑ 260 Buford McGee	.01	.05
❑ 261 Cleveland Gary	.01	.05
❑ 262 Jackie Slater	.01	.05
❑ 263 Henry Ellard	.02	.10
❑ 264 Alvin Wright	.01	.05
❑ 265 Darryl Henley RC	.01	.05
❑ 266 Damone Johnson RC	.01	.05
❑ 267 Frank Stams	.01	.05
❑ 268 Jerry Gray	.01	.05
❑ 269 Jim Everett	.02	.10
❑ 270 Pat Terrell	.01	.05
❑ 271 Todd Lyght RC	.01	.05
❑ 272 Aaron Cox	.01	.05
❑ 273 Barry Sanders LL	.20	.50
❑ 274 Jerry Rice LL	.15	.40
❑ 275 Derrick Thomas LL	.08	.25
❑ 276 Mark Carrier DB LL	.02	.10
❑ 277 Warren Moon LL	.08	.25
❑ 278 Randall Cunningham LL	.02	.10
❑ 279 Nick Lowery LL	.01	.05
❑ 280 Clarence Verdin LL	.01	.05
❑ 281 Thurman Thomas LL	.08	.25
❑ 282 Mike Horan LL	.01	.05
❑ 283 Flipper Anderson LL	.01	.05
❑ 284 John Offerdahl	.01	.05
❑ 285 Dan Marino UER	.50	1.25
❑ 286 Mark Clayton	.02	.10
❑ 287 Tony Paige	.01	.05
❑ 288 Keith Sims	.01	.05
❑ 289 Jeff Cross	.01	.05
❑ 290 Pete Stoyanovich	.01	.05
❑ 291 Ferrell Edmunds	.01	.05
❑ 292 Reggie Roby	.01	.05
❑ 293 Louis Oliver	.01	.05
❑ 294 Jarvis Williams	.01	.05
❑ 295 Sammie Smith	.01	.05
❑ 296 Richmond Webb	.01	.05
❑ 297 J.B. Brown	.01	.05
❑ 298 Jim C.Jensen	.01	.05
❑ 299 Mark Duper	.02	.10
❑ 300 David Griggs	.01	.05
❑ 301 Randal Hill RC	.02	.10
❑ 302 Aaron Craver RC	.01	.05
❑ 303 Keith Millard	.01	.05
❑ 304 Steve Jordan	.01	.05
❑ 305 Anthony Carter	.02	.10
❑ 306 Mike Merriweather	.01	.05
❑ 307 Audray McMillian RC UER	.01	.05
❑ 308 Randall McDaniel	.02	.10
❑ 309 Gary Zimmerman	.02	.10
❑ 310 Carl Lee	.01	.05
❑ 311 Reggie Rutland	.01	.05
❑ 312 Hassan Jones	.01	.05
❑ 313 Kirk Lowdermilk UER	.01	.05
❑ 314 Herschel Walker	.02	.10
❑ 315 Chris Doleman	.01	.05
❑ 316 Joey Browner	.01	.05
❑ 317 Wade Wilson	.02	.10
❑ 318 Henry Thomas	.01	.05
❑ 319 Rich Gannon	.08	.25
❑ 320 Al Noga UER	.01	.05
❑ 321 Pat Harlow RC	.01	.05
❑ 322 Bruce Armstrong	.01	.05
❑ 323 Maurice Hurst	.01	.05
❑ 324 Brent Williams	.01	.05
❑ 325 Chris Singleton	.01	.05
❑ 326 Jason Staurovsky	.01	.05
❑ 327 Marvin Allen	.01	.05
❑ 328 Hart Lee Dykes	.01	.05
❑ 329 Johnny Rembert	.01	.05
❑ 330 Andre Tippett	.01	.05
❑ 331 Greg McMurtry	.01	.05
❑ 332 John Stephens	.01	.05
❑ 333 Ray Agnew	.01	.05
❑ 334 Tommy Hodson	.01	.05
❑ 335 Ronnie Lippett	.01	.05
❑ 336 Marv Cook	.01	.05
❑ 337 Tommy Barnhardt RC	.01	.05
❑ 338 Dalton Hilliard	.01	.05
❑ 339 Sam Mills	.01	.05
❑ 340 Morten Andersen	.01	.05
❑ 341 Stan Brock	.01	.05
❑ 342 Brett Maxie	.01	.05
❑ 343 Steve Walsh	.01	.05
❑ 344 Vaughan Johnson	.01	.05
❑ 345 Rickey Jackson	.01	.05
❑ 346 Renaldo Turnbull	.01	.05
❑ 347 Joel Hilgenberg	.01	.05
❑ 348 Toi Cook RC	.01	.05
❑ 349 Robert Massey	.01	.05
❑ 350 Pat Swilling	.02	.10
❑ 351 Eric Martin	.01	.05
❑ 352 Rueben Mayes UER	.01	.05
❑ 353 Vince Buck	.01	.05
❑ 354 Brett Perriman	.08	.25
❑ 355 Wesley Carroll RC	.01	.05
❑ 356 Jarrod Bunch RC	.01	.05
❑ 357 Pepper Johnson	.01	.05
❑ 358 Dave Meggett	.02	.10
❑ 359 Mark Collins	.01	.05
❑ 360 Sean Landeta	.01	.05
❑ 361 Maurice Carthon	.01	.05
❑ 362 Mike Fox UER	.01	.05
❑ 363 Jeff Hostetler	.02	.10
❑ 364 Phil Simms	.02	.10
❑ 365 Leonard Marshall	.01	.05
❑ 366 Gary Reasons	.01	.05
❑ 367 Rodney Hampton	.08	.25
❑ 368 Greg Jackson RC	.01	.05
❑ 369 Jumbo Elliott	.01	.05
❑ 370 Bob Kratch RC	.01	.05
❑ 371 Lawrence Taylor	.08	.25
❑ 372 Erik Howard	.01	.05
❑ 373 Carl Banks	.01	.05
❑ 374 Stephen Baker	.01	.05
❑ 375 Mark Ingram	.02	.10
❑ 376 Browning Nagle RC	.01	.05
❑ 377 Jeff Lageman	.01	.05
❑ 378 Ken O'Brien	.01	.05
❑ 379 Al Toon	.02	.10
❑ 380 Joe Prokop	.01	.05
❑ 381 Tony Stargell	.01	.05
❑ 382 Blair Thomas	.01	.05
❑ 383 Erik McMillan	.01	.05
❑ 384 Dennis Byrd	.01	.05
❑ 385 Freeman McNeil	.01	.05
❑ 386 Brad Baxter	.01	.05
❑ 387 Mark Boyer	.01	.05
❑ 388 Terance Mathis	.02	.10
❑ 389 Jim Sweeney	.01	.05
❑ 390 Kyle Clifton	.01	.05
❑ 391 Pat Leahy	.01	.05
❑ 392 Rob Moore	.08	.25
❑ 393 James Hasty	.01	.05
❑ 394 Blaise Bryant	.01	.05
❑ 395A Jesse Campbell ERR RC	.40	1.00
❑ 395B Jesse Campbell COR RC	.01	.05
❑ 396 Keith Jackson	.02	.10
❑ 397 Jerome Brown	.01	.05
❑ 398 Keith Byars	.01	.05
❑ 399 Seth Joyner	.02	.10
❑ 400 Mike Bellamy	.01	.05
❑ 401 Fred Barnett	.08	.25
❑ 402 Reggie Singletary RC	.01	.05
❑ 403 Reggie White	.08	.25
❑ 404 Randall Cunningham	.08	.25
❑ 405 Byron Evans	.01	.05
❑ 406 Wes Hopkins	.01	.05
❑ 407 Ben Smith	.01	.05
❑ 408 Roger Ruzek	.01	.05
❑ 409 Eric Allen UER	.01	.05
❑ 410 Anthony Toney UER	.01	.05
❑ 411 Clyde Simmons	.01	.05
❑ 412 Andre Waters	.01	.05
❑ 413 Calvin Williams	.02	.10
❑ 414 Eric Swann RC	.08	.25
❑ 415 Eric Hill	.01	.05
❑ 416 Tim McDonald	.01	.05
❑ 417 Luis Sharpe	.01	.05
❑ 418 Ernie Jones UER	.01	.05
❑ 419 Ken Harvey	.02	.10
❑ 420 Ricky Proehl	.01	.05
❑ 421 Johnny Johnson	.01	.05
❑ 422 Anthony Bell	.01	.05
❑ 423 Timm Rosenbach	.01	.05
❑ 424 Rich Camarillo	.01	.05
❑ 425 Walter Reeves	.01	.05
❑ 426 Freddie Joe Nunn	.01	.05
❑ 427 Anthony Thompson UER	.01	.05

❑ 428 Bill Lewis .01 .05
❑ 429 Jim Wahler RC .01 .05
❑ 430 Cedric Mack .01 .05
❑ 431 Mike Jones DE RC .01 .05
❑ 432 Ernie Mills RC .02 .10
❑ 433 Tim Worley .01 .05
❑ 434 Greg Lloyd .08 .25
❑ 435 Dermontti Dawson .01 .05
❑ 436 Louis Lipps .01 .05
❑ 437 Eric Green .01 .05
❑ 438 Donald Evans .01 .05
❑ 439 D.J. Johnson .01 .05
❑ 440 Tunch Ilkin .01 .05
❑ 441 Bubby Brister .01 .05
❑ 442 Chris Calloway .01 .05
❑ 443 David Little .01 .05
❑ 444 Thomas Everett .01 .05
❑ 445 Carnell Lake .01 .05
❑ 446 Rod Woodson .08 .25
❑ 447 Gary Anderson K .01 .05
❑ 448 Merril Hoge .01 .05
❑ 449 Gerald Williams .01 .05
❑ 450 Eric Moten RC .01 .05
❑ 451 Marion Butts .02 .10
❑ 452 Leslie O'Neal .02 .10
❑ 453 Ronnie Harmon .01 .05
❑ 454 Gill Byrd .01 .05
❑ 455 Junior Seau .08 .25
❑ 456 Nate Lewis RC .01 .05
❑ 457 Leo Goeas .01 .05
❑ 458 Burt Grossman .01 .05
❑ 459 Courtney Hall .01 .05
❑ 460 Anthony Miller .02 .10
❑ 461 Gary Plummer .01 .05
❑ 462 Billy Joe Tolliver .01 .05
❑ 463 Lee Williams .01 .05
❑ 464 Arthur Cox .01 .05
❑ 465 John Kidd UER .01 .05
❑ 466 Frank Cornish .01 .05
❑ 467 John Carney .01 .05
❑ 468 Eric Bieniemy RC .01 .05
❑ 469 Don Griffin .01 .05
❑ 470 Jerry Rice .30 .75
❑ 471 Keith DeLong .01 .05
❑ 472 John Taylor .02 .10
❑ 473 Brent Jones .08 .25
❑ 474 Pierce Holt .01 .05
❑ 475 Kevin Fagan .01 .05
❑ 476 Bill Romanowski .01 .05
❑ 477 Dexter Carter .01 .05
❑ 478 Guy McIntyre .01 .05
❑ 479 Joe Montana .50 1.25
❑ 480 Charles Haley .02 .10
❑ 481 Mike Cofer .01 .05
❑ 482 Jesse Sapolu .01 .05
❑ 483 Eric Davis .01 .05
❑ 484 Mike Sherrard .01 .05
❑ 485 Steve Young .30 .75
❑ 486 Darryl Pollard .01 .05
❑ 487 Tom Rathman .01 .05
❑ 488 Michael Carter .01 .05
❑ 489 Ricky Watters RC .60 1.50
❑ 490 John Johnson RC .01 .05
❑ 491 Eugene Robinson .01 .05
❑ 492 Andy Heck .01 .05
❑ 493 John L. Williams .01 .05
❑ 494 Norm Johnson .01 .05
❑ 495 David Wyman .01 .05
❑ 496 Derrick Fenner UER .01 .05
❑ 497 Rick Donnelly .01 .05
❑ 498 Tony Woods .01 .05
❑ 499 Derrick Loville RC .01 .05
❑ 500 Dave Krieg .02 .10
❑ 501 Joe Nash .01 .05
❑ 502 Brian Blades .02 .10
❑ 503 Cortez Kennedy .08 .25
❑ 504 Jeff Bryant .01 .05
❑ 505 Tommy Kane .01 .05
❑ 506 Travis McNeal .01 .05
❑ 507 Terry Wooden .01 .05
❑ 508 Chris Warren .08 .25
❑ 509A Dan McGwire ERR RC .01 .05
❑ 509B Dan McGwire COR RC .01 .05
❑ 510 Mark Robinson .01 .05
❑ 511 Ron Hall .01 .05
❑ 512 Paul Gruber .01 .05
❑ 513 Harry Hamilton .01 .05
❑ 514 Keith McCants .01 .05
❑ 515 Reggie Cobb .01 .05
❑ 516 Steve Christie UER .01 .05
❑ 517 Broderick Thomas .01 .05
❑ 518 Mark Carrier WR .08 .25
❑ 519 Vinny Testaverde .02 .10
❑ 520 Ricky Reynolds .01 .05
❑ 521 Jesse Anderson .01 .05
❑ 522 Reuben Davis .01 .05
❑ 523 Wayne Haddix .01 .05
❑ 524 Gary Anderson RB UER .01 .05
❑ 525 Bruce Hill .01 .05
❑ 526 Kevin Murphy .01 .05
❑ 527 Lawrence Dawsey RC .02 .10
❑ 528 Ricky Ervins RC .02 .10
❑ 529 Charles Mann .01 .05
❑ 530 Jim Lachey .01 .05
❑ 531 Mark Rypien UER .02 .10
❑ 532 Darrell Green .01 .05
❑ 533 Stan Humphries .08 .25
❑ 534 Jeff Bostic UER .01 .05
❑ 535 Earnest Byner .01 .05
❑ 536 Art Monk UER .02 .10
❑ 537 Don Warren .01 .05
❑ 538 Darryl Grant .01 .05
❑ 539 Wilber Marshall .01 .05
❑ 540 Kurt Gouveia RC .01 .05
❑ 541 Markus Koch .01 .05
❑ 542 Andre Collins .01 .05
❑ 543 Chip Lohmiller .01 .05
❑ 544 Alvin Walton .01 .05
❑ 545 Gary Clark .08 .25
❑ 546 Ricky Sanders .01 .05
❑ 547 Redskins vs. Eagles .01 .05
❑ 548 Bengals vs. Oilers .01 .05
❑ 549 Dolphins vs. Chiefs .01 .05
❑ 550 Bears vs. Saints UER .01 .05
❑ 551 Playoffs/Thurman Thomas .02 .10
❑ 552 49ers vs. Redskins .01 .05
❑ 553 Giants vs. Bears .01 .05
❑ 554 Playoffs/Bo Jackson .02 .10
❑ 555 AFC Championship .01 .05
❑ 556 NFC Championship .01 .05
❑ 557 Super Bowl XXV .01 .05
❑ 558 Checklist 1-140 .01 .05
❑ 559 Checklist 141-280 .01 .05
❑ 560 Checklist 281-420 UER .01 .05
❑ 561 Checklist 421-561 UER .01 .05

1992 Bowman

❑ COMPLETE SET (573) 25.00 50.00
❑ 1 Reggie White .40 1.00
❑ 2 Johnny Meads .08 .25
❑ 3 Chip Lohmiller .08 .25
❑ 4 James Lofton .20 .50
❑ 5 Ray Horton .08 .25
❑ 6 Rich Moran .08 .25
❑ 7 Howard Cross .08 .25
❑ 8 Mike Horan .08 .25
❑ 9 Erik Kramer .20 .50
❑ 10 Steve Wisniewski .08 .25
❑ 11 Michael Haynes .20 .50
❑ 12 Donald Evans .08 .25
❑ 13 Michael Irvin FOIL .40 1.00
❑ 14 Gary Zimmerman .08 .25
❑ 15 John Friesz .20 .50
❑ 16 Mark Carrier WR .40 1.00
❑ 17 Mark Duper .08 .25
❑ 18 James Thornton .08 .25
❑ 19 Jon Hand .08 .25
❑ 20 Sterling Sharpe .40 1.00
❑ 21 Jacob Green .08 .25
❑ 22 Wesley Carroll .08 .25
❑ 23 Clay Matthews .20 .50
❑ 24 Kevin Greene .20 .50
❑ 25 Brad Baxter .08 .25
❑ 26 Don Griffin .08 .25
❑ 27 Robert Delpino .60 1.50
❑ 28 Lee Johnson .08 .25
❑ 29 Jim Wahler .08 .25
❑ 30 Leonard Russell .20 .50
❑ 31 Eric Moore .08 .25
❑ 32 Dino Hackett .08 .25
❑ 33 Simon Fletcher .08 .25
❑ 34 Al Edwards .08 .25
❑ 35 Brad Edwards .00 .25
❑ 36 James Joseph .08 .25
❑ 37 Rodney Peete .20 .50
❑ 38 Ricky Reynolds .08 .25
❑ 39 Eddie Anderson .08 .25
❑ 40 Ken Clarke .08 .25
❑ 41 Tony Bennett .20 .50
❑ 42 Larry Brown DB .08 .25
❑ 43 Ray Childress .08 .25
❑ 44 Mike Kenn .08 .25
❑ 45 Vestee Jackson .08 .25
❑ 46 Neil O'Donnell .20 .50
❑ 47 Bill Brooks .08 .25
❑ 48 Kevin Butler .08 .25
❑ 49 Joe Phillips .08 .25
❑ 50 Cortez Kennedy .20 .50
❑ 51 Rickey Jackson .08 .25
❑ 52 Vinnie Clark .08 .25
❑ 53 Michael Jackson .20 .50
❑ 54 Ernie Jones .08 .25
❑ 55 Tom Newberry .08 .25
❑ 56 Pat Harlow .08 .25
❑ 57 Craig Taylor .08 .25
❑ 58 Joe Prokop .08 .25
❑ 59 Warren Moon FOIL SP .75 2.00
❑ 60 Jeff Lageman .08 .25
❑ 61 Neil Smith .40 1.00
❑ 62 Jim Jeffcoat .08 .25
❑ 63 Bill Fralic .08 .25
❑ 64 Mark Schlereth RC .08 .25
❑ 65 Keith Byars .08 .25
❑ 66 Jeff Hostetler .20 .50
❑ 67 Joey Browner .08 .25
❑ 68 Bobby Hebert FOIL SP .60 1.50
❑ 69 Keith Sims .08 .25
❑ 70 Warren Moon .40 1.00
❑ 71 Pio Sagapolutele RC .08 .25
❑ 72 Cornelius Bennett .20 .50
❑ 73 Greg Davis .08 .25
❑ 74 Ronnie Harmon .08 .25
❑ 75 Ron Hall .08 .25
❑ 76 Howie Long .40 1.00
❑ 77 Greg Lewis .08 .25
❑ 78 Carnell Lake .08 .25
❑ 79 Ray Crockett .08 .25
❑ 80 Tom Waddle .08 .25
❑ 81 Vincent Brown .08 .25
❑ 82 Bill Brooks .20 .50
❑ 83 John L. Williams .08 .25
❑ 84 Floyd Turner .08 .25
❑ 85 Scott Radecic .08 .25
❑ 86 Anthony Munoz .20 .50
❑ 87 Lonnie Young .08 .25
❑ 88 Dexter Carter .08 .25
❑ 89 Tony Zendejas .08 .25
❑ 90 Tim Jorden .08 .25
❑ 91 LeRoy Butler .08 .25
❑ 92 Richard Brown RC .08 .25
❑ 93 Erric Pegram .20 .50
❑ 94 Sean Landeta .08 .25
❑ 95 Clyde Simmons .08 .25
❑ 96 Martin Mayhew .08 .25
❑ 97 Jarvis Williams .08 .25
❑ 98 Barry Word .08 .25
❑ 99 John Taylor FOIL .20 .50
❑ 100 Emmitt Smith 3.00 8.00
❑ 101 Leon Seals .08 .25
❑ 102 Marion Butts .08 .25
❑ 103 Mike Merriweather .08 .25
❑ 104 Ernest Givins .20 .50
❑ 105 Wymon Henderson .08 .25
❑ 106 Robert Wilson .08 .25
❑ 107 Bobby Hebert .08 .25
❑ 108 Terry McDaniel .08 .25
❑ 109 Jerry Ball .08 .25
❑ 110 John Taylor .20 .50
❑ 111 Hob Moore .20 .50
❑ 112 Thurman Thomas FOIL .40 1.00
❑ 113 Checklist 1-115 .08 .25
❑ 114 Brian Blades .20 .50
❑ 115 Larry Kelm .08 .25
❑ 116 James Francis .08 .25

❑ 117 Rod Woodson	.40	1.00
❑ 118 Trace Armstrong	.08	.25
❑ 119 Eugene Daniel	.08	.25
❑ 120 Andre Tippett	.08	.25
❑ 121 Chris Jacke	.08	.25
❑ 122 Jessie Tuggle	.08	.25
❑ 123 Chris Chandler	.40	1.00
❑ 124 Tim Johnson	.08	.25
❑ 125 Mark Collins	.08	.25
❑ 126 Aeneas Williams SP	.60	1.50
❑ 127 James Jones DT	.08	.25
❑ 128 George Jamison	.08	.25
❑ 129 Deron Cherry	.08	.25
❑ 130 Mark Clayton	.20	.50
❑ 131 Keith DeLong	.08	.25
❑ 132 Marcus Allen	.40	1.00
❑ 133 Joe Walter RC	.08	.25
❑ 134 Reggie Rutland	.08	.25
❑ 135 Kent Hull	.08	.25
❑ 136 Jeff Feagles	.08	.25
❑ 137 Ronnie Lott FOIL SP	.75	2.00
❑ 138 Henry Rolling	.08	.25
❑ 139 Gary Anderson RB	.08	.25
❑ 140 Morten Andersen	.08	.25
❑ 141 Cris Dishman	.08	.25
❑ 142 David Treadwell	.08	.25
❑ 143 Kevin Gogan	.08	.25
❑ 144 James Hasty	.08	.25
❑ 145 Robert Delpino	.08	.25
❑ 146 Patrick Hunter	.08	.25
❑ 147 Gary Anderson K	.08	.25
❑ 148 Chip Banks	.08	.25
❑ 149 Dan Fike	.08	.25
❑ 150 Chris Miller	.20	.50
❑ 151 Hugh Millen	.08	.25
❑ 152 Courtney Hall	.08	.25
❑ 153 Gary Clark	.20	.50
❑ 154 Michael Brooks	.08	.25
❑ 155 Jay Hilgenberg	.08	.25
❑ 156 Tim McDonald	.08	.25
❑ 157 Andre Tippett	.20	.50
❑ 158 Doug Riesenberg	.08	.25
❑ 159 Bill Maas	.08	.25
❑ 160 Fred Barnett	.20	.50
❑ 161 Pierce Holt	.08	.25
❑ 162 Brian Noble	.08	.25
❑ 163 Harold Green	.08	.25
❑ 164 Joel Hilgenberg	.08	.25
❑ 165 Mervyn Fernandez	.08	.25
❑ 166 John Offerdahl	.08	.25
❑ 167 Shane Conlan	.08	.25
❑ 168 Mark Higgs FOIL SP	.60	1.50
❑ 169 Bubba McDowell	.08	.25
❑ 170 Barry Sanders	2.50	6.00
❑ 171 Larry Roberts	.08	.25
❑ 172 Herschel Walker	.20	.50
❑ 173 Steve McMichael	.20	.50
❑ 174 Kelly Stouffer	.08	.25
❑ 175 Louis Lipps	.08	.25
❑ 176 Jim Everett	.20	.50
❑ 177 Tony Tolbert	.08	.25
❑ 178 Mike Baab	.08	.25
❑ 179 Eric Swann	.20	.50
❑ 180 Emmitt Smith FOIL SP	5.00	12.00
❑ 181 Tim Brown	.40	1.00
❑ 182 Dennis Smith	.08	.25
❑ 183 Moe Gardner	.08	.25
❑ 184 Derrick Walker	.08	.25
❑ 185 Reyna Thompson	.08	.25
❑ 186 Esera Tuaolo	.08	.25
❑ 187 Jeff Wright	.08	.25
❑ 188 Mark Rypien	.08	.25
❑ 189 Quinn Early	.20	.50
❑ 190 Christian Okoye	.08	.25
❑ 191 Keith Jackson	.20	.50
❑ 192 Doug Smith	.08	.25
❑ 193 John Elway FOIL	4.00	10.00
❑ 194 Reggie Cobb	.08	.25
❑ 195 Reggie Roby	.08	.25
❑ 196 Clarence Verdin	.08	.25
❑ 197 Jim Breech	.08	.25
❑ 198 Jim Sweeney	.08	.25
❑ 199 Marv Cook	.08	.25
❑ 200 Ronnie Lott	.20	.50
❑ 201 Mel Gray	.20	.50
❑ 202 Maury Buford	.08	.25
❑ 203 Lorenzo Lynch	.08	.25
❑ 204 Jesse Sapolu	.08	.25
❑ 205 Steve Jordan	.08	.25
❑ 206 Don Majkowski	.08	.25
❑ 207 Flipper Anderson	.08	.25
❑ 208 Ed King	.08	.25
❑ 209 Tony Woods	.08	.25
❑ 210 Ron Heller	.08	.25
❑ 211 Greg Kragen	.08	.25
❑ 212 Scott Case	.08	.25
❑ 213 Tommy Barnhardt	.08	.25
❑ 214 Charles Mann	.08	.25
❑ 215 David Griggs	.08	.25
❑ 216 Kenneth Davis FOIL SP	.60	1.50
❑ 217 Lamar Lathon	.08	.25
❑ 218 Nate Odomes	.08	.25
❑ 219 Vinny Testaverde	.20	.50
❑ 220 Rod Bernstine	.08	.25
❑ 221 Barry Sanders FOIL	4.00	10.00
❑ 222 Carlton Haselrig RC	.08	.25
❑ 223 Steve Beuerlein	.20	.50
❑ 224 John Alt	.08	.25
❑ 225 Pepper Johnson	.08	.25
❑ 226 Checklist 116-230	.08	.25
❑ 227 Irv Eatman	.08	.25
❑ 228 Greg Townsend	.08	.25
❑ 229 Mark Jackson	.08	.25
❑ 230 Robert Blackmon	.08	.25
❑ 231 Terry Allen	.40	1.00
❑ 232 Bennie Blades	.08	.25
❑ 233 Sam Mills	.40	1.00
❑ 234 Richmond Webb	.08	.25
❑ 235 Richard Dent	.20	.50
❑ 236 Alonzo Mitz RC	.08	.25
❑ 237 Steve Young	2.00	5.00
❑ 238 Pat Swilling	.08	.25
❑ 239 James Campen	.08	.25
❑ 240 Earnest Byner	.08	.25
❑ 241 Pat Terrell	.08	.25
❑ 242 Carwell Gardner	.08	.25
❑ 243 Charles McRae	.08	.25
❑ 244 Vince Newsome	.08	.25
❑ 245 Eric Hill	.08	.25
❑ 246 Steve Young FOIL	2.00	5.00
❑ 247 Nate Lewis	.08	.25
❑ 248 William Fuller	.08	.25
❑ 249 Andre Waters	.08	.25
❑ 250 Dean Biasucci	.08	.25
❑ 251 Andre Rison	.20	.50
❑ 252 Brent Williams	.08	.25
❑ 253 Todd McNair	.08	.25
❑ 254 Jeff Davidson RC	.08	.25
❑ 255 Art Monk	.20	.50
❑ 256 Kirk Lowdermilk	.08	.25
❑ 257 Bob Golic	.08	.25
❑ 258 Michael Irvin	.40	1.00
❑ 259 Eric Green	.08	.25
❑ 260 David Fulcher	.20	.50
❑ 261 Damone Johnson	.08	.25
❑ 262 Marc Spindler	.08	.25
❑ 263 Alfred Williams	.08	.25
❑ 264 Donnie Elder	.08	.25
❑ 265 Keith McKeller	.08	.25
❑ 266 Steve Bono RC	.40	1.00
❑ 267 Jumbo Elliott	.08	.25
❑ 268 Randy Hilliard RC	.08	.25
❑ 269 Rufus Porter	.08	.25
❑ 270 Neal Anderson	.08	.25
❑ 271 Dalton Hilliard	.08	.25
❑ 272 Michael Zordich RC	.08	.25
❑ 273 Cornelius Bennett FOIL	.20	.50
❑ 274 Louie Aguiar RC	.08	.25
❑ 275 Aaron Craver	.08	.25
❑ 276 Tony Bennett	.08	.25
❑ 277 Terry Wooden	.08	.25
❑ 278 Mike Munchak	.20	.50
❑ 279 Chris Hinton	.08	.25
❑ 280 John Elway	2.50	6.00
❑ 281 Randall McDaniel	.08	.25
❑ 282 Brad Baxter	.20	.50
❑ 283 Wes Hopkins	.08	.25
❑ 284 Scott Davis	.08	.25
❑ 285 Mark Tuinei	.08	.25
❑ 286 Broderick Thompson	.08	.25
❑ 287 Henry Ellard	.20	.50
❑ 288 Adrian Cooper	.08	.25
❑ 289 Don Warren	.08	.25
❑ 290 Rodney Hampton	.20	.50
❑ 291 Kevin Ross	.08	.25
❑ 292 Mark Carrier DB	.08	.25
❑ 293 Ian Beckles	.08	.25
❑ 294 Gene Atkins	.08	.25
❑ 295 Mark Rypien FOIL	.20	.50
❑ 296 Eric Metcalf	.20	.50
❑ 297 Howard Ballard	.08	.25
❑ 298 Nate Newton	.08	.25
❑ 299 Dan Owens	.08	.25
❑ 300 Tim McGee	.08	.25
❑ 301 Greg McMurtry	.08	.25
❑ 302 Walter Reeves	.08	.25
❑ 303 Jeff Herrod	.08	.25
❑ 304 Darren Comeaux	.08	.25
❑ 305 Pete Stoyanovich	.08	.25
❑ 306 Johnny Holland	.08	.25
❑ 307 Jay Novacek	.20	.50
❑ 308 Steve Broussard	.08	.25
❑ 309 Darrell Green	.08	.25
❑ 310 Sam Mills	.08	.25
❑ 311 Tim Barnett	.08	.25
❑ 312 Steve Atwater	.08	.25
❑ 313 Tom Waddle FOIL	.20	.50
❑ 314 Felix Wright	.08	.25
❑ 315 Sean Jones	.08	.25
❑ 316 Jim Harbaugh	.40	1.00
❑ 317 Eric Allen	.08	.25
❑ 318 Don Mosebar	.08	.25
❑ 319 Rob Taylor	.08	.25
❑ 320 Terance Mathis	.20	.50
❑ 321 Leroy Hoard	.20	.50
❑ 322 Kenneth Davis	.08	.25
❑ 323 Guy McIntyre	.08	.25
❑ 324 Deron Cherry	.20	.50
❑ 325 Tunch Ilkin	.08	.25
❑ 326 Willie Green	.08	.25
❑ 327 Darryl Henley	.08	.25
❑ 328 Shawn Jefferson	.08	.25
❑ 329 Greg Jackson	.08	.25
❑ 330 John Roper	.08	.25
❑ 331 Bill Lewis	.08	.25
❑ 332 Rodney Holman	.08	.25
❑ 333 Bruce Armstrong	.08	.25
❑ 334 Robb Thomas	.08	.25
❑ 335 Alvin Harper	.20	.50
❑ 336 Brian Jordan	.20	.50
❑ 337 Morten Andersen	.20	.50
❑ 338 Dermontti Dawson	.08	.25
❑ 339 Checklist 231-345	.08	.25
❑ 340 Louis Oliver	.08	.25
❑ 341 Paul McJulien RC	.08	.25
❑ 342 Karl Mecklenburg	.08	.25
❑ 343 Lawrence Dawsey	.20	.50
❑ 344 Kyle Clifton	.08	.25
❑ 345 Jeff Bostic	.08	.25
❑ 346 Cris Carter	.60	1.50
❑ 347 Al Smith	.08	.25
❑ 348 Mark Kelso	.08	.25
❑ 349 Art Monk FOIL	.40	1.00
❑ 350 Michael Carter	.08	.25
❑ 351 Ethan Horton	.08	.25
❑ 352 Andy Heck	.08	.25
❑ 353 Gill Fenerty	.08	.25
❑ 354 David Brandon RC	.08	.25
❑ 355 Anthony Johnson	.40	1.00
❑ 356 Mike Golic	.08	.25
❑ 357 Ferrell Edmunds	.08	.25
❑ 358 Dennis Gibson	.08	.25
❑ 359 Gill Byrd	.08	.25
❑ 360 Todd Lyght	.08	.25
❑ 361 Jayice Pearson RC	.08	.25
❑ 362 John Rade	.08	.25
❑ 363 Keith Van Horne	.08	.25
❑ 364 John Kasay	.08	.25
❑ 365 Broderick Thomas	.60	1.50
❑ 366 Ken Harvey	.08	.25
❑ 367 Rich Gannon	.40	1.00
❑ 368 Darrell Thompson	.08	.25
❑ 369 Jon Vaughn	.08	.25
❑ 370 Jesse Solomon	.08	.25
❑ 371 Erik McMillan	.08	.25
❑ 372 Bruce Matthews	.08	.25
❑ 373 Wilber Marshall	.08	.25
❑ 374 Brian Blades	.60	1.50
❑ 375 Vance Johnson	.08	.25
❑ 376 Eddie Brown	.08	.25
❑ 377 Don Beebe	.08	.25
❑ 378 Brent Jones	.20	.50
❑ 379 Matt Bahr	.08	.25
❑ 380 Dwight Stone	.08	.25
❑ 381 Tony Casillas	.08	.25
❑ 382 Jay Schroeder	.08	.25
❑ 383 Byron Evans	.08	.25

❑ 384 Dan Saleaumua .08 .25
❑ 385 Wendell Davis .08 .25
❑ 386 Ron Holmes .08 .25
❑ 387 George Thomas RC .08 .25
❑ 388 Ray Berry .08 .25
❑ 389 Eric Martin .08 .25
❑ 390 Kevin Mack .08 .25
❑ 391 Natu Tuatagaloa RC .08 .25
❑ 392 Bill Romanowski .08 .25
❑ 393 Nick Bell FOIL SP .60 1.50
❑ 394 Grant Feasel .08 .25
❑ 395 Eugene Lockhart .08 .25
❑ 396 Lorenzo White .08 .25
❑ 397 Mike Farr .08 .25
❑ 398 Eric Bieniemy .08 .25
❑ 399 Kevin Murphy .08 .25
❑ 400 Luis Sharpe .08 .25
❑ 401 Jessie Tuggle .60 1.50
❑ 402 Cleveland Gary .08 .25
❑ 403 Tony Mandarich .08 .25
❑ 404 Bryan Cox .20 .50
❑ 405 Marvin Washington .08 .25
❑ 406 Fred Stokes .08 .25
❑ 407 Duane Bickett .08 .25
❑ 408 Leonard Marshall .08 .25
❑ 409 Barry Foster .20 .50
❑ 410 Thurman Thomas .40 1.00
❑ 411 Willie Gault .20 .50
❑ 412 Vinson Smith RC .08 .25
❑ 413 Mark Bortz .08 .25
❑ 414 Johnny Johnson .08 .25
❑ 415 Rodney Hampton FOIL .40 1.00
❑ 416 Steve Wallace .08 .25
❑ 417 Fuad Reveiz .08 .25
❑ 418 Derrick Thomas .20 .50
❑ 419 Jackie Harris RC .40 1.00
❑ 420 Derek Russell .08 .25
❑ 421 David Grant .08 .25
❑ 422 Tommy Kane .08 .25
❑ 423 Stan Brock .08 .25
❑ 424 Haywood Jeffires .20 .50
❑ 425 Broderick Thomas .08 .25
❑ 426 John Kidd .08 .25
❑ 427 Shawn McCarthy RC .20 .50
❑ 428 Jim Arnold .08 .25
❑ 429 Scott Fulhage .08 .25
❑ 430 Jackie Slater .08 .25
❑ 431 Scott Galbraith RC .08 .25
❑ 432 Roger Ruzek .08 .25
❑ 433 Irving Fryar .20 .50
❑ 434A D.Thomas FOIL ERR 494 .40 1.00
❑ 434B D.Thomas FOIL COR .40 1.00
❑ 435 D.J. Johnson .08 .25
❑ 436 Jim C.Jensen .08 .25
❑ 437 James Washington .08 .25
❑ 438 Phil Hansen .08 .25
❑ 439 Rohn Stark .08 .25
❑ 440 Jarrod Bunch .08 .25
❑ 441 Todd Marinovich .08 .25
❑ 442 Brett Perriman .40 1.00
❑ 443 Eugene Robinson .08 .25
❑ 444 Robert Massey .08 .25
❑ 445 Nick Lowery .08 .25
❑ 446 Rickey Dixon .08 .25
❑ 447 Jim Lachey .08 .25
❑ 448 Johnny Hector .20 .50
❑ 449 Gary Plummer .08 .25
❑ 450 Robert Brown .08 .25
❑ 451 Gaston Green .08 .25
❑ 452 Checklist 346-459 .08 .25
❑ 453 Darion Conner .08 .25
❑ 454 Mike Cofer .08 .25
❑ 455 Craig Heyward .20 .50
❑ 456 Anthony Carter .20 .50
❑ 457 Pat Coleman RC .08 .25
❑ 458 Jeff Bryant .08 .25
❑ 459 Mark Gunn RC .08 .25
❑ 460 Stan Thomas .08 .25
❑ 461 Simon Fletcher .60 1.50
❑ 462 Ray Agnew .08 .25
❑ 463 Jessie Hester .08 .25
❑ 464 Rob Burnett .08 .25
❑ 465 Mike Croel .08 .25
❑ 466 Mike Pitts .08 .25
❑ 467 Darryl Talley .08 .25
❑ 468 Rich Camarillo .08 .25
❑ 469 Reggie White FOIL .40 1.00
❑ 470 Nick Bell .08 .25
❑ 471 Tracy Hayworth RC .08 .25
❑ 472 Eric Thomas .08 .25
❑ 473 Paul Gruber .08 .25
❑ 474 David Richards .08 .25
❑ 475 T.J. Turner .08 .25
❑ 476 Mark Ingram .08 .25
❑ 477 Tim Grunhard .08 .25
❑ 478 Marion Butts FOIL .20 .50
❑ 479 Tom Rathman .08 .25
❑ 480 Brian Mitchell .20 .50
❑ 481 Bryce Paup .40 1.00
❑ 482 Mike Pritchard .20 .50
❑ 483 Ken Norton Jr. .20 .50
❑ 484 Roman Phifer .08 .25
❑ 485 Greg Lloyd .20 .50
❑ 486 Brett Maxie .08 .25
❑ 487 Richard Dent FOIL SP .60 1.50
❑ 488 Curtis Duncan .08 .25
❑ 489 Chris Burkett .08 .25
❑ 490 Travis McNeal .08 .25
❑ 491 Carl Lee .08 .25
❑ 492 Clarence Kay .08 .25
❑ 493 Tom Thayer .08 .25
❑ 494 Erik Kramer FOIL SP .75 2.00
❑ 495 Perry Kemp .08 .25
❑ 496 Jeff Jaeger .08 .25
❑ 497 Eric Sanders .08 .25
❑ 498 Burt Grossman .08 .25
❑ 499 Ben Smith .08 .25
❑ 500 Keith McCants .08 .25
❑ 501 John Stephens .08 .25
❑ 502 John Rienstra .08 .25
❑ 503 Jim Ritcher .08 .25
❑ 504 Harris Barton .08 .25
❑ 505 Andre Rison FOIL SP .75 2.00
❑ 506 Chris Martin .08 .25
❑ 507 Freddie Joe Nunn .08 .25
❑ 508 Mark Higgs .08 .25
❑ 509 Norm Johnson .08 .25
❑ 510 Stephen Baker .08 .25
❑ 511 Ricky Sanders .08 .25
❑ 512 Ray Donaldson .08 .25
❑ 513 David Fulcher .08 .25
❑ 514 Gerald Williams .08 .25
❑ 515 Toi Cook .08 .25
❑ 516 Chris Warren .40 1.00
❑ 517 Jeff Gossett .08 .25
❑ 518 Ken Lanier .08 .25
❑ 519 Haywood Jeffires FOIL SP .75 2.00
❑ 520 Kevin Glover .08 .25
❑ 521 Mo Lewis .08 .25
❑ 522 Bern Brostek .08 .25
❑ 523 Bo Orlando RC .08 .25
❑ 524 Mike Saxon .08 .25
❑ 525 Seth Joyner .08 .25
❑ 526 John Carney .08 .25
❑ 527 Jeff Cross .08 .25
❑ 528 Gary Anderson K FOIL SP .60 1.50
❑ 529 Chuck Cecil .08 .25
❑ 530 Tim Green .08 .25
❑ 531 Kevin Porter .08 .25
❑ 532 Chris Spielman .20 .50
❑ 533 Willie Drewrey .08 .25
❑ 534 Chris Singleton UER .08 .25
❑ 535 Matt Stover .08 .25
❑ 536 Andre Collins .08 .25
❑ 537 Erik Howard .08 .25
❑ 538 Steve Tasker .20 .50
❑ 539 Anthony Thompson .08 .25
❑ 540 Charles Haley .20 .50
❑ 541 Mike Merriweather .20 .50
❑ 542 Henry Thomas .08 .25
❑ 543 Scott Stephen .08 .25
❑ 544 Bruce Kozerski .08 .25
❑ 545 Tim McKyer .08 .25
❑ 546 Chris Doleman .08 .25
❑ 547 Riki Ellison .08 .25
❑ 548 Mike Prior .08 .25
❑ 549 Dwayne Harper .08 .25
❑ 550 Bubby Brister .08 .25
❑ 551 Dave Meggett .20 .50
❑ 552 Greg Montgomery .08 .25
❑ 553 Kevin Mack .20 .50
❑ 554 Mark Stepnoski .20 .50
❑ 555 Kenny Walker .08 .25
❑ 556 Eric Moten .08 .25
❑ 557 Michael Stewart .08 .25
❑ 558 Calvin Williams .20 .50
❑ 559 Johnny Hector .08 .25
❑ 560 Tony Paige .08 .25
❑ 561 Tim Newton .08 .25
❑ 562 Brad Muster .08 .25
❑ 563 Aeneas Williams .20 .50
❑ 564 Herman Moore .40 1.00
❑ 565 Checklist 460-573 .08 .25
❑ 566 Jerome Henderson .08 .25
❑ 567 Danny Copeland .08 .25
❑ 568 Alexander Wright .20 .50
❑ 569 Tim Harris .08 .25
❑ 570 Jonathan Hayes .08 .25
❑ 571 Tony Jones T .08 .25
❑ 572 Carlton Bailey RC .08 .25
❑ 573 Vaughan Johnson .08 .25

1993 Bowman

❑ COMPLETE SET (423) 10.00 25.00
❑ 1 Troy Aikman FOIL 1.50 3.00
❑ 2 John Parrella RC .07 .20
❑ 3 Dana Stubblefield RC .30 .75
❑ 4 Mark Higgs .07 .20
❑ 5 Tom Carter RC .15 .40
❑ 6 Nate Lewis .07 .20
❑ 7 Vaughn Hebron RC .07 .20
❑ 8 Ernest Givins .15 .40
❑ 9 Vince Buck .07 .20
❑ 10 Levon Kirkland .07 .20
❑ 11 J.J. Birden .07 .20
❑ 12 Steve Jordan .07 .20
❑ 13 Simon Fletcher .07 .20
❑ 14 Willie Green .07 .20
❑ 15 Pepper Johnson .07 .20
❑ 16 Roger Harper RC .07 .20
❑ 17 Rob Moore .15 .40
❑ 18 David Lang .07 .20
❑ 19 David Klingler .07 .20
❑ 20 Garrison Hearst RC .75 2.00
❑ 21 Anthony Johnson .15 .40
❑ 22 Eric Curry RC .15 .40
❑ 23 Nolan Harrison .07 .20
❑ 24 Earl Dotson RC .07 .20
❑ 25 Leonard Russell .15 .40
❑ 26 Doug Riesenberg .07 .20
❑ 27 Dwayne Harper .07 .20
❑ 28 Richard Dent .15 .40
❑ 29 Victor Bailey RC .07 .20
❑ 30 Junior Seau .30 .75
❑ 31 Steve Tasker .15 .40
❑ 32 Kurt Gouveia .07 .20
❑ 33 Renaldo Turnbull UER .07 .20
❑ 34 Dale Carter .07 .20
❑ 35 Russell Maryland .07 .20
❑ 36 Dana Hall .07 .20
❑ 37 Marco Coleman .07 .20
❑ 38 Greg Montgomery .07 .20
❑ 39 Deon Figures RC .07 .20
❑ 40 Troy Drayton RC .15 .40
❑ 41 Eric Metcalf .15 .40
❑ 42 Michael Husted RC .07 .20
❑ 43 Harry Newsome .07 .20
❑ 44 Kelvin Pritchett .07 .20
❑ 45 Andre Rison FOIL .30 .75
❑ 46 John Copeland RC .15 .40
❑ 47 Greg Biekert RC .07 .20
❑ 48 Johnny Johnson .07 .20
❑ 49 Chuck Cecil .07 .20
❑ 50 Rick Mirer RC .60 1.50
❑ 51 Rod Bernstine .07 .20
❑ 52 Steve McMichael .15 .40
❑ 53 Roosevelt Potts RC .07 .20
❑ 54 Mike Sherrard .07 .20
❑ 55 Terrell Buckley .07 .20
❑ 56 Eugene Chung .07 .20
❑ 57 Kimble Anders RC .30 .75
❑ 58 Daryl Johnston .30 .75
❑ 59 Harris Barton .07 .20
❑ 60 Thurman Thomas FOIL .60 1.50

❑ 61 Eric Martin .07 .20
❑ 62 Reggie Brooks RC .15 .40
❑ 63 Eric Bieniemy .07 .20
❑ 64 John Offerdahl .07 .20
❑ 65 Wilber Marshall .07 .20
❑ 66 Mark Carrier WR .15 .40
❑ 67 Merril Hoge .07 .20
❑ 68 Cris Carter .30 .75
❑ 69 Marty Thompson RC .07 .20
❑ 70 Randall Cunningham FOIL .60 1.50
❑ 71 Winston Moss .07 .20
❑ 72 Doug Pelfrey RC .07 .20
❑ 73 Jackie Slater .07 .20
❑ 74 Pierce Holt .07 .20
❑ 75 Hardy Nickerson .15 .40
❑ 76 Chris Burkett .07 .20
❑ 77 Michael Brandon .07 .20
❑ 78 Tom Waddle .07 .20
❑ 79 Walter Reeves .07 .20
❑ 80 Lawrence Taylor FOIL .30 .75
❑ 81 Wayne Simmons RC .07 .20
❑ 82 Brent Williams .07 .20
❑ 83 Shannon Sharpe .30 .75
❑ 84 Robert Blackmon .07 .20
❑ 85 Keith Jackson .15 .40
❑ 86 A.J. Johnson .07 .20
❑ 87 Ryan McNeil RC .30 .75
❑ 88 Michael Dean Perry .15 .40
❑ 89 Russell Copeland RC .15 .40
❑ 90 Sam Mills .07 .20
❑ 91 Courtney Hall .07 .20
❑ 92 Gino Torretta RC .15 .40
❑ 93 Artie Smith RC .07 .20
❑ 94 David Whitmore .07 .20
❑ 95 Charles Haley .15 .40
❑ 96 Rod Woodson .30 .75
❑ 97 Lorenzo White .07 .20
❑ 98 Tom Scott RC .07 .20
❑ 99 Tyji Armstrong .07 .20
❑ 100 Boomer Esiason .15 .40
❑ 101 Rocket Ismail FOIL .30 .75
❑ 102 Mark Carrier DB .07 .20
❑ 103 Broderick Thompson .07 .20
❑ 104 Bob Whitfield .07 .20
❑ 105 Ben Coleman RC .07 .20
❑ 106 Jon Vaughn .07 .20
❑ 107 Marcus Buckley RC .07 .20
❑ 108 Cleveland Gary .07 .20
❑ 109 Ashley Ambrose .07 .20
❑ 110 Reggie White FOIL .60 1.50
❑ 111 Arthur Marshall RC .07 .20
❑ 112 Greg McMurtry .07 .20
❑ 113 Mike Johnson .07 .20
❑ 114 Tim McGee .07 .20
❑ 115 John Carney .07 .20
❑ 116 Neil Smith .30 .75
❑ 117 Mark Stepnoski .07 .20
❑ 118 Don Beebe .07 .20
❑ 119 Scott Mitchell .30 .75
❑ 120 Randall McDaniel .07 .20
❑ 121 Chidi Ahanotu RC .07 .20
❑ 122 Ray Childress .07 .20
❑ 123 Tony McGee RC .15 .40
❑ 124 Marc Boutte .07 .20
❑ 125 Ronnie Lott .15 .40
❑ 126 Jason Elam RC .30 .75
❑ 127 Martin Harrison RC .07 .20
❑ 128 Leonard Renfro RC .07 .20
❑ 129 Jessie Armstead RC .15 .40
❑ 130 Quentin Coryatt .15 .40
❑ 131 Luis Sharpe .07 .20
❑ 132 Bill Maas .07 .20
❑ 133 Jesse Solomon .07 .20
❑ 134 Kevin Greene .15 .40
❑ 135 Derek Brown RBK RC .15 .40
❑ 136 Greg Townsend .07 .20
❑ 137 Neal Anderson .07 .20
❑ 138 John L. Williams .07 .20
❑ 139 Vincent Brisby RC .30 .75
❑ 140 Barry Sanders FOIL 2.00 5.00
❑ 141 Charles Mann .07 .20
❑ 142 Ken Norton .15 .40
❑ 143 Eric Moten .07 .20
❑ 144 John Alt .07 .20
❑ 145 Dan Footman RC .07 .20
❑ 146 Bill Brooks .07 .20
❑ 147 James Thornton .07 .20
❑ 148 Martin Mayhew .07 .20
❑ 149 Andy Harmon .15 .40
❑ 150 Dan Marino FOIL 2.50 6.00
❑ 151 Micheal Barrow RC .30 .75
❑ 152 Flipper Anderson .07 .20
❑ 153 Jackie Harris .07 .20
❑ 154 Todd Kelly RC .07 .20
❑ 155 Dan Williams RC .07 .20
❑ 156 Harold Green .07 .20
❑ 157 David Treadwell .07 .20
❑ 158 Chris Doleman .07 .20
❑ 159 Eric Hill .07 .20
❑ 160 Lincoln Kennedy RC .07 .20
❑ 161 Devon McDonald RC .07 .20
❑ 162 Natrone Means RC .30 .75
❑ 163 Rick Hamilton RC .07 .20
❑ 164 Kelvin Martin .07 .20
❑ 165 Jeff Hostetler .15 .40
❑ 166 Mark Brunell RC 1.50 4.00
❑ 167 Tim Barnett .07 .20
❑ 168 Ray Crockett .07 .20
❑ 169 William Perry .15 .40
❑ 170 Michael Irvin .30 .75
❑ 171 Marvin Washington .07 .20
❑ 172 Irving Fryar .15 .40
❑ 173 Scott Sisson RC .07 .20
❑ 174 Gary Anderson K .07 .20
❑ 175 Bruce Smith .30 .75
❑ 176 Clyde Simmons .07 .20
❑ 177 Russell White RC .15 .40
❑ 178 Irv Smith RC .07 .20
❑ 179 Mark Wheeler .07 .20
❑ 180 Warren Moon .30 .75
❑ 181 Del Speer RC .07 .20
❑ 182 Henry Thomas .07 .20
❑ 183 Keith Kartz .07 .20
❑ 184 Ricky Ervins .07 .20
❑ 185 Phil Simms .15 .40
❑ 186 Tim Brown .30 .75
❑ 187 Willis Peguese .07 .20
❑ 188 Rich Moran .07 .20
❑ 189 Robert Jones .07 .20
❑ 190 Craig Heyward .15 .40
❑ 191 Ricky Watters .30 .75
❑ 192 Stan Humphries .15 .40
❑ 193 Larry Webster .07 .20
❑ 194 Brad Baxter .07 .20
❑ 195 Randal Hill .07 .20
❑ 196 Robert Porcher .07 .20
❑ 197 Patrick Robinson RC .07 .20
❑ 198 Ferrell Edmunds .07 .20
❑ 199 Melvin Jenkins .07 .20
❑ 200 Joe Montana FOIL 2.50 6.00
❑ 201 Marv Cook .07 .20
❑ 202 Henry Ellard .15 .40
❑ 203 Calvin Williams .15 .40
❑ 204 Craig Erickson .15 .40
❑ 205 Steve Atwater .07 .20
❑ 206 Najee Mustafaa .07 .20
❑ 207 Darryl Talley .07 .20
❑ 208 Jarrod Bunch .07 .20
❑ 209 Tim McDonald .07 .20
❑ 210 Patrick Bates RC .07 .20
❑ 211 Sean Jones .07 .20
❑ 212 Leslie O'Neal .15 .40
❑ 213 Mike Golic .07 .20
❑ 214 Mark Clayton .07 .20
❑ 215 Leonard Marshall .07 .20
❑ 216 Curtis Conway RC .60 1.50
❑ 217 Andre Hastings RC .15 .40
❑ 218 Barry Word .07 .20
❑ 219 Will Wolford .07 .20
❑ 220 Desmond Howard .15 .40
❑ 221 Rickey Jackson .07 .20
❑ 222 Alvin Harper .15 .40
❑ 223 William White .07 .20
❑ 224 Steve Broussard .07 .20
❑ 225 Aeneas Williams .07 .20
❑ 226 Michael Brooks .07 .20
❑ 227 Reggie Cobb .07 .20
❑ 228 Derrick Walker .07 .20
❑ 229 Marcus Allen .30 .75
❑ 230 Jerry Ball .07 .20
❑ 231 J.B. Brown .07 .20
❑ 232 Terry McDaniel .07 .20
❑ 233 LeRoy Butler .07 .20
❑ 234 Kyle Clifton .07 .20
❑ 235 Henry Jones .07 .20
❑ 236 Shane Conlan .07 .20
❑ 237 Michael Bates RC .07 .20
❑ 238 Vincent Brown .07 .20
❑ 239 William Fuller .07 .20
❑ 240 Ricardo McDonald .07 .20
❑ 241 Gary Zimmerman .07 .20
❑ 242 Fred Barnett .15 .40
❑ 243 Elvis Grbac RC 1.50 4.00
❑ 244 Myron Baker RC .07 .20
❑ 245 Steve Emtman .07 .20
❑ 246 Mike Compton RC .30 .75
❑ 247 Mark Jackson .07 .20
❑ 248 Santo Stephens RC .07 .20
❑ 249 Tommie Agee .07 .20
❑ 250 Broderick Thomas .07 .20
❑ 251 Fred Baxter RC .07 .20
❑ 252 Andre Collins .07 .20
❑ 253 Ernest Dye RC .07 .20
❑ 254 Raylee Johnson RC .15 .40
❑ 255 Rickey Dixon .07 .20
❑ 256 Ron Heller .07 .20
❑ 257 Joel Steed .07 .20
❑ 258 Everett Lindsay RC .07 .20
❑ 259 Tony Smith RB .07 .20
❑ 260 Sterling Sharpe UER .30 .75
❑ 261 Tommy Vardell .07 .20
❑ 262 Morten Andersen .07 .20
❑ 263 Eddie Robinson .07 .20
❑ 264 Jerome Bettis RC 4.00 8.00
❑ 265 Alonzo Spellman .07 .20
❑ 266 Harvey Williams .15 .40
❑ 267 Jason Belser RC .07 .20
❑ 268 Derek Russell .07 .20
❑ 269 Derrick Lassic RC .07 .20
❑ 270 Steve Young FOIL 1.50 3.00
❑ 271 Adrian Murrell RC .30 .75
❑ 272 Lewis Tillman .07 .20
❑ 273 O.J.McDuffie RC .30 .75
❑ 274 Marty Carter .07 .20
❑ 275 Ray Seals .07 .20
❑ 276 Earnest Byner .07 .20
❑ 277 Marion Butts .07 .20
❑ 278 Chris Spielman .15 .40
❑ 279 Carl Pickens .15 .40
❑ 280 Drew Bledsoe RC 2.50 6.00
❑ 281 Mark Kelso .07 .20
❑ 282 Eugene Robinson .07 .20
❑ 283 Eric Allen .07 .20
❑ 284 Ethan Horton .07 .20
❑ 285 Greg Lloyd .15 .40
❑ 286 Anthony Carter .15 .40
❑ 287 Edgar Bennett .30 .75
❑ 288 Bobby Hebert .07 .20
❑ 289 Haywood Jeffires .15 .40
❑ 290 Glyn Milburn RC .30 .75
❑ 291 Bernie Kosar .15 .40
❑ 292 Jumbo Elliott .07 .20
❑ 293 Jessie Hester .07 .20
❑ 294 Brent Jones .15 .40
❑ 295 Carl Banks .07 .20
❑ 296 Brian Washington .07 .20
❑ 297 Steve Beuerlein .15 .40
❑ 298 John Lynch RC .75 2.00
❑ 299 Troy Vincent .07 .20
❑ 300 Emmitt Smith FOIL 2.50 5.00
❑ 301 Chris Zorich .07 .20
❑ 302 Wade Wilson .07 .20
❑ 303 Darrien Gordon RC .07 .20
❑ 304 Fred Stokes .07 .20
❑ 305 Nick Lowery .07 .20
❑ 306 Rodney Peete .07 .20
❑ 307 Chris Warren .15 .40
❑ 308 Herschel Walker .15 .40
❑ 309 Aundray Bruce .07 .20
❑ 310 Barry Foster FOIL .15 .40
❑ 311 George Teague RC .15 .40
❑ 312 Darryl Williams .07 .20
❑ 313 Thomas Smith RC .15 .40
❑ 314 Dennis Brown .07 .20
❑ 315 Marvin Jones RC .15 .40
❑ 316 Andre Tippett .07 .20
❑ 317 Demetrius DuBose RC .07 .20
❑ 318 Kirk Lowdermilk .07 .20
❑ 319 Shane Dronett .07 .20
❑ 320 Terry Kirby RC .30 .75
❑ 321 Qadry Ismail RC .30 .75
❑ 322 Lorenzo Lynch .07 .20
❑ 323 Willie Drewrey .07 .20
❑ 324 Jessie Tuggle .07 .20
❑ 325 Leroy Hoard .15 .40
❑ 326 Mark Collins .07 .20
❑ 327 Darrell Green .07 .20

Card	Low	High
❑ 328 Anthony Miller	.15	.40
❑ 329 Brad Muster	.07	.20
❑ 330 Jim Kelly FOIL	.60	1.50
❑ 331 Sean Gilbert	.15	.40
❑ 332 Tim McKyer	.07	.20
❑ 333 Scott Mersereau	.07	.20
❑ 334 Willie Davis	.30	.75
❑ 335 Brett Favre FOIL	3.00	6.00
❑ 336 Kevin Gogan	.07	.20
❑ 337 Jim Harbaugh	.30	.75
❑ 338 James Trapp RC	.07	.20
❑ 339 Pete Stoyanovich	.07	.20
❑ 340 Jerry Rice FOIL	1.50	3.00
❑ 341 Gary Anderson RB	.07	.20
❑ 342 Carlton Gray RC	.07	.20
❑ 343 Dermontti Dawson	.07	.20
❑ 344 Ray Buchanan RC	.30	.75
❑ 345 Derrick Fenner	.07	.20
❑ 346 Dennis Smith	.07	.20
❑ 347 Todd Rucci RC	.07	.20
❑ 348 Seth Joyner	.07	.20
❑ 349 Jim McMahon	.15	.40
❑ 350 Rodney Hampton	.15	.40
❑ 351 Al Smith	.07	.20
❑ 352 Steve Everitt RC	.07	.20
❑ 353 Vinnie Clark	.07	.20
❑ 354 Eric Swann	.15	.40
❑ 355 Brian Mitchell	.15	.40
❑ 356 Will Shields RC	.30	.75
❑ 357 Cornelius Bennett	.15	.40
❑ 358 Darrin Smith RC	.15	.40
❑ 359 Chris Mims	.07	.20
❑ 360 Blair Thomas	.07	.20
❑ 361 Dennis Gibson	.07	.20
❑ 362 Santana Dotson	.15	.40
❑ 363 Mark Ingram	.07	.20
❑ 364 Don Mosebar	.07	.20
❑ 365 Ty Detmer	.30	.75
❑ 366 Bob Christian RC	.07	.20
❑ 367 Adrian Hardy	.07	.20
❑ 368 Vaughan Johnson	.07	.20
❑ 369 Jim Everett	.15	.40
❑ 370 Ricky Sanders	.07	.20
❑ 371 Jonathan Hayes	.07	.20
❑ 372 Bruce Matthews	.07	.20
❑ 373 Darren Drozdov RC	.30	.75
❑ 374 Scott Brumfield RC	.07	.20
❑ 375 Cortez Kennedy	.15	.40
❑ 376 Tim Harris	.07	.20
❑ 377 Neil O'Donnell	.30	.75
❑ 378 Robert Smith RC	1.25	3.00
❑ 379 Mike Caldwell RC	.07	.20
❑ 380 Burt Grossman	.07	.20
❑ 381 Corey Miller	.07	.20
❑ 382 Kevin Williams RC	.15	.40
❑ 383 Ken Harvey	.07	.20
❑ 384 Greg Robinson RC	.07	.20
❑ 385 Harold Alexander RC	.07	.20
❑ 386 Andre Reed	.15	.40
❑ 387 Reggie Langhorne	.07	.20
❑ 388 Courtney Hawkins	.07	.20
❑ 389 James Hasty	.07	.20
❑ 390 Pat Swilling	.07	.20
❑ 391 Chris Slade RC	.15	.40
❑ 392 Keith Byars	.07	.20
❑ 393 Dalton Hilliard	.07	.20
❑ 394 David Williams	.07	.20
❑ 395 Terry Obee RC	.07	.20
❑ 396 Heath Sherman	.07	.20
❑ 397 John Taylor	.15	.40
❑ 398 Irv Eatman	.07	.20
❑ 399 Johnny Holland	.07	.20
❑ 400 John Elway FOIL	2.50	6.00
❑ 401 Clay Matthews	.15	.40
❑ 402 Dave Meggett	.07	.20
❑ 403 Eric Green	.07	.20
❑ 404 Bryan Cox	.07	.20
❑ 405 Jay Novacek	.15	.40
❑ 406 Kenneth Davis	.07	.20
❑ 407 Lamar Thomas RC	.07	.20
❑ 408 Lance Gunn RC	.07	.20
❑ 409 Audray McMillian	.07	.20
❑ 410 Derrick Thomas FOIL	.60	1.50
❑ 411 Rufus Porter	.07	.20
❑ 412 Coleman Rudolph RC	.07	.20
❑ 413 Mark Rypien	.07	.20
❑ 414 Duane Bickett	.07	.20
❑ 415 Chris Singleton	.07	.20
❑ 416 Mitch Lyons RC	.07	.20
❑ 417 Bill Fralic	.07	.20
❑ 418 Gary Plummer	.07	.20
❑ 419 Ricky Proehl	.07	.20
❑ 420 Howie Long	.30	.75
❑ 421 Willie Roaf RC	.30	.75
❑ 422 Checklist 1-212	.07	.20
❑ 423 Checklist 213-423	.07	.20

1994 Bowman

Card	Low	High
❑ COMPLETE SET (390)	20.00	50.00
❑ 1 Dan Wilkinson RC	.15	.40
❑ 2 Marshall Faulk RC	6.00	15.00
❑ 3 Heath Shuler RC	.30	.75
❑ 4 Willie McGinest RC	.30	.75
❑ 5 Trent Dilfer RC	1.25	3.00
❑ 6 Brent Jones	.15	.40
❑ 7 Sam Adams RC	.15	.40
❑ 8 Randy Baldwin	.07	.20
❑ 9 Jamir Miller RC	.15	.40
❑ 10 John Thierry RC	.07	.20
❑ 11 Aaron Glenn RC	.30	.75
❑ 12 Joe Johnson RC	.07	.20
❑ 13 Bernard Williams RC	.07	.20
❑ 14 Wayne Gandy RC	.07	.20
❑ 15 Aaron Taylor RC	.07	.20
❑ 16 Charles Johnson RC	.30	.75
❑ 17 Dewayne Washington RC	.15	.40
❑ 18 Bernie Kosar	.15	.40
❑ 19 Johnnie Morton RC	1.00	2.50
❑ 20 Rob Fredrickson RC	.15	.40
❑ 21 Shante Carver RC	.07	.20
❑ 22 Thomas Lewis RC	.15	.40
❑ 23 Greg Hill RC	.30	.75
❑ 24 Cris Dishman	.07	.20
❑ 25 Jeff Burris RC	.15	.40
❑ 26 Isaac Davis RC	.07	.20
❑ 27 Bert Emanuel RC	.30	.75
❑ 28 Allen Aldridge RC	.07	.20
❑ 29 Kevin Lee RC	.07	.20
❑ 30 Chris Brantley RC	.07	.20
❑ 31 Rich Braham RC	.07	.20
❑ 32 Ricky Watters	.15	.40
❑ 33 Quentin Coryatt	.07	.20
❑ 34 Hardy Nickerson	.15	.40
❑ 35 Johnny Johnson	.07	.20
❑ 36 Ken Harvey	.07	.20
❑ 37 Chris Zorich	.07	.20
❑ 38 Chris Warren	.15	.40
❑ 39 David Palmer RC	.30	.75
❑ 40 Chris Miller	.07	.20
❑ 41 Ken Ruettgers	.07	.20
❑ 42 Joe Panos RC	.07	.20
❑ 43 Mario Bates RC	.30	.75
❑ 44 Harry Colon	.07	.20
❑ 45 Barry Foster	.07	.20
❑ 46 Steve Tasker	.15	.40
❑ 47 Richmond Webb	.07	.20
❑ 48 James Folston RC	.07	.20
❑ 49 Erik Williams	.07	.20
❑ 50 Rodney Hampton	.15	.40
❑ 51 Derek Russell	.07	.20
❑ 52 Greg Montgomery	.07	.20
❑ 53 Anthony Phillips	.07	.20
❑ 54 Andre Coleman RC	.07	.20
❑ 55 Gary Brown	.07	.20
❑ 56 Neil Smith	.15	.40
❑ 57 Myron Baker	.07	.20
❑ 58 Sean Dawkins RC	.30	.75
❑ 59 Marvin Washington	.07	.20
❑ 60 Steve Beuerlein	.15	.40
❑ 61 Brentson Buckner RC	.07	.20
❑ 62 William Gaines RC	.07	.20
❑ 63 LeShon Johnson RC	.15	.40
❑ 64 Errict Rhett RC	.30	.75
❑ 65 Jim Everett	.15	.40
❑ 66 Desmond Howard	.15	.40

Card	Low	High
❑ 67 Jack Del Rio	.07	.20
❑ 68 Isaac Bruce RC	6.00	12.00
❑ 69 Van Malone RC	.07	.20
❑ 70 Jim Kelly	.30	.75
❑ 71 Leon Lett	.07	.20
❑ 72 Greg Robinson	.07	.20
❑ 73 Ryan Yarborough RC	.07	.20
❑ 74 Terry Wooden	.07	.20
❑ 75 Eric Allen	.07	.20
❑ 76 Ernest Givins	.15	.40
❑ 77 Marcus Spears RC	.07	.20
❑ 78 Thomas Randolph RC	.07	.20
❑ 79 Willie Clark RC	.07	.20
❑ 80 John Elway	1.50	4.00
❑ 81 Aubrey Beavers RC	.07	.20
❑ 82 Jeff Cothran RC	.07	.20
❑ 83 Norm Johnson	.07	.20
❑ 84 Donnell Bennett RC	.30	.75
❑ 85 Phillippi Sparks	.07	.20
❑ 86 Scott Mitchell	.15	.40
❑ 87 Bucky Brooks RC	.07	.20
❑ 88 Courtney Hawkins	.07	.20
❑ 89 Kevin Greene	.15	.40
❑ 90 Doug Nussmeier RC	.07	.20
❑ 91 Floyd Turner	.07	.20
❑ 92 Anthony Newman	.07	.20
❑ 93 Vinny Testaverde	.15	.40
❑ 94 Ronnie Lott	.15	.40
❑ 95 Troy Aikman	.75	2.00
❑ 96 John Taylor	.15	.40
❑ 97 Henry Ellard	.15	.40
❑ 98 Carl Lee	.07	.20
❑ 99 Terry McDaniel	.07	.20
❑ 100 Joe Montana	1.50	4.00
❑ 101 David Klingler	.07	.20
❑ 102 Bruce Walker RC	.07	.20
❑ 103 Rick Cunningham RC	.07	.20
❑ 104 Robert Delpino	.07	.20
❑ 105 Mark Ingram	.07	.20
❑ 106 Leslie O'Neal	.07	.20
❑ 107 Darrell Thompson	.07	.20
❑ 108 Dave Meggett	.07	.20
❑ 109 Chris Gardocki	.07	.20
❑ 110 Andre Rison	.15	.40
❑ 111 Kelvin Martin	.07	.20
❑ 112 Marcus Robertson	.07	.20
❑ 113 Jason Gildon RC	1.25	3.00
❑ 114 Mel Gray	.07	.20
❑ 115 Tommy Vardell	.07	.20
❑ 116 Dexter Carter	.07	.20
❑ 117 Scottie Graham RC	.15	.40
❑ 118 Horace Copeland	.07	.20
❑ 119 Cornelius Bennett	.15	.40
❑ 120 Chris Maumalanga RC	.07	.20
❑ 121 Mo Lewis	.07	.20
❑ 122 Toby Wright RC	.07	.20
❑ 123 George Hegamin RC	.07	.20
❑ 124 Chip Lohmiller	.07	.20
❑ 125 Calvin Jones RC	.07	.20
❑ 126 Steve Shine	.07	.20
❑ 127 Chuck Levy RC	.07	.20
❑ 128 Sam Mills	.07	.20
❑ 129 Terance Mathis	.15	.40
❑ 130 Randall Cunningham	.30	.75
❑ 131 John Fina	.07	.20
❑ 132 Reggie White	.30	.75
❑ 133 Tom Waddle	.07	.20
❑ 134 Chris Calloway	.07	.20
❑ 135 Kevin Mawae RC	.30	.75
❑ 136 Lake Dawson RC	.15	.40
❑ 137 Alai Kalaniubalu	.07	.20
❑ 138 Tom Nalen RC	.30	.75
❑ 139 Cody Carlson	.07	.20
❑ 140 Dan Marino	1.50	4.00
❑ 141 Harris Barton	.07	.20
❑ 142 Don Mosebar	.07	.20
❑ 143 Romeo Bandison	.07	.20
❑ 144 Bruce Smith	.30	.75
❑ 145 Warren Moon	.30	.75
❑ 146 David Lutz	.07	.20
❑ 147 Dermontti Dawson	.07	.20
❑ 148 Ricky Proehl	.07	.20
❑ 149 Lou Benfatti RC	.07	.20
❑ 150 Craig Erickson	.07	.20
❑ 151 Sean Gilbert	.07	.20
❑ 152 Zefross Moss	.07	.20
❑ 153 Darnay Scott RC	.50	1.25
❑ 154 Courtney Hall	.07	.20
❑ 155 Brian Mitchell	.07	.20

❑ 156 Joe Burch UER RC	.07	.20
❑ 157 Terry Mickens	.07	.20
❑ 158 Jay Novacek	.15	.40
❑ 159 Chris Gedney	.07	.20
❑ 160 Bruce Matthews	.07	.20
❑ 161 Marlo Perry RC	.07	.20
❑ 162 Vince Buck	.07	.20
❑ 163 Michael Bates	.07	.20
❑ 164 Willie Davis	.15	.40
❑ 165 Mike Pritchard	.07	.20
❑ 166 Doug Riesenberg	.07	.20
❑ 167 Herschel Walker	.15	.40
❑ 168 Tim Ruddy RC	.07	.20
❑ 169 William Floyd RC	.30	.75
❑ 170 John Randle	.15	.40
❑ 171 Winston Moss	.07	.20
❑ 172 Thurman Thomas	.30	.75
❑ 173 Eric England RC	.07	.20
❑ 174 Vincent Brisby	.15	.40
❑ 175 Greg Lloyd	.15	.40
❑ 176 Paul Gruber	.07	.20
❑ 177 Brad Ottis RC	.07	.20
❑ 178 George Teague	.07	.20
❑ 179 Willie Jackson RC	.30	.75
❑ 180 Barry Sanders	1.25	3.00
❑ 181 Brian Washington	.07	.20
❑ 182 Michael Jackson	.15	.40
❑ 183 Jason Mathews RC	.07	.20
❑ 184 Chester McGlockton	.07	.20
❑ 185 Tydus Winans RC	.07	.20
❑ 186 Michael Haynes	.15	.40
❑ 187 Erik Kramer	.15	.40
❑ 188 Chris Doleman	.07	.20
❑ 189 Haywood Jeffires	.15	.40
❑ 190 Larry Whigham RC	.07	.20
❑ 191 Shawn Jefferson	.07	.20
❑ 192 Pete Stoyanovich	.07	.20
❑ 193 Rod Bernstine	.07	.20
❑ 194 William Thomas	.07	.20
❑ 195 Marcus Allen	.30	.75
❑ 196 Dave Brown	.15	.40
❑ 197 Harold Bishop RC	.07	.20
❑ 198 Lorenzo Lynch	.07	.20
❑ 199 Dwight Stone	.07	.20
❑ 200 Jerry Rice	.75	2.00
❑ 201 Rocket Ismail	.15	.40
❑ 202 LeRoy Butler	.07	.20
❑ 203 Glenn Parker	.07	.20
❑ 204 Bruce Armstrong	.07	.20
❑ 205 Shane Conlan	.07	.20
❑ 206 Russell Maryland	.07	.20
❑ 207 Herman Moore	.30	.75
❑ 208 Eric Martin	.07	.20
❑ 209 John Friesz	.15	.40
❑ 210 Boomer Esiason	.15	.40
❑ 211 Jim Harbaugh	.30	.75
❑ 212 Harold Green	.07	.20
❑ 213 Perry Klein RC	.07	.20
❑ 214 Eric Metcalf	.15	.40
❑ 215 Steve Everitt	.07	.20
❑ 216 Victor Bailey	.07	.20
❑ 217 Lincoln Kennedy	.07	.20
❑ 218 Glyn Milburn	.15	.40
❑ 219 John Copeland	.07	.20
❑ 220 Drew Bledsoe	.75	2.00
❑ 221 Kevin Williams WR	.15	.40
❑ 222 Roosevelt Potts	.07	.20
❑ 223 Troy Drayton	.07	.20
❑ 224 Terry Kirby	.30	.75
❑ 225 Ronald Moore	.07	.20
❑ 226 Tyrone Hughes	.15	.40
❑ 227 Wayne Simmons	.07	.20
❑ 228 Tony McGee	.07	.20
❑ 229 Derek Brown RBK	.07	.20
❑ 230 Jason Elam	.15	.40
❑ 231 Qadry Ismail	.30	.75
❑ 232 O.J.McDuffie	.30	.75
❑ 233 Mike Caldwell	.07	.20
❑ 234 Reggie Brooks	.15	.40
❑ 235 Rick Mirer	.30	.75
❑ 236 Steve Tovar	.07	.20
❑ 237 Patrick Robinson	.07	.20
❑ 238 Tom Carter	.07	.20
❑ 239 Ben Coates	.15	.40
❑ 240 Jerome Bettis	.50	1.25
❑ 241 Garrison Hearst	.30	.75
❑ 242 Natrone Means	.30	.75
❑ 243 Dana Stubblefield	.15	.40
❑ 244 Willie Roaf	.07	.20
❑ 245 Cortez Kennedy	.15	.40
❑ 246 Todd Steussie RC	.15	.40
❑ 247 Pat Coleman	.07	.20
❑ 248 David Wyman	.07	.20
❑ 249 Jeremy Lincoln	.07	.20
❑ 250 Carlester Crumpler	.07	.20
❑ 251 Dale Carter	.07	.20
❑ 252 Corey Raymond RC	.07	.20
❑ 253 Bryan Cox	.07	.20
❑ 254 Charlie Garner RC	1.25	3.00
❑ 255 Jeff Hostetler	.15	.40
❑ 256 Shane Bonham RC	.07	.20
❑ 257 Thomas Everett	.07	.20
❑ 258 John Jackson T	.07	.20
❑ 259 Terry Irving RC	.07	.20
❑ 260 Corey Sawyer	.15	.40
❑ 261 Rob Waldrop	.07	.20
❑ 262 Curtis Conway	.30	.75
❑ 263 Winfred Tubbs RC	.15	.40
❑ 264 Sean Jones	.07	.20
❑ 265 James Washington	.07	.20
❑ 266 Lonnie Johnson RC	.07	.20
❑ 267 Rob Moore	.15	.40
❑ 268 Flipper Anderson	.07	.20
❑ 269 Jon Hand	.07	.20
❑ 270 Joe Patton RC	.07	.20
❑ 271 Howard Ballard	.07	.20
❑ 272 Fernando Smith RC	.07	.20
❑ 273 Jessie Tuggle	.07	.20
❑ 274 John Alt	.07	.20
❑ 275 Corey Miller	.07	.20
❑ 276 Gus Frerotte RC	1.25	3.00
❑ 277 Jeff Cross	.07	.20
❑ 278 Kevin Smith	.07	.20
❑ 279 Corey Louchiey RC	.07	.20
❑ 280 Micheal Barrow	.07	.20
❑ 281 Jim Flanigan RC	.15	.40
❑ 282 Calvin Williams	.15	.40
❑ 283 Jeff Jaeger	.07	.20
❑ 284 John Reece RC	.07	.20
❑ 285 Jason Hanson	.07	.20
❑ 286 Kurt Haws RC	.07	.20
❑ 287 Eric Davis	.07	.20
❑ 288 Maurice Hurst	.07	.20
❑ 289 Kirk Lowdermilk	.07	.20
❑ 290 Rod Woodson	.15	.40
❑ 291 Andre Reed	.15	.40
❑ 292 Vince Workman	.07	.20
❑ 293 Wayne Martin	.07	.20
❑ 294 Keith Lyle RC	.07	.20
❑ 295 Brett Favre	1.50	4.00
❑ 296 Doug Brien RC	.07	.20
❑ 297 Junior Seau	.30	.75
❑ 298 Randall McDaniel	.07	.20
❑ 299 Johnny Mitchell	.07	.20
❑ 300 Emmitt Smith	1.25	3.00
❑ 301 Michael Brooks	.07	.20
❑ 302 Steve Jackson	.07	.20
❑ 303 Jeff George	.30	.75
❑ 304 Irving Fryar	.15	.40
❑ 305 Derrick Thomas	.30	.75
❑ 306 Dante Jones	.07	.20
❑ 307 Darrell Green	.07	.20
❑ 308 Mark Bavaro	.07	.20
❑ 309 Eugene Robinson	.07	.20
❑ 310 Shannon Sharpe	.15	.40
❑ 311 Michael Timpson	.07	.20
❑ 312 Kevin Mitchell RC	.07	.20
❑ 313 Stevon Moore	.07	.20
❑ 314 Eric Swann	.15	.40
❑ 315 James Bostic RC	.30	.75
❑ 316 Robert Brooks	.30	.75
❑ 317 Pete Pierson RC	.07	.20
❑ 318 Jim Sweeney	.07	.20
❑ 319 Anthony Smith	.07	.20
❑ 320 Rohn Stark	.07	.20
❑ 321 Gary Anderson K	.07	.20
❑ 322 Robert Porcher	.07	.20
❑ 323 Darryl Talley	.07	.20
❑ 324 Stan Humphries	.15	.40
❑ 325 Shelly Hammonds RC	.07	.20
❑ 326 Jim McMahon	.15	.40
❑ 327 Lamont Warren RC	.07	.20
❑ 328 Chris Penn RC	.07	.20
❑ 329 Tony Woods	.07	.20
❑ 330 Raymont Harris RC	.30	.75
❑ 331 Mitch Davis RC	.07	.20
❑ 332 Michael Irvin	.30	.75
❑ 333 Kent Graham	.15	.40
❑ 334 Brian Blades	.15	.40
❑ 335 Lomas Brown	.07	.20
❑ 336 Willie Drewrey	.07	.20
❑ 337 Russell Freeman	.07	.20
❑ 338 Eric Zomalt RC	.07	.20
❑ 339 Santana Dotson	.15	.40
❑ 340 Sterling Sharpe	.15	.40
❑ 341 Ray Crittenden RC	.07	.20
❑ 342 Perry Carter RC	.07	.20
❑ 343 Austin Robbins	.07	.20
❑ 344 Mike Wells DT RC	.07	.20
❑ 345 Toddrick McIntosh RC	.07	.20
❑ 346 Mark Carrier WR	.15	.40
❑ 347 Eugene Daniel	.07	.20
❑ 348 Tre Johnson RC	.07	.20
❑ 349 D.J. Johnson	.07	.20
❑ 350 Steve Young	.60	1.50
❑ 351 Jim Pyne RC	.07	.20
❑ 352 Jocelyn Borgella RC	.07	.20
❑ 353 Pat Carter	.07	.20
❑ 354 Sam Rogers RC	.07	.20
❑ 355 Jason Sehorn RC	.50	1.25
❑ 356 Darren Carrington	.07	.20
❑ 357 Lamar Smith RC	1.50	4.00
❑ 358 James Burton RC	.07	.20
❑ 359 Darrin Smith	.07	.20
❑ 360 Marco Coleman	.07	.20
❑ 361 Webster Slaughter	.07	.20
❑ 362 Lewis Tillman	.07	.20
❑ 363 David Alexander	.07	.20
❑ 364 Bradford Banta RC	.07	.20
❑ 365 Erric Pegram	.07	.20
❑ 366 Mike Fox	.07	.20
❑ 367 Jeff Lageman	.07	.20
❑ 368 Kurt Gouveia	.07	.20
❑ 369 Tim Brown	.30	.75
❑ 370 Seth Joyner	.07	.20
❑ 371 Irv Eatman	.07	.20
❑ 372 Dorsey Levens RC	1.50	4.00
❑ 373 Anthony Pleasant	.07	.20
❑ 374 Henry Jones	.07	.20
❑ 375 Cris Carter	.40	1.00
❑ 376 Morten Andersen	.07	.20
❑ 377 Neil O'Donnell	.30	.75
❑ 378 Tyronne Drakeford RC	.07	.20
❑ 379 John Carney	.07	.20
❑ 380 Vincent Brown	.07	.20
❑ 381 J.J. Birden	.07	.20
❑ 382 Chris Spielman	.15	.40
❑ 383 Mark Bortz	.07	.20
❑ 384 Ray Childress	.07	.20
❑ 385 Carlton Bailey	.07	.20
❑ 386 Charles Haley	.15	.40
❑ 387 Shane Dronett	.07	.20
❑ 388 Jon Vaughn	.07	.20
❑ 389 Checklist 1-195	.07	.20
❑ 390 Checklist 196-390	.07	.20

1995 Bowman

❑ COMPLETE SET (357)	25.00	60.00
❑ 1 Ki-Jana Carter RC	.30	.75
❑ 2 Tony Boselli RC	.30	.75
❑ 3 Steve McNair RC	3.00	8.00
❑ 4 Michael Westbrook RC	.25	.60
❑ 5 Kerry Collins RC	2.00	5.00
❑ 6 Kevin Carter RC	.30	.75
❑ 7 Mike Mamula RC	.07	.20
❑ 8 Joey Galloway RC	1.50	4.00
❑ 9 Kyle Brady RC	.30	.75
❑ 10 J.J. Stokes RC	.30	.75
❑ 11 Derrick Alexander DE RC	.07	.20
❑ 12 Warren Sapp RC	1.50	4.00
❑ 13 Mark Fields RC	.30	.75
❑ 14 Ruben Brown RC	.30	.75
❑ 15 Ellis Johnson RC	.07	.20
❑ 16 Hugh Douglas RC	.30	.75

❑ 17 Mike Pelton RC .07 .20
❑ 18 Napoleon Kaufman RC 1.25 3.00
❑ 19 James O. Stewart RC 1.00 2.50
❑ 20 Luther Elliss RC .07 .20
❑ 21 Rashaan Salaam RC .15 .40
❑ 22 Tyrone Poole RC .30 .75
❑ 23 Ty Law RC 1.25 3.00
❑ 24 Korey Stringer RC .25 .60
❑ 25 Billy Milner RC .07 .20
❑ 26 Devin Bush RC .07 .20
❑ 27 Mark Bruener RC .15 .40
❑ 28 Derrick Brooks RC 1.50 4.00
❑ 29 Blake Brockermeyer RC .07 .20
❑ 30 Alundis Brice RC .07 .20
❑ 31 Trezelle Jenkins RC .07 .20
❑ 32 Craig Newsome RC .07 .20
❑ 33 Fred Barnett .10 .30
❑ 34 Ray Childress .05 .15
❑ 35 Chris Miller .05 .15
❑ 36 Charles Haley .10 .30
❑ 37 Ray Crittenden .05 .15
❑ 38 Gus Frerotte .10 .30
❑ 39 Jeff George .10 .30
❑ 40 Dan Marino 1.25 3.00
❑ 41 Shawn Lee .05 .15
❑ 42 Herman Moore .25 .60
❑ 43 Chris Calloway .05 .15
❑ 44 Jeff Graham .05 .15
❑ 45 Ray Buchanan .05 .15
❑ 46 Doug Pelfrey .05 .15
❑ 47 Lake Dawson .10 .30
❑ 48 Glenn Parker .05 .15
❑ 49 Terry McDaniel .05 .15
❑ 50 Rod Woodson .10 .30
❑ 51 Santana Dotson .05 .15
❑ 52 Anthony Miller .10 .30
❑ 53 Bo Orlando .05 .15
❑ 54 David Palmer .10 .30
❑ 55 William Floyd .10 .30
❑ 56 Edgar Bennett .10 .30
❑ 57 Jeff Blake RC 1.00 2.50
❑ 58 Anthony Pleasant .05 .15
❑ 59 Quinn Early .10 .30
❑ 60 Bobby Houston .05 .15
❑ 61 Terrell Fletcher RC .07 .20
❑ 62 Gary Brown .05 .15
❑ 63 Dwayne Sabb .05 .15
❑ 64 Roman Phifer .05 .15
❑ 65 Sherman Williams RC .07 .20
❑ 66 Roosevelt Potts .05 .15
❑ 67 Darnay Scott .10 .30
❑ 68 Charlie Garner .25 .60
❑ 69 Bert Emanuel .25 .60
❑ 70 Herschel Walker .10 .30
❑ 71 Lorenzo Styles RC .07 .20
❑ 72 Andre Coleman .05 .15
❑ 73 Tyronne Drakeford .05 .15
❑ 74 Jay Novacek .10 .30
❑ 75 Raymont Harris .05 .15
❑ 76 Tamarick Vanover RC .30 .75
❑ 77 Tom Carter .05 .15
❑ 78 Eric Green .05 .15
❑ 79 Patrick Hunter .05 .15
❑ 80 Jeff Hostetler .10 .30
❑ 81 Robert Blackmon .05 .15
❑ 82 Anthony Cook RC .07 .20
❑ 83 Craig Erickson .05 .15
❑ 84 Glyn Milburn .05 .15
❑ 85 Greg Lloyd .10 .30
❑ 86 Brent Jones .05 .15
❑ 87 Barrett Brooks RC .07 .20
❑ 88 Alvin Harper .05 .15
❑ 89 Sean Jones .05 .15
❑ 90 Cris Carter .25 .60
❑ 91 Russell Copeland .05 .15
❑ 92 Frank Sanders RC .30 .75
❑ 93 Mo Lewis .05 .15
❑ 94 Michael Haynes .10 .30
❑ 95 Andre Rison .10 .30
❑ 96 Jesse James RC .07 .20
❑ 97 Stan Humphries .10 .30
❑ 98 James Hasty .05 .15
❑ 99 Ricardo McDonald .05 .15
❑ 100 Jerry Rice .60 1.50
❑ 101 Chris Hudson RC .07 .20
❑ 102 Dave Meggett .05 .15
❑ 103 Brian Mitchell .05 .15
❑ 104 Mike Johnson .05 .15
❑ 105 Kordell Stewart RC 1.50 4.00
❑ 106 Michael Brooks .05 .15
❑ 107 Steve Walsh .05 .15
❑ 108 Eric Metcalf .10 .30
❑ 109 Ricky Watters .10 .30
❑ 110 Brett Favre 1.25 3.00
❑ 111 Aubrey Beavers .05 .15
❑ 112 Brian Williams LB RC .07 .20
❑ 113 Eugene Robinson .05 .15
❑ 114 Matt O'Dwyer RC .07 .20
❑ 115 Micheal Barrow .05 .15
❑ 116 Rocket Ismail .10 .30
❑ 117 Scott Gragg RC .07 .20
❑ 118 Leon Lett .05 .15
❑ 119 Reggie Roby .05 .15
❑ 120 Marshall Faulk .75 2.00
❑ 121 Jack Jackson RC .07 .20
❑ 122 Keith Byars .05 .15
❑ 123 Eric Hill .05 .15
❑ 124 Todd Sauerbrun RC .07 .20
❑ 125 Dexter Carter .05 .15
❑ 126 Vinny Testaverde .10 .30
❑ 127 Shane Conlan .05 .15
❑ 128 Terrance Shaw RC .07 .20
❑ 129 Willie Roaf .05 .15
❑ 130 Jim Kelly .25 .60
❑ 131 Neil O'Donnell .10 .30
❑ 132 Ray McElroy RC .07 .20
❑ 133 Ed McDaniel .05 .15
❑ 134 Brian Gelzheiser RC .07 .20
❑ 135 Marcus Allen .25 .60
❑ 136 Carl Pickens .10 .30
❑ 137 Mike Verstegan RC .07 .20
❑ 138 Chris Mims .05 .15
❑ 139 Darryl Pounds RC .07 .20
❑ 140 Emmitt Smith 1.25 2.50
❑ 141 Mike Frederick RC .07 .20
❑ 142 Henry Ellard .10 .30
❑ 143 Willie McGinest .10 .30
❑ 144 Michael Roan RC .07 .20
❑ 145 Chris Spielman .10 .30
❑ 146 Darryl Talley .05 .15
❑ 147 Randall Cunningham .25 .60
❑ 148 Andrew Greene RC .07 .20
❑ 149 George Teague .05 .15
❑ 150 Tyrone Hughes .10 .30
❑ 151 Ron Davis RC .07 .20
❑ 152 Stevon Moore .05 .15
❑ 153 Merton Hanks .05 .15
❑ 154 Darren Perry .05 .15
❑ 155 Dave Brown .10 .30
❑ 156 Mike Morton RC .07 .20
❑ 157 Seth Joyner .05 .15
❑ 158 Bryan Cox .05 .15
❑ 159 Corey Fuller RC .07 .20
❑ 160 John Elway 1.25 3.00
❑ 161 Dewayne Washington .10 .30
❑ 162 Chris Warren .10 .30
❑ 163 Jeff Kopp RC .07 .20
❑ 164 Sean Dawkins .10 .30
❑ 165 Mark Carrier DB .05 .15
❑ 166 Andre Hastings .10 .30
❑ 167 Derek West RC .07 .20
❑ 168 Glenn Montgomery .05 .15
❑ 169 Trent Dilfer .25 .60
❑ 170 Rob Johnson RC 1.00 2.50
❑ 171 Todd Scott .05 .15
❑ 172 Charles Johnson .10 .30
❑ 173 Kez McCorvey RC .07 .20
❑ 174 Rob Fredrickson .05 .15
❑ 175 Corey Sawyer .05 .15
❑ 176 Brett Perriman .10 .30
❑ 177 Ken Dilger RC .30 .75
❑ 178 Dana Stubblefield .10 .30
❑ 179 Eric Allen .05 .15
❑ 180 Drew Bledsoe .40 1.00
❑ 181 Tyrone Davis RC .07 .20
❑ 182 Reggie Brooks .10 .30
❑ 183 Dale Carter .10 .30
❑ 184 William Henderson RC 1.25 3.00
❑ 185 Reggie White .25 .60
❑ 186 Lorenzo White .05 .15
❑ 187 Leslie O'Neal .10 .30
❑ 188 Stoney Case RC .07 .20
❑ 189 Jeff Burns .05 .15
❑ 190 Leroy Hoard .05 .15
❑ 191 Thomas Randolph .05 .15
❑ 192 Rodney Thomas RC .15 .40
❑ 193 Quentin Coryatt .10 .30
❑ 194 Terry Wooden .05 .15
❑ 195 David Sloan RC .07 .20
❑ 196 Bernie Parmalee .10 .30
❑ 197 Zack Crockett RC .15 .40
❑ 198 Troy Aikman .60 1.50
❑ 199 Bruce Smith .25 .60
❑ 200 Eric Zeier RC .30 .75
❑ 201 Anthony Smith .05 .15
❑ 202 Jake Reed .10 .30
❑ 203 Hardy Nickerson .05 .15
❑ 204 Patrick Riley RC .07 .20
❑ 205 Bruce Matthews .05 .15
❑ 206 Larry Centers .10 .30
❑ 207 Troy Drayton .05 .15
❑ 208 John Burrough RC .07 .20
❑ 209 Jason Elam .10 .30
❑ 210 Donnell Woolford .05 .15
❑ 211 Sam Shade RC .07 .20
❑ 212 Kevin Greene .10 .30
❑ 213 Ronald Moore .05 .15
❑ 214 Shane Hannah RC .07 .20
❑ 215 Jim Everett .05 .15
❑ 216 Scott Mitchell .10 .30
❑ 217 Antonio Freeman RC 1.25 3.00
❑ 218 Tony McGee .05 .15
❑ 219 Clay Matthews .10 .30
❑ 220 Neil Smith .10 .30
❑ 221 Mark Williams FOIL .15 .40
❑ 222 Derrick Graham FOIL .15 .40
❑ 223 Mike Hollis FOIL .15 .40
❑ 224 Darion Conner FOIL .15 .40
❑ 225 Steve Beuerlein FOIL .15 .40
❑ 226 Rod Smith DB FOIL .15 .40
❑ 227 James Williams LB FOIL .15 .40
❑ 228 Bob Christian FOIL .15 .40
❑ 229 Jeff Lageman FOIL .15 .40
❑ 230 Frank Reich FOIL .15 .40
❑ 231 Harry Colon FOIL .15 .40
❑ 232 Carlton Bailey FOIL .15 .40
❑ 233 Mickey Washington FOIL .15 .40
❑ 234 Shawn Bouwens FOIL .15 .40
❑ 235 Don Beebe FOIL .15 .40
❑ 236 Kelvin Pritchett FOIL .15 .40
❑ 237 Tommy Barnhardt FOIL .15 .40
❑ 238 Mike Dumas FOIL .15 .40
❑ 239 Brett Maxie FOIL .15 .40
❑ 240 Desmond Howard FOIL .15 .40
❑ 241 Sam Mills FOIL .15 .40
❑ 242 Keith Goganious FOIL .15 .40
❑ 243 Bubba McDowell FOIL .15 .40
❑ 244 Vinnie Clark FOIL .15 .40
❑ 245 Lamar Lathon FOIL .15 .40
❑ 246 Bryan Barker FOIL .15 .40
❑ 247 Darren Carrington FOIL .15 .40
❑ 248 Jay Barker RC .07 .20
❑ 249 Eric Davis .05 .15
❑ 250 Heath Shuler .10 .30
❑ 251 Donta Jones RC .07 .20
❑ 252 LeRoy Butler .05 .15
❑ 253 Michael Zordich .05 .15
❑ 254 Cortez Kennedy .10 .30
❑ 255 Brian DeMarco RC .07 .20
❑ 256 Randal Hill .05 .15
❑ 257 Michael Irvin .25 .60
❑ 258 Natrone Means .10 .30
❑ 259 Linc Harden RC .07 .20
❑ 260 Jerome Bettis .25 .60
❑ 261 Tony Bennett .05 .15
❑ 262 Dameian Jeffries RC .07 .20
❑ 263 Cornelius Bennett .10 .30
❑ 264 Chris Zorich .05 .15
❑ 265 Bobby Taylor RC .30 .75
❑ 266 Terrell Buckley .05 .15
❑ 267 Troy Dumas RC .07 .20
❑ 268 Rodney Hampton .10 .30
❑ 269 Steve Everitt .05 .15
❑ 270 Mel Gray .05 .15
❑ 271 Antonio Armstrong RC .07 .20
❑ 272 Jim Harbaugh .10 .30
❑ 273 Gary Clark .05 .15
❑ 274 Tau Pupua RC .07 .20
❑ 275 Warren Moon .10 .30
❑ 276 Corey Croom .05 .15
❑ 277 Tony Berti RC .07 .20
❑ 278 Shannon Sharpe .10 .30
❑ 279 Boomer Esiason .10 .30
❑ 280 Aeneas Williams .05 .15
❑ 281 Lethon Flowers RC .07 .20
❑ 282 Derek Brown TE .05 .15
❑ 283 Charlie Williams RC .07 .20

Card	Low	High
❑ 284 Dan Wilkinson	.10	.30
❑ 285 Mike Sherrard	.05	.15
❑ 286 Evan Pilgrim RC	.07	.20
❑ 287 Kimble Anders	10	.30
❑ 288 Greg Jefferson RC	.07	.20
❑ 289 Ken Norton	.10	.30
❑ 290 Terance Mathis	.10	.30
❑ 291 Torey Hunter RC	.07	.20
❑ 292 Ken Harvey	.05	.15
❑ 293 Irving Fryar	.10	.30
❑ 294 Michael Reed RC	.07	.20
❑ 295 Andre Reed	.10	.30
❑ 296 Vencie Glenn	.05	.15
❑ 297 Corey Swinson	.05	.15
❑ 298 Harvey Williams	.05	.15
❑ 299 Willie Davis	.10	.30
❑ 300 Barry Sanders	1.00	2.50
❑ 301 Curtis Martin RC	3.00	8.00
❑ 302 Johnny Mitchell	.05	.15
❑ 303 Daryl Johnston	.10	.30
❑ 304 Lorenzo Lynch	.05	.15
❑ 305 Christian Fauria RC	.15	.40
❑ 306 Sean Gilbert	.10	.30
❑ 307 Ray Zellars RC	.15	.40
❑ 308 William Strong RC	.07	.20
❑ 309 Jack Del Rio	.05	.15
❑ 310 Junior Seau	.25	.60
❑ 311 Justin Armour RC	.07	.20
❑ 312 Eric Bjornson RC	.07	.20
❑ 313 Vincent Brown	.05	.15
❑ 314 Darius Holland RC	.07	.20
❑ 315 Chad May RC	.07	.20
❑ 316 Simon Fletcher	.05	.15
❑ 317 Roell Preston RC	.10	.30
❑ 318 John Thierry	.05	.15
❑ 319 Orlando Thomas RC	.07	.20
❑ 320 Zach Wiegert RC	.07	.20
❑ 321 Derrick Alexander WR	.25	.60
❑ 322 Chris Cowart RC	.07	.20
❑ 323 Chris Sanders RC	.15	.40
❑ 324 Robert Brooks	.25	.60
❑ 325 Todd Collins RC	1.00	2.50
❑ 326 Ken Irvin RC	.07	.20
❑ 327 Erric Pegram	.10	.30
❑ 328 Damien Covington RC	.07	.20
❑ 329 Brendan Stai RC	.07	.20
❑ 330 James A.Stewart RC	.07	.20
❑ 331 Jessie Tuggle	.05	.15
❑ 332 Marco Coleman	.05	.15
❑ 333 Steve Young	.50	1.25
❑ 334 Greg Hill	.10	.30
❑ 335 Darryl Williams	.05	.15
❑ 336 Calvin Williams	.10	.30
❑ 337 Cris Dishman	.05	.15
❑ 338 Anthony Morgan	.05	.15
❑ 339 Renaldo Turnbull	.05	.15
❑ 340 Rick Mirer	.10	.30
❑ 341 Tim Brown	.25	.60
❑ 342 Dennis Gibson	.05	.15
❑ 343 Brad Baxter	.05	.15
❑ 344 Henry Jones	.05	.15
❑ 345 Johnny Bailey	.05	.15
❑ 346 Rocket Ismail	.10	.30
❑ 347 Richmond Webb	.05	.15
❑ 348 Robert Jones	.05	.15
❑ 349 Garrison Hearst	.25	.60
❑ 350 Errict Rhett	.10	.30
❑ 351 Steve Atwater	.05	.15
❑ 352 Joe Cain	.05	.15
❑ 353 Ben Coates	.10	.30
❑ 354 Aaron Glenn	.05	.15
❑ 355 Antonio Langham	.05	.15
❑ 356 Eugene Daniel	.05	.15
❑ 357 Tim Bowens	.05	.15

1998 Bowman

Card	Low	High
❑ COMPLETE SET (220)	20.00	50.00
❑ 1 Peyton Manning RC	12.50	25.00
❑ 2 Keith Brooking RC	.60	1.50
❑ 3 Duane Starks RC	.30	.75
❑ 4 Takeo Spikes RC	.60	1.50
❑ 5 Andre Wadsworth RC	.50	1.25
❑ 6 Greg Ellis RC	.30	.75
❑ 7 Brian Griese RC	1.25	3.00
❑ 8 Germane Crowell RC	.50	1.25
❑ 9 Jerome Pathon RC	.60	1.50
❑ 10 Ryan Leaf RC	.60	1.50
❑ 11 Fred Taylor RC	1.00	2.50
❑ 12 Robert Edwards RC	.50	1.25
❑ 13 Grant Wistrom RC	.50	1.25
❑ 14 Robert Holcombe RC	.50	1.25
❑ 15 Tim Dwight RC	.60	1.50
❑ 16 Jacquez Green RC	.50	1.25
❑ 17 Marcus Nash RC	.30	.75
❑ 18 Jason Peter RC	.30	.75
❑ 19 Anthony Simmons RC	.50	1.25
❑ 20 Curtis Enis RC	.30	.75
❑ 21 John Avery RC	.50	1.25
❑ 22 Pat Johnson RC	.50	1.25
❑ 23 Joe Jurevicius RC	.60	1.50
❑ 24 Brian Simmons RC	.50	1.25
❑ 25 Kevin Dyson RC	.60	1.50
❑ 26 Skip Hicks RC	.50	1.25
❑ 27 Hines Ward RC	3.00	8.00
❑ 28 Tavian Banks RC	.50	1.25
❑ 29 Ahman Green RC	2.00	5.00
❑ 30 Tony Simmons RC	.50	1.25
❑ 31 Charles Johnson	.10	.30
❑ 32 Freddie Jones	.10	.30
❑ 33 Joey Galloway	.20	.50
❑ 34 Tony Banks	.20	.50
❑ 35 Jake Plummer	.30	.75
❑ 36 Reidel Anthony	.20	.50
❑ 37 Steve McNair	.30	.75
❑ 38 Michael Westbrook	.20	.50
❑ 39 Chris Sanders	.10	.30
❑ 40 Isaac Bruce	.30	.75
❑ 41 Charlie Garner	.20	.50
❑ 42 Wayne Chrebet	.30	.75
❑ 43 Michael Strahan	.20	.50
❑ 44 Brad Johnson	.30	.75
❑ 45 Mike Alstott	.30	.75
❑ 46 Tony Gonzalez	.30	.75
❑ 47 Johnnie Morton	.20	.50
❑ 48 Darnay Scott	.20	.50
❑ 49 Rae Carruth	.10	.30
❑ 50 Terrell Davis	.30	.75
❑ 51 Jermaine Lewis	.20	.50
❑ 52 Frank Sanders	.20	.50
❑ 53 Byron Hanspard	.10	.30
❑ 54 Gus Frerotte	.10	.30
❑ 55 Terry Glenn	.30	.75
❑ 56 J.J. Stokes	.20	.50
❑ 57 Will Blackwell	.10	.30
❑ 58 Keyshawn Johnson	.30	.75
❑ 59 Tiki Barber	.30	.75
❑ 60 Dorsey Levens	.30	.75
❑ 61 Zach Thomas	.30	.75
❑ 62 Corey Dillon	.30	.75
❑ 63 Antowain Smith	.30	.75
❑ 64 Michael Sinclair	.10	.30
❑ 65 Rod Smith	.20	.50
❑ 66 Trent Dilfer	.30	.75
❑ 67 Warren Sapp	.20	.50
❑ 68 Charles Way	.10	.30
❑ 69 Tamarick Vanover	.10	.30
❑ 70 Drew Bledsoe	.50	1.25
❑ 71 John Mobley	.10	.30
❑ 72 Kerry Collins	.20	.50
❑ 73 Peter Boulware	.10	.30
❑ 74 Simeon Rice	.20	.50
❑ 75 Eddie George	.30	.75
❑ 76 Fred Lane	.10	.30
❑ 77 Jamal Anderson	.30	.75
❑ 78 Antonio Freeman	.30	.75
❑ 79 Jason Sehorn	.20	.50
❑ 80 Curtis Martin	.30	.75
❑ 81 Bobby Hoying	.20	.50
❑ 82 Garrison Hearst	.30	.75
❑ 83 Glenn Foley	.20	.50
❑ 84 Danny Kanell	.20	.50
❑ 85 Kordell Stewart	.30	.75
❑ 86 O.J. McDuffie	.20	.50
❑ 87 Marvin Harrison	.30	.75
❑ 88 Bobby Engram	.20	.50

Card	Low	High
❑ 89 Chris Slade	.10	.30
❑ 90 Warrick Dunn	.30	.75
❑ 91 Ricky Watters	.20	.50
❑ 92 Rickey Dudley	.10	.30
❑ 93 Terrell Owens	.30	.75
❑ 94 Karim Abdul-Jabbar	.30	.75
❑ 95 Napoleon Kaufman	.30	.75
❑ 96 Darrell Green	.20	.50
❑ 97 Levon Kirkland	.10	.30
❑ 98 Jeff George	.20	.50
❑ 99 Andre Hastings	.10	.30
❑ 100 John Elway	1.25	3.00
❑ 101 John Randle	.20	.50
❑ 102 Andre Rison	.20	.50
❑ 103 Keenan McCardell	.20	.50
❑ 104 Marshall Faulk	.40	1.00
❑ 105 Emmitt Smith	1.00	2.50
❑ 106 Robert Brooks	.20	.50
❑ 107 Scott Mitchell	.20	.50
❑ 108 Shannon Sharpe	.20	.50
❑ 109 Deion Sanders	.30	.75
❑ 110 Jerry Rice	.60	1.50
❑ 111 Erik Kramer	.10	.30
❑ 112 Michael Jackson	.10	.30
❑ 113 Aeneas Williams	.10	.30
❑ 114 Terry Allen	.30	.75
❑ 115 Steve Young	.40	1.00
❑ 116 Warren Moon	.30	.75
❑ 117 Junior Seau	.30	.75
❑ 118 Jerome Bettis	.30	.75
❑ 119 Irving Fryar	.20	.50
❑ 120 Barry Sanders	1.00	2.50
❑ 121 Tim Brown	.30	.75
❑ 122 Chad Brown	.10	.30
❑ 123 Ben Coates	.20	.50
❑ 124 Robert Smith	.30	.75
❑ 125 Brett Favre	1.25	3.00
❑ 126 Derrick Thomas	.30	.75
❑ 127 Reggie White	.30	.75
❑ 128 Troy Aikman	.60	1.50
❑ 129 Jeff Blake	.20	.50
❑ 130 Mark Brunell	.30	.75
❑ 131 Curtis Conway	.20	.50
❑ 132 Wesley Walls	.20	.50
❑ 133 Thurman Thomas	.30	.75
❑ 134 Chris Chandler	.20	.50
❑ 135 Dan Marino	1.25	3.00
❑ 136 Larry Centers	.10	.30
❑ 137 Shawn Jefferson	.10	.30
❑ 138 Andre Reed	.20	.50
❑ 139 Jake Reed	.20	.50
❑ 140 Cris Carter	.30	.75
❑ 141 Elvis Grbac	.20	.50
❑ 142 Mark Chmura	.20	.50
❑ 143 Michael Irvin	.30	.75
❑ 144 Carl Pickens	.20	.50
❑ 145 Herman Moore	.20	.50
❑ 146 Marvin Jones	.10	.30
❑ 147 Terance Mathis	.20	.50
❑ 148 Rob Moore	.20	.50
❑ 149 Bruce Smith	.20	.50
❑ 150 Rob Johnson CL	.10	.30
❑ 151 Leslie Shepherd	.10	.30
❑ 152 Chris Spielman	.10	.30
❑ 153 Tony McGee	.10	.30
❑ 154 Kevin Smith	.10	.30
❑ 155 Bill Romanowski	.10	.30
❑ 156 Stephen Boyd	.10	.30
❑ 157 James Stewart	.20	.50
❑ 158 Jason Taylor	.20	.50
❑ 159 Troy Drayton	.10	.30
❑ 160 Mark Fields	.10	.30
❑ 161 Jessie Armstead	.10	.30
❑ 162 James Jett	.20	.50
❑ 163 Bobby Taylor	.10	.30
❑ 164 Kimble Anders	.20	.50
❑ 165 Jimmy Smith	.20	.50
❑ 166 Quentin Coryatt	.10	.30
❑ 167 Bryant Westbrook	.10	.30
❑ 168 Neil Smith	.20	.50
❑ 169 Darren Woodson	.10	.30
❑ 170 Ray Buchanan	.10	.30
❑ 171 Earl Holmes	.10	.30
❑ 172 Ray Lewis	.30	.75
❑ 173 Steve Broussard	.10	.30
❑ 174 Derrick Brooks	.30	.75
❑ 175 Ken Harvey	.10	.30
❑ 176 Darryll Lewis	.10	.30
❑ 177 Derrick Rodgers	.10	.30

❑ 178 James McKnight .30 .75
❑ 179 Cris Dishman .10 .30
❑ 180 Hardy Nickerson .10 .30
❑ 181 Charles Woodson RC .75 2.00
❑ 182 Randy Moss RC 6.00 15.00
❑ 183 Stephen Alexander RC .50 1.25
❑ 184 Samari Rolle RC .30 .75
❑ 185 Jamie Duncan RC .30 .75
❑ 186 Lance Schulters RC .30 .75
❑ 187 Tony Parrish RC .60 1.50
❑ 188 Corey Chavous RC .60 1.50
❑ 189 Jammi German RC .30 .75
❑ 190 Sam Cowart RC .50 1.25
❑ 191 Donald Hayes RC .50 1.25
❑ 192 R.W. McQuarters RC .50 1.25
❑ 193 Az-Zahir Hakim RC .60 1.50
❑ 194 Chris Fuamatu-Ma'afala RC .50 1.25
❑ 195 Allen Rossum RC .50 1.25
❑ 196 Jon Ritchie RC .50 1.25
❑ 197 Blake Spence RC .30 .75
❑ 198 Brian Alford RC .30 .75
❑ 199 Fred Weary RC .30 .75
❑ 200 Rod Rutledge RC .30 .75
❑ 201 Michael Myers RC .30 .75
❑ 202 Rashaan Shehee RC .50 1.25
❑ 203 Donovin Darius RC .50 1.25
❑ 204 E.G. Green RC .50 1.25
❑ 205 Vonnie Holliday RC .50 1.25
❑ 206 Charlie Batch RC .60 1.50
❑ 207 Michael Pittman RC .75 2.00
❑ 208 Artrell Hawkins RC .30 .75
❑ 209 Jonathan Quinn RC .60 1.50
❑ 210 Kailee Wong RC .30 .75
❑ 211 DeShea Townsend RC .30 .75
❑ 212 Patrick Surtain RC .60 1.50
❑ 213 Brian Kelly RC .50 1.25
❑ 214 Tebucky Jones RC .30 .75
❑ 215 Pete Gonzalez RC .30 .75
❑ 216 Shaun Williams RC .50 1.25
❑ 217 Scott Frost RC .30 .75
❑ 218 Leonard Little RC .60 1.50
❑ 219 Alonzo Mayes RC .30 .75
❑ 220 Cordell Taylor RC .30 .75

1999 Bowman

❑ COMPLETE SET (220) 15.00 40.00
❑ 1 Dan Marino 1.00 2.50
❑ 2 Michael Westbrook .20 .50
❑ 3 Yancey Thigpen .10 .30
❑ 4 Tony Martin .20 .50
❑ 5 Michael Strahan .20 .50
❑ 6 Dedric Ward .10 .30
❑ 7 Joey Galloway .20 .50
❑ 8 Bobby Engram .20 .50
❑ 9 Frank Sanders .20 .50
❑ 10 Jake Plummer .20 .50
❑ 11 Eddie Kennison .20 .50
❑ 12 Curtis Martin .30 .75
❑ 13 Chris Spielman .10 .30
❑ 14 Trent Dilfer .20 .50
❑ 15 Tim Biakabutuka .20 .50
❑ 16 Elvis Grbac .20 .50
❑ 17 Charlie Batch .30 .75
❑ 18 Takeo Spikes .10 .30
❑ 19 Tony Banks .20 .50
❑ 20 Doug Flutie .30 .75
❑ 21 Ty Law .20 .50
❑ 22 Isaac Bruce .30 .75
❑ 23 James Jett .20 .50
❑ 24 Kent Graham .10 .30
❑ 25 Derrick Mayes .10 .30
❑ 26 Amani Toomer .10 .30
❑ 27 Ray Lewis .30 .75
❑ 28 Shawn Springs .10 .30
❑ 29 Warren Sapp .10 .30
❑ 30 Jamal Anderson .30 .75
❑ 31 Byron Bam Morris .10 .30
❑ 32 Johnnie Morton .10 .30
❑ 33 Terance Mathis .10 .30
❑ 34 Terrell Davis .30 .75
❑ 35 John Randle .20 .50
❑ 36 Vinny Testaverde .10 .30
❑ 37 Junior Seau .30 .75
❑ 38 Reidel Anthony .20 .50
❑ 39 Brad Johnson .10 .30
❑ 40 Emmitt Smith .60 1.50
❑ 41 Mo Lewis .10 .30
❑ 42 Terry Glenn .30 .75
❑ 43 Dorsey Levens .30 .75
❑ 44 Thurman Thomas .20 .50
❑ 45 Rob Moore .20 .50
❑ 46 Corey Dillon .30 .75
❑ 47 Jessie Armstead .10 .30
❑ 48 Marshall Faulk .40 1.00
❑ 49 Charles Woodson .10 .30
❑ 50 John Elway 1.00 2.50
❑ 51 Kevin Dyson .20 .50
❑ 52 Tony Simmons .10 .30
❑ 53 Keenan McCardell .20 .50
❑ 54 O.J. Santiago .10 .30
❑ 55 Jermaine Lewis .20 .50
❑ 56 Herman Moore .20 .50
❑ 57 Gary Brown .10 .30
❑ 58 Jim Harbaugh .20 .50
❑ 59 Mike Alstott .30 .75
❑ 60 Brett Favre 1.00 2.50
❑ 61 Tim Brown .30 .75
❑ 62 Steve McNair .30 .75
❑ 63 Ben Coates .20 .50
❑ 64 Jerome Pathon .10 .30
❑ 65 Ray Buchanan .10 .30
❑ 66 Troy Aikman .60 1.50
❑ 67 Andre Reed .20 .50
❑ 68 Bubby Brister .10 .30
❑ 69 Karim Abdul-Jabbar .20 .50
❑ 70 Peyton Manning 1.00 2.50
❑ 71 Charles Johnson .10 .30
❑ 72 Natrone Means .20 .50
❑ 73 Michael Sinclair .10 .30
❑ 74 Skip Hicks .10 .30
❑ 75 Derrick Alexander .20 .50
❑ 76 Wayne Chrebet .20 .50
❑ 77 Rod Smith .20 .50
❑ 78 Carl Pickens .20 .50
❑ 79 Adrian Murrell .20 .50
❑ 80 Fred Taylor .30 .75
❑ 81 Eric Moulds .30 .75
❑ 82 Lawrence Phillips .20 .50
❑ 83 Marvin Harrison .30 .75
❑ 84 Cris Carter .30 .75
❑ 85 Ike Hilliard .10 .30
❑ 86 Hines Ward .30 .75
❑ 87 Terrell Owens .30 .75
❑ 88 Ricky Proehl .10 .30
❑ 89 Bert Emanuel .20 .50
❑ 90 Randy Moss .75 2.00
❑ 91 Aaron Glenn .10 .30
❑ 92 Robert Smith .30 .75
❑ 93 Andre Hastings .10 .30
❑ 94 Jake Reed .20 .50
❑ 95 Curtis Enis .10 .30
❑ 96 Andre Wadsworth .10 .30
❑ 97 Ed McCaffrey .20 .50
❑ 98 Zach Thomas .30 .75
❑ 99 Kerry Collins .20 .50
❑ 100 Drew Bledsoe .40 1.00
❑ 101 Germane Crowell .10 .30
❑ 102 Bryan Still .10 .30
❑ 103 Chad Brown .10 .30
❑ 104 Jacquez Green .10 .30
❑ 105 Garrison Hearst .20 .50
❑ 106 Napoleon Kaufman .30 .75
❑ 107 Ricky Watters .20 .50
❑ 108 O.J. McDuffie .20 .50
❑ 109 Keyshawn Johnson .30 .75
❑ 110 Jerome Bettis .30 .75
❑ 111 Duce Staley .30 .75
❑ 112 Curtis Conway .20 .50
❑ 113 Chris Chandler .20 .50
❑ 114 Marcus Nash .10 .30
❑ 115 Stephen Alexander .10 .30
❑ 116 Darnay Scott .10 .30
❑ 117 Bruce Smith .20 .50
❑ 118 Priest Holmes .50 1.25
❑ 119 Mark Brunell .30 .75
❑ 120 Jerry Rice .60 1.50
❑ 121 Randall Cunningham .30 .75
❑ 122 Scott Mitchell .10 .30
❑ 123 Antonio Freeman .30 .75
❑ 124 Kordell Stewart .20 .50
❑ 125 Jon Kitna .30 .75
❑ 126 Ahman Green .30 .75
❑ 127 Warrick Dunn .30 .75
❑ 128 Robert Brooks .20 .50
❑ 129 Derrick Thomas .30 .75
❑ 130 Steve Young .40 1.00
❑ 131 Peter Boulware .10 .30
❑ 132 Michael Irvin .20 .50
❑ 133 Shannon Sharpe .10 .30
❑ 134 Jimmy Smith .20 .50
❑ 135 John Avery .10 .30
❑ 136 Fred Lane .10 .30
❑ 137 Trent Green .30 .75
❑ 138 Andre Rison .20 .50
❑ 139 Antowain Smith .10 .30
❑ 140 Eddie George .30 .75
❑ 141 Jeff Blake .20 .50
❑ 142 Rocket Ismail .20 .50
❑ 143 Rickey Dudley .10 .30
❑ 144 Courtney Hawkins .10 .30
❑ 145 Mikhael Ricks .10 .30
❑ 146 J.J. Stokes .20 .50
❑ 147 Levon Kirkland .10 .30
❑ 148 Deion Sanders .30 .75
❑ 149 Barry Sanders 1.00 2.50
❑ 150 Tiki Barber .30 .75
❑ 151 David Boston RC .75 2.00
❑ 152 Chris McAlister RC .60 1.50
❑ 153 Peerless Price RC .75 2.00
❑ 154 D'Wayne Bates RC .60 1.50
❑ 155 Cade McNown RC .60 1.50
❑ 156 Akili Smith RC .60 1.50
❑ 157 Kevin Johnson RC .75 2.00
❑ 158 Tim Couch RC .75 2.00
❑ 159 Sedrick Irvin RC .30 .75
❑ 160 Chris Claiborne RC .30 .75
❑ 161 Edgerrin James RC 3.00 8.00
❑ 162 Mike Cloud RC .60 1.50
❑ 163 Cecil Collins RC .30 .75
❑ 164 James Johnson RC .60 1.50
❑ 165 Rob Konrad RC .75 2.00
❑ 166 Daunte Culpepper RC 3.00 8.00
❑ 167 Kevin Faulk RC .75 2.00
❑ 168 Donovan McNabb RC 4.00 10.00
❑ 169 Troy Edwards RC .60 1.50
❑ 170 Amos Zereoue RC .75 2.00
❑ 171 Karsten Bailey RC .60 1.50
❑ 172 Brock Huard RC .75 2.00
❑ 173 Joe Germaine RC .60 1.50
❑ 174 Torry Holt RC 2.00 5.00
❑ 175 Shaun King RC .60 1.50
❑ 176 Jevon Kearse RC 1.25 3.00
❑ 177 Champ Bailey RC 1.00 2.50
❑ 178 Ebenezer Ekuban RC .60 1.50
❑ 179 Andy Katzenmoyer .60 1.50
❑ 180 Antoine Winfield RC .60 1.50
❑ 181 Jermaine Fazande RC .60 1.50
❑ 182 Ricky Williams RC 1.50 4.00
❑ 183 Joel Makovicka RC .75 2.00
❑ 184 Reginald Kelly RC .30 .75
❑ 185 Brandon Stokley RC 1.00 2.50
❑ 186 L.C. Stevens RC .30 .75
❑ 187 Marty Booker RC .75 2.00
❑ 188 Jerry Azumah .75 2.00
❑ 189 Ted White RC .30 .75
❑ 190 Scott Covington RC .75 2.00
❑ 191 Tim Alexander RC .30 .75
❑ 192 Darrin Chiaverini RC .60 1.50
❑ 193 Dat Nguyen RC .75 2.00
❑ 194 Wane McGarity RC .30 .75
❑ 195 Al Wilson RC .75 2.00
❑ 196 Travis McGriff RC .30 .75
❑ 197 Stacey Mack RC .75 2.00
❑ 198 Antuan Edwards RC .30 .75
❑ 199 Aaron Brooks RC 1.50 4.00
❑ 200 De'Mond Parker RC .30 .75
❑ 201 Jed Weaver RC .30 .75
❑ 202 Madre Hill RC .30 .75
❑ 203 Jim Kleinsasser RC .75 2.00
❑ 204 Michael Bishop RC .75 2.00
❑ 205 Michael Basnight RC .30 .75
❑ 206 Sean Bennett RC .30 .75
❑ 207 Dameane Douglas RC .60 1.50
❑ 208 Na Brown RC .60 1.50

209 Patrick Kerney RC	.75	2.00
210 Malcolm Johnson RC	.30	.75
211 Dre Bly RC	.75	2.00
212 Terry Jackson RC	.60	1.50
213 Eugene Baker RC	.30	.75
214 Autry Denson RC	.60	1.50
215 Darnell McDonald RC	.60	1.50
216 Charlie Rogers RC	.60	1.50
217 Joe Montgomery RC	.60	1.50
218 Cecil Martin RC	.60	1.50
219 Larry Parker RC	.75	2.00
220 Mike Peterson RC	.75	2.00

2000 Bowman

COMPLETE SET (240)	30.00	80.00
1 Eddie George	.25	.60
2 Ike Hilliard	.15	.40
3 Terrell Owens	.25	.60
4 James Stewart	.15	.40
5 Joey Galloway	.15	.40
6 Jake Reed	.15	.40
7 Derrick Alexander	.15	.40
8 Jeff George	.15	.40
9 Kerry Collins	.15	.40
10 Tony Gonzalez	.15	.40
11 Marcus Robinson	.25	.60
12 Charles Woodson	.15	.40
13 Germane Crowell	.08	.25
14 Yancey Thigpen	.08	.25
15 Tony Martin	.15	.40
16 Frank Sanders	.15	.40
17 Napoleon Kaufman	.15	.40
18 Jay Fiedler	.25	.60
19 Patrick Jeffers	.25	.60
20 Steve McNair	.25	.60
21 Herman Moore	.15	.40
22 Tim Brown	.25	.60
23 Olandis Gary	.25	.60
24 Corey Dillon	.25	.60
25 Warren Sapp	.15	.40
26 Curtis Enis	.08	.25
27 Vinny Testaverde	.15	.40
28 Tim Biakabutuka	.15	.40
29 Kevin Johnson	.25	.60
30 Charlie Batch	.25	.60
31 Jermaine Fazande	.08	.25
32 Shaun King	.08	.25
33 Errict Rhett	.15	.40
34 O.J. McDuffie	.15	.40
35 Bruce Smith	.15	.40
36 Antonio Freeman	.25	.60
37 Tim Couch	.15	.40
38 Duce Staley	.25	.60
39 Jeff Blake	.15	.40
40 Jim Harbaugh	.15	.40
41 Jeff Graham	.08	.25
42 Drew Bledsoe	.30	.75
43 Mike Alstott	.25	.60
44 Terance Mathis	.15	.40
45 Antowain Smith	.15	.40
46 Johnnie Morton	.15	.40
47 Chris Chandler	.15	.40
48 Keith Poole	.15	.40
49 Ricky Watters	.15	.40
50 Darnay Scott	.15	.40
51 Damon Huard	.25	.60
52 Peerless Price	.15	.40
53 Brian Griese	.25	.60
54 Frank Wycheck	.08	.25
55 Kevin Dyson	.15	.40
56 Junior Seau	.25	.60
57 Curtis Conway	.15	.40
58 Jamal Anderson	.25	.60
59 Jim Miller	.08	.25
60 Rob Johnson	.08	.25
61 Mark Brunell	.25	.60
62 Wayne Chrebet	.15	.40
63 James Johnson	.08	.25
64 Sean Dawkins	.08	.25
65 Stephen Davis	.25	.60
66 Daunte Culpepper	.30	.75
67 Doug Flutie	.25	.60
68 Pete Mitchell	.08	.25
69 Bill Schroeder	.15	.40
70 Terrence Wilkins	.08	.25
71 Cade McNown	.08	.25
72 Muhsin Muhammad	.15	.40
73 E.G. Green	.08	.25
74 Edgerrin James	.40	1.00
75 Troy Edwards	.08	.25
76 Terry Glenn	.15	.40
77 Tony Banks	.15	.40
78 Derrick Mayes	.15	.40
79 Curtis Martin	.25	.60
80 Kordell Stewart	.15	.40
81 Amani Toomer	.15	.40
82 Dorsey Levens	.15	.40
83 Brad Johnson	.25	.60
84 Ed McCaffrey	.25	.60
85 Charlie Garner	.15	.40
86 Brett Favre	.75	2.00
87 J.J. Stokes	.15	.40
88 Steve Young	.30	.75
89 Jonathan Linton	.08	.25
90 Isaac Bruce	.25	.60
91 Shawn Jefferson	.08	.25
92 Rod Smith	.15	.40
93 Champ Bailey	.15	.40
94 Ricky Williams	.25	.60
95 Priest Holmes	.30	.75
96 Corey Bradford	.15	.40
97 Eric Moulds	.25	.60
98 Warrick Dunn	.25	.60
99 Jevon Kearse	.25	.60
100 Albert Connell	.08	.25
101 Az-Zahir Hakim	.08	.25
102 Marvin Harrison	.25	.60
103 Qadry Ismail	.15	.40
104 Oronde Gadsden	.15	.40
105 Rob Moore	.15	.40
106 Marshall Faulk	.30	.75
107 Steve Beuerlein	.08	.25
108 Torry Holt	.25	.60
109 Donovan McNabb	.40	1.00
110 Rich Gannon	.25	.60
111 Jerome Bettis	.25	.60
112 Peyton Manning	.60	1.50
113 Cris Carter	.25	.60
114 Jake Plummer	.15	.40
115 Kent Graham	.08	.25
116 Keenan McCardell	.15	.40
117 Tim Dwight	.25	.60
118 Fred Taylor	.25	.60
119 Jerry Rice	.50	1.25
120 Michael Westbrook	.15	.40
121 Kurt Warner	.50	1.25
122 Jimmy Smith	.15	.40
123 Emmitt Smith	.50	1.25
124 Terrell Davis	.25	.60
125 Randy Moss	.50	1.25
126 Akili Smith	.08	.25
127 Rocket Ismail	.15	.40
128 Jon Kitna	.25	.60
129 Elvis Grbac	.15	.40
130 Wesley Walls	.08	.25
131 Torrance Small	.08	.25
132 Tyrone Wheatley	.15	.40
133 Carl Pickens	.15	.40
134 Zach Thomas	.25	.60
135 Jacquez Green	.08	.25
136 Robert Smith	.25	.60
137 Keyshawn Johnson	.25	.60
138 Matthew Hatchette	.08	.25
139 Troy Aikman	.50	1.25
140 Charles Johnson	.15	.40
141 Terry Battle EP	.12	.30
142 Pepe Pearson EP RC	.30	.75
143 Cory Sauter EP	.12	.30
144 Brian Shay EP	.12	.30
145 Marcus Crandell EP RC	.20	.50
146 Danny Wuerffel EP	.20	.50
147 L.C. Stevens EP	.12	.30
148 Ted White EP	.12	.30
149 Matt Lytle EP RC	.20	.50
150 Vershan Jackson EP RC	.12	.30
151 Mario Bailey EP	.12	.30
152 Darryl Daniel EP RC	.20	.50
153 Sean Morey EP RC	.20	.50
154 Jim Kubiak EP RC	.20	.50
155 Aaron Stecker EP RC	.30	.75
156 Damon Dunn EP RC	.20	.50
157 Kevin Daft EP	.12	.30
158 Corey Thomas EP	.12	.30
159 Deon Mitchell EP RC	.20	.50
160 Todd Floyd EP RC	.12	.30
161 Norman Miller EP RC	.12	.30
162 Jeremaine Copeland EP	.12	.30
163 Michael Blair EP	.12	.30
164 Ron Powlus EP RC	.30	.75
165 Pat Barnes EP	.20	.50
166 Dez White RC	.40	1.00
167 Trung Canidate RC	.30	.75
168 Thomas Jones RC	.60	1.50
169 Courtney Brown RC	.40	1.00
170 Jamal Lewis RC	1.00	2.50
171 Chris Redman RC	.30	.75
172 Ron Dayne RC	.40	1.00
173 Chad Pennington RC	1.00	2.50
174 Plaxico Burress RC	.75	2.00
175 R.Jay Soward RC	.30	.75
176 Travis Taylor RC	.40	1.00
177 Shaun Alexander RC	1.25	3.00
178 Brian Urlacher RC	1.50	4.00
179 Danny Farmer RC	.30	.75
180 Tee Martin RC	.40	1.00
181 Sylvester Morris RC	.30	.75
182 Curtis Keaton RC	.30	.75
183 Peter Warrick RC	.40	1.00
184 Anthony Becht RC	.40	1.00
185 Travis Prentice RC	.40	1.00
186 J.R. Redmond RC	.30	.75
187 Bubba Franks RC	.40	1.00
188 Ron Dugans RC	.20	.50
189 Reuben Droughns RC	.50	1.25
190 Corey Simon RC	.40	1.00
191 Joe Hamilton RC	.30	.75
192 Laveranues Coles RC	.50	1.25
193 Todd Pinkston RC	.40	1.00
194 Jerry Porter RC	.50	1.25
195 Dennis Northcutt RC	.40	1.00
196 Tim Rattay RC	.40	1.00
197 Giovanni Carmazzi RC	.20	.50
198 Mareno Philyaw RC	.20	.50
199 Avion Black RC	.30	.75
200 Chafie Fields RC	.20	.50
201 Rondell Mealey RC	.20	.50
202 Troy Walters RC	.40	1.00
203 Frank Moreau RC	.30	.75
204 Vaughn Sanders RC	.20	.50
205 Sherrod Gideon RC	.20	.50
206 Doug Chapman RC	.30	.75
207 Marcus Knight RC	.30	.75
208 Jamel White RC	.30	.75
209 Windrell Hayes RC	.30	.75
210 Reggie Jones RC	.40	1.00
211 Jarious Jackson RC	.30	.75
212 Ronney Jenkins RC	.30	.75
213 Quinton Spotwood RC	.20	.50
214 Rob Morris RC	.30	.75
215 Gari Scott RC	.20	.50
216 Kevin Thompson RC	.20	.50
217 Trevor Insley RC	.20	.50
218 Frank Murphy RC	.20	.50
219 Patrick Pass RC	.30	.75
220 Mike Anderson RC	.50	1.25
221 Derrius Thompson RC	.40	1.00
222 John Abraham RC	.40	1.00
223 Dante Hall RC	.75	2.00
224 Chad Morton RC	.40	1.00
225 Ahmed Plummer RC	.40	1.00
226 Julian Peterson RC	.40	1.00
227 Mike Green RC	.30	.75
228 Michael Wiley RC	.30	.75
229 Spergon Wynn RC	.30	.75
230 Trevor Gaylor RC	.30	.75
231 Doug Johnson RC	.40	1.00
232 Marc Bulger RC	.75	2.00
233 Ron Dixon RC	.30	.75
234 Aaron Shea RC	.30	.75
235 Thomas Hamner RC	.20	.50
236 Tom Brady RC	20.00	50.00
237 Deltha O'Neal RC	.40	1.00
238 Todd Husak RC	.40	1.00

❑ 239 Erron Kinney RC	.40	1.00
❑ 240 JaJuan Dawson RC	.20	.50

2001 Bowman

❑ COMPLETE SET (275)	35.00	70.00
❑ 1 Emmitt Smith	.60	1.50
❑ 2 James Stewart	.15	.40
❑ 3 Jeff Graham	.15	.40
❑ 4 Keyshawn Johnson	.20	.50
❑ 5 Stephen Davis	.20	.50
❑ 6 Chad Lewis	.15	.40
❑ 7 Drew Bledsoe	.25	.60
❑ 8 Fred Taylor	.25	.60
❑ 9 Mike Anderson	.20	.50
❑ 10 Tony Gonzalez	.20	.50
❑ 11 Aaron Brooks	.20	.50
❑ 12 Vinny Testaverde	.20	.50
❑ 13 Jerome Bettis	.25	.60
❑ 14 Marshall Faulk	.25	.60
❑ 15 Jeff Garcia	.20	.50
❑ 16 Terry Glenn	.20	.50
❑ 17 Jay Fiedler	.20	.50
❑ 18 Ahman Green	.25	.60
❑ 19 Cade McNown	.20	.50
❑ 20 Rob Johnson	.20	.50
❑ 21 Jamal Anderson	.20	.50
❑ 22 Corey Dillon	.20	.50
❑ 23 Jake Plummer	.20	.50
❑ 24 Rod Smith	.20	.50
❑ 25 Trent Green	.25	.60
❑ 26 Ricky Williams	.25	.60
❑ 27 Charlie Garner	.20	.50
❑ 28 Shaun Alexander	.25	.60
❑ 29 Jeff George	.20	.50
❑ 30 Torry Holt	.20	.50
❑ 31 James Thrash	.20	.50
❑ 32 Rich Gannon	.20	.50
❑ 33 Ron Dayne	.20	.50
❑ 34 Dedric Ward	.15	.40
❑ 35 Edgerrin James	.25	.60
❑ 36 Cris Carter	.25	.60
❑ 37 Derrick Mason	.20	.50
❑ 38 Brad Johnson	.20	.50
❑ 39 Charlie Batch	.20	.50
❑ 40 Joey Galloway	.20	.50
❑ 41 James Allen	.15	.40
❑ 42 Tim Biakabutuka	.15	.40
❑ 43 Ray Lewis	.25	.60
❑ 44 David Boston	.15	.40
❑ 45 Kevin Johnson	.15	.40
❑ 46 Jimmy Smith	.20	.50
❑ 47 Joe Horn	.20	.50
❑ 48 Terrell Owens	.25	.60
❑ 49 Eddie George	.25	.60
❑ 50 Brett Favre	.75	2.00
❑ 51 Wayne Chrebet	.20	.50
❑ 52 Hines Ward	.25	.60
❑ 53 Warrick Dunn	.25	.60
❑ 54 Matt Hasselbeck	.25	.60
❑ 55 Tiki Barber	.25	.60
❑ 56 Lamar Smith	.20	.50
❑ 57 Tim Couch	.15	.40
❑ 58 Eric Moulds	.20	.50
❑ 59 Shawn Jefferson	.15	.40
❑ 60 Donald Hayes	.15	.40
❑ 61 Brian Urlacher	.30	.75
❑ 62 Steve McNair	.25	.60
❑ 63 Kurt Warner	.30	.75
❑ 64 Tim Brown	.25	.60
❑ 65 Troy Brown	.20	.50
❑ 66 Albert Connell	.15	.40
❑ 67 Peyton Manning	.60	1.50
❑ 68 Peter Warrick	.20	.50
❑ 69 Elvis Grbac	.20	.50
❑ 70 Chris Chandler	.20	.50
❑ 71 Akili Smith	.15	.40
❑ 72 Keenan McCardell	.20	.50
❑ 73 Kerry Collins	.20	.50
❑ 74 Junior Seau	.25	.60
❑ 75 Donovan McNabb	.30	.75
❑ 76 Tony Banks	.15	.40
❑ 77 Steve Beuerlein	.20	.50
❑ 78 Daunte Culpepper	.25	.60
❑ 79 Darrell Jackson	.20	.50
❑ 80 Isaac Bruce	.25	.60
❑ 81 Tyrone Wheatley	.20	.50
❑ 82 Derrick Alexander	.15	.40
❑ 83 Germane Crowell	.15	.40
❑ 84 Jon Kitna	.20	.50
❑ 85 Jamal Lewis	.25	.60
❑ 86 Ed McCaffrey	.20	.50
❑ 87 Mark Brunell	.25	.60
❑ 88 Jeff Blake	.20	.50
❑ 89 Duce Staley	.20	.50
❑ 90 Doug Flutie	.25	.60
❑ 91 Kordell Stewart	.20	.50
❑ 92 Randy Moss	.30	.75
❑ 93 Marvin Harrison	.25	.60
❑ 94 Muhsin Muhammad	.20	.50
❑ 95 Brian Griese	.20	.50
❑ 96 Antonio Freeman	.25	.60
❑ 97 Amani Toomer	.20	.50
❑ 98 Oronde Gadsden	.15	.40
❑ 99 Curtis Martin	.25	.60
❑ 100 Jerry Rice	.50	1.25
❑ 101 Michael Pittman	.20	.50
❑ 102 Shannon Sharpe	.25	.60
❑ 103 Peerless Price	.15	.40
❑ 104 Bill Schroeder	.20	.50
❑ 105 Ike Hilliard	.20	.50
❑ 106 Freddie Jones	.15	.40
❑ 107 Tai Streets	.15	.40
❑ 108 Ricky Watters	.20	.50
❑ 109 Az-Zahir Hakim	.15	.40
❑ 110 Jacquez Green	.15	.40
❑ 111 Bobby Shaw	.15	.40
❑ 112 Johnnie Morton	.20	.50
❑ 113 Laveranues Coles	.25	.60
❑ 114 Chad Pennington	.25	.60
❑ 115 Champ Bailey	.25	.60
❑ 116 Charles Woodson	.25	.60
❑ 117 Curtis Conway	.20	.50
❑ 118 Marcus Robinson	.20	.50
❑ 119 Michael Westbrook	.15	.40
❑ 120 Mike Alstott	.20	.50
❑ 121 Priest Holmes	.25	.60
❑ 122 Qadry Ismail	.20	.50
❑ 123 Rocket Ismail	.20	.50
❑ 124 Shawn Bryson	.15	.40
❑ 125 Jeff Lewis	.15	.40
❑ 126 Jeremy Mcdaniel	.15	.40
❑ 127 Terance Mathis	.15	.40
❑ 128 Travis Prentice	.15	.40
❑ 129 Warren Sapp	.20	.50
❑ 130 Jevon Kearse	.20	.50
❑ 131 George Layne RC	.30	.75
❑ 132 Correll Buckhalter RC	.50	1.25
❑ 133 Tony Stewart RC	.40	1.00
❑ 134 Chris Barnes RC	.30	.75
❑ 135 A.J. Feeley RC	.40	1.00
❑ 136 Margin Hooks RC	.30	.75
❑ 137 Anthony Henry RC	.50	1.25
❑ 138 Dwight Smith RC	.30	.75
❑ 139 Torrance Marshall RC	.40	1.00
❑ 140 Gary Baxter RC	.40	1.00
❑ 141 Derek Combs RC	.30	.75
❑ 142 Marcus Bell DT RC	.30	.75
❑ 143 Delawrence Grant RC	.30	.75
❑ 144 Jameel Cook RC	.40	1.00
❑ 145 Eric Downing RC	.30	.75
❑ 146 Marlon McCree RC	.30	.75
❑ 147 Tay Cody RC	.30	.75
❑ 148 Mario Monds RC	.30	.75
❑ 149 Kenny Smith RC	.30	.75
❑ 150 Sedrick Hodge RC	.30	.75
❑ 151 Marcus Stroud RC	.40	1.00
❑ 152 Steve Smith RC	1.25	3.00
❑ 153 Tyrone Robertson RC	.30	.75
❑ 154 James Reed RC	.30	.75
❑ 155 Kris Kocurek RC	.30	.75
❑ 156 Dan O'Leary RC	.30	.75
❑ 157 Harold Blackmon RC	.30	.75
❑ 158 Fred Smoot RC	.50	1.25
❑ 159 Billy Baber RC	.30	.75
❑ 160 Jarrod Cooper RC	.40	1.00
❑ 161 Travis Henry RC	.50	1.25
❑ 162 David Terrell RC	.40	1.00
❑ 163 Josh Heupel RC	.50	1.25
❑ 164 Drew Brees RC	5.00	12.00
❑ 165 T.J. Houshmandzadeh RC	.75	2.00
❑ 166 Rod Gardner RC	.40	1.00
❑ 167 Richard Seymour RC	.50	1.25
❑ 168 Koren Robinson RC	.50	1.25
❑ 169 Scotty Anderson RC	.40	1.00
❑ 170 Marques Tuiasosopo RC	.40	1.00
❑ 171 John Capel RC	.30	.75
❑ 172 LaMont Jordan RC	.50	1.25
❑ 173 James Jackson RC	.40	1.00
❑ 174 Bobby Newcombe RC	.40	1.00
❑ 175 Anthony Thomas RC	.50	1.25
❑ 176 Dan Alexander RC	.40	1.00
❑ 177 Quincy Carter RC	.40	1.00
❑ 178 Morlon Greenwood RC	.30	.75
❑ 179 Robert Ferguson RC	.50	1.25
❑ 180 Sage Rosenfels RC	.50	1.25
❑ 181 Michael Stone RC	.30	.75
❑ 182 Chris Weinke RC	.40	1.00
❑ 183 Travis Minor RC	.40	1.00
❑ 184 Gerard Warren RC	.40	1.00
❑ 185 Jamar Fletcher RC	.30	.75
❑ 186 Andre Carter RC	.50	1.25
❑ 187 Deuce McAllister RC	.60	1.50
❑ 188 Dan Morgan RC	.50	1.25
❑ 189 Todd Heap RC	.50	1.25
❑ 190 Snoop Minnis RC	.40	1.00
❑ 191 Will Allen RC	.50	1.25
❑ 192 Freddie Mitchell RC	.30	.75
❑ 193 Rudi Johnson RC	.50	1.25
❑ 194 Kevan Barlow RC	.40	1.00
❑ 195 Jamie Winborn RC	.40	1.00
❑ 196 Onomo Ojo RC	.30	.75
❑ 197 Leonard Davis RC	.40	1.00
❑ 198 Santana Moss RC	.75	2.00
❑ 199 Chris Chambers RC	.75	2.00
❑ 200 Michael Vick RC	1.00	2.50
❑ 201 Michael Bennett RC	.50	1.25
❑ 202 Mike McMahon RC	.40	1.00
❑ 203 Jonathan Carter RC	.30	.75
❑ 204 Jamal Reynolds RC	.40	1.00
❑ 205 Justin Smith RC	.50	1.25
❑ 206 Quincy Morgan RC	.40	1.00
❑ 207 Chad Johnson RC	1.25	3.00
❑ 208 Jesse Palmer RC	.50	1.25
❑ 209 Reggie Wayne RC	1.25	3.00
❑ 210 LaDainian Tomlinson RC	5.00	12.00
❑ 211 Andre King RC	.30	.75
❑ 212 Richmond Flowers RC	.30	.75
❑ 213 Derrick Blaylock RC	.40	1.00
❑ 214 Cedrick Wilson RC	.50	1.25
❑ 215 Zeke Moreno RC	.40	1.00
❑ 216 Tommy Polley RC	.40	1.00
❑ 217 Damione Lewis RC	.40	1.00
❑ 218 Aaron Schobel RC	.50	1.25
❑ 219 Alge Crumpler RC	.50	1.25
❑ 220 Nate Clements RC	.50	1.25
❑ 221 Quentin McCord RC	.40	1.00
❑ 222 Ken-Yon Rambo RC	.30	.75
❑ 223 Milton Wynn RC	.30	.75
❑ 224 Derrick Gibson RC	.30	.75
❑ 225 Chris Taylor RC	.30	.75
❑ 226 Corey Hall RC	.30	.75
❑ 227 Vinny Sutherland RC	.30	.75
❑ 228 Kendrell Bell RC	.50	1.25
❑ 229 Casey Hampton RC	.40	1.00
❑ 230 Demetric Evans RC	.30	.75
❑ 231 Brian Allen RC	.30	.75
❑ 232 Rodney Bailey RC	.30	.75
❑ 233 Otis Leverette RC	.30	.75
❑ 234 Ron Edwards RC	.30	.75
❑ 235 Michael Jameson RC	.30	.75
❑ 236 Markus Steele RC	.30	.75
❑ 237 Jimmy Williams RC	.30	.75
❑ 238 Roger Knight RC	.30	.75
❑ 239 Randy Garner RC	.30	.75
❑ 240 Raymond Perryman RC	.30	.75
❑ 241 Karon Riley RC	.30	.75
❑ 242 Adam Archuleta RC	.40	1.00
❑ 243 Arnold Jackson RC	.30	.75
❑ 244 Ryan Pickett RC	.30	.75
❑ 245 Shad Meier RC	.30	.75
❑ 246 Reggie Germany RC	.30	.75
❑ 247 Justin McCareins RC	.40	1.00
❑ 248 Idrees Bashir RC	.30	.75
❑ 249 Josh Booty RC	.40	1.00

Card	Low	High
❑ 250 Eddie Berlin RC	.30	.75
❑ 251 Heath Evans RC	.40	1.00
❑ 252 Alex Bannister RC	.30	.75
❑ 253 Corey Alston RC	.30	.75
❑ 254 Reggie White RC	.30	.75
❑ 255 Orlando Huff RC	.30	.75
❑ 256 Ken Lucas RC	.40	1.00
❑ 257 Matt Stewart RC	.30	.75
❑ 258 Cedric Scott RC	.30	.75
❑ 259 Ronney Daniels RC	.30	.75
❑ 260 Kevin Kasper RC	.40	1.00
❑ 261 Tony Driver RC	.40	1.00
❑ 262 Kyle Vanden Bosch RC	.50	1.25
❑ 263 T.J. Turner RC	.30	.75
❑ 264 Eric Westmoreland RC	.30	.75
❑ 265 Ronald Flemons RC	.30	.75
❑ 266 Eric Kelly RC	.30	.75
❑ 267 Moran Norris RC	.30	.75
❑ 268 Damerien McCants RC	.40	1.00
❑ 269 James Boyd RC	.30	.75
❑ 270 Keith Adams RC	.30	.75
❑ 271 Brandon Manumaleuna RC	.40	1.00
❑ 272 Dee Brown RC	.30	.75
❑ 273 Ross Kolodziej RC	.30	.75
❑ 274 Boo Williams RC	.40	1.00
❑ 275 Patrick Chukwurah RC	.30	.75

2002 Bowman

Card	Low	High
❑ COMPLETE SET (275)	20.00	50.00
❑ 1 Emmitt Smith	.60	1.50
❑ 2 Drew Brees	.40	1.00
❑ 3 Duce Staley	.20	.50
❑ 4 Curtis Martin	.25	.60
❑ 5 Isaac Bruce	.25	.60
❑ 6 Stephen Davis	.20	.50
❑ 7 Darrell Jackson	.20	.50
❑ 8 James Stewart	.15	.40
❑ 9 Tim Couch	.15	.40
❑ 10 Travis Henry	.20	.50
❑ 11 Thomas Jones	.20	.50
❑ 12 Jamal Lewis	.20	.50
❑ 13 Chris Chambers	.25	.60
❑ 14 Jeff Blake	.20	.50
❑ 15 Plaxico Burress	.20	.50
❑ 16 Michael Pittman	.20	.50
❑ 17 Jeff Garcia	.20	.50
❑ 18 Tim Brown	.25	.60
❑ 19 Kent Graham	.15	.40
❑ 20 Shannon Sharpe	.25	.60
❑ 21 Corey Dillon	.20	.50
❑ 22 Muhsin Muhammad	.20	.50
❑ 23 Tony Gonzalez	.20	.50
❑ 24 Qadry Ismail	.20	.50
❑ 25 Mike McMahon	.15	.40
❑ 26 Edgerrin James	.25	.60
❑ 27 Daunte Culpepper	.20	.50
❑ 28 Deuce McAllister	.25	.60
❑ 29 Kerry Collins	.20	.50
❑ 30 Eddie George	.20	.50
❑ 31 Torry Holt	.25	.60
❑ 32 Todd Pinkston	.15	.40
❑ 33 Quincy Carter	.15	.40
❑ 34 Rod Smith	.20	.50
❑ 35 Michael Vick	.25	.60
❑ 36 Jim Miller	.20	.50
❑ 37 Troy Brown	.20	.50
❑ 38 Wayne Chrebet	.20	.50
❑ 39 Curtis Conway	.20	.50
❑ 40 Reidel Anthony	.15	.40
❑ 41 Mark Brunell	.20	.50
❑ 42 Chris Weinke	.15	.40
❑ 43 Eric Moulds	.20	.50
❑ 44 Ike Hilliard	.20	.50
❑ 45 Jay Fiedler	.20	.50
❑ 46 Keyshawn Johnson	.20	.50
❑ 47 Rod Gardner	.15	.40
❑ 48 Chris Redman	.15	.40
❑ 49 James Allen	.15	.40
❑ 50 Kordell Stewart	.20	.50
❑ 51 Priest Holmes	.25	.60
❑ 52 Anthony Thomas	.20	.50
❑ 53 Peter Warrick	.20	.50
❑ 54 Jake Plummer	.20	.50
❑ 55 Jerry Rice	.50	1.25
❑ 56 Joe Horn	.20	.50
❑ 57 Derrick Mason	.20	.50
❑ 58 Kurt Warner	.25	.60
❑ 59 Antowain Smith	.20	.50
❑ 60 Randy Moss	.25	.60
❑ 61 Warrick Dunn	.20	.50
❑ 62 Laveranues Coles	.25	.60
❑ 63 LaDainian Tomlinson	.40	1.00
❑ 64 Michael Westbrook	.15	.40
❑ 65 Travis Taylor	.15	.40
❑ 66 Brian Griese	.20	.50
❑ 67 Bill Schroeder	.20	.50
❑ 68 Ahman Green	.20	.50
❑ 69 Jimmy Smith	.20	.50
❑ 70 Charlie Garner	.20	.50
❑ 71 Terrell Owens	.25	.60
❑ 72 Brad Johnson	.20	.50
❑ 73 James Thrash	.20	.50
❑ 74 Marvin Harrison	.25	.60
❑ 75 Brett Favre	.60	1.50
❑ 76 Rocket Ismail	.20	.50
❑ 77 David Boston	.15	.40
❑ 78 Jermaine Lewis	.15	.40
❑ 79 Aaron Brooks	.20	.50
❑ 80 Shaun Alexander	.25	.60
❑ 81 Steve McNair	.25	.60
❑ 82 Marshall Faulk	.25	.60
❑ 83 Terrell Davis	.25	.60
❑ 84 Corey Bradford	.15	.40
❑ 85 David Terrell	.20	.50
❑ 86 Kevin Johnson	.15	.40
❑ 87 Jon Kitna	.20	.50
❑ 88 Az-Zahir Hakim	.15	.40
❑ 89 Drew Bledsoe	.25	.60
❑ 90 Garrison Hearst	.20	.50
❑ 91 Doug Flutie	.25	.60
❑ 92 Jerome Bettis	.25	.60
❑ 93 Vinny Testaverde	.20	.50
❑ 94 Tiki Barber	.25	.60
❑ 95 Johnnie Morton	.20	.50
❑ 96 Lamar Smith	.20	.50
❑ 97 Marcus Robinson	.20	.50
❑ 98 Fred Taylor	.25	.60
❑ 99 Tom Brady	.60	1.50
❑ 100 Peyton Manning	.50	1.25
❑ 101 Donovan McNabb	.30	.75
❑ 102 Rich Gannon	.20	.50
❑ 103 Hines Ward	.25	.60
❑ 104 Michael Bennett	.20	.50
❑ 105 Ricky Williams	.25	.60
❑ 106 Germane Crowell	.15	.40
❑ 107 Joey Galloway	.20	.50
❑ 108 Amani Toomer	.20	.50
❑ 109 Trent Green	.20	.50
❑ 110 Terry Glenn	.20	.50
❑ 111 Donte Stallworth RC	.50	1.25
❑ 112 Mike Williams RC	.30	.75
❑ 113 Kurt Kittner RC	.30	.75
❑ 114 Josh Reed RC	.40	1.00
❑ 115 Raonall Smith RC	.30	.75
❑ 116 David Garrard RC	.75	2.00
❑ 117 Eric Crouch RC	.50	1.25
❑ 118 Bryan Thomas RC	.30	.75
❑ 119 Levi Jones RC	.30	.75
❑ 120 Andre Davis RC	.40	1.00
❑ 121 Herb Haygood RC	.30	.75
❑ 122 Josh McCown RC	.50	1.25
❑ 123 Quentin Jammer RC	.50	1.25
❑ 124 Cliff Russell RC	.30	.75
❑ 125 Jeremy Shockey RC	.75	2.00
❑ 126 Jamin Elliott RC	.30	.75
❑ 127 Roy Williams RC	.60	1.50
❑ 128 Marquise Walker RC	.30	.75
❑ 129 Kalimba Edwards RC	.40	1.00
❑ 130 Daniel Graham RC	.40	1.00
❑ 131 Freddie Milons RC	.30	.75
❑ 132 Anthony Weaver RC	.30	.75
❑ 133 Jake Schifino RC	.30	.75
❑ 134 Antonio Bryant RC	.60	1.50
❑ 135 DeShaun Foster RC	.50	1.25
❑ 136 Antwaan Randle El RC	.50	1.25
❑ 137 William Green RC	.40	1.00
❑ 138 Ed Reed RC	1.50	4.00
❑ 139 Maurice Morris RC	.50	1.25
❑ 140 Joey Harrington RC	.50	1.25
❑ 141 T.J. Duckett RC	.50	1.25
❑ 142 Javon Walker RC	.50	1.25
❑ 143 Albert Haynesworth RC	.50	1.25
❑ 144 Julius Peppers RC	.75	2.00
❑ 145 Clinton Portis RC	1.25	3.00
❑ 146 Craig Nall RC	.40	1.00
❑ 147 Ashley Lelie RC	.50	1.25
❑ 148 Reche Caldwell RC	.50	1.25
❑ 149 Rohan Davey RC	.50	1.25
❑ 150 Patrick Ramsey RC	.50	1.25
❑ 151 Jabar Gaffney RC	.50	1.25
❑ 152 Tank Williams RC	.40	1.00
❑ 153 Ron Johnson RC	.40	1.00
❑ 154 Ladell Betts RC	.50	1.25
❑ 155 Brian Westbrook RC	1.50	4.00
❑ 156 Jamar Martin RC	.40	1.00
❑ 157 Travis Stephens RC	.30	.75
❑ 158 Tim Carter RC	.40	1.00
❑ 159 Darrell Hill RC	.30	.75
❑ 160 Luke Staley RC	.30	.75
❑ 161 Randy Fasani RC	.40	1.00
❑ 162 Matt Schobel RC	.50	1.25
❑ 163 Jon McGraw RC	.30	.75
❑ 164 Dwight Freeney RC	.75	2.00
❑ 165 Chad Hutchinson RC	.30	.75
❑ 166 Adrian Peterson RC	.50	1.25
❑ 167 Josh Scobey RC	.40	1.00
❑ 168 Jonathan Wells RC	.50	1.25
❑ 169 Sam Simmons RC	.30	.75
❑ 170 Jerramy Stevens RC	.50	1.25
❑ 171 Jason McAddley RC	.40	1.00
❑ 172 Ken Simonton RC	.30	.75
❑ 173 Chester Taylor RC	.75	2.00
❑ 174 Brandon Doman RC	.30	.75
❑ 175 Javin Hunter RC	.30	.75
❑ 176 Eddie Drummond RC	.30	.75
❑ 177 Andre Lott RC	.30	.75
❑ 178 Travis Fisher RC	.40	1.00
❑ 179 Jarvis Green RC	.30	.75
❑ 180 Ross Tucker RC	.30	.75
❑ 181 Lamont Brightful RC	.30	.75
❑ 182 Rocky Calmus RC	.40	1.00
❑ 183 Wes Pate RC	.30	.75
❑ 184 Lamar Gordon RC	.50	1.25
❑ 185 Terry Jones RC	.30	.75
❑ 186 Kyle Johnson RC	.30	.75
❑ 187 Daryl Jones RC	.30	.75
❑ 188 Tellis Redmon RC	.30	.75
❑ 189 Howard Green RC	.30	.75
❑ 190 Jarrod Baxter RC	.30	.75
❑ 191 Delvon Flowers RC	.30	.75
❑ 192 Kevin Curtis RC	.30	.75
❑ 193 Kelly Campbell RC	.40	1.00
❑ 194 Eddie Freeman RC	.30	.75
❑ 195 Atrews Bell RC	.30	.75
❑ 196 Omar Easy RC	.40	1.00
❑ 197 Jeremy Allen RC	.30	.75
❑ 198 Andra Davis RC	.30	.75
❑ 199 Jack Brewer RC	.30	.75
❑ 200 Mike Rumph RC	.30	.75
❑ 201 Seth Burford RC	.30	.75
❑ 202 Marquand Manuel RC	.30	.75
❑ 203 Marques Anderson RC	.40	1.00
❑ 204 Ben Leber RC	.30	.75
❑ 205 Ryan Denney RC	.30	.75
❑ 206 Justin Peelle RC	.30	.75
❑ 207 Lito Sheppard RC	.50	1.25
❑ 208 Damien Anderson RC	.40	1.00
❑ 209 Lamont Thompson RC	.40	1.00
❑ 210 David Priestley RC	.30	.75
❑ 211 Michael Lewis RC	.50	1.25
❑ 212 Lee Mays RC	.30	.75
❑ 213 Alan Harper RC	.30	.75
❑ 214 Verron Haynes RC	.40	1.00
❑ 215 Chris Hope RC	.50	1.25
❑ 216 David Thornton RC	.30	.75
❑ 217 Derek Ross RC	.40	1.00
❑ 218 Brett Keisel RC	.75	2.00
❑ 219 Joseph Jefferson RC	.30	.75
❑ 220 Andre Goodman RC	.30	.75
❑ 221 Robert Royal RC	.50	1.25
❑ 222 Sheldon Brown RC	.50	1.25
❑ 223 DeVeren Johnson RC	.30	.75
❑ 224 Rock Cartwright RC	.50	1.25
❑ 225 Quincy Monk RC	.30	.75

❑ 226 Nick Rogers RC	.30	.75
❑ 227 Kendall Simmons RC	.30	.75
❑ 228 Joe Burns RC	.30	.75
❑ 229 Wesly Mallard RC	.30	.75
❑ 230 Chris Cash RC	.30	.75
❑ 231 David Givens RC	.50	1.25
❑ 232 John Owens RC	.30	.75
❑ 233 Jarrett Ferguson RC	.30	.75
❑ 234 Randy McMichael RC	.50	1.25
❑ 235 Chris Baker RC	.30	.75
❑ 236 Rashad Bauman RC	.30	.75
❑ 237 Matt Murphy RC	.30	.75
❑ 238 LaVar Glover RC	.40	1.00
❑ 239 Steve Bellisari RC	.30	.75
❑ 240 Chad Williams RC	.30	.75
❑ 241 Kevin Thomas RC	.30	.75
❑ 242 Carlos Hall RC	.30	.75
❑ 243 Nick Greisen RC	.30	.75
❑ 244 Justin Bannan RC	.30	.75
❑ 245 Charles Hill RC	.30	.75
❑ 246 Mark Anelli RC	.30	.75
❑ 247 Coy Wire RC	.40	1.00
❑ 248 Darnell Sanders RC	.30	.75
❑ 249 Larry Foote RC	.75	2.00
❑ 250 David Carr RC	.50	1.25
❑ 251 Ricky Williams RC	.40	1.00
❑ 252 Napoleon Harris RC	.40	1.00
❑ 253 Ennis Haywood RC	.30	.75
❑ 254 Keyuo Craver RC	.30	.75
❑ 255 Kahlil Hill RC	.30	.75
❑ 256 J.T. O'Sullivan RC	.50	1.25
❑ 257 Woody Dantzler RC	.40	1.00
❑ 258 Phillip Buchanon RC	.50	1.25
❑ 259 Charles Grant RC	.50	1.25
❑ 260 Dusty Bonner RC	.30	.75
❑ 261 James Allen RC	.30	.75
❑ 262 Ronald Curry RC	.50	1.25
❑ 263 Deion Branch RC	.50	1.25
❑ 264 Larry Ned RC	.30	.75
❑ 265 Mel Mitchell RC	.30	.75
❑ 266 Kendall Newson RC	.30	.75
❑ 267 Shaun Hill RC	.60	1.50
❑ 268 David Pugh RC	.30	.75
❑ 269 Dante Wesley RC	.30	.75
❑ 270 Josh Mallard RC	.30	.75
❑ 271 Akin Ayodele RC	.40	1.00
❑ 272 Pete Hunter RC	.30	.75
❑ 273 Kevin McCadam RC	.30	.75
❑ 274 Jeff Kelly RC	.30	.75
❑ 275 John Henderson RC	.50	1.25

2004 Bowman

❑ COMPLETE SET (275)	30.00	60.00
❑ 1 Brett Favre	.75	2.00
❑ 2 Jay Fiedler	.10	.30
❑ 3 Andre Davis	.10	.30
❑ 4 Travis Henry	.20	.50
❑ 5 Jimmy Smith	.20	.50
❑ 6 Santana Moss	.20	.50
❑ 7 Correll Buckhalter	.20	.50
❑ 8 Randy Moss	.30	.75
❑ 9 Edgerrin James	.30	.75
❑ 10 Marc Bulger	.30	.75
❑ 11 Derrick Mason	.20	.50
❑ 12 Mark Brunell	.20	.50
❑ 13 Donte' Stallworth	.20	.50
❑ 14 Deion Branch	.30	.75
❑ 15 Jake Plummer	.20	.50
❑ 16 Steve Smith	.30	.75
❑ 17 Jon Kitna	.20	.50
❑ 18 Andre Johnson	.30	.75
❑ 19 A.J. Feeley	.30	.75
❑ 20 Drew Bledsoe	.30	.75
❑ 21 Antonio Bryant	.30	.75
❑ 22 Reggie Wayne	.20	.50
❑ 23 Thomas Jones	.20	.50
❑ 24 Alge Crumpler	.20	.50
❑ 25 Anquan Boldin	.30	.75
❑ 26 Tim Rattay	.10	.30
❑ 27 Charlie Garner	.20	.50
❑ 28 James Thrash	.10	.30
❑ 29 Koren Robinson	.20	.50
❑ 30 Terrell Owens	.30	.75
❑ 31 Amani Toomer	.20	.50
❑ 32 Kelly Campbell	.10	.30
❑ 33 Patrick Ramsey	.20	.50
❑ 34 Plaxico Burress	.20	.50
❑ 35 Chad Pennington	.30	.75
❑ 36 Fred Taylor	.20	.50
❑ 37 Domanick Davis	.25	.60
❑ 38 DeShaun Foster	.20	.50
❑ 39 T.J. Duckett	.20	.50
❑ 40 Ahman Green	.30	.75
❑ 41 Lee Suggs	.30	.75
❑ 42 Tony Gonzalez	.20	.50
❑ 43 Rich Gannon	.20	.50
❑ 44 Kevan Barlow	.20	.50
❑ 45 Torry Holt	.30	.75
❑ 46 Aaron Brooks	.20	.50
❑ 47 Tyrone Calico	.20	.50
❑ 48 Keenan McCardell	.10	.30
❑ 49 Hines Ward	.30	.75
❑ 50 LaDainian Tomlinson	.40	1.00
❑ 51 Dante Hall	.30	.75
❑ 52 Marcus Pollard	.10	.30
❑ 53 Corey Dillon	.20	.50
❑ 54 Justin McCareins	.10	.30
❑ 55 Stephen Davis	.20	.50
❑ 56 Jeff Garcia	.30	.75
❑ 57 Ashley Lelie	.20	.50
❑ 58 Javon Walker	.20	.50
❑ 59 Kyle Boller	.30	.75
❑ 60 Chad Johnson	.30	.75
❑ 61 Anthony Thomas	.20	.50
❑ 62 Byron Leftwich	.40	1.00
❑ 63 David Boston	.20	.50
❑ 64 Onterrio Smith	.20	.50
❑ 65 Deuce McAllister	.30	.75
❑ 66 Antwaan Randle El	.30	.75
❑ 67 Justin Fargas	.20	.50
❑ 68 Laveranues Coles	.20	.50
❑ 69 Quincy Morgan	.20	.50
❑ 70 Priest Holmes	.40	1.00
❑ 71 Robert Ferguson	.10	.30
❑ 72 Charles Rogers	.20	.50
❑ 73 Drew Brees	.30	.75
❑ 74 Matt Hasselbeck	.20	.50
❑ 75 Peyton Manning	.50	1.25
❑ 76 Rudi Johnson	.20	.50
❑ 77 Jake Delhomme	.30	.75
❑ 78 Tiki Barber	.30	.75
❑ 79 Brad Johnson	.20	.50
❑ 80 Steve McNair	.30	.75
❑ 81 Willis McGahee	.30	.75
❑ 82 Josh McCown	.20	.50
❑ 83 Garrison Hearst	.20	.50
❑ 84 Quincy Carter	.20	.50
❑ 85 Ricky Williams	.30	.75
❑ 86 Trent Green	.20	.50
❑ 87 Curtis Martin	.30	.75
❑ 88 Jerry Porter	.20	.50
❑ 89 Brian Westbrook	.20	.50
❑ 90 Clinton Portis	.30	.75
❑ 91 Eric Moulds	.20	.50
❑ 92 Marcel Shipp	.20	.50
❑ 93 Joey Harrington	.30	.75
❑ 94 David Carr	.30	.75
❑ 95 Marvin Harrison	.30	.75
❑ 96 Joe Horn	.20	.50
❑ 97 Chris Chambers	.20	.50
❑ 98 Darrell Jackson	.20	.50
❑ 99 Eddie George	.20	.50
❑ 100 Donovan McNabb	.40	1.00
❑ 101 Marshall Faulk	.30	.75
❑ 102 Rex Grossman	.30	.75
❑ 103 Tai Streets	.10	.30
❑ 104 Jeremy Shockey	.30	.75
❑ 105 Jamal Lewis	.30	.75
❑ 106 Tom Brady	.75	2.00
❑ 107 Shaun Alexander	.30	.75
❑ 108 Carson Palmer	.40	1.00
❑ 109 Daunte Culpepper	.30	.75
❑ 110 Michael Vick	.60	1.50
❑ 111 Eli Manning RC	5.00	12.00
❑ 112 Kevin Jones RC	.60	1.50
❑ 113 Philip Rivers RC	2.50	6.00
❑ 114 Ben Roethlisberger RC	6.00	15.00
❑ 115 Roy Williams RC	.75	2.00
❑ 116 Tommie Harris RC	.60	1.50
❑ 117 Vontez Duff RC	.40	1.00
❑ 118 Karlos Dansby RC	.60	1.50
❑ 119 Thomas Tapeh RC	.50	1.25
❑ 120 Matt Schaub RC	1.50	4.00
❑ 121 Dexter Reid RC	.40	1.00
❑ 122 Jonathan Smith RC	.40	1.00
❑ 123 Ricardo Colclough RC	.60	1.50
❑ 124 Jeff Dugan RC	.40	1.00
❑ 125 Larry Fitzgerald RC	2.50	6.00
❑ 126 Gibril Wilson RC	.60	1.50
❑ 127 Sean Taylor RC	.60	1.50
❑ 128 Marquise Hill RC	.40	1.00
❑ 129 Ernest Wilford RC	.50	1.25
❑ 130 Cedric Cobbs RC	.60	1.50
❑ 131 Rich Gardner RC	.50	1.25
❑ 132 Chris Cooley RC	.60	1.50
❑ 133 Kenechi Udeze RC	.60	1.50
❑ 134 John Navarre RC	.50	1.25
❑ 135 Ben Troupe RC	.60	1.50
❑ 136 Dave Ball RC	.40	1.00
❑ 137 Antwan Odom RC	.60	1.50
❑ 138 Stuart Schweigert RC	.50	1.25
❑ 139 Derek Abney RC	.40	1.00
❑ 140 Keary Colbert RC	.50	1.25
❑ 141 Jeris McIntyre RC	.40	1.00
❑ 142 Matt Kranchick RC	.60	1.50
❑ 143 Rodney Leisle RC	.40	1.00
❑ 144 Vince Wilfork RC	.60	1.50
❑ 145 Lee Evans RC	.75	2.00
❑ 146 Darnell Dockett RC	.40	1.00
❑ 147 Jeremy LeSueur RC	.40	1.00
❑ 148 Gilbert Gardner RC	.40	1.00
❑ 149 Amon Gordon RC	.40	1.00
❑ 150 Darius Watts RC	.50	1.25
❑ 151 Junior Siavii RC	.60	1.50
❑ 152 Igor Olshansky RC	.60	1.50
❑ 153 Courtney Watson RC	.50	1.25
❑ 154 D.J. Williams RC	.60	1.50
❑ 155 Mewelde Moore RC	.60	1.50
❑ 156 Teddy Lehman RC	.60	1.50
❑ 157 Nathan Vasher RC	.60	1.50
❑ 158 Randy Starks RC	.40	1.00
❑ 159 Isaac Sopoaga RC	.40	1.00
❑ 160 Drew Henson RC	.40	1.00
❑ 161 Erik Coleman RC	.50	1.25
❑ 162 Robert Kent RC	.40	1.00
❑ 163 Jammal Lord RC	.40	1.00
❑ 164 Richard Seigler RC	.40	1.00
❑ 165 Jeff Smoker RC	.50	1.25
❑ 166 Niko Koutouvides RC	.40	1.00
❑ 167 Adimchinobe Echemandu RC	.50	1.25
❑ 168 Matt Mauck RC	.50	1.25
❑ 169 Brandon Miree RC	.40	1.00
❑ 170 Dunta Robinson RC	.60	1.50
❑ 171 B.J. Symons RC	.60	1.50
❑ 172 Courtney Anderson RC	.40	1.00
❑ 173 Bruce Perry RC	.40	1.00
❑ 174 Shaun Phillips RC	.50	1.25
❑ 175 Greg Jones RC	.60	1.50
❑ 176 Ryan Krause RC	.40	1.00
❑ 177 Charlie Anderson RC	.40	1.00
❑ 178 Tank Johnson RC	.50	1.25
❑ 179 Dwan Edwards RC	.40	1.00
❑ 180 Julius Jones RC	.75	2.00
❑ 181 Chad Lavalais RC	.40	1.00
❑ 182 Tim Anderson RC	.60	1.50
❑ 183 Jarrett Payton RC	.60	1.50
❑ 184 Matt Ware RC	.60	1.50
❑ 185 DeAngelo Hall RC	.60	1.50
❑ 186 Ben Hartsock RC	.60	1.50
❑ 187 Bradlee Van Pelt RC	.60	1.50
❑ 188 Michael Boulware RC	.60	1.50
❑ 189 Keith Smith RC	.40	1.00
❑ 190 Michael Jenkins RC	.60	1.50
❑ 191 Quincy Wilson RC	.50	1.25
❑ 192 Dontarrious Thomas RC	.50	1.25
❑ 193 Sloan Thomas RC	.50	1.25
❑ 194 Tony Hargrove RC	.40	1.00
❑ 195 Ben Watson RC	.60	1.50
❑ 196 Craig Krenzel RC	.60	1.50
❑ 197 Jason Babin RC	.50	1.25
❑ 198 Jim Sorgi RC	.60	1.50
❑ 199 Triandos Luke RC	.40	1.00
❑ 200 Kellen Winslow RC	.75	2.00
❑ 201 Patrick Crayton RC	.75	2.00

❑ 202 Michael Waddell RC	.40	1.00
❑ 203 Chris Gamble RC	.50	1.25
❑ 204 Josh Harris RC	.40	1.00
❑ 205 Devard Darling RC	.50	1.25
❑ 206 Shawntae Spencer RC	.40	1.00
❑ 207 Will Smith RC	.60	1.50
❑ 208 Samie Parker RC	.50	1.25
❑ 209 Darrion Scott RC	.60	1.50
❑ 210 Chris Perry RC	.60	1.50
❑ 211 P.K. Sam RC	.40	1.00
❑ 212 Wes Welker RC	1.50	4.00
❑ 213 Ryan Dinwiddie RC	.40	1.00
❑ 214 Rod Davis RC	.40	1.00
❑ 215 Casey Clausen RC	.50	1.25
❑ 216 Clarence Moore RC	.60	1.50
❑ 217 D.J. Hackett RC	.60	1.50
❑ 218 Casey Bramlet RC	.40	1.00
❑ 219 Jared Lorenzen RC	.50	1.25
❑ 220 Devery Henderson RC	.60	1.50
❑ 221 Sean Jones RC	.50	1.25
❑ 222 Maurice Mann RC	.40	1.00
❑ 223 Jared Allen RC	1.50	4.00
❑ 224 Bruce Thornton RC	.40	1.00
❑ 225 Tatum Bell RC	.60	1.50
❑ 226 Leon Joe RC	.40	1.00
❑ 227 Tim Euhus RC	.40	1.00
❑ 228 John Standeford RC	.40	1.00
❑ 229 Reggie Torbor RC	.40	1.00
❑ 230 Rashaun Woods RC	.40	1.00
❑ 231 Jason Shivers RC	.40	1.00
❑ 232 Jason Peters RC	.50	1.25
❑ 233 Ahmad Carroll RC	.60	1.50
❑ 234 Jason David RC	.60	1.50
❑ 235 Keyaron Fox RC	.50	1.25
❑ 236 Corey Williams RC	.50	1.25
❑ 237 Raheem Orr RC	.40	1.00
❑ 238 Carlos Francis RC	.40	1.00
❑ 239 Von Hutchins RC	.40	1.00
❑ 240 Marcus Tubbs RC	.60	1.50
❑ 241 Daryl Smith RC	.60	1.50
❑ 242 Robert Gallery RC	.60	1.50
❑ 243 Sean Tufts RC	.40	1.00
❑ 244 Marquis Cooper RC	.60	1.50
❑ 245 Bernard Berrian RC	.60	1.50
❑ 246 Derrick Strait RC	.50	1.25
❑ 247 Travis LaBoy RC	.60	1.50
❑ 248 Johnnie Morant RC	.50	1.25
❑ 249 Caleb Miller RC	.40	1.00
❑ 250 Michael Clayton RC	.60	1.50
❑ 251 Will Poole RC	.60	1.50
❑ 252 Andy Hall RC	.50	1.25
❑ 253 Demorrio Williams RC	.60	1.50
❑ 254 Chris Thompson RC	.40	1.00
❑ 255 Derrick Hamilton RC	.40	1.00
❑ 256 Glenn Earl RC	.40	1.00
❑ 257 Jonathan Vilma RC	.60	1.50
❑ 258 Donnell Washington RC	.50	1.25
❑ 259 Drew Carter RC	.60	1.50
❑ 260 Steven Jackson RC	1.50	4.00
❑ 261 Jamaar Taylor RC	.40	1.00
❑ 262 Nate Lawrie RC	.40	1.00
❑ 263 Cody Pickett RC	.50	1.25
❑ 264 Keiwan Ratliff RC	.40	1.00
❑ 265 Luke McCown RC	.60	1.50
❑ 266 Jerricho Cotchery RC	.60	1.50
❑ 267 Joey Thomas RC	.40	1.00
❑ 268 Shawn Andrews RC	.60	1.50
❑ 269 Derrick Ward RC	.60	1.50
❑ 270 Reggie Williams RC	.60	1.50
❑ 271 Rod Rutherford RC	.40	1.00
❑ 272 Michael Turner RC	1.50	4.00
❑ 273 Michael Gaines RC	.40	1.00
❑ 274 Will Allen RC	.50	1.25
❑ 275 J.P. Losman RC	.60	1.50

2005 Bowman

❑ COMP.SET w/o AU's (270)	25.00	60.00
❑ 1 Peyton Manning	.50	1.25
❑ 2 Antonio Gates	.30	.75
❑ 3 Priest Holmes	.30	.75
❑ 4 Anquan Boldin	.25	.60
❑ 5 Donovan McNabb	.30	.75
❑ 6 Drew Bennett	.25	.60
❑ 7 Michael Vick	.30	.75
❑ 8 David Carr	.25	.60
❑ 9 Drew Brees	.30	.75
❑ 10 Trent Green	.25	.60
❑ 11 Drew Bledsoe	.30	.75
❑ 12 Randy Moss	.30	.75
❑ 13 Terrell Owens	.30	.75
❑ 14 Donte Stallworth	.25	.60
❑ 15 Alge Crumpler	.25	.60
❑ 16 Jake Plummer	.25	.60
❑ 17 Curtis Martin	.30	.75
❑ 18 Jason Witten	.30	.75
❑ 19 Tom Brady	.60	1.50
❑ 20 Thomas Jones	.25	.60
❑ 21 Tiki Barber	.30	.75
❑ 22 Maurice Carthon CO	.20	.50
❑ 23 Rex Grossman	.30	.75
❑ 24 Brett Favre	.75	2.00
❑ 25 Marshall Faulk	.30	.75
❑ 26 LaMont Jordan	.25	.60
❑ 27 Kurt Warner	.30	.75
❑ 28 Corey Dillon	.25	.60
❑ 29 Julius Jones	.30	.75
❑ 30 Ahman Green	.30	.75
❑ 31 Jamal Lewis	.25	.60
❑ 32 Ben Roethlisberger	.75	2.00
❑ 33 Keary Colbert	.20	.50
❑ 34 Mike Nolan CO RC	.25	.60
❑ 35 Joey Harrington	.30	.75
❑ 36 Brian Westbrook	.30	.75
❑ 37 Domanick Davis	.20	.50
❑ 38 Carson Palmer	.30	.75
❑ 39 Stephen Davis	.25	.60
❑ 40 Eli Manning	.60	1.50
❑ 41 Edgerrin James	.25	.60
❑ 42 Jonathan Vilma	.25	.60
❑ 43 Brad Childress CO RC	.25	.60
❑ 44 Willis McGahee	.30	.75
❑ 45 Steve McNair	.30	.75
❑ 46 Plaxico Burress	.25	.60
❑ 47 Rudi Johnson	.25	.60
❑ 48 Jerry Porter	.25	.60
❑ 49 Chad Pennington	.30	.75
❑ 50 Charles Rogers	.20	.50
❑ 51 Patrick Ramsey	.25	.60
❑ 52 Dwight Freeney	.25	.60
❑ 53 Brian Griese	.25	.60
❑ 54 Jerome Bettis	.30	.75
❑ 55 Tim Lewis CO	.20	.50
❑ 56 Aaron Brooks	.20	.50
❑ 57 Matt Hasselbeck	.25	.60
❑ 58 Chris Chambers	.25	.60
❑ 59 Kyle Boller	.25	.60
❑ 60 Brandon Lloyd	.20	.50
❑ 61 Marc Bulger	.25	.60
❑ 62 Isaac Bruce	.25	.60
❑ 63 Jake Delhomme	.30	.75
❑ 64 Chad Johnson	.25	.60
❑ 65 Shaun Alexander	.30	.75
❑ 66 Kevin Jones	.25	.60
❑ 67 Eric Moulds	.25	.60
❑ 68 Laveranues Coles	.25	.60
❑ 69 A.J. Feeley	.20	.50
❑ 70 Sean Taylor	.25	.60
❑ 71 Romeo Crennel CO RC	.30	.75
❑ 72 Ashley Lelie	.20	.50
❑ 73 Nick Saban CO RC	.25	.60
❑ 74 Deuce McAllister	.30	.75
❑ 75 Kerry Collins	.25	.60
❑ 76 Chris Brown	.25	.60
❑ 77 Steven Jackson	.40	1.00
❑ 78 Nate Burleson	.25	.60
❑ 79 LaDainian Tomlinson	.40	1.00
❑ 80 Darrell Jackson	.25	.60
❑ 81 Torry Holt	.25	.60
❑ 82 Lee Suggs	.25	.60
❑ 83 Lee Evans	.25	.60
❑ 84 Santana Moss	.25	.60
❑ 85 Jeremy Shockey	.30	.75
❑ 86 Hines Ward	.30	.75
❑ 87 Muhsin Muhammad	.25	.60
❑ 88 Daunte Culpepper	.30	.75
❑ 89 Deion Branch	.25	.60
❑ 90 DeShaun Foster	.25	.60
❑ 91 Travis Henry	.25	.60
❑ 92 Jerry Rice	.60	1.50
❑ 93 Reggie Wayne	.25	.60
❑ 94 Roy Williams WR	.30	.75
❑ 95 Michael Jenkins	.25	.60
❑ 96 Tatum Bell	.25	.60
❑ 97 Andre Johnson	.25	.60
❑ 98 Dante Hall	.25	.60
❑ 99 Javon Walker	.25	.60
❑ 100 Larry Fitzgerald	.30	.75
❑ 101 Joe Horn	.25	.60
❑ 102 Marvin Harrison	.30	.75
❑ 103 Fred Taylor	.30	.75
❑ 104 Byron Leftwich	.25	.60
❑ 105 Tony Gonzalez	.25	.60
❑ 106 T.J. Houshmandzadeh	.25	.60
❑ 107 J.P. Losman	.25	.60
❑ 108 Michael Clayton	.25	.60
❑ 109 Clinton Portis	.30	.75
❑ 110 Ted Cottrell CO RC	.20	.50
❑ 111 Braylon Edwards RC	1.50	4.00
❑ 112 Aaron Rodgers RC	2.00	5.00
❑ 113 Ronnie Brown RC	2.00	5.00
❑ 114 Alex Smith QB RC	.60	1.50
❑ 115 Cadillac Williams RC	1.00	2.50
❑ 116 Ciatrick Fason RC	.50	1.25
❑ 117 Derrick Johnson RC	.60	1.50
❑ 118 Carlos Rogers RC	.60	1.50
❑ 119 Ryan Moats RC	.50	1.25
❑ 120 Alvin Pearman RC	.40	1.00
❑ 121 Stefan LeFors RC	.50	1.25
❑ 122 Brandon Jacobs RC	.75	2.00
❑ 123 Kyle Orton RC	1.00	2.50
❑ 124 Marion Barber RC	2.00	5.00
❑ 125 Mark Bradley RC	.50	1.25
❑ 126 Travis Johnson RC	.40	1.00
❑ 127 Antrel Rolle RC	.60	1.50
❑ 128 Jason Campbell RC	1.00	2.50
❑ 129 DeMarcus Ware RC	1.00	2.50
❑ 130 Frank Gore RC	1.25	3.00
❑ 131 Justin Miller RC	.50	1.25
❑ 132 J.J. Arrington RC	.60	1.50
❑ 133 Marcus Spears RC	.60	1.50
❑ 134 Roddy White RC	.75	2.00
❑ 135 Fabian Washington RC	.60	1.50
❑ 136 Vincent Jackson RC	.75	2.00
❑ 137 Erasmus James RC	.50	1.25
❑ 138 Roscoe Parrish RC	.50	1.25
❑ 139 Airese Currie RC	.50	1.25
❑ 140 Heath Miller RC	1.25	3.00
❑ 141 Mike Patterson RC	.50	1.25
❑ 142 Troy Williamson RC	.60	1.50
❑ 143 Terrence Murphy RC	.40	1.00
❑ 144 Dan Orlovsky RC	.60	1.50
❑ 145 Eric Shelton RC	.50	1.25
❑ 146 Thomas Davis RC	.50	1.25
❑ 147 Cedric Benson RC	.60	1.50
❑ 148 Noah Herron RC	.60	1.50
❑ 149 Vernand Morency RC	.50	1.25
❑ 150 Darren Sproles RC	.75	2.00
❑ 151 Alex Smith TE RC	.60	1.50
❑ 152 Mark Clayton RC	.60	1.50
❑ 153 Craphonso Thorpe RC	.50	1.25
❑ 154 Mike Williams	.50	1.25
❑ 155 Anthony Davis RC	.50	1.25
❑ 156 Charlie Frye RC	.60	1.50
❑ 157 Fred Gibson RC	.50	1.25
❑ 158 Reggie Brown RC	.50	1.25
❑ 159 Andrew Walter RC	.50	1.25
❑ 160 Adam Jones RC	.50	1.25
❑ 161 David Greene RC	.50	1.25
❑ 162 Maurice Clarett	.50	1.25
❑ 163 Courtney Roby RC	.50	1.25
❑ 164 Derek Anderson RC	.60	1.50
❑ 165 Matt Jones RC	.60	1.50
❑ 166 Chris Henry RC	.60	1.50
❑ 167 Shaun Cody RC	.50	1.25
❑ 168 Khalif Barnes RC	.40	1.00
❑ 169 Matt Roth RC	.60	1.50
❑ 170 Lionel Gates RC	.40	1.00
❑ 171 Kevin Burnett RC	.50	1.25
❑ 172 Taylor Stubblefield RC	.40	1.00
❑ 173 Zach Tuiasosopo RC	.40	1.00
❑ 174 Alex Barron RC	.40	1.00
❑ 175 Mike Nugent RC	.50	1.25
❑ 176 Barrett Ruud RC	.60	1.50
❑ 177 Brock Berlin RC	.50	1.25

❑ 178 Kirk Morrison RC .60 1.50
❑ 179 David Pollack RC .50 1.25
❑ 180 Ryan Fitzpatrick RC .60 1.50
❑ 181 Kay-Jay Harris RC .50 1.25
❑ 182 Dan Cody RC .60 1.50
❑ 183 Chad Owens RC .60 1.50
❑ 184 Stanley Wilson RC .50 1.25
❑ 185 Rasheed Marshall RC .50 1.25
❑ 186 Bryant McFadden RC .50 1.25
❑ 187 Joel Dreessen RC .50 1.25
❑ 188 Donte Nicholson RC .50 1.25
❑ 189 Scott Starks RC .50 1.25
❑ 190 Walter Reyes RC .40 1.00
❑ 191 Stanford Routt RC .50 1.25
❑ 192 Lance Mitchell RC .50 1.25
❑ 193 Rian Wallace RC .50 1.25
❑ 194 Timmy Chang RC .50 1.25
❑ 195 Oshiomogho Atogwe RC .40 1.00
❑ 196 Larry Brackins RC .40 1.00
❑ 197 Jovan Witherspoon RC .40 1.00
❑ 198 Boomer Grigsby RC .60 1.50
❑ 199 Darryl Blackstock RC .40 1.00
❑ 200 Jerome Mathis RC .60 1.50
❑ 201 Ellis Hobbs RC .60 1.50
❑ 202 Dante Ridgeway RC .40 1.00
❑ 203 James Kilian RC .40 1.00
❑ 204 Patrick Estes RC .40 1.00
❑ 205 Justin Tuck RC .75 2.00
❑ 206 Channing Crowder RC .50 1.25
❑ 207 Dustin Fox RC .60 1.50
❑ 208 Marlin Jackson RC .50 1.25
❑ 209 Luis Castillo RC .60 1.50
❑ 210 Paris Warren RC .50 1.25
❑ 211 J.R. Russell RC .40 1.00
❑ 212 Cedric Houston RC .60 1.50
❑ 213 Corey Webster RC .60 1.50
❑ 214 Craig Bragg RC .40 1.00
❑ 215 Tab Perry RC .60 1.50
❑ 216 Ryan Riddle RC .40 1.00
❑ 217 Gino Guidugli RC .40 1.00
❑ 218 Deandra Cobb RC .50 1.25
❑ 219 Travis Daniels RC .50 1.25
❑ 220 Marcus Maxwell RC .40 1.00
❑ 221 Eric King RC .40 1.00
❑ 222 Matt Cassel RC 2.00 5.00
❑ 223 Justin Green RC .60 1.50
❑ 224 Steve Savoy RC .40 1.00
❑ 225 Shawne Merriman RC .60 1.50
❑ 226 Damien Nash RC .50 1.25
❑ 227 T.A. McLendon RC .40 1.00
❑ 228 Vincent Fuller RC .50 1.25
❑ 229 Jordan Beck RC .50 1.25
❑ 230 Lofa Tatupu RC .60 1.50
❑ 231 Will Peoples RC .50 1.25
❑ 232 Chad Friehauf RC .50 1.25
❑ 233 Brady Poppinga RC .60 1.50
❑ 234 Anttaj Hawthorne RC .50 1.25
❑ 235 Adrian McPherson RC .50 1.25
❑ 236 Nick Collins RC .60 1.50
❑ 237 Roydell Williams RC .50 1.25
❑ 238 Craig Ochs RC .50 1.25
❑ 239 Billy Bajema RC .40 1.00
❑ 240 Jon Goldsberry RC .60 1.50
❑ 241 Jared Newberry RC .50 1.25
❑ 242 Odell Thurman RC .60 1.50
❑ 243 Kelvin Hayden RC .50 1.25
❑ 244 Jamaal Brimmer RC .40 1.00
❑ 245 Jonathan Babineaux RC .50 1.25
❑ 246 Bo Scaife RC .50 1.25
❑ 247 Chris Spencer RC .60 1.50
❑ 248 Manuel White RC .50 1.25
❑ 249 Josh Davis RC .40 1.00
❑ 250 Bryan Randall RC .50 1.25
❑ 251 James Butler RC .50 1.25
❑ 252 Harry Williams RC .50 1.25
❑ 253 Leroy Hill RC .60 1.50
❑ 254 Josh Bullocks RC .60 1.50
❑ 255 Alfred Fincher RC .50 1.25
❑ 256 Antonio Perkins RC .50 1.25
❑ 257 Bobby Purify RC .50 1.25
❑ 258 Rick Razzano RC .40 1.00
❑ 259 Darrent Williams RC .60 1.50
❑ 260 Darian Durant RC .60 1.50
❑ 261 Fred Amey RC .50 1.25
❑ 262 Ronald Bartell RC .50 1.25
❑ 263 Kerry Rhodes RC .60 1.50
❑ 264 Jerome Carter RC .40 1.00
❑ 265 Marcus Randall RC .50 1.25
❑ 266 Nehemiah Broughton RC .50 1.25
❑ 267 Keron Henry RC .40 1.00
❑ 268 Jerome Collins RC .50 1.25
❑ 269 Trent Cole RC .60 1.50
❑ 270 Alphonso Hodge RC .40 1.00
❑ 271 Brandon Jones RC .60 1.50
❑ 272 Chase Lyman RC .40 1.00
❑ 273 Marviel Underwood RC .50 1.25
❑ 274 Maurice Washington RC .40 1.00
❑ 275 Madison Hedgecock RC .60 1.50

2006 Bowman

❑ COMPLETE SET (275) 25.00 60.00
❑ 1 Plaxico Burress .25 .60
❑ 2 Lee Evans .25 .60
❑ 3 Shaun Alexander .25 .60
❑ 4 Muhsin Muhammad .25 .60
❑ 5 Jamal Lewis .25 .60
❑ 6 Brett Favre .60 1.50
❑ 7 Jake Plummer .25 .60
❑ 8 Clinton Portis .30 .75
❑ 9 Deuce McAllister .25 .60
❑ 10 Rod Marinelli CO RC .20 .50
❑ 11 Tom Brady .50 1.25
❑ 12 Torry Holt .25 .60
❑ 13 T.J. Houshmandzadeh .25 .60
❑ 14 Rudi Johnson .25 .60
❑ 15 Priest Holmes .25 .60
❑ 16 Tatum Bell .20 .50
❑ 17 Carson Palmer .30 .75
❑ 18 Jeremy Shockey .30 .75
❑ 19 Willis McGahee .30 .75
❑ 20 Shawne Merriman .25 .60
❑ 21 Alge Crumpler .25 .60
❑ 22 Terrell Owens .30 .75
❑ 23 Marion Barber .30 .75
❑ 24 Fred Taylor .25 .60
❑ 25 Dante Hall .25 .60
❑ 26 Steve Smith .30 .75
❑ 27 Mike McCarthy CO RC .20 .50
❑ 28 Brad Johnson .25 .60
❑ 29 Reggie Wayne .25 .60
❑ 30 David Carr .20 .50
❑ 31 DeShaun Foster .25 .60
❑ 32 Julius Jones .25 .60
❑ 33 Tony Gonzalez .25 .60
❑ 34 Chad Johnson .25 .60
❑ 35 Javon Walker .25 .60
❑ 36 Curtis Martin .30 .75
❑ 37 Marc Bulger .25 .60
❑ 38 Peyton Manning .50 1.25
❑ 39 LaMont Jordan .25 .60
❑ 40 LaDainian Tomlinson .40 1.00
❑ 41 Tiki Barber .30 .75
❑ 42 Darrell Jackson .25 .60
❑ 43 Byron Leftwich .25 .60
❑ 44 J.P. Losman .25 .60
❑ 45 Dwight Freeney .25 .60
❑ 46 Kevin Jones .25 .60
❑ 47 Drew Brees .30 .75
❑ 48 Isaac Bruce .25 .60
❑ 49 Hines Ward .30 .75
❑ 50 Drew Bledsoe .30 .75
❑ 51 Randy Moss .30 .75
❑ 52 Roy Williams WR .30 .75
❑ 53 Edgerrin James .25 .60
❑ 54 Donte Stallworth .25 .60
❑ 55 Odell Thurman .20 .50
❑ 56 Chester Taylor .25 .60
❑ 57 Ahman Green .25 .60
❑ 58 Steven Jackson .30 .75
❑ 59 Randy McMichael .20 .50
❑ 60 Larry Fitzgerald .30 .75
❑ 61 Ben Roethlisberger .50 1.25
❑ 62 Charlie Frye .25 .60
❑ 63 Daunte Culpepper .30 .75
❑ 64 Keary Colbert .25 .60
❑ 65 Santana Moss .25 .60
❑ 66 Patrick Ramsey .25 .60
❑ 67 Mark Clayton .25 .60
❑ 68 Jonathan Vilma .25 .60
❑ 69 Gary Kubiak CO .20 .50
❑ 70 Michael Jenkins .25 .60
❑ 71 Jake Delhomme .25 .60
❑ 72 Marvin Harrison .30 .75
❑ 73 Aaron Rodgers .30 .75
❑ 74 Trent Green .25 .60
❑ 75 Andre Johnson .25 .60
❑ 76 Chris Chambers .25 .60
❑ 77 Matt Hasselbeck .25 .60
❑ 78 Chris Brown .25 .60
❑ 79 Reggie Brown .20 .50
❑ 80 Eli Manning .40 1.00
❑ 81 Warrick Dunn .25 .60
❑ 82 Kurt Warner .30 .75
❑ 83 Corey Dillon .25 .60
❑ 84 Antonio Gates .30 .75
❑ 85 Anquan Boldin .25 .60
❑ 86 Terry Glenn .25 .60
❑ 87 Donovan McNabb .30 .75
❑ 88 Steve McNair .25 .60
❑ 89 Drew Bennett .25 .60
❑ 90 Jason Witten .30 .75
❑ 91 Alex Smith QB .25 .60
❑ 92 Joe Horn .25 .60
❑ 93 Eric Moulds .25 .60
❑ 94 Domanick Davis .25 .60
❑ 95 Billy Volek .20 .50
❑ 96 Deion Branch .25 .60
❑ 97 Chris Cooley .25 .60
❑ 98 Todd Heap UER .25 .60
❑ 99 Larry Johnson .25 .60
❑ 100 Chad Pennington .25 .60
❑ 101 Willie Parker .40 1.00
❑ 102 Brandon Lloyd .25 .60
❑ 103 Cadillac Williams .30 .75
❑ 104 Rod Smith .25 .60
❑ 105 Philip Rivers .30 .75
❑ 106 Ronnie Brown .30 .75
❑ 107 Reuben Droughns .25 .60
❑ 108 Braylon Edwards .30 .75
❑ 109 Joey Galloway .25 .60
❑ 110 Michael Vick .30 .75
❑ 111 Reggie Bush RC 1.50 4.00
❑ 112 Matt Leinart RC 1.00 2.50
❑ 113 Vince Young RC 1.50 4.00
❑ 114 Jay Cutler RC 1.50 4.00
❑ 115 Santonio Holmes RC 1.50 4.00
❑ 116 LenDale White RC .75 2.00
❑ 117 DeAngelo Williams RC 1.25 3.00
❑ 118 Mario Williams RC .75 2.00
❑ 119 A.J. Hawk RC 1.00 2.50
❑ 120 Joseph Addai RC .75 2.00
❑ 121 Leonard Pope RC .60 1.50
❑ 122 Tamba Hali RC .60 1.50
❑ 123 Bruce Gradkowski RC .60 1.50
❑ 124 Jerome Harrison RC .60 1.50
❑ 125 Jason Allen RC .50 1.25
❑ 126 Laurence Maroney RC .75 2.00
❑ 127 Mathias Kiwanuka RC .75 2.00
❑ 128 Brodrick Bunkley RC .50 1.25
❑ 129 Brian Calhoun RC .50 1.25
❑ 130 Bobby Carpenter RC .50 1.25
❑ 131 Johnathan Joseph RC .50 1.25
❑ 132 Maurice Stovall RC .50 1.25
❑ 133 Anthony Fasano RC .60 1.50
❑ 134 Travis Wilson RC .40 1.00
❑ 135 Chad Jackson RC .50 1.25
❑ 136 D'Brickashaw Ferguson RC .60 1.50
❑ 137 Tarvaris Jackson RC .60 1.50
❑ 138 Omar Jacobs RC .40 1.00
❑ 139 Reggie McNeal RC .50 1.25
❑ 140 Jerious Norwood RC .60 1.50
❑ 141 Haloti Ngata RC .60 1.50
❑ 142 Jason Avant RC .60 1.50
❑ 143 Brandon Marshall RC .60 1.50
❑ 144 Tye Hill RC .50 1.25
❑ 145 Manny Lawson RC .60 1.50
❑ 146 Brandon Williams RC .50 1.25
❑ 147 Demetrius Williams RC .50 1.25
❑ 148 Michael Huff RC .60 1.50
❑ 149 Mike Hass RC .60 1.50
❑ 150 Vernon Davis RC .60 1.50
❑ 151 Donte Whitner RC .60 1.50
❑ 152 Marcedes Lewis RC .60 1.50
❑ 153 Michael Robinson RC .50 1.25

❑ 154 Maurice Drew RC	1.25	3.00
❑ 155 Sinorice Moss RC	.60	1.50
❑ 156 Brodie Croyle RC	.60	1.50
❑ 157 Derek Hagan RC	.50	1.25
❑ 158 Chad Greenway RC	.60	1.50
❑ 159 Kellen Clemens RC	.60	1.50
❑ 160 Skyler Green RC	.40	1.00
❑ 161 Devin Hester RC	1.25	3.00
❑ 162 Jeremy Bloom RC	.50	1.25
❑ 163 Ashton Youboty RC	.50	1.25
❑ 164 Kamerion Wimbley RC	.60	1.50
❑ 165 Charlie Whitehurst RC	.60	1.50
❑ 166 Devin Aromashodu RC	.60	1.50
❑ 167 Darnell Bing RC	.50	1.25
❑ 168 Adam Jennings RC	.50	1.25
❑ 169 Joe Klopfenstein RC	.50	1.25
❑ 170 Jeff Webb RC	.50	1.25
❑ 171 D.J. Shockley RC	.50	1.25
❑ 172 Daniel Bullocks RC	.60	1.50
❑ 173 Marcus Vick RC	.40	1.00
❑ 174 Greg Jennings RC	1.00	2.50
❑ 175 David Thomas RC	.60	1.50
❑ 176 Thomas Howard RC	.50	1.25
❑ 177 Todd Watkins RC	.40	1.00
❑ 178 Leon Washington RC	.75	2.00
❑ 179 Winston Justice RC	.60	1.50
❑ 180 Lawrence Vickers RC	.50	1.25
❑ 181 Bernard Pollard RC	.50	1.25
❑ 182 Davin Joseph RC	.50	1.25
❑ 183 Abdul Hodge RC	.50	1.25
❑ 184 Pat Watkins RC	.60	1.50
❑ 185 Jon Alston RC	.40	1.00
❑ 186 Ernie Sims RC	.50	1.25
❑ 187 Jovon Bouknight RC	.50	1.25
❑ 188 D'Qwell Jackson RC	.50	1.25
❑ 189 Wali Lundy RC	.60	1.50
❑ 190 Corey Bramlet RC	.50	1.25
❑ 191 Jonathan Orr RC	.50	1.25
❑ 192 Gerald Riggs RC	.50	1.25
❑ 193 Antonio Cromartie RC	.60	1.50
❑ 194 Will Blackmon RC	.60	1.50
❑ 195 Chris Gocong RC	.50	1.25
❑ 196 David Pittman RC	.50	1.25
❑ 197 Quinn Sypniewski RC	.50	1.25
❑ 198 A.J. Nicholson RC	.40	1.00
❑ 199 Richard Marshall RC	.50	1.25
❑ 200 Kevin McMahan RC	.50	1.25
❑ 201 Cedric Humes RC	.50	1.25
❑ 202 J.D. Runnels RC	.50	1.25
❑ 203 Darryl Tapp RC	.50	1.25
❑ 204 Charles Davis RC	.50	1.25
❑ 205 Brad Smith RC	.60	1.50
❑ 206 Tim Massaquoi RC	.50	1.25
❑ 207 Nate Salley RC	.50	1.25
❑ 208 Matt Shelton RC	.60	1.50
❑ 209 Brett Basanez RC	.60	1.50
❑ 210 Demario Minter RC	.50	1.25
❑ 211 Marques Hagans RC	.50	1.25
❑ 212 Rocky Mcintosh RC	.60	1.50
❑ 213 Anthony Mix RC	.50	1.25
❑ 214 Hank Baskett RC	.60	1.50
❑ 215 Jimmy Williams RC	.60	1.50
❑ 216 Andre Hall RC	.50	1.25
❑ 217 Cody Hodges RC	.50	1.25
❑ 218 Greg Lee RC	.40	1.00
❑ 219 Danieal Manning RC	.60	1.50
❑ 220 Jason Hatcher RC	.50	1.25
❑ 221 Ben Obomanu RC	.50	1.25
❑ 222 Dusty Dvoracek RC	.60	1.50
❑ 223 Ingle Martin RC	.50	1.25
❑ 224 Marcus McNeill RC	.50	1.25
❑ 225 DeMeco Ryans RC	.75	2.00
❑ 226 Dwayne Slay RC	.50	1.25
❑ 227 Domenik Hixon RC	.60	1.50
❑ 228 John David Washington RC	.50	1.25
❑ 229 P.J. Daniels RC	.40	1.00
❑ 230 Kelly Jennings RC	.60	1.50
❑ 231 Josh Betts RC	.50	1.25
❑ 232 Marques Colston RC	1.50	4.00
❑ 233 John McCargo RC	.50	1.25
❑ 234 P.J. Pope RC	.60	1.50
❑ 235 Gabe Watson RC	.40	1.00
❑ 236 Paul Pinegar RC	.40	1.00
❑ 237 Ray Edwards RC	.60	1.50
❑ 238 Elvis Dumervil RC	.60	1.50
❑ 239 Travis Lulay RC	.50	1.25
❑ 240 Alan Zemaitis RC	.60	1.50
❑ 241 Bennie Brazell RC	.50	1.25
❑ 242 Jeff King RC	.50	1.25
❑ 243 Damien Rhodes RC	.50	1.25
❑ 244 Orien Harris RC	.50	1.25
❑ 245 David Anderson RC	.50	1.25
❑ 246 Roman Harper RC	.50	1.25
❑ 247 Garrett Mills RC	.50	1.25
❑ 248 Anthony Schlegel RC	.50	1.25
❑ 249 David Kirtman RC	.50	1.25
❑ 250 Omar Gaither RC	.50	1.25
❑ 251 Freddie Keiaho RC	.50	1.25
❑ 252 J.J. Outlaw RC	.50	1.25
❑ 253 Willie Reid RC	.50	1.25
❑ 254 Tony Scheffler RC	.60	1.50
❑ 255 Dee Webb RC	.50	1.25
❑ 256 Drew Olson RC	.40	1.00
❑ 257 Tim Day RC	.50	1.25
❑ 258 Martin Nance RC	.50	1.25
❑ 259 Spencer Havner RC	.50	1.25
❑ 260 Ko Simpson RC	.50	1.25
❑ 261 Jesse Mahelona RC	.50	1.25
❑ 262 Owen Daniels RC	.60	1.50
❑ 263 Mike Bell RC	.60	1.50
❑ 264 Anwar Phillips RC	.50	1.25
❑ 265 Erik Meyer RC	.50	1.25
❑ 266 Delanie Walker RC	.50	1.25
❑ 267 Dominique Byrd RC	.50	1.25
❑ 268 Eric Smith RC	.50	1.25
❑ 269 Darrell Hackney RC	.50	1.25
❑ 270 Freddie Roach RC	.50	1.25
❑ 271 James Anderson RC	.40	1.00
❑ 272 Anthony Smith RC	.60	1.50
❑ 273 Quinton Ganther RC	.40	1.00
❑ 274 Nick Mangold RC	.50	1.25
❑ 275 Gerris Wilkinson RC	.40	1.00

2007 Bowman

❑ COMPLETE SET (275)	25.00	60.00
❑ 1 Matt Leinart	.30	.75
❑ 2 Matt Schaub	.25	.60
❑ 3 Jason Campbell	.25	.60
❑ 4 Steve McNair	.25	.60
❑ 5 J.P. Losman	.20	.50
❑ 6 Jake Delhomme	.25	.60
❑ 7 Rex Grossman	.25	.60
❑ 8 Carson Palmer	.30	.75
❑ 9 Tony Romo	.50	1.25
❑ 10 Jay Cutler	.30	.75
❑ 11 Brett Favre	.60	1.50
❑ 12 Peyton Manning	.50	1.25
❑ 13 Trent Green	.25	.60
❑ 14 Tom Brady	.60	1.50
❑ 15 Drew Brees	.30	.75
❑ 16 Eli Manning	.30	.75
❑ 17 Chad Pennington	.25	.60
❑ 18 Donovan McNabb	.30	.75
❑ 19 Ben Roethlisberger	.40	1.00
❑ 20 Philip Rivers	.30	.75
❑ 21 Alex Smith QB	.30	.75
❑ 22 Matt Hasselbeck	.25	.60
❑ 23 Marc Bulger	.25	.60
❑ 24 Vince Young	.30	.75
❑ 25 Edgerrin James	.25	.60
❑ 26 Warrick Dunn	.25	.60
❑ 27 Jamal Lewis	.25	.60
❑ 28 Willis McGahee	.25	.60
❑ 29 DeShaun Foster	.25	.60
❑ 30 DeAngelo Williams	.30	.75
❑ 31 Cedric Benson	.25	.60
❑ 32 Thomas Jones	.25	.60
❑ 33 Rudi Johnson	.25	.60
❑ 34 Julius Jones	.25	.60
❑ 35 Dominic Rhodes	.25	.60
❑ 36 Joseph Addai	.30	.75
❑ 37 Fred Taylor	.25	.60
❑ 38 Maurice Jones-Drew	.30	.75
❑ 39 Larry Johnson	.25	.60
❑ 40 Ronnie Brown	.25	.60
❑ 41 Chester Taylor	.20	.50
❑ 42 Laurence Maroney	.30	.75
❑ 43 Deuce McAllister	.25	.60
❑ 44 Reggie Bush	.40	1.00
❑ 45 Brandon Jacobs	.25	.60
❑ 46 Brian Westbrook	.25	.60
❑ 47 Willie Parker	.25	.60
❑ 48 LaDainian Tomlinson	.40	1.00
❑ 49 Frank Gore	.30	.75
❑ 50 Shaun Alexander	.25	.60
❑ 51 Steven Jackson	.30	.75
❑ 52 Cadillac Williams	.25	.60
❑ 53 Clinton Portis	.25	.60
❑ 54 Michael Turner	.30	.75
❑ 55 Anquan Boldin	.25	.60
❑ 56 Larry Fitzgerald	.30	.75
❑ 57 Derrick Mason	.20	.50
❑ 58 Lee Evans	.25	.60
❑ 59 Steve Smith	.25	.60
❑ 60 Muhsin Muhammad	.25	.60
❑ 61 Chad Johnson	.25	.60
❑ 62 T.J. Houshmandzadeh	.25	.60
❑ 63 Braylon Edwards	.25	.60
❑ 64 Terrell Owens	.30	.75
❑ 65 Terry Glenn	.25	.60
❑ 66 Javon Walker	.25	.60
❑ 67 Mike Furrey	.25	.60
❑ 68 Roy Williams WR	.25	.60
❑ 69 Donald Driver	.30	.75
❑ 70 Greg Jennings	.25	.60
❑ 71 Andre Johnson	.25	.60
❑ 72 Reggie Wayne	.25	.60
❑ 73 Marvin Harrison	.30	.75
❑ 74 Matt Jones	.25	.60
❑ 75 Chris Chambers	.25	.60
❑ 76 Troy Williamson	.20	.50
❑ 77 Devery Henderson	.20	.50
❑ 78 Joe Horn	.25	.60
❑ 79 Marques Colston	.30	.75
❑ 80 Plaxico Burress	.25	.60
❑ 81 Amani Toomer	.25	.60
❑ 82 Jerricho Cotchery	.20	.50
❑ 83 Laveranues Coles	.25	.60
❑ 84 Randy Moss	.30	.75
❑ 85 Donte Stallworth	.25	.60
❑ 86 Reggie Brown	.20	.50
❑ 87 Hines Ward	.30	.75
❑ 88 Santonio Holmes	.25	.60
❑ 89 Keenan McCardell	.20	.50
❑ 90 Eric Parker	.20	.50
❑ 91 Arnaz Battle	.20	.50
❑ 92 Antonio Bryant	.25	.60
❑ 93 Deion Branch	.25	.60
❑ 94 Darrell Jackson	.25	.60
❑ 95 Kevin Curtis	.20	.50
❑ 96 Torry Holt	.25	.60
❑ 97 Isaac Bruce	.25	.60
❑ 98 Antwaan Randle El	.20	.50
❑ 99 Santana Moss	.25	.60
❑ 100 Alge Crumpler	.25	.60
❑ 101 Kellen Winslow	.25	.60
❑ 102 Tony Gonzalez	.25	.60
❑ 103 Jeremy Shockey	.25	.60
❑ 104 Antonio Gates	.25	.60
❑ 105 Vernon Davis	.25	.60
❑ 106 Tarvaris Jackson	.25	.60
❑ 107 Travis Henry	.25	.60
❑ 108 Drew Bennett	.20	.50
❑ 109 Todd Heap	.20	.50
❑ 110 Byron Leftwich	.25	.60
❑ 111 JaMarcus Russell RC	.75	2.00
❑ 112 Brady Quinn RC	1.25	3.00
❑ 113 Drew Stanton RC	.50	1.25
❑ 114 Troy Smith RC	.75	2.00
❑ 115 Kevin Kolb RC	1.00	2.50
❑ 116 Trent Edwards RC	1.00	2.50
❑ 117 John Beck RC	.60	1.50
❑ 118 Jordan Palmer RC	.60	1.50
❑ 119 Chris Leak RC	.50	1.25
❑ 120 Isaiah Stanback RC	.60	1.50
❑ 121 Tyler Palko RC	.50	1.25
❑ 122 Jared Zabransky RC	.60	1.50
❑ 123 Jeff Rowe RC	.50	1.25
❑ 124 Zac Taylor RC	.60	1.50
❑ 125 Lester Ricard RC	.60	1.50
❑ 126 Adrian Peterson RC	6.00	15.00
❑ 127 Marshawn Lynch RC	1.00	2.50
❑ 128 Brandon Jackson RC	.60	1.50
❑ 129 Michael Bush RC	.60	1.50

❑ 130 Kenny Irons RC	.60	1.50
❑ 131 Antonio Pittman RC	.60	1.50
❑ 132 Tony Hunt RC	.60	1.50
❑ 133 Darius Walker RC	.50	1.25
❑ 134 Dwayne Wright RC	.50	1.25
❑ 135 Lorenzo Booker RC	.60	1.50
❑ 136 Kenneth Darby RC	.60	1.50
❑ 137 Chris Henry RB RC	.50	1.25
❑ 138 Selvin Young RC	.60	1.50
❑ 139 Brian Leonard RC	.50	1.25
❑ 140 Ahmad Bradshaw RC	.75	2.00
❑ 141 Gary Russell RC	.50	1.25
❑ 142 Kolby Smith RC	.60	1.50
❑ 143 Thomas Clayton RC	.50	1.25
❑ 144 Garrett Wolfe RC	.60	1.50
❑ 145 Calvin Johnson RC	1.50	4.00
❑ 146 Ted Ginn Jr. RC	1.00	2.50
❑ 147 Dwayne Jarrett RC	.60	1.50
❑ 148 Dwayne Bowe RC	1.00	2.50
❑ 149 Sidney Rice RC	1.25	3.00
❑ 150 Robert Meachem RC	.60	1.50
❑ 151 Anthony Gonzalez RC	.75	2.00
❑ 152 Craig Buster Davis RC	.60	1.50
❑ 153 Aundrae Allison RC	.50	1.25
❑ 154 Chansi Stuckey RC	.60	1.50
❑ 155 David Clowney RC	.60	1.50
❑ 156 Steve Smith USC RC	1.00	2.50
❑ 157 Courtney Taylor RC	.50	1.25
❑ 158 Paul Williams RC	.50	1.25
❑ 159 Johnnie Lee Higgins RC	.60	1.50
❑ 160 Rhema McKnight RC	.50	1.25
❑ 161 Jason Hill RC	.60	1.50
❑ 162 Dallas Baker RC	.50	1.25
❑ 163 Greg Olsen RC	.75	2.00
❑ 164 Yamon Figurs RC	.40	1.00
❑ 165 Scott Chandler RC	.50	1.25
❑ 166 Matt Spaeth RC	.60	1.50
❑ 167 Ben Patrick RC	.50	1.25
❑ 168 Clark Harris RC	.60	1.50
❑ 169 Martrez Milner RC	.50	1.25
❑ 170 Joe Newton RC	.50	1.25
❑ 171 Alan Branch RC	.50	1.25
❑ 172 Amobi Okoye RC	.60	1.50
❑ 173 DeMarcus Tank Tyler RC	.50	1.25
❑ 174 Justin Harrell RC	.60	1.50
❑ 175 Brandon Mebane RC	.50	1.25
❑ 176 Gaines Adams RC	.60	1.50
❑ 177 Jamaal Anderson RC	.50	1.25
❑ 178 Adam Carriker RC	.50	1.25
❑ 179 Jarvis Moss RC	.60	1.50
❑ 180 Charles Johnson RC	.40	1.00
❑ 181 Anthony Spencer RC	.60	1.50
❑ 182 Quentin Moses RC	.50	1.25
❑ 183 LaMarr Woodley RC	.60	1.50
❑ 184 Victor Abiamiri RC	.60	1.50
❑ 185 Ray McDonald RC	.50	1.25
❑ 186 Tim Crowder RC	.60	1.50
❑ 187 Patrick Willis RC	1.00	2.50
❑ 188 Brandon Siler RC	.50	1.25
❑ 189 David Harris RC	.50	1.25
❑ 190 Buster Davis RC	.50	1.25
❑ 191 Lawrence Timmons RC	.60	1.50
❑ 192 Paul Posluszny RC	.75	2.00
❑ 193 Jon Beason RC	.60	1.50
❑ 194 Rufus Alexander RC	.60	1.50
❑ 195 Earl Everett RC	.50	1.25
❑ 196 Stewart Bradley RC	.60	1.50
❑ 197 Prescott Burgess RC	.50	1.25
❑ 198 Leon Hall RC	.60	1.50
❑ 199 Darrelle Revis RC	.75	2.00
❑ 200 Aaron Ross RC	.60	1.50
❑ 201 Daymeion Hughes RC	.50	1.25
❑ 202 Marcus McCauley RC	.50	1.25
❑ 203 Chris Houston RC	.50	1.25
❑ 204 Tanard Jackson RC	.40	1.00
❑ 205 Jonathan Wade RC	.50	1.25
❑ 206 Josh Wilson RC	.50	1.25
❑ 207 Eric Wright RC	.60	1.50
❑ 208 A.J. Davis RC	.40	1.00
❑ 209 David Irons RC	.40	1.00
❑ 210 LaRon Landry RC	.75	2.00
❑ 211 Reggie Nelson RC	.50	1.25
❑ 212 Michael Griffin RC	.60	1.50
❑ 213 Brandon Meriweather RC	.60	1.50
❑ 214 Eric Weddle RC	.50	1.25
❑ 215 Aaron Rouse RC	.60	1.50
❑ 216 Josh Gattis RC	.40	1.00
❑ 217 Joe Thomas RC	.60	1.50
❑ 218 Levi Brown RC	.60	1.50
❑ 219 Tony Ugoh RC	.50	1.25
❑ 220 Ryan Kalil RC	.50	1.25
❑ 221 Joe Staley RC	.50	1.25
❑ 222 Steve Breaston RC	.60	1.50
❑ 223 Jacoby Jones RC	.60	1.50
❑ 224 Ryne Robinson RC	.50	1.25
❑ 225 Chris Davis RC	.50	1.25
❑ 226 Le'Ron McClain RC	.60	1.50
❑ 227 Joel Filani RC	.50	1.25
❑ 228 Gerald Alexander RC	.40	1.00
❑ 229 Justise Hairston RC	.50	1.25
❑ 230 Nate Ilaoa RC	.60	1.50
❑ 231 Brett Ratliff RC	.60	1.50
❑ 232 Kyle Steffes RC	.40	1.00
❑ 233 Jesse Pellot-Rosa RC	.40	1.00
❑ 234 Roy Hall RC	.60	1.50
❑ 235 Brannon Condren RC	.40	1.00
❑ 236 Clint Session RC	.50	1.25
❑ 237 Dan Bazuin RC	.50	1.25
❑ 238 Michael Okwo RC	.50	1.25
❑ 239 Kevin Payne RC	.40	1.00
❑ 240 Legedu Naanee RC	.60	1.50
❑ 241 Jarrett Hicks RC	.50	1.25
❑ 242 Sonny Shackelford RC	.50	1.25
❑ 243 Arron Sears RC	.50	1.25
❑ 244 Justin Durant RC	.50	1.25
❑ 245 Ikaika Alma-Francis RC	.60	1.50
❑ 246 Sabby Piscitelli RC	.60	1.50
❑ 247 Quincy Black RC	.60	1.50
❑ 248 Jay Alford RC	1.00	2.50
❑ 249 Anthony Waters RC	.50	1.25
❑ 250 Laurent Robinson RC	.60	1.50
❑ 251 Brian Robison RC	.60	1.50
❑ 252 Jay Moore RC	.50	1.25
❑ 253 Stephen Nicholas RC	.50	1.25
❑ 254 John Bowie RC	.40	1.00
❑ 255 Brian Smith RC	.40	1.00
❑ 256 Marvin White RC	.40	1.00
❑ 257 Fred Bennett RC	.40	1.00
❑ 258 Kevin Boss RC	1.00	2.50
❑ 259 Dante Rosario RC	.60	1.50
❑ 260 Brent Celek RC	.60	1.50
❑ 261 Orenthal O'Neal RC	.40	1.00
❑ 262 Reagan Mauia RC	.40	1.00
❑ 263 Deon Anderson RC	.50	1.25
❑ 264 Tyler Ecker RC	.50	1.25
❑ 265 Michael Allan RC	.40	1.00
❑ 266 Jordan Kent RC	.50	1.25
❑ 267 John Broussard RC	.50	1.25
❑ 268 Chandler Williams RC	.50	1.25
❑ 269 Jason Snelling RC	.50	1.25
❑ 270 Derek Stanley RC	.50	1.25
❑ 271 Zach Miller RC	.60	1.50
❑ 272 Ramzee Robinson RC	.40	1.00
❑ 273 Michael Johnson RC	.50	1.25
❑ 274 Syndric Steptoe RC	.50	1.25
❑ 275 Tarell Brown RC	.40	1.00

2008 Bowman

❑ COMPLETE SET (275)	30.00	60.00
❑ 1 Drew Brees	.25	.60
❑ 2 Tom Brady	.40	1.00
❑ 3 Peyton Manning	.40	1.00
❑ 4 Carson Palmer	.25	.60
❑ 5 Ben Roethlisberger	.30	.75
❑ 6 Eli Manning	.25	.60
❑ 7 Tony Romo	.40	1.00
❑ 8 Vince Young	.20	.50
❑ 9 Matt Hasselbeck	.20	.50
❑ 10 David Garrard	.20	.50
❑ 11 Jay Cutler	.25	.60
❑ 12 Derek Anderson	.20	.50
❑ 13 Philip Rivers	.25	.60
❑ 14 Donovan McNabb	.25	.60
❑ 15 Matt Leinart	.25	.60
❑ 16 Jason Campbell	.20	.50
❑ 17 JaMarcus Russell	.25	.60
❑ 18 Jeff Garcia	.20	.50
❑ 19 Brodie Croyle	.20	.50
❑ 20 Marc Bulger	.20	.50
❑ 21 Trent Edwards	.25	.60
❑ 22 Kyle Boller	.15	.40
❑ 23 Tarvaris Jackson	.20	.50
❑ 24 Matt Schaub	.20	.50
❑ 25 Aaron Rodgers	.25	.60
❑ 26 Steven Jackson	.25	.60
❑ 27 Willie Parker	.20	.50
❑ 28 Clinton Portis	.20	.50
❑ 29 Adrian Peterson	.50	1.25
❑ 30 LaDainian Tomlinson	.30	.75
❑ 31 Marion Barber	.25	.60
❑ 32 Brian Westbrook	.20	.50
❑ 33 Fred Taylor	.20	.50
❑ 34 Marshawn Lynch	.25	.60
❑ 35 Joseph Addai	.25	.60
❑ 36 Willis McGahee	.20	.50
❑ 37 Frank Gore	.20	.50
❑ 38 Julius Jones	.20	.50
❑ 39 Thomas Jones	.20	.50
❑ 40 Cedric Benson	.20	.50
❑ 41 LenDale White	.20	.50
❑ 42 Ryan Grant	.25	.60
❑ 43 Laurence Maroney	.20	.50
❑ 44 Brandon Jacobs	.20	.50
❑ 45 Jamal Lewis	.20	.50
❑ 46 Larry Johnson	.20	.50
❑ 47 Rudi Johnson	.20	.50
❑ 48 Ahmad Bradshaw	.20	.50
❑ 49 Justin Fargas	.15	.40
❑ 50 Reggie Bush	.25	.60
❑ 51 Maurice Jones-Drew	.20	.50
❑ 52 Michael Turner	.25	.60
❑ 53 Ronnie Brown	.20	.50
❑ 54 DeAngelo Williams	.20	.50
❑ 55 Edgerrin James	.20	.50
❑ 56 Chad Johnson	.20	.50
❑ 57 Reggie Wayne	.20	.50
❑ 58 Anquan Boldin	.20	.50
❑ 59 Randy Moss	.25	.60
❑ 60 Plaxico Burress	.20	.50
❑ 61 Terrell Owens	.25	.60
❑ 62 Andre Johnson	.20	.50
❑ 63 Larry Fitzgerald	.25	.60
❑ 64 Braylon Edwards	.20	.50
❑ 65 Steve Smith	.20	.50
❑ 66 Greg Jennings	.20	.50
❑ 67 Torry Holt	.20	.50
❑ 68 T.J. Houshmandzadeh	.20	.50
❑ 69 Jerricho Cotchery	.15	.40
❑ 70 Joey Galloway	.20	.50
❑ 71 Santonio Holmes	.20	.50
❑ 72 Lee Evans	.20	.50
❑ 73 Dwayne Bowe	.20	.50
❑ 74 Laurent Robinson	.15	.40
❑ 75 Wes Welker	.25	.60
❑ 76 Roy Williams WR	.20	.50
❑ 77 Brandon Marshall	.20	.50
❑ 78 Hines Ward	.20	.50
❑ 79 Donald Driver	.20	.50
❑ 80 Calvin Johnson	.25	.60
❑ 81 Marques Colston	.20	.50
❑ 82 Chris Chambers	.20	.50
❑ 83 Amani Toomer	.20	.50
❑ 84 Bernard Berrian	.20	.50
❑ 85 Sidney Rice	.25	.60
❑ 86 Anthony Gonzalez	.20	.50
❑ 87 Steve Smith USC	.20	.50
❑ 88 Ted Ginn Jr.	.20	.50
❑ 89 Isaac Bruce	.20	.50
❑ 90 Derrick Mason	.15	.40
❑ 91 Roddy White	.20	.50
❑ 92 Bobby Engram	.15	.40
❑ 93 Reggie Williams	.20	.50
❑ 94 Donte Stallworth	.20	.50
❑ 95 Santana Moss	.15	.40
❑ 96 Laveranues Coles	.20	.50
❑ 97 Jerry Porter	.20	.50
❑ 98 Shaun McDonald	.15	.40
❑ 99 Dallas Clark	.20	.50
❑ 100 Tony Gonzalez	.20	.50
❑ 101 Kellen Winslow	.20	.50
❑ 102 Antonio Gates	.20	.50
❑ 103 Jason Witten	.25	.60
❑ 104 Chris Cooley	.20	.50
❑ 105 Brett Favre	1.25	3.00

❑ 106 Bob Sanders	.20	.50
❑ 107 John Harbaugh CO	.15	.40
❑ 108 Jon Kitna	.20	.50
❑ 109 Tony Sparano CO	.15	.40
❑ 110 Mike Smith CO	.15	.40
❑ 111 Ryan Clady RC	.60	1.50
❑ 112 Branden Albert RC	.60	1.50
❑ 113 Gosder Cherilus RC	.50	1.25
❑ 114 Duane Brown RC	.50	1.25
❑ 115 Brandon Flowers RC	.60	1.50
❑ 116 Quentin Groves RC	.50	1.25
❑ 117 Jason Jones RC	.60	1.50
❑ 118 Kendall Langford RC	.60	1.50
❑ 119 Brad Cottam RC	.60	1.50
❑ 120 Antwaun Molden RC	.50	1.25
❑ 121 Bryan Smith RC	.50	1.25
❑ 122 DaJuan Morgan RC	.50	1.25
❑ 123 Craig Stevens RC	.50	1.25
❑ 125 Andre Fluellen RC	.50	1.25
❑ 126 Cliff Avril RC	.50	1.25
❑ 127 Tyvon Branch RC	.50	1.25
❑ 128 Justin King RC	.50	1.25
❑ 129 Jeremy Thompson RC	.40	1.00
❑ 130 William Hayes RC	.40	1.00
❑ 131 Will Franklin RC	.50	1.25
❑ 132 Marcus Smith RC	.50	1.25
❑ 133 Dwight Lowery RC	.50	1.25
❑ 134 Reggie Corner RC	.40	1.00
❑ 135 Kenny Iwebema RC	.40	1.00
❑ 136 Quintin Demps RC	.60	1.50
❑ 137 Jack Williams RC	.40	1.00
❑ 138 Craig Steltz RC	.50	1.25
❑ 139 Bryan Kehl RC	.50	1.25
❑ 140 Justin Tryon RC	.40	1.00
❑ 141 Arman Shields RC	.50	1.25
❑ 142 Paul Hubbard RC	.50	1.25
❑ 143 Jonathan Wilhite RC	.50	1.25
❑ 144 Thomas DeCoud RC	.40	1.00
❑ 145 Derek Fine RC	.50	1.25
❑ 146 Stanford Keglar RC	.40	1.00
❑ 147 Kenneth Moore RC	.50	1.25
❑ 148 Robert James RC	.40	1.00
❑ 149 Jalen Parmele RC	.50	1.25
❑ 150 Brandon Carr RC	.50	1.25
❑ 151 Gary Barnidge RC	.50	1.25
❑ 152 Zack Bowman RC	.50	1.25
❑ 153 Lex Hilliard RC	.60	1.50
❑ 154 Mario Urrutia RC	.50	1.25
❑ 155 Adrian Arrington RC	.50	1.25
❑ 156 Jerome Felton RC	.40	1.00
❑ 157 Chaz Schilens RC	.60	1.50
❑ 158 Steve Johnson RC	.60	1.50
❑ 159 Tim Hightower RC	.75	2.00
❑ 160 Alex Brink RC	.60	1.50
❑ 161 Brett Swain RC	.50	1.25
❑ 162 Matt Slater RC	.60	1.50
❑ 163 Justin Harper RC	.50	1.25
❑ 164 Kevin Robinson RC	.50	1.25
❑ 165 Pierre Garcon RC	1.00	2.50
❑ 166 Matt Ryan RC	2.50	6.00
❑ 167 Brian Brohm RC	.60	1.50
❑ 168 Andre Woodson RC	.60	1.50
❑ 169 Chad Henne RC	1.00	2.50
❑ 170 Joe Flacco RC	2.00	5.00
❑ 171 John David Booty RC	.60	1.50
❑ 172 Colt Brennan RC	1.00	2.50
❑ 173 Dennis Dixon RC	.60	1.50
❑ 174 Erik Ainge RC	.60	1.50
❑ 175 Josh Johnson RC	.60	1.50
❑ 176 Kevin O'Connell RC	.60	1.50
❑ 178 Jaymar Johnson RC	.50	1.25
❑ 179 Marcus Thomas RC	.50	1.25
❑ 180 Darren McFadden RC	1.25	3.00
❑ 181 Rashard Mendenhall RC	1.25	3.00
❑ 182 Jonathan Stewart RC	1.25	3.00
❑ 183 Felix Jones RC	1.25	3.00
❑ 184 Jamaal Charles RC	1.00	2.50
❑ 185 Chris Johnson RC	2.00	5.00
❑ 186 Ray Rice RC	1.25	3.00
❑ 187 Mike Hart RC	.60	1.50
❑ 188 Kevin Smith RC	1.00	2.50
❑ 189 Steve Slaton RC	.75	2.00
❑ 190 Matt Forte RC	1.25	3.00
❑ 191 Tashard Choice RC	.60	1.50
❑ 192 Cory Boyd RC	.50	1.25
❑ 193 Allen Patrick RC	.50	1.25
❑ 194 Thomas Brown RC	.60	1.50
❑ 195 Justin Forsett RC	.60	1.50
❑ 196 Harry Douglas RC	.50	1.25

❑ 197 DeSean Jackson RC	1.25	3.00
❑ 198 Malcolm Kelly RC	.60	1.50
❑ 200 Mario Manningham RC	.60	1.50
❑ 201 James Hardy RC	.50	1.25
❑ 202 Early Doucet RC	.60	1.50
❑ 203 Donnie Avery RC	.75	2.00
❑ 204 Dexter Jackson RC	.60	1.50
❑ 205 Devin Thomas RC	.60	1.50
❑ 206 Jordy Nelson RC	.75	2.00
❑ 207 Keenan Burton RC	.50	1.25
❑ 208 Earl Bennett RC	.60	1.50
❑ 209 Jerome Simpson RC	.50	1.25
❑ 210 Andre Caldwell RC	.60	1.50
❑ 211 Josh Morgan RC	.60	1.50
❑ 212 Eddie Royal RC	1.00	2.50
❑ 213 Fred Davis RC	.60	1.50
❑ 214 John Carlson RC	.60	1.50
❑ 215 Martellus Bennett RC	.60	1.50
❑ 216 Martin Rucker RC	.50	1.25
❑ 217 Jermichael Finley RC	.60	1.50
❑ 218 Dustin Keller RC	.60	1.50
❑ 219 Jacob Tamme RC	.60	1.50
❑ 220 Kellen Davis RC	.40	1.00
❑ 221 Owen Schmitt RC	.60	1.50
❑ 222 Jacob Hester RC	.60	1.50
❑ 223 Chris Williams RC	.50	1.25
❑ 225 Sam Baker RC	.40	1.00
❑ 226 Jeff Otah RC	.50	1.25
❑ 227 Glenn Dorsey RC	.60	1.50
❑ 228 Sedrick Ellis RC	.60	1.50
❑ 229 Kentwan Balmer RC	.50	1.25
❑ 230 Pat Sims RC	.50	1.25
❑ 231 Marcus Harrison RC	.60	1.50
❑ 232 Dre Moore RC	.50	1.25
❑ 233 Paul Smith RC	.60	1.50
❑ 234 Trevor Laws RC	.60	1.50
❑ 236 Vernon Gholston RC	.60	1.50
❑ 237 Derrick Harvey RC	.50	1.25
❑ 238 Calais Campbell RC	.50	1.25
❑ 239 Phillip Merling RC	.50	1.25
❑ 240 Chris Ellis RC	.50	1.25
❑ 241 Lawrence Jackson RC	.50	1.25
❑ 242 Dan Connor RC	.60	1.50
❑ 243 Curtis Lofton RC	.60	1.50
❑ 244 Jerod Mayo RC	.75	2.00
❑ 245 Tavares Gooden RC	.50	1.25
❑ 246 Kyle Wright RC	.50	1.25
❑ 247 Philip Wheeler RC	.60	1.50
❑ 248 Marcus Monk RC	.60	1.50
❑ 249 Jonathan Goff RC	.50	1.25
❑ 250 Keith Rivers RC	.60	1.50
❑ 251 Lavelle Hawkins RC	.50	1.25
❑ 252 Xavier Adibi RC	.50	1.25
❑ 253 Chauncey Washington RC	.50	1.25
❑ 254 Bruce Davis RC	.60	1.50
❑ 255 Jordon Dizon RC	.60	1.50
❑ 256 Shawn Crable RC	.60	1.50
❑ 257 Geno Hayes RC	.40	1.00
❑ 258 D.Rodgers-Cromartie RC	.60	1.50
❑ 259 Chevis Jackson RC	.50	1.25
❑ 260 Terrence Wheatley RC	.50	1.25
❑ 261 Mike Jenkins RC	.60	1.50
❑ 262 Aqib Talib RC	.60	1.50
❑ 263 Leodis McKelvin RC	.60	1.50
❑ 264 Terrell Thomas RC	.50	1.25
❑ 265 Reggie Smith RC	.50	1.25
❑ 266 Antoine Cason RC	.60	1.50
❑ 267 Patrick Lee RC	.60	1.50
❑ 268 Tracy Porter RC	.75	2.00
❑ 269 Charles Godfrey RC	.50	1.25
❑ 270 Kenny Phillips RC	.60	1.50
❑ 271 Marcus Henry RC	.50	1.25
❑ 272 DJ Hall RC	.50	1.25
❑ 273 Xavier Omon RC	.60	1.50
❑ 274 Tyrell Johnson RC	.60	1.50
❑ 275 Ryan Torain RC	.60	1.50

1998 Bowman Chrome

❑ COMPLETE SET (220)	50.00	100.00
❑ 1 Peyton Manning RC	20.00	40.00
❑ 2 Keith Brooking RC	1.50	4.00
❑ 3 Duane Starks RC	.75	2.00
❑ 4 Takeo Spikes RC	1.50	4.00
❑ 5 Andre Wadsworth RC	1.25	3.00
❑ 6 Greg Ellis RC	.75	2.00
❑ 7 Brian Griese RC	3.00	8.00
❑ 8 Germane Crowell RC	1.25	3.00
❑ 9 Jerome Pathon RC	1.50	4.00
❑ 10 Ryan Leaf RC	1.50	4.00
❑ 11 Fred Taylor RC	2.50	6.00
❑ 12 Robert Edwards RC	1.25	3.00
❑ 13 Grant Wistrom RC	1.25	3.00
❑ 14 Robert Holcombe RC	1.25	3.00
❑ 15 Tim Dwight RC	1.50	4.00
❑ 16 Jacquez Green RC	1.25	3.00
❑ 17 Marcus Nash RC	.75	2.00
❑ 18 Jason Peter RC	.75	2.00
❑ 19 Anthony Simmons RC	1.25	3.00
❑ 20 Curtis Enis RC	.75	2.00
❑ 21 John Avery RC	1.25	3.00
❑ 22 Pat Johnson RC	1.25	3.00
❑ 23 Joe Jurevicius RC	1.50	4.00
❑ 24 Brian Simmons RC	1.25	3.00
❑ 25 Kevin Dyson RC	1.50	4.00
❑ 26 Skip Hicks RC	1.25	3.00
❑ 27 Hines Ward RC	7.50	15.00
❑ 28 Tavian Banks RC	1.25	3.00
❑ 29 Ahman Green RC	4.00	10.00
❑ 30 Tony Simmons RC	1.25	3.00
❑ 31 Charles Johnson	.20	.50
❑ 32 Freddie Jones	.20	.50
❑ 33 Joey Galloway	.30	.75
❑ 34 Tony Banks	.30	.75
❑ 35 Jake Plummer	.50	1.25
❑ 36 Reidel Anthony	.30	.75
❑ 37 Steve McNair	.50	1.25
❑ 38 Michael Westbrook	.30	.75
❑ 39 Chris Sanders	.20	.50
❑ 40 Isaac Bruce	.20	.50
❑ 41 Charlie Garner	.30	.75
❑ 42 Wayne Chrebet	.50	1.25
❑ 43 Michael Strahan	.30	.75
❑ 44 Brad Johnson	.50	1.25
❑ 45 Mike Alstott	.20	.50
❑ 46 Tony Gonzalez	.50	1.25
❑ 47 Johnnie Morton	.30	.75
❑ 48 Darnay Scott	.30	.75
❑ 49 Rae Carruth	.20	.50
❑ 50 Terrell Davis	.50	1.25
❑ 51 Jermaine Lewis	.30	.75
❑ 52 Frank Sanders	.30	.75
❑ 53 Byron Hanspard	.20	.50
❑ 54 Gus Frerotte	.20	.50
❑ 55 Terry Glenn	.50	1.25
❑ 56 J.J. Stokes	.30	.75
❑ 57 Will Blackwell	.20	.50
❑ 58 Keyshawn Johnson	.50	1.25
❑ 59 Tiki Barber	.50	1.25
❑ 60 Dorsey Levens	.50	1.25
❑ 61 Zach Thomas	.50	1.25
❑ 62 Corey Dillon	.50	1.25
❑ 63 Antowain Smith	.50	1.25
❑ 64 Michael Sinclair	.20	.50
❑ 65 Rod Smith	.30	.75
❑ 66 Trent Dilfer	.50	1.25
❑ 67 Warren Sapp	.30	.75
❑ 68 Charles Way	.20	.50
❑ 69 Tamarick Vanover	.20	.50
❑ 70 Drew Bledsoe	.75	2.00
❑ 71 John Mobley	.20	.50
❑ 72 Kerry Collins	.30	.75
❑ 73 Peter Boulware	.20	.50

	Card	Low	High
❑	74 Simeon Rice	.30	.75
❑	75 Eddie George	.50	1.25
❑	76 Fred Lane	.20	.50
❑	77 Jamal Anderson	.50	1.25
❑	78 Antonio Freeman	.50	1.25
❑	79 Jason Sehorn	.30	.75
❑	80 Curtis Martin	.50	1.25
❑	81 Bobby Hoying	.30	.75
❑	82 Garrison Hearst	.50	1.25
❑	83 Glenn Foley	.30	.75
❑	84 Danny Kanell	.30	.75
❑	85 Kordell Stewart	.50	1.25
❑	86 O.J. McDuffie	.30	.75
❑	87 Marvin Harrison	.50	1.25
❑	88 Bobby Engram	.30	.75
❑	89 Chris Slade	.20	.50
❑	90 Warrick Dunn	.50	1.25
❑	91 Ricky Watters	.30	.75
❑	92 Rickey Dudley	.20	.50
❑	93 Terrell Owens	.50	1.25
❑	94 Karim Abdul-Jabbar	.50	1.25
❑	95 Napoleon Kaufman	.50	1.25
❑	96 Darrell Green	.30	.75
❑	97 Levon Kirkland	.20	.50
❑	98 Jeff George	.30	.75
❑	99 Andre Hastings	.20	.50
❑	100 John Elway	2.00	5.00
❑	101 John Randle	.30	.75
❑	102 Andre Rison	.30	.75
❑	103 Keenan McCardell	.30	.75
❑	104 Marshall Faulk	.60	1.50
❑	105 Emmitt Smith	1.50	4.00
❑	106 Robert Brooks	.30	.75
❑	107 Scott Mitchell	.30	.75
❑	108 Shannon Sharpe	.30	.75
❑	109 Deion Sanders	.50	1.25
❑	110 Jerry Rice	1.00	2.50
❑	111 Erik Kramer	.20	.50
❑	112 Michael Jackson	.20	.50
❑	113 Aeneas Williams	.20	.50
❑	114 Terry Allen	.50	1.25
❑	115 Steve Young	.60	1.50
❑	116 Warren Moon	.50	1.25
❑	117 Junior Seau	.50	1.25
❑	118 Jerome Bettis	.50	1.25
❑	119 Irving Fryar	.30	.75
❑	120 Barry Sanders	1.50	4.00
❑	121 Tim Brown	.20	.50
❑	122 Chad Brown	.20	.50
❑	123 Ben Coates	.30	.75
❑	124 Robert Smith	.50	1.25
❑	125 Brett Favre	2.00	5.00
❑	126 Derrick Thomas	.50	1.25
❑	127 Reggie White	.50	1.25
❑	128 Troy Aikman	1.00	2.50
❑	129 Jeff Blake	.30	.75
❑	130 Mark Brunell	.50	1.25
❑	131 Curtis Conway	.30	.75
❑	132 Wesley Walls	.30	.75
❑	133 Thurman Thomas	.50	1.25
❑	134 Chris Chandler	.30	.75
❑	135 Dan Marino	2.00	5.00
❑	136 Larry Centers	.20	.50
❑	137 Shawn Jefferson	.20	.50
❑	138 Andre Reed	.30	.75
❑	139 Jake Reed	.30	.75
❑	140 Cris Carter	.50	1.25
❑	141 Elvis Grbac	.30	.75
❑	142 Mark Chmura	.30	.75
❑	143 Michael Irvin	.50	1.25
❑	144 Carl Pickens	.30	.75
❑	145 Herman Moore	.30	.75
❑	146 Marvin Jones	.20	.50
❑	147 Terance Mathis	.30	.75
❑	148 Rob Moore	.30	.75
❑	149 Bruce Smith	.30	.75
❑	150 Rob Johnson CL	.20	.50
❑	151 Leslie Shepherd	.20	.50
❑	152 Chris Spielman	.20	.50
❑	153 Tony McGee	.20	.50
❑	154 Kevin Smith	.20	.50
❑	155 Bill Romanowski	.20	.50
❑	156 Stephen Boyd	.20	.50
❑	157 James Stewart	.30	.75
❑	158 Jason Taylor	.30	.75
❑	159 Troy Drayton	.20	.50
❑	160 Mark Fields	.20	.50
❑	161 Jessie Armstead	.20	.50
❑	162 James Jett	.30	.75
❑	163 Bobby Taylor	.20	.50
❑	164 Kimble Anders	.30	.75
❑	165 Jimmy Smith	.30	.75
❑	166 Quentin Coryatt	.20	.50
❑	167 Bryant Westbrook	.20	.50
❑	168 Neil Smith	.30	.75
❑	169 Darren Woodson	.20	.50
❑	170 Ray Buchanan	.20	.50
❑	171 Earl Holmes	.20	.50
❑	172 Ray Lewis	.50	1.25
❑	173 Steve Broussard	.20	.50
❑	174 Derrick Brooks	.50	1.25
❑	175 Ken Harvey	.20	.50
❑	176 Darryll Lewis	.20	.50
❑	177 Derrick Rodgers	.20	.50
❑	178 James McKnight	.50	1.25
❑	179 Cris Dishman	.20	.50
❑	180 Hardy Nickerson	.20	.50
❑	181 Charles Woodson RC	2.00	5.00
❑	182 Randy Moss RC	10.00	25.00
❑	183 Stephen Alexander RC	1.25	3.00
❑	184 Samari Rolle RC	.75	2.00
❑	185 Jamie Duncan RC	.75	2.00
❑	186 Lance Schulters RC	.75	2.00
❑	187 Tony Parrish RC	1.50	4.00
❑	188 Corey Chavous RC	1.50	4.00
❑	189 Jammi German RC	.75	2.00
❑	190 Sam Cowart RC	1.25	3.00
❑	191 Donald Hayes RC	1.25	3.00
❑	192 R.W. McQuarters RC	1.25	3.00
❑	193 Az-Zahir Hakim RC	1.50	4.00
❑	194 Chris Fuamatu-Ma'afala RC	1.25	3.00
❑	195 Allen Rossum RC	.75	2.00
❑	196 Jon Ritchie RC	1.25	3.00
❑	197 Blake Spence RC	.75	2.00
❑	198 Brian Alford RC	.75	2.00
❑	199 Fred Weary RC	.75	2.00
❑	200 Rod Rutledge RC	.75	2.00
❑	201 Michael Myers RC	.75	2.00
❑	202 Rashaan Shehee RC	1.25	3.00
❑	203 Donovin Darius RC	1.25	3.00
❑	204 E.G. Green RC	1.25	3.00
❑	205 Vonnie Holliday RC	1.25	3.00
❑	206 Charlie Batch RC	1.50	4.00
❑	207 Michael Pittman RC	1.50	4.00
❑	208 Artrell Hawkins RC	.75	2.00
❑	209 Jonathan Quinn RC	1.50	4.00
❑	210 Kailee Wong RC	.75	2.00
❑	211 Deshea Townsend RC	.75	2.00
❑	212 Patrick Surtain RC	1.50	4.00
❑	213 Brian Kelly RC	1.25	3.00
❑	214 Tebucky Jones RC	.75	2.00
❑	215 Pete Gonzalez RC	.75	2.00
❑	216 Shaun Williams RC	1.25	3.00
❑	217 Scott Frost RC	.75	2.00
❑	218 Leonard Little RC	1.50	4.00
❑	219 Alonzo Mayes RC	.75	2.00
❑	220 Cordell Taylor RC	.75	2.00

1999 Bowman Chrome

	Card	Low	High
❑	COMPLETE SET (220)	40.00	80.00
❑	1 Dan Marino	1.50	4.00
❑	2 Michael Westbrook	.30	.75
❑	3 Yancey Thigpen	.20	.50
❑	4 Tony Martin	.30	.75
❑	5 Michael Strahan	.30	.75
❑	6 Dedric Ward	.20	.50
❑	7 Joey Galloway	.30	.75
❑	8 Bobby Engram	.30	.75
❑	9 Frank Sanders	.30	.75
❑	10 Jake Plummer	.30	.75
❑	11 Eddie Kennison	.30	.75
❑	12 Curtis Martin	.50	1.25
❑	13 Chris Spielman	.20	.50
❑	14 Trent Dilfer	.30	.75
❑	15 Tim Biakabutuka	.30	.75
❑	16 Elvis Grbac	.30	.75
❑	17 Charlie Batch	.50	1.25
❑	18 Takeo Spikes	.20	.50
❑	19 Tony Banks	.30	.75
❑	20 Doug Flutie	.50	1.25
❑	21 Ty Law	.30	.75
❑	22 Isaac Bruce	.50	1.25
❑	23 James Jett	.30	.75
❑	24 Kent Graham	.20	.50
❑	25 Derrick Mayes	.20	.50
❑	26 Amani Toomer	.20	.50
❑	27 Ray Lewis	.50	1.25
❑	28 Shawn Springs	.20	.50
❑	29 Warren Sapp	.20	.50
❑	30 Jamal Anderson	.50	1.25
❑	31 Byron Bam Morris	.20	.50
❑	32 Johnnie Morton	.20	.50
❑	33 Terance Mathis	.20	.50
❑	34 Terrell Davis	.50	1.25
❑	35 John Randle	.30	.75
❑	36 Vinny Testaverde	.20	.50
❑	37 Junior Seau	.50	1.25
❑	38 Reidel Anthony	.30	.75
❑	39 Brad Johnson	.20	.50
❑	40 Emmitt Smith	1.00	2.50
❑	41 Mo Lewis	.20	.50
❑	42 Terry Glenn	.50	1.25
❑	43 Dorsey Levens	.50	1.25
❑	44 Thurman Thomas	.30	.75
❑	45 Rob Moore	.30	.75
❑	46 Corey Dillon	.50	1.25
❑	47 Jessie Armstead	.20	.50
❑	48 Marshall Faulk	.60	1.50
❑	49 Charles Woodson	.20	.50
❑	50 John Elway	1.50	4.00
❑	51 Kevin Dyson	.30	.75
❑	52 Tony Simmons	.20	.50
❑	53 Keenan McCardell	.30	.75
❑	54 O.J. Santiago	.20	.50
❑	55 Jermaine Lewis	.30	.75
❑	56 Herman Moore	.30	.75
❑	57 Gary Brown	.20	.50
❑	58 Jim Harbaugh	.30	.75
❑	59 Mike Alstott	.50	1.25
❑	60 Brett Favre	1.50	4.00
❑	61 Tim Brown	.50	1.25
❑	62 Steve McNair	.20	.50
❑	63 Ben Coates	.30	.75
❑	64 Jerome Pathon	.20	.50
❑	65 Ray Buchanan	.20	.50
❑	66 Troy Aikman	1.00	2.50
❑	67 Andre Reed	.30	.75
❑	68 Bubby Brister	.20	.50
❑	69 Karim Abdul-Jabbar	.30	.75
❑	70 Peyton Manning	1.50	4.00
❑	71 Charles Johnson	.20	.50
❑	72 Natrone Means	.30	.75
❑	73 Michael Sinclair	.20	.50
❑	74 Skip Hicks	.20	.50
❑	75 Derrick Alexander	.20	.50
❑	76 Wayne Chrebet	.30	.75
❑	77 Rod Smith	.30	.75
❑	78 Carl Pickens	.30	.75
❑	79 Adrian Murrell	.30	.75
❑	80 Fred Taylor	.50	1.25
❑	81 Eric Moulds	.50	1.25
❑	82 Lawrence Phillips	.30	.75
❑	83 Marvin Harrison	.50	1.25
❑	84 Cris Carter	.50	1.25
❑	85 Ike Hilliard	.20	.50
❑	86 Hines Ward	.50	1.25
❑	87 Terrell Owens	.50	1.25
❑	88 Ricky Proehl	.20	.50
❑	89 Bert Emanuel	.30	.75
❑	90 Randy Moss	1.25	3.00
❑	91 Aaron Glenn	.20	.50
❑	92 Robert Smith	.50	1.25
❑	93 Andre Hastings	.20	.50
❑	94 Jake Reed	.30	.75
❑	95 Curtis Enis	.20	.50
❑	96 Andre Wadsworth	.20	.50
❑	97 Ed McCaffrey	.30	.75
❑	98 Zach Thomas	.50	1.25
❑	99 Kerry Collins	.30	.75
❑	100 Drew Bledsoe	.60	1.50
❑	101 Germane Crowell	.20	.50
❑	102 Bryan Still	.20	.50
❑	103 Chad Brown	.20	.50
❑	104 Jacquez Green	.20	.50

Card	Low	High
❑ 105 Garrison Hearst	.30	.75
❑ 106 Napoleon Kaufman	.50	1.25
❑ 107 Ricky Watters	.30	.75
❑ 108 O.J. McDuffie	.30	.75
❑ 109 Keyshawn Johnson	.50	1.25
❑ 110 Jerome Bettis	.50	1.25
❑ 111 Duce Staley	.50	1.25
❑ 112 Curtis Conway	.30	.75
❑ 113 Chris Chandler	.30	.75
❑ 114 Marcus Nash	.20	.50
❑ 115 Stephen Alexander	.20	.50
❑ 116 Darnay Scott	.30	.75
❑ 117 Bruce Smith	.30	.75
❑ 118 Priest Holmes	.75	2.00
❑ 119 Mark Brunell	.50	1.25
❑ 120 Jerry Rice	1.00	2.50
❑ 121 Randall Cunningham	.50	1.25
❑ 122 Scott Mitchell	.20	.50
❑ 123 Antonio Freeman	.50	1.25
❑ 124 Kordell Stewart	.30	.75
❑ 125 Jon Kitna	.50	1.25
❑ 126 Ahman Green	.50	1.25
❑ 127 Warrick Dunn	.50	1.25
❑ 128 Robert Brooks	.30	.75
❑ 129 Derrick Thomas	.50	1.25
❑ 130 Steve Young	.60	1.50
❑ 131 Peter Boulware	.20	.50
❑ 132 Michael Irvin	.30	.75
❑ 133 Shannon Sharpe	.30	.75
❑ 134 Jimmy Smith	.30	.75
❑ 135 John Avery	.20	.50
❑ 136 Fred Lane	.20	.50
❑ 137 Trent Green	.50	1.25
❑ 138 Andre Rison	.30	.75
❑ 139 Antowain Smith	.50	1.25
❑ 140 Eddie George	.50	1.25
❑ 141 Jeff Blake	.30	.75
❑ 142 Rocket Ismail	.30	.75
❑ 143 Rickey Dudley	.20	.50
❑ 144 Courtney Hawkins	.20	.50
❑ 145 Mikhael Ricks	.20	.50
❑ 146 J.J. Stokes	.30	.75
❑ 147 Levon Kirkland	.20	.50
❑ 148 Deion Sanders	.50	1.25
❑ 149 Barry Sanders	1.50	4.00
❑ 150 Tiki Barber	.50	1.25
❑ 151 David Boston RC	.75	2.00
❑ 152 Chris McAlister RC	.50	1.25
❑ 153 Peerless Price RC	.75	2.00
❑ 154 D'Wayne Bates RC	.50	1.25
❑ 155 Cade McNown RC	.50	1.25
❑ 156 Akili Smith RC	.50	1.25
❑ 157 Kevin Johnson RC	.75	2.00
❑ 158 Tim Couch RC	.75	2.00
❑ 159 Sedrick Irvin RC	.40	1.00
❑ 160 Chris Claiborne RC	.40	1.00
❑ 161 Edgerrin James RC	4.00	10.00
❑ 162 Mike Cloud RC	.50	1.25
❑ 163 Cecil Collins RC	.40	1.00
❑ 164 James Johnson RC	.50	1.25
❑ 165 Rob Konrad RC	.75	2.00
❑ 166 Daunte Culpepper RC	4.00	10.00
❑ 167 Kevin Faulk RC	.75	2.00
❑ 168 Donovan McNabb RC	5.00	12.00
❑ 169 Troy Edwards RC	.50	1.25
❑ 170 Amos Zereoue RC	.75	2.00
❑ 171 Karsten Bailey RC	.50	1.25
❑ 172 Brock Huard RC	.75	2.00
❑ 173 Joe Germaine RC	.50	1.25
❑ 174 Torry Holt RC	2.50	6.00
❑ 175 Shaun King RC	.50	1.25
❑ 176 Jevon Kearse RC	1.50	4.00
❑ 177 Champ Bailey RC	1.25	3.00
❑ 178 Ebenezer Ekuban RC	.50	1.25
❑ 179 Andy Katzenmoyer RC	.50	1.25
❑ 180 Antoine Winfield RC	.50	1.25
❑ 181 Jermaine Fazande RC	.50	1.25
❑ 182 Ricky Williams RC	2.00	5.00
❑ 183 Joel Makovicka RC	.75	2.00
❑ 184 Reginald Kelly RC	.50	1.25
❑ 185 Brandon Stokley RC	1.00	2.50
❑ 186 L.C. Stevens RC	.40	1.00
❑ 187 Marty Booker RC	.75	2.00
❑ 188 Jerry Azumah RC	.50	1.25
❑ 189 Ted White RC	.40	1.00
❑ 190 Scott Covington RC	.75	2.00
❑ 191 Tim Alexander RC	.40	1.00
❑ 192 Darrin Chiaverini RC	.50	1.25
❑ 193 Dat Nguyen RC	.75	2.00
❑ 194 Wane McGarity RC	.40	1.00
❑ 195 Al Wilson RC	.75	2.00
❑ 196 Travis McGriff RC	.40	1.00
❑ 197 Stacey Mack RC	.75	2.00
❑ 198 Antuan Edwards RC	.40	1.00
❑ 199 Aaron Brooks RC	2.00	5.00
❑ 200 De'Mond Parker RC	.40	1.00
❑ 201 Jed Weaver RC	.40	1.00
❑ 202 Madre Hill RC	.40	1.00
❑ 203 Jim Kleinsasser RC	.75	2.00
❑ 204 Michael Bishop RC	.75	2.00
❑ 205 Michael Basnight RC	.40	1.00
❑ 206 Sean Bennett RC	.40	1.00
❑ 207 Dameane Douglas RC	.50	1.25
❑ 208 Na Brown RC	.50	1.25
❑ 209 Patrick Kerney RC	.75	2.00
❑ 210 Malcolm Johnson RC	.40	1.00
❑ 211 Dre Bly RC	.75	2.00
❑ 212 Terry Jackson RC	.50	1.25
❑ 213 Eugene Baker RC	.40	1.00
❑ 214 Autry Denson RC	.50	1.25
❑ 215 Darnell McDonald RC	.50	1.25
❑ 216 Charlie Rogers RC	.50	1.25
❑ 217 Joe Montgomery RC	.50	1.25
❑ 218 Cecil Martin RC	.50	1.25
❑ 219 Larry Parker RC	.75	2.00
❑ 220 Mike Peterson RC	.50	1.25

2000 Bowman Chrome

Card	Low	High
❑ 1 Eddie George	.40	1.00
❑ 2 Ike Hilliard	.25	.60
❑ 3 Terrell Owens	.40	1.00
❑ 4 James Stewart	.25	.60
❑ 5 Joey Galloway	.25	.60
❑ 6 Jake Reed	.15	.40
❑ 7 Derrick Alexander	.25	.60
❑ 8 Jeff George	.25	.60
❑ 9 Kerry Collins	.25	.60
❑ 10 Tony Gonzalez	.25	.60
❑ 11 Marcus Robinson	.40	1.00
❑ 12 Charles Woodson	.25	.60
❑ 13 Germane Crowell	.15	.40
❑ 14 Yancey Thigpen	.15	.40
❑ 15 Tony Martin	.15	.40
❑ 16 Frank Sanders	.25	.60
❑ 17 Napoleon Kaufman	.25	.60
❑ 18 Jay Fiedler	.40	1.00
❑ 19 Patrick Jeffers	.40	1.00
❑ 20 Steve McNair	.40	1.00
❑ 21 Herman Moore	.25	.60
❑ 22 Tim Brown	.40	1.00
❑ 23 Olandis Gary	.40	1.00
❑ 24 Corey Dillon	.40	1.00
❑ 25 Warren Sapp	.25	.60
❑ 26 Curtis Enis	.15	.40
❑ 27 Vinny Testaverde	.25	.60
❑ 28 Tim Biakabutuka	.25	.60
❑ 29 Kevin Johnson	.40	1.00
❑ 30 Charlie Batch	.40	1.00
❑ 31 Jermaine Fazande	.25	.60
❑ 32 Shaun King	.15	.40
❑ 33 Errict Rhett	.25	.60
❑ 34 O.J. McDuffie	.25	.60
❑ 35 Bruce Smith	.25	.60
❑ 36 Antonio Freeman	.40	1.00
❑ 37 Tim Couch	.25	.60
❑ 38 Duce Staley	.40	1.00
❑ 39 Jeff Blake	.25	.60
❑ 40 Jim Harbaugh	.25	.60
❑ 41 Jeff Graham	.15	.40
❑ 42 Drew Bledsoe	.50	1.25
❑ 43 Mike Alstott	.40	1.00
❑ 44 Terance Mathis	.25	.60
❑ 45 Antowain Smith	.25	.60
❑ 46 Johnnie Morton	.25	.60
❑ 47 Chris Chandler	.25	.60
❑ 48 Keith Poole	.15	.40
❑ 49 Ricky Watters	.25	.60
❑ 50 Darnay Scott	.15	.40
❑ 51 Damon Huard	.25	.60
❑ 52 Peerless Price	.25	.60
❑ 53 Brian Griese	.40	1.00
❑ 54 Frank Wycheck	.25	.60
❑ 55 Kevin Dyson	.25	.60
❑ 56 Junior Seau	.40	1.00
❑ 57 Curtis Conway	.25	.60
❑ 58 Jamal Anderson	.40	1.00
❑ 59 Jim Miller	.15	.40
❑ 60 Rob Johnson	.25	.60
❑ 61 Mark Brunell	.40	1.00
❑ 62 Wayne Chrebet	.25	.60
❑ 63 James Johnson	.15	.40
❑ 64 Sean Dawkins	.15	.40
❑ 65 Stephen Davis	.40	1.00
❑ 66 Daunte Culpepper	.50	1.25
❑ 67 Doug Flutie	.40	1.00
❑ 68 Pete Mitchell	.15	.40
❑ 69 Bill Schroeder	.15	.40
❑ 70 Terrence Wilkins	.15	.40
❑ 71 Cade McNown	.15	.40
❑ 72 Muhsin Muhammad	.25	.60
❑ 73 E.G. Green	.15	.40
❑ 74 Edgerrin James	.60	1.50
❑ 75 Troy Edwards	.15	.40
❑ 76 Terry Glenn	.25	.60
❑ 77 Tony Banks	.25	.60
❑ 78 Derrick Mayes	.25	.60
❑ 79 Curtis Martin	.40	1.00
❑ 80 Kordell Stewart	.25	.60
❑ 81 Amani Toomer	.25	.60
❑ 82 Dorsey Levens	.25	.60
❑ 83 Brad Johnson	.40	1.00
❑ 84 Ed McCaffrey	.40	1.00
❑ 85 Charlie Garner	.25	.60
❑ 86 Brett Favre	1.25	3.00
❑ 87 J.J. Stokes	.25	.60
❑ 88 Steve Young	.50	1.25
❑ 89 Jonathan Linton	.15	.40
❑ 90 Isaac Bruce	.40	1.00
❑ 91 Shawn Jefferson	.15	.40
❑ 92 Rod Smith	.25	.60
❑ 93 Champ Bailey	.25	.60
❑ 94 Ricky Williams	.40	1.00
❑ 95 Priest Holmes	.50	1.25
❑ 96 Corey Bradford	.25	.60
❑ 97 Eric Moulds	.40	1.00
❑ 98 Warrick Dunn	.40	1.00
❑ 99 Jevon Kearse	.40	1.00
❑ 100 Albert Connell	.15	.40
❑ 101 Az-Zahir Hakim	.15	.40
❑ 102 Marvin Harrison	.40	1.00
❑ 103 Qadry Ismail	.25	.60
❑ 104 Oronde Gadsden	.25	.60
❑ 105 Rob Moore	.25	.60
❑ 106 Marshall Faulk	.60	1.50
❑ 107 Steve Beuerlein	.25	.60
❑ 108 Torry Holt	.40	1.00
❑ 109 Donovan McNabb	.60	1.50
❑ 110 Rich Gannon	.40	1.00
❑ 111 Jerome Bettis	.40	1.00
❑ 112 Peyton Manning	1.00	2.50
❑ 113 Cris Carter	.40	1.00
❑ 114 Jake Plummer	.25	.60
❑ 115 Kent Graham	.15	.40
❑ 116 Keenan McCardell	.25	.60
❑ 117 Tim Dwight	.40	1.00
❑ 118 Fred Taylor	.40	1.00
❑ 119 Jerry Rice	.75	2.00
❑ 120 Michael Westbrook	.25	.60
❑ 121 Kurt Warner	.75	2.00
❑ 122 Jimmy Smith	.25	.60
❑ 123 Emmitt Smith	.75	2.00
❑ 124 Terrell Davis	.40	1.00
❑ 125 Randy Moss	.75	2.00
❑ 126 Akili Smith	.15	.40
❑ 127 Rocket Ismail	.25	.60
❑ 128 Jon Kitna	.40	1.00
❑ 129 Elvis Grbac	.25	.60
❑ 130 Wesley Walls	.15	.40
❑ 131 Torrance Small	.15	.40
❑ 132 Tyrone Wheatley	.25	.60
❑ 133 Carl Pickens	.15	.40
❑ 134 Zach Thomas	.40	1.00
❑ 135 Jacquez Green	.15	.40
❑ 136 Robert Smith	.40	1.00

☐ 137 Keyshawn Johnson .40 1.00
☐ 138 Matthew Hatchette .15 .40
☐ 139 Troy Aikman .75 2.00
☐ 140 Charles Johnson .25 .60
☐ 141 Terry Battle EP .40 1.00
☐ 142 Pepe Pearson EP RC .75 2.00
☐ 143 Cory Sauter EP .40 1.00
☐ 144 Brian Shay EP .40 1.00
☐ 145 Marcus Crandell EP RC .60 1.50
☐ 146 Danny Wuerffel EP .60 1.50
☐ 147 L.C. Stevens EP .40 1.00
☐ 148 Ted White EP .40 1.00
☐ 149 Matt Lytle EP RC .60 1.50
☐ 150 Vershan Jackson EP RC .40 1.00
☐ 151 Mario Bailey EP .40 1.00
☐ 152 Darryl Daniel EP RC .60 1.50
☐ 153 Sean Morey EP RC .60 1.50
☐ 154 Jim Kubiak EP RC .60 1.50
☐ 155 Aaron Stecker EP RC .75 2.00
☐ 156 Damon Dunn EP RC .60 1.50
☐ 157 Kevin Daft EP .40 1.00
☐ 158 Corey Thomas EP .40 1.00
☐ 159 Deon Mitchell EP RC .60 1.50
☐ 160 Todd Floyd EP RC .40 1.00
☐ 161 Norman Miller EP RC .40 1.00
☐ 162 Jeremaine Copeland EP .40 1.00
☐ 163 Michael Blair EP .40 1.00
☐ 164 Ron Powlus EP RC .75 2.00
☐ 165 Pat Barnes EP .60 1.50
☐ 166 Dez White RC 1.50 4.00
☐ 167 Trung Canidate SP RC 10.00 25.00
☐ 168 Thomas Jones SP RC 20.00 40.00
☐ 169 Courtney Brown SP RC 12.50 30.00
☐ 170 Jamal Lewis SP RC 20.00 50.00
☐ 171 Chris Redman SP RC 10.00 25.00
☐ 172 Ron Dayne SP RC 12.50 30.00
☐ 173 Chad Pennington SP RC 20.00 50.00
☐ 174 Plaxico Burress SP RC 20.00 50.00
☐ 175 R.Jay Soward SP RC 10.00 25.00
☐ 176 Travis Taylor SP RC 12.50 30.00
☐ 177 Shaun Alexander SP RC 15.00 40.00
☐ 178 Brian Urlacher RC 10.00 20.00
☐ 179 Danny Farmer RC 1.25 3.00
☐ 180 Tee Martin SP RC 12.50 30.00
☐ 181 Sylvester Morris SP RC 10.00 25.00
☐ 182 Curtis Keaton RC 1.25 3.00
☐ 183 Peter Warrick SP RC 12.50 30.00
☐ 184 Anthony Becht RC 1.50 4.00
☐ 185 Travis Prentice SP RC 12.50 30.00
☐ 186 J.R. Redmond SP RC 10.00 25.00
☐ 187 Bubba Franks SP RC 12.50 30.00
☐ 188 Ron Dugans SP RC 7.50 20.00
☐ 189 Reuben Droughns RC 2.00 5.00
☐ 190 Corey Simon RC .75 2.00
☐ 191 Joe Hamilton RC 1.25 3.00
☐ 192 Laveranues Coles RC 2.00 5.00
☐ 193 Todd Pinkston SP RC 12.50 30.00
☐ 194 Jerry Porter SP RC 20.00 50.00
☐ 195 Dennis Northcutt RC 1.50 4.00
☐ 196 Tim Rattay RC 1.50 4.00
☐ 197 Giovanni Carmazzi RC .75 2.00
☐ 198 Mareno Philyaw RC .75 2.00
☐ 199 Avion Black RC 1.25 3.00
☐ 200 Chafie Fields RC .75 2.00
☐ 201 Rondell Mealey RC .75 2.00
☐ 202 Troy Walters RC 1.50 4.00
☐ 203 Frank Moreau RC 1.25 3.00
☐ 204 Vaughn Sanders RC .75 2.00
☐ 205 Sherrod Gideon RC .75 2.00
☐ 206 Doug Chapman RC 1.25 3.00
☐ 207 Marcus Knight RC 1.25 3.00
☐ 208 Jamel White RC 1.25 3.00
☐ 209 Windrell Hayes RC 1.25 3.00
☐ 210 Reggie Jones RC .75 2.00
☐ 211 Jarious Jackson RC 1.25 3.00
☐ 212 Ronney Jenkins RC 1.25 3.00
☐ 213 Quinton Spotwood RC .75 2.00
☐ 214 Rob Morris RC 1.25 3.00
☐ 215 Gari Scott RC .75 2.00
☐ 216 Kevin Thompson RC .75 2.00
☐ 217 Trevor Insley RC .75 2.00
☐ 218 Frank Murphy RC .75 2.00
☐ 219 Patrick Pass RC 1.25 3.00
☐ 220 Mike Anderson RC 1.00 2.50
☐ 221 Derrius Thompson RC 1.50 4.00
☐ 222 John Abraham RC 2.50 6.00
☐ 223 Dante Hall RC 3.00 8.00
☐ 224 Chad Morton RC 1.50 4.00
☐ 225 Ahmed Plummer RC 1.50 4.00
☐ 226 Julian Peterson RC 1.50 4.00
☐ 227 Mike Green RC 1.25 3.00
☐ 228 Michael Wiley RC 1.25 3.00
☐ 229 Spergon Wynn RC 1.25 3.00
☐ 230 Trevor Gaylor RC 1.25 3.00
☐ 231 Doug Johnson RC 1.50 4.00
☐ 232 Marc Bulger RC 3.00 8.00
☐ 233 Ron Dixon RC 1.25 3.00
☐ 234 Aaron Shea RC .60 1.50
☐ 235 Thomas Hamner RC .75 2.00
☐ 236 Tom Brady RC 40.00 100.00
☐ 237 Deltha O'Neal RC 1.50 4.00
☐ 238 Todd Husak RC 1.50 4.00
☐ 239 Erron Kinney RC 1.50 4.00
☐ 240 JaJuan Dawson RC .75 2.00
☐ 241 Nick Williams .40 1.00
☐ 242 Deon Grant RC 1.25 3.00
☐ 243 Brad Hoover RC 1.25 3.00
☐ 244 Kamil Loud .15 .40
☐ 245 Rashard Anderson RC 1.25 3.00
☐ 246 Clint Stoerner RC .60 1.50
☐ 247 Antwan Harris RC .75 2.00
☐ 248 Jason Webster RC .75 2.00
☐ 249 Kevin McDougal RC 1.25 3.00
☐ 250 Tony Scott RC .75 2.00
☐ 251 Thabiti Davis RC .75 2.00
☐ 252 Ian Gold RC 1.25 3.00
☐ 253 Sammy Morris RC 1.50 4.00
☐ 254 Raynoch Thompson RC 1.25 3.00
☐ 255 Jeremy McDaniel .40 1.00
☐ 256 Terrelle Smith RC 1.25 3.00
☐ 257 Deon Dyer RC 1.25 3.00
☐ 258 Na'il Diggs RC 1.25 3.00
☐ 259 Brandon Short RC 1.25 3.00
☐ 260 Mike Brown RC 3.00 8.00
☐ 261 John Engelberger RC 1.25 3.00
☐ 262 Rogers Beckett RC 1.25 3.00
☐ 263 JaJuan Seider RC .75 2.00
☐ 264 Desmond Kitchings RC 1.25 3.00
☐ 265 Reggie Davis RC 1.25 3.00
☐ 266 Corey Moore RC .75 2.00
☐ 267 Cornelius Griffin RC 1.25 3.00
☐ 268 Stockar McDougle RC .75 2.00
☐ 269 James Williams RC 1.25 3.00
☐ 270 Darrell Jackson RC 2.50 6.00

2001 Bowman Chrome

☐ COMP.SET w/o SP's (110) 10.00 25.00
☐ 1 Emmitt Smith 1.00 2.50
☐ 2 James Stewart .25 .60
☐ 3 Jeff Graham .25 .60
☐ 4 Keyshawn Johnson .30 .75
☐ 5 Stephen Davis .30 .75
☐ 6 Chad Lewis .25 .60
☐ 7 Drew Bledsoe .40 1.00
☐ 8 Fred Taylor .40 1.00
☐ 9 Mike Anderson .30 .75
☐ 10 Tony Gonzalez .30 .75
☐ 11 Aaron Brooks .30 .75
☐ 12 Vinny Testaverde .30 .75
☐ 13 Jerome Bettis .40 1.00
☐ 14 Marshall Faulk .40 1.00
☐ 15 Jeff Garcia .30 .75
☐ 16 Terry Glenn .30 .75
☐ 17 Jay Fiedler .30 .75
☐ 18 Ahman Green .40 1.00
☐ 19 Cade McNown .30 .75
☐ 20 Rob Johnson .30 .75
☐ 21 Jamal Anderson .30 .75
☐ 22 Corey Dillon .30 .75
☐ 23 Jake Plummer .30 .75
☐ 24 Rod Smith .30 .75
☐ 25 Trent Green .40 1.00
☐ 26 Ricky Williams .40 1.00
☐ 27 Charlie Garner .30 .75
☐ 28 Shaun Alexander .40 1.00
☐ 29 Jeff George .30 .75
☐ 30 Torry Holt .30 .75
☐ 31 James Thrash .30 .75
☐ 32 Rich Gannon .30 .75
☐ 33 Ron Dayne .30 .75
☐ 34 Dedric Ward .25 .60
☐ 35 Edgerrin James .40 1.00
☐ 36 Cris Carter .40 1.00
☐ 37 Derrick Mason .30 .75
☐ 38 Brad Johnson .30 .75
☐ 39 Charlie Batch .30 .75
☐ 40 Joey Galloway .30 .75
☐ 41 James Allen .25 .60
☐ 42 Tim Biakabutuka .25 .60
☐ 43 Ray Lewis .40 1.00
☐ 44 David Boston .25 .60
☐ 45 Kevin Johnson .25 .60
☐ 46 Jimmy Smith .30 .75
☐ 47 Joe Horn .30 .75
☐ 48 Terrell Owens .40 1.00
☐ 49 Eddie George .40 1.00
☐ 50 Brett Favre 1.25 3.00
☐ 51 Wayne Chrebet .30 .75
☐ 52 Hines Ward .40 1.00
☐ 53 Warrick Dunn .40 1.00
☐ 54 Matt Hasselbeck .40 1.00
☐ 55 Tiki Barber .40 1.00
☐ 56 Lamar Smith .30 .75
☐ 57 Tim Couch .25 .60
☐ 58 Eric Moulds .30 .75
☐ 59 Shawn Jefferson .25 .60
☐ 60 Donald Hayes .25 .60
☐ 61 Brian Urlacher .50 1.25
☐ 62 Steve McNair .40 1.00
☐ 63 Kurt Warner .50 1.25
☐ 64 Tim Brown .40 1.00
☐ 65 Troy Brown .30 .75
☐ 66 Albert Connell .25 .60
☐ 67 Peyton Manning 1.00 2.50
☐ 68 Peter Warrick .30 .75
☐ 69 Elvis Grbac .30 .75
☐ 70 Chris Chandler .30 .75
☐ 71 Akili Smith .25 .60
☐ 72 Keenan McCardell .30 .75
☐ 73 Kerry Collins .30 .75
☐ 74 Junior Seau .40 1.00
☐ 75 Donovan McNabb .50 1.25
☐ 76 Tony Banks .25 .60
☐ 77 Steve Beuerlein .30 .75
☐ 78 Daunte Culpepper .40 1.00
☐ 79 Darrell Jackson .30 .75
☐ 80 Isaac Bruce .40 1.00
☐ 81 Tyrone Wheatley .30 .75
☐ 82 Derrick Alexander .25 .60
☐ 83 Germane Crowell .25 .60
☐ 84 Jon Kitna .30 .75
☐ 85 Jamal Lewis .40 1.00
☐ 86 Ed McCaffrey .30 .75
☐ 87 Mark Brunell .40 1.00
☐ 88 Jeff Blake .30 .75
☐ 89 Duce Staley .30 .75
☐ 90 Doug Flutie .40 1.00
☐ 91 Kordell Stewart .30 .75
☐ 92 Randy Moss .50 1.25
☐ 93 Marvin Harrison .40 1.00
☐ 94 Muhsin Muhammad .30 .75
☐ 95 Brian Griese .30 .75
☐ 96 Antonio Freeman .40 1.00
☐ 97 Amani Toomer .30 .75
☐ 98 Oronde Gadsden .25 .60
☐ 99 Curtis Martin .40 1.00
☐ 100 Jerry Rice .75 2.00
☐ 101 Michael Pittman .30 .75
☐ 102 Shannon Sharpe .40 1.00
☐ 103 Peerless Price .25 .60
☐ 104 Bill Schroeder .30 .75
☐ 105 Ike Hilliard .30 .75
☐ 106 Freddie Jones .25 .60
☐ 107 Tai Streets .25 .60
☐ 108 Ricky Watters .30 .75
☐ 109 Az-Zahir Hakim .25 .60
☐ 110 Jacquez Green .25 .60
☐ 111 George Layne RC 2.00 5.00
☐ 112 Correll Buckhalter RC 3.00 8.00
☐ 113 Tony Stewart RC 2.50 6.00
☐ 114 Chris Barnes RC 2.00 5.00
☐ 115 A.J. Feeley RC 2.50 6.00
☐ 116 Margin Hooks RC 2.00 5.00
☐ 117 Anthony Henry RC 3.00 8.00

Card		
❑ 118 Dwight Smith RC	2.00	5.00
❑ 119 Torrance Marshall RC	2.50	6.00
❑ 120 Gary Baxter RC	2.50	6.00
❑ 121 Derek Combs RC	2.00	5.00
❑ 122 Marcus Bell RC	2.00	5.00
❑ 123 DeLawrence Grant RC	2.00	5.00
❑ 124 Jameel Cook RC	2.50	6.00
❑ 125 Eric Downing RC	2.00	5.00
❑ 126 Marlon McCree RC	2.00	5.00
❑ 127 Tay Cody RC	2.00	5.00
❑ 128 Mario Monds RC	2.00	5.00
❑ 129 Kenny Smith RC	2.00	5.00
❑ 130 Sedrick Hodge RC	2.00	5.00
❑ 131 Marcus Stroud RC	2.50	6.00
❑ 132 Steve Smith RC	10.00	25.00
❑ 133 Tyrone Robertson RC	2.00	5.00
❑ 134 James Reed RC	2.00	5.00
❑ 135 Kris Kocurek RC	2.00	5.00
❑ 136 Dan O'Leary RC	2.00	5.00
❑ 137 Harold Blackmon RC	2.00	5.00
❑ 138 Fred Smoot RC	3.00	8.00
❑ 139 Billy Baber RC	2.00	5.00
❑ 140 Jarrod Cooper RC	2.50	6.00
❑ 141 Travis Henry RC	3.00	8.00
❑ 142 David Terrell RC	2.50	6.00
❑ 143 Josh Heupel RC	3.00	8.00
❑ 144 Drew Brees RC	30.00	60.00
❑ 145 T.J. Houshmandzadeh RC	5.00	12.00
❑ 146 Rod Gardner RC	2.50	6.00
❑ 147 Richard Seymour RC	3.00	8.00
❑ 148 Koren Robinson RC	3.00	8.00
❑ 149 Scotty Anderson RC	2.50	6.00
❑ 150 Marques Tuiasosopo RC	2.50	6.00
❑ 151 John Capel RC	2.00	5.00
❑ 152 LaMont Jordan RC	3.00	8.00
❑ 153 James Jackson RC	2.50	6.00
❑ 154 Bobby Newcombe RC	2.50	6.00
❑ 155 Anthony Thomas RC	3.00	8.00
❑ 156 Dan Alexander RC	2.50	6.00
❑ 157 Quincy Carter RC	2.50	6.00
❑ 158 Morlon Greenwood RC	2.00	5.00
❑ 159 Robert Ferguson RC	3.00	8.00
❑ 160 Sage Rosenfels RC	3.00	8.00
❑ 161 Michael Stone RC	2.00	5.00
❑ 162 Chris Weinke RC	2.50	6.00
❑ 163 Travis Minor RC	2.50	6.00
❑ 164 Gerard Warren RC	2.50	6.00
❑ 165 Jamar Fletcher RC	2.00	5.00
❑ 166 Andre Carter RC	3.00	8.00
❑ 167 Deuce McAllister RC	4.00	10.00
❑ 168 Dan Morgan RC	3.00	8.00
❑ 169 Todd Heap RC	3.00	8.00
❑ 170 Snoop Minnis RC	2.50	6.00
❑ 171 Will Allen RC	3.00	8.00
❑ 172 Freddie Mitchell RC	2.00	5.00
❑ 173 Rudi Johnson RC	3.00	8.00
❑ 174 Kevan Barlow RC	2.50	6.00
❑ 175 Jamie Winborn RC	2.50	6.00
❑ 176 Onome Ojo RC	2.00	5.00
❑ 177 Leonard Davis RC	2.50	6.00
❑ 178 Santana Moss RC	5.00	12.00
❑ 179 Chris Chambers RC	5.00	12.00
❑ 180 Michael Vick RC	8.00	20.00
❑ 181 Michael Bennett RC	3.00	8.00
❑ 182 Mike McMahon RC	2.50	6.00
❑ 183 Jonathan Carter RC	2.00	5.00
❑ 184 Jamal Reynolds RC	2.50	6.00
❑ 185 Justin Smith RC	3.00	8.00
❑ 186 Quincy Morgan RC	2.50	6.00
❑ 187 Chad Johnson RC	10.00	25.00
❑ 188 Jesse Palmer RC	3.00	8.00
❑ 189 Reggie Wayne RC	10.00	25.00
❑ 190 LaDainian Tomlinson RC	30.00	80.00
❑ 191 Andre King RC	2.00	5.00
❑ 192 Richmond Flowers RC	2.00	5.00
❑ 193 Derrick Blaylock RC	2.50	6.00
❑ 194 Cedrick Wilson RC	3.00	8.00
❑ 195 Zeke Moreno RC	2.50	6.00
❑ 196 Tommy Polley RC	2.50	6.00
❑ 197 Damione Lewis RC	2.50	6.00
❑ 198 Aaron Schobel RC	3.00	8.00
❑ 199 Alge Crumpler RC	3.00	8.00
❑ 200 Nate Clements RC	3.00	8.00
❑ 201 Quentin McCord RC	2.50	6.00
❑ 202 Ken-Yon Rambo RC	2.00	5.00
❑ 203 Milton Wynn RC	2.00	5.00
❑ 204 Derrick Gibson RC	2.00	5.00
❑ 205 Chris Taylor RC	2.00	5.00
❑ 206 Corey Hall RC	2.00	5.00
❑ 207 Vinny Sutherland RC	2.00	5.00
❑ 208 Kendrell Bell RC	3.00	8.00
❑ 209 Casey Hampton RC	2.50	6.00
❑ 210 Demetric Evans RC	2.00	5.00
❑ 211 Brian Allen RC	2.00	5.00
❑ 212 Rodney Bailey RC	2.00	5.00
❑ 213 Otis Leverette RC	2.00	5.00
❑ 214 Ron Edwards RC	2.00	5.00
❑ 215 Michael Jameson RC	2.00	5.00
❑ 216 Markus Steele RC	2.00	5.00
❑ 217 Jimmy Williams RC	2.00	5.00
❑ 218 Roger Knight RC	2.00	5.00
❑ 219 Randy Garner RC	2.00	5.00
❑ 220 Raymond Perryman RC	2.00	5.00
❑ 221 Karon Riley RC	2.00	5.00
❑ 222 Adam Archuleta RC	2.50	6.00
❑ 223 Arnold Jackson RC	2.00	5.00
❑ 224 Ryan Pickett RC	2.00	5.00
❑ 225 Shad Meier RC	2.00	5.00
❑ 226 Heggie Germany RC	2.00	5.00
❑ 227 Justin McCareins RC	2.50	6.00
❑ 228 Idrees Bashir RC	2.00	5.00
❑ 229 Josh Booty RC	2.50	6.00
❑ 230 Eddie Berlin RC	2.00	5.00
❑ 231 Heath Evans RC	2.50	6.00
❑ 232 Alex Bannister RC	2.00	5.00
❑ 233 Corey Alston RC	2.00	5.00
❑ 234 Reggie White RC	2.00	5.00
❑ 235 Orlando Huff RC	2.00	5.00
❑ 236 Ken Lucas RC	2.50	6.00
❑ 237 Matt Stewart RC	2.00	5.00
❑ 238 Cedric Scott RC	2.00	5.00
❑ 239 Ronney Daniels RC	2.00	5.00
❑ 240 Kevin Kasper RC	2.50	6.00
❑ 241 Tony Driver RC	2.50	6.00
❑ 242 Kyle Vanden Bosch RC	3.00	8.00
❑ 243 T.J. Turner RC	2.00	5.00
❑ 244 Eric Westmoreland RC	2.00	5.00
❑ 245 Ronald Flemons RC	2.00	5.00
❑ 246 Eric Kelly RC	2.00	5.00
❑ 247 Moran Norris RC	2.00	5.00
❑ 248 Damerien McCants RC	2.50	6.00
❑ 249 James Boyd RC	2.00	5.00
❑ 250 Keith Adams RC	2.00	5.00
❑ 251 Brandon Manumaleuna RC	2.50	6.00
❑ 252 Dee Brown RC	2.00	5.00
❑ 253 Ross Kolodziej RC	2.00	5.00
❑ 254 Boo Williams RC	2.50	6.00
❑ 255 Patrick Chukwurah RC	2.00	5.00

2002 Bowman Chrome

Card		
❑ COMP.SET w/o SP's (110)	10.00	25.00
❑ 1 Emmitt Smith	1.00	2.50
❑ 2 Drew Brees	.60	1.50
❑ 3 Duce Staley	.30	.75
❑ 4 Curtis Martin	.40	1.00
❑ 5 Isaac Bruce	.40	1.00
❑ 6 Stephen Davis	.30	.75
❑ 7 Darrell Jackson	.30	.75
❑ 8 James Stewart	.25	.60
❑ 9 Tim Couch	.25	.60
❑ 10 Travis Henry	.30	.75
❑ 11 Thomas Jones	.30	.75
❑ 12 Jamal Lewis	.30	.75
❑ 13 Chris Chambers	.40	1.00
❑ 14 Jeff Blake	.30	.75
❑ 15 Plaxico Burress	.30	.75
❑ 16 Michael Pittman	.30	.75
❑ 17 Jeff Garcia	.30	.75
❑ 18 Tim Brown	.40	1.00
❑ 19 Kent Graham	.25	.60
❑ 20 Shannon Sharpe	.40	1.00
❑ 21 Corey Dillon	.30	.75
❑ 22 Muhsin Muhammad	.30	.75
❑ 23 Tony Gonzalez	.30	.75
❑ 24 Qadry Ismail	.30	.75
❑ 25 Mike McMahon	.25	.60
❑ 26 Edgerrin James	.40	1.00
❑ 27 Daunte Culpepper	.30	.75
❑ 28 Deuce McAllister	.40	1.00
❑ 29 Kerry Collins	.30	.75
❑ 30 Eddie George	.30	.75
❑ 31 Torry Holt	.40	1.00
❑ 32 Todd Pinkston	.25	.60
❑ 33 Quincy Carter	.25	.60
❑ 34 Rod Smith	.30	.75
❑ 35 Michael Vick	.40	1.00
❑ 36 Jim Miller	.30	.75
❑ 37 Troy Brown	.30	.75
❑ 38 Wayne Chrebet	.30	.75
❑ 39 Curtis Conway	.30	.75
❑ 40 Reidel Anthony	.25	.60
❑ 41 Mark Brunell	.30	.75
❑ 42 Chris Weinke	.25	.60
❑ 43 Eric Moulds	.30	.75
❑ 44 Ike Hilliard	.30	.75
❑ 45 Jay Fiedler	.30	.75
❑ 46 Keyshawn Johnson	.30	.75
❑ 47 Rod Gardner	.25	.60
❑ 48 Chris Redman	.25	.60
❑ 49 James Allen	.25	.60
❑ 50 Kordell Stewart	.30	.75
❑ 51 Priest Holmes	.40	1.00
❑ 52 Anthony Thomas	.30	.75
❑ 53 Peter Warrick	.30	.75
❑ 54 Jake Plummer	.30	.75
❑ 55 Jerry Rice	.75	2.00
❑ 56 Joe Horn	.30	.75
❑ 57 Derrick Mason	.30	.75
❑ 58 Kurt Warner	.40	1.00
❑ 59 Antowain Smith	.30	.75
❑ 60 Randy Moss	.40	1.00
❑ 61 Warrick Dunn	.30	.75
❑ 62 Laveranues Coles	.40	1.00
❑ 63 LaDainian Tomlinson	.60	1.50
❑ 64 Michael Westbrook	.25	.60
❑ 65 Travis Taylor	.25	.60
❑ 66 Brian Griese	.30	.75
❑ 67 Bill Schroeder	.30	.75
❑ 68 Ahman Green	.30	.75
❑ 69 Jimmy Smith	.30	.75
❑ 70 Charlie Garner	.30	.75
❑ 71 Terrell Owens	.40	1.00
❑ 72 Brad Johnson	.30	.75
❑ 73 James Thrash	.30	.75
❑ 74 Marvin Harrison	.40	1.00
❑ 75 Brett Favre	1.00	2.50
❑ 76 Rocket Ismail	.30	.75
❑ 77 David Boston	.25	.60
❑ 78 Jermaine Lewis	.25	.60
❑ 79 Aaron Brooks	.30	.75
❑ 80 Shaun Alexander	.40	1.00
❑ 81 Steve McNair	.40	1.00
❑ 82 Marshall Faulk	.40	1.00
❑ 83 Terrell Davis	.40	1.00
❑ 84 Corey Bradford	.25	.60
❑ 85 David Terrell	.25	.60
❑ 86 Kevin Johnson	.25	.60
❑ 87 Jon Kitna	.30	.75
❑ 88 Az-Zahir Hakim	.25	.60
❑ 89 Drew Bledsoe	.40	1.00
❑ 90 Garrison Hearst	.30	.75
❑ 91 Doug Flutie	.40	1.00
❑ 92 Jerome Bettis	.40	1.00
❑ 93 Vinny Testaverde	.30	.75
❑ 94 Tiki Barber	.40	1.00
❑ 95 Johnnie Morton	.30	.75
❑ 96 Lamar Smith	.30	.75
❑ 97 Marcus Robinson	.30	.75
❑ 98 Fred Taylor	.40	1.00
❑ 99 Tom Brady	1.00	2.50
❑ 100 Peyton Manning	.75	2.00
❑ 101 Donovan McNabb	.50	1.25
❑ 102 Rich Gannon	.30	.75
❑ 103 Hines Ward	.40	1.00
❑ 104 Michael Bennett	.30	.75
❑ 105 Ricky Williams	.40	1.00
❑ 106 Germane Crowell	.25	.60
❑ 107 Joey Galloway	.30	.75
❑ 108 Amani Toomer	.30	.75
❑ 109 Trent Green	.30	.75
❑ 110 Terry Glenn	.30	.75
❑ 111 Donte Stallworth RC	1.50	4.00
❑ 112 Mike Williams RC	1.00	2.50
❑ 113 Kurt Kittner RC	1.00	2.50

Card		
❑ 114 Josh Reed RC	1.25	3.00
❑ 115 Raonall Smith RC	1.00	2.50
❑ 116 David Garrard RC	2.50	6.00
❑ 117 Eric Crouch RC	1.50	4.00
❑ 118 Levi Jones RC	1.00	2.50
❑ 119 Quentin Jammer RC	1.50	4.00
❑ 120 Cliff Russell RC	1.00	2.50
❑ 121 Jamin Elliott RC	1.00	2.50
❑ 122 Roy Williams RC	2.00	5.00
❑ 123 Marquise Walker RC	1.00	2.50
❑ 124 Kalimba Edwards RC	1.25	3.00
❑ 125 Daniel Graham RC	1.25	3.00
❑ 126 Anthony Weaver RC	1.00	2.50
❑ 127 Antonio Bryant RC	2.00	5.00
❑ 128 DeShaun Foster RC	1.50	4.00
❑ 129 Antwaan Randle El RC	1.50	4.00
❑ 130 William Green RC	1.25	3.00
❑ 131 Joey Harrington RC	1.50	4.00
❑ 132 T.J. Duckett RC	1.50	4.00
❑ 133 Javon Walker RC	1.50	4.00
❑ 134 Albert Haynesworth RC	1.50	4.00
❑ 135 Julius Peppers RC	2.50	6.00
❑ 136 Clinton Portis RC	4.00	10.00
❑ 137 Ashley Lelie RC	1.50	4.00
❑ 138 Reche Caldwell RC	1.50	4.00
❑ 139 Rohan Davey RC	1.50	4.00
❑ 140 Patrick Ramsey RC	1.50	4.00
❑ 141 Ron Johnson RC	1.25	3.00
❑ 142 Jamar Martin RC	1.25	3.00
❑ 143 Travis Stephens RC	1.00	2.50
❑ 143AU Travis Stephens AU	4.00	10.00
❑ 144 Darrell Hill RC	1.00	2.50
❑ 145 Jon McGraw RC	1.00	2.50
❑ 146 Javin Hunter RC	1.00	2.50
❑ 146AU Javin Hunter AU	4.00	10.00
❑ 147 Eddie Drummond RC	1.00	2.50
❑ 148 Andre Lott RC	1.00	2.50
❑ 149 Travis Fisher RC	1.25	3.00
❑ 150 Lamont Brightful RC	1.00	2.50
❑ 151 Rocky Calmus RC	1.25	3.00
❑ 152 Wes Pate RC	1.00	2.50
❑ 152AU Wes Pate AU	4.00	10.00
❑ 153 Lamar Gordon RC	1.50	4.00
❑ 154 Terry Jones RC	1.00	2.50
❑ 155 Kyle Johnson RC	1.00	2.50
❑ 155AU Kyle Johnson AU	4.00	10.00
❑ 156 Daryl Jones RC	1.00	2.50
❑ 157 Tellis Redmon RC	1.00	2.50
❑ 158 Jarrod Baxter RC	1.00	2.50
❑ 159 Delvon Flowers RC	1.00	2.50
❑ 160 Kelly Campbell RC	1.25	3.00
❑ 161 Eddie Freeman RC	1.00	2.50
❑ 162 Atrews Bell RC	1.00	2.50
❑ 163 Omar Easy RC	1.25	3.00
❑ 164 Jeremy Allen RC	1.00	2.50
❑ 165 Andra Davis RC	1.00	2.50
❑ 166 Mike Rumph RC	1.00	2.50
❑ 167 Seth Burford RC	1.00	2.50
❑ 168 Marquand Manuel RC	1.00	2.50
❑ 169 Marques Anderson RC	1.25	3.00
❑ 170 Ben Leber RC	1.00	2.50
❑ 171 Ryan Denney RC	1.00	2.50
❑ 172 Justin Peelle RC	1.00	2.50
❑ 173 Lito Sheppard RC	1.50	4.00
❑ 174 Damien Anderson RC	1.25	3.00
❑ 175 Lamont Thompson RC	1.25	3.00
❑ 176 David Priestley RC	1.00	2.50
❑ 177 Michael Lewis RC	1.50	4.00
❑ 178 Lee Mays RC	1.00	2.50
❑ 179 Alan Harper RC	1.00	2.50
❑ 180 Verron Haynes RC	1.25	3.00
❑ 181 Chris Hope RC	1.50	4.00
❑ 182 Derek Ross RC	1.25	3.00
❑ 183 Joseph Jefferson RC	1.00	2.50
❑ 184 Carlos Hall RC	1.00	2.50
❑ 185 Robert Royal RC	1.50	4.00
❑ 186 Sheldon Brown RC	1.50	4.00
❑ 187 DeVeren Johnson RC	1.00	2.50
❑ 188 Rock Cartwright RC	1.50	4.00
❑ 189 Kendall Simmons RC	1.00	2.50
❑ 190 Joe Burns RC	1.00	2.50
❑ 191 David Givens RC	1.50	4.00
❑ 192 John Owens RC	1.00	2.50
❑ 193 Jarrett Ferguson RC	1.00	2.50
❑ 194 Randy McMichael RC	1.50	4.00
❑ 195 Chris Baker RC	1.00	2.50
❑ 196 Rashad Bauman RC	1.00	2.50
❑ 197 Matt Murphy RC	1.00	2.50
❑ 198 Steve Bellisari RC	1.00	2.50
❑ 199 Jeff Kelly RC	1.00	2.50
❑ 200 Mark Anelli RC	1.00	2.50
❑ 201 Darnell Sanders RC	1.00	2.50
❑ 202 Coy Wire RC	1.25	3.00
❑ 203 Ricky Williams RC	1.25	3.00
❑ 204 Napoleon Harris RC	1.25	3.00
❑ 205 Ennis Haywood RC	1.00	2.50
❑ 206 Keyuo Craver RC	1.00	2.50
❑ 207 Kahlil Hill RC	1.00	2.50
❑ 208 J.T. O'Sullivan RC	1.50	4.00
❑ 209 Woody Dantzler RC	1.25	3.00
❑ 210 Phillip Buchanon RC	1.50	4.00
❑ 211 Charles Grant RC	1.50	4.00
❑ 212 Dusty Bonner RC	1.00	2.50
❑ 213 James Allen RC	1.00	2.50
❑ 214 Ronald Curry RC	1.50	4.00
❑ 215 Deion Branch RC	1.50	4.00
❑ 216 Larry Ned RC	1.00	2.50
❑ 217 Kendall Newson RC	1.00	2.50
❑ 218 Shaun Hill RC	2.00	5.00
❑ 219 Akin Ayodele RC	1.25	3.00
❑ 220 John Henderson RC	1.50	4.00
❑ 221 Andre Davis AU A RC	5.00	12.00
❑ 222 Bryan Thomas AU A RC	4.00	10.00
❑ 223 Brian Westbrook AU C RC	40.00	80.00
❑ 224 Chad Hutchinson AU C RC	4.00	10.00
❑ 225 Craig Nall AU D RC	5.00	12.00
❑ 226 David Carr AU A RC	10.00	25.00
❑ 227 Dwight Freeney AU D RC	25.00	40.00
❑ 228 Adrian Peterson AU A RC	8.00	20.00
❑ 229 Randy Fasani AU E RC	5.00	12.00
❑ 230 Ed Reed AU A RC	35.00	60.00
❑ 231 Freddie Milons AU B RC	4.00	10.00
❑ 232 Herb Haygood AU E RC	4.00	10.00
❑ 233 Jabar Gaffney AU A RC	6.00	15.00
❑ 234 Josh McCown AU A RC	12.00	30.00
❑ 235 Jeremy Shockey AU A RC	15.00	40.00
❑ 236 Jake Schifino AU F RC	4.00	10.00
❑ 237 Josh Scobey AU E RC	5.00	12.00
❑ 238 Jonathan Wells AU D RC	6.00	15.00
❑ 239 Ladell Betts AU A RC	8.00	20.00
❑ 240 Luke Staley AU E RC	4.00	10.00
❑ 241 Maurice Morris AU B RC	6.00	15.00
❑ 242 Matt Schobel AU D RC	6.00	15.00
❑ 243 Sam Simmons AU C RC	4.00	10.00
❑ 244 Tim Carter AU A RC	5.00	12.00
❑ 245 Tank Williams AU E RC	5.00	12.00
❑ 246 Jerramy Stevens AU A RC	6.00	15.00
❑ 247 Jason McAddley AU C RC	5.00	12.00
❑ 248 Ken Simonton AU D RC	4.00	10.00
❑ 249 Chester Taylor AU F RC	10.00	25.00
❑ 250 Brandon Doman AU C RC	4.00	10.00

2003 Bowman Chrome

Card		
❑ COMP.SET w/o SP's (110)	10.00	25.00
❑ COMP.SET w/o AU's (220)	50.00	100.00
❑ 1 Brett Favre	1.00	2.50
❑ 2 Jeremy Shockey	.40	1.00
❑ 3 Fred Taylor	.40	1.00
❑ 4 Rich Gannon	.30	.75
❑ 5 Joey Galloway	.30	.75
❑ 6 Ray Lewis	.40	1.00
❑ 7 Jeff Blake	.30	.75
❑ 8 Stacey Mack	.25	.60
❑ 9 Matt Hasselbeck	.30	.75
❑ 10 Laveranues Coles	.30	.75
❑ 11 Brad Johnson	.30	.75
❑ 12 Tommy Maddox	.30	.75
❑ 13 Curtis Martin	.40	1.00
❑ 14 Tom Brady	1.00	2.50
❑ 15 Ricky Williams	.30	.75
❑ 16 Stephen Davis	.30	.75
❑ 17 Chad Johnson	.40	1.00
❑ 18 Joey Harrington	.30	.75
❑ 19 Tony Gonzalez	.30	.75
❑ 20 Peerless Price	.25	.60
❑ 21 LaDainian Tomlinson	.50	1.25
❑ 22 James Thrash	.25	.60
❑ 23 Charlie Garner	.30	.75
❑ 24 Eddie George	.30	.75
❑ 25 Terrell Owens	.40	1.00
❑ 26 Brian Urlacher	.60	1.50
❑ 27 Eric Moulds	.30	.75
❑ 28 Emmitt Smith	1.00	2.50
❑ 29 Tim Couch	.25	.60
❑ 30 Jake Plummer	.30	.75
❑ 31 Marvin Harrison	.40	1.00
❑ 32 Chris Chambers	.30	.75
❑ 33 Tiki Barber	.40	1.00
❑ 34 Kurt Warner	.40	1.00
❑ 35 Michael Pittman	.25	.60
❑ 36 Kevin Dyson	.30	.75
❑ 37 Clinton Portis	.50	1.25
❑ 38 Peyton Manning	.75	2.00
❑ 39 Travis Taylor	.25	.60
❑ 40 Jeff Garcia	.40	1.00
❑ 41 Patrick Ramsey	.30	.75
❑ 42 Shaun Alexander	.40	1.00
❑ 43 Joe Horn	.30	.75
❑ 44 Daunte Culpepper	.40	1.00
❑ 45 Travis Henry	.30	.75
❑ 46 Brian Finneran	.25	.60
❑ 47 William Green	.25	.60
❑ 48 Kordell Stewart	.30	.75
❑ 49 Reggie Wayne	.30	.75
❑ 50 Priest Holmes	.40	1.00
❑ 51 Jay Fiedler	.30	.75
❑ 52 Corey Dillon	.30	.75
❑ 53 Jamal Lewis	.40	1.00
❑ 54 Mark Brunell	.30	.75
❑ 55 Santana Moss	.30	.75
❑ 56 Duce Staley	.30	.75
❑ 57 Torry Holt	.40	1.00
❑ 58 Rod Gardner	.25	.60
❑ 59 Kerry Collins	.30	.75
❑ 60 Randy Moss	.40	1.00
❑ 61 Jerry Porter	.30	.75
❑ 62 Plaxico Burress	.40	1.00
❑ 63 Steve McNair	.40	1.00
❑ 64 Muhsin Muhammad	.30	.75
❑ 65 Drew Bledsoe	.40	1.00
❑ 66 T.J. Duckett	.30	.75
❑ 67 Ahman Green	.40	1.00
❑ 68 Rod Smith	.30	.75
❑ 69 Jimmy Smith	.30	.75
❑ 70 Trent Green	.30	.75
❑ 71 Tim Brown	.40	1.00
❑ 72 Jerome Bettis	.40	1.00
❑ 73 Isaac Bruce	.40	1.00
❑ 74 Derrick Mason	.30	.75
❑ 75 Donovan McNabb	.40	1.00
❑ 76 Deuce McAllister	.40	1.00
❑ 77 Zach Thomas	.40	1.00
❑ 78 Garrison Hearst	.30	.75
❑ 79 Koren Robinson	.30	.75
❑ 80 Marshall Faulk	.40	1.00
❑ 81 Keyshawn Johnson	.40	1.00
❑ 82 Jake Delhomme	.40	1.00
❑ 83 Marty Booker	.30	.75
❑ 84 James Stewart	.30	.75
❑ 85 Corey Bradford	.25	.60
❑ 86 Derrius Thompson	.25	.60
❑ 87 Edgerrin James	.40	1.00
❑ 88 Darrell Jackson	.30	.75
❑ 89 Hines Ward	.40	1.00
❑ 90 David Boston	.25	.60
❑ 91 Curtis Conway	.25	.60
❑ 92 David Patten	.25	.60
❑ 93 Michael Bennett	.30	.75
❑ 94 Todd Pinkston	.25	.60
❑ 95 Jerry Rice	.75	2.00
❑ 96 Jon Kitna	.30	.75
❑ 97 Ed McCaffrey	.30	.75
❑ 98 Donald Driver	.40	1.00
❑ 99 Anthony Thomas	.30	.75
❑ 100 Michael Vick	.40	1.00
❑ 101 Terry Glenn	.30	.75
❑ 102 Quincy Morgan	.25	.60
❑ 103 David Carr	.40	1.00
❑ 104 Troy Brown	.30	.75
❑ 105 Aaron Brooks	.30	.75
❑ 106 Amani Toomer	.30	.75
❑ 107 Drew Brees	.40	1.00
❑ 108 Chad Hutchinson	.25	.60
❑ 109 Warrick Dunn	.30	.75

❑ 110 Chad Pennington	.40	1.00
❑ 111 Brian St.Pierre RC	2.00	5.00
❑ 112 Keenan Howry RC	1.25	3.00
❑ 113 Sultan McCullough RC	1.25	3.00
❑ 114 Terence Newman RC	2.00	5.00
❑ 115 Kelley Washington RC	1.50	4.00
❑ 116 Musa Smith RC	1.50	4.00
❑ 117 Victor Hobson RC	1.25	3.00
❑ 118 Travis Anglin RC	1.25	3.00
❑ 119 Artose Pinner RC	1.25	3.00
❑ 120 Rashean Mathis RC	1.50	4.00
❑ 121 DeWayne White RC	1.25	3.00
❑ 122 Kevin Curtis RC	2.00	5.00
❑ 123 Tyrone Calico RC	1.50	4.00
❑ 124 Ricky Manning RC	1.50	4.00
❑ 125 Cory Redding RC	1.50	4.00
❑ 126 Dallas Clark RC	4.00	10.00
❑ 127 Marcus Trufant RC	2.00	5.00
❑ 128 Terrell Suggs RC	2.50	6.00
❑ 129 Aaron Walker RC	1.50	4.00
❑ 130 Calvin Pace RC	1.50	4.00
❑ 131 Ken Dorsey RC	1.50	4.00
❑ 132 Earnest Graham RC	2.00	5.00
❑ 133 Cecil Sapp RC	1.25	3.00
❑ 134 William Joseph RC	1.25	3.00
❑ 135 Anquan Boldin RC	5.00	12.00
❑ 136 Justin Griffith RC	1.50	4.00
❑ 137 Teyo Johnson RC	1.50	4.00
❑ 138 Chris Crocker RC	1.50	4.00
❑ 139 Doug Gabriel RC	1.50	4.00
❑ 140 Terry Pierce RC	1.25	3.00
❑ 141 Bradie James RC	2.00	5.00
❑ 142 Terrence Edwards RC	1.25	3.00
❑ 143 E.J. Henderson RC	1.50	4.00
❑ 144 Tony Romo RC	20.00	40.00
❑ 145 DeWayne Robertson RC	1.50	4.00
❑ 146 Dwone Hicks RC	1.25	3.00
❑ 147 Carl Ford RC	1.25	3.00
❑ 148 Ken Hamlin RC	2.00	5.00
❑ 149 Adrian Madise RC	1.25	3.00
❑ 150 Siddeeq Shabazz RC	1.25	3.00
❑ 151 Dave Ragone RC	1.25	3.00
❑ 152 Mike Seidman RC	1.25	3.00
❑ 153 DeAndrew Rubin RC	1.25	3.00
❑ 154 Mike Pinkard RC	1.25	3.00
❑ 155 Nate Burleson RC	1.50	4.00
❑ 156 Angelo Crowell RC	1.50	4.00
❑ 157 J.R. Tolver RC	1.50	4.00
❑ 158 Osi Umenyiora RC	3.00	8.00
❑ 159 Nick Barnett RC	2.00	5.00
❑ 160 Brandon Drumm RC	1.25	3.00
❑ 161 Rien Long RC	1.25	3.00
❑ 162 Zuriel Smith RC	1.25	3.00
❑ 163 Onterrio Smith RC	1.50	4.00
❑ 164 Kenny Peterson RC	1.50	4.00
❑ 165 Chaun Thompson RC	1.25	3.00
❑ 166 Terrence Holt RC	1.50	4.00
❑ 167 Ovie Mughelli RC	1.25	3.00
❑ 168 Bethel Johnson RC	1.50	4.00
❑ 169 Avon Cobourne RC	1.25	3.00
❑ 170 Andre Woolfolk RC	1.50	4.00
❑ 171 George Wrighster RC	1.25	3.00
❑ 172 Justin Fargas RC	2.00	5.00
❑ 173 Marquel Blackwell RC	1.25	3.00
❑ 174 Walter Young RC	1.25	3.00
❑ 175 Kawika Mitchell RC	2.00	5.00
❑ 176 Drayton Florence RC	1.50	4.00
❑ 177 Jeremi Johnson RC	1.25	3.00
❑ 178 Lee Suggs RC	1.50	4.00
❑ 179 David Kircus RC	2.00	5.00
❑ 180 Rex Grossman RC	2.00	5.00
❑ 180AU Rex Grossman AU B	15.00	40.00
❑ 181 Jon Olinger RC	1.25	3.00
❑ 182 Dan Curley RC	1.25	3.00
❑ 183 Andrew Pinnock RC	1.50	4.00
❑ 184 Kirk Farmer RC	1.50	4.00
❑ 185 Charles Rogers RC	1.50	4.00
❑ 186 Alonzo Jackson RC	1.25	3.00
❑ 187 Trent Smith RC	1.50	4.00
❑ 188 Seneca Wallace RC	2.00	5.00
❑ 189 Shane Walton RC	1.25	3.00
❑ 190 Chris Brown RC	2.00	5.00
❑ 191 Dahrran Diedrick RC	1.25	3.00
❑ 192 Juston Wood RC	1.25	3.00
❑ 193 Mike Doss RC	2.00	5.00
❑ 194 Visanthe Shiancoe RC	2.00	5.00
❑ 195 Andre Johnson RC	4.00	10.00
❑ 196 Dennis Weathersby RC	1.25	3.00
❑ 197 Chris Davis RC	1.50	4.00
❑ 198 LaTarence Dunbar RC	1.25	3.00
❑ 199 Eugene Wilson RC	2.00	5.00
❑ 200 Ryan Hoag RC	1.25	3.00
❑ 201 Chris Simms RC	2.00	5.00
❑ 202 Curt Anes RC	1.25	3.00
❑ 203 Taco Wallace RC	1.25	3.00
❑ 204 David Tyree RC	2.00	5.00
❑ 205 Nate Hybl RC	1.50	4.00
❑ 206 Willis McGahee RC	4.00	10.00
❑ 207 Casey Moore RC	1.25	3.00
❑ 208 Pisa Tinoisamoa RC	2.00	5.00
❑ 209 Willie Ponder RC	1.25	3.00
❑ 210 Donald Lee RC	1.50	4.00
❑ 211 Nnamdi Asomugha RC	2.00	5.00
❑ 212 Sammy Davis RC	1.50	4.00
❑ 213 Joffrey Reynolds RC	1.25	3.00
❑ 214 Eddie Moore RC	1.25	3.00
❑ 215 Tony Hollings RC	1.50	4.00
❑ 216 Nick Maddox RC	1.25	3.00
❑ 217 Kevin Walter RC	2.00	5.00
❑ 218 Dan Klecko RC	1.50	4.00
❑ 219 Antwan Peek RC	1.25	3.00
❑ 220 Tyler Brayton RC	1.50	4.00
❑ 221 Byron Leftwich AU B RC	10.00	25.00
❑ 222 Bobby Wade AU D RC	5.00	12.00
❑ 223 Jerome McDougle AU C RC	5.00	12.00
❑ 224 Michael Haynes AU D RC	4.00	10.00
❑ 225 Taylor Jacobs AU C RC	6.00	15.00
❑ 226 Shaun McDonald AU D RC	6.00	15.00
❑ 228 Talman Gardner AU D RC	4.00	10.00
❑ 229 Domanick Davis AU D RC	6.00	15.00
❑ 230 Jason Witten AU D RC	30.00	50.00
❑ 231 Kyle Boller AU B RC	8.00	20.00
❑ 232 L.J. Smith AU C RC	8.00	20.00
❑ 233 Boss Bailey AU C RC	6.00	15.00
❑ 234 Billy McMullen AU D RC	4.00	10.00
❑ 235 Larry Johnson AU B RC	15.00	40.00
❑ 236 Kareem Kelly AU E RC	4.00	10.00
❑ 237 Carson Palmer AU A RC	150.00	300.00
❑ 238 Quentin Griffin AU D RC	5.00	12.00
❑ 239 Kevin Garrett AU E RC	4.00	10.00
❑ 240 Charles Tillman AU E RC	8.00	20.00
❑ 241 Arnaz Battle AU D RC	8.00	20.00
❑ 242 Brooks Bollinger AU E RC	6.00	15.00
❑ 243 LaBrandon Toefield AU D RC	5.00	12.00
❑ 244 Sam Aiken AU D RC	6.00	15.00
❑ 245 Justin Gage AU D RC	6.00	15.00
❑ 246 Gibran Hamdan AU D RC	4.00	10.00

2004 Bowman Chrome

❑ COMP.SET w/o SP's (220)	100.00	175.00
❑ COMP.SET w/o RC's (110)	12.50	30.00
❑ ROOKIE AU/199 GROUP A ODDS 1:603		
❑ ROOKIE AU GROUP B ODDS 1:1293		
❑ ROOKIE AU GROUP C ODDS 1:359		
❑ ROOKIE AU GROUP D ODDS 1:21		
❑ 1 Brett Favre	1.00	2.50
❑ 2 Jay Fiedler	.25	.60
❑ 3 Andre Davis	.25	.60
❑ 4 Travis Henry	.30	.75
❑ 5 Jimmy Smith	.30	.75
❑ 6 Santana Moss	.30	.75
❑ 7 Correll Buckhalter	.30	.75
❑ 8 Randy Moss	.40	1.00
❑ 9 Edgerrin James	.40	1.00
❑ 10 Marc Bulger	.30	.75
❑ 11 Derrick Mason	.30	.75
❑ 12 Mark Brunell	.30	.75
❑ 13 Donte Stallworth	.30	.75
❑ 14 Deion Branch	.30	.75
❑ 15 Jake Plummer	.30	.75
❑ 16 Steve Smith	.40	1.00
❑ 17 Jon Kitna	.30	.75
❑ 18 Andre Johnson	.40	1.00
❑ 19 A.J. Feeley	.30	.75
❑ 20 Drew Bledsoe	.40	1.00
❑ 21 Antonio Bryant	.40	1.00
❑ 22 Reggie Wayne	.30	.75
❑ 23 Thomas Jones	.30	.75
❑ 24 Alge Crumpler	.30	.75
❑ 25 Anquan Boldin	.40	1.00
❑ 26 Tim Rattay	.25	.60
❑ 27 Charlie Garner	.30	.75
❑ 28 James Thrash	.25	.60
❑ 29 Koren Robinson	.40	1.00
❑ 30 Terrell Owens	.40	1.00
❑ 31 Amani Toomer	.30	.75
❑ 32 Kelly Campbell	.25	.60
❑ 33 Patrick Ramsey	.30	.75
❑ 34 Plaxico Burress	.30	.75
❑ 35 Chad Pennington	.40	1.00
❑ 36 Fred Taylor	.30	.75
❑ 37 Domanick Davis	.30	.75
❑ 38 DeShaun Foster	.30	.75
❑ 39 T.J. Duckett	.30	.75
❑ 40 Ahman Green	.40	1.00
❑ 41 Lee Suggs	.40	1.00
❑ 42 Tony Gonzalez	.40	1.00
❑ 43 Rich Gannon	.30	.75
❑ 44 Kevan Barlow	.30	.75
❑ 45 Torry Holt	.40	1.00
❑ 46 Aaron Brooks	.30	.75
❑ 47 Tyrone Calico	.30	.75
❑ 48 Keenan McCardell	.25	.60
❑ 49 Hines Ward	.40	1.00
❑ 50 LaDainian Tomlinson	.50	1.25
❑ 51 Dante Hall	.30	.75
❑ 52 Marcus Pollard	.25	.60
❑ 53 Corey Dillon	.30	.75
❑ 54 Justin McCareins	.25	.60
❑ 55 Stephen Davis	.30	.75
❑ 56 Jeff Garcia	.40	1.00
❑ 57 Ashley Lelie	.30	.75
❑ 58 Javon Walker	.30	.75
❑ 59 Kyle Boller	.30	.75
❑ 60 Chad Johnson	.30	.75
❑ 61 Anthony Thomas	.30	.75
❑ 62 Byron Leftwich	.40	1.00
❑ 63 David Boston	.25	.60
❑ 64 Onterrio Smith	.25	.60
❑ 65 Deuce McAllister	.40	1.00
❑ 66 Antwaan Randle El	.30	.75
❑ 67 Justin Fargas	.30	.75
❑ 68 Laveranues Coles	.30	.75
❑ 69 Quincy Morgan	.25	.60
❑ 70 Priest Holmes	.40	1.00
❑ 71 Robert Ferguson	.25	.60
❑ 72 Charles Rogers	.30	.75
❑ 73 Drew Brees	.40	1.00
❑ 74 Matt Hasselbeck	.40	1.00
❑ 75 Peyton Manning	.75	2.00
❑ 76 Rudi Johnson	.30	.75
❑ 77 Jake Delhomme	.30	.75
❑ 78 Tiki Barber	.40	1.00
❑ 79 Brad Johnson	.30	.75
❑ 80 Steve McNair	.40	1.00
❑ 81 Willis McGahee	.40	1.00
❑ 82 Josh McCown	.30	.75
❑ 83 Garrison Hearst	.30	.75
❑ 84 Quincy Carter	.25	.60
❑ 85 Ricky Williams	.40	1.00
❑ 86 Trent Green	.30	.75
❑ 87 Curtis Martin	.40	1.00
❑ 88 Jerry Porter	.30	.75
❑ 89 Brian Westbrook	.40	1.00
❑ 90 Clinton Portis	.40	1.00
❑ 91 Eric Moulds	.30	.75
❑ 92 Marcel Shipp	.40	1.00
❑ 93 Joey Harrington	.30	.75
❑ 94 David Carr	.30	.75
❑ 95 Marvin Harrison	.40	1.00
❑ 96 Joe Horn	.30	.75
❑ 97 Chris Chambers	.30	.75
❑ 98 Darrell Jackson	.30	.75
❑ 99 Eddie George	.30	.75
❑ 100 Donovan McNabb	.40	1.00
❑ 101 Marshall Faulk	.40	1.00
❑ 102 Rex Grossman	.40	1.00
❑ 103 Tai Streets	.25	.60
❑ 104 Jeremy Shockey	.30	.75
❑ 105 Jamal Lewis	.30	.75
❑ 106 Tom Brady	1.00	2.50
❑ 107 Shaun Alexander	.40	1.00
❑ 108 Carson Palmer	.50	1.25
❑ 109 Daunte Culpepper	.40	1.00

Card	Low	High
❑ 110 Michael Vick	.40	1.00
❑ 111 Roethlis AU/199 RC	150.00	300.00
❑ 112 Tommie Harris RC	1.50	4.00
❑ 113 Thomas Tapeh RC	1.25	3.00
❑ 114 Matt Schaub RC	4.00	10.00
❑ 115 Jonathan Smith RC	1.00	2.50
❑ 116 Ricardo Colclough RC	1.50	4.00
❑ 117 Jeff Dugan RC	1.00	2.50
❑ 118 Larry Fitzgerald RC	5.00	12.00
❑ 119 Gibril Wilson RC	1.50	4.00
❑ 120 Sean Taylor RC	1.50	4.00
❑ 121 Marquise Hill RC	1.00	2.50
❑ 122 Cedric Cobbs RC	1.25	3.00
❑ 123 Rich Gardner RC	1.25	3.00
❑ 124 Chris Cooley RC	1.50	4.00
❑ 125 Ben Troupe RC	1.25	3.00
❑ 126 Antwan Odom RC	1.50	4.00
❑ 127 Stuart Schweigert RC	1.25	3.00
❑ 128 Derek Abney RC	1.00	2.50
❑ 129 Keary Colbert RC	1.25	3.00
❑ 130 Jeris McIntyre RC	1.00	2.50
❑ 131 Matt Kranchick RC	1.50	4.00
❑ 132 Rodney Leisle RC	1.00	2.50
❑ 133 Vince Wilfork RC	1.50	4.00
❑ 134 Darnell Dockett RC	1.00	2.50
❑ 135 Jeremy LeSueur RC	1.00	2.50
❑ 136 Gilbert Gardner RC	1.00	2.50
❑ 137 Amon Gordon RC	1.00	2.50
❑ 138 Darius Watts RC	1.25	3.00
❑ 139 Junior Siavii RC	1.00	2.50
❑ 140 Igor Olshansky RC	1.50	4.00
❑ 141 Mewelde Moore RC	1.50	4.00
❑ 142 Nathan Vasher RC	1.50	4.00
❑ 143 Randy Starks RC	1.00	2.50
❑ 144 Isaac Sopoaga RC	1.00	2.50
❑ 145 Drew Henson RC	1.00	2.50
❑ 146 Erik Coleman RC	1.25	3.00
❑ 147 Robert Kent RC	1.00	2.50
❑ 148 Jammal Lord RC	1.00	2.50
❑ 149 Richard Seigler RC	1.00	2.50
❑ 150 Niko Koutouvides RC	1.00	2.50
❑ 151 Brandon Miree RC	1.00	2.50
❑ 152 Dunta Robinson RC	1.25	3.00
❑ 153 Courtney Anderson RC	1.00	2.50
❑ 154 Bruce Perry RC	1.00	2.50
❑ 155 Shaun Phillips RC	1.25	3.00
❑ 156 Greg Jones RC	1.50	4.00
❑ 157 Tank Johnson RC	1.25	3.00
❑ 158 Dwan Edwards RC	1.00	2.50
❑ 159 Julius Jones RC	2.00	5.00
❑ 160 Chad Lavalais RC	1.00	2.50
❑ 161 Tim Anderson RC	1.25	3.00
❑ 162 Jarrett Payton RC	1.25	3.00
❑ 163 Matt Ware RC	1.50	4.00
❑ 164 DeAngelo Hall RC	1.50	4.00
❑ 165 Ben Hartsock RC	1.25	3.00
❑ 166 Keith Smith RC	1.00	2.50
❑ 167 Michael Jenkins RC	1.50	4.00
❑ 168 Quincy Wilson RC	1.25	3.00
❑ 169 Dontarrious Thomas RC	1.25	3.00
❑ 170 Tony Hargrove RC	1.00	2.50
❑ 171 Ben Watson RC	1.50	4.00
❑ 172 Triandos Luke RC	1.00	2.50
❑ 173 Kellen Winslow RC	2.00	5.00
❑ 174 Patrick Crayton RC	2.00	5.00
❑ 175 Devard Darling RC	1.25	3.00
❑ 176 Shawntae Spencer RC	1.00	2.50
❑ 177 Will Smith RC	1.50	4.00
❑ 178 Darrion Scott RC	1.25	3.00
❑ 179 Wes Welker RC	4.00	10.00
❑ 180 Ryan Dinwiddie RC	1.00	2.50
❑ 181 Rod Davis RC	1.00	2.50
❑ 182 Casey Clausen RC	1.25	3.00
❑ 183 Clarence Moore RC	1.25	3.00
❑ 184 D.J. Hackett RC	1.50	4.00
❑ 185 Devery Henderson RC	1.50	4.00
❑ 186 Sean Jones RC	1.25	3.00
❑ 187 Bruce Thornton RC	1.00	2.50
❑ 188 Tatum Bell RC	1.50	4.00
❑ 189 Tim Euhus RC	1.00	2.50
❑ 190 John Standeford RC	1.00	2.50
❑ 191 Reggie Torbor RC	1.00	2.50
❑ 192 Rashaun Woods RC	1.00	2.50
❑ 193 Jason Shivers RC	1.00	2.50
❑ 194 Ahmad Carroll RC	1.50	4.00
❑ 195 Keyaron Fox RC	1.25	3.00
❑ 196 Von Hutchins RC	1.00	2.50
❑ 197 Marcus Tubbs RC	1.00	2.50
❑ 198 Daryl Smith RC	1.25	3.00

Card	Low	High
❑ 199 Robert Gallery RC	1.50	4.00
❑ 200 Marquis Cooper RC	1.50	4.00
❑ 201 Bernard Berrian RC	1.50	4.00
❑ 202 Derrick Strait RC	1.25	3.00
❑ 203 Travis LaBoy RC	1.25	3.00
❑ 204 Caleb Miller RC	1.00	2.50
❑ 205 Michael Clayton RC	1.50	4.00
❑ 206 Will Poole RC	1.50	4.00
❑ 207 Derrick Hamilton RC	1.00	2.50
❑ 208 Glenn Earl RC	1.00	2.50
❑ 209 Donnell Washington RC	1.25	3.00
❑ 210 Nate Lawrie RC	1.00	2.50
❑ 211 Keiwan Ratliff RC	1.00	2.50
❑ 212 Luke McCown RC	1.50	4.00
❑ 213 Joey Thomas RC	1.00	2.50
❑ 214 Shawn Andrews RC	1.25	3.00
❑ 215 Derrick Ward RC	1.50	4.00
❑ 216 Reggie Williams RC	1.50	4.00
❑ 217 Rod Rutherford RC	1.00	2.50
❑ 218 Michael Gaines RC	1.00	2.50
❑ 219 Will Allen RC	1.25	3.00
❑ 220 J.P. Losman RC	1.50	4.00
❑ 221 Roy Williams AU/199 RC	25.00	60.00
❑ 222 Kevin Jones AU/199 RC	15.00	40.00
❑ 223 Philip Rivers AU/199 RC	75.00	150.00
❑ 224 Steven Jackson AU/199 RC	60.00	120.00
❑ 225 Eli Manning AU/199 RC	100.00	200.00
❑ 226 Cody Pickett AU D RC	5.00	12.00
❑ 227 P.K. Sam AU D RC	4.00	10.00
❑ 228 Maurice Mann AU D RC	4.00	10.00
❑ 229 Andy Hall AU D RC	5.00	12.00
❑ 230 Chris Perry AU D RC	6.00	15.00
❑ 231 Ernest Wilford AU C RC	5.00	12.00
❑ 232 Kenechi Udeze AU D RC	6.00	15.00
❑ 233 Michael Boulware AU D RC	6.00	15.00
❑ 234 B.J. Symons AU D RC	4.00	10.00
❑ 235 Jared Lorenzen AU D RC	5.00	12.00
❑ 236 Matt Mauck AU D RC	5.00	12.00
❑ 237 Carlos Francis AU D RC	4.00	10.00
❑ 238 Michael Turner AU D RC	20.00	50.00
❑ 239 Lee Evans AU B RC	20.00	40.00
❑ 240 Jerricho Cotchery AU D RC	10.00	20.00
❑ 241 John Navarre AU D RC	5.00	12.00
❑ 242 Jonathan Vilma AU D RC	7.50	25.00
❑ 243 Josh Harris AU D RC	4.00	10.00
❑ 244 Jeff Smoker AU C RC	5.00	12.00
❑ 245 Jamaar Taylor AU D RC	4.00	10.00

2005 Bowman Chrome

Card	Low	High
❑ COMP.SET w/o AU's (220)	40.00	100.00
❑ COMP.SET w/o RC's (110)	12.50	30.00
❑ ROOK.AU GROUP A ODDS 1:381 H, 1:1011 R		
❑ ROOK.AU GROUP B ODDS 1:156 H, 1:449 R		
❑ ROOK.AU GROUP C ODDS 1:318 H, 1:899 R		
❑ ROOK.AU GROUP D ODDS 1:296 H, 1:899 R		
❑ ROOK.AU GROUP E ODDS 1:281 H, 1:809 R		
❑ ROOK.AU GROUP F ODDS 1:132 H, 404 R		
❑ ROOK.AU GROUP G ODDS 1:39 H, 1:108 R		
❑ ROOKIE AU/199 ODDS 1:685 H, 1:1348 R		
❑ UNPRICED PRINT.PLATE 1/1 ODDS 1:975 H		
❑ 1 Peyton Manning	.60	1.50
❑ 2 Priest Holmes	.40	1.00
❑ 3 Anquan Boldin	.30	.75
❑ 4 Michael Vick	.40	1.00
❑ 5 Drew Brees	.40	1.00
❑ 6 Terrell Owens	.40	1.00
❑ 7 Curtis Martin	.40	1.00
❑ 8 Tom Brady	.75	2.00
❑ 9 Maurice Carthon CO	.25	.60
❑ 10 Brett Favre	1.00	2.50
❑ 11 Marshall Faulk	.40	1.00
❑ 12 Corey Dillon	.30	.75
❑ 13 Julius Jones	.40	1.00
❑ 14 Jamal Lewis	.30	.75
❑ 15 Keary Colbert	.25	.60
❑ 16 Joey Harrington	.40	1.00
❑ 17 Domanick Davis	.25	.60
❑ 18 Eli Manning	.75	2.00
❑ 19 Brad Childress CO	.30	.75
❑ 20 Steve McNair	.40	1.00
❑ 21 Plaxico Burress	.30	.75
❑ 22 Chad Pennington	.40	1.00
❑ 23 Patrick Ramsey	.30	.75
❑ 24 Brian Griese	.30	.75
❑ 25 Matt Hasselbeck	.30	.75
❑ 26 Chris Chambers	.30	.75
❑ 27 Marc Bulger	.30	.75
❑ 28 Jake Delhomme	.40	1.00
❑ 29 Shaun Alexander	.40	1.00
❑ 30 Laveranues Coles	.30	.75
❑ 31 A.J. Feeley	.25	.60
❑ 32 Ashley Lelie	.25	.60
❑ 33 Deuce McAllister	.40	1.00
❑ 34 Chris Brown	.30	.75
❑ 35 Nate Burleson	.30	.75
❑ 36 Darrell Jackson	.30	.75
❑ 37 Lee Evans	.30	.75
❑ 38 Jeremy Shockey	.40	1.00
❑ 39 Muhsin Muhammad	.30	.75
❑ 40 Deion Branch	.30	.75
❑ 41 DeShaun Foster	.30	.75
❑ 42 Reggie Wayne	.30	.75
❑ 43 Michael Jenkins	.30	.75
❑ 44 Andre Johnson	.30	.75
❑ 45 Javon Walker	.30	.75
❑ 46 Joe Horn	.30	.75
❑ 47 Fred Taylor	.40	1.00
❑ 48 Tony Gonzalez	.30	.75
❑ 49 J.P. Losman	.30	.75
❑ 50 Clinton Portis	.40	1.00
❑ 51 Randy Moss	.40	1.00
❑ 52 Jake Plummer	.30	.75
❑ 53 Tiki Barber	.40	1.00
❑ 54 Edgerrin James	.30	.75
❑ 55 Jerome Bettis	.40	1.00
❑ 56 Brandon Lloyd	.25	.60
❑ 57 Romeo Crennel CO	.40	1.00
❑ 58 Antonio Gates	.40	1.00
❑ 59 Donovan McNabb	.40	1.00
❑ 60 Drew Bennett	.30	.75
❑ 61 David Carr	.30	.75
❑ 62 Trent Green	.30	.75
❑ 63 Drew Bledsoe	.40	1.00
❑ 64 Donte Stallworth	.30	.75
❑ 65 Alge Crumpler	.30	.75
❑ 66 Jason Witten	.40	1.00
❑ 67 Thomas Jones	.30	.75
❑ 68 Rex Grossman	.40	1.00
❑ 69 LaMont Jordan	.30	.75
❑ 70 Kurt Warner	.40	1.00
❑ 71 Ahman Green	.40	1.00
❑ 72 Ben Roethlisberger	1.00	2.50
❑ 73 Mike Nolan CO	.30	.75
❑ 74 Brian Westbrook	.40	1.00
❑ 75 Carson Palmer	.40	1.00
❑ 76 Stephen Davis	.30	.75
❑ 77 Jonathan Vilma	.30	.75
❑ 78 Willis McGahee	.40	1.00
❑ 79 Rudi Johnson	.30	.75
❑ 80 Jerry Porter	.30	.75
❑ 81 Charles Rogers	.25	.60
❑ 82 Dwight Freeney	.30	.75
❑ 83 Tim Lewis CO	.25	.60
❑ 84 Aaron Brooks	.25	.60
❑ 85 Kyle Boller	.30	.75
❑ 86 Isaac Bruce	.30	.75
❑ 87 Chad Johnson	.30	.75
❑ 88 Kevin Jones	.30	.75
❑ 89 Eric Moulds	.30	.75
❑ 90 Sean Taylor	.30	.75
❑ 91 Chris Perry	.25	.60
❑ 92 Kerry Collins	.30	.75
❑ 93 Steven Jackson	.50	1.25
❑ 94 LaDainian Tomlinson	.50	1.25
❑ 95 Torry Holt	.30	.75
❑ 96 Lee Suggs	.30	.75
❑ 97 Santana Moss	.30	.75
❑ 98 Hines Ward	.40	1.00
❑ 99 Daunte Culpepper	.40	1.00
❑ 100 Travis Henry	.30	.75
❑ 101 Ricky Williams	.30	.75
❑ 102 Roy Williams WR	.40	1.00
❑ 103 Tatum Bell	.30	.75
❑ 104 Dante Hall	.30	.75
❑ 105 Larry Fitzgerald	.40	1.00

❑ 106 Marvin Harrison .40 1.00
❑ 107 Byron Leftwich .30 .75
❑ 108 T.J. Houshmandzadeh .30 .75
❑ 109 Michael Clayton .30 .75
❑ 110 Ted Cottrell CO .25 .60
❑ 111 Carlos Rogers RC 1.25 3.00
❑ 112 Kyle Orton RC 2.00 5.00
❑ 113 Marion Barber RC 4.00 10.00
❑ 114 Mark Bradley RC 1.00 2.50
❑ 115 Travis Johnson RC .75 2.00
❑ 116 Antrel Rolle RC 1.25 3.00
❑ 117 Jason Campbell RC 2.00 5.00
❑ 118 Justin Miller RC 1.00 2.50
❑ 119 J.J. Arrington RC 1.25 3.00
❑ 120 Marcus Spears RC 1.25 3.00
❑ 121 Vincent Jackson RC 1.50 4.00
❑ 122 Erasmus James RC 1.00 2.50
❑ 123 Heath Miller RC 2.50 6.00
❑ 124 Eric Shelton RC 1.00 2.50
❑ 125 Cedric Benson RC 1.25 3.00
❑ 126 Mark Clayton RC 1.25 3.00
❑ 127 Anthony Davis RC 1.00 2.50
❑ 128 Charlie Frye RC 1.25 3.00
❑ 129 Fred Gibson RC 1.00 2.50
❑ 130 Reggie Brown RC 1.00 2.50
❑ 131 Andrew Walter RC 1.00 2.50
❑ 132 Adam Jones RC 1.00 2.50
❑ 133 David Greene RC 1.00 2.50
❑ 134 Maurice Clarett 1.00 2.50
❑ 135 Roscoe Parrish RC 1.00 2.50
❑ 136 Chris Henry RC 1.25 3.00
❑ 137 Mike Nugent RC 1.00 2.50
❑ 138 Kevin Burnett RC 1.00 2.50
❑ 139 Matt Roth RC 1.25 3.00
❑ 140 Barrett Ruud RC 1.25 3.00
❑ 141 Kirk Morrison RC 1.25 3.00
❑ 142 Brock Berlin RC 1.00 2.50
❑ 143 Bryant McFadden RC 1.00 2.50
❑ 144 Scott Starks RC 1.00 2.50
❑ 145 Stanford Routt RC 1.00 2.50
❑ 146 Oshiomogho Atogwe RC .75 2.00
❑ 147 Jovan Witherspoon RC .75 2.00
❑ 148 Boomer Grigsby RC 1.25 3.00
❑ 149 Lance Mitchell RC 1.00 2.50
❑ 150 Darryl Blackstock RC .75 2.00
❑ 151 Ellis Hobbs RC 1.25 3.00
❑ 152 James Kilian RC .75 2.00
❑ 153 Willie Parker 1.25 3.00
❑ 154 Justin Tuck RC 1.50 4.00
❑ 155 Luis Castillo RC 1.25 3.00
❑ 156 Paris Warren RC 1.00 2.50
❑ 157 Corey Webster RC 1.25 3.00
❑ 158 Tab Perry RC 1.25 3.00
❑ 159 Rian Wallace RC 1.00 2.50
❑ 160 Joel Dreessen RC 1.00 2.50
❑ 161 Khalif Barnes RC .75 2.00
❑ 162 David Pollack RC 1.00 2.50
❑ 163 Zach Tuiasosopo RC .75 2.00
❑ 164 Ryan Riddle RC .75 2.00
❑ 165 Travis Daniels RC 1.00 2.50
❑ 166 Eric King RC .75 2.00
❑ 167 Justin Green RC 1.25 3.00
❑ 168 Manuel White RC 1.00 2.50
❑ 169 Jordan Beck RC 1.00 2.50
❑ 170 Lofa Tatupu RC 1.25 3.00
❑ 171 Will Peoples RC 1.00 2.50
❑ 172 Chad Friehauf RC 1.00 2.50
❑ 173 Brady Poppinga RC 1.25 3.00
❑ 174 Anttaj Hawthorne RC 1.00 2.50
❑ 175 Nick Collins RC 1.25 3.00
❑ 176 Craig Ochs RC 1.00 2.50
❑ 177 Billy Bajema RC .75 2.00
❑ 178 Jon Goldsberry RC 1.25 3.00
❑ 179 Jared Newberry RC 1.00 2.50
❑ 180 Odell Thurman RC 1.25 3.00
❑ 181 Kelvin Hayden RC 1.00 2.50
❑ 182 Jamaal Brimmer RC .75 2.00
❑ 183 Jonathan Babineaux RC 1.00 2.50
❑ 184 Bo Scaife RC 1.00 2.50
❑ 185 Bryan Randall RC 1.00 2.50
❑ 186 James Butler RC 1.00 2.50
❑ 187 Harry Williams RC 1.00 2.50
❑ 188 Leroy Hill RC 1.25 3.00
❑ 189 Josh Bullocks RC 1.25 3.00
❑ 190 Alfred Fincher RC 1.00 2.50
❑ 191 Antonio Perkins RC 1.00 2.50
❑ 192 Bobby Purify RC 1.00 2.50
❑ 193 Darrent Williams RC 1.25 3.00
❑ 194 Darian Durant RC 1.25 3.00
❑ 195 Fred Amey RC 1.00 2.50
❑ 196 Ronald Bartell RC 1.00 2.50
❑ 197 Kerry Rhodes RC 1.25 3.00
❑ 198 Jerome Carter RC .75 2.00
❑ 199 Roddy White RC 1.50 4.00
❑ 200 Nehemiah Broughton RC 1.00 2.50
❑ 201 Keron Henry RC .75 2.00
❑ 202 Jerome Collins RC 1.00 2.50
❑ 203 Trent Cole RC 1.25 3.00
❑ 204 Alphonso Hodge RC .75 2.00
❑ 205 Marviel Underwood RC 1.00 2.50
❑ 206 Marlin Jackson RC 1.00 2.50
❑ 207 Madison Hedgecock RC 1.25 3.00
❑ 208 Chris Spencer RC 1.25 3.00
❑ 209 Vincent Fuller RC 1.00 2.50
❑ 210 Marcus Maxwell RC .75 2.00
❑ 211 Dustin Fox RC 1.25 3.00
❑ 212 Timmy Chang RC 1.00 2.50
❑ 213 Walter Reyes RC .75 2.00
❑ 214 Donte Nicholson RC 1.00 2.50
❑ 215 Stanley Wilson RC 1.00 2.50
❑ 216 Dan Cody RC 1.25 3.00
❑ 217 Alex Barron RC .75 2.00
❑ 218 Taylor Stubblefield RC .75 2.00
❑ 219 Shaun Cody RC 1.00 2.50
❑ 220 Steve Savoy RC .75 2.00
❑ 221 Aaron Rodgers AU/199 RC 90.00 150.00
❑ 222 Alex Smith QB AU/199 RC 40.00 80.00
❑ 223 Bray.Edwards AU/199 RC 40.00 100.00
❑ 224 Cadill.Williams AU/199 RC 40.00 80.00
❑ 225 Mike Williams AU/199 15.00 40.00
❑ 226 Ronnie Brown AU/199 RC 50.00 120.00
❑ 227 T.Williamson AU/199 RC 15.00 40.00
❑ 228 Dante Ridgeway AU B RC 4.00 10.00
❑ 229 Channing Crowder AU G RC 5.00 12.00
❑ 230 Chase Lyman AU E RC 4.00 10.00
❑ 231 Courtney Roby AU F RC 5.00 12.00
❑ 232 Damien Nash AU G RC 5.00 12.00
❑ 233 Dan Orlovsky AU C RC 6.00 15.00
❑ 234 Fabian Washington AU B RC 6.00 15.00
❑ 235 Shawne Merriman AU B RC 15.00 40.00
❑ 236 Cedric Houston AU G RC 6.00 15.00
❑ 237 Alex Smith TE AU D RC 6.00 15.00
❑ 238 Brandon Jones AU B RC 6.00 15.00
❑ 239 Alvin Pearman AU G RC 4.00 10.00
❑ 240 Derek Anderson AU C RC 12.00 30.00
❑ 241 J.R. Russell AU G RC 4.00 10.00
❑ 242 Jerome Mathis AU F RC 6.00 15.00
❑ 243 Josh Davis AU A RC 4.00 10.00
❑ 244 Kay-Jay Harris AU G RC 5.00 12.00
❑ 245 Rasheed Marshall AU F RC 5.00 12.00
❑ 246 Matt Jones AU/199 RC 15.00 40.00
❑ 247 Chad Owens AU G RC 6.00 15.00
❑ 248 Larry Brackins AU A RC 4.00 10.00
❑ 249 Matt Cassel AU G RC 15.00 40.00
❑ 250 Noah Herron AU G RC 6.00 15.00
❑ 251 Roydell Williams AU G RC 5.00 12.00
❑ 252 Ryan Fitzpatrick AU F RC 6.00 15.00
❑ 253 Derrick Johnson AU E RC 6.00 15.00
❑ 254 DeMarcus Ware AU D RC 15.00 30.00
❑ 255 Brandon Jacobs AU A RC 20.00 40.00
❑ 256 Craig Bragg AU G RC 4.00 10.00
❑ 257 Ryan Moats AU G RC 5.00 12.00
❑ 258 Stefan LeFors AU G RC 5.00 12.00
❑ 259 Frank Gore AU B RC 20.00 50.00
❑ DSB Bogut/A.Smith QB AU/100 50.00 120.00

2006 Bowman Chrome

❑ COMPLETE SET (275) 100.00 200.00
❑ COMP.SHORT SET (55) 15.00 40.00
❑ COMP.VET SET (110) 8.00 20.00
❑ 1 Devin Aromashodu RC .75 2.00
❑ 2 Daniel Bullocks RC .75 2.00
❑ 3 Winston Justice RC .75 2.00
❑ 4 Lawrence Vickers RC .60 1.50
❑ 5 Bernard Pollard RC .60 1.50
❑ 6 Abdul Hodge RC .60 1.50
❑ 7 Jovon Bouknight RC .60 1.50
❑ 8 Wali Lundy RC .75 2.00
❑ 9 Jonathan Orr RC .60 1.50
❑ 10 Gerald Riggs RC .60 1.50
❑ 11 Chris Gocong RC .60 1.50
❑ 12 David Kirtman RC .60 1.50
❑ 13 Quinn Sypniewski RC .60 1.50
❑ 14 Richard Marshall RC .60 1.50
❑ 15 Darryl Tapp RC .60 1.50
❑ 16 Charles Davis RC .60 1.50
❑ 17 Tim Massaquoi RC .60 1.50
❑ 18 DeMario Minter RC .60 1.50
❑ 19 Hank Baskett RC .75 2.00
❑ 20 Andre Hall RC .60 1.50
❑ 21 Cody Hodges RC .60 1.50
❑ 22 Greg Lee RC .50 1.25
❑ 23 Danieal Manning RC .75 2.00
❑ 24 Jason Hatcher RC .60 1.50
❑ 25 Ben Obomanu RC .60 1.50
❑ 26 Dusty Dvoracek RC .75 2.00
❑ 27 Domenik Hixon RC .75 2.00
❑ 28 Josh Betts RC .60 1.50
❑ 29 Marques Colston RC 2.00 5.00
❑ 30 P.J. Pope RC .75 2.00
❑ 31 Gabe Watson RC .50 1.25
❑ 32 Alan Zemaitis RC .75 2.00
❑ 33 Jeff King RC .60 1.50
❑ 34 Damien Rhodes RC .60 1.50
❑ 35 Orien Harris RC .60 1.50
❑ 36 David Anderson RC .60 1.50
❑ 37 Garrett Mills RC .60 1.50
❑ 38 Anthony Schlegel RC .60 1.50
❑ 39 Omar Gaither RC .60 1.50
❑ 40 Freddie Keiaho RC .60 1.50
❑ 41 J.J. Outlaw RC .60 1.50
❑ 42 Tony Scheffler RC .75 2.00
❑ 43 Dee Webb RC .60 1.50
❑ 44 Drew Olson RC .50 1.25
❑ 45 Martin Nance RC .60 1.50
❑ 46 Ko Simpson RC .60 1.50
❑ 47 Jesse Mahelona RC .60 1.50
❑ 48 Owen Daniels RC .75 2.00
❑ 49 Delanie Walker RC .60 1.50
❑ 50 Eric Smith RC .60 1.50
❑ 51 Darrell Hackney RC .60 1.50
❑ 52 Freddie Roach RC .60 1.50
❑ 53 James Anderson RC .50 1.25
❑ 54 Anthony Smith RC .75 2.00
❑ 55 Gerris Wilkinson RC .50 1.25
❑ 56 Tamba Hali RC 1.50 4.00
❑ 57 Jerome Harrison RC 1.50 4.00
❑ 58 Jason Allen RC 1.25 3.00
❑ 59 Brodrick Bunkley RC 1.25 3.00
❑ 60 Bobby Carpenter RC 1.25 3.00
❑ 61 Johnathan Joseph RC 1.25 3.00
❑ 62 Travis Wilson RC 1.00 2.50
❑ 63 Reggie McNeal RC 1.25 3.00
❑ 64 Haloti Ngata RC 1.50 4.00
❑ 65 Manny Lawson RC 1.50 4.00
❑ 66 Donte Whitner RC 1.50 4.00
❑ 67 Derek Hagan RC 1.25 3.00
❑ 68 Devin Hester RC 3.00 8.00
❑ 69 Jeremy Bloom RC 1.25 3.00
❑ 70 Ashton Youboty RC 1.25 3.00
❑ 71 Kamerion Wimbley RC 1.50 4.00
❑ 72 Charlie Whitehurst RC 1.50 4.00
❑ 73 Darnell Bing RC 1.25 3.00
❑ 74 Adam Jennings RC 1.25 3.00
❑ 75 Tim Day RC 1.25 3.00
❑ 76 Jeff Webb RC 1.25 3.00
❑ 77 D.J. Shockley RC 1.25 3.00
❑ 78 Marcus Vick RC 1.00 2.50
❑ 79 Thomas Howard RC 1.25 3.00
❑ 80 Todd Watkins RC 1.00 2.50
❑ 81 Davin Joseph RC 1.25 3.00
❑ 82 Pat Watkins RC 1.50 4.00
❑ 83 Jon Alston RC 1.00 2.50
❑ 84 Ernie Sims RC 1.25 3.00
❑ 85 D'Qwell Jackson RC 1.25 3.00
❑ 86 Corey Bramlet RC 1.25 3.00
❑ 87 Antonio Cromartie RC 1.50 4.00
❑ 88 A.J. Nicholson RC 1.00 2.50
❑ 89 Kevin McMahan RC 1.25 3.00
❑ 90 J.D. Runnels RC 1.25 3.00
❑ 91 Nate Salley RC 1.25 3.00
❑ 92 Matt Shelton RC 1.50 4.00
❑ 93 Brett Basanez RC 1.50 4.00
❑ 94 Rocky McIntosh RC 1.50 4.00

Card	Low	High
❑ 95 Anthony Mix RC	1.25	3.00
❑ 96 Jimmy Williams RC	1.50	4.00
❑ 97 Marcus McNeill RC	1.25	3.00
❑ 98 DeMeco Ryans RC	2.00	5.00
❑ 99 Dwayne Slay RC	1.25	3.00
❑ 100 John David Washington RC	1.25	3.00
❑ 101 P.J. Daniels RC	1.00	2.50
❑ 102 Kelly Jennings RC	1.50	4.00
❑ 103 John McCargo RC	1.25	3.00
❑ 104 Paul Pinegar RC	1.00	2.50
❑ 105 Ray Edwards RC	1.50	4.00
❑ 106 Elvis Dumervil RC	1.50	4.00
❑ 107 Travis Lulay RC	1.25	3.00
❑ 108 Bennie Brazell RC	1.25	3.00
❑ 109 Dominique Byrd RC	1.25	3.00
❑ 110 Nick Mangold RC	1.25	3.00
❑ 111 Plaxico Burress	.30	.75
❑ 112 Shaun Alexander	.30	.75
❑ 113 Muhsin Muhammad	.30	.75
❑ 114 Jake Plummer	.30	.75
❑ 115 Deuce McAllister	.30	.75
❑ 116 T.J. Houshmandzadeh	.30	.75
❑ 117 Carson Palmer	.40	1.00
❑ 118 Willis McGahee	.40	1.00
❑ 119 Terrell Owens	.40	1.00
❑ 120 Fred Taylor	.30	.75
❑ 121 Dante Hall	.30	.75
❑ 122 Brad Johnson	.30	.75
❑ 123 Reggie Wayne	.30	.75
❑ 124 DeShaun Foster	.30	.75
❑ 125 Tony Gonzalez	.30	.75
❑ 126 Javon Walker	.30	.75
❑ 127 Marc Bulger	.30	.75
❑ 128 LaDainian Tomlinson	.50	1.25
❑ 129 Byron Leftwich	.30	.75
❑ 130 Dwight Freeney	.30	.75
❑ 131 Kevin Jones	.30	.75
❑ 132 Hines Ward	.40	1.00
❑ 133 Randy Moss	.40	1.00
❑ 134 Edgerrin James	.30	.75
❑ 135 Ahman Green	.30	.75
❑ 136 Steven Jackson	.40	1.00
❑ 137 Ben Roethlisberger	.60	1.50
❑ 138 Daunte Culpepper	.40	1.00
❑ 139 Santana Moss	.30	.75
❑ 140 Jonathan Vilma	.30	.75
❑ 141 Gary Kubiak CO	.25	.60
❑ 142 Marvin Harrison	.40	1.00
❑ 143 Trent Green	.30	.75
❑ 144 Chris Chambers	.30	.75
❑ 145 Chris Brown	.30	.75
❑ 146 Eli Manning	.50	1.25
❑ 147 Corey Dillon	.30	.75
❑ 148 Anquan Boldin	.30	.75
❑ 149 Donovan McNabb	.40	1.00
❑ 150 Drew Bennett	.30	.75
❑ 151 Jason Witten	.40	1.00
❑ 152 Eric Moulds	.30	.75
❑ 153 Billy Volek	.25	.60
❑ 154 Chris Cooley	.30	.75
❑ 155 Larry Johnson	.30	.75
❑ 156 Willie Parker	.50	1.25
❑ 157 Cadillac Williams	.40	1.00
❑ 158 Philip Rivers	.40	1.00
❑ 159 Reuben Droughns	.30	.75
❑ 160 Joey Galloway	.30	.75
❑ 161 Lee Evans	.30	.75
❑ 162 Jamal Lewis	.30	.75
❑ 163 Brett Favre	.75	2.00
❑ 164 Clinton Portis	.40	1.00
❑ 165 Rod Marinelli CO	.25	.60
❑ 166 Tom Brady	.60	1.50
❑ 167 Torry Holt	.30	.75
❑ 168 Rudi Johnson	.30	.75
❑ 169 Priest Holmes	.30	.75
❑ 170 Tatum Bell	.25	.60
❑ 171 Jeremy Shockey	.40	1.00
❑ 172 Shawne Merriman	.30	.75
❑ 173 Alge Crumpler	.30	.75
❑ 174 Marion Barber	.40	1.00
❑ 175 Steve Smith	.40	1.00
❑ 176 Mike McCarthy CO	.25	.60
❑ 177 David Carr	.25	.60
❑ 178 Julius Jones	.30	.75
❑ 179 Chad Johnson	.30	.75
❑ 180 Curtis Martin	.40	1.00
❑ 181 Peyton Manning	.60	1.50
❑ 182 LaMont Jordan	.30	.75
❑ 183 Tiki Barber	.40	1.00
❑ 184 Darrell Jackson	.30	.75
❑ 185 J.P. Losman	.30	.75
❑ 186 Drew Brees	.40	1.00
❑ 187 Isaac Bruce	.30	.75
❑ 188 Drew Bledsoe	.40	1.00
❑ 189 Roy Williams WR	.40	1.00
❑ 190 Donte Stallworth	.30	.75
❑ 191 Odell Thurman	.25	.60
❑ 192 Chester Taylor	.30	.75
❑ 193 Randy McMichael	.25	.60
❑ 194 Larry Fitzgerald	.40	1.00
❑ 195 Charlie Frye	.30	.75
❑ 196 Keary Colbert	.30	.75
❑ 197 Patrick Ramsey	.30	.75
❑ 198 Mark Clayton	.30	.75
❑ 199 Michael Jenkins	.30	.75
❑ 200 Jake Delhomme	.30	.75
❑ 201 Aaron Rodgers	.40	1.00
❑ 202 Andre Johnson	.30	.75
❑ 203 Matt Hasselbeck	.30	.75
❑ 204 Reggie Brown	.25	.60
❑ 205 Warrick Dunn	.30	.75
❑ 206 Kurt Warner	.40	1.00
❑ 207 Antonio Gates	.40	1.00
❑ 208 Terry Glenn	.30	.75
❑ 209 Steve McNair	.30	.75
❑ 210 Alex Smith QB	.30	.75
❑ 211 Joe Horn	.30	.75
❑ 212 Domanick Davis	.30	.75
❑ 213 Deion Branch	.30	.75
❑ 214 Todd Heap	.30	.75
❑ 215 Chad Pennington	.30	.75
❑ 216 Brandon Lloyd	.30	.75
❑ 217 Rod Smith	.30	.75
❑ 218 Ronnie Brown	.40	1.00
❑ 219 Braylon Edwards	.40	1.00
❑ 220 Michael Vick	.40	1.00
❑ 221 Vince Young RC	4.00	10.00
❑ 222 Jay Cutler RC	4.00	10.00
❑ 223 Reggie Bush RC	4.00	10.00
❑ 224 Matt Leinart RC	2.50	6.00
❑ 225 Vernon Davis RC	1.50	4.00
❑ 226 A.J. Hawk RC	2.50	6.00
❑ 227 Santonio Holmes RC	4.00	10.00
❑ 228 DeAngelo Williams RC	3.00	8.00
❑ 229 LenDale White RC	2.00	5.00
❑ 230 Sinorice Moss RC	1.50	4.00
❑ 231 Joseph Addai RC	2.00	5.00
❑ 232 Mike Bell RC	1.50	4.00
❑ 233 Will Blackmon RC	1.50	4.00
❑ 234 Brian Calhoun RC	1.25	3.00
❑ 235 Kellen Clemens RC	1.50	4.00
❑ 236 Brodie Croyle RC	1.50	4.00
❑ 237 Maurice Drew RC	3.00	8.00
❑ 238 Anthony Fasano RC	1.50	4.00
❑ 239 D'Brickashaw Ferguson RC	1.50	4.00
❑ 240 Quinton Ganther RC	1.00	2.50
❑ 241 Bruce Gradkowski RC	1.50	4.00
❑ 242 Skyler Green RC	1.00	2.50
❑ 243 Chad Greenway RC	1.50	4.00
❑ 244 Marques Hagans RC	1.25	3.00
❑ 245 Michael Huff RC	1.50	4.00
❑ 246 Cedric Humes RC	1.25	3.00
❑ 247 Tarvaris Jackson RC	1.50	4.00
❑ 248 Omar Jacobs RC	1.00	2.50
❑ 249 Greg Jennings RC	2.50	6.00
❑ 250 Mathias Kiwanuka RC	2.00	5.00
❑ 251 Joe Klopfenstein RC	1.25	3.00
❑ 252 Marcedes Lewis RC	1.50	4.00
❑ 253 Brandon Marshall RC	1.50	4.00
❑ 254 Ingle Martin RC	1.25	3.00
❑ 255 Dontrell Moore RC	1.25	3.00
❑ 256 Jerious Norwood RC	1.50	4.00
❑ 257 Leonard Pope RC	1.50	4.00
❑ 258 Willie Reid RC	1.25	3.00
❑ 259 Michael Robinson RC	1.25	3.00
❑ 260 Brad Smith RC	1.50	4.00
❑ 261 Maurice Stovall RC	1.25	3.00
❑ 262 David Thomas RC	1.50	4.00
❑ 263 Leon Washington RC	2.00	5.00
❑ 264 Brandon Williams RC	1.25	3.00
❑ 265 Demetrius Williams RC	1.25	3.00
❑ 266 Tye Hill RC	1.25	3.00
❑ 267 Mike Hass RC	1.50	4.00
❑ 268 Jason Avant RC	1.50	4.00
❑ 269 Chad Jackson RC	1.25	3.00
❑ 270 Laurence Maroney RC	2.00	5.00
❑ 271 Anwar Phillips RC	1.25	3.00
❑ 272 David Kirtman RC	1.25	3.00
❑ 273 Roman Harper RC	1.25	3.00
❑ 274 Spencer Havner RC	1.25	3.00
❑ 275 Erik Meyer RC	1.25	3.00

2007 Bowman Chrome

Card	Low	High
❑ COMPLETE SET (220)	40.00	100.00
❑ COMP.SHORT SET (55)	8.00	20.00
❑ COMP.VET SET (110)	6.00	15.00
❑ 1-55 INSERTED IN BOWMAN PACKS		
❑ BC1 Kenny Irons RC	.60	1.50
❑ BC2 David Clowney RC	.60	1.50
❑ BC3 Courtney Taylor RC	.50	1.25
❑ BC4 Amobi Okoye RC	.60	1.50
❑ BC5 Jamaal Anderson RC	.50	1.25
❑ BC6 Adam Carriker RC	.50	1.25
❑ BC7 Jarvis Moss RC	.60	1.50
❑ BC8 Anthony Spencer RC	.60	1.50
❑ BC9 Jon Beason RC	.60	1.50
❑ BC10 Darrelle Revis RC	.75	2.00
❑ BC11 Aaron Ross RC	.60	1.50
❑ BC12 Reggie Nelson RC	.50	1.25
❑ BC13 Michael Griffin RC	.60	1.50
❑ BC14 Brandon Meriweather RC	.60	1.50
❑ BC15 Tyler Palko RC	.50	1.25
❑ BC16 Jared Zabransky RC	.60	1.50
❑ BC17 Lester Ricard RC	.60	1.50
❑ BC18 Darius Walker RC	.50	1.25
❑ BC19 Ahmad Bradshaw RC	.75	2.00
❑ BC20 Thomas Clayton RC	.50	1.25
❑ BC21 Rhema McKnight RC	.50	1.25
❑ BC22 Scott Chandler RC	.50	1.25
❑ BC23 Matt Spaeth RC	.60	1.50
❑ BC24 Ben Patrick RC	.50	1.25
❑ BC25 Clark Harris RC	.60	1.50
❑ BC26 Martrez Milner RC	.50	1.25
❑ BC27 Joe Newton RC	.50	1.25
❑ BC28 DeMarcus Tank Tyler RC	.50	1.25
❑ BC29 Justin Harrell RC	.60	1.50
❑ BC30 LaMarr Woodley RC	.60	1.50
❑ BC31 David Harris RC	.50	1.25
❑ BC32 Buster Davis RC	.50	1.25
❑ BC33 Rufus Alexander RC	.60	1.50
❑ BC34 Earl Everett RC	.50	1.25
❑ BC35 Stewart Bradley RC	.60	1.50
❑ BC36 Prescott Burgess RC	.50	1.25
❑ BC37 Daymeion Hughes RC	.50	1.25
❑ BC38 Marcus McCauley RC	.50	1.25
❑ BC39 Chris Houston RC	.50	1.25
❑ BC40 David Irons RC	.40	1.00
❑ BC41 Levi Brown RC	.60	1.50
❑ BC42 Joe Staley RC	.50	1.25
❑ BC43 Steve Breaston RC	.60	1.50
❑ BC44 Le'Ron McClain RC	.60	1.50
❑ BC45 Joel Filani RC	.50	1.25
❑ BC46 Justise Hairston RC	.50	1.25
❑ BC47 Nate Ilaoa RC	.60	1.50
❑ BC48 Brett Ratliff RC	.60	1.50
❑ BC49 Roy Hall RC	.60	1.50
❑ BC50 Legedu Naanee RC	.60	1.50
❑ BC51 Jarrett Hicks RC	.50	1.25
❑ BC52 Sonny Shackelford RC	.50	1.25
❑ BC53 Jordan Kent RC	.50	1.25
❑ BC54 John Broussard RC	.50	1.25
❑ BC55 Chandler Williams RC	.50	1.25
❑ BC56 JaMarcus Russell RC	2.00	5.00
❑ BC57 Brady Quinn RC	3.00	8.00
❑ BC58 Drew Stanton RC	1.25	3.00
❑ BC59 Troy Smith RC	2.00	5.00
❑ BC60 Kevin Kolb RC	2.50	6.00
❑ BC61 Trent Edwards RC	2.50	6.00
❑ BC62 John Beck RC	1.50	4.00
❑ BC63 Jordan Palmer RC	1.50	4.00
❑ BC64 Chris Leak RC	1.25	3.00
❑ BC65 Adrian Peterson RC	12.00	30.00
❑ BC66 Marshawn Lynch RC	2.50	6.00
❑ BC67 Brandon Jackson RC	1.50	4.00

Card		
❑ BC68 Michael Bush RC	1.50	4.00
❑ BC69 Antonio Pittman RC	1.50	4.00
❑ BC70 Tony Hunt RC	1.50	4.00
❑ BC71 Lorenzo Booker RC	1.50	4.00
❑ BC72 Chris Henry RC	1.25	3.00
❑ BC73 Brian Leonard RC	1.25	3.00
❑ BC74 Garrett Wolfe RC	1.50	4.00
❑ BC75 Calvin Johnson RC	4.00	10.00
❑ BC76 Ted Ginn RC	2.50	6.00
❑ BC77 Dwayne Jarrett RC	1.50	4.00
❑ BC78 Dwayne Bowe RC	2.50	6.00
❑ BC79 Sidney Rice RC	3.00	8.00
❑ BC80 Robert Meachem RC	1.50	4.00
❑ BC81 Anthony Gonzalez RC	2.00	5.00
❑ BC82 Craig Buster Davis RC	1.50	4.00
❑ BC83 Aundrae Allison RC	1.25	3.00
❑ BC84 Chansi Stuckey RC	1.50	4.00
❑ BC85 Alan Branch RC	1.25	3.00
❑ BC86 Steve Smith USC RC	2.50	6.00
❑ BC87 Paul Williams RC	1.25	3.00
❑ BC88 Johnnie Lee Higgins RC	1.50	4.00
❑ BC89 Jason Hill RC	1.50	4.00
❑ BC90 Greg Olsen RC	2.00	5.00
❑ BC91 Yamon Figurs RC	1.00	2.50
❑ BC92 Gaines Adams RC	1.50	4.00
❑ BC93 Patrick Willis RC	2.50	6.00
❑ BC94 Joe Thomas RC	1.50	4.00
❑ BC95 Isaiah Stanback RC	1.50	4.00
❑ BC96 Paul Posluszny RC	2.00	5.00
❑ BC97 Jeff Rowe RC	1.25	3.00
❑ BC98 Zac Taylor RC	1.50	4.00
❑ BC99 Dwayne Wright RC	1.25	3.00
❑ BC100 Kenneth Darby RC	1.50	4.00
❑ BC101 Selvin Young RC	1.50	4.00
❑ BC102 Gary Russell RC	1.25	3.00
❑ BC103 Kolby Smith RC	1.50	4.00
❑ BC104 Dallas Baker RC	1.25	3.00
❑ BC105 Jacoby Jones RC	1.50	4.00
❑ BC106 Ryne Robinson RC	1.25	3.00
❑ BC107 Chris Davis RC	1.25	3.00
❑ BC108 Laron Landry RC	2.00	5.00
❑ BC109 Leon Hall RC	1.50	4.00
❑ BC110 Lawrence Timmons RC	1.50	4.00
❑ BC111 Matt Leinart	.40	1.00
❑ BC112 Jason Campbell	.30	.75
❑ BC113 J.P. Losman	.25	.60
❑ BC114 Rex Grossman	.30	.75
❑ BC115 Tony Romo	.60	1.50
❑ BC116 Brett Favre	.75	2.00
❑ BC117 Trent Green	.30	.75
❑ BC118 Drew Brees	.40	1.00
❑ BC119 Chad Pennington	.30	.75
❑ BC120 Ben Roethlisberger	.50	1.25
❑ BC121 Alex Smith QB	.40	1.00
❑ BC122 Marc Bulger	.30	.75
❑ BC123 Edgerrin James	.30	.75
❑ BC124 Jamal Lewis	.30	.75
❑ BC125 DeShaun Foster	.30	.75
❑ BC126 Cedric Benson	.30	.75
❑ BC127 Rudi Johnson	.30	.75
❑ BC128 Dominic Rhodes	.30	.75
❑ BC129 Fred Taylor	.30	.75
❑ BC130 Larry Johnson	.30	.75
❑ BC131 Chester Taylor	.25	.60
❑ BC132 Deuce McAllister	.30	.75
❑ BC133 Brandon Jacobs	.30	.75
❑ BC134 Willie Parker	.30	.75
❑ BC135 Frank Gore	.40	1.00
❑ BC136 Steven Jackson	.40	1.00
❑ BC137 Clinton Portis	.30	.75
❑ BC138 Anquan Boldin	.30	.75
❑ BC139 Derrick Mason	.25	.60
❑ BC140 Steve Smith	.30	.75
❑ BC141 Chad Johnson	.30	.75
❑ BC142 Braylon Edwards	.30	.75
❑ BC143 Terry Glenn	.30	.75
❑ BC144 Mike Furrey	.30	.75
❑ BC145 Donald Driver	.40	1.00
❑ BC146 Andre Johnson	.30	.75
❑ BC147 Marvin Harrison	.40	1.00
❑ BC148 Chris Chambers	.30	.75
❑ BC149 Devery Henderson	.25	.60
❑ BC150 Marques Colston	.40	1.00
❑ BC151 Amani Toomer	.30	.75
❑ BC152 Laveranues Coles	.30	.75
❑ BC153 Donte Stallworth	.30	.75
❑ BC154 Hines Ward	.40	1.00
❑ BC155 Keenan McCardell	.25	.60
❑ BC156 Arnaz Battle	.25	.60
❑ BC157 Deion Branch	.30	.75
❑ BC158 Kevin Curtis	.25	.60
❑ BC159 Isaac Bruce	.30	.75
❑ BC160 Santana Moss	.30	.75
❑ BC161 Kellen Winslow	.30	.75
❑ BC162 Jeremy Shockey	.30	.75
❑ BC163 Vernon Davis	.30	.75
❑ BC164 Travis Henry	.30	.75
❑ BC165 Todd Heap	.25	.60
❑ BC166 Matt Schaub	.30	.75
❑ BC167 Steve McNair	.30	.75
❑ BC168 Jake Delhomme	.30	.75
❑ BC169 Carson Palmer	.40	1.00
❑ BC170 Jay Cutler	.40	1.00
❑ BC171 Peyton Manning	.60	1.50
❑ BC172 Tom Brady	.75	2.00
❑ BC173 Eli Manning	.40	1.00
❑ BC174 Donovan Mcnabb	.40	1.00
❑ BC175 Philip Rivers	.40	1.00
❑ BC176 Matt Hasselbeck	.30	.75
❑ BC177 Vince Young	.40	1.00
❑ BC178 Warrick Dunn	.30	.75
❑ BC179 Willis McGahee	.30	.75
❑ BC180 DeAngelo Williams	.40	1.00
❑ BC181 Thomas Jones	.30	.75
❑ BC182 Julius Jones	.30	.75
❑ BC183 Joseph Addai	.40	1.00
❑ BC184 Maurice Jones-Drew	.40	1.00
❑ BC185 Ronnie Brown	.30	.75
❑ BC186 Laurence Maroney	.40	1.00
❑ BC187 Reggie Bush	.50	1.25
❑ BC188 Brian Westbrook	.30	.75
❑ BC189 LaDainian Tomlinson	.50	1.25
❑ BC190 Shaun Alexander	.30	.75
❑ BC191 Cadillac Williams	.30	.75
❑ BC192 Michael Turner	.40	1.00
❑ BC193 Larry Fitzgerald	.40	1.00
❑ BC194 Lee Evans	.30	.75
❑ BC195 Muhsin Muhammad	.30	.75
❑ BC196 T.J. Houshmandzadeh	.30	.75
❑ BC197 Terrell Owens	.40	1.00
❑ BC198 Javon Walker	.30	.75
❑ BC199 Roy Williams WR	.30	.75
❑ BC200 Greg Jennings	.30	.75
❑ BC201 Reggie Wayne	.30	.75
❑ BC202 Matt Jones	.30	.75
❑ BC203 Troy Williamson	.25	.60
❑ BC204 Joe Horn	.30	.75
❑ BC205 Plaxico Burress	.30	.75
❑ BC206 Jerricho Cotchery	.25	.60
❑ BC207 Randy Moss	.40	1.00
❑ BC208 Reggie Brown	.25	.60
❑ BC209 Santonio Holmes	.30	.75
❑ BC210 Eric Parker	.25	.60
❑ BC211 Antonio Bryant	.30	.75
❑ BC212 Darrell Jackson	.30	.75
❑ BC213 Torry Holt	.30	.75
❑ BC214 Antwaan Randle El	.25	.60
❑ BC215 Alge Crumpler	.30	.75
❑ BC216 Tony Gonzalez	.30	.75
❑ BC217 Antonio Gates	.30	.75
❑ BC218 Tarvaris Jackson	.30	.75
❑ BC219 Drew Bennett	.25	.60
❑ BC220 Byron Leftwich	.30	.75

2009 Bowman Chrome

Card		
❑ COMPLETE SET (165)	40.00	100.00
❑ 1 Drew Brees	.30	.75
❑ 2 Ben Roethlisberger	.50	1.25
❑ 3 Eli Manning	.30	.75
❑ 4 Tony Romo	.50	1.25
❑ 5 Philip Rivers	.30	.75
❑ 6 Aaron Rodgers	.30	.75
❑ 7 Marc Bulger	.25	.60
❑ 8 Jay Cutler	.30	.75
❑ 9 Matt Ryan	.30	.75
❑ 10 Tom Brady	.50	1.25
❑ 11 Carson Palmer	.30	.75
❑ 12 Peyton Manning	.50	1.25
❑ 13 Kerry Collins	.25	.60
❑ 14 Kurt Warner	.30	.75
❑ 15 Jason Campbell	.25	.60
❑ 16 Chad Pennington	.25	.60
❑ 17 Trent Edwards	.25	.60
❑ 18 Matt Schaub	.25	.60
❑ 19 Donovan McNabb	.30	.75
❑ 20 Jared Allen	.30	.75
❑ 21 Kyle Orton	.25	.60
❑ 22 JaMarcus Russell	.25	.60
❑ 23 Joe Flacco	.30	.75
❑ 24 Jake Delhomme	.25	.60
❑ 25 David Garrard	.25	.60
❑ 26 Matt Cassel	.25	.60
❑ 27 Derek Anderson	.25	.60
❑ 28 Steven Jackson	.25	.60
❑ 29 Clinton Portis	.25	.60
❑ 30 Adrian Peterson	.60	1.50
❑ 31 LaDainian Tomlinson	.30	.75
❑ 32 Marion Barber	.30	.75
❑ 33 Brian Westbrook	.25	.60
❑ 34 Frank Gore	.25	.60
❑ 35 Chris Johnson	.30	.75
❑ 36 Michael Turner	.25	.60
❑ 37 Brandon Jacobs	.25	.60
❑ 38 Steve Slaton	.25	.60
❑ 39 Matt Forte	.30	.75
❑ 40 Leon Washington	.25	.60
❑ 41 Fred Taylor	.25	.60
❑ 42 Joseph Addai	.30	.75
❑ 43 Willis McGahee	.25	.60
❑ 44 Marshawn Lynch	.25	.60
❑ 45 Thomas Jones	.25	.60
❑ 46 DeAngelo Williams	.30	.75
❑ 47 Earnest Graham	.20	.50
❑ 48 Jamal Lewis	.25	.60
❑ 49 John Carlson	.25	.60
❑ 50 Ryan Grant	.25	.60
❑ 51 Ronnie Brown	.25	.60
❑ 52 Jonathan Stewart	.25	.60
❑ 53 Kevin Boss	.20	.50
❑ 54 Darren McFadden	.30	.75
❑ 55 Maurice Jones-Drew	.25	.60
❑ 56 LenDale White	.25	.60
❑ 57 Pierre Thomas	.25	.60
❑ 58 LaMarr Woodley	.20	.50
❑ 59 Warrick Dunn	.25	.60
❑ 60 Sammy Morris	.20	.50
❑ 61 Reggie Bush	.30	.75
❑ 62 Kevin Smith	.25	.60
❑ 63 Ricky Williams	.25	.60
❑ 64 Felix Jones	.30	.75
❑ 65 Anquan Boldin	.25	.60
❑ 66 Andre Johnson	.25	.60
❑ 67 Larry Fitzgerald	.30	.75
❑ 68 Steve Smith	.25	.60
❑ 69 Greg Jennings	.30	.75
❑ 70 Santana Moss	.25	.60
❑ 71 Brandon Marshall	.25	.60
❑ 72 T.J. Houshmandzadeh	.25	.60
❑ 73 Eddie Royal	.25	.60
❑ 74 Chad Ochocinco	.25	.60
❑ 75 Troy Polamalu	.30	.75
❑ 76 Terrell Owens	.30	.75
❑ 77 Braylon Edwards	.25	.60
❑ 78 Randy Moss	.30	.75
❑ 79 Reggie Wayne	.25	.60
❑ 80 Wes Welker	.30	.75
❑ 81 Roddy White	.25	.60
❑ 82 Dwayne Bowe	.25	.60
❑ 83 Lance Moore	.25	.60
❑ 84 Tim Hightower	.25	.60
❑ 85 Antonio Bryant	.25	.60
❑ 86 Jerricho Cotchery	.20	.50
❑ 87 Laveranues Coles	.25	.60
❑ 88 Derrick Mason	.20	.50
❑ 89 Peyton Hillis	.20	.50
❑ 90 Greg Camarillo	.25	.60
❑ 91 DeSean Jackson	.25	.60
❑ 92 Ed Reed	.25	.60
❑ 93 Lee Evans	.25	.60
❑ 94 Hines Ward	.25	.60
❑ 95 Calvin Johnson	.30	.75
❑ 96 Steve Smith USC	.25	.60
❑ 97 Bernard Berrian	.25	.60
❑ 98 Chris Cooley	.25	.60

❑ 99 Tony Gonzalez	.25	.60
❑ 100 Kevin Walter	.25	.60
❑ 101 Antonio Gates	.25	.60
❑ 102 Jason Witten	.30	.75
❑ 103 Dallas Clark	.25	.60
❑ 104 Joey Porter	.25	.60
❑ 105 Patrick Willis	.25	.60
❑ 106 DeMarcus Ware	.25	.60
❑ 107 James Harrison	.30	.75
❑ 108 Charles Woodson	.25	.60
❑ 109 Oshiomogho Atogwe	.20	.50
❑ 110 Justin Tuck	.25	.60
❑ 111 Matthew Stafford RC	3.00	8.00
❑ 112 Josh Freeman RC	2.00	5.00
❑ 113 Nate Davis RC	1.00	2.50
❑ 114 Rhett Bomar RC	.75	2.00
❑ 115 Mark Sanchez RC	4.00	10.00
❑ 116 Chris Wells RC	2.50	6.00
❑ 117 Javon Ringer RC	1.00	2.50
❑ 118 Deon Butler RC	1.00	2.50
❑ 119 Brandon Pettigrew RC	1.25	3.00
❑ 120 LeSean McCoy RC	2.00	5.00
❑ 121 Darrius Heyward-Bey RC	1.50	4.00
❑ 122 Ramses Barden RC	.75	2.00
❑ 123 Derrick Williams RC	1.00	2.50
❑ 124 Hakeem Nicks RC	2.00	5.00
❑ 125 Aaron Curry RC	1.25	3.00
❑ 126 Patrick Turner RC	.75	2.00
❑ 127 Knowshon Moreno RC	2.50	6.00
❑ 128 Brian Robiskie RC	1.00	2.50
❑ 129 Stephen McGee RC	1.00	2.50
❑ 130 Kenny Britt RC	1.50	4.00
❑ 131 Mohamed Massaquoi RC	1.00	2.50
❑ 132 Donald Brown RC	2.00	5.00
❑ 133 Juaquin Iglesias RC	1.00	2.50
❑ 134 Andre Brown RC	.75	2.00
❑ 135 Michael Crabtree RC	2.50	6.00
❑ 136 Glen Coffee RC	1.25	3.00
❑ 137 Shonn Greene RC	2.00	5.00
❑ 138 Percy Harvin RC	3.00	8.00
❑ 139 Pat White RC	1.50	4.00
❑ 140 Jeremy Maclin RC	2.00	5.00
❑ 141 Jason Smith RC	.75	2.00
❑ 142 Tyson Jackson RC	1.00	2.50
❑ 143 Mike Wallace RC	2.00	5.00
❑ 144 Mike Thomas RC	1.00	2.50
❑ 145 B.J. Raji RC	1.25	3.00
❑ 146 Aaron Maybin RC	1.00	2.50
❑ 147 Brian Orakpo RC	1.25	3.00
❑ 148 Malcolm Jenkins RC	1.00	2.50
❑ 149 Brian Cushing RC	1.25	3.00
❑ 150 Brian Hartline RC	1.00	2.50
❑ 151 Mike Goodson RC	1.00	2.50
❑ 152 Louis Murphy RC	1.00	2.50
❑ 153 Austin Collie RC	2.00	5.00
❑ 154 Gartrell Johnson RC	.75	2.00
❑ 155 Johnny Knox RC	1.50	4.00
❑ 156 Kenny McKinley RC	1.00	2.50
❑ 157 Jarett Dillard RC	1.00	2.50
❑ 158 Brooks Foster RC	.75	2.00
❑ 159 Tom Brandstater RC	1.00	2.50
❑ 160 Mike Teel RC	1.00	2.50
❑ 161 Cedric Peerman RC	.75	2.00
❑ 162 Brandon Gibson RC	1.00	2.50
❑ 163 James Davis RC	1.00	2.50
❑ 164 Curtis Painter RC	1.00	2.50
❑ 165 Brandon Tate RC	.75	2.00

2009 Bowman Draft

❑ COMPLETE SET (220)	20.00	40.00
❑ 1 Drew Brees	.25	.60
❑ 2 Ben Roethlisberger	.40	1.00
❑ 3 Eli Manning	.25	.60
❑ 4 Tony Romo	.40	1.00
❑ 5 Philip Rivers	.25	.60
❑ 6 Aaron Rodgers	.25	.60
❑ 7 Brett Favre	.60	1.50
❑ 8 Jay Cutler	.25	.60
❑ 9 Matt Ryan	.25	.60
❑ 10 Tom Brady	.40	1.00
❑ 11 Carson Palmer	.25	.60
❑ 12 Peyton Manning	.40	1.00
❑ 13 Kerry Collins	.20	.50
❑ 14 Kurt Warner	.25	.60
❑ 15 Jason Campbell	.20	.50
❑ 16 Chad Pennington	.20	.50
❑ 17 Trent Edwards	.20	.50
❑ 18 Matt Schaub	.20	.50
❑ 19 Donovan McNabb	.25	.60
❑ 20 Jared Allen	.25	.60
❑ 21 Kyle Orton	.20	.50
❑ 22 JaMarcus Russell	.20	.50
❑ 23 Joe Flacco	.25	.60
❑ 24 Jake Delhomme	.20	.50
❑ 25 David Garrard	.20	.50
❑ 26 Matt Cassel	.20	.50
❑ 27 Derek Anderson	.20	.50
❑ 28 Steven Jackson	.20	.50
❑ 29 Clinton Portis	.20	.50
❑ 30 Adrian Peterson	.50	1.25
❑ 31 LaDainian Tomlinson	.25	.60
❑ 32 Marion Barber	.25	.60
❑ 33 Brian Westbrook	.20	.50
❑ 34 Frank Gore	.20	.50
❑ 35 Chris Johnson	.25	.60
❑ 36 Michael Turner	.20	.50
❑ 37 Brandon Jacobs	.20	.50
❑ 38 Steve Slaton	.20	.50
❑ 39 Matt Forte	.25	.60
❑ 40 Leon Washington	.20	.50
❑ 41 Fred Taylor	.20	.50
❑ 42 Joseph Addai	.25	.60
❑ 43 Willis McGahee	.20	.50
❑ 44 Marshawn Lynch	.20	.50
❑ 45 Thomas Jones	.20	.50
❑ 46 DeAngelo Williams	.25	.60
❑ 47 Earnest Graham	.15	.40
❑ 48 Jamal Lewis	.20	.50
❑ 49 John Carlson	.20	.50
❑ 50 Ryan Grant	.20	.50
❑ 51 Ronnie Brown	.20	.50
❑ 52 Jonathan Stewart	.20	.50
❑ 53 Kevin Boss	.15	.40
❑ 54 Darren McFadden	.25	.60
❑ 55 Maurice Jones-Drew	.20	.50
❑ 56 LenDale White	.20	.50
❑ 57 Pierre Thomas	.20	.50
❑ 58 LaMarr Woodley	.15	.40
❑ 59 Warrick Dunn	.20	.50
❑ 60 Sammy Morris	.15	.40
❑ 61 Reggie Bush	.25	.60
❑ 62 Kevin Smith	.20	.50
❑ 63 Ricky Williams	.20	.50
❑ 64 Felix Jones	.25	.60
❑ 65 Anquan Boldin	.20	.50
❑ 66 Andre Johnson	.20	.50
❑ 67 Larry Fitzgerald	.25	.60
❑ 68 Steve Smith	.20	.50
❑ 69 Greg Jennings	.25	.60
❑ 70 Santana Moss	.20	.50
❑ 71 Brandon Marshall	.20	.50
❑ 72 T.J. Houshmandzadeh	.20	.50
❑ 73 Eddie Royal	.20	.50
❑ 74 Chad Johnson	.20	.50
❑ 75 Troy Polamalu	.25	.60
❑ 76 Terrell Owens	.25	.60
❑ 77 Braylon Edwards	.20	.50
❑ 78 Randy Moss	.25	.60
❑ 79 Reggie Wayne	.20	.50
❑ 80 Wes Welker	.25	.60
❑ 81 Roddy White	.20	.50
❑ 82 Dwayne Bowe	.20	.50
❑ 83 Lance Moore	.20	.50
❑ 84 Tim Hightower	.20	.50
❑ 85 Antonio Bryant	.20	.50
❑ 86 Jerricho Cotchery	.15	.40
❑ 87 Laveranues Coles	.20	.50
❑ 88 Derrick Mason	.15	.40
❑ 89 Peyton Hillis	.15	.40
❑ 90 Greg Camarillo	.20	.50
❑ 91 DeSean Jackson	.20	.50
❑ 92 Ed Reed	.20	.50
❑ 93 Lee Evans	.20	.50
❑ 94 Hines Ward	.20	.50
❑ 95 Calvin Johnson	.25	.60
❑ 96 Steve Smith USC	.20	.50
❑ 97 Bernard Berrian	.20	.50
❑ 98 Chris Cooley	.20	.50
❑ 99 Tony Gonzalez	.20	.50
❑ 100 Kevin Walter	.20	.50
❑ 101 Antonio Gates	.20	.50
❑ 102 Jason Witten	.25	.60
❑ 103 Dallas Clark	.20	.50
❑ 104 Joey Porter	.20	.50
❑ 105 Patrick Willis	.20	.50
❑ 106 DeMarcus Ware	.20	.50
❑ 107 James Harrison	.25	.60
❑ 108 Charles Woodson	.20	.50
❑ 109 Oshiomogho Atogwe	.15	.40
❑ 110 Justin Tuck	.20	.50
❑ 111 Matthew Stafford RC	2.00	5.00
❑ 112 Brian Orakpo RC	.75	2.00
❑ 113 Michael Oher RC	1.25	3.00
❑ 114 Michael Crabtree RC	1.50	4.00
❑ 115 Andre Smith RC	.60	1.50
❑ 116 Knowshon Moreno RC	1.50	4.00
❑ 117 Aaron Curry RC	.75	2.00
❑ 118 Gartrell Johnson RC	.50	1.25
❑ 119 Jason Smith RC	.50	1.25
❑ 120 James Laurinaitis RC	.75	2.00
❑ 121 Chris Wells RC	1.50	4.00
❑ 122 Glen Coffee RC	.75	2.00
❑ 123 Eugene Monroe RC	.50	1.25
❑ 124 Rey Maualuga RC	1.00	2.50
❑ 125 Malcolm Jenkins RC	.60	1.50
❑ 126 Michael Johnson RC	.40	1.00
❑ 127 Javon Ringer RC	.60	1.50
❑ 128 B.J. Raji RC	.75	2.00
❑ 129 Donald Brown RC	1.25	3.00
❑ 130 Clint Sintim RC	.60	1.50
❑ 131 Brian Cushing RC	.75	2.00
❑ 132 Brandon Pettigrew RC	.75	2.00
❑ 133 Alphonso Smith RC	.50	1.25
❑ 134 Vontae Davis RC	.60	1.50
❑ 135 Jeremy Maclin RC	1.25	3.00
❑ 136 John Parker Wilson RC	.60	1.50
❑ 137 Peria Jerry RC	.50	1.25
❑ 138 Chase Coffman RC	.50	1.25
❑ 139 Darius Butler RC	.60	1.50
❑ 140 Jamon Meredith RC	.50	1.25
❑ 141 Alex Mack RC	.50	1.25
❑ 142 Jarett Dillard RC	.60	1.50
❑ 143 Mike Mickens RC	.50	1.25
❑ 144 William Moore RC	.50	1.25
❑ 145 Austin Collie RC	1.25	3.00
❑ 146 Fili Moala RC	.50	1.25
❑ 147 Percy Harvin RC	2.00	5.00
❑ 148 Jared Cook Jr. RC	.50	1.25
❑ 149 Rashad Jennings RC	.60	1.50
❑ 150 Rhett Bomar RC	.50	1.25
❑ 151 Sen'Derrick Marks RC	.40	1.00
❑ 152 Duke Robinson RC	.40	1.00
❑ 153 Everette Brown RC	.60	1.50
❑ 154 Darrius Heyward-Bey RC	1.00	2.50
❑ 155 Jeremy Childs RC	.50	1.25
❑ 156 Darius Passmore RC	.50	1.25
❑ 157 Brooks Foster RC	.50	1.25
❑ 158 Tyson Jackson RC	.60	1.50
❑ 159 James Casey RC	.50	1.25
❑ 160 Marcus Freeman RC	.60	1.50
❑ 161 Max Unger RC	.50	1.25
❑ 162 Josh Freeman RC	1.25	3.00
❑ 163 Victor Harris RC	.60	1.50
❑ 164 Derrick Williams RC	.60	1.50
❑ 165 Jonathan Luigs RC	.40	1.00
❑ 166 Graham Harrell RC	.60	1.50
❑ 167 Pat White RC	1.00	2.50
❑ 168 Chase Daniel RC	.75	2.00
❑ 169 Mike Goodson RC	.60	1.50
❑ 170 LeSean McCoy RC	1.25	3.00
❑ 171 James Davis RC	.60	1.50
❑ 172 Ramses Barden RC	.50	1.25
❑ 173 Juaquin Iglesias RC	.60	1.50
❑ 174 Cedric Peerman RC	.50	1.25
❑ 175 Kenny Britt RC	1.00	2.50
❑ 176 Marlon Lucky RC	.50	1.25
❑ 177 Mohamed Massaquoi RC	.60	1.50
❑ 178 Louis Murphy RC	.60	1.50
❑ 179 Tyrell Sutton RC	.50	1.25
❑ 180 Andre Brown RC	.50	1.25
❑ 181 Brandon Tate RC	.50	1.25
❑ 182 Kory Sheets RC	.50	1.25
❑ 183 Arian Foster RC	.60	1.50
❑ 184 Demetrius Byrd RC	.50	1.25
❑ 185 Hunter Cantwell RC	.60	1.50
❑ 186 Brandon Gibson RC	.60	1.50
❑ 187 Brian Robiskie RC	.60	1.50
❑ 188 Dannell Ellerbe RC	.50	1.25
❑ 189 Cornelius Ingram RC	.40	1.00
❑ 190 Mark Sanchez RC	2.50	6.00
❑ 191 Kenny McKinley RC	.60	1.50
❑ 192 Travis Beckum RC	.50	1.25
❑ 193 Jeremiah Johnson RC	.60	1.50
❑ 194 P.J. Hill RC	.50	1.25
❑ 195 Deon Butler RC	.60	1.50
❑ 196 Clay Matthews RC	1.00	2.50
❑ 197 Patrick Chung RC	.60	1.50
❑ 198 Patrick Turner RC	.50	1.25

Card		
❑ 199 Darry Beckwith RC	.50	1.25
❑ 200 Nate Davis RC	.60	1.50
❑ 201 Stephen McGee RC	.60	1.50
❑ 202 Aaron Kelly RC	.50	1.25
❑ 203 Ian Johnson RC	.60	1.50
❑ 204 Brian Hoyer RC	.60	1.50
❑ 205 Shonn Greene RC	1.25	3.00
❑ 206 Sammie Stroughter RC	.60	1.50
❑ 207 Cullen Harper RC	.60	1.50
❑ 208 Devin Moore RC	.50	1.25
❑ 209 Quan Cosby RC	.50	1.25
❑ 210 Hakeem Nicks RC	1.25	3.00
❑ 211 Kevin Ellison RC	.50	1.25
❑ 212 Phil Loadholt RC	.50	1.25
❑ 213 Scott McKillop RC	.50	1.25
❑ 214 Brad Lester RC	.40	1.00
❑ 215 Michael Hamlin RC	.50	1.25
❑ 216 Fenuki Tupou RC	.40	1.00
❑ 217 Terrance Taylor RC	.60	1.50
❑ 218 Zack Follett RC	.40	1.00
❑ 219 Aaron Maybin RC	.60	1.50
❑ 220 Worrell Williams RC	.50	1.25

1995 Bowman's Best

Card		
❑ COMPLETE SET (180)	40.00	100.00
❑ R1 Ki-Jana Carter RC	.60	1.50
❑ R2 Tony Boselli RC	.60	1.50
❑ R3 Steve McNair RC	6.00	15.00
❑ R4 Michael Westbrook RC	.60	1.50
❑ R5 Kerry Collins RC	2.50	6.00
❑ R6 Kevin Carter RC	.60	1.50
❑ R7 Mike Mamula RC	.15	.40
❑ R8 Joey Galloway RC	2.50	6.00
❑ R9 Kyle Brady RC	.60	1.50
❑ R10 Ray McElroy RC	.15	.40
❑ R11 Derrick Alexander DE RC	.15	.40
❑ R12 Warren Sapp RC	2.50	6.00
❑ R13 Mark Fields RC	.60	1.50
❑ R14 Ruben Brown RC	.60	1.50
❑ R15 Ellis Johnson RC	.15	.40
❑ R16 Hugh Douglas RC	.60	1.50
❑ R17 Alundis Brice RC	.15	.40
❑ R18 Napoleon Kaufman RC	2.00	5.00
❑ R19 James O. Stewart RC	1.25	3.00
❑ R20 Luther Elliss RC	.15	.40
❑ R21 Rashaan Salaam RC	.30	.75
❑ R22 Tyrone Poole RC	.60	1.50
❑ R23 Ty Law RC	1.50	4.00
❑ R24 Korey Stringer RC	.50	1.25
❑ R25 Billy Milner RC	.15	.40
❑ R26 Roell Preston RC	.30	.75
❑ R27 Mark Bruener RC	.30	.75
❑ R28 Derrick Brooks RC	2.50	6.00
❑ R29 Blake Brockermeyer RC	.15	.40
❑ R30 Mike Frederick RC	.15	.40
❑ R31 Trezelle Jenkins RC	.15	.40
❑ R32 Craig Newsome RC	.15	.40
❑ R33 Matt O'Dwyer RC	.15	.40
❑ R34 Terrance Shaw RC	.15	.40
❑ R35 Anthony Cook RC	.15	.40
❑ R36 Darick Holmes RC	.30	.75
❑ R37 Cory Raymer RC	.15	.40
❑ R38 Zach Wiegert RC	.15	.40
❑ R39 Sam Shade RC	.15	.40
❑ R40 Brian DeMarco RC	.15	.40
❑ R41 Ron Davis RC	.15	.40
❑ R42 Orlando Thomas RC	.15	.40
❑ R43 Derek West RC	.15	.40
❑ R44 Ray Zellars RC	.30	.75
❑ R45 Todd Collins RC	2.00	5.00
❑ R46 Linc Harden RC	.15	.40
❑ R47 Frank Sanders RC	.60	1.50
❑ R48 Ken Dilger RC	.60	1.50
❑ R49 Barrett Robbins RC	.15	.40
❑ R50 Bobby Taylor RC	1.00	2.50
❑ R51 Terrell Fletcher RC	.15	.40
❑ R52 Jack Jackson RC	.15	.40
❑ R53 Jeff Kopp RC	.15	.40
❑ R54 Brendan Stai RC	.15	.40
❑ R55 Corey Fuller RC	.15	.40
❑ R56 Todd Sauerbrun RC	.15	.40
❑ R57 Dameian Jeffries RC	.15	.40
❑ R58 Troy Dumas RC	.15	.40
❑ R59 Charlie Williams RC	.15	.40
❑ R60 Kordell Stewart RC	2.50	6.00
❑ R61 Jay Barker RC	.15	.40
❑ R62 Jesse James RC	.15	.40
❑ R63 Shane Hannah RC	.15	.40
❑ R64 Rob Johnson RC	1.50	4.00
❑ R65 Darius Holland RC	.15	.40
❑ R66 William Henderson RC	2.00	5.00
❑ R67 Chris Sanders RC	.30	.75
❑ R68 Darryl Pounds RC	.15	.40
❑ R69 Melvin Tuten RC	.15	.40
❑ R70 David Sloan RC	.15	.40
❑ R71 Chris Hudson RC	.15	.40
❑ R72 William Strong RC	.15	.40
❑ R73 Brian Williams LB RC	.15	.40
❑ R74 Curtis Martin RC	6.00	15.00
❑ R75 Mike Verstegen RC	.15	.40
❑ R76 Justin Armour RC	.15	.40
❑ R77 Lorenzo Styles RC	.15	.40
❑ R78 Oliver Gibson RC	.15	.40
❑ R79 Zack Crockett RC	.30	.75
❑ R80 Tau Pupua RC	.15	.40
❑ R81 Tamarick Vanover RC	.60	1.50
❑ R82 Steve McLaughlin RC	.15	.40
❑ R83 Sean Harris RC	.15	.40
❑ R84 Eric Zeier RC	.60	1.50
❑ R85 Rodney Young RC	.15	.40
❑ R86 Chad May RC	.15	.40
❑ R87 Evan Pilgrim RC	.15	.40
❑ R88 James A.Stewart RC	.15	.40
❑ R89 Torey Hunter RC	.15	.40
❑ R90 Antonio Freeman RC	1.50	4.00
❑ V1 Rob Moore	.25	.60
❑ V2 Craig Heyward	.25	.60
❑ V3 Jim Kelly	.50	1.25
❑ V4 John Kasay	.10	.30
❑ V5 Jeff Graham	.10	.30
❑ V6 Jeff Blake RC	1.00	2.50
❑ V7 Antonio Langham	.10	.30
❑ V8 Troy Aikman	1.25	3.00
❑ V9 Simon Fletcher	.10	.30
❑ V10 Barry Sanders	2.00	5.00
❑ V11 Edgar Bennett	.25	.60
❑ V12 Ray Childress	.10	.30
❑ V13 Ray Buchanan	.10	.30
❑ V14 Desmond Howard	.25	.60
❑ V15 Dale Carter	.25	.60
❑ V16 Troy Vincent	.10	.30
❑ V17 David Palmer	.25	.60
❑ V18 Ben Coates	.25	.60
❑ V19 Derek Brown TE	.10	.30
❑ V20 Dave Brown	.25	.60
❑ V21 Mo Lewis	.10	.30
❑ V22 Harvey Williams	.10	.30
❑ V23 Randall Cunningham	.50	1.25
❑ V24 Kevin Greene	.25	.60
❑ V25 Junior Seau	.50	1.25
❑ V26 Merton Hanks	.10	.30
❑ V27 Cortez Kennedy	.25	.60
❑ V28 Troy Drayton	.10	.30
❑ V29 Hardy Nickerson	.10	.30
❑ V30 Brian Mitchell	.10	.30
❑ V31 Raymont Harris	.10	.30
❑ V32 Keith Goganious	.10	.30
❑ V33 Andre Reed	.25	.60
❑ V34 Terance Mathis	.25	.60
❑ V35 Garrison Hearst	.50	1.25
❑ V36 Glyn Milburn	.10	.30
❑ V37 Emmitt Smith	2.00	5.00
❑ V38 Vinny Testaverde	.25	.60
❑ V39 Darnay Scott	.25	.60
❑ V40 Mickey Washington	.10	.30
❑ V41 Craig Erickson	.10	.30
❑ V42 Chris Chandler	.50	1.25
❑ V43 Brett Favre	2.50	6.00
❑ V44 Scott Mitchell	.25	.60
❑ V45 Chris Slade	.10	.30
❑ V46 Warren Moon	.25	.60
❑ V47 Dan Marino	2.50	6.00
❑ V48 Greg Hill	.25	.60
❑ V49 Rocket Ismail	.25	.60
❑ V50 Bobby Houston	.10	.30
❑ V51 Rodney Hampton	.25	.60
❑ V52 Jim Everett	.10	.30
❑ V53 Rick Mirer	.25	.60
❑ V54 Steve Young	1.00	2.50
❑ V55 Dennis Gibson	.10	.30
❑ V56 Rod Woodson	.25	.60
❑ V57 Calvin Williams	.25	.60
❑ V58 Tom Carter	.10	.30
❑ V59 Trent Dilfer	.50	1.25
❑ V60 Shane Conlan	.10	.30
❑ V61 Cornelius Bennett	.25	.60
❑ V62 Eric Metcalf	.25	.60
❑ V63 Frank Reich	.10	.30
❑ V64 Eric Hill	.10	.30
❑ V65 Erik Kramer	.10	.30
❑ V66 Michael Irvin	.50	1.25
❑ V67 Tony McGee	.10	.30
❑ V68 Andre Rison	.25	.60
❑ V69 Shannon Sharpe	.25	.60
❑ V70 Quentin Coryatt	.25	.60
❑ V71 Robert Brooks	.50	1.25
❑ V72 Steve Beuerlein	.25	.60
❑ V73 Herman Moore	.50	1.25
❑ V74 Jack Del Rio	.10	.30
❑ V75 Dave Meggett	.10	.30
❑ V76 Pete Stoyanovich	.10	.30
❑ V77 Neil Smith	.25	.60
❑ V78 Corey Miller	.10	.30
❑ V79 Tim Brown	.50	1.25
❑ V80 Tyrone Hughes	.25	.60
❑ V81 Boomer Esiason	.25	.60
❑ V82 Natrone Means	.25	.60
❑ V83 Chris Warren	.25	.60
❑ V84 Byron Bam Morris	.10	.30
❑ V85 Jerry Rice	1.25	3.00
❑ V86 Michael Zordich	.10	.30
❑ V87 Errict Rhett	.25	.60
❑ V88 Henry Ellard	.25	.60
❑ V89 Chris Miller	.10	.30
❑ V90 John Elway	2.50	6.00

1996 Bowman's Best

Card		
❑ COMPLETE SET (180)	40.00	80.00
❑ 1 Emmitt Smith	1.25	3.00
❑ 2 Kordell Stewart	.30	.75
❑ 3 Mark Chmura	.20	.50
❑ 4 Sean Dawkins	.10	.30
❑ 5 Steve Young	.60	1.50
❑ 6 Tamarick Vanover	.20	.50
❑ 7 Scott Mitchell	.20	.50
❑ 8 Aaron Hayden	.10	.30
❑ 9 William Thomas	.10	.30
❑ 10 Dan Marino	1.50	4.00
❑ 11 Curtis Conway	.30	.75
❑ 12 Steve Atwater	.10	.30
❑ 13 Derrick Brooks	.30	.75
❑ 14 Rick Mirer	.20	.50
❑ 15 Mark Brunell	.40	1.00
❑ 16 Garrison Hearst	.20	.50
❑ 17 Eric Turner	.10	.30
❑ 18 Mark Carrier WR	.10	.30
❑ 19 Darnay Scott	.20	.50
❑ 20 Steve McNair	.60	1.50
❑ 21 Jim Everett	.10	.30
❑ 22 Wayne Chrebet	.40	1.00
❑ 23 Ben Coates	.20	.50
❑ 24 Harvey Williams	.10	.30
❑ 25 Michael Westbrook	.30	.75
❑ 26 Kevin Carter	.10	.30
❑ 27 Dave Brown	.10	.30
❑ 28 Jake Reed	.20	.50
❑ 29 Thurman Thomas	.30	.75
❑ 30 Jeff George	.20	.50
❑ 31 Carnell Lake	.10	.30
❑ 32 J.J. Stokes	.30	.75
❑ 33 Jay Novacek	.10	.30

Card	Low	High
☐ 34 Brett Perriman	.10	.30
☐ 35 Robert Brooks	.30	.75
☐ 36 Neil Smith	.20	.50
☐ 37 Chris Zorich	.10	.30
☐ 38 Micheal Barrow	.10	.30
☐ 39 Quentin Coryatt	.10	.30
☐ 40 Kerry Collins	.30	.75
☐ 41 Aeneas Williams	.10	.30
☐ 42 James O.Stewart	.20	.50
☐ 43 Warren Moon	.20	.50
☐ 44 Willie McGinest	.10	.30
☐ 45 Rodney Hampton	.20	.50
☐ 46 Jeff Hostetler	.10	.30
☐ 47 Darrell Green	.10	.30
☐ 48 Warren Sapp	.10	.30
☐ 49 Troy Drayton	.10	.30
☐ 50 Junior Seau	.30	.75
☐ 51 Mike Mamula	.10	.30
☐ 52 Antonio Langham	.10	.30
☐ 53 Eric Metcalf	.10	.30
☐ 54 Adrian Murrell	.20	.50
☐ 55 Joey Galloway	.30	.75
☐ 56 Anthony Miller	.20	.50
☐ 57 Carl Pickens	.20	.50
☐ 58 Bruce Smith	.20	.50
☐ 59 Merton Hanks	.10	.30
☐ 60 Troy Aikman	.75	2.00
☐ 61 Erik Kramer	.10	.30
☐ 62 Tyrone Poole	.10	.30
☐ 63 Michael Jackson	.20	.50
☐ 64 Rob Moore	.20	.50
☐ 65 Marcus Allen	.30	.75
☐ 66 Orlando Thomas	.10	.30
☐ 67 Dave Meggett	.10	.30
☐ 68 Trent Dilfer	.30	.75
☐ 69 Herman Moore	.20	.50
☐ 70 Brett Favre	1.50	4.00
☐ 71 Blaine Bishop	.10	.30
☐ 72 Eric Allen	.10	.30
☐ 73 Bernie Parmalee	.10	.30
☐ 74 Kyle Brady	.10	.30
☐ 75 Terry McDaniel	.10	.30
☐ 76 Rodney Peete	.10	.30
☐ 77 Yancey Thigpen	.20	.50
☐ 78 Stan Humphries	.20	.50
☐ 79 Craig Heyward	.10	.30
☐ 80 Rashaan Salaam	.20	.50
☐ 81 Shannon Sharpe	.20	.50
☐ 82 Jim Harbaugh	.20	.50
☐ 83 Vinnie Clark	.10	.30
☐ 84 Steve Bono	.10	.30
☐ 85 Drew Bledsoe	.40	1.00
☐ 86 Ken Norton	.10	.30
☐ 87 Brian Mitchell	.10	.30
☐ 88 Hardy Nickerson	.10	.30
☐ 89 Todd Lyght	.10	.30
☐ 90 Barry Sanders	1.25	3.00
☐ 91 Robert Blackmon	.10	.00
☐ 92 Larry Centers	.20	.50
☐ 93 Jim Kelly	.30	.75
☐ 94 Lamar Lathon	.10	.30
☐ 95 Cris Carter	.30	.75
☐ 96 Hugh Douglas	.20	.50
☐ 97 Michael Strahan	.20	.50
☐ 98 Lee Woodall	.10	.30
☐ 99 Michael Irvin	.30	.75
☐ 100 Marshall Faulk	.40	1.00
☐ 101 Terance Mathis	.10	.30
☐ 102 Eric Zeier	.10	.30
☐ 103 Marty Carter	.10	.30
☐ 104 Steve Tovar	.10	.30
☐ 105 Isaac Bruce	.30	.75
☐ 106 Tony Martin	.20	.50
☐ 107 Dale Carter	.10	.30
☐ 108 Terry Kirby	.20	.50
☐ 109 Tyrone Hughes	.10	.30
☐ 110 Bryce Paup	.10	.30
☐ 111 Errict Rhett	.20	.50
☐ 112 Ricky Watters	.20	.50
☐ 113 Chris Chandler	.20	.50
☐ 114 Edgar Bennett	.20	.50
☐ 115 John Elway	1.50	4.00
☐ 116 Sam Mills	.10	.30
☐ 117 Seth Joyner	.10	.30
☐ 118 Jeff Lageman	.10	.30
☐ 119 Chris Calloway	.10	.30
☐ 120 Curtis Martin	.00	1.50
☐ 121 Ken Harvey	.10	.30
☐ 122 Eugene Daniel	.10	.30
☐ 123 Tim Brown	.30	.75
☐ 124 Mo Lewis	.10	.30
☐ 125 Jeff Blake	.30	.75
☐ 126 Jessie Tuggle	.10	.30
☐ 127 Vinny Testaverde	.20	.50
☐ 128 Chris Warren	.20	.50
☐ 129 Terrell Davis	.60	1.50
☐ 130 Greg Lloyd	.20	.50
☐ 131 Deion Sanders	.40	1.00
☐ 132 Derrick Thomas	.30	.75
☐ 133 Darryll Lewis	.10	.30
☐ 134 Reggie White	.30	.75
☐ 135 Jerry Rice	.75	2.00
☐ 136 Tony Banks RC	.30	.75
☐ 137 Derrick Mayes RC	.30	.75
☐ 138 Leeland McElroy RC	.20	.50
☐ 139 Bryan Still RC	.20	.50
☐ 140 Tim Biakabutuka RC	.30	.75
☐ 141 Rickey Dudley RC	.30	.75
☐ 142 Tory James RC	.20	.50
☐ 143 Lawyer Milloy RC	.50	1.25
☐ 144 Mike Ulufale RC	.10	.30
☐ 145 Bobby Engram RC	.30	.75
☐ 146 Willie Anderson RC	.10	.30
☐ 147 Terrell Owens RC	6.00	15.00
☐ 148 Jonathan Ogden RC	.30	.75
☐ 149 Darrius Johnson RC	.10	.30
☐ 150 Kevin Hardy RC	.30	.75
☐ 151 Simeon Rice RC	.60	1.50
☐ 152 Alex Molden RC	.10	.30
☐ 153 Cedric Jones RC	.10	.30
☐ 154 Duane Clemons RC	.10	.30
☐ 155 Karim Abdul-Jabbar RC	.30	.75
☐ 156 Dedric Mathis RC	.10	.30
☐ 157 John Michels RC	.10	.30
☐ 158 Winslow Oliver RC	.10	.30
☐ 159 Stepfret Williams RC	.10	.30
☐ 160 Eddie Kennison RC	.30	.75
☐ 161 Marcus Coleman RC	.10	.30
☐ 162 Tedy Bruschi RC	7.50	20.00
☐ 163 Detron Smith RC	.10	.30
☐ 164 Ray Lewis RC	12.50	25.00
☐ 165 Marvin Harrison RC	6.00	15.00
☐ 166 Je'rod Cherry RC	.10	.30
☐ 167 Jerris McPhail RC	.10	.30
☐ 168 Eric Moulds RC	2.00	5.00
☐ 169 Walt Harris RC	.10	.30
☐ 170 Eddie George RC	3.00	8.00
☐ 171 Jermaine Lewis RC	.30	.75
☐ 172 Jeff Lewis RC	.20	.50
☐ 173 Ray Mickens RC	.10	.30
☐ 174 Amani Toomer RC	2.00	5.00
☐ 175 Zach Thomas RC	1.25	3.00
☐ 176 Lawrence Phillips RC	.20	.50
☐ 177 John Mobley RC	.10	.30
☐ 178 Anthony Dorsett RC	.10	.30
☐ 179 DeRon Jenkins RC	.10	.30
☐ 180 Keyshawn Johnson RC	2.50	6.00

1997 Bowman's Best

Card	Low	High
☐ COMPLETE SET (125)	12.50	30.00
☐ 1 Brett Favre	1.50	4.00
☐ 2 Larry Centers	.25	.60
☐ 3 Trent Dilfer	.40	1.00
☐ 4 Rodney Hampton	.25	.60
☐ 5 Wesley Walls	.25	.60
☐ 6 Jerome Bettis	.40	1.00
☐ 7 Keyshawn Johnson	.40	1.00
☐ 8 Keenan McCardell	.25	.60
☐ 9 Terry Allen	.40	1.00
☐ 10 Troy Aikman	.75	2.00
☐ 11 Tony Banks	.25	.60
☐ 12 Ty Detmer	.25	.60
☐ 13 Chris Chandler	.25	.60
☐ 14 Marshall Faulk	.50	1.25
☐ 15 Heath Shuler	.15	.40
☐ 16 Stan Humphries	.25	.60
☐ 17 Bryan Cox	.15	.40
☐ 18 Chris Spielman	.15	.40
☐ 19 Derrick Thomas	.40	1.00
☐ 20 Steve Young	.50	1.25
☐ 21 Desmond Howard	.25	.60
☐ 22 Jeff Blake	.25	.60
☐ 23 Michael Jackson	.25	.60
☐ 24 Cris Carter	.40	1.00
☐ 25 Joey Galloway	.25	.60
☐ 26 Simeon Rice	.25	.60
☐ 27 Reggie White	.40	1.00
☐ 28 Dave Brown	.15	.40
☐ 29 Mike Alstott	.40	1.00
☐ 30 Emmitt Smith	1.25	3.00
☐ 31 Anthony Johnson	.15	.40
☐ 32 Mark Brunell	.50	1.25
☐ 33 Ricky Watters	.25	.60
☐ 34 Terrell Davis	.50	1.25
☐ 35 Ben Coates	.25	.60
☐ 36 Gus Frerotte	.15	.40
☐ 37 Andre Reed	.25	.60
☐ 38 Isaac Bruce	.40	1.00
☐ 39 Junior Seau	.40	1.00
☐ 40 Eddie George	.40	1.00
☐ 41 Adrian Murrell	.25	.60
☐ 42 Jake Reed	.25	.60
☐ 43 Karim Abdul-Jabbar	.25	.60
☐ 44 Scott Mitchell	.25	.60
☐ 45 Ki-Jana Carter	.15	.40
☐ 46 Curtis Conway	.25	.60
☐ 47 Jim Harbaugh	.25	.60
☐ 48 Tim Brown	.40	1.00
☐ 49 Mario Bates	.15	.40
☐ 50 Jerry Rice	.75	2.00
☐ 51 Byron Bam Morris	.15	.40
☐ 52 Marcus Allen	.40	1.00
☐ 53 Errict Rhett	.15	.40
☐ 54 Steve McNair	.50	1.25
☐ 55 Kerry Collins	.40	1.00
☐ 56 Bert Emanuel	.25	.60
☐ 57 Curtis Martin	.50	1.25
☐ 58 Bryce Paup	.15	.40
☐ 59 Brad Johnson	.40	1.00
☐ 60 John Elway	1.50	4.00
☐ 61 Natrone Means	.25	.60
☐ 62 Deion Sanders	.40	1.00
☐ 63 Tony Martin	.25	.60
☐ 64 Michael Westbrook	.25	.60
☐ 65 Chris Calloway	.15	.40
☐ 66 Antonio Freeman	.40	1.00
☐ 67 Rob Johnson	.40	1.00
☐ 68 Kent Graham	.15	.40
☐ 69 O.J. McDuffie	.25	.60
☐ 70 Barry Sanders	1.25	3.00
☐ 71 Chris Warren	.25	.60
☐ 72 Kordell Stewart	.40	1.00
☐ 73 Thurman Thomas	.40	1.00
☐ 74 Marvin Harrison	.40	1.00
☐ 75 Carl Pickens	.25	.60
☐ 76 Brent Jones	.15	.40
☐ 77 Irving Fryar	.25	.60
☐ 78 Neil O'Donnell	.25	.60
☐ 79 Elvis Grbac	.25	.60
☐ 80 Drew Bledsoe	.50	1.25
☐ 81 Shannon Sharpe	.25	.60
☐ 82 Vinny Testaverde	.25	.60
☐ 83 Chris Sanders	.15	.40
☐ 84 Herman Moore	.25	.60
☐ 85 Jeff George	.25	.60
☐ 86 Bruce Smith	.25	.60
☐ 87 Robert Smith	.25	.60
☐ 88 Kevin Hardy	.15	.40
☐ 89 Kevin Greene	.25	.60
☐ 90 Dan Marino	1.50	4.00
☐ 91 Michael Irvin	.40	1.00
☐ 92 Garrison Hearst	.25	.60
☐ 93 Lake Dawson	.15	.40
☐ 94 Lawrence Phillips	.15	.40
☐ 95 Terry Glenn	.40	1.00
☐ 96 Jake Plummer RC	2.50	6.00
☐ 97 Byron Hanspard RC	.25	.60
☐ 98 Bryant Westbrook RC	.15	.40
☐ 99 Troy Davis RC	.25	.60
☐ 100 Danny Wuerffel RC	.40	1.00
☐ 101 Tony Gonzalez RC	1.50	4.00
☐ 102 Jim Druckenmiller RC	.25	.60
☐ 103 Kevin Lockett RC	.25	.60
☐ 104 Renaldo Wynn RC	.15	.40

Card	Low	High
❑ 105 James Farrior RC	.40	1.00
❑ 106 Rae Carruth RC	.15	.40
❑ 107 Tom Knight RC	.15	.40
❑ 108 Corey Dillon RC	3.00	8.00
❑ 109 Kenny Holmes RC	.40	1.00
❑ 110 Orlando Pace RC	.40	1.00
❑ 111 Reidel Anthony RC	.40	1.00
❑ 112 Chad Scott RC	.25	.60
❑ 113 Antowain Smith RC	1.25	3.00
❑ 114 David LaFleur RC	.15	.40
❑ 115 Yatil Green RC	.25	.60
❑ 116 Darrell Russell RC	.15	.40
❑ 117 Joey Kent RC	.40	1.00
❑ 118 Darnell Autry RC	.25	.60
❑ 119 Peter Boulware RC	.40	1.00
❑ 120 Shawn Springs RC	.25	.60
❑ 121 Ike Hilliard RC	.60	1.50
❑ 122 Dwayne Rudd RC	.40	1.00
❑ 123 Reinard Wilson RC	.25	.60
❑ 124 Michael Booker RC	.15	.40
❑ 125 Warrick Dunn RC	1.50	4.00

1998 Bowman's Best

Card	Low	High
❑ COMPLETE SET (125)	30.00	80.00
❑ 1 Emmitt Smith	1.25	3.00
❑ 2 Reggie White	.40	1.00
❑ 3 Jake Plummer	.40	1.00
❑ 4 Ike Hilliard	.15	.40
❑ 5 Isaac Bruce	.15	.40
❑ 6 Trent Dilfer	.40	1.00
❑ 7 Ricky Watters	.25	.60
❑ 8 Jeff George	.25	.60
❑ 9 Wayne Chrebet	.40	1.00
❑ 10 Brett Favre	1.50	4.00
❑ 11 Terry Allen	.40	1.00
❑ 12 Bert Emanuel	.15	.40
❑ 13 Andre Reed	.25	.60
❑ 14 Andre Rison	.25	.60
❑ 15 Jeff Blake	.25	.60
❑ 16 Steve McNair	.40	1.00
❑ 17 Joey Galloway	.25	.60
❑ 18 Irving Fryar	.25	.60
❑ 19 Dorsey Levens	.40	1.00
❑ 20 Jerry Rice	.75	2.00
❑ 21 Kerry Collins	.25	.60
❑ 22 Michael Jackson	.15	.40
❑ 23 Kordell Stewart	.40	1.00
❑ 24 Junior Seau	.40	1.00
❑ 25 Jimmy Smith	.25	.60
❑ 26 Michael Westbrook	.25	.60
❑ 27 Eddie George	.40	1.00
❑ 28 Cris Carter	.40	1.00
❑ 29 Jason Sehorn	.25	.60
❑ 30 Warrick Dunn	.40	1.00
❑ 31 Garrison Hearst	.40	1.00
❑ 32 Erik Kramer	.15	.40
❑ 33 Chris Chandler	.25	.60
❑ 34 Michael Irvin	.40	1.00
❑ 35 Marshall Faulk	.50	1.25
❑ 36 Warren Moon	.40	1.00
❑ 37 Rickey Dudley	.15	.40
❑ 38 Drew Bledsoe	.60	1.50
❑ 39 Antowain Smith	.40	1.00
❑ 40 Terrell Davis	.40	1.00
❑ 41 Gus Frerotte	.15	.40
❑ 42 Robert Brooks	.25	.60
❑ 43 Tony Banks	.25	.60
❑ 44 Terrell Owens	.40	1.00
❑ 45 Edgar Bennett	.15	.40
❑ 46 Rob Moore	.25	.60
❑ 47 J.J. Stokes	.25	.60
❑ 48 Yancey Thigpen	.15	.40
❑ 49 Elvis Grbac	.25	.60
❑ 50 John Elway	1.50	4.00
❑ 51 Charles Johnson	.15	.40
❑ 52 Karim Abdul-Jabbar	.40	1.00
❑ 53 Carl Pickens	.25	.60
❑ 54 Peter Boulware	.15	.40
❑ 55 Chris Warren	.15	.40
❑ 56 Terance Mathis	.25	.60
❑ 57 Andre Hastings	.15	.40
❑ 58 Jake Reed	.25	.60
❑ 59 Mike Alstott	.15	.40
❑ 60 Mark Brunell	.40	1.00
❑ 61 Herman Moore	.25	.60
❑ 62 Troy Aikman	.75	2.00
❑ 63 Fred Lane	.15	.40
❑ 64 Rod Smith	.25	.60
❑ 65 Terry Glenn	.40	1.00
❑ 66 Jerome Bettis	.40	1.00
❑ 67 Derrick Thomas	.40	1.00
❑ 68 Marvin Harrison	.40	1.00
❑ 69 Adrian Murrell	.15	.40
❑ 70 Curtis Martin	.40	1.00
❑ 71 Bobby Hoying	.25	.60
❑ 72 Darrell Green	.25	.60
❑ 73 Sean Dawkins	.15	.40
❑ 74 Robert Smith	.40	1.00
❑ 75 Antonio Freeman	.40	1.00
❑ 76 Scott Mitchell	.25	.60
❑ 77 Curtis Conway	.25	.60
❑ 78 Rae Carruth	.15	.40
❑ 79 Jamal Anderson	.40	1.00
❑ 80 Dan Marino	1.50	4.00
❑ 81 Brad Johnson	.40	1.00
❑ 82 Danny Kanell	.25	.60
❑ 83 Charlie Garner	.25	.60
❑ 84 Rob Johnson	.25	.60
❑ 85 Natrone Means	.25	.60
❑ 86 Tim Brown	.40	1.00
❑ 87 Keyshawn Johnson	.40	1.00
❑ 88 Ben Coates	.25	.60
❑ 89 Derrick Alexander	.25	.60
❑ 90 Steve Young	.50	1.25
❑ 91 Shannon Sharpe	.25	.60
❑ 92 Corey Dillon	.40	1.00
❑ 93 Bruce Smith	.25	.60
❑ 94 Errict Rhett	.25	.60
❑ 95 Jim Harbaugh	.15	.40
❑ 96 Napoleon Kaufman	.40	1.00
❑ 97 Glenn Foley	.25	.60
❑ 98 Tony Gonzalez	.40	1.00
❑ 99 Keenan McCardell	.25	.60
❑ 100 Barry Sanders	1.25	3.00
❑ 101 Charles Woodson RC	1.25	3.00
❑ 102 Tim Dwight RC	1.00	2.50
❑ 103 Marcus Nash RC	.50	1.25
❑ 104 Joe Jurevicius RC	1.00	2.50
❑ 105 Jacquez Green RC	.75	2.00
❑ 106 Kevin Dyson RC	1.00	2.50
❑ 107 Keith Brooking RC	1.00	2.50
❑ 108 Andre Wadsworth RC	.75	2.00
❑ 109 Randy Moss RC	6.00	15.00
❑ 110 Robert Edwards RC	.75	2.00
❑ 111 Pat Johnson RC	.75	2.00
❑ 112 Peyton Manning RC	12.50	25.00
❑ 113 Duane Starks RC	.50	1.25
❑ 114 Grant Wistrom RC	.75	2.00
❑ 115 Anthony Simmons RC	.75	2.00
❑ 116 Takeo Spikes RC	1.00	2.50
❑ 117 Tony Simmons RC	.75	2.00
❑ 118 Jerome Pathon RC	1.00	2.50
❑ 119 Ryan Leaf RC	1.00	2.50
❑ 120 Skip Hicks RC	.75	2.00
❑ 121 Curtis Enis RC	.50	1.25
❑ 122 Germane Crowell RC	.75	2.00
❑ 123 John Avery RC	.75	2.00
❑ 124 Hines Ward RC	5.00	10.00
❑ 125 Fred Taylor RC	1.50	4.00

1999 Bowman's Best

Card	Low	High
❑ COMPLETE SET (133)	30.00	80.00
❑ 1 Randy Moss	1.00	2.50
❑ 2 Skip Hicks	.15	.40
❑ 3 Robert Smith	.40	1.00
❑ 4 Drew Bledsoe	.50	1.25
❑ 5 Tim Brown	.40	1.00
❑ 6 Marshall Faulk	.50	1.25
❑ 7 Terance Mathis	.25	.60
❑ 8 Sean Dawkins	.15	.40
❑ 9 Ed McCaffrey	.25	.60
❑ 10 Jamal Anderson	.40	1.00
❑ 11 Antonio Freeman	.40	1.00
❑ 12 Terry Kirby	.25	.60
❑ 13 Vinny Testaverde	.25	.60
❑ 14 Eddie George	.40	1.00
❑ 15 Ricky Watters	.25	.60
❑ 16 Johnnie Morton	.25	.60
❑ 17 Natrone Means	.25	.60
❑ 18 Terry Glenn	.40	1.00
❑ 19 Michael Westbrook	.25	.60
❑ 20 Doug Flutie	.40	1.00
❑ 21 Jake Plummer	.25	.60
❑ 22 Darnay Scott	.25	.60
❑ 23 Andre Rison	.25	.60
❑ 24 Jon Kitna	.40	1.00
❑ 25 Dan Marino	1.25	3.00
❑ 26 Ike Hilliard	.25	.60
❑ 27 Warrick Dunn	.40	1.00
❑ 28 Jerome Bettis	.40	1.00
❑ 29 Curtis Conway	.25	.60
❑ 30 Emmitt Smith	.75	2.00
❑ 31 Jimmy Smith	.25	.60
❑ 32 Isaac Bruce	.40	1.00
❑ 33 Jerry Rice	.75	2.00
❑ 34 Curtis Martin	.40	1.00
❑ 35 Steve McNair	.40	1.00
❑ 36 Jeff Blake	.25	.60
❑ 37 Rob Moore	.25	.60
❑ 38 Dorsey Levens	.40	1.00
❑ 39 Terrell Davis	.40	1.00
❑ 40 John Elway	1.25	3.00
❑ 41 Trent Dilfer	.25	.60
❑ 42 Joey Galloway	.25	.60
❑ 43 Keyshawn Johnson	.40	1.00
❑ 44 O.J. McDuffie	.25	.60
❑ 45 Fred Taylor	.40	1.00
❑ 46 Andre Reed	.25	.60
❑ 47 Frank Sanders	.25	.60
❑ 48 Keenan McCardell	.25	.60
❑ 49 Elvis Grbac	.25	.60
❑ 50 Barry Sanders	1.25	3.00
❑ 51 Terrell Owens	.40	1.00
❑ 52 Trent Green	.40	1.00
❑ 53 Brad Johnson	.40	1.00
❑ 54 Rich Gannon	.40	1.00
❑ 55 Randall Cunningham	.40	1.00
❑ 56 Tony Martin	.25	.60
❑ 57 Rod Smith	.25	.60
❑ 58 Eric Moulds	.40	1.00
❑ 59 Yancey Thigpen	.15	.40
❑ 60 Brett Favre	1.25	3.00
❑ 61 Cris Carter	.40	1.00
❑ 62 Marvin Harrison	.40	1.00
❑ 63 Chris Chandler	.25	.60
❑ 64 Antowain Smith	.40	1.00
❑ 65 Carl Pickens	.25	.60
❑ 66 Shannon Sharpe	.25	.60
❑ 67 Mike Alstott	.40	1.00
❑ 68 J.J. Stokes	.25	.60
❑ 69 Ben Coates	.25	.60
❑ 70 Peyton Manning	1.25	3.00
❑ 71 Duce Staley	.40	1.00
❑ 72 Michael Irvin	.25	.60
❑ 73 Tim Biakabutuka	.25	.60
❑ 74 Priest Holmes	.60	1.50
❑ 75 Steve Young	.50	1.25
❑ 76 Jerome Pathon	.25	.60
❑ 77 Wayne Chrebet	.40	1.00
❑ 78 Bert Emanuel	.15	.40
❑ 79 Curtis Enis	.15	.40
❑ 80 Mark Brunell	.40	1.00
❑ 81 Herman Moore	.25	.60
❑ 82 Corey Dillon	.40	1.00
❑ 83 Jim Harbaugh	.25	.60
❑ 84 Gary Brown	.15	.40
❑ 85 Kordell Stewart	.25	.60
❑ 86 Garrison Hearst	.25	.60
❑ 87 Rocket Ismail	.25	.60
❑ 88 Charlie Batch	.40	1.00

Card	Low	High
❑ 89 Napoleon Kaufman	.40	1.00
❑ 90 Troy Aikman	.75	2.00
❑ 91 Brett Favre BP	.60	1.50
❑ 92 Randy Moss BP	.50	1.25
❑ 93 Terrell Davis BP	.40	1.00
❑ 94 Barry Sanders BP	.60	1.50
❑ 95 Peyton Manning BP	.60	1.50
❑ 96 Troy Edwards BP	.25	.60
❑ 97 Cade McNown BP	.25	.60
❑ 98 Edgerrin James BP	1.00	2.50
❑ 99 Torry Holt BP	.40	1.00
❑ 100 Tim Couch BP	.40	1.00
❑ 101 Chris Claiborne RC	.40	1.00
❑ 102 Brock Huard RC	.75	2.00
❑ 103 Amos Zereoue RC	.75	2.00
❑ 104 Sedrick Irvin RC	.40	1.00
❑ 105 Kevin Faulk RC	.75	2.00
❑ 106 Ebenezer Ekuban RC	.40	1.00
❑ 107 Daunte Culpepper RC	3.00	8.00
❑ 108 Rob Konrad RC	.60	1.50
❑ 109 James Johnson RC	.60	1.50
❑ 110 Kurt Warner RC	4.00	10.00
❑ 111 Mike Cloud RC	.60	1.50
❑ 112 Andy Katzenmoyer RC	.60	1.50
❑ 113 Jevon Kearse RC	1.25	3.00
❑ 114 Akili Smith RC	.60	1.50
❑ 115 Edgerrin James RC	3.00	8.00
❑ 116 Cecil Collins RC	.40	1.00
❑ 117 Chris McAlister RC	.60	1.50
❑ 118 Donovan McNabb RC	4.00	10.00
❑ 119 Kevin Johnson RC	.75	2.00
❑ 120 Torry Holt RC	2.00	5.00
❑ 121 Antoine Winfield RC	.60	1.50
❑ 122 Michael Bishop RC	.75	2.00
❑ 123 Joe Germaine RC	.60	1.50
❑ 124 David Boston RC	.75	2.00
❑ 125 D'Wayne Bates RC	.60	1.50
❑ 126 Champ Bailey RC	1.00	2.50
❑ 127 Cade McNown RC	.60	1.50
❑ 128 Shaun King RC	.60	1.50
❑ 129 Peerless Price RC	.75	2.00
❑ 130 Troy Edwards RC	.60	1.50
❑ 131 Karsten Bailey RC	.60	1.50
❑ 132 Tim Couch RC	.75	2.00
❑ 133 Ricky Williams RC	1.50	4.00
❑ C1 Rookie Class Photo	3.00	8.00

2000 Bowman's Best

Card	Low	High
❑ COMPLETE SET (150)	250.00	500.00
❑ 1 Troy Edwards	.10	.30
❑ 2 Kurt Warner	.60	1.50
❑ 3 Steve McNair	.30	.75
❑ 4 Terry Glenn	.20	.50
❑ 5 Charlie Batch	.30	.75
❑ 6 Patrick Jeffers	.30	.75
❑ 7 Jake Plummer	.20	.50
❑ 8 Derrick Alexander	.20	.50
❑ 9 Joey Galloway	.20	.50
❑ 10 Tony Banks	.20	.50
❑ 11 Robert Smith	.30	.75
❑ 12 Jerry Rice	.60	1.50
❑ 13 Jeff Garcia	.30	.75
❑ 14 Michael Westbrook	.20	.50
❑ 15 Curtis Conway	.20	.50
❑ 16 Brian Griese	.30	.75
❑ 17 Peyton Manning	.75	2.00
❑ 18 Daunte Culpepper	.40	1.00
❑ 19 Frank Sanders	.20	.50
❑ 20 Muhsin Muhammad	.20	.50
❑ 21 Corey Dillon	.30	.75
❑ 22 Brett Favre	1.00	2.50
❑ 23 Warrick Dunn	.30	.75
❑ 24 Tim Brown	.30	.75
❑ 25 Kerry Collins	.20	.50
❑ 26 Brad Johnson	.30	.75
❑ 27 Rocket Ismail	.20	.50
❑ 28 Jamal Anderson	.30	.75
❑ 29 Jimmy Smith	.20	.50
❑ 30 Torry Holt	.30	.75
❑ 31 Duce Staley	.30	.75
❑ 32 Drew Bledsoe	.40	1.00
❑ 33 Jerome Bettis	.30	.75
❑ 34 Keyshawn Johnson	.30	.75
❑ 35 Fred Taylor	.30	.75
❑ 36 Akili Smith	.10	.30
❑ 37 Rob Johnson	.20	.50
❑ 38 Elvis Grbac	.20	.50
❑ 39 Antonio Freeman	.30	.75
❑ 40 Curtis Enis	.10	.30
❑ 41 Terance Mathis	.20	.50
❑ 42 Terrell Davis	.30	.75
❑ 43 Randy Moss	.60	1.50
❑ 44 Jon Kitna	.30	.75
❑ 45 Curtis Martin	.30	.75
❑ 46 Terrell Owens	.30	.75
❑ 47 Robert Smith	.30	.75
❑ 48 Albert Connell	.10	.30
❑ 49 Edgerrin James	.50	1.25
❑ 50 Tony Gonzalez	.20	.50
❑ 51 Eric Moulds	.30	.75
❑ 52 Natrone Means	.20	.50
❑ 53 Carl Pickens	.20	.50
❑ 54 Mark Brunell	.30	.75
❑ 55 Rob Moore	.20	.50
❑ 56 Marshall Faulk	.40	1.00
❑ 57 Stephen Davis	.30	.75
❑ 58 Rich Gannon	.30	.75
❑ 59 Ricky Williams	.30	.75
❑ 60 Emmitt Smith	.60	1.50
❑ 61 Germane Crowell	.10	.30
❑ 62 Doug Flutie	.30	.75
❑ 63 O.J. McDuffie	.20	.50
❑ 64 Chris Chandler	.20	.50
❑ 65 Qadry Ismail	.20	.50
❑ 66 Tim Couch	.20	.50
❑ 67 James Stewart	.20	.50
❑ 68 Marvin Harrison	.30	.75
❑ 69 Cris Carter	.30	.75
❑ 70 Cade McNown	.10	.30
❑ 71 Marcus Robinson	.30	.75
❑ 72 Steve Beuerlein	.20	.50
❑ 73 Jevon Kearse	.30	.75
❑ 74 Eddie George	.30	.75
❑ 75 Donovan McNabb	.50	1.25
❑ 76 Jeff Blake	.20	.50
❑ 77 Wayne Chrebet	.20	.50
❑ 78 Kordell Stewart	.20	.50
❑ 79 Steve Young	.40	1.00
❑ 80 Mike Alstott	.30	.75
❑ 81 Ricky Watters	.20	.50
❑ 82 Charlie Garner	.20	.50
❑ 83 Troy Aikman	.60	1.50
❑ 84 Dorsey Levens	.20	.50
❑ 85 Ike Hilliard	.20	.50
❑ 86 Shaun King	.10	.30
❑ 87 Isaac Bruce	.30	.75
❑ 88 Tyrone Wheatley	.20	.50
❑ 89 Amani Toomer	.20	.50
❑ 90 Ed McCaffrey	.30	.75
❑ 91 E.James/M.Faulk BP	.30	.75
❑ 92 D.Bledsoe/B.Johnson BP	.30	.75
❑ 93 J.Smith/R.Moss BP	.40	1.00
❑ 94 E.George/S.Davis BP	.20	.50
❑ 95 M.Brunell/T.Aikman BP	.40	1.00
❑ 96 M.Harrison/C.Carter BP	.30	.75
❑ 97 C.Martin/E.Smith BP	.40	1.00
❑ 98 T.Brown/I.Bruce BP	.20	.50
❑ 99 F.Taylor/R.Williams BP	.30	.75
❑ 100 K.Warner/P.Manning BP	.40	1.00
❑ 101 Shaun Alexander RC	8.00	20.00
❑ 102 Thomas Jones RC	5.00	12.00
❑ 103 Courtney Brown RC	3.00	8.00
❑ 104 Curtis Keaton RC	2.50	6.00
❑ 105 Jerry Porter RC	4.00	10.00
❑ 106 Corey Simon RC	3.00	8.00
❑ 107 Dez White RC	3.00	8.00
❑ 108 Jamal Lewis RC	6.00	15.00
❑ 109 Ron Dayne RC	3.00	8.00
❑ 110 R.Jay Soward RC	2.50	6.00
❑ 111 Tee Martin RC	3.00	8.00
❑ 112 Brian Urlacher RC	10.00	25.00
❑ 113 Reuben Droughns RC	4.00	10.00
❑ 114 Travis Taylor RC	3.00	8.00
❑ 115 Plaxico Burress RC	6.00	15.00
❑ 116 Chad Pennington RC	6.00	15.00
❑ 117 Sylvester Morris RC	2.50	6.00
❑ 118 Ron Dugans RC	1.50	4.00
❑ 119 Joe Hamilton RC	2.50	6.00
❑ 120 Chris Redman RC	2.50	6.00
❑ 121 Trung Canidate RC	2.50	6.00
❑ 122 J.R. Redmond RC	2.50	6.00
❑ 123 Danny Farmer RC	2.50	6.00
❑ 124 Todd Pinkston RC	3.00	8.00
❑ 125 Dennis Northcutt RC	3.00	8.00
❑ 126 Laveranues Coles RC	4.00	10.00
❑ 127 Bubba Franks RC	3.00	8.00
❑ 128 Travis Prentice RC	2.50	6.00
❑ 129 Peter Warrick RC	3.00	8.00
❑ 130 Anthony Becht RC	3.00	8.00
❑ 131 Ike Charlton RC	1.50	4.00
❑ 132 Shaun Ellis RC	3.00	8.00
❑ 133 Sean Morey RC	2.50	6.00
❑ 134 Sebastian Janikowski RC	3.00	8.00
❑ 135 Aaron Stecker RC	3.00	8.00
❑ 136 Ronney Jenkins RC	2.50	6.00
❑ 137 Jamel White RC	2.50	6.00
❑ 138 Nick Williams	1.50	4.00
❑ 139 Andy McCullough	1.50	4.00
❑ 140 Kevin Daft	1.50	4.00
❑ 141 Thomas Hamner RC	1.50	4.00
❑ 142 Tim Rattay RC	3.00	8.00
❑ 143 Spergon Wynn RC	2.50	6.00
❑ 144 Brandon Short RC	2.50	6.00
❑ 145 Chad Morton RC	3.00	8.00
❑ 146 Gari Scott RC	1.50	4.00
❑ 147 Frank Murphy RC	1.50	4.00
❑ 148 James Williams RC	2.50	6.00
❑ 149 Windrell Hayes RC	2.50	6.00
❑ 150 Doug Johnson RC	3.00	8.00

2001 Bowman's Best

Card	Low	High
❑ COMP.SET w/o SP's (100)	7.50	20.00
❑ 1 Jerry Rice	.60	1.50
❑ 2 Doug Flutie	.30	.75
❑ 3 Drew Bledsoe	.30	.75
❑ 4 Edgerrin James	.30	.75
❑ 5 Muhsin Muhammad	.25	.60
❑ 6 Charlie Batch	.25	.60
❑ 7 Marshall Faulk	.30	.75
❑ 8 Trent Green	.30	.75
❑ 9 Rich Gannon	.25	.60
❑ 10 Emmitt Smith	.75	2.00
❑ 11 Steve McNair	.30	.75
❑ 12 Darrell Jackson	.25	.60
❑ 13 Amani Toomer	.25	.60
❑ 14 Jimmy Smith	.25	.60
❑ 15 Kevin Johnson	.20	.50
❑ 16 Ray Lewis	.30	.75
❑ 17 Peter Warrick	.25	.60
❑ 18 Cris Carter	.30	.75
❑ 19 Jerome Bettis	.30	.75
❑ 20 Keyshawn Johnson	.25	.60
❑ 21 Joey Galloway	.25	.60
❑ 22 Chris Chandler	.25	.60
❑ 23 Brett Favre	1.00	2.50
❑ 24 Aaron Brooks	.25	.60
❑ 25 Kurt Warner	.40	1.00
❑ 26 Jeff Graham	.20	.50
❑ 27 Curtis Martin	.30	.75
❑ 28 Mike Anderson	.25	.60
❑ 29 Eric Moulds	.25	.60
❑ 30 David Boston	.20	.50
❑ 31 Elvis Grbac	.25	.60
❑ 32 James Stewart	.20	.50
❑ 33 Randy Moss	.40	1.00
❑ 34 Donovan McNabb	.40	1.00
❑ 35 Matt Hasselbeck	.30	.75
❑ 36 Stephen Davis	.25	.60
❑ 37 Brad Johnson	.25	.60
❑ 38 Jamal Anderson	.25	.60
❑ 39 Tim Biakabutuka	.20	.50

❑ 40 Antonio Freeman	.30	.75
❑ 41 Mark Brunell	.30	.75
❑ 42 Tiki Barber	.30	.75
❑ 43 Charlie Garner	.25	.60
❑ 44 Eddie George	.30	.75
❑ 45 Ricky Williams	.30	.75
❑ 46 Rob Johnson	.25	.60
❑ 47 Jake Plummer	.25	.60
❑ 48 Peyton Manning	.75	2.00
❑ 49 Lamar Smith	.25	.60
❑ 50 Corey Dillon	.25	.60
❑ 51 Derrick Alexander	.20	.50
❑ 52 Troy Brown	.25	.60
❑ 53 Wayne Chrebet	.25	.60
❑ 54 Shaun Alexander	.30	.75
❑ 55 Jeff George	.25	.60
❑ 56 Tim Brown	.30	.75
❑ 57 Brian Griese	.25	.60
❑ 58 Cade McNown	.25	.60
❑ 59 Jamal Lewis	.30	.75
❑ 60 Germane Crowell	.20	.50
❑ 61 Junior Seau	.30	.75
❑ 62 Warrick Dunn	.30	.75
❑ 63 Isaac Bruce	.30	.75
❑ 64 Terry Glenn	.25	.60
❑ 65 Fred Taylor	.30	.75
❑ 66 Tim Couch	.20	.50
❑ 67 Akili Smith	.20	.50
❑ 68 Tony Gonzalez	.25	.60
❑ 69 Kerry Collins	.25	.60
❑ 70 James Thrash	.25	.60
❑ 71 Terrell Owens	.30	.75
❑ 72 Derrick Mason	.25	.60
❑ 73 Tyrone Wheatley	.25	.60
❑ 74 Oronde Gadsden	.20	.50
❑ 75 Ahman Green	.30	.75
❑ 76 Jon Kitna	.25	.60
❑ 77 Tony Banks	.20	.50
❑ 78 Marvin Harrison	.30	.75
❑ 79 Daunte Culpepper	.30	.75
❑ 80 Vinny Testaverde	.25	.60
❑ 81 Chad Lewis	.20	.50
❑ 82 Torry Holt	.25	.60
❑ 83 Jeff Garcia	.25	.60
❑ 84 Rod Smith	.25	.60
❑ 85 Marcus Robinson	.25	.60
❑ 86 Keenan McCardell	.25	.60
❑ 87 Joe Horn	.25	.60
❑ 88 Kordell Stewart	.25	.60
❑ 89 Jay Fiedler	.25	.60
❑ 90 Ed McCaffrey	.25	.60
❑ 91 E.George/S.Davis	.30	.75
❑ 92 P.Manning/J.Garcia	.75	2.00
❑ 93 R.Smith/T.Holt	.25	.60
❑ 94 E.James/M.Faulk	.30	.75
❑ 95 E.Grbac/D.Culpepper	.30	.75
❑ 96 M.Harrison/R.Moss	.40	1.00
❑ 97 M.Anderson/E.Smith	.75	2.00
❑ 98 B.Griese/K.Warner	.40	1.00
❑ 99 M.Muhammad/E.McCaffrey	.25	.60
❑ 100 E.Moulds/T.Owens	.30	.75
❑ 101 David Terrell JSY RC	2.50	6.00
❑ 102 Kevan Barlow JSY RC	2.50	6.00
❑ 103 Quincy Morgan JSY RC	2.50	6.00
❑ 104 Chris Weinke JSY RC	2.50	6.00
❑ 105 Josh Heupel JSY RC	3.00	8.00
❑ 106 Chris Chambers JSY RC	5.00	12.00
❑ 107 Reggie Wayne JSY RC	8.00	20.00
❑ 108 Gerard Warren JSY RC	2.50	6.00
❑ 109 Freddie Mitchell JSY RC	2.00	5.00
❑ 110 Anthony Thomas JSY RC	3.00	8.00
❑ 111 Robert Ferguson JSY RC	3.00	8.00
❑ 112 Deuce McAllister JSY RC	4.00	10.00
❑ 113 Travis Henry JSY RC	3.00	8.00
❑ 114 Rod Gardner JSY RC	2.50	6.00
❑ 115 Michael Bennett JSY RC	3.00	8.00
❑ 116 Santana Moss JSY RC	5.00	12.00
❑ 117 Chad Johnson JSY RC	8.00	20.00
❑ 118 Jesse Palmer JSY RC	3.00	8.00
❑ 119 James Jackson JSY RC	2.50	6.00
❑ 120 Dan Morgan JSY RC	3.00	8.00
❑ 121 Drew Brees RC	12.50	30.00
❑ 122 Travis Minor RC	1.50	4.00
❑ 123 Quincy Carter RC	1.50	4.00
❑ 124 LaDainian Tomlinson RC	15.00	40.00
❑ 125 Michael Vick RC	4.00	10.00
❑ 126 Ryan Pickett RC	1.25	3.00
❑ 127 Mike McMahon RC	1.50	4.00
❑ 128 Alex Bannister RC	1.25	3.00
❑ 129 A.J. Feeley RC	1.50	4.00
❑ 130 Shad Meier RC	1.25	3.00
❑ 131 Jamie Winborn RC	1.50	4.00
❑ 132 Fred Smoot RC	2.00	5.00
❑ 133 Milton Wynn RC	1.25	3.00
❑ 134 Onome Ojo RC	1.25	3.00
❑ 135 Jonathan Carter RC	1.25	3.00
❑ 136 Todd Heap RC	2.00	5.00
❑ 137 Bobby Newcombe RC	1.50	4.00
❑ 138 Tony Stewart RC	1.50	4.00
❑ 139 Torrance Marshall RC	1.50	4.00
❑ 140 Jamal Reynolds RC	1.50	4.00
❑ 141 Jamar Fletcher RC	1.25	3.00
❑ 142 Richard Seymour RC	2.00	5.00
❑ 143 Tay Cody RC	1.25	3.00
❑ 144 Koren Robinson RC	2.00	5.00
❑ 145 Eddie Berlin RC	1.25	3.00
❑ 146 Damione Lewis RC	1.50	4.00
❑ 147 Marques Tuiasosopo RC	1.50	4.00
❑ 148 Snoop Minnis RC	1.50	4.00
❑ 149 Chris Barnes RC	1.25	3.00
❑ 150 Leonard Davis RC	1.50	4.00
❑ 151 Vinny Sutherland RC	1.25	3.00
❑ 152 Rudi Johnson RC	2.00	5.00
❑ 153 Derrick Gibson RC	1.25	3.00
❑ 154 Dan Alexander RC	1.50	4.00
❑ 155 Damerien McCants RC	1.50	4.00
❑ 156 Adam Archuleta RC	1.50	4.00
❑ 157 Correll Buckhalter RC	2.00	5.00
❑ 158 LaMont Jordan RC	2.00	5.00
❑ 159 Quentin McCord RC	1.50	4.00
❑ 160 Justin Smith RC	2.00	5.00
❑ 161 Nate Clements RC	2.00	5.00
❑ 162 Alge Crumpler RC	2.00	5.00
❑ 163 Dan O'Leary RC	1.25	3.00
❑ 164 Sage Rosenfels RC	2.00	5.00
❑ 165 Andre Carter RC	2.00	5.00
❑ 166 Marcus Stroud RC	1.50	4.00
❑ 167 Will Allen RC	2.00	5.00
❑ 168 Tommy Polley RC	1.50	4.00
❑ 169 Justin McCareins RC	1.50	4.00
❑ 170 Josh Booty RC	1.50	4.00

2002 Bowman's Best

❑ COMP.SET w/o SP's (90)	15.00	40.00
❑ 1 Peyton Manning	1.00	2.50
❑ 2 Chris Weinke	.30	.75
❑ 3 Daunte Culpepper	.40	1.00
❑ 4 Deuce McAllister	.50	1.25
❑ 5 Duce Staley	.40	1.00
❑ 6 Koren Robinson	.30	.75
❑ 7 Emmitt Smith	1.25	3.00
❑ 8 Jamal Lewis	.40	1.00
❑ 9 Jake Plummer	.40	1.00
❑ 10 Tim Brown	.50	1.25
❑ 11 LaDainian Tomlinson	.75	2.00
❑ 12 Derrick Mason	.40	1.00
❑ 13 Keyshawn Johnson	.40	1.00
❑ 14 Priest Holmes	.50	1.25
❑ 15 Marcus Robinson	.40	1.00
❑ 16 Drew Bledsoe	.50	1.25
❑ 17 Troy Brown	.40	1.00
❑ 18 Ahman Green	.40	1.00
❑ 19 Edgerrin James	.50	1.25
❑ 20 Hines Ward	.50	1.25
❑ 21 Marshall Faulk	.50	1.25
❑ 22 Rod Gardner	.30	.75
❑ 23 Amani Toomer	.40	1.00
❑ 24 Ricky Williams	.50	1.25
❑ 25 Peter Warrick	.40	1.00
❑ 26 Ray Lewis	.50	1.25
❑ 27 Warrick Dunn	.40	1.00
❑ 28 Jermaine Lewis	.30	.75
❑ 29 Mark Brunell	.40	1.00
❑ 30 Randy Moss	.50	1.25
❑ 31 Laveranues Coles	.50	1.25
❑ 32 Kordell Stewart	.40	1.00
❑ 33 Darrell Jackson	.40	1.00
❑ 34 Jeff Garcia	.40	1.00
❑ 35 Eddie George	.40	1.00
❑ 36 Tim Dwight	.40	1.00
❑ 37 Trent Green	.40	1.00
❑ 38 Quincy Carter	.30	.75
❑ 39 Mike McMahon	.30	.75
❑ 40 Corey Dillon	.40	1.00
❑ 41 Corey Bradford	.30	.75
❑ 42 Aaron Brooks	.40	1.00
❑ 43 Todd Pinkston	.30	.75
❑ 44 Isaac Bruce	.50	1.25
❑ 45 Shane Matthews	.30	.75
❑ 46 Eric Moulds	.40	1.00
❑ 47 Anthony Thomas	.40	1.00
❑ 48 David Boston	.30	.75
❑ 49 Kevin Johnson	.30	.75
❑ 50 Brett Favre	1.25	3.00
❑ 51 Ron Dayne	.40	1.00
❑ 52 Donovan McNabb	.60	1.50
❑ 53 Brad Johnson	.40	1.00
❑ 54 Garrison Hearst	.40	1.00
❑ 55 Jimmy Smith	.40	1.00
❑ 56 Muhsin Muhammad	.40	1.00
❑ 57 Michael Vick	.50	1.25
❑ 58 Kerry Collins	.40	1.00
❑ 59 Jerome Bettis	.50	1.25
❑ 60 Trent Dilfer	.40	1.00
❑ 61 Torry Holt	.50	1.25
❑ 62 Stephen Davis	.40	1.00
❑ 63 Steve McNair	.50	1.25
❑ 64 Marvin Harrison	.50	1.25
❑ 65 Zach Thomas	.50	1.25
❑ 66 Antowain Smith	.40	1.00
❑ 67 Joe Horn	.40	1.00
❑ 68 Jim Miller	.40	1.00
❑ 69 Travis Taylor	.30	.75
❑ 70 James Allen	.30	.75
❑ 71 Tom Brady	1.25	3.00
❑ 72 Tiki Barber	.50	1.25
❑ 73 Doug Flutie	.50	1.25
❑ 74 Rich Gannon	.40	1.00
❑ 75 Kurt Warner	.50	1.25
❑ 76 Michael Pittman	.40	1.00
❑ 77 Curtis Martin	.50	1.25
❑ 78 Plaxico Burress	.40	1.00
❑ 79 Terrell Owens	.50	1.25
❑ 80 Tony Gonzalez	.40	1.00
❑ 81 Michael Bennett	.40	1.00
❑ 82 Brian Griese	.40	1.00
❑ 83 Tim Couch	.30	.75
❑ 84 Shaun Alexander	.50	1.25
❑ 85 Drew Brees	.75	2.00
❑ 86 Vinny Testaverde	.40	1.00
❑ 87 Chris Chambers	.50	1.25
❑ 88 David Terrell	.40	1.00
❑ 89 Rod Smith	.40	1.00
❑ 90 Jerry Rice	1.00	2.50
❑ 91 David Carr JSY RC	3.00	8.00
❑ 92 Joey Harrington JSY RC	3.00	8.00
❑ 93 Marquise Walker JSY RC	2.00	5.00
❑ 94 Ladell Betts JSY RC	3.00	8.00
❑ 95 David Garrard JSY RC	5.00	12.00
❑ 96 Antwaan Randle El JSY RC	3.00	8.00
❑ 97 Antonio Bryant JSY RC	4.00	10.00
❑ 98 Eric Crouch JSY RC	3.00	8.00
❑ 99 Tim Carter JSY RC	2.50	6.00
❑ 100 William Green JSY RC	2.50	6.00
❑ 101 Rohan Davey JSY RC	3.00	8.00
❑ 102 Julius Peppers JSY RC	5.00	12.00
❑ 103 Donte Stallworth JSY RC	3.00	8.00
❑ 104 Ashley Lelie JSY RC	3.00	8.00
❑ 105 Jeremy Shockey JSY RC	5.00	12.00
❑ 106 Javon Walker JSY RC	3.00	8.00
❑ 107 Patrick Ramsey JSY RC	3.00	8.00
❑ 108 Roy Williams JSY RC	4.00	10.00
❑ 109 T.J. Duckett JSY RC	3.00	8.00
❑ 110 Jabar Gaffney JSY RC	3.00	8.00
❑ 111 Andre Davis JSY RC	2.50	6.00
❑ 112 Reche Caldwell JSY RC	3.00	8.00
❑ 113 Josh McCown JSY RC	3.00	8.00
❑ 114 Maurice Morris JSY RC	3.00	8.00
❑ 115 Ron Johnson JSY RC	2.50	6.00
❑ 116 DeShaun Foster JSY RC	3.00	8.00
❑ 117 Clinton Portis JSY RC	8.00	20.00
❑ 118 Aaron Lockett AU RC	3.00	8.00
❑ 119 Robert Thomas AU RC	3.00	8.00
❑ 121 Atrews Bell AU RC	3.00	8.00

❑ 122 Brandon Doman AU RC 3.00 8.00
❑ 124 Bryan Thomas AU RC 3.00 8.00
❑ 125 Bryant McKinnie AU RC 3.00 8.00
❑ 126 Chad Hutchinson AU RC 3.00 8.00
❑ 127 Charles Grant AU RC 5.00 12.00
❑ 128 Chester Taylor AU RC 8.00 20.00
❑ 129 Craig Nall AU RC 4.00 10.00
❑ 130 Deion Branch AU RC 5.00 12.00
❑ 131 Doug Jolley AU RC 3.00 8.00
❑ 132 Dwight Freeney AU RC 20.00 40.00
❑ 133 Ed Reed AU RC 25.00 50.00
❑ 134 Freddie Milons AU RC 3.00 8.00
❑ 135 Herb Haygood AU RC 3.00 8.00
❑ 136 J.T. O'Sullivan AU RC 5.00 12.00
❑ 137 Jake Schifino AU RC 3.00 8.00
❑ 138 Jason McAddley AU RC 4.00 10.00
❑ 139 Jeff Kelly AU RC 3.00 8.00
❑ 140 Jerramy Stevens AU RC 5.00 12.00
❑ 141 John Henderson AU RC 5.00 12.00
❑ 142 Jonathan Wells AU RC 5.00 12.00
❑ 143 Josh Scobey AU RC 4.00 10.00
❑ 144 Kelly Campbell AU RC 4.00 10.00
❑ 145 Kahlil Hill AU RC 3.00 8.00
❑ 146 Kalimba Edwards AU RC 4.00 10.00
❑ 147 Ken Simonton AU RC 3.00 8.00
❑ 148 Kurt Kittner AU RC 3.00 8.00
❑ 149 Lamar Gordon AU RC 5.00 12.00
❑ 150 Leonard Henry AU RC 3.00 8.00
❑ 151 Lito Sheppard AU RC 5.00 12.00
❑ 152 Luke Staley AU RC 3.00 8.00
❑ 153 Matt Schobel AU RC 5.00 12.00
❑ 154 Mike Rumph AU RC 3.00 8.00
❑ 155 Najeh Davenport AU RC 5.00 12.00
❑ 156 Napoleon Harris AU RC 4.00 10.00
❑ 158 Quentin Jammer AU RC 5.00 12.00
❑ 159 Randy Fasani AU RC 4.00 10.00
❑ 160 Ronald Curry AU RC 5.00 12.00
❑ 161 Ryan Sims AU RC 5.00 12.00
❑ 162 Sam Simmons AU RC 3.00 8.00
❑ 163 Seth Burford AU RC 3.00 8.00
❑ 164 Tellis Redmon AU RC 3.00 8.00
❑ 165 Terry Charles AU RC 3.00 8.00
❑ 166 Tracey Wistrom AU RC 4.00 10.00
❑ 167 Verron Haynes AU RC 4.00 10.00
❑ 168 Wes Pate AU RC 3.00 8.00
❑ 169 Wendell Bryant AU RC 3.00 8.00
❑ 170 Damien Anderson AU RC 4.00 10.00

2004 Bowman's Best

❑ COMP.SET w/o SP's (100) 25.00 50.00
❑ RC JSY GROUP A ODDS 1:130
❑ RC JSY GROUP B ODDS 1:236
❑ RC JSY GROUP C ODDS 1:86
❑ RC JSY GROUP D ODDS 1:38
❑ RC JSY GROUP E ODDS 1:31
❑ RC JSY GROUP F ODDS 1:27
❑ RC JSY GROUP G ODDS 1:50
❑ RC JSY GROUP H ODDS 1:89
❑ RC JSY GROUP I ODDS 1:29
❑ RC AU/199 STATED ODDS 1:311
❑ RC AU STATED ODDS 1:3
❑ 1 Brett Favre 1.25 3.00
❑ 2 Chris Chambers .40 1.00
❑ 3 Kyle Boller .40 1.00
❑ 4 Brian Urlacher .50 1.25
❑ 5 Marvin Harrison .50 1.25
❑ 6 Matt Hasselbeck .50 1.25
❑ 7 Aaron Brooks .40 1.00
❑ 8 Curtis Martin .50 1.25
❑ 9 Keenan McCardell .30 .75
❑ 10 Terrell Owens .50 1.25
❑ 11 Jimmy Smith .40 1.00
❑ 12 Garrison Hearst .40 1.00
❑ 13 Joe Horn .40 1.00
❑ 14 David Carr .40 1.00
❑ 15 Tom Brady 1.25 3.00
❑ 16 Shaun Alexander .50 1.25
❑ 17 Tommy Maddox .40 1.00
❑ 18 Tiki Barber .50 1.25
❑ 19 Trent Green .40 1.00
❑ 20 Anquan Boldin .50 1.25
❑ 21 Peerless Price .40 1.00
❑ 22 Jake Delhomme .40 1.00
❑ 23 Eric Moulds .40 1.00
❑ 24 Quincy Carter .30 .75
❑ 25 Steve McNair .50 1.25
❑ 26 Tim Rattay .30 .75
❑ 27 Laveranues Coles .40 1.00
❑ 28 Corey Dillon .40 1.00
❑ 29 Byron Leftwich .50 1.25
❑ 30 Chad Pennington .50 1.25
❑ 31 Koren Robinson .50 1.25
❑ 32 Plaxico Burress .40 1.00
❑ 33 Steve Smith .50 1.25
❑ 34 Warrick Dunn .40 1.00
❑ 35 Jamal Lewis .40 1.00
❑ 36 Charles Rogers .40 1.00
❑ 37 Tony Gonzalez .50 1.25
❑ 38 Jake Plummer .40 1.00
❑ 39 Chad Johnson .40 1.00
❑ 40 Peyton Manning 1.00 2.50
❑ 41 Daunte Culpepper .50 1.25
❑ 42 Fred Taylor .40 1.00
❑ 43 Amani Toomer .40 1.00
❑ 44 Santana Moss .40 1.00
❑ 45 Deuce McAllister .50 1.25
❑ 46 Rex Grossman .50 1.25
❑ 47 Ray Lewis .50 1.25
❑ 48 Hines Ward .50 1.25
❑ 49 Darrell Jackson .40 1.00
❑ 50 Randy Moss .50 1.25
❑ 51 Carson Palmer .60 1.50
❑ 52 Rod Smith .40 1.00
❑ 53 Drew Bledsoe .50 1.25
❑ 54 Brad Johnson .40 1.00
❑ 55 Travis Henry .40 1.00
❑ 56 Joey Harrington .40 1.00
❑ 57 Edgerrin James .50 1.25
❑ 58 Kurt Warner .50 1.25
❑ 59 Josh McCown .40 1.00
❑ 60 Clinton Portis .50 1.25
❑ 61 Brian Westbrook .50 1.25
❑ 62 Marc Bulger .40 1.00
❑ 63 Charlie Garner .40 1.00
❑ 64 Torry Holt .50 1.25
❑ 65 LaDainian Tomlinson .60 1.50
❑ 66 Mark Brunell .40 1.00
❑ 67 Derrick Mason .40 1.00
❑ 68 Andre Johnson .50 1.25
❑ 69 Keyshawn Johnson .40 1.00
❑ 70 Ahman Green .50 1.25
❑ 71 Rudi Johnson .40 1.00
❑ 72 Stephen Davis .40 1.00
❑ 73 Jeff Garcia .50 1.25
❑ 74 Michael Strahan .40 1.00
❑ 75 Michael Vick .50 1.25
❑ 76 Ricky Williams .50 1.25
❑ 77 Domanick Davis .40 1.00
❑ 78 Priest Holmes .50 1.25
❑ 79 Marshall Faulk .50 1.25
❑ 80 Donovan McNabb .50 1.25
❑ 81 Dunta Robinson RC 1.25 3.00
❑ 82 Robert Gallery RC 1.50 4.00
❑ 83 Ben Troupe RC 1.25 3.00
❑ 84 Antwan Odom RC 1.50 4.00
❑ 85 Brandon Miree RC 1.00 2.50
❑ 86 Darnell Dockett RC 1.00 2.50
❑ 87 Vince Wilfork RC 1.50 4.00
❑ 88 Randy Starks RC 1.00 2.50
❑ 89 Chris Cooley RC 1.50 4.00
❑ 90 Dwan Edwards RC 1.00 2.50
❑ 91 Patrick Crayton RC 2.00 5.00
❑ 92 Sean Jones RC 1.25 3.00
❑ 93 Sean Ryan RC 1.00 2.50
❑ 94 Chris Gamble RC 1.25 3.00
❑ 95 Will Smith RC 1.50 4.00
❑ 96 Sloan Thomas RC 1.25 3.00
❑ 97 Tim Euhus RC 1.00 2.50
❑ 98 Tommie Harris RC 1.50 4.00
❑ 99 Will Poole RC 1.50 4.00
❑ 100 Karlos Dansby RC 1.50 4.00
❑ 101 Bernard Berrian JSY RC D 2.50 6.00
❑ 102 DeAngelo Hall JSY RC A 2.50 6.00
❑ 103 Mewelde Moore JSY RC G 2.50 6.00
❑ 104 Rashaun Woods JSY RC G 1.50 4.00
❑ 105 Reggie Williams JSY RC 2.50 6.00
❑ 106 Derrick Hamilton JSY RC F 1.50 4.00
❑ 107 Kellen Winslow JSY RC C 6.00 15.00
❑ 108 Devard Darling JSY RC D 2.00 5.00
❑ 109 Michael Clayton JSY RC B 2.50 6.00
❑ 110 Larry Fitzgerald JSY RC E 6.00 15.00
❑ 111 Greg Jones JSY RC E 2.50 6.00
❑ 112 Chris Perry JSY RC H 2.50 6.00
❑ 113 Lee Evans JSY RC F 3.00 8.00
❑ 114 Tatum Bell JSY RC E 2.50 6.00
❑ 115 Steven Jackson JSY RC I 6.00 15.00
❑ 116 Matt Schaub JSY RC A 6.00 15.00
❑ 117 Ben Troupe JSY 2.00 5.00
❑ 118 Devery Henderson JSY RC F 2.50 6.00
❑ 119 Ben Watson JSY RC E 2.50 6.00
❑ 120 J.P. Losman JSY RC I 2.50 6.00
❑ 121 Keary Colbert JSY RC F 2.00 5.00
❑ 122 Darius Watts JSY RC C 2.00 5.00
❑ 123 Cedric Cobbs JSY RC D 2.00 5.00
❑ 124 Luke McCown JSY RC A 2.50 6.00
❑ 125 Michael Jenkins JSY RC A 2.50 6.00
❑ 126 Eli Manning AU/199 RC 75.00 150.00
❑ 127 Roy Williams AU/199 RC 25.00 60.00
❑ 128 Kevin Jones AU/199 RC 15.00 40.00
❑ 129 Philip Rivers AU/199 RC 50.00 100.00
❑ 130 Roethlisbergr AU/199 RC 125.00 200.00
❑ 131 Carlos Francis AU RC 3.00 8.00
❑ 132 Bradlee Van Pelt AU RC 4.00 10.00
❑ 133 Michael Turner AU RC 20.00 40.00
❑ 134 Kenechi Udeze AU RC 5.00 12.00
❑ 135 Jeff Smoker AU RC 4.00 10.00
❑ 136 Josh Harris AU RC 3.00 8.00
❑ 137 Derrick Strait AU RC 4.00 10.00
❑ 138 Jonathan Vilma AU RC 5.00 12.00
❑ 139 Triandos Luke AU RC 3.00 8.00
❑ 140 Jim Sorgi AU RC 5.00 12.00
❑ 141 Ryan Krause AU RC 3.00 8.00
❑ 142 Julius Jones AU RC 15.00 40.00
❑ 143 Mark Jones AU RC 3.00 8.00
❑ 144 P.K. Sam AU RC 3.00 8.00
❑ 145 B.J. Symons AU RC 3.00 8.00
❑ 146 A. Echemandu AU RC 4.00 10.00
❑ 147 Casey Bramlet AU RC 3.00 8.00
❑ 148 Clarence Moore AU RC 4.00 10.00
❑ 149 D.J. Williams AU RC 5.00 12.00
❑ 150 Jeris McIntyre AU RC 3.00 8.00
❑ 151 Jerricho Cotchery AU RC 6.00 15.00
❑ 152 Andy Hall AU RC 4.00 10.00
❑ 153 Samie Parker AU RC 4.00 10.00
❑ 154 Maurice Mann AU RC 3.00 8.00
❑ 155 Jonathan Smith AU RC 3.00 8.00
❑ 156 Derrick Ward AU RC 6.00 15.00
❑ 157 D.J. Hackett AU RC 6.00 15.00
❑ 158 Craig Krenzel AU RC 5.00 12.00
❑ 159 Jared Lorenzen AU RC 4.00 10.00
❑ 160 Cody Pickett AU RC 4.00 10.00
❑ 161 Jamaar Taylor AU RC 3.00 8.00
❑ 162 Michael Boulware AU RC 5.00 12.00
❑ 163 Matt Mauck AU RC 4.00 10.00
❑ 164 John Navarre AU RC 4.00 10.00
❑ 165 Ahmad Carroll AU RC 5.00 12.00
❑ 166 Bruce Perry AU RC 3.00 8.00
❑ 167 Erik Jensen AU RC 3.00 8.00
❑ 168 Matt Kranchick AU RC 5.00 12.00
❑ 169 Courtney Anderson AU RC 3.00 8.00
❑ 170 Nate Lawrie AU RC 3.00 8.00
❑ 171 Thomas Tapeh AU RC 4.00 10.00
❑ 172 Courtney Watson AU RC 4.00 10.00
❑ 173 Drew Carter AU RC 5.00 12.00
❑ 174 Ricardo Colclough AU RC 5.00 12.00
❑ 175 Dontarrious Thomas AU RC 4.00 10.00
❑ 176 Ernest Wilford AU RC 4.00 10.00
❑ 177 Quincy Wilson AU RC 4.00 10.00
❑ 178 Derek Abney AU RC 3.00 8.00
❑ 179 Jeff Dugan AU RC 3.00 8.00
❑ 180 Ben Hartsock AU RC 4.00 10.00
❑ 181 Matt Kegel AU RC 5.00 12.00
❑ 182 Derrick Knight AU RC 3.00 8.00
❑ 183 Teddy Lehman AU RC 4.00 10.00
❑ 184 Johnnie Morant AU RC 4.00 10.00
❑ 185A B.Sanders AU RC Long AU 100.00 150.00
❑ 185B B.Sanders AU RC Short AU 50.00 100.00
❑ 186 Michael Gaines AU RC 3.00 8.00
❑ 187 Daryl Smith AU RC 4.00 10.00
❑ 188 Jason Babin AU RC 4.00 10.00

2005 Bowman's Best

❑ COMP.SET w/o SPs (100) 15.00 40.00
❑ ROOKIE JSY STATED ODDS 1:14
❑ ROOKIE JSY PRINT RUN 799 SER.#'d SETS
❑ ROOKIE AU/999 STATED ODDS 1:8
❑ ROOKIE AU/199 STATED ODDS 1:296
❑ ROOKIE AU PRINT RUN 999 SER.#'d SETS
❑ UNPRICED GOLD PRINT RUN 1 SET
❑ UNPRICED PRINT.PLATE PRINT RUN 1 SET
❑ 1 Tiki Barber .40 1.00
❑ 2 Peyton Manning .60 1.50
❑ 3 Tony Gonzalez .30 .75
❑ 4 Terrell Owens .40 1.00
❑ 5 Brett Favre 1.00 2.50
❑ 6 Rudi Johnson .30 .75
❑ 7 Hines Ward .40 1.00
❑ 8 Andre Johnson .30 .75
❑ 9 Tom Brady .75 2.00
❑ 10 LaDainian Tomlinson .50 1.25
❑ 11 Daunte Culpepper .40 1.00
❑ 12 Muhsin Muhammad .30 .75
❑ 13 Dwight Freeney .30 .75
❑ 14 Curtis Martin .40 1.00
❑ 15 Eli Manning .75 2.00
❑ 16 Willis McGahee .40 1.00
❑ 17 Steve McNair .40 1.00
❑ 18 Jamal Lewis .30 .75
❑ 19 Reggie Wayne .30 .75
❑ 20 Trent Green .30 .75
❑ 21 Isaac Bruce .30 .75
❑ 22 Edgerrin James .30 .75
❑ 23 Marc Bulger .30 .75
❑ 24 Torry Holt .30 .75
❑ 25 Deuce McAllister .40 1.00
❑ 26 Jake Plummer .30 .75
❑ 27 Randy Moss .40 1.00
❑ 28 Drew Brees .40 1.00
❑ 29 Ahman Green .40 1.00
❑ 30 Marvin Harrison .40 1.00
❑ 31 Michael Vick .40 1.00
❑ 32 Julius Jones .40 1.00
❑ 33 Matt Hasselbeck .30 .75
❑ 34 Priest Holmes .40 1.00
❑ 35 Drew Bennett .30 .75
❑ 36 Donovan McNabb .40 1.00
❑ 37 Chad Johnson .30 .75
❑ 38 Fred Taylor .40 1.00
❑ 39 Chris Brown .30 .75
❑ 40 Jake Delhomme .40 1.00
❑ 41 Joe Horn .30 .75
❑ 42 Chad Pennington .40 1.00
❑ 43 Corey Dillon .30 .75
❑ 44 Byron Leftwich .30 .75
❑ 45 Javon Walker .30 .75
❑ 46 Ben Roethlisberger 1.00 2.50
❑ 47 Eric Moulds .30 .75
❑ 48 Domanick Davis .25 .60
❑ 49 Steven Jackson .50 1.25
❑ 50 Shaun Alexander .40 1.00
❑ 51 Stanford Routt RC 1.25 3.00
❑ 52 Marion Barber RC 5.00 12.00
❑ 53 Matt Roth RC 1.50 4.00
❑ 54 James Kilian RC 1.00 2.50
❑ 55 Alex Barron RC 1.00 2.50
❑ 56 Madison Hedgecock RC 1.50 4.00
❑ 57 Patrick Estes RC 1.00 2.50
❑ 58 Bryant McFadden RC 1.25 3.00
❑ 59 Dan Cody RC 1.50 4.00
❑ 60 Justin Miller RC 1.25 3.00
❑ 61 Paris Warren RC 1.25 3.00
❑ 62 Marcus Spears RC 1.50 4.00
❑ 63 Odell Thurman RC 1.50 4.00
❑ 64 Craphonso Thorpe RC 1.25 3.00
❑ 65 Dustin Fox RC 1.50 4.00
❑ 66 David Pollack RC 1.25 3.00
❑ 67 Anthony Davis RC 1.25 3.00
❑ 68 Mike Nugent RC 1.25 3.00
❑ 69 David Greene RC 1.25 3.00
❑ 70 Rick Razzano RC 1.00 2.50
❑ 70AU Rick Razzano AU 3.00 8.00
❑ 71 Mike Patterson RC 1.25 3.00
❑ 72 Derek Anderson RC 1.50 4.00
❑ 72AU Derek Anderson AU 10.00 25.00
❑ 73 Marlin Jackson RC 1.25 3.00
❑ 73AU Marlin Jackson AU 4.00 10.00
❑ 74 Boomer Grigsby RC 1.50 4.00
❑ 75 Kevin Burnett RC 1.25 3.00
❑ 76 Ryan Riddle RC 1.00 2.50
❑ 77 Brock Berlin RC 1.25 3.00
❑ 78 Khalif Barnes RC 1.00 2.50
❑ 79 Marcus Maxwell RC 1.00 2.50
❑ 80 Fred Gibson RC 1.25 3.00
❑ 81 T.A. McLendon RC 1.00 2.50
❑ 82 Kirk Morrison RC 1.50 4.00
❑ 83 Sean Considine RC 1.00 2.50
❑ 84 Luis Castillo RC 1.50 4.00
❑ 85 Darryl Blackstock RC 1.00 2.50
❑ 86 Airese Currie RC 1.25 3.00
❑ 87 Corey Webster RC 1.50 4.00
❑ 88 Kurt Campbell RC 1.00 2.50
❑ 89 Ellis Hobbs RC 1.50 4.00
❑ 90 Timmy Chang RC 1.25 3.00
❑ 91 Travis Johnson RC 1.00 2.50
❑ 92 Eric Moore RC 1.00 2.50
❑ 93 Barrett Ruud RC 1.50 4.00
❑ 94 Erasmus James RC 1.25 3.00
❑ 95 Anttaj Hawthorne RC 1.25 3.00
❑ 96 Manuel White RC 1.25 3.00
❑ 97 Rian Wallace RC 1.25 3.00
❑ 98 Justin Tuck RC 2.00 5.00
❑ 99 Travis Daniels RC 1.25 3.00
❑ 100 Donte Nicholson RC 1.25 3.00
❑ 101 Matt Jones JSY RC 2.50 6.00
❑ 102 J.J. Arrington JSY RC 2.50 6.00
❑ 103 Mark Bradley JSY RC 2.00 5.00
❑ 104 Reggie Brown JSY RC 2.00 5.00
❑ 105 Jason Campbell JSY RC 4.00 10.00
❑ 106 Maurice Clarett JSY 2.00 5.00
❑ 107 Mark Clayton JSY RC 2.50 6.00
❑ 108 Braylon Edwards JSY RC 6.00 15.00
❑ 109 Ciatrick Fason JSY RC 2.00 5.00
❑ 110 Charlie Frye JSY RC 2.50 6.00
❑ 111 Frank Gore JSY RC 5.00 12.00
❑ 112 Vincent Jackson JSY RC 3.00 8.00
❑ 113 Adam Jones JSY RC 2.00 5.00
❑ 114 Stefan LeFors JSY 2.00 5.00
❑ 114AU Stefan LeFors AU RC 4.00 10.00
❑ 115 Ryan Moats JSY 2.00 5.00
❑ 115AU Ryan Moats AU RC 4.00 10.00
❑ 116 Vernand Morency JSY RC 2.00 5.00
❑ 117 Terrence Murphy JSY RC 1.50 4.00
❑ 118 Kyle Orton JSY RC 4.00 10.00
❑ 119 Roscoe Parrish JSY RC 2.00 5.00
❑ 120 Courtney Roby JSY RC 2.00 5.00
❑ 121 Carlos Rogers JSY RC 2.50 6.00
❑ 122 Antrel Rolle JSY RC 2.50 6.00
❑ 123 Eric Shelton JSY RC 2.00 5.00
❑ 124 Andrew Walter JSY RC 2.00 5.00
❑ 125 Roddy White JSY RC 3.00 8.00
❑ 126 Cadillac Williams JSY RC 4.00 10.00
❑ 127 Troy Williamson JSY RC 2.50 6.00
❑ 128 Cedric Benson AU/199 RC 15.00 40.00
❑ 129 Aaron Rodgers AU/199 RC 75.00 135.00
❑ 130 Alex Smith QB AU/199 RC 60.00 120.00
❑ 131 Mike Williams AU/199 8.00 20.00
❑ 132 Ronnie Brown AU/199 RC 50.00 120.00
❑ 133 Adrian McPherson AU RC 4.00 10.00
❑ 134 Brandon Jacobs AU RC 12.50 30.00
❑ 135 Chad Owens AU RC 5.00 12.00
❑ 136 Chase Lyman AU RC 3.00 8.00
❑ 137 Chris Henry AU RC 5.00 12.00
❑ 138 Craig Bragg AU RC 3.00 8.00
❑ 139 Damien Nash AU RC 4.00 10.00
❑ 140 Dante Ridgeway AU RC 3.00 8.00
❑ 141 Darren Sproles AU RC 10.00 20.00
❑ 142 Deandra Cobb AU RC 4.00 10.00
❑ 143 Gino Guidugli AU RC 3.00 8.00
❑ 144 J.R. Russell AU RC 3.00 8.00
❑ 145 Jerome Mathis AU RC 5.00 12.00
❑ 146 Josh Davis AU RC 3.00 8.00
❑ 147 Kay-Jay Harris AU RC 4.00 10.00
❑ 148 Larry Brackins AU RC 3.00 8.00
❑ 149 Matt Cassel AU RC 15.00 40.00
❑ 150 Noah Herron AU RC 5.00 12.00
❑ 151 Rasheed Marshall AU RC 4.00 10.00
❑ 152 Roydell Williams AU RC 4.00 10.00
❑ 153 Ryan Fitzpatrick AU RC 5.00 12.00
❑ 154 Steve Savoy AU RC 3.00 8.00
❑ 155 Tab Perry AU RC 5.00 12.00
❑ 156 Shawne Merriman AU RC 5.00 12.00
❑ 157 Charles Frederick AU RC 4.00 10.00
❑ 158 Alvin Pearman AU RC 3.00 8.00
❑ 159 Channing Crowder AU RC 4.00 10.00
❑ 160 Fabian Washington AU RC 5.00 12.00
❑ 161 Dan Orlovsky AU RC 5.00 12.00
❑ 162 Derrick Johnson AU RC 5.00 12.00
❑ 163 Alex Smith TE AU RC 5.00 12.00
❑ 164 Cedric Houston AU RC 5.00 12.00
❑ 165 Brandon Jones AU RC 5.00 12.00
❑ 166 DeMarcus Ware AU RC 12.50 25.00
❑ 167 Lionel Gates AU RC 3.00 8.00

1996 Donruss

❑ COMPLETE SET (240) 7.50 20.00
❑ 1 Barry Sanders .60 1.50
❑ 2 Flipper Anderson .02 .10
❑ 3 Ben Coates .07 .20
❑ 4 Rob Johnson .15 .40
❑ 5 Rodney Hampton .07 .20
❑ 6 Desmond Howard .07 .20
❑ 7 Craig Heyward .02 .10
❑ 8 Alvin Harper .02 .10
❑ 9 Todd Collins .07 .20
❑ 10 Ken Norton Jr. .02 .10
❑ 11 Stan Humphries .07 .20
❑ 12 Aeneas Williams .02 .10
❑ 13 Jeff Hostetler .02 .10
❑ 14 Frank Sanders .07 .20
❑ 15 J.J. Birden .02 .10
❑ 16 Bryce Paup .02 .10
❑ 17 Bill Brooks .02 .10
❑ 18 Kevin Williams .02 .10
❑ 19 Boomer Esiason .07 .20
❑ 20 O.J. McDuffie .07 .20
❑ 21 Eric Swann .02 .10
❑ 22 Neil Smith .07 .20
❑ 23 Charlie Garner .07 .20
❑ 24 Greg Lloyd .07 .20
❑ 25 Willie Jackson .07 .20
❑ 26 Shawn Jefferson .02 .10
❑ 27 Rodney Peete .02 .10
❑ 28 Michael Westbrook .15 .40
❑ 29 J.J. Stokes .15 .40
❑ 30 Troy Aikman .40 1.00
❑ 31 Sean Dawkins .02 .10
❑ 32 Larry Centers .07 .20
❑ 33 Herschel Walker .07 .20
❑ 34 Stoney Case .02 .10
❑ 35 Kevin Greene .07 .20
❑ 36 Quinn Early .02 .10
❑ 37 Fred Barnett .02 .10
❑ 38 Andre Coleman .02 .10
❑ 39 Mark Chmura .07 .20
❑ 40 Adrian Murrell .07 .20
❑ 41 Roosevelt Potts .02 .10
❑ 42 Jay Novacek .02 .10
❑ 43 Derrick Alexander .07 .20
❑ 44 Ken Dilger .07 .20
❑ 45 Rob Moore .07 .20
❑ 46 Cris Carter .15 .40
❑ 47 Jeff Blake .15 .40
❑ 48 Derek Loville .02 .10
❑ 49 Tyrone Wheatley .07 .20
❑ 50 Terrell Fletcher .02 .10
❑ 51 Sherman Williams .02 .10
❑ 52 Justin Armour .02 .10
❑ 53 Kordell Stewart .15 .40
❑ 54 Tim Brown .15 .40
❑ 55 Kevin Carter .02 .10
❑ 56 Andre Rison .07 .20

Card		
❑ 57 James O.Stewart	.07	.20
❑ 58 Brent Jones	.02	.10
❑ 59 Erik Kramer	.02	.10
❑ 60 Floyd Turner	.02	.10
❑ 61 Ricky Watters	.07	.20
❑ 62 Hardy Nickerson	.02	.10
❑ 63 Aaron Craver	.02	.10
❑ 64 Dave Krieg	.02	.10
❑ 65 Warren Moon	.07	.20
❑ 66 Wayne Chrebet	.20	.50
❑ 67 Napoleon Kaufman	.15	.40
❑ 68 Terance Mathis	.02	.10
❑ 69 Chad May	.02	.10
❑ 70 Andre Reed	.07	.20
❑ 71 Reggie White	.15	.40
❑ 72 Brett Favre	.75	2.00
❑ 73 Chris Zorich	.02	.10
❑ 74 Kerry Collins	.15	.40
❑ 75 Herman Moore	.07	.20
❑ 76 Yancey Thigpen	.07	.20
❑ 77 Glenn Foley	.07	.20
❑ 78 Quentin Coryatt	.02	.10
❑ 79 Terry Kirby	.07	.20
❑ 80 Edgar Bennett	.07	.20
❑ 81 Mark Brunell	.25	.60
❑ 82 Heath Shuler	.07	.20
❑ 83 Gus Frerotte	.07	.20
❑ 84 Deion Sanders	.25	.60
❑ 85 Calvin Williams	.02	.10
❑ 86 Junior Seau	.15	.40
❑ 87 Jim Kelly	.15	.40
❑ 88 Daryl Johnston	.07	.20
❑ 89 Irving Fryar	.07	.20
❑ 90 Brian Blades	.02	.10
❑ 91 Willie Davis	.02	.10
❑ 92 Jerome Bettis	.15	.40
❑ 93 Marcus Allen	.15	.40
❑ 94 Jeff Graham	.02	.10
❑ 95 Rick Mirer	.07	.20
❑ 96 Harvey Williams	.02	.10
❑ 97 Steve Atwater	.02	.10
❑ 98 Carl Pickens	.07	.20
❑ 99 Darick Holmes	.02	.10
❑ 100 Bruce Smith	.07	.20
❑ 101 Vinny Testaverde	.07	.20
❑ 102 Thurman Thomas	.15	.40
❑ 103 Drew Bledsoe	.25	.60
❑ 104 Bernie Parmalee	.02	.10
❑ 105 Greg Hill	.07	.20
❑ 106 Steve McNair	.30	.75
❑ 107 Andre Hastings	.02	.10
❑ 108 Eric Metcalf	.02	.10
❑ 109 Kimble Anders	.07	.20
❑ 110 Steve Tasker	.02	.10
❑ 111 Mark Carrier WR	.02	.10
❑ 112 Jerry Rice	.40	1.00
❑ 113 Joey Galloway	.15	.40
❑ 114 Robert Smith	.07	.20
❑ 115 Hugh Douglas	.07	.20
❑ 116 Willie McGinest	.02	.10
❑ 117 Terrell Davis	.30	.75
❑ 118 Cortez Kennedy	.02	.10
❑ 119 Marshall Faulk	.20	.50
❑ 120 Michael Haynes	.02	.10
❑ 121 Isaac Bruce	.15	.40
❑ 122 Brian Mitchell	.02	.10
❑ 123 Bryan Cox	.02	.10
❑ 124 Tamarick Vanover	.07	.20
❑ 125 William Floyd	.07	.20
❑ 126 Chris Chandler	.07	.20
❑ 127 Carnell Lake	.02	.10
❑ 128 Aaron Bailey	.02	.10
❑ 129 Darnay Scott	.07	.20
❑ 130 Darren Woodson	.07	.20
❑ 131 Ernie Mills	.02	.10
❑ 132 Charles Haley	.07	.20
❑ 133 Rocket Ismail	.02	.10
❑ 134 Bert Emanuel	.07	.20
❑ 135 Lake Dawson	.02	.10
❑ 136 Jake Reed	.07	.20
❑ 137 Dave Brown	.02	.10
❑ 138 Steve Bono	.02	.10
❑ 139 Terry Allen	.07	.20
❑ 140 Errict Rhett	.07	.20
❑ 141 Rod Woodson	.07	.20
❑ 142 Charles Johnson	.02	.10
❑ 143 Emmitt Smith	.60	1.50
❑ 144 Ki-Jana Carter	.07	.20
❑ 145 Garrison Hearst	.07	.20
❑ 146 Rashaan Salaam	.07	.20
❑ 147 Tony Boselli	.02	.10
❑ 148 Derrick Thomas	.15	.40
❑ 149 Mark Seay	.02	.10
❑ 150 Derrick Alexander	.02	.10
❑ 151 Christian Fauria	.02	.10
❑ 152 Aaron Hayden	.02	.10
❑ 153 Chris Warren	.07	.20
❑ 154 Dave Meggett	.02	.10
❑ 155 Jeff George	.07	.20
❑ 156 Jackie Harris	.02	.10
❑ 157 Michael Irvin	.15	.40
❑ 158 Scott Mitchell	.07	.20
❑ 160 Trent Dilfer	.15	.40
❑ 160 Kyle Brady	.02	.10
❑ 161 Dan Marino	.75	2.00
❑ 162 Curtis Martin	.30	.75
❑ 163 Mario Bates	.07	.20
❑ 164 Erric Pegram	.02	.10
❑ 165 Eric Zeier	.02	.10
❑ 166 Rodney Thomas	.02	.10
❑ 167 Neil O'Donnell	.07	.20
❑ 168 Warren Sapp	.02	.10
❑ 169 Jim Harbaugh	.07	.20
❑ 170 Henry Ellard	.02	.10
❑ 171 Anthony Miller	.07	.20
❑ 172 Derrick Moore	.02	.10
❑ 173 John Elway	.75	2.00
❑ 174 Vincent Brisby	.02	.10
❑ 175 Antonio Freeman	.15	.40
❑ 176 Chris Sanders	.07	.20
❑ 177 Steve Young	.30	.75
❑ 178 Shannon Sharpe	.07	.20
❑ 179 Brett Perriman	.02	.10
❑ 180 Orlando Thomas	.02	.10
❑ 181 Eric Bjornson	.02	.10
❑ 182 Natrone Means	.07	.20
❑ 183 Jim Everett	.02	.10
❑ 184 Curtis Conway	.15	.40
❑ 185 Robert Brooks	.15	.40
❑ 186 Tony Martin	.07	.20
❑ 187 Mark Carrier DB	.02	.10
❑ 188 LeShon Johnson	.02	.10
❑ 189 Bernie Kosar	.02	.10
❑ 190 Ray Zellars	.02	.10
❑ 191 Steve Walsh	.02	.10
❑ 192 Craig Erickson	.02	.10
❑ 193 Tommy Maddox	.15	.40
❑ 194 Leslie O'Neal	.02	.10
❑ 195 Harold Green	.02	.10
❑ 196 Steve Beuerlein	.07	.20
❑ 197 Ronald Moore	.02	.10
❑ 198 Leslie Shepherd	.02	.10
❑ 199 Leroy Hoard	.02	.10
❑ 200 Michael Jackson	.07	.20
❑ 201 Will Moore	.02	.10
❑ 202 Ricky Ervins	.02	.10
❑ 203 Keith Jennings	.02	.10
❑ 204 Eric Green	.02	.10
❑ 205 Mark Rypien	.02	.10
❑ 206 Torrance Small	.02	.10
❑ 207 Sean Gilbert	.02	.10
❑ 208 Mike Alstott RC	.40	1.00
❑ 209 Willie Anderson RC	.02	.10
❑ 210 Alex Molden RC	.02	.10
❑ 211 Jonathan Ogden RC	.15	.40
❑ 212 Stepfret Williams RC	.07	.20
❑ 213 Jeff Lewis RC	.07	.20
❑ 214 Regan Upshaw RC	.02	.10
❑ 215 Daryl Gardener RC	.02	.10
❑ 216 Danny Kanell RC	.15	.40
❑ 217 John Mobley RC	.02	.10
❑ 218 Reggie Brown LB RC	.02	.10
❑ 219 Muhsin Muhammad RC	.40	1.00
❑ 220 Kevin Hardy RC	.15	.40
❑ 221 Stanley Pritchett RC	.07	.20
❑ 222 Cedric Jones RC	.02	.10
❑ 223 Marco Battaglia RC	.02	.10
❑ 224 Duane Clemons RC	.02	.10
❑ 225 Jerald Moore RC	.07	.20
❑ 226 Simeon Rice RC	.40	1.00
❑ 227 Chris Darkins RC	.02	.10
❑ 228 Bobby Hoying RC	.15	.40
❑ 229 Stephen Davis RC	.60	1.50
❑ 230 Walt Harris RC	.02	.10
❑ 231 Jermane Mayberry RC	.02	.10
❑ 232 Tony Brackens RC	.15	.40
❑ 233 Eric Moulds RC	.50	1.25
❑ 234 Alex Van Dyke RC	.07	.20
❑ 235 Marvin Harrison RC	1.00	2.50
❑ 236 Rickey Dudley RC	.15	.40
❑ 237 Terrell Owens RC	1.00	2.50
❑ 238 Jerry Rice CL	.15	.40
❑ 239 Dan Marino CL	.15	.40
❑ 240 Emmitt Smith CL	.15	.40

1997 Donruss

Card		
❑ COMPLETE SET (230)	7.50	20.00
❑ 1 Dan Marino	.75	2.00
❑ 2 Brett Favre	.75	2.00
❑ 3 Emmitt Smith	.60	1.50
❑ 4 Eddie George	.20	.50
❑ 5 Karim Abdul-Jabbar	.10	.30
❑ 6 Terrell Davis	.25	.60
❑ 7 Curtis Martin	.25	.60
❑ 8 Drew Bledsoe	.25	.60
❑ 9 Jerry Rice	.40	1.00
❑ 10 Troy Aikman	.40	1.00
❑ 11 Barry Sanders	.60	1.50
❑ 12 Mark Brunell	.25	.60
❑ 13 Kerry Collins	.20	.50
❑ 14 Steve Young	.25	.60
❑ 15 Kordell Stewart	.20	.50
❑ 16 Eddie Kennison	.10	.30
❑ 17 Terry Glenn	.20	.50
❑ 18 John Elway	.75	2.00
❑ 19 Joey Galloway	.10	.30
❑ 20 Deion Sanders	.20	.50
❑ 21 Keyshawn Johnson	.20	.50
❑ 22 Lawrence Phillips	.07	.20
❑ 23 Ricky Watters	.10	.30
❑ 24 Marvin Harrison	.20	.50
❑ 25 Bobby Engram	.10	.30
❑ 26 Marshall Faulk	.25	.60
❑ 27 Carl Pickens	.10	.30
❑ 28 Isaac Bruce	.20	.50
❑ 29 Herman Moore	.10	.30
❑ 30 Jerome Bettis	.20	.50
❑ 31 Rashaan Salaam	.07	.20
❑ 32 Errict Rhett	.07	.20
❑ 33 Tim Biakabutuka	.10	.30
❑ 34 Robert Brooks	.10	.30
❑ 35 Antonio Freeman	.20	.50
❑ 36 Steve McNair	.25	.60
❑ 37 Jeff Blake	.10	.30
❑ 38 Tony Banks	.10	.30
❑ 39 Terrell Owens	.25	.60
❑ 40 Eric Moulds	.20	.50
❑ 41 Leeland McElroy	.07	.20
❑ 42 Chris Sanders	.07	.20
❑ 43 Thurman Thomas	.20	.50
❑ 44 Bruce Smith	.10	.30
❑ 45 Reggie White	.20	.50
❑ 46 Chris Warren	.10	.30
❑ 47 J.J. Stokes	.10	.30
❑ 48 Ben Coates	.10	.30
❑ 49 Tim Brown	.20	.50
❑ 50 Marcus Allen	.20	.50
❑ 51 Michael Irvin	.20	.50
❑ 52 William Floyd	.10	.30
❑ 53 Ken Dilger	.07	.20
❑ 54 Bobby Taylor	.07	.20
❑ 55 Keenan McCardell	.10	.30
❑ 56 Raymont Harris	.07	.20
❑ 57 Keith Byars	.07	.20
❑ 58 O.J. McDuffie	.10	.30
❑ 59 Robert Smith	.10	.30
❑ 60 Bert Emanuel	.10	.30
❑ 61 Rick Mirer	.07	.20
❑ 62 Vinny Testaverde	.10	.30
❑ 63 Kyle Brady	.07	.20
❑ 64 Mark Bruener	.07	.20
❑ 65 Neil O'Donnell	.10	.30
❑ 66 Anthony Johnson	.07	.20
❑ 67 Ken Norton	.07	.20

Card		
❑ 68 Warren Sapp	.10	.30
❑ 69 Amani Toomer	.10	.30
❑ 70 Simeon Rice	.10	.30
❑ 71 Kevin Hardy	.07	.20
❑ 72 Junior Seau	.20	.50
❑ 73 Neil Smith	.10	.30
❑ 74 LeShon Johnson	.07	.20
❑ 75 Quinn Early	.07	.20
❑ 76 Andre Reed	.10	.30
❑ 77 Jake Reed	.10	.30
❑ 78 Elvis Grbac	.10	.30
❑ 79 Tyrone Wheatley	.10	.30
❑ 80 Adrian Murrell	.10	.30
❑ 81 Fred Barnett	.07	.20
❑ 82 Darrell Green	.10	.30
❑ 83 Stan Humphries	.10	.30
❑ 84 Troy Drayton	.07	.20
❑ 85 Steve Atwater	.07	.20
❑ 86 Quentin Coryatt	.07	.20
❑ 87 Dan Wilkinson	.07	.20
❑ 88 Scott Mitchell	.10	.30
❑ 89 Willie McGinest	.07	.20
❑ 90 Kevin Smith	.07	.20
❑ 91 Gus Frerotte	.07	.20
❑ 92 Byron Bam Morris	.07	.20
❑ 93 Darick Holmes	.07	.20
❑ 94 Zach Thomas	.20	.50
❑ 95 Tom Carter	.07	.20
❑ 96 Cortez Kennedy	.07	.20
❑ 97 Kevin Williams	.07	.20
❑ 98 Michael Haynes	.07	.20
❑ 99 Lamont Warren	.07	.20
❑ 100 Jeff Graham	.07	.20
❑ 101 Alex Van Dyke	.07	.20
❑ 102 Jim Everett	.07	.20
❑ 103 Chris Chandler	.10	.30
❑ 104 Qadry Ismail	.10	.30
❑ 105 Ray Zellars	.07	.20
❑ 106 Chris T. Jones	.07	.20
❑ 107 Charlie Garner	.10	.30
❑ 108 Bobby Hoying	.10	.30
❑ 109 Mark Chmura	.10	.30
❑ 110 Cris Carter	.20	.50
❑ 111 Darnay Scott	.10	.30
❑ 112 Anthony Miller	.07	.20
❑ 113 Desmond Howard	.10	.30
❑ 114 Terance Mathis	.10	.30
❑ 115 Rodney Hampton	.10	.30
❑ 116 Napoleon Kaufman	.20	.50
❑ 117 Jim Harbaugh	.10	.30
❑ 118 Shannon Sharpe	.10	.30
❑ 119 Irving Fryar	.10	.30
❑ 120 Garrison Hearst	.10	.30
❑ 121 Terry Allen	.20	.50
❑ 122 Larry Centers	.10	.30
❑ 123 Sean Dawkins	.07	.20
❑ 124 Jeff George	.10	.30
❑ 125 Tony Martin	.10	.30
❑ 126 Mike Alstott	.20	.50
❑ 127 Rickey Dudley	.10	.30
❑ 128 Kevin Carter	.07	.20
❑ 129 Derrick Alexander WR	.10	.30
❑ 130 Greg Lloyd	.07	.20
❑ 131 Bryce Paup	.07	.20
❑ 132 Derrick Thomas	.20	.50
❑ 133 Greg Hill	.07	.20
❑ 134 Jamal Anderson	.20	.50
❑ 135 Curtis Conway	.10	.30
❑ 136 Frank Sanders	.10	.30
❑ 137 Brett Perriman	.07	.20
❑ 138 Edgar Bennett	.10	.30
❑ 139 Wayne Chrebet	.20	.50
❑ 140 Natrone Means	.10	.30
❑ 141 Eric Metcalf	.10	.30
❑ 142 Trent Dilfer	.20	.50
❑ 143 Terry Kirby	.10	.30
❑ 144 Johnnie Morton	.10	.30
❑ 145 Dale Carter	.07	.20
❑ 146 Michael Westbrook	.10	.30
❑ 147 Stanley Pritchett	.07	.20
❑ 148 Todd Collins	.07	.20
❑ 149 Tamarick Vanover	.10	.30
❑ 150 Kevin Greene	.10	.30
❑ 151 Lamar Lathon	.07	.20
❑ 152 Muhsin Muhammad	.10	.30
❑ 153 Dorsey Levens	.20	.50
❑ 154 Rod Woodson	.10	.30
❑ 155 Brent Jones	.07	.20
❑ 156 Michael Jackson	.10	.30
❑ 157 Shawn Jefferson	.07	.20
❑ 158 Kimble Anders	.10	.30
❑ 159 Sean Gilbert	.07	.20
❑ 160 Carnell Lake	.07	.20
❑ 161 Darren Woodson	.07	.20
❑ 162 Dave Meggett	.07	.20
❑ 163 Henry Ellard	.07	.20
❑ 164 Eric Swann	.07	.20
❑ 165 Tony Boselli	.07	.20
❑ 166 Daryl Johnston	.10	.30
❑ 167 Willie Jackson	.07	.20
❑ 168 Wesley Walls	.10	.30
❑ 169 Mario Bates	.07	.20
❑ 170 Lake Dawson	.07	.20
❑ 171 Mike Mamula	.07	.20
❑ 172 Ed McCaffrey	.10	.30
❑ 173 Tony Brackens	.07	.20
❑ 174 Craig Heyward	.07	.20
❑ 175 Harvey Williams	.07	.20
❑ 176 Dave Brown	.07	.20
❑ 177 Aaron Glenn	.07	.20
❑ 178 Jeff Hostetler	.07	.20
❑ 179 Alvin Harper	.07	.20
❑ 180 Ty Detmer	.10	.30
❑ 181 James Jett	.10	.30
❑ 182 James O.Stewart	.10	.30
❑ 183 Warren Moon	.20	.50
❑ 184 Herschel Walker	.10	.30
❑ 185 Ki-Jana Carter	.07	.20
❑ 186 Leslie O'Neal	.07	.20
❑ 187 Danny Kanell	.07	.20
❑ 188 Eric Bjornson	.07	.20
❑ 189 Alex Molden	.07	.20
❑ 190 Bryant Young	.07	.20
❑ 191 Merton Hanks	.07	.20
❑ 192 Heath Shuler	.07	.20
❑ 193 Brian Blades	.07	.20
❑ 194 Steve Bono	.10	.30
❑ 195 Wayne Simmons	.07	.20
❑ 196 Warrick Dunn RC	.60	1.50
❑ 197 Peter Boulware RC	.20	.50
❑ 198 David LaFleur RC	.07	.20
❑ 199 Shawn Springs RC	.10	.30
❑ 200 Reidel Anthony RC	.20	.50
❑ 201 Jim Druckenmiller RC	.10	.30
❑ 202 Orlando Pace RC	.20	.50
❑ 203 Yatil Green RC	.10	.30
❑ 204 Bryant Westbrook RC	.07	.20
❑ 205 Tiki Barber RC	1.25	3.00
❑ 206 James Farrior RC	.20	.50
❑ 207 Rae Carruth RC	.07	.20
❑ 208 Danny Wuerffel RC	.20	.50
❑ 209 Corey Dillon RC	1.25	3.00
❑ 210 Ike Hilliard RC	.30	.75
❑ 211 Tony Gonzalez RC	.60	1.50
❑ 212 Antowain Smith RC	.50	1.25
❑ 213 Pat Barnes RC	.20	.50
❑ 214 Troy Davis RC	.10	.30
❑ 215 Byron Hanspard RC	.10	.30
❑ 216 Joey Kent RC	.20	.50
❑ 217 Jake Plummer RC	1.00	2.50
❑ 218 Kenny Holmes RC	.20	.50
❑ 219 Darnell Autry RC	.10	.30
❑ 220 Darrell Russell RC	.07	.20
❑ 221 Walter Jones RC	.20	.50
❑ 222 Dwayne Rudd RC	.20	.50
❑ 223 Tom Knight RC	.07	.20
❑ 224 Kevin Lockett RC	.10	.30
❑ 225 Will Blackwell RC	.10	.30
❑ 226 Dan Marino CL	.15	.40
❑ 227 Brett Favre CL	.15	.40
❑ 228 Emmitt Smith CL	.20	.50
❑ 229 Barry Sanders CL	.20	.50
❑ 230 Jerry Rice CL	.08	.25
❑ P1 Drew Bledsoe Promo	.40	1.00
❑ P2 Mark Brunell Promo	.40	1.00
❑ P3 Barry Sanders Promo	.60	1.50

1999 Donruss

Card		
❑ COMPLETE SET (200)	40.00	100.00
❑ COMP.SET w/o SP's (150)	10.00	20.00
❑ 1 Jake Plummer	.15	.40
❑ 2 Rob Moore	.15	.40
❑ 3 Adrian Murrell	.15	.40
❑ 4 Frank Sanders	.15	.40
❑ 5 Jamal Anderson	.25	.60
❑ 6 Tim Dwight	.15	.40
❑ 7 Terance Mathis	.15	.40
❑ 8 Chris Chandler	.15	.40
❑ 9 Byron Hanspard	.08	.25
❑ 10 Priest Holmes	.40	1.00
❑ 11 Jermaine Lewis	.15	.40
❑ 12 Errict Rhett	.15	.40
❑ 13 Doug Flutie	.25	.60
❑ 14 Eric Moulds	.25	.60
❑ 15 Antowain Smith	.25	.60
❑ 16 Thurman Thomas	.15	.40
❑ 17 Andre Reed	.15	.40
❑ 18 Bruce Smith	.15	.40
❑ 19 Tim Biakabutuka	.15	.40
❑ 20 Rae Carruth	.08	.25
❑ 21 Muhsin Muhammad	.15	.40
❑ 22 Curtis Enis	.08	.25
❑ 23 Curtis Conway	.15	.40
❑ 24 Bobby Engram	.15	.40
❑ 25 Corey Dillon	.25	.60
❑ 26 Carl Pickens	.15	.40
❑ 27 Jeff Blake	.15	.40
❑ 28 Darnay Scott	.15	.40
❑ 29 Ty Detmer	.15	.40
❑ 30 Leslie Shepherd	.08	.25
❑ 31 Emmitt Smith	.50	1.25
❑ 32 Troy Aikman	.50	1.25
❑ 33 Michael Irvin	.15	.40
❑ 34 Deion Sanders	.25	.60
❑ 35 Rocket Ismail	.15	.40
❑ 36 John Elway	.75	2.00
❑ 37 Terrell Davis	.25	.60
❑ 38 Ed McCaffrey	.15	.40
❑ 39 Shannon Sharpe	.15	.40
❑ 40 Rod Smith	.15	.40
❑ 41 Bubby Brister	.08	.25
❑ 42 Brian Griese	.25	.60
❑ 43 Barry Sanders	.75	2.00
❑ 44 Charlie Batch	.25	.60
❑ 45 Herman Moore	.15	.40
❑ 46 Germane Crowell	.08	.25
❑ 47 Johnnie Morton	.15	.40
❑ 48 Ron Rivers	.08	.25
❑ 49 Brett Favre	.75	2.00
❑ 50 Antonio Freeman	.25	.60
❑ 51 Dorsey Levens	.25	.60
❑ 52 Mark Chmura	.08	.25
❑ 53 Corey Bradford	.25	.60
❑ 54 Bill Schroeder	.25	.60
❑ 55 Peyton Manning ERR	.75	2.00
❑ 56 Marvin Harrison	.25	.60
❑ 57 E.G. Green	.08	.25
❑ 58 Fred Taylor	.25	.60
❑ 59 Mark Brunell	.25	.60
❑ 60 Tavian Banks	.08	.25
❑ 61 Jimmy Smith	.15	.40
❑ 62 Keenan McCardell	.15	.40
❑ 63 Warren Moon	.25	.60
❑ 64 Derrick Alexander WR	.15	.40
❑ 65 Byron Bam Morris	.08	.25
❑ 66 Elvis Grbac	.15	.40
❑ 67 Andre Rison	.15	.40
❑ 68 Dan Marino	.75	2.00
❑ 69 Karim Abdul-Jabbar	.15	.40
❑ 70 O.J. McDuffie	.15	.40
❑ 71 Tony Martin	.08	.25
❑ 72 Randy Moss	.60	1.50

Card	Low	High
73 Cris Carter	.25	.60
74 Randall Cunningham	.25	.60
75 Robert Smith	.25	.60
76 Jeff George	.15	.40
77 Jake Reed	.15	.40
78 Terry Allen	.15	.40
79 Drew Bledsoe	.30	.75
80 Terry Glenn	.25	.60
81 Ben Coates	.15	.40
82 Tony Simmons	.08	.25
83 Cam Cleeland	.08	.25
84 Eddie Kennison	.15	.40
85 Kerry Collins	.08	.25
86 Ike Hilliard	.08	.25
87 Gary Brown	.08	.25
88 Joe Jurevicius	.15	.40
89 Kent Graham	.08	.25
90 Wayne Chrebet	.15	.40
91 Keyshawn Johnson	.25	.60
92 Curtis Martin	.25	.60
93 Vinny Testaverde	.15	.40
94 Tim Brown	.25	.60
95 Napoleon Kaufman	.25	.60
96 Charles Woodson	.25	.60
97 Tyrone Wheatley	.15	.40
98 Rich Gannon	.25	.60
99 Charles Johnson	.08	.25
100 Duce Staley	.25	.60
101 Kordell Stewart	.15	.40
102 Jerome Bettis	.25	.60
103 Hines Ward	.25	.60
104 Ryan Leaf	.25	.60
105 Natrone Means	.15	.40
106 Jim Harbaugh	.15	.40
107 Junior Seau	.25	.60
108 Mikhael Ricks	.08	.25
109 Jerry Rice	.50	1.25
110 Steve Young	.30	.75
111 Garrison Hearst	.15	.40
112 Terrell Owens	.25	.60
113 Lawrence Phillips	.15	.40
114 J.J. Stokes	.15	.40
115 Sean Dawkins	.08	.25
116 Derrick Mayes	.08	.25
117 Joey Galloway	.15	.40
118 Jon Kitna	.25	.60
119 Ahman Green	.25	.60
120 Ricky Watters	.15	.40
121 Isaac Bruce	.25	.60
122 Marshall Faulk	.30	.75
123 Az-Zahir Hakim	.08	.25
124 Warrick Dunn	.25	.60
125 Mike Alstott	.25	.60
126 Trent Dilfer	.15	.40
127 Reidel Anthony	.15	.40
128 Jacquez Green	.08	.25
129 Warren Sapp	.15	.40
130 Eddie George	.25	.60
131 Steve McNair	.25	.60
132 Kevin Dyson	.15	.40
133 Yancey Thigpen	.08	.25
134 Frank Wycheck	.08	.25
135 Stephen Davis	.25	.60
136 Brad Johnson	.25	.60
137 Skip Hicks	.08	.25
138 Michael Westbrook	.15	.40
139 Darrell Green	.08	.25
140 Albert Connell	.08	.25
141 Tim Couch RC	.75	2.00
142 Donovan McNabb RC	3.00	8.00
143 Akili Smith RC	.60	1.50
144 Edgerrin James RC	2.50	6.00
145 Ricky Williams RC	1.25	3.00
146 Torry Holt RC	1.50	4.00
147 Champ Bailey RC	1.00	2.50
148 David Boston RC	.75	2.00
149 Andy Katzenmoyer RC	.60	1.50
150 Chris McAlister RC	.60	1.50
151 Daunte Culpepper RC	2.50	6.00
152 Cade McNown RC	.60	1.50
153 Troy Edwards RC	.60	1.50
154 Kevin Johnson RC	.75	2.00
155 James Johnson RC	.60	1.50
156 Rob Konrad RC	.60	1.50
157 Jim Kleinsasser RC	.75	2.00
158 Kevin Faulk RC	.75	2.00
159 Joe Montgomery RC	.60	1.50
160 Shaun King RC	.60	1.50
161 Peerless Price RC	.75	2.00
162 Mike Cloud RC	.60	1.50
163 Jermaine Fazande RC	.60	1.50
164 D'Wayne Bates RC	.60	1.50
165 Brock Huard RC	.75	2.00
166 Marty Booker RC	.75	2.00
167 Karsten Bailey RC	.60	1.50
168 Shawn Bryson RC	.75	2.00
169 Jeff Paulk RC	.40	1.00
170 Travis McGriff RC	.40	1.00
171 Amos Zereoue RC	.75	2.00
172 Craig Yeast RC	.60	1.50
173 Joe Germaine RC	.60	1.50
174 Dameane Douglas RC	.60	1.50
175 Brandon Stokley RC	1.00	2.50
176 Larry Parker RC	.75	2.00
177 Joel Makovicka RC	.75	2.00
178 Wane McGarity RC	.40	1.00
179 Na Brown RC	.60	1.50
180 Cecil Collins RC	.40	1.00
181 Nick Williams RC	.60	1.50
182 Charlie Rogers RC	.60	1.50
183 Darrin Chiaverini RC	.60	1.50
184 Terry Jackson RC	.60	1.50
185 De'Mond Parker RC	.40	1.00
186 Sedrick Irvin RC	.40	1.00
187 MarTay Jenkins RC	.75	2.00
188 Kurt Warner RC	5.00	12.00
189 Michael Bishop RC	.75	2.00
190 Sean Bennett RC	.40	1.00
191 Jamal Anderson CL	.08	.25
192 Eric Moulds CL	.08	.25
193 Terrell Davis CL	.25	.60
194 John Elway CL	.30	.75
195 Barry Sanders CL	.30	.75
196 Peyton Manning CL	.30	.75
197 Fred Taylor CL	.25	.60
198 Dan Marino CL	.30	.75
199 Randy Moss CL	.25	.60
200 Terrell Owens CL	.15	.40

2000 Donruss

Card	Low	High
COMPLETE SET (250)	150.00	400.00
COMP.SET w/o SP's (150)	7.50	20.00
1 Jake Plummer	.10	.30
2 Frank Sanders	.10	.30
3 Rob Moore	.10	.30
4 David Boston	.20	.50
5 Tim Dwight	.20	.50
6 Jamal Anderson	.20	.50
7 Chris Chandler	.10	.30
8 Terance Mathis	.10	.30
9 Tony Banks	.10	.30
10 Jermaine Lewis	.10	.30
11 Shannon Sharpe	.10	.30
12 Trent Dilfer	.10	.30
13 Qadry Ismail	.10	.30
14 Eric Moulds	.20	.50
15 Doug Flutie	.20	.50
16 Antowain Smith	.10	.30
17 Jonathan Linton	.07	.20
18 Peerless Price	.10	.30
19 Rob Johnson	.10	.30
20 Natrone Means	.10	.30
21 Muhsin Muhammad	.10	.30
22 Wesley Walls	.10	.30
23 Tim Biakabutuka	.10	.30
24 Steve Beuerlein	.10	.30
25 Patrick Jeffers	.20	.50
26 Curtis Enis	.07	.20
27 Cade McNown	.07	.20
28 Bobby Engram	.10	.30
29 Marcus Robinson	.20	.50
30 Marty Booker	.10	.30
31 Corey Dillon	.20	.50
32 Darnay Scott	.10	.30
33 Carl Pickens	.10	.30
34 Akili Smith	.07	.20
35 Michael Basnight	.07	.20
36 Tim Couch	.10	.30
37 Kevin Johnson	.20	.50
38 Karim Abdul-Jabbar	.10	.30
39 Errict Rhett	.10	.30
40 Darrin Chiaverini	.07	.20
41 Emmitt Smith	.40	1.00
42 Troy Aikman	.40	1.00
43 Joey Galloway	.10	.30
44 Randall Cunningham	.20	.50
45 Michael Irvin	.10	.30
46 Rocket Ismail	.10	.30
47 Jason Tucker	.07	.20
48 Terrell Davis	.20	.50
49 John Elway	.60	1.50
50 Olandis Gary	.10	.30
51 Ed McCaffrey	.20	.50
52 Rod Smith	.10	.30
53 Brian Griese	.20	.50
54 Charlie Batch	.20	.50
55 Barry Sanders	.50	1.25
56 Herman Moore	.10	.30
57 Johnnie Morton	.10	.30
58 Germane Crowell	.07	.20
59 James Stewart	.10	.30
60 Brett Favre	.60	1.50
61 Dorsey Levens	.10	.30
62 Antonio Freeman	.20	.50
63 Corey Bradford	.10	.30
64 Bill Schroeder	.10	.30
65 E.G. Green	.07	.20
66 Peyton Manning	.50	1.25
67 Edgerrin James	.30	.75
68 Marvin Harrison	.20	.50
69 Terrence Wilkins	.07	.20
70 Mark Brunell	.20	.50
71 Fred Taylor	.20	.50
72 Keenan McCardell	.10	.30
73 Jimmy Smith	.10	.30
74 Warren Moon	.20	.50
75 Elvis Grbac	.10	.30
76 Tony Gonzalez	.10	.30
77 Dan Marino	.60	1.50
78 O.J. McDuffie	.10	.30
79 Tony Martin	.10	.30
80 James Johnson	.07	.20
81 Thurman Thomas	.10	.30
82 Randy Moss	.40	1.00
83 Daunte Culpepper	.25	.60
84 Cris Carter	.20	.50
85 Robert Smith	.20	.50
86 John Randle	.10	.30
87 Drew Bledsoe	.25	.60
88 Terry Glenn	.10	.30
89 Kevin Faulk	.10	.30
90 Ricky Williams	.20	.50
91 Jeff Blake	.10	.30
92 Jake Reed	.10	.30
93 Amani Toomer	.10	.30
94 Kerry Collins	.10	.30
95 Tiki Barber	.20	.50
96 Ike Hilliard	.10	.30
97 Curtis Martin	.20	.50
98 Vinny Testaverde	.10	.30
99 Wayne Chrebet	.10	.30
100 Ray Lucas	.10	.30
101 Charles Woodson	.10	.30
102 Napoleon Kaufman	.10	.30
103 Tim Brown	.20	.50
104 Tyrone Wheatley	.10	.30
105 Rich Gannon	.20	.50
106 Duce Staley	.20	.50
107 Donovan McNabb	.30	.75
108 Amos Zereoue	.20	.50
109 Kordell Stewart	.10	.30
110 Jerome Bettis	.20	.50
111 Troy Edwards	.07	.20
112 Ryan Leaf	.10	.30
113 Junior Seau	.20	.50
114 Jim Harbaugh	.10	.30
115 Jermaine Fazande	.07	.20
116 Curtis Conway	.10	.30
117 Steve Young	.25	.60
118 Jerry Rice	.40	1.00
119 Terrell Owens	.20	.50
120 Charlie Garner	.10	.30
121 Jeff Garcia	.20	.50
122 Jon Kitna	.20	.50

Card		
❑ 123 Derrick Mayes	.10	.30
❑ 124 Ricky Watters	.10	.30
❑ 125 Kurt Warner	.40	1.00
❑ 126 Marshall Faulk	.25	.60
❑ 127 Torry Holt	.20	.50
❑ 128 Az-Zahir Hakim	.10	.30
❑ 129 Isaac Bruce	.20	.50
❑ 130 Mike Alstott	.20	.50
❑ 131 Warrick Dunn	.20	.50
❑ 132 Shaun King	.07	.20
❑ 133 Keyshawn Johnson	.20	.50
❑ 134 Jacquez Green	.07	.20
❑ 135 Reidel Anthony	.10	.30
❑ 136 Warren Sapp	.10	.30
❑ 137 Eddie George	.20	.50
❑ 138 Steve McNair	.20	.50
❑ 139 Yancey Thigpen	.07	.20
❑ 140 Kevin Dyson	.10	.30
❑ 141 Frank Wycheck	.10	.30
❑ 142 Jevon Kearse	.20	.50
❑ 143 Stephen Davis	.20	.50
❑ 144 Skip Hicks	.07	.20
❑ 145 Brad Johnson	.20	.50
❑ 146 Bruce Smith	.10	.30
❑ 147 Michael Westbrook	.10	.30
❑ 148 Albert Connell	.07	.20
❑ 149 Jeff George	.10	.30
❑ 150 Deion Sanders	.20	.50
❑ 151 Courtney Brown RC	2.50	6.00
❑ 152 Corey Simon RC	2.50	6.00
❑ 153 Brian Urlacher RC	10.00	25.00
❑ 154 Shaun Ellis RC	2.50	6.00
❑ 155 John Abraham RC	2.50	6.00
❑ 156 Deltha O'Neal RC	2.50	6.00
❑ 157 Ahmed Plummer RC	2.50	6.00
❑ 158 Chris Hovan RC	2.00	5.00
❑ 159 Rob Morris RC	2.00	5.00
❑ 160 Keith Bulluck RC	2.50	6.00
❑ 161 Darren Howard RC	2.00	5.00
❑ 162 John Engelberger RC	2.00	5.00
❑ 163 Raynoch Thompson RC	2.00	5.00
❑ 164 Cornelius Griffin RC	2.00	5.00
❑ 165 William Bartee RC	2.00	5.00
❑ 166 Fred Robbins RC	1.25	3.00
❑ 167 Micheal Boireau RC	1.25	3.00
❑ 168 Brandon Short RC	2.00	5.00
❑ 169 Jacoby Shepherd RC	1.25	3.00
❑ 170 Peter Warrick RC	2.50	6.00
❑ 171 Jamal Lewis RC	6.00	15.00
❑ 172 Thomas Jones RC	4.00	10.00
❑ 173 Plaxico Burress RC	5.00	12.00
❑ 174 Travis Taylor RC	2.50	6.00
❑ 175 Ron Dayne RC	2.50	6.00
❑ 176 Bubba Franks RC	2.50	6.00
❑ 177 Sebastian Janikowski RC	2.50	6.00
❑ 178 Chad Pennington RC	6.00	15.00
❑ 179 Shaun Alexander RC	8.00	20.00
❑ 180 Sylvester Morris RC	2.00	5.00
❑ 181 Anthony Becht RC	2.50	6.00
❑ 182 R.Jay Soward RC	2.00	5.00
❑ 183 Trung Canidate RC	2.00	5.00
❑ 184 Dennis Northcutt RC	2.50	6.00
❑ 185 Todd Pinkston RC	2.50	6.00
❑ 186 Jerry Porter RC	3.00	8.00
❑ 187 Travis Prentice RC	2.00	5.00
❑ 188 Giovanni Carmazzi RC	1.25	3.00
❑ 189 Ron Dugans RC	1.25	3.00
❑ 190 Erron Kinney RC	2.50	6.00
❑ 191 Dez White RC	2.50	6.00
❑ 192 Chris Cole RC	2.00	5.00
❑ 193 Ron Dixon RC	2.00	5.00
❑ 194 Chris Redman RC	2.00	5.00
❑ 195 J.R. Redmond RC	2.00	5.00
❑ 196 Laveranues Coles RC	3.00	8.00
❑ 197 JaJuan Dawson RC	1.25	3.00
❑ 198 Darrell Jackson RC	5.00	12.00
❑ 199 Reuben Droughns RC	3.00	8.00
❑ 200 Doug Chapman RC	2.00	5.00
❑ 201 Terrelle Smith RC	2.00	5.00
❑ 202 Curtis Keaton RC	2.00	5.00
❑ 203 Gari Scott RC	1.25	3.00
❑ 204 Danny Farmer RC	2.00	5.00
❑ 205 Hank Poteat RC	2.00	5.00
❑ 206 Ben Kelly RC	1.25	3.00
❑ 207 Corey Moore RC	1.25	3.00
❑ 208 Na'il Diggs RC	2.00	5.00
❑ 209 Aaron Shea RC	2.00	5.00
❑ 210 Trevor Gaylor RC	2.00	5.00
❑ 211 Julian Peterson RC	2.50	6.00
❑ 212 Frank Moreau RC	2.00	5.00
❑ 213 Deon Dyer RC	2.00	5.00
❑ 214 Avion Black RC	2.00	5.00
❑ 215 Paul Smith RC	2.00	5.00
❑ 216 Michael Wiley RC	2.00	5.00
❑ 217 Dante Hall RC	5.00	12.00
❑ 218 Mike Brown RC	4.00	10.00
❑ 219 Sammy Morris RC	2.50	6.00
❑ 220 Billy Volek RC	4.00	10.00
❑ 221 Tee Martin RC	2.50	6.00
❑ 222 Troy Walters RC	2.50	6.00
❑ 223 Chad Morton RC	2.50	6.00
❑ 224 Erik Flowers RC	2.00	5.00
❑ 225 Ronney Jenkins RC	2.00	5.00
❑ 226 Thomas Hamner RC	1.25	3.00
❑ 227 Mareno Philyaw RC	1.25	3.00
❑ 228 James Williams RC	2.00	5.00
❑ 229 Mike Anderson RC	3.00	8.00
❑ 230 Tom Brady RC	100.00	200.00
❑ 231 Mike Green RC	2.00	5.00
❑ 232 Todd Husak RC	2.50	6.00
❑ 233 Tim Rattay RC	2.50	6.00
❑ 234 Jarious Jackson RC	2.00	5.00
❑ 235 Joe Hamilton RC	2.00	5.00
❑ 236 Shyrone Stith RC	2.00	5.00
❑ 237 Rondell Mealey RC	1.25	3.00
❑ 238 Demario Brown RC	1.25	3.00
❑ 239 Chris Coleman RC	2.50	6.00
❑ 240 Dwayne Goodrich RC	1.25	3.00
❑ 241 Drew Haddad RC	1.25	3.00
❑ 242 Doug Johnson RC	2.50	6.00
❑ 243 Windrell Hayes RC	2.00	5.00
❑ 244 Charles Lee RC	1.25	3.00
❑ 245 Kevin McDougal RC	2.00	5.00
❑ 246 Spergon Wynn RC	2.00	5.00
❑ 247 Shockmain Davis RC	1.25	3.00
❑ 248 Jamel White RC	2.00	5.00
❑ 249 Bashir Yamini RC	1.25	3.00
❑ 250 Kwame Cavil RC	1.25	3.00

2002 Donruss

Card		
❑ COMPLETE SET (300)	60.00	120.00
❑ COMP.SET w/o SP's (200)	7.50	20.00
❑ 1 Jake Plummer	.15	.40
❑ 2 David Boston	.12	.30
❑ 3 MarTay Jenkins	.12	.30
❑ 4 Thomas Jones	.15	.40
❑ 5 Frank Sanders	.12	.30
❑ 6 Shawn Jefferson	.12	.30
❑ 7 Alge Crumpler	.15	.40
❑ 8 Michael Vick	.20	.50
❑ 9 Jamal Anderson	.15	.40
❑ 10 Warrick Dunn	.15	.40
❑ 11 Peter Boulware	.15	.40
❑ 12 Jamal Lewis	.15	.40
❑ 13 Jeff Blake	.15	.40
❑ 14 Travis Taylor	.12	.30
❑ 15 Ray Lewis	.20	.50
❑ 16 Todd Heap	.15	.40
❑ 17 Nate Clements	.12	.30
❑ 18 Alex Van Pelt	.12	.30
❑ 19 Reggie Germany	.12	.30
❑ 20 Larry Centers	.15	.40
❑ 21 Eric Moulds	.15	.40
❑ 22 Travis Henry	.15	.40
❑ 23 Wesley Walls	.15	.40
❑ 24 Steve Smith	.20	.50
❑ 25 Lamar Smith	.15	.40
❑ 26 Patrick Jeffers	.15	.40
❑ 27 Chris Weinke	.12	.30
❑ 28 Muhsin Muhammad	.15	.40
❑ 29 Marcus Robinson	.15	.40
❑ 30 Jim Miller	.15	.40
❑ 31 Anthony Thomas	.15	.40
❑ 32 David Terrell	.12	.30
❑ 33 Brian Urlacher	.25	.60
❑ 34 Marty Booker	.15	.40
❑ 35 Darnay Scott	.15	.40
❑ 36 Jon Kitna	.15	.40
❑ 37 Chad Johnson	.20	.50
❑ 38 T.J. Houshmandzadeh	.20	.50
❑ 39 Corey Dillon	.15	.40
❑ 40 Peter Warrick	.15	.40
❑ 41 Gerard Warren	.12	.30
❑ 42 Anthony Henry	.12	.30
❑ 43 Quincy Morgan	.12	.30
❑ 44 JaJuan Dawson	.12	.30
❑ 45 Tim Couch	.12	.30
❑ 46 Kevin Johnson	.12	.30
❑ 47 James Jackson	.12	.30
❑ 48 La'Roi Glover	.12	.30
❑ 49 Anthony Wright	.12	.30
❑ 50 Rocket Ismail	.15	.40
❑ 51 Troy Hambrick	.12	.30
❑ 52 Emmitt Smith	.50	1.25
❑ 53 Quincy Carter	.12	.30
❑ 54 Joey Galloway	.15	.40
❑ 55 Shannon Sharpe	.20	.50
❑ 56 Kevin Kasper	.12	.30
❑ 57 Olandis Gary	.15	.40
❑ 58 Brian Griese	.15	.40
❑ 59 Rod Smith	.15	.40
❑ 60 Terrell Davis	.20	.50
❑ 61 Ed McCaffrey	.15	.40
❑ 62 Mike Anderson	.15	.40
❑ 63 Bill Schroeder	.15	.40
❑ 64 Scotty Anderson	.12	.30
❑ 65 Mike McMahon	.12	.30
❑ 66 James Stewart	.12	.30
❑ 67 Az-Zahir Hakim	.12	.30
❑ 68 Germane Crowell	.12	.30
❑ 69 Kabeer Gbaja-Biamila	.15	.40
❑ 70 LeRoy Butler	.15	.40
❑ 71 Antonio Freeman	.20	.50
❑ 72 Bubba Franks	.15	.40
❑ 73 Brett Favre	.50	1.25
❑ 74 Ahman Green	.15	.40
❑ 75 Terry Glenn	.15	.40
❑ 76 Jamie Sharper	.15	.40
❑ 77 Tony Simmons	.12	.30
❑ 78 James Allen	.12	.30
❑ 79 Terrence Wilkins	.12	.30
❑ 80 Dominic Rhodes	.15	.40
❑ 81 Qadry Ismail	.15	.40
❑ 82 Peyton Manning	.40	1.00
❑ 83 Edgerrin James	.20	.50
❑ 84 Marvin Harrison	.20	.50
❑ 85 Reggie Wayne	.20	.50
❑ 86 Fred Taylor	.20	.50
❑ 87 Elvis Joseph	.12	.30
❑ 88 Mark Brunell	.15	.40
❑ 89 Keenan McCardell	.15	.40
❑ 90 Jimmy Smith	.15	.40
❑ 91 Kyle Brady	.12	.30
❑ 92 Derrick Alexander	.15	.40
❑ 93 Johnnie Morton	.15	.40
❑ 94 Trent Green	.15	.40
❑ 95 Priest Holmes	.20	.50
❑ 96 Tony Gonzalez	.15	.40
❑ 97 Snoop Minnis	.12	.30
❑ 98 Travis Minor	.15	.40
❑ 99 Oronde Gadsden	.12	.30
❑ 100 Jay Fiedler	.15	.40
❑ 101 Chris Chambers	.20	.50
❑ 102 Ricky Williams	.20	.50
❑ 103 Zach Thomas	.20	.50
❑ 104 Byron Chamberlain	.12	.30
❑ 105 Todd Bouman	.12	.30
❑ 106 Daunte Culpepper	.15	.40
❑ 107 Michael Bennett	.15	.40
❑ 108 Randy Moss	.20	.50
❑ 109 Cris Carter	.20	.50
❑ 110 David Patten	.12	.30
❑ 111 Donald Hayes	.12	.30
❑ 112 Tom Brady	.50	1.25
❑ 113 Antowain Smith	.15	.40
❑ 114 Troy Brown	.15	.40
❑ 115 Drew Bledsoe	.20	.50
❑ 116 Bryan Cox	.15	.40
❑ 117 Boo Williams	.12	.30
❑ 118 Aaron Brooks	.15	.40
❑ 119 Deuce McAllister	.20	.50
❑ 120 Joe Horn	.15	.40
❑ 121 Amani Toomer	.15	.40
❑ 122 Ron Dayne	.15	.40

Card	Lo	Hi
❑ 123 Kerry Collins	.15	.40
❑ 124 Ike Hilliard	.15	.40
❑ 125 Tiki Barber	.20	.50
❑ 126 Michael Strahan	.20	.50
❑ 127 Chad Pennington	.20	.50
❑ 128 Santana Moss	.15	.40
❑ 129 LaMont Jordan	.15	.40
❑ 130 Curtis Martin	.20	.50
❑ 131 Wayne Chrebet	.15	.40
❑ 132 Laveranues Coles	.20	.50
❑ 133 Vinny Testaverde	.15	.40
❑ 134 Charles Woodson	.20	.50
❑ 135 Tyrone Wheatley	.15	.40
❑ 136 Jerry Porter	.15	.40
❑ 137 Rich Gannon	.15	.40
❑ 138 Charlie Garner	.15	.40
❑ 139 Tim Brown	.20	.50
❑ 140 Jerry Rice	.40	1.00
❑ 141 James Thrash	.15	.40
❑ 142 Todd Pinkston	.12	.30
❑ 143 A.J. Feeley	.15	.40
❑ 144 Donovan McNabb	.25	.60
❑ 145 Duce Staley	.15	.40
❑ 146 Freddie Mitchell	.12	.30
❑ 147 Correll Buckhalter	.15	.40
❑ 148 Casey Hampton	.12	.30
❑ 149 Hines Ward	.20	.50
❑ 150 Chris Fuamatu-Ma'afala	.12	.30
❑ 151 Jerome Bettis	.20	.50
❑ 152 Kordell Stewart	.15	.40
❑ 153 Plaxico Burress	.15	.40
❑ 154 Kendrell Bell	.12	.30
❑ 155 Trevor Gaylor	.12	.30
❑ 156 Curtis Conway	.15	.40
❑ 157 Doug Flutie	.20	.50
❑ 158 Drew Brees	.30	.75
❑ 159 LaDainian Tomlinson	.30	.75
❑ 160 Junior Seau	.20	.50
❑ 161 Bryant Young	.12	.30
❑ 162 Andre Carter	.12	.30
❑ 163 Eric Johnson	.12	.30
❑ 164 Jeff Garcia	.15	.40
❑ 165 Garrison Hearst	.15	.40
❑ 166 Terrell Owens	.20	.50
❑ 167 Kevan Barlow	.12	.30
❑ 168 Levon Kirkland	.12	.30
❑ 169 Ricky Watters	.15	.40
❑ 170 Trent Dilfer	.15	.40
❑ 171 Shaun Alexander	.20	.50
❑ 172 Koren Robinson	.12	.30
❑ 173 Darrell Jackson	.15	.40
❑ 174 Adam Archuleta	.12	.30
❑ 175 Aeneas Williams	.15	.40
❑ 176 Trung Canidate	.12	.30
❑ 177 Kurt Warner	.20	.50
❑ 178 Marshall Faulk	.20	.50
❑ 179 Torry Holt	.20	.50
❑ 180 Isaac Bruce	.20	.50
❑ 181 John Lynch	.15	.40
❑ 182 Joe Jurevicius	.15	.40
❑ 183 Brad Johnson	.15	.40
❑ 184 Rob Johnson	.15	.40
❑ 185 Keyshawn Johnson	.15	.40
❑ 186 Mike Alstott	.15	.40
❑ 187 Warren Sapp	.15	.40
❑ 188 Drew Bennett	.15	.40
❑ 189 Frank Wycheck	.12	.30
❑ 190 Kevin Dyson	.15	.40
❑ 191 Steve McNair	.20	.50
❑ 192 Eddie George	.15	.40
❑ 193 Jevon Kearse	.15	.40
❑ 194 Derrick Mason	.15	.40
❑ 195 Champ Bailey	.20	.50
❑ 196 Darrell Green	.20	.50
❑ 197 Bruce Smith	.20	.50
❑ 198 Jacquez Green	.12	.30
❑ 199 Stephen Davis	.15	.40
❑ 200 Rod Gardner	.12	.30
❑ 201 David Carr RC	1.00	2.50
❑ 202 Joey Harrington RC	1.00	2.50
❑ 203 Patrick Ramsey RC	1.00	2.50
❑ 204 Kurt Kittner RC	.60	1.50
❑ 205 Rohan Davey RC	1.00	2.50
❑ 206 Josh McCown RC	1.00	2.50
❑ 207 David Garrard RC	1.50	4.00
❑ 208 Randy Fasani RC	.75	2.00
❑ 209 Atrews Bell RC	.60	1.50
❑ 210 Brandon Doman RC	.60	1.50
❑ 211 Eric Crouch RC	1.00	2.50
❑ 212 Woody Dantzler RC	.75	2.00
❑ 213 Chad Hutchinson RC	.60	1.50
❑ 214 Zak Kustok RC	.60	1.50
❑ 215 Ronald Curry RC	1.00	2.50
❑ 216 William Green RC	.75	2.00
❑ 217 T.J. Duckett RC	1.00	2.50
❑ 218 Clinton Portis RC	2.50	6.00
❑ 219 DeShaun Foster RC	1.00	2.50
❑ 220 Lamar Gordon RC	1.00	2.50
❑ 221 Jonathan Wells RC	1.00	2.50
❑ 222 Adrian Peterson RC	1.00	2.50
❑ 223 Ladell Betts RC	1.00	2.50
❑ 224 Maurice Morris RC	1.00	2.50
❑ 225 Brian Westbrook RC	3.00	8.00
❑ 226 Luke Staley RC	.60	1.50
❑ 227 Travis Stephens RC	.60	1.50
❑ 228 Craig Nall RC	.75	2.00
❑ 229 Chester Taylor RC	1.50	4.00
❑ 230 Ken Simonton RC	.60	1.50
❑ 231 Verron Haynes RC	.75	2.00
❑ 232 Tellis Redmon RC	.60	1.50
❑ 233 J.T. O'Sullivan RC	1.00	2.50
❑ 234 Major Applewhite RC	1.00	2.50
❑ 235 Ricky Williams RC	.75	2.00
❑ 236 James Mungro RC	1.00	2.50
❑ 237 Josh Scobey RC	.75	2.00
❑ 238 Najeh Davenport RC	1.00	2.50
❑ 239 Dicenzo Miller RC	.60	1.50
❑ 240 Ennis Haywood RC	.60	1.50
❑ 241 Jabar Gaffney RC	1.00	2.50
❑ 242 Antonio Bryant RC	1.25	3.00
❑ 243 Donte Stallworth RC	1.00	2.50
❑ 244 Josh Reed RC	.75	2.00
❑ 245 Ashley Lelie RC	1.00	2.50
❑ 246 Reche Caldwell RC	1.00	2.50
❑ 247 Marquise Walker RC	.60	1.50
❑ 248 Javon Walker RC	1.00	2.50
❑ 249 Andre Davis RC	.75	2.00
❑ 250 Antwaan Randle El RC	1.00	2.50
❑ 251 Kelly Campbell RC	.75	2.00
❑ 252 Cliff Russell RC	.60	1.50
❑ 253 Kahlil Hill RC	.60	1.50
❑ 254 Ron Johnson RC	.75	2.00
❑ 255 Deion Branch RC	1.00	2.50
❑ 256 Brian Poli-Dixon RC	.60	1.50
❑ 257 Freddie Milons RC	.60	1.50
❑ 258 Lee Mays RC	.60	1.50
❑ 259 Tim Carter RC	.75	2.00
❑ 260 Terry Charles RC	.60	1.50
❑ 261 Jamar Martin RC	.75	2.00
❑ 262 Jason McAddley RC	.75	2.00
❑ 263 Chris Hope RC	1.00	2.50
❑ 264 Howard Green RC	.60	1.50
❑ 265 Jeremy Shockey RC	1.50	4.00
❑ 266 Daniel Graham RC	.75	2.00
❑ 267 Eddie Freeman RC	.60	1.50
❑ 268 Julius Peppers RC	1.50	4.00
❑ 269 Kalimba Edwards RC	.75	2.00
❑ 270 Dwight Freeney RC	1.50	4.00
❑ 271 Dennis Johnson RC	.60	1.50
❑ 272 Alex Brown RC	1.00	2.50
❑ 273 Bryan Thomas RC	.60	1.50
❑ 274 Bryan Fletcher RC	.60	1.50
❑ 275 Will Overstreet RC	.60	1.50
❑ 276 Ryan Denney RC	.60	1.50
❑ 277 Charles Grant RC	1.00	2.50
❑ 278 John Henderson RC	1.00	2.50
❑ 279 Albert Haynesworth RC	1.00	2.50
❑ 280 Wendell Bryant RC	.60	1.50
❑ 281 Ryan Sims RC	1.00	2.50
❑ 282 Anthony Weaver RC	.60	1.50
❑ 283 Larry Tripplett RC	.60	1.50
❑ 284 Alan Harper RC	.60	1.50
❑ 285 Napoleon Harris RC	.75	2.00
❑ 286 Robert Thomas RC	.60	1.50
❑ 287 Levar Fisher RC	.60	1.50
❑ 288 Andra Davis RC	.60	1.50
❑ 289 Quentin Jammer RC	1.00	2.50
❑ 290 Phillip Buchanon RC	1.00	2.50
❑ 291 Keyuo Craver RC	.60	1.50
❑ 292 Lito Sheppard RC	1.00	2.50
❑ 293 Rocky Calmus RC	.75	2.00
❑ 294 Mike Rumph RC	.60	1.50
❑ 295 Mike Echols RC	.60	1.50
❑ 296 Joseph Jefferson RC	.60	1.50
❑ 297 Roy Williams RC	1.25	3.00
❑ 298 Ed Reed RC	3.00	8.00
❑ 299 Michael Lewis RC	1.00	2.50
❑ 300 Eddie Drummond RC	.60	1.50

2001 Donruss Classics

Card	Lo	Hi
❑ COMP.SET w/o SPs (100)	7.50	20.00
❑ 1 David Boston	.20	.50
❑ 2 Jake Plummer	.25	.60
❑ 3 Thomas Jones	.25	.60
❑ 4 Jamal Anderson	.25	.60
❑ 5 Chris Redman	.30	.75
❑ 6 Elvis Grbac	.25	.60
❑ 7 Jamal Lewis	.30	.75
❑ 8 Qadry Ismail	.25	.60
❑ 9 Ray Lewis	.30	.75
❑ 10 Shannon Sharpe	.30	.75
❑ 11 Travis Taylor	.20	.50
❑ 12 Eric Moulds	.25	.60
❑ 13 Rob Johnson	.25	.60
❑ 14 Muhsin Muhammad	.25	.60
❑ 15 Brian Urlacher	.40	1.00
❑ 16 Cade McNown	.25	.60
❑ 17 Marcus Robinson	.25	.60
❑ 18 Akili Smith	.20	.50
❑ 19 Corey Dillon	.25	.60
❑ 20 Peter Warrick	.25	.60
❑ 21 Courtney Brown	.20	.50
❑ 22 Tim Couch	.20	.50
❑ 23 Emmitt Smith	.75	2.00
❑ 24 Brian Griese	.25	.60
❑ 25 Ed McCaffery	.25	.60
❑ 26 Olandis Gary	.20	.50
❑ 27 Mike Anderson	.25	.60
❑ 28 Rod Smith	.25	.60
❑ 29 Terrell Davis	.30	.75
❑ 30 Charlie Batch	.25	.60
❑ 31 James Stewart	.20	.50
❑ 32 Ahman Green	.30	.75
❑ 33 Antonio Freeman	.30	.75
❑ 34 Brett Favre	1.00	2.50
❑ 35 Edgerrin James	.30	.75
❑ 36 Marvin Harrison	.30	.75
❑ 37 Peyton Manning	.75	2.00
❑ 38 Fred Taylor	.30	.75
❑ 39 Jimmy Smith	.25	.60
❑ 40 Keenan McCardell	.25	.60
❑ 41 Mark Brunell	.30	.75
❑ 42 Sylvester Morris	.20	.50
❑ 43 Tony Gonzalez	.25	.60
❑ 44 Zach Thomas	.30	.75
❑ 45 Jay Fiedler	.25	.60
❑ 46 Lamar Smith	.25	.60
❑ 47 Cris Carter	.30	.75
❑ 48 Daunte Culpepper	.30	.75
❑ 49 Randy Moss	.40	1.00
❑ 50 Drew Bledsoe	.30	.75
❑ 51 Terry Glenn	.25	.60
❑ 52 Aaron Brooks	.25	.60
❑ 53 Joe Horn	.25	.60
❑ 54 Ricky Williams	.30	.75
❑ 55 Amani Toomer	.25	.60
❑ 56 Ike Hilliard	.25	.60
❑ 57 Kerry Collins	.25	.60
❑ 58 Ron Dayne	.25	.60
❑ 59 Tiki Barber	.30	.75
❑ 60 Chad Pennington	.30	.75
❑ 61 Curtis Martin	.30	.75
❑ 62 Laveranues Coles	.30	.75
❑ 63 Vinny Testaverde	.25	.60
❑ 64 Wayne Chrebet	.25	.60
❑ 65 Charles Woodson	.30	.75
❑ 66 Rich Gannon	.25	.60
❑ 67 Tim Brown	.30	.75
❑ 68 Tyrone Wheatley	.25	.60
❑ 69 Corey Simon	.20	.50
❑ 70 Donovan McNabb	.40	1.00
❑ 71 Duce Staley	.25	.60
❑ 72 Jerome Bettis	.30	.75
❑ 73 Plaxico Burress	.25	.60

Card		
❑ 74 Doug Flutie	.30	.75
❑ 75 Junior Seau	.30	.75
❑ 76 Jeff Garcia	.25	.60
❑ 77 Jerry Rice	.60	1.50
❑ 78 Giovanni Carmazzi	.20	.50
❑ 79 Terrell Owens	.30	.75
❑ 80 Darrell Jackson	.25	.60
❑ 81 Ricky Watters	.25	.60
❑ 82 Shaun Alexander	.30	.75
❑ 83 Isaac Bruce	.30	.75
❑ 84 Kurt Warner	.40	1.00
❑ 85 Marshall Faulk	.30	.75
❑ 86 Torry Holt	.25	.60
❑ 87 Brad Johnson	.25	.60
❑ 88 Keyshawn Johnson	.25	.60
❑ 89 Mike Alstott	.25	.60
❑ 90 Shaun King	.20	.50
❑ 91 Warren Sapp	.25	.60
❑ 92 Warrick Dunn	.30	.75
❑ 93 Eddie George	.30	.75
❑ 94 Jevon Kearse	.25	.60
❑ 95 Steve McNair	.30	.75
❑ 96 Jeff George	.25	.60
❑ 97 Stephen Davis	.25	.60
❑ 98 Charlie Garner	.25	.60
❑ 99 Trent Dilfer	.25	.60
❑ 100 Troy Aikman	.50	1.25
❑ 101 Michael Vick RC	5.00	12.00
❑ 102 Drew Brees RC	12.00	30.00
❑ 103 Chris Weinke RC	2.00	5.00
❑ 104 Mike McMahon RC	2.00	5.00
❑ 105 Jesse Palmer RC	2.50	6.00
❑ 106 Quincy Carter RC	2.00	5.00
❑ 107 Josh Heupel RC	2.50	6.00
❑ 108 Tim Hasselbeck RC	2.00	5.00
❑ 109 LaDainian Tomlinson RC	15.00	40.00
❑ 110 Deuce McAllister RC	3.00	8.00
❑ 111 Michael Bennett RC	2.50	6.00
❑ 112 Anthony Thomas RC	2.50	6.00
❑ 113 LaMont Jordan RC	2.50	6.00
❑ 114 Travis Henry RC	2.50	6.00
❑ 115 Kevan Barlow RC	2.00	5.00
❑ 116 Travis Minor RC	2.00	5.00
❑ 117 Rudi Johnson RC	2.50	6.00
❑ 118 David Allen RC	1.50	4.00
❑ 119 Heath Evans RC	2.00	5.00
❑ 120 Moran Norris RC	1.50	4.00
❑ 121 David Terrell RC	2.00	5.00
❑ 122 Koren Robinson RC	2.50	6.00
❑ 123 Rod Gardner RC	2.00	5.00
❑ 124 Santana Moss RC	4.00	10.00
❑ 125 Freddie Mitchell RC	1.50	4.00
❑ 126 Reggie Wayne RC	6.00	15.00
❑ 127 Quincy Morgan RC	2.00	5.00
❑ 128 Chad Johnson RC	6.00	15.00
❑ 129 Robert Ferguson RC	2.50	6.00
❑ 130 Chris Chambers RC	4.00	10.00
❑ 131 Snoop Minnis RC	2.00	5.00
❑ 132 Eddie Berlin RC	1.50	4.00
❑ 133 Alex Bannister RC	1.50	4.00
❑ 134 Todd Heap RC	2.50	6.00
❑ 135 Alge Crumpler RC	2.50	6.00
❑ 136 Justin Smith RC	2.50	6.00
❑ 137 Andre Carter RC	2.50	6.00
❑ 138 Jamal Reynolds RC	2.00	5.00
❑ 139 Richard Seymour RC	2.50	6.00
❑ 140 Marcus Stroud RC	2.00	5.00
❑ 141 Casey Hampton RC	2.00	5.00
❑ 142 Gerard Warren RC	2.00	5.00
❑ 143 Torrance Marshall RC	2.00	5.00
❑ 144 Brian Allen RC	1.50	4.00
❑ 145 Morlon Greenwood RC	1.50	4.00
❑ 146 Keith Adams RC	1.50	4.00
❑ 147 Will Allen RC	2.50	6.00
❑ 148 Nate Clements RC	2.50	6.00
❑ 149 Adam Archuleta RC	2.00	5.00
❑ 150 Hakim Akbar RC	1.50	4.00
❑ 151 James Lofton	.50	1.25
❑ 152 Jim Kelly	1.00	2.50
❑ 153 Gale Sayers	1.00	2.50
❑ 154 Mike Singletary	.75	2.00
❑ 155 Boomer Esiason	.60	1.50
❑ 156 Charlie Joiner	.50	1.25
❑ 157 Ken Anderson	.60	1.50
❑ 158 Y.A. Tittle	.75	2.00
❑ 159 Jim Brown	1.25	3.00
❑ 160 Otto Graham	.60	1.50
❑ 161 Ozzie Newsome	.50	1.25
❑ 162 Drew Pearson	.60	1.50
❑ 163 Lance Alworth	.60	1.50
❑ 164 Roger Staubach	1.25	3.00
❑ 165 Tony Dorsett	.75	2.00
❑ 166 John Elway	2.00	5.00
❑ 167 Barry Sanders	2.00	5.00
❑ 168 Bart Starr	1.50	4.00
❑ 169 Paul Hornung	.75	2.00
❑ 170 Earl Campbell	.75	2.00
❑ 171 Warren Moon	.75	2.00
❑ 172 Johnny Unitas	1.50	4.00
❑ 173 Deacon Jones	.60	1.50
❑ 174 Eric Dickerson	.60	1.50
❑ 175 Bob Griese	.75	2.00
❑ 176 Dan Marino	2.50	6.00
❑ 177 Larry Csonka	.75	2.00
❑ 178 Paul Warfield	.60	1.50
❑ 179 Fran Tarkenton	1.00	2.50
❑ 180 Archie Manning	.60	1.50
❑ 181 Frank Gifford	.75	2.00
❑ 182 Lawrence Taylor	.75	2.00
❑ 183 Dan Fouts	.75	2.00
❑ 184 Don Maynard	.60	1.50
❑ 185 Joe Namath	1.25	3.00
❑ 186 Fred Biletnikoff	.75	2.00
❑ 187 Marcus Allen	.75	2.00
❑ 188 Jim Plunkett	.60	1.50
❑ 189 Franco Harris	.75	2.00
❑ 190 Terry Bradshaw	1.25	3.00
❑ 191 Joe Montana	2.50	6.00
❑ 192 Roger Craig	.60	1.50
❑ 193 Steve Young	1.00	2.50
❑ 194 Dwight Clark	.60	1.50
❑ 195 Steve Largent	.75	2.00
❑ 196 Art Monk	.60	1.50
❑ 197 Charley Taylor	.60	1.50
❑ 198 Joe Theismann	.75	2.00
❑ 199 Sammy Baugh	.75	2.00
❑ 200 Sonny Jurgensen	.75	2.00

2002 Donruss Classics

Card		
❑ COMP.SET w/o SP's (100)	7.50	20.00
❑ 1 David Boston	.20	.50
❑ 2 Jake Plummer	.25	.60
❑ 3 Jamal Anderson	.25	.60
❑ 4 Michael Vick	.30	.75
❑ 5 Chris Weinke	.20	.50
❑ 6 Muhsin Muhammad	.25	.60
❑ 7 Steve Smith	.30	.75
❑ 8 Anthony Thomas	.25	.60
❑ 9 David Terrell	.25	.60
❑ 10 Brian Urlacher	.40	1.00
❑ 11 Marty Booker	.25	.60
❑ 12 Quincy Carter	.20	.50
❑ 13 Emmitt Smith	.75	2.00
❑ 14 Mike McMahon	.20	.50
❑ 15 James Stewart	.20	.50
❑ 16 Brett Favre	.75	2.00
❑ 17 Ahman Green	.25	.60
❑ 18 Antonio Freeman	.30	.75
❑ 19 Michael Bennett	.25	.60
❑ 20 Randy Moss	.30	.75
❑ 21 Cris Carter	.30	.75
❑ 22 Daunte Culpepper	.25	.60
❑ 23 Aaron Brooks	.25	.60
❑ 24 Ricky Williams	.30	.75
❑ 25 Deuce McAllister	.30	.75
❑ 26 Kerry Collins	.25	.60
❑ 27 Michael Strahan	.30	.75
❑ 28 Donovan McNabb	.40	1.00
❑ 29 Duce Staley	.25	.60
❑ 30 Freddie Mitchell	.20	.50
❑ 31 Correll Buckhalter	.25	.60
❑ 32 Jeff Garcia	.25	.60
❑ 33 Terrell Owens	.30	.75
❑ 34 Garrison Hearst	.25	.60
❑ 35 Marshall Faulk	.30	.75
❑ 36 Isaac Bruce	.30	.75
❑ 37 Kurt Warner	.30	.75
❑ 38 Torry Holt	.30	.75
❑ 39 Brad Johnson	.25	.60
❑ 40 Keyshawn Johnson	.25	.60
❑ 41 Mike Alstott	.25	.60
❑ 42 Warrick Dunn	.25	.60
❑ 43 Stephen Davis	.25	.60
❑ 44 Rod Gardner	.20	.50
❑ 45 Bruce Smith	.30	.75
❑ 46 Elvis Grbac	.25	.60
❑ 47 Ray Lewis	.30	.75
❑ 48 Jamal Lewis	.25	.60
❑ 49 Rob Johnson	.25	.60
❑ 50 Eric Moulds	.25	.60
❑ 51 Travis Henry	.25	.60
❑ 52 Corey Dillon	.25	.60
❑ 53 Peter Warrick	.25	.60
❑ 54 Tim Couch	.20	.50
❑ 55 James Jackson	.20	.50
❑ 56 Kevin Johnson	.20	.50
❑ 57 Brian Griese	.25	.60
❑ 58 Terrell Davis	.30	.75
❑ 59 Rod Smith	.25	.60
❑ 60 Mike Anderson	.25	.60
❑ 61 Peyton Manning	.60	1.50
❑ 62 Marvin Harrison	.30	.75
❑ 63 Edgerrin James	.30	.75
❑ 64 Dominic Rhodes	.25	.60
❑ 65 Mark Brunell	.25	.60
❑ 66 Fred Taylor	.30	.75
❑ 67 Jimmy Smith	.25	.60
❑ 68 Tony Gonzalez	.25	.60
❑ 69 Trent Green	.25	.60
❑ 70 Priest Holmes	.30	.75
❑ 71 Snoop Minnis	.20	.50
❑ 72 Jay Fiedler	.25	.60
❑ 73 Lamar Smith	.25	.60
❑ 74 Chris Chambers	.30	.75
❑ 75 Tom Brady	.75	2.00
❑ 76 Drew Bledsoe	.30	.75
❑ 77 Antowain Smith	.25	.60
❑ 78 Troy Brown	.25	.60
❑ 79 Vinny Testaverde	.25	.60
❑ 80 Curtis Martin	.30	.75
❑ 81 Wayne Chrebet	.25	.60
❑ 82 Laveranues Coles	.30	.75
❑ 83 Tim Brown	.30	.75
❑ 84 Jerry Rice	.60	1.50
❑ 85 Rich Gannon	.25	.60
❑ 86 Charlie Garner	.25	.60
❑ 87 Kordell Stewart	.25	.60
❑ 88 Jerome Bettis	.30	.75
❑ 89 Kendrell Bell	.20	.50
❑ 90 Plaxico Burress	.25	.60
❑ 91 Drew Brees	.50	1.25
❑ 92 LaDainian Tomlinson	.50	1.25
❑ 93 Doug Flutie	.30	.75
❑ 94 Shaun Alexander	.30	.75
❑ 95 Matt Hasselbeck	.30	.75
❑ 96 Koren Robinson	.20	.50
❑ 97 Steve McNair	.30	.75
❑ 98 Eddie George	.25	.60
❑ 99 Derrick Mason	.25	.60
❑ 100 Jevon Kearse	.25	.60
❑ 101 Joe Montana	3.00	8.00
❑ 102 Joe Namath	2.00	5.00
❑ 103 Warren Moon	1.25	3.00
❑ 104 Dan Marino	3.00	8.00
❑ 105 Steve Bartkowski	1.00	2.50
❑ 106 John Elway	2.50	6.00
❑ 107 Troy Aikman	2.00	5.00
❑ 108 Steve Young	1.50	4.00
❑ 109 Terry Bradshaw	2.00	5.00
❑ 110 Bart Starr	2.50	6.00
❑ 111 Bert Jones	.75	2.00
❑ 112 Craig Morton	1.00	2.50
❑ 113 Bob Griese	1.25	3.00
❑ 114 Dan Fouts	1.25	3.00
❑ 115 Phil Simms	1.00	2.50
❑ 116 Jim McMahon	1.25	3.00
❑ 117 Joe Theismann	1.25	3.00
❑ 118 Ken Stabler	1.50	4.00
❑ 119 Johnny Unitas	2.00	5.00
❑ 120 Roger Staubach	2.00	5.00
❑ 121 Len Dawson	1.25	3.00
❑ 122 Tony Dorsett	1.25	3.00
❑ 123 Gale Sayers	1.50	4.00
❑ 124 Jim Kelly	1.50	4.00

Card	Low	High
❑ 125 Herschel Walker	1.00	2.50
❑ 126 John Riggins	1.25	3.00
❑ 127 Eric Dickerson	1.00	2.50
❑ 128 Franco Harris	1.25	3.00
❑ 129 Earl Campbell	1.25	3.00
❑ 130 Thurman Thomas	1.25	3.00
❑ 131 Barry Sanders	2.00	5.00
❑ 132 Marcus Allen	1.25	3.00
❑ 134 Natrone Means	.75	2.00
❑ 135 Steve Largent	1.25	3.00
❑ 136 Don Maynard	1.00	2.50
❑ 137 Henry Ellard	.75	2.00
❑ 138 Sterling Sharpe	1.00	2.50
❑ 139 Art Monk	1.00	2.50
❑ 140 Andre Reed	1.00	2.50
❑ 141 Raymond Berry	1.00	2.50
❑ 142 Ozzie Newsome	1.00	2.50
❑ 143 William Perry	1.00	2.50
❑ 144 Deacon Jones	1.00	2.50
❑ 145 Howie Long	1.25	3.00
❑ 146 L.C. Greenwood	1.00	2.50
❑ 147 Ronnie Lott	1.25	3.00
❑ 148 Dick Butkus	2.00	5.00
❑ 149 Fran Tarkenton	1.25	3.00
❑ 150 Mike Singletary	1.25	3.00
❑ 151 David Carr RC	2.00	5.00
❑ 152 Joey Harrington RC	2.00	5.00
❑ 153 Patrick Ramsey RC	2.00	5.00
❑ 154 Kurt Kittner RC	1.25	3.00
❑ 155 DeShaun Foster RC	2.00	5.00
❑ 156 William Green RC	1.50	4.00
❑ 157 Clinton Portis RC	5.00	12.00
❑ 158 T.J. Duckett RC	2.00	5.00
❑ 159 Cliff Russell RC	1.25	3.00
❑ 160 Antonio Bryant RC	2.50	6.00
❑ 161 Donte Stallworth RC	2.00	5.00
❑ 162 Reche Caldwell RC	2.00	5.00
❑ 163 Jabar Gaffney RC	2.00	5.00
❑ 164 Ashley Lelie RC	2.00	5.00
❑ 165 Andre Davis RC	1.50	4.00
❑ 166 Josh Reed RC	1.50	4.00
❑ 167 Ron Johnson RC	1.50	4.00
❑ 168 Kelly Campbell RC	1.50	4.00
❑ 169 Javon Walker RC	2.00	5.00
❑ 170 Antwaan Randle El RC	2.00	5.00
❑ 171 Marquise Walker RC	1.25	3.00
❑ 172 Jeremy Shockey RC	3.00	8.00
❑ 173 Jerramy Stevens RC	2.00	5.00
❑ 174 Daniel Graham RC	1.50	4.00
❑ 175 Julius Peppers RC	3.00	8.00
❑ 176 Kalimba Edwards RC	1.50	4.00
❑ 177 Alex Brown RC	2.00	5.00
❑ 178 Will Overstreet RC	1.25	3.00
❑ 179 Dwight Freeney RC	3.00	8.00
❑ 180 John Henderson RC	2.00	5.00
❑ 181 Ryan Sims RC	2.00	5.00
❑ 182 Albert Haynesworth RC	2.00	5.00
❑ 183 Wendell Bryant RC	1.25	3.00
❑ 184 Anthony Weaver RC	1.25	3.00
❑ 185 Napoleon Harris RC	1.50	4.00
❑ 186 Robert Thomas RC	1.25	3.00
❑ 187 Quentin Jammer RC	2.00	5.00
❑ 188 Ed Reed RC	6.00	15.00
❑ 189 Roy Williams RC	2.50	6.00
❑ 190 Phillip Buchanon RC	2.00	5.00
❑ 191 Lito Sheppard RC	2.00	5.00
❑ 192 Mike Rumph RC	1.25	3.00
❑ 193 Keyuo Craver RC	1.25	3.00
❑ 194 Randy Fasani RC	1.50	4.00
❑ 195 Rohan Davey RC	2.00	5.00
❑ 196 Chad Hutchinson RC	1.25	3.00
❑ 197 Eric Crouch RC	2.00	5.00
❑ 198 Lamar Gordon RC	2.00	5.00
❑ 199 Brian Westbrook RC	6.00	15.00
❑ 200 Adrian Peterson RC	2.00	5.00

2004 Donruss Classics

Card	Low	High
❑ COMP.SET w/o SP's (100)	7.50	20.00
❑ 1 Anquan Boldin	.30	.75
❑ 2 Emmitt Smith	.75	2.00
❑ 3 Michael Vick	.30	.75
❑ 4 Peerless Price	.25	.60
❑ 5 Warrick Dunn	.25	.60
❑ 6 Jamal Lewis	.25	.60
❑ 7 Kyle Boller	.25	.60
❑ 8 Terrell Suggs	.20	.50
❑ 9 Todd Heap	.25	.60
❑ 10 Drew Bledsoe	.30	.75
❑ 11 Travis Henry	.25	.60
❑ 12 DeShaun Foster	.25	.60
❑ 13 Jake Delhomme	.25	.60
❑ 14 Stephen Davis	.25	.60
❑ 15 Steve Smith	.30	.75
❑ 16 Anthony Thomas	.25	.60
❑ 17 Brian Urlacher	.30	.75
❑ 18 Rex Grossman	.30	.75
❑ 19 Chad Johnson	.25	.60
❑ 20 Carson Palmer	.40	1.00
❑ 21 Rudi Johnson	.25	.60
❑ 22 Andre Davis	.20	.50
❑ 23 Lee Suggs	.30	.75
❑ 24 Quincy Carter	.20	.50
❑ 25 Roy Williams S	.25	.60
❑ 26 Clinton Portis	.30	.75
❑ 27 Jake Plummer	.25	.60
❑ 28 Rod Smith	.25	.60
❑ 29 Charles Rogers	.25	.60
❑ 30 Joey Harrington	.25	.60
❑ 31 Ahman Green	.30	.75
❑ 32 Brett Favre	.75	2.00
❑ 33 Javon Walker	.25	.60
❑ 34 Andre Johnson	.30	.75
❑ 35 David Carr	.25	.60
❑ 36 Domanick Davis	.25	.60
❑ 37 Edgerrin James	.30	.75
❑ 38 Marvin Harrison	.30	.75
❑ 39 Peyton Manning	.60	1.50
❑ 40 Reggie Wayne	.25	.60
❑ 41 Byron Leftwich	.30	.75
❑ 42 Fred Taylor	.25	.60
❑ 43 Jimmy Smith	.25	.60
❑ 44 Priest Holmes	.30	.75
❑ 45 Dante Hall	.25	.60
❑ 46 Tony Gonzalez	.30	.75
❑ 47 Trent Green	.25	.60
❑ 48 Chris Chambers	.25	.60
❑ 49 Ricky Williams	.30	.75
❑ 50 Zach Thomas	.30	.75
❑ 51 Daunte Culpepper	.30	.75
❑ 52 Michael Bennett	.25	.60
❑ 53 Randy Moss	.30	.75
❑ 54 Deion Branch	.25	.60
❑ 55 Adam Vinatieri	.30	.75
❑ 56 Tedy Bruschi	.30	.75
❑ 57 Tom Brady	.75	2.00
❑ 58 Aaron Brooks	.25	.60
❑ 59 Deuce McAllister	.30	.75
❑ 60 Donte' Stallworth	.25	.60
❑ 61 Joe Horn	.25	.60
❑ 62 Jeremy Shockey	.25	.60
❑ 63 Kerry Collins	.25	.60
❑ 64 Michael Strahan	.25	.60
❑ 65 Tiki Barber	.30	.75
❑ 66 Chad Pennington	.30	.75
❑ 67 Curtis Martin	.30	.75
❑ 68 Santana Moss	.25	.60
❑ 69 Jerry Rice	.60	1.50
❑ 70 Charles Woodson	.30	.75
❑ 71 Rod Woodson	.25	.60
❑ 72 Tim Brown	.30	.75
❑ 73 Brian Westbrook	.30	.75
❑ 74 Correll Buckhalter	.25	.60
❑ 75 Donovan McNabb	.30	.75
❑ 76 Antwaan Randle El	.25	.60
❑ 77 Hines Ward	.30	.75
❑ 78 Kendrell Bell	.20	.50
❑ 79 David Boston	.20	.50
❑ 80 Drew Brees	.30	.75
❑ 81 LaDainian Tomlinson	.40	1.00
❑ 82 Jeff Garcia	.30	.75
❑ 83 Kevan Barlow	.25	.60
❑ 84 Terrell Owens	.30	.75
❑ 85 Koren Robinson	.30	.75
❑ 86 Matt Hasselbeck	.30	.75
❑ 87 Shaun Alexander	.30	.75
❑ 88 Isaac Bruce	.25	.60
❑ 89 Marc Bulger	.25	.60
❑ 90 Marshall Faulk	.30	.75
❑ 91 Torry Holt	.30	.75
❑ 92 Brad Johnson	.25	.60
❑ 93 Keenan McCardell	.20	.50
❑ 94 Keyshawn Johnson	.25	.60
❑ 95 Derrick Mason	.25	.60
❑ 96 Eddie George	.25	.60
❑ 97 Steve McNair	.30	.75
❑ 98 LaVar Arrington	.25	.60
❑ 99 Laveranues Coles	.25	.60
❑ 100 Patrick Ramsey	.25	.60
❑ 101 Archie Manning	.75	2.00
❑ 102 Bart Starr	2.00	5.00
❑ 103 Bo Jackson	1.25	3.00
❑ 104 Bob Griese	.75	2.00
❑ 105 Christian Okoye	.50	1.25
❑ 106 Daryl Johnston	.75	2.00
❑ 107 Deacon Jones	.60	1.50
❑ 108 Deion Sanders	.75	2.00
❑ 109 Dick Butkus	1.25	3.00
❑ 110 Lynn Swann	1.00	2.50
❑ 111 Don Maynard	.60	1.50
❑ 112 Don Shula	.75	2.00
❑ 113 Franco Harris	1.00	2.50
❑ 114 Fred Biletnikoff	.75	2.00
❑ 115 Gale Sayers	1.00	2.50
❑ 116 George Blanda	.75	2.00
❑ 117 Herman Edwards	.60	1.50
❑ 118 Herschel Walker	.60	1.50
❑ 119 Jack Lambert	1.00	2.50
❑ 120 James Lofton	.50	1.25
❑ 121 Jim Plunkett	.60	1.50
❑ 122 Jim Thorpe	.75	2.00
❑ 123 Joe Greene	.75	2.00
❑ 124 John Riggins	1.00	2.50
❑ 125 L.C. Greenwood	.60	1.50
❑ 126 Larry Csonka	.75	2.00
❑ 127 Leroy Kelly	.60	1.50
❑ 128 Walter Payton	3.00	8.00
❑ 129 Marcus Allen	.75	2.00
❑ 130 Mark Bavaro	.50	1.25
❑ 131 Mel Blount	.60	1.50
❑ 132 Michael Irvin	.75	2.00
❑ 133 Mike Ditka	.75	2.00
❑ 134 Mike Singletary	.75	2.00
❑ 135 Ozzie Newsome	.60	1.50
❑ 136 Paul Hornung	.75	2.00
❑ 137 Paul Warfield	.60	1.50
❑ 138 Randall Cunningham	.60	1.50
❑ 139 Ray Nitschke	.75	2.00
❑ 140 Reggie White	.75	2.00
❑ 141 Richard Dent	.50	1.25
❑ 142 Sammy Baugh	.75	2.00
❑ 143 Sonny Jurgensen	.60	1.50
❑ 144 Sterling Sharpe	.60	1.50
❑ 145 Steve Largent	.75	2.00
❑ 146 Terrell Davis	.75	2.00
❑ 147 Terry Bradshaw	1.25	3.00
❑ 148 Thurman Thomas	.60	1.50
❑ 149 Tony Dorsett	.75	2.00
❑ 150 Warren Moon	.60	1.50
❑ 151 John Navarre RC	1.50	4.00
❑ 152 Derek Abney RC	1.25	3.00
❑ 153 Ryan Dinwiddie RC	1.25	3.00
❑ 154 Bruce Perry/100 RC	7.50	20.00
❑ 155 A. Echemandu RC	1.50	4.00
❑ 156 Troy Fleming RC	1.25	3.00
❑ 157 Brandon Miree RC	1.25	3.00
❑ 158 Jarrett Payton RC	1.50	4.00
❑ 159 Ben Hartsock RC	1.50	4.00
❑ 160 Chris Cooley RC	2.00	5.00
❑ 161 Derrick Ward RC	2.00	5.00
❑ 162 Triandos Luke RC	1.25	3.00

2005 Donruss Classics

Card		
❑ COMP.SET w/o SP's (100)	7.50	20.00
❑ 101-150 LEG PRINT RUN 1000 SER.#'d SETS		
❑ 151-175 PRINT RUN 1999 SER.#'d SETS		
❑ 176-200 PRINT RUN 1499 SER.#'d SETS		
❑ 201-225 PRINT RUN 999 SER.#'d SETS		
❑ 226-250 AU PRINT RUN 499 SER.#'d SETS		
❑ 1 Kurt Warner	.30	.75
❑ 2 Josh McCown	.25	.60
❑ 3 Larry Fitzgerald	.30	.75
❑ 4 Alge Crumpler	.25	.60
❑ 5 Michael Vick	.30	.75
❑ 6 Warrick Dunn	.25	.60
❑ 7 Todd Heap	.25	.60
❑ 8 Jamal Lewis	.25	.60
❑ 9 Kyle Boller	.25	.60
❑ 10 Drew Bledsoe	.30	.75
❑ 11 Lee Evans	.25	.60
❑ 12 Willis McGahee	.30	.75
❑ 13 Steve Smith	.30	.75
❑ 14 Jake Delhomme	.30	.75
❑ 15 Muhsin Muhammad	.25	.60
❑ 16 Brian Urlacher	.30	.75
❑ 17 Rex Grossman	.30	.75
❑ 18 Thomas Jones	.25	.60
❑ 19 Carson Palmer	.30	.75
❑ 20 Chad Johnson	.25	.60
❑ 21 Rudi Johnson	.25	.60
❑ 22 Antonio Bryant	.25	.60
❑ 23 Kellen Winslow Jr.	.30	.75
❑ 24 Lee Suggs	.25	.60
❑ 25 Julius Jones	.30	.75
❑ 26 Keyshawn Johnson	.25	.60
❑ 27 Roy Williams S	.25	.60
❑ 28 Jake Plummer	.25	.60
❑ 29 Rod Smith	.25	.60
❑ 30 Tatum Bell	.25	.60
❑ 31 Joey Harrington	.30	.75
❑ 32 Kevin Jones	.25	.60
❑ 33 Roy Williams WR	.30	.75
❑ 34 Ahman Green	.30	.75
❑ 35 Brett Favre	.75	2.00
❑ 36 Javon Walker	.25	.60
❑ 37 Andre Johnson	.25	.60
❑ 38 David Carr	.25	.60
❑ 39 Domanick Davis	.20	.50
❑ 40 Edgerrin James	.25	.60
❑ 41 Marvin Harrison	.30	.75
❑ 42 Peyton Manning	.50	1.25
❑ 43 Reggie Wayne	.25	.60
❑ 44 Byron Leftwich	.25	.60
❑ 45 Fred Taylor	.30	.75
❑ 46 Jimmy Smith	.25	.60
❑ 47 Priest Holmes	.30	.75
❑ 48 Tony Gonzalez	.25	.60
❑ 49 Trent Green	.25	.60
❑ 50 A.J. Feeley	.20	.50
❑ 51 Chris Chambers	.25	.60
❑ 52 Zach Thomas	.30	.75
❑ 53 Daunte Culpepper	.30	.75
❑ 54 Michael Bennett	.25	.60
❑ 55 Randy Moss	.30	.75
❑ 56 Corey Dillon	.25	.60
❑ 57 David Givens	.25	.60
❑ 58 Tom Brady	.60	1.50
❑ 59 Aaron Brooks	.20	.50
❑ 60 Deuce McAllister	.30	.75
❑ 61 Joe Horn	.25	.60
❑ 62 Eli Manning	.60	1.50
❑ 63 Jeremy Shockey	.30	.75
❑ 64 Tiki Barber	.30	.75
❑ 65 Chad Pennington	.30	.75
❑ 66 Curtis Martin	.30	.75
❑ 67 Santana Moss	.25	.60
❑ 68 Jerry Porter	.25	.60
❑ 69 Kerry Collins	.25	.60
❑ 70 J.P. Losman	.25	.60
❑ 71 Brian Westbrook	.30	.75
❑ 72 Donovan McNabb	.30	.75
❑ 73 Terrell Owens	.30	.75
❑ 74 Ben Roethlisberger	.75	2.00
❑ 75 Duce Staley	.25	.60
❑ 76 Hines Ward	.30	.75
❑ 77 Jerome Bettis	.30	.75
❑ 78 Antonio Gates	.30	.75
❑ 79 Drew Brees	.30	.75
❑ 80 LaDainian Tomlinson	.40	1.00
❑ 81 Brandon Lloyd	.20	.50
❑ 82 Kevan Barlow	.20	.50
❑ 83 Laveranues Coles	.25	.60
❑ 84 Darrell Jackson	.25	.60
❑ 85 Jerry Rice	.60	1.50
❑ 86 Matt Hasselbeck	.25	.60
❑ 87 Shaun Alexander	.30	.75
❑ 88 Isaac Bruce	.25	.60
❑ 89 Marc Bulger	.25	.60
❑ 90 Steven Jackson	.40	1.00
❑ 91 Torry Holt	.25	.60
❑ 92 Brian Griese	.25	.60
❑ 93 Michael Clayton	.25	.60
❑ 94 Mike Alstott	.25	.60
❑ 95 Chris Brown	.25	.60
❑ 96 Drew Bennett	.25	.60
❑ 97 Steve McNair	.30	.75
❑ 98 Clinton Portis	.30	.75
❑ 99 LaVar Arrington	.30	.75
❑ 100 Patrick Ramsey	.25	.60
❑ 101 Don Shula	1.25	3.00
❑ 102 James Lofton	1.00	2.50
❑ 103 Thurman Thomas	1.50	4.00
❑ 104 Gale Sayers	2.00	5.00
❑ 105 Mike Singletary	1.50	4.00
❑ 106 Boomer Esiason	1.25	3.00
❑ 107 Cris Collinsworth	1.25	3.00
❑ 108 Ickey Woods	1.00	2.50
❑ 109 Jim Brown	2.00	5.00
❑ 110 Leroy Kelly	1.25	3.00
❑ 111 Ozzie Newsome	1.25	3.00
❑ 112 Paul Warfield	1.25	3.00
❑ 113 Deion Sanders	2.00	5.00
❑ 114 Herschel Walker	1.25	3.00
❑ 115 Mike Ditka	1.50	4.00
❑ 116 Michael Irvin	1.50	4.00
❑ 117 Roger Staubach	2.50	6.00
❑ 118 Tony Dorsett	1.25	3.00
❑ 119 Troy Aikman	2.00	5.00
❑ 120 John Elway	3.00	8.00
❑ 121 Barry Sanders	2.50	6.00
❑ 122 Bart Starr	2.50	6.00
❑ 123 Paul Hornung	1.50	4.00
❑ 124 Sterling Sharpe	1.25	3.00
❑ 125 Warren Moon	1.50	4.00
❑ 126 Christian Okoye	1.00	2.50
❑ 127 Marcus Allen	1.50	4.00
❑ 128 Deacon Jones	1.25	3.00
❑ 129 Bob Griese	1.50	4.00
❑ 130 Dan Marino	4.00	10.00
❑ 131 Fran Tarkenton	1.50	4.00
❑ 132 Y.A. Tittle	1.50	4.00
❑ 133 Don Maynard	1.25	3.00
❑ 134 Joe Namath	2.50	6.00
❑ 135 Jim Plunkett	1.25	3.00
❑ 136 Bo Jackson	2.00	5.00
❑ 137 Herman Edwards	1.00	2.50
❑ 138 Randall Cunningham	1.25	3.00
❑ 139 Franco Harris	1.50	4.00
❑ 140 Jack Lambert	1.50	4.00
❑ 141 Joe Greene	1.50	4.00
❑ 142 L.C. Greenwood	1.25	3.00
❑ 143 Terry Bradshaw	2.50	6.00
❑ 144 Dan Fouts	1.50	4.00
❑ 145 Joe Montana	4.00	10.00
❑ 146 John Taylor	1.25	3.00
❑ 147 Roger Craig	1.50	4.00
❑ 148 Steve Young	2.00	5.00
❑ 149 Steve Largent	1.50	4.00
❑ 150 Sonny Jurgensen	1.25	3.00
❑ 151 Adam Jones RC	1.50	4.00
❑ 152 Antrel Rolle RC	2.00	5.00
❑ 153 Carlos Rogers RC	2.00	5.00
❑ 154 DeMarcus Ware RC	3.00	8.00
❑ 155 Shawne Merriman RC	2.00	5.00
❑ 156 Thomas Davis RC	1.50	4.00
❑ 157 Derrick Johnson RC	2.00	5.00
❑ 163 Clarence Moore RC	1.50	4.00
❑ 164 D.J. Hackett RC	2.00	5.00
❑ 165 Mark Jones RC	1.25	3.00
❑ 166 Sloan Thomas RC	1.50	4.00
❑ 167 Jamaar Taylor RC	1.25	3.00
❑ 168 Casey Bramlet RC	1.25	3.00
❑ 169 Drew Carter RC	2.00	5.00
❑ 170 Antwan Odom RC	2.00	5.00
❑ 171 Marquise Hill RC	1.25	3.00
❑ 172 Ricardo Colclough RC	2.00	5.00
❑ 173 Keith Smith RC	1.25	3.00
❑ 174 Joey Thomas RC	1.25	3.00
❑ 175 Stuart Schweigert RC	1.50	4.00
❑ 176 Cody Pickett RC	2.00	5.00
❑ 177 B.J. Symons RC	1.50	4.00
❑ 178 Matt Mauck RC	2.00	5.00
❑ 179 Bradlee Van Pelt RC	2.00	5.00
❑ 180 Jim Sorgi RC	2.50	6.00
❑ 181 Ernest Wilford RC	2.00	5.00
❑ 182 Bernard Berrian RC	2.50	6.00
❑ 183 Darius Watts RC	2.00	5.00
❑ 184 Derrick Hamilton RC	1.50	4.00
❑ 185 Jerricho Cotchery RC	2.50	6.00
❑ 186 Jeris McIntyre RC	1.50	4.00
❑ 187 Carlos Francis RC	1.50	4.00
❑ 188 Maurice Mann RC	1.50	4.00
❑ 189 Randy Starks RC	1.50	4.00
❑ 190 Darnell Dockett RC	1.50	4.00
❑ 191 Marcus Tubbs RC	1.50	4.00
❑ 192 Daryl Smith RC	2.00	5.00
❑ 193 Karlos Dansby RC	2.50	6.00
❑ 194 Michael Boulware RC	2.50	6.00
❑ 195 Teddy Lehman RC	2.00	5.00
❑ 196 Will Poole RC	2.50	6.00
❑ 197 Derrick Strait RC	2.00	5.00
❑ 198 Ahmad Carroll RC	2.50	6.00
❑ 199 Jeremy LeSueur RC	1.50	4.00
❑ 200 Bob Sanders RC	6.00	15.00
❑ 201 J.P. Losman RC	2.50	6.00
❑ 202 Matt Schaub RC	6.00	15.00
❑ 203 Josh Harris RC	1.50	4.00
❑ 204 Luke McCown RC	2.50	6.00
❑ 205 Quincy Wilson RC	2.00	5.00
❑ 206 Michael Turner RC	6.00	15.00
❑ 207 Mewelde Moore RC	2.50	6.00
❑ 208 Cedric Cobbs RC	2.00	5.00
❑ 209 Ben Watson RC	2.50	6.00
❑ 210 Michael Jenkins RC	2.50	6.00
❑ 211 Devery Henderson RC	2.50	6.00
❑ 212 Johnnie Morant RC	2.00	5.00
❑ 213 Keary Colbert RC	2.00	5.00
❑ 214 Devard Darling RC	2.00	5.00
❑ 215 P.K. Sam RC	1.50	4.00
❑ 216 Samie Parker RC	2.00	5.00
❑ 217 Jason Babin RC	2.00	5.00
❑ 218 Tommie Harris RC	2.50	6.00
❑ 219 Vince Wilfork RC	2.50	6.00
❑ 220 Jonathan Vilma RC	2.50	6.00
❑ 221 D.J. Williams RC	2.50	6.00
❑ 222 Chris Gamble RC	2.00	5.00
❑ 223 Matt Ware RC	2.50	6.00
❑ 224 Shawntae Spencer RC	1.50	4.00
❑ 225 Sean Jones RC	2.00	5.00
❑ 226 Drew Henson RC	2.00	5.00
❑ 227 Ben Roethlisberger RC	25.00	60.00
❑ 228 Eli Manning RC	20.00	50.00
❑ 229 Philip Rivers RC	12.00	30.00
❑ 230 Steven Jackson RC	8.00	20.00
❑ 231 Kevin Jones RC	3.00	8.00
❑ 232 Chris Perry RC	3.00	8.00
❑ 233 Greg Jones RC	3.00	8.00
❑ 234 Tatum Bell RC	3.00	8.00
❑ 235 Jeff Smoker RC	2.50	6.00
❑ 236 Julius Jones RC	4.00	10.00
❑ 237 Kellen Winslow RC	4.00	10.00
❑ 238 Ben Troupe RC	2.50	6.00
❑ 239 Larry Fitzgerald RC	10.00	25.00
❑ 240 Craig Krenzel RC	3.00	8.00
❑ 241 Roy Williams RC	4.00	10.00
❑ 242 Reggie Williams RC	3.00	8.00
❑ 243 Michael Clayton RC	3.00	8.00
❑ 244 Lee Evans RC	4.00	10.00
❑ 245 Rashaun Woods RC	2.00	5.00
❑ 246 Kenechi Udeze RC	3.00	8.00
❑ 247 Will Smith RC	3.00	8.00
❑ 248 DeAngelo Hall RC	3.00	8.00
❑ 249 Dunta Robinson RC	2.50	6.00
❑ 250 Sean Taylor RC	3.00	8.00

❑ 158 Travis Johnson RC 1.25 3.00
❑ 159 David Pollack RC 1.50 4.00
❑ 160 Erasmus James RC 1.50 4.00
❑ 161 Marcus Spears RC 2.00 5.00
❑ 162 Fabian Washington RC 2.00 5.00
❑ 163 Luis Castillo RC 2.00 5.00
❑ 164 Marlin Jackson RC 1.50 4.00
❑ 165 Mike Patterson RC 1.50 4.00
❑ 166 Brodney Pool RC 1.50 4.00
❑ 167 Barrett Ruud RC 2.00 5.00
❑ 168 Shaun Cody RC 1.50 4.00
❑ 169 Stanford Routt RC 1.50 4.00
❑ 170 Josh Bullocks RC 2.00 5.00
❑ 171 Kevin Burnett RC 1.50 4.00
❑ 172 Corey Webster RC 2.00 5.00
❑ 173 Lofa Tatupu RC 2.00 5.00
❑ 174 Justin Miller RC 1.50 4.00
❑ 175 Odell Thurman RC 2.00 5.00
❑ 176 Heath Miller RC 5.00 12.00
❑ 177 Vernand Morency RC 2.00 5.00
❑ 178 Ryan Moats RC 2.00 5.00
❑ 179 Courtney Roby RC 2.00 5.00
❑ 180 Alex Smith TE RC 2.50 6.00
❑ 181 Kevin Everett RC 2.50 6.00
❑ 182 Brandon Jones RC 2.50 6.00
❑ 183 Maurice Clarett 2.00 5.00
❑ 184 Marion Barber RC 8.00 20.00
❑ 185 Brandon Jacobs RC 3.00 8.00
❑ 186 Matt Cassel RC 5.00 12.00
❑ 187 Stefan LeFors RC 2.00 5.00
❑ 188 Alvin Pearman RC 1.50 4.00
❑ 189 James Kilian RC 1.50 4.00
❑ 190 Airese Currie RC 2.00 5.00
❑ 191 Damien Nash RC 2.00 5.00
❑ 192 Dan Orlovsky RC 2.50 6.00
❑ 193 Larry Brackins RC 1.50 4.00
❑ 194 Rasheed Marshall RC 2.00 5.00
❑ 195 Marcus Maxwell RC 1.50 4.00
❑ 196 LeRon McCoy RC 1.50 4.00
❑ 197 Harry Williams RC 2.00 5.00
❑ 198 Noah Herron RC 2.50 6.00
❑ 199 Tab Perry RC 2.50 6.00
❑ 200 Chad Owens RC 2.50 6.00
❑ 201 Alex Smith QB RC 2.50 6.00
❑ 202 Ronnie Brown RC 8.00 20.00
❑ 203 Braylon Edwards RC 6.00 15.00
❑ 204 Cedric Benson RC 2.50 6.00
❑ 205 Cadillac Williams RC 4.00 10.00
❑ 206 Troy Williamson RC 2.50 6.00
❑ 207 Mike Williams 2.00 5.00
❑ 208 Matt Jones RC 2.50 6.00
❑ 209 Mark Clayton RC 2.50 6.00
❑ 210 Aaron Rodgers RC 8.00 20.00
❑ 211 Jason Campbell RC 4.00 10.00
❑ 212 Roddy White RC 3.00 8.00
❑ 213 Reggie Brown RC 2.00 5.00
❑ 214 Mark Bradley RC 2.00 5.00
❑ 215 J.J. Arrington RC 2.50 6.00
❑ 216 Eric Shelton RC 2.00 5.00
❑ 217 Roscoe Parrish RC 2.00 5.00
❑ 218 Terrence Murphy RC 1.50 4.00
❑ 219 Vincent Jackson RC 3.00 8.00
❑ 220 Frank Gore RC 5.00 12.00
❑ 221 Charlie Frye RC 2.50 6.00
❑ 222 Andrew Walter RC 2.00 5.00
❑ 223 David Greene RC 2.00 5.00
❑ 224 Kyle Orton RC 4.00 10.00
❑ 225 Ciatrick Fason RC 2.00 5.00
❑ 226 Cedric Houston AU RC 6.00 15.00
❑ 227 Dante Ridgeway AU RC 4.00 10.00
❑ 228 Craig Bragg AU RC 4.00 10.00
❑ 229 Deandra Cobb AU RC 5.00 12.00
❑ 230 Derek Anderson AU RC 12.00 30.00
❑ 231 Paris Warren AU RC 5.00 12.00
❑ 232 Lionel Gates AU RC 4.00 10.00
❑ 233 Anthony Davis AU RC 5.00 12.00
❑ 234 Ryan Fitzpatrick AU RC 6.00 15.00
❑ 235 J.R. Russell AU RC 4.00 10.00
❑ 236 Dan Cody AU RC 6.00 15.00
❑ 237 Bryant McFadden AU RC 5.00 12.00
❑ 238 Adrian McPherson AU RC 5.00 12.00
❑ 239 Chris Henry AU RC 6.00 15.00
❑ 240 Craphonso Thorpe AU RC 5.00 12.00
❑ 241 Darren Sproles AU RC 15.00 25.00
❑ 242 Fred Gibson AU RC 5.00 12.00
❑ 243 Jerome Mathis AU RC 6.00 15.00
❑ 244 Josh Davis AU RC 4.00 10.00
❑ 245 Kay Jay Harris AU RC 5.00 12.00
❑ 246 Matt Roth AU RC 6.00 15.00
❑ 247 Roydell Williams AU RC 5.00 12.00
❑ 248 Steve Savoy AU RC 4.00 10.00
❑ 249 T.A. McLendon AU RC 4.00 10.00
❑ 250 Taylor Stubblefield AU RC 4.00 10.00

2006 Donruss Classics

❑ COMP.SET w/o SP's (100) 7.50 20.00
❑ LEGEND PRINT RUN 1000 SER.#'d SETS
❑ 1 Anquan Boldin .25 .60
❑ 2 Kurt Warner .30 .75
❑ 3 Larry Fitzgerald .30 .75
❑ 4 Marcel Shipp .20 .50
❑ 5 Alge Crumpler .25 .60
❑ 6 Michael Vick .30 .75
❑ 7 Warrick Dunn .25 .60
❑ 8 Jamal Lewis .25 .60
❑ 9 Kyle Boller .25 .60
❑ 10 Eric Moulds .25 .60
❑ 11 J.P. Losman .25 .60
❑ 12 Willis McGahee .30 .75
❑ 13 Jake Delhomme .25 .60
❑ 14 Stephen Davis .25 .60
❑ 15 Steve Smith .30 .75
❑ 16 Cedric Benson .25 .60
❑ 17 Kyle Orton .25 .60
❑ 18 Muhsin Muhammad .25 .60
❑ 19 Thomas Jones .25 .60
❑ 20 Carson Palmer .30 .75
❑ 21 Chad Johnson .25 .60
❑ 22 Rudi Johnson .25 .60
❑ 23 T.J. Houshmandzadeh .25 .60
❑ 24 Braylon Edwards .30 .75
❑ 25 Reuben Droughns .25 .60
❑ 26 Trent Dilfer .25 .60
❑ 27 Drew Bledsoe .30 .75
❑ 28 Julius Jones .25 .60
❑ 29 Keyshawn Johnson .25 .60
❑ 30 Terry Glenn .25 .60
❑ 31 Ashley Lelie .20 .50
❑ 32 Jake Plummer .25 .60
❑ 33 Tatum Bell .20 .50
❑ 34 Joey Harrington .20 .50
❑ 35 Kevin Jones .25 .60
❑ 36 Roy Williams WR .30 .75
❑ 37 Aaron Rodgers .30 .75
❑ 38 Brett Favre .60 1.50
❑ 39 Samkon Gado .30 .75
❑ 40 Andre Johnson .25 .60
❑ 41 David Carr .20 .50
❑ 42 Domanick Davis .25 .60
❑ 43 Edgerrin James .25 .60
❑ 44 Marvin Harrison .30 .75
❑ 45 Peyton Manning .50 1.25
❑ 46 Reggie Wayne .25 .60
❑ 47 Byron Leftwich .25 .60
❑ 48 Fred Taylor .25 .60
❑ 49 Jimmy Smith .25 .60
❑ 50 Matt Jones .25 .60
❑ 51 Larry Johnson .25 .60
❑ 52 Tony Gonzalez .25 .60
❑ 53 Trent Green .25 .60
❑ 54 Chris Chambers .25 .60
❑ 55 Ricky Williams .20 .50
❑ 56 Ronnie Brown .30 .75
❑ 57 Daunte Culpepper .30 .75
❑ 58 Mewelde Moore .20 .50
❑ 59 Nate Burleson .25 .60
❑ 60 Corey Dillon .25 .60
❑ 61 Deion Branch .25 .60
❑ 62 Tom Brady .50 1.25
❑ 63 Aaron Brooks .25 .60
❑ 64 Deuce McAllister .25 .60
❑ 65 Donte Stallworth .25 .60
❑ 66 Eli Manning .40 1.00
❑ 67 Plaxico Burress .25 .60
❑ 68 Tiki Barber .30 .75
❑ 69 Chad Pennington .25 .60
❑ 70 Curtis Martin .30 .75
❑ 71 Laveranues Coles .25 .60
❑ 72 Kerry Collins .25 .60
❑ 73 LaMont Jordan .25 .60
❑ 74 Randy Moss .30 .75
❑ 75 Brian Westbrook .25 .60
❑ 76 Donovan McNabb .30 .75
❑ 77 Reggie Brown .20 .50
❑ 78 Ben Roethlisberger .50 1.25
❑ 79 Hines Ward .30 .75
❑ 80 Willie Parker .40 1.00
❑ 81 Antonio Gates .30 .75
❑ 82 Drew Brees .30 .75
❑ 83 LaDainian Tomlinson .40 1.00
❑ 84 Alex Smith QB .25 .60
❑ 85 Frank Gore .30 .75
❑ 86 Darrell Jackson .25 .60
❑ 87 Matt Hasselbeck .25 .60
❑ 88 Shaun Alexander .25 .60
❑ 89 Marc Bulger .25 .60
❑ 90 Steven Jackson .30 .75
❑ 91 Torry Holt .25 .60
❑ 92 Cadillac Williams .30 .75
❑ 93 Joey Galloway .25 .60
❑ 94 Michael Clayton .25 .60
❑ 95 Chris Brown .25 .60
❑ 96 Steve McNair .25 .60
❑ 97 Drew Bennett .25 .60
❑ 98 Clinton Portis .30 .75
❑ 99 Mark Brunell .25 .60
❑ 100 Santana Moss .25 .60
❑ 101 Brodie Croyle/999 RC 2.50 6.00
❑ 102 Omar Jacobs/1499 RC 1.50 4.00
❑ 103 Charlie Whitehurst/999 RC 2.50 6.00
❑ 104 Tarvaris Jackson/999 RC 2.50 6.00
❑ 105 Kellen Clemens/999 RC 2.50 6.00
❑ 106 Vince Young/599 RC 8.00 20.00
❑ 107 Reggie McNeal/1499 RC 2.00 5.00
❑ 108 Marcus Vick/1499 RC 1.50 4.00
❑ 109 DonTrell Moore/1499 RC 2.00 5.00
❑ 110 Willie Reid/1499 RC 2.00 5.00
❑ 111 Matt Leinart/599 RC 5.00 12.00
❑ 112 Jay Cutler/599 RC 8.00 20.00
❑ 113 Brad Smith/1499 RC 2.50 6.00
❑ 114 Joseph Addai/599 RC 4.00 10.00
❑ 115 DeAngelo Williams/599 RC 6.00 15.00
❑ 116 Laurence Maroney/599 RC 4.00 10.00
❑ 117 Jerious Norwood/999 RC 2.50 6.00
❑ 118 Claude Wroten/1499 RC 1.50 4.00
❑ 119 Antonio Cromartie/1499 RC 2.50 6.00
❑ 120 Maurice Drew/999 RC 5.00 12.00
❑ 121 Anwar Phillips/1499 RC 2.00 5.00
❑ 122 LenDale White/599 RC 4.00 10.00
❑ 123 Reggie Bush/599 RC 8.00 20.00
❑ 124 Cedric Humes/1499 RC 2.00 5.00
❑ 125 Jerome Harrison/1499 RC 2.50 6.00
❑ 126 Brian Calhoun/999 RC 2.00 5.00
❑ 127 Joe Klopfenstein/999 RC 2.00 5.00
❑ 128 Leonard Pope/1499 RC 2.50 6.00
❑ 129 Vernon Davis/599 RC 3.00 8.00
❑ 130 Anthony Fasano/999 RC 2.50 6.00
❑ 131 Marcedes Lewis/999 RC 2.50 6.00
❑ 132 Dominique Byrd/1499 RC 2.00 5.00
❑ 133 Derek Hagan/1499 RC 2.00 5.00
❑ 134 Pat Watkins/1499 RC 2.50 6.00
❑ 135 Todd Watkins/1499 RC 1.50 4.00
❑ 136 Jeremy Bloom/1499 RC 2.00 5.00
❑ 137 Chad Jackson/599 RC 2.50 6.00
❑ 138 Devin Hester/1499 RC 5.00 12.00
❑ 139 Sinorice Moss/599 RC 3.00 8.00
❑ 140 Jason Avant/1499 RC 2.50 6.00
❑ 141 Maurice Stovall/1499 RC 2.00 5.00
❑ 142 Santonio Holmes/599 RC 8.00 20.00
❑ 143 Travis Wilson/999 RC 1.50 4.00
❑ 144 Demetrius Williams/1499 RC 2.00 5.00
❑ 145 Bernard Pollard/1499 RC 2.00 5.00
❑ 146 Michael Robinson/1499 RC 2.00 5.00
❑ 147 Brandon Marshall/1499 RC 2.50 6.00
❑ 148 Greg Jennings/999 RC 4.00 10.00
❑ 149 Brandon Williams/1499 RC 2.00 5.00
❑ 150 Jonathan Orr/1499 RC 2.00 5.00
❑ 151 David Thomas/1499 RC 2.50 6.00
❑ 152 Skyler Green/1499 RC 1.50 4.00
❑ 153 Mario Williams/499 RC 4.00 10.00
❑ 154 Ernie Sims/999 RC 2.00 5.00
❑ 155 A.J. Hawk/599 RC 5.00 12.00
❑ 156 Donte Whitner/1499 RC 2.50 6.00
❑ 157 Michael Huff/999 RC 2.50 6.00

Card	Low	High
❑ 158 Leon Washington/1499 RC	3.00	8.00
❑ 159 P.J. Daniels/1499 RC	1.50	4.00
❑ 160 Cory Rodgers/1499 RC	2.50	6.00
❑ 161 Tony Scheffler AU/499 RC	8.00	20.00
❑ 162 Paul Pinegar AU/999 RC	3.00	8.00
❑ 163 D.J. Shockley AU/599 RC	5.00	12.00
❑ 164 Ben Obomanu AU/899 RC	4.00	10.00
❑ 165 Adam Jennings AU/599 RC	5.00	12.00
❑ 166 Brandon Kirsch AU/999 RC	4.00	10.00
❑ 167 Mike Bell AU/999 RC	5.00	12.00
❑ 168 De'Arrius Howard AU/999 RC	5.00	12.00
❑ 169 Martin Nance AU/999 RC	4.00	10.00
❑ 170 Miles Austin AU/999 RC	50.00	80.00
❑ 171 Wendell Mathis AU/999 RC	4.00	10.00
❑ 172 Gerald Riggs AU/995 RC	4.00	10.00
❑ 173 Hank Baskett AU/999 RC	5.00	12.00
❑ 174 Greg Lee AU/999 RC	3.00	8.00
❑ 175 Quinton Ganther AU/799 RC	3.00	8.00
❑ 176 Garrett Mills/1499 RC	2.00	5.00
❑ 177 Jeff Webb AU/599 RC	5.00	12.00
❑ 178 Delanie Walker AU/599 RC	5.00	12.00
❑ 179 D'Brick. Ferguson AU/599 RC	6.00	15.00
❑ 180 Mathias Kiwanuka AU/499 RC	8.00	20.00
❑ 181 Kamerion Wimbley AU/499 RC	6.00	15.00
❑ 182 Tamba Hali AU/499 RC	6.00	15.00
❑ 183 Brodrick Bunkley AU/499 RC	5.00	12.00
❑ 184 Gabe Watson/1499 RC	1.50	4.00
❑ 185 Haloti Ngata AU/499 RC	6.00	15.00
❑ 186 DeMeco Ryans AU/599 RC	8.00	20.00
❑ 187 A.J. Nicholson/1499 RC	1.50	4.00
❑ 188 Abdul Hodge AU/999 RC	5.00	12.00
❑ 189 Chad Greenway AU/499 RC	6.00	15.00
❑ 190 D'Qwell Jackson AU/599 RC	5.00	12.00
❑ 191 Manny Lawson AU/499 RC	6.00	15.00
❑ 192 Bobby Carpenter AU/499 RC	5.00	12.00
❑ 193 Jon Alston AU/999 RC	3.00	8.00
❑ 194 Thomas Howard AU/599 RC	5.00	12.00
❑ 195 Tye Hill AU/499 RC	5.00	12.00
❑ 196 Kelly Jennings AU/499 RC	6.00	15.00
❑ 197 Ashton Youboty AU/999 RC	4.00	10.00
❑ 198 Alan Zemaitis AU/999 RC	5.00	12.00
❑ 199 Johnathan Joseph AU/499 RC	5.00	12.00
❑ 200 Jimmy Williams AU/599 RC	6.00	15.00
❑ 201 Ko Simpson AU/999 RC	4.00	10.00
❑ 202 Jason Allen AU/499 RC	5.00	12.00
❑ 203 Darnell Bing AU/999 RC	4.00	10.00
❑ 204 Erik Meyer AU/999 RC	4.00	10.00
❑ 205 Bruce Gradkowski AU/499 RC	6.00	15.00
❑ 206 Darrell Hackney AU/999 RC	4.00	10.00
❑ 207 Derrick Ross AU/799 RC	4.00	10.00
❑ 207 Drew Olson AU/999 RC	3.00	8.00
❑ 209 Taurean Henderson AU/999 RC	5.00	12.00
❑ 210 Andre Hall AU/999 RC	4.00	10.00
❑ 211 Devin Aromashodu AU/899 RC	6.00	15.00
❑ 212 Mike Hass AU/599 RC	6.00	15.00
❑ 213 Ingle Martin AU/499 RC	5.00	12.00
❑ 214 Marques Hagans AU/499 RC	5.00	12.00
❑ 215 Wali Lundy AU/499 RC	6.00	15.00
❑ 216 Domenik Hixon AU/499 RC	6.00	15.00
❑ 217 Ethan Kilmer AU/899 RC	5.00	12.00
❑ 218 Bennie Brazell/1499 RC	2.00	5.00
❑ 219 David Anderson/1499 RC	2.00	5.00
❑ 220 Marques Colston AU/770 RC	25.00	50.00
❑ 221 Kevin McMahan AU/999 RC	4.00	10.00
❑ 222 Anthony Mix/1499 RC	2.00	5.00
❑ 223 John McCargo AU/499 RC	5.00	12.00
❑ 224 Rocky McIntosh/1499 RC	2.50	6.00
❑ 225 Cedric Griffin AU/599 RC	5.00	12.00
❑ 226 Barry Sanders	2.50	6.00
❑ 227 Bart Starr	2.50	6.00
❑ 228 Bo Jackson	2.00	5.00
❑ 229 Bob Griese	1.50	4.00
❑ 230 Bobby Layne	1.50	4.00
❑ 231 Boomer Esiason	1.25	3.00
❑ 232 Bulldog Turner	1.25	3.00
❑ 233 Dan Marino	3.00	8.00
❑ 234 Deacon Jones	1.25	3.00
❑ 235 Derrick Thomas	2.50	6.00
❑ 236 Dick Butkus	2.00	5.00
❑ 237 Don Meredith	1.50	4.00
❑ 238 Eric Dickerson	1.25	3.00
❑ 239 Fran Tarkenton	2.00	5.00
❑ 240 Fred Biletnikoff	1.50	4.00
❑ 241 Gale Sayers	2.00	5.00
❑ 242 Harvey Martin	1.00	2.50
❑ 243 Herman Edwards	1.25	3.00
❑ 244 Jack Lambert	1.50	4.00
❑ 245 Jim Brown	2.00	5.00
❑ 246 Jim Kelly	2.00	5.00
❑ 247 Jim Plunkett	1.25	3.00
❑ 248 Jim Thorpe	2.00	5.00
❑ 249 Joe Montana	3.00	8.00
❑ 250 John Elway	2.50	6.00
❑ 251 John Riggins	1.50	4.00
❑ 252 Johnny Unitas	2.50	6.00
❑ 253 Len Dawson	1.50	4.00
❑ 254 Marcus Allen	1.50	4.00
❑ 255 Mike Singletary	1.50	4.00
❑ 256 Ozzie Newsome	1.25	3.00
❑ 257 Phil Simms	1.25	3.00
❑ 258 Ray Nitschke	1.50	4.00
❑ 259 Red Grange	2.00	5.00
❑ 260 Roger Staubach	2.50	6.00
❑ 261 Ronnie Lott	1.25	3.00
❑ 262 Steve Largent	1.50	4.00
❑ 263 Terry Bradshaw	2.50	6.00
❑ 264 Troy Aikman	2.00	5.00
❑ 265 Walter Payton	3.00	8.00
❑ 266 Bill Dudley	1.25	3.00
❑ 267 Joe Perry	1.25	3.00
❑ 268 Charley Trippi	1.00	2.50
❑ 269 Paul Lowe	1.00	2.50
❑ 270 Clem Daniels	1.00	2.50
❑ 271 Ken Kavanaugh	1.00	2.50
❑ 272 Andre Reed	1.25	3.00
❑ 273 Steve Van Buren	1.25	3.00
❑ 274 Jim Taylor	1.50	4.00

2007 Donruss Classics

Card	Low	High
❑ COMP.SET w/o SP's (100)	7.50	20.00
❑ 1 Anquan Boldin	.25	.60
❑ 2 Edgerrin James	.25	.60
❑ 3 Larry Fitzgerald	.30	.75
❑ 4 Matt Leinart	.30	.75
❑ 5 Alge Crumpler	.25	.60
❑ 6 Michael Vick	.30	.75
❑ 7 Warrick Dunn	.25	.60
❑ 8 Todd Heap	.20	.50
❑ 9 Mark Clayton	.25	.60
❑ 10 Steve McNair	.25	.60
❑ 11 J.P. Losman	.20	.50
❑ 12 Lee Evans	.25	.60
❑ 13 Willis McGahee	.25	.60
❑ 14 DeAngelo Williams	.30	.75
❑ 15 Jake Delhomme	.25	.60
❑ 16 Steve Smith	.25	.60
❑ 17 Brian Urlacher	.30	.75
❑ 18 Muhsin Muhammad	.25	.60
❑ 19 Rex Grossman	.25	.60
❑ 20 Thomas Jones	.25	.60
❑ 21 Carson Palmer	.30	.75
❑ 22 Chad Johnson	.25	.60
❑ 23 Rudi Johnson	.25	.60
❑ 24 T.J. Houshmandzadeh	.25	.60
❑ 25 Braylon Edwards	.25	.60
❑ 26 Charlie Frye	.25	.60
❑ 27 Julius Jones	.25	.60
❑ 28 Terrell Owens	.30	.75
❑ 29 Tony Romo	.50	1.25
❑ 30 Javon Walker	.25	.60
❑ 31 Jay Cutler	.30	.75
❑ 32 Mike Bell	.25	.60
❑ 33 Jon Kitna	.20	.50
❑ 34 Kevin Jones	.20	.50
❑ 35 Roy Williams WR	.25	.60
❑ 36 Brett Favre	.60	1.50
❑ 37 Donald Driver	.30	.75
❑ 38 Ahman Green	.25	.60
❑ 39 Andre Johnson	.25	.60
❑ 40 Matt Schaub	.25	.60
❑ 41 Eric Moulds	.25	.60
❑ 42 Joseph Addai	.30	.75
❑ 43 Marvin Harrison	.30	.75
❑ 44 Peyton Manning	.50	1.25
❑ 45 Reggie Wayne	.25	.60
❑ 46 Byron Leftwich	.25	.60
❑ 47 Fred Taylor	.25	.60
❑ 48 Maurice Jones-Drew	.30	.75
❑ 49 Larry Johnson	.25	.60
❑ 50 Tony Gonzalez	.25	.60
❑ 51 Trent Green	.25	.60
❑ 52 Chris Chambers	.25	.60
❑ 53 Daunte Culpepper	.25	.60
❑ 54 Ronnie Brown	.25	.60
❑ 55 Chester Taylor	.20	.50
❑ 56 Tarvaris Jackson	.25	.60
❑ 57 Travis Taylor	.20	.50
❑ 58 Tom Brady	.60	1.50
❑ 59 Corey Dillon	.25	.60
❑ 60 Laurence Maroney	.30	.75
❑ 61 Deuce McAllister	.25	.60
❑ 62 Drew Brees	.30	.75
❑ 63 Marques Colston	.30	.75
❑ 64 Reggie Bush	.40	1.00
❑ 65 Eli Manning	.30	.75
❑ 66 Jeremy Shockey	.25	.60
❑ 67 Plaxico Burress	.25	.60
❑ 68 Chad Pennington	.25	.60
❑ 69 Laveranues Coles	.25	.60
❑ 70 Leon Washington	.25	.60
❑ 71 LaMont Jordan	.25	.60
❑ 72 Michael Huff	.25	.60
❑ 73 Randy Moss	.30	.75
❑ 74 Brian Westbrook	.25	.60
❑ 75 Donovan McNabb	.30	.75
❑ 76 Reggie Brown	.20	.50
❑ 77 Ben Roethlisberger	.40	1.00
❑ 78 Hines Ward	.30	.75
❑ 79 Willie Parker	.25	.60
❑ 80 Antonio Gates	.25	.60
❑ 81 LaDainian Tomlinson	.40	1.00
❑ 82 Philip Rivers	.30	.75
❑ 83 Alex Smith QB	.30	.75
❑ 84 Frank Gore	.30	.75
❑ 85 Vernon Davis	.25	.60
❑ 86 Darrell Jackson	.25	.60
❑ 87 Matt Hasselbeck	.25	.60
❑ 88 Shaun Alexander	.25	.60
❑ 89 Marc Bulger	.25	.60
❑ 90 Steven Jackson	.30	.75
❑ 91 Torry Holt	.25	.60
❑ 92 Bruce Gradkowski	.20	.50
❑ 93 Cadillac Williams	.25	.60
❑ 94 Joey Galloway	.25	.60
❑ 95 Drew Bennett	.20	.50
❑ 96 Vince Young	.30	.75
❑ 97 Travis Henry	.25	.60
❑ 98 Clinton Portis	.25	.60
❑ 99 Jason Campbell	.25	.60
❑ 100 Santana Moss	.25	.60
❑ 101 Archie Manning	2.00	5.00
❑ 103 Bill Bates	1.50	4.00
❑ 104 Bob Hayes	2.50	6.00
❑ 105 Bob Lilly	1.50	4.00
❑ 106 Bobby Mitchell	1.50	4.00
❑ 108 Charley Taylor	1.50	4.00
❑ 109 Charlie Joiner	1.50	4.00
❑ 110 Cliff Harris	1.25	3.00
❑ 111 Cris Collinsworth	1.50	4.00
❑ 112 Dan Fouts	2.00	5.00
❑ 113 Daryle Lamonica	1.25	3.00
❑ 114 Dave Casper	1.50	4.00
❑ 115 Don Maynard	1.50	4.00
❑ 116 Earl Campbell	2.00	5.00
❑ 117 Forrest Gregg	1.25	3.00
❑ 118 Franco Harris	2.00	5.00
❑ 120 Gale Sayers	2.50	6.00
❑ 121 Gene Upshaw	1.25	3.00
❑ 122 George Blanda	1.50	4.00
❑ 123 Hugh McElhenny	1.50	4.00
❑ 124 Jack Youngblood	1.50	4.00
❑ 125 Boyd Dowler	1.25	3.00
❑ 126 Jan Stenerud	1.25	3.00
❑ 127 Jim McMahon	2.50	6.00
❑ 128 Harlon Hill	1.25	3.00
❑ 129 Joe Namath	2.50	6.00
❑ 130 Joe Theismann	2.00	5.00
❑ 131 John Mackey	1.50	4.00
❑ 133 Kellen Winslow	1.50	4.00
❑ 134 Ken Stabler	2.50	6.00
❑ 135 Lenny Moore	1.50	4.00
❑ 136 Lou Groza	1.50	4.00
❑ 137 Mark Duper	1.25	3.00
❑ 138 Michael Irvin	1.50	4.00

❑ 139 Paul Warfield 1.50 4.00
❑ 140 Randall Cunningham 1.50 4.00
❑ 141 Roger Craig 1.50 4.00
❑ 142 Ron Mix 1.25 3.00
❑ 143 Roosevelt Brown 1.25 3.00
❑ 144 Roosevelt Grier 1.25 3.00
❑ 145 Sam Huff 1.50 4.00
❑ 146 Sammy Baugh 2.00 5.00
❑ 147 Sterling Sharpe 1.50 4.00
❑ 148 Tim Brown 2.00 5.00
❑ 149 Y.A. Tittle 2.00 5.00
❑ 150 Yale Lary 1.25 3.00
❑ 151 JaMarcus Russell/599 RC 5.00 12.00
❑ 152 Brady Quinn/599 RC 8.00 20.00
❑ 153 Kevin Kolb/1499 RC 4.00 10.00
❑ 154 John Beck/1499 RC 2.50 6.00
❑ 155 Drew Stanton/1499 RC 2.00 5.00
❑ 156 Trent Edwards/1499 RC 4.00 10.00
❑ 157 Isaiah Stanback/1499 RC 2.50 6.00
❑ 158 Troy Smith/1499 RC 3.00 8.00
❑ 159 Adrian Peterson/599 RC 30.00 80.00
❑ 160 Marshawn Lynch/599 RC 6.00 15.00
❑ 161 Kenny Irons/599 RC 4.00 10.00
❑ 162 Chris Henry/599 RC 3.00 8.00
❑ 163 Brian Leonard/599 RC 3.00 8.00
❑ 164 Brandon Jackson/599 RC 4.00 10.00
❑ 165 Lorenzo Booker/599 RC 4.00 10.00
❑ 166 Tony Hunt/599 RC 4.00 10.00
❑ 167 Garrett Wolfe/599 RC 4.00 10.00
❑ 168 Michael Bush/599 RC 4.00 10.00
❑ 169 Antonio Pittman/1499 RC 2.50 6.00
❑ 170 Kolby Smith/1499 RC 2.50 6.00
❑ 171 DeShawn Wynn/1499 RC 2.50 6.00
❑ 172 Calvin Johnson/599 RC 10.00 25.00
❑ 173 Ted Ginn Jr.RC/599 RC 6.00 15.00
❑ 174 Dwayne Bowe/599 RC 6.00 15.00
❑ 175 Robert Meachem/599 RC 4.00 10.00
❑ 176 Craig Buster Davis/599 RC 4.00 10.00
❑ 177 Anthony Gonzalez/599 RC 5.00 12.00
❑ 178 Sidney Rice/1499 RC 5.00 12.00
❑ 179 Dwayne Jarrett/1499 RC 2.50 6.00
❑ 180 Steve Smith USC/1499 RC 4.00 10.00
❑ 181 Jacoby Jones/1499 RC 2.50 6.00
❑ 182 Yamon Figurs/1499 RC 1.50 4.00
❑ 183 Laurent Robinson/1499 RC 2.50 6.00
❑ 184 Jason Hill/1499 RC 2.50 6.00
❑ 185 James Jones/1499 RC 2.50 6.00
❑ 186 Mike Walker/1499 RC 2.50 6.00
❑ 187 Paul Williams/1499 RC 2.00 5.00
❑ 188 Johnnie Lee Higgins/1499 RC 2.50 6.00
❑ 189 Chris Davis/1499 RC 2.00 5.00
❑ 190 Aundrae Allison/1499 RC 2.00 5.00
❑ 191 David Clowney/1499 RC 2.50 6.00
❑ 192 Courtney Taylor/1499 RC 2.00 5.00
❑ 193 Dallas Baker/1499 RC 2.00 5.00
❑ 194 Greg Olsen/1499 RC 3.00 8.00
❑ 195 Zach Miller/1499 RC 2.50 6.00
❑ 196 Amobi Okoye/1499 RC 2.50 6.00
❑ 197 Alan Branch/1499 RC 2.00 5.00
❑ 198 Gaines Adams/1499 RC 2.50 6.00
❑ 199 Jamaal Anderson/1499 RC 2.00 5.00
❑ 200 Adam Carriker/1499 RC 2.00 5.00
❑ 201 Jarvis Moss/1499 RC 2.50 6.00
❑ 202 Anthony Spencer/1499 RC 2.50 6.00
❑ 203 LaMarr Woodley/1499 RC 2.50 6.00
❑ 204 Tim Crowder/1499 RC 2.50 6.00
❑ 205 Victor Abiamiri/1499 RC 2.50 6.00
❑ 206 Patrick Willis/1499 RC 4.00 10.00
❑ 207 David Harris/1499 RC 2.00 5.00
❑ 208 Lawrence Timmons/1499 RC 2.50 6.00
❑ 209 Jon Beason/1499 RC 2.50 6.00
❑ 210 Paul Posluszny/1499 RC 3.00 8.00
❑ 211 Leon Hall/1499 RC 2.50 6.00
❑ 212 Aaron Ross/1499 RC 2.50 6.00
❑ 213 Chris Houston/1499 RC 2.00 5.00
❑ 214 Eric Wright/1499 RC 2.50 6.00
❑ 215 Josh Wilson/1499 RC 2.00 5.00
❑ 216 LaRon Landry/1499 RC 3.00 8.00
❑ 217 Michael Griffin/1499 RC 2.50 6.00
❑ 218 Reggie Nelson/1499 RC 2.00 5.00
❑ 219 Brandon Meriweather/1499 RC 2.50 6.00
❑ 220 Sabby Piscitelli/1499 RC 2.50 6.00
❑ 221 Jordan Palmer AU/499 RC 8.00 20.00
❑ 222 Jon Cornish AU/999 RC 4.00 10.00
❑ 223 Jared Zabransky AU/499 RC 8.00 20.00
❑ 224 Jarrett Hicks AU/999 RC 4.00 10.00
❑ 225 Kenneth Darby AU/499 RC 8.00 20.00
❑ 226 Steve Breaston AU/499 RC 8.00 20.00
❑ 227 Matt Spaeth AU/499 RC 8.00 20.00
❑ 228 Stewart Bradley AU/499 RC 8.00 20.00
❑ 229 Tymere Zimmerman AU/999 RC 4.00 10.00
❑ 230 Kenny Scott AU/999 RC 3.00 8.00
❑ 231 Chris Leak AU/499 RC 6.00 15.00
❑ 232 Ronnie McGill AU/999 RC 4.00 10.00
❑ 233 D.Tyler AU/499 RC EXCH 6.00 15.00
❑ 234 Syndric Steptoe AU/499 RC 6.00 15.00
❑ 235 C.Johnson AU/499 RC EXCH 5.00 12.00
❑ 236 Chansi Stuckey AU/499 RC 8.00 20.00
❑ 237 Nate Ilaoa AU/499 RC 8.00 20.00
❑ 238 Buster Davis AU/499 RC EXCH 6.00 15.00
❑ 239 Aaron Fairooz AU/999 RC 4.00 10.00
❑ 240 Jeff Rowe AU/499 RC 6.00 15.00
❑ 241 Rhema McKnight AU/999 RC 4.00 10.00
❑ 242 Danny Ware AU/999 RC 5.00 12.00
❑ 243 Tyler Palko AU/999 RC 4.00 10.00
❑ 244 Syvelle Newton AU/999 RC 4.00 10.00
❑ 245 Michael Okwo AU/499 RC 6.00 15.00
❑ 246 Brandon Siler AU/999 RC 4.00 10.00
❑ 247 Ryan McBean AU/999 RC 5.00 12.00
❑ 248 Ray McDonald AU/499 RC 6.00 15.00
❑ 249 David Ball AU/999 RC 3.00 8.00
❑ 250 Alonzo Coleman AU/999 RC 4.00 10.00
❑ 251 H.B. Blades AU/999 RC 4.00 10.00
❑ 252 Thomas Clayton AU/499 RC 6.00 15.00
❑ 253 Darius Walker AU/499 RC 6.00 15.00
❑ 254 Jordan Kent AU/499 RC EXCH 6.00 15.00
❑ 255 Dwayne Wright AU/499 RC 6.00 15.00
❑ 256 Rufus Alexander AU/999 RC 5.00 12.00
❑ 257 Gary Russell AU/999 RC 4.00 10.00
❑ 258 Aaron Rouse AU/499 RC 8.00 20.00
❑ 259 Joel Filani AU/499 RC 6.00 15.00
❑ 260 Zak DeOssie AU/999 RC 4.00 10.00
❑ 261 Scott Chandler AU/499 RC 6.00 15.00
❑ 262 Jerard Rabb AU/999 RC EXCH 4.00 10.00
❑ 263 Tim Shaw AU/999 RC 4.00 10.00
❑ 264 Jemalle Cornelius AU/999 RC 4.00 10.00
❑ 265 Ahmad Bradshaw AU/499 RC 15.00 40.00
❑ 266 Earl Everett AU/999 RC 4.00 10.00
❑ 267 D'Juan Woods AU/999 RC 4.00 10.00
❑ 268 Toby Korrodi AU/999 RC 4.00 10.00
❑ 269 Ryne Robinson AU/499 RC 6.00 15.00
❑ 270 Selvin Young AU/999 RC 10.00 25.00
❑ 271 Marcus McCauley AU/499 RC 6.00 15.00
❑ 272 Daymeion Hughes AU/499 RC 6.00 15.00
❑ 273 A.J. Davis AU/999 RC 3.00 8.00
❑ 274 David Irons AU/999 RC 3.00 8.00
❑ 275 Josh Gattis AU/999 RC 3.00 8.00

2008 Donruss Classics

❑ COMP.SET w/o SP's (100) 7.50 20.00
❑ 1 Edgerrin James .25 .60
❑ 2 Larry Fitzgerald .30 .75
❑ 3 Matt Leinart .30 .75
❑ 4 Warrick Dunn .25 .60
❑ 5 Roddy White .25 .60
❑ 6 Alge Crumpler .25 .60
❑ 7 Willis McGahee .25 .60
❑ 8 Mark Clayton .25 .60
❑ 9 Derrick Mason .20 .50
❑ 10 Trent Edwards .30 .75
❑ 11 Marshawn Lynch .30 .75
❑ 12 Lee Evans .25 .60
❑ 13 DeAngelo Williams .25 .60
❑ 14 DeShaun Foster .25 .60
❑ 15 Steve Smith .25 .60
❑ 16 Cedric Benson .25 .60
❑ 17 Bernard Berrian .25 .60
❑ 18 Greg Olsen .25 .60
❑ 19 Carson Palmer .30 .75
❑ 20 Chad Johnson .25 .60
❑ 21 T.J. Houshmandzadeh .25 .60
❑ 22 Rudi Johnson .25 .60
❑ 23 Brady Quinn .30 .75
❑ 24 Jamal Lewis .25 .60
❑ 25 Braylon Edwards .25 .60
❑ 26 Tony Romo .50 1.25
❑ 27 Terrell Owens .30 .75
❑ 28 Jason Witten .30 .75
❑ 29 Marion Barber .30 .75
❑ 30 Jay Cutler .30 .75
❑ 31 Brandon Marshall .25 .60
❑ 32 Brandon Stokley .25 .60
❑ 33 Jon Kitna .25 .60
❑ 34 Roy Williams WR .25 .60
❑ 35 Shaun McDonald .20 .50
❑ 36 Aaron Rodgers .30 .75
❑ 37 Greg Jennings .25 .60
❑ 38 Ryan Grant .30 .75
❑ 39 Matt Schaub .25 .60
❑ 40 Andre Johnson .25 .60
❑ 41 Kevin Walter .25 .60
❑ 42 Peyton Manning .50 1.25
❑ 43 Reggie Wayne .25 .60
❑ 44 Joseph Addai .30 .75
❑ 45 Dallas Clark .25 .60
❑ 46 David Garrard .25 .60
❑ 47 Fred Taylor .25 .60
❑ 48 Maurice Jones-Drew .25 .60
❑ 49 Larry Johnson .25 .60
❑ 50 Tony Gonzalez .25 .60
❑ 51 Dwayne Bowe .25 .60
❑ 52 Ronnie Brown .25 .60
❑ 53 Ted Ginn Jr. .25 .60
❑ 54 John Beck .20 .50
❑ 55 Tarvaris Jackson .25 .60
❑ 56 Adrian Peterson .60 1.50
❑ 57 Chester Taylor .20 .50
❑ 58 Tom Brady .50 1.25
❑ 59 Randy Moss .30 .75
❑ 60 Wes Welker .30 .75
❑ 61 Laurence Maroney .25 .60
❑ 62 Drew Brees .30 .75
❑ 63 Marques Colston .25 .60
❑ 64 Reggie Bush .30 .75
❑ 65 Eli Manning .30 .75
❑ 66 Plaxico Burress .25 .60
❑ 67 Brandon Jacobs .25 .60
❑ 68 Kellen Clemens .25 .60
❑ 69 Jerricho Cotchery .20 .50
❑ 70 Thomas Jones .25 .60
❑ 71 Justin Fargas .20 .50
❑ 72 Jerry Porter .25 .60
❑ 73 JaMarcus Russell .30 .75
❑ 74 Donovan McNabb .30 .75
❑ 75 Brian Westbrook .25 .60
❑ 76 Kevin Curtis .20 .50
❑ 77 Ben Roethlisberger .40 1.00
❑ 78 Willie Parker .25 .60
❑ 79 Hines Ward .25 .60
❑ 80 Philip Rivers .30 .75
❑ 81 LaDainian Tomlinson .40 1.00
❑ 82 Antonio Gates .25 .60
❑ 83 Frank Gore .25 .60
❑ 84 Vernon Davis .20 .50
❑ 85 Devin Hester .30 .75
❑ 86 Matt Hasselbeck .25 .60
❑ 87 Julius Jones .25 .60
❑ 88 Deion Branch .25 .60
❑ 89 Marc Bulger .25 .60
❑ 90 Steven Jackson .30 .75
❑ 91 Torry Holt .25 .60
❑ 92 Jeff Garcia .25 .60
❑ 93 Earnest Graham .20 .50
❑ 94 Joey Galloway .25 .60
❑ 95 Vince Young .25 .60
❑ 96 LenDale White .25 .60
❑ 97 Roydell Williams .20 .50
❑ 98 Jason Campbell .25 .60
❑ 99 Chris Cooley .25 .60
❑ 100 Clinton Portis .25 .60
❑ 101 Jay Novacek 1.50 4.00
❑ 102 Knute Rockne 3.00 8.00
❑ 103 Tom Landry 2.50 6.00
❑ 104 Sammy Baugh 2.00 5.00
❑ 105 Willie Lanier 1.25 3.00
❑ 106 Ken Strong 1.25 3.00
❑ 107 Marion Motley 1.50 4.00
❑ 108 Tom Fears 1.25 3.00
❑ 109 Bob Waterfield 1.50 4.00
❑ 110 Hank Stram 1.50 4.00
❑ 111 Elroy Hirsch 1.50 4.00
❑ 112 Dick Lane 1.25 3.00
❑ 113 Jim Parker 1.25 3.00
❑ 114 Red Grange 2.50 6.00

Card	Low	High
❑ 115 Bobby Layne	2.00	5.00
❑ 116 Norm Van Brocklin	1.50	4.00
❑ 117 Michael Irvin	1.50	4.00
❑ 118 Steve Largent	2.00	5.00
❑ 119 Dick Butkus	2.50	6.00
❑ 120 Ray Nitschke	2.00	5.00
❑ 121 Lawrence Taylor	2.00	5.00
❑ 122 Bob Lilly	1.50	4.00
❑ 123 Mike Singletary	2.00	5.00
❑ 124 Y.A. Tittle	2.00	5.00
❑ 125 Steve Young	2.50	6.00
❑ 126 Tim Brown	2.00	5.00
❑ 127 Joe Greene	2.00	5.00
❑ 128 Paul Krause	1.25	3.00
❑ 129 Troy Aikman	2.50	6.00
❑ 130 Bo Jackson	2.50	6.00
❑ 131 George Blanda	2.00	5.00
❑ 132 Charlie Joiner	1.25	3.00
❑ 133 Walter Payton	4.00	10.00
❑ 134 Jack Youngblood	1.25	3.00
❑ 135 Ozzie Newsome	1.50	4.00
❑ 136 Dan Marino	4.00	10.00
❑ 137 John Elway	3.00	8.00
❑ 138 Joe Montana	4.00	10.00
❑ 139 Barry Sanders	3.00	8.00
❑ 140 Doak Walker	2.00	5.00
❑ 141 Lem Barney	1.25	3.00
❑ 142 Bert Bell	1.25	3.00
❑ 143 Bulldog Turner	1.50	4.00
❑ 144 Greasy Neale	1.25	3.00
❑ 145 Ernie Stautner	1.25	3.00
❑ 146 Frank Gatski	1.25	3.00
❑ 148 Leo Nomellini	1.25	3.00
❑ 150 Otto Graham	2.00	5.00
❑ 151 B. Flowers AU/499 RC	6.00	15.00
❑ 152 Tracy Porter AU/499 RC	12.50	25.00
❑ 153 Terrell Thomas RC	2.00	5.00
❑ 154 Chevis Jackson AU/375 RC	5.00	12.00
❑ 155 Reggie Smith AU/499 RC	5.00	12.00
❑ 156 Phillip Merling RC	2.00	5.00
❑ 157 Calais Campbell RC	2.00	5.00
❑ 158 Quentin Groves RC	2.00	5.00
❑ 159 Pat Sims RC	2.00	5.00
❑ 160 Dan Connor RC	2.50	6.00
❑ 161 Shawn Crable AU/436 RC	6.00	15.00
❑ 162 Xavier Adibi RC	2.00	5.00
❑ 163 Jerod Mayo RC	3.00	8.00
❑ 164 Jordon Dizon RC	2.50	6.00
❑ 165 Jake Long RC	2.50	6.00
❑ 166 Matt Ryan RC	10.00	25.00
❑ 167 Brian Brohm RC	2.50	6.00
❑ 168 Chad Henne RC	4.00	10.00
❑ 169 Dennis Dixon RC	2.50	6.00
❑ 170 Erik Ainge RC	2.50	6.00
❑ 171 Colt Brennan RC	4.00	10.00
❑ 172 Andre Woodson RC	2.50	6.00
❑ 173 Marcus Thomas RC	2.00	5.00
❑ 174 Darren McFadden RC	5.00	12.00
❑ 175 Jonathan Stewart RC	5.00	12.00
❑ 176 Felix Jones RC	5.00	12.00
❑ 177 Rashard Mendenhall RC	5.00	12.00
❑ 178 Tashard Choice RC	2.50	6.00
❑ 179 Ryan Torain AU/499 RC	15.00	30.00
❑ 180 Tim Hightower RC	3.00	8.00
❑ 181 Craig Steltz AU/499 RC	5.00	12.00
❑ 182 Caleb Campbell RC	2.50	6.00
❑ 183 Dustin Keller RC	2.50	6.00
❑ 184 John Carlson RC	2.50	6.00
❑ 185 Fred Davis RC	2.50	6.00
❑ 186 Martellus Bennett AU/499 RC	6.00	15.00
❑ 187 Donnie Avery RC	3.00	8.00
❑ 188 Devin Thomas RC	2.50	6.00
❑ 189 Jordy Nelson RC	3.00	8.00
❑ 190 James Hardy RC	2.00	5.00
❑ 191 Eddie Royal RC	4.00	10.00
❑ 192 Jerome Simpson RC	2.00	5.00
❑ 193 DeSean Jackson RC	5.00	12.00
❑ 194 Malcolm Kelly RC	2.50	6.00
❑ 195 Limas Sweed RC	2.50	6.00
❑ 196 Earl Bennett RC	2.50	6.00
❑ 197 Early Doucet RC	2.50	6.00
❑ 198 Harry Douglas RC	2.00	5.00
❑ 199 Mario Manningham RC	2.50	6.00
❑ 200 Andre Caldwell RC	2.50	6.00
❑ 201 Leodis McKelvin AU/499 RC	6.00	15.00
❑ 202 Antoine Cason AU/499 RC	6.00	15.00
❑ 203 D.Rodgers-Crom AU/499 RC	6.00	15.00
❑ 204 Aqib Talib RC	2.50	6.00
❑ 205 Mike Jenkins RC	2.50	6.00
❑ 206 Vernon Gholston AU/499 RC	6.00	15.00
❑ 207 Derrick Harvey AU/499 RC	5.00	12.00
❑ 208 L.Jackson AU/499 RC	5.00	12.00
❑ 209 Chris Long AU/499 RC	6.00	15.00
❑ 210 Kentwan Balmer AU/499 RC	5.00	12.00
❑ 211 Glenn Dorsey RC	2.50	6.00
❑ 212 Sedrick Ellis RC	2.50	6.00
❑ 213 Jacob Hester AU/499 RC	6.00	15.00
❑ 214 Owen Schmitt AU/499 RC	6.00	15.00
❑ 215 Peyton Hillis AU/499 RC	6.00	15.00
❑ 216 Kenny Phillips RC	2.50	6.00
❑ 217 Curtis Lofton AU/499 RC	6.00	15.00
❑ 218 Keith Rivers AU/499 RC	6.00	15.00
❑ 219 Joe Flacco AU/399 RC	35.00	60.00
❑ 220 Matt Flynn AU/499 RC	6.00	15.00
❑ 221 Kevin O'Connell AU/499 RC	6.00	15.00
❑ 222 John D.Booty AU/349 RC	6.00	15.00
❑ 223 Josh Johnson AU/399 RC	6.00	15.00
❑ 224 Matt Forte AU/499 RC	25.00	40.00
❑ 225 Thomas Brown AU/499 RC	6.00	15.00
❑ 226 C.Washington AU/499 RC	5.00	12.00
❑ 227 Justin Forsett AU/499 RC	6.00	15.00
❑ 228 Cory Boyd AU/499 RC	5.00	12.00
❑ 229 Allen Patrick AU/499 RC	5.00	12.00
❑ 230 Chris Johnson AU/499 RC	30.00	60.00
❑ 231 Ray Rice AU/499 RC	10.00	25.00
❑ 232 K.Smith AU/99 RC EXCH	30.00	60.00
❑ 233 Mike Hart AU/499 RC	6.00	15.00
❑ 234 Jamaal Charles AU/499 RC	10.00	25.00
❑ 235 Steve Slaton AU/99 RC	20.00	50.00
❑ 236 Brad Cottam AU/499 RC	6.00	15.00
❑ 237 Jermichael Finley AU/499 RC	10.00	20.00
❑ 238 Martin Rucker AU/499 RC	5.00	12.00
❑ 239 Jacob Tamme AU/499 RC	6.00	15.00
❑ 240 Kellen Davis AU/499 RC	4.00	10.00
❑ 241 Will Franklin AU/499 RC	5.00	12.00
❑ 242 Marcus Smith AU/499RC	5.00	12.00
❑ 243 Keenan Burton RC	2.00	5.00
❑ 244 Josh Morgan AU/499 RC	6.00	15.00
❑ 245 Kevin Robinson RC	2.00	5.00
❑ 246 Paul Hubbard AU/499 RC	5.00	12.00
❑ 247 Adrian Arrington RC	2.00	5.00
❑ 248 Marcus Monk AU/499 RC	6.00	15.00
❑ 249 Lavelle Hawkins AU/499 RC	5.00	12.00
❑ 250 Dexter Jackson AU/499 RC	6.00	15.00

2009 Donruss Classics

Card	Low	High
❑ COMP.SET w/o SP's (100)	7.50	20.00
❑ 1 Anquan Boldin	.25	.60
❑ 2 Kurt Warner	.30	.75
❑ 3 Larry Fitzgerald	.30	.75
❑ 4 Steve Breaston	.25	.60
❑ 5 Matt Ryan	.30	.75
❑ 6 Michael Turner	.25	.60
❑ 7 Roddy White	.25	.60
❑ 8 Joe Flacco	.30	.75
❑ 9 Willis McGahee	.25	.60
❑ 10 Derrick Mason	.20	.50
❑ 11 Lee Evans	.25	.60
❑ 12 Marshawn Lynch	.25	.60
❑ 13 DeAngelo Williams	.30	.75
❑ 14 Jake Delhomme	.25	.60
❑ 15 Jonathan Stewart	.25	.60
❑ 16 Steve Smith	.25	.60
❑ 17 Greg Olsen	.20	.50
❑ 18 Kyle Orton	.25	.60
❑ 19 Matt Forte	.30	.75
❑ 20 Carson Palmer	.30	.75
❑ 21 Chad Ochocinco	.25	.60
❑ 22 T.J. Houshmandzadeh	.25	.60
❑ 23 Brady Quinn	.25	.60
❑ 24 Braylon Edwards	.25	.60
❑ 25 Jamal Lewis	.25	.60
❑ 26 Kellen Winslow Jr.	.25	.60
❑ 27 Felix Jones	.30	.75
❑ 28 Roy Williams WR	.25	.60
❑ 29 Marion Barber	.30	.75
❑ 30 Tony Romo	.50	1.25
❑ 31 Brandon Marshall	.25	.60
❑ 32 Eddie Royal	.25	.60
❑ 33 Jay Cutler	.30	.75
❑ 34 Calvin Johnson	.30	.75
❑ 35 Kevin Smith	.25	.60
❑ 36 Aaron Rodgers	.30	.75
❑ 37 Donald Driver	.25	.60
❑ 38 Ryan Grant	.25	.60
❑ 39 Andre Johnson	.25	.60
❑ 40 Matt Schaub	.25	.60
❑ 41 Steve Slaton	.25	.60
❑ 42 Anthony Gonzalez	.25	.60
❑ 43 Joseph Addai	.30	.75
❑ 44 Peyton Manning	.50	1.25
❑ 45 Reggie Wayne	.25	.60
❑ 46 David Garrard	.25	.60
❑ 47 Maurice Jones-Drew	.25	.60
❑ 48 Marcedes Lewis	.20	.50
❑ 49 Dwayne Bowe	.25	.60
❑ 50 Larry Johnson	.25	.60
❑ 51 Chad Pennington	.25	.60
❑ 52 Ronnie Brown	.25	.60
❑ 53 Ricky Williams	.25	.60
❑ 54 Adrian Peterson	.60	1.50
❑ 55 Bernard Berrian	.25	.60
❑ 56 Chester Taylor	.20	.50
❑ 57 Laurence Maroney	.25	.60
❑ 58 Randy Moss	.30	.75
❑ 59 Tom Brady	.50	1.25
❑ 60 Drew Brees	.30	.75
❑ 61 Marques Colston	.25	.60
❑ 62 Reggie Bush	.30	.75
❑ 63 Brandon Jacobs	.25	.60
❑ 64 Kevin Boss	.20	.50
❑ 65 Eli Manning	.30	.75
❑ 66 Kellen Clemens	.20	.50
❑ 67 Jerricho Cotchery	.20	.50
❑ 68 Laveranues Coles	.25	.60
❑ 69 Thomas Jones	.25	.60
❑ 70 JaMarcus Russell	.25	.60
❑ 71 Justin Fargas	.20	.50
❑ 72 Darren McFadden	.30	.75
❑ 73 Brian Westbrook	.25	.60
❑ 74 Donovan McNabb	.30	.75
❑ 75 Kevin Curtis	.20	.50
❑ 76 Ben Roethlisberger	.50	1.25
❑ 77 Heath Miller	.25	.60
❑ 78 Santonio Holmes	.25	.60
❑ 79 Willie Parker	.25	.60
❑ 80 Antonio Gates	.25	.60
❑ 81 LaDainian Tomlinson	.30	.75
❑ 82 Philip Rivers	.30	.75
❑ 83 Frank Gore	.25	.60
❑ 84 Isaac Bruce	.25	.60
❑ 85 Deion Branch	.25	.60
❑ 86 Julius Jones	.25	.60
❑ 87 Matt Hasselbeck	.25	.60
❑ 88 Marc Bulger	.25	.60
❑ 89 Steven Jackson	.25	.60
❑ 90 Donnie Avery	.25	.60
❑ 91 Antonio Bryant	.25	.60
❑ 92 Earnest Graham	.20	.50
❑ 93 Derrick Ward	.25	.60
❑ 94 Chris Johnson	.30	.75
❑ 95 Justin Gage	.20	.50
❑ 96 LenDale White	.25	.60
❑ 97 Chris Cooley	.20	.50
❑ 98 Clinton Portis	.25	.60
❑ 99 Jason Campbell	.25	.60
❑ 100 Santana Moss	.25	.60
❑ 101 Alan Page	1.50	4.00
❑ 102 Andre Reed	1.50	4.00
❑ 103 Barry Sanders	3.00	8.00
❑ 104 Billy Sims	1.50	4.00
❑ 105 Bo Jackson	2.50	6.00
❑ 106 Bob Lilly	1.50	4.00
❑ 107 Bobby Layne	2.00	5.00
❑ 108 Carl Eller	1.25	3.00
❑ 109 Chuck Bednarik	1.50	4.00
❑ 110 Ace Parker	1.25	3.00
❑ 111 Cliff Harris	1.50	4.00
❑ 112 Danny White	1.50	4.00
❑ 113 Daryl Johnston	2.00	5.00
❑ 114 Dave Casper	1.25	3.00
❑ 115 Earl Campbell	2.00	5.00
❑ 116 Emmitt Smith	3.00	8.00
❑ 117 Eric Dickerson	1.50	4.00

❑ 118 Franco Harris	2.00	5.00
❑ 119 Gale Sayers	2.50	6.00
❑ 121 Jack Youngblood	1.25	3.00
❑ 122 Jay Novacek	1.50	4.00
❑ 123 Jerry Rice	3.00	8.00
❑ 124 Jim Brown	2.50	6.00
❑ 125 Jim Kelly	2.00	5.00
❑ 126 Jim McMahon	1.50	4.00
❑ 127 Joe Greene	2.00	5.00
❑ 128 Joe Montana	4.00	10.00
❑ 129 John Stallworth	1.50	4.00
❑ 130 Lawrence Taylor	2.00	5.00
❑ 131 Lou Groza	1.50	4.00
❑ 132 Marion Motley	1.50	4.00
❑ 133 Merlin Olsen	1.50	4.00
❑ 134 Michael Irvin	1.50	4.00
❑ 135 Mike Singletary	2.00	5.00
❑ 136 Phil Simms	1.50	4.00
❑ 137 Reggie White	2.00	5.00
❑ 138 Roger Craig	1.50	4.00
❑ 139 Roger Staubach	2.50	6.00
❑ 140 Sid Luckman	1.50	4.00
❑ 141 Steve Young	2.50	6.00
❑ 142 Ted Hendricks	1.25	3.00
❑ 143 Thurman Thomas	2.00	5.00
❑ 144 Tim Brown	2.00	5.00
❑ 145 Tom Landry	2.50	6.00
❑ 146 Tony Dorsett	2.00	5.00
❑ 147 Troy Aikman	2.50	6.00
❑ 148 Walter Payton	4.00	10.00
❑ 149 William Perry	1.50	4.00
❑ 150 Y.A. Tittle	2.00	5.00
❑ 151 Aaron Curry RC	2.50	6.00
❑ 152 Aaron Kelly AU/999 RC	4.00	10.00
❑ 153 Aaron Maybin RC	2.00	5.00
❑ 154 Alphonso Smith RC	1.50	4.00
❑ 155 Andre Brown AU/299 RC	5.00	12.00
❑ 156 Andre Smith RC	2.00	5.00
❑ 157 Arian Foster RC	2.00	5.00
❑ 158 Austin Collie AU/399 RC	15.00	30.00
❑ 159 B.J. Raji RC	2.50	6.00
❑ 160 Brandon Gibson AU/499 RC	6.00	15.00
❑ 161 Brandon Pettigrew RC	2.50	6.00
❑ 162 Brandon Tate AU/399 RC	5.00	12.00
❑ 163 Brian Cushing RC	2.50	6.00
❑ 164 Brian Hartline RC	2.00	5.00
❑ 165 Brian Orakpo RC	2.50	6.00
❑ 166 Brian Robiskie RC	2.00	5.00
❑ 167 Brooks Foster AU/399 RC	5.00	12.00
❑ 168 Cameron Morrah RC	1.25	3.00
❑ 169 Cedric Peerman AU/499 RC	5.00	12.00
❑ 170 Chase Coffman AU/299 RC	5.00	12.00
❑ 171 Chris Wells RC	5.00	12.00
❑ 172 Clay Matthews RC	3.00	8.00
❑ 173 Clint Sintim AU/299 RC	6.00	15.00
❑ 174 Cody Brown RC	1.50	4.00
❑ 175 Cornelius Ingram AU/399 RC	4.00	10.00
❑ 176 Darcel McBath RC	2.00	5.00
❑ 177 Darius Butler RC	2.00	5.00
❑ 178 D.Passmore AU/999 RC EXCH	4.00	10.00
❑ 179 Darrius Heyward-Bey RC	3.00	0.00
❑ 180 Demetrius Byrd RC	1.50	4.00
❑ 181 Deon Butler AU/399 RC	6.00	15.00
❑ 182 Derrick Williams AU/299 RC	6.00	15.00
❑ 183 Devin Moore AU/999 RC	4.00	10.00
❑ 184 D. Edison AU/499 RC	4.00	10.00
❑ 185 Donald Brown RC	4.00	10.00
❑ 186 Eugene Monroe RC	1.50	4.00
❑ 187 Everette Brown RC	2.00	5.00
❑ 188 Gartrell Johnson RC	1.50	4.00
❑ 189 Glen Coffee RC	2.50	6.00
❑ 190 Graham Harrell AU/999 RC	5.00	12.00
❑ 191 Hakeem Nicks RC	4.00	10.00
❑ 192 H.Cantwell AU/999 RC EXCH	5.00	12.00
❑ 193 Ian Johnson RC	2.00	5.00
❑ 194 Jairus Byrd RC	2.50	6.00
❑ 195 James Casey AU/299 RC	5.00	12.00
❑ 196 James Davis RC	2.00	5.00
❑ 197 James Laurinaitis RC	2.50	6.00
❑ 198 Jared Cook AU/299 RC	5.00	12.00
❑ 199 Jarett Dillard AU/299 RC	6.00	15.00
❑ 200 Jason Smith RC	1.50	4.00
❑ 201 Javon Ringer RC	2.00	5.00
❑ 202 J.Johnson AU/999 RC	5.00	12.00
❑ 203 Jeremy Childs RC	1.50	4.00
❑ 204 Jeremy Maclin RC	4.00	10.00
❑ 205 John Parker Wilson AU/999 RC	5.00	12.00
❑ 206 Johnny Knox AU/399 RC	10.00	20.00
❑ 207 Josh Freeman RC	4.00	10.00
❑ 208 Juaquin Iglesias AU/399 RC	6.00	15.00
❑ 209 Kenny Britt RC	3.00	8.00
❑ 210 Kenny McKinley AU/399 RC	6.00	15.00
❑ 211 Kevin Ogletree AU/999 RC	6.00	15.00
❑ 212 Knowshon Moreno RC	5.00	12.00
❑ 213 Kory Sheets AU/999 RC	4.00	10.00
❑ 214 Larry English RC	2.00	5.00
❑ 215 LeSean McCoy RC	4.00	10.00
❑ 216 Louis Delmas RC	2.00	5.00
❑ 217 Louis Murphy RC	2.00	5.00
❑ 218 Malcolm Jenkins RC	2.00	5.00
❑ 219 Mark Sanchez RC	8.00	20.00
❑ 220 Matthew Stafford RC	6.00	15.00
❑ 221 Michael Crabtree RC	5.00	12.00
❑ 222 Michael Mitchell RC	2.00	5.00
❑ 223 Mike Goodson AU/299 RC	6.00	15.00
❑ 224 Mike Thomas AU/299 RC	6.00	15.00
❑ 225 Mike Wallace AU/299 RC	15.00	30.00
❑ 226 Mohamed Massaquoi RC	2.00	5.00
❑ 227 Nate Davis AU/299 RC	12.50	25.00
❑ 228 Nathan Brown AU/999 RC	4.00	10.00
❑ 229 Pat White RC	3.00	8.00
❑ 230 Patrick Chung RC	2.00	5.00
❑ 231 Patrick Turner AU/399 RC	5.00	12.00
❑ 232 Percy Harvin RC	6.00	15.00
❑ 233 Peria Jerry RC	1.50	4.00
❑ 234 Quan Cosby AU/999 RC	4.00	10.00
❑ 235 Quinten Lawrence RC	1.50	4.00
❑ 236 Quinn Johnson AU/699 RC	4.00	10.00
❑ 237 Ramses Barden AU/299 RC	5.00	12.00
❑ 238 Rashad Jennings AU/499 RC	6.00	15.00
❑ 239 Rey Maualuga AU/299 RC	10.00	25.00
❑ 240 Rhett Bomar AU/299 RC	5.00	12.00
❑ 241 Richard Quinn RC	1.50	4.00
❑ 242 Shawn Nelson AU/499 RC	5.00	12.00
❑ 243 Shonn Greene RC	4.00	10.00
❑ 244 Stephen McGee AU/299 RC	12.50	25.00
❑ 245 Tom Brandstater AU/299 RC	6.00	15.00
❑ 246 Tony Fiammetta AU/699 RC	4.00	10.00
❑ 247 Travis Beckum AU/499 RC	5.00	12.00
❑ 248 Tyrell Sutton AU/999 RC	4.00	10.00
❑ 249 Tyson Jackson RC	2.00	5.00
❑ 250 Vontae Davis RC	2.00	5.00

1999 Donruss Elite

❑ COMPLETE SET (200)	40.00	100.00
❑ COMP.SET w/o SP's (160)	15.00	30.00
❑ 1 Warren Moon	.50	1.25
❑ 2 Terry Allen UER	.30	.75
❑ 3 Jeff George	.30	.75
❑ 4 Brett Favre	1.50	4.00
❑ 5 Rob Moore	.30	.75
❑ 6 Bubby Brister	.20	.50
❑ 7 John Elway	1.50	4.00
❑ 8 Troy Aikman	1.00	2.50
❑ 9 Steve McNair	.50	1.25
❑ 10 Charlie Batch	.50	1.25
❑ 11 Elvis Grbac	.30	.75
❑ 12 Trent Dilfer	.30	.75
❑ 13 Kerry Collins	.30	.75
❑ 14 Neil O'Donnell	.20	.50
❑ 15 Tony Simmons	.20	.50
❑ 16 Ryan Leaf	.50	1.25
❑ 17 Bobby Hoying	.30	.75
❑ 18 Marvin Harrison	.50	1.25
❑ 19 Keyshawn Johnson	.50	1.25
❑ 20 Cris Carter	.50	1.25
❑ 21 Deion Sanders	.50	1.25
❑ 22 Emmitt Smith UER	1.00	2.50
❑ 23 Antowain Smith	.50	1.25
❑ 24 Terry Fair	.20	.50
❑ 25 Robert Holcombe	.20	.50
❑ 26 Napoleon Kaufman	.50	1.25
❑ 27 Eddie George	.50	1.25
❑ 28 Corey Dillon	.50	1.25
❑ 29 Adrian Murrell	.30	.75
❑ 30 Charles Way	.20	.50
❑ 31 Amp Lee	.20	.50
❑ 32 Ricky Watters	.30	.75
❑ 33 Gary Brown	.20	.50
❑ 34 Thurman Thomas	.30	.75
❑ 35 Pat Johnson	.20	.50
❑ 36 Jerome Bettis	.50	1.25
❑ 37 Muhsin Muhammad	.30	.75
❑ 38 Kimble Anders	.30	.75
❑ 39 Curtis Enis	.20	.50
❑ 40 Mike Alstott	.50	1.25
❑ 41 Charles Johnson	.20	.50
❑ 42 Chris Warren	.20	.50
❑ 43 Tony Banks	.30	.75
❑ 44 Leroy Hoard	.20	.50
❑ 45 Chris Fuamatu-Ma'afala	.20	.50
❑ 46 Michael Irvin	.50	1.25
❑ 47 Robert Edwards	.20	.50
❑ 48 Hines Ward	.50	1.25
❑ 49 Trent Green	.50	1.25
❑ 50 Eric Zeier	.20	.50
❑ 51 Sean Dawkins	.20	.50
❑ 52 Yancey Thigpen	.20	.50
❑ 53 Jacquez Green	.20	.50
❑ 54 Zach Thomas	.50	1.25
❑ 55 Junior Seau	.50	1.25
❑ 56 Darnay Scott	.20	.50
❑ 57 Kent Graham	.20	.50
❑ 58 O.J. Santiago	.20	.50
❑ 59 Tony Gonzalez	.50	1.25
❑ 60 Ty Detmer	.20	.50
❑ 61 Albert Connell	.20	.50
❑ 62 James Jett	.30	.75
❑ 63 Bert Emanuel	.30	.75
❑ 64 Derrick Alexander WR	.30	.75
❑ 65 Wesley Walls	.30	.75
❑ 66 Jake Reed	.30	.75
❑ 67 Randall Cunningham	.50	1.25
❑ 68 Leslie Shepherd	.20	.50
❑ 69 Mark Chmura	.20	.50
❑ 70 Bobby Engram	.30	.75
❑ 71 Rickey Dudley	.20	.50
❑ 72 Darick Holmes	.20	.50
❑ 73 Andre Reed	.30	.75
❑ 74 Az-Zahir Hakim	.20	.50
❑ 75 Cameron Cleeland	.20	.50
❑ 76 Lamar Thomas	.20	.50
❑ 77 Oronde Gadsden	.30	.75
❑ 78 Ben Coates	.30	.75
❑ 79 Bruce Smith	.30	.75
❑ 80 Jerry Rice	1.00	2.50
❑ 81 Tim Brown	.50	1.25
❑ 82 Michael Westbrook	.30	.75
❑ 83 J.J. Stokes	.30	.75
❑ 84 Shannon Sharpe	.30	.75
❑ 85 Reidel Anthony	.30	.75
❑ 86 Antonio Freeman	.50	1.25
❑ 87 Keenan McCardell	.30	.75
❑ 88 Terry Glenn	.50	1.25
❑ 89 Andre Rison	.30	.75
❑ 90 Neil Smith	.30	.75
❑ 91 Terrance Mathis	.30	.75
❑ 92 Rocket Ismail	.30	.75
❑ 93 Byron Bam Morris	.20	.50
❑ 94 Ike Hilliard	.20	.50
❑ 95 Eddie Kennison	.30	.75
❑ 96 Tavian Banks	.20	.50
❑ 97 Yatil Green	.20	.50
❑ 98 Frank Wycheck	.20	.50
❑ 99 Warren Sapp UER	.20	.50
❑ 100 Germane Crowell	.20	.50
❑ 101 Curtis Martin	1.00	2.50
❑ 102 John Avery	.40	1.00
❑ 103 Eric Moulds	1.00	2.50
❑ 104 Randy Moss	3.00	8.00
❑ 105 Terrell Owens	1.00	2.50
❑ 106 Vinny Testaverde	.60	1.50
❑ 107 Doug Flutie	.50	1.25
❑ 108 Mark Brunell	.50	1.25
❑ 109 Isaac Bruce UER	1.00	2.50
❑ 110 Kordell Stewart	.60	1.50
❑ 111 Drew Bledsoe	1.25	3.00
❑ 112 Chris Chandler	.60	1.50
❑ 113 Dan Marino	3.00	8.00
❑ 114 Brian Griese	1.00	2.50
❑ 115 Carl Pickens	.60	1.50
❑ 116 Jake Plummer	.60	1.50
❑ 117 Natrone Means	.60	1.50
❑ 118 Peyton Manning	4.00	10.00

❑ 119 Garrison Hearst	1.00	2.50
❑ 120 Barry Sanders	3.00	8.00
❑ 121 Steve Young	1.25	3.00
❑ 122 Rashaan Shehee	.40	1.00
❑ 123 Ed McCaffrey	.60	1.50
❑ 124 Charles Woodson	1.00	2.50
❑ 125 Dorsey Levens	1.00	2.50
❑ 126 Robert Smith	1.00	2.50
❑ 127 Greg Hill	.40	1.00
❑ 128 Fred Taylor	1.00	2.50
❑ 129 Marcus Nash	.40	1.00
❑ 130 Terrell Davis	1.00	2.50
❑ 131 Ahman Green	1.00	2.50
❑ 132 Jamal Anderson	1.00	2.50
❑ 133 Karim Abdul-Jabbar	.60	1.50
❑ 134 Jermaine Lewis	.60	1.50
❑ 135 Jerome Pathon	.60	1.50
❑ 136 Brad Johnson	1.00	2.50
❑ 137 Herman Moore	.60	1.50
❑ 138 Tim Dwight	1.00	2.50
❑ 139 Johnnie Morton	.40	1.00
❑ 140 Marshall Faulk	1.25	3.00
❑ 141 Frank Sanders	.60	1.50
❑ 142 Kevin Dyson	.60	1.50
❑ 143 Curtis Conway	.60	1.50
❑ 144 Derrick Mayes	.40	1.00
❑ 145 O.J. McDuffie	.60	1.50
❑ 146 Joe Jurevicius	.60	1.50
❑ 147 Jon Kitna	1.00	2.50
❑ 148 Joey Galloway	.60	1.50
❑ 149 Jimmy Smith	.60	1.50
❑ 150 Skip Hicks	.40	1.00
❑ 151 Rod Smith	.60	1.50
❑ 152 Duce Staley	1.00	2.50
❑ 153 James Stewart	.40	1.00
❑ 154 Rob Johnson	.60	1.50
❑ 155 Mikhael Ricks	.40	1.00
❑ 156 Wayne Chrebet	.60	1.50
❑ 157 Robert Brooks	.60	1.50
❑ 158 Tim Biakabutuka	.60	1.50
❑ 159 Priest Holmes	1.25	4.00
❑ 160 Warrick Dunn	1.00	2.50
❑ 161 Champ Bailey RC	2.00	5.00
❑ 162 D'Wayne Bates RC	1.00	2.50
❑ 163 Michael Bishop RC	1.25	3.00
❑ 164 David Boston RC	1.25	3.00
❑ 165 Na Brown RC	1.00	2.50
❑ 166 Chris Claiborne RC	.60	1.50
❑ 167 Joe Montgomery RC	1.00	2.50
❑ 168 Mike Cloud RC	1.00	2.50
❑ 169 Travis McGriff RC	.60	1.50
❑ 170 Tim Couch RC	1.25	3.00
❑ 171 Daunte Culpepper RC	5.00	12.00
❑ 172 Autry Denson RC	1.00	2.50
❑ 173 Jermaine Fazande RC	1.00	2.50
❑ 174 Troy Edwards RC	1.00	2.50
❑ 175 Kevin Faulk RC	1.25	3.00
❑ 176 Dee Miller UER RC	.60	1.50
❑ 177 Brock Huard RC	1.25	3.00
❑ 178 Torry Holt RC	3.00	8.00
❑ 179 Sedrick Irvin RC	.60	1.50
❑ 180 Edgerrin James RC	5.00	12.00
❑ 181 Joe Germaine RC	1.00	2.50
❑ 182 James Johnson RC	1.00	2.50
❑ 183 Kevin Johnson RC	1.00	2.50
❑ 184 Andy Katzenmoyer RC	1.00	2.50
❑ 185 Jevon Kearse RC	2.50	6.00
❑ 186 Shaun King RC	1.00	2.50
❑ 187 Rob Konrad RC	1.25	3.00
❑ 188 Jim Kleinsasser RC	1.25	3.00
❑ 189 Chris McAlister RC	1.00	2.50
❑ 190 Donovan McNabb RC	6.00	15.00
❑ 191 Cade McNown RC	1.00	2.50
❑ 192 De'Mond Parker RC	.40	1.00
❑ 193 Craig Yeast RC	1.00	2.50
❑ 194 Shawn Bryson RC	1.25	3.00
❑ 195 Peerless Price RC	1.25	3.00
❑ 196 Darnell McDonald RC	1.00	2.50
❑ 197 Akili Smith RC	.60	1.50
❑ 198 Tai Streets RC	1.25	3.00
❑ 199 Ricky Williams RC	2.50	6.00
❑ 200 Amos Zereoue RC	1.00	2.50

2000 Donruss Elite

❑ COMPLETE SET (200)	300.00	500.00
❑ 1 Jake Plummer	.20	.50
❑ 2 David Boston	.30	.75
❑ 3 Rob Moore	.20	.50
❑ 4 Chris Chandler	.20	.50
❑ 5 Tim Dwight	.30	.75
❑ 6 Terance Mathis	.20	.50
❑ 7 Jamal Anderson	.30	.75
❑ 8 Priest Holmes	.40	1.00
❑ 9 Tony Banks	.20	.50
❑ 10 Shannon Sharpe	.20	.50
❑ 11 Qadry Ismail	.20	.50
❑ 12 Eric Moulds	.30	.75
❑ 13 Doug Flutie	.30	.75
❑ 14 Antowain Smith	.20	.50
❑ 15 Peerless Price	.20	.50
❑ 16 Muhsin Muhammad	.20	.50
❑ 17 Tim Biakabutuka	.20	.50
❑ 18 Patrick Jeffers	.30	.75
❑ 19 Steve Beuerlein	.20	.50
❑ 20 Wesley Walls	.10	.30
❑ 21 Curtis Enis	.10	.30
❑ 22 Marcus Robinson	.30	.75
❑ 23 Carl Pickens	.20	.50
❑ 24 Corey Dillon	.30	.75
❑ 25 Akili Smith	.10	.30
❑ 26 Darnay Scott	.20	.50
❑ 27 Kevin Johnson	.30	.75
❑ 28 Errict Rhett	.20	.50
❑ 29 Emmitt Smith	.60	1.50
❑ 30 Deion Sanders	.30	.75
❑ 31 Troy Aikman	.60	1.50
❑ 32 Joey Galloway	.20	.50
❑ 33 Michael Irvin	.20	.50
❑ 34 Rocket Ismail	.20	.50
❑ 35 Jason Tucker	.10	.30
❑ 36 Ed McCaffrey	.30	.75
❑ 37 Rod Smith	.20	.50
❑ 38 Brian Griese	.30	.75
❑ 39 Terrell Davis	.30	.75
❑ 40 Olandis Gary	.30	.75
❑ 41 Charlie Batch	.30	.75
❑ 42 Johnnie Morton	.20	.50
❑ 43 Herman Moore	.20	.50
❑ 44 James Stewart	.20	.50
❑ 45 Dorsey Levens	.20	.50
❑ 46 Antonio Freeman	.30	.75
❑ 47 Brett Favre	1.00	2.50
❑ 48 Bill Schroeder	.20	.50
❑ 49 Peyton Manning	.75	2.00
❑ 50 Keenan McCardell	.20	.50
❑ 51 Fred Taylor	.30	.75
❑ 52 Jimmy Smith	.20	.50
❑ 53 Elvis Grbac	.20	.50
❑ 54 Tony Gonzalez	.20	.50
❑ 55 Derrick Alexander	.20	.50
❑ 56 Dan Marino	1.00	2.50
❑ 57 Tony Martin	.20	.50
❑ 58 James Johnson	.10	.30
❑ 59 Damon Huard	.30	.75
❑ 60 Thurman Thomas	.20	.50
❑ 61 Robert Smith	.30	.75
❑ 62 Randall Cunningham	.30	.75
❑ 63 Jeff George	.20	.50
❑ 64 Terry Glenn	.20	.50
❑ 65 Drew Bledsoe	.40	1.00
❑ 66 Jeff Blake	.20	.50
❑ 67 Amani Toomer	.20	.50
❑ 68 Kerry Collins	.20	.50
❑ 69 Joe Montgomery	.10	.30
❑ 70 Vinny Testaverde	.20	.50
❑ 71 Ray Lucas	.20	.50
❑ 72 Keyshawn Johnson	.30	.75
❑ 73 Wayne Chrebet	.20	.50
❑ 74 Napoleon Kaufman	.20	.50
❑ 75 Tim Brown	.30	.75
❑ 76 Rich Gannon	.30	.75
❑ 77 Duce Staley	.30	.75
❑ 78 Kordell Stewart	.20	.50
❑ 79 Jerome Bettis	.30	.75
❑ 80 Troy Edwards	.10	.30
❑ 81 Natrone Means	.10	.30
❑ 82 Curtis Conway	.20	.50
❑ 83 Jim Harbaugh	.20	.50
❑ 84 Junior Seau	.30	.75
❑ 85 Jermaine Fazande	.10	.30
❑ 86 Terrell Owens	.30	.75
❑ 87 Charlie Garner	.20	.50
❑ 88 Steve Young	.40	1.00
❑ 89 Jeff Garcia	.30	.75
❑ 90 Derrick Mayes	.20	.50
❑ 91 Ricky Watters	.20	.50
❑ 92 Az-Zahir Hakim	.20	.50
❑ 93 Torry Holt	.30	.75
❑ 94 Warren Sapp	.20	.50
❑ 95 Mike Alstott	.30	.75
❑ 96 Warrick Dunn	.30	.75
❑ 97 Kevin Dyson	.20	.50
❑ 98 Bruce Smith	.20	.50
❑ 99 Albert Connell	.10	.30
❑ 100 Michael Westbrook	.20	.50
❑ 101 Cade McNown	.10	.30
❑ 102 Tim Couch	.75	2.00
❑ 103 John Elway	2.50	6.00
❑ 104 Barry Sanders	2.00	5.00
❑ 105 Germane Crowell	.50	1.25
❑ 106 Marvin Harrison	.75	2.00
❑ 107 Edgerrin James	1.25	3.00
❑ 108 Mark Brunell	.75	2.00
❑ 109 Randy Moss	1.50	4.00
❑ 110 Cris Carter	.75	2.00
❑ 111 Daunte Culpepper	1.00	2.50
❑ 112 Ricky Williams	.30	.75
❑ 113 Curtis Martin	.75	2.00
❑ 114 Donovan McNabb	1.25	3.00
❑ 115 Jerry Rice	1.50	4.00
❑ 116 Jon Kitna	.75	2.00
❑ 117 Isaac Bruce	.75	2.00
❑ 118 Marshall Faulk	1.00	2.50
❑ 119 Kurt Warner	1.50	4.00
❑ 120 Shaun King	.10	.30
❑ 121 Eddie George	.75	2.00
❑ 122 Steve McNair	.75	2.00
❑ 123 Jevon Kearse	.75	2.00
❑ 124 Stephen Davis	.75	2.00
❑ 125 Brad Johnson	.75	2.00
❑ 126 Mike Anderson RC	1.00	2.50
❑ 127 Peter Warrick RC	2.00	5.00
❑ 128 Courtney Brown RC	.75	2.00
❑ 129 Plaxico Burress RC	4.00	10.00
❑ 130 Corey Simon RC	2.00	5.00
❑ 131 Thomas Jones RC	3.00	8.00
❑ 132 Travis Taylor RC	.75	2.00
❑ 133 Shaun Alexander RC	8.00	20.00
❑ 134 Deon Grant RC	1.50	4.00
❑ 135 Chris Redman RC	1.50	4.00
❑ 136 Chad Pennington RC	5.00	12.00
❑ 137 Jamal Lewis RC	5.00	12.00
❑ 138 Brian Urlacher RC	10.00	25.00
❑ 139 Keith Bulluck RC	2.00	5.00
❑ 140 Bubba Franks RC	2.00	5.00
❑ 141 Dez White RC	2.00	5.00
❑ 142 Na'il Diggs RC	1.50	4.00
❑ 143 Ahmed Plummer RC	2.00	5.00
❑ 144 Ron Dayne RC	2.00	5.00
❑ 145 Shaun Ellis RC	2.00	5.00
❑ 146 Sylvester Morris RC	1.50	4.00
❑ 147 Deltha O'Neal RC	2.00	5.00
❑ 148 Raynoch Thompson RC	1.50	4.00
❑ 149 R.Jay Soward RC	1.50	4.00
❑ 150 Mario Edwards RC	1.50	4.00
❑ 151 John Engelberger RC	1.50	4.00
❑ 152 Dwayne Goodrich RC	2.00	5.00
❑ 153 Sherrod Gideon RC	1.00	2.50
❑ 154 John Abraham RC	2.00	5.00
❑ 155 Ben Kelly RC	2.00	5.00
❑ 156 Travis Prentice RC	1.50	4.00
❑ 157 Darrell Jackson RC	4.00	10.00
❑ 158 Giovanni Carmazzi RC	1.00	2.50
❑ 159 Anthony Lucas RC	1.00	2.50
❑ 160 Danny Farmer RC	1.50	4.00
❑ 161 Dennis Northcutt RC	2.00	5.00
❑ 162 Troy Walters RC	2.00	5.00

❑ 163 Laveranues Coles RC	2.50	6.00
❑ 164 Tee Martin RC	2.00	5.00
❑ 165 J.R. Redmond RC	1.50	4.00
❑ 166 Tim Rattay RC	2.00	5.00
❑ 167 Jerry Porter RC	2.50	6.00
❑ 168 Sebastian Janikowski RC	2.00	5.00
❑ 169 Michael Wiley RC	1.50	4.00
❑ 170 Reuben Droughns RC	2.50	6.00
❑ 171 Trung Canidate RC	1.50	4.00
❑ 172 Shyrone Stith RC	2.00	5.00
❑ 173 Chris Hovan RC	1.50	4.00
❑ 174 Brandon Short RC	2.00	5.00
❑ 175 Mark Roman RC	1.50	4.00
❑ 176 Trevor Gaylor RC	1.50	4.00
❑ 177 Chris Cole RC	1.50	4.00
❑ 178 Hank Poteat RC	1.50	4.00
❑ 179 Darren Howard RC	1.50	4.00
❑ 180 Rob Morris RC	2.00	5.00
❑ 181 Spergon Wynn RC	1.50	4.00
❑ 182 Marc Bulger RC	5.00	10.00
❑ 183 Tom Brady RC	75.00	150.00
❑ 184 Todd Husak RC	2.00	5.00
❑ 185 Gari Scott RC	1.00	2.50
❑ 186 Erron Kinney RC	1.50	4.00
❑ 187 Julian Peterson RC	2.00	5.00
❑ 188 Sammy Morris RC	2.00	5.00
❑ 189 Rondell Mealey RC	1.00	2.50
❑ 190 Doug Chapman RC	1.50	4.00
❑ 191 Ron Dugans RC	1.00	2.50
❑ 192 Deon Dyer RC	1.50	4.00
❑ 193 Fred Robbins RC	1.00	2.50
❑ 194 Ike Charlton RC	2.00	5.00
❑ 195 Mareno Philyaw RC	1.00	2.50
❑ 196 Thomas Hamner RC	1.00	2.50
❑ 197 Jarious Jackson RC	1.50	4.00
❑ 198 Anthony Becht RC	2.00	5.00
❑ 199 Joe Hamilton RC	1.50	4.00
❑ 200 Todd Pinkston RC	2.00	5.00

2001 Donruss Elite

❑ COMP.SET w/o SP's (100)	7.50	20.00
❑ 1 David Boston	.15	.40
❑ 2 Jake Plummer	.20	.50
❑ 3 Thomas Jones	.20	.50
❑ 4 Jamal Anderson	.20	.50
❑ 5 Chris Redman	.25	.60
❑ 6 Jamal Lewis	.25	.60
❑ 7 Shannon Sharpe	.25	.60
❑ 8 Travis Taylor	.15	.40
❑ 9 Trent Dilfer	.20	.50
❑ 10 Doug Flutie	.25	.60
❑ 11 Eric Moulds	.20	.50
❑ 12 Rob Johnson	.20	.50
❑ 13 Muhsin Muhammad	.20	.50
❑ 14 Steve Beuerlein	.20	.50
❑ 15 Brian Urlacher	.30	.75
❑ 16 Cade McNown	.20	.50
❑ 17 Marcus Robinson	.20	.50
❑ 18 Akili Smith	.15	.40
❑ 19 Corey Dillon	.20	.50
❑ 20 Peter Warrick	.20	.50
❑ 21 Kevin Johnson	.15	.40
❑ 22 Tim Couch	.15	.40
❑ 23 Emmitt Smith	.60	1.50
❑ 24 Troy Aikman	.40	1.00
❑ 25 Brian Griese	.20	.50
❑ 26 John Elway	.60	1.50
❑ 27 Mike Anderson	.20	.50
❑ 28 Rod Smith	.20	.50
❑ 29 Terrell Davis	.25	.60
❑ 30 Barry Sanders	.60	1.50
❑ 31 Charlie Batch	.20	.50
❑ 32 James Stewart	.15	.40
❑ 33 Ahman Green	.25	.60
❑ 34 Antonio Freeman	.25	.60
❑ 35 Brett Favre	.75	2.00
❑ 36 Edgerrin James	.25	.60
❑ 37 Marvin Harrison	.25	.60
❑ 38 Peyton Manning	.60	1.50
❑ 39 Fred Taylor	.25	.60
❑ 40 Jimmy Smith	.20	.50
❑ 41 Keenan McCardell	.20	.50
❑ 42 Mark Brunell	.25	.60
❑ 43 Derrick Alexander	.15	.40
❑ 44 Elvis Grbac	.20	.50
❑ 45 Sylvester Morris	.15	.40
❑ 46 Tony Gonzalez	.20	.50
❑ 47 Dan Marino	.75	2.00
❑ 48 Jay Fiedler	.20	.50
❑ 49 Lamar Smith	.20	.50
❑ 50 Oronde Gadsden	.15	.40
❑ 51 Cris Carter	.25	.60
❑ 52 Daunte Culpepper	.25	.60
❑ 53 Randy Moss	.30	.75
❑ 54 Robert Smith	.20	.50
❑ 55 Drew Bledsoe	.25	.60
❑ 56 Terry Glenn	.20	.50
❑ 57 Aaron Brooks	.20	.50
❑ 58 Joe Horn	.20	.50
❑ 59 Ricky Williams	.25	.60
❑ 60 Amani Toomer	.20	.50
❑ 61 Ike Hilliard	.20	.50
❑ 62 Kerry Collins	.20	.50
❑ 63 Ron Dayne	.20	.50
❑ 64 Tiki Barber	.25	.60
❑ 65 Chad Pennington	.25	.60
❑ 66 Curtis Martin	.25	.60
❑ 67 Vinny Testaverde	.20	.50
❑ 68 Wayne Chrebet	.20	.50
❑ 69 Rich Gannon	.20	.50
❑ 70 Tim Brown	.25	.60
❑ 71 Tyrone Wheatley	.20	.50
❑ 72 Donovan McNabb	.30	.75
❑ 73 Jerome Bettis	.25	.60
❑ 74 Plaxico Burress	.20	.50
❑ 75 Junior Seau	.25	.60
❑ 76 Charlie Garner	.20	.50
❑ 77 Jeff Garcia	.20	.50
❑ 78 Jerry Rice	.50	1.25
❑ 79 Terrell Owens	.25	.60
❑ 80 Darrell Jackson	.20	.50
❑ 81 Ricky Watters	.20	.50
❑ 82 Shaun Alexander	.25	.60
❑ 83 Isaac Bruce	.25	.60
❑ 84 Kurt Warner	.30	.75
❑ 85 Marshall Faulk	.25	.60
❑ 86 Torry Holt	.20	.50
❑ 87 Trent Green	.25	.60
❑ 88 Keyshawn Johnson	.20	.50
❑ 89 Shaun King	.15	.40
❑ 90 Warren Sapp	.20	.50
❑ 91 Warrick Dunn	.25	.60
❑ 92 Eddie George	.25	.60
❑ 93 Jevon Kearse	.20	.50
❑ 94 Steve McNair	.25	.60
❑ 95 Albert Connell	.15	.40
❑ 96 Jeff George	.20	.50
❑ 97 Brad Johnson	.20	.50
❑ 98 Bruce Smith	.25	.60
❑ 99 Michael Westbrook	.15	.40
❑ 100 Stephen Davis	.20	.50
❑ 101 Michael Vick RC	8.00	20.00
❑ 102 Drew Brees RC	20.00	50.00
❑ 103 Chris Weinke RC	3.00	8.00
❑ 104 Quincy Carter RC	3.00	8.00
❑ 105 Sage Rosenfels RC	4.00	10.00
❑ 106 Josh Heupel RC	4.00	10.00
❑ 107 Tony Driver RC	3.00	8.00
❑ 108 Ben Leard RC	2.50	6.00
❑ 109 Marques Tuiasosopo RC	3.00	8.00
❑ 110 Tim Hasselbeck RC	3.00	8.00
❑ 111 Mike McMahon RC	3.00	8.00
❑ 112 Deuce McAllister RC	5.00	12.00
❑ 113 LaMont Jordan RC	4.00	10.00
❑ 114 LaDainian Tomlinson RC	25.00	60.00
❑ 115 James Jackson RC	3.00	8.00
❑ 116 Anthony Thomas RC	4.00	10.00
❑ 117 Travis Henry RC	4.00	10.00
❑ 118 DeAngelo Evans RC	3.00	8.00
❑ 119 Travis Minor RC	3.00	8.00
❑ 120 Rudi Johnson RC	4.00	10.00
❑ 121 Michael Bennett RC	4.00	10.00
❑ 122 Kevan Barlow RC	3.00	8.00
❑ 123 Dan Alexander RC	3.00	8.00
❑ 124 David Allen RC	2.50	6.00
❑ 125 Correll Buckhalter RC	4.00	10.00
❑ 126 David Rivers RC	2.50	6.00
❑ 127 Reggie White RC	2.50	6.00
❑ 128 Moran Norris RC	2.50	6.00
❑ 129 Ja'Mar Toombs RC	2.50	6.00
❑ 130 Jason McKinley RC	2.50	6.00
❑ 131 Scotty Anderson RC	3.00	8.00
❑ 132 Dustin McClintock RC	3.00	8.00
❑ 133 Heath Evans RC	3.00	8.00
❑ 134 David Terrell RC	3.00	8.00
❑ 135 Santana Moss RC	6.00	15.00
❑ 136 Rod Gardner RC	3.00	8.00
❑ 137 Quincy Morgan RC	3.00	8.00
❑ 138 Freddie Mitchell RC	2.50	6.00
❑ 139 Boo Williams RC	3.00	8.00
❑ 140 Reggie Wayne RC	10.00	25.00
❑ 141 Ronney Daniels RC	2.50	6.00
❑ 142 Bobby Newcombe RC	3.00	8.00
❑ 143 Reggie Germany/250 RC	3.00	8.00
❑ 144 Jesse Palmer RC	4.00	10.00
❑ 145 Robert Ferguson RC	4.00	10.00
❑ 146 Ken-Yon Rambo RC	2.50	6.00
❑ 147 Alex Bannister RC	2.50	6.00
❑ 148 Koren Robinson RC	4.00	10.00
❑ 149 Chad Johnson RC	10.00	25.00
❑ 150 Chris Chambers RC	6.00	15.00
❑ 151 Javon Green RC	2.50	6.00
❑ 152 Snoop Minnis RC	3.00	8.00
❑ 153 Vinny Sutherland RC	2.50	6.00
❑ 154 Cedrick Wilson RC	4.00	10.00
❑ 155 John Capel/250 RC	3.00	8.00
❑ 156 T.J. Houshmandzadeh RC	6.00	15.00
❑ 157 Todd Heap RC	4.00	10.00
❑ 158 Alge Crumpler RC	4.00	10.00
❑ 159 Jabari Holloway RC	3.00	8.00
❑ 160 Marcellus Rivers RC	2.50	6.00
❑ 161 Rashon Burns RC	2.50	6.00
❑ 162 Tony Stewart RC	3.00	8.00
❑ 163 Jevaris Johnson RC	2.50	6.00
❑ 164 Jamal Reynolds RC	3.00	8.00
❑ 165 Andre Carter RC	4.00	10.00
❑ 166 David Warren RC	2.50	6.00
❑ 167 Justin Smith RC	4.00	10.00
❑ 168 Josh Booty RC	3.00	8.00
❑ 169 Karon Riley RC	2.50	6.00
❑ 170 Cedric Scott RC	2.50	6.00
❑ 171 Kenny Smith RC	2.50	6.00
❑ 172 Richard Seymour RC	4.00	10.00
❑ 173 Willie Howard RC	2.50	6.00
❑ 174 Markus Steele RC	2.50	6.00
❑ 175 Marcus Stroud RC	3.00	8.00
❑ 176 Damione Lewis RC	3.00	8.00
❑ 177 Casey Hampton RC	3.00	8.00
❑ 178 Ennis Davis RC	2.50	6.00
❑ 179 Gerard Warren RC	3.00	8.00
❑ 180 Tommy Polley RC	3.00	8.00
❑ 181 Kendrell Bell/250 RC	5.00	12.00
❑ 182 Dan Morgan RC	4.00	10.00
❑ 183 Morlon Greenwood RC	2.50	6.00
❑ 184 Quinton Caver/250	3.00	8.00
❑ 185 Keith Adams RC	2.50	6.00
❑ 186 Brian Allen RC	2.50	6.00
❑ 187 Carlos Polk RC	2.50	6.00
❑ 188 Torrance Marshall RC	3.00	8.00
❑ 189 Jamie Winborn RC	3.00	8.00
❑ 190 Jamar Fletcher RC	2.50	6.00
❑ 191 Ken Lucas RC	3.00	8.00
❑ 192 Fred Smoot RC	4.00	10.00
❑ 193 Nate Clements RC	4.00	10.00
❑ 194 Will Allen RC	4.00	10.00
❑ 195 Willie Middlebrooks/250 RC	4.00	10.00
❑ 196 Gary Baxter RC	3.00	8.00
❑ 197 Derrick Gibson RC	2.50	6.00
❑ 198 Robert Carswell/250 RC	3.00	8.00
❑ 199 Hakim Akbar RC	2.50	6.00
❑ 200 Adam Archuleta RC	3.00	8.00

2002 Donruss Elite

Card	Low	High
COMP.SET w/o SP's (100)	7.50	20.00
1 Elvis Grbac	.20	.50
2 Jamal Lewis	.20	.50
3 Ray Lewis	.25	.60
4 Travis Henry	.20	.50
5 Eric Moulds	.20	.50
6 Corey Dillon	.20	.50
7 Peter Warrick	.20	.50
8 Tim Couch	.15	.40
9 James Jackson	.15	.40
10 Kevin Johnson	.15	.40
11 Mike Anderson	.20	.50
12 Terrell Davis	.25	.60
13 Brian Griese	.20	.50
14 Rod Smith	.20	.50
15 Marvin Harrison	.25	.60
16 Reggie Wayne	.25	.60
17 Dominic Rhodes	.20	.50
18 Edgerrin James	.25	.60
19 Mark Brunell	.20	.50
20 Keenan McCardell	.20	.50
21 Jimmy Smith	.20	.50
22 Tony Gonzalez	.20	.50
23 Trent Green	.20	.50
24 Priest Holmes	.25	.60
25 Snoop Minnis	.15	.40
26 Chris Chambers	.25	.60
27 Jay Fiedler	.20	.50
28 Travis Minor	.20	.50
29 Lamar Smith	.20	.50
30 Tom Brady	.60	1.50
31 Troy Brown	.20	.50
32 Antowain Smith	.20	.50
33 Laveranues Coles	.25	.60
34 Curtis Martin	.25	.60
35 Vinny Testaverde	.20	.50
36 Wayne Chrebet	.20	.50
37 Tim Brown	.25	.60
38 Rich Gannon	.20	.50
39 Jerry Rice	.50	1.25
40 Charlie Garner	.20	.50
41 Jerome Bettis	.25	.60
42 Plaxico Burress	.20	.50
43 Kordell Stewart	.20	.50
44 Kendrell Bell	.15	.40
45 Doug Flutie	.25	.60
46 LaDainian Tomlinson	.40	1.00
47 Junior Seau	.25	.60
48 Drew Brees	.40	1.00
49 Shaun Alexander	.25	.60
50 Koren Robinson	.15	.40
51 Ricky Watters	.20	.50
52 Eddie George	.20	.50
53 Derrick Mason	.20	.50
54 Steve McNair	.25	.60
55 David Boston	.15	.40
56 Jake Plummer	.20	.50
57 Chris Chandler	.20	.50
58 Jamal Anderson	.20	.50
59 Michael Vick	.25	.60
60 Wesley Walls	.20	.50
61 Chris Weinke	.15	.40
62 David Terrell	.20	.50
63 Anthony Thomas	.20	.50
64 Brian Urlacher	.30	.75
65 Quincy Carter	.15	.40
66 Rocket Ismail	.20	.50
67 Emmitt Smith	.60	1.50
68 James Stewart	.15	.40
69 Germane Crowell	.15	.40
70 Mike McMahon	.15	.40
71 Brett Favre	.60	1.50
72 Ahman Green	.20	.50
73 Antonio Freeman	.25	.60
74 Michael Bennett	.20	.50
75 Cris Carter	.25	.60
76 Daunte Culpepper	.20	.50
77 Randy Moss	.25	.60
78 Aaron Brooks	.20	.50
79 Deuce McAllister	.25	.60
80 Ricky Williams	.25	.60
81 Kerry Collins	.20	.50
82 Ron Dayne	.20	.50
83 Amani Toomer	.20	.50
84 Correll Buckhalter	.20	.50
85 James Thrash	.20	.50
86 Freddie Mitchell	.15	.40
87 Duce Staley	.20	.50
88 Jeff Garcia	.20	.50
89 Garrison Hearst	.20	.50
90 Terrell Owens	.25	.60
91 Isaac Bruce	.25	.60
92 Marshall Faulk	.25	.60
93 Torry Holt	.25	.60
94 Kurt Warner	.25	.60
95 Mike Alstott	.20	.50
96 Brad Johnson	.20	.50
97 Keyshawn Johnson	.20	.50
98 Stephen Davis	.20	.50
99 Rod Gardner	.15	.40
100 Tony Banks	.15	.40
101 David Carr RC	5.00	12.00
102 Joey Harrington RC	5.00	12.00
103 Rohan Davey RC	5.00	12.00
104 Chad Hutchinson RC	3.00	8.00
105 Patrick Ramsey RC	5.00	12.00
106 Kurt Kittner RC	3.00	8.00
107 Eric Crouch RC	5.00	12.00
108 David Garrard RC	8.00	20.00
109 Ronald Curry RC	5.00	12.00
110 Zak Kustok RC	3.00	8.00
111 Woody Dantzler RC	4.00	10.00
112 Wes Pate RC	3.00	8.00
113 Brian Westbrook RC	15.00	40.00
114 Josh McCown RC	5.00	12.00
115 Travis Stephens RC	3.00	8.00
116 Luke Staley RC	3.00	8.00
117 William Green RC	4.00	10.00
118 Clinton Portis RC	12.00	30.00
119 DeShaun Foster RC	5.00	12.00
120 Verron Haynes RC	4.00	10.00
121 T.J. Duckett RC	5.00	12.00
122 Antwoine Womack RC	3.00	8.00
123 Leonard Henry RC	3.00	8.00
124 Lamar Gordon RC	5.00	12.00
125 Adrian Peterson RC	5.00	12.00
126 Chester Taylor RC	8.00	20.00
127 Damien Anderson RC	4.00	10.00
128 Maurice Morris RC	5.00	12.00
129 Ricky Williams RC	4.00	10.00
130 Terry Charles RC	3.00	8.00
131 Demontray Carter RC	3.00	8.00
132 Jason McAddley RC	4.00	10.00
133 Ladell Betts RC	5.00	12.00
134 Cortlen Johnson RC	3.00	8.00
135 James Mungro RC	5.00	12.00
136 Atrews Bell RC	3.00	8.00
137 Josh Scobey RC	4.00	10.00
138 Justin Peelle RC	3.00	8.00
139 Najeh Davenport RC	5.00	12.00
140 Josh Reed RC	4.00	10.00
141 Marquise Walker RC	3.00	8.00
142 Jabar Gaffney RC	5.00	12.00
143 Antwaan Randle El RC	5.00	12.00
144 Ashley Lelie RC	5.00	12.00
145 Tavon Mason RC	3.00	8.00
146 Antonio Bryant RC	6.00	15.00
147 Javon Walker RC	5.00	12.00
148 Kelly Campbell RC	4.00	10.00
149 Ron Johnson RC	4.00	10.00
150 Andre Davis RC	4.00	10.00
151 Cliff Russell RC	3.00	8.00
152 Reche Caldwell RC	5.00	12.00
153 Kyle Johnson RC	3.00	8.00
154 Freddie Milons RC	3.00	8.00
155 Brian Poli-Dixon RC	3.00	8.00
156 David Thornton RC	3.00	8.00
157 Bryan Thomas RC	3.00	8.00
158 Kahlil Hill RC	3.00	8.00
159 Deion Branch RC	5.00	12.00
160 Akin Ayodele RC	4.00	10.00
161 Donte Stallworth RC	5.00	12.00
162 Tim Carter RC	4.00	10.00
163 Kenyon Coleman RC	3.00	8.00
164 Jeremy Shockey RC	8.00	20.00
165 Eddie Freeman RC	3.00	8.00
166 Tracey Wistrom RC	4.00	10.00
167 Daniel Graham RC	4.00	10.00
168 Julius Peppers RC	8.00	20.00
169 Alex Brown RC	5.00	12.00
170 Dwight Freeney RC	8.00	20.00
171 Kalimba Edwards RC	4.00	10.00
172 Dennis Johnson RC	3.00	8.00
173 Travis Fisher RC	4.00	10.00
174 John Henderson RC	5.00	12.00
175 Anthony Weaver RC	3.00	8.00
176 Ryan Sims RC	5.00	12.00
177 Alan Harper RC	3.00	8.00
178 Larry Tripplett RC	3.00	8.00
179 Wendell Bryant RC	3.00	8.00
180 Albert Haynesworth RC	5.00	12.00
181 Levar Fisher RC	3.00	8.00
182 Andra Davis RC	3.00	8.00
183 Joseph Jefferson RC	3.00	8.00
184 Lamont Thompson RC	4.00	10.00
185 Robert Thomas RC	3.00	8.00
186 Michael Lewis RC	5.00	12.00
187 Rocky Calmus RC	4.00	10.00
188 Napoleon Harris RC	4.00	10.00
189 Lito Sheppard RC	5.00	12.00
190 Quentin Jammer RC	5.00	12.00
191 Roy Williams RC	6.00	15.00
192 Marques Anderson RC	4.00	10.00
193 Chris Hope RC	5.00	12.00
194 Raonall Smith RC	3.00	8.00
195 Mike Rumph RC	3.00	8.00
196 James Allen RC	3.00	8.00
197 Ed Reed RC	15.00	40.00
198 Mike Williams RC	3.00	8.00
199 Phillip Buchanon RC	5.00	12.00
200 Bryant McKinnie RC	3.00	8.00

2004 Donruss Elite

Card	Low	High
COMP.SET w/o SP's (100)	7.50	20.00
ROOKIE PRINT RUN 500 SER.#'d SETS		
1 Emmitt Smith	1.00	2.50
2 Anquan Boldin	.40	1.00
3 Michael Vick	.40	1.00
4 Peerless Price	.30	.75
5 T.J. Duckett	.30	.75
6 Warrick Dunn	.30	.75
7 Jamal Lewis	.30	.75
8 Kyle Boller	.30	.75
9 Todd Heap	.30	.75
10 Ray Lewis	.40	1.00
11 Drew Bledsoe	.40	1.00
12 Eric Moulds	.30	.75
13 Travis Henry	.30	.75
14 Jake Delhomme	.30	.75
15 Stephen Davis	.30	.75
16 Steve Smith	.40	1.00
17 Anthony Thomas	.30	.75
18 Brian Urlacher	.40	1.00
19 Rex Grossman	.40	1.00
20 Chad Johnson	.30	.75
21 Carson Palmer	.50	1.25
22 Rudi Johnson	.30	.75
23 Peter Warrick	.30	.75
24 Andre Davis	.25	.60
25 Tim Couch	.30	.75
26 Quincy Carter	.25	.60
27 Roy Williams S	.30	.75
28 Terence Newman	.30	.75
29 Clinton Portis	.40	1.00
30 Jake Plummer	.30	.75
31 Rod Smith	.30	.75
32 Charles Rogers	.30	.75
33 Joey Harrington	.30	.75
34 Ahman Green	.40	1.00

Card		
35 Brett Favre	1.00	2.50
36 Javon Walker	.30	.75
37 Andre Johnson	.40	1.00
38 David Carr	.30	.75
39 Domanick Davis	.30	.75
40 Edgerrin James	.40	1.00
41 Marvin Harrison	.40	1.00
42 Peyton Manning	.75	2.00
43 Reggie Wayne	.30	.75
44 Byron Leftwich	.40	1.00
45 Fred Taylor	.30	.75
46 Jimmy Smith	.30	.75
47 Priest Holmes	.40	1.00
48 Tony Gonzalez	.40	1.00
49 Trent Green	.30	.75
50 Chris Chambers	.30	.75
51 Ricky Williams	.40	1.00
52 Zach Thomas	.40	1.00
53 Daunte Culpepper	.40	1.00
54 Michael Bennett	.30	.75
55 Moe Williams	.25	.60
56 Randy Moss	.40	1.00
57 Deion Branch	.30	.75
58 Tom Brady	1.00	2.50
59 Tedy Bruschi	.40	1.00
60 Aaron Brooks	.30	.75
61 Deuce McAllister	.40	1.00
62 Joe Horn	.30	.75
63 Jeremy Shockey	.30	.75
64 Kerry Collins	.30	.75
65 Michael Strahan	.30	.75
66 Tiki Barber	.40	1.00
67 Chad Pennington	.40	1.00
68 Curtis Martin	.40	1.00
69 Santana Moss	.30	.75
70 Jerry Porter	.30	.75
71 Jerry Rice	.75	2.00
72 Tim Brown	.40	1.00
73 Brian Westbrook	.40	1.00
74 Correll Buckhalter	.30	.75
75 Donovan McNabb	.40	1.00
76 Hines Ward	.40	1.00
77 Kendrell Bell	.25	.60
78 Plaxico Burress	.30	.75
79 David Boston	.25	.60
80 Drew Brees	.40	1.00
81 LaDainian Tomlinson	.50	1.25
82 Jeff Garcia	.40	1.00
83 Kevan Barlow	.30	.75
84 Terrell Owens	.40	1.00
85 Koren Robinson	.40	1.00
86 Matt Hasselbeck	.40	1.00
87 Shaun Alexander	.40	1.00
88 Isaac Bruce	.30	.75
89 Marc Bulger	.30	.75
90 Marshall Faulk	.40	1.00
91 Torry Holt	.40	1.00
92 Brad Johnson	.30	.75
93 Derrick Brooks	.30	.75
94 Keenan McCardell	.25	.00
95 Derrick Mason	.30	.75
96 Eddie George	.30	.75
97 Steve McNair	.40	1.00
98 Jevon Kearse	.30	.75
99 Laveranues Coles	.30	.75
100 Patrick Ramsey	.30	.75
101 Adimchinobe Echemandu RC	2.50	6.00
102 Ahmad Carroll RC	3.00	8.00
103 Antwan Odom RC	3.00	8.00
104 B.J. Johnson RC	2.00	5.00
105 Ben Roethlisberger RC	25.00	60.00
106 Ben Troupe RC	2.50	6.00
107 Ben Watson RC	3.00	8.00
108 Bernard Berrian RC	3.00	8.00
109 Bob Sanders RC	8.00	20.00
110 Brandon Everage RC	2.00	5.00
111 Brandon Miree RC	2.00	5.00
112 Carlos Francis RC	2.00	5.00
113 Cedric Cobbs RC	2.50	6.00
114 Chad Lavalais RC	2.00	5.00
115 Chris Collins RC	2.00	5.00
116 Chris Gamble RC	2.50	6.00
117 Chris Perry RC	3.00	8.00
118 Cody Pickett RC	2.50	6.00
119 Craig Krenzel RC	3.00	8.00
120 D.J. Hackett RC	3.00	8.00
121 D.J. Williams RC	3.00	8.00
122 Darius Watts RC	2.50	6.00
123 Darnell Dockett RC	2.00	5.00
124 DeAngelo Hall RC	3.00	8.00
125 Derek Abney RC	2.00	5.00
126 Derrick Hamilton RC	2.00	5.00
127 Derrick Strait RC	2.50	6.00
128 Devard Darling RC	2.50	6.00
129 Devery Henderson RC	3.00	8.00
130 Dontarrious Thomas RC	2.50	6.00
131 Drew Henson RC	2.00	5.00
132 Dunta Robinson RC	2.50	6.00
133 Dwan Edwards RC	2.00	5.00
134 Eli Manning RC	20.00	50.00
135 Ernest Wilford RC	2.50	6.00
136 Fred Russell RC	2.50	6.00
137 Greg Jones RC	3.00	8.00
138 Igor Olshansky RC	3.00	8.00
139 J.P. Losman RC	3.00	8.00
140 Jared Lorenzen RC	2.50	6.00
141 Jarrett Payton RC	2.50	6.00
142 Jason Babin RC	2.50	6.00
143 Jason Fife RC	2.00	5.00
144 Jeff Smoker RC	2.50	6.00
145 Jeremy LeSueur RC	2.00	5.00
146 Jerricho Cotchery RC	3.00	8.00
147 John Navarre RC	2.50	6.00
148 John Standeford RC	2.00	5.00
149 Johnnie Morant RC	2.50	6.00
150 Jonathan Vilma RC	3.00	8.00
151 Josh Davis RC	2.50	6.00
152 Josh Harris RC	2.00	5.00
153 Julius Jones RC	4.00	10.00
154 Justin Jenkins RC	2.00	5.00
155 Karlos Dansby RC	3.00	8.00
156 Keary Colbert RC	2.50	6.00
157 Keith Smith RC	2.00	5.00
158 Keiwan Ratliff RC	2.00	5.00
159 Kellen Winslow RC	4.00	10.00
160 Kendrick Starling RC	2.00	5.00
161 Kenechi Udeze RC	3.00	8.00
162 Kevin Jones RC	3.00	8.00
163 Larry Fitzgerald RC	10.00	25.00
164 Lee Evans RC	4.00	10.00
165 Luke McCown RC	3.00	8.00
166 Marquise Hill RC	2.00	5.00
167 Matt Schaub RC	8.00	20.00
168 Matt Ware RC	3.00	8.00
169 Matt Mauck RC	2.50	6.00
170 Maurice Mann RC	2.00	5.00
171 Mewelde Moore RC	3.00	8.00
172 Michael Boulware RC	3.00	8.00
173 Michael Clayton RC	3.00	8.00
174 Michael Jenkins RC	3.00	8.00
175 Michael Turner RC	8.00	20.00
176 B.J. Symons RC	2.00	5.00
177 Nathan Vasher RC	3.00	8.00
178 P.K. Sam RC	2.00	5.00
179 Philip Rivers RC	12.00	30.00
180 Quincy Wilson RC	2.50	6.00
181 Ran Carthon RC	2.00	5.00
182 Randy Starks RC	2.00	5.00
183 Rashaun Woods RC	2.00	5.00
184 Reggie Williams RC	3.00	8.00
185 Ricardo Colclough RC	3.00	8.00
186 Robert Kent RC	2.00	5.00
187 Roy Williams RC	4.00	10.00
188 Samie Parker RC	2.50	6.00
189 Scott Rislov RC	2.00	5.00
190 Sean Jones RC	2.50	6.00
191 Sean Taylor RC	3.00	8.00
192 Steven Jackson RC	8.00	20.00
193 Stuart Schweigert RC	2.50	6.00
194 Tatum Bell RC	3.00	8.00
195 Teddy Lehman RC	2.50	6.00
196 Tommie Harris RC	3.00	8.00
197 Troy Fleming RC	2.00	5.00
198 Vince Wilfork RC	3.00	8.00
199 Will Poole RC	3.00	8.00
200 Will Smith RC	3.00	8.00

2005 Donruss Elite

Card		
COMP.SET w/o SP's (100)	7.50	20.00
101-200 PRINT RUN 499 SER.#'d SETS		
1 Kurt Warner	.40	1.00
2 Larry Fitzgerald	.40	1.00
3 Anquan Boldin	.30	.75
4 Emmitt Smith	.75	2.00
5 Michael Vick	.40	1.00
6 Warrick Dunn	.30	.75
7 Alge Crumpler	.30	.75
8 Jamal Lewis	.30	.75
9 Kyle Boller	.30	.75
10 Ray Lewis	.40	1.00
11 Drew Bledsoe	.40	1.00
12 Willis McGahee	.40	1.00
13 Travis Henry	.30	.75
14 Eric Moulds	.30	.75
15 Rex Grossman	.40	1.00
16 Brian Urlacher	.40	1.00
17 Thomas Jones	.30	.75
18 Carson Palmer	.40	1.00
19 Rudi Johnson	.30	.75
20 Chad Johnson	.30	.75
21 J.P. Losman	.30	.75
22 Lee Suggs	.30	.75
23 Antonio Bryant	.30	.75
24 Julius Jones	.40	1.00
25 Roy Williams S	.30	.75
26 Keyshawn Johnson	.30	.75
27 Jake Plummer	.30	.75
28 Tatum Bell	.30	.75
29 Rod Smith	.30	.75
30 Joey Harrington	.40	1.00
31 Kevin Jones	.30	.75
32 Roy Williams WR	.40	1.00
33 Brett Favre	1.00	2.50
34 Ahman Green	.40	1.00
35 Javon Walker	.30	.75
36 David Carr	.30	.75
37 Andre Johnson	.30	.75
38 Domanick Davis	.25	.60
39 Peyton Manning	.60	1.50
40 Edgerrin James	.30	.75
41 Brandon Stokley	.25	.60
42 Reggie Wayne	.30	.75
43 Marvin Harrison	.40	1.00
44 Byron Leftwich	.30	.75
45 Jimmy Smith	.30	.75
46 Fred Taylor	.40	1.00
47 Trent Green	.30	.75
48 Priest Holmes	.40	1.00
49 Tony Gonzalez	.30	.75
50 A.J. Feeley	.25	.60
51 Chris Chambers	.30	.75
52 Daunte Culpepper	.40	1.00
53 Randy Moss	.40	1.00
54 Onterrio Smith	.25	.60
55 Corey Dillon	.30	.75
56 Tom Brady	.75	2.00
57 David Givens	.30	.75
58 Aaron Brooks	.25	.60
59 Deuce McAllister	.40	1.00
60 Joe Horn	.30	.75
61 Eli Manning	.75	2.00
62 Tiki Barber	.40	1.00
63 Jeremy Shockey	.40	1.00
64 Chad Pennington	.40	1.00
65 Curtis Martin	.40	1.00
66 Santana Moss	.30	.75
67 Kerry Collins	.30	.75
68 Jerry Porter	.30	.75
69 Donovan McNabb	.40	1.00
70 Terrell Owens	.40	1.00
71 Brian Westbrook	.40	1.00
72 Ben Roethlisberger	1.00	2.50

Card		
❑ 73 Plaxico Burress	.30	.75
❑ 74 Hines Ward	.40	1.00
❑ 75 Jerome Bettis	.40	1.00
❑ 76 Duce Staley	.30	.75
❑ 77 Antonio Gates	.40	1.00
❑ 78 Drew Brees	.40	1.00
❑ 79 LaDainian Tomlinson	.50	1.25
❑ 80 Brandon Lloyd	.25	.60
❑ 81 Kevan Barlow	.25	.60
❑ 82 Matt Hasselbeck	.30	.75
❑ 83 Shaun Alexander	.40	1.00
❑ 84 Darrell Jackson	.30	.75
❑ 85 Jerry Rice	.75	2.00
❑ 86 Marc Bulger	.30	.75
❑ 87 Marshall Faulk	.40	1.00
❑ 88 Steven Jackson	.50	1.25
❑ 89 Isaac Bruce	.30	.75
❑ 90 Torry Holt	.30	.75
❑ 91 Michael Clayton	.30	.75
❑ 92 Brian Griese	.30	.75
❑ 93 Mike Alstott	.30	.75
❑ 94 Steve McNair	.40	1.00
❑ 95 Derrick Mason	.30	.75
❑ 96 Chris Brown	.30	.75
❑ 97 Drew Bennett	.30	.75
❑ 98 Patrick Ramsey	.30	.75
❑ 99 Clinton Portis	.40	1.00
❑ 100 LaVar Arrington	.40	1.00
❑ 101 Aaron Rodgers RC	12.00	30.00
❑ 102 Adam Jones RC	3.00	8.00
❑ 103 Adrian McPherson RC	3.00	8.00
❑ 104A Alex Smith TE ERR RC	4.00	10.00
❑ 104B Alex Smith TE COR RC	4.00	10.00
❑ 105A Alex Smith QB ERR RC	4.00	10.00
❑ 105B Alex Smith QB COR RC	4.00	10.00
❑ 106 Alvin Pearman RC	2.50	6.00
❑ 107 Andrew Walter RC	3.00	8.00
❑ 108 Anthony Davis RC	3.00	8.00
❑ 109 Antrel Rolle RC	4.00	10.00
❑ 110 Anttaj Hawthorne RC	3.00	8.00
❑ 111 Brandon Browner RC	2.50	6.00
❑ 112 Brandon Jacobs RC	5.00	12.00
❑ 113 Braylon Edwards RC	10.00	25.00
❑ 114 Brock Berlin RC	3.00	8.00
❑ 115 Brandon Jones RC	4.00	10.00
❑ 116 Bryant McFadden RC	3.00	8.00
❑ 117 Carlos Rogers RC	4.00	10.00
❑ 118 Cadillac Williams RC	6.00	15.00
❑ 119 Cedric Benson RC	4.00	10.00
❑ 120 Cedric Houston RC	4.00	10.00
❑ 121 Channing Crowder RC	3.00	8.00
❑ 122 Charles Frederick RC	3.00	8.00
❑ 123 Charlie Frye RC	4.00	10.00
❑ 124 Chase Lyman RC	2.50	6.00
❑ 125 Chris Henry RC	4.00	10.00
❑ 126 Chris Rix RC	3.00	8.00
❑ 127 Ciatrick Fason RC	3.00	8.00
❑ 128 Corey Webster RC	4.00	10.00
❑ 129 Courtney Roby RC	3.00	8.00
❑ 130 Craig Bragg RC	2.50	6.00
❑ 131 Craphonso Thorpe RC	3.00	8.00
❑ 132 Damien Nash RC	3.00	8.00
❑ 133 Dan Cody RC	4.00	10.00
❑ 134 Dan Orlovsky RC	4.00	10.00
❑ 135 Dante Ridgeway RC	2.50	6.00
❑ 136 Darian Durant RC	4.00	10.00
❑ 137 Darren Sproles RC	5.00	12.00
❑ 138 Darryl Blackstock RC	2.50	6.00
❑ 139 David Greene RC	3.00	8.00
❑ 140 David Pollack RC	3.00	8.00
❑ 141 DeMarcus Ware RC	6.00	15.00
❑ 142 Derek Anderson RC	4.00	10.00
❑ 143 Derrick Johnson RC	4.00	10.00
❑ 144 Erasmus James RC	3.00	8.00
❑ 145 Eric Shelton RC	3.00	8.00
❑ 146 Ernest Shazor RC	3.00	8.00
❑ 147 Fabian Washington RC	4.00	10.00
❑ 148 Frank Gore UER RC	8.00	20.00
❑ 149 Fred Amey RC	3.00	8.00
❑ 150 Fred Gibson RC	3.00	8.00
❑ 151 Maurice Clarett	3.00	8.00
❑ 152 Gino Guidugli RC	2.50	6.00
❑ 153 Heath Miller RC	8.00	20.00
❑ 154 J.J. Arrington RC	4.00	10.00
❑ 155 J.R. Russell RC	2.50	6.00
❑ 156 Jason Campbell RC	6.00	15.00
❑ 157 Jason White RC	4.00	10.00
❑ 158 Jerome Mathis RC	4.00	10.00
❑ 159 Josh Bullocks RC	4.00	10.00
❑ 160 Josh Davis RC	2.50	6.00
❑ 161 Justin Miller RC	3.00	8.00
❑ 162 Justin Tuck RC	5.00	12.00
❑ 163 Kay-Jay Harris RC	3.00	8.00
❑ 164 Kevin Burnett RC	3.00	8.00
❑ 165 Kyle Orton RC	6.00	15.00
❑ 166 Larry Brackins RC	2.50	6.00
❑ 167 Marcus Spears RC	4.00	10.00
❑ 168 Marion Barber RC	12.00	30.00
❑ 169 Mark Bradley RC	3.00	8.00
❑ 170 Mark Clayton RC	4.00	10.00
❑ 171 Marlin Jackson RC	3.00	8.00
❑ 172 Matt Jones RC	4.00	10.00
❑ 173 Matt Roth RC	4.00	10.00
❑ 174 Mike Patterson RC	3.00	8.00
❑ 175 Mike Williams	3.00	8.00
❑ 176 Airese Currie RC	3.00	8.00
❑ 177 Reggie Brown RC	3.00	8.00
❑ 178 Roddy White RC	5.00	12.00
❑ 179 Ronnie Brown RC	12.00	30.00
❑ 180 Roscoe Parrish RC	3.00	8.00
❑ 181 Roydell Williams RC	3.00	8.00
❑ 182 Ryan Fitzpatrick RC	4.00	10.00
❑ 183 Rasheed Marshall RC	3.00	8.00
❑ 184 Ryan Moats RC	3.00	8.00
❑ 185 Shaun Cody RC	3.00	8.00
❑ 186 Shawne Merriman RC	4.00	10.00
❑ 187 Chad Owens RC	4.00	10.00
❑ 188 Stefan LeFors RC	3.00	8.00
❑ 189 Steve Savoy RC	2.50	6.00
❑ 190 T.A. McLendon RC	2.50	6.00
❑ 191 Tab Perry RC	4.00	10.00
❑ 192 Taylor Stubblefield RC	2.50	6.00
❑ 193 Terrence Murphy RC	2.50	6.00
❑ 194 Thomas Davis RC	3.00	8.00
❑ 195 Timmy Chang RC	3.00	8.00
❑ 196 Travis Johnson RC	2.50	6.00
❑ 197 Troy Williamson RC	4.00	10.00
❑ 198 Vernand Morency RC	3.00	8.00
❑ 199 Vincent Jackson RC	5.00	12.00
❑ 200 Walter Reyes RC	2.50	6.00

2006 Donruss Elite

Card		
❑ COMP.SET w/o RC's (100)	7.50	20.00
❑ ROOKIE PRINT RUN 599 SER.#'d SETS		
❑ 1 Anquan Boldin	.30	.75
❑ 2 Kurt Warner	.40	1.00
❑ 3 Larry Fitzgerald	.40	1.00
❑ 4 Marcel Shipp	.25	.60
❑ 5 Alge Crumpler	.30	.75
❑ 6 Michael Vick	.40	1.00
❑ 7 Warrick Dunn	.30	.75
❑ 8 Derrick Mason	.30	.75
❑ 9 Jamal Lewis	.30	.75
❑ 10 Kyle Boller	.30	.75
❑ 11 J.P. Losman	.30	.75
❑ 12 Lee Evans	.30	.75
❑ 13 Willis McGahee	.40	1.00
❑ 14 Jake Delhomme	.30	.75
❑ 15 Stephen Davis	.30	.75
❑ 16 Steve Smith	.40	1.00
❑ 17 Cedric Benson	.30	.75
❑ 18 Kyle Orton	.30	.75
❑ 19 Thomas Jones	.30	.75
❑ 20 Carson Palmer	.40	1.00
❑ 21 Chad Johnson	.30	.75
❑ 22 Rudi Johnson	.30	.75
❑ 23 Braylon Edwards	.40	1.00
❑ 24 Reuben Droughns	.30	.75
❑ 25 Trent Dilfer	.30	.75
❑ 26 Drew Bledsoe	.40	1.00
❑ 27 Julius Jones	.30	.75
❑ 28 Keyshawn Johnson	.30	.75
❑ 29 Jake Plummer	.30	.75
❑ 30 Rod Smith	.30	.75
❑ 31 Tatum Bell	.25	.60
❑ 32 Joey Harrington	.25	.60
❑ 33 Kevin Jones	.30	.75
❑ 34 Roy Williams WR	.40	1.00
❑ 35 Aaron Rodgers	.40	1.00
❑ 36 Brett Favre	.75	2.00
❑ 37 Ahman Green	.30	.75
❑ 38 Andre Johnson	.30	.75
❑ 39 David Carr	.25	.60
❑ 40 Domanick Davis	.30	.75
❑ 41 Edgerrin James	.30	.75
❑ 42 Marvin Harrison	.40	1.00
❑ 43 Peyton Manning	.60	1.50
❑ 44 Byron Leftwich	.30	.75
❑ 45 Fred Taylor	.30	.75
❑ 46 Jimmy Smith	.30	.75
❑ 47 Matt Jones	.30	.75
❑ 48 Larry Johnson	.30	.75
❑ 49 Tony Gonzalez	.30	.75
❑ 50 Trent Green	.30	.75
❑ 51 Chris Chambers	.30	.75
❑ 52 Ricky Williams	.25	.60
❑ 53 Ronnie Brown	.40	1.00
❑ 54 Randy McMichael	.25	.60
❑ 55 Daunte Culpepper	.40	1.00
❑ 56 Mewelde Moore	.25	.60
❑ 57 Nate Burleson	.30	.75
❑ 58 Corey Dillon	.30	.75
❑ 59 Deion Branch	.30	.75
❑ 60 Tom Brady	.60	1.50
❑ 61 Aaron Brooks	.30	.75
❑ 62 Deuce McAllister	.30	.75
❑ 63 Donte Stallworth	.30	.75
❑ 64 Eli Manning	.50	1.25
❑ 65 Jeremy Shockey	.40	1.00
❑ 66 Plaxico Burress	.30	.75
❑ 67 Tiki Barber	.40	1.00
❑ 68 Chad Pennington	.30	.75
❑ 69 Curtis Martin	.40	1.00
❑ 70 Laveranues Coles	.30	.75
❑ 71 Kerry Collins	.30	.75
❑ 72 LaMont Jordan	.30	.75
❑ 73 Randy Moss	.40	1.00
❑ 74 Donovan McNabb	.40	1.00
❑ 75 Reggie Brown	.25	.60
❑ 76 Brian Westbrook	.30	.75
❑ 77 Ben Roethlisberger	.60	1.50
❑ 78 Duce Staley	.25	.60
❑ 79 Hines Ward	.40	1.00
❑ 80 Antonio Gates	.40	1.00
❑ 81 Drew Brees	.40	1.00
❑ 82 LaDainian Tomlinson	.50	1.25
❑ 83 Alex Smith QB	.30	.75
❑ 84 Kevan Barlow	.30	.75
❑ 85 Brandon Lloyd	.30	.75
❑ 86 Darrell Jackson	.30	.75
❑ 87 Matt Hasselbeck	.30	.75
❑ 88 Shaun Alexander	.30	.75
❑ 89 Marc Bulger	.30	.75
❑ 90 Steven Jackson	.40	1.00
❑ 91 Torry Holt	.30	.75
❑ 92 Cadillac Williams	.40	1.00
❑ 93 Joey Galloway	.30	.75
❑ 94 Michael Clayton	.30	.75
❑ 95 Chris Brown	.30	.75
❑ 96 Drew Bennett	.30	.75
❑ 97 Steve McNair	.30	.75
❑ 98 Clinton Portis	.40	1.00
❑ 99 Mark Brunell	.30	.75
❑ 100 Santana Moss	.30	.75
❑ 101 A.J. Hawk RC	8.00	20.00
❑ 102 Abdul Hodge RC	4.00	10.00
❑ 103 Adam Jennings RC	4.00	10.00
❑ 104 Alan Zemaitis RC	5.00	12.00
❑ 105 Andre Hall RC	4.00	10.00
❑ 106 Anthony Fasano RC	5.00	12.00
❑ 107 Anthony Mix RC	4.00	10.00
❑ 108 Ashton Youboty RC	4.00	10.00
❑ 109 Miles Austin RC	12.00	30.00
❑ 110 Barrick Nealy RC	4.00	10.00
❑ 111 Ben Obomanu RC	4.00	10.00
❑ 112 Bobby Carpenter RC	4.00	10.00
❑ 113 Brad Smith RC	5.00	12.00
❑ 114 Brandon Kirsch RC	4.00	10.00
❑ 115 Brandon Marshall RC	5.00	12.00
❑ 116 Brandon Williams RC	4.00	10.00
❑ 117 Brett Elliott RC	5.00	12.00
❑ 118 Brian Calhoun RC	4.00	10.00
❑ 119 Brodie Croyle RC	5.00	12.00
❑ 120 Brodrick Bunkley RC	4.00	10.00

Card	Low	High
❑ 121 Bruce Gradkowski RC	5.00	12.00
❑ 122 Cedric Griffin RC	4.00	10.00
❑ 123 Cedric Humes RC	4.00	10.00
❑ 124 Chad Greenway RC	5.00	12.00
❑ 125 Chad Jackson RC	4.00	10.00
❑ 126 Charlie Whitehurst RC	5.00	12.00
❑ 127 Cory Rodgers RC	5.00	12.00
❑ 128 D.J. Shockley RC	4.00	10.00
❑ 129 Darnell Bing RC	4.00	10.00
❑ 130 Darrell Hackney RC	4.00	10.00
❑ 131 David Thomas RC	5.00	12.00
❑ 132 D'Brickashaw Ferguson RC	5.00	12.00
❑ 133 DeAngelo Williams RC	10.00	25.00
❑ 134 De'Arrius Howard RC	5.00	12.00
❑ 135 Dee Webb RC	4.00	10.00
❑ 136 Delanie Walker RC	4.00	10.00
❑ 137 DeMeco Ryans RC	6.00	15.00
❑ 138 Demetrius Williams RC	4.00	10.00
❑ 139 Derek Hagan RC	4.00	10.00
❑ 140 Derrick Ross RC	4.00	10.00
❑ 141 Devin Aromashodu RC	5.00	12.00
❑ 142 Devin Hester RC	10.00	25.00
❑ 143 Dominique Byrd RC	4.00	10.00
❑ 144 Donte Whitner RC	5.00	12.00
❑ 145 DonTrell Moore RC	4.00	10.00
❑ 146 D'Qwell Jackson RC	4.00	10.00
❑ 147 Drew Olson RC	3.00	8.00
❑ 148 Eric Winston RC	3.00	8.00
❑ 149 Erik Meyer RC	4.00	10.00
❑ 150 Ernie Sims RC	4.00	10.00
❑ 151 Gabe Watson RC	3.00	8.00
❑ 152 Gerald Riggs RC	4.00	10.00
❑ 153 Ryan Gilbert RC	4.00	10.00
❑ 154 Greg Jennings RC	8.00	20.00
❑ 155 Greg Lee RC	3.00	8.00
❑ 156 Haloti Ngata RC	5.00	12.00
❑ 157 Hank Baskett RC	5.00	12.00
❑ 158 Ingle Martin RC	4.00	10.00
❑ 159 Jason Allen RC	4.00	10.00
❑ 160 Jason Avant RC	5.00	12.00
❑ 161 Jason Carter RC	4.00	10.00
❑ 162 Jay Cutler RC	12.00	30.00
❑ 163 Jeff King RC	4.00	10.00
❑ 164 Jeff Webb RC	4.00	10.00
❑ 165 Jeremy Bloom RC	4.00	10.00
❑ 166 Jerious Norwood RC	5.00	12.00
❑ 167 Jerome Harrison RC	5.00	12.00
❑ 168 Jimmy Williams RC	5.00	12.00
❑ 169 Joe Klopfenstein RC	4.00	10.00
❑ 170 Jon Alston RC	3.00	8.00
❑ 171 Johnathan Joseph RC	4.00	10.00
❑ 172 Jonathan Orr RC	4.00	10.00
❑ 173 Joseph Addai RC	6.00	15.00
❑ 174 Kai Parham RC	5.00	12.00
❑ 175 Kamerion Wimbley RC	5.00	12.00
❑ 176 Kellen Clemens RC	5.00	12.00
❑ 177 Kelly Jennings RC	5.00	12.00
❑ 178 Kent Smith RC	5.00	12.00
❑ 179 Ko Simpson RC	4.00	10.00
❑ 180 Laurence Maroney RC	6.00	15.00
❑ 181 Lawrence Vickers RC	4.00	10.00
❑ 182 LenDale White RC	6.00	15.00
❑ 183 Leon Washington RC	6.00	15.00
❑ 184 Leonard Pope RC	5.00	12.00
❑ 185 Manny Lawson RC	5.00	12.00
❑ 186 Marcedes Lewis RC	5.00	12.00
❑ 187 Marcus Vick RC	3.00	8.00
❑ 188 Mario Williams RC	6.00	15.00
❑ 189 Marques Colston RC	12.00	30.00
❑ 190 Martin Nance RC	4.00	10.00
❑ 191 Mathias Kiwanuka RC	6.00	15.00
❑ 192 Matt Leinart RC	8.00	20.00
❑ 193 Maurice Drew RC	10.00	25.00
❑ 194 Maurice Stovall RC	4.00	10.00
❑ 195 Michael Huff RC	5.00	12.00
❑ 196 Michael Robinson RC	4.00	10.00
❑ 197 Mike Bell RC	5.00	12.00
❑ 198 Mike Hass RC	5.00	12.00
❑ 199 Omar Jacobs RC	3.00	8.00
❑ 200 Owen Daniels RC	5.00	12.00
❑ 201 P.J. Daniels RC	3.00	8.00
❑ 202 Paul Pinegar RC	3.00	8.00
❑ 203 Quinton Ganther RC	3.00	8.00
❑ 204 Reggie Bush RC	12.00	30.00
❑ 205 Reggie McNeal RC	4.00	10.00
❑ 206 Rodrique Wright RC	3.00	8.00
❑ 207 Santonio Holmes RC	12.00	30.00
❑ 208 Sinorice Moss RC	5.00	12.00
❑ 209 Skyler Green RC	3.00	8.00
❑ 210 Tamba Hali RC	5.00	12.00
❑ 211 Tarvaris Jackson RC	5.00	12.00
❑ 212 Taurean Henderson RC	5.00	12.00
❑ 213 Terrence Whitehead RC	4.00	10.00
❑ 214 Tim Day RC	4.00	10.00
❑ 215 Todd Watkins RC	3.00	8.00
❑ 216 Tony Scheffler RC	5.00	12.00
❑ 217 Travis Lulay RC	4.00	10.00
❑ 218 Travis Wilson RC	3.00	8.00
❑ 219 Tye Hill RC	4.00	10.00
❑ 220 Vernon Davis RC	5.00	12.00
❑ 221 Vince Young RC	12.00	30.00
❑ 222 Wali Lundy RC	5.00	12.00
❑ 223 Wendell Mathis RC	4.00	10.00
❑ 224 Willie Reid RC	4.00	10.00
❑ 225 Winston Justice RC	5.00	12.00

2007 Donruss Elite

Card	Low	High
❑ COMP.SET w/o RC's (100)	7.50	20.00
❑ 1 Anquan Boldin	.30	.75
❑ 2 Edgerrin James	.30	.75
❑ 3 Matt Leinart	.40	1.00
❑ 4 Alge Crumpler	.30	.75
❑ 5 Michael Vick	.40	1.00
❑ 6 Jerious Norwood	.30	.75
❑ 7 Warrick Dunn	.30	.75
❑ 8 Jamal Lewis	.30	.75
❑ 9 Mark Clayton	.30	.75
❑ 10 Steve McNair	.30	.75
❑ 11 J.P. Losman	.25	.60
❑ 12 Lee Evans	.30	.75
❑ 13 Willis McGahee	.30	.75
❑ 14 DeAngelo Williams	.40	1.00
❑ 15 Jake Delhomme	.30	.75
❑ 16 Steve Smith	.30	.75
❑ 17 Bernard Berrian	.25	.60
❑ 18 Rex Grossman	.30	.75
❑ 19 Thomas Jones	.30	.75
❑ 20 Carson Palmer	.40	1.00
❑ 21 Chad Johnson	.30	.75
❑ 22 Rudi Johnson	.30	.75
❑ 23 T.J. Houshmandzadeh	.30	.75
❑ 24 Braylon Edwards	.30	.75
❑ 25 Charlie Frye	.30	.75
❑ 26 Reuben Droughns	.30	.75
❑ 27 Julius Jones	.30	.75
❑ 28 Terrell Owens	.40	1.00
❑ 29 Tony Romo	.60	1.50
❑ 30 Javon Walker	.30	.75
❑ 31 Jay Cutler	.40	1.00
❑ 32 Mike Bell	.30	.75
❑ 33 Jon Kitna	.25	.60
❑ 34 Kevin Jones	.25	.60
❑ 35 Roy Williams WR	.30	.75
❑ 36 Brett Favre	.75	2.00
❑ 37 Donald Driver	.40	1.00
❑ 38 Ahman Green	.30	.75
❑ 39 Andre Johnson	.30	.75
❑ 40 Matt Schaub	.30	.75
❑ 41 Wali Lundy	.25	.60
❑ 42 Joseph Addai	.40	1.00
❑ 43 Marvin Harrison	.40	1.00
❑ 44 Peyton Manning	.60	1.50
❑ 45 Reggie Wayne	.30	.75
❑ 46 Byron Leftwich	.30	.75
❑ 47 Fred Taylor	.30	.75
❑ 48 Maurice Jones-Drew	.40	1.00
❑ 49 Larry Johnson	.30	.75
❑ 50 Tony Gonzalez	.30	.75
❑ 51 Trent Green	.30	.75
❑ 52 Chris Chambers	.30	.75
❑ 53 Daunte Culpepper	.30	.75
❑ 54 Ronnie Brown	.30	.75
❑ 55 Chester Taylor	.25	.60
❑ 56 Tarvaris Jackson	.30	.75
❑ 57 Travis Taylor	.25	.60
❑ 58 Tom Brady	.75	2.00
❑ 59 Corey Dillon	.30	.75
❑ 60 Laurence Maroney	.40	1.00
❑ 61 Deuce McAllister	.30	.75
❑ 62 Drew Brees	.40	1.00
❑ 63 Marques Colston	.40	1.00
❑ 64 Reggie Bush	.50	1.25
❑ 65 Brandon Jacobs	.30	.75
❑ 66 Eli Manning	.40	1.00
❑ 67 Jeremy Shockey	.30	.75
❑ 68 Chad Pennington	.30	.75
❑ 69 Laveranues Coles	.30	.75
❑ 70 Leon Washington	.30	.75
❑ 71 Ronald Curry	.30	.75
❑ 72 LaMont Jordan	.30	.75
❑ 73 Randy Moss	.40	1.00
❑ 74 Brian Westbrook	.30	.75
❑ 75 Donovan McNabb	.40	1.00
❑ 76 Reggie Brown	.25	.60
❑ 77 Ben Roethlisberger	.50	1.25
❑ 78 Hines Ward	.40	1.00
❑ 79 Willie Parker	.30	.75
❑ 80 Antonio Gates	.30	.75
❑ 81 LaDainian Tomlinson	.50	1.25
❑ 82 Philip Rivers	.40	1.00
❑ 83 Alex Smith QB	.40	1.00
❑ 84 Frank Gore	.40	1.00
❑ 85 Vernon Davis	.30	.75
❑ 86 Darrell Jackson	.30	.75
❑ 87 Matt Hasselbeck	.30	.75
❑ 88 Shaun Alexander	.30	.75
❑ 89 Marc Bulger	.30	.75
❑ 90 Steven Jackson	.40	1.00
❑ 91 Torry Holt	.30	.75
❑ 92 Chris Simms	.25	.60
❑ 93 Cadillac Williams	.30	.75
❑ 94 Joey Galloway	.30	.75
❑ 95 Drew Bennett	.25	.60
❑ 96 LenDale White	.30	.75
❑ 97 Vince Young	.40	1.00
❑ 98 Clinton Portis	.30	.75
❑ 99 Jason Campbell	.30	.75
❑ 100 Santana Moss	.30	.75
❑ 101 A.J. Davis RC	3.00	8.00
❑ 102 Aaron Ross RC	5.00	12.00
❑ 103 Aaron Rouse RC	5.00	12.00
❑ 104 Adam Carriker RC	4.00	10.00
❑ 105 Adrian Peterson RC	25.00	60.00
❑ 106 Ahmad Bradshaw RC	6.00	15.00
❑ 107 Alan Branch RC	4.00	10.00
❑ 108 Amobi Okoye RC	5.00	12.00
❑ 109 Anthony Gonzalez RC	6.00	15.00
❑ 110 Anthony Spencer RC	5.00	12.00
❑ 111 Antonio Pittman RC	5.00	12.00
❑ 112 Aundrae Allison RC	4.00	10.00
❑ 113 Brady Quinn RC	10.00	25.00
❑ 114 Brandon Jackson RC	5.00	12.00
❑ 115 Brandon Meriweather RC	5.00	12.00
❑ 116 Brandon Siler RC	4.00	10.00
❑ 117 Brian Leonard RC	4.00	10.00
❑ 118 Calvin Johnson RC	12.00	30.00
❑ 119 Chanci Stuckey RC	5.00	12.00
❑ 120 Chris Davis RC	4.00	10.00
❑ 121 Chris Henry RC	4.00	10.00
❑ 122 Chris Houston RC	4.00	10.00
❑ 123 Chris Leak RC	4.00	10.00
❑ 124 Courtney Taylor RC	4.00	10.00
❑ 125 Craig Buster Davis RC	5.00	12.00
❑ 126 Dallas Baker RC	4.00	10.00
❑ 127 Darius Walker RC	4.00	10.00
❑ 128 Darrelle Revis RC	6.00	15.00
❑ 129 David Ball RC	3.00	8.00
❑ 130 David Clowney RC	5.00	12.00
❑ 131 David Harris RC	4.00	10.00
❑ 132 DeShawn Wynn RC	5.00	12.00
❑ 133 D'Juan Woods RC	4.00	10.00
❑ 134 Drew Stanton RC	4.00	10.00
❑ 135 Dwayne Bowe RC	8.00	20.00
❑ 136 Dwayne Jarrett RC	5.00	12.00
❑ 137 Dwayne Wright RC	4.00	10.00
❑ 138 Eric Weddle RC	4.00	10.00
❑ 139 Gaines Adams RC	5.00	12.00
❑ 140 Garrett Wolfe RC	5.00	12.00
❑ 141 Gary Russell RC	4.00	10.00
❑ 142 Greg Olsen RC	6.00	15.00
❑ 143 H.B. Blades RC	4.00	10.00
❑ 144 Isaiah Stanback RC	5.00	12.00
❑ 145 Jacoby Jones RC	5.00	12.00
❑ 146 Jamaal Anderson RC	4.00	10.00

Card	Low	High
❑ 147 JaMarcus Russell RC	20.00	40.00
❑ 148 James Jones RC	5.00	12.00
❑ 149 Jared Zabransky RC	5.00	12.00
❑ 150 Jarrett Hicks RC	4.00	10.00
❑ 151 Jarvis Moss RC	5.00	12.00
❑ 152 Jason Hill RC	5.00	12.00
❑ 153 Jason Snelling RC	4.00	10.00
❑ 154 Jeff Rowe RC	4.00	10.00
❑ 155 Joel Filani RC	4.00	10.00
❑ 156 John Beck RC	5.00	12.00
❑ 157 Johnnie Lee Higgins RC	5.00	12.00
❑ 158 Jon Beason RC	5.00	12.00
❑ 159 Jon Cornish RC	4.00	10.00
❑ 160 Jonathan Wade RC	4.00	10.00
❑ 161 Jordan Kent RC	4.00	10.00
❑ 162 Jordan Palmer RC	5.00	12.00
❑ 163 Kenneth Darby RC	5.00	12.00
❑ 164 Kenny Irons RC	5.00	12.00
❑ 165 Kevin Kolb RC	8.00	20.00
❑ 166 Kolby Smith RC	5.00	12.00
❑ 167 LaRon Landry RC	6.00	15.00
❑ 168 Laurent Robinson RC	5.00	12.00
❑ 169 Lawrence Timmons RC	5.00	12.00
❑ 170 Leon Hall RC	5.00	12.00
❑ 171 Lorenzo Booker RC	5.00	12.00
❑ 172 Marshawn Lynch RC	8.00	20.00
❑ 173 Matt Trannon RC	4.00	10.00
❑ 174 Michael Bush RC	5.00	12.00
❑ 175 Michael Griffin RC	5.00	12.00
❑ 176 Mike Walker RC	5.00	12.00
❑ 177 Nate Ilaoa RC	5.00	12.00
❑ 178 Patrick Willis RC	8.00	20.00
❑ 179 Paul Posluszny RC	6.00	15.00
❑ 180 Paul Williams RC	4.00	10.00
❑ 181 Reggie Nelson RC	4.00	10.00
❑ 182 Rhema McKnight RC	4.00	10.00
❑ 183 Robert Meachem RC	5.00	12.00
❑ 184 Rufus Alexander RC	5.00	12.00
❑ 185 Ryan Moore RC	4.00	10.00
❑ 186 Selvin Young RC	5.00	12.00
❑ 187 Sidney Rice RC	10.00	25.00
❑ 188 Steve Breaston RC	5.00	12.00
❑ 189 Steve Smith USC RC	8.00	20.00
❑ 190 Syvelle Newton RC	4.00	10.00
❑ 191 DeMarcus Tank Tyler RC	4.00	10.00
❑ 192 Ted Ginn Jr. RC	8.00	20.00
❑ 193 Tony Hunt RC	5.00	12.00
❑ 194 Trent Edwards RC	8.00	20.00
❑ 195 Troy Smith RC	6.00	15.00
❑ 196 Tyler Palko RC	4.00	10.00
❑ 197 Tymere Zimmerman RC	4.00	10.00
❑ 198 Yamon Figurs RC	3.00	8.00
❑ 199 Zac Taylor RC	5.00	12.00
❑ 200 Zach Miller RC	5.00	12.00

2008 Donruss Elite

Card	Low	High
❑ COMP.SET w/o RC's (100)	7.50	20.00
❑ 1 Anquan Boldin	.30	.75
❑ 2 Edgerrin James	.30	.75
❑ 3 Larry Fitzgerald	.40	1.00
❑ 4 Matt Leinart	.40	1.00
❑ 5 Alge Crumpler	.30	.75
❑ 6 Warrick Dunn	.30	.75
❑ 7 Roddy White	.30	.75
❑ 8 Willis McGahee	.30	.75
❑ 9 Todd Heap	.25	.60
❑ 10 Derrick Mason	.25	.60
❑ 11 Marshawn Lynch	.40	1.00
❑ 12 Trent Edwards	.40	1.00
❑ 13 Lee Evans	.30	.75
❑ 14 Steve Smith	.30	.75
❑ 15 DeShaun Foster	.30	.75
❑ 16 DeAngelo Williams	.30	.75
❑ 17 Cedric Benson	.30	.75
❑ 18 Bernard Berrian	.30	.75
❑ 19 Devin Hester	.40	1.00
❑ 20 Carson Palmer	.40	1.00
❑ 21 T.J. Houshmandzadeh	.30	.75
❑ 22 Chad Johnson	.30	.75
❑ 23 Jamal Lewis	.30	.75
❑ 24 Braylon Edwards	.30	.75
❑ 25 Kellen Winslow	.30	.75
❑ 26 Tony Romo	.60	1.50
❑ 27 Terrell Owens	.40	1.00
❑ 28 Jason Witten	.40	1.00
❑ 29 Jay Cutler	.40	1.00
❑ 30 Travis Henry	.30	.75
❑ 31 Brandon Marshall	.30	.75
❑ 32 Jon Kitna	.30	.75
❑ 33 Roy Williams WR	.30	.75
❑ 34 Calvin Johnson	.40	1.00
❑ 35 Brett Favre	1.00	2.50
❑ 36 Greg Jennings	.30	.75
❑ 37 Ryan Grant	.40	1.00
❑ 38 Matt Schaub	.30	.75
❑ 39 Ahman Green	.30	.75
❑ 40 Andre Johnson	.30	.75
❑ 41 Peyton Manning	.60	1.50
❑ 42 Reggie Wayne	.30	.75
❑ 43 Marvin Harrison	.40	1.00
❑ 44 Joseph Addai	.40	1.00
❑ 45 David Garrard	.30	.75
❑ 46 Fred Taylor	.30	.75
❑ 47 Reggie Williams	.30	.75
❑ 48 Larry Johnson	.30	.75
❑ 49 Tony Gonzalez	.30	.75
❑ 50 Dwayne Bowe	.30	.75
❑ 51 Derek Hagan	.25	.60
❑ 52 Ronnie Brown	.30	.75
❑ 53 Ted Ginn Jr.	.30	.75
❑ 54 Tarvaris Jackson	.30	.75
❑ 55 Chester Taylor	.25	.60
❑ 56 Adrian Peterson	.75	2.00
❑ 57 Tom Brady	.60	1.50
❑ 58 Laurence Maroney	.30	.75
❑ 59 Randy Moss	.40	1.00
❑ 60 Wes Welker	.40	1.00
❑ 61 Drew Brees	.40	1.00
❑ 62 Reggie Bush	.40	1.00
❑ 63 Marques Colston	.30	.75
❑ 64 Eli Manning	.40	1.00
❑ 65 Brandon Jacobs	.30	.75
❑ 66 Plaxico Burress	.30	.75
❑ 67 Thomas Jones	.30	.75
❑ 68 Jerricho Cotchery	.25	.60
❑ 69 Laveranues Coles	.30	.75
❑ 70 JaMarcus Russell	.40	1.00
❑ 71 Justin Fargas	.25	.60
❑ 72 Jerry Porter	.30	.75
❑ 73 Donovan McNabb	.40	1.00
❑ 74 Brian Westbrook	.30	.75
❑ 75 Kevin Curtis	.25	.60
❑ 76 Ben Roethlisberger	.50	1.25
❑ 77 Willie Parker	.30	.75
❑ 78 Santonio Holmes	.30	.75
❑ 79 Hines Ward	.30	.75
❑ 80 Philip Rivers	.40	1.00
❑ 81 LaDainian Tomlinson	.50	1.25
❑ 82 Antonio Gates	.30	.75
❑ 83 Frank Gore	.30	.75
❑ 84 Arnaz Battle	.25	.60
❑ 85 Vernon Davis	.25	.60
❑ 86 Matt Hasselbeck	.30	.75
❑ 87 Shaun Alexander	.30	.75
❑ 88 Deion Branch	.30	.75
❑ 89 Marc Bulger	.30	.75
❑ 90 Torry Holt	.30	.75
❑ 91 Steven Jackson	.40	1.00
❑ 92 Jeff Garcia	.30	.75
❑ 93 Joey Galloway	.30	.75
❑ 94 Earnest Graham	.25	.60
❑ 95 Vince Young	.30	.75
❑ 96 LenDale White	.30	.75
❑ 97 Roydell Williams	.25	.60
❑ 98 Clinton Portis	.30	.75
❑ 99 Chris Cooley	.30	.75
❑ 100 Santana Moss	.25	.60
❑ 101 Matt Ryan AU/199 RC	60.00	120.00
❑ 102 Brian Brohm AU/199 RC	12.00	30.00
❑ 103 Chad Henne AU/199 RC	20.00	50.00
❑ 104 Andre Woodson AU/249 RC	8.00	20.00
❑ 105 Joe Flacco AU/299 RC	40.00	80.00
❑ 106 John David Booty/999 RC	2.50	6.00
❑ 107 Josh Johnson/999 RC	2.50	6.00
❑ 108 Erik Ainge AU/299 RC	8.00	20.00
❑ 109 Colt Brennan AU/249 RC	30.00	80.00
❑ 110 Dennis Dixon AU/299 RC	8.00	20.00
❑ 111 Kevin O'Connell/999 RC	2.50	6.00
❑ 112 Matt Flynn/999 RC	2.50	6.00
❑ 113 Bernard Morris/999 RC	2.00	5.00
❑ 114 Sam Keller/999 RC	2.50	6.00
❑ 115 Paul Smith/999 RC	2.50	6.00
❑ 116 Darren McFadden AU/199 RC	40.00	80.00
❑ 117 Jonathan Stewart AU/199 RC	30.00	60.00
❑ 118 R.Mendenhall AU/199 RC	50.00	100.00
❑ 119 Felix Jones AU/199 RC	40.00	80.00
❑ 120 Chris Johnson/999 RC	8.00	20.00
❑ 121 Jamaal Charles/999 RC	4.00	10.00
❑ 122 Ray Rice/999 RC	5.00	12.00
❑ 123 Steve Slaton/999 RC	3.00	8.00
❑ 124 Mike Hart/999 RC	2.50	6.00
❑ 125 Matt Forte AU/299 RC	35.00	60.00
❑ 126 Tashard Choice AU/299 RC	12.50	25.00
❑ 127 Kevin Smith/999 RC	4.00	10.00
❑ 128 Allen Patrick/999 RC	2.00	5.00
❑ 129 Thomas Brown/999 RC	2.50	6.00
❑ 130 Justin Forsett AU/299 RC	8.00	20.00
❑ 131 Cory Boyd AU/299 RC	6.00	15.00
❑ 132 Dantrell Savage/999 RC	2.50	6.00
❑ 133 Kalvin McRae/999 RC	2.00	5.00
❑ 134 Darrell Strong AU/299 RC	6.00	15.00
❑ 135 Owen Schmitt AU/299 RC	8.00	20.00
❑ 136 Peyton Hillis AU/299 RC	8.00	20.00
❑ 137 Jacob Hester AU/299 RC	8.00	20.00
❑ 138 Fred Davis/999 RC	2.50	6.00
❑ 139 Martellus Bennett AU/299 RC	8.00	20.00
❑ 140 John Carlson AU/299 RC	8.00	20.00
❑ 141 Martin Rucker/999 RC	2.00	5.00
❑ 142 Brad Cottam AU/299 RC	8.00	20.00
❑ 143 Jermichael Finley/999 RC	2.50	6.00
❑ 144 Jacob Tamme/999 RC	2.50	6.00
❑ 145 Dustin Keller AU/299 RC	10.00	25.00
❑ 146 Kellen Davis/999 RC	1.50	4.00
❑ 147 DeSean Jackson AU/249 RC	20.00	40.00
❑ 148 James Hardy AU/299 RC	6.00	15.00
❑ 149 Malcolm Kelly AU/249 RC	8.00	20.00
❑ 150 Early Doucet AU/199 RC	8.00	20.00
❑ 151 Limas Sweed AU/249 RC	8.00	20.00
❑ 152 Andre Caldwell AU/299 RC	8.00	20.00
❑ 153 M.Manningham AU/299 RC	12.50	25.00
❑ 154 Devin Thomas AU/299 RC	8.00	20.00
❑ 155 Donnie Avery AU/299 RC	10.00	25.00
❑ 156 Earl Bennett AU/299 RC	8.00	20.00
❑ 157 Eddie Royal AU/249 RC	12.00	30.00
❑ 158 Lavelle Hawkins AU/299 RC	6.00	15.00
❑ 159 DJ Hall/999 RC	2.00	5.00
❑ 160 Adarius Bowman/999 RC	2.00	5.00
❑ 161 Jordy Nelson AU/249 RC	10.00	25.00
❑ 162 Harry Douglas AU/299 RC	6.00	15.00
❑ 163 Jerome Simpson AU/299 RC	6.00	15.00
❑ 164 Dorien Bryant/999 RC	2.00	5.00
❑ 165 Will Franklin/999 RC	2.00	5.00
❑ 166 Keenan Burton/999 RC	2.00	5.00
❑ 167 Kevin Robinson/999 RC	2.00	5.00
❑ 168 Paul Hubbard AU/299 RC	6.00	15.00
❑ 169 Davone Bess/999 RC	3.00	8.00
❑ 170 Adrian Arrington/999 RC	2.00	5.00
❑ 171 Dexter Jackson AU/299 RC	8.00	20.00
❑ 172 Ryan Grice-Mullen/999 RC	2.50	6.00
❑ 173 Darius Reynaud/999 RC	2.00	5.00
❑ 174 Josh Morgan AU/299 RC	8.00	20.00
❑ 175 Anthony Alridge/999 RC	2.00	5.00
❑ 176 Jason Rivers/999 RC	2.50	6.00
❑ 177 Marcus Smith AU/299 RC	6.00	15.00
❑ 178 Mark Bradford/999 RC	2.00	5.00
❑ 179 Marcus Monk AU/299 RC	8.00	20.00
❑ 180 Chris Long/999 RC	2.50	6.00
❑ 181 Vernon Gholston/999 RC	2.50	6.00
❑ 182 Derrick Harvey/999 RC	2.00	5.00
❑ 183 Glenn Dorsey/999 RC	2.50	6.00
❑ 184 Sedrick Ellis/999 RC	2.50	6.00
❑ 185 Dan Connor AU/299 RC	8.00	20.00
❑ 186 Curtis Lofton/999 RC	2.50	6.00
❑ 187 Keith Rivers AU/299 RC	8.00	20.00
❑ 188 Xavier Adibi/999 RC	2.00	5.00
❑ 189 Ali Highsmith/999 RC	1.50	4.00
❑ 190 Quentin Groves AU/299 RC	6.00	15.00
❑ 191 Erin Henderson/999 RC	2.00	5.00
❑ 192 Mike Jenkins/999 RC	2.50	6.00
❑ 193 Antoine Cason AU/299 RC	8.00	20.00
❑ 194 D.Rodgers-Cromartie/999 RC	2.50	6.00
❑ 195 Leodis McKelvin/999 RC	2.50	6.00
❑ 196 Aqib Talib/999 RC	2.50	6.00
❑ 197 Reggie Smith/999 RC	2.00	5.00

❑ 198 Tracy Porter AU/299 RC 15.00 30.00
❑ 199 Terrell Thomas AU/299 RC 6.00 15.00
❑ 200 Kenny Phillips/999 RC 2.50 6.00

2009 Donruss Elite

❑ COMP.SET w/o RC's (100) 7.50 20.00
❑ 1 Kurt Warner .40 1.00
❑ 2 Larry Fitzgerald .40 1.00
❑ 3 Anquan Boldin .30 .75
❑ 4 Tim Hightower .30 .75
❑ 5 Roddy White .30 .75
❑ 6 Michael Turner .30 .75
❑ 7 Matt Ryan .40 1.00
❑ 8 Willis McGahee .30 .75
❑ 9 Joe Flacco .40 1.00
❑ 10 Trent Edwards .30 .75
❑ 11 Marshawn Lynch .30 .75
❑ 12 Lee Evans .30 .75
❑ 13 Steve Smith .30 .75
❑ 14 DeAngelo Williams .40 1.00
❑ 15 Jake Delhomme .30 .75
❑ 16 Jonathan Stewart .30 .75
❑ 17 Devin Hester .40 1.00
❑ 18 Kyle Orton .30 .75
❑ 19 Matt Forte .40 1.00
❑ 20 Carson Palmer .40 1.00
❑ 21 Chad Ochocinco .30 .75
❑ 22 T.J. Houshmandzadeh .30 .75
❑ 23 Brady Quinn .30 .75
❑ 24 Jamal Lewis .30 .75
❑ 25 Kellen Winslow .30 .75
❑ 26 Braylon Edwards .30 .75
❑ 27 Tony Romo .60 1.50
❑ 28 Terrell Owens .40 1.00
❑ 29 Marion Barber .40 1.00
❑ 30 Jason Witten .40 1.00
❑ 31 Jay Cutler .40 1.00
❑ 32 Brandon Marshall .30 .75
❑ 33 Eddie Royal .30 .75
❑ 34 Calvin Johnson .40 1.00
❑ 35 Kevin Smith .30 .75
❑ 36 Aaron Rodgers .40 1.00
❑ 37 Ryan Grant .30 .75
❑ 38 Greg Jennings .40 1.00
❑ 39 Matt Schaub .30 .75
❑ 40 Andre Johnson .30 .75
❑ 41 Steve Slaton .30 .75
❑ 42 Peyton Manning .60 1.50
❑ 43 Joseph Addai .40 1.00
❑ 44 Reggie Wayne .30 .75
❑ 45 Dallas Clark .30 .75
❑ 46 David Garrard .30 .75
❑ 47 Marcedes Lewis .25 .60
❑ 48 Maurice Jones-Drew .30 .75
❑ 49 Larry Johnson .30 .75
❑ 50 Dwayne Bowe .30 .75
❑ 51 Chad Pennington .30 .75
❑ 52 Ronnie Brown .30 .75
❑ 53 Greg Camarillo .30 .75
❑ 54 Bernard Berrian .30 .75
❑ 55 Adrian Peterson .75 2.00
❑ 56 Chester Taylor .25 .60
❑ 57 Tom Brady .60 1.50
❑ 58 Randy Moss .40 1.00
❑ 59 Wes Welker .40 1.00
❑ 60 Drew Brees .40 1.00
❑ 61 Reggie Bush .40 1.00
❑ 62 Jeremy Shockey .25 .60
❑ 63 Eli Manning .40 1.00
❑ 64 Amani Toomer .30 .75
❑ 65 Brandon Jacobs .30 .75
❑ 66 Kellen Clemens .25 .60
❑ 67 Jerricho Cotchery .25 .60
❑ 68 Laveranues Coles .30 .75
❑ 69 Thomas Jones .30 .75
❑ 70 JaMarcus Russell .30 .75
❑ 71 Justin Fargas .25 .60
❑ 72 Zach Miller .25 .60
❑ 73 Donovan McNabb .40 1.00
❑ 74 Brian Westbrook .30 .75
❑ 75 DeSean Jackson .30 .75
❑ 76 Ben Roethlisberger .60 1.50
❑ 77 Willie Parker .30 .75
❑ 78 Hines Ward .30 .75
❑ 79 Heath Miller .30 .75
❑ 80 Philip Rivers .40 1.00
❑ 81 LaDainian Tomlinson .40 1.00
❑ 82 Vincent Jackson .30 .75
❑ 83 Frank Gore .30 .75
❑ 84 Isaac Bruce .30 .75
❑ 85 Matt Hasselbeck .30 .75
❑ 86 Deion Branch .30 .75
❑ 87 John Carlson .30 .75
❑ 88 Marc Bulger .30 .75
❑ 89 Steven Jackson .30 .75
❑ 90 Donnie Avery .30 .75
❑ 91 Derrick Ward .30 .75
❑ 92 Earnest Graham .25 .60
❑ 93 Antonio Bryant .30 .75
❑ 94 Kerry Collins .30 .75
❑ 95 Justin Gage .25 .60
❑ 96 Chris Johnson .40 1.00
❑ 97 Jason Campbell .30 .75
❑ 98 Clinton Portis .30 .75
❑ 99 Santana Moss .30 .75
❑ 100 Chris Cooley .30 .75
❑ 101 Aaron Curry RC 3.00 8.00
❑ 102 Aaron Kelly AU/999 RC 5.00 12.00
❑ 103 Aaron Maybin RC 2.50 6.00
❑ 104 Alphonso Smith RC 2.00 5.00
❑ 105 Andre Brown AU/299 RC 5.00 12.00
❑ 106 Arian Foster RC 2.50 6.00
❑ 107 Austin Collie AU/299 RC 15.00 30.00
❑ 108 B.J. Raji RC 3.00 8.00
❑ 109 Brandon Gibson AU/499 RC 6.00 15.00
❑ 110 Brandon Pettigrew RC 3.00 8.00
❑ 111 Brandon Tate AU/299 RC 5.00 12.00
❑ 112 Brian Cushing AU/299 RC 10.00 25.00
❑ 113 Brian Hartline RC 2.50 6.00
❑ 114 Brian Orakpo AU/299 RC 8.00 20.00
❑ 115 Brian Robiskie RC 2.50 6.00
❑ 116 Brooks Foster AU/499 RC 5.00 12.00
❑ 117 Cameron Morrah RC 1.50 4.00
❑ 118 Cedric Peerman AU/499 RC 5.00 12.00
❑ 119 Chase Coffman AU/299 RC 5.00 12.00
❑ 120 Chip Vaughn RC 1.50 4.00
❑ 121 Chris Wells RC 6.00 15.00
❑ 122 Clay Matthews AU/299 RC 10.00 25.00
❑ 123 Clint Sintim AU/299 RC 6.00 15.00
❑ 124 Connor Barwin RC 2.00 5.00
❑ 125 Cornelius Ingram AU/499 RC 4.00 10.00
❑ 126 D.J. Moore RC 2.00 5.00
❑ 127 Darius Passmore RC 2.00 5.00
❑ 128 Darrius Heyward-Bey RC 4.00 10.00
❑ 129 Dometrius Byrd RC 2.00 5.00
❑ 130 Deon Butler AU/299 RC 6.00 15.00
❑ 131 Derrick Williams RC 2.50 6.00
❑ 132 Devin Moore AU/999 RC 5.00 12.00
❑ 133 Dominique Edison AU/499 RC 4.00 10.00
❑ 134 Donald Brown RC 5.00 12.00
❑ 135 Everette Brown AU/299 RC 6.00 15.00
❑ 136 Glen Coffee RC 3.00 8.00
❑ 137 Graham Harrell AU/999 RC 6.00 15.00
❑ 138 Hakeem Nicks RC 5.00 12.00
❑ 139 Hunter Cantwell RC 2.50 6.00
❑ 140 Ian Johnson RC 2.50 6.00
❑ 141 James Casey AU/499 RC 5.00 12.00
❑ 142 James Davis RC 2.50 6.00
❑ 143 James Laurinaitis AU/299 RC 8.00 20.00
❑ 144 Jared Cook AU/299 RC 5.00 12.00
❑ 145 Jarett Dillard RC 2.50 6.00
❑ 146 Javon Ringer RC 2.50 6.00
❑ 147 Jeremiah Johnson AU/999 RC 6.00 15.00
❑ 148 Jeremy Childs RC 2.00 5.00
❑ 149 Jeremy Maclin RC 5.00 12.00
❑ 150 John Parker Wilson AU/999 RC 6.00 15.00
❑ 151 Johnny Knox AU/499 RC 10.00 25.00
❑ 152 Josh Freeman RC 5.00 12.00
❑ 153 Juaquin Iglesias RC 2.50 6.00
❑ 154 Kenny Britt RC 4.00 10.00
❑ 155 Kenny McKinley AU/499 RC 6.00 15.00
❑ 156 Kevin Ogletree AU/999 RC 6.00 15.00
❑ 157 Knowshon Moreno RC 6.00 15.00
❑ 158 Kory Sheets AU/999 RC 5.00 12.00
❑ 159 Larry English AU/299 RC 10.00 20.00
❑ 160 LeSean McCoy RC 5.00 12.00
❑ 161 Louis Delmas RC 2.50 6.00
❑ 162 Louis Murphy RC 2.50 6.00
❑ 163 Malcolm Jenkins RC 2.50 6.00
❑ 164 Mark Sanchez RC 10.00 25.00
❑ 165 Matthew Stafford RC 8.00 20.00
❑ 166 Bear Pascoe RC 2.50 6.00
❑ 167 Michael Crabtree RC 6.00 15.00
❑ 168 Michael Johnson RC 1.50 4.00
❑ 169 Mike Goodson AU/299 RC 6.00 15.00
❑ 170 Mike Thomas RC 2.50 6.00
❑ 171 Mike Wallace RC 5.00 12.00
❑ 172 Mohamed Massaquoi RC 2.50 6.00
❑ 173 Nate Davis AU/299 RC 6.00 15.00
❑ 174 Nathan Brown AU/999 RC 5.00 12.00
❑ 175 P.J. Hill AU/999 RC 5.00 12.00
❑ 176 Pat White RC 4.00 10.00
❑ 177 Patrick Chung RC 2.50 6.00
❑ 178 Patrick Turner AU/299 RC 5.00 12.00
❑ 179 Percy Harvin RC 8.00 20.00
❑ 180 Peria Jerry RC 2.00 5.00
❑ 181 Quan Cosby AU/999 RC 5.00 12.00
❑ 182 Quinn Johnson AU/499 RC 5.00 12.00
❑ 183 Ramses Barden AU/299 RC 5.00 12.00
❑ 184 Rashad Jennings AU/499 RC 6.00 15.00
❑ 185 Rashad Johnson RC 2.00 5.00
❑ 186 Rey Maualuga RC 4.00 10.00
❑ 187 Rhett Bomar RC 2.00 5.00
❑ 188 Gartrell Johnson RC 2.00 5.00
❑ 189 Sammie Stroughter RC 2.50 6.00
❑ 190 Sean Smith RC 2.50 6.00
❑ 191 Shawn Nelson AU/499 RC 5.00 12.00
❑ 192 Shonn Greene RC 5.00 12.00
❑ 193 Stephen McGee RC 2.50 6.00
❑ 194 Tom Brandstater AU/299 RC 6.00 15.00
❑ 195 Tony Fiammetta AU/499 RC 5.00 12.00
❑ 196 Travis Beckum AU/299 RC 5.00 12.00
❑ 197 Tyrell Sutton RC 2.00 5.00
❑ 198 Tyson Jackson RC 2.50 6.00
❑ 199 Vontae Davis AU/299 RC 6.00 15.00
❑ 200 William Moore RC 2.00 5.00
❑ 201 Andre Smith RC 1.50 4.00
❑ 202 Asher Allen RC 1.25 3.00
❑ 203 Brandon Underwood RC 1.50 4.00
❑ 204 Alex Mack RC 1.25 3.00
❑ 205 Captain Munnerlyn RC 1.25 3.00
❑ 206 Chris Clemons RC 1.00 2.50
❑ 207 Cody Brown RC 1.25 3.00
❑ 208 Coye Francies RC 1.00 2.50
❑ 209 Eric Wood RC 1.25 3.00
❑ 210 Darcel McBath RC 1.50 4.00
❑ 211 Darius Butler RC 1.50 4.00
❑ 212 Darry Beckwith RC 1.25 3.00
❑ 213 David Bruton RC 1.25 3.00
❑ 214 Sherrod Martin RC 1.25 3.00
❑ 215 Eben Britton RC 1.25 3.00
❑ 216 Richard Quinn RC 1.25 3.00
❑ 217 Eugene Monroe RC 1.25 3.00
❑ 218 Evander Hood RC 2.50 6.00
❑ 219 Fili Moala RC 1.25 3.00
❑ 220 Duke Robinson RC 1.00 2.50
❑ 221 Gerald McRath RC 1.25 3.00
❑ 222 Herman Johnson RC 1.25 3.00
❑ 223 Jairus Byrd RC 2.00 5.00
❑ 224 Jamon Meredith RC 1.25 3.00
❑ 225 Jarron Gilbert RC 1.25 3.00
❑ 226 Jason Phillips RC 1.25 3.00
❑ 227 Jason Smith RC 1.25 3.00
❑ 228 Jason Williams RC 1.50 4.00
❑ 229 Jasper Brinkley RC 1.25 3.00
❑ 230 Anthony Hill RC 1.00 2.50
❑ 231 Kaluka Maiava RC 1.50 4.00
❑ 232 Keenan Lewis RC 1.50 4.00
❑ 233 Kraig Urbik RC 1.25 3.00
❑ 234 Lawrence Sidbury RC 1.00 2.50
❑ 235 Marcus Freeman RC 1.50 4.00
❑ 236 Michael Hamlin RC 1.25 3.00
❑ 237 Michael Oher RC 3.00 8.00
❑ 238 Mike Mickens RC 1.25 3.00
❑ 239 Nic Harris RC 1.25 3.00
❑ 240 Paul Kruger RC 1.25 3.00
❑ 241 Phil Loadholt RC 1.25 3.00
❑ 242 Robert Ayers RC 1.50 4.00
❑ 243 Ron Brace RC 1.25 3.00
❑ 244 Scott McKillop RC 1.25 3.00
❑ 245 Sen'Derrick Marks RC 1.00 2.50
❑ 246 Troy Kropog RC 1.00 2.50
❑ 247 Tyrone McKenzie RC 1.25 3.00
❑ 248 Victor Harris RC 1.50 4.00
❑ 249 William Beatty RC 1.00 2.50
❑ 250 Zack Follett RC 1.00 2.50

2009 Donruss Gridiron Gear

Card	Low	High
❑ COMP.SET w/o RC's (100)	10.00	25.00
❑ 1 Aaron Rodgers	.30	.75
❑ 2 Adrian Peterson	.60	1.50
❑ 3 Andre Johnson	.25	.60
❑ 4 Anthony Gonzalez	.25	.60
❑ 5 Antonio Bryant	.25	.60
❑ 6 Antonio Gates	.25	.60
❑ 7 Ben Roethlisberger	.50	1.25
❑ 8 Bernard Berrian	.25	.60
❑ 9 Brady Quinn	.25	.60
❑ 10 Brandon Jacobs	.25	.60
❑ 11 Brandon Marshall	.25	.60
❑ 12 Braylon Edwards	.25	.60
❑ 13 Brian Urlacher	.30	.75
❑ 14 Brian Westbrook	.25	.60
❑ 15 Calvin Johnson	.30	.75
❑ 16 Carson Palmer	.30	.75
❑ 17 Chad Ochocinco	.25	.60
❑ 18 Chad Pennington	.25	.60
❑ 19 Chris Cooley	.25	.60
❑ 20 Chris Johnson	.30	.75
❑ 21 Clinton Portis	.25	.60
❑ 22 Darren McFadden	.30	.75
❑ 23 Daunte Culpepper	.25	.60
❑ 24 David Garrard	.25	.60
❑ 25 DeAngelo Williams	.30	.75
❑ 26 Derrick Ward	.25	.60
❑ 27 DeSean Jackson	.25	.60
❑ 28 Donnie Avery	.25	.60
❑ 29 Donovan McNabb	.30	.75
❑ 30 Drew Brees	.30	.75
❑ 31 Dwayne Bowe	.25	.60
❑ 32 Eddie Royal	.25	.60
❑ 33 Eli Manning	.30	.75
❑ 34 Frank Gore	.25	.60
❑ 35 Greg Olsen	.20	.50
❑ 36 Greg Jennings	.30	.75
❑ 37 Jake Delhomme	.25	.60
❑ 38 Jamal Lewis	.25	.60
❑ 39 JaMarcus Russell	.25	.60
❑ 40 Jason Campbell	.25	.60
❑ 41 Jason Witten	.30	.75
❑ 42 Jay Cutler	.30	.75
❑ 43 Jerricho Cotchery	.20	.50
❑ 44 Joe Flacco	.30	.75
❑ 45 Joseph Addai	.30	.75
❑ 46 Josh Morgan	.20	.50
❑ 47 Julius Jones	.25	.60
❑ 48 Kellen Winslow Jr.	.25	.60
❑ 49 Kerry Collins	.25	.60
❑ 50 Kevin Boss	.20	.50
❑ 51 Kevin Smith	.25	.60
❑ 52 Kurt Warner	.30	.75
❑ 53 Kyle Orton	.25	.60
❑ 54 LaDainian Tomlinson	.30	.75
❑ 55 Larry Fitzgerald	.30	.75
❑ 56 Larry Johnson	.25	.60
❑ 57 Laurence Maroney	.25	.60
❑ 58 Laveranues Coles	.25	.60
❑ 59 Lee Evans	.25	.60
❑ 60 LenDale White	.25	.60
❑ 61 Leon Washington	.25	.60
❑ 62 Marc Bulger	.25	.60
❑ 63 Marion Barber	.30	.75
❑ 64 Marques Colston	.25	.60
❑ 65 Marshawn Lynch	.25	.60
❑ 66 Matt Cassel	.25	.60
❑ 67 Matt Forte	.30	.75
❑ 68 Matt Hasselbeck	.25	.60
❑ 69 Matt Ryan	.30	.75
❑ 70 Matt Schaub	.25	.60
❑ 71 Maurice Jones-Drew	.25	.60
❑ 72 Michael Turner	.25	.60
❑ 73 Peyton Manning	.50	1.25
❑ 74 Philip Rivers	.30	.75
❑ 75 Randy Moss	.30	.75
❑ 76 Ray Rice	.30	.75
❑ 77 Reggie Bush	.30	.75
❑ 78 Reggie Wayne	.25	.60
❑ 79 Ricky Williams	.25	.60
❑ 80 Roddy White	.25	.60
❑ 81 Ronnie Brown	.25	.60
❑ 82 Ryan Grant	.25	.60
❑ 83 Santonio Holmes	.25	.60
❑ 84 Steve Breaston	.25	.60
❑ 85 Steve Slaton	.25	.60
❑ 86 Steve Smith	.25	.60
❑ 87 Steven Jackson	.25	.60
❑ 88 T.J. Houshmandzadeh	.25	.60
❑ 89 Brett Favre	5.00	12.00
❑ 90 Terrell Owens	.30	.75
❑ 91 Tom Brady	.50	1.25
❑ 92 Tony Gonzalez	.25	.60
❑ 93 Tony Romo	.50	1.25
❑ 94 Torry Holt	.25	.60
❑ 95 Vernon Davis	.20	.50
❑ 96 Vincent Jackson	.25	.60
❑ 97 Wes Welker	.30	.75
❑ 98 Willie Parker	.25	.60
❑ 99 Willis McGahee	.25	.60
❑ 100 Zach Miller	.20	.50
❑ 101 Aaron Brown RC	2.00	5.00
❑ 102 Aaron Kelly RC	1.50	4.00
❑ 103 Aaron Maybin RC	2.00	5.00
❑ 104 Alex Mack RC	1.50	4.00
❑ 105 Alphonso Smith RC	1.50	4.00
❑ 106 Andre Smith RC	2.00	5.00
❑ 107 Anthony Hill RC	1.25	3.00
❑ 108 Arian Foster RC	2.00	5.00
❑ 109 Austin Collie RC	4.00	10.00
❑ 110 B.J. Raji RC	2.50	6.00
❑ 111 Bear Pascoe RC	2.00	5.00
❑ 112 Bernard Scott RC	2.00	5.00
❑ 113 Bradley Fletcher RC	1.50	4.00
❑ 114 Brandon Gibson RC	2.00	5.00
❑ 115 Brandon Tate RC	1.50	4.00
❑ 116 Brian Cushing RC	2.50	6.00
❑ 117 Brian Hartline RC	2.00	5.00
❑ 118 Brian Orakpo RC	2.50	6.00
❑ 119 Brooks Foster RC	1.50	4.00
❑ 120 Cameron Morrah RC	1.25	3.00
❑ 121 Cedric Peerman RC	1.50	4.00
❑ 122 Chase Coffman RC	1.50	4.00
❑ 123 Chase Daniel RC	2.50	6.00
❑ 124 Chris Ogbonnaya RC	2.00	5.00
❑ 125 Clay Matthews RC	3.00	8.00
❑ 126 Clint Sintim RC	2.00	5.00
❑ 127 Cody Brown RC	1.50	4.00
❑ 128 Connor Barwin RC	1.50	4.00
❑ 129 Cornelius Ingram RC	1.25	3.00
❑ 130 Curtis Painter RC	2.00	5.00
❑ 131 Dan Gronkowski RC	1.25	3.00
❑ 132 Darcel McBath RC	2.00	5.00
❑ 133 Darius Butler RC	2.00	5.00
❑ 134 David Johnson RC	1.50	4.00
❑ 135 David Veikune RC	1.50	4.00
❑ 136 Davon Drew RC	1.50	4.00
❑ 137 DeAndre Levy RC	2.00	5.00
❑ 138 Demetrius Byrd RC	1.50	4.00
❑ 139 Derek Cox RC	2.00	5.00
❑ 140 Devin Moore RC	1.50	4.00
❑ 141 Dominique Edison RC	1.25	3.00
❑ 142 Eddie Williams RC	1.50	4.00
❑ 143 Eric Wood RC	1.50	4.00
❑ 144 Eugene Monroe RC	1.50	4.00
❑ 145 Evander Hood RC	3.00	8.00
❑ 146 Everette Brown RC	2.00	5.00
❑ 147 Frank Summers RC	2.00	5.00
❑ 148 Fui Vakapuna RC	1.50	4.00
❑ 149 Gartrell Johnson RC	1.50	4.00
❑ 150 Hunter Cantwell RC	2.00	5.00
❑ 151 James Casey RC	1.50	4.00
❑ 152 James Davis RC	2.00	5.00
❑ 153 James Laurinaitis RC	2.50	6.00
❑ 154 Jared Cook RC	1.50	4.00
❑ 155 Jarett Dillard RC	2.00	5.00
❑ 156 Jairus Byrd RC	2.50	6.00
❑ 157 Jason Williams RC	2.00	5.00
❑ 158 Javarris Williams RC	1.50	4.00
❑ 159 Jeremy Childs RC	1.50	4.00
❑ 160 John Nalbone RC	1.25	3.00
❑ 161 John Phillips RC	2.00	5.00
❑ 162 Johnny Knox RC	3.00	8.00
❑ 163 Julian Edelman RC	8.00	20.00
❑ 164 Keith Null RC	2.00	5.00
❑ 165 Kenny McKinley RC	2.00	5.00
❑ 166 Kevin Ogletree RC	2.00	5.00
❑ 167 Kory Sheets RC	1.50	4.00
❑ 168 Lardarius Webb RC	2.00	5.00
❑ 169 Larry English RC	2.00	5.00
❑ 170 Louis Delmas RC	2.00	5.00
❑ 171 Louis Murphy RC	2.00	5.00
❑ 172 Malcolm Jenkins RC	2.00	5.00
❑ 173 Manuel Johnson RC	1.50	4.00
❑ 174 Marko Mitchell RC	1.50	4.00
❑ 175 Michael Mitchell RC	2.00	5.00
❑ 176 Michael Oher RC	4.00	10.00
❑ 177 Mike Goodson RC	2.00	5.00
❑ 178 Mike Teel RC	2.00	5.00
❑ 179 P.J. Hill RC	1.50	4.00
❑ 180 Patrick Chung RC	2.00	5.00
❑ 181 Peria Jerry RC	1.50	4.00
❑ 182 Quan Cosby RC	1.50	4.00
❑ 183 Quinn Johnson RC	1.50	4.00
❑ 184 Quinten Lawrence RC	1.50	4.00
❑ 185 Rashad Jennings RC	2.00	5.00
❑ 186 Rey Maualuga RC	3.00	8.00
❑ 187 Richard Quinn RC	1.50	4.00
❑ 188 Robert Ayers RC	2.00	5.00
❑ 189 Ron Brace RC	1.50	4.00
❑ 190 Sammie Stroughter RC	2.00	5.00
❑ 191 Sean Smith RC	2.00	5.00
❑ 192 Shawn Nelson RC	1.50	4.00
❑ 193 Sherrod Martin RC	1.50	4.00
❑ 194 Tiquan Underwood RC	1.50	4.00
❑ 195 Tom Brandstater RC	2.00	5.00
❑ 196 Tony Fiammetta RC	1.50	4.00
❑ 197 Travis Beckum RC	1.50	4.00
❑ 198 Tyrell Sutton RC	1.50	4.00
❑ 199 Vontae Davis RC	2.00	5.00
❑ 200 William Moore RC	1.50	4.00
❑ 201 Mark Sanchez JSY AU RC	60.00	120.00
❑ 202 Chris Wells JSY AU RC	25.00	60.00
❑ 203 M.Stafford JSY AU RC	40.00	80.00
❑ 204 Donald Brown JSY AU RC	20.00	50.00
❑ 205 Hakeem Nicks JSY AU RC	20.00	50.00
❑ 206 M.Crabtree JSY AU RC	25.00	60.00
❑ 207 B.Pettigrew JSY AU RC	12.00	30.00
❑ 208 Ramses Barden JSY AU RC	8.00	20.00
❑ 209 Kenny Britt JSY AU RC	15.00	40.00
❑ 210 Deon Butler JSY AU RC	10.00	25.00
❑ 211 J.Iglesias JSY AU RC	10.00	25.00
❑ 212 Jeremy Maclin JSY AU RC	20.00	50.00
❑ 213 Glen Coffee JSY AU/99 RC	12.00	30.00
❑ 214 Jason Smith JSY AU RC	8.00	20.00
❑ 215 Patrick Turner JSY AU RC	8.00	20.00
❑ 216 K.Moreno JSY AU RC	25.00	60.00
❑ 217 M.Massaquoi JSY AU RC	10.00	25.00
❑ 218 Shonn Greene JSY AU RC	20.00	50.00
❑ 219 Nate Davis JSY AU RC	10.00	25.00
❑ 220 LeSean McCoy JSY AU RC	20.00	50.00
❑ 221 Pat White JSY AU RC	15.00	40.00
❑ 222 Percy Harvin JSY AU RC	40.00	80.00
❑ 223 Tyson Jackson JSY AU RC	10.00	25.00
❑ 224 Javon Ringer JSY AU RC	10.00	25.00
❑ 225 Mike Wallace JSY AU RC	20.00	50.00
❑ 226 Josh Freeman JSY AU/98 RC	20.00	50.00
❑ 227 Stephen McGee JSY AU RC	10.00	25.00
❑ 228 Mike Thomas JSY AU RC	10.00	25.00
❑ 229 Brian Robiskie JSY AU RC	10.00	25.00
❑ 230 Aaron Curry JSY AU RC	12.00	30.00
❑ 231 Andre Brown JSY AU RC	8.00	20.00
❑ 232 Derrick Williams JSY AU RC	10.00	25.00
❑ 233 D.Heyward-Bey JSY AU RC	15.00	40.00
❑ 234 Rhett Bomar JSY AU RC	8.00	20.00

2009 Donruss Rookies and Stars

Card	Low	High
❑ COMP.SET w/o SP's (100)	8.00	20.00
❑ 1 Kurt Warner	.30	.75
❑ 2 Larry Fitzgerald	.30	.75
❑ 3 Steve Breaston	.25	.60
❑ 4 Matt Ryan	.30	.75
❑ 5 Michael Turner	.25	.60
❑ 6 Roddy White	.25	.60
❑ 7 Derrick Mason	.20	.50
❑ 8 Joe Flacco	.30	.75
❑ 9 Willis McGahee	.25	.60
❑ 10 Lee Evans	.25	.60
❑ 11 Marshawn Lynch	.25	.60
❑ 12 Trent Edwards	.25	.60
❑ 13 DeAngelo Williams	.30	.75
❑ 14 Jake Delhomme	.25	.60
❑ 15 Jonathan Stewart	.25	.60
❑ 16 Steve Smith	.25	.60
❑ 17 Greg Olsen	.20	.50
❑ 18 Kyle Orton	.25	.60
❑ 19 Matt Forte	.30	.75
❑ 20 Carson Palmer	.30	.75
❑ 21 Chad Ochocinco	.25	.60
❑ 22 T.J. Houshmandzadeh	.25	.60
❑ 23 Brady Quinn	.25	.60
❑ 24 Braylon Edwards	.25	.60
❑ 25 Jamal Lewis	.25	.60
❑ 26 Jason Witten	.30	.75
❑ 27 Marion Barber	.30	.75
❑ 28 Tony Romo	.50	1.25
❑ 29 Brandon Marshall	.25	.60
❑ 30 Jay Cutler	.30	.75
❑ 31 Eddie Royal	.25	.60
❑ 32 Calvin Johnson	.30	.75
❑ 33 Daunte Culpepper	.25	.60
❑ 34 Kevin Smith	.25	.60
❑ 35 Aaron Rodgers	.30	.75
❑ 36 Greg Jennings	.30	.75
❑ 37 Ryan Grant	.25	.60
❑ 38 Andre Johnson	.25	.60
❑ 39 Matt Schaub	.25	.60
❑ 40 Owen Daniels	.20	.50
❑ 41 Steve Slaton	.25	.60
❑ 42 Anthony Gonzalez	.25	.60
❑ 43 Joseph Addai	.30	.75
❑ 44 Peyton Manning	.50	1.25
❑ 45 Reggie Wayne	.25	.60
❑ 46 David Garrard	.25	.60
❑ 47 Marcedes Lewis	.20	.50
❑ 48 Maurice Jones-Drew	.25	.60
❑ 49 Dwayne Bowe	.25	.60
❑ 50 Larry Johnson	.25	.60
❑ 51 Tony Gonzalez	.25	.60
❑ 52 Chad Pennington	.25	.60
❑ 53 Ricky Williams	.25	.60
❑ 54 Ronnie Brown	.25	.60
❑ 55 Adrian Peterson	.60	1.50
❑ 56 Bernard Berrian	.25	.60
❑ 57 Tarvaris Jackson	.25	.60
❑ 58 Laurence Maroney	.25	.60
❑ 59 Tom Brady	.50	1.25
❑ 60 Wes Welker	.30	.75
❑ 61 Drew Brees	.30	.75
❑ 62 Marques Colston	.25	.60
❑ 63 Reggie Bush	.30	.75
❑ 64 Brandon Jacobs	.25	.60
❑ 65 Eli Manning	.30	.75
❑ 66 Kevin Boss	.20	.50
❑ 67 Thomas Jones	.25	.60
❑ 68 Jerricho Cotchery	.20	.50
❑ 69 Leon Washington	.25	.60
❑ 70 Darren McFadden	.30	.75
❑ 71 JaMarcus Russell	.25	.60
❑ 72 Zach Miller	.20	.50
❑ 73 Brian Westbrook	.25	.60
❑ 74 DeSean Jackson	.25	.60
❑ 75 Donovan McNabb	.30	.75
❑ 76 Ben Roethlisberger	.50	1.25
❑ 77 Heath Miller	.25	.60
❑ 78 Santonio Holmes	.25	.60
❑ 79 Willie Parker	.25	.60
❑ 80 LaDainian Tomlinson	.30	.75
❑ 81 Philip Rivers	.30	.75
❑ 82 Vincent Jackson	.25	.60
❑ 83 Frank Gore	.25	.60
❑ 84 Shaun Hill	.25	.60
❑ 85 Vernon Davis	.20	.50
❑ 86 John Carlson	.25	.60
❑ 87 Julius Jones	.25	.60
❑ 88 Matt Hasselbeck	.25	.60
❑ 89 Marc Bulger	.25	.60
❑ 90 Steven Jackson	.25	.60
❑ 91 Torry Holt	.25	.60
❑ 92 Antonio Bryant	.25	.60
❑ 93 Cadillac Williams	.25	.60
❑ 94 Kellen Winslow	.25	.60
❑ 95 Chris Johnson	.30	.75
❑ 96 Kerry Collins	.25	.60
❑ 97 LenDale White	.25	.60
❑ 98 Chris Cooley	.25	.60
❑ 99 Clinton Portis	.25	.60
❑ 100 Jason Campbell	.25	.60
❑ 101 Santonio Holmes ELE	1.25	3.00
❑ 102 Willie Parker ELE	1.25	3.00
❑ 103 Kurt Warner ELE	1.50	4.00
❑ 104 Brian Westbrook ELE	1.25	3.00
❑ 105 Tim Hightower ELE	1.25	3.00
❑ 106 Donovan McNabb ELE	1.50	4.00
❑ 107 Wes Welker ELE	1.50	4.00
❑ 108 Randy Moss ELE	1.50	4.00
❑ 109 Philip Rivers ELE	1.50	4.00
❑ 110 Antonio Gates ELE	1.25	3.00
❑ 111 Thomas Jones ELE	1.25	3.00
❑ 112 Brandon Marshall ELE	1.25	3.00
❑ 113 Nate Burleson ELE	1.00	2.50
❑ 114 Leon Washington ELE	1.25	3.00
❑ 115 Brandon Jacobs ELE	1.25	3.00
❑ 116 Aaron Kelly RC	1.50	4.00
❑ 117 Aaron Maybin RC	2.00	5.00
❑ 118 Alphonso Smith RC	1.50	4.00
❑ 119 Andre Smith RC	2.00	5.00
❑ 120 Arian Foster RC	2.00	5.00
❑ 121 Asher Allen RC	1.50	4.00
❑ 122 Austin Collie RC	4.00	10.00
❑ 123 B.J. Raji RC	2.50	6.00
❑ 124 Bradley Fletcher RC	1.50	4.00
❑ 125 Brandon Gibson RC	2.00	5.00
❑ 126 Brian Cushing RC	2.50	6.00
❑ 127 Brian Hartline RC	2.00	5.00
❑ 128 Brian Orakpo RC	2.50	6.00
❑ 129 Brooks Foster RC	1.50	4.00
❑ 130 Cameron Morrah RC	1.25	3.00
❑ 131 Cedric Peerman RC	1.50	4.00
❑ 132 Chase Coffman RC	1.50	4.00
❑ 133 Chip Vaughn RC	1.25	3.00
❑ 134 Chris Owens RC	1.50	4.00
❑ 135 Clay Matthews RC	3.00	8.00
❑ 136 Clint Sintim RC	2.00	5.00
❑ 137 Cody Brown RC	1.50	4.00
❑ 138 Connor Barwin RC	1.50	4.00
❑ 139 Cornelius Ingram RC	1.25	3.00
❑ 140 Darcel McBath RC	2.00	5.00
❑ 141 Darius Butler RC	2.00	5.00
❑ 142 Darius Passmore RC	1.50	4.00
❑ 143 David Bruton RC	1.50	4.00
❑ 144 DeAndre Levy RC	2.00	5.00
❑ 145 Demetrius Byrd RC	1.50	4.00
❑ 146 Devin Moore RC	1.50	4.00
❑ 147 Dominique Edison RC	1.25	3.00
❑ 148 Eugene Monroe RC	1.50	4.00
❑ 149 Evander Hood RC	3.00	8.00
❑ 150 Everette Brown RC	2.00	5.00
❑ 151 Brandon Tate RC	1.50	4.00
❑ 152 Graham Harrell RC	2.00	5.00
❑ 153 Hunter Cantwell RC	2.00	5.00
❑ 154 Jairus Byrd RC	2.50	6.00
❑ 155 James Casey RC	1.50	4.00
❑ 156 James Laurinaitis RC	2.50	6.00
❑ 157 Jared Cook RC	1.50	4.00
❑ 158 Jarett Dillard RC	2.00	5.00
❑ 159 Jason Williams RC	2.00	5.00
❑ 160 Jeremiah Johnson RC	2.00	5.00
❑ 161 Jeremy Childs RC	1.50	4.00
❑ 162 Jerraud Powers RC	1.50	4.00
❑ 163 John Parker Wilson RC	2.00	5.00
❑ 164 Johnny Knox RC	3.00	8.00
❑ 165 Kaluka Maiava RC	2.00	5.00
❑ 166 Keenan Lewis RC	2.00	5.00
❑ 167 Kenny McKinley RC	2.00	5.00
❑ 168 Kevin Barnes RC	1.50	4.00
❑ 169 Kevin Ogletree RC	2.00	5.00
❑ 170 Kory Sheets RC	1.50	4.00
❑ 171 Lardarius Webb RC	2.00	5.00
❑ 172 Larry English RC	2.00	5.00
❑ 173 Louis Delmas RC	2.00	5.00
❑ 174 Louis Murphy RC	2.00	5.00
❑ 175 Malcolm Jenkins RC	2.00	5.00
❑ 176 Michael Mitchell RC	2.00	5.00
❑ 177 Mike Goodson RC	2.00	5.00
❑ 178 Nathan Brown RC	1.50	4.00
❑ 179 P.J. Hill RC	1.50	4.00
❑ 180 Patrick Chung RC	2.00	5.00
❑ 181 Peria Jerry RC	1.50	4.00
❑ 182 Quan Cosby RC	1.50	4.00
❑ 183 Quinn Johnson RC	1.50	4.00
❑ 184 Rashad Jennings RC	2.00	5.00
❑ 185 Rashad Johnson RC	1.50	4.00
❑ 186 Rey Maualuga RC	3.00	8.00
❑ 187 Richard Quinn RC	1.50	4.00
❑ 188 Robert Ayers RC	2.00	5.00
❑ 189 Ryan Mouton RC	1.50	4.00
❑ 190 Sean Smith RC	2.00	5.00
❑ 191 Sen'Derrick Marks RC	1.25	3.00
❑ 192 Shawn Nelson RC	1.50	4.00
❑ 193 Sherrod Martin RC	1.50	4.00
❑ 194 Tom Brandstater RC	2.00	5.00
❑ 195 Tony Fiammetta RC	1.50	4.00
❑ 196 Travis Beckum RC	1.50	4.00
❑ 197 Tyrell Sutton RC	1.50	4.00
❑ 198 Tyrone McKenzie RC	1.50	4.00
❑ 199 Vontae Davis RC	2.00	5.00
❑ 200 William Moore RC	1.50	4.00
❑ 201 Matthew Stafford AU RC	50.00	100.00
❑ 202 Jason Smith AU RC	8.00	20.00
❑ 203 Tyson Jackson AU RC	10.00	25.00
❑ 204 Aaron Curry AU RC	12.00	30.00
❑ 205 Mark Sanchez AU RC	60.00	120.00
❑ 206 Darrius Heyward-Bey AU RC	15.00	40.00
❑ 207 Michael Crabtree AU RC	40.00	80.00
❑ 208 Knowshon Moreno AU RC	40.00	80.00
❑ 209 Josh Freeman AU RC	20.00	50.00
❑ 210 Jeremy Maclin AU RC	20.00	50.00
❑ 211 Brandon Pettigrew AU RC	12.00	30.00
❑ 212 Percy Harvin AU RC	50.00	100.00
❑ 213 Donald Brown AU RC	20.00	50.00
❑ 214 Hakeem Nicks AU RC	20.00	50.00
❑ 215 Kenny Britt AU RC	15.00	40.00
❑ 216 Chris Wells AU RC	25.00	60.00
❑ 217 Brian Robiskie AU RC	10.00	25.00
❑ 218 Pat White AU RC	25.00	60.00
❑ 219 Mohamed Massaquoi AU RC	10.00	25.00
❑ 220 LeSean McCoy AU RC	20.00	50.00
❑ 221 Shonn Greene AU RC	20.00	50.00
❑ 222 Glen Coffee AU RC	12.00	30.00
❑ 223 Derrick Williams AU RC	10.00	25.00
❑ 224 Javon Ringer AU RC	10.00	25.00
❑ 225 Mike Wallace AU RC	20.00	50.00
❑ 226 Ramses Barden AU RC	8.00	20.00
❑ 227 Patrick Turner AU RC	8.00	20.00
❑ 228 Deon Butler AU RC	10.00	25.00
❑ 229 Juaquin Iglesias AU RC	10.00	25.00
❑ 230 Stephen McGee AU RC	10.00	25.00
❑ 231 Mike Thomas AU RC	10.00	25.00
❑ 232 Andre Brown AU RC	8.00	20.00
❑ 233 Rhett Bomar AU RC	8.00	20.00
❑ 234 Nate Davis AU RC	10.00	25.00

2006 Donruss Threads

Card	Low	High
❑ COMP.SET w/o RC's (150)	10.00	25.00
❑ 1 Braylon Edwards	.40	1.00
❑ 2 Jason Witten	.40	1.00
❑ 3 Julius Jones	.30	.75
❑ 4 Roy Williams S	.30	.75
❑ 5 Terry Glenn	.30	.75
❑ 6 Ashley Lelie	.25	.60
❑ 7 Kevin Jones	.30	.75
❑ 8 Mike Williams	.30	.75
❑ 9 Roy Williams WR	.40	1.00
❑ 10 Aaron Rodgers	.40	1.00
❑ 11 Tatum Bell	.25	.60
❑ 12 Samkon Gado	.40	1.00
❑ 13 Corey Bradford	.25	.60
❑ 14 Dallas Clark	.30	.75
❑ 15 Matt Jones	.30	.75
❑ 16 Larry Johnson	.30	.75
❑ 17 Byron Leftwich	.30	.75
❑ 18 Fred Taylor	.30	.75
❑ 19 Anquan Boldin	.30	.75
❑ 20 Kurt Warner	.40	1.00
❑ 21 Larry Fitzgerald	.40	1.00
❑ 22 Alge Crumpler	.30	.75
❑ 23 Michael Vick	.40	1.00
❑ 24 Warrick Dunn	.30	.75
❑ 25 Jamal Lewis	.30	.75
❑ 26 Ray Lewis	.40	1.00
❑ 27 Eric Moulds	.30	.75
❑ 28 Josh Reed	.25	.60
❑ 29 Lee Evans	.30	.75
❑ 30 Steve Smith	.40	1.00
❑ 31 Brian Urlacher	.40	1.00
❑ 32 Thomas Jones	.30	.75
❑ 33 Chad Johnson	.30	.75
❑ 34 Rudi Johnson	.30	.75
❑ 35 T.J. Houshmandzadeh	.30	.75
❑ 36 Reuben Droughns	.30	.75
❑ 37 Drew Bledsoe	.40	1.00
❑ 38 Keyshawn Johnson	.30	.75
❑ 39 Jake Plummer	.30	.75
❑ 40 Rod Smith	.30	.75
❑ 41 Mike Anderson	.30	.75
❑ 42 Joey Harrington	.25	.60
❑ 43 Brett Favre	.75	2.00
❑ 44 Donald Driver	.40	1.00
❑ 45 Javon Walker	.30	.75
❑ 46 Andre Johnson	.30	.75
❑ 47 David Carr	.25	.60
❑ 48 Domanick Davis	.30	.75
❑ 49 Edgerrin James	.30	.75
❑ 50 Marvin Harrison	.40	1.00
❑ 51 Peyton Manning	.60	1.50
❑ 52 Reggie Wayne	.30	.75
❑ 53 Jimmy Smith	.30	.75
❑ 54 Tony Gonzalez	.30	.75
❑ 55 Trent Green	.30	.75
❑ 56 Eddie Kennison	.25	.60
❑ 57 Chris Chambers	.30	.75
❑ 58 Zach Thomas	.40	1.00
❑ 59 Daunte Culpepper	.40	1.00
❑ 60 Corey Dillon	.30	.75
❑ 61 Deion Branch	.30	.75
❑ 62 Tedy Bruschi	.40	1.00
❑ 63 Tom Brady	.60	1.50
❑ 64 Deuce McAllister	.30	.75
❑ 65 Donte Stallworth	.30	.75
❑ 66 Jeremy Shockey	.40	1.00
❑ 67 Tiki Barber	.40	1.00
❑ 68 Chad Pennington	.30	.75
❑ 69 Curtis Martin	.40	1.00
❑ 70 Donovan McNabb	.40	1.00
❑ 71 Antwaan Randle El	.30	.75
❑ 72 Hines Ward	.40	1.00
❑ 73 Antonio Gates	.40	1.00
❑ 74 Drew Brees	.40	1.00
❑ 75 Keenan McCardell	.30	.75
❑ 76 LaDainian Tomlinson	.50	1.25
❑ 77 Alex Smith QB	.30	.75
❑ 78 Brandon Lloyd	.30	.75
❑ 79 Frank Gore	.40	1.00
❑ 80 Kevan Barlow	.30	.75
❑ 81 Darrell Jackson	.30	.75
❑ 82 Joe Jurevicius	.25	.60
❑ 83 Matt Hasselbeck	.30	.75
❑ 84 Shaun Alexander	.30	.75
❑ 85 Shaun McDonald	.25	.60
❑ 86 Marc Bulger	.30	.75
❑ 87 Steven Jackson	.40	1.00
❑ 88 Torry Holt	.30	.75
❑ 89 Cadillac Williams	.40	1.00
❑ 90 Chris Simms	.30	.75
❑ 91 Joey Galloway	.30	.75
❑ 92 Michael Clayton	.30	.75
❑ 93 Chris Brown	.30	.75
❑ 94 Drew Bennett	.30	.75
❑ 95 Steve McNair	.30	.75
❑ 96 Tyrone Calico	.25	.60
❑ 97 Clinton Portis	.40	1.00
❑ 98 David Patten	.25	.60
❑ 99 Mark Brunell	.30	.75
❑ 100 Santana Moss	.30	.75
❑ 101 Randy McMichael	.25	.60
❑ 102 Ronnie Brown	.40	1.00
❑ 103 Mewelde Moore	.25	.60
❑ 104 Nate Burleson	.30	.75
❑ 105 Troy Williamson	.30	.75
❑ 106 David Givens	.30	.75
❑ 107 Aaron Brooks	.30	.75
❑ 108 Laveranues Coles	.30	.75
❑ 109 Justin McCareins	.25	.60
❑ 110 Kerry Collins	.30	.75
❑ 111 LaMont Jordan	.30	.75
❑ 112 Randy Moss	.40	1.00
❑ 113 Jerry Porter	.30	.75
❑ 114 Brian Westbrook	.30	.75
❑ 115 Plaxico Burress	.30	.75
❑ 116 Joe Horn	.30	.75
❑ 117 Eli Manning	.50	1.25
❑ 118 Reggie Brown	.25	.60
❑ 119 Ryan Moats	.30	.75
❑ 120 Ben Roethlisberger	.60	1.50
❑ 121 Willie Parker	.50	1.25
❑ 122 Marcus Pollard	.25	.60
❑ 123 Bubba Franks	.25	.60
❑ 124 Jabar Gaffney	.25	.60
❑ 125 Brandon Stokley	.30	.75
❑ 126 Ernest Wilford	.25	.60
❑ 127 Dante Hall	.30	.75
❑ 128 Marty Booker	.25	.60
❑ 129 Samie Parker	.25	.60
❑ 130 J.J. Arrington	.25	.60
❑ 131 Marcel Shipp	.25	.60
❑ 132 Michael Jenkins	.30	.75
❑ 133 T.J. Duckett	.25	.60
❑ 134 Derrick Mason	.30	.75
❑ 135 Kyle Boller	.30	.75
❑ 136 Mark Clayton	.30	.75
❑ 137 Willis McGahee	.40	1.00
❑ 138 DeShaun Foster	.30	.75
❑ 139 Jake Delhomme	.30	.75
❑ 140 Julius Peppers	.30	.75
❑ 141 Keary Colbert	.30	.75
❑ 142 Stephen Davis	.30	.75
❑ 143 Todd Heap	.30	.75
❑ 144 J.P. Losman	.30	.75
❑ 145 Muhsin Muhammad	.30	.75
❑ 146 Carson Palmer	.40	1.00
❑ 147 Cedric Benson	.30	.75
❑ 148 Rex Grossman	.40	1.00
❑ 149 Charlie Frye	.30	.75
❑ 150 Dennis Northcutt	.25	.60
❑ 151 Mathias Kiwanuka RC	3.00	8.00
❑ 152 Ingle Martin RC	2.00	5.00
❑ 153 Reggie McNeal RC	2.00	5.00
❑ 154 Bruce Gradkowski RC	2.50	6.00
❑ 155 D.J. Shockley RC	2.00	5.00
❑ 156 Paul Pinegar RC	1.50	4.00
❑ 157 Brandon Kirsch RC	2.00	5.00
❑ 158 P.J. Daniels RC	1.50	4.00
❑ 159 Marques Hagans RC	2.00	5.00
❑ 160 Jerome Harrison RC	2.50	6.00
❑ 161 Wali Lundy RC	2.50	6.00
❑ 162 Cedric Humes RC	2.00	5.00
❑ 163 Quinton Ganther RC	1.50	4.00
❑ 164 Mike Bell RC	2.50	6.00
❑ 165 John David Washington RC	2.00	5.00
❑ 166 Anthony Fasano RC	2.50	6.00
❑ 167 Tony Scheffler RC	2.50	6.00
❑ 168 Leonard Pope RC	2.50	6.00
❑ 169 David Thomas RC	2.50	6.00
❑ 170 Dominique Byrd RC	2.00	5.00
❑ 171 Devin Hester RC	5.00	12.00
❑ 172 Willie Reid RC	2.00	5.00
❑ 173 Brad Smith RC	2.50	6.00
❑ 174 Cory Rodgers RC	2.50	6.00
❑ 175 Domenik Hixon RC	2.50	6.00
❑ 176 Jeremy Bloom RC	2.00	5.00
❑ 177 Jonathan Orr RC	2.00	5.00
❑ 178 Jeff Webb RC	2.00	5.00
❑ 179 Ethan Kilmer RC	2.50	6.00
❑ 180 Bennie Brazell RC	2.00	5.00
❑ 181 David Anderson RC	2.00	5.00
❑ 182 Kevin McMahan RC	2.00	5.00
❑ 183 Anthony Mix RC	2.00	5.00
❑ 184 D'Brickashaw Ferguson RC	2.50	6.00
❑ 185 Kamerion Wimbley RC	2.50	6.00
❑ 186 Tamba Hali RC	2.50	6.00
❑ 187 Haloti Ngata RC	2.50	6.00
❑ 188 Brodrick Bunkley RC	2.00	5.00
❑ 189 John McCargo RC	2.00	5.00
❑ 190 Claude Wroten RC	1.50	4.00
❑ 191 Gabe Watson RC	1.50	4.00
❑ 192 D'Qwell Jackson RC	2.00	5.00
❑ 193 Abdul Hodge RC	2.00	5.00
❑ 194 Ernie Sims RC	2.00	5.00
❑ 195 Chad Greenway RC	2.50	6.00
❑ 196 Bobby Carpenter RC	2.00	5.00
❑ 197 Manny Lawson RC	2.50	6.00
❑ 198 DeMeco Ryans RC	3.00	8.00
❑ 199 Rocky McIntosh RC	2.50	6.00
❑ 200 Thomas Howard RC	2.00	5.00
❑ 201 Jon Alston RC	1.50	4.00
❑ 202 A.J. Nicholson RC	1.50	4.00
❑ 203 Tye Hill RC	2.00	5.00
❑ 204 Antonio Cromartie RC	2.50	6.00
❑ 205 Johnathan Joseph RC	2.00	5.00
❑ 206 Kelly Jennings RC	2.50	6.00
❑ 207 Ashton Youboty RC	2.00	5.00
❑ 208 Alan Zemaitis RC	2.50	6.00
❑ 209 Jason Allen RC	2.00	5.00
❑ 210 Cedric Griffin RC	2.00	5.00
❑ 211 Ko Simpson RC	2.00	5.00
❑ 212 Pat Watkins RC	2.50	6.00
❑ 213 Donte Whitner RC	2.50	6.00
❑ 214 Bernard Pollard RC	2.00	5.00
❑ 215 Darnell Bing RC	2.00	5.00
❑ 216 Marcus Vick RC	1.50	4.00
❑ 217 Roman Harper RC	2.00	5.00
❑ 218 Anthony Smith RC	2.50	6.00
❑ 219 Daniel Bullocks RC	2.50	6.00
❑ 220 Eric Smith RC	2.00	5.00
❑ 221 Danieal Manning RC	2.50	6.00
❑ 222 Anthony Schlegel RC	2.00	5.00
❑ 223 Dusty Dvoracek RC	2.50	6.00
❑ 224 Darryl Tapp RC	2.00	5.00
❑ 225 Chris Gocong RC	2.00	5.00
❑ 226 Brandon Williams AU/240 RC	15.00	40.00
❑ 227 Michael Robinson AU/240 RC	15.00	40.00
❑ 228 Vernon Davis AU/100 RC	20.00	50.00
❑ 229 Brandon Marshall AU/240 RC	30.00	60.00
❑ 230 Travis Wilson AU/180 RC	12.00	30.00
❑ 231 Maurice Stovall AU/140 RC	15.00	40.00
❑ 232 Matt Leinart AU/140 RC	30.00	80.00
❑ 233 Ch.Whitehurst AU/200 RC	20.00	50.00
❑ 234 Derek Hagan AU/100 RC	15.00	40.00
❑ 235 Jason Avant AU/150 RC	20.00	50.00
❑ 236 Jerious Norwood AU/210 RC	20.00	50.00
❑ 237 Sinorice Moss AU/100 RC	20.00	50.00
❑ 238 Marcedes Lewis AU/100 RC	20.00	50.00
❑ 239 Maurice Drew AU/100 RC	40.00	100.00
❑ 240 Kellen Clemens AU/210 RC	20.00	50.00
❑ 241 Leon Washington AU/200 RC	25.00	60.00
❑ 242 Brian Calhoun AU/140 RC	15.00	40.00
❑ 243 A.J. Hawk AU/100 RC	30.00	80.00
❑ 244 DeAn.Williams AU/160 RC	40.00	100.00
❑ 245 Chad Jackson AU/140 RC	15.00	40.00
❑ 246 L.Maroney AU/140 RC	25.00	60.00
❑ 247 Michael Huff AU/100 RC	20.00	50.00
❑ 248 Joe Klopfenstein AU/240 RC	15.00	40.00
❑ 249 Dem.Williams AU/160 RC	15.00	40.00
❑ 250 Reggie Bush AU/100 RC	75.00	150.00
❑ 251 Omar Jacobs AU/120 RC	12.00	30.00
❑ 252 Santonio Holmes AU/120 RC	50.00	120.00
❑ 253 Mario Williams AU/160 RC	25.00	60.00
❑ 254 LenDale White AU/100 RC	25.00	60.00
❑ 255 Vince Young AU/100 RC	50.00	120.00
❑ 256 Tarvaris Jackson AU/210 RC	20.00	50.00
❑ 257 Jay Cutler AU/120 RC	90.00	150.00
❑ 258 Joseph Addai AU/100 RC	25.00	60.00
❑ 259 Brodie Croyle AU/120 RC	20.00	50.00
❑ 260 Greg Jennings AU/240 RC	30.00	80.00
❑ 261 Erik Meyer AU RC	4.00	10.00
❑ 262 Drew Olson AU RC	3.00	8.00
❑ 263 Darrell Hackney AU RC	4.00	10.00
❑ 264 Andre Hall AU RC	4.00	10.00
❑ 265 Taurean Henderson AU RC	5.00	12.00
❑ 266 Derrick Ross AU RC	4.00	10.00

❑ 267 De'Arrius Howard AU RC 5.00 12.00
❑ 268 Wendell Mathis AU RC 4.00 10.00
❑ 269 Gerald Riggs AU RC 4.00 10.00
❑ 270 Garrett Mills AU RC 4.00 10.00
❑ 271 Jai Lewis AU RC 4.00 10.00
❑ 272 Skyler Green AU RC 3.00 8.00
❑ 273 Mike Hass AU RC 5.00 12.00
❑ 274 Delanie Walker AU RC 4.00 10.00
❑ 275 Adam Jennings AU RC 4.00 10.00
❑ 276 Todd Watkins AU RC 3.00 8.00
❑ 277 Devin Aromashodu AU RC 6.00 15.00
❑ 278 Ben Obomanu AU RC 4.00 10.00
❑ 279 Marques Colston AU RC 20.00 50.00
❑ 280 Miles Austin AU RC 60.00 100.00
❑ 281 Martin Nance AU RC 4.00 10.00
❑ 282 Greg Lee AU RC 3.00 8.00
❑ 283 Hank Baskett AU RC 5.00 12.00
❑ 284 Jimmy Williams AU RC 5.00 12.00
❑ 285 Anwar Phillips AU RC 4.00 10.00

2007 Donruss Threads

❑ COMP.SET w/o RC's (150) 10.00 25.00
❑ 1 Anquan Boldin .30 .75
❑ 2 Larry Fitzgerald .40 1.00
❑ 3 Alge Crumpler .30 .75
❑ 4 Michael Vick .40 1.00
❑ 5 Steve McNair .30 .75
❑ 6 Ray Lewis .40 1.00
❑ 7 Keyshawn Johnson .30 .75
❑ 8 Steve Smith .30 .75
❑ 9 Brian Urlacher .40 1.00
❑ 10 Muhsin Muhammad .30 .75
❑ 11 Chad Johnson .30 .75
❑ 12 Rudi Johnson .30 .75
❑ 13 T.J. Houshmandzadeh .30 .75
❑ 14 Terry Glenn .30 .75
❑ 15 Terrell Owens .40 1.00
❑ 16 Jon Kitna .25 .60
❑ 17 Brett Favre .75 2.00
❑ 18 Peyton Manning .60 1.50
❑ 19 Fred Taylor .30 .75
❑ 20 Eddie Kennison .25 .60
❑ 21 Larry Johnson .30 .75
❑ 22 Tony Gonzalez .30 .75
❑ 23 Trent Green .30 .75
❑ 24 Chris Chambers .30 .75
❑ 25 Marty Booker .25 .60
❑ 26 Tom Brady .75 2.00
❑ 27 Donte Stallworth .30 .75
❑ 28 Deuce McAllister .30 .75
❑ 29 Drew Brees .40 1.00
❑ 30 Reuben Droughns .30 .75
❑ 31 Jeremy Shockey .30 .75
❑ 32 Plaxico Burress .30 .75
❑ 33 Chad Pennington .30 .75
❑ 34 Jerricho Cotchery .25 .60
❑ 35 Laveranues Coles .30 .75
❑ 36 LaMont Jordan .30 .75
❑ 37 Brian Westbrook UER .30 .75
❑ 38 Donovan McNabb .40 1.00
❑ 39 Hines Ward .40 1.00
❑ 40 Antonio Gates .30 .75
❑ 41 LaDainian Tomlinson .50 1.25
❑ 42 Arnaz Battle .25 .60
❑ 43 Darrell Jackson .30 .75
❑ 44 Deion Branch .30 .75
❑ 45 Matt Hasselbeck .30 .75
❑ 46 Jerramy Stevens .25 .60
❑ 47 Shaun Alexander .30 .75
❑ 48 Isaac Bruce .30 .75
❑ 49 Marc Bulger .30 .75
❑ 50 Drew Bennett .25 .60
❑ 51 Torry Holt .30 .75
❑ 52 Joey Galloway .30 .75
❑ 53 Mike Alstott .30 .75
❑ 54 Travis Henry .30 .75
❑ 55 Clinton Portis .30 .75
❑ 56 Santana Moss .30 .75
❑ 57 Edgerrin James .30 .75
❑ 58 Matt Leinart .40 1.00
❑ 59 Jerious Norwood .30 .75
❑ 60 Warrick Dunn .30 .75
❑ 61 Mark Clayton .30 .75
❑ 62 J.P. Losman .25 .60
❑ 63 Josh Reed .25 .60
❑ 64 Lee Evans .30 .75
❑ 65 DeAngelo Williams .40 1.00
❑ 66 DeShaun Foster .30 .75
❑ 67 Jake Delhomme .30 .75
❑ 68 Bernard Berrian .25 .60
❑ 69 Cedric Benson .30 .75
❑ 70 Rex Grossman .30 .75
❑ 71 Carson Palmer .40 1.00
❑ 72 Braylon Edwards .30 .75
❑ 73 Kellen Winslow .30 .75
❑ 74 Charlie Frye .30 .75
❑ 75 Julius Jones .30 .75
❑ 76 Marion Barber .40 1.00
❑ 77 Javon Walker .30 .75
❑ 78 Jay Cutler .40 1.00
❑ 79 Mike Bell .30 .75
❑ 80 Donald Driver .40 1.00
❑ 81 Greg Jennings .30 .75
❑ 82 Andre Johnson .30 .75
❑ 83 Matt Schaub .30 .75
❑ 84 Wali Lundy .25 .60
❑ 85 Joseph Addai .40 1.00
❑ 86 Marvin Harrison .40 1.00
❑ 87 Kevin Jones .25 .60
❑ 88 Roy Williams WR .30 .75
❑ 89 Mike Furrey .30 .75
❑ 90 A.J. Hawk .40 1.00
❑ 91 Reggie Wayne .30 .75
❑ 92 Dallas Clark .25 .60
❑ 93 Byron Leftwich .30 .75
❑ 94 Maurice Jones-Drew .40 1.00
❑ 95 Reggie Williams .30 .75
❑ 96 Tony Romo .60 1.50
❑ 97 Daunte Culpepper .30 .75
❑ 98 Ronnie Brown .30 .75
❑ 99 Chester Taylor .25 .60
❑ 100 Travis Taylor .25 .60
❑ 101 Ben Watson .25 .60
❑ 102 Laurence Maroney .40 1.00
❑ 103 Bo Scaife .25 .60
❑ 104 Peerless Price .25 .60
❑ 105 Marques Colston .40 1.00
❑ 106 Reggie Bush .50 1.25
❑ 107 Brandon Jacobs .30 .75
❑ 108 Eli Manning .40 1.00
❑ 109 Leon Washington .30 .75
❑ 110 Kevan Barlow .30 .75
❑ 111 Randy Moss .40 1.00
❑ 112 Troy Polamalu .40 1.00
❑ 113 Willie Parker .30 .75
❑ 114 Santonio Holmes .30 .75
❑ 115 Philip Rivers .40 1.00
❑ 116 Shawne Merriman .30 .75
❑ 117 Alex Smith QB .40 1.00
❑ 118 Frank Gore .40 1.00
❑ 119 Vernon Davis .30 .75
❑ 120 Reggie Brown .25 .60
❑ 121 Ben Roethlisberger .60 1.50
❑ 122 Steven Jackson .40 1.00
❑ 123 Bruce Gradkowski .25 .60
❑ 124 Cadillac Williams .30 .75
❑ 125 Chris Cooley .30 .75
❑ 126 Michael Jenkins .30 .75
❑ 127 Demetrius Williams .25 .60
❑ 128 Roy Williams S .30 .75
❑ 129 Owen Daniels .25 .60
❑ 130 Hank Baskett .30 .75
❑ 131 Marcedes Lewis .25 .60
❑ 132 Brandon Marshall .30 .75
❑ 133 John Madsen .25 .60
❑ 134 Michael Huff .30 .75
❑ 135 Joe Klopfenstein .25 .60
❑ 136 Vincent Jackson .25 .60
❑ 137 Todd Heap .25 .60
❑ 138 Tarvaris Jackson .30 .75
❑ 139 Troy Williamson .25 .60
❑ 140 Ronald Curry .30 .75
❑ 141 Ahman Green .30 .75
❑ 142 LenDale White .30 .75
❑ 143 Vince Young .40 1.00
❑ 144 Thomas Jones .30 .75
❑ 145 Jamal Lewis .30 .75
❑ 146 Joe Horn .30 .75
❑ 147 Tatum Bell .25 .60
❑ 148 Willis McGahee .30 .75
❑ 149 Jason Campbell .30 .75
❑ 150 Ladell Betts .25 .60
❑ 151 John Broussard RC 2.00 5.00
❑ 152 Michael Allan RC 1.50 4.00
❑ 153 Tyler Thigpen RC 2.50 6.00
❑ 154 Chandler Williams RC 2.00 5.00
❑ 155 Eric Weddle RC 2.00 5.00
❑ 156 Derek Stanley RC 2.00 5.00
❑ 157 Justise Hairston RC 2.00 5.00
❑ 158 Johnathan Holland RC 2.00 5.00
❑ 159 Legedu Naanee RC 2.50 6.00
❑ 160 Courtney Taylor RC 2.00 5.00
❑ 161 David Irons RC 1.50 4.00
❑ 162 Joel Filani RC 2.00 5.00
❑ 163 H.B. Blades RC 2.00 5.00
❑ 164 Rufus Alexander RC 2.50 6.00
❑ 165 Roy Hall RC 2.50 6.00
❑ 166 Eric Frampton RC 2.00 5.00
❑ 167 Tim Shaw RC 2.00 5.00
❑ 168 Tymere Zimmerman RC 2.00 5.00
❑ 169 Jeff Rowe RC 2.00 5.00
❑ 170 Josh Gattis RC 1.50 4.00
❑ 171 Brandon Myles RC 2.00 5.00
❑ 172 Earl Everett RC 2.00 5.00
❑ 173 Steve Breaston RC 2.50 6.00
❑ 174 Ryan McBean RC 2.50 6.00
❑ 175 Scott Chandler RC 2.00 5.00
❑ 176 Chris Davis RC 2.00 5.00
❑ 177 Fred Bennett RC 1.50 4.00
❑ 178 Ryne Robinson RC 2.00 5.00
❑ 179 Zak DeOssie RC 2.00 5.00
❑ 180 Dwayne Wright RC 2.00 5.00
❑ 181 A.J. Davis RC 1.50 4.00
❑ 182 Ray McDonald RC 2.00 5.00
❑ 183 Daymeion Hughes RC 2.00 5.00
❑ 184 Michael Okwo RC 2.00 5.00
❑ 185 Aaron Rouse RC 2.50 6.00
❑ 186 Stewart Bradley RC 2.50 6.00
❑ 187 Jonathan Wade RC 2.00 5.00
❑ 188 Charles Johnson RC 1.50 4.00
❑ 189 Demarcus Tank Tyler RC 2.00 5.00
❑ 190 Mike Walker RC 2.50 6.00
❑ 191 James Jones RC 2.50 6.00
❑ 192 Matt Spaeth RC 2.50 6.00
❑ 193 Laurent Robinson RC 2.50 6.00
❑ 194 Jacoby Jones RC 2.50 6.00
❑ 195 Marcus McCauley RC 2.00 5.00
❑ 196 Buster Davis RC 2.00 5.00
❑ 197 Quentin Moses RC 2.00 5.00
❑ 198 Sabby Piscitelli RC 2.50 6.00
❑ 199 Dan Bazuin RC 2.00 5.00
❑ 200 Ikaika Alama-Francis RC 2.50 6.00
❑ 201 Victor Abiamiri RC 2.50 6.00
❑ 202 Tim Crowder RC 2.50 6.00
❑ 203 Josh Wilson RC 2.00 5.00
❑ 204 Eric Wright RC 2.50 6.00
❑ 205 David Harris RC 2.00 5.00
❑ 206 LaMarr Woodley RC 2.50 6.00
❑ 207 Chris Houston RC 2.00 5.00
❑ 208 Zach Miller RC 2.50 6.00
❑ 209 Aaron Fairooz RC 2.00 5.00
❑ 210 Alan Branch RC 2.00 5.00
❑ 211 Anthony Spencer RC 2.50 6.00
❑ 212 Jon Beason RC 2.50 6.00
❑ 213 Brandon Meriweather RC 2.50 6.00
❑ 214 Reggie Nelson RC 2.00 5.00
❑ 215 Aaron Ross RC 2.50 6.00
❑ 216 Michael Griffin RC 2.50 6.00
❑ 217 Ronnie McGill RC 2.00 5.00
❑ 218 Jarvis Moss RC 2.50 6.00
❑ 219 Darrelle Revis RC 3.00 8.00
❑ 220 Lawrence Timmons RC 2.50 6.00
❑ 221 Adam Carriker RC 2.00 5.00
❑ 222 Amobi Okoye RC 2.50 6.00
❑ 223 Jamaal Anderson RC 2.00 5.00
❑ 224 Syvelle Newton RC 2.00 5.00
❑ 225 Levi Brown RC 2.50 6.00
❑ 226 Chansi Stuckey AU/499 RC 6.00 15.00
❑ 227 Nate Ilaoa AU/999 RC 5.00 12.00
❑ 228 Brandon Siler AU/198 RC 5.00 12.00
❑ 229 Jason Snelling AU/999 RC 4.00 10.00
❑ 230 Kenneth Darby AU/999 RC 5.00 12.00
❑ 231 A.Bradshaw AU/999 RC 12.00 30.00
❑ 232 Thomas Clayton AU/763 RC 4.00 10.00

❑ 233 D.Baker AU/499 RC UER 5.00 12.00
❑ 234 Ben Patrick AU/849 RC 4.00 10.00
❑ 235 Jordan Kent AU/999 RC 4.00 10.00
❑ 236 Jordan Palmer AU/299 RC 6.00 15.00
❑ 237 Chris Leak AU/299 RC 5.00 12.00
❑ 238 Jon Cornish AU/876 RC 4.00 10.00
❑ 239 J.Zabransky AU/299 RC 6.00 15.00
❑ 240 R.McKnight AU/999 RC 4.00 10.00
❑ 241 Selvin Young AU/999 RC 8.00 20.00
❑ 242 Gary Russell AU/981 RC 4.00 10.00
❑ 243 Jerard Rabb AU/999 RC 4.00 10.00
❑ 244 J.Cornelius AU/581 RC 5.00 12.00
❑ 245 A.Coleman AU/781 RC 4.00 10.00
❑ 246 Danny Ware AU/999 RC 5.00 12.00
❑ 247 David Ball AU/999 RC 3.00 8.00
❑ 248 D'Juan Woods AU/456 RC 5.00 12.00
❑ 249 S.Steptoe AU/676 RC 4.00 10.00
❑ 250 Jarrett Hicks AU/999 RC 4.00 10.00
❑ 251 T.Edwards/140 AU RC 30.00 80.00
❑ 252 M.Lynch/100 AU RC 50.00 100.00
❑ 253 Chris Henry/105 AU RC 15.00 40.00
❑ 254 Paul Williams/200 AU RC 15.00 40.00
❑ 255 Sidney Rice/100 AU RC 40.00 100.00
❑ 256 A.Peterson/120 AU RC 175.00 350.00
❑ 257 Drew Stanton/140 AU RC 15.00 40.00
❑ 258 C.Johnson/105 AU RC 75.00 150.00
❑ 259 Yamon Figurs/150 AU RC 12.00 30.00
❑ 260 Troy Smith/100 AU RC 25.00 60.00
❑ 261 Brian Leonard/210 AU RC 15.00 40.00
❑ 262 Greg Olsen/125 AU RC 25.00 60.00
❑ 263 Kenny Irons/100 AU RC 20.00 50.00
❑ 264 Joe Thomas/120 AU RC 20.00 50.00
❑ 265 Brady Quinn/125 AU RC 50.00 120.00
❑ 266 B.Jackson/140 AU RC 20.00 50.00
❑ 267 Steve Smith/150 AU RC 40.00 80.00
❑ 268 Dwayne Jarrett/140 AU RC 20.00 50.00
❑ 269 Ted Ginn/100 AU RC 30.00 80.00
❑ 270 John Beck/120 AU RC 20.00 50.00
❑ 271 Lorenzo Booker/150 AU RC 20.0050.00
❑ 272 Antonio Pittman/105 AU RC 20.0050.00
❑ 273 R.Meachem/140 AU RC 20.00 50.00
❑ 274 Dwayne Bowe/100 AU RC 30.00 80.00
❑ 275 A.Gonzalez/160 AU RC 25.00 60.00
❑ 276 J.Russell/140 AU RC 40.00 100.00
❑ 277 Michael Bush/120 AU RC 20.00 50.00
❑ 278 J.Lee Higgins/175 AU RC 20.00 50.00
❑ 279 Kevin Kolb/100 AU RC 30.00 80.00
❑ 280 Gaines Adams/150 AU RC 20.00 50.00
❑ 281 Patrick Willis/150 AU RC 30.00 80.00
❑ 282 Jason Hill/120 AU RC 20.00 50.00
❑ 283 I.Stanback/200 AU RC 20.00 50.00
❑ 284 Kolby Smith/125 AU RC 20.00 50.00
❑ 285 Leon Hall/120 AU RC 20.00 50.00
❑ 286 Darius Walker/180 AU RC 15.00 40.00
❑ 287 D.Clowney/175 AU RC 20.00 50.00
❑ 288 LaRon Landry/150 AU RC 25.00 60.00
❑ 289 Paul Posluszny/180 AU RC 25.0060.00
❑ 290 Garrett Wolfe/125 AU RC 20.00 50.00
❑ 291 Tony Hunt/120 AU RC EXCH 20.00 50.00
❑ 292 Craig Davis/150 AU RC EXCH 20.00 50.00
❑ 293 D.Wynn/120 AU RC 20.00 50.00
❑ 294 Aundrae Allison/175 AU RC 15.0040.00

2008 Donruss Threads

❑ COMP.SET w/o RC's (150) 10.00 25.00
❑ 1 Anquan Boldin .25 .60
❑ 2 Larry Fitzgerald .30 .75
❑ 3 Warrick Dunn .25 .60
❑ 4 Derrick Mason .20 .50
❑ 5 Steve Smith .25 .60
❑ 6 Brian Urlacher .30 .75
❑ 7 Chad Johnson .25 .60
❑ 8 Terrell Owens .30 .75
❑ 9 Tony Gonzalez .25 .60
❑ 10 Rex Grossman .25 .60
❑ 11 Torry Holt .25 .60
❑ 12 Isaac Bruce .25 .60
❑ 13 Jeff Garcia .25 .60
❑ 14 Santana Moss .20 .50
❑ 15 LaDainian Tomlinson .40 1.00
❑ 16 Matt Hasselbeck .25 .60
❑ 17 Julius Jones .25 .60
❑ 18 Earnest Graham .20 .50
❑ 19 Joey Galloway .25 .60
❑ 20 Ike Hilliard .20 .50
❑ 21 Vince Young .25 .60
❑ 22 Jason Taylor .25 .60
❑ 23 Tom Brady .50 1.25
❑ 24 Randy Moss .30 .75
❑ 25 Donte Stallworth .25 .60
❑ 26 Deuce McAllister .25 .60
❑ 27 Eli Manning .30 .75
❑ 28 Michael Strahan .25 .60
❑ 29 Thomas Jones .25 .60
❑ 30 Laveranues Coles .25 .60
❑ 31 Jerry Porter .25 .60
❑ 32 Correll Buckhalter .25 .60
❑ 33 Donovan McNabb .30 .75
❑ 34 Hines Ward .25 .60
❑ 35 Tony Scheffler .20 .50
❑ 36 Jason Witten .30 .75
❑ 37 DeMarcus Ware .25 .60
❑ 38 Jay Cutler .30 .75
❑ 39 Brandon Marshall .25 .60
❑ 40 Brandon Stokley .25 .60
❑ 41 Selvin Young .20 .50
❑ 42 Jon Kitna .25 .60
❑ 43 Roy Williams WR .25 .60
❑ 44 Shaun McDonald .20 .50
❑ 45 Calvin Johnson .30 .75
❑ 46 Aaron Rodgers .30 .75
❑ 47 Ryan Grant .30 .75
❑ 48 Donald Driver .25 .60
❑ 49 Greg Jennings .25 .60
❑ 50 James Jones .20 .50
❑ 51 Matt Schaub .25 .60
❑ 52 Owen Daniels .20 .50
❑ 53 Andre Johnson .25 .60
❑ 54 Kevin Walter .25 .60
❑ 55 Ahman Green .25 .60
❑ 56 Peyton Manning .50 1.25
❑ 57 Marvin Harrison .30 .75
❑ 58 Joseph Addai .30 .75
❑ 59 Reggie Wayne .25 .60
❑ 60 Dallas Clark .25 .60
❑ 61 David Garrard .25 .60
❑ 62 Fred Taylor .25 .60
❑ 63 Maurice Jones-Drew .25 .60
❑ 64 Reggie Williams .25 .60
❑ 65 Larry Johnson .25 .60
❑ 66 Kolby Smith .20 .50
❑ 67 Dwayne Bowe .25 .60
❑ 68 Ted Ginn Jr. .25 .60
❑ 69 Ronnie Brown .25 .60
❑ 70 John Beck .20 .50
❑ 71 Tarvaris Jackson .25 .60
❑ 72 Adrian Peterson .60 1.50
❑ 73 Chester Taylor .20 .50
❑ 74 Sidney Rice .30 .75
❑ 75 Wes Welker .30 .75
❑ 76 Laurence Maroney .25 .60
❑ 77 Drew Brees .30 .75
❑ 78 Reggie Bush .30 .75
❑ 79 Marques Colston .25 .60
❑ 80 Brandon Jacobs .25 .60
❑ 81 Plaxico Burress .25 .60
❑ 82 Derrick Ward .25 .60
❑ 83 Kellen Clemens .25 .60
❑ 84 Leon Washington .25 .60
❑ 85 Jerricho Cotchery .20 .50
❑ 86 Matt Leinart .30 .75
❑ 87 Edgerrin James .25 .60
❑ 88 JaMarcus Russell .30 .75
❑ 89 Justin Fargas .20 .50
❑ 90 Alge Crumpler .25 .60
❑ 91 Jerious Norwood .25 .60
❑ 92 Roddy White .25 .60
❑ 93 Ronald Curry .25 .60
❑ 94 Willis McGahee .25 .60
❑ 95 Mark Clayton .25 .60
❑ 96 Brian Westbrook .25 .60
❑ 97 Kevin Curtis .20 .50
❑ 98 Ed Reed .25 .60
❑ 99 Ray Lewis .30 .75
❑ 100 Reggie Brown .20 .50
❑ 101 Trent Edwards .30 .75
❑ 102 Marshawn Lynch .30 .75
❑ 103 Ben Roethlisberger .50 1.25
❑ 104 Willie Parker .25 .60
❑ 105 Lee Evans .25 .60
❑ 106 Josh Reed .20 .50
❑ 107 Santonio Holmes .25 .60
❑ 108 Jake Delhomme .25 .60
❑ 109 DeShaun Foster .25 .60
❑ 110 Heath Miller .20 .50
❑ 111 Philip Rivers .30 .75
❑ 112 DeAngelo Williams .25 .60
❑ 113 Drew Carter .20 .50
❑ 114 Adrian Peterson Bears .20 .50
❑ 115 Antonio Gates .25 .60
❑ 116 Shawne Merriman .25 .60
❑ 117 Bernard Berrian .25 .60
❑ 118 Cedric Benson .25 .60
❑ 119 Vincent Jackson .20 .50
❑ 120 Alex Smith QB .25 .60
❑ 121 Devin Hester .30 .75
❑ 122 Carson Palmer .30 .75
❑ 123 Frank Gore .25 .60
❑ 124 T.J. Houshmandzadeh .25 .60
❑ 125 Rudi Johnson .25 .60
❑ 126 Vernon Davis .20 .50
❑ 127 Patrick Willis .25 .60
❑ 128 Kenny Watson .20 .50
❑ 129 Derek Anderson .25 .60
❑ 130 Jamal Lewis .25 .60
❑ 131 Kellen Winslow .25 .60
❑ 132 Maurice Morris .20 .50
❑ 133 Nate Burleson .20 .50
❑ 134 Braylon Edwards .25 .60
❑ 135 Josh Cribbs .30 .75
❑ 136 Deion Branch .25 .60
❑ 137 Marc Bulger .25 .60
❑ 138 Tony Romo .50 1.25
❑ 139 Marion Barber .30 .75
❑ 140 Steven Jackson .30 .75
❑ 141 Randy McMichael .20 .50
❑ 142 Cadillac Williams .25 .60
❑ 143 LenDale White .25 .60
❑ 144 Chris Brown .20 .50
❑ 145 Roydell Williams .20 .50
❑ 146 Justin Gage .20 .50
❑ 147 Jason Campbell .25 .60
❑ 148 Clinton Portis .25 .60
❑ 149 Chris Cooley .25 .60
❑ 150 Ladell Betts .20 .50
❑ 151 A.Arrington AU/299 RC 4.00 10.00
❑ 152 Alex Brink/999 RC 2.50 6.00
❑ 153 Ali Highsmith AU/999 RC 3.00 8.00
❑ 154 Anthony Alridge AU/999 RC 4.00 10.00
❑ 155 Antoine Cason/999 RC 2.50 6.00
❑ 156 Antwaun Molden/999 RC 2.00 5.00
❑ 157 Aqib Talib/999 RC 2.50 6.00
❑ 158 Arman Shields/999 RC 2.00 5.00
❑ 159 Brad Cottam AU/299 RC 5.00 12.00
❑ 160 Brandon Flowers/999 RC 2.50 6.00
❑ 161 Bruce Davis/999 RC 2.50 6.00
❑ 162 Calais Campbell AU/299 RC 4.00 10.00
❑ 163 Caleb Campbell AU/299 RC 6.00 15.00
❑ 164 Charles Godfrey/999 RC 2.00 5.00
❑ 165 Ch.Washington AU/299 RC 4.00 10.00
❑ 166 Chevis Jackson AU/299 RC 4.00 10.00
❑ 167 Cory Boyd AU/299 RC 4.00 10.00
❑ 168 Craig Steltz AU/299 RC 4.00 10.00
❑ 169 Craig Stevens/999 RC 2.00 5.00
❑ 170 Curtis Lofton AU/299 RC 5.00 12.00
❑ 171 DaJuan Morgan/999 RC 2.00 5.00
❑ 172 Dantrell Savage AU/999 RC 5.00 12.00
❑ 173 Darius Reynaud AU/999 RC 4.00 10.00
❑ 174 Darrell Strong AU/999 RC 4.00 10.00
❑ 175 Davone Bess AU/999 RC 6.00 15.00
❑ 176 Derek Fine/999 RC 2.00 5.00
❑ 177 Derrick Harvey/999 RC 2.00 5.00
❑ 178 DJ Hall AU/999 RC 4.00 10.00
❑ 179 D.Rodgers-Cromartie/999 RC 2.50 6.00
❑ 180 Erin Henderson AU/999 RC 4.00 10.00
❑ 181 E.Wheelwright AU/755 RC 4.00 10.00
❑ 182 Fred Davis/999 RC 2.50 6.00
❑ 183 Gary Barnidge/999 RC 2.00 5.00
❑ 184 Joe Jon Finley/999 RC 2.00 5.00
❑ 185 Jacob Hester AU/299 RC 5.00 12.00
❑ 186 Jacob Tamme/999 RC 2.50 6.00
❑ 187 Jalen Parmele/999 RC 2.00 5.00
❑ 188 Jamar Adams AU/775 RC 4.00 10.00
❑ 189 Jason Rivers AU/999 RC 5.00 12.00

❑ 190 Jaymar Johnson/999 RC 2.00 5.00
❑ 191 Jed Collins AU/999 RC 4.00 10.00
❑ 192 Jermichael Finley/999 RC 2.50 6.00
❑ 193 Jerod Mayo/999 RC 3.00 8.00
❑ 194 John Carlson/999 RC 2.50 6.00
❑ 195 Jonathan Hefney AU/928 RC 4.00 10.00
❑ 196 Jordon Dizon AU/299 RC 6.00 15.00
❑ 197 Josh Morgan AU/499 RC 8.00 20.00
❑ 198 Justin Forsett AU/299 RC 5.00 12.00
❑ 199 Justin Harper/999 RC 2.00 5.00
❑ 200 Kalvin McRae AU/999 RC 4.00 10.00
❑ 201 Keenan Burton/999 RC 2.00 5.00
❑ 202 Kellen Davis AU/299 RC 3.00 8.00
❑ 203 Kenneth Moore/999 RC 2.00 5.00
❑ 204 Kentwan Balmer/999 RC 2.00 5.00
❑ 205 Kevin Robinson AU/299 RC 4.00 10.00
❑ 206 Lawrence Jackson/999 RC 2.00 5.00
❑ 207 Leodis McKelvin/999 RC 2.50 6.00
❑ 208 Marcus Henry/999 RC 2.00 5.00
❑ 209 Marcus Monk AU/350 RC 5.00 12.00
❑ 210 Marcus Smith AU/299 RC 4.00 10.00
❑ 211 M.Thomas AU/299 RC EXCH 4.00 10.00
❑ 212 Mario Urrutia/999 RC 2.00 5.00
❑ 213 Mark Bradford AU/999 RC 4.00 10.00
❑ 214 Martellus Bennett/999 RC 2.50 6.00
❑ 215 Martin Rucker AU/299 RC 4.00 10.00
❑ 216 Matt Sherry/999 RC 2.00 5.00
❑ 217 Owen Schmitt AU/199 RC 5.00 12.00
❑ 218 Pat Sims/999 RC 2.00 5.00
❑ 219 Patrick Lee/999 RC 2.50 6.00
❑ 220 Paul Hubbard AU/699 RC 4.00 10.00
❑ 221 Paul Smith AU/999 RC 5.00 12.00
❑ 222 Peyton Hillis AU/299 RC 5.00 12.00
❑ 223 Phillip Merling/999 RC 2.00 5.00
❑ 224 Philip Wheeler/999 RC 2.50 6.00
❑ 225 Pierre Garcon/999 RC 4.00 10.00
❑ 226 Quentin Groves AU/299 RC 4.00 10.00
❑ 227 Reggie Smith/999 RC 2.00 5.00
❑ 228 R.Grice-Mullen AU/999 RC 5.00 12.00
❑ 229 Ryan Torain AU/199 RC 8.00 20.00
❑ 230 Sam Keller AU/999 RC 5.00 12.00
❑ 231 Sedrick Ellis/999 RC 2.50 6.00
❑ 232 Shawn Crable AU/299 RC 6.00 15.00
❑ 233 A.Bowman AU/999 RC 4.00 10.00
❑ 234 Simeon Castille AU/805 RC 4.00 10.00
❑ 235 Steve Johnson/999 RC 2.50 6.00
❑ 236 Tavares Gooden/999 RC 2.00 5.00
❑ 237 Terrell Thomas/999 RC 2.00 5.00
❑ 238 Terrence Wheatley/999 RC 2.00 5.00
❑ 239 Robert Killebrew AU/830 RC 4.00 10.00
❑ 240 Thomas Brown/999 RC 2.50 6.00
❑ 241 Tim Hightower AU/299 RC 15.00 30.00
❑ 242 Tom Zbikowski/999 RC 2.50 6.00
❑ 243 Tom Santi/999 RC 2.00 5.00
❑ 244 Bernard Morris AU/999 RC 4.00 10.00
❑ 245 Tracy Porter AU/299 RC 15.00 30.00
❑ 246 Vernon Gholston/999 RC 2.50 6.00
❑ 247 Will Franklin AU/199 RC 4.00 10.00
❑ 248 Xavier Adibi/999 RC 2.00 5.00
❑ 249 Xavier Omon/999 RC 2.50 6.00
❑ 250 Zackary Bowman/999 RC 2.00 5.00
❑ 251 Brian Brohm AU/100 RC 20.00 50.00
❑ 252 Chad Henne AU/100 RC 40.00 80.00
❑ 253 Chris Long AU/100 RC 20.00 50.00
❑ 254 Donnie Avery AU/100 RC 25.00 60.00
❑ 255 Eddie Royal AU/100 RC 30.00 60.00
❑ 256 Felix Jones AU/100 RC 40.00 100.00
❑ 257 James Hardy AU/100 RC 20.00 50.00
❑ 258 J.David Booty AU/100 RC 20.00 50.00
❑ 259 K.Smith AU/100 RC EXCH 30.00 60.00
❑ 260 Malcolm Kelly AU/100 RC 20.00 50.00
❑ 261 Matt Forte AU/100 RC 50.00 100.00
❑ 262 Matt Ryan AU/100 RC 100.00 200.00
❑ 263 Ray Rice AU/100 RC 40.00 80.00
❑ 264 DeS.Jackson AU/105 RC 40.00 80.00
❑ 265 Andre Caldwell AU/120 RC 12.00 30.00
❑ 266 D.McFadden AU/120 RC 40.00 100.00
❑ 267 Dustin Keller AU/120 RC 20.00 50.00
❑ 268 Early Doucet AU/120 RC 15.00 40.00
❑ 269 Glenn Dorsey AU/120 RC 30.00 60.00
❑ 270 Jake Long AU/120 RC 20.00 50.00
❑ 271 Joe Flacco AU/120 RC 75.00 150.00
❑ 272 Kevin O'Connell AU/120 RC 20.00 50.00
❑ 273 Steve Slaton AU/120 RC 25.00 60.00
❑ 274 L.Sweed AU/125 RC EXCH 20.00 50.00
❑ 275 Earl Bennett AU/140 RC 20.00 50.00
❑ 276 Chris Johnson AU/140 RC 60.00 120.00
❑ 277 Dexter Jackson AU/140 RC 20.00 50.00
❑ 278 Harry Douglas AU/140 RC 15.00 40.00
❑ 279 Jamaal Charles AU/140 RC 30.00 60.00
❑ 280 Jerome Simpson AU/140 RC 20.00 50.00
❑ 281 J.Stewart AU/140 RC 40.00 80.00
❑ 282 Devin Thomas AU/150 RC 20.00 50.00
❑ 283 Jordy Nelson AU/150 RC 25.00 60.00
❑ 284 M.Manningham AU/150 RC 30.00 60.00
❑ 285 R.Mendenhall AU/150 RC 40.00 80.00
❑ 286 Dennis Dixon AU/100 RC 20.00 50.00
❑ 287 Erik Ainge AU/100 RC EXCH 20.00 50.00
❑ 288 Mike Hart AU/100 RC 20.00 50.00
❑ 289 M.Jenkins AU/105 RC EXCH 20.00 50.00
❑ 290 Dan Connor AU/120 RC 20.00 50.00
❑ 291 Dorien Bryant AU/120 RC 15.00 40.00
❑ 292 Keith Rivers AU/120 RC 15.00 40.00
❑ 293 K.Phillips AU/120 RC EXCH 20.00 50.00
❑ 294 Matt Flynn AU/125 RC 20.00 50.00
❑ 295 Lavelle Hawkins AU/140 RC 15.00 40.00
❑ 296 Allen Patrick AU/140 RC 12.00 30.00
❑ 297 Andre Woodson AU/140 RC 15.00 40.00
❑ 298 Colt Brennan AU/140 RC 30.00 60.00
❑ 299 Josh Johnson AU/140 RC 15.00 40.00
❑ 300 Tashard Choice AU/150 RC 30.00 60.00

2009 Donruss Threads

❑ COMP.SET w/o RC's (100) 8.00 20.00
❑ 1 Kurt Warner .30 .75
❑ 2 Larry Fitzgerald .30 .75
❑ 3 Tim Hightower .25 .60
❑ 4 Matt Ryan .30 .75
❑ 5 Michael Turner .25 .60
❑ 6 Roddy White .25 .60
❑ 7 Derrick Mason .20 .50
❑ 8 Joe Flacco .30 .75
❑ 9 Willis McGahee .25 .60
❑ 10 Lee Evans .25 .60
❑ 11 Marshawn Lynch .25 .60
❑ 12 Terrell Owens .30 .75
❑ 13 DeAngelo Williams .30 .75
❑ 14 Jake Delhomme .25 .60
❑ 15 Jonathan Stewart .25 .60
❑ 16 Steve Smith .25 .60
❑ 17 Greg Olsen .20 .50
❑ 18 Kyle Orton .25 .60
❑ 19 Matt Forte .30 .75
❑ 20 Carson Palmer .30 .75
❑ 21 Cedric Benson .25 .60
❑ 22 Chad Ochocinco .25 .60
❑ 23 Brady Quinn .25 .60
❑ 24 Braylon Edwards .25 .60
❑ 25 Jamal Lewis .25 .60
❑ 26 Marion Barber .30 .75
❑ 27 Roy Williams WR .25 .60
❑ 28 Tony Romo .50 1.25
❑ 29 Brandon Marshall .25 .60
❑ 30 Jay Cutler .30 .75
❑ 31 Correll Buckhalter .20 .50
❑ 32 Calvin Johnson .30 .75
❑ 33 Daunte Culpepper .25 .60
❑ 34 Kevin Smith .25 .60
❑ 35 Aaron Rodgers .30 .75
❑ 36 Greg Jennings .30 .75
❑ 37 Ryan Grant .25 .60
❑ 38 Andre Johnson .25 .60
❑ 39 Matt Schaub .25 .60
❑ 40 Steve Slaton .25 .60
❑ 41 Anthony Gonzalez .25 .60
❑ 42 Joseph Addai .30 .75
❑ 43 Peyton Manning .50 1.25
❑ 44 Reggie Wayne .25 .60
❑ 45 David Garrard .25 .60
❑ 46 Marcedes Lewis .20 .50
❑ 47 Maurice Jones-Drew .25 .60
❑ 48 Dwayne Bowe .25 .60
❑ 49 Larry Johnson .25 .60
❑ 50 Matt Cassel .25 .60
❑ 51 Tony Gonzalez .25 .60
❑ 52 Chad Pennington .25 .60
❑ 53 Ricky Williams .25 .60
❑ 54 Ronnie Brown .25 .60
❑ 55 Adrian Peterson .60 1.50
❑ 56 Bernard Berrian .25 .60
❑ 57 Visanthe Shiancoe .20 .50
❑ 58 Laurence Maroney .25 .60
❑ 59 Tom Brady .50 1.25
❑ 60 Wes Welker .30 .75
❑ 61 Randy Moss .30 .75
❑ 62 Drew Brees .30 .75
❑ 63 Marques Colston .25 .60
❑ 64 Reggie Bush .30 .75
❑ 65 Brandon Jacobs .25 .60
❑ 66 Eli Manning .30 .75
❑ 67 Kevin Boss .20 .50
❑ 68 Thomas Jones .25 .60
❑ 69 Jerricho Cotchery .20 .50
❑ 70 Leon Washington .25 .60
❑ 71 Darren McFadden .30 .75
❑ 72 JaMarcus Russell .25 .60
❑ 73 Zach Miller .20 .50
❑ 74 Brian Westbrook .25 .60
❑ 75 DeSean Jackson .25 .60
❑ 76 Donovan McNabb .30 .75
❑ 77 Ben Roethlisberger .50 1.25
❑ 78 Santonio Holmes .25 .60
❑ 79 Willie Parker .25 .60
❑ 80 LaDainian Tomlinson .30 .75
❑ 81 Philip Rivers .30 .75
❑ 82 Vincent Jackson .25 .60
❑ 83 Frank Gore .25 .60
❑ 84 Shaun Hill .25 .60
❑ 85 Vernon Davis .20 .50
❑ 86 Julius Jones .25 .60
❑ 87 Matt Hasselbeck .25 .60
❑ 88 T.J. Houshmandzadeh .25 .60
❑ 89 Marc Bulger .25 .60
❑ 90 Steven Jackson .25 .60
❑ 91 Torry Holt .25 .60
❑ 92 Antonio Bryant .25 .60
❑ 93 Derrick Ward .25 .60
❑ 94 Kellen Winslow Jr. .25 .60
❑ 95 Chris Johnson .30 .75
❑ 96 Kerry Collins .25 .60
❑ 97 LenDale White .25 .60
❑ 98 Chris Cooley .25 .60
❑ 99 Clinton Portis .25 .60
❑ 100 Jason Campbell .25 .60
❑ 101 Aaron Brown RC 2.50 6.00
❑ 102 Aaron Kelly AU/199 RC 4.00 10.00
❑ 103 Aaron Maybin RC 2.50 6.00
❑ 104 Alphonso Smith RC 2.00 5.00
❑ 105 Andre Smith RC 2.50 6.00
❑ 106 Anthony Hill RC 1.50 4.00
❑ 107 Arian Foster RC 2.50 6.00
❑ 108 Asher Allen RC 2.00 5.00
❑ 109 Austin Collie AU/149 RC 15.00 30.00
❑ 110 Bernard Scott RC 2.50 6.00
❑ 111 Bradley Fletcher RC 2.00 5.00
❑ 112 Brandon Gibson AU/199 RC 5.00 12.00
❑ 113 Brian Hartline RC 2.50 6.00
❑ 114 Brooks Foster AU/199 RC 4.00 10.00
❑ 115 Cameron Morrah AU/499 RC 3.00 8.00
❑ 116 Chase Daniel RC 2.50 6.00
❑ 117 Chip Vaughn RC 1.50 4.00
❑ 118 Chris Ogbonnaya RC 2.50 6.00
❑ 119 Chris Owens RC 2.00 5.00
❑ 120 Clay Matthews AU/199 RC 8.00 20.00
❑ 121 Clint Sintim AU/99 RC 6.00 15.00
❑ 122 Cody Brown RC 2.00 5.00
❑ 123 Connor Barwin RC 2.00 5.00
❑ 124 Cornelius Ingram AU/199 RC 3.00 8.00
❑ 125 Curtis Painter RC 2.50 6.00
❑ 126 Darcel McBath RC 2.50 6.00
❑ 127 Darius Butler RC 2.50 6.00
❑ 128 Darius Passmore AU/199 RC 4.00 10.00
❑ 129 David Bruton RC 2.00 5.00
❑ 130 David Johnson RC 2.00 5.00
❑ 131 DeAndre Levy RC 2.50 6.00
❑ 132 D.Byrd AU/499 RC EXCH 4.00 10.00
❑ 133 Devin Moore AU/249 RC 4.00 10.00
❑ 134 Davon Drew RC 2.00 5.00
❑ 135 D.Edison AU/199 RC 3.00 8.00
❑ 136 Eddie Williams RC 2.00 5.00
❑ 137 Eugene Monroe RC 2.00 5.00
❑ 138 Evander Hood RC 4.00 10.00
❑ 139 Gartrell Johnson RC 2.00 5.00
❑ 140 Gerald McRath RC 2.00 5.00
❑ 141 Glover Quin RC 2.00 5.00
❑ 142 Graham Harrell RC 2.50 6.00
❑ 143 Hunter Cantwell RC 2.50 6.00
❑ 144 Ian Johnson RC 2.50 6.00
❑ 145 Jairus Byrd RC 3.00 8.00
❑ 146 James Casey AU/199 RC 4.00 10.00
❑ 147 James Davis RC 2.50 6.00
❑ 148 James Laurinaitis AU/199 RC 6.0015.00
❑ 149 Jarett Dillard AU/499 RC 5.00 12.00
❑ 150 Jason Phillips RC 2.00 5.00
❑ 151 Jason Williams RC 2.50 6.00
❑ 152 Jasper Brinkley RC 2.00 5.00
❑ 153 Javarris Williams RC 2.00 5.00
❑ 154 Jeremy Childs RC 2.00 5.00

❑ 155 Jerraud Powers RC 2.00 5.00
❑ 156 John Phillips RC 2.50 6.00
❑ 157 Johnny Knox AU/199 RC 15.00 30.00
❑ 158 Kaluka Maiava RC 2.50 6.00
❑ 159 Keenan Lewis RC 2.50 6.00
❑ 160 Keith Null RC 2.50 6.00
❑ 161 Kenny McKinley AU/199 RC 5.00 12.00
❑ 162 Kevin Barnes RC 2.00 5.00
❑ 163 Kevin Huber RC 1.50 4.00
❑ 164 Kevin Ogletree AU/199 RC 8.00 20.00
❑ 165 Lardarius Webb RC 2.50 6.00
❑ 166 Larry English AU/199 RC 5.00 12.00
❑ 167 Louis Delmas RC 2.50 6.00
❑ 168 Louis Murphy AU/299 RC 8.00 20.00
❑ 169 Manuel Johnson RC 2.00 5.00
❑ 170 Marcus Freeman RC 2.50 6.00
❑ 171 Marko Mitchell RC 2.00 5.00
❑ 172 Bear Pascoe RC 2.50 6.00
❑ 173 Michael Mitchell RC 2.50 6.00
❑ 174 Mike Goodson AU/399 RC 5.00 12.00
❑ 175 Nathan Brown AU/149 RC 5.00 12.00
❑ 176 Nic Harris RC 2.00 5.00
❑ 177 P.J. Hill AU/199 RC 4.00 10.00
❑ 178 Patrick Chung RC 2.50 6.00
❑ 179 Peria Jerry RC 2.00 5.00
❑ 180 Quan Cosby AU/149 RC 5.00 12.00
❑ 181 Quinn Johnson AU/149 RC 5.00 12.00
❑ 182 Quinten Lawrence RC 2.00 5.00
❑ 183 Rashad Johnson RC 2.00 5.00
❑ 184 Richard Quinn RC 2.00 5.00
❑ 185 Robert Ayers RC 2.50 6.00
❑ 186 Ryan Mouton RC 2.00 5.00
❑ 187 Sammie Stroughter RC 2.50 6.00
❑ 188 Scott McKillop RC 2.00 5.00
❑ 189 Sean Smith RC 2.50 6.00
❑ 190 Sen'Derrick Marks RC 1.50 4.00
❑ 191 S.Nelson AU/149 RC EXCH 5.00 12.00
❑ 192 Sherrod Martin RC 2.00 5.00
❑ 193 Stanley Arnoux RC 2.00 5.00
❑ 194 Tiquan Underwood RC 2.00 5.00
❑ 195 Tony Fiammetta AU/199 RC 4.00 10.00
❑ 196 Travis Beckum AU/249 RC 4.00 10.00
❑ 197 Tyrell Sutton AU/499 RC 6.00 15.00
❑ 198 Tyrone McKenzie RC 2.00 5.00
❑ 199 Victor Butler RC 2.00 5.00
❑ 200 William Moore RC 2.00 5.00
❑ 201 Aaron Curry AU/275 RC 12.00 30.00
❑ 202 Andre Brown AU/175 RC 8.00 20.00
❑ 203 B.J. Raji AU/392 RC 12.00 30.00
❑ 204 B.Pettigrew AU/180 RC 12.00 30.00
❑ 205 Brandon Tate AU/200 RC 8.00 20.00
❑ 206 Brian Cushing AU/280 RC 12.00 30.00
❑ 207 Brian Orakpo AU/258 RC 12.00 30.00
❑ 208 Brian Robiskie AU/200 RC 10.00 25.00
❑ 209 Cedric Peerman AU/385 RC 8.00 20.00
❑ 210 Chase Coffman AU/385 RC 8.00 20.00
❑ 211 Chris Wells AU/175 RC 30.00 80.00
❑ 212 D.Heyward-Bey AU/250 RC 15.00 40.00
❑ 213 Derrick Williams AU/200 RC 10.00 25.00
❑ 214 Donald Brown AU/175 RC 20.00 50.00
❑ 215 Everette Brown AU/275 RC 10.00 25.00
❑ 216 G.Coffee AU/270 RC EXCH 12.00 30.00
❑ 217 Hakeem Nicks AU/175 RC 20.00 50.00
❑ 218 Tyson Jackson AU/350 RC 10.00 25.00
❑ 219 Deon Butler AU/300 RC 10.00 25.00
❑ 220 Jared Cook AU/396 RC 8.00 20.00
❑ 221 Javon Ringer AU/180 RC 10.00 25.00
❑ 222 J.Johnson AU/175 RC 10.00 25.00
❑ 223 Jeremy Maclin AU/180 RC 20.00 50.00
❑ 224 J.Parker Wilson AU/180 RC 10.00 25.00
❑ 225 Josh Freeman AU/175 RC 20.00 50.00
❑ 226 Juaquin Iglesias AU/200 RC 10.00 25.00
❑ 227 K. Britt AU/175 RC EXCH 15.00 40.00
❑ 228 K.Moreno AU/180 RC 40.00 80.00
❑ 229 Kory Sheets AU/390 RC 8.00 20.00
❑ 230 LeSean McCoy AU/175 RC 20.00 50.00
❑ 231 Malcolm Jenkins AU/280 RC 10.00 25.00
❑ 232 Mark Sanchez AU/175 RC 75.00 150.00
❑ 233 M.Stafford AU/160 RC 50.00 120.00
❑ 234 M.Crabtree AU/160 RC 50.00 100.00
❑ 235 Jason Smith AU/250 RC 8.00 20.00
❑ 236 Mike Thomas AU/390 RC 10.00 25.00
❑ 237 Mike Wallace AU/350 RC 20.00 50.00
❑ 238 M.Massaquoi AU/180 RC 10.00 25.00
❑ 239 Nate Davis AU/125 RC 10.00 25.00
❑ 240 Pat White AU/125 RC 30.00 60.00
❑ 241 Patrick Turner AU/300 RC 8.00 20.00
❑ 242 Percy Harvin AU/180 RC 50.00 100.00
❑ 243 Ramses Barden AU/300 RC 8.00 20.00
❑ 244 R.Jennings AU/160 RC 10.00 25.00
❑ 245 Rey Maualuga AU/280 RC 15.00 40.00
❑ 246 Rhett Bomar AU/175 RC 8.00 20.00
❑ 247 Shonn Greene AU/180 RC 20.00 50.00
❑ 248 Stephen McGee AU/200 RC 10.00 25.00
❑ 249 T.Brandstater AU/385 RC 10.00 25.00
❑ 250 Vontae Davis AU/275 RC 10.00 25.00
❑ 251 Brett Favre 20.00 40.00

1992 Finest

❑ COMPLETE SET (45) 7.50 20.00
❑ 1 Neal Anderson .20 .50
❑ 2 Cornelius Bennett .20 .50
❑ 3 Marion Butts .10 .30
❑ 4 Anthony Carter .20 .50
❑ 5 Mike Croel .10 .30
❑ 6 John Elway 2.00 5.00
❑ 7 Jim Everett .20 .50
❑ 8 Ernest Givins .10 .30
❑ 9 Rodney Hampton .20 .50
❑ 10 Alvin Harper .10 .30
❑ 11 Michael Irvin .40 1.00
❑ 12 Rickey Jackson .10 .30
❑ 13 Seth Joyner .10 .30
❑ 14 James Lofton .20 .50
❑ 15 Ronnie Lott .20 .50
❑ 16 Eric Metcalf .20 .50
❑ 17 Chris Miller .20 .50
❑ 18 Art Monk .20 .50
❑ 19 Warren Moon .40 1.00
❑ 20 Rob Moore .20 .50
❑ 21 Anthony Munoz .20 .50
❑ 22 Christian Okoye .10 .30
❑ 23 Andre Rison .20 .50
❑ 24 Leonard Russell .10 .30
❑ 25 Mark Rypien .20 .50
❑ 26 Barry Sanders 2.00 5.00
❑ 27 Emmitt Smith 2.50 6.00
❑ 28 Pat Swilling .10 .30
❑ 29 John Taylor .20 .50
❑ 30 Derrick Thomas .40 1.00
❑ 31 Thurman Thomas .40 1.00
❑ 32 Reggie White .40 1.00
❑ 33 Rod Woodson .40 1.00
❑ 34 Edgar Bennett .20 .50
❑ 35 Terrell Buckley .10 .30
❑ 36 Keith Hamilton .20 .50
❑ 37 Amp Lee .10 .30
❑ 38 Ricardo McDonald .10 .30
❑ 39 Chris Mims .10 .30
❑ 40 Robert Porcher .40 1.00
❑ 41 Leon Searcy .10 .30
❑ 42 Siran Stacy .10 .30
❑ 43 Tommy Vardell .10 .30
❑ 44 Bob Whitfield .10 .30
❑ NNO Checklist .10 .30

1994 Finest

❑ COMPLETE SET (220) 15.00 40.00
❑ 1 Emmitt Smith 2.50 6.00
❑ 2 Calvin Williams .25 .60
❑ 3 Mark Collins .10 .30
❑ 4 Steve McMichael .25 .60
❑ 5 Jim Kelly .50 1.25
❑ 6 Michael Dean Perry .25 .60
❑ 7 Wayne Simmons .10 .30
❑ 8 Rocket Ismail .25 .60
❑ 9 Mark Rypien .10 .30
❑ 10 Brian Blades .25 .60
❑ 11 Barry Word .10 .30
❑ 12 Jerry Rice 1.50 4.00
❑ 13 Derrick Fenner .10 .30
❑ 14 Karl Mecklenburg .10 .30
❑ 15 Reggie Cobb .10 .30
❑ 16 Eric Swann .25 .60
❑ 17 Neil Smith .25 .60
❑ 18 Barry Foster .10 .30
❑ 19 Willie Roaf .10 .30
❑ 20 Troy Drayton .10 .30
❑ 21 Warren Moon .50 1.25
❑ 22 Richmond Webb .10 .30
❑ 23 Anthony Miller .25 .60
❑ 24 Chris Slade .10 .30
❑ 25 Mel Gray .10 .30
❑ 26 Ronnie Lott .25 .60
❑ 27 Andre Rison .25 .60
❑ 28 Jeff George .50 1.25
❑ 29 John Copeland .10 .30
❑ 30 Derrick Thomas .50 1.25
❑ 31 Sterling Sharpe .25 .60
❑ 32 Chris Doleman .10 .30
❑ 33 Monte Coleman .10 .30
❑ 34 Mark Bavaro .10 .30
❑ 35 Kevin Williams WR .25 .60
❑ 36 Eric Metcalf .25 .60
❑ 37 Brent Jones .25 .60
❑ 38 Steve Tasker .25 .60
❑ 39 Dave Meggett .10 .30
❑ 40 Howie Long .50 1.25
❑ 41 Rick Mirer .50 1.25
❑ 42 Jerome Bettis 1.50 4.00
❑ 43 Marion Butts .10 .30
❑ 44 Barry Sanders 2.50 6.00
❑ 45 Jason Elam .25 .60
❑ 46 Broderick Thomas .10 .30
❑ 47 Derek Brown RBK .10 .30
❑ 48 Lorenzo White .10 .30
❑ 49 Neil O'Donnell .50 1.25
❑ 50 Chris Burkett .10 .30
❑ 51 John Offerdahl .10 .30
❑ 52 Rohn Stark .10 .30
❑ 53 Neal Anderson .10 .30
❑ 54 Steve Beuerlein .25 .60
❑ 55 Bruce Armstrong .10 .30
❑ 56 Lincoln Kennedy .10 .30
❑ 57 Darrell Green .10 .30
❑ 58 Ricardo McDonald .10 .30
❑ 59 Chris Warren .25 .60
❑ 60 Mark Jackson .10 .30
❑ 61 Pepper Johnson .10 .30
❑ 62 Chris Spielman .25 .60
❑ 63 Marcus Allen .50 1.25
❑ 64 Jim Everett .25 .60
❑ 65 Greg Townsend .10 .30
❑ 66 Cris Carter .60 1.50
❑ 67 Don Beebe .10 .30
❑ 68 Reggie Langhorne .10 .30
❑ 69 Randall Cunningham .50 1.25
❑ 70 Johnny Holland .10 .30
❑ 71 Morten Andersen .10 .30
❑ 72 Leonard Marshall .10 .30
❑ 73 Keith Jackson .10 .30
❑ 74 Leslie O'Neal .10 .30
❑ 75 Hardy Nickerson .25 .60
❑ 76 Dan Williams .10 .30
❑ 77 Steve Young 1.25 3.00
❑ 78 Deon Figures .10 .30
❑ 79 Michael Irvin .50 1.25
❑ 80 Luis Sharpe .10 .30
❑ 81 Andre Tippett .10 .30
❑ 82 Ricky Sanders .10 .30
❑ 83 Erric Pegram .10 .30
❑ 84 Albert Lewis .10 .30
❑ 85 Anthony Blaylock .10 .30
❑ 86 Pat Swilling .10 .30
❑ 87 Duane Bickett .10 .30
❑ 88 Myron Guyton .10 .30
❑ 89 Clay Matthews .10 .30
❑ 90 Jim McMahon .25 .60
❑ 91 Bruce Smith .50 1.25
❑ 92 Reggie White .50 1.25

Card		
93 Shannon Sharpe	.25	.60
94 Rickey Jackson	.10	.30
95 Ronnie Harmon	.10	.30
96 Terry McDaniel	.10	.30
97 Bryan Cox	.10	.30
98 Webster Slaughter	.10	.30
99 Boomer Esiason	.25	.60
100 Tim Krumrie	.10	.30
101 Cortez Kennedy	.25	.60
102 Henry Ellard	.25	.60
103 Clyde Simmons	.10	.30
104 Craig Erickson	.10	.30
105 Eric Green	.10	.30
106 Gary Clark	.25	.60
107 Jay Novacek	.25	.60
108 Dana Stubblefield	.25	.60
109 Mike Johnson	.10	.30
110 Ray Crockett	.10	.30
111 Leonard Russell	.10	.30
112 Robert Smith	.50	1.25
113 Art Monk	.25	.60
114 Ray Childress	.10	.30
115 O.J.McDuffie	.50	1.25
116 Tim Brown	.50	1.25
117 Kevin Ross	.10	.30
118 Richard Dent	.25	.60
119 John Elway	3.00	8.00
120 James Hasty	.10	.30
121 Gary Plummer	.10	.30
122 Pierce Holt	.10	.30
123 Eric Martin	.10	.30
124 Brett Favre	3.00	8.00
125 Cornelius Bennett	.25	.60
126 Jessie Hester	.10	.30
127 Lewis Tillman	.10	.30
128 Qadry Ismail	.50	1.25
129 Jay Schroeder	.10	.30
130 Curtis Conway	.50	1.25
131 Santana Dotson	.25	.60
132 Nick Lowery	.10	.30
133 Lomas Brown	.10	.30
134 Reggie Roby	.10	.30
135 John L. Williams	.10	.30
136 Vinny Testaverde	.25	.60
137 Seth Joyner	.10	.30
138 Ethan Horton	.10	.30
139 Jackie Slater	.10	.30
140 Rod Bernstine	.10	.30
141 Rob Moore	.25	.60
142 Dan Marino	3.00	8.00
143 Ken Harvey	.10	.30
144 Ernest Givins	.25	.60
145 Russell Maryland	.10	.30
146 Drew Bledsoe	1.25	3.00
147 Kevin Greene	.25	.60
148 Bobby Hebert	.10	.30
149 Junior Seau	.50	1.25
150 Tim McDonald	.10	.30
151 Thurman Thomas	.50	1.25
152 Phil Simms	.25	.60
153 Terrell Buckley	.10	.30
154 Sam Mills	.10	.30
155 Anthony Carter	.25	.60
156 Kelvin Martin	.10	.30
157 Shane Conlan	.10	.30
158 Irving Fryar	.25	.60
159 Demetrius DuBose	.10	.30
160 David Klingler	.10	.30
161 Herman Moore	.50	1.25
162 Jeff Hostetler	.25	.60
163 Tommy Vardell	.10	.30
164 Craig Heyward	.25	.60
165 Wilber Marshall	.10	.30
166 Quentin Coryatt	.10	.30
167 Glyn Milburn	.25	.60
168 Fred Barnett	.25	.60
169 Charles Haley	.25	.60
170 Carl Banks	.10	.30
171 Ricky Proehl	.10	.30
172 Joe Montana	3.00	8.00
173 Johnny Mitchell	.10	.30
174 Andre Reed	.25	.60
175 Marco Coleman	.10	.30
176 Vaughan Johnson	.10	.30
177 Carl Pickens	.25	.60
178 Dwight Stone	.10	.30
179 Ricky Watters	.25	.60
180 Michael Haynes	.25	.60
181 Roger Craig	.25	.60
182 Cleveland Gary	.10	.30
183 Steve Emtman	.10	.30
184 Patrick Bates	.10	.30
185 Mark Carrier WR	.25	.60
186 Brad Hopkins	.10	.30
187 Dennis Smith	.10	.30
188 Natrone Means	.50	1.25
189 Michael Jackson	.25	.60
190 Ken Norton Jr.	.25	.60
191 Carlton Gray	.10	.30
192 Edgar Bennett	.50	1.25
193 Lawrence Taylor	.50	1.25
194 Marv Cook	.10	.30
195 Eric Curry	.10	.30
196 Victor Bailey	.10	.30
197 Ryan McNeil	.10	.30
198 Rod Woodson	.25	.60
199 Earnest Byner	.10	.30
200 Marvin Jones	.10	.30
201 Thomas Smith	.10	.30
202 Troy Aikman	1.50	4.00
203 Audray McMillian	.10	.30
204 Wade Wilson	.10	.30
205 George Teague	.10	.30
206 Deion Sanders	.75	2.00
207 Will Shields	.25	.60
208 John Taylor	.25	.60
209 Jim Harbaugh	.50	1.25
210 Micheal Barrow	.10	.30
211 Harold Green	.10	.30
212 Steve Everitt	.10	.30
213 Flipper Anderson	.10	.30
214 Rodney Hampton	.25	.60
215 Steve Atwater	.10	.30
216 James Trapp	.10	.30
217 Terry Kirby	.50	1.25
218 Garrison Hearst	.50	1.25
219 Jeff Bryant	.10	.30
220 Roosevelt Potts	.10	.30

1995 Finest

Card		
COMPLETE SET (275)	30.00	80.00
COMP.SERIES 1 (165)	10.00	20.00
COMP.SERIES 2 (110)	25.00	60.00
1 Natrone Means	.25	.60
2 Dave Meggett	.08	.25
3 Tim Bowens	.08	.25
4 Jay Novacek	.25	.60
5 Michael Jackson	.25	.60
6 Calvin Williams	.25	.60
7 Neil Smith	.25	.60
8 Chris Gardocki	.08	.25
9 Jeff Burris	.08	.25
10 Warren Moon	.25	.60
11 Gary Anderson K	.08	.25
12 Bert Emanuel	.50	1.25
13 Rick Tuten	.08	.25
14 Steve Wallace	.08	.25
15 Marion Butts	.08	.25
16 Johnnie Morton	.25	.60
17 Rob Moore	.25	.60
18 Wayne Gandy	.08	.25
19 Quentin Coryatt	.25	.60
20 Richmond Webb	.08	.25
21 Errict Rhett	.25	.60
22 Joe Johnson	.08	.25
23 Gary Brown	.08	.25
24 Jeff Hostetler	.25	.60
25 Larry Centers	.25	.60
26 Tom Carter	.08	.25
27 Steve Atwater	.08	.25
28 Doug Pelfrey	.08	.25
29 Bryce Paup	.25	.60
30 Erik Williams	.08	.25
31 Henry Jones	.08	.25
32 Stanley Richard	.08	.25
33 Marcus Allen	.50	1.25
34 Antonio Langham	.08	.25
35 Lewis Tillman	.08	.25
36 Thomas Randolph	.08	.25
37 Byron Bam Morris	.08	.25
38 David Palmer	.25	.60
39 Ricky Watters	.25	.60
40 Brett Perriman	.25	.60
41 Will Wolford	.08	.25
42 Burt Grossman	.08	.25
43 Vincent Brisby	.08	.25
44 Ronnie Lott	.25	.60
45 Brian Blades	.25	.60
46 Brent Jones	.08	.25
47 Anthony Newman	.08	.25
48 Willie Roaf	.08	.25
49 Paul Gruber	.08	.25
50 Jeff George	.25	.60
51 Jamir Miller	.08	.25
52 Anthony Miller	.25	.60
53 Darrell Green	.08	.25
54 Steve Wisniewski	.08	.25
55 Dan Wilkinson	.25	.60
56 Brett Favre	2.00	5.00
57 Leslie O'Neal	.25	.60
58 Keith Byars	.08	.25
59 James Washington	.08	.25
60 Andre Reed	.25	.60
61 Ken Norton Jr.	.25	.60
62 John Randle	.25	.60
63 Lake Dawson	.25	.60
64 Greg Montgomery	.08	.25
65 Erric Pegram	.25	.60
66 Steve Everitt	.08	.25
67 Chris Brantley	.08	.25
68 Rod Woodson	.25	.60
69 Eugene Robinson	.08	.25
70 Dave Brown	.25	.60
71 Ricky Reynolds	.08	.25
72 Rohn Stark	.08	.25
73 Randal Hill	.08	.25
74 Brian Washington	.08	.25
75 Heath Shuler	.25	.60
76 Darion Conner	.08	.25
77 Terry McDaniel	.08	.25
78 Al Del Greco	.08	.25
79 Allen Aldridge	.08	.25
80 Trace Armstrong	.08	.25
81 Darnay Scott	.25	.60
82 Charlie Garner	.50	1.25
83 Harold Bishop	.08	.25
84 Reggie White	.50	1.25
85 Shawn Jefferson	.08	.25
86 Irving Spikes	.25	.60
87 Mel Gray	.08	.25
88 D.J. Johnson	.08	.25
89 Daryl Johnston	.25	.60
90 Joe Montana	2.00	5.00
91 Michael Strahan	.50	1.25
92 Robert Blackmon	.08	.25
93 Ryan Yarborough	.25	.60
94 Terry Allen	.25	.60
95 Michael Haynes	.25	.60
96 Jim Harbaugh	.25	.60
97 Micheal Barrow	.08	.25
98 John Thierry	.08	.25
99 Seth Joyner	.08	.25
100 Deion Sanders	.75	2.00
101 Eric Turner	.08	.25
102 LeShon Johnson	.25	.60
103 John Copeland	.08	.25
104 Cornelius Bennett	.25	.60
105 Sean Gilbert	.25	.60
106 Herschel Walker	.25	.60
107 Henry Ellard	.25	.60
108 Neil O'Donnell	.25	.60
109 Charles Wilson	.08	.25
110 Willie McGinest	.25	.60
111 Tim Brown	.50	1.25
112 Simon Fletcher	.08	.25
113 Broderick Thomas	.08	.25
114 Tom Waddle	.08	.25
115 Jessie Tuggle	.08	.25
116 Maurice Hurst	.08	.25
117 Aubrey Beavers	.08	.25
118 Donnell Bennett	.25	.60
119 Shante Carver	.08	.25
120 Eric Metcalf	.25	.60
121 John Carney	.08	.25

Card		
❑ 122 Thomas Lewis	.25	.60
❑ 123 Johnny Mitchell	.08	.25
❑ 124 Trent Dilfer	.50	1.25
❑ 125 Marshall Faulk	1.25	3.00
❑ 126 Ernest Givins	.08	.25
❑ 127 Aeneas Williams	.08	.25
❑ 128 Bucky Brooks	.08	.25
❑ 129 Todd Steussie	.08	.25
❑ 130 Randall Cunningham	.50	1.25
❑ 131 Reggie Brooks	.25	.60
❑ 132 Morten Andersen	.08	.25
❑ 133 James Jett	.25	.60
❑ 134 George Teague	.08	.25
❑ 135 John Taylor	.08	.25
❑ 136 Charles Johnson	.25	.60
❑ 137 Isaac Bruce	1.00	2.50
❑ 138 Jason Elam	.25	.60
❑ 139 Carl Pickens	.25	.60
❑ 140 Chris Warren	.25	.60
❑ 141 Bruce Armstrong	.08	.25
❑ 142 Mark Carrier DB	.08	.25
❑ 143 Irving Fryar	.25	.60
❑ 144 Van Malone	.08	.25
❑ 145 Charles Haley	.25	.60
❑ 146 Chris Calloway	.08	.25
❑ 147 J.J. Birden	.08	.25
❑ 148 Tony Bennett	.08	.25
❑ 149 Lincoln Kennedy	.08	.25
❑ 150 Stan Humphries	.25	.60
❑ 151 Hardy Nickerson	.08	.25
❑ 152 Randall McDaniel	.08	.25
❑ 153 Marcus Robertson	.08	.25
❑ 154 Ronald Moore	.08	.25
❑ 155 Thurman Thomas	.50	1.25
❑ 156 Tommy Vardell	.08	.25
❑ 157 Ken Ruettgers	.08	.25
❑ 158 Rob Fredrickson	.08	.25
❑ 159 Johnny Bailey	.08	.25
❑ 160 Greg Lloyd	.25	.60
❑ 161 David Alexander	.08	.25
❑ 162 Kevin Mawae	.08	.25
❑ 163 Derek Brown RBK	.08	.25
❑ 164 William Floyd	.25	.60
❑ 165 Aaron Glenn	.08	.25
❑ 166 Joey Galloway RC	3.00	8.00
❑ 167 Troy Drayton	.08	.25
❑ 168 Dermontti Dawson	.25	.60
❑ 169 Ronald Moore	.08	.25
❑ 170 Dan Marino	2.00	5.00
❑ 171 Dennis Gibson	.08	.25
❑ 172 Raymont Harris	.08	.25
❑ 173 Shannon Sharpe	.25	.60
❑ 174 Kevin Williams	.25	.60
❑ 175 Jim Everett	.08	.25
❑ 176 Rocket Ismail	.25	.60
❑ 177 Mark Fields RC	.50	1.25
❑ 178 George Koonce	.08	.25
❑ 179 Chris Hudson	.08	.25
❑ 180 Jerry Rice	1.00	2.50
❑ 181 Dewayne Washington	.25	.60
❑ 182 Dale Carter	.25	.60
❑ 183 Pete Stoyanovich	.08	.25
❑ 184 Blake Brockermeyer	.08	.25
❑ 185 Troy Aikman	1.00	2.50
❑ 186 Jeff Blake RC	1.00	2.50
❑ 187 Troy Vincent	.08	.25
❑ 188 Lamar Lathon	.08	.25
❑ 189 Tony Boselli	.50	1.25
❑ 190 Emmitt Smith	1.50	4.00
❑ 191 Bobby Houston	.08	.25
❑ 192 Edgar Bennett	.25	.60
❑ 193 Derrick Brooks RC	3.00	8.00
❑ 194 Ricky Proehl	.08	.25
❑ 195 Rodney Hampton	.25	.60
❑ 196 Dave Krieg	.08	.25
❑ 197 Vinny Testaverde	.25	.60
❑ 198 Erik Kramer	.08	.25
❑ 199 Ben Coates	.25	.60
❑ 200 Steve Young	.75	2.00
❑ 201 Glyn Milburn	.08	.25
❑ 202 Bryan Cox	.08	.25
❑ 203 Luther Elliss	.08	.25
❑ 204 Mark McMillian	.08	.25
❑ 205 Jerome Bettis	.50	1.25
❑ 206 Craig Heyward	.25	.60
❑ 207 Ray Buchanan	.08	.25
❑ 208 Kimble Anders	.25	.60
❑ 209 Kevin Greene	.25	.60
❑ 210 Eric Allen	.08	.25
❑ 211 Ricardo McDonald	.08	.25
❑ 212 Ruben Brown RC	.60	1.50
❑ 213 Harvey Williams	.08	.25
❑ 214 Broderick Thomas	.08	.25
❑ 215 Frank Reich	.08	.25
❑ 216 Frank Sanders RC	.60	1.50
❑ 217 Craig Newsome	.08	.25
❑ 218 Merton Hanks	.08	.25
❑ 219 Chris Miller	.08	.25
❑ 220 John Elway	2.00	5.00
❑ 221 Ernest Givins	.08	.25
❑ 222 Boomer Esiason	.25	.60
❑ 223 Reggie Roby	.08	.25
❑ 224 Qadry Ismail	.25	.60
❑ 225 Ki-Jana Carter RC	.60	1.50
❑ 226 Leon Lett	.08	.25
❑ 227 Eric Hill	.08	.25
❑ 228 Scott Mitchell	.25	.60
❑ 229 Craig Erickson	.08	.25
❑ 230 Drew Bledsoe	.75	2.00
❑ 231 Sean Landeta	.08	.25
❑ 232 Barrett Brooks	.08	.25
❑ 233 Brian Mitchell	.08	.25
❑ 234 Tyrone Poole	.50	1.25
❑ 235 Desmond Howard	.25	.60
❑ 236 Wayne Simmons	.08	.25
❑ 237 Michael Westbrook RC	.60	1.50
❑ 238 Quinn Early	.25	.60
❑ 239 Willie Davis	.25	.60
❑ 240 Rashaan Salaam RC	.30	.75
❑ 241 Devin Bush	.08	.25
❑ 242 Dana Stubblefield	.25	.60
❑ 243 Dexter Carter	.08	.25
❑ 244 Shane Conlan	.08	.25
❑ 245 Keith Elias RC	.08	.25
❑ 246 Robert Brooks	.50	1.25
❑ 247 Garrison Hearst	.50	1.25
❑ 248 Eric Zeier RC	.60	1.50
❑ 249 Nate Newton	.25	.60
❑ 250 Barry Sanders	1.50	4.00
❑ 251 Dave Meggett	.08	.25
❑ 252 Courtney Hawkins	.08	.25
❑ 253 Cortez Kennedy	.25	.60
❑ 254 Mario Bates	.25	.60
❑ 255 Junior Seau	.50	1.25
❑ 256 Brian Washington	.08	.25
❑ 257 Darius Holland	.08	.25
❑ 258 Jeff Graham	.08	.25
❑ 259 Rob Moore	.25	.60
❑ 260 Andre Rison	.25	.60
❑ 261 Kerry Collins RC	4.00	8.00
❑ 262 Roosevelt Potts	.08	.25
❑ 263 Cris Carter	.50	1.25
❑ 264 Curtis Martin RC	6.00	15.00
❑ 265 Rick Mirer	.25	.60
❑ 266 Mo Lewis	.08	.25
❑ 267 Mike Sherrard	.08	.25
❑ 268 Herman Moore	.50	1.25
❑ 269 Eric Metcalf	.25	.60
❑ 270 Ray Childress	.08	.25
❑ 271 Chris Slade	.08	.25
❑ 272 Michael Irvin	.50	1.25
❑ 273 Jim Kelly	.50	1.25
❑ 274 Terance Mathis	.25	.60
❑ 275 LeRoy Butler	.08	.25

1996 Finest

Card		
❑ COMPLETE SET (359)	150.00	300.00
❑ COMP.SERIES 1 (191)	100.00	200.00
❑ COMP.SERIES 2 (168)	50.00	100.00
❑ COMP.BRONZE SER.1 (110)	15.00	40.00
❑ COMP.BRONZE SER.2 (110)	15.00	40.00
❑ B2 Jay Novacek B	.25	.60
❑ B3 Ray Buchanan B	.10	.30
❑ B5 Phil Hansen B	.10	.30
❑ B6 Mike Mamula B	.10	.30
❑ B9 Bernie Parmalee B	.10	.30
❑ B10 Herman Moore B	.25	.60
❑ B11 Shawn Jefferson B	.10	.30
❑ B12 Chris Doleman B	.10	.30
❑ B13 Erik Kramer B	.25	.60
❑ B15 Orlando Thomas B	.10	.30
❑ B16 Terrell Davis B	1.50	4.00
❑ B18 Roman Phifer B	.10	.30
❑ B19 Trent Dilfer B	.25	.60
❑ B21 Darnay Scott B	.25	.60
❑ B22 Steve McNair B	1.50	4.00
❑ B23 Lamar Lathon B	.10	.30
❑ B26 Thomas Randolph B	.10	.30
❑ B27 Michael Jackson B	.25	.60
❑ B28 Seth Joyner B	.10	.30
❑ B29 Jeff Lageman B	.10	.30
❑ B30 Darryl Williams B	.10	.30
❑ B32 Erric Pegram B	.25	.60
❑ B34 Sean Dawkins B	.25	.60
❑ B38 Dan Saleaumua B UER 28	.10	.30
❑ B39 Henry Thomas B	.10	.30
❑ B43 Pat Swilling B	.10	.30
❑ B44 Marty Carter B	.10	.30
❑ B45 Anthony Miller B	.25	.60
❑ B48 Chris Warren B	.25	.60
❑ B49 Derek Brown RBK B	.10	.30
❑ B51 Blaine Bishop B	.10	.30
❑ B52 Jake Reed B	.25	.60
❑ B55 Vencie Glenn B	.10	.30
❑ B58 Derrick Alexander WR B	.25	.60
❑ B64 Jessie Tuggle B	.10	.30
❑ B65 Terrance Shaw B	.10	.30
❑ B66 David Sloan B	.25	.60
❑ B68 Brent Jones B	.10	.30
❑ B70 William Thomas B	.10	.30
❑ B71 Robert Smith B	.25	.60
❑ B72 Wayne Simmons B	.10	.30
❑ B73 Jim Harbaugh B	.25	.60
❑ B76 Wayne Chrebet B	.40	1.00
❑ B77 Chris Hudson B	.10	.30
❑ B79 Stevon Moore B	.10	.30
❑ B80 Chris Calloway B	.10	.30
❑ B81 Tom Carter B	.10	.30
❑ B82 Dave Meggett B	.10	.30
❑ B83 Sam Mills B	.25	.60
❑ B86 Renaldo Turnbull B	.10	.30
❑ B87 Derrick Brooks B	.40	1.00
❑ B89 Eugene Robinson B	.10	.30
❑ B91 Rodney Thomas B	.10	.30
❑ B92 Dan Wilkinson B	.10	.30
❑ B93 Mark Fields B	.10	.30
❑ B94 Warren Sapp B	.10	.30
❑ B95 Curtis Martin B	1.50	4.00
❑ B97 Ray Crockett B	.10	.30
❑ B98 Ed McDaniel B	.10	.30
❑ B101 Craig Heyward B	.10	.30
❑ B102 Ellis Johnson B	.10	.30
❑ B104 O.J. McDuffie B	.25	.60
❑ B105 J.J. Stokes B	.40	1.00
❑ B106 Mo Lewis B	.10	.30
❑ B108 Rob Moore B	.25	.60
❑ B110 Tyrone Wheatley B	.25	.60
❑ B111 Ken Harvey B	.10	.30
❑ B113 Willie Green B	.10	.30
❑ B114 Willie Davis B	.25	.60
❑ B115 Andy Harmon B	.10	.30
❑ B117 Bryan Cox B	.10	.30
❑ B119 Bert Emanuel B	.25	.60
❑ B120 Greg Lloyd B	.25	.60
❑ B122 Willie Jackson B	.25	.60
❑ B123 Lorenzo Lynch B	.10	.30
❑ B124 Pepper Johnson B	.10	.30
❑ B128 Tyrone Poole B	.10	.30
❑ B129 Neil Smith B	.25	.60
❑ B130 Eddie Robinson B	.10	.30
❑ B131 Bryce Paup B	.25	.60
❑ B134 Troy Aikman B	2.00	5.00
❑ B136 Chris Sanders B	.25	.60
❑ B138 Jim Everett B	.10	.30
❑ B139 Frank Sanders B	.25	.60
❑ B141 Cortez Kennedy B	.25	.60
❑ B143 Derrick Alexander DE B	.10	.30
❑ B144 Rob Fredrickson B	.10	.30
❑ B145 Chris Zorich B	.10	.30
❑ B146 Devin Bush B	.10	.30
❑ B149 Troy Vincent B	.10	.30
❑ B151 Deion Sanders B	1.00	2.50
❑ B152 James O. Stewart B	.25	.60
❑ B156 Lawrence Dawsey B	.10	.30

Card	Low	High
❑ B157 Robert Brooks B	.40	1.00
❑ B158 Rashaan Salaam B	.25	.60
❑ B161 Tim Brown B	.25	.60
❑ B162 Brendan Stai B	.10	.30
❑ B163 Sean Gilbert B	.10	.30
❑ B169 Calvin Williams B	.25	.60
❑ B171 Ruben Brown B	.10	.30
❑ B172 Eric Green B	.10	.30
❑ B175 Jerry Rice B	2.00	5.00
❑ B176 Bruce Smith B	.40	1.00
❑ B177 Mark Bruener B	.10	.30
❑ B179 Lamont Warren B	.10	.30
❑ B180 Tamarick Vanover B	.40	1.00
❑ B182 Scott Mitchell B	.25	.60
❑ B186 Terry Wooden B	.10	.30
❑ B187 Ken Norton B	.25	.60
❑ B188 Jeff Herrod B	.10	.30
❑ B192 Gus Frerotte B	.25	.60
❑ B194 Brett Maxie B	.10	.30
❑ B198 Eddie Kennison B RC	.40	1.00
❑ B201 Marcus Jones B RC	.10	.30
❑ B202 Terry Allen B	.25	.60
❑ B203 Leroy Hoard B	.10	.30
❑ B205 Reggie White B	.40	1.00
❑ B206 Larry Centers B	.25	.60
❑ B208 Vincent Brisby B	.10	.30
❑ B209 Michael Timpson B	.10	.30
❑ B211 John Mobley B RC	.10	.30
❑ B212 Clay Matthews B	.25	.60
❑ B213 Shannon Sharpe B	.25	.60
❑ B214 Tony Bennett B	.10	.30
❑ B216 Mickey Washington B	.10	.30
❑ B217 Fred Barnett B	.25	.60
❑ B218 Michael Haynes B	.25	.60
❑ B219 Stan Humphries B	.25	.60
❑ B221 Winston Moss B	.10	.30
❑ B222 Tim Biakabutuka B RC	.40	1.00
❑ B223 Leeland McElroy B RC	.25	.60
❑ B224 Vinnie Clark B	.10	.30
❑ B225 Keyshawn Johnson B RC	2.00	5.00
❑ B228 Tony Woods B	.10	.30
❑ B231 Anthony Pleasant B	.10	.30
❑ B232 Jeff George B	.25	.60
❑ B233 Curtis Conway B	.40	1.00
❑ B235 Jeff Lewis B RC	.25	.60
❑ B236 Edgar Bennett B	.25	.60
❑ B237 Regan Upshaw B RC	.10	.30
❑ B238 William Fuller B	.10	.30
❑ B241 Willie Anderson B RC	.10	.30
❑ B242 Derrick Thomas B	.40	1.00
❑ B243 Marvin Harrison B RC	6.00	15.00
❑ B244 Darion Conner B	.10	.30
❑ B245 Antonio Langham B	.10	.30
❑ B246 Rodney Peete B	.10	.30
❑ B247 Tim McDonald B	.10	.30
❑ B248 Robert Jones B	.10	.30
❑ B251 Mark Carrier DB B	.10	.30
❑ B252 Stephen Grant B	.10	.30
❑ B254 Jeff Hostetler B	.25	.60
❑ B255 Darrell Green B	.10	.30
❑ B261 Eric Swann B	.25	.60
❑ B263 Irv Smith B	.10	.30
❑ B264 Tim McKyer B	.10	.30
❑ B266 Sean Jones B	.10	.30
❑ B271 Yancey Thigpen B	.25	.60
❑ B273 Quentin Coryatt B	.10	.30
❑ B274 Hardy Nickerson B	.10	.30
❑ B275 Ricardo McDonald B	.10	.30
❑ B277 Robert Blackmon B	.10	.30
❑ B279 Alonzo Spellman B	.10	.30
❑ B281 Rickey Dudley B RC	.40	1.00
❑ B282 Joe Cain B	.10	.30
❑ B284 John Randle B	.25	.60
❑ B286 Vinny Testaverde B	.25	.60
❑ B289 Henry Jones B	.10	.30
❑ B290 Simeon Rice B RC	1.00	2.50
❑ B295 Leslie O'Neal B	.10	.30
❑ B297 Greg Hill B	.25	.60
❑ B301 Eric Metcalf B	.25	.60
❑ B303 Jerome Woods B RC	.10	.30
❑ B306 Anthony Smith B	.10	.30
❑ B307 Darren Perry B	.10	.30
❑ B311 James Hasty B	.10	.30
❑ B312 Cris Carter B	.40	1.00
❑ B314 Lawrence Phillips B RC	.25	.60
❑ B317 Aeneas Williams B	.10	.30
❑ B318 Eric Hill B	.10	.30
❑ B319 Kevin Hardy B RC	.40	1.00
❑ B321 Chris Chandler B	.25	.60
❑ B322 Rocket Ismail B	.25	.60
❑ B323 Anthony Parker B	.10	.30
❑ B324 John Thierry B	.10	.30
❑ B325 Micheal Barrow B	.10	.30
❑ B326 Henry Ford B	.10	.30
❑ B327 Aaron Hayden B RC	.10	.30
❑ B328 Terance Mathis B	.10	.30
❑ B329 Kirk Pointer B RC	.10	.30
❑ B330 Ray Mickens B RC	.10	.30
❑ B331 Jermane Mayberry B RC	.10	.30
❑ B332 Mario Bates B	.25	.60
❑ B333 Carlton Gray B	.10	.30
❑ B334 Derek Loville B	.10	.30
❑ B335 Mike Alstott B RC	2.00	5.00
❑ B336 Eric Guliford B	.10	.30
❑ B337 Marvcus Patton B	.10	.30
❑ B338 Terrell Owens B RC	6.00	15.00
❑ B339 Lance Johnstone B RC	.25	.60
❑ B340 Lake Dawson B	.25	.60
❑ B341 Winslow Oliver B RC	.10	.30
❑ B342 Adrian Murrell B	.25	.60
❑ B343 Jason Belser B	.10	.30
❑ B344 Brian Dawkins B RC	2.50	6.00
❑ B345 Reggie Brown B RC	.10	.30
❑ B346 Shaun Gayle B	.10	.30
❑ B347 Tony Brackens B RC	.40	1.00
❑ B348 Thomas Lewis B	.10	.30
❑ B349 Kelvin Pritchett B	.10	.30
❑ B350 Bobby Engram B RC	.40	1.00
❑ B351 Moe Williams B RC	1.00	2.50
❑ B352 Thomas Smith B	.10	.30
❑ B353 Dexter Carter B	.10	.30
❑ B354 Qadry Ismail B	.25	.60
❑ B355 Marco Battaglia B RC	.10	.30
❑ B356 Levon Kirkland B	.10	.30
❑ B357 Eric Allen B	.10	.30
❑ B358 Bobby Hoying B RC	.40	1.00
❑ B359 Checklist B	.10	.30
❑ G1 Kordell Stewart G	2.00	5.00
❑ G7 Kimble Anders G	.60	1.50
❑ G8 Merton Hanks G	.60	1.50
❑ G17 Rick Mirer G	1.25	3.00
❑ G33 Craig Newsome G	.60	1.50
❑ G36 Bryce Paup G	1.25	3.00
❑ G40 Dan Marino G	10.00	25.00
❑ G42 Andre Coleman G	.60	1.50
❑ G47 Kevin Carter G	.60	1.50
❑ G60 Mark Brunell G	2.00	5.00
❑ G61 David Palmer G	1.25	3.00
❑ G75 Carnell Lake G	.60	1.50
❑ G96 Joey Galloway G	2.00	5.00
❑ G112 Melvin Tuten G	.60	1.50
❑ G121 Aaron Glenn G	.60	1.50
❑ G132 Brett Favre G	10.00	25.00
❑ G133 Ken Dilger G	1.25	3.00
❑ G140 Barry Sanders G	7.50	20.00
❑ G142 Glyn Milburn G	.60	1.50
❑ G148 Brett Perriman G	1.25	3.00
❑ G160 Kerry Collins G	2.00	5.00
❑ G164 Lee Woodall G	.60	1.50
❑ G173 Marshall Faulk G	2.50	6.00
❑ G178 Troy Aikman G	5.00	12.00
❑ G190 Drew Bledsoe G	2.00	5.00
❑ G191 Checklist G	.60	1.50
❑ G193 Michael Irvin G	2.00	5.00
❑ G196 Warren Moon G	1.25	3.00
❑ G200 Steve Young G	5.00	12.00
❑ G207 Alex Van Dyke G RC	1.25	3.00
❑ G220 Cris Carter G	2.00	5.00
❑ G230 John Elway G	10.00	25.00
❑ G234 Charles Haley G	1.25	3.00
❑ G240 Jim Kelly G	2.00	5.00
❑ G250 Rodney Hampton G	1.25	3.00
❑ G256 Errict Rhett G	1.25	3.00
❑ G257 Alex Molden G	.60	1.50
❑ G260 Kevin Hardy G	1.25	3.00
❑ G267 Bryant Young G	1.25	3.00
❑ G268 Jeff Blake G	2.00	5.00
❑ G270 Keyshawn Johnson G	2.00	5.00
❑ G278 Junior Seau G	2.00	5.00
❑ G285 Terry Kirby G	1.25	3.00
❑ G293 Hugh Douglas G	1.25	3.00
❑ G296 Reggie White G	2.00	5.00
❑ G298 Elvis Grbac G	2.00	5.00
❑ G300 Emmitt Smith G	7.50	20.00
❑ G309 Ricky Watters G	1.25	3.00
❑ S4 Brett Favre S	6.00	15.00
❑ S14 Chester McGlockton S	.30	.75
❑ S20 Tyrone Hughes S	.30	.75
❑ S24 Ty Law S	1.25	3.00
❑ S25 Brian Mitchell S	.30	.75
❑ S31 Darren Woodson S	.60	1.50
❑ S35 Brian Mitchell S	.30	.75
❑ S37 Dana Stubblefield S	.60	1.50
❑ S41 Kerry Collins S	1.25	3.00
❑ S46 Orlando Thomas S	.30	.75
❑ S50 Jerry Rice S	3.00	8.00
❑ S53 Willie McGinest S	.30	.75
❑ S54 Blake Brockermeyer S	.30	.75
❑ S56 Michael Westbrook S	1.25	3.00
❑ S57 Garrison Hearst S	1.25	3.00
❑ S59 Kyle Brady S	.60	1.50
❑ S62 Tim Brown S	.60	1.50
❑ S60 Jeff Graham S	.30	.75
❑ S67 Dan Marino S	6.00	15.00
❑ S69 Tamarick Vanover S	1.25	3.00
❑ S74 Daryl Johnston S	.60	1.50
❑ S78 Frank Sanders S	.60	1.50
❑ S84 Darryll Lewis S	.30	.75
❑ S85 Carl Pickens S	.60	1.50
❑ S88 Jerome Bettis S	1.25	3.00
❑ S90 Terrell Davis S	2.50	6.00
❑ S99 Napoleon Kaufman S	1.25	3.00
❑ S100 Rashaan Salaam S	.60	1.50
❑ S103 Barry Sanders S	6.00	15.00
❑ S107 Tony Boselli S	.60	1.50
❑ S109 Eric Zeier S	.60	1.50
❑ S116 Bruce Smith S	1.25	3.00
❑ S118 Zack Crockett S	.30	.75
❑ S125 Joey Galloway S	1.25	3.00
❑ S126 Heath Shuler S	.60	1.50
❑ S127 Curtis Martin S	2.50	6.00
❑ S135 Greg Lloyd S	.60	1.50
❑ S137 Marshall Faulk S	1.50	4.00
❑ S147 Tyrone Poole S	.30	.75
❑ S150 J.J. Stokes S	1.25	3.00
❑ S153 Drew Bledsoe S	1.25	3.00
❑ S154 Terry McDaniel S	.30	.75
❑ S155 Terrell Fletcher S	.30	.75
❑ S159 Dave Brown S	.30	.75
❑ S165 Jim Harbaugh S	.60	1.50
❑ S166 Larry Brown S	.30	.75
❑ S167 Neil Smith S	.60	1.50
❑ S168 Herman Moore S	.60	1.50
❑ S170 Deion Sanders S	2.00	5.00
❑ S174 Mark Chmura S	.60	1.50
❑ S181 Chris Warren S	.60	1.50
❑ S183 Robert Brooks S	1.25	3.00
❑ S184 Steve McNair S	2.50	6.00
❑ S185 Kordell Stewart S	1.25	3.00
❑ S189 Charlie Garner S	.60	1.50
❑ S195 Harvey Williams S	.30	.75
❑ S197 Jeff George S	.60	1.50
❑ S199 Ricky Watters S	.60	1.50
❑ S204 Steve Bono S	.60	1.50
❑ S210 Jeff Blake S	1.25	3.00
❑ S215 Phillippi Sparks S	.30	.75
❑ S226 William Floyd S	.60	1.50
❑ S227 Troy Drayton S	.30	.75
❑ S229 Rodney Hampton S	.60	1.50
❑ S239 Duane Clemons S RC	.30	.75
❑ S249 Curtis Conway S	1.25	3.00
❑ S253 John Mobley S	.30	.75
❑ S258 Chris Slade S	.30	.75
❑ S259 Derrick Thomas S	1.25	3.00
❑ S262 Eric Metcalf S	.60	1.50
❑ S265 Emmitt Smith S	5.00	12.00
❑ S269 Jeff Hostetler S	.60	1.50
❑ S272 Thurman Thomas S	1.25	3.00
❑ S276 Steve Atwater S	.30	.75
❑ S280 Isaac Bruce S	1.25	3.00
❑ S283 Neil O'Donnell S	.60	1.50
❑ S287 Jim Kelly S	1.25	3.00
❑ S288 Lawrence Phillips S	1.25	3.00
❑ S291 Terance Mathis S	.30	.75
❑ S292 Errict Rhett S	.60	1.50
❑ S294 Santo Stephens S	.30	.75
❑ S299 Walt Harris S RC	.30	.75
❑ S302 Jamir Miller S	.30	.75
❑ S304 Ben Coates S	.60	1.50
❑ S305 Marcus Allen S	1.25	3.00
❑ S308 Jonathan Ogden S RC	1.25	3.00
❑ S310 John Elway S	6.00	15.00
❑ S313 Irving Fryar S	.60	1.50
❑ S315 Junior Seau S	1.25	3.00
❑ S316 Alex Molden S RC	.30	.75
❑ S320 Steve Young S	2.50	6.00

1997 Finest

Card		
COMPLETE SET (350)	250.00	500.00
COMP.SERIES 1 SET (175)	125.00	250.00
COMP.SERIES 2 SET (175)	125.00	250.00
COMP.BRONZE SET (200)	25.00	60.00
COMP.BRONZE SER.1 (100)	10.00	25.00
COMP.BRONZE SER.2 (100)	15.00	40.00
1 Mark Brunell B	.75	2.00
2 Chris Slade B	.25	.60
3 Chris Doleman B	.25	.60
4 Chris Hudson B	.25	.60
5 Karim Abdul-Jabbar B	.40	1.00
6 Darren Perry B	.25	.60
7 Daryl Johnston B	.40	1.00
8 Rob Moore B UER	.40	1.00
9 Robert Smith B	.40	1.00
10 Terry Allen B	.60	1.50
11 Jason Dunn B	.25	.60
12 Henry Thomas B	.25	.60
13 Rod Stephens B	.25	.60
14 Ray Mickens B	.25	.60
15 Ty Detmer B	.40	1.00
16 Fred Barnett B	.25	.60
17 Derrick Alexander WR B	.40	1.00
18 Marcus Robertson B	.25	.60
19 Robert Blackmon B	.25	.60
20 Isaac Bruce B	.60	1.50
21 Chester McGlockton B	.25	.60
22 Stan Humphries B	.40	1.00
23 Lonnie Marts B	.25	.60
24 Jason Sehorn B	.40	1.00
25 Bobby Engram B UER	.40	1.00
26 Brett Perriman B UER	.25	.60
27 Stevon Moore B	.25	.60
28 Jamal Anderson B	.60	1.50
29 Wayne Martin B	.25	.60
30 Michael Irvin B UER	.60	1.50
31 Thomas Smith B	.25	.60
32 Tony Brackens B	.25	.60
33 Eric Davis B	.25	.60
34 James O.Stewart B	.40	1.00
35 Ki-Jana Carter B	.25	.60
36 Ken Norton B	.25	.60
37 William Thomas B	.25	.60
38 Tim Brown B	.60	1.50
39 Lawrence Phillips B	.25	.60
40 Ricky Watters B	.40	1.00
41 Tony Bennett B	.25	.60
42 Jessie Armstead B	.25	.60
43 Trent Dilfer B	.60	1.50
44 Rodney Hampton B	.40	1.00
45 Sam Mills B	.25	.60
46 Rodney Harrison B RC	1.25	3.00
47 Rob Fredrickson B	.25	.60
48 Eric Hill B	.25	.60
49 Bennie Blades B	.25	.60
50 Eddie George B	.60	1.50
51 Dave Brown B	.25	.60
52 Raymont Harris B	.25	.60
53 Steve Tovar B	.25	.60
54 Thurman Thomas B	.60	1.50
55 Leeland McElroy B	.25	.60
56 Brian Mitchell B UER	.25	.60
57 Eric Allen B	.25	.60
58 Vinny Testaverde B	.40	1.00
59 Marvin Washington B	.25	.60
60 Junior Seau B	.60	1.50
61 Bert Emanuel B	.40	1.00
62 Kevin Carter B	.25	.60
63 Mark Carrier DB B	.25	.60
64 Andre Coleman B	.25	.60
65 Chris Warren B	.40	1.00
66 Aeneas Williams B	.25	.60
67 Eugene Robinson B	.25	.60
68 Darren Woodson B	.25	.60
69 Anthony Johnson B	.25	.60
70 Terry Glenn B	.60	1.50
71 Troy Vincent B	.25	.60
72 John Copeland B	.25	.60
73 Warren Sapp B	.40	1.00
74 Bobby Hebert B	.25	.60
75 Jeff Hostetler B	.25	.60
76 Willie Davis B	.25	.60
77 Mickey Washington B	.25	.60
78 Cortez Kennedy B	.25	.60
79 Michael Strahan B	.40	1.00
80 Jerome Bettis B	.60	1.50
81 Andre Hastings B UER	.25	.60
82 Simeon Rice B	.40	1.00
83 Cornelius Bennett B	.25	.60
84 Napoleon Kaufman B	.60	1.50
85 Jim Harbaugh B	.40	1.00
86 Aaron Hayden B	.25	.60
87 Gus Frerotte B	.25	.60
88 Jeff Blake B	.40	1.00
89 Anthony Miller B UER	.25	.60
90 Deion Sanders B	.60	1.50
91 Curtis Conway B	.40	1.00
92 William Floyd B	.40	1.00
93 Eric Moulds B UER	.60	1.50
94 Mel Gray B	.25	.60
95 Andre Rison B UER	.40	1.00
96 Eugene Daniel B	.25	.60
97 Jason Belser B	.25	.60
98 Mike Mamula B	.25	.60
99 Jim Everett B	.25	.60
100 Checklist B	.25	.60
101 Drew Bledsoe S	1.50	4.00
102 Shannon Sharpe S	.75	2.00
103 Ken Harvey S	.50	1.25
104 Isaac Bruce S	1.25	3.00
105 Terry Allen S	1.25	3.00
106 Lawyer Milloy S	.75	2.00
107 Ashley Ambrose S	.50	1.25
108 Alfred Williams S	.50	1.25
109 Hugh Douglas S	.50	1.25
110 Junior Seau S	1.25	3.00
111 Kordell Stewart S	1.25	3.00
112 Adrian Murrell S	.75	2.00
113 Byron Bam Morris S	.50	1.25
114 Terrell Buckley S	.50	1.25
115 Dan Marino S	5.00	12.00
116 Willie Clay S	.50	1.25
117 Neil Smith S	.75	2.00
118 Blaine Bishop S	.50	1.25
119 John Mobley S	.50	1.25
120 Herman Moore S	.75	2.00
121 Keyshawn Johnson S	1.25	3.00
122 Boomer Esiason S	.75	2.00
123 Marshall Faulk S	1.50	4.00
124 Keith Jackson S	.50	1.25
125 Ricky Watters S	.75	2.00
126 Carl Pickens S	.75	2.00
127 Cris Carter S	1.25	3.00
128 Mike Alstott S	1.25	3.00
129 Simeon Rice S	.75	2.00
130 Troy Aikman S	2.50	6.00
131 Tamarick Vanover S	.75	2.00
132 Marquez Pope S	.50	1.25
133 Winslow Oliver S	.50	1.25
134 Edgar Bennett S	.75	2.00
135 Dave Meggett S	.50	1.25
136 Marcus Allen S	1.25	3.00
137 Jerry Rice S	2.50	6.00
138 Steve Atwater S	.50	1.25
139 Tim McDonald S	.50	1.25
140 Barry Sanders S	4.00	10.00
141 Eddie George S	1.25	3.00
142 Wesley Walls S	.50	1.25
143 Jerome Bettis S	1.25	3.00
144 Kevin Greene S	.75	2.00
145 Terrell Davis S	1.50	4.00
146 Gus Frerotte S	.75	2.00
147 Joey Galloway S	.75	2.00
148 Vinny Testaverde S	.75	2.00
149 Hardy Nickerson S	.50	1.25
150 Brett Favre S	5.00	12.00
151 Desmond Howard G	.60	1.50
152 Keyshawn Johnson G	2.00	5.00
153 Tony Banks G	2.00	5.00
154 Chris Spielman G	.60	1.50
155 Reggie White G	2.00	5.00
156 Zach Thomas G	2.00	5.00
157 Carl Pickens G	1.25	3.00
158 Karim Abdul-Jabbar G	2.00	5.00
159 Chad Brown G	.60	1.50
160 Kerry Collins G	2.00	5.00
161 Marvin Harrison G	2.00	5.00
162 Steve Young G	2.50	6.00
163 Deion Sanders G	2.00	5.00
164 Trent Dilfer G	2.00	5.00
165 Barry Sanders G	6.00	15.00
166 Cris Carter G	2.00	5.00
167 Keenan McCardell G	1.25	3.00
168 Terry Glenn G	2.00	5.00
169 Emmitt Smith G	6.00	15.00
170 John Elway G	7.50	20.00
171 Jerry Rice G	4.00	10.00
172 Troy Aikman G	4.00	10.00
173 Curtis Martin G	2.50	6.00
174 Darrell Green G	.60	1.50
175 Mark Brunell G	2.50	6.00
176 Corey Dillon B RC	5.00	12.00
177 Tyrone Poole B	.25	.60
178 Anthony Pleasant B	.25	.60
179 Frank Sanders B	.40	1.00
180 Troy Aikman B	1.50	3.00
181 Bill Romanowski B	.25	.60
182 Ty Law B	.40	1.00
183 Orlando Thomas B	.25	.60
184 Quentin Coryatt B	.25	.60
185 Kenny Holmes B RC	.50	1.25
186 Bryant Young B	.25	.60
187 Michael Sinclair B	.25	.60
188 Mike Tomczak B	.25	.60
189 Bobby Taylor B	.25	.60
190 Brett Favre B	3.00	6.00
191 Kent Graham B	.25	.60
192 Jessie Tuggle B	.25	.60
193 Jimmy Smith B	.40	1.00
194 Greg Hill B	.25	.60
195 Yatil Green B RC	.30	.75
196 Mark Fields B	.25	.60
197 Phillippi Sparks B	.25	.60
198 Aaron Glenn B	.25	.60
199 Pat Swilling B	.25	.60
200 Barry Sanders B	2.00	5.00
201 Mark Chmura B	.40	1.00
202 Marco Coleman B	.25	.60
203 Merton Hanks B	.25	.60
204 Brian Blades B	.25	.60
205 Errict Rhett B	.25	.60
206 Henry Ellard B	.25	.60
207 Andre Reed B	.40	1.00
208 Bryan Cox B	.25	.60
209 Darnay Scott B	.40	1.00
210 John Elway B	3.00	6.00
211 Glyn Milburn B	.25	.60
212 Don Beebe B	.25	.60
213 Kevin Lockett B RC	.30	.75
214 Dorsey Levens B	.60	1.50
215 Kordell Stewart B	.60	1.50
216 Larry Centers B	.40	1.00
217 Cris Carter B	.60	1.50
218 Willie McGinest B	.25	.60
219 Renaldo Wynn B RC	.10	.30
220 Jerry Rice B	1.50	3.00
221 Reidel Anthony B RC	.30	.75
222 Mark Carrier WR B	.25	.60
223 Quinn Early B	.25	.60
224 Chris Sanders B	.25	.60
225 Shawn Springs B RC	.30	.75
226 Kevin Smith B	.25	.60
227 Ben Coates B	.40	1.00
228 Tyrone Wheatley B	.40	1.00
229 Antonio Freeman B	.60	1.50
230 Dan Marino B	3.00	6.00
231 Dwayne Rudd B RC	.50	1.25
232 Leslie O'Neal B	.25	.60
233 Brent Jones B	.25	.60
234 Jake Plummer B RC	4.00	10.00
235 Kerry Collins B	.60	1.50
236 Rashaan Salaam B	.25	.60
237 Tyrone Braxton B	.25	.60
238 Herman Moore B	.40	1.00
239 Keyshawn Johnson B	.60	1.50
240 Drew Bledsoe B	.75	2.00
241 Rickey Dudley B	.40	1.00
242 Antowain Smith B RC	2.00	5.00
243 Jeff Lageman B	.25	.60
244 Chris T. Jones B	.25	.60
245 Steve Young B	.75	2.00
246 Eddie Robinson B	.25	.60

Card		
❑ 247 Chad Cota B	.25	.60
❑ 248 Michael Jackson B	.40	1.00
❑ 249 Robert Porcher B	.25	.60
❑ 250 Reggie White B	.60	1.50
❑ 251 Carnell Lake B	.25	.60
❑ 252 Chris Calloway B	.25	.60
❑ 253 Terance Mathis B	.40	1.00
❑ 254 Carl Pickens B	.40	1.00
❑ 255 Curtis Martin B	.75	2.00
❑ 256 Jeff Graham B	.25	.60
❑ 257 Regan Upshaw RC B	.10	.30
❑ 258 Sean Gilbert B	.25	.60
❑ 259 Will Blackwell B RC	.30	.75
❑ 260 Emmitt Smith B	2.50	5.00
❑ 261 Reinard Wilson B RC	.30	.75
❑ 262 Darrell Russell B RC	.10	.30
❑ 263 Wayne Chrebet B	.40	1.00
❑ 264 Kevin Hardy B	.25	.60
❑ 265 Shannon Sharpe B	.40	1.00
❑ 266 Harvey Williams B	.25	.60
❑ 267 John Randle B	.40	1.00
❑ 268 Tim Bowens B	.25	.60
❑ 269 Tony Gonzalez B RC	2.50	6.00
❑ 270 Warrick Dunn B RC	2.50	6.00
❑ 271 Sean Dawkins B	.25	.60
❑ 272 Darryll Lewis B	.25	.60
❑ 273 Alonzo Spellman B	.25	.60
❑ 274 Mark Collins B	.25	.60
❑ 275 Checklist Card B	.25	.60
❑ 276 Pat Barnes S RC	.75	2.00
❑ 277 Dana Stubblefield S	.75	2.00
❑ 278 Dan Wilkinson S	.50	1.25
❑ 279 Bryce Paup S	.50	1.25
❑ 280 Kerry Collins S	1.25	3.00
❑ 281 Derrick Brooks S	1.25	3.00
❑ 282 Walter Jones S RC	1.25	3.00
❑ 283 Terry McDaniel S	.50	1.25
❑ 284 James Farrior S RC	1.25	3.00
❑ 285 Curtis Martin S	1.50	4.00
❑ 286 O.J. McDuffie S	.75	2.00
❑ 287 Natrone Means S	.75	2.00
❑ 288 Bryant Westbrook S RC	.75	2.00
❑ 289 Peter Boulware S RC	1.25	3.00
❑ 290 Emmitt Smith S	4.00	10.00
❑ 291 Joey Kent S RC	1.25	3.00
❑ 292 Eddie Kennison S	.75	2.00
❑ 293 LeRoy Butler S	.50	1.25
❑ 294 Dale Carter S	.50	1.25
❑ 295 Jim Druckenmiller S RC	.75	2.00
❑ 296 Byron Hanspard S RC	.75	2.00
❑ 297 Jeff Blake S	.75	2.00
❑ 298 Levon Kirkland S	.50	1.25
❑ 299 Michael Westbrook S	.75	2.00
❑ 300 John Elway S	5.00	12.00
❑ 301 Lamar Lathon S	.50	1.25
❑ 302 Ray Lewis S	2.00	5.00
❑ 303 Steve McNair S	1.50	4.00
❑ 304 Shawn Springs S	.75	2.00
❑ 305 Karim Abdul-Jabbar S	.75	2.00
❑ 306 Orlando Pace S RC	1.25	3.00
❑ 307 Scott Mitchell S	.50	1.25
❑ 308 Walt Harris S	.50	1.25
❑ 309 Bruce Smith S	.75	2.00
❑ 310 Reggie White S	1.25	3.00
❑ 311 Eric Swann S	.50	1.25
❑ 312 Derrick Thomas S	1.25	3.00
❑ 313 Tony Martin S	.75	2.00
❑ 314 Darrell Russell S RC	.75	2.00
❑ 315 Mark Brunell S	1.50	4.00
❑ 316 Trent Dilfer S	1.25	3.00
❑ 317 Irving Fryar S	.50	1.25
❑ 318 Amani Toomer S	.75	2.00
❑ 319 Jake Reed S	.75	2.00
❑ 320 Steve Young S	1.50	4.00
❑ 321 Troy Davis S RC	.75	2.00
❑ 322 Jim Harbaugh S	.75	2.00
❑ 323 Neil O'Donnell S	.50	1.25
❑ 324 Terry Glenn S	1.25	3.00
❑ 325 Deion Sanders S	1.25	3.00
❑ 326 Gus Frerotte G	1.25	3.00
❑ 327 Tom Knight G RC	1.25	3.00
❑ 328 Peter Boulware G	1.25	3.00
❑ 329 Jerome Bettis G	2.00	5.00
❑ 330 Orlando Pace G	2.00	5.00
❑ 331 Darnell Autry G RC	1.25	3.00
❑ 332 Ike Hilliard G RC	5.00	12.00
❑ 333 David LaFleur G RC	.60	1.50
❑ 334 Jim Harbaugh G	1.25	3.00
❑ 335 Eddie George G	2.00	5.00
❑ 336 Vinny Testaverde G	1.25	3.00
❑ 337 Terry Allen G	1.25	3.00
❑ 338 Jim Druckenmiller G	1.25	3.00
❑ 339 Ricky Watters G	1.25	3.00
❑ 340 Brett Favre G	7.50	20.00
❑ 341 Simeon Rice G	1.25	3.00
❑ 342 Shannon Sharpe G	1.25	3.00
❑ 343 Kordell Stewart G	2.00	5.00
❑ 344 Isaac Bruce G	2.00	5.00
❑ 345 Drew Bledsoe G	2.50	6.00
❑ 346 Jeff Blake G	1.25	3.00
❑ 347 Herman Moore G	1.25	3.00
❑ 348 Junior Seau G	2.00	5.00
❑ 349 Rae Carruth G RC	.60	1.50
❑ 350 Dan Marino G	7.50	20.00
❑ P5 K.Abdul-Jabbar Promo	.60	1.50
❑ P32 Tony Brackens Promo	.60	1.50
❑ P45 Sam Mills Promo	.60	1.50
❑ P70 Terry Glenn Promo	.60	1.50
❑ P87 Gus Frerotte Promo	.60	1.50

1998 Finest

Card		
❑ COMPLETE SET (270)	30.00	80.00
❑ COMP.SERIES 1 (150)	20.00	50.00
❑ COMP.SERIES 2 (120)	12.50	30.00
❑ 1 John Elway	1.50	4:00
❑ 2 Terance Mathis	.25	.60
❑ 3 Jermaine Lewis	.25	.60
❑ 4 Fred Lane	.15	.40
❑ 5 Simeon Rice	.25	.60
❑ 6 David Dunn	.15	.40
❑ 7 Dexter Coakley	.15	.40
❑ 8 Carl Pickens	.25	.60
❑ 9 Antonio Freeman	.40	1.00
❑ 10 Herman Moore	.25	.60
❑ 11 Kevin Hardy	.15	.40
❑ 12 Tony Gonzalez	.40	1.00
❑ 13 O.J. McDuffie	.25	.60
❑ 14 David Palmer	.15	.40
❑ 15 Lawyer Milloy	.25	.60
❑ 16 Danny Kanell	.25	.60
❑ 17 Randal Hill	.15	.40
❑ 18 Chris Slade	.15	.40
❑ 19 Charlie Garner	.25	.60
❑ 20 Mark Brunell	.40	1.00
❑ 21 Donnell Woolford	.15	.40
❑ 22 Freddie Jones	.15	.40
❑ 23 Ken Norton	.15	.40
❑ 24 Tony Banks	.25	.60
❑ 25 Isaac Bruce	.40	1.00
❑ 26 Willie Davis	.15	.40
❑ 27 Cris Dishman	.15	.40
❑ 28 Aeneas Williams	.15	.40
❑ 29 Michael Booker	.15	.40
❑ 30 Cris Carter	.40	1.00
❑ 31 Michael McCrary	.15	.40
❑ 32 Eric Moulds	.40	1.00
❑ 33 Rae Carruth	.15	.40
❑ 34 Bobby Engram	.25	.60
❑ 35 Jeff Blake	.25	.60
❑ 36 Deion Sanders	.40	1.00
❑ 37 Rod Smith	.25	.60
❑ 38 Bryant Westbrook	.15	.40
❑ 39 Mark Chmura	.25	.60
❑ 40 Tim Brown	.40	1.00
❑ 41 Bobby Taylor	.15	.40
❑ 42 James Stewart	.25	.60
❑ 43 Kimble Anders	.25	.60
❑ 44 Karim Abdul-Jabbar	.40	1.00
❑ 45 Willie McGinest	.15	.40
❑ 46 Jessie Armstead	.15	.40
❑ 47 Brad Johnson	.40	1.00
❑ 48 Greg Lloyd	.15	.40
❑ 49 Stephen Davis	.15	.40
❑ 50 Jerome Bettis	.40	1.00
❑ 51 Warren Sapp	.25	.60
❑ 52 Horace Copeland	.15	.40
❑ 53 Chad Brown	.15	.40
❑ 54 Chris Canty	.15	.40
❑ 55 Robert Smith	.40	1.00
❑ 56 Pete Mitchell	.15	.40
❑ 57 Aaron Bailey	.15	.40
❑ 58 Robert Porcher	.15	.40
❑ 59 John Mobley	.15	.40
❑ 60 Tony Martin	.25	.60
❑ 61 Michael Irvin	.40	1.00
❑ 62 Charles Way	.15	.40
❑ 63 Raymont Harris	.15	.40
❑ 64 Chuck Smith	.15	.40
❑ 65 Larry Centers	.15	.40
❑ 66 Greg Hill	.15	.40
❑ 67 Kenny Holmes	.15	.40
❑ 68 John Lynch	.25	.60
❑ 69 Michael Sinclair	.15	.40
❑ 70 Steve Young	.50	1.25
❑ 71 Michael Strahan	.25	.60
❑ 72 Levon Kirkland	.15	.40
❑ 73 Rickey Dudley	.15	.40
❑ 74 Marcus Allen	.40	1.00
❑ 75 John Randle	.25	.60
❑ 76 Erik Kramer	.15	.40
❑ 77 Neil Smith	.25	.60
❑ 78 Byron Hanspard	.15	.40
❑ 79 Quinn Early	.15	.40
❑ 80 Warren Moon	.40	1.00
❑ 81 William Thomas	.15	.40
❑ 82 Ben Coates	.25	.60
❑ 83 Lake Dawson	.15	.40
❑ 84 Steve McNair	.40	1.00
❑ 85 Gus Frerotte	.15	.40
❑ 86 Rodney Harrison	.25	.60
❑ 87 Reggie White	.40	1.00
❑ 88 Derrick Thomas	.40	1.00
❑ 89 Dale Carter	.15	.40
❑ 90 Warrick Dunn	.40	1.00
❑ 91 Will Blackwell	.15	.40
❑ 92 Troy Vincent	.15	.40
❑ 93 Johnnie Morton	.25	.60
❑ 94 David LaFleur	.15	.40
❑ 95 Tony McGee	.15	.40
❑ 96 Lonnie Johnson	.15	.40
❑ 97 Thurman Thomas	.40	1.00
❑ 98 Chris Chandler	.25	.60
❑ 99 Jamal Anderson	.40	1.00
❑ 100 Checklist	.15	.40
❑ 101 Marshall Faulk	.60	1.50
❑ 102 Chris Calloway	.15	.40
❑ 103 Chris Spielman	.15	.40
❑ 104 Zach Thomas	.40	1.00
❑ 105 Jeff George	.25	.60
❑ 106 Darrell Russell	.15	.40
❑ 107 Darryll Lewis	.15	.40
❑ 108 Reidel Anthony	.25	.60
❑ 109 Terrell Owens	.40	1.00
❑ 110 Rob Moore	.25	.60
❑ 111 Darrell Green	.25	.60
❑ 112 Merton Hanks	.15	.40
❑ 113 Shawn Jefferson	.15	.40
❑ 114 Chris Sanders	.15	.40
❑ 115 Scott Mitchell	.25	.60
❑ 116 Vaughn Hebron	.15	.40
❑ 117 Ed McCaffrey	.25	.60
❑ 118 Bruce Smith	.25	.60
❑ 119 Peter Boulware	.15	.40
❑ 120 Brett Favre	1.50	4.00
❑ 121 Peyton Manning RC	15.00	40.00
❑ 122 Brian Griese RC	2.00	5.00
❑ 123 Tavian Banks RC	.60	1.50
❑ 124 Duane Starks RC	.40	1.00
❑ 125 Robert Holcombe RC	.60	1.50
❑ 126 Brian Simmons RC	.60	1.50
❑ 127 Skip Hicks RC	.60	1.50
❑ 128 Keith Brooking RC	1.00	2.50
❑ 129 Ahman Green RC	2.50	6.00
❑ 130 Jerome Pathon RC	1.00	2.50
❑ 131 Curtis Enis RC	.40	1.00
❑ 132 Grant Wistrom RC	.60	1.50
❑ 133 Germane Crowell RC	.60	1.50
❑ 134 Jacquez Green RC	.60	1.50
❑ 135 Randy Moss RC	8.00	20.00
❑ 136 Jason Peter RC	.40	1.00
❑ 137 John Avery RC	.60	1.50
❑ 138 Takeo Spikes RC	1.00	2.50
❑ 139 Pat Johnson RC	.60	1.50
❑ 140 Andre Wadsworth RC	.60	1.50

Card		
❑ 141 Fred Taylor RC	1.50	4.00
❑ 142 Charles Woodson RC	1.25	3.00
❑ 143 Marcus Nash RC	.40	1.00
❑ 144 Robert Edwards RC	.60	1.50
❑ 145 Kevin Dyson RC	1.00	2.50
❑ 146 Joe Jurevicius RC	1.00	2.50
❑ 147 Anthony Simmons RC	.60	1.50
❑ 148 Hines Ward RC	5.00	10.00
❑ 149 Greg Ellis RC	.40	1.00
❑ 150 Ryan Leaf RC	1.00	2.50
❑ 151 Jerry Rice	.75	2.00
❑ 152 Tony Martin	.25	.60
❑ 153 Checklist	.15	.40
❑ 154 Rob Johnson	.25	.60
❑ 155 Shannon Sharpe	.25	.60
❑ 156 Bert Emanuel	.25	.60
❑ 157 Eric Metcalf	.15	.40
❑ 158 Natrone Means	.25	.60
❑ 159 Derrick Alexander	.25	.60
❑ 160 Emmitt Smith	1.25	3.00
❑ 161 Jeff Burris	.15	.40
❑ 162 Chris Warren	.25	.60
❑ 163 Corey Fuller	.15	.40
❑ 164 Courtney Hawkins	.15	.40
❑ 165 James McKnight	.40	1.00
❑ 166 Shawn Springs	.15	.40
❑ 167 Wayne Martin	.15	.40
❑ 168 Michael Westbrook	.25	.60
❑ 169 Michael Jackson	.15	.40
❑ 170 Dan Marino	1.50	4.00
❑ 171 Amp Lee	.15	.40
❑ 172 James Jett	.25	.60
❑ 173 Ty Law	.25	.60
❑ 174 Kerry Collins	.25	.60
❑ 175 Robert Brooks	.25	.60
❑ 176 Blaine Bishop	.15	.40
❑ 177 Stephen Boyd	.15	.40
❑ 178 Keyshawn Johnson	.40	1.00
❑ 179 Deon Figures	.15	.40
❑ 180 Allen Aldridge	.15	.40
❑ 181 Corey Miller	.15	.40
❑ 182 Chad Lewis	.25	.60
❑ 183 Derrick Rodgers	.15	.40
❑ 184 Troy Drayton	.15	.40
❑ 185 Darren Woodson	.15	.40
❑ 186 Ken Dilger	.15	.40
❑ 187 Elvis Grbac	.25	.60
❑ 188 Terrell Fletcher	.15	.40
❑ 189 Frank Sanders	.25	.60
❑ 190 Curtis Martin	.40	1.00
❑ 191 Derrick Brooks	.40	1.00
❑ 192 Darrien Gordon	.15	.40
❑ 193 Andre Reed	.25	.60
❑ 194 Darnay Scott	.25	.60
❑ 195 Curtis Conway	.25	.60
❑ 196 Tim McDonald	.15	.40
❑ 197 Sean Dawkins	.15	.40
❑ 198 Napoleon Kaufman	.40	1.00
❑ 199 Willie Clay	.15	.40
❑ 200 Terrell Davis	.40	1.00
❑ 201 Wesley Walls	.25	.60
❑ 202 Santana Dotson	.15	.40
❑ 203 Frank Wycheck	.15	.40
❑ 204 Wayne Chrebet	.40	1.00
❑ 205 Andre Rison	.25	.60
❑ 206 Jason Sehorn	.25	.60
❑ 207 Jessie Tuggle	.15	.40
❑ 208 Kevin Turner	.15	.40
❑ 209 Jason Taylor	.25	.60
❑ 210 Yancey Thigpen	.15	.40
❑ 211 Jake Reed	.25	.60
❑ 212 Carnell Lake	.15	.40
❑ 213 Joey Galloway	.25	.60
❑ 214 Andre Hastings	.15	.40
❑ 215 Terry Allen	.40	1.00
❑ 216 Jim Harbaugh	.25	.60
❑ 217 Tony Banks	.25	.60
❑ 218 Greg Clark	.15	.40
❑ 219 Corey Dillon	.40	1.00
❑ 220 Troy Aikman	.75	2.00
❑ 221 Antowain Smith	.40	1.00
❑ 222 Steve Atwater	.15	.40
❑ 223 Trent Dilfer	.40	1.00
❑ 224 Junior Seau	.40	1.00
❑ 225 Garrison Hearst	.40	1.00
❑ 226 Eric Allen	.15	.40
❑ 227 Chad Cota	.15	.40
❑ 228 Vinny Testaverde	.25	.60
❑ 229 Duce Staley	.50	1.25
❑ 230 Drew Bledsoe	.60	1.50
❑ 231 Charles Johnson	.15	.40
❑ 232 Jake Plummer	.40	1.00
❑ 233 Errict Rhett	.25	.60
❑ 234 Doug Evans	.15	.40
❑ 235 Phillippi Sparks	.15	.40
❑ 236 Ashley Ambrose	.15	.40
❑ 237 Bryan Cox	.15	.40
❑ 238 Kevin Smith	.15	.40
❑ 239 Hardy Nickerson	.15	.40
❑ 240 Terry Glenn	.40	1.00
❑ 241 Lee Woodall	.15	.40
❑ 242 Andre Coleman	.15	.40
❑ 243 Michael Bates	.15	.40
❑ 244 Mark Fields	.15	.40
❑ 245 Eddie Kennison	.25	.60
❑ 246 Dana Stubblefield	.15	.40
❑ 247 Bobby Hoying	.25	.60
❑ 248 Mo Lewis	.15	.40
❑ 249 Derrick Mayes	.25	.60
❑ 250 Eddie George	.40	1.00
❑ 251 Mike Alstott	.40	1.00
❑ 252 J.J. Stokes	.25	.60
❑ 253 Adrian Murrell	.25	.60
❑ 254 Kevin Greene	.25	.60
❑ 255 LeRoy Butler	.15	.40
❑ 256 Glenn Foley	.25	.60
❑ 257 Jimmy Smith	.25	.60
❑ 258 Tiki Barber	.40	1.00
❑ 259 Irving Fryar	.25	.60
❑ 260 Ricky Watters	.25	.60
❑ 261 Jeff Graham	.15	.40
❑ 262 Kordell Stewart	.40	1.00
❑ 263 Rod Woodson	.25	.60
❑ 264 Leslie Shepherd	.15	.40
❑ 265 Ryan McNeil	.15	.40
❑ 266 Ike Hilliard	.25	.60
❑ 267 Keenan McCardell	.25	.60
❑ 268 Marvin Harrison	.40	1.00
❑ 269 Dorsey Levens	.40	1.00
❑ 270 Barry Sanders	1.25	3.00

1999 Finest

Card		
❑ COMPLETE SET (175)	30.00	80.00
❑ COMP.SET w/o SPs (124)	15.00	30.00
❑ 1 Peyton Manning	1.25	3.00
❑ 2 Priest Holmes	.60	1.50
❑ 3 Kordell Stewart	.25	.60
❑ 4 Shannon Sharpe	.25	.60
❑ 5 Andre Rison	.25	.60
❑ 6 Rickey Dudley	.15	.40
❑ 7 Duce Staley	.40	1.00
❑ 8 Randall Cunningham	.40	1.00
❑ 9 Warrick Dunn	.40	1.00
❑ 10 Dan Marino	1.25	3.00
❑ 11 Kevin Greene	.15	.40
❑ 12 Garrison Hearst	.25	.60
❑ 13 Eric Moulds	.40	1.00
❑ 14 Marvin Harrison	.40	1.00
❑ 15 Eddie George	.40	1.00
❑ 16 Vinny Testaverde	.25	.60
❑ 17 Brad Johnson	.40	1.00
❑ 18 Derrick Thomas	.40	1.00
❑ 19 Chris Chandler	.25	.60
❑ 20 Troy Aikman	.75	2.00
❑ 21 Terance Mathis	.25	.60
❑ 22 Terrell Owens	.40	1.00
❑ 23 Junior Seau	.40	1.00
❑ 24 Cris Carter	.40	1.00
❑ 25 Fred Taylor	.40	1.00
❑ 26 Adrian Murrell	.25	.60
❑ 27 Terry Glenn	.40	1.00
❑ 28 Rod Smith	.25	.60
❑ 29 Darnay Scott	.25	.60
❑ 30 Brett Favre	1.25	3.00
❑ 31 Cam Cleeland	.15	.40
❑ 32 Ricky Watters	.25	.60
❑ 33 Derrick Alexander	.25	.60
❑ 34 Bruce Smith	.25	.60
❑ 35 Steve McNair	.40	1.00
❑ 36 Wayne Chrebet	.25	.60
❑ 37 Herman Moore	.25	.60
❑ 38 Bert Emanuel	.25	.60
❑ 39 Michael Irvin	.25	.60
❑ 40 Steve Young	.50	1.25
❑ 41 Napoleon Kaufman	.40	1.00
❑ 42 Tim Biakabutuka	.25	.60
❑ 43 Isaac Bruce	.40	1.00
❑ 44 J.J. Stokes	.25	.60
❑ 45 Antonio Freeman	.40	1.00
❑ 46 John Randle	.25	.60
❑ 47 Frank Sanders	.25	.60
❑ 48 O.J. McDuffie	.25	.60
❑ 49 Keenan McCardell	.25	.60
❑ 50 Randy Moss	1.00	2.50
❑ 51 Ed McCaffrey	.25	.60
❑ 52 Yancey Thigpen	.15	.40
❑ 53 Curtis Conway	.25	.60
❑ 54 Mike Alstott	.40	1.00
❑ 55 Deion Sanders	.40	1.00
❑ 56 Dorsey Levens	.40	1.00
❑ 57 Joey Galloway	.25	.60
❑ 58 Natrone Means	.25	.60
❑ 59 Tim Brown	.40	1.00
❑ 60 Jerry Rice	.75	2.00
❑ 61 Robert Smith	.40	1.00
❑ 62 Carl Pickens	.25	.60
❑ 63 Ben Coates	.25	.60
❑ 64 Jerome Bettis	.40	1.00
❑ 65 Corey Dillon	.40	1.00
❑ 66 Curtis Martin	.40	1.00
❑ 67 Jimmy Smith	.25	.60
❑ 68 Keyshawn Johnson	.40	1.00
❑ 69 Charlie Batch	.40	1.00
❑ 70 Jamal Anderson	.40	1.00
❑ 71 Mark Brunell	.40	1.00
❑ 72 Antowain Smith	.40	1.00
❑ 73 Aeneas Williams	.15	.40
❑ 74 Wesley Walls	.25	.60
❑ 75 Jake Plummer	.25	.60
❑ 76 Oronde Gadsden	.25	.60
❑ 77 Gary Brown	.15	.40
❑ 78 Peter Boulware	.15	.40
❑ 79 Stephen Alexander	.15	.40
❑ 80 Barry Sanders	1.25	3.00
❑ 81 Warren Sapp	.25	.60
❑ 82 Michael Sinclair	.15	.40
❑ 83 Freddie Jones	.15	.40
❑ 84 Ike Hilliard	.15	.40
❑ 85 Jake Reed	.25	.60
❑ 86 Tim Dwight	.40	1.00
❑ 87 Johnnie Morton	.25	.60
❑ 88 Robert Brooks	.25	.60
❑ 89 Rocket Ismail	.25	.60
❑ 90 Emmitt Smith	.75	2.00
❑ 91 Ricky Proehl	.15	.40
❑ 92 James Jett	.25	.60
❑ 93 Karim Abdul-Jabbar	.25	.60
❑ 94 Mark Chmura	.15	.40
❑ 95 Andre Reed	.25	.60
❑ 96 Michael Westbrook	.25	.60
❑ 97 Michael Strahan	.25	.60
❑ 98 Chad Brown	.15	.40
❑ 99 Trent Dilfer	.25	.60
❑ 100 Terrell Davis	.40	1.00
❑ 101 Aaron Glenn	.15	.40
❑ 102 Skip Hicks	.15	.40
❑ 103 Tony Gonzalez	.40	1.00
❑ 104 Ty Law	.25	.60
❑ 105 Jermaine Lewis	.25	.60
❑ 106 Ray Lewis	.40	1.00
❑ 107 Zach Thomas	.40	1.00
❑ 108 Reidel Anthony	.25	.60
❑ 109 Levon Kirkland	.15	.40
❑ 110 Drew Bledsoe	.50	1.25
❑ 111 Bobby Engram	.25	.60
❑ 112 Jerome Pathon	.15	.40
❑ 113 Muhsin Muhammad	.25	.60
❑ 114 Vonnie Holliday	.15	.40
❑ 115 Bill Romanowski	.15	.40
❑ 116 Marshall Faulk	.50	1.25
❑ 117 Ty Detmer	.25	.60
❑ 118 Mo Lewis	.15	.40
❑ 119 Charles Woodson	.40	1.00
❑ 120 Doug Flutie	.40	1.00

Card		
❑ 121 Jon Kitna	.40	1.00
❑ 122 Courtney Hawkins	.15	.40
❑ 123 Trent Green	.40	1.00
❑ 124 John Elway	1.25	3.00
❑ 125 Barry Sanders GM	2.00	5.00
❑ 126 Brett Favre GM	2.00	5.00
❑ 127 Curtis Martin GM	.60	1.50
❑ 128 Dan Marino GM	2.00	5.00
❑ 129 Eddie George GM	.40	1.00
❑ 130 Emmitt Smith GM	2.00	5.00
❑ 131 Jamal Anderson GM	.60	1.50
❑ 132 Jerry Rice GM	1.25	3.00
❑ 133 John Elway GM	2.00	5.00
❑ 134 Terrell Davis GM	1.00	2.50
❑ 135 Troy Aikman GM	1.25	3.00
❑ 136 Skip Hicks SN	.15	.40
❑ 137 Charles Woodson SN	.40	1.00
❑ 138 Charlie Batch SN	1.00	2.50
❑ 139 Curtis Enis SN	.60	1.50
❑ 140 Fred Taylor SN	1.00	2.50
❑ 141 Jake Plummer SN	.60	1.50
❑ 142 Peyton Manning SN	2.00	5.00
❑ 143 Randy Moss SN	1.50	4.00
❑ 144 Corey Dillon SN	.60	1.50
❑ 145 Priest Holmes SN	.60	1.50
❑ 146 Warrick Dunn SN	.60	1.50
❑ 147 Jevon Kearse RC	1.50	4.00
❑ 148 Chris Claiborne RC	.60	1.50
❑ 149 Akili Smith RC	.60	1.50
❑ 150 Brock Huard RC	1.25	3.00
❑ 151 Daunte Culpepper RC	4.00	10.00
❑ 152 Edgerrin James RC	4.00	10.00
❑ 153 Cecil Collins RC	.60	1.50
❑ 154 Kevin Faulk RC	1.25	3.00
❑ 155 Amos Zereoue RC	1.25	3.00
❑ 156 James Johnson RC	1.00	2.50
❑ 157 Sedrick Irvin RC	.60	1.50
❑ 158 Ricky Williams RC	2.00	5.00
❑ 159 Mike Cloud RC	1.00	2.50
❑ 160 Chris McAlister	.60	1.50
❑ 161 Rob Konrad RC	1.00	2.50
❑ 162 Champ Bailey RC	1.25	3.00
❑ 163 Ebenezer Ekuban RC	1.00	2.50
❑ 164 Tim Couch RC	1.25	3.00
❑ 165 Cade McNown RC	1.00	2.50
❑ 166 Donovan McNabb RC	5.00	12.00
❑ 167 Joe Germaine RC	1.00	2.50
❑ 168 Shaun King RC	1.00	2.50
❑ 169 Peerless Price RC	1.25	3.00
❑ 170 Kevin Johnson RC	1.00	2.50
❑ 171 Troy Edwards RC	1.00	2.50
❑ 172 Karsten Bailey RC	1.00	2.50
❑ 173 David Boston RC	1.25	3.00
❑ 174 D'Wayne Bates RC	1.00	2.50
❑ 175 Torry Holt RC	2.50	6.00

2000 Finest

Card		
❑ COMPLETE SET (205)	150.00	400.00
❑ 1 Tim Dwight	.30	.75
❑ 2 Cade McNown	.10	.30
❑ 3 Drew Bledsoe	.40	1.00
❑ 4 Torry Holt	.30	.75
❑ 5 Derrick Mayes	.20	.50
❑ 6 Vinny Testaverde	.20	.50
❑ 7 Patrick Jeffers	.30	.75
❑ 8 Dorsey Levens	.20	.50
❑ 9 James Johnson	.10	.30
❑ 10 Champ Bailey	.20	.50
❑ 11 Jeff George	.20	.50
❑ 12 Shawn Jefferson	.10	.30
❑ 13 Terrence Wilkins	.10	.30
❑ 14 J.J. Stokes	.20	.50
❑ 15 Doug Flutie	.30	.75
❑ 16 Corey Dillon	.30	.75
❑ 17 Rod Smith	.20	.50
❑ 18 Jimmy Smith	.20	.50
❑ 19 Amani Toomer	.20	.50
❑ 20 Curtis Conway	.20	.50
❑ 21 Brad Johnson	.30	.75
❑ 22 Edgerrin James	.50	1.25
❑ 23 Derrick Alexander	.20	.50
❑ 24 Terrell Owens	.30	.75
❑ 25 Kurt Warner	.60	1.50
❑ 26 Frank Sanders	.20	.50
❑ 27 Tony Banks	.20	.50
❑ 28 Troy Aikman	.60	1.50
❑ 29 Curtis Enis	.10	.30
❑ 30 Eddie George	.30	.75
❑ 31 Bill Schroeder	.20	.50
❑ 32 Kent Graham	.10	.30
❑ 33 Mike Alstott	.30	.75
❑ 34 Steve Young	.40	1.00
❑ 35 Jacquez Green	.10	.30
❑ 36 Frank Wycheck	.10	.30
❑ 37 Kerry Collins	.20	.50
❑ 38 Stephen Davis	.30	.75
❑ 39 Tony Gonzalez	.20	.50
❑ 40 Tyrone Wheatley	.20	.50
❑ 41 Brett Favre	1.00	2.50
❑ 42 Joey Galloway	.20	.50
❑ 43 Terrell Davis	.30	.75
❑ 44 Marvin Harrison	.30	.75
❑ 45 Zach Thomas	.30	.75
❑ 46 Jerry Rice	.60	1.50
❑ 47 Keyshawn Johnson	.30	.75
❑ 48 Rob Johnson	.20	.50
❑ 49 Rocket Ismail	.20	.50
❑ 50 Elvis Grbac	.20	.50
❑ 51 Warrick Dunn	.30	.75
❑ 52 Jevon Kearse	.30	.75
❑ 53 Albert Connell	.10	.30
❑ 54 Muhsin Muhammad	.20	.50
❑ 55 Carl Pickens	.20	.50
❑ 56 Peyton Manning	.75	2.00
❑ 57 Daunte Culpepper	.40	1.00
❑ 58 Ike Hilliard	.20	.50
❑ 59 Steve McNair	.30	.75
❑ 60 Sean Dawkins	.10	.30
❑ 61 Steve Beuerlein	.20	.50
❑ 62 Priest Holmes	.40	1.00
❑ 63 Jim Harbaugh	.20	.50
❑ 64 Germane Crowell	.10	.30
❑ 65 Cris Carter	.30	.75
❑ 66 Jamal Anderson	.30	.75
❑ 67 Kevin Johnson	.30	.75
❑ 68 Herman Moore	.20	.50
❑ 69 Ricky Williams	.30	.75
❑ 70 Rich Gannon	.30	.75
❑ 71 Isaac Bruce	.30	.75
❑ 72 Peerless Price	.20	.50
❑ 73 Az-Zahir Hakim	.20	.50
❑ 74 Mark Brunell	.30	.75
❑ 75 Rob Moore	.20	.50
❑ 76 Antowain Smith	.20	.50
❑ 77 Tim Biakabutuka	.20	.50
❑ 78 Ed McCaffrey	.30	.75
❑ 79 Tony Martin	.20	.50
❑ 80 Marcus Robinson	.30	.75
❑ 81 Kevin Dyson	.20	.50
❑ 82 Wesley Walls	.10	.30
❑ 83 Chris Chandler	.20	.50
❑ 84 Keenan McCardell	.20	.50
❑ 85 Napoleon Kaufman	.20	.50
❑ 86 Emmitt Smith	.60	1.50
❑ 87 James Stewart	.20	.50
❑ 88 Tim Brown	.30	.75
❑ 89 Ricky Watters	.20	.50
❑ 90 Johnnie Morton	.20	.50
❑ 91 Jake Plummer	.20	.50
❑ 92 Olandis Gary	.30	.75
❑ 93 Jerome Bettis	.30	.75
❑ 94 Terry Glenn	.20	.50
❑ 95 Kordell Stewart	.20	.50
❑ 96 Charlie Garner	.20	.50
❑ 97 Yancey Thigpen	.10	.30
❑ 98 Michael Westbrook	.20	.50
❑ 99 Bobby Engram	.20	.50
❑ 100 Eric Moulds	.30	.75
❑ 101 Darnay Scott	.20	.50
❑ 102 Antonio Freeman	.30	.75
❑ 103 Wayne Chrebet	.20	.50
❑ 104 Akili Smith	.10	.30
❑ 105 Jeff Blake	.20	.50
❑ 106 Curtis Martin	.30	.75
❑ 107 Errict Rhett	.20	.50
❑ 108 Damon Huard	.30	.75
❑ 109 Jeff Graham	.10	.30
❑ 110 Terance Mathis	.20	.50
❑ 111 Jon Kitna	.30	.75
❑ 112 Tim Couch	.20	.50
❑ 113 Fred Taylor	.30	.75
❑ 114 Qadry Ismail	.20	.50
❑ 115 Donovan McNabb	.50	1.25
❑ 116 Charles Johnson	.20	.50
❑ 117 Troy Edwards	.10	.30
❑ 118 Shaun King	.10	.30
❑ 119 Charlie Batch	.30	.75
❑ 120 Robert Smith	.30	.75
❑ 121 Marshall Faulk	.40	1.00
❑ 122 Brian Griese	.30	.75
❑ 123 O.J. McDuffie	.20	.50
❑ 124 Randy Moss	.60	1.50
❑ 125 Duce Staley	.30	.75
❑ 126 Peter Warrick RC	3.00	8.00
❑ 127 Dez White RC	3.00	8.00
❑ 128 Ron Dayne RC	3.00	8.00
❑ 129 J.R. Redmond RC	2.50	6.00
❑ 130 Thomas Jones RC	5.00	12.00
❑ 131 Plaxico Burress RC	6.00	15.00
❑ 132 Reuben Droughns RC	4.00	10.00
❑ 133 Shaun Alexander RC	6.00	15.00
❑ 134 Ron Dugans RC	2.50	6.00
❑ 135 Travis Prentice RC	2.50	6.00
❑ 136 Joe Hamilton RC	2.50	6.00
❑ 137 Curtis Keaton RC	2.50	6.00
❑ 138 Chris Redman RC	2.50	6.00
❑ 139 Chad Pennington RC	7.50	20.00
❑ 140 Travis Taylor RC	3.00	8.00
❑ 141 Bubba Franks RC	3.00	8.00
❑ 142 Dennis Northcutt RC	3.00	8.00
❑ 143 Jerry Porter RC	4.00	10.00
❑ 144 Sylvester Morris RC	2.50	6.00
❑ 145 Anthony Becht RC	3.00	8.00
❑ 146 Trung Canidate RC	2.50	6.00
❑ 147 Jamal Lewis RC	7.50	20.00
❑ 148 R.Jay Soward RC	2.50	6.00
❑ 149 Tee Martin RC	3.00	8.00
❑ 150 Courtney Brown RC	3.00	8.00
❑ 151 Brian Urlacher RC	12.50	30.00
❑ 152 Danny Farmer RC	2.50	6.00
❑ 153 Laveranues Coles RC	4.00	10.00
❑ 154 Todd Pinkston RC	3.00	8.00
❑ 155 Corey Simon RC	3.00	8.00
❑ 156 Spergon Wynn RC	2.50	6.00
❑ 157 Tim Rattay RC	3.00	8.00
❑ 158 Todd Husak RC	3.00	8.00
❑ 159 Aaron Shea RC	2.50	6.00
❑ 160 Giovanni Carmazzi RC	2.50	6.00
❑ 161 Trevor Gaylor RC	2.50	6.00
❑ 162 JaJuan Dawson RC	2.50	6.00
❑ 163 Jarious Jackson RC	2.50	6.00
❑ 164 Chris Samuels RC	2.50	6.00
❑ 165 Rob Morris RC	2.50	6.00
❑ 166 P.Warrick/R.Moss IF	.75	2.00
❑ 167 R.Moss/P.Warrick IF	.75	2.00
❑ 168 T.Prentice/S.Davis IF	.60	1.50
❑ 169 S.Davis/T.Prentice IF	.60	1.50
❑ 170 C.Redman/K.Warner IF	.60	1.50
❑ 171 K.Warner/C.Redman IF	.60	1.50
❑ 172 Syl.Morris/J.Smith IF	.60	1.50
❑ 173 J.Smith/Syl.Morris IF	.60	1.50
❑ 174 C.Pennington/P.Manning IF	1.50	4.00
❑ 175 P.Manning/C.Pennington IF	1.50	4.00
❑ 176 R.Soward/M.Harrison IF	.60	1.50
❑ 177 M.Harrison/R.Soward IF	.60	1.50
❑ 178 R.Dayne/J.Anderson IF	.60	1.50
❑ 179 J.Anderson/R.Dayne IF	.60	1.50
❑ 180 S.Alexander/E.George IF	1.00	2.50
❑ 181 E.George/S.Alexander IF	.75	2.00
❑ 182 C.Brown/B.Smith IF	.60	1.50
❑ 183 B.Smith/C.Brown IF	.60	1.50
❑ 184 J.Lewis/E.James IF	1.25	3.00
❑ 185 E.James/J.Lewis IF	1.25	3.00
❑ 186 T.Canidate/E.Smith IF	1.25	3.00
❑ 187 E.Smith/T.Canidate IF	1.25	3.00
❑ 188 T.Taylor/C.Carter IF	.75	2.00
❑ 189 C.Carter/T.Taylor IF	.75	2.00
❑ 190 C.Keaton/M.Faulk IF	.75	2.00
❑ 191 M.Faulk/C.Keaton IF	.75	2.00
❑ 192 P.Burress/J.Rice IF	1.25	3.00
❑ 193 J.Rice/P.Burress IF	1.25	3.00
❑ 194 T.Jones/T.Davis IF	.75	2.00
❑ 195 T.Davis/T.Jones IF	.75	2.00
❑ 196 Peyton Manning GM	2.00	5.00

Card	Low	High
❑ 197 Randy Moss GM	1.50	4.00
❑ 198 Terrell Davis GM	.60	1.50
❑ 199 Marshall Faulk GM	1.00	2.50
❑ 200 Edgerrin James GM	1.50	4.00
❑ 201 Emmitt Smith GM	1.50	4.00
❑ 202 Ricky Williams GM	.60	1.50
❑ 203 Kurt Warner GM	1.25	3.00
❑ 204 Eddie George GM	.60	1.50
❑ 205 Brett Favre GM	2.50	6.00

2001 Finest

Card	Low	High
❑ COMP.SET w/o SP's (100)	20.00	40.00
❑ 1 Eddie George	.40	1.00
❑ 2 Jay Fiedler	.30	.75
❑ 3 Peter Warrick	.30	.75
❑ 4 Vinny Testaverde	.30	.75
❑ 5 Charles Johnson	.25	.60
❑ 6 Ahman Green	.40	1.00
❑ 7 Isaac Bruce	.40	1.00
❑ 8 Junior Seau	.40	1.00
❑ 9 Daunte Culpepper	.40	1.00
❑ 10 Ike Hilliard	.30	.75
❑ 11 Tony Banks	.25	.60
❑ 12 Steve Beuerlein	.30	.75
❑ 13 Jamal Anderson	.30	.75
❑ 14 Tyrone Wheatley	.30	.75
❑ 15 Sylvester Morris	.25	.60
❑ 16 Edgerrin James	.40	1.00
❑ 17 Shaun King	.25	.60
❑ 18 Terrell Owens	.40	1.00
❑ 19 Donovan Mcnabb	.50	1.25
❑ 20 Cade Mcnown	.30	.75
❑ 21 Elvis Grbac	.30	.75
❑ 22 James Stewart	.25	.60
❑ 23 Joe Horn	.30	.75
❑ 24 Randy Moss	.50	1.25
❑ 25 Matt Hasselbeck	.40	1.00
❑ 26 Jerome Bettis	.40	1.00
❑ 27 Bill Schroeder	.30	.75
❑ 28 Jake Plummer	.30	.75
❑ 29 Rod Smith	.30	.75
❑ 30 Akili Smith	.25	.60
❑ 31 Jimmy Smith	.30	.75
❑ 32 Oronde Gadsden	.25	.60
❑ 33 Kerry Collins	.30	.75
❑ 34 Warrick Dunn	.40	1.00
❑ 35 Jeff Graham	.25	.60
❑ 36 Ray Lewis	.40	1.00
❑ 37 Joey Galloway	.30	.75
❑ 38 Tim Brown	.40	1.00
❑ 39 Derrick Alexander	.25	.60
❑ 40 Jerry Rice	.75	2.00
❑ 41 Muhsin Muhammad	.30	.75
❑ 42 Shawn Jefferson	.25	.60
❑ 43 Curtis Martin	.40	1.00
❑ 44 Terry Glenn	.30	.75
❑ 45 Marvin Harrison	.40	1.00
❑ 46 Mike Anderson	.30	.75
❑ 47 Stephen Davis	.30	.75
❑ 48 Chad Lewis	.25	.60
❑ 49 Fred Taylor	.40	1.00
❑ 50 Corey Dillon	.30	.75
❑ 51 Charlie Batch	.30	.75
❑ 52 Kevin Johnson	.25	.60
❑ 53 Brett Favre	1.25	3.00
❑ 54 Marshall Faulk	.40	1.00
❑ 55 Kordell Stewart	.30	.75
❑ 56 Steve McNair	.40	1.00
❑ 57 Jeff Blake	.30	.75
❑ 58 Eric Moulds	.30	.75
❑ 59 Emmitt Smith	1.00	2.50
❑ 60 David Boston	.25	.60
❑ 61 Cris Carter	.40	1.00
❑ 62 Peyton Manning	1.00	2.50
❑ 63 Keyshawn Johnson	.30	.75
❑ 64 Doug Flutie	.40	1.00
❑ 65 Drew Bledsoe	.40	1.00
❑ 66 Ricky Williams	.40	1.00
❑ 67 Keenan Mccardell	.30	.75
❑ 68 Brian Urlacher	.50	1.25
❑ 69 Jamal Lewis	.40	1.00
❑ 70 Ed McCaffrey	.30	.75
❑ 71 Antonio Freeman	.40	1.00
❑ 72 Darrell Jackson	.30	.75
❑ 73 Jeff George	.30	.75
❑ 74 Chris Chandler	.30	.75
❑ 75 Germane Crowell	.25	.60
❑ 76 Tim Biakabutuka	.25	.60
❑ 77 Jon Kitna	.30	.75
❑ 78 Troy Brown	.30	.75
❑ 79 Lamar Smith	.30	.75
❑ 80 Derrick Mason	.30	.75
❑ 81 Hines Ward	.40	1.00
❑ 82 Mark Brunell	.40	1.00
❑ 83 Trent Dilfer	.30	.75
❑ 84 Tim Couch	.25	.60
❑ 85 Donald Hayes	.25	.60
❑ 86 Amani Toomer	.30	.75
❑ 87 Tony Gonzalez	.30	.75
❑ 88 Rich Gannon	.30	.75
❑ 89 Rob Johnson	.30	.75
❑ 90 Torry Holt	.30	.75
❑ 91 Jeff Garcia	.30	.75
❑ 92 Kurt Warner	.50	1.25
❑ 93 Aaron Brooks	.30	.75
❑ 94 Brian Griese	.30	.75
❑ 95 James Allen	.25	.60
❑ 96 Wayne Chrebet	.30	.75
❑ 97 Tiki Barber	.40	1.00
❑ 98 Brad Johnson	.30	.75
❑ 99 Ricky Watters	.30	.75
❑ 100 Charlie Garner	.30	.75
❑ 101 Andre Carter RC	3.00	8.00
❑ 102 Dan Morgan RC	3.00	8.00
❑ 103 Gerard Warren RC	2.50	6.00
❑ 104 Jesse Palmer RC	3.00	8.00
❑ 105 Josh Heupel RC	3.00	8.00
❑ 106 Justin Smith RC	3.00	8.00
❑ 107 LaMont Jordan RC	3.00	8.00
❑ 108 Leonard Davis RC	2.50	6.00
❑ 109 Marques Tuiasosopo RC	2.50	6.00
❑ 110 Snoop Minnis RC	2.50	6.00
❑ 111 Quincy Carter RC	2.50	6.00
❑ 112 Quincy Morgan RC	2.50	6.00
❑ 113 Richard Seymour RC	3.00	8.00
❑ 114 Rudi Johnson RC	3.00	8.00
❑ 115 Sage Rosenfels RC	3.00	8.00
❑ 116 Todd Heap RC	3.00	8.00
❑ 117 Travis Minor RC	2.50	6.00
❑ 118 Will Allen RC	3.00	8.00
❑ 119 Jamal Reynolds RC	2.50	6.00
❑ 120 Scotty Anderson RC	2.50	6.00
❑ 121 Anthony Thomas RC	3.00	8.00
❑ 122 Chad Johnson RC	8.00	20.00
❑ 123 Chris Chambers RC	5.00	12.00
❑ 124 Chris Weinke RC	2.50	6.00
❑ 125 David Terrell RC	2.50	6.00
❑ 126 Deuce McAllister RC	4.00	10.00
❑ 127 Drew Brees RC	25.00	50.00
❑ 128 Freddie Mitchell RC	2.00	5.00
❑ 129 James Jackson RC	2.50	6.00
❑ 130 Kevan Barlow RC	2.50	6.00
❑ 131 Koren Robinson RC	3.00	8.00
❑ 132 LaDainian Tomlinson RC	40.00	80.00
❑ 133 Michael Bennett RC	3.00	8.00
❑ 134 Michael Vick RC	6.00	15.00
❑ 135 Mike McMahon RC	2.50	6.00
❑ 136 Reggie Wayne RC	8.00	20.00
❑ 137 Robert Ferguson RC	3.00	8.00
❑ 138 Rod Gardner RC	2.50	6.00
❑ 139 Santana Moss RC	5.00	12.00
❑ 140 Travis Henry RC	3.00	8.00

2002 Finest

Card	Low	High
❑ COMP.SET w/o SP's (62)	15.00	40.00
❑ 1 Peyton Manning	1.00	2.50
❑ 2 Troy Brown	.40	1.00
❑ 3 Curtis Martin	.50	1.25
❑ 4 Kordell Stewart	.40	1.00
❑ 5 Michael Pittman	.40	1.00
❑ 6 Rod Gardner	.30	.75
❑ 7 Germane Crowell	.30	.75
❑ 8 Terrell Davis	.50	1.25
❑ 9 Eric Moulds	.40	1.00
❑ 10 Jake Plummer	.40	1.00
❑ 11 Tony Gonzalez	.40	1.00
❑ 12 Ricky Williams	.50	1.25
❑ 13 Deuce McAllister	.50	1.25
❑ 14 Jerry Rice	1.00	2.50
❑ 15 Torry Holt	.50	1.25
❑ 16 Michael Vick	.50	1.25
❑ 17 David Terrell	.40	1.00
❑ 18 Terry Glenn	.40	1.00
❑ 19 Mark Brunell	.40	1.00
❑ 20 Vinny Testaverde	.40	1.00
❑ 21 Jerome Bettis	.50	1.25
❑ 22 Randy Moss	.50	1.25
❑ 23 Marvin Harrison	.50	1.25
❑ 24 Chris Weinke	.30	.75
❑ 25 Tiki Barber	.50	1.25
❑ 26 Corey Bradford	.30	.75
❑ 27 David Boston	.30	.75
❑ 28 Emmitt Smith	1.25	3.00
❑ 29 Santana Moss	.40	1.00
❑ 30 Brian Griese	.40	1.00
❑ 31 Priest Holmes	.50	1.25
❑ 32 Rich Gannon	.40	1.00
❑ 33 Antowain Smith	.40	1.00
❑ 34 Marcus Robinson	.40	1.00
❑ 35 Warrick Dunn	.40	1.00
❑ 36 Daunte Culpepper	.40	1.00
❑ 37 Shaun Alexander	.50	1.25
❑ 38 Kurt Warner	.50	1.25
❑ 39 Quincy Carter	.30	.75
❑ 40 Ray Lewis	.50	1.25
❑ 41 Aaron Brooks	.40	1.00
❑ 42 Plaxico Burress	.40	1.00
❑ 43 Jamal Lewis	.40	1.00
❑ 44 Ahman Green	.40	1.00
❑ 45 Rod Smith	.40	1.00
❑ 46 Tim Couch	.30	.75
❑ 47 Muhsin Muhammad	.40	1.00
❑ 48 Drew Bledsoe	.50	1.25
❑ 49 Anthony Thomas	.40	1.00
❑ 50 Tom Brady	1.25	3.00
❑ 51 Trent Green	.40	1.00
❑ 52 Charlie Garner	.40	1.00
❑ 53 Darrell Jackson	.40	1.00
❑ 54 Mike McMahon	.30	.75
❑ 55 Donovan McNabb	.60	1.50
❑ 56 Fred Taylor	.50	1.25
❑ 57 Corey Dillon	.40	1.00
❑ 58 Keyshawn Johnson	.40	1.00
❑ 59 Drew Brees	.75	2.00
❑ 60 Steve McNair	.50	1.25
❑ 61 Jimmy Smith	.40	1.00
❑ 62 Terrell Owens	.50	1.25
❑ 63 Eddie George JSY/499	6.00	15.00
❑ 64 Jeff Garcia JSY/999	5.00	12.00
❑ 65 LaDain Tomlinson JSY/999	10.00	25.00
❑ 66 Cris Carter JSY/499	8.00	20.00
❑ 67 Chris Chambers JSY/499	8.00	20.00
❑ 68 Brian Urlacher JSY/999	8.00	20.00
❑ 69 Tim Brown JSY/999	6.00	15.00
❑ 70 Marshall Faulk JSY/999	6.00	15.00
❑ 71 Stephen Davis JSY/999	5.00	12.00
❑ 72 Jevon Kearse JSY/999	5.00	12.00
❑ 73 Edgerrin James JSY/999	6.00	15.00

- ❑ 74 Mike Anderson JSY/999 5.00 12.00
- ❑ 75 Warren Sapp JSY/499 6.00 15.00
- ❑ 76 Brett Favre JSY/499 20.00 50.00
- ❑ 77 Julius Peppers RC 2.00 5.00
- ❑ 78 Tim Carter RC 1.00 2.50
- ❑ 79 Travis Stephens RC .75 2.00
- ❑ 80 Jabar Gaffney RC 1.25 3.00
- ❑ 81 Cliff Russell RC .75 2.00
- ❑ 82 Reche Caldwell RC 1.25 3.00
- ❑ 83 Maurice Morris RC 1.25 3.00
- ❑ 84 Antwaan Randle El RC 1.25 3.00
- ❑ 85 Ladell Betts RC 1.25 3.00
- ❑ 86 Daniel Graham RC 1.00 2.50
- ❑ 87 Jeremy Shockey RC 2.00 5.00
- ❑ 88 Mike Williams RC .75 2.00
- ❑ 89 Josh McCown RC 1.25 3.00
- ❑ 90 Rohan Davey RC 1.25 3.00
- ❑ 91 David Garrard RC 2.00 5.00
- ❑ 92 Dwight Freeney RC 2.00 5.00
- ❑ 93 Leonard Henry RC .75 2.00
- ❑ 94 Albert Haynesworth RC 1.25 3.00
- ❑ 95 Herb Haygood RC .75 2.00
- ❑ 96 Kurt Kittner RC .75 2.00
- ❑ 97 Jason McAddley RC 1.00 2.50
- ❑ 98 Bryan Thomas RC .75 2.00
- ❑ 99 Wendell Bryant RC .75 2.00
- ❑ 100 Mike Rumph RC .75 2.00
- ❑ 101 Chad Hutchinson RC .75 2.00
- ❑ 102 Brian Westbrook RC 4.00 10.00
- ❑ 103 Deion Branch RC 1.25 3.00
- ❑ 104 John Henderson RC 1.25 3.00
- ❑ 105 Jerramy Stevens RC 1.25 3.00
- ❑ 106 Tracey Wistrom RC 1.00 2.50
- ❑ 107 Phillip Buchanon RC 1.25 3.00
- ❑ 108 Matt Schobel RC 1.25 3.00
- ❑ 109 Ed Reed RC 4.00 10.00
- ❑ 110 Randy Fasani RC 1.00 2.50
- ❑ 111 Josh Scobey RC 1.00 2.50
- ❑ 112 Luke Staley RC .75 2.00
- ❑ 113 Anthony Weaver RC .75 2.00
- ❑ 114 Kyle Johnson RC .75 2.00
- ❑ 115 David Carr AU RC 8.00 20.00
- ❑ 116 Joey Harrington AU RC 8.00 20.00
- ❑ 117 Donte Stallworth AU RC 8.00 20.00
- ❑ 118 Ashley Lelie AU RC 8.00 20.00
- ❑ 119 Patrick Ramsey AU RC 8.00 20.00
- ❑ 120 William Green AU RC 6.00 15.00
- ❑ 121 Josh Reed AU RC 6.00 15.00
- ❑ 122 Clinton Portis AU RC 25.00 50.00
- ❑ 123 Antonio Bryant AU RC 10.00 25.00
- ❑ 124 Javon Walker AU RC 8.00 20.00
- ❑ 125 Roy Williams AU RC 10.00 25.00
- ❑ 126 Marquise Walker AU RC 5.00 12.00
- ❑ 127 Quentin Jammer AU RC 8.00 20.00
- ❑ 128 DeShaun Foster AU RC 8.00 20.00
- ❑ 129 Andre Davis AU RC 6.00 15.00
- ❑ 130 Ron Johnson AU RC 6.00 15.00
- ❑ 131 Lamar Gordon AU RC 8.00 20.00
- ❑ 132 T.J. Duckett AU/300 RC 8.00 20.00
- ❑ 133 Freddie Milons AU RC 5.00 12.00
- ❑ 134 Eric Crouch AU RC 8.00 20.00
- ❑ 135 Adrian Peterson AU RC 8.00 20.00
- ❑ 136 Damien Anderson AU RC 6.00 15.00

2003 Finest

- ❑ COMP.SET w/o SP's (100) 20.00 50.00
- ❑ 1 Chad Pennington .40 1.00
- ❑ 2 Tommy Maddox .30 .75
- ❑ 3 Brett Favre 1.00 2.50
- ❑ 4 Eric Moulds .30 .75
- ❑ 5 Randy Moss .40 1.00
- ❑ 6 Duce Staley .30 .75
- ❑ 7 Derrick Mason .30 .75
- ❑ 8 Shaun Alexander .40 1.00
- ❑ 9 Peyton Manning .75 2.00
- ❑ 10 Kerry Collins .30 .75
- ❑ 11 Joe Horn .30 .75
- ❑ 12 Laveranues Coles .30 .75
- ❑ 13 Marty Booker .30 .75
- ❑ 14 Emmitt Smith 1.00 2.50
- ❑ 15 Edgerrin James .40 1.00
- ❑ 16 Aaron Brooks .30 .75
- ❑ 17 Curtis Martin .40 1.00
- ❑ 18 Hines Ward .40 1.00
- ❑ 19 Rod Smith .30 .75
- ❑ 20 Priest Holmes .40 1.00
- ❑ 21 Jerry Rice .75 2.00
- ❑ 22 Peerless Price .25 .60
- ❑ 23 Mark Brunell .30 .75
- ❑ 24 Trent Green .30 .75
- ❑ 25 David Boston .25 .60
- ❑ 26 Chris Chambers .30 .75
- ❑ 27 Marshall Faulk .40 1.00
- ❑ 28 Fred Taylor .40 1.00
- ❑ 29 Tim Couch .25 .60
- ❑ 30 Amani Toomer .30 .75
- ❑ 31 Travis Henry .30 .75
- ❑ 32 Jeff Blake .30 .75
- ❑ 33 Troy Brown .30 .75
- ❑ 34 Charlie Garner .30 .75
- ❑ 35 Tom Brady 1.00 2.50
- ❑ 36 Warrick Dunn .30 .75
- ❑ 37 Plaxico Burress .40 1.00
- ❑ 38 Marvin Harrison .40 1.00
- ❑ 39 Clinton Portis .50 1.25
- ❑ 40 Deuce McAllister .40 1.00
- ❑ 41 Matt Hasselbeck .30 .75
- ❑ 42 Jeff Garcia .40 1.00
- ❑ 43 David Carr .40 1.00
- ❑ 44 Ahman Green .40 1.00
- ❑ 45 Eddie George .30 .75
- ❑ 46 Drew Brees .40 1.00
- ❑ 47 Tiki Barber .40 1.00
- ❑ 48 Jay Fiedler .30 .75
- ❑ 49 Curtis Conway .25 .60
- ❑ 50 Steve McNair .40 1.00
- ❑ 51 Donald Driver .40 1.00
- ❑ 52 Jake Plummer .30 .75
- ❑ 53 Jamal Lewis .40 1.00
- ❑ 54 Corey Dillon .30 .75
- ❑ 55 Stephen Davis .30 .75
- ❑ 56 Terrell Owens .40 1.00
- ❑ 57 Torry Holt .40 1.00
- ❑ 58 Chad Johnson .40 1.00
- ❑ 59 Chad Hutchinson .25 .60
- ❑ 60 Kurt Warner .40 1.00
- ❑ 61 Troy Polamalu RC 8.00 20.00
- ❑ 62 Eugene Wilson RC 1.25 3.00
- ❑ 63 Juston Wood RC .75 2.00
- ❑ 64 Anquan Boldin RC 3.00 8.00
- ❑ 65 Doug Gabriel RC 1.00 2.50
- ❑ 66 Domanick Davis RC 1.25 3.00
- ❑ 67 J.R. Tolver RC 1.00 2.50
- ❑ 68 Jerome McDougle RC .75 2.00
- ❑ 69 Keenan Howry RC .75 2.00
- ❑ 70 Teyo Johnson RC 1.00 2.50
- ❑ 71 Bethel Johnson RC 1.00 2.50
- ❑ 72 Ken Hamlin RC 1.25 3.00
- ❑ 73 L.J. Smith RC 1.25 3.00
- ❑ 74 Rashean Mathis RC 1.00 2.50
- ❑ 75 Arnaz Battle RC 1.25 3.00
- ❑ 76 B.J. Askew RC 1.00 2.50
- ❑ 77 Mike Doss RC 1.25 3.00
- ❑ 78 Kevin Curtis RC 1.25 3.00
- ❑ 79 Terence Newman RC 1.25 3.00
- ❑ 80 Shaun McDonald RC 1.25 3.00
- ❑ 81 Kevin Williams RC 1.25 3.00
- ❑ 82 Nate Burleson RC 1.00 2.50
- ❑ 83 Tyrone Calico RC 1.00 2.50
- ❑ 84 DeWayne White RC .75 2.00
- ❑ 85 Marcus Trufant RC 1.25 3.00
- ❑ 86 Nick Barnett RC 1.25 3.00
- ❑ 87 Bennie Joppru RC .75 2.00
- ❑ 88 Andre Woolfolk RC 1.00 2.50
- ❑ 89 Billy McMullen RC .75 2.00
- ❑ 90 Boss Bailey RC 1.00 2.50
- ❑ 91 William Joseph RC .75 2.00
- ❑ 92 Michael Haynes RC .75 2.00
- ❑ 93 DeWayne Robertson RC 1.00 2.50
- ❑ 94 LaTarence Dunbar RC .75 2.00
- ❑ 95 David Tyree RC 1.25 3.00
- ❑ 96 Walter Young RC .75 2.00
- ❑ 97 E.J. Henderson RC 1.00 2.50
- ❑ 98 Ty Warren RC 1.25 3.00
- ❑ 99 Zuriel Smith RC .75 2.00
- ❑ 100 Brock Forsey RC 1.00 2.50
- ❑ 101 Ricky Williams JSY C 4.00 10.00
- ❑ 102 Drew Bledsoe JSY C 5.00 12.00
- ❑ 103 Joey Harrington JSY C 4.00 10.00
- ❑ 104 Tim Brown JSY C 5.00 12.00
- ❑ 105 Brian Urlacher JSY C 8.00 20.00
- ❑ 106 Zach Thomas JSY C 5.00 12.00
- ❑ 107 Jeremy Shockey JSY C 5.00 12.00
- ❑ 108 Michael Strahan JSY A 5.00 12.00
- ❑ 109 Jason Taylor JSY C 4.00 10.00
- ❑ 110 Donovan McNabb JSY C 5.00 12.00
- ❑ 111 LaDainian Tomlinson JSY B 8.00 20.00
- ❑ 112 Rich Gannon JSY C 4.00 10.00
- ❑ 113 Brad Johnson JSY C 4.00 10.00
- ❑ 114 Daunte Culpepper JSY C 5.00 12.00
- ❑ 115 Michael Vick JSY C 5.00 12.00
- ❑ 116 Jimmy Smith JSY B 5.00 12.00
- ❑ 117 Keyshawn Johnson JSY C 5.00 12.00
- ❑ 118 Keith Brooking JSY C 4.00 10.00
- ❑ 119 Carson Palmer AU/399 RC 40.00 80.00
- ❑ 120 Byron Leftwich AU/399 RC 12.00 30.00
- ❑ 121 Chris Simms AU/399 RC 10.00 25.00
- ❑ 122 Kyle Boller AU/399 RC 10.00 25.00
- ❑ 123 Justin Fargas AU RC 6.00 15.00
- ❑ 124 Seneca Wallace AU RC 6.00 15.00
- ❑ 125 Larry Johnson AU RC 8.00 20.00
- ❑ 126 Kareem Kelly AU RC 4.00 10.00
- ❑ 127 Willis McGahee AU/399 RC 20.00 40.00
- ❑ 128 Kelley Washington AU RC 5.00 12.00
- ❑ 129 Brian St.Pierre AU RC 6.00 15.00
- ❑ 130 Kliff Kingsbury AU RC 5.00 12.00
- ❑ 131 Ken Dorsey AU RC 5.00 12.00
- ❑ 132 Bryant Johnson AU RC 6.00 15.00
- ❑ 133 Dallas Clark AU RC 20.00 40.00
- ❑ 134 Chris Brown AU RC 6.00 15.00
- ❑ 135 Taylor Jacobs AU RC 5.00 12.00
- ❑ 136 Artose Pinner AU RC 4.00 10.00
- ❑ 137 Lee Suggs AU RC 5.00 12.00
- ❑ 138 LaBrandon Toefield AU RC 5.00 12.00
- ❑ 139 Jason Witten AU RC 25.00 40.00
- ❑ 140 Brad Banks AU RC 5.00 12.00
- ❑ 141 Earnest Graham AU RC 8.00 20.00
- ❑ 142 Bobby Wade AU RC 5.00 12.00
- ❑ 143 Talman Gardner AU RC 4.00 10.00
- ❑ 144 Justin Gage AU RC 6.00 15.00
- ❑ 145 Sam Aiken AU RC 6.00 15.00
- ❑ 146 Musa Smith AU RC 5.00 12.00
- ❑ 147 Terrell Suggs AU RC 8.00 20.00
- ❑ 148 Brandon Lloyd AU RC 6.00 15.00
- ❑ 150 Rex Grossman AU RC 6.00 15.00

2004 Finest

- ❑ COMP.SET w/o SP's (100) 15.00 40.00
- ❑ COMP.SET w/o RC's (60) 5.00 12.00
- ❑ 108-134 AU/399 RC STATED ODDS 1:120
- ❑ 108-134 AU/999 RC STATED ODDS 1:12
- ❑ 1 Steve McNair .30 .75
- ❑ 2 Corey Dillon .25 .60
- ❑ 3 Joey Harrington .25 .60
- ❑ 4 Travis Henry .25 .60
- ❑ 5 Donovan McNabb .30 .75
- ❑ 6 Jamal Lewis .25 .60
- ❑ 7 Jeff Garcia .30 .75
- ❑ 8 Fred Taylor .25 .60
- ❑ 9 Aaron Brooks .25 .60
- ❑ 10 Marc Bulger .25 .60
- ❑ 11 Keenan McCardell .20 .50
- ❑ 12 David Carr .25 .60
- ❑ 13 Charles Rogers .25 .60
- ❑ 14 Ray Lewis .30 .75
- ❑ 15 Priest Holmes .30 .75
- ❑ 16 Curtis Martin .30 .75
- ❑ 17 Plaxico Burress .25 .60
- ❑ 18 Shaun Alexander .30 .75
- ❑ 19 Brad Johnson .25 .60
- ❑ 20 Marvin Harrison .30 .75

Card		
❑ 21 Rod Smith	.25	.60
❑ 22 Jake Delhomme	.25	.60
❑ 23 Santana Moss	.25	.60
❑ 24 Trent Green	.25	.60
❑ 25 Michael Vick	.30	.75
❑ 26 Tim Rattay	.20	.50
❑ 27 Chris Chambers	.25	.60
❑ 28 Robert Ferguson	.20	.50
❑ 29 Tiki Barber	.30	.75
❑ 30 Terrell Owens	.30	.75
❑ 31 Marshall Faulk	.30	.75
❑ 32 Quincy Carter	.20	.50
❑ 33 Stephen Davis	.25	.60
❑ 34 Josh McCown	.25	.60
❑ 35 Jeremy Shockey	.25	.60
❑ 36 Tommy Maddox	.25	.60
❑ 37 Derrick Mason	.25	.60
❑ 38 Kerry Collins	.25	.60
❑ 39 Jimmy Smith	.25	.60
❑ 40 Chad Pennington	.30	.75
❑ 41 Domanick Davis	.25	.60
❑ 42 Darrell Jackson	.25	.60
❑ 43 Steve Smith	.30	.75
❑ 44 Drew Bledsoe	.30	.75
❑ 45 Deuce McAllister	.30	.75
❑ 46 Jerry Porter	.25	.60
❑ 47 Peerless Price	.25	.60
❑ 48 Eric Moulds	.25	.60
❑ 49 Garrison Hearst	.25	.60
❑ 50 Brett Favre	.75	2.00
❑ 51 Amani Toomer	.25	.60
❑ 52 Andre Johnson	.30	.75
❑ 53 Edgerrin James	.30	.75
❑ 54 Rex Grossman	.30	.75
❑ 55 Daunte Culpepper	.30	.75
❑ 56 Tony Gonzalez	.30	.75
❑ 57 Byron Leftwich	.30	.75
❑ 58 Mark Brunell	.25	.60
❑ 59 Laveranues Coles	.25	.60
❑ 60 Matt Hasselbeck	.30	.75
❑ 61 Chris Gamble RC	.60	1.50
❑ 62 Michael Turner RC	2.00	5.00
❑ 63 Julius Jones RC	1.00	2.50
❑ 64 Dunta Robinson RC	.60	1.50
❑ 65 Sean Taylor RC	.75	2.00
❑ 66 Ahmad Carroll RC	.75	2.00
❑ 67 Derrick Strait RC	.60	1.50
❑ 68 Dontarrious Thomas RC	.60	1.50
❑ 69 Jason Babin RC	.60	1.50
❑ 70 Reggie Williams RC	.75	2.00
❑ 71 Dwan Edwards RC	.50	1.25
❑ 72 Rashaun Woods RC	.50	1.25
❑ 73 Ricardo Colclough RC	.75	2.00
❑ 74 Will Smith RC	.75	2.00
❑ 75 Kellen Winslow RC	1.00	2.50
❑ 76 Roy Williams RC	1.00	2.50
❑ 77 B.J. Symons RC	.50	1.25
❑ 78 Carlos Francis RC	.50	1.25
❑ 79 Triandos Luke RC	.50	1.25
❑ 80 Drew Henson RC	.50	1.25
❑ 81 Keiwan Ratliff RC	.50	1.25
❑ 82 Will Poole RC	.75	2.00
❑ 83 Tommie Harris RC	.75	2.00
❑ 84 Steven Jackson RC	2.00	5.00
❑ 85 Greg Jones RC	.75	2.00
❑ 86 Vince Wilfork RC	.75	2.00
❑ 87 DeAngelo Hall RC	.75	2.00
❑ 88 Daryl Smith RC	.60	1.50
❑ 89 Teddy Lehman RC	.60	1.50
❑ 90 Casey Bramlet RC	.50	1.25
❑ 91 Marcus Tubbs RC	.50	1.25
❑ 92 Andy Hall RC	.60	1.50
❑ 93 Jim Sorgi RC	.75	2.00
❑ 94 Kenechi Udeze RC	.75	2.00
❑ 95 Darius Watts RC	.60	1.50
❑ 96 Tank Johnson RC	.60	1.50
❑ 97 Matt Mauck RC	.60	1.50
❑ 98 Bradlee Van Pelt RC	.60	1.50
❑ 99 D.J. Williams RC	.75	2.00
❑ 100 Larry Fitzgerald RC	2.50	6.00
❑ 101 Peyton Manning JSY	6.00	15.00
❑ 102 Clinton Portis JSY	3.00	8.00
❑ 103 Chad Johnson JSY	2.50	6.00
❑ 104 Randy Moss JSY	3.00	8.00
❑ 105 Tom Brady JSY	8.00	20.00
❑ 106 LaDainian Tomlinson JSY	4.00	10.00
❑ 107 Ahman Green JSY	3.00	8.00
❑ 108 Roethlisberger AU/399 RC	100.00	200.00
❑ 109 Philip Rivers AU/399 RC	50.00	100.00
❑ 110 Eli Manning AU/399 RC	75.00	150.00
❑ 111 Kevin Jones AU/399 RC	8.00	20.00
❑ 112 Bernard Berrian AU RC	6.00	15.00
❑ 113 Jeff Smoker AU RC	5.00	12.00
❑ 114 Mewelde Moore AU RC	6.00	15.00
❑ 115 Michael Clayton AU RC	6.00	15.00
❑ 116 Jonathan Vilma AU RC	6.00	15.00
❑ 117 Johnnie Morant AU RC	5.00	12.00
❑ 118 Devard Darling AU RC	5.00	12.00
❑ 119 Cedric Cobbs AU RC	5.00	12.00
❑ 120 Chris Perry AU/399 RC	8.00	20.00
❑ 121 Ernest Wilford AU RC	5.00	12.00
❑ 122 Michael Jenkins AU RC	6.00	15.00
❑ 123 Jerricho Cotchery AU RC	6.00	15.00
❑ 124 P.K. Sam AU RC	4.00	10.00
❑ 125 Tatum Bell AU RC	6.00	15.00
❑ 126 Derrick Hamilton AU RC	4.00	10.00
❑ 127 Luke McCown AU RC	6.00	15.00
❑ 128 Devery Henderson AU RC	6.00	15.00
❑ 129 Craig Krenzel AU RC	6.00	15.00
❑ 130 J.P. Losman AU RC	6.00	15.00
❑ 131 Lee Evans AU RC	8.00	20.00
❑ 132 Matt Schaub AU RC	20.00	50.00
❑ 133 Robert Gallery AU RC	6.00	15.00
❑ 134 Keary Colbert AU RC	5.00	12.00

2005 Finest

Card		
❑ COMP.SET w/o AUs (150)	25.00	60.00
❑ 1 Muhsin Muhammad	.25	.60
❑ 2 Kevin Jones	.25	.60
❑ 3 Eli Manning	.60	1.50
❑ 4 Kevan Barlow	.20	.50
❑ 5 Randy Moss	.30	.75
❑ 6 Brian Griese	.25	.60
❑ 7 Dante Hall	.25	.60
❑ 8 Chris Brown	.25	.60
❑ 9 Antonio Gates	.30	.75
❑ 10 Champ Bailey	.25	.60
❑ 11 Eric Moulds	.25	.60
❑ 12 Ray Lewis	.30	.75
❑ 13 Larry Fitzgerald	.30	.75
❑ 14 Byron Leftwich	.25	.60
❑ 15 Marvin Harrison	.30	.75
❑ 16 Stephen Davis	.25	.60
❑ 17 Laveranues Coles	.25	.60
❑ 18 Shaun Alexander	.30	.75
❑ 19 Drew Bledsoe	.30	.75
❑ 20 Sean Taylor	.25	.60
❑ 21 Deuce McAllister	.30	.75
❑ 22 Nate Burleson	.25	.60
❑ 23 A.J. Feeley	.20	.50
❑ 24 Jerome Bettis	.30	.75
❑ 25 Torry Holt	.25	.60
❑ 26 LaDainian Tomlinson	.40	1.00
❑ 27 Travis Henry	.25	.60
❑ 28 T.J. Houshmandzadeh	.25	.60
❑ 29 Fred Taylor	.30	.75
❑ 30 Michael Jenkins	.25	.60
❑ 31 Edgerrin James	.25	.60
❑ 32 Terrell Owens	.30	.75
❑ 33 Jason Witten	.30	.75
❑ 34 Clinton Portis	.30	.75
❑ 35 Deion Branch	.25	.60
❑ 36 Priest Holmes	.30	.75
❑ 37 Javon Walker	.25	.60
❑ 38 Rex Grossman	.30	.75
❑ 39 Domanick Davis	.20	.50
❑ 40 Allen Rossum	.20	.50
❑ 41 Dwight Freeney	.25	.60
❑ 42 Jimmy Smith	.25	.60
❑ 43 Tiki Barber	.30	.75
❑ 44 Steve McNair	.30	.75
❑ 45 Steven Jackson	.40	1.00
❑ 46 Joe Horn	.25	.60
❑ 47 Randy McMichael	.20	.50
❑ 48 J.P. Losman	.25	.60
❑ 49 Warrick Dunn	.25	.60
❑ 50 Tatum Bell	.25	.60
❑ 51 Roy Williams WR	.30	.75
❑ 52 Curtis Martin	.30	.75
❑ 53 Donovan McNabb	.30	.75
❑ 54 LaMont Jordan	.25	.60
❑ 55 Marc Bulger	.25	.60
❑ 56 Drew Bennett	.25	.60
❑ 57 Julius Jones	.30	.75
❑ 58 Santana Moss	.25	.60
❑ 59 Michael Bennett	.25	.60
❑ 60 Tony Gonzalez	.25	.60
❑ 61 Jamal Lewis	.25	.60
❑ 62 Keary Colbert	.20	.50
❑ 63 Carson Palmer	.30	.75
❑ 64 Dunta Robinson	.20	.50
❑ 65 Brandon Stokley	.20	.50
❑ 66 Brett Favre	.75	2.00
❑ 67 Jonathan Vilma	.25	.60
❑ 68 Darrell Jackson	.25	.60
❑ 69 Michael Pittman	.20	.50
❑ 70 Drew Brees	.30	.75
❑ 71 Amani Toomer	.25	.60
❑ 72 Corey Dillon	.25	.60
❑ 73 Willis McGahee	.30	.75
❑ 74 Michael Vick	.30	.75
❑ 75 Chad Johnson	.25	.60
❑ 76 Anquan Boldin	.25	.60
❑ 77 Kerry Collins	.25	.60
❑ 78 Marshall Faulk	.30	.75
❑ 79 Roy Williams S	.25	.60
❑ 80 Trent Green	.25	.60
❑ 81 Chris Gamble	.20	.50
❑ 82 Ahman Green	.30	.75
❑ 83 Todd Heap	.25	.60
❑ 84 Brandon Lloyd	.20	.50
❑ 85 Andre Johnson	.25	.60
❑ 86 Lee Suggs	.25	.60
❑ 87 Plaxico Burress	.25	.60
❑ 88 Hines Ward	.30	.75
❑ 89 Rod Smith	.25	.60
❑ 90 Joey Harrington	.30	.75
❑ 91 Derrick Mason	.25	.60
❑ 92 Rudi Johnson	.25	.60
❑ 93 Isaac Bruce	.25	.60
❑ 94 Chris Chambers	.25	.60
❑ 95 Matt Hasselbeck	.25	.60
❑ 96 Donte Stallworth	.25	.60
❑ 97 Philip Rivers	.30	.75
❑ 98 Michael Clayton	.25	.60
❑ 99 Alge Crumpler	.25	.60
❑ 100 Chad Pennington	.30	.75
❑ 101 Brian Westbrook	.30	.75
❑ 102 Daunte Culpepper	.30	.75
❑ 103 Jeremy Shockey	.30	.75
❑ 104 Jerry Porter	.25	.60
❑ 105 Tom Brady	.60	1.50
❑ 106 Lee Evans	.25	.60
❑ 107 Jake Delhomme	.30	.75
❑ 108 Ben Roethlisberger	.75	2.00
❑ 109 Jake Plummer	.25	.60
❑ 110 Charles Rogers	.20	.50
❑ 111 Patrick Ramsey	.25	.60
❑ 112 Reggie Wayne	.25	.60
❑ 113 Reuben Droughns	.20	.50
❑ 114 Aaron Brooks	.20	.50
❑ 115 David Carr	.25	.60
❑ 116 Thomas Jones	.25	.60
❑ 117 Ashley Lelie	.20	.50
❑ 118 Donald Driver	.30	.75
❑ 119 Billy Volek	.25	.60
❑ 120 Peyton Manning	.50	1.25
❑ 121 Frank Gore RC	2.00	5.00
❑ 122 Adam Jones RC	.75	2.00
❑ 123 Antrel Rolle RC	1.00	2.50
❑ 124 Roddy White RC	1.25	3.00
❑ 125 Derrick Johnson RC	1.00	2.50
❑ 126 Troy Williamson RC	1.00	2.50
❑ 127 Maurice Clarett	.75	2.00
❑ 128 Dan Orlovsky RC	1.00	2.50
❑ 129 Andrew Walter RC	.75	2.00
❑ 130 Reggie Brown RC	.75	2.00
❑ 131 Matt Jones RC	1.00	2.50
❑ 132 David Greene RC	.75	2.00
❑ 133 Jerome Mathis RC	1.00	2.50
❑ 134 Thomas Davis RC	.75	2.00
❑ 135 Roscoe Parrish RC	.75	2.00
❑ 136 Ciatrick Fason RC	.75	2.00
❑ 137 David Pollack RC	.75	2.00

❑ 138 Kyle Orton RC 1.50 4.00
❑ 139 Heath Miller RC 2.00 5.00
❑ 140 Courtney Roby RC .75 2.00
❑ 141 Terrence Murphy RC .60 1.50
❑ 142 DeMarcus Ware RC 1.50 4.00
❑ 143 Fabian Washington RC 1.00 2.50
❑ 144 J.J. Arrington RC 1.00 2.50
❑ 145 Fred Gibson RC .75 2.00
❑ 146 Carlos Rogers RC 1.00 2.50
❑ 147 Eric Shelton RC .75 2.00
❑ 148 Craphonso Thorpe RC .75 2.00
❑ 149 Anthony Davis RC .75 2.00
❑ 150 Marion Barber RC 3.00 8.00
❑ 151 Aaron Rodgers AU/299 RC 60.00 100.00
❑ 152 Alex Smith QB AU/299 RC 30.00 60.00
❑ 153 Braylon Edwards AU/299 RC 30.00 60.00
❑ 154 Cadillac Williams AU/299 RC 30.00 60.00
❑ 155 Cedric Benson AU/299 RC 15.00 40.00
❑ 156 Charlie Frye AU/299 RC 12.00 30.00
❑ 157 Jason Campbell AU/299 RC 25.00 60.00
❑ 158 Mark Clayton AU/299 RC 15.00 40.00
❑ 159 Mike Williams AU/299 10.00 25.00
❑ 160 Ronnie Brown AU/299 RC 40.00 80.00
❑ 161 Alex Smith TE AU RC 5.00 12.00
❑ 162 Alvin Pearman AU RC 3.00 8.00
❑ 163 Brandon Jacobs AU RC 12.00 30.00
❑ 164 Channing Crowder AU RC 4.00 10.00
❑ 165 Chris Henry AU RC 5.00 12.00
❑ 166 Courtney Roby AU RC 4.00 10.00
❑ 167 Derek Anderson AU RC 10.00 25.00
❑ 168 Mark Bradley AU RC 4.00 10.00
❑ 169 Ryan Fitzpatrick AU RC 5.00 12.00
❑ 170 Ryan Moats AU RC 4.00 10.00
❑ 171 Stefan LeFors AU RC 4.00 10.00
❑ 172 Steve Savoy AU RC 3.00 8.00
❑ 173 Tab Perry AU RC 5.00 12.00
❑ 174 Timmy Chang AU RC 4.00 10.00
❑ 175 Vincent Jackson AU RC 10.00 20.00
❑ 176 Charles Frederick AU RC 4.00 10.00
❑ 177 Kay-Jay Harris AU RC 4.00 10.00
❑ 178 Darren Sproles AU RC 10.00 20.00
❑ 179 Adrian McPherson AU RC 4.00 10.00
❑ 180 Craig Bragg AU RC 3.00 8.00
❑ 181 J.R. Russell AU RC 3.00 8.00
❑ 182 Gino Guidugli AU RC 3.00 8.00
❑ 183 Vernand Morency AU RC 4.00 10.00

2006 Finest

❑ COMP.SET w/o AU's (150) 12.50 30.00
❑ 1 Muhsin Muhammad .25 .60
❑ 2 Kevin Jones .25 .60
❑ 3 Eli Manning .40 1.00
❑ 4 Marion Barber .30 .75
❑ 5 Randy Moss .30 .75
❑ 6 Odell Thurman .20 .50
❑ 7 Dante Hall .25 .60
❑ 8 Chris Brown .25 .60
❑ 9 Antonio Gates .30 .75
❑ 10 Champ Bailey .25 .60
❑ 11 Eric Moulds .25 .60
❑ 12 Ray Lewis .30 .75
❑ 13 Larry Fitzgerald .30 .75
❑ 14 Byron Leftwich .25 .60
❑ 15 Marvin Harrison .30 .75
❑ 16 Larry Johnson .25 .60
❑ 17 Steve Smith .30 .75
❑ 18 Shaun Alexander .25 .60
❑ 19 Drew Bledsoe .30 .75
❑ 20 Joey Galloway .25 .60
❑ 21 Deuce McAllister .25 .60
❑ 22 Ben Obomanu RC 1.25 3.00
❑ 23 Chester Taylor .25 .60
❑ 24 Delanie Walker RC 1.25 3.00
❑ 25 Torry Holt .25 .60
❑ 26 LaDainian Tomlinson .40 1.00
❑ 27 Derrick Mason .25 .60
❑ 28 T.J. Houshmandzadeh .25 .60
❑ 29 Fred Taylor .25 .60
❑ 30 Michael Jenkins .25 .60
❑ 31 Edgerrin James .25 .60
❑ 32 Terrell Owens .30 .75
❑ 33 Jason Witten .30 .75
❑ 34 Clinton Portis .30 .75
❑ 35 Deion Branch .25 .60
❑ 36 Priest Holmes .25 .60
❑ 37 Quinton Ganther RC 1.00 2.50
❑ 38 Kurt Warner .30 .75
❑ 39 Domanick Davis .25 .60
❑ 40 Chris Simms .25 .60
❑ 41 Dwight Freeney .25 .60
❑ 42 Daniel Bullocks RC 1.50 4.00
❑ 43 Tiki Barber .30 .75
❑ 44 Steve McNair .25 .60
❑ 45 Steven Jackson .30 .75
❑ 46 Joe Horn .25 .60
❑ 47 Randy McMichael .20 .50
❑ 48 Cedric Humes RC 1.25 3.00
❑ 49 Warrick Dunn .25 .60
❑ 50 Tatum Bell .20 .50
❑ 51 P.J. Pope RC 1.50 4.00
❑ 52 Curtis Martin .30 .75
❑ 53 Donovan McNabb .30 .75
❑ 54 LaMont Jordan .25 .60
❑ 55 Marc Bulger .25 .60
❑ 56 Drew Bennett .25 .60
❑ 57 Julius Jones .25 .60
❑ 58 Santana Moss .25 .60
❑ 59 Ronnie Brown .30 .75
❑ 60 Tony Gonzalez .25 .60
❑ 61 Jamal Lewis .25 .60
❑ 62 D.J. Shockley RC 1.25 3.00
❑ 63 Carson Palmer .30 .75
❑ 64 Jonathan Orr RC 1.25 3.00
❑ 65 Brandon Stokley .25 .60
❑ 66 Brett Favre .60 1.50
❑ 67 Jonathan Vilma .25 .60
❑ 68 Darrell Jackson .25 .60
❑ 69 Brian Urlacher .30 .75
❑ 70 Drew Brees .30 .75
❑ 71 Mike Williams .25 .60
❑ 72 Corey Dillon .25 .60
❑ 73 Willis McGahee .30 .75
❑ 74 Michael Vick .30 .75
❑ 75 Chad Johnson .25 .60
❑ 76 Anquan Boldin .25 .60
❑ 77 Shawne Merriman .25 .60
❑ 78 Willie Parker .40 1.00
❑ 79 Roy Williams S .25 .60
❑ 80 Trent Green .25 .60
❑ 81 Chris Gamble .20 .50
❑ 82 Ahman Green .25 .60
❑ 83 Todd Heap .25 .60
❑ 84 Brett Basanez RC 1.50 4.00
❑ 85 Andre Johnson .25 .60
❑ 86 Abdul Hodge RC 1.25 3.00
❑ 87 Plaxico Burress .25 .60
❑ 88 Hines Ward .30 .75
❑ 89 Rod Smith .25 .60
❑ 90 Cadillac Williams .30 .75
❑ 91 Braylon Edwards .30 .75
❑ 92 Rudi Johnson .25 .60
❑ 93 Isaac Bruce .25 .60
❑ 94 Chris Chambers .25 .60
❑ 95 Matt Hasselbeck .25 .60
❑ 96 Donte Stallworth .25 .60
❑ 97 Philip Rivers .30 .75
❑ 98 Will Blackmon RC 1.50 4.00
❑ 99 Alge Crumpler .25 .60
❑ 100 Chad Pennington .25 .60
❑ 101 Darnell Bing RC 1.25 3.00
❑ 102 Daunte Culpepper .30 .75
❑ 103 Jeremy Shockey .30 .75
❑ 104 Jerry Porter .25 .60
❑ 105 Tom Brady .50 1.25
❑ 106 Jeff Webb RC 1.25 3.00
❑ 107 Jake Delhomme .25 .60
❑ 108 Ben Roethlisberger .50 1.25
❑ 109 Jake Plummer .25 .60
❑ 110 Paul Pinegar RC 1.00 2.50
❑ 111 Kevin McMahan RC 1.25 3.00
❑ 112 Reggie Wayne .25 .60
❑ 113 Bennie Brazell RC 1.25 3.00
❑ 114 Todd Watkins RC 1.00 2.50
❑ 115 David Carr .20 .50
❑ 116 Cory Rodgers RC 1.50 4.00
❑ 117 Leon Washington RC 2.00 5.00
❑ 118 Michael Strahan .25 .60
❑ 119 P.J. Daniels RC 1.00 2.50
❑ 120 Peyton Manning .50 1.25
❑ 121 Brandon Marshall RC 1.50 4.00
❑ 122 Jerome Harrison RC 1.50 4.00
❑ 123 Mario Williams RC 2.00 5.00
❑ 124 Ernie Sims RC 1.25 3.00
❑ 125 Devin Hester RC 3.00 8.00
❑ 126 Jimmy Williams RC 1.50 4.00
❑ 127 Charlie Whitehurst RC 1.50 4.00
❑ 128 Jason Avant RC 1.50 4.00
❑ 129 Marcus Vick RC 1.00 2.50
❑ 130 Mathias Kiwanuka RC 2.00 5.00
❑ 131 Brodrick Bunkley RC 1.25 3.00
❑ 132 Reggie McNeal RC 1.25 3.00
❑ 133 Dominique Byrd RC 1.25 3.00
❑ 134 Jason Allen RC 1.25 3.00
❑ 135 D'Qwell Jackson RC 1.25 3.00
❑ 136 Donte Whitner RC 1.50 4.00
❑ 137 Willie Reid RC 1.25 3.00
❑ 138 Kamerion Wimbley RC 1.50 4.00
❑ 139 Martin Nance RC 1.25 3.00
❑ 140 Haloti Ngata RC 1.50 4.00
❑ 141 Devin Aromashodu RC 1.50 4.00
❑ 142 Jeremy Bloom RC 1.25 3.00
❑ 143 Manny Lawson RC 1.50 4.00
❑ 144 Johnathan Joseph RC 1.25 3.00
❑ 145 Brad Smith RC 1.50 4.00
❑ 146 Thomas Howard RC 1.25 3.00
❑ 147 Demetrius Williams RC 1.25 3.00
❑ 148 Antonio Cromartie RC 1.50 4.00
❑ 149 Bobby Carpenter RC 1.25 3.00
❑ 150 Tamba Hali RC 1.50 4.00
❑ 151 Reggie Bush AU/199 RC 50.00 100.00
❑ 152 Matt Leinart AU/199 RC 15.00 40.00
❑ 153 Vince Young AU/199 RC 25.00 60.00
❑ 154 Jay Cutler AU/199 RC 50.00 100.00
❑ 155 S.Holmes AU/199 RC 25.00 60.00
❑ 156 LenDale White AU/199 RC 12.00 30.00
❑ 157 DeA.Williams AU/199 RC 20.00 50.00
❑ 158 Sinorice Moss AU/199 RC 10.00 25.00
❑ 159 Vernon Davis AU/199 RC 10.00 25.00
❑ 160 Joseph Addai AU/199 RC 12.00 30.00
❑ 161 Omar Jacobs AU/199 RC 6.00 15.00
❑ 162 Chad Jackson AU/199 RC 8.00 20.00
❑ 163 Chad Greenway AU RC 5.00 12.00
❑ 164 Maurice Drew AU RC 10.00 25.00
❑ 165 D.Ferguson AU RC 5.00 12.00
❑ 166 Anthony Fasano AU RC 5.00 12.00
❑ 167 Derek Hagan AU/199 RC 8.00 20.00
❑ 168 A.J. Hawk AU/199 RC 15.00 40.00
❑ 169 David Thomas AU RC 5.00 12.00
❑ 170 Brian Calhoun AU RC 4.00 10.00
❑ 171 Kellen Clemens AU RC 5.00 12.00
❑ 172 Tarvaris Jackson AU RC 5.00 12.00
❑ 173 Maurice Stovall AU RC 4.00 10.00
❑ 174 Michael Huff AU/199 RC 10.00 25.00
❑ 175 Greg Jennings AU RC 8.00 20.00
❑ 176 Joe Klopfenstein AU RC 4.00 10.00
❑ 177 Leonard Pope AU RC 5.00 12.00
❑ 178 Michael Robinson AU RC 4.00 10.00
❑ 179 Ingle Martin AU RC 4.00 10.00
❑ 180 Wali Lundy AU RC 5.00 12.00
❑ 181 Drew Olson AU RC 3.00 8.00
❑ 182 Jerious Norwood AU RC 5.00 12.00
❑ 183 Travis Wilson AU RC 3.00 8.00
❑ 184 Tye Hill AU RC 4.00 10.00
❑ 185 Brandon Williams AU RC 4.00 10.00
❑ 186 Marques Hagans AU RC 4.00 10.00

2007 Finest

❑ COMPLETE SET (150) 30.00 60.00
❑ 1 Peyton Manning .50 1.25
❑ 2 Drew Brees .30 .75
❑ 3 Donovan McNabb .30 .75

Card	Low	High
❑ 4 Tony Romo	.50	1.25
❑ 5 Carson Palmer	.30	.75
❑ 6 Mark Bulger	.25	.60
❑ 7 Philip Rivers	.30	.75
❑ 8 Tom Brady	.60	1.50
❑ 9 J.P. Losman	.20	.50
❑ 10 Steve McNair	.25	.60
❑ 11 Eli Manning	.30	.75
❑ 12 Matt Hasselbeck	.25	.60
❑ 13 Alex Smith QB	.30	.75
❑ 14 Ben Roethlisberger	.40	1.00
❑ 15 Matt Leinart	.30	.75
❑ 16 Rex Grossman	.25	.60
❑ 17 Brett Favre	.60	1.50
❑ 18 Vince Young	.30	.75
❑ 19 Jay Cutler	.30	.75
❑ 20 Chad Pennington	.25	.60
❑ 21 LaDainian Tomlinson	.40	1.00
❑ 22 Larry Johnson	.25	.60
❑ 23 Frank Gore	.30	.75
❑ 24 Steven Jackson	.30	.75
❑ 25 Willie Parker	.25	.60
❑ 26 Rudi Johnson	.25	.60
❑ 27 Brian Westbrook	.25	.60
❑ 28 Chester Taylor	.20	.50
❑ 29 Travis Henry	.25	.60
❑ 30 Thomas Jones	.25	.60
❑ 31 Edgerrin James	.25	.60
❑ 32 Fred Taylor	.25	.60
❑ 33 Warrick Dunn	.25	.60
❑ 34 Jamal Lewis	.25	.60
❑ 35 Julius Jones	.25	.60
❑ 36 Joseph Addai	.30	.75
❑ 37 Ahman Green	.25	.60
❑ 38 Deuce McAllister	.25	.60
❑ 39 Ronnie Brown	.25	.60
❑ 40 Maurice Jones-Drew	.30	.75
❑ 41 DeShaun Foster	.25	.60
❑ 42 Shaun Alexander	.25	.60
❑ 43 Cadillac Williams	.25	.60
❑ 44 Laurence Maroney	.30	.75
❑ 45 Cedric Benson	.25	.60
❑ 46 Dominic Rhodes	.25	.60
❑ 47 Jerious Norwood	.25	.60
❑ 48 Brandon Jacobs	.25	.60
❑ 49 DeAngelo Williams	.30	.75
❑ 50 Willis McGahee	.25	.60
❑ 51 Clinton Portis	.25	.60
❑ 52 Chad Johnson	.25	.60
❑ 53 Marvin Harrison	.30	.75
❑ 54 Roy Williams WR	.25	.60
❑ 55 Reggie Wayne	.25	.60
❑ 56 Donald Driver	.30	.75
❑ 57 Lee Evans	.25	.60
❑ 58 Anquan Boldin	.25	.60
❑ 59 Torry Holt	.25	.60
❑ 60 Terrell Owens	.30	.75
❑ 61 Steve Smith	.25	.60
❑ 62 Andre Johnson	.25	.60
❑ 63 Laveraneus Coles	.25	.60
❑ 64 Javon Walker	.25	.60
❑ 65 T.J. Houshmandzadeh	.25	.60
❑ 66 Marques Colston	.30	.75
❑ 67 Terry Glenn	.25	.60
❑ 68 Plaxico Burress	.25	.60
❑ 69 Hines Ward	.30	.75
❑ 70 Jerricho Cotchery	.20	.50
❑ 71 Larry Fitzgerald	.30	.75
❑ 72 Braylon Edwards	.25	.60
❑ 73 Santana Moss	.25	.60
❑ 74 Santonio Holmes	.25	.60
❑ 75 Mike Furrey	.25	.60
❑ 76 Isaac Bruce	.25	.60
❑ 77 Derrick Mason	.20	.50
❑ 78 Randy Moss	.30	.75
❑ 79 Greg Jennings	.25	.60
❑ 80 Devin Hester	.30	.75
❑ 81 Muhsin Muhammad	.25	.60
❑ 82 Kellen Winslow	.25	.60
❑ 83 Todd Heap	.20	.50
❑ 84 Tony Gonzalez	.25	.60
❑ 85 Antonio Gates	.25	.60
❑ 86 Jeremy Shockey	.25	.60
❑ 87 Jason Witten	.30	.75
❑ 88 Randy McMichael	.20	.50
❑ 89 Alge Crumpler	.25	.60
❑ 90 L.J. Smith	.20	.50
❑ 91 Champ Bailey	.25	.60
❑ 92 DeAngelo Hall	.25	.60
❑ 93 Asante Samuel	.20	.50
❑ 94 Julius Peppers	.25	.60
❑ 95 Jason Taylor	.20	.50
❑ 96 Michael Strahan	.25	.60
❑ 97 Shawne Merriman	.25	.60
❑ 98 Brian Urlacher	.30	.75
❑ 99 Troy Polamalu	.30	.75
❑ 100 Ed Reed	.25	.60
❑ 101 JaMarcus Russell RC	2.00	5.00
❑ 102 Brady Quinn RC	3.00	8.00
❑ 103 John Beck RC	1.50	4.00
❑ 104 Kevin Kolb RC	2.50	6.00
❑ 105 Trent Edwards RC	2.50	6.00
❑ 106 Troy Smith RC	2.00	5.00
❑ 107 Drew Stanton RC	1.25	3.00
❑ 108 Chris Leak RC	1.25	3.00
❑ 109 Jordan Palmer RC	1.50	4.00
❑ 110 Drew Tate RC	1.25	3.00
❑ 111 Isaiah Stanback RC	1.50	4.00
❑ 112 Adrian Peterson RC	12.00	30.00
❑ 113 Marshawn Lynch RC	2.50	6.00
❑ 114 Brandon Jackson RC	1.50	4.00
❑ 115 Kenny Irons RC	1.50	4.00
❑ 116 Michael Bush RC	1.25	3.00
❑ 117 Lorenzo Booker RC	1.50	4.00
❑ 118 Brian Leonard RC	1.25	3.00
❑ 119 Garrett Wolfe RC	1.50	4.00
❑ 120 Antonio Pittman RC	1.50	4.00
❑ 121 Selvin Young RC	1.50	4.00
❑ 122 Chris Henry RB RC	1.25	3.00
❑ 123 Tony Hunt RC	1.50	4.00
❑ 124 Kenneth Darby RC	1.50	4.00
❑ 125 Kolby Smith RC	1.50	4.00
❑ 126 Darius Walker RC	1.25	3.00
❑ 127 Greg Olsen RC	2.00	5.00
❑ 128 Dwayne Bowe RC	2.50	6.00
❑ 129 Craig Buster Davis RC	1.50	4.00
❑ 130 Ted Ginn Jr. RC	2.50	6.00
❑ 131 Anthony Gonzalez RC	2.00	5.00
❑ 132 Yamon Figurs RC	1.00	2.50
❑ 133 Jason Hill RC	1.50	4.00
❑ 134 Dwayne Jarrett RC	1.50	4.00
❑ 135 Calvin Johnson RC	4.00	10.00
❑ 136 Robert Meachem RC	1.50	4.00
❑ 137 Sidney Rice RC	3.00	8.00
❑ 138 Steve Smith USC RC	2.50	6.00
❑ 139 Paul Williams RC	1.25	3.00
❑ 140 Steve Breaston RC	1.50	4.00
❑ 141 David Clowney RC	1.50	4.00
❑ 142 Aundrae Allison RC	1.25	3.00
❑ 143 Ryne Robinson RC	1.25	3.00
❑ 144 Joe Thomas RC	1.50	4.00
❑ 145 Leon Hall RC	1.50	4.00
❑ 146 Gaines Adams RC	1.50	4.00
❑ 147 LaRon Landry RC	2.00	5.00
❑ 148 Amobi Okoye RC	1.50	4.00
❑ 149 Patrick Willis RC	2.50	6.00
❑ 150 Lawrence Timmons RC	1.50	4.00

2008 Finest

Card	Low	High
❑ COMP.SET w/o RC's (100)	10.00	25.00
❑ 1 Drew Brees	.30	.75
❑ 2 Tom Brady	.50	1.25
❑ 3 Peyton Manning	.50	1.25
❑ 4 Carson Palmer	.30	.75
❑ 5 Ben Roethlisberger	.50	1.25
❑ 6 Tony Romo	.50	1.25
❑ 7 Vince Young	.25	.60
❑ 8 David Garrard	.25	.60
❑ 9 Jeff Garcia	.25	.60
❑ 10 Derek Anderson	.25	.60
❑ 11 Matt Hasselbeck	.25	.60
❑ 12 Donovan McNabb	.30	.75
❑ 13 Philip Rivers	.30	.75
❑ 14 Jay Cutler	.30	.75
❑ 15 Matt Leinart	.30	.75
❑ 16 Jason Campbell	.25	.60
❑ 17 Matt Schaub	.25	.60
❑ 18 Jon Kitna	.25	.60
❑ 19 Marc Bulger	.25	.60
❑ 20 Eli Manning	.30	.75
❑ 21 Willie Parker	.25	.60
❑ 22 Clinton Portis	.25	.60
❑ 23 Adrian Peterson	.60	1.50
❑ 24 LaDainian Tomlinson	.40	1.00
❑ 25 Marion Barber	.30	.75
❑ 26 Brian Westbrook	.25	.60
❑ 27 Fred Taylor	.25	.60
❑ 28 Marshawn Lynch	.30	.75
❑ 29 Joseph Addai	.30	.75
❑ 30 Willis McGahee	.25	.60
❑ 31 Frank Gore	.25	.60
❑ 32 Larry Johnson	.25	.60
❑ 33 Jamal Lewis	.25	.60
❑ 34 Edgerrin James	.25	.60
❑ 35 Thomas Jones	.25	.60
❑ 36 Brandon Jacobs	.25	.60
❑ 37 LenDale White	.25	.60
❑ 38 Justin Fargas	.20	.50
❑ 39 Ryan Grant	.30	.75
❑ 40 Earnest Graham	.20	.50
❑ 41 Laurence Maroney	.25	.60
❑ 42 Steven Jackson	.30	.75
❑ 43 DeAngelo Williams	.25	.60
❑ 44 Shaun Alexander	.25	.60
❑ 45 Maurice Jones-Drew	.25	.60
❑ 46 Reggie Bush	.30	.75
❑ 47 Chester Taylor	.20	.50
❑ 48 Rudi Johnson	.25	.60
❑ 49 Ronnie Brown	.25	.60
❑ 50 Travis Henry	.25	.60
❑ 51 Cedric Benson	.25	.60
❑ 52 Chad Johnson	.25	.60
❑ 53 Reggie Wayne	.25	.60
❑ 54 Anquan Boldin	.25	.60
❑ 55 Randy Moss	.30	.75
❑ 56 Plaxico Burress	.25	.60
❑ 57 Terrell Owens	.30	.75
❑ 58 Andre Johnson	.25	.60
❑ 59 Larry Fitzgerald	.30	.75
❑ 60 Braylon Edwards	.25	.60
❑ 61 Steve Smith	.25	.60
❑ 62 Wes Welker	.30	.75
❑ 63 T.J. Houshmandzadeh	.25	.60
❑ 64 Derrick Mason	.20	.50
❑ 65 Brandon Marshall	.25	.60
❑ 66 Marques Colston	.25	.60
❑ 67 Bobby Engram	.20	.50
❑ 68 Torry Holt	.25	.60
❑ 69 Roddy White	.25	.60
❑ 70 Jerricho Cotchery	.20	.50
❑ 71 Donald Driver	.25	.60
❑ 72 Roy Williams WR	.25	.60
❑ 73 Hines Ward	.25	.60
❑ 74 Santonio Holmes	.25	.60
❑ 75 Joey Galloway	.25	.60
❑ 76 Greg Jennings	.25	.60
❑ 77 Dwayne Bowe	.25	.60
❑ 78 Calvin Johnson	.30	.75
❑ 79 Santana Moss	.20	.50
❑ 80 Kevin Curtis	.20	.50
❑ 81 Chris Chambers	.25	.60
❑ 82 Kellen Winslow	.25	.60
❑ 83 Tony Gonzalez	.25	.60
❑ 84 Antonio Gates	.25	.60
❑ 85 Jeremy Shockey	.25	.60
❑ 86 Jason Witten	.30	.75
❑ 87 Chris Cooley	.25	.60
❑ 88 Owen Daniels	.20	.50
❑ 89 Dallas Clark	.25	.60
❑ 90 Vernon Davis	.20	.50
❑ 91 Antonio Cromartie	.20	.50
❑ 92 Marcus Trufant	.20	.50
❑ 93 Terence Newman	.20	.50
❑ 94 Osi Umenyiora	.20	.50
❑ 95 Mario Williams	.25	.60
❑ 96 Patrick Willis	.25	.60
❑ 97 Shawne Merriman	.25	.60
❑ 98 DeMarcus Ware	.25	.60
❑ 99 Ed Reed	.25	.60
❑ 100 Bob Sanders	.25	.60
❑ 101 Erik Ainge RC	2.00	5.00
❑ 102 John David Booty RC	2.00	5.00
❑ 103 Colt Brennan RC	3.00	8.00
❑ 104 Brian Brohm RC	2.00	5.00

Card	Low	High
❑ 105 Joe Flacco RC	6.00	15.00
❑ 106 Chad Henne RC	3.00	8.00
❑ 107 Josh Johnson RC	2.00	5.00
❑ 108 Anthony Morelli RC	2.00	5.00
❑ 109 Matt Ryan RC	8.00	20.00
❑ 110 Andre Woodson RC	2.00	5.00
❑ 111 Kyle Wright RC	1.50	4.00
❑ 112 Jamaal Charles RC	3.00	8.00
❑ 113 Tashard Choice RC	2.00	5.00
❑ 114 Matt Forte RC	4.00	10.00
❑ 115 Mike Hart RC	2.00	5.00
❑ 116 Chris Johnson RC	6.00	15.00
❑ 117 Felix Jones RC	4.00	10.00
❑ 118 Darren McFadden RC	4.00	10.00
❑ 119 Rashard Mendenhall RC	4.00	10.00
❑ 120 Allen Patrick RC	1.50	4.00
❑ 121 Ray Rice RC	4.00	10.00
❑ 122 Dustin Keller RC	2.00	5.00
❑ 123 Steve Slaton RC	2.50	6.00
❑ 124 Kevin Smith RC	3.00	8.00
❑ 125 Jonathan Stewart RC	4.00	10.00
❑ 126 Kevin O'Connell RC	2.00	5.00
❑ 127 Adrian Arrington RC	1.50	4.00
❑ 128 Donnie Avery RC	2.50	6.00
❑ 129 Earl Bennett RC	2.00	5.00
❑ 130 Dexter Jackson RC	2.00	5.00
❑ 131 Jerome Simpson RC	1.50	4.00
❑ 132 Keenan Burton RC	1.50	4.00
❑ 133 Andre Caldwell RC	2.00	5.00
❑ 134 Early Doucet RC	2.00	5.00
❑ 135 Harry Douglas RC	1.50	4.00
❑ 136 James Hardy RC	1.50	4.00
❑ 137 Jordy Nelson RC	2.50	6.00
❑ 138 DeSean Jackson RC	4.00	10.00
❑ 139 Malcolm Kelly RC	2.00	5.00
❑ 140 Mario Manningham RC	2.00	5.00
❑ 141 Limas Sweed RC	2.00	5.00
❑ 142 Eddie Royal RC	3.00	8.00
❑ 143 Devin Thomas RC	2.00	5.00
❑ 144 John Carlson RC	2.00	5.00
❑ 145 Chris Long RC	2.00	5.00
❑ 146 Vernon Gholston RC	2.00	5.00
❑ 147 D.Rodgers-Cromartie RC	2.00	5.00
❑ 148 Keith Rivers RC	2.00	5.00
❑ 149 Jake Long RC	2.00	5.00
❑ 150 Glenn Dorsey RC	2.00	5.00
❑ 151 Brett Favre SP	20.00	40.00

2009 Finest

Card	Low	High
❑ COMP.SET w/o AU's (100)	30.00	80.00
❑ 1 Larry Fitzgerald	.30	.75
❑ 2 Willis McGahee	.25	.60
❑ 3 Darren McFadden	.30	.75
❑ 4 Brett Favre	5.00	12.00
❑ 5 Brian Westbrook	.25	.60
❑ 6 Anquan Boldin	.25	.60
❑ 7 Hines Ward	.25	.60
❑ 8 Drew Brees	.30	.75
❑ 9 Terrell Owens	.30	.75
❑ 10 Matt Ryan	.30	.75
❑ 11 Steve Slaton	.25	.60
❑ 12 Matt Cassel	.25	.60
❑ 13 Clinton Portis	.25	.60
❑ 14 Kurt Warner	.30	.75
❑ 15 Santana Moss	.25	.60
❑ 16 Steven Jackson	.25	.60
❑ 17 Brandon Jacobs	.25	.60
❑ 18 LaDainian Tomlinson	.30	.75
❑ 19 DeAngelo Williams	.30	.75
❑ 20 Marion Barber	.30	.75
❑ 21 Randy Moss	.30	.75
❑ 22 Aaron Rodgers	.30	.75
❑ 23 Jay Cutler	.30	.75
❑ 24 Chad Ochocinco	.25	.60
❑ 25 Adrian Peterson	.60	1.50
❑ 26 Joe Flacco	.30	.75
❑ 27 Chris Johnson	.30	.75
❑ 28 Reggie Wayne	.25	.60
❑ 29 Tom Brady	.50	1.25
❑ 30 Steve Smith	.25	.60
❑ 31 Braylon Edwards	.25	.60
❑ 32 Donovan McNabb	.30	.75
❑ 33 Michael Turner	.25	.60
❑ 34 Michael Vick	1.25	3.00
❑ 35 Eli Manning	.30	.75
❑ 36 Brandon Marshall	.25	.60
❑ 37 Roy Williams WR	.25	.60
❑ 38 Reggie Bush	.30	.75
❑ 39 Philip Rivers	.30	.75
❑ 40 Marshawn Lynch	.25	.60
❑ 41 Tony Romo	.50	1.25
❑ 42 Jonathan Stewart	.25	.60
❑ 43 Matt Forte	.30	.75
❑ 44 Ryan Grant	.25	.60
❑ 45 Ben Roethlisberger	.50	1.25
❑ 46 Dwayne Bowe	.25	.60
❑ 47 Antonio Gates	.25	.60
❑ 48 Maurice Jones-Drew	.25	.60
❑ 49 DeSean Jackson	.25	.60
❑ 50 Calvin Johnson	.30	.75
❑ 51 Joseph Addai	.30	.75
❑ 52 Eddie Royal	.25	.60
❑ 53 Andre Johnson	.25	.60
❑ 54 Jason Witten	.30	.75
❑ 55 Ronnie Brown	.25	.60
❑ 56 T.J. Houshmandzadeh	.25	.60
❑ 57 Frank Gore	.25	.60
❑ 58 LenDale White	.25	.60
❑ 59 Greg Jennings	.30	.75
❑ 60 Peyton Manning	.50	1.25
❑ 61 Josh Freeman RC	2.00	5.00
❑ 62 Shonn Greene RC	2.00	5.00
❑ 63 Mike Wallace RC	2.00	5.00
❑ 64 Javon Ringer RC	1.00	2.50
❑ 65 Hakeem Nicks RC	2.00	5.00
❑ 66 Brandon Pettigrew RC	1.25	3.00
❑ 67 Brian Robiskie RC	1.00	2.50
❑ 68 Chris Wells RC	2.50	6.00
❑ 69 Pat White RC	1.50	4.00
❑ 70 Michael Crabtree RC	2.50	6.00
❑ 71 Mike Thomas RC	1.00	2.50
❑ 72 Nate Davis RC	1.00	2.50
❑ 73 Percy Harvin RC	3.00	8.00
❑ 74 Tyson Jackson RC	1.00	2.50
❑ 75 Darrius Heyward-Bey RC	1.50	4.00
❑ 76 Aaron Curry RC	1.25	3.00
❑ 77 Juaquin Iglesias RC	1.00	2.50
❑ 78 Mohamed Massaquoi RC	1.00	2.50
❑ 79 Andre Brown RC	.75	2.00
❑ 80 Mark Sanchez RC	4.00	10.00
❑ 81 Jason Smith RC	.75	2.00
❑ 82 Patrick Turner RC	.75	2.00
❑ 83 Donald Brown RC	2.00	5.00
❑ 84 Derrick Williams RC	1.00	2.50
❑ 85 Jeremy Maclin RC	2.00	5.00
❑ 86 Rhett Bomar RC	.75	2.00
❑ 87 Glen Coffee RC	1.25	3.00
❑ 88 James Davis RC	1.00	2.50
❑ 89 Jarett Dillard RC	1.00	2.50
❑ 90 Knowshon Moreno RC	2.50	6.00
❑ 91 Kenny Britt RC	1.50	4.00
❑ 92 Stephen McGee RC	1.00	2.50
❑ 93 Austin Collie RC	2.00	5.00
❑ 94 Gartrell Johnson RC	.75	2.00
❑ 95 LeSean McCoy RC	2.00	5.00
❑ 96 Deon Butler RC	1.00	2.50
❑ 97 Brandon Tate RC	.75	2.00
❑ 98 Tom Brandstater RC	1.00	2.50
❑ 99 Ramses Barden RC	.75	2.00
❑ 100 Matthew Stafford RC	3.00	8.00
❑ 101 James Laurinaitis AU/330*	10.00	25.00
❑ 102 James Casey AU/495*	6.00	15.00
❑ 103 Brian Cushing AU/476*	10.00	25.00
❑ 105 Austin Collie AU/486*	20.00	40.00
❑ 106 Johnny Knox AU/408*	15.00	40.00
❑ 107 Chris Wells AU/245*	20.00	50.00
❑ 108 Quan Cosby AU/495*	6.00	15.00
❑ 109 Cedric Peerman AU/476*	6.00	15.00
❑ 110 Chase Coffman AU/378*	6.00	15.00
❑ 112 Glen Coffee AU/384*	10.00	25.00
❑ 113 Gartrell Johnson AU/476*	6.00	15.00
❑ 114 Rashad Jennings AU/464*	8.00	20.00
❑ 115 James Davis AU/495*	8.00	20.00
❑ 116 Jarett Dillard AU/476*	8.00	20.00
❑ 117 Jeremy Maclin AU/234*	20.00	50.00
❑ 119 Rey Maualuga AU/368*	10.00	25.00
❑ 120 Kenny Britt AU/245*	12.00	30.00
❑ 121 LeSean McCoy AU/245*	15.00	40.00
❑ 122 Nate Davis AU/495*	8.00	20.00
❑ 123 Percy Harvin AU/288*	40.00	80.00
❑ 124 Patrick Turner AU/384*	8.00	20.00
❑ 128 Shonn Greene AU/486*	15.00	40.00
❑ 129 Stephen McGee AU/395*	8.00	20.00
❑ 130 Tom Brandstater AU/187*	8.00	20.00

1995 Flair

Card	Low	High
❑ COMPLETE SET (220)	12.50	30.00
❑ 1 Larry Centers	.15	.40
❑ 2 Garrison Hearst	.30	.75
❑ 3 Seth Joyner	.07	.20
❑ 4 Dave Krieg	.07	.20
❑ 5 Rob Moore	.15	.40
❑ 6 Frank Sanders RC	.30	.75
❑ 7 Eric Swann	.15	.40
❑ 8 Devin Bush	.07	.20
❑ 9 Chris Doleman	.07	.20
❑ 10 Bert Emanuel	.30	.75
❑ 11 Jeff George	.15	.40
❑ 12 Craig Heyward	.15	.40
❑ 13 Terance Mathis	.15	.40
❑ 14 Eric Metcalf	.15	.40
❑ 15 Cornelius Bennett	.15	.40
❑ 16 Jeff Burris	.07	.20
❑ 17 Todd Collins RC	1.00	2.50
❑ 18 Russell Copeland	.07	.20
❑ 19 Jim Kelly	.30	.75
❑ 20 Andre Reed	.15	.40
❑ 21 Bruce Smith	.30	.75
❑ 22 Don Beebe	.07	.20
❑ 23 Mark Carrier WR	.15	.40
❑ 24 Kerry Collins RC	1.00	2.50
❑ 25 Barry Foster	.15	.40
❑ 26 Pete Metzelaars	.07	.20
❑ 27 Tyrone Poole	.30	.75
❑ 28 Frank Reich	.07	.20
❑ 29 Curtis Conway	.30	.75
❑ 30 Chris Gedney	.07	.20
❑ 31 Jeff Graham	.07	.20
❑ 32 Raymont Harris	.07	.20
❑ 33 Erik Kramer	.07	.20
❑ 34 Rashaan Salaam RC	.15	.40
❑ 35 Lewis Tillman	.07	.20
❑ 36 Michael Timpson	.07	.20
❑ 37 Jeff Blake RC	.40	1.00
❑ 38 Ki-Jana Carter RC	.30	.75
❑ 39 Tony McGee	.07	.20
❑ 40 Carl Pickens	.15	.40
❑ 41 Corey Sawyer	.07	.20
❑ 42 Darnay Scott	.15	.40
❑ 43 Dan Wilkinson	.15	.40
❑ 44 Derrick Alexander WR	.30	.75
❑ 45 Leroy Hoard	.07	.20
❑ 46 Michael Jackson	.15	.40
❑ 47 Antonio Langham	.07	.20
❑ 48 Andre Rison	.15	.40
❑ 49 Vinny Testaverde	.15	.40
❑ 50 Eric Turner	.07	.20
❑ 51 Troy Aikman	.75	2.00
❑ 52 Charles Haley	.15	.40
❑ 53 Michael Irvin	.30	.75
❑ 54 Daryl Johnston	.15	.40
❑ 55 Leon Lett	.07	.20
❑ 56 Jay Novacek	.15	.40
❑ 57 Emmitt Smith	1.25	3.00
❑ 58 Kevin Williams WR	.15	.40
❑ 59 Steve Atwater	.07	.20
❑ 60 Rod Bernstine	.07	.20
❑ 61 John Elway	1.50	4.00
❑ 62 Glyn Milburn	.07	.20
❑ 63 Anthony Miller	.15	.40
❑ 64 Mike Pritchard	.07	.20

Card		
❑ 65 Shannon Sharpe	.15	.40
❑ 66 Scott Mitchell	.15	.40
❑ 67 Herman Moore	.30	.75
❑ 68 Johnnie Morton	.15	.40
❑ 69 Brett Perriman	.15	.40
❑ 70 Barry Sanders	1.25	3.00
❑ 71 Chris Spielman	.15	.40
❑ 72 Edgar Bennett	.15	.40
❑ 73 Robert Brooks	.30	.75
❑ 74 Brett Favre	1.50	4.00
❑ 75 LeShon Johnson	.15	.40
❑ 76 Sean Jones	.07	.20
❑ 77 George Teague	.07	.20
❑ 78 Reggie White	.30	.75
❑ 79 Micheal Barrow	.07	.20
❑ 80 Gary Brown	.07	.20
❑ 81 Mel Gray	.07	.20
❑ 82 Haywood Jeffires	.07	.20
❑ 83 Steve McNair RC	1.50	4.00
❑ 84 Rodney Thomas RC	.15	.40
❑ 85 Trev Alberts	.07	.20
❑ 86 Flipper Anderson	.07	.20
❑ 87 Tony Bennett	.07	.20
❑ 88 Quentin Coryatt	.15	.40
❑ 89 Sean Dawkins	.15	.40
❑ 90 Craig Erickson	.07	.20
❑ 91 Marshall Faulk	1.00	2.50
❑ 92 Steve Beuerlein	.15	.40
❑ 93 Tony Boselli RC	.30	.75
❑ 94 Reggie Cobb	.07	.20
❑ 95 Ernest Givins	.07	.20
❑ 96 Desmond Howard	.15	.40
❑ 97 Jeff Lageman	.07	.20
❑ 98 James O. Stewart RC	.60	1.50
❑ 99 Marcus Allen	.30	.75
❑ 100 Steve Bono	.15	.40
❑ 101 Dale Carter	.15	.40
❑ 102 Willie Davis	.15	.40
❑ 103 Lake Dawson	.15	.40
❑ 104 Greg Hill	.15	.40
❑ 105 Neil Smith	.15	.40
❑ 106 Tim Bowens	.07	.20
❑ 107 Bryan Cox	.07	.20
❑ 108 Irving Fryar	.15	.40
❑ 109 Eric Green	.07	.20
❑ 110 Terry Kirby	.15	.40
❑ 111 Dan Marino	1.50	4.00
❑ 112 O.J. McDuffie	.30	.75
❑ 113 Bernie Parmalee	.15	.40
❑ 114 Derrick Alexander DE RC	.07	.20
❑ 115 Cris Carter	.30	.75
❑ 116 Qadry Ismail	.15	.40
❑ 117 Warren Moon	.15	.40
❑ 118 Jake Reed	.15	.40
❑ 119 Robert Smith	.30	.75
❑ 120 Dewayne Washington	.15	.40
❑ 121 Drew Bledsoe	.50	1.25
❑ 122 Vincent Brisby	.07	.20
❑ 123 Ben Coates	.15	.40
❑ 124 Curtis Martin RC	1.50	4.00
❑ 125 Willie McGinest	.15	.40
❑ 126 Dave Meggett	.07	.20
❑ 127 Chris Slade UER 126	.07	.20
❑ 128 Eric Allen	.07	.20
❑ 129 Mario Bates	.15	.40
❑ 130 Jim Everett	.07	.20
❑ 131 Michael Haynes	.15	.40
❑ 132 Tyrone Hughes	.15	.40
❑ 133 Renaldo Turnbull	.07	.20
❑ 134 Ray Zellars RC	.15	.40
❑ 135 Michael Brooks	.07	.20
❑ 136 Dave Brown	.15	.40
❑ 137 Rodney Hampton	.15	.40
❑ 138 Thomas Lewis	.15	.40
❑ 139 Mike Sherrard	.07	.20
❑ 140 Herschel Walker	.15	.40
❑ 141 Tyrone Wheatley RC	.60	1.50
❑ 142 Kyle Brady RC	.30	.75
❑ 143 Boomer Esiason	.15	.40
❑ 144 Aaron Glenn	.07	.20
❑ 145 Mo Lewis	.07	.20
❑ 146 Johnny Mitchell	.07	.20
❑ 147 Ronald Moore	.07	.20
❑ 148 Joe Aska	.15	.40
❑ 149 Tim Brown	.30	.75
❑ 150 Jeff Hostetler	.15	.40
❑ 151 Rocket Ismail	.15	.40
❑ 152 Napoleon Kaufman RC	.60	1.50
❑ 153 Chester McGlockton	.15	.40

Card		
❑ 154 Harvey Williams	.07	.20
❑ 155 Fred Barnett	.15	.40
❑ 156 Randall Cunningham	.30	.75
❑ 157 Charlie Garner	.30	.75
❑ 158 Mike Mamula RC	.07	.20
❑ 159 Kevin Turner	.07	.20
❑ 160 Ricky Watters	.15	.40
❑ 161 Calvin Williams	.15	.40
❑ 162 Mark Bruener RC	.15	.40
❑ 163 Kevin Greene	.15	.40
❑ 164 Charles Johnson	.15	.40
❑ 165 Greg Lloyd	.15	.40
❑ 166 Byron Bam Morris	.07	.20
❑ 167 Neil O'Donnell	.15	.40
❑ 168 Kordell Stewart RC	.75	2.00
❑ 169 John L. Williams	.07	.20
❑ 170 Rod Woodson	.15	.40
❑ 171 Jerome Bettis	.30	.75
❑ 172 Isaac Bruce	.50	1.25
❑ 173 Kevin Carter RC	.30	.75
❑ 174 Troy Drayton	.07	.20
❑ 175 Sean Gilbert	.15	.40
❑ 176 Carlos Jenkins	.07	.20
❑ 177 Todd Lyght	.07	.20
❑ 178 Chris Miller	.07	.20
❑ 179 Andre Coleman	.07	.20
❑ 180 Stan Humphries	.15	.40
❑ 181 Shawn Jefferson	.07	.20
❑ 182 Natrone Means	.15	.40
❑ 183 Leslie O'Neal	.15	.40
❑ 184 Junior Seau	.30	.75
❑ 185 Mark Seay	.15	.40
❑ 186 William Floyd	.15	.40
❑ 187 Merton Hanks	.07	.20
❑ 188 Brent Jones	.07	.20
❑ 189 Ken Norton	.15	.40
❑ 190 Jerry Rice	.75	2.00
❑ 191 Deion Sanders	.40	1.00
❑ 192 J.J. Stokes RC	.30	.75
❑ 193 Dana Stubblefield	.15	.40
❑ 194 Steve Young	.60	1.50
❑ 195 Sam Adams	.07	.20
❑ 196 Brian Blades	.15	.40
❑ 197 Joey Galloway RC	.75	2.00
❑ 198 Cortez Kennedy	.15	.40
❑ 199 Rick Mirer	.15	.40
❑ 200 Chris Warren	.15	.40
❑ 201 Derrick Brooks RC	.75	2.00
❑ 202 Lawrence Dawsey	.07	.20
❑ 203 Trent Dilfer	.30	.75
❑ 204 Alvin Harper	.07	.20
❑ 205 Jackie Harris	.07	.20
❑ 206 Courtney Hawkins	.07	.20
❑ 207 Hardy Nickerson	.07	.20
❑ 208 Errict Rhett	.15	.40
❑ 209 Warren Sapp RC	.75	2.00
❑ 210 Terry Allen	.15	.40
❑ 211 Tom Carter	.07	.20
❑ 212 Henry Ellard	.15	.40
❑ 213 Darrell Green	.07	.20
❑ 214 Brian Mitchell	.07	.20
❑ 215 Heath Shuler	.15	.40
❑ 216 Michael Westbrook RC	.30	.75
❑ 217 Tydus Winans	.07	.20
❑ 218 Checklist	.07	.20
❑ 219 Checklist	.07	.20
❑ 220 Checklist	.15	.40
❑ S1 Michael Irvin Sample	.50	1.25

2002 Flair

Card		
❑ COMP.SET w/o SP's (90)	10.00	25.00
❑ 1 Jeff Garcia	.40	1.00
❑ 2 Jevon Kearse	.40	1.00
❑ 3 Chris Weinke	.30	.75
❑ 4 Ray Lewis	.50	1.25
❑ 5 Donovan McNabb	.60	1.50
❑ 6 Tiki Barber	.50	1.25
❑ 7 Rich Gannon	.40	1.00
❑ 8 Jamal Anderson	.40	1.00
❑ 9 Curtis Martin	.50	1.25
❑ 10 Darrell Jackson	.40	1.00
❑ 11 Ricky Williams	.50	1.25
❑ 12 Drew Brees	.75	2.00
❑ 13 Mark Brunell	.40	1.00
❑ 14 Johnnie Morton	.40	1.00
❑ 15 Quincy Carter	.30	.75
❑ 16 Brian Urlacher	.60	1.50
❑ 17 Peerless Price	.30	.75
❑ 18 Drew Bledsoe	.50	1.25
❑ 19 Aaron Brooks	.40	1.00
❑ 20 Derrick Mason	.40	1.00
❑ 21 Charlie Garner	.40	1.00
❑ 22 Mike Alstott	.40	1.00
❑ 23 Freddie Mitchell	.30	.75
❑ 24 Isaac Bruce	.50	1.25
❑ 25 Hines Ward	.50	1.25
❑ 26 Doug Flutie	.50	1.25
❑ 27 Terrell Owens	.50	1.25
❑ 28 Peyton Manning	1.00	2.50
❑ 29 Ron Dayne	.40	1.00
❑ 30 Peter Warrick	.40	1.00
❑ 31 Randy Moss	.50	1.25
❑ 32 Priest Holmes	.50	1.25
❑ 33 Joey Galloway	.40	1.00
❑ 34 Jimmy Smith	.40	1.00
❑ 35 Marvin Harrison	.50	1.25
❑ 36 Junior Seau	.50	1.25
❑ 37 Zach Thomas	.50	1.25
❑ 38 Antowain Smith	.40	1.00
❑ 39 Marty Booker	.40	1.00
❑ 40 Deuce McAllister	.50	1.25
❑ 41 Rod Smith	.40	1.00
❑ 42 Michael Westbrook	.30	.75
❑ 43 Antonio Freeman	.50	1.25
❑ 44 Kerry Collins	.40	1.00
❑ 45 Koren Robinson	.30	.75
❑ 46 Jamal Lewis	.40	1.00
❑ 47 Duce Staley	.40	1.00
❑ 48 Jerome Bettis	.50	1.25
❑ 49 David Terrell	.40	1.00
❑ 50 Daunte Culpepper	.40	1.00
❑ 51 Tim Couch	.30	.75
❑ 52 Brian Griese	.40	1.00
❑ 53 Marshall Faulk	.50	1.25
❑ 54 Brad Johnson	.40	1.00
❑ 55 Eddie George	.40	1.00
❑ 56 Kurt Warner	.50	1.25
❑ 57 Steve McNair	.50	1.25
❑ 58 Stephen Davis	.40	1.00
❑ 59 Corey Dillon	.40	1.00
❑ 60 Troy Brown	.40	1.00
❑ 61 Warrick Dunn	.40	1.00
❑ 62 Ed McCaffrey	.40	1.00
❑ 63 Amani Toomer	.40	1.00
❑ 64 Rod Gardner	.30	.75
❑ 65 Mike McMahon	.30	.75
❑ 66 Wayne Chrebet	.40	1.00
❑ 67 Jake Plummer	.40	1.00
❑ 68 Edgerrin James	.50	1.25
❑ 69 Eric Moulds	.40	1.00
❑ 70 Tony Gonzalez	.40	1.00
❑ 71 Marcus Robinson	.40	1.00
❑ 72 Muhsin Muhammad	.40	1.00
❑ 73 Trent Dilfer	.40	1.00
❑ 74 Kevin Johnson	.30	.75
❑ 75 Fred Taylor	.50	1.25
❑ 76 Terrell Davis	.50	1.25
❑ 77 Emmitt Smith	1.25	3.00
❑ 78 Az-Zahir Hakim	.30	.75
❑ 79 Tim Brown	.50	1.25
❑ 80 Jerry Rice	1.00	2.50
❑ 81 Warren Sapp	.40	1.00
❑ 82 Michael Strahan	.50	1.25
❑ 83 Garrison Hearst	.40	1.00
❑ 84 David Boston	.30	.75
❑ 85 Michael Vick	.50	1.25
❑ 86 Anthony Thomas	.40	1.00
❑ 87 Ahman Green	.40	1.00
❑ 88 Chris Chambers	.50	1.25
❑ 89 Tom Brady	1.25	3.00
❑ 90 Plaxico Burress	.40	1.00
❑ 91 LaDainian Tomlinson	.75	2.00
❑ 92 Shaun Alexander	.50	1.25
❑ 93 Torry Holt	.50	1.25
❑ 94 Kordell Stewart	.40	1.00

❑ 95 Chad Pennington .50 1.25
❑ 96 Chris Redman .30 .75
❑ 97 Kendrell Bell .30 .75
❑ 98 Michael Bennett .40 1.00
❑ 99 Joe Horn .40 1.00
❑ 100 Brett Favre 1.25 3.00
❑ 101 David Carr RC 2.00 5.00
❑ 102 Joey Harrington RC 2.00 5.00
❑ 103 Ashley Lelie RC 2.00 5.00
❑ 104 Javon Walker RC 2.00 5.00
❑ 105 Reche Caldwell RC 2.00 5.00
❑ 106 Andre Davis RC 1.50 4.00
❑ 107 William Green RC 1.50 4.00
❑ 108 Antonio Bryant RC 2.50 6.00
❑ 109 Clinton Portis RC 5.00 12.00
❑ 110 Luke Staley RC 1.25 3.00
❑ 111 Josh Reed RC 1.50 4.00
❑ 112 Ron Johnson RC 1.50 4.00
❑ 113 Lamar Gordon RC 1.50 4.00
❑ 114 Cliff Russell RC 1.25 3.00
❑ 115 Eric Crouch RC 2.00 5.00
❑ 116 Ladell Betts RC 2.00 5.00
❑ 117 Patrick Ramsey RC 2.00 5.00
❑ 118 Adrian Peterson RC 2.00 5.00
❑ 119 DeShaun Foster RC 2.00 5.00
❑ 120 Tim Carter RC 1.50 4.00
❑ 121 Jabar Gaffney RC 2.00 5.00
❑ 122 T.J. Duckett RC 2.00 5.00
❑ 123 Julius Peppers RC 3.00 8.00
❑ 124 Rohan Davey RC 2.00 5.00
❑ 125 Antwaan Randle El RC 2.00 5.00
❑ 126 Jeremy Shockey RC 3.00 8.00
❑ 127 Donte Stallworth RC 2.00 5.00
❑ 128 Marquise Walker RC 1.25 3.00
❑ 129 Brian Westbrook RC 6.00 15.00
❑ 130 Randy Fasani RC 1.50 4.00
❑ 131 Jonathan Wells RC 2.00 5.00
❑ 132 Travis Stephens RC 1.25 3.00
❑ 133 Daniel Graham RC 1.50 4.00
❑ 134 Maurice Morris RC 2.00 5.00
❑ 135 David Garrard RC 3.00 8.00

2004 Flair

❑ COMP.SET w/o SP's (60) 20.00 40.00
❑ ROOKIE STATED ODDS 1:100 RETAIL
❑ ROOKIE PRINT RUN 799 SER.#'d SETS
❑ 1 Clinton Portis .60 1.50
❑ 2 Deuce McAllister .60 1.50
❑ 3 Marshall Faulk .60 1.50
❑ 4 Tom Brady 1.50 4.00
❑ 5 Ahman Green .60 1.50
❑ 6 LaDainian Tomlinson .75 2.00
❑ 7 Lee Suggs .60 1.50
❑ 8 Amani Toomer .50 1.25
❑ 9 Priest Holmes .60 1.50
❑ 10 Peerless Price .50 1.25
❑ 11 Warren Sapp .50 1.25
❑ 12 Andre Davis .40 1.00
❑ 13 Chad Pennington .60 1.50
❑ 14 Quincy Carter .40 1.00
❑ 15 Santana Moss .50 1.25
❑ 16 Antonio Bryant .60 1.50
❑ 17 Jerry Porter .50 1.25
❑ 18 Laveranues Coles .50 1.25
❑ 19 Daunte Culpepper .60 1.50
❑ 20 Stephen Davis .50 1.25
❑ 21 Rich Gannon .50 1.25
❑ 22 Chad Johnson .50 1.25
❑ 23 Ashley Lelie .50 1.25
❑ 24 Ray Lewis .60 1.50
❑ 25 Joey Harrington .50 1.25
❑ 26 Brian Westbrook .60 1.50
❑ 27 Marvin Harrison .60 1.50
❑ 28 Torry Holt .60 1.50
❑ 29 Kevan Barlow .50 1.25
❑ 30 Peyton Manning 1.25 3.00
❑ 31 Andre Johnson .60 1.50
❑ 32 Steve Smith .60 1.50
❑ 33 Troy Brown .50 1.25
❑ 34 Brian Urlacher .60 1.50
❑ 35 Anquan Boldin .60 1.50
❑ 36 Matt Hasselbeck .60 1.50
❑ 37 Edgerrin James .60 1.50
❑ 38 Dante Hall .50 1.25
❑ 39 Brad Johnson .50 1.25
❑ 40 Jamal Lewis .50 1.25
❑ 41 Rudi Johnson .50 1.25
❑ 42 Michael Strahan .50 1.25
❑ 43 Donovan McNabb .60 1.50
❑ 44 Steve McNair .60 1.50
❑ 45 Ricky Williams .60 1.50
❑ 46 Jake Delhomme .50 1.25
❑ 47 Patrick Ramsey .50 1.25
❑ 48 Randy Moss .60 1.50
❑ 49 David Carr .50 1.25
❑ 50 Jeff Garcia .60 1.50
❑ 51 Shaun Alexander .60 1.50
❑ 52 Byron Leftwich .60 1.50
❑ 53 Michael Vick .60 1.50
❑ 54 Brett Favre 1.50 4.00
❑ 55 Hines Ward .60 1.50
❑ 56 Chris Chambers .50 1.25
❑ 57 Eddie George .50 1.25
❑ 58 Eric Moulds .50 1.25
❑ 59 Plaxico Burress .50 1.25
❑ 60 Charles Rogers .50 1.25
❑ 61 Eli Manning RC 10.00 25.00
❑ 62 Larry Fitzgerald RC 5.00 12.00
❑ 63 Chris Perry RC 1.50 4.00
❑ 64 Ben Roethlisberger RC 12.00 30.00
❑ 65 Roy Williams RC 2.00 5.00
❑ 66 Kellen Winslow RC 2.00 5.00
❑ 67 Steven Jackson RC 4.00 10.00
❑ 68 Kevin Jones RC 1.50 4.00
❑ 69 Reggie Williams RC 1.50 4.00
❑ 70 Michael Clayton RC 1.50 4.00
❑ 71 Rashaun Woods RC 1.00 2.50
❑ 72 Ben Troupe RC 1.25 3.00
❑ 73 Greg Jones RC 1.50 4.00
❑ 74 J.P. Losman RC 1.50 4.00
❑ 75 Philip Rivers RC 6.00 15.00
❑ 76 Michael Jenkins RC 1.50 4.00
❑ 77 Darius Watts RC 1.25 3.00
❑ 78 Michael Turner RC 4.00 10.00
❑ 79 Lee Evans RC 2.00 5.00
❑ 80 Drew Henson RC 1.00 2.50
❑ 81 Luke McCown RC 1.50 4.00
❑ 82 Julius Jones RC 2.00 5.00
❑ 83 Bernard Berrian RC 1.50 4.00
❑ 84 Keary Colbert RC 1.25 3.00
❑ 85 Tatum Bell RC 1.50 4.00

1999 Flair Showcase

❑ COMPLETE SET (192) 300.00 600.00
❑ COMP.SET w/o SPs (160) 20.00 50.00
❑ 1 Troy Aikman PW .75 2.00
❑ 2 Jamal Anderson PW .15 .40
❑ 3 Charlie Batch PW .40 1.00
❑ 4 Jerome Bettis PW .15 .40
❑ 5 Drew Bledsoe PW .50 1.25
❑ 6 Mark Brunell PW .40 1.00
❑ 7 Randall Cunningham PW .40 1.00
❑ 8 Terrell Davis PW .40 1.00
❑ 9 Corey Dillon PW .40 1.00
❑ 10 Warrick Dunn PW .40 1.00
❑ 11 Curtis Enis PW .15 .40
❑ 12 Marshall Faulk PW .50 1.25
❑ 13 Brett Favre PW 1.25 3.00
❑ 14 Doug Flutie PW .40 1.00
❑ 15 Eddie George PW .40 1.00
❑ 16 Brian Griese PW .40 1.00
❑ 17 Keyshawn Johnson PW .40 1.00
❑ 18 Peyton Manning PW 1.25 3.00
❑ 19 Dan Marino PW 1.25 3.00
❑ 20 Curtis Martin PW .40 1.00
❑ 21 Steve McNair PW .40 1.00
❑ 22 Randy Moss PW 1.00 2.50
❑ 23 Terrell Owens PW .40 1.00
❑ 24 Jake Plummer PW .25 .60
❑ 25 Jerry Rice PW .75 2.00
❑ 26 Barry Sanders PW 1.25 3.00
❑ 27 Antowain Smith PW .40 1.00
❑ 28 Emmitt Smith PW .75 2.00
❑ 29 Kordell Stewart PW .25 .60
❑ 30 J.J. Stokes PW .25 .60
❑ 31 Fred Taylor PW .40 1.00
❑ 32 Steve Young PW .50 1.25
❑ 33 Troy Aikman PN .75 2.00
❑ 34 Mike Alstott PN .40 1.00
❑ 35 Jamal Anderson PN .40 1.00
❑ 36 Charlie Batch PN .40 1.00
❑ 37 Jerome Bettis PN .40 1.00
❑ 38 Drew Bledsoe PN .50 1.25
❑ 39 Mark Brunell PN .40 1.00
❑ 40 Cris Carter PN .40 1.00
❑ 41 Mark Chmura PN .15 .40
❑ 42 Wayne Chrebet PN .25 .60
❑ 43 Kerry Collins PN .15 .40
❑ 44 Randall Cunningham PN .40 1.00
❑ 45 Terrell Davis PN .40 1.00
❑ 46 Trent Dilfer PN .25 .60
❑ 47 Corey Dillon PN .40 1.00
❑ 48 Warrick Dunn PN .40 1.00
❑ 49 Kevin Dyson PN .25 .60
❑ 50 Curtis Enis PN .15 .40
❑ 51 Marshall Faulk PN .50 1.25
❑ 52 Brett Favre PN 1.25 3.00
❑ 53 Doug Flutie PN .40 1.00
❑ 54 Antonio Freeman PN .40 1.00
❑ 55 Eddie George PN .40 1.00
❑ 56 Terry Glenn PN .40 1.00
❑ 57 Tony Gonzalez PN .40 1.00
❑ 58 Elvis Grbac PN .25 .60
❑ 59 Jacquez Green PN .15 .40
❑ 60 Brian Griese PN .40 1.00
❑ 61 Marvin Harrison PN .40 1.00
❑ 62 Garrison Hearst PN .25 .60
❑ 63 Skip Hicks PN .15 .40
❑ 64 Priest Holmes PN .60 1.50
❑ 65 Michael Irvin PN .25 .60
❑ 66 Brad Johnson PN .25 .60
❑ 67 Keyshawn Johnson PN .40 1.00
❑ 68 Napoleon Kaufman PN .40 1.00
❑ 69 Dorsey Levens PN .40 1.00
❑ 70 Peyton Manning PN 1.25 3.00
❑ 71 Dan Marino PN 1.25 3.00
❑ 72 Curtis Martin PN .40 1.00
❑ 73 Ed McCaffrey PN .25 .60
❑ 74 Keenan McCardell PN .25 .60
❑ 75 O.J. McDuffie PN .25 .60
❑ 76 Steve McNair PN .40 1.00
❑ 77 Scott Mitchell PN .15 .40
❑ 78 Randy Moss PN 1.00 2.50
❑ 79 Eric Moulds PN .40 1.00
❑ 80 Terrell Owens PN .40 1.00
❑ 81 Lawrence Phillips PN .25 .60
❑ 82 Jake Plummer PN .25 .60
❑ 83 Jerry Rice PN .75 2.00
❑ 84 Andre Rison PN .25 .60
❑ 85 Barry Sanders PN 1.25 3.00
❑ 86 Shannon Sharpe PN .25 .60
❑ 87 Antowain Smith PN .40 1.00
❑ 88 Emmitt Smith PN .75 2.00
❑ 89 Rod Smith PN .25 .60
❑ 90 Duce Staley PN .40 1.00
❑ 91 Kordell Stewart PN .25 .60
❑ 92 J.J. Stokes PN .25 .60
❑ 93 Fred Taylor PN .40 1.00
❑ 94 Vinny Testaverde PN .25 .60
❑ 95 Ricky Watters PN .25 .60
❑ 96 Steve Young PN .50 1.25
❑ 97 Mike Alstott .40 1.00
❑ 98 Jamal Anderson .40 1.00
❑ 99 Charlie Batch .40 1.00
❑ 100 Jerome Bettis .40 1.00
❑ 101 Tim Biakabutuka .25 .60
❑ 102 Drew Bledsoe .50 1.25
❑ 103 Tim Brown .40 1.00
❑ 104 Mark Brunell .40 1.00
❑ 105 Cris Carter .40 1.00
❑ 106 Chris Chandler .25 .60

❑ 107 Mark Chmura	.15	.40
❑ 108 Wayne Chrebet	.25	.60
❑ 109 Ben Coates	.25	.60
❑ 110 Kerry Collins	.25	.60
❑ 111 Randall Cunningham	.40	1.00
❑ 112 Trent Dilfer	.25	.60
❑ 113 Corey Dillon	.40	1.00
❑ 114 Warrick Dunn	.40	1.00
❑ 115 Kevin Dyson	.25	.60
❑ 116 Curtis Enis	.15	.40
❑ 117 Marshall Faulk	.50	1.25
❑ 118 Doug Flutie	.40	1.00
❑ 119 Antonio Freeman	.40	1.00
❑ 120 Joey Galloway	.25	.60
❑ 121 Rich Gannon	.40	1.00
❑ 122 Eddie George	.40	1.00
❑ 123 Terry Glenn	.40	1.00
❑ 124 Tony Gonzalez	.40	1.00
❑ 125 Elvis Grbac	.25	.60
❑ 126 Jacquez Green	.15	.40
❑ 127 Brian Griese	.40	1.00
❑ 128 Marvin Harrison	.40	1.00
❑ 129 Garrison Hearst	.25	.60
❑ 130 Skip Hicks	.15	.40
❑ 131 Priest Holmes	.60	1.50
❑ 132 Michael Irvin	.25	.60
❑ 133 Brad Johnson	.25	.60
❑ 134 Napoleon Kaufman	.40	1.00
❑ 135 Terry Kirby	.15	.40
❑ 136 Dorsey Levens	.40	1.00
❑ 137 Curtis Martin	.40	1.00
❑ 138 Ed McCaffrey	.25	.60
❑ 139 Keenan McCardell	.25	.60
❑ 140 O.J. McDuffie	.25	.60
❑ 141 Steve McNair	.40	1.00
❑ 142 Natrone Means	.25	.60
❑ 143 Scott Mitchell	.15	.40
❑ 144 Herman Moore	.25	.60
❑ 145 Eric Moulds	.40	1.00
❑ 146 Terrell Owens	.40	1.00
❑ 147 Lawrence Phillips	.25	.60
❑ 148 Jerry Rice	.75	2.00
❑ 149 Andre Rison	.25	.60
❑ 150 Deion Sanders	.40	1.00
❑ 151 Shannon Sharpe	.25	.60
❑ 152 Antowain Smith	.40	1.00
❑ 153 Rod Smith	.25	.60
❑ 154 Duce Staley	.40	1.00
❑ 155 Kordell Stewart	.25	.60
❑ 156 J.J. Stokes	.25	.60
❑ 157 Vinny Testaverde	.25	.60
❑ 158 Yancey Thigpen	.15	.40
❑ 159 Ricky Watters	.25	.60
❑ 160 Steve Young	.50	1.25
❑ 161 Troy Aikman SP	6.00	12.00
❑ 162 Champ Bailey RC	5.00	12.00
❑ 163 Karsten Bailey RC	3.00	8.00
❑ 164 D'Wayne Bates RC	3.00	8.00
❑ 165 David Boston RC	4.00	10.00
❑ 166 Mike Cloud RC	3.00	8.00
❑ 167 Cecil Collins RC	2.00	5.00
❑ 168 Tim Couch RC	4.00	10.00
❑ 169 Daunte Culpepper RC	15.00	40.00
❑ 170 Terrell Davis SP	2.50	6.00
❑ 171 Troy Edwards RC	3.00	8.00
❑ 172 Kevin Faulk RC	4.00	10.00
❑ 173 Brett Favre SP	10.00	20.00
❑ 174 Torry Holt RC	10.00	25.00
❑ 175 Sedrick Irvin RC	2.00	5.00
❑ 176 Edgerrin James RC	15.00	40.00
❑ 177 James Johnson RC	3.00	8.00
❑ 178 Kevin Johnson RC	4.00	10.00
❑ 179 Keyshawn Johnson SP	2.00	5.00
❑ 180 Peyton Manning SP	10.00	20.00
❑ 181 Dan Marino SP	10.00	20.00
❑ 182 Donovan McNabb RC	20.00	50.00
❑ 183 Cade McNown RC	3.00	8.00
❑ 184 Joe Montgomery RC	3.00	8.00
❑ 185 Randy Moss SP	6.00	15.00
❑ 186 Jake Plummer SP	2.50	6.00
❑ 187 Peerless Price RC	4.00	10.00
❑ 188 Barry Sanders SP	10.00	20.00
❑ 189 Akili Smith RC	3.00	8.00
❑ 190 Emmitt Smith SP	6.00	12.00
❑ 191 Fred Taylor SP	3.00	8.00
❑ 192 Ricky Williams RC	7.50	20.00
❑ P24 Jake Plummer PW Promo	.40	1.00
❑ P82 Jake Plummer PN Promo	.40	1.00
❑ P147 Jake Plummer Promo	.40	1.00

2006 Flair Showcase

❑ COMP.SET w/o SP's (100)	8.00	20.00
❑ 1 Edgerrin James	.25	.60
❑ 2 Larry Fitzgerald	.30	.75
❑ 3 Anquan Boldin	.25	.60
❑ 4 Michael Vick	.30	.75
❑ 5 Warrick Dunn	.25	.60
❑ 6 Roddy White	.25	.60
❑ 7 Steve McNair	.25	.60
❑ 8 Jamal Lewis	.25	.60
❑ 9 Derrick Mason	.25	.60
❑ 10 Willis McGahee	.30	.75
❑ 11 Lee Evans	.25	.60
❑ 12 J.P. Losman	.25	.60
❑ 13 Jake Delhomme	.25	.60
❑ 14 DeShaun Foster	.25	.60
❑ 15 Steve Smith	.30	.75
❑ 16 Rex Grossman	.30	.75
❑ 17 Thomas Jones	.25	.60
❑ 18 Muhsin Muhammad	.25	.60
❑ 19 Brian Urlacher	.30	.75
❑ 20 Carson Palmer	.30	.75
❑ 21 Rudi Johnson	.25	.60
❑ 22 Chad Johnson	.25	.60
❑ 23 Charlie Frye	.25	.60
❑ 24 Reuben Droughns	.25	.60
❑ 25 Braylon Edwards	.30	.75
❑ 26 Drew Bledsoe	.30	.75
❑ 27 Julius Jones	.25	.60
❑ 28 Terrell Owens	.30	.75
❑ 29 Jake Plummer	.25	.60
❑ 30 Tatum Bell	.20	.50
❑ 31 Javon Walker	.25	.60
❑ 32 Kevin Jones	.25	.60
❑ 33 Roy Williams WR	.30	.75
❑ 34 Mike Williams	.25	.60
❑ 35 Brett Favre	.60	1.50
❑ 36 Ahman Green	.25	.60
❑ 37 Donald Driver	.30	.75
❑ 38 David Carr	.20	.50
❑ 39 Eric Moulds	.25	.60
❑ 40 Andre Johnson	.25	.60
❑ 41 Peyton Manning	.50	1.25
❑ 42 Marvin Harrison	.30	.75
❑ 43 Reggie Wayne	.25	.60
❑ 44 Byron Leftwich	.25	.60
❑ 45 Fred Taylor	.25	.60
❑ 46 Ernest Wilford	.20	.50
❑ 47 Trent Green	.25	.60
❑ 48 Larry Johnson	.25	.60
❑ 49 Tony Gonzalez	.25	.60
❑ 50 Eddie Kennison	.20	.50
❑ 51 Daunte Culpepper	.30	.75
❑ 52 Ronnie Brown	.30	.75
❑ 53 Chris Chambers	.25	.60
❑ 54 Brad Johnson	.25	.60
❑ 55 Chester Taylor	.25	.60
❑ 56 Troy Williamson	.25	.60
❑ 57 Tom Brady	.50	1.25
❑ 58 Corey Dillon	.25	.60
❑ 59 Troy Brown	.20	.50
❑ 60 Drew Brees	.30	.75
❑ 61 Deuce McAllister	.25	.60
❑ 62 Joe Horn	.25	.60
❑ 63 Eli Manning	.40	1.00
❑ 64 Tiki Barber	.30	.75
❑ 65 Plaxico Burress	.25	.60
❑ 66 Jeremy Shockey	.30	.75
❑ 67 Chad Pennington	.25	.60
❑ 68 Curtis Martin	.30	.75
❑ 69 Laveranues Coles	.25	.60
❑ 70 Aaron Brooks	.25	.60
❑ 71 LaMont Jordan	.25	.60
❑ 72 Randy Moss	.30	.75
❑ 73 Jerry Porter	.25	.60
❑ 74 Donovan McNabb	.30	.75
❑ 75 Brian Westbrook	.25	.60
❑ 76 Reggie Brown	.20	.50
❑ 77 Ben Roethlisberger	.50	1.25
❑ 78 Willie Parker	.40	1.00
❑ 79 Hines Ward	.30	.75
❑ 80 Philip Rivers	.30	.75
❑ 81 LaDainian Tomlinson	.40	1.00
❑ 82 Antonio Gates	.30	.75
❑ 83 Alex Smith QB	.25	.60
❑ 84 Frank Gore	.30	.75
❑ 85 Antonio Bryant	.25	.60
❑ 86 Matt Hasselbeck	.25	.60
❑ 87 Shaun Alexander	.25	.60
❑ 88 Nate Burleson	.25	.60
❑ 89 Marc Bulger	.25	.60
❑ 90 Steven Jackson	.30	.75
❑ 91 Torry Holt	.25	.60
❑ 92 Chris Simms	.25	.60
❑ 93 Cadillac Williams	.30	.75
❑ 94 Joey Galloway	.25	.60
❑ 95 Kerry Collins	.25	.60
❑ 96 David Givens	.25	.60
❑ 97 Drew Bennett	.25	.60
❑ 98 Mark Brunell	.25	.60
❑ 99 Clinton Portis	.30	.75
❑ 100 Santana Moss	.25	.60
❑ 101 Todd Watkins RC	1.50	4.00
❑ 102 Adam Jennings RC	2.00	5.00
❑ 103 David Pittman RC	2.00	5.00
❑ 104 Dawan Landry RC	2.50	6.00
❑ 105 Ko Simpson RC	2.00	5.00
❑ 106 James Anderson RC	1.50	4.00
❑ 107 Dusty Dvoracek RC	2.50	6.00
❑ 108 Jamar Williams RC	2.00	5.00
❑ 109 Bennie Brazell RC	2.00	5.00
❑ 110 Leon Williams RC	2.00	5.00
❑ 111 Lawrence Vickers RC	2.00	5.00
❑ 112 Elvis Dumervil RC	2.50	6.00
❑ 113 Domenik Hixon RC	2.50	6.00
❑ 114 Antoine Bethea RC	3.00	8.00
❑ 115 David Anderson RC	2.00	5.00
❑ 116 Freddie Keiaho RC	2.00	5.00
❑ 117 Clint Ingram RC	2.50	6.00
❑ 118 Jeff Webb RC	2.00	5.00
❑ 119 Devin Aromashodu RC	2.50	6.00
❑ 120 Mike Hass RC	2.50	6.00
❑ 121 Josh Lay RC	1.50	4.00
❑ 122 Marques Colston RC	6.00	15.00
❑ 123 Gerris Wilkinson RC	1.50	4.00
❑ 124 Barry Cofield RC	2.50	6.00
❑ 125 Guy Whimper RC	1.50	4.00
❑ 126 Nick Mangold RC	1.25	3.00
❑ 127 Anthony Schlegel RC	2.00	5.00
❑ 128 Eric Smith RC	2.00	5.00
❑ 129 Darnell Bing RC	2.00	5.00
❑ 130 Anthony Smith RC	2.50	6.00
❑ 131 Charlie Whitehurst RC	2.50	6.00
❑ 132 Delanie Walker RC	2.00	5.00
❑ 133 Marcus Hudson RC	2.00	5.00
❑ 134 David Kirtman RC	2.00	5.00
❑ 135 Victor Adeyanju RC	2.00	5.00
❑ 136 Davin Joseph RC	2.00	5.00
❑ 137 Marcus McNeill RC	2.00	5.00
❑ 138 Calvin Lowry RC	2.50	6.00
❑ 139 Stephen Tulloch RC	2.00	5.00
❑ 140 Tema Nande RC	2.00	5.00
❑ 141 Jonathan Orr RC	2.00	5.00
❑ 142 Jon Alston RC	1.50	4.00
❑ 143 Jimmy Williams RC	3.00	8.00
❑ 144 D.J. Shockley RC	2.50	6.00
❑ 145 Demetrius Williams RC	2.50	6.00
❑ 146 P.J. Daniels RC	2.00	5.00
❑ 147 Quinn Sypniewski RC	2.50	6.00
❑ 148 Ashton Youboty RC	2.50	6.00
❑ 149 Richard Marshall RC	2.50	6.00
❑ 150 Jeff King RC	2.50	6.00
❑ 151 Danieal Manning RC	3.00	8.00
❑ 152 Reggie McNeal RC	2.50	6.00
❑ 153 D'Qwell Jackson RC	2.50	6.00
❑ 154 Jerome Harrison RC	3.00	8.00
❑ 155 Skyler Green RC	2.00	5.00
❑ 156 Brandon Marshall RC	3.00	8.00
❑ 157 Daniel Bullocks RC	3.00	8.00
❑ 158 Abdul Hodge RC	2.50	6.00
❑ 159 Cory Rodgers RC	3.00	8.00
❑ 160 Ingle Martin RC	2.50	6.00
❑ 161 Stephen Gostkowski RC	5.00	12.00
❑ 162 Wali Lundy RC	3.00	8.00

Card		
❑ 163 Bernard Pollard RC	2.50	6.00
❑ 164 Marcus Vick RC	2.00	5.00
❑ 165 Cedric Griffin RC	2.50	6.00
❑ 166 Garrett Mills RC	2.50	6.00
❑ 167 Roman Harper RC	2.50	6.00
❑ 168 Brad Smith RC	3.00	8.00
❑ 169 Leon Washington RC	4.00	10.00
❑ 170 Ahmad Brooks RC	2.50	6.00
❑ 171 Thomas Howard RC	2.50	6.00
❑ 172 Jason Avant RC	3.00	8.00
❑ 173 Jeremy Bloom RC	2.50	6.00
❑ 174 Omar Jacobs RC	2.00	5.00
❑ 175 Mike Bell RC	3.00	8.00
❑ 176 Cedric Humes RC	2.50	6.00
❑ 177 Michael Robinson RC	2.50	6.00
❑ 178 Ben Obomanu RC	2.50	6.00
❑ 179 Darryl Tapp RC	2.50	6.00
❑ 180 Claude Wroten RC	2.00	5.00
❑ 181 Dominique Byrd RC	2.50	6.00
❑ 182 Marques Hagans RC	2.50	6.00
❑ 183 Bruce Gradkowski RC	3.00	8.00
❑ 184 Rocky McIntosh RC	3.00	8.00
❑ 185 Leonard Pope RC	3.00	8.00
❑ 186 Jerious Norwood RC	3.00	8.00
❑ 187 Haloti Ngata RC	3.00	8.00
❑ 188 Donte Whitner RC	3.00	8.00
❑ 189 John McCargo RC	2.50	6.00
❑ 190 Devin Hester RC	6.00	15.00
❑ 191 Johnathan Joseph RC	2.50	6.00
❑ 192 Kamerion Wimbley RC	3.00	8.00
❑ 193 Travis Wilson RC	2.00	5.00
❑ 194 Bobby Carpenter RC	2.50	6.00
❑ 195 Anthony Fasano RC	3.00	8.00
❑ 196 Tony Scheffler RC	3.00	8.00
❑ 197 Ernie Sims RC	2.50	6.00
❑ 198 Brian Calhoun RC	2.50	6.00
❑ 199 A.J. Hawk RC	5.00	12.00
❑ 200 Greg Jennings RC	5.00	12.00
❑ 201 Mario Williams RC	4.00	10.00
❑ 202 DeMeco Ryans RC	4.00	10.00
❑ 203 Marcedes Lewis RC	3.00	8.00
❑ 204 Maurice Drew RC	6.00	15.00
❑ 205 Tamba Hali RC	3.00	8.00
❑ 206 Brodie Croyle RC	3.00	8.00
❑ 207 Jason Allen RC	2.50	6.00
❑ 208 Derek Hagan RC	2.50	6.00
❑ 209 Chad Greenway RC	3.00	8.00
❑ 210 Tarvaris Jackson RC	3.00	8.00
❑ 211 Chad Jackson RC	2.50	6.00
❑ 212 David Thomas RC	3.00	8.00
❑ 213 Mathias Kiwanuka RC	4.00	10.00
❑ 214 Sinorice Moss RC	3.00	8.00
❑ 215 D'Brickashaw Ferguson RC	3.00	8.00
❑ 216 Kellen Clemens RC	3.00	8.00
❑ 217 Michael Huff RC	3.00	8.00
❑ 218 Brodrick Bunkley RC	2.50	6.00
❑ 219 Willie Reid RC	2.50	6.00
❑ 220 Antonio Cromartie RC	3.00	8.00
❑ 221 Manny Lawson RC	3.00	8.00
❑ 222 Brandon Williams RC	2.50	6.00
❑ 223 Kelly Jennings RC	3.00	8.00
❑ 224 Tye Hill RC	2.50	6.00
❑ 225 Joe Klopfenstein RC	2.50	6.00
❑ 226 Maurice Stovall RC	2.50	6.00
❑ 227 Matt Leinart RC	6.00	15.00
❑ 228 DeAngelo Williams RC	8.00	20.00
❑ 229 Jay Cutler RC	10.00	25.00
❑ 230 Joseph Addai RC	5.00	12.00
❑ 231 Laurence Maroney RC	5.00	12.00
❑ 232 Reggie Bush RC	10.00	25.00
❑ 233 Santonio Holmes RC	10.00	25.00
❑ 234 Vernon Davis RC	4.00	10.00
❑ 235 Vince Young RC	10.00	25.00
❑ 236 LenDale White RC	5.00	12.00
❑ 237 Edgerrin James	1.25	3.00
❑ 238 Michael Vick	1.50	4.00
❑ 239 Jamal Lewis	1.25	3.00
❑ 240 Willis McGahee	1.50	4.00
❑ 241 Steve Smith	1.50	4.00
❑ 242 Brian Urlacher	1.50	4.00
❑ 243 Carson Palmer	1.50	4.00
❑ 244 Charlie Frye	1.25	3.00
❑ 245 Terrell Owens	1.50	4.00
❑ 246 Jake Plummer	1.25	3.00
❑ 247 Kevin Jones	1.25	3.00
❑ 248 Brett Favre	3.00	8.00
❑ 249 David Carr	1.00	2.50
❑ 250 Peyton Manning	2.50	6.00
❑ 251 Byron Leftwich	1.25	3.00
❑ 252 Larry Johnson	1.25	3.00
❑ 253 Daunte Culpepper	1.50	4.00
❑ 254 Brad Johnson	1.25	3.00
❑ 255 Tom Brady	2.50	6.00
❑ 256 Drew Brees	1.50	4.00
❑ 257 Eli Manning	2.00	5.00
❑ 258 Curtis Martin	1.50	4.00
❑ 259 Randy Moss	1.50	4.00
❑ 260 Donovan McNabb	1.50	4.00
❑ 261 Ben Roethlisberger	2.50	6.00
❑ 262 LaDainian Tomlinson	2.00	5.00
❑ 263 Alex Smith QB	1.25	3.00
❑ 264 Shaun Alexander	1.25	3.00
❑ 265 Marc Bulger	1.25	3.00
❑ 266 Cadillac Williams	1.50	4.00
❑ 267 Drew Bennett	1.25	3.00
❑ 268 Clinton Portis	1.50	4.00

1960 Fleer

Card		
❑ COMPLETE SET (132)	500.00	750.00
❑ WRAPPER (5-CENT)	20.00	25.00
❑ 1 Harvey White RC !	12.00	20.00
❑ 2 Tom Corky Tharp RC	2.00	3.50
❑ 3 Dan McGrew RC	2.00	3.50
❑ 4 Bob White RC	2.00	3.50
❑ 5 Dick Jamieson RC	2.00	3.50
❑ 6 Sam Salerno RC	2.00	3.50
❑ 7 Sid Gillman CO RC	12.00	20.00
❑ 8 Ben Preston RC	2.00	3.50
❑ 9 George Blanch RC	2.00	3.50
❑ 10 Bob Stransky RC	2.00	3.50
❑ 11 Fran Curci RC	2.00	3.50
❑ 12 George Shirkey RC	2.00	3.50
❑ 13 Paul Larson	2.00	3.50
❑ 14 John Stolte RC	2.00	3.50
❑ 15 Serafino Fazio RC	2.50	5.00
❑ 16 Tom Dimitroff RC	2.00	3.50
❑ 17 Elbert Dubenion RC	6.00	12.00
❑ 18 Hogan Wharton RC	2.00	3.50
❑ 19 Tom O'Connell	2.00	3.50
❑ 20 Sammy Baugh CO	30.00	50.00
❑ 21 Tony Sardisco RC	2.00	3.50
❑ 22 Alan Cann RC	2.00	3.50
❑ 23 Mike Hudock RC	2.00	3.50
❑ 24 Bill Atkins RC	2.00	3.50
❑ 25 Charlie Jackson RC	2.00	3.50
❑ 26 Frank Tripucka	3.00	6.00
❑ 27 Tony Teresa RC	2.00	3.50
❑ 28 Joe Amstutz RC	2.00	3.50
❑ 29 Bob Fee RC	2.00	3.50
❑ 30 Jim Baldwin RC	2.00	3.50
❑ 31 Jim Yates RC	2.00	3.50
❑ 32 Don Flynn RC	2.00	3.50
❑ 33 Ken Adamson RC	2.00	3.50
❑ 34 Ron Drzewiecki	2.00	3.50
❑ 35 J.W. Slack RC	2.00	3.50
❑ 36 Bob Yates RC	2.00	3.50
❑ 37 Gary Cobb RC	2.00	3.50
❑ 38 Jacky Lee RC	2.50	5.00
❑ 39 Jack Spikes RC	2.50	5.00
❑ 40 Jim Padgett RC	2.00	3.50
❑ 41 Jack Larscheid UER RC	2.00	3.50
❑ 42 Bob Reifsnyder RC	2.00	3.50
❑ 43 Fran Rogel	2.00	3.50
❑ 44 Ray Moss RC	2.00	3.50
❑ 45 Tony Banfield RC	2.50	5.00
❑ 46 George Herring RC	2.00	3.50
❑ 47 Willie Smith RC	2.00	3.50
❑ 48 Buddy Allen RC	2.00	3.50
❑ 49 Bill Brown LB RC	2.00	3.50
❑ 50 Ken Ford RC	2.00	3.50
❑ 51 Billy Kinard RC	2.00	3.50
❑ 52 Buddy Mayfield RC	2.00	3.50
❑ 53 Bill Krisher RC	2.00	3.50
❑ 54 Frank Bernardi RC	2.00	3.50
❑ 55 Lou Saban CO RC	2.50	5.00
❑ 56 Gene Cockrell RC	2.00	3.50
❑ 57 Sam Sanders RC	2.00	3.50
❑ 58 George Blanda	30.00	50.00
❑ 59 Sherrill Headrick RC	2.50	5.00
❑ 60 Carl Larpenter RC	2.00	3.50
❑ 61 Gene Prebola RC	2.00	3.50
❑ 62 Dick Chorovich RC	2.00	3.50
❑ 63 Bob McNamara RC	2.00	3.50
❑ 64 Tom Saidock RC	2.00	3.50
❑ 65 Willie Evans RC	2.00	3.50
❑ 66 Billy Cannon RC UER	10.00	20.00
❑ 67 Sam McCord RC	2.00	3.50
❑ 68 Mike Simmons RC	2.00	3.50
❑ 69 Jim Swink RC	2.50	5.00
❑ 70 Don Hitt RC	2.00	3.50
❑ 71 Gerhard Schwedes RC	2.00	3.50
❑ 72 Thurlow Cooper RC	2.00	3.50
❑ 73 Abner Haynes RC	10.00	20.00
❑ 74 Billy Shoemake RC	2.00	3.50
❑ 75 Marv Lasater RC	2.00	3.50
❑ 76 Paul Lowe RC	7.50	15.00
❑ 77 Bruce Hartman RC	2.00	3.50
❑ 78 Blanche Martin RC	2.00	3.50
❑ 79 Gene Grabosky RC	2.00	3.50
❑ 80 Lou Rymkus CO	2.50	5.00
❑ 81 Chris Burford RC	4.00	8.00
❑ 82 Don Allen RC	2.00	3.50
❑ 83 Bob Nelson C RC	2.00	3.50
❑ 84 Jim Woodard RC	2.00	3.50
❑ 85 Tom Rychlec RC	2.00	3.50
❑ 86 Bob Cox RC	2.00	3.50
❑ 87 Jerry Cornelison RC	2.00	3.50
❑ 88 Jack Work	2.00	3.50
❑ 89 Sam DeLuca RC	2.00	3.50
❑ 90 Rommie Loudd RC	2.00	3.50
❑ 91 Teddy Edmondson RC	2.00	3.50
❑ 92 Buster Ramsey CO	2.00	3.50
❑ 93 Doug Asad RC	2.00	3.50
❑ 94 Jimmy Harris	2.00	3.50
❑ 95 Larry Cundiff RC	2.00	3.50
❑ 96 Richie Lucas RC	3.00	6.00
❑ 97 Don Norwood RC	2.00	3.50
❑ 98 Larry Grantham RC	2.50	5.00
❑ 99 Bill Mathis RC	3.00	6.00
❑ 100 Mel Branch RC	2.50	5.00
❑ 101 Marvin Terrell RC	2.00	3.50
❑ 102 Charlie Flowers RC	2.00	3.50
❑ 103 John McMullan RC	2.00	3.50
❑ 104 Charlie Kaaihue RC	2.00	3.50
❑ 105 Joe Schaffer RC	2.00	3.50
❑ 106 Al Day RC	2.00	3.50
❑ 107 Johnny Carson	2.00	3.50
❑ 108 Alan Goldstein RC	2.00	3.50
❑ 109 Doug Cline RC	2.00	3.50
❑ 110 Al Carmichael	2.00	3.50
❑ 111 Bob Dee RC	2.00	3.50
❑ 112 John Bredice RC	2.00	3.50
❑ 113 Don Floyd RC	2.00	3.50
❑ 114 Ronnie Cain RC	2.00	3.50
❑ 115 Stan Flowers RC	2.00	3.50
❑ 116 Hank Stram CO RC	25.00	40.00
❑ 117 Bob Dougherty RC	2.00	3.50
❑ 118 Ron Mix RC	25.00	40.00
❑ 119 Roger Ellis RC	2.00	3.50
❑ 120 Elvin Caldwell RC	2.00	3.50
❑ 121 Bill Kimber RC	2.00	3.50
❑ 122 Jim Matheny RC	2.00	3.50
❑ 123 Curley Johnson RC	2.00	3.50
❑ 124 Jack Kemp RC	75.00	150.00
❑ 125 Ed Denk RC	2.00	3.50
❑ 126 Jerry McFarland RC	2.00	3.50
❑ 127 Dan Lanphear RC	2.00	3.50
❑ 128 Paul Maguire RC	10.00	18.00
❑ 129 Ray Collins	2.00	3.50
❑ 130 Ron Burton RC	3.00	6.00
❑ 131 Eddie Erdelatz CO RC	2.00	3.50
❑ 132 Ron Beagle RC !	7.50	15.00

1961 Fleer

Card		
❑ COMPLETE SET (220)	1000.00	1600.00
❑ WRAPPER (5-CENT, SER.1)	20.00	25.00
❑ WRAPPER (5-CENT, SER.2)	25.00	30.00
❑ 1 Ed Brown !	7.50	15.00
❑ 2 Rick Casares	3.00	6.00
❑ 3 Willie Galimore	3.00	6.00
❑ 4 Jim Dooley	2.50	4.00
❑ 5 Harlon Hill	2.50	4.00
❑ 6 Stan Jones	3.50	7.00
❑ 7 J.C. Caroline	2.50	4.00
❑ 8 Joe Fortunato	2.50	4.00
❑ 9 Doug Atkins	4.00	8.00
❑ 10 Milt Plum	3.00	6.00
❑ 11 Jim Brown	90.00	150.00
❑ 12 Bobby Mitchell	5.00	10.00
❑ 13 Ray Renfro	3.00	6.00
❑ 14 Gern Nagler	2.50	4.00
❑ 15 Jim Shofner	2.50	4.00
❑ 16 Vince Costello	2.50	4.00
❑ 17 Galen Fiss RC	2.50	4.00
❑ 18 Walt Michaels	3.00	6.00
❑ 19 Bob Gain	2.50	4.00
❑ 20 Mal Hammack	2.50	4.00
❑ 21 Frank Mestnik RC	2.50	4.00
❑ 22 Bobby Joe Conrad	3.00	6.00
❑ 23 John David Crow	3.00	6.00
❑ 24 Sonny Randle RC	3.00	6.00
❑ 25 Don Gillis	2.50	4.00
❑ 26 Jerry Norton	2.50	4.00
❑ 27 Bill Stacy RC	2.50	4.00
❑ 28 Leo Sugar	2.50	4.00
❑ 29 Frank Fuller	2.50	4.00
❑ 30 Johnny Unitas	35.00	60.00
❑ 31 Alan Ameche	3.50	7.00
❑ 32 Lenny Moore	7.50	15.00
❑ 33 Raymond Berry	7.50	15.00
❑ 34 Jim Mutscheller	2.50	4.00
❑ 35 Jim Parker	3.50	7.00
❑ 36 Bill Pellington	2.50	4.00
❑ 37 Gino Marchetti	5.00	10.00
❑ 38 Gene Lipscomb	3.50	7.00
❑ 39 Art Donovan	7.50	15.00
❑ 40 Eddie LeBaron	3.00	6.00
❑ 41 Don Meredith RC	90.00	150.00
❑ 42 Don McIlhenny	2.50	4.00
❑ 43 L.G. Dupre	2.50	4.00
❑ 44 Fred Dugan RC	2.50	4.00
❑ 45 Billy Howton	3.00	6.00
❑ 46 Duane Putnam	2.50	4.00
❑ 47 Gene Cronin	2.50	4.00
❑ 48 Jerry Tubbs	2.50	4.00
❑ 49 Clarence Peaks	2.50	4.00
❑ 50 Ted Dean RC	2.50	4.00
❑ 51 Tommy McDonald	4.00	8.00
❑ 52 Bill Barnes	2.50	4.00
❑ 53 Pete Retzlaff	3.00	6.00
❑ 54 Bobby Walston	2.50	4.00
❑ 55 Chuck Bednarik	6.00	12.00
❑ 56 Maxie Baughan RC	3.00	6.00
❑ 57 Bob Pellegrini	2.50	4.00
❑ 58 Jesse Richardson	2.50	4.00
❑ 59 John Brodie RC	30.00	50.00
❑ 60 J.D. Smith RB	3.00	6.00
❑ 61 Ray Norton RC	2.50	4.00
❑ 62 Monty Stickles RC	2.50	4.00
❑ 63 Bob St.Clair	3.50	7.00
❑ 64 Dave Baker RC	2.50	4.00
❑ 65 Abe Woodson	2.50	4.00
❑ 66 Matt Hazeltine	2.50	4.00
❑ 67 Leo Nomellini	5.00	10.00
❑ 68 Charley Conerly	5.00	10.00
❑ 69 Kyle Rote	3.50	7.00
❑ 70 Jack Stroud RC	2.50	4.00
❑ 71 Roosevelt Brown	3.50	7.00
❑ 72 Jim Patton	2.50	4.00
❑ 73 Erich Barnes	2.50	4.00
❑ 74 Sam Huff	7.50	15.00
❑ 75 Andy Robustelli	5.00	10.00
❑ 76 Dick Modzelewski RC	2.50	4.00
❑ 77 Roosevelt Grier	3.50	7.00
❑ 78 Earl Morrall	3.50	7.00
❑ 79 Jim Ninowski	2.50	4.00
❑ 80 Nick Pietrosante RC	3.00	6.00
❑ 81 Howard Cassady	3.00	6.00
❑ 82 Jim Gibbons	2.50	4.00
❑ 83 Gail Cogdill RC	3.00	6.00
❑ 84 Dick Lane	3.50	7.00
❑ 85 Yale Lary	3.50	7.00
❑ 86 Joe Schmidt	4.00	8.00
❑ 87 Darris McCord	2.50	4.00
❑ 88 Bart Starr	35.00	60.00
❑ 89 Jim Taylor	30.00	50.00
❑ 90 Paul Hornung	30.00	55.00
❑ 91 Tom Moore RC	4.00	8.00
❑ 92 Boyd Dowler RC	7.50	15.00
❑ 93 Max McGee	4.00	8.00
❑ 94 Forrest Gregg	5.00	10.00
❑ 95 Jerry Kramer	5.00	10.00
❑ 96 Jim Ringo	4.00	8.00
❑ 97 Bill Forester	3.00	6.00
❑ 98 Frank Ryan	3.00	6.00
❑ 99 Ollie Matson	6.00	12.00
❑ 100 Jon Arnett	3.00	6.00
❑ 101 Dick Bass RC	3.00	6.00
❑ 102 Jim Phillips	2.50	4.00
❑ 103 Del Shofner	3.00	6.00
❑ 104 Art Hunter	2.50	4.00
❑ 105 Lindon Crow	2.50	4.00
❑ 106 Les Richter	3.00	6.00
❑ 107 Lou Michaels	2.50	4.00
❑ 108 Ralph Guglielmi	2.50	4.00
❑ 109 Don Bosseler	2.50	4.00
❑ 110 John Olszewski	2.50	4.00
❑ 111 Bill Anderson	2.50	4.00
❑ 112 Joe Walton	2.50	4.00
❑ 113 Jim Schrader	2.50	4.00
❑ 114 Gary Glick	2.50	4.00
❑ 115 Ralph Felton	2.50	4.00
❑ 116 Bob Toneff	2.50	4.00
❑ 117 Bobby Layne	25.00	40.00
❑ 118 John Henry Johnson	4.00	8.00
❑ 119 Tom Tracy	3.00	6.00
❑ 120 Jimmy Orr RC	3.50	7.00
❑ 121 John Nisby	2.50	4.00
❑ 122 Dean Derby	2.50	4.00
❑ 123 John Reger	2.50	4.00
❑ 124 George Tarasovic	2.50	4.00
❑ 125 Ernie Stautner	5.00	10.00
❑ 126 George Shaw	2.50	4.00
❑ 127 Hugh McElhenny	6.00	12.00
❑ 128 Dick Haley RC	2.50	4.00
❑ 129 Dave Middleton	2.50	4.00
❑ 130 Perry Richards RC	2.50	4.00
❑ 131 Gene Johnson DB RC	2.50	4.00
❑ 132 Don Joyce RC	2.50	4.00
❑ 133 Johnny Green RC	4.00	8.00
❑ 134 Wray Carlton RC	4.00	8.00
❑ 135 Richie Lucas	4.00	8.00
❑ 136 Elbert Dubenion !	4.00	8.00
❑ 137 Tom Rychlec	3.50	6.00
❑ 138 Mack Yoho RC	3.50	6.00
❑ 139 Phil Blazer RC	3.50	6.00
❑ 140 Dan McGrew	3.50	6.00
❑ 141 Bill Atkins	3.50	6.00
❑ 142 Archie Matsos RC	3.50	6.00
❑ 143 Gene Grabosky	3.50	6.00
❑ 144 Frank Tripucka	5.00	10.00
❑ 145 Al Carmichael	3.50	6.00
❑ 146 Bob McNamara	3.50	6.00
❑ 147 Lionel Taylor RC	7.50	15.00
❑ 148 Eldon Danenhauer RC	3.50	6.00
❑ 149 Willie Smith	3.50	6.00
❑ 150 Carl Larpenter	3.50	6.00
❑ 151 Ken Adamson	3.50	6.00
❑ 152 Goose Gonsoulin UER RC	5.00	10.00
❑ 153 Joe Young RC	3.50	6.00
❑ 154 Gordy Holz RC	3.50	6.00
❑ 155 Jack Kemp	50.00	80.00
❑ 156 Charlie Flowers	3.50	6.00
❑ 157 Paul Lowe	5.00	10.00
❑ 158 Don Norton RC	3.50	6.00
❑ 159 Howard Clark RC	3.50	6.00
❑ 160 Paul Maguire	7.50	15.00
❑ 161 Ernie Wright RC	4.00	8.00
❑ 162 Ron Mix	7.50	15.00
❑ 163 Fred Cole RC	3.50	6.00
❑ 164 Jim Sears RC	3.50	6.00
❑ 165 Volney Peters	3.50	6.00
❑ 166 George Blanda	25.00	45.00
❑ 167 Jacky Lee	4.00	8.00
❑ 168 Bob White	3.50	6.00
❑ 169 Doug Cline	3.50	6.00
❑ 170 Dave Smith RB RC	3.50	6.00
❑ 171 Billy Cannon	7.50	15.00
❑ 172 Bill Groman RC	3.50	6.00
❑ 173 Al Jamison RC	3.50	6.00
❑ 174 Jim Norton RC	3.50	6.00
❑ 175 Dennit Morris RC	3.50	6.00
❑ 176 Don Floyd	3.50	6.00
❑ 177 Butch Songin	3.50	6.00
❑ 178 Billy Lott RC	3.50	6.00
❑ 179 Ron Burton	5.00	10.00
❑ 180 Jim Colclough RC	3.50	6.00
❑ 181 Charley Leo RC	3.50	6.00
❑ 182 Walt Cudzik RC	3.50	6.00
❑ 183 Fred Bruney	3.50	6.00
❑ 184 Ross O'Hanley RC	3.50	6.00
❑ 185 Tony Sardisco	3.50	6.00
❑ 186 Harry Jacobs RC	3.50	6.00
❑ 187 Bob Dee	3.50	6.00
❑ 188 Tom Flores RC	15.00	30.00
❑ 189 Jack Larscheid	3.50	6.00
❑ 190 Dick Christy RC	3.50	6.00
❑ 191 Alan Miller RC	3.50	6.00
❑ 192 James Smith	3.50	6.00
❑ 193 Gerald Burch RC	3.50	6.00
❑ 194 Gene Prebola	3.50	6.00
❑ 195 Alan Goldstein	3.50	6.00
❑ 196 Don Manoukian RC	3.50	6.00
❑ 197 Jim Otto RC	40.00	75.00
❑ 198 Wayne Crow	3.50	6.00
❑ 199 Cotton Davidson RC	4.00	8.00
❑ 200 Randy Duncan RC	4.00	8.00
❑ 201 Jack Spikes	4.00	8.00
❑ 202 Johnny Robinson RC	7.50	15.00
❑ 203 Abner Haynes	7.50	15.00
❑ 204 Chris Burford	4.00	8.00
❑ 205 Bill Krisher	3.50	6.00
❑ 206 Marvin Terrell	3.50	6.00
❑ 207 Jimmy Harris	3.50	6.00
❑ 208 Mel Branch	4.00	8.00
❑ 209 Paul Miller	3.50	6.00
❑ 210 Al Dorow	3.50	6.00
❑ 211 Dick Jamieson	3.50	6.00
❑ 212 Pete Hart RC	3.50	6.00
❑ 213 Bill Shockley RC	3.50	6.00
❑ 214 Dewey Bohling RC	3.50	6.00
❑ 215 Don Maynard RC	40.00	80.00
❑ 216 Bob Mischak RC	3.50	6.00
❑ 217 Mike Hudock	3.50	6.00
❑ 218 Bob Reifsnyder	3.50	6.00
❑ 219 Tom Saidock	3.50	6.00
❑ 220 Sid Youngelman !	12.00	20.00

1962 Fleer

Card		
❑ COMPLETE SET (88)	500.00	900.00
❑ WRAPPER (5-CENT)	100.00	200.00
❑ 1 Billy Lott	8.00	16.00
❑ 2 Ron Burton	5.00	10.00
❑ 3 Gino Cappelletti RC	7.50	15.00
❑ 4 Babe Parilli	5.00	10.00
❑ 5 Jim Colclough	3.50	7.00
❑ 6 Tony Sardisco	3.50	7.00
❑ 7 Walt Cudzik	3.50	7.00
❑ 8 Bob Dee	3.50	7.00
❑ 9 Tommy Addison RC	4.00	8.00
❑ 10 Harry Jacobs	3.50	7.00
❑ 11 Ross O'Hanley	3.50	7.00
❑ 12 Art Baker	3.50	7.00

❑ 13 Johnny Green 3.50 7.00
❑ 14 Elbert Dubenion 5.00 10.00
❑ 15 Tom Rychlec 3.50 7.00
❑ 16 Billy Shaw RC 20.00 40.00
❑ 17 Ken Rice 3.50 7.00
❑ 18 Bill Atkins 3.50 7.00
❑ 19 Richie Lucas 4.00 8.00
❑ 20 Archie Matsos 3.50 7.00
❑ 21 Laverne Torczon 3.50 7.00
❑ 22 Warren Rabb RC UER 3.50 7.00
❑ 23 Jack Spikes 4.00 8.00
❑ 24 Cotton Davidson 4.00 8.00
❑ 25 Abner Haynes 7.50 15.00
❑ 26 Jimmy Saxton RC 3.50 7.00
❑ 27 Chris Burford 4.00 8.00
❑ 28 Bill Miller RC 3.50 7.00
❑ 29 Sherrill Headrick 4.00 8.00
❑ 30 E.J.Holub RC 4.00 8.00
❑ 31 Jerry Mays RC 5.00 10.00
❑ 32 Mel Branch 4.00 8.00
❑ 33 Paul Rochester RC 3.50 7.00
❑ 34 Frank Tripucka 5.00 10.00
❑ 35 Gene Mingo 3.50 7.00
❑ 36 Lionel Taylor 6.00 12.00
❑ 37 Ken Adamson 3.50 7.00
❑ 38 Eldon Danenhauer 3.50 7.00
❑ 39 Goose Gonsoulin 5.00 10.00
❑ 40 Gordy Holz 3.50 7.00
❑ 41 Bud McFadin 4.00 8.00
❑ 42 Jim Stinnette RC 3.50 7.00
❑ 43 Bob Hudson RC 3.50 7.00
❑ 44 George Herring 3.50 7.00
❑ 45 Charley Tolar RC 3.50 7.00
❑ 46 George Blanda 30.00 50.00
❑ 47 Billy Cannon 7.50 15.00
❑ 48 Charlie Hennigan RC 7.50 15.00
❑ 49 Bill Groman 3.50 7.00
❑ 50 Al Jamison 3.50 7.00
❑ 51 Tony Banfield 3.50 7.00
❑ 52 Jim Norton 3.50 7.00
❑ 53 Dennit Morris 3.50 7.00
❑ 54 Don Floyd 3.50 7.00
❑ 55 Ed Husmann UER RC 3.50 7.00
❑ 56 Robert Brooks RC 3.50 7.00
❑ 57 Al Dorow 3.50 7.00
❑ 58 Dick Christy 3.50 7.00
❑ 59 Don Maynard 30.00 50.00
❑ 60 Art Powell 5.00 10.00
❑ 61 Mike Hudock 3.50 7.00
❑ 62 Bill Mathis 4.00 8.00
❑ 63 Butch Songin 3.50 7.00
❑ 64 Larry Grantham 3.50 7.00
❑ 65 Nick Mumley RC 3.50 7.00
❑ 66 Tom Saidock 3.50 7.00
❑ 67 Alan Miller 3.50 7.00
❑ 68 Tom Flores 7.50 15.00
❑ 69 Bob Coolbaugh 3.50 7.00
❑ 70 George Fleming RC 3.50 7.00
❑ 71 Wayne Hawkins RC 4.00 8.00
❑ 72 Jim Otto 25.00 40.00
❑ 73 Wayne Crow 3.50 7.00
❑ 74 Fred Williamson RC 18.00 30.00
❑ 75 Tom Louderback RC 3.50 7.00
❑ 76 Volney Peters 3.50 7.00
❑ 77 Charley Powell RC 3.50 7.00
❑ 78 Don Norton 3.50 7.00
❑ 79 Jack Kemp 75.00 125.00
❑ 80 Paul Lowe 5.00 10.00
❑ 81 Dave Kocourek 3.50 7.00
❑ 82 Ron Mix 7.50 15.00
❑ 83 Ernie Wright 5.00 10.00
❑ 84 Dick Harris RC 3.50 7.00
❑ 85 Bill Hudson RC 3.50 7.00
❑ 86 Ernie Ladd RC 15.00 25.00
❑ 87 Earl Faison RC 4.00 8.00
❑ 88 Don Nory ! 9.00 18.00

1963 Fleer

❑ COMPLETE SET (88) 1200.00 1800.00
❑ WRAPPER (5-CENT) 60.00 120.00
❑ 1 Larry Garron RC 10.00 20.00
❑ 2 Babe Parilli 5.00 10.00
❑ 3 Ron Burton 6.00 12.00
❑ 4 Jim Colclough 4.00 8.00
❑ 5 Gino Cappelletti 6.00 12.00
❑ 6 Charles Long SP RC 75.00 150.00
❑ 7 Billy Neighbors RC 4.00 8.00
❑ 8 Dick Felt RC 4.00 8.00
❑ 9 Tommy Addison 4.00 8.00
❑ 10 Nick Buoniconti RC 45.00 80.00
❑ 11 Larry Eisenhauer RC 4.00 8.00
❑ 12 Bill Mathis 4.00 8.00
❑ 13 Lee Grosscup RC 5.00 10.00
❑ 14 Dick Christy 4.00 8.00
❑ 15 Don Maynard 30.00 50.00
❑ 16 Alex Kroll RC 4.00 8.00
❑ 17 Bob Mischak 4.00 8.00
❑ 18 Dainard Paulson RC 4.00 8.00
❑ 19 Lee Riley 4.00 8.00
❑ 20 Larry Grantham 5.00 10.00
❑ 21 Hubert Bobo RC 4.00 8.00
❑ 22 Nick Mumley 4.00 8.00
❑ 23 Cookie Gilchrist RC 30.00 50.00
❑ 24 Jack Kemp 75.00 150.00
❑ 25 Wray Carlton 4.00 8.00
❑ 26 Elbert Dubenion 5.00 10.00
❑ 27 Ernie Warlick RC 5.00 10.00
❑ 28 Billy Shaw 7.50 15.00
❑ 29 Ken Rice 4.00 8.00
❑ 30 Booker Edgerson RC 4.00 8.00
❑ 31 Ray Abruzzese RC 4.00 8.00
❑ 32 Mike Stratton RC 7.50 15.00
❑ 33 Tom Sestak RC 6.00 12.00
❑ 34 Charley Tolar 4.00 8.00
❑ 35 Dave Smith RB 4.00 8.00
❑ 36 George Blanda 30.00 55.00
❑ 37 Billy Cannon 7.50 15.00
❑ 38 Charlie Hennigan 5.00 10.00
❑ 39 Bob Talamini RC 4.00 8.00
❑ 40 Jim Norton 4.00 8.00
❑ 41 Tony Banfield 4.00 8.00
❑ 42 Doug Cline 4.00 8.00
❑ 43 Don Floyd 4.00 8.00
❑ 44 Ed Husmann 4.00 8.00
❑ 45 Curtis McClinton RC 7.50 15.00
❑ 46 Jack Spikes 5.00 10.00
❑ 47 Len Dawson RC 150.00 250.00
❑ 48 Abner Haynes 7.50 15.00
❑ 49 Chris Burford 5.00 10.00
❑ 50 Fred Arbanas RC 6.00 12.00
❑ 51 Johnny Robinson 5.00 10.00
❑ 52 E.J. Holub 5.00 10.00
❑ 53 Sherrill Headrick 5.00 10.00
❑ 54 Mel Branch 5.00 10.00
❑ 55 Jerry Mays 5.00 10.00
❑ 56 Cotton Davidson 5.00 10.00
❑ 57 Clem Daniels RC 7.50 15.00
❑ 58 Bo Roberson RC 5.00 10.00
❑ 59 Art Powell 6.00 12.00
❑ 60 Bob Coolbaugh 4.00 8.00
❑ 61 Wayne Hawkins 4.00 8.00
❑ 62 Jim Otto 18.00 30.00
❑ 63 Fred Williamson 10.00 20.00
❑ 64 Bob Dougherty SP 60.00 120.00
❑ 65 Dalva Allen RC 4.00 8.00
❑ 66 Chuck McMurtry RC 4.00 8.00
❑ 67 Gerry McDougall RC 4.00 8.00
❑ 68 Tobin Rote 5.00 10.00
❑ 69 Paul Lowe 6.00 12.00
❑ 70 Keith Lincoln RC 25.00 40.00
❑ 71 Dave Kocourek 4.00 8.00
❑ 72 Lance Alworth RC 125.00 250.00
❑ 73 Ron Mix 15.00 25.00
❑ 74 Charley McNeil RC 4.00 8.00
❑ 75 Emil Karas RC 4.00 8.00
❑ 76 Ernie Ladd 10.00 20.00
❑ 77 Earl Faison 4.00 8.00
❑ 78 Jim Stinnette 4.00 8.00
❑ 79 Frank Tripucka 6.00 12.00
❑ 80 Don Stone RC 4.00 8.00
❑ 81 Bob Scarpitto RC 4.00 8.00
❑ 82 Lionel Taylor 6.00 12.00
❑ 83 Jerry Tarr RC 4.00 8.00
❑ 84 Eldon Danenhauer 4.00 8.00
❑ 85 Goose Gonsoulin 5.00 10.00
❑ 86 Jim Fraser RC 4.00 8.00
❑ 87 Chuck Gavin RC 4.00 8.00
❑ 88 Bud McFadin ! 10.00 20.00
❑ NNO Checklist SP ! 250.00 350.00

1990 Fleer

❑ COMPLETE SET (400) 4.00 10.00
❑ 1 Harris Barton .01 .04
❑ 2 Chet Brooks .01 .04
❑ 3 Michael Carter .01 .04
❑ 4 Mike Cofer UER .01 .04
❑ 5 Roger Craig .02 .10
❑ 6 Kevin Fagan RC .01 .04
❑ 7 Charles Haley UER .02 .10
❑ 8 Pierce Holt RC .01 .04
❑ 9 Ronnie Lott .02 .10
❑ 10A Joe Montana ERR .50 1.25
❑ 10B Joe Montana COR .50 1.25
❑ 11 Bubba Paris .01 .04
❑ 12 Tom Rathman .01 .04
❑ 13 Jerry Rice .30 .75
❑ 14 John Taylor .08 .25
❑ 15 Keena Turner .01 .04
❑ 16 Michael Walter .01 .04
❑ 17 Steve Young .20 .50
❑ 18 Steve Atwater .01 .04
❑ 19 Tyrone Braxton .01 .04
❑ 20 Michael Brooks RC .01 .04
❑ 21 John Elway .50 1.25
❑ 22 Simon Fletcher .01 .04
❑ 23 Bobby Humphrey .01 .04
❑ 24 Mark Jackson .01 .04
❑ 25 Vance Johnson .01 .04
❑ 26 Greg Kragen .01 .04
❑ 27 Ken Lanier RC .01 .04
❑ 28 Karl Mecklenburg .01 .04
❑ 29 Orson Mobley RC .01 .04
❑ 30 Steve Sewell .01 .04
❑ 31 Dennis Smith .01 .04
❑ 32 David Treadwell .01 .04
❑ 33 Flipper Anderson .01 .04
❑ 34 Greg Bell .01 .04
❑ 35 Henry Ellard .02 .10
❑ 36 Jim Everett .02 .10
❑ 37 Jerry Gray .01 .04
❑ 38 Kevin Greene .02 .10
❑ 39 Pete Holohan .01 .04
❑ 40 LeRoy Irvin .01 .04
❑ 41 Mike Lansford .01 .04
❑ 42 Buford McGee RC .01 .04
❑ 43 Tom Newberry .01 .04
❑ 44 Vince Newsome RC .01 .04
❑ 45 Jackie Slater .01 .04
❑ 46 Mike Wilcher .01 .04
❑ 47 Matt Bahr .01 .04
❑ 48 Brian Brennan .01 .04
❑ 49 Thane Gash RC .01 .04
❑ 50 Mike Johnson .01 .04
❑ 51 Bernie Kosar .02 .10
❑ 52 Reggie Langhorne .01 .04
❑ 53 Tim Manoa .01 .04
❑ 54 Clay Matthews .02 .10
❑ 55 Eric Metcalf .08 .25

Card	Low	High
❑ 56 Frank Minnifield	.01	.04
❑ 57 Gregg Rakoczy UER RC	.01	.04
❑ 58 Webster Slaughter	.02	.10
❑ 59 Bryan Wagner	.01	.04
❑ 60 Felix Wright	.01	.04
❑ 61 Raul Allegre	.01	.04
❑ 62 Ottis Anderson UER	.02	.10
❑ 63 Carl Banks	.01	.04
❑ 64 Mark Bavaro	.01	.04
❑ 65 Maurice Carthon	.01	.04
❑ 66 Mark Collins UER	.01	.04
❑ 67 Jeff Hostetler RC	.08	.25
❑ 68 Erik Howard	.01	.04
❑ 69 Pepper Johnson	.01	.04
❑ 70 Sean Landeta	.01	.04
❑ 71 Lionel Manuel	.01	.04
❑ 72 Leonard Marshall	.01	.04
❑ 73 Dave Meggett	.02	.10
❑ 74 Bart Oates	.01	.04
❑ 75 Doug Riesenberg RC	.01	.04
❑ 76 Phil Simms	.02	.10
❑ 77 Lawrence Taylor	.08	.25
❑ 78 Eric Allen	.01	.04
❑ 79 Jerome Brown	.01	.04
❑ 80 Keith Byars	.01	.04
❑ 81 Cris Carter	.20	.50
❑ 82A Byron Evans ERR RC	.05	.15
❑ 82B Randall Cunningham	.05	.15
❑ 83A Ron Heller ERR RC	.05	.15
❑ 83B Byron Evans COR RC	.05	.15
❑ 84 Ron Heller COR RC	.01	.04
❑ 85 Terry Hoage RC	.01	.04
❑ 86 Keith Jackson	.02	.10
❑ 87 Seth Joyner	.02	.10
❑ 88 Mike Quick	.01	.04
❑ 89 Mike Schad	.01	.04
❑ 90 Clyde Simmons	.01	.04
❑ 91 John Teltschik	.01	.04
❑ 92 Anthony Toney	.01	.04
❑ 93 Reggie White	.08	.25
❑ 94 Ray Berry	.01	.04
❑ 95 Joey Browner	.01	.04
❑ 96 Anthony Carter	.02	.10
❑ 97 Chris Doleman	.01	.04
❑ 98 Rick Fenney	.01	.04
❑ 99 Rich Gannon RC	.60	1.50
❑ 100 Hassan Jones	.01	.04
❑ 101 Steve Jordan	.01	.04
❑ 102 Rich Karlis	.01	.04
❑ 103 Andre Ware RC	.08	.25
❑ 104 Kirk Lowdermilk	.01	.04
❑ 105 Keith Millard	.01	.04
❑ 106 Scott Studwell	.01	.04
❑ 107 Herschel Walker	.02	.10
❑ 108 Wade Wilson	.02	.10
❑ 109 Gary Zimmerman	.02	.10
❑ 110 Don Beebe	.02	.10
❑ 111 Cornelius Bennett	.02	.10
❑ 112 Shane Conlan	.01	.04
❑ 113 Jim Kelly	.08	.25
❑ 114 Scott Norwood UER	.01	.04
❑ 115 Mark Kelso UER	.01	.04
❑ 116 Larry Kinnebrew	.01	.04
❑ 117 Pete Metzelaars	.01	.04
❑ 118 Scott Radecic	.01	.04
❑ 119 Andre Reed	.08	.25
❑ 120 Jim Ritcher RC	.01	.04
❑ 121 Bruce Smith	.08	.25
❑ 122 Leonard Smith	.01	.04
❑ 123 Art Still	.01	.04
❑ 124 Thurman Thomas	.08	.25
❑ 125 Steve Brown	.01	.04
❑ 126 Ray Childress	.01	.04
❑ 127 Ernest Givins	.02	.10
❑ 128 John Grimsley	.01	.04
❑ 129 Alonzo Highsmith	.01	.04
❑ 130 Drew Hill	.01	.04
❑ 131 Bruce Matthews	.02	.10
❑ 132 Johnny Meads	.01	.04
❑ 133 Warren Moon UER	.08	.25
❑ 134 Mike Munchak	.02	.10
❑ 135 Mike Rozier	.01	.04
❑ 136 Dean Steinkuhler	.01	.04
❑ 137 Lorenzo White	.01	.04
❑ 138 Tony Zendejas	.01	.04
❑ 139 Gary Anderson K	.01	.04
❑ 140 Bubby Brister	.01	.04
❑ 141 Thomas Everett	.01	.04
❑ 142 Derek Hill	.01	.04
❑ 143 Merril Hoge	.01	.04
❑ 144 Tim Johnson	.01	.04
❑ 145 Louis Lipps	.02	.10
❑ 146 David Little	.01	.04
❑ 147 Greg Lloyd	.08	.25
❑ 148 Mike Mularkey	.01	.04
❑ 149 John Rienstra RC	.01	.04
❑ 150 Gerald Williams UER RC	.01	.04
❑ 151 Keith Willis UER	.01	.04
❑ 152 Rod Woodson	.08	.25
❑ 153 Tim Worley	.01	.04
❑ 154 Gary Clark	.08	.25
❑ 155 Darryl Grant	.01	.04
❑ 156 Darrell Green	.02	.10
❑ 157 Joe Jacoby	.01	.04
❑ 158 Jim Lachey	.01	.04
❑ 159 Chip Lohmiller	.01	.04
❑ 160 Charles Mann	.01	.04
❑ 161 Wilber Marshall	.01	.04
❑ 162 Mark May	.01	.04
❑ 163 Ralf Mojsiejenko	.01	.04
❑ 164 Art Monk UER	.02	.10
❑ 165 Gerald Riggs	.02	.10
❑ 166 Mark Rypien	.02	.10
❑ 167 Ricky Sanders	.01	.04
❑ 168 Don Warren	.01	.04
❑ 169 Robert Brown RC	.01	.04
❑ 170 Blair Bush	.01	.04
❑ 171 Brent Fullwood	.01	.04
❑ 172 Tim Harris	.01	.04
❑ 173 Chris Jacke	.01	.04
❑ 174 Perry Kemp	.01	.04
❑ 175 Don Majkowski	.01	.04
❑ 176 Tony Mandarich	.01	.04
❑ 177 Mark Murphy	.01	.04
❑ 178 Brian Noble	.01	.04
❑ 179 Ken Ruettgers	.01	.04
❑ 180 Sterling Sharpe	.08	.25
❑ 181 Ed West RC	.01	.04
❑ 182 Keith Woodside	.01	.04
❑ 183 Morten Andersen	.01	.04
❑ 184 Stan Brock	.01	.04
❑ 185 Jim Dombrowski RC	.01	.04
❑ 186 John Fourcade	.01	.04
❑ 187 Bobby Hebert	.01	.04
❑ 188 Craig Heyward	.02	.10
❑ 189 Dalton Hilliard	.01	.04
❑ 190 Rickey Jackson	.02	.10
❑ 191 Buford Jordan	.01	.04
❑ 192 Eric Martin	.01	.04
❑ 193 Robert Massey	.01	.04
❑ 194 Sam Mills	.02	.10
❑ 195 Pat Swilling	.02	.10
❑ 196 Jim Wilks	.01	.04
❑ 197 John Alt RC	.01	.04
❑ 198 Walker Lee Ashley	.01	.04
❑ 199 Steve DeBerg	.01	.04
❑ 200 Leonard Griffin	.01	.04
❑ 201 Albert Lewis	.01	.04
❑ 202 Nick Lowery	.01	.04
❑ 203 Bill Maas	.01	.04
❑ 204 Pete Mandley	.01	.04
❑ 205 Chris Martin RC	.01	.04
❑ 206 Christian Okoye	.01	.04
❑ 207 Stephone Paige	.01	.04
❑ 208 Kevin Porter RC	.01	.04
❑ 209 Derrick Thomas	.08	.25
❑ 210 Lewis Billups	.01	.04
❑ 211 James Brooks	.02	.10
❑ 212 Jason Buck	.01	.04
❑ 213 Rickey Dixon RC	.01	.04
❑ 214 Boomer Esiason	.02	.10
❑ 215 David Fulcher	.01	.04
❑ 216 Rodney Holman	.01	.04
❑ 217 Lee Johnson	.01	.04
❑ 218 Tim Krumrie	.01	.04
❑ 219 Tim McGee	.01	.04
❑ 220 Anthony Munoz	.02	.10
❑ 221 Bruce Reimers RC	.01	.04
❑ 222 Leon White	.01	.04
❑ 223 Ickey Woods	.01	.04
❑ 224 Harvey Armstrong RC	.01	.04
❑ 225 Michael Ball RC	.01	.04
❑ 226 Chip Banks	.01	.04
❑ 227 Pat Beach	.01	.04
❑ 228 Duane Bickett	.01	.04
❑ 229 Bill Brooks	.01	.04
❑ 230 Jon Hand	.01	.04
❑ 231 Andre Rison	.08	.25
❑ 232 Rohn Stark	.01	.04
❑ 233 Donnell Thompson	.01	.04
❑ 234 Jack Trudeau	.01	.04
❑ 235 Clarence Verdin	.01	.04
❑ 236 Mark Clayton	.02	.10
❑ 237 Jeff Cross	.01	.04
❑ 238 Jeff Dellenbach RC	.01	.04
❑ 239 Mark Duper	.02	.10
❑ 240 Ferrell Edmunds	.01	.04
❑ 241 Hugh Green UER	.01	.04
❑ 242 E.J. Junior	.01	.04
❑ 243 Marc Logan	.01	.04
❑ 244 Dan Marino	.50	1.25
❑ 245 John Offerdahl	.01	.04
❑ 246 Reggie Roby	.01	.04
❑ 247 Sammie Smith	.01	.04
❑ 248 Pete Stoyanovich	.01	.04
❑ 249 Marcus Allen	.08	.25
❑ 250 Eddie Anderson RC	.01	.04
❑ 251 Steve Beuerlein	.02	.10
❑ 252 Mike Dyal	.01	.04
❑ 253 Mervyn Fernandez	.01	.04
❑ 254 Bob Golic	.01	.04
❑ 255 Mike Harden	.01	.04
❑ 256 Bo Jackson	.10	.30
❑ 257 Howie Long UER	.08	.25
❑ 258 Don Mosebar	.01	.04
❑ 259 Jay Schroeder	.01	.04
❑ 260 Steve Smith	.01	.04
❑ 261 Greg Townsend	.01	.04
❑ 262 Lionel Washington	.01	.04
❑ 263 Brian Blades	.02	.10
❑ 264 Jeff Bryant	.01	.04
❑ 265 Grant Feasel RC	.01	.04
❑ 266 Jacob Green	.01	.04
❑ 267 James Jefferson	.01	.04
❑ 268 Norm Johnson	.01	.04
❑ 269 Dave Krieg UER	.02	.10
❑ 270 Travis McNeal	.01	.04
❑ 271 Joe Nash	.01	.04
❑ 272 Rufus Porter	.01	.04
❑ 273 Kelly Stouffer	.01	.04
❑ 274 John L. Williams	.01	.04
❑ 275 Jim Arnold	.01	.04
❑ 276 Jerry Ball	.01	.04
❑ 277 Bennie Blades	.01	.04
❑ 278 Lomas Brown	.01	.04
❑ 279 Michael Cofer	.01	.04
❑ 280 Bob Gagliano	.01	.04
❑ 281 Richard Johnson	.01	.04
❑ 282 Eddie Murray	.01	.04
❑ 283 Rodney Peete	.02	.10
❑ 284 Barry Sanders	.50	1.25
❑ 285 Eric Sanders	.01	.04
❑ 286 Chris Spielman	.08	.25
❑ 287 Eric Williams RC	.01	.04
❑ 288 Neal Anderson	.02	.10
❑ 289A Kevin Butler P/P	.08	.25
❑ 289B Kevin Butler K/P	.08	.25
❑ 289C Kevin Butler P/K	.08	.25
❑ 289D Kevin Butler K/K	.01	.04
❑ 290 Jim Covert	.01	.04
❑ 291 Richard Dent	.02	.10
❑ 292 Dennis Gentry	.01	.04
❑ 293 Jim Harbaugh	.08	.25
❑ 294 Jay Hilgenberg	.01	.04
❑ 295 Vestee Jackson	.01	.04
❑ 296 Steve McMichael	.02	.10
❑ 297 Ron Morris	.01	.04
❑ 298 Brad Muster	.01	.04
❑ 299 Mike Singletary	.02	.10
❑ 300 James Thornton UER	.01	.04
❑ 301 Mike Tomczak	.02	.10
❑ 302 Keith Van Horne	.01	.04
❑ 303 Chris Bahr UER	.01	.04
❑ 304 Martin Bayless RC	.01	.04
❑ 305 Marion Butts	.02	.10
❑ 306 Gill Byrd	.01	.04
❑ 307 Arthur Cox	.01	.04
❑ 308 Burt Grossman	.01	.04
❑ 309 Jamie Holland	.01	.04
❑ 310 Jim McMahon	.02	.10
❑ 311 Anthony Miller	.08	.25
❑ 312 Leslie O'Neal	.02	.10
❑ 313 Billy Ray Smith	.01	.04
❑ 314 Tim Spencer	.01	.04
❑ 315 Broderick Thompson RC	.01	.04
❑ 316 Lee Williams	.01	.04
❑ 317 Bruce Armstrong	.01	.04

Card		
❑ 318 Tim Goad RC	.01	.04
❑ 319 Steve Grogan	.02	.10
❑ 320 Roland James	.01	.04
❑ 321 Cedric Jones	.01	.04
❑ 322 Fred Marion	.01	.04
❑ 323 Stanley Morgan	.01	.04
❑ 324 Robert Perryman	.01	.04
❑ 325 Johnny Rembert	.01	.04
❑ 326 Ed Reynolds	.01	.04
❑ 327 Kenneth Sims	.01	.04
❑ 328 John Stephens	.01	.04
❑ 329 Danny Villa RC	.01	.04
❑ 330 Robert Awalt	.01	.04
❑ 331 Anthony Bell	.01	.04
❑ 332 Rich Camarillo	.01	.04
❑ 333 Earl Ferrell	.01	.04
❑ 334 Roy Green	.02	.10
❑ 335 Gary Hogeboom	.01	.04
❑ 336 Cedric Mack	.01	.04
❑ 337 Freddie Joe Nunn	.01	.04
❑ 338 Luis Sharpe	.01	.04
❑ 339 Vai Sikahema	.01	.04
❑ 340 J.T. Smith	.01	.04
❑ 341 Tom Tupa RC	.01	.04
❑ 342 Percy Snow RC	.01	.04
❑ 343 Mark Carrier WR	.08	.25
❑ 344 Randy Grimes	.01	.04
❑ 345 Paul Gruber	.01	.04
❑ 346 Ron Hall	.01	.04
❑ 347 Jeff George RC	.20	.50
❑ 348 Bruce Hill UER	.01	.04
❑ 349 William Howard UER	.01	.04
❑ 350 Donald Igwebuike	.01	.04
❑ 351 Chris Mohr RC	.01	.04
❑ 352 Winston Moss RC	.01	.04
❑ 353 Ricky Reynolds	.01	.04
❑ 354 Mark Robinson	.01	.04
❑ 355 Lars Tate	.01	.04
❑ 356 Vinny Testaverde	.02	.10
❑ 357 Broderick Thomas	.01	.04
❑ 358 Troy Benson	.01	.04
❑ 359 Jeff Criswell RC	.01	.04
❑ 360 Tony Eason	.01	.04
❑ 361 James Hasty	.01	.04
❑ 362 Johnny Hector	.01	.04
❑ 363 Bobby Humphery UER	.01	.04
❑ 364 Pat Leahy	.01	.04
❑ 365 Erik McMillan	.01	.04
❑ 366 Freeman McNeil	.01	.04
❑ 367 Ken O'Brien	.01	.04
❑ 368 Ron Stallworth	.01	.04
❑ 369 Al Toon	.02	.10
❑ 370 Blair Thomas RC	.01	.04
❑ 371 Aundray Bruce	.01	.04
❑ 372 Tony Casillas	.01	.04
❑ 373 Shawn Collins	.01	.04
❑ 374 Evan Cooper	.01	.04
❑ 375 Bill Fralic	.01	.04
❑ 376 Scott Funhage	.01	.04
❑ 377 Mike Gann	.01	.04
❑ 378 Ron Heller TE	.01	.04
❑ 379 Keith Jones	.01	.04
❑ 380 Mike Kenn	.01	.04
❑ 381 Chris Miller	.08	.25
❑ 382 Deion Sanders UER	.20	.50
❑ 383 John Settle	.01	.04
❑ 384 Troy Aikman	.30	.75
❑ 385 Bill Bates	.02	.10
❑ 386 Willie Broughton	.01	.04
❑ 387 Steve Folsom	.01	.04
❑ 388 Ray Horton UER	.01	.04
❑ 389 Michael Irvin	.08	.25
❑ 390 Jim Jeffcoat	.01	.04
❑ 391 Eugene Lockhart	.01	.04
❑ 392 Kelvin Martin RC	.01	.04
❑ 393 Nate Newton	.02	.10
❑ 394 Mike Saxon UER	.01	.04
❑ 395 Derrick Shepard	.01	.04
❑ 396 Steve Walsh	.02	.10
❑ 397 Joe Montana/Rice MVP's	.30	.75
❑ 398 Checklist Card UER	.01	.04
❑ 399 Checklist Card UER	.01	.04
❑ 400 Checklist Card	.01	.04

1990 Fleer Update

Card		
❑ COMP.FACT.SET (120)	12.50	25.00
❑ U1 Albert Bentley	.02	.08
❑ U2 Dean Biasucci	.02	.08
❑ U3 Ray Donaldson	.02	.08
❑ U4 Jeff George	.50	1.25
❑ U5 Ray Agnew RC	.02	.08
❑ U6 Greg McMurtry RC	.02	.08
❑ U7 Chris Singleton RC	.02	.08
❑ U8 James Francis RC	.02	.08
❑ U9 Harold Green RC	.10	.30
❑ U10 John Elliott	.02	.08
❑ U11 Rodney Hampton RC	.10	.30
❑ U12 Gary Reasons	.02	.08
❑ U13 Lewis Tillman	.02	.08
❑ U14 Everson Walls	.02	.08
❑ U15 David Alexander RC	.02	.08
❑ U16 Jim McMahon	.05	.15
❑ U17 Ben Smith RC	.02	.08
❑ U18 Andre Waters	.02	.08
❑ U19 Calvin Williams RC	.05	.15
❑ U20 Earnest Byner	.02	.08
❑ U21 Andre Collins RC	.02	.08
❑ U22 Russ Grimm	.02	.08
❑ U23 Stan Humphries RC	.10	.30
❑ U24 Martin Mayhew RC	.02	.08
❑ U25 Barry Foster RC	.10	.30
❑ U26 Eric Green RC	.05	.15
❑ U27 Tunch Ilkin	.02	.08
❑ U28 Hardy Nickerson	.05	.15
❑ U29 Jerrol Williams	.02	.08
❑ U30 Mike Baab	.02	.08
❑ U31 Leroy Hoard RC	.20	.50
❑ U32 Eddie Johnson RC	.02	.08
❑ U33 William Fuller	.05	.15
❑ U34 Haywood Jeffires RC	.10	.30
❑ U35 Don Maggs RC	.02	.08
❑ U36 Allen Pinkett	.02	.08
❑ U37 Robert Awalt	.02	.08
❑ U38 Dennis McKinnon	.02	.08
❑ U39 Ken Norton Jr. RC	.10	.30
❑ U40 Emmitt Smith RC	7.50	20.00
❑ U41 Alexander Wright RC	.02	.08
❑ U42 Eric Hill	.02	.08
❑ U43 Johnny Johnson RC	.05	.15
❑ U44 Timm Rosenbach	.02	.08
❑ U45 Anthony Thompson RC	.02	.08
❑ U46 Dexter Carter RC	.02	.00
❑ U47 Eric Davis UER RC	.05	.15
❑ U48 Keith DeLong	.02	.08
❑ U49 Brent Jones RC	.10	.30
❑ U50 Darryl Pollard RC	.02	.08
❑ U51 Steve Wallace RC	.10	.30
❑ U52 Bern Brostek RC	.02	.08
❑ U53 Aaron Cox	.02	.08
❑ U54 Cleveland Gary	.02	.08
❑ U55 Fred Strickland RC	.02	.08
❑ U56 Pat Terrell RC	.02	.08
❑ U57 Steve Broussard RC	.02	.08
❑ U58 Scott Case	.02	.08
❑ U59 Brian Jordan RC	.05	.15
❑ U60 Andre Rison	.10	.30
❑ U61 Kevin Haverdink	.02	.08
❑ U62 Rueben Mayes	.02	.08
❑ U63 Steve Walsh	.05	.15
❑ U64 Greg Bell	.02	.08
❑ U65 Tim Brown	.10	.30
❑ U66 Willie Gault	.05	.15
❑ U67 Vance Mueller RC	.02	.08
❑ U68 Bill Pickel	.02	.08
❑ U69 Aaron Wallace RC	.02	.08
❑ U70 Glenn Parker RC	.02	.08
❑ U71 Frank Reich	.10	.30
❑ U72 Leon Seals RC	.02	.08
❑ U73 Darryl Talley	.02	.08
❑ U74 Brad Baxter RC	.02	.08
❑ U75 Jeff Criswell	.02	.08
❑ U76 Jeff Lageman	.02	.08
❑ U77 Rob Moore RC	.60	1.50
❑ U78 Blair Thomas	.05	.15
❑ U79 Louis Oliver	.02	.08
❑ U80 Tony Paige	.02	.08
❑ U81 Richmond Webb RC	.02	.08
❑ U82 Robert Blackmon RC	.02	.08
❑ U83 Derrick Fenner RC	.02	.08
❑ U84 Andy Heck	.02	.08
❑ U85 Cortez Kennedy RC	.10	.30
❑ U86 Terry Wooden RC	.02	.08
❑ U87 Jeff Donaldson	.02	.08
❑ U88 Tim Grunhard RC	.02	.08
❑ U89 Emile Harry RC	.02	.08
❑ U90 Dan Saleaumua	.02	.08
❑ U91 Percy Snow	.02	.08
❑ U92 Andre Ware	.10	.30
❑ U93 Darrell Fullington RC	.02	.08
❑ U94 Mike Merriweather	.02	.08
❑ U95 Henry Thomas	.02	.08
❑ U96 Robert Brown	.02	.08
❑ U97 LeRoy Butler RC	.10	.30
❑ U98 Anthony Dilweg	.02	.08
❑ U99 Darrell Thompson RC	.02	.08
❑ U100 Keith Woodside	.02	.08
❑ U101 Gary Plummer	.02	.08
❑ U102 Junior Seau RC	2.00	5.00
❑ U103 Billy Joe Tolliver	.02	.08
❑ U104 Mark Vlasic	.02	.08
❑ U105 Gary Anderson RB	.02	.08
❑ U106 Ian Beckles RC	.02	.08
❑ U107 Reggie Cobb RC	.02	.08
❑ U108 Keith McCants RC	.02	.08
❑ U109 Mark Bortz RC	.02	.08
❑ U110 Maury Buford	.02	.08
❑ U111 Mark Carrier RC DB	.10	.30
❑ U112 Dan Hampton	.05	.15
❑ U113 William Perry	.05	.15
❑ U114 Ron Rivera	.02	.08
❑ U115 Lemuel Stinson	.02	.08
❑ U116 Melvin Bratton RC	.02	.08
❑ U117 Gary Kubiak RC	.10	.30
❑ U118 Alton Montgomery RC	.02	.08
❑ U119 Ricky Nattiel	.02	.08
❑ U120 Checklist 1-132	.02	.08

1991 Fleer

Card		
❑ COMPLETE SET (432)	4.00	8.00
❑ 1 Shane Conlan	.01	.05
❑ 2 John Davis RC	.01	.05
❑ 3 Kent Hull	.01	.05
❑ 4 James Lofton	.02	.10
❑ 5 Keith McKeller	.01	.05
❑ 6 Scott Norwood	.01	.05
❑ 7 Nate Odomes	.01	.05
❑ 8 Andre Reed	.02	.10
❑ 9 Jim Ritcher	.01	.05
❑ 10 Leon Seals	.01	.05
❑ 11 Bruce Smith	.08	.25
❑ 12 Leonard Smith	.01	.05
❑ 13 Steve Tasker	.02	.10
❑ 14 Thurman Thomas	.08	.25
❑ 15 Lewis Billups	.01	.05
❑ 16 James Brooks	.02	.10
❑ 17 Eddie Brown	.01	.05
❑ 18 Carl Carter	.01	.05
❑ 19 Boomer Esiason	.02	.10
❑ 20 James Francis	.01	.05
❑ 21 David Fulcher	.01	.05
❑ 22 Harold Green	.02	.10
❑ 23 Rodney Holman	.01	.05
❑ 24 Bruce Kozerski	.01	.05
❑ 25 Tim McGee	.01	.05
❑ 26 Anthony Munoz	.02	.10

Card	Low	High
❑ 27 Bruce Reimers	.01	.05
❑ 28 Ickey Woods	.01	.05
❑ 29 Carl Zander	.01	.05
❑ 30 Mike Baab	.01	.05
❑ 31 Brian Brennan	.01	.05
❑ 32 Rob Burnett RC	.02	.10
❑ 33 Paul Farren	.01	.05
❑ 34 Thane Gash	.01	.05
❑ 35 David Grayson	.01	.05
❑ 36 Mike Johnson	.01	.05
❑ 37 Reggie Langhorne	.01	.05
❑ 38 Kevin Mack	.01	.05
❑ 39 Eric Metcalf	.02	.10
❑ 40 Frank Minnifield	.01	.05
❑ 41 Gregg Rakoczy	.01	.05
❑ 42 Felix Wright	.01	.05
❑ 43 Steve Atwater	.01	.05
❑ 44 Michael Brooks	.01	.05
❑ 45 John Elway	.50	1.25
❑ 46 Simon Fletcher	.01	.05
❑ 47 Bobby Humphrey	.01	.05
❑ 48 Mark Jackson	.01	.05
❑ 49 Keith Kartz	.01	.05
❑ 50 Clarence Kay	.01	.05
❑ 51 Greg Kragen	.01	.05
❑ 52 Karl Mecklenburg	.01	.05
❑ 53 Warren Powers	.01	.05
❑ 54 Dennis Smith	.01	.05
❑ 55 Jim Szymanski	.01	.05
❑ 56 David Treadwell	.01	.05
❑ 57 Michael Young	.01	.05
❑ 58 Ray Childress	.01	.05
❑ 59 Curtis Duncan	.01	.05
❑ 60 William Fuller	.02	.10
❑ 61 Ernest Givins	.02	.10
❑ 62 Drew Hill	.01	.05
❑ 63 Haywood Jeffires	.02	.10
❑ 64 Richard Johnson DB	.01	.05
❑ 65 Sean Jones	.02	.10
❑ 66 Don Maggs	.01	.05
❑ 67 Bruce Matthews	.02	.10
❑ 68 Johnny Meads	.01	.05
❑ 69 Greg Montgomery	.01	.05
❑ 70 Warren Moon	.08	.25
❑ 71 Mike Munchak	.02	.10
❑ 72 Allen Pinkett	.01	.05
❑ 73 Lorenzo White	.01	.05
❑ 74 Pat Beach	.01	.05
❑ 75 Albert Bentley	.01	.05
❑ 76 Dean Biasucci	.01	.05
❑ 77 Duane Bickett	.01	.05
❑ 78 Bill Brooks	.01	.05
❑ 79 Sam Clancy	.01	.05
❑ 80 Ray Donaldson	.01	.05
❑ 81 Jeff George	.08	.25
❑ 82 Alan Grant	.01	.05
❑ 83 Jessie Hester	.01	.05
❑ 84 Jeff Herrod	.01	.05
❑ 85 Rohn Stark	.01	.05
❑ 86 Jack Trudeau	.01	.05
❑ 87 Clarence Verdin	.01	.05
❑ 88 John Alt	.01	.05
❑ 89 Steve DeBerg	.01	.05
❑ 90 Tim Grunhard	.01	.05
❑ 91 Dino Hackett	.01	.05
❑ 92 Jonathan Hayes	.01	.05
❑ 93 Albert Lewis	.01	.05
❑ 94 Nick Lowery	.01	.05
❑ 95 Bill Maas UER	.01	.05
❑ 96 Christian Okoye	.01	.05
❑ 97 Stephone Paige	.01	.05
❑ 98 Kevin Porter	.01	.05
❑ 99 David Szott	.01	.05
❑ 100 Derrick Thomas	.08	.25
❑ 101 Barry Word FFC	.01	.05
❑ 102 Marcus Allen	.08	.25
❑ 103 Thomas Benson	.01	.05
❑ 104 Tim Brown	.08	.25
❑ 105 Riki Ellison	.01	.05
❑ 106 Mervyn Fernandez	.01	.05
❑ 107 Willie Gault	.02	.10
❑ 108 Bob Golic	.01	.05
❑ 109 Ethan Horton FFC	.01	.05
❑ 110 Bo Jackson	.10	.30
❑ 111 Howie Long	.08	.25
❑ 112 Don Mosebar	.01	.05
❑ 113 Jerry Robinson	.01	.05
❑ 114 Jay Schroeder	.01	.05
❑ 115 Steve Smith	.01	.05
❑ 116 Greg Townsend	.01	.05
❑ 117 Steve Wisniewski	.01	.05
❑ 118 Mark Clayton	.02	.10
❑ 119 Mark Duper	.02	.10
❑ 120 Ferrell Edmunds	.01	.05
❑ 121 Hugh Green	.01	.05
❑ 122 David Griggs	.01	.05
❑ 123 Jim C. Jensen	.01	.05
❑ 124 Dan Marino	.50	1.25
❑ 125 Tim McKyer	.01	.05
❑ 126 John Offerdahl	.01	.05
❑ 127 Louis Oliver	.01	.05
❑ 128 Tony Paige	.01	.05
❑ 129 Reggie Roby	.01	.05
❑ 130 Keith Sims	.01	.05
❑ 131 Sammie Smith	.01	.05
❑ 132 Pete Stoyanovich	.01	.05
❑ 133 Richmond Webb	.01	.05
❑ 134 Bruce Armstrong	.01	.05
❑ 135 Vincent Brown	.01	.05
❑ 136 Hart Lee Dykes	.01	.05
❑ 137 Irving Fryar	.02	.10
❑ 138 Tim Goad	.01	.05
❑ 139 Tommy Hodson	.01	.05
❑ 140 Maurice Hurst	.01	.05
❑ 141 Ronnie Lippett	.01	.05
❑ 142 Greg McMurtry	.01	.05
❑ 143 Ed Reynolds	.01	.05
❑ 144 John Stephens	.01	.05
❑ 145 Andre Tippett	.01	.05
❑ 146 Danny Villa	.01	.05
❑ 147 Brad Baxter	.01	.05
❑ 148 Kyle Clifton	.01	.05
❑ 149 Jeff Criswell	.01	.05
❑ 150 James Hasty	.01	.05
❑ 151 Jeff Lageman	.01	.05
❑ 152 Pat Leahy	.01	.05
❑ 153 Rob Moore	.08	.25
❑ 154 Al Toon	.02	.10
❑ 155 Gary Anderson K	.01	.05
❑ 156 Bubby Brister	.01	.05
❑ 157 Chris Calloway	.01	.05
❑ 158 Donald Evans	.01	.05
❑ 159 Eric Green	.01	.05
❑ 160 Bryan Hinkle	.01	.05
❑ 161 Merril Hoge	.01	.05
❑ 162 Tunch Ilkin	.01	.05
❑ 163 Louis Lipps	.01	.05
❑ 164 David Little	.01	.05
❑ 165 Mike Mularkey	.01	.05
❑ 166 Gerald Williams	.01	.05
❑ 167 Warren Williams	.01	.05
❑ 168 Rod Woodson	.08	.25
❑ 169 Tim Worley	.01	.05
❑ 170 Martin Bayless	.01	.05
❑ 171 Marion Butts	.02	.10
❑ 172 Gill Byrd	.01	.05
❑ 173 Frank Cornish	.01	.05
❑ 174 Arthur Cox	.01	.05
❑ 175 Burt Grossman	.01	.05
❑ 176 Anthony Miller	.02	.10
❑ 177 Leslie O'Neal	.02	.10
❑ 178 Gary Plummer	.01	.05
❑ 179 Junior Seau	.08	.25
❑ 180 Billy Joe Tolliver	.01	.05
❑ 181 Derrick Walker RC	.01	.05
❑ 182 Lee Williams	.01	.05
❑ 183 Robert Blackmon	.01	.05
❑ 184 Brian Blades	.02	.10
❑ 185 Grant Feasel	.01	.05
❑ 186 Derrick Fenner	.01	.05
❑ 187 Andy Heck	.01	.05
❑ 188 Norm Johnson	.01	.05
❑ 189 Tommy Kane	.01	.05
❑ 190 Cortez Kennedy	.08	.25
❑ 191 Dave Krieg	.02	.10
❑ 192 Travis McNeal	.01	.05
❑ 193 Eugene Robinson	.01	.05
❑ 194 Chris Warren FFC	.08	.25
❑ 195 John L. Williams	.01	.05
❑ 196 Steve Broussard	.01	.05
❑ 197 Scott Case	.01	.05
❑ 198 Shawn Collins	.01	.05
❑ 199 Darion Conner UER	.01	.05
❑ 200 Tory Epps	.01	.05
❑ 201 Bill Fralic	.01	.05
❑ 202 Michael Haynes FFC	.08	.25
❑ 203 Chris Hinton	.01	.05
❑ 204 Keith Jones	.01	.05
❑ 205 Brian Jordan	.02	.10
❑ 206 Mike Kenn	.01	.05
❑ 207 Chris Miller	.02	.10
❑ 208 Andre Rison	.02	.10
❑ 209 Mike Rozier	.01	.05
❑ 210 Deion Sanders	.15	.40
❑ 211 Gary Wilkins	.01	.05
❑ 212 Neal Anderson	.02	.10
❑ 213 Trace Armstrong	.01	.05
❑ 214 Mark Bortz	.01	.05
❑ 215 Kevin Butler	.01	.05
❑ 216 Mark Carrier DB	.02	.10
❑ 217 Wendell Davis FFC	.01	.05
❑ 218 Richard Dent	.02	.10
❑ 219 Dennis Gentry	.01	.05
❑ 220 Jim Harbaugh	.08	.25
❑ 221 Jay Hilgenberg	.01	.05
❑ 222 Steve McMichael	.02	.10
❑ 223 Ron Morris	.01	.05
❑ 224 Brad Muster	.01	.05
❑ 225 Mike Singletary	.02	.10
❑ 226 James Thornton	.01	.05
❑ 227 Tommie Agee	.01	.05
❑ 228 Troy Aikman	.30	.75
❑ 229 Jack Del Rio	.02	.10
❑ 230 Issiac Holt	.01	.05
❑ 231 Ray Horton	.01	.05
❑ 232 Jim Jeffcoat	.01	.05
❑ 233 Eugene Lockhart	.01	.05
❑ 234 Kelvin Martin	.01	.05
❑ 235 Nate Newton	.02	.10
❑ 236 Mike Saxon	.01	.05
❑ 237 Emmitt Smith	1.00	2.50
❑ 238A Daniel Stubbs	.02	.10
❑ 238B Daniel Stubbs	.02	.10
❑ 239 Jim Arnold	.01	.05
❑ 240 Jerry Ball	.01	.05
❑ 241 Bennie Blades	.01	.05
❑ 242 Lomas Brown	.01	.05
❑ 243 Robert Clark	.01	.05
❑ 244 Mike Cofer	.01	.05
❑ 245 Mel Gray	.02	.10
❑ 246 Rodney Peete	.02	.10
❑ 247 Barry Sanders	.50	1.25
❑ 248 Andre Ware	.02	.10
❑ 249 Matt Brock RC	.01	.05
❑ 250 Robert Brown	.01	.05
❑ 251 Anthony Dilweg	.01	.05
❑ 252 Johnny Holland	.01	.05
❑ 253 Tim Harris	.01	.05
❑ 254 Chris Jacke	.01	.05
❑ 255 Perry Kemp	.01	.05
❑ 256 Don Majkowski UER	.01	.05
❑ 257 Tony Mandarich	.01	.05
❑ 258 Mark Murphy	.01	.05
❑ 259 Brian Noble	.01	.05
❑ 260 Jeff Query	.01	.05
❑ 261 Sterling Sharpe	.08	.25
❑ 262 Ed West	.01	.05
❑ 263 Keith Woodside	.01	.05
❑ 264 Flipper Anderson	.01	.05
❑ 265 Aaron Cox	.01	.05
❑ 266 Henry Ellard	.02	.10
❑ 267 Jim Everett	.02	.10
❑ 268 Cleveland Gary	.01	.05
❑ 269 Kevin Greene	.02	.10
❑ 270 Pete Holohan	.01	.05
❑ 271 Mike Lansford	.01	.05
❑ 272 Duval Love RC	.01	.05
❑ 273 Buford McGee	.01	.05
❑ 274 Tom Newberry	.01	.05
❑ 275 Jackie Slater	.01	.05
❑ 276 Frank Stams	.01	.05
❑ 277 Alfred Anderson	.01	.05
❑ 278 Joey Browner	.01	.05
❑ 279 Anthony Carter	.02	.10
❑ 280 Chris Doleman	.01	.05
❑ 281 Rick Fenney	.01	.05
❑ 282 Rich Gannon	.08	.25
❑ 283 Hassan Jones	.01	.05
❑ 284 Steve Jordan	.01	.05
❑ 285 Carl Lee	.01	.05
❑ 286 Randall McDaniel	.02	.10
❑ 287 Keith Millard	.01	.05
❑ 288 Herschel Walker	.02	.10
❑ 289 Wade Wilson	.02	.10
❑ 290 Gary Zimmerman	.02	.10
❑ 291 Morten Andersen	.01	.05
❑ 292 Jim Dombrowski	.01	.05

❑ 293 Gill Fenerty	.01	.05
❑ 294 Craig Heyward	.02	.10
❑ 295 Dalton Hilliard	.01	.05
❑ 296 Rickey Jackson	.01	.05
❑ 297 Vaughan Johnson	.01	.05
❑ 298 Eric Martin	.01	.05
❑ 299 Robert Massey	.01	.05
❑ 300 Rueben Mayes	.01	.05
❑ 301 Sam Mills	.01	.05
❑ 302 Brett Perriman	.08	.25
❑ 303 Pat Swilling	.02	.10
❑ 304 Steve Walsh	.01	.05
❑ 305 Ottis Anderson	.02	.10
❑ 306 Matt Bahr	.01	.05
❑ 307 Mark Bavaro	.01	.05
❑ 308 Maurice Carthon	.01	.05
❑ 309 Mark Collins	.01	.05
❑ 310 John Elliott	.01	.05
❑ 311 Rodney Hampton	.08	.25
❑ 312 Jeff Hostetler	.02	.10
❑ 313 Erik Howard	.01	.05
❑ 314 Pepper Johnson	.01	.05
❑ 315 Sean Landeta	.01	.05
❑ 316 Dave Meggett	.02	.10
❑ 317 Bart Oates	.01	.05
❑ 318 Phil Simms	.02	.10
❑ 319 Lawrence Taylor	.08	.25
❑ 320 Reyna Thompson	.01	.05
❑ 321 Everson Walls	.01	.05
❑ 322 Eric Allen	.01	.05
❑ 323 Fred Barnett FFC	.08	.25
❑ 324 Jerome Brown	.01	.05
❑ 325 Keith Byars	.01	.05
❑ 326 Randall Cunningham	.08	.25
❑ 327 Byron Evans	.01	.05
❑ 328 Ron Heller	.01	.05
❑ 329 Keith Jackson	.02	.10
❑ 330 Seth Joyner	.02	.10
❑ 331 Heath Sherman	.01	.05
❑ 332 Clyde Simmons	.01	.05
❑ 333 Ben Smith	.01	.05
❑ 334 Anthony Toney	.01	.05
❑ 335 Andre Waters	.01	.05
❑ 336 Reggie White	.08	.25
❑ 337 Calvin Williams	.02	.10
❑ 338 Anthony Bell	.01	.05
❑ 339 Rich Camarillo	.01	.05
❑ 340 Roy Green	.01	.05
❑ 341 Tim Jorden RC	.01	.05
❑ 342 Cedric Mack	.01	.05
❑ 343 Dexter Manley	.01	.05
❑ 344 Freddie Joe Nunn	.01	.05
❑ 345 Ricky Proehl	.01	.05
❑ 346 Tootie Robbins	.01	.05
❑ 347 Timm Rosenbach	.01	.05
❑ 348 Luis Sharpe	.01	.05
❑ 349 Vai Sikahema	.01	.05
❑ 350 Anthony Thompson	.01	.05
❑ 351 Lonnie Young	.01	.05
❑ 352 Dexter Carter	.01	.05
❑ 353 Mike Cofer	.01	.05
❑ 354 Kevin Fagan	.01	.05
❑ 355 Don Griffin	.01	.05
❑ 356 Charles Haley UER	.02	.10
❑ 357 Pierce Holt	.01	.05
❑ 358 Brent Jones	.08	.25
❑ 359 Guy McIntyre	.01	.05
❑ 360 Joe Montana	.50	1.25
❑ 361 Darryl Pollard	.01	.05
❑ 362 Tom Rathman	.01	.05
❑ 363 Jerry Rice	.30	.75
❑ 364 Bill Romanowski	.01	.05
❑ 365 John Taylor	.02	.10
❑ 366 Steve Wallace	.02	.10
❑ 367 Steve Young	.30	.75
❑ 368 Gary Anderson RB	.01	.05
❑ 369 Ian Beckles	.01	.05
❑ 370 Mark Carrier WR	.08	.25
❑ 371 Reggie Cobb	.01	.05
❑ 372 Reuben Davis	.01	.05
❑ 373 Randy Grimes	.01	.05
❑ 374 Wayne Haddix	.01	.05
❑ 375 Ron Hall	.01	.05
❑ 376 Harry Hamilton	.01	.05
❑ 377 Bruce Hill	.01	.05
❑ 378 Keith McCants	.01	.05
❑ 379 Bruce Perkins	.01	.05
❑ 380 Vinny Testaverde UER	.02	.10
❑ 381 Broderick Thomas	.01	.05
❑ 382 Jeff Bostic	.01	.05
❑ 383 Earnest Byner	.01	.05
❑ 384 Gary Clark	.08	.25
❑ 385 Darryl Grant	.01	.05
❑ 386 Darrell Green	.01	.05
❑ 387 Stan Humphries	.08	.25
❑ 388 Jim Lachey	.01	.05
❑ 389 Charles Mann	.01	.05
❑ 390 Wilber Marshall	.01	.05
❑ 391 Art Monk	.02	.10
❑ 392 Gerald Riggs	.01	.05
❑ 393 Mark Rypien	.02	.10
❑ 394 Ricky Sanders	.01	.05
❑ 395 Don Warren	.01	.05
❑ 396 Bruce Smith HIT	.02	.10
❑ 397 Reggie White HIT	.02	.10
❑ 398 Lawrence Taylor HIT	.02	.10
❑ 399 David Fulcher HIT	.01	.05
❑ 400 Derrick Thomas HIT	.02	.10
❑ 401 Mark Carrier DB HIT	.01	.05
❑ 402 Mike Singletary HIT	.02	.10
❑ 403 Charles Haley HIT	.01	.05
❑ 404 Jeff Cross HIT	.01	.05
❑ 405 Leslie O'Neal HIT	.02	.10
❑ 406 Tim Harris HIT	.01	.05
❑ 407 Steve Atwater HIT	.01	.05
❑ 408 Joe Montana LL UER	.20	.50
❑ 409 Randall Cunningham LL	.02	.10
❑ 410 Warren Moon LL	.02	.10
❑ 411 Andre Rison LL UER 412	.02	.10
❑ 412 Haywood Jeffires LL	.02	.10
❑ 413 Stephone Paige LL	.01	.05
❑ 414 Phil Simms LL	.02	.10
❑ 415 Barry Sanders LL	.20	.50
❑ 416 Bo Jackson LL	.02	.10
❑ 417 Thurman Thomas LL	.02	.10
❑ 418 Emmitt Smith LL	.50	1.25
❑ 419 John L. Williams LL	.01	.05
❑ 420 Nick Bell RC	.01	.05
❑ 421 Eric Bieniemy RC	.01	.05
❑ 422 Mike Dumas UER RC	.01	.05
❑ 423 Russell Maryland RC	.08	.25
❑ 424 Derek Russell RC	.01	.05
❑ 425 Chris Smith RC	.01	.05
❑ 426 Mike Stonebreaker RP	.01	.05
❑ 427 Pat Tyrance RP	.01	.05
❑ 428 Kenny Walker RC	.01	.05
❑ 429 Checklist 1-108 UER	.01	.05
❑ 430 Checklist 109-216	.01	.05
❑ 431 Checklist 217-324	.01	.05
❑ 432 Checklist 325-432	.01	.05

1992 Fleer

❑ COMPLETE SET (480)	5.00	10.00
❑ 1 Steve Broussard	.01	.05
❑ 2 Rick Bryan	.01	.05
❑ 3 Scott Case	.01	.05
❑ 4 Tory Epps	.01	.05
❑ 5 Bill Fralic	.01	.05
❑ 6 Moe Gardner	.01	.05
❑ 7 Michael Haynes	.02	.10
❑ 8 Chris Hinton	.01	.05
❑ 9 Brian Jordan	.02	.10
❑ 10 Mike Kenn	.01	.05
❑ 11 Tim McKyer	.01	.05
❑ 12 Chris Miller	.02	.10
❑ 13 Erric Pegram	.02	.10
❑ 14 Mike Pritchard	.02	.10
❑ 15 Andre Rison	.02	.10
❑ 16 Jessie Tuggle	.01	.05
❑ 17 Carlton Bailey RC	.02	.10
❑ 18 Howard Ballard	.01	.05
❑ 19 Don Beebe	.01	.05
❑ 20 Cornelius Bennett	.02	.10
❑ 21 Shane Conlan	.01	.05
❑ 22 Kent Hull	.01	.05
❑ 23 Mark Kelso	.01	.05
❑ 24 James Lofton	.02	.10
❑ 25 Keith McKeller	.01	.05
❑ 26 Scott Norwood	.01	.05
❑ 27 Nate Odomes	.01	.05
❑ 28 Frank Reich	.02	.10
❑ 29 Jim Ritcher	.01	.05
❑ 30 Leon Seals	.01	.05
❑ 31 Darryl Talley	.01	.05
❑ 32 Steve Tasker	.02	.10
❑ 33 Thurman Thomas	.08	.25
❑ 34 Will Wolford	.01	.05
❑ 35 Neal Anderson	.01	.05
❑ 36 Trace Armstrong	.01	.05
❑ 37 Mark Carrier DB	.01	.05
❑ 38 Richard Dent	.02	.10
❑ 39 Shaun Gayle	.01	.05
❑ 40 Jim Harbaugh	.08	.25
❑ 41 Jay Hilgenberg	.01	.05
❑ 42 Darren Lewis	.01	.05
❑ 43 Steve McMichael	.02	.10
❑ 44 Brad Muster	.01	.05
❑ 45 William Perry	.02	.10
❑ 46 John Roper	.01	.05
❑ 47 Lemuel Stinson	.01	.05
❑ 48 Stan Thomas	.01	.05
❑ 49 Keith Van Horne	.01	.05
❑ 50 Tom Waddle	.01	.05
❑ 51 Donnell Woolford	.01	.05
❑ 52 Chris Zorich	.02	.10
❑ 53 Eddie Brown	.01	.05
❑ 54 James Francis	.01	.05
❑ 55 David Fulcher	.01	.05
❑ 56 David Grant	.01	.05
❑ 57 Harold Green	.01	.05
❑ 58 Rodney Holman	.01	.05
❑ 59 Lee Johnson	.01	.05
❑ 60 Tim Krumrie	.01	.05
❑ 61 Anthony Munoz	.02	.10
❑ 62 Joe Walter RC	.01	.05
❑ 63 Mike Baab	.01	.05
❑ 64 Stephen Braggs	.01	.05
❑ 65 Richard Brown RC	.01	.05
❑ 66 Dan Fike	.01	.05
❑ 67 Scott Galbraith RC	.01	.05
❑ 68 Randy Hilliard RC	.01	.05
❑ 69 Michael Jackson	.02	.10
❑ 70 Tony Jones T	.01	.05
❑ 71 Ed King	.01	.05
❑ 72 Kevin Mack	.01	.05
❑ 73 Clay Matthews	.02	.10
❑ 74 Eric Metcalf	.02	.10
❑ 75 Vince Newsome	.01	.05
❑ 76 John Rienstra	.01	.05
❑ 77 Steve Beuerlein	.02	.10
❑ 78 Larry Brown DB	.01	.05
❑ 79 Tony Casillas	.01	.05
❑ 80 Alvin Harper	.02	.10
❑ 81 Issiac Holt	.01	.05
❑ 82 Ray Horton	.01	.05
❑ 83 Michael Irvin	.08	.25
❑ 84 Daryl Johnston	.08	.25
❑ 85 Kelvin Martin	.01	.05
❑ 86 Nate Newton	.02	.10
❑ 87 Ken Norton	.02	.10
❑ 88 Jay Novacek	.02	.10
❑ 89 Emmitt Smith	.60	1.50
❑ 90 Vinson Smith RC	.01	.05
❑ 91 Mark Stepnoski	.02	.10
❑ 92 Steve Atwater	.01	.05
❑ 93 Mike Croel	.01	.05
❑ 94 John Elway	.50	1.25
❑ 95 Simon Fletcher	.01	.05
❑ 96 Gaston Green	.01	.05
❑ 97 Mark Jackson	.01	.05
❑ 98 Keith Kartz	.01	.05
❑ 99 Greg Kragen	.01	.05
❑ 100 Greg Lewis	.01	.05
❑ 101 Karl Mecklenburg	.01	.05
❑ 102 Derek Russell	.01	.05
❑ 103 Steve Sewell	.01	.05
❑ 104 Dennis Smith	.01	.05
❑ 105 David Treadwell	.01	.05
❑ 106 Kenny Walker	.01	.05
❑ 107 Doug Widell	.01	.05
❑ 108 Michael Young	.01	.05
❑ 109 Jerry Ball	.01	.05
❑ 110 Bennie Blades	.01	.05
❑ 111 Lomas Brown	.01	.05

Card	Low	High
❑ 112 Scott Conover RC	.01	.05
❑ 113 Ray Crockett	.01	.05
❑ 114 Mike Farr	.01	.05
❑ 115 Mel Gray	.02	.10
❑ 116 Willie Green	.01	.05
❑ 117 Tracy Hayworth RC	.01	.05
❑ 118 Erik Kramer	.02	.10
❑ 119 Herman Moore	.08	.25
❑ 120 Dan Owens	.01	.05
❑ 121 Rodney Peete	.02	.10
❑ 122 Brett Perriman	.08	.25
❑ 123 Barry Sanders	.50	1.25
❑ 124 Chris Spielman	.02	.10
❑ 125 Marc Spindler	.01	.05
❑ 126 Tony Bennett	.01	.05
❑ 127 Matt Brock	.01	.05
❑ 128 LeRoy Butler	.01	.05
❑ 129 Johnny Holland	.01	.05
❑ 130 Perry Kemp	.01	.05
❑ 131 Don Majkowski	.01	.05
❑ 132 Mark Murphy	.01	.05
❑ 133 Brian Noble	.01	.05
❑ 134 Bryce Paup	.08	.25
❑ 135 Sterling Sharpe	.08	.25
❑ 136 Scott Stephen	.01	.05
❑ 137 Darrell Thompson	.01	.05
❑ 138 Mike Tomczak	.01	.05
❑ 139 Esera Tuaolo	.01	.05
❑ 140 Keith Woodside	.01	.05
❑ 141 Ray Childress	.01	.05
❑ 142 Cris Dishman	.01	.05
❑ 143 Curtis Duncan	.01	.05
❑ 144 John Flannery	.01	.05
❑ 145 William Fuller	.02	.10
❑ 146 Ernest Givins	.02	.10
❑ 147 Haywood Jeffires	.02	.10
❑ 148 Sean Jones	.02	.10
❑ 149 Lamar Lathon	.01	.05
❑ 150 Bruce Matthews	.01	.05
❑ 151 Bubba McDowell	.01	.05
❑ 152 Johnny Meads	.01	.05
❑ 153 Warren Moon	.08	.25
❑ 154 Mike Munchak	.02	.10
❑ 155 Al Smith	.01	.05
❑ 156 Doug Smith	.01	.05
❑ 157 Lorenzo White	.01	.05
❑ 158 Michael Ball	.01	.05
❑ 159 Chip Banks	.01	.05
❑ 160 Duane Bickett	.01	.05
❑ 161 Bill Brooks	.01	.05
❑ 162 Ken Clark	.01	.05
❑ 163 Jon Hand	.01	.05
❑ 164 Jeff Herrod	.01	.05
❑ 165 Jessie Hester	.01	.05
❑ 166 Scott Radecic	.01	.05
❑ 167 Rohn Stark	.01	.05
❑ 168 Clarence Verdin	.01	.05
❑ 169 John Alt	.01	.05
❑ 170 Tim Barnett	.01	.05
❑ 171 Tim Grunhard	.01	.05
❑ 172 Dino Hackett	.01	.05
❑ 173 Jonathan Hayes	.01	.05
❑ 174 Bill Maas	.01	.05
❑ 175 Chris Martin	.01	.05
❑ 176 Christian Okoye	.01	.05
❑ 177 Stephone Paige	.01	.05
❑ 178 Jayice Pearson RC	.01	.05
❑ 179 Kevin Porter	.01	.05
❑ 180 Kevin Ross	.01	.05
❑ 181 Dan Saleaumua	.01	.05
❑ 182 Tracy Simien RC	.01	.05
❑ 183 Neil Smith	.08	.25
❑ 184 Derrick Thomas	.08	.25
❑ 185 Robb Thomas	.01	.05
❑ 186 Mark Vlasic	.01	.05
❑ 187 Barry Word	.01	.05
❑ 188 Marcus Allen	.08	.25
❑ 189 Eddie Anderson	.01	.05
❑ 190 Nick Bell	.01	.05
❑ 191 Tim Brown	.08	.25
❑ 192 Scott Davis	.01	.05
❑ 193 Riki Ellison	.01	.05
❑ 194 Mervyn Fernandez	.01	.05
❑ 195 Willie Gault	.02	.10
❑ 196 Jeff Gossett	.01	.05
❑ 197 Ethan Horton	.01	.05
❑ 198 Jeff Jaeger	.01	.05
❑ 199 Howie Long	.08	.25
❑ 200 Ronnie Lott	.02	.10
❑ 201 Todd Marinovich	.01	.05
❑ 202 Don Mosebar	.01	.05
❑ 203 Jay Schroeder	.01	.05
❑ 204 Greg Townsend	.01	.05
❑ 205 Lionel Washington	.01	.05
❑ 206 Steve Wisniewski	.01	.05
❑ 207 Flipper Anderson	.01	.05
❑ 208 Bern Brostek	.01	.05
❑ 209 Robert Delpino	.01	.05
❑ 210 Henry Ellard	.02	.10
❑ 211 Jim Everett	.02	.10
❑ 212 Cleveland Gary	.01	.05
❑ 213 Kevin Greene	.02	.10
❑ 214 Darryl Henley	.01	.05
❑ 215 Damone Johnson	.01	.05
❑ 216 Larry Kelm	.01	.05
❑ 217 Todd Lyght	.01	.05
❑ 218 Jackie Slater	.01	.05
❑ 219 Michael Stewart	.01	.05
❑ 220 Pat Terrell UER	.01	.05
❑ 221 Robert Young	.01	.05
❑ 222 Mark Clayton	.02	.10
❑ 223 Bryan Cox	.02	.10
❑ 224 Aaron Craver	.01	.05
❑ 225 Jeff Cross	.01	.05
❑ 226 Mark Duper	.01	.05
❑ 227 Harry Galbreath	.01	.05
❑ 228 David Griggs	.01	.05
❑ 229 Mark Higgs	.01	.05
❑ 230 Vestee Jackson	.01	.05
❑ 231 John Offerdahl	.01	.05
❑ 232 Louis Oliver	.01	.05
❑ 233 Tony Paige	.01	.05
❑ 234 Reggie Roby	.01	.05
❑ 235 Sammie Smith	.01	.05
❑ 236 Pete Stoyanovich	.01	.05
❑ 237 Richmond Webb	.01	.05
❑ 238 Terry Allen	.08	.25
❑ 239 Ray Berry	.01	.05
❑ 240 Joey Browner	.01	.05
❑ 241 Anthony Carter	.02	.10
❑ 242 Cris Carter	.20	.50
❑ 243 Chris Doleman	.01	.05
❑ 244 Rich Gannon	.08	.25
❑ 245 Tim Irwin	.01	.05
❑ 246 Steve Jordan	.01	.05
❑ 247 Carl Lee	.01	.05
❑ 248 Randall McDaniel	.02	.10
❑ 249 Mike Merriweather	.01	.05
❑ 250 Harry Newsome	.01	.05
❑ 251 John Randle	.02	.10
❑ 252 Henry Thomas	.01	.05
❑ 253 Herschel Walker	.02	.10
❑ 254 Ray Agnew	.01	.05
❑ 255 Bruce Armstrong	.01	.05
❑ 256 Vincent Brown	.01	.05
❑ 257 Marv Cook	.01	.05
❑ 258 Irving Fryar	.02	.10
❑ 259 Pat Harlow	.01	.05
❑ 260 Tommy Hodson	.01	.05
❑ 261 Maurice Hurst	.01	.05
❑ 262 Ronnie Lippett	.01	.05
❑ 263 Eugene Lockhart	.01	.05
❑ 264 Greg McMurtry	.01	.05
❑ 265 Hugh Millen	.01	.05
❑ 266 Leonard Russell	.02	.10
❑ 267 Andre Tippett	.01	.05
❑ 268 Brent Williams	.01	.05
❑ 269 Morten Andersen	.01	.05
❑ 270 Gene Atkins	.01	.05
❑ 271 Wesley Carroll	.01	.05
❑ 272 Jim Dombrowski	.01	.05
❑ 273 Quinn Early	.02	.10
❑ 274 Gill Fenerty	.01	.05
❑ 275 Bobby Hebert	.01	.05
❑ 276 Joel Hilgenberg	.01	.05
❑ 277 Rickey Jackson	.01	.05
❑ 278 Vaughan Johnson	.01	.05
❑ 279 Eric Martin	.01	.05
❑ 280 Brett Maxie	.01	.05
❑ 281 Fred McAfee RC	.01	.05
❑ 282 Sam Mills	.01	.05
❑ 283 Pat Swilling	.02	.10
❑ 284 Floyd Turner	.01	.05
❑ 285 Steve Walsh	.01	.05
❑ 286 Frank Warren	.01	.05
❑ 287 Stephen Baker	.01	.05
❑ 288 Maurice Carthon	.01	.05
❑ 289 Mark Collins	.01	.05
❑ 290 John Elliott	.01	.05
❑ 291 Myron Guyton	.01	.05
❑ 292 Rodney Hampton	.02	.10
❑ 293 Jeff Hostetler	.02	.10
❑ 294 Mark Ingram	.01	.05
❑ 295 Pepper Johnson	.01	.05
❑ 296 Sean Landeta	.01	.05
❑ 297 Leonard Marshall	.01	.05
❑ 298 Dave Meggett	.02	.10
❑ 299 Bart Oates	.01	.05
❑ 300 Phil Simms	.02	.10
❑ 301 Reyna Thompson	.01	.05
❑ 302 Lewis Tillman	.01	.05
❑ 303 Brad Baxter	.01	.05
❑ 304 Kyle Clifton	.01	.05
❑ 305 James Hasty	.01	.05
❑ 306 Joe Kelly	.01	.05
❑ 307 Jeff Lageman	.01	.05
❑ 308 Mo Lewis	.01	.05
❑ 309 Erik McMillan	.01	.05
❑ 310 Rob Moore	.02	.10
❑ 311 Tony Stargell	.01	.05
❑ 312 Jim Sweeney	.01	.05
❑ 313 Marvin Washington	.01	.05
❑ 314 Lonnie Young	.01	.05
❑ 315 Eric Allen	.01	.05
❑ 316 Fred Barnett	.08	.25
❑ 317 Jerome Brown	.01	.05
❑ 318 Keith Byars	.01	.05
❑ 319 Wes Hopkins	.01	.05
❑ 320 Keith Jackson	.02	.10
❑ 321 James Joseph	.01	.05
❑ 322 Seth Joyner	.02	.10
❑ 323 Jeff Kemp	.01	.05
❑ 324 Roger Ruzek	.01	.05
❑ 325 Clyde Simmons	.01	.05
❑ 326 William Thomas	.01	.05
❑ 327 Reggie White	.08	.25
❑ 328 Calvin Williams	.02	.10
❑ 329 Rich Camarillo	.01	.05
❑ 330 Ken Harvey	.01	.05
❑ 331 Eric Hill	.01	.05
❑ 332 Johnny Johnson	.01	.05
❑ 333 Ernie Jones	.01	.05
❑ 334 Tim Jorden	.01	.05
❑ 335 Tim McDonald	.01	.05
❑ 336 Freddie Joe Nunn	.01	.05
❑ 337 Luis Sharpe	.01	.05
❑ 338 Eric Swann	.02	.10
❑ 339 Aeneas Williams	.02	.10
❑ 340 Gary Anderson K	.01	.05
❑ 341 Bubby Brister	.01	.05
❑ 342 Adrian Cooper	.01	.05
❑ 343 Barry Foster	.02	.10
❑ 344 Eric Green	.01	.05
❑ 345 Bryan Hinkle	.01	.05
❑ 346 Tunch Ilkin	.01	.05
❑ 347 Carnell Lake	.01	.05
❑ 348 Louis Lipps	.01	.05
❑ 349 David Little	.01	.05
❑ 350 Greg Lloyd	.02	.10
❑ 351 Neil O'Donnell	.08	.25
❑ 352 Dwight Stone	.01	.05
❑ 353 Rod Woodson	.08	.25
❑ 354 Rod Bernstine	.01	.05
❑ 355 Eric Bieniemy	.01	.05
❑ 356 Marion Butts	.01	.05
❑ 357 Gill Byrd	.01	.05
❑ 358 John Friesz	.02	.10
❑ 359 Burt Grossman	.01	.05
❑ 360 Courtney Hall	.01	.05
❑ 361 Ronnie Harmon	.01	.05
❑ 362 Shawn Jefferson	.01	.05
❑ 363 Nate Lewis	.01	.05
❑ 364 Craig McEwen RC	.01	.05
❑ 365 Eric Moten	.01	.05
❑ 366 Joe Phillips	.01	.05
❑ 367 Gary Plummer	.01	.05
❑ 368 Henry Rolling	.01	.05
❑ 369 Broderick Thompson	.01	.05
❑ 370 Harris Barton	.01	.05
❑ 371 Steve Bono RC	.08	.25
❑ 372 Todd Bowles	.01	.05
❑ 373 Dexter Carter	.01	.05
❑ 374 Michael Carter	.01	.05
❑ 375 Mike Cofer	.01	.05
❑ 376 Keith DeLong	.01	.05
❑ 377 Charles Haley	.02	.10
❑ 378 Merton Hanks	.02	.10

Card		
❑ 379 Tim Harris	.01	.05
❑ 380 Brent Jones	.02	.10
❑ 381 Guy McIntyre	.01	.05
❑ 382 Tom Rathman	.01	.05
❑ 383 Bill Romanowski	.01	.05
❑ 384 Jesse Sapolu	.01	.05
❑ 385 John Taylor	.02	.10
❑ 386 Steve Young	.25	.60
❑ 387 Robert Blackmon	.01	.05
❑ 388 Brian Blades	.02	.10
❑ 389 Jacob Green	.01	.05
❑ 390 Dwayne Harper	.01	.05
❑ 391 Andy Heck	.01	.05
❑ 392 Tommy Kane	.01	.05
❑ 393 John Kasay	.01	.05
❑ 394 Cortez Kennedy	.02	.10
❑ 395 Bryan Millard	.01	.05
❑ 396 Rufus Porter	.01	.05
❑ 397 Eugene Robinson	.01	.05
❑ 398 John L. Williams	.01	.05
❑ 399 Terry Wooden	.01	.05
❑ 400 Gary Anderson RB	.01	.05
❑ 401 Ian Beckles	.01	.05
❑ 402 Mark Carrier WR	.02	.10
❑ 403 Reggie Cobb	.01	.05
❑ 404 Lawrence Dawsey	.02	.10
❑ 405 Ron Hall	.01	.05
❑ 406 Keith McCants	.01	.05
❑ 407 Charles McRae	.01	.05
❑ 408 Tim Newton	.01	.05
❑ 409 Jesse Solomon	.01	.05
❑ 410 Vinny Testaverde	.02	.10
❑ 411 Broderick Thomas	.01	.05
❑ 412 Robert Wilson	.01	.05
❑ 413 Jeff Bostic	.01	.05
❑ 414 Earnest Byner	.01	.05
❑ 415 Gary Clark	.08	.25
❑ 416 Andre Collins	.01	.05
❑ 417 Brad Edwards	.01	.05
❑ 418 Kurt Gouveia	.01	.05
❑ 419 Darrell Green	.01	.05
❑ 420 Joe Jacoby	.01	.05
❑ 421 Jim Lachey	.01	.05
❑ 422 Chip Lohmiller	.01	.05
❑ 423 Charles Mann	.01	.05
❑ 424 Wilber Marshall	.01	.05
❑ 425 Ron Middleton RC	.01	.05
❑ 426 Brian Mitchell	.02	.10
❑ 427 Art Monk	.02	.10
❑ 428 Mark Rypien	.01	.05
❑ 429 Ricky Sanders	.01	.05
❑ 430 Mark Schlereth RC	.01	.05
❑ 431 Fred Stokes	.01	.05
❑ 432 Edgar Bennett RC	.08	.25
❑ 433 Brian Bollinger RC	.01	.05
❑ 434 Joe Bowden RC	.01	.05
❑ 435 Terrell Buckley RC	.01	.05
❑ 436 Willie Clay RC	.01	.05
❑ 437 Steve Gordon RC	.01	.05
❑ 438 Keith Hamilton RC	.02	.10
❑ 439 Carlos Huerta	.01	.05
❑ 440 Matt LaBounty RC	.01	.05
❑ 441 Amp Lee RC	.01	.05
❑ 442 Ricardo McDonald RC	.01	.05
❑ 443 Chris Mims RC	.02	.10
❑ 444 Michael Moody RC	.01	.05
❑ 445 Patrick Rowe RC	.01	.05
❑ 446 Leon Searcy RC	.02	.10
❑ 447 Siran Stacy RC	.01	.05
❑ 448 Kevin Turner RC	.01	.05
❑ 449 Tommy Vardell RC	.02	.10
❑ 450 Bob Whitfield RC	.01	.05
❑ 451 Darryl Williams RC	.01	.05
❑ 452 Thurman Thomas LL	.02	.10
❑ 453 Emmitt Smith LL	.30	.75
❑ 454 Haywood Jeffires LL	.01	.05
❑ 455 Michael Irvin LL	.02	.10
❑ 456 Mark Clayton LL	.01	.05
❑ 457 Barry Sanders LL	.25	.60
❑ 458 Pete Stoyanovich LL	.01	.05
❑ 459 Chip Lohmiller LL	.01	.05
❑ 460 William Fuller LL	.01	.05
❑ 461 Pat Swilling LL	.01	.05
❑ 462 Ronnie Lott LL	.01	.05
❑ 463 Ray Crockett LL	.01	.05
❑ 464 Tim McKyer LL	.01	.05
❑ 465 Aeneas Williams LL	.01	.05
❑ 466 Rod Woodson LL	.02	.10
❑ 467 Mel Gray LL	.01	.05
❑ 468 Nate Lewis LL	.01	.05
❑ 469 Steve Young LL	.10	.30
❑ 470 Reggie Roby LL	.01	.05
❑ 471 John Elway PV	.25	.60
❑ 472 Ronnie Lott PV	.01	.05
❑ 473 Art Monk PV UER	.01	.05
❑ 474 Warren Moon PV	.02	.10
❑ 475 Emmitt Smith PV	.30	.75
❑ 476 Thurman Thomas PV	.02	.10
❑ 477 Checklist 1-120	.01	.05
❑ 478 Checklist 121-240	.01	.05
❑ 479 Checklist 241-360	.01	.05
❑ 480 Checklist 361-480	.01	.05

1993 Fleer

Card		
❑ COMPLETE SET (500)	10.00	20.00
❑ 1 Dan Saleaumua	.01	.05
❑ 2 Bryan Cox	.01	.05
❑ 3 Dermontti Dawson	.01	.05
❑ 4 Michael Jackson	.02	.10
❑ 5 Calvin Williams	.02	.10
❑ 6 Terry McDaniel	.01	.05
❑ 7 Jack Del Rio	.01	.05
❑ 8 Steve Atwater	.01	.05
❑ 9 Ernie Jones	.01	.05
❑ 10 Brad Muster	.01	.05
❑ 11 Harold Green	.01	.05
❑ 12 Eric Bieniemy	.01	.05
❑ 13 Eric Dorsey	.01	.05
❑ 14 Fred Barnett	.02	.10
❑ 15 Cleveland Gary	.01	.05
❑ 16 Darion Conner	.01	.05
❑ 17 Jerry Ball	.01	.05
❑ 18 Tony Casillas	.01	.05
❑ 19 Brian Blades	.02	.10
❑ 20 Tony Bennett	.01	.05
❑ 21 Reggie Cobb	.01	.05
❑ 22 Kurt Gouveia	.01	.05
❑ 23 Greg McMurtry	.01	.05
❑ 24 Kyle Clifton	.01	.05
❑ 25 Trace Armstrong	.01	.05
❑ 26 Terry Allen	.08	.25
❑ 27 Steve Bono	.02	.10
❑ 28 Barry Word	.01	.05
❑ 29 Mark Duper	.01	.05
❑ 30 Nate Newton	.02	.10
❑ 31 Will Wolford	.01	.05
❑ 32 Curtis Duncan	.01	.05
❑ 33 Nick Bell	.01	.05
❑ 34 Don Beebe	.01	.05
❑ 35 Mike Croel	.01	.05
❑ 36 Rich Camarillo	.01	.05
❑ 37 Wade Wilson	.01	.05
❑ 38 John Taylor	.02	.10
❑ 39 Marion Butts	.01	.05
❑ 40 Rodney Hampton	.02	.10
❑ 41 Seth Joyner	.01	.05
❑ 42 Wilber Marshall	.01	.05
❑ 43 Bobby Hebert	.01	.05
❑ 44 Bennie Blades	.01	.05
❑ 45 Thomas Everett	.01	.05
❑ 46 Ricky Sanders	.01	.05
❑ 47 Matt Brock	.01	.05
❑ 48 Lawrence Dawsey	.01	.05
❑ 49 Brad Edwards	.01	.05
❑ 50 Vincent Brown	.01	.05
❑ 51 Jeff Lageman	.01	.05
❑ 52 Mark Carrier DB	.01	.05
❑ 53 Cris Carter	.08	.25
❑ 54 Brent Jones	.02	.10
❑ 55 Barry Foster	.02	.10
❑ 56 Derrick Thomas	.08	.25
❑ 57 Scott Zolak	.01	.05
❑ 58 Mark Stepnoski	.01	.05
❑ 59 Eric Metcalf	.02	.10
❑ 60 Al Smith	.01	.05
❑ 61 Ronnie Harmon	.01	.05
❑ 62 Cornelius Bennett	.02	.10
❑ 63 Karl Mecklenburg	.01	.05
❑ 64 Chris Chandler	.02	.10
❑ 65 Toi Cook	.01	.05
❑ 66 Tim Krumrie	.01	.05
❑ 67 Gill Byrd	.01	.05
❑ 68 Mark Jackson	.01	.05
❑ 69 Tim Harris	.01	.05
❑ 70 Shane Conlan	.01	.05
❑ 71 Moe Gardner	.01	.05
❑ 72 Lomas Brown	.01	.05
❑ 73 Charles Haley	.02	.10
❑ 74 Mark Rypien	.01	.05
❑ 75 LeRoy Butler	.01	.05
❑ 76 Steve DeBerg	.01	.05
❑ 77 Darrell Green	.01	.05
❑ 78 Marv Cook	.01	.05
❑ 79 Chris Burkett	.01	.05
❑ 80 Richard Dent	.02	.10
❑ 81 Roger Craig	.02	.10
❑ 82 Amp Lee	.01	.05
❑ 83 Eric Green	.01	.05
❑ 84 Willie Davis	.08	.25
❑ 85 Mark Higgs	.01	.05
❑ 86 Carlton Haselrig	.01	.05
❑ 87 Tommy Vardell	.01	.05
❑ 88 Haywood Jeffires	.02	.10
❑ 89 Tim Brown	.08	.25
❑ 90 Randall McDaniel	.02	.10
❑ 91 John Elway	.60	1.50
❑ 92 Ken Harvey	.01	.05
❑ 93 Joel Hilgenberg	.01	.05
❑ 94 Steve Wallace	.01	.05
❑ 95 Stan Humphries	.02	.10
❑ 96 Greg Jackson	.01	.05
❑ 97 Clyde Simmons	.01	.05
❑ 98 Jim Everett	.02	.10
❑ 99 Michael Haynes	.02	.10
❑ 100 Mel Gray	.02	.10
❑ 101 Alvin Harper	.02	.10
❑ 102 Art Monk	.02	.10
❑ 103 Brett Favre	.75	2.00
❑ 104 Keith McCants	.01	.05
❑ 105 Charles Mann	.01	.05
❑ 106 Leonard Russell	.02	.10
❑ 107 Mo Lewis	.01	.05
❑ 108 Shaun Gayle	.01	.05
❑ 109 Chris Doleman	.01	.05
❑ 110 Tim McDonald	.01	.05
❑ 111 Louis Oliver	.01	.05
❑ 112 Greg Lloyd	.02	.10
❑ 113 Chip Banks	.01	.05
❑ 114 Sean Jones	.01	.05
❑ 115 Ethan Horton	.01	.05
❑ 116 Kenneth Davis	.01	.05
❑ 117 Simon Fletcher	.01	.05
❑ 118 Johnny Johnson	.01	.05
❑ 119 Vaughan Johnson	.01	.05
❑ 120 Derrick Fenner	.01	.05
❑ 121 Nate Lewis	.01	.05
❑ 122 Pepper Johnson	.01	.05
❑ 123 Heath Sherman	.01	.05
❑ 124 Darryl Henley	.01	.05
❑ 125 Pierce Holt	.01	.05
❑ 126 Herman Moore	.08	.25
❑ 127 Michael Irvin	.08	.25
❑ 128 Tommy Kane	.01	.05
❑ 129 Jackie Harris	.01	.05
❑ 130 Hardy Nickerson	.02	.10
❑ 131 Chip Lohmiller	.01	.05
❑ 132 Andre Tippett	.01	.05
❑ 133 Leonard Marshall	.01	.05
❑ 134 Craig Heyward	.02	.10
❑ 135 Anthony Carter	.02	.10
❑ 136 Tom Rathman	.01	.05
❑ 137 Lorenzo White	.01	.05
❑ 138 Nick Lowery	.01	.05
❑ 139 John Offerdahl	.01	.05
❑ 140 Neil O'Donnell	.08	.25
❑ 141 Clarence Verdin	.01	.05
❑ 142 Ernest Givins	.02	.10
❑ 143 Todd Marinovich	.01	.05
❑ 144 Jeff Wright	.01	.05
❑ 145 Michael Brooks	.01	.05
❑ 146 Freddie Joe Nunn	.01	.05
❑ 147 William Perry	.02	.10
❑ 148 Daniel Stubbs	.01	.05
❑ 149 Morten Andersen	.01	.05

Card		
❑ 150 Dave Meggett	.01	.05
❑ 151 Andre Waters	.01	.05
❑ 152 Todd Lyght	.01	.05
❑ 153 Chris Miller	.02	.10
❑ 154 Rodney Peete	.01	.05
❑ 155 Jim Jeffcoat	.01	.05
❑ 156 Cortez Kennedy	.02	.10
❑ 157 Johnny Holland	.01	.05
❑ 158 Ricky Reynolds	.01	.05
❑ 159 Kevin Greene	.02	.10
❑ 160 Jeff Herrod	.01	.05
❑ 161 Bruce Matthews	.01	.05
❑ 162 Anthony Smith	.01	.05
❑ 163 Henry Jones	.01	.05
❑ 164 Rob Burnett	.01	.05
❑ 165 Eric Swann	.02	.10
❑ 166 Tom Waddle	.01	.05
❑ 167 Alfred Williams	.01	.05
❑ 168 Darren Carrington RC	.01	.05
❑ 169 Mike Sherrard	.01	.05
❑ 170 Frank Reich	.02	.10
❑ 171 Anthony Newman RC	.01	.05
❑ 172 Mike Pritchard	.02	.10
❑ 173 Andre Ware	.01	.05
❑ 174 Daryl Johnston	.08	.25
❑ 175 Rufus Porter	.01	.05
❑ 176 Reggie White	.08	.25
❑ 177 Charles Mincy RC	.01	.05
❑ 178 Pete Stoyanovich	.01	.05
❑ 179 Rod Woodson	.08	.25
❑ 180 Anthony Johnson	.02	.10
❑ 181 Cody Carlson	.01	.05
❑ 182 Gaston Green	.01	.05
❑ 183 Audray McMillian	.01	.05
❑ 184 Mike Johnson	.01	.05
❑ 185 Aeneas Williams	.01	.05
❑ 186 Jarrod Bunch	.01	.05
❑ 187 Dennis Smith	.01	.05
❑ 188 Quinn Early	.02	.10
❑ 189 James Hasty	.01	.05
❑ 190 Darryl Talley	.01	.05
❑ 191 Jon Vaughn	.01	.05
❑ 192 Andre Rison	.02	.10
❑ 193 Kelvin Pritchett	.01	.05
❑ 194 Ken Norton Jr.	.02	.10
❑ 195 Chris Warren	.02	.10
❑ 196 Sterling Sharpe	.08	.25
❑ 197 Christian Okoye	.01	.05
❑ 198 Richmond Webb	.01	.05
❑ 199 James Francis	.01	.05
❑ 200 Reggie Langhorne	.01	.05
❑ 201 J.J. Birden	.01	.05
❑ 202 Aaron Wallace	.01	.05
❑ 203 Henry Thomas	.01	.05
❑ 204 Clay Matthews	.02	.10
❑ 205 Robert Massey	.01	.05
❑ 206 Donnell Woolford	.01	.05
❑ 207 Ricky Watters	.08	.25
❑ 208 Wayne Martin	.01	.05
❑ 209 Rob Moore	.02	.10
❑ 210 Steve Tasker	.02	.10
❑ 211 Jackie Slater	.01	.05
❑ 212 Steve Young	.30	.75
❑ 213 Barry Sanders	.50	1.25
❑ 214 Jay Novacek	.02	.10
❑ 215 Eugene Robinson	.01	.05
❑ 216 Duane Bickett	.01	.05
❑ 217 Broderick Thomas	.01	.05
❑ 218 David Fulcher	.01	.05
❑ 219 Rohn Stark	.01	.05
❑ 220 Warren Moon	.08	.25
❑ 221 Steve Wisniewski	.01	.05
❑ 222 Nate Odomes	.01	.05
❑ 223 Shannon Sharpe	.08	.25
❑ 224 Byron Evans	.01	.05
❑ 225 Mark Collins	.01	.05
❑ 226 Rod Bernstine	.01	.05
❑ 227 Sam Mills	.01	.05
❑ 228 Marvin Washington	.01	.05
❑ 229 Thurman Thomas	.08	.25
❑ 230 Brent Williams	.01	.05
❑ 231 Jessie Tuggle	.01	.05
❑ 232 Chris Spielman	.02	.10
❑ 233 Emmitt Smith	.60	1.50
❑ 234 John L. Williams	.01	.05
❑ 235 Jeff Cross	.01	.05
❑ 236 Chris Doleman AW	.01	.05
❑ 237 John Elway AW	.30	.75
❑ 238 Barry Foster AW	.01	.05
❑ 239 Cortez Kennedy AW	.01	.05
❑ 240 Steve Young AW	.15	.40
❑ 241 Barry Foster LL	.01	.05
❑ 242 Warren Moon LL	.01	.05
❑ 243 Sterling Sharpe LL	.01	.05
❑ 244 Emmitt Smith LL	.30	.75
❑ 245 Thurman Thomas LL	.02	.10
❑ 246 Michael Irvin PV	.02	.10
❑ 247 Steve Young PV	.15	.40
❑ 248 Barry Foster PV	.01	.05
❑ 249 Checklist	.01	.05
❑ 250 Checklist	.01	.05
❑ 251 Checklist	.01	.05
❑ 252 Checklist	.01	.05
❑ 253 Troy Aikman AW	.15	.40
❑ 254 Jason Hanson AW	.01	.05
❑ 255 Carl Pickens AW	.02	.10
❑ 256 Santana Dotson AW	.01	.05
❑ 257 Dale Carter AW	.01	.05
❑ 258 Clyde Simmons LL	.01	.05
❑ 259 Audray McMillian LL	.01	.05
❑ 260 Henry Jones LL	.01	.05
❑ 261 Deion Sanders LL	.08	.25
❑ 262 Haywood Jeffires LL	.01	.05
❑ 263 Deion Sanders PV	.08	.25
❑ 264 Andre Reed PV	.02	.10
❑ 265 Vince Workman	.01	.05
❑ 266 Robert Brown	.01	.05
❑ 267 Ray Agnew	.01	.05
❑ 268 Ronnie Lott	.02	.10
❑ 269 Wesley Carroll	.01	.05
❑ 270 John Randle	.02	.10
❑ 271 Rodney Culver	.01	.05
❑ 272 David Alexander	.01	.05
❑ 273 Troy Aikman	.30	.75
❑ 274 Bernie Kosar	.02	.10
❑ 275 Scott Case	.01	.05
❑ 276 Dan McGwire	.01	.05
❑ 277 John Alt	.01	.05
❑ 278 Dan Marino	.60	1.50
❑ 279 Santana Dotson	.02	.10
❑ 280 Johnny Mitchell	.01	.05
❑ 281 Alonzo Spellman	.01	.05
❑ 282 Adrian Cooper	.01	.05
❑ 283 Gary Clark	.02	.10
❑ 284 Vance Johnson	.01	.05
❑ 285 Eric Martin	.01	.05
❑ 286 Jesse Solomon	.01	.05
❑ 287 Carl Banks	.01	.05
❑ 288 Harris Barton	.01	.05
❑ 289 Jim Harbaugh	.08	.25
❑ 290 Bubba McDowell	.01	.05
❑ 291 Anthony McDowell RC	.01	.05
❑ 292 Terrell Buckley	.01	.05
❑ 293 Bruce Armstrong	.01	.05
❑ 294 Kurt Barber	.01	.05
❑ 295 Reginald Jones	.01	.05
❑ 296 Steve Jordan	.01	.05
❑ 297 Kerry Cash	.01	.05
❑ 298 Ray Crockett	.01	.05
❑ 299 Keith Byars	.01	.05
❑ 300 Russell Maryland	.01	.05
❑ 301 Johnny Bailey	.01	.05
❑ 302 Vinnie Clark	.01	.05
❑ 303 Terry Wooden	.01	.05
❑ 304 Harvey Williams	.02	.10
❑ 305 Marco Coleman	.01	.05
❑ 306 Mark Wheeler	.01	.05
❑ 307 Greg Townsend	.01	.05
❑ 308 Tim McGee	.01	.05
❑ 309 Donald Evans	.01	.05
❑ 310 Randal Hill	.01	.05
❑ 311 Kenny Walker	.01	.05
❑ 312 Dalton Hilliard	.01	.05
❑ 313 Howard Ballard	.01	.05
❑ 314 Phil Simms	.02	.10
❑ 315 Jerry Rice	.40	1.00
❑ 316 Courtney Hall	.01	.05
❑ 317 Darren Lewis	.01	.05
❑ 318 Greg Montgomery	.01	.05
❑ 319 Paul Gruber	.01	.05
❑ 320 George Koonce RC	.01	.05
❑ 321 Eugene Chung	.01	.05
❑ 322 Mike Brim	.01	.05
❑ 323 Patrick Hunter	.01	.05
❑ 324 Todd Scott	.01	.05
❑ 325 Steve Emtman	.01	.05
❑ 326 Andy Harmon RC	.02	.10
❑ 327 Larry Brown DB	.01	.05
❑ 328 Chuck Cecil	.01	.05
❑ 329 Tim McKyer	.01	.05
❑ 330 Jeff Bryant	.01	.05
❑ 331 Tim Barnett	.01	.05
❑ 332 Irving Fryar	.02	.10
❑ 333 Tyji Armstrong	.01	.05
❑ 334 Brad Baxter	.01	.05
❑ 335 Shane Collins	.01	.05
❑ 336 Jeff Graham	.02	.10
❑ 337 Ricky Proehl	.01	.05
❑ 338 Tommy Maddox	.08	.25
❑ 339 Jim Dombrowski	.01	.05
❑ 340 Bill Brooks	.01	.05
❑ 341 Dave Brown RC	.08	.25
❑ 342 Eric Davis	.01	.05
❑ 343 Leslie O'Neal	.02	.10
❑ 344 Jim Morrissey	.01	.05
❑ 345 Mike Munchak	.02	.10
❑ 346 Ron Hall	.01	.05
❑ 347 Brian Noble	.01	.05
❑ 348 Chris Singleton	.01	.05
❑ 349 Boomer Esiason	.02	.10
❑ 350 Ray Roberts	.01	.05
❑ 351 Gary Zimmerman	.01	.05
❑ 352 Quentin Coryatt	.02	.10
❑ 353 Willie Green	.01	.05
❑ 354 Randall Cunningham	.08	.25
❑ 355 Kevin Smith	.02	.10
❑ 356 Michael Dean Perry	.02	.10
❑ 357 Tim Green	.01	.05
❑ 358 Dwayne Harper	.01	.05
❑ 359 Dale Carter	.01	.05
❑ 360 Keith Jackson	.02	.10
❑ 361 Martin Mayhew	.01	.05
❑ 362 Brian Washington	.01	.05
❑ 363 Earnest Byner	.01	.05
❑ 364 D.J. Johnson	.01	.05
❑ 365 Timm Rosenbach	.01	.05
❑ 366 Doug Widell	.01	.05
❑ 367 Vaughn Dunbar	.01	.05
❑ 368 Phil Hansen	.01	.05
❑ 369 Mike Fox	.01	.05
❑ 370 Dana Hall	.01	.05
❑ 371 Junior Seau	.08	.25
❑ 372 Steve McMichael	.02	.10
❑ 373 Eddie Robinson	.01	.05
❑ 374 Milton Mack RC	.01	.05
❑ 375 Mike Prior	.01	.05
❑ 376 Jerome Henderson	.01	.05
❑ 377 Scott Mersereau	.01	.05
❑ 378 Neal Anderson	.01	.05
❑ 379 Harry Newsome	.01	.05
❑ 380 John Baylor	.01	.05
❑ 381 Bill Fralic	.01	.05
❑ 382 Mark Bavaro	.01	.05
❑ 383 Robert Jones	.01	.05
❑ 384 Tyronne Stowe	.01	.05
❑ 385 Deion Sanders	.20	.50
❑ 386 Robert Blackmon	.01	.05
❑ 387 Neil Smith	.08	.25
❑ 388 Mark Ingram	.01	.05
❑ 389 Mark Carrier WR	.02	.10
❑ 390 Browning Nagle	.01	.05
❑ 391 Ricky Ervins	.01	.05
❑ 392 Carnell Lake	.01	.05
❑ 393 Luis Sharpe	.01	.05
❑ 394 Greg Kragen	.01	.05
❑ 395 Tommy Barnhardt	.01	.05
❑ 396 Mark Kelso	.01	.05
❑ 397 Kent Graham RC	.08	.25
❑ 398 Bill Romanowski	.01	.05
❑ 399 Anthony Miller	.02	.10
❑ 400 John Roper	.01	.05
❑ 401 Lamar Rogers	.01	.05
❑ 402 Troy Auzenne	.01	.05
❑ 403 Webster Slaughter	.01	.05
❑ 404 David Brandon	.01	.05
❑ 405 Chris Hinton	.01	.05
❑ 406 Andy Heck	.01	.05
❑ 407 Tracy Simien	.01	.05
❑ 408 Troy Vincent	.01	.05
❑ 409 Jason Hanson	.01	.05
❑ 410 Rod Jones CB RC	.01	.05
❑ 411 Al Noga	.01	.05
❑ 412 Ernie Mills	.01	.05
❑ 413 Willie Gault	.01	.05
❑ 414 Henry Ellard	.02	.10
❑ 415 Rickey Jackson	.01	.05
❑ 416 Bruce Smith	.08	.25

❑ 417 Derek Brown TE	.01	.05
❑ 418 Kevin Fagan	.01	.05
❑ 419 Gary Plummer	.01	.05
❑ 420 Wendell Davis	.01	.05
❑ 421 Craig Thompson	.01	.05
❑ 422 Wes Hopkins	.01	.05
❑ 423 Ray Childress	.01	.05
❑ 424 Pat Harlow	.01	.05
❑ 425 Howie Long	.08	.25
❑ 426 Shane Dronett	.01	.05
❑ 427 Sean Salisbury	.01	.05
❑ 428 Dwight Hollier RC	.01	.05
❑ 429 Brett Perriman	.08	.25
❑ 430 Donald Hollas RC	.01	.05
❑ 431 Jim Lachey	.01	.05
❑ 432 Darren Perry	.01	.05
❑ 433 Lionel Washington	.01	.05
❑ 434 Sean Gilbert	.02	.10
❑ 435 Gene Atkins	.01	.05
❑ 436 Jim Kelly	.08	.25
❑ 437 Ed McCaffrey	.08	.25
❑ 438 Don Griffin	.01	.05
❑ 439 Jerrol Williams	.01	.05
❑ 440 Bryce Paup	.02	.10
❑ 441 Darryl Williams	.01	.05
❑ 442 Vai Sikahema	.01	.05
❑ 443 Cris Dishman	.01	.05
❑ 444 Kevin Mack	.01	.05
❑ 445 Winston Moss	.01	.05
❑ 446 Tyrone Braxton	.01	.05
❑ 447 Mike Merriweather	.01	.05
❑ 448 Tony Paige	.01	.05
❑ 449 Robert Porcher	.01	.05
❑ 450 Ricardo McDonald	.01	.05
❑ 451 Danny Copeland	.01	.05
❑ 452 Tony Tolbert	.01	.05
❑ 453 Eric Dickerson	.02	.10
❑ 454 Flipper Anderson	.01	.05
❑ 455 Dave Krieg	.02	.10
❑ 456 Brad Lamb RC	.01	.05
❑ 457 Bart Oates	.01	.05
❑ 458 Guy McIntyre	.01	.05
❑ 459 Stanley Richard	.01	.05
❑ 460 Edgar Bennett	.08	.25
❑ 461 Pat Carter	.01	.05
❑ 462 Eric Allen	.01	.05
❑ 463 William Fuller	.01	.05
❑ 464 James Jones DT	.01	.05
❑ 465 Chester McGlockton	.02	.10
❑ 466 Charles Dimry	.01	.05
❑ 467 Tim Grunhard	.01	.05
❑ 468 Jarvis Williams	.01	.05
❑ 469 Tracy Scroggins	.01	.05
❑ 470 David Klingler	.01	.05
❑ 471 Andre Collins	.01	.05
❑ 472 Erik Williams	.01	.05
❑ 473 Eddie Anderson	.01	.05
❑ 474 Marc Boutte	.01	.05
❑ 475 Joe Montana	.60	1.50
❑ 476 Andre Reed	.02	.10
❑ 477 Lawrence Taylor	.08	.25
❑ 478 Jeff George	.08	.25
❑ 479 Chris Mims	.01	.05
❑ 480 Ken Ruettgers	.01	.05
❑ 481 Roman Phifer	.01	.05
❑ 482 William Thomas	.01	.05
❑ 483 Lamar Lathon	.01	.05
❑ 484 Vinny Testaverde	.02	.10
❑ 485 Mike Kenn	.01	.05
❑ 486 Greg Lewis	.01	.05
❑ 487 Chris Martin	.01	.05
❑ 488 Maurice Hurst	.01	.05
❑ 489 Pat Swilling	.01	.05
❑ 490 Carl Pickens	.02	.10
❑ 491 Tony Smith RB	.01	.05
❑ 492 James Washington	.01	.05
❑ 493 Jeff Hostetler	.02	.10
❑ 494 Jeff Chadwick	.01	.05
❑ 495 Kevin Ross	.01	.05
❑ 496 Jim Ritcher	.01	.05
❑ 497 Jessie Hester	.01	.05
❑ 498 Burt Grossman	.01	.05
❑ 499 Keith Van Horne	.01	.05
❑ 500 Gerald Robinson	.01	.05
❑ P1 Promo Panel	2.00	5.00

1994 Fleer

❑ COMPLETE SET (480)	10.00	20.00
❑ 1 Michael Bankston	.01	.05
❑ 2 Steve Beuerlein	.02	.10
❑ 3 John Booty	.01	.05
❑ 4 Rich Camarillo	.01	.05
❑ 5 Chuck Cecil	.01	.05
❑ 6 Larry Centers	.08	.25
❑ 7 Gary Clark	.02	.10
❑ 8 Garrison Hearst	.08	.25
❑ 9 Eric Hill	.01	.05
❑ 10 Randal Hill	.01	.05
❑ 11 Ronald Moore	.01	.05
❑ 12 Ricky Proehl	.01	.05
❑ 13 Luis Sharpe	.01	.05
❑ 14 Clyde Simmons	.01	.05
❑ 15 Tyronne Stowe	.01	.05
❑ 16 Eric Swann	.02	.10
❑ 17 Aeneas Williams	.01	.05
❑ 18 Darion Conner	.01	.05
❑ 19 Moe Gardner	.01	.05
❑ 20 Jumpy Geathers	.01	.05
❑ 21 Jeff George	.08	.25
❑ 22 Roger Harper	.01	.05
❑ 23 Bobby Hebert	.01	.05
❑ 24 Pierce Holt	.01	.05
❑ 25 D.J. Johnson	.01	.05
❑ 26 Mike Kenn	.01	.05
❑ 27 Lincoln Kennedy	.01	.05
❑ 28 Erric Pegram	.01	.05
❑ 29 Mike Pritchard	.01	.05
❑ 30 Andre Rison	.02	.10
❑ 31 Deion Sanders	.20	.50
❑ 32 Tony Smith RB	.01	.05
❑ 33 Jesse Solomon	.01	.05
❑ 34 Jessie Tuggle	.01	.05
❑ 35 Don Beebe	.01	.05
❑ 36 Cornelius Bennett	.02	.10
❑ 37 Bill Brooks	.01	.05
❑ 38 Kenneth Davis	.01	.05
❑ 39 John Fina	.01	.05
❑ 40 Phil Hansen	.01	.05
❑ 41 Kent Hull	.01	.05
❑ 42 Henry Jones	.01	.05
❑ 43 Jim Kelly	.08	.25
❑ 44 Pete Metzelaars	.01	.05
❑ 45 Marvcus Patton	.01	.05
❑ 46 Andre Reed	.02	.10
❑ 47 Frank Reich	.02	.10
❑ 48 Bruce Smith	.08	.25
❑ 49 Thomas Smith	.01	.05
❑ 50 Darryl Talley	.01	.05
❑ 51 Steve Tasker	.02	.10
❑ 52 Thurman Thomas	.08	.25
❑ 53 Jeff Wright	.01	.05
❑ 54 Neal Anderson	.01	.05
❑ 55 Trace Armstrong	.01	.05
❑ 56 Troy Auzenne	.01	.05
❑ 57 Joe Cain RC	.01	.05
❑ 58 Mark Carrier DB	.01	.05
❑ 59 Curtis Conway	.08	.25
❑ 60 Richard Dent	.02	.10
❑ 61 Shaun Gayle	.01	.05
❑ 62 Andy Heck	.01	.05
❑ 63 Dante Jones	.01	.05
❑ 64 Erik Kramer	.02	.10
❑ 65 Steve McMichael	.02	.10
❑ 66 Terry Obee	.01	.05
❑ 67 Vinson Smith	.01	.05
❑ 68 Alonzo Spellman	.01	.05
❑ 69 Tom Waddle	.01	.05
❑ 70 Donnell Woolford	.01	.05
❑ 71 Tim Worley	.01	.05
❑ 72 Chris Zorich	.01	.05
❑ 73 Mike Brim	.01	.05

❑ 74 John Copeland	.01	.05
❑ 75 Derrick Fenner	.01	.05
❑ 76 James Francis	.01	.05
❑ 77 Harold Green	.01	.05
❑ 78 Rod Jones CB	.01	.05
❑ 79 David Klingler	.01	.05
❑ 80 Bruce Kozerski	.01	.05
❑ 81 Tim Krumrie	.01	.05
❑ 82 Ricardo McDonald	.01	.05
❑ 83 Tim McGee	.01	.05
❑ 84 Tony McGee	.01	.05
❑ 85 Louis Oliver	.01	.05
❑ 86 Carl Pickens	.02	.10
❑ 87 Jeff Query	.01	.05
❑ 88 Daniel Stubbs	.01	.05
❑ 89 Steve Tovar	.01	.05
❑ 90 Alfred Williams	.01	.05
❑ 91 Darryl Williams	.01	.05
❑ 92 Rob Burnett	.01	.05
❑ 93 Mark Carrier WR	.02	.10
❑ 94 Leroy Hoard	.01	.05
❑ 95 Michael Jackson	.02	.10
❑ 96 Mike Johnson	.01	.05
❑ 97 Pepper Johnson	.01	.05
❑ 98 Tony Jones T	.01	.05
❑ 99 Clay Matthews	.01	.05
❑ 100 Eric Metcalf	.02	.10
❑ 101 Stevon Moore	.01	.05
❑ 102 Michael Dean Perry	.02	.10
❑ 103 Anthony Pleasant	.01	.05
❑ 104 Vinny Testaverde	.02	.10
❑ 105 Eric Turner	.01	.05
❑ 106 Tommy Vardell	.01	.05
❑ 107 Troy Aikman	.40	1.00
❑ 108 Larry Brown DB	.01	.05
❑ 109 Dixon Edwards	.01	.05
❑ 110 Charles Haley	.02	.10
❑ 111 Alvin Harper	.02	.10
❑ 112 Michael Irvin	.08	.25
❑ 113 Jim Jeffcoat	.01	.05
❑ 114 Daryl Johnston	.02	.10
❑ 115 Leon Lett	.01	.05
❑ 116 Russell Maryland	.01	.05
❑ 117 Nate Newton	.01	.05
❑ 118 Ken Norton Jr.	.02	.10
❑ 119 Jay Novacek	.02	.10
❑ 120 Darrin Smith	.01	.05
❑ 121 Emmitt Smith	.60	1.50
❑ 122 Kevin Smith	.01	.05
❑ 123 Mark Stepnoski	.01	.05
❑ 124 Tony Tolbert	.01	.05
❑ 125 Erik Williams	.01	.05
❑ 126 Kevin Williams WR	.02	.10
❑ 127 Darren Woodson	.02	.10
❑ 128 Steve Atwater	.01	.05
❑ 129 Rod Bernstine	.01	.05
❑ 130 Ray Crockett	.01	.05
❑ 131 Mike Croel	.01	.05
❑ 132 Robert Delpino	.01	.05
❑ 133 Shane Dronett	.01	.05
❑ 134 Jason Elam	.02	.10
❑ 135 John Elway	.75	2.00
❑ 136 Simon Fletcher	.01	.05
❑ 137 Greg Kragen	.01	.05
❑ 138 Karl Mecklenburg	.01	.05
❑ 139 Glyn Milburn	.02	.10
❑ 140 Anthony Miller	.02	.10
❑ 141 Derek Russell	.01	.05
❑ 142 Shannon Sharpe	.02	.10
❑ 143 Dennis Smith	.01	.05
❑ 144 Dan Williams	.01	.05
❑ 145 Gary Zimmerman	.01	.05
❑ 146 Bennie Blades	.01	.05
❑ 147 Lomas Brown	.01	.05
❑ 148 Bill Fralic	.01	.05
❑ 149 Mel Gray	.01	.05
❑ 150 Willie Green	.01	.05
❑ 151 Jason Hanson	.01	.05
❑ 152 Robert Massey	.01	.05
❑ 153 Ryan McNeil	.01	.05
❑ 154 Scott Mitchell	.02	.10
❑ 155 Derrick Moore	.01	.05
❑ 156 Herman Moore	.08	.25
❑ 157 Brett Perriman	.02	.10
❑ 158 Robert Porcher	.01	.05
❑ 159 Kelvin Pritchett	.01	.05
❑ 160 Barry Sanders	.60	1.50
❑ 161 Tracy Scroggins	.01	.05
❑ 162 Chris Spielman	.02	.10

Card		
❑ 163 Pat Swilling	.01	.05
❑ 164 Edgar Bennett	.08	.25
❑ 165 Robert Brooks	.08	.25
❑ 166 Terrell Buckley	.01	.05
❑ 167 LeRoy Butler	.01	.05
❑ 168 Brett Favre	.75	2.00
❑ 169 Harry Galbreath	.01	.05
❑ 170 Jackie Harris	.01	.05
❑ 171 Johnny Holland	.01	.05
❑ 172 Chris Jacke	.01	.05
❑ 173 George Koonce	.01	.05
❑ 174 Bryce Paup	.02	.10
❑ 175 Ken Ruettgers	.01	.05
❑ 176 Sterling Sharpe	.02	.10
❑ 177 Wayne Simmons	.01	.05
❑ 178 George Teague	.01	.05
❑ 179 Darrell Thompson	.01	.05
❑ 180 Reggie White	.08	.25
❑ 181 Gary Brown	.01	.05
❑ 182 Cody Carlson	.01	.05
❑ 183 Ray Childress	.01	.05
❑ 184 Cris Dishman	.01	.05
❑ 185 Ernest Givins	.02	.10
❑ 186 Haywood Jeffires	.02	.10
❑ 187 Sean Jones	.01	.05
❑ 188 Lamar Lathon	.01	.05
❑ 189 Bruce Matthews	.01	.05
❑ 190 Bubba McDowell	.01	.05
❑ 191 Glenn Montgomery	.01	.05
❑ 192 Greg Montgomery	.01	.05
❑ 193 Warren Moon	.08	.25
❑ 194 Bo Orlando	.01	.05
❑ 195 Marcus Robertson	.01	.05
❑ 196 Eddie Robinson	.01	.05
❑ 197 Webster Slaughter	.01	.05
❑ 198 Lorenzo White	.01	.05
❑ 199 John Baylor	.01	.05
❑ 200 Jason Belser	.01	.05
❑ 201 Tony Bennett	.01	.05
❑ 202 Dean Biasucci	.01	.05
❑ 203 Ray Buchanan	.01	.05
❑ 204 Kerry Cash	.01	.05
❑ 205 Quentin Coryatt	.01	.05
❑ 206 Eugene Daniel	.01	.05
❑ 207 Steve Emtman	.01	.05
❑ 208 Jon Hand	.01	.05
❑ 209 Jim Harbaugh	.08	.25
❑ 210 Jeff Herrod	.01	.05
❑ 211 Anthony Johnson	.02	.10
❑ 212 Roosevelt Potts	.01	.05
❑ 213 Rohn Stark	.01	.05
❑ 214 Will Wolford	.01	.05
❑ 215 Marcus Allen	.08	.25
❑ 216 John Alt	.01	.05
❑ 217 Kimble Anders	.02	.10
❑ 218 J.J. Birden	.01	.05
❑ 219 Dale Carter	.01	.05
❑ 220 Keith Cash	.01	.05
❑ 221 Tony Casillas	.01	.05
❑ 222 Willie Davis	.02	.10
❑ 223 Tim Grunhard	.01	.05
❑ 224 Nick Lowery	.01	.05
❑ 225 Charles Mincy	.01	.05
❑ 226 Joe Montana	.75	2.00
❑ 227 Dan Saleaumua	.01	.05
❑ 228 Tracy Simien	.01	.05
❑ 229 Neil Smith	.02	.10
❑ 230 Derrick Thomas	.08	.25
❑ 231 Eddie Anderson	.01	.05
❑ 232 Tim Brown	.08	.25
❑ 233 Nolan Harrison	.01	.05
❑ 234 Jeff Hostetler	.02	.10
❑ 235 Rocket Ismail	.02	.10
❑ 236 Jeff Jaeger	.01	.05
❑ 237 James Jett	.01	.05
❑ 238 Joe Kelly	.01	.05
❑ 239 Albert Lewis	.01	.05
❑ 240 Terry McDaniel	.01	.05
❑ 241 Chester McGlockton	.01	.05
❑ 242 Winston Moss	.01	.05
❑ 243 Gerald Perry	.01	.05
❑ 244 Greg Robinson	.01	.05
❑ 245 Anthony Smith	.01	.05
❑ 246 Steve Smith	.01	.05
❑ 247 Greg Townsend	.01	.05
❑ 248 Lionel Washington	.01	.05
❑ 249 Steve Wisniewski	.01	.05
❑ 250 Alexander Wright	.01	.05
❑ 251 Flipper Anderson	.01	.05
❑ 252 Jerome Bettis	.20	.50
❑ 253 Marc Boutte	.01	.05
❑ 254 Shane Conlan	.01	.05
❑ 255 Troy Drayton	.01	.05
❑ 256 Henry Ellard	.02	.10
❑ 257 Sean Gilbert	.01	.05
❑ 258 Nate Lewis	.01	.05
❑ 259 Todd Lyght	.01	.05
❑ 260 Chris Miller	.01	.05
❑ 261 Anthony Newman	.01	.05
❑ 262 Roman Phifer	.01	.05
❑ 263 Henry Rolling	.01	.05
❑ 264 T.J.Rubley RC	.01	.05
❑ 265 Jackie Slater	.01	.05
❑ 266 Fred Stokes	.01	.05
❑ 267 Robert Young	.01	.05
❑ 268 Gene Atkins	.01	.05
❑ 269 J.B. Brown	.01	.05
❑ 270 Keith Byars	.01	.05
❑ 271 Marco Coleman	.01	.05
❑ 272 Bryan Cox	.01	.05
❑ 273 Jeff Cross	.01	.05
❑ 274 Irving Fryar	.02	.10
❑ 275 Mark Higgs	.01	.05
❑ 276 Dwight Hollier	.01	.05
❑ 277 Mark Ingram	.01	.05
❑ 278 Keith Jackson	.01	.05
❑ 279 Terry Kirby	.08	.25
❑ 280 Bernie Kosar	.02	.10
❑ 281 Dan Marino	.75	2.00
❑ 282 O.J.McDuffie	.08	.25
❑ 283 Keith Sims	.01	.05
❑ 284 Pete Stoyanovich	.01	.05
❑ 285 Troy Vincent	.01	.05
❑ 286 Richmond Webb	.01	.05
❑ 287 Terry Allen	.02	.10
❑ 288 Anthony Carter	.02	.10
❑ 289 Cris Carter	.20	.50
❑ 290 Jack Del Rio	.01	.05
❑ 291 Chris Doleman	.01	.05
❑ 292 Vencie Glenn	.01	.05
❑ 293 Scottie Graham RC	.02	.10
❑ 294 Chris Hinton	.01	.05
❑ 295 Qadry Ismail	.08	.25
❑ 296 Carlos Jenkins	.01	.05
❑ 297 Steve Jordan	.01	.05
❑ 298 Carl Lee	.01	.05
❑ 299 Randall McDaniel	.02	.10
❑ 300 John Randle	.02	.10
❑ 301 Todd Scott	.01	.05
❑ 302 Robert Smith	.08	.25
❑ 303 Fred Strickland	.01	.05
❑ 304 Henry Thomas	.01	.05
❑ 305 Bruce Armstrong	.01	.05
❑ 306 Harlon Barnett	.01	.05
❑ 307 Drew Bledsoe	.30	.75
❑ 308 Vincent Brown	.01	.05
❑ 309 Ben Coates	.02	.10
❑ 310 Todd Collins	.01	.05
❑ 311 Myron Guyton	.01	.05
❑ 312 Pat Harlow	.01	.05
❑ 313 Maurice Hurst	.01	.05
❑ 314 Leonard Russell	.01	.05
❑ 315 Chris Slade	.01	.05
❑ 316 Michael Timpson	.01	.05
❑ 317 Andre Tippett	.01	.05
❑ 318 Morten Andersen	.01	.05
❑ 319 Derek Brown RBK	.01	.05
❑ 320 Vince Buck	.01	.05
❑ 321 Toi Cook	.01	.05
❑ 322 Quinn Early	.02	.10
❑ 323 Jim Everett	.02	.10
❑ 324 Michael Haynes	.02	.10
❑ 325 Tyrone Hughes	.02	.10
❑ 326 Rickey Jackson	.01	.05
❑ 327 Vaughan Johnson	.01	.05
❑ 328 Eric Martin	.01	.05
❑ 329 Wayne Martin	.01	.05
❑ 330 Sam Mills	.01	.05
❑ 331 Willie Roaf	.01	.05
❑ 332 Irv Smith	.01	.05
❑ 333 Keith Taylor	.01	.05
❑ 334 Renaldo Turnbull	.01	.05
❑ 335 Carlton Bailey	.01	.05
❑ 336 Michael Brooks	.01	.05
❑ 337 Jarrod Bunch	.01	.05
❑ 338 Chris Calloway	.01	.05
❑ 339 Mark Collins	.01	.05
❑ 340 Howard Cross	.01	.05
❑ 341 Stacey Dillard RC	.01	.05
❑ 342 John Elliott	.01	.05
❑ 343 Rodney Hampton	.02	.10
❑ 344 Greg Jackson	.01	.05
❑ 345 Mark Jackson	.01	.05
❑ 346 Dave Meggett	.01	.05
❑ 347 Corey Miller	.01	.05
❑ 348 Mike Sherrard	.01	.05
❑ 349 Phil Simms	.02	.10
❑ 350 Lewis Tillman	.01	.05
❑ 351 Brad Baxter	.01	.05
❑ 352 Kyle Clifton	.01	.05
❑ 353 Boomer Esiason	.02	.10
❑ 354 James Hasty	.01	.05
❑ 355 Bobby Houston	.01	.05
❑ 356 Johnny Johnson	.01	.05
❑ 357 Jeff Lageman	.01	.05
❑ 358 Mo Lewis	.01	.05
❑ 359 Ronnie Lott	.02	.10
❑ 360 Leonard Marshall	.01	.05
❑ 361 Johnny Mitchell	.01	.05
❑ 362 Rob Moore	.02	.10
❑ 363 Eric Thomas	.01	.05
❑ 364 Brian Washington	.01	.05
❑ 365 Marvin Washington	.01	.05
❑ 366 Eric Allen	.01	.05
❑ 367 Fred Barnett	.02	.10
❑ 368 Bubby Brister	.01	.05
❑ 369 Randall Cunningham	.08	.25
❑ 370 Byron Evans	.01	.05
❑ 371 William Fuller	.01	.05
❑ 372 Andy Harmon	.01	.05
❑ 373 Seth Joyner	.01	.05
❑ 374 William Perry	.02	.10
❑ 375 Leonard Renfro	.01	.05
❑ 376 Heath Sherman	.01	.05
❑ 377 Ben Smith	.01	.05
❑ 378 William Thomas	.01	.05
❑ 379 Herschel Walker	.02	.10
❑ 380 Calvin Williams	.02	.10
❑ 381 Chad Brown	.01	.05
❑ 382 Dermontti Dawson	.01	.05
❑ 383 Deon Figures	.01	.05
❑ 384 Barry Foster	.01	.05
❑ 385 Jeff Graham	.01	.05
❑ 386 Eric Green	.01	.05
❑ 387 Kevin Greene	.02	.10
❑ 388 Carlton Haselrig	.01	.05
❑ 389 Levon Kirkland	.01	.05
❑ 390 Carnell Lake	.01	.05
❑ 391 Greg Lloyd	.02	.10
❑ 392 Neil O'Donnell	.08	.25
❑ 393 Darren Perry	.01	.05
❑ 394 Dwight Stone	.01	.05
❑ 395 Leroy Thompson	.01	.05
❑ 396 Rod Woodson	.02	.10
❑ 397 Marion Butts	.01	.05
❑ 398 John Carney	.01	.05
❑ 399 Darren Carrington	.01	.05
❑ 400 Burt Grossman	.01	.05
❑ 401 Courtney Hall	.01	.05
❑ 402 Ronnie Harmon	.01	.05
❑ 403 Stan Humphries	.02	.10
❑ 404 Shawn Jefferson	.01	.05
❑ 405 Vance Johnson	.01	.05
❑ 406 Chris Mims	.01	.05
❑ 407 Leslie O'Neal	.01	.05
❑ 408 Stanley Richard	.01	.05
❑ 409 Junior Seau	.08	.25
❑ 410 Harris Barton	.01	.05
❑ 411 Dennis Brown	.01	.05
❑ 412 Eric Davis	.01	.05
❑ 413 Merton Hanks	.02	.10
❑ 414 John Johnson	.01	.05
❑ 415 Brent Jones	.02	.10
❑ 416 Marc Logan	.01	.05
❑ 417 Tim McDonald	.01	.05
❑ 418 Gary Plummer	.01	.05
❑ 419 Tom Rathman	.01	.05
❑ 420 Jerry Rice	.40	1.00
❑ 421 Bill Romanowski	.01	.05
❑ 422 Jesse Sapolu	.01	.05
❑ 423 Dana Stubblefield	.02	.10
❑ 424 John Taylor	.02	.10
❑ 425 Steve Wallace	.01	.05
❑ 426 Ted Washington	.01	.05
❑ 427 Ricky Watters	.02	.10
❑ 428 Troy Wilson RC	.01	.05
❑ 429 Steve Young	.30	.75

❑ 430 Howard Ballard .01 .05
❑ 431 Michael Bates .01 .05
❑ 432 Robert Blackmon .01 .05
❑ 433 Brian Blades .02 .10
❑ 434 Ferrell Edmunds .01 .05
❑ 435 Carlton Gray .01 .05
❑ 436 Patrick Hunter .01 .05
❑ 437 Cortez Kennedy .02 .10
❑ 438 Kelvin Martin .01 .05
❑ 439 Rick Mirer .08 .25
❑ 440 Nate Odomes .01 .05
❑ 441 Ray Roberts .01 .05
❑ 442 Eugene Robinson .01 .05
❑ 443 Rod Stephens .01 .05
❑ 444 Chris Warren .02 .10
❑ 445 John L. Williams .01 .05
❑ 446 Terry Wooden .01 .05
❑ 447 Marty Carter .01 .05
❑ 448 Reggie Cobb .01 .05
❑ 449 Lawrence Dawsey .01 .05
❑ 450 Santana Dotson .02 .10
❑ 451 Craig Erickson .01 .05
❑ 452 Thomas Everett .01 .05
❑ 453 Paul Gruber .01 .05
❑ 454 Courtney Hawkins .01 .05
❑ 455 Martin Mayhew .01 .05
❑ 456 Hardy Nickerson .02 .10
❑ 457 Ricky Reynolds .01 .05
❑ 458 Vince Workman .01 .05
❑ 459 Reggie Brooks .02 .10
❑ 460 Earnest Byner .01 .05
❑ 461 Andre Collins .01 .05
❑ 462 Brad Edwards .01 .05
❑ 463 Kurt Gouveia .01 .05
❑ 464 Darrell Green .01 .05
❑ 465 Ken Harvey .01 .05
❑ 466 Ethan Horton .01 .05
❑ 467 A.J. Johnson .01 .05
❑ 468 Tim Johnson .01 .05
❑ 469 Jim Lachey .01 .05
❑ 470 Chip Lohmiller .01 .05
❑ 471 Art Monk .02 .10
❑ 472 Sterling Palmer RC .01 .05
❑ 473 Mark Rypien .01 .05
❑ 474 Ricky Sanders .01 .05
❑ 475 Checklist 1-106 .01 .05
❑ 476 Checklist 107-214 .01 .05
❑ 477 Checklist 215-317 .01 .05
❑ 478 Checklist 318-409 .01 .05
❑ 479 Checklist 410-480/Inserts .01 .05
❑ 480 Inserts Checklist .01 .05
❑ P244 Jerome Bettis Promo .40 1.00

1995 Fleer

❑ COMPLETE SET (400) 10.00 25.00
❑ 1 Michael Bankston .02 .10
❑ 2 Larry Centers .07 .20
❑ 3 Gary Clark .02 .10
❑ 4 Eric Hill .02 .10
❑ 5 Seth Joyner .02 .10
❑ 6 Dave Krieg .02 .10
❑ 7 Lorenzo Lynch .02 .10
❑ 8 Jamir Miller .02 .10
❑ 9 Ronald Moore .02 .10
❑ 10 Ricky Proehl .02 .10
❑ 11 Clyde Simmons .02 .10
❑ 12 Eric Swann .07 .20
❑ 13 Aeneas Williams .02 .10
❑ 14 J.J. Birden .02 .10
❑ 15 Chris Doleman .02 .10
❑ 16 Bert Emanuel .10 .30
❑ 17 Jumpy Geathers .02 .10
❑ 18 Jeff George .07 .20
❑ 19 Roger Harper .02 .10
❑ 20 Craig Heyward .07 .20
❑ 21 Pierce Holt .02 .10
❑ 22 D.J. Johnson .02 .10
❑ 23 Terance Mathis .07 .20
❑ 24 Clay Matthews .07 .20
❑ 25 Andre Rison .07 .20
❑ 26 Chuck Smith .02 .10
❑ 27 Jessie Tuggle .02 .10
❑ 28 Cornelius Bennett .07 .20
❑ 29 Bucky Brooks .02 .10
❑ 30 Jeff Burris .02 .10
❑ 31 Russell Copeland .02 .10
❑ 32 Matt Darby .02 .10
❑ 33 Phil Hansen .02 .10
❑ 34 Henry Jones .02 .10
❑ 35 Jim Kelly .10 .30
❑ 36 Mark Maddox RC .02 .10
❑ 37 Bryce Paup .07 .20
❑ 38 Andre Reed .07 .20
❑ 39 Bruce Smith .10 .30
❑ 40 Darryl Talley .02 .10
❑ 41 Dewell Brewer RC .02 .10
❑ 42 Mike Fox .02 .10
❑ 43 Eric Guliford .02 .10
❑ 44 Lamar Lathon .02 .10
❑ 45 Pete Metzelaars .02 .10
❑ 46 Sam Mills .07 .20
❑ 47 Frank Reich .02 .10
❑ 48 Rod Smith DB .07 .20
❑ 49 Jack Trudeau .02 .10
❑ 50 Trace Armstrong .02 .10
❑ 51 Joe Cain .02 .10
❑ 52 Mark Carrier DB .02 .10
❑ 53 Curtis Conway .10 .30
❑ 54 Shaun Gayle .02 .10
❑ 55 Jeff Graham .02 .10
❑ 56 Raymont Harris .02 .10
❑ 57 Erik Kramer .02 .10
❑ 58 Lewis Tillman .02 .10
❑ 59 Tom Waddle .02 .10
❑ 60 Steve Walsh .02 .10
❑ 61 Donnell Woolford .02 .10
❑ 62 Chris Zorich .02 .10
❑ 63 Jeff Blake RC .25 .60
❑ 64 Mike Brim .02 .10
❑ 65 Steve Broussard .02 .10
❑ 66 James Francis .02 .10
❑ 67 Ricardo McDonald .02 .10
❑ 68 Tony McGee .02 .10
❑ 70 Darnay Scott .07 .20
❑ 71 Steve Tovar .02 .10
❑ 72 Dan Wilkinson .07 .20
❑ 73 Alfred Williams .02 .10
❑ 74 Darryl Williams .02 .10
❑ 75 Derrick Alexander WR .10 .30
❑ 76 Randy Baldwin .02 .10
❑ 77 Carl Banks .02 .10
❑ 78 Rob Burnett .02 .10
❑ 79 Steve Everitt .02 .10
❑ 80 Leroy Hoard .02 .10
❑ 81 Michael Jackson .07 .20
❑ 82 Pepper Johnson .02 .10
❑ 83 Tony Jones T .02 .10
❑ 84 Antonio Langham .02 .10
❑ 85 Eric Metcalf .07 .20
❑ 86 Stevon Moore .02 .10
❑ 87 Anthony Pleasant .02 .10
❑ 88 Vinny Testaverde .07 .20
❑ 89 Eric Turner .02 .10
❑ 90 Troy Aikman .40 1.00
❑ 91 Charles Haley .07 .20
❑ 92 Michael Irvin .10 .30
❑ 93 Daryl Johnston .07 .20
❑ 94 Robert Jones .02 .10
❑ 95 Leon Lett .02 .10
❑ 96 Russell Maryland .02 .10
❑ 97 Nate Newton .07 .20
❑ 98 Jay Novacek .07 .20
❑ 99 Darrin Smith .02 .10
❑ 100 Emmitt Smith .60 1.50
❑ 101 Kevin Smith .02 .10
❑ 102 Erik Williams .02 .10
❑ 103 Kevin Williams WR .07 .20
❑ 104 Darren Woodson .07 .20
❑ 105 Elijah Alexander .02 .10
❑ 106 Steve Atwater .02 .10
❑ 107 Ray Crockett .02 .10
❑ 108 Shane Dronett .02 .10
❑ 109 Jason Elam .07 .20
❑ 110 John Elway .75 2.00
❑ 111 Simon Fletcher .02 .10
❑ 112 Glyn Milburn .02 .10
❑ 113 Anthony Miller .07 .20
❑ 114 Michael Dean Perry .02 .10
❑ 115 Mike Pritchard .02 .10
❑ 116 Derek Russell .02 .10
❑ 117 Leonard Russell .02 .10
❑ 118 Shannon Sharpe .07 .20
❑ 119 Gary Zimmerman .02 .10
❑ 120 Bennie Blades .02 .10
❑ 121 Lomas Brown .02 .10
❑ 122 Willie Clay .02 .10
❑ 123 Mike Johnson .02 .10
❑ 124 Robert Massey .02 .10
❑ 125 Scott Mitchell .07 .20
❑ 126 Herman Moore .10 .30
❑ 127 Brett Perriman .07 .20
❑ 128 Robert Porcher .02 .10
❑ 129 Barry Sanders .60 1.50
❑ 130 Chris Spielman .07 .20
❑ 131 Henry Thomas .02 .10
❑ 132 Edgar Bennett .07 .20
❑ 134 LeRoy Butler .02 .10
❑ 135 Brett Favre .75 2.00
❑ 136 Sean Jones .02 .10
❑ 137 John Jurkovic .02 .10
❑ 138 George Koonce .02 .10
❑ 139 Wayne Simmons .02 .10
❑ 140 George Teague .02 .10
❑ 141 Reggie White .10 .30
❑ 142 Micheal Barrow .02 .10
❑ 143 Gary Brown .02 .10
❑ 144 Cody Carlson .02 .10
❑ 145 Ray Childress .02 .10
❑ 146 Cris Dishman .02 .10
❑ 147 Ernest Givins .02 .10
❑ 148 Mel Gray .02 .10
❑ 149 Darryll Lewis .02 .10
❑ 150 Bruce Matthews .02 .10
❑ 151 Marcus Robertson .02 .10
❑ 152 Webster Slaughter .02 .10
❑ 153 Al Smith .02 .10
❑ 154 Mark Stepnoski .02 .10
❑ 155 Trev Alberts .02 .10
❑ 156 Flipper Anderson .02 .10
❑ 157 Jason Belser .02 .10
❑ 158 Tony Bennett .02 .10
❑ 159 Ray Buchanan .02 .10
❑ 160 Quentin Coryatt .07 .20
❑ 161 Sean Dawkins .07 .20
❑ 162 Steve Emtman .02 .10
❑ 163 Marshall Faulk .50 1.25
❑ 164 Stephen Grant RC .02 .10
❑ 165 Jim Harbaugh .07 .20
❑ 166 Jeff Herrod .02 .10
❑ 167 Tony Siragusa .02 .10
❑ 168 Steve Beuerlein .07 .20
❑ 169 Darren Carrington .02 .10
❑ 170 Reggie Cobb .02 .10
❑ 171 Kelvin Martin .02 .10
❑ 172 Kelvin Pritchett .02 .10
❑ 173 Joel Smeenge .02 .10
❑ 174 James Williams LB .02 .10
❑ 175 Marcus Allen .10 .30
❑ 176 Kimble Anders .07 .20
❑ 177 Dale Carter .07 .20
❑ 178 Mark Collins .02 .10
❑ 179 Willie Davis .07 .20
❑ 180 Lake Dawson .07 .20
❑ 181 Greg Hill .07 .20
❑ 182 Darren Mickell .02 .10
❑ 183 Joe Montana .75 2.00
❑ 184 Tracy Simien .02 .10
❑ 185 Neil Smith .07 .20
❑ 186 William White .02 .10
❑ 187 Greg Biekert .02 .10
❑ 188 Tim Brown .10 .30
❑ 189 Rob Fredrickson .02 .10
❑ 190 Andrew Glover RC .02 .10
❑ 191 Nolan Harrison .02 .10
❑ 192 Jeff Hostetler .07 .20
❑ 193 Rocket Ismail .07 .20
❑ 194 Terry McDaniel .02 .10
❑ 195 Chester McGlockton .07 .20
❑ 196 Winston Moss .02 .10
❑ 197 Anthony Smith .02 .10
❑ 198 Harvey Williams .02 .10
❑ 199 Steve Wisniewski .02 .10
❑ 200 Johnny Bailey .02 .10
❑ 201 Jerome Bettis .10 .30

❑ 202 Isaac Bruce	.20	.50
❑ 203 Shane Conlan	.02	.10
❑ 204 Troy Drayton	.02	.10
❑ 205 Sean Gilbert	.07	.20
❑ 206 Jessie Hester	.02	.10
❑ 207 Jimmie Jones	.02	.10
❑ 208 Todd Lyght	.02	.10
❑ 209 Chris Miller	.02	.10
❑ 210 Roman Phifer	.02	.10
❑ 211 Marquez Pope	.02	.10
❑ 212 Robert Young	.02	.10
❑ 213 Gene Atkins	.02	.10
❑ 214 Aubrey Beavers	.02	.10
❑ 215 Tim Bowens	.02	.10
❑ 216 Bryan Cox	.02	.10
❑ 217 Jeff Cross	.02	.10
❑ 218 Irving Fryar	.07	.20
❑ 219 Eric Green	.02	.10
❑ 220 Mark Ingram	.02	.10
❑ 221 Terry Kirby	.07	.20
❑ 222 Dan Marino	.75	2.00
❑ 223 O.J. McDuffie	.10	.30
❑ 224 Bernie Parmalee	.07	.20
❑ 225 Keith Sims	.02	.10
❑ 226 Irving Spikes	.07	.20
❑ 227 Michael Stewart	.02	.10
❑ 228 Troy Vincent	.02	.10
❑ 229 Richmond Webb	.02	.10
❑ 230 Terry Allen	.07	.20
❑ 231 Cris Carter	.10	.30
❑ 232 Jack Del Rio	.02	.10
❑ 233 Vencie Glenn	.02	.10
❑ 234 Qadry Ismail	.07	.20
❑ 235 Carlos Jenkins	.02	.10
❑ 236 Ed McDaniel	.02	.10
❑ 237 Randall McDaniel	.05	.15
❑ 238 Warren Moon	.07	.20
❑ 239 Anthony Parker	.02	.10
❑ 240 John Randle	.07	.20
❑ 241 Jake Reed	.07	.20
❑ 242 Fuad Reveiz	.02	.10
❑ 243 Broderick Thomas	.02	.10
❑ 244 Dewayne Washington	.07	.20
❑ 245 Bruce Armstrong	.02	.10
❑ 246 Drew Bledsoe	.25	.60
❑ 247 Vincent Brisby	.02	.10
❑ 248 Vincent Brown	.02	.10
❑ 249 Marion Butts	.02	.10
❑ 250 Ben Coates	.07	.20
❑ 251 Tim Goad	.02	.10
❑ 252 Myron Guyton	.02	.10
❑ 253 Maurice Hurst	.02	.10
❑ 254 Mike Jones	.02	.10
❑ 255 Willie McGinest	.07	.20
❑ 256 Dave Meggett	.02	.10
❑ 257 Ricky Reynolds	.02	.10
❑ 258 Chris Slade	.07	.20
❑ 259 Michael Timpson	.02	.10
❑ 260 Mario Bates	.07	.20
❑ 261 Derek Brown RBK	.02	.10
❑ 262 Darion Conner	.02	.10
❑ 263 Quinn Early	.07	.20
❑ 264 Jim Everett	.02	.10
❑ 265 Michael Haynes	.07	.20
❑ 266 Tyrone Hughes	.07	.20
❑ 267 Joe Johnson	.02	.10
❑ 268 Wayne Martin	.02	.10
❑ 269 Willie Roaf	.02	.10
❑ 270 Irv Smith	.02	.10
❑ 271 Jimmy Spencer	.02	.10
❑ 272 Winfred Tubbs	.02	.10
❑ 273 Renaldo Turnbull	.02	.10
❑ 274 Michael Brooks	.02	.10
❑ 275 Dave Brown	.07	.20
❑ 276 Chris Calloway	.02	.10
❑ 277 Jesse Campbell	.02	.10
❑ 278 Howard Cross	.02	.10
❑ 279 John Elliott	.02	.10
❑ 280 Keith Hamilton	.02	.10
❑ 281 Rodney Hampton	.07	.20
❑ 282 Thomas Lewis	.07	.20
❑ 283 Thomas Randolph	.02	.10
❑ 284 Mike Sherrard	.02	.10
❑ 285 Michael Strahan	.10	.30
❑ 286 Brad Baxter	.02	.10
❑ 287 Tony Casillas	.02	.10
❑ 288 Kyle Clifton	.02	.10
❑ 289 Boomer Esiason	.07	.20
❑ 290 Aaron Glenn	.02	.10
❑ 291 Bobby Houston	.02	.10
❑ 292 Johnny Johnson	.02	.10
❑ 293 Jeff Lageman	.02	.10
❑ 294 Mo Lewis	.02	.10
❑ 295 Johnny Mitchell	.02	.10
❑ 296 Rob Moore	.07	.20
❑ 297 Marcus Turner	.02	.10
❑ 298 Marvin Washington	.02	.10
❑ 299 Eric Allen	.02	.10
❑ 300 Fred Barnett	.07	.20
❑ 301 Randall Cunningham	.10	.30
❑ 302 Byron Evans	.02	.10
❑ 303 William Fuller	.02	.10
❑ 304 Charlie Garner	.10	.30
❑ 305 Andy Harmon	.02	.10
❑ 306 Greg Jackson	.02	.10
❑ 307 Bill Romanowski	.02	.10
❑ 308 William Thomas	.02	.10
❑ 309 Herschel Walker	.07	.20
❑ 310 Calvin Williams	.07	.20
❑ 311 Michael Zordich	.02	.10
❑ 312 Chad Brown	.07	.20
❑ 313 Dermontti Dawson	.07	.20
❑ 314 Barry Foster	.07	.20
❑ 315 Kevin Greene	.07	.20
❑ 316 Charles Johnson	.07	.20
❑ 317 Levon Kirkland	.02	.10
❑ 318 Carnell Lake	.02	.10
❑ 319 Greg Lloyd	.07	.20
❑ 320 Byron Bam Morris	.02	.10
❑ 321 Neil O'Donnell	.07	.20
❑ 322 Darren Perry	.02	.10
❑ 323 Ray Seals	.02	.10
❑ 324 John L. Williams	.02	.10
❑ 325 Rod Woodson	.07	.20
❑ 326 John Carney	.02	.10
❑ 327 Andre Coleman	.02	.10
❑ 328 Courtney Hall	.02	.10
❑ 329 Ronnie Harmon	.02	.10
❑ 330 Dwayne Harper	.02	.10
❑ 331 Stan Humphries	.07	.20
❑ 332 Shawn Jefferson	.02	.10
❑ 333 Tony Martin	.07	.20
❑ 334 Natrone Means	.07	.20
❑ 335 Chris Mims	.02	.10
❑ 336 Leslie O'Neal	.07	.20
❑ 337 Alfred Pupunu RC	.02	.10
❑ 338 Junior Seau	.10	.30
❑ 339 Mark Seay	.07	.20
❑ 340 Eric Davis	.02	.10
❑ 341 William Floyd	.07	.20
❑ 342 Merton Hanks	.02	.10
❑ 343 Rickey Jackson	.02	.10
❑ 344 Brent Jones	.02	.10
❑ 345 Tim McDonald	.02	.10
❑ 346 Ken Norton Jr.	.07	.20
❑ 347 Gary Plummer	.02	.10
❑ 348 Jerry Rice	.40	1.00
❑ 349 Deion Sanders	.15	.40
❑ 350 Jesse Sapolu	.02	.10
❑ 351 Dana Stubblefield	.07	.20
❑ 352 John Taylor	.02	.10
❑ 353 Steve Wallace	.02	.10
❑ 354 Ricky Watters	.07	.20
❑ 355 Lee Woodall	.02	.10
❑ 356 Bryant Young	.07	.20
❑ 357 Steve Young	.30	.75
❑ 358 Sam Adams	.02	.10
❑ 359 Howard Ballard	.02	.10
❑ 360 Robert Blackmon	.02	.10
❑ 361 Brian Blades	.07	.20
❑ 362 Carlton Gray	.02	.10
❑ 363 Cortez Kennedy	.07	.20
❑ 364 Rick Mirer	.07	.20
❑ 365 Eugene Robinson	.02	.10
❑ 366 Chris Warren	.07	.20
❑ 367 Terry Wooden	.02	.10
❑ 368 Brad Culpepper	.02	.10
❑ 369 Lawrence Dawsey	.02	.10
❑ 370 Trent Dilfer	.10	.30
❑ 371 Santana Dotson	.02	.10
❑ 372 Craig Erickson	.02	.10
❑ 373 Thomas Everett	.02	.10
❑ 374 Paul Gruber	.02	.10
❑ 375 Alvin Harper	.02	.10
❑ 376 Jackie Harris	.02	.10
❑ 377 Courtney Hawkins	.02	.10
❑ 378 Martin Mayhew	.02	.10
❑ 379 Hardy Nickerson	.02	.10
❑ 380 Errict Rhett	.07	.20
❑ 381 Charles Wilson	.02	.10
❑ 382 Reggie Brooks	.07	.20
❑ 383 Tom Carter	.02	.10
❑ 384 Andre Collins	.02	.10
❑ 385 Henry Ellard	.07	.20
❑ 386 Ricky Ervins	.02	.10
❑ 387 Darrell Green	.02	.10
❑ 388 Ken Harvey	.02	.10
❑ 389 Brian Mitchell	.02	.10
❑ 390 Stanley Richard	.02	.10
❑ 391 Heath Shuler	.07	.20
❑ 392 Rod Stephens	.02	.10
❑ 393 Tyronne Stowe	.02	.10
❑ 394 Tydus Winans	.02	.10
❑ 395 Tony Woods	.02	.10
❑ 396 Checklist	.02	.10
❑ 397 Checklist	.02	.10
❑ 398 Checklist	.02	.10
❑ 399 Checklist	.02	.10
❑ 400 Checklist	.02	.10

1996 Fleer

❑ COMPLETE SET (200)	7.50	20.00
❑ 1 Garrison Hearst	.07	.20
❑ 2 Rob Moore	.07	.20
❑ 3 Frank Sanders	.07	.20
❑ 4 Eric Swann	.02	.10
❑ 5 Aeneas Williams	.02	.10
❑ 6 Jeff George	.07	.20
❑ 7 Craig Heyward	.02	.10
❑ 8 Terance Mathis	.02	.10
❑ 9 Eric Metcalf	.02	.10
❑ 10 Michael Jackson	.07	.20
❑ 11 Andre Rison	.07	.20
❑ 12 Vinny Testaverde	.07	.20
❑ 13 Eric Turner	.02	.10
❑ 14 Darick Holmes	.02	.10
❑ 15 Jim Kelly	.10	.30
❑ 16 Bryce Paup	.02	.10
❑ 17 Bruce Smith	.07	.20
❑ 18 Thurman Thomas	.10	.30
❑ 19 Kerry Collins	.10	.30
❑ 20 Lamar Lathon	.02	.10
❑ 21 Derrick Moore	.02	.10
❑ 22 Tyrone Poole	.02	.10
❑ 23 Curtis Conway	.10	.30
❑ 24 Bryan Cox	.02	.10
❑ 25 Erik Kramer	.02	.10
❑ 26 Rashaan Salaam	.07	.20
❑ 27 Jeff Blake	.10	.30
❑ 28 Ki-Jana Carter	.07	.20
❑ 29 Carl Pickens	.07	.20
❑ 30 Darnay Scott	.07	.20
❑ 31 Troy Aikman	.30	.75
❑ 32 Charles Haley	.07	.20
❑ 33 Michael Irvin	.10	.30
❑ 34 Daryl Johnston	.07	.20
❑ 35 Jay Novacek	.02	.10
❑ 36 Deion Sanders	.15	.40
❑ 37 Emmitt Smith	.50	1.25
❑ 38 Steve Atwater	.02	.10
❑ 39 Terrell Davis	.25	.60
❑ 40 John Elway	.60	1.50
❑ 41 Anthony Miller	.07	.20
❑ 42 Shannon Sharpe	.07	.20
❑ 43 Scott Mitchell	.07	.20
❑ 44 Herman Moore	.07	.20
❑ 45 Johnnie Morton	.07	.20
❑ 46 Brett Perriman	.02	.10
❑ 47 Barry Sanders	.50	1.25
❑ 48 Edgar Bennett	.07	.20
❑ 49 Robert Brooks	.10	.30
❑ 50 Mark Chmura	.07	.20
❑ 51 Brett Favre	.60	1.50
❑ 52 Reggie White	.10	.30

Card		
❑ 53 Mel Gray	.02	.10
❑ 54 Steve McNair	.25	.60
❑ 55 Chris Sanders	.07	.20
❑ 56 Rodney Thomas	.02	.10
❑ 57 Quentin Coryatt	.02	.10
❑ 58 Sean Dawkins	.02	.10
❑ 59 Ken Dilger	.07	.20
❑ 60 Marshall Faulk	.15	.40
❑ 61 Jim Harbaugh	.07	.20
❑ 62 Tony Boselli	.02	.10
❑ 63 Mark Brunell	.20	.50
❑ 64 Natrone Means	.07	.20
❑ 65 James O.Stewart	.07	.20
❑ 66 Marcus Allen	.10	.30
❑ 67 Steve Bono	.02	.10
❑ 68 Neil Smith	.07	.20
❑ 69 Derrick Thomas	.10	.30
❑ 70 Tamarick Vanover	.07	.20
❑ 71 Fred Barnett	.02	.10
❑ 72 Eric Green	.02	.10
❑ 73 Dan Marino	.60	1.50
❑ 74 O.J. McDuffie	.07	.20
❑ 75 Bernie Parmalee	.02	.10
❑ 76 Cris Carter	.10	.30
❑ 77 Qadry Ismail	.07	.20
❑ 78 Warren Moon	.07	.20
❑ 79 Jake Reed	.07	.20
❑ 80 Robert Smith	.07	.20
❑ 81 Drew Bledsoe	.20	.50
❑ 82 Vincent Brisby	.02	.10
❑ 83 Ben Coates	.07	.20
❑ 84 Curtis Martin	.25	.60
❑ 85 Dave Meggett	.02	.10
❑ 86 Mario Bates	.07	.20
❑ 87 Jim Everett	.02	.10
❑ 88 Michael Haynes	.02	.10
❑ 89 Renaldo Turnbull	.02	.10
❑ 90 Dave Brown	.02	.10
❑ 91 Rodney Hampton	.07	.20
❑ 92 Thomas Lewis	.02	.10
❑ 93 Tyrone Wheatley	.07	.20
❑ 94 Kyle Brady	.02	.10
❑ 95 Hugh Douglas	.07	.20
❑ 96 Aaron Glenn	.02	.10
❑ 97 Jeff Graham	.02	.10
❑ 98 Adrian Murrell	.07	.20
❑ 99 Neil O'Donnell	.07	.20
❑ 100 Tim Brown	.10	.30
❑ 101 Jeff Hostetler	.02	.10
❑ 102 Napoleon Kaufman	.10	.30
❑ 103 Chester McGlockton	.02	.10
❑ 104 Harvey Williams	.02	.10
❑ 105 William Fuller	.02	.10
❑ 106 Charlie Garner	.07	.20
❑ 107 Ricky Watters	.07	.20
❑ 108 Calvin Williams	.02	.10
❑ 109 Jerome Bettis	.10	.30
❑ 110 Greg Lloyd	.07	.20
❑ 111 Byron Bam Morris	.02	.10
❑ 112 Kordell Stewart	.10	.30
❑ 113 Yancey Thigpen	.07	.20
❑ 114 Rod Woodson	.07	.20
❑ 115 Isaac Bruce	.10	.30
❑ 116 Troy Drayton	.02	.10
❑ 117 Leslie O'Neal	.02	.10
❑ 118 Steve Walsh	.02	.10
❑ 119 Marco Coleman	.02	.10
❑ 120 Aaron Hayden	.02	.10
❑ 121 Stan Humphries	.07	.20
❑ 122 Junior Seau	.10	.30
❑ 123 William Floyd	.07	.20
❑ 124 Brent Jones	.02	.10
❑ 125 Ken Norton	.02	.10
❑ 126 Jerry Rice	.30	.75
❑ 127 J.J. Stokes	.10	.30
❑ 128 Steve Young	.25	.60
❑ 129 Brian Blades	.02	.10
❑ 130 Joey Galloway	.10	.30
❑ 131 Rick Mirer	.07	.20
❑ 132 Chris Warren	.07	.20
❑ 133 Trent Dilfer	.10	.30
❑ 134 Alvin Harper	.02	.10
❑ 135 Hardy Nickerson	.02	.10
❑ 136 Errict Rhett	.07	.20
❑ 137 Terry Allen	.07	.20
❑ 138 Henry Ellard	.02	.10
❑ 139 Heath Shuler	.07	.20
❑ 140 Michael Westbrook	.10	.30
❑ 141 Karim Abdul-Jabbar RC	.10	.30
❑ 142 Mike Alstott RC	.40	1.00
❑ 143 Marco Battaglia RC	.02	.10
❑ 144 Tim Biakabutuka RC	.10	.30
❑ 145 Tony Brackens RC	.10	.30
❑ 146 Duane Clemons RC	.02	.10
❑ 147 Ernie Conwell RC	.02	.10
❑ 148 Chris Darkins RC	.02	.10
❑ 149 Stephen Davis RC	.60	1.50
❑ 150 Brian Dawkins RC	.50	1.25
❑ 151 Rickey Dudley RC	.10	.30
❑ 152 Jason Dunn RC	.07	.20
❑ 153 Bobby Engram RC	.10	.30
❑ 154 Daryl Gardener RC	.02	.10
❑ 155 Eddie George RC	.50	1.25
❑ 156 Terry Glenn RC	.40	1.00
❑ 157 Kevin Hardy RC	.10	.30
❑ 158 Walt Harris RC	.02	.10
❑ 159 Marvin Harrison RC	1.00	2.50
❑ 160 Bobby Hoying RC	.10	.30
❑ 161 Keyshawn Johnson RC	.40	1.00
❑ 162 Cedric Jones RC	.02	.10
❑ 163 Marcus Jones RC	.02	.10
❑ 164 Eddie Kennison RC	.10	.30
❑ 165 Ray Lewis RC	1.00	2.50
❑ 166 Derrick Mayes RC	.10	.30
❑ 167 Leeland McElroy RC	.07	.20
❑ 168 Johnny McWilliams RC	.07	.20
❑ 169 John Mobley RC	.02	.10
❑ 170 Alex Molden RC	.02	.10
❑ 171 Eric Moulds RC	.50	1.25
❑ 172 Muhsin Muhammad RC UER	.40	1.00
❑ 173 Jonathan Ogden RC	.10	.30
❑ 174 Lawrence Phillips RC	.10	.30
❑ 175 Stanley Pritchett RC	.07	.20
❑ 176 Simeon Rice RC	.30	.75
❑ 177 Bryan Still RC	.07	.20
❑ 178 Amani Toomer RC	.40	1.00
❑ 179 Regan Upshaw RC	.02	.10
❑ 180 Alex Van Dyke RC	.07	.20
❑ 181 Barry Sanders PFW	.25	.60
❑ 182 Marcus Allen PFW	.10	.30
❑ 183 Bryce Paup PFW	.02	.10
❑ 184 Jerry Rice PFW	.15	.40
❑ 185 D.Howard/B.Christian PFW	.07	.20
❑ 186 Leon Lett PFW	.02	.10
❑ 187 Brett Favre PFW	.30	.75
❑ 188 G.Lloyd/D.Thomas PFW	.02	.10
❑ 189 Jeff Blake PFW	.07	.20
❑ 190 Emmitt Smith PFW	.25	.60
❑ 191 J.Elway/J.Hostetler PFW	.15	.40
❑ 192 Chiefs PFW	.02	.10
❑ 193 Marshall Faulk PFW	.10	.30
❑ 194 T.Aikman/S.Young PFW	.15	.40
❑ 195 Dan Marino PFW	.30	.75
❑ 196 Donta Jones PFW	.02	.10
❑ 197 Jim Kelly PFW	.10	.30
❑ 198 Checklist	.02	.10
❑ 199 Checklist	.02	.10
❑ 200 Checklist	.02	.10
❑ P1 Promo Sheet/WFloyd/TDil/Favre	1.50	4.00

1997 Fleer

Card		
❑ COMPLETE SET (450)	15.00	40.00
❑ 1 Mark Brunell	.40	1.00
❑ 2 Andre Reed	.20	.50
❑ 3 Darrell Green	.20	.50
❑ 4 Mario Bates	.10	.30
❑ 5 Eddie George	.30	.75
❑ 6 Cris Carter	.30	.75
❑ 7 Terrell Owens	.40	1.00
❑ 8 Bill Romanowski	.10	.30
❑ 9 Isaac Bruce	.30	.75
❑ 10 Eric Curry	.10	.30
❑ 11 Danny Kanell	.10	.30
❑ 12 Ki-Jana Carter	.10	.30
❑ 13 Antonio Freeman	.30	.75
❑ 14 Ricky Watters	.20	.50
❑ 15 Ty Law	.20	.50
❑ 16 Alonzo Spellman	.10	.30
❑ 17 Kordell Stewart	.30	.75
❑ 18 Jerry Rice	.60	1.50
❑ 19 Derrick Alexander WR	.20	.50
❑ 20 Barry Sanders	1.00	2.50
❑ 21 Keyshawn Johnson	.30	.75
❑ 22 Emmitt Smith	1.00	2.50
❑ 23 Ricky Proehl	.10	.30
❑ 24 Daryl Gardener	.10	.30
❑ 25 Dan Saleaumua	.10	.30
❑ 26 Kevin Greene	.20	.50
❑ 27 Junior Seau	.30	.75
❑ 28 Randall McDaniel	.10	.30
❑ 29 Marshall Faulk	.40	1.00
❑ 30 Lorenzo Lynch	.10	.30
❑ 31 Terance Mathis	.20	.50
❑ 32 Warren Sapp	.20	.50
❑ 33 Chris Sanders	.10	.30
❑ 34 Tom Carter	.10	.30
❑ 35 Aeneas Williams	.10	.30
❑ 36 Lawrence Phillips	.10	.30
❑ 37 John Elway	1.25	3.00
❑ 38 Stanley Richard	.10	.30
❑ 39 Darryl Williams	.10	.30
❑ 40 Phillippi Sparks	.10	.30
❑ 41 Tedy Bruschi	.60	1.50
❑ 42 Merton Hanks	.10	.30
❑ 43 Ray Lewis	.50	1.25
❑ 44 Erik Williams	.10	.30
❑ 45 Jason Gildon	.10	.30
❑ 46 George Koonce	.10	.30
❑ 47 Louis Oliver	.10	.30
❑ 48 Muhsin Muhammad	.20	.50
❑ 49 Daryl Hobbs	.10	.30
❑ 50 Terry Glenn	.30	.75
❑ 51 Marvin Harrison	.30	.75
❑ 52 Brian Dawkins	.30	.75
❑ 53 Dale Carter	.10	.30
❑ 54 Alex Molden	.10	.30
❑ 55 Raymont Harris	.10	.30
❑ 56 Jeff Burris	.10	.30
❑ 57 Don Beebe	.10	.30
❑ 58 Jamir Miller	.10	.30
❑ 59 Carl Pickens	.20	.50
❑ 60 Antonio London	.10	.30
❑ 61 Courtney Hall	.10	.30
❑ 62 Derrick Brooks	.30	.75
❑ 63 Chris Boniol	.10	.30
❑ 64 Jeff Lageman	.10	.30
❑ 65 Roy Barker	.10	.30
❑ 66 Devin Bush	.10	.30
❑ 67 Aaron Glenn	.10	.30
❑ 68 Wayne Simmons	.10	.30
❑ 69 Steve Atwater	.10	.30
❑ 70 Jimmie Jones	.10	.30
❑ 71 Mark Carrier WR	.10	.30
❑ 72 Chris Chandler	.20	.50
❑ 73 Andy Harmon	.10	.30
❑ 74 John Friesz	.10	.30
❑ 75 Karim Abdul-Jabbar	.20	.50
❑ 76 Levon Kirkland	.10	.30
❑ 77 Torrance Small	.10	.30
❑ 78 Harvey Williams	.10	.30
❑ 79 Chris Calloway	.10	.30
❑ 80 Vinny Testaverde	.20	.50
❑ 81 Bryant Young	.10	.30
❑ 82 Ray Buchanan	.10	.30
❑ 83 Robert Smith	.20	.50
❑ 84 Robert Brooks	.20	.50
❑ 85 Ray Crockett	.10	.30
❑ 86 Bennie Blades	.10	.30
❑ 87 Mark Carrier DB	.10	.30
❑ 88 Mike Tomczak	.10	.30
❑ 89 Darick Holmes	.10	.30
❑ 90 Drew Bledsoe	.40	1.00
❑ 91 Darren Woodson	.10	.30
❑ 92 Dan Wilkinson	.10	.30
❑ 93 Charles Way	.10	.30
❑ 94 Ray Farmer	.10	.30
❑ 95 Marcus Allen	.30	.75
❑ 96 Marco Coleman	.10	.30
❑ 97 Zach Thomas	.30	.75
❑ 98 Wesley Walls	.20	.50
❑ 99 Frank Wycheck	.10	.30
❑ 100 Troy Aikman	.60	1.50
❑ 101 Clyde Simmons	.10	.30
❑ 102 Courtney Hawkins	.10	.30

❑ 103 Chuck Smith .10 .30
❑ 104 Neil O'Donnell .20 .50
❑ 105 Kevin Carter .10 .30
❑ 106 Chris Slade .10 .30
❑ 107 Jessie Armstead .10 .30
❑ 108 Sean Dawkins .10 .30
❑ 109 Robert Blackmon .10 .30
❑ 110 Kevin Smith .10 .30
❑ 111 Lonnie Johnson .10 .30
❑ 112 Craig Newsome .10 .30
❑ 113 Jonathan Ogden .10 .30
❑ 114 Chris Zorich .10 .30
❑ 115 Tim Brown .30 .75
❑ 116 Fred Barnett .10 .30
❑ 117 Michael Haynes .10 .30
❑ 118 Eric Hill .10 .30
❑ 119 Ronnie Harmon .10 .30
❑ 120 Sean Gilbert .10 .30
❑ 121 Derrick Alexander DE .10 .30
❑ 122 Derrick Thomas .30 .75
❑ 123 Tyrone Wheatley .20 .50
❑ 124 Cortez Kennedy .10 .30
❑ 125 Jeff George .20 .50
❑ 126 Chad Cota .10 .30
❑ 127 Gary Zimmerman .10 .30
❑ 128 Johnnie Morton .20 .50
❑ 129 Chad Brown .10 .30
❑ 130 Marvcus Patton .10 .30
❑ 131 James O.Stewart .20 .50
❑ 132 Terry Kirby .20 .50
❑ 133 Chris Mims .10 .30
❑ 134 William Thomas .10 .30
❑ 135 Steve Tasker .10 .30
❑ 136 Jason Belser .10 .30
❑ 137 Bryan Cox .10 .30
❑ 138 Jessie Tuggle .10 .30
❑ 139 Ashley Ambrose .10 .30
❑ 140 Mark Chmura .20 .50
❑ 141 Jeff Hostetler .10 .30
❑ 142 Rich Owens .10 .30
❑ 143 Willie Davis .10 .30
❑ 144 Hardy Nickerson .10 .30
❑ 145 Curtis Martin .40 1.00
❑ 146 Ken Norton .10 .30
❑ 147 Victor Green .10 .30
❑ 148 Anthony Miller .10 .30
❑ 149 John Kasay .10 .30
❑ 150 O.J. McDuffie .20 .50
❑ 151 Darren Perry .10 .30
❑ 152 Luther Elliss .10 .30
❑ 153 Greg Hill .10 .30
❑ 154 John Randle .20 .50
❑ 155 Stephen Grant .10 .30
❑ 156 Leon Lett .10 .30
❑ 157 Darrien Gordon .10 .30
❑ 158 Ray Zellars .10 .30
❑ 159 Michael Jackson .20 .50
❑ 160 Leslie O'Neal .10 .30
❑ 161 Bruce Smith .20 .50
❑ 162 Santana Dotson .10 .30
❑ 163 Bobby Hebert .10 .30
❑ 164 Keith Hamilton .10 .30
❑ 165 Tony Boselli .10 .30
❑ 166 Alfred Williams .10 .30
❑ 167 Ty Detmer .20 .50
❑ 168 Chester McGlockton .10 .30
❑ 169 William Floyd .20 .50
❑ 170 Bruce Matthews .10 .30
❑ 171 Simeon Rice .20 .50
❑ 172 Scott Mitchell .20 .50
❑ 173 Ricardo McDonald .10 .30
❑ 174 Tyrone Poole .10 .30
❑ 175 Greg Lloyd .10 .30
❑ 176 Bruce Armstrong .10 .30
❑ 177 Erik Kramer .10 .30
❑ 178 Kimble Anders .20 .50
❑ 179 Lamar Smith .30 .75
❑ 180 Tony Tolbert .10 .30
❑ 181 Joe Aska .10 .30
❑ 182 Eric Allen .10 .30
❑ 183 Eric Turner .10 .30
❑ 184 Brad Johnson .30 .75
❑ 185 Tony Martin .20 .50
❑ 186 Mike Mamula .10 .30
❑ 187 Irving Spikes .10 .30
❑ 188 Keith Jackson .10 .30
❑ 189 Carlton Bailey .10 .30
❑ 190 Tyrone Braxton .10 .30
❑ 191 Chad Bratzke .10 .30
❑ 192 Adrian Murrell .20 .50
❑ 193 Roman Phifer .10 .30
❑ 194 Todd Collins .10 .30
❑ 195 Chris Warren .20 .50
❑ 196 Kevin Hardy .10 .30
❑ 197 Rick Mirer .10 .30
❑ 198 Cornelius Bennett .10 .30
❑ 199 Jimmy Hitchcock .10 .30
❑ 200 Michael Irvin .30 .75
❑ 201 Quentin Coryatt .10 .30
❑ 202 Reggie White .30 .75
❑ 203 Larry Centers .20 .50
❑ 204 Rodney Thomas .10 .30
❑ 205 Dana Stubblefield .10 .30
❑ 206 Rod Woodson .20 .50
❑ 207 Rhett Hall .10 .30
❑ 208 Steve Tovar .10 .30
❑ 209 Michael Westbrook .20 .50
❑ 210 Steve Wisniewski .10 .30
❑ 211 Carlester Crumpler .10 .30
❑ 212 Elvis Grbac .20 .50
❑ 213 Tim Bowens .10 .30
❑ 214 Robert Porcher .10 .30
❑ 215 John Carney .10 .30
❑ 216 Anthony Newman .10 .30
❑ 217 Earnest Byner .10 .30
❑ 218 Dewayne Washington .10 .30
❑ 219 Willie Green .10 .30
❑ 220 Terry Allen .30 .75
❑ 221 William Fuller .10 .30
❑ 222 Al Del Greco .10 .30
❑ 223 Trent Dilfer .30 .75
❑ 224 Michael Dean Perry .10 .30
❑ 225 Larry Allen .10 .30
❑ 226 Mark Bruener .10 .30
❑ 227 Clay Matthews .10 .30
❑ 228 Reuben Brown .10 .30
❑ 229 Edgar Bennett .20 .50
❑ 230 Neil Smith .20 .50
❑ 231 Ken Harvey .10 .30
❑ 232 Kyle Brady .10 .30
❑ 233 Corey Miller .10 .30
❑ 234 Tony Siragusa .10 .30
❑ 235 Todd Sauerbrun .10 .30
❑ 236 Daniel Stubbs .10 .30
❑ 237 Robb Thomas .10 .30
❑ 238 Jimmy Smith .20 .50
❑ 239 Marquez Pope .10 .30
❑ 240 Tim Biakabutuka .20 .50
❑ 241 Jamie Asher .10 .30
❑ 242 Steve McNair .40 1.00
❑ 243 Harold Green .10 .30
❑ 244 Frank Sanders .20 .50
❑ 245 Joe Johnson .10 .30
❑ 246 Eric Bieniemy .10 .30
❑ 247 Kevin Turner .10 .30
❑ 248 Rickey Dudley .20 .50
❑ 249 Orlando Thomas .10 .30
❑ 250 Dan Marino 1.25 3.00
❑ 251 Deion Sanders .30 .75
❑ 252 Dan Williams .10 .30
❑ 253 Sam Gash .10 .30
❑ 254 Lonnie Marts .10 .30
❑ 255 Mo Lewis .10 .30
❑ 256 Charles Johnson .20 .50
❑ 257 Chris Jacke .10 .30
❑ 258 Keenan McCardell .20 .50
❑ 259 Donnell Woolford .10 .30
❑ 260 Terrance Shaw .10 .30
❑ 261 Jason Dunn .10 .30
❑ 262 Willie McGinest .10 .30
❑ 263 Ken Dilger .10 .30
❑ 264 Keith Lyle .10 .30
❑ 265 Antonio Langham .10 .30
❑ 266 Carlton Gray .10 .30
❑ 267 LeShon Johnson .10 .30
❑ 268 Thurman Thomas .30 .75
❑ 269 Jesse Campbell .10 .30
❑ 270 Carnell Lake .10 .30
❑ 271 Cris Dishman .10 .30
❑ 272 Kevin Williams .10 .30
❑ 273 Troy Brown .20 .50
❑ 274 William Roaf .10 .30
❑ 275 Terrell Davis .40 1.00
❑ 276 Herman Moore .20 .50
❑ 277 Walt Harris .10 .30
❑ 278 Mark Collins .10 .30
❑ 279 Bert Emanuel .20 .50
❑ 280 Qadry Ismail .20 .50
❑ 281 Phil Hansen .10 .30
❑ 282 Steve Young .40 1.00
❑ 283 Michael Sinclair .10 .30
❑ 284 Jeff Graham .10 .30
❑ 285 Sam Mills .10 .30
❑ 286 Terry McDaniel .10 .30
❑ 287 Eugene Robinson .10 .30
❑ 288 Tony Bennett .10 .30
❑ 289 Daryl Johnston .20 .50
❑ 290 Eric Swann .10 .30
❑ 291 Byron Bam Morris .10 .30
❑ 292 Thomas Lewis .10 .30
❑ 293 Terrell Fletcher .10 .30
❑ 294 Gus Frerotte .10 .30
❑ 295 Stanley Pritchett .10 .30
❑ 296 Mike Alstott .30 .75
❑ 297 Will Shields .10 .30
❑ 298 Errict Rhett .10 .30
❑ 299 Garrison Hearst .20 .50
❑ 300 Kerry Collins .30 .75
❑ 301 Darryll Lewis .10 .30
❑ 302 Chris T. Jones .10 .30
❑ 303 Yancey Thigpen .20 .50
❑ 304 Jackie Harris .10 .30
❑ 305 Steve Christie .10 .30
❑ 306 Gilbert Brown .20 .50
❑ 307 Terry Wooden .10 .30
❑ 308 Pete Mitchell .10 .30
❑ 309 Tim McDonald .10 .30
❑ 310 Jake Reed .20 .50
❑ 311 Ed McCaffrey .20 .50
❑ 312 Chris Doleman .10 .30
❑ 313 Eric Metcalf .20 .50
❑ 314 Ricky Reynolds .10 .30
❑ 315 David Sloan .10 .30
❑ 316 Marvin Washington .10 .30
❑ 317 Herschel Walker .20 .50
❑ 318 Michael Timpson .10 .30
❑ 319 Blaine Bishop .10 .30
❑ 320 Irv Smith .10 .30
❑ 321 Seth Joyner .10 .30
❑ 322 Terrell Buckley .10 .30
❑ 323 Michael Strahan .20 .50
❑ 324 Sam Adams .10 .30
❑ 325 Leslie Shepherd .10 .30
❑ 326 James Jett .20 .50
❑ 327 Anthony Pleasant .10 .30
❑ 328 Lee Woodall .10 .30
❑ 329 Shannon Sharpe .20 .50
❑ 330 Jamal Anderson .30 .75
❑ 331 Andre Hastings .10 .30
❑ 332 Troy Vincent .10 .30
❑ 333 Sean LaChapelle .10 .30
❑ 334 Winslow Oliver .10 .30
❑ 335 Sean Jones .10 .30
❑ 336 Darnay Scott .20 .50
❑ 337 Todd Lyght .10 .30
❑ 338 Leonard Russell .10 .30
❑ 339 Nate Newton .10 .30
❑ 340 Zack Crockett .10 .30
❑ 341 Amp Lee .10 .30
❑ 342 Bobby Engram .20 .50
❑ 343 Mike Hollis .10 .30
❑ 344 Rodney Hampton .20 .50
❑ 345 Mel Gray .10 .30
❑ 346 Van Malone .10 .30
❑ 347 Aaron Craver .10 .30
❑ 348 Jim Everett .10 .30
❑ 349 Trace Armstrong .10 .30
❑ 350 Pat Swilling .10 .30
❑ 351 Brent Jones .10 .30
❑ 352 Chris Spielman .10 .30
❑ 353 Brett Perriman .10 .30
❑ 354 Brian Kinchen .10 .30
❑ 355 Joey Galloway .20 .50
❑ 356 Henry Ellard .10 .30
❑ 357 Ben Coates .20 .50
❑ 358 Dorsey Levens .30 .75
❑ 359 Charlie Garner .20 .50
❑ 360 Erric Pegram .10 .30
❑ 361 Anthony Johnson .10 .30
❑ 362 Rashaan Salaam .10 .30
❑ 363 Jeff Blake .20 .50
❑ 364 Kent Graham .10 .30
❑ 365 Broderick Thomas .10 .30
❑ 366 Richmond Webb .10 .30
❑ 367 Alfred Pupunu .10 .30
❑ 368 Mark Stepnoski .10 .30
❑ 369 David Dunn .10 .30

Card	Low	High
❑ 370 Bobby Houston	.10	.30
❑ 371 Anthony Parker	.10	.30
❑ 372 Quinn Early	.10	.30
❑ 373 LeRoy Butler	.10	.30
❑ 374 Kurt Gouveia	.10	.30
❑ 375 Greg Biekert	.10	.30
❑ 376 Jim Harbaugh	.20	.50
❑ 377 Eric Bjornson	.10	.30
❑ 378 Craig Heyward	.10	.30
❑ 379 Steve Bono	.20	.50
❑ 380 Tony Banks	.20	.50
❑ 381 John Mobley	.10	.30
❑ 382 Irving Fryar	.20	.50
❑ 383 Dermontti Dawson	.10	.30
❑ 384 Eric Davis	.10	.30
❑ 385 Natrone Means	.20	.50
❑ 386 Jason Sehorn	.20	.50
❑ 387 Michael McCrary	.10	.30
❑ 388 Corwin Brown	.10	.30
❑ 389 Kevin Glover	.10	.30
❑ 390 Jerris McPhail	.10	.30
❑ 391 Bobby Taylor	.10	.30
❑ 392 Tony McGee	.10	.30
❑ 393 Curtis Conway	.20	.50
❑ 394 Napoleon Kaufman	.30	.75
❑ 395 Brian Blades	.10	.30
❑ 396 Richard Dent	.10	.30
❑ 397 Dave Brown	.10	.30
❑ 398 Stan Humphries	.20	.50
❑ 399 Stevon Moore	.10	.30
❑ 400 Brett Favre	1.50	3.00
❑ 401 Jerome Bettis	.30	.75
❑ 402 Darrin Smith	.10	.30
❑ 403 Chris Penn	.10	.30
❑ 404 Rob Moore	.20	.50
❑ 405 Micheal Barrow	.10	.30
❑ 406 Tony Brackens	.10	.30
❑ 407 Wayne Martin	.10	.30
❑ 408 Warren Moon	.30	.75
❑ 409 Jason Elam	.20	.50
❑ 410 J.J. Birden	.10	.30
❑ 411 Hugh Douglas	.10	.30
❑ 412 Lamar Lathon	.10	.30
❑ 413 John Kidd	.10	.30
❑ 414 Bryce Paup	.10	.30
❑ 415 Shawn Jefferson	.10	.30
❑ 416 Leeland McElroy SS	.10	.30
❑ 417 Elbert Shelley SS	.10	.30
❑ 418 Jermaine Lewis SS	.20	.50
❑ 419 Eric Moulds SS	.30	.75
❑ 420 Michael Bates SS	.10	.30
❑ 421 John Mangum SS	.10	.30
❑ 422 Corey Sawyer SS	.10	.30
❑ 423 Jim Schwantz SS RC	.10	.30
❑ 424 Rod Smith WR SS	.30	.75
❑ 425 Glyn Milburn SS	.10	.30
❑ 426 Desmond Howard SS	.20	.50
❑ 427 John Henry Mills SS RC	.10	.30
❑ 428 Cary Blanchard SS RC	.10	.30
❑ 429 Chris Hudson SS	.10	.30
❑ 430 Tamarick Vanover SS	.20	.50
❑ 431 Kirby Dar Dar SS RC	.20	.50
❑ 432 David Palmer SS	.10	.30
❑ 433 Dave Meggett SS	.10	.30
❑ 434 Tyrone Hughes SS	.10	.30
❑ 435 Amani Toomer SS	.20	.50
❑ 436 Wayne Chrebet SS	.20	.50
❑ 437 Carl Kidd RC SS	.10	.30
❑ 438 Derrick Witherspoon SS	.10	.30
❑ 439 Jahine Arnold SS	.10	.30
❑ 440 Andre Coleman SS	.10	.30
❑ 441 Jeff Wilkins SS	.10	.30
❑ 442 Jay Bellamy SS RC	.10	.30
❑ 443 Eddie Kennison SS	.20	.50
❑ 444 Nilo Silvan SS	.10	.30
❑ 445 Brian Mitchell SS	.10	.30
❑ 446 Garrison Hearst CL	.20	.50
❑ 447 Napoleon Kaufman CL	.30	.75
❑ 448 Brian Mitchell CL	.10	.30
❑ 449 Rodney Hampton CL	.10	.30
❑ 450 Edgar Bennett CL	.10	.30
❑ S1 Mark Chmura Sample	.40	1.00
❑ AU1 Reggie White AUTO	75.00	125.00

2006 Fleer

Card	Low	High
❑ COMPLETE SET (200)	20.00	50.00
❑ COMP.SET w/o RC's (100)	6.00	15.00
❑ 1 Anquan Boldin	.15	.40
❑ 2 Larry Fitzgerald	.20	.50
❑ 3 J.J. Arrington	.12	.30
❑ 4 Michael Vick	.20	.50
❑ 5 Warrick Dunn	.15	.40
❑ 6 Roddy White	.15	.40
❑ 7 Jamal Lewis	.15	.40
❑ 8 Kyle Boller	.15	.40
❑ 9 Derrick Mason	.15	.40
❑ 10 Willis McGahee	.20	.50
❑ 11 J.P. Losman	.15	.40
❑ 12 Lee Evans	.15	.40
❑ 13 Steve Smith	.20	.50
❑ 14 Jake Delhomme	.15	.40
❑ 15 DeShaun Foster	.15	.40
❑ 16 Rex Grossman	.20	.50
❑ 17 Brian Urlacher	.20	.50
❑ 18 Thomas Jones	.15	.40
❑ 19 Carson Palmer	.20	.50
❑ 20 Chad Johnson	.15	.40
❑ 21 Rudi Johnson	.15	.40
❑ 22 Charlie Frye	.15	.40
❑ 23 Braylon Edwards	.20	.50
❑ 24 Reuben Droughns	.15	.40
❑ 25 Julius Jones	.15	.40
❑ 26 Drew Bledsoe	.20	.50
❑ 27 Terry Glenn	.15	.40
❑ 28 Jake Plummer	.15	.40
❑ 29 Tatum Bell	.12	.30
❑ 30 Champ Bailey	.15	.40
❑ 31 Rod Smith	.15	.40
❑ 32 Roy Williams WR	.20	.50
❑ 33 Kevin Jones	.15	.40
❑ 34 Mike Williams	.15	.40
❑ 35 Brett Favre	.40	1.00
❑ 36 Ahman Green	.15	.40
❑ 37 Javon Walker	.15	.40
❑ 38 David Carr	.12	.30
❑ 39 Andre Johnson	.15	.40
❑ 40 Domanick Davis	.15	.40
❑ 41 Peyton Manning	.30	.75
❑ 42 Edgerrin James	.15	.40
❑ 43 Marvin Harrison	.20	.50
❑ 44 Reggie Wayne	.15	.40
❑ 45 Byron Leftwich	.15	.40
❑ 46 Fred Taylor	.15	.40
❑ 47 Ernest Wilford	.12	.30
❑ 48 Larry Johnson	.15	.40
❑ 49 Trent Green	.15	.40
❑ 50 Tony Gonzalez	.15	.40
❑ 51 Ronnie Brown	.20	.50
❑ 52 Ricky Williams	.12	.30
❑ 53 Chris Chambers	.15	.40
❑ 54 Daunte Culpepper	.20	.50
❑ 55 Troy Williamson	.15	.40
❑ 56 Brad Johnson	.15	.40
❑ 57 Tom Brady	.30	.75
❑ 58 Deion Branch	.15	.40
❑ 59 Corey Dillon	.15	.40
❑ 60 Deuce McAllister	.15	.40
❑ 61 Donte Stallworth	.15	.40
❑ 62 Joe Horn	.15	.40
❑ 63 Eli Manning	.25	.60
❑ 64 Tiki Barber	.20	.50
❑ 65 Plaxico Burress	.15	.40
❑ 66 Jeremy Shockey	.20	.50
❑ 67 Chad Pennington	.15	.40
❑ 68 Curtis Martin	.20	.50
❑ 69 Laveranues Coles	.15	.40
❑ 70 Randy Moss	.20	.50
❑ 71 Aaron Brooks	.15	.40
❑ 72 LaMont Jordan	.15	.40

Card	Low	High
❑ 73 Donovan McNabb	.20	.50
❑ 74 Brian Westbrook	.15	.40
❑ 75 Terrell Owens	.20	.50
❑ 76 Ben Roethlisberger	.30	.75
❑ 77 Hines Ward	.20	.50
❑ 78 Willie Parker	.25	.60
❑ 79 Heath Miller	.15	.40
❑ 80 LaDainian Tomlinson	.25	.60
❑ 81 Drew Brees	.20	.50
❑ 82 Antonio Gates	.20	.50
❑ 83 Alex Smith QB	.15	.40
❑ 84 Antonio Bryant	.15	.40
❑ 85 Frank Gore	.20	.50
❑ 86 Shaun Alexander	.15	.40
❑ 87 Matt Hasselbeck	.15	.40
❑ 88 Darrell Jackson	.15	.40
❑ 89 Marc Bulger	.15	.40
❑ 90 Steven Jackson	.20	.50
❑ 91 Torry Holt	.15	.40
❑ 92 Cadillac Williams	.20	.50
❑ 93 Chris Simms	.15	.40
❑ 94 Joey Galloway	.15	.40
❑ 95 Steve McNair	.15	.40
❑ 96 Chris Brown	.15	.40
❑ 97 Drew Bennett	.15	.40
❑ 98 Clinton Portis	.20	.50
❑ 99 Santana Moss	.15	.40
❑ 100 Mark Brunell	.15	.40
❑ 101 A.J. Hawk RC	1.25	3.00
❑ 102 A.J. Nicholson RC	.50	1.25
❑ 103 Abdul Hodge RC	.60	1.50
❑ 104 Andre Hall RC	.60	1.50
❑ 105 Anthony Fasano RC	.75	2.00
❑ 106 Antonio Cromartie RC	.75	2.00
❑ 107 Ashton Youboty RC	.60	1.50
❑ 108 Bobby Carpenter RC	.60	1.50
❑ 109 Brad Smith RC	.75	2.00
❑ 110 Greg Jennings RC	1.25	3.00
❑ 111 Brandon Williams RC	.60	1.50
❑ 112 Brian Calhoun RC	.60	1.50
❑ 113 Brodie Croyle RC	.75	2.00
❑ 114 Brodrick Bunkley RC	.60	1.50
❑ 115 Bruce Gradkowski RC	.75	2.00
❑ 116 Chad Greenway RC	.75	2.00
❑ 117 Chad Jackson RC	.60	1.50
❑ 118 Charles Davis RC	.60	1.50
❑ 119 Charles Gordon RC	.60	1.50
❑ 120 Charlie Whitehurst RC	.75	2.00
❑ 121 Claude Wroten RC	.50	1.25
❑ 122 Cory Rodgers RC	.75	2.00
❑ 123 D.J. Shockley RC	.60	1.50
❑ 124 Darnell Bing RC	.60	1.50
❑ 125 Darrell Hackney RC	.60	1.50
❑ 126 David Thomas RC	.75	2.00
❑ 127 D'Brickashaw Ferguson RC	.75	2.00
❑ 128 DeAngelo Williams RC	1.50	4.00
❑ 129 DeMeco Ryans RC	1.00	2.50
❑ 130 Demetrius Williams RC	.60	1.50
❑ 131 Derek Hagan RC	.60	1.50
❑ 132 Devin Hester RC	1.50	4.00
❑ 133 Dominique Byrd RC	.60	1.50
❑ 134 DonTrell Moore RC	.60	1.50
❑ 135 D'Qwell Jackson RC	.60	1.50
❑ 136 Drew Olson RC	.50	1.25
❑ 137 Elvis Dumervil RC	.75	2.00
❑ 138 Ernie Sims RC	.60	1.50
❑ 139 Garrett Mills RC	.60	1.50
❑ 140 Gerald Riggs RC	.60	1.50
❑ 141 Greg Lee RC	.50	1.25
❑ 142 Haloti Ngata RC	.75	2.00
❑ 143 Hank Baskett RC	.75	2.00
❑ 144 Jason Allen RC	.60	1.50
❑ 145 Jason Avant RC	.75	2.00
❑ 146 Jay Cutler RC	2.00	5.00
❑ 147 Jeff Webb RC	.60	1.50
❑ 148 Jeremy Bloom RC	.60	1.50
❑ 149 Jerome Harrison RC	.75	2.00
❑ 150 Jimmy Williams RC	.75	2.00
❑ 151 Joe Klopfenstein RC	.60	1.50
❑ 152 Johnathan Joseph RC	.60	1.50
❑ 153 Joseph Addai RC	1.00	2.50
❑ 154 Jovon Bouknight RC	.60	1.50
❑ 155 Kai Parham RC	.75	2.00
❑ 156 Kamerion Wimbley RC	.75	2.00
❑ 157 Kellen Clemens RC	.75	2.00
❑ 158 Kelly Jennings RC	.75	2.00
❑ 159 Ko Simpson RC	.60	1.50
❑ 160 Laurence Maroney RC	1.00	2.50
❑ 161 Lawrence Vickers RC	.60	1.50

Card		
❑ 162 LenDale White RC	1.00	2.50
❑ 163 Leon Washington RC	1.00	2.50
❑ 164 Leonard Pope RC	.75	2.00
❑ 165 Manny Lawson RC	.75	2.00
❑ 166 Marcedes Lewis RC	.75	2.00
❑ 167 Marcus McNeill RC	.60	1.50
❑ 168 Donte Whitner RC	.75	2.00
❑ 169 Mario Williams RC	1.00	2.50
❑ 170 Martin Nance RC	.60	1.50
❑ 171 Mathias Kiwanuka RC	1.00	2.50
❑ 172 Matt Bernstein RC	.50	1.25
❑ 173 Matt Leinart RC	1.25	3.00
❑ 174 Maurice Drew RC	1.50	4.00
❑ 175 Maurice Stovall RC	.60	1.50
❑ 176 Michael Huff RC	.75	2.00
❑ 177 Michael Robinson RC	.60	1.50
❑ 178 Mike Hass RC	.75	2.00
❑ 179 Omar Jacobs RC	.50	1.25
❑ 180 Orien Harris RC	.60	1.50
❑ 181 Owen Daniels RC	.75	2.00
❑ 182 Miles Austin RC	2.00	5.00
❑ 183 Reggie Bush RC	2.00	5.00
❑ 184 Reggie McNeal RC	.60	1.50
❑ 185 Santonio Holmes RC	2.00	5.00
❑ 186 Sinorice Moss RC	.75	2.00
❑ 187 Skyler Green RC	.50	1.25
❑ 188 Tony Scheffler RC	.75	2.00
❑ 189 Tamba Hali RC	.75	2.00
❑ 190 Tarvaris Jackson RC	.75	2.00
❑ 191 Thomas Howard RC	.60	1.50
❑ 192 Tim Day RC	.60	1.50
❑ 193 Todd Watkins RC	.50	1.25
❑ 194 Travis Wilson RC	.50	1.25
❑ 195 Tye Hill RC	.60	1.50
❑ 196 Vernon Davis RC	.75	2.00
❑ 197 Vince Young RC	2.00	5.00
❑ 198 Wali Lundy RC	.75	2.00
❑ 199 Will Blackmon RC	.75	2.00
❑ 200 Winston Justice RC	.75	2.00

1997 Fleer Goudey

Card		
❑ COMPLETE SET (150)	6.00	15.00
❑ 1 Michael Jackson	.10	.30
❑ 2 Ray Lewis	.30	.75
❑ 3 Vinny Testaverde	.10	.30
❑ 4 Eric Turner	.07	.20
❑ 5 Jim Kelly	.20	.50
❑ 6 Bryce Paup	.07	.20
❑ 7 Andre Reed	.10	.30
❑ 8 Bruce Smith	.10	.30
❑ 9 Thurman Thomas	.20	.50
❑ 10 Jeff Blake	.10	.30
❑ 11 Ki-Jana Carter	.07	.20
❑ 12 Carl Pickens	.10	.30
❑ 13 Darnay Scott	.10	.30
❑ 14 Terrell Davis	.25	.60
❑ 15 John Elway	.75	2.00
❑ 16 Anthony Miller	.07	.20
❑ 17 John Mobley	.07	.20
❑ 18 Shannon Sharpe	.10	.30
❑ 19 Chris Chandler	.10	.30
❑ 20 Eddie George	.20	.50
❑ 21 Steve McNair	.25	.60
❑ 22 Chris Sanders	.07	.20
❑ 23 Quentin Coryatt	.07	.20
❑ 24 Sean Dawkins	.07	.20
❑ 25 Ken Dilger	.07	.20
❑ 26 Marshall Faulk	.25	.60
❑ 27 Jim Harbaugh	.10	.30
❑ 28 Marvin Harrison	.20	.50
❑ 29 Tony Brackens	.07	.20
❑ 30 Mark Brunell	.25	.60
❑ 31 Kevin Hardy	.07	.20
❑ 32 Keenan McCardell	.10	.30
❑ 33 James O.Stewart	.10	.30
❑ 34 Marcus Allen	.20	.50
❑ 35 Steve Bono	.10	.30
❑ 36 Dale Carter	.07	.20
❑ 37 Neil Smith	.10	.30
❑ 38 Derrick Thomas	.20	.50
❑ 39 Tamarick Vanover	.10	.30
❑ 40 Karim Abdul-Jabbar	.10	.30
❑ 41 Dan Marino	.75	2.00
❑ 42 O.J. McDuffie	.10	.30
❑ 43 Stanley Pritchett	.07	.20
❑ 44 Zach Thomas	.20	.50
❑ 45 Drew Bledsoe	.25	.60
❑ 46 Ben Coates	.10	.30
❑ 47 Terry Glenn	.20	.50
❑ 48 Shawn Jefferson	.07	.20
❑ 49 Curtis Martin	.25	.60
❑ 50 Dave Meggett	.07	.20
❑ 51 Hugh Douglas	.07	.20
❑ 52 Keyshawn Johnson	.20	.50
❑ 53 Adrian Murrell	.10	.30
❑ 54 Tim Brown	.20	.50
❑ 55 Rickey Dudley	.10	.30
❑ 56 Jeff Hostetler	.07	.20
❑ 57 Napoleon Kaufman	.20	.50
❑ 58 Chester McGlockton	.07	.20
❑ 59 Jerome Bettis	.20	.50
❑ 60 Andre Hastings	.07	.20
❑ 61 Greg Lloyd	.07	.20
❑ 62 Kordell Stewart	.20	.50
❑ 63 Yancey Thigpen	.10	.30
❑ 64 Rod Woodson	.10	.30
❑ 65 Andre Coleman	.07	.20
❑ 66 Stan Humphries	.10	.30
❑ 67 Tony Martin	.10	.30
❑ 68 Leonard Russell	.07	.20
❑ 69 Junior Seau	.20	.50
❑ 70 Brian Blades	.07	.20
❑ 71 Joey Galloway	.10	.30
❑ 72 Chris Warren	.10	.30
❑ 73 Larry Centers	.10	.30
❑ 74 Leeland McElroy	.07	.20
❑ 75 Simeon Rice	.10	.30
❑ 76 Frank Sanders	.10	.30
❑ 77 Eric Swann	.07	.20
❑ 78 Jamal Anderson	.20	.50
❑ 79 Bert Emanuel	.10	.30
❑ 80 Terance Mathis	.10	.30
❑ 81 Eric Metcalf	.10	.30
❑ 82 Tim Biakabutuka	.10	.30
❑ 83 Kerry Collins	.20	.50
❑ 84 Kevin Greene	.10	.30
❑ 85 Muhsin Muhammad	.10	.30
❑ 86 Wesley Walls	.10	.30
❑ 87 Curtis Conway	.10	.30
❑ 88 Bryan Cox	.07	.20
❑ 89 Walt Harris	.07	.20
❑ 90 Erik Kramer	.07	.20
❑ 91 Rashaan Salaam	.07	.20
❑ 92 Troy Aikman	.40	1.00
❑ 93 Michael Irvin	.20	.50
❑ 94 Daryl Johnston	.10	.30
❑ 95 Leon Lett	.07	.20
❑ 96 Deion Sanders	.20	.50
❑ 97 Emmitt Smith	.60	1.50
❑ 98 Scott Mitchell	.10	.30
❑ 99 Herman Moore	.10	.30
❑ 100 Johnnie Morton	.10	.30
❑ 101 Brett Perriman	.07	.20
❑ 102 Barry Sanders	.60	1.50
❑ 103 Edgar Bennett	.10	.30
❑ 104 Robert Brooks	.10	.30
❑ 105 Brett Favre	.75	2.00
❑ 106 Antonio Freeman	.20	.50
❑ 107 Keith Jackson	.07	.20
❑ 108 Reggie White	.20	.50
❑ 109 Cris Carter	.20	.50
❑ 110 Warren Moon	.20	.50
❑ 111 John Randle	.10	.30
❑ 112 Jake Reed	.10	.30
❑ 113 Robert Smith	.10	.30
❑ 114 Jim Everett	.07	.20
❑ 115 Michael Haynes	.07	.20
❑ 116 Alex Molden	.07	.20
❑ 117 Ray Zellars	.07	.20
❑ 118 Chris Calloway	.07	.20
❑ 119 Rodney Hampton	.10	.30
❑ 120 Phillippi Sparks	.07	.20
❑ 121 Amani Toomer	.10	.30
❑ 122 Ty Detmer	.10	.30
❑ 123 Jason Dunn	.07	.20
❑ 124 Irving Fryar	.10	.30
❑ 125 Chris T. Jones	.07	.20
❑ 126 Ricky Watters	.10	.30
❑ 127 Tony Banks	.10	.30
❑ 128 Isaac Bruce	.20	.50
❑ 129 Eddie Kennison	.10	.30
❑ 130 Lawrence Phillips	.07	.20
❑ 131 Merton Hanks	.07	.20
❑ 132 Terry Kirby	.10	.30
❑ 133 Ken Norton	.07	.20
❑ 134 Jerry Rice	.40	1.00
❑ 135 J.J. Stokes	.10	.30
❑ 136 Steve Young	.25	.60
❑ 137 Alvin Harper	.07	.20
❑ 138 Jackie Harris	.07	.20
❑ 139 Hardy Nickerson	.07	.20
❑ 140 Errict Rhett	.07	.20
❑ 141 Terry Allen	.20	.50
❑ 142 Henry Ellard	.07	.20
❑ 143 Gus Frerotte	.07	.20
❑ 144 Brian Mitchell	.07	.20
❑ 145 Michael Westbrook	.10	.30
❑ 146 Chuck Bednarik	.10	.30
❑ 146AU Chuck Bednarik AUTO	20.00	50.00
❑ 147 Y.A. Tittle	.10	.30
❑ 147AU Y.A. Tittle AUTO	20.00	50.00
❑ 148 Checklist	.07	.20
❑ 149 Checklist	.07	.20
❑ 150 Checklist	.07	.20
❑ P1 Brett Favre Promo	.75	2.00

1997 Fleer Goudey II

Card		
❑ COMPLETE SET (150)	7.50	20.00
❑ 1 Gale Sayers SP	.20	.50
❑ 1AU Gale Sayers AUTO	40.00	100.00
❑ 1RT Gale Sayers Rare Trad.	4.00	8.00
❑ 2 Vinny Testaverde	.10	.30
❑ 3 Jeff George	.10	.30
❑ 4 Brett Favre	.75	2.00
❑ 5 Eddie Kennison	.10	.30
❑ 6 Ken Norton	.07	.20
❑ 7 John Elway	.75	2.00
❑ 8 Troy Aikman	.40	1.00
❑ 9 Steve McNair	.25	.60
❑ 10 Kordell Stewart	.20	.50
❑ 11 Drew Bledsoe	.25	.60
❑ 12 Kerry Collins	.20	.50
❑ 13 Dan Marino	.75	2.00
❑ 14 Brad Johnson	.20	.50
❑ 15 Todd Collins	.07	.20
❑ 16 Ki-Jana Carter	.07	.20
❑ 17 Pat Barnes RC	.20	.50
❑ 18 Aeneas Williams	.07	.20
❑ 19 Keyshawn Johnson	.20	.50
❑ 20 Barry Sanders	.60	1.50
❑ 21 Tiki Barber RC	1.25	3.00
❑ 22 Emmitt Smith	.60	1.50
❑ 23 Kevin Hardy	.07	.20
❑ 24 Mario Bates	.07	.20
❑ 25 Ricky Watters	.10	.30
❑ 26 Chris Canty RC	.07	.20
❑ 27 Eddie George	.20	.50
❑ 28 Curtis Martin	.25	.60
❑ 29 Adrian Murrell	.10	.30
❑ 30 Terrell Davis	.25	.60
❑ 31 Rashaan Salaam	.07	.20
❑ 32 Marcus Allen	.20	.50
❑ 33 Karim Abdul-Jabbar	.20	.50
❑ 34 Thurman Thomas	.20	.50
❑ 35 Marvin Harrison	.20	.50
❑ 36 Jerome Bettis	.20	.50
❑ 37 Larry Centers	.10	.30
❑ 38 Stan Humphries	.10	.30
❑ 39 Lawrence Phillips	.07	.20
❑ 40 Gale Sayers SP	.20	.50
❑ 40AU Gale Sayers AUTO	40.00	100.00
❑ 40RT Gale Sayers Rare Trad.	4.00	8.00
❑ 41 Henry Ellard	.07	.20

- ❑ 42 Chris Warren .10 .30
- ❑ 43 Robert Brooks .10 .30
- ❑ 44 Sedrick Shaw RC .10 .30
- ❑ 45 Muhsin Muhammad .10 .30
- ❑ 46 Napoleon Kaufman .20 .50
- ❑ 47 Reidel Anthony RC .20 .50
- ❑ 48 Jamal Anderson .20 .50
- ❑ 49 Scott Mitchell .10 .30
- ❑ 50 Mark Brunell .25 .60
- ❑ 51 William Thomas .07 .20
- ❑ 52 Bryan Cox .07 .20
- ❑ 53 Carl Pickens .10 .30
- ❑ 54 Chris Spielman .07 .20
- ❑ 55 Junior Seau .20 .50
- ❑ 56 Hardy Nickerson .07 .20
- ❑ 57 Dwayne Rudd RC .20 .50
- ❑ 58 Peter Boulware RC .20 .50
- ❑ 59 Jim Druckenmiller RC .10 .30
- ❑ 60 Michael Westbrook .10 .30
- ❑ 61 Shawn Springs RC .10 .30
- ❑ 62 Zach Thomas .20 .50
- ❑ 63 David LaFleur RC .07 .20
- ❑ 64 Darrell Russell RC .07 .20
- ❑ 65 Jake Plummer RC 1.00 2.50
- ❑ 66 Tim Biakabutuka .10 .30
- ❑ 67 Tyrone Wheatley .10 .30
- ❑ 68 Elvis Grbac .10 .30
- ❑ 69 Antonio Freeman .20 .50
- ❑ 70 Wayne Chrebet .20 .50
- ❑ 71 Walter Jones RC .20 .50
- ❑ 72 Marshall Faulk .25 .60
- ❑ 73 Jason Dunn .07 .20
- ❑ 74 Darnay Scott .10 .30
- ❑ 75 Errict Rhett .07 .20
- ❑ 76 Orlando Pace RC .20 .50
- ❑ 77 Natrone Means .10 .30
- ❑ 78 Bruce Smith .10 .30
- ❑ 79 Jamie Sharper RC .10 .30
- ❑ 80 Jerry Rice .40 1.00
- ❑ 81 Tim Brown .20 .50
- ❑ 82 Brian Mitchell .07 .20
- ❑ 83 Andre Reed .10 .30
- ❑ 84 Herman Moore .10 .30
- ❑ 85 Rob Moore .10 .30
- ❑ 86 Rae Carruth RC .07 .20
- ❑ 87 Bert Emanuel .10 .30
- ❑ 88 Michael Irvin .20 .50
- ❑ 89 Mark Chmura .10 .30
- ❑ 90 Tony Brackens .07 .20
- ❑ 91 Kevin Greene .10 .30
- ❑ 92 Reggie White .20 .50
- ❑ 93 Derrick Thomas .20 .50
- ❑ 94 Troy Davis RC .10 .30
- ❑ 95 Greg Lloyd .07 .20
- ❑ 96 Cortez Kennedy .07 .20
- ❑ 97 Simeon Rice .10 .30
- ❑ 98 Terrell Owens .25 .60
- ❑ 99 Hugh Douglas .07 .20
- ❑ 100 Terry Glenn .20 .50
- ❑ 101 Jim Harbaugh .10 .30
- ❑ 102 Shannon Sharpe .10 .00
- ❑ 103 Joey Kent RC .20 .50
- ❑ 104 Jeff Blake .10 .30
- ❑ 105 Terry Allen .20 .50
- ❑ 106 Cris Carter .20 .50
- ❑ 107 Amani Toomer .10 .30
- ❑ 108 Derrick Alexander WR .10 .30
- ❑ 109 Darnell Autry RC .10 .30
- ❑ 110 Irving Fryar .10 .30
- ❑ 111 Bryant Westbrook RC .07 .20
- ❑ 112 Tony Banks .10 .30
- ❑ 113 Michael Booker RC .07 .20
- ❑ 114 Yatil Green RC .10 .30
- ❑ 115 James Farrior RC .20 .50
- ❑ 116 Warrick Dunn RC .60 1.50
- ❑ 117 Greg Hill .07 .20
- ❑ 118 Tony Martin .10 .30
- ❑ 119 Chris Sanders .07 .20
- ❑ 120 Charles Johnson .10 .30
- ❑ 121 John Mobley .07 .20
- ❑ 122 Keenan McCardell .10 .30
- ❑ 123 Willie McGinest .07 .20
- ❑ 124 O.J. McDuffie .10 .30
- ❑ 125 Deion Sanders .20 .50
- ❑ 126 Curtis Conway .10 .30
- ❑ 127 Desmond Howard .10 .30
- ❑ 128 Johnnie Morton .10 .30
- ❑ 129 Ike Hilliard RC .30 .75
- ❑ 130 Gus Frerotte .07 .20
- ❑ 131 Tom Knight .07 .20
- ❑ 132 Sean Dawkins .07 .20
- ❑ 133 Isaac Bruce .20 .50
- ❑ 134 Wesley Walls .10 .30
- ❑ 135 Danny Wuerffel RC .20 .50
- ❑ 136 Tony Gonzalez RC .60 1.50
- ❑ 137 Ben Coates .10 .30
- ❑ 138 Joey Galloway .10 .30
- ❑ 139 Michael Jackson .10 .30
- ❑ 140 Steve Young .25 .60
- ❑ 141 Corey Dillon RC 1.25 3.00
- ❑ 142 Jake Reed .10 .30
- ❑ 143 Edgar Bennett .10 .30
- ❑ 144 Ty Detmer .10 .30
- ❑ 145 Darrell Green .10 .30
- ❑ 146 Antowain Smith RC .50 1.25
- ❑ 147 Mike Alstott .20 .50
- ❑ 148 Checklist .07 .20
- ❑ 149 Checklist .07 .20
- ❑ 150 Gale Sayers SP .20 .50
- ❑ 150AU Gale Sayers AUTO 40.00 100.00
- ❑ 150RT Gale Sayers Rare Trad. 4.00 8.00
- ❑ P92 Reggie White Promo .20 .50

1998 Fleer Tradition

- ❑ COMPLETE SET (250) 20.00 40.00
- ❑ 1 Brett Favre .75 2.00
- ❑ 2 Barry Sanders .60 1.50
- ❑ 3 John Elway .75 2.00
- ❑ 4 Emmitt Smith .60 1.50
- ❑ 5 Dan Marino .75 2.00
- ❑ 6 Eddie George .20 .50
- ❑ 7 Jerry Rice .40 1.00
- ❑ 8 Jake Plummer .20 .50
- ❑ 9 Joey Galloway .10 .30
- ❑ 10 Mike Alstott .20 .50
- ❑ 11 Brian Mitchell .07 .20
- ❑ 12 Keyshawn Johnson .20 .50
- ❑ 13 Jerald Moore .07 .20
- ❑ 14 Randal Hill .07 .20
- ❑ 15 Byron Hanspard .07 .20
- ❑ 16 Jeff George .10 .30
- ❑ 17 Terry Glenn .20 .50
- ❑ 18 Jerome Bettis .20 .50
- ❑ 19 Curtis Conway .10 .30
- ❑ 20 Fred Lane .07 .20
- ❑ 21 Isaac Bruce .20 .50
- ❑ 22 Tiki Barber .20 .50
- ❑ 23 Bobby Hoying .10 .30
- ❑ 24 Marcus Allen .20 .50
- ❑ 25 Dana Stubblefield .07 .20
- ❑ 26 Peter Boulware .07 .20
- ❑ 27 John Randle .10 .30
- ❑ 28 Jason Sehorn .10 .30
- ❑ 29 Rod Smith .10 .30
- ❑ 30 Michael Sinclair .07 .20
- ❑ 31 Marshall Faulk .25 .60
- ❑ 32 Karl Williams .07 .20
- ❑ 33 Kordell Stewart .20 .50
- ❑ 34 Corey Dillon .20 .50
- ❑ 35 Bryant Young .07 .20
- ❑ 36 Charlie Garner .10 .30
- ❑ 37 Andre Reed .10 .30
- ❑ 38 Ray Buchanan .07 .20
- ❑ 39 Brett Perriman .07 .20
- ❑ 40 Leon Lett .07 .20
- ❑ 41 Keenan McCardell .10 .30
- ❑ 42 Eric Swann .07 .20
- ❑ 43 Leslie Shepherd .07 .20
- ❑ 44 Curtis Martin .20 .50
- ❑ 45 Andre Rison .10 .30
- ❑ 46 Keith Lyle .07 .20
- ❑ 47 Rae Carruth .07 .20
- ❑ 48 William Henderson .10 .30
- ❑ 49 Sean Dawkins .07 .20
- ❑ 50 Terrell Davis .20 .50
- ❑ 51 Tim Brown .20 .50
- ❑ 52 Willie McGinest .07 .20
- ❑ 53 Jermaine Lewis .10 .30
- ❑ 54 Ricky Watters .10 .30
- ❑ 55 Freddie Jones .07 .20
- ❑ 56 Robert Smith .20 .50
- ❑ 57 Reidel Anthony .10 .30
- ❑ 58 James Stewart .10 .30
- ❑ 59 Earl Holmes RC .20 .50
- ❑ 60 Dale Carter .07 .20
- ❑ 61 Michael Irvin .20 .50
- ❑ 62 Jason Taylor .10 .30
- ❑ 63 Eric Metcalf .07 .20
- ❑ 64 LeRoy Butler .07 .20
- ❑ 65 Jamal Anderson .20 .50
- ❑ 66 Jamie Asher .07 .20
- ❑ 67 Chris Sanders .07 .20
- ❑ 68 Warren Sapp .10 .30
- ❑ 69 Ray Zellars .07 .20
- ❑ 70 Carl Pickens .10 .30
- ❑ 71 Garrison Hearst .20 .50
- ❑ 72 Eddie Kennison .10 .30
- ❑ 73 John Mobley .07 .20
- ❑ 74 Rob Johnson .10 .30
- ❑ 75 William Thomas .07 .20
- ❑ 76 Drew Bledsoe .30 .75
- ❑ 77 Micheal Barrow .07 .20
- ❑ 78 Jim Harbaugh .10 .30
- ❑ 79 Terry McDaniel .07 .20
- ❑ 80 Johnnie Morton .10 .30
- ❑ 81 Danny Kanell .10 .30
- ❑ 82 Larry Centers .07 .20
- ❑ 83 Courtney Hawkins .07 .20
- ❑ 84 Tony Brackens .07 .20
- ❑ 85 Tony Gonzalez .20 .50
- ❑ 86 Aaron Glenn .07 .20
- ❑ 87 Cris Carter .20 .50
- ❑ 88 Chuck Smith .07 .20
- ❑ 89 Tamarick Vanover .07 .20
- ❑ 90 Karim Abdul-Jabbar .20 .50
- ❑ 91 Bryant Westbrook .07 .20
- ❑ 92 Mike Pritchard .07 .20
- ❑ 93 Darren Woodson .07 .20
- ❑ 94 Wesley Walls .10 .30
- ❑ 95 Tony Banks .10 .30
- ❑ 96 Michael Westbrook .10 .30
- ❑ 97 Shannon Sharpe .10 .30
- ❑ 98 Jeff Blake .10 .30
- ❑ 99 Terrell Owens .20 .50
- ❑ 100 Warrick Dunn .20 .50
- ❑ 101 Levon Kirkland .07 .20
- ❑ 102 Frank Wycheck .07 .20
- ❑ 103 Gus Frerotte .07 .20
- ❑ 104 Simeon Rice .10 .30
- ❑ 105 Shawn Jefferson .07 .20
- ❑ 106 Irving Fryar .10 .30
- ❑ 107 Michael McCrary .07 .20
- ❑ 108 Robert Brooks .10 .30
- ❑ 109 Chris Chandler .10 .30
- ❑ 110 Junior Seau .20 .50
- ❑ 111 O.J. McDuffie .10 .30
- ❑ 112 Glenn Foley .10 .30
- ❑ 113 Darryl Williams .07 .20
- ❑ 114 Elvis Grbac .10 .30
- ❑ 115 Napoleon Kaufman .20 .50
- ❑ 116 Anthony Miller .07 .20
- ❑ 117 Troy Davis .07 .20
- ❑ 118 Charles Way .07 .20
- ❑ 119 Scott Mitchell .10 .30
- ❑ 120 Ken Harvey .07 .20
- ❑ 121 Tyrone Hughes .07 .20
- ❑ 122 Mark Brunell .20 .50
- ❑ 123 David Palmer .07 .20
- ❑ 124 Rob Moore .10 .30
- ❑ 125 Kerry Collins .10 .30
- ❑ 126 Will Blackwell .07 .20
- ❑ 127 Ray Crockett .07 .20
- ❑ 128 Leslie O'Neal .07 .20
- ❑ 129 Antowain Smith .20 .50
- ❑ 130 Carlester Crumpler .07 .20
- ❑ 131 Michael Jackson .07 .20
- ❑ 132 Trent Dilfer .20 .50
- ❑ 133 Dan Williams .07 .20
- ❑ 134 Dorsey Levens .20 .50
- ❑ 135 Ty Law .10 .30
- ❑ 136 Rickey Dudley .07 .20
- ❑ 137 Jessie Tuggle .07 .20
- ❑ 138 Darrien Gordon .07 .20
- ❑ 139 Kevin Turner .07 .20

Card	Low	High
❑ 140 Willie Davis	.07	.20
❑ 141 Zach Thomas	.20	.50
❑ 142 Tony McGee	.07	.20
❑ 143 Dexter Coakley	.07	.20
❑ 144 Troy Brown	.10	.30
❑ 145 Leeland McElroy	.07	.20
❑ 146 Michael Strahan	.10	.30
❑ 147 Ken Dilger	.07	.20
❑ 148 Bryce Paup	.07	.20
❑ 149 Herman Moore	.10	.30
❑ 150 Reggie White	.20	.50
❑ 151 Dewayne Washington	.07	.20
❑ 152 Natrone Means	.10	.30
❑ 153 Ben Coates	.10	.30
❑ 154 Bert Emanuel	.10	.30
❑ 155 Steve Young	.25	.60
❑ 156 Jimmy Smith	.10	.30
❑ 157 Darrell Green	.10	.30
❑ 158 Troy Aikman	.40	1.00
❑ 159 Greg Hill	.07	.20
❑ 160 Raymont Harris	.07	.20
❑ 161 Troy Drayton	.07	.20
❑ 162 Stevon Moore	.07	.20
❑ 163 Warren Moon	.20	.50
❑ 164 Wayne Martin	.07	.20
❑ 165 Jason Gildon	.07	.20
❑ 166 Chris Calloway	.07	.20
❑ 167 Aeneas Williams	.07	.20
❑ 168 Michael Bates	.07	.20
❑ 169 Hugh Douglas	.07	.20
❑ 170 Brad Johnson	.20	.50
❑ 171 Bruce Smith	.10	.30
❑ 172 Neil Smith	.10	.30
❑ 173 James McKnight	.20	.50
❑ 174 Robert Porcher	.07	.20
❑ 175 Merton Hanks	.07	.20
❑ 176 Ki-Jana Carter	.07	.20
❑ 177 Mo Lewis	.07	.20
❑ 178 Chester McGlockton	.07	.20
❑ 179 Zack Crockett	.07	.20
❑ 180 Derrick Thomas	.20	.50
❑ 181 J.J. Stokes	.10	.30
❑ 182 Derrick Rodgers	.07	.20
❑ 183 Daryl Johnston	.10	.30
❑ 184 Chris Penn	.07	.20
❑ 185 Steve Atwater	.07	.20
❑ 186 Amp Lee	.07	.20
❑ 187 Frank Sanders	.10	.30
❑ 188 Chris Slade	.07	.20
❑ 189 Mark Chmura	.10	.30
❑ 190 Kimble Anders	.10	.30
❑ 191 Charles Johnson	.07	.20
❑ 192 William Floyd	.07	.20
❑ 193 Jay Graham	.07	.20
❑ 194 Hardy Nickerson	.07	.20
❑ 195 Terry Allen	.20	.50
❑ 196 James Jett	.10	.30
❑ 197 Jessie Armstead	.07	.20
❑ 198 Yancey Thigpen	.10	.30
❑ 199 Terance Mathis	.10	.30
❑ 200 Steve McNair	.20	.50
❑ 201 Wayne Chrebet	.20	.50
❑ 202 Jamir Miller	.07	.20
❑ 203 Duce Staley	.25	.60
❑ 204 Deion Sanders	.20	.50
❑ 205 Carnell Lake	.07	.20
❑ 206 Ed McCaffrey	.10	.30
❑ 207 Shawn Springs	.07	.20
❑ 208 Tony Martin	.10	.30
❑ 209 Jerris McPhail	.07	.20
❑ 210 Darnay Scott	.10	.30
❑ 211 Jake Reed	.10	.30
❑ 212 Adrian Murrell	.10	.30
❑ 213 Quinn Early	.07	.20
❑ 214 Marvin Harrison	.20	.50
❑ 215 Ryan McNeil	.07	.20
❑ 216 Derrick Alexander	.10	.30
❑ 217 Ray Lewis	.20	.50
❑ 218 Antonio Freeman	.20	.50
❑ 219 Dwayne Rudd	.07	.20
❑ 220 Muhsin Muhammad	.10	.30
❑ 221 Kevin Hardy	.07	.20
❑ 222 Andre Hastings	.07	.20
❑ 223 John Avery RC	.30	.75
❑ 224 Keith Brooking RC	.50	1.25
❑ 225 Kevin Dyson RC	.50	1.25
❑ 226 Robert Edwards RC	.30	.75
❑ 227 Greg Ellis RC	.20	.50
❑ 228 Curtis Enis RC	.20	.50
❑ 229 Terry Fair RC	.30	.75
❑ 230 Ahman Green RC	1.50	4.00
❑ 231 Jacquez Green RC	.30	.75
❑ 232 Brian Griese RC	1.25	3.00
❑ 233 Skip Hicks RC	.30	.75
❑ 234 Ryan Leaf RC	.50	1.25
❑ 235 Peyton Manning RC	7.50	15.00
❑ 236 R.W. McQuarters RC	.30	.75
❑ 237 Randy Moss RC	4.00	10.00
❑ 238 Marcus Nash RC	.20	.50
❑ 239 Anthony Simmons RC	.30	.75
❑ 240 Brian Simmons RC	.30	.75
❑ 241 Takeo Spikes RC	.50	1.25
❑ 242 Duane Starks RC	.20	.50
❑ 243 Fred Taylor RC	.75	2.00
❑ 244 Andre Wadsworth RC	.30	.75
❑ 245 Shaun Williams RC	.30	.75
❑ 246 Grant Wistrom RC	.30	.75
❑ 247 Charles Woodson RC	.60	1.50
❑ 248 Checklist	.07	.20
❑ 249 Checklist	.07	.20
❑ 250 Checklist	.07	.20

1999 Fleer Tradition

Card	Low	High
❑ COMPLETE SET (300)	20.00	40.00
❑ 1 Randy Moss	.50	1.25
❑ 2 Peyton Manning	.60	1.50
❑ 3 Barry Sanders	.60	1.50
❑ 4 Terrell Davis	.20	.50
❑ 5 Brett Favre	.60	1.50
❑ 6 Fred Taylor	.20	.50
❑ 7 Jake Plummer	.10	.30
❑ 8 John Elway	.60	1.50
❑ 9 Emmitt Smith	.40	1.00
❑ 10 Kerry Collins	.10	.30
❑ 11 Peter Boulware	.07	.20
❑ 12 Jamal Anderson	.20	.50
❑ 13 Doug Flutie	.20	.50
❑ 14 Michael Bates	.07	.20
❑ 15 Corey Dillon	.20	.50
❑ 16 Curtis Conway	.10	.30
❑ 17 Ty Detmer	.10	.30
❑ 18 Robert Brooks	.10	.30
❑ 19 Dale Carter	.07	.20
❑ 20 Charlie Batch	.20	.50
❑ 21 Ken Dilger	.07	.20
❑ 22 Troy Aikman	.40	1.00
❑ 23 Tavian Banks	.07	.20
❑ 24 Cris Carter	.20	.50
❑ 25 Derrick Alexander WR	.10	.30
❑ 26 Chris Bordano RC	.07	.20
❑ 27 Karim Abdul-Jabbar	.10	.30
❑ 28 Jessie Armstead	.07	.20
❑ 29 Drew Bledsoe	.25	.60
❑ 30 Brian Dawkins	.20	.50
❑ 31 Wayne Chrebet	.10	.30
❑ 32 Garrison Hearst	.10	.30
❑ 33 Eric Allen	.07	.20
❑ 34 Tony Banks	.10	.30
❑ 35 Jerome Bettis	.20	.50
❑ 36 Stephen Alexander	.07	.20
❑ 37 Rodney Harrison	.07	.20
❑ 38 Mike Alstott	.20	.50
❑ 39 Chad Brown	.07	.20
❑ 40 Johnny McWilliams	.07	.20
❑ 41 Kevin Dyson	.10	.30
❑ 42 Keith Brooking	.07	.20
❑ 43 Jim Harbaugh	.10	.30
❑ 44 Bobby Engram	.10	.30
❑ 45 John Holecek	.07	.20
❑ 46 Steve Beuerlein	.07	.20
❑ 47 Tony McGee	.07	.20
❑ 48 Greg Ellis	.07	.20
❑ 49 Corey Fuller	.07	.20
❑ 50 Stephen Boyd	.07	.20
❑ 51 Marshall Faulk	.25	.60
❑ 52 LeRoy Butler	.07	.20
❑ 53 Reggie Barlow	.07	.20
❑ 54 Randall Cunningham	.20	.50
❑ 55 Aeneas Williams	.07	.20
❑ 56 Kimble Anders	.10	.30
❑ 57 Cam Cleeland	.07	.20
❑ 58 John Avery	.07	.20
❑ 59 Gary Brown	.07	.20
❑ 60 Ben Coates	.10	.30
❑ 61 Koy Detmer	.07	.20
❑ 62 Bryan Cox	.07	.20
❑ 63 Edgar Bennett	.07	.20
❑ 64 Tim Brown	.20	.50
❑ 65 Isaac Bruce	.20	.50
❑ 66 Eddie George	.20	.50
❑ 67 Reidel Anthony	.10	.30
❑ 68 Charlie Jones	.07	.20
❑ 69 Terry Allen	.10	.30
❑ 70 Joey Galloway	.10	.30
❑ 71 Jamir Miller	.07	.20
❑ 72 Will Blackwell	.07	.20
❑ 73 Ray Buchanan	.07	.20
❑ 74 Priest Holmes	.30	.75
❑ 75 Michael Irvin	.10	.30
❑ 76 Jonathan Linton	.07	.20
❑ 77 Curtis Enis	.07	.20
❑ 78 Neil O'Donnell	.10	.30
❑ 79 Tim Biakabutuka	.10	.30
❑ 80 Terry Kirby	.07	.20
❑ 81 Germane Crowell	.07	.20
❑ 82 Jason Elam	.07	.20
❑ 83 Mark Chmura	.07	.20
❑ 84 Marvin Harrison	.20	.50
❑ 85 Jimmy Hitchcock	.07	.20
❑ 86 Tony Brackens	.07	.20
❑ 87 Sean Dawkins	.07	.20
❑ 88 Tony Gonzalez	.20	.50
❑ 89 Kent Graham	.07	.20
❑ 90 Oronde Gadsden	.10	.30
❑ 91 Hugh Douglas	.07	.20
❑ 92 Robert Edwards	.07	.20
❑ 93 R.W. McQuarters	.07	.20
❑ 94 Aaron Glenn	.07	.20
❑ 95 Kevin Carter	.07	.20
❑ 96 Rickey Dudley	.07	.20
❑ 97 Derrick Brooks	.20	.50
❑ 98 Mark Bruener	.07	.20
❑ 99 Darrell Green	.07	.20
❑ 100 Jessie Tuggle	.07	.20
❑ 101 Freddie Jones	.07	.20
❑ 102 Rob Moore	.10	.30
❑ 103 Ahman Green	.20	.50
❑ 104 Chris Chandler	.10	.30
❑ 105 Steve McNair	.20	.50
❑ 106 Kevin Greene	.07	.20
❑ 107 Jermaine Lewis	.10	.30
❑ 108 Erik Kramer	.07	.20
❑ 109 Eric Moulds	.20	.50
❑ 110 Terry Fair	.07	.20
❑ 111 Carl Pickens	.10	.30
❑ 112 La'Roi Glover RC	.50	1.25
❑ 113 Chris Spielman	.07	.20
❑ 114 Leroy Hoard	.07	.20
❑ 115 Mark Brunell	.20	.50
❑ 116 Patrick Jeffers RC	1.50	3.00
❑ 117 Elvis Grbac	.10	.30
❑ 118 Ike Hilliard	.07	.20
❑ 119 Sam Madison	.07	.20
❑ 120 Terrell Owens	.20	.50
❑ 121 Rich Gannon	.20	.50
❑ 122 Skip Hicks	.07	.20
❑ 123 Eric Green	.07	.20
❑ 124 Trent Dilfer	.10	.30
❑ 125 Terry Glenn	.20	.50
❑ 126 Trent Green	.20	.50
❑ 127 Charles Johnson	.07	.20
❑ 128 Adrian Murrell	.10	.30
❑ 129 Jason Gildon	.07	.20
❑ 130 Tim Dwight	.20	.50
❑ 131 Ryan Leaf	.20	.50
❑ 132 Rocket Ismail	.10	.30
❑ 133 Jon Kitna	.20	.50
❑ 134 Alonzo Mayes	.07	.20
❑ 135 Yancey Thigpen	.07	.20
❑ 136 David LaFleur	.07	.20
❑ 137 Ray Lewis	.20	.50
❑ 138 Herman Moore	.10	.30
❑ 139 Brian Griese	.20	.50
❑ 140 Antonio Freeman	.20	.50

Card	Low	High
❑ 141 Darnay Scott	.07	.20
❑ 142 Ed McDaniel	.07	.20
❑ 143 Andre Reed	.10	.30
❑ 144 Andre Hastings	.07	.20
❑ 145 Chris Warren	.07	.20
❑ 146 Kevin Hardy	.07	.20
❑ 147 Joe Jurevicius	.10	.30
❑ 148 Jerome Pathon	.07	.20
❑ 149 Duce Staley	.20	.50
❑ 150 Dan Marino	.60	1.50
❑ 151 Jerry Rice	.40	1.00
❑ 152 Byron Bam Morris	.07	.20
❑ 153 Az-Zahir Hakim	.07	.20
❑ 154 Ty Law	.10	.30
❑ 155 Warrick Dunn	.20	.50
❑ 156 Keyshawn Johnson	.20	.50
❑ 157 Brian Mitchell	.07	.20
❑ 158 James Jett	.10	.30
❑ 159 Fred Lane	.07	.20
❑ 160 Courtney Hawkins	.07	.20
❑ 161 Andre Wadsworth	.07	.20
❑ 162 Natrone Means	.10	.30
❑ 163 Andrew Glover	.07	.20
❑ 164 Anthony Simmons	.07	.20
❑ 165 Leon Lett	.07	.20
❑ 166 Frank Wycheck	.07	.20
❑ 167 Barry Minter	.07	.20
❑ 168 Michael McCrary	.07	.20
❑ 169 Johnnie Morton	.10	.30
❑ 170 Jay Riemersma	.07	.20
❑ 171 Vonnie Holliday	.07	.20
❑ 172 Brian Simmons	.07	.20
❑ 173 Joe Johnson	.07	.20
❑ 174 Ed McCaffrey	.10	.30
❑ 175 Jason Sehorn	.07	.20
❑ 176 Keenan McCardell	.10	.30
❑ 177 Bobby Taylor	.07	.20
❑ 178 Andre Rison	.10	.30
❑ 179 Greg Hill	.07	.20
❑ 180 O.J. McDuffie	.10	.30
❑ 181 Darren Woodson	.07	.20
❑ 182 Willie McGinest	.07	.20
❑ 183 J.J. Stokes	.10	.30
❑ 184 Leon Johnson	.07	.20
❑ 185 Bert Emanuel	.10	.30
❑ 186 Napoleon Kaufman	.20	.50
❑ 187 Leslie Shepherd	.07	.20
❑ 188 Levon Kirkland	.07	.20
❑ 189 Simeon Rice	.10	.30
❑ 190 Mikhael Ricks	.07	.20
❑ 191 Robert Smith	.20	.50
❑ 192 Michael Sinclair	.07	.20
❑ 193 Muhsin Muhammad	.10	.30
❑ 194 Duane Starks	.07	.20
❑ 195 Terance Mathis	.10	.30
❑ 196 Antowain Smith	.20	.50
❑ 197 Tony Parrish	.07	.20
❑ 198 Takeo Spikes	.07	.20
❑ 199 Ernie Mills	.07	.20
❑ 200 John Mobley	.07	.20
❑ 202 Pete Mitchell	.07	.20
❑ 203 Darick Holmes	.07	.20
❑ 204 Derrick Thomas	.20	.50
❑ 205 David Palmer	.07	.20
❑ 206 Jason Taylor	.07	.20
❑ 207 Sammy Knight	.07	.20
❑ 208 Dwayne Rudd	.07	.20
❑ 209 Lawyer Milloy	.10	.30
❑ 210 Michael Strahan	.10	.30
❑ 211 Mo Lewis	.07	.20
❑ 212 William Thomas	.07	.20
❑ 213 Darrell Russell	.07	.20
❑ 214 Brad Johnson	.20	.50
❑ 215 Kordell Stewart	.10	.30
❑ 216 Robert Holcombe	.07	.20
❑ 217 Junior Seau	.20	.50
❑ 218 Jacquez Green	.07	.20
❑ 219 Shawn Springs	.07	.20
❑ 220 Michael Westbrook	.10	.30
❑ 221 Rod Woodson	.10	.30
❑ 222 Frank Sanders	.10	.30
❑ 223 Bruce Smith	.10	.30
❑ 224 Eugene Robinson	.07	.20
❑ 225 Bill Romanowski	.07	.20
❑ 226 Wesley Walls	.10	.30
❑ 227 Jimmy Smith	.10	.30
❑ 228 Deion Sanders	.20	.50
❑ 229 Lamar Thomas	.07	.20
❑ 230 Dorsey Levens	.20	.50
❑ 231 Tony Simmons	.07	.20
❑ 232 John Randle	.10	.30
❑ 233 Curtis Martin	.20	.50
❑ 234 Bryant Young	.07	.20
❑ 235 Charles Woodson	.20	.50
❑ 236 Charles Way	.07	.20
❑ 237 Zach Thomas	.20	.50
❑ 238 Ricky Proehl	.07	.20
❑ 239 Ricky Watters	.10	.30
❑ 240 Hardy Nickerson	.07	.20
❑ 241 Shannon Sharpe	.10	.30
❑ 242 O.J. Santiago	.07	.20
❑ 243 Vinny Testaverde	.10	.30
❑ 244 Roell Preston	.07	.20
❑ 245 James Stewart	.10	.30
❑ 246 Jake Reed	.10	.30
❑ 247 Steve Young	.25	.60
❑ 248 Shaun Williams	.07	.20
❑ 249 Rod Smith	.10	.30
❑ 250 Warren Sapp	.10	.30
❑ 251 Champ Bailey RC	.60	1.50
❑ 252 Karsten Bailey RC	.30	.75
❑ 253 D'Wayne Bates RC	.30	.75
❑ 254 Michael Bishop RC	.50	1.25
❑ 255 David Boston RC	.50	1.25
❑ 256 Na Brown RC	.30	.75
❑ 257 Fernando Bryant RC	.30	.75
❑ 258 Shawn Bryson RC	.50	1.25
❑ 259 Darrin Chiaverini RC	.30	.75
❑ 260 Chris Claiborne RC	.15	.40
❑ 261 Mike Cloud RC	.30	.75
❑ 262 Cecil Collins RC	.15	.40
❑ 263 Tim Couch RC	.50	1.25
❑ 264 Scott Covington RC	.50	1.25
❑ 265 Daunte Culpepper RC	2.00	5.00
❑ 266 Antuan Edwards RC	.15	.40
❑ 267 Troy Edwards RC	.30	.75
❑ 268 Ebenezer Ekuban RC	.30	.75
❑ 269 Kevin Faulk RC	.50	1.25
❑ 270 Jermaine Fazande RC	.30	.75
❑ 271 Joe Germaine RC	.30	.75
❑ 272 Martin Gramatica RC	.15	.40
❑ 273 Torry Holt RC	1.25	3.00
❑ 274 Brock Huard RC	.50	1.25
❑ 275 Sedrick Irvin RC	.15	.40
❑ 276 Sheldon Jackson RC	.30	.75
❑ 277 Edgerrin James RC	2.00	5.00
❑ 278 James Johnson RC	.30	.75
❑ 279 Kevin Johnson RC	.50	1.25
❑ 280 Malcolm Johnson RC	.15	.40
❑ 281 Andy Katzenmoyer RC	.30	.75
❑ 282 Jevon Kearse RC	.75	2.00
❑ 283 Patrick Kerney RC	.50	1.25
❑ 284 Shaun King RC	.30	.75
❑ 285 Jim Kleinsasser RC	.50	1.25
❑ 286 Rob Konrad RC	.50	1.25
❑ 287 Chris McAlister RC	.30	.75
❑ 288 Donovan McNabb RC	2.50	6.00
❑ 289 Cade McNown RC	.30	.75
❑ 290 Dee Miller RC	.15	.40
❑ 291 Joe Montgomery RC	.30	.75
❑ 292 De'Mond Parker RC	.15	.40
❑ 293 Peerless Price RC	.50	1.25
❑ 294 Akili Smith RC	.30	.75
❑ 295 Justin Swift RC	.15	.40
❑ 296 Jerame Tuman RC	.50	1.25
❑ 297 Ricky Williams RC	1.00	2.50
❑ 298 Antoine Winfield	.30	.75
❑ 299 Craig Yeast RC	.30	.75
❑ 300 Amos Zereoue RC	.50	1.25
❑ P6 Fred Taylor Promo	.40	1.00

2000 Fleer Tradition

Card	Low	High
❑ COMPLETE SET (400)	25.00	60.00
❑ 1 Kevin Johnson	.20	.50
❑ 2 Chris Chandler	.10	.30
❑ 3 Peerless Price	.10	.30
❑ 4 Andre Rison	.10	.30
❑ 5 Curtis Enis	.07	.20
❑ 6 Tim Couch	.10	.30
❑ 7 Brian Dawkins	.20	.50
❑ 8 Akili Smith	.07	.20
❑ 9 Kevin Faulk	.10	.30
❑ 10 Joey Galloway	.10	.30
❑ 11 Bill Romanowski	.07	.20
❑ 12 Charlie Batch	.20	.50
❑ 13 Terrence Wilkins	.07	.20
❑ 14 Kevin Hardy	.07	.20
❑ 15 Cade McNown	.07	.20
❑ 16 Elvis Grbac	.10	.30
❑ 17 Cris Carter	.20	.50
❑ 18 Willie McGinest	.07	.20
❑ 19 Michael Bishop	.07	.20
❑ 20 Lee Woodall	.07	.20
❑ 21 Jake Reed	.10	.30
❑ 22 Bryan Cox	.07	.20
❑ 23 Chris Sanders	.07	.20
❑ 24 Tavian Banks	.07	.20
❑ 25 Levon Kirkland	.07	.20
❑ 26 James Hundon	.07	.20
❑ 27 Junior Seau	.20	.50
❑ 28 Darren Woodson	.07	.20
❑ 29 Kevin Carter	.07	.20
❑ 30 Joe Jurevicius	.07	.20
❑ 31 John Lynch	.10	.30
❑ 32 Steve McNair	.20	.50
❑ 33 Jake Plummer	.10	.30
❑ 34 Antonio Freeman	.20	.50
❑ 35 Peter Boulware	.07	.20
❑ 36 Brad Johnson	.20	.50
❑ 37 Bobby Engram	.10	.30
❑ 38 David Boston	.20	.50
❑ 39 Jason Tucker	.07	.20
❑ 40 Troy Brown	.10	.30
❑ 41 Brian Griese	.20	.50
❑ 42 Dorsey Levens	.10	.30
❑ 43 Cornelius Bennett	.07	.20
❑ 44 Donovan McNabb	.30	.75
❑ 45 Rob Johnson	.10	.30
❑ 46 Robert Smith	.20	.50
❑ 47 Stanley Pritchett	.07	.20
❑ 48 Tedy Bruschi	.20	.50
❑ 49 Dan Marino	.60	1.50
❑ 50 Amani Toomer	.10	.30
❑ 51 Aaron Glenn	.07	.20
❑ 52 Rickey Dudley	.07	.20
❑ 53 Tim Brown	.20	.50
❑ 54 Jim Harbaugh	.10	.30
❑ 55 Terrell Owens	.20	.50
❑ 56 Jason Sehorn	.07	.20
❑ 57 Cortez Kennedy	.07	.20
❑ 58 London Fletcher RC	.10	.30
❑ 59 Simeon Rice	.10	.30
❑ 60 Shaun King	.07	.20
❑ 61 Stephen Davis	.20	.50
❑ 62 Andre Wadsworth	.07	.20
❑ 63 Kyle Brady	.07	.20
❑ 64 Priest Holmes	.25	.60
❑ 65 Patrick Jeffers	.20	.50
❑ 66 Barry Minter	.07	.20
❑ 67 Curtis Martin	.20	.50
❑ 68 Darrin Chiaverini	.07	.20
❑ 69 Robert Thomas	.07	.20
❑ 70 Samari Rolle	.07	.20
❑ 71 Robert Porcher	.07	.20
❑ 72 Jerry Rice	.40	1.00
❑ 73 Bill Schroeder	.10	.30
❑ 74 Chad Bratzke	.07	.20
❑ 75 Tony Brackens	.07	.20
❑ 76 O.J. McDuffie	.10	.30
❑ 77 John Randle	.10	.30
❑ 78 Michael Pittman	.07	.20
❑ 79 Drew Bledsoe	.25	.60
❑ 80 Ike Hilliard	.10	.30
❑ 81 Victor Green	.07	.20
❑ 82 Duce Staley	.20	.50
❑ 83 Bruce Smith	.10	.30
❑ 84 Amos Zereoue	.20	.50
❑ 85 Charlie Garner	.10	.30
❑ 86 Shawn Springs	.07	.20
❑ 87 Kurt Warner	.40	1.00
❑ 88 Eddie George	.20	.50
❑ 89 Michael Westbrook	.10	.30
❑ 90 Dexter Coakley	.07	.20
❑ 91 Rob Moore	.10	.30

Card	Low	High
❑ 92 Duane Starks	.07	.20
❑ 93 Steve Beuerlein	.10	.30
❑ 94 Marty Booker	.10	.30
❑ 95 Karim Abdul-Jabbar	.10	.30
❑ 96 Troy Aikman	.40	1.00
❑ 97 Germane Crowell	.07	.20
❑ 98 Matt Hasselbeck	.10	.30
❑ 99 E.G. Green	.07	.20
❑ 100 Mark Brunell	.20	.50
❑ 101 Tony Martin	.10	.30
❑ 102 Darrell Green	.07	.20
❑ 103 Ricky Williams	.20	.50
❑ 104 Michael Strahan	.10	.30
❑ 105 Vinny Testaverde	.10	.30
❑ 106 Charles Johnson	.10	.30
❑ 107 Hines Ward	.20	.50
❑ 108 Bryant Young	.07	.20
❑ 109 Mo Lewis	.07	.20
❑ 110 Greg Clark	.07	.20
❑ 111 Jon Kitna	.20	.50
❑ 112 Jacquez Green	.07	.20
❑ 113 Kevin Dyson	.10	.30
❑ 114 Stephen Alexander	.07	.20
❑ 115 Cam Cleeland	.07	.20
❑ 116 Keith Poole	.07	.20
❑ 117 Az-Zahir Hakim	.10	.30
❑ 118 Tim Dwight	.20	.50
❑ 119 Corey Bradford	.07	.20
❑ 120 Carlos Emmons	.07	.20
❑ 121 Trent Dilfer	.10	.30
❑ 122 Lance Schulters	.07	.20
❑ 123 Byron Hanspard	.07	.20
❑ 124 Tim Biakabutuka	.10	.30
❑ 125 Eddie Kennison	.10	.30
❑ 126 Terry Kirby	.07	.20
❑ 127 Mike McKenzie	.07	.20
❑ 128 Fred Beasley	.07	.20
❑ 129 Chad Brown	.07	.20
❑ 130 Terrell Davis	.20	.50
❑ 131 Herman Moore	.10	.30
❑ 132 Vonnie Holliday	.07	.20
❑ 133 Jim Miller	.07	.20
❑ 134 Peyton Manning	.50	1.25
❑ 135 Derrick Alexander	.10	.30
❑ 136 Oronde Gadsden	.10	.30
❑ 137 Robert Griffith	.07	.20
❑ 138 Troy Edwards	.07	.20
❑ 139 Damon Huard	.20	.50
❑ 140 Jessie Armstead	.07	.20
❑ 141 Charles Woodson	.10	.30
❑ 142 Troy Vincent	.07	.20
❑ 143 Natrone Means	.07	.20
❑ 144 Jeff Garcia	.20	.50
❑ 145 Terry Glenn	.10	.30
❑ 146 Marshall Faulk	.25	.60
❑ 147 Pat Johnson	.07	.20
❑ 148 Frank Wycheck	.07	.20
❑ 149 Champ Bailey	.10	.30
❑ 150 Jamal Anderson	.20	.50
❑ 151 Doug Flutie	.20	.50
❑ 152 Michael Bates	.07	.20
❑ 153 Corey Dillon	.20	.50
❑ 154 Keith McKenzie	.07	.20
❑ 155 Orpheus Roye	.07	.20
❑ 156 Olandis Gary	.20	.50
❑ 157 Johnnie Morton	.10	.30
❑ 158 Brett Favre	.60	1.50
❑ 159 Adrian Murrell	.07	.20
❑ 160 Fred Taylor	.20	.50
❑ 161 Tony Gonzalez	.10	.30
❑ 162 Zach Thomas	.20	.50
❑ 163 Randy Moss	.40	1.00
❑ 164 Marcus Robinson	.20	.50
❑ 165 Tiki Barber	.20	.50
❑ 166 Rich Gannon	.20	.50
❑ 167 Jeremiah Trotter RC	.60	1.50
❑ 168 Jermaine Fazande	.07	.20
❑ 169 Steve Young	.25	.60
❑ 170 Isaac Bruce	.20	.50
❑ 171 Warrick Dunn	.20	.50
❑ 172 Yancey Thigpen	.07	.20
❑ 173 Rod Smith	.10	.30
❑ 174 Albert Connell	.07	.20
❑ 175 Freddie Jones	.07	.20
❑ 176 Terance Mathis	.10	.30
❑ 177 Eric Moulds	.20	.50
❑ 178 Brian Mitchell	.07	.20
❑ 179 Wesley Walls	.07	.20
❑ 180 Carl Pickens	.10	.30
❑ 181 Errict Rhett	.10	.30
❑ 182 Madre Hill	.07	.20
❑ 183 Jason Elam	.07	.20
❑ 184 Greg Ellis	.07	.20
❑ 185 David Sloan	.07	.20
❑ 186 Edgerrin James	.30	.75
❑ 187 Jimmy Smith	.10	.30
❑ 188 Tony Richardson RC	.10	.30
❑ 189 James Hasty	.07	.20
❑ 190 Sam Madison	.07	.20
❑ 191 Tony Simmons	.07	.20
❑ 192 Andre Hastings	.07	.20
❑ 193 Keyshawn Johnson	.20	.50
❑ 194 Na Brown	.07	.20
❑ 195 Napoleon Kaufman	.10	.30
❑ 196 Torrance Small	.07	.20
❑ 197 Curtis Conway	.10	.30
❑ 198 Jeff Graham	.07	.20
❑ 199 Jason Hanson	.07	.20
❑ 200 Derrick Mayes	.10	.30
❑ 201 Torry Holt	.20	.50
❑ 202 Warren Sapp	.10	.30
❑ 203 Kimble Anders	.07	.20
❑ 204 Blaine Bishop	.07	.20
❑ 205 Leroy Hoard	.07	.20
❑ 206 Larry Centers	.07	.20
❑ 207 O.J. Santiago	.07	.20
❑ 208 Antowain Smith	.10	.30
❑ 209 Chuck Smith	.07	.20
❑ 210 Takeo Spikes	.07	.20
❑ 211 Rocket Ismail	.10	.30
❑ 212 Ed McCaffrey	.20	.50
❑ 213 Karsten Bailey	.07	.20
❑ 214 Terry Fair	.07	.20
❑ 215 Ken Dilger	.07	.20
❑ 216 Jamie Martin	.10	.30
❑ 217 Cris Dishman	.07	.20
❑ 218 Jay Fiedler	.10	.30
❑ 219 Lawyer Milloy	.10	.30
❑ 220 Jake Delhomme RC	1.25	3.00
❑ 221 Wayne Chrebet	.10	.30
❑ 222 Darrell Russell	.07	.20
❑ 223 Christian Fauria	.07	.20
❑ 224 Jerome Bettis	.20	.50
❑ 225 Ryan Leaf	.10	.30
❑ 226 Ricky Watters	.10	.30
❑ 227 Keenan McCardell	.10	.30
❑ 228 Grant Wistrom	.07	.20
❑ 229 Jevon Kearse	.20	.50
❑ 230 Frank Sanders	.10	.30
❑ 231 Shannon Sharpe	.10	.30
❑ 232 Jonathan Linton	.07	.20
❑ 233 Alonzo Mayes	.07	.20
❑ 234 Jason Garrett	.07	.20
❑ 235 Kordell Stewart	.10	.30
❑ 236 David LaFleur	.07	.20
❑ 237 Kenny Bynum	.07	.20
❑ 238 Byron Chamberlain	.07	.20
❑ 239 Tyrone Davis	.07	.20
❑ 240 Jerome Pathon	.10	.30
❑ 241 Alvis Whitted	.07	.20
❑ 242 Kevin Lockett	.07	.20
❑ 243 Matthew Hatchette	.07	.20
❑ 244 Rod Woodson	.10	.30
❑ 245 Joe Horn	.10	.30
❑ 246 Ronnie Powell	.07	.20
❑ 247 Dedric Ward	.07	.20
❑ 248 James Johnson	.07	.20
❑ 249 James Jett	.07	.20
❑ 250 Bobby Shaw RC	.20	.50
❑ 251 J.J. Stokes	.10	.30
❑ 252 Paul Shields RC	.07	.20
❑ 253 Sean Dawkins	.07	.20
❑ 254 Hardy Nickerson	.07	.20
❑ 255 Stephen Boyd	.07	.20
❑ 256 Chris Warren	.07	.20
❑ 257 Kerry Collins	.10	.30
❑ 258 Isaac Byrd	.07	.20
❑ 259 Bobby Hoying	.07	.20
❑ 260 Daunte Culpepper	.25	.60
❑ 261 Moe Williams	.10	.30
❑ 262 Kamil Loud	.07	.20
❑ 263 Derrick Brooks	.20	.50
❑ 264 Jay Riemersma	.07	.20
❑ 265 Ray Lucas	.10	.30
❑ 266 Jason Gildon	.07	.20
❑ 267 James Stewart	.10	.30
❑ 268 Marcellus Wiley	.07	.20
❑ 269 Craig Yeast	.07	.20
❑ 270 Michael Basnight	.07	.20
❑ 271 Tyrone Wheatley	.10	.30
❑ 272 Martin Gramatica	.07	.20
❑ 273 Phillip Daniels RC	.10	.30
❑ 274 Richard Huntley	.07	.20
❑ 275 Muhsin Muhammad	.10	.30
❑ 276 Todd Lyght	.07	.20
❑ 277 Carlester Crumpler	.07	.20
❑ 278 Jeff Lewis	.07	.20
❑ 279 Jeff George	.10	.30
❑ 280 Jeff Blake	.10	.30
❑ 281 Michael McCrary	.07	.20
❑ 282 Shawn Jefferson	.07	.20
❑ 283 Mark Bruener	.07	.20
❑ 284 Donnie Abraham	.07	.20
❑ 285 Yatil Green	.07	.20
❑ 286 Jermaine Lewis	.07	.20
❑ 287 Rob Fredrickson	.07	.20
❑ 288 Thurman Thomas	.10	.30
❑ 289 Kent Graham	.07	.20
❑ 290 Darnay Scott	.10	.30
❑ 291 Tony Graziani	.07	.20
❑ 292 Qadry Ismail	.10	.30
❑ 293 Aeneas Williams	.07	.20
❑ 294 Marvin Harrison	.20	.50
❑ 295 Jimmy Hitchcock	.07	.20
❑ 296 Bob Christian	.07	.20
❑ 297 Pete Mitchell	.07	.20
❑ 298 Mike Alstott	.20	.50
❑ 299 Emmitt Smith	.40	1.00
❑ 300 Trevor Pryce	.07	.20
❑ 301 Tony Banks	.10	.30
❑ 302 Mikhael Ricks	.07	.20
❑ 303 Randall Cunningham	.20	.50
❑ 304 Thomas Jones RC	.50	1.25
❑ 305 Mark Simoneau RC	.25	.60
❑ 306 Jamal Lewis RC	.75	2.00
❑ 307 Kwame Cavil RC	.15	.40
❑ 308 Rashard Anderson RC	.25	.60
❑ 309 Brian Urlacher RC	1.25	3.00
❑ 310 Peter Warrick RC	.30	.75
❑ 311 Courtney Brown RC	.30	.75
❑ 312 Michael Wiley RC	.25	.60
❑ 313 Chris Cole RC	.25	.60
❑ 314 Reuben Droughns RC	.30	.75
❑ 315 Bubba Franks RC	.30	.75
❑ 316 Rob Morris RC	.25	.60
❑ 317 R.Jay Soward RC	.25	.60
❑ 318 Sylvester Morris RC	.25	.60
❑ 319 Ben Kelly RC	.15	.40
❑ 320 Doug Chapman RC	.25	.60
❑ 321 J.R. Redmond RC	.25	.60
❑ 322 Darren Howard RC	.25	.60
❑ 323 Ron Dayne RC	.30	.75
❑ 324 Chad Pennington RC	.75	2.00
❑ 325 Jerry Porter RC	.30	.75
❑ 326 Corey Simon RC	.30	.75
❑ 327 Plaxico Burress RC	.60	1.50
❑ 328 Trung Canidate RC	.25	.60
❑ 329 Rogers Beckett RC	.25	.60
❑ 330 Giovanni Carmazzi RC	.15	.40
❑ 331 Shaun Alexander RC	1.00	2.50
❑ 332 Joe Hamilton RC	.25	.60
❑ 333 Keith Bulluck RC	.30	.75
❑ 334 Todd Husak RC	.30	.75
❑ 335 D.Walker RC/R.Thompson RC	.25	.60
❑ 336 M.Philyaw RC/A.Midget RC	.15	.40
❑ 337 C.Redman RC/T.Taylor RC	.30	.75
❑ 338 Sam.Morris RC/A.Black RC	.30	.75
❑ 339 D.Grant RC/A.McKinley RC	.25	.60
❑ 340 D.White RC/F.Murphy RC	.30	.75
❑ 341 C.Keaton RC/R.Dugans RC	.30	.75
❑ 342 Prentice RC/Northcutt RC	.25	.60
❑ 343 O.Grant RC/D.Goodrich RC	.15	.40
❑ 344 D.O'Neal RC/I.Gold RC	.30	.75
❑ 345 S.McDougle RC/B.Green RC	.15	.40
❑ 346 A.Lucas RC/N.Diggs RC	.25	.60
❑ 347 M.Washington RC/D.Kendra RC	.25	.60
❑ 348 T.Slaughter RC/S.Stith RC	.25	.60
❑ 349 W.Bartee RC/F.Moreau RC	.25	.60
❑ 350 D.Dyer RC/T.Wade RC	.25	.60
❑ 351 C.Hovan RC/T.Walters	.30	.75
❑ 352 T.Brady RC/Stachelski RC	12.50	30.00
❑ 353 M.Bulger RC/T.Smith RC	.60	1.50
❑ 354 C.Griffin RC/R.Dixon RC	.25	.60
❑ 355 L.Coles RC/A.Becht RC	.30	.75
❑ 356 Janikowski RC/Lechler RC	.30	.75
❑ 357 T.Pinkston RC/G.Scott RC	.30	.75
❑ 358 D.Farmer RC/T.Martin RC	.25	.60

Card		
❑ 359 B.Young RC/J.Shepherd RC	.25	.60
❑ 360 J.Seider RC/T.Gaylor RC	.25	.60
❑ 361 T.Rattay RC/C.Fields RC	.30	.75
❑ 362 D.Jackson RC/J.Williams RC	.50	1.25
❑ 363 N.Webster RC/J.Whalen RC	.15	.40
❑ 364 E.Kinney RC/C.Coleman RC	.30	.75
❑ 365 C.Samuels RC/L.Murray RC	.25	.60
❑ 366 Cardinals IA/Plummer	.10	.30
❑ 367 Falcons IA/Chandlr/Andrson	.10	.30
❑ 368 Ravens IA/Boulware	.07	.20
❑ 369 Bills IA/Flutie	.10	.30
❑ 370 Panthers IA/Beuerlein	.10	.30
❑ 371 Bears IA/McNown	.07	.20
❑ 372 Bengals IA/Dillon	.10	.30
❑ 373 Browns IA/Couch	.10	.30
❑ 374 Cowboys IA/Smith	.20	.50
❑ 375 Broncos IA/Gary	.10	.30
❑ 376 Lions IA/Batch	.10	.30
❑ 377 Packers IA/Levens	.10	.30
❑ 378 Colts IA/James	.25	.60
❑ 379 Jaguars IA/Brackens	.07	.20
❑ 380 Chiefs IA/Grbac	.07	.20
❑ 381 Dolphins IA/Marino	.30	.75
❑ 382 Vikings IA/Rob.Smith	.10	.30
❑ 383 Patriots IA/Bledsoe	.10	.30
❑ 384 Saints IA/Williams	.20	.50
❑ 385 Giants IA/Armstead	.07	.20
❑ 386 Jets IA/Martin	.10	.30
❑ 387 Raiders IA/Kaufman	.10	.30
❑ 388 Eagles IA/McNabb	.10	.30
❑ 389 Steelers IA/Bettis	.10	.30
❑ 390 Rams IA/Faulk	.20	.50
❑ 391 Chargers IA/Fazande	.07	.20
❑ 392 49ers IA/Garner	.10	.30
❑ 393 Seahawks IA/Kennedy	.07	.20
❑ 394 Buccaneers IA/Alstott	.10	.30
❑ 395 Titans IA/McNair	.10	.30
❑ 396 Redskins IA/S.Davis	.10	.30
❑ 397 Tim Couch CL	.10	.30
❑ 398 Peyton Manning CL	.25	.60
❑ 399 Kurt Warner CL	.20	.50
❑ 400 Randy Moss CL	.20	.50

2001 Fleer Tradition

Card		
❑ COMPLETE SET (450)	20.00	40.00
❑ 1 Thomas Jones	.20	.50
❑ 2 Bruce Smith	.25	.60
❑ 3 Marvin Harrison	.25	.60
❑ 4 Darrell Jackson	.20	.50
❑ 5 Trent Green	.25	.60
❑ 6 Wesley Walls	.15	.40
❑ 7 Jimmy Smith	.20	.50
❑ 8 Isaac Bruce	.25	.60
❑ 9 Jamal Anderson	.20	.50
❑ 10 Marty Booker	.20	.50
❑ 11 Elvis Grbac	.20	.50
❑ 12 Joe Jurevicius	.15	.40
❑ 13 Reidel Anthony	.15	.40
❑ 14 Darnay Scott	.20	.50
❑ 15 Oronde Gadsden	.15	.40
❑ 16 Shawn Bryson	.15	.40
❑ 17 Jonathan Ogden	.20	.50
❑ 18 Aaron Shea	.15	.40
❑ 19 Randy Moss	.30	.75
❑ 20 Eddie George	.25	.60
❑ 21 Stephen Davis	.20	.50
❑ 22 Emmitt Smith	.60	1.50
❑ 23 Willie McGinest	.15	.40
❑ 24 Trent Dilfer	.20	.50
❑ 25 Peter Boulware	.15	.40
❑ 26 Rod Smith	.20	.50
❑ 27 Ricky Williams	.25	.60
❑ 28 Albert Connell	.15	.40
❑ 29 Robert Porcher	.15	.40
❑ 30 Jessie Armstead	.15	.40
❑ 31 Shane Matthews	.15	.40
❑ 32 Eric Moulds	.20	.50
❑ 33 Kurt Schulz	.15	.40
❑ 34 Richie Anderson	.15	.40
❑ 35 Ron Dugans	.15	.40
❑ 36 Steve Beuerlein	.20	.50
❑ 37 Darren Sharper	.20	.50
❑ 38 Andre Rison	.20	.50
❑ 39 Courtney Brown	.15	.40
❑ 40 Eddie Kennison	.20	.50
❑ 41 Ken Dilger	.15	.40
❑ 42 Charles Johnson	.15	.40
❑ 43 Dexter Coakley	.15	.40
❑ 44 Akili Smith	.15	.40
❑ 45 R.Jay Soward	.15	.40
❑ 46 Danny Farmer	.15	.40
❑ 47 Dez White	.20	.50
❑ 48 Olandis Gary	.15	.40
❑ 49 Wali Rainer	.15	.40
❑ 50 Derrick Alexander	.15	.40
❑ 51 Donnie Abraham	.15	.40
❑ 52 David Sloan	.15	.40
❑ 53 Larry Allen	.20	.50
❑ 54 Sam Madison	.15	.40
❑ 55 Troy Edwards	.15	.40
❑ 56 Ryan Longwell	.20	.50
❑ 57 Brian Griese	.20	.50
❑ 58 John Randle	.20	.50
❑ 59 Reggie Jones	.15	.40
❑ 60 Mike Peterson	.15	.40
❑ 61 Bill Romanowski	.20	.50
❑ 62 Kevin Faulk	.20	.50
❑ 63 Tai Streets	.15	.40
❑ 64 Tony Brackens	.15	.40
❑ 65 James Stewart	.15	.40
❑ 66 Joe Horn	.20	.50
❑ 67 Kurt Warner	.30	.75
❑ 68 Eric Hicks RC	.25	.60
❑ 69 Bryan Westbrook	.15	.40
❑ 70 Tiki Barber	.25	.60
❑ 71 Frank Sanders	.15	.40
❑ 72 Olindo Mare	.15	.40
❑ 73 Bill Schroeder	.20	.50
❑ 74 Anthony Becht	.15	.40
❑ 75 Rob Johnson	.20	.50
❑ 76 Troy Brown	.20	.50
❑ 77 Chad Bratzke	.15	.40
❑ 78 Rickey Dudley	.15	.40
❑ 79 Doug Johnson	.15	.40
❑ 80 Joe Johnson	.15	.40
❑ 81 Keenan McCardell	.20	.50
❑ 82 Tim Brown	.25	.60
❑ 83 Blaine Bishop	.15	.40
❑ 84 Ron Dixon	.15	.40
❑ 85 Michael Cloud	.15	.40
❑ 86 Todd Pinkston	.15	.40
❑ 87 Shannon Sharpe	.25	.60
❑ 88 Marvin Jones	.15	.40
❑ 89 Zach Thomas	.25	.60
❑ 90 Kordell Stewart	.20	.50
❑ 91 Champ Bailey	.25	.60
❑ 92 Jacquez Green	.15	.40
❑ 93 Daunte Culpepper	.25	.60
❑ 94 Freddie Jones	.15	.40
❑ 95 Donald Hayes	.15	.40
❑ 96 Rich Gannon	.20	.50
❑ 97 Ty Law	.20	.50
❑ 98 Grant Wistrom	.15	.40
❑ 99 James Allen	.15	.40
❑ 100 Corey Simon	.15	.40
❑ 101 Jeff Blake	.20	.50
❑ 102 Bryant Young	.20	.50
❑ 103 Craig Yeast	.15	.40
❑ 104 Bobby Shaw	.15	.40
❑ 105 Kerry Collins	.20	.50
❑ 106 Brock Huard	.15	.40
❑ 107 JaJuan Dawson	.15	.40
❑ 108 Jeff Graham	.15	.40
❑ 109 Chad Pennington	.25	.60
❑ 110 Jake Plummer	.20	.50
❑ 111 James McKnight	.15	.40
❑ 112 Terrell Owens	.25	.60
❑ 113 Mo Lewis	.15	.40
❑ 114 Jeremy McDaniel	.15	.40
❑ 115 Ed McCaffrey	.20	.50
❑ 116 Ricky Watters	.20	.50
❑ 117 Jerry Porter	.15	.40
❑ 118 Shawn Jefferson	.15	.40
❑ 119 Charlie Batch	.20	.50
❑ 120 Justin Watson	.15	.40
❑ 121 Donovan McNabb	.30	.75
❑ 122 Shaun King	.15	.40
❑ 123 Brett Favre	.75	2.00
❑ 124 Ronald McKinnon	.15	.40
❑ 125 Richard Huntley	.15	.40
❑ 126 Ray Lewis	.25	.60
❑ 127 Jerome Pathon	.15	.40
❑ 128 Sam Cowart	.15	.40
❑ 129 Ryan Leaf	.15	.40
❑ 130 Greg Clark	.15	.40
❑ 131 Tony Boselli	.20	.50
❑ 132 Frank Wycheck	.15	.40
❑ 133 Charlie Garner	.20	.50
❑ 134 Tony Siragusa	.20	.50
❑ 135 Sylvester Morris	.15	.40
❑ 136 Qadry Ismail	.20	.50
❑ 137 Jon Kitna	.20	.50
❑ 138 James Thrash	.20	.50
❑ 139 Lamar Smith	.20	.50
❑ 140 Brad Johnson	.20	.50
❑ 141 London Fletcher	.15	.40
❑ 142 Tim Biakabutuka	.15	.40
❑ 143 Ed McDaniel	.15	.40
❑ 144 Tony Parrish	.15	.40
❑ 145 David Boston	.15	.40
❑ 146 Brian Urlacher	.30	.75
❑ 147 Drew Bledsoe	.25	.60
❑ 148 David Patten	.15	.40
❑ 149 Marcellus Wiley	.15	.40
❑ 150 Peter Warrick	.20	.50
❑ 151 La'Roi Glover	.15	.40
❑ 152 Troy Aikman	.40	1.00
❑ 153 Chris Chandler	.20	.50
❑ 154 Travis Prentice	.15	.40
❑ 155 Ike Hilliard	.20	.50
❑ 156 John Mobley	.15	.40
❑ 157 Warren Sapp	.20	.50
❑ 158 Joey Galloway	.20	.50
❑ 159 Laveranues Coles	.25	.60
❑ 160 Germane Crowell	.15	.40
❑ 161 Jamal Lewis	.25	.60
❑ 162 Mike Anderson	.20	.50
❑ 163 Charles Woodson	.25	.60
❑ 164 Antonio Freeman	.25	.60
❑ 165 Derrick Mason	.20	.50
❑ 166 Chris Claiborne	.15	.40
❑ 167 Brian Mitchell	.20	.50
❑ 168 Mike Vanderjagt	.15	.40
❑ 169 Rod Woodson	.25	.60
❑ 170 Doug Chapman	.15	.40
❑ 171 John Lynch	.20	.50
❑ 172 Kevin Hardy	.15	.40
❑ 173 Sam Shade	.15	.40
❑ 174 Edgerrin James	.25	.60
❑ 175 Brian Dawkins	.20	.50
❑ 176 Donnie Edwards	.15	.40
❑ 177 Patrick Jeffers	.15	.40
❑ 178 Mark Brunell	.25	.60
❑ 179 Junior Seau	.25	.60
❑ 180 Trace Armstrong	.15	.40
❑ 181 Marcus Robinson	.20	.50
❑ 182 Tony Gonzalez	.20	.50
❑ 183 J.J. Stokes	.15	.40
❑ 184 Jake Reed	.20	.50
❑ 185 Corey Dillon	.20	.50
❑ 186 Jay Fiedler	.20	.50
❑ 187 Christian Fauria	.15	.40
❑ 188 Sammy Knight	.15	.40
❑ 189 Kevin Johnson	.15	.40
❑ 190 Matthew Hatchette	.15	.40
❑ 191 Az-Zahir Hakim	.15	.40
❑ 192 Keith Hamilton	.15	.40
❑ 193 Darren Woodson	.20	.50
❑ 194 Terry Glenn	.20	.50
❑ 195 Simeon Rice	.20	.50
❑ 196 Keyshawn Johnson	.20	.50
❑ 197 Terrell Davis	.25	.60
❑ 198 William Roaf	.20	.50
❑ 199 Doug Flutie	.25	.60
❑ 200 Kevin Carter	.15	.40
❑ 201 Stephen Boyd	.15	.40
❑ 202 Michael Strahan	.25	.60
❑ 203 Ray Buchanan	.15	.40
❑ 204 Tyrone Wheatley	.20	.50
❑ 205 Jason Hanson	.15	.40
❑ 206 Wayne Chrebet	.20	.50
❑ 207 Samari Rolle	.15	.40
❑ 208 Duce Staley	.20	.50
❑ 209 Dorsey Levens	.20	.50

Card	Low	High
❑ 210 Sebastian Janikowski	.20	.50
❑ 211 Duane Starks	.15	.40
❑ 212 Jason Gildon	.20	.50
❑ 213 Terrence Wilkins	.15	.40
❑ 214 Eric Allen	.20	.50
❑ 215 Deion Sanders	.25	.60
❑ 216 Curtis Conway	.20	.50
❑ 217 Fred Taylor	.25	.60
❑ 218 Troy Vincent	.20	.50
❑ 219 Mike Minter RC	.20	.50
❑ 220 Jeff Garcia	.20	.50
❑ 221 Tony Richardson	.15	.40
❑ 222 Jerome Bettis	.25	.60
❑ 223 Chad Morton	.15	.40
❑ 224 Tony Horne	.15	.40
❑ 225 Dave Moore	.15	.40
❑ 226 Victor Green	.15	.40
❑ 227 Chris Sanders	.15	.40
❑ 228 Marshall Faulk	.25	.60
❑ 229 Cris Carter	.25	.60
❑ 230 Rodney Harrison	.20	.50
❑ 231 Tim Couch	.15	.40
❑ 232 Antowain Smith	.20	.50
❑ 233 Lawyer Milloy	.20	.50
❑ 234 Lance Schulters	.15	.40
❑ 235 Michael Wiley	.15	.40
❑ 236 Steve McNair	.25	.00
❑ 237 Aaron Brooks	.20	.50
❑ 238 Anthony Simmons	.15	.40
❑ 239 Dwayne Carswell	.15	.40
❑ 240 Priest Holmes	.25	.60
❑ 241 Amani Toomer	.20	.50
❑ 242 Aeneas Williams	.20	.50
❑ 243 MarTay Jenkins	.15	.40
❑ 244 Jeff George	.20	.50
❑ 245 Vinny Testaverde	.20	.50
❑ 246 Peerless Price	.15	.40
❑ 247 Bubba Franks	.20	.50
❑ 248 Randall Cunningham	.25	.60
❑ 249 Aaron Glenn	.20	.50
❑ 250 Terance Mathis	.15	.40
❑ 251 Peyton Manning	.60	1.50
❑ 252 Terrell Buckley	.20	.50
❑ 253 Greg Biekert	.15	.40
❑ 254 Martin Gramatica	.15	.40
❑ 255 Kyle Brady	.15	.40
❑ 256 Johnnie Morton	.20	.50
❑ 257 Jeremiah Trotter	.15	.40
❑ 258 Travis Taylor	.15	.40
❑ 259 Frank Moreau	.15	.40
❑ 260 LeRoy Butler	.20	.50
❑ 261 Plaxico Burress	.20	.50
❑ 262 Randall Godfrey	.15	.40
❑ 263 Jason Taylor	.25	.60
❑ 264 Jeff Burris	.15	.40
❑ 265 Jim Harbaugh	.20	.50
❑ 266 Marco Coleman	.15	.40
❑ 267 Robert Smith	.20	.50
❑ 268 Mike Hollis	.15	.40
❑ 269 Jerry Rice	.50	1.25
❑ 270 Muhsin Muhammad	.20	.50
❑ 271 J.R. Redmond	.15	.40
❑ 272 Brian Walker	.15	.40
❑ 273 Orlando Pace	.20	.50
❑ 274 Cade McNown	.20	.50
❑ 275 Darren Howard	.15	.40
❑ 276 Ron Dayne	.20	.50
❑ 277 Shaun Alexander	.25	.60
❑ 278 Brandon Bennett	.15	.40
❑ 279 Jason Sehorn	.20	.50
❑ 280 Matt Hasselbeck	.25	.60
❑ 281 Michael Pittman	.20	.50
❑ 282 Dennis Northcutt	.15	.40
❑ 283 Dedric Ward	.15	.40
❑ 284 Curtis Martin	.25	.60
❑ 285 Sammy Morris	.20	.50
❑ 286 Rocket Ismail	.20	.50
❑ 287 Jon Ritchie	.15	.40
❑ 288 Shaun Ellis	.15	.40
❑ 289 Tim Dwight	.20	.50
❑ 290 Trevor Pryce	.15	.40
❑ 291 Warrick Dunn	.25	.60
❑ 292 Napoleon Kaufman	.15	.40
❑ 293 Mike Alstott	.20	.50
❑ 294 Herman Moore	.20	.50
❑ 295 Chad Lewis	.15	.40
❑ 296 Hugh Douglas	.15	.40
❑ 297 Chris Redman	.25	.60
❑ 298 Ahman Green	.25	.60
❑ 299 Hines Ward	.25	.60
❑ 300 Mark Bruener	.20	.50
❑ 301 Jevon Kearse	.20	.50
❑ 302 Jermaine Fazande	.15	.40
❑ 303 Terrell Fletcher	.15	.40
❑ 304 Torry Holt	.20	.50
❑ 305 Chris McAlister	.15	.40
❑ 306 Jason Elam	.20	.50
❑ 307 Fred Beasley	.15	.40
❑ 308 Frank Wycheck UH	.15	.40
❑ 309 Michael McCrary UH	.15	.40
❑ 310 Mark Brunell UH	.25	.60
❑ 311 Tim Couch UH	.15	.40
❑ 312 Takeo Spikes UH	.15	.40
❑ 313 Jerome Bettis UH	.25	.60
❑ 314 Zach Thomas UH	.25	.60
❑ 315 Drew Bledsoe UH	.25	.60
❑ 316 Wayne Chrebet UH	.20	.50
❑ 317 Jay Riemersma UH	.15	.40
❑ 318 Marvin Harrison UH	.25	.60
❑ 319 Ed McCaffrey UH	.20	.50
❑ 320 Tony Gonzalez UH	.20	.50
❑ 321 Tim Brown UH	.25	.60
❑ 322 Junior Seau UH	.25	.60
❑ 323 Shawn Springs UH	.15	.40
❑ 324 Troy Aikman UH	.40	1.00
❑ 325 Pat Tillman UH RC	8.00	20.00
❑ 326 David Akers UH RC	.15	.40
❑ 327 Michael Strahan UH	.25	.60
❑ 328 Darrell Green UH	.25	.60
❑ 329 Kurt Warner UH	.30	.75
❑ 330 Jeff Garcia UH	.20	.50
❑ 331 Aaron Brooks UH	.20	.50
❑ 332 Jamal Anderson UH	.20	.50
❑ 333 Brad Hoover UH	.20	.50
❑ 334 Cris Carter UH	.25	.60
❑ 335 Derrick Brooks UH	.25	.60
❑ 336 Antonio Freeman UH	.25	.60
❑ 337 Luther Elliss UH	.15	.40
❑ 338 James Allen UH	.15	.40
❑ 339 Arizona Cardinals TC	.20	.50
❑ 340 Atlanta Falcons TC	.20	.50
❑ 341 Baltimore Ravens TC	.15	.40
❑ 342 Buffalo Bills TC	.15	.40
❑ 343 Carolina Panthers TC	.15	.40
❑ 344 Chicago Bears TC	.25	.60
❑ 345 Cincinnati Bengals TC	.20	.50
❑ 346 Cleveland Browns TC	.15	.40
❑ 347 Cowboys TC/Emmitt	.30	.75
❑ 348 Denver Broncos TC	.20	.50
❑ 349 Detroit Lions TC	.15	.40
❑ 350 Packers TC/Favre	.40	1.00
❑ 351 Colts TC/James	.20	.50
❑ 352 Jacksonville Jaguars TC	.20	.50
❑ 353 Kansas City Chiefs TC	.15	.40
❑ 354 Miami Dolphins TC	.20	.50
❑ 355 Minnesota Vikings TC	.25	.60
❑ 356 New England Patriots TC	.25	.60
❑ 357 New Orleans Saints TC	.15	.40
❑ 358 New York Giants TC	.20	.50
❑ 359 New York Jets TC	.20	.50
❑ 360 Oakland Raiders TC	.20	.50
❑ 361 Philadelphia Eagles TC	.25	.60
❑ 362 Pittsburgh Steelers TC	.25	.60
❑ 363 San Diego Chargers TC	.15	.40
❑ 364 San Francisco 49ers TC	.15	.40
❑ 365 Seattle Seahawks TC	.15	.40
❑ 366 Rams TC/Warner	.25	.60
❑ 367 Tampa Bay Buccaneers TC	.20	.50
❑ 368 Tennessee Titans TC	.20	.50
❑ 369 Washington Redskins TC	.15	.60
❑ 370 Buffalo Bills TL	.15	.40
❑ 371 Indianapolis Colts TL	.25	.60
❑ 372 Miami Dolphins TL	.15	.40
❑ 373 New England Patriots TL	.20	.50
❑ 374 New York Jets TL	.20	.50
❑ 375 Baltimore Ravens TL	.20	.50
❑ 376 Cincinnati Bengals TL	.15	.40
❑ 377 Cleveland Browns TL	.15	.40
❑ 378 Jacksonville Jaguars TL	.20	.50
❑ 379 Pittsburgh Steelers TL	.25	.60
❑ 380 Tennessee Titans TL	.20	.50
❑ 381 Denver Broncos TL	.20	.50
❑ 382 Kansas City Chiefs TL	.20	.50
❑ 383 Oakland Raiders TL	.20	.50
❑ 384 San Diego Chargers TL	.20	.50
❑ 385 Seattle Seahawks TL	.15	.40
❑ 386 Arizona Cardinals TL	.15	.40
❑ 387 Dallas Cowboys TL	.25	.60
❑ 388 New York Giants TL	.20	.50
❑ 389 Philadelphia Eagles TL	.20	.50
❑ 390 Washington Redskins TL	.20	.50
❑ 391 Chicago Bears TL	.15	.40
❑ 392 Detroit Lions TL	.15	.40
❑ 393 Green Bay Packers TL	.25	.60
❑ 394 Minnesota Vikings TL	.25	.60
❑ 395 Tampa Bay Buccaneers TL	.20	.50
❑ 396 Atlanta Falcons TL	.15	.40
❑ 397 Carolina Panthers TL	.15	.40
❑ 398 New Orleans Saints TL	.20	.50
❑ 399 San Francisco 49ersTL	.20	.50
❑ 400 St. Louis Rams TL	.25	.60
❑ 401 Michael Vick RC	.75	2.00
❑ 402 Drew Brees RC	3.00	8.00
❑ 403 Michael Bennett RC	.40	1.00
❑ 404 David Terrell RC	.30	.75
❑ 405 Deuce McAllister RC	.50	1.25
❑ 406 Santana Moss RC	.60	1.50
❑ 407 Koren Robinson RC	.40	1.00
❑ 408 Chris Weinke RC	.30	.75
❑ 409 Reggie Wayne RC	1.00	2.50
❑ 410 Rod Gardner RC	.30	.75
❑ 411 James Jackson RC	.30	.75
❑ 412 Travis Henry RC	.40	1.00
❑ 413 Josh Heupel RC	.40	1.00
❑ 414 LaDainian Tomlinson RC	3.00	8.00
❑ 415 Chad Johnson RC	1.00	2.50
❑ 416 Sage Rosenfels RC	.40	1.00
❑ 417 Quincy Morgan RC	.30	.75
❑ 418 Ken-Yon Rambo RC	.25	.60
❑ 419 LaMont Jordan RC	.40	1.00
❑ 420 Anthony Thomas RC	.40	1.00
❑ 421 Dave Dickenson RC	.30	.75
❑ 422 Travis Minor RC	.30	.75
❑ 423 Kevan Barlow RC	.30	.75
❑ 424 Chris Chambers RC	.60	1.50
❑ 425 Richard Seymour RC	.40	1.00
❑ 426 Gerard Warren RC	.30	.75
❑ 427 Jamar Fletcher RC	.25	.60
❑ 428 Freddie Mitchell RC	.25	.60
❑ 429 Jamal Reynolds RC	.30	.75
❑ 430 Marques Tuiasosopo RC	.30	.75
❑ 431 Snoop Minnis RC	.30	.75
❑ 432 Mike McMahon RC	.30	.75
❑ 433 Robert Ferguson RC	.40	1.00
❑ 434 Ronney Daniels RC	.25	.60
❑ 435 Rudi Johnson RC	.40	1.00
❑ 436 Vinny Sutherland RC	.25	.60
❑ 437 Josh Booty RC	.30	.75
❑ 438 Reggie White RC	.25	.60
❑ 439 Todd Heap RC	.40	1.00
❑ 440 Justin Smith RC	.40	1.00
❑ 441 Andre Carter RC	.40	1.00
❑ 442 Bobby Newcombe RC	.30	.75
❑ 443 Alex Bannister RC	.25	.60
❑ 444 Correll Buckhalter RC	.40	1.00
❑ 445 Quincy Carter RC	.30	.75
❑ 446 Jesse Palmer RC	.40	1.00
❑ 447 Heath Evans RC	.30	.75
❑ 448 Dan Morgan RC	.40	1.00
❑ 449 Justin McCareins RC	.30	.75
❑ 450 Alge Crumpler RC	.40	1.00

2001 Fleer Tradition Glossy

Card	Low	High
❑ COMP.SET w/o SP's (400)	20.00	40.00
❑ 1 Thomas Jones	.25	.60
❑ 2 Bruce Smith	.30	.75
❑ 3 Marvin Harrison	.30	.75
❑ 4 Darrell Jackson	.25	.60
❑ 5 Trent Green	.30	.75
❑ 6 Wesley Walls	.20	.50
❑ 7 Jimmy Smith	.25	.60
❑ 8 Isaac Bruce	.30	.75

Card		
❑ 9 Jamal Anderson	.25	.60
❑ 10 Marty Booker	.25	.60
❑ 11 Elvis Grbac	.25	.60
❑ 12 Joe Jurevicius	.20	.50
❑ 13 Reidel Anthony	.20	.50
❑ 14 Darnay Scott	.25	.60
❑ 15 Oronde Gadsden	.20	.50
❑ 16 Shawn Bryson	.20	.50
❑ 17 Jonathan Ogden	.25	.60
❑ 18 Aaron Shea	.20	.50
❑ 19 Randy Moss	.40	1.00
❑ 20 Eddie George	.30	.75
❑ 21 Stephen Davis	.25	.60
❑ 22 Emmitt Smith	.75	2.00
❑ 23 Willie McGinest	.20	.50
❑ 24 Trent Dilfer	.25	.60
❑ 25 Peter Boulware	.20	.50
❑ 26 Rod Smith	.25	.60
❑ 27 Ricky Williams	.30	.75
❑ 28 Albert Connell	.20	.50
❑ 29 Robert Porcher	.20	.50
❑ 30 Jessie Armstead	.20	.50
❑ 31 Shane Matthews	.20	.50
❑ 32 Eric Moulds	.25	.60
❑ 33 Kurt Schulz	.20	.50
❑ 34 Richie Anderson	.20	.50
❑ 35 Ron Dugans	.20	.50
❑ 36 Steve Beuerlein	.25	.60
❑ 37 Darren Sharper	.25	.60
❑ 38 Andre Rison	.25	.60
❑ 39 Courtney Brown	.20	.50
❑ 40 Eddie Kennison	.25	.60
❑ 41 Ken Dilger	.20	.50
❑ 42 Charles Johnson	.20	.50
❑ 43 Dexter Coakley	.20	.50
❑ 44 Akili Smith	.20	.50
❑ 45 R.Jay Soward	.20	.50
❑ 46 Danny Farmer	.20	.50
❑ 47 Dez White	.25	.60
❑ 48 Olandis Gary	.20	.50
❑ 49 Wali Rainer	.20	.50
❑ 50 Derrick Alexander	.20	.50
❑ 51 Donnie Abraham	.20	.50
❑ 52 David Sloan	.20	.50
❑ 53 Larry Allen	.25	.60
❑ 54 Sam Madison	.20	.50
❑ 55 Troy Edwards	.20	.50
❑ 56 Ryan Longwell	.25	.60
❑ 57 Brian Griese	.25	.60
❑ 58 John Randle	.25	.60
❑ 59 Reggie Jones	.20	.50
❑ 60 Mike Peterson	.20	.50
❑ 61 Bill Romanowski	.25	.60
❑ 62 Kevin Faulk	.25	.60
❑ 63 Tai Streets	.20	.50
❑ 64 Tony Brackens	.20	.50
❑ 65 James Stewart	.20	.50
❑ 66 Joe Horn	.25	.60
❑ 67 Kurt Warner	.40	1.00
❑ 68 Eric Hicks RC	.30	.75
❑ 69 Bryan Westbrook	.20	.50
❑ 70 Tiki Barber	.30	.75
❑ 71 Frank Sanders	.20	.50
❑ 72 Olindo Mare	.20	.50
❑ 73 Bill Schroeder	.25	.60
❑ 74 Anthony Becht	.20	.50
❑ 75 Rob Johnson	.25	.60
❑ 76 Troy Brown	.25	.60
❑ 77 Chad Bratzke	.20	.50
❑ 78 Rickey Dudley	.20	.50
❑ 79 Doug Johnson	.20	.50
❑ 80 Joe Johnson	.20	.50
❑ 81 Keenan McCardell	.25	.60
❑ 82 Tim Brown	.30	.75
❑ 83 Blaine Bishop	.20	.50
❑ 84 Ron Dixon	.20	.50
❑ 85 Michael Cloud	.20	.50
❑ 86 Todd Pinkston	.20	.50
❑ 87 Shannon Sharpe	.30	.75
❑ 88 Marvin Jones	.20	.50
❑ 89 Zach Thomas	.30	.75
❑ 90 Kordell Stewart	.25	.60
❑ 91 Champ Bailey	.30	.75
❑ 92 Jacquez Green	.20	.50
❑ 93 Daunte Culpepper	.30	.75
❑ 94 Freddie Jones	.20	.50
❑ 95 Donald Hayes	.20	.50
❑ 96 Rich Gannon	.25	.60
❑ 97 Ty Law	.25	.60
❑ 98 Grant Wistrom	.20	.50
❑ 99 James Allen	.20	.50
❑ 100 Corey Simon	.20	.50
❑ 101 Jeff Blake	.25	.60
❑ 102 Bryant Young	.25	.60
❑ 103 Craig Yeast	.20	.50
❑ 104 Bobby Shaw	.20	.50
❑ 105 Kerry Collins	.25	.60
❑ 106 Brock Huard	.20	.50
❑ 107 JaJuan Dawson	.20	.50
❑ 108 Jeff Graham	.20	.50
❑ 109 Chad Pennington	.30	.75
❑ 110 Jake Plummer	.25	.60
❑ 111 James McKnight	.20	.50
❑ 112 Terrell Owens	.30	.75
❑ 113 Mo Lewis	.20	.50
❑ 114 Jeremy McDaniel	.20	.50
❑ 115 Ed McCaffrey	.25	.60
❑ 116 Ricky Watters	.25	.60
❑ 117 Jerry Porter	.20	.50
❑ 118 Shawn Jefferson	.20	.50
❑ 119 Charlie Batch	.25	.60
❑ 120 Justin Watson	.20	.50
❑ 121 Donovan McNabb	.40	1.00
❑ 122 Shaun King	.20	.50
❑ 123 Brett Favre	1.00	2.50
❑ 124 Ronald McKinnon	.20	.50
❑ 125 Richard Huntley	.20	.50
❑ 126 Ray Lewis	.30	.75
❑ 127 Jerome Pathon	.20	.50
❑ 128 Sam Cowart	.20	.50
❑ 129 Ryan Leaf	.20	.50
❑ 130 Greg Clark	.20	.50
❑ 131 Tony Boselli	.25	.60
❑ 132 Frank Wycheck	.20	.50
❑ 133 Charlie Garner	.25	.60
❑ 134 Tony Siragusa	.25	.60
❑ 135 Sylvester Morris	.20	.50
❑ 136 Qadry Ismail	.25	.60
❑ 137 Jon Kitna	.25	.60
❑ 138 James Thrash	.25	.60
❑ 139 Lamar Smith	.25	.60
❑ 140 Brad Johnson	.25	.60
❑ 141 London Fletcher	.20	.50
❑ 142 Tim Biakabutuka	.20	.50
❑ 143 Ed McDaniel	.20	.50
❑ 144 Tony Parrish	.20	.50
❑ 145 David Boston	.20	.50
❑ 146 Brian Urlacher	.40	1.00
❑ 147 Drew Bledsoe	.30	.75
❑ 148 David Patten	.20	.50
❑ 149 Marcellus Wiley	.20	.50
❑ 150 Peter Warrick	.25	.60
❑ 151 La'Roi Glover	.20	.50
❑ 152 Troy Aikman	.50	1.25
❑ 153 Chris Chandler	.25	.60
❑ 154 Travis Prentice	.20	.50
❑ 155 Ike Hilliard	.25	.60
❑ 156 John Mobley	.20	.50
❑ 157 Warren Sapp	.25	.60
❑ 158 Joey Galloway	.25	.60
❑ 159 Laveranues Coles	.30	.75
❑ 160 Germane Crowell	.20	.50
❑ 161 Jamal Lewis	.30	.75
❑ 162 Mike Anderson	.25	.60
❑ 163 Charles Woodson	.30	.75
❑ 164 Antonio Freeman	.30	.75
❑ 165 Derrick Mason	.25	.60
❑ 166 Chris Claiborne	.20	.50
❑ 167 Brian Mitchell	.25	.60
❑ 168 Mike Vanderjagt	.20	.50
❑ 169 Rod Woodson	.30	.75
❑ 170 Doug Chapman	.20	.50
❑ 171 John Lynch	.25	.60
❑ 172 Kevin Hardy	.20	.50
❑ 173 Sam Shade	.20	.50
❑ 174 Edgerrin James	.30	.75
❑ 175 Brian Dawkins	.25	.60
❑ 176 Donnie Edwards	.20	.50
❑ 177 Patrick Jeffers	.20	.50
❑ 178 Mark Brunell	.30	.75
❑ 179 Junior Seau	.30	.75
❑ 180 Trace Armstrong	.20	.50
❑ 181 Marcus Robinson	.25	.60
❑ 182 Tony Gonzalez	.25	.60
❑ 183 J.J. Stokes	.20	.50
❑ 184 Jake Reed	.25	.60
❑ 185 Corey Dillon	.25	.60
❑ 186 Jay Fiedler	.25	.60
❑ 187 Christian Fauria	.20	.50
❑ 188 Sammy Knight	.20	.50
❑ 189 Kevin Johnson	.20	.50
❑ 190 Matthew Hatchette	.20	.50
❑ 191 Az-Zahir Hakim	.20	.50
❑ 192 Keith Hamilton	.20	.50
❑ 193 Darren Woodson	.25	.60
❑ 194 Terry Glenn	.25	.60
❑ 195 Simeon Rice	.25	.60
❑ 196 Keyshawn Johnson	.25	.60
❑ 197 Terrell Davis	.30	.75
❑ 198 William Roaf	.25	.60
❑ 199 Doug Flutie	.30	.75
❑ 200 Kevin Carter	.20	.50
❑ 201 Stephen Boyd	.20	.50
❑ 202 Michael Strahan	.30	.75
❑ 203 Ray Buchanan	.20	.50
❑ 204 Tyrone Wheatley	.25	.60
❑ 205 Jason Hanson	.20	.50
❑ 206 Wayne Chrebet	.25	.60
❑ 207 Samari Rolle	.20	.50
❑ 208 Duce Staley	.25	.60
❑ 209 Dorsey Levens	.25	.60
❑ 210 Sebastian Janikowski	.25	.60
❑ 211 Duane Starks	.20	.50
❑ 212 Jason Gildon	.25	.60
❑ 213 Terrence Wilkins	.20	.50
❑ 214 Eric Allen	.25	.60
❑ 215 Deion Sanders	.30	.75
❑ 216 Curtis Conway	.25	.60
❑ 217 Fred Taylor	.30	.75
❑ 218 Troy Vincent	.25	.60
❑ 219 Mike Minter	.25	.60
❑ 220 Jeff Garcia	.25	.60
❑ 221 Tony Richardson	.20	.50
❑ 222 Jerome Bettis	.30	.75
❑ 223 Chad Morton	.20	.50
❑ 224 Tony Horne	.20	.50
❑ 225 Dave Moore	.20	.50
❑ 226 Victor Green	.20	.50
❑ 227 Chris Sanders	.20	.50
❑ 228 Marshall Faulk	.30	.75
❑ 229 Cris Carter	.30	.75
❑ 230 Rodney Harrison	.25	.60
❑ 231 Tim Couch	.20	.50
❑ 232 Antowain Smith	.25	.60
❑ 233 Lawyer Milloy	.25	.60
❑ 234 Lance Schulters	.20	.50
❑ 235 Michael Wiley	.20	.50
❑ 236 Steve McNair	.30	.75
❑ 237 Aaron Brooks	.25	.60
❑ 238 Anthony Simmons	.20	.50
❑ 239 Dwayne Carswell	.20	.50
❑ 240 Priest Holmes	.30	.75
❑ 241 Amani Toomer	.25	.60
❑ 242 Aeneas Williams	.25	.60
❑ 243 MarTay Jenkins	.20	.50
❑ 244 Jeff George	.25	.60
❑ 245 Vinny Testaverde	.25	.60
❑ 246 Peerless Price	.20	.50
❑ 247 Bubba Franks	.25	.60
❑ 248 Randall Cunningham	.30	.75
❑ 249 Aaron Glenn	.25	.60
❑ 250 Terance Mathis	.20	.50
❑ 251 Peyton Manning	.75	2.00
❑ 252 Terrell Buckley	.25	.60
❑ 253 Greg Biekert	.20	.50
❑ 254 Martin Gramatica	.20	.50
❑ 255 Kyle Brady	.20	.50
❑ 256 Johnnie Morton	.25	.60
❑ 257 Jeremiah Trotter	.20	.50
❑ 258 Travis Taylor	.20	.50
❑ 259 Frank Moreau	.20	.50
❑ 260 LeRoy Butler	.25	.60
❑ 261 Plaxico Burress	.25	.60
❑ 262 Randall Godfrey	.20	.50
❑ 263 Jason Taylor	.30	.75
❑ 264 Jeff Burris	.20	.50
❑ 265 Jim Harbaugh	.25	.60
❑ 266 Marco Coleman	.20	.50
❑ 267 Robert Smith	.25	.60
❑ 268 Mike Hollis	.20	.50
❑ 269 Jerry Rice	.60	1.50
❑ 270 Muhsin Muhammad	.25	.60
❑ 271 J.R. Redmond	.20	.50
❑ 272 Brian Walker	.20	.50
❑ 273 Orlando Pace	.25	.60
❑ 274 Cade McNown	.25	.60
❑ 275 Darren Howard	.20	.50

Card		
276 Ron Dayne	.25	.60
277 Shaun Alexander	.30	.75
278 Brandon Bennett	.20	.50
279 Jason Sehorn	.25	.60
280 Matt Hasselbeck	.30	.75
281 Michael Pittman	.25	.60
282 Dennis Northcutt	.20	.50
283 Dedric Ward	.20	.50
284 Curtis Martin	.30	.75
285 Sammy Morris	.25	.60
286 Rocket Ismail	.25	.60
287 Jon Ritchie	.20	.50
288 Shaun Ellis	.20	.50
289 Tim Dwight	.25	.60
290 Trevor Pryce	.20	.50
291 Warrick Dunn	.30	.75
292 Napoleon Kaufman	.20	.50
293 Mike Alstott	.25	.60
294 Herman Moore	.25	.60
295 Chad Lewis	.20	.50
296 Hugh Douglas	.20	.50
297 Chris Redman	.30	.75
298 Ahman Green	.30	.75
299 Hines Ward	.30	.75
300 Mark Bruener	.25	.60
301 Jevon Kearse	.25	.60
302 Jermaine Fazande	.20	.50
303 Terrell Fletcher	.20	.50
304 Torry Holt	.25	.60
305 Chris McAlister	.20	.50
306 Jason Elam	.25	.60
307 Fred Beasley	.20	.50
308 Frank Wycheck UH	.20	.50
309 Michael McCrary UH	.20	.50
310 Mark Brunell UH	.30	.75
311 Tim Couch UH	.20	.50
312 Takeo Spikes UH	.20	.50
313 Jerome Bettis UH	.30	.75
314 Zach Thomas UH	.30	.75
315 Drew Bledsoe UH	.30	.75
316 Wayne Chrebet UH	.25	.60
317 Jay Riemersma UH	.20	.50
318 Marvin Harrison UH	.30	.75
319 Ed McCaffrey UH	.25	.60
320 Tony Gonzalez UH	.25	.60
321 Tim Brown UH	.30	.75
322 Junior Seau UH	.30	.75
323 Shawn Springs UH	.20	.50
324 Troy Aikman UH	.50	1.25
325 Pat Tillman UH RC	8.00	20.00
326 David Akers UH RC	.20	.50
327 Michael Strahan UH	.30	.75
328 Darrell Green UH	.30	.75
329 Kurt Warner UH	.40	1.00
330 Jeff Garcia UH	.25	.60
331 Aaron Brooks UH	.25	.60
332 Jamal Anderson UH	.25	.60
333 Brad Hoover UH	.25	.60
334 Cris Carter UH	.30	.75
335 Derrick Brooks UH	.30	.75
336 Antonio Freeman UH	.30	.75
337 Luther Elliss UH	.20	.50
338 James Allen UH	.20	.50
339 Arizona Cardinals TC	.25	.60
340 Atlanta Falcons TC	.25	.60
341 Baltimore Ravens TC	.20	.50
342 Buffalo Bills TC	.20	.50
343 Carolina Panthers TC	.20	.50
344 Chicago Bears TC	.30	.75
345 Cincinnati Bengals TC	.25	.60
346 Cleveland Browns TC	.20	.50
347 Cowboys TC/Emmitt	.40	1.00
348 Denver Broncos TC	.25	.60
349 Detroit Lions TC	.20	.50
350 Packers TC/Favre	.50	1.25
351 Colts TC/James	.30	.75
352 Jacksonville Jaguars TC	.30	.75
353 Kansas City Chiefs TC	.20	.50
354 Miami Dolphins TC	.25	.60
355 Minnesota Vikings TC	.30	.75
356 New England Patriots TC	.30	.75
357 New Orleans Saints TC	.25	.60
358 New York Giants TC	.25	.60
359 New York Jets TC	.25	.60
360 Oakland Raiders TC	.25	.60
361 Philadelphia Eagles TC	.30	.75
362 Pittsburgh Steelers TC	.25	.60
363 San Diego Chargers TC	.20	.50
364 San Francisco 49ers TC	.20	.50
365 Seattle Seahawks TC	.20	.50
366 Rams TC/Warner	.30	.75
367 Tampa Bay Buccaneers TC	.25	.60
368 Tennessee Titans TC	.25	.60
369 Washington Redskins TC	.25	.60
370 Buffalo Bills TL	.25	.60
371 Indianapolis Colts TL	.30	.75
372 Miami Dolphins TL	.20	.50
373 New England Patriots TL	.25	.60
374 New York Jets TL	.25	.60
375 Baltimore Ravens TL	.25	.60
376 Cincinnati Bengals TL	.20	.50
377 Cleveland Browns TL	.20	.50
378 Jacksonville Jaguars TL	.25	.60
379 Pittsburgh Steelers TL	.25	.60
380 Tennessee Titans TL	.25	.60
381 Denver Broncos TL	.25	.60
382 Kansas City Chiefs TL	.25	.60
383 Oakland Raiders TL	.25	.60
384 San Diego Chargers TL	.25	.60
385 Seattle Seahawks TL	.20	.50
386 Arizona Cardinals TL	.20	.50
387 Dallas Cowboys TL	.30	.75
388 New York Giants TL	.25	.60
389 Philadelphia Eagles TL	.25	.60
390 Washington Redskins TL	.25	.60
391 Chicago Bears TL	.20	.50
392 Detroit Lions TL	.20	.50
393 Green Bay Packers TL	.30	.75
394 Minnesota Vikings TL	.30	.75
395 Tampa Bay Buccaneers TL	.25	.60
396 Atlanta Falcons TL	.20	.50
397 Carolina Panthers TL	.20	.50
398 New Orleans Saints TL	.25	.60
399 San Francisco 49ersTL	.25	.60
400 St. Louis Rams TL	.30	.75
401 Michael Vick RC	2.50	6.00
402 Drew Brees RC	8.00	20.00
403 Michael Bennett RC	1.25	3.00
404 David Terrell RC	1.00	2.50
405 Deuce McAllister RC	1.50	4.00
406 Santana Moss RC	2.00	5.00
407 Koren Robinson RC	1.25	3.00
408 Chris Weinke RC	1.00	2.50
409 Reggie Wayne RC	3.00	8.00
410 Rod Gardner RC	1.00	2.50
411 James Jackson RC	1.00	2.50
412 Travis Henry RC	1.25	3.00
413 Josh Heupel RC	1.25	3.00
414 LaDainian Tomlinson RC	10.00	25.00
415 Chad Johnson RC	3.00	8.00
416 Sage Rosenfels RC	1.25	3.00
417 Quincy Morgan RC	1.00	2.50
418 Ken-Yon Rambo RC	.75	2.00
419 LaMont Jordan RC	1.25	3.00
420 Anthony Thomas RC	1.25	3.00
421 Dave Dickenson RC	1.00	2.50
422 Travis Minor RC	1.00	2.50
423 Kevan Barlow RC	1.00	2.50
424 Chris Chambers RC	2.00	5.00
425 Richard Seymour RC	1.25	3.00
426 Gerard Warren RC	1.00	2.50
427 Jamar Fletcher RC	.75	2.00
428 Freddie Mitchell RC	.75	2.00
429 Jamal Reynolds RC	1.00	2.50
430 Marques Tuiasosopo RC	1.00	2.50
431 Snoop Minnis RC	1.00	2.50
432 Mike McMahon RC	1.00	2.50
433 Robert Ferguson RC	1.25	3.00
434 Ronney Daniels RC	.75	2.00
435 Rudi Johnson RC	1.25	3.00
436 Vinny Sutherland RC	.75	2.00
437 Josh Booty RC	1.00	2.50
438 Reggie White RC	.75	2.00
439 Todd Heap RC	1.25	3.00
440 Justin Smith RC	1.25	3.00
441 Andre Carter RC	1.25	3.00
442 Bobby Newcombe RC	1.00	2.50
443 Alex Bannister RC	.75	2.00
444 Correll Buckhalter RC	1.25	3.00
445 Quincy Carter RC	1.00	2.50
446 Jesse Palmer RC	1.25	3.00
447 Heath Evans RC	1.00	2.50
448 Dan Morgan RC	1.25	3.00
449 Justin McCareins RC	1.00	2.50
450 Alge Crumpler RC	1.25	3.00

2002 Fleer Tradition

Card		
COMPLETE SET (300)	30.00	80.00
1 Jeff Garcia	.20	.50
2 Brian Simmons	.15	.40
3 Kordell Stewart	.20	.50
4 Chris Weinke	.15	.40
5 Donovan McNabb	.30	.75
6 Antoine Winfield	.15	.40
7 Ray Lewis	.25	.60
8 Drew Brees	.40	1.00
9 Frank Sanders	.15	.40
10 Rich Gannon	.20	.50
11 Jamal Anderson	.20	.50
12 Curtis Martin	.25	.60
13 Darrell Jackson	.20	.50
14 Micheal Barrow	.15	.40
15 Jeff Wilkins	.15	.40
16 Ricky Williams	.25	.60
17 Brad Johnson	.20	.50
18 Tedy Bruschi	.25	.60
19 Frank Wycheck	.15	.40
20 Byron Chamberlain	.15	.40
21 Terry Glenn	.20	.50
22 James McKnight	.15	.40
23 Thomas Jones	.20	.50
24 Jamie Sharper	.20	.50
25 Trent Green	.20	.50
26 Mike Rucker RC	.25	.60
27 Mark Brunell	.20	.50
28 Takeo Spikes	.15	.40
29 Dominic Rhodes	.20	.50
30 Jim Miller	.20	.50
31 Corey Bradford	.15	.40
32 Jamir Miller	.15	.40
33 Johnnie Morton	.20	.50
34 Rocket Ismail	.20	.50
35 Mike Anderson	.20	.50
36 James Allen	.15	.40
37 Quincy Carter	.15	.40
38 Germane Crowell	.15	.40
39 Quincy Morgan	.15	.40
40 Kabeer Gbaja-Biamila	.20	.50
41 Reggie Wayne	.25	.60
42 Brian Urlacher	.30	.75
43 Stacey Mack	.15	.40
44 Justin Smith	.15	.40
45 Snoop Minnis	.15	.40
46 Donald Hayes	.15	.40
47 Jay Fiedler	.20	.50
48 Nate Clements	.15	.40
49 Drew Bledsoe	.25	.60
50 Peter Boulware	.20	.50
51 Lawyer Milloy	.20	.50
52 Michael Pittman	.20	.50
53 Aaron Brooks	.20	.50
54 Maurice Smith	.15	.40
55 Ike Hilliard	.20	.50
56 Derrick Mason	.20	.50
57 LaMont Jordan	.20	.50
58 Charlie Garner	.20	.50
59 Mike Alstott	.20	.50
60 Freddie Mitchell	.15	.40
61 Isaac Bruce	.25	.60
62 Hines Ward	.25	.60
63 John Randle	.20	.50
64 Doug Flutie	.25	.60
65 Terrell Owens	.25	.60
66 Garrison Hearst	.20	.50
67 Rodney Harrison	.20	.50
68 Koren Robinson	.15	.40
69 Amos Zereoue	.15	.40
70 Aeneas Williams	.20	.50
71 Hugh Douglas	.15	.40
72 Jacquez Green	.15	.40
73 Sebastian Janikowski	.15	.40

Card		
74 Kevin Dyson	.20	.50
75 Terance Mathis	.15	.40
76 Vinny Testaverde	.20	.50
77 Kwamie Lassiter	.15	.40
78 Ron Dayne	.20	.50
79 Jonathan Ogden	.20	.50
80 Charlie Clemons RC	.15	.40
81 Peter Warrick	.20	.50
82 Adam Vinatieri	.25	.60
83 Ted Washington	.15	.40
85 Rosevelt Colvin RC	.30	.75
86 Oronde Gadsden	.15	.40
87 Anthony Henry	.15	.40
88 Priest Holmes	.25	.60
89 Joey Galloway	.20	.50
90 Jimmy Smith	.20	.50
91 Bill Romanowski	.20	.50
92 Chris Claiborne	.15	.40
93 Marvin Harrison	.25	.60
94 Vonnie Holliday	.15	.40
95 Darren Sharper	.20	.50
96 Chad Bratzke	.15	.40
97 James Stewart	.15	.40
98 Fred Taylor	.25	.60
99 Jason Elam	.20	.50
100 Keyshawn Johnson	.20	.50
101 Dexter Coakley	.15	.40
102 Zach Thomas	.25	.60
103 Jamel White	.15	.40
104 Antowain Smith	.20	.50
105 Marty Booker	.20	.50
106 Deuce McAllister	.25	.60
107 Adam Archuleta	.15	.40
108 Rod Smith	.20	.50
109 Tony Boselli	.20	.50
110 Joe Johnson	.15	.40
111 Simeon Rice	.15	.40
112 Cory Schlesinger	.15	.40
113 La'Roi Glover	.15	.40
114 Tiki Barber	.25	.60
115 Michael Westbrook	.15	.40
116 Antonio Freeman	.25	.60
117 Kerry Collins	.20	.50
118 Laveranues Coles	.25	.60
119 Jay Feely	.15	.40
120 Champ Bailey	.25	.60
121 Peyton Manning	.50	1.25
122 Chad Pennington	.25	.60
123 Anthony Dorsett	.15	.40
124 Jamal Lewis	.20	.50
125 Marcus Pollard	.15	.40
126 Charles Woodson	.25	.60
127 Duce Staley	.20	.50
128 Travis Henry	.20	.50
129 Tony Brackens	.15	.40
130 Jeremiah Trotter	.15	.40
131 Jerome Bettis	.25	.60
132 Chad Johnson	.25	.60
133 Lamar Smith	.20	.50
134 Joey Porter	.20	.50
135 Curtis Conway	.20	.50
136 David Terrell	.15	.40
137 Daunte Culpepper	.20	.50
138 Chris Fuamatu-Ma'afala	.15	.40
139 J.J. Stokes	.15	.40
140 Tim Couch	.15	.40
141 Ty Law	.20	.50
142 Vinny Sutherland	.15	.40
143 Trung Canidate	.15	.40
144 Larry Allen	.15	.40
145 Darren Howard	.15	.40
146 Ricky Watters	.20	.50
147 Grant Wistrom	.20	.50
148 Brian Griese	.20	.50
149 Jason Sehorn	.20	.50
150 Marshall Faulk	.25	.60
151 Martin Gramatica	.15	.40
152 Robert Porcher	.15	.40
153 Richie Anderson	.15	.40
154 Derrick Brooks	.25	.60
155 Jevon Kearse	.20	.50
156 Bill Schroeder	.20	.50
157 Marvin Jones	.15	.40
158 Eddie George	.20	.50
159 Keith Brooking	.15	.40
160 Ryan Longwell	.15	.40
161 Brian Dawkins	.20	.50
162 Chris Redman	.15	.40
163 Az-Zahir Hakim	.15	.40
164 James Thrash	.20	.50
165 Rob Johnson	.20	.50
166 Hardy Nickerson	.15	.40
167 Chad Scott	.15	.40
168 Jon Kitna	.20	.50
169 Donnie Edwards	.15	.40
170 Andre Carter	.15	.40
171 Warrick Holdman	.15	.40
172 Jason Taylor	.25	.60
173 Levon Kirkland	.15	.40
174 Mike Brown	.20	.50
175 David Patten	.15	.40
176 Kurt Warner	.25	.60
177 Fred Smoot	.20	.50
178 Dat Nguyen	.15	.40
179 Joe Horn	.20	.50
180 John Lynch	.20	.50
181 Troy Hambrick	.15	.40
182 John Carney	.15	.40
183 Wesley Walls	.20	.50
184 Deltha O'Neal	.15	.40
185 Joe Jurevicius	.20	.50
186 Steve McNair	.25	.60
187 Scotty Anderson	.15	.40
188 John Abraham	.20	.50
189 Stephen Davis	.20	.50
190 Nate Wayne	.15	.40
191 Corey Simon	.15	.40
192 Joel Makovicka	.15	.40
193 Rob Morris	.15	.40
194 Correll Buckhalter	.20	.50
195 Qadry Ismail	.20	.50
196 Keenan McCardell	.20	.50
197 Jason Gildon	.20	.50
198 Peerless Price	.15	.40
199 Tony Richardson	.15	.40
200 Kevan Barlow	.15	.40
201 Corey Dillon	.20	.50
202 Sam Madison	.15	.40
203 Chad Brown	.15	.40
204 Dez White	.15	.40
205 Troy Brown	.20	.50
206 Orlando Pace	.20	.50
207 Jermaine Lewis	.15	.40
208 Willie Jackson	.15	.40
209 Warrick Dunn	.20	.50
210 James Jackson	.15	.40
211 Sammy Knight	.15	.40
212 Ronde Barber	.20	.50
213 Ed McCaffrey	.20	.50
214 Amani Toomer	.20	.50
215 Rod Gardner	.15	.40
216 Mike McMahon	.15	.40
217 Wayne Chrebet	.20	.50
218 Jake Plummer	.20	.50
219 Bubba Franks	.20	.50
220 Shane Lechler	.15	.40
221 Travis Taylor	.15	.40
222 Edgerrin James	.25	.60
223 David Akers	.15	.40
224 Eric Moulds	.20	.50
225 Mike Vanderjagt	.15	.40
226 Kendrell Bell	.15	.40
227 Darnay Scott	.20	.50
228 Tony Gonzalez	.20	.50
229 Marcellus Wiley	.15	.40
230 Marcus Robinson	.20	.50
231 Muhsin Muhammad	.20	.50
232 Trent Dilfer	.20	.50
233 Kevin Johnson	.15	.40
234 Travis Minor	.20	.50
235 London Fletcher	.15	.40
236 Reggie Swinton	.15	.40
237 Michael Bennett	.20	.50
238 Brett Favre DD	.50	1.25
239 Terrell Davis DD	.20	.50
240 Emmitt Smith DD	.50	1.25
241 Shannon Sharpe DD	.20	.50
242 Cris Carter DD	.20	.50
243 Tim Brown DD	.20	.50
244 Jerry Rice DD	.40	1.00
245 Bruce Smith DD	.20	.50
246 Warren Sapp DD	.15	.40
247 Michael Strahan DD	.20	.50
248 Junior Seau DD	.20	.50
249 Darrell Green DD	.20	.50
250 Rod Woodson DD	.20	.50
251 David Boston BB	.15	.40
252 Michael Vick BB	.20	.50
253 Anthony Thomas BB	.15	.40
254 Ahman Green BB	.15	.40
255 Chris Chambers BB	.20	.50
256 Tom Brady BB	.50	1.25
257 Plaxico Burress BB	.15	.40
258 LaDainian Tomlinson BB	.30	.75
259 Shaun Alexander BB	.20	.50
260 Torry Holt BB	.20	.50
261 Julius Peppers RC	1.00	2.50
262 William Green RC	.50	1.25
263 Joey Harrington RC	.60	1.50
264 Jabar Gaffney RC	.60	1.50
265 T.J. Duckett RC	.60	1.50
266 Antwaan Randle El RC	.60	1.50
267 Javon Walker RC	.60	1.50
268 David Carr RC	.60	1.50
269 DeShaun Foster RC	.60	1.50
270 Donte Stallworth RC	.60	1.50
271 Antonio Bryant RC	.75	2.00
272 Clinton Portis RC	1.50	4.00
273 Josh Reed RC	.50	1.25
274 Ashley Lelie RC	.60	1.50
275 Patrick Ramsey RC	.60	1.50
276 J.Wells RC/A.Peterson RC	.60	1.50
277 Q.Jammer RC/R.Williams RC	.75	2.00
278 J.Shockey RC/D.Graham RC	.50	1.25
279 E.Crouch RC/Applewhite RC	.60	1.50
280 Buchanon RC/Sheppard RC	.60	1.50
281 K.Hill RC/D.Branch RC	.60	1.50
282 R.Sims RC/W.Bryant RC	.60	1.50
283 J.Scobey RC/Westbrook RC	2.00	5.00
284 L.Betts RC/O.Easy RC	.60	1.50
285 A.Davis RC/D.Jones RC	.50	1.25
286 C.Russell RC/C.Taylor RC	1.00	2.50
287 McAddley RC/J.McCown RC	.60	1.50
288 D.Garrard RC/R.Davey RC	1.00	2.50
289 M.Walker RC/R.Johnson RC	.50	1.25
290 L.Staley RC/L.Gordon RC	.60	1.50
291 R.Caldwell RC/L.Mays RC	.60	1.50
292 R.Thomas RC/N.Harris RC	.50	1.25
293 M.Morris RC/J.Stevens RC	.60	1.50
294 K.Kittner RC/R.Fasani RC	.50	1.25
295 R.Calmus RC/J.Schifino RC	.50	1.25
296 T.Carter RC/F.Milons RC	.50	1.25
297 Wistrom RC/Stephens RC	.50	1.25
298 M.Williams RC/D.Freeney RC	1.00	2.50
299 Hendersn RC/Hayneswrth RC	.60	1.50
300 N.Davenport RC/C.Nall RC	.60	1.50

2003 Fleer Tradition

Card		
COMPLETE SET (300)	15.00	40.00
1 Aaron Glenn	.15	.40
2 Jerry Rice	.50	1.25
3 Chad Hutchinson	.15	.40
4 Kris Jenkins	.15	.40
5 Ed Reed	.25	.60
6 Ed McCaffrey	.20	.50
7 Rod Gardner	.15	.40
8 Aaron Brooks	.20	.50
9 Chad Pennington	.25	.60
10 Jevon Kearse	.20	.50
11 Kurt Warner	.25	.60
12 Eddie George	.20	.50
13 Ron Dugans	.15	.40
14 Adam Vinatieri	.25	.60
15 Jimmy Smith	.20	.50
16 Chad Johnson	.25	.60
17 Kyle Brady	.15	.40
18 Eddie Kennison	.15	.40
19 Joe Jurevicius	.20	.50
20 Ronde Barber	.20	.50
21 Adam Archuleta	.15	.40
22 Champ Bailey	.20	.50
23 Joe Horn	.20	.50
24 Ladell Betts	.20	.50
25 Edgerrin James	.25	.60

❑ 26 Rosevelt Colvin .20 .50
❑ 27 Ahman Green .25 .60
❑ 28 Joey Porter .25 .60
❑ 29 Charles Woodson .20 .50
❑ 30 Lance Schulters .15 .40
❑ 31 Edgerton Hartwell .15 .40
❑ 32 Joey Galloway .20 .50
❑ 33 Roy Williams .25 .60
❑ 34 Al Wilson .20 .50
❑ 35 Charlie Garner .20 .50
❑ 36 John Lynch .20 .50
❑ 37 La'Roi Glover .15 .40
❑ 38 Emmitt Smith .60 1.50
❑ 39 Ryan Longwell .20 .50
❑ 40 Alge Crumpler .20 .50
❑ 41 John Abraham .20 .50
❑ 42 Chris Hovan .20 .50
❑ 43 Laveranues Coles .20 .50
❑ 44 Eric Hicks .15 .40
❑ 45 Johnnie Morton .20 .50
❑ 46 Sam Madison .20 .50
❑ 47 Amani Toomer .20 .50
❑ 48 Chris Redman .15 .40
❑ 49 Jon Kitna .20 .50
❑ 50 Leonard Little .15 .40
❑ 51 Eric Moulds .20 .50
❑ 52 Santana Moss .20 .50
❑ 53 Amos Zereoue .15 .40
❑ 54 Jonathan Wells .15 .40
❑ 55 Chris Chambers .20 .50
❑ 56 London Fletcher .15 .40
❑ 57 Frank Wycheck .15 .40
❑ 58 Josh McCown .20 .50
❑ 59 Shannon Sharpe .20 .50
❑ 60 Andre Carter .15 .40
❑ 61 Corey Dillon .20 .50
❑ 62 Josh Reed .15 .40
❑ 63 Marc Boerigter .15 .40
❑ 64 Fred Smoot .15 .40
❑ 65 Shaun Alexander .25 .60
❑ 66 Andre Davis .15 .40
❑ 67 Julian Peterson .15 .40
❑ 68 Corey Bradford .15 .40
❑ 69 Marc Bulger .25 .60
❑ 70 Fred Taylor .25 .60
❑ 71 Junior Seau .25 .60
❑ 72 Simeon Rice .20 .50
❑ 73 Anthony Thomas .20 .50
❑ 74 Correll Buckhalter .20 .50
❑ 75 Justin Smith .20 .50
❑ 76 Marcel Shipp .15 .40
❑ 77 Garrison Hearst .20 .50
❑ 78 Stacey Mack .15 .40
❑ 79 Antowain Smith .20 .50
❑ 80 Kabeer Gbaja-Biamila .20 .50
❑ 81 Curtis Martin .25 .60
❑ 82 Marcellus Wiley .15 .40
❑ 83 Gary Walker .15 .40
❑ 84 Kalimba Edwards .15 .40
❑ 85 Stephen Davis .20 .50
❑ 86 Antwaan Randle El .20 .50
❑ 87 Curtis Conway .15 .40
❑ 88 Keith Brooking .20 .50
❑ 89 Mark Word RC .15 .40
❑ 90 Greg Ellis .25 .60
❑ 91 Steve McNair .25 .60
❑ 92 Ashley Lelie .15 .40
❑ 93 Kelly Holcomb .15 .40
❑ 94 Darrell Jackson .20 .50
❑ 95 Mark Brunell .20 .50
❑ 96 Hugh Douglas .20 .50
❑ 97 Kendrell Bell .15 .40
❑ 98 Steve Smith .25 .60
❑ 99 Bill Schroeder .15 .40
❑ 100 Darren Howard .20 .50
❑ 101 Kevan Barlow .15 .40
❑ 102 Marshall Faulk .25 .60
❑ 103 Ike Hilliard .20 .50
❑ 104 T.J. Duckett .20 .50
❑ 105 Bobby Taylor .20 .50
❑ 106 Kevin Carter .20 .50
❑ 107 Darren Sharper .20 .50
❑ 108 Marty Booker .20 .50
❑ 109 Isaac Bruce .25 .60
❑ 110 Kevin Hardy .15 .40
❑ 111 Tai Streets .15 .40
❑ 112 Brad Johnson .20 .50
❑ 113 Daunte Culpepper .25 .60
❑ 114 Kevin Johnson .15 .40
❑ 115 Matt Hasselbeck .20 .50
❑ 116 Jabar Gaffney .15 .40
❑ 117 Takeo Spikes .15 .40
❑ 118 Brett Favre .60 1.50
❑ 119 Keyshawn Johnson .25 .60
❑ 120 David Akers .20 .50
❑ 121 Maurice Morris .15 .40
❑ 122 Jake Delhomme .25 .60
❑ 123 Kordell Stewart .20 .50
❑ 124 Terrell Davis .25 .60
❑ 125 Brian Kelly .15 .40
❑ 126 David Terrell .15 .40
❑ 127 Koren Robinson .20 .50
❑ 128 Michael Strahan .20 .50
❑ 129 Jake Plummer .20 .50
❑ 130 Terrell Owens .25 .60
❑ 131 Brian Urlacher .40 1.00
❑ 132 David Patten .15 .40
❑ 133 Michael Vick .25 .60
❑ 134 Jamal Lewis .25 .60
❑ 135 Terry Glenn .20 .50
❑ 136 Brian Simmons .15 .40
❑ 137 David Boston .15 .40
❑ 138 Michael Bennett .20 .50
❑ 139 James Stewart .20 .50
❑ 140 Tiki Barber .25 .60
❑ 141 Brian Griese .20 .50
❑ 142 Deion Branch .20 .50
❑ 143 Mike Peterson .15 .40
❑ 144 James Mungro .15 .40
❑ 145 Tim Couch .15 .40
❑ 146 Brian Dawkins .20 .50
❑ 147 Dennis Northcutt .15 .40
❑ 148 Mike Alstott .25 .60
❑ 149 James Thrash .15 .40
❑ 150 Tim Brown .25 .60
❑ 151 Brian Finneran .15 .40
❑ 152 Derrick Brooks .20 .50
❑ 153 Muhsin Muhammad .20 .50
❑ 154 Jason Elam .20 .50
❑ 155 Tim Dwight .15 .40
❑ 156 Bruce Smith .20 .50
❑ 157 Derrick Mason .20 .50
❑ 158 Napoleon Harris .15 .40
❑ 159 Jason Gildon .20 .50
❑ 160 Todd Heap .20 .50
❑ 161 Aaron Schobel .20 .50
❑ 162 Derrius Thompson .15 .40
❑ 163 Nate Clements .20 .50
❑ 164 Jason McAddley .15 .40
❑ 165 Todd Pinkston .15 .40
❑ 166 Bubba Franks .20 .50
❑ 167 Deuce McAllister .25 .60
❑ 168 Patrick Surtain .15 .40
❑ 169 Javon Walker .20 .50
❑ 170 Tom Brady .60 1.50
❑ 171 Dexter Coakley .20 .50
❑ 172 Patrick Kerney .20 .50
❑ 173 Jay Fiedler .20 .50
❑ 174 Tommy Maddox .20 .50
❑ 175 Donald Driver .25 .60
❑ 176 Patrick Ramsey .20 .50
❑ 177 Olandis Gary .20 .50
❑ 178 Tony Gonzalez .20 .50
❑ 179 Donnie Edwards .15 .40
❑ 180 Peter Boulware .20 .50
❑ 181 Jeff Blake .20 .50
❑ 182 Torry Holt .25 .60
❑ 183 Donovan McNabb .25 .60
❑ 184 Peter Warrick .20 .50
❑ 185 Jeff Garcia .25 .60
❑ 186 Travis Henry .20 .50
❑ 187 Doug Jolley .15 .40
❑ 188 Peyton Manning .50 1.25
❑ 189 Jerome Bettis .25 .60
❑ 190 Travis Taylor .15 .40
❑ 191 Drew Brees .25 .60
❑ 192 Phillip Buchanon .15 .40
❑ 193 Jerramy Stevens .20 .50
❑ 194 Trent Green .20 .50
❑ 195 Duce Staley .20 .50
❑ 196 Plaxico Burress .25 .60
❑ 197 Jerry Porter .20 .50
❑ 198 Trevor Pryce .20 .50
❑ 199 Dwight Freeney .20 .50
❑ 200 Quincy Morgan .15 .40
❑ 201 Troy Vincent .20 .50
❑ 202 Randy McMichael .15 .40
❑ 203 Troy Hambrick .15 .40
❑ 204 Randy Moss .25 .60
❑ 205 Troy Brown .20 .50
❑ 206 Ray Lewis .25 .60
❑ 207 Trung Canidate .15 .40
❑ 208 Raynoch Thompson .15 .40
❑ 209 Ty Law .20 .50
❑ 210 Reggie Wayne .20 .50
❑ 211 Warren Sapp .20 .50
❑ 212 Richard Seymour .20 .50
❑ 213 Warrick Dunn .20 .50
❑ 214 Robert Ferguson .15 .40
❑ 215 Wayne Chrebet .20 .50
❑ 216 Rod Coleman RC .15 .40
❑ 217 Will Allen .20 .50
❑ 218 Rod Woodson .25 .60
❑ 219 Zach Thomas .25 .60
❑ 220 Rod Smith .20 .50
❑ 221 Ricky Williams .20 .50
❑ 222 LaDainian Tomlinson .30 .75
❑ 223 Priest Holmes .25 .60
❑ 224 Rich Gannon .20 .50
❑ 225 Drew Bledsoe .25 .60
❑ 226 Kerry Collins .20 .50
❑ 227 Marvin Harrison .25 .60
❑ 228 Hines Ward .25 .60
❑ 229 Peerless Price .15 .40
❑ 230 Jason Taylor .20 .50
❑ 231 Jeremy Shockey .25 .60
❑ 232 Clinton Portis .30 .75
❑ 233 Antonio Bryant .25 .60
❑ 234 Donte Stallworth .20 .50
❑ 235 David Carr .25 .60
❑ 236 Joey Harrington .20 .50
❑ 237 William Green .15 .40
❑ 238 Julius Peppers .25 .60
❑ 239 Shipp/Thompson/Wilson .12 .30
❑ 240 Vick/Dunn/Finner/Brooking .20 .50
❑ 241 Lewis/Hartwell/Taylor/Reed .20 .50
❑ 242 Bled/Henry/Mould/Fletch .20 .50
❑ 243 Peppers/Smith/Muhammad .20 .50
❑ 244 Booker/Urlacher/Thomas .30 .75
❑ 245 Dillon/Smith/Johnson/Kitna .20 .50
❑ 246 Couch/Green/Morgan/Word .12 .30
❑ 247 Hutchinson/Galloway /Williams/Ellis .20 .50
❑ 248 Portis/Smith/Wilson .25 .60
❑ 249 Harring/Stew/Schr/Edwards .15 .40
❑ 250 Favre/Green/Driver/KGB .50 1.25
❑ 251 Carr/Wells/Bradford/Glenn .20 .50
❑ 252 Mann/James/Harr/Freen .40 1.00
❑ 253 Brunell/Taylor/Smith/McCree .12 .30
❑ 254 Green/Holmes/Kenn/Hicks .20 .50
❑ 255 Wilms/Chamb/Thom/Tayl .20 .50
❑ 256 Culp/Benn/Moss/Williams .20 .50
❑ 257 Brady/Smith/Brown/Vina .50 1.25
❑ 258 Brooks/McAllister/Horn/Howard .20 .50
❑ 259 Collins/Barber/Toomer/Strahan .20 .50
❑ 260 Pennington/Martin/Chrebet /Abraham .20 .50
❑ 261 Gannon/Garn/Rice/Woods .15 .40
❑ 262 McNabb/Staley/Pinkston/Taylor .20 .50
❑ 263 Maddox/Zereoue/Ward /Gildon/Porter .20 .50
❑ 264 Brees/Tomlinson/Edwards .25 .60
❑ 265 Garcia/Hearst/Owens/Carter .20 .50
❑ 266 Hasselbeck/Alexander /Robin/Tongue .12 .30
❑ 267 Bulger/Faulk/Holt/Little .20 .50
❑ 268 B.John/Key.John/S.Rice/Kelly .15 .40
❑ 269 McNair/George/Mason /Schulters .20 .50
❑ 270 Ramsey/Gardner/Smoot .15 .40
❑ 271 Carson Palmer RC 2.00 5.00
❑ 272 Kyle Boller RC .50 1.25
❑ 273 Byron Leftwich RC .60 1.50
❑ 274 Willis McGahee RC 1.00 2.50
❑ 275 Larry Johnson RC .60 1.50
❑ 276 Charles Rogers RC .40 1.00
❑ 277 Andre Johnson RC 1.00 2.50
❑ 278 Bryant Johnson RC .50 1.25
❑ 279 Rex Grossman RC .50 1.25
❑ 280 Taylor Jacobs RC .40 1.00
❑ 281 Rober RC/Sull RC/Will RC .50 1.25
❑ 282 Jopp RC/Davis RC/Rag RC .50 1.25
❑ 283 Witt RC/Clark RC/Smith RC 1.25 3.00
❑ 284 Edwds RC/Smith RC/Bail RC .40 1.00
❑ 285 SuggsRC/BrownRC/SmithRC .50 1.25
❑ 286 Griff RC/Pinn RC/Askew RC .40 1.00
❑ 287 Farg RC/Gabr RC/Johns RC .50 1.25

❑ 288 Kenn RC/Joseph RC/Warr RC	.50	1.25
❑ 289 Sug RC/Hayn RC/McDo RC	.60	1.50
❑ 290 Wash RC/Curt RC/Burles RC	.50	1.25
❑ 291 Wall RC/Dors RC/Simms RC	.50	1.25
❑ 292 Wade RC/Aik RC/Gage RC	.50	1.25
❑ 293 McCull RC/Sapp RC/Grah RC	.50	1.25
❑ 294 Kelly RC/Gard RC/Tolv RC	.40	1.00
❑ 295 Johns RC/Bold RC/Calic RC	1.25	3.00
❑ 296 Lloyd RC/McM RC/McD RC	.50	1.25
❑ 297 Kels RC/White RC/Doss RC	.30	.75
❑ 298 Newm RC/Truf RC/Wool RC	.50	1.25
❑ 299 Romo RC/King.RC/St.P RC	6.00	12.00
❑ 300 Pinn RC/Toef RC/Cobou RC	.40	1.00

2004 Fleer Tradition

❑ COMPLETE SET (360)	50.00	100.00
❑ COMP.SET w/o SP's (330)	15.00	30.00
❑ 1 Dolphins TL	.15	.40
❑ 2 Bills TL	.15	.40
❑ 3 Patriots TL	.30	.75
❑ 4 Jets TL	.15	.40
❑ 5 Colts TL	.30	.75
❑ 6 Jaguars TL	.15	.40
❑ 7 Titans TL	.08	.25
❑ 8 Texans TL	.15	.40
❑ 9 Raiders TL	.25	.60
❑ 10 Broncos TL	.15	.40
❑ 11 Chiefs TL	.15	.40
❑ 12 Chargers TL	.20	.50
❑ 13 Steelers TL	.25	.60
❑ 14 Browns TL	.08	.25
❑ 15 Bengals TL	.15	.40
❑ 16 Ravens TL	.15	.40
❑ 17 Eagles TL	.15	.40
❑ 18 Giants TL	.15	.40
❑ 19 Redskins TL	.15	.40
❑ 20 Cowboys TL	.15	.40
❑ 21 Vikings TL	.25	.60
❑ 22 Packers TL	.30	.75
❑ 23 Bears TL	.25	.60
❑ 24 Lions TL	.15	.40
❑ 25 49ers TL	.15	.40
❑ 26 Rams TL	.15	.40
❑ 27 Seahawks TL	.15	.40
❑ 28 Cardinals TL	.08	.25
❑ 29 Panthers TL	.15	.40
❑ 30 BuccaneersTL	.08	.25
❑ 31 Falcons TL	.08	.25
❑ 32 Saints TL	.15	.40
❑ 33 Anquan Boldin	.20	.50
❑ 34 Michael Vick	.20	.50
❑ 35 Kyle Boller	.15	.40
❑ 36 Aeneas Williams	.12	.30
❑ 37 Jake Delhomme	.15	.40
❑ 38 Rex Grossman	.20	.50
❑ 39 Carson Palmer	.25	.60
❑ 40 Quincy Morgan	.12	.30
❑ 41 Terry Glenn	.15	.40
❑ 42 Jake Plummer	.15	.40
❑ 43 Joey Harrington	.15	.40
❑ 44 Brett Favre	.50	1.25
❑ 45 Jeff Garcia	.20	.50
❑ 46 Peyton Manning	.40	1.00
❑ 47 Byron Leftwich	.20	.50
❑ 48 Trent Green	.15	.40
❑ 49 A.J. Feeley	.15	.40
❑ 50 Daunte Culpepper	.20	.50
❑ 51 Tom Brady	.50	1.25
❑ 52 Aaron Brooks	.15	.40
❑ 53 Kerry Collins	.15	.40
❑ 54 Chad Pennington	.20	.50
❑ 55 Rich Gannon	.15	.40
❑ 56 Donovan McNabb	.20	.50
❑ 57 Tommy Maddox	.15	.40
❑ 58 Drew Brees	.20	.50
❑ 59 Terrell Owens	.20	.50
❑ 60 Matt Hasselbeck	.20	.50
❑ 61 Kurt Warner	.20	.50
❑ 62 Brad Johnson	.15	.40
❑ 63 Jerome Bettis	.20	.50
❑ 64 Keith Bulluck	.12	.30
❑ 65 Rod Gardner	.12	.30
❑ 66 Eddie George	.15	.40
❑ 67 Warren Sapp	.15	.40
❑ 68 Marc Bulger	.15	.40
❑ 69 Shaun Alexander	.20	.50
❑ 70 Tai Streets	.12	.30
❑ 71 LaDainian Tomlinson	.25	.60
❑ 72 Steve McNair	.20	.50
❑ 73 Brian Westbrook	.20	.50
❑ 74 Jerry Rice	.40	1.00
❑ 75 Santana Moss	.15	.40
❑ 76 Moe Williams	.12	.30
❑ 77 Deuce McAllister	.20	.50
❑ 78 Adam Vinatieri	.20	.50
❑ 79 Randy Moss	.20	.50
❑ 80 Ricky Williams	.20	.50
❑ 81 Priest Holmes	.20	.50
❑ 82 Jimmy Smith	.15	.40
❑ 83 Edgerrin James	.20	.50
❑ 84 Andre Johnson	.20	.50
❑ 85 Ahman Green	.20	.50
❑ 86 Charles Rogers	.15	.40
❑ 87 Champ Bailey	.15	.40
❑ 88 Roy Williams S	.15	.40
❑ 89 Tim Couch	.15	.40
❑ 90 Corey Dillon	.15	.40
❑ 91 Thomas Jones	.15	.40
❑ 92 Stephen Davis	.15	.40
❑ 93 Travis Henry	.15	.40
❑ 94 Jamal Lewis	.15	.40
❑ 95 Warrick Dunn	.15	.40
❑ 96 Emmitt Smith	.50	1.25
❑ 97 Mark Brunell	.15	.40
❑ 98 Willis McGahee	.20	.50
❑ 99 Duce Staley	.15	.40
❑ 100 Lee Suggs	.20	.50
❑ 101 Rod Smith	.15	.40
❑ 102 Marvin Harrison	.20	.50
❑ 103 Larry Johnson	.30	.75
❑ 104 Michael Bennett	.15	.40
❑ 105 Donte Stallworth	.15	.40
❑ 106 DeShaun Foster	.15	.40
❑ 107 Hines Ward	.20	.50
❑ 108 T.J. Duckett	.15	.40
❑ 109 Brian Urlacher	.20	.50
❑ 110 Boss Bailey	.12	.30
❑ 111 Tim Brown	.20	.50
❑ 112 David Boston	.12	.30
❑ 113 Marshall Faulk	.20	.50
❑ 114 Jason Witten	.20	.50
❑ 115 Richard Seymour	.12	.30
❑ 116 Domanick Davis	.15	.40
❑ 117 Jon Kitna	.15	.40
❑ 118 Ray Lewis	.20	.50
❑ 119 Tedy Bruschi	.20	.50
❑ 120 Chris Chambers	.15	.40
❑ 121 Freddie Mitchell	.12	.30
❑ 122 Amani Toomer	.15	.40
❑ 123 Curtis Martin	.20	.50
❑ 124 Eric Moulds	.15	.40
❑ 125 Darrell Jackson	.15	.40
❑ 126 Clinton Portis	.20	.50
❑ 127 Jay Fiedler	.12	.30
❑ 128 Todd Heap	.15	.40
❑ 129 Dexter Jackson	.12	.30
❑ 130 James Jackson	.12	.30
❑ 131 Shannon Sharpe	.15	.40
❑ 132 Donald Driver	.20	.50
❑ 133 Billy Miller	.12	.30
❑ 134 Dante Hall	.15	.40
❑ 135 Onterrio Smith	.12	.30
❑ 136 Joe Horn	.15	.40
❑ 137 Shaun Ellis	.12	.30
❑ 138 L.J. Smith	.15	.40
❑ 139 Jerry Porter	.15	.40
❑ 140 Reggie Wayne	.15	.40
❑ 141 Derrick Brooks	.15	.40
❑ 142 Terrell Suggs	.12	.30
❑ 143 Randy McMichael	.12	.30
❑ 144 Mike Alstott	.15	.40
❑ 145 Nate Poole RC	.20	.50
❑ 146 Chris Brown	.15	.40
❑ 147 Torry Holt	.20	.50
❑ 148 Adewale Ogunleye	.15	.40
❑ 149 Peter Warrick	.15	.40
❑ 150 Alge Crumpler	.15	.40
❑ 151 Charlie Garner	.15	.40
❑ 152 Jeremy Shockey	.15	.40
❑ 153 Simeon Rice	.15	.40
❑ 154 Julian Peterson	.15	.40
❑ 155 Patrick Ramsey	.15	.40
❑ 156 Shawn Springs	.12	.30
❑ 157 Marcus Stroud	.12	.30
❑ 158 Keyshawn Johnson	.15	.40
❑ 159 Steve Smith	.20	.50
❑ 160 Ty Law	.15	.40
❑ 161 Derrick Mason	.15	.40
❑ 162 Josh Reed	.20	.50
❑ 163 Fred Smoot	.12	.30
❑ 164 Muhsin Muhammad	.15	.40
❑ 165 Justin Gage	.15	.40
❑ 166 Chad Johnson	.15	.40
❑ 167 Dennis Northcutt	.12	.30
❑ 168 Jooy Galloway	.15	.40
❑ 169 Ashley Lelie	.15	.40
❑ 170 Casey Fitzsimmons	.12	.30
❑ 171 Dwight Freeney	.20	.50
❑ 172 Nick Barnett	.15	.40
❑ 173 LaBrandon Toefield	.12	.30
❑ 174 Jabar Gaffney	.15	.40
❑ 175 Tony Gonzalez	.20	.50
❑ 176 Zach Thomas	.20	.50
❑ 177 Nate Burleson	.15	.40
❑ 178 Deion Branch	.15	.40
❑ 179 Boo Williams	.12	.30
❑ 180 Michael Strahan	.15	.40
❑ 181 Anthony Becht	.12	.30
❑ 182 Charles Woodson	.20	.50
❑ 183 Sheldon Brown	.12	.30
❑ 184 Kendrell Bell	.12	.30
❑ 185 Kassim Osgood	.12	.30
❑ 186 Tony Parrish	.12	.30
❑ 187 Marcel Shipp	.20	.50
❑ 188 Bobby Engram	.15	.40
❑ 189 Keith Brooking	.12	.30
❑ 190 Isaac Bruce	.15	.40
❑ 191 Travis Taylor	.12	.30
❑ 192 Charles Lee	.12	.30
❑ 193 Takeo Spikes	.12	.30
❑ 194 Justin McCareins	.12	.30
❑ 195 Julius Peppers	.15	.40
❑ 196 LaVar Arrington	.15	.40
❑ 197 Dez White	.15	.40
❑ 198 Rudi Johnson	.15	.40
❑ 199 Andre Davis	.12	.30
❑ 200 Quincy Carter	.12	.30
❑ 201 Quentin Griffin	.15	.40
❑ 202 Dallas Clark	.20	.50
❑ 203 Artose Pinner	.12	.30
❑ 204 Kevin Johnson	.12	.30
❑ 205 Kabeer Gbaja-Biamila	.15	.40
❑ 206 Marcus Coleman	.12	.30
❑ 207 Johnnie Morton	.15	.40
❑ 208 Jason Taylor	.20	.50
❑ 209 Kevin Williams	.12	.30
❑ 210 David Givens	.15	.40
❑ 211 Charles Grant	.12	.30
❑ 212 Ike Hilliard	.15	.40
❑ 213 Wayne Chrebet	.15	.40
❑ 214 Teyo Johnson	.15	.40
❑ 215 Brian Dawkins	.15	.40
❑ 216 Antwaan Randle El	.15	.40
❑ 217 Eric Parker	.15	.40
❑ 218 Josh McCown	.15	.40
❑ 219 Tim Rattay	.12	.30
❑ 220 Brian Finneran	.12	.30
❑ 221 Chad Brown	.12	.30
❑ 222 Ed Reed	.15	.40
❑ 223 Dane Looker	.15	.40
❑ 224 Aaron Schobel	.12	.30
❑ 225 Joe Jurevicius	.12	.30
❑ 226 Ricky Manning	.12	.30
❑ 227 Jevon Kearse	.15	.40
❑ 228 Laveranues Coles	.15	.40
❑ 229 Kelley Washington	.12	.30
❑ 230 William Green	.12	.30
❑ 231 Terence Newman	.15	.40
❑ 232 Bryant Johnson	.15	.40
❑ 233 Peerless Price	.15	.40
❑ 234 Peter Boulware	.15	.40
❑ 235 Drew Bledsoe	.20	.50
❑ 236 Kris Jenkins	.15	.40
❑ 237 Marty Booker	.15	.40

Card	Low	High
❑ 238 Matt Schobel	.12	.30
❑ 239 Earl Little	.12	.30
❑ 240 Antonio Bryant	.20	.50
❑ 241 Al Wilson	.12	.30
❑ 242 Dre Bly	.12	.30
❑ 243 Javon Walker	.15	.40
❑ 244 David Carr	.15	.40
❑ 245 Mike Vanderjagt	.12	.30
❑ 246 Fred Taylor	.15	.40
❑ 247 Eddie Kennison	.15	.40
❑ 248 Patrick Surtain	.12	.30
❑ 249 Jim Kleinsasser	.12	.30
❑ 250 Daniel Graham	.12	.30
❑ 251 Jerome Pathon	.12	.30
❑ 252 Tiki Barber	.20	.50
❑ 253 John Abraham	.12	.30
❑ 254 Justin Fargas	.15	.40
❑ 255 Correll Buckhalter	.15	.40
❑ 256 Plaxico Burress	.15	.40
❑ 257 Quentin Jammer	.12	.30
❑ 258 Kevan Barlow	.15	.40
❑ 259 Koren Robinson	.20	.50
❑ 260 Leonard Little	.12	.30
❑ 261 John Lynch	.15	.40
❑ 262 Tyrone Calico	.15	.40
❑ 263 Taylor Jacobs	.12	.30
❑ 264 Joey Porter	.15	.40
❑ 265 Freddie Jones	.12	.30
❑ 266 Marcus Pollard	.12	.30
❑ 267 Mike Peterson	.12	.30
❑ 268 Justin Griffith	.12	.30
❑ 269 Shawn Bryson	.12	.30
❑ 270 Will Allen	.12	.30
❑ 271 Antonio Gates	.20	.50
❑ 272 Chris McAlister	.12	.30
❑ 273 Tony Hollings	.12	.30
❑ 274 Cedrick Wilson	.12	.30
❑ 275 Adam Archuleta	.12	.30
❑ 276 London Fletcher	.12	.30
❑ 277 Drew Bennett	.15	.40
❑ 278 Rod Smart	.15	.40
❑ 279 LaMont Jordan	.20	.50
❑ 280 Jerry Azumah	.12	.30
❑ 281 Bubba Franks	.15	.40
❑ 282 Troy Edwards	.12	.30
❑ 283 Willie McGinest	.15	.40
❑ 284 Morten Andersen	.12	.30
❑ 285 Dat Nguyen	.12	.30
❑ 286 Samari Rolle	.12	.30
❑ 287 Brian Simmons	.12	.30
❑ 288 Chike Okeafor	.15	.40
❑ 289 Rodney Harrison	.15	.40
❑ 290 Jason Elam	.15	.40
❑ 291 Tim Dwight	.15	.40
❑ 292 Corey Bradford	.15	.40
❑ 293 Charles Tillman	.15	.40
❑ 294 Tim Carter	.12	.30
❑ 295 Ahmed Plummer	.12	.30
❑ 296 Troy Walters	.12	.30
❑ 297 Michael Lewis	.15	.40
❑ 298 Tory James	.12	.30
❑ 299 Doug Flutie	.20	.50
❑ 300 Az-Zahir Hakim	.12	.30
❑ 301 Itula Mili	.12	.30
❑ 302 Jamie Sharper	.12	.30
❑ 303 Vonnie Holliday	.12	.30
❑ 304 Brian Russell RC	.20	.50
❑ 305 Bryan Gilmore	.12	.30
❑ 306 Darren Sharper	.15	.40
❑ 307 Kyle Brady	.15	.40
❑ 308 David Tyree	.20	.50
❑ 309 Andre Carter	.12	.30
❑ 310 Lawyer Milloy	.12	.30
❑ 311 David Terrell	.12	.30
❑ 312 Richie Anderson	.12	.30
❑ 313 Darren Howard	.12	.30
❑ 314 Sebastian Janikowski	.12	.30
❑ 315 Kimo von Oelhoffen	.12	.30
❑ 316 Donnie Edwards	.15	.40
❑ 317 Brandon Lloyd	.12	.30
❑ 318 Robert Ferguson	.12	.30
❑ 319 Derek Smith	.12	.30
❑ 320 Anthony Thomas	.15	.40
❑ 321 Ken Hamlin	.12	.30
❑ 322 Ronde Barber	.15	.40
❑ 323 Erron Kinney	.12	.30
❑ 324 Tom Brady AW	.40	1.00
❑ 325 Peyton Manning AW	.30	.75
❑ 326 Steve McNair AW	.15	.40
❑ 327 Jamal Lewis AW	.12	.30
❑ 328 Ray Lewis AW	.15	.40
❑ 329 Anquan Boldin AW	.15	.40
❑ 330 Terrell Suggs AW	.10	.25
❑ 331 Eli Manning RC	5.00	12.00
❑ 332 Larry Fitzgerald RC	2.50	6.00
❑ 333 Ben Roethlisberger RC	6.00	15.00
❑ 334 Tatum Bell RC	.75	2.00
❑ 335 Roy Williams RC	1.00	2.50
❑ 336 Drew Henson RC	.50	1.25
❑ 337 Philip Rivers RC	4.00	10.00
❑ 338 Rashaun Woods RC	.50	1.25
❑ 339 Kevin Jones RC	.75	2.00
❑ 340 Sean Taylor RC	.75	2.00
❑ 341 Steven Jackson RC	2.00	5.00
❑ 342 Kellen Winslow RC	1.00	2.50
❑ 343 Chris Perry RC	.75	2.00
❑ 344 J.P. Losman RC	.75	2.00
❑ 345 Greg Jones RC	.75	2.00
❑ 346 Reggie Williams RC	.75	2.00
❑ 347 Michael Clayton RC	.75	2.00
❑ 348 Jonathan Vilma RC	.75	2.00
❑ 349 Julius Jones RC	1.00	2.50
❑ 350 Michael Jenkins RC	.75	2.00
❑ 351 E.Manning/Rivers/Roethlis.	12.50	25.00
❑ 352 Fitzgerald/Re.Will/Ro.Will.	3.00	8.00
❑ 353 Evans RC/Berr.RC/Ham.RC	1.00	2.50
❑ 354 Ude.RC/Poole RC/Colb.RC	.75	2.00
❑ 355 Gamb.RC/Rob.RC/Hall RC	.75	2.00
❑ 356 Trou.RC/Wats.RC/Harts.RC	.75	2.00
❑ 357 Darl.RC/Morant RC/Wilf.RC	.60	1.50
❑ 358 McCo.RC/Pick.RC/Sch.RC	2.00	5.00
❑ 359 Bell/Turn.RC/Cobbs RC	2.00	5.00
❑ 360 Moore RC/Wils.RC/Kni.RC	.75	2.00

1999 Leaf Certified

Card	Low	High
❑ COMPLETE SET (225)	100.00	200.00
❑ COMP.SET w/o RCs 175)	15.00	40.00
❑ 1 Simeon Rice	.25	.60
❑ 2 Frank Sanders	.25	.60
❑ 3 Andre Wadsworth	.15	.40
❑ 4 Larry Centers	.15	.40
❑ 5 Byron Hanspard	.15	.40
❑ 6 Terance Mathis	.25	.60
❑ 7 O.J. Santiago	.15	.40
❑ 8 Chris Calloway	.15	.40
❑ 9 Michael Jackson	.15	.40
❑ 10 Rod Woodson	.25	.60
❑ 11 Pat Johnson	.15	.40
❑ 12 Rob Johnson	.25	.60
❑ 13 Andre Reed	.25	.60
❑ 14 Tim Biakabutuka	.25	.60
❑ 15 Rae Carruth	.15	.40
❑ 16 Fred Lane	.15	.40
❑ 17 Muhsin Muhammad	.25	.60
❑ 18 Wesley Walls	.25	.60
❑ 19 Edgar Bennett	.15	.40
❑ 20 Curtis Conway	.25	.60
❑ 21 Bobby Engram	.25	.60
❑ 22 Jeff Blake	.25	.60
❑ 23 Darnay Scott	.15	.40
❑ 24 Ty Detmer	.25	.60
❑ 25 Sedrick Shaw	.15	.40
❑ 26 Leslie Shepherd	.15	.40
❑ 27 Terry Kirby	.15	.40
❑ 28 Chris Warren	.15	.40
❑ 29 Rocket Ismail	.25	.60
❑ 30 Marcus Nash	.15	.40
❑ 31 Neil Smith	.25	.60
❑ 32 Bubby Brister	.15	.40
❑ 33 Brian Griese	.40	1.00
❑ 34 Germane Crowell	.15	.40
❑ 35 Johnnie Morton	.25	.60
❑ 36 Gus Frerotte	.15	.40
❑ 37 Robert Brooks	.25	.60
❑ 38 Mark Chmura	.15	.40
❑ 39 Derrick Mayes	.15	.40
❑ 40 Jerome Pathon	.15	.40
❑ 41 Jimmy Smith	.25	.60
❑ 42 James Stewart	.25	.60
❑ 43 Tavian Banks	.15	.40
❑ 44 Derrick Alexander WR	.25	.60
❑ 45 Kimble Anders	.25	.60
❑ 46 Elvis Grbac	.25	.60
❑ 47 Derrick Thomas	.40	1.00
❑ 48 Byron Bam Morris	.15	.40
❑ 49 Tony Gonzalez	.40	1.00
❑ 50 John Avery	.15	.40
❑ 51 Tyrone Wheatley	.25	.60
❑ 52 Zach Thomas	.40	1.00
❑ 53 Lamar Thomas	.15	.40
❑ 54 Jeff George	.25	.60
❑ 55 John Randle	.25	.60
❑ 56 Jake Reed	.25	.60
❑ 57 Leroy Hoard	.15	.40
❑ 58 Robert Edwards	.15	.40
❑ 59 Ben Coates	.25	.60
❑ 60 Tony Simmons	.15	.40
❑ 61 Shawn Jefferson	.15	.40
❑ 62 Eddie Kennison	.25	.60
❑ 63 Lamar Smith	.25	.60
❑ 64 Tiki Barber	.40	1.00
❑ 65 Kerry Collins	.25	.60
❑ 66 Ike Hilliard	.15	.40
❑ 67 Gary Brown	.15	.40
❑ 68 Joe Jurevicius	.25	.60
❑ 69 Kent Graham	.15	.40
❑ 70 Dedric Ward	.15	.40
❑ 71 Terry Allen	.25	.60
❑ 72 Neil O'Donnell	.25	.60
❑ 73 Desmond Howard	.25	.60
❑ 74 James Jett	.25	.60
❑ 75 Jon Ritchie	.15	.40
❑ 76 Rickey Dudley	.15	.40
❑ 77 Charles Johnson	.15	.40
❑ 78 Chris Fuamatu-Ma'afala	.15	.40
❑ 79 Hines Ward	.40	1.00
❑ 80 Ryan Leaf	.40	1.00
❑ 81 Jim Harbaugh	.25	.60
❑ 82 Junior Seau	.40	1.00
❑ 83 Mikhael Ricks	.15	.40
❑ 84 J.J. Stokes	.25	.60
❑ 85 Ahman Green	.40	1.00
❑ 86 Tony Banks	.25	.60
❑ 87 Robert Holcombe	.15	.40
❑ 88 Az-Zahir Hakim	.15	.40
❑ 89 Greg Hill	.15	.40
❑ 90 Trent Green	.40	1.00
❑ 91 Eric Zeier	.15	.40
❑ 92 Reidel Anthony	.25	.60
❑ 93 Bert Emanuel	.25	.60
❑ 94 Warren Sapp	.15	.40
❑ 95 Kevin Dyson	.25	.60
❑ 96 Yancey Thigpen	.15	.40
❑ 97 Frank Wycheck	.15	.40
❑ 98 Michael Westbrook	.25	.60
❑ 99 Albert Connell	.15	.40
❑ 100 Darrell Green	.15	.40
❑ 101 Rob Moore	.25	.60
❑ 102 Adrian Murrell	.25	.60
❑ 103 Jake Plummer	.40	1.00
❑ 104 Chris Chandler	.25	.60
❑ 105 Jamal Anderson	.40	1.00
❑ 106 Tim Dwight	.40	1.00
❑ 107 Jermaine Lewis	.40	1.00
❑ 108 Priest Holmes	1.00	2.50
❑ 109 Bruce Smith	.40	1.00
❑ 110 Eric Moulds	.40	1.00
❑ 111 Antowain Smith	.60	1.50
❑ 112 Curtis Enis	.40	1.00
❑ 113 Corey Dillon	.60	1.50
❑ 114 Michael Irvin	.40	1.00
❑ 115 Ed McCaffrey	.40	1.00
❑ 116 Shannon Sharpe	.40	1.00
❑ 117 Terrell Davis	.60	1.50
❑ 118 Charlie Batch	.60	1.50
❑ 119 Antonio Freeman	.40	1.00
❑ 120 Dorsey Levens	.40	1.00
❑ 121 Marvin Harrison	.60	1.50
❑ 122 Peyton Manning	2.00	5.00
❑ 123 Keenan McCardell	.40	1.00
❑ 124 Fred Taylor	.60	1.50
❑ 125 Andre Rison	.40	1.00
❑ 126 O.J. McDuffie	.40	1.00
❑ 127 Karim Abdul-Jabbar	.40	1.00

Card		
❑ 128 Randy Moss	1.50	4.00
❑ 129 Terry Glenn	.40	1.00
❑ 130 Vinny Testaverde	.40	1.00
❑ 131 Keyshawn Johnson	.40	1.00
❑ 132 Curtis Martin	.40	1.00
❑ 133 Wayne Chrebet	.40	1.00
❑ 134 Napoleon Kaufman	.40	1.00
❑ 135 Charles Woodson	.40	1.00
❑ 136 Duce Staley	.60	1.50
❑ 137 Kordell Stewart	.40	1.00
❑ 138 Terrell Owens	.60	1.50
❑ 139 Ricky Watters	.40	1.00
❑ 140 Joey Galloway	.40	1.00
❑ 141 Jon Kitna	.40	1.00
❑ 142 Isaac Bruce	.60	1.50
❑ 143 Jacquez Green	.40	1.00
❑ 144 Warrick Dunn	.40	1.00
❑ 145 Mike Alstott	.40	1.00
❑ 146 Trent Dilfer	.40	1.00
❑ 147 Steve McNair	.40	1.00
❑ 148 Eddie George	.60	1.50
❑ 149 Skip Hicks	.40	1.00
❑ 150 Brad Johnson	.60	1.50
❑ 151 Doug Flutie	.60	1.50
❑ 152 Thurman Thomas	.40	1.00
❑ 153 Carl Pickens	.40	1.00
❑ 154 Emmitt Smith	2.00	5.00
❑ 155 Troy Aikman	2.00	5.00
❑ 156 Deion Sanders	.60	1.50
❑ 157 John Elway	3.00	8.00
❑ 158 Rod Smith	.40	1.00
❑ 159 Barry Sanders	3.00	8.00
❑ 160 Herman Moore	.60	1.50
❑ 161 Brett Favre	3.00	8.00
❑ 162 Mark Brunell	.60	1.50
❑ 163 Warren Moon	.60	1.50
❑ 164 Dan Marino	3.00	8.00
❑ 165 Randall Cunningham	.60	1.50
❑ 166 Robert Smith	.60	1.50
❑ 167 Cris Carter	.60	1.50
❑ 168 Drew Bledsoe	1.25	3.00
❑ 169 Tim Brown	.60	1.50
❑ 170 Jerome Bettis	.60	1.50
❑ 171 Natrone Means	.40	1.00
❑ 172 Jerry Rice	2.00	5.00
❑ 173 Steve Young	1.25	3.00
❑ 174 Garrison Hearst	.60	1.50
❑ 175 Marshall Faulk	1.25	3.00
❑ 176 David Boston RC	2.00	5.00
❑ 177 Jeff Paulk RC	.75	2.00
❑ 178 Reginald Kelly RC	.75	2.00
❑ 179 Scott Covington RC	2.00	5.00
❑ 180 Chris McAlister RC	1.25	3.00
❑ 181 Shawn Bryson RC	2.00	5.00
❑ 182 Peerless Price RC	2.00	5.00
❑ 183 Cade McNown RC	1.25	3.00
❑ 184 Michael Bishop RC	2.00	5.00
❑ 185 D'Wayne Bates RC	1.25	3.00
❑ 186 Marty Booker RC	2.00	5.00
❑ 187 Akili Smith RC	.75	2.00
❑ 188 Craig Yeast RC	1.25	3.00
❑ 189 Tim Couch RC	2.00	5.00
❑ 190 Kevin Johnson RC	2.00	5.00
❑ 191 Wane McGarity RC	.75	2.00
❑ 192 Olandis Gary RC	2.00	5.00
❑ 193 Travis McGriff RC	.75	2.00
❑ 194 Sedrick Irvin RC	.75	2.00
❑ 195 Chris Claiborne RC	.75	2.00
❑ 196 De'Mond Parker RC	.75	2.00
❑ 197 Dee Miller RC	.75	2.00
❑ 198 Edgerrin James RC	6.00	15.00
❑ 199 Mike Cloud RC	1.25	3.00
❑ 200 Larry Parker RC	2.00	5.00
❑ 201 Cecil Collins RC	.75	2.00
❑ 202 James Johnson RC	1.25	3.00
❑ 203 Rob Konrad RC	2.00	5.00
❑ 204 Daunte Culpepper RC	6.00	15.00
❑ 205 Jim Kleinsasser RC	2.00	5.00
❑ 206 Kevin Faulk RC	2.00	5.00
❑ 207 Andy Katzenmoyer RC	1.25	3.00
❑ 208 Ricky Williams RC	3.00	8.00
❑ 209 Joe Montgomery RC	1.25	3.00
❑ 210 Sean Bennett RC	.75	2.00
❑ 211 Dameane Douglas RC	2.00	5.00
❑ 212 Donovan McNabb RC	7.50	20.00
❑ 213 Na Brown RC	1.25	3.00
❑ 214 Amos Zereoue RC	2.00	5.00
❑ 215 Troy Edwards RC	1.25	3.00
❑ 216 Jermaine Fazande RC	1.25	3.00
❑ 217 Tai Streets RC	2.00	5.00
❑ 218 Brock Huard RC	2.00	5.00
❑ 219 Charlie Rogers RC	1.25	3.00
❑ 220 Karsten Bailey RC	1.25	3.00
❑ 221 Joe Germaine RC	1.25	3.00
❑ 222 Torry Holt RC	4.00	10.00
❑ 223 Shaun King RC	1.25	3.00
❑ 224 Jevon Kearse RC	3.00	8.00
❑ 225 Champ Bailey RC	2.50	6.00

2000 Leaf Certified

Card		
❑ COMP.SET w/o RC's (150)	15.00	40.00
❑ 1 Frank Sanders	.15	.40
❑ 2 Rob Moore	.25	.60
❑ 3 Simeon Rice	.25	.60
❑ 4 David Boston	.40	1.00
❑ 5 Tim Dwight	.40	1.00
❑ 6 Jamal Anderson	.40	1.00
❑ 7 Chris Chandler	.15	.40
❑ 8 Terance Mathis	.25	.60
❑ 9 Priest Holmes	.50	1.25
❑ 10 Rod Woodson	.25	.60
❑ 11 Tony Banks	.15	.40
❑ 12 Jermaine Lewis	.15	.40
❑ 13 Shannon Sharpe	.15	.40
❑ 14 Qadry Ismail	.25	.60
❑ 15 Doug Flutie	.40	1.00
❑ 16 Antowain Smith	.25	.60
❑ 17 Peerless Price	.25	.60
❑ 18 Rob Johnson	.15	.40
❑ 19 Muhsin Muhammad	.25	.60
❑ 20 Wesley Walls	.15	.40
❑ 21 Tim Biakabutuka	.15	.40
❑ 22 Steve Beuerlein	.15	.40
❑ 23 Patrick Jeffers	.15	.40
❑ 24 Natrone Means	.15	.40
❑ 25 Curtis Enis	.15	.40
❑ 26 Bobby Engram	.15	.40
❑ 27 Marcus Robinson	.40	1.00
❑ 28 Eddie Kennison	.15	.40
❑ 29 Marty Booker	.25	.60
❑ 30 Darnay Scott	.15	.40
❑ 31 Carl Pickens	.15	.40
❑ 32 Karim Abdul-Jabbar	.15	.40
❑ 33 Errict Rhett	.15	.40
❑ 34 Darrin Chiaverini	.15	.40
❑ 35 Randall Cunningham	.15	.40
❑ 36 Michael Irvin	.15	.40
❑ 37 Rocket Ismail	.15	.40
❑ 38 Ed McCaffrey	.40	1.00
❑ 39 Rod Smith	.15	.40
❑ 40 Herman Moore	.25	.60
❑ 41 Johnnie Morton	.15	.40
❑ 42 James Stewart	.15	.40
❑ 43 Bill Schroeder	.25	.60
❑ 44 Ahman Green	.40	1.00
❑ 45 Terrence Wilkins	.15	.40
❑ 46 Keenan McCardell	.15	.40
❑ 47 Derrick Alexander	.15	.40
❑ 48 Elvis Grbac	.15	.40
❑ 49 Tony Gonzalez	.15	.40
❑ 50 O.J. McDuffie	.15	.40
❑ 51 Tony Martin	.15	.40
❑ 52 James Johnson	.15	.40
❑ 53 Thurman Thomas	.15	.40
❑ 54 Jay Fiedler	.40	1.00
❑ 55 Damon Huard	.15	.40
❑ 56 Leroy Hoard	.15	.40
❑ 57 Terry Glenn	.25	.60
❑ 58 Kevin Faulk	.15	.40
❑ 59 Jeff Blake	.15	.40
❑ 60 Jake Reed	.15	.40
❑ 61 Amani Toomer	.15	.40
❑ 62 Kerry Collins	.15	.40
❑ 63 Ike Hilliard	.15	.40
❑ 64 Joe Montgomery	.15	.40
❑ 65 Vinny Testaverde	.15	.40
❑ 66 Wayne Chrebet	.15	.40
❑ 67 Ray Lucas	.25	.60
❑ 68 Napoleon Kaufman	.25	.60
❑ 69 Charles Woodson	.15	.40
❑ 70 Tyrone Wheatley	.15	.40
❑ 71 Rich Gannon	.40	1.00
❑ 72 Duce Staley	.40	1.00
❑ 73 Kordell Stewart	.25	.60
❑ 74 Jerome Bettis	.40	1.00
❑ 75 Troy Edwards	.15	.40
❑ 76 Junior Seau	.40	1.00
❑ 77 Jim Harbaugh	.15	.40
❑ 78 Curtis Conway	.25	.60
❑ 79 Jermaine Fazande	.15	.40
❑ 80 Terrell Owens	.40	1.00
❑ 81 Charlie Garner	.25	.60
❑ 82 Garrison Hearst	.15	.40
❑ 83 Jeff Garcia	.40	1.00
❑ 84 Derrick Mayes	.15	.40
❑ 85 Az-Zahir Hakim	.15	.40
❑ 86 Mike Alstott	.40	1.00
❑ 87 Warrick Dunn	.40	1.00
❑ 88 Jacquez Green	.15	.40
❑ 89 Warren Sapp	.15	.40
❑ 90 Yancey Thigpen	.15	.40
❑ 91 Kevin Dyson	.15	.40
❑ 92 Frank Wycheck	.15	.40
❑ 93 Jevon Kearse	.40	1.00
❑ 94 Adrian Murrell	.15	.40
❑ 95 Bruce Smith	.15	.40
❑ 96 Michael Westbrook	.15	.40
❑ 97 Albert Connell	.15	.40
❑ 98 Champ Bailey	.25	.60
❑ 99 Jeff George	.15	.40
❑ 100 Deion Sanders	.40	1.00
❑ 101 Jake Plummer	.40	1.00
❑ 102 Eric Moulds	.60	1.50
❑ 103 Cade McNown	.15	.40
❑ 104 Corey Dillon	.60	1.50
❑ 105 Akili Smith	.25	.60
❑ 106 Tim Couch	.40	1.00
❑ 107 Kevin Johnson	.60	1.50
❑ 108 Emmitt Smith	1.25	3.00
❑ 109 Troy Aikman	1.25	3.00
❑ 110 Joey Galloway	.40	1.00
❑ 111 John Elway	2.00	5.00
❑ 112 Terrell Davis	.40	1.00
❑ 113 Olandis Gary	.60	1.50
❑ 114 Brian Griese	.40	1.00
❑ 115 Charlie Batch	.60	1.50
❑ 116 Barry Sanders	1.50	4.00
❑ 117 Germane Crowell	.25	.60
❑ 118 Brett Favre	2.00	5.00
❑ 119 Dorsey Levens	.25	.60
❑ 120 Antonio Freeman	.60	1.50
❑ 121 Peyton Manning	1.50	4.00
❑ 122 Edgerrin James	1.00	2.50
❑ 123 Marvin Harrison	.60	1.50
❑ 124 Mark Brunell	.40	1.00
❑ 125 Fred Taylor	.40	1.00
❑ 126 Jimmy Smith	.40	1.00
❑ 127 Dan Marino	2.00	5.00
❑ 128 Randy Moss	1.25	3.00
❑ 129 Daunte Culpepper	.75	2.00
❑ 130 Cris Carter	.60	1.50
❑ 131 Robert Smith	.60	1.50
❑ 132 Drew Bledsoe	.75	2.00
❑ 133 Ricky Williams	.40	1.00
❑ 134 Curtis Martin	.60	1.50
❑ 135 Tim Brown	.60	1.50
❑ 136 Donovan McNabb	1.00	2.50
❑ 137 Jerry Rice	1.25	3.00
❑ 138 Steve Young	.75	2.00
❑ 139 Jon Kitna	.60	1.50
❑ 140 Ricky Watters	.25	.60
❑ 141 Kurt Warner	1.25	3.00
❑ 142 Marshall Faulk	.75	2.00
❑ 143 Torry Holt	.60	1.50
❑ 144 Isaac Bruce	.60	1.50
❑ 145 Shaun King	.15	.40
❑ 146 Keyshawn Johnson	.60	1.50
❑ 147 Eddie George	.40	1.00
❑ 148 Steve McNair	.60	1.50
❑ 149 Stephen Davis	.60	1.50
❑ 150 Brad Johnson	.60	1.50
❑ 151 Rogers Beckett RC	1.50	4.00
❑ 152 Erik Flowers RC	1.50	4.00
❑ 153 Demario Brown RC	1.00	2.50

Card	Low	High
❑ 154 Doug Johnson RC	2.00	5.00
❑ 155 Deon Grant RC	1.50	4.00
❑ 156 Ian Gold RC	1.50	4.00
❑ 157 Brian Urlacher RC	7.50	20.00
❑ 158 Frank Murphy RC	1.00	2.50
❑ 159 James Whalen RC	1.00	2.50
❑ 160 JaJuan Dawson RC	1.00	2.50
❑ 161 William Bartee RC	1.50	4.00
❑ 162 Aaron Shea RC	.40	1.00
❑ 163 Deltha O'Neal RC	2.00	5.00
❑ 164 Jarious Jackson RC	1.50	4.00
❑ 165 Muneer Moore RC	1.00	2.50
❑ 166 Hank Poteat RC	1.50	4.00
❑ 167 Jacoby Shepherd RC	1.00	2.50
❑ 168 Ben Kelly RC	1.00	2.50
❑ 169 Orantes Grant RC	1.00	2.50
❑ 170 Chris Hovan RC	1.50	4.00
❑ 171 Leon Murray RC	1.00	2.50
❑ 172 Marc Bulger RC	4.00	10.00
❑ 173 Chad Morton RC	2.00	5.00
❑ 174 Na'il Diggs RC	1.50	4.00
❑ 175 Shaun Ellis RC	2.00	5.00
❑ 176 John Abraham RC	2.00	5.00
❑ 177 Fred Robbins RC	1.00	2.50
❑ 178 Marcus Knight RC	1.50	4.00
❑ 179 Thomas Hamner RC	1.00	2.50
❑ 180 Cornelius Griffin RC	1.50	4.00
❑ 181 Raynoch Thompson RC	1.50	4.00
❑ 182 Paul Smith RC	1.50	4.00
❑ 183 Ahmed Plummer RC	2.00	5.00
❑ 184 John Engelberger RC	1.50	4.00
❑ 185 Darren Howard RC	1.50	4.00
❑ 186 Corey Moore RC	1.00	2.50
❑ 187 Joe Hamilton RC	1.50	4.00
❑ 188 Rob Morris RC	1.50	4.00
❑ 189 Keith Bulluck RC	2.00	5.00
❑ 190 Todd Husak RC	2.00	5.00
❑ 191 Mareno Philyaw RC	1.25	3.00
❑ 192 Kwame Cavil RC	1.25	3.00
❑ 193 Sammy Morris RC	2.50	6.00
❑ 194 Avion Black RC	2.00	5.00
❑ 195 Bashir Yamini RC	1.25	3.00
❑ 196 Curtis Keaton RC	2.00	5.00
❑ 197 Mike Anderson RC	3.00	8.00
❑ 198 Bubba Franks RC	2.50	6.00
❑ 199 Anthony Lucas RC	1.25	3.00
❑ 200 Rondell Mealey RC	1.25	3.00
❑ 201 Terrelle Smith RC	2.00	5.00
❑ 202 Frank Moreau RC	2.00	5.00
❑ 203 Deon Dyer RC	2.00	5.00
❑ 204 Quinton Spotwood RC	1.25	3.00
❑ 205 Troy Walters RC	4.00	10.00
❑ 206 Doug Chapman RC	2.00	5.00
❑ 207 Tom Brady RC	100.00	200.00
❑ 208 Sherrod Gideon RC	1.25	3.00
❑ 209 Ron Dixon RC	2.00	5.00
❑ 210 Anthony Becht RC	2.50	6.00
❑ 211 James Williams RC	2.00	5.00
❑ 212 Sebastian Janikowski RC	2.50	6.00
❑ 213 Corey Simon RC	2.50	6.00
❑ 214 Gari Scott RC	1.25	3.00
❑ 215 Dante Hall RC	5.00	12.00
❑ 216 Tim Rattay RC	2.50	6.00
❑ 217 Chafie Fields RC	1.25	3.00
❑ 218 Trung Canidate RC	2.00	5.00
❑ 219 Chris Coleman RC	2.50	6.00
❑ 220 Erron Kinney RC	2.50	6.00
❑ 221 Thomas Jones RC	6.00	15.00
❑ 222 Travis Taylor RC	4.00	10.00
❑ 223 Chris Redman RC	3.00	8.00
❑ 224 Jamal Lewis RC	10.00	25.00
❑ 225 Dez White RC	4.00	10.00
❑ 226 Peter Warrick RC	4.00	10.00
❑ 227 Ron Dugans RC	3.00	8.00
❑ 228 Courtney Brown RC	4.00	10.00
❑ 229 Travis Prentice RC	3.00	8.00
❑ 230 Dennis Northcutt RC	4.00	10.00
❑ 231 Michael Wiley RC	3.00	8.00
❑ 232 Chris Cole RC	3.00	8.00
❑ 233 Reuben Droughns RC	4.00	10.00
❑ 234 R.Jay Soward RC	3.00	8.00
❑ 235 Shyrone Stith RC	3.00	8.00
❑ 236 Sylvester Morris RC	3.00	8.00
❑ 237 J.R. Redmond RC	3.00	8.00
❑ 238 Ron Dayne RC	4.00	10.00
❑ 239 Chad Pennington RC	10.00	25.00
❑ 240 Laveranues Coles RC	5.00	12.00
❑ 241 Jerry Porter RC	4.00	10.00
❑ 242 Todd Pinkston RC	4.00	10.00
❑ 243 Plaxico Burress RC	7.50	20.00
❑ 244 Danny Farmer RC	3.00	8.00
❑ 245 Tee Martin RC	4.00	10.00
❑ 246 Trevor Gaylor RC	3.00	8.00
❑ 247 Giovanni Carmazzi RC	3.00	8.00
❑ 248 Darrell Jackson RC	5.00	12.00
❑ 249 Shaun Alexander RC	10.00	25.00
❑ 250 Chris Samuels RC	3.00	8.00

2001 Leaf Certified Materials

Card	Low	High
❑ COMP.SET w/o SPs (100)	12.50	30.00
❑ 1 Aaron Brooks	.30	.75
❑ 2 Ahman Green	.40	1.00
❑ 3 Akili Smith	.25	.60
❑ 4 Amani Toomer	.30	.75
❑ 5 Antonio Freeman	.40	1.00
❑ 6 Barry Sanders	1.00	2.50
❑ 7 Brad Johnson	.30	.75
❑ 8 Brett Favre	1.25	3.00
❑ 9 Brian Griese	.30	.75
❑ 10 Brian Urlacher	.50	1.25
❑ 11 Bruce Smith	.40	1.00
❑ 12 Cade McNown	.30	.75
❑ 13 Chad Pennington	.40	1.00
❑ 14 Charlie Batch	.30	.75
❑ 15 Charlie Garner	.30	.75
❑ 16 Corey Dillon	.30	.75
❑ 17 Cris Carter	.40	1.00
❑ 18 Curtis Martin	.40	1.00
❑ 19 Dan Marino	1.25	3.00
❑ 20 Darrell Jackson	.30	.75
❑ 21 Daunte Culpepper	.40	1.00
❑ 22 David Boston	.25	.60
❑ 23 Derrick Alexander	.25	.60
❑ 24 Donovan McNabb	.50	1.25
❑ 25 Dorsey Levens	.30	.75
❑ 26 Doug Flutie	.40	1.00
❑ 27 Drew Bledsoe	.40	1.00
❑ 28 Ed McCaffrey	.30	.75
❑ 29 Eddie George	.40	1.00
❑ 30 Edgerrin James	.40	1.00
❑ 31 Elvis Grbac	.30	.75
❑ 32 Emmitt Smith	1.00	2.50
❑ 33 Eric Moulds	.30	.75
❑ 34 Frank Wycheck	.25	.60
❑ 35 Fred Taylor	.40	1.00
❑ 36 Ike Hilliard	.30	.75
❑ 37 Isaac Bruce	.40	1.00
❑ 38 Jacquez Green	.25	.60
❑ 39 Jake Plummer	.30	.75
❑ 40 Jamal Anderson	.30	.75
❑ 41 Jamal Lewis	.40	1.00
❑ 42 James Stewart	.25	.60
❑ 43 Jay Fiedler	.30	.75
❑ 44 Jeff Garcia	.30	.75
❑ 45 Jeff George	.30	.75
❑ 46 Jerome Bettis	.40	1.00
❑ 47 Jerry Rice	.75	2.00
❑ 48 Jevon Kearse	.30	.75
❑ 49 Jimmy Smith	.30	.75
❑ 50 Joe Horn	.30	.75
❑ 51 Joey Galloway	.30	.75
❑ 52 John Elway	1.00	2.50
❑ 53 Junior Seau	.40	1.00
❑ 54 Keenan McCardell	.30	.75
❑ 55 Kerry Collins	.30	.75
❑ 56 Keyshawn Johnson	.30	.75
❑ 57 Kurt Warner	.50	1.25
❑ 58 Lamar Smith	.30	.75
❑ 59 Laveranues Coles	.40	1.00
❑ 60 Marcus Robinson	.30	.75
❑ 61 Mark Brunell	.40	1.00
❑ 62 Marshall Faulk	.40	1.00
❑ 63 Marvin Harrison	.40	1.00
❑ 64 Matt Hasselbeck	.40	1.00
❑ 65 Mike Alstott	.30	.75
❑ 66 Mike Anderson	.30	.75
❑ 67 Muhsin Muhammad	.30	.75
❑ 68 Peter Warrick	.30	.75
❑ 69 Peyton Manning	1.00	2.50
❑ 70 Plaxico Burress	.30	.75
❑ 71 Randy Moss	.50	1.25
❑ 72 Ray Lewis	.40	1.00
❑ 73 Rich Gannon	.30	.75
❑ 74 Ricky Watters	.30	.75
❑ 75 Ricky Williams	.40	1.00
❑ 76 Rob Johnson	.30	.75
❑ 77 Rod Smith	.30	.75
❑ 78 Ron Dayne	.30	.75
❑ 79 Shannon Sharpe	.40	1.00
❑ 80 Shaun Alexander	.40	1.00
❑ 81 Stephen Davis	.30	.75
❑ 82 Steve McNair	.40	1.00
❑ 83 Steve Young	.50	1.25
❑ 84 Sylvester Morris	.25	.60
❑ 85 Terrell Davis	.40	1.00
❑ 86 Terrell Owens	.40	1.00
❑ 87 Terry Glenn	.30	.75
❑ 88 Thomas Jones	.30	.75
❑ 89 Tiki Barber	.40	1.00
❑ 90 Tim Brown	.40	1.00
❑ 91 Tim Couch	.25	.60
❑ 92 Tony Gonzalez	.30	.75
❑ 93 Torry Holt	.30	.75
❑ 94 Travis Taylor	.25	.60
❑ 95 Troy Aikman	.60	1.50
❑ 96 Tyrone Wheatley	.30	.75
❑ 97 Vinny Testaverde	.30	.75
❑ 98 Warren Sapp	.30	.75
❑ 99 Warrick Dunn	.40	1.00
❑ 100 Wayne Chrebet	.30	.75
❑ 101 Chris Taylor RC	2.50	6.00
❑ 102 Ken-Yon Rambo RC	2.50	6.00
❑ 103 Correll Buckhalter RC	4.00	10.00
❑ 104 A.J. Feeley RC	3.00	8.00
❑ 105 Josh Booty RC	3.00	8.00
❑ 106 LaMont Jordan RC	4.00	10.00
❑ 107 Alge Crumpler RC	4.00	10.00
❑ 108 Jamal Reynolds RC	3.00	8.00
❑ 109 Nate Clements RC	4.00	10.00
❑ 110 Will Allen RC	4.00	10.00
❑ 111 Santana Moss FF RC	8.00	20.00
❑ 112 Chad Johnson FF RC	12.00	30.00
❑ 113 Chris Chambers FF RC	8.00	20.00
❑ 114 David Terrell FF RC	4.00	10.00
❑ 115 Freddie Mitchell FF RC	3.00	8.00
❑ 116 Koren Robinson FF RC	5.00	12.00
❑ 117 Quincy Morgan FF RC	4.00	10.00
❑ 118 Reggie Wayne FF RC	12.00	30.00
❑ 119 Robert Ferguson FF RC	5.00	12.00
❑ 120 Rod Gardner FF RC	4.00	10.00
❑ 121 Snoop Minnis FF RC	4.00	10.00
❑ 122 Josh Heupel FF RC	5.00	12.00
❑ 123 Anthony Thomas FF RC	5.00	12.00
❑ 124 Deuce McAllister FF RC	6.00	15.00
❑ 125 James Jackson FF RC	4.00	10.00
❑ 126 Travis Minor FF RC	4.00	10.00
❑ 127 Kevan Barlow FF RC	4.00	10.00
❑ 128 LaDain Tomlinson FF RC	30.00	80.00
❑ 129 Todd Heap FF RC	5.00	12.00
❑ 130 Michael Bennett FF RC	5.00	12.00
❑ 131 Rudi Johnson FF RC	5.00	12.00
❑ 132 Travis Henry FF RC	5.00	12.00
❑ 133 Michael Vick FF RC	10.00	25.00
❑ 134 Drew Brees FF RC	25.00	60.00
❑ 135 Chris Weinke FF RC	4.00	10.00
❑ 136 Quincy Carter FF RC	4.00	10.00
❑ 137 Mike McMahon FF RC	4.00	10.00
❑ 138 Jesse Palmer FF RC	5.00	12.00
❑ 139 Marq Tuiasosopo FF RC	4.00	10.00
❑ 140 Dan Morgan FF RC	5.00	12.00
❑ 141 Gerard Warren FF RC	4.00	10.00
❑ 142 Leonard Davis FF RC	4.00	10.00
❑ 143 Andre Carter FF RC	5.00	12.00
❑ 144 Justin Smith FF RC	5.00	12.00
❑ 145 Sage Rosenfels FF RC	5.00	12.00

2002 Leaf Certified

❑ COMP.SET w/o SP's (100)	10.00	25.00
❑ 1 David Boston	.25	.60
❑ 2 Jake Plummer	.30	.75
❑ 3 Michael Vick	.40	1.00
❑ 4 Jamal Anderson	.30	.75
❑ 5 Chris Redman	.25	.60
❑ 6 Ray Lewis	.40	1.00
❑ 7 Eric Moulds	.30	.75
❑ 8 Travis Henry	.30	.75
❑ 9 Nate Clements	.25	.60
❑ 10 Chris Weinke	.25	.60
❑ 11 Muhsin Muhammad	.30	.75
❑ 12 Wesley Walls	.30	.75
❑ 13 Anthony Thomas	.30	.75
❑ 14 Brian Urlacher	.50	1.25
❑ 15 Dez White	.25	.60
❑ 16 Corey Dillon	.30	.75
❑ 17 Peter Warrick	.30	.75
❑ 18 Tim Couch	.25	.60
❑ 19 Kevin Johnson	.25	.60
❑ 20 James Jackson	.25	.60
❑ 21 Emmitt Smith	1.00	2.50
❑ 22 Quincy Carter	.25	.60
❑ 23 Brian Griese	.30	.75
❑ 24 Ed McCaffrey	.30	.75
❑ 25 Rod Smith	.30	.75
❑ 26 Terrell Davis	.40	1.00
❑ 27 Mike Anderson	.30	.75
❑ 28 Germane Crowell	.25	.60
❑ 29 James Stewart	.25	.60
❑ 30 Charlie Batch	.30	.75
❑ 31 Antonio Freeman	.40	1.00
❑ 32 Brett Favre	1.00	2.50
❑ 33 Ahman Green	.30	.75
❑ 34 LeRoy Butler	.30	.75
❑ 35 Edgerrin James	.40	1.00
❑ 36 Marvin Harrison	.40	1.00
❑ 37 Peyton Manning	.75	2.00
❑ 38 Fred Taylor	.40	1.00
❑ 39 Jimmy Smith	.30	.75
❑ 40 Mark Brunell	.30	.75
❑ 41 Keenan McCardell	.30	.75
❑ 42 Tony Gonzalez	.30	.75
❑ 43 Priest Holmes	.40	1.00
❑ 44 Jay Fiedler	.30	.75
❑ 45 Chris Chambers	.40	1.00
❑ 46 Zach Thomas	.40	1.00
❑ 47 Travis Minor	.30	.75
❑ 48 Cris Carter	.40	1.00
❑ 49 Daunte Culpepper	.30	.75
❑ 50 Randy Moss	.40	1.00
❑ 51 Drew Bledsoe	.40	1.00
❑ 52 Tom Brady	1.00	2.50
❑ 53 Antowain Smith	.30	.75
❑ 54 Troy Brown	.30	.75
❑ 55 Aaron Brooks	.30	.75
❑ 56 Ricky Williams	.40	1.00
❑ 57 Ron Dayne	.30	.75
❑ 58 Kerry Collins	.30	.75
❑ 59 Michael Strahan	.40	1.00
❑ 60 Amani Toomer	.30	.75
❑ 61 Chad Pennington	.40	1.00
❑ 62 Curtis Martin	.40	1.00
❑ 63 Vinny Testaverde	.30	.75
❑ 64 Wayne Chrebet	.30	.75
❑ 65 Charles Woodson	.40	1.00
❑ 66 Rich Gannon	.30	.75
❑ 67 Tim Brown	.40	1.00
❑ 68 Jerry Rice	.75	2.00
❑ 69 Tyrone Wheatley	.30	.75
❑ 70 Donovan McNabb	.50	1.25
❑ 71 Duce Staley	.30	.75
❑ 72 Todd Pinkston	.25	.60
❑ 73 Correll Buckhalter	.30	.75
❑ 74 Jerome Bettis	.40	1.00
❑ 75 Kordell Stewart	.30	.75
❑ 76 Plaxico Burress	.30	.75
❑ 77 Hines Ward	.40	1.00
❑ 78 Junior Seau	.40	1.00
❑ 79 LaDainian Tomlinson	.60	1.50
❑ 80 Doug Flutie	.40	1.00
❑ 81 Terrell Owens	.40	1.00
❑ 82 Jeff Garcia	.30	.75
❑ 83 Ricky Watters	.30	.75
❑ 84 Shaun Alexander	.40	1.00
❑ 85 Koren Robinson	.25	.60
❑ 86 Isaac Bruce	.40	1.00
❑ 87 Kurt Warner	.40	1.00
❑ 88 Marshall Faulk	.40	1.00
❑ 89 Torry Holt	.40	1.00
❑ 90 Keyshawn Johnson	.30	.75
❑ 91 Mike Alstott	.30	.75
❑ 92 Warren Sapp	.30	.75
❑ 93 Brad Johnson	.30	.75
❑ 94 Eddie George	.30	.75
❑ 95 Jevon Kearse	.30	.75
❑ 96 Steve McNair	.40	1.00
❑ 97 Derrick Mason	.30	.75
❑ 98 Frank Wycheck	.25	.60
❑ 99 Champ Bailey	.40	1.00
❑ 100 Stephen Davis	.30	.75
❑ 101 Ladell Betts JSY RC	3.00	8.00
❑ 102 Antonio Bryant JSY RC	4.00	10.00
❑ 103 Reche Caldwell JSY RC	3.00	8.00
❑ 104 David Carr JSY RC	3.00	8.00
❑ 105 Tim Carter JSY RC	2.50	6.00
❑ 106 Eric Crouch JSY RC	3.00	8.00
❑ 107 Rohan Davey JSY RC	3.00	8.00
❑ 108 Andre Davis JSY RC	2.50	6.00
❑ 109 T.J. Duckett JSY RC	3.00	8.00
❑ 110 DeShaun Foster JSY RC	3.00	8.00
❑ 111 Jabar Gaffney JSY RC	3.00	8.00
❑ 112 Daniel Graham JSY RC	2.50	6.00
❑ 113 William Green FB RC	2.50	6.00
❑ 114 Joey Harrington JSY RC	3.00	8.00
❑ 115 David Garrard JSY RC	5.00	12.00
❑ 116 Ron Johnson JSY RC	2.50	6.00
❑ 117 Ashley Lelie JSY RC	3.00	8.00
❑ 118 Josh McCown JSY RC	3.00	8.00
❑ 119 Maurice Morris JSY RC	3.00	8.00
❑ 120 Julius Peppers JSY RC	5.00	12.00
❑ 121 Clinton Portis JSY RC	8.00	20.00
❑ 122 Patrick Ramsey JSY RC	3.00	8.00
❑ 123 Antwaan Randle El JSY RC	3.00	8.00
❑ 124 Josh Reed JSY RC	2.50	6.00
❑ 125 Cliff Russell JSY RC	2.00	5.00
❑ 126 Jeremy Shockey JSY RC	5.00	12.00
❑ 127 Donte Stallworth JSY RC	3.00	8.00
❑ 128 Travis Stephens JSY RC	2.00	5.00
❑ 129 Javon Walker JSY RC	3.00	8.00
❑ 130 Marquise Walker JSY RC	2.00	5.00
❑ 131 Roy Williams JSY RC	4.00	10.00
❑ 132 Mike Williams JSY RC	2.00	5.00

2004 Leaf Certified Materials

❑ COMP.SET w/o SP's (150)	12.50	30.00
❑ 151-200 PRINT RUN 1000 SER.#'d SETS		
❑ 201-233 PRINT RUN 1250 SER.#'d SETS		
❑ UNPRICED MIRROR BLACK #'d OF 1		
❑ UNPRICED MIRROR EMERALD #'d OF 5		
❑ 1 Anquan Boldin	.40	1.00
❑ 2 Emmitt Smith	1.00	2.50
❑ 3 Josh McCown	.30	.75
❑ 4 Marcel Shipp	.40	1.00
❑ 5 Michael Vick	.40	1.00
❑ 6 Peerless Price	.30	.75
❑ 7 T.J. Duckett	.30	.75
❑ 8 Warrick Dunn	.30	.75
❑ 9 Jamal Lewis	.30	.75
❑ 10 Kyle Boller	.30	.75
❑ 11 Ray Lewis	.40	1.00
❑ 12 Terrell Suggs	.25	.60
❑ 13 Todd Heap	.30	.75
❑ 14 Drew Bledsoe	.40	1.00
❑ 15 Eric Moulds	.30	.75
❑ 16 Travis Henry	.30	.75
❑ 17 Julius Peppers	.30	.75
❑ 18 Muhsin Muhammad	.30	.75
❑ 19 Stephen Davis	.30	.75
❑ 20 Anthony Thomas	.30	.75
❑ 21 Brian Urlacher	.40	1.00
❑ 22 Rex Grossman	.40	1.00
❑ 23 Chad Johnson	.30	.75
❑ 24 Corey Dillon	.30	.75
❑ 25 Peter Warrick	.30	.75
❑ 26 Jeff Garcia	.40	1.00
❑ 27 Tim Couch	.30	.75
❑ 28 William Green	.25	.60
❑ 29 Antonio Bryant	.40	1.00
❑ 30 Keyshawn Johnson	.30	.75
❑ 31 Quincy Carter	.25	.60
❑ 32 Roy Williams S	.30	.75
❑ 33 Terence Newman	.30	.75
❑ 34 Ashley Lelie	.30	.75
❑ 35 Ed McCaffrey	.40	1.00
❑ 36 Jake Plummer	.30	.75
❑ 37 Mike Anderson	.30	.75
❑ 38 Rod Smith	.30	.75
❑ 39 Charles Rogers	.30	.75
❑ 40 Joey Harrington	.30	.75
❑ 41 Ahman Green	.40	1.00
❑ 42 Brett Favre	1.00	2.50
❑ 43 Donald Driver	.40	1.00
❑ 44 Javon Walker	.30	.75
❑ 45 Robert Ferguson	.25	.60
❑ 46 Andre Johnson	.40	1.00
❑ 47 David Carr	.30	.75
❑ 48 Edgerrin James	.40	1.00
❑ 49 Marvin Harrison	.40	1.00
❑ 50 Peyton Manning	.75	2.00
❑ 51 Reggie Wayne	.30	.75
❑ 52 Byron Leftwich	.40	1.00
❑ 53 Fred Taylor	.30	.75
❑ 54 Jimmy Smith	.30	.75
❑ 55 Dante Hall	.30	.75
❑ 56 Priest Holmes	.40	1.00
❑ 57 Tony Gonzalez	.40	1.00
❑ 58 Trent Green	.30	.75
❑ 59 A.J. Feeley	.30	.75
❑ 60 Chris Chambers	.30	.75
❑ 61 David Boston	.25	.60
❑ 62 Jason Taylor	.40	1.00
❑ 63 Jay Fiedler	.25	.60
❑ 64 Junior Seau	.40	1.00
❑ 65 Randy McMichael	.25	.60
❑ 66 Ricky Williams	.40	1.00
❑ 67 Zach Thomas	.40	1.00
❑ 68 Daunte Culpepper	.40	1.00
❑ 69 Michael Bennett	.30	.75
❑ 70 Randy Moss	.40	1.00
❑ 71 Tom Brady	1.00	2.50
❑ 72 Troy Brown	.30	.75
❑ 73 Ty Law	.30	.75
❑ 74 Aaron Brooks	.30	.75
❑ 75 Deuce McAllister	.40	1.00
❑ 76 Donte Stallworth	.30	.75
❑ 77 Amani Toomer	.30	.75
❑ 78 Jeremy Shockey	.30	.75
❑ 79 Kerry Collins	.30	.75
❑ 80 Michael Strahan	.30	.75
❑ 81 Tiki Barber	.40	1.00
❑ 82 Chad Pennington	.40	1.00
❑ 83 Curtis Martin	.40	1.00
❑ 84 Justin McCareins	.25	.60
❑ 85 Santana Moss	.30	.75
❑ 86 Charles Woodson	.40	1.00
❑ 87 Jerry Rice	.75	2.00
❑ 88 Rich Gannon	.30	.75
❑ 89 Tim Brown	.40	1.00
❑ 90 Warren Sapp	.30	.75
❑ 91 Correll Buckhalter	.30	.75
❑ 92 Donovan McNabb	.40	1.00
❑ 93 Freddie Mitchell	.25	.60
❑ 94 Jevon Kearse	.30	.75
❑ 95 Terrell Owens	.40	1.00
❑ 96 Antwaan Randle El	.30	.75
❑ 97 Duce Staley	.30	.75

Card		
❑ 98 Hines Ward	.40	1.00
❑ 99 Jerome Bettis	.40	1.00
❑ 100 Plaxico Burress	.30	.75
❑ 101 Doug Flutie	.40	1.00
❑ 102 LaDainian Tomlinson	.50	1.25
❑ 103 Koren Robinson	.40	1.00
❑ 104 Matt Hasselbeck	.40	1.00
❑ 105 Shaun Alexander	.40	1.00
❑ 106 Isaac Bruce	.30	.75
❑ 107 Kurt Warner	.40	1.00
❑ 108 Marc Bulger	.30	.75
❑ 109 Marshall Faulk	.40	1.00
❑ 110 Torry Holt	.40	1.00
❑ 111 Brad Johnson	.30	.75
❑ 112 Mike Alstott	.30	.75
❑ 113 Derrick Mason	.30	.75
❑ 114 Drew Bennett	.30	.75
❑ 115 Eddie George	.30	.75
❑ 116 Frank Wycheck	.30	.75
❑ 117 Keith Bulluck	.25	.60
❑ 118 Steve McNair	.40	1.00
❑ 119 Tyrone Calico	.30	.75
❑ 120 Clinton Portis	.40	1.00
❑ 121 LaVar Arrington	.30	.75
❑ 122 Laveranues Coles	.30	.75
❑ 123 Mark Brunell	.30	.75
❑ 124 Patrick Ramsey	.30	.75
❑ 125 Rod Gardner	.25	.60
❑ 126 Jake Plummer FLB	.30	.75
❑ 127 Thomas Jones FLB	.30	.75
❑ 128 Priest Holmes FLB	.40	1.00
❑ 129 Jim Kelly FLB	.60	1.50
❑ 130 Doug Flutie FLB	.40	1.00
❑ 131 Walter Payton FLB	2.50	6.00
❑ 132 Troy Aikman FLB	1.00	2.50
❑ 133 John Elway FLB	1.50	4.00
❑ 134 Barry Sanders FLB	1.50	4.00
❑ 135 Mark Brunell FLB	.30	.75
❑ 136 Earl Campbell FLB	.60	1.50
❑ 137 Joe Montana FLB	2.00	5.00
❑ 138 Dan Marino FLB	2.00	5.00
❑ 139 Curtis Martin FLB	.40	1.00
❑ 140 Drew Bledsoe FLB	.40	1.00
❑ 141 Ricky Williams FLB	.40	1.00
❑ 142 Junior Seau FLB	.40	1.00
❑ 143 Charlie Garner FLB	.30	.75
❑ 144 Jerry Rice FLB	.75	2.00
❑ 145 Ahman Green FLB	.40	1.00
❑ 146 Jerome Bettis FLB	.40	1.00
❑ 147 Trent Green FLB	.30	.75
❑ 148 Warrick Dunn FLB	.30	.75
❑ 149 Deion Sanders FLB	.40	1.00
❑ 150 Stephen Davis FLB	.30	.75
❑ 151 Adimchinobe Echemandu AU RC	4.00	10.00
❑ 152 Ahmad Carroll RC	2.50	6.00
❑ 153 Andy Hall AU RC	4.00	10.00
❑ 154 B.J. Johnson AU RC	4.00	10.00
❑ 155 B.J. Symons AU RC	6.00	15.00
❑ 156 Bradlee Van Pelt AU RC	8.00	20.00
❑ 157 Brandon Miree AU RC	4.00	10.00
❑ 158 Bruce Perry AU RC	6.00	15.00
❑ 159 Carlos Francis AU RC	4.00	10.00
❑ 160 Casey Bramlet AU RC	4.00	10.00
❑ 161 Chris Gamble RC	2.00	5.00
❑ 162 Clarence Moore AU RC	6.00	15.00
❑ 163 Cody Pickett AU RC	6.00	15.00
❑ 164 Craig Krenzel AU RC	6.00	15.00
❑ 165 D.J. Hackett RC	2.50	6.00
❑ 166 D.J. Williams RC	2.50	6.00
❑ 167 Derrick Ward AU RC	6.00	15.00
❑ 168 Drew Carter AU RC	6.00	15.00
❑ 169 Ernest Wilford RC	2.00	5.00
❑ 170 Drew Henson RC	1.50	4.00
❑ 171 Jamaar Taylor AU RC	6.00	15.00
❑ 172 Jared Lorenzen AU RC	4.00	10.00
❑ 173 Jarrett Payton AU RC	6.00	15.00
❑ 174 Jason Babin AU RC	6.00	15.00
❑ 175 Jeff Smoker AU RC	6.00	15.00
❑ 176 Jeris McIntyre AU RC	4.00	10.00
❑ 177 Jerricho Cotchery RC	2.50	6.00
❑ 178 Jim Sorgi AU RC	6.00	15.00
❑ 179 John Navarre AU RC	6.00	15.00
❑ 180 Patrick Crayton AU RC	10.00	20.00
❑ 181 Johnnie Morant RC	2.00	5.00
❑ 182 Sean Taylor RC	2.50	6.00
❑ 183 Jonathan Vilma RC	2.50	6.00
❑ 184 Josh Harris RC	1.50	4.00
❑ 185 Kenechi Udeze RC	2.50	6.00
❑ 186 Mark Jones AU RC	4.00	10.00
❑ 187 Matt Mauck AU RC	6.00	15.00
❑ 188 Maurice Mann AU RC	4.00	10.00
❑ 189 Michael Turner RC	6.00	15.00
❑ 190 P.K. Sam RC	1.50	4.00
❑ 191 Quincy Wilson RC	2.00	5.00
❑ 192 Ran Carthon AU RC	4.00	10.00
❑ 193 Ryan Krause AU RC	4.00	10.00
❑ 194 Samie Parker RC	2.00	5.00
❑ 195 Sloan Thomas AU RC	4.00	10.00
❑ 196 Tommie Harris RC	2.50	6.00
❑ 197 Triandos Luke AU RC	6.00	15.00
❑ 198 Troy Fleming AU RC	4.00	10.00
❑ 199 Vince Wilfork RC	2.50	6.00
❑ 200 Will Smith RC	2.50	6.00
❑ 201 Larry Fitzgerald JSY RC	7.50	20.00
❑ 202 DeAngelo Hall JSY RC	4.00	10.00
❑ 203 Matt Schaub JSY RC	7.50	20.00
❑ 204 Michael Jenkins JSY RC	3.00	8.00
❑ 205 Devard Darling JSY RC	3.00	8.00
❑ 206 J.P. Losman JSY RC	4.00	10.00
❑ 207 Lee Evans JSY RC	4.00	10.00
❑ 208 Keary Colbert JSY RC	3.00	8.00
❑ 209 Bernard Berrian JSY RC	4.00	10.00
❑ 210 Chris Perry JSY RC	4.00	10.00
❑ 211 Kellen Winslow JSY RC	5.00	12.00
❑ 212 Luke McCown JSY RC	3.00	8.00
❑ 213 Julius Jones JSY RC	7.50	20.00
❑ 214 Darius Watts JSY RC	3.00	8.00
❑ 215 Tatum Bell JSY RC	5.00	12.00
❑ 216 Kevin Jones JSY RC	5.00	12.00
❑ 217 Roy Williams JSY RC	6.00	15.00
❑ 218 Dunta Robinson JSY RC	3.00	8.00
❑ 219 Greg Jones JSY RC	4.00	10.00
❑ 220 Reggie Williams JSY RC	4.00	10.00
❑ 221 Mewelde Moore JSY RC	3.00	8.00
❑ 222 Ben Watson JSY RC	3.00	8.00
❑ 223 Cedric Cobbs JSY RC	3.00	8.00
❑ 224 Devery Henderson JSY RC	3.00	8.00
❑ 225 Eli Manning JSY RC	15.00	30.00
❑ 226 Robert Gallery JSY RC	3.00	8.00
❑ 227 Ben Roethlisberger JSY RC	15.00	40.00
❑ 228 Philip Rivers JSY RC	7.50	20.00
❑ 229 Derrick Hamilton JSY RC	3.00	8.00
❑ 230 Rashaun Woods JSY RC	3.00	8.00
❑ 231 Steven Jackson JSY RC	7.50	20.00
❑ 232 Michael Clayton JSY RC	4.00	10.00
❑ 233 Ben Troupe JSY RC	3.00	8.00

2005 Leaf Certified Materials

Card		
❑ COMP.SET w/o RCs (150)	15.00	40.00
❑ 151-200 PRINT RUN 1000 SER.#'d SETS		
❑ 1 Anquan Boldin	.30	.75
❑ 2 Josh McCown	.30	.75
❑ 3 Larry Fitzgerald	.40	1.00
❑ 4 Michael Vick	.40	1.00
❑ 5 Peerless Price	.25	.60
❑ 6 T.J. Duckett	.25	.60
❑ 7 Warrick Dunn	.30	.75
❑ 8 Jamal Lewis	.30	.75
❑ 9 Kyle Boller	.30	.75
❑ 10 Todd Heap	.30	.75
❑ 11 Ray Lewis	.40	1.00
❑ 12 Terrell Suggs	.30	.75
❑ 13 Drew Bledsoe	.40	1.00
❑ 14 Eric Moulds	.30	.75
❑ 15 J.P. Losman	.30	.75
❑ 16 Lee Evans	.30	.75
❑ 17 Willis McGahee	.40	1.00
❑ 18 DeShaun Foster	.30	.75
❑ 19 Jake Delhomme	.40	1.00
❑ 20 Steve Smith	.40	1.00
❑ 21 Brian Urlacher	.40	1.00
❑ 22 Rex Grossman	.40	1.00
❑ 23 Carson Palmer	.40	1.00
❑ 24 Chad Johnson	.30	.75
❑ 25 Rudi Johnson	.30	.75
❑ 26 Kellen Winslow Jr.	.40	1.00
❑ 27 Kelly Holcomb	.25	.60
❑ 28 Lee Suggs	.30	.75
❑ 29 William Green	.25	.60
❑ 30 Julius Jones	.40	1.00
❑ 31 Keyshawn Johnson	.30	.75
❑ 32 Roy Williams S	.30	.75
❑ 33 Terence Newman	.25	.60
❑ 34 Ashley Lelie	.25	.60
❑ 35 Champ Bailey	.30	.75
❑ 36 Darius Watts	.25	.60
❑ 37 Jake Plummer	.30	.75
❑ 38 Tatum Bell	.30	.75
❑ 39 Charles Rogers	.25	.60
❑ 40 Joey Harrington	.40	1.00
❑ 41 Kevin Jones	.30	.75
❑ 42 Roy Williams WR	.40	1.00
❑ 43 Ahman Green	.40	1.00
❑ 44 Brett Favre	1.00	2.50
❑ 45 Javon Walker	.30	.75
❑ 46 Robert Ferguson	.30	.75
❑ 47 Andre Johnson	.30	.75
❑ 48 David Carr	.30	.75
❑ 49 Domanick Davis	.25	.60
❑ 50 Dallas Clark	.30	.75
❑ 51 Edgerrin James	.30	.75
❑ 52 Marvin Harrison	.40	1.00
❑ 53 Peyton Manning	.60	1.50
❑ 54 Reggie Wayne	.30	.75
❑ 55 Byron Leftwich	.30	.75
❑ 56 Fred Taylor	.40	1.00
❑ 57 Jimmy Smith	.30	.75
❑ 58 Reggie Williams	.30	.75
❑ 59 Priest Holmes	.40	1.00
❑ 60 Tony Gonzalez	.30	.75
❑ 61 Trent Green	.30	.75
❑ 62 Chris Chambers	.30	.75
❑ 63 Jason Taylor	.30	.75
❑ 64 Junior Seau	.40	1.00
❑ 65 Zach Thomas	.40	1.00
❑ 66 Daunte Culpepper	.40	1.00
❑ 67 Michael Bennett	.30	.75
❑ 68 Randy Moss	.40	1.00
❑ 69 Corey Dillon	.30	.75
❑ 70 Tom Brady	.75	2.00
❑ 71 Deion Branch	.30	.75
❑ 72 Aaron Brooks	.25	.60
❑ 73 Deuce McAllister	.40	1.00
❑ 74 Donte Stallworth	.30	.75
❑ 75 Joe Horn	.30	.75
❑ 76 Eli Manning	.75	2.00
❑ 77 Jeremy Shockey	.40	1.00
❑ 78 Michael Strahan	.30	.75
❑ 79 Tiki Barber	.40	1.00
❑ 80 Anthony Becht	.25	.60
❑ 81 Chad Pennington	.40	1.00
❑ 82 Curtis Martin	.40	1.00
❑ 83 Justin McCareins	.25	.60
❑ 84 Laveranues Coles	.30	.75
❑ 85 Santana Moss	.30	.75
❑ 86 Shaun Ellis	.25	.60
❑ 87 Jerry Porter	.30	.75
❑ 88 Brian Westbrook	.40	1.00
❑ 89 Chad Lewis	.25	.60
❑ 90 Donovan McNabb	.40	1.00
❑ 91 Freddie Mitchell	.25	.60
❑ 92 Hugh Douglas	.25	.60
❑ 93 Jevon Kearse	.30	.75
❑ 94 Terrell Owens	.40	1.00
❑ 95 Todd Pinkston	.25	.60
❑ 96 Antwaan Randle El	.30	.75
❑ 97 Ben Roethlisberger	1.00	2.50
❑ 98 Duce Staley	.30	.75
❑ 99 Hines Ward	.40	1.00
❑ 100 Jerome Bettis	.40	1.00
❑ 101 Antonio Gates	.40	1.00
❑ 102 Drew Brees	.40	1.00
❑ 103 LaDainian Tomlinson	.50	1.25
❑ 104 Kevan Barlow	.25	.60
❑ 105 Darrell Jackson	.30	.75
❑ 106 Koren Robinson	.30	.75
❑ 107 Matt Hasselbeck	.30	.75
❑ 108 Shaun Alexander	.40	1.00
❑ 109 Marc Bulger	.30	.75
❑ 110 Steven Jackson	.50	1.25
❑ 111 Torry Holt	.30	.75

❑ 112 Michael Clayton .30 .75
❑ 113 Chris Brown .30 .75
❑ 114 Drew Bennett .30 .75
❑ 115 Keith Bulluck .25 .60
❑ 116 Steve McNair .40 1.00
❑ 117 Clinton Portis .40 1.00
❑ 118 LaVar Arrington .40 1.00
❑ 119 John Riggins .50 1.25
❑ 120 Sean Taylor .30 .75
❑ 121 Jake Plummer .30 .75
❑ 122 Thomas Jones .30 .75
❑ 123 Doug Flutie .40 1.00
❑ 124 Walter Payton 1.25 3.00
❑ 125 Corey Dillon .30 .75
❑ 126 Troy Aikman .60 1.50
❑ 127 Terrell Davis .40 1.00
❑ 128 Marshall Faulk .40 1.00
❑ 129 Dan Marino 1.25 3.00
❑ 130 Thurman Thomas .50 1.25
❑ 131 Warren Moon .50 1.25
❑ 132 Curtis Martin .40 1.00
❑ 133 Drew Bledsoe .40 1.00
❑ 134 Kerry Collins .30 .75
❑ 135 Keyshawn Johnson .30 .75
❑ 136 A.J. Feeley .25 .60
❑ 137 Duce Staley .30 .75
❑ 138 Junior Seau .40 1.00
❑ 139 Jerry Rice .75 2.00
❑ 140 Steve Young .60 1.50
❑ 141 Jerome Bettis .40 1.00
❑ 142 Kurt Warner .40 1.00
❑ 143 Trent Green .30 .75
❑ 144 Keyshawn Johnson .30 .75
❑ 145 Warren Sapp .30 .75
❑ 146 Warrick Dunn .30 .75
❑ 147 Jevon Kearse .30 .75
❑ 148 Deion Sanders .60 1.50
❑ 149 Laveranues Coles .30 .75
❑ 150 Stephen Davis .30 .75
❑ 151 Cedric Benson RC 2.00 5.00
❑ 152 Mike Williams 1.50 4.00
❑ 153 DeMarcus Ware RC 3.00 8.00
❑ 154 Shawne Merriman RC 2.00 5.00
❑ 155 Thomas Davis RC 1.50 4.00
❑ 156 Derrick Johnson RC 2.00 5.00
❑ 157 Travis Johnson RC 1.25 3.00
❑ 158 David Pollack RC 1.50 4.00
❑ 159 Erasmus James RC 1.50 4.00
❑ 160 Marcus Spears RC 2.00 5.00
❑ 161 Fabian Washington RC 2.00 5.00
❑ 162 Aaron Rodgers RC 6.00 15.00
❑ 163 Marlin Jackson RC 1.50 4.00
❑ 164 Heath Miller RC 4.00 10.00
❑ 165 Matt Roth RC 2.00 5.00
❑ 166 Dan Cody RC 2.00 5.00
❑ 167 Bryant McFadden RC 1.50 4.00
❑ 168 Chris Henry RC 2.00 5.00
❑ 169 David Greene RC 1.50 4.00
❑ 170 Brandon Jones RC 2.00 5.00
❑ 171 Marion Barber RC 6.00 15.00
❑ 172 Brandon Jacobs RC 2.50 6.00
❑ 173 Jerome Mathis RC 2.00 5.00
❑ 174 Craphonso Thorpe RC 1.50 4.00
❑ 175 Alvin Pearman RC 1.25 3.00
❑ 176 Darren Sproles RC 2.50 6.00
❑ 177 Fred Gibson RC 1.50 4.00
❑ 178 Roydell Williams RC 1.50 4.00
❑ 179 Airese Currie RC 1.50 4.00
❑ 180 Damien Nash RC 1.50 4.00
❑ 181 Dan Orlovsky RC 2.00 5.00
❑ 182 Adrian McPherson RC 1.50 4.00
❑ 183 Larry Brackins RC 1.25 3.00
❑ 184 Rasheed Marshall RC 1.50 4.00
❑ 185 Cedric Houston RC 2.00 5.00
❑ 186 Chad Owens RC 2.00 5.00
❑ 187 Tab Perry RC 2.00 5.00
❑ 188 Dante Ridgeway RC 1.25 3.00
❑ 189 Craig Bragg RC 1.25 3.00
❑ 190 Deandra Cobb RC 1.50 4.00
❑ 191 Derek Anderson RC 2.00 5.00
❑ 192 Paris Warren RC 1.50 4.00
❑ 193 Lionel Gates RC 1.25 3.00
❑ 194 Anthony Davis RC 1.50 4.00
❑ 195 Ryan Fitzpatrick RC 2.00 5.00
❑ 196 J.R. Russell RC 1.25 3.00
❑ 197 Jason White RC 2.00 5.00
❑ 198 Kay-Jay Harris RC 1.50 4.00
❑ 199 T.A. McLendon RC 1.25 3.00
❑ 200 Taylor Stubblefield RC 1.25 3.00
❑ 201 Adam Jones JSY/1499 RC 2.50 6.00
❑ 202 Alex Smith QB JSY/499 RC 12.50 30.00
❑ 203 Andrew Walter JSY/1249 RC 2.50 6.00
❑ 204 Antrel Rolle JSY/999 RC 3.00 8.00
❑ 205 Braylon Edwards JSY /499 RC 10.00 25.00
❑ 206 Cadillac Williams JSY /499 RC 12.50 30.00
❑ 207 Carlos Rogers JSY/1499 RC 2.00 5.00
❑ 208 Charlie Frye JSY/1499 RC 2.00 5.00
❑ 209 Ciatrick Fason JSY/1499 RC 2.50 6.00
❑ 210 Courtney Roby JSY/1249 RC 2.50 6.00
❑ 211 Eric Shelton JSY/999 RC 2.50 6.00
❑ 212 Frank Gore JSY/999 RC 5.00 12.00
❑ 213 J.J. Arrington JSY/499 RC 4.00 10.00
❑ 214 Kyle Orton JSY/1499 RC 5.00 12.00
❑ 215 Jason Campbell JSY/749 RC 5.00 12.00
❑ 216 Mark Bradley JSY/999 RC 2.50 6.00
❑ 217 Mark Clayton JSY/499 RC 4.00 10.00
❑ 218 Matt Jones JSY/749 RC 4.00 10.00
❑ 219 Maurice Clarett JSY/999 2.50 6.00
❑ 220 Reggie Brown JSY/999 RC 2.50 6.00
❑ 221 Roddy White JSY/749 RC 4.00 10.00
❑ 222 Ronnie Brown JSY/499 RC 12.50 30.00
❑ 223 Roscoe Parrish JSY/999 RC 2.50 6.00
❑ 224 Ryan Moats JSY/999 RC 2.50 6.00
❑ 225 Stefan LeFors JSY/1499 RC 2.50 6.00
❑ 226 Terrence Murphy JSY /1499 RC 2.00 5.00
❑ 227 Troy Williamson JSY/749 RC 4.00 10.00
❑ 228 Vernand Morency JSY /1499 RC 2.50 6.00
❑ 229 Vincent Jackson JSY /1499 RC 4.00 10.00

2006 Leaf Certified Materials

❑ COMP.SET w/o SP's (150) 15.00 40.00
❑ 1 Anquan Boldin .30 .75
❑ 2 Edgerrin James .30 .75
❑ 3 Kurt Warner .40 1.00
❑ 4 Larry Fitzgerald .40 1.00
❑ 5 Alge Crumpler .30 .75
❑ 6 Brian Finneran .25 .60
❑ 7 Michael Jenkins .30 .75
❑ 8 Michael Vick .40 1.00
❑ 9 Warrick Dunn .30 .75
❑ 10 Derrick Mason .30 .75
❑ 11 Jamal Lewis .30 .75
❑ 12 Kyle Boller .30 .75
❑ 13 Todd Heap .30 .75
❑ 14 Mark Clayton .30 .75
❑ 15 Eric Moulds .30 .75
❑ 16 J.P. Losman .30 .75
❑ 17 Josh Reed .25 .60
❑ 18 Lee Evans .30 .75
❑ 19 Willis McGahee .40 1.00
❑ 20 DeShaun Foster .30 .75
❑ 21 Jake Delhomme .30 .75
❑ 22 Stephen Davis .30 .75
❑ 23 Keary Colbert .30 .75
❑ 24 Steve Smith .40 1.00
❑ 25 Brian Urlacher .40 1.00
❑ 26 Cedric Benson .30 .75
❑ 27 Muhsin Muhammad .30 .75
❑ 28 Rex Grossman .40 1.00
❑ 29 Thomas Jones .30 .75
❑ 30 Carson Palmer .40 1.00
❑ 31 Chad Johnson .30 .75
❑ 32 Rudi Johnson .30 .75
❑ 33 T.J. Houshmandzadeh .30 .75
❑ 34 Charlie Frye .30 .75
❑ 35 Dennis Northcutt .25 .60
❑ 36 Braylon Edwards .40 1.00
❑ 37 Reuben Droughns .30 .75
❑ 38 Drew Bledsoe .40 1.00
❑ 39 Julius Jones .30 .75
❑ 40 Terrell Owens .40 1.00
❑ 41 Jason Witten .40 1.00
❑ 42 Terry Glenn .30 .75
❑ 43 Roy Williams S .30 .75
❑ 44 Jake Plummer .30 .75
❑ 45 Rod Smith .30 .75
❑ 46 Tatum Bell .25 .60
❑ 47 Ashley Lelie .25 .60
❑ 48 Josh McCown .30 .75
❑ 49 Kevin Jones .30 .75
❑ 50 Mike Williams .30 .75
❑ 51 Roy Williams WR .40 1.00
❑ 52 Ahman Green .30 .75
❑ 53 Brett Favre .75 2.00
❑ 54 Aaron Rodgers .40 1.00
❑ 55 Samkon Gado .40 1.00
❑ 56 Donald Driver .40 1.00
❑ 57 Robert Ferguson .25 .60
❑ 58 Andre Johnson .30 .75
❑ 59 David Carr .25 .60
❑ 60 Domanick Davis .30 .75
❑ 61 Dallas Clark .30 .75
❑ 62 Marvin Harrison .40 1.00
❑ 63 Peyton Manning .60 1.50
❑ 64 Reggie Wayne .30 .75
❑ 65 Brandon Stokley .30 .75
❑ 66 Byron Leftwich .30 .75
❑ 67 Fred Taylor .30 .75
❑ 68 Jimmy Smith .30 .75
❑ 69 Matt Jones .30 .75
❑ 70 Larry Johnson .30 .75
❑ 71 Tony Gonzalez .30 .75
❑ 72 Trent Green .30 .75
❑ 73 Eddie Kennison .25 .60
❑ 74 Samie Parker .25 .60
❑ 75 Chris Chambers .30 .75
❑ 76 Daunte Culpepper .40 1.00
❑ 77 Randy McMichael .25 .60
❑ 78 Ronnie Brown .40 1.00
❑ 79 Marty Booker .25 .60
❑ 80 Zach Thomas .40 1.00
❑ 81 Brad Johnson .30 .75
❑ 82 Mewelde Moore .25 .60
❑ 83 Nate Burleson .30 .75
❑ 84 Troy Williamson .30 .75
❑ 85 Deion Branch .30 .75
❑ 86 Tom Brady .60 1.50
❑ 87 Corey Dillon .30 .75
❑ 88 Daniel Graham .25 .60
❑ 89 Troy Brown .25 .60
❑ 90 Deuce McAllister .30 .75
❑ 91 Donte Stallworth .30 .75
❑ 92 Drew Brees .40 1.00
❑ 93 Joe Horn .30 .75
❑ 94 Devery Henderson .25 .60
❑ 95 Eli Manning .50 1.25
❑ 96 Jeremy Shockey .40 1.00
❑ 97 Plaxico Burress .30 .75
❑ 98 Amani Toomer .30 .75
❑ 99 Tiki Barber .40 1.00
❑ 100 Chad Pennington .30 .75
❑ 101 Curtis Martin .40 1.00
❑ 102 Laveranues Coles .30 .75
❑ 103 Justin McCareins .25 .60
❑ 104 Jerry Porter .30 .75
❑ 105 LaMont Jordan .30 .75
❑ 106 Doug Gabriel .25 .60
❑ 107 Randy Moss .40 1.00
❑ 108 Brian Westbrook .30 .75
❑ 109 Donovan McNabb .40 1.00
❑ 110 Reggie Brown .25 .60
❑ 111 Chad Lewis .25 .60
❑ 112 Ryan Moats .30 .75
❑ 113 Jevon Kearse .30 .75
❑ 114 Ben Roethlisberger .60 1.50
❑ 115 Heath Miller .30 .75
❑ 116 Hines Ward .40 1.00
❑ 117 Willie Parker .50 1.25
❑ 118 Troy Polamalu .50 1.25
❑ 119 Antonio Gates .40 1.00
❑ 120 Eric Parker .25 .60
❑ 121 Keenan McCardell .30 .75
❑ 122 LaDainian Tomlinson .50 1.25
❑ 123 Philip Rivers .40 1.00
❑ 124 Alex Smith QB .30 .75
❑ 125 Antonio Bryant .30 .75
❑ 126 Frank Gore .40 1.00

Card	Low	High
❑ 127 Kevan Barlow	.30	.75
❑ 128 Darrell Jackson	.30	.75
❑ 129 Jerramy Stevens	.30	.75
❑ 130 Matt Hasselbeck	.30	.75
❑ 131 Shaun Alexander	.30	.75
❑ 132 Isaac Bruce	.30	.75
❑ 133 Marc Bulger	.30	.75
❑ 134 Marshall Faulk	.30	.75
❑ 135 Steven Jackson	.40	1.00
❑ 136 Torry Holt	.30	.75
❑ 137 Cadillac Williams	.40	1.00
❑ 138 Chris Simms	.30	.75
❑ 139 Joey Galloway	.30	.75
❑ 140 Michael Clayton	.30	.75
❑ 141 Brandon Jones	.25	.60
❑ 142 Chris Brown	.30	.75
❑ 143 Drew Bennett	.30	.75
❑ 144 Tyrone Calico	.25	.60
❑ 145 Steve McNair	.30	.75
❑ 146 Antwaan Randle El	.30	.75
❑ 147 Clinton Portis	.40	1.00
❑ 148 Mark Brunell	.30	.75
❑ 149 Santana Moss	.30	.75
❑ 150 Jason Campbell	.30	.75
❑ 151 Brodie Croyle/500 RC	3.00	8.00
❑ 152 Greg Jennings/500 RC	5.00	12.00
❑ 153 Joseph Addai/500 RC	4.00	10.00
❑ 154 Bennie Brazell/1000 RC	1.50	4.00
❑ 155 David Thomas/500 RC	3.00	8.00
❑ 156 Marques Colston/1000 RC	5.00	12.00
❑ 157 Reggie McNeal/500 RC	2.50	6.00
❑ 158 D.J. Shockley/1000 RC	1.50	4.00
❑ 159 Dominique Byrd/500 RC	2.50	6.00
❑ 160 Antonio Cromartie/1000 RC	2.00	5.00
❑ 161 Donte Whitner/1000 RC	2.00	5.00
❑ 162 Anwar Phillips/1000 RC	1.50	4.00
❑ 163 A.J. Nicholson/1000 RC	1.25	3.00
❑ 164 De'Arrius Howard/500 RC	3.00	8.00
❑ 165 Erik Meyer/500 RC	2.50	6.00
❑ 166 Darrell Hackney/1000 RC	1.50	4.00
❑ 167 Paul Pinegar/500 RC	2.00	5.00
❑ 168 Brandon Kirsch/500 RC	2.50	6.00
❑ 169 Quinton Ganther/1000 RC	1.25	3.00
❑ 170 Andre Hall/1000 RC	1.50	4.00
❑ 171 Derrick Ross/1000 RC	1.50	4.00
❑ 172 Mike Bell/1000 RC	2.00	5.00
❑ 173 Wendell Mathis/500 RC	2.50	6.00
❑ 174 Garrett Mills/500 RC	2.50	6.00
❑ 175 David Anderson/1000 RC	1.50	4.00
❑ 176 Kevin McMahan/1000 RC	1.50	4.00
❑ 177 Martin Nance/1000 RC	1.50	4.00
❑ 178 Greg Lee/500 RC	2.00	5.00
❑ 179 Anthony Mix/500 RC	2.50	6.00
❑ 180 D.Ferguson/500 RC	3.00	8.00
❑ 181 Tamba Hali/500 RC	3.00	8.00
❑ 182 Haloti Ngata/1000 RC	2.00	5.00
❑ 183 Claude Wroten/1000 RC	1.25	3.00
❑ 184 Gabe Watson/1000 RC	1.25	3.00
❑ 185 D'Qwell Jackson/1000 RC	1.50	4.00
❑ 186 Abdul Hodge/500 RC	2.50	6.00
❑ 187 Chad Greenway/500 RC	3.00	8.00
❑ 188 Bobby Carpenter/1000 RC	1.50	4.00
❑ 189 DeMeco Ryans/500 RC	4.00	10.00
❑ 190 Rocky McIntosh/500 RC	3.00	8.00
❑ 191 Thomas Howard/1000 RC	1.50	4.00
❑ 192 Jon Alston/500 RC	2.00	5.00
❑ 193 Jimmy Williams/1000 RC	2.00	5.00
❑ 194 Ashton Youboty/500 RC	2.50	6.00
❑ 195 Alan Zemaitis/1000 RC	2.00	5.00
❑ 196 Cedric Griffin/500 RC	2.50	6.00
❑ 197 Ko Simpson/1000 RC	1.50	4.00
❑ 198 Pat Watkins/500 RC	3.00	8.00
❑ 199 Bernard Pollard/1000 RC	1.50	4.00
❑ 200 Jay Cutler/500 RC	5.00	12.00
❑ 201 Chad Jackson JSY/1400 RC	3.00	8.00
❑ 202 L.Maroney JSY/550 RC	4.00	10.00
❑ 203 Tar.Jackson JSY/1400 RC	2.50	6.00
❑ 204 Michael Huff JSY/1400 RC	2.50	6.00
❑ 205 Mario Williams JSY/1400 RC	3.00	8.00
❑ 206 Mar.Lewis JSY/1400 RC	2.50	6.00
❑ 207 Maurice Drew JSY/1400 RC	5.00	12.00
❑ 208 Vince Young JSY/550 RC	8.00	20.00
❑ 209 LenDale White JSY/550 RC	5.00	12.00
❑ 210 Reggie Bush JSY/550 RC	8.00	20.00
❑ 211 Matt Leinart JSY/550 RC	5.00	12.00
❑ 212 M.Robinson JSY/1400 RC	3.00	8.00
❑ 213 Vernon Davis JSY/550 RC	5.00	12.00
❑ 214 Br.Williams JSY/1400 RC	2.00	5.00
❑ 215 Derek Hagan JSY/1400 RC	3.00	8.00
❑ 216 Jason Avant JSY/1400 RC	2.50	6.00
❑ 217 B.Marshall JSY/1400 RC	3.00	8.00
❑ 218 Omar Jacobs JSY/1400 RC	3.00	8.00
❑ 219 Santonio Holmes JSY/550 RC	6.00	15.00
❑ 220 J.Norwood JSY/1400 RC	2.50	6.00
❑ 221 Dem.Williams JSY/1400 RC	3.00	8.00
❑ 222 Sinorice Moss JSY/1400 RC	3.00	8.00
❑ 223 L.Washington JSY/1400 RC	3.00	8.00
❑ 224 Kellen Clemens JSY/900 RC	2.50	6.00
❑ 225 A.J. Hawk JSY/550 RC	8.00	20.00
❑ 226 Maurice Stovall JSY/1400 RC	3.00	8.00
❑ 227 DeA.Williams JSY/550 RC	6.00	15.00
❑ 228 C.Whitehurst JSY/1400 RC	2.50	6.00
❑ 229 Travis Wilson JSY/1400 RC	3.00	8.00
❑ 230 J.Klopfenstein JSY/1400 RC	3.00	8.00
❑ 231 Brian Calhoun JSY/1400 RC	3.00	8.00
❑ 232 Barry Sanders JSY/150	10.00	25.00
❑ 233 Jerry Rice JSY/150	8.00	20.00
❑ 234 Dan Marino JSY/150	12.00	30.00
❑ 235 Earl Campbell JSY/150	6.00	15.00
❑ 236 Jim Brown JSY/100	10.00	25.00
❑ 237 Joe Montana JSY/125	10.00	25.00
❑ 238 Troy Aikman JSY/150	8.00	20.00
❑ 239 Walter Payton JSY/100	15.00	40.00
❑ 240 Terry Bradshaw JSY/150	10.00	25.00
❑ 241 John Elway JSY/150	10.00	25.00
❑ 242 Fred Biletnikoff JSY/100	6.00	15.00
❑ 243 Lance Alworth JSY/125	6.00	15.00
❑ 244 Ronnie Lott JSY/150	6.00	15.00
❑ 245 Yale Lary JSY/125	6.00	15.00
❑ 246 Bart Starr JSY/80	12.00	30.00
❑ 247 Doak Walker JSY/75	10.00	25.00
❑ 248 Gale Sayers JSY/100	8.00	20.00
❑ 249 Bo Jackson JSY/150	6.00	15.00
❑ 250 Roger Staubach JSY/125	10.00	25.00
❑ 251 Dick Butkus JSY/150	8.00	20.00

2007 Leaf Certified Materials

Card	Low	High
❑ COMP.SET w/o SP's (150)	15.00	40.00
❑ 1 Tony Romo	.60	1.50
❑ 2 Julius Jones	.30	.75
❑ 3 Terry Glenn	.30	.75
❑ 4 Terrell Owens	.40	1.00
❑ 5 Jason Witten	.40	1.00
❑ 6 Patrick Crayton	.25	.60
❑ 7 Eli Manning	.40	1.00
❑ 8 Plaxico Burress	.30	.75
❑ 9 Jeremy Shockey	.30	.75
❑ 10 Brandon Jacobs	.30	.75
❑ 11 Sinorice Moss	.30	.75
❑ 12 Donovan McNabb	.40	1.00
❑ 13 Brian Westbrook	.30	.75
❑ 14 Reggie Brown	.25	.60
❑ 15 Hank Baskett	.30	.75
❑ 16 Jason Campbell	.30	.75
❑ 17 Clinton Portis	.30	.75
❑ 18 Santana Moss	.30	.75
❑ 19 Chris Cooley	.25	.60
❑ 20 Ladell Betts	.25	.60
❑ 21 Rex Grossman	.30	.75
❑ 22 Cedric Benson	.30	.75
❑ 23 Bernard Berrian	.25	.60
❑ 24 Devin Hester	.40	1.00
❑ 25 Brian Urlacher	.40	1.00
❑ 26 Jon Kitna	.25	.60
❑ 27 Roy Williams WR	.30	.75
❑ 28 Mike Furrey	.30	.75
❑ 29 Tatum Bell	.25	.60
❑ 30 Brett Favre	.75	2.00
❑ 31 Donald Driver	.40	1.00
❑ 32 Greg Jennings	.30	.75
❑ 33 Nick Barnett	.25	.60
❑ 34 Tarvaris Jackson	.30	.75
❑ 35 Chester Taylor	.25	.60
❑ 36 Troy Williamson	.25	.60
❑ 37 Michael Vick	.40	1.00
❑ 38 Warrick Dunn	.30	.75
❑ 39 Joe Horn	.30	.75
❑ 40 Michael Jenkins	.30	.75
❑ 41 Alge Crumpler	.30	.75
❑ 42 Jerious Norwood	.30	.75
❑ 43 Jake Delhomme	.30	.75
❑ 44 DeShaun Foster	.30	.75
❑ 45 Steve Smith	.30	.75
❑ 46 DeAngelo Williams	.40	1.00
❑ 47 Drew Brees	.40	1.00
❑ 48 Deuce McAllister	.30	.75
❑ 49 Marques Colston	.40	1.00
❑ 50 Devery Henderson	.25	.60
❑ 51 Reggie Bush	.50	1.25
❑ 52 Cadillac Williams	.30	.75
❑ 53 Joey Galloway	.30	.75
❑ 54 Michael Clayton	.30	.75
❑ 55 Derrick Brooks	.30	.75
❑ 56 Matt Leinart	.40	1.00
❑ 57 Edgerrin James	.30	.75
❑ 58 Anquan Boldin	.30	.75
❑ 59 Larry Fitzgerald	.40	1.00
❑ 60 Marc Bulger	.30	.75
❑ 61 Steven Jackson	.40	1.00
❑ 62 Torry Holt	.30	.75
❑ 63 Isaac Bruce	.30	.75
❑ 64 Randy McMichael	.25	.60
❑ 65 Drew Bennett	.25	.60
❑ 66 Alex Smith QB	.40	1.00
❑ 67 Frank Gore	.40	1.00
❑ 68 Vernon Davis	.30	.75
❑ 69 Darrell Jackson	.30	.75
❑ 70 Matt Hasselbeck	.30	.75
❑ 71 Shaun Alexander	.30	.75
❑ 72 Deion Branch	.30	.75
❑ 73 Nate Burleson	.25	.60
❑ 74 J.P. Losman	.25	.60
❑ 75 Anthony Thomas	.25	.60
❑ 76 Lee Evans	.30	.75
❑ 77 Josh Reed	.25	.60
❑ 78 Daunte Culpepper	.30	.75
❑ 79 Ronnie Brown	.30	.75
❑ 80 Chris Chambers	.30	.75
❑ 81 Marty Booker	.25	.60
❑ 82 Jason Taylor	.25	.60
❑ 83 Zach Thomas	.30	.75
❑ 84 Tom Brady	.75	2.00
❑ 85 Laurence Maroney	.40	1.00
❑ 86 Randy Moss	.40	1.00
❑ 87 Ben Watson	.25	.60
❑ 88 Donte Stallworth	.30	.75
❑ 89 Tedy Bruschi	.40	1.00
❑ 90 Chad Pennington	.30	.75
❑ 91 Thomas Jones	.30	.75
❑ 92 Laveranues Coles	.30	.75
❑ 93 Jerricho Cotchery	.25	.60
❑ 94 Leon Washington	.30	.75
❑ 95 Steve McNair	.30	.75
❑ 96 Willis McGahee	.30	.75
❑ 97 Demetrius Williams	.25	.60
❑ 98 Todd Heap	.25	.60
❑ 99 Ray Lewis	.40	1.00
❑ 100 Mark Clayton	.30	.75
❑ 101 Carson Palmer	.40	1.00
❑ 102 Rudi Johnson	.30	.75
❑ 103 Chad Johnson	.30	.75
❑ 104 T.J. Houshmandzadeh	.30	.75
❑ 105 Charlie Frye	.30	.75
❑ 106 Braylon Edwards	.30	.75
❑ 107 Kellen Winslow	.30	.75
❑ 108 Jamal Lewis	.30	.75
❑ 109 Ben Roethlisberger	.50	1.25
❑ 110 Willie Parker	.30	.75
❑ 111 Hines Ward	.40	1.00
❑ 112 Heath Miller	.25	.60
❑ 113 Troy Polamalu	.40	1.00
❑ 114 Ahman Green	.30	.75
❑ 115 Andre Johnson	.30	.75
❑ 116 Matt Schaub	.30	.75
❑ 117 DeMeco Ryans	.30	.75
❑ 118 Peyton Manning	.60	1.50
❑ 119 Joseph Addai	.40	1.00
❑ 120 Marvin Harrison	.40	1.00
❑ 121 Reggie Wayne	.30	.75
❑ 122 Dallas Clark	.25	.60
❑ 123 Byron Leftwich	.30	.75
❑ 124 Fred Taylor	.30	.75

- ❑ 125 Matt Jones .30 .75
- ❑ 126 Reggie Williams .30 .75
- ❑ 127 Marcedes Lewis .25 .60
- ❑ 128 Maurice Jones-Drew .40 1.00
- ❑ 129 Ernest Wilford .25 .60
- ❑ 130 Vince Young .40 1.00
- ❑ 131 LenDale White .30 .75
- ❑ 132 Brandon Jones .25 .60
- ❑ 133 Jay Cutler .40 1.00
- ❑ 134 Travis Henry .30 .75
- ❑ 135 Javon Walker .30 .75
- ❑ 136 Rod Smith .30 .75
- ❑ 137 Champ Bailey .30 .75
- ❑ 138 Mike Bell .30 .75
- ❑ 139 Brandon Marshall .30 .75
- ❑ 140 Larry Johnson .30 .75
- ❑ 141 Eddie Kennison .25 .60
- ❑ 142 Tony Gonzalez .30 .75
- ❑ 143 Brodie Croyle .30 .75
- ❑ 144 LaMont Jordan .30 .75
- ❑ 145 Ronald Curry .30 .75
- ❑ 146 Philip Rivers .40 1.00
- ❑ 147 LaDainian Tomlinson .50 1.25
- ❑ 148 Michael Turner .40 1.00
- ❑ 149 Antonio Gates .30 .75
- ❑ 150 Shawne Merriman .30 .75
- ❑ 151 Aaron Ross RC 2.00 5.00
- ❑ 152 Adam Carriker RC 1.50 4.00
- ❑ 153 Ahmad Bradshaw RC 2.50 6.00
- ❑ 154 Alan Branch RC 1.50 4.00
- ❑ 155 Chansi Stuckey RC 2.00 5.00
- ❑ 156 Charles Johnson RC 1.25 3.00
- ❑ 157 Chris Leak RC 1.50 4.00
- ❑ 158 Jarvis Moss RC 2.00 5.00
- ❑ 159 Dan Bazuin RC 1.50 4.00
- ❑ 160 David Harris RC 1.50 4.00
- ❑ 161 Dwayne Wright RC 1.50 4.00
- ❑ 162 Eric Frampton RC 1.50 4.00
- ❑ 163 Eric Wright RC 2.00 5.00
- ❑ 164 Jared Zabransky RC 2.00 5.00
- ❑ 165 Jason Snelling RC 1.50 4.00
- ❑ 166 Jordan Palmer RC 2.00 5.00
- ❑ 167 Kenneth Darby RC 2.00 5.00
- ❑ 168 LaMarr Woodley RC 2.00 5.00
- ❑ 169 LaRon Landry RC 2.50 6.00
- ❑ 170 Lawrence Timmons RC 2.00 5.00
- ❑ 171 Leon Hall RC 2.00 5.00
- ❑ 172 Michael Griffin RC 2.00 5.00
- ❑ 173 Mike Walker RC 2.00 5.00
- ❑ 174 Paul Posluszny RC 2.50 6.00
- ❑ 175 Thomas Clayton RC 1.50 4.00
- ❑ 176 Amobi Okoye AU RC 5.00 12.00
- ❑ 177 Anthony Spencer AU RC 5.00 12.00
- ❑ 178 Aundrae Allison AU RC 4.00 10.00
- ❑ 179 Ben Patrick AU RC 4.00 10.00
- ❑ 180 Brandon Meriweather AU RC 5.00 12.00
- ❑ 181 Chris Davis AU RC 4.00 10.00
- ❑ 182 Chris Houston AU RC 4.00 10.00
- ❑ 183 Craig Buster Davis AU RC EXCH
- ❑ 184 Dallas Baker AU RC 4.00 10.00
- ❑ 185 Darius Walker AU RC 4.00 10.00
- ❑ 186 Darrelle Revis AU RC 6.00 15.00
- ❑ 187 David Clowney AU RC 5.00 12.00
- ❑ 188 DeShawn Wynn AU RC 5.00 12.00
- ❑ 189 Ikaika Alama-Francis AU RC 5.00 12.00
- ❑ 190 Isaiah Stanback AU RC 5.00 12.00
- ❑ 191 Jacoby Jones AU RC 5.00 12.00
- ❑ 192 Jamaal Anderson AU RC 4.00 10.00
- ❑ 193 James Jones AU RC 5.00 12.00
- ❑ 194 Courtney Taylor AU RC 4.00 10.00
- ❑ 195 Jon Beason AU RC 5.00 12.00
- ❑ 196 Jonathan Wade AU RC 4.00 10.00
- ❑ 197 Josh Wilson AU RC 4.00 10.00
- ❑ 198 Kolby Smith AU RC 5.00 12.00
- ❑ 199 Laurent Robinson AU RC 5.00 12.00
- ❑ 200 Reggie Nelson AU RC 4.00 10.00
- ❑ 201 Dwayne Jarrett JSY RC 3.00 8.00
- ❑ 202 Johnnie Lee Higgins JSY RC 3.00 8.00
- ❑ 203 Michael Bush JSY RC 3.00 8.00
- ❑ 204 Antonio Pittman JSY RC 3.00 8.00
- ❑ 205 Patrick Willis JSY RC 5.00 12.00
- ❑ 206 Gaines Adams JSY RC 3.00 8.00
- ❑ 207 Tony Hunt JSY RC 3.00 8.00
- ❑ 208 Chris Henry RB JSY RC 2.50 6.00
- ❑ 209 John Beck JSY RC 3.00 8.00
- ❑ 210 Dwayne Bowe JSY RC 5.00 12.00
- ❑ 211 Brian Leonard JSY RC 2.50 6.00
- ❑ 212 Anthony Gonzalez JSY RC 4.00 10.00
- ❑ 213 Trent Edwards JSY RC 5.00 12.00
- ❑ 214 Jason Hill JSY RC 3.00 8.00
- ❑ 215 JaMarcus Russell JSY/849 RC 8.00 20.00
- ❑ 216 Ted Ginn Jr. JSY RC 5.00 12.00
- ❑ 217 Paul Williams JSY RC 2.50 6.00
- ❑ 218 Garrett Wolfe JSY RC 3.00 8.00
- ❑ 219 Adrian Peterson JSY/849 RC 12.00 30.00
- ❑ 220 Kevin Kolb JSY RC 5.00 12.00
- ❑ 221 Marshawn Lynch JSY/849 RC 5.00 12.00
- ❑ 222 Steve Smith USC JSY RC 5.00 12.00
- ❑ 223 Greg Olsen JSY RC 4.00 10.00
- ❑ 224 Kenny Irons JSY RC 3.00 8.00
- ❑ 225 Brandon Jackson JSY RC 3.00 8.00
- ❑ 226 Yamon Figurs JSY RC 2.00 5.00
- ❑ 227 Lorenzo Booker JSY RC 3.00 8.00
- ❑ 228 Drew Stanton JSY RC 2.50 6.00
- ❑ 229 Brady Quinn JSY/849 RC 6.00 15.00
- ❑ 230 Joe Thomas JSY RC 3.00 8.00
- ❑ 231 Robert Meachem JSY RC 3.00 8.00
- ❑ 232 Troy Smith JSY RC 4.00 10.00
- ❑ 233 Sidney Rice JSY RC 6.00 15.00
- ❑ 234 Calvin Johnson JSY/849 RC 10.00 25.00
- ❑ 235 Bart Starr JSY 12.00 30.00
- ❑ 236 Bob Griese JSY 8.00 20.00
- ❑ 237 Bobby Layne/50 JSY 10.00 25.00
- ❑ 238 Bulldog Turner JSY 8.00 20.00
- ❑ 239 Earl Campbell JKT 8.00 20.00
- ❑ 240 Franco Harris JSY 8.00 20.00
- ❑ 241 James Lofton JSY 5.00 12.00
- ❑ 242 Jim McMahon JSY 10.00 25.00
- ❑ 243 Jim Thorpe JSY 60.00 100.00
- ❑ 244 Joe Namath JSY 10.00 25.00
- ❑ 246 Lou Groza JSY 6.00 15.00
- ❑ 247 Ray Nitschke JSY 10.00 25.00
- ❑ 248 Ron Mix JSY 5.00 12.00
- ❑ 249 Roosevelt Brown JSY 5.00 12.00
- ❑ 250 Sam Huff JSY 6.00 15.00
- ❑ 251 Sammy Baugh JSY 20.00 40.00
- ❑ 252 Sid Luckman JSY 15.00 30.00
- ❑ 253 Otto Graham JSY 15.00 30.00
- ❑ 254 Y.A. Tittle JSY 8.00 20.00

2008 Leaf Certified Materials

- ❑ COMP.SET w/o SP's (150) 15.00 40.00
- ❑ 1 Matt Leinart .40 1.00
- ❑ 2 Larry Fitzgerald .40 1.00
- ❑ 3 Anquan Boldin .30 .75
- ❑ 4 Edgerrin James .30 .75
- ❑ 5 Jerious Norwood .30 .75
- ❑ 6 Roddy White .30 .75
- ❑ 7 Joe Horn .30 .75
- ❑ 8 Michael Turner .40 1.00
- ❑ 9 Willis McGahee .30 .75
- ❑ 10 Derrick Mason .25 .60
- ❑ 11 Mark Clayton .30 .75
- ❑ 12 Demetrius Williams .25 .60
- ❑ 13 Trent Edwards .40 1.00
- ❑ 14 Marshawn Lynch .40 1.00
- ❑ 15 Lee Evans .30 .75
- ❑ 16 Steve Smith .30 .75
- ❑ 17 DeAngelo Williams .30 .75
- ❑ 18 Julius Peppers .30 .75
- ❑ 19 Jake Delhomme .30 .75
- ❑ 20 Adrian Peterson .25 .60
- ❑ 21 Greg Olsen .30 .75
- ❑ 22 Devin Hester .40 1.00
- ❑ 23 Brian Urlacher .40 1.00
- ❑ 24 Rex Grossman .30 .75
- ❑ 25 Carson Palmer .40 1.00
- ❑ 26 Chad Johnson .30 .75
- ❑ 27 T.J. Houshmandzadeh .30 .75
- ❑ 28 Rudi Johnson .30 .75
- ❑ 29 Derek Anderson .30 .75
- ❑ 30 Jamal Lewis .30 .75
- ❑ 31 Kellen Winslow .30 .75
- ❑ 32 Braylon Edwards .30 .75
- ❑ 33 Tony Romo .60 1.50
- ❑ 34 Terrell Owens .40 1.00
- ❑ 35 Marion Barber .40 1.00
- ❑ 36 Jason Witten .40 1.00
- ❑ 37 Jay Cutler .40 1.00
- ❑ 38 Selvin Young .25 .60
- ❑ 39 Brandon Marshall .30 .75
- ❑ 40 Brandon Stokley .30 .75
- ❑ 41 Jon Kitna .30 .75
- ❑ 42 Roy Williams WR .30 .75
- ❑ 43 Calvin Johnson .40 1.00
- ❑ 44 Mike Furrey .30 .75
- ❑ 45 Aaron Rodgers .40 1.00
- ❑ 46 Ryan Grant .40 1.00
- ❑ 47 Greg Jennings .30 .75
- ❑ 48 Donald Driver .30 .75
- ❑ 49 Matt Schaub .30 .75
- ❑ 50 Ahman Green .30 .75
- ❑ 51 Andre Johnson .30 .75
- ❑ 52 Kevin Walter .30 .75
- ❑ 53 DeMeco Ryans .30 .75
- ❑ 54 Peyton Manning .60 1.50
- ❑ 55 Joseph Addai .40 1.00
- ❑ 56 Marvin Harrison .40 1.00
- ❑ 57 Reggie Wayne .30 .75
- ❑ 58 Dallas Clark .30 .75
- ❑ 59 Anthony Gonzalez .30 .75
- ❑ 60 David Garrard .30 .75
- ❑ 61 Fred Taylor .30 .75
- ❑ 62 Maurice Jones-Drew .30 .75
- ❑ 63 Reggie Williams .30 .75
- ❑ 64 Marcedes Lewis .25 .60
- ❑ 65 Matt Jones .30 .75
- ❑ 66 Jerry Porter .30 .75
- ❑ 67 Brodie Croyle .30 .75
- ❑ 68 Larry Johnson .30 .75
- ❑ 69 Kolby Smith .25 .60
- ❑ 70 Tony Gonzalez .30 .75
- ❑ 71 Dwayne Bowe .30 .75
- ❑ 72 John Beck .25 .60
- ❑ 73 Ronnie Brown .30 .75
- ❑ 74 Ted Ginn Jr. .30 .75
- ❑ 75 Derek Hagan .25 .60
- ❑ 76 Jason Taylor .30 .75
- ❑ 77 Bernard Berrian .30 .75
- ❑ 78 Tarvaris Jackson .30 .75
- ❑ 79 Adrian Peterson .75 2.00
- ❑ 80 Chester Taylor .25 .60
- ❑ 81 Sidney Rice .40 1.00
- ❑ 82 Tom Brady .60 1.50
- ❑ 83 Randy Moss .40 1.00
- ❑ 84 Laurence Maroney .30 .75
- ❑ 85 Wes Welker .40 1.00
- ❑ 86 Drew Brees .40 1.00
- ❑ 87 Reggie Bush .40 1.00
- ❑ 88 Deuce McAllister .30 .75
- ❑ 89 Marques Colston .30 .75
- ❑ 90 Eli Manning .40 1.00
- ❑ 91 Plaxico Burress .30 .75
- ❑ 92 Brandon Jacobs .30 .75
- ❑ 93 Amani Toomer .30 .75
- ❑ 94 Jeremy Shockey .30 .75
- ❑ 95 Steve Smith USC .30 .75
- ❑ 96 Michael Strahan .30 .75
- ❑ 97 Kellen Clemens .30 .75
- ❑ 98 Leon Washington .30 .75
- ❑ 99 Jerricho Cotchery .25 .60
- ❑ 100 Laveranues Coles .30 .75
- ❑ 101 Thomas Jones .30 .75
- ❑ 102 Javon Walker .30 .75
- ❑ 103 JaMarcus Russell .40 1.00
- ❑ 104 Justin Fargas .25 .60
- ❑ 105 Michael Bush .30 .75
- ❑ 106 Zach Miller .30 .75
- ❑ 107 Donovan McNabb .40 1.00
- ❑ 108 Brian Westbrook .30 .75
- ❑ 109 Kevin Curtis .25 .60
- ❑ 110 Reggie Brown .25 .60
- ❑ 111 Greg Lewis .25 .60
- ❑ 112 Ben Roethlisberger .60 1.50
- ❑ 113 Willie Parker .30 .75
- ❑ 114 Hines Ward .30 .75
- ❑ 115 Santonio Holmes .30 .75
- ❑ 116 Philip Rivers .40 1.00
- ❑ 117 LaDainian Tomlinson .50 1.25
- ❑ 118 Vincent Jackson .25 .60
- ❑ 119 Antonio Gates .30 .75
- ❑ 120 Brett Favre 2.50 6.00

Card		
❑ 121 Alex Smith QB	.30	.75
❑ 122 Frank Gore	.30	.75
❑ 123 Michael Robinson	.25	.60
❑ 124 Vernon Davis	.25	.60
❑ 125 Isaac Bruce	.30	.75
❑ 126 Patrick Willis	.30	.75
❑ 127 Matt Hasselbeck	.30	.75
❑ 128 Nate Burleson	.25	.60
❑ 129 Deion Branch	.30	.75
❑ 130 Julius Jones	.30	.75
❑ 131 Marc Bulger	.30	.75
❑ 132 Steven Jackson	.40	1.00
❑ 133 Torry Holt	.30	.75
❑ 134 Warrick Dunn	.30	.75
❑ 135 Jeff Garcia	.30	.75
❑ 136 Cadillac Williams	.30	.75
❑ 137 Earnest Graham	.25	.60
❑ 138 Joey Galloway	.30	.75
❑ 139 Michael Clayton	.30	.75
❑ 140 Vince Young	.30	.75
❑ 141 LenDale White	.30	.75
❑ 142 Justin Gage	.25	.60
❑ 143 Roydell Williams	.25	.60
❑ 144 Alge Crumpler	.30	.75
❑ 145 Brandon Jones	.25	.60
❑ 146 Jason Campbell	.30	.75
❑ 147 Clinton Portis	.30	.75
❑ 148 Ladell Betts	.25	.60
❑ 149 Santana Moss	.25	.60
❑ 150 Chris Cooley	.30	.75
❑ 151 Adrian Arrington AU/999 RC	3.00	8.00
❑ 152 Andre Woodson RC	1.50	4.00
❑ 153 Antoine Cason AU/749 RC	4.00	10.00
❑ 154 Aqib Talib AU/999 RC	4.00	10.00
❑ 155 Brad Cottam AU/999 RC	4.00	10.00
❑ 156 Brandon Flowers AU/899 RC	4.00	10.00
❑ 157 Chauncey Washington AU /799 RC	3.00	8.00
❑ 158 Chevis Jackson RC	1.25	3.00
❑ 159 Colt Brennan RC	2.50	6.00
❑ 160 Curtis Lofton AU/999 RC	4.00	10.00
❑ 161 Dan Connor RC	1.50	4.00
❑ 162 Dennis Dixon RC	1.50	4.00
❑ 163 Derrick Harvey RC	1.25	3.00
❑ 164 D.Rodgers-Cromartie RC	1.50	4.00
❑ 165 Erik Ainge AU/699 RC	4.00	10.00
❑ 166 Fred Davis AU/999 RC	4.00	10.00
❑ 167 Jacob Hester AU/399 RC	5.00	12.00
❑ 168 Jermichael Finley RC	1.50	4.00
❑ 169 Jerod Mayo RC	2.00	5.00
❑ 170 John Carlson RC	1.50	4.00
❑ 171 Josh Johnson RC	1.50	4.00
❑ 172 Jordon Dizon AU/299 RC	5.00	12.00
❑ 173 Josh Morgan RC	1.50	4.00
❑ 174 Justin Forsett AU/649 RC	4.00	10.00
❑ 175 Keenan Burton RC	1.25	3.00
❑ 176 Keith Rivers RC	1.50	4.00
❑ 177 Kenny Phillips RC	1.50	4.00
❑ 178 Kevin Robinson AU/999 RC	3.00	8.00
❑ 179 Lavelle Hawkins RC	1.25	3.00
❑ 180 Leodis McKelvin AU/999 RC	4.00	10.00
❑ 181 Marcus Smith RC	1.25	3.00
❑ 182 Marcus Thomas AU/499 RC	4.00	10.00
❑ 183 Martellus Bennett RC	1.50	4.00
❑ 184 Matt Flynn RC	1.50	4.00
❑ 185 Mike Jenkins RC	1.50	4.00
❑ 186 Mike Hart RC	1.50	4.00
❑ 187 Paul Hubbard RC	1.25	3.00
❑ 188 Peyton Hillis AU/499 RC	5.00	12.00
❑ 189 Quentin Groves AU/275 RC	4.00	10.00
❑ 190 Reggie Smith RC	1.25	3.00
❑ 191 Ryan Torain AU/299 RC	5.00	12.00
❑ 192 Sedrick Ellis RC	1.50	4.00
❑ 193 Shawn Crable RC	1.50	4.00
❑ 194 Tashard Choice AU/999 RC	7.50	15.00
❑ 195 Terrell Thomas AU/999 RC	3.00	8.00
❑ 196 Thomas Brown AU/999 RC	4.00	10.00
❑ 197 Tim Hightower AU/499 RC	8.00	20.00
❑ 198 Tracy Porter AU/999 RC	8.00	20.00
❑ 199 Vernon Gholston AU/999 RC	4.00	10.00
❑ 200 Will Franklin AU/249 RC	4.00	10.00
❑ 201 Andre Caldwell JSY RC	2.50	6.00
❑ 202 Dustin Keller JSY RC	2.50	6.00
❑ 203 Earl Bennett JSY RC	2.50	6.00
❑ 204 Early Doucet JSY RC	2.50	6.00
❑ 205 Glenn Dorsey JSY RC	2.50	6.00
❑ 206 Harry Douglas JSY RC	2.00	5.00
❑ 207 John David Booty JSY RC	2.50	6.00
❑ 208 Kevin O'Connell JSY RC	2.50	6.00
❑ 209 Darren McFadden JSY RC	8.00	20.00
❑ 210 Jonathan Stewart JSY RC	5.00	12.00
❑ 211 Felix Jones JSY RC	8.00	20.00
❑ 212 R.Mendenhall JSY RC	5.00	12.00
❑ 213 Chris Johnson JSY RC	8.00	20.00
❑ 214 Matt Forte JSY RC	5.00	12.00
❑ 215 Ray Rice JSY RC	5.00	12.00
❑ 216 Kevin Smith JSY RC	4.00	10.00
❑ 217 Jamaal Charles JSY RC	4.00	10.00
❑ 218 Steve Slaton JSY RC	3.00	8.00
❑ 219 Matt Ryan JSY RC	8.00	20.00
❑ 220 Joe Flacco JSY RC	8.00	20.00
❑ 221 Brian Brohm JSY RC	2.50	6.00
❑ 222 Chad Henne JSY RC	4.00	10.00
❑ 223 Donnie Avery JSY RC	3.00	8.00
❑ 224 Devin Thomas JSY RC	2.50	6.00
❑ 225 Jordy Nelson JSY RC	3.00	8.00
❑ 226 James Hardy JSY RC	2.00	5.00
❑ 227 Eddie Royal JSY RC	4.00	10.00
❑ 228 DeSean Jackson JSY RC	5.00	12.00
❑ 229 Malcolm Kelly JSY RC	2.50	6.00
❑ 230 Limas Sweed JSY RC	2.50	6.00
❑ 231 Mario Manningham JSY RC	2.50	6.00
❑ 232 Jerome Simpson JSY RC	2.00	5.00
❑ 233 Dexter Jackson JSY RC	2.50	6.00
❑ 234 Jake Long JSY RC	2.50	6.00
❑ 235 Bart Starr JSY	10.00	25.00
❑ 236 Johnny Unitas JSY/75	12.00	30.00
❑ 237 Brett Favre JSY	12.00	30.00
❑ 238 Tom Landry JSY	12.00	30.00
❑ 239 Hank Stram JSY	6.00	15.00
❑ 240 Chuck Foreman JSY	4.00	10.00
❑ 241 Dan Marino JSY	12.00	30.00
❑ 242 Andre Reed JSY	5.00	12.00
❑ 243 Frank Gifford JSY/50	6.00	15.00
❑ 244 John Riggins JSY	5.00	12.00
❑ 245 John Stallworth JSY	5.00	12.00
❑ 246 John Elway JSY	10.00	25.00
❑ 247 Emmitt Smith JSY	12.00	30.00
❑ 248 Randall Cunningham JSY	6.00	15.00
❑ 249 Reggie White JSY	6.00	15.00
❑ 250 John Matuszak JSY	6.00	15.00
❑ 251 Troy Aikman JSY	8.00	20.00
❑ 252 Billy Sims JSY	5.00	12.00
❑ 253 Willie Brown JSY	4.00	10.00
❑ 254 Barry Sanders JSY	10.00	25.00
❑ 255 Walter Payton JSY	12.00	30.00

2000 Leaf Limited

Card		
❑ COMP.SET w/o SPs (200)	60.00	120.00
❑ 1 Ben Coates	.20	.50
❑ 2 Joe Horn	.30	.75
❑ 3 Jonathan Linton	.20	.50
❑ 4 Derrick Mason	.30	.75
❑ 5 Ray Lucas	.30	.75
❑ 6 Brock Huard	.30	.75
❑ 7 Frank Wycheck	.20	.50
❑ 8 Michael Strahan	.30	.75
❑ 9 Jessie Armstead	.20	.50
❑ 10 Stephen Alexander	.20	.50
❑ 11 Larry Centers	.20	.50
❑ 12 Michael Pittman	.20	.50
❑ 13 Priest Holmes	.60	1.50
❑ 14 Jermaine Lewis	.30	.75
❑ 15 Jay Riemersma	.20	.50
❑ 16 Wesley Walls	.20	.50
❑ 17 Curtis Enis	.20	.50
❑ 18 Bobby Engram	.30	.75
❑ 19 Jim Miller	.20	.50
❑ 20 Eddie Kennison	.30	.75
❑ 21 Errict Rhett	.20	.50
❑ 22 Chris Warren	.20	.50
❑ 23 Byron Chamberlain	.20	.50
❑ 24 Desmond Howard	.20	.50
❑ 25 Lamar Smith	.30	.75
❑ 26 Robert Porcher	.20	.50
❑ 27 Corey Bradford	.30	.75
❑ 28 Donald Driver	.50	1.25
❑ 29 Ahman Green	.50	1.25
❑ 30 Ken Dilger	.20	.50
❑ 31 James McKnight	.30	.75
❑ 32 Kimble Anders	.20	.50
❑ 33 Zach Thomas	.50	1.25
❑ 34 James Johnson	.20	.50
❑ 35 Lawyer Milloy	.30	.75
❑ 36 Ty Law	.30	.75
❑ 37 Willie McGinest	.20	.50
❑ 38 Jason Sehorn	.30	.75
❑ 39 Andre Rison	.30	.75
❑ 40 Rickey Dudley	.20	.50
❑ 41 Patrick Jeffers	.50	1.25
❑ 42 Darrell Russell	.20	.50
❑ 43 Charles Johnson	.30	.75
❑ 44 Michael Westbrook	.30	.75
❑ 45 Levon Kirkland	.20	.50
❑ 46 Ryan Leaf	.30	.75
❑ 47 Sean Dawkins	.20	.50
❑ 48 Todd Lyght	.20	.50
❑ 49 Kevin Carter	.20	.50
❑ 50 Neil O'Donnell	.20	.50
❑ 51 Randall Cunningham	.60	1.50
❑ 52 Oronde Gadsden	.40	1.00
❑ 53 O.J. McDuffie	.40	1.00
❑ 54 Jake Reed	.40	1.00
❑ 55 Brian Mitchell	.25	.60
❑ 56 Kordell Stewart	.40	1.00
❑ 57 Derrick Mayes	.40	1.00
❑ 58 Az-Zahir Hakim	.25	.60
❑ 59 Jacquez Green	.25	.60
❑ 60 Andre Reed	.40	1.00
❑ 61 Deion Sanders	.60	1.50
❑ 62 Frank Sanders	.40	1.00
❑ 63 Rob Moore	.40	1.00
❑ 64 Shawn Jefferson	.25	.60
❑ 65 Pat Johnson	.25	.60
❑ 66 Peter Boulware	.25	.60
❑ 67 Donald Hayes	.25	.60
❑ 68 Marty Booker	.40	1.00
❑ 69 Leslie Shepherd	.25	.60
❑ 70 Jason Tucker	.25	.60
❑ 71 Johnnie Morton	.40	1.00
❑ 72 Germane Crowell	.25	.60
❑ 73 Herman Moore	.40	1.00
❑ 74 Bill Schroeder	.40	1.00
❑ 75 E.G. Green	.25	.60
❑ 76 Jerome Pathon	.40	1.00
❑ 77 Tony Brackens	.25	.60
❑ 78 Tony Richardson RC	.25	.60
❑ 79 Sam Madison	.25	.60
❑ 80 Jeff George	.40	1.00
❑ 81 Matthew Hatchette	.25	.60
❑ 82 Kevin Faulk	.40	1.00
❑ 83 Jeff Blake	.40	1.00
❑ 84 Ike Hilliard	.40	1.00
❑ 85 Napoleon Kaufman	.40	1.00
❑ 86 Charles Woodson	.40	1.00
❑ 87 Na Brown	.25	.60
❑ 88 Hines Ward	.60	1.50
❑ 89 Troy Edwards	.25	.60
❑ 90 Curtis Conway	.40	1.00
❑ 91 Junior Seau	.60	1.50
❑ 92 Jim Harbaugh	.40	1.00
❑ 93 J.J. Stokes	.40	1.00
❑ 94 Jon Kitna	.60	1.50
❑ 95 Reidel Anthony	.25	.60
❑ 96 Warrick Dunn	.60	1.50
❑ 97 Carl Pickens	.40	1.00
❑ 98 Yancey Thigpen	.25	.60
❑ 99 Albert Connell	.25	.60
❑ 100 Irving Fryar	.40	1.00
❑ 101 Qadry Ismail	.50	1.25
❑ 102 Shannon Sharpe	.50	1.25
❑ 103 Joey Galloway	.50	1.25
❑ 104 Ed McCaffrey	.75	2.00
❑ 105 Rod Smith	.50	1.25
❑ 106 Terrell Owens	.75	2.00
❑ 107 Warren Sapp	.50	1.25
❑ 108 Jevon Kearse	.75	2.00
❑ 109 Bruce Smith	.50	1.25
❑ 110 Champ Bailey	.50	1.25
❑ 111 David Boston	.75	2.00
❑ 112 Tim Dwight	.75	2.00
❑ 113 Terance Mathis	.50	1.25
❑ 114 Tony Banks	.50	1.25
❑ 115 Shawn Bryson	.30	.75

Card		
❑ 116 Peerless Price	.50	1.25
❑ 117 Muhsin Muhammad	.50	1.25
❑ 118 Tim Biakabutuka	.50	1.25
❑ 119 Steve Beuerlein	.50	1.25
❑ 120 Corey Dillon	.75	2.00
❑ 121 Kevin Johnson	.75	2.00
❑ 122 Rocket Ismail	.50	1.25
❑ 123 Charlie Batch	.75	2.00
❑ 124 James Stewart	.50	1.25
❑ 125 Terrence Wilkins	.30	.75
❑ 126 Keenan McCardell	.50	1.25
❑ 127 Mark Brunell	.75	2.00
❑ 128 Fred Taylor	.75	2.00
❑ 129 Derrick Alexander	.50	1.25
❑ 130 Tony Gonzalez	.50	1.25
❑ 131 Warren Moon	.75	2.00
❑ 132 Thurman Thomas	.50	1.25
❑ 133 Tony Martin	.50	1.25
❑ 134 Jay Fiedler	.75	2.00
❑ 135 John Randle	.50	1.25
❑ 136 Troy Brown	.50	1.25
❑ 137 Amani Toomer	.50	1.25
❑ 138 Kerry Collins	.50	1.25
❑ 139 Tiki Barber	.75	2.00
❑ 140 Wayne Chrebet	.50	1.25
❑ 141 Tyrone Wheatley	.50	1.25
❑ 142 Duce Staley	.75	2.00
❑ 143 Jermaine Fazande	.30	.75
❑ 144 Charlie Garner	.50	1.25
❑ 145 Torry Holt	.75	2.00
❑ 146 Mike Alstott	.75	2.00
❑ 147 Shaun King	.20	.50
❑ 148 Darrell Green	.30	.75
❑ 149 Brad Johnson	.75	2.00
❑ 150 Olandis Gary	.75	2.00
❑ 151 Jake Plummer	.60	1.50
❑ 152 Chris Chandler	.60	1.50
❑ 153 Jamal Anderson	1.00	2.50
❑ 154 Eric Moulds	1.00	2.50
❑ 155 Doug Flutie	1.00	2.50
❑ 156 Rob Johnson	.60	1.50
❑ 157 Marcus Robinson	1.00	2.50
❑ 158 Cade McNown	.40	1.00
❑ 159 Akili Smith	.40	1.00
❑ 160 Tim Couch	.60	1.50
❑ 161 Emmitt Smith	2.00	5.00
❑ 162 Troy Aikman	2.00	5.00
❑ 163 Brian Griese	1.00	2.50
❑ 164 John Elway	3.00	8.00
❑ 165 Terrell Davis	1.00	2.50
❑ 166 Dorsey Levens	.60	1.50
❑ 167 Antonio Freeman	1.00	2.50
❑ 168 Brett Favre	3.00	8.00
❑ 169 Marvin Harrison	1.00	2.50
❑ 170 Peyton Manning	2.50	6.00
❑ 171 Edgerrin James	1.50	4.00
❑ 172 Jimmy Smith	.60	1.50
❑ 173 Elvis Grbac	.60	1.50
❑ 174 Dan Marino	3.00	8.00
❑ 175 Randy Moss	2.00	5.00
❑ 176 Cris Carter	1.00	2.50
❑ 177 Robert Smith	1.00	2.50
❑ 178 Daunte Culpepper	1.25	3.00
❑ 179 Terry Glenn	.60	1.50
❑ 180 Drew Bledsoe	1.25	3.00
❑ 181 Ricky Williams	.50	1.25
❑ 182 Jake Delhomme RC	3.00	8.00
❑ 183 Curtis Martin	1.00	2.50
❑ 184 Vinny Testaverde	.60	1.50
❑ 185 Tim Brown	1.00	2.50
❑ 186 Rich Gannon	1.00	2.50
❑ 187 Donovan McNabb	1.25	3.00
❑ 188 Jerome Bettis	1.00	2.50
❑ 189 Bobby Shaw RC	1.00	2.50
❑ 190 Jerry Rice	2.00	5.00
❑ 191 Steve Young	1.25	3.00
❑ 192 Jeff Garcia	1.00	2.50
❑ 193 Ricky Watters	.40	1.00
❑ 194 Isaac Bruce	1.00	2.50
❑ 195 Marshall Faulk	1.25	3.00
❑ 196 Kurt Warner	2.00	5.00
❑ 197 Keyshawn Johnson	1.00	2.50
❑ 198 Eddie George	1.00	2.50
❑ 199 Steve McNair	1.00	2.50
❑ 200 Stephen Davis	1.00	2.50
❑ 201 Bobby Brooks RC	1.25	3.00
❑ 202 Cornelius Griffin RC	1.50	4.00
❑ 203 Danny Clark RC	1.50	4.00
❑ 204 Pat Dennis RC	1.25	3.00
❑ 205 Tommy Hendricks RC	2.00	5.00
❑ 206 Fred Jones RC	1.25	3.00
❑ 207 Isaiah Kacyvenski RC	1.25	3.00
❑ 208 Keith Miller RC	1.25	3.00
❑ 209 Andre O' Neal RC	1.25	3.00
❑ 210 Justin Snow RC	1.25	3.00
❑ 211 Armegis Spearman RC	1.50	4.00
❑ 212 Lester Towns RC	1.25	3.00
❑ 213 Antonio Wilson RC	1.25	3.00
❑ 214 Greg Wesley RC	2.00	5.00
❑ 215 Jabari Issa RC	1.25	3.00
❑ 216 Darwin Walker RC	1.25	3.00
❑ 217 Reggie Grimes RC	1.25	3.00
❑ 218 Rian Lindell RC	1.25	3.00
❑ 219 Chris Combs RC	1.25	3.00
❑ 220 Rashard Anderson RC	1.50	4.00
❑ 221 Erik Flowers RC	1.50	4.00
❑ 222 Corey Moore RC	1.25	3.00
❑ 223 Rob Meier RC	1.25	3.00
❑ 224 John Milem RC	1.25	3.00
❑ 225 Jeremiah Parker RC	1.25	3.00
❑ 226 Neil Rackers RC	2.00	5.00
❑ 227 Josh Taves RC	1.50	4.00
❑ 228 Mao Tosi RC	1.25	3.00
❑ 229 Gary Berry RC	1.25	3.00
❑ 230 Matt Bowen RC	1.25	3.00
❑ 231 Ralph Brown RC	1.25	3.00
❑ 232 Tony Darden RC	1.25	3.00
❑ 233 Arturo Freeman RC	1.25	3.00
❑ 234 David Gibson RC	1.25	3.00
❑ 235 Demario Brown RC	1.25	3.00
❑ 236 Deveron Harper RC	1.25	3.00
❑ 237 Johnnie Harris RC	1.25	3.00
❑ 238 Marcus Knight RC	1.50	4.00
❑ 239 Ronnie Heard RC	1.50	4.00
❑ 240 Eric Johnson RC	1.50	4.00
❑ 241 John Keith RC	1.25	3.00
❑ 242 Anthony Malbrough RC	1.25	3.00
❑ 243 Anthony Mitchell RC	1.25	3.00
❑ 244 Aric Morris RC	1.25	3.00
❑ 245 Bobby Myers RC	1.25	3.00
❑ 246 Erik Olson RC	1.25	3.00
❑ 247 Lewis Sanders RC	1.25	3.00
❑ 248 Tony Scott RC	1.25	3.00
❑ 249 David Terrell RC	1.25	3.00
❑ 250 Travares Tillman RC	1.25	3.00
❑ 251 David Stachelski RC	1.50	4.00
❑ 252 Darren Howard RC	2.00	5.00
❑ 253 Frank Chamberlin RC	1.50	4.00
❑ 254 Na'il Diggs RC	2.00	5.00
❑ 255 Orantes Grant RC	1.50	4.00
❑ 256 Barrett Green RC	1.50	4.00
❑ 257 Kory Minor RC	1.50	4.00
❑ 258 Deon Grant RC	2.00	5.00
❑ 259 Mark Simoneau RC	2.00	5.00
❑ 260 Raynoch Thompson RC	2.00	5.00
❑ 261 Kenyatta Wright RC	1.50	4.00
❑ 262 Marcus Bell LB RC	1.50	4.00
❑ 263 Jack Golden RC	1.50	4.00
❑ 264 Thomas Hamner RC	1.50	4.00
❑ 265 Sekou Sanyika RC	1.50	4.00
❑ 266 Marcus Washington RC	2.00	5.00
❑ 267 Tim Seder RC	2.00	5.00
❑ 268 Paul Edinger RC	2.50	6.00
❑ 269 Michael Boireau RC	1.50	4.00
❑ 270 Byron Frisch RC	1.50	4.00
❑ 271 Ketric Sanford RC	1.50	4.00
❑ 272 Frank Murphy RC	1.50	4.00
❑ 273 Robaire Smith RC	1.50	4.00
❑ 274 Adalius Thomas RC	6.00	15.00
❑ 275 William Bartee RC	2.00	5.00
❑ 276 Robert Bean RC	2.00	5.00
❑ 277 Tyrone Carter RC	2.50	6.00
❑ 278 Iko Charlton RC	1.50	4.00
❑ 279 Mario Edwards RC	2.00	5.00
❑ 280 Dwayne Goodrich RC	1.50	4.00
❑ 281 Michael Hawthorne RC	1.50	4.00
❑ 282 Kareem Larrimore RC	1.50	4.00
❑ 283 Mark Roman RC	2.00	5.00
❑ 284 Jacoby Shepherd RC	1.50	4.00
❑ 285 Jason Webster RC	1.50	4.00
❑ 286 Jimmy Wyrick RC	1.50	4.00
❑ 287 Rashidi Barnes RC	1.50	4.00
❑ 288 David Barrett RC	1.50	4.00
❑ 289 Ainsley Battles RC	1.50	4.00
❑ 290 Lamar Chapman RC	1.50	4.00
❑ 291 Todd Franz RC	1.50	4.00
❑ 292 Michael Green RC	1.50	4.00
❑ 293 Antwan Harris RC	1.50	4.00
❑ 294 Brandon Jennings RC	1.50	4.00
❑ 295 Darrick Vaughn RC	1.50	4.00
❑ 296 David Macklin RC	1.50	4.00
❑ 297 Bobby Brown RC	1.50	4.00
❑ 298 Reggie Stephens RC	1.50	4.00
❑ 299 Kenoy Kennedy RC	1.50	4.00
❑ 300 Raion Hill RC	1.50	4.00
❑ 301 Windrell Hayes RC	3.00	8.00
❑ 302 DaShon Polk RC	2.50	6.00
❑ 303 Tywan Mitchell RC	3.00	8.00
❑ 304 Casey Crawford RC	2.50	6.00
❑ 305 Hank Poteat RC	3.00	8.00
❑ 306 Mondriel Fulcher RC	2.50	6.00
❑ 307 Cory Geason RC	2.50	6.00
❑ 308 James Hill RC	2.50	6.00
❑ 309 Brian Jennings RC	2.50	6.00
❑ 310 John Jones RC	3.00	8.00
❑ 311 Anthony Lucas RC	2.50	6.00
❑ 312 Mike Leach RC	2.50	6.00
❑ 313 Dustin Lyman RC	2.50	6.00
❑ 314 Derek Rackley RC	2.50	6.00
❑ 315 Sebastian Janikowski RC	4.00	10.00
❑ 316 Brad St.Louis RC	2.50	6.00
❑ 317 Jay Tant RC	2.50	6.00
❑ 318 Austin Wheatley RC	2.50	6.00
❑ 319 Jermaine Wiggins RC	4.00	10.00
❑ 320 Todd Yoder RC	3.00	8.00
❑ 321 Deon Dyer RC	3.00	8.00
❑ 322 Jim Finn	2.50	6.00
❑ 323 Herbert Goodman RC	3.00	8.00
❑ 324 Mike Green RC	3.00	8.00
❑ 325 Dante Hall RC	6.00	15.00
❑ 326 Thabiti Davis RC	2.50	6.00
❑ 327 Kevin Houser RC	3.00	8.00
❑ 328 Jonas Lewis RC	2.50	6.00
❑ 329 Chad Morton RC	4.00	10.00
❑ 330 Patrick Pass RC	3.00	8.00
❑ 331 Maurice Smith RC	4.00	10.00
❑ 332 Paul Smith RC	3.00	8.00
❑ 333 Terrelle Smith RC	3.00	8.00
❑ 334 Craig Walendy RC	2.50	6.00
❑ 335 Jamel White RC	3.00	8.00
❑ 336 Jarious Jackson RC	3.00	8.00
❑ 337 Matt Lytle RC	3.00	8.00
❑ 338 Ron Powlus RC	4.00	10.00
❑ 339 Ian Gold RC	3.00	8.00
❑ 340 Brandon Short RC	3.00	8.00
❑ 341 T.J. Slaughter RC	2.50	6.00
❑ 342 Nate Webster RC	2.50	6.00
❑ 343 John Engelberger RC	3.00	8.00
❑ 344 Rogers Beckett RC	3.00	8.00
❑ 345 Mike Brown RC	6.00	15.00
❑ 346 Anthony Wright RC	4.00	10.00
❑ 347 Danny Farmer RC	3.00	8.00
❑ 348 Clint Stoerner RC	3.00	8.00
❑ 349 Julian Peterson RC	4.00	10.00
❑ 350 Ahmed Plummer RC	4.00	10.00
❑ 351 Avion Black RC	4.00	10.00
❑ 352 Kwame Cavil RC	3.00	8.00
❑ 353 Chris Cole RC	4.00	10.00
❑ 354 Chris Coleman RC	3.00	8.00
❑ 355 Trevor Gaylor RC	4.00	10.00
❑ 356 Damon Hodge RC	4.00	10.00
❑ 357 Darrell Jackson RC	10.00	25.00
❑ 358 Reggie Jones RC	3.00	8.00
❑ 359 Charles Lee RC	3.00	8.00
❑ 360 Jerry Porter RC	5.00	12.00
❑ 361 Bobby Shaw	4.00	10.00
❑ 362 Ron Dugans RC	3.00	8.00
❑ 363 James Williams RC	4.00	10.00
❑ 364 Bashir Yamini RC	3.00	8.00
❑ 365 Anthony Becht RC	5.00	12.00
❑ 366 Erron Kinney RC	5.00	12.00
❑ 367 Aaron Shea RC	4.00	10.00
❑ 368 Chris Samuels RC	4.00	10.00
❑ 369 Trung Canidate RC	4.00	10.00
❑ 370 Obafemi Ayanbadejo RC	4.00	10.00
❑ 371 Doug Chapman RC	4.00	10.00
❑ 372 Ronney Jenkins RC	4.00	10.00
❑ 373 Curtis Keaton RC	4.00	10.00
❑ 374 Kevin McDougal RC	4.00	10.00
❑ 375 Frank Moreau RC	4.00	10.00
❑ 376 Aaron Stecker RC	5.00	12.00
❑ 377 Shyrone Stith RC	4.00	10.00
❑ 378 Tom Brady RC	175.00	350.00
❑ 379 Giovanni Carmazzi RC	3.00	8.00
❑ 380 Joe Hamilton RC	4.00	10.00
❑ 381 Todd Husak RC	5.00	12.00
❑ 382 Doug Johnson RC	5.00	12.00

Card	Low	High
❑ 383 Tee Martin RC	5.00	12.00
❑ 384 Chad Pennington RC	25.00	60.00
❑ 385 Tim Rattay RC	5.00	12.00
❑ 386 Chris Redman RC	4.00	10.00
❑ 387 Billy Volek RC	5.00	12.00
❑ 388 Spergon Wynn RC	4.00	10.00
❑ 389 John Abraham RC	5.00	12.00
❑ 390 Keith Bulluck RC	5.00	12.00
❑ 391 Rob Morris RC	4.00	10.00
❑ 392 JaJuan Dawson RC	3.00	8.00
❑ 393 Chris Hovan RC	4.00	10.00
❑ 394 Shaun Ellis RC	5.00	12.00
❑ 395 Deltha O'Neal RC	5.00	12.00
❑ 396 Gari Scott RC	3.00	8.00
❑ 397 Dialleo Burks RC	3.00	8.00
❑ 398 Shockmain Davis RC	3.00	8.00
❑ 399 Brad Hoover RC	4.00	10.00
❑ 400 Brian Finneran RC	5.00	12.00
❑ 401 Sylvester Morris J/FB/750 RC	4.00	10.00
❑ 402 Denn Northcutt J/FB/500 RC	5.00	12.00
❑ 403 Todd Pinkston J/FB/100 RC	7.50	20.00
❑ 404 Larry Foster J/FB/500 RC	5.00	12.00
❑ 405 R.Jay Soward J/FB/1000 RC	4.00	10.00
❑ 406 Travis Taylor J/FB/250 RC	7.50	20.00
❑ 407 Peter Warrick J/FB/1000 RC	6.00	15.00
❑ 408 Dez White J/FB/1000 RC	6.00	15.00
❑ 409 Ron Dayne J/FB/1000 RC	7.50	20.00
❑ 410 Thomas Jones J/FB/500 RC	10.00	25.00
❑ 411 Jamal Lewis J/FB/1000 RC	12.50	30.00
❑ 412 Sammy Morris J/FB/500 RC	6.00	15.00
❑ 413 Travis Prentice J/FB/500 RC	5.00	12.00
❑ 414 J.R. Redmond J/FB/250 RC	6.00	15.00
❑ 415 Michael Wiley FB/1000 RC	5.00	12.00
❑ 416 Laver Coles J/FB/250 RC	15.00	40.00
❑ 417 Bubba Franks J/FB/500 RC	6.00	15.00
❑ 418 Mike Anderson J/FB/250 RC	10.00	25.00
❑ 419 Plaxico Burress J/FB/250 RC	25.00	50.00
❑ 420 Ron Dixon J/FB/1000 RC	5.00	12.00
❑ 421 Troy Walters J/FB/1000 RC	5.00	12.00
❑ 422 Sha Alexander J/FB/1000 RC	10.00	25.00
❑ 423 Brian Urlacher J/FB/1000 RC	15.00	40.00
❑ 424 Corey Simon J/FB/1000 RC	5.00	12.00
❑ 425 Courtney Brown J/FB/500 RC	6.00	15.00

2003 Leaf Limited

Card	Low	High
❑ COMP.SET w/o SP's (100)	100.00	250.00
❑ 1 Emmitt Smith	4.00	10.00
❑ 2 Michael Vick	1.50	4.00
❑ 3 Peerless Price	1.00	2.50
❑ 4 T.J. Duckett	1.25	3.00
❑ 5 Jamal Lewis	1.50	4.00
❑ 6 Drew Bledsoe	1.50	4.00
❑ 7 Eric Moulds	1.25	3.00
❑ 8 Travis Henry	1.25	3.00
❑ 9 Jim Kelly	2.00	5.00
❑ 10 Julius Peppers	1.50	4.00
❑ 11 Dick Butkus	2.50	6.00
❑ 12 Mike Singletary	1.50	4.00
❑ 13 Walter Payton	5.00	12.00
❑ 14 Anthony Thomas	1.25	3.00
❑ 15 Brian Urlacher	2.50	6.00
❑ 16 Marty Booker	1.25	3.00
❑ 17 Corey Dillon	1.25	3.00
❑ 18 Jim Thorpe	2.00	5.00
❑ 19 Jim Brown	2.50	6.00
❑ 20 Tim Couch	1.00	2.50
❑ 21 William Green	1.00	2.50
❑ 22 Deion Sanders	1.50	4.00
❑ 23 Michael Irvin	1.50	4.00
❑ 24 Roger Staubach	2.50	6.00
❑ 25 Troy Aikman	2.00	5.00
❑ 26 Tony Dorsett	1.50	4.00
❑ 27 Antonio Bryant	1.50	4.00
❑ 28 Clinton Portis	2.00	5.00
❑ 29 Jake Plummer	1.25	3.00
❑ 30 Rod Smith	1.25	3.00
❑ 31 Barry Sanders	4.00	10.00
❑ 32 Doak Walker	1.50	4.00
❑ 33 Joey Harrington	1.25	3.00
❑ 34 Bart Starr	2.50	6.00
❑ 35 Ahman Green	1.50	4.00
❑ 36 Brett Favre	4.00	10.00
❑ 37 Donald Driver	1.50	4.00
❑ 38 David Carr	1.50	4.00
❑ 39 Don Shula	1.50	4.00
❑ 40 Johnny Unitas	3.00	8.00
❑ 41 Edgerrin James	1.50	4.00
❑ 42 Marvin Harrison	1.50	4.00
❑ 43 Peyton Manning	3.00	8.00
❑ 44 Fred Taylor	1.50	4.00
❑ 45 Jimmy Smith	1.25	3.00
❑ 46 Mark Brunell	1.25	3.00
❑ 47 Marcus Allen	1.50	4.00
❑ 48 Priest Holmes	1.50	4.00
❑ 49 Tony Gonzalez	1.25	3.00
❑ 50 Trent Green	1.25	3.00
❑ 51 Dan Marino	5.00	12.00
❑ 52 Bob Griese	1.50	4.00
❑ 53 Chris Chambers	1.25	3.00
❑ 54 Ricky Williams	1.25	3.00
❑ 55 Fran Tarkenton	1.50	4.00
❑ 56 Daunte Culpepper	1.50	4.00
❑ 57 Michael Bennett	1.25	3.00
❑ 58 Randy Moss	1.50	4.00
❑ 59 Tom Brady	4.00	10.00
❑ 60 Aaron Brooks	1.25	3.00
❑ 61 Deuce McAllister	1.50	4.00
❑ 62 Donte Stallworth	1.25	3.00
❑ 63 Mark Bavaro	1.25	3.00
❑ 64 Jeremy Shockey	1.50	4.00
❑ 65 Kerry Collins	1.25	3.00
❑ 66 Tiki Barber	1.50	4.00
❑ 67 Joe Namath	2.50	6.00
❑ 68 Chad Pennington	1.50	4.00
❑ 69 Curtis Martin	1.50	4.00
❑ 70 Jerry Porter	1.25	3.00
❑ 71 Jerry Rice	3.00	8.00
❑ 72 Rich Gannon	1.25	3.00
❑ 73 Tim Brown	1.50	4.00
❑ 74 Donovan McNabb	1.50	4.00
❑ 75 Terry Bradshaw	2.50	6.00
❑ 76 Antwaan Randle El	1.25	3.00
❑ 77 Plaxico Burress	1.50	4.00
❑ 78 Tommy Maddox	1.25	3.00
❑ 79 David Boston	1.00	2.50
❑ 80 Drew Brees	1.50	4.00
❑ 81 LaDainian Tomlinson	2.00	5.00
❑ 82 Joe Montana	5.00	12.00
❑ 83 Steve Young	2.00	5.00
❑ 84 Jeff Garcia	1.50	4.00
❑ 85 Terrell Owens	1.50	4.00
❑ 86 Koren Robinson	1.25	3.00
❑ 87 Matt Hasselbeck	1.25	3.00
❑ 88 Shaun Alexander	1.50	4.00
❑ 89 Isaac Bruce	1.50	4.00
❑ 90 Kurt Warner	1.50	4.00
❑ 91 Marshall Faulk	1.50	4.00
❑ 92 Torry Holt	1.50	4.00
❑ 93 Brad Johnson	1.25	3.00
❑ 94 Keyshawn Johnson	1.50	4.00
❑ 95 Earl Campbell	1.50	4.00
❑ 96 Eddie George	1.25	3.00
❑ 97 Steve McNair	1.50	4.00
❑ 98 John Riggins	1.50	4.00
❑ 99 Laveranues Coles	1.25	3.00
❑ 100 Patrick Ramsey	1.25	3.00
❑ 101 LaTarence Dunbar RC	1.50	4.00
❑ 102 Sam Aiken RC	2.50	6.00
❑ 103 Bobby Wade RC	2.00	5.00
❑ 104 Justin Gage RC	2.50	6.00
❑ 105 Lee Suggs RC	2.00	5.00
❑ 106 Jason Witten RC	6.00	15.00
❑ 107 Quentin Griffin RC	2.00	5.00
❑ 108 Domanick Davis RC	2.50	6.00
❑ 109 LaBrandon Toefield RC	2.00	5.00
❑ 110 J.R. Tolver RC	2.00	5.00
❑ 111 Kliff Kingsbury RC	2.00	5.00
❑ 112 Talman Gardner RC	1.50	4.00
❑ 113 Teyo Johnson RC	2.00	5.00
❑ 114 Billy McMullen RC	1.50	4.00
❑ 115 L.J. Smith RC	2.50	6.00
❑ 116 Brian St.Pierre RC	2.50	6.00
❑ 117 Brandon Lloyd RC	2.50	6.00
❑ 118 Seneca Wallace RC	2.50	6.00
❑ 119 Kevin Curtis RC	2.50	6.00
❑ 120 Shaun McDonald RC	2.50	6.00
❑ 121 Terrell Suggs RC	3.00	8.00
❑ 122 Terence Newman RC	2.50	6.00
❑ 123 Tony Romo RC	25.00	50.00
❑ 124 DeWayne Robertson RC	2.00	5.00
❑ 125 Marcus Trufant RC	2.50	6.00
❑ 126 Artose Pinner AU RC	6.00	15.00
❑ 127 Bryant Johnson AU RC	10.00	25.00
❑ 128 Kelley Washington AU RC	8.00	20.00
❑ 129 Dallas Clark AU RC	25.00	50.00
❑ 130 Onterrio Smith AU RC	8.00	20.00
❑ 131 Tony Hollings AU RC	8.00	20.00
❑ 132 Tyrone Calico AU RC	8.00	20.00
❑ 133 Carson Palmer AU RC	50.00	100.00
❑ 134 Byron Leftwich AU RC	12.00	30.00
❑ 135 Rex Grossman AU RC	10.00	25.00
❑ 136 Kyle Boller AU RC	10.00	25.00
❑ 137 Chris Simms AU RC	10.00	25.00
❑ 138 Dave Ragone AU RC	6.00	15.00
❑ 139 Ken Dorsey AU RC	8.00	20.00
❑ 140 Willis McGahee AU RC	20.00	50.00
❑ 141 Larry Johnson AU RC	12.00	30.00
❑ 142 Musa Smith AU RC	8.00	20.00
❑ 143 Chris Brown AU RC	10.00	25.00
❑ 144 Charles Rogers AU RC	8.00	20.00
❑ 145 Andre Johnson AU RC	35.00	60.00
❑ 146 Taylor Jacobs AU RC	8.00	20.00
❑ 147 Anquan Boldin AU RC	40.00	80.00
❑ 148 Bethel Johnson AU RC	8.00	20.00
❑ 149 Justin Fargas AU RC	10.00	25.00
❑ 150 Nate Burleson AU RC	8.00	20.00

2004 Leaf Limited

Card	Low	High
❑ 201-233 JSY AU PRINT RUN 150		
❑ 1 A.J. Feeley	1.25	3.00
❑ 2 Aaron Brooks	1.25	3.00
❑ 3 Ahman Green	1.50	4.00
❑ 4 Andre Johnson	1.50	4.00
❑ 5 Anquan Boldin	1.50	4.00
❑ 6 Antwaan Randle El	1.25	3.00
❑ 7 Ashley Lelie	1.25	3.00
❑ 8 Brad Johnson	1.25	3.00
❑ 9 Brett Favre	4.00	10.00
❑ 10 Brian Urlacher	1.50	4.00
❑ 11 Brian Westbrook	1.50	4.00
❑ 12 Byron Leftwich	1.50	4.00
❑ 13 Carson Palmer	2.00	5.00
❑ 14 Chad Johnson	1.25	3.00
❑ 15 Chad Pennington	1.50	4.00
❑ 16 Charlie Garner	1.25	3.00
❑ 17 Charles Rogers	1.25	3.00
❑ 18 Chris Brown	1.25	3.00
❑ 19 Chris Chambers	1.25	3.00
❑ 20 Clinton Portis	1.50	4.00
❑ 21 Corey Dillon	1.25	3.00
❑ 22 Deion Sanders	1.50	4.00
❑ 23 Curtis Martin	1.50	4.00
❑ 24 Daunte Culpepper	1.50	4.00
❑ 25 David Terrell	1.00	2.50
❑ 26 David Carr	1.25	3.00
❑ 27 Deion Branch	1.25	3.00
❑ 28 Derrick Mason	1.25	3.00
❑ 29 DeShaun Foster	1.25	3.00
❑ 30 Deuce McAllister	1.50	4.00
❑ 31 Domanick Davis	1.25	3.00
❑ 32 Donovan McNabb	1.50	4.00
❑ 33 Donte Stallworth	1.25	3.00
❑ 34 Drew Bledsoe	1.50	4.00
❑ 35 Duce Staley	1.25	3.00
❑ 36 Eddie George	1.25	3.00
❑ 37 Edgerrin James	1.50	4.00
❑ 38 Emmitt Smith	4.00	10.00
❑ 39 Eric Moulds	1.25	3.00
❑ 40 Fred Taylor	1.25	3.00
❑ 41 Hines Ward	1.50	4.00
❑ 42 Isaac Bruce	1.25	3.00

❑ 43 Jake Delhomme 1.25 3.00
❑ 44 Jake Plummer 1.25 3.00
❑ 45 Javon Walker 1.25 3.00
❑ 46 Jeff Garcia 1.50 4.00
❑ 47 Jeremy Shockey 1.25 3.00
❑ 48 Jerome Bettis 1.50 4.00
❑ 49 Jerry Porter 1.25 3.00
❑ 50 Jerry Rice 3.00 8.00
❑ 51 Jevon Kearse 1.25 3.00
❑ 52 Jimmy Smith 1.25 3.00
❑ 53 Joe Horn 1.25 3.00
❑ 54 Joey Harrington 1.25 3.00
❑ 55 Josh McCown 1.25 3.00
❑ 56 Kevan Barlow 1.25 3.00
❑ 57 Koren Robinson 1.50 4.00
❑ 58 Kyle Boller 1.25 3.00
❑ 59 LaDainian Tomlinson 2.00 5.00
❑ 60 LaVar Arrington 1.25 3.00
❑ 61 Laveranues Coles 1.25 3.00
❑ 62 Lee Suggs 1.50 4.00
❑ 63 Marc Bulger 1.25 3.00
❑ 64 Mark Brunell 1.25 3.00
❑ 65 Marshall Faulk 1.50 4.00
❑ 66 Marvin Harrison 1.50 4.00
❑ 67 Matt Hasselbeck 1.50 4.00
❑ 68 Michael Bennett 1.25 3.00
❑ 69 Michael Strahan 1.25 3.00
❑ 70 Michael Vick 1.50 4.00
❑ 71 Peerless Price 1.25 3.00
❑ 72 Peter Warrick 1.25 3.00
❑ 73 Peyton Manning 3.00 8.00
❑ 74 Priest Holmes 1.50 4.00
❑ 75 Quentin Griffin 1.25 3.00
❑ 76 Randy Moss 1.50 4.00
❑ 77 Ray Lewis 1.50 4.00
❑ 78 Rex Grossman 1.50 4.00
❑ 79 Lamar Gordon 1.00 2.50
❑ 80 Rod Smith 1.25 3.00
❑ 81 Roy Williams S 1.25 3.00
❑ 82 Rudi Johnson 1.25 3.00
❑ 83 Santana Moss 1.25 3.00
❑ 84 Shaun Alexander 1.50 4.00
❑ 85 Stephen Davis 1.25 3.00
❑ 86 Steve McNair 1.50 4.00
❑ 87 Steve Smith 1.50 4.00
❑ 88 T.J. Duckett 1.25 3.00
❑ 89 Terrell Owens 1.50 4.00
❑ 90 Thomas Jones 1.25 3.00
❑ 91 Tiki Barber 1.50 4.00
❑ 92 Tim Brown 1.50 4.00
❑ 93 Tom Brady 4.00 10.00
❑ 94 Tony Gonzalez 1.50 4.00
❑ 95 Torry Holt 1.50 4.00
❑ 96 Travis Henry 1.25 3.00
❑ 97 Trent Green 1.25 3.00
❑ 98 Warren Sapp 1.25 3.00
❑ 99 William Green 1.00 2.50
❑ 100 Willis McGahee 1.50 4.00
❑ 101 Barry Sanders 5.00 12.00
❑ 102 Bart Starr 5.00 12.00
❑ 103 Bo Jackson 3.00 8.00
❑ 104 Bob Griese 2.00 5.00
❑ 105 Bronko Nagurski 2.00 5.00
❑ 106 Dan Marino 6.00 15.00
❑ 107 Deion Sanders 2.00 5.00
❑ 108 Dick Butkus 3.00 8.00
❑ 109 Doak Walker 2.00 5.00
❑ 110 Don Maynard 1.50 4.00
❑ 111 Don Shula 2.00 5.00
❑ 112 Earl Campbell 2.00 5.00
❑ 113 Fran Tarkenton 2.00 5.00
❑ 114 Franco Harris 2.50 6.00
❑ 115 Fred Biletnikoff 2.00 5.00
❑ 116 Gale Sayers 2.50 6.00
❑ 117 Herman Edwards 1.50 4.00
❑ 118 Jim Brown 3.00 8.00
❑ 119 Jim Kelly 2.00 5.00
❑ 120 Jim Thorpe 2.00 5.00
❑ 121 Jimmy Johnson 1.50 4.00
❑ 122 Joe Greene 2.00 5.00
❑ 123 Joe Montana 6.00 15.00
❑ 124 Joe Namath 3.00 8.00
❑ 125 John Elway 5.00 12.00
❑ 126 John Riggins 2.50 6.00
❑ 127 Johnny Unitas 5.00 12.00
❑ 128 Larry Csonka 2.00 5.00
❑ 129 Lawrence Taylor 2.50 6.00
❑ 130 Marcus Allen 2.00 5.00
❑ 131 Mark Bavaro 1.25 3.00
❑ 132 Michael Irvin 2.00 5.00
❑ 133 Mike Ditka 2.00 5.00
❑ 134 Mike Singletary 2.00 5.00
❑ 135 Ozzie Newsome 1.50 4.00
❑ 136 Paul Warfield 1.50 4.00
❑ 137 Randall Cunningham 1.50 4.00
❑ 138 Ray Nitschke 2.00 5.00
❑ 139 Red Grange 2.00 5.00
❑ 140 Reggie White 2.00 5.00
❑ 141 Roger Staubach 3.00 8.00
❑ 142 Sterling Sharpe 1.50 4.00
❑ 143 Steve Largent 2.00 5.00
❑ 144 Terrell Davis 2.00 5.00
❑ 145 Terry Bradshaw 3.00 8.00
❑ 146 Thurman Thomas 1.50 4.00
❑ 147 Tony Dorsett 2.00 5.00
❑ 148 Troy Aikman 3.00 8.00
❑ 149 Walter Payton 8.00 20.00
❑ 150 Warren Moon 1.50 4.00
❑ 151 Ahmad Carroll RC 4.00 10.00
❑ 152 Andy Hall RC 3.00 8.00
❑ 153 Antwan Odom RC 4.00 10.00
❑ 154 B.J. Symons RC 2.50 6.00
❑ 155 Carlos Francis RC 2.50 6.00
❑ 156 Casey Bramlet RC 2.50 6.00
❑ 157 Chris Cooley RC 4.00 10.00
❑ 158 Chris Gamble RC 3.00 8.00
❑ 159 Clarence Moore RC 3.00 8.00
❑ 160 Cody Pickett RC 3.00 8.00
❑ 161 Courtney Watson RC 3.00 8.00
❑ 162 Craig Krenzel RC 4.00 10.00
❑ 163 D.J. Hackett RC 4.00 10.00
❑ 164 D.J. Williams RC 4.00 10.00
❑ 165 Derrick Strait RC 3.00 8.00
❑ 166 Dontarrious Thomas RC 3.00 8.00
❑ 167 Drew Henson RC 2.50 6.00
❑ 168 Ernest Wilford RC 3.00 8.00
❑ 169 Jamaar Taylor RC 2.50 6.00
❑ 170 Jason Babin RC 3.00 8.00
❑ 171 Jeff Smoker RC 3.00 8.00
❑ 172 Jerricho Cotchery RC 4.00 10.00
❑ 173 Jim Sorgi RC 4.00 10.00
❑ 174 Joey Thomas RC 2.50 6.00
❑ 175 John Navarre RC 3.00 8.00
❑ 176 Johnnie Morant RC 3.00 8.00
❑ 177 Jonathan Vilma RC 4.00 10.00
❑ 178 Josh Harris RC 2.50 6.00
❑ 179 Keiwan Ratliff RC 2.50 6.00
❑ 180 Kenechi Udeze RC 4.00 10.00
❑ 181 Kris Wilson RC 3.00 8.00
❑ 182 Marcus Tubbs RC 2.50 6.00
❑ 183 Marquise Hill RC 2.50 6.00
❑ 184 Matt Mauck RC 3.00 8.00
❑ 185 Maurice Mann RC 2.50 6.00
❑ 186 Michael Boulware RC 4.00 10.00
❑ 187 Michael Turner RC 10.00 25.00
❑ 188 P.K. Sam RC 2.50 6.00
❑ 189 Patrick Crayton RC 5.00 12.00
❑ 190 Ricardo Colclough RC 4.00 10.00
❑ 191 Richard Smith RC 2.50 6.00
❑ 192 Samie Parker RC 3.00 8.00
❑ 193 Sean Taylor RC 4.00 10.00
❑ 194 Teddy Lehman RC 3.00 8.00
❑ 195 Thomas Tapeh RC 3.00 8.00
❑ 196 Tommie Harris RC 4.00 10.00
❑ 197 Triandos Luke RC 2.50 6.00
❑ 198 Troy Fleming RC 2.50 6.00
❑ 199 Vince Wilfork RC 4.00 10.00
❑ 200 Will Smith RC 4.00 10.00
❑ 201 Larry Fitzgerald JSY AU RC 60.00 100.00
❑ 202 DeAngelo Hall JSY AU RC 12.00 30.00
❑ 203 Matt Schaub JSY AU RC 30.00 80.00
❑ 204 Michael Jenkins JSY AU RC 12.0030.00
❑ 205 Devard Darling JSY AU RC 10.0025.00
❑ 206 J.P. Losman JSY AU RC 12.00 30.00
❑ 207 Lee Evans JSY AU RC 15.00 40.00
❑ 208 Keary Colbert JSY AU RC 10.00 25.00
❑ 209 Bernard Berrian JSY AU RC 12.0030.00
❑ 210 Chris Perry JSY AU RC 12.00 30.00
❑ 211 K.Winslow JSY AU RC 15.00 40.00
❑ 212 Luke McCown JSY AU RC 12.00 30.00
❑ 213 Julius Jones JSY AU RC 15.00 40.00
❑ 214 Darius Watts JSY AU RC 10.00 25.00
❑ 215 Tatum Bell JSY AU RC 12.00 30.00
❑ 216 Kevin Jones JSY AU RC 12.00 30.00
❑ 217 Roy Will.WR JSY AU RC 15.00 40.00
❑ 218 Dunta Robinson JSY AU RC 10.0025.00
❑ 219 Greg Jones JSY AU RC 12.00 30.00
❑ 220 Reggie Williams JSY AU RC 12.0030.00
❑ 221 Mewelde Moore JSY AU RC 12.0030.00
❑ 222 Ben Watson JSY AU RC 12.00 30.00
❑ 223 Cedric Cobbs JSY AU RC 10.00 25.00
❑ 224 Devery Henderson JSY AU RC 12.00 30.00
❑ 225 Eli Manning JSY AU RC 100.00 175.00
❑ 226 Robert Gallery JSY AU RC 12.00 30.00
❑ 227 Roethlisberger JSY AU RC 125.00 200.00
❑ 228 Philip Rivers JSY AU RC 60.00 120.00
❑ 229 Derrick Hamilton JSY AU RC 8.0020.00
❑ 230 Rashaun Woods JSY AU RC 8.0020.00
❑ 231 Stev.Jackson JSY AU RC 30.00 80.00
❑ 232 Michael Clayton JSY AU RC 12.0030.00
❑ 233 Ben Troupe JSY AU RC 10.00 25.00

2005 Leaf Limited

❑ 1-150 PRINT RUN 599 SER.#'d SETS
❑ 151-200 ROOKIE PRINT RUN 250
❑ 201-229 JSY AU PRINT RUN 100 SETS
❑ UNPRICED PLATINUM SER.#'d TO 1
❑ 1 Anquan Boldin 1.25 3.00
❑ 2 Kurt Warner 1.50 4.00
❑ 3 Larry Fitzgerald 1.50 4.00
❑ 4 Alge Crumpler 1.25 3.00
❑ 5 Michael Vick 1.50 4.00
❑ 6 Warrick Dunn 1.25 3.00
❑ 7 Jamal Lewis 1.25 3.00
❑ 8 Kyle Boller 1.25 3.00
❑ 9 Ray Lewis 1.50 4.00
❑ 10 Derrick Mason 1.25 3.00
❑ 11 J.P. Losman 1.25 3.00
❑ 12 Lee Evans 1.25 3.00
❑ 13 Willis McGahee 1.50 4.00
❑ 14 DeShaun Foster 1.25 3.00
❑ 15 Jake Delhomme 1.50 4.00
❑ 16 Steve Smith 1.50 4.00
❑ 17 Brian Urlacher 1.50 4.00
❑ 18 Rex Grossman 1.50 4.00
❑ 19 Muhsin Muhammad 1.25 3.00
❑ 20 Carson Palmer 1.50 4.00
❑ 21 Chad Johnson 1.25 3.00
❑ 22 Rudi Johnson 1.25 3.00
❑ 23 Antonio Bryant 1.25 3.00
❑ 24 Lee Suggs 1.25 3.00
❑ 25 Trent Dilfer 1.25 3.00
❑ 26 Drew Bledsoe 1.50 4.00
❑ 27 Julius Jones 1.50 4.00
❑ 28 Keyshawn Johnson 1.25 3.00
❑ 29 Roy Williams S 1.25 3.00
❑ 30 Ashley Lelie 1.00 2.50
❑ 31 Jake Plummer 1.25 3.00
❑ 32 Tatum Bell 1.25 3.00
❑ 33 Rod Smith 1.25 3.00
❑ 34 Joey Harrington 1.50 4.00
❑ 35 Kevin Jones 1.25 3.00
❑ 36 Roy Williams WR 1.50 4.00
❑ 37 Ahman Green 1.50 4.00
❑ 38 Brett Favre 4.00 10.00
❑ 39 Javon Walker 1.25 3.00
❑ 40 Andre Johnson 1.25 3.00
❑ 41 David Carr 1.25 3.00
❑ 42 Domanick Davis 1.00 2.50
❑ 43 Edgerrin James 1.25 3.00
❑ 44 Marvin Harrison 1.50 4.00
❑ 45 Peyton Manning 2.50 6.00
❑ 46 Reggie Wayne 1.25 3.00
❑ 47 Byron Leftwich 1.25 3.00
❑ 48 Fred Taylor 1.50 4.00
❑ 49 Jimmy Smith 1.25 3.00
❑ 50 Priest Holmes 1.50 4.00
❑ 51 Tony Gonzalez 1.25 3.00
❑ 52 Trent Green 1.25 3.00
❑ 53 Chris Chambers 1.25 3.00
❑ 54 Ricky Williams 1.25 3.00

Card	Low	High
❑ 55 Daunte Culpepper	1.50	4.00
❑ 56 Nate Burleson	1.25	3.00
❑ 57 Michael Bennett	1.25	3.00
❑ 58 Corey Dillon	1.25	3.00
❑ 59 Deion Branch	1.25	3.00
❑ 60 Tom Brady	3.00	8.00
❑ 61 Aaron Brooks	1.00	2.50
❑ 62 Deuce McAllister	1.50	4.00
❑ 63 Joe Horn	1.25	3.00
❑ 64 Eli Manning	3.00	8.00
❑ 65 Jeremy Shockey	1.50	4.00
❑ 66 Plaxico Burress	1.25	3.00
❑ 67 Tiki Barber	1.50	4.00
❑ 68 Chad Pennington	1.50	4.00
❑ 69 Curtis Martin	1.50	4.00
❑ 70 Laveranues Coles	1.25	3.00
❑ 71 Kerry Collins	1.25	3.00
❑ 72 LaMont Jordan	1.25	3.00
❑ 73 Randy Moss	1.50	4.00
❑ 74 Brian Westbrook	1.50	4.00
❑ 75 Donovan McNabb	1.50	4.00
❑ 76 Terrell Owens	1.50	4.00
❑ 77 Ben Roethlisberger	4.00	10.00
❑ 78 Duce Staley	1.25	3.00
❑ 79 Hines Ward	1.50	4.00
❑ 80 Jerome Bettis	1.50	4.00
❑ 81 Antonio Gates	1.50	4.00
❑ 82 Drew Brees	1.50	4.00
❑ 83 LaDainian Tomlinson	2.00	5.00
❑ 84 Brandon Lloyd	1.00	2.50
❑ 85 Kevan Barlow	1.00	2.50
❑ 86 Darrell Jackson	1.25	3.00
❑ 87 Matt Hasselbeck	1.25	3.00
❑ 88 Shaun Alexander	1.50	4.00
❑ 89 Marc Bulger	1.25	3.00
❑ 90 Steven Jackson	2.00	5.00
❑ 91 Torry Holt	1.25	3.00
❑ 92 Brian Griese	1.25	3.00
❑ 93 Michael Clayton	1.25	3.00
❑ 94 Chris Brown	1.25	3.00
❑ 95 Drew Bennett	1.25	3.00
❑ 96 Steve McNair	1.50	4.00
❑ 97 Clinton Portis	1.50	4.00
❑ 98 LaVar Arrington	1.50	4.00
❑ 99 Patrick Ramsey	1.25	3.00
❑ 100 Santana Moss	1.25	3.00
❑ 101 Barry Sanders	3.00	8.00
❑ 102 Bart Starr	3.00	8.00
❑ 103 Bo Jackson	2.50	6.00
❑ 104 Brian Piccolo	2.50	6.00
❑ 105 Bob Griese	2.00	5.00
❑ 106 Dan Fouts	2.00	5.00
❑ 107 Dan Marino	5.00	12.00
❑ 108 Deacon Jones	1.50	4.00
❑ 109 Doak Walker	2.00	5.00
❑ 110 Don Maynard	1.50	4.00
❑ 111 Don Meredith	2.00	5.00
❑ 112 Don Shula	1.50	4.00
❑ 113 Earl Campbell	2.00	5.00
❑ 114 Eric Dickerson	1.50	4.00
❑ 115 Fran Tarkenton	2.00	5.00
❑ 116 Franco Harris	2.00	5.00
❑ 117 Gale Sayers	2.50	6.00
❑ 118 Jack Lambert	2.00	5.00
❑ 119 James Lofton	1.25	3.00
❑ 120 Jim Brown	2.50	6.00
❑ 121 Jim Kelly	2.50	6.00
❑ 122 Jim Thorpe	2.50	6.00
❑ 123 Joe Greene	2.00	5.00
❑ 124 Joe Montana	5.00	12.00
❑ 125 Joe Namath	3.00	8.00
❑ 126 John Elway	4.00	10.00
❑ 127 John Riggins	2.00	5.00
❑ 128 Johnny Unitas	3.00	8.00
❑ 129 Lawrence Taylor	2.00	5.00
❑ 130 Leroy Kelly	1.50	4.00
❑ 131 Marcus Allen	2.00	5.00
❑ 132 Michael Irvin	2.00	5.00
❑ 133 Mike Ditka	2.00	5.00
❑ 134 Mike Singletary	2.00	5.00
❑ 135 Ozzie Newsome	1.50	4.00
❑ 136 Paul Hornung	2.00	5.00
❑ 137 Paul Warfield	1.50	4.00
❑ 138 Randall Cunningham	1.50	4.00
❑ 139 Red Grange	2.50	6.00
❑ 140 Roger Staubach	3.00	8.00
❑ 141 Sammy Baugh	2.00	5.00
❑ 142 Sonny Jurgensen	1.50	4.00
❑ 143 Steve Largent	2.00	5.00
❑ 144 Steve Young	2.50	6.00
❑ 145 Terrell Davis	2.00	5.00
❑ 146 Terry Bradshaw	3.00	8.00
❑ 147 Tony Dorsett	1.50	4.00
❑ 148 Troy Aikman	2.50	6.00
❑ 149 Walter Payton	5.00	12.00
❑ 150 Warren Moon	2.00	5.00
❑ 151 Aaron Rodgers RC	10.00	25.00
❑ 152 Adrian McPherson RC	2.50	6.00
❑ 153 Airese Currie RC	2.50	6.00
❑ 154 Alvin Pearman RC	2.00	5.00
❑ 155 Anthony Davis RC	2.50	6.00
❑ 156 Brandon Jacobs RC	4.00	10.00
❑ 157 Brandon Jones RC	3.00	8.00
❑ 158 Cedric Benson RC	3.00	8.00
❑ 159 Cedric Houston RC	3.00	8.00
❑ 160 Chad Owens RC	3.00	8.00
❑ 161 Chris Henry RC	3.00	8.00
❑ 162 Nate Washington RC	3.00	8.00
❑ 163 Craig Bragg RC	2.00	5.00
❑ 164 Craphonso Thorpe RC	2.50	6.00
❑ 165 Damien Nash RC	2.50	6.00
❑ 166 Dan Orlovsky RC	3.00	8.00
❑ 167 Dante Ridgeway RC	2.00	5.00
❑ 168 Darren Sproles RC	4.00	10.00
❑ 169 David Greene RC	2.50	6.00
❑ 170 David Pollack RC	2.50	6.00
❑ 171 Deandra Cobb RC	2.50	6.00
❑ 172 DeMarcus Ware RC	5.00	12.00
❑ 173 Derek Anderson RC	3.00	8.00
❑ 174 Derrick Johnson RC	3.00	8.00
❑ 175 Erasmus James RC	2.50	6.00
❑ 176 Fabian Washington RC	3.00	8.00
❑ 177 Fred Gibson RC	2.50	6.00
❑ 178 Harry Williams RC	2.50	6.00
❑ 179 Heath Miller RC	6.00	15.00
❑ 180 J.R. Russell RC	2.00	5.00
❑ 181 James Kilian RC	2.00	5.00
❑ 182 Jerome Mathis RC	3.00	8.00
❑ 183 Larry Brackins RC	2.00	5.00
❑ 184 LeRon McCoy RC	2.00	5.00
❑ 185 Lionel Gates RC	2.00	5.00
❑ 186 Marcus Spears RC	3.00	8.00
❑ 187 Marion Barber RC	10.00	25.00
❑ 188 Marlin Jackson RC	2.50	6.00
❑ 189 Matt Cassel RC	6.00	15.00
❑ 190 Mike Williams	2.50	6.00
❑ 191 Noah Herron RC	3.00	8.00
❑ 192 Paris Warren RC	2.50	6.00
❑ 193 Rasheed Marshall RC	2.50	6.00
❑ 194 Roscoe Crosby RC	2.00	5.00
❑ 195 Roydell Williams RC	2.50	6.00
❑ 196 Ryan Fitzpatrick RC	3.00	8.00
❑ 197 Shawne Merriman RC	3.00	8.00
❑ 198 Tab Perry RC	3.00	8.00
❑ 199 Thomas Davis RC	2.50	6.00
❑ 200 Travis Johnson RC	2.00	5.00
❑ 201 Adam Jones JSY AU RC	8.00	20.00
❑ 202 Alex Smith QB JSY AU RC	10.00	25.00
❑ 203 Andrew Walter JSY AU RC	8.00	20.00
❑ 204 Antrel Rolle JSY AU RC	10.00	25.00
❑ 205 Braylon Edwards JSY AU RC	25.00	60.00
❑ 206 Cadillac Williams JSY AU RC	15.00	40.00
❑ 207 Carlos Rogers JSY AU RC	10.00	25.00
❑ 208 Charlie Frye JSY AU RC	10.00	25.00
❑ 209 Ciatrick Fason JSY AU RC	8.00	20.00
❑ 210 Courtney Roby JSY AU RC	8.00	20.00
❑ 211 Eric Shelton JSY AU RC	8.00	20.00
❑ 212 Frank Gore JSY AU RC	20.00	50.00
❑ 213 J.J. Arrington JSY AU RC	10.00	25.00
❑ 214 Kyle Orton JSY AU RC	15.00	30.00
❑ 215 Jason Campbell JSY AU RC	15.00	40.00
❑ 216 Mark Bradley JSY AU RC	8.00	20.00
❑ 217 Mark Clayton JSY AU RC	10.00	25.00
❑ 218 Matt Jones JSY AU RC	10.00	25.00
❑ 219 Maurice Clarett JSY AU	8.00	20.00
❑ 220 Reggie Brown JSY AU RC	8.00	20.00
❑ 221 Ronnie Brown JSY AU RC	30.00	80.00
❑ 222 Roddy White JSY AU RC	20.00	35.00
❑ 223 Ryan Moats JSY AU RC	8.00	20.00
❑ 224 Roscoe Parrish JSY AU RC	8.00	20.00
❑ 225 Stefan LeFors JSY AU RC	8.00	20.00
❑ 226 Terrence Murphy JSY AU RC	6.00	15.00
❑ 227 Troy Williamson JSY AU RC	10.00	25.00
❑ 228 Vernand Morency JSY AU RC	8.00	20.00
❑ 229 Vincent Jackson JSY AU RC	15.00	30.00

2006 Leaf Limited

Card	Low	High
❑ 1 Alex Smith QB	1.25	3.00
❑ 2 Antonio Bryant	1.25	3.00
❑ 3 Frank Gore	1.50	4.00
❑ 4 Rex Grossman	1.50	4.00
❑ 5 Thomas Jones	1.25	3.00
❑ 6 Cedric Benson	1.25	3.00
❑ 7 Carson Palmer	1.50	4.00
❑ 8 Chad Johnson	1.25	3.00
❑ 9 Rudi Johnson	1.25	3.00
❑ 10 T.J. Houshmandzadeh	1.25	3.00
❑ 11 J.P. Losman	1.25	3.00
❑ 12 Lee Evans	1.25	3.00
❑ 13 Willis McGahee	1.50	4.00
❑ 14 Jake Plummer	1.25	3.00
❑ 15 Javon Walker	1.25	3.00
❑ 16 Rod Smith	1.25	3.00
❑ 17 Tatum Bell	1.00	2.50
❑ 18 Braylon Edwards	1.50	4.00
❑ 19 Charlie Frye	1.25	3.00
❑ 20 Reuben Droughns	1.25	3.00
❑ 21 Cadillac Williams	1.50	4.00
❑ 22 Chris Simms	1.25	3.00
❑ 23 Joey Galloway	1.25	3.00
❑ 24 Anquan Boldin	1.25	3.00
❑ 25 Edgerrin James	1.25	3.00
❑ 26 Kurt Warner	1.50	4.00
❑ 27 Larry Fitzgerald	1.50	4.00
❑ 28 Antonio Gates	1.50	4.00
❑ 29 Keenan McCardell	1.25	3.00
❑ 30 LaDainian Tomlinson	2.00	5.00
❑ 31 Philip Rivers	1.50	4.00
❑ 32 Eddie Kennison	1.00	2.50
❑ 33 Larry Johnson	1.25	3.00
❑ 34 Priest Holmes	1.25	3.00
❑ 35 Trent Green	1.25	3.00
❑ 36 Tony Gonzalez	1.25	3.00
❑ 37 Dallas Clark	1.25	3.00
❑ 38 Marvin Harrison	1.50	4.00
❑ 39 Peyton Manning	2.50	6.00
❑ 40 Reggie Wayne	1.25	3.00
❑ 41 Drew Bledsoe	1.50	4.00
❑ 42 Julius Jones	1.25	3.00
❑ 43 Roy Williams S	1.25	3.00
❑ 44 Terrell Owens	1.50	4.00
❑ 45 Terry Glenn	1.25	3.00
❑ 46 Chris Chambers	1.25	3.00
❑ 47 Daunte Culpepper	1.50	4.00
❑ 48 Marty Booker	1.00	2.50
❑ 49 Ronnie Brown	1.50	4.00
❑ 50 Brian Westbrook	1.25	3.00
❑ 51 Donovan McNabb	1.50	4.00
❑ 52 Jevon Kearse	1.25	3.00
❑ 53 Reggie Brown	1.00	2.50
❑ 54 Alge Crumpler	1.25	3.00
❑ 55 Michael Vick	1.50	4.00
❑ 56 Warrick Dunn	1.25	3.00
❑ 57 Eli Manning	2.00	5.00
❑ 58 Jeremy Shockey	1.50	4.00
❑ 59 Plaxico Burress	1.25	3.00
❑ 60 Tiki Barber	1.50	4.00
❑ 61 Byron Leftwich	1.25	3.00
❑ 62 Fred Taylor	1.25	3.00
❑ 63 Jimmy Smith	1.25	3.00
❑ 64 Matt Jones	1.25	3.00
❑ 65 Josh McCown	1.25	3.00
❑ 66 Roy Williams WR	1.50	4.00
❑ 67 Kevin Jones	1.25	3.00
❑ 68 Aaron Rodgers	1.50	4.00
❑ 69 Brett Favre	3.00	8.00
❑ 70 Robert Ferguson	1.00	2.50
❑ 71 Samkon Gado	1.50	4.00
❑ 72 Ahman Green	1.25	3.00
❑ 73 DeShaun Foster	1.25	3.00
❑ 74 Jake Delhomme	1.25	3.00

❑ 75 Keary Colbert 1.25 3.00
❑ 76 Steve Smith 1.50 4.00
❑ 77 Corey Dillon 1.25 3.00
❑ 78 Deion Branch 1.25 3.00
❑ 79 Tedy Bruschi 1.50 4.00
❑ 80 Tom Brady 2.50 6.00
❑ 81 Jerry Porter 1.25 3.00
❑ 82 Randy Moss 1.50 4.00
❑ 83 LaMont Jordan 1.25 3.00
❑ 84 Isaac Bruce 1.25 3.00
❑ 85 Marc Bulger 1.25 3.00
❑ 86 Steven Jackson 1.50 4.00
❑ 87 Torry Holt 1.25 3.00
❑ 88 Derrick Mason 1.25 3.00
❑ 89 Mark Clayton 1.25 3.00
❑ 90 Steve McNair 1.25 3.00
❑ 91 Jamal Lewis 1.25 3.00
❑ 92 Antwaan Randle El 1.25 3.00
❑ 93 Clinton Portis 1.50 4.00
❑ 94 Santana Moss 1.25 3.00
❑ 95 Chad Pennington 1.25 3.00
❑ 96 Laveranues Coles 1.25 3.00
❑ 97 Curtis Martin 1.50 4.00
❑ 98 Mewelde Moore 1.00 2.50
❑ 99 Troy Williamson 1.25 3.00
❑ 100 Brad Johnson 1.25 3.00
❑ 101 Darrell Jackson 1.25 3.00
❑ 102 Matt Hasselbeck 1.25 3.00
❑ 103 Nate Burleson 1.25 3.00
❑ 104 Shaun Alexander 1.25 3.00
❑ 105 Ben Roethlisberger 2.50 6.00
❑ 106 Hines Ward 1.50 4.00
❑ 107 Willie Parker 2.00 5.00
❑ 108 Donte Stallworth 1.25 3.00
❑ 109 Drew Brees 1.50 4.00
❑ 110 Deuce McAllister 1.25 3.00
❑ 111 Andre Johnson 1.25 3.00
❑ 112 David Carr 1.00 2.50
❑ 113 Domanick Davis 1.25 3.00
❑ 114 Eric Moulds 1.25 3.00
❑ 115 David Givens 1.25 3.00
❑ 116 Drew Bennett 1.25 3.00
❑ 117 Chris Brown 1.25 3.00
❑ 118 Bob Griese 2.00 5.00
❑ 119 Daryle Lamonica 1.25 3.00
❑ 120 Dave Casper 1.25 3.00
❑ 121 Don Meredith 2.00 5.00
❑ 122 Herschel Walker 1.50 4.00
❑ 123 Jack Lambert 2.00 5.00
❑ 124 Jackie Smith 1.25 3.00
❑ 125 Jim Otto 1.25 3.00
❑ 126 John Riggins 2.00 5.00
❑ 127 John Stallworth 1.50 4.00
❑ 128 Lawrence Taylor 2.00 5.00
❑ 129 Lester Hayes 1.25 3.00
❑ 130 L.C. Greenwood 1.50 4.00
❑ 131 Paul Warfield 1.50 4.00
❑ 132 Barry Sanders 3.00 8.00
❑ 133 Bart Starr 3.00 8.00
❑ 134 Billy Sims 1.50 4.00
❑ 135 Bulldog Turner 1.50 4.00
❑ 136 Deion Sanders 2.50 6.00
❑ 137 Dutch Clark 1.50 4.00
❑ 138 Forrest Gregg 1.25 3.00
❑ 139 Gale Sayers 2.50 6.00
❑ 140 Jim Brown 2.50 6.00
❑ 141 Jim Thorpe 2.50 6.00
❑ 142 Joe Montana 4.00 10.00
❑ 143 John Elway 3.00 8.00
❑ 144 Johnny Unitas 3.00 8.00
❑ 145 Lance Alworth 1.50 4.00
❑ 146 Raymond Berry 1.50 4.00
❑ 147 Doak Walker 2.00 5.00
❑ 148 Red Grange 2.50 6.00
❑ 149 Walter Payton 4.00 10.00
❑ 150 Yale Lary 1.25 3.00
❑ 151 Adam Jennings RC 2.50 6.00
❑ 152 Alan Zemaitis RC 3.00 8.00
❑ 153 Patrick Cobbs RC 2.50 6.00
❑ 154 Anthony Schlegel RC 2.50 6.00
❑ 155 Anthony Smith RC 3.00 8.00
❑ 156 Antonio Cromartie RC 3.00 8.00
❑ 157 Ashton Youboty RC 2.50 6.00
❑ 158 Bennie Brazell RC 2.50 6.00
❑ 159 Bernard Pollard RC 2.50 6.00
❑ 160 Brodrick Bunkley RC 2.50 6.00
❑ 161 Calvin Lowry RC 3.00 8.00
❑ 162 Cedric Griffin RC 2.50 6.00
❑ 163 Cedric Humes RC 2.50 6.00
❑ 164 Charles Davis RC 2.50 6.00
❑ 165 Chris Gocong RC 2.50 6.00
❑ 166 Claude Wroten RC 2.00 5.00
❑ 167 Clint Ingram RC 3.00 8.00
❑ 168 D.J. Shockley RC 2.50 6.00
❑ 169 Danieal Manning RC 3.00 8.00
❑ 170 Daniel Bullocks RC 3.00 8.00
❑ 171 Darnell Bing RC 2.50 6.00
❑ 172 Chris Hannon RC 2.50 6.00
❑ 173 Darryl Tapp RC 2.50 6.00
❑ 174 David Anderson RC 2.50 6.00
❑ 175 David Kirtman RC 2.50 6.00
❑ 176 David Pittman RC 2.50 6.00
❑ 177 Davin Joseph RC 2.50 6.00
❑ 178 Sam Hurd RC 5.00 12.00
❑ 179 Delanie Walker RC 2.50 6.00
❑ 180 DeMeco Ryans RC 4.00 10.00
❑ 181 Derrick Ross RC 2.50 6.00
❑ 182 Devin Hester RC 6.00 15.00
❑ 183 Domenik Hixon RC 3.00 8.00
❑ 184 Dominique Byrd RC 2.50 6.00
❑ 185 Donte Whitner RC 3.00 8.00
❑ 186 D'Qwell Jackson RC 2.50 6.00
❑ 187 Dusty Dvoracek RC 3.00 8.00
❑ 188 Eric Smith RC 2.50 6.00
❑ 189 Fred Evans RC 2.50 6.00
❑ 190 Ernie Sims RC 2.50 6.00
❑ 191 Ethan Kilmer RC 3.00 8.00
❑ 192 Freddie Keiaho RC 2.50 6.00
❑ 193 Frostee Rucker RC 2.50 6.00
❑ 194 Gabe Watson RC 2.00 5.00
❑ 195 Garrett Mills RC 2.50 6.00
❑ 196 Dawan Landry RC 3.00 8.00
❑ 197 Gerris Wilkinson RC 2.00 5.00
❑ 198 Jarrad Page RC 3.00 8.00
❑ 199 Haloti Ngata RC 3.00 8.00
❑ 200 Hank Baskett RC 3.00 8.00
❑ 201 Jai Lewis RC 2.50 6.00
❑ 202 Jamar Williams RC 2.50 6.00
❑ 203 James Anderson RC 2.00 5.00
❑ 204 Jason Allen RC 2.50 6.00
❑ 205 Jason Hatcher RC 2.50 6.00
❑ 206 Chris Barclay RC 2.50 6.00
❑ 207 J.D. Runnels RC 2.50 6.00
❑ 208 Jeff King RC 2.50 6.00
❑ 209 Jeffrey Webb RC 2.50 6.00
❑ 210 Jerome Harrison RC 3.00 8.00
❑ 211 Jimmy Williams RC 3.00 8.00
❑ 212 John David Washington RC 2.50 6.00
❑ 213 Jon Alston RC 2.00 5.00
❑ 214 Johnathan Joseph RC 2.50 6.00
❑ 215 Kamerion Wimbley RC 3.00 8.00
❑ 216 Kelly Jennings RC 3.00 8.00
❑ 217 Charles Sharon RC 2.50 6.00
❑ 218 Ko Simpson RC 2.50 6.00
❑ 219 Lawrence Vickers RC 2.50 6.00
❑ 220 Leon Williams RC 2.50 6.00
❑ 221 Leonard Pope RC 3.00 8.00
❑ 222 Marques Colston RC 10.00 25.00
❑ 223 Martin Nance RC 2.50 6.00
❑ 224 Mathias Kiwanuka RC 4.00 10.00
❑ 225 Mike Bell RC 3.00 8.00
❑ 226 Mike Hass RC 3.00 8.00
❑ 227 Miles Austin RC 8.00 20.00
❑ 228 Nate Salley RC 2.50 6.00
❑ 229 Nick Mangold RC 2.50 6.00
❑ 230 Owen Daniels RC 3.00 8.00
❑ 231 Shaun Bodiford RC 2.50 6.00
❑ 232 Quinn Sypniewski RC 2.50 6.00
❑ 233 Quinton Ganther RC 2.00 5.00
❑ 234 Richard Marshall RC 2.50 6.00
❑ 235 Rocky McIntosh RC 3.00 8.00
❑ 236 Roman Harper RC 2.50 6.00
❑ 237 Stephen Tulloch RC 2.50 6.00
❑ 238 Brett Basanez RC 3.00 8.00
❑ 239 Tamba Hali RC 3.00 8.00
❑ 240 Brett Elliott RC 3.00 8.00
❑ 241 Thomas Howard RC 2.50 6.00
❑ 242 Tim Jennings RC 2.50 6.00
❑ 243 Jason Carter RC 2.50 6.00
❑ 244 Todd Watkins RC 2.00 5.00
❑ 245 Tony Scheffler RC 3.00 8.00
❑ 246 Tye Hill RC 2.50 6.00
❑ 247 Victor Adeyanju RC 2.50 6.00
❑ 248 Wendell Mathis RC 2.50 6.00
❑ 249 Will Blackmon RC 3.00 8.00
❑ 250 Willie Reid RC 2.50 6.00
❑ 251 Mario Williams JSY AU RC 10.00 25.00
❑ 252 Reggie Bush JSY AU RC 60.00 120.00
❑ 253 Vince Young JSY AU RC 40.00 80.00
❑ 254 A.J. Hawk JSY AU RC 20.00 50.00
❑ 255 Vernon Davis JSY AU RC 8.00 20.00
❑ 256 Michael Huff JSY AU RC 8.00 20.00
❑ 257 Matt Leinart JSY AU RC 30.00 60.00
❑ 258 Jay Cutler AU RC 60.00 120.00
❑ 259 L.Maroney JSY AU RC 20.00 50.00
❑ 260 Santonio Holmes JSY AU RC 25.00 50.00
❑ 261 DeA.Williams JSY AU RC 30.00 60.00
❑ 262 Marcedes Lewis JSY AU RC 8.00 20.00
❑ 263 Joseph Addai AU RC 25.00 60.00
❑ 264 Chad Jackson JSY AU RC 6.00 15.00
❑ 265 Sinorice Moss JSY AU RC 8.00 20.00
❑ 266 LenDale White JSY AU RC 10.00 25.00
❑ 267 Kellen Clemens JSY AU RC 8.00 20.00
❑ 268 Greg Jennings AU RC 20.00 40.00
❑ 269 Joe Klopfenstein JSY AU RC 6.00 15.00
❑ 270 Maurice Drew JSY AU RC 30.00 60.00
❑ 271 Tarvaris Jackson JSY AU RC 8.00 20.00
❑ 272 Brian Calhoun JSY AU RC 6.00 15.00
❑ 273 Travis Wilson JSY AU RC 5.00 12.00
❑ 274 Jerious Norwood JSY AU RC 12.00 30.00
❑ 275 C.Whitehurst JSY AU RC 8.00 20.00
❑ 276 Derek Hagan JSY AU RC 6.00 15.00
❑ 277 Brandon Williams JSY AU RC 6.00 15.00
❑ 278 Brodie Croyle AU RC 8.00 20.00
❑ 279 Maurice Stovall JSY AU RC 6.00 15.00
❑ 280 Michael Robinson JSY AU RC 6.00 15.00
❑ 281 Jason Avant JSY AU RC 8.00 20.00
❑ 282 Dem.Williams JSY AU RC 6.00 15.00
❑ 283 Leon Washington JSY AU RC 15.00 30.00
❑ 284 Brandon Marshall JSY AU RC 12.50 25.00
❑ 285 Omar Jacobs JSY AU RC 5.00 12.00
❑ 286 Anthony Fasano AU RC 12.50 25.00
❑ 287 Ingle Martin AU RC 6.00 15.00
❑ 288 Reggie McNeal AU RC 6.00 15.00
❑ 289 Brad Smith AU RC 8.00 20.00
❑ 290 Jeremy Bloom AU RC 6.00 15.00
❑ 291 Bruce Gradkowski AU RC 8.00 20.00
❑ 292 P.J. Daniels AU RC 5.00 12.00
❑ 293 Cory Rodgers AU RC 8.00 20.00
❑ 294 Skyler Green AU RC 5.00 12.00
❑ 295 Bobby Carpenter AU RC 6.00 15.00
❑ 296 Arom/Obom/Mix AU/100 12.50 25.00
❑ 297 Hodge/Greenway AU/100 20.00 40.00
❑ 298 M.Will/McCar/Lwsn AU/100 20.00 50.00
❑ 299 Fasano/Stovall AU/50 20.00 40.00
❑ 300 Hawk/Carpenter AU/50 30.00 80.00
❑ 301 Leinart/Bush/Wht AU/25 150.00 300.00
❑ 302 Young/Thomas AU/50 30.00 80.00
❑ 303 Olson/Drew/Lewis AU/100 35.00 60.00
❑ 304 Hagans/Lundy/Ferg AU/100 20.00 40.00
❑ 305 Calhn/Willms/Orr AU/100 20.00 40.00
❑ TC Steve Smith TC/500 2.50 6.00
❑ TCA Steve Smith TC AU/50 20.00 40.00

2007 Leaf Limited

❑ 1 Anquan Boldin 1.25 3.00
❑ 2 Edgerrin James 1.25 3.00
❑ 3 Larry Fitzgerald 1.50 4.00
❑ 4 Matt Leinart 1.50 4.00
❑ 5 Alge Crumpler 1.25 3.00
❑ 6 Warrick Dunn 1.25 3.00
❑ 7 Jerious Norwood 1.25 3.00
❑ 8 Willis McGahee 1.25 3.00
❑ 9 Steve McNair 1.25 3.00
❑ 10 Mark Clayton 1.25 3.00
❑ 11 Anthony Thomas 1.00 2.50
❑ 12 J.P. Losman 1.00 2.50
❑ 13 Lee Evans 1.25 3.00
❑ 14 Jake Delhomme 1.25 3.00
❑ 15 Steve Smith 1.25 3.00
❑ 16 DeAngelo Williams 1.50 4.00
❑ 17 Rex Grossman 1.25 3.00
❑ 18 Cedric Benson 1.25 3.00
❑ 19 Bernard Berrian 1.00 2.50

❑ 20 Carson Palmer	1.50	4.00
❑ 21 Chad Johnson	1.25	3.00
❑ 22 Rudi Johnson	1.25	3.00
❑ 23 T.J. Houshmandzadeh	1.25	3.00
❑ 24 Kellen Winslow	1.25	3.00
❑ 25 Braylon Edwards	1.25	3.00
❑ 26 Jamal Lewis	1.25	3.00
❑ 27 Julius Jones	1.25	3.00
❑ 28 Terrell Owens	1.50	4.00
❑ 29 Tony Romo	2.50	6.00
❑ 30 Jay Cutler	1.50	4.00
❑ 31 Javon Walker	1.25	3.00
❑ 32 Travis Henry	1.25	3.00
❑ 33 Tatum Bell	1.00	2.50
❑ 34 Roy Williams WR	1.25	3.00
❑ 35 Jon Kitna	1.00	2.50
❑ 36 Brett Favre	3.00	8.00
❑ 37 Donald Driver	1.50	4.00
❑ 38 Greg Jennings	1.25	3.00
❑ 39 Matt Schaub	1.25	3.00
❑ 40 Andre Johnson	1.25	3.00
❑ 41 Ahman Green	1.25	3.00
❑ 42 Peyton Manning	2.50	6.00
❑ 43 Marvin Harrison	1.50	4.00
❑ 44 Reggie Wayne	1.25	3.00
❑ 45 Joseph Addai	1.50	4.00
❑ 46 David Garrard	1.25	3.00
❑ 47 Fred Taylor	1.25	3.00
❑ 48 Maurice Jones-Drew	1.50	4.00
❑ 49 Brodie Croyle	1.25	3.00
❑ 50 Larry Johnson	1.25	3.00
❑ 51 Tony Gonzalez	1.25	3.00
❑ 52 Trent Green	1.25	3.00
❑ 53 Ronnie Brown	1.25	3.00
❑ 54 Chris Chambers	1.25	3.00
❑ 55 Tarvaris Jackson	1.25	3.00
❑ 56 Troy Williamson	1.00	2.50
❑ 57 Chester Taylor	1.00	2.50
❑ 58 Tom Brady	3.00	8.00
❑ 59 Randy Moss	1.50	4.00
❑ 60 Laurence Maroney	1.50	4.00
❑ 61 Donte Stallworth	1.25	3.00
❑ 62 Drew Brees	1.50	4.00
❑ 63 Deuce McAllister	1.25	3.00
❑ 64 Reggie Bush	2.00	5.00
❑ 65 Marques Colston	1.50	4.00
❑ 66 Eli Manning	1.50	4.00
❑ 67 Jeremy Shockey	1.25	3.00
❑ 68 Brandon Jacobs	1.25	3.00
❑ 69 Chad Pennington	1.25	3.00
❑ 70 Thomas Jones	1.25	3.00
❑ 71 Laveranues Coles	1.25	3.00
❑ 72 Jerry Porter	1.25	3.00
❑ 73 LaMont Jordan	1.25	3.00
❑ 74 Donovan McNabb	1.50	4.00
❑ 75 Brian Westbrook	1.25	3.00
❑ 76 Reggie Brown	1.00	2.50
❑ 77 Ben Roethlisberger	2.50	6.00
❑ 78 Hines Ward	1.50	4.00
❑ 79 Willie Parker	1.25	3.00
❑ 80 Philip Rivers	1.50	4.00
❑ 81 Antonio Gates	1.25	3.00
❑ 82 LaDainian Tomlinson	2.00	5.00
❑ 83 Alex Smith QB	1.50	4.00
❑ 84 Darrell Jackson	1.25	3.00
❑ 85 Frank Gore	1.50	4.00
❑ 86 Matt Hasselbeck	1.25	3.00
❑ 87 Shaun Alexander	1.25	3.00
❑ 88 Deion Branch	1.25	3.00
❑ 89 Marc Bulger	1.25	3.00
❑ 90 Steven Jackson	1.50	4.00
❑ 91 Torry Holt	1.25	3.00
❑ 92 Jeff Garcia	1.25	3.00
❑ 93 Cadillac Williams	1.25	3.00
❑ 94 Joey Galloway	1.25	3.00
❑ 95 Vince Young	1.50	4.00
❑ 96 Brandon Jones	1.00	2.50
❑ 97 LenDale White	1.25	3.00
❑ 98 Jason Campbell	1.25	3.00
❑ 99 Clinton Portis	1.25	3.00
❑ 100 Santana Moss	1.25	3.00
❑ 101 Alan Page	2.00	5.00
❑ 102 Barry Sanders	5.00	12.00
❑ 103 Bart Starr	5.00	12.00
❑ 104 Bill Dudley	2.50	6.00
❑ 105 Billy Howton	2.00	5.00
❑ 106 Bob Griese	3.00	8.00
❑ 107 Bobby Layne	3.00	8.00
❑ 108 Boyd Dowler	2.00	5.00
❑ 109 Charley Taylor	2.50	6.00
❑ 110 Charley Trippi	2.00	5.00
❑ 111 Charlie Joiner	2.50	6.00
❑ 112 Chuck Bednarik	2.50	6.00
❑ 113 Cris Collinsworth	2.50	6.00
❑ 114 Dan Fouts	3.00	8.00
❑ 115 Dan Hampton	2.50	6.00
❑ 116 Dan Marino	6.00	15.00
❑ 117 Dante Lavelli	2.00	5.00
❑ 118 Darrell Green	2.50	6.00
❑ 119 Daryle Lamonica	2.00	5.00
❑ 120 Deacon Jones	2.50	6.00
❑ 121 Dick Butkus	4.00	10.00
❑ 122 Doak Walker	2.50	6.00
❑ 123 Don Maynard	2.50	6.00
❑ 124 Don Perkins	2.00	5.00
❑ 125 Dutch Clark	2.50	6.00
❑ 126 Earl Campbell	3.00	8.00
❑ 127 Forrest Gregg	2.00	5.00
❑ 128 Fran Tarkenton	4.00	10.00
❑ 129 Franco Harris	3.00	8.00
❑ 130 Fred Biletnikoff	3.00	8.00
❑ 131 Gale Sayers	4.00	10.00
❑ 132 Gene Upshaw	2.00	5.00
❑ 133 George Blanda	2.50	6.00
❑ 134 Harlon Hill	2.00	5.00
❑ 135 Jack Lambert	3.00	8.00
❑ 136 Jack Youngblood	2.50	6.00
❑ 137 James Lofton	2.00	5.00
❑ 138 Jan Stenerud	2.00	5.00
❑ 139 Jethro Pugh	2.00	5.00
❑ 140 Jim Brown	4.00	10.00
❑ 141 Jim Kelly	4.00	10.00
❑ 142 Jim McMahon	4.00	10.00
❑ 143 Jim Otto	2.00	5.00
❑ 144 Jim Thorpe	4.00	10.00
❑ 145 Jimmy Orr	2.00	5.00
❑ 146 Joe Greene	3.00	8.00
❑ 147 Joe Montana	6.00	15.00
❑ 148 Joe Namath	4.00	10.00
❑ 149 Joe Theismann	3.00	8.00
❑ 150 John Elway	5.00	12.00
❑ 151 John Mackey	2.50	6.00
❑ 152 John Riggins	2.50	6.00
❑ 153 John Stallworth	2.50	6.00
❑ 154 Johnny Morris	2.00	5.00
❑ 155 Johnny Unitas	5.00	12.00
❑ 156 Kellen Winslow Sr.	2.50	6.00
❑ 157 Ken Stabler	4.00	10.00
❑ 158 Lance Alworth	2.50	6.00
❑ 159 Larry Csonka	3.00	8.00
❑ 160 Larry Little	2.00	5.00
❑ 161 Lee Roy Selmon	2.50	6.00
❑ 162 Len Dawson	3.00	8.00
❑ 163 Lou Groza	2.50	6.00
❑ 164 Lydell Mitchell	2.00	5.00
❑ 165 Marcus Allen	3.00	8.00
❑ 166 Mark Duper	2.00	5.00
❑ 167 Merlin Olsen	2.50	6.00
❑ 168 Mike Singletary	3.00	8.00
❑ 169 Ollie Matson	2.50	6.00
❑ 170 Otto Graham	3.00	8.00
❑ 171 Ozzie Newsome	2.50	6.00
❑ 172 Paul Hornung	3.00	8.00
❑ 173 Paul Warfield	2.50	6.00
❑ 174 Phil Simms	2.50	6.00
❑ 175 Randall Cunningham	2.50	6.00
❑ 176 Ray Nitschke	3.00	8.00
❑ 177 Raymond Berry	2.50	6.00
❑ 178 Red Grange	4.00	10.00
❑ 179 Rick Casares	2.00	5.00
❑ 180 Ron Mix	2.00	5.00
❑ 181 Roger Craig	2.50	6.00
❑ 182 Roger Staubach	5.00	12.00
❑ 183 Rosey Brown	2.00	5.00
❑ 184 Rosey Grier	2.00	5.00
❑ 185 Ronnie Lott	2.50	6.00
❑ 186 Sam Huff	2.50	6.00
❑ 187 Sammy Baugh	3.00	8.00
❑ 188 Sid Luckman	3.00	8.00
❑ 189 Sonny Jurgensen	2.50	6.00
❑ 190 Sterling Sharpe	2.50	6.00
❑ 191 Steve Largent	3.00	8.00
❑ 192 Steve Young	4.00	10.00
❑ 193 Ted Hendricks	2.50	6.00
❑ 194 Thurman Thomas	2.50	6.00
❑ 195 Tim Brown	3.00	8.00
❑ 196 Tiki Barber	3.00	8.00
❑ 197 Troy Aikman	4.00	10.00
❑ 198 Walter Payton	6.00	15.00
❑ 199 Willie Brown	2.50	6.00
❑ 200 Elroy Hirsch	2.50	6.00
❑ 201 Brandon McDonald RC	2.00	5.00
❑ 202 David Irons RC	2.00	5.00
❑ 203 Fred Bennett RC	2.00	5.00
❑ 204 Nick Graham RC	2.50	6.00
❑ 205 Rashad Barksdale RC	2.00	5.00
❑ 206 Tanard Jackson RC	2.00	5.00
❑ 207 Tarell Brown RC	2.00	5.00
❑ 208 Usama Young RC	2.50	6.00
❑ 209 William Gay RC	2.50	6.00
❑ 210 Jarvis Moss RC	3.00	8.00
❑ 211 Le'Ron McClain RC	3.00	8.00
❑ 212 Kevin Payne RC	2.00	5.00
❑ 213 Adam Hayward RC	2.50	6.00
❑ 214 Brandon Siler RC	2.50	6.00
❑ 215 Chad Nkang RC	2.00	5.00
❑ 216 Clint Session RC	2.50	6.00
❑ 217 Desmond Bishop RC	2.50	6.00
❑ 218 Edmond Miles RC	2.50	6.00
❑ 219 H.B. Blades RC	2.50	6.00
❑ 220 Justin Durant RC	2.50	6.00
❑ 221 Justin Rogers RC	3.00	8.00
❑ 222 Nate Harris RC	2.50	6.00
❑ 223 Quincy Black RC	3.00	8.00
❑ 224 Quinton Culberson RC	2.00	5.00
❑ 225 Ramon Guzman RC	2.00	5.00
❑ 226 Stephen Nicholas RC	2.50	6.00
❑ 227 Tim Shaw RC	2.50	6.00
❑ 228 Tony Taylor RC	2.50	6.00
❑ 229 Zak DeOssie RC	2.50	6.00
❑ 230 Mason Crosby RC	3.00	8.00
❑ 231 Nick Folk RC	3.00	8.00
❑ 232 Matt Gutierrez RC	3.00	8.00
❑ 233 Matt Moore RC	4.00	10.00
❑ 234 Tyler Thigpen RC	3.00	8.00
❑ 235 Clifton Dawson RC	3.00	8.00
❑ 236 Gary Russell RC	2.50	6.00
❑ 237 Kenton Keith RC	3.00	8.00
❑ 238 Pierre Thomas RC	12.00	30.00
❑ 239 Gerald Alexander RC	2.00	5.00
❑ 240 John Wendling RC	2.50	6.00
❑ 241 Eric Frampton RC	2.50	6.00
❑ 242 Eric Weddle RC	2.50	6.00
❑ 243 Daniel Coats RC	2.50	6.00
❑ 244 Michael Matthews RC	2.50	6.00
❑ 245 Biren Ealy RC	2.50	6.00
❑ 246 Bobby Sippio RC	2.50	6.00
❑ 247 Glenn Holt RC	2.50	6.00
❑ 248 John Broussard RC	2.50	6.00
❑ 249 Legedu Naanee RC	3.00	8.00
❑ 250 Syndric Steptoe RC	2.50	6.00
❑ 251 Levi Brown AU RC	5.00	12.00
❑ 252 Jamaal Anderson AU RC	4.00	10.00
❑ 253 Amobi Okoye AU RC	5.00	12.00
❑ 254 Adam Carriker AU RC	4.00	10.00
❑ 255 Darrelle Revis AU RC	6.00	15.00
❑ 256 Michael Griffin AU RC	5.00	12.00
❑ 257 Aaron Ross AU RC	5.00	12.00
❑ 258 Brandon Meriweather AU RC	5.00	12.00
❑ 259 Jon Beason AU RC	5.00	12.00
❑ 260 Anthony Spencer AU RC	5.00	12.00
❑ 261 Alan Branch No AU RC	2.50	6.00
❑ 262 Chris Houston AU RC	4.00	10.00
❑ 263 LaMarr Woodley AU RC	10.00	20.00
❑ 264 David Harris AU RC	4.00	10.00
❑ 265 Eric Wright No AU RC	3.00	8.00
❑ 266 Josh Wilson AU RC	4.00	10.00
❑ 267 Tim Crowder AU RC	5.00	12.00
❑ 268 Victor Abiamiri AU RC	5.00	12.00
❑ 269 Ikaika Alama-Francis AU RC	5.00	12.00
❑ 270 Dan Bazuin AU RC	4.00	10.00
❑ 271 Sabby Piscitelli AU RC	5.00	12.00
❑ 272 Quentin Moses AU RC	4.00	10.00
❑ 273 Buster Davis AU RC	4.00	10.00
❑ 274 Marcus McCauley AU RC	4.00	10.00
❑ 275 Matt Spaeth AU RC	5.00	12.00
❑ 276 Demarcus Tank Tyler No AU RC	2.50	6.00
❑ 277 Charles Johnson No AU RC	2.00	5.00
❑ 278 Jonathan Wade AU RC	4.00	10.00
❑ 279 Stewart Bradley AU RC	5.00	12.00
❑ 280 Aaron Rouse AU RC	5.00	12.00
❑ 281 Michael Okwo AU RC	4.00	10.00
❑ 282 Daymeion Hughes AU RC	4.00	10.00
❑ 283 Ray McDonald AU RC	4.00	10.00
❑ 284 Thomas Clayton AU RC	4.00	10.00
❑ 285 DeShawn Wynn AU RC	5.00	12.00
❑ 286 Jason Snelling AU RC	4.00	10.00

❑ 287 Kenneth Darby AU RC 5.00 12.00
❑ 288 Ahmad Bradshaw AU/291 RC 15.00 40.00
❑ 289 Nate Ilaoa AU/203 RC 5.00 12.00
❑ 290 Joel Filani AU RC 4.00 10.00
❑ 291 Courtney Taylor AU RC 4.00 10.00
❑ 292 Jordan Kent AU/245 RC 4.00 10.00
❑ 293 Dallas Baker AU RC 4.00 10.00
❑ 294 Roy Hall AU RC 5.00 12.00
❑ 295 Chansi Stuckey AU RC 5.00 12.00
❑ 296 Scott Chandler AU RC 4.00 10.00
❑ 297 Ben Patrick AU RC 4.00 10.00
❑ 298 Chris Leak AU RC 4.00 10.00
❑ 299 Jared Zabransky AU RC 5.00 12.00
❑ 300 Selvin Young AU/194 RC 12.00 30.00
❑ 301 Adrian Peterson JSY AU RC 175.00 300.00
❑ 302 Anthony Gonzalez JSY AU RC 25.00 50.00
❑ 303 Antonio Pittman JSY AU RC 8.00 20.00
❑ 304 Aundrae Allison AU RC 6.00 15.00
❑ 305 Brady Quinn JSY AU RC 50.00 120.00
❑ 306 Brandon Jackson JSY AU RC 8.00 20.00
❑ 307 Brian Leonard JSY AU RC 6.00 15.00
❑ 308 Calvin Johnson JSY AU RC 40.00 100.00
❑ 309 Chris Davis AU RC 6.00 15.00
❑ 310 Chris Henry RB JSY AU RC 6.00 15.00
❑ 311 Craig Buster Davis EXCH
❑ 312 David Clowney AU RC 8.00 20.00
❑ 313 Drew Stanton JSY AU RC 6.00 15.00
❑ 314 Dwayne Bowe JSY AU RC 25.00 50.00
❑ 315 Dwayne Jarrett JSY AU RC 8.00 20.00
❑ 316 Dwayne Wright AU RC 6.00 15.00
❑ 317 Gaines Adams JSY AU RC 8.00 20.00
❑ 318 Garrett Wolfe JSY AU RC 8.00 20.00
❑ 319 Greg Olsen JSY AU RC 12.00 30.00
❑ 320 Isaiah Stanback AU RC 8.00 20.00
❑ 321 Jacoby Jones AU RC 8.00 20.00
❑ 322 JaMarcus Russell JSY AU RC 25.00 60.00
❑ 323 James Jones AU RC 8.00 20.00
❑ 324 Jason Hill JSY AU RC 8.00 20.00
❑ 325 Jeff Rowe AU RC 6.00 15.00
❑ 326 Joe Thomas EXCH
❑ 327 John Beck JSY AU RC 8.00 20.00
❑ 328 J.Lee Higgins JSY AU RC 8.00 20.00
❑ 329 Jordan Palmer AU RC 8.00 20.00
❑ 330 Kenny Irons JSY No AU RC 8.00 20.00
❑ 331 Kevin Kolb JSY AU RC 15.00 40.00
❑ 332 Kolby Smith AU RC 8.00 20.00
❑ 333 LaRon Landry AU RC 10.00 25.00
❑ 334 Laurent Robinson AU RC 8.00 20.00
❑ 335 Lawrence Timmons AU RC 8.00 20.00
❑ 336 Leon Hall AU RC 8.00 20.00
❑ 337 Lorenzo Booker JSY AU RC 8.00 20.00
❑ 338 Marshawn Lynch JSY AU RC 40.00 80.00
❑ 339 Michael Bush JSY AU RC 8.00 20.00
❑ 340 Mike Walker AU RC 8.00 20.00
❑ 341 Patrick Willis JSY AU RC 20.00 50.00
❑ 342 Paul Posluszny AU RC 10.00 25.00
❑ 343 Paul Williams JSY AU RC 6.00 15.00
❑ 344 Reggie Nelson AU RC 6.00 15.00
❑ 345 Robert Meachem JSY AU RC 8.00 20.00
❑ 346 Ryne Robinson AU RC 6.00 15.00
❑ 347 Sidney Rice JSY AU RC 15.00 40.00
❑ 348 Steve Breaston AU RC 8.00 20.00
❑ 349 Steve Smith USC JSY AU RC 20.00 40.00
❑ 350 Ted Ginn Jr. JSY AU RC 15.00 40.00
❑ 351 Tony Hunt JSY AU RC 8.00 20.00
❑ 352 Trent Edwards JSY AU RC 12.00 30.00
❑ 353 Troy Smith JSY AU RC 12.00 30.00
❑ 354 Yamon Figurs JSY AU RC 5.00 12.00
❑ 355 Zach Miller AU RC 8.00 20.00

1998 Leaf Rookies and Stars

❑ COMPLETE SET (300) 125.00 250.00
❑ 1 Keyshawn Johnson .25 .60
❑ 2 Marvin Harrison .25 .60
❑ 3 Eddie Kennison .15 .40
❑ 4 Bryant Young .08 .25
❑ 5 Darren Woodson .08 .25
❑ 6 Tyrone Wheatley .15 .40
❑ 7 Michael Westbrook .15 .40
❑ 8 Charles Way .08 .25
❑ 9 Ricky Watters .15 .40
❑ 10 Chris Warren .15 .40
❑ 11 Wesley Walls .15 .40
❑ 12 Tamarick Vanover .08 .25
❑ 13 Zach Thomas .25 .60
❑ 14 Derrick Thomas .25 .60
❑ 15 Yancey Thigpen .08 .25
❑ 16 Vinny Testaverde .15 .40
❑ 17 Dana Stubblefield .08 .25
❑ 18 J.J. Stokes .15 .40
❑ 19 James Stewart .15 .40
❑ 20 Jeff George .15 .40
❑ 21 John Randle .15 .40
❑ 22 Gary Brown .08 .25
❑ 23 Ed McCaffrey .15 .40
❑ 24 James Jett .15 .40
❑ 25 Rob Johnson .15 .40
❑ 26 Daryl Johnston .15 .40
❑ 27 Jermaine Lewis .15 .40
❑ 28 Tony Martin .15 .40
❑ 29 Derrick Mayes .15 .40
❑ 30 Keenan McCardell .15 .40
❑ 31 O.J. McDuffie .15 .40
❑ 32 Chris Chandler .15 .40
❑ 33 Doug Flutie .25 .60
❑ 34 Scott Mitchell .15 .40
❑ 35 Warren Moon .25 .60
❑ 36 Rob Moore .15 .40
❑ 37 Johnnie Morton .15 .40
❑ 38 Neil O'Donnell .15 .40
❑ 39 Rich Gannon .25 .60
❑ 40 Andre Reed .15 .40
❑ 41 Jake Reed .15 .40
❑ 42 Errict Rhett .15 .40
❑ 43 Simeon Rice .15 .40
❑ 44 Andre Rison .15 .40
❑ 45 Eric Moulds .25 .60
❑ 46 Frank Sanders .15 .40
❑ 47 Darnay Scott .15 .40
❑ 48 Junior Seau .25 .60
❑ 49 Shannon Sharpe .15 .40
❑ 50 Bruce Smith .15 .40
❑ 51 Jimmy Smith .15 .40
❑ 52 Robert Smith .25 .60
❑ 53 Derrick Alexander .15 .40
❑ 54 Kimble Anders .15 .40
❑ 55 Jamal Anderson .25 .60
❑ 56 Mario Bates .15 .40
❑ 57 Edgar Bennett .08 .25
❑ 58 Tim Biakabutuka .15 .40
❑ 59 Ki-Jana Carter .08 .25
❑ 60 Larry Centers .08 .25
❑ 61 Mark Chmura .15 .40
❑ 62 Wayne Chrebet .25 .60
❑ 63 Ben Coates .15 .40
❑ 64 Curtis Conway .15 .40
❑ 65 Randall Cunningham .25 .60
❑ 66 Rickey Dudley .08 .25
❑ 67 Bert Emanuel .15 .40
❑ 68 Bobby Engram .15 .40
❑ 69 William Floyd .08 .25
❑ 70 Irving Fryar .15 .40
❑ 71 Elvis Grbac .15 .40
❑ 72 Kevin Greene .15 .40
❑ 73 Jim Harbaugh .15 .40
❑ 74 Raymont Harris .08 .25
❑ 75 Garrison Hearst .25 .60
❑ 76 Greg Hill .08 .25
❑ 77 Desmond Howard .15 .40
❑ 78 Bobby Hoying .15 .40
❑ 79 Michael Jackson .08 .25
❑ 80 Terry Allen .25 .60
❑ 81 Jerome Bettis .25 .60
❑ 82 Jeff Blake .15 .40
❑ 83 Robert Brooks .15 .40
❑ 84 Tim Brown .25 .60
❑ 85 Isaac Bruce .25 .60
❑ 86 Cris Carter .25 .60
❑ 87 Ty Detmer .15 .40
❑ 88 Trent Dilfer .25 .60
❑ 89 Marshall Faulk .30 .75
❑ 90 Antonio Freeman .25 .60
❑ 91 Gus Frerotte .08 .25
❑ 92 Joey Galloway .15 .40
❑ 93 Michael Irvin .25 .60
❑ 94 Brad Johnson .25 .60
❑ 95 Danny Kanell .15 .40
❑ 96 Napoleon Kaufman .25 .60
❑ 97 Dorsey Levens .25 .60
❑ 98 Natrone Means .15 .40
❑ 99 Herman Moore .15 .40
❑ 100 Adrian Murrell .15 .40
❑ 101 Carl Pickens .15 .40
❑ 102 Rod Smith .15 .40
❑ 103 Thurman Thomas .25 .60
❑ 104 Reggie White .25 .60
❑ 105 Jim Druckenmiller .08 .25
❑ 106 Antowain Smith .25 .60
❑ 107 Reidel Anthony .15 .40
❑ 108 Ike Hilliard .15 .40
❑ 109 Rae Carruth .08 .25
❑ 110 Troy Davis .08 .25
❑ 111 Terance Mathis .15 .40
❑ 112 Brett Favre 1.00 2.50
❑ 113 Dan Marino 1.00 2.50
❑ 114 Emmitt Smith .75 2.00
❑ 115 Barry Sanders .75 2.00
❑ 116 Eddie George .25 .60
❑ 117 Drew Bledsoe .40 1.00
❑ 118 Troy Aikman .50 1.25
❑ 119 Terrell Davis .25 .60
❑ 120 John Elway 1.00 2.50
❑ 121 Mark Brunell .25 .60
❑ 122 Jerry Rice .50 1.25
❑ 123 Kordell Stewart .25 .60
❑ 124 Steve McNair .25 .60
❑ 125 Curtis Martin .25 .60
❑ 126 Steve Young .30 .75
❑ 127 Kerry Collins .15 .40
❑ 128 Terry Glenn .25 .60
❑ 129 Deion Sanders .25 .60
❑ 130 Mike Alstott .25 .60
❑ 131 Tony Banks .15 .40
❑ 132 Karim Abdul-Jabbar .25 .60
❑ 133 Terrell Owens .25 .60
❑ 134 Yatil Green .08 .25
❑ 135 Tony Gonzalez .25 .60
❑ 136 Byron Hanspard .08 .25
❑ 137 David LaFleur .08 .25
❑ 138 Danny Wuerffel .15 .40
❑ 139 Tiki Barber .25 .60
❑ 140 Peter Boulware .08 .25
❑ 141 Will Blackwell .08 .25
❑ 142 Warrick Dunn .25 .60
❑ 143 Corey Dillon .25 .60
❑ 144 Jake Plummer .25 .60
❑ 145 Neil Smith .15 .40
❑ 146 Charles Johnson .08 .25
❑ 147 Fred Lane .08 .25
❑ 148 Dan Wilkinson .08 .25
❑ 149 Ken Norton Jr. .08 .25
❑ 150 Stephen Davis .08 .25
❑ 151 Gilbert Brown .08 .25
❑ 152 Kenny Bynum RC .08 .25
❑ 153 Derrick Cullors .08 .25
❑ 154 Charlie Garner .15 .40
❑ 155 Jeff Graham .08 .25
❑ 156 Warren Sapp .15 .40
❑ 157 Jerald Moore .08 .25
❑ 158 Sean Dawkins .08 .25
❑ 159 Charlie Jones .08 .25
❑ 160 Kevin Lockett .08 .25
❑ 161 James McKnight .25 .60
❑ 162 Chris Penn .08 .25
❑ 163 Leslie Shepherd .08 .25
❑ 164 Karl Williams .08 .25
❑ 165 Mark Bruener .08 .25
❑ 166 Ernie Conwell .08 .25
❑ 167 Ken Dilger .08 .25
❑ 168 Troy Drayton .08 .25
❑ 169 Freddie Jones .08 .25
❑ 170 Dale Carter .08 .25
❑ 171 Charles Woodson RC 3.00 8.00
❑ 172 Alonzo Mayes RC 1.00 2.50
❑ 173 Andre Wadsworth RC 1.50 4.00
❑ 174 Grant Wistrom RC 1.50 4.00
❑ 175 Greg Ellis RC 1.00 2.50
❑ 176 Chris Howard RC 1.00 2.50
❑ 177 Keith Brooking RC 2.50 6.00
❑ 178 Takeo Spikes RC 2.50 6.00
❑ 179 Anthony Simmons RC 1.50 4.00
❑ 180 Brian Simmons RC 1.50 4.00

❑ 181 Sam Cowart RC	1.50	4.00
❑ 182 Ken Oxendine RC	1.00	2.50
❑ 183 Vonnie Holliday RC	1.50	4.00
❑ 184 Terry Fair RC	1.50	4.00
❑ 185 Shaun Williams RC	1.50	4.00
❑ 186 Tremayne Stephens RC	1.00	2.50
❑ 187 Duane Starks RC	1.00	2.50
❑ 188 Jason Peter RC	1.00	2.50
❑ 189 Tebucky Jones RC	1.00	2.50
❑ 190 Donovin Darius RC	1.50	4.00
❑ 191 R.W. McQuarters RC	1.50	4.00
❑ 192 Corey Chavous RC	2.50	6.00
❑ 193 Cameron Cleeland RC	1.00	2.50
❑ 194 Stephen Alexander RC	1.50	4.00
❑ 195 Rod Rutledge RC	1.00	2.50
❑ 196 Scott Frost RC	1.00	2.50
❑ 197 Fred Beasley RC	1.00	2.50
❑ 198 Dorian Boose RC	1.00	2.50
❑ 199 Randy Moss RC	12.00	30.00
❑ 200 Jacquez Green RC	1.50	4.00
❑ 201 Marcus Nash RC	1.00	2.50
❑ 202 Hines Ward RC	12.50	25.00
❑ 203 Kevin Dyson RC	2.50	6.00
❑ 204 E.G. Green RC	1.50	4.00
❑ 205 Germane Crowell RC	1.50	4.00
❑ 206 Joe Jurevicius RC	2.50	6.00
❑ 207 Tony Simmons RC	1.50	4.00
❑ 208 Tim Dwight RC	2.50	6.00
❑ 209 Az-Zahir Hakim RC	2.50	6.00
❑ 210 Jerome Pathon RC	2.50	6.00
❑ 211 Pat Johnson RC	1.50	4.00
❑ 212 Mikhael Ricks RC	1.50	4.00
❑ 213 Donald Hayes RC	1.50	4.00
❑ 214 Jammi German RC	1.00	2.50
❑ 215 Larry Shannon RC	1.00	2.50
❑ 216 Brian Alford RC	1.00	2.50
❑ 217 Curtis Enis RC	1.00	2.50
❑ 218 Fred Taylor RC	4.00	10.00
❑ 219 Robert Edwards RC	1.50	4.00
❑ 220 Ahman Green RC	5.00	12.00
❑ 221 Tavian Banks RC	1.50	4.00
❑ 222 Skip Hicks RC	1.50	4.00
❑ 223 Robert Holcombe RC	1.50	4.00
❑ 224 John Avery RC	1.50	4.00
❑ 225 Chris Fuamatu-Ma'afala RC	1.50	4.00
❑ 226 Michael Pittman RC	4.00	8.00
❑ 227 Rashaan Shehee RC	1.50	4.00
❑ 228 Jonathan Linton RC	1.50	4.00
❑ 229 Jon Ritchie RC	1.50	4.00
❑ 230 Chris Floyd RC	1.00	2.50
❑ 231 Wilmont Perry RC	1.00	2.50
❑ 232 Raymond Priester RC	1.00	2.50
❑ 233 Peyton Manning RC	25.00	50.00
❑ 234 Ryan Leaf RC	2.50	6.00
❑ 235 Brian Griese RC	5.00	12.00
❑ 236 Jeff Ogden RC	2.50	6.00
❑ 237 Charlie Batch RC	2.50	6.00
❑ 238 Moses Moreno RC	1.00	2.50
❑ 239 Jonathan Quinn RC	2.50	6.00
❑ 240 Flozell Adams RC	1.00	2.50
❑ 241 Brett Favre PT	5.00	12.00
❑ 242 Dan Marino PT	5.00	12.00
❑ 243 Emmitt Smith PT	4.00	10.00
❑ 244 Barry Sanders PT	4.00	10.00
❑ 245 Eddie George PT	1.00	2.50
❑ 246 Drew Bledsoe PT	2.00	5.00
❑ 247 Troy Aikman PT	2.50	6.00
❑ 248 Terrell Davis PT	1.00	2.50
❑ 249 John Elway PT	5.00	12.00
❑ 250 Carl Pickens PT	1.00	2.50
❑ 251 Jerry Rice PT	2.50	6.00
❑ 252 Kordell Stewart PT	1.00	2.50
❑ 253 Steve McNair PT	1.00	2.50
❑ 254 Curtis Martin PT	1.00	2.50
❑ 255 Steve Young PT	1.50	4.00
❑ 256 Herman Moore PT	1.00	2.50
❑ 257 Dorsey Levens PT	1.00	2.50
❑ 258 Deion Sanders PT	1.00	2.50
❑ 259 Napoleon Kaufman PT	1.00	2.50
❑ 260 Warrick Dunn PT	1.00	2.50
❑ 261 Corey Dillon PT	1.00	2.50
❑ 262 Jerome Bettis PT	1.00	2.50
❑ 263 Tim Brown PT	1.00	2.50
❑ 264 Cris Carter PT	1.00	2.50
❑ 265 Antonio Freeman PT	1.00	2.50
❑ 266 Randy Moss PT	6.00	15.00
❑ 267 Curtis Enis PT	1.00	2.50
❑ 268 Fred Taylor PT	1.50	4.00
❑ 269 Robert Edwards PT	1.00	2.50
❑ 270 Peyton Manning PT	12.50	25.00
❑ 271 Barry Sanders TL	.40	1.00
❑ 272 Eddie George TL	.15	.40
❑ 273 Troy Aikman TL	.25	.60
❑ 274 Mark Brunell TL	.25	.60
❑ 275 Kordell Stewart TL	.25	.60
❑ 276 Tim Biakabutuka TL	.08	.25
❑ 277 Terry Glenn TL	.08	.25
❑ 278 Mike Alstott TL	.08	.25
❑ 279 Tony Banks TL	.08	.25
❑ 280 Karim Abdul-Jabbar TL	.08	.25
❑ 281 Terrell Owens TL	.15	.40
❑ 282 Byron Hanspard TL	.08	.25
❑ 283 Jake Plummer TL	.15	.40
❑ 284 Terry Allen TL	.08	.25
❑ 285 Jeff Blake TL	.08	.25
❑ 286 Brad Johnson TL	.08	.25
❑ 287 Danny Kanell TL	.08	.25
❑ 288 Natrone Means TL	.08	.25
❑ 289 Rod Smith TL	.08	.25
❑ 290 Thurman Thomas TL	.08	.25
❑ 291 Reggie White TL	.08	.25
❑ 292 Troy Davis TL	.08	.25
❑ 293 Curtis Conway TL	.08	.25
❑ 294 Irving Fryar TL	.08	.25
❑ 295 Jim Harbaugh TL	.08	.25
❑ 296 Andre Rison TL	.08	.25
❑ 297 Ricky Watters TL	.08	.25
❑ 298 Keyshawn Johnson TL	.08	.25
❑ 299 Jeff George TL	.08	.25
❑ 300 Marshall Faulk TL	.25	.60

1999 Leaf Rookies and Stars

❑ COMPLETE SET (300)	75.00	150.00
❑ COMP.SET w/o SP's (200)	15.00	30.00
❑ 1 Frank Sanders	.15	.40
❑ 2 Adrian Murrell	.15	.40
❑ 3 Rob Moore	.15	.40
❑ 4 Simeon Rice	.15	.40
❑ 5 Michael Pittman	.08	.25
❑ 6 Jake Plummer	.15	.40
❑ 7 Chris Chandler	.15	.40
❑ 8 Tim Dwight	.15	.40
❑ 9 Chris Calloway	.08	.25
❑ 10 Terance Mathis	.15	.40
❑ 11 Jamal Anderson	.25	.60
❑ 12 Byron Hanspard	.08	.25
❑ 13 O.J. Santiago	.08	.25
❑ 14 Ken Oxendine	.08	.25
❑ 15 Priest Holmes	.40	1.00
❑ 16 Scott Mitchell	.08	.25
❑ 17 Tony Banks	.15	.40
❑ 18 Patrick Johnson	.08	.25
❑ 19 Rod Woodson	.15	.40
❑ 20 Jermaine Lewis	.15	.40
❑ 21 Errict Rhett	.15	.40
❑ 22 Stoney Case	.08	.25
❑ 23 Andre Reed	.15	.40
❑ 24 Eric Moulds	.15	.40
❑ 25 Rob Johnson	.15	.40
❑ 26 Doug Flutie	.25	.60
❑ 27 Bruce Smith	.15	.40
❑ 28 Jay Riemersma	.08	.25
❑ 29 Antowain Smith	.08	.25
❑ 30 Thurman Thomas	.15	.40
❑ 31 Jonathan Linton	.08	.25
❑ 32 Muhsin Muhammad	.15	.40
❑ 33 Rae Carruth	.08	.25
❑ 34 Wesley Walls	.15	.40
❑ 35 Fred Lane	.08	.25
❑ 36 Kevin Greene	.08	.25
❑ 37 Tim Biakabutuka	.15	.40
❑ 38 Curtis Enis	.08	.25
❑ 39 Shane Matthews	.15	.40
❑ 40 Bobby Engram	.15	.40
❑ 41 Curtis Conway	.15	.40
❑ 42 Marcus Robinson	.50	1.25
❑ 43 Darnay Scott	.08	.25
❑ 44 Carl Pickens	.15	.40
❑ 45 Corey Dillon	.25	.60
❑ 46 Jeff Blake	.15	.40
❑ 47 Terry Kirby	.08	.25
❑ 48 Ty Detmer	.15	.40
❑ 49 Leslie Shepherd	.08	.25
❑ 50 Karim Abdul-Jabbar	.15	.40
❑ 51 Emmitt Smith	.50	1.25
❑ 52 Deion Sanders	.25	.60
❑ 53 Michael Irvin	.15	.40
❑ 54 Rocket Ismail	.15	.40
❑ 55 David LaFleur	.08	.25
❑ 56 Troy Aikman	.50	1.25
❑ 57 Ed McCaffrey	.15	.40
❑ 58 Rod Smith	.15	.40
❑ 59 Shannon Sharpe	.15	.40
❑ 60 Brian Griese	.25	.60
❑ 61 John Elway	.75	2.00
❑ 62 Bubby Brister	.08	.25
❑ 63 Neil Smith	.15	.40
❑ 64 Terrell Davis	.25	.60
❑ 65 John Avery	.08	.25
❑ 66 Derek Loville	.08	.25
❑ 67 Ron Rivers	.08	.25
❑ 68 Herman Moore	.15	.40
❑ 69 Johnnie Morton	.15	.40
❑ 70 Charlie Batch	.25	.60
❑ 71 Barry Sanders	.75	2.00
❑ 72 Germane Crowell	.08	.25
❑ 73 Greg Hill	.08	.25
❑ 74 Gus Frerotte	.15	.40
❑ 75 Corey Bradford	.08	.25
❑ 76 Dorsey Levens	.25	.60
❑ 77 Antonio Freeman	.25	.60
❑ 78 Mark Chmura	.08	.25
❑ 79 Brett Favre	.75	2.00
❑ 80 Bill Schroeder	.15	.40
❑ 81 Matt Hasselbeck	.25	.60
❑ 82 E.G. Green	.08	.25
❑ 83 Ken Dilger	.08	.25
❑ 84 Jerome Pathon	.08	.25
❑ 85 Marvin Harrison	.25	.60
❑ 86 Peyton Manning	.75	2.00
❑ 87 Tavian Banks	.08	.25
❑ 88 Keenan McCardell	.15	.40
❑ 89 Mark Brunell	.25	.60
❑ 90 Fred Taylor	.25	.60
❑ 91 Jimmy Smith	.15	.40
❑ 92 James Stewart	.15	.40
❑ 93 Kyle Brady	.08	.25
❑ 94 Derrick Thomas	.25	.60
❑ 95 Rashaan Shehee	.08	.25
❑ 96 Derrick Alexander WR	.15	.40
❑ 97 Byron Bam Morris	.08	.25
❑ 98 Andre Rison	.15	.40
❑ 99 Elvis Grbac	.15	.40
❑ 100 Tony Gonzalez	.25	.60
❑ 101 Donnell Bennett	.08	.25
❑ 102 Warren Moon	.25	.60
❑ 103 Zach Thomas	.25	.60
❑ 104 Oronde Gadsden	.15	.40
❑ 105 Dan Marino	.75	2.00
❑ 106 O.J. McDuffie	.15	.40
❑ 107 Tony Martin	.15	.40
❑ 108 Randy Moss	.60	1.50
❑ 109 Cris Carter	.25	.60
❑ 110 Robert Smith	.25	.60
❑ 111 Randall Cunningham	.25	.60
❑ 112 Jake Reed	.15	.40
❑ 113 John Randle	.15	.40
❑ 114 Leroy Hoard	.08	.25
❑ 115 Jeff George	.15	.40
❑ 116 Ty Law	.15	.40
❑ 117 Shawn Jefferson	.08	.25
❑ 118 Troy Brown	.15	.40
❑ 119 Robert Edwards	.08	.25
❑ 120 Tony Simmons	.08	.25
❑ 121 Terry Glenn	.25	.60
❑ 122 Ben Coates	.15	.40
❑ 123 Drew Bledsoe	.30	.75
❑ 124 Terry Allen	.15	.40
❑ 125 Cameron Cleeland	.08	.25
❑ 126 Eddie Kennison	.15	.40
❑ 127 Amani Toomer	.08	.25
❑ 128 Kerry Collins	.15	.40

❑ 129 Joe Jurevicius	.15	.40
❑ 130 Tiki Barber	.25	.60
❑ 131 Ike Hilliard	.08	.25
❑ 132 Michael Strahan	.15	.40
❑ 133 Gary Brown	.08	.25
❑ 134 Jason Sehorn	.08	.25
❑ 135 Curtis Martin	.25	.60
❑ 136 Vinny Testaverde	.15	.40
❑ 137 Dedric Ward	.08	.25
❑ 138 Keyshawn Johnson	.25	.60
❑ 139 Wayne Chrebet	.15	.40
❑ 140 Tyrone Wheatley	.15	.40
❑ 141 Napoleon Kaufman	.25	.60
❑ 142 Tim Brown	.25	.60
❑ 143 Rickey Dudley	.08	.25
❑ 144 Jon Ritchie	.08	.25
❑ 145 James Jett	.08	.25
❑ 146 Rich Gannon	.25	.60
❑ 147 Charles Woodson	.25	.60
❑ 148 Charles Johnson	.08	.25
❑ 149 Duce Staley	.25	.60
❑ 150 Will Blackwell	.08	.25
❑ 151 Kordell Stewart	.15	.40
❑ 152 Jerome Bettis	.25	.60
❑ 153 Hines Ward	.25	.60
❑ 154 Richard Huntley	.15	.40
❑ 155 Natrone Means	.15	.40
❑ 156 Mikhael Ricks	.08	.25
❑ 157 Junior Seau	.25	.60
❑ 158 Jim Harbaugh	.15	.40
❑ 159 Ryan Leaf	.25	.60
❑ 160 Erik Kramer	.08	.25
❑ 161 Terrell Owens	.25	.60
❑ 162 J.J. Stokes	.15	.40
❑ 163 Lawrence Phillips	.15	.40
❑ 164 Charlie Garner	.15	.40
❑ 165 Jerry Rice	.50	1.25
❑ 166 Garrison Hearst	.15	.40
❑ 167 Steve Young	.30	.75
❑ 168 Derrick Mayes	.15	.40
❑ 169 Ahman Green	.25	.60
❑ 170 Joey Galloway	.15	.40
❑ 171 Ricky Watters	.15	.40
❑ 172 Jon Kitna	.25	.60
❑ 173 Sean Dawkins	.08	.25
❑ 174 Az-Zahir Hakim	.08	.25
❑ 175 Robert Holcombe	.08	.25
❑ 176 Isaac Bruce	.25	.60
❑ 177 Amp Lee	.08	.25
❑ 178 Marshall Faulk	.30	.75
❑ 179 Trent Green	.25	.60
❑ 180 Eric Zeier	.15	.40
❑ 181 Bert Emanuel	.15	.40
❑ 182 Jacquez Green	.08	.25
❑ 183 Reidel Anthony	.15	.40
❑ 184 Warren Sapp	.08	.25
❑ 185 Mike Alstott	.25	.60
❑ 186 Warrick Dunn	.25	.60
❑ 187 Trent Dilfer	.25	.60
❑ 188 Neil O'Donnell	.15	.40
❑ 189 Eddie George	.25	.60
❑ 190 Yancey Thigpen	.08	.25
❑ 191 Steve McNair	.25	.60
❑ 192 Kevin Dyson	.15	.40
❑ 193 Frank Wycheck	.08	.25
❑ 194 Stephen Davis	.25	.60
❑ 195 Stephen Alexander	.08	.25
❑ 196 Darrell Green	.08	.25
❑ 197 Skip Hicks	.08	.25
❑ 198 Brad Johnson	.25	.60
❑ 199 Michael Westbrook	.15	.40
❑ 200 Albert Connell	.08	.25
❑ 201 David Boston RC	1.50	3.00
❑ 202 Joel Makovicka RC	1.50	3.00
❑ 203 Chris Greisen RC	1.25	2.50
❑ 204 Jeff Paulk RC	.75	1.50
❑ 205 Reginald Kelly RC	1.25	2.50
❑ 206 Chris McAlister RC	1.25	2.50
❑ 207 Brandon Stokley RC	1.50	4.00
❑ 208 Antoine Winfield RC	1.25	2.50
❑ 209 Bobby Collins RC	.75	1.50
❑ 210 Peerless Price RC	1.50	3.00
❑ 211 Shawn Bryson RC	1.50	3.00
❑ 212 Sheldon Jackson RC	1.25	2.50
❑ 213 Kamil Loud RC	.75	1.50
❑ 214 D'Wayne Bates RC	1.25	2.50
❑ 215 Jerry Azumah RC	1.25	2.50
❑ 216 Marty Booker RC	1.50	3.00
❑ 217 Cade McNown RC	1.25	2.50
❑ 218 James Allen RC	1.50	3.00
❑ 219 Nick Williams RC	1.25	2.50
❑ 220 Akili Smith RC	1.25	2.50
❑ 221 Craig Yeast RC	1.25	2.50
❑ 222 Damon Griffen RC	1.25	2.50
❑ 223 Scott Covington RC	1.50	3.00
❑ 224 Michael Basnight RC	.75	1.50
❑ 225 Ronnie Powell RC	.75	1.50
❑ 226 Rahim Abdullah RC	1.25	2.50
❑ 227 Tim Couch RC	1.50	3.00
❑ 228 Kevin Johnson RC	1.50	3.00
❑ 229 Darrin Chiaverini RC	1.25	2.50
❑ 230 Mark Campbell RC	1.25	2.50
❑ 231 Mike Lucky RC	1.25	2.50
❑ 232 Robert Thomas RC	1.25	2.50
❑ 233 Ebenezer Ekuban RC	1.25	2.50
❑ 234 Dat Nguyen RC	1.50	3.00
❑ 235 Wane McGarity RC	.75	1.50
❑ 236 Jason Tucker RC	1.25	2.50
❑ 237 Olandis Gary RC	1.50	3.00
❑ 238 Al Wilson RC	1.50	3.00
❑ 239 Travis McGriff RC	.75	1.50
❑ 240 Desmond Clark RC	1.50	3.00
❑ 241 Andre Cooper RC	.75	1.50
❑ 242 Chris Watson RC	.75	1.50
❑ 243 Sedrick Irvin RC	.75	1.50
❑ 244 Chris Claiborne RC	.75	1.50
❑ 245 Cory Sauter RC	.75	1.50
❑ 246 Brock Olivo RC	.75	1.50
❑ 247 De'Mond Parker RC	.75	1.50
❑ 248 Aaron Brooks RC	2.50	6.00
❑ 249 Antuan Edwards RC	1.25	2.50
❑ 250 Basil Mitchell RC	.75	1.50
❑ 251 Terrence Wilkins RC	1.25	2.50
❑ 252 Edgerrin James RC	6.00	15.00
❑ 253 Fernando Bryant RC	1.25	2.50
❑ 254 Mike Cloud RC	1.25	2.50
❑ 255 Larry Parker RC	1.50	3.00
❑ 256 Rob Konrad RC	1.50	3.00
❑ 257 Cecil Collins RC	.75	1.50
❑ 258 James Johnson RC	1.25	2.50
❑ 259 Jim Kleinsasser RC	1.50	3.00
❑ 260 Daunte Culpepper RC	6.00	15.00
❑ 261 Michael Bishop RC	1.50	3.00
❑ 262 Andy Katzenmoyer RC	1.25	2.50
❑ 263 Kevin Faulk RC	1.50	3.00
❑ 264 Brett Bech RC	.75	1.50
❑ 265 Ricky Williams RC	3.00	8.00
❑ 266 Sean Bennett RC	.75	1.50
❑ 267 Joe Montgomery RC	1.25	2.50
❑ 268 Dan Campbell RC	.75	1.50
❑ 269 Ray Lucas RC	1.50	3.00
❑ 270 Scott Dreisbach RC	1.25	2.50
❑ 271 Jed Weaver RC	.75	1.50
❑ 272 Dameane Douglas RC	1.25	2.50
❑ 273 Cecil Martin RC	1.25	2.50
❑ 274 Donovan McNabb RC	7.50	20.00
❑ 275 Na Brown RC	1.25	2.50
❑ 276 Jerame Tuman RC	1.50	3.00
❑ 277 Amos Zereoue RC	1.50	3.00
❑ 278 Troy Edwards RC	1.25	2.50
❑ 279 Jermaine Fazande RC	1.25	2.50
❑ 280 Steve Heiden RC	1.50	3.00
❑ 281 Jeff Garcia RC	7.50	20.00
❑ 282 Terry Jackson RC	1.25	2.50
❑ 283 Charlie Rogers RC	1.25	2.50
❑ 284 Brock Huard RC	1.50	3.00
❑ 285 Karsten Bailey RC	1.25	2.50
❑ 286 Lamar King RC	.75	1.50
❑ 287 Justin Watson RC	.75	1.50
❑ 288 Kurt Warner RC	7.50	20.00
❑ 289 Torry Holt RC	5.00	12.00
❑ 290 Joe Germaine RC	1.25	2.50
❑ 291 Dre' Bly RC	1.50	3.00
❑ 292 Martin Gramatica RC	.75	1.50
❑ 293 Rabih Abdullah RC	1.25	2.50
❑ 294 Shaun King RC	1.25	2.50
❑ 295 Anthony McFarland RC	1.25	2.50
❑ 296 Darnell McDonald RC	1.25	2.50
❑ 297 Kevin Daft RC	1.25	2.50
❑ 298 Jevon Kearse RC	3.00	8.00
❑ 299 Mike Sellers	.08	.25
❑ 300 Champ Bailey RC	2.50	6.00

2000 Leaf Rookies and Stars

❑ COMP.SET w/o SP's (100)	6.00	15.00
❑ 1 Jake Plummer	.15	.40
❑ 2 David Boston	.25	.60
❑ 3 Tim Dwight	.25	.60
❑ 4 Jamal Anderson	.25	.60
❑ 5 Chris Chandler	.15	.40
❑ 6 Tony Banks	.15	.40
❑ 7 Qadry Ismail	.15	.40
❑ 8 Eric Moulds	.25	.60
❑ 9 Doug Flutie	.25	.60
❑ 10 Lamar Smith	.15	.40
❑ 11 Peerless Price	.15	.40
❑ 12 Rob Johnson	.15	.40
❑ 13 Reggie White	.25	.60
❑ 14 Muhsin Muhammad	.15	.40
❑ 15 Steve Beuerlein	.15	.40
❑ 16 Cade McNown	.08	.25
❑ 17 Derrick Alexander	.15	.40
❑ 18 Marcus Robinson	.25	.60
❑ 19 Corey Dillon	.25	.60
❑ 20 Akili Smith	.08	.25
❑ 21 Tim Couch	.15	.40
❑ 22 Kevin Johnson	.25	.60
❑ 23 Emmitt Smith	.50	1.25
❑ 24 Troy Aikman	.50	1.25
❑ 25 Joey Galloway	.15	.40
❑ 26 Rocket Ismail	.15	.40
❑ 27 John Elway	.75	2.00
❑ 28 Terrell Davis	.25	.60
❑ 29 Brian Griese	.25	.60
❑ 30 Olandis Gary	.25	.60
❑ 31 Ed McCaffrey	.25	.60
❑ 32 Rod Smith	.15	.40
❑ 33 Barry Sanders	.60	1.50
❑ 34 Charlie Batch	.25	.60
❑ 35 Germane Crowell	.08	.25
❑ 36 James Stewart	.15	.40
❑ 37 Brett Favre	.75	2.00
❑ 38 Dorsey Levens	.15	.40
❑ 39 Antonio Freeman	.25	.60
❑ 40 Peyton Manning	.60	1.50
❑ 41 Edgerrin James	.40	1.00
❑ 42 Marvin Harrison	.25	.60
❑ 43 Fred Taylor	.25	.60
❑ 44 Mark Brunell	.25	.60
❑ 45 Jimmy Smith	.15	.40
❑ 46 Elvis Grbac	.15	.40
❑ 47 Tony Gonzalez	.15	.40
❑ 48 Dan Marino	.75	2.00
❑ 49 Joe Horn	.15	.40
❑ 50 Jay Fiedler	.25	.60
❑ 51 James Allen	.15	.40
❑ 52 Randy Moss	.50	1.25
❑ 53 Daunte Culpepper	.30	.75
❑ 54 Cris Carter	.25	.60
❑ 55 Robert Smith	.25	.60
❑ 56 Drew Bledsoe	.30	.75
❑ 57 Terry Glenn	.25	.60
❑ 58 Ricky Williams	.25	.60
❑ 59 Amani Toomer	.15	.40
❑ 60 Kerry Collins	.15	.40
❑ 61 Curtis Martin	.25	.60
❑ 62 Vinny Testaverde	.15	.40
❑ 63 Wayne Chrebet	.15	.40
❑ 64 Tim Brown	.25	.60
❑ 65 Tyrone Wheatley	.15	.40
❑ 66 Rich Gannon	.25	.60
❑ 67 Donovan McNabb	.40	1.00
❑ 68 Duce Staley	.25	.60
❑ 69 Jerome Bettis	.25	.60
❑ 70 Donald Hayes	.08	.25
❑ 71 Junior Seau	.25	.60

Card	Low	High
❑ 72 Jermaine Fazande	.08	.25
❑ 73 Jerry Rice	.50	1.25
❑ 74 Steve Young	.30	.75
❑ 75 Terrell Owens	.25	.60
❑ 76 Charlie Garner	.15	.40
❑ 77 Jeff Garcia	.25	.60
❑ 78 Tim Biakabutuka	.15	.40
❑ 79 Tiki Barber	.25	.60
❑ 80 Ricky Watters	.15	.40
❑ 81 Kurt Warner	.50	1.25
❑ 82 Marshall Faulk	.30	.75
❑ 83 Isaac Bruce	.25	.60
❑ 84 Torry Holt	.25	.60
❑ 85 Mike Alstott	.25	.60
❑ 86 Warrick Dunn	.25	.60
❑ 87 Shaun King	.08	.25
❑ 88 Keyshawn Johnson	.25	.60
❑ 89 Warren Sapp	.15	.40
❑ 90 Eddie George	.25	.60
❑ 91 Jevon Kearse	.25	.60
❑ 92 Steve McNair	.25	.60
❑ 93 Carl Pickens	.15	.40
❑ 94 Deion Sanders	.25	.60
❑ 95 Stephen Davis	.25	.60
❑ 96 Brad Johnson	.25	.60
❑ 97 Bruce Smith	.15	.40
❑ 98 Michael Wcotbrook	.15	.40
❑ 99 Albert Connell	.08	.25
❑ 100 Jeff George	.15	.40
❑ 101 Thomas Jones RC	5.00	12.00
❑ 102 Bashir Yamini RC	2.00	5.00
❑ 103 Jamal Lewis RC	8.00	20.00
❑ 104 Travis Taylor RC	3.00	8.00
❑ 105 Chris Redman RC	2.50	6.00
❑ 106 Avion Black RC	2.50	6.00
❑ 107 Sammy Morris RC	3.00	8.00
❑ 108 Dez White RC	3.00	8.00
❑ 109 Peter Warrick RC	3.00	8.00
❑ 110 Ron Dugans RC	2.00	5.00
❑ 111 Curtis Keaton RC	2.50	6.00
❑ 112 Danny Farmer RC	2.50	6.00
❑ 113 Courtney Brown RC	3.00	8.00
❑ 114 Dennis Northcutt RC	3.00	8.00
❑ 115 Travis Prentice RC	2.50	6.00
❑ 116 JaJuan Dawson RC	2.00	5.00
❑ 117 Spergon Wynn RC	2.50	6.00
❑ 118 Michael Wiley RC	2.50	6.00
❑ 119 Chris Cole RC	2.50	6.00
❑ 120 Mike Anderson RC	5.00	12.00
❑ 121 Muneer Moore RC	2.00	5.00
❑ 122 Reuben Droughns RC	3.00	8.00
❑ 123 Bubba Franks RC	3.00	8.00
❑ 124 Anthony Lucas RC	2.00	5.00
❑ 125 Charles Lee RC	2.00	5.00
❑ 126 R.Jay Soward RC	2.50	6.00
❑ 127 Shyrone Stith RC	2.50	6.00
❑ 128 Sylvester Morris RC	2.50	6.00
❑ 129 Frank Moreau RC	2.50	6.00
❑ 130 Dante Hall RC	4.00	10.00
❑ 131 Doug Chapman RC	2.50	6.00
❑ 132 Troy Walters RC	3.00	8.00
❑ 133 J.R. Redmond RC	2.50	6.00
❑ 134 Tom Brady RC	100.00	200.00
❑ 135 Terrelle Smith RC	2.50	6.00
❑ 136 Chad Morton RC	3.00	8.00
❑ 137 Ron Dayne RC	3.00	8.00
❑ 138 Ron Dixon RC	2.50	6.00
❑ 139 Chad Pennington RC	8.00	20.00
❑ 140 Anthony Becht RC	3.00	8.00
❑ 141 Laveranues Coles RC	4.00	10.00
❑ 142 Windrell Hayes RC	2.50	6.00
❑ 143 Sebastian Janikowski RC	3.00	8.00
❑ 144 Jerry Porter RC	3.00	8.00
❑ 145 Corey Simon RC	3.00	8.00
❑ 146 Todd Pinkston RC	3.00	8.00
❑ 147 Gari Scott RC	2.00	5.00
❑ 148 Plaxico Burress RC	6.00	15.00
❑ 149 Tee Martin RC	3.00	8.00
❑ 150 Trevor Gaylor RC	2.50	6.00
❑ 151 Ronney Jenkins RC	2.50	6.00
❑ 152 Giovanni Carmazzi RC	2.00	5.00
❑ 153 Tim Rattay RC	3.00	8.00
❑ 154 Shaun Alexander RC	8.00	20.00
❑ 155 Darrell Jackson RC	4.00	10.00
❑ 156 James Williams RC	2.50	6.00
❑ 157 Trung Canidate RC	2.50	6.00
❑ 158 Joe Hamilton RC	2.50	6.00
❑ 159 Erron Kinney RC	3.00	8.00
❑ 160 Todd Husak RC	3.00	8.00
❑ 161 Raynoch Thompson RC	2.50	6.00
❑ 162 Darwin Walker RC	2.00	5.00
❑ 163 Jay Tant RC	2.00	5.00
❑ 164 Doug Johnson RC	3.00	8.00
❑ 165 Robert Bean RC	2.50	6.00
❑ 166 Mark Simoneau RC	2.50	6.00
❑ 167 John Jones RC	2.50	6.00
❑ 168 Obafemi Ayanbadejo RC	2.50	6.00
❑ 169 Mike Brown RC	4.00	10.00
❑ 170 Shockmain Davis RC	2.00	5.00
❑ 171 Erik Flowers RC	2.50	6.00
❑ 172 Corey Moore RC	2.00	5.00
❑ 173 Drew Haddad RC	2.00	5.00
❑ 174 Kwame Cavil RC	2.00	5.00
❑ 175 Pat Dennis RC	2.00	5.00
❑ 176 Rashard Anderson RC	2.50	6.00
❑ 177 Brian Finneran RC	3.00	8.00
❑ 178 Na'il Diggs RC	2.50	6.00
❑ 179 Marc Bulger RC	6.00	15.00
❑ 180 Mondriel Fulcher RC	2.00	5.00
❑ 181 Dwayne Carswell	2.00	5.00
❑ 182 Brian Urlacher RC	10.00	25.00
❑ 183 Paul Edinger RC	3.00	8.00
❑ 184 Karon Coleman RC	2.50	6.00
❑ 185 Aaron Shea RC	2.50	6.00
❑ 186 Fabien Bownes RC	2.00	5.00
❑ 187 Damon Hodge RC	2.50	6.00
❑ 188 Dwayne Goodrich RC	2.00	5.00
❑ 189 Clint Stoerner RC	2.50	6.00
❑ 190 James Whalen RC	2.00	5.00
❑ 191 Deltha O'Neal RC	3.00	8.00
❑ 192 Ian Gold RC	2.50	6.00
❑ 193 Kenoy Kennedy RC	2.00	5.00
❑ 194 Jarious Jackson RC	2.50	6.00
❑ 195 Leroy Fields RC	2.00	5.00
❑ 196 Barrett Green RC	2.00	5.00
❑ 197 Joey Jamison RC	2.00	5.00
❑ 198 Rondell Mealey RC	2.00	5.00
❑ 199 Rob Morris RC	2.50	6.00
❑ 200 Marcus Washington RC	2.50	6.00
❑ 201 Trevor Insley RC	2.00	5.00
❑ 202 Jamel White RC	2.50	6.00
❑ 203 Kevin McDougal RC	2.50	6.00
❑ 204 Ibn Green RC	2.00	5.00
❑ 205 T.J. Slaughter RC	2.00	5.00
❑ 206 Emanuel Smith RC	2.00	5.00
❑ 207 Herbert Goodman RC	2.50	6.00
❑ 208 William Bartee RC	2.50	6.00
❑ 209 Orantes Grant RC	2.00	5.00
❑ 210 Brad Hoover RC	2.50	6.00
❑ 211 Deon Dyer RC	2.50	6.00
❑ 212 Jonas Lewis RC	2.00	5.00
❑ 213 Chris Hovan RC	2.50	6.00
❑ 214 Fred Robbins RC	2.00	5.00
❑ 215 Michael Boireau RC	2.00	5.00
❑ 216 Giles Cole RC	2.00	5.00
❑ 217 Dave Stachelski RC	2.00	5.00
❑ 218 Patrick Pass RC	2.50	6.00
❑ 219 Darren Howard RC	2.50	6.00
❑ 220 Austin Wheatley RC	2.00	5.00
❑ 221 Kevin Houser RC	2.50	6.00
❑ 222 Rian Lindell RC	2.00	5.00
❑ 223 Jake Delhomme RC	12.00	30.00
❑ 224 Cornelius Griffin RC	2.50	6.00
❑ 225 Shaun Ellis RC	3.00	8.00
❑ 226 John Abraham RC	3.00	8.00
❑ 227 Travares Tillman RC	2.00	5.00
❑ 228 Julian Peterson RC	3.00	8.00
❑ 229 Marcus Knight RC	2.50	6.00
❑ 230 Thomas Hamner RC	2.00	5.00
❑ 231 Hank Poteat RC	2.50	6.00
❑ 232 Neil Rackers RC	3.00	8.00
❑ 233 Bobby Shaw RC	2.50	6.00
❑ 234 Rogers Beckett RC	2.50	6.00
❑ 235 Reggie Jones RC	2.00	5.00
❑ 236 Tim Seder RC	2.50	6.00
❑ 237 Durell Price RC	2.00	5.00
❑ 238 Ahmed Plummer RC	3.00	8.00
❑ 239 John Engelberger RC	2.50	6.00
❑ 240 Paul Smith RC	2.50	6.00
❑ 241 Chafie Fields RC	2.00	5.00
❑ 242 Kevin Feterik RC	2.00	5.00
❑ 243 Jacoby Shepherd RC	2.00	5.00
❑ 244 Nate Webster RC	2.00	5.00
❑ 245 Ketric Sanford RC	2.00	5.00
❑ 246 Tavarus Hogans RC	2.00	5.00
❑ 247 Keith Bulluck RC	3.00	8.00
❑ 248 Mike Green RC	2.50	6.00
❑ 249 Chris Coleman RC	3.00	8.00
❑ 250 Demario Brown RC	2.00	5.00
❑ 251 Billy Volek RC	4.00	10.00
❑ 252 Mareno Philyaw RC	2.00	5.00
❑ 253 Ethan Howell RC	2.00	5.00
❑ 254 Chris Samuels RC	2.50	6.00
❑ 255 Brandon Short RC	2.50	6.00
❑ 256 Maurice Smith RC	2.50	6.00
❑ 257 Frank Murphy RC	2.00	5.00
❑ 258 Darrick Vaughn RC	2.00	5.00
❑ 259 Payton Williams RC	2.00	5.00
❑ 260 JaJuan Seider RC	2.00	5.00
❑ 261 Antonio Banks EP RC	.75	2.00
❑ 262 Jonathan Brown EP RC	.75	2.00
❑ 263 Ontiwaun Carter EP RC	.75	2.00
❑ 264 Jeremaine Copeland EP	.75	2.00
❑ 265 Ralph Dawkins EP RC	1.25	3.00
❑ 266 Marques Douglas EP RC	.75	2.00
❑ 267 Kevin Drake EP RC	.75	2.00
❑ 268 Damon Dunn EP RC	1.25	3.00
❑ 269 Todd Floyd EP RC	.75	2.00
❑ 270 Tony Graziani EP	1.25	3.00
❑ 271 Derrick Ham EP RC	1.25	3.00
❑ 272 Duane Hawthorne EP RC	1.25	3.00
❑ 273 Alonzo Johnson EP RC	.75	2.00
❑ 274 Mark Kacmarynski EP RC	.75	2.00
❑ 275 Eric Kresser EP	.75	2.00
❑ 276 Jim Kubiak EP RC	1.25	3.00
❑ 277 Blaine McElmurry EP RC	.75	2.00
❑ 278 Scott Milanovich EP	1.25	3.00
❑ 279 Norman Miller EP RC	.75	2.00
❑ 280 Sean Morey EP RC	1.25	3.00
❑ 281 Jeff Ogden EP	1.25	3.00
❑ 282 Pepe Pearson EP RC	1.25	3.00
❑ 283 Ron Powlus EP RC	1.50	4.00
❑ 284 Jason Shelley EP RC	.75	2.00
❑ 285 Ben Snell EP RC	.75	2.00
❑ 286 Aaron Stecker EP RC	1.50	4.00
❑ 287 L.C. Stevens EP	.75	2.00
❑ 288 Mike Sutton EP RC	.75	2.00
❑ 289 Damian Vaughn EP RC	.75	2.00
❑ 290 Ted White EP	.75	2.00
❑ 291 Marcus Crandell EP RC	1.25	3.00
❑ 292 Darryl Daniel EP RC	1.25	3.00
❑ 293 Jesse Haynes EP	.75	2.00
❑ 294 Matt Lytle EP RC	1.25	3.00
❑ 295 Deon Mitchell EP RC	1.25	3.00
❑ 296 Kendrick Nord EP RC	.75	2.00
❑ 297 Ronnie Powell EP	.75	2.00
❑ 298 Selucio Sanford EP RC	1.25	3.00
❑ 299 Corey Thomas EP	.75	2.00
❑ 300 Vershan Jackson EP RC	.75	2.00
❑ 301 Michael Vick XRC	10.00	25.00
❑ 302 Drew Brees XRC	20.00	50.00
❑ 303 Quincy Carter XRC	4.00	10.00
❑ 304 Marques Tuiasosopa XRC	4.00	10.00
❑ 305 Chris Weinke XRC	4.00	10.00
❑ 306 LaDainian Tomlinson XRC	20.00	50.00
❑ 307 Deuce McAllister XRC	5.00	12.00
❑ 308 Michael Bennett XRC	4.00	10.00
❑ 309 Anthony Thomas XRC	4.00	10.00
❑ 310 LaMont Jordan XRC	5.00	12.00
❑ 311 David Terrell XRC	4.00	10.00
❑ 312 Koren Robinson XRC	4.00	10.00
❑ 313 Rod Gardner XRC	4.00	10.00
❑ 314 Santana Moss XRC	6.00	15.00
❑ 315 Freddie Mitchell XRC	2.50	6.00
❑ 316 Gerard Warren XRC	3.00	8.00
❑ 317 Justin Smith XRC	4.00	10.00
❑ 318 Richard Seymour XRC	5.00	12.00
❑ 319 Andre Carter XRC	3.00	8.00
❑ 320 Jamal Reynolds XRC	2.50	6.00

2001 Leaf Rookies and Stars

Card	Low	High
❑ COMP.SET w/o SP's (100)	7.50	20.00
❑ 1 Aaron Brooks	.20	.50
❑ 2 Ahman Green	.25	.60
❑ 3 Antonio Freeman	.25	.60
❑ 4 Brad Johnson	.20	.50
❑ 5 Brett Favre	.75	2.00
❑ 6 Brian Griese	.20	.50
❑ 7 Brian Urlacher	.30	.75
❑ 8 Bruce Smith	.25	.60
❑ 9 Cade McNown	.20	.50
❑ 10 Chad Pennington	.25	.60
❑ 11 Champ Bailey	.25	.60
❑ 12 Charles Woodson	.25	.60
❑ 13 Charlie Batch	.20	.50
❑ 14 Charlie Garner	.20	.50
❑ 15 Corey Dillon	.20	.50
❑ 16 Cris Carter	.25	.60
❑ 17 Curtis Martin	.25	.60
❑ 18 Dan Marino	.75	2.00
❑ 19 Daunte Culpepper	.25	.60
❑ 20 David Boston	.15	.40
❑ 21 Deion Sanders	.25	.60
❑ 22 Donovan McNabb	.30	.75
❑ 23 Doug Flutie	.25	.60
❑ 24 Drew Bledsoe	.25	.60
❑ 25 Duce Staley	.20	.50
❑ 26 Ed McCaffrey	.20	.50
❑ 27 Eddie George	.25	.60
❑ 28 Edgerrin James	.25	.60
❑ 29 Elvis Grbac	.20	.50
❑ 30 Emmitt Smith	.60	1.50
❑ 31 Eric Moulds	.20	.50
❑ 32 Fred Taylor	.25	.60
❑ 33 Germane Crowell	.15	.40
❑ 34 Ike Hilliard	.20	.50
❑ 35 Isaac Bruce	.25	.60
❑ 36 Jake Plummer	.20	.50
❑ 37 Jamal Anderson	.20	.50
❑ 38 Jamal Lewis	.25	.60
❑ 39 James Allen	.15	.40
❑ 40 James Stewart	.15	.40
❑ 41 Jay Fiedler	.20	.50
❑ 42 Jeff Garcia	.20	.50
❑ 43 Jeff George	.20	.50
❑ 44 Jeff Lewis	.15	.40
❑ 45 Jerome Bettis	.25	.60
❑ 46 Jerry Rice	.50	1.25
❑ 47 Jevon Kearse	.20	.50
❑ 48 Jimmy Smith	.20	.50
❑ 49 Joey Galloway	.20	.50
❑ 50 John Elway	.60	1.50
❑ 51 Junior Seau	.25	.60
❑ 52 Keenan McCardell	.20	.50
❑ 53 Kerry Collins	.20	.50
❑ 54 Kevin Johnson	.15	.40
❑ 55 Keyshawn Johnson	.20	.50
❑ 56 Kordell Stewart	.20	.50
❑ 57 Kurt Warner	.30	.75
❑ 58 Lamar Smith	.20	.50
❑ 59 Marcus Robinson	.20	.50
❑ 60 Mark Brunell	.25	.60
❑ 61 Marshall Faulk	.25	.60
❑ 62 Marvin Harrison	.25	.60
❑ 63 Matt Hasselbeck	.25	.60
❑ 64 Mike Alstott	.20	.50
❑ 65 Mike Anderson	.20	.50
❑ 66 Muhsin Muhammad	.20	.50
❑ 67 Peter Warrick	.20	.50
❑ 68 Peyton Manning	.60	1.50
❑ 69 Priest Holmes	.25	.60
❑ 70 Randy Moss	.30	.75
❑ 71 Ray Lewis	.25	.60
❑ 72 Rich Gannon	.20	.50
❑ 73 Ricky Watters	.20	.50
❑ 74 Ricky Williams	.25	.60
❑ 75 Rob Johnson	.20	.50
❑ 76 Rod Smith	.20	.50
❑ 77 Ron Dayne	.20	.50
❑ 78 Shannon Sharpe	.25	.60
❑ 79 Shaun Alexander	.25	.60
❑ 80 Stephen Davis	.20	.50
❑ 81 Steve McNair	.25	.60
❑ 82 Steve Young	.30	.75
❑ 83 Sylvester Morris	.15	.40
❑ 84 Terrell Davis	.25	.60
❑ 85 Terrell Owens	.25	.60
❑ 86 Thomas Jones	.20	.50
❑ 87 Tim Brown	.25	.60
❑ 88 Tim Couch	.15	.40
❑ 89 Tony Banks	.15	.40
❑ 90 Tony Gonzalez	.20	.50
❑ 91 Torry Holt	.20	.50
❑ 92 Travis Taylor	.15	.40
❑ 93 Trent Green	.25	.60
❑ 94 Troy Aikman	.40	1.00
❑ 95 Tyrone Wheatley	.20	.50
❑ 96 Vinny Testaverde	.20	.50
❑ 97 Warren Sapp	.20	.50
❑ 98 Warrick Dunn	.25	.60
❑ 99 Wayne Chrebet	.20	.50
❑ 100 Zach Thomas	.25	.60
❑ 101 A.J. Feeley RC	1.50	4.00
❑ 102 Josh Booty RC	1.50	4.00
❑ 103 Roderick Robinson RC	1.25	3.00
❑ 104 Renaldo Hill RC	1.50	4.00
❑ 105 Harold Blackmon RC	1.25	3.00
❑ 106 Rudi Johnson RC	2.00	5.00
❑ 107 Curtis Fuller RC	1.25	3.00
❑ 108 Dan Alexander RC	1.50	4.00
❑ 109 Anthony Thomas RPS	2.00	5.00
❑ 110 Travis Minor RPS	1.50	4.00
❑ 111 Heath Evans RC	1.50	4.00
❑ 112 Joe Walker RC	1.25	3.00
❑ 113 Moran Norris RC	1.25	3.00
❑ 114 Quincy Carter RPS	1.50	4.00
❑ 115 Michael Vick RPS	2.50	6.00
❑ 116 Vinny Sutherland RC	1.25	3.00
❑ 117 Scotty Anderson RC	1.50	4.00
❑ 118 Eddie Berlin RC	1.25	3.00
❑ 119 Jonathan Carter RC	1.25	3.00
❑ 120 Monty Beisel RC	1.25	3.00
❑ 121 T.J. Houshmandzadeh RC	3.00	8.00
❑ 122 Rodney Bailey RC	1.25	3.00
❑ 123 Reggie Germany RC	1.25	3.00
❑ 124 Ellis Wyms RC	1.25	3.00
❑ 125 Koren Robinson RPS	2.00	5.00
❑ 126 Antonio Pierce RC	4.00	10.00
❑ 127 Arnold Jackson RC	1.25	3.00
❑ 128 Andre Rone RC	1.25	3.00
❑ 129 Richard Newsome RC	1.25	3.00
❑ 130 Ifeanyi Ohalete RC	1.25	3.00
❑ 131 Dan O'Leary RC	1.25	3.00
❑ 132 Shad Meier RC	1.25	3.00
❑ 133 Jay Feely RC	2.00	5.00
❑ 134 Brandon Manumaleuna RC	1.50	4.00
❑ 135 Riall Johnson RC	1.25	3.00
❑ 136 Snoop Minnis RPS	1.50	4.00
❑ 137 Jermaine Hampton RC	1.25	3.00
❑ 138 Johnny Huggins RC	1.25	3.00
❑ 139 Marcellus Rivers RC	1.25	3.00
❑ 140 Andre Carter RPS	2.00	5.00
❑ 141 Michael Stone RC	1.25	3.00
❑ 142 Tony Dixon RC	1.50	4.00
❑ 143 Bhawoh Jue RC	1.50	4.00
❑ 144 Will Peterson RC	1.50	4.00
❑ 145 Anthony Henry RC	2.00	5.00
❑ 146 Marques Tuiasosopo RPS	1.50	4.00
❑ 147 Reggie Swinton RC	1.25	3.00
❑ 148 Robert Carswell RC	1.25	3.00
❑ 149 Freddie Mitchell RPS	1.25	3.00
❑ 150 Idrees Bashir RC	1.25	3.00
❑ 151 James Boyd RC	1.25	3.00
❑ 152 Chris Chambers RPS	2.00	5.00
❑ 153 Aaron Schobel RC	2.00	5.00
❑ 154 Dominic Raiola RC	1.25	3.00
❑ 155 Derrick Burgess RC	2.00	5.00
❑ 156 DeLawrence Grant RC	1.25	3.00
❑ 157 Karon Riley RC	1.25	3.00
❑ 158 Cedric Scott RC	1.25	3.00
❑ 159 Patrick Washington RC	1.25	3.00
❑ 160 Eric Johnson RC	2.00	5.00
❑ 161 Tevita Ofahengaue RC	1.25	3.00
❑ 162 Chris Cooper RC	1.25	3.00
❑ 163 Fred Wakefield RC	1.25	3.00
❑ 164 Kenny Smith RC	1.25	3.00
❑ 165 Marcus Bell RC	1.25	3.00
❑ 166 Mario Fatafehi RC	1.25	3.00
❑ 167 Anthony Herron RC	1.25	3.00
❑ 168 Joe Tafoya RC	1.25	3.00
❑ 169 Morlon Greenwood RC	1.25	3.00
❑ 170 Orlando Huff RC	1.25	3.00
❑ 171 Carlos Polk RC	1.25	3.00
❑ 172 Edgerton Hartwell RC	1.25	3.00
❑ 173 Zeke Moreno RC	1.50	4.00
❑ 174 Alex Lincoln RC	1.25	3.00
❑ 175 Quinton Caver RC	1.25	3.00
❑ 176 Matt Stewart RC	1.25	3.00
❑ 177 Markus Steele RC	1.25	3.00
❑ 178 Dwight Smith RC	1.25	3.00
❑ 179 Reggie Wayne RPS	3.00	8.00
❑ 180 Jerametrius Butler RC	1.25	3.00
❑ 181 Jason Doering RC	1.25	3.00
❑ 182 John Howell RC	1.25	3.00
❑ 183 Alvin Porter RC	1.25	3.00
❑ 184 Eric Downing RC	1.25	3.00
❑ 185 John Nix RC	1.25	3.00
❑ 186 Tim Baker RC	1.25	3.00
❑ 187 Robert Garza RC	1.25	3.00
❑ 188 Randy Chevrier RC	1.25	3.00
❑ 189 Drew Brees RPS	6.00	15.00
❑ 190 Shawn Worthen RC	1.25	3.00
❑ 191 Drew Bennett RC	2.00	5.00
❑ 192 Marlon McCree RC	1.25	3.00
❑ 193 David Terrell RPS	1.50	4.00
❑ 194 Jeff Backus RC	1.25	3.00
❑ 195 Otis Leverette RC	1.25	3.00
❑ 196 Jason Glenn RC	1.25	3.00
❑ 197 Rashad Holman RC	1.25	3.00
❑ 198 T.J. Turner RC	1.25	3.00
❑ 199 Lynn Scott RC	1.25	3.00
❑ 200 Bill Gramatica RC	1.25	3.00
❑ 201 Michael Vick RC	6.00	15.00
❑ 202 Drew Brees RC	15.00	40.00
❑ 203 Quincy Carter RC	2.50	6.00
❑ 204 Jesse Palmer RC	3.00	8.00
❑ 205 Mike McMahon RC	2.50	6.00
❑ 206 Dave Dickenson RC	2.50	6.00
❑ 207 Jameel Cook RC	2.50	6.00
❑ 208 Marques Tuiasosopo RC	2.50	6.00
❑ 209 Chris Weinke RC	2.50	6.00
❑ 210 Sage Rosenfels RC	3.00	8.00
❑ 211 Josh Heupel RC	3.00	8.00
❑ 212 LaDainian Tomlinson RC	20.00	50.00
❑ 213 Michael Bennett RC	3.00	8.00
❑ 214 Anthony Thomas RC	3.00	8.00
❑ 215 Travis Henry RC	3.00	8.00
❑ 216 James Jackson RC	2.50	6.00
❑ 217 Correll Buckhalter RC	3.00	8.00
❑ 218 Derrick Blaylock RC	2.50	6.00
❑ 219 Dee Brown RC	2.00	5.00
❑ 220 LeVar Woods RC	2.50	6.00
❑ 221 Deuce McAllister RC	4.00	10.00
❑ 222 LaMont Jordan RC	3.00	8.00
❑ 223 Kevan Barlow RC	2.50	6.00
❑ 224 Travis Minor RC	2.50	6.00
❑ 225 David Terrell RC	2.50	6.00
❑ 226 Koren Robinson RC	3.00	8.00
❑ 227 Rod Gardner RC	2.50	6.00
❑ 228 Santana Moss RC	5.00	12.00
❑ 229 Freddie Mitchell RC	2.00	5.00
❑ 230 Reggie Wayne RC	8.00	20.00
❑ 231 Quincy Morgan RC	2.50	6.00
❑ 232 Chris Chambers RC	5.00	12.00
❑ 233 Steve Smith RC	8.00	20.00
❑ 234 Snoop Minnis RC	2.50	6.00
❑ 235 Justin McCareins RC	2.50	6.00
❑ 236 Onome Ojo RC	2.00	5.00
❑ 237 Damerien McCants RC	2.50	6.00
❑ 238 Mike McMahon RPS	2.50	6.00
❑ 239 Cedrick Wilson RC	3.00	8.00
❑ 240 Kevin Kasper RC	2.50	0.00
❑ 241 Chris Taylor RC	2.00	5.00
❑ 242 Ken-Yon Rambo RC	2.00	5.00
❑ 243 Richmond Flowers RC	2.00	5.00
❑ 244 Andre King RC	2.00	5.00
❑ 245 Boo Williams RC	2.50	6.00
❑ 246 Adrian Wilson RC	4.00	10.00
❑ 247 Cory Bird RC	2.50	6.00
❑ 248 Alex Bannister RC	2.00	5.00
❑ 249 Elvis Joseph RC	2.00	5.00
❑ 250 Chad Johnson RC	8.00	20.00
❑ 251 Robert Ferguson RC	3.00	8.00
❑ 252 David Martin RC	2.00	5.00
❑ 253 Quentin McCord RC	2.50	6.00
❑ 254 Todd Heap RC	3.00	8.00
❑ 255 Alge Crumpler RC	3.00	8.00
❑ 256 Nate Clements RC	3.00	8.00
❑ 257 Will Allen RC	3.00	8.00
❑ 258 Willie Middlebrooks RC	2.50	6.00
❑ 259 Fred Smoot RC	3.00	8.00
❑ 260 Andre Dyson RC	2.00	5.00
❑ 261 Gary Baxter RC	2.50	6.00
❑ 262 Jamar Fletcher RC	2.00	5.00
❑ 263 Ken Lucas RC	2.50	6.00
❑ 264 Tay Cody RC	2.00	5.00
❑ 265 Eric Kelly RC	2.00	5.00
❑ 266 Adam Archuleta RC	2.50	6.00

❑ 267 Derrick Gibson RC	2.00	5.00
❑ 268 Jarrod Cooper RC	2.50	6.00
❑ 269 Hakim Akbar RC	2.00	5.00
❑ 270 Tony Driver RC	2.50	6.00
❑ 271 Justin Smith RC	3.00	8.00
❑ 272 Andre Carter RC	3.00	8.00
❑ 273 Jamal Reynolds RC	2.50	6.00
❑ 274 Gerard Warren RC	2.50	6.00
❑ 275 Richard Seymour RC	3.00	8.00
❑ 276 Damione Lewis RC	2.50	6.00
❑ 277 Casey Hampton RC	2.50	6.00
❑ 278 Marcus Stroud RC	2.50	6.00
❑ 279 Benjamin Gay RC	2.50	6.00
❑ 280 Shaun Rogers RC	3.00	8.00
❑ 281 Dan Morgan RC	3.00	8.00
❑ 282 Kendrell Bell RC	3.00	8.00
❑ 283 Tommy Polley RC	2.50	6.00
❑ 284 Jamie Winborn RC	2.50	6.00
❑ 285 Sedrick Hodge RC	2.00	5.00
❑ 286 Torrance Marshall RC	2.50	6.00
❑ 287 Eric Westmoreland RC	2.00	5.00
❑ 288 Brian Allen RC	2.00	5.00
❑ 289 Brandon Spoon RC	2.50	6.00
❑ 290 Henry Burris RC	3.00	8.00
❑ 291 Leonard Davis RC	2.50	6.00
❑ 292 Kenyatta Walker RC	2.00	5.00
❑ 293 Cedric James RC	2.00	5.00
❑ 294 Sean Brewer RC	2.00	5.00
❑ 295 Jason Brookins RC	3.00	8.00
❑ 296 Kyle Vanden Bosch RC	3.00	8.00
❑ 297 Nick Goings RC	3.00	8.00
❑ 298 Kris Jenkins RC	3.00	8.00
❑ 299 Dominic Rhodes RC	3.00	8.00
❑ 300 Leonard Myers RC	2.00	5.00

2002 Leaf Rookies and Stars

❑ COMPLETE SET (300)	100.00	250.00
❑ COMP.SET w/o SP's (100)	10.00	25.00
❑ 1 Jake Plummer	.25	.60
❑ 2 David Boston	.20	.50
❑ 3 Thomas Jones	.25	.60
❑ 4 Michael Vick	.30	.75
❑ 5 Warrick Dunn	.25	.60
❑ 6 Jamal Lewis	.25	.60
❑ 7 Chris Redman	.20	.50
❑ 8 Ray Lewis	.30	.75
❑ 9 Drew Bledsoe	.30	.75
❑ 10 Travis Henry	.25	.60
❑ 11 Eric Moulds	.25	.60
❑ 12 Steve Smith	.30	.75
❑ 13 Chris Weinke	.20	.50
❑ 14 Lamar Smith	.25	.60
❑ 15 Anthony Thomas	.25	.60
❑ 16 David Terrell	.20	.50
❑ 17 Brian Urlacher	.40	1.00
❑ 18 Corey Dillon	.25	.60
❑ 19 Michael Westbrook	.20	.50
❑ 20 Peter Warrick	.25	.60
❑ 21 Tim Couch	.20	.50
❑ 22 James Jackson	.20	.50
❑ 23 Kevin Johnson	.20	.50
❑ 24 Quincy Carter	.20	.50
❑ 25 Joey Galloway	.25	.60
❑ 26 Emmitt Smith	.75	2.00
❑ 27 Terrell Davis	.30	.75
❑ 28 Brian Griese	.25	.60
❑ 29 Ed McCaffrey	.25	.60
❑ 30 Rod Smith	.25	.60
❑ 31 Mike McMahon	.20	.50
❑ 32 Germane Crowell	.20	.50
❑ 33 Az-Zahir Hakim	.20	.50
❑ 34 Terry Glenn	.25	.60
❑ 35 Brett Favre	.75	2.00
❑ 36 Ahman Green	.25	.60
❑ 37 James Allen	.20	.50
❑ 38 Corey Bradford	.20	.50
❑ 39 Peyton Manning	.60	1.50
❑ 40 Edgerrin James	.30	.75
❑ 41 Marvin Harrison	.30	.75
❑ 42 Qadry Ismail	.25	.60
❑ 43 Fred Taylor	.30	.75
❑ 44 Mark Brunell	.25	.60
❑ 45 Jimmy Smith	.25	.60
❑ 46 Priest Holmes	.30	.75
❑ 47 Tony Gonzalez	.25	.60
❑ 48 Trent Green	.25	.60
❑ 49 Johnnie Morton	.25	.60
❑ 50 Chris Chambers	.30	.75
❑ 51 Ricky Williams	.30	.75
❑ 52 Zach Thomas	.30	.75
❑ 53 Randy Moss	.30	.75
❑ 54 Michael Bennett	.25	.60
❑ 55 Derrick Alexander	.25	.60
❑ 56 Daunte Culpepper	.25	.60
❑ 57 Tom Brady	.75	2.00
❑ 58 Troy Brown	.25	.60
❑ 59 Antowain Smith	.25	.60
❑ 60 Joe Horn	.25	.60
❑ 61 Aaron Brooks	.25	.60
❑ 62 Deuce McAllister	.30	.75
❑ 63 Kerry Collins	.25	.60
❑ 64 Amani Toomer	.25	.60
❑ 65 Michael Strahan	.30	.75
❑ 66 Laveranues Coles	.30	.75
❑ 67 Vinny Testaverde	.25	.60
❑ 68 Curtis Martin	.30	.75
❑ 69 Rich Gannon	.25	.60
❑ 70 Tim Brown	.30	.75
❑ 71 Jerry Rice	.60	1.50
❑ 72 Donovan McNabb	.40	1.00
❑ 73 Freddie Mitchell	.20	.50
❑ 74 Duce Staley	.25	.60
❑ 75 Kordell Stewart	.25	.60
❑ 76 Jerome Bettis	.30	.75
❑ 77 Plaxico Burress	.25	.60
❑ 78 Drew Brees	.50	1.25
❑ 79 LaDainian Tomlinson	.50	1.25
❑ 80 Junior Seau	.30	.75
❑ 81 Jeff Garcia	.25	.60
❑ 82 Garrison Hearst	.25	.60
❑ 83 Terrell Owens	.30	.75
❑ 84 Shaun Alexander	.30	.75
❑ 85 Koren Robinson	.20	.50
❑ 86 Kurt Warner	.30	.75
❑ 87 Marshall Faulk	.30	.75
❑ 88 Isaac Bruce	.30	.75
❑ 89 Torry Holt	.30	.75
❑ 90 Rob Johnson	.25	.60
❑ 91 Brad Johnson	.25	.60
❑ 92 Keyshawn Johnson	.25	.60
❑ 93 Mike Alstott	.25	.60
❑ 94 Eddie George	.25	.60
❑ 95 Steve McNair	.30	.75
❑ 96 Derrick Mason	.25	.60
❑ 97 Jevon Kearse	.25	.60
❑ 98 Stephen Davis	.25	.60
❑ 99 Sage Rosenfels	.25	.60
❑ 100 Rod Gardner	.20	.50
❑ 101 Adrian Peterson RC	1.50	4.00
❑ 102 Nick Rolovich RC	1.00	2.50
❑ 103 Lew Thomas RC	1.00	2.50
❑ 104 David Carr RC	1.50	4.00
❑ 105 Daryl Jones RC	1.00	2.50
❑ 106 Brandon Doman RC	1.00	2.50
❑ 107 Ed Reed RC	5.00	12.00
❑ 108 Tellis Redmon RC	1.00	2.50
❑ 109 Andra Davis RC	1.00	2.50
❑ 110 Kendall Newson RC	1.00	2.50
❑ 111 Joe Burns RC	1.00	2.50
❑ 112 Maurice Morris RC	1.50	4.00
❑ 113 Craig Nall RC	1.25	3.00
❑ 114 Phillip Buchanon RC	1.50	4.00
❑ 115 Mike Echols RC	1.00	2.50
❑ 116 Terry Jones Jr. RC	1.00	2.50
❑ 117 Anthony Weaver RC	1.00	2.50
❑ 118 Jeb Putzier RC	1.50	4.00
❑ 119 Tony Fisher RC	1.25	3.00
❑ 120 Joey Harrington RC	1.50	4.00
❑ 121 Lamar Gordon RC	1.50	4.00
❑ 122 Tracey Wistrom RC	1.25	3.00
❑ 123 Ashley Lelie RC	1.50	4.00
❑ 124 Will Witherspoon RC	1.50	4.00
❑ 125 Travis Stephens RC	1.00	2.50
❑ 126 J.T. O'Sullivan RC	1.50	4.00
❑ 127 Brian Westbrook RC	5.00	12.00
❑ 128 James Mungro RC	1.50	4.00
❑ 129 Lamont Thompson RC	1.25	3.00
❑ 130 Jarrod Baxter RC	1.00	2.50
❑ 131 Andre Lott RC	1.00	2.50
❑ 132 Steve Bellisari RC	1.00	2.50
❑ 133 David Garrard RC	2.50	6.00
❑ 134 Michael Lewis RC	1.50	4.00
❑ 135 James Allen RC	1.00	2.50
❑ 136 Bryant McKinnie RC	1.00	2.50
❑ 137 Marques Anderson RC	1.25	3.00
❑ 138 Rohan Davey RC	1.50	4.00
❑ 139 Kyle Johnson RC	1.00	2.50
❑ 140 Dusty Bonner RC	1.00	2.50
❑ 141 DeShaun Foster RC	1.50	4.00
❑ 142 Chad Hutchinson RC	1.00	2.50
❑ 143 Jack Brewer RC	1.00	2.50
❑ 144 Eddie Freeman RC	1.00	2.50
❑ 145 Seth Burford RC	1.00	2.50
❑ 146 Roosevelt Williams RC	1.00	2.50
❑ 147 Jamin Elliott RC	1.00	2.50
❑ 148 Charles Grant RC	1.50	4.00
❑ 149 Jeff Kelly RC	1.00	2.50
❑ 150 Cliff Russell RC	1.00	2.50
❑ 151 Josh Scobey RC	1.25	3.00
❑ 152 Tank Williams RC	1.25	3.00
❑ 153 Larry Tripplett RC	1.00	2.50
❑ 154 Clinton Portis RC	4.00	10.00
❑ 155 Javin Hunter RC	1.00	2.50
❑ 156 Deveren Johnson RC	1.00	2.50
❑ 157 Reche Caldwell RC	1.50	4.00
❑ 158 Ronald Curry RC	1.50	4.00
❑ 159 Chris Hope RC	1.50	4.00
❑ 160 Damien Anderson RC	1.25	3.00
❑ 161 Saleem Rasheed RC	1.00	2.50
❑ 162 Albert Haynesworth RC	1.50	4.00
❑ 163 Bryan Gilmore RC	1.00	2.50
❑ 164 Wes Pate RC	1.00	2.50
❑ 165 Deion Branch RC	1.50	4.00
❑ 166 Ben Leber RC	1.00	2.50
❑ 167 Andre Davis RC	1.25	3.00
❑ 168 Darrell Hill RC	1.00	2.50
❑ 169 Rodney Wright RC	1.00	2.50
❑ 170 Demontray Carter RC	1.00	2.50
❑ 171 Zak Kustok RC	1.00	2.50
❑ 172 James Wofford RC	1.00	2.50
❑ 173 David Priestley RC	1.00	2.50
❑ 174 Donte Stallworth RC	1.50	4.00
❑ 175 Marc Boerigter RC	1.50	4.00
❑ 176 Freddie Milons RC	1.00	2.50
❑ 177 John Simon RC	1.00	2.50
❑ 178 Josh Norman RC	1.00	2.50
❑ 179 Jabar Gaffney RC	1.50	4.00
❑ 180 Doug Jolley RC	1.00	2.50
❑ 181 Preston Parsons RC	1.00	2.50
❑ 182 Chris Baker RC	1.00	2.50
❑ 183 Javon Walker RC	1.50	4.00
❑ 184 Justin Peelle RC	1.00	2.50
❑ 185 Josh Reed RC	1.25	3.00
❑ 186 Omar Easy RC	1.25	3.00
❑ 187 Jerramy Stevens RC	1.50	4.00
❑ 188 Shaun Hill RC	2.00	5.00
❑ 189 David Thornton RC	1.00	2.50
❑ 190 John Henderson RC	1.50	4.00
❑ 191 Verron Haynes RC	1.25	3.00
❑ 192 Dennis Johnson RC	1.00	2.50
❑ 193 Napoleon Harris RC	1.25	3.00
❑ 194 Jonathan Wells RC	1.50	4.00
❑ 195 Howard Green RC	1.00	2.50
❑ 196 Travis Fisher RC	1.25	3.00
❑ 197 Anton Palepoi RC	1.00	2.50
❑ 198 Ed Stansbury RC	1.00	2.50
❑ 199 Josh McCown RC	1.50	4.00
❑ 200 Alex Brown RC	1.50	4.00
❑ 201 Joseph Jefferson RC	1.00	2.50
❑ 202 Julius Peppers RC	2.50	6.00
❑ 203 Larry Ned RC	1.00	2.50
❑ 204 Rock Cartwright RC	1.50	4.00
❑ 205 Kalimba Edwards RC	1.25	3.00
❑ 206 Matt Schobel RC	1.50	4.00
❑ 207 Maurice Jackson RC	1.00	2.50
❑ 208 Kelly Campbell RC	1.25	3.00
❑ 209 Mel Mitchell RC	1.00	2.50
❑ 210 Ken Simonton RC	1.00	2.50
❑ 211 Brian Allen RC	1.00	2.50
❑ 212 Darnell Sanders RC	1.00	2.50
❑ 213 Jesse Chatman RC	1.00	2.50
❑ 214 Keyuo Craver RC	1.00	2.50

❑ 215 Chester Taylor RC	2.50	6.00
❑ 216 Kurt Kittner RC	1.00	2.50
❑ 217 Derek Ross RC	1.25	3.00
❑ 218 Charles Hill RC	1.00	2.50
❑ 219 Jarvis Green RC	1.00	2.50
❑ 220 Mike Jenkins RC	1.00	2.50
❑ 221 Robert Royal RC	1.50	4.00
❑ 222 Ladell Betts RC	1.50	4.00
❑ 223 Antwoine Womack RC	1.00	2.50
❑ 224 Raonall Smith RC	1.00	2.50
❑ 225 Charles Stackhouse RC	1.00	2.50
❑ 226 Quinn Gray RC	1.25	3.00
❑ 227 Lito Sheppard RC	1.50	4.00
❑ 228 Ryan Van Dyke RC	1.00	2.50
❑ 229 Will Overstreet RC	1.00	2.50
❑ 230 Leonard Henry RC	1.00	2.50
❑ 231 Dorsett Davis RC	1.00	2.50
❑ 232 Marquand Manuel RC	1.00	2.50
❑ 233 Luke Staley RC	1.00	2.50
❑ 234 Carlos Hall RC	1.00	2.50
❑ 235 Marcus Brady RC	1.00	2.50
❑ 236 Ryan Denney RC	1.00	2.50
❑ 237 Eric McCoo RC	1.00	2.50
❑ 238 Major Applewhite RC	1.50	4.00
❑ 239 Adam Tate RC	1.00	2.50
❑ 240 Marquise Walker RC	1.00	2.50
❑ 241 John Flowers RC	1.00	2.50
❑ 242 Levar Fisher RC	1.00	2.50
❑ 243 Ricky Williams RC	1.25	3.00
❑ 244 Mike Rumph RC	1.00	2.50
❑ 245 Delvin Joyce RC	1.00	2.50
❑ 246 Bryan Thomas RC	1.00	2.50
❑ 247 Mike Williams RC	1.00	2.50
❑ 248 Sam Brandon RC	1.00	2.50
❑ 249 Eddie Drummond RC	1.00	2.50
❑ 250 Najeh Davenport RC	1.50	4.00
❑ 251 Brian Williams RC	1.00	2.50
❑ 252 Scott Fujita RC	1.50	4.00
❑ 253 Dwight Freeney RC	2.50	6.00
❑ 254 Herb Haygood RC	1.00	2.50
❑ 255 Patrick Ramsey RC	1.50	4.00
❑ 256 Atnaf Harris RC	1.00	2.50
❑ 257 Jason McAddley RC	1.25	3.00
❑ 258 Pete Rebstock RC	1.00	2.50
❑ 259 Quentin Jammer RC	1.50	4.00
❑ 260 Luke Butkus RC	1.00	2.50
❑ 261 Jeremy Allen RC	1.00	2.50
❑ 262 Jake Schifino RC	1.00	2.50
❑ 263 Randy Fasani RC	1.25	3.00
❑ 264 Bryan Fletcher RC	1.00	2.50
❑ 265 Jeremy Shockey RC	2.50	6.00
❑ 266 Kevin Bentley RC	1.00	2.50
❑ 267 Jon McGraw RC	1.00	2.50
❑ 268 Robert Thomas RC	1.00	2.50
❑ 269 Coy Wire RC	1.25	3.00
❑ 270 Brian Poli-Dixon RC	1.00	2.50
❑ 271 Willie Offord RC	1.00	2.50
❑ 272 Rocky Calmus RC	1.25	3.00
❑ 273 Sheldon Brown RC	1.50	4.00
❑ 274 Terry Charles RC	1.00	2.50
❑ 275 Ron Johnson RC	1.25	3.00
❑ 276 Roy Williams RC	2.00	5.00
❑ 277 Sam Simmons RC	1.00	2.50
❑ 278 Andre Goodman RC	1.00	2.50
❑ 279 Ryan Sims RC	1.50	4.00
❑ 280 Antwaan Randle El RC	1.50	4.00
❑ 281 Alan Harper RC	1.00	2.50
❑ 282 Tavon Mason RC	1.00	2.50
❑ 283 Kahlil Hill RC	1.00	2.50
❑ 284 Antonio Bryant RC	2.00	5.00
❑ 285 Akin Ayodele RC	1.25	3.00
❑ 286 T.J. Duckett RC	1.50	4.00
❑ 287 Kenyon Coleman RC	1.00	2.50
❑ 288 Tim Carter RC	1.25	3.00
❑ 289 Lamont Brightful RC	1.00	2.50
❑ 290 Trev Faulk RC	1.00	2.50
❑ 291 Randy McMichael RC	1.50	4.00
❑ 292 Daniel Graham RC	1.25	3.00
❑ 293 Wendell Bryant RC	1.00	2.50
❑ 294 Jamar Martin RC	1.25	3.00
❑ 295 Chris Luzar RC	1.00	2.50
❑ 296 William Green RC	1.25	3.00
❑ 297 Lee Mays RC	1.00	2.50
❑ 298 Eric Crouch RC	1.50	4.00
❑ 299 Steve Smith RC	1.00	2.50
❑ 300 Woody Dantzler RC	1.25	3.00

2003 Leaf Rookies and Stars

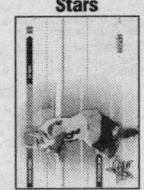

❑ COMP.SET w/o SP's (100)	7.50	20.00
❑ 1 Emmitt Smith	.75	2.00
❑ 2 Michael Vick	.30	.75
❑ 3 Peerless Price	.20	.50
❑ 4 T.J. Duckett	.25	.60
❑ 5 Warrick Dunn	.25	.60
❑ 6 Jamal Lewis	.30	.75
❑ 7 Ray Lewis	.30	.75
❑ 8 Drew Bledsoe	.30	.75
❑ 9 Eric Moulds	.25	.60
❑ 10 Josh Reed	.20	.50
❑ 11 Travis Henry	.25	.60
❑ 12 Julius Peppers	.30	.75
❑ 13 Anthony Thomas	.25	.60
❑ 14 Brian Urlacher	.50	1.25
❑ 15 Marty Booker	.25	.60
❑ 16 Kordell Stewart	.25	.60
❑ 17 Corey Dillon	.25	.60
❑ 18 Chad Johnson	.30	.75
❑ 19 Tim Couch	.20	.50
❑ 20 William Green	.20	.50
❑ 21 Antonio Bryant	.30	.75
❑ 22 Roy Williams	.30	.75
❑ 23 Ashley Lelie	.20	.50
❑ 24 Clinton Portis	.40	1.00
❑ 25 Ed McCaffrey	.25	.60
❑ 26 Jake Plummer	.25	.60
❑ 27 Rod Smith	.25	.60
❑ 28 Joey Harrington	.25	.60
❑ 29 Ahman Green	.30	.75
❑ 30 Brett Favre	.75	2.00
❑ 31 Donald Driver	.30	.75
❑ 32 Javon Walker	.25	.60
❑ 33 David Carr	.30	.75
❑ 34 Edgerrin James	.30	.75
❑ 35 Marvin Harrison	.30	.75
❑ 36 Peyton Manning	.60	1.50
❑ 37 Fred Taylor	.30	.75
❑ 38 Jimmy Smith	.25	.60
❑ 39 Mark Brunell	.25	.60
❑ 40 Priest Holmes	.30	.75
❑ 41 Tony Gonzalez	.25	.60
❑ 42 Trent Green	.25	.60
❑ 43 Chris Chambers	.25	.60
❑ 44 Jay Fiedler	.25	.60
❑ 45 Junior Seau	.30	.75
❑ 46 Ricky Williams	.25	.60
❑ 47 Zach Thomas	.30	.75
❑ 48 Daunte Culpepper	.30	.75
❑ 49 Michael Bennett	.25	.60
❑ 50 Randy Moss	.30	.75
❑ 51 Tom Brady	.75	2.00
❑ 52 Troy Brown	.25	.60
❑ 53 Aaron Brooks	.25	.60
❑ 54 Deuce McAllister	.30	.75
❑ 55 Donte Stallworth	.25	.60
❑ 56 Joe Horn	.25	.60
❑ 57 Jeremy Shockey	.30	.75
❑ 58 Kerry Collins	.25	.60
❑ 59 Michael Strahan	.25	.60
❑ 60 Tiki Barber	.30	.75
❑ 61 Chad Pennington	.30	.75
❑ 62 Curtis Martin	.30	.75
❑ 63 Santana Moss	.25	.60
❑ 64 Charles Woodson	.25	.60
❑ 65 Jerry Rice	.60	1.50
❑ 66 Rich Gannon	.25	.60
❑ 67 Tim Brown	.30	.75
❑ 68 Donovan McNabb	.30	.75
❑ 69 Antwaan Randle El	.25	.60
❑ 70 Tommy Maddox	.25	.60
❑ 71 Jerome Bettis	.30	.75
❑ 72 Kendrell Bell	.20	.50
❑ 73 Plaxico Burress	.30	.75
❑ 74 David Boston	.20	.50
❑ 75 Drew Brees	.30	.75
❑ 76 LaDainian Tomlinson	.40	1.00
❑ 77 Kevan Barlow	.20	.50
❑ 78 Jeff Garcia	.30	.75
❑ 79 Terrell Owens	.30	.75
❑ 80 Matt Hasselbeck	.25	.60
❑ 81 Koren Robinson	.25	.60
❑ 82 Shaun Alexander	.30	.75
❑ 83 Isaac Bruce	.30	.75
❑ 84 Kurt Warner	.30	.75
❑ 85 Marshall Faulk	.30	.75
❑ 86 Torry Holt	.30	.75
❑ 87 Brad Johnson	.25	.60
❑ 88 Keyshawn Johnson	.30	.75
❑ 89 Mike Alstott	.30	.75
❑ 90 Warren Sapp	.25	.60
❑ 91 Eddie George	.25	.60
❑ 92 Jevon Kearse	.25	.60
❑ 93 Steve McNair	.30	.75
❑ 94 Laveranues Coles	.25	.60
❑ 95 Rod Gardner	.20	.50
❑ 96 Patrick Ramsey	.25	.60
❑ 97 Boller/Suggs/Smith CL	.25	.60
❑ 98 R.Grossman/T.Jacobs CL	.10	.25
❑ 99 A.Boldin/B.Johnson CL	.25	.60
❑ 100 T.Calico/C.Brown CL	.20	.50
❑ 101 Charles Tillman RC	2.00	5.00
❑ 102 Justin Griffith RC	1.25	3.00
❑ 103 Ovie Mughelli RC	1.00	2.50
❑ 104 Chris Edmonds RC	1.00	2.50
❑ 105 Jeremi Johnson RC	1.00	2.50
❑ 106 Malaefou MacKenzie RC	1.00	2.50
❑ 107 James Lynch RC	1.00	2.50
❑ 108 B.J. Askew RC	1.25	3.00
❑ 109 Andrew Pinnock RC	1.25	3.00
❑ 110 Chris Davis RC	1.25	3.00
❑ 111 Dan Curley RC	1.00	2.50
❑ 112 Lenny Walls RC	1.00	2.50
❑ 113 Travis Fisher RC	1.25	3.00
❑ 114 Ahmaad Galloway RC	1.25	3.00
❑ 115 Joe Smith RC	1.25	3.00
❑ 116 Reno Mahe RC	1.25	3.00
❑ 117 Torrie Cox RC	1.00	2.50
❑ 118 Kerry Carter RC	1.00	2.50
❑ 119 Dwone Hicks RC	1.00	2.50
❑ 120 Cato June RC	2.00	5.00
❑ 121 Terry Pierce RC	1.00	2.50
❑ 122 Eddie Moore RC	1.00	2.50
❑ 123 Mike Seidman RC	1.00	2.50
❑ 124 Michael Nattiel RC	1.00	2.50
❑ 125 Casey Fitzsimmons RC	1.25	3.00
❑ 126 George Wrighster RC	1.00	2.50
❑ 127 Mike Pinkard RC	1.00	2.50
❑ 128 Donald Lee RC	1.25	3.00
❑ 129 Sean Berton RC	1.00	2.50
❑ 130 Soloman Bates RC	1.00	2.50
❑ 131 Zach Hilton RC	1.25	3.00
❑ 132 Antonio Gates RC	15.00	30.00
❑ 133 Aaron Walker RC	1.25	3.00
❑ 134 Richard Angulo RC	1.00	2.50
❑ 135 Will Heller RC	1.25	3.00
❑ 136 Theo Sanders RC	1.00	2.50
❑ 137 Jimmy Farris RC	1.00	2.50
❑ 138 Ryan Nece RC	1.25	3.00
❑ 139 Antonio Brown RC	1.00	2.50
❑ 140 Clarence Coleman RC	1.00	2.50
❑ 141 Lawrence Hamilton RC	1.00	2.50
❑ 142 C.J. Jones RC	1.00	2.50
❑ 143 Frisman Jackson RC	1.25	3.00
❑ 144 Antonio Chatman RC	1.50	4.00
❑ 145 Rocky Boiman RC	1.25	3.00
❑ 146 Tron LaFavor RC	1.00	2.50
❑ 147 Derick Armstrong RC	1.25	3.00
❑ 148 J.J. Moses RC	1.00	2.50
❑ 149 Aaron Moorehead RC	1.25	3.00
❑ 150 Brad Pyatt RC	1.00	2.50
❑ 151 Arland Bruce RC	1.00	2.50
❑ 152 Chris Horn RC	1.25	3.00
❑ 153 Kareem Kelly RC	1.00	2.50
❑ 154 Talman Gardner RC	1.00	2.50
❑ 155 David Tyree RC	1.50	4.00
❑ 156 Willie Ponder RC	1.00	2.50
❑ 157 Greg Lewis RC	3.00	8.00
❑ 158 Eric Parker RC	1.50	4.00
❑ 159 Kassim Osgood RC	1.50	4.00
❑ 160 Jason Willis RC	1.00	2.50

❑ 161 Akbar Gbaja-Biamila RC 1.25 3.00
❑ 162 Mike Furrey RC 4.00 10.00
❑ 163 Chris Kelsay RC 1.25 3.00
❑ 164 Cory Redding RC 1.25 3.00
❑ 165 Kenny Peterson RC 1.25 3.00
❑ 166 Osi Umenyiora RC 2.50 6.00
❑ 167 Tyler Brayton RC 1.25 3.00
❑ 168 DeWayne White RC 1.00 2.50
❑ 169 Kevin Williams RC 1.50 4.00
❑ 170 Dan Klecko RC 1.25 3.00
❑ 171 Johnathan Sullivan RC 1.00 2.50
❑ 172 William Joseph RC 1.00 2.50
❑ 173 Rien Long RC 1.00 2.50
❑ 174 Angelo Crowell RC 1.25 3.00
❑ 175 Chaun Thompson RC 1.00 2.50
❑ 176 Bradie James RC 1.50 4.00
❑ 177 Antwan Peek RC 1.00 2.50
❑ 178 Kawika Mitchell RC 1.50 4.00
❑ 179 Cie Grant RC 1.25 3.00
❑ 180 E.J. Henderson RC 1.25 3.00
❑ 181 Victor Hobson RC 1.00 2.50
❑ 182 Alonzo Jackson RC 1.00 2.50
❑ 183 Matt Wilhelm RC 1.25 3.00
❑ 184 Pisa Tinoisamoa RC 1.50 4.00
❑ 185 Ricky Manning RC 1.25 3.00
❑ 186 Dennis Weathersby RC 1.00 2.50
❑ 187 Donald Strickland RC 1.00 2.50
❑ 188 Asante Samuel RC 3.00 8.00
❑ 189 Eugene Wilson RC 1.50 4.00
❑ 190 Nnamdi Asomugha RC 1.50 4.00
❑ 191 Ike Taylor RC 3.00 8.00
❑ 192 Drayton Florence RC 1.25 3.00
❑ 193 DeJuan Groce RC 1.50 4.00
❑ 194 Shane Walton RC 1.00 2.50
❑ 195 Terrence Holt RC 1.25 3.00
❑ 196 Rashean Mathis RC 1.25 3.00
❑ 197 Julian Battle RC 1.25 3.00
❑ 198 Hanik Milligan RC 1.00 2.50
❑ 199 Terrence Kiel RC 1.25 3.00
❑ 200 David Kircus RC 1.50 4.00
❑ 201 Lee Suggs RC 1.50 4.00
❑ 202 Charles Rogers RC 1.50 4.00
❑ 203 Brandon Lloyd RC 2.00 5.00
❑ 204 Terrence Edwards RC 1.25 3.00
❑ 205 Tony Romo RC 25.00 50.00
❑ 206 Brooks Bollinger RC 2.00 5.00
❑ 207 Jerome McDougle RC 1.25 3.00
❑ 208 Jimmy Kennedy RC 1.50 4.00
❑ 209 Ken Dorsey RC 1.50 4.00
❑ 210 Kirk Farmer RC 1.50 4.00
❑ 211 Mike Doss RC 2.00 5.00
❑ 212 Chris Simms RC 2.00 5.00
❑ 213 Cecil Sapp RC 1.25 3.00
❑ 214 Justin Gage RC 2.00 5.00
❑ 215 Sam Aiken RC 2.00 5.00
❑ 216 Doug Gabriel RC 1.50 4.00
❑ 217 Jason Witten RC 5.00 12.00
❑ 218 Bennie Joppru RC 1.25 3.00
❑ 219 Jason Gesser RC 1.50 4.00
❑ 220 Brock Forsey RC 1.50 4.00
❑ 221 Quentin Griffin RC 1.50 4.00
❑ 222 Avon Cobourne RC 1.25 3.00
❑ 223 Domanick Davis RC 2.00 5.00
❑ 224 Boss Bailey RC 1.50 4.00
❑ 225 Tony Hollings RC 1.50 4.00
❑ 226 LaBrandon Toefield RC 1.50 4.00
❑ 227 Arlen Harris RC 1.25 3.00
❑ 228 Sultan McCullough RC 1.25 3.00
❑ 229 Visanthe Shiancoe RC 2.00 5.00
❑ 230 L.J. Smith RC 2.00 5.00
❑ 231 LaTarence Dunbar RC 1.25 3.00
❑ 232 Walter Young RC 1.25 3.00
❑ 233 Bobby Wade RC 1.50 4.00
❑ 234 Zuriel Smith RC 1.25 3.00
❑ 235 Adrian Madise RC 1.25 3.00
❑ 236 Ken Hamlin RC 2.00 5.00
❑ 237 Carl Ford RC 1.25 3.00
❑ 238 Cortez Hankton RC 1.50 4.00
❑ 239 J.R. Tolver RC 1.50 4.00
❑ 240 Keenan Howry RC 1.25 3.00
❑ 241 Billy McMullen RC 1.25 3.00
❑ 242 Arnaz Battle RC 2.00 5.00
❑ 243 Shaun McDonald RC 2.00 5.00
❑ 244 Andre Woolfolk RC 1.50 4.00
❑ 245 Sammy Davis RC 1.50 4.00
❑ 246 Calvin Pace RC 1.50 4.00
❑ 247 Michael Haynes RC 1.25 3.00
❑ 248 Ty Warren RC 2.00 5.00
❑ 249 Nick Barnett RC 2.00 5.00
❑ 250 Troy Polamalu RC 15.00 30.00
❑ 251 Carson Palmer JSY RC 12.00 30.00
❑ 252 Byron Leftwich JSY RC 4.00 10.00
❑ 253 Kyle Boller JSY RC 3.00 8.00
❑ 254 Rex Grossman JSY RC 3.00 8.00
❑ 255 Dave Ragone JSY RC 2.00 5.00
❑ 256 Brian St.Pierre JSY RC 3.00 8.00
❑ 257 Kliff Kingsbury JSY RC 2.50 6.00
❑ 258 Seneca Wallace JSY RC 3.00 8.00
❑ 259 Larry Johnson JSY RC 4.00 10.00
❑ 260 Willis McGahee JSY RC 6.00 15.00
❑ 261 Justin Fargas JSY RC 3.00 8.00
❑ 262 Onterrio Smith JSY RC 2.50 6.00
❑ 263 Chris Brown JSY RC 3.00 8.00
❑ 264 Musa Smith JSY RC 2.50 6.00
❑ 265 Artose Pinner JSY RC 2.00 5.00
❑ 266 Andre Johnson JSY RC 6.00 15.00
❑ 267 Kelley Washington JSY RC 2.50 6.00
❑ 268 Taylor Jacobs JSY RC 2.50 6.00
❑ 269 Bryant Johnson JSY RC 3.00 8.00
❑ 270 Tyrone Calico JSY RC 2.50 6.00
❑ 271 Anquan Boldin JSY RC 8.00 20.00
❑ 272 Bethel Johnson JSY RC 2.50 6.00
❑ 273 Nate Burleson JSY RC 2.50 6.00
❑ 274 Kevin Curtis JSY RC 3.00 8.00
❑ 275 Dallas Clark JSY RC 6.00 15.00
❑ 276 Teyo Johnson JSY RC 2.50 6.00
❑ 277 Terrell Suggs JSY RC 4.00 10.00
❑ 278 DeWayne Robertson JSY RC 2.50 6.00
❑ 279 Terence Newman JSY RC 3.00 8.00
❑ 280 Marcus Trufant JSY RC 3.00 8.00
❑ 281 C.Palmer/B.Leftwich JSY 4.00 10.00
❑ 282 R.Grossman/B.St.Pierre JSY 3.00 8.00
❑ 283 K.Boller/D.Ragone JSY 3.00 8.00
❑ 284 K.Kingsbury/S.Wallace JSY 3.00 8.00
❑ 285 L.Johnson/W.McGahee JSY 6.00 15.00
❑ 286 J.Fargas/O.Smith JSY 3.00 8.00
❑ 287 C.Brown/M.Smith JSY 3.00 8.00
❑ 288 A.Pinner/A.Johnson JSY 6.00 15.00
❑ 289 K.Washington/T.Jacobs JSY 2.50 6.00
❑ 290 B.Johnson/T.Calico JSY 3.00 8.00
❑ 291 A.Boldin/B.Johnson JSY 8.00 20.00
❑ 292 N.Burleson/K.Curtis JSY 3.00 8.00
❑ 293 D.Clark/T.Johnson JSY 6.00 15.00
❑ 294 T.Suggs/D.Robertson JSY 4.00 10.00
❑ 295 T.Newman/M.Trufant JSY 3.00 8.00

2004 Leaf Rookies and Stars

❑ COMP.SET w/o SP's (200) 30.00 60.00
❑ COMP.SET w/o RC's (100) 7.50 20.00
❑ 251-283 JSY PRINT RUN 750 SER.#'d SETS
❑ 284-299 PRINT RUN 500 SER.#'d SETS
❑ 1 Anquan Boldin .30 .75
❑ 2 Emmitt Smith .75 2.00
❑ 3 Josh McCown .25 .60
❑ 4 Michael Vick .30 .75
❑ 5 Peerless Price .25 .60
❑ 6 T.J. Duckett .25 .60
❑ 7 Warrick Dunn .25 .60
❑ 8 Jamal Lewis .25 .60
❑ 9 Kyle Boller .25 .60
❑ 10 Ray Lewis .30 .75
❑ 11 Drew Bledsoe .30 .75
❑ 12 Eric Moulds .25 .60
❑ 13 Travis Henry .25 .60
❑ 14 Jake Delhomme .25 .60
❑ 15 Stephen Davis .25 .60
❑ 16 Steve Smith .30 .75
❑ 17 Brian Urlacher .30 .75
❑ 18 Rex Grossman .30 .75
❑ 19 Thomas Jones .25 .60
❑ 20 Carson Palmer .40 1.00
❑ 21 Chad Johnson .25 .60
❑ 22 Rudi Johnson .25 .60
❑ 23 Jeff Garcia .30 .75
❑ 24 William Green .20 .50
❑ 25 Keyshawn Johnson .25 .60
❑ 26 Terence Newman .25 .60
❑ 27 Roy Williams S .25 .60
❑ 28 Jake Plummer .25 .60
❑ 29 Quentin Griffin .25 .60
❑ 30 Rod Smith .25 .60
❑ 31 Charles Rogers .25 .60
❑ 32 Joey Harrington .25 .60
❑ 33 Ahman Green .30 .75
❑ 34 Brett Favre .75 2.00
❑ 35 Javon Walker .25 .60
❑ 36 Andre Johnson .30 .75
❑ 37 David Carr .25 .60
❑ 38 Domanick Davis .25 .60
❑ 39 Edgerrin James .30 .75
❑ 40 Marvin Harrison .30 .75
❑ 41 Peyton Manning .60 1.50
❑ 42 Byron Leftwich .30 .75
❑ 43 Fred Taylor .25 .60
❑ 44 Jimmy Smith .25 .60
❑ 45 Priest Holmes .30 .75
❑ 46 Tony Gonzalez .30 .75
❑ 47 Trent Green .25 .60
❑ 48 A.J. Feeley .25 .60
❑ 49 Chris Chambers .25 .60
❑ 50 Deion Sanders .30 .75
❑ 51 Daunte Culpepper .30 .75
❑ 52 Michael Bennett .25 .60
❑ 53 Randy Moss .30 .75
❑ 54 Corey Dillon .25 .60
❑ 55 Deion Branch .25 .60
❑ 56 Tom Brady .75 2.00
❑ 57 Aaron Brooks .25 .60
❑ 58 Deuce McAllister .30 .75
❑ 59 Joe Horn .25 .60
❑ 60 Jeremy Shockey .25 .60
❑ 61 Michael Strahan .25 .60
❑ 62 Tiki Barber .30 .75
❑ 63 Chad Pennington .30 .75
❑ 64 Curtis Martin .30 .75
❑ 65 Santana Moss .25 .60
❑ 66 Jerry Porter .25 .60
❑ 67 Jerry Rice .60 1.50
❑ 68 Warren Sapp .25 .60
❑ 69 Donovan McNabb .30 .75
❑ 70 Jevon Kearse .25 .60
❑ 71 Terrell Owens .30 .75
❑ 72 Duce Staley .25 .60
❑ 73 Hines Ward .30 .75
❑ 74 Jerome Bettis .30 .75
❑ 75 LaDainian Tomlinson .40 1.00
❑ 76 Kevan Barlow .25 .60
❑ 77 Tim Rattay .20 .50
❑ 78 Koren Robinson .30 .75
❑ 79 Matt Hasselbeck .30 .75
❑ 80 Shaun Alexander .30 .75
❑ 81 Isaac Bruce .25 .60
❑ 82 Marc Bulger .25 .60
❑ 83 Marshall Faulk .30 .75
❑ 84 Torry Holt .30 .75
❑ 85 Brad Johnson .25 .60
❑ 86 Derrick Brooks .25 .60
❑ 87 Chris Brown .25 .60
❑ 88 Derrick Mason .25 .60
❑ 89 Eddie George .25 .60
❑ 90 Steve McNair .30 .75
❑ 91 Clinton Portis .30 .75
❑ 92 LaVar Arrington .25 .60
❑ 93 Laveranues Coles .25 .60
❑ 94 Mark Brunell .25 .60
❑ 95 Hall/Schaub/Jenkins CL .50 1.25
❑ 96 Losman/L.Evans CL .25 .60
❑ 97 Winslow Jr./L.McCown CL .25 .60
❑ 98 D.Watts/T.Bell CL .20 .50
❑ 99 K.Jones/Ro.Will. CL .25 .60
❑ 100 G.Jones/Re.Will. CL .20 .50
❑ 101 Darnell Dockett RC 1.00 2.50
❑ 102 Karlos Dansby RC 1.50 4.00
❑ 103 Larry Croom RC 1.00 2.50
❑ 104 Chad Lavalais RC 1.00 2.50
❑ 105 Demorrio Williams RC 1.50 4.00
❑ 106 B.J. Sams RC 1.25 3.00
❑ 107 Dwan Edwards RC 1.00 2.50
❑ 108 Jason Peters RC 1.25 3.00
❑ 109 Shaud Williams RC 1.25 3.00
❑ 110 Tim Anderson RC 1.25 3.00
❑ 111 Tim Euhus RC 1.00 2.50

❑ 112 Michael Gaines RC 1.00 2.50
❑ 113 Rod Rutherford RC 1.00 2.50
❑ 114 Leon Joe RC 1.00 2.50
❑ 115 Nathan Vasher RC 1.50 4.00
❑ 116 Caleb Miller RC 1.00 2.50
❑ 117 Jamall Broussard RC 1.00 2.50
❑ 118 Keiwan Ratliff RC 1.00 2.50
❑ 119 Landon Johnson RC 1.00 2.50
❑ 120 Madieu Williams RC 1.00 2.50
❑ 121 Matthias Askew RC 1.00 2.50
❑ 122 Robert Geathers RC 1.00 2.50
❑ 123 Richard Alston RC 1.00 2.50
❑ 124 Bruce Thornton RC 1.00 2.50
❑ 125 Patrick Crayton RC 2.00 5.00
❑ 126 Bradlee Van Pelt RC 1.25 3.00
❑ 127 Charlie Adams RC 1.00 2.50
❑ 128 Nate Jackson RC 1.00 2.50
❑ 129 Roc Alexander RC 1.00 2.50
❑ 130 Romar Crenshaw RC 1.00 2.50
❑ 131 Keith Smith RC 1.00 2.50
❑ 132 Joey Thomas RC 1.00 2.50
❑ 133 Kelvin Kight RC 1.00 2.50
❑ 134 Scott McBrien RC 1.25 3.00
❑ 135 Andrae Thurman RC 1.00 2.50
❑ 136 Derick Armstrong 1.00 2.50
❑ 137 Glenn Earl RC 1.00 2.50
❑ 138 Kendrick Starling RC 1.00 2.50
❑ 139 Ben Hartsock RC 1.25 3.00
❑ 140 Gilbert Gardner RC 1.00 2.50
❑ 141 Jason David RC 1.00 2.50
❑ 142 Daryl Smith RC 1.25 3.00
❑ 143 Jared Allen RC 4.00 10.00
❑ 144 Jeris McIntyre RC 1.00 2.50
❑ 145 John Booth RC 1.00 2.50
❑ 146 Jonathan Smith RC 1.00 2.50
❑ 147 Junior Siavii RC 1.00 2.50
❑ 148 Keyaron Fox RC 1.25 3.00
❑ 149 Kris Wilson RC 1.25 3.00
❑ 150 Doug Easlick RC 1.00 2.50
❑ 151 Fred Russell RC 1.25 3.00
❑ 152 Tony Bua RC 1.00 2.50
❑ 153 Will Poole RC 1.50 4.00
❑ 154 Ben Nelson RC 1.00 2.50
❑ 155 Brock Lesnar RC 4.00 10.00
❑ 156 Butchie Wallace RC 1.00 2.50
❑ 157 Darrion Scott RC 1.25 3.00
❑ 158 Dontarrious Thomas RC 1.25 3.00
❑ 159 Richard Owens RC 1.00 2.50
❑ 160 Rod Davis RC 1.00 2.50
❑ 161 Dexter Reid RC 1.00 2.50
❑ 162 Kory Chapman RC 1.00 2.50
❑ 163 Marquise Hill RC 1.00 2.50
❑ 164 Courtney Watson RC 1.25 3.00
❑ 165 Mike Karney RC 1.25 3.00
❑ 166 Gibril Wilson RC 1.50 4.00
❑ 167 Reggie Torbor RC 1.00 2.50
❑ 168 Darrell McClover RC 1.00 2.50
❑ 169 Derrick Strait RC 1.25 3.00
❑ 170 Erik Coleman RC 1.25 3.00
❑ 171 Johnathan Reese RC 1.00 2.50
❑ 172 Rashad Washington RC 1.00 2.50
❑ 173 Courtney Anderson RC 1.00 2.50
❑ 174 Stuart Schweigert RC 1.25 3.00
❑ 175 J.R. Reed RC 1.00 2.50
❑ 176 Justin Jenkins RC 1.00 2.50
❑ 177 Matt Ware RC 1.50 4.00
❑ 178 Nate Lawrie RC 1.00 2.50
❑ 179 Thomas Tapeh RC 1.25 3.00
❑ 180 Matt Kranchick RC 1.50 4.00
❑ 181 Willie Parker RC 6.00 15.00
❑ 182 Igor Olshansky RC 1.50 4.00
❑ 183 Ryan Krause RC 1.00 2.50
❑ 184 Shaun Phillips RC 1.25 3.00
❑ 185 Wes Welker RC 5.00 12.00
❑ 186 Richard Seigler RC 1.00 2.50
❑ 187 Shawntae Spencer RC 1.00 2.50
❑ 188 Marcus Tubbs RC 1.00 2.50
❑ 189 Niko Koutouvides RC 1.00 2.50
❑ 190 Brandon Chillar RC 1.25 3.00
❑ 191 Tony Hargrove RC 1.00 2.50
❑ 192 Mark Jones RC 1.00 2.50
❑ 193 Marquis Cooper RC 1.50 4.00
❑ 194 Antwan Odom RC 1.50 4.00
❑ 195 Michael Waddell RC 1.00 2.50
❑ 196 Randy Starks RC 1.00 2.50
❑ 197 Rich Gardner RC 1.25 3.00
❑ 198 Travis Laboy RC 1.25 3.00
❑ 199 Vick King RC 1.00 2.50
❑ 200 Chris Cooley RC 1.50 4.00
❑ 201 Adimchinobe Echemandu RC 2.00 5.00
❑ 202 Ahmad Carroll RC 2.50 6.00
❑ 203 Andy Hall RC 2.00 5.00
❑ 204 B.J. Johnson RC 1.50 4.00
❑ 205 B.J. Symons RC 1.50 4.00
❑ 206 Brandon Miree RC 1.50 4.00
❑ 207 Bruce Perry RC 1.50 4.00
❑ 208 Carlos Francis RC 1.50 4.00
❑ 209 Casey Bramlet RC 1.50 4.00
❑ 210 Chris Gamble RC 2.00 5.00
❑ 211 Clarence Moore RC 2.00 5.00
❑ 212 Cody Pickett RC 2.00 5.00
❑ 213 Craig Krenzel RC 2.50 6.00
❑ 214 D.J. Hackett RC 2.50 6.00
❑ 215 D.J. Williams RC 2.50 6.00
❑ 216 Derrick Ward RC 2.50 6.00
❑ 217 Drew Carter RC 2.50 6.00
❑ 218 Drew Henson RC 1.50 4.00
❑ 219 Ernest Wilford RC 2.00 5.00
❑ 220 Jamaar Taylor RC 1.50 4.00
❑ 221 Jared Lorenzen RC 2.00 5.00
❑ 222 Jarrett Payton RC 2.00 5.00
❑ 223 Jason Babin RC 2.00 5.00
❑ 224 Jeff Smoker RC 2.00 5.00
❑ 225 Jerricho Cotchery RC 2.50 6.00
❑ 226 Jim Sorgi RC 2.50 6.00
❑ 227 John Navarre RC 2.00 5.00
❑ 228 Johnnie Morant RC 2.00 5.00
❑ 229 Jonathan Vilma RC 2.50 6.00
❑ 230 Josh Harris RC 1.50 4.00
❑ 231 Kenechi Udeze RC 2.50 6.00
❑ 232 Matt Mauck RC 2.00 5.00
❑ 233 Maurice Mann RC 1.50 4.00
❑ 234 Michael Turner RC 6.00 15.00
❑ 235 P.K. Sam RC 1.50 4.00
❑ 236 Quincy Wilson RC 2.00 5.00
❑ 237 Ran Carthon RC 1.50 4.00
❑ 238 Ricardo Colclough RC 2.50 6.00
❑ 239 Samie Parker RC 2.00 5.00
❑ 240 Sean Jones RC 2.00 5.00
❑ 241 Sean Taylor RC 2.50 6.00
❑ 242 Sloan Thomas RC 2.00 5.00
❑ 243 Tommie Harris RC 2.50 6.00
❑ 244 Triandos Luke RC 1.50 4.00
❑ 245 Troy Fleming RC 1.50 4.00
❑ 246 Vince Wilfork RC 2.50 6.00
❑ 247 Will Smith RC 2.50 6.00
❑ 248 Michael Boulware RC 2.50 6.00
❑ 249 Richard Smith RC 1.50 4.00
❑ 250 Teddy Lehman RC 2.00 5.00
❑ 251 Larry Fitzgerald JSY RC 10.00 25.00
❑ 252 DeAngelo Hall JSY RC 3.00 8.00
❑ 253 Matt Schaub JSY RC 8.00 20.00
❑ 254 Michael Jenkins JSY RC 3.00 8.00
❑ 255 Devard Darling JSY RC 2.50 6.00
❑ 256 J.P. Losman JSY RC 3.00 8.00
❑ 257 Lee Evans JSY RC 4.00 10.00
❑ 258 Keary Colbert JSY RC 2.50 6.00
❑ 259 Bernard Berrian JSY RC 3.00 8.00
❑ 260 Chris Perry JSY RC 3.00 8.00
❑ 261 Kellen Winslow Jr. JSY RC 4.00 10.00
❑ 262 Luke McCown JSY RC 3.00 8.00
❑ 263 Julius Jones JSY RC 4.00 10.00
❑ 264 Darius Watts JSY RC 2.50 6.00
❑ 265 Tatum Bell JSY RC 3.00 8.00
❑ 266 Kevin Jones JSY RC 3.00 8.00
❑ 267 Roy Williams JSY RC 4.00 10.00
❑ 268 Dunta Robinson JSY RC 2.50 6.00
❑ 269 Greg Jones JSY RC 3.00 8.00
❑ 270 Reggie Williams JSY RC 3.00 8.00
❑ 271 Mewelde Moore JSY RC 3.00 8.00
❑ 272 Ben Watson JSY RC 3.00 8.00
❑ 273 Cedric Cobbs JSY RC 2.50 6.00
❑ 274 Devery Henderson JSY RC 3.00 8.00
❑ 275 Eli Manning JSY RC 12.00 30.00
❑ 276 Robert Gallery JSY RC 3.00 8.00
❑ 277 Ben Roethlisberger JSY RC 15.00 40.00
❑ 278 Philip Rivers JSY RC 12.00 30.00
❑ 279 Derrick Hamilton JSY RC 2.00 5.00
❑ 280 Rashaun Woods JSY RC 2.00 5.00
❑ 281 Steven Jackson JSY RC 8.00 20.00
❑ 282 Michael Clayton JSY RC 3.00 8.00
❑ 283 Ben Troupe JSY RC 2.50 6.00
❑ 284 E.Manning/Rivers JSY 15.00 30.00
❑ 285 Fitzgerald/Ro.Williams JSY 10.00 25.00
❑ 286 Winslow Jr./G.Jones JSY 4.00 10.00
❑ 287 D.Hall/D.Robinson JSY 3.00 8.00
❑ 288 Re.Williams/Darling JSY 3.00 8.00
❑ 289 Roethlisberger/Losman JSY 15.00 40.00
❑ 290 Clayton/Henderson JSY 3.00 8.00
❑ 291 S.Jackson/Perry JSY 8.00 20.00
❑ 292 L.Evans/M.Jenkins JSY 4.00 10.00
❑ 293 R.Woods/T.Bell JSY 3.00 8.00
❑ 294 K.Jones/Berrian JSY 3.00 8.00
❑ 295 Watson/Troupe JSY 3.00 8.00
❑ 296 J.Jones/M.Moore JSY 4.00 10.00
❑ 297 M.Schaub/Hamilton JSY 8.00 20.00
❑ 298 L.McCown/Watts JSY 3.00 8.00
❑ 299 Colbert/Cobbs JSY 2.50 6.00

2005 Leaf Rookies and Stars

❑ COMP.SET w/o RC's (100) 7.50 20.00
❑ 201-250 RC PRINT RUN 799 SER.#'d SETS
❑ 251-279 JSY PRINT RUN 750 SER.#'d SETS
❑ 280-293 JSY DUAL PRINT RUN 500 SER.#'d SETS
❑ 1 Anquan Boldin .25 .60
❑ 2 Kurt Warner .30 .75
❑ 3 Larry Fitzgerald .30 .75
❑ 4 Michael Vick .30 .75
❑ 5 T.J. Duckett .20 .50
❑ 6 Warrick Dunn .25 .60
❑ 7 Jamal Lewis .25 .60
❑ 8 Kyle Boller .25 .60
❑ 9 Ray Lewis .30 .75
❑ 10 Derrick Mason .25 .60
❑ 11 J.P. Losman .25 .60
❑ 12 Lee Evans .25 .60
❑ 13 Willis McGahee .30 .75
❑ 14 DeShaun Foster .25 .60
❑ 15 Jake Delhomme .30 .75
❑ 16 Steve Smith .30 .75
❑ 17 Brian Urlacher .30 .75
❑ 18 Rex Grossman .30 .75
❑ 19 Muhsin Muhammad .25 .60
❑ 20 Carson Palmer .30 .75
❑ 21 Chad Johnson .25 .60
❑ 22 Rudi Johnson .25 .60
❑ 23 Lee Suggs .25 .60
❑ 24 Drew Bledsoe .30 .75
❑ 25 Julius Jones .30 .75
❑ 26 Keyshawn Johnson .25 .60
❑ 27 Roy Williams S .25 .60
❑ 28 Ashley Lelie .20 .50
❑ 29 Jake Plummer .25 .60
❑ 30 Rod Smith .25 .60
❑ 31 Tatum Bell .25 .60
❑ 32 Joey Harrington .30 .75
❑ 33 Kevin Jones .25 .60
❑ 34 Roy Williams WR .30 .75
❑ 35 Ahman Green .30 .75
❑ 36 Brett Favre .75 2.00
❑ 37 Javon Walker .25 .60
❑ 38 Andre Johnson .25 .60
❑ 39 David Carr .25 .60
❑ 40 Domanick Davis .20 .50
❑ 41 Edgerrin James .25 .60
❑ 42 Marvin Harrison .30 .75
❑ 43 Peyton Manning .50 1.25
❑ 44 Reggie Wayne .25 .60
❑ 45 Byron Leftwich .25 .60
❑ 46 Fred Taylor .30 .75
❑ 47 Jimmy Smith .25 .60
❑ 48 Priest Holmes .30 .75
❑ 49 Tony Gonzalez .25 .60
❑ 50 Trent Green .25 .60
❑ 51 Chris Chambers .25 .60
❑ 52 Daunte Culpepper .30 .75
❑ 53 Michael Bennett .25 .60
❑ 54 Nate Burleson .25 .60
❑ 55 Corey Dillon .25 .60
❑ 56 Deion Branch .25 .60
❑ 57 Tom Brady .60 1.50

❑ 58 Aaron Brooks .20 .50
❑ 59 Deuce McAllister .30 .75
❑ 60 Joe Horn .25 .60
❑ 61 Eli Manning .60 1.50
❑ 62 Jeremy Shockey .30 .75
❑ 63 Tiki Barber .30 .75
❑ 64 Plaxico Burress .25 .60
❑ 65 Chad Pennington .30 .75
❑ 66 Curtis Martin .30 .75
❑ 67 Laveranues Coles .25 .60
❑ 68 Jerry Porter .25 .60
❑ 69 Kerry Collins .25 .60
❑ 70 LaMont Jordan .25 .60
❑ 71 Randy Moss .30 .75
❑ 72 Brian Westbrook .30 .75
❑ 73 Donovan McNabb .30 .75
❑ 74 Terrell Owens .30 .75
❑ 75 Ben Roethlisberger .75 2.00
❑ 76 Duce Staley .25 .60
❑ 77 Hines Ward .30 .75
❑ 78 Jerome Bettis .30 .75
❑ 79 Antonio Gates .30 .75
❑ 80 Drew Brees .30 .75
❑ 81 LaDainian Tomlinson .40 1.00
❑ 82 Kevan Barlow .20 .50
❑ 83 Darrell Jackson .25 .60
❑ 84 Matt Hasselbeck .25 .60
❑ 85 Shaun Alexander .30 .75
❑ 86 Marc Bulger .25 .60
❑ 87 Steven Jackson .40 1.00
❑ 88 Torry Holt .25 .60
❑ 89 Brian Griese .25 .60
❑ 90 Michael Clayton .25 .60
❑ 91 Chris Brown .25 .60
❑ 92 Drew Bennett .25 .60
❑ 93 Steve McNair .30 .75
❑ 94 Clinton Portis .30 .75
❑ 95 LaVar Arrington .30 .75
❑ 96 Santana Moss .25 .60
❑ 97 A.Smith QB CL/F.Gore .60 1.50
❑ 98 B.Edwards CL/C.Frye .75 2.00
❑ 99 C.Fason CL/T.Williamson .30 .75
❑ 100 C.Rogers CL/J.Campbell .50 1.25
❑ 101 Travis Johnson RC 1.00 2.50
❑ 102 Alex Smith TE RC 1.50 4.00
❑ 103 Channing Crowder RC 1.25 3.00
❑ 104 Craig Bragg RC 1.00 2.50
❑ 105 Darrent Williams RC 1.50 4.00
❑ 106 Derrick Wimbush RC 1.25 3.00
❑ 107 Josh Cribbs RC 6.00 15.00
❑ 108 Luis Castillo RC 1.50 4.00
❑ 109 Matt Roth RC 1.50 4.00
❑ 110 Mike Patterson RC 1.25 3.00
❑ 111 Fred Gibson RC 1.25 3.00
❑ 112 Marcus Spears RC 1.50 4.00
❑ 113 Brodney Pool RC 1.25 3.00
❑ 114 Barrett Ruud RC 1.50 4.00
❑ 115 Stanford Routt RC 1.25 3.00
❑ 116 Josh Bullocks RC 1.50 4.00
❑ 117 Kevin Burnett RC 1.25 3.00
❑ 118 Corey Webster RC 1.50 4.00
❑ 119 Lofa Tatupu RC 1.50 4.00
❑ 120 Mike Nugent RC 1.25 3.00
❑ 121 Jim Leonhard RC 1.25 3.00
❑ 122 Ronald Bartell RC 1.25 3.00
❑ 123 Nick Collins RC 1.50 4.00
❑ 124 Justin Miller RC 1.25 3.00
❑ 125 Jonathan Babineaux RC 1.25 3.00
❑ 126 Kelvin Hayden RC 1.25 3.00
❑ 127 Matt McCoy RC 1.25 3.00
❑ 128 Oshiomogho Atogwe RC 1.00 2.50
❑ 129 Stanley Wilson RC 1.25 3.00
❑ 130 Justin Tuck RC 2.00 5.00
❑ 131 Eric Green RC 1.00 2.50
❑ 132 Karl Paymah RC 1.25 3.00
❑ 133 Kirk Morrison RC 1.50 4.00
❑ 134 Dustin Fox RC 1.50 4.00
❑ 135 Alfred Fincher RC 1.25 3.00
❑ 136 Chris Henry RC 1.50 4.00
❑ 137 Ellis Hobbs RC 1.50 4.00
❑ 138 Scott Starks RC 1.25 3.00
❑ 139 Jordan Beck RC 1.25 3.00
❑ 140 Vincent Burns RC 1.00 2.50
❑ 141 Darryl Blackstock RC 1.00 2.50
❑ 142 Domonique Foxworth RC 1.25 3.00
❑ 143 Leroy Hill RC 1.50 4.00
❑ 144 Cedric Killings RC 1.00 2.50
❑ 145 Leonard Weaver RC 1.00 2.50
❑ 146 Sean Considine RC 1.00 2.50
❑ 147 Antonio Perkins RC 1.25 3.00
❑ 148 Travis Daniels RC 1.25 3.00
❑ 149 Vincent Fuller RC 1.25 3.00
❑ 150 Manuel White RC 1.25 3.00
❑ 151 Kerry Rhodes RC 1.50 4.00
❑ 152 Brady Poppinga RC 1.50 4.00
❑ 153 Chris Canty RC 1.50 4.00
❑ 154 James Sanders RC 1.00 2.50
❑ 155 Matt Giordano RC 1.25 3.00
❑ 156 Boomer Grigsby RC 1.50 4.00
❑ 157 Donte Nicholson RC 1.25 3.00
❑ 158 Jerome Collins RC 1.25 3.00
❑ 159 Trent Cole RC 1.50 4.00
❑ 160 Alphonso Hodge RC 1.00 2.50
❑ 161 Jonathan Welsh RC 1.00 2.50
❑ 162 Adam Seward RC 1.25 3.00
❑ 163 Robert McCune RC 1.25 3.00
❑ 164 Eric King RC 1.00 2.50
❑ 165 Gerald Sensabaugh RC 1.50 4.00
❑ 166 Justin Green RC 1.50 4.00
❑ 167 Jeb Huckeba RC 1.25 3.00
❑ 168 Michael Boley RC 1.00 2.50
❑ 169 Andre Maddox RC 1.00 2.50
❑ 170 Rian Wallace RC 1.25 3.00
❑ 171 Michael Hawkins RC 1.00 2.50
❑ 172 Lance Mitchell RC 1.25 3.00
❑ 173 Ryan Claridge RC 1.00 2.50
❑ 174 James Butler RC 1.25 3.00
❑ 175 Ryan Riddle RC 1.00 2.50
❑ 176 Bo Scaife RC 1.25 3.00
❑ 177 Chris Harris RC 1.25 3.00
❑ 178 C.C. Brown RC 1.00 2.50
❑ 179 Pat Thomas RC 1.00 2.50
❑ 180 Derrick Johnson CB RC 1.00 2.50
❑ 181 Joel Dreessen RC 1.25 3.00
❑ 182 Rick Razzano RC 1.00 2.50
❑ 183 Nehemiah Broughton RC 1.25 3.00
❑ 184 Marcus Maxwell RC 1.00 2.50
❑ 185 Harry Williams RC 1.25 3.00
❑ 186 Patrick Estes RC 1.00 2.50
❑ 187 Billy Bajema RC 1.00 2.50
❑ 188 Madison Hedgecock RC 1.50 4.00
❑ 189 Manuel Wright RC 1.25 3.00
❑ 190 Roscoe Crosby RC 1.00 2.50
❑ 191 Wesley Duke RC 1.25 3.00
❑ 192 Ronnie Cruz RC 1.00 2.50
❑ 193 Adam Bergen RC 1.00 2.50
❑ 194 B.J. Ward RC 1.00 2.50
❑ 195 Stephen Spach RC 1.00 2.50
❑ 196 Marviel Underwood RC 1.25 3.00
❑ 197 John Bronson RC 1.00 2.50
❑ 198 Zak Keasey RC 1.25 3.00
❑ 199 Gregg Guenther RC 1.00 2.50
❑ 200 Jerome Carter RC 1.00 2.50
❑ 201 Aaron Rodgers RC 6.00 15.00
❑ 202 Adrian McPherson RC 1.50 4.00
❑ 203 Alvin Pearman RC 1.25 3.00
❑ 204 Airese Currie RC 1.50 4.00
❑ 205 Anthony Davis RC 1.50 4.00
❑ 206 Brandon Jacobs RC 2.50 6.00
❑ 207 Brandon Jones RC 2.00 5.00
❑ 208 Bryant McFadden RC 1.50 4.00
❑ 209 Cedric Benson RC 2.00 5.00
❑ 210 Cedric Houston RC 2.00 5.00
❑ 211 Chad Owens RC 2.00 5.00
❑ 212 Chris Henry 2.00 5.00
❑ 213 Craphonso Thorpe RC 1.50 4.00
❑ 214 Damien Nash RC 1.50 4.00
❑ 215 Dan Cody RC 2.00 5.00
❑ 216 Dan Orlovsky RC 2.00 5.00
❑ 217 Dante Ridgeway RC 1.25 3.00
❑ 218 Darren Sproles RC 2.50 6.00
❑ 219 David Greene RC 1.50 4.00
❑ 220 David Pollack RC 1.50 4.00
❑ 221 Deandra Cobb RC 1.50 4.00
❑ 222 DeMarcus Ware RC 3.00 8.00
❑ 223 Derek Anderson RC 2.00 5.00
❑ 224 Derrick Johnson RC 2.00 5.00
❑ 225 Fabian Washington RC 2.00 5.00
❑ 226 Roydell Williams RC 1.50 4.00
❑ 227 Heath Miller RC 4.00 10.00
❑ 228 J.R. Russell RC 1.25 3.00
❑ 229 James Kilian RC 1.25 3.00
❑ 230 Jerome Mathis RC 2.00 5.00
❑ 231 Larry Brackins RC 1.25 3.00
❑ 232 LeRon McCoy RC 1.25 3.00
❑ 233 Lionel Gates RC 1.25 3.00
❑ 234 Marion Barber RC 6.00 15.00
❑ 235 Marlin Jackson RC 1.50 4.00
❑ 236 Matt Cassel RC 4.00 10.00
❑ 237 Mike Williams 1.50 4.00
❑ 238 Nate Washington RC 2.00 5.00
❑ 239 Noah Herron RC 2.00 5.00
❑ 240 Fred Amey RC 1.50 4.00
❑ 241 Paris Warren RC 1.50 4.00
❑ 242 Rasheed Marshall RC 1.50 4.00
❑ 243 Ryan Fitzpatrick RC 2.00 5.00
❑ 244 Shaun Cody RC 1.50 4.00
❑ 245 Shawne Merriman RC 2.00 5.00
❑ 246 Tab Perry RC 2.00 5.00
❑ 247 Thomas Davis RC 1.50 4.00
❑ 248 Tyson Thompson RC 2.00 5.00
❑ 249 Chris Carr RC 1.50 4.00
❑ 250 Odell Thurman RC 2.00 5.00
❑ 251 Adam Jones JSY RC 2.00 5.00
❑ 252 Alex Smith QB JSY RC 2.50 6.00
❑ 253 Andrew Walter JSY RC 2.00 5.00
❑ 254 Antrel Rolle JSY RC 2.50 6.00
❑ 255 Braylon Edwards JSY RC 6.00 15.00
❑ 256 Carlos Rogers JSY RC 2.50 6.00
❑ 257 Cadillac Williams JSY RC 4.00 10.00
❑ 258 Charlie Frye JSY RC 2.50 6.00
❑ 259 Ciatrick Fason JSY RC 2.00 5.00
❑ 260 Courtney Roby JSY RC 2.00 5.00
❑ 261 Eric Shelton JSY RC 2.00 5.00
❑ 262 Frank Gore JSY RC 5.00 12.00
❑ 263 J.J. Arrington JSY RC 2.50 6.00
❑ 264 Jason Campbell JSY RC 4.00 10.00
❑ 265 Kyle Orton JSY RC 4.00 10.00
❑ 266 Mark Clayton JSY RC 2.50 6.00
❑ 267 Mark Bradley JSY RC 2.00 5.00
❑ 268 Matt Jones JSY RC 2.50 6.00
❑ 269 Maurice Clarett JSY 2.00 5.00
❑ 270 Reggie Brown JSY RC 2.00 5.00
❑ 271 Roddy White JSY RC 3.00 8.00
❑ 272 Ronnie Brown JSY RC 8.00 20.00
❑ 273 Roscoe Parrish JSY RC 2.00 5.00
❑ 274 Ryan Moats JSY RC 2.00 5.00
❑ 275 Stefan LeFors JSY RC 2.00 5.00
❑ 276 Terrence Murphy JSY RC 2.00 5.00
❑ 277 Troy Williamson JSY RC 2.50 6.00
❑ 278 Vernand Morency JSY RC 2.00 5.00
❑ 279 Vincent Jackson JSY RC 3.00 8.00
❑ 280 A.Smith QB J/J.Campbell J 4.00 10.00
❑ 281 R.Brown J/C.Williams J 8.00 20.00
❑ 282 B.Edwards J/T.Williamson J 6.00 15.00
❑ 283 A.Jones J/A.Rolle J 2.00 5.00
❑ 284 R.Parrish J/F.Gore J 5.00 12.00
❑ 285 C.Frye J/A.Walter J 2.00 5.00
❑ 286 J.Arrington J/E.Shelton J 2.50 6.00
❑ 287 C.Rogers J/K.Orton J 4.00 10.00
❑ 288 M.Clayton J/M.Bradley J 2.00 5.00
❑ 289 R.White J/Re.Brown J 2.00 5.00
❑ 290 T.Murphy J/C.Roby J 2.00 5.00
❑ 291 M.Clarett J/C.Fason J 2.00 5.00
❑ 292 R.Moats J/S.LeFors J 2.00 5.00
❑ 293 M.Jones J/V.Jackson J 3.00 8.00

2006 Leaf Rookies and Stars

❑ COMP.SET w/o RC's (100) 8.00 20.00
❑ 1 Anquan Boldin .20 .50
❑ 2 Edgerrin James .20 .50
❑ 3 Kurt Warner .25 .60
❑ 4 Larry Fitzgerald .25 .60
❑ 5 Alge Crumpler .20 .50
❑ 6 Michael Vick .25 .60
❑ 7 Warrick Dunn .20 .50
❑ 8 Derrick Mason .20 .50
❑ 9 Jamal Lewis .20 .50
❑ 10 Mike Anderson .20 .50
❑ 11 Josh Reed .15 .40
❑ 12 Lee Evans .20 .50
❑ 13 Willis McGahee .25 .60

Card	Low	High
❑ 14 DeShaun Foster	.20	.50
❑ 15 Jake Delhomme	.20	.50
❑ 16 Keyshawn Johnson	.20	.50
❑ 17 Steve Smith	.25	.60
❑ 18 Cedric Benson	.20	.50
❑ 19 Muhsin Muhammad	.20	.50
❑ 20 Rex Grossman	.25	.60
❑ 21 Carson Palmer	.25	.60
❑ 22 Chad Johnson	.20	.50
❑ 23 Rudi Johnson	.20	.50
❑ 24 T.J. Houshmandzadeh	.20	.50
❑ 25 Charlie Frye	.20	.50
❑ 26 Joe Jurevicius	.15	.40
❑ 27 Reuben Droughns	.20	.50
❑ 28 Drew Bledsoe	.25	.60
❑ 29 Julius Jones	.20	.50
❑ 30 Terrell Owens	.25	.60
❑ 31 Terry Glenn	.20	.50
❑ 32 Jake Plummer	.20	.50
❑ 33 Rod Smith	.20	.50
❑ 34 Tatum Bell	.15	.40
❑ 35 Josh McCown	.20	.50
❑ 36 Kevin Jones	.20	.50
❑ 37 Roy Williams WR	.25	.60
❑ 38 Ahman Green	.20	.50
❑ 39 Brett Favre	.50	1.25
❑ 40 Donald Driver	.25	.60
❑ 41 Robert Ferguson	.15	.40
❑ 42 Samkon Gado	.25	.60
❑ 43 Andre Johnson	.20	.50
❑ 44 David Carr	.15	.40
❑ 45 Domanick Davis	.20	.50
❑ 46 Eric Moulds	.20	.50
❑ 47 Marvin Harrison	.25	.60
❑ 48 Peyton Manning	.40	1.00
❑ 49 Reggie Wayne	.20	.50
❑ 50 Dallas Clark	.20	.50
❑ 51 Fred Taylor	.20	.50
❑ 52 Byron Leftwich	.20	.50
❑ 53 Jimmy Smith	.20	.50
❑ 54 Larry Johnson	.20	.50
❑ 55 Tony Gonzalez	.20	.50
❑ 56 Trent Green	.20	.50
❑ 57 Eddie Kennison	.15	.40
❑ 58 Chris Chambers	.20	.50
❑ 59 Daunte Culpepper	.25	.60
❑ 60 Ronnie Brown	.25	.60
❑ 61 Chester Taylor	.20	.50
❑ 62 Brad Johnson	.20	.50
❑ 63 Deion Branch	.20	.50
❑ 64 Corey Dillon	.20	.50
❑ 65 Tom Brady	.40	1.00
❑ 66 Deuce McAllister	.20	.50
❑ 67 Donte Stallworth	.20	.50
❑ 68 Drew Brees	.25	.60
❑ 69 Eli Manning	.30	.75
❑ 70 Plaxico Burress	.20	.50
❑ 71 Tiki Barber	.25	.60
❑ 72 Chad Pennington	.20	.50
❑ 73 Curtis Martin	.25	.60
❑ 74 Laveranues Coles	.20	.50
❑ 75 Aaron Brooks	.20	.50
❑ 76 LaMont Jordan	.20	.50
❑ 77 Randy Moss	.25	.60
❑ 78 Brian Westbrook	.20	.50
❑ 79 Donovan McNabb	.25	.60
❑ 80 Jabar Gaffney	.15	.40
❑ 81 Hines Ward	.25	.60
❑ 82 Ben Roethlisberger	.40	1.00
❑ 83 Willie Parker	.30	.75
❑ 84 Antonio Gates	.25	.60
❑ 85 LaDainian Tomlinson	.30	.75
❑ 86 Philip Rivers	.25	.60
❑ 87 Alex Smith QB	.20	.50
❑ 88 Antonio Bryant	.20	.50
❑ 89 Kevan Barlow	.20	.50
❑ 90 Darrell Jackson	.20	.50
❑ 91 Matt Hasselbeck	.20	.50
❑ 92 Shaun Alexander	.20	.50
❑ 93 Torry Holt	.20	.50
❑ 94 Steven Jackson	.25	.60
❑ 95 Cadillac Williams	.25	.60
❑ 96 Joey Galloway	.20	.50
❑ 97 David Givens	.20	.50
❑ 98 Drew Bennett	.20	.50
❑ 99 Antwaan Randle El	.20	.50
❑ 100 Clinton Portis	.25	.60
❑ 101 Kamerion Wimbley RC	1.50	4.00
❑ 102 Mathias Kiwanuka RC	2.00	5.00
❑ 103 Reggie McNeal RC	1.25	3.00
❑ 104 Claude Wroten RC	1.00	2.50
❑ 105 Gabe Watson RC	1.00	2.50
❑ 106 D'Qwell Jackson RC	1.25	3.00
❑ 107 Todd Watkins RC	1.00	2.50
❑ 108 Bennie Brazell RC	1.25	3.00
❑ 109 David Anderson RC	1.25	3.00
❑ 110 John David Washington RC	1.25	3.00
❑ 111 Marques Hagans RC	1.25	3.00
❑ 112 Kevin Youngblood RC	1.00	2.50
❑ 113 Ben Obomanu RC	1.25	3.00
❑ 114 Jamal Jones RC	1.00	2.50
❑ 115 Nick Mangold RC	1.25	3.00
❑ 116 Davin Joseph RC	1.25	3.00
❑ 117 Erik Meyer RC	1.25	3.00
❑ 118 Taurean Henderson RC	1.50	4.00
❑ 119 A.J. Nicholson RC	1.00	2.50
❑ 120 Thomas Howard RC	1.25	3.00
❑ 121 Jon Alston RC	1.00	2.50
❑ 122 Ashton Youboty RC	1.25	3.00
❑ 123 Alan Zemaitis RC	1.50	4.00
❑ 124 Lawrence Vickers RC	1.25	3.00
❑ 125 J.D. Runnels RC	1.25	3.00
❑ 126 Ray Perkins RC	1.25	3.00
❑ 127 Jeff King RC	1.25	3.00
❑ 128 Quinn Sypniewski RC	1.25	3.00
❑ 129 Jason Carter RC	1.25	3.00
❑ 130 Malcom Floyd RC	2.00	5.00
❑ 131 Mike Jennings RC	1.25	3.00
❑ 132 Chris Gocong RC	1.25	3.00
❑ 133 Frostee Rucker RC	1.25	3.00
❑ 134 Jason Hatcher RC	1.25	3.00
❑ 135 Victor Adeyanju RC	1.25	3.00
❑ 136 Elvis Dumervil RC	1.50	4.00
❑ 137 Ray Edwards RC	1.50	4.00
❑ 138 Anthony Schlegel RC	1.25	3.00
❑ 139 Freddie Keiaho RC	1.25	3.00
❑ 140 Gerris Wilkinson RC	1.00	2.50
❑ 141 Leon Williams RC	1.25	3.00
❑ 142 Stephen Tulloch RC	1.25	3.00
❑ 143 Jamar Williams RC	1.25	3.00
❑ 144 Clint Ingram RC	1.50	4.00
❑ 145 James Anderson RC	1.00	2.50
❑ 146 Darrell Hackney RC	1.25	3.00
❑ 147 Paul Pinegar RC	1.00	2.50
❑ 148 Brandon Kirsch RC	1.25	3.00
❑ 149 Andre Hall RC	1.25	3.00
❑ 150 De'Arrius Howard RC	1.50	4.00
❑ 151 Cedric Humes RC	1.25	3.00
❑ 152 Wendell Mathis RC	1.25	3.00
❑ 153 Gerald Riggs RC	1.25	3.00
❑ 154 Quinton Ganther RC	1.00	2.50
❑ 155 Martin Nance RC	1.25	3.00
❑ 156 Greg Lee RC	1.00	2.50
❑ 157 Jai Lewis RC	1.25	3.00
❑ 158 Cory Rodgers RC	1.50	4.00
❑ 159 Mike Espy RC	1.50	4.00
❑ 160 Chris Barclay RC	1.25	3.00
❑ 161 DeMeco Ryans RC	2.00	5.00
❑ 162 Rocky McIntosh RC	1.50	4.00
❑ 163 David Kirtman RC	1.25	3.00
❑ 164 Skyler Green RC	1.00	2.50
❑ 165 Will Blackmon RC	1.50	4.00
❑ 166 Darryl Tapp RC	1.25	3.00
❑ 167 Dusty Dvoracek RC	1.50	4.00
❑ 168 Richard Marshall RC	1.25	3.00
❑ 169 Tim Jennings RC	1.25	3.00
❑ 170 David Pittman RC	1.25	3.00
❑ 171 DeMario Minter RC	1.25	3.00
❑ 172 Marcus Maxey RC	1.25	3.00
❑ 173 Roman Harper RC	1.25	3.00
❑ 174 Anthony Smith RC	1.50	4.00
❑ 175 Nate Salley RC	1.25	3.00
❑ 176 Mike Hass RC	1.50	4.00
❑ 177 Greg Blue RC	1.25	3.00
❑ 178 Daniel Bullocks RC	1.50	4.00
❑ 179 Danieal Manning RC	1.50	4.00
❑ 180 Calvin Lowry RC	1.50	4.00
❑ 181 Eric Smith RC	1.25	3.00
❑ 182 Jimmy Williams RC	1.50	4.00
❑ 183 Cedric Griffin RC	1.25	3.00
❑ 184 Ko Simpson RC	1.25	3.00
❑ 185 Pat Watkins RC	1.50	4.00
❑ 186 Marcus Vick RC	1.00	2.50
❑ 187 Bernard Pollard RC	1.25	3.00
❑ 188 Darnell Bing RC	1.25	3.00
❑ 189 Cory Ross RC	1.50	4.00
❑ 190 Patrick Cobbs RC	1.25	3.00
❑ 191 Montell Owens RC	1.25	3.00
❑ 192 Chris Hannon RC	1.25	3.00
❑ 193 John Madsen RC	1.50	4.00
❑ 194 Shaun Bodiford RC	1.25	3.00
❑ 195 Fred Evans RC	1.25	3.00
❑ 196 Cletis Gordon RC	.75	2.00
❑ 197 Jarrad Page RC	1.50	4.00
❑ 198 Brett Elliott RC	1.50	4.00
❑ 199 Brett Basanez RC	1.50	4.00
❑ 200 Drew Olson RC	1.00	2.50
❑ 201 Jay Cutler RC	5.00	12.00
❑ 202 Brodie Croyle RC	2.00	5.00
❑ 203 Ingle Martin RC	1.50	4.00
❑ 204 Derrick Ross RC	1.50	4.00
❑ 205 Bruce Gradkowski RC	2.00	5.00
❑ 206 D.J. Shockley RC	1.50	4.00
❑ 207 Joseph Addai RC	2.50	6.00
❑ 208 P.J. Daniels RC	1.25	3.00
❑ 209 Marques Colston RC	5.00	12.00
❑ 210 Jerome Harrison RC	2.00	5.00
❑ 211 Wali Lundy RC	2.00	5.00
❑ 212 Mike Bell RC	2.00	5.00
❑ 213 Miles Austin RC	5.00	12.00
❑ 214 Anthony Fasano RC	2.00	5.00
❑ 215 Tony Scheffler RC	2.00	5.00
❑ 216 Leonard Pope RC	2.00	5.00
❑ 217 David Thomas RC	2.00	5.00
❑ 218 Dominique Byrd RC	1.50	4.00
❑ 219 Garrett Mills RC	1.50	4.00
❑ 220 Hank Baskett RC	2.00	5.00
❑ 221 Greg Jennings RC	3.00	8.00
❑ 222 Devin Hester RC	4.00	10.00
❑ 223 Willie Reid RC	1.50	4.00
❑ 224 Brad Smith RC	2.00	5.00
❑ 225 Sam Hurd RC	3.00	8.00
❑ 226 Owen Daniels RC	2.00	5.00
❑ 227 Domenik Hixon RC	2.00	5.00
❑ 228 Jeremy Bloom RC	1.50	4.00
❑ 229 Dawan Landry RC	2.00	5.00
❑ 230 Jonathan Orr RC	1.50	4.00
❑ 231 Delanie Walker RC	1.50	4.00
❑ 232 Adam Jennings RC	1.50	4.00
❑ 233 Jeffrey Webb RC	1.50	4.00
❑ 234 Ethan Kilmer RC	2.00	5.00
❑ 235 Tye Hill RC	1.50	4.00
❑ 236 Jason Allen RC	1.50	4.00
❑ 237 Antonio Cromartie RC	2.00	5.00
❑ 238 D'Brickashaw Ferguson RC	2.00	5.00
❑ 239 Tamba Hali RC	2.00	5.00
❑ 240 Haloti Ngata RC	2.00	5.00
❑ 241 Brodrick Bunkley RC	1.50	4.00
❑ 242 John McCargo RC	1.50	4.00
❑ 243 Johnathan Joseph RC	1.50	4.00
❑ 244 Kelly Jennings RC	2.00	5.00
❑ 245 Donte Whitner RC	2.00	5.00
❑ 246 Abdul Hodge RC	1.50	4.00
❑ 247 Ernie Sims RC	1.50	4.00
❑ 248 Chad Greenway RC	2.00	5.00
❑ 249 Bobby Carpenter RC	1.50	4.00
❑ 250 Manny Lawson RC	2.00	5.00
❑ 251 Matt Leinart JSY/599 RC	5.00	12.00
❑ 252 Kellen Clemens JSY RC	2.50	6.00
❑ 253 Tarvaris Jackson JSY RC	2.50	6.00
❑ 254 Charlie Whitehurst JSY RC	2.50	6.00
❑ 255 DeAn.Williams JSY/599 RC	6.00	15.00
❑ 256 Maurice Drew JSY RC	5.00	12.00
❑ 257 Brian Calhoun JSY RC	2.00	5.00
❑ 258 Jerious Norwood JSY RC	2.50	6.00
❑ 259 Vernon Davis JSY RC	2.50	6.00
❑ 260 Joe Klopfenstein JSY RC	2.00	5.00
❑ 261 Sinorice Moss JSY RC	2.50	6.00
❑ 262 Derek Hagan JSY RC	2.00	5.00
❑ 263 Brandon Williams JSY RC	2.00	5.00
❑ 264 Michael Robinson JSY RC	2.00	5.00
❑ 265 Jason Avant JSY RC	2.50	6.00
❑ 266 Brandon Marshall JSY RC	2.50	6.00
❑ 267 Demetrius Williams JSY RC	2.00	5.00
❑ 268 Mario Williams JSY RC	3.00	8.00
❑ 269 Michael Huff JSY RC	2.50	6.00
❑ 270 Chad Jackson JSY RC	2.00	5.00
❑ 271 V.Young JSY AU/249 RC	40.00	80.00
❑ 272 O.Jacobs JSY AU/449 RC	6.00	15.00
❑ 273 R.Bush JSY AU/99 RC	75.00	150.00
❑ 274 L.Maroney JSY AU/99 RC	30.00	80.00
❑ 275 L.White JSY AU/249 RC	15.00	40.00
❑ 276 L.Washington JSY AU/199 RC	15.00	30.00
❑ 277 M.Lewis JSY AU/449 RC	6.00	15.00
❑ 278 S.Holmes JSY AU/449 RC	25.00	40.00
❑ 279 T.Wilson JSY AU/449 RC	4.00	10.00

❑ 280 M.Stovall JSY AU/99 RC 6.00 15.00
❑ 281 A.J. Hawk JSY AU/99 RC 30.00 60.00

2007 Leaf Rookies and Stars

❑ COMP.SET w/o SP's (100) 10.00 25.00
❑ 1 Tony Romo .50 1.25
❑ 2 Julius Jones .25 .60
❑ 3 Terrell Owens .30 .75
❑ 4 Eli Manning .30 .75
❑ 5 Plaxico Burress .25 .60
❑ 6 Jeremy Shockey .25 .60
❑ 7 Brandon Jacobs .25 .60
❑ 8 Donovan McNabb .30 .75
❑ 9 Brian Westbrook .25 .60
❑ 10 Reggie Brown .20 .50
❑ 11 Jason Campbell .25 .60
❑ 12 Clinton Portis .25 .60
❑ 13 Santana Moss .25 .60
❑ 14 Rex Grossman .25 .60
❑ 15 Cedric Benson .25 .60
❑ 16 Muhsin Muhammad .25 .60
❑ 17 Jon Kitna .20 .50
❑ 18 Roy Williams WR .25 .60
❑ 19 Tatum Bell .20 .50
❑ 20 Brett Favre .60 1.50
❑ 21 Vernand Morency .25 .60
❑ 22 Donald Driver .30 .75
❑ 23 Tarvaris Jackson .25 .60
❑ 24 Chester Taylor .20 .50
❑ 25 Troy Williamson .20 .50
❑ 26 Jerious Norwood .25 .60
❑ 27 Warrick Dunn .25 .60
❑ 28 Alge Crumpler .25 .60
❑ 29 Jake Delhomme .25 .60
❑ 30 DeShaun Foster .25 .60
❑ 31 Steve Smith .25 .60
❑ 32 Drew Brees .30 .75
❑ 33 Deuce McAllister .25 .60
❑ 34 Marques Colston .30 .75
❑ 35 Reggie Bush .40 1.00
❑ 36 Jeff Garcia .25 .60
❑ 37 Cadillac Williams .25 .60
❑ 38 Joey Galloway .25 .60
❑ 39 Matt Leinart .30 .75
❑ 40 Edgerrin James .25 .60
❑ 41 Anquan Boldin .25 .60
❑ 42 Larry Fitzgerald .30 .75
❑ 43 Marc Bulger .25 .60
❑ 44 Steven Jackson .30 .75
❑ 45 Torry Holt .25 .60
❑ 46 Alex Smith QB .30 .75
❑ 47 Frank Gore .30 .75
❑ 48 Vernon Davis .25 .60
❑ 49 Matt Hasselbeck .25 .60
❑ 50 Shaun Alexander .25 .60
❑ 51 Deion Branch .25 .60
❑ 52 J.P. Losman .20 .50
❑ 53 Anthony Thomas .20 .50
❑ 54 Lee Evans .25 .60
❑ 55 Trent Green .25 .60
❑ 56 Ronnie Brown .25 .60
❑ 57 Chris Chambers .25 .60
❑ 58 Tom Brady .60 1.50
❑ 59 Laurence Maroney .30 .75
❑ 60 Randy Moss .30 .75
❑ 61 Chad Pennington .25 .60
❑ 62 Jerricho Cotchery .20 .50
❑ 63 Leon Washington .25 .60
❑ 64 Steve McNair .25 .60
❑ 65 Willis McGahee .25 .60
❑ 66 Mark Clayton .25 .60
❑ 67 Carson Palmer .30 .75
❑ 68 Rudi Johnson .25 .60
❑ 69 Chad Johnson .25 .60
❑ 70 T.J. Houshmandzadeh .25 .60
❑ 71 Charlie Frye .25 .60
❑ 72 Braylon Edwards .25 .60
❑ 73 Jamal Lewis .25 .60
❑ 74 Ben Roethlisberger .50 1.25
❑ 75 Willie Parker .25 .60
❑ 76 Hines Ward .30 .75
❑ 77 Ahman Green .25 .60
❑ 78 Andre Johnson .25 .60
❑ 79 Matt Schaub .25 .60
❑ 80 Peyton Manning .50 1.25
❑ 81 Joseph Addai .30 .75
❑ 82 Marvin Harrison .30 .75
❑ 83 Reggie Wayne .25 .60
❑ 84 Byron Leftwich .25 .60
❑ 85 Fred Taylor .25 .60
❑ 86 Maurice Jones-Drew .30 .75
❑ 87 Vince Young .30 .75
❑ 88 LenDale White .25 .60
❑ 89 Brandon Jones .20 .50
❑ 90 Jay Cutler .30 .75
❑ 91 Javon Walker .25 .60
❑ 92 Mike Bell .25 .60
❑ 93 Larry Johnson .25 .60
❑ 94 Tony Gonzalez .25 .60
❑ 95 Brodie Croyle .25 .60
❑ 96 LaMont Jordan .25 .60
❑ 97 Dominic Rhodes .25 .60
❑ 98 Philip Rivers .30 .75
❑ 99 LaDainian Tomlinson .40 1.00
❑ 100 Antonio Gates .25 .60
❑ 101 Drew Brees ELE 1.50 4.00
❑ 102 Reggie Bush ELE 2.00 5.00
❑ 103 Brett Favre ELE 3.00 8.00
❑ 104 Marvin Harrison ELE 1.50 4.00
❑ 105 Eli Manning ELE 1.50 4.00
❑ 106 Willie Parker ELE 1.25 3.00
❑ 107 Brian Westbrook ELE 1.25 3.00
❑ 108 Tom Brady ELE 3.00 8.00
❑ 109 Jay Cutler ELE 1.50 4.00
❑ 110 Rudi Johnson ELE 1.25 3.00
❑ 111 J.P. Losman ELE 1.00 2.50
❑ 112 Laurence Maroney ELE 1.50 4.00
❑ 113 Carson Palmer ELE 1.50 4.00
❑ 114 Ben Roethlisberger ELE 2.50 6.00
❑ 115 Brian Urlacher ELE 1.50 4.00
❑ 116 A.J. Davis RC 1.25 3.00
❑ 117 Usama Young RC 1.50 4.00
❑ 118 Aaron Rouse RC 2.00 5.00
❑ 119 Ahmad Bradshaw RC 2.50 6.00
❑ 120 Alan Branch RC 1.50 4.00
❑ 121 Alonzo Coleman RC 1.50 4.00
❑ 122 Amobi Okoye RC 2.00 5.00
❑ 123 Anthony Spencer RC 2.00 5.00
❑ 124 Deon Anderson RC 1.50 4.00
❑ 125 Justin Durant RC 1.50 4.00
❑ 126 Brandon Siler RC 1.50 4.00
❑ 127 Buster Davis RC 1.50 4.00
❑ 128 Charles Johnson RC 1.25 3.00
❑ 129 Courtney Taylor RC 1.50 4.00
❑ 130 Dallas Baker RC 1.50 4.00
❑ 131 Dan Bazuin RC 1.50 4.00
❑ 132 Danny Ware RC 2.00 5.00
❑ 133 Darius Walker RC 1.50 4.00
❑ 134 David Ball RC 1.25 3.00
❑ 135 David Harris RC 1.50 4.00
❑ 136 David Irons RC 1.25 3.00
❑ 137 Daymeion Hughes RC 1.50 4.00
❑ 138 Anthony Waters RC 1.50 4.00
❑ 139 Antwan Barnes RC 1.50 4.00
❑ 140 Eric Frampton RC 1.50 4.00
❑ 141 Eric Weddle RC 1.50 4.00
❑ 142 Eric Wright RC 2.00 5.00
❑ 143 Fred Bennett RC 1.25 3.00
❑ 144 Gary Russell RC 1.50 4.00
❑ 145 H.B. Blades RC 1.50 4.00
❑ 146 Jacoby Jones RC 2.00 5.00
❑ 147 Clifton Dawson RC 2.00 5.00
❑ 148 Kevin Boss RC 3.00 8.00
❑ 149 Jarvis Moss RC 2.00 5.00
❑ 150 Gerald Alexander RC 1.25 3.00
❑ 151 Jeff Rowe RC 1.50 4.00
❑ 152 Tanard Jackson RC 1.25 3.00
❑ 153 Joel Filani RC 1.50 4.00
❑ 154 Jon Abbate RC 1.25 3.00
❑ 155 Jon Beason RC 2.00 5.00
❑ 156 Marcus Mason RC 2.00 5.00
❑ 157 Jonathan Wade RC 1.50 4.00
❑ 158 Dante Rosario RC 2.00 5.00
❑ 159 Josh Wilson RC 1.50 4.00
❑ 160 Kenneth Darby RC 2.00 5.00
❑ 161 Biren Ealy RC 1.50 4.00
❑ 162 LaMarr Woodley RC 2.00 5.00
❑ 163 Levi Brown RC 2.00 5.00
❑ 164 Marcus McCauley RC 1.50 4.00
❑ 165 Matt Spaeth RC 2.00 5.00
❑ 166 Michael Okwo RC 1.50 4.00
❑ 167 Mike Walker RC 2.00 5.00
❑ 168 Quentin Moses RC 1.50 4.00
❑ 169 Ray McDonald RC 1.50 4.00
❑ 170 Reggie Ball RC 1.50 4.00
❑ 171 Justin Harrell RC 2.00 5.00
❑ 172 Ed Johnson RC 1.50 4.00
❑ 173 Rufus Alexander RC 2.00 5.00
❑ 174 Ryan McBean RC 2.00 5.00
❑ 175 Ryne Robinson RC 1.50 4.00
❑ 176 Sabby Piscitelli RC 2.00 5.00
❑ 177 Scott Chandler RC 1.50 4.00
❑ 178 Selvin Young RC 2.00 5.00
❑ 179 Steve Breaston RC 2.00 5.00
❑ 180 Stewart Bradley RC 2.00 5.00
❑ 181 Turk McBride RC 1.50 4.00
❑ 182 Demarcus Tank Tyler RC 1.50 4.00
❑ 183 Tim Crowder RC 2.00 5.00
❑ 184 Tim Shaw RC 1.50 4.00
❑ 185 Kenton Keith RC 2.00 5.00
❑ 186 Tyler Palko RC 1.50 4.00
❑ 187 Mason Crosby RC 2.00 5.00
❑ 188 Pierre Thomas RC 6.00 15.00
❑ 189 Victor Abiamiri RC 2.00 5.00
❑ 190 Zak DeOssie RC 1.50 4.00
❑ 191 Tyler Thigpen RC 2.00 5.00
❑ 192 Tony Ugoh RC 1.50 4.00
❑ 193 Michael Allan RC 1.25 3.00
❑ 194 Martrez Milner RC 1.50 4.00
❑ 195 John Broussard RC 1.50 4.00
❑ 196 Roy Hall RC 2.00 5.00
❑ 197 Matt Gutierrez RC 2.00 5.00
❑ 198 Legedu Naanee RC 2.00 5.00
❑ 199 Derek Stanley RC 1.50 4.00
❑ 200 Quincy Black RC 2.00 5.00
❑ 201 Trent Edwards/99 AU RC 20.00 50.00
❑ 202 Marshawn Lynch/99 AU RC 30.00 60.00
❑ 203 Chris Henry/99 AU RC 10.00 25.00
❑ 204 Paul Williams/299 AU RC 6.00 15.00
❑ 206 A.Peterson/99 AU RC 200.00 350.00
❑ 207 Drew Stanton/99 AU RC 10.00 25.00
❑ 208 Calvin Johnson/99 AU RC 60.00 120.00
❑ 209 Yamon Figurs/99 AU RC 8.00 20.00
❑ 210 Troy Smith/99 AU RC 15.00 40.00
❑ 211 Garrett Wolfe/249 AU RC 8.00 20.00
❑ 212 Greg Olsen/99 AU RC 15.00 40.00
❑ 213 Joe Thomas/99 AU RC 12.00 30.00
❑ 214 Brady Quinn/99 AU RC 50.00 100.00
❑ 215 Ted Ginn Jr./99 AU RC 20.00 50.00
❑ 216 John Beck/99 AU RC 12.00 30.00
❑ 218 Robert Meachem/99 AU RC 12.00 30.00
❑ 219 JaMarcus Russell/99 AU RC 15.00 40.00
❑ 221 Kevin Kolb/99 AU RC 20.00 50.00
❑ 223 Patrick Willis/99 AU RC 20.00 50.00
❑ 224 Jason Hill/249 AU RC 8.00 20.00
❑ 225 Brandon Jackson/99 AU RC 12.00 30.00
❑ 226 David Clowney/299 AU RC 8.00 20.00
❑ 228 Leon Hall/99 AU RC 12.00 30.00
❑ 229 Dwayne Bowe/99 AU RC 20.00 50.00
❑ 230 Kolby Smith/299 AU RC 10.00 25.00
❑ 232 Dwayne Jarrett/99 AU RC 12.00 30.00
❑ 233 Lorenzo Booker/99 AU RC 12.00 30.00
❑ 234 A.Gonzalez/99 AU RC 15.00 40.00
❑ 235 J.Lee Higgins/99 AU RC 12.00 30.00
❑ 236 Isaiah Stanback/299 AU RC 8.00 20.00
❑ 237 LaRon Landry/249 AU RC 10.00 25.00
❑ 238 Paul Posluszny/99 AU RC 15.00 40.00
❑ 239 Brian Leonard/99 AU RC 10.00 25.00
❑ 242 Aundrae Allison/249 AU RC 6.00 15.00
❑ 244 Jamaal Anderson/249 AU RC 6.00 15.00
❑ 245 Adam Carriker/99 AU RC 10.00 25.00
❑ 246 Darrelle Revis/99 AU RC 15.00 40.00
❑ 247 L.Timmons/99 AU RC 12.00 30.00
❑ 248 Michael Griffin/299 AU RC 8.00 20.00
❑ 250 Reggie Nelson/99 AU RC 10.00 25.00
❑ 252 Zach Miller/99 AU RC 12.00 30.00
❑ 253 Chris Houston/299 AU RC 6.00 15.00
❑ 255 Laurent Robinson/299 AU RC 8.00 20.00
❑ 256 James Jones/246 AU RC 8.00 20.00
❑ 258 Chris Davis/249 AU RC 6.00 15.00
❑ 259 Thomas Clayton/299 AU RC 6.00 15.00
❑ 260 Jordan Palmer/99 AU RC 12.00 30.00

Card	Low	High
❑ 261 Jordan Kent/299 AU RC	6.00	15.00
❑ 262 Chansi Stuckey/299 AU RC	8.00	20.00
❑ 263 Nate Ilaoa/299 AU RC	8.00	20.00
❑ 264 Chris Leak/99 AU RC	10.00	25.00
❑ 265 Jared Zabransky/99 AU RC	12.00	30.00
❑ 266 Syndric Steptoe/299 AU RC	6.00	15.00

2008 Leaf Rookies and Stars

Card	Low	High
❑ COMP.SET w/o SP's (100)	10.00	25.00
❑ 1 Matt Leinart	.30	.75
❑ 2 Larry Fitzgerald	.30	.75
❑ 3 Anquan Boldin	.25	.60
❑ 4 Edgerrin James	.25	.60
❑ 5 Roddy White	.25	.60
❑ 6 Michael Turner	.30	.75
❑ 7 Willis McGahee	.25	.60
❑ 8 Derrick Mason	.20	.50
❑ 9 Demetrius Williams	.20	.50
❑ 10 Trent Edwards	.30	.75
❑ 11 Marshawn Lynch	.30	.75
❑ 12 Lee Evans	.25	.60
❑ 13 Steve Smith	.25	.60
❑ 14 DeAngelo Williams	.25	.60
❑ 15 Julius Peppers	.25	.60
❑ 16 Greg Olsen	.25	.60
❑ 17 Devin Hester	.30	.75
❑ 18 Rex Grossman	.25	.60
❑ 19 Carson Palmer	.30	.75
❑ 20 Chad Johnson	.25	.60
❑ 21 T.J. Houshmandzadeh	.25	.60
❑ 22 Chris Perry	.20	.50
❑ 23 Derek Anderson	.25	.60
❑ 24 Kellen Winslow	.25	.60
❑ 25 Braylon Edwards	.25	.60
❑ 26 Tony Romo	.50	1.25
❑ 27 Terrell Owens	.30	.75
❑ 28 Marion Barber	.30	.75
❑ 29 Jay Cutler	.30	.75
❑ 30 Brandon Stokley	.25	.60
❑ 31 Jon Kitna	.25	.60
❑ 32 Roy Williams WR	.25	.60
❑ 33 Calvin Johnson	.30	.75
❑ 34 Aaron Rodgers	.30	.75
❑ 35 Ryan Grant	.30	.75
❑ 36 Donald Driver	.25	.60
❑ 37 Matt Schaub	.25	.60
❑ 38 Andre Johnson	.25	.60
❑ 39 Kevin Walter	.25	.60
❑ 40 Peyton Manning	.50	1.25
❑ 41 Joseph Addai	.30	.75
❑ 42 Reggie Wayne	.25	.60
❑ 43 Dallas Clark	.25	.60
❑ 44 David Garrard	.25	.60
❑ 45 Fred Taylor	.25	.60
❑ 46 Maurice Jones-Drew	.25	.60
❑ 47 Reggie Williams	.25	.60
❑ 48 Brodie Croyle	.25	.60
❑ 49 Larry Johnson	.25	.60
❑ 50 Tony Gonzalez	.25	.60
❑ 51 Chad Pennington	.25	.60
❑ 52 Ronnie Brown	.25	.60
❑ 53 Ted Ginn Jr.	.25	.60
❑ 54 Tarvaris Jackson	.25	.60
❑ 55 Adrian Peterson	.60	1.50
❑ 56 Sidney Rice	.30	.75
❑ 57 Tom Brady	.50	1.25
❑ 58 Randy Moss	.30	.75
❑ 59 Laurence Maroney	.25	.60
❑ 60 Drew Brees	.30	.75
❑ 61 Reggie Bush	.30	.75
❑ 62 Deuce McAllister	.25	.60
❑ 63 Eli Manning	.30	.75
❑ 64 Plaxico Burress	.25	.60
❑ 65 Brandon Jacobs	.25	.60
❑ 66 Brett Favre	2.00	5.00
❑ 67 Leon Washington	.25	.60
❑ 68 Laveranues Coles	.25	.60
❑ 69 JaMarcus Russell	.30	.75
❑ 70 Justin Fargas	.20	.50
❑ 71 Zach Miller	.25	.60
❑ 72 Donovan McNabb	.30	.75
❑ 73 Brian Westbrook	.25	.60
❑ 74 Reggie Brown	.20	.50
❑ 75 Ben Roethlisberger	.40	1.00
❑ 76 Willie Parker	.25	.60
❑ 77 Santonio Holmes	.25	.60
❑ 78 Philip Rivers	.30	.75
❑ 79 LaDainian Tomlinson	.40	1.00
❑ 80 Vincent Jackson	.20	.50
❑ 81 Antonio Gates	.25	.60
❑ 82 J.T. O'Sullivan	.20	.50
❑ 83 Frank Gore	.25	.60
❑ 84 Vernon Davis	.20	.50
❑ 85 Matt Hasselbeck	.25	.60
❑ 86 Deion Branch	.25	.60
❑ 87 Julius Jones	.25	.60
❑ 88 Marc Bulger	.25	.60
❑ 89 Steven Jackson	.30	.75
❑ 90 Torry Holt	.25	.60
❑ 91 Warrick Dunn	.25	.60
❑ 92 Jeff Garcia	.25	.60
❑ 93 Joey Galloway	.25	.60
❑ 94 Vince Young	.25	.60
❑ 95 LenDale White	.25	.60
❑ 96 Roydell Williams	.20	.50
❑ 97 Jason Campbell	.25	.60
❑ 98 Clinton Portis	.25	.60
❑ 99 Santana Moss	.20	.50
❑ 100 Ladell Betts	.20	.50
❑ 101 Trent Edwards ELE	1.50	4.00
❑ 102 Marshawn Lynch ELE	1.50	4.00
❑ 103 Braylon Edwards ELE	1.25	3.00
❑ 104 Carson Palmer ELE	1.50	4.00
❑ 105 Tom Brady ELE	2.50	6.00
❑ 106 Matt Hasselbeck ELE	1.25	3.00
❑ 107 Nate Burleson ELE	1.00	2.50
❑ 108 Fred Taylor ELE	1.25	3.00
❑ 109 David Garrard ELE	1.25	3.00
❑ 110 Maurice Jones-Drew ELE	1.25	3.00
❑ 111 Devin Hester ELE	1.50	4.00
❑ 112 Willie Parker ELE	1.25	3.00
❑ 113 Ben Roethlisberger ELE	2.00	5.00
❑ 114 Ryan Grant ELE	1.50	4.00
❑ 115 Eli Manning ELE	1.50	4.00
❑ 116 Adrian Arrington RC	1.50	4.00
❑ 117 Ali Highsmith RC	1.25	3.00
❑ 118 Anthony Alridge RC	1.50	4.00
❑ 119 Antoine Cason RC	2.00	5.00
❑ 120 Aqib Talib RC	2.00	5.00
❑ 121 Brad Cottam RC	2.00	5.00
❑ 122 Brandon Flowers RC	2.00	5.00
❑ 123 Calais Campbell RC	1.50	4.00
❑ 124 Chauncey Washington RC	1.50	4.00
❑ 125 Chevis Jackson RC	1.50	4.00
❑ 126 Cory Boyd RC	1.50	4.00
❑ 127 Craig Steltz RC	1.50	4.00
❑ 128 Curtis Lofton RC	2.00	5.00
❑ 129 DJ Hall RC	1.50	4.00
❑ 130 Dantrell Savage RC	2.00	5.00
❑ 131 Dorius Reynaud RC	1.50	4.00
❑ 132 Darrell Strong RC	1.50	4.00
❑ 133 Davone Bess RC	2.50	6.00
❑ 134 Derrick Harvey RC	1.50	4.00
❑ 135 D.Rodgers-Cromartie RC	2.00	5.00
❑ 136 Erin Henderson RC	1.50	4.00
❑ 137 Ernie Wheelwright RC	1.50	4.00
❑ 138 Fred Davis RC	2.00	5.00
❑ 139 Joe Jon Finley RC	1.50	4.00
❑ 140 Jacob Hester RC	2.00	5.00
❑ 141 Jacob Tamme RC	2.00	5.00
❑ 142 Jamar Adams RC	1.50	4.00
❑ 143 Jason Rivers RC	2.00	5.00
❑ 144 Jed Collins RC	1.50	4.00
❑ 145 Jermichael Finley RC	2.00	5.00
❑ 146 John Carlson RC	2.00	5.00
❑ 147 Jonathan Hefney RC	1.50	4.00
❑ 148 Jordon Dizon RC	2.00	5.00
❑ 149 Josh Morgan RC	2.00	5.00
❑ 150 Justin Forsett RC	2.00	5.00
❑ 151 Kalvin McRae RC	1.50	4.00
❑ 152 Keenan Burton RC	1.50	4.00
❑ 153 Kellen Davis RC	1.25	3.00
❑ 154 Kentwan Balmer RC	1.50	4.00
❑ 155 Kevin Robinson RC	1.50	4.00
❑ 156 Lawrence Jackson RC	1.50	4.00
❑ 157 Leodis McKelvin RC	2.00	5.00
❑ 158 Marcus Monk RC	2.00	5.00
❑ 159 Marcus Smith RC	1.50	4.00
❑ 160 Marcus Thomas RC	1.50	4.00
❑ 161 Mark Bradford RC	1.50	4.00
❑ 162 Martellus Bennett RC	2.00	5.00
❑ 163 Martin Rucker RC	1.50	4.00
❑ 164 Mike Jenkins RC	2.00	5.00
❑ 165 Owen Schmitt RC	2.00	5.00
❑ 166 Pat Sims RC	1.50	4.00
❑ 167 Paul Hubbard RC	1.50	4.00
❑ 168 Paul Smith RC	2.00	5.00
❑ 169 Peyton Hillis RC	2.00	5.00
❑ 170 Phillip Merling RC	1.50	4.00
❑ 171 Quentin Groves RC	1.50	4.00
❑ 172 Reggie Smith RC	1.50	4.00
❑ 173 Ryan Grice-Mullen RC	2.00	5.00
❑ 174 Ryan Torain RC	2.00	5.00
❑ 175 Sam Keller RC	2.00	5.00
❑ 176 Sedrick Ellis RC	2.00	5.00
❑ 177 Shawn Crable RC	2.00	5.00
❑ 178 Simeon Castille RC	1.50	4.00
❑ 179 Terrell Thomas RC	1.50	4.00
❑ 180 Thomas Brown RC	2.00	5.00
❑ 181 Tim Hightower RC	2.50	6.00
❑ 182 Tracy Porter RC	2.50	6.00
❑ 183 Vernon Gholston RC	2.00	5.00
❑ 184 Will Franklin RC	1.50	4.00
❑ 185 Xavier Adibi RC	1.50	4.00
❑ 186 Alex Brink RC	2.00	5.00
❑ 187 Jalen Parmele RC	1.50	4.00
❑ 188 Xavier Omon RC	2.00	5.00
❑ 189 Craig Stevens RC	1.50	4.00
❑ 190 Derek Fine RC	1.50	4.00
❑ 191 Gary Barnidge RC	1.50	4.00
❑ 192 Arman Shields RC	1.50	4.00
❑ 193 Kenneth Moore RC	1.50	4.00
❑ 194 Marcus Henry RC	1.50	4.00
❑ 195 Jaymar Johnson RC	1.50	4.00
❑ 196 Pierre Garcon RC	3.00	8.00
❑ 197 Patrick Lee RC	2.00	5.00
❑ 198 Terrence Wheatley RC	1.50	4.00
❑ 199 Tavares Gooden RC	1.50	4.00
❑ 200 Bruce Davis RC	2.00	5.00
❑ 201 Allen Patrick AU/268 RC	6.00	15.00
❑ 202 Andre Caldwell AU/116 RC	10.00	25.00
❑ 203 Andre Woodson AU/219 RC	8.00	20.00
❑ 204 Brian Brohm AU/99 RC	12.00	30.00
❑ 206 C.Henne AU/99 RC EXCH	20.00	50.00
❑ 207 Chris Johnson AU/166 RC	60.00	100.00
❑ 208 Chris Long AU/99 RC EXCH	12.00	30.00
❑ 209 Colt Brennan AU/213 RC	25.00	50.00
❑ 210 Dan Connor AU/270 RC	8.00	20.00
❑ 211 Darren McFadden AU/99 RC	30.00	80.00
❑ 212 Dennis Dixon AU/218 RC	8.00	20.00
❑ 213 DeSean Jackson AU/119 RC	20.00	50.00
❑ 214 Devin Thomas AU/118 RC	10.00	25.00
❑ 215 Dexter Jackson AU/132 RC	10.00	25.00
❑ 216 Donnie Avery AU/129 RC	12.00	30.00
❑ 217 Dustin Keller AU/116 RC	10.00	25.00
❑ 218 Earl Bennett AU/118 RC	15.00	30.00
❑ 219 Early Doucet AU/106 RC	10.00	25.00
❑ 220 Eddie Royal AU/126 RC	25.00	50.00
❑ 221 Erik Ainge AU/271 RC	8.00	20.00
❑ 222 Felix Jones AU/99 RC	30.00	80.00
❑ 223 Glenn Dorsey AU/99 RC	12.00	30.00
❑ 224 Harry Douglas AU/99 RC	10.00	25.00
❑ 225 Jake Long AU/99 RC	12.00	30.00
❑ 226 Jamaal Charles AU/118 RC	15.00	40.00
❑ 227 James Hardy AU/118 RC	8.00	20.00
❑ 228 Jerod Mayo AU/52 RC	30.00	60.00
❑ 229 Jerome Simpson AU/117 RC	8.00	20.00
❑ 230 Joe Flacco AU/99 RC	60.00	120.00
❑ 231 John David Booty AU/118 RC	10.00	25.00
❑ 232 Jonathan Stewart AU/99 RC	30.00	60.00
❑ 233 Jordy Nelson AU/99 RC	15.00	40.00
❑ 234 Josh Johnson AU/268 RC	8.00	20.00
❑ 235 Keith Rivers AU/263 RC	6.00	15.00
❑ 236 K.Phillips AU/99 RC EXCH	10.00	25.00
❑ 237 Kevin O'Connell AU/142 RC	10.00	25.00
❑ 238 Kevin Smith AU/117 RC	15.00	40.00
❑ 239 Lavelle Hawkins AU/273 RC	6.00	15.00
❑ 240 Limas Sweed AU/103 RC	10.00	25.00
❑ 241 Malcolm Kelly AU/108 RC	10.00	25.00
❑ 242 M.Manningham AU/118 RC	15.00	30.00
❑ 243 Matt Flynn AU/263 RC	8.00	20.00
❑ 244 Matt Forte AU/107 RC	50.00	80.00

❑ 245 Matt Ryan AU/99 RC 90.00 150.00
❑ 246 Mike Hart AU/263 RC EXCH 8.00 20.00
❑ 247 R.Mendenhall AU/99 RC 25.00 50.00
❑ 248 Ray Rice AU/105 RC 20.00 50.00
❑ 249 Steve Slaton AU/118 RC 20.00 50.00
❑ 250 Tashard Choice AU/270 RC 15.00 30.00

2009 Limited

❑ 1 Kurt Warner 1.50 4.00
❑ 2 Larry Fitzgerald 1.50 4.00
❑ 3 Tim Hightower 1.25 3.00
❑ 4 Matt Ryan 1.50 4.00
❑ 5 Michael Turner 1.25 3.00
❑ 6 Roddy White 1.25 3.00
❑ 7 Tony Gonzalez 1.25 3.00
❑ 8 Mark Clayton 1.00 2.50
❑ 9 Joe Flacco 1.50 4.00
❑ 10 Willis McGahee 1.25 3.00
❑ 11 Lee Evans 1.25 3.00
❑ 12 Marshawn Lynch 1.25 3.00
❑ 13 Terrell Owens 1.50 4.00
❑ 14 DeAngelo Williams 1.50 4.00
❑ 15 Jake Delhomme 1.25 3.00
❑ 16 Steve Smith 1.25 3.00
❑ 17 Brian Urlacher 1.50 4.00
❑ 18 Greg Olsen 1.00 2.50
❑ 19 Jay Cutler 1.50 4.00
❑ 20 Matt Forte 1.50 4.00
❑ 21 Carson Palmer 1.50 4.00
❑ 22 Cedric Benson 1.25 3.00
❑ 23 Chad Ochocinco 1.25 3.00
❑ 24 Brady Quinn 1.25 3.00
❑ 25 Braylon Edwards 1.25 3.00
❑ 26 Jamal Lewis 1.25 3.00
❑ 27 Marion Barber 1.50 4.00
❑ 28 Roy Williams WR 1.25 3.00
❑ 29 Tony Romo 2.50 6.00
❑ 30 Eddie Royal 1.25 3.00
❑ 31 Kyle Orton 1.25 3.00
❑ 32 LaMont Jordan 1.00 2.50
❑ 33 Calvin Johnson 1.50 4.00
❑ 34 Daunte Culpepper 1.25 3.00
❑ 35 Kevin Smith 1.25 3.00
❑ 36 Aaron Rodgers 1.50 4.00
❑ 37 Greg Jennings 1.50 4.00
❑ 38 Ryan Grant 1.25 3.00
❑ 39 Andre Johnson 1.25 3.00
❑ 40 Matt Schaub 1.25 3.00
❑ 41 Steve Slaton 1.25 3.00
❑ 42 Anthony Gonzalez 1.25 3.00
❑ 43 Joseph Addai 1.50 4.00
❑ 44 Peyton Manning 2.50 6.00
❑ 45 Reggie Wayne 1.25 3.00
❑ 46 David Garrard 1.25 3.00
❑ 47 Maurice Jones-Drew 1.25 3.00
❑ 48 Torry Holt 1.25 3.00
❑ 49 Dwayne Bowe 1.25 3.00
❑ 50 Larry Johnson 1.25 3.00
❑ 51 Matt Cassel 1.25 3.00
❑ 52 Chad Pennington 1.25 3.00
❑ 53 Ronnie Brown 1.25 3.00
❑ 54 Ricky Williams 1.25 3.00
❑ 55 Adrian Peterson 3.00 8.00
❑ 56 Bernard Berrian 1.25 3.00
❑ 57 Brett Favre Vikings 10.00 25.00
❑ 58 Laurence Maroney 1.25 3.00
❑ 59 Randy Moss 1.50 4.00
❑ 60 Tom Brady 2.50 6.00
❑ 61 Wes Welker 1.50 4.00
❑ 62 Drew Brees 1.50 4.00
❑ 63 Marques Colston 1.25 3.00
❑ 64 Reggie Bush 1.50 4.00
❑ 65 Brandon Jacobs 1.25 3.00
❑ 66 Eli Manning 1.50 4.00
❑ 67 Kevin Boss 1.00 2.50
❑ 68 Jerricho Cotchery 1.00 2.50
❑ 69 Leon Washington 1.25 3.00
❑ 70 Darren McFadden 1.50 4.00
❑ 71 JaMarcus Russell 1.25 3.00
❑ 72 Zach Miller 1.00 2.50
❑ 73 Brian Westbrook 1.25 3.00
❑ 74 DeSean Jackson 1.25 3.00
❑ 75 Donovan McNabb 1.50 4.00
❑ 76 Ben Roethlisberger 2.50 6.00
❑ 77 Santonio Holmes 1.25 3.00
❑ 78 Willie Parker 1.25 3.00
❑ 79 Antonio Gates 1.25 3.00
❑ 80 LaDainian Tomlinson 1.50 4.00
❑ 81 Philip Rivers 1.50 4.00
❑ 82 Vincent Jackson 1.25 3.00
❑ 83 Frank Gore 1.25 3.00
❑ 84 Isaac Bruce 1.25 3.00
❑ 85 Vernon Davis 1.00 2.50
❑ 86 Julius Jones 1.25 3.00
❑ 87 Matt Hasselbeck 1.25 3.00
❑ 88 T.J. Houshmandzadeh 1.25 3.00
❑ 89 Donnie Avery 1.25 3.00
❑ 90 Marc Bulger 1.25 3.00
❑ 91 Steven Jackson 1.25 3.00
❑ 92 Antonio Bryant 1.25 3.00
❑ 93 Derrick Ward 1.25 3.00
❑ 94 Kellen Winslow Jr. 1.25 3.00
❑ 95 Chris Johnson 1.50 4.00
❑ 96 Kerry Collins 1.25 3.00
❑ 97 LenDale White 1.25 3.00
❑ 98 Chris Cooley 1.25 3.00
❑ 99 Clinton Portis 1.25 3.00
❑ 100 Jason Campbell 1.25 3.00
❑ 101 Archie Manning 2.00 5.00
❑ 102 Bart Starr 3.00 8.00
❑ 103 Billy Howton 1.25 3.00
❑ 104 Bob Griese 2.00 5.00
❑ 105 Bob Lilly 1.50 4.00
❑ 106 Brett Favre Jets 4.00 10.00
❑ 107 Carl Eller 1.25 3.00
❑ 108 Charley Taylor 1.25 3.00
❑ 109 Charley Trippi 1.25 3.00
❑ 110 Chuck Bednarik 1.50 4.00
❑ 111 Dan Fouts 2.00 5.00
❑ 112 Dan Marino 3.00 8.00
❑ 113 Deacon Jones 1.50 4.00
❑ 114 Don Maynard 1.50 4.00
❑ 115 Emmitt Smith 2.50 6.00
❑ 116 Fran Tarkenton 2.00 5.00
❑ 117 Fred Biletnikoff 2.00 5.00
❑ 118 Garo Yepremian 1.25 3.00
❑ 119 George Blanda 1.50 4.00
❑ 120 Hugh McElhenny 1.25 3.00
❑ 121 Jack Lambert 2.00 5.00
❑ 122 James Lofton 1.25 3.00
❑ 123 Jan Stenerud 1.25 3.00
❑ 124 Jerry Rice 2.50 6.00
❑ 125 Jethro Pugh 1.25 3.00
❑ 126 Jim Brown 2.50 6.00
❑ 127 Jim Otto 1.25 3.00
❑ 128 Joe Greene 2.00 5.00
❑ 129 Joe Montana 3.00 8.00
❑ 130 Joe Namath 2.50 6.00
❑ 131 John Elway 2.50 6.00
❑ 132 John Stallworth 1.50 4.00
❑ 133 Lance Alworth 1.50 4.00
❑ 134 Lenny Moore 1.50 4.00
❑ 135 Phil Simms 1.50 4.00
❑ 136 Raymond Berry 1.50 4.00
❑ 137 Roger Staubach 2.50 6.00
❑ 138 Ted Hendricks 1.25 3.00
❑ 139 Tiki Barber 1.25 3.00
❑ 140 Troy Aikman 2.00 5.00
❑ 141 Willie Brown 1.25 3.00
❑ 142 Walter Payton 4.00 10.00
❑ 143 Jim Thorpe 2.50 6.00
❑ 144 Doak Walker 2.00 5.00
❑ 145 Ace Parker 1.25 3.00
❑ 146 Don Perkins 1.25 3.00
❑ 147 Sammy Baugh 2.00 5.00
❑ 148 Jim McMahon 1.50 4.00
❑ 149 Jim Kelly 1.50 4.00
❑ 150 Barry Sanders 2.50 6.00
❑ 151 Aaron Brown RC/399 2.00 5.00
❑ 152 Aaron Kelly AU/399 RC 4.00 10.00
❑ 153 Aaron Maybin AU/99 RC EXCH 15.00 30.00
❑ 154 Austin Collie AU/399 RC 12.50 25.00
❑ 155 B.J. Raji AU/399 RC 6.00 15.00
❑ 156 Bernard Scott RC/399 2.00 5.00
❑ 157 Brandon Gibson AU/399 RC 5.00 12.00
❑ 158 Brandon Tate AU/399 RC 4.00 10.00
❑ 159 Brian Cushing AU/199 RC 6.00 15.00
❑ 160 Brian Hartline RC/399 2.00 5.00
❑ 161 Brian Orakpo AU/249 RC 6.00 15.00
❑ 162 Brooks Foster AU/399 RC 4.00 10.00
❑ 163 Cameron Morrah AU/399 RC 3.00 8.00
❑ 164 Cedric Peerman AU/199 RC 4.00 10.00
❑ 165 Chase Coffman AU/399 RC 4.00 10.00
❑ 166 Chris Ogbonnaya RC/399 2.00 5.00
❑ 167 Clay Matthews AU/299 RC 8.00 20.00
❑ 168 Clint Sintim AU/149 RC 6.00 15.00
❑ 169 Cornelius Ingram AU/399 RC 3.00 8.00
❑ 170 Demetrius Byrd AU/99 RC 5.00 12.00
❑ 171 Devin Moore AU/299 RC 4.00 10.00
❑ 172 D.Edison AU/399 RC 3.00 8.00
❑ 173 Everette Brown AU/399 RC 5.00 12.00
❑ 174 Gartrell Johnson RC/399 1.50 4.00
❑ 175 Hunter Cantwell AU/149 RC 6.00 15.00
❑ 176 James Casey AU/399 RC 4.00 10.00
❑ 177 James Laurinaitis AU/299 RC 6.00 15.00
❑ 178 Jared Cook AU/399 RC 4.00 10.00
❑ 179 Jarett Dillard AU/399 RC 5.00 12.00
❑ 180 Johnny Knox AU/399 RC 8.00 20.00
❑ 181 Kenny McKinley AU/399 RC 5.00 12.00
❑ 182 Kevin Ogletree AU/249 RC 6.00 15.00
❑ 183 Kory Sheets AU/99 RC 5.00 12.00
❑ 184 Larry English AU/249 RC 5.00 12.00
❑ 185 L.Murphy AU/99 RC EXCH 10.00 25.00
❑ 186 Malcolm Jenkins AU/249 RC 5.00 12.00
❑ 187 Mike Goodson AU/299 RC 5.00 12.00
❑ 188 Nathan Brown AU/399 RC 4.00 10.00
❑ 189 P.J. Hill AU/399 RC 4.00 10.00
❑ 190 Quan Cosby AU/249 RC 4.00 10.00
❑ 191 Quinn Johnson AU/399 RC 4.00 10.00
❑ 192 Rashad Jennings AU/199 RC 5.00 12.00
❑ 193 Rey Maualuga AU/399 RC 8.00 20.00
❑ 194 S.Nelson AU/99 RC EXCH 5.00 12.00
❑ 195 Tiquan Underwood RC/399 1.50 4.00
❑ 196 Tom Brandstater AU/149 RC 6.00 15.00
❑ 197 T.Fiammetta AU/399 RC 4.00 10.00
❑ 198 Travis Beckum AU/399 RC 4.00 10.00
❑ 199 Tyrell Sutton AU/399 RC 4.00 10.00
❑ 200 Vontae Davis AU/399 RC 5.00 12.00
❑ 201 Glen Coffee JSY AU RC 10.00 25.00
❑ 202 M.Crabtree JSY AU RC 50.00 100.00
❑ 203 Nate Davis JSY AU RC 8.00 20.00
❑ 204 Javon Ringer JSY AU RC 8.00 20.00
❑ 205 K.Britt JSY AU RC EXCH 12.00 30.00
❑ 206 Mike Wallace JSY AU RC 25.00 50.00
❑ 207 Jeremy Maclin JSY AU RC 15.00 40.00
❑ 208 LeSean McCoy JSY AU RC 15.00 40.00
❑ 209 Donald Brown JSY AU RC 15.00 40.00
❑ 210 Mike Thomas JSY AU RC 8.00 20.00
❑ 211 Tyson Jackson JSY AU RC 8.00 20.00
❑ 212 Josh Freeman JSY AU RC 15.00 40.00
❑ 213 D.Heyward-Bey JSY AU RC 12.00 30.00
❑ 214 Aaron Curry JSY AU RC 10.00 25.00
❑ 215 Deon Butler JSY AU RC 8.00 20.00
❑ 216 Jason Smith JSY AU RC 8.00 20.00
❑ 217 Juaquin Iglesias JSY AU RC 8.00 20.00
❑ 218 Stephen McGee JSY AU RC 8.00 20.00
❑ 219 Andre Brown JSY AU RC 6.00 15.00
❑ 220 H.Nicks JSY AU RC EXCH 15.00 40.00
❑ 221 Ramses Barden JSY AU RC 6.00 15.00
❑ 222 Rhett Bomar JSY AU RC 6.00 15.00
❑ 223 Percy Harvin JSY AU RC 60.00 120.00
❑ 224 Pat White JSY AU RC 12.00 30.00
❑ 225 Patrick Turner JSY AU RC 6.00 15.00
❑ 226 Chris Wells JSY AU RC 20.00 50.00
❑ 227 Mark Sanchez JSY AU RC 60.00 120.00
❑ 228 Shonn Greene JSY AU RC 15.00 40.00
❑ 229 Brian Robiskie JSY AU RC 8.00 20.00
❑ 230 Massaquoi JSY AU RC EXCH 8.00 20.00
❑ 231 B.Pettigrew JSY AU RC 10.00 25.00
❑ 232 Derrick Williams JSY AU RC 8.00 20.00
❑ 233 M.Stafford JSY AU RC 50.00 100.00
❑ 234 K.Moreno JSY AU RC 40.00 80.00

1991 Pacific

❑ COMPLETE SET (660) 7.50 15.00
❑ COMP.SERIES 1 (550) 4.00 8.00
❑ COMP.FACT.SER.1 (550) 5.00 10.00
❑ COMP.SERIES 2 (110) 4.00 8.00
❑ COMP.FACT.SER.2 (110) 6.00 12.00
❑ COMP.CHECKLIST SET (5) 7.50 15.00
❑ 1 Deion Sanders .15 .40
❑ 2 Steve Broussard .01 .05
❑ 3 Aundray Bruce .01 .05
❑ 4 Rick Bryan .01 .05
❑ 5 John Rade .01 .05
❑ 6 Scott Case .01 .05
❑ 7 Tony Casillas .01 .05
❑ 8 Shawn Collins .01 .05
❑ 9 Darion Conner .01 .05
❑ 10 Tory Epps .01 .05
❑ 11 Bill Fralic .01 .05
❑ 12 Mike Gann .01 .05
❑ 13 Tim Green UER .01 .05
❑ 14 Chris Hinton .01 .05
❑ 15 Houston Hoover UER .01 .05
❑ 16 Chris Miller .02 .10
❑ 17 Andre Rison .02 .10
❑ 18 Mike Rozier .01 .05
❑ 19 Jessie Tuggle .01 .05
❑ 20 Don Beebe .01 .05
❑ 21 Ray Bentley .01 .05
❑ 22 Shane Conlan .01 .05
❑ 23 Kent Hull .01 .05
❑ 24 Mark Kelso .01 .05
❑ 25 James Lofton UER .02 .10
❑ 26 Scott Norwood .01 .05
❑ 27 Andre Reed .02 .10
❑ 28 Leonard Smith .01 .05
❑ 29 Bruce Smith .08 .25
❑ 30 Leon Seals .01 .05
❑ 31 Darryl Talley .01 .05
❑ 32 Steve Tasker .02 .10
❑ 33 Thurman Thomas .08 .25
❑ 34 James Williams .01 .05
❑ 35 Will Wolford .01 .05
❑ 36 Frank Reich .02 .10
❑ 37 Jeff Wright RC .01 .05
❑ 38 Neal Anderson .02 .10
❑ 39 Trace Armstrong .01 .05
❑ 40 Johnny Bailey UER .01 .05
❑ 41 Mark Bortz UER .01 .05
❑ 42 Cap Boso RC .01 .05
❑ 43 Kevin Butler .01 .05
❑ 44 Mark Carrier DB .02 .10
❑ 45 Jim Covert .01 .05
❑ 46 Wendell Davis .01 .05
❑ 47 Richard Dent .02 .10
❑ 48 Shaun Gayle .01 .05
❑ 49 Jim Harbaugh .08 .25
❑ 50 Jay Hilgenberg .01 .05
❑ 51 Brad Muster .01 .05
❑ 52 William Perry .02 .10
❑ 53 Mike Singletary UER .02 .10
❑ 54 Peter Tom Willis .01 .05
❑ 55 Donnell Woolford .01 .05
❑ 56 Steve McMichael .02 .10
❑ 57 Eric Ball .01 .05
❑ 58 Lewis Billups .01 .05
❑ 59 Jim Breech .01 .05
❑ 60 James Brooks .02 .10
❑ 61 Eddie Brown .01 .05
❑ 62 Rickey Dixon .01 .05
❑ 63 Boomer Esiason .02 .10
❑ 64 James Francis .01 .05
❑ 65 David Fulcher .01 .05
❑ 66 David Grant .01 .05
❑ 67 Harold Green UER .01 .05
❑ 68 Rodney Holman .01 .05
❑ 69 Stanford Jennings .01 .05
❑ 70A Tim Krumrie ERR .20 .50
❑ 70B Tim Krumrie COR .10 .30
❑ 71 Tim McGee .01 .05
❑ 72 Anthony Munoz .02 .10
❑ 73 Mitchell Price RC .01 .05
❑ 74 Eric Thomas .01 .05
❑ 75 Ickey Woods .01 .05
❑ 76 Mike Baab .01 .05
❑ 77 Thane Gash .01 .05
❑ 78 David Grayson .01 .05
❑ 79 Mike Johnson .01 .05
❑ 80 Reggie Langhorne .01 .05
❑ 81 Kevin Mack .01 .05
❑ 82 Clay Matthews .02 .10
❑ 83A Eric Metcalf ERR .20 .50
❑ 83B Eric Metcalf COR .10 .30
❑ 84 Frank Minnifield .01 .05
❑ 85 Mike Oliphant .01 .05
❑ 86 Mike Pagel .01 .05
❑ 87 John Talley .01 .05
❑ 88 Lawyer Tillman .01 .05
❑ 89 Gregg Rakoczy UER .01 .05
❑ 90 Bryan Wagner .01 .05
❑ 91 Rob Burnett RC .02 .10
❑ 92 Tommie Agee .01 .05
❑ 93 Troy Aikman UER .30 .75
❑ 94A Bill Bates ERR .20 .50
❑ 94B Bill Bates COR .10 .30
❑ 95 Jack Del Rio .02 .10
❑ 96 Issiac Holt UER .01 .05
❑ 97 Michael Irvin .08 .25
❑ 98 Jim Jeffcoat UER .01 .05
❑ 99 Jimmie Jones .01 .05
❑ 100 Kelvin Martin .01 .05
❑ 101 Nate Newton .02 .10
❑ 102 Danny Noonan .01 .05
❑ 103 Ken Norton Jr. .02 .10
❑ 104 Jay Novacek .08 .25
❑ 105 Mike Saxon .01 .05
❑ 106 Derrick Shepard .01 .05
❑ 107 Emmitt Smith 1.00 2.50
❑ 108 Daniel Stubbs .01 .05
❑ 109 Tony Tolbert .01 .05
❑ 110 Alexander Wright .01 .05
❑ 111 Steve Atwater .01 .05
❑ 112 Melvin Bratton .01 .05
❑ 113 Tyrone Braxton UER .01 .05
❑ 114 Alphonso Carreker .01 .05
❑ 115 John Elway .50 1.25
❑ 116 Simon Fletcher .01 .05
❑ 117 Bobby Humphrey .01 .05
❑ 118 Mark Jackson .01 .05
❑ 119 Vance Johnson .01 .05
❑ 120 Greg Kragen UER .01 .05
❑ 121 Karl Mecklenburg UER .01 .05
❑ 122A Orsen Mobley ERR .20 .50
❑ 122B Orson Mobley COR .02 .10
❑ 123 Alton Montgomery .01 .05
❑ 124 Ricky Nattiel .01 .05
❑ 125 Steve Sewell .01 .05
❑ 126 Shannon Sharpe .20 .50
❑ 127 Dennis Smith .01 .05
❑ 128A Andre Townsend ERR RC .20 .50
❑ 128B Andrew Townsend COR RC .02 .10
❑ 129 Mike Horan .01 .05
❑ 130 Jerry Ball .01 .05
❑ 131 Bennie Blades .01 .05
❑ 132 Lomas Brown .01 .05
❑ 133 Jeff Campbell UER .01 .05
❑ 134 Robert Clark .01 .05
❑ 135 Michael Cofer .01 .05
❑ 136 Dennis Gibson .01 .05
❑ 137 Mel Gray .02 .10
❑ 138 LeRoy Irvin UER .01 .05
❑ 139 George Jamison RC .01 .05
❑ 140 Richard Johnson .01 .05
❑ 141 Eddie Murray .01 .05
❑ 142 Dan Owens .01 .05
❑ 143 Rodney Peete .02 .10
❑ 144 Barry Sanders .50 1.25
❑ 145 Chris Spielman .02 .10
❑ 146 Marc Spindler .01 .05
❑ 147 Andre Ware .02 .10
❑ 148 William White .01 .05
❑ 149 Tony Bennett .02 .10
❑ 150 Robert Brown .01 .05
❑ 151 LeRoy Butler .02 .10
❑ 152 Anthony Dilweg .01 .05
❑ 153 Michael Haddix .01 .05
❑ 154 Ron Hallstrom .01 .05
❑ 155 Tim Harris .01 .05
❑ 156 Johnny Holland .01 .05
❑ 157 Chris Jacke .01 .05
❑ 158 Perry Kemp .01 .05
❑ 159 Mark Lee .01 .05
❑ 160 Don Majkowski .01 .05
❑ 161 Tony Mandarich UER .01 .05
❑ 162 Mark Murphy .01 .05
❑ 163 Brian Noble .01 .05
❑ 164 Shawn Patterson .01 .05
❑ 165 Jeff Query .01 .05
❑ 166 Sterling Sharpe .08 .25
❑ 167 Darrell Thompson .01 .05
❑ 168 Ed West .01 .05
❑ 169 Ray Childress UER .01 .05
❑ 170A Cris Dishman ERR RC .02 .10
❑ 170B Cris Dishman ERR/COR RC .02 .10
❑ 170C Cris Dishman COR RC .02 .10
❑ 171 Curtis Duncan .01 .05
❑ 172 William Fuller .02 .10
❑ 173 Ernest Givins UER .02 .10
❑ 174 Drew Hill .01 .05
❑ 175A Haywood Jeffires ERR .08 .25
❑ 175B Haywood Jeffires COR .08 .25
❑ 176 Sean Jones .02 .10
❑ 177 Lamar Lathon .01 .05
❑ 178 Bruce Matthews .02 .10
❑ 179 Bubba McDowell .01 .05
❑ 180 Johnny Meads .01 .05
❑ 181 Warren Moon UER .08 .25
❑ 182 Mike Munchak .02 .10
❑ 183 Allen Pinkett .01 .05
❑ 184 Dean Steinkuhler UER .01 .05
❑ 185 Lorenzo White UER .01 .05
❑ 186A John Grimsley ERR .20 .50
❑ 186B John Grimsley COR .02 .10
❑ 187 Pat Beach .01 .05
❑ 188 Albert Bentley .01 .05
❑ 189 Dean Biasucci .01 .05
❑ 190 Duane Bickett .01 .05
❑ 191 Bill Brooks .01 .05
❑ 192 Eugene Daniel .01 .05
❑ 193 Jeff George .08 .25
❑ 194 Jon Hand .01 .05
❑ 195 Jeff Herrod .01 .05
❑ 196A Jessie Hester ERR Jesse .10 .30
❑ 196B Jessie Hester ERR .02 .10
❑ 197 Mike Prior .01 .05
❑ 198 Stacey Simmons .01 .05
❑ 199 Rohn Stark .01 .05
❑ 200 Pat Tomberlin .01 .05
❑ 201 Clarence Verdin .01 .05
❑ 202 Keith Taylor .01 .05
❑ 203 Jack Trudeau .01 .05
❑ 204 Chip Banks .01 .05
❑ 205 John Alt .01 .05
❑ 206 Deron Cherry .01 .05
❑ 207 Steve DeBerg .01 .05
❑ 208 Tim Grunhard .01 .05
❑ 209 Albert Lewis .01 .05
❑ 210 Nick Lowery UER .01 .05
❑ 211 Bill Maas .01 .05
❑ 212 Chris Martin .01 .05
❑ 213 Todd McNair .01 .05
❑ 214 Christian Okoye .01 .05
❑ 215 Stephone Paige .01 .05
❑ 216 Steve Pelluer .01 .05
❑ 217 Kevin Porter .01 .05
❑ 218 Kevin Ross .01 .05
❑ 219 Dan Saleaumua .01 .05
❑ 220 Neil Smith .08 .25
❑ 221 David Szott UER .01 .05
❑ 222 Derrick Thomas .08 .25
❑ 223 Barry Word .01 .05
❑ 224 Percy Snow .01 .05
❑ 225 Marcus Allen .08 .25
❑ 226 Eddie Anderson UER .01 .05
❑ 227 Steve Beuerlein UER .02 .10
❑ 228A Tim Brown ERR NPO .08 .25
❑ 228B Tim Brown COR .08 .25
❑ 229 Scott Davis .01 .05
❑ 230 Mike Dyal .01 .05
❑ 231 Mervyn Fernandez UER .01 .05
❑ 232 Willie Gault UER .01 .05
❑ 233 Ethan Horton UER .01 .05
❑ 234 Bo Jackson UER .10 .30
❑ 235 Howie Long .08 .25

Card		
❑ 236 Terry McDaniel	.01	.05
❑ 237 Max Montoya	.01	.05
❑ 238 Don Mosebar	.01	.05
❑ 239 Jay Schroeder	.01	.05
❑ 240 Steve Smith	.01	.05
❑ 241 Greg Townsend	.01	.05
❑ 242 Aaron Wallace	.01	.05
❑ 243 Lionel Washington	.01	.05
❑ 244A Steve Wisniewski ERR	.02	.10
❑ 244B Steve Wisniewski ERR/COR	.30	.75
❑ 244C Steve Wisniewski COR	.02	.10
❑ 245 Flipper Anderson	.01	.05
❑ 246 Latin Berry RC	.01	.05
❑ 247 Robert Delpino	.01	.05
❑ 248 Marcus Dupree	.01	.05
❑ 249 Henry Ellard	.02	.10
❑ 250 Jim Everett	.02	.10
❑ 251 Cleveland Gary	.01	.05
❑ 252 Jerry Gray	.01	.05
❑ 253 Kevin Greene	.02	.10
❑ 254 Pete Holohan UER	.01	.05
❑ 255 Buford McGee	.01	.05
❑ 256 Tom Newberry	.01	.05
❑ 257A Irv Pankey ERR	.20	.50
❑ 257B Irv Pankey COR	.02	.10
❑ 258 Jackie Slater	.01	.05
❑ 259 Doug Smith	.01	.05
❑ 260 Frank Stams	.01	.05
❑ 261 Michael Stewart	.01	.05
❑ 262 Fred Strickland	.01	.05
❑ 263 J.B. Brown UER	.01	.05
❑ 264 Mark Clayton	.02	.10
❑ 265 Jeff Cross	.01	.05
❑ 266 Mark Dennis RC	.01	.05
❑ 267 Mark Duper	.02	.10
❑ 268 Ferrell Edmunds	.01	.05
❑ 269 Dan Marino	.50	1.25
❑ 270 John Offerdahl	.01	.05
❑ 271 Louis Oliver	.01	.05
❑ 272 Tony Paige	.01	.05
❑ 273 Reggie Roby	.01	.05
❑ 274 Sammie Smith	.01	.05
❑ 275 Keith Sims	.01	.05
❑ 276 Brian Sochia	.01	.05
❑ 277 Pete Stoyanovich	.01	.05
❑ 278 Richmond Webb	.01	.05
❑ 279 Jarvis Williams	.01	.05
❑ 280 Tim McKyer	.01	.05
❑ 281A Jim C. Jensen ERR	.20	.50
❑ 281B Jim C. Jensen COR	.02	.10
❑ 282 Scott Secules RC	.01	.05
❑ 283 Ray Berry	.01	.05
❑ 284 Joey Browner UER	.01	.05
❑ 285 Anthony Carter	.02	.10
❑ 286A Cris Carter ERR Chris	.20	.50
❑ 286B Cris Carter ERR/COR Chris	.60	1.50
❑ 286C Cris Carter COR	.20	.50
❑ 287 Chris Doleman	.01	.05
❑ 288 Mark Dusbabek UER	.01	.05
❑ 289 Hassan Jones	.01	.05
❑ 290 Steve Jordan	.01	.05
❑ 291 Carl Lee	.01	.05
❑ 292 Kirk Lowdermilk	.01	.05
❑ 293 Randall McDaniel	.02	.10
❑ 294 Mike Merriweather	.01	.05
❑ 295A Keith Millard UER	.07	.20
❑ 295B Keith Millard COR	1.00	2.50
❑ 296 Al Noga UER	.01	.05
❑ 297 Scott Studwell UER	.01	.05
❑ 298 Henry Thomas	.01	.05
❑ 299 Herschel Walker	.02	.10
❑ 300 Gary Zimmerman	.02	.10
❑ 301 Rich Gannon	.08	.25
❑ 302 Wade Wilson UER	.02	.10
❑ 303 Vincent Brown	.01	.05
❑ 304 Marv Cook	.01	.05
❑ 305 Hart Lee Dykes	.01	.05
❑ 306 Irving Fryar	.02	.10
❑ 307 Tommy Hodson UER	.01	.05
❑ 308 Maurice Hurst	.01	.05
❑ 309 Ronnie Lippett UER	.01	.05
❑ 310 Fred Marion	.01	.05
❑ 311 Greg McMurtry	.01	.05
❑ 312 Johnny Rembert	.01	.05
❑ 313 Chris Singleton	.01	.05
❑ 314 Ed Reynolds	.01	.05
❑ 315 Andre Tippett	.01	.05
❑ 316 Garin Veris	.01	.05
❑ 317 Brent Williams	.01	.05
❑ 318A John Stephens ERR	.02	.10
❑ 318B John Stephens ERR/COR	.30	.75
❑ 318C John Stephens COR	.02	.10
❑ 319 Sammy Martin	.01	.05
❑ 320 Bruce Armstrong	.01	.05
❑ 321A Morten Andersen ERR	.10	.30
❑ 321B Morten Andersen ERR/COR	.30	.75
❑ 321C Morten Andersen COR	.02	.10
❑ 322 Gene Atkins UER	.01	.05
❑ 323 Vince Buck	.01	.05
❑ 324 John Fourcade	.01	.05
❑ 325 Kevin Haverdink	.01	.05
❑ 326 Bobby Hebert	.01	.05
❑ 327 Craig Heyward	.02	.10
❑ 328 Dalton Hilliard	.01	.05
❑ 329 Rickey Jackson	.01	.05
❑ 330A Vaughan Johnson ERR	.07	.20
❑ 330B Vaughan Johnson COR	1.00	2.50
❑ 331 Eric Martin	.01	.05
❑ 332 Wayne Martin	.01	.05
❑ 333 Rueben Mayes UER	.01	.05
❑ 334 Sam Mills	.01	.05
❑ 335 Brett Perriman	.08	.25
❑ 336 Pat Swilling	.02	.10
❑ 337 Renaldo Turnbull	.01	.05
❑ 338 Lonzell Hill	.01	.05
❑ 339 Steve Walsh	.01	.05
❑ 340 Carl Banks UER	.01	.05
❑ 341 Mark Bavaro UER	.01	.05
❑ 342 Maurice Carthon	.01	.05
❑ 343 Pat Harlow RC	.01	.05
❑ 344 Eric Dorsey	.01	.05
❑ 345 John Elliott	.01	.05
❑ 346 Rodney Hampton	.08	.25
❑ 347 Jeff Hostetler	.02	.10
❑ 348 Erik Howard UER	.01	.05
❑ 349 Pepper Johnson	.01	.05
❑ 350A Sean Landeta ERR	.02	.10
❑ 350B Sean Landeta COR	.20	.50
❑ 351 Leonard Marshall	.01	.05
❑ 352 Dave Meggett	.02	.10
❑ 353A Bart Oates ERR	.02	.10
❑ 353B Bart Oates ERR/COR	.30	.75
❑ 353C Bart Oates COR	.02	.10
❑ 354 Gary Reasons	.01	.05
❑ 355 Phil Simms	.02	.10
❑ 356 Lawrence Taylor	.08	.25
❑ 357 Reyna Thompson	.01	.05
❑ 358 Brian Williams OL UER	.01	.05
❑ 359 Matt Bahr	.01	.05
❑ 360 Mark Ingram	.02	.10
❑ 361 Brad Baxter	.01	.05
❑ 362 Mark Boyer	.01	.05
❑ 363 Dennis Byrd	.01	.05
❑ 364 Dave Cadigan UER	.01	.05
❑ 365 Kyle Clifton	.01	.05
❑ 366 James Hasty	.01	.05
❑ 367 Joe Kelly UER	.01	.05
❑ 368 Jeff Lageman	.01	.05
❑ 369 Pat Leahy UER	.01	.05
❑ 370 Terance Mathis	.02	.10
❑ 371 Erik McMillan	.01	.05
❑ 372 Rob Moore	.08	.25
❑ 373 Ken O'Brien	.01	.05
❑ 374 Tony Stargell	.01	.05
❑ 375 Jim Sweeney UER	.01	.05
❑ 376 Al Toon	.02	.10
❑ 377 Johnny Hector	.01	.05
❑ 378 Jeff Criswell	.01	.05
❑ 379 Mike Haight RC	.01	.05
❑ 380 Troy Benson	.01	.05
❑ 381 Eric Allen	.01	.05
❑ 382 Fred Barnett	.08	.25
❑ 383 Jerome Brown	.01	.05
❑ 384 Keith Byars	.01	.05
❑ 385 Randall Cunningham	.08	.25
❑ 386 Byron Evans	.01	.05
❑ 387 Wes Hopkins	.01	.05
❑ 388 Keith Jackson	.02	.10
❑ 389 Seth Joyner UER	.02	.10
❑ 390 Bobby Wilson RC	.01	.05
❑ 391 Heath Sherman	.01	.05
❑ 392 Clyde Simmons UER	.01	.05
❑ 393 Ben Smith	.01	.05
❑ 394 Andre Waters	.01	.05
❑ 395 Reggie White UER	.08	.25
❑ 396 Calvin Williams	.02	.10
❑ 397 Al Harris	.01	.05
❑ 398 Anthony Toney	.01	.05
❑ 399 Mike Quick	.01	.05
❑ 400 Anthony Bell	.01	.05
❑ 401 Rich Camarillo	.01	.05
❑ 402 Roy Green	.01	.05
❑ 403 Ken Harvey	.02	.10
❑ 404 Eric Hill	.01	.05
❑ 405 Garth Jax UER RC	.01	.05
❑ 406 Ernie Jones	.01	.05
❑ 407A Cedric Mack ERR	.07	.20
❑ 407B Cedric Mack COR	1.00	2.50
❑ 408 Dexter Manley	.01	.05
❑ 409 Tim McDonald	.01	.05
❑ 410 Freddie Joe Nunn	.01	.05
❑ 411 Ricky Proehl	.01	.05
❑ 412 Moe Gardner RC	.01	.05
❑ 413 Timm Rosenbach	.01	.05
❑ 414 Luis Sharpe UER	.01	.05
❑ 415 Vai Sikahema UER	.01	.05
❑ 416 Anthony Thompson	.01	.05
❑ 417 Ron Wolfley UER	.01	.05
❑ 418 Lonnie Young	.01	.05
❑ 419 Gary Anderson K	.01	.05
❑ 420 Bubby Brister	.01	.05
❑ 421 Thomas Everett	.01	.05
❑ 422 Eric Green	.01	.05
❑ 423 Delton Hall	.01	.05
❑ 424 Bryan Hinkle	.01	.05
❑ 425 Merril Hoge	.01	.05
❑ 426 Carnell Lake	.01	.05
❑ 427 Louis Lipps	.01	.05
❑ 428 David Little	.01	.05
❑ 429 Greg Lloyd	.08	.25
❑ 430 Mike Mularkey	.01	.05
❑ 431 Keith Willis UER	.01	.05
❑ 432 Dwayne Woodruff	.01	.05
❑ 433 Rod Woodson	.08	.25
❑ 434 Tim Worley	.01	.05
❑ 435 Warren Williams	.01	.05
❑ 436 Terry Long UER	.01	.05
❑ 437 Martin Bayless	.01	.05
❑ 438 Jarrod Bunch RC	.01	.05
❑ 439 Marion Butts	.02	.10
❑ 440 Gill Byrd UER	.01	.05
❑ 441 Arthur Cox	.01	.05
❑ 442 John Friesz	.08	.25
❑ 443 Leo Goeas	.01	.05
❑ 444 Burt Grossman	.01	.05
❑ 445 Courtney Hall UER	.01	.05
❑ 446 Ronnie Harmon	.01	.05
❑ 447 Nate Lewis RC	.01	.05
❑ 448 Anthony Miller	.02	.10
❑ 449 Leslie O'Neal	.02	.10
❑ 450 Gary Plummer	.01	.05
❑ 451 Junior Seau	.08	.25
❑ 452 Billy Ray Smith	.01	.05
❑ 453 Billy Joe Tolliver	.01	.05
❑ 454 Broderick Thompson	.01	.05
❑ 455 Lee Williams	.01	.05
❑ 456 Michael Carter	.01	.05
❑ 457 Mike Cofer	.01	.05
❑ 458 Kevin Fagan	.01	.05
❑ 459 Charles Haley	.02	.10
❑ 460 Pierce Holt	.01	.05
❑ 461 Johnnie Jackson UER RC	.01	.05
❑ 462 Brent Jones	.08	.25
❑ 463 Guy McIntyre	.01	.05
❑ 464 Joe Montana	.50	1.25
❑ 465A Bubba Paris ERR	.02	.10
❑ 465B Bubba Paris ERR/COR	.20	.50
❑ 465C Bubba Paris COR	.02	.10
❑ 466 Tom Rathman UER	.01	.05
❑ 467 Jerry Rice UER	.30	.75
❑ 468 Mike Sherrard	.01	.05
❑ 469 John Taylor UER	.02	.10
❑ 470 Steve Young	.30	.75
❑ 471 Dennis Brown	.01	.05
❑ 472 Dexter Carter	.01	.05
❑ 473 Bill Romanowski	.01	.05
❑ 474 Dave Waymer	.01	.05
❑ 475 Robert Blackmon	.01	.05
❑ 476 Derrick Fenner	.01	.05
❑ 477 Nesby Glasgow UER	.01	.05
❑ 478 Jacob Green	.01	.05
❑ 479 Andy Heck	.01	.05
❑ 480 Norm Johnson UER	.01	.05
❑ 481 Tommy Kane	.01	.05
❑ 482 Cortez Kennedy	.08	.25
❑ 483A Dave Krieg ERR	.07	.20
❑ 483B Dave Krieg COR	1.00	2.50

Card		
❑ 484 Bryan Millard	.01	.05
❑ 485 Joe Nash	.01	.05
❑ 486 Rufus Porter	.01	.05
❑ 487 Eugene Robinson	.01	.05
❑ 488 Mike Tice RC	.01	.05
❑ 489 Chris Warren	.08	.25
❑ 490 John L. Williams UER	.01	.05
❑ 491 Terry Wooden	.01	.05
❑ 492 Tony Woods	.01	.05
❑ 493 Brian Blades	.02	.10
❑ 494 Paul Skansi	.01	.05
❑ 495 Gary Anderson RB	.01	.05
❑ 496 Mark Carrier WR	.08	.25
❑ 497 Chris Chandler	.08	.25
❑ 498 Steve Christie	.01	.05
❑ 499 Reggie Cobb	.01	.05
❑ 500 Reuben Davis	.01	.05
❑ 501 Willie Drewrey UER	.01	.05
❑ 502 Randy Grimes	.01	.05
❑ 503 Paul Gruber	.01	.05
❑ 504 Wayne Haddix	.01	.05
❑ 505 Ron Hall	.01	.05
❑ 506 Harry Hamilton	.01	.05
❑ 507 Bruce Hill	.01	.05
❑ 508 Eugene Marve	.01	.05
❑ 509 Keith McCants	.01	.05
❑ 510 Winston Moss	.01	.05
❑ 511 Kevin Murphy	.01	.05
❑ 512 Mark Robinson	.01	.05
❑ 513 Vinny Testaverde	.02	.10
❑ 514 Broderick Thomas	.01	.05
❑ 515A Jeff Bostic UER	.02	.10
❑ 515B Jeff Bostic UER	.02	.10
❑ 516 Todd Bowles	.01	.05
❑ 517 Earnest Byner	.01	.05
❑ 518 Gary Clark	.08	.25
❑ 519 Craig Erickson RC	.08	.25
❑ 520 Darryl Grant	.01	.05
❑ 521 Darrell Green	.01	.05
❑ 522 Russ Grimm	.01	.05
❑ 523 Stan Humphries	.08	.25
❑ 524 Joe Jacoby UER	.01	.05
❑ 525 Jim Lachey	.01	.05
❑ 526 Chip Lohmiller	.01	.05
❑ 527 Charles Mann	.01	.05
❑ 528 Wilber Marshall	.01	.05
❑ 529A Art Monk	.02	.10
❑ 529B Art Monk	.02	.10
❑ 530 Tracy Rocker	.01	.05
❑ 531 Mark Rypien	.02	.10
❑ 532 Ricky Sanders UER	.01	.05
❑ 533 Alvin Walton UER	.01	.05
❑ 534 Todd Marinovich UER RC	.01	.05
❑ 535 Mike Dumas RC	.01	.05
❑ 536A Russell Maryland ERR RC	.08	.25
❑ 536B Russell Maryland COR RC	.08	.25
❑ 537 Eric Turner UER RC	.02	.10
❑ 538 Ernie Mills RC	.02	.10
❑ 539 Ed King RC	.01	.05
❑ 540 Mike Stonebreaker	.01	.05
❑ 541 Chris Zorich RC	.08	.25
❑ 542A Mike Croel ERR RC	.01	.05
❑ 542B Mike Croel COR RC	.01	.05
❑ 543 Eric Moten RC	.01	.05
❑ 544 Dan McGwire RC	.01	.05
❑ 545 Keith Cash RC	.01	.05
❑ 546 Kenny Walker UER RC	.01	.05
❑ 547 Leroy Hoard UER	.02	.10
❑ 548 Luis Cristobal UER	.01	.05
❑ 549 Stacy Danley	.01	.05
❑ 550 Todd Lyght RC	.01	.05
❑ 551 Brett Favre RC	3.00	8.00
❑ 552 Mike Pritchard RC	.08	.25
❑ 553 Moe Gardner	.01	.05
❑ 554 Tim McKyer	.01	.05
❑ 555 Erric Pegram RC	.08	.25
❑ 556 Norm Johnson	.01	.05
❑ 557 Bruce Pickens RC	.01	.05
❑ 558 Henry Jones RC	.02	.10
❑ 559 Phil Hansen RC	.01	.05
❑ 560 Cornelius Bennett	.02	.10
❑ 561 Stan Thomas	.01	.05
❑ 562 Chris Zorich	.02	.10
❑ 563 Anthony Morgan RC	.01	.05
❑ 564 Darren Lewis RC	.01	.05
❑ 565 Mike Stonebreaker	.01	.05
❑ 566 Alfred Williams RC	.01	.05
❑ 567 Lamar Rogers RC	.01	.05
❑ 568 Erik Wilhelm UER RC	.01	.05
❑ 569 Ed King	.01	.05
❑ 570 Michael Jackson WR RC	.08	.25
❑ 571 James Jones RC	.01	.05
❑ 572 Russell Maryland	.08	.25
❑ 573 Dixon Edwards RC	.01	.05
❑ 574 Darrick Brownlow RC	.01	.05
❑ 575 Larry Brown DB RC	.02	.10
❑ 576 Mike Croel	.01	.05
❑ 577 Keith Traylor RC	.01	.05
❑ 578 Kenny Walker	.01	.05
❑ 579 Reggie Johnson RC	.01	.05
❑ 580 Herman Moore RC	.08	.25
❑ 581 Kelvin Pritchett RC	.02	.10
❑ 582 Kevin Scott RC	.01	.05
❑ 583 Vinnie Clark RC	.01	.05
❑ 584 Esera Tuaolo RC	.01	.05
❑ 585 Don Davey	.01	.05
❑ 586 Blair Kiel RC	.01	.05
❑ 587 Mike Dumas	.01	.05
❑ 588 Darryll Lewis RC	.02	.10
❑ 589 John Flannery RC	.01	.05
❑ 590 Kevin Donnalley RC	.01	.05
❑ 591 Shane Curry	.01	.05
❑ 592 Mark Vander Poel RC	.01	.05
❑ 593 Dave McCloughan	.01	.05
❑ 594 Mel Agee RC	.01	.05
❑ 595 Kerry Cash RC	.01	.05
❑ 596 Harvey Williams RC	.08	.25
❑ 597 Joe Valerio	.01	.05
❑ 598 Tim Barnett UER RC	.01	.05
❑ 599 Todd Marinovich	.02	.10
❑ 600 Nick Bell RC	.01	.05
❑ 601 Roger Craig	.02	.10
❑ 602 Ronnie Lott	.02	.10
❑ 603 Mike Jones RC LB	.01	.05
❑ 604 Todd Lyght	.01	.05
❑ 605 Roman Phifer RC	.01	.05
❑ 606 David Lang RC	.01	.05
❑ 607 Aaron Craver RC	.01	.05
❑ 608 Mark Higgs RC	.01	.05
❑ 609 Chris Green	.01	.05
❑ 610 Randy Baldwin RC	.01	.05
❑ 611 Pat Harlow	.01	.05
❑ 612 Leonard Russell RC	.08	.25
❑ 613 Jerome Henderson RC	.01	.05
❑ 614 Scott Zolak RC	.01	.05
❑ 615 Jon Vaughn RC	.01	.05
❑ 616 Harry Colon RC	.01	.05
❑ 617 Wesley Carroll RC	.01	.05
❑ 618 Quinn Early	.02	.10
❑ 619 Reginald Jones RC	.01	.05
❑ 620 Jarrod Bunch	.01	.05
❑ 621 Kanavis McGhee RC	.01	.05
❑ 622 Ed McCaffrey RC	.75	2.00
❑ 623 Browning Nagle RC	.01	.05
❑ 624 Mo Lewis RC	.02	.10
❑ 625 Blair Thomas	.01	.05
❑ 626 Antone Davis RC	.01	.05
❑ 627 Jim McMahon	.02	.10
❑ 628 Scott Kowalkowski RC	.01	.05
❑ 629 Brad Goebel RC	.01	.05
❑ 630 William Thomas RC	.01	.05
❑ 631 Eric Swann RC	.08	.25
❑ 632 Mike Jones DE RC	.01	.05
❑ 633 Aeneas Williams RC	.08	.25
❑ 634 Dexter Davis RC	.01	.05
❑ 635 Tom Tupa UER	.01	.05
❑ 636 Johnny Johnson	.01	.05
❑ 637 Randal Hill RC	.02	.10
❑ 638 Jeff Graham RC	.08	.25
❑ 639 Ernie Mills	.01	.05
❑ 640 Adrian Cooper RC	.01	.05
❑ 641 Stanley Richard RC	.01	.05
❑ 642 Eric Bieniemy RC	.01	.05
❑ 643 Eric Moten	.01	.05
❑ 644 Shawn Jefferson RC	.02	.10
❑ 645 Ted Washington RC	.01	.05
❑ 646 John Johnson RC	.01	.05
❑ 647 Dan McGwire	.01	.05
❑ 648 Doug Thomas RC	.01	.05
❑ 649 David Daniels RC	.01	.05
❑ 650 John Kasay RC	.02	.10
❑ 651 Jeff Kemp	.01	.05
❑ 652 Charles McRae RC	.01	.05
❑ 653 Lawrence Dawsey RC	.02	.10
❑ 654 Robert Wilson RC	.01	.05
❑ 655 Dexter Manley	.01	.05
❑ 656 Chuck Weatherspoon	.01	.05
❑ 657 Tim Ryan G RC	.01	.05
❑ 658 Bobby Wilson	.01	.05
❑ 659 Ricky Ervins RC	.02	.10
❑ 660 Matt Millen	.02	.10

1992 Pacific

Card		
❑ COMPLETE SET (660)	6.00	15.00
❑ COMP.FACT.SET (690)	10.00	25.00
❑ COMP.SERIES 1 (330)	3.00	8.00
❑ COMP.SERIES 2 (330)	3.00	8.00
❑ COMP.CHECKLIST SET (5)	1.50	3.00
❑ 1 Steve Broussard	.01	.05
❑ 2 Darion Conner	.01	.05
❑ 3 Tory Epps	.01	.05
❑ 4 Michael Haynes	.02	.10
❑ 5 Chris Hinton	.01	.05
❑ 6 Mike Kenn	.01	.05
❑ 7 Tim McKyer	.01	.05
❑ 8 Chris Miller	.02	.10
❑ 9 Erric Pegram	.02	.10
❑ 10 Mike Pritchard	.02	.10
❑ 11 Moe Gardner	.01	.05
❑ 12 Tim Green	.01	.05
❑ 13 Norm Johnson	.01	.05
❑ 14 Don Beebe	.01	.05
❑ 15 Cornelius Bennett	.02	.10
❑ 16 Al Edwards	.01	.05
❑ 17 Mark Kelso	.01	.05
❑ 18 James Lofton	.02	.10
❑ 19 Frank Reich	.02	.10
❑ 20 Leon Seals	.01	.05
❑ 21 Darryl Talley	.01	.05
❑ 22 Thurman Thomas	.08	.25
❑ 23 Kent Hull	.01	.05
❑ 24 Jeff Wright	.01	.05
❑ 25 Nate Odomes	.01	.05
❑ 26 Carwell Gardner	.01	.05
❑ 27 Neal Anderson	.01	.05
❑ 28 Mark Carrier DB	.01	.05
❑ 29 Johnny Bailey	.01	.05
❑ 30 Jim Harbaugh	.08	.25
❑ 31 Jay Hilgenberg	.01	.05
❑ 32 William Perry	.02	.10
❑ 33 Wendell Davis	.01	.05
❑ 34 Donnell Woolford	.01	.05
❑ 35 Keith Van Horne	.01	.05
❑ 36 Shaun Gayle	.01	.05
❑ 37 Tom Waddle	.01	.05
❑ 38 Chris Zorich	.02	.10
❑ 39 Tom Thayer	.01	.05
❑ 40 Rickey Dixon	.01	.05
❑ 41 James Francis	.01	.05
❑ 42 David Fulcher	.01	.05
❑ 43 Reggie Rembert	.01	.05
❑ 44 Anthony Munoz	.02	.10
❑ 45 Harold Green	.01	.05
❑ 46 Mitchell Price	.01	.05
❑ 47 Rodney Holman	.01	.05
❑ 48 Bruce Kozerski	.01	.05
❑ 49 Bruce Reimers	.01	.05
❑ 50 Erik Wilhelm	.01	.05
❑ 51 Harlon Barnett	.01	.05
❑ 52 Mike Johnson	.01	.05
❑ 53 Brian Brennan	.01	.05
❑ 54 Ed King	.01	.05
❑ 55 Reggie Langhorne	.01	.05
❑ 56 James Jones DT	.01	.05
❑ 57 Mike Baab	.01	.05
❑ 58 Dan Fike	.01	.05
❑ 59 Frank Minnifield	.01	.05
❑ 60 Clay Matthews	.02	.10
❑ 61 Kevin Mack	.01	.05
❑ 62 Tony Casillas	.01	.05
❑ 63 Jay Novacek	.02	.10
❑ 64 Larry Brown DB	.01	.05
❑ 65 Michael Irvin	.08	.25
❑ 66 Jack Del Rio	.01	.05

Card		
❑ 67 Ken Willis	.01	.05
❑ 68 Emmitt Smith	.60	1.50
❑ 69 Alan Veingrad	.01	.05
❑ 70 John Gesek	.01	.05
❑ 71 Steve Beuerlein	.02	.10
❑ 72 Vinson Smith RC	.01	.05
❑ 73 Steve Atwater	.01	.05
❑ 74 Mike Croel	.01	.05
❑ 75 John Elway	.50	1.25
❑ 76 Gaston Green	.01	.05
❑ 77 Mike Horan	.01	.05
❑ 78 Vance Johnson	.01	.05
❑ 79 Karl Mecklenburg	.01	.05
❑ 80 Shannon Sharpe	.08	.25
❑ 81 David Treadwell	.01	.05
❑ 82 Kenny Walker	.01	.05
❑ 83 Greg Lewis	.01	.05
❑ 84 Shawn Moore	.01	.05
❑ 85 Alton Montgomery	.01	.05
❑ 86 Michael Young	.01	.05
❑ 87 Jerry Ball	.01	.05
❑ 88 Bennie Blades	.01	.05
❑ 89 Mel Gray	.02	.10
❑ 90 Herman Moore	.08	.25
❑ 91 Erik Kramer	.02	.10
❑ 92 Willie Green	.01	.05
❑ 93 George Jamison	.01	.05
❑ 94 Chris Spielman	.02	.10
❑ 95 Kelvin Pritchett	.01	.05
❑ 96 William White	.01	.05
❑ 97 Mike Utley	.02	.10
❑ 98 Tony Bennett	.01	.05
❑ 99 LeRoy Butler	.01	.05
❑ 100 Vinnie Clark	.01	.05
❑ 101 Ron Hallstrom	.01	.05
❑ 102 Chris Jacke	.01	.05
❑ 103 Tony Mandarich	.01	.05
❑ 104 Sterling Sharpe	.08	.25
❑ 105 Don Majkowski	.01	.05
❑ 106 Johnny Holland	.01	.05
❑ 107 Esera Tuaolo	.01	.05
❑ 108 Darrell Thompson	.01	.05
❑ 109 Bubba McDowell	.01	.05
❑ 110 Curtis Duncan	.01	.05
❑ 111 Lamar Lathon	.01	.05
❑ 112 Drew Hill	.01	.05
❑ 113 Bruce Matthews	.01	.05
❑ 114 Bo Orlando RC	.01	.05
❑ 115 Don Maggs	.01	.05
❑ 116 Lorenzo White	.01	.05
❑ 117 Ernest Givins	.02	.10
❑ 118 Tony Jones WR	.01	.05
❑ 119 Dean Steinkuhler	.01	.05
❑ 120 Dean Biasucci	.01	.05
❑ 121 Duane Bickett	.01	.05
❑ 122 Bill Brooks	.01	.05
❑ 123 Ken Clark	.01	.05
❑ 124 Jessie Hester	.01	.05
❑ 125 Anthony Johnson	.02	.10
❑ 126 Chip Banks	.01	.05
❑ 127 Mike Prior	.01	.05
❑ 128 Rohn Stark	.01	.05
❑ 129 Jeff Herrod	.01	.05
❑ 130 Clarence Verdin	.01	.05
❑ 131 Tim Manoa	.01	.05
❑ 132 Brian Baldinger RC	.01	.05
❑ 133 Tim Barnett	.01	.05
❑ 134 J.J. Birden	.01	.05
❑ 135 Deron Cherry	.01	.05
❑ 136 Steve DeBerg	.01	.05
❑ 137 Nick Lowery	.01	.05
❑ 138 Todd McNair	.01	.05
❑ 139 Christian Okoye	.01	.05
❑ 140 Mark Vlasic	.01	.05
❑ 141 Dan Saleaumua	.01	.05
❑ 142 Neil Smith	.08	.25
❑ 143 Robb Thomas	.01	.05
❑ 144 Eddie Anderson	.01	.05
❑ 145 Nick Bell	.01	.05
❑ 146 Tim Brown	.08	.25
❑ 147 Roger Craig	.02	.10
❑ 148 Jeff Gossett	.01	.05
❑ 149 Ethan Horton	.01	.05
❑ 150 Jamie Holland	.01	.05
❑ 151 Jeff Jaeger	.01	.05
❑ 152 Todd Marinovich	.01	.05
❑ 153 Marcus Allen	.08	.25
❑ 154 Steve Smith	.01	.05
❑ 155 Flipper Anderson	.01	.05
❑ 156 Robert Delpino	.01	.05
❑ 157 Cleveland Gary	.01	.05
❑ 158 Kevin Greene	.02	.10
❑ 159 Dale Hatcher	.01	.05
❑ 160 Duval Love	.01	.05
❑ 161 Ron Brown	.01	.05
❑ 162 Jackie Slater	.01	.05
❑ 163 Doug Smith	.01	.05
❑ 164 Aaron Cox	.01	.05
❑ 165 Larry Kelm	.01	.05
❑ 166 Mark Clayton	.02	.10
❑ 167 Louis Oliver	.01	.05
❑ 168 Mark Higgs	.01	.05
❑ 169 Aaron Craver	.01	.05
❑ 170 Sammie Smith	.01	.05
❑ 171 Tony Paige	.01	.05
❑ 172 Jeff Cross	.01	.05
❑ 173 David Griggs	.01	.05
❑ 174 Richmond Webb	.01	.05
❑ 175 Vestee Jackson	.01	.05
❑ 176 Jim C. Jensen	.01	.05
❑ 177 Anthony Carter	.02	.10
❑ 178 Cris Carter	.20	.50
❑ 179 Chris Doleman	.01	.05
❑ 180 Rich Gannon	.08	.25
❑ 181 Al Noga	.01	.05
❑ 182 Randall McDaniel	.02	.10
❑ 183 Todd Scott	.01	.05
❑ 184 Henry Thomas	.01	.05
❑ 185 Felix Wright	.01	.05
❑ 186 Gary Zimmerman	.01	.05
❑ 187 Herschel Walker	.02	.10
❑ 188 Vincent Brown	.01	.05
❑ 189 Harry Colon	.01	.05
❑ 190 Irving Fryar	.02	.10
❑ 191 Marv Cook	.01	.05
❑ 192 Leonard Russell	.02	.10
❑ 193 Hugh Millen	.01	.05
❑ 194 Pat Harlow	.01	.05
❑ 195 Jon Vaughn	.01	.05
❑ 196 Ben Coates RC	.30	.75
❑ 197 Johnny Rembert	.01	.05
❑ 198 Greg McMurtry	.01	.05
❑ 199 Morten Andersen	.01	.05
❑ 200 Tommy Barnhardt	.01	.05
❑ 201 Bobby Hebert	.01	.05
❑ 202 Dalton Hilliard	.01	.05
❑ 203 Sam Mills	.01	.05
❑ 204 Pat Swilling	.01	.05
❑ 205 Rickey Jackson	.01	.05
❑ 206 Stan Brock	.01	.05
❑ 207 Reginald Jones	.01	.05
❑ 208 Gill Fenerty	.01	.05
❑ 209 Eric Martin	.01	.05
❑ 210 Matt Bahr	.01	.05
❑ 211 Rodney Hampton	.02	.10
❑ 212 Jeff Hostetler	.02	.10
❑ 213 Pepper Johnson	.01	.05
❑ 214 Leonard Marshall	.01	.05
❑ 215 Doug Riesenberg	.01	.05
❑ 216 Stephen Baker	.01	.05
❑ 217 Mike Fox	.01	.05
❑ 218 Bart Oates	.01	.05
❑ 219 Everson Walls	.01	.05
❑ 220 Gary Reasons	.01	.05
❑ 221 Jeff Lageman	.01	.05
❑ 222 Joe Kelly	.01	.05
❑ 223 Mo Lewis	.01	.05
❑ 224 Tony Stargell	.01	.05
❑ 225 Jim Sweeney	.01	.05
❑ 226 Freeman McNeil	.02	.10
❑ 227 Brian Washington	.01	.05
❑ 228 Johnny Hector	.01	.05
❑ 229 Terance Mathis	.02	.10
❑ 230 Rob Moore	.02	.10
❑ 231 Brad Baxter	.01	.05
❑ 232 Eric Allen	.01	.05
❑ 233 Fred Barnett	.02	.10
❑ 234 Jerome Brown	.01	.05
❑ 235 Keith Byars	.01	.05
❑ 236 William Thomas	.01	.05
❑ 237 Jessie Small	.01	.05
❑ 238 Robert Drummond	.01	.05
❑ 239 Reggie White	.08	.25
❑ 240 James Joseph	.01	.05
❑ 241 Brad Goebel	.01	.05
❑ 242 Clyde Simmons	.01	.05
❑ 243 Rich Camarillo	.01	.05
❑ 244 Ken Harvey	.01	.05
❑ 245 Garth Jax	.01	.05
❑ 246 Johnny Johnson	.01	.05
❑ 247 Mike Jones	.01	.05
❑ 248 Ernie Jones	.01	.05
❑ 249 Tom Tupa	.01	.05
❑ 250 Ron Wolfley	.01	.05
❑ 251 Luis Sharpe	.01	.05
❑ 252 Eric Swann	.02	.10
❑ 253 Anthony Thompson	.01	.05
❑ 254 Gary Anderson K	.01	.05
❑ 255 Dermontti Dawson	.01	.05
❑ 256 Jeff Graham	.08	.25
❑ 257 Eric Green	.01	.05
❑ 258 Louis Lipps	.01	.05
❑ 259 Neil O'Donnell	.02	.10
❑ 260 Rod Woodson	.08	.25
❑ 261 Dwight Stone	.01	.05
❑ 262 Aaron Jones	.01	.05
❑ 263 Keith Willis	.01	.05
❑ 264 Ernie Mills	.01	.05
❑ 265 Martin Bayless	.01	.05
❑ 266 Rod Bernstine	.01	.05
❑ 267 John Carney	.01	.05
❑ 268 John Friesz	.02	.10
❑ 269 Nate Lewis	.01	.05
❑ 270 Shawn Jefferson	.01	.05
❑ 271 Burt Grossman	.01	.05
❑ 272 Eric Moten	.01	.05
❑ 273 Gary Plummer	.01	.05
❑ 274 Henry Rolling	.01	.05
❑ 275 Steve Hendrickson RC	.01	.05
❑ 276 Michael Carter	.01	.05
❑ 277 Steve Bono RC	.08	.25
❑ 278 Dexter Carter	.01	.05
❑ 279 Mike Cofer	.01	.05
❑ 280 Charles Haley	.02	.10
❑ 281 Tom Rathman	.01	.05
❑ 282 Guy McIntyre	.01	.05
❑ 283 John Taylor	.02	.10
❑ 284 Dave Waymer	.01	.05
❑ 285 Steve Wallace	.01	.05
❑ 286 Jamie Williams	.01	.05
❑ 287 Brian Blades	.02	.10
❑ 288 Jeff Bryant	.01	.05
❑ 289 Grant Feasel	.01	.05
❑ 290 Jacob Green	.01	.05
❑ 291 Andy Heck	.01	.05
❑ 292 Kelly Stouffer	.01	.05
❑ 293 John Kasay	.01	.05
❑ 294 Cortez Kennedy	.02	.10
❑ 295 Bryan Millard	.01	.05
❑ 296 Eugene Robinson	.01	.05
❑ 297 Tony Woods	.01	.05
❑ 298 Jesse Anderson UER	.01	.05
❑ 299 Gary Anderson RB	.01	.05
❑ 300 Mark Carrier WR	.02	.10
❑ 301 Reggie Cobb	.01	.05
❑ 302 Robert Wilson	.01	.05
❑ 303 Jesse Solomon	.01	.05
❑ 304 Broderick Thomas	.01	.05
❑ 305 Lawrence Dawsey	.02	.10
❑ 306 Charles McRae	.01	.05
❑ 307 Paul Gruber	.01	.05
❑ 308 Vinny Testaverde	.02	.10
❑ 309 Brian Mitchell	.02	.10
❑ 310 Darrell Green	.01	.05
❑ 311 Art Monk	.02	.10
❑ 312 Russ Grimm	.01	.05
❑ 313 Mark Rypien	.01	.05
❑ 314 Bobby Wilson	.01	.05
❑ 315 Wilber Marshall	.01	.05
❑ 316 Gerald Riggs	.01	.05
❑ 317 Chip Lohmiller	.01	.05
❑ 318 Joe Jacoby	.01	.05
❑ 319 Martin Mayhew	.01	.05
❑ 320 Amp Lee RC	.01	.05
❑ 321 Terrell Buckley RC	.01	.05
❑ 322 Tommy Vardell RC	.01	.05
❑ 323 Ricardo McDonald RC	.01	.05
❑ 324 Joe Bowden RC	.01	.05
❑ 325 Darryl Williams RC	.01	.05
❑ 326 Carlos Huerta	.01	.05
❑ 327 Patrick Rowe RC	.01	.05
❑ 328 Siran Stacy RC	.01	.05
❑ 329 Dexter McNabb RC	.01	.05
❑ 330 Willie Clay RC	.01	.05
❑ 331 Oliver Barnett	.01	.05
❑ 332 Aundray Bruce	.01	.05
❑ 333 Ken Tippins RC	.01	.05

Card		
❑ 334 Jessie Tuggle	.01	.05
❑ 335 Brian Jordan	.02	.10
❑ 336 Andre Rison	.02	.10
❑ 337 Houston Hoover	.01	.05
❑ 338 Bill Fralic	.01	.05
❑ 339 Pat Chaffey RC	.01	.05
❑ 340 Keith Jones	.01	.05
❑ 341 Jamie Dukes RC	.01	.05
❑ 342 Chris Mohr	.01	.05
❑ 343 John Davis	.01	.05
❑ 344 Ray Bentley	.01	.05
❑ 345 Scott Norwood	.01	.05
❑ 346 Shane Conlan	.01	.05
❑ 347 Steve Tasker	.02	.10
❑ 348 Will Wolford	.01	.05
❑ 349 Gary Baldinger RC	.01	.05
❑ 350 Kirby Jackson	.01	.05
❑ 351 Jamie Mueller	.01	.05
❑ 352 Pete Metzelaars	.01	.05
❑ 353 Richard Dent	.02	.10
❑ 354 Ron Rivera	.01	.05
❑ 355 Jim Morrissey	.01	.05
❑ 356 John Roper	.01	.05
❑ 357 Steve McMichael	.02	.10
❑ 358 Ron Morris	.01	.05
❑ 359 Darren Lewis	.01	.05
❑ 360 Anthony Morgan	.01	.05
❑ 361 Stan Thomas	.01	.05
❑ 362 James Thornton	.01	.05
❑ 363 Brad Muster	.01	.05
❑ 364 Tim Krumrie	.01	.05
❑ 365 Lee Johnson	.01	.05
❑ 366 Eric Ball	.01	.05
❑ 367 Alonzo Mitz RC	.01	.05
❑ 368 David Grant	.01	.05
❑ 369 Lynn James	.01	.05
❑ 370 Lewis Billups	.01	.05
❑ 371 Jim Breech	.01	.05
❑ 372 Alfred Williams	.01	.05
❑ 373 Wayne Haddix	.01	.05
❑ 374 Tim McGee	.01	.05
❑ 375 Michael Jackson	.02	.10
❑ 376 Leroy Hoard	.02	.10
❑ 377 Tony Jones T	.01	.05
❑ 378 Vince Newsome	.01	.05
❑ 379 Todd Philcox RC	.01	.05
❑ 380 Eric Metcalf	.02	.10
❑ 381 John Rienstra	.01	.05
❑ 382 Matt Stover	.01	.05
❑ 383 Brian Hansen	.01	.05
❑ 384 Joe Morris	.01	.05
❑ 385 Anthony Pleasant	.01	.05
❑ 386 Mark Stepnoski	.01	.05
❑ 387 Erik Williams	.01	.05
❑ 388 Jimmie Jones	.01	.05
❑ 389 Kevin Gogan	.01	.05
❑ 390 Manny Hendrix RC	.01	.05
❑ 391 Issiac Holt	.01	.05
❑ 392 Ken Norton	.02	.10
❑ 393 Tommie Agee	.01	.05
❑ 394 Alvin Harper	.02	.10
❑ 395 Alexander Wright	.01	.05
❑ 396 Mike Saxon	.01	.05
❑ 397 Michael Brooks	.01	.05
❑ 398 Bobby Humphrey	.01	.05
❑ 399 Ken Lanier	.01	.05
❑ 400 Steve Sewell	.01	.05
❑ 401 Robert Perryman	.01	.05
❑ 402 Wymon Henderson	.01	.05
❑ 403 Keith Kartz	.01	.05
❑ 404 Clarence Kay	.01	.05
❑ 405 Keith Traylor	.01	.05
❑ 406 Doug Widell	.01	.05
❑ 407 Dennis Smith	.01	.05
❑ 408 Marc Spindler	.01	.05
❑ 409 Lomas Brown	.01	.05
❑ 410 Robert Clark	.01	.05
❑ 411 Eric Andolsek	.01	.05
❑ 412 Mike Farr	.01	.05
❑ 413 Ray Crockett	.01	.05
❑ 414 Jeff Campbell	.01	.05
❑ 415 Dan Owens	.01	.05
❑ 416 Jim Arnold	.01	.05
❑ 417 Barry Sanders	.50	1.25
❑ 418 Eddie Murray	.01	.05
❑ 419 Vince Workman	.01	.05
❑ 420 Ed West	.01	.05
❑ 421 Charles Wilson	.01	.05
❑ 422 Perry Kemp	.01	.05
❑ 423 Chuck Cecil	.01	.05
❑ 424 James Campen	.01	.05
❑ 425 Robert Brown	.01	.05
❑ 426 Brian Noble	.01	.05
❑ 427 Rich Moran	.01	.05
❑ 428 Vai Sikahema	.01	.05
❑ 429 Allen Rice	.01	.05
❑ 430 Haywood Jeffires	.02	.10
❑ 431 Warren Moon	.08	.25
❑ 432 Greg Montgomery	.01	.05
❑ 433 Sean Jones	.01	.05
❑ 434 Richard Johnson CB	.01	.05
❑ 435 Al Smith	.01	.05
❑ 436 Johnny Meads	.01	.05
❑ 437 William Fuller	.01	.05
❑ 438 Mike Munchak	.02	.10
❑ 439 Ray Childress	.01	.05
❑ 440 Cody Carlson	.01	.05
❑ 441 Scott Radecic	.01	.05
❑ 442 Quintus McDonald RC	.01	.05
❑ 443 Eugene Daniel	.01	.05
❑ 444 Mark Herrmann RC	.01	.05
❑ 445 John Baylor RC	.01	.05
❑ 446 Dave McCloughan	.01	.05
❑ 447 Mark Vander Poel	.01	.05
❑ 448 Randy Dixon	.01	.05
❑ 449 Keith Taylor	.01	.05
❑ 450 Alan Grant	.01	.05
❑ 451 Tony Siragusa	.01	.05
❑ 452 Rich Baldinger	.01	.05
❑ 453 Derrick Thomas	.08	.25
❑ 454 Bill Jones RC	.01	.05
❑ 455 Troy Stradford	.01	.05
❑ 456 Barry Word	.01	.05
❑ 457 Tim Grunhard	.01	.05
❑ 458 Chris Martin	.01	.05
❑ 459 Jayice Pearson RC	.01	.05
❑ 460 Dino Hackett	.01	.05
❑ 461 David Lutz	.01	.05
❑ 462 Albert Lewis	.01	.05
❑ 463 Fred Jones RC	.01	.05
❑ 464 Winston Moss	.01	.05
❑ 465 Sam Graddy RC	.01	.05
❑ 466 Steve Wisniewski	.01	.05
❑ 467 Jay Schroeder	.01	.05
❑ 468 Ronnie Lott	.02	.10
❑ 469 Willie Gault	.02	.10
❑ 470 Greg Townsend	.01	.05
❑ 471 Max Montoya	.01	.05
❑ 472 Howie Long	.08	.25
❑ 473 Lionel Washington	.01	.05
❑ 474 Riki Ellison	.01	.05
❑ 475 Tom Newberry	.01	.05
❑ 476 Damone Johnson	.01	.05
❑ 477 Pat Terrell	.01	.05
❑ 478 Marcus Dupree	.01	.05
❑ 479 Todd Lyght	.01	.05
❑ 480 Buford McGee	.01	.05
❑ 481 Bern Brostek	.01	.05
❑ 482 Jim Price	.01	.05
❑ 483 Robert Young	.01	.05
❑ 484 Tony Zondojas	.01	.05
❑ 485 Robert Bailey RC	.01	.05
❑ 486 Alvin Wright	.01	.05
❑ 487 Pat Carter	.01	.05
❑ 488 Pete Stoyanovich	.01	.05
❑ 489 Reggie Roby	.01	.05
❑ 490 Harry Galbreath	.01	.05
❑ 491 Mike McGruder RC	.01	.05
❑ 492 J.B. Brown	.01	.05
❑ 493 E.J. Junior	.01	.05
❑ 494 Ferrell Edmunds	.01	.05
❑ 495 Scott Secules	.01	.05
❑ 496 Greg Baty RC	.01	.05
❑ 497 Mike Iaquaniello	.01	.05
❑ 498 Keith Sims	.01	.05
❑ 499 John Randle	.02	.10
❑ 500 Joey Browner	.01	.05
❑ 501 Steve Jordan	.01	.05
❑ 502 Darrin Nelson	.01	.05
❑ 503 Audray McMillian	.01	.05
❑ 504 Harry Newsome	.01	.05
❑ 505 Hassan Jones	.01	.05
❑ 506 Ray Berry	.01	.05
❑ 507 Mike Merriweather	.01	.05
❑ 508 Leo Lewis	.01	.05
❑ 509 Tim Irwin	.01	.05
❑ 510 Kirk Lowdermilk	.01	.05
❑ 511 Alfred Anderson	.01	.05
❑ 512 Michael Timpson RC	.01	.05
❑ 513 Jerome Henderson	.01	.05
❑ 514 Andre Tippett	.01	.05
❑ 515 Chris Singleton	.01	.05
❑ 516 John Stephens	.01	.05
❑ 517 Ronnie Lippett	.01	.05
❑ 518 Bruce Armstrong	.01	.05
❑ 519 Marion Hobby RC	.01	.05
❑ 520 Tim Goad	.01	.05
❑ 521 Mickey Washington RC	.01	.05
❑ 522 Fred Smerlas	.01	.05
❑ 523 Wayne Martin	.01	.05
❑ 524 Frank Warren	.01	.05
❑ 525 Floyd Turner	.01	.05
❑ 526 Wesley Carroll	.01	.05
❑ 527 Gene Atkins	.01	.05
❑ 528 Vaughan Johnson	.01	.05
❑ 529 Hoby Brenner	.01	.05
❑ 530 Renaldo Turnbull	.01	.05
❑ 531 Joel Hilgenberg	.01	.05
❑ 532 Craig Heyward	.02	.10
❑ 533 Vince Buck	.01	.05
❑ 534 Jim Dombrowski	.01	.05
❑ 535 Fred McAfee RC	.01	.05
❑ 536 Phil Simms	.02	.10
❑ 537 Lewis Tillman	.01	.05
❑ 538 John Elliott	.01	.05
❑ 539 Dave Meggett	.02	.10
❑ 540 Mark Collins	.01	.05
❑ 541 Ottis Anderson	.02	.10
❑ 542 Bobby Abrams RC	.01	.05
❑ 543 Sean Landeta	.01	.05
❑ 544 Brian Williams OL	.01	.05
❑ 545 Erik Howard	.01	.05
❑ 546 Mark Ingram	.01	.05
❑ 547 Kanavis McGhee	.01	.05
❑ 548 Kyle Clifton	.01	.05
❑ 549 Marvin Washington	.01	.05
❑ 550 Jeff Criswell	.01	.05
❑ 551 Dave Cadigan	.01	.05
❑ 552 Chris Burkett	.01	.05
❑ 553 Erik McMillan	.01	.05
❑ 554 James Hasty	.01	.05
❑ 555 Louie Aguiar RC	.01	.05
❑ 556 Troy Johnson RC	.01	.05
❑ 557 Troy Taylor RC	.01	.05
❑ 558 Pat Kelly RC	.01	.05
❑ 559 Heath Sherman	.01	.05
❑ 560 Roger Ruzek	.01	.05
❑ 561 Andre Waters	.01	.05
❑ 562 Izel Jenkins	.01	.05
❑ 563 Keith Jackson	.02	.10
❑ 564 Byron Evans	.01	.05
❑ 565 Wes Hopkins	.01	.05
❑ 566 Rich Miano	.01	.05
❑ 567 Seth Joyner	.01	.05
❑ 568 Thomas Sanders	.01	.05
❑ 569 David Alexander	.01	.05
❑ 570 Jeff Kemp	.01	.05
❑ 571 Jock Jones RC	.01	.05
❑ 572 Craig Patterson RC	.01	.05
❑ 573 Robert Massey	.01	.05
❑ 574 Bill Lewis	.01	.05
❑ 575 Freddie Joe Nunn	.01	.05
❑ 576 Aeneas Williams	.02	.10
❑ 577 John Jackson WR	.01	.05
❑ 578 Tim McDonald	.01	.05
❑ 579 Michael Zordich RC	.01	.05
❑ 580 Eric Hill	.01	.05
❑ 581 Lorenzo Lynch	.01	.05
❑ 582 Vernice Smith RC	.01	.05
❑ 583 Greg Lloyd	.02	.10
❑ 584 Carnell Lake	.01	.05
❑ 585 Hardy Nickerson	.02	.10
❑ 586 Delton Hall	.01	.05
❑ 587 Gerald Williams	.01	.05
❑ 588 Bryan Hinkle	.01	.05
❑ 589 Barry Foster	.02	.10
❑ 590 Bubby Brister	.02	.10
❑ 591 Rick Strom RC	.01	.05
❑ 592 David Little	.01	.05
❑ 593 Leroy Thompson RC	.01	.05
❑ 594 Eric Bieniemy	.01	.05
❑ 595 Courtney Hall	.01	.05
❑ 596 George Thornton	.01	.05
❑ 597 Donnie Elder	.01	.05
❑ 598 Billy Ray Smith	.01	.05
❑ 599 Gill Byrd	.01	.05
❑ 600 Marion Butts	.01	.05

❑ 601 Ronnie Harmon .01 .05
❑ 602 Anthony Shelton .01 .05
❑ 603 Mark May .01 .05
❑ 604 Craig McEwen RC .01 .05
❑ 605 Steve Young .25 .60
❑ 606 Keith Henderson .01 .05
❑ 607 Pierce Holt .01 .05
❑ 608 Roy Foster .01 .05
❑ 609 Don Griffin .01 .05
❑ 610 Harry Sydney .01 .05
❑ 611 Todd Bowles .01 .05
❑ 612 Ted Washington .01 .05
❑ 613 Johnnie Jackson .01 .05
❑ 614 Jesse Sapolu .01 .05
❑ 615 Brent Jones .02 .10
❑ 616 Travis McNeal .01 .05
❑ 617 Darrick Brilz RC .01 .05
❑ 618 Terry Wooden .01 .05
❑ 619 Tommy Kane .01 .05
❑ 620 Nesby Glasgow .01 .05
❑ 621 Dwayne Harper .01 .05
❑ 622 Rick Tuten .01 .05
❑ 623 Chris Warren .02 .10
❑ 624 John L. Williams .01 .05
❑ 625 Rufus Porter .01 .05
❑ 626 David Daniels .01 .05
❑ 627 Keith McCants .01 .05
❑ 628 Reuben Davis .01 .05
❑ 629 Mark Royals .01 .05
❑ 630 Marty Carter RC .01 .05
❑ 631 Ian Beckles .01 .05
❑ 632 Ron Hall .01 .05
❑ 633 Eugene Marve .01 .05
❑ 634 Willie Drewrey .01 .05
❑ 635 Tom McHale RC .01 .05
❑ 636 Kevin Murphy .01 .05
❑ 637 Robert Hardy RC .01 .05
❑ 638 Ricky Sanders .01 .05
❑ 639 Gary Clark .02 .10
❑ 640 Andre Collins .01 .05
❑ 641 Brad Edwards .01 .05
❑ 642 Monte Coleman .01 .05
❑ 643 Clarence Vaughn RC .01 .05
❑ 644 Fred Stokes .01 .05
❑ 645 Charles Mann .01 .05
❑ 646 Earnest Byner .01 .05
❑ 647 Jim Lachey .01 .05
❑ 648 Jeff Bostic .01 .05
❑ 649 Chris Mims RC .01 .05
❑ 650 George Williams RC .01 .05
❑ 651 Ed Cunningham RC .01 .05
❑ 652 Tony Smith WR RC .01 .05
❑ 653 Will Furrer RC .01 .05
❑ 654 Matt Elliott RC .01 .05
❑ 655 Mike Mooney RC .01 .05
❑ 656 Eddie Blake RC .01 .05
❑ 657 Leon Searcy RC .01 .05
❑ 658 Kevin Turner RC .01 .05
❑ 659 Keith Hamilton RC .02 .10
❑ 660 Alan Haller RC .01 .05

1993 Pacific

❑ COMPLETE SET (440) 10.00 20.00
❑ 1 Emmitt Smith .60 1.50
❑ 2 Troy Aikman .30 .75
❑ 3 Larry Brown DB .01 .05
❑ 4 Tony Casillas .01 .05
❑ 5 Thomas Everett .01 .05
❑ 6 Alvin Harper .02 .10
❑ 7 Michael Irvin .08 .25
❑ 8 Charles Haley .02 .10
❑ 9 Leon Lett RC .02 .10
❑ 10 Kevin Smith .02 .10
❑ 11 Robert Jones .01 .05
❑ 12 Jimmy Smith .08 .25
❑ 13 Derrick Gainer RC .01 .05
❑ 14 Lin Elliott .01 .05
❑ 15 William Thomas .01 .05
❑ 16 Clyde Simmons .01 .05
❑ 17 Seth Joyner .01 .05
❑ 18 Randall Cunningham .08 .25
❑ 19 Byron Evans .01 .05
❑ 20 Fred Barnett .02 .10
❑ 21 Calvin Williams .02 .10
❑ 22 James Joseph .01 .05
❑ 23 Heath Sherman .01 .05
❑ 24 Siran Stacy .01 .05
❑ 25 Andy Harmon .02 .10
❑ 26 Eric Allen .01 .05
❑ 27 Herschel Walker .02 .10
❑ 28 Vai Sikahema .01 .05
❑ 29 Earnest Byner .01 .05
❑ 30 Jeff Bostic .01 .05
❑ 31 Monte Coleman .01 .05
❑ 32 Ricky Ervins .01 .05
❑ 33 Darrell Green .01 .05
❑ 34 Mark Schlereth .01 .05
❑ 35 Mark Rypien .01 .05
❑ 36 Art Monk .02 .10
❑ 37 Brian Mitchell .02 .10
❑ 38 Chip Lohmiller .01 .05
❑ 39 Charles Mann .01 .05
❑ 40 Shane Collins .01 .05
❑ 41 Jim Lachey .01 .05
❑ 42 Desmond Howard .02 .10
❑ 43 Rodney Hampton .02 .10
❑ 44 Dave Brown RC .08 .25
❑ 45 Mark Collins .01 .05
❑ 46 Jarrod Bunch .01 .05
❑ 47 William Roberts .01 .05
❑ 48 Sean Landeta .01 .05
❑ 49 Lawrence Taylor .08 .25
❑ 50 Ed McCaffrey .08 .25
❑ 51 Bart Oates .01 .05
❑ 52 Pepper Johnson .01 .05
❑ 53 Eric Dorsey .01 .05
❑ 54 Erik Howard .01 .05
❑ 55 Phil Simms .02 .10
❑ 56 Derek Brown TE .01 .05
❑ 57 Johnny Bailey .01 .05
❑ 58 Rich Camarillo .01 .05
❑ 59 Larry Centers RC .08 .25
❑ 60 Chris Chandler .02 .10
❑ 61 Randal Hill .01 .05
❑ 62 Ricky Proehl .01 .05
❑ 63 Freddie Joe Nunn .01 .05
❑ 64 Robert Massey .01 .05
❑ 65 Aeneas Williams .01 .05
❑ 66 Luis Sharpe .01 .05
❑ 67 Eric Swann .02 .10
❑ 68 Timm Rosenbach .01 .05
❑ 69 Anthony Edwards RC .01 .05
❑ 70 Greg Davis .01 .05
❑ 71 Terry Allen .08 .25
❑ 72 Anthony Carter .02 .10
❑ 73 Cris Carter .08 .25
❑ 74 Roger Craig .02 .10
❑ 75 Jack Del Rio .01 .05
❑ 76 Chris Doleman .01 .05
❑ 77 Rich Gannon .08 .25
❑ 78 Hassan Jones .01 .05
❑ 79 Steve Jordan .01 .05
❑ 80 Randall McDaniel .02 .10
❑ 81 Sean Salisbury .01 .05
❑ 82 Harry Newsome .01 .05
❑ 83 Carlos Jenkins .01 .05
❑ 84 Jake Reed .08 .25
❑ 85 Edgar Bennett .08 .25
❑ 86 Tony Bennett .01 .05
❑ 87 Terrell Buckley .01 .05
❑ 88 Ty Detmer .08 .25
❑ 89 Brett Favre .75 2.00
❑ 90 Chris Jacke .01 .05
❑ 91 Sterling Sharpe .08 .25
❑ 92 James Campen .01 .05
❑ 93 Brian Noble .01 .05
❑ 94 Lester Archambeau RC .01 .05
❑ 95 Harry Sydney .01 .05
❑ 96 Corey Harris .01 .05
❑ 97 Don Majkowski .01 .05
❑ 98 Ken Ruettgers .01 .05
❑ 99 Lomas Brown .01 .05
❑ 100 Jason Hanson .01 .05
❑ 101 Robert Porcher .01 .05
❑ 102 Chris Spielman .02 .10
❑ 103 Erik Kramer .02 .10
❑ 104 Tracy Scroggins .01 .05
❑ 105 Rodney Peete .01 .05
❑ 106 Barry Sanders .50 1.25
❑ 107 Herman Moore .08 .25
❑ 108 Brett Perriman .08 .25
❑ 109 Mel Gray .02 .10
❑ 110 Dennis Gibson .01 .05
❑ 111 Bennie Blades .01 .05
❑ 112 Andre Ware .01 .05
❑ 113 Gary Anderson RB .01 .05
❑ 114 Tyji Armstrong .01 .05
❑ 115 Reggie Cobb .01 .05
❑ 116 Marty Carter .01 .05
❑ 117 Lawrence Dawsey .01 .05
❑ 118 Steve DeBerg .01 .05
❑ 119 Ron Hall .01 .05
❑ 120 Courtney Hawkins .01 .05
❑ 121 Broderick Thomas .01 .05
❑ 122 Keith McCants .01 .05
❑ 123 Bruce Reimers .01 .05
❑ 124 Darrick Brownlow .01 .05
❑ 125 Mark Wheeler .01 .05
❑ 126 Ricky Reynolds .01 .05
❑ 127 Neal Anderson .01 .05
❑ 128 Trace Armstrong .01 .05
❑ 129 Mark Carrier DB .01 .05
❑ 130 Richard Dent .02 .10
❑ 131 Wendell Davis .01 .05
❑ 132 Darren Lewis .01 .05
❑ 133 Tom Waddle .01 .05
❑ 134 Jim Harbaugh .08 .25
❑ 135 Steve McMichael .02 .10
❑ 136 William Perry .02 .10
❑ 137 Alonzo Spellman .01 .05
❑ 138 John Roper .01 .05
❑ 139 Peter Tom Willis .01 .05
❑ 140 Dante Jones .01 .05
❑ 141 Harris Barton .01 .05
❑ 142 Michael Carter .01 .05
❑ 143 Eric Davis .01 .05
❑ 144 Dana Hall .01 .05
❑ 145 Amp Lee .01 .05
❑ 146 Don Griffin .01 .05
❑ 147 Jerry Rice .40 1.00
❑ 148 Ricky Watters .08 .25
❑ 149 Steve Young .30 .75
❑ 150 Bill Romanowski .01 .05
❑ 151 Klaus Wilmsmeyer .01 .05
❑ 152 Steve Bono .02 .10
❑ 153 Tom Rathman .01 .05
❑ 154 Odessa Turner .01 .05
❑ 155 Morten Andersen .01 .05
❑ 156 Richard Cooper .01 .05
❑ 157 Toi Cook .01 .05
❑ 158 Quinn Early .02 .10
❑ 159 Vaughn Dunbar .01 .05
❑ 160 Rickey Jackson .01 .05
❑ 161 Wayne Martin .01 .05
❑ 162 Hoby Brenner .01 .05
❑ 163 Joel Hilgenberg .01 .05
❑ 164 Mike Buck .01 .05
❑ 165 Torrance Small .01 .05
❑ 166 Eric Martin .01 .05
❑ 167 Vaughan Johnson .01 .05
❑ 168 Sam Mills .01 .05
❑ 169 Steve Broussard .01 .05
❑ 170 Darion Conner .01 .05
❑ 171 Drew Hill .01 .05
❑ 172 Chris Hinton .01 .05
❑ 173 Chris Miller .02 .10
❑ 174 Tim McKyer .01 .05
❑ 175 Norm Johnson .01 .05
❑ 176 Mike Pritchard .02 .10
❑ 177 Andre Rison .02 .10
❑ 178 Deion Sanders .20 .50
❑ 179 Tony Smith RB .01 .05
❑ 180 Bruce Pickens .01 .05
❑ 181 Michael Haynes .02 .10
❑ 182 Jessie Tuggle .01 .05
❑ 183 Marc Boutte .01 .05
❑ 184 Don Bracken .01 .05
❑ 185 Bern Brostek .01 .05
❑ 186 Henry Ellard .02 .10
❑ 187 Jim Everett .02 .10
❑ 188 Sean Gilbert .02 .10
❑ 189 Cleveland Gary .01 .05
❑ 190 Todd Kinchen .01 .05
❑ 191 Pat Terrell .01 .05

❑ 192 Jackie Slater .01 .05
❑ 193 David Lang .01 .05
❑ 194 Flipper Anderson .01 .05
❑ 195 Tony Zendejas .01 .05
❑ 196 Roman Phifer .01 .05
❑ 197 Steve Christie .01 .05
❑ 198 Cornelius Bennett .02 .10
❑ 199 Phil Hansen .01 .05
❑ 200 Don Beebe .01 .05
❑ 201 Mark Kelso .01 .05
❑ 202 Bruce Smith .08 .25
❑ 203 Darryl Talley .01 .05
❑ 204 Andre Reed .02 .10
❑ 205 Mike Lodish .01 .05
❑ 206 Jim Kelly .08 .25
❑ 207 Thurman Thomas .08 .25
❑ 208 Kenneth Davis .01 .05
❑ 209 Frank Reich .02 .10
❑ 210 Kent Hull .01 .05
❑ 211 Marco Coleman .01 .05
❑ 212 Bryan Cox .01 .05
❑ 213 Jeff Cross .01 .05
❑ 214 Mark Higgs .01 .05
❑ 215 Keith Jackson .02 .10
❑ 216 Scott Miller .01 .05
❑ 217 John Offerdahl .01 .05
❑ 218 Dan Marino .60 1.50
❑ 219 Keith Sims .01 .05
❑ 220 Chuck Klingbeil .01 .05
❑ 221 Troy Vincent .01 .05
❑ 222 Mike Williams WR RC .01 .05
❑ 223 Pete Stoyanovich .01 .05
❑ 224 J.B. Brown .01 .05
❑ 225 Ashley Ambrose .01 .05
❑ 226 Jason Belser RC .01 .05
❑ 227 Jeff George .08 .25
❑ 228 Quentin Coryatt .02 .10
❑ 229 Duane Bickett .01 .05
❑ 230 Steve Emtman .01 .05
❑ 231 Anthony Johnson .02 .10
❑ 232 Rohn Stark .01 .05
❑ 233 Jessie Hester .01 .05
❑ 234 Reggie Langhorne .01 .05
❑ 235 Clarence Verdin .01 .05
❑ 236 Dean Biasucci .01 .05
❑ 237 Jack Trudeau .01 .05
❑ 238 Tony Siragusa .01 .05
❑ 239 Chris Burkett .01 .05
❑ 240 Brad Baxter .01 .05
❑ 241 Rob Moore .02 .10
❑ 242 Browning Nagle .01 .05
❑ 243 Jim Sweeney .01 .05
❑ 244 Kurt Barber .01 .05
❑ 245 Siupeli Malamala RC .01 .05
❑ 246 Mike Brim .01 .05
❑ 247 Mo Lewis .01 .05
❑ 248 Johnny Mitchell .01 .05
❑ 249 Ken Whisenhunt RC .10 .30
❑ 250 James Hasty .01 .05
❑ 251 Kyle Clifton .01 .05
❑ 252 Terance Mathis .02 .10
❑ 253 Ray Agnew .01 .05
❑ 254 Eugene Chung .01 .05
❑ 255 Marv Cook .01 .05
❑ 256 Johnny Rembert .01 .05
❑ 257 Maurice Hurst .01 .05
❑ 258 Jon Vaughn .01 .05
❑ 259 Leonard Russell .02 .10
❑ 260 Pat Harlow .01 .05
❑ 261 Andre Tippett .01 .05
❑ 262 Michael Timpson .01 .05
❑ 263 Greg McMurtry .01 .05
❑ 264 Chris Singleton .01 .05
❑ 265 Reggie Redding RC .01 .05
❑ 266 Walter Stanley .01 .05
❑ 267 Gary Anderson K .01 .05
❑ 268 Merril Hoge .01 .05
❑ 269 Barry Foster .02 .10
❑ 270 Charles Davenport .01 .05
❑ 271 Jeff Graham .02 .10
❑ 272 Adrian Cooper .01 .05
❑ 273 David Little .01 .05
❑ 274 Neil O'Donnell .08 .25
❑ 275 Rod Woodson .08 .25
❑ 276 Ernie Mills .01 .05
❑ 277 Dwight Stone .01 .05
❑ 278 Darren Perry .01 .05
❑ 279 Dermontti Dawson .01 .05
❑ 280 Carlton Haselrig .01 .05
❑ 281 Pat Coleman .01 .05
❑ 282 Ernest Givins .02 .10
❑ 283 Warren Moon .08 .25
❑ 284 Haywood Jeffires .02 .10
❑ 285 Cody Carlson .01 .05
❑ 286 Ray Childress .01 .05
❑ 287 Bruce Matthews .01 .05
❑ 288 Webster Slaughter .01 .05
❑ 289 Bo Orlando .01 .05
❑ 290 Lorenzo White .01 .05
❑ 291 Eddie Robinson .01 .05
❑ 292 Bubba McDowell .01 .05
❑ 293 Bucky Richardson .01 .05
❑ 294 Sean Jones .01 .05
❑ 295 David Brandon .01 .05
❑ 296 Shawn Collins .01 .05
❑ 297 Lawyer Tillman .01 .05
❑ 298 Bob Dahl .01 .05
❑ 299 Kevin Mack .01 .05
❑ 300 Bernie Kosar .02 .10
❑ 301 Tommy Vardell .01 .05
❑ 302 Jay Hilgenberg .01 .05
❑ 303 Michael Dean Perry .02 .10
❑ 304 Michael Jackson .02 .10
❑ 305 Eric Metcalf .02 .10
❑ 306 Rico Smith RC .01 .05
❑ 307 Stevon Moore RC .01 .05
❑ 308 Leroy Hoard .02 .10
❑ 309 Eric Ball .01 .05
❑ 310 Derrick Fenner .01 .05
❑ 311 James Francis .01 .05
❑ 312 Ricardo McDonald .01 .05
❑ 313 Tim Krumrie .01 .05
❑ 314 Carl Pickens .02 .10
❑ 315 David Klingler .01 .05
❑ 316 Donald Hollas RC .01 .05
❑ 317 Harold Green .01 .05
❑ 318 Daniel Stubbs .01 .05
❑ 319 Alfred Williams .01 .05
❑ 320 Darryl Williams .01 .05
❑ 321 Mike Arthur RC .01 .05
❑ 322 Leonard Wheeler .01 .05
❑ 323 Gill Byrd .01 .05
❑ 324 Eric Bieniemy .01 .05
❑ 325 Marion Butts .01 .05
❑ 326 John Carney .01 .05
❑ 327 Stan Humphries .02 .10
❑ 328 Ronnie Harmon .01 .05
❑ 329 Junior Seau .08 .25
❑ 330 Nate Lewis .01 .05
❑ 331 Harry Swayne .01 .05
❑ 332 Leslie O'Neal .02 .10
❑ 333 Eric Moten .01 .05
❑ 334 Blaise Winter RC .01 .05
❑ 335 Anthony Miller .02 .10
❑ 336 Gary Plummer .01 .05
❑ 337 Willie Davis .08 .25
❑ 338 J.J. Birden .01 .05
❑ 339 Tim Barnett .01 .05
❑ 340 Dave Krieg .02 .10
❑ 341 Barry Word .01 .05
❑ 342 Tracy Simien .01 .05
❑ 343 Christian Okoye .01 .05
❑ 344 Todd McNair .01 .05
❑ 345 Dan Saleaumua .01 .05
❑ 346 Derrick Thomas .08 .25
❑ 347 Harvey Williams .02 .10
❑ 348 Kimble Anders RC .08 .25
❑ 349 Tim Grunhard .01 .05
❑ 350 Tony Hargain UER RC .01 .05
❑ 351 Simon Fletcher .01 .05
❑ 352 John Elway .60 1.50
❑ 353 Mike Croel .01 .05
❑ 354 Steve Atwater .01 .05
❑ 355 Tommy Maddox .08 .25
❑ 356 Karl Mecklenburg .01 .05
❑ 357 Shane Dronett .01 .05
❑ 358 Kenny Walker .01 .05
❑ 359 Reggie Rivers RC .01 .05
❑ 360 Cedric Tillman RC .01 .05
❑ 361 Arthur Marshall RC .01 .05
❑ 362 Greg Lewis .01 .05
❑ 363 Shannon Sharpe .08 .25
❑ 364 Doug Widell .01 .05
❑ 365 Todd Marinovich .01 .05
❑ 366 Nick Bell .01 .05
❑ 367 Eric Dickerson .02 .10
❑ 368 Max Montoya .01 .05
❑ 369 Winston Moss .01 .05
❑ 370 Howie Long .08 .25
❑ 371 Willie Gault .01 .05
❑ 372 Tim Brown .08 .25
❑ 373 Steve Smith .01 .05
❑ 374 Steve Wisniewski .01 .05
❑ 375 Alexander Wright .01 .05
❑ 376 Ethan Horton .01 .05
❑ 377 Napoleon McCallum .01 .05
❑ 378 Terry McDaniel .01 .05
❑ 379 Patrick Hunter .01 .05
❑ 380 Robert Blackmon .01 .05
❑ 381 John Kasay .01 .05
❑ 382 Cortez Kennedy .02 .10
❑ 383 Andy Heck .01 .05
❑ 384 Bill Hitchcock RC .01 .05
❑ 385 Rick Mirer RC .08 .25
❑ 386 Jeff Bryant .01 .05
❑ 387 Eugene Robinson .01 .05
❑ 388 John L. Williams .01 .05
❑ 389 Chris Warren .02 .10
❑ 390 Rufus Porter .01 .05
❑ 391 Joe Tofflemire RC .01 .05
❑ 392 Dan McGwire .01 .05
❑ 393 Boomer Esiason .02 .10
❑ 394 Brad Muster .01 .05
❑ 395 James Lofton .02 .10
❑ 396 Tim McGee .01 .05
❑ 397 Steve Beuerlein .02 .10
❑ 398 Gaston Green .01 .05
❑ 399 Bill Brooks .01 .05
❑ 400 Ronnie Lott .02 .10
❑ 401 Jay Schroeder .01 .05
❑ 402 Marcus Allen .08 .25
❑ 403 Kevin Greene .02 .10
❑ 404 Kirk Lowdermilk .01 .05
❑ 405 Hugh Millen .01 .05
❑ 406 Pat Swilling .01 .05
❑ 407 Bobby Hebert .01 .05
❑ 408 Carl Banks .01 .05
❑ 409 Jeff Hostetler .02 .10
❑ 410 Leonard Marshall .01 .05
❑ 411 Ken O'Brien .01 .05
❑ 412 Joe Montana .60 1.50
❑ 413 Reggie White .08 .25
❑ 414 Gary Clark .02 .10
❑ 415 Johnny Johnson .01 .05
❑ 416 Tim McDonald .01 .05
❑ 417 Pierce Holt .01 .05
❑ 418 Gino Torretta RC .02 .10
❑ 419 Glyn Milburn RC .08 .25
❑ 420 O.J.McDuffie RC .08 .25
❑ 421 Coleman Rudolph RC .01 .05
❑ 422 Reggie Brooks RC .02 .10
❑ 423 Garrison Hearst RC .25 .60
❑ 424 Leonard Renfro RC .01 .05
❑ 425 Kevin Williams RC WR .08 .25
❑ 426 Demetrius DuBose RC .01 .05
❑ 427 Elvis Grbac RC .50 1.25
❑ 428 Lincoln Kennedy RC .01 .05
❑ 429 Carlton Gray RC .01 .05
❑ 430 Micheal Barrow RC .08 .25
❑ 431 George Teague RC .02 .10
❑ 432 Curtis Conway RC .15 .40
❑ 433 Natrone Means RC .08 .25
❑ 434 Jerome Bettis RC 2.00 5.00
❑ 435 Drew Bledsoe RC .75 2.00
❑ 436 Robert Smith RC .40 1.00
❑ 437 Deon Figures RC .01 .05
❑ 438 Qadry Ismail RC .08 .25
❑ 439 Chris Slade RC .02 .10
❑ 440 Dana Stubblefield RC .08 .25

1994 Pacific

❑ COMPLETE SET (450) 15.00 30.00
❑ 1 Troy Aikman .40 1.00
❑ 2 Charles Haley .02 .10

Card		
❑ 3 Alvin Harper	.02	.10
❑ 4 Michael Irvin	.08	.25
❑ 5 Jim Jeffcoat	.01	.05
❑ 6 Daryl Johnston	.02	.10
❑ 7 Robert Jones	.01	.05
❑ 8 Brock Marion RC	.08	.25
❑ 9 Russell Maryland	.01	.05
❑ 10 Ken Norton	.02	.10
❑ 11 Jay Novacek	.02	.10
❑ 12 Emmitt Smith	.60	1.50
❑ 13 Kevin Smith	.01	.05
❑ 14 Tony Tolbert	.01	.05
❑ 15 Kevin Williams WR	.02	.10
❑ 16 Don Beebe	.01	.05
❑ 17 Cornelius Bennett	.02	.10
❑ 18 Bill Brooks	.01	.05
❑ 19 Steve Christie	.01	.05
❑ 20 Russell Copeland	.01	.05
❑ 21 Kenneth Davis	.01	.05
❑ 22 Kent Hull	.01	.05
❑ 23 Jim Kelly	.08	.25
❑ 24 Pete Metzelaars	.01	.05
❑ 25 Andre Reed	.02	.10
❑ 26 Frank Reich	.02	.10
❑ 27 Bruce Smith	.08	.25
❑ 28 Darryl Talley	.01	.05
❑ 29 Steve Tasker	.02	.10
❑ 30 Thurman Thomas	.08	.25
❑ 31 Steve Bono	.02	.10
❑ 32 Dexter Carter	.01	.05
❑ 33 Kevin Fagan	.01	.05
❑ 34 Dana Hall	.01	.05
❑ 35 Brent Jones	.02	.10
❑ 36 Amp Lee	.01	.05
❑ 37 Marc Logan	.01	.05
❑ 38 Tim McDonald	.01	.05
❑ 39 Guy McIntyre	.01	.05
❑ 40 Tom Rathman	.01	.05
❑ 41 Jerry Rice	.40	1.00
❑ 42 Dana Stubblefield	.02	.10
❑ 43 Steve Wallace	.01	.05
❑ 44 Ricky Watters	.02	.10
❑ 45 Steve Young	.30	.75
❑ 46 Marcus Allen	.08	.25
❑ 47 Kimble Anders	.02	.10
❑ 48 Tim Barnett	.01	.05
❑ 49 J.J. Birden	.01	.05
❑ 50 Dale Carter	.01	.05
❑ 51 Jonathan Hayes	.01	.05
❑ 52 Dave Krieg	.02	.10
❑ 53 Albert Lewis	.01	.05
❑ 54 Nick Lowery	.01	.05
❑ 55 Joe Montana	.75	2.00
❑ 56 Neil Smith	.02	.10
❑ 57 John Stephens	.01	.05
❑ 58 Derrick Thomas	.08	.25
❑ 59 Harvey Williams	.02	.10
❑ 60 Micheal Barrow	.01	.05
❑ 61 Gary Brown	.01	.05
❑ 62 Cody Carlson	.01	.05
❑ 63 Ray Childress	.01	.05
❑ 64 Curtis Duncan	.01	.05
❑ 65 Ernest Givins	.02	.10
❑ 66 Haywood Jeffires	.02	.10
❑ 67 Wilber Marshall	.01	.05
❑ 68 Bubba McDowell	.01	.05
❑ 69 Warren Moon	.08	.25
❑ 70 Mike Munchak	.02	.10
❑ 71 Marcus Robertson	.01	.05
❑ 72 Webster Slaughter	.01	.05
❑ 73 Gary Wellman RC	.01	.05
❑ 74 Lorenzo White	.01	.05
❑ 75 Ray Crockett	.01	.05
❑ 76 Jason Hanson	.01	.05
❑ 77 Rodney Holman	.01	.05
❑ 78 George Jamison	.01	.05
❑ 79 Erik Kramer	.02	.10
❑ 80 Ryan McNeil	.01	.05
❑ 81 Derrick Moore	.01	.05
❑ 82 Herman Moore	.08	.25
❑ 83 Rodney Peete	.01	.05
❑ 84 Brett Perriman	.02	.10
❑ 85 Barry Sanders	.60	1.50
❑ 86 Chris Spielman	.02	.10
❑ 87 Pat Swilling	.01	.05
❑ 88 Vernon Turner	.01	.05
❑ 89 Andre Ware	.01	.05
❑ 90 Michael Brooks	.01	.05
❑ 91 Dave Brown	.02	.10
❑ 92 Derek Brown TE	.01	.05
❑ 93 Jarrod Bunch	.01	.05
❑ 94 Chris Calloway	.01	.05
❑ 95 Kent Graham	.02	.10
❑ 96 Rodney Hampton	.02	.10
❑ 97 Mark Jackson	.01	.05
❑ 98 Ed McCaffrey	.08	.25
❑ 99 Dave Meggett	.01	.05
❑ 100 Aaron Pierce	.01	.05
❑ 101 Mike Sherrard	.01	.05
❑ 102 Phil Simms	.02	.10
❑ 103 Lewis Tillman	.01	.05
❑ 104 Eddie Anderson	.01	.05
❑ 105 Patrick Bates	.01	.05
❑ 106 Nick Bell	.01	.05
❑ 107 Tim Brown	.08	.25
❑ 108 Willie Gault	.01	.05
❑ 109 Jeff Gossett	.01	.05
❑ 110 Ethan Horton	.01	.05
❑ 111 Jeff Hostetler	.02	.10
❑ 112 Rocket Ismail	.02	.10
❑ 113 Chester McGlockton	.01	.05
❑ 114 Anthony Smith	.01	.05
❑ 115 Steve Smith	.01	.05
❑ 116 Greg Townsend	.01	.05
❑ 117 Steve Wisniewski	.01	.05
❑ 118 Alexander Wright	.01	.05
❑ 119 Steve Atwater	.01	.05
❑ 120 Rod Bernstine	.01	.05
❑ 121 Mike Croel	.01	.05
❑ 122 Shane Dronett	.01	.05
❑ 123 Jason Elam	.02	.10
❑ 124 John Elway	.75	2.00
❑ 125 Brian Habib	.01	.05
❑ 126 Rondell Jones	.01	.05
❑ 127 Tommy Maddox	.08	.25
❑ 128 Karl Mecklenburg	.01	.05
❑ 129 Glyn Milburn	.02	.10
❑ 130 Derek Russell	.01	.05
❑ 131 Shannon Sharpe	.02	.10
❑ 132 Dennis Smith	.01	.05
❑ 133 Edgar Bennett	.08	.25
❑ 134 Tony Bennett	.01	.05
❑ 135 Robert Brooks	.08	.25
❑ 136 Terrell Buckley	.01	.05
❑ 137 LeRoy Butler	.01	.05
❑ 138 Mark Clayton	.01	.05
❑ 139 Ty Detmer	.02	.10
❑ 140 Brett Favre	.75	2.00
❑ 141 John Jurkovic RC	.02	.10
❑ 142 Bryce Paup	.02	.10
❑ 143 Sterling Sharpe	.02	.10
❑ 144 George Teague	.01	.05
❑ 145 Darrell Thompson	.01	.05
❑ 146 Ed West	.01	.05
❑ 147 Reggie White	.08	.25
❑ 148 Terry Allen	.02	.10
❑ 149 Anthony Carter	.02	.10
❑ 150 Cris Carter	.20	.50
❑ 151 Roger Craig	.02	.10
❑ 152 Jack Del Rio	.01	.05
❑ 153 Chris Doleman	.01	.05
❑ 154 Scottie Graham RC	.02	.10
❑ 155 Eric Guliford RC	.01	.05
❑ 156 Qadry Ismail	.08	.25
❑ 157 Steve Jordan	.01	.05
❑ 158 Randall McDaniel	.02	.10
❑ 159 Jim McMahon	.02	.10
❑ 160 Audray McMillian	.01	.05
❑ 161 Sean Salisbury	.01	.05
❑ 162 Robert Smith	.08	.25
❑ 163 Henry Thomas	.01	.05
❑ 164 Gary Anderson K	.01	.05
❑ 165 Deon Figures	.01	.05
❑ 166 Barry Foster	.01	.05
❑ 167 Jeff Graham	.01	.05
❑ 168 Kevin Greene	.02	.10
❑ 169 Dave Hoffman	.01	.05
❑ 170 Merril Hoge	.01	.05
❑ 171 Gary Jones	.01	.05
❑ 172 Greg Lloyd	.02	.10
❑ 173 Ernie Mills	.01	.05
❑ 174 Neil O'Donnell	.08	.25
❑ 175 Darren Perry	.01	.05
❑ 176 Leon Searcy	.01	.05
❑ 177 Leroy Thompson	.01	.05
❑ 178 Willie Williams RC	.01	.05
❑ 179 Rod Woodson	.02	.10
❑ 180 Keith Byars	.01	.05
❑ 181 Marco Coleman	.01	.05
❑ 182 Bryan Cox	.01	.05
❑ 183 Irving Fryar	.02	.10
❑ 184 John Grimsley	.01	.05
❑ 185 Mark Higgs	.01	.05
❑ 186 Mark Ingram	.01	.05
❑ 187 Keith Jackson	.01	.05
❑ 188 Terry Kirby	.08	.25
❑ 189 Dan Marino	.75	2.00
❑ 190 O.J.McDuffie	.08	.25
❑ 191 Scott Mitchell	.02	.10
❑ 192 Pete Stoyanovich	.01	.05
❑ 193 Troy Vincent	.01	.05
❑ 194 Richmond Webb	.01	.05
❑ 195 Brad Baxter	.01	.05
❑ 196 Chris Burkett	.01	.05
❑ 197 Rob Carpenter WR	.01	.05
❑ 198 Boomer Esiason	.02	.10
❑ 199 Johnny Johnson	.01	.05
❑ 200 Jeff Lageman	.01	.05
❑ 201 Mo Lewis	.01	.05
❑ 202 Ronnie Lott	.02	.10
❑ 203 Leonard Marshall	.01	.05
❑ 204 Terance Mathis	.02	.10
❑ 205 Johnny Mitchell	.01	.05
❑ 206 Rob Moore	.02	.10
❑ 207 Anthony Prior	.01	.05
❑ 208 Blair Thomas	.01	.05
❑ 209 Brian Washington	.01	.05
❑ 210 Eric Bieniemy	.01	.05
❑ 211 Marion Butts	.01	.05
❑ 212 Gill Byrd	.01	.05
❑ 213 John Carney	.01	.05
❑ 214 Darren Carrington	.01	.05
❑ 215 John Friesz	.02	.10
❑ 216 Ronnie Harmon	.01	.05
❑ 217 Stan Humphries	.02	.10
❑ 218 Nate Lewis	.01	.05
❑ 219 Natrone Means	.08	.25
❑ 220 Anthony Miller	.02	.10
❑ 221 Chris Mims	.01	.05
❑ 222 Eric Moten	.01	.05
❑ 223 Leslie O'Neal	.01	.05
❑ 224 Junior Seau	.08	.25
❑ 225 Morten Andersen	.01	.05
❑ 226 Gene Atkins	.01	.05
❑ 227 Derek Brown RBK	.01	.05
❑ 228 Toi Cook	.01	.05
❑ 229 Vaughn Dunbar	.01	.05
❑ 230 Quinn Early	.02	.10
❑ 231 Reggie Freeman	.01	.05
❑ 232 Tyrone Hughes	.02	.10
❑ 233 Rickey Jackson	.01	.05
❑ 234 Eric Martin	.01	.05
❑ 235 Sam Mills	.01	.05
❑ 236 Brad Muster	.01	.05
❑ 237 Torrance Small	.01	.05
❑ 238 Irv Smith	.01	.05
❑ 239 Wade Wilson	.01	.05
❑ 240 Eric Allen	.01	.05
❑ 241 Victor Bailey	.01	.05
❑ 242 Fred Barnett	.02	.10
❑ 243 Mark Bavaro	.01	.05
❑ 244 Bubby Brister	.02	.10
❑ 245 Randall Cunningham	.08	.25
❑ 246 Antone Davis	.01	.05
❑ 247 Britt Hager RC	.01	.05
❑ 248 Vaughn Hebron	.01	.05
❑ 249 James Joseph	.01	.05
❑ 250 Seth Joyner	.01	.05
❑ 251 Rich Miano	.01	.05
❑ 252 Heath Sherman	.01	.05
❑ 253 Clyde Simmons	.01	.05
❑ 254 Herschel Walker	.02	.10
❑ 255 Calvin Williams	.02	.10
❑ 256 Jerry Ball	.01	.05
❑ 257 Mark Carrier WR	.02	.10
❑ 258 Michael Jackson	.02	.10
❑ 259 Mike Johnson	.01	.05
❑ 260 James Jones DT	.01	.05
❑ 261 Brian Kinchen	.01	.05
❑ 262 Clay Matthews	.01	.05
❑ 263 Eric Metcalf	.02	.10
❑ 264 Stevon Moore	.01	.05
❑ 265 Michael Dean Perry	.02	.10
❑ 266 Todd Philcox	.01	.05
❑ 267 Anthony Pleasant	.01	.05
❑ 268 Vinny Testaverde	.02	.10
❑ 269 Eric Turner	.01	.05

Card	Low	High
❑ 270 Tommy Vardell	.01	.05
❑ 271 Neal Anderson	.01	.05
❑ 272 Trace Armstrong	.01	.05
❑ 273 Mark Carrier DB	.01	.05
❑ 274 Bob Christian	.01	.05
❑ 275 Curtis Conway	.08	.25
❑ 276 Richard Dent	.02	.10
❑ 277 Robert Green	.01	.05
❑ 278 Jim Harbaugh	.08	.25
❑ 279 Craig Heyward	.02	.10
❑ 280 Terry Obee	.01	.05
❑ 281 Alonzo Spellman	.01	.05
❑ 282 Tom Waddle	.01	.05
❑ 283 Peter Tom Willis	.01	.05
❑ 284 Donnell Woolford	.01	.05
❑ 285 Tim Worley	.01	.05
❑ 286 Chris Zorich	.01	.05
❑ 287 Steve Broussard	.01	.05
❑ 288 Darion Conner	.01	.05
❑ 289 Jumpy Geathers	.01	.05
❑ 290 Michael Haynes	.02	.10
❑ 291 Bobby Hebert	.01	.05
❑ 292 Lincoln Kennedy	.01	.05
❑ 293 Chris Miller	.01	.05
❑ 294 David Mims RC	.01	.05
❑ 295 Erric Pegram	.01	.05
❑ 296 Mike Pritchard	.01	.05
❑ 297 Andre Rison	.02	.10
❑ 298 Deion Sanders	.20	.50
❑ 299 Chuck Smith	.01	.05
❑ 300 Tony Smith RB	.01	.05
❑ 301 Johnny Bailey	.01	.05
❑ 302 Steve Beuerlein	.02	.10
❑ 303 Chuck Cecil	.01	.05
❑ 304 Chris Chandler	.02	.10
❑ 305 Gary Clark	.02	.10
❑ 306 Rick Cunningham RC	.01	.05
❑ 307 Ken Harvey	.01	.05
❑ 308 Garrison Hearst	.08	.25
❑ 309 Randal Hill	.01	.05
❑ 310 Robert Massey	.01	.05
❑ 311 Ronald Moore	.01	.05
❑ 312 Ricky Proehl	.01	.05
❑ 313 Eric Swann	.02	.10
❑ 314 Aeneas Williams	.01	.05
❑ 315 Michael Bates	.01	.05
❑ 316 Brian Blades	.02	.10
❑ 317 Carlton Gray	.01	.05
❑ 318 Paul Green RC	.01	.05
❑ 319 Patrick Hunter	.01	.05
❑ 320 John Kasay	.01	.05
❑ 321 Cortez Kennedy	.02	.10
❑ 322 Kelvin Martin	.01	.05
❑ 323 Dan McGwire	.01	.05
❑ 324 Rick Mirer	.08	.25
❑ 325 Eugene Robinson	.01	.05
❑ 326 Rick Tuten	.01	.05
❑ 327 Chris Warren	.02	.10
❑ 328 John L. Williams	.01	.05
❑ 329 Reggie Cobb	.01	.05
❑ 330 Horace Copeland	.01	.05
❑ 331 Lawrence Dawsey	.01	.05
❑ 332 Santana Dotson	.02	.10
❑ 333 Craig Erickson	.01	.05
❑ 334 Hon Hall	.01	.05
❑ 335 Courtney Hawkins	.01	.05
❑ 336 Keith McCants	.01	.05
❑ 337 Hardy Nickerson	.02	.10
❑ 338 Mazio Royster RC	.01	.05
❑ 339 Broderick Thomas	.01	.05
❑ 340 Casey Weldon RC	.08	.25
❑ 341 Mark Wheeler	.01	.05
❑ 342 Vince Workman	.01	.05
❑ 343 Flipper Anderson	.01	.05
❑ 344 Jerome Bettis	.20	.50
❑ 345 Richard Buchanan	.01	.05
❑ 346 Shane Conlan	.01	.05
❑ 347 Troy Drayton	.01	.05
❑ 348 Henry Ellard	.02	.10
❑ 349 Jim Everett	.02	.10
❑ 350 Cleveland Gary	.01	.05
❑ 351 Sean Gilbert	.01	.05
❑ 352 David Lang	.01	.05
❑ 353 Todd Lyght	.01	.05
❑ 354 T.J. Rubley	.01	.05
❑ 355 Jackie Slater	.01	.05
❑ 356 Russell White	.02	.10
❑ 357 Bruce Armstrong	.01	.05
❑ 358 Drew Bledsoe	.30	.75
❑ 359 Vincent Brisby	.02	.10
❑ 360 Vincent Brown	.01	.05
❑ 361 Ben Coates	.02	.10
❑ 362 Marv Cook	.01	.05
❑ 363 Ray Crittenden RC	.01	.05
❑ 364 Corey Croom RC	.01	.05
❑ 365 Pat Harlow	.01	.05
❑ 366 Dion Lambert	.01	.05
❑ 367 Greg McMurtry	.01	.05
❑ 368 Leonard Russell	.01	.05
❑ 369 Scott Secules	.01	.05
❑ 370 Chris Slade	.01	.05
❑ 371 Michael Timpson	.01	.05
❑ 372 Kevin Turner	.01	.05
❑ 373 Ashley Ambrose	.01	.05
❑ 374 Dean Biasucci	.01	.05
❑ 375 Duane Bickett	.01	.05
❑ 376 Quentin Coryatt	.01	.05
❑ 377 Rodney Culver	.01	.05
❑ 378 Sean Dawkins RC	.08	.25
❑ 379 Jeff George	.08	.25
❑ 380 Jeff Herrod	.01	.05
❑ 381 Jessie Hester	.01	.05
❑ 382 Anthony Johnson	.02	.10
❑ 383 Reggie Langhorne	.01	.05
❑ 384 Roosevelt Potts	.01	.05
❑ 385 William Schultz RC	.01	.05
❑ 386 Rohn Stark	.01	.05
❑ 387 Clarence Verdin	.01	.05
❑ 388 Carl Banks	.01	.05
❑ 389 Reggie Brooks	.02	.10
❑ 390 Earnest Byner	.01	.05
❑ 391 Tom Carter	.01	.05
❑ 392 Cary Conklin	.01	.05
❑ 393 Pat Eilers RC	.01	.05
❑ 394 Ricky Ervins	.01	.05
❑ 395 Rich Gannon	.08	.25
❑ 396 Darrell Green	.01	.05
❑ 397 Desmond Howard	.02	.10
❑ 398 Chip Lohmiller	.01	.05
❑ 399 Sterling Palmer RC	.01	.05
❑ 400 Mark Rypien	.01	.05
❑ 401 Ricky Sanders	.01	.05
❑ 402 Johnny Thomas CB	.01	.05
❑ 403 John Copeland	.01	.05
❑ 404 Derrick Fenner	.01	.05
❑ 405 Alex Gordon	.01	.05
❑ 406 Harold Green	.01	.05
❑ 407 Lance Gunn	.01	.05
❑ 408 David Klingler	.01	.05
❑ 409 Ricardo McDonald	.01	.05
❑ 410 Tim McGee	.01	.05
❑ 411 Reggie Rembert	.01	.05
❑ 412 Patrick Robinson	.01	.05
❑ 413 Jay Schroeder	.01	.05
❑ 414 Erik Wilhelm	.01	.05
❑ 415 Alfred Williams	.01	.05
❑ 416 Darryl Williams	.01	.05
❑ 417 Sam Adams RC	.02	.10
❑ 418 Mario Bates RC	.08	.25
❑ 419 James Bostic RC	.08	.25
❑ 420 Bucky Brooks RC	.01	.05
❑ 421 Jeff Burris RC	.02	.10
❑ 422 Shante Carver RC	.01	.05
❑ 423 Jeff Cothran RC	.01	.05
❑ 424 Lake Dawson RC	.02	.10
❑ 425 Trent Dilfer RC	.50	1.25
❑ 426 Marshall Faulk RC	2.00	5.00
❑ 427 Cory Fleming RC	.01	.05
❑ 428 William Floyd RC	.08	.25
❑ 429 Glenn Foley RC	.08	.25
❑ 430 Rob Fredrickson RC	.02	.10
❑ 431 Charlie Garner RC	.50	1.25
❑ 432 Greg Hill RC	.08	.25
❑ 433 Charles Johnson RC	.08	.25
❑ 434 Calvin Jones RC	.01	.05
❑ 435 Jimmy Klingler RC	.01	.05
❑ 436 Antonio Langham RC	.02	.10
❑ 437 Kevin Lee RC	.01	.05
❑ 438 Chuck Levy RC	.01	.05
❑ 439 Willie McGinest RC	.08	.25
❑ 440 Jamir Miller RC	.02	.10
❑ 441 Johnnie Morton RC	.20	.50
❑ 442 David Palmer RC	.08	.25
❑ 443 Errict Rhett RC	.08	.25
❑ 444 Corey Sawyer RC	.02	.10
❑ 445 Darnay Scott RC	.20	.50
❑ 446 Heath Shuler RC	.08	.25
❑ 447 Lamar Smith RC	.50	1.25
❑ 448 Dan Wilkinson RC	.02	.10
❑ 449 Bernard Williams RC	.01	.05
❑ 450 Bryant Young RC	.15	.40
❑ P1 Sterling Sharpe Promo	.30	.75

1995 Pacific

Card	Low	High
❑ COMPLETE SET (450)	10.00	25.00
❑ 1 Randy Baldwin	.02	.10
❑ 2 Tommy Barnhardt	.02	.10
❑ 3 Tim McKyer	.02	.10
❑ 4 Sam Mills	.07	.20
❑ 5 Brian O'Neal	.02	.10
❑ 6 Frank Reich	.02	.10
❑ 7 Jack Trudeau	.02	.10
❑ 8 Vernon Turner	.02	.10
❑ 9 Kerry Collins RC	.75	2.00
❑ 10 Shawn King	.02	.10
❑ 11 Steve Beuerlein	.07	.20
❑ 12 Derek Brown TE	.02	.10
❑ 13 Reggie Clark	.02	.10
❑ 14 Reggie Cobb	.02	.10
❑ 15 Desmond Howard	.07	.20
❑ 16 Jeff Lageman	.02	.10
❑ 17 Kelvin Pritchett	.02	.10
❑ 18 Cedric Tillman	.02	.10
❑ 19 Tony Boselli RC	.10	.30
❑ 20 James O. Stewart RC	.50	1.25
❑ 21 Eric Davis	.02	.10
❑ 22 William Floyd	.07	.20
❑ 23 Elvis Grbac	.10	.30
❑ 24 Brent Jones	.02	.10
❑ 25 Ken Norton, Jr.	.07	.20
❑ 26 Bart Oates	.02	.10
❑ 27 Jerry Rice	.40	1.00
❑ 28 Deion Sanders	.15	.40
❑ 29 John Taylor	.02	.10
❑ 30 Adam Walker RC	.02	.10
❑ 31 Steve Wallace	.02	.10
❑ 32 Ricky Watters	.07	.20
❑ 33 Lee Woodall	.02	.10
❑ 34 Bryant Young	.07	.20
❑ 35 Steve Young	.30	.75
❑ 36 J.J. Stokes RC	.10	.30
❑ 37 Troy Aikman	.40	1.00
❑ 38 Larry Allen	.07	.20
❑ 39 Chris Boniol RC	.02	.10
❑ 40 Lincoln Coleman	.02	.10
❑ 41 Charles Haley	.07	.20
❑ 42 Alvin Harper	.02	.10
❑ 43 Chad Hennings	.07	.20
❑ 44 Michael Irvin	.10	.30
❑ 45 Daryl Johnston	.07	.20
❑ 46 Leon Lett	.02	.10
❑ 47 Nate Newton	.07	.20
❑ 48 Jay Novacek	.07	.20
❑ 49 Emmitt Smith	.60	1.50
❑ 50 James Washington	.02	.10
❑ 51 Kevin Williams	.07	.20
❑ 52 Sherman Williams RC	.02	.10
❑ 53 Barry Foster	.07	.20
❑ 54 Eric Green	.02	.10
❑ 55 Kevin Greene	.07	.20
❑ 56 Andre Hastings	.07	.20
❑ 57 Charles Johnson	.07	.20
❑ 58 Greg Lloyd	.07	.20
❑ 59 Ernie Mills	.02	.10
❑ 60 Byron Bam Morris	.02	.10
❑ 61 Neil O'Donnell	.07	.20
❑ 62 Darren Perry	.02	.10
❑ 63 Yancey Thigpen RC	.07	.20
❑ 64 Mike Tomczak	.02	.10
❑ 65 John L. Williams	.02	.10
❑ 66 Rod Woodson	.07	.20
❑ 67 Mark Bruener RC	.07	.20
❑ 68 Kordell Stewart RC	.60	1.50
❑ 69 Jeff Brohm RC	.02	.10

Card		
❑ 70 Andre Coleman	.02	.10
❑ 71 Reuben Davis	.02	.10
❑ 72 Dennis Gibson	.02	.10
❑ 73 Darrien Gordon	.02	.10
❑ 74 Stan Humphries	.07	.20
❑ 75 Shawn Jefferson	.02	.10
❑ 76 Tony Martin	.07	.20
❑ 77 Natrone Means	.07	.20
❑ 78 Shannon Mitchell RC	.02	.10
❑ 79 Leslie O'Neal	.07	.20
❑ 80 Alfred Pupunu	.02	.10
❑ 81 Stanley Richard	.02	.10
❑ 82 Junior Seau	.10	.30
❑ 83 Mark Seay	.07	.20
❑ 84 Derrick Alexander WR	.10	.30
❑ 85 Carl Banks	.02	.10
❑ 86 Isaac Booth	.02	.10
❑ 87 Rob Burnett	.02	.10
❑ 88 Earnest Byner	.02	.10
❑ 89 Steve Everitt	.02	.10
❑ 90 Leroy Hoard	.02	.10
❑ 91 Pepper Johnson	.02	.10
❑ 92 Antonio Langham	.02	.10
❑ 93 Eric Metcalf	.07	.20
❑ 94 Anthony Pleasant	.02	.10
❑ 95 Frank Stams	.02	.10
❑ 96 Vinny Testaverde	.07	.20
❑ 97 Eric Turner	.02	.10
❑ 98 Mike Miller RC	.02	.10
❑ 99 Craig Powell RC	.02	.10
❑ 100 Gene Atkins	.02	.10
❑ 101 Aubrey Beavers	.02	.10
❑ 102 Tim Bowens	.02	.10
❑ 103 Keith Byars	.02	.10
❑ 104 Bryan Cox	.02	.10
❑ 105 Aaron Craver	.02	.10
❑ 106 Jeff Cross	.02	.10
❑ 107 Irving Fryar	.07	.20
❑ 108 Dan Marino	.75	2.00
❑ 109 O.J. McDuffie	.10	.30
❑ 110 Bernie Parmalee	.07	.20
❑ 111 James Saxon	.02	.10
❑ 112 Keith Sims	.02	.10
❑ 113 Irving Spikes	.07	.20
❑ 114 Pete Mitchell RC	.07	.20
❑ 115 Terry Allen	.07	.20
❑ 116 Cris Carter	.10	.30
❑ 117 Adrian Cooper	.02	.10
❑ 118 Bernard Dafney	.02	.10
❑ 119 Jack Del Rio	.02	.10
❑ 120 Vencie Glenn	.02	.10
❑ 121 Qadry Ismail	.07	.20
❑ 122 Carlos Jenkins	.02	.10
❑ 123 Andrew Jordan	.02	.10
❑ 124 Ed McDaniel	.02	.10
❑ 125 Warren Moon	.07	.20
❑ 126 David Palmer	.07	.20
❑ 127 John Randle	.07	.20
❑ 128 Jake Reed	.07	.20
❑ 129 Derrick Alexander DE RC	.02	.10
❑ 130 Chad May RC	.02	.10
❑ 131 Korey Stringer RC	.10	.30
❑ 132 Bruce Armstrong	.02	.10
❑ 133 Drew Bledsoe	.25	.60
❑ 134 Vincent Brisby	.02	.10
❑ 135 Troy Brown	.10	.30
❑ 136 Vincent Brown	.02	.10
❑ 137 Marion Butts	.02	.10
❑ 138 Ben Coates	.07	.20
❑ 139 Ray Crittenden	.02	.10
❑ 140 Maurice Hurst	.02	.10
❑ 141 Aaron Jones	.02	.10
❑ 142 Willie McGinest	.07	.20
❑ 143 Marty Moore RC	.10	.30
❑ 144 Mike Pitts	.02	.10
❑ 145 Leroy Thompson	.02	.10
❑ 146 Michael Timpson	.02	.10
❑ 147 Bennie Blades	.02	.10
❑ 148 Jocelyn Borgella	.02	.10
❑ 149 Anthony Carter	.07	.20
❑ 150 Willie Clay	.02	.10
❑ 151 Mel Gray	.02	.10
❑ 152 Mike Johnson	.02	.10
❑ 153 Dave Krieg	.02	.10
❑ 154 Robert Massey	.02	.10
❑ 155 Scott Mitchell	.07	.20
❑ 156 Herman Moore	.10	.30
❑ 157 Johnnie Morton	.07	.20
❑ 158 Barry Sanders	.60	1.50
❑ 159 Chris Spielman	.07	.20
❑ 160 Broderick Thomas	.02	.10
❑ 161 Cory Schlesinger RC	.07	.20
❑ 162 Marcus Allen	.10	.30
❑ 163 Donnell Bennett	.07	.20
❑ 164 J.J. Birden	.02	.10
❑ 165 Matt Blundin RC	.02	.10
❑ 166 Steve Bono	.07	.20
❑ 167 Dale Carter	.07	.20
❑ 168 Lake Dawson	.07	.20
❑ 169 Ron Dickerson	.02	.10
❑ 170 Lin Elliott	.02	.10
❑ 171 Jaime Fields	.02	.10
❑ 172 Greg Hill	.07	.20
❑ 173 Danan Hughes	.02	.10
❑ 174 Neil Smith	.07	.20
❑ 175 Steve Stenstrom RC	.02	.10
❑ 176 Edgar Bennett	.07	.20
❑ 177 Robert Brooks	.10	.30
❑ 178 Mark Brunell	.25	.60
❑ 179 Doug Evans RC	.10	.30
❑ 180 Brett Favre	.75	2.00
❑ 181 Corey Harris	.02	.10
❑ 182 LeShon Johnson	.07	.20
❑ 183 Sean Jones	.02	.10
❑ 184 Lenny McGill RC	.02	.10
❑ 185 Terry Mickens	.02	.10
❑ 186 Sterling Sharpe	.07	.20
❑ 187 Joe Sims	.02	.10
❑ 188 Darrell Thompson	.02	.10
❑ 189 Reggie White	.10	.30
❑ 190 Craig Newsome RC	.02	.10
❑ 191 Tim Brown	.10	.30
❑ 192 Vince Evans	.02	.10
❑ 193 Rob Fredrickson	.02	.10
❑ 194 Andrew Glover RC	.02	.10
❑ 195 Jeff Hostetler	.07	.20
❑ 196 Rocket Ismail	.07	.20
❑ 197 Jeff Jaeger	.02	.10
❑ 198 James Jett	.07	.20
❑ 199 Chester McGlockton	.07	.20
❑ 200 Don Mosebar	.02	.10
❑ 201 Tom Rathman	.02	.10
❑ 202 Harvey Williams	.02	.10
❑ 203 Steve Wisniewski	.02	.10
❑ 204 Alexander Wright	.02	.10
❑ 205 Napoleon Kaufman RC	.50	1.25
❑ 206 Trace Armstrong	.02	.10
❑ 207 Curtis Conway	.10	.30
❑ 208 Raymont Harris	.02	.10
❑ 209 Erik Kramer	.02	.10
❑ 210 Nate Lewis	.02	.10
❑ 211 Shane Matthews RC	.10	.30
❑ 212 John Thierry	.02	.10
❑ 213 Lewis Tillman	.02	.10
❑ 214 Tom Waddle	.02	.10
❑ 215 Steve Walsh	.02	.10
❑ 216 James Williams T RC	.02	.10
❑ 217 Donnell Woolford	.02	.10
❑ 218 Chris Zorich	.02	.10
❑ 219 Rashaan Salaam RC	.07	.20
❑ 220 John Booty	.02	.10
❑ 221 Michael Brooks	.02	.10
❑ 222 Dave Brown	.07	.20
❑ 223 Chris Calloway	.02	.10
❑ 224 Gary Downs	.02	.10
❑ 225 Kent Graham	.07	.20
❑ 226 Keith Hamilton	.02	.10
❑ 227 Rodney Hampton	.07	.20
❑ 228 Brian Kozlowski	.02	.10
❑ 229 Thomas Lewis	.07	.20
❑ 230 Dave Meggett	.02	.10
❑ 231 Aaron Pierce	.02	.10
❑ 232 Mike Sherrard	.02	.10
❑ 233 Phillippi Sparks	.02	.10
❑ 234 Tyrone Wheatley RC	.50	1.25
❑ 235 Trev Alberts	.02	.10
❑ 236 Aaron Bailey RC	.02	.10
❑ 237 Jason Belser	.02	.10
❑ 238 Tony Bennett	.02	.10
❑ 239 Kerry Cash	.02	.10
❑ 240 Marshall Faulk	.50	1.25
❑ 241 Stephen Grant	.02	.10
❑ 242 Jeff Herrod	.02	.10
❑ 243 Ronald Humphrey	.02	.10
❑ 244 Kirk Lowdermilk	.02	.10
❑ 245 Don Majkowski	.02	.10
❑ 246 Tony McCoy	.02	.10
❑ 247 Floyd Turner	.02	.10
❑ 248 Lamont Warren	.02	.10
❑ 249 Zack Crockett RC	.07	.20
❑ 250 Michael Bankston	.02	.10
❑ 251 Larry Centers	.07	.20
❑ 252 Gary Clark	.02	.10
❑ 253 Ed Cunningham	.02	.10
❑ 254 Garrison Hearst	.10	.30
❑ 255 Eric Hill	.02	.10
❑ 256 Terry Irving	.02	.10
❑ 257 Lorenzo Lynch	.02	.10
❑ 258 Jamir Miller	.02	.10
❑ 259 Ronald Moore	.02	.10
❑ 260 Terry Samuels	.02	.10
❑ 261 Jay Schroeder	.02	.10
❑ 262 Eric Swann	.07	.20
❑ 263 Aeneas Williams	.02	.10
❑ 264 Frank Sanders RC	.10	.30
❑ 265 Morten Andersen	.02	.10
❑ 266 Mario Bates	.07	.20
❑ 267 Derek Brown RBK	.02	.10
❑ 268 Darion Conner	.02	.10
❑ 269 Quinn Early	.07	.20
❑ 270 Jim Everett	.02	.10
❑ 271 Michael Haynes	.07	.20
❑ 272 Wayne Martin	.02	.10
❑ 273 Derrell Mitchell RC	.02	.10
❑ 274 Lorenzo Neal	.02	.10
❑ 275 Jimmy Spencer	.02	.10
❑ 276 Winfred Tubbs	.02	.10
❑ 277 Renaldo Turnbull	.02	.10
❑ 278 Jeff Uhlenhake	.02	.10
❑ 279 Steve Atwater	.02	.10
❑ 280 Keith Burns RC	.02	.10
❑ 281 Butler By'Not'e RC	.07	.20
❑ 282 Jeff Campbell	.02	.10
❑ 283 Derrick Clark RC	.02	.10
❑ 284 Shane Dronett	.02	.10
❑ 285 Jason Elam	.07	.20
❑ 286 John Elway	.75	2.00
❑ 287 Jerry Evans	.02	.10
❑ 288 Karl Mecklenburg	.02	.10
❑ 289 Glyn Milburn	.02	.10
❑ 290 Anthony Miller	.07	.20
❑ 291 Tom Rouen	.02	.10
❑ 292 Leonard Russell	.02	.10
❑ 293 Shannon Sharpe	.07	.20
❑ 294 Steve Russ RC	.02	.10
❑ 295 Mel Agee	.02	.10
❑ 296 Lester Archambeau	.02	.10
❑ 297 Bert Emanuel	.10	.30
❑ 298 Jeff George	.07	.20
❑ 299 Craig Heyward	.07	.20
❑ 300 Bobby Hebert	.02	.10
❑ 301 D.J. Johnson	.02	.10
❑ 302 Mike Kenn	.02	.10
❑ 303 Terance Mathis	.07	.20
❑ 304 Clay Matthews	.07	.20
❑ 305 Erric Pegram	.07	.20
❑ 306 Andre Rison	.07	.20
❑ 307 Chuck Smith	.02	.10
❑ 308 Jessie Tuggle	.02	.10
❑ 309 Lorenzo Styles RC	.02	.10
❑ 310 Cornelius Bennett	.07	.20
❑ 311 Bill Brooks	.02	.10
❑ 312 Jeff Burris	.02	.10
❑ 313 Carwell Gardner	.02	.10
❑ 314 Kent Hull	.02	.10
❑ 315 Yonel Jourdain	.02	.10
❑ 316 Jim Kelly	.10	.30
❑ 317 Vince Marrow	.02	.10
❑ 318 Pete Metzelaars	.02	.10
❑ 319 Andre Reed	.07	.20
❑ 320 Kurt Schulz RC	.02	.10
❑ 321 Bruce Smith	.10	.30
❑ 322 Darryl Talley	.02	.10
❑ 323 Matt Darby	.02	.10
❑ 324 Justin Armour RC	.02	.10
❑ 325 Todd Collins RC	.50	1.25
❑ 326 David Alexander DE	.02	.10
❑ 327 Eric Allen	.02	.10
❑ 328 Fred Barnett	.07	.20
❑ 329 Randall Cunningham	.10	.30
❑ 330 William Fuller	.02	.10
❑ 331 Charlie Garner	.10	.30
❑ 332 Vaughn Hebron	.02	.10
❑ 333 James Joseph	.02	.10
❑ 334 Bill Romanowski	.02	.10
❑ 335 Ken Rose	.02	.10
❑ 336 Jeff Snyder	.02	.10

Card	Low	High
❑ 337 William Thomas	.02	.10
❑ 338 Herschel Walker	.07	.20
❑ 339 Calvin Williams	.07	.20
❑ 340 Dave Barr RC	.02	.10
❑ 341 Chidi Ahanotu	.02	.10
❑ 342 Barney Bussey	.02	.10
❑ 343 Horace Copeland	.02	.10
❑ 344 Trent Dilfer	.10	.30
❑ 345 Craig Erickson	.02	.10
❑ 346 Paul Gruber	.02	.10
❑ 347 Courtney Hawkins	.02	.10
❑ 348 Lonnie Marts	.02	.10
❑ 349 Martin Mayhew	.02	.10
❑ 350 Hardy Nickerson	.02	.10
❑ 351 Errict Rhett	.07	.20
❑ 352 Lamar Thomas	.02	.10
❑ 353 Charles Wilson	.02	.10
❑ 354 Vince Workman	.02	.10
❑ 355 Derrick Brooks RC	.60	1.50
❑ 356 Warren Sapp RC	.60	1.50
❑ 357 Sam Adams	.02	.10
❑ 358 Michael Bates	.02	.10
❑ 359 Brian Blades	.07	.20
❑ 360 Carlton Gray	.02	.10
❑ 361 Bill Hitchcock	.02	.10
❑ 362 Cortez Kennedy	.07	.20
❑ 363 Rick Mirer	.07	.20
❑ 364 Eugene Robinson	.02	.10
❑ 365 Michael Sinclair	.02	.10
❑ 366 Steve Smith	.02	.10
❑ 367 Bob Spitulski	.02	.10
❑ 368 Rick Tuten	.02	.10
❑ 369 Chris Warren	.07	.20
❑ 370 Terrence Warren	.02	.10
❑ 371 Christian Fauria RC	.07	.20
❑ 372 Joey Galloway RC	.60	1.50
❑ 373 Boomer Esiason	.07	.20
❑ 374 Aaron Glenn	.02	.10
❑ 375 Victor Green RC	.02	.10
❑ 376 Johnny Johnson	.02	.10
❑ 377 Mo Lewis	.02	.10
❑ 378 Ronnie Lott	.07	.20
❑ 379 Nick Lowery	.02	.10
❑ 380 Johnny Mitchell	.02	.10
❑ 381 Rob Moore	.07	.20
❑ 382 Adrian Murrell	.07	.20
❑ 383 Anthony Prior	.02	.10
❑ 384 Brian Washington	.02	.10
❑ 385 Matt Willig RC	.02	.10
❑ 386 Kyle Brady RC	.10	.30
❑ 387 Flipper Anderson	.02	.10
❑ 388 Johnny Bailey	.02	.10
❑ 389 Jerome Bettis	.10	.30
❑ 390 Isaac Bruce	.20	.50
❑ 391 Shane Conlan	.02	.10
❑ 392 Troy Drayton	.02	.10
❑ 393 D'Marco Farr	.02	.10
❑ 394 Jessie Hester	.02	.10
❑ 395 Todd Kinchen	.02	.10
❑ 396 Ron Middleton	.02	.10
❑ 397 Chris Miller	.02	.10
❑ 398 Marquez Pope	.02	.10
❑ 399 Robert Young	.02	.10
❑ 400 Tony Zendejas	.02	.10
❑ 401 Kevin Carter RC	.10	.30
❑ 402 Reggie Brooks	.07	.20
❑ 403 Tom Carter	.02	.10
❑ 404 Andre Collins	.02	.10
❑ 405 Pat Eilers	.02	.10
❑ 406 Henry Ellard	.07	.20
❑ 407 Ricky Ervins	.02	.10
❑ 408 Gus Frerotte	.07	.20
❑ 409 Ken Harvey	.02	.10
❑ 410 Jim Lachey	.02	.10
❑ 411 Brian Mitchell	.02	.10
❑ 412 Reggie Roby	.02	.10
❑ 413 Heath Shuler	.07	.20
❑ 414 Tyronne Stowe	.02	.10
❑ 415 Tydus Winans	.02	.10
❑ 416 Cory Raymer RC	.02	.10
❑ 417 Michael Westbrook RC	.10	.30
❑ 418 Jeff Blake RC	.30	.75
❑ 419 Steve Broussard	.02	.10
❑ 420 Dave Cadigan	.02	.10
❑ 421 Jeff Cothran	.02	.10
❑ 422 Derrick Fenner	.02	.10
❑ 423 James Francis	.02	.10
❑ 424 Lee Johnson	.02	.10
❑ 425 Louis Oliver	.02	.10
❑ 426 Carl Pickens	.07	.20
❑ 427 Jeff Query	.02	.10
❑ 428 Corey Sawyer	.02	.10
❑ 429 Darnay Scott	.07	.20
❑ 430 Dan Wilkinson	.07	.20
❑ 431 Alfred Williams	.02	.10
❑ 432 Ki-Jana Carter RC	.10	.30
❑ 433 David Dunn RC	.02	.10
❑ 434 John Walsh RC	.02	.10
❑ 435 Gary Brown	.02	.10
❑ 436 Pat Carter	.02	.10
❑ 437 Ray Childress	.02	.10
❑ 438 Ernest Givins	.02	.10
❑ 439 Haywood Jeffires	.02	.10
❑ 440 Lamar Lathon	.02	.10
❑ 441 Bruce Matthews	.02	.10
❑ 442 Marcus Robertson	.02	.10
❑ 443 Eddie Robinson	.02	.10
❑ 444 Malcolm Seabron RC	.02	.10
❑ 445 Webster Slaughter	.02	.10
❑ 446 Al Smith	.02	.10
❑ 447 Billy Joe Tolliver	.02	.10
❑ 448 Lorenzo White	.02	.10
❑ 449 Steve McNair RC	1.25	3.00
❑ 450 Rodney Thomas RC	.07	.20
❑ P1 Natrone Means Promo	.40	1.00
❑ P1J Natrone Means Promo	.40	1.00

1996 Pacific

Card	Low	High
❑ COMPLETE SET (450)	20.00	40.00
❑ 1 Jeff Feagles	.02	.10
❑ 2 Rob Moore	.07	.20
❑ 3 Clyde Simmons	.02	.10
❑ 4 Mike Buck	.02	.10
❑ 5 Aeneas Williams	.02	.10
❑ 6 Simeon Rice RC	.40	1.00
❑ 7 Garrison Hearst	.07	.20
❑ 8 Eric Swann	.02	.10
❑ 9 Dave Krieg	.02	.10
❑ 10 Leeland McElroy RC	.07	.20
❑ 11 Oscar McBride	.02	.10
❑ 12 Frank Sanders	.07	.20
❑ 13 Larry Centers	.07	.20
❑ 14 Seth Joyner	.02	.10
❑ 15 Stevie Anderson	.02	.10
❑ 16 Craig Heyward	.02	.10
❑ 17 Devin Bush	.02	.10
❑ 18 Eric Metcalf	.02	.10
❑ 19 Jeff George	.07	.20
❑ 20 Richard Huntley RC	.07	.20
❑ 21 Jamal Anderson RC	.20	.50
❑ 22 Bert Emanuel	.07	.20
❑ 23 Terance Mathis	.02	.10
❑ 24 Roman Fortin	.02	.10
❑ 25 Jessie Tuggle	.02	.10
❑ 26 Morten Andersen	.02	.10
❑ 27 Chris Doleman	.02	.10
❑ 28 D.J. Johnson	.02	.10
❑ 29 Kevin Ross	.02	.10
❑ 30 Michael Jackson	.07	.20
❑ 31 Eric Zeier	.02	.10
❑ 32 Jonathan Ogden RC	.15	.40
❑ 33 Eric Turner	.02	.10
❑ 34 Andre Rison	.07	.20
❑ 35 Lorenzo White	.02	.10
❑ 36 Earnest Byner	.02	.10
❑ 37 Derrick Alexander WR	.07	.20
❑ 38 Brian Kinchen	.02	.10
❑ 39 Anthony Pleasant	.02	.10
❑ 40 Vinny Testaverde	.07	.20
❑ 41 Pepper Johnson	.02	.10
❑ 42 Frank Hartley	.02	.10
❑ 43 Craig Powell	.02	.10
❑ 44 Leroy Hoard	.02	.10
❑ 45 Kent Hull	.02	.10
❑ 46 Bryce Paup	.02	.10
❑ 47 Andre Reed	.07	.20
❑ 48 Darick Holmes	.02	.10
❑ 49 Russell Copeland	.02	.10
❑ 50 Jerry Ostroski	.02	.10
❑ 51 Chris Green	.02	.10
❑ 52 Eric Moulds RC	.50	1.25
❑ 53 Justin Armour	.02	.10
❑ 54 Jim Kelly	.15	.40
❑ 55 Cornelius Bennett	.02	.10
❑ 56 Steve Tasker	.02	.10
❑ 57 Thurman Thomas	.15	.40
❑ 58 Bruce Smith	.07	.20
❑ 59 Todd Collins	.07	.20
❑ 60 Shawn King	.02	.10
❑ 61 Don Beebe	.02	.10
❑ 62 John Kasay	.02	.10
❑ 63 Tim McKyer	.02	.10
❑ 64 Darion Conner	.02	.10
❑ 65 Pete Metzelaars	.02	.10
❑ 66 Derrick Moore	.02	.10
❑ 67 Blake Brockermeyer	.02	.10
❑ 68 Tim Biakabutuka RC	.15	.40
❑ 69 Sam Mills	.02	.10
❑ 70 Vince Workman	.02	.10
❑ 71 Kerry Collins	.15	.40
❑ 72 Carlton Bailey	.02	.10
❑ 73 Mark Carrier WR	.02	.10
❑ 74 Donnell Woolford	.02	.10
❑ 75 Walt Harris RC	.02	.10
❑ 76 John Thierry	.02	.10
❑ 77 Al Fontenot RC	.02	.10
❑ 78 Lewis Tillman	.02	.10
❑ 79 Curtis Conway	.15	.40
❑ 80 Chris Zorich	.02	.10
❑ 81 Mark Carrier DB	.02	.10
❑ 82 Bobby Engram RC	.15	.40
❑ 83 Alonzo Spellman	.02	.10
❑ 84 Rashaan Salaam	.07	.20
❑ 85 Michael Timpson	.02	.10
❑ 86 Nate Lewis	.02	.10
❑ 87 James Williams T	.02	.10
❑ 88 Jeff Graham	.02	.10
❑ 89 Erik Kramer	.02	.10
❑ 90 Willie Anderson	.02	.10
❑ 91 Tony McGee	.02	.10
❑ 92 Marco Battaglia	.02	.10
❑ 93 Dan Wilkinson	.02	.10
❑ 94 John Walsh	.02	.10
❑ 95 Eric Bieniemy	.02	.10
❑ 96 Ricardo McDonald	.02	.10
❑ 97 Carl Pickens	.07	.20
❑ 98 Kevin Sargent	.02	.10
❑ 99 David Dunn	.02	.10
❑ 100 Jeff Blake	.15	.40
❑ 101 Harold Green	.02	.10
❑ 102 James Francis	.02	.10
❑ 103 John Copeland	.02	.10
❑ 104 Darnay Scott	.07	.20
❑ 105 Darren Woodson	.07	.20
❑ 106 Jay Novacek	.02	.10
❑ 107 Charles Haley	.07	.20
❑ 108 Mark Tuinei	.02	.10
❑ 109 Michael Irvin	.15	.40
❑ 110 Troy Aikman	.40	1.00
❑ 111 Chris Boniol	.02	.10
❑ 112 Sherman Williams	.02	.10
❑ 113 Deion Sanders	.25	.60
❑ 114 Emmitt Smith	.60	1.50
❑ 115 Eric Bjornson	.02	.10
❑ 116 Nate Newton	.02	.10
❑ 117 Larry Allen	.02	.10
❑ 118 Kevin Williams	.02	.10
❑ 119 Leon Lett	.02	.10
❑ 120 John Mobley	.02	.10
❑ 121 Anthony Miller	.07	.20
❑ 122 Brian Habib	.02	.10
❑ 123 Aaron Craver	.02	.10
❑ 124 Glyn Milburn	.02	.10
❑ 125 Shannon Sharpe	.07	.20
❑ 126 Steve Atwater	.02	.10
❑ 127 Jason Elam	.07	.20
❑ 128 John Elway	.75	2.00
❑ 129 Reggie Rivers	.02	.10
❑ 130 Mike Pritchard	.02	.10
❑ 131 Vance Johnson	.02	.10
❑ 132 Terrell Davis	.30	.75
❑ 133 Tyrone Braxton	.02	.10
❑ 134 Ed McCaffrey	.07	.20
❑ 135 Brett Perriman	.02	.10

❑ 136 Chris Spielman .02 .10
❑ 137 Luther Elliss .02 .10
❑ 138 Johnnie Morton .07 .20
❑ 139 Zefross Moss .02 .10
❑ 140 Barry Sanders .60 1.50
❑ 141 Lomas Brown .02 .10
❑ 142 Cory Schlesinger .02 .10
❑ 143 Jason Hanson .02 .10
❑ 144 Kevin Glover .02 .10
❑ 145 Ron Rivers RC .07 .20
❑ 146 Aubrey Matthews .02 .10
❑ 147 Reggie Brown LB RC .02 .10
❑ 148 Herman Moore .07 .20
❑ 149 Scott Mitchell .07 .20
❑ 150 Brett Favre .75 2.00
❑ 151 Sean Jones .02 .10
❑ 152 LeRoy Butler .02 .10
❑ 153 Mark Chmura .07 .20
❑ 154 Derrick Mayes RC .15 .40
❑ 155 Mark Ingram .02 .10
❑ 156 Antonio Freeman .15 .40
❑ 157 Chris Darkins RC .02 .10
❑ 158 Robert Brooks .15 .40
❑ 159 William Henderson .15 .40
❑ 160 George Koonce .02 .10
❑ 161 Craig Newsome .02 .10
❑ 162 Darius Holland .02 .10
❑ 163 George Teague .02 .10
❑ 164 Edgar Bennett .07 .20
❑ 165 Reggie White .15 .40
❑ 166 Micheal Barrow .02 .10
❑ 167 Mel Gray .02 .10
❑ 168 Anthony Dorsett .02 .10
❑ 169 Roderick Lewis .02 .10
❑ 170 Henry Ford .02 .10
❑ 171 Mark Stepnoski .02 .10
❑ 172 Chris Sanders .07 .20
❑ 173 Anthony Cook .02 .10
❑ 174 Eddie Robinson .02 .10
❑ 175 Steve McNair .30 .75
❑ 176 Haywood Jeffires .02 .10
❑ 177 Eddie George RC .50 1.25
❑ 178 Marion Butts .02 .10
❑ 179 Malcolm Seabron .02 .10
❑ 180 Rodney Thomas .02 .10
❑ 181 Ken Dilger .07 .20
❑ 182 Zack Crockett .02 .10
❑ 183 Tony Bennett .02 .10
❑ 184 Quentin Coryatt .02 .10
❑ 185 Marshall Faulk .20 .50
❑ 186 Sean Dawkins .02 .10
❑ 187 Jim Harbaugh .07 .20
❑ 188 Eugene Daniel .02 .10
❑ 189 Roosevelt Potts .02 .10
❑ 190 Lamont Warren .02 .10
❑ 191 Will Wolford .02 .10
❑ 192 Tony Siragusa .02 .10
❑ 193 Aaron Bailey .02 .10
❑ 194 Trev Alberts .02 .10
❑ 195 Kevin Hardy .07 .20
❑ 196 Greg Spann .02 .10
❑ 197 Steve Beuerlein .07 .20
❑ 198 Steve Taneyhill .02 .10
❑ 199 Vaughn Dunbar .02 .10
❑ 200 Mark Brunell .25 .60
❑ 201 Bernard Carter .02 .10
❑ 202 James O. Stewart .07 .20
❑ 203 Tony Boselli .02 .10
❑ 204 Chris Doering .02 .10
❑ 205 Willie Jackson .07 .20
❑ 206 Tony Brackens RC .15 .40
❑ 207 Ernest Givins .02 .10
❑ 208 Le'Shai Maston .02 .10
❑ 209 Pete Mitchell .07 .20
❑ 210 Desmond Howard .07 .20
❑ 211 Vinnie Clark .02 .10
❑ 212 Jeff Lageman .02 .10
❑ 213 Derrick Walker .02 .10
❑ 214 Dan Saleaumua .02 .10
❑ 215 Derrick Thomas .15 .40
❑ 216 Neil Smith .07 .20
❑ 217 Willie Davis .02 .10
❑ 218 Mark Collins .02 .10
❑ 219 Lake Dawson .02 .10
❑ 220 Greg Hill .07 .20
❑ 221 Anthony Davis .02 .10
❑ 222 Kimble Anders .07 .20
❑ 223 Webster Slaughter .02 .10
❑ 224 Tamarick Vanover .07 .20
❑ 225 Marcus Allen .15 .40
❑ 226 Steve Bono .02 .10
❑ 227 Will Shields .02 .10
❑ 228 Karim Abdul-Jabbar RC .15 .40
❑ 229 Tim Bowens .02 .10
❑ 230 Keith Sims .02 .10
❑ 231 Terry Kirby .07 .20
❑ 232 Gene Atkins .02 .10
❑ 233 Dan Marino .75 2.00
❑ 234 Richmond Webb .02 .10
❑ 235 Gary Clark .02 .10
❑ 236 O.J. McDuffie .07 .20
❑ 237 Marco Coleman .02 .10
❑ 238 Bernie Parmalee .02 .10
❑ 239 Randal Hill .02 .10
❑ 240 Bryan Cox .02 .10
❑ 241 Irving Fryar .07 .20
❑ 242 Derrick Alexander DE .02 .10
❑ 243 Qadry Ismail .07 .20
❑ 244 Warren Moon .07 .20
❑ 245 Cris Carter .15 .40
❑ 246 Chad May .02 .10
❑ 247 Robert Smith .07 .20
❑ 248 Fuad Reveiz .02 .10
❑ 249 Orlando Thomas .02 .10
❑ 250 Chris Hinton .02 .10
❑ 251 Jack Del Rio .02 .10
❑ 252 Moe Williams RB RC .40 1.00
❑ 253 Roy Barker .02 .10
❑ 254 Jake Reed .07 .20
❑ 255 Adrian Cooper .02 .10
❑ 256 Curtis Martin .30 .75
❑ 257 Ben Coates .07 .20
❑ 258 Drew Bledsoe .25 .60
❑ 259 Maurice Hurst .02 .10
❑ 260 Troy Brown .15 .40
❑ 261 Bruce Armstrong .02 .10
❑ 262 Myron Guyton .02 .10
❑ 263 Dave Meggett .02 .10
❑ 264 Terry Glenn RC .40 1.00
❑ 265 Chris Slade .02 .10
❑ 266 Vincent Brisby .02 .10
❑ 267 Willie McGinest .02 .10
❑ 268 Vincent Brown .02 .10
❑ 269 Will Moore .02 .10
❑ 270 Jay Barker .02 .10
❑ 271 Ray Zellars .02 .10
❑ 272 Derek Brown RBK .02 .10
❑ 273 William Roaf .02 .10
❑ 274 Quinn Early .02 .10
❑ 275 Michael Haynes .02 .10
❑ 276 Rufus Porter .02 .10
❑ 277 Renaldo Turnbull .02 .10
❑ 278 Wayne Martin .02 .10
❑ 279 Tyrone Hughes .02 .10
❑ 280 Irv Smith .02 .10
❑ 281 Eric Allen .02 .10
❑ 282 Mark Fields .02 .10
❑ 283 Mario Bates .07 .20
❑ 284 Jim Everett .02 .10
❑ 285 Vince Buck .02 .10
❑ 286 Alex Molden RC .02 .10
❑ 287 Tyrone Wheatley .07 .20
❑ 288 Chris Calloway .02 .10
❑ 289 Jessie Armstead .02 .10
❑ 290 Arthur Marshall .02 .10
❑ 291 Aaron Pierce .02 .10
❑ 292 Dave Brown .02 .10
❑ 293 Rodney Hampton .07 .20
❑ 294 Jumbo Elliott .02 .10
❑ 295 Mike Sherrard .02 .10
❑ 296 Howard Cross .02 .10
❑ 297 Michael Brooks .02 .10
❑ 298 Herschel Walker .07 .20
❑ 299 Danny Kanell RC .15 .40
❑ 300 Keith Elias .02 .10
❑ 301 Bobby Houston .02 .10
❑ 302 Dexter Carter .02 .10
❑ 303 Tony Casillas .02 .10
❑ 304 Kyle Brady .02 .10
❑ 305 Glenn Foley .07 .20
❑ 306 Ronald Moore .02 .10
❑ 307 Ryan Yarborough .02 .10
❑ 308 Aaron Glenn .02 .10
❑ 309 Adrian Murrell .07 .20
❑ 310 Boomer Esiason .07 .20
❑ 311 Kyle Clifton .02 .10
❑ 312 Wayne Chrebet .25 .60
❑ 313 Erik Howard .02 .10
❑ 314 Keyshawn Johnson RC .40 1.00
❑ 315 Marvin Washington .02 .10
❑ 316 Johnny Mitchell .02 .10
❑ 317 Alex Van Dyke RC .07 .20
❑ 318 Billy Joe Hobert .07 .20
❑ 319 Andrew Glover .02 .10
❑ 320 Vince Evans .02 .10
❑ 321 Chester McGlockton .02 .10
❑ 322 Pat Swilling .02 .10
❑ 323 Rocket Ismail .02 .10
❑ 324 Eddie Anderson .02 .10
❑ 325 Rickey Dudley RC .15 .40
❑ 326 Steve Wisniewski .02 .10
❑ 327 Harvey Williams .02 .10
❑ 328 Napoleon Kaufman .15 .40
❑ 329 Tim Brown .15 .40
❑ 330 Jeff Hostetler .02 .10
❑ 331 Anthony Smith .02 .10
❑ 332 Terry McDaniel .02 .10
❑ 333 Charlie Garner .07 .20
❑ 334 Ricky Watters .07 .20
❑ 335 Brian Dawkins RC .50 1.25
❑ 336 Randall Cunningham .15 .40
❑ 337 Gary Anderson .02 .10
❑ 338 Calvin Williams .02 .10
❑ 339 Chris T. Jones .07 .20
❑ 340 Bobby Hoying RC .15 .40
❑ 341 William Fuller .02 .10
❑ 342 William Thomas .02 .10
❑ 343 Mike Mamula .02 .10
❑ 344 Fred Barnett .02 .10
❑ 345 Rodney Peete .02 .10
❑ 346 Mark McMillian .02 .10
❑ 347 Bobby Taylor .02 .10
❑ 348 Yancey Thigpen .07 .20
❑ 349 Neil O'Donnell .07 .20
❑ 350 Rod Woodson .07 .20
❑ 351 Kordell Stewart .15 .40
❑ 352 Dermontti Dawson .02 .10
❑ 353 Norm Johnson .02 .10
❑ 354 Ernie Mills .02 .10
❑ 355 Byron Bam Morris .02 .10
❑ 356 Mark Bruener .02 .10
❑ 357 Kevin Greene .07 .20
❑ 358 Greg Lloyd .07 .20
❑ 359 Andre Hastings .02 .10
❑ 360 Erric Pegram .02 .10
❑ 361 Carnell Lake .02 .10
❑ 362 Dwayne Harper .02 .10
❑ 363 Ronnie Harmon .02 .10
❑ 364 Leslie O'Neal .02 .10
❑ 365 John Carney .02 .10
❑ 366 Stan Humphries .07 .20
❑ 367 Brian Roche RC .02 .10
❑ 368 Terrell Fletcher .02 .10
❑ 369 Shaun Gayle .02 .10
❑ 370 Alfred Pupunu .02 .10
❑ 371 Shawn Jefferson .02 .10
❑ 372 Junior Seau .15 .40
❑ 373 Mark Seay .02 .10
❑ 374 Aaron Hayden .02 .10
❑ 375 Tony Martin .07 .20
❑ 376 Steve Young .30 .75
❑ 377 J.J. Stokes .15 .40
❑ 378 Jerry Rice .40 1.00
❑ 379 Derek Loville .02 .10
❑ 380 Lee Woodall .02 .10
❑ 381 Terrell Owens RC 1.00 2.50
❑ 382 Elvis Grbac .07 .20
❑ 383 Ricky Ervins .02 .10
❑ 384 Eric Davis .02 .10
❑ 385 Dana Stubblefield .07 .20
❑ 386 Gary Plummer .02 .10
❑ 387 Tim McDonald .02 .10
❑ 388 William Floyd .07 .20
❑ 389 Ken Norton Jr. .02 .10
❑ 390 Merton Hanks .02 .10
❑ 391 Bart Oates .02 .10
❑ 392 Brent Jones .02 .10
❑ 393 Steve Broussard .02 .10
❑ 394 Robert Blackmon .02 .10
❑ 395 Rick Tuten .02 .10
❑ 396 Pete Kendall .02 .10
❑ 397 John Friesz .02 .10
❑ 398 Terry Wooden .02 .10
❑ 399 Rick Mirer .07 .20
❑ 400 Chris Warren .07 .20
❑ 401 Joey Galloway .15 .40
❑ 402 Howard Ballard .02 .10

❑ 403 Jason Kyle	.02	.10
❑ 404 Kevin Mawae	.02	.10
❑ 405 Mack Strong	.15	.40
❑ 406 Reggie Brown RBK RC	.02	.10
❑ 407 Cortez Kennedy	.02	.10
❑ 408 Sean Gilbert	.02	.10
❑ 409 J.T. Thomas	.02	.10
❑ 410 Shane Conlan	.02	.10
❑ 411 Johnny Bailey	.02	.10
❑ 412 Mark Rypien	.02	.10
❑ 413 Leonard Russell	.02	.10
❑ 414 Troy Drayton	.02	.10
❑ 415 Jerome Bettis	.15	.40
❑ 416 Jessie Hester	.02	.10
❑ 417 Isaac Bruce	.15	.40
❑ 418 Roman Phifer	.02	.10
❑ 419 Todd Kinchen	.02	.10
❑ 420 Alexander Wright	.02	.10
❑ 421 Marcus Jones RC	.02	.10
❑ 422 Horace Copeland	.02	.10
❑ 423 Eric Curry	.02	.10
❑ 424 Courtney Hawkins	.02	.10
❑ 425 Alvin Harper	.02	.10
❑ 426 Derrick Brooks	.15	.40
❑ 427 Errict Rhett	.07	.20
❑ 428 Trent Dilfer	.15	.40
❑ 429 Hardy Nickerson	.02	.10
❑ 430 Brad Culpepper	.02	.10
❑ 431 Warren Sapp	.02	.10
❑ 432 Reggie Roby	.02	.10
❑ 433 Santana Dotson	.02	.10
❑ 434 Jerry Ellison	.02	.10
❑ 435 Lawrence Dawsey	.02	.10
❑ 436 Heath Shuler	.07	.20
❑ 437 Stanley Richard	.07	.20
❑ 438 Rod Stephens	.02	.10
❑ 439 Stephen Davis RC	.60	1.50
❑ 440 Terry Allen	.07	.20
❑ 441 Michael Westbrook	.15	.40
❑ 442 Ken Harvey	.02	.10
❑ 443 Coleman Bell	.02	.10
❑ 444 Marvcus Patton	.02	.10
❑ 445 Gus Frerotte	.07	.20
❑ 446 Leslie Shepherd	.02	.10
❑ 447 Tom Carter	.02	.10
❑ 448 Brian Mitchell	.02	.10
❑ 449 Darrell Green	.02	.10
❑ 450A Tony Woods	.02	.10
❑ 450B Chris Warren Promo	.20	.50
❑ CW1 Chris Warren Promo	.40	1.00

1997 Pacific

❑ COMPLETE SET (450)	15.00	30.00
❑ 1 Lomas Brown	.07	.20
❑ 2 Pat Carter	.07	.20
❑ 3 Larry Centers	.10	.30
❑ 4 Matt Darby	.07	.20
❑ 5 Marcus Dowdell	.07	.20
❑ 6 Aaron Graham	.07	.20
❑ 7 Kent Graham	.07	.20
❑ 8 LeShon Johnson	.07	.20
❑ 9 Seth Joyner	.07	.20
❑ 10 Leeland McElroy	.07	.20
❑ 11 Rob Moore	.10	.30
❑ 12 Simeon Rice	.10	.30
❑ 13 Eric Swann	.07	.20
❑ 14 Aeneas Williams	.07	.20
❑ 15 Morten Andersen	.07	.20
❑ 16 Jamal Anderson	.20	.50
❑ 17 Lester Archambeau	.07	.20
❑ 18 Cornelius Bennett	.07	.20
❑ 19 J.J. Birden	.07	.20
❑ 20 Antone Davis	.07	.20
❑ 21 Bert Emanuel	.10	.30
❑ 22 Travis Hall RC	.07	.20
❑ 23 Bobby Hebert	.07	.20
❑ 24 Craig Heyward	.07	.20
❑ 25 Terance Mathis	.10	.30
❑ 26 Tim McKyer	.07	.20
❑ 27 Eric Metcalf	.10	.30
❑ 28 Jessie Tuggle	.07	.20
❑ 29 Derrick Alexander WR	.10	.30
❑ 30 Orlando Brown	.07	.20
❑ 31 Rob Burnett	.07	.20
❑ 32 Earnest Byner	.07	.20
❑ 33 Ray Ethridge	.07	.20
❑ 34 Steve Everitt	.07	.20
❑ 35 Carwell Gardner	.07	.20
❑ 36 Michael Jackson	.10	.30
❑ 37 Jermaine Lewis	.20	.50
❑ 38 Stevon Moore	.07	.20
❑ 39 Byron Bam Morris	.07	.20
❑ 40 Jonathan Ogden	.07	.20
❑ 41 Vinny Testaverde	.10	.30
❑ 42 Todd Collins	.07	.20
❑ 43 Russell Copeland	.07	.20
❑ 44 Quinn Early	.07	.20
❑ 45 John Fina	.07	.20
❑ 46 Phil Hansen	.07	.20
❑ 47 Eric Moulds	.20	.50
❑ 48 Bryce Paup	.07	.20
❑ 49 Andre Reed	.10	.30
❑ 50 Kurt Schulz	.07	.20
❑ 51 Bruce Smith	.10	.30
❑ 52 Chris Spielman	.07	.20
❑ 53 Steve Tasker	.07	.20
❑ 54 Thurman Thomas	.20	.50
❑ 55 Carlton Bailey	.07	.20
❑ 56 Michael Bates	.07	.20
❑ 57 Blake Brockermeyer	.07	.20
❑ 58 Mark Carrier WR	.07	.20
❑ 59 Kerry Collins	.20	.50
❑ 60 Eric Davis	.07	.20
❑ 61 Kevin Greene	.10	.30
❑ 62 Rocket Ismail	.10	.30
❑ 63 Anthony Johnson	.07	.20
❑ 64 Shawn King	.07	.20
❑ 65 Greg Kragen	.07	.20
❑ 66 Sam Mills	.07	.20
❑ 67 Tyrone Poole	.07	.20
❑ 68 Wesley Walls	.10	.30
❑ 69 Mark Carrier DB	.07	.20
❑ 70 Curtis Conway	.10	.30
❑ 71 Bobby Engram	.10	.30
❑ 72 Jim Flanigan	.07	.20
❑ 73 Al Fontenot	.07	.20
❑ 74 Raymont Harris	.07	.20
❑ 75 Walt Harris	.07	.20
❑ 76 Andy Heck	.07	.20
❑ 77 Dave Krieg	.07	.20
❑ 78 Rashaan Salaam	.07	.20
❑ 79 Vinson Smith	.07	.20
❑ 80 Alonzo Spellman	.07	.20
❑ 81 Michael Timpson	.07	.20
❑ 82 James Williams	.07	.20
❑ 83 Ashley Ambrose	.07	.20
❑ 84 Eric Bieniemy	.07	.20
❑ 85 Jeff Blake	.10	.30
❑ 86 Ki-Jana Carter	.07	.20
❑ 87 John Copeland	.07	.20
❑ 88 David Dunn	.07	.20
❑ 89 Jeff Hill	.07	.20
❑ 90 Ricardo McDonald	.07	.20
❑ 91 Tony McGee	.07	.20
❑ 92 Greg Myers	.07	.20
❑ 93 Carl Pickens	.10	.30
❑ 94 Corey Sawyer	.07	.20
❑ 95 Darnay Scott	.10	.30
❑ 96 Dan Wilkinson	.07	.20
❑ 97 Troy Aikman	.40	1.00
❑ 98 Larry Allen	.07	.20
❑ 99 Eric Bjornson	.07	.20
❑ 100 Ray Donaldson	.07	.20
❑ 101 Michael Irvin	.20	.50
❑ 102 Daryl Johnston	.10	.30
❑ 103 Nate Newton	.07	.20
❑ 104 Deion Sanders	.20	.50
❑ 105 Jim Schwantz RC	.07	.20
❑ 106 Emmitt Smith	.60	1.50
❑ 107 Broderick Thomas	.07	.20
❑ 108 Tony Tolbert	.07	.20
❑ 109 Erik Williams	.07	.20
❑ 110 Sherman Williams	.07	.20
❑ 111 Darren Woodson	.07	.20
❑ 112 Steve Atwater	.07	.20
❑ 113 Aaron Craver	.07	.20
❑ 114 Ray Crockett	.07	.20
❑ 115 Terrell Davis	.25	.60
❑ 116 Jason Elam	.10	.30
❑ 117 John Elway	.75	2.00
❑ 118 Todd Kinchen	.07	.20
❑ 119 Ed McCaffrey	.10	.30
❑ 120 Anthony Miller	.07	.20
❑ 121 John Mobley	.07	.20
❑ 122 Michael Dean Perry	.07	.20
❑ 123 Reggie Rivers	.07	.20
❑ 124 Shannon Sharpe	.10	.30
❑ 125 Alfred Williams	.07	.20
❑ 126 Reggie Brown LB	.10	.30
❑ 127 Luther Elliss	.07	.20
❑ 128 Kevin Glover	.07	.20
❑ 129 Jason Hanson	.07	.20
❑ 130 Pepper Johnson	.07	.20
❑ 131 Glyn Milburn	.07	.20
❑ 132 Scott Mitchell	.10	.30
❑ 133 Herman Moore	.10	.30
❑ 134 Johnnie Morton	.10	.30
❑ 135 Brett Perriman	.07	.20
❑ 136 Robert Porcher	.07	.20
❑ 137 Ron Rivers	.07	.20
❑ 138 Barry Sanders	.60	1.50
❑ 139 Henry Thomas	.07	.20
❑ 140 Don Beebe	.07	.20
❑ 141 Edgar Bennett	.10	.30
❑ 142 Robert Brooks	.10	.30
❑ 143 LeRoy Butler	.07	.20
❑ 144 Mark Chmura	.10	.30
❑ 145 Brett Favre	.75	2.00
❑ 146 Antonio Freeman	.20	.50
❑ 147 Chris Jacke	.07	.20
❑ 148 Travis Jervey	.10	.30
❑ 149 Sean Jones	.07	.20
❑ 150 Dorsey Levens	.20	.50
❑ 151 John Michels	.07	.20
❑ 152 Craig Newsome	.07	.20
❑ 153 Eugene Robinson	.07	.20
❑ 154 Reggie White	.20	.50
❑ 155 Micheal Barrow	.07	.20
❑ 156 Blaine Bishop	.07	.20
❑ 157 Chris Chandler	.10	.30
❑ 158 Anthony Cook	.07	.20
❑ 159 Malcolm Floyd	.07	.20
❑ 160 Eddie George	.20	.50
❑ 161 Roderick Lewis	.07	.20
❑ 162 Steve McNair	.25	.60
❑ 163 John Henry Mills RC	.07	.20
❑ 164 Derek Russell	.07	.20
❑ 165 Chris Sanders	.07	.20
❑ 166 Mark Stepnoski	.07	.20
❑ 167 Frank Wycheck	.07	.20
❑ 168 Robert Young	.07	.20
❑ 169 Trev Alberts	.07	.20
❑ 170 Aaron Bailey	.07	.20
❑ 171 Tony Bennett	.07	.20
❑ 172 Ray Buchanan	.07	.20
❑ 173 Quentin Coryatt	.07	.20
❑ 174 Eugene Daniel	.07	.20
❑ 175 Sean Dawkins	.07	.20
❑ 176 Ken Dilger	.07	.20
❑ 177 Marshall Faulk	.25	.60
❑ 178 Jim Harbaugh	.10	.30
❑ 179 Marvin Harrison	.20	.50
❑ 180 Paul Justin	.07	.20
❑ 181 Lamont Warren	.07	.20
❑ 182 Bernard Whittington	.07	.20
❑ 183 Tony Boselli	.07	.20
❑ 184 Tony Brackens	.07	.20
❑ 185 Mark Brunell	.25	.60
❑ 186 Brian DeMarco	.07	.20
❑ 187 Rich Griffith	.07	.20
❑ 188 Kevin Hardy	.07	.20
❑ 189 Willie Jackson	.07	.20
❑ 190 Jeff Lageman	.07	.20
❑ 191 Keenan McCardell	.10	.30
❑ 192 Natrone Means	.10	.30
❑ 193 Pete Mitchell	.07	.20
❑ 194 Joel Smeenge	.07	.20
❑ 195 Jimmy Smith	.10	.30
❑ 196 James O.Stewart	.10	.30
❑ 197 Marcus Allen	.20	.50
❑ 198 John Alt	.07	.20
❑ 199 Kimble Anders	.10	.30
❑ 200 Steve Bono	.10	.30
❑ 201 Vaughn Booker	.07	.20

Card		
❑ 202 Dale Carter	.07	.20
❑ 203 Mark Collins	.07	.20
❑ 204 Greg Hill	.07	.20
❑ 205 Joe Horn	.20	.50
❑ 206 Dan Saleaumua	.07	.20
❑ 207 Will Shields	.07	.20
❑ 208 Neil Smith	.10	.30
❑ 209 Derrick Thomas	.20	.50
❑ 210 Tamarick Vanover	.10	.30
❑ 211 Karim Abdul-Jabbar	.10	.30
❑ 212 Fred Barnett	.07	.20
❑ 213 Tim Bowens	.07	.20
❑ 214 Kirby Dar Dar RC	.10	.30
❑ 215 Troy Drayton	.07	.20
❑ 216 Craig Erickson	.07	.20
❑ 217 Daryl Gardener	.07	.20
❑ 218 Randal Hill	.07	.20
❑ 219 Dan Marino	.75	2.00
❑ 220 O.J. McDuffie	.10	.30
❑ 221 Bernie Parmalee	.07	.20
❑ 222 Stanley Pritchett	.07	.20
❑ 223 Daniel Stubbs	.07	.20
❑ 224 Zach Thomas	.20	.50
❑ 225 Derrick Alexander DE	.07	.20
❑ 226 Cris Carter	.20	.50
❑ 227 Jeff Christy	.07	.20
❑ 228 Qadry Ismail	.10	.30
❑ 229 Brad Johnson	.20	.50
❑ 230 Andrew Jordan	.07	.20
❑ 231 Randall McDaniel	.07	.20
❑ 232 David Palmer	.07	.20
❑ 233 John Randle	.10	.30
❑ 234 Jake Reed	.10	.30
❑ 235 Scott Sisson	.07	.20
❑ 236 Korey Stringer	.07	.20
❑ 237 Darryl Talley	.07	.20
❑ 238 Orlando Thomas	.07	.20
❑ 239 Bruce Armstrong	.07	.20
❑ 240 Drew Bledsoe	.25	.60
❑ 241 Willie Clay	.07	.20
❑ 242 Ben Coates	.10	.30
❑ 243 Ferric Collons RC	.07	.20
❑ 244 Terry Glenn	.20	.50
❑ 245 Jerome Henderson	.07	.20
❑ 246 Shawn Jefferson	.07	.20
❑ 247 Dietrich Jells	.07	.20
❑ 248 Ty Law	.10	.30
❑ 249 Curtis Martin	.25	.60
❑ 250 Willie McGinest	.07	.20
❑ 251 Dave Meggett	.07	.20
❑ 252 Lawyer Milloy	.10	.30
❑ 253 Chris Slade	.07	.20
❑ 254 Je'rod Cherry	.07	.20
❑ 255 Jim Everett	.07	.20
❑ 256 Mark Fields	.07	.20
❑ 257 Michael Haynes	.07	.20
❑ 258 Tyrone Hughes	.07	.20
❑ 259 Haywood Jeffires	.07	.20
❑ 260 Wayne Martin	.07	.20
❑ 261 Mark McMillian	.07	.20
❑ 262 Rufus Porter	.07	.20
❑ 263 William Roaf	.07	.20
❑ 264 Torrance Small	.07	.20
❑ 265 Renaldo Turnbull	.07	.20
❑ 266 Ray Zellars	.07	.20
❑ 267 Jessie Armstead	.07	.20
❑ 268 Chad Bratzke	.07	.20
❑ 269 Dave Brown	.07	.20
❑ 270 Chris Calloway	.07	.20
❑ 271 Howard Cross	.07	.20
❑ 272 Lawrence Dawsey	.07	.20
❑ 273 Rodney Hampton	.10	.30
❑ 274 Danny Kanell	.07	.20
❑ 275 Arthur Marshall	.07	.20
❑ 276 Aaron Pierce	.07	.20
❑ 277 Phillippi Sparks	.07	.20
❑ 278 Amani Toomer	.10	.30
❑ 279 Charles Way	.07	.20
❑ 280 Richie Anderson	.10	.30
❑ 281 Fred Baxter	.07	.20
❑ 282 Wayne Chrebet	.20	.50
❑ 283 Kyle Clifton	.07	.20
❑ 284 Jumbo Elliott	.07	.20
❑ 285 Aaron Glenn	.07	.20
❑ 286 Jeff Graham	.07	.20
❑ 287 Bobby Hamilton RC	.07	.20
❑ 288 Keyshawn Johnson	.20	.50
❑ 289 Adrian Murrell	.10	.30
❑ 290 Neil O'Donnell	.10	.30
❑ 291 Webster Slaughter	.07	.20
❑ 292 Alex Van Dyke	.07	.20
❑ 293 Marvin Washington	.07	.20
❑ 294 Joe Aska	.07	.20
❑ 295 Jerry Ball	.07	.20
❑ 296 Tim Brown	.20	.50
❑ 297 Rickey Dudley	.10	.30
❑ 298 Pat Harlow	.07	.20
❑ 299 Nolan Harrison	.07	.20
❑ 300 Billy Joe Hobert	.10	.30
❑ 301 James Jett	.10	.30
❑ 302 Napoleon Kaufman	.20	.50
❑ 303 Lincoln Kennedy	.07	.20
❑ 304 Albert Lewis	.07	.20
❑ 305 Chester McGlockton	.07	.20
❑ 306 Pat Swilling	.07	.20
❑ 307 Steve Wisniewski	.07	.20
❑ 308 Darion Conner	.07	.20
❑ 309 Ty Detmer	.10	.30
❑ 310 Jason Dunn	.07	.20
❑ 311 Irving Fryar	.10	.30
❑ 312 James Fuller	.07	.20
❑ 313 William Fuller	.07	.20
❑ 314 Charlie Garner	.10	.30
❑ 315 Bobby Hoying	.10	.30
❑ 316 Tom Hutton	.07	.20
❑ 317 Chris T. Jones	.07	.20
❑ 318 Mike Mamula	.07	.20
❑ 319 Mark Seay	.07	.20
❑ 320 Bobby Taylor	.07	.20
❑ 321 Ricky Watters	.10	.30
❑ 322 Jahine Arnold	.07	.20
❑ 323 Jerome Bettis	.20	.50
❑ 324 Chad Brown	.07	.20
❑ 325 Mark Bruener	.07	.20
❑ 326 Andre Hastings	.07	.20
❑ 327 Norm Johnson	.07	.20
❑ 328 Levon Kirkland	.07	.20
❑ 329 Carnell Lake	.07	.20
❑ 330 Greg Lloyd	.07	.20
❑ 331 Ernie Mills	.07	.20
❑ 332 Orpheus Roye RC	.07	.20
❑ 333 Kordell Stewart	.20	.50
❑ 334 Yancey Thigpen	.10	.30
❑ 335 Mike Tomczak	.07	.20
❑ 336 Rod Woodson	.10	.30
❑ 337 Tony Banks	.10	.30
❑ 338 Bern Brostek	.07	.20
❑ 339 Isaac Bruce	.20	.50
❑ 340 Ernie Conwell	.07	.20
❑ 341 Keith Crawford	.07	.20
❑ 342 Wayne Gandy	.07	.20
❑ 343 Harold Green	.07	.20
❑ 344 Carlos Jenkins	.07	.20
❑ 345 Jimmie Jones	.07	.20
❑ 346 Eddie Kennison	.10	.30
❑ 347 Todd Lyght	.07	.20
❑ 348 Leslie O'Neal	.07	.20
❑ 349 Lawrence Phillips	.07	.20
❑ 350 Greg Robinson	.07	.20
❑ 351 Darren Bennett	.07	.20
❑ 352 Lewis Bush	.07	.20
❑ 353 Eric Castle	.07	.20
❑ 354 Terrell Fletcher	.07	.20
❑ 355 Darrien Gordon	.07	.20
❑ 356 Kurt Gouveia	.07	.20
❑ 357 Aaron Hayden	.07	.20
❑ 358 Stan Humphries	.10	.30
❑ 359 Tony Martin	.10	.30
❑ 360 Vaughn Parker RC	.07	.20
❑ 361 Brian Roche	.07	.20
❑ 362 Leonard Russell	.07	.20
❑ 363 Junior Seau	.20	.50
❑ 364 Roy Barker	.07	.20
❑ 365 Harris Barton	.07	.20
❑ 366 Dexter Carter	.07	.20
❑ 367 Chris Doleman	.07	.20
❑ 368 Tyronne Drakeford	.07	.20
❑ 369 Elvis Grbac	.10	.30
❑ 370 Derek Loville	.07	.20
❑ 371 Tim McDonald	.07	.20
❑ 372 Ken Norton	.07	.20
❑ 373 Terrell Owens	.25	.60
❑ 374 Gary Plummer	.07	.20
❑ 375 Jerry Rice	.40	1.00
❑ 376 Dana Stubblefield	.07	.20
❑ 377 Lee Woodall	.07	.20
❑ 378 Steve Young	.25	.60
❑ 379 Robert Blackmon	.07	.20
❑ 380 Brian Blades	.07	.20
❑ 381 Carlester Crumpler	.07	.20
❑ 382 Christian Fauria	.07	.20
❑ 383 John Friesz	.07	.20
❑ 384 Joey Galloway	.10	.30
❑ 385 Derrick Graham	.07	.20
❑ 386 Cortez Kennedy	.07	.20
❑ 387 Warren Moon	.20	.50
❑ 388 Winston Moss	.07	.20
❑ 389 Mike Pritchard	.07	.20
❑ 390 Michael Sinclair	.07	.20
❑ 391 Lamar Smith	.20	.50
❑ 392 Chris Warren	.10	.30
❑ 393 Chidi Ahanotu	.07	.20
❑ 394 Mike Alstott	.20	.50
❑ 395 Reggie Brooks	.07	.20
❑ 396 Trent Dilfer	.20	.50
❑ 397 Jerry Ellison	.07	.20
❑ 398 Paul Gruber	.07	.20
❑ 399 Alvin Harper	.07	.20
❑ 400 Courtney Hawkins	.07	.20
❑ 401 Dave Moore	.07	.20
❑ 402 Errict Rhett	.07	.20
❑ 403 Warren Sapp	.10	.30
❑ 404 Nilo Silvan	.07	.20
❑ 405 Regan Upshaw	.07	.20
❑ 406 Casey Weldon	.07	.20
❑ 407 Terry Allen	.20	.50
❑ 408 Jamie Asher	.07	.20
❑ 409 Bill Brooks	.07	.20
❑ 410 Tom Carter	.07	.20
❑ 411 Henry Ellard	.07	.20
❑ 412 Gus Frerotte	.07	.20
❑ 413 Darrell Green	.10	.30
❑ 414 Ken Harvey	.07	.20
❑ 415 Tre Johnson	.07	.20
❑ 416 Brian Mitchell	.07	.20
❑ 417 Rich Owens	.07	.20
❑ 418 Heath Shuler	.07	.20
❑ 419 Michael Westbrook	.10	.30
❑ 420 Tony Woods RC	.07	.20
❑ 421 Reidel Anthony RC	.20	.50
❑ 422 Darnell Autry RC	.10	.30
❑ 423 Tiki Barber RC	1.25	3.00
❑ 424 Pat Barnes RC	.20	.50
❑ 425 Terry Battle RC	.07	.20
❑ 426 Will Blackwell RC	.10	.30
❑ 427 Peter Boulware RC	.20	.50
❑ 428 Rae Carruth RC	.07	.20
❑ 429 Troy Davis RC	.10	.30
❑ 430 Jim Druckenmiller RC	.10	.30
❑ 431 Warrick Dunn RC	.60	1.50
❑ 432 Marc Edwards RC	.07	.20
❑ 433 James Farrior RC	.20	.50
❑ 434 Yatil Green RC	.10	.30
❑ 435 Byron Hanspard RC	.10	.30
❑ 436 Ike Hilliard RC	.30	.75
❑ 437 David LaFleur RC	.07	.20
❑ 438 Kevin Lockett RC	.10	.30
❑ 439 Sam Madison RC	.20	.50
❑ 440 Brian Manning RC	.10	.30
❑ 441 Orlando Pace RC	.20	.50
❑ 442 Jake Plummer RC	1.00	2.50
❑ 443 Chad Scott RC	.10	.30
❑ 444 Sedrick Shaw RC	.10	.30
❑ 445 Antowain Smith RC	.50	1.25
❑ 446 Shawn Springs RC	.10	.30
❑ 447 Ross Verba RC	.07	.20
❑ 448 Bryant Westbrook RC	.07	.20
❑ 449 Renaldo Wynn RC	.07	.20
❑ 450 Jimmy Johnson CO	.10	.30
❑ S1 Mark Brunell Sample	.40	1.00

1998 Pacific

Card		
❑ COMPLETE SET (450)	25.00	60.00
❑ 1 Mario Bates	.15	.40

Card		
❑ 2 Lomas Brown	.08	.25
❑ 3 Larry Centers	.08	.25
❑ 4 Chris Gedney	.08	.25
❑ 5 Terry Irving	.08	.25
❑ 6 Tom Knight	.08	.25
❑ 7 Eric Metcalf	.08	.25
❑ 8 Jamir Miller	.08	.25
❑ 9 Rob Moore	.15	.40
❑ 10 Joe Nedney	.08	.25
❑ 11 Jake Plummer	.25	.60
❑ 12 Simeon Rice	.15	.40
❑ 13 Frank Sanders	.15	.40
❑ 14 Eric Swann	.08	.25
❑ 15 Aeneas Williams	.08	.25
❑ 16 Morten Andersen	.08	.25
❑ 17 Jamal Anderson	.25	.60
❑ 18 Michael Booker	.08	.25
❑ 19 Keith Brooking RC	.60	1.50
❑ 20 Ray Buchanan	.08	.25
❑ 21 Devin Bush	.08	.25
❑ 22 Chris Chandler	.15	.40
❑ 23 Tony Graziani	.08	.25
❑ 24 Harold Green	.08	.25
❑ 25 Byron Hanspard	.08	.25
❑ 26 Todd Kinchen	.08	.25
❑ 27 Tony Martin	.15	.40
❑ 28 Terance Mathis	.15	.40
❑ 29 Eugene Robinson	.08	.25
❑ 30 O.J. Santiago	.08	.25
❑ 31 Chuck Smith	.08	.25
❑ 32 Jessie Tuggle	.08	.25
❑ 33 Bob Whitfield	.08	.25
❑ 34 Peter Boulware	.08	.25
❑ 35 Jay Graham	.08	.25
❑ 36 Eric Green	.08	.25
❑ 37 Jim Harbaugh	.15	.40
❑ 38 Michael Jackson	.08	.25
❑ 39 Jermaine Lewis	.15	.40
❑ 40 Ray Lewis	.25	.60
❑ 41 Michael McCrary	.08	.25
❑ 42 Stevon Moore	.08	.25
❑ 43 Jonathan Ogden	.08	.25
❑ 44 Errict Rhett	.15	.40
❑ 45 Matt Stover	.08	.25
❑ 46 Rod Woodson	.15	.40
❑ 47 Eric Zeier	.15	.40
❑ 48 Ruben Brown	.08	.25
❑ 49 Steve Christie	.08	.25
❑ 50 Quinn Early	.08	.25
❑ 51 John Fina	.08	.25
❑ 52 Doug Flutie	.25	.60
❑ 53 Phil Hansen	.08	.25
❑ 54 Lonnie Johnson	.08	.25
❑ 55 Rob Johnson	.15	.40
❑ 56 Henry Jones	.08	.25
❑ 57 Eric Moulds	.25	.60
❑ 58 Andre Reed	.15	.40
❑ 59 Antowain Smith	.25	.60
❑ 60 Bruce Smith	.15	.40
❑ 61 Thurman Thomas	.25	.60
❑ 62 Ted Washington	.08	.25
❑ 63 Michael Bates	.08	.25
❑ 64 Tim Biakabutuka	.15	.40
❑ 65 Blake Brockermeyer	.08	.25
❑ 66 Mark Carrier	.08	.25
❑ 67 Rae Carruth	.08	.25
❑ 68 Kerry Collins	.15	.40
❑ 69 Doug Evans	.08	.25
❑ 70 William Floyd	.08	.25
❑ 71 Sean Gilbert	.08	.25
❑ 72 Rocket Ismail	.08	.25
❑ 73 John Kasay	.08	.25
❑ 74 Fred Lane	.08	.25
❑ 75 Lamar Lathon	.08	.25
❑ 76 Muhsin Muhammad	.15	.40
❑ 77 Wesley Walls	.15	.40
❑ 78 Edgar Bennett	.08	.25
❑ 79 Tom Carter	.08	.25
❑ 80 Curtis Conway	.15	.40
❑ 81 Bobby Engram	.15	.40
❑ 82 Curtis Enis RC	.30	.75
❑ 83 Jim Flanigan	.08	.25
❑ 84 Walt Harris	.08	.25
❑ 85 Jeff Jaeger	.08	.25
❑ 86 Erik Kramer	.08	.25
❑ 87 John Mangum	.08	.25
❑ 88 Glyn Milburn	.08	.25
❑ 89 Barry Minter	.08	.25
❑ 90 Chris Penn	.08	.25
❑ 91 Todd Sauerbrun	.08	.25
❑ 92 James Williams	.08	.25
❑ 93 Ashley Ambrose	.08	.25
❑ 94 Willie Anderson	.08	.25
❑ 95 Eric Bieniemy	.08	.25
❑ 96 Jeff Blake	.15	.40
❑ 97 Ki-Jana Carter	.08	.25
❑ 98 John Copeland	.08	.25
❑ 99 Corey Dillon	.25	.60
❑ 100 Tony McGee	.08	.25
❑ 101 Neil O'Donnell	.15	.40
❑ 102 Carl Pickens	.15	.40
❑ 103 Kevin Sargent	.08	.25
❑ 104 Darnay Scott	.15	.40
❑ 105 Takeo Spikes RC	.60	1.50
❑ 106 Troy Aikman	.50	1.25
❑ 107 Larry Allen	.08	.25
❑ 108 Eric Bjornson	.08	.25
❑ 109 Billy Davis	.08	.25
❑ 110 Jason Garrett RC	.50	1.25
❑ 111 Michael Irvin	.25	.60
❑ 112 Daryl Johnston	.15	.40
❑ 113 David LaFleur	.08	.25
❑ 114 Everett McIver	.08	.25
❑ 115 Ernie Mills	.08	.25
❑ 116 Nate Newton	.08	.25
❑ 117 Deion Sanders	.25	.60
❑ 118 Emmitt Smith	.75	2.00
❑ 119 Kevin Smith	.08	.25
❑ 120 Erik Williams	.08	.25
❑ 121 Steve Atwater	.08	.25
❑ 122 Tyrone Braxton	.08	.25
❑ 123 Ray Crockett	.08	.25
❑ 124 Terrell Davis	.25	.60
❑ 125 Jason Elam	.08	.25
❑ 126 John Elway	1.00	2.50
❑ 127 Willie Green	.08	.25
❑ 128 Brian Griese RC	1.25	3.00
❑ 129 Tony Jones	.08	.25
❑ 130 Ed McCaffrey	.15	.40
❑ 131 John Mobley	.08	.25
❑ 132 Tom Nalen	.08	.25
❑ 133 Marcus Nash RC	.30	.75
❑ 134 Bill Romanowski	.08	.25
❑ 135 Shannon Sharpe	.15	.40
❑ 136 Neil Smith	.15	.40
❑ 137 Rod Smith	.15	.40
❑ 138 Keith Traylor	.08	.25
❑ 139 Stephen Boyd	.08	.25
❑ 140 Mark Carrier DB	.08	.25
❑ 141 Charlie Batch RC	.60	1.50
❑ 142 Jason Hanson	.08	.25
❑ 143 Scott Mitchell	.15	.40
❑ 144 Herman Moore	.15	.40
❑ 145 Johnnie Morton	.15	.40
❑ 146 Robert Porcher	.08	.25
❑ 147 Ron Rivers	.08	.25
❑ 148 Barry Sanders	.75	2.00
❑ 149 Tracy Scroggins	.08	.25
❑ 150 David Sloan	.08	.25
❑ 151 Tommy Vardell	.08	.25
❑ 152 Kerwin Waldroup	.08	.25
❑ 153 Bryant Westbrook	.08	.25
❑ 154 Robert Brooks	.15	.40
❑ 155 Gilbert Brown	.08	.25
❑ 156 LeRoy Butler	.08	.25
❑ 157 Mark Chmura	.15	.40
❑ 158 Earl Dotson	.08	.25
❑ 159 Santana Dotson	.08	.25
❑ 160 Brett Favre	1.00	2.50
❑ 161 Antonio Freeman	.25	.60
❑ 162 Raymont Harris	.08	.25
❑ 163 William Henderson	.15	.40
❑ 164 Vonnie Holliday RC	.50	1.25
❑ 165 George Koonce	.08	.25
❑ 166 Dorsey Levens	.25	.60
❑ 167 Derrick Mayes	.15	.40
❑ 168 Craig Newsome	.08	.25
❑ 169 Ross Verba	.08	.25
❑ 170 Reggie White	.25	.60
❑ 171 Elijah Alexander	.08	.25
❑ 172 Aaron Bailey	.08	.25
❑ 173 Jason Belser	.08	.25
❑ 174 Robert Blackmon	.08	.25
❑ 175 Zack Crockett	.08	.25
❑ 176 Ken Dilger	.08	.25
❑ 177 Marshall Faulk	.30	.75
❑ 178 Tarik Glenn	.08	.25
❑ 179 Marvin Harrison	.25	.60
❑ 180 Tony Mandarich	.08	.25
❑ 181 Peyton Manning RC	7.50	15.00
❑ 182 Marcus Pollard	.08	.25
❑ 183 Lamont Warren	.08	.25
❑ 184 Tavian Banks RC	.50	1.25
❑ 185 Reggie Barlow	.08	.25
❑ 186 Tony Boselli	.08	.25
❑ 187 Tony Brackens	.08	.25
❑ 188 Mark Brunell	.25	.60
❑ 189 Kevin Hardy	.08	.25
❑ 190 Mike Hollis	.08	.25
❑ 191 Jeff Lageman	.08	.25
❑ 192 Keenan McCardell	.15	.40
❑ 193 Pete Mitchell	.08	.25
❑ 194 Bryce Paup	.08	.25
❑ 195 Leon Searcy	.08	.25
❑ 196 Jimmy Smith	.15	.40
❑ 197 James Stewart	.15	.40
❑ 198 Fred Taylor RC	1.00	2.50
❑ 199 Renaldo Wynn	.08	.25
❑ 200 Derrick Alexander WR	.15	.40
❑ 201 Kimble Anders	.15	.40
❑ 202 Donnell Bennett	.08	.25
❑ 203 Dale Carter	.08	.25
❑ 204 Anthony Davis	.08	.25
❑ 205 Rich Gannon	.25	.60
❑ 206 Tony Gonzalez	.25	.60
❑ 207 Elvis Grbac	.15	.40
❑ 208 James Hasty	.08	.25
❑ 209 Leslie O'Neal	.08	.25
❑ 210 Andre Rison	.15	.40
❑ 211 Rashaan Shehee RC	.50	1.25
❑ 212 Will Shields	.08	.25
❑ 213 Pete Stoyanovich	.08	.25
❑ 214 Derrick Thomas	.25	.60
❑ 215 Tamarick Vanover	.08	.25
❑ 216 Karim Abdul-Jabbar	.25	.60
❑ 217 Trace Armstrong	.08	.25
❑ 218 John Avery RC	.50	1.25
❑ 219 Tim Bowens	.08	.25
❑ 220 Terrell Buckley	.08	.25
❑ 221 Troy Drayton	.08	.25
❑ 222 Daryl Gardener	.08	.25
❑ 223 Damon Huard RC	1.25	3.00
❑ 224 Charles Jordan	.08	.25
❑ 225 Dan Marino	1.00	2.50
❑ 226 O.J. McDuffie	.15	.40
❑ 227 Bernie Parmalee	.08	.25
❑ 228 Stanley Pritchett	.08	.25
❑ 229 Derrick Rodgers	.08	.25
❑ 230 Lamar Thomas	.08	.25
❑ 231 Zach Thomas	.25	.60
❑ 232 Richmond Webb	.08	.25
❑ 233 Derrick Alexander DE	.08	.25
❑ 234 Jerry Ball	.08	.25
❑ 235 Cris Carter	.25	.60
❑ 236 Randall Cunningham	.25	.60
❑ 237 Charles Evans	.08	.25
❑ 238 Corey Fuller	.08	.25
❑ 239 Andrew Glover	.08	.25
❑ 240 Leroy Hoard	.08	.25
❑ 241 Brad Johnson	.25	.60
❑ 242 Ed McDaniel	.08	.25
❑ 243 Randall McDaniel	.08	.25
❑ 244 Randy Moss RC	4.00	10.00
❑ 245 John Randle	.15	.40
❑ 246 Jake Reed	.15	.40
❑ 247 Dwayne Rudd	.08	.25
❑ 248 Robert Smith	.25	.60
❑ 249 Bruce Armstrong	.08	.25
❑ 250 Drew Bledsoe	.40	1.00
❑ 251 Vincent Brisby	.08	.25
❑ 252 Tedy Bruschi	.50	1.25
❑ 253 Ben Coates	.15	.40
❑ 254 Derrick Cullors	.08	.25
❑ 255 Terry Glenn	.25	.60
❑ 256 Shawn Jefferson	.08	.25
❑ 257 Ted Johnson	.08	.25
❑ 258 Ty Law	.15	.40
❑ 259 Willie McGinest	.08	.25
❑ 260 Lawyer Milloy	.15	.40
❑ 261 Sedrick Shaw	.08	.25
❑ 262 Chris Slade	.08	.25
❑ 263 Troy Davis	.08	.25
❑ 264 Mark Fields	.08	.25
❑ 265 Andre Hastings	.08	.25
❑ 266 Billy Joe Hobert	.08	.25
❑ 267 Qadry Ismail	.15	.40
❑ 268 Tony Johnson	.08	.25

❑ 269 Sammy Knight RC .25 .60
❑ 270 Wayne Martin .08 .25
❑ 271 Chris Naeole .08 .25
❑ 272 Keith Poole .08 .25
❑ 273 William Roaf .08 .25
❑ 274 Pio Sagapolutele .08 .25
❑ 275 Danny Wuerffel .15 .40
❑ 276 Ray Zellars .08 .25
❑ 277 Jessie Armstead .08 .25
❑ 278 Tiki Barber .25 .60
❑ 279 Chris Calloway .08 .25
❑ 280 Percy Ellsworth .08 .25
❑ 281 Sam Garnes RC .30 .75
❑ 282 Kent Graham .08 .25
❑ 283 Ike Hilliard .15 .40
❑ 284 Danny Kanell .15 .40
❑ 285 Corey Miller .08 .25
❑ 286 Phillippi Sparks .08 .25
❑ 287 Michael Strahan .15 .40
❑ 288 Amani Toomer .15 .40
❑ 289 Charles Way .08 .25
❑ 290 Tyrone Wheatley .15 .40
❑ 291 Tito Wooten .08 .25
❑ 292 Kyle Brady .08 .25
❑ 293 Keith Byars .08 .25
❑ 294 Wayne Chrebet .25 .60
❑ 295 John Elliott .08 .25
❑ 296 Glenn Foley .15 .40
❑ 297 Aaron Glenn .08 .25
❑ 298 Keyshawn Johnson .25 .60
❑ 299 Curtis Martin .25 .60
❑ 300 Otis Smith .08 .25
❑ 301 Vinny Testaverde .15 .40
❑ 302 Alex Van Dyke .08 .25
❑ 303 Dedric Ward .08 .25
❑ 304 Greg Biekert .08 .25
❑ 305 Tim Brown .25 .60
❑ 306 Rickey Dudley .08 .25
❑ 307 Jeff George .15 .40
❑ 308 Pat Harlow .08 .25
❑ 309 Desmond Howard .15 .40
❑ 310 James Jett .15 .40
❑ 311 Napoleon Kaufman .25 .60
❑ 312 Lincoln Kennedy .08 .25
❑ 313 Russell Maryland .08 .25
❑ 314 Darrell Russell .08 .25
❑ 315 Eric Turner .08 .25
❑ 316 Steve Wisniewski .08 .25
❑ 317 Charles Woodson RC .75 2.00
❑ 318 James Darling RC .30 .75
❑ 319 Jason Dunn .08 .25
❑ 320 Irving Fryar .15 .40
❑ 321 Charlie Garner .15 .40
❑ 322 Jeff Graham .08 .25
❑ 323 Bobby Hoying .15 .40
❑ 324 Chad Lewis .15 .40
❑ 325 Rodney Peete .08 .25
❑ 326 Freddie Solomon .08 .25
❑ 327 Duce Staley .30 .75
❑ 328 Bobby Taylor .08 .25
❑ 329 William Thomas .08 .25
❑ 330 Kevin Turner .08 .25
❑ 331 Troy Vincent .08 .25
❑ 332 Jerome Bettis .25 .60
❑ 333 Will Blackwell .08 .25
❑ 334 Mark Bruener .08 .25
❑ 335 Andre Coleman .08 .25
❑ 336 Dermontti Dawson .08 .25
❑ 337 Jason Gildon .08 .25
❑ 338 Courtney Hawkins .08 .25
❑ 339 Charles Johnson .08 .25
❑ 340 Levon Kirkland .08 .25
❑ 341 Carnell Lake .08 .25
❑ 342 Tim Lester .08 .25
❑ 343 Joel Steed .08 .25
❑ 344 Kordell Stewart .25 .60
❑ 345 Will Wolford .08 .25
❑ 346 Tony Banks .15 .40
❑ 347 Isaac Bruce .25 .60
❑ 348 Ernie Conwell .08 .25
❑ 349 D'Marco Farr .08 .25
❑ 350 Wayne Gandy .08 .25
❑ 351 Jerome Pathon RC .60 1.50
❑ 352 Eddie Kennison .15 .40
❑ 353 Amp Lee .08 .25
❑ 354 Keith Lyle .08 .25
❑ 355 Ryan McNeil .08 .25
❑ 356 Jerald Moore .08 .25
❑ 357 Orlando Pace .08 .25
❑ 358 Roman Phifer .08 .25
❑ 359 David Thompson RC .30 .75
❑ 360 Darren Bennett .08 .25
❑ 361 John Carney .08 .25
❑ 362 Marco Coleman .08 .25
❑ 363 Terrell Fletcher .08 .25
❑ 364 William Fuller .08 .25
❑ 365 Charlie Jones .08 .25
❑ 366 Freddie Jones .08 .25
❑ 367 Ryan Leaf RC .60 1.50
❑ 368 Natrone Means .15 .40
❑ 369 Junior Seau .25 .60
❑ 370 Terrance Shaw .08 .25
❑ 371 Tremayne Stephens RC .30 .75
❑ 372 Bryan Still .08 .25
❑ 373 Aaron Taylor .08 .25
❑ 374 Greg Clark .08 .25
❑ 375 Ty Detmer .15 .40
❑ 376 Jim Druckenmiller .08 .25
❑ 377 Marc Edwards .08 .25
❑ 378 Merton Hanks .08 .25
❑ 379 Garrison Hearst .25 .60
❑ 380 Chuck Levy .08 .25
❑ 381 Ken Norton .08 .25
❑ 382 Terrell Owens .25 .60
❑ 383 Marquez Pope .08 .25
❑ 384 Jerry Rice .50 1.25
❑ 385 Irv Smith .08 .25
❑ 386 J.J. Stokes .15 .40
❑ 387 Iheanyi Uwaezuoke .08 .25
❑ 388 Bryant Young .08 .25
❑ 389 Steve Young .30 .75
❑ 390 Sam Adams .08 .25
❑ 391 Chad Brown .08 .25
❑ 392 Christian Fauria .08 .25
❑ 393 Joey Galloway .15 .40
❑ 394 Ahman Green RC 1.50 4.00
❑ 395 Walter Jones .08 .25
❑ 396 Cortez Kennedy .08 .25
❑ 397 Jon Kitna .25 .60
❑ 398 James McKnight .25 .60
❑ 399 Warren Moon .25 .60
❑ 400 Mike Pritchard .08 .25
❑ 401 Michael Sinclair .08 .25
❑ 402 Shawn Springs .08 .25
❑ 403 Ricky Watters .15 .40
❑ 404 Darryl Williams .08 .25
❑ 405 Mike Alstott .25 .60
❑ 406 Reidel Anthony .15 .40
❑ 407 Derrick Brooks .25 .60
❑ 408 Brad Culpepper .08 .25
❑ 409 Trent Dilfer .25 .60
❑ 410 Warrick Dunn .25 .60
❑ 411 Bert Emanuel .15 .40
❑ 412 Jacquez Green RC .50 1.25
❑ 413 Paul Gruber .08 .25
❑ 414 Patrick Hape RC .50 1.25
❑ 415 Dave Moore .08 .25
❑ 416 Hardy Nickerson .08 .25
❑ 417 Warren Sapp .15 .40
❑ 418 Robb Thomas .08 .25
❑ 419 Regan Upshaw .08 .25
❑ 420 Karl Williams .08 .25
❑ 421 Blaine Bishop .08 .25
❑ 422 Anthony Cook .08 .25
❑ 423 Willie Davis .08 .25
❑ 424 Al Del Greco .08 .25
❑ 425 Kevin Dyson .25 .60
❑ 426 Henry Ford .08 .25
❑ 427 Eddie George .25 .60
❑ 428 Jackie Harris .08 .25
❑ 429 Steve McNair .25 .60
❑ 430 Chris Sanders .08 .25
❑ 431 Mark Stepnoski .08 .25
❑ 432 Yancey Thigpen .08 .25
❑ 433 Barron Wortham .08 .25
❑ 434 Frank Wycheck .08 .25
❑ 435 Stephen Alexander RC .50 1.25
❑ 436 Terry Allen .25 .60
❑ 437 Jamie Asher .08 .25
❑ 438 Bob Dahl .08 .25
❑ 439 Stephen Davis .08 .25
❑ 440 Cris Dishman .08 .25
❑ 441 Gus Frerotte .08 .25
❑ 442 Darrell Green .15 .40
❑ 443 Trent Green .30 .75
❑ 444 Ken Harvey .08 .25
❑ 445 Skip Hicks RC .50 1.25
❑ 446 Jeff Hostetler .08 .25
❑ 447 Brian Mitchell .08 .25
❑ 448 Leslie Shepherd .08 .25
❑ 449 Michael Westbrook .15 .40
❑ 450 Dan Wilkinson .08 .25
❑ S1 Warrick Dunn Sample .40 1.00

1999 Pacific

❑ COMPLETE SET (450) 30.00 80.00
❑ 1 Mario Bates .08 .25
❑ 2 Larry Centers .08 .25
❑ 3 Chris Gedney .08 .25
❑ 4 Kwamie Lassiter RC .25 .60
❑ 5 Johnny McWilliams .08 .25
❑ 6 Eric Metcalf .08 .25
❑ 7 Rob Moore .15 .40
❑ 8 Adrian Murrell .15 .40
❑ 9 Jake Plummer .15 .40
❑ 10 Simeon Rice .15 .40
❑ 11 Frank Sanders .15 .40
❑ 12 Andre Wadsworth .08 .25
❑ 13 Aeneas Williams .08 .25
❑ 14 M.Pittman/R.Anderson RC .50 1.25
❑ 15 Morten Andersen .08 .25
❑ 16 Jamal Anderson .25 .60
❑ 17 Lester Archambeau .08 .25
❑ 18 Chris Chandler .15 .40
❑ 19 Bob Christian .08 .25
❑ 20 Steve DeBerg .08 .25
❑ 21 Tim Dwight .25 .60
❑ 22 Tony Martin .15 .40
❑ 23 Terance Mathis .15 .40
❑ 24 Eugene Robinson .08 .25
❑ 25 O.J. Santiago .08 .25
❑ 26 Chuck Smith .08 .25
❑ 27 Jessie Tuggle .08 .25
❑ 28 Jammi German/Ken Oxendine .08 .25
❑ 29 Peter Boulware .08 .25
❑ 30 Jay Graham .08 .25
❑ 31 Jim Harbaugh .15 .40
❑ 32 Priest Holmes .40 1.00
❑ 33 Michael Jackson .08 .25
❑ 34 Jermaine Lewis .15 .40
❑ 35 Ray Lewis .25 .60
❑ 36 Michael McCrary .08 .25
❑ 37 Jonathan Ogden .08 .25
❑ 38 Errict Rhett .08 .25
❑ 39 James Roe RC .40 1.00
❑ 40 Floyd Turner .08 .25
❑ 41 Rod Woodson .15 .40
❑ 42 Eric Zeier .08 .25
❑ 43 W.Richardson/P.Johnson .08 .25
❑ 44 Ruben Brown .08 .25
❑ 45 Quinn Early .08 .25
❑ 46 Doug Flutie .25 .60
❑ 47 Sam Gash .08 .25
❑ 48 Phil Hansen .08 .25
❑ 49 Lonnie Johnson .08 .25
❑ 50 Rob Johnson .15 .40
❑ 51 Eric Moulds .25 .60
❑ 52 Andre Reed .15 .40
❑ 53 Jay Riemersma .08 .25
❑ 54 Antowain Smith .25 .60
❑ 55 Bruce Smith .15 .40
❑ 56 Thurman Thomas .15 .40
❑ 57 Ted Washington .08 .25
❑ 58 J.Linton/Kamil Loud RC .40 1.00
❑ 59 Michael Bates .08 .25
❑ 60 Steve Beuerlein .08 .25
❑ 61 Tim Biakabutuka .15 .40
❑ 62 Mark Carrier WR .08 .25
❑ 63 Eric Davis .08 .25
❑ 64 William Floyd .08 .25
❑ 65 Sean Gilbert .08 .25
❑ 66 Kevin Greene .08 .25
❑ 67 Rocket Ismail .15 .40
❑ 68 Anthony Johnson .08 .25

Card		
❑ 69 Fred Lane	.08	.25
❑ 70 Muhsin Muhammad	.15	.40
❑ 71 Winslow Oliver	.08	.25
❑ 72 Wesley Walls	.15	.40
❑ 73 D.Craig RC/S.Matthews	.60	1.50
❑ 74 Edgar Bennett	.08	.25
❑ 75 Curtis Conway	.15	.40
❑ 76 Bobby Engram	.15	.40
❑ 77 Curtis Enis	.08	.25
❑ 78 Ty Hallock RC	.40	1.00
❑ 79 Walt Harris	.08	.25
❑ 80 Jeff Jaeger	.08	.25
❑ 81 Erik Kramer	.08	.25
❑ 82 Glyn Milburn	.08	.25
❑ 83 Chris Penn	.08	.25
❑ 84 Steve Stenstrom	.08	.25
❑ 85 Ryan Wetnight	.08	.25
❑ 86 James Allen RC/Moreno	.60	1.50
❑ 87 Ashley Ambrose	.08	.25
❑ 88 Brandon Bennett RC	.40	1.00
❑ 89 Eric Bieniemy	.08	.25
❑ 90 Jeff Blake	.15	.40
❑ 91 Corey Dillon	.25	.60
❑ 92 Paul Justin	.08	.25
❑ 93 Eric Kresser RC	.40	1.00
❑ 94 Tremain Mack	.08	.25
❑ 95 Tony McGee	.08	.25
❑ 96 Neil O'Donnell	.15	.40
❑ 97 Carl Pickens	.15	.40
❑ 98 Darnay Scott	.08	.25
❑ 99 Takeo Spikes	.08	.25
❑ 100 Ty Detmer	.08	.25
❑ 101 Chris Gardocki	.08	.25
❑ 102 Damon Gibson	.08	.25
❑ 103 Antonio Langham	.08	.25
❑ 104 Jerris McPhail	.08	.25
❑ 105 Irv Smith	.08	.25
❑ 106 Freddie Solomon	.08	.25
❑ 107 S.Milanovich/Fred Brock RC	.40	1.00
❑ 108 Troy Aikman	.50	1.25
❑ 109 Larry Allen	.08	.25
❑ 110 Eric Bjornson	.08	.25
❑ 111 Billy Davis	.08	.25
❑ 112 Michael Irvin	.15	.40
❑ 113 David LaFleur	.08	.25
❑ 114 Ernie Mills	.08	.25
❑ 115 Nate Newton	.08	.25
❑ 116 Deion Sanders	.25	.60
❑ 117 Emmitt Smith	.50	1.25
❑ 118 Chris Warren	.08	.25
❑ 119 Bubby Brister	.15	.40
❑ 120 Terrell Davis	.25	.60
❑ 121 Jason Elam	.08	.25
❑ 122 John Elway	.75	2.00
❑ 123 Willie Green	.08	.25
❑ 124 Howard Griffith	.08	.25
❑ 125 Vaughn Hebron	.08	.25
❑ 126 Ed McCaffrey	.15	.40
❑ 127 John Mobley	.08	.25
❑ 128 Bill Romanowski	.08	.25
❑ 129 Shannon Sharpe	.15	.40
❑ 130 Neil Smith	.15	.40
❑ 131 Rod Smith	.15	.40
❑ 132 Brian Griese/M.Nash	.25	.60
❑ 133 Charlie Batch	.25	.60
❑ 134 Stephen Boyd	.08	.25
❑ 135 Mark Carrier DB	.08	.25
❑ 136 Germane Crowell	.08	.25
❑ 137 Terry Fair	.08	.25
❑ 138 Jason Hanson	.08	.25
❑ 139 Greg Jeffries RC	.40	1.00
❑ 140 Herman Moore	.15	.40
❑ 141 Johnnie Morton	.15	.40
❑ 142 Robert Porcher	.08	.25
❑ 143 Ron Rivers	.08	.25
❑ 144 Barry Sanders	.75	2.00
❑ 145 Tommy Vardell	.08	.25
❑ 146 Bryant Westbrook	.08	.25
❑ 147 Robert Brooks	.15	.40
❑ 148 LeRoy Butler	.08	.25
❑ 149 Mark Chmura	.08	.25
❑ 150 Tyrone Davis	.08	.25
❑ 151 Brett Favre	.75	2.00
❑ 152 Antonio Freeman	.25	.60
❑ 153 Raymont Harris	.08	.25
❑ 154 Vonnie Holliday	.08	.25
❑ 155 Darick Holmes	.08	.25
❑ 156 Dorsey Levens	.25	.60
❑ 157 Brian Manning	.08	.25
❑ 158 Derrick Mayes	.08	.25
❑ 159 Roell Preston	.08	.25
❑ 160 Jeff Thomason	.08	.25
❑ 161 Tyrone Williams	.08	.25
❑ 162 C.Bradford/Michael Blair RC	.60	1.50
❑ 163 Aaron Bailey	.08	.25
❑ 164 Ken Dilger	.08	.25
❑ 165 Marshall Faulk	.30	.75
❑ 166 E.G. Green	.08	.25
❑ 167 Marvin Harrison	.25	.60
❑ 168 Craig Heyward	.08	.25
❑ 169 Peyton Manning	.75	2.00
❑ 170 Jerome Pathon	.15	.40
❑ 171 Marcus Pollard	.08	.25
❑ 172 Torrance Small	.08	.25
❑ 173 Mike Vanderjagt	.08	.25
❑ 174 Lamont Warren	.08	.25
❑ 175 Tavian Banks	.08	.25
❑ 176 Reggie Barlow	.08	.25
❑ 177 Tony Boselli	.08	.25
❑ 178 Tony Brackens	.08	.25
❑ 179 Mark Brunell	.25	.60
❑ 180 Kevin Hardy	.08	.25
❑ 181 Damon Jones	.08	.25
❑ 182 Jamie Martin	.25	.60
❑ 183 Keenan McCardell	.15	.40
❑ 184 Pete Mitchell	.08	.25
❑ 185 Bryce Paup	.08	.25
❑ 186 Jimmy Smith	.15	.40
❑ 187 Fred Taylor	.25	.60
❑ 188 Alvis Whitted/Chris Howard	.08	.25
❑ 189 Derrick Alexander WR	.15	.40
❑ 190 Kimble Anders	.15	.40
❑ 191 Donnell Bennett	.08	.25
❑ 192 Dale Carter	.08	.25
❑ 193 Rich Gannon	.25	.60
❑ 194 Tony Gonzalez	.25	.60
❑ 195 Elvis Grbac	.15	.40
❑ 196 Joe Horn	.15	.40
❑ 197 Kevin Lockett	.08	.25
❑ 198 Byron Bam Morris	.08	.25
❑ 199 Andre Rison	.15	.40
❑ 200 Derrick Thomas	.25	.60
❑ 201 Tamarick Vanover	.08	.25
❑ 202 G.Favors/R.Shehee	.08	.25
❑ 203 Karim Abdul-Jabbar	.15	.40
❑ 204 Trace Armstrong	.08	.25
❑ 205 John Avery	.08	.25
❑ 206 Lorenzo Bromell RC	.25	.60
❑ 207 Terrell Buckley	.08	.25
❑ 208 Oronde Gadsden	.15	.40
❑ 209 Sam Madison	.08	.25
❑ 210 Dan Marino	.75	2.00
❑ 211 O.J. McDuffie	.15	.40
❑ 212 Ed Perry RC	.25	.60
❑ 213 Jason Taylor	.08	.25
❑ 214 Lamar Thomas	.08	.25
❑ 215 Zach Thomas	.25	.60
❑ 216 H.Lusk/Nate Jacquet RC	.40	1.00
❑ 217 T.Doxzon RC/D.Huard	.60	1.50
❑ 218 Gary Anderson	.08	.25
❑ 219 Cris Carter	.25	.60
❑ 220 Randall Cunningham	.25	.60
❑ 221 Andrew Glover	.08	.25
❑ 222 Matthew Hatchette	.08	.25
❑ 223 Brad Johnson	.25	.60
❑ 224 Ed McDaniel	.08	.25
❑ 225 Randall McDaniel	.08	.25
❑ 226 Randy Moss	.60	1.50
❑ 227 David Palmer	.08	.25
❑ 228 John Randle	.15	.40
❑ 229 Jake Reed	.15	.40
❑ 230 Robert Smith	.25	.60
❑ 231 Todd Steussie	.08	.25
❑ 232 S.Colinet RC/K.Mays	.08	.25
❑ 233 J.Fiedler RC/T.Bouman RC	1.50	4.00
❑ 234 Drew Bledsoe	.30	.75
❑ 235 Troy Brown	.15	.40
❑ 236 Ben Coates	.15	.40
❑ 237 Derrick Cullors	.08	.25
❑ 238 Robert Edwards	.08	.25
❑ 239 Terry Glenn	.25	.60
❑ 240 Shawn Jefferson	.08	.25
❑ 241 Ty Law	.15	.40
❑ 242 Lawyer Milloy	.15	.40
❑ 243 Lovett Purnell RC	.40	1.00
❑ 244 Sedrick Shaw	.08	.25
❑ 245 Tony Simmons	.08	.25
❑ 246 Chris Slade	.08	.25
❑ 247 R.Rutledge/Anth.Ladd RC	.40	1.00
❑ 248 Chris Floyd/Harold Shaw	.08	.25
❑ 249 Ink Aleaga RC	.40	1.00
❑ 250 Cameron Cleeland	.08	.25
❑ 251 Kerry Collins	.15	.40
❑ 252 Troy Davis	.08	.25
❑ 253 Sean Dawkins	.08	.25
❑ 254 Mark Fields	.08	.25
❑ 255 Andre Hastings	.08	.25
❑ 256 Sammy Knight	.08	.25
❑ 257 Keith Poole	.08	.25
❑ 258 William Roaf	.08	.25
❑ 259 Lamar Smith	.15	.40
❑ 260 Danny Wuerffel	.08	.25
❑ 261 J.Wilcox RC/B.Bech RC	.40	1.00
❑ 262 Chris Bordano RC/W.Perry	.40	1.00
❑ 263 Jessie Armstead	.08	.25
❑ 264 Tiki Barber	.25	.60
❑ 265 Chad Bratzke	.08	.25
❑ 266 Gary Brown	.08	.25
❑ 267 Chris Calloway	.08	.25
❑ 268 Howard Cross	.08	.25
❑ 269 Kent Graham	.08	.25
❑ 270 Ike Hilliard	.08	.25
❑ 271 Danny Kanell	.15	.40
❑ 272 Michael Strahan	.15	.40
❑ 273 Amani Toomer	.08	.25
❑ 274 Charles Way	.08	.25
❑ 275 Greg Comella RC/M.Cherry	.60	1.50
❑ 276 Kyle Brady	.08	.25
❑ 277 Keith Byars	.08	.25
❑ 278 Chad Cascadden	.08	.25
❑ 279 Wayne Chrebet	.15	.40
❑ 280 Bryan Cox	.08	.25
❑ 281 Glenn Foley	.15	.40
❑ 282 Aaron Glenn	.08	.25
❑ 283 Keyshawn Johnson	.25	.60
❑ 284 Leon Johnson	.08	.25
❑ 285 Mo Lewis	.08	.25
❑ 286 Curtis Martin	.25	.60
❑ 287 Otis Smith	.08	.25
❑ 288 Vinny Testaverde	.15	.40
❑ 289 Dedric Ward	.08	.25
❑ 290 Tim Brown	.25	.60
❑ 291 Rickey Dudley	.08	.25
❑ 292 Jeff George	.15	.40
❑ 293 Desmond Howard	.15	.40
❑ 294 James Jett	.15	.40
❑ 295 Lance Johnstone	.08	.25
❑ 296 Randy Jordan	.08	.25
❑ 297 Napoleon Kaufman	.25	.60
❑ 298 Lincoln Kennedy	.08	.25
❑ 299 Terry Mickens	.08	.25
❑ 300 Darrell Russell	.08	.25
❑ 301 Harvey Williams	.08	.25
❑ 302 Ch.Woodson/Ritchie	.25	.60
❑ 303 R.Williams/J.Williams	.08	.25
❑ 304 Koy Detmer	.08	.25
❑ 305 Hugh Douglas	.08	.25
❑ 306 Jason Dunn	.08	.25
❑ 307 Irving Fryar	.15	.40
❑ 308 Charlie Garner	.15	.40
❑ 309 Jeff Graham	.08	.25
❑ 310 Bobby Hoying	.15	.40
❑ 311 Rodney Peete	.08	.25
❑ 312 Allen Rossum	.08	.25
❑ 313 Duce Staley	.25	.60
❑ 314 William Thomas	.08	.25
❑ 315 Kevin Turner	.08	.25
❑ 316 K.Sinceno RC/C.Walker RC	.40	1.00
❑ 317 Jahine Arnold	.08	.25
❑ 318 Jerome Bettis	.25	.60
❑ 319 Will Blackwell	.08	.25
❑ 320 Mark Bruener	.08	.25
❑ 321 Dermontti Dawson	.08	.25
❑ 322 Chris Fuamatu-Ma'afala	.08	.25
❑ 323 Courtney Hawkins	.08	.25
❑ 324 Richard Huntley	.15	.40
❑ 325 Charles Johnson	.08	.25
❑ 326 Levon Kirkland	.08	.25
❑ 327 Kordell Stewart	.15	.40
❑ 328 Hines Ward	.25	.60
❑ 329 Dewayne Washington	.08	.25
❑ 330 Tony Banks	.15	.40
❑ 331 Steve Bono	.08	.25
❑ 332 Isaac Bruce	.25	.60
❑ 333 June Henley RC	.50	1.25
❑ 334 Robert Holcombe	.08	.25
❑ 335 Mike Jones LB	.08	.25

❑ 336 Eddie Kennison	.15	.40
❑ 337 Amp Lee	.08	.25
❑ 338 Jerald Moore	.08	.25
❑ 339 Ricky Proehl	.08	.25
❑ 340 J.T. Thomas	.08	.25
❑ 341 Derrick Harris/Az-Zahir Hakim	.15	.40
❑ 342 Roland Williams/Grant Wistrom	.08	.25
❑ 343 Kurt Warner RC/T.Horne !	5.00	12.00
❑ 344 Terrell Fletcher	.08	.25
❑ 345 Greg Jackson	.08	.25
❑ 346 Charlie Jones	.08	.25
❑ 347 Freddie Jones	.08	.25
❑ 348 Ryan Leaf	.25	.60
❑ 349 Natrone Means	.15	.40
❑ 350 Mikhael Ricks	.08	.25
❑ 351 Junior Seau	.25	.60
❑ 352 Bryan Still	.08	.25
❑ 353 T.Stephens/R.Thelwell RC	.50	1.25
❑ 354 Greg Clark	.08	.25
❑ 355 Marc Edwards	.08	.25
❑ 356 Merton Hanks	.08	.25
❑ 357 Garrison Hearst	.15	.40
❑ 358 R.W. McQuarters	.08	.25
❑ 359 Ken Norton Jr.	.08	.25
❑ 360 Terrell Owens	.25	.60
❑ 361 Jerry Rice	.50	1.25
❑ 362 J.J. Stokes	.15	.40
❑ 363 Bryant Young	.08	.25
❑ 364 Steve Young	.30	.75
❑ 365 Chad Brown	.08	.25
❑ 366 Christian Fauria	.08	.25
❑ 367 Joey Galloway	.15	.40
❑ 368 Ahman Green	.25	.60
❑ 369 Cortez Kennedy	.08	.25
❑ 370 Jon Kitna	.25	.60
❑ 371 James McKnight	.15	.40
❑ 372 Mike Pritchard	.08	.25
❑ 373 Michael Sinclair	.08	.25
❑ 374 Shawn Springs	.08	.25
❑ 375 Ricky Watters	.15	.40
❑ 376 Darryl Williams	.08	.25
❑ 377 R.Wilson/K.Joseph RC	.60	1.50
❑ 378 Mike Alstott	.25	.60
❑ 379 Reidel Anthony	.15	.40
❑ 380 Derrick Brooks	.25	.60
❑ 381 Trent Dilfer	.25	.60
❑ 382 Warrick Dunn	.25	.60
❑ 383 Bert Emanuel	.15	.40
❑ 384 Jacquez Green	.08	.25
❑ 385 Patrick Hape	.08	.25
❑ 386 John Lynch	.15	.40
❑ 387 Dave Moore	.08	.25
❑ 388 Hardy Nickerson	.08	.25
❑ 389 Warren Sapp	.15	.40
❑ 390 Karl Williams	.08	.25
❑ 391 Blaine Bishop	.08	.25
❑ 392 Joe Bowden	.08	.25
❑ 393 Isaac Byrd RC	.40	1.00
❑ 394 Willie Davis	.08	.25
❑ 395 Al Del Greco	.08	.25
❑ 396 Kevin Dyson	.15	.40
❑ 397 Eddie George	.25	.60
❑ 398 Jackie Harris	.08	.25
❑ 399 Dave Krieg	.08	.25
❑ 400 Steve McNair	.25	.60
❑ 401 Michael Roan	.08	.25
❑ 402 Yancey Thigpen	.08	.25
❑ 403 Frank Wycheck	.08	.25
❑ 404 Derrick Mason/Steve Matthews	.15	.40
❑ 405 Stephen Alexander	.08	.25
❑ 406 Terry Allen	.15	.40
❑ 407 Jamie Asher	.08	.25
❑ 408 Stephen Davis	.25	.60
❑ 409 Darrell Green	.08	.25
❑ 410 Trent Green	.25	.60
❑ 411 Skip Hicks	.08	.25
❑ 412 Brian Mitchell	.08	.25
❑ 413 Leslie Shepherd	.08	.25
❑ 414 Michael Westbrook	.15	.40
❑ 415 T.Hardy/Rabih Abdullah RC	.40	1.00
❑ 416 C.Thomas RC/M.Quinn RC	.40	1.00
❑ 417 J.Quinn/Kelly Holcomb RC	3.00	8.00
❑ 418 Brian Alford/Blake Spence	.40	1.00
❑ 419 Andy Haase RC/Carlos King	.40	1.00
❑ 420 James Thrash RC/K.Hankton	.60	1.50
❑ 421 F.Beasley/Itula Mili RC	.50	1.25
❑ 422 Champ Bailey RC	.75	2.00
❑ 423 D'Wayne Bates RC	.50	1.25
❑ 424 Michael Bishop RC	.60	1.50
❑ 425 David Boston RC	.60	1.50
❑ 426 Shawn Bryson RC	.60	1.50
❑ 427 Tim Couch RC	.60	1.50
❑ 428 Scott Covington RC	.60	1.50
❑ 429 Daunte Culpepper RC	2.50	6.00
❑ 430 Autry Denson RC	.50	1.25
❑ 431 Troy Edwards RC	.50	1.25
❑ 432 Kevin Faulk RC	.60	1.50
❑ 433 Joe Germaine RC	.50	1.25
❑ 434 Torry Holt RC	1.50	4.00
❑ 435 Brock Huard RC	.60	1.50
❑ 436 Sedrick Irvin RC	.40	1.00
❑ 437 Edgerrin James RC	2.50	6.00
❑ 438 Andy Katzenmoyer RC	.50	1.25
❑ 439 Shaun King RC	.50	1.25
❑ 440 Rob Konrad RC	.50	1.25
❑ 441 Donovan McNabb RC	3.00	8.00
❑ 442 Cade McNown RC	.50	1.25
❑ 443 Billy Miller RC	.40	1.00
❑ 444 Dee Miller RC	.40	1.00
❑ 445 Sirr Parker RC	.40	1.00
❑ 446 Peerless Price RC	.60	1.50
❑ 447 Akili Smith RC	.50	1.25
❑ 448 Tai Streets RC	.60	1.50
❑ 449 Ricky Williams RC	1.25	3.00
❑ 450 Amos Zereoue RC	.60	1.50
❑ S1 Warrick Dunn Sample	.25	.60

2000 Pacific

❑ COMPLETE SET (450)	25.00	60.00
❑ 1 Mario Bates	.08	.25
❑ 2 David Boston	.25	.60
❑ 3 Rob Fredrickson	.08	.25
❑ 4 Terry Hardy	.08	.25
❑ 5 Rob Moore	.15	.40
❑ 6 Adrian Murrell	.15	.40
❑ 7 Michael Pittman	.08	.25
❑ 8 Jake Plummer	.15	.40
❑ 9 Simeon Rice	.15	.40
❑ 10 Frank Sanders	.15	.40
❑ 11 Aeneas Williams	.08	.25
❑ 12 M.Cody/A.McCullough	.08	.25
❑ 13 D.McKinley RC/J.Makovicka	.25	.60
❑ 14 Jamal Anderson	.25	.60
❑ 15 Chris Calloway	.08	.25
❑ 16 Chris Chandler	.15	.40
❑ 17 Bob Christian	.08	.25
❑ 18 Tim Dwight	.25	.60
❑ 19 Jammi German	.08	.25
❑ 20 Ronnie Harris	.08	.25
❑ 21 Terance Mathis	.15	.40
❑ 22 Ken Oxendine	.08	.25
❑ 23 O.J. Santiago	.08	.25
❑ 24 Bob Whitfield	.08	.25
❑ 25 E.Baker/R.Kelly	.08	.25
❑ 26 Justin Armour	.08	.25
❑ 27 Tony Banks	.15	.40
❑ 28 Peter Boulware	.08	.25
❑ 29 Stoney Case	.08	.25
❑ 30 Priest Holmes	.30	.75
❑ 31 Qadry Ismail	.15	.40
❑ 32 Patrick Johnson	.08	.25
❑ 33 Michael McCrary	.08	.25
❑ 34 Jonathan Ogden	.08	.25
❑ 35 Errict Rhett	.15	.40
❑ 36 Duane Starks	.08	.25
❑ 37 Doug Flutie	.25	.60
❑ 38 Rob Johnson	.15	.40
❑ 39 Jonathan Linton	.08	.25
❑ 40 Eric Moulds	.25	.60
❑ 41 Peerless Price	.15	.40
❑ 42 Andre Reed	.15	.40
❑ 43 Jay Riemersma	.08	.25
❑ 44 Antowain Smith	.15	.40
❑ 45 Bruce Smith	.15	.40
❑ 46 Thurman Thomas	.15	.40
❑ 47 Kevin Williams	.08	.25
❑ 48 B.Collins/S.Jackson	.08	.25
❑ 49 Michael Bates	.08	.25
❑ 50 Steve Beuerlein	.15	.40
❑ 51 Tim Biakabutuka	.15	.40
❑ 52 Antonio Edwards	.08	.25
❑ 53 Donald Hayes	.08	.25
❑ 54 Patrick Jeffers	.25	.60
❑ 55 Anthony Johnson	.08	.25
❑ 56 Jeff Lewis	.08	.25
❑ 57 Eric Metcalf	.08	.25
❑ 58 Muhsin Muhammad	.15	.40
❑ 59 Jason Peter	.08	.25
❑ 60 Wesley Walls	.08	.25
❑ 61 John Allred	.08	.25
❑ 62 Marty Booker	.15	.40
❑ 63 Curtis Conway	.15	.40
❑ 64 Bobby Engram	.08	.25
❑ 65 Curtis Enis	.08	.25
❑ 66 Shane Matthews	.15	.40
❑ 67 Cade McNown	.08	.25
❑ 68 Glyn Milburn	.08	.25
❑ 69 Jim Miller	.08	.25
❑ 70 Marcus Robinson	.25	.60
❑ 71 Ryan Wetnight	.08	.25
❑ 72 J.Allen/M.Brooks	.15	.40
❑ 73 Jeff Blake	.15	.40
❑ 74 Corey Dillon	.25	.60
❑ 75 Rodney Heath RC	.15	.40
❑ 76 Willie Jackson	.08	.25
❑ 77 Tremain Mack	.08	.25
❑ 78 Tony McGee	.08	.25
❑ 79 Carl Pickens	.15	.40
❑ 80 Darnay Scott	.15	.40
❑ 81 Akili Smith	.08	.25
❑ 82 Takeo Spikes	.08	.25
❑ 83 Craig Yeast	.08	.25
❑ 84 M.Basnight/N.Williams	.08	.25
❑ 85 Karim Abdul-Jabbar	.15	.40
❑ 86 Darrin Chiaverini	.08	.25
❑ 87 Tim Couch	.15	.40
❑ 88 Marc Edwards	.08	.25
❑ 89 Kevin Johnson	.25	.60
❑ 90 Terry Kirby	.08	.25
❑ 91 Daylon McCutcheon	.08	.25
❑ 92 Jamir Miller	.08	.25
❑ 93 Leslie Shepherd	.08	.25
❑ 94 Irv Smith	.08	.25
❑ 95 M.Campbell/J.Dearth	.08	.25
❑ 96 Z.Davis RC/D.Dunn RC	.15	.40
❑ 97 M.Hill/T.Saleh RC	.08	.25
❑ 98 Troy Aikman	.50	1.25
❑ 99 Eric Bjornson	.08	.25
❑ 100 Dexter Coakley	.08	.25
❑ 101 Greg Ellis	.08	.25
❑ 102 Rocket Ismail	.15	.40
❑ 103 David LaFleur	.08	.25
❑ 104 Ernie Mills	.08	.25
❑ 105 Jeff Ogden	.15	.40
❑ 106 R.Neufeld RC/R.Thomas	.15	.40
❑ 107 Deion Sanders	.25	.60
❑ 108 Emmitt Smith	.50	1.25
❑ 109 Chris Warren	.08	.25
❑ 110 M.Lucky/J.Tucker	.08	.25
❑ 111 Byron Chamberlain	.08	.25
❑ 112 Terrell Davis	.25	.60
❑ 113 Jason Elam	.08	.25
❑ 114 Olandis Gary	.25	.60
❑ 115 Brian Griese	.25	.60
❑ 116 Ed McCaffrey	.25	.60
❑ 117 Trevor Pryce	.08	.25
❑ 118 Bill Romanowski	.08	.25
❑ 119 Shannon Sharpe	.15	.40
❑ 120 Rod Smith	.15	.40
❑ 121 Al Wilson	.08	.25
❑ 122 A.Cooper/C.Watson	.08	.25
❑ 123 Charlie Batch	.25	.60
❑ 124 Stephen Boyd	.08	.25
❑ 125 Chris Claiborne	.08	.25
❑ 126 Germane Crowell	.08	.25
❑ 127 Terry Fair	.08	.25
❑ 128 Gus Frerotte	.08	.25
❑ 129 Jason Hanson	.08	.25
❑ 130 Greg Hill	.08	.25
❑ 131 Herman Moore	.15	.40
❑ 132 Johnnie Morton	.15	.40
❑ 133 Barry Sanders	.60	1.50
❑ 134 David Sloan	.08	.25
❑ 135 B.Olivo/C.Sauter	.08	.25

Card	Low	High
❑ 136 Corey Bradford	.15	.40
❑ 137 Tyrone Davis	.08	.25
❑ 138 Brett Favre	.75	2.00
❑ 139 Antonio Freeman	.25	.60
❑ 140 Vonnie Holliday	.08	.25
❑ 141 Dorsey Levens	.15	.40
❑ 142 Keith McKenzie	.08	.25
❑ 143 Mike McKenzie	.08	.25
❑ 144 Bill Schroeder	.15	.40
❑ 145 Jeff Thomason	.08	.25
❑ 146 Frank Winters	.08	.25
❑ 147 Cornelius Bennett	.08	.25
❑ 148 Tony Blevins RC	.15	.40
❑ 149 Chad Bratzke	.08	.25
❑ 150 Ken Dilger	.08	.25
❑ 151 Tarik Glenn	.08	.25
❑ 152 E.G. Green	.08	.25
❑ 153 Marvin Harrison	.25	.60
❑ 154 Edgerrin James	.40	1.00
❑ 155 Peyton Manning	.60	1.50
❑ 156 Jerome Pathon	.15	.40
❑ 157 Marcus Pollard	.08	.25
❑ 158 Terrence Wilkins	.08	.25
❑ 159 I.Jones RC/P.Shields RC	.25	.60
❑ 160 Reggie Barlow	.08	.25
❑ 161 Aaron Beasley	.08	.25
❑ 162 Tony Boselli	.08	.25
❑ 163 Tony Brackens	.08	.25
❑ 164 Kyle Brady	.08	.25
❑ 165 Mark Brunell	.25	.60
❑ 166 Jay Fiedler	.25	.60
❑ 167 Kevin Hardy	.08	.25
❑ 168 Carnell Lake	.08	.25
❑ 169 Keenan McCardell	.15	.40
❑ 170 Jonathan Quinn	.08	.25
❑ 171 Jimmy Smith	.15	.40
❑ 172 James Stewart	.15	.40
❑ 173 Fred Taylor	.25	.60
❑ 174 L.Jackson RC/S.Mack	.25	.60
❑ 175 Derrick Alexander	.15	.40
❑ 176 Donnell Bennett	.08	.25
❑ 177 Donnie Edwards	.08	.25
❑ 178 Tony Gonzalez	.15	.40
❑ 179 Elvis Grbac	.15	.40
❑ 180 James Hasty	.08	.25
❑ 181 Joe Horn	.15	.40
❑ 182 Lonnie Johnson	.08	.25
❑ 183 Kevin Lockett	.08	.25
❑ 184 Larry Parker	.08	.25
❑ 185 Tony Richardson RC	.15	.40
❑ 186 Rashaan Shehee	.08	.25
❑ 187 Tamarick Vanover	.08	.25
❑ 188 Trace Armstrong	.08	.25
❑ 189 Oronde Gadsden	.15	.40
❑ 190 Damon Huard	.25	.60
❑ 191 Nate Jacquet	.08	.25
❑ 192 James Johnson	.08	.25
❑ 193 Rob Konrad	.08	.25
❑ 194 Sam Madison	.08	.25
❑ 195 Dan Marino	.75	2.00
❑ 196 Tony Martin	.15	.40
❑ 197 O.J. McDuffie	.15	.40
❑ 198 Stanley Pritchett	.08	.25
❑ 199 Tim Ruddy	.08	.25
❑ 200 Patrick Surtain	.08	.25
❑ 201 Zach Thomas	.25	.60
❑ 202 Cris Carter	.25	.60
❑ 203 Duane Clemons	.08	.25
❑ 204 Carlester Crumpler	.08	.25
❑ 205 Daunte Culpepper	.30	.75
❑ 206 Jeff George	.15	.40
❑ 207 Matthew Hatchette	.08	.25
❑ 208 Leroy Hoard	.08	.25
❑ 209 Randy Moss	.50	1.25
❑ 210 John Randle	.15	.40
❑ 211 Jake Reed	.15	.40
❑ 212 Robert Smith	.25	.60
❑ 213 Robert Tate	.08	.25
❑ 214 Terry Allen	.15	.40
❑ 215 Bruce Armstrong	.08	.25
❑ 216 Drew Bledsoe	.30	.75
❑ 217 Ben Coates	.08	.25
❑ 218 Kevin Faulk	.15	.40
❑ 219 Terry Glenn	.15	.40
❑ 220 Shawn Jefferson	.08	.25
❑ 221 Andy Katzenmoyer	.08	.25
❑ 222 Ty Law	.15	.40
❑ 223 Willie McGinest	.08	.25
❑ 224 Lawyer Milloy	.15	.40
❑ 225 Tony Simmons	.08	.25
❑ 226 M.Bishop/S.Morey RC	.15	.40
❑ 227 Cameron Cleeland	.08	.25
❑ 228 Troy Davis	.08	.25
❑ 229 Jake Delhomme RC	1.25	3.00
❑ 230 Andre Hastings	.08	.25
❑ 231 Eddie Kennison	.15	.40
❑ 232 Wilmont Perry	.08	.25
❑ 233 Dino Philyaw	.08	.25
❑ 234 Keith Poole	.08	.25
❑ 235 William Roaf	.08	.25
❑ 236 Billy Joe Tolliver	.08	.25
❑ 237 Fred Weary	.08	.25
❑ 238 Ricky Williams	.25	.60
❑ 239 Franklin RC/M.Powell RC	.25	.60
❑ 240 Jessie Armstead	.08	.25
❑ 241 Tiki Barber	.25	.60
❑ 242 Daniel Campbell	.08	.25
❑ 243 Kerry Collins	.15	.40
❑ 244 Percy Ellsworth	.08	.25
❑ 245 Kent Graham	.08	.25
❑ 246 Ike Hilliard	.15	.40
❑ 247 Cedric Jones	.08	.25
❑ 248 Bashir Levingston RC	.25	.60
❑ 249 Pete Mitchell	.08	.25
❑ 250 Michael Strahan	.15	.40
❑ 251 Amani Toomer	.08	.25
❑ 252 Charles Way	.08	.25
❑ 253 Andre Weathers RC	.15	.40
❑ 254 Richie Anderson	.15	.40
❑ 255 Wayne Chrebet	.15	.40
❑ 256 Marcus Coleman	.08	.25
❑ 257 Bryan Cox	.08	.25
❑ 258 Jason Fabini RC	.15	.40
❑ 259 Robert Farmer RC	.25	.60
❑ 260 Keyshawn Johnson	.25	.60
❑ 261 Ray Lucas	.15	.40
❑ 262 Curtis Martin	.25	.60
❑ 263 Kevin Mawae	.08	.25
❑ 264 Eric Ogbogu	.08	.25
❑ 265 Bernie Parmalee	.08	.25
❑ 266 Vinny Testaverde	.15	.40
❑ 267 Dedric Ward	.08	.25
❑ 268 Eric Barton RC	.15	.40
❑ 269 Tim Brown	.25	.60
❑ 270 Tony Bryant	.08	.25
❑ 271 Rickey Dudley	.08	.25
❑ 272 Rich Gannon	.25	.60
❑ 273 Bobby Hoying	.15	.40
❑ 274 James Jett	.08	.25
❑ 275 Napoleon Kaufman	.15	.40
❑ 276 Jon Ritchie	.08	.25
❑ 277 Darrell Russell	.08	.25
❑ 278 Kenny Shedd	.08	.25
❑ 279 Marquis Walker RC	.15	.40
❑ 280 Tyrone Wheatley	.15	.40
❑ 281 Charles Woodson	.15	.40
❑ 282 Luther Broughton RC	.15	.40
❑ 283 Al Harris RC	.08	.25
❑ 284 Greg Jefferson	.08	.25
❑ 285 Dietrich Jells	.08	.25
❑ 286 Charles Johnson	.15	.40
❑ 287 Chad Lewis	.08	.25
❑ 288 Mike Mamula	.08	.25
❑ 289 Donovan McNabb	.40	1.00
❑ 290 Doug Pederson	.08	.25
❑ 291 Allen Rossum	.08	.25
❑ 292 Torrance Small	.08	.25
❑ 293 Duce Staley	.25	.60
❑ 294 Jerome Bettis	.25	.60
❑ 295 Kris Brown	.08	.25
❑ 296 Mark Bruener	.08	.25
❑ 297 Troy Edwards	.08	.25
❑ 298 Jason Gildon	.08	.25
❑ 299 Richard Huntley	.08	.25
❑ 300 Bobby Shaw RC	.25	.60
❑ 301 Scott Shields RC	.15	.40
❑ 302 Kordell Stewart	.15	.40
❑ 303 Hines Ward	.25	.60
❑ 304 Amos Zereoue	.25	.60
❑ 305 M.Cushing RC/J.Tuman	.15	.40
❑ 306 P.Gonzalez/A.Wright RC	.60	1.50
❑ 307 Isaac Bruce	.25	.60
❑ 308 Kevin Carter	.08	.25
❑ 309 Marshall Faulk	.30	.75
❑ 310 London Fletcher RC	.15	.40
❑ 311 Joe Germaine	.08	.25
❑ 312 Az-Zahir Hakim	.15	.40
❑ 313 Torry Holt	.25	.60
❑ 314 Tony Horne	.08	.25
❑ 315 Mike Jones LB	.08	.25
❑ 316 Dexter McCleon RC	.25	.60
❑ 317 Orlando Pace	.08	.25
❑ 318 Ricky Proehl	.08	.25
❑ 319 Kurt Warner	.50	1.25
❑ 320 Roland Williams	.08	.25
❑ 321 Grant Wistrom	.08	.25
❑ 322 J.Hodgins RC/J.Watson	.08	.25
❑ 323 Jermaine Fazande	.08	.25
❑ 324 Jeff Graham	.08	.25
❑ 325 Jim Harbaugh	.15	.40
❑ 326 Raylee Johnson	.08	.25
❑ 327 Charlie Jones	.08	.25
❑ 328 Freddie Jones	.08	.25
❑ 329 Natrone Means	.08	.25
❑ 330 Chris Penn	.08	.25
❑ 331 Mikhael Ricks	.08	.25
❑ 332 Junior Seau	.25	.60
❑ 333 R.Davis RC/R.Reed RC	.15	.40
❑ 334 Fred Beasley	.08	.25
❑ 335 Brentson Buckner	.08	.25
❑ 336 Greg Clark	.08	.25
❑ 337 Dave Fiore RC	.08	.25
❑ 338 Charlie Garner	.15	.40
❑ 339 Mark Harris RC	.25	.60
❑ 340 Ramos McDonald RC	.15	.40
❑ 341 Terrell Owens	.25	.60
❑ 342 Jerry Rice	.50	1.25
❑ 343 Lance Schulters	.08	.25
❑ 344 J.J. Stokes	.15	.40
❑ 345 Bryant Young	.08	.25
❑ 346 Steve Young	.30	.75
❑ 347 Jeff Garcia	.25	.60
❑ 348 Fabien Bownes RC	.08	.25
❑ 349 Chad Brown	.08	.25
❑ 350 Reggie Brown	.08	.25
❑ 351 Sean Dawkins	.08	.25
❑ 352 Christian Fauria	.08	.25
❑ 353 Ahman Green	.25	.60
❑ 354 Walter Jones	.08	.25
❑ 355 Cortez Kennedy	.08	.25
❑ 356 Jon Kitna	.25	.60
❑ 357 Derrick Mayes	.15	.40
❑ 358 Charlie Rogers	.08	.25
❑ 359 Shawn Springs	.08	.25
❑ 360 Ricky Watters	.15	.40
❑ 361 Donne Abraham	.08	.25
❑ 362 Mike Alstott	.25	.60
❑ 363 Reidel Anthony	.08	.25
❑ 364 Ronde Barber	.08	.25
❑ 365 Derrick Brooks	.25	.60
❑ 366 Warrick Dunn	.25	.60
❑ 367 Jacquez Green	.08	.25
❑ 368 Marcus Jones	.08	.25
❑ 369 Shaun King	.08	.25
❑ 370 John Lynch	.15	.40
❑ 371 Warren Sapp	.15	.40
❑ 372 Steve White RC	.08	.25
❑ 373 M.Gramatica/K.McLeod RC	.15	.40
❑ 374 Blaine Bishop	.08	.25
❑ 375 Al Del Greco	.08	.25
❑ 376 Kevin Dyson	.15	.40
❑ 377 Eddie George	.25	.60
❑ 378 Jevon Kearse	.25	.60
❑ 379 Derrick Mason	.15	.40
❑ 380 Bruce Matthews	.08	.25
❑ 381 Steve McNair	.25	.60
❑ 382 Neil O'Donnell	.08	.25
❑ 383 Yancey Thigpen	.08	.25
❑ 384 Frank Wycheck	.08	.25
❑ 385 K.Daft/L.Brown	.08	.25
❑ 386 Stephen Alexander	.08	.25
❑ 387 Champ Bailey	.15	.40
❑ 388 Larry Centers	.08	.25
❑ 389 Marco Coleman	.08	.25
❑ 390 Albert Connell	.08	.25
❑ 391 Stephen Davis	.25	.60
❑ 392 Irving Fryar	.15	.40
❑ 393 Skip Hicks	.08	.25
❑ 394 Brad Johnson	.25	.60
❑ 395 Michael Westbrook	.15	.40
❑ 396 O.Ayanbadejo RC /L.Gordon RC	.15	.40
❑ 397 D.Driver/R.Powell	.25	.60
❑ 398 T.Bouman/J.Brigham RC	.25	.60
❑ 399 B.Huard/S.Bonner	.08	.25
❑ 400 M.Sellers/S.George RC	.15	.40
❑ 401 Shaun Alexander RC	1.50	4.00

Card		
❑ 402 LaVar Arrington RC	1.00	2.50
❑ 403 Tom Brady RC	15.00	40.00
❑ 404 Demario Brown RC	.25	.60
❑ 405 Plaxico Burress RC	1.00	2.50
❑ 406 Trung Canidate RC	.40	1.00
❑ 407 Giovanni Carmazzi RC	.25	.60
❑ 408 Kwame Cavil RC	.25	.60
❑ 409 Chrys Chukwuma RC	.50	1.25
❑ 410 Ron Dayne RC	.50	1.25
❑ 411 Reuben Droughns RC	.60	1.50
❑ 412 Ron Dugans RC	.25	.60
❑ 413 Deon Dyer RC	.40	1.00
❑ 414 Danny Farmer RC	.40	1.00
❑ 415 Chafie Fields RC	.25	.60
❑ 416 Trevor Gaylor RC	.40	1.00
❑ 417 Sherrod Gideon RC	.25	.60
❑ 418 Joey Goodspeed RC	.25	.60
❑ 419 Joe Hamilton RC	.40	1.00
❑ 420 Tony Hartley RC	.25	.60
❑ 421 Todd Husak RC	.50	1.25
❑ 422 Trevor Insley RC	.25	.60
❑ 423 Thomas Jones RC	.75	2.00
❑ 424 Marcus Knight RC	.40	1.00
❑ 425 Jamal Lewis RC	1.25	3.00
❑ 426 Anthony Lucas RC	.60	1.50
❑ 427 Tee Martin RC	.50	1.25
❑ 428 Rondell Mealey RC	.25	.60
❑ 429 Sylvester Morris RC	.40	1.00
❑ 430 Chad Morton RC	.50	1.25
❑ 431 Dennis Northcutt RC	.50	1.25
❑ 432 Chad Pennington RC	1.25	3.00
❑ 433 Rodnick Phillips RC	.25	.60
❑ 434 Mareno Philyaw RC	.25	.60
❑ 435 Jerry Porter RC	.60	1.50
❑ 436 Travis Prentice RC	.40	1.00
❑ 437 Tim Rattay RC	.50	1.25
❑ 438 Chris Redman RC	.40	1.00
❑ 439 J.R. Redmond RC	.40	1.00
❑ 440 Gari Scott RC	.25	.60
❑ 441 Keith Smith RC	.25	.60
❑ 442 Terrelle Smith RC	.40	1.00
❑ 443 R.Jay Soward RC	.40	1.00
❑ 444 Quinton Spotwood RC	.25	.60
❑ 445 Shyrone Stith RC	.40	1.00
❑ 446 Travis Taylor RC	.50	1.25
❑ 447 Troy Walters RC	.50	1.25
❑ 448 Peter Warrick RC	.50	1.25
❑ 449 Dez White RC	.50	1.25
❑ 450 Michael Wiley RC	.40	1.00

2001 Pacific

Card		
❑ COMP.SET w/o SP's (450)	25.00	50.00
❑ 1 David Boston	.15	.40
❑ 2 Mac Cody	.15	.40
❑ 3 Chris Gedney	.15	.40
❑ 4 Chris Greisen	.15	.40
❑ 5 Terry Hardy	.15	.40
❑ 6 MarTay Jenkins	.15	.40
❑ 7 Thomas Jones	.20	.50
❑ 8 Joel Makovicka	.15	.40
❑ 9 Tywan Mitchell	.15	.40
❑ 10 Rob Moore	.15	.40
❑ 11 Michael Pittman	.20	.50
❑ 12 Jake Plummer	.20	.50
❑ 13 Frank Sanders	.15	.40
❑ 14 Aeneas Williams	.20	.50
❑ 15 Jamal Anderson	.20	.50
❑ 16 Eugene Baker	.15	.40
❑ 17 Chris Chandler	.20	.50
❑ 18 Tim Dwight	.20	.50
❑ 19 Brian Finneran	.20	.50
❑ 20 Jammi German	.15	.40
❑ 21 Shawn Jefferson	.15	.40
❑ 22 Doug Johnson	.15	.40
❑ 23 Danny Kanell	.20	.50
❑ 24 Reggie Kelly	.15	.40
❑ 25 Terance Mathis	.15	.40
❑ 26 Derek Rackley	.15	.40
❑ 27 Ron Rivers	.15	.40
❑ 28 Maurice Smith	.15	.40
❑ 29 Sam Adams	.15	.40
❑ 30 Obafemi Ayanbadejo	.15	.40
❑ 31 Tony Banks	.15	.40
❑ 32 Trent Dilfer	.20	.50
❑ 33 Sam Gash	.15	.40
❑ 34 Priest Holmes	.25	.60
❑ 35 Qadry Ismail	.20	.50
❑ 36 Pat Johnson	.15	.40
❑ 37 Jamal Lewis	.25	.60
❑ 38 Jermaine Lewis	.15	.40
❑ 39 Ray Lewis	.25	.60
❑ 40 Chris Redman	.25	.60
❑ 41 Shannon Sharpe	.25	.60
❑ 42 Brandon Stokley	.20	.50
❑ 43 Travis Taylor	.15	.40
❑ 44 Shawn Bryson	.15	.40
❑ 45 Kwame Cavil	.15	.40
❑ 46 Sam Cowart	.15	.40
❑ 47 Doug Flutie	.25	.60
❑ 48 Rob Johnson	.20	.50
❑ 49 Jonathan Linton	.15	.40
❑ 50 Jeremy McDaniel	.15	.40
❑ 51 Sammy Morris	.20	.50
❑ 52 Eric Moulds	.20	.50
❑ 53 Peerless Price	.15	.40
❑ 54 Jay Riemersma	.15	.40
❑ 55 Antowain Smith	.20	.50
❑ 56 Chris Watson	.15	.40
❑ 57 Marcellus Wiley	.15	.40
❑ 58 Michael Bates	.15	.40
❑ 59 Steve Beuerlein	.20	.50
❑ 60 Tim Biakabutuka	.15	.40
❑ 61 Isaac Byrd	.15	.40
❑ 62 Dameyune Craig	.15	.40
❑ 63 William Floyd	.15	.40
❑ 64 Karl Hankton	.15	.40
❑ 65 Donald Hayes	.15	.40
❑ 66 Chris Hetherington RC	.15	.40
❑ 67 Brad Hoover	.20	.50
❑ 68 Patrick Jeffers	.15	.40
❑ 69 Muhsin Muhammad	.20	.50
❑ 70 Iheanyi Uwaezuoke	.15	.40
❑ 71 Wesley Walls	.15	.40
❑ 72 James Allen	.15	.40
❑ 73 Marlon Barnes	.15	.40
❑ 74 D'Wayne Bates	.15	.40
❑ 75 Marty Booker	.20	.50
❑ 76 Macey Brooks	.15	.40
❑ 77 Bobby Engram	.20	.50
❑ 78 Curtis Enis	.15	.40
❑ 79 Mark Hartsell RC	.15	.40
❑ 80 Eddie Kennison	.20	.50
❑ 81 Shane Matthews	.15	.40
❑ 82 Cade McNown	.20	.50
❑ 83 Jim Miller	.20	.50
❑ 84 Marcus Robinson	.20	.50
❑ 85 Brian Urlacher	.30	.75
❑ 86 Dez White	.20	.50
❑ 87 Brandon Bennett	.15	.40
❑ 88 Steve Bush RC	.15	.40
❑ 89 Corey Dillon	.20	.50
❑ 90 Ron Dugans	.15	.40
❑ 91 Danny Farmer	.15	.40
❑ 92 Damon Griffin	.15	.40
❑ 93 Clif Groce	.15	.40
❑ 94 Curtis Keaton	.15	.40
❑ 95 Scott Mitchell	.15	.40
❑ 96 Darnay Scott	.20	.50
❑ 97 Akili Smith	.15	.40
❑ 98 Peter Warrick	.20	.50
❑ 99 Nick Williams	.15	.40
❑ 100 Craig Yeast	.15	.40
❑ 101 Bobby Brown	.15	.40
❑ 102 Darrin Chiaverini	.15	.40
❑ 103 Tim Couch	.15	.40
❑ 104 JaJuan Dawson	.15	.40
❑ 105 Marc Edwards	.15	.40
❑ 106 Kevin Johnson	.15	.40
❑ 107 Dennis Northcutt	.15	.40
❑ 108 David Patten	.15	.40
❑ 109 Doug Pederson	.15	.40
❑ 110 Travis Prentice	.15	.40
❑ 111 Errict Rhett	.20	.50
❑ 112 Aaron Shea	.15	.40
❑ 113 Kevin Thompson	.15	.40
❑ 114 Jamel White	.15	.40
❑ 115 Spergon Wynn	.15	.40
❑ 116 Troy Aikman	.40	1.00
❑ 117 Chris Brazzell	.15	.40
❑ 118 Randall Cunningham	.25	.60
❑ 119 Jackie Harris	.20	.50
❑ 120 Damon Hodge	.15	.40
❑ 121 Rocket Ismail	.20	.50
❑ 122 David LaFleur	.15	.40
❑ 123 Wane McGarity	.15	.40
❑ 124 James McKnight	.15	.40
❑ 125 Emmitt Smith	.60	1.50
❑ 126 Clint Stoerner	.20	.50
❑ 127 Jason Tucker	.15	.40
❑ 128 Michael Wiley	.15	.40
❑ 129 Anthony Wright	.15	.40
❑ 130 Mike Anderson	.20	.50
❑ 131 Dwayne Carswell	.15	.40
❑ 132 Byron Chamberlain	.15	.40
❑ 133 Desmond Clark	.20	.50
❑ 134 Chris Cole	.15	.40
❑ 135 KaRon Coleman	.15	.40
❑ 136 Terrell Davis	.25	.60
❑ 137 Gus Frerotte	.20	.50
❑ 138 Olandis Gary	.15	.40
❑ 139 Brian Griese	.20	.50
❑ 140 Howard Griffith	.15	.40
❑ 141 Jarious Jackson	.15	.40
❑ 142 Ed McCaffrey	.20	.50
❑ 143 Scottie Montgomery RC	.15	.40
❑ 144 Rod Smith	.20	.50
❑ 145 Charlie Batch	.20	.50
❑ 146 Stoney Case	.15	.40
❑ 147 Germane Crowell	.15	.40
❑ 148 Larry Foster	.15	.40
❑ 149 Desmond Howard	.20	.50
❑ 150 Sedrick Irvin	.15	.40
❑ 151 Herman Moore	.20	.50
❑ 152 Johnnie Morton	.20	.50
❑ 153 Robert Porcher	.15	.40
❑ 154 Cory Sauter	.15	.40
❑ 155 Cory Schlesinger	.15	.40
❑ 156 David Sloan	.15	.40
❑ 157 Brian Stablein	.15	.40
❑ 158 James Stewart	.15	.40
❑ 159 Corey Bradford	.15	.40
❑ 160 Tyrone Davis	.15	.40
❑ 161 Donald Driver	.25	.60
❑ 162 Brett Favre	.75	2.00
❑ 163 Bubba Franks	.20	.50
❑ 164 Antonio Freeman	.25	.60
❑ 165 Herbert Goodman	.15	.40
❑ 166 Ahman Green	.25	.60
❑ 167 Matt Hasselbeck	.25	.60
❑ 168 William Henderson	.20	.50
❑ 169 Charles Lee	.15	.40
❑ 170 Dorsey Levens	.20	.50
❑ 171 Bill Schroeder	.20	.50
❑ 172 Darren Sharper	.20	.50
❑ 173 Matt Snider	.15	.40
❑ 174 Danny Wuerffel	.20	.50
❑ 175 Ken Dilger	.15	.40
❑ 176 Jim Finn	.15	.40
❑ 177 Lennox Gordon	.15	.40
❑ 178 E.G. Green	.15	.40
❑ 179 Marvin Harrison	.25	.60
❑ 180 Kelly Holcomb	.20	.50
❑ 181 Trevor Insley	.15	.40
❑ 182 Edgerrin James	.25	.60
❑ 183 Peyton Manning	.60	1.50
❑ 184 Kevin McDougal	.15	.40
❑ 185 Jerome Pathon	.15	.40
❑ 186 Marcus Pollard	.15	.40
❑ 187 Justin Snow	.15	.40
❑ 188 Terrence Wilkins	.15	.40
❑ 189 Reggie Barlow	.15	.40
❑ 190 Kyle Brady	.15	.40
❑ 191 Mark Brunell	.25	.60
❑ 192 Kevin Hardy	.15	.40
❑ 193 Anthony Johnson	.15	.40
❑ 194 Stacey Mack	.15	.40
❑ 195 Jamie Martin	.15	.40
❑ 196 Keenan McCardell	.20	.50
❑ 197 Daimon Shelton	.15	.40
❑ 198 Jimmy Smith	.20	.50
❑ 199 R.Jay Soward	.15	.40
❑ 200 Shyrone Stith	.15	.40
❑ 201 Fred Taylor	.25	.60
❑ 202 Alvis Whitted	.15	.40

Card		
❑ 203 Jermaine Williams	.15	.40
❑ 204 Derrick Alexander	.15	.40
❑ 205 Kimble Anders	.15	.40
❑ 206 Donnell Bennett	.15	.40
❑ 207 Mike Cloud	.15	.40
❑ 208 Todd Collins	.15	.40
❑ 209 Tony Gonzalez	.20	.50
❑ 210 Elvis Grbac	.20	.50
❑ 211 Dante Hall	.25	.60
❑ 212 Kevin Lockett	.15	.40
❑ 213 Warren Moon	.25	.60
❑ 214 Frank Moreau	.15	.40
❑ 215 Sylvester Morris	.15	.40
❑ 216 Larry Parker	.15	.40
❑ 217 Tony Richardson	.15	.40
❑ 218 Trace Armstrong	.15	.40
❑ 219 Autry Denson	.15	.40
❑ 220 Bert Emanuel	.15	.40
❑ 221 Jay Fiedler	.20	.50
❑ 222 Oronde Gadsden	.15	.40
❑ 223 Damon Huard	.20	.50
❑ 224 James Johnson	.15	.40
❑ 225 Rob Konrad	.15	.40
❑ 226 Tony Martin	.20	.50
❑ 227 O.J. McDuffie	.15	.40
❑ 228 Mike Quinn	.15	.40
❑ 229 Lamar Smith	.20	.50
❑ 230 Jason Taylor	.25	.60
❑ 231 Thurman Thomas	.25	.60
❑ 232 Zach Thomas	.25	.60
❑ 233 Todd Bouman	.15	.40
❑ 234 Bubby Brister	.20	.50
❑ 235 Cris Carter	.25	.60
❑ 236 Daunte Culpepper	.25	.60
❑ 237 John Davis RC	.15	.40
❑ 238 Robert Griffith	.15	.40
❑ 239 Matthew Hatchette	.15	.40
❑ 240 Jim Kleinsasser	.20	.50
❑ 241 Randy Moss	.30	.75
❑ 242 John Randle	.20	.50
❑ 243 Robert Smith	.20	.50
❑ 244 Chris Walsh RC	.15	.40
❑ 245 Troy Walters	.15	.40
❑ 246 Moe Williams	.15	.40
❑ 247 Michael Bishop	.20	.50
❑ 248 Drew Bledsoe	.25	.60
❑ 249 Troy Brown	.20	.50
❑ 250 Tedy Bruschi	.25	.60
❑ 251 Tony Carter	.15	.40
❑ 252 Shockmain Davis	.15	.40
❑ 253 Kevin Faulk	.20	.50
❑ 254 Terry Glenn	.20	.50
❑ 255 Ty Law	.20	.50
❑ 256 Lawyer Milloy	.20	.50
❑ 257 J.R. Redmond	.15	.40
❑ 258 Harold Shaw	.15	.40
❑ 259 Tony Simmons	.15	.40
❑ 260 Jermaine Wiggins	.15	.40
❑ 261 Jeff Blake	.20	.50
❑ 262 Aaron Brooks	.20	.50
❑ 263 Cam Cleeland	.15	.40
❑ 264 Andrew Glover	.15	.40
❑ 265 La'Roi Glover	.15	.40
❑ 266 Joe Horn	.20	.50
❑ 267 Kevin Houser	.15	.40
❑ 268 Willie Jackson	.15	.40
❑ 269 Jerald Moore	.15	.40
❑ 270 Chad Morton	.15	.40
❑ 271 Keith Poole	.15	.40
❑ 272 Terrelle Smith	.15	.40
❑ 273 Ricky Williams	.25	.60
❑ 274 Robert Wilson	.15	.40
❑ 275 Jessie Armstead	.15	.40
❑ 276 Tiki Barber	.25	.60
❑ 277 Mike Cherry	.15	.40
❑ 278 Kerry Collins	.20	.50
❑ 279 Greg Comella	.15	.40
❑ 280 Thabiti Davis	.15	.40
❑ 281 Ron Dayne	.20	.50
❑ 282 Ron Dixon	.15	.40
❑ 283 Ike Hilliard	.20	.50
❑ 284 Joe Jurevicius	.15	.40
❑ 285 Jason Sehorn	.20	.50
❑ 286 Michael Strahan	.25	.60
❑ 287 Amani Toomer	.20	.50
❑ 288 Craig Walendy	.15	.40
❑ 289 Damon Washington RC	.15	.40
❑ 290 Richie Anderson	.15	.40
❑ 291 Anthony Becht	.15	.40
❑ 292 Wayne Chrebet	.20	.50
❑ 293 Laveranues Coles	.25	.60
❑ 294 Bryan Cox	.20	.50
❑ 295 Marvin Jones	.15	.40
❑ 296 Mo Lewis	.15	.40
❑ 297 Ray Lucas	.15	.40
❑ 298 Curtis Martin	.25	.60
❑ 299 Bernie Parmalee	.15	.40
❑ 300 Chad Pennington	.25	.60
❑ 301 Jerald Sowell	.15	.40
❑ 302 Dwight Stone	.15	.40
❑ 303 Vinny Testaverde	.20	.50
❑ 304 Dedric Ward	.15	.40
❑ 305 Tim Brown	.25	.60
❑ 306 Zack Crockett	.15	.40
❑ 307 Scott Dreisbach	.15	.40
❑ 308 Rickey Dudley	.15	.40
❑ 309 David Dunn	.15	.40
❑ 310 Mondriel Fulcher	.15	.40
❑ 311 Rich Gannon	.20	.50
❑ 312 James Jett	.15	.40
❑ 313 Randy Jordan	.20	.50
❑ 314 Napoleon Kaufman	.15	.40
❑ 315 Rodney Peete	.15	.40
❑ 316 Jerry Porter	.15	.40
❑ 317 Andre Rison	.20	.50
❑ 318 Tyrone Wheatley	.20	.50
❑ 319 Charles Woodson	.25	.60
❑ 320 Darnell Autry	.15	.40
❑ 321 Na Brown	.15	.40
❑ 322 Hugh Douglas	.15	.40
❑ 323 Charles Johnson	.15	.40
❑ 324 Chad Lewis	.15	.40
❑ 325 Cecil Martin	.15	.40
❑ 326 Donovan McNabb	.30	.75
❑ 327 Brian Mitchell	.20	.50
❑ 328 Todd Pinkston	.15	.40
❑ 329 Ron Powlus	.20	.50
❑ 330 Stanley Pritchett	.15	.40
❑ 331 Torrance Small	.15	.40
❑ 332 Duce Staley	.20	.50
❑ 333 Troy Vincent	.20	.50
❑ 334 Chris Warren	.20	.50
❑ 335 Jerome Bettis	.25	.60
❑ 336 Plaxico Burress	.20	.50
❑ 337 Troy Edwards	.15	.40
❑ 338 Chris Fuamatu-Ma'afala	.15	.40
❑ 339 Cory Geason	.15	.40
❑ 340 Kent Graham	.20	.50
❑ 341 Courtney Hawkins	.15	.40
❑ 342 Richard Huntley	.15	.40
❑ 343 Tee Martin	.20	.50
❑ 344 Bobby Shaw	.15	.40
❑ 345 Kordell Stewart	.20	.50
❑ 346 Hines Ward	.25	.60
❑ 347 Destry Wright RC	.15	.40
❑ 348 Amos Zereoue	.15	.40
❑ 349 Isaac Bruce	.25	.60
❑ 350 Trung Canidate	.15	.40
❑ 351 Marshall Faulk	.25	.60
❑ 352 London Fletcher	.15	.40
❑ 353 Joe Germaine	.15	.40
❑ 354 Trent Green	.25	.60
❑ 355 Az-Zahir Hakim	.15	.40
❑ 356 James Hodgins	.15	.40
❑ 357 Robert Holcombe	.15	.40
❑ 358 Torry Holt	.20	.50
❑ 359 Tony Horne	.15	.40
❑ 360 Ricky Proehl	.15	.40
❑ 361 Chris Thomas RC	.15	.40
❑ 362 Kurt Warner	.30	.75
❑ 363 Justin Watson	.15	.40
❑ 364 Kenny Bynum	.15	.40
❑ 365 Robert Chancey	.15	.40
❑ 366 Curtis Conway	.20	.50
❑ 367 Jermaine Fazande	.15	.40
❑ 368 Terrell Fletcher	.15	.40
❑ 369 Trevor Gaylor	.15	.40
❑ 370 Jeff Graham	.15	.40
❑ 371 Jim Harbaugh	.20	.50
❑ 372 Rodney Harrison	.20	.50
❑ 373 Ronney Jenkins	.15	.40
❑ 374 Freddie Jones	.15	.40
❑ 375 Reggie Jones	.15	.40
❑ 376 Ryan Leaf	.15	.40
❑ 377 Junior Seau	.25	.60
❑ 378 Fred Beasley	.15	.40
❑ 379 Greg Clark	.15	.40
❑ 380 Jeff Garcia	.20	.50
❑ 381 Charlie Garner	.20	.50
❑ 382 Terry Jackson	.15	.40
❑ 383 Brian Jennings	.15	.40
❑ 384 Travis Jervey	.15	.40
❑ 385 Jonas Lewis	.15	.40
❑ 386 Terrell Owens	.25	.60
❑ 387 Jerry Rice	.50	1.25
❑ 388 Paul Smith	.15	.40
❑ 389 J.J. Stokes	.15	.40
❑ 390 Tai Streets	.15	.40
❑ 391 Justin Swift	.15	.40
❑ 392 Shaun Alexander	.25	.60
❑ 393 Karsten Bailey	.15	.40
❑ 394 Chad Brown	.15	.40
❑ 395 Sean Dawkins	.15	.40
❑ 396 Christian Fauria	.15	.40
❑ 397 Brock Huard	.15	.40
❑ 398 Darrell Jackson	.20	.50
❑ 399 Jon Kitna	.20	.50
❑ 400 Derrick Mayes	.15	.40
❑ 401 Itula Mili	.15	.40
❑ 402 Charlie Rogers	.15	.40
❑ 403 Mack Strong	.20	.50
❑ 404 Ricky Watters	.20	.50
❑ 405 James Williams WR	.15	.40
❑ 406 Rabih Abdullah	.15	.40
❑ 407 Mike Alstott	.20	.50
❑ 408 Reidel Anthony	.15	.40
❑ 409 Derrick Brooks	.25	.60
❑ 410 Warrick Dunn	.25	.60
❑ 411 Jacquez Green	.15	.40
❑ 412 Joe Hamilton	.15	.40
❑ 413 Keyshawn Johnson	.20	.50
❑ 414 Shaun King	.15	.40
❑ 415 Charles Kirby RC	.15	.40
❑ 416 Warren Sapp	.20	.50
❑ 417 Aaron Stecker	.15	.40
❑ 418 Todd Yoder	.15	.40
❑ 419 Eric Zeier	.15	.40
❑ 420 Chris Coleman	.15	.40
❑ 421 Kevin Dyson	.20	.50
❑ 422 Eddie George	.25	.60
❑ 423 Jevon Kearse	.20	.50
❑ 424 Erron Kinney	.15	.40
❑ 425 Mike Leach	.15	.40
❑ 426 Derrick Mason	.20	.50
❑ 427 Steve McNair	.25	.60
❑ 428 Lorenzo Neal	.20	.50
❑ 429 Carl Pickens	.20	.50
❑ 430 Chris Sanders	.15	.40
❑ 431 Yancey Thigpen	.15	.40
❑ 432 Rodney Thomas	.15	.40
❑ 433 Frank Wycheck	.15	.40
❑ 434 Stephen Alexander	.15	.40
❑ 435 Champ Bailey	.25	.60
❑ 436 Larry Centers	.20	.50
❑ 437 Albert Connell	.15	.40
❑ 438 Stephen Davis	.20	.50
❑ 439 Zeron Flemister RC	.15	.40
❑ 440 Irving Fryar	.20	.50
❑ 441 Jeff George	.20	.50
❑ 442 Skip Hicks	.15	.40
❑ 443 Todd Husak	.15	.40
❑ 444 Brad Johnson	.20	.50
❑ 445 Adrian Murrell	.20	.50
❑ 446 Deion Sanders	.25	.60
❑ 447 Mike Sellers	.15	.40
❑ 448 Derrius Thompson	.15	.40
❑ 449 James Thrash	.20	.50
❑ 450 Michael Westbrook	.15	.40
❑ 451 Alex Bannister AU/1750 RC	4.00	10.00
❑ 452 Kevan Barlow AU/1500 RC	5.00	12.00
❑ 453 Drew Brees AU/1000 RC	50.00	100.00
❑ 454 Travis Henry AU/1500 RC	6.00	15.00
❑ 455 Chad Johnson AU/1750 RC	12.50	30.00
❑ 456 M.McMahon AU/1000 RC	5.00	12.00
❑ 457 B.Newcombe AU/1750 RC	5.00	12.00
❑ 458 Sage Rosenfels AU/1000 RC	6.00	15.00
❑ 459 L.Tomlinson AU/1500 RC	50.00	100.00
❑ 460 Chris Weinke AU/1000 RC	5.00	12.00
❑ 461 Tay Cody RC	.75	2.00
❑ 462 Adam Archuleta RC	1.00	2.50
❑ 463 Will Allen RC	1.25	3.00
❑ 464 Moran Norris RC	.75	2.00
❑ 465 Tommy Polley RC	1.00	2.50
❑ 466 Ennis Davis RC	.75	2.00
❑ 467 Jamar Fletcher RC	.75	2.00
❑ 468 Derrick Gibson RC	.75	2.00
❑ 469 Sedrick Hodge RC	.75	2.00

Card	Low	High
❑ 470 Willie Howard RC	.75	2.00
❑ 471 Steve Hutchinson RC	1.00	2.50
❑ 472 Michael Stone RC	.75	2.00
❑ 473 Vinny Sutherland/1750 RC	1.00	2.50
❑ 474 Joe Tafoya RC	.75	2.00
❑ 475 Maurice Williams RC	.75	2.00
❑ 476 Pork Chop Womack RC	.75	2.00
❑ 477 Chad Ward RC	.75	2.00
❑ 478 Scotty Anderson/1750 RC	1.25	3.00
❑ 479 Gary Baxter RC	1.00	2.50
❑ 480 M.Tuiasosopo/1000 RC	2.00	5.00
❑ 481 Tim Hasselbeck/1000 RC	2.00	5.00
❑ 482 Clevan Thomas RC	.75	2.00
❑ 483 Marcus Stroud RC	1.00	2.50
❑ 484 John Schlecht RC	.75	2.00
❑ 485 Brandon Spoon RC	1.00	2.50
❑ 486 Alex Lincoln RC	.75	2.00
❑ 487 Anthony Thomas/1750 RC	1.50	4.00
❑ 488 Freddie Mitchell/1750 RC	1.00	2.50
❑ 489 Brian Allen RC	.75	2.00
❑ 490 Zeke Moreno RC	1.00	2.50
❑ 491 Tony Driver RC	1.00	2.50
❑ 492 Kynan Forney RC	.75	2.00
❑ 493 Reggie Wayne/1750 RC	4.00	10.00
❑ 494 Larry Casher RC	.75	2.00
❑ 495 Fred Wakefield RC	.75	2.00
❑ 496 Jeff Backus RC	.75	2.00
❑ 497 Jarrod Cooper RC	1.00	2.50
❑ 498 Heath Evans RC	1.00	2.50
❑ 499 James Jackson/1500 RC	1.25	3.00
❑ 500 Jabari Holloway RC	1.00	2.50
❑ 501 Quincy Morgan/1750 RC	1.25	3.00
❑ 502 Josh Booty/1000 RC	2.00	5.00
❑ 503 Ja'Mar Toombs RC	.75	2.00
❑ 504 Jason McKinley/1000 RC	1.50	4.00
❑ 505 Reggie White/1500 RC	1.00	2.50
❑ 506 Todd Heap/1750 RC	1.50	4.00
❑ 507 Rudi Johnson/1500 RC	1.50	4.00
❑ 508 Snoop Minnis/1750 RC	1.25	3.00
❑ 509 David Terrell/1750 RC	1.25	3.00
❑ 510 Torrance Marshall RC	1.00	2.50
❑ 511 Michael Bennett/1500 RC	1.50	4.00
❑ 512 Chris Chambers/1750 RC	2.50	6.00
❑ 513 Ben Leard/1000 RC	1.50	4.00
❑ 514 Rod Gardner/1750 RC	1.25	3.00
❑ 515 Michael Vick/1000 RC	5.00	12.00
❑ 516 Josh Heupel/1000 RC	2.50	6.00
❑ 517 Jesse Palmer/1000 RC	2.50	6.00
❑ 518 Quincy Carter/1000 RC	2.00	5.00
❑ 519 A.J. Feeley/1000 RC	2.00	5.00
❑ 520 David Rivers/1000 RC	1.50	4.00
❑ 521 Deuce McAllister/1500 RC	2.00	5.00
❑ 522 LaMont Jordan/1500 RC	1.50	4.00
❑ 523 David Allen/1500 RC	1.00	2.50
❑ 524 Correll Buckhalter/1500 RC	1.50	4.00
❑ 525 Travis Minor/1500	1.25	3.00
❑ 526 Koren Robinson/1750 RC	1.50	4.00
❑ 527 Santana Moss/1750 RC	2.50	6.00
❑ 528 Robert Ferguson/1750 RC	1.50	4.00
❑ 529 T.J.Houshmndzdh/1750 RC	2.50	6.00
❑ 530 Cedrick Wilson/1750 RC	1.50	4.00

2002 Pacific

Card	Low	High
❑ COMPLETE SET (500)	50.00	100.00
❑ 1 David Boston	.15	.40
❑ 2 Arnold Jackson	.15	.40
❑ 3 MarTay Jenkins	.15	.40
❑ 4 Thomas Jones	.20	.50
❑ 5 Kwamie Lassiter	.15	.40
❑ 6 Joel Makovicka	.15	.40
❑ 7 Ronald McKinnon	.15	.40
❑ 8 Tywan Mitchell	.15	.40
❑ 9 Michael Pittman	.20	.50
❑ 10 Jake Plummer	.20	.50
❑ 11 Frank Sanders	.15	.40
❑ 12 Kyle Vanden Bosch	.20	.50
❑ 13 Jamal Anderson	.20	.50
❑ 14 Keith Brooking	.15	.40
❑ 15 Chris Chandler	.20	.50
❑ 16 Bob Christian	.15	.40
❑ 17 Alge Crumpler	.20	.50
❑ 18 Brian Finneran	.20	.50
❑ 19 Shawn Jefferson	.15	.40
❑ 20 Patrick Kerney	.15	.40
❑ 21 Terance Mathis	.15	.40
❑ 22 Maurice Smith	.15	.40
❑ 23 Rodney Thomas	.20	.50
❑ 24 Darrick Vaughn	.15	.40
❑ 25 Michael Vick	.25	.60
❑ 26 Sam Adams	.15	.40
❑ 27 Terry Allen	.20	.50
❑ 28 Obafemi Ayanbadejo	.15	.40
❑ 29 Peter Boulware	.20	.50
❑ 30 Jason Brookins	.15	.40
❑ 31 Randall Cunningham	.20	.50
❑ 32 Elvis Grbac	.20	.50
❑ 33 Todd Heap	.20	.50
❑ 34 Qadry Ismail	.20	.50
❑ 35 Jamal Lewis	.20	.50
❑ 36 Ray Lewis	.25	.60
❑ 37 Chris Redman	.15	.40
❑ 38 Shannon Sharpe	.25	.60
❑ 39 Brandon Stokley	.20	.50
❑ 40 Travis Taylor	.15	.40
❑ 41 Moe Williams	.15	.40
❑ 42 Rod Woodson	.25	.60
❑ 43 Shawn Bryson	.15	.40
❑ 44 Larry Centers	.20	.50
❑ 45 Nate Clements	.15	.40
❑ 46 London Fletcher	.15	.40
❑ 47 Reggie Germany	.15	.40
❑ 48 Travis Henry	.20	.50
❑ 49 Jeremy McDaniel	.15	.40
❑ 50 Sammy Morris	.20	.50
❑ 51 Eric Moulds	.20	.50
❑ 52 Peerless Price	.15	.40
❑ 53 Jay Riemersma	.15	.40
❑ 54 Alex Van Pelt	.15	.40
❑ 55 Tim Biakabutuka	.20	.50
❑ 56 Isaac Byrd	.15	.40
❑ 57 Doug Evans	.15	.40
❑ 58 Donald Hayes	.15	.40
❑ 59 Chris Hetherington	.15	.40
❑ 60 Brad Hoover	.15	.40
❑ 61 Richard Huntley	.15	.40
❑ 62 Patrick Jeffers	.20	.50
❑ 63 Matt Lytle	.15	.40
❑ 64 Dan Morgan	.15	.40
❑ 65 Muhsin Muhammad	.20	.50
❑ 66 Mike Rucker RC	.25	.60
❑ 67 Steve Smith	.25	.60
❑ 68 Wesley Walls	.20	.50
❑ 69 Chris Weinke	.15	.40
❑ 70 James Allen	.15	.40
❑ 71 Fred Baxter	.15	.40
❑ 72 Marty Booker	.20	.50
❑ 73 Mike Brown	.20	.50
❑ 74 Rosevelt Colvin RC	.30	.75
❑ 75 Phillip Daniels	.15	.40
❑ 76 Leon Johnson	.15	.40
❑ 77 Shane Matthews	.15	.40
❑ 78 Jim Miller	.20	.50
❑ 79 Tony Parrish	.15	.40
❑ 80 Marcus Robinson	.20	.50
❑ 81 David Terrell	.20	.50
❑ 82 Anthony Thomas	.20	.50
❑ 83 Brian Urlacher	.30	.75
❑ 84 Ted Washington	.15	.40
❑ 85 Dez White	.15	.40
❑ 86 Brandon Bennett	.15	.40
❑ 87 Corey Dillon	.20	.50
❑ 88 Ron Dugans	.15	.40
❑ 89 Danny Farmer	.15	.40
❑ 90 T.J. Houshmandzadeh	.25	.60
❑ 91 Chad Johnson	.25	.60
❑ 92 Curtis Keaton	.15	.40
❑ 93 Jon Kitna	.20	.50
❑ 94 Tony McGee	.20	.50
❑ 95 Lorenzo Neal	.20	.50
❑ 96 Darnay Scott	.20	.50
❑ 97 Akili Smith	.20	.50
❑ 98 Justin Smith	.15	.40
❑ 99 Takeo Spikes	.15	.40
❑ 100 Peter Warrick	.20	.50
❑ 101 Tim Couch	.15	.40
❑ 102 JaJuan Dawson	.15	.40
❑ 103 Benjamin Gay	.15	.40
❑ 104 Anthony Henry	.15	.40
❑ 105 James Jackson	.15	.40
❑ 106 Kevin Johnson	.15	.40
❑ 107 Andre King	.15	.40
❑ 108 Jamir Miller	.15	.40
❑ 109 Quincy Morgan	.15	.40
❑ 110 Dennis Northcutt	.15	.40
❑ 111 O.J. Santiago	.15	.40
❑ 112 Jamel White	.15	.40
❑ 113 Quincy Carter	.15	.40
❑ 114 Darrin Chiaverini	.15	.40
❑ 115 Dexter Coakley	.15	.40
❑ 116 Joey Galloway	.20	.50
❑ 117 Troy Hambrick	.15	.40
❑ 118 Rocket Ismail	.20	.50
❑ 119 Dat Nguyen	.15	.40
❑ 120 Ken-Yon Rambo	.15	.40
❑ 121 Emmitt Smith	.60	1.50
❑ 122 Reggie Swinton	.15	.40
❑ 123 Robert Thomas	.15	.40
❑ 124 Michael Wiley	.15	.40
❑ 125 Anthony Wright	.15	.40
❑ 126 Mike Anderson	.20	.50
❑ 127 Dwayne Carswell	.15	.40
❑ 128 Desmond Clark	.20	.50
❑ 129 Chris Cole	.15	.40
❑ 130 Terrell Davis	.25	.60
❑ 131 Gus Frerotte	.20	.50
❑ 132 Olandis Gary	.20	.50
❑ 133 Brian Griese	.20	.50
❑ 134 Kevin Kasper	.15	.40
❑ 135 Ed McCaffrey	.20	.50
❑ 136 Phil McGeoghan RC	.15	.40
❑ 137 John Mobley	.15	.40
❑ 138 Scottie Montgomery	.15	.40
❑ 139 Deltha O'Neal	.15	.40
❑ 140 Trevor Pryce	.15	.40
❑ 141 Rod Smith	.20	.50
❑ 142 Al Wilson	.20	.50
❑ 143 Scotty Anderson	.15	.40
❑ 144 Charlie Batch	.20	.50
❑ 145 Aveion Cason	.15	.40
❑ 146 Germane Crowell	.15	.40
❑ 147 Reuben Droughns	.20	.50
❑ 148 Bert Emanuel	.20	.50
❑ 149 Larry Foster	.15	.40
❑ 150 Az-Zahir Hakim	.15	.40
❑ 151 Desmond Howard	.20	.50
❑ 152 Mike McMahon	.15	.40
❑ 153 Herman Moore	.20	.50
❑ 154 Johnnie Morton	.20	.50
❑ 155 Robert Porcher	.15	.40
❑ 156 Cory Schlesinger	.15	.40
❑ 157 David Sloan	.15	.40
❑ 158 James Stewart	.15	.40
❑ 159 Lamont Warren	.15	.40
❑ 160 Donald Driver	.25	.60
❑ 161 Brett Favre	.60	1.50
❑ 162 Bubba Franks	.20	.50
❑ 163 Antonio Freeman	.25	.60
❑ 164 Kabeer Gbaja-Biamila	.20	.50
❑ 165 Terry Glenn	.20	.50
❑ 166 Ahman Green	.20	.50
❑ 167 William Henderson	.20	.50
❑ 168 Dorsey Levens	.20	.50
❑ 169 David Martin	.15	.40
❑ 170 Rondell Mealey	.15	.40
❑ 171 Bill Schroeder	.20	.50
❑ 172 Darren Sharper	.20	.50
❑ 173 Avion Black	.15	.40
❑ 174 Tony Boselli	.20	.50
❑ 175 Corey Bradford	.15	.40
❑ 176 Marcus Coleman	.15	.40
❑ 177 Leomont Evans	.15	.40
❑ 178 Aaron Glenn	.15	.40
❑ 179 Trevor Insley	.15	.40
❑ 180 Jermaine Lewis	.15	.40
❑ 181 Anthony Malbrough	.15	.40
❑ 182 Frank Moreau	.15	.40
❑ 183 Mike Quinn	.15	.40
❑ 184 Charlie Rogers	.15	.40
❑ 185 Jamie Sharper	.20	.50
❑ 186 Matt Snider	.15	.40
❑ 187 Gary Walker	.15	.40
❑ 188 Kevin Williams RC	.40	1.00
❑ 189 Kailee Wong	.15	.40
❑ 190 Chad Bratzke	.15	.40

Card		
❑ 191 Ken Dilger	.20	.50
❑ 192 Marvin Harrison	.25	.60
❑ 193 Edgerrin James	.25	.60
❑ 194 Kevin McDougal	.15	.40
❑ 195 Rob Morris	.15	.40
❑ 196 Jerome Pathon	.15	.40
❑ 197 Marcus Pollard	.15	.40
❑ 198 Dominic Rhodes	.20	.50
❑ 199 Marcus Washington	.15	.40
❑ 200 Reggie Wayne	.25	.60
❑ 201 Terrence Wilkins	.15	.40
❑ 202 Tony Brackens	.15	.40
❑ 203 Kyle Brady	.15	.40
❑ 204 Mark Brunell	.20	.50
❑ 205 Donovin Darius	.15	.40
❑ 206 Sean Dawkins	.20	.50
❑ 207 Damon Gibson	.15	.40
❑ 208 Elvis Joseph	.15	.40
❑ 209 Stacey Mack	.15	.40
❑ 210 Keenan McCardell	.20	.50
❑ 211 Hardy Nickerson	.15	.40
❑ 212 Jonathan Quinn	.15	.40
❑ 213 Micah Ross RC	.15	.40
❑ 214 Jimmy Smith	.20	.50
❑ 215 Fred Taylor	.25	.60
❑ 216 Patrick Washington	.15	.40
❑ 217 Derrick Alexander	.20	.50
❑ 218 Mike Cloud	.15	.40
❑ 219 Donnie Edwards	.15	.40
❑ 220 Tony Gonzalez	.20	.50
❑ 221 Trent Green	.20	.50
❑ 222 Dante Hall	.20	.50
❑ 223 Priest Holmes	.25	.60
❑ 224 Eddie Kennison	.20	.50
❑ 225 Snoop Minnis	.15	.40
❑ 226 Larry Parker	.15	.40
❑ 227 Marvcus Patton	.15	.40
❑ 228 Tony Richardson	.15	.40
❑ 229 Mikhael Ricks	.15	.40
❑ 230 Chris Chambers	.25	.60
❑ 231 Jay Fiedler	.20	.50
❑ 232 Oronde Gadsden	.15	.40
❑ 233 Rob Konrad	.15	.40
❑ 234 Sam Madison	.15	.40
❑ 235 Brock Marion	.15	.40
❑ 236 James McKnight	.15	.40
❑ 237 Travis Minor	.20	.50
❑ 238 Jeff Ogden	.20	.50
❑ 239 Lamar Smith	.20	.50
❑ 240 Jason Taylor	.25	.60
❑ 241 Zach Thomas	.25	.60
❑ 242 Dedric Ward	.15	.40
❑ 243 Ricky Williams	.25	.60
❑ 244 Michael Bennett	.20	.50
❑ 245 Todd Bouman	.15	.40
❑ 246 Cris Carter	.25	.60
❑ 247 Byron Chamberlain	.15	.40
❑ 248 Doug Chapman	.15	.40
❑ 249 Kenny Clark RC	.15	.40
❑ 250 Daunte Culpepper	.20	.50
❑ 251 Nate Jacquet	.15	.40
❑ 252 Jim Kleinsasser	.25	.60
❑ 253 Harold Morrow	.15	.40
❑ 254 Randy Moss	.25	.60
❑ 255 Jake Reed	.20	.50
❑ 256 Spergon Wynn	.15	.40
❑ 257 Drew Bledsoe	.25	.60
❑ 258 Tom Brady	.60	1.50
❑ 259 Troy Brown	.20	.50
❑ 260 Fred Coleman	.15	.40
❑ 261 Marc Edwards	.15	.40
❑ 262 Kevin Faulk	.20	.50
❑ 263 Bobby Hamilton	.15	.40
❑ 264 Ty Law	.20	.50
❑ 265 Lawyer Milloy	.20	.50
❑ 266 David Patten	.15	.40
❑ 267 J.R. Redmond	.15	.40
❑ 268 Antowain Smith	.20	.50
❑ 269 Adam Vinatieri	.25	.60
❑ 270 Jermaine Wiggins	.15	.40
❑ 271 Aaron Brooks	.20	.50
❑ 272 Cam Cleeland	.15	.40
❑ 273 Charlie Clemons RC	.15	.40
❑ 274 James Fenderson RC	.15	.40
❑ 275 La'Roi Glover	.15	.40
❑ 276 Joe Horn	.20	.50
❑ 277 Willie Jackson	.15	.40
❑ 278 Sammy Knight	.15	.40
❑ 279 Michael Lewis	.25	.60
❑ 280 Deuce McAllister	.25	.60
❑ 281 Terrelle Smith	.15	.40
❑ 282 Boo Williams	.15	.40
❑ 283 Robert Wilson	.15	.40
❑ 284 Tiki Barber	.25	.60
❑ 285 Micheal Barrow	.15	.40
❑ 286 Kerry Collins	.20	.50
❑ 287 Greg Comella	.15	.40
❑ 288 Thabiti Davis	.15	.40
❑ 289 Ron Dayne	.20	.50
❑ 290 Ron Dixon	.15	.40
❑ 291 Ike Hilliard	.20	.50
❑ 292 Joe Jurevicius	.20	.50
❑ 293 Michael Strahan	.25	.60
❑ 294 Amani Toomer	.20	.50
❑ 295 Damon Washington	.15	.40
❑ 296 John Abraham	.20	.50
❑ 297 Richie Anderson	.15	.40
❑ 298 Anthony Becht	.15	.40
❑ 299 Wayne Chrebet	.20	.50
❑ 300 Laveranues Coles	.25	.60
❑ 301 James Farrior	.20	.50
❑ 302 Marvin Jones	.15	.40
❑ 303 LaMont Jordan	.20	.50
❑ 304 Curtis Martin	.25	.60
❑ 305 Santana Moss	.20	.50
❑ 306 Chad Pennington	.25	.60
❑ 307 Kevin Swayne	.15	.40
❑ 308 Vinny Testaverde	.20	.50
❑ 309 Craig Yeast	.15	.40
❑ 310 Greg Biekert	.15	.40
❑ 311 Tim Brown	.25	.60
❑ 312 Zack Crockett	.15	.40
❑ 313 Rich Gannon	.20	.50
❑ 314 Charlie Garner	.20	.50
❑ 315 Sebastian Janikowski	.15	.40
❑ 316 Randy Jordan	.15	.40
❑ 317 Terry Kirby	.15	.40
❑ 318 Jerry Porter	.20	.50
❑ 319 Jerry Rice	.50	1.25
❑ 320 Jon Ritchie	.15	.40
❑ 321 Tyrone Wheatley	.20	.50
❑ 322 Roland Williams	.15	.40
❑ 323 Charles Woodson	.25	.60
❑ 324 Correll Buckhalter	.20	.50
❑ 325 Brian Dawkins	.20	.50
❑ 326 Hugh Douglas	.15	.40
❑ 327 A.J. Feeley	.20	.50
❑ 328 Chad Lewis	.15	.40
❑ 329 Cecil Martin	.15	.40
❑ 330 Brian Mitchell	.20	.50
❑ 331 Freddie Mitchell	.15	.40
❑ 332 Todd Pinkston	.15	.40
❑ 333 Rod Smart RC	.20	.50
❑ 334 Duce Staley	.20	.50
❑ 335 James Thrash	.20	.50
❑ 336 Jeremiah Trotter	.15	.40
❑ 337 Troy Vincent	.20	.50
❑ 338 Kendrell Bell	.15	.40
❑ 339 Jerome Bettis	.25	.60
❑ 340 Demetrius Brown RC	.15	.40
❑ 341 Plaxico Burress	.20	.50
❑ 342 Troy Edwards	.15	.40
❑ 343 Chris Fuamatu-Ma'afala	.15	.40
❑ 344 Jason Gildon	.20	.50
❑ 345 Earl Holmes	.15	.40
❑ 346 Joey Porter	.20	.50
❑ 347 Chad Scott	.15	.40
❑ 348 Bobby Shaw	.15	.40
❑ 349 Kordell Stewart	.20	.50
❑ 350 Hines Ward	.25	.60
❑ 351 Amos Zereoue	.15	.40
❑ 352 Adam Archuleta	.15	.40
❑ 353 Dre' Bly	.15	.40
❑ 354 Isaac Bruce	.25	.60
❑ 355 Trung Canidate	.15	.40
❑ 356 Ernie Conwell	.15	.40
❑ 357 Marshall Faulk	.25	.60
❑ 358 Torry Holt	.25	.60
❑ 359 Leonard Little	.20	.50
❑ 360 Yo Murphy	.15	.40
❑ 361 Ricky Proehl	.20	.50
❑ 362 Kurt Warner	.25	.60
❑ 363 Aeneas Williams	.20	.50
❑ 364 Drew Brees	.40	1.00
❑ 365 Curtis Conway	.20	.50
❑ 366 Tim Dwight	.20	.50
❑ 367 Terrell Fletcher	.15	.40
❑ 368 Doug Flutie	.25	.60
❑ 369 Jeff Graham	.15	.40
❑ 370 Rodney Harrison	.20	.50
❑ 371 Ronney Jenkins	.15	.40
❑ 372 Raylee Johnson	.15	.40
❑ 373 Freddie Jones	.15	.40
❑ 374 Ryan McNeil	.15	.40
❑ 375 Junior Seau	.25	.60
❑ 376 LaDainian Tomlinson	.40	1.00
❑ 377 Marcellus Wiley	.15	.40
❑ 378 Kevan Barlow	.15	.40
❑ 379 Fred Beasley	.15	.40
❑ 380 Zack Bronson RC	.15	.40
❑ 381 Andre Carter	.15	.40
❑ 382 Jeff Garcia	.20	.50
❑ 383 Garrison Hearst	.20	.50
❑ 384 Terry Jackson	.15	.40
❑ 385 Eric Johnson	.15	.40
❑ 386 Saladin McCullough RC	.15	.40
❑ 387 Terrell Owens	.25	.60
❑ 388 Ahmed Plummer	.15	.40
❑ 389 J.J. Stokes	.15	.40
❑ 390 Tai Streets	.15	.40
❑ 391 Vinny Sutherland	.15	.40
❑ 392 Bryant Young	.15	.40
❑ 393 Shaun Alexander	.25	.60
❑ 394 Chad Brown	.15	.40
❑ 395 Kerwin Cook RC	.15	.40
❑ 396 Trent Dilfer	.20	.50
❑ 397 Bobby Engram	.20	.50
❑ 398 Christian Fauria	.15	.40
❑ 399 Matt Hasselbeck	.25	.60
❑ 400 Darrell Jackson	.20	.50
❑ 401 John Randle	.20	.50
❑ 402 Koren Robinson	.15	.40
❑ 403 Anthony Simmons	.15	.40
❑ 404 Mack Strong	.15	.40
❑ 405 Ricky Watters	.20	.50
❑ 406 James Williams WR	.15	.40
❑ 407 Mike Alstott	.20	.50
❑ 408 Ronde Barber	.20	.50
❑ 409 Derrick Brooks	.25	.60
❑ 410 Jameel Cook	.15	.40
❑ 411 Warrick Dunn	.20	.50
❑ 412 Jacquez Green	.15	.40
❑ 413 Brad Johnson	.20	.50
❑ 414 Keyshawn Johnson	.20	.50
❑ 415 Rob Johnson	.20	.50
❑ 416 John Lynch	.20	.50
❑ 417 Dave Moore	.15	.40
❑ 418 Warren Sapp	.20	.50
❑ 419 Aaron Stecker	.15	.40
❑ 420 Karl Williams	.15	.40
❑ 421 Drew Bennett	.20	.50
❑ 422 Eddie Berlin	.15	.40
❑ 423 Rafael Cooper RC	.15	.40
❑ 424 Kevin Dyson	.20	.50
❑ 425 Eddie George	.20	.50
❑ 426 Mike Green	.15	.40
❑ 427 Skip Hicks	.15	.40
❑ 428 Jevon Kearse	.20	.50
❑ 429 Erron Kinney	.15	.40
❑ 430 Derrick Mason	.20	.50
❑ 431 Justin McCareins	.20	.50
❑ 432 Steve McNair	.25	.60
❑ 433 Neil O'Donnell	.20	.50
❑ 434 Frank Wycheck	.15	.40
❑ 435 Reidel Anthony	.15	.40
❑ 436 Jessie Armstead	.15	.40
❑ 437 Champ Bailey	.25	.60
❑ 438 Tony Banks	.15	.40
❑ 439 Michael Bates	.15	.40
❑ 440 Donnell Bennett	.15	.40
❑ 441 Ki-Jana Carter	.20	.50
❑ 442 Stephen Davis	.20	.50
❑ 443 Zeron Flemister	.15	.40
❑ 444 Rod Gardner	.15	.40
❑ 445 Kevin Lockett	.15	.40
❑ 446 Eric Metcalf	.15	.40
❑ 447 Sage Rosenfels	.20	.50
❑ 448 Fred Smoot	.20	.50
❑ 449 Michael Westbrook	.15	.40
❑ 450 Danny Wuerffel	.20	.50
❑ 451 Jason McAddley RC	.50	1.25
❑ 452 Freddie Milons RC	.40	1.00
❑ 453 Bryan Thomas RC	.40	1.00
❑ 454 Levi Jones RC	.40	1.00
❑ 455 William Green RC	.50	1.25
❑ 456 Luke Staley RC	.40	1.00
❑ 457 Daniel Graham RC	.50	1.25

Card		
❑ 458 David Garrard RC	1.00	2.50
❑ 459 Reche Caldwell RC	.60	1.50
❑ 460 Andra Davis RC	.40	1.00
❑ 461 Lito Sheppard RC	.60	1.50
❑ 462 Chris Hope RC	.60	1.50
❑ 463 Javon Walker RC	.60	1.50
❑ 464 David Carr RC	.60	1.50
❑ 465 Alan Harper RC	.40	1.00
❑ 466 Adrian Peterson RC	.60	1.50
❑ 467 Kelly Campbell RC	.50	1.25
❑ 468 Ashley Lelie RC	.60	1.50
❑ 469 Kurt Kittner RC	.40	1.00
❑ 470 Antwaan Randle El RC	.60	1.50
❑ 471 Ladell Betts RC	.60	1.50
❑ 472 Josh Reed RC	.50	1.25
❑ 473 Clinton Portis RC	1.50	4.00
❑ 474 Ron Johnson RC	.50	1.25
❑ 475 Eric Crouch RC	.60	1.50
❑ 476 Tracey Wistrom RC	.50	1.25
❑ 477 David Neill RC	.40	1.00
❑ 478 Ronald Curry RC	.60	1.50
❑ 479 Lamar Gordon RC	.60	1.50
❑ 480 Damien Anderson RC	.50	1.25
❑ 481 Napoleon Harris RC	.50	1.25
❑ 482 Zak Kustok RC	.40	1.00
❑ 483 Rocky Calmus RC	.50	1.25
❑ 484 Roy Williams RC	.75	2.00
❑ 485 Joey Harrington RC	.60	1.50
❑ 486 Maurice Morris RC	.60	1.50
❑ 487 Antonio Bryant RC	.75	2.00
❑ 488 Josh McCown RC	.60	1.50
❑ 489 John Henderson RC	.60	1.50
❑ 490 Quentin Jammer RC	.60	1.50
❑ 491 Mike Williams RC	.40	1.00
❑ 492 Patrick Ramsey RC	.60	1.50
❑ 493 Kenyon Coleman RC	.40	1.00
❑ 494 DeShaun Foster RC	.60	1.50
❑ 495 Brian Poli-Dixon RC	.40	1.00
❑ 496 Cliff Russell RC	.40	1.00
❑ 497 Brian Westbrook RC	2.00	5.00
❑ 498 Andre Davis RC	.50	1.25
❑ 499 Larry Tripplett RC	.40	1.00
❑ 500 Lamont Thompson RC	.50	1.25
❑ 501 T.J. Duckett RC	.60	1.50
❑ 502 Dameon Hunter RC	.40	1.00
❑ 503 Javin Hunter RC	.40	1.00
❑ 504 Tellis Redmon RC	.40	1.00
❑ 505 Chester Taylor RC	1.00	2.50
❑ 506 Randy Fasani RC	.50	1.25
❑ 507 Julius Peppers RC	1.00	2.50
❑ 508 Jamin Elliott RC	.40	1.00
❑ 509 Chad Hutchinson RC	.40	1.00
❑ 510 Eddie Drummond RC	.40	1.00
❑ 511 Craig Nall RC	.50	1.25
❑ 512 Jabar Gaffney RC	.60	1.50
❑ 513 Jonathan Wells RC	.60	1.50
❑ 514 Shaun Hill RC	.75	2.00
❑ 515 Deion Branch RC	.60	1.50
❑ 516 Rohan Davey RC	.60	1.50
❑ 517 J.T. O'Sullivan RC	.60	1.50
❑ 518 Tim Carter RC	.50	1.25
❑ 519 Daryl Jones RC	.40	1.00
❑ 520 Jeremy Shockey RC	1.00	2.50
❑ 521 Seth Burford RC	.40	1.00
❑ 522 Brandon Doman RC	.40	1.00
❑ 523 Jerramy Stevens RC	.60	1.50
❑ 524 Travis Stephens RC	.40	1.00
❑ 525 Marquise Walker RC	.40	1.00

1964 Philadelphia

Card		
❑ COMPLETE SET (198)	600.00	900.00
❑ WRAPPER (1-CENT)	35.00	60.00
❑ WRAPPER (5-CENT)	10.00	20.00
❑ 1 Raymond Berry	10.00	20.00
❑ 2 Tom Gilburg	1.25	2.50
❑ 3 John Mackey RC	18.00	30.00
❑ 4 Gino Marchetti	2.50	5.00
❑ 5 Jim Martin	1.25	2.50
❑ 6 Tom Matte RC	3.00	6.00
❑ 7 Jimmy Orr	1.50	3.00
❑ 8 Jim Parker	2.00	4.00
❑ 9 Bill Pellington	1.25	2.50
❑ 10 Alex Sandusky	1.25	2.50
❑ 11 Dick Szymanski	1.25	2.50
❑ 12 Johnny Unitas	25.00	45.00
❑ 13 Baltimore Colts	1.50	3.00
❑ 14 Colts Play/Don Shula	20.00	35.00
❑ 15 Doug Atkins	2.50	5.00
❑ 16 Ronnie Bull	1.25	2.50
❑ 17 Mike Ditka	25.00	40.00
❑ 18 Joe Fortunato	1.25	2.50
❑ 19 Willie Galimore	1.50	3.00
❑ 20 Joe Marconi	1.25	2.50
❑ 21 Bennie McRae RC	1.25	2.50
❑ 22 Johnny Morris	1.25	2.50
❑ 23 Richie Petitbon	1.25	2.50
❑ 24 Mike Pyle RC	1.25	2.50
❑ 25 Roosevelt Taylor RC	2.00	4.00
❑ 26 Bill Wade	1.50	3.00
❑ 27 Chicago Bears	1.50	3.00
❑ 28 Bears Play/George Halas	6.00	12.00
❑ 29 Johnny Brewer RC	1.25	2.50
❑ 30 Jim Brown	50.00	90.00
❑ 31 Gary Collins RC	4.00	8.00
❑ 32 Vince Costello	1.25	2.50
❑ 33 Galen Fiss	1.25	2.50
❑ 34 Bill Glass	1.25	2.50
❑ 35 Ernie Green RC	1.50	3.00
❑ 36 Rich Kreitling	1.25	2.50
❑ 37 John Morrow	1.25	2.50
❑ 38 Frank Ryan	1.50	3.00
❑ 39 Charlie Scales RC	1.25	2.50
❑ 40 Dick Schafrath RC	1.25	2.50
❑ 41 Cleveland Browns	1.50	3.00
❑ 42 Cleveland Browns Play	1.25	2.50
❑ 43 Don Bishop	1.25	2.50
❑ 44 Frank Clarke RC	1.50	3.00
❑ 45 Mike Connelly	1.25	2.50
❑ 46 Lee Folkins RC	1.25	2.50
❑ 47 Cornell Green RC	4.00	8.00
❑ 48 Bob Lilly	25.00	40.00
❑ 49 Amos Marsh	1.25	2.50
❑ 50 Tommy McDonald	2.50	5.00
❑ 51 Don Meredith	20.00	35.00
❑ 52 Pettis Norman RC	1.50	3.00
❑ 53 Don Perkins	2.00	4.00
❑ 54 Guy Reese RC	1.25	2.50
❑ 55 Dallas Cowboys	2.00	4.00
❑ 56 Cowboys Play/T.Landry	12.00	20.00
❑ 57 Terry Barr	1.25	2.50
❑ 58 Roger Brown	1.50	3.00
❑ 59 Gail Cogdill	1.25	2.50
❑ 60 John Gordy RC	1.25	2.50
❑ 61 Dick Lane	2.00	4.00
❑ 62 Yale Lary	2.00	4.00
❑ 63 Dan Lewis	1.25	2.50
❑ 64 Darris McCord	1.25	2.50
❑ 65 Earl Morrall	1.50	3.00
❑ 66 Joe Schmidt	2.50	5.00
❑ 67 Pat Studstill RC	1.50	3.00
❑ 68 Wayne Walker RC	1.50	3.00
❑ 69 Detroit Lions	1.50	3.00
❑ 70 Detroit Lions	1.25	2.50
❑ 71 Herb Adderley RC	20.00	35.00
❑ 72 Willie Davis RC	18.00	30.00
❑ 73 Forrest Gregg	2.50	5.00
❑ 74 Paul Hornung	20.00	35.00
❑ 75 Hank Jordan	2.50	5.00
❑ 76 Jerry Kramer	3.00	6.00
❑ 77 Tom Moore	1.50	3.00
❑ 78 Jim Ringo	2.50	5.00
❑ 79 Bart Starr	35.00	60.00
❑ 80 Jim Taylor	15.00	25.00
❑ 81 Jesse Whittenton RC	1.50	3.00
❑ 82 Willie Wood	4.00	8.00
❑ 83 Green Bay Packers	3.00	6.00
❑ 84 Packers Play/Lombardi	20.00	35.00
❑ 85 Jon Arnett	1.25	2.50
❑ 86 Pervis Atkins RC	1.25	2.50
❑ 87 Dick Bass	1.50	3.00
❑ 88 Carroll Dale	2.00	4.00
❑ 89 Roman Gabriel	3.00	6.00
❑ 90 Ed Meador	1.25	2.50
❑ 91 Merlin Olsen RC	30.00	50.00
❑ 92 Jack Pardee RC	2.00	4.00
❑ 93 Jim Phillips	1.25	2.50
❑ 94 Carver Shannon RC	1.25	2.50
❑ 95 Frank Varrichione	1.25	2.50
❑ 96 Danny Villanueva	1.25	2.50
❑ 97 Los Angeles Rams	1.50	3.00
❑ 98 Los Angeles Rams Play	1.25	2.50
❑ 99 Grady Alderman RC	1.50	3.00
❑ 100 Larry Bowie RC	1.25	2.50
❑ 101 Bill Brown RC	3.00	6.00
❑ 102 Paul Flatley RC	1.25	2.50
❑ 103 Rip Hawkins	1.25	2.50
❑ 104 Jim Marshall	4.00	8.00
❑ 105 Tommy Mason	1.50	3.00
❑ 106 Jim Prestel	1.25	2.50
❑ 107 Jerry Reichow	1.25	2.50
❑ 108 Ed Sharockman	1.25	2.50
❑ 109 Fran Tarkenton	20.00	35.00
❑ 110 Mick Tingelhoff RC	3.00	6.00
❑ 111 Minnesota Vikings	1.50	3.00
❑ 112 Vikings Play/Van Brock.	2.00	4.00
❑ 113 Erich Barnes	1.25	2.50
❑ 114 Roosevelt Brown	2.00	4.00
❑ 115 Don Chandler	1.25	2.50
❑ 116 Darrell Dess	1.25	2.50
❑ 117 Frank Gifford	20.00	35.00
❑ 118 Dick James	1.25	2.50
❑ 119 Jim Katcavage	1.25	2.50
❑ 120 John Lovetere RC	1.25	2.50
❑ 121 Dick Lynch RC	1.50	3.00
❑ 122 Jim Patton	1.25	2.50
❑ 123 Del Shofner	1.25	2.50
❑ 124 Y.A.Tittle	10.00	20.00
❑ 125 New York Giants	1.50	3.00
❑ 126 New York Giants Play	1.25	2.50
❑ 127 Sam Baker	1.25	2.50
❑ 128 Maxie Baughan	1.25	2.50
❑ 129 Timmy Brown	1.50	3.00
❑ 130 Mike Clark RC	1.25	2.50
❑ 131 Irv Cross RC	1.50	3.00
❑ 132 Ted Dean	1.25	2.50
❑ 133 Ron Goodwin RC	1.25	2.50
❑ 134 King Hill	1.25	2.50
❑ 135 Clarence Peaks	1.25	2.50
❑ 136 Pete Retzlaff	1.50	3.00
❑ 137 Jim Schrader	1.25	2.50
❑ 138 Norm Snead	1.50	3.00
❑ 139 Philadelphia Eagles	1.50	3.00
❑ 140 Philadelphia Eagles Play	1.25	2.50
❑ 141 Gary Ballman RC	1.25	2.50
❑ 142 Charley Bradshaw RC	1.25	2.50
❑ 143 Ed Brown	1.50	3.00
❑ 144 John Henry Johnson	2.00	4.00
❑ 145 Joe Krupa	1.25	2.50
❑ 146 Bill Mack	1.25	2.50
❑ 147 Lou Michaels	1.25	2.50
❑ 148 Buzz Nutter	1.25	2.50
❑ 149 Myron Pottios	1.25	2.50
❑ 150 John Reger	1.25	2.50
❑ 151 Mike Sandusky	1.25	2.50
❑ 152 Clendon Thomas	1.25	2.50
❑ 153 Pittsburgh Steelers	1.50	3.00
❑ 154 Pittsburgh Steelers Play	1.25	2.50
❑ 155 Kermit Alexander RC	1.50	3.00
❑ 156 Bernie Casey	1.50	3.00
❑ 157 Dan Colchico	1.25	2.50
❑ 158 Clyde Conner	1.25	2.50
❑ 159 Tommy Davis	1.25	2.50
❑ 160 Matt Hazeltine	1.25	2.50
❑ 161 Jim Johnson RC	10.00	20.00
❑ 162 Don Lisbon RC	1.25	2.50
❑ 163 Lamar McHan	1.25	2.50
❑ 164 Bob St.Clair	2.00	4.00
❑ 165 J.D. Smith	1.25	2.50
❑ 166 Abe Woodson	1.25	2.50
❑ 167 San Francisco 49ers	1.50	3.00
❑ 168 San Francisco 49ers Play	1.25	2.50
❑ 169 Garland Boyette UER RC	1.25	2.50
❑ 170 Bobby Joe Conrad	1.50	3.00
❑ 171 Bob DeMarco RC	1.25	2.50
❑ 172 Ken Gray RC	1.25	2.50
❑ 173 Jimmy Hill	1.25	2.50
❑ 174 Charlie Johnson	1.50	3.00
❑ 175 Ernie McMillan	1.25	2.50
❑ 176 Dale Meinert RC	1.25	2.50
❑ 177 Luke Owens RC	1.25	2.50
❑ 178 Sonny Randle	1.25	2.50
❑ 179 Joe Robb RC	1.25	2.50
❑ 180 Bill Stacy	1.25	2.50
❑ 181 St. Louis Cardinals	1.50	3.00

Card	Low	High
❑ 182 St. Louis Cardinals Play	1.25	2.50
❑ 183 Bill Barnes	1.25	2.50
❑ 184 Don Bosseler	1.25	2.50
❑ 185 Sam Huff	3.00	6.00
❑ 186 Sonny Jurgensen	10.00	20.00
❑ 187 Bob Khayat RC	1.25	2.50
❑ 188 Riley Mattson	1.25	2.50
❑ 189 Bobby Mitchell	3.00	6.00
❑ 190 John Nisby	1.25	2.50
❑ 191 Vince Promuto	1.25	2.50
❑ 192 Joe Rutgens RC	1.25	2.50
❑ 193 Lonnie Sanders RC	1.25	2.50
❑ 194 Jim Steffen RC	1.25	2.50
❑ 195 Washington Redskins	1.50	3.00
❑ 196 Washington Redskins Play	1.25	2.50
❑ 197 Checklist 1 UER	18.00	30.00
❑ 198 Checklist 2 UER	30.00	55.00

1965 Philadelphia

Card	Low	High
❑ COMPLETE SET (198)	500.00	800.00
❑ WRAPPER (5-CENT)	10.00	20.00
❑ 1 Colts Team	7.50	15.00
❑ 2 Raymond Berry	5.00	10.00
❑ 3 Bob Boyd DB	1.00	2.00
❑ 4 Wendell Harris	1.00	2.00
❑ 5 Jerry Logan RC	1.00	2.00
❑ 6 Tony Lorick RC	1.00	2.00
❑ 7 Lou Michaels	1.00	2.00
❑ 8 Lenny Moore	4.00	8.00
❑ 9 Jimmy Orr	1.50	3.00
❑ 10 Jim Parker	2.00	4.00
❑ 11 Dick Szymanski	1.00	2.00
❑ 12 Johnny Unitas	25.00	40.00
❑ 13 Bob Vogel RC	1.00	2.00
❑ 14 Colts Play/Don Shula	12.00	20.00
❑ 15 Chicago Bears	1.50	3.00
❑ 16 Jon Arnett	1.00	2.00
❑ 17 Doug Atkins	2.50	5.00
❑ 18 Rudy Bukich RC	1.50	3.00
❑ 19 Mike Ditka	25.00	40.00
❑ 20 Dick Evey RC	1.00	2.00
❑ 21 Joe Fortunato	1.00	2.00
❑ 22 Bobby Joe Green RC	1.00	2.00
❑ 23 Johnny Morris	1.00	2.00
❑ 24 Mike Pyle	1.00	2.00
❑ 25 Roosevelt Taylor	1.50	3.00
❑ 26 Bill Wade	1.50	3.00
❑ 27 Bob Wetoska RC	1.00	2.00
❑ 28 Bears Play/George Halas	4.00	8.00
❑ 29 Cleveland Browns	1.50	3.00
❑ 30 Walter Beach RC	1.00	2.00
❑ 31 Jim Brown	50.00	80.00
❑ 32 Gary Collins	1.50	3.00
❑ 33 Bill Glass	1.00	2.00
❑ 34 Ernie Green	1.00	2.00
❑ 35 Jim Houston RC	1.00	2.00
❑ 36 Dick Modzelewski	1.00	2.00
❑ 37 Bernie Parrish	1.00	2.00
❑ 38 Walter Roberts RC	1.00	2.00
❑ 39 Frank Ryan	1.50	3.00
❑ 40 Dick Schafrath	1.00	2.00
❑ 41 Paul Warfield RC	50.00	90.00
❑ 42 Cleveland Browns	1.00	2.00
❑ 43 Dallas Cowboys	1.50	3.00
❑ 44 Frank Clarke	1.50	3.00
❑ 45 Mike Connelly	1.00	2.00
❑ 46 Buddy Dial	1.00	2.00
❑ 47 Bob Lilly	20.00	35.00
❑ 48 Tony Liscio RC	1.00	2.00
❑ 49 Tommy McDonald	2.50	5.00
❑ 50 Don Meredith	15.00	25.00
❑ 51 Pettis Norman	1.00	2.00
❑ 52 Don Perkins	2.00	4.00
❑ 53 Mel Renfro RC	25.00	40.00
❑ 54 Jim Ridlon	1.00	2.00
❑ 55 Jerry Tubbs	1.00	2.00
❑ 56 Cowboys Play/T.Landry	7.50	15.00
❑ 57 Detroit Lions	1.50	3.00
❑ 58 Terry Barr	1.00	2.00
❑ 59 Roger Brown	1.00	2.00
❑ 60 Gail Cogdill	1.00	2.00
❑ 61 Jim Gibbons	1.00	2.00
❑ 62 John Gordy	1.00	2.00
❑ 63 Yale Lary	2.00	4.00
❑ 64 Dick LeBeau RC	2.50	6.00
❑ 65 Earl Morrall	1.50	3.00
❑ 66 Nick Pietrosante	1.00	2.00
❑ 67 Pat Studstill	1.00	2.00
❑ 68 Wayne Walker	1.50	3.00
❑ 69 Tom Watkins RC	1.00	2.00
❑ 70 Detroit Lions	1.50	3.00
❑ 71 Green Bay Packers	4.00	8.00
❑ 72 Herb Adderley	4.00	8.00
❑ 73 Willie Davis DE	4.00	8.00
❑ 74 Boyd Dowler	2.00	4.00
❑ 75 Forrest Gregg	2.50	5.00
❑ 76 Paul Hornung	20.00	35.00
❑ 77 Hank Jordan	2.50	5.00
❑ 78 Tom Moore	1.50	3.00
❑ 79 Ray Nitschke	12.00	20.00
❑ 80 Elijah Pitts RC	4.00	8.00
❑ 81 Bart Starr	30.00	50.00
❑ 82 Jim Taylor	12.00	20.00
❑ 83 Willie Wood	3.00	6.00
❑ 84 Packers Play/Lombardi	12.00	20.00
❑ 85 Los Angeles Rams	1.50	3.00
❑ 86 Dick Bass	1.50	3.00
❑ 87 Roman Gabriel	2.50	5.00
❑ 88 Roosevelt Grier	2.00	4.00
❑ 89 Deacon Jones	5.00	10.00
❑ 90 Lamar Lundy RC	2.00	4.00
❑ 91 Marlin McKeever	1.00	2.00
❑ 92 Ed Meador	1.00	2.00
❑ 93 Bill Munson RC	2.00	4.00
❑ 94 Merlin Olsen	7.50	15.00
❑ 95 Bobby Smith RC	1.00	2.00
❑ 96 Frank Varrichione	1.00	2.00
❑ 97 Ben Wilson RC	1.00	2.00
❑ 98 Los Angeles Rams	1.00	2.00
❑ 99 Minnesota Vikings	1.50	3.00
❑ 100 Grady Alderman	1.00	2.00
❑ 101 Hal Bedsole RC	1.00	2.00
❑ 102 Bill Brown	1.50	3.00
❑ 103 Bill Butler RC	1.00	2.00
❑ 104 Fred Cox RC	1.50	3.00
❑ 105 Carl Eller RC	18.00	30.00
❑ 106 Paul Flatley	1.00	2.00
❑ 107 Jim Marshall	3.00	6.00
❑ 108 Tommy Mason	1.00	2.00
❑ 109 George Rose RC	1.00	2.00
❑ 110 Fran Tarkenton	15.00	25.00
❑ 111 Mick Tingelhoff	1.50	3.00
❑ 112 Vikings Play/Van Brock.	2.00	4.00
❑ 113 New York Giants	1.50	3.00
❑ 114 Erich Barnes	1.00	2.00
❑ 115 Roosevelt Brown	2.00	4.00
❑ 116 Clarence Childs RC	1.00	2.00
❑ 117 Jerry Hillebrand	1.00	2.00
❑ 118 Greg Larson RC	1.00	2.00
❑ 119 Dick Lynch	1.00	2.00
❑ 120 Joe Morrison RC	2.00	4.00
❑ 121 Lou Slaby RC	1.00	2.00
❑ 122 Aaron Thomas RC	1.00	2.00
❑ 123 Steve Thurlow RC	1.00	2.00
❑ 124 Ernie Wheelwright RC	1.00	2.00
❑ 125 Gary Wood RC	1.50	3.00
❑ 126 New York Giants	1.00	2.00
❑ 127 Philadelphia Eagles	1.50	3.00
❑ 128 Sam Baker	1.00	2.00
❑ 129 Maxie Baughan	1.00	2.00
❑ 130 Timmy Brown	1.50	3.00
❑ 131 Jack Concannon RC	1.00	2.00
❑ 132 Irv Cross	1.50	3.00
❑ 133 Earl Gros	1.00	2.00
❑ 134 Dave Lloyd RC	1.00	2.00
❑ 135 Floyd Peters RC	1.00	2.00
❑ 136 Nate Ramsey RC	1.00	2.00
❑ 137 Pete Retzlaff	1.50	3.00
❑ 138 Jim Ringo	2.00	4.00
❑ 139 Norm Snead	2.00	4.00
❑ 140 Philadelphia Eagles	1.00	2.00
❑ 141 Pittsburgh Steelers	1.50	3.00
❑ 142 John Baker	1.00	2.00
❑ 143 Gary Ballman	1.00	2.00
❑ 144 Charley Bradshaw	1.00	2.00
❑ 145 Ed Brown	1.00	2.00
❑ 146 Dick Haley	1.00	2.00
❑ 147 John Henry Johnson	2.00	4.00
❑ 148 Brady Keys RC	1.00	2.00
❑ 149 Ray Lemek	1.00	2.00
❑ 150 Ben McGee RC	1.00	2.00
❑ 151 Clarence Peaks UER	1.00	2.00
❑ 152 Myron Pottios	1.00	2.00
❑ 153 Clendon Thomas	1.00	2.00
❑ 154 Pittsburgh Steelers	1.00	2.00
❑ 155 St. Louis Cardinals	1.50	3.00
❑ 156 Jim Bakken RC	1.50	3.00
❑ 157 Joe Childress	1.00	2.00
❑ 158 Bobby Joe Conrad	1.50	3.00
❑ 159 Bob DeMarco	1.00	2.00
❑ 160 Pat Fischer RC	2.00	4.00
❑ 161 Irv Goode RC	1.00	2.00
❑ 162 Ken Gray	1.00	2.00
❑ 163 Charlie Johnson	1.50	3.00
❑ 164 Bill Koman	1.00	2.00
❑ 165 Dale Meinert	1.00	2.00
❑ 166 Jerry Stovall RC	1.50	3.00
❑ 167 Abe Woodson	1.00	2.00
❑ 168 St. Louis Cardinals	1.00	2.00
❑ 169 San Francisco 49ers	1.50	3.00
❑ 170 Kermit Alexander	1.00	2.00
❑ 171 John Brodie	5.00	10.00
❑ 172 Bernie Casey	1.50	3.00
❑ 173 John David Crow	1.50	3.00
❑ 174 Tommy Davis	1.00	2.00
❑ 175 Matt Hazeltine	1.00	2.00
❑ 176 Jim Johnson	2.00	4.00
❑ 177 Charlie Krueger RC	1.00	2.00
❑ 178 Roland Lakes RC	1.00	2.00
❑ 179 George Mira RC	1.50	3.00
❑ 180 Dave Parks RC	1.50	3.00
❑ 181 John Thomas RC	1.00	2.00
❑ 182 49ers Play/Christiansen	1.00	2.00
❑ 183 Washington Redskins	1.50	3.00
❑ 184 Pervis Atkins	1.00	2.00
❑ 185 Preston Carpenter	1.00	2.00
❑ 186 Angelo Coia	1.00	2.00
❑ 187 Sam Huff	3.00	6.00
❑ 188 Sonny Jurgensen	7.50	15.00
❑ 189 Paul Krause RC	15.00	30.00
❑ 190 Jim Martin	1.00	2.00
❑ 191 Bobby Mitchell	2.50	5.00
❑ 192 John Nisby	1.00	2.00
❑ 193 John Paluck	1.00	2.00
❑ 194 Vince Promuto	1.00	2.00
❑ 195 Charley Taylor RC	30.00	50.00
❑ 196 Washington Redskins	1.00	2.00
❑ 197 Checklist 1	15.00	30.00
❑ 198 Checklist 2 UER	25.00	50.00

1966 Philadelphia

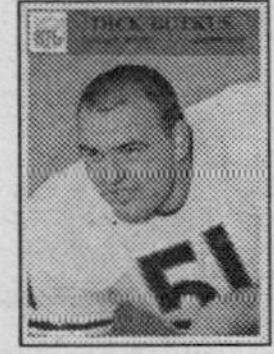

Card	Low	High
❑ COMPLETE SET (198)	600.00	900.00
❑ WRAPPER (5-CENT)	10.00	20.00
❑ 1 Falcons Insignia	6.00	12.00
❑ 2 Larry Benz RC	1.00	2.00
❑ 3 Dennis Claridge RC	1.00	2.00
❑ 4 Perry Lee Dunn RC	1.00	2.00
❑ 5 Dan Grimm RC	1.00	2.00
❑ 6 Alex Hawkins	1.00	2.00
❑ 7 Ralph Heck RC	1.00	2.00
❑ 8 Frank Lasky RC	1.00	2.00
❑ 9 Guy Reese	1.00	2.00
❑ 10 Bob Richards RC	1.00	2.00
❑ 11 Ron Smith RC	1.00	2.00
❑ 12 Ernie Wheelwright	1.00	2.00
❑ 13 Falcons Roster	1.50	3.00
❑ 14 Baltimore Colts	1.50	3.00
❑ 15 Raymond Berry	4.00	8.00
❑ 16 Bob Boyd DB	1.00	2.00
❑ 17 Jerry Logan	1.00	2.00
❑ 18 John Mackey	3.00	6.00

❑ 19 Tom Matte 2.00 4.00
❑ 20 Lou Michaels 1.00 2.00
❑ 21 Lenny Moore 4.00 8.00
❑ 22 Jimmy Orr 1.50 3.00
❑ 23 Jim Parker 2.00 4.00
❑ 24 Johnny Unitas 30.00 50.00
❑ 25 Bob Vogel 1.00 2.00
❑ 26 Colts Play/Moore/Parker 2.00 4.00
❑ 27 Chicago Bears 1.50 3.00
❑ 28 Doug Atkins 2.00 4.00
❑ 29 Rudy Bukich 1.00 2.00
❑ 30 Ronnie Bull 1.00 2.00
❑ 31 Dick Butkus RC 150.00 250.00
❑ 32 Mike Ditka 20.00 35.00
❑ 33 Joe Fortunato 1.00 2.00
❑ 34 Bobby Joe Green 1.00 2.00
❑ 35 Roger LeClerc 1.00 2.00
❑ 36 Johnny Morris 1.00 2.00
❑ 37 Mike Pyle 1.00 2.00
❑ 38 Gale Sayers RC 125.00 225.00
❑ 39 Bears Play/G.Sayers 20.00 35.00
❑ 40 Cleveland Browns 1.50 3.00
❑ 41 Jim Brown 50.00 80.00
❑ 42 Gary Collins 1.50 3.00
❑ 43 Ross Fichtner RC 1.00 2.00
❑ 44 Ernie Green 1.00 2.00
❑ 45 Gene Hickerson RC 15.00 25.00
❑ 46 Jim Houston 1.00 2.00
❑ 47 John Morrow 1.00 2.00
❑ 48 Walter Roberts 1.00 2.00
❑ 49 Frank Ryan 1.50 3.00
❑ 50 Dick Schafrath 1.00 2.00
❑ 51 Paul Wiggin RC 1.00 2.00
❑ 52 Cleveland Browns 1.00 2.00
❑ 53 Dallas Cowboys 1.50 3.00
❑ 54 George Andrie UER RC 2.00 4.00
❑ 55 Frank Clarke 1.50 3.00
❑ 56 Mike Connelly 1.00 2.00
❑ 57 Cornell Green 2.00 4.00
❑ 58 Bob Hayes RC 35.00 60.00
❑ 59 Chuck Howley RC 12.50 25.00
❑ 60 Bob Lilly 12.00 20.00
❑ 61 Don Meredith 15.00 25.00
❑ 62 Don Perkins 1.50 3.00
❑ 63 Mel Renfro 7.50 15.00
❑ 64 Danny Villanueva 1.00 2.00
❑ 65 Dallas Cowboys 1.00 2.00
❑ 66 Detroit Lions 1.50 3.00
❑ 67 Roger Brown 1.00 2.00
❑ 68 John Gordy 1.00 2.00
❑ 69 Alex Karras 5.00 10.00
❑ 70 Dick LeBeau 1.00 2.00
❑ 71 Amos Marsh 1.00 2.00
❑ 72 Milt Plum 1.50 3.00
❑ 73 Bobby Smith 1.00 2.00
❑ 74 Wayne Rasmussen RC 1.00 2.00
❑ 75 Pat Studstill 1.00 2.00
❑ 76 Wayne Walker 1.00 2.00
❑ 77 Tom Watkins 1.00 2.00
❑ 78 Detroit Lions 1.00 2.00
❑ 79 Green Bay Packers 3.00 6.00
❑ 80 Herb Adderley 3.00 6.00
❑ 81 Lee Roy Caffey RC 2.00 4.00
❑ 82 Don Chandler 1.50 3.00
❑ 83 Willie Davis DE 3.00 6.00
❑ 84 Boyd Dowler 2.00 4.00
❑ 85 Forrest Gregg 2.00 4.00
❑ 86 Tom Moore 1.50 3.00
❑ 87 Ray Nitschke 7.50 15.00
❑ 88 Bart Starr 30.00 50.00
❑ 89 Jim Taylor 12.00 20.00
❑ 90 Willie Wood 3.00 6.00
❑ 91 Green Bay Packers 1.00 2.00
❑ 92 Los Angeles Rams 1.50 3.00
❑ 93 Willie Brown RC 1.00 2.00
❑ 94 Roman Gabriel/D.Bass 2.00 4.00
❑ 95 Bruce Gossett RC 1.50 3.00
❑ 96 Deacon Jones 3.00 6.00
❑ 97 Tommy McDonald 2.50 5.00
❑ 98 Marlin McKeever 1.00 2.00
❑ 99 Aaron Martin RC 1.00 2.00
❑ 100 Ed Meador 1.00 2.00
❑ 101 Bill Munson 1.50 3.00
❑ 102 Merlin Olsen 4.00 8.00
❑ 103 Jim Stiger RC 1.00 2.00
❑ 104 Rams Play/W.Brown 1.50 3.00
❑ 105 Minnesota Vikings 1.50 3.00
❑ 106 Grady Alderman 1.00 2.00
❑ 107 Bill Brown 1.50 3.00
❑ 108 Fred Cox 1.00 2.00
❑ 109 Paul Flatley 1.00 2.00
❑ 110 Rip Hawkins 1.00 2.00
❑ 111 Tommy Mason 1.00 2.00
❑ 112 Ed Sharockman 1.00 2.00
❑ 113 Gordon Smith RC 1.00 2.00
❑ 114 Fran Tarkenton 15.00 30.00
❑ 115 Mick Tingelhoff 1.50 3.00
❑ 116 Bobby Walden RC 1.00 2.00
❑ 117 Minnesota Vikings 1.00 2.00
❑ 118 New York Giants 1.50 3.00
❑ 119 Roosevelt Brown 2.00 4.00
❑ 120 Henry Carr RC 1.50 3.00
❑ 121 Clarence Childs 1.00 2.00
❑ 122 Tucker Frederickson RC 1.50 3.00
❑ 123 Jerry Hillebrand 1.00 2.00
❑ 124 Greg Larson 1.00 2.00
❑ 125 Spider Lockhart RC 1.50 3.00
❑ 126 Dick Lynch 1.00 2.00
❑ 127 Earl Morrall/Scholtz 1.50 3.00
❑ 128 Joe Morrison 1.00 2.00
❑ 129 Steve Thurlow 1.00 2.00
❑ 130 New York Giants 1.00 2.00
❑ 131 Philadelphia Eagles 1.50 3.00
❑ 132 Sam Baker 1.00 2.00
❑ 133 Maxie Baughan 1.00 2.00
❑ 134 Bob Brown OT RC 7.50 15.00
❑ 135 Timmy Brown 1.50 3.00
❑ 136 Irv Cross 1.50 3.00
❑ 137 Earl Gros 1.00 2.00
❑ 138 Ray Poage RC 1.00 2.00
❑ 139 Nate Ramsey 1.00 2.00
❑ 140 Pete Retzlaff 1.50 3.00
❑ 141 Jim Ringo 2.00 4.00
❑ 142 Norm Snead 2.00 4.00
❑ 143 Philadelphia Eagles 1.00 2.00
❑ 144 Pittsburgh Steelers 1.50 3.00
❑ 145 Gary Ballman 1.00 2.00
❑ 146 Charley Bradshaw 1.00 2.00
❑ 147 Jim Butler RC 1.00 2.00
❑ 148 Mike Clark 1.00 2.00
❑ 149 Dick Hoak RC 1.00 2.00
❑ 150 Roy Jefferson RC 1.50 3.00
❑ 151 Frank Lambert RC 1.00 2.00
❑ 152 Mike Lind RC 1.00 2.00
❑ 153 Bill Nelsen RC 2.00 4.00
❑ 154 Clarence Peaks 1.00 2.00
❑ 155 Clendon Thomas 1.00 2.00
❑ 156 Pittsburgh Steelers 1.00 2.00
❑ 157 St. Louis Cardinals 1.50 3.00
❑ 158 Jim Bakken 1.00 2.00
❑ 159 Bobby Joe Conrad 1.50 3.00
❑ 160 Willis Crenshaw RC 1.00 2.00
❑ 161 Bob DeMarco 1.00 2.00
❑ 162 Pat Fischer 1.50 3.00
❑ 163 Charlie Johnson 1.50 3.00
❑ 164 Dale Meinert 1.00 2.00
❑ 165 Sonny Randle 1.00 2.00
❑ 166 Sam Silas RC 1.00 2.00
❑ 167 Bill Triplett RC 1.00 2.00
❑ 168 Larry Wilson 2.00 4.00
❑ 169 St. Louis Cardinals 1.00 2.00
❑ 170 San Francisco 49ers 1.50 3.00
❑ 171 Kermit Alexander 1.00 2.00
❑ 172 Bruce Bosley 1.00 2.00
❑ 173 John Brodie 3.00 6.00
❑ 174 Bernie Casey 1.50 3.00
❑ 175 John David Crow 2.00 4.00
❑ 176 Tommy Davis 1.00 2.00
❑ 177 Jim Johnson 2.00 4.00
❑ 178 Gary Lewis RC 1.00 2.00
❑ 179 Dave Parks 1.00 2.00
❑ 180 Walter Rock RC 1.50 3.00
❑ 181 Ken Willard RC 2.00 4.00
❑ 182 San Francisco 49ers 1.00 2.00
❑ 183 Washington Redskins 1.50 3.00
❑ 184 Rickie Harris RC 1.00 2.00
❑ 185 Sonny Jurgensen 4.00 8.00
❑ 186 Paul Krause 3.00 6.00
❑ 187 Bobby Mitchell 3.00 6.00
❑ 188 Vince Promuto 1.00 2.00
❑ 189 Pat Richter RC 1.00 2.00
❑ 190 Joe Rutgens 1.00 2.00
❑ 191 Johnny Sample 1.00 2.00
❑ 192 Lonnie Sanders 1.00 2.00
❑ 193 Jim Steffen 1.00 2.00
❑ 194 Charley Taylor 7.50 15.00
❑ 195 Washington Redskins 1.00 2.00
❑ 196 Referee Signals 1.50 3.00
❑ 197 Checklist 1 12.50 25.00
❑ 198 Checklist 2 UER 25.00 50.00

1967 Philadelphia

❑ COMPLETE SET (198) 425.00 650.00
❑ WRAPPER (5-CENT) 10.00 20.00
❑ 1 Falcons Team 5.00 10.00
❑ 2 Junior Coffey RC 1.50 3.00
❑ 3 Alex Hawkins 1.00 2.00
❑ 4 Randy Johnson RC 1.50 3.00
❑ 5 Lou Kirouac RC 1.00 2.00
❑ 6 Billy Martin RC 1.00 2.00
❑ 7 Tommy Nobis RC 10.00 20.00
❑ 8 Jerry Richardson RC 2.00 4.00
❑ 9 Marion Rushing RC 1.00 2.00
❑ 10 Ron Smith 1.00 2.00
❑ 11 Ernie Wheelwright UER 1.00 2.00
❑ 12 Atlanta Falcons 1.00 2.00
❑ 13 Baltimore Colts 1.50 3.00
❑ 14 Raymond Berry UER 3.50 7.00
❑ 15 Bob Boyd DB 1.00 2.00
❑ 16 Ordell Braase RC 1.00 2.00
❑ 17 Alvin Haymond RC 1.00 2.00
❑ 18 Tony Lorick 1.00 2.00
❑ 19 Lenny Lyles RC 1.00 2.00
❑ 20 John Mackey 2.50 5.00
❑ 21 Tom Matte 1.50 3.00
❑ 22 Lou Michaels 1.00 2.00
❑ 23 Johnny Unitas 25.00 40.00
❑ 24 Baltimore Colts 1.00 2.00
❑ 25 Chicago Bears 1.50 3.00
❑ 26 Rudy Bukich UER 1.00 2.00
❑ 27 Ronnie Bull 1.00 2.00
❑ 28 Dick Butkus 45.00 75.00
❑ 29 Mike Ditka 18.00 30.00
❑ 30 Dick Gordon RC 1.50 3.00
❑ 31 Roger LeClerc 1.00 2.00
❑ 32 Bennie McRae 1.00 2.00
❑ 33 Richie Petitbon 1.00 2.00
❑ 34 Mike Pyle 1.00 2.00
❑ 35 Gale Sayers 45.00 75.00
❑ 36 Chicago Bears 1.00 2.00
❑ 37 Cleveland Browns 1.50 3.00
❑ 38 Johnny Brewer 1.00 2.00
❑ 39 Gary Collins 1.50 3.00
❑ 40 Ross Fichtner 1.00 2.00
❑ 41 Ernie Green 1.00 2.00
❑ 42 Gene Hickerson 2.50 5.00
❑ 43 Leroy Kelly RC 25.00 40.00
❑ 44 Frank Ryan 1.50 3.00
❑ 45 Dick Schafrath 1.00 2.00
❑ 46 Paul Warfield 10.00 18.00
❑ 47 John Wooten RC 1.00 2.00
❑ 48 Cleveland Browns 1.00 2.00
❑ 49 Dallas Cowboys 1.50 3.00
❑ 50 George Andrie 1.00 2.00
❑ 51 Cornell Green 1.50 3.00
❑ 52 Bob Hayes 10.00 20.00
❑ 53 Chuck Howley 2.00 4.00
❑ 54 Lee Roy Jordan RC 12.00 20.00
❑ 55 Bob Lilly 7.50 15.00
❑ 56 Dave Manders RC 1.00 2.00
❑ 57 Don Meredith 15.00 25.00
❑ 58 Dan Reeves RC 18.00 30.00
❑ 59 Mel Renfro 3.00 6.00
❑ 60 Dallas Cowboys 1.50 3.00
❑ 61 Detroit Lions 1.50 3.00
❑ 62 Roger Brown 1.50 3.00
❑ 63 Gail Cogdill 1.00 2.00
❑ 64 John Gordy 1.00 2.00
❑ 65 Ron Kramer 1.00 2.00
❑ 66 Dick LeBeau 1.00 2.00
❑ 67 Mike Lucci RC 2.00 4.00
❑ 68 Amos Marsh 1.00 2.00
❑ 69 Tom Nowatzke RC 1.00 2.00
❑ 70 Pat Studstill 1.00 2.00

Card	Low	High
❑ 71 Karl Sweetan RC	1.00	2.00
❑ 72 Detroit Lions	1.00	2.00
❑ 73 Green Bay Packers	2.50	5.00
❑ 74 Herb Adderley UER	3.00	6.00
❑ 75 Lee Roy Caffey	1.50	3.00
❑ 76 Willie Davis DE	2.50	5.00
❑ 77 Forrest Gregg	2.00	4.00
❑ 78 Hank Jordan	2.00	4.00
❑ 79 Ray Nitschke	6.00	12.00
❑ 80 Dave Robinson RC	3.00	6.00
❑ 81 Bob Skoronski RC	1.50	3.00
❑ 82 Bart Starr	30.00	50.00
❑ 83 Willie Wood	2.50	5.00
❑ 84 Green Bay Packers	1.50	3.00
❑ 85 Los Angeles Rams	1.50	3.00
❑ 86 Dick Bass	1.50	3.00
❑ 87 Maxie Baughan	1.00	2.00
❑ 88 Roman Gabriel	2.00	4.00
❑ 89 Bruce Gossett	1.00	2.00
❑ 90 Deacon Jones	2.50	5.00
❑ 91 Tommy McDonald	2.50	5.00
❑ 92 Marlin McKeever	1.00	2.00
❑ 93 Tom Moore	1.00	2.00
❑ 94 Merlin Olsen	3.00	6.00
❑ 95 Clancy Williams RC	1.00	2.00
❑ 96 Los Angeles Rams	1.00	2.00
❑ 97 Minnesota Vikings	1.50	3.00
❑ 98 Grady Alderman	1.00	2.00
❑ 99 Bill Brown	1.50	3.00
❑ 100 Fred Cox	1.00	2.00
❑ 101 Paul Flatley	1.00	2.00
❑ 102 Dale Hackbart RC	1.00	2.00
❑ 103 Jim Marshall	2.00	4.00
❑ 104 Tommy Mason	1.00	2.00
❑ 105 Milt Sunde RC	1.00	2.00
❑ 106 Fran Tarkenton	10.00	20.00
❑ 107 Mick Tingelhoff	1.50	3.00
❑ 108 Minnesota Vikings	1.00	2.00
❑ 109 New York Giants	1.50	3.00
❑ 110 Henry Carr	1.00	2.00
❑ 111 Clarence Childs	1.00	2.00
❑ 112 Allen Jacobs RC	1.00	2.00
❑ 113 Homer Jones RC	1.50	3.00
❑ 114 Tom Kennedy RC	1.00	2.00
❑ 115 Spider Lockhart	1.00	2.00
❑ 116 Joe Morrison	1.00	2.00
❑ 117 Francis Peay RC	1.00	2.00
❑ 118 Jeff Smith LB RC	1.00	2.00
❑ 119 Aaron Thomas	1.00	2.00
❑ 120 New York Giants	1.00	2.00
❑ 121 Saints Insignia	1.50	3.00
❑ 122 Charley Bradshaw	1.00	2.00
❑ 123 Paul Hornung	12.50	25.00
❑ 124 Elbert Kimbrough RC	1.00	2.00
❑ 125 Earl Leggett RC	1.00	2.00
❑ 126 Obert Logan RC	1.00	2.00
❑ 127 Riley Mattson	1.00	2.00
❑ 128 John Morrow	1.00	2.00
❑ 129 Bob Scholtz RC	1.00	2.00
❑ 130 Dave Whitsell RC	1.00	2.00
❑ 131 Gary Wood	1.00	2.00
❑ 132 Saints Roster UER 121	1.50	3.00
❑ 133 Philadelphia Eagles	1.50	3.00
❑ 134 Sam Baker	1.00	2.00
❑ 135 Bob Brown OT	2.00	5.00
❑ 136 Timmy Brown	1.50	3.00
❑ 137 Earl Gros	1.00	2.00
❑ 138 Dave Lloyd	1.00	2.00
❑ 139 Floyd Peters	1.00	2.00
❑ 140 Pete Retzlaff	1.50	3.00
❑ 141 Joe Scarpati RC	1.00	2.00
❑ 142 Norm Snead	1.50	3.00
❑ 143 Jim Skaggs RC	1.00	2.00
❑ 144 Philadelphia Eagles	1.00	2.00
❑ 145 Pittsburgh Steelers	1.50	3.00
❑ 146 Bill Asbury RC	1.00	2.00
❑ 147 John Baker	1.00	2.00
❑ 148 Gary Ballman	1.00	2.00
❑ 149 Mike Clark	1.00	2.00
❑ 150 Riley Gunnels	1.00	2.00
❑ 151 John Hilton RC	1.00	2.00
❑ 152 Roy Jefferson	1.50	3.00
❑ 153 Brady Keys	1.00	2.00
❑ 154 Ben McGee	1.00	2.00
❑ 155 Bill Nelsen	1.50	3.00
❑ 156 Pittsburgh Steelers	1.00	2.00
❑ 157 St. Louis Cardinals	1.50	3.00
❑ 158 Jim Bakken	1.00	2.00
❑ 159 Bobby Joe Conrad	1.50	3.00
❑ 160 Ken Gray	1.00	2.00
❑ 161 Charlie Johnson	1.50	3.00
❑ 162 Joe Robb	1.00	2.00
❑ 163 Johnny Roland RC	1.50	3.00
❑ 164 Roy Shivers RC	1.00	2.00
❑ 165 Jackie Smith RC	7.50	15.00
❑ 166 Jerry Stovall	1.00	2.00
❑ 167 Larry Wilson	2.00	4.00
❑ 168 St. Louis Cardinals	1.00	2.00
❑ 169 San Francisco 49ers	1.50	3.00
❑ 170 Kermit Alexander	1.00	2.00
❑ 171 Bruce Bosley	1.00	2.00
❑ 172 John Brodie	3.00	6.00
❑ 173 Bernie Casey	1.50	3.00
❑ 174 Tommy Davis	1.00	2.00
❑ 175 Howard Mudd RC	2.00	4.00
❑ 176 Dave Parks	1.00	2.00
❑ 177 John Thomas	1.00	2.00
❑ 178 Dave Wilcox RC	12.50	25.00
❑ 179 Ken Willard	1.50	3.00
❑ 180 San Francisco 49ers	1.00	2.00
❑ 181 Washington Redskins	1.50	3.00
❑ 182 Charlie Gogolak RC	1.00	2.00
❑ 183 Chris Hanburger RC	2.50	5.00
❑ 184 Len Hauss RC	1.50	3.00
❑ 185 Sonny Jurgensen	3.50	7.00
❑ 186 Bobby Mitchell	2.50	5.00
❑ 187 Brig Owens RC	1.00	2.00
❑ 188 Jim Shorter RC	1.00	2.00
❑ 189 Jerry Smith RC	1.50	3.00
❑ 190 Charley Taylor	4.00	8.00
❑ 191 A.D. Whitfield RC	1.00	2.00
❑ 192 Washington Redskins	1.00	2.00
❑ 193 Browns Play/Leroy Kelly	3.00	6.00
❑ 194 New York Giants PC	1.00	2.00
❑ 195 Atlanta Falcons PC	1.00	2.00
❑ 196 Referee Signals	1.50	3.00
❑ 197 Checklist 1	12.00	20.00
❑ 198 Checklist 2 UER	20.00	40.00

2009 Philadelphia

Card	Low	High
❑ COMP.SET w/o SP's (200)	25.00	50.00
❑ 1 Kurt Warner	.30	.75
❑ 2 Matt Leinart	.25	.60
❑ 3 Edgerrin James	.25	.60
❑ 4 Tim Hightower	.25	.60
❑ 5 Larry Fitzgerald	.30	.75
❑ 6 Anquan Boldin	.25	.60
❑ 7 Karlos Dansby	.20	.50
❑ 8 Steve Breaston	.25	.60
❑ 9 Matt Ryan	.30	.75
❑ 10 Michael Turner	.25	.60
❑ 11 Jerious Norwood	.25	.60
❑ 12 Roddy White	.25	.60
❑ 13 John Abraham	.20	.50
❑ 14 Harry Douglas	.20	.50
❑ 15 Michael Jenkins	.20	.50
❑ 16 Joe Flacco	.30	.75
❑ 17 Willis McGahee	.25	.60
❑ 18 Ray Rice	.30	.75
❑ 19 Derrick Mason	.20	.50
❑ 20 Ray Lewis	.30	.75
❑ 21 Terrell Suggs	.20	.50
❑ 22 Trent Edwards	.25	.60
❑ 23 Marshawn Lynch	.25	.60
❑ 24 Lee Evans	.25	.60
❑ 25 Josh Reed	.20	.50
❑ 26 Paul Posluszny	.25	.60
❑ 27 Jake Delhomme	.25	.60
❑ 28 Jonathan Stewart	.25	.60
❑ 29 DeAngelo Williams	.30	.75
❑ 30 Steve Smith	.25	.60
❑ 31 Muhsin Muhammad	.25	.60
❑ 32 Jon Beason	.20	.50
❑ 33 Julius Peppers	.25	.60
❑ 34 Kyle Orton	.25	.60
❑ 35 Matt Forte	.30	.75
❑ 36 Devin Hester	.30	.75
❑ 37 Brian Urlacher	.30	.75
❑ 38 Lance Briggs	.25	.60
❑ 39 Charles Tillman	.20	.50
❑ 40 Greg Olsen	.20	.50
❑ 41 Carson Palmer	.30	.75
❑ 42 Chris Perry	.20	.50
❑ 43 T.J. Houshmandzadeh	.25	.60
❑ 44 Chad Ocho Cinco	.25	.60
❑ 45 Dhani Jones	.20	.50
❑ 46 Brady Quinn	.25	.60
❑ 47 Jamal Lewis	.25	.60
❑ 48 Braylon Edwards	.25	.60
❑ 49 Kellen Winslow	.25	.60
❑ 50 D'Qwell Jackson	.20	.50
❑ 51 Shaun Rogers	.20	.50
❑ 52 Tony Romo	.50	1.25
❑ 53 Marion Barber	.30	.75
❑ 54 Jason Witten	.30	.75
❑ 55 Terrell Owens	.30	.75
❑ 56 Felix Jones	.30	.75
❑ 57 Roy Williams WR	.25	.60
❑ 58 DeMarcus Ware	.25	.60
❑ 59 Zach Thomas	.25	.60
❑ 60 Jay Cutler	.30	.75
❑ 61 Tony Scheffler	.20	.50
❑ 62 Brandon Marshall	.25	.60
❑ 63 Eddie Royal	.25	.60
❑ 64 D.J. Williams	.20	.50
❑ 65 Ronald Curry	.20	.50
❑ 66 Kevin Smith	.25	.60
❑ 67 Rudi Johnson	.20	.50
❑ 68 Calvin Johnson	.30	.75
❑ 69 Ernie Sims	.20	.50
❑ 70 DeWayne White	.20	.50
❑ 71 Aaron Rodgers	.30	.75
❑ 72 Ryan Grant	.25	.60
❑ 73 Greg Jennings	.30	.75
❑ 74 Donald Driver	.25	.60
❑ 75 A.J. Hawk	.25	.60
❑ 76 Aaron Kampman	.25	.60
❑ 77 Nick Collins	.20	.50
❑ 78 Matt Schaub	.25	.60
❑ 79 Steve Slaton	.25	.60
❑ 80 Andre Johnson	.25	.60
❑ 81 Owen Daniels	.20	.50
❑ 82 Kevin Walter	.25	.60
❑ 83 Mario Williams	.25	.60
❑ 84 Peyton Manning	.50	1.25
❑ 85 Joseph Addai	.30	.75
❑ 86 Reggie Wayne	.25	.60
❑ 87 Dwight Freeney	.25	.60
❑ 88 Anthony Gonzalez	.25	.60
❑ 89 Dallas Clark	.25	.60
❑ 90 Robert Mathis	.20	.50
❑ 91 David Garrard	.25	.60
❑ 92 Maurice Jones-Drew	.25	.60
❑ 93 Marcedes Lewis	.20	.50
❑ 94 Rashean Mathis	.20	.50
❑ 95 Mike Peterson	.20	.50
❑ 96 Matt Cassel	.25	.60
❑ 97 Larry Johnson	.25	.60
❑ 98 Jamaal Charles	.25	.60
❑ 99 Dwayne Bowe	.25	.60
❑ 100 Tony Gonzalez	.25	.60
❑ 101 Chad Pennington	.25	.60
❑ 102 Ronnie Brown	.25	.60
❑ 103 Ted Ginn	.25	.60
❑ 104 Greg Camarillo	.25	.60
❑ 105 Joey Porter	.25	.60
❑ 106 Adrian Peterson	.60	1.50
❑ 107 Bernard Berrian	.25	.60
❑ 108 Bobby Wade	.20	.50
❑ 109 Kevin Williams	.20	.50
❑ 110 Jared Allen	.30	.75
❑ 111 Gus Frerotte	.20	.50
❑ 112 Tom Brady	.50	1.25
❑ 113 Sammy Morris	.20	.50
❑ 114 Randy Moss	.30	.75
❑ 115 Wes Welker	.30	.75
❑ 116 Jerod Mayo	.25	.60
❑ 117 Brandon Meriweather	.20	.50
❑ 118 Drew Brees	.30	.75
❑ 119 Reggie Bush	.30	.75
❑ 120 Robert Meachem	.25	.60
❑ 121 Devery Henderson	.20	.50
❑ 122 Lance Moore	.25	.60
❑ 123 Jeremy Shockey	.20	.50

Card		
❑ 124 Jonathan Vilma	.20	.50
❑ 125 Marques Colston	.25	.60
❑ 126 Eli Manning	.30	.75
❑ 127 Brandon Jacobs	.25	.60
❑ 128 Osi Umenyiora	.25	.60
❑ 129 Steve Smith USC	.25	.60
❑ 130 Justin Tuck	.25	.60
❑ 131 Mathias Kiwanuka	.20	.50
❑ 132 Bart Scott	.20	.50
❑ 133 Thomas Jones	.25	.60
❑ 134 Laveranues Coles	.25	.60
❑ 135 Jerricho Cotchery	.20	.50
❑ 136 Chansi Stuckey	.20	.50
❑ 137 JaMarcus Russell	.25	.60
❑ 138 Darren McFadden	.30	.75
❑ 139 Zach Miller	.20	.50
❑ 140 Gibril Wilson	.20	.50
❑ 141 Justin Fargas	.20	.50
❑ 142 Donovan McNabb	.30	.75
❑ 143 Brian Westbrook	.25	.60
❑ 144 Correll Buckhalter	.20	.50
❑ 145 DeSean Jackson	.25	.60
❑ 146 Quintin Mikell RC	.30	.75
❑ 147 Asante Samuel	.20	.50
❑ 148 Hank Baskett	.20	.50
❑ 149 Ben Roethlisberger	.50	1.25
❑ 150 Willie Parker	.25	.60
❑ 151 Santonio Holmes	.25	.60
❑ 152 Hines Ward	.25	.60
❑ 153 James Harrison	.30	.75
❑ 154 Troy Polamalu	.30	.75
❑ 155 LaMarr Woodley	.20	.50
❑ 156 Philip Rivers	.30	.75
❑ 157 LaDainian Tomlinson	.30	.75
❑ 158 Vincent Jackson	.25	.60
❑ 159 Antonio Gates	.25	.60
❑ 160 Chris Chambers	.25	.60
❑ 161 Antonio Cromartie	.20	.50
❑ 162 Shaun Hill	.25	.60
❑ 163 Frank Gore	.25	.60
❑ 164 Isaac Bruce	.25	.60
❑ 165 Patrick Willis	.25	.60
❑ 166 Takeo Spikes	.20	.50
❑ 167 Arnaz Battle	.20	.50
❑ 168 Matt Hasselbeck	.25	.60
❑ 169 Julius Jones	.25	.60
❑ 170 John Carlson	.25	.60
❑ 171 Lofa Tatupu	.25	.60
❑ 172 Julian Peterson	.20	.50
❑ 173 Patrick Kerney	.20	.50
❑ 174 Marc Bulger	.25	.60
❑ 175 Steven Jackson	.25	.60
❑ 176 Donnie Avery	.25	.60
❑ 177 Torry Holt	.25	.60
❑ 178 Chris Long	.25	.60
❑ 179 Oshiomogho Atogwe	.20	.50
❑ 180 Leonard Little	.20	.50
❑ 181 Jeff Garcia	.25	.60
❑ 182 Earnest Graham	.20	.50
❑ 183 Warrick Dunn	.25	.60
❑ 184 Antonio Bryant	.25	.60
❑ 185 Barrett Ruud	.20	.50
❑ 186 Ronde Barber	.20	.50
❑ 187 Vince Young	.25	.60
❑ 188 Kerry Collins	.25	.60
❑ 189 Chris Johnson	.30	.75
❑ 190 LenDale White	.25	.60
❑ 191 Bo Scaife	.20	.50
❑ 192 Albert Haynesworth	.20	.50
❑ 193 Cortland Finnegan	.20	.50
❑ 194 Jason Campbell	.25	.60
❑ 195 Clinton Portis	.25	.60
❑ 196 Santana Moss	.25	.60
❑ 197 Chris Cooley	.25	.60
❑ 198 Antwaan Randle El	.20	.50
❑ 199 London Fletcher	.20	.50
❑ 200 DeAngelo Hall	.25	.60
❑ 201 Matthew Stafford RC	5.00	12.00
❑ 202 Knowshon Moreno RC	4.00	10.00
❑ 203 Patrick Turner RC	1.25	3.00
❑ 204 Mike Goodson RC	1.50	4.00
❑ 205 Darrius Heyward-Bey RC	2.50	6.00
❑ 206 Javon Ringer RC	1.50	4.00
❑ 207 Aaron Curry RC	2.00	5.00
❑ 208 Brian Orakpo RC	2.00	5.00
❑ 209 Brandon Pettigrew RC	2.00	5.00
❑ 210 Michael Johnson RC	1.00	2.50
❑ 211 Rey Maualuga RC	2.50	6.00
❑ 212 William Moore RC	1.25	3.00
❑ 213 James Laurinaitis RC	2.00	5.00
❑ 214 Brian Cushing RC	2.00	5.00
❑ 215 Malcolm Jenkins RC	1.50	4.00
❑ 216 Alphonso Smith RC	1.25	3.00
❑ 217 Chase Coffman RC	1.25	3.00
❑ 218 Brian Robiskie RC	1.50	4.00
❑ 219 Marcus Freeman RC	1.50	4.00
❑ 220 Juaquin Iglesias RC	1.50	4.00
❑ 221 Vontae Davis RC	1.50	4.00
❑ 222 Michael Crabtree RC	4.00	10.00
❑ 223 Chris Wells RC	4.00	10.00
❑ 224 Mark Sanchez RC	6.00	15.00
❑ 225 Jeremy Maclin RC	3.00	8.00
❑ 226 Nathan Brown RC	1.25	3.00
❑ 227 LeSean McCoy RC	3.00	8.00
❑ 228 Percy Harvin RC	5.00	12.00
❑ 229 Jarett Dillard RC	1.25	3.00
❑ 230 Travis Beckum RC	1.25	3.00
❑ 231 Devin Moore RC	1.25	3.00
❑ 232 Graham Harrell RC	1.50	4.00
❑ 233 Demetrius Byrd RC	1.25	3.00
❑ 234 Aaron Kelly RC	1.25	3.00
❑ 235 Pat White RC	2.50	6.00
❑ 236 Shonn Greene RC	3.00	8.00
❑ 237 James Davis RC	1.50	4.00
❑ 238 P.J. Hill RC	1.25	3.00
❑ 239 Eben Britton RC	1.25	3.00
❑ 240 B.J. Raji RC	2.00	5.00
❑ 241 Ian Johnson RC	1.50	4.00
❑ 242 Quan Cosby RC	1.25	3.00
❑ 243 Darius Butler RC	1.50	4.00
❑ 244 Kenny Britt RC	2.50	6.00
❑ 245 Curtis Painter RC	1.50	4.00
❑ 246 Sen'Derrick Marks RC	1.00	2.50
❑ 247 Larry English RC	1.50	4.00
❑ 248 Sean Smith RC	1.50	4.00
❑ 249 Victor Harris RC	1.50	4.00
❑ 250 Everette Brown RC	1.50	4.00
❑ 251 Darry Beckwith RC	1.25	3.00
❑ 252 Mike Wallace RC	3.00	8.00
❑ 253 Derrick Williams RC	1.50	4.00
❑ 254 Clint Sintim RC	1.50	4.00
❑ 255 Mike Mickens RC	1.25	3.00
❑ 256 Patrick Chung RC	1.50	4.00
❑ 257 Aaron Maybin RC	1.50	4.00
❑ 258 Matt Shaughnessy RC	1.25	3.00
❑ 259 Fili Moala RC	1.25	3.00
❑ 260 Tyson Jackson RC	1.50	4.00
❑ 261 Peria Jerry RC	1.25	3.00
❑ 262 Rhett Bomar RC	1.25	3.00
❑ 263 Michael Oher RC	3.00	8.00
❑ 264 Eugene Monroe RC	1.25	3.00
❑ 265 Alex Mack RC	1.25	3.00
❑ 266 Duke Robinson RC	1.00	2.50
❑ 267 Josh Freeman RC	3.00	8.00
❑ 268 Jason Smith RC	1.25	3.00
❑ 269 Herman Johnson RC	1.25	3.00
❑ 270 Stephen McGee RC	1.50	4.00
❑ 271 Hakeem Nicks RC	3.00	8.00
❑ 272 Alex Boone RC	1.50	4.00
❑ 273 Rashad Jennings RC	1.50	4.00
❑ 274 Brandon Tate RC	1.25	3.00
❑ 275 Donald Brown RC	3.00	8.00
❑ 276 Alan Page	2.00	5.00
❑ 277 Lem Barney	1.50	4.00
❑ 278 Phil Simms	2.00	5.00
❑ 279 Jim Kelly	2.50	6.00
❑ 280 Jack Youngblood	1.50	4.00
❑ 281 Alex Karras	2.00	5.00
❑ 282 Fred Biletnikoff	2.50	6.00
❑ 283 Earl Campbell	2.50	6.00
❑ 284 Darrell Green	2.00	5.00
❑ 285 Steve Young	3.00	8.00
❑ 286 Ron Yary	1.50	4.00
❑ 287 Thurman Thomas	2.50	6.00
❑ 288 Lawrence Taylor	2.50	6.00
❑ 289 Steve Largent	2.50	6.00
❑ 290 Roger Staubach	3.00	8.00
❑ 291 Troy Aikman	3.00	8.00
❑ 292 John Elway	4.00	10.00
❑ 293 Tom Rathman	1.50	4.00
❑ 294 Fran Tarkenton	2.50	6.00
❑ 295 Terry Bradshaw	4.00	10.00
❑ 296 Barry Sanders	4.00	10.00
❑ 297 Merlin Olsen	2.00	5.00
❑ 298 Roger Craig	2.00	5.00
❑ 299 Ken Anderson	2.00	5.00
❑ 300 Jerry Rice	4.00	10.00
❑ 301 Barack Obama	1.50	4.00
❑ 302 Barack Obama	1.50	4.00
❑ 303 Barack Obama	1.50	4.00
❑ 304 Barack Obama	1.50	4.00
❑ 305 Barack Obama	1.50	4.00
❑ 306 Barack Obama	1.50	4.00
❑ 307 Barack Obama	1.50	4.00
❑ 308 Barack Obama	1.50	4.00
❑ 309 Barack Obama	1.50	4.00
❑ 310 Barack Obama	1.50	4.00
❑ 311 Barack Obama	1.50	4.00
❑ 312 Barack Obama	1.50	4.00
❑ 313 Barack Obama	1.50	4.00
❑ 314 Barack Obama	1.50	4.00
❑ 315 Barack Obama	1.50	4.00
❑ 316 Barack Obama	1.50	4.00
❑ 317 Barack Obama	1.50	4.00
❑ 318 Barack Obama	1.50	4.00
❑ 319 Barack Obama	1.50	4.00
❑ 320 Barack Obama	1.50	4.00
❑ 321 Barack Obama	1.50	4.00
❑ 322 Barack Obama	1.50	4.00
❑ 323 Barack Obama	1.50	4.00
❑ 324 Barack Obama	1.50	4.00
❑ 325 Barack Obama	1.50	4.00
❑ 326 Woodstock 40th Anniversary	1.25	3.00
❑ 327 Woodstock 40th Anniversary	1.25	3.00
❑ 328 Woodstock 40th Anniversary	1.25	3.00
❑ 329 Woodstock 40th Anniversary	1.25	3.00
❑ 330 Woodstock 40th Anniversary	1.25	3.00
❑ 331 The Vietnam War	1.25	3.00
❑ 332 The Vietnam War	1.25	3.00
❑ 333 The Vietnam War	1.25	3.00
❑ 334 The Vietnam War	1.25	3.00
❑ 335 The Vietnam War	1.25	3.00
❑ 336 The Vietnam War	1.25	3.00
❑ 337 The Vietnam War	1.25	3.00
❑ 338 The Vietnam War	1.25	3.00
❑ 339 The Vietnam War	1.25	3.00
❑ 340 The Vietnam War	1.25	3.00
❑ 341 Humphrey/McCarthy	1.25	3.00
❑ 342 Goldwater/Rockefeller	1.25	3.00
❑ 343 Rockefeller/Reagan	2.00	5.00
❑ 344 R.Nixon/Rockefeller	1.50	4.00
❑ 345 L.Johnson/Lodge	1.25	3.00
❑ 346 S.Agnew/E.Muskie	1.25	3.00
❑ 347 J.F.Kennedy/Humphrey	2.00	5.00
❑ 348 P.Brown/R.Nixon	1.50	4.00
❑ 349 R.Reagan/P.Brown	2.00	5.00
❑ 350 Humphrey/W.Miller	1.25	3.00
❑ 351 J.F.Kennedy/R.Nixon	2.00	5.00
❑ 352 Anquan Boldin IA	1.25	3.00
❑ 353 Kurt Warner IA	1.50	4.00
❑ 354 Larry Fitzgerald IA	1.50	4.00
❑ 355 Roddy White IA	1.25	3.00
❑ 356 Matt Ryan IA	1.50	4.00
❑ 357 Michael Turner IA	1.25	3.00
❑ 358 Ray Lewis IA	1.50	4.00
❑ 359 Marshawn Lynch IA	1.25	3.00
❑ 360 DeAngelo Williams IA	1.50	4.00
❑ 361 Steve Smith IA	1.25	3.00
❑ 362 Julius Peppers IA	1.25	3.00
❑ 363 Brian Urlacher IA	1.50	4.00
❑ 364 T.J. Houshmandzadeh IA	1.25	3.00
❑ 365 DeMarcus Ware IA	1.25	3.00
❑ 366 Tony Romo IA	2.50	6.00
❑ 367 Marion Barber IA	1.50	4.00
❑ 368 Brandon Marshall IA	1.25	3.00
❑ 369 Jay Cutler IA	1.50	4.00
❑ 370 Calvin Johnson IA	1.50	4.00
❑ 371 Greg Jennings IA	1.50	4.00
❑ 372 Andre Johnson IA	1.25	3.00
❑ 373 Peyton Manning IA	2.50	6.00
❑ 374 Bob Sanders IA	1.25	3.00
❑ 375 Reggie Wayne IA	1.25	3.00
❑ 376 Maurice Jones-Drew IA	1.25	3.00
❑ 377 Dwayne Bowe IA	1.25	3.00
❑ 378 Ronnie Brown IA	1.25	3.00
❑ 379 Adrian Peterson IA	3.00	8.00
❑ 380 Randy Moss IA	1.50	4.00
❑ 381 Tom Brady IA	2.50	6.00
❑ 382 Drew Brees IA	1.50	4.00
❑ 383 Justin Tuck IA	1.25	3.00
❑ 384 Eli Manning IA	1.50	4.00
❑ 385 Brett Favre IA	4.00	10.00
❑ 386 Darren McFadden IA	1.50	4.00
❑ 387 Brian Dawkins IA	1.25	3.00
❑ 388 Donovan McNabb IA	1.50	4.00
❑ 389 Brian Westbrook IA	1.25	3.00
❑ 390 Troy Polamalu IA	1.50	4.00

Card		
❑ 391 Ben Roethlisberger IA	2.50	6.00
❑ 392 Philip Rivers IA	1.50	4.00
❑ 393 LaDainian Tomlinson IA	1.50	4.00
❑ 394 Frank Gore IA	1.25	3.00
❑ 395 Julian Peterson IA	1.00	2.50
❑ 396 Steven Jackson IA	1.25	3.00
❑ 397 Derrick Brooks IA	1.25	3.00
❑ 398 Darren Sproles IA	1.25	3.00
❑ 399 Chris Johnson IA	1.50	4.00
❑ 400 Clinton Portis IA	1.25	3.00

1991 Pinnacle

Card		
❑ COMPLETE SET (415)	7.50	20.00
❑ 1 Warren Moon	.15	.40
❑ 2 Morten Andersen	.02	.10
❑ 3 Rohn Stark	.02	.10
❑ 4 Mark Bortz	.02	.10
❑ 5 Mark Higgs RC	.02	.10
❑ 6 Troy Aikman	.75	2.00
❑ 7 John Elway	1.25	3.00
❑ 8 Neal Anderson	.07	.20
❑ 9 Chris Doleman	.02	.10
❑ 10 Jay Schroeder	.02	.10
❑ 11 Sterling Sharpe	.15	.40
❑ 12 Steve DeBerg	.02	.10
❑ 13 Ronnie Lott	.07	.20
❑ 14 Sean Landeta	.02	.10
❑ 15 Jim Everett	.07	.20
❑ 16 Jim Breech	.02	.10
❑ 17 Barry Foster	.07	.20
❑ 18 Mike Merriweather	.02	.10
❑ 19 Eric Metcalf	.07	.20
❑ 20 Mark Carrier DB	.07	.20
❑ 21 James Brooks	.07	.20
❑ 22 Nate Odomes	.02	.10
❑ 23 Rodney Hampton	.15	.40
❑ 24 Chris Miller	.07	.20
❑ 25 Roger Craig	.07	.20
❑ 26 Louis Oliver	.02	.10
❑ 27 Allen Pinkett	.02	.10
❑ 28 Bubby Brister	.02	.10
❑ 29 Reyna Thompson	.02	.10
❑ 30 Issiac Holt	.02	.10
❑ 31 Steve Broussard	.02	.10
❑ 32 Christian Okoye	.02	.10
❑ 33 Dave Meggett	.07	.20
❑ 34 Andre Reed	.07	.20
❑ 35 Shane Conlan	.02	.10
❑ 36 Eric Ball	.02	.10
❑ 37 Johnny Bailey	.02	.10
❑ 38 Don Majkowski	.02	.10
❑ 39 Gerald Williams	.02	.10
❑ 40 Kevin Mack	.02	.10
❑ 41 Jeff Herrod	.02	.10
❑ 42 Emmitt Smith	2.50	6.00
❑ 43 Wendell Davis	.02	.10
❑ 44 Lorenzo White	.02	.10
❑ 45 Andre Rison	.07	.20
❑ 46 Jerry Gray	.02	.10
❑ 47 Dennis Smith	.02	.10
❑ 48 Gaston Green	.02	.10
❑ 49 Dermontti Dawson	.02	.10
❑ 50 Jeff Hostetler	.07	.20
❑ 51 Nick Lowery	.02	.10
❑ 52 Merril Hoge	.02	.10
❑ 53 Bobby Hebert	.02	.10
❑ 54 Scott Case	.02	.10
❑ 55 Jack Del Rio	.07	.20
❑ 56 Cornelius Bennett	.07	.20
❑ 57 Tony Mandarich	.02	.10
❑ 58 Bill Brooks	.02	.10
❑ 59 Jessie Tuggle	.02	.10
❑ 60 Hugh Millen RC	.02	.10
❑ 61 Tony Bennett	.07	.20
❑ 62 Cris Dishman RC	.02	.10
❑ 63 Darryl Henley RC	.02	.10
❑ 64 Duane Bickett	.02	.10
❑ 65 Jay Hilgenberg	.02	.10
❑ 66 Joe Montana	1.25	3.00
❑ 67 Bill Fralic	.02	.10
❑ 68 Sam Mills	.02	.10
❑ 69 Bruce Armstrong	.02	.10
❑ 70 Dan Marino	1.25	3.00
❑ 71 Jim Lachey	.02	.10
❑ 72 Rod Woodson	.15	.40
❑ 73 Simon Fletcher	.02	.10
❑ 74 Bruce Matthews	.07	.20
❑ 75 Howie Long	.15	.40
❑ 76 John Friesz	.15	.40
❑ 77 Karl Mecklenburg	.02	.10
❑ 78 John L. Williams UER	.02	.10
❑ 79 Rob Burnett RC	.07	.20
❑ 80 Anthony Carter	.07	.20
❑ 81 Henry Ellard	.07	.20
❑ 82 Don Beebe	.02	.10
❑ 83 Louis Lipps	.02	.10
❑ 84 Greg McMurtry	.02	.10
❑ 85 Will Wolford	.02	.10
❑ 86 Eric Green	.02	.10
❑ 87 Irving Fryar	.07	.20
❑ 88 John Offerdahl	.02	.10
❑ 89 John Alt	.02	.10
❑ 90 Tom Tupa	.02	.10
❑ 91 Don Mosebar	.02	.10
❑ 92 Jeff George	.20	.50
❑ 93 Vinny Testaverde	.07	.20
❑ 94 Greg Townsend	.02	.10
❑ 95 Derrick Fenner	.02	.10
❑ 96 Brian Mitchell	.07	.20
❑ 97 Herschel Walker	.07	.20
❑ 98 Ricky Proehl	.02	.10
❑ 99 Mark Clayton	.07	.20
❑ 100 Derrick Thomas	.15	.40
❑ 101 Jim Harbaugh	.15	.40
❑ 102 Barry Word	.02	.10
❑ 103 Jerry Rice	.75	2.00
❑ 104 Keith Byars	.02	.10
❑ 105 Marion Butts	.07	.20
❑ 106 Rich Moran	.02	.10
❑ 107 Thurman Thomas	.15	.40
❑ 108 Stephone Paige	.02	.10
❑ 109 D.J. Johnson	.02	.10
❑ 110 William Perry	.07	.20
❑ 111 Haywood Jeffires	.07	.20
❑ 112 Rodney Peete	.07	.20
❑ 113 Andy Heck	.02	.10
❑ 114 Kevin Ross	.02	.10
❑ 115 Michael Carter	.02	.10
❑ 116 Tim McKyer	.02	.10
❑ 117 Kenneth Davis	.02	.10
❑ 118 Richmond Webb	.02	.10
❑ 119 Rich Camarillo	.02	.10
❑ 120 James Francis	.02	.10
❑ 121 Craig Heyward	.07	.20
❑ 122 Hardy Nickerson	.07	.20
❑ 123 Michael Brooks	.02	.10
❑ 124 Fred Barnett	.15	.40
❑ 125 Cris Carter	.40	1.00
❑ 126 Brian Jordan	.07	.20
❑ 127 Pat Leahy	.02	.10
❑ 128 Kevin Greene	.07	.20
❑ 129 Trace Armstrong	.02	.10
❑ 130 Eugene Lockhart	.02	.10
❑ 131 Albert Lewis	.02	.10
❑ 132 Ernie Jones	.02	.10
❑ 133 Eric Martin	.02	.10
❑ 134 Anthony Thompson	.02	.10
❑ 135 Tim Krumrie	.02	.10
❑ 136 James Lofton	.07	.20
❑ 137 John Taylor	.07	.20
❑ 138 Jeff Cross	.02	.10
❑ 139 Tommy Kane	.02	.10
❑ 140 Robb Thomas	.02	.10
❑ 141 Gary Anderson K	.02	.10
❑ 142 Mark Murphy	.02	.10
❑ 143 Rickey Jackson	.02	.10
❑ 144 Ken O'Brien	.02	.10
❑ 145 Ernest Givins	.07	.20
❑ 146 Jessie Hester	.02	.10
❑ 147 Deion Sanders	.30	.75
❑ 148 Keith Henderson RC	.02	.10
❑ 149 Chris Singleton	.02	.10
❑ 150 Rod Bernstine	.02	.10
❑ 151 Quinn Early	.07	.20
❑ 152 Boomer Esiason	.07	.20
❑ 153 Mike Gann	.02	.10
❑ 154 Dino Hackett	.02	.10
❑ 155 Perry Kemp	.02	.10
❑ 156 Mark Ingram	.07	.20
❑ 157 Daryl Johnston	.30	.75
❑ 158 Eugene Daniel	.02	.10
❑ 159 Dalton Hilliard	.02	.10
❑ 160 Rufus Porter	.02	.10
❑ 161 Tunch Ilkin	.02	.10
❑ 162 James Hasty	.02	.10
❑ 163 Keith McKeller	.02	.10
❑ 164 Heath Sherman	.02	.10
❑ 165 Vai Sikahema	.02	.10
❑ 166 Pat Terrell	.02	.10
❑ 167 Anthony Munoz	.07	.20
❑ 168 Brad Edwards RC	.02	.10
❑ 169 Tom Rathman	.02	.10
❑ 170 Steve McMichael	.07	.20
❑ 171 Vaughan Johnson	.02	.10
❑ 172 Nate Lewis RC	.02	.10
❑ 173 Mark Rypien	.07	.20
❑ 174 Rob Moore	.20	.50
❑ 175 Tim Green	.02	.10
❑ 176 Tony Casillas	.02	.10
❑ 177 Jon Hand	.02	.10
❑ 178 Todd McNair	.02	.10
❑ 179 Toi Cook RC	.02	.10
❑ 180 Eddie Brown	.02	.10
❑ 181 Mark Jackson	.02	.10
❑ 182 Pete Stoyanovich	.02	.10
❑ 183 Bryce Paup RC	.15	.40
❑ 184 Anthony Miller	.07	.20
❑ 185 Dan Saleaumua	.02	.10
❑ 186 Guy McIntyre	.02	.10
❑ 187 Broderick Thomas	.02	.10
❑ 188 Frank Warren	.02	.10
❑ 189 Drew Hill	.02	.10
❑ 190 Reggie White	.15	.40
❑ 191 Chris Hinton	.02	.10
❑ 192 David Little	.02	.10
❑ 193 David Fulcher	.02	.10
❑ 194 Clarence Verdin	.02	.10
❑ 195 Junior Seau	.25	.60
❑ 196 Blair Thomas	.02	.10
❑ 197 Stan Brock	.02	.10
❑ 198 Gary Clark	.15	.40
❑ 199 Michael Irvin	.15	.40
❑ 200 Ronnie Harmon	.02	.10
❑ 201 Steve Young	.75	2.00
❑ 202 Brian Noble	.02	.10
❑ 203 Dan Stryzinski	.02	.10
❑ 204 Darryl Talley	.02	.10
❑ 205 David Alexander	.02	.10
❑ 206 Pat Swilling	.07	.20
❑ 207 Gary Plummer	.02	.10
❑ 208 Robert Delpino	.02	.10
❑ 209 Norm Johnson	.02	.10
❑ 210 Mike Singletary	.07	.20
❑ 211 Anthony Johnson	.15	.40
❑ 212 Eric Allen	.02	.10
❑ 213 Gill Fenerty	.02	.10
❑ 214 Neil Smith	.15	.40
❑ 215 Joe Phillips	.02	.10
❑ 216 Ottis Anderson	.07	.20
❑ 217 LeRoy Butler	.07	.20
❑ 218 Ray Childress	.02	.10
❑ 219 Rodney Holman	.02	.10
❑ 220 Kevin Fagan	.02	.10
❑ 221 Bruce Smith	.15	.40
❑ 222 Brad Muster	.02	.10
❑ 223 Mike Horan	.02	.10
❑ 224 Steve Atwater	.02	.10
❑ 225 Rich Gannon	.20	.50
❑ 226 Anthony Pleasant	.02	.10
❑ 227 Steve Jordan	.02	.10
❑ 228 Lomas Brown	.02	.10
❑ 229 Jackie Slater	.02	.10
❑ 230 Brad Baxter	.02	.10
❑ 231 Joe Morris	.02	.10
❑ 232 Marcus Allen	.15	.40
❑ 233 Chris Warren	.15	.40
❑ 234 Johnny Johnson	.02	.10
❑ 235 Phil Simms	.07	.20
❑ 236 Dave Krieg	.07	.20
❑ 237 Jim McMahon	.07	.20
❑ 238 Richard Dent	.07	.20
❑ 239 John Washington RC	.02	.10
❑ 240 Sammie Smith	.02	.10
❑ 241 Brian Brennan	.02	.10

Card		
❑ 242 Cortez Kennedy	.15	.40
❑ 243 Tim McDonald	.02	.10
❑ 244 Charles Haley	.07	.20
❑ 245 Joey Browner	.02	.10
❑ 246 Eddie Murray	.02	.10
❑ 247 Bob Golic	.02	.10
❑ 248 Myron Guyton	.02	.10
❑ 249 Dennis Byrd	.02	.10
❑ 250 Barry Sanders	1.25	3.00
❑ 251 Clay Matthews	.07	.20
❑ 252 Pepper Johnson	.02	.10
❑ 253 Eric Swann RC	.15	.40
❑ 254 Lamar Lathon	.02	.10
❑ 255 Andre Tippett	.02	.10
❑ 256 Tom Newberry	.02	.10
❑ 257 Kyle Clifton	.02	.10
❑ 258 Leslie O'Neal	.07	.20
❑ 259 Bubba McDowell	.02	.10
❑ 260 Scott Davis	.02	.10
❑ 261 Wilber Marshall	.02	.10
❑ 262 Marv Cook	.02	.10
❑ 263 Jeff Lageman	.02	.10
❑ 264 Michael Young	.02	.10
❑ 265 Gary Zimmerman	.02	.10
❑ 266 Mike Munchak	.07	.20
❑ 267 David Treadwell	.02	.10
❑ 268 Steve Wisniewski	.02	.10
❑ 269 Mark Duper	.07	.20
❑ 270 Chris Spielman	.07	.20
❑ 271 Brett Perriman	.15	.40
❑ 272 Lionel Washington	.02	.10
❑ 273 Lawrence Taylor	.15	.40
❑ 274 Mark Collins	.02	.10
❑ 275 Mark Carrier WR	.15	.40
❑ 276 Paul Gruber	.02	.10
❑ 277 Earnest Byner	.02	.10
❑ 278 Andre Collins	.02	.10
❑ 279 Reggie Cobb	.02	.10
❑ 280 Art Monk	.07	.20
❑ 281 Henry Jones RC	.07	.20
❑ 282 Mike Pritchard RC	.15	.40
❑ 283 Moe Gardner RC	.02	.10
❑ 284 Chris Zorich RC	.15	.40
❑ 285 Keith Traylor RC	.02	.10
❑ 286 Mike Dumas RC	.02	.10
❑ 287 Ed King RC	.02	.10
❑ 288 Russell Maryland RC	.15	.40
❑ 289 Alfred Williams RC	.02	.10
❑ 290 Derek Russell RC	.02	.10
❑ 291 Vinnie Clark RC	.02	.10
❑ 292 Mike Croel RC	.02	.10
❑ 293 Todd Marinovich RC	.02	.10
❑ 294 Phil Hansen RC	.02	.10
❑ 295 Aaron Craver RC	.02	.10
❑ 296 Nick Bell RC	.02	.10
❑ 297 Kenny Walker RC	.02	.10
❑ 298 Roman Phifer RC	.02	.10
❑ 299 Kanavis McGhee RC	.02	.10
❑ 300 Ricky Ervins RC	.07	.20
❑ 301 Jim Price RC	.02	.10
❑ 302 John Johnson RC	.02	.10
❑ 303 George Thornton RC	.02	.10
❑ 304 Huey Richardson RC	.02	.10
❑ 305 Harry Colon RC	.02	.10
❑ 306 Antone Davis RC	.02	.10
❑ 307 Todd Lyght RC	.02	.10
❑ 308 Bryan Cox RC	.15	.40
❑ 309 Brad Goebel RC	.02	.10
❑ 310 Eric Moten RC	.02	.10
❑ 311 John Kasay RC	.07	.20
❑ 312 Esera Tuaolo RC	.02	.10
❑ 313 Bobby Wilson RC	.02	.10
❑ 314 Mo Lewis RC	.07	.20
❑ 315 Harvey Williams RC	.15	.40
❑ 316 Mike Stonebreaker	.02	.10
❑ 317 Charles McRae RC	.02	.10
❑ 318 John Flannery RC	.02	.10
❑ 319 Ted Washington RC	.02	.10
❑ 320 Stanley Richard RC	.02	.10
❑ 321 Browning Nagle RC	.02	.10
❑ 322 Ed McCaffrey RC	2.00	5.00
❑ 323 Jeff Graham RC	.15	.40
❑ 324 Stan Thomas	.02	.10
❑ 325 Lawrence Dawsey RC	.07	.20
❑ 326 Eric Bieniemy RC	.02	.10
❑ 327 Tim Barnett RC	.02	.10
❑ 328 Erric Pegram RC	.15	.40
❑ 329 Lamar Rogers RC	.02	.10
❑ 330 Ernie Mills RC	.07	.20
❑ 331 Pat Harlow RC	.02	.10
❑ 332 Greg Lewis RC	.02	.10
❑ 333 Jarrod Bunch RC	.02	.10
❑ 334 Dan McGwire RC	.02	.10
❑ 335 Randal Hill RC	.07	.20
❑ 336 Leonard Russell RC	.15	.40
❑ 337 Carnell Lake	.02	.10
❑ 338 Brian Blades	.07	.20
❑ 339 Darrell Green	.02	.10
❑ 340 Bobby Humphrey	.02	.10
❑ 341 Mervyn Fernandez	.02	.10
❑ 342 Ricky Sanders	.02	.10
❑ 343 Keith Jackson	.07	.20
❑ 344 Carl Banks	.02	.10
❑ 345 Gill Byrd	.02	.10
❑ 346 Al Toon	.07	.20
❑ 347 Stephen Baker	.02	.10
❑ 348 Randall Cunningham	.15	.40
❑ 349 Flipper Anderson	.02	.10
❑ 350 Jay Novacek	.15	.40
❑ 351 Steve Young/B.Smith HH	.15	.40
❑ 352 Barry Sanders/Browner HH	.30	.75
❑ 353 Joe Montana/M.Carrier HH	.30	.75
❑ 354 Thurman Thomas/L.Taylor	.07	.20
❑ 355 Jerry Rice/Darr.Green HH	.20	.50
❑ 356 Warren Moon Tech	.07	.20
❑ 357 Anthony Munoz TECH	.02	.10
❑ 358 Barry Sanders Tech	.50	1.25
❑ 359 Jerry Rice Tech	.50	1.25
❑ 360 Joey Browner TECH	.02	.10
❑ 361 Morten Andersen TECH	.02	.10
❑ 362 Sean Landeta TECH	.02	.10
❑ 363 Thurman Thomas GW	.15	.40
❑ 364 Emmitt Smith GW	1.25	3.00
❑ 365 Gaston Green GW	.02	.10
❑ 366 Barry Sanders GW	.50	1.25
❑ 367 Christian Okoye GW	.02	.10
❑ 368 Earnest Byner GW	.02	.10
❑ 369 Neal Anderson GW	.02	.10
❑ 370 Herschel Walker GW	.07	.20
❑ 371 Rodney Hampton GW	.15	.40
❑ 372 Darryl Talley IDOL	.02	.10
❑ 373 Mark Carrier IDOL	.02	.10
❑ 374 Jim Breech IDOL	.02	.10
❑ 375 R.Hampton/O.Anderson ID	.02	.10
❑ 376 Kevin Mack IDOL	.02	.10
❑ 377 S.Jordan/O.Robertson ID	.02	.10
❑ 378 B.Esiason/B.Jones ID	.02	.10
❑ 379 Steve DeBerg IDOL	.07	.20
❑ 380 Al Toon IDOL	.02	.10
❑ 381 Ronnie Lott/C.Taylor ID	.07	.20
❑ 382 Henry Ellard IDOL	.02	.10
❑ 383 Troy Aikman/Staubach ID	.50	1.25
❑ 384 T.Thomas/E.Campbell ID	.15	.40
❑ 385 Dan Marino/Bradshaw ID	.60	1.50
❑ 386 Howie Long/Joe Greene ID	.07	.20
❑ 387 Franco Harris IR	.07	.20
❑ 388 Esera Tuaolo	.02	.10
❑ 389 Super Bowl XXVI	.02	.10
❑ 390 Charles Mann	.02	.10
❑ 391 Kenny Walker Succeed	.02	.10
❑ 392 Reggie Roby	.02	.10
❑ 393 Bruce Pickens RC	.02	.10
❑ 394 Ray Childress SIDE	.02	.10
❑ 395 Karl Mecklenburg SIDE	.02	.10
❑ 396 Dean Biasucci SIDE	.02	.10
❑ 397 John Alt SIDE	.02	.10
❑ 398 Marcus Allen SL	.07	.20
❑ 399 John Offerdahl SIDE	.02	.10
❑ 400 Richard Tardits RC	.02	.10
❑ 401 Al Toon SIDE	.02	.10
❑ 402 Joey Browner SIDE	.02	.10
❑ 403 Spencer Tillman RC	.02	.10
❑ 404 Jay Novacek SIDE	.07	.20
❑ 405 Stephen Braggs SIDE	.02	.10
❑ 406 Mike Tice RC	.02	.10
❑ 407 Kevin Greene SIDE	.07	.20
❑ 408 Reggie White SIDE	.07	.20
❑ 409 Brian Noble SIDE	.02	.10
❑ 410 Bart Oates SIDE	.02	.10
❑ 411 Art Monk SIDE	.07	.20
❑ 412 Ron Wolfley SIDE	.02	.10
❑ 413 Louis Lipps SIDE	.02	.10
❑ 414 Dante Jones SIDE RC	.07	.20
❑ 415 Kenneth Davis SIDE	.02	.10
❑ P1 Emmitt Smith Promo	12.50	25.00

1992 Pinnacle

Card		
❑ COMPLETE SET (360)	12.50	25.00
❑ 1 Reggie White	.20	.50
❑ 2 Eric Green	.05	.15
❑ 3 Craig Heyward	.10	.30
❑ 4 Phil Simms	.10	.30
❑ 5 Pepper Johnson	.05	.15
❑ 6 Sean Landeta	.05	.15
❑ 7 Dino Hackett	.05	.15
❑ 8 Andre Ware	.05	.15
❑ 9 Ricky Nattiel	.05	.15
❑ 10 Jim Price	.05	.15
❑ 11 Jim Ritcher	.05	.15
❑ 12 Kelly Stouffer	.05	.15
❑ 13 Ray Crockett	.05	.15
❑ 14 Steve Tasker	.10	.30
❑ 15 Barry Sanders	1.25	3.00
❑ 16 Pat Swilling	.05	.15
❑ 17 Moe Gardner	.05	.15
❑ 18 Steve Young	.75	2.00
❑ 19 Chris Spielman	.10	.30
❑ 20 Richard Dent	.10	.30
❑ 21 Anthony Munoz	.10	.30
❑ 22 Thurman Thomas	.20	.50
❑ 23 Ricky Sanders	.05	.15
❑ 24 Steve Atwater	.05	.15
❑ 25 Tony Tolbert	.05	.15
❑ 26 Haywood Jeffires	.10	.30
❑ 27 Duane Bickett	.05	.15
❑ 28 Tim McDonald	.05	.15
❑ 29 Cris Carter	.30	.75
❑ 30 Derrick Thomas	.20	.50
❑ 31 Hugh Millen	.05	.15
❑ 32 Bart Oates	.05	.15
❑ 33 Darryl Talley	.05	.15
❑ 34 Marion Butts	.05	.15
❑ 35 Pete Stoyanovich	.05	.15
❑ 36 Ronnie Lott	.10	.30
❑ 37 Simon Fletcher	.05	.15
❑ 38 Morten Andersen	.05	.15
❑ 39 Clyde Simmons	.05	.15
❑ 40 Mark Rypien	.05	.15
❑ 41 Henry Ellard	.10	.30
❑ 42 Michael Irvin	.20	.50
❑ 43 Louis Lipps	.05	.15
❑ 44 John L. Williams	.05	.15
❑ 45 Broderick Thomas	.05	.15
❑ 46 Don Majkowski	.05	.15
❑ 47 William Perry	.10	.30
❑ 48 David Fulcher	.05	.15
❑ 49 Tony Bennett	.05	.15
❑ 50 Clay Matthews	.10	.30
❑ 51 Warren Moon	.20	.50
❑ 52 Bruce Armstrong	.05	.15
❑ 53 Bill Brooks	.05	.15
❑ 54 Greg Townsend	.05	.15
❑ 55 Steve Broussard	.05	.15
❑ 56 Mel Gray	.10	.30
❑ 57 Kevin Mack	.05	.15
❑ 58 Emmitt Smith	2.00	4.00
❑ 59 Mike Croel	.05	.15
❑ 60 Brian Mitchell	.10	.30
❑ 61 Bennie Blades	.05	.15
❑ 62 Carnell Lake	.05	.15
❑ 63 Cornelius Bennett	.10	.30
❑ 64 Darrell Thompson	.05	.15
❑ 65 Jessie Hester	.05	.15
❑ 66 Marv Cook	.05	.15
❑ 67 Tim Brown	.20	.50
❑ 68 Mark Duper	.05	.15
❑ 69 Robert Delpino	.05	.15
❑ 70 Eric Martin	.05	.15
❑ 71 Wendell Davis	.05	.15
❑ 72 Vaughan Johnson	.05	.15
❑ 73 Brian Blades	.10	.30

Card		
❑ 74 Ed King	.05	.15
❑ 75 Gaston Green	.05	.15
❑ 76 Christian Okoye	.05	.15
❑ 77 Rohn Stark	.05	.15
❑ 78 Kevin Greene	.10	.30
❑ 79 Jay Novacek	.10	.30
❑ 80 Chip Lohmiller	.05	.15
❑ 81 Cris Dishman	.05	.15
❑ 82 Ethan Horton	.05	.15
❑ 83 Pat Harlow	.05	.15
❑ 84 Mark Ingram	.05	.15
❑ 85 Mark Carrier DB	.05	.15
❑ 86 Sam Mills	.05	.15
❑ 87 Mark Higgs	.05	.15
❑ 88 Keith Jackson	.10	.30
❑ 89 Gary Anderson K	.05	.15
❑ 90 Ken Harvey	.05	.15
❑ 91 Anthony Carter	.10	.30
❑ 92 Randall McDaniel	.05	.15
❑ 93 Johnny Johnson	.05	.15
❑ 94 Shane Conlan	.05	.15
❑ 95 Sterling Sharpe	.20	.50
❑ 96 Guy McIntyre	.05	.15
❑ 97 Albert Lewis	.05	.15
❑ 98 Chris Doleman	.05	.15
❑ 99 Andre Rison	.10	.30
❑ 100 Bobby Hebert	.05	.15
❑ 101 Dan Owens	.05	.15
❑ 102 Rodney Hampton	.10	.30
❑ 103 Ernie Jones	.05	.15
❑ 104 Reggie Cobb	.05	.15
❑ 105 Wilber Marshall	.05	.15
❑ 106 Mike Munchak	.10	.30
❑ 107 Cortez Kennedy	.10	.30
❑ 108 Todd Lyght	.05	.15
❑ 109 Burt Grossman	.05	.15
❑ 110 Ferrell Edmunds	.05	.15
❑ 111 Jim Everett	.10	.30
❑ 112 Hardy Nickerson	.10	.30
❑ 113 Andre Tippett	.05	.15
❑ 114 Ronnie Harmon	.05	.15
❑ 115 Andre Waters	.05	.15
❑ 116 Ernest Givins	.10	.30
❑ 117 Eric Hill	.05	.15
❑ 118 Erric Pegram	.10	.30
❑ 119 Jarrod Bunch	.05	.15
❑ 120 Marcus Allen	.20	.50
❑ 121 Barry Foster	.10	.30
❑ 122 Kent Hull	.05	.15
❑ 123 Neal Anderson	.05	.15
❑ 124 Stephen Braggs	.05	.15
❑ 125 Nick Lowery	.05	.15
❑ 126 Jeff Hostetler	.10	.30
❑ 127 Michael Carter	.05	.15
❑ 128 Don Warren	.05	.15
❑ 129 Brad Baxter	.05	.15
❑ 130 John Taylor	.10	.30
❑ 131 Harold Green	.05	.15
❑ 132 Mike Merriweather	.05	.15
❑ 133 Gary Clark	.20	.50
❑ 134 Vince Buck	.05	.15
❑ 135 Dan Saleaumua	.05	.15
❑ 136 Gary Zimmerman	.05	.15
❑ 137 Richmond Webb	.05	.15
❑ 138 Art Monk	.10	.30
❑ 139 Mervyn Fernandez	.05	.15
❑ 140 Mark Jackson	.05	.15
❑ 141 Freddie Joe Nunn	.05	.15
❑ 142 Jeff Lageman	.05	.15
❑ 143 Kenny Walker	.05	.15
❑ 144 Mark Carrier WR	.10	.30
❑ 145 Jon Vaughn	.05	.15
❑ 146 Greg Davis	.05	.15
❑ 147 Bubby Brister	.05	.15
❑ 148 Mo Lewis	.05	.15
❑ 149 Howie Long	.20	.50
❑ 150 Rod Bernstine	.05	.15
❑ 151 Nick Bell	.05	.15
❑ 152 Terry Allen	.20	.50
❑ 153 William Fuller	.05	.15
❑ 154 Dexter Carter	.05	.15
❑ 155 Gene Atkins	.05	.15
❑ 156 Don Beebe	.05	.15
❑ 157 Mark Collins	.05	.15
❑ 158 Jerry Ball	.05	.15
❑ 159 Fred Barnett	.20	.50
❑ 160 Rodney Holman	.05	.15
❑ 161 Stephen Baker	.05	.15
❑ 162 Jeff Graham	.20	.50
❑ 163 Leonard Russell	.10	.30
❑ 164 Jeff Gossett	.05	.15
❑ 165 Vinny Testaverde	.10	.30
❑ 166 Maurice Hurst	.05	.15
❑ 167 Louis Oliver	.05	.15
❑ 168 Jim Morrissey	.05	.15
❑ 169 Greg Kragen	.05	.15
❑ 170 Andre Collins	.05	.15
❑ 171 Dave Meggett	.10	.30
❑ 172 Keith Henderson	.05	.15
❑ 173 Vince Newsome	.05	.15
❑ 174 Chris Hinton	.05	.15
❑ 175 James Hasty	.05	.15
❑ 176 John Offordahl	.05	.15
❑ 177 Lomas Brown	.05	.15
❑ 178 Neil O'Donnell	.10	.30
❑ 179 Leonard Marshall	.05	.15
❑ 180 Bubba McDowell	.05	.15
❑ 181 Herman Moore	.20	.50
❑ 182 Rob Moore	.10	.30
❑ 183 Earnest Byner	.05	.15
❑ 184 Keith McCants	.05	.15
❑ 185 Floyd Turner	.05	.15
❑ 186 Steve Jordan	.05	.15
❑ 187 Nate Odomes	.05	.15
❑ 188 Jeff Herrod	.05	.15
❑ 189 Jim Harbaugh	.20	.50
❑ 190 Jessie Tuggle	.05	.15
❑ 191 Al Smith	.05	.15
❑ 192 Lawrence Dawsey	.10	.30
❑ 193 Steve Bono RC	.20	.50
❑ 194 Greg Lloyd	.10	.30
❑ 195 Steve Wisniewski	.05	.15
❑ 196 Larry Kelm	.05	.15
❑ 197 Tommy Kane	.05	.15
❑ 198 Mark Schlereth RC	.05	.15
❑ 199 Ray Childress	.05	.15
❑ 200 Vincent Brown	.05	.15
❑ 201 Rodney Peete	.10	.30
❑ 202 Dennis Smith	.05	.15
❑ 203 Bruce Matthews	.05	.15
❑ 204 Rickey Jackson	.05	.15
❑ 205 Eric Allen	.05	.15
❑ 206 Rich Camarillo	.05	.15
❑ 207 Jim Lachey	.05	.15
❑ 208 Kevin Ross	.05	.15
❑ 209 Irving Fryar	.10	.30
❑ 210 Mark Clayton	.10	.30
❑ 211 Keith Byars	.05	.15
❑ 212 John Elway	1.25	3.00
❑ 213 Harris Barton	.05	.15
❑ 214 Aeneas Williams	.10	.30
❑ 215 Rich Gannon	.20	.50
❑ 216 Toi Cook	.05	.15
❑ 217 Rod Woodson	.20	.50
❑ 218 Gary Anderson RB	.05	.15
❑ 219 Reggie Roby	.05	.15
❑ 220 Karl Mecklenburg	.05	.15
❑ 221 Rufus Porter	.05	.15
❑ 222 Jon Hand	.05	.15
❑ 223 Tim Barnett	.05	.15
❑ 224 Eric Swann	.10	.30
❑ 225 Eugene Robinson	.05	.15
❑ 226 Michael Young	.05	.15
❑ 227 Frank Warren	.05	.15
❑ 228 Mike Kenn	.05	.15
❑ 229 Tim Green	.05	.15
❑ 230 Barry Word	.05	.15
❑ 231 Mike Pritchard	.10	.30
❑ 232 John Kasay	.05	.15
❑ 233 Derek Russell	.05	.15
❑ 234 Jim Breech	.05	.15
❑ 235 Pierce Holt	.05	.15
❑ 236 Tim Krumrie	.05	.15
❑ 237 William Roberts	.05	.15
❑ 238 Erik Kramer	.10	.30
❑ 239 Brett Perriman	.20	.50
❑ 240 Reyna Thompson	.05	.15
❑ 241 Chris Miller	.10	.30
❑ 242 Drew Hill	.05	.15
❑ 243 Curtis Duncan	.05	.15
❑ 244 Seth Joyner	.05	.15
❑ 245 Ken Norton Jr.	.10	.30
❑ 246 Calvin Williams	.10	.30
❑ 247 James Joseph	.05	.15
❑ 248 Bennie Thompson RC	.05	.15
❑ 249 Tunch Ilkin	.05	.15
❑ 250 Brad Edwards	.05	.15
❑ 251 Jeff Jaeger	.05	.15
❑ 252 Gill Byrd	.05	.15
❑ 253 Jeff Feagles	.05	.15
❑ 254 Jamie Dukes RC	.05	.15
❑ 255 Greg McMurtry	.05	.15
❑ 256 Anthony Johnson	.10	.30
❑ 257 Lamar Lathon	.05	.15
❑ 258 John Roper	.05	.15
❑ 259 Lorenzo White	.05	.15
❑ 260 Brian Noble	.05	.15
❑ 261 Chris Singleton	.05	.15
❑ 262 Todd Marinovich	.05	.15
❑ 263 Jay Hilgenberg	.05	.15
❑ 264 Kyle Clifton	.05	.15
❑ 265 Tony Casillas	.05	.15
❑ 266 James Francis	.05	.15
❑ 267 Eddie Anderson	.05	.15
❑ 268 Tim Harris	.05	.15
❑ 269 James Lofton	.10	.30
❑ 270 Jay Schroeder	.05	.15
❑ 271 Ed West	.05	.15
❑ 272 Don Mosebar	.05	.15
❑ 273 Jackie Slater	.05	.15
❑ 274 Fred McAfee RC	.05	.15
❑ 275 Steve Sewell	.05	.15
❑ 276 Charles Mann	.05	.15
❑ 277 Ron Hall	.05	.15
❑ 278 Darrell Green	.05	.15
❑ 279 Jeff Cross	.05	.15
❑ 280 Jeff Wright	.05	.15
❑ 281 Issiac Holt	.05	.15
❑ 282 Dermontti Dawson	.05	.15
❑ 283 Michael Haynes	.10	.30
❑ 284 Tony Mandarich	.05	.15
❑ 285 Leroy Hoard	.10	.30
❑ 286 Darryl Henley	.05	.15
❑ 287 Tim McGee	.05	.15
❑ 288 Willie Gault	.10	.30
❑ 289 Dalton Hilliard	.05	.15
❑ 290 Tim McKyer	.05	.15
❑ 291 Tom Waddle	.05	.15
❑ 292 Eric Thomas	.05	.15
❑ 293 Herschel Walker	.10	.30
❑ 294 Donnell Woolford	.05	.15
❑ 295 James Brooks	.10	.30
❑ 296 Brad Muster	.05	.15
❑ 297 Brent Jones	.10	.30
❑ 298 Erik Howard	.05	.15
❑ 299 Alvin Harper	.10	.30
❑ 300 Joey Browner	.05	.15
❑ 301 Jack Del Rio	.05	.15
❑ 302 Cleveland Gary	.05	.15
❑ 303 Brett Favre	3.00	6.00
❑ 304 Freeman McNeil	.05	.15
❑ 305 Willie Green	.05	.15
❑ 306 Percy Snow	.05	.15
❑ 307 Neil Smith	.20	.50
❑ 308 Eric Bieniemy	.05	.15
❑ 309 Keith Traylor	.05	.15
❑ 310 Ernie Mills	.05	.15
❑ 311 Will Wolford	.05	.15
❑ 312 Robert Young	.05	.15
❑ 313 Anthony Smith	.05	.15
❑ 314 Robert Porcher RC	.20	.50
❑ 315 Leon Searcy RC	.05	.15
❑ 316 Amp Lee RC	.05	.15
❑ 317 Siran Stacy RC	.05	.15
❑ 318 Patrick Rowe RC	.05	.15
❑ 319 Chris Mims RC	.05	.15
❑ 320 Matt Elliott RC	.05	.15
❑ 321 Ricardo McDonald RC	.05	.15
❑ 322 Keith Hamilton RC	.10	.30
❑ 323 Edgar Bennett RC	.20	.50
❑ 324 Chris Hakel RC	.05	.15
❑ 325 Dexter McNabb RC	.05	.15
❑ 326 Rod Milstead RC	.05	.15
❑ 327 Joe Bowden RC	.05	.15
❑ 328 Brian Bollinger RC	.05	.15
❑ 329 Darryl Williams RC	.05	.15
❑ 330 Tommy Vardell RC	.05	.15
❑ 331 Glenn Parker SIDE	.05	.15
❑ 332 Herschel Walker SIDE	.05	.15
❑ 333 Mike Cofer SIDE	.05	.15
❑ 334 Mark Rypien SIDE	.05	.15
❑ 335 Andre Rison GW	.10	.30
❑ 336 Henry Ellard GW	.05	.15
❑ 337 Rob Moore GW	.05	.15
❑ 338 Fred Barnett GW	.05	.15
❑ 339 Mark Clayton GW	.05	.15
❑ 340 Eric Martin GW	.05	.15

Card		
❑ 341 Irving Fryar GW	.05	.15
❑ 342 Tim Brown GW	.10	.30
❑ 343 Sterling Sharpe GW	.10	.30
❑ 344 Gary Clark GW	.05	.15
❑ 345 John Mackey HOF	.05	.15
❑ 346 Lem Barney HOF	.05	.15
❑ 347 John Riggins HOF	.10	.30
❑ 348 Marion Butts IDOL	.05	.15
❑ 349 Jeff Lageman IDOL	.05	.15
❑ 350 Eric Green IDOL	.05	.15
❑ 351 Reggie White/Bob.Jones I	.10	.30
❑ 352 Marv Cook IDOL	.05	.15
❑ 353 John Elway/Staubach ID	.50	1.25
❑ 354 Steve Tasker IDOL	.05	.15
❑ 355 Nick Lowery IDOL	.05	.15
❑ 356 Mark Clayton/Warfield ID	.05	.15
❑ 357 Warren Moon/R.Gabriel ID	.10	.30
❑ 358 Eric Metcalf	.10	.30
❑ 359 Charles Haley	.10	.30
❑ 360 Terrell Buckley RC	.05	.15
❑ P1 Promo Panel	2.00	5.00

1993 Pinnacle

Card		
❑ COMPLETE SET (360)	7.50	20.00
❑ 1 Brett Favre	1.25	3.00
❑ 2 Tommy Vardell	.02	.10
❑ 3 Jarrod Bunch	.02	.10
❑ 4 Mike Croel	.02	.10
❑ 5 Morten Andersen	.02	.10
❑ 6 Barry Foster	.07	.20
❑ 7 Chris Spielman	.07	.20
❑ 8 Jim Jeffcoat	.02	.10
❑ 9 Ken Ruettgers	.02	.10
❑ 10 Cris Dishman	.02	.10
❑ 11 Ricky Watters	.15	.40
❑ 12 Alfred Williams	.02	.10
❑ 13 Mark Kelso	.02	.10
❑ 14 Moe Gardner	.02	.10
❑ 15 Terry Allen	.15	.40
❑ 16 Willie Gault	.02	.10
❑ 17 Bubba McDowell	.02	.10
❑ 18 Brian Mitchell	.07	.20
❑ 19 Karl Mecklenburg	.02	.10
❑ 20 Jim Everett	.07	.20
❑ 21 Bobby Humphrey	.02	.10
❑ 22 Tim Krumrie	.02	.10
❑ 23 Ken Norton Jr.	.07	.20
❑ 24 Wendell Davis	.02	.10
❑ 25 Brad Baxter	.02	.10
❑ 26 Mel Gray	.07	.20
❑ 27 Jon Vaughn	.02	.10
❑ 28 James Hasty	.02	.10
❑ 29 Chris Warren	.07	.20
❑ 30 Tim Harris	.02	.10
❑ 31 Eric Metcalf	.07	.20
❑ 32 Rob Moore	.07	.20
❑ 33 Charles Haley	.07	.20
❑ 34 Leonard Marshall	.02	.10
❑ 35 Jeff Graham	.07	.20
❑ 36 Eugene Robinson	.02	.10
❑ 37 Darryl Talley	.02	.10
❑ 38 Brent Jones	.07	.20
❑ 39 Reggie Roby	.02	.10
❑ 40 Bruce Armstrong	.02	.10
❑ 41 Audray McMillian	.02	.10
❑ 42 Bern Brostek	.02	.10
❑ 43 Tony Bennett	.02	.10
❑ 44 Albert Lewis	.02	.10
❑ 45 Derrick Thomas	.15	.40
❑ 46 Cris Carter	.15	.40
❑ 47 Richmond Webb	.02	.10
❑ 48 Sean Landeta	.02	.10
❑ 49 Cleveland Gary	.02	.10
❑ 50 Mark Carrier DB	.02	.10
❑ 51 Lawrence Dawsey	.02	.10
❑ 52 Lamar Lathon	.02	.10
❑ 53 Nick Bell	.02	.10
❑ 54 Curtis Duncan	.02	.10
❑ 55 Irving Fryar	.07	.20
❑ 56 Seth Joyner	.02	.10
❑ 57 Jay Novacek	.07	.20
❑ 58 John L. Williams	.02	.10
❑ 59 Amp Lee	.02	.10
❑ 60 Marion Butts	.02	.10
❑ 61 Clyde Simmons	.02	.10
❑ 62 Rich Gannon	.15	.40
❑ 63 Anthony Johnson	.07	.20
❑ 64 Dave Meggett	.02	.10
❑ 65 James Francis	.02	.10
❑ 66 Trace Armstrong	.02	.10
❑ 67 Mo Lewis	.02	.10
❑ 68 Cornelius Bennett	.07	.20
❑ 69 Mark Duper	.02	.10
❑ 70 Frank Reich	.07	.20
❑ 71 Eric Green	.02	.10
❑ 72 Bruce Matthews	.02	.10
❑ 73 Steve Broussard	.02	.10
❑ 74 Anthony Carter	.07	.20
❑ 75 Sterling Sharpe	.15	.40
❑ 76 Mike Kenn	.02	.10
❑ 77 Andre Rison	.07	.20
❑ 78 Todd Marinovich	.02	.10
❑ 79 Vincent Brown	.02	.10
❑ 80 Harold Green	.02	.10
❑ 81 Art Monk	.07	.20
❑ 82 Reggie Cobb	.02	.10
❑ 83 Johnny Johnson	.02	.10
❑ 84 Tommy Kane	.02	.10
❑ 85 Rohn Stark	.02	.10
❑ 86 Steve Tasker	.07	.20
❑ 87 Ronnie Harmon	.02	.10
❑ 88 Pepper Johnson	.02	.10
❑ 89 Hardy Nickerson	.07	.20
❑ 90 Alvin Harper	.07	.20
❑ 91 Louis Oliver	.02	.10
❑ 92 Rod Woodson	.15	.40
❑ 93 Sam Mills	.02	.10
❑ 94 Randall McDaniel	.05	.15
❑ 95 Johnny Holland	.02	.10
❑ 96 Jackie Slater	.02	.10
❑ 97 Don Mosebar	.02	.10
❑ 98 Andre Ware	.02	.10
❑ 99 Kelvin Martin	.02	.10
❑ 100 Emmitt Smith	1.00	2.50
❑ 101 Michael Brooks	.02	.10
❑ 102 Dan Saleaumua	.02	.10
❑ 103 John Elway	1.00	2.50
❑ 104 Henry Jones	.02	.10
❑ 105 William Perry	.07	.20
❑ 106 James Lofton	.07	.20
❑ 107 Carnell Lake	.02	.10
❑ 108 Chip Lohmiller	.02	.10
❑ 109 Andre Tippett	.02	.10
❑ 110 Barry Word	.02	.10
❑ 111 Haywood Jeffires	.07	.20
❑ 112 Kenny Walker	.02	.10
❑ 113 John Randle	.07	.20
❑ 114 Donnell Woolford	.02	.10
❑ 115 Johnny Bailey	.02	.10
❑ 116 Marcus Allen	.15	.40
❑ 117 Mark Jackson	.02	.10
❑ 118 Ray Agnew	.02	.10
❑ 119 Gill Byrd	.02	.10
❑ 120 Kyle Clifton	.02	.10
❑ 121 Marv Cook	.02	.10
❑ 122 Jerry Ball	.02	.10
❑ 123 Steve Jordan	.02	.10
❑ 124 Shannon Sharpe	.15	.40
❑ 125 Brian Blades	.07	.20
❑ 126 Rodney Hampton	.07	.20
❑ 127 Bobby Hebert	.02	.10
❑ 128 Jessie Tuggle	.02	.10
❑ 129 Tom Newberry	.02	.10
❑ 130 Keith McCants	.02	.10
❑ 131 Richard Dent	.07	.20
❑ 132 Herman Moore	.15	.40
❑ 133 Michael Irvin	.15	.40
❑ 134 Ernest Givins	.07	.20
❑ 135 Mark Rypien	.02	.10
❑ 136 Leonard Russell	.07	.20
❑ 137 Reggie White	.15	.40
❑ 138 Thurman Thomas	.15	.40
❑ 139 Nick Lowery	.02	.10
❑ 140 Al Smith	.02	.10
❑ 141 Jackie Harris	.02	.10
❑ 142 Duane Bickett	.02	.10
❑ 143 Lawyer Tillman	.02	.10
❑ 144 Steve Wisniewski	.02	.10
❑ 145 Derrick Fenner	.02	.10
❑ 146 Harris Barton	.02	.10
❑ 147 Rich Camarillo	.02	.10
❑ 148 John Offerdahl	.02	.10
❑ 149 Mike Johnson	.02	.10
❑ 150 Ricky Reynolds	.02	.10
❑ 151 Fred Barnett	.07	.20
❑ 152 Nate Newton	.07	.20
❑ 153 Chris Doleman	.02	.10
❑ 154 Todd Scott	.02	.10
❑ 155 Tim McKyer	.02	.10
❑ 156 Ken Harvey	.02	.10
❑ 157 Jeff Feagles	.02	.10
❑ 158 Vince Workman	.02	.10
❑ 159 Bart Oates	.02	.10
❑ 160 Chris Miller	.07	.20
❑ 161 Pete Stoyanovich	.02	.10
❑ 162 Steve Wallace	.02	.10
❑ 163 Dermontti Dawson	.02	.10
❑ 164 Kenneth Davis	.02	.10
❑ 165 Mike Munchak	.07	.20
❑ 166 George Jamison	.02	.10
❑ 167 Christian Okoye	.02	.10
❑ 168 Chris Hinton	.02	.10
❑ 169 Vaughan Johnson	.02	.10
❑ 170 Gaston Green	.02	.10
❑ 171 Kevin Greene	.07	.20
❑ 172 Rob Burnett	.02	.10
❑ 173 Norm Johnson	.02	.10
❑ 174 Eric Hill	.02	.10
❑ 175 Lomas Brown	.02	.10
❑ 176 Chip Banks	.02	.10
❑ 177 Greg Townsend	.02	.10
❑ 178 David Fulcher	.02	.10
❑ 179 Gary Anderson RB	.02	.10
❑ 180 Brian Washington	.02	.10
❑ 181 Brett Perriman	.15	.40
❑ 182 Chris Chandler	.07	.20
❑ 183 Phil Hansen	.02	.10
❑ 184 Mark Clayton	.02	.10
❑ 185 Frank Warren	.02	.10
❑ 186 Tim Brown	.15	.40
❑ 187 Mark Stepnoski	.02	.10
❑ 188 Bryan Cox	.02	.10
❑ 189 Gary Zimmerman	.02	.10
❑ 190 Neil O'Donnell	.15	.40
❑ 191 Anthony Smith	.02	.10
❑ 192 Craig Heyward	.07	.20
❑ 193 Keith Byars	.02	.10
❑ 194 Sean Salisbury	.02	.10
❑ 195 Todd Lyght	.02	.10
❑ 196 Jessie Hester	.02	.10
❑ 197 Rufus Porter	.02	.10
❑ 198 Steve Christie	.02	.10
❑ 199 Nate Lewis	.02	.10
❑ 200 Barry Sanders	.75	2.00
❑ 201 Michael Haynes	.07	.20
❑ 202 John Taylor	.07	.20
❑ 203 John Friesz	.07	.20
❑ 204 William Fuller	.02	.10
❑ 205 Dennis Smith	.02	.10
❑ 206 Adrian Cooper	.02	.10
❑ 207 Henry Thomas	.02	.10
❑ 208 Gerald Williams	.02	.10
❑ 209 Chris Burkett	.02	.10
❑ 210 Broderick Thomas	.02	.10
❑ 211 Marvin Washington	.02	.10
❑ 212 Bennie Blades	.02	.10
❑ 213 Tony Casillas	.02	.10
❑ 214 Bubby Brister	.02	.10
❑ 215 Don Griffin	.02	.10
❑ 216 Jeff Cross	.02	.10
❑ 217 Derrick Walker	.02	.10
❑ 218 Lorenzo White	.02	.10
❑ 219 Ricky Sanders	.02	.10
❑ 220 Rickey Jackson	.02	.10
❑ 221 Simon Fletcher	.02	.10
❑ 222 Troy Vincent	.02	.10
❑ 223 Gary Clark	.07	.20
❑ 224 Stanley Richard	.02	.10
❑ 225 Dave Krieg	.07	.20
❑ 226 Warren Moon	.15	.40
❑ 227 Reggie Langhorne	.02	.10
❑ 228 Kent Hull	.02	.10
❑ 229 Ferrell Edmunds	.02	.10
❑ 230 Cortez Kennedy	.07	.20

❑ 231 Hugh Millen .02 .10
❑ 232 Eugene Chung .02 .10
❑ 233 Rodney Peete .02 .10
❑ 234 Tom Waddle .02 .10
❑ 235 David Klingler .02 .10
❑ 236 Mark Carrier WR .07 .20
❑ 237 Jay Schroeder .02 .10
❑ 238 James Jones DT .02 .10
❑ 239 Phil Simms .07 .20
❑ 240 Steve Atwater .02 .10
❑ 241 Jeff Herrod .02 .10
❑ 242 Dale Carter .02 .10
❑ 243 Glenn Cadrez RC .02 .10
❑ 244 Wayne Martin .02 .10
❑ 245 Willie Davis .15 .40
❑ 246 Lawrence Taylor .15 .40
❑ 247 Stan Humphries .07 .20
❑ 248 Byron Evans .02 .10
❑ 249 Wilber Marshall .02 .10
❑ 250 Michael Bankston RC .02 .10
❑ 251 Steve McMichael .07 .20
❑ 252 Brad Edwards .02 .10
❑ 253 Will Wolford .02 .10
❑ 254 Paul Gruber .02 .10
❑ 255 Steve Young .50 1.25
❑ 256 Chuck Cecil .02 .10
❑ 257 Pierce Holt .02 .10
❑ 258 Anthony Miller .07 .20
❑ 259 Carl Banks .02 .10
❑ 260 Brad Muster .02 .10
❑ 261 Clay Matthews .07 .20
❑ 262 Rod Bernstine .02 .10
❑ 263 Tim Barnett .02 .10
❑ 264 Greg Lloyd .07 .20
❑ 265 Sean Jones .02 .10
❑ 266 J.J. Birden .02 .10
❑ 267 Tim McDonald .02 .10
❑ 268 Charles Mann .02 .10
❑ 269 Bruce Smith .15 .40
❑ 270 Sean Gilbert .07 .20
❑ 271 Ricardo McDonald .02 .10
❑ 272 Jeff Hostetler .07 .20
❑ 273 Russell Maryland .02 .10
❑ 274 Dave Brown RC .15 .40
❑ 275 Ronnie Lott .07 .20
❑ 276 Jim Kelly .15 .40
❑ 277 Joe Montana 1.00 2.50
❑ 278 Eric Allen .02 .10
❑ 279 Browning Nagle .02 .10
❑ 280 Neal Anderson .02 .10
❑ 281 Troy Aikman .50 1.25
❑ 282 Ed McCaffrey .15 .40
❑ 283 Robert Jones .02 .10
❑ 284 Dalton Hilliard .02 .10
❑ 285 Johnny Mitchell .02 .10
❑ 286 Jay Hilgenberg .02 .10
❑ 287 Eric Martin .02 .10
❑ 288 Steve Emtman .02 .10
❑ 289 Vaughn Dunbar .02 .10
❑ 290 Mark Wheeler .02 .10
❑ 291 Leslie O'Neal .07 .20
❑ 292 Jerry Rice .60 1.50
❑ 293 Neil Smith .15 .40
❑ 294 Kerry Cash .02 .10
❑ 295 Dan McGwire .02 .10
❑ 296 Carl Pickens .07 .20
❑ 297 Terrell Buckley .02 .10
❑ 298 Randall Cunningham .15 .40
❑ 299 Santana Dotson .07 .20
❑ 300 Keith Jackson .07 .20
❑ 301 Jim Lachey .02 .10
❑ 302 Dan Marino 1.00 2.50
❑ 303 Lee Williams .02 .10
❑ 304 Burt Grossman .02 .10
❑ 305 Kevin Mack .02 .10
❑ 306 Pat Swilling .02 .10
❑ 307 Arthur Marshall RC .02 .10
❑ 308 Jim Harbaugh .15 .40
❑ 309 Kurt Barber .02 .10
❑ 310 Harvey Williams .07 .20
❑ 311 Ricky Ervins .02 .10
❑ 312 Flipper Anderson .02 .10
❑ 313 Bernie Kosar .07 .20
❑ 314 Boomer Esiason .07 .20
❑ 315 Deion Sanders .30 .75
❑ 316 Ray Childress .02 .10
❑ 317 Howie Long .15 .40
❑ 318 Henry Ellard .07 .20
❑ 319 Marco Coleman .02 .10
❑ 320 Chris Mims .02 .10
❑ 321 Quentin Coryatt .07 .20
❑ 322 Jason Hanson .02 .10
❑ 323 Ricky Proehl .02 .10
❑ 324 Randal Hill .02 .10
❑ 325 Vinny Testaverde .07 .20
❑ 326 Jeff George .15 .40
❑ 327 Junior Seau .15 .40
❑ 328 Earnest Byner .02 .10
❑ 329 Andre Reed .07 .20
❑ 330 Phillippi Sparks .02 .10
❑ 331 Kevin Ross .02 .10
❑ 332 Clarence Verdin .02 .10
❑ 333 Darryl Henley .02 .10
❑ 334 Dana Hall .02 .10
❑ 335 Greg McMurtry .02 .10
❑ 336 Ron Hall .02 .10
❑ 337 Darrell Green .02 .10
❑ 338 Carlton Bailey .02 .10
❑ 339 Irv Eatman .02 .10
❑ 340 Greg Kragen .02 .10
❑ 341 Wade Wilson .02 .10
❑ 342 Klaus Wilmsmeyer .02 .10
❑ 343 Derek Brown TE .02 .10
❑ 344 Erik Williams .02 .10
❑ 345 Jim McMahon .07 .20
❑ 346 Mike Sherrard .02 .10
❑ 347 Mark Bavaro .02 .10
❑ 348 Anthony Munoz .07 .20
❑ 349 Eric Dickerson .07 .20
❑ 350 Steve Beuerlein .07 .20
❑ 351 Tim McGee .02 .10
❑ 352 Terry McDaniel .02 .10
❑ 353 Dan Fouts HOF .02 .10
❑ 354 Chuck Noll HOF .07 .20
❑ 355 Bill Walsh HOF RC .07 .20
❑ 356 Larry Little HOF .02 .10
❑ 357 Todd Marinovich HH .02 .10
❑ 358 Jeff George HH .15 .40
❑ 359 Bernie Kosar HH .07 .20
❑ 360 Rob Moore HH .07 .20
❑ NNO Franco Harris AU/3000 12.50 25.00

1994 Pinnacle

❑ COMPLETE SET (270) 8.00 20.00
❑ 1 Deion Sanders .20 .50
❑ 2 Eric Metcalf .07 .20
❑ 3 Barry Sanders .75 2.00
❑ 4 Ernest Givins .07 .20
❑ 5 Phil Simms .07 .20
❑ 6 Rod Woodson .07 .20
❑ 7 Michael Irvin .15 .40
❑ 8 Cortez Kennedy .07 .20
❑ 9 Eric Martin .02 .10
❑ 10 Jeff Hostetler .07 .20
❑ 11 Sterling Sharpe .07 .20
❑ 12 John Elway 1.00 2.50
❑ 13 Neal Anderson .02 .10
❑ 14 Terry Kirby .15 .40
❑ 15 Jim Everett .07 .20
❑ 16 Lawrence Dawsey .02 .10
❑ 17 Kelvin Martin .02 .10
❑ 18 Tim McGee .02 .10
❑ 19 Cris Carter .20 .50
❑ 20 Ronnie Harmon .02 .10
❑ 21 Jim Kelly .15 .40
❑ 22 Steve Young .40 1.00
❑ 23 Johnny Johnson .02 .10
❑ 24 Sean Gilbert .02 .10
❑ 25 Brian Mitchell .02 .10
❑ 26 Carl Pickens .07 .20
❑ 27 Tim Brown .15 .40
❑ 28 Reggie Langhorne .02 .10
❑ 29 Webster Slaughter .02 .10
❑ 30 Alvin Harper .07 .20
❑ 31 Andre Rison .07 .20
❑ 32 Derrick Thomas .15 .40
❑ 33 Irving Fryar .07 .20
❑ 34 Vinny Testaverde .07 .20
❑ 35 Steve Beuerlein .07 .20
❑ 36 Brett Favre 1.00 2.50
❑ 37 Barry Foster .02 .10
❑ 38 Vaughan Johnson .02 .10
❑ 39 Carlton Bailey .02 .10
❑ 40 Steve Emtman .02 .10
❑ 41 Anthony Miller .07 .20
❑ 42 Jeff Cross .02 .10
❑ 43 Trace Armstrong .02 .10
❑ 44 Derek Russell .02 .10
❑ 45 Vincent Brisby .07 .20
❑ 46 Mark Jackson .02 .10
❑ 47 Eugene Robinson .02 .10
❑ 48 John Friesz .07 .20
❑ 49 Scott Mitchell .07 .20
❑ 50 Steve Atwater .02 .10
❑ 51 Ken Norton .07 .20
❑ 52 Vincent Brown .02 .10
❑ 53 Morten Andersen .02 .10
❑ 54 Gary Anderson K .02 .10
❑ 55 Eric Curry .02 .10
❑ 56 Henry Jones .02 .10
❑ 57 Flipper Anderson .02 .10
❑ 58 Pat Swilling .02 .10
❑ 59 Erric Pegram .02 .10
❑ 60 Bruce Matthews .02 .10
❑ 61 Willie Davis .07 .20
❑ 62 O.J.McDuffie .15 .40
❑ 63 Qadry Ismail .15 .40
❑ 64 Anthony Smith .02 .10
❑ 65 Eric Allen .02 .10
❑ 66 Marion Butts .02 .10
❑ 67 Chris Miller .02 .10
❑ 68 Terrell Buckley .02 .10
❑ 69 Thurman Thomas .15 .40
❑ 70 Roosevelt Potts .02 .10
❑ 71 Tony McGee .02 .10
❑ 72 Jason Hanson .02 .10
❑ 73 Victor Bailey .02 .10
❑ 74 Albert Lewis .02 .10
❑ 75 Nate Odomes .02 .10
❑ 76 Ben Coates .07 .20
❑ 77 Warren Moon .15 .40
❑ 78 Derek Brown RBK .02 .10
❑ 79 David Klingler .02 .10
❑ 80 Cleveland Gary .02 .10
❑ 81 Emmitt Smith .75 2.00
❑ 82 Jay Novacek .07 .20
❑ 83 Dana Stubblefield .07 .20
❑ 84 Michael Brooks .02 .10
❑ 85 James Jett .02 .10
❑ 86 J.J. Birden .02 .10
❑ 87 William Fuller .02 .10
❑ 88 Glyn Milburn .07 .20
❑ 89 Tim Worley .02 .10
❑ 90 Brett Perriman .07 .20
❑ 91 Randall Cunningham .15 .40
❑ 92 Drew Bledsoe .40 1.00
❑ 93 Jerome Bettis .25 .60
❑ 94 Boomer Esiason .07 .20
❑ 95 Garrison Hearst .15 .40
❑ 96 Bruce Smith .15 .40
❑ 97 Jackie Harris .02 .10
❑ 98 Jeff George .15 .40
❑ 99 Tom Waddle .02 .10
❑ 100 John Copeland .02 .10
❑ 101 Bobby Hebert .02 .10
❑ 102 Joe Montana 1.00 2.50
❑ 103 Herman Moore .15 .40
❑ 104 Rick Mirer .15 .40
❑ 105 Ricky Watters .07 .20
❑ 106 Neil O'Donnell .15 .40
❑ 107 Herschel Walker .07 .20
❑ 108 Rob Moore .07 .20
❑ 109 Reggie Brooks .07 .20
❑ 110 Tommy Vardell .02 .10
❑ 111 Eric Green .02 .10
❑ 112 Stan Humphries .07 .20
❑ 113 Greg Robinson .02 .10
❑ 114 Eric Swann .07 .20
❑ 115 Courtney Hawkins .02 .10
❑ 116 Andre Reed .07 .20
❑ 117 Steve McMichael .07 .20
❑ 118 Gary Brown .02 .10
❑ 119 Terry Allen .07 .20
❑ 120 Dan Marino 1.00 2.50

❑ 121 Gary Clark .07 .20
❑ 122 Chris Warren .07 .20
❑ 123 Pierce Holt .02 .10
❑ 124 Anthony Carter .07 .20
❑ 125 Quentin Coryatt .02 .10
❑ 126 Harold Green .02 .10
❑ 127 Leonard Russell .02 .10
❑ 128 Tim McDonald .02 .10
❑ 129 Chris Spielman .07 .20
❑ 130 Cody Carlson .02 .10
❑ 131 Ronald Moore .02 .10
❑ 132 Renaldo Turnbull .02 .10
❑ 133 Ronnie Lott .07 .20
❑ 134 Natrone Means .15 .40
❑ 135 Keith Byars .02 .10
❑ 136 Henry Ellard .07 .20
❑ 137 Steve Jordan .02 .10
❑ 138 Calvin Williams .07 .20
❑ 139 Brian Blades .07 .20
❑ 140 Michael Jackson .07 .20
❑ 141 Charles Haley .07 .20
❑ 142 Curtis Conway .15 .40
❑ 143 Nick Lowery .02 .10
❑ 144 Bill Brooks .02 .10
❑ 145 Michael Haynes .07 .20
❑ 146 Willie Green .02 .10
❑ 147 Duane Bickett .02 .10
❑ 148 Shannon Sharpe .07 .20
❑ 149 Ricky Proehl .02 .10
❑ 150 Troy Aikman .50 1.25
❑ 151 Mike Sherrard .02 .10
❑ 152 Reggie Cobb .02 .10
❑ 153 Norm Johnson .02 .10
❑ 154 Neil Smith .07 .20
❑ 155 James Francis .02 .10
❑ 156 Greg McMurtry .02 .10
❑ 157 Greg Townsend .02 .10
❑ 158 Mel Gray .02 .10
❑ 159 Rocket Ismail .07 .20
❑ 160 Leslie O'Neal .02 .10
❑ 161 Johnny Mitchell .02 .10
❑ 162 Brent Jones .07 .20
❑ 163 Chris Doleman .02 .10
❑ 164 Seth Joyner .02 .10
❑ 165 Marco Coleman .02 .10
❑ 166 Mark Higgs .02 .10
❑ 167 John L. Williams .02 .10
❑ 168 Darrell Green .02 .10
❑ 169 Mark Carrier WR .07 .20
❑ 170 Reggie White .15 .40
❑ 171 Darryl Talley .02 .10
❑ 172 Russell Maryland .02 .10
❑ 173 Mark Collins .02 .10
❑ 174 Chris Jacke .02 .10
❑ 175 Richard Dent .07 .20
❑ 176 John Taylor .07 .20
❑ 177 Rodney Hampton .07 .20
❑ 178 Dwight Stone .02 .10
❑ 179 Cornelius Bennett .07 .20
❑ 180 Cris Dishman .02 .10
❑ 181 Jerry Rice .50 1.25
❑ 182 Rod Bernstine .02 .10
❑ 183 Keith Hamilton .02 .10
❑ 184 Keith Jackson .02 .10
❑ 185 Craig Erickson .02 .10
❑ 186 Marcus Allen .15 .40
❑ 187 Marcus Robertson .02 .10
❑ 188 Junior Seau .15 .40
❑ 189 LeShon Johnson RC .07 .20
❑ 190 Perry Klein RC .02 .10
❑ 191 Bryant Young RC .25 .60
❑ 192 Byron Bam Morris RC .07 .20
❑ 193 Jeff Cothran RC .02 .10
❑ 194 Lamar Smith RC .60 1.50
❑ 195 Calvin Jones RC .02 .10
❑ 196 James Bostic RC .15 .40
❑ 197 Dan Wilkinson RC .07 .20
❑ 198 Marshall Faulk RC 2.50 6.00
❑ 199 Heath Shuler RC .15 .40
❑ 200 Willie McGinest RC .15 .40
❑ 201 Trev Alberts RC .07 .20
❑ 202 Trent Dilfer RC .60 1.50
❑ 203 Sam Adams RC .07 .20
❑ 204 Charles Johnson RC .15 .40
❑ 205 Johnnie Morton RC .60 1.50
❑ 206 Thomas Lewis RC .07 .20
❑ 207 Greg Hill RC .15 .40
❑ 208 William Floyd RC .15 .40
❑ 209 Derrick Alexander WR RC .15 .40
❑ 210 Darnay Scott RC .30 .75
❑ 211 Lake Dawson RC .07 .20
❑ 212 Errict Rhett RC .15 .40
❑ 213 Kevin Lee RC .02 .10
❑ 214 Chuck Levy RC .02 .10
❑ 215 David Palmer RC .15 .40
❑ 216 Ryan Yarborough RC .02 .10
❑ 217 Charlie Garner RC .60 1.50
❑ 218 Mario Bates RC .15 .40
❑ 219 Jamir Miller RC .07 .20
❑ 220 Bucky Brooks RC .02 .10
❑ 221 Donnell Bennett RC .15 .40
❑ 222 Kevin Greene .07 .20
❑ 223 LeRoy Butler .02 .10
❑ 224 Anthony Pleasant .02 .10
❑ 225 Steve Christie .02 .10
❑ 226 Bill Romanowski .02 .10
❑ 227 Darren Carrington .02 .10
❑ 228 Chester McGlockton .02 .10
❑ 229 Jack Del Rio .02 .10
❑ 230 Kevin Smith .02 .10
❑ 231 Chris Zorich .02 .10
❑ 232 Donnell Woolford .02 .10
❑ 233 Tony Casillas .02 .10
❑ 234 Terry McDaniel .02 .10
❑ 235 Ray Childress .02 .10
❑ 236 John Randle .07 .20
❑ 237 Clyde Simmons .02 .10
❑ 238 Dante Jones .02 .10
❑ 239 Karl Mecklenburg .02 .10
❑ 240 Daryl Johnston .07 .20
❑ 241 Hardy Nickerson .07 .20
❑ 242 Jeff Lageman .02 .10
❑ 243 Lewis Tillman .02 .10
❑ 244 Jim McMahon .07 .20
❑ 245 Mike Pritchard .02 .10
❑ 246 Harvey Williams .07 .20
❑ 247 Sean Jones .02 .10
❑ 248 Stevon Moore .02 .10
❑ 249 Pete Metzelaars .02 .10
❑ 250 Mike Johnson .02 .10
❑ 251 Chris Slade .02 .10
❑ 252 Jessie Hester .02 .10
❑ 253 Louis Oliver .02 .10
❑ 254 Ken Harvey .02 .10
❑ 255 Bryan Cox .02 .10
❑ 256 Erik Kramer .07 .20
❑ 257 Andy Harmon .02 .10
❑ 258 Rickey Jackson .02 .10
❑ 259 Mark Carrier DB .02 .10
❑ 260 Greg Lloyd .07 .20
❑ 261 Robert Brooks .15 .40
❑ 262 Dave Brown .07 .20
❑ 263 Dennis Smith .02 .10
❑ 264 Michael Dean Perry .07 .20
❑ 265 Dan Saleaumua .02 .10
❑ 266 Mo Lewis .02 .10
❑ 267 AFC Checklist .02 .10
❑ 268 AFC Checklist .02 .10
❑ 269 NFC Checklist .02 .10
❑ 270 NFC Checklist .02 .10
❑ 271SP Jerry Rice TD King SP 4.00 8.00
❑ NNO Drew Bledsoe Pin.Passer 15.00 40.00

1995 Pinnacle

❑ COMPLETE SET (250) 8.00 20.00
❑ 1 Reggie White .15 .40
❑ 2 Troy Aikman .40 1.00
❑ 3 Willie Davis .07 .20
❑ 4 Jerry Rice .40 1.00
❑ 5 Bruce Smith .15 .40
❑ 6 Keith Byars .02 .10
❑ 7 Chris Warren .07 .20
❑ 8 Erik Kramer .02 .10
❑ 9 Leon Lett .02 .10
❑ 10 Greg Lloyd .07 .20
❑ 11 Jackie Harris .02 .10
❑ 12 Irving Fryar .07 .20
❑ 13 Rodney Hampton .07 .20
❑ 14 Michael Irvin .15 .40
❑ 15 Michael Haynes .07 .20
❑ 16 Irving Spikes .07 .20
❑ 17 Calvin Williams .07 .20
❑ 18 Ken Norton Jr. .07 .20
❑ 19 Herman Moore .15 .40
❑ 20 Lewis Tillman .02 .10
❑ 21 Cortez Kennedy .07 .20
❑ 22 Dan Marino .75 2.00
❑ 23 Erric Pegram .07 .20
❑ 24 Tim Brown .15 .40
❑ 25 Jeff Blake RC .30 .75
❑ 26 Brett Favre .75 2.00
❑ 27 Garrison Hearst .15 .40
❑ 28 Ronnie Harmon .02 .10
❑ 29 Qadry Ismail .07 .20
❑ 30 Ben Coates .07 .20
❑ 31 Deion Sanders .25 .60
❑ 32 John Elway .75 2.00
❑ 33 Natrone Means .07 .20
❑ 34 Derrick Alexander WR .15 .40
❑ 35 Craig Heyward .07 .20
❑ 36 Jake Reed .07 .20
❑ 37 Steve Walsh .02 .10
❑ 38 John Randle .07 .20
❑ 39 Barry Sanders .60 1.50
❑ 40 Tydus Winans .02 .10
❑ 41 Thomas Lewis .07 .20
❑ 42 Jim Kelly .15 .40
❑ 43 Gus Frerotte .07 .20
❑ 44 Cris Carter .15 .40
❑ 45 Kevin Williams WR .07 .20
❑ 46 Dave Meggett .02 .10
❑ 47 Pat Swilling .02 .10
❑ 48 Neil O'Donnell .07 .20
❑ 49 Terance Mathis .07 .20
❑ 50 Desmond Howard .07 .20
❑ 51 Bryant Young .07 .20
❑ 52 Stan Humphries .07 .20
❑ 53 Alvin Harper .02 .10
❑ 54 Henry Ellard .07 .20
❑ 55 Jessie Hester .02 .10
❑ 56 Lorenzo White .02 .10
❑ 57 John Friesz .07 .20
❑ 58 Anthony Smith .02 .10
❑ 59 Bert Emanuel .15 .40
❑ 60 Gary Clark .02 .10
❑ 61 Bill Brooks .02 .10
❑ 62 Steve Young .30 .75
❑ 63 Jerome Bettis .15 .40
❑ 64 John Taylor .02 .10
❑ 65 Ricky Proehl .02 .10
❑ 66 Junior Seau .15 .40
❑ 67 Bubby Brister .02 .10
❑ 68 Neil Smith .07 .20
❑ 69 Dan McGwire .02 .10
❑ 70 Brett Perriman .07 .20
❑ 71 Chris Spielman .07 .20
❑ 72 Jeff George .07 .20
❑ 73 Emmitt Smith .40 1.00
❑ 74 Chris Penn .02 .10
❑ 75 Derrick Fenner .02 .10
❑ 76 Reggie Brooks .07 .20
❑ 77 Chris Chandler .07 .20
❑ 78 Rod Woodson .07 .20
❑ 79 Isaac Bruce .25 .60
❑ 80 Reggie Cobb .02 .10
❑ 81 Bryce Paup .07 .20
❑ 82 Warren Moon .07 .20
❑ 83 Bryan Reeves .02 .10
❑ 84 Lake Dawson .07 .20
❑ 85 Larry Centers .07 .20
❑ 86 Marshall Faulk .50 1.25
❑ 87 Jim Harbaugh .07 .20
❑ 88 Ray Childress .02 .10
❑ 89 Eric Metcalf .07 .20
❑ 90 Ernie Mills .02 .10
❑ 91 Lamar Lathon .02 .10
❑ 92 Errict Rhett .07 .20
❑ 93 David Klingler .07 .20
❑ 94 Vincent Brown .02 .10
❑ 95 Andre Rison .07 .20
❑ 96 Brian Mitchell .02 .10
❑ 97 Mark Rypien .02 .10
❑ 98 Eugene Robinson .02 .10
❑ 99 Eric Green .02 .10

Card	Low	High
❑ 100 Rocket Ismail	.07	.20
❑ 101 Flipper Anderson	.02	.10
❑ 102 Randall Cunningham	.15	.40
❑ 103 Ricky Watters	.07	.20
❑ 104 Amp Lee	.02	.10
❑ 105 Ernest Givins	.02	.10
❑ 106 Daryl Johnston	.07	.20
❑ 107 Dave Krieg	.02	.10
❑ 108 Dana Stubblefield	.07	.20
❑ 109 Torrance Small	.02	.10
❑ 110 Yancey Thigpen RC	.07	.20
❑ 111 Chester McGlockton	.07	.20
❑ 112 Craig Erickson	.02	.10
❑ 113 Herschel Walker	.07	.20
❑ 114 Mike Sherrard	.02	.10
❑ 115 Tony McGee	.02	.10
❑ 116 Adrian Murrell	.07	.20
❑ 117 Frank Reich	.02	.10
❑ 118 Hardy Nickerson	.02	.10
❑ 119 Andre Reed	.07	.20
❑ 120 Leonard Russell	.02	.10
❑ 121 Eric Allen	.02	.10
❑ 122 Jeff Hostetler	.07	.20
❑ 123 Barry Foster	.07	.20
❑ 124 Anthony Miller	.07	.20
❑ 125 Shawn Jefferson	.02	.10
❑ 126 Richie Anderson RC	.20	.50
❑ 127 Steve Bono	.07	.20
❑ 128 Seth Joyner	.02	.10
❑ 129 Darnay Scott	.07	.20
❑ 130 Johnny Mitchell	.02	.10
❑ 131 Eric Swann	.07	.20
❑ 132 Drew Bledsoe	.25	.60
❑ 133 Marcus Allen	.15	.40
❑ 134 Carl Pickens	.07	.20
❑ 135 Michael Brooks	.02	.10
❑ 136 John L. Williams	.02	.10
❑ 137 Steve Beuerlein	.07	.20
❑ 138 Robert Smith	.15	.40
❑ 139 O.J. McDuffie	.15	.40
❑ 140 Haywood Jeffires	.02	.10
❑ 141 Aeneas Williams	.02	.10
❑ 142 Rick Mirer	.07	.20
❑ 143 William Floyd	.07	.20
❑ 144 Fred Barnett	.07	.20
❑ 145 Leroy Hoard	.02	.10
❑ 146 Terry Kirby	.07	.20
❑ 147 Boomer Esiason	.07	.20
❑ 148 Ken Harvey	.02	.10
❑ 149 Cleveland Gary	.02	.10
❑ 150 Brian Blades	.07	.20
❑ 151 Eric Turner	.02	.10
❑ 152 Vinny Testaverde	.07	.20
❑ 153 Ronald Moore UER	.02	.10
❑ 154 Curtis Conway	.15	.40
❑ 155 Johnnie Morton	.07	.20
❑ 156 Kenneth Davis	.02	.10
❑ 157 Scott Mitchell	.07	.20
❑ 158 Sean Gilbert	.07	.20
❑ 159 Shannon Sharpe	.07	.20
❑ 160 Mark Seay	.07	.20
❑ 161 Cornelius Bennett	.07	.20
❑ 162 Heath Shuler	.07	.20
❑ 163 Byron Bam Morris	.02	.10
❑ 164 Robert Brooks	.15	.40
❑ 165 Glyn Milburn	.02	.10
❑ 166 Gary Brown	.02	.10
❑ 167 Jim Everett	.02	.10
❑ 168 Steve Atwater	.02	.10
❑ 169 Darren Woodson	.07	.20
❑ 170 Mark Ingram	.02	.10
❑ 171 Donnell Woolford	.02	.10
❑ 172 Trent Dilfer	.15	.40
❑ 173 Charlie Garner	.15	.40
❑ 174 Charles Johnson	.07	.20
❑ 175 Mike Pritchard	.02	.10
❑ 176 Derek Brown RBK	.02	.10
❑ 177 Chris Miller	.02	.10
❑ 178 Charles Haley	.07	.20
❑ 179 J.J. Birden	.02	.10
❑ 180 Jeff Graham	.02	.10
❑ 181 Bernie Parmalee	.07	.20
❑ 182 Mark Brunell	.25	.60
❑ 183 Greg Hill	.07	.20
❑ 184 Michael Timpson	.02	.10
❑ 185 Terry Allen	.07	.20
❑ 186 Ricky Ervins	.02	.10
❑ 187 Dave Brown	.07	.20
❑ 188 Dan Wilkinson	.07	.20
❑ 189 Jay Novacek	.07	.20
❑ 190 Harvey Williams	.02	.10
❑ 191 Mario Bates	.07	.20
❑ 192 Steve Young LAW	.20	.50
❑ 193 Joe Montana	.75	2.00
❑ 194 Steve Young PP	.20	.50
❑ 195 Troy Aikman PP	.25	.60
❑ 196 Drew Bledsoe PP	.15	.40
❑ 197 Dan Marino PP	.40	1.00
❑ 198 John Elway PP	.40	1.00
❑ 199 Brett Favre PP	.40	1.00
❑ 200 Heath Shuler PP	.07	.20
❑ 201 Warren Moon PP	.02	.10
❑ 202 Jim Kelly PP	.15	.40
❑ 203 Jeff Hostetler PP	.07	.20
❑ 204 Rick Mirer PP	.07	.20
❑ 205 Dave Brown PP	.07	.20
❑ 206 Randall Cunningham PP	.07	.20
❑ 207 Neil O'Donnell PP	.07	.20
❑ 208 Jim Everett PP	.02	.10
❑ 209 Ki-Jana Carter RC	.15	.40
❑ 210 Steve McNair RC	1.25	3.00
❑ 211 Michael Westbrook RC	.15	.40
❑ 212 Kerry Collins RC	.75	2.00
❑ 213 Joey Galloway RC	.60	1.50
❑ 214 Kyle Brady RC	.15	.40
❑ 215 J.J. Stokes RC	.15	.40
❑ 216 Tyrone Wheatley RC	.50	1.25
❑ 217 Rashaan Salaam RC	.07	.20
❑ 218 Napoleon Kaufman RC	.50	1.25
❑ 219 Frank Sanders RC	.15	.40
❑ 220 Stoney Case RC	.02	.10
❑ 221 Todd Collins RC	.50	1.25
❑ 222 Warren Sapp RC	.60	1.50
❑ 223 Sherman Williams RC	.02	.10
❑ 224 Rob Johnson RC	.40	1.00
❑ 225 Mark Bruener RC	.07	.20
❑ 226 Derrick Brooks RC	.60	1.50
❑ 227 Chad May RC	.02	.10
❑ 228 James A.Stewart RC	.02	.10
❑ 229 Ray Zellars RC	.07	.20
❑ 230 Dave Barr RC	.02	.10
❑ 231 Kordell Stewart RC	.60	1.50
❑ 232 Jimmy Oliver RC	.02	.10
❑ 233 Tony Boselli RC	.15	.40
❑ 234 James O. Stewart RC	.50	1.25
❑ 235 Derrick Alexander DE RC	.02	.10
❑ 236 Lovell Pinkney RC	.02	.10
❑ 237 John Walsh RC	.02	.10
❑ 238 Tyrone Davis RC	.02	.10
❑ 239 Joe Aska RC	.02	.10
❑ 240 Korey Stringer RC	.10	.30
❑ 241 Hugh Douglas RC	.15	.40
❑ 242 Christian Fauria RC	.07	.20
❑ 243 Terrell Fletcher RC	.02	.10
❑ 244 Dan Marino CL	.25	.60
❑ 245 Drew Bledsoe CL	.15	.40
❑ 246 John Elway CL	.15	.40
❑ 247 Emmitt Smith CL	.20	.50
❑ 248 Steve Young CL	.15	.40
❑ 249 Barry Sanders CL	.25	.60
❑ 250 Jerry Rice/Seau CL	.15	.40
❑ 251SP Deion Sanders SP	1.50	4.00

1996 Pinnacle

Card	Low	High
❑ COMPLETE SET (200)	8.00	20.00
❑ 1 Emmitt Smith	.60	1.50
❑ 2 Robert Brooks	.15	.40
❑ 3 Joey Galloway	.15	.40
❑ 4 Dan Marino	.75	2.00
❑ 5 Frank Sanders	.07	.20
❑ 6 Cris Carter	.15	.40
❑ 7 Jeff Blake	.15	.40
❑ 8 Steve McNair	.30	.75
❑ 9 Tamarick Vanover	.07	.20
❑ 10 Andre Reed	.07	.20
❑ 11 Junior Seau	.15	.40
❑ 12 Alvin Harper	.02	.10
❑ 13 Trent Dilfer	.15	.40
❑ 14 Kordell Stewart	.15	.40
❑ 15 Kyle Brady	.02	.10
❑ 16 Charles Haley	.07	.20
❑ 17 Greg Lloyd	.07	.20
❑ 18 Mario Bates	.07	.20
❑ 19 Shannon Sharpe	.07	.20
❑ 20 Scott Mitchell	.07	.20
❑ 21 Craig Heyward	.02	.10
❑ 22 Marcus Allen	.15	.40
❑ 23 Curtis Martin	.30	.75
❑ 24 Drew Bledsoe	.25	.60
❑ 25 Jerry Rice	.40	1.00
❑ 26 Charlie Garner	.07	.20
❑ 27 Michael Irvin	.15	.40
❑ 28 Curtis Conway	.15	.40
❑ 29 Terrell Davis	.30	.75
❑ 30 Jeff Hostetler	.02	.10
❑ 31 Neil O'Donnell	.07	.20
❑ 32 Errict Rhett	.07	.20
❑ 33 Stan Humphries	.07	.20
❑ 34 Jeff Graham	.02	.10
❑ 35 Floyd Turner	.02	.10
❑ 36 Vincent Brisby	.02	.10
❑ 37 Steve Young	.30	.75
❑ 38 Carl Pickens	.07	.20
❑ 39 Terance Mathis	.02	.10
❑ 40 Brett Favre	.75	2.00
❑ 41 Ki-Jana Carter	.07	.20
❑ 42 Jim Everett	.02	.10
❑ 43 Marshall Faulk	.20	.50
❑ 44 William Floyd	.07	.20
❑ 45 Deion Sanders	.25	.60
❑ 46 Garrison Hearst	.07	.20
❑ 47 Chris Sanders	.07	.20
❑ 48 Isaac Bruce	.15	.40
❑ 49 Natrone Means	.07	.20
❑ 50 Troy Aikman	.40	1.00
❑ 51 Ben Coates	.07	.20
❑ 52 Tony Martin	.07	.20
❑ 53 Rod Woodson	.07	.20
❑ 54 Edgar Bennett	.07	.20
❑ 55 Eric Zeier	.02	.10
❑ 56 Steve Bono	.02	.10
❑ 57 Tim Brown	.15	.40
❑ 58 Kevin Williams	.02	.10
❑ 59 Erik Kramer	.02	.10
❑ 60 Jim Kelly	.15	.40
❑ 61 Larry Centers	.07	.20
❑ 62 Terrell Fletcher	.02	.10
❑ 63 Michael Westbrook	.15	.40
❑ 64 Kerry Collins	.15	.40
❑ 65 Jay Novacek	.02	.10
❑ 66 J.J. Stokes	.15	.40
❑ 67 John Elway	.75	2.00
❑ 68 Jim Harbaugh	.07	.20
❑ 69 Aeneas Williams	.02	.10
❑ 70 Tyrone Wheatley	.07	.20
❑ 71 Chris Warren	.07	.20
❑ 72 Rodney Thomas	.02	.10
❑ 73 Jeff George	.07	.20
❑ 74 Rick Mirer	.07	.20
❑ 75 Yancey Thigpen	.07	.20
❑ 76 Herman Moore	.07	.20
❑ 77 Gus Frerotte	.07	.20
❑ 78 Anthony Miller	.07	.20
❑ 79 Ricky Watters	.07	.20
❑ 80 Sherman Williams	.02	.10
❑ 81 Hardy Nickerson	.02	.10
❑ 82 Henry Ellard	.02	.10
❑ 83 Aaron Craver	.02	.10
❑ 84 Rodney Peete	.02	.10
❑ 85 Eric Metcalf	.02	.10
❑ 86 Brian Blades	.02	.10
❑ 87 Rob Moore	.07	.20
❑ 88 Kimble Anders	.07	.20
❑ 89 Harvey Williams	.02	.10
❑ 90 Thurman Thomas	.15	.40
❑ 91 Dave Brown	.02	.10
❑ 92 Terry Allen	.07	.20
❑ 93 Ken Norton Jr.	.02	.10
❑ 94 Reggie White	.15	.40
❑ 95 Mark Chmura	.07	.20
❑ 96 Bert Emanuel	.07	.20
❑ 97 Brett Perriman	.02	.10
❑ 98 Antonio Freeman	.15	.40
❑ 99 Brian Mitchell	.02	.10

Card		
❑ 100 Orlando Thomas	.02	.10
❑ 101 Aaron Hayden	.02	.10
❑ 102 Quinn Early	.02	.10
❑ 103 Lovell Pinkney	.02	.10
❑ 104 Napoleon Kaufman	.15	.40
❑ 105 Daryl Johnston	.07	.20
❑ 106 Steve Tasker	.02	.10
❑ 107 Brent Jones	.02	.10
❑ 108 Mark Brunell	.25	.60
❑ 109 Leslie O'Neal	.02	.10
❑ 110 Irving Fryar	.07	.20
❑ 111 Jim Miller	.15	.40
❑ 112 Sean Dawkins	.02	.10
❑ 113 Boomer Esiason	.07	.20
❑ 114 Heath Shuler	.07	.20
❑ 115 Bruce Smith	.07	.20
❑ 116 Russell Maryland	.02	.10
❑ 117 Jake Reed	.07	.20
❑ 118 O.J. McDuffie	.07	.20
❑ 119 Erik Williams	.02	.10
❑ 120 Willie McGinest	.02	.10
❑ 121 Terry Kirby	.07	.20
❑ 122 Fred Barnett	.02	.10
❑ 123 Andre Hastings	.02	.10
❑ 124 Dale Hellestrae	.02	.10
❑ 125 Darren Woodson	.07	.20
❑ 126 Steve Atwater	.02	.10
❑ 127 Quentin Coryatt	.02	.10
❑ 128 Derrick Thomas	.15	.40
❑ 129 Nate Newton	.02	.10
❑ 130 Kevin Greene	.07	.20
❑ 131 Barry Sanders	.60	1.50
❑ 132 Warren Moon	.07	.20
❑ 133 Rashaan Salaam	.07	.20
❑ 134 Rodney Hampton	.07	.20
❑ 135 James O.Stewart	.07	.20
❑ 136 Erric Pegram	.02	.10
❑ 137 Bryan Cox	.02	.10
❑ 138 Adrian Murrell	.07	.20
❑ 139 Robert Smith	.07	.20
❑ 140 Bernie Parmalee	.02	.10
❑ 141 Bryce Paup	.02	.10
❑ 142 Darick Holmes	.02	.10
❑ 143 Hugh Douglas	.07	.20
❑ 144 Ken Dilger	.07	.20
❑ 145 Derek Loville	.02	.10
❑ 146 Horace Copeland	.02	.10
❑ 147 Wayne Chrebet	.25	.60
❑ 148 Andre Coleman	.02	.10
❑ 149 Greg Hill	.07	.20
❑ 150 Eric Swann	.02	.10
❑ 151 Tyrone Hughes	.02	.10
❑ 152 Ernie Mills	.02	.10
❑ 153 Terry Glenn RC	.50	1.25
❑ 154 Cedric Jones RC	.02	.10
❑ 155 Leeland McElroy RC	.07	.20
❑ 156 Bobby Engram RC	.15	.40
❑ 157 Willie Anderson RC	.02	.10
❑ 158 Mike Alstott RC	.50	1.25
❑ 159 Alex Van Dyke RC	.07	.20
❑ 160 Jeff Lewis RC	.07	.20
❑ 161 Keyshawn Johnson RC	.50	1.25
❑ 162 Regan Upshaw RC	.02	.10
❑ 163 Eric Moulds RC	.60	1.50
❑ 164 Tim Biakabutuka RC	.15	.40
❑ 165 Kevin Hardy RC	.15	.40
❑ 166 Marvin Harrison RC	1.25	3.00
❑ 167 Karim Abdul-Jabbar RC	.15	.40
❑ 168 Tony Brackens RC	.15	.40
❑ 169 Stepfret Williams RC	.07	.20
❑ 170 Eddie George RC	.60	1.50
❑ 171 Lawrence Phillips RC	.15	.40
❑ 172 Danny Kanell RC	.15	.40
❑ 173 Derrick Mayes RC	.15	.40
❑ 174 Daryl Gardener RC	.02	.10
❑ 175 Jonathan Ogden RC	.15	.40
❑ 176 Alex Molden RC	.02	.10
❑ 177 Chris Darkins RC	.02	.10
❑ 178 Stephen Davis RC	.75	2.00
❑ 179 Rickey Dudley RC	.15	.40
❑ 180 Eddie Kennison RC	.15	.40
❑ 181 Simeon Rice RC	.40	1.00
❑ 182 Bobby Hoying RC	.15	.40
❑ 183 Troy Aikman BF6	.20	.50
❑ 184 Emmitt Smith BF6	.40	1.00
❑ 185 Michael Irvin BF6	.07	.20
❑ 186 Deion Sanders BF6	.15	.40
❑ 187 Daryl Johnston BF6	.07	.20
❑ 188 Jay Novacek BF6	.02	.10
❑ 189 Steve Young BF6	.15	.40
❑ 190 Jerry Rice BF6	.20	.50
❑ 191 J.J. Stokes BF6	.15	.40
❑ 192 Ken Norton BF6	.02	.10
❑ 193 William Floyd BF6	.07	.20
❑ 194 Brent Jones BF6	.02	.10
❑ 195 Dan Marino CL	.15	.40
❑ 196 Brett Favre CL	.15	.40
❑ 197 Emmitt Smith CL	.15	.40
❑ 198 Barry Sanders CL	.15	.40
❑ 199 ESmith/Mar/Fav/BSand CL	.15	.40
❑ 200 Brett Favre PackBack	.75	2.00

1997 Pinnacle

Card		
❑ COMPLETE SET (200)	7.50	20.00
❑ 1 Brett Favre	.75	2.00
❑ 2 Dan Marino	.75	2.00
❑ 3 Emmitt Smith	.60	1.50
❑ 4 Steve Young	.25	.60
❑ 5 Drew Bledsoe	.25	.60
❑ 6 Eddie George	.20	.50
❑ 7 Barry Sanders	.60	1.50
❑ 8 Jerry Rice	.40	1.00
❑ 9 John Elway	.75	2.00
❑ 10 Troy Aikman	.40	1.00
❑ 11 Kerry Collins	.20	.50
❑ 12 Rick Mirer	.07	.20
❑ 13 Jim Harbaugh	.10	.30
❑ 14 Elvis Grbac	.10	.30
❑ 15 Gus Frerotte	.07	.20
❑ 16 Neil O'Donnell	.10	.30
❑ 17 Jeff George	.10	.30
❑ 18 Kordell Stewart	.20	.50
❑ 19 Junior Seau	.20	.50
❑ 20 Vinny Testaverde	.10	.30
❑ 21 Terry Glenn	.20	.50
❑ 22 Anthony Johnson	.07	.20
❑ 23 Boomer Esiason	.10	.30
❑ 24 Terrell Owens	.25	.60
❑ 25 Natrone Means	.10	.30
❑ 26 Marcus Allen	.20	.50
❑ 27 James Jett	.10	.30
❑ 28 Chris T. Jones	.07	.20
❑ 29 Stan Humphries	.10	.30
❑ 30 Keith Byars	.07	.20
❑ 31 John Friesz	.07	.20
❑ 32 Mike Alstott	.20	.50
❑ 33 Eddie Kennison	.10	.30
❑ 34 Eric Moulds	.20	.50
❑ 35 Frank Sanders	.10	.30
❑ 36 Daryl Johnston	.10	.30
❑ 37 Cris Carter	.20	.50
❑ 38 Errict Rhett	.07	.20
❑ 39 Ben Coates	.10	.30
❑ 40 Shannon Sharpe	.10	.30
❑ 41 Jamal Anderson	.20	.50
❑ 42 Tim Biakabutuka	.10	.30
❑ 43 Jeff Blake	.10	.30
❑ 44 Michael Irvin	.20	.50
❑ 45 Terrell Davis	.25	.60
❑ 46 Byron Bam Morris	.07	.20
❑ 47 Rashaan Salaam	.07	.20
❑ 48 Adrian Murrell	.10	.30
❑ 49 Ty Detmer	.10	.30
❑ 50 Terry Allen	.20	.50
❑ 51 Mark Brunell	.25	.60
❑ 52 O.J. McDuffie	.10	.30
❑ 53 Willie McGinest	.07	.20
❑ 54 Chris Warren	.10	.30
❑ 55 Trent Dilfer	.20	.50
❑ 56 Jerome Bettis	.20	.50
❑ 57 Tamarick Vanover	.10	.30
❑ 58 Ki-Jana Carter	.07	.20
❑ 59 Ray Zellars	.07	.20
❑ 60 J.J. Stokes	.10	.30
❑ 61 Cornelius Bennett	.07	.20
❑ 62 Scott Mitchell	.10	.30
❑ 63 Tyrone Wheatley	.10	.30
❑ 64 Steve McNair	.25	.60
❑ 65 Tony Banks	.10	.30
❑ 66 James O.Stewart	.10	.30
❑ 67 Robert Smith	.10	.30
❑ 68 Thurman Thomas	.20	.50
❑ 69 Mark Chmura	.10	.30
❑ 70 Napoleon Kaufman	.20	.50
❑ 71 Ken Norton	.07	.20
❑ 72 Herschel Walker	.10	.30
❑ 73 Joey Galloway	.10	.30
❑ 74 Neil Smith	.10	.30
❑ 75 Simeon Rice	.10	.30
❑ 76 Michael Jackson	.10	.30
❑ 77 Muhsin Muhammad	.10	.30
❑ 78 Kevin Hardy	.07	.20
❑ 79 Irving Fryar	.10	.30
❑ 80 Jeff Hostetler	.07	.20
❑ 81 Eric Swann	.07	.20
❑ 82 Jim Everett	.07	.20
❑ 83 Karim Abdul-Jabbar	.20	.50
❑ 84 Garrison Hearst	.10	.30
❑ 85 Lawrence Phillips	.07	.20
❑ 86 Bryan Cox	.07	.20
❑ 87 Larry Centers	.10	.30
❑ 88 Wesley Walls	.10	.30
❑ 89 Curtis Conway	.10	.30
❑ 90 Darnay Scott	.10	.30
❑ 91 Anthony Miller	.07	.20
❑ 92 Edgar Bennett	.10	.30
❑ 93 Willie Green	.07	.20
❑ 94 Kent Graham	.07	.20
❑ 95 Dave Brown	.07	.20
❑ 96 Wayne Chrebet	.20	.50
❑ 97 Ricky Watters	.10	.30
❑ 98 Tony Martin	.10	.30
❑ 99 Warren Moon	.20	.50
❑ 100 Curtis Martin	.25	.60
❑ 101 Dorsey Levens	.20	.50
❑ 102 Jim Pyne	.07	.20
❑ 103 Antonio Freeman	.20	.50
❑ 104 Leeland McElroy	.07	.20
❑ 105 Isaac Bruce	.20	.50
❑ 106 Chris Sanders	.07	.20
❑ 107 Tim Brown	.20	.50
❑ 108 Greg Lloyd	.07	.20
❑ 109 Terrell Buckley	.07	.20
❑ 110 Deion Sanders	.20	.50
❑ 111 Carl Pickens	.10	.30
❑ 112 Bobby Engram	.10	.30
❑ 113 Andre Reed	.10	.30
❑ 114 Terance Mathis	.10	.30
❑ 115 Herman Moore	.10	.30
❑ 116 Robert Brooks	.10	.30
❑ 117 Ken Dilger	.07	.20
❑ 118 Keenan McCardell	.10	.30
❑ 119 Andre Hastings	.07	.20
❑ 120 Willie Davis	.07	.20
❑ 121 Bruce Smith	.10	.30
❑ 122 Rob Moore	.10	.30
❑ 123 Johnnie Morton	.10	.30
❑ 124 Sean Dawkins	.07	.20
❑ 125 Mario Bates	.07	.20
❑ 126 Henry Ellard	.07	.20
❑ 127 Derrick Alexander WR	.10	.30
❑ 128 Kevin Greene	.10	.30
❑ 129 Derrick Thomas	.20	.50
❑ 130 Rod Woodson	.10	.30
❑ 131 Rodney Hampton	.10	.30
❑ 132 Marshall Faulk	.25	.60
❑ 133 Michael Westbrook	.10	.30
❑ 134 Erik Kramer	.07	.20
❑ 135 Todd Collins	.07	.20
❑ 136 Bill Romanowski	.07	.20
❑ 137 Jake Reed	.10	.30
❑ 138 Heath Shuler	.07	.20
❑ 139 Keyshawn Johnson	.20	.50
❑ 140 Marvin Harrison	.20	.50
❑ 141 Andre Rison	.10	.30
❑ 142 Zach Thomas	.20	.50
❑ 143 Eric Metcalf	.10	.30
❑ 144 Amani Toomer	.10	.30
❑ 145 Desmond Howard	.10	.30
❑ 146 Jimmy Smith	.10	.30
❑ 147 Brad Johnson	.20	.50
❑ 148 Troy Vincent	.07	.20
❑ 149 Bryce Paup	.07	.20
❑ 150 Reggie White	.20	.50

❑ 151 Jake Plummer RC 1.00 2.50
❑ 152 Darnell Autry RC .10 .30
❑ 153 Tiki Barber RC 1.25 3.00
❑ 154 Pat Barnes RC .20 .50
❑ 155 Orlando Pace RC .20 .50
❑ 156 Peter Boulware RC .20 .50
❑ 157 Shawn Springs RC .10 .30
❑ 158 Troy Davis RC .10 .30
❑ 159 Ike Hilliard RC .30 .75
❑ 160 Jim Druckenmiller RC .10 .30
❑ 161 Warrick Dunn RC .50 1.50
❑ 162 James Farrior RC .20 .50
❑ 163 Tony Gonzalez RC .60 1.50
❑ 164 Darrell Russell RC .07 .20
❑ 165 Byron Hanspard RC .10 .30
❑ 166 Corey Dillon RC 1.25 3.00
❑ 167 Kenny Holmes RC .20 .50
❑ 168 Walter Jones RC .20 .50
❑ 169 Danny Wuerffel RC .20 .50
❑ 170 Tom Knight RC .07 .20
❑ 171 David LaFleur RC .07 .20
❑ 172 Kevin Lockett RC .10 .30
❑ 173 Will Blackwell RC .10 .30
❑ 174 Reidel Anthony RC .20 .50
❑ 175 Dwayne Rudd RC .20 .50
❑ 176 Yatil Green RC .10 .30
❑ 177 Antowain Smith RC .50 1.25
❑ 178 Rae Carruth RC .07 .20
❑ 179 Bryant Westbrook RC .07 .20
❑ 180 Reinard Wilson RC .10 .30
❑ 181 Joey Kent RC .20 .50
❑ 182 Renaldo Wynn RC .07 .20
❑ 183 Brett Favre I .40 1.00
❑ 184 Emmitt Smith I .30 .75
❑ 185 Dan Marino I .40 1.00
❑ 186 Troy Aikman I .20 .50
❑ 187 Jerry Rice I .20 .50
❑ 188 Drew Bledsoe I .10 .30
❑ 189 Eddie George I .20 .50
❑ 190 Terry Glenn I .10 .30
❑ 191 John Elway I .40 1.00
❑ 192 Steve Young I .10 .30
❑ 193 Mark Brunell I .20 .50
❑ 194 Barry Sanders I .30 .75
❑ 195 Kerry Collins I .10 .30
❑ 196 Curtis Martin I .20 .50
❑ 197 Terrell Davis I .20 .50
❑ 198 Bledsoe/KCollins/Marino CL .20 .50
❑ 199 SYoung/Brunell/JGeorge CL .07 .20
❑ 200 Aikman/Elway/Mirer CL .07 .20

1992 Playoff

❑ COMPLETE SET (150) 10.00 25.00
❑ 1 Emmitt Smith 4.00 8.00
❑ 2 Steve Young 1.50 3.00
❑ 3 Jack Del Rio .08 .25
❑ 4 Bobby Hebert .08 .25
❑ 5 Shannon Sharpe .30 .75
❑ 6 Gary Clark .30 .75
❑ 7 Christian Okoye .08 .25
❑ 8 Ernest Givins .15 .40
❑ 9 Mike Horan .08 .25
❑ 10 Dennis Gentry .08 .25
❑ 11 Michael Irvin .30 .75
❑ 12 Eric Floyd .08 .25
❑ 13 Brent Jones .15 .40
❑ 14 Anthony Carter .15 .40
❑ 15 Tony Martin .15 .40
❑ 16 Greg Lewis UER .08 .25
❑ 17 Todd McNair .08 .25
❑ 18 Earnest Byner .08 .25
❑ 19 Steve Beuerlein .15 .40
❑ 20 Roger Craig .15 .40
❑ 21 Mark Higgs .08 .25
❑ 22 Guy McIntyre .08 .25
❑ 23 Don Warren .08 .25
❑ 24 Alvin Harper .15 .40
❑ 25 Mark Jackson .08 .25
❑ 26 Chris Doleman .08 .25
❑ 27 Jesse Sapolu .08 .25
❑ 28 Tony Tolbert .08 .25
❑ 29 Wendell Davis .08 .25
❑ 30 Dan Saleaumua .08 .25
❑ 31 Jeff Bostic .08 .25
❑ 32 Jay Novacek .15 .40
❑ 33 Cris Carter .40 1.00
❑ 34 Tony Paige .08 .25
❑ 35 Greg Kragen .08 .25
❑ 36 Jeff Dellenbach .08 .25
❑ 37 Keith DeLong .08 .25
❑ 38 Todd Scott .08 .25
❑ 39 Jeff Feagles .08 .25
❑ 40 Mike Saxon .08 .25
❑ 41 Martin Mayhew .08 .25
❑ 42 Steve Bono RC .30 .75
❑ 43 Willie Davis RC .15 .40
❑ 44 Mark Stepnoski .15 .40
❑ 45 Harry Newsome .08 .25
❑ 46 Thane Gash .08 .25
❑ 47 Gaston Green .08 .25
❑ 48 James Washington .08 .25
❑ 49 Kenny Walker .08 .25
❑ 50 Jeff Davidson RC .08 .25
❑ 51 Shane Conlan .08 .25
❑ 52 Richard Dent .15 .40
❑ 53 Haywood Jeffires .15 .40
❑ 54 Harry Galbreath .08 .25
❑ 55 Terry Allen .30 .75
❑ 56 Tommy Barnhardt .08 .25
❑ 57 Mike Golic .08 .25
❑ 58 Dalton Hilliard .08 .25
❑ 59 Danny Copeland .08 .25
❑ 60 Jerry Fontenot RC .08 .25
❑ 61 Kelvin Martin .08 .25
❑ 62 Mark Kelso .08 .25
❑ 63 Wymon Henderson .08 .25
❑ 64 Mark Rypien .08 .25
❑ 65 Bobby Humphrey .08 .25
❑ 66 Rich Gannon UER .30 .75
❑ 67 Darren Lewis .08 .25
❑ 68 Barry Foster .15 .40
❑ 69 Ken Norton Jr. .15 .40
❑ 70 James Lofton .15 .40
❑ 71 Trace Armstrong .08 .25
❑ 72 Vestee Jackson .08 .25
❑ 73 Clyde Simmons .08 .25
❑ 74 Brad Muster .08 .25
❑ 75 Cornelius Bennett .15 .40
❑ 76 Mike Merriweather .08 .25
❑ 77 John Elway 1.50 4.00
❑ 78 Herschel Walker .15 .40
❑ 79 Hassan Jones UER .08 .25
❑ 80 Jim Harbaugh .30 .75
❑ 81 Issiac Holt .08 .25
❑ 82 David Alexander .08 .25
❑ 83 Brian Mitchell .15 .40
❑ 84 Mark Tuinei .08 .25
❑ 85 Tom Rathman .08 .25
❑ 86 Reggie White .30 .75
❑ 87 William Perry .15 .40
❑ 88 Jeff Wright .08 .25
❑ 89 Keith Kartz .08 .25
❑ 90 Andre Waters .08 .25
❑ 91 Darryl Talley .08 .25
❑ 92 Morten Andersen .08 .25
❑ 93 Tom Waddle .08 .25
❑ 94 Felix Wright UER .08 .25
❑ 95 Keith Jackson .15 .40
❑ 96 Art Monk .15 .40
❑ 97 Seth Joyner .08 .25
❑ 98 Steve McMichael .15 .40
❑ 99 Thurman Thomas .30 .75
❑ 100 Warren Moon .30 .75
❑ 101 Tony Casillas .08 .25
❑ 102 Vance Johnson .08 .25
❑ 103 Doug Dawson RC .08 .25
❑ 104 Bill Maas .08 .25
❑ 105 Mark Clayton .15 .40
❑ 106 Hoby Brenner .08 .25
❑ 107 Gary Anderson K .08 .25
❑ 108 Marc Logan .08 .25
❑ 109 Ricky Sanders .08 .25
❑ 110 Vai Sikahema .08 .25
❑ 111 Neil Smith .30 .75
❑ 112 Cody Carlson .08 .25
❑ 113 Jimmie Jones .08 .25
❑ 114 Pat Swilling .08 .25
❑ 115 Neil O'Donnell .15 .40
❑ 116 Chip Lohmiller .08 .25
❑ 117 Mike Croel .08 .25
❑ 118 Pete Metzelaars .08 .25
❑ 119 Ray Childress .08 .25
❑ 120 Fred Banks .08 .25
❑ 121 Derek Kennard .08 .25
❑ 122 Daryl Johnston .30 .75
❑ 123 Lorenzo White UER .08 .25
❑ 124 Hardy Nickerson .15 .40
❑ 125 Derrick Thomas .30 .75
❑ 126 Steve Walsh .08 .25
❑ 127 Doug Widell .08 .25
❑ 128 Calvin Williams .15 .40
❑ 129 Tim Harris .08 .25
❑ 130 Rod Woodson .30 .75
❑ 131 Craig Heyward .15 .40
❑ 132 Barry Word .08 .25
❑ 133 Mark Duper .08 .25
❑ 134 Tim Johnson .08 .25
❑ 135 John Gesek .08 .25
❑ 136 Steve Jackson .08 .25
❑ 137 Dave Krieg .15 .40
❑ 138 Barry Sanders 1.50 4.00
❑ 139 Michael Haynes .15 .40
❑ 140 Eric Metcalf .15 .40
❑ 141 Stan Humphries .30 .75
❑ 142 Sterling Sharpe .30 .75
❑ 143 Todd Marinovich .08 .25
❑ 144 Rodney Hampton .15 .40
❑ 145 Rodney Peete .15 .40
❑ 146 Darryl Williams RC .08 .25
❑ 147 Darren Perry RC .08 .25
❑ 148 Terrell Buckley RC .08 .25
❑ 149 Amp Lee RC .08 .25
❑ 150 Ricky Watters .30 .75

1993 Playoff

❑ COMPLETE SET (315) 10.00 25.00
❑ 1 Troy Aikman .60 1.50
❑ 2 Jerry Rice .75 2.00
❑ 3 Keith Jackson .07 .20
❑ 4 Sean Gilbert .07 .20
❑ 5 Jim Kelly .15 .40
❑ 6 Junior Seau .15 .40
❑ 7 Deion Sanders .40 1.00
❑ 8 Joe Montana 1.25 0.00
❑ 9 Terrell Buckley .02 .10
❑ 10 Emmitt Smith 1.25 3.00
❑ 11 Pete Stoyanovich .02 .10
❑ 12 Randall Cunningham .15 .40
❑ 13 Boomer Esiason .07 .20
❑ 14 Mike Saxon .02 .10
❑ 15 Chuck Cecil .02 .10
❑ 16 Vinny Testaverde .07 .20
❑ 17 Jeff Hostetler .07 .20
❑ 18 Mark Clayton .02 .10
❑ 19 Nick Bell .02 .10
❑ 20 Frank Reich .07 .20
❑ 21 Henry Ellard .07 .20
❑ 22 Andre Reed .07 .20
❑ 23 Mark Ingram .02 .10
❑ 24 Mike Brim .02 .10
❑ 25A Bernie Kosar ERR Kozar .07 .20
❑ 25B Bernie Kosar COR .07 .20
❑ 26 Jeff George .15 .40
❑ 27 Tommy Maddox .15 .40
❑ 28 Kent Graham RC .15 .40
❑ 29 David Klingler .02 .10
❑ 30 Robert Delpino .02 .10
❑ 31 Kevin Fagan .02 .10
❑ 32 Mark Bavaro .02 .10
❑ 33 Harold Green .02 .10
❑ 34 Shawn McCarthy .02 .10

Card	Player	Low	High
❑ 35	Ricky Proehl	.02	.10
❑ 36	Eugene Robinson	.02	.10
❑ 37	Phil Simms	.07	.20
❑ 38	David Lang	.02	.10
❑ 39	Santana Dotson	.07	.20
❑ 40	Brett Perriman	.15	.40
❑ 41	Jim Harbaugh	.15	.40
❑ 42	Keith Byars	.02	.10
❑ 43	Quentin Coryatt	.07	.20
❑ 44	Louis Oliver	.02	.10
❑ 45	Howie Long	.15	.40
❑ 46	Mike Sherrard	.02	.10
❑ 47	Earnest Byner	.02	.10
❑ 48	Neil Smith	.15	.40
❑ 49	Audray McMillian	.02	.10
❑ 50	Vaughn Dunbar	.02	.10
❑ 51	Ronnie Lott	.07	.20
❑ 52	Clyde Simmons	.02	.10
❑ 53	Kevin Scott	.02	.10
❑ 54	Bubby Brister	.02	.10
❑ 55	Randal Hill	.02	.10
❑ 56	Pat Swilling	.02	.10
❑ 57	Steve Beuerlein	.07	.20
❑ 58	Gary Clark	.07	.20
❑ 59	Brian Noble	.02	.10
❑ 60	Leslie O'Neal	.07	.20
❑ 61	Vincent Brown	.02	.10
❑ 62	Edgar Bennett	.15	.40
❑ 63	Anthony Carter	.07	.20
❑ 64	Glenn Cadrez UER RC	.02	.10
❑ 65	Dalton Hilliard	.02	.10
❑ 66	James Lofton	.07	.20
❑ 67	Walter Stanley	.02	.10
❑ 68	Tim Harris	.02	.10
❑ 69	Carl Banks	.02	.10
❑ 70	Andre Ware	.02	.10
❑ 71	Karl Mecklenburg	.02	.10
❑ 72	Russell Maryland	.02	.10
❑ 73	Leroy Thompson	.02	.10
❑ 74	Tommy Kane	.02	.10
❑ 75	Dan Marino	1.25	3.00
❑ 76	Darrell Fullington	.02	.10
❑ 77	Jessie Tuggle	.02	.10
❑ 78	Bruce Smith	.15	.40
❑ 79	Neal Anderson	.02	.10
❑ 80	Kevin Mack	.02	.10
❑ 81	Shane Dronett	.02	.10
❑ 82	Nick Lowery	.02	.10
❑ 83	Sheldon White	.02	.10
❑ 84	Flipper Anderson	.02	.10
❑ 85	Jeff Herrod	.02	.10
❑ 86	Dwight Stone	.02	.10
❑ 87	Dave Krieg	.07	.20
❑ 88	Bryan Cox	.02	.10
❑ 89	Greg McMurtry	.02	.10
❑ 90	Rickey Jackson	.02	.10
❑ 91	Ernie Mills	.02	.10
❑ 92	Browning Nagle	.02	.10
❑ 93	John Taylor	.07	.20
❑ 94	Eric Dickerson	.07	.20
❑ 95	Johnny Holland	.02	.10
❑ 96	Anthony Miller	.07	.20
❑ 97	Fred Barnett	.07	.20
❑ 98	Ricky Ervins UER	.02	.10
❑ 99	Leonard Russell	.07	.20
❑ 100	Lawrence Taylor	.15	.40
❑ 101	Tony Casillas	.02	.10
❑ 102	John Elway	1.25	3.00
❑ 103	Bennie Blades	.02	.10
❑ 104	Harry Sydney	.02	.10
❑ 105	Bubba McDowell	.02	.10
❑ 106	Todd McNair	.02	.10
❑ 107	Steve Smith	.02	.10
❑ 108	Jim Everett	.07	.20
❑ 109	Bobby Humphrey	.02	.10
❑ 110	Rich Gannon	.15	.40
❑ 111	Marv Cook	.02	.10
❑ 112	Wayne Martin	.02	.10
❑ 113	Sean Landeta	.02	.10
❑ 114	Brad Baxter UER	.02	.10
❑ 115	Reggie White	.15	.40
❑ 116	Johnny Johnson	.02	.10
❑ 117	Jeff Graham	.07	.20
❑ 118	Darren Carrington RC	.02	.10
❑ 119	Ricky Watters	.15	.40
❑ 120	Art Monk	.07	.20
❑ 121	Cornelius Bennett	.07	.20
❑ 122	Wade Wilson	.02	.10
❑ 123	Daniel Stubbs	.02	.10
❑ 124	Brad Muster	.02	.10
❑ 125	Mike Tomczak	.02	.10
❑ 126	Jay Novacek	.07	.20
❑ 127	Shannon Sharpe	.15	.40
❑ 128	Rodney Peete	.02	.10
❑ 129	Daryl Johnston	.15	.40
❑ 130	Warren Moon	.15	.40
❑ 131	Willie Gault	.02	.10
❑ 132	Tony Martin	.15	.40
❑ 133	Terry Allen	.15	.40
❑ 134	Hugh Millen	.02	.10
❑ 135	Rob Moore	.07	.20
❑ 136	Andy Harmon RC	.07	.20
❑ 137	Kelvin Martin	.02	.10
❑ 138	Rod Woodson	.15	.40
❑ 139	Nate Lewis	.02	.10
❑ 140	Darryl Talley	.02	.10
❑ 141	Guy McIntyre	.02	.10
❑ 142	John L. Williams	.02	.10
❑ 143	Brad Edwards	.02	.10
❑ 144	Trace Armstrong	.02	.10
❑ 145	Kenneth Davis	.02	.10
❑ 146	Clay Matthews	.07	.20
❑ 147	Gaston Green	.02	.10
❑ 148	Chris Spielman	.07	.20
❑ 149	Cody Carlson	.02	.10
❑ 150	Derrick Thomas	.15	.40
❑ 151	Terry McDaniel	.02	.10
❑ 152	Kevin Greene	.07	.20
❑ 153	Roger Craig	.07	.20
❑ 154	Craig Heyward	.07	.20
❑ 155	Rodney Hampton	.07	.20
❑ 156	Heath Sherman	.02	.10
❑ 157	Mark Stepnoski	.02	.10
❑ 158	Chris Chandler	.07	.20
❑ 159	Rod Bernstine	.02	.10
❑ 160	Pierce Holt	.02	.10
❑ 161	Wilber Marshall	.02	.10
❑ 162	Reggie Cobb	.02	.10
❑ 163	Tom Rathman	.02	.10
❑ 164	Michael Haynes	.07	.20
❑ 165	Nate Odomes	.02	.10
❑ 166	Tom Waddle	.02	.10
❑ 167	Eric Ball	.02	.10
❑ 168	Brett Favre	1.50	4.00
❑ 169	Michael Jackson	.07	.20
❑ 170	Lorenzo White	.02	.10
❑ 171	Cleveland Gary	.02	.10
❑ 172	Jay Schroeder	.02	.10
❑ 173	Tony Paige	.02	.10
❑ 174	Jack Del Rio	.02	.10
❑ 175	Jon Vaughn	.02	.10
❑ 176	Morten Andersen UER	.02	.10
❑ 177	Chris Burkett	.02	.10
❑ 178	Vai Sikahema	.02	.10
❑ 179	Ronnie Harmon	.02	.10
❑ 180	Amp Lee	.02	.10
❑ 181	Chip Lohmiller	.02	.10
❑ 182	Steve Broussard	.02	.10
❑ 183	Don Beebe	.02	.10
❑ 184	Tommy Vardell	.02	.10
❑ 185	Keith Jennings	.02	.10
❑ 186	Simon Fletcher	.02	.10
❑ 187	Mel Gray	.07	.20
❑ 188	Vince Workman	.02	.10
❑ 189	Haywood Jeffires	.07	.20
❑ 190	Barry Word	.02	.10
❑ 191	Ethan Horton	.02	.10
❑ 192	Mark Higgs	.02	.10
❑ 193	Irving Fryar	.07	.20
❑ 194	Charles Haley	.07	.20
❑ 195	Steve Bono	.07	.20
❑ 196	Mike Golic	.02	.10
❑ 197	Gary Anderson K	.02	.10
❑ 198	Sterling Sharpe	.15	.40
❑ 199	Andre Tippett	.02	.10
❑ 200	Thurman Thomas	.15	.40
❑ 201	Chris Miller	.07	.20
❑ 202	Henry Jones	.02	.10
❑ 203	Mo Lewis	.02	.10
❑ 204	Marion Butts	.02	.10
❑ 205	Mike Johnson	.02	.10
❑ 206	Alvin Harper	.07	.20
❑ 207	Ray Childress	.02	.10
❑ 208	Anthony Johnson	.07	.20
❑ 209	Tony Bennett	.02	.10
❑ 210	Anthony Newman RC	.02	.10
❑ 211	Christian Okoye	.02	.10
❑ 212	Marcus Allen	.15	.40
❑ 213	Jackie Harris	.02	.10
❑ 214	Mark Duper	.02	.10
❑ 215	Cris Carter	.15	.40
❑ 216	John Stephens	.02	.10
❑ 217	Barry Sanders	1.00	2.50
❑ 218A	H.Moore ERR Sherman	.50	1.25
❑ 218B	Herman Moore COR	1.00	2.50
❑ 219	Marvin Washington	.02	.10
❑ 220	Calvin Williams	.07	.20
❑ 221	John Randle	.07	.20
❑ 222	Marco Coleman	.02	.10
❑ 223	Eric Martin	.02	.10
❑ 224	Dave Meggett	.02	.10
❑ 225	Brian Washington	.02	.10
❑ 226	Barry Foster	.07	.20
❑ 227	Michael Zordich	.02	.10
❑ 228	Stan Humphries	.07	.20
❑ 229	Mike Cofer	.02	.10
❑ 230	Chris Warren	.07	.20
❑ 231	Keith McCants	.02	.10
❑ 232	Mark Rypien	.02	.10
❑ 233	James Francis	.02	.10
❑ 234	Andre Rison	.07	.20
❑ 235	William Perry	.07	.20
❑ 236	Chip Banks	.02	.10
❑ 237	Willie Davis	.15	.40
❑ 238	Chris Doleman	.02	.10
❑ 239	Tim Brown	.15	.40
❑ 240	Darren Perry	.02	.10
❑ 241	Johnny Bailey	.02	.10
❑ 242	Ernest Givins	.07	.20
❑ 243	John Carney	.02	.10
❑ 244	Cortez Kennedy	.07	.20
❑ 245	Lawrence Dawsey	.02	.10
❑ 246	Martin Mayhew	.02	.10
❑ 247	Shane Conlan	.02	.10
❑ 248	J.J. Birden	.02	.10
❑ 249	Quinn Early	.07	.20
❑ 250	Michael Irvin	.15	.40
❑ 251	Neil O'Donnell	.15	.40
❑ 252	Stan Gelbaugh	.02	.10
❑ 253	Drew Hill	.02	.10
❑ 254	Wendell Davis	.02	.10
❑ 255	Tim Johnson	.02	.10
❑ 256	Seth Joyner	.02	.10
❑ 257	Derrick Fenner	.02	.10
❑ 258	Steve Young	.60	1.50
❑ 259	Jackie Slater	.02	.10
❑ 260	Eric Metcalf	.07	.20
❑ 261	Rufus Porter	.02	.10
❑ 262	Ken Norton Jr.	.07	.20
❑ 263	Tim McDonald	.02	.10
❑ 264	Mark Jackson	.02	.10
❑ 265	Hardy Nickerson	.07	.20
❑ 266	Anthony Munoz	.07	.20
❑ 267	Mark Carrier WR	.07	.20
❑ 268	Mike Pritchard	.07	.20
❑ 269	Steve Emtman	.02	.10
❑ 270	Ricky Sanders	.02	.10
❑ 271	Robert Massey	.02	.10
❑ 272	Pete Metzelaars	.02	.10
❑ 273	Reggie Langhorne	.02	.10
❑ 274	Tim McGee	.02	.10
❑ 275	Reggie Rivers RC	.02	.10
❑ 276	Jimmie Jones	.02	.10
❑ 277	Lorenzo White TB	.02	.10
❑ 278	Emmitt Smith TB	.75	2.00
❑ 279	Thurman Thomas TB	.15	.40
❑ 280	Barry Sanders TB	.60	1.50
❑ 281	Rodney Hampton TB	.07	.20
❑ 282	Barry Foster TB	.07	.20
❑ 283	Troy Aikman PC	.40	1.00
❑ 284	Michael Irvin PC	.07	.20
❑ 285	Brett Favre PC	1.00	2.50
❑ 286	Sterling Sharpe PC	.07	.20
❑ 287	Steve Young PC	.40	1.00
❑ 288	Jerry Rice PC	.50	1.25
❑ 289	Stan Humphries PC	.07	.20
❑ 290	Anthony Miller PC	.07	.20
❑ 291	Dan Marino PC	.75	2.00
❑ 292	Keith Jackson PC	.02	.10
❑ 293	Patrick Bates RC	.02	.10
❑ 294	Jerome Bettis RC	4.00	10.00
❑ 295	Drew Bledsoe RC	2.50	6.00
❑ 296	Tom Carter RC	.07	.20
❑ 297	Curtis Conway RC	.40	1.00
❑ 298	John Copeland RC	.07	.20
❑ 299	Eric Curry RC	.02	.10
❑ 300	Reggie Brooks RC	.07	.20

Card		
❑ 301 Steve Everitt RC	.02	.10
❑ 302 Deon Figures RC	.02	.10
❑ 303 Garrison Hearst RC	.75	2.00
❑ 304 Qadry Ismail UER RC	.15	.40
❑ 305 Marvin Jones RC	.02	.10
❑ 306 Lincoln Kennedy RC	.02	.10
❑ 307 O.J.McDuffie RC	.15	.40
❑ 308 Rick Mirer RC	.15	.40
❑ 309 Wayne Simmons RC	.02	.10
❑ 310 Irv Smith RC	.02	.10
❑ 311 Robert Smith RC	1.25	3.00
❑ 312 Dana Stubblefield RC	.15	.40
❑ 313 George Teague RC	.07	.20
❑ 314 Dan Williams RC	.02	.10
❑ 315 Kevin Williams RC WR	.15	.40
❑ NNO Santa Claus	.75	2.00

1994 Playoff

Card		
❑ COMPLETE SET (336)	12.50	30.00
❑ 1 Joe Montana	1.50	4.00
❑ 2 Derrick Thomas	.20	.50
❑ 3 Dan Marino	1.50	4.00
❑ 4 Cris Carter	.30	.75
❑ 5 Boomer Esiason	.10	.30
❑ 6 Bruce Smith	.20	.50
❑ 7 Andre Rison	.10	.30
❑ 8 Curtis Conway	.20	.50
❑ 9 Michael Irvin	.20	.50
❑ 10 Shannon Sharpe	.10	.30
❑ 11 Pat Swilling	.05	.15
❑ 12 John Parrella	.05	.15
❑ 13 Mel Gray	.05	.15
❑ 14 Ray Childress	.05	.15
❑ 15 Willie Davis	.10	.30
❑ 16 Rocket Ismail	.10	.30
❑ 17 Jim Everett	.10	.30
❑ 18 Mark Higgs	.05	.15
❑ 19 Trace Armstrong	.05	.15
❑ 20 Jim Kelly	.20	.50
❑ 21 Rob Burnett	.05	.15
❑ 22 Jay Novacek	.10	.30
❑ 23 Robert Delpino	.05	.15
❑ 24 Brett Perriman	.10	.30
❑ 25 Troy Aikman	.75	2.00
❑ 26 Reggie White	.20	.50
❑ 27 Lorenzo White	.05	.15
❑ 28 Bubba McDowell	.05	.15
❑ 29 Steve Emtman	.05	.15
❑ 30 Brett Favre	1.50	4.00
❑ 31 Derek Russell	.05	.15
❑ 32 Jeff Hostetler	.10	.30
❑ 33 Henry Ellard	.10	.30
❑ 34 Jack Del Rio	.05	.15
❑ 35 Mike Saxon	.05	.15
❑ 36 Rickey Jackson	.05	.15
❑ 37 Phil Simms	.10	.30
❑ 38 Quinn Early	.10	.30
❑ 39 Russell Copeland	.05	.15
❑ 40 Carl Pickens	.10	.30
❑ 41 Lance Gunn	.05	.15
❑ 42 Bernie Kosar	.10	.30
❑ 43 John Elway	1.50	4.00
❑ 44 George Teague	.05	.15
❑ 45 Nick Lowery	.05	.15
❑ 46 Haywood Jeffires	.10	.30
❑ 47 Will Shields	.05	.15
❑ 48 Daryl Johnston	.10	.30
❑ 49 Pete Metzelaars	.05	.15
❑ 50 Warren Moon	.20	.50
❑ 51 Cornelius Bennett	.10	.30
❑ 52 Vinny Testaverde	.10	.30
❑ 53 John Mangum RC	.05	.15
❑ 54 Tommy Vardell	.05	.15
❑ 55 Lincoln Coleman RC	.05	.15
❑ 56 Karl Mecklenburg	.05	.15
❑ 57 Jackie Harris	.05	.15
❑ 58 Curtis Duncan	.05	.15
❑ 59 Quentin Coryatt	.05	.15
❑ 60 Tim Brown	.20	.50
❑ 61 Irving Fryar	.10	.30
❑ 62 Sean Gilbert	.05	.15
❑ 63 Qadry Ismail	.20	.50
❑ 64 Irv Smith	.05	.15
❑ 65 Mark Jackson	.05	.15
❑ 66 Ronnie Lott	.10	.30
❑ 67 Henry Jones	.05	.15
❑ 68 Horace Copeland	.05	.15
❑ 69 John Copeland	.05	.15
❑ 70 Mark Carrier WR	.10	.30
❑ 71 Michael Jackson	.10	.30
❑ 72 Jason Elam	.10	.30
❑ 73 Rod Bernstine	.05	.15
❑ 74 Wayne Simmons	.05	.15
❑ 75 Cody Carlson	.05	.15
❑ 76 Alexander Wright	.05	.15
❑ 77 Shane Conlan	.05	.15
❑ 78 Keith Jackson	.05	.15
❑ 79 Sean Salisbury	.05	.15
❑ 80 Vaughan Johnson	.05	.15
❑ 81 Rob Moore	.10	.30
❑ 82 Andre Reed	.10	.30
❑ 83 David Klingler	.05	.15
❑ 84 Jim Harbaugh	.20	.50
❑ 85 John Jett RC	.05	.15
❑ 86 Sterling Sharpe	.10	.30
❑ 87 Webster Slaughter	.05	.15
❑ 88 J.J. Birden	.05	.15
❑ 89 O.J.McDuffie	.20	.50
❑ 90 Andre Tippett	.05	.15
❑ 91 Don Beebe	.05	.15
❑ 92 Mark Stepnoski	.05	.15
❑ 93 Neil Smith	.10	.30
❑ 94 Terry Kirby	.20	.50
❑ 95 Wade Wilson	.05	.15
❑ 96 Darryl Talley	.05	.15
❑ 97 Anthony Smith	.05	.15
❑ 98 Willie Roaf	.05	.15
❑ 99 Mo Lewis	.05	.15
❑ 100 James Washington	.05	.15
❑ 101 Nate Odomes	.05	.15
❑ 102 Chris Gedney	.05	.15
❑ 103 Joe Walter	.05	.15
❑ 104 Alvin Harper	.10	.30
❑ 105 Simon Fletcher	.05	.15
❑ 106 Rodney Peete	.05	.15
❑ 107 Terrell Buckley	.05	.15
❑ 108 Jeff George	.20	.50
❑ 109 James Jett	.05	.15
❑ 110 Tony Casillas	.05	.15
❑ 111 Marco Coleman	.05	.15
❑ 112 Anthony Carter	.10	.30
❑ 113 Lincoln Kennedy	.05	.15
❑ 114 Chris Calloway	.05	.15
❑ 115 Randall Cunningham	.20	.50
❑ 116 Steve Beuerlein	.10	.30
❑ 117 Neil O'Donnell	.20	.50
❑ 118 Stan Humphries	.10	.30
❑ 119 John Taylor	.10	.30
❑ 120 Cortez Kennedy	.10	.30
❑ 121 Santana Dotson	.10	.30
❑ 122 Thomas Smith	.05	.15
❑ 123 Kevin Williams WR	.10	.30
❑ 124 Andre Ware	.05	.15
❑ 125 Ethan Horton	.05	.15
❑ 126 Mike Sherrard	.05	.15
❑ 127 Fred Barnett	.10	.30
❑ 128 Ricky Proehl	.05	.15
❑ 129 Kevin Greene	.10	.30
❑ 130 John Carney	.05	.15
❑ 131 Tim McDonald	.05	.15
❑ 132 Rick Mirer	.20	.50
❑ 133 Blair Thomas	.05	.15
❑ 134 Hardy Nickerson	.10	.30
❑ 135 Heath Sherman	.05	.15
❑ 136 Andre Hastings	.10	.30
❑ 137 Randal Hill	.05	.15
❑ 138 Mike Cofer	.05	.15
❑ 139 Brian Blades	.10	.30
❑ 140 Earnest Byner	.05	.15
❑ 141 Bill Bates	.10	.30
❑ 142 Junior Seau	.20	.50
❑ 143 Johnny Bailey	.05	.15
❑ 144 Dwight Stone	.05	.15
❑ 145 Todd Kelly	.05	.15
❑ 146 Tyrone Montgomery	.05	.15
❑ 147 Herschel Walker	.10	.30
❑ 148 Gary Clark	.10	.30
❑ 149 Eric Green	.05	.15
❑ 150 Steve Young	.60	1.50
❑ 151 Anthony Miller	.10	.30
❑ 152 Dana Stubblefield	.10	.30
❑ 153 Dean Wells RC	.05	.15
❑ 154 Vincent Brisby	.10	.30
❑ 155 Chris Chandler	.10	.30
❑ 156 Clyde Simmons	.05	.15
❑ 157 Rod Woodson	.10	.30
❑ 158 Nate Lewis	.05	.15
❑ 159 Martin Harrison	.05	.15
❑ 160 Kelvin Martin	.05	.15
❑ 161 Craig Erickson	.05	.15
❑ 162 Johnny Mitchell	.05	.15
❑ 163 Calvin Williams	.10	.30
❑ 164 Deon Figures	.05	.15
❑ 165 Tom Rathman	.05	.15
❑ 166 Rick Hamilton	.05	.15
❑ 167 John L. Williams	.05	.15
❑ 168 Demetrius DuBose	.05	.15
❑ 169 Michael Brooks	.05	.15
❑ 170 Marion Butts	.05	.15
❑ 171 Brent Jones	.10	.30
❑ 172 Bobby Hebert	.05	.15
❑ 173 Brad Edwards	.05	.15
❑ 174 David Wyman	.05	.15
❑ 175 Herman Moore	.20	.50
❑ 176 LeRoy Butler	.05	.15
❑ 177 Reggie Langhorne	.05	.15
❑ 178 Dave Krieg	.10	.30
❑ 179 Patrick Bates	.05	.15
❑ 180 Erik Kramer	.10	.30
❑ 181 Troy Drayton	.05	.15
❑ 182 Dave Meggett	.05	.15
❑ 183 Eric Allen	.05	.15
❑ 184 Mark Bavaro	.05	.15
❑ 185 Leslie O'Neal	.05	.15
❑ 186 Jerry Rice	.75	2.00
❑ 187 Desmond Howard	.10	.30
❑ 188 Deion Sanders	.30	.75
❑ 189 Bill Maas	.05	.15
❑ 190 Frank Wycheck RC	.75	2.00
❑ 191 Ernest Givins	.10	.30
❑ 192 Terry McDaniel	.05	.15
❑ 193 Bryan Cox	.05	.15
❑ 194 Guy McIntyre	.05	.15
❑ 195 Pierce Holt	.05	.15
❑ 196 Fred Stokes	.05	.15
❑ 197 Mike Pritchard	.05	.15
❑ 198 Terry Obee	.05	.15
❑ 199 Mark Collins	.05	.15
❑ 200 Drew Bledsoe	.50	1.25
❑ 201 Barry Word	.05	.15
❑ 202 Derrick Lassic	.05	.15
❑ 203 Chris Spielman	.10	.30
❑ 204 John Jurkovic RC	.10	.30
❑ 205 Ken Norton Jr.	.10	.30
❑ 206 Dale Carter	.05	.15
❑ 207 Chris Doleman	.05	.15
❑ 208 Keith Hamilton	.05	.15
❑ 209 Andy Harmon	.05	.15
❑ 210 John Friesz	.10	.30
❑ 211 Steve Bono	.10	.30
❑ 212 Mark Rypien	.05	.15
❑ 213 Ricky Sanders	.05	.15
❑ 214 Michael Haynes	.10	.30
❑ 215 Todd McNair	.05	.15
❑ 216 Leon Lett	.05	.15
❑ 217 Scott Mitchell	.10	.30
❑ 218 Mike Morris RC	.05	.15
❑ 219 Darrin Smith	.05	.15
❑ 220 Jim McMahon	.10	.30
❑ 221 Garrison Hearst	.20	.50
❑ 222 Leroy Thompson	.05	.15
❑ 223 Darren Carrington	.05	.15
❑ 224 Pete Stoyanovich	.05	.15
❑ 225 Chris Miller	.05	.15
❑ 226 Bruce Smith SP	.10	.30
❑ 227 Simon Fletcher SP	.05	.15
❑ 228 Reggie White SP	.20	.50
❑ 229 Neil Smith SP	.10	.30
❑ 230 Chris Doleman SP	.05	.15
❑ 231 Keith Hamilton SP	.05	.15
❑ 232 Dana Stubblefield SP	.05	.15
❑ 233 Erric Pegram GA	.05	.15
❑ 234 Thurman Thomas GA	.20	.50
❑ 235 Lewis Tillman GA	.05	.15

❑ 236 Harold Green GA	.05	.15
❑ 237 Eric Metcalf GA	.10	.30
❑ 238 Emmitt Smith GA	1.25	3.00
❑ 239 Glyn Milburn GA	.10	.30
❑ 240 Barry Sanders GA	1.25	3.00
❑ 241 Edgar Bennett GA	.10	.30
❑ 242 Gary Brown GA	.05	.15
❑ 243 Roosevelt Potts GA	.05	.15
❑ 244 Marcus Allen GA	.20	.50
❑ 245 Greg Robinson GA	.05	.15
❑ 246 Jerome Bettis GA	.30	.75
❑ 247 Keith Byars GA	.05	.15
❑ 248 Robert Smith GA	.20	.50
❑ 249 Leonard Russell GA	.05	.15
❑ 250 Derek Brown RBK GA	.05	.15
❑ 251 Rodney Hampton GA	.10	.30
❑ 252 Johnny Johnson GA	.05	.15
❑ 253 Vaughn Hebron GA	.05	.15
❑ 254 Ronald Moore GA	.05	.15
❑ 255 Barry Foster GA	.05	.15
❑ 256 Natrone Means GA	.20	.50
❑ 257 Ricky Watters GA	.10	.30
❑ 258 Chris Warren GA	.20	.50
❑ 259 Vince Workman GA	.05	.15
❑ 260 Reggie Brooks GA	.05	.15
❑ 261 Carolina Panthers	.15	.40
❑ 262 Jacksonville Jaguars	.15	.40
❑ 263 Troy Aikman SB	.40	1.00
❑ 264 Barry Sanders SB	.60	1.50
❑ 265 Emmitt Smith SB	.60	1.50
❑ 266 Michael Irvin SB	.20	.50
❑ 267 Jerry Rice SB	.40	1.00
❑ 268 Shannon Sharpe SB	.10	.30
❑ 269 Bob Kratch SB	.05	.15
❑ 270 Howard Ballard SB	.05	.15
❑ 271 Erik Williams SB	.05	.15
❑ 272 Guy McIntyre SB	.05	.15
❑ 273 Kevin Williams WR SB	.10	.30
❑ 274 Mel Gray SB	.05	.15
❑ 275 Eddie Murray SB	.05	.15
❑ 276 Mark Stepnoski SB	.05	.15
❑ 277 Tommy Barnhardt SB	.05	.15
❑ 278 Derrick Thomas SB	.10	.30
❑ 279 Ken Norton Jr. SB	.10	.30
❑ 280 Chris Spielman SB	.05	.15
❑ 281 Deion Sanders SB	.20	.50
❑ 282 Mark Collins SB	.05	.15
❑ 283 Bruce Smith SB	.10	.30
❑ 284 Reggie White SB	.20	.50
❑ 285 Sean Gilbert SB	.05	.15
❑ 286 Cortez Kennedy SB	.10	.30
❑ 287 Steve Atwater SB	.05	.15
❑ 288 Tim McDonald SB	.05	.15
❑ 289 Jerome Bettis SB	.30	.75
❑ 290 Dana Stubblefield SB	.10	.30
❑ 291 Bert Emanuel RC	.20	.50
❑ 292 Jeff Burris RC	.10	.30
❑ 293 Bucky Brooks RC	.05	.15
❑ 294 Dan Wilkinson RC	.10	.30
❑ 295 Darnay Scott RC	.40	1.00
❑ 296 Derrick Alexander WR RC	.20	.50
❑ 297 Antonio Langham RC	.10	.30
❑ 298 Shante Carver RC	.05	.15
❑ 299 Shelby Hill RC	.05	.15
❑ 300 Larry Allen RC	.20	.50
❑ 301 Johnnie Morton RC	.75	2.00
❑ 302 Van Malone RC	.05	.15
❑ 303 Aaron Taylor RC	.05	.15
❑ 304 Marshall Faulk RC	2.50	6.00
❑ 305 Eric Mahlum RC	.05	.15
❑ 306 Trev Alberts RC	.10	.30
❑ 307 Greg Hill RC	.20	.50
❑ 308 Donnell Bennett RC	.20	.50
❑ 309 Rob Fredrickson RC	.10	.30
❑ 310 James Folston RC	.05	.15
❑ 311 Isaac Bruce RC	2.00	5.00
❑ 312 Tim Ruddy RC	.05	.15
❑ 313 Aubrey Beavers RC	.05	.15
❑ 314 David Palmer RC	.20	.50
❑ 315 Dewayne Washington RC	.10	.30
❑ 316 Willie McGinest RC	.20	.50
❑ 317 Mario Bates RC	.20	.50
❑ 318 Kevin Lee RC	.05	.15
❑ 319 Jason Sehorn RC	.30	.75
❑ 320 Thomas Randolph RC	.05	.15
❑ 321 Ryan Yarborough RC	.05	.15
❑ 322 Bernard Williams RC	.05	.15
❑ 323 Chuck Levy RC	.05	.15
❑ 324 Jamir Miller RC	.10	.30
❑ 325 Charles Johnson RC	.20	.50
❑ 326 Bryant Young RC	.30	.75
❑ 327 William Floyd RC	.20	.50
❑ 328 Kevin Mitchell RC	.05	.15
❑ 329 Sam Adams RC	.10	.30
❑ 330 Kevin Mawae RC	.20	.50
❑ 331 Errict Rhett RC	.20	.50
❑ 332 Trent Dilfer RC	.60	1.50
❑ 333 Heath Shuler RC	.20	.50
❑ 334 Aaron Glenn RC	.20	.50
❑ 335 Todd Steussie RC	.10	.30
❑ 336 Toby Wright RC	.05	.15
❑ NNO Gale Sayers Play.Club	1.50	4.00
❑ NNO Gale Sayers AUTO	25.00	60.00

1993 Playoff Contenders

❑ COMPLETE SET (150)	7.50	20.00
❑ 1 Brett Favre	1.50	3.00
❑ 2 Thurman Thomas	.15	.40
❑ 3 Barry Word	.02	.10
❑ 4 Herman Moore	.15	.40
❑ 5 Reggie Langhorne	.02	.10
❑ 6 Wilber Marshall	.02	.10
❑ 7 Ricky Watters	.15	.40
❑ 8 Marcus Allen	.15	.40
❑ 9 Jeff Hostetler	.07	.20
❑ 10 Steve Young	.40	1.00
❑ 11 Bobby Hebert	.02	.10
❑ 12 David Klingler	.02	.10
❑ 13 Craig Heyward	.07	.20
❑ 14 Andre Reed	.07	.20
❑ 15 Tommy Vardell	.02	.10
❑ 16 Anthony Carter	.07	.20
❑ 17 Mel Gray	.07	.20
❑ 18 Dan Marino	1.00	2.50
❑ 19 Haywood Jeffires	.07	.20
❑ 20 Joe Montana	1.00	2.50
❑ 21 Tim Brown	.15	.40
❑ 22 Jim McMahon	.07	.20
❑ 23 Scott Mitchell	.15	.40
❑ 24 Rickey Jackson	.02	.10
❑ 25 Troy Aikman	.60	1.50
❑ 26 Rodney Hampton	.07	.20
❑ 27 Fred Barnett	.07	.20
❑ 28 Gary Clark	.07	.20
❑ 29 Barry Foster	.07	.20
❑ 30 Brian Blades	.07	.20
❑ 31 Tim McDonald	.02	.10
❑ 32 Kelvin Martin	.02	.10
❑ 33 Henry Jones	.02	.10
❑ 34 Erric Pegram	.07	.20
❑ 35 Don Beebe	.02	.10
❑ 36 Eric Metcalf	.07	.20
❑ 37 Charles Haley	.07	.20
❑ 38 Robert Delpino	.02	.10
❑ 39 Leonard Russell UER	.07	.20
❑ 40 Jackie Harris	.02	.10
❑ 41 Ernest Givins	.07	.20
❑ 42 Willie Davis	.15	.40
❑ 43 Alexander Wright	.02	.10
❑ 44 Keith Byars	.02	.10
❑ 45 Dave Meggett	.02	.10
❑ 46 Johnny Johnson	.02	.10
❑ 47 Mark Bavaro	.02	.10
❑ 48 Seth Joyner	.02	.10
❑ 49 Junior Seau	.15	.40
❑ 50 Emmitt Smith	1.25	2.50
❑ 51 Shannon Sharpe	.15	.40
❑ 52 Rodney Peete	.02	.10
❑ 53 Andre Rison	.07	.20
❑ 54 Cornelius Bennett	.07	.20
❑ 55 Mark Carrier WR	.07	.20
❑ 56 Mark Clayton	.02	.10
❑ 57 Warren Moon	.15	.40
❑ 58 J.J. Birden	.02	.10
❑ 59 Howie Long	.15	.40
❑ 60 Irving Fryar	.07	.20
❑ 61 Mark Jackson	.02	.10
❑ 62 Eric Martin	.02	.10
❑ 63 Herschel Walker	.07	.20
❑ 64 Cortez Kennedy	.07	.20
❑ 65 Steve Beuerlein	.07	.20
❑ 66 Jim Kelly	.15	.40
❑ 67 Bernie Kosar Cowboys	.07	.20
❑ 68 Pat Swilling	.02	.10
❑ 69 Michael Irvin	.15	.40
❑ 70 Harvey Williams	.07	.20
❑ 71 Steve Smith	.02	.10
❑ 72 Wade Wilson	.02	.10
❑ 73 Phil Simms	.07	.20
❑ 74 Vinny Testaverde	.07	.20
❑ 75 Barry Sanders	1.00	2.50
❑ 76 Ken Norton Jr.	.07	.20
❑ 77 Rod Woodson	.15	.40
❑ 78 Webster Slaughter	.02	.10
❑ 79 Derrick Thomas	.15	.40
❑ 80 Mike Sherrard	.02	.10
❑ 81 Calvin Williams	.07	.20
❑ 82 Jay Novacek	.07	.20
❑ 83 Michael Brooks	.02	.10
❑ 84 Randall Cunningham	.15	.40
❑ 85 Chris Warren	.07	.20
❑ 86 Johnny Mitchell	.02	.10
❑ 87 Jim Harbaugh	.15	.40
❑ 88 Rod Bernstine	.02	.10
❑ 89 John Elway	1.00	2.50
❑ 90 Jerry Rice	.60	1.50
❑ 91 Brent Jones	.07	.20
❑ 92 Cris Carter	.15	.40
❑ 93 Alvin Harper	.07	.20
❑ 94 Horace Copeland RC	.07	.20
❑ 95 Rocket Ismail	.07	.20
❑ 96 Darrin Smith RC	.07	.20
❑ 97 Reggie Brooks RC	.07	.20
❑ 98 Demetrius DuBose RC	.02	.10
❑ 99 Eric Curry RC	.02	.10
❑ 100 Rick Mirer RC	.15	.40
❑ 101 Carlton Gray UER RC	.02	.10
❑ 102 Dana Stubblefield RC	.15	.40
❑ 103 Todd Kelly RC	.02	.10
❑ 104 Natrone Means RC	.15	.40
❑ 105 Darrien Gordon RC	.02	.10
❑ 106 Deon Figures RC	.02	.10
❑ 107 Garrison Hearst RC	.50	1.25
❑ 108 Ronald Moore RC	.07	.20
❑ 109 Leonard Renfro RC	.02	.10
❑ 110 Lester Holmes	.02	.10
❑ 111 Vaughn Hebron RC	.02	.10
❑ 112 Marvin Jones RC	.02	.10
❑ 113 Irv Smith RC	.02	.10
❑ 114 Willie Roaf RC	.07	.20
❑ 115 Derek Brown RBK RC	.07	.20
❑ 116 Vincent Brisby RC	.15	.40
❑ 117 Drew Bledsoe RC	1.50	4.00
❑ 118 Gino Torretta RC	.07	.20
❑ 119 Robert Smith RC	.75	2.00
❑ 120 Qadry Ismail RC	.15	.40
❑ 121 O.J.McDuffie RC	.15	.40
❑ 122 Terry Kirby RC	.15	.40
❑ 123 Troy Drayton RC	.07	.20
❑ 124 Jerome Bettis RC	2.50	6.00
❑ 125 Patrick Bates RC	.02	.10
❑ 126 Roosevelt Potts RC	.02	.10
❑ 127 Tom Carter RC	.07	.20
❑ 128 Patrick Robinson RC	.02	.10
❑ 129 Brad Hopkins RC	.02	.10
❑ 130 George Teague RC	.07	.20
❑ 131 Wayne Simmons RC	.02	.10
❑ 132 Mark Brunell RC	1.00	2.50
❑ 133 Ryan McNeil RC	.15	.40
❑ 134 Dan Williams RC	.02	.10
❑ 135 Glyn Milburn RC	.15	.40
❑ 136 Kevin Williams RC WR	.15	.40
❑ 137 Derrick Lassic RC	.02	.10
❑ 138 Steve Everitt RC	.02	.10
❑ 139 Lance Gunn RC	.02	.10
❑ 140 John Copeland RC	.07	.20
❑ 141 Curtis Conway RC	.40	1.00
❑ 142 Thomas Smith RC	.07	.20
❑ 143 Russell Copeland RC	.07	.20
❑ 144 Lincoln Kennedy RC	.02	.10
❑ 145 Boomer Esiason CL	.02	.10
❑ 146 Neil Smith CL	.02	.10
❑ 147 Jack Del Rio CL	.02	.10
❑ 148 Morten Andersen CL	.02	.10

Card		
❑ 149 Sterling Sharpe CL	.07	.20
❑ 150 Reggie White CL	.07	.20

1994 Playoff Contenders

Card		
❑ COMPLETE SET (120)	7.50	20.00
❑ 1 Drew Bledsoe	.40	1.00
❑ 2 Barry Sanders	1.00	2.50
❑ 3 Jerry Rice	.60	1.50
❑ 4 Rod Woodson	.07	.20
❑ 5 Irving Fryar	.07	.20
❑ 6 Charles Haley	.07	.20
❑ 7 Chris Warren	.07	.20
❑ 8 Craig Erickson	.02	.10
❑ 9 Eric Metcalf	.07	.20
❑ 10 Marcus Allen	.15	.40
❑ 11 Chris Miller	.02	.10
❑ 12 Andre Rison	.07	.20
❑ 13 Art Monk	.07	.20
❑ 14 Calvin Williams	.07	.20
❑ 15 Shannon Sharpe	.07	.20
❑ 16 Rodney Hampton	.07	.20
❑ 17 Marion Butts	.02	.10
❑ 18 John Jurkovic RC	.07	.20
❑ 19 Jim Kelly	.15	.40
❑ 20 Emmitt Smith	1.00	2.50
❑ 21 Jeff Hostetler	.07	.20
❑ 22 Barry Foster	.02	.10
❑ 23 Boomer Esiason	.07	.20
❑ 24 Jim Harbaugh	.15	.40
❑ 25 Joe Montana	1.25	3.00
❑ 26 Jeff George	.15	.40
❑ 27 Warren Moon	.15	.40
❑ 28 Steve Young	.50	1.25
❑ 29 Randall Cunningham	.15	.40
❑ 30 Shawn Jefferson	.02	.10
❑ 31 Cortez Kennedy	.07	.20
❑ 32 Reggie Brooks	.07	.20
❑ 33 Alvin Harper	.07	.20
❑ 34 Brent Jones	.07	.20
❑ 35 O.J.McDuffie	.15	.40
❑ 36 Jerome Bettis	.25	.60
❑ 37 Daryl Johnston	.07	.20
❑ 38 Herman Moore	.15	.40
❑ 39 Dave Meggett	.02	.10
❑ 40 Reggie White	.15	.40
❑ 41 Junior Seau	.15	.40
❑ 42 Dan Marino	1.25	3.00
❑ 43 Scott Mitchell	.07	.20
❑ 44 John Elway	1.25	3.00
❑ 45 Troy Aikman	.60	1.50
❑ 46 Terry Allen	.07	.20
❑ 47 David Klingler	.02	.10
❑ 48 Stan Humphries	.07	.20
❑ 49 Rick Mirer	.15	.40
❑ 50 Neil O'Donnell	.15	.40
❑ 51 Keith Jackson	.02	.10
❑ 52 Ricky Watters	.07	.20
❑ 53 Dave Brown	.07	.20
❑ 54 Neil Smith	.07	.20
❑ 55 Johnny Mitchell	.02	.10
❑ 56 Jackie Harris	.02	.10
❑ 57 Terry Kirby	.15	.40
❑ 58 Willie Davis	.07	.20
❑ 59 Rob Moore	.07	.20
❑ 60 Nate Newton	.02	.10
❑ 61 Deion Sanders	.30	.75
❑ 62 John Taylor	.07	.20
❑ 63 Sterling Sharpe	.07	.20
❑ 64 Natrone Means	.15	.40
❑ 65 Steve Beuerlein	.07	.20
❑ 66 Erik Kramer	.07	.20
❑ 67 Qadry Ismail	.15	.40
❑ 68 Johnny Johnson	.02	.10
❑ 69 Herschel Walker	.07	.20
❑ 70 Mark Stepnoski	.02	.10
❑ 71 Brett Favre	1.25	3.00
❑ 72 Dana Stubblefield	.07	.20
❑ 73 Bruce Smith	.15	.40
❑ 74 Leroy Hoard	.02	.10
❑ 75 Steve Walsh	.02	.10
❑ 76 Jay Novacek	.07	.20
❑ 77 Derrick Thomas	.15	.40
❑ 78 Keith Byars	.02	.10
❑ 79 Ben Coates	.07	.20
❑ 80 Lorenzo Neal	.02	.10
❑ 81 Ronnie Lott	.07	.20
❑ 82 Tim Brown	.15	.40
❑ 83 Michael Irvin	.15	.40
❑ 84 Ronald Moore	.02	.10
❑ 85 Andre Reed	.07	.20
❑ 86 James Jett	.02	.10
❑ 87 Curtis Conway	.15	.40
❑ 88 Bernie Parmalee RC	.15	.40
❑ 89 Keith Cash	.02	.10
❑ 90 Russell Copeland	.02	.10
❑ 91 Kevin Williams WR	.07	.20
❑ 92 Gary Brown	.02	.10
❑ 93 Thurman Thomas	.15	.40
❑ 94 Jamir Miller RC	.07	.20
❑ 95 Bert Emanuel RC	.15	.40
❑ 96 Bucky Brooks RC	.02	.10
❑ 97 Jeff Burris RC	.07	.20
❑ 98 Antonio Langham RC	.07	.20
❑ 99 Derrick Alexander WR RC	.15	.40
❑ 100 Dan Wilkinson RC	.07	.20
❑ 101 Shante Carver RC	.02	.10
❑ 102 Johnnie Morton RC	.75	2.00
❑ 103 LeShon Johnson RC	.07	.20
❑ 104 Marshall Faulk RC	2.50	6.00
❑ 105 Greg Hill RC	.15	.40
❑ 106 Lake Dawson RC	.07	.20
❑ 107 Irving Spikes RC	.07	.20
❑ 108 David Palmer RC	.15	.40
❑ 109 Willie McGinest RC	.15	.40
❑ 110 Joe Johnson RC	.02	.10
❑ 111 Aaron Glenn RC	.15	.40
❑ 112 Charlie Garner RC	.60	1.50
❑ 113 Charles Johnson RC	.15	.40
❑ 114 Byron Bam Morris RC	.07	.20
❑ 115 Bryant Young RC	.25	.60
❑ 116 William Floyd RC	.15	.40
❑ 117 Trent Dilfer RC	.60	1.50
❑ 118 Errict Rhett RC	.15	.40
❑ 119 Heath Shuler RC	.15	.40
❑ 120 Gus Frerotte RC	.75	2.00

1995 Playoff Contenders

Card		
❑ COMPLETE SET (150)	10.00	25.00
❑ 1 Steve Young	.40	1.00
❑ 2 Jeff Blake RC	.30	.75
❑ 3 Rick Mirer	.07	.20
❑ 4 Brett Favre	1.25	2.50
❑ 5 Heath Shuler	.07	.20
❑ 6 Steve Bono	.07	.20
❑ 7 John Elway	1.00	2.50
❑ 8 Troy Aikman	.50	1.25
❑ 9 Rodney Peete	.02	.10
❑ 10 Gus Frerotte	.07	.20
❑ 11 Drew Bledsoe	.30	.75
❑ 12 Jim Kelly	.15	.40
❑ 13 Dan Marino	1.00	2.50
❑ 14 Errict Rhett	.07	.20
❑ 15 Jeff Hostetler	.07	.20
❑ 16 Erik Kramer	.02	.10
❑ 17 Jim Everett	.02	.10
❑ 18 Elvis Grbac	.15	.40
❑ 19 Scott Mitchell	.07	.20
❑ 20 Barry Sanders	.75	2.00
❑ 21 Deion Sanders	.30	.75
❑ 22 Emmitt Smith	.75	2.00
❑ 23 Garrison Hearst	.15	.40
❑ 24 Mario Bates	.07	.20
❑ 25 Mark Brunell	.30	.75
❑ 26 Robert Smith	.15	.40
❑ 27 Rodney Hampton	.07	.20
❑ 28 Marshall Faulk	.60	1.50
❑ 29 Greg Hill	.07	.20
❑ 30 Bernie Parmalee	.07	.20
❑ 31 Natrone Means	.07	.20
❑ 32 Marcus Allen	.15	.40
❑ 33 Byron Bam Morris	.02	.10
❑ 34 Edgar Bennett	.07	.20
❑ 35 Vincent Brisby	.02	.10
❑ 36 Jerome Bettis	.15	.40
❑ 37 Craig Heyward	.07	.20
❑ 38 Anthony Miller	.07	.20
❑ 39 Curtis Conway	.15	.40
❑ 40 William Floyd	.07	.20
❑ 41 Chris Warren	.07	.20
❑ 42 Terry Kirby	.07	.20
❑ 43 Herschel Walker	.07	.20
❑ 44 Eric Metcalf	.07	.20
❑ 45 Darnay Scott	.07	.20
❑ 46 Jackie Harris	.02	.10
❑ 47 Dana Stubblefield	.07	.20
❑ 48 Daryl Johnston	.07	.20
❑ 49 Dave Meggett	.02	.10
❑ 50 Ricky Watters	.07	.20
❑ 51 Ken Norton	.07	.20
❑ 52 Boomer Esiason	.07	.20
❑ 53 Lake Dawson	.07	.20
❑ 54 Eric Green	.02	.10
❑ 55 Junior Seau	.15	.40
❑ 56 Yancey Thigpen RC	.15	.40
❑ 57 James Jett	.07	.20
❑ 58 Leonard Russell	.02	.10
❑ 59 Brent Jones	.02	.10
❑ 60 Trent Dilfer	.15	.40
❑ 61 Terance Mathis	.07	.20
❑ 62 Jeff George	.07	.20
❑ 63 Alvin Harper	.02	.10
❑ 64 Terry Allen	.07	.20
❑ 65 Stan Humphries	.07	.20
❑ 66 Robert Green	.02	.10
❑ 67 Bryce Paup	.07	.20
❑ 68 Tamarick Vanover RC	.15	.40
❑ 69 Desmond Howard	.07	.20
❑ 70 Derek Loville	.02	.10
❑ 71 Dave Brown	.07	.20
❑ 72 Carl Pickens	.07	.20
❑ 73 Gary Clark	.02	.10
❑ 74 Gary Brown	.02	.10
❑ 75 Brett Perriman	.07	.20
❑ 76 Charlie Garner	.15	.40
❑ 77 Ben Coates	.07	.20
❑ 78 Bruce Smith	.15	.40
❑ 79 Erric Pegram	.07	.20
❑ 80 Jerry Rice	.50	1.25
❑ 81 Tim Brown	.15	.40
❑ 82 John Taylor	.02	.10
❑ 83 Will Moore	.02	.10
❑ 84 Jay Novacek	.07	.20
❑ 85 Kevin Williams	.07	.20
❑ 86 Rocket Ismail	.07	.20
❑ 87 Robert Brooks	.15	.40
❑ 88 Michael Irvin	.15	.40
❑ 89 Mark Chmura	.15	.40
❑ 90 Shannon Sharpe	.07	.20
❑ 91 Henry Ellard	.07	.20
❑ 92 Reggie White	.15	.40
❑ 93 Isaac Bruce	.30	.75
❑ 94 Charles Haley	.07	.20
❑ 95 Jake Reed	.07	.20
❑ 96 Pete Metzelaars	.02	.10
❑ 97 Dave Krieg	.02	.10
❑ 98 Tony Martin	.07	.20
❑ 99 Charles Jordan RC	.07	.20
❑ 100 Bert Emanuel	.15	.40
❑ 101 Andre Rison	.07	.20
❑ 102 Jeff Graham	.02	.10
❑ 103 O.J. McDuffie	.15	.40
❑ 104 Randall Cunningham	.15	.40
❑ 105 Harvey Williams	.02	.10
❑ 106 Cris Carter	.15	.40
❑ 107 Irving Fryar	.07	.20
❑ 108 Jim Harbaugh	.07	.20
❑ 109 Bernie Kosar	.02	.10
❑ 110 Charles Johnson	.07	.20
❑ 111 Warren Moon	.07	.20
❑ 112 Neil O'Donnell	.07	.20
❑ 113 Fred Barnett	.07	.20

❑ 114 Herman Moore	.15	.40
❑ 115 Chris Miller	.02	.10
❑ 116 Vinny Testaverde	.07	.20
❑ 117 Craig Erickson	.02	.10
❑ 118 Qadry Ismail	.07	.20
❑ 119 Willie Davis	.07	.20
❑ 120 Michael Jackson	.07	.20
❑ 121 Stoney Case RC	.15	.40
❑ 122 Frank Sanders RC	.15	.40
❑ 123 Todd Collins RC	1.00	2.50
❑ 124 Kerry Collins RC	.75	2.00
❑ 125 Sherman Williams RC	.02	.10
❑ 126 Terrell Davis RC	1.00	2.50
❑ 127 Luther Elliss RC	.02	.10
❑ 128 Steve McNair RC	1.25	3.00
❑ 129 Chris Sanders RC	.15	.40
❑ 130 Ki-Jana Carter RC	.15	.40
❑ 131 Rodney Thomas RC	.15	.40
❑ 132 Tony Boselli RC	.15	.40
❑ 133 Rob Johnson RC	.40	1.00
❑ 134 James O. Stewart RC	.50	1.25
❑ 135 Chad May RC	.02	.10
❑ 136 Eric Bjornson RC	.07	.20
❑ 137 Tyrone Wheatley RC	.50	1.25
❑ 138 Kyle Brady RC	.15	.40
❑ 139 Curtis Martin RC	1.25	3.00
❑ 140 Eric Zeier RC	.15	.40
❑ 141 Ray Zellars RC	.07	.20
❑ 142 Napoleon Kaufman RC	.50	1.25
❑ 143 Mike Mamula RC	.07	.20
❑ 144 Mark Bruener RC	.07	.20
❑ 145 Kordell Stewart RC	.60	1.50
❑ 146 J.J. Stokes RC	.15	.40
❑ 147 Joey Galloway RC	.60	1.50
❑ 148 Warren Sapp RC	.60	1.50
❑ 149 Michael Westbrook RC	.15	.40
❑ 150 Rashaan Salaam RC	.15	.40

1997 Playoff Contenders

❑ COMPLETE SET (150)	15.00	40.00
❑ 1 Kent Graham	.15	.40
❑ 2 Leeland McElroy	.15	.40
❑ 3 Rob Moore	.25	.60
❑ 4 Frank Sanders	.25	.60
❑ 5 Jake Plummer RC	2.00	5.00
❑ 6 Chris Chandler	.25	.60
❑ 7 Bert Emanuel	.25	.60
❑ 8 O.J. Santiago RC	.25	.60
❑ 9 Byron Hanspard RC	.25	.60
❑ 10 Vinny Testaverde	.25	.60
❑ 11 Michael Jackson	.25	.60
❑ 12 Earnest Byner	.15	.40
❑ 13 Jermaine Lewis	.40	1.00
❑ 14 Derrick Alexander WR	.25	.60
❑ 15 Jay Graham RC	.25	.60
❑ 16 Todd Collins	.15	.40
❑ 17 Thurman Thomas	.40	1.00
❑ 18 Bruce Smith	.25	.60
❑ 19 Andre Reed	.25	.60
❑ 20 Quinn Early	.15	.40
❑ 21 Antowain Smith RC	1.00	2.50
❑ 22 Kerry Collins	.40	1.00
❑ 23 Tim Biakabutuka	.25	.60
❑ 24 Anthony Johnson	.15	.40
❑ 25 Wesley Walls	.25	.60
❑ 26 Fred Lane RC	.25	.60
❑ 27 Rae Carruth RC	.15	.40
❑ 28 Raymont Harris	.15	.40
❑ 29 Rick Mirer	.15	.40
❑ 30 Darnell Autry RC	.25	.60
❑ 31 Jeff Blake	.25	.60
❑ 32 Ki-Jana Carter	.15	.40
❑ 33 Carl Pickens	.25	.60
❑ 34 Darnay Scott	.25	.60
❑ 35 Corey Dillon RC	2.50	6.00
❑ 36 Troy Aikman	.75	2.00
❑ 37 Emmitt Smith	1.25	3.00
❑ 38 Michael Irvin	.40	1.00
❑ 39 Deion Sanders	.40	1.00
❑ 40 Anthony Miller	.15	.40
❑ 41 Eric Bjornson	.15	.40
❑ 42 David LaFleur RC	.15	.40
❑ 43 John Elway	1.50	4.00
❑ 44 Terrell Davis	.50	1.25
❑ 45 Shannon Sharpe	.25	.60
❑ 46 Ed McCaffrey	.25	.60
❑ 47 Rod Smith WR	.40	1.00
❑ 48 Scott Mitchell	.25	.60
❑ 49 Barry Sanders	1.25	3.00
❑ 50 Herman Moore	.25	.60
❑ 51 Brett Favre	1.50	4.00
❑ 52 Dorsey Levens	.40	1.00
❑ 53 William Henderson	.25	.60
❑ 54 Derrick Mayes	.25	.60
❑ 55 Antonio Freeman	.40	1.00
❑ 56 Robert Brooks	.25	.60
❑ 57 Mark Chmura	.25	.60
❑ 58 Reggie White	.40	1.00
❑ 59 Darren Sharper RC	10.00	20.00
❑ 60 Jim Harbaugh	.25	.60
❑ 61 Marshall Faulk	.50	1.25
❑ 62 Marvin Harrison	.40	1.00
❑ 63 Mark Brunell	.50	1.25
❑ 64 Natrone Means	.25	.60
❑ 65 Jimmy Smith	.25	.60
❑ 66 Keenan McCardell	.25	.60
❑ 67 Elvis Grbac	.25	.60
❑ 68 Greg Hill	.15	.40
❑ 69 Marcus Allen	.40	1.00
❑ 70 Andre Rison	.25	.60
❑ 71 Kimble Anders	.25	.60
❑ 72 Tony Gonzalez RC	1.25	3.00
❑ 73 Pat Barnes RC	.40	1.00
❑ 74 Dan Marino	1.50	4.00
❑ 75 Karim Abdul-Jabbar	.25	.60
❑ 76 Zach Thomas	.40	1.00
❑ 77 O.J. McDuffie	.25	.60
❑ 78 Brian Manning RC	.15	.40
❑ 79 Brad Johnson	.40	1.00
❑ 80 Cris Carter	.40	1.00
❑ 81 Jake Reed	.25	.60
❑ 82 Robert Smith	.25	.60
❑ 83 Drew Bledsoe	.50	1.25
❑ 84 Curtis Martin	.50	1.25
❑ 85 Ben Coates	.25	.60
❑ 86 Terry Glenn	.40	1.00
❑ 87 Shawn Jefferson	.15	.40
❑ 88 Heath Shuler	.15	.40
❑ 89 Mario Bates	.15	.40
❑ 90 Andre Hastings	.15	.40
❑ 91 Troy Davis RC	.25	.60
❑ 92 Danny Wuerffel RC	.40	1.00
❑ 93 Dave Brown	.15	.40
❑ 94 Chris Calloway	.15	.40
❑ 95 Tiki Barber RC	2.50	6.00
❑ 96 Mike Cherry RC	.15	.40
❑ 97 Neil O'Donnell	.25	.60
❑ 98 Keyshawn Johnson	.40	1.00
❑ 99 Adrian Murrell	.25	.60
❑ 100 Wayne Chrebet	.40	1.00
❑ 101 Dedric Ward RC	.25	.60
❑ 102 Leon Johnson RC	.25	.60
❑ 103 Jeff George	.25	.60
❑ 104 Napoleon Kaufman	.40	1.00
❑ 105 Tim Brown	.40	1.00
❑ 106 James Jett	.25	.60
❑ 107 Ty Detmer	.25	.60
❑ 108 Ricky Watters	.25	.60
❑ 109 Irving Fryar	.25	.60
❑ 110 Michael Timpson	.15	.40
❑ 111 Chad Lewis RC	.75	2.00
❑ 112 Kordell Stewart	.40	1.00
❑ 113 Jerome Bettis	.40	1.00
❑ 114 Charles Johnson	.25	.60
❑ 115 George Jones RC	.25	.60
❑ 116 Will Blackwell RC	.25	.60
❑ 117 Stan Humphries	.25	.60
❑ 118 Junior Seau	.40	1.00
❑ 119 Freddie Jones RC	.25	.60
❑ 120 Steve Young	.50	1.25
❑ 121 Jerry Rice	.75	2.00
❑ 122 Garrison Hearst	.25	.60
❑ 123 William Floyd	.25	.60
❑ 124 Terrell Owens	.50	1.25
❑ 125 J.J. Stokes	.25	.60
❑ 126 Marc Edwards RC	.15	.40
❑ 127 Jim Druckenmiller RC	.25	.60
❑ 128 Warren Moon	.40	1.00
❑ 129 Chris Warren	.25	.60
❑ 130 Joey Galloway	.25	.60
❑ 131 Shawn Springs RC	.25	.60
❑ 132 Tony Banks	.25	.60
❑ 133 Lawrence Phillips	.15	.40
❑ 134 Isaac Bruce	.40	1.00
❑ 135 Eddie Kennison	.25	.60
❑ 136 Orlando Pace RC	.40	1.00
❑ 137 Trent Dilfer	.40	1.00
❑ 138 Mike Alstott	.40	1.00
❑ 139 Horace Copeland	.15	.40
❑ 140 Jackie Harris	.15	.40
❑ 141 Warrick Dunn RC	1.25	3.00
❑ 142 Reidel Anthony RC	.40	1.00
❑ 143 Steve McNair	.50	1.25
❑ 144 Eddie George	.40	1.00
❑ 145 Chris Sanders	.15	.40
❑ 146 Gus Frerotte	.15	.40
❑ 147 Terry Allen	.40	1.00
❑ 148 Henry Ellard	.15	.40
❑ 149 Leslie Shepherd	.15	.40
❑ 150 Michael Westbrook	.25	.60
❑ S1 Terrell Davis Sample	.75	2.00

1998 Playoff Contenders Ticket

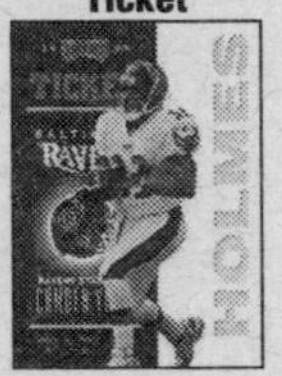

❑ COMP.SET w/o SPs (80)	25.00	60.00
❑ 1 Rob Moore	.50	1.25
❑ 2 Jake Plummer	.75	2.00
❑ 3 Jamal Anderson	.75	2.00
❑ 4 Terance Mathis	.50	1.25
❑ 5 Priest Holmes RC	15.00	40.00
❑ 6 Michael Jackson	.30	.75
❑ 7 Eric Zeier	.50	1.25
❑ 8 Andre Reed	.50	1.25
❑ 9 Antowain Smith	.75	2.00
❑ 10 Bruce Smith	.50	1.25
❑ 11 Thurman Thomas	.75	2.00
❑ 12 Rocket Ismail	.30	.75
❑ 13 Wesley Walls	.50	1.25
❑ 14 Curtis Conway	.50	1.25
❑ 15 Jeff Blake	.50	1.25
❑ 16 Corey Dillon	.75	2.00
❑ 17 Carl Pickens	.50	1.25
❑ 18 Troy Aikman	1.50	4.00
❑ 19 Michael Irvin	.75	2.00
❑ 20 Ernie Mills	.30	.75
❑ 21 Deion Sanders	.75	2.00
❑ 22 Emmitt Smith	2.50	6.00
❑ 23 Terrell Davis	.75	2.00
❑ 24 John Elway	3.00	8.00
❑ 25 Neil Smith	.50	1.25
❑ 26 Rod Smith WR	.50	1.25
❑ 27 Herman Moore	.50	1.25
❑ 28 Johnnie Morton	.50	1.25
❑ 29 Barry Sanders	2.50	6.00
❑ 30 Robert Brooks	.50	1.25
❑ 31 Brett Favre	3.00	8.00
❑ 32 Antonio Freeman	.75	2.00
❑ 33 Dorsey Levens	.75	2.00
❑ 34 Reggie White	.75	2.00
❑ 35 Marshall Faulk	1.00	2.50
❑ 36 Mark Brunell	.75	2.00
❑ 37 Jimmy Smith	.50	1.25
❑ 38 James Stewart	.50	1.25
❑ 39 Donnell Bennett	.30	.75
❑ 40 Andre Rison	.50	1.25
❑ 41 Derrick Thomas	.75	2.00
❑ 42 Karim Abdul-Jabbar	.75	2.00
❑ 43 Dan Marino	3.00	8.00
❑ 44 Cris Carter	.75	2.00
❑ 45 Brad Johnson	.75	2.00

❑ 46 Robert Smith .75 2.00
❑ 47 Drew Bledsoe 1.25 3.00
❑ 48 Terry Glenn .75 2.00
❑ 49 Lamar Smith .50 1.25
❑ 50 Ike Hilliard .50 1.25
❑ 51 Danny Kanell .50 1.25
❑ 52 Wayne Chrebet .75 2.00
❑ 53 Keyshawn Johnson .75 2.00
❑ 54 Curtis Martin .75 2.00
❑ 55 Tim Brown .75 2.00
❑ 56 Rickey Dudley .30 .75
❑ 57 Jeff George .50 1.25
❑ 58 Napoleon Kaufman .75 2.00
❑ 59 Irving Fryar .50 1.25
❑ 60 Jerome Bettis .75 2.00
❑ 61 Charles Johnson .30 .75
❑ 62 Kordell Stewart .75 2.00
❑ 63 Natrone Means .50 1.25
❑ 64 Bryan Still .30 .75
❑ 65 Garrison Hearst .75 2.00
❑ 66 Jerry Rice 1.50 4.00
❑ 67 Steve Young 1.00 2.50
❑ 68 Joey Galloway .50 1.25
❑ 69 Warren Moon .75 2.00
❑ 70 Ricky Watters .50 1.25
❑ 71 Isaac Bruce .75 2.00
❑ 72 Mike Alstott .75 2.00
❑ 73 Reidel Anthony .50 1.25
❑ 74 Trent Dilfer .75 2.00
❑ 75 Warrick Dunn .75 2.00
❑ 76 Warren Sapp .50 1.25
❑ 77 Eddie George .75 2.00
❑ 78 Steve McNair .75 2.00
❑ 79 Terry Allen .75 2.00
❑ 80 Gus Frerotte .30 .75
❑ 81 Andre Wadsworth AU/500* 10.00 25.00
❑ 82 Tim Dwight AU/500* 15.00 40.00
❑ 83 Curtis Enis AU/400* 15.00 40.00
❑ 85 Charlie Batch AU/500* 15.00 40.00
❑ 86 Germane Crowell AU/500* 10.00 25.00
❑ 87 Pey.Manning AU/200* 2000.00 3000.00
❑ 88 Jerome Pathon AU/500* 15.00 40.00
❑ 89 Fred Taylor AU/500* 60.00 120.00
❑ 90 Tavian Banks AU/500* 10.00 25.00
❑ 92 Randy Moss AU/300* 250.00 500.00
❑ 93 Robert Edwards AU/500* 10.00 25.00
❑ 94 Hines Ward AU/500* 150.00 250.00
❑ 95 Ryan Leaf AU/200* 25.00 50.00
❑ 96 Mikhael Ricks AU/500* 10.00 25.00
❑ 97 Ahman Green AU/500* 25.00 60.00
❑ 98 Jacquez Green AU/500* 10.00 25.00
❑ 99 Kevin Dyson AU/500* 15.00 40.00
❑ 100 Skip Hicks AU/500* 10.00 25.00
❑ 103 C.Fuamatu-Ma'afala AU/500* 10.00 25.00

1999 Playoff Contenders SSD

❑ COMPLETE SET (205) 750.00 1500.00
❑ COMP.SET w/o SP's (141) 25.00 60.00
❑ 1 Randy Moss 2.00 5.00
❑ 2 Randall Cunningham .75 2.00
❑ 3 Cris Carter .75 2.00
❑ 4 Robert Smith .75 2.00
❑ 5 Jake Reed .50 1.25
❑ 6 Albert Connell .30 .75
❑ 7 Jeff George .50 1.25
❑ 8 Brett Favre 2.50 6.00
❑ 9 Antonio Freeman .75 2.00
❑ 10 Dorsey Levens .75 2.00
❑ 11 Mark Chmura .50 1.25
❑ 12 Mike Alstott .75 2.00
❑ 13 Warrick Dunn .75 2.00
❑ 14 Trent Dilfer .50 1.25
❑ 15 Jacquez Green .30 .75
❑ 16 Reidel Anthony .30 .75
❑ 17 Warren Sapp .50 1.25
❑ 18 Amani Toomer .30 .75
❑ 19 Curtis Enis .30 .75
❑ 20 Curtis Conway .50 1.25
❑ 21 Bobby Engram .50 1.25
❑ 22 Barry Sanders 2.50 6.00
❑ 23 Charlie Batch .75 2.00
❑ 24 Herman Moore .50 1.25
❑ 25 Johnnie Morton .50 1.25
❑ 26 Greg Hill .30 .75
❑ 27 Germane Crowell .30 .75
❑ 28 Kerry Collins .50 1.25
❑ 29 Ike Hilliard .30 .75
❑ 30 Joe Jurevicius .50 1.25
❑ 31 Stephen Davis .75 2.00
❑ 32 Brad Johnson .75 2.00
❑ 33 Skip Hicks .30 .75
❑ 34 Michael Westbrook .50 1.25
❑ 35 Jake Plummer .50 1.25
❑ 36 Adrian Murrell .30 .75
❑ 37 Frank Sanders .50 1.25
❑ 38 Rob Moore .50 1.25
❑ 39 Gary Brown .30 .75
❑ 40 Duce Staley .75 2.00
❑ 41 Charles Johnson .50 1.25
❑ 42 Emmitt Smith 1.50 4.00
❑ 43 Troy Aikman 1.50 4.00
❑ 44 Michael Irvin .50 1.25
❑ 45 Deion Sanders .75 2.00
❑ 46 Rocket Ismail .50 1.25
❑ 47 Jerry Rice 1.50 4.00
❑ 48 Terrell Owens .75 2.00
❑ 49 Steve Young 1.00 2.50
❑ 50 Garrison Hearst .50 1.25
❑ 51 J.J. Stokes .50 1.25
❑ 52 Lawrence Phillips .50 1.25
❑ 53 Jamal Anderson .75 2.00
❑ 54 Chris Chandler .50 1.25
❑ 55 Terance Mathis .50 1.25
❑ 56 Tim Dwight .75 2.00
❑ 57 Charlie Garner .50 1.25
❑ 58 Chris Calloway .50 1.25
❑ 59 Eddie Kennison .50 1.25
❑ 60 Billy Joe Hobert .30 .75
❑ 61 Tim Biakabutuka .50 1.25
❑ 62 Muhsin Muhammad .50 1.25
❑ 63 Olandis Gary AU/1825* RC 5.00 12.00
❑ 64 Wesley Walls .50 1.25
❑ 65 Isaac Bruce .75 2.00
❑ 66 Marshall Faulk 1.00 2.50
❑ 67 Kordell Stewart .50 1.25
❑ 68 Jerome Bettis .75 2.00
❑ 69 Hines Ward .75 2.00
❑ 70 Corey Dillon .75 2.00
❑ 71 Carl Pickens .50 1.25
❑ 72 Darnay Scott .50 1.25
❑ 73 Steve McNair .75 2.00
❑ 74 Eddie George .75 2.00
❑ 75 Yancey Thigpen .30 .75
❑ 76 Kevin Dyson .50 1.25
❑ 77 Fred Taylor .75 2.00
❑ 78 Mark Brunell .75 2.00
❑ 79 Jimmy Smith .50 1.25
❑ 80 Keenan McCardell .50 1.25
❑ 81 James Stewart .50 1.25
❑ 82 Jermaine Lewis .50 1.25
❑ 83 Priest Holmes 1.25 3.00
❑ 84 Stoney Case .30 .75
❑ 85 Errict Rhett .50 1.25
❑ 86 Bill Schroeder .75 2.00
❑ 87 Terry Kirby .30 .75
❑ 88 Leslie Shepherd .30 .75
❑ 89 Terrence Wilkins AU/825* RC 4.00 10.00
❑ 90 Dan Marino 2.50 6.00
❑ 91 O.J. McDuffie .50 1.25
❑ 92 Karim Abdul-Jabbar .50 1.25
❑ 93 Zach Thomas .75 2.00
❑ 94 Terry Allen .50 1.25
❑ 95 Tony Martin .50 1.25
❑ 96 Drew Bledsoe 1.00 2.50
❑ 97 Terry Glenn .75 2.00
❑ 98 Ben Coates .50 1.25
❑ 99 Tony Simmons .30 .75
❑ 100 Curtis Martin .75 2.00
❑ 101 Keyshawn Johnson .75 2.00
❑ 102 Vinny Testaverde .50 1.25
❑ 103 Wayne Chrebet .75 2.00
❑ 104 Peyton Manning 2.50 6.00
❑ 105 Marvin Harrison .75 2.00
❑ 106 E.G. Green .30 .75
❑ 107 Doug Flutie .75 2.00
❑ 108 Thurman Thomas .50 1.25
❑ 109 Andre Reed .50 1.25
❑ 110 Eric Moulds .75 2.00
❑ 111 Antowain Smith .75 2.00
❑ 112 Bruce Smith .50 1.25
❑ 113 Terrell Davis .75 2.00
❑ 114 John Elway 2.50 6.00
❑ 115 Ed McCaffrey .50 1.25
❑ 116 Rod Smith .50 1.25
❑ 117 Shannon Sharpe .50 1.25
❑ 118 Jeff Garcia AU/325* RC 40.00 80.00
❑ 119 Brian Griese .75 2.00
❑ 120 Justin Watson AU/325* RC 6.00 15.00
❑ 121 Bubby Brister .50 1.25
❑ 122 Ryan Leaf .75 2.00
❑ 123 Natrone Means .50 1.25
❑ 124 Mikhael Ricks .30 .75
❑ 125 Junior Seau .75 2.00
❑ 126 Jim Harbaugh .50 1.25
❑ 127 Andre Rison .50 1.25
❑ 128 Elvis Grbac .50 1.25
❑ 129 Bam Morris .30 .75
❑ 130 Rashaan Shehee .30 .75
❑ 131 Warren Moon .75 2.00
❑ 132 Tony Gonzalez .75 2.00
❑ 133 Derrick Alexander .50 1.25
❑ 134 Jon Kitna .75 2.00
❑ 135 Ricky Watters .50 1.25
❑ 136 Joey Galloway .50 1.25
❑ 137 Ahman Green .75 2.00
❑ 138 Derrick Mayes .50 1.25
❑ 139 Tyrone Wheatley .50 1.25
❑ 140 Napoleon Kaufman .75 2.00
❑ 141 Tim Brown .75 2.00
❑ 142 Charles Woodson .75 2.00
❑ 143 Rich Gannon .75 2.00
❑ 144 Rickey Dudley .30 .75
❑ 145 Az-Zahir Hakim .30 .75
❑ 146 Kurt Warner AU/1825* RC 90.00 175.00
❑ 147 Sean Bennett AU/1325* RC 3.00 8.00
❑ 148 B.Stokley AU/1325* RC 6.00 15.00
❑ 149 Amos Zereoue AU/1325* RC 4.00 10.00
❑ 150 Brock Huard AU/1325* RC 5.00 12.00
❑ 151 Tim Couch AU/1025* RC 8.00 20.00
❑ 152 Ricky Williams AU/725* RC 25.00 50.00
❑ 153 D.McNabb AU/525* RC 40.00 100.00
❑ 154 Edgerrin James AU/525* RC 30.00 60.00
❑ 155 Torry Holt AU/1025* RC 30.00 60.00
❑ 156 D.Culpepper AU/1025* RC 20.00 50.00
❑ 157 Akili Smith AU/1025* RC 4.00 10.00
❑ 158 Champ Bailey AU/1725* RC 12.50 30.00
❑ 159 C.Claiborne AU/1825* RC 4.00 10.00
❑ 160A C McAlister No AU/1825* RC 5.00 12.00
❑ 160B Jason Tucker AU/1825* 3.00 8.00
❑ 161 Troy Edwards AU/1225* RC 4.00 10.00
❑ 162 Jevon Kearse AU/325* RC 20.00 50.00
❑ 163 D.McDonald AU/1825* RC 3.00 8.00
❑ 164 David Boston AU/1025* RC 4.00 10.00
❑ 165 Peerless Price AU/1325* RC 5.00 12.00
❑ 166 C.Collins AU/1025* RC 3.00 8.00
❑ 167 Rob Konrad AU/1325* RC 3.00 8.00
❑ 168 Cade McNown AU/1025* RC 4.00 10.00
❑ 169 Shawn Bryson AU/1825* RC 3.00 8.00
❑ 170 Kevin Faulk AU/1325* RC 10.00 25.00
❑ 171 Corby Jones AU/1825* RC 3.00 8.00
❑ 172A J.Johnson No AU/1325* RC 3.00 8.00
❑ 172B Patrick Jeffers AU/1325* 4.00 10.00
❑ 173 Autry Denson AU/1825* RC 3.00 8.00
❑ 174 Sedrick Irvin AU/1825* RC 3.00 8.00
❑ 175 M.Bishop AU/1825* RC 4.00 10.00
❑ 176 Joe Germaine AU/825* RC 4.00 10.00
❑ 177 D.Parker AU/1325* RC 3.00 8.00
❑ 178A Shaun King No AU/1825* RC 4.00 10.00
❑ 178B Ray Lucas AU/1825* 5.00 12.00
❑ 179 D'Wayne Bates AU/1825* RC 4.00 10.00
❑ 180 Tai Streets AU/1825* RC 4.00 10.00
❑ 181 Na Brown AU/1825* RC 3.00 8.00
❑ 182 Desmond Clark AU/1825* RC 5.00 12.00
❑ 183 Jim Kleinsasser AU/1825* RC 4.00 8.00
❑ 184 Kevin Johnson AU/1325* RC 5.00 12.00
❑ 185 Joe Montgomery AU/1325* RC 3.00 8.00
❑ 186 John Elway PT 4.00 10.00
❑ 187 Dan Marino PT 4.00 10.00
❑ 188 Jerry Rice PT 2.50 6.00
❑ 189 Barry Sanders PT 4.00 10.00
❑ 190 Steve Young PT 1.50 4.00

❑ 191 Doug Flutie PT 1.00 2.50
❑ 192 Troy Aikman PT 2.50 6.00
❑ 193 Drew Bledsoe PT 1.50 4.00
❑ 194 Brett Favre PT 4.00 10.00
❑ 195 Randall Cunningham PT 1.00 2.50
❑ 196 Terrell Davis PT 1.00 2.50
❑ 197 Kordell Stewart PT 1.00 2.50
❑ 198 Keyshawn Johnson PT 1.00 2.50
❑ 199 Jake Plummer PT 1.00 2.50
❑ 200 Peyton Manning PT 4.00 10.00
❑ 201 Jay Fiedler AU/1825* 5.00 12.00
❑ 202 Kevin Daft AU/325* 6.00 15.00

2000 Playoff Contenders

❑ COMP.SET w/o SP's (100) 7.50 20.00
❑ 1 David Boston .30 .75
❑ 2 Jake Plummer .20 .50
❑ 3 Chris Chandler .20 .50
❑ 4 Jamal Anderson .30 .75
❑ 5 Tim Dwight .30 .75
❑ 6 Qadry Ismail .20 .50
❑ 7 Tony Banks .20 .50
❑ 8 Lamar Smith .20 .50
❑ 9 Doug Flutie .30 .75
❑ 10 Eric Moulds .30 .75
❑ 11 Peerless Price .20 .50
❑ 12 Rob Johnson .20 .50
❑ 13 Muhsin Muhammad .20 .50
❑ 14 Reggie White .30 .75
❑ 15 Steve Beuerlein .20 .50
❑ 16 Cade McNown .10 .30
❑ 17 Derrick Alexander .20 .50
❑ 18 Marcus Robinson .20 .50
❑ 19 Akili Smith .10 .30
❑ 20 Corey Dillon .30 .75
❑ 21 Kevin Johnson .30 .75
❑ 22 Tim Couch .20 .50
❑ 23 Emmitt Smith .60 1.50
❑ 24 Joey Galloway .20 .50
❑ 25 Rocket Ismail .20 .50
❑ 26 Troy Aikman .60 1.50
❑ 27 Brian Griese .30 .75
❑ 28 Ed McCaffrey .30 .75
❑ 29 John Elway 1.00 2.50
❑ 30 Olandis Gary .30 .75
❑ 31 Rod Smith .20 .50
❑ 32 Terrell Davis .30 .75
❑ 33 Charlie Batch .30 .75
❑ 34 Germane Crowell .10 .30
❑ 35 James Stewart .20 .50
❑ 36 Barry Sanders .75 2.00
❑ 37 Antonio Freeman .30 .75
❑ 38 Brett Favre 1.00 2.50
❑ 39 Dorsey Levens .20 .50
❑ 40 Edgerrin James .50 1.25
❑ 41 Marvin Harrison .30 .75
❑ 42 Peyton Manning .75 2.00
❑ 43 Fred Taylor .30 .75
❑ 44 Jimmy Smith .20 .50
❑ 45 Mark Brunell .30 .75
❑ 46 Elvis Grbac .20 .50
❑ 47 Tony Gonzalez .20 .50
❑ 48 Dan Marino 1.00 2.50
❑ 49 Joe Horn .20 .50
❑ 50 Jay Fiedler .30 .75
❑ 51 Thurman Thomas .20 .50
❑ 52 Cris Carter .30 .75
❑ 53 Daunte Culpepper .40 1.00
❑ 54 Randy Moss .60 1.50
❑ 55 Robert Smith .30 .75
❑ 56 Drew Bledsoe .40 1.00
❑ 57 Terry Glenn .20 .50
❑ 58 Ricky Williams .30 .75
❑ 59 Amani Toomer .10 .30
❑ 60 Kerry Collins .20 .50
❑ 61 Curtis Martin .30 .75
❑ 62 Vinny Testaverde .20 .50
❑ 63 Wayne Chrebet .20 .50
❑ 64 Rich Gannon .30 .75
❑ 65 Tim Brown .30 .75
❑ 66 Tyrone Wheatley .20 .50
❑ 67 Donovan McNabb .50 1.25
❑ 68 Duce Staley .30 .75
❑ 69 Jerome Bettis .30 .75
❑ 70 Jermaine Fazande .10 .30
❑ 71 Junior Seau .30 .75
❑ 72 Donald Hayes .10 .30
❑ 73 Charlie Garner .20 .50
❑ 74 Jeff Garcia .30 .75
❑ 75 Jerry Rice .60 1.50
❑ 76 Steve Young .40 1.00
❑ 77 Terrell Owens .30 .75
❑ 78 Tiki Barber .30 .75
❑ 79 Tim Biakabutuka .20 .50
❑ 80 Ricky Watters .20 .50
❑ 81 Isaac Bruce .30 .75
❑ 82 Kurt Warner .60 1.50
❑ 83 Marshall Faulk .40 1.00
❑ 84 Torry Holt .30 .75
❑ 85 Keyshawn Johnson .30 .75
❑ 86 Mike Alstott .30 .75
❑ 87 Shaun King .10 .30
❑ 88 Warren Sapp .20 .50
❑ 89 Warrick Dunn .30 .75
❑ 90 Eddie George .30 .75
❑ 91 Jevon Kearse .30 .75
❑ 92 Steve McNair .30 .75
❑ 93 Carl Pickens .20 .50
❑ 94 Albert Connell .10 .30
❑ 95 Brad Johnson .30 .75
❑ 96 Bruce Smith .20 .50
❑ 97 Deion Sanders .30 .75
❑ 98 Jeff George .20 .50
❑ 99 Michael Westbrook .20 .50
❑ 100 Stephen Davis .30 .75
❑ 101 Courtney Brown AU RC 5.00 12.00
❑ 102 Corey Simon AU RC 5.00 12.00
❑ 103 Brian Urlacher AU RC 40.00 80.00
❑ 104 Deon Grant AU RC 4.00 10.00
❑ 105 Peter Warrick AU RC 5.00 12.00
❑ 106 Jamal Lewis AU RC 10.00 25.00
❑ 107 Thomas Jones unsigned 12.50 25.00
❑ 108 Plaxico Burress AU RC 6.00 15.00
❑ 109 Travis Taylor AU RC 5.00 12.00
❑ 110 Ron Dayne AU RC 5.00 12.00
❑ 111 Bubba Franks AU RC 5.00 12.00
❑ 112 Chad Pennington AU RC 12.00 30.00
❑ 113 Shaun Alexander AU RC 10.00 25.00
❑ 114 Sylvester Morris AU RC 4.00 10.00
❑ 115 Mike Anderson AU RC 5.00 12.00
❑ 116 R.Jay Soward AU RC 3.00 8.00
❑ 117 Trung Canidate AU RC 4.00 10.00
❑ 118 Dennis Northcutt AU RC 4.00 10.00
❑ 119 Todd Pinkston AU RC 4.00 10.00
❑ 120 Jerry Porter AU RC 5.00 12.00
❑ 121 Travis Prentice AU RC 4.00 10.00
❑ 122 Giovanni Carmazzi AU RC 3.00 8.00
❑ 123 Ron Dugans AU RC 3.00 8.00
❑ 124 Dez White AU RC 5.00 12.00
❑ 125 Chris Cole AU RC 3.00 8.00
❑ 126 Ron Dixon AU RC 4.00 10.00
❑ 127 Chris Redman AU RC 5.00 12.00
❑ 128 J.R. Redmond AU RC 4.00 10.00
❑ 129 Laveranues Coles AU RC 6.00 15.00
❑ 130 JaJuan Dawson AU RC 3.00 8.00
❑ 131 Darrell Jackson AU RC 5.00 12.00
❑ 132 Reuben Droughns AU RC 5.00 12.00
❑ 133 Doug Chapman AU RC 4.00 10.00
❑ 134 Curtis Keaton AU RC 4.00 10.00
❑ 135 Gari Scott AU RC 3.00 8.00
❑ 136 Danny Farmer AU RC 4.00 10.00
❑ 137 Trevor Gaylor AU RC 4.00 10.00
❑ 138 Avion Black AU RC 3.00 8.00
❑ 139 Michael Wiley AU RC 4.00 10.00
❑ 140 Sammy Morris AU RC 5.00 12.00
❑ 141 Tee Martin AU RC 5.00 12.00
❑ 142 Troy Walters AU RC 5.00 12.00
❑ 143 Marc Bulger AU RC 15.00 40.00
❑ 144 Tom Brady AU RC 500.00 1000.00
❑ 145 Todd Husak AU RC 4.00 10.00
❑ 146 Tim Rattay AU RC 5.00 12.00
❑ 147 Jarious Jackson AU RC 4.00 10.00
❑ 148 Joe Hamilton AU RC 4.00 10.00
❑ 149 Shyrone Stith AU RC 4.00 10.00
❑ 150 Kwame Cavil AU RC 3.00 8.00
❑ 151 Antonio Banks ET AU RC 2.50 6.00
❑ 152 Jonathan Brown ET AU RC 2.50 6.00
❑ 153 Ontiwaun Carter ET AU RC 2.50 6.00
❑ 154 Jeremaine Copeland ET 2.50 6.00
❑ 155 Ralph Dawkins ET AU RC 3.00 8.00
❑ 156 Marques Douglas ET AU RC 2.50 6.00
❑ 157 Kevin Drake ET AU RC 2.50 6.00
❑ 158 Damon Dunn ET AU RC 3.00 8.00
❑ 159 Todd Floyd ET AU RC 2.50 6.00
❑ 160 Tony Graziani ET AU 3.00 8.00
❑ 162 Duane Hawthorne ET AU RC 3.00 8.00
❑ 163 Alonzo Johnson ET AU RC 2.50 6.00
❑ 164 Mark Kacmarynski ET AU RC 2.50 6.00
❑ 165 Eric Kresser ET AU 2.50 6.00
❑ 166 Jim Kubiak ET AU RC 3.00 8.00
❑ 167 Blaine McElmurry ET AU RC 2.50 6.00
❑ 168 Scott Milanovich ET AU 3.00 8.00
❑ 169 Norman Miller ET AU RC 2.50 6.00
❑ 170 Sean Morey ET AU RC 3.00 8.00
❑ 171 Jeff Ogden ET AU 3.00 8.00
❑ 172 Pepe Pearson ET AU RC 3.00 8.00
❑ 173 Ron Powlus ET AU RC 3.00 8.00
❑ 174 Jason Shelley ET AU RC 3.00 8.00
❑ 175 Ben Snell ET AU RC 3.00 8.00
❑ 176 Aaron Stecker ET AU RC 3.00 8.00
❑ 177 L.C. Stevens ET AU 2.50 6.00
❑ 178 Mike Sutton ET AU RC 2.50 6.00
❑ 179 Damian Vaughn ET AU RC 2.50 6.00
❑ 180 Ted White ET AU 2.50 6.00
❑ 181 Marcus Crandell ET AU RC 3.00 8.00
❑ 182 Darryl Daniel ET AU RC 3.00 8.00
❑ 183 Jesse Haynes ET AU 2.50 6.00
❑ 184 Matt Lytle ET AU RC 3.00 8.00
❑ 185 Deon Mitchell ET AU RC 3.00 8.00
❑ 186 Kendrick Nord ET AU RC 2.50 6.00
❑ 188 Selucio Sanford ET AU RC 3.00 8.00
❑ 189 Corey Thomas ET AU 2.50 6.00
❑ 190 Vershan Jackson ET AU RC 2.50 6.00
❑ 191 Jake Plummer PT AU 8.00 20.00
❑ 192 Jim Kelly PT AU 20.00 40.00
❑ 193 Bernie Kosar PT AU 10.00 25.00
❑ 194 Marvin Harrison PT AU 12.50 30.00
❑ 196 Kerry Collins PT AU 8.00 20.00
❑ 197 Kurt Warner PT AU 20.00 40.00
❑ 198 Jevon Kearse PT AU 8.00 20.00
❑ 199 Brad Johnson PT AU 6.00 15.00
❑ 200 Jeff George PT AU 6.00 15.00

2001 Playoff Contenders

❑ COMP.SET w/o RC's (100) 10.00 25.00
❑ 1 David Boston .20 .50
❑ 2 Jake Plummer .25 .60
❑ 3 Jamal Anderson .25 .60
❑ 4 Chris Chandler .25 .60
❑ 5 Elvis Grbac .25 .60
❑ 6 Brandon Stokley .25 .60
❑ 7 Travis Taylor .20 .50
❑ 8 Ray Lewis .30 .75
❑ 9 Rob Johnson .25 .60
❑ 10 Eric Moulds .25 .60
❑ 11 Tim Biakabutuka .20 .50
❑ 12 Muhsin Muhammad .25 .60
❑ 13 James Allen .20 .50
❑ 14 Brian Urlacher .40 1.00
❑ 15 Peter Warrick .25 .60
❑ 16 Corey Dillon .25 .60
❑ 17 Tim Couch .20 .50
❑ 18 Kevin Johnson .20 .50
❑ 19 Rickey Dudley .20 .50
❑ 20 Emmitt Smith .75 2.00
❑ 21 Joey Galloway .25 .60
❑ 22 Brian Griese .25 .60
❑ 23 Terrell Davis .30 .75
❑ 24 Mike Anderson .25 .60
❑ 25 Ed McCaffrey .25 .60
❑ 26 Rod Smith .25 .60

❑ 27 Charlie Batch .25 .60
❑ 28 James Stewart .20 .50
❑ 29 Germane Crowell .20 .50
❑ 30 Johnnie Morton .25 .60
❑ 31 Brett Favre 1.00 2.50
❑ 32 Ahman Green .30 .75
❑ 33 Antonio Freeman .30 .75
❑ 34 Peyton Manning .75 2.00
❑ 35 Edgerrin James .30 .75
❑ 36 Marvin Harrison .30 .75
❑ 37 Jerome Pathon .20 .50
❑ 38 Mark Brunell .30 .75
❑ 39 Fred Taylor .30 .75
❑ 40 Keenan McCardell .25 .60
❑ 41 Jimmy Smith .25 .60
❑ 42 Trent Green .30 .75
❑ 43 Priest Holmes .30 .75
❑ 44 Tony Gonzalez .25 .60
❑ 45 Derrick Alexander .20 .50
❑ 46 Jay Fiedler .25 .60
❑ 47 Lamar Smith .25 .60
❑ 48 Zach Thomas .30 .75
❑ 49 Oronde Gadsden .20 .50
❑ 50 Daunte Culpepper .30 .75
❑ 51 Randy Moss .40 1.00
❑ 52 Cris Carter .30 .75
❑ 53 Drew Bledsoe .30 .75
❑ 54 J.R. Redmond .20 .50
❑ 55 Troy Brown .25 .60
❑ 56 Aaron Brooks .25 .60
❑ 57 Ricky Williams .30 .75
❑ 58 Joe Horn .25 .60
❑ 59 Kerry Collins .25 .60
❑ 60 Tiki Barber .30 .75
❑ 61 Ron Dayne .25 .60
❑ 62 Ike Hilliard .25 .60
❑ 63 Vinny Testaverde .25 .60
❑ 64 Curtis Martin .30 .75
❑ 65 Wayne Chrebet .25 .60
❑ 66 Laveranues Coles .30 .75
❑ 67 Rich Gannon .25 .60
❑ 68 Tyrone Wheatley .25 .60
❑ 69 Tim Brown .30 .75
❑ 70 Jerry Rice .60 1.50
❑ 71 Donovan McNabb .40 1.00
❑ 72 Duce Staley .25 .60
❑ 73 Todd Pinkston .20 .50
❑ 74 Kordell Stewart .25 .60
❑ 75 Jerome Bettis .30 .75
❑ 76 Plaxico Burress .25 .60
❑ 77 Doug Flutie .30 .75
❑ 78 Junior Seau .30 .75
❑ 79 Jeff Garcia .25 .60
❑ 80 Garrison Hearst .25 .60
❑ 81 Terrell Owens .30 .75
❑ 82 Matt Hasselbeck .30 .75
❑ 83 Ricky Watters .25 .60
❑ 84 Shaun Alexander .30 .75
❑ 85 Darrell Jackson .25 .60
❑ 86 Kurt Warner .40 1.00
❑ 87 Marshall Faulk .30 .75
❑ 88 Isaac Bruce .30 .75
❑ 89 Torry Holt .25 .60
❑ 90 Brad Johnson .25 .60
❑ 91 Keyshawn Johnson .25 .60
❑ 92 Warrick Dunn .30 .75
❑ 93 Warren Sapp .25 .60
❑ 94 Steve McNair .30 .75
❑ 95 Eddie George .30 .75
❑ 96 Derrick Mason .25 .60
❑ 97 Jevon Kearse .25 .60
❑ 98 Stephen Davis .25 .60
❑ 99 Bruce Smith .30 .75
❑ 100 Michael Westbrook .20 .50
❑ 101 Adam Archuleta/50* RC 30.00 80.00
❑ 102 Alex Bannister AU RC 3.00 8.00
❑ 103 Alge Crumpler AU RC 6.00 15.00
❑ 104 Andre Carter AU/100* RC 15.00 40.00
❑ 105 Anthony Thomas AU/600* RC 5.00 12.00
❑ 106 Ben Leard AU RC 3.00 8.00
❑ 107 Bobby Newcombe AU RC 4.00 10.00
❑ 108 Brian Allen AU RC 3.00 8.00
❑ 109 Carlos Polk AU RC 3.00 8.00
❑ 110 Casey Hampton No Auto RC 4.00 10.00
❑ 111 Cedric Scott AU RC 3.00 8.00
❑ 112 Cedrick Wilson AU RC 5.00 12.00
❑ 113 Chad Johnson AU RC 40.00 80.00
❑ 114 C.Chambers AU/170* RC 75.00 150.00
❑ 115 Chris Weinke AU/350* RC 4.00 10.00
❑ 116 C.Buckhalter AU/590* RC 10.00 25.00
❑ 117 Damione Lewis AU RC 4.00 10.00
❑ 118 Dan Morgan AU RC 5.00 12.00
❑ 119 Daniel Guy AU RC 3.00 8.00
❑ 120 David Allen AU RC 3.00 8.00
❑ 121 David Terrell AU/500* RC 4.00 10.00
❑ 122 Ken Lucas AU/276* RC 4.00 10.00
❑ 123 D.McAllister AU/500* RC 20.00 50.00
❑ 124 Drew Brees AU/500* RC 400.00 550.00
❑ 125 Eddie Berlin AU RC 3.00 8.00
❑ 126 Boo Williams AU/50* RC 30.00 80.00
❑ 127 Ennis Davis AU RC 3.00 8.00
❑ 128 Freddie Mitchell AU RC 3.00 8.00
❑ 129 Gary Baxter AU RC 4.00 10.00
❑ 130 Gerard Warren AU/200* RC 6.00 15.00
❑ 131 Hakim Akbar AU RC 3.00 8.00
❑ 132 Heath Evans AU RC 4.00 10.00
❑ 133 Jabari Holloway AU RC 4.00 10.00
❑ 134 Jamal Reynolds AU/500* RC 4.00 10.00
❑ 135 James Jackson AU RC 4.00 10.00
❑ 136 Jamie Winborn AU RC 4.00 10.00
❑ 137 Javon Green AU RC 3.00 8.00
❑ 138 Jesse Palmer AU RC 5.00 12.00
❑ 139 Dominic Rhodes AU/300* RC 8.00 20.00
❑ 140 Josh Heupel AU/150* RC 15.00 40.00
❑ 141 Justin Smith AU RC 5.00 12.00
❑ 142 Karon Riley AU RC 3.00 8.00
❑ 143 Keith Adams/50* RC 25.00 60.00
❑ 144 Kendrell Bell AU RC 5.00 12.00
❑ 145 Kenny Smith AU RC 3.00 8.00
❑ 146 Ken.Walker AU/50* RC 25.00 60.00
❑ 147 Ken-Yon Rambo AU RC 3.00 8.00
❑ 148 Kevan Barlow AU RC 4.00 10.00
❑ 149 Koren Robinson AU/400* RC 5.00 12.00
❑ 150 L.Tomlinson AU/600 RC 200.00 400.00
❑ 151 LaMont Jordan AU/50* RC 50.00 120.00
❑ 152 Leonard Davis/50* RC 40.00 100.00
❑ 153 Marcus Stroud AU RC 4.00 10.00
❑ 154 Marques Tuiasosopo AU RC 4.00 10.00
❑ 155 Snoop Minnis AU/295* RC 4.00 10.00
❑ 156 Michael Bennett AU/600* RC 6.00 15.00
❑ 157 Michael Vick AU/327* RC 90.00 150.00
❑ 158 Mike McMahon AU/529* RC 4.00 10.00
❑ 159 Moran Norris AU RC 3.00 8.00
❑ 160 Morlon Greenwood AU RC 3.00 8.00
❑ 161 Nate Clements/50* RC 40.00 100.00
❑ 162 Quincy Carter AU SP RC 15.00 40.00
❑ 163 Quincy Morgan AU RC 4.00 10.00
❑ 164 Jamar Fletcher/50* RC 25.00 60.00
❑ 165 Reggie Germany AU RC 3.00 8.00
❑ 166 Reggie Wayne AU/400* RC 90.00 150.00
❑ 167 Reggie White AU RC 3.00 8.00
❑ 168 Richard Seymour/50* RC 40.00 100.00
❑ 169 Robert Carswell/50* RC 25.00 60.00
❑ 170 Robert Ferguson AU RC 5.00 12.00
❑ 171 Rod Gardner AU/75* RC 30.00 80.00
❑ 172 Ronney Daniels AU RC 3.00 8.00
❑ 173 Rudi Johnson AU RC 15.00 40.00
❑ 174 Sage Rosenfels AU/400* RC 8.00 20.00
❑ 175 Santana Moss AU/500* RC 15.00 40.00
❑ 176 Shaun Rogers AU RC 5.00 12.00
❑ 177 Houshmandzadeh AU RC 25.00 50.00
❑ 178 Tim Hasselbeck AU RC 4.00 10.00
❑ 179 Todd Heap AU/169* RC 40.00 80.00
❑ 180 Tony Stewart AU RC 4.00 10.00
❑ 181 Torrance Marshall AU RC 4.00 10.00
❑ 182 Travis Henry AU/369* RC 10.00 25.00
❑ 183 Travis Minor AU RC 4.00 10.00
❑ 184 Vinny Sutherland AU RC 3.00 8.00
❑ 185 Will Allen AU RC 5.00 12.00
❑ 186 Willie Howard AU RC 3.00 8.00
❑ 187 W.Middlebrooks/50* RC 30.00 80.00
❑ 188 Derrick Blaylock AU/200* RC 6.00 15.00
❑ 189 A.J. Feeley AU/200* RC 6.00 15.00
❑ 190 Steve Smith AU/300* RC 100.00 200.00
❑ 191 Onome Ojo AU/200* RC 5.00 12.00
❑ 192 Dee Brown AU/300* RC 3.00 8.00
❑ 193 Kevin Kasper AU/200* RC 6.00 15.00
❑ 194 Dave Dickenson AU/300* RC 4.00 10.00
❑ 195 Chris Barnes AU/200* RC 5.00 12.00
❑ 196 Scotty Anderson AU/300* RC 4.00 10.00
❑ 197 Chris Taylor AU/300* RC 3.00 8.00
❑ 198 Cedric James AU/300* RC 3.00 8.00
❑ 199 Justin McCareins AU/200* RC 6.00 15.00
❑ 200 Tommy Polley AU/200* RC 6.00 15.00

2002 Playoff Contenders

❑ COMP.SET w/o SP's (100) 10.00 25.00
❑ 1 Drew Bledsoe .30 .75
❑ 2 Travis Henry .25 .60
❑ 3 Eric Moulds .25 .60
❑ 4 Chris Chambers .30 .75
❑ 5 Ricky Williams .30 .75
❑ 6 Zach Thomas .30 .75
❑ 7 Tom Brady .75 2.00
❑ 8 Antowain Smith .25 .60
❑ 9 Troy Brown .25 .60
❑ 10 Curtis Martin .30 .75
❑ 11 Vinny Testaverde .25 .60
❑ 12 Chad Pennington .30 .75
❑ 13 Jeff Blake .25 .60
❑ 14 Jamal Lewis .25 .60
❑ 15 Ray Lewis .30 .75
❑ 16 Michael Westbrook .20 .50
❑ 17 Corey Dillon .25 .60
❑ 18 Peter Warrick .25 .60
❑ 19 Tim Couch .20 .50
❑ 20 Quincy Morgan .20 .50
❑ 21 Kevin Johnson .20 .50
❑ 22 Kordell Stewart .25 .60
❑ 23 Plaxico Burress .25 .60
❑ 24 Jerome Bettis .30 .75
❑ 25 James Allen .20 .50
❑ 26 Corey Bradford .20 .50
❑ 27 Mark Brunell .25 .60
❑ 28 Fred Taylor .30 .75
❑ 29 Jimmy Smith .25 .60
❑ 30 Peyton Manning .60 1.50
❑ 31 Reggie Wayne .30 .75
❑ 32 Marvin Harrison .30 .75
❑ 33 Edgerrin James .30 .75
❑ 34 Steve McNair .30 .75
❑ 35 Eddie George .25 .60
❑ 36 Jevon Kearse .25 .60
❑ 37 Derrick Mason .25 .60
❑ 38 Brian Griese .25 .60
❑ 39 Terrell Davis .30 .75
❑ 40 Ed McCaffrey .25 .60
❑ 41 Rod Smith .25 .60
❑ 42 Trent Green .25 .60
❑ 43 Priest Holmes .30 .75
❑ 44 Johnnie Morton .25 .60
❑ 45 Tony Gonzalez .25 .60
❑ 46 Rich Gannon .25 .60
❑ 47 Tim Brown .30 .75
❑ 48 Jerry Rice .60 1.50
❑ 49 Charlie Garner .25 .60
❑ 50 Drew Brees .50 1.25
❑ 51 LaDainian Tomlinson .50 1.25
❑ 52 Junior Seau .30 .75
❑ 53 Quincy Carter .20 .50
❑ 54 Emmitt Smith .75 2.00
❑ 55 Joey Galloway .25 .60
❑ 56 Kerry Collins .25 .60
❑ 57 Tiki Barber .30 .75
❑ 58 Michael Strahan .30 .75
❑ 59 Donovan McNabb .40 1.00
❑ 60 Duce Staley .25 .60
❑ 61 Antonio Freeman .30 .75
❑ 62 Derrius Thompson .20 .50
❑ 63 Stephen Davis .25 .60
❑ 64 Rod Gardner .20 .50
❑ 65 Anthony Thomas .25 .60
❑ 66 Marty Booker .25 .60
❑ 67 Brian Urlacher .40 1.00
❑ 68 James Stewart .20 .50
❑ 69 Az-Zahir Hakim .20 .50
❑ 70 Brett Favre .75 2.00
❑ 71 Ahman Green .25 .60
❑ 72 Donald Driver .30 .75
❑ 73 Daunte Culpepper .25 .60

Card	Low	High
74 Michael Bennett	.25	.60
75 Randy Moss	.30	.75
76 Michael Vick	.30	.75
77 Warrick Dunn	.25	.60
78 Chris Weinke	.20	.50
79 Lamar Smith	.25	.60
80 Steve Smith	.30	.75
81 Aaron Brooks	.25	.60
82 Deuce McAllister	.30	.75
83 Joe Horn	.25	.60
84 Brad Johnson	.25	.60
85 Keyshawn Johnson	.25	.60
86 Mike Alstott	.25	.60
87 Warren Sapp	.25	.60
88 Jake Plummer	.25	.60
89 Thomas Jones	.25	.60
90 David Boston	.20	.50
91 Kurt Warner	.30	.75
92 Marshall Faulk	.30	.75
93 Isaac Bruce	.30	.75
94 Torry Holt	.30	.75
95 Jeff Garcia	.25	.60
96 Garrison Hearst	.25	.60
97 Kevan Barlow	.20	.50
98 Terrell Owens	.30	.75
99 Trent Dilfer	.25	.60
100 Shaun Alexander	.30	.75
101 Adrian Peterson AU/360 RC	6.00	15.00
102 A.Haynesworth No Auto RC	8.00	20.00
103 Alex Brown AU/410 RC	6.00	15.00
104 Andra Davis AU/510 RC	3.00	8.00
105 Andre Davis AU/360 RC	5.00	12.00
106 Andre Lott AU/750 RC	3.00	8.00
107 Anthony Weaver AU/450 RC	3.00	8.00
108 Antonio Bryant AU/165 RC	15.00	40.00
109 A.Randle El AU/135 RC	15.00	40.00
110 Ashley Lelie AU/360 RC	6.00	15.00
111 Brian Poli-Dixon AU/460 RC	3.00	8.00
112 B.Westbrook AU/600 RC	50.00	100.00
113 Bryant McKinnie AU/600 RC	3.00	8.00
114 C Hutchinson AU/450 RC	3.00	8.00
115 Charles Grant AU/450 RC	5.00	12.00
116 Chester Taylor AU/315 RC	12.00	30.00
117 Cliff Russell AU/545 RC	3.00	8.00
118 Clinton Portis AU/360 RC	40.00	80.00
119 R.McMichael AU/400 RC	6.00	15.00
120 D.Anderson AU/460 RC	4.00	10.00
121 Daniel Graham AU/185 RC	6.00	15.00
122 David Carr AU/250 RC	10.00	25.00
123 David Garrard AU/310 RC	30.00	60.00
124 Deion Branch AU/650 RC	5.00	12.00
125 John Simon AU/400 RC	4.00	10.00
126 DeShaun Foster AU/310 RC	8.00	20.00
127 Donte Stallworth AU/302 RC	6.00	15.00
128 Dwight Freeney AU/410 RC	35.00	60.00
129 Ed Reed AU/550 RC	40.00	80.00
130 Eric Crouch AU/280 RC	8.00	20.00
131 Freddie Milons AU/380 RC	4.00	10.00
132 Jabar Gaffney AU/315 RC	6.00	15.00
133 Javon Walker AU/435 RC	6.00	15.00
134 J.Shockey AU/160 RC	60.00	100.00
135 Jerramy Stevens AU/250 RC	8.00	20.00
136 Joey Harrington AU/250 RC	8.00	20.00
137 John Henderson AU/560 RC	5.00	12.00
138 Jonathan Wells AU/485 RC	5.00	12.00
139 Josh McCown AU/595 RC	5.00	12.00
140 Josh Reed AU/290 RC	6.00	15.00
141 Josh Scobey AU/615 RC	4.00	10.00
142 Julius Peppers AU/40 RC	350.00	600.00
143 Kalimba Edwards AU/510 RC	4.00	10.00
144 Kelly Campbell AU/360 RC	5.00	12.00
145 Ken Simonton AU/650 RC	3.00	8.00
146 Keyuo Craver AU/850 RC	3.00	8.00
147 Kahlil Hill AU/850 RC	3.00	8.00
148 Kurt Kittner AU/235 RC	5.00	12.00
149 Ladell Betts AU/600 RC	8.00	20.00
150 Lamar Gordon AU/600 RC	5.00	12.00
151 Levar Fisher AU/760 RC	3.00	8.00
152 Lito Sheppard AU/410 RC	10.00	25.00
153 Luke Staley AU/360 RC	4.00	10.00
154 Marquise Walker AU/330 RC	4.00	10.00
155 Maurice Morris AU/153 RC	15.00	40.00
156 Mike Rumph AU/510 RC	3.00	8.00
157 Mike Williams AU/500 RC	3.00	8.00
158 Najeh Davenport AU/460 RC	5.00	12.00
159 Napoleon Harris AU/900 RC	4.00	10.00
160 Patrick Ramsey AU/575 RC	5.00	12.00
161 Buchanon No AU/310 RC	10.00	25.00
162 Quentin Jammer AU/300 RC	8.00	20.00
163 Randy Fasani AU/500 RC	4.00	10.00
164 Reche Caldwell AU/340 RC	6.00	15.00
165 Robert Thomas AU/460 RC	3.00	8.00
166 Rocky Calmus AU/385 RC	5.00	12.00
167 Rohan Davey AU/295 RC	8.00	20.00
168 Ron Johnson AU/385 RC	5.00	12.00
169 Roy Williams AU/250 RC	20.00	40.00
170 Ryan Sims No AU/360 RC	6.00	15.00
171 Tavon Mason AU/690 RC	3.00	8.00
172 Terry Charles AU/750 RC	3.00	8.00
173 T.J. Duckett AU/335 RC	8.00	20.00
174 Tim Carter AU/600 RC	4.00	10.00
175 Travis Stephens AU/170 RC	5.00	12.00
176 Trev Faulk AU/600 RC	3.00	8.00
177 Wendell Bryant AU/560 RC	3.00	8.00
178 William Green AU/317 RC	5.00	12.00
179 Woody Dantzler AU/185 RC	6.00	15.00
180 Tony Fisher AU/340 RC	5.00	12.00
181 Javin Hunter AU/400 RC	4.00	10.00
182 Daryl Jones AU/400 RC	4.00	10.00
183 Jesse Chatman AU/400 RC	4.00	10.00
184 J.T. O'Sullivan AU/340 RC	6.00	15.00
185 Josh Norman AU/340 RC	4.00	10.00
186 James Mungro AU/100 RC	25.00	50.00

2003 Playoff Contenders

Card	Low	High
COMP.SET w/o SP's (100)	7.50	20.00
1 Roy Williams	.30	.75
2 Antonio Bryant	.30	.75
3 Jeremy Shockey	.30	.75
4 Kerry Collins	.25	.60
5 Tiki Barber	.30	.75
6 Michael Strahan	.25	.60
7 Donovan McNabb	.30	.75
8 Duce Staley	.25	.60
9 Todd Pinkston	.20	.50
10 Patrick Ramsey	.25	.60
11 Laveranues Coles	.25	.60
12 Rod Gardner	.20	.50
13 Drew Bledsoe	.30	.75
14 Travis Henry	.25	.60
15 Eric Moulds	.25	.60
16 Josh Reed	.20	.50
17 Ricky Williams	.25	.60
18 Jay Fiedler	.25	.60
19 Chris Chambers	.25	.60
20 Zach Thomas	.30	.75
21 Junior Seau	.30	.75
22 Tom Brady	.75	2.00
23 Troy Brown	.25	.60
24 Chad Pennington	.30	.75
25 Curtis Martin	.30	.75
26 Santana Moss	.25	.60
27 Emmitt Smith	.75	2.00
28 Jeff Garcia	.30	.75
29 Terrell Owens	.30	.75
30 Kevan Barlow	.20	.50
31 Shaun Alexander	.30	.75
32 Matt Hasselbeck	.25	.60
33 Koren Robinson	.25	.60
34 Kurt Warner	.30	.75
35 Marshall Faulk	.30	.75
36 Torry Holt	.30	.75
37 Isaac Bruce	.30	.75
38 Clinton Portis	.40	1.00
39 Jake Plummer	.25	.60
40 Rod Smith	.25	.60
41 Ed McCaffrey	.25	.60
42 Ashley Lelie	.20	.50
43 Priest Holmes	.30	.75
44 Trent Green	.25	.60
45 Tony Gonzalez	.25	.60
46 Jerry Rice	.60	1.50
47 Rich Gannon	.25	.60
48 Tim Brown	.30	.75
49 Jerry Porter	.25	.60
50 Charles Woodson	.25	.60
51 LaDainian Tomlinson	.40	1.00
52 Drew Brees	.30	.75
53 David Boston	.20	.50
54 Brian Urlacher	.50	1.25
55 Kordell Stewart	.25	.60
56 Marty Booker	.25	.60
57 Joey Harrington	.25	.60
58 Brett Favre	.75	2.00
59 Ahman Green	.30	.75
60 Donald Driver	.30	.75
61 Javon Walker	.25	.60
62 Randy Moss	.30	.75
63 Daunte Culpepper	.30	.75
64 Michael Bennett	.25	.60
65 Jamal Lewis	.30	.75
66 Ray Lewis	.30	.75
67 Corey Dillon	.25	.60
68 Chad Johnson	.30	.75
69 William Green	.20	.50
70 Tim Couch	.20	.50
71 Quincy Morgan	.20	.50
72 Plaxico Burress	.30	.75
73 Tommy Maddox	.25	.60
74 Hines Ward	.30	.75
75 Antwaan Randle El	.25	.60
76 Michael Vick	.30	.75
77 Peerless Price	.20	.50
78 Warrick Dunn	.25	.60
79 T.J. Duckett	.25	.60
80 Julius Peppers	.30	.75
81 Stephen Davis	.25	.60
82 Deuce McAllister	.30	.75
83 Aaron Brooks	.25	.60
84 Joe Horn	.25	.60
85 Donte Stallworth	.25	.60
86 Mike Alstott	.30	.75
87 Brad Johnson	.25	.60
88 Keyshawn Johnson	.30	.75
89 Warren Sapp	.25	.60
90 David Carr	.30	.75
91 Jabar Gaffney	.20	.50
92 Peyton Manning	.60	1.50
93 Edgerrin James	.30	.75
94 Marvin Harrison	.30	.75
95 Mark Brunell	.25	.60
96 Fred Taylor	.30	.75
97 Jimmy Smith	.25	.60
98 Steve McNair	.30	.75
99 Eddie George	.25	.60
100 Jevon Kearse	.25	.60
101 Lee Suggs AU/499 RC	5.00	12.00
102 Charles Rogers AU/204 RC	15.00	40.00
103 Brandon Lloyd AU/589 RC	6.00	15.00
104 Terrence Edwards AU/399 RC	4.00	10.00
105 Mike Pinkard AU/849 RC	4.00	10.00
106 DeWayne White AU/524 RC	4.00	10.00
107 Jero McDougle AU/339 RC	4.00	10.00
108 Jimmy Kennedy AU/514 RC	5.00	12.00
109 William Joseph AU/764 RC	4.00	10.00
110 E.J. Henderson AU/774 RC	5.00	12.00
111 Mike Doss AU/574 RC	6.00	15.00
112A C.Simms Blu AU/310 RC	15.00	40.00
112B C.Simms Blk AU/79 RC	40.00	80.00
113 Cecil Sapp AU/474 RC	4.00	10.00
114 Justin Gage AU/579 RC	6.00	15.00
115 Sam Aiken AU/664 RC	6.00	15.00
116 Doug Gabriel AU/389 RC	5.00	12.00
117 Jason Witten AU/599 RC	75.00	125.00
118 Bennie Joppru AU/449 RC	4.00	10.00
119 Chris Kelsay AU/864 RC	5.00	12.00
120 John.Sullivan/924 RC	2.50	6.00
121 Kevin Williams AU/764 RC	10.00	20.00
122 Rien Long AU/849 RC	4.00	10.00
123 Kenny Peterson/674 RC	3.00	8.00
124 Boss Bailey AU/564 RC	5.00	12.00
125 Denn Weathersby AU/774 RC	4.00	10.00
126A Car.Palmer Blk AU/36 RC	350.00	600.00
126B Car.Palmer Blu AU/158 RC	200.00	400.00
127 Byron Leftwich AU/169 RC	20.00	50.00
128 Kyle Boller AU/439 RC	7.50	20.00
129 Rex Grossman AU/494 RC	15.00	40.00
130 Dave Ragone AU/344 RC	4.00	10.00
131 Brian St.Pierre AU/554 RC	6.00	15.00
132 Kliff Kingsbury AU/879 RC	5.00	12.00
133 Seneca Wallace AU/864 RC	10.00	25.00
134 Larry Johnson AU/344 RC	25.00	50.00
135 Will McGahee AU/369 RC	15.00	40.00
136 Justin Fargas AU/354 RC	10.00	25.00

❑ 137 Onterrio Smith AU/414 RC 5.00 12.00
❑ 138 Chris Brown AU/279 RC 7.50 20.00
❑ 139 Musa Smith AU/379 RC 5.00 12.00
❑ 140 Artose Pinner AU/364 RC 4.00 10.00
❑ 141 Andre Johnson AU/199 RC 100.00 175.00
❑ 142 Kell Washington AU/472 RC 5.00 12.00
❑ 143 Taylor Jacobs AU/349 RC 5.00 12.00
❑ 144 Bryant Johnson AU/389 RC 6.00 15.00
❑ 145 Tyrone Calico AU/499 RC 5.00 12.00
❑ 146 Anquan Boldin AU/524 RC 40.00 80.00
❑ 147 Bethel Johnson AU/484 RC 5.00 12.00
❑ 148 Nate Burleson AU/549 RC 5.00 12.00
❑ 149 Kevin Curtis AU/455 RC 10.00 25.00
❑ 150 Dallas Clark AU/539 RC 40.00 80.00
❑ 151 Teyo Johnson AU/389 RC 5.00 12.00
❑ 152 Terrell Suggs AU/564 RC 10.00 25.00
❑ 153 DeWayne Robertson/689 RC 3.00 8.00
❑ 154 Terence Newman AU/364 RC 12.00 30.00
❑ 155 Marcus Trufant AU/739 RC 6.00 15.00
❑ 156 Tony Romo AU/999 RC 200.00 350.00
❑ 157 Brooks Bollinger AU/974 RC 6.00 15.00
❑ 158 Ken Dorsey AU/774 RC 5.00 12.00
❑ 159 Kirk Farmer AU/999 RC 5.00 12.00
❑ 160 Jason Gesser AU/999 RC 5.00 12.00
❑ 161 Brock Forsey AU/999 RC 5.00 12.00
❑ 162 Quentin Griffin AU/999 RC 5.00 12.00
❑ 163 Avon Cobourne AU/974 RC 4.00 10.00
❑ 164 Domanick Davis AU/999 RC 6.00 15.00
❑ 165 Tony Hollings AU/974 RC 5.00 12.00
❑ 166 LaBran.Toefield AU/799 RC 5.00 12.00
❑ 167 Arlen Harris AU/974 RC 4.00 10.00
❑ 168 Sult McCullough AU/989 RC 4.00 10.00
❑ 169 Visant Shiancoe AU/999 RC 10.00 20.00
❑ 170 L.J. Smith AU/974 RC 6.00 15.00
❑ 171 LaTaren Dunbar AU/999 RC 4.00 10.00
❑ 172 Walter Young AU/889 RC 4.00 10.00
❑ 173 Bobby Wade AU/989 RC 5.00 12.00
❑ 174 Zuriel Smith AU/989 RC 4.00 10.00
❑ 175 Adrian Madise AU/999 RC 4.00 10.00
❑ 176 Ken Hamlin AU/989 RC 6.00 15.00
❑ 177 Carl Ford AU/999 RC 4.00 10.00
❑ 178 Cortez Hankton AU/989 RC 5.00 12.00
❑ 179 J.R. Tolver AU/889 RC 5.00 12.00
❑ 180 Keenan Howry AU/999 RC 4.00 10.00
❑ 181 Billy McMullen AU/899 RC 4.00 10.00
❑ 182 Arnaz Battle AU/989 RC 7.50 20.00
❑ 183 Shaun McDonald AU/899 RC 6.00 15.00
❑ 184 Andre Woolfolk AU/989 RC 5.00 12.00
❑ 185 Sammy Davis AU/999 RC 5.00 12.00
❑ 186 Calvin Pace AU/999 RC 5.00 12.00
❑ 187 Michael Haynes AU/999 RC 4.00 10.00
❑ 188 Ty Warren AU/999 RC 6.00 15.00
❑ 189 Nick Barnett AU/999 RC 12.50 25.00
❑ 190 Troy Polamalu AU/989 RC 125.00 200.00
❑ 191 Eric Parker AU/589 RC 6.00 15.00
❑ 192 Justin Griffith AU/589 RC 5.00 12.00
❑ 193 David Tyree AU/599 RC 10.00 25.00
❑ 194 Pisa Tinoisamoa/599 RC 4.00 10.00
❑ 195 Rashean Mathis AU/589 RC 5.00 12.00
❑ 196 Mike Sherman AU/574 RC 10.00 25.00
❑ 197 Dave Wannstedt AU/574 RC 7.50 20.00
❑ 198 Dick Vermeil AU/574 RC 10.00 25.00
❑ 199 Tony Dungy AU/574 RC 30.00 60.00
❑ 200 Mike Martz AU/574 RC 7.50 20.00

2004 Playoff Contenders

❑ COMP.SET w/o SP's (100) 7.50 20.00
❑ 1 Anquan Boldin .30 .75
❑ 2 Emmitt Smith .75 2.00
❑ 3 Josh McCown .25 .60
❑ 4 Michael Vick .30 .75
❑ 5 Peerless Price .25 .60
❑ 6 T.J. Duckett .25 .60
❑ 7 Warrick Dunn .25 .60
❑ 8 Jamal Lewis .25 .60
❑ 9 Kyle Boller .25 .60
❑ 10 Ray Lewis .30 .75
❑ 11 Drew Bledsoe .30 .75
❑ 12 Eric Moulds .25 .60
❑ 13 Travis Henry .25 .60
❑ 14 Willis McGahee .30 .75
❑ 15 DeShaun Foster .25 .60
❑ 16 Jake Delhomme .25 .60
❑ 17 Stephen Davis .25 .60
❑ 18 Steve Smith .30 .75
❑ 19 Brian Urlacher .30 .75
❑ 20 Rex Grossman .30 .75
❑ 21 Thomas Jones .25 .60
❑ 22 Carson Palmer .40 1.00
❑ 23 Chad Johnson .25 .60
❑ 24 Rudi Johnson .25 .60
❑ 25 Jeff Garcia .30 .75
❑ 26 Lee Suggs .30 .75
❑ 27 William Green .20 .50
❑ 28 Keyshawn Johnson .25 .60
❑ 29 Roy Williams S .25 .60
❑ 30 Eddie George .25 .60
❑ 31 Ashley Lelie .25 .60
❑ 32 Jake Plummer .25 .60
❑ 33 Quentin Griffin .25 .60
❑ 34 Rod Smith .25 .60
❑ 35 Charles Rogers .25 .60
❑ 36 Joey Harrington .25 .60
❑ 37 Ahman Green .30 .75
❑ 38 Brett Favre .75 2.00
❑ 39 Javon Walker .25 .60
❑ 40 Andre Johnson .30 .75
❑ 41 David Carr .25 .60
❑ 42 Domanick Davis .25 .60
❑ 43 Edgerrin James .30 .75
❑ 44 Marvin Harrison .30 .75
❑ 45 Peyton Manning .60 1.50
❑ 46 Byron Leftwich .30 .75
❑ 47 Fred Taylor .25 .60
❑ 48 Jimmy Smith .25 .60
❑ 49 Priest Holmes .30 .75
❑ 50 Tony Gonzalez .30 .75
❑ 51 Trent Green .25 .60
❑ 52 A.J. Feeley .25 .60
❑ 53 Chris Chambers .25 .60
❑ 54 Deion Sanders .30 .75
❑ 55 Daunte Culpepper .30 .75
❑ 56 Michael Bennett .25 .60
❑ 57 Randy Moss .30 .75
❑ 58 Corey Dillon .25 .60
❑ 59 Deion Branch .25 .60
❑ 60 Tom Brady .75 2.00
❑ 61 Aaron Brooks .25 .60
❑ 62 Deuce McAllister .30 .75
❑ 63 Donte Stallworth .25 .60
❑ 64 Joe Horn .25 .60
❑ 65 Amani Toomer .25 .60
❑ 66 Jeremy Shockey .25 .60
❑ 67 Michael Strahan .25 .60
❑ 68 Tiki Barber .30 .75
❑ 69 Chad Pennington .30 .75
❑ 70 Curtis Martin .30 .75
❑ 71 Santana Moss .25 .60
❑ 72 Jerry Porter .25 .60
❑ 73 Jerry Rice .60 1.50
❑ 74 Warren Sapp .25 .60
❑ 75 Brian Westbrook .30 .75
❑ 76 Donovan McNabb .30 .75
❑ 77 Jevon Kearse .25 .60
❑ 78 Terrell Owens .30 .75
❑ 79 Antwaan Randle El .25 .60
❑ 80 Hines Ward .30 .75
❑ 81 Jerome Bettis .30 .75
❑ 82 LaDainian Tomlinson .40 1.00
❑ 83 Kevan Barlow .25 .60
❑ 84 Tim Rattay .20 .50
❑ 85 Koren Robinson .30 .75
❑ 86 Matt Hasselbeck .30 .75
❑ 87 Shaun Alexander .30 .75
❑ 88 Isaac Bruce .25 .60
❑ 89 Marc Bulger .25 .60
❑ 90 Marshall Faulk .30 .75
❑ 91 Torry Holt .30 .75
❑ 92 Brad Johnson .25 .60
❑ 93 Mike Alstott .25 .60
❑ 94 Chris Brown .25 .60
❑ 95 Derrick Mason .25 .60
❑ 96 Steve McNair .30 .75
❑ 97 Clinton Portis .30 .75
❑ 98 LaVar Arrington .25 .60
❑ 99 Laveranues Coles .25 .60
❑ 100 Mark Brunell .25 .60
❑ 101 Adimchinobe Echemandu AU RC 5.00 12.00
❑ 102 Ahmad Carroll AU/574* RC 6.00 15.00
❑ 103 Andy Hall AU RC 5.00 12.00
❑ 104 B.J. Johnson AU RC 4.00 10.00
❑ 105 B.J. Symons AU RC 4.00 10.00
❑ 106 Roethlisberger AU/541* RC 175.00 300.00
❑ 107 Ben Troupe AU/540* RC 5.00 12.00
❑ 108 Ben Watson AU/660* RC 6.00 15.00
❑ 109 Bernard Berrian AU/653* RC 10.00 25.00
❑ 110 Brandon Miree AU RC 4.00 10.00
❑ 111 Bruce Perry AU RC 4.00 10.00
❑ 112 Carlos Francis AU RC 4.00 10.00
❑ 113 Casey Bramlet AU RC 4.00 10.00
❑ 114 Cedric Cobbs AU/630* RC 5.00 12.00
❑ 115 Chris Gamble AU/490* RC 5.00 12.00
❑ 116 Chris Perry AU/478* RC 8.00 20.00
❑ 117 Clarence Moore AU RC 5.00 12.00
❑ 118 Cody Pickett AU RC 5.00 12.00
❑ 119 Craig Krenzel AU RC 6.00 15.00
❑ 120 D.J. Hackett AU/325* RC 8.00 20.00
❑ 121 D.J. Williams AU/490* RC 6.00 15.00
❑ 122 Darius Watts AU RC 5.00 12.00
❑ 123 DeAngelo Hall AU RC 10.00 25.00
❑ 124 Derrick Hamilton AU/373* RC 5.00 12.00
❑ 125 Derrick Ward AU RC 10.00 25.00
❑ 126 Devard Darling AU/325* RC 6.00 15.00
❑ 127 D.Henderson AU/475* RC 10.00 25.00
❑ 128 Drew Carter AU RC 6.00 15.00
❑ 129 Drew Henson AU/415* RC 4.00 10.00
❑ 130 D.Robinson AU/660* RC 5.00 12.00
❑ 131 Eli Manning AU/372* RC 125.00 250.00
❑ 132 Ernest Wilford AU/365* RC 8.00 20.00
❑ 133 Greg Jones AU/553* RC 8.00 20.00
❑ 134 J.P. Losman AU/358* RC 10.00 25.00
❑ 135 Jamaar Taylor AU RC 4.00 10.00
❑ 136 Jared Lorenzen AU RC 5.00 12.00
❑ 137 Jarrett Payton AU RC 5.00 12.00
❑ 138 Jason Babin AU RC 5.00 12.00
❑ 139 Jeff Smoker AU RC 5.00 12.00
❑ 140 J.Cotchery AU/325* RC 10.00 25.00
❑ 141 Jim Sorgi AU RC 6.00 15.00
❑ 142 John Navarre AU RC 5.00 12.00
❑ 143 Johnnie Morant AU/325* RC 6.00 15.00
❑ 144 Jonathan Vilma AU SP RC 6.00 15.00
❑ 145 Josh Harris AU/555* RC 4.00 10.00
❑ 146 Julius Jones AU/252* RC 25.00 50.00
❑ 147 Keary Colbert AU/495* RC 5.00 12.00
❑ 148 Kel.Winslow AU/135* RC 40.00 100.00
❑ 149 Kenechi Udeze AU/475* RC 6.00 15.00
❑ 150 Kevin Jones AU/327* RC 10.00 25.00
❑ 151 L.Fitzgerald AU/50* RC 500.00 800.00
❑ 152 Lee Evans AU/375* RC 12.00 30.00
❑ 153 Luke McCown AU/543* RC 6.00 15.00
❑ 154 Matt Mauck AU RC 5.00 12.00
❑ 155 Matt Schaub AU/367* RC 50.00 100.00
❑ 156 Maurice Mann AU RC 4.00 10.00
❑ 157 Mewelde Moore AU/435* RC 10.00 25.00
❑ 158 Michael Clayton AU/325* RC 10.00 25.00
❑ 159 Michael Jenkins AU/412* RC 10.00 25.00
❑ 160 M.Turner AU/535* RC 30.00 80.00
❑ 161 P.K. Sam AU/300* RC 5.00 12.00
❑ 162 Philip Rivers AU/556* RC 90.00 150.00
❑ 163 Quincy Wilson AU/350* RC 6.00 15.00
❑ 164 Ran Carthon AU RC 4.00 10.00
❑ 165 Rashaun Woods AU RC 4.00 10.00
❑ 166 Re.Williams AU/336* RC 10.00 25.00
❑ 167 R.Colclough AU/640* RC 6.00 15.00
❑ 168 Robert Gallery AU/310* RC 10.00 25.00
❑ 169 Roy Williams AU/564* RC 15.00 40.00
❑ 170 Samie Parker AU/356* RC 6.00 15.00
❑ 171 Sean Jones AU RC 5.00 12.00
❑ 172 S.Taylor/575* RC No Auto 8.00 20.00
❑ 173 Sloan Thomas AU RC 5.00 12.00
❑ 174 Steven Jackson AU/333* RC 40.00 80.00
❑ 175 Tatum Bell AU/539* RC 8.00 20.00
❑ 176 Tommie Harris AU/365* RC 8.00 20.00
❑ 177 Triandos Luke AU RC 4.00 10.00
❑ 178 Troy Fleming AU RC 4.00 10.00
❑ 179 Vince Wilfork AU/315* RC 8.00 20.00
❑ 180 Will Smith AU/565* RC 6.00 15.00
❑ 181 Marcus Tubbs AU RC 4.00 10.00
❑ 182 Michael Boulware AU RC 6.00 15.00
❑ 183 Kris Wilson AU RC 5.00 12.00
❑ 184 Richard Smith AU RC 4.00 10.00
❑ 185 Teddy Lehman AU RC 5.00 12.00
❑ 186 Chris Cooley AU RC 35.00 60.00

❑ 187 Thomas Tapeh AU RC 5.00 12.00
❑ 188A Willie Parker Blk AU RC 25.00 60.00
❑ 188B Willie Parker Blu AU RC 50.00 100.00
❑ 189 Patrick Crayton AU RC 15.00 30.00
❑ 190 Kendrick Starling AU RC 4.00 10.00
❑ 191 B.J. Sams AU RC 5.00 12.00
❑ 192 Derick Armstrong AU RC 4.00 10.00
❑ 193 Wes Welker AU RC 40.00 80.00
❑ 194 Erik Coleman AU RC 5.00 12.00
❑ 195 Gibril Wilson AU RC 6.00 15.00
❑ 196 Andy Reid AU/335* RC 10.00 25.00
❑ 197 Brian Billick AU/585* RC 8.00 20.00
❑ 198 Jeff Fisher AU/585* RC 10.00 25.00
❑ 199 Jon Gruden AU/585* RC 8.00 20.00
❑ 200 Marvin Lewjs AU/585* RC 8.00 20.00

2005 Playoff Contenders

❑ COMP.SET w/o RC's (100) 7.50 20.00
❑ AU PRINT RUNS ANNOUNCED BY PLAYOFF
❑ UNPRICED CHAMPION.PRINT RUN 1 SET
❑ 1 Anquan Boldin .25 .60
❑ 2 Kurt Warner .30 .75
❑ 3 Larry Fitzgerald .30 .75
❑ 4 Michael Vick .30 .75
❑ 5 T.J. Duckett .20 .50
❑ 6 Warrick Dunn .25 .60
❑ 7 Derrick Mason .25 .60
❑ 8 Jamal Lewis .25 .60
❑ 9 Kyle Boller .25 .60
❑ 10 Ray Lewis .30 .75
❑ 11 J.P. Losman .25 .60
❑ 12 Lee Evans .25 .60
❑ 13 Willis McGahee .30 .75
❑ 14 DeShaun Foster .25 .60
❑ 15 Jake Delhomme .30 .75
❑ 16 Steve Smith .30 .75
❑ 17 Brian Urlacher .30 .75
❑ 18 Muhsin Muhammad .25 .60
❑ 19 Rex Grossman .30 .75
❑ 20 Carson Palmer .30 .75
❑ 21 Chad Johnson .25 .60
❑ 22 Rudi Johnson .25 .60
❑ 23 Lee Suggs .25 .60
❑ 24 Trent Dilfer .25 .60
❑ 25 Drew Bledsoe .30 .75
❑ 26 Jason Witten .30 .75
❑ 27 Julius Jones .30 .75
❑ 28 Keyshawn Johnson .25 .60
❑ 29 Ashley Lelie .20 .50
❑ 30 Jake Plummer .25 .60
❑ 31 Rod Smith .25 .60
❑ 32 Tatum Bell .25 .60
❑ 33 Joey Harrington .30 .75
❑ 34 Kevin Jones .25 .60
❑ 35 Roy Williams WR .30 .75
❑ 36 Ahman Green .30 .75
❑ 37 Brett Favre .75 2.00
❑ 38 Javon Walker .25 .60
❑ 39 Andre Johnson .25 .60
❑ 40 David Carr .25 .60
❑ 41 Domanick Davis .20 .50
❑ 42 Edgerrin James .25 .60
❑ 43 Marvin Harrison .30 .75
❑ 44 Peyton Manning .50 1.25
❑ 45 Reggie Wayne .25 .60
❑ 46 Byron Leftwich .25 .60
❑ 47 Fred Taylor .30 .75
❑ 48 Jimmy Smith .25 .60
❑ 49 Priest Holmes .30 .75
❑ 50 Tony Gonzalez .25 .60
❑ 51 Trent Green .25 .60
❑ 52 Chris Chambers .25 .60
❑ 53 Ricky Williams .25 .60
❑ 54 Daunte Culpepper .30 .75
❑ 55 Michael Bennett .25 .60
❑ 56 Nate Burleson .25 .60
❑ 57 Corey Dillon .25 .60
❑ 58 Deion Branch .25 .60
❑ 59 Tom Brady .60 1.50
❑ 60 Aaron Brooks .20 .50
❑ 61 Deuce McAllister .30 .75
❑ 62 Joe Horn .25 .60
❑ 63 Eli Manning .60 1.50
❑ 64 Jeremy Shockey .30 .75
❑ 65 Plaxico Burress .25 .60
❑ 66 Tiki Barber .30 .75
❑ 67 Chad Pennington .30 .75
❑ 68 Curtis Martin .30 .75
❑ 69 Laveranues Coles .25 .60
❑ 70 Kerry Collins .25 .60
❑ 71 LaMont Jordan .25 .60
❑ 72 Randy Moss .30 .75
❑ 73 Brian Westbrook .30 .75
❑ 74 Donovan McNabb .30 .75
❑ 75 Terrell Owens .30 .75
❑ 76 Ben Roethlisberger .75 2.00
❑ 77 Duce Staley .25 .60
❑ 78 Hines Ward .30 .75
❑ 79 Jerome Bettis .30 .75
❑ 80 Antonio Gates .30 .75
❑ 81 Drew Brees .30 .75
❑ 82 LaDainian Tomlinson .40 1.00
❑ 83 Brandon Lloyd .20 .50
❑ 84 Kevan Barlow .20 .50
❑ 85 Darrell Jackson .25 .60
❑ 86 Matt Hasselbeck .25 .60
❑ 87 Shaun Alexander .30 .75
❑ 88 Isaac Bruce .25 .60
❑ 89 Marc Bulger .25 .60
❑ 90 Steven Jackson .40 1.00
❑ 91 Torry Holt .25 .60
❑ 92 Brian Griese .25 .60
❑ 93 Derrick Brooks .25 .60
❑ 94 Chris Brown .25 .60
❑ 95 Drew Bennett .25 .60
❑ 96 Steve McNair .30 .75
❑ 97 Travis Henry .25 .60
❑ 98 Clinton Portis .30 .75
❑ 99 LaVar Arrington .30 .75
❑ 100 Santana Moss .25 .60
❑ 101 Aaron Rodgers AU/530* RC 125.00 200.00
❑ 102 Adam Jones AU RC 10.00 25.00
❑ 103 A.McPherson AU/365* RC 20.00 40.00
❑ 104 Alvin Pearman AU RC 4.00 10.00
❑ 105 Airese Currie AU RC 5.00 12.00
❑ 106 Alex Smith QB AU/401* RC 30.00 60.00
❑ 107 Andrew Walter AU/99* RC 50.00 120.00
❑ 108 Anthony Davis AU/366* RC 8.00 20.00
❑ 109 Antrel Rolle AU RC 6.00 15.00
❑ 110 Brandon Jacobs AU RC 20.00 40.00
❑ 111 Brandon Jones AU RC 6.00 15.00
❑ 112 Braylon Edwards AU RC 20.00 50.00
❑ 113 Bryant McFadden AU/315* RC 8.00 20.00
❑ 114 Carlos Rogers AU RC 10.00 25.00
❑ 115 Cad.Williams AU/380* RC 30.00 60.00
❑ 116 Cedric Benson AU/289* RC 30.0060.00
❑ 117 C.Houston AU/116* RC 75.00 150.00
❑ 118 Chad Owens AU RC 6.00 15.00
❑ 119 Charlie Frye AU RC 6.00 15.00
❑ 120 Chris Henry AU RC 6.00 15.00
❑ 121 Ciatrick Fason AU RC 5.00 12.00
❑ 122 Courtney Roby AU RC 5.00 12.00
❑ 123 Craig Bragg AU/425* RC 8.00 20.00
❑ 124 C.Thorpe AU/416* RC 5.00 12.00
❑ 125 Damien Nash AU RC 5.00 12.00
❑ 126 Dan Cody AU/315* RC 8.00 20.00
❑ 127 Dan Orlovsky AU RC 6.00 15.00
❑ 128 Dante Ridgeway AU/373* RC 4.00 10.00
❑ 129 Darren Sproles AU/454* RC 20.00 50.00
❑ 130 David Greene AU RC 5.00 12.00
❑ 131 David Pollack AU RC 5.00 12.00
❑ 132 Deandra Cobb AU/440* RC 5.00. 12.00
❑ 133 DeMarcus Ware AU RC 20.00 40.00
❑ 134 Derek Anderson AU/450* RC 15.00 40.00
❑ 135 Derrick Johnson AU RC 10.00 25.00
❑ 136 Erasmus James AU RC 5.00 12.00
❑ 137 Eric Shelton AU RC 5.00 12.00
❑ 138 Fabian Washington AU RC 6.00 15.00
❑ 139 Frank Gore AU RC 30.00 60.00
❑ 140 Fred Gibson AU/476* RC 5.00 12.00
❑ 141 Heath Miller AU/510* RC 20.00 50.00
❑ 142 J.J. Arrington AU/465* RC 8.00 20.00
❑ 143 J.R. Russell AU/489* RC 4.00 10.00
❑ 144 Jason Campbell AU RC 20.00 40.00
❑ 145 Jason White AU RC 6.00 15.00
❑ 146 Jerome Mathis AU/416* RC 6.00 15.00
❑ 147 Josh Davis AU RC 4.00 10.00
❑ 148 Kay-Jay Harris AU RC 5.00 12.00
❑ 149 Kyle Orton AU RC 20.00 40.00
❑ 150 Larry Brackins AU RC 4.00 10.00
❑ 151 Lionel Gates AU/241* RC 8.00 20.00
❑ 152 Marion Barber AU RC 50.00 100.00
❑ 153 Mark Bradley AU RC 5.00 12.00
❑ 154 Mark Clayton AU/494* RC 10.00 25.00
❑ 155 Marlin Jackson AU RC 5.00 12.00
❑ 156 Matt Jones AU/165* RC 30.00 60.00
❑ 157 Matt Roth AU RC 6.00 15.00
❑ 158 Maurice Clarett AU/89* 40.00 100.00
❑ 159 Mike Williams AU/73* 40.00 100.00
❑ 160 Paris Warren AU/241* RC 10.00 25.00
❑ 161 Rasheed Marshall AU RC 5.00 12.00
❑ 162 Reggie Brown AU/528* RC 5.00 12.00
❑ 163 Roddy White AU RC 15.00 30.00
❑ 164 Ronnie Brown AU/550* RC 40.00 80.00
❑ 165 Roscoe Parrish AU RC 5.00 12.00
❑ 166 Royd.Williams AU/491* RC 5.00 12.00
❑ 167 R.Fitzpatrick AU/284* RC 10.00 25.00
❑ 168 Ryan Moats AU RC 5.00 12.00
❑ 169 Shaun Cody AU RC 5.00 12.00
❑ 170 Shawne Merriman AU RC 20.00 50.00
❑ 171 Stefan LeFors AU RC 5.00 12.00
❑ 172 Steve Savoy AU RC 4.00 10.00
❑ 173 T.A. McLendon AU RC 4.00 10.00
❑ 174 Tab Perry AU RC 6.00 15.00
❑ 175 Taylor Stubblefield AU RC 4.00 10.00
❑ 176 Terrence Murphy AU RC 4.00 10.00
❑ 177 Thomas Davis AU RC 5.00 12.00
❑ 178 Travis Johnson AU RC 4.00 10.00
❑ 179 T.Williamson AU/402* RC 10.00 25.00
❑ 180 Vernand Morency AU RC 5.00 12.00
❑ 181 Vincent Jackson AU RC 15.00 30.00
❑ 182 Alex Smith TE AU RC 6.00 15.00
❑ 183 Channing Crowder AU RC 5.00 12.00
❑ 184 Darrent Williams AU RC 15.00 40.00
❑ 185 Derrick Wimbush AU RC 5.00 12.00
❑ 186 James Kilian AU RC 4.00 10.00
❑ 187 Josh Cribbs AU RC 30.00 60.00
❑ 188 LeRon McCoy AU RC 4.00 10.00
❑ 189 Luis Castillo AU RC 6.00 15.00
❑ 190 Matt Cassel AU RC 15.00 40.00
❑ 191 Mike Patterson AU RC 5.00 12.00
❑ 192 Nate Washington AU RC 10.00 20.00
❑ 193 Noah Herron AU RC 6.00 15.00
❑ 194 Fred Amey AU RC 5.00 12.00
❑ 195 Tyson Thompson AU RC 6.00 15.00
❑ 196 Mike Nugent AU RC 5.00 12.00
❑ 197 Odell Thurman AU RC 8.00 20.00
❑ 198 Chris Carr AU RC 5.00 12.00
❑ 199 Bo Scaife AU RC 5.00 12.00
❑ 200 Billy Bajema AU RC 4.00 10.00

2006 Playoff Contenders

❑ COMP.SET w/o RC's (100) 8.00 20.00
❑ 1 Anquan Boldin .25 .60
❑ 2 Edgerrin James .25 .60
❑ 3 Larry Fitzgerald .30 .75
❑ 4 Alge Crumpler .25 .60
❑ 5 Michael Vick .30 .75
❑ 6 Warrick Dunn .25 .60
❑ 7 Steve McNair .25 .60
❑ 8 Mark Clayton .25 .60
❑ 9 Derrick Mason .25 .60
❑ 10 Lee Evans .25 .60
❑ 11 Willis McGahee .30 .75
❑ 12 Jake Delhomme .25 .60
❑ 13 Keyshawn Johnson .25 .60
❑ 14 Steve Smith .30 .75
❑ 15 Cedric Benson .25 .60
❑ 16 Brian Urlacher .30 .75
❑ 17 Thomas Jones .25 .60
❑ 18 Carson Palmer .30 .75

❑ 19 Chad Johnson .25 .60
❑ 20 Rudi Johnson .25 .60
❑ 21 T.J. Houshmandzadeh .25 .60
❑ 22 Charlie Frye .25 .60
❑ 23 Braylon Edwards .30 .75
❑ 24 Reuben Droughns .25 .60
❑ 25 Tony Romo .75 2.00
❑ 26 Julius Jones .25 .60
❑ 27 Roy Williams S .25 .60
❑ 28 Terrell Owens .30 .75
❑ 29 Javon Walker .25 .60
❑ 30 Rod Smith .25 .60
❑ 31 Tatum Bell .20 .50
❑ 32 Roy Williams WR .30 .75
❑ 33 Kevin Jones .25 .60
❑ 34 Brett Favre .60 1.50
❑ 35 Robert Ferguson .20 .50
❑ 36 Samkon Gado .30 .75
❑ 37 Andre Johnson .25 .60
❑ 38 David Carr .20 .50
❑ 39 Domanick Davis .25 .60
❑ 40 Eric Moulds .25 .60
❑ 41 Dallas Clark .25 .60
❑ 42 Marvin Harrison .30 .75
❑ 43 Peyton Manning .50 1.25
❑ 44 Reggie Wayne .25 .60
❑ 45 Matt Jones .25 .60
❑ 46 Byron Leftwich .25 .60
❑ 47 Fred Taylor .25 .60
❑ 48 Larry Johnson .25 .60
❑ 49 Priest Holmes .25 .60
❑ 50 Tony Gonzalez .25 .60
❑ 51 Trent Green .25 .60
❑ 52 Chris Chambers .25 .60
❑ 53 Daunte Culpepper .30 .75
❑ 54 Ronnie Brown .30 .75
❑ 55 Chester Taylor .25 .60
❑ 56 Brad Johnson .25 .60
❑ 57 Corey Dillon .25 .60
❑ 58 Deion Branch .25 .60
❑ 59 Tom Brady .50 1.25
❑ 60 Tedy Bruschi .30 .75
❑ 61 Deuce McAllister .25 .60
❑ 62 Donte Stallworth .25 .60
❑ 63 Drew Brees .30 .75
❑ 64 Eli Manning .40 1.00
❑ 65 Jeremy Shockey .30 .75
❑ 66 Tiki Barber .30 .75
❑ 67 Chad Pennington .25 .60
❑ 68 Curtis Martin .30 .75
❑ 69 Laveranues Coles .25 .60
❑ 70 Randy Moss .30 .75
❑ 71 LaMont Jordan .25 .60
❑ 72 Jerry Porter .25 .60
❑ 73 Donovan McNabb .30 .75
❑ 74 Reggie Brown .20 .50
❑ 75 Ben Roethlisberger .50 1.25
❑ 76 Hines Ward .30 .75
❑ 77 Willie Parker .40 1.00
❑ 78 Antonio Gates .30 .75
❑ 79 Philip Rivers .30 .75
❑ 80 LaDainian Tomlinson .40 1.00
❑ 81 Alex Smith QB .25 .60
❑ 82 Antonio Bryant .25 .60
❑ 83 Kevan Barlow .25 .60
❑ 84 Darrell Jackson .25 .60
❑ 85 Matt Hasselbeck .25 .60
❑ 86 Nate Burleson .25 .60
❑ 87 Shaun Alexander .25 .60
❑ 88 Marc Bulger .25 .60
❑ 89 Steven Jackson .30 .75
❑ 90 Isaac Bruce .25 .60
❑ 91 Torry Holt .25 .60
❑ 92 Cadillac Williams .30 .75
❑ 93 Chris Simms .25 .60
❑ 94 Joey Galloway .25 .60
❑ 95 Chris Brown .25 .60
❑ 96 David Givens .25 .60
❑ 97 Drew Bennett .25 .60
❑ 98 Clinton Portis .30 .75
❑ 99 Santana Moss .25 .60
❑ 100 Mark Brunell .25 .60
❑ 101 Malcom Floyd AU RC 12.50 25.00
❑ 102 Bart Scott AU RC 10.00 25.00
❑ 103 Reggie McNeal AU/457* RC 5.00 12.00
❑ 104 Domenik Hixon AU/586* RC 8.00 20.00
❑ 105 Vince Young AU/487* RC 50.00 100.00
❑ 106 Marcedes Lewis AU RC 6.00 15.00
❑ 107 Wali Lundy AU400* RC 10.00 25.00
❑ 108 Tarvaris Jackson AU RC 10.00 25.00
❑ 109 Ko Simpson AU RC 5.00 12.00
❑ 110 Jason Allen AU RC 5.00 12.00
❑ 111 Anthony Fasano AU RC 6.00 15.00
❑ 112 Joe Klopfenstein AU RC 5.00 12.00
❑ 113 Marques Hagans AU RC 5.00 12.00
❑ 114 Jason Avant AU RC 6.00 15.00
❑ 115 Santonio Holmes AU RC 35.00 60.00
❑ 116 Marcus Vick AU/149* RC 40.00 100.00
❑ 117 Antonio Cromartie AU/322* RC 10.00 25.00
❑ 118 DeAngelo Williams AU RC 30.00 60.00
❑ 119 Laurence Maroney AU RC 15.00 40.00
❑ 120 Daniel Bullocks AU RC 6.00 15.00
❑ 121 Jonathan Orr AU RC 5.00 12.00
❑ 122 Mike Bell AU RC 10.00 25.00
❑ 123 Kellen Clemens AU RC 8.00 20.00
❑ 124 Tim Jennings AU RC 5.00 12.00
❑ 125 Cory Rodgers AU RC 6.00 15.00
❑ 126 Jerome Harrison AU RC 15.00 30.00
❑ 127 Brad Smith AU/570* RC 8.00 20.00
❑ 128 Jeff Webb AU/250* RC 5.00 12.00
❑ 129 Will Blackmon AU RC 6.00 15.00
❑ 130 Quinton Ganther AU RC 4.00 10.00
❑ 131 Drew Olson AU RC 4.00 10.00
❑ 132 Omar Jacobs AU RC 4.00 10.00
❑ 133 Adam Jennings AU RC 5.00 12.00
❑ 134 Cedric Humes AU RC 5.00 12.00
❑ 135 Derrick Ross AU/250* RC 40.00 80.00
❑ 136 Charlie Whitehurst AU RC 6.00 15.00
❑ 137 Bobby Carpenter AU RC 5.00 12.00
❑ 138 Darryl Tapp AU RC 5.00 12.00
❑ 139 A.J. Hawk AU/399* RC 25.00 50.00
❑ 140 Bruce Gradkowski AU RC 8.00 20.00
❑ 141 Chad Greenway AU RC 6.00 15.00
❑ 142 John David Washington AU RC 5.00 12.00
❑ 143 Kamerion Wimbley AU RC 6.00 15.00
❑ 144 LenDale White AU/549* RC 20.00 40.00
❑ 145 Johnathan Joseph AU/549* RC 5.00 12.00
❑ 146 Maurice Drew AU RC 25.00 60.00
❑ 147 Brandon Marshall AU/608* RC 25.00 50.00
❑ 148 Vernon Davis AU/537* RC 15.00 40.00
❑ 149 Joseph Addai AU RC 25.00 50.00
❑ 150 Bennie Brazell AU RC 5.00 12.00
❑ 151 D.J. Shockley AU RC 5.00 12.00
❑ 152 Jay Cutler AU/501* RC 60.00 120.00
❑ 153 Wendell Mathis AU RC 5.00 12.00
❑ 154 Demetrius Williams AU RC 5.00 12.00
❑ 155 Dusty Dvoracek AU RC 6.00 15.00
❑ 156 DeMario Minter AU RC 5.00 12.00
❑ 157 Marcus Maxey AU RC 5.00 12.00
❑ 158 Brodie Croyle AU RC 10.00 25.00
❑ 159 Jeremy Bloom AU/473* RC 8.00 20.00
❑ 160 Todd Watkins AU RC 4.00 10.00
❑ 161 Cory Ross AU RC 6.00 15.00
❑ 162 Tamba Hali AU/500* RC 10.00 25.00
❑ 163 P.J. Daniels AU/555* RC 4.00 10.00
❑ 164 Brandon Williams AU RC 5.00 12.00
❑ 165 Devin Hester AU RC 40.00 80.00
❑ 166 Kelly Jennings AU/393* RC 6.00 15.00
❑ 167 Dawan Landry AU RC 6.00 15.00
❑ 168 Greg Jennings AU RC 20.00 40.00
❑ 169 Mathias Kiwanuka AU RC 8.00 20.00
❑ 170 Leon Washington AU RC 20.00 50.00
❑ 171 Richard Marshall AU RC 5.00 12.00
❑ 172 Haloti Ngata AU RC 6.00 15.00
❑ 173 Sinorice Moss AU RC 6.00 15.00
❑ 174 Greg Blue AU RC 5.00 12.00
❑ 175 Chris Barclay AU RC 5.00 12.00
❑ 176 D'Qwell Jackson AU RC 5.00 12.00
❑ 177 Eric Smith AU RC 5.00 12.00
❑ 178 Ethan Kilmer AU RC 6.00 15.00
❑ 179 Mike Hass AU RC 6.00 15.00
❑ 180 Derek Hagan AU RC 5.00 12.00
❑ 181 Travis Wilson AU RC 4.00 10.00
❑ 182 Reggie Bush AU/645* RC 60.00 120.00
❑ 183 Maurice Stovall AU/579* RC 10.00 25.00
❑ 184 Skyler Green AU RC 4.00 10.00
❑ 185 Calvin Lowry AU RC 6.00 15.00
❑ 186 Jerious Norwood AU RC 15.00 40.00
❑ 187 Brodrick Bunkley AU/518* RC 5.00 12.00
❑ 188 Ernie Sims AU/611* RC 5.00 12.00
❑ 189 Ingle Martin AU RC 5.00 12.00
❑ 190 Anthony Mix AU RC 5.00 12.00
❑ 191 Patrick Cobbs AU RC 5.00 12.00
❑ 192 Delanie Walker AU/212* RC 40.00 80.00
❑ 193 Gabe Watson AU RC 4.00 10.00
❑ 194 Willie Reid AU/515* RC 5.00 12.00
❑ 195 Michael Huff AU RC 10.00 25.00
❑ 196 Mario Williams AU/395* RC 12.00 30.00
❑ 197 Chad Jackson AU RC 5.00 12.00
❑ 198 David Kirtman AU RC 5.00 12.00
❑ 199 Brian Calhoun AU/407* RC 8.00 20.00
❑ 200 Michael Robinson AU/512* RC 8.00 20.00
❑ 201 D.Ferguson AU/386* RC 10.00 25.00
❑ 202 Donte Whitner AU/518* RC 6.00 15.00
❑ 203 Roman Harper AU RC 5.00 12.00
❑ 204 Manny Lawson AU RC 6.00 15.00
❑ 205 DeMeco Ryans AU RC 10.00 25.00
❑ 206 Anthony Smith AU RC 8.00 20.00
❑ 207 Thomas Howard AU RC 5.00 12.00
❑ 208 John McCargo AU RC 5.00 12.00
❑ 209 David Pittman AU RC 5.00 12.00
❑ 210 Danieal Manning AU RC 6.00 15.00
❑ 211 Nate Salley AU RC 5.00 12.00
❑ 212 Jimmy Williams AU/524* RC 6.00 15.00
❑ 213 Rocky McIntosh AU RC 6.00 15.00
❑ 214 Montell Owens AU RC 5.00 12.00
❑ 215 Devin Aromashodu AU RC 8.00 20.00
❑ 216 Ben Obomanu AU RC 5.00 12.00
❑ 217 David Anderson AU RC 5.00 12.00
❑ 218 Marques Colston AU RC 30.00 60.00
❑ 219 Miles Austin AU RC 50.00 80.00
❑ 220 Tony Scheffler AU/526* RC 12.00 30.00
❑ 221 Leonard Pope AU/495* RC 6.00 15.00
❑ 222 David Thomas AU RC 6.00 15.00
❑ 223 Dominique Byrd AU RC 5.00 12.00
❑ 224 Owen Daniels AU RC 6.00 15.00
❑ 225 Garrett Mills AU RC 5.00 12.00
❑ 226 Hank Baskett AU RC 6.00 15.00
❑ 227 Jason Carter AU RC 5.00 12.00
❑ 228 Sam Hurd AU RC 10.00 25.00
❑ 229 Charles Sharon AU/250* RC 40.00 80.00
❑ 230 Chris Hannon AU RC 5.00 12.00
❑ 231 John Madsen AU RC 6.00 15.00
❑ 232 Shaun Bodiford AU RC 5.00 12.00
❑ 233 Mike Espy AU RC 6.00 15.00
❑ 234 Abdul Hodge AU RC 5.00 12.00
❑ 235 Anthony Montgomery AU RC 5.00 12.00
❑ 236 Matt Leinart AU/567* RC 50.00 80.00
❑ 237 Bernard Pollard AU/307* RC 10.00 25.00
❑ 238 Pat Watkins AU/343* RC 10.00 25.00
❑ 239 Cedric Griffin AU/357* RC 10.00 25.00
❑ 240 A.J. Nicholson AU RC 4.00 10.00
❑ 241 Claude Wroten AU/306* RC 20.00 50.00
❑ 242 Tye Hill AU/368* RC 10.00 25.00

2007 Playoff Contenders

❑ COMP.SET W/O RC's (100) 8.00 20.00
❑ 1 Edgerrin James .25 .60
❑ 2 Larry Fitzgerald .30 .75
❑ 3 Anquan Boldin .25 .60
❑ 4 Matt Leinart .30 .75
❑ 5 Joey Harrington .25 .60
❑ 6 Warrick Dunn .25 .60
❑ 7 Joe Horn .25 .60
❑ 8 Steve McNair .25 .60
❑ 9 Willis McGahee .25 .60
❑ 10 Derrick Mason .20 .50
❑ 11 J.P. Losman .20 .50
❑ 12 Lee Evans .25 .60
❑ 13 Josh Reed .20 .50
❑ 14 Jake Delhomme .25 .60
❑ 15 DeShaun Foster .25 .60
❑ 16 Steve Smith .25 .60
❑ 17 Rex Grossman .25 .60
❑ 18 Bernard Berrian .20 .50
❑ 19 Cedric Benson .25 .60
❑ 20 Carson Palmer .30 .75
❑ 21 Chad Johnson .25 .60
❑ 22 T.J. Houshmandzadeh .25 .60
❑ 23 Rudi Johnson .25 .60
❑ 24 Braylon Edwards .25 .60
❑ 25 Kellen Winslow .25 .60
❑ 26 Jamal Lewis .25 .60
❑ 27 Tony Romo .50 1.25

Card	Low	High
❑ 28 Terrell Owens	.30	.75
❑ 29 Jason Witten	.30	.75
❑ 30 Julius Jones	.25	.60
❑ 31 Jay Cutler	.30	.75
❑ 32 Javon Walker	.25	.60
❑ 33 Travis Henry	.25	.60
❑ 34 Jon Kitna	.20	.50
❑ 35 Roy Williams WR	.25	.60
❑ 36 Tatum Bell	.20	.50
❑ 37 Brett Favre	.60	1.50
❑ 38 Donald Driver	.30	.75
❑ 39 Greg Jennings	.25	.60
❑ 40 Matt Schaub	.25	.60
❑ 41 Ahman Green	.25	.60
❑ 42 Andre Johnson	.25	.60
❑ 43 Peyton Manning	.50	1.25
❑ 44 Joseph Addai	.30	.75
❑ 45 Marvin Harrison	.30	.75
❑ 46 Reggie Wayne	.25	.60
❑ 47 David Garrard	.25	.60
❑ 48 Fred Taylor	.25	.60
❑ 49 Maurice Jones-Drew	.30	.75
❑ 50 Larry Johnson	.25	.60
❑ 51 Damon Huard	.25	.60
❑ 52 Tony Gonzalez	.25	.60
❑ 53 Trent Green	.25	.60
❑ 54 Ronnie Brown	.25	.60
❑ 55 Chris Chambers	.25	.60
❑ 56 Troy Williamson	.20	.50
❑ 57 Tarvaris Jackson	.25	.60
❑ 58 Chester Taylor	.20	.50
❑ 59 Tom Brady	.60	1.50
❑ 60 Randy Moss	.30	.75
❑ 61 Laurence Maroney	.30	.75
❑ 62 Drew Brees	.30	.75
❑ 63 Deuce McAllister	.25	.60
❑ 64 Reggie Bush	.40	1.00
❑ 65 Eli Manning	.30	.75
❑ 66 Brandon Jacobs	.25	.60
❑ 67 Plaxico Burress	.25	.60
❑ 68 Chad Pennington	.25	.60
❑ 69 Laveranues Coles	.25	.60
❑ 70 Thomas Jones	.25	.60
❑ 71 Ronald Curry	.25	.60
❑ 72 LaMont Jordan	.25	.60
❑ 73 Jerry Porter	.25	.60
❑ 74 Donovan McNabb	.30	.75
❑ 75 Brian Westbrook	.25	.60
❑ 76 Ben Roethlisberger	.50	1.25
❑ 77 Willie Parker	.25	.60
❑ 78 Hines Ward	.30	.75
❑ 79 LaDainian Tomlinson	.40	1.00
❑ 80 Philip Rivers	.30	.75
❑ 81 Antonio Gates	.25	.60
❑ 82 Alex Smith QB	.30	.75
❑ 83 Frank Gore	.30	.75
❑ 84 Darrell Jackson	.25	.60
❑ 85 Vernon Davis	.25	.60
❑ 86 Deion Branch	.25	.60
❑ 87 Matt Hasselbeck	.25	.60
❑ 88 Shaun Alexander	.25	.60
❑ 89 Marc Bulger	.25	.60
❑ 90 Steven Jackson	.30	.75
❑ 91 Torry Holt	.25	.60
❑ 92 Jeff Garcia	.25	.60
❑ 93 Cadillac Williams	.25	.60
❑ 94 Joey Galloway	.25	.60
❑ 95 Vince Young	.30	.75
❑ 96 Chris Brown	.20	.50
❑ 97 Brandon Jones	.20	.50
❑ 98 Jason Campbell	.25	.60
❑ 99 Clinton Portis	.25	.60
❑ 100 Santana Moss	.25	.60
❑ 101 Aaron Ross AU RC	10.00	25.00
❑ 102 Aaron Rouse AU RC	8.00	20.00
❑ 103 Adam Carriker AU/333* RC	15.00	40.00
❑ 104 Adrian Peterson AU/355* RC	200.00	400.00
❑ 105 Ahmad Bradshaw No AU RC	2.00	5.00
❑ 106 Alan Branch No AU RC	1.25	3.00
❑ 107 Amobi Okoye AU RC	8.00	20.00
❑ 108 Anthony Gonzalez AU RC	25.00	50.00
❑ 109 Anthony Spencer AU RC	8.00	20.00
❑ 110 Antonio Pittman AU RC	8.00	20.00
❑ 111 Aundrae Allison AU RC	6.00	15.00
❑ 112 Ben Patrick AU RC	6.00	15.00
❑ 113 Biren Ealy AU RC	6.00	15.00
❑ 114 Bobby Sippio AU RC	6.00	15.00
❑ 115 Brady Quinn AU/534* RC	40.00	80.00
❑ 116 Brandon Jackson AU RC	8.00	20.00
❑ 117 Brandon Mebane AU RC	6.00	15.00
❑ 118 Brandon Meriweather AU RC	8.00	20.00
❑ 119 Brandon Siler AU RC	6.00	15.00
❑ 120 Brian Leonard AU RC	6.00	15.00
❑ 121 Brian Robison AU RC	8.00	20.00
❑ 122 Buster Davis AU/246* RC	15.00	40.00
❑ 123 C.Johnson AU/525* RC	50.00	100.00
❑ 124 Chansi Stuckey AU/502* RC	8.00	20.00
❑ 126 Chris Davis AU RC	6.00	15.00
❑ 127 Chris Henry RB AU RC	6.00	15.00
❑ 128 Chris Houston AU RC	6.00	15.00
❑ 129 Clifton Ryan AU RC	6.00	15.00
❑ 130 Clifton Dawson AU RC	8.00	20.00
❑ 131 Courtney Taylor AU RC	6.00	15.00
❑ 132 Craig Buster Davis No AU RC	1.50	4.00
❑ 133 Dallas Baker AU RC	6.00	15.00
❑ 134 Dan Bazuin AU/198* RC	25.00	50.00
❑ 135 Daymeion Hughes AU/383* RC	10.00	25.00
❑ 136 Dante Rosario AU RC	8.00	20.00
❑ 137 David Irons AU/198* RC	15.00	40.00
❑ 138 Darrelle Revis AU/533* RC	15.00	25.00
❑ 139 David Clowney AU/410* RC	8.00	20.00
❑ 140 David Harris AU RC	6.00	15.00
❑ 141 DeShawn Wynn AU/429* RC	8.00	20.00
❑ 142 Drew Stanton AU RC	6.00	15.00
❑ 143 Dwayne Bowe AU RC	25.00	50.00
❑ 144 Dwayne Jarrett AU/484* RC	8.00	20.00
❑ 145 Dwayne Wright AU/410* RC	6.00	15.00
❑ 146 Ed Johnson AU RC	6.00	15.00
❑ 147 Eric Frampton AU/452* RC	6.00	15.00
❑ 148 Eric Weddle AU RC	6.00	15.00
❑ 149 Eric Wright No AU RC	1.50	4.00
❑ 150 Fred Bennett AU RC	5.00	12.00
❑ 151 Gaines Adams AU RC	8.00	20.00
❑ 152 Garrett Wolfe AU RC	10.00	25.00
❑ 153 Glenn Holt AU RC	6.00	15.00
❑ 154 Glenn Martinez AU RC	8.00	20.00
❑ 155 Greg Olsen AU RC	12.00	30.00
❑ 156 Greg Peterson AU RC	6.00	15.00
❑ 157 H.B. Blades AU/383* RC	6.00	15.00
❑ 158 I.Alama-Francis AU/222* RC	15.00	40.00
❑ 159 Isaiah Stanback AU/510* RC	8.00	20.00
❑ 160 Jacoby Jones AU/435* RC	10.00	25.00
❑ 161 J.Anderson AU/123* RC SP	50.00	100.00
❑ 162 JaMarcus Russell AU RC	25.00	60.00
❑ 163 James Jones AU RC	15.00	40.00
❑ 164 J.Zabransky AU/347* RC	15.00	40.00
❑ 165 Jarvis Moss AU/227* RC	15.00	40.00
❑ 166 Jason Hill AU RC SP	8.00	20.00
❑ 167 Jeff Rowe AU/362* RC	10.00	25.00
❑ 168 Joe Thomas AU/129* RC	60.00	100.00
❑ 169 Joel Filani AU/483* RC	6.00	15.00
❑ 170 John Beck AU RC	8.00	20.00
❑ 171 John Broussard AU RC	6.00	15.00
❑ 172 Johnnie Lee Higgins AU RC	8.00	20.00
❑ 173 Jon Beason AU RC	8.00	20.00
❑ 175 Jordan Kent AU RC	6.00	15.00
❑ 176 Josh Wilson AU/501* RC	6.00	15.00
❑ 177 Justin Durant AU RC	6.00	15.00
❑ 178 Kenneth Darby AU RC	8.00	20.00
❑ 179 Kenny Irons No AU/50* RC	125.00	250.00
❑ 180 Kenton Keith AU RC	8.00	20.00
❑ 181 Kevin Kolb AU RC	25.00	40.00
❑ 182 Keyunta Dawson AU RC	6.00	15.00
❑ 183 Kolby Smith AU/444* RC	8.00	20.00
❑ 184 LaMarr Woodley AU RC	10.00	25.00
❑ 185 LaRon Landry AU RC	12.00	30.00
❑ 186 Laurent Robinson AU RC	8.00	20.00
❑ 187 Lawrence Timmons AU RC	8.00	20.00
❑ 188 Legedu Naanee AU RC	8.00	20.00
❑ 189 Leon Hall AU RC	8.00	20.00
❑ 190 Levi Brown AU/369* RC	8.00	20.00
❑ 191 Lorenzo Booker AU RC	8.00	20.00
❑ 192 Marcus McCauley AU/386* RC	15.00	40.00
❑ 193 Marcus Thomas AU RC	6.00	15.00
❑ 194 Marshawn Lynch AU/533* RC	20.00	50.00
❑ 195 Martrez Milner AU RC	6.00	15.00
❑ 196 Mason Crosby AU RC	8.00	20.00
❑ 197 Matt Gutierrez AU RC	8.00	20.00
❑ 198 Matt Moore AU RC	25.00	40.00
❑ 199 Matt Spaeth AU/237* RC	15.00	40.00
❑ 200 Michael Bush AU RC	12.00	30.00
❑ 201 Michael Griffin AU RC	8.00	20.00
❑ 202 Michael Okwo AU/261* RC	10.00	25.00
❑ 203 Mike Walker AU/248* RC	30.00	60.00
❑ 204 Nick Folk AU RC	8.00	20.00
❑ 205 Patrick Willis AU/239* RC	30.00	60.00
❑ 206 Paul Posluszny AU RC	12.00	30.00
❑ 207 Paul Williams AU RC	6.00	15.00
❑ 208 Pierre Thomas AU RC	25.00	40.00
❑ 209 Quentin Moses AU/498* RC	6.00	15.00
❑ 210 Ray McDonald AU/519* RC	6.00	15.00
❑ 211 Reggie Ball AU RC	6.00	15.00
❑ 212 Reggie Nelson AU RC	6.00	15.00
❑ 213 Robert Meachem AU RC	20.00	40.00
❑ 214 Roy Hall AU RC	8.00	20.00
❑ 215 Rufus Alexander AU RC	8.00	20.00
❑ 216 Ryne Robinson AU/430* RC	6.00	15.00
❑ 217 Sabby Piscitelli AU/337* RC	10.00	25.00
❑ 218 Scott Chandler AU RC	6.00	15.00
❑ 220 Sidney Rice AU/529* RC	30.00	50.00
❑ 221 Stephen Nicholas AU RC	6.00	15.00
❑ 222 Steve Breaston AU/274* RC	15.00	40.00
❑ 223 Steve Smith AU/541 RC	20.00	40.00
❑ 224 Stewart Bradley AU RC	8.00	20.00
❑ 225 Syndric Steptoe AU/149* RC	25.00	60.00
❑ 226 Tanard Jackson No AU RC	1.00	2.50
❑ 227 Ted Ginn AU/519 RC	20.00	50.00
❑ 228 Thomas Clayton AU RC	6.00	15.00
❑ 229 Tim Crowder AU/454* RC	8.00	20.00
❑ 230 Tim Shaw AU/408* RC	6.00	15.00
❑ 231 Tony Hunt AU RC	8.00	20.00
❑ 232 Trent Edwards AU RC	15.00	40.00
❑ 233 Troy Smith AU RC	12.00	30.00
❑ 234 Turk McBride AU RC	6.00	15.00
❑ 235 Tyler Palko AU RC	6.00	15.00
❑ 236 Tyler Thigpen AU RC	8.00	20.00
❑ 237 Victor Abiamiri AU/449* RC	8.00	20.00
❑ 238 Yamon Figurs AU RC	5.00	12.00
❑ 239 Zak DeOssie AU RC	6.00	15.00
❑ 240 Zach Miller AU RC	8.00	20.00

2008 Playoff Contenders

Card	Low	High
❑ COMP.SET w/o RC's (100)	8.00	20.00
❑ 1 Kurt Warner	.30	.75
❑ 2 Larry Fitzgerald	.30	.75
❑ 3 Anquan Boldin	.25	.60
❑ 4 Edgerrin James	.25	.60
❑ 5 Jerious Norwood	.25	.60
❑ 6 Roddy White	.25	.60
❑ 7 Michael Turner	.30	.75
❑ 8 Willis McGahee	.25	.60
❑ 9 Derrick Mason	.20	.50
❑ 10 Le'Ron McClain	.30	.75
❑ 11 Trent Edwards	.30	.75
❑ 12 Marshawn Lynch	.30	.75
❑ 13 Lee Evans	.25	.60
❑ 14 Steve Smith	.25	.60
❑ 15 DeAngelo Williams	.25	.60
❑ 16 Jake Delhomme	.25	.60
❑ 17 Greg Olsen	.25	.60
❑ 18 Devin Hester	.30	.75
❑ 19 Kyle Orton	.25	.60
❑ 20 Carson Palmer	.30	.75
❑ 21 Chad Johnson	.25	.60
❑ 22 T.J. Houshmandzadeh	.25	.60
❑ 23 Chris Perry	.20	.50
❑ 24 Derek Anderson	.25	.60
❑ 25 Jamal Lewis	.25	.60
❑ 26 Braylon Edwards	.25	.60
❑ 27 Tony Romo	.50	1.25
❑ 28 Terrell Owens	.30	.75
❑ 29 Marion Barber	.30	.75
❑ 30 Jason Witten	.30	.75
❑ 31 Jay Cutler	.30	.75
❑ 32 Selvin Young	.20	.50
❑ 33 Brandon Marshall	.25	.60
❑ 34 Jon Kitna	.25	.60
❑ 35 Roy Williams WR	.25	.60
❑ 36 Calvin Johnson	.30	.75
❑ 37 Aaron Rodgers	.30	.75
❑ 38 Ryan Grant	.30	.75
❑ 39 Greg Jennings	.25	.60
❑ 40 Matt Schaub	.25	.60
❑ 41 Ahman Green	.25	.60

❑ 42 Andre Johnson .25 .60
❑ 43 Peyton Manning .50 1.25
❑ 44 Joseph Addai .30 .75
❑ 45 Reggie Wayne .25 .60
❑ 46 David Garrard .25 .60
❑ 47 Fred Taylor .25 .60
❑ 48 Maurice Jones-Drew .25 .60
❑ 49 Brodie Croyle .25 .60
❑ 50 Larry Johnson .25 .60
❑ 51 Tony Gonzalez .25 .60
❑ 52 Chad Pennington .25 .60
❑ 53 Ronnie Brown .25 .60
❑ 54 Ted Ginn Jr. .25 .60
❑ 55 Tarvaris Jackson .25 .60
❑ 56 Adrian Peterson .60 1.50
❑ 57 Chester Taylor .20 .50
❑ 58 Tom Brady .50 1.25
❑ 59 Randy Moss .30 .75
❑ 60 Laurence Maroney .25 .60
❑ 61 Drew Brees .30 .75
❑ 62 Reggie Bush .30 .75
❑ 63 Marques Colston .25 .60
❑ 64 Eli Manning .30 .75
❑ 65 Plaxico Burress .25 .60
❑ 66 Brandon Jacobs .25 .60
❑ 67 Brett Favre 1.50 4.00
❑ 68 Leon Washington .25 .60
❑ 69 Laveranues Coles .25 .60
❑ 70 Javon Walker .25 .60
❑ 71 JaMarcus Russell .30 .75
❑ 72 Justin Fargas .20 .50
❑ 73 Donovan McNabb .30 .75
❑ 74 Brian Westbrook .25 .60
❑ 75 Kevin Curtis .20 .50
❑ 76 Ben Roethlisberger .50 1.25
❑ 77 Willie Parker .25 .60
❑ 78 Santonio Holmes .25 .60
❑ 79 Philip Rivers .30 .75
❑ 80 LaDainian Tomlinson .40 1.00
❑ 81 Vincent Jackson .20 .50
❑ 82 Antonio Gates .25 .60
❑ 83 J.T. O'Sullivan .20 .50
❑ 84 Frank Gore .25 .60
❑ 85 Isaac Bruce .25 .60
❑ 86 Matt Hasselbeck .25 .60
❑ 87 Deion Branch .25 .60
❑ 88 Julius Jones .25 .60
❑ 89 Marc Bulger .25 .60
❑ 90 Steven Jackson .30 .75
❑ 91 Torry Holt .25 .60
❑ 92 Warrick Dunn .25 .60
❑ 93 Jeff Garcia .25 .60
❑ 94 Joey Galloway .25 .60
❑ 95 Vince Young .25 .60
❑ 96 LenDale White .25 .60
❑ 97 Justin Gage .20 .50
❑ 98 Jason Campbell .25 .60
❑ 99 Clinton Portis .25 .60
❑ 100 Chris Cooley .25 .60
❑ 101 Adrian Arrington AU RC 6.00 15.00
❑ 102 Ali Highsmith AU/214* RC 25.00 40.00
❑ 103 Allen Patrick AU RC 6.00 15.00
❑ 104 Andre Caldwell AU RC 8.00 20.00
❑ 105 Andre Woodson AU/250* RC 12.00 30.00
❑ 106 Antoine Cason AU RC 8.00 20.00
❑ 107 Aqib Talib AU RC 8.00 20.00
❑ 108 Brad Cottam AU/132* RC 30.00 60.00
❑ 109 Brandon Flowers AU/192* RC 30.00 60.00
❑ 110 Brian Brohm AU RC 10.00 25.00
❑ 111 Calais Campbell AU RC 6.00 15.00
❑ 112 Chad Henne AU RC 30.00 60.00
❑ 113 C.Washington AU/114* RC 50.00 100.00
❑ 114 Chevis Jackson AU RC 6.00 15.00
❑ 115 Chris Johnson AU RC 100.00 175.00
❑ 116 Chris Long AU RC 8.00 20.00
❑ 117 Colt Brennan AU RC 25.00 50.00
❑ 118 Craig Steltz AU RC 6.00 15.00
❑ 119 Curtis Lofton AU RC 8.00 20.00
❑ 120 Dan Connor AU RC 8.00 20.00
❑ 121 Dantrell Savage AU/76* RC 50.00 100.00
❑ 122 Darius Reynaud AU RC 6.00 15.00
❑ 123 Darren McFadden AU RC 25.00 60.00
❑ 124 Davone Bess AU RC 10.00 25.00
❑ 125 Dennis Dixon AU RC 20.00 40.00
❑ 126 Derrick Harvey AU RC 6.00 15.00
❑ 127 DeSean Jackson AU RC 35.00 60.00
❑ 128 Devin Thomas AU RC 10.00 25.00
❑ 129 Dexter Jackson AU RC 8.00 20.00
❑ 130 D.Rodgers-Cromartie AU RC 8.00 20.00
❑ 131 Donnie Avery AU RC 10.00 25.00
❑ 132 Dustin Keller AU RC 10.00 25.00
❑ 133 Earl Bennett AU RC 12.00 30.00
❑ 134 Early Doucet AU/113* RC 35.00 60.00
❑ 135 Eddie Royal AU RC 15.00 40.00
❑ 136 Erik Ainge AU/107* RC 25.00 60.00
❑ 137 Erin Henderson AU/158* RC 25.00 60.00
❑ 138 Felix Jones AU RC 30.00 80.00
❑ 139 Fred Davis AU RC 8.00 20.00
❑ 140 Glenn Dorsey AU RC 8.00 20.00
❑ 141 Harry Douglas AU RC 6.00 15.00
❑ 142 Jacob Hester AU RC 8.00 20.00
❑ 143 Jacob Tamme AU RC 8.00 20.00
❑ 144 Jake Long AU/163* RC 15.00 40.00
❑ 145 Jamaal Charles AU RC 20.00 40.00
❑ 146 James Hardy AU RC 6.00 15.00
❑ 147 Jed Collins AU/30* RC 250.00 400.00
❑ 148 Jermichael Finley AU/231* RC 25.00 50.00
❑ 149 Jerod Mayo AU RC 12.00 30.00
❑ 150 Jerome Simpson AU RC 6.00 15.00
❑ 151 Joe Flacco AU/220* RC 100.00 200.00
❑ 152 John Carlson AU RC 8.00 20.00
❑ 153 John David Booty AU RC 10.00 25.00
❑ 154A J.Stewart AU Blk RC 30.00 80.00
❑ 154B J.Stewart AU Blu RC 50.00 120.00
❑ 155 Jordon Dizon AU/188* RC 20.00 40.00
❑ 156 Jordy Nelson AU RC 10.00 25.00
❑ 157 Josh Johnson AU RC 8.00 20.00
❑ 158 Josh Morgan AU RC 10.00 25.00
❑ 159 Justin Forsett AU RC 12.50 25.00
❑ 160 Keenan Burton AU RC 6.00 15.00
❑ 161 Keith Rivers AU RC 10.00 25.00
❑ 162 Kellen Davis AU RC 5.00 12.00
❑ 163 Kenny Phillips AU RC 8.00 20.00
❑ 164 Kentwan Balmer AU RC 6.00 15.00
❑ 165 Kevin O'Connell AU RC 8.00 20.00
❑ 166 Kevin Smith AU RC 15.00 40.00
❑ 167 Lavelle Hawkins AU RC 6.00 15.00
❑ 168 Lawrence Jackson AU RC 6.00 15.00
❑ 169 Leodis McKelvin AU RC 8.00 20.00
❑ 170 Limas Sweed AU RC 8.00 20.00
❑ 171 Malcolm Kelly AU/141* RC 40.00 80.00
❑ 172 Marcus Smith AU RC EXCH 6.00 15.00
❑ 173 Marcus Thomas AU/165* RC 15.00 40.00
❑ 174 Mario Manningham AU RC 12.00 30.00
❑ 175 Martellus Bennett AU RC 8.00 20.00
❑ 176 Martin Rucker AU RC 6.00 15.00
❑ 177 Matt Flynn AU RC 8.00 20.00
❑ 178 Matt Forte AU RC 25.00 60.00
❑ 179 Matt Ryan AU/246* RC 125.00 250.00
❑ 180 Mike Hart AU RC 8.00 20.00
❑ 181 Mike Jenkins AU RC 8.00 20.00
❑ 182 Owen Schmitt AU RC 8.00 20.00
❑ 183 Pat Sims AU RC 6.00 15.00
❑ 184 Peyton Hillis AU/113* RC 25.00 60.00
❑ 185 Phillip Merling AU/100* RC 30.00 80.00
❑ 186 Quentin Groves AU RC 6.00 15.00
❑ 187 Rashard Mendenhall AU RC 30.00 60.00
❑ 188 Ray Rice AU RC 30.00 60.00
❑ 189 Reggie Smith AU/196* RC 20.00 40.00
❑ 190 Ryan Torain AU/70* RC 60.00 120.00
❑ 191 Sedrick Ellis AU RC 8.00 20.00
❑ 192 Steve Slaton AU RC 20.00 40.00
❑ 193 Tashard Choice AU RC 20.00 40.00
❑ 194 Terrell Thomas AU RC 6.00 15.00
❑ 195 Thomas Brown AU/151* RC 20.00 40.00
❑ 196 Tim Hightower AU RC 10.00 25.00
❑ 197 Vernon Gholston AU RC 8.00 20.00
❑ 198 Will Franklin AU RC 6.00 15.00
❑ 199 Xavier Adibi AU RC 6.00 15.00
❑ 200 B.Witherspoon AU/150* RC 30.00 60.00
❑ 201 Caleb Hanie AU RC 6.00 15.00
❑ 202 Charles Godfrey AU RC 6.00 15.00
❑ 203 Chaz Schilens AU RC 15.00 30.00
❑ 204 Chris Horton AU RC 8.00 20.00
❑ 205 Derek Fine AU RC 6.00 15.00
❑ 206 Zackary Bowman AU RC 6.00 15.00
❑ 207 Dwight Lowery AU RC 6.00 15.00
❑ 208 Jalen Parmele AU RC 6.00 15.00
❑ 209 Jerome Felton AU RC 5.00 12.00
❑ 210 Kendall Langford AU RC 8.00 20.00
❑ 211 Kregg Lumpkin AU RC 6.00 15.00
❑ 212 Marcus Henry AU RC 6.00 15.00
❑ 213 Matt Slater AU RC 8.00 20.00
❑ 214 Mike Cox AU RC 6.00 15.00
❑ 215 Mike Tolbert AU/199* RC 20.00 40.00
❑ 216 Pierre Garcon AU RC 50.00 80.00
❑ 217 Quintin Demps AU RC 8.00 20.00
❑ 218 Sam Baker AU RC 5.00 12.00
❑ 219 Steve Johnson AU RC 8.00 20.00
❑ 220 Tavares Gooden AU RC 6.00 15.00
❑ 221 Terrence Wheatley AU RC 6.00 15.00
❑ 222 Tom Santi AU RC 6.00 15.00
❑ 223 Tom Zbikowski AU/149* RC 25.0060.00
❑ 224 Tyvon Branch AU RC 6.00 15.00
❑ 225 Xavier Omon AU/124* RC 30.00 60.00

2009 Playoff Contenders

❑ COMP.SET w/o RC's (100) 10.00 25.00
❑ 1 Kurt Warner .30 .75
❑ 2 Larry Fitzgerald .30 .75
❑ 3 Tim Hightower .25 .60
❑ 4 Matt Ryan .30 .75
❑ 5 Michael Turner .25 .60
❑ 6 Roddy White .25 .60
❑ 7 Tony Gonzalez .25 .60
❑ 8 Joe Flacco .30 .75
❑ 9 Mark Clayton .20 .50
❑ 10 Willis McGahee .25 .60
❑ 11 Lee Evans .25 .60
❑ 12 Marshawn Lynch .25 .60
❑ 13 Terrell Owens .30 .75
❑ 14 DeAngelo Williams .30 .75
❑ 15 Jake Delhomme .25 .60
❑ 16 Steve Smith .25 .60
❑ 17 Devin Hester .30 .75
❑ 18 Greg Olsen .20 .50
❑ 19 Jay Cutler .30 .75
❑ 20 Matt Forte .30 .75
❑ 21 Carson Palmer .30 .75
❑ 22 Chad Ochocinco .25 .60
❑ 23 Cedric Benson .25 .60
❑ 24 Josh Cribbs .30 .75
❑ 25 Braylon Edwards .25 .60
❑ 26 Jamal Lewis .25 .60
❑ 27 Roy Williams WR .25 .60
❑ 28 Marion Barber .30 .75
❑ 29 Tony Romo .50 1.25
❑ 30 Brandon Marshall .25 .60
❑ 31 Eddie Royal .25 .60
❑ 32 Kyle Orton .25 .60
❑ 33 Calvin Johnson .30 .75
❑ 34 Bryant Johnson .20 .50
❑ 35 Kevin Smith .25 .60
❑ 36 Aaron Rodgers .30 .75
❑ 37 Greg Jennings .30 .75
❑ 38 Ryan Grant .25 .60
❑ 39 Andre Johnson .25 .60
❑ 40 Matt Schaub .25 .60
❑ 41 Steve Slaton .25 .60
❑ 42 Anthony Gonzalez .25 .60
❑ 43 Joseph Addai .30 .75
❑ 44 Peyton Manning .50 1.25
❑ 45 Reggie Wayne .25 .60
❑ 46 David Garrard .25 .60
❑ 47 Maurice Jones-Drew .25 .60
❑ 48 Torry Holt .25 .60
❑ 49 Dwayne Bowe .25 .60
❑ 50 Jamaal Charles .25 .60
❑ 51 Matt Cassel .25 .60
❑ 52 Chad Henne .30 .75
❑ 53 Ted Ginn .25 .60
❑ 54 Ronnie Brown .25 .60
❑ 55 Adrian Peterson .60 1.50
❑ 56 Bernard Berrian .25 .60
❑ 57 Brett Favre 4.00 10.00
❑ 58 Randy Moss .30 .75
❑ 59 Tom Brady .50 1.25
❑ 60 Laurence Maroney .25 .60
❑ 61 Drew Brees .30 .75
❑ 62 Marques Colston .25 .60
❑ 63 Reggie Bush .30 .75
❑ 64 Brandon Jacobs .25 .60
❑ 65 Eli Manning .30 .75
❑ 66 Steve Smith USC .25 .60
❑ 67 Jerricho Cotchery .20 .50
❑ 68 Leon Washington .25 .60
❑ 69 Thomas Jones .25 .60
❑ 70 Darren McFadden .30 .75
❑ 71 JaMarcus Russell .25 .60
❑ 72 Zach Miller .20 .50
❑ 73 Brian Westbrook .25 .60
❑ 74 DeSean Jackson .25 .60
❑ 75 Donovan McNabb .30 .75
❑ 76 Ben Roethlisberger .50 1.25
❑ 77 Santonio Holmes .25 .60
❑ 78 Willie Parker .25 .60
❑ 79 Antonio Gates .25 .60
❑ 80 LaDainian Tomlinson .30 .75

❑ 81 Philip Rivers .30 .75
❑ 82 Vincent Jackson .25 .60
❑ 83 Frank Gore .25 .60
❑ 84 Josh Morgan .20 .50
❑ 85 Vernon Davis .20 .50
❑ 86 Julius Jones .25 .60
❑ 87 Matt Hasselbeck .25 .60
❑ 88 T.J. Houshmandzadeh .25 .60
❑ 89 Donnie Avery .25 .60
❑ 90 Marc Bulger .25 .60
❑ 91 Steven Jackson .25 .60
❑ 92 Antonio Bryant .25 .60
❑ 93 Derrick Ward .25 .60
❑ 94 Kellen Winslow Jr. .25 .60
❑ 95 Bo Scaife .20 .50
❑ 96 Chris Johnson .30 .75
❑ 97 Kerry Collins .25 .60
❑ 98 Chris Cooley .25 .60
❑ 99 Clinton Portis .25 .60
❑ 100 Santana Moss .25 .60
❑ 101 Matthew Stafford AU/540* RC 60.00 120.00
❑ 102 Jason Smith AU/237* RC 15.00 40.00
❑ 103 Tyson Jackson AU/443* RC 8.00 20.00
❑ 104 Aaron Curry AU RC 12.00 30.00
❑ 105 Mark Sanchez AU RC 125.00 200.00
❑ 106 D.Heyward-Bey AU RC 12.00 30.00
❑ 107 Crabtree AU/539* RC EXCH 60.00 120.00
❑ 108 Knowshon Moreno AU/445* RC 40.00 80.00
❑ 109 Josh Freeman AU RC 25.00 50.00
❑ 110 Jeremy Maclin AU/278* RC 30.00 60.00
❑ 111 Brandon Pettigrew AU RC 10.00 25.00
❑ 112 P.Harvin AU/497* RC EXCH 60.00 120.00
❑ 113 Donald Brown AU/465* RC 25.00 50.00
❑ 114 H.Nicks AU/318* RC EXCH 30.00 60.00
❑ 115 Kenny Britt AU RC EXCH 20.00 40.00
❑ 116 Chris Wells AU/531* RC 30.00 60.00
❑ 117 B.Robiskie AU RC EXCH 10.00 25.00
❑ 118 Pat White AU RC 12.00 30.00
❑ 119 Mohamed Massaquoi AU RC 15.00 30.00
❑ 120 L.McCoy AU RC EXCH 25.00 50.00
❑ 121 Shonn Greene AU RC 30.00 50.00
❑ 122 Glen Coffee AU RC EXCH 15.00 30.00
❑ 123 D.Williams AU RC EXCH 10.00 25.00
❑ 124 Mike Wallace AU RC 20.00 40.00
❑ 125 Ramses Barden AU RC 6.00 15.00
❑ 126 Patrick Turner AU RC 6.00 15.00
❑ 127 Deon Butler AU RC 8.00 20.00
❑ 128 Juaquin Iglesias AU/467* RC 8.00 20.00
❑ 129 Stephen McGee AU RC 10.00 25.00
❑ 130 Mike Thomas AU RC 8.00 20.00
❑ 131 Andre Brown AU/363* RC 10.00 25.00
❑ 132 Rhett Bomar AU RC 6.00 15.00
❑ 133 Nate Davis AU RC 10.00 25.00
❑ 134 Javon Ringer AU RC 8.00 20.00
❑ 135 Aaron Brown AU RC 6.00 15.00
❑ 136 Aaron Kelly AU/21* RC 400.00 600.00
❑ 137 A.Maybin AU/99* RC EXCH 50.00 100.00
❑ 138 A.Smith AU/99* RC EXCH 40.00 80.00
❑ 139 Anthony Hill AU RC 5.00 12.00
❑ 140 Vontae Davis AU RC 8.00 20.00
❑ 141 Austin Collie AU RC 20.00 40.00
❑ 142 B.J. Raji AU RC 12.00 30.00
❑ 143 Bernard Scott AU RC 10.00 25.00
❑ 144 Brandon Gibson AU RC 8.00 20.00
❑ 145 B.Myers AU/99* RC EXCH 60.00 120.00
❑ 146 Brandon Tate AU RC 6.00 15.00
❑ 147 Brian Cushing AU/151* RC 60.00 120.00
❑ 148 Brian Hartline AU RC 8.00 20.00
❑ 149 Brian Hoyer AU RC 8.00 20.00
❑ 150 Brian Orakpo AU/199* RC 30.00 60.00
❑ 151 Brooks Foster AU RC 6.00 15.00
❑ 152 Cameron Morrah AU RC 5.00 12.00
❑ 153 Captain Munnerlyn AU RC 6.00 15.00
❑ 154 Chase Coffman AU RC 6.00 15.00
❑ 155 Chase Daniel AU RC 10.00 25.00
❑ 156 Clay Matthews AU RC 20.00 40.00
❑ 157 Clint Sintim AU/247* RC 8.00 20.00
❑ 158 Cornelius Ingram AU RC 5.00 12.00
❑ 159 Curtis Painter AU RC 10.00 25.00
❑ 160 David Johnson AU RC 6.00 15.00
❑ 161 Demetrius Byrd AU/505* RC 6.00 15.00
❑ 162 Dominique Edison AU RC 5.00 12.00
❑ 163 Everette Brown AU RC 8.00 20.00
❑ 164 Frank Summers AU RC 8.00 20.00
❑ 165 Gartrell Johnson AU RC 5.00 12.00
❑ 166 Hunter Cantwell AU/281* RC 8.00 20.00
❑ 167 Jake O'Connell AU RC 5.00 12.00
❑ 168 James Casey AU RC 6.00 15.00
❑ 169 James Laurinaitis AU RC 10.00 25.00
❑ 170 Jared Cook AU RC 6.00 15.00
❑ 171 Jarett Dillard AU RC 6.00 15.00
❑ 172 Zach Miller AU RC 6.00 15.00
❑ 173 John Nalbone AU RC 5.00 12.00
❑ 174 John Phillips AU RC 10.00 25.00
❑ 175 Johnny Knox AU RC 12.00 30.00
❑ 176 Julian Edelman AU RC 20.00 40.00
❑ 177 Keith Null AU RC 8.00 20.00
❑ 178 Kenny McKinley AU RC 8.00 20.00
❑ 179 Kevin Ogletree AU/493* RC 20.00 40.00
❑ 180 Kory Sheets AU/449* RC 6.00 15.00
❑ 181 Lardarius Webb AU RC 8.00 20.00
❑ 182 L.Stephens-Howling AU RC 15.00 30.00
❑ 183 Larry English AU/510* RC 8.00 20.00
❑ 184 Louis Delmas AU RC 10.00 25.00
❑ 185 L.Murphy AU/99* RC EXCH 60.00 100.00
❑ 186 Malcolm Jenkins AU/393* RC 8.00 20.00
❑ 187 Manuel Johnson AU RC 6.00 15.00
❑ 188 Marko Mitchell AU RC 6.00 15.00
❑ 189 Mike Teel AU RC 8.00 20.00
❑ 190 Goodson AU/99* RC EXCH 50.00 100.00
❑ 191 Nick Miller AU RC 5.00 12.00
❑ 192 P.J. Hill AU RC 6.00 15.00
❑ 193 Quan Cosby AU/311* RC 12.00 30.00
❑ 194 Quinn Johnson AU RC 6.00 15.00
❑ 195 Rashad Jennings AU RC 8.00 20.00
❑ 196 Rey Maualuga AU/157* RC 50.00 100.00
❑ 197 Richard Quinn AU RC 6.00 15.00
❑ 198 Mouton AU/99* RC EXCH 50.00 100.00
❑ 199 Sammie Stroughter AU RC 8.00 20.00
❑ 200 Sean Smith AU RC 8.00 20.00
❑ 201 Nelson AU/99* RC EXCH 30.00 80.00
❑ 202 Sherrod Martin AU RC 6.00 15.00
❑ 203 Stefan Logan AU RC 10.00 25.00
❑ 204 Brandstater AU/63* RC 125.00 250.00
❑ 205 Tony Fiammetta AU RC 6.00 15.00
❑ 206 Travis Beckum AU RC 6.00 15.00
❑ 207 Tyrell Sutton AU/440* RC 15.00 30.00
❑ 208 J.Davis AU/99* RC EXCH 60.00 120.00
❑ 209 M.Oher AU/99* RC EXCH 90.00 150.00

1998 Playoff Prestige Hobby

❑ COMP.HOBBY SET (200) 40.00 100.00
❑ 1 John Elway 3.00 8.00
❑ 2 Steve Atwater .30 .75
❑ 3 Terrell Davis .75 2.00
❑ 4 Bill Romanowski .30 .75
❑ 5 Rod Smith .50 1.25
❑ 6 Shannon Sharpe .50 1.25
❑ 7 Ed McCaffrey .50 1.25
❑ 8 Neil Smith .50 1.25
❑ 9 Brett Favre 3.00 8.00
❑ 10 Dorsey Levens .75 2.00
❑ 11 LeRoy Butler .30 .75
❑ 12 Antonio Freeman .75 2.00
❑ 13 Robert Brooks .50 1.25
❑ 14 Mark Chmura .50 1.25
❑ 15 Gilbert Brown .30 .75
❑ 16 Kordell Stewart .75 2.00
❑ 17 Jerome Bettis .75 2.00
❑ 18 Carnell Lake .30 .75
❑ 19 Dermontti Dawson .30 .75
❑ 20 Charles Johnson .30 .75
❑ 21 Greg Lloyd .30 .75
❑ 22 Levon Kirkland .30 .75
❑ 23 Steve Young 1.00 2.50
❑ 24 Jim Druckenmiller .30 .75
❑ 25 Garrison Hearst .75 2.00
❑ 26 Merton Hanks .30 .75
❑ 27 Ken Norton .30 .75
❑ 28 Jerry Rice 1.50 4.00
❑ 29 Terrell Owens .75 2.00
❑ 30 J.J. Stokes .50 1.25
❑ 31 Trent Dilfer .75 2.00
❑ 32 Warrick Dunn .75 2.00
❑ 33 Mike Alstott .75 2.00
❑ 34 Reidel Anthony .50 1.25
❑ 35 Warren Sapp .50 1.25
❑ 36 Elvis Grbac .50 1.25
❑ 37 Kimble Anders .50 1.25
❑ 38 Ted Popson .30 .75
❑ 39 Derrick Thomas .75 2.00
❑ 40 Tony Gonzalez .75 2.00
❑ 41 Andre Rison .50 1.25
❑ 42 Derrick Alexander .50 1.25
❑ 43 Brad Johnson .75 2.00
❑ 44 Robert Smith .75 2.00
❑ 45 Randall McDaniel .30 .75
❑ 46 Cris Carter .75 2.00
❑ 47 Jake Reed .50 1.25
❑ 48 John Randle .50 1.25
❑ 49 Drew Bledsoe 1.25 3.00
❑ 50 Willie Clay .30 .75
❑ 51 Chris Slade .30 .75
❑ 52 Willie McGinest .30 .75
❑ 53 Shawn Jefferson .30 .75
❑ 54 Ben Coates .50 1.25
❑ 55 Terry Glenn .75 2.00
❑ 56 Jason Hanson .30 .75
❑ 57 Scott Mitchell .50 1.25
❑ 58 Barry Sanders 2.50 6.00
❑ 59 Herman Moore .50 1.25
❑ 60 Johnnie Morton .50 1.25
❑ 61 Mark Brunell .75 2.00
❑ 62 James Stewart .50 1.25
❑ 63 Tony Boselli .30 .75
❑ 64 Jimmy Smith .50 1.25
❑ 65 Keenan McCardell .50 1.25
❑ 66 Dan Marino 3.00 8.00
❑ 67 Troy Drayton .30 .75
❑ 68 Bernie Parmalee .30 .75
❑ 69 Karim Abdul-Jabbar .75 2.00
❑ 70 Zach Thomas .75 2.00
❑ 71 O.J. McDuffie .50 1.25
❑ 72 Tim Bowens .30 .75
❑ 73 Danny Kanell .50 1.25
❑ 74 Tiki Barber .75 2.00
❑ 75 Tyrone Wheatley .50 1.25
❑ 76 Charles Way .30 .75
❑ 77 Jason Sehorn .50 1.25
❑ 78 Ike Hilliard .50 1.25
❑ 79 Michael Strahan .50 1.25
❑ 80 Troy Aikman 1.50 4.00
❑ 81 Deion Sanders .75 2.00
❑ 82 Emmitt Smith 2.50 6.00
❑ 83 Darren Woodson .30 .75
❑ 84 Daryl Johnston .50 1.25
❑ 85 Michael Irvin .75 2.00
❑ 86 David LaFleur .30 .75
❑ 87 Glenn Foley .50 1.25
❑ 88 Neil O'Donnell .50 1.25
❑ 89 Keyshawn Johnson .75 2.00
❑ 90 Aaron Glenn .30 .75
❑ 91 Wayne Chrebet .75 2.00
❑ 92 Curtis Martin .75 2.00
❑ 93 Steve McNair .75 2.00
❑ 94 Eddie George .75 2.00
❑ 95 Bruce Matthews .30 .75
❑ 96 Frank Wycheck .30 .75
❑ 97 Yancey Thigpen .30 .75
❑ 98 Gus Frerotte .30 .75
❑ 99 Terry Allen .75 2.00
❑ 100 Michael Westbrook .50 1.25
❑ 101 Jamie Asher .30 .75
❑ 102 Marshall Faulk 1.00 2.50
❑ 103 Zack Crockett .30 .75
❑ 104 Ken Dilger .30 .75
❑ 105 Marvin Harrison .75 2.00
❑ 106 Chris Chandler .50 1.25
❑ 107 Byron Hanspard .30 .75
❑ 108 Jamal Anderson .75 2.00
❑ 109 Terance Mathis .50 1.25
❑ 110 Peter Boulware .30 .75
❑ 111 Michael Jackson .30 .75
❑ 112 Jim Harbaugh .50 1.25
❑ 113 Errict Rhett .50 1.25
❑ 114 Antowain Smith .75 2.00
❑ 115 Thurman Thomas .75 2.00
❑ 116 Bruce Smith .50 1.25
❑ 117 Doug Flutie .75 2.00
❑ 118 Rob Johnson .50 1.25
❑ 119 Kerry Collins .50 1.25
❑ 120 Fred Lane .30 .75

❑ 121 Wesley Walls .50 1.25
❑ 122 William Floyd .30 .75
❑ 123 Kevin Greene .50 1.25
❑ 124 Erik Kramer .30 .75
❑ 125 Darnell Autry .30 .75
❑ 126 Curtis Conway .50 1.25
❑ 127 Edgar Bennett .30 .75
❑ 128 Jeff Blake .50 1.25
❑ 129 Corey Dillon .75 2.00
❑ 130 Carl Pickens .50 1.25
❑ 131 Darnay Scott .50 1.25
❑ 132 Jake Plummer .75 2.00
❑ 133 Larry Centers .30 .75
❑ 134 Frank Sanders .50 1.25
❑ 135 Rob Moore .50 1.25
❑ 136 Adrian Murrell .50 1.25
❑ 137 Troy Davis .30 .75
❑ 138 Ray Zellars .30 .75
❑ 139 Willie Roaf .30 .75
❑ 140 Andre Hastings .30 .75
❑ 141 Jeff George .50 1.25
❑ 142 Napoleon Kaufman .75 2.00
❑ 143 Desmond Howard .50 1.25
❑ 144 Tim Brown .75 2.00
❑ 145 James Jett .50 1.25
❑ 146 Rickey Dudley .30 .75
❑ 147 Bobby Hoying .50 1.25
❑ 148 Duce Staley 1.00 2.50
❑ 149 Charlie Garner .50 1.25
❑ 150 Irving Fryar .50 1.25
❑ 151 Chris T. Jones .30 .75
❑ 152 Tony Banks .50 1.25
❑ 153 Craig Heyward .30 .75
❑ 154 Isaac Bruce .75 2.00
❑ 155 Eddie Kennison .50 1.25
❑ 156 Junior Seau .75 2.00
❑ 157 Tony Martin .50 1.25
❑ 158 Freddie Jones .30 .75
❑ 159 Natrone Means .50 1.25
❑ 160 Warren Moon .75 2.00
❑ 161 Steve Broussard .30 .75
❑ 162 Joey Galloway .50 1.25
❑ 163 Brian Blades .30 .75
❑ 164 Ricky Watters .50 1.25
❑ 165 Peyton Manning RC 12.50 25.00
❑ 166 Ryan Leaf RC 1.25 3.00
❑ 167 Andre Wadsworth RC 1.00 2.50
❑ 168 Charles Woodson RC 1.50 4.00
❑ 169 Curtis Enis RC .60 1.50
❑ 170 Fred Taylor RC 2.00 5.00
❑ 171 Kevin Dyson RC 1.25 3.00
❑ 172 Robert Edwards RC 1.00 2.50
❑ 173 Randy Moss RC 6.00 15.00
❑ 174 R.W. McQuarters RC 1.00 2.50
❑ 175 John Avery RC 1.00 2.50
❑ 176 Marcus Nash RC .60 1.50
❑ 177 Jerome Pathon RC 1.25 3.00
❑ 178 Jacquez Green RC 1.00 2.50
❑ 179 Robert Holcombe RC 1.00 2.50
❑ 180 Pat Johnson RC 1.00 2.50
❑ 181 Germane Crowell RC 1.00 2.50
❑ 182 Tony Simmons RC 1.00 2.50
❑ 183 Joe Jurevicius RC 1.25 3.00
❑ 184 Mikhael Ricks RC 1.00 2.50
❑ 185 Charlie Batch RC 1.25 3.00
❑ 186 Jon Ritchie RC 1.00 2.50
❑ 187 Scott Frost RC .60 1.50
❑ 188 Skip Hicks RC 1.00 2.50
❑ 189 Brian Alford RC .60 1.50
❑ 190 E.G. Green RC 1.00 2.50
❑ 191 Jammi German RC .60 1.50
❑ 192 Ahman Green RC 2.50 6.00
❑ 193 Chris Floyd RC .60 1.50
❑ 194 Larry Shannon RC .60 1.50
❑ 195 Jonathan Quinn RC 1.25 3.00
❑ 196 Rashaan Shehee RC 1.00 2.50
❑ 197 Brian Griese RC 2.50 6.00
❑ 198 Hines Ward RC 5.00 10.00
❑ 199 Michael Pittman RC 2.00 4.00
❑ 200 Az-Zahir Hakim RC 1.25 3.00

1999 Playoff Prestige EXP

❑ COMPLETE SET (200) 25.00 50.00
❑ 1 Anthony McFarland RC .60 1.50
❑ 2 Al Wilson RC .40 1.00
❑ 3 Jevon Kearse RC 1.00 2.50
❑ 4 Aaron Brooks RC 1.25 3.00
❑ 5 Travis McGriff RC .30 .75
❑ 6 Jeff Paulk RC .30 .75
❑ 7 Shawn Bryson RC .60 1.50
❑ 8 Karsten Bailey RC .40 1.00
❑ 9 Mike Cloud RC .40 1.00
❑ 10 James Johnson RC .40 1.00
❑ 11 Tai Streets RC .60 1.50
❑ 12 Jermaine Fazande RC .40 1.00
❑ 13 Ebenezer Ekuban RC .40 1.00
❑ 14 Joe Montgomery RC .40 1.00
❑ 15 Craig Yeast RC .40 1.00
❑ 16 Joe Germaine RC .40 1.00
❑ 17 Andy Katzenmoyer RC .40 1.00
❑ 18 Kevin Faulk RC .60 1.50
❑ 19 Chris McAlister RC .40 1.00
❑ 20 Sedrick Irvin RC .30 .75
❑ 21 Brock Huard RC .60 1.50
❑ 22 Cade McNown RC .40 1.00
❑ 23 Shaun King RC .40 1.00
❑ 24 Amos Zereoue RC .60 1.50
❑ 25 Dameane Douglas RC .40 1.00
❑ 26 D'Wayne Bates RC .40 1.00
❑ 27 Kevin Johnson RC .60 1.50
❑ 28 Rob Konrad RC .60 1.50
❑ 29 Troy Edwards RC .40 1.00
❑ 30 Peerless Price RC .60 1.50
❑ 31 Daunte Culpepper RC 2.50 6.00
❑ 32 Akili Smith RC .40 1.00
❑ 33 David Boston RC .60 1.50
❑ 34 Chris Claiborne RC .30 .75
❑ 35 Torry Holt RC 1.50 4.00
❑ 36 Champ Bailey RC .75 2.00
❑ 37 Edgerrin James RC 2.50 6.00
❑ 38 Donovan McNabb RC 3.00 8.00
❑ 39 Ricky Williams RC 1.25 3.00
❑ 40 Tim Couch RC .60 1.50
❑ 41 Charles Woodson RP .40 1.00
❑ 42 Skip Hicks RP .15 .40
❑ 43 Brian Griese RP .40 1.00
❑ 44 Tim Dwight RP .40 1.00
❑ 45 Ryan Leaf RP .25 .60
❑ 46 Curtis Enis RP .15 .40
❑ 47 Charlie Batch RP .40 1.00
❑ 48 Fred Taylor RP .40 1.00
❑ 49 Peyton Manning RP .60 1.50
❑ 50 Randy Moss RP .50 1.25
❑ 51 Jim Harbaugh .25 .60
❑ 52 Warren Moon .40 1.00
❑ 53 Jeff George .25 .60
❑ 54 Rich Gannon .40 1.00
❑ 55 Scott Mitchell .15 .40
❑ 56 Kerry Collins .25 .60
❑ 57 Brad Johnson .40 1.00
❑ 58 Charles Johnson .15 .40
❑ 59 Chris Calloway .15 .40
❑ 60 Tyrone Wheatley .25 .60
❑ 61 Michael Westbrook .25 .60
❑ 62 Skip Hicks .15 .40
❑ 63 Terry Allen .25 .60
❑ 64 Albert Connell .15 .40
❑ 65 Kevin Dyson .25 .60
❑ 66 Frank Wycheck .15 .40
❑ 67 Yancey Thigpen .15 .40
❑ 68 Steve McNair .40 1.00
❑ 69 Eddie George .40 1.00
❑ 70 Eric Zeier .15 .40
❑ 71 Jacquez Green .15 .40
❑ 72 Reidel Anthony .25 .60
❑ 73 Warren Sapp .25 .60
❑ 74 Mike Alstott .40 1.00
❑ 75 Warrick Dunn .40 1.00
❑ 76 Trent Dilfer .25 .60
❑ 77 Ahman Green .40 1.00
❑ 78 Joey Galloway .25 .60
❑ 79 Ricky Watters .25 .60
❑ 80 Jon Kitna .40 1.00
❑ 81 Amp Lee .15 .40
❑ 82 Isaac Bruce .40 1.00
❑ 83 Robert Holcombe .15 .40
❑ 84 Greg Hill .15 .40
❑ 85 Marshall Faulk .50 1.25
❑ 86 Trent Green .40 1.00
❑ 87 J.J. Stokes .25 .60
❑ 88 Terrell Owens .40 1.00
❑ 89 Jerry Rice .75 2.00
❑ 90 Garrison Hearst .25 .60
❑ 91 Steve Young .50 1.25
❑ 92 Junior Seau .40 1.00
❑ 93 Mikhael Ricks .15 .40
❑ 94 Natrone Means .25 .60
❑ 95 Ryan Leaf .40 1.00
❑ 96 Courtney Hawkins .15 .40
❑ 97 Chris Fuamatu-Ma'afala UER .15 .40
❑ 98 Jerome Bettis .40 1.00
❑ 99 Kordell Stewart .25 .60
❑ 100 Bobby Hoying .25 .60
❑ 101 Charlie Garner .25 .60
❑ 102 Duce Staley .40 1.00
❑ 103 Charles Woodson .40 1.00
❑ 104 James Jett .25 .60
❑ 105 Rickey Dudley .15 .40
❑ 106 Tim Brown .40 1.00
❑ 107 Napoleon Kaufman .40 1.00
❑ 108 Wayne Chrebet .25 .60
❑ 109 Keyshawn Johnson .40 1.00
❑ 110 Vinny Testaverde .25 .60
❑ 111 Curtis Martin .40 1.00
❑ 112 Joe Jurevicius .25 .60
❑ 113 Tiki Barber .40 1.00
❑ 114 Ike Hilliard .15 .40
❑ 115 Kent Graham .15 .40
❑ 116 Gary Brown .15 .40
❑ 117 Lamar Smith .25 .60
❑ 118 Eddie Kennison .25 .60
❑ 119 Cam Cleeland .15 .40
❑ 120 Tony Simmons .15 .40
❑ 121 Ben Coates .25 .60
❑ 122 Darick Holmes .15 .40
❑ 123 Terry Glenn .40 1.00
❑ 124 Drew Bledsoe .50 1.25
❑ 125 Leroy Hoard .15 .40
❑ 126 Jake Reed .25 .60
❑ 127 Randy Moss 1.00 2.50
❑ 128 Cris Carter .40 1.00
❑ 129 Robert Smith .40 1.00
❑ 130 Randall Cunningham .40 1.00
❑ 131 Lamar Thomas .15 .40
❑ 132 John Avery .15 .40
❑ 133 O.J. McDuffie .25 .60
❑ 134 Dan Marino 1.25 3.00
❑ 135 Karim Abdul-Jabbar .25 .60
❑ 136 Rashaan Shehee .15 .40
❑ 137 Derrick Alexander WR .25 .60
❑ 138 Byron Bam Morris .15 .40
❑ 139 Andre Rison .25 .60
❑ 140 Elvis Grbac .25 .60
❑ 141 Tavian Banks .15 .40
❑ 142 Keenan McCardell .25 .60
❑ 143 Jimmy Smith .25 .60
❑ 144 Fred Taylor .40 1.00
❑ 145 Mark Brunell .40 1.00
❑ 146 Jerome Pathon .15 .40
❑ 147 Marvin Harrison .40 1.00
❑ 148 Peyton Manning 1.25 3.00
❑ 149 Robert Brooks .25 .60
❑ 150 Mark Chmura .15 .40
❑ 151 Antonio Freeman .40 1.00
❑ 152 Dorsey Levens .40 1.00
❑ 153 Brett Favre 1.25 3.00
❑ 154 Johnnie Morton .25 .60
❑ 155 Germane Crowell .15 .40
❑ 156 Barry Sanders 1.25 3.00
❑ 157 Herman Moore .25 .60
❑ 158 Charlie Batch .40 1.00
❑ 159 Marcus Nash .15 .40
❑ 160 Shannon Sharpe .25 .60

Card		
❑ 161 Rod Smith	.25	.60
❑ 162 Ed McCaffrey	.25	.60
❑ 163 Terrell Davis	.40	1.00
❑ 164 John Elway	1.25	3.00
❑ 165 Ernie Mills	.15	.40
❑ 166 Michael Irvin	.25	.60
❑ 167 Deion Sanders	.40	1.00
❑ 168 Emmitt Smith	.75	2.00
❑ 169 Troy Aikman	.75	2.00
❑ 170 Chris Spielman	.15	.40
❑ 171 Terry Kirby	.15	.40
❑ 172 Ty Detmer	.25	.60
❑ 173 Leslie Shepherd	.15	.40
❑ 174 Darnay Scott	.15	.40
❑ 175 Jeff Blake	.25	.60
❑ 176 Carl Pickens	.25	.60
❑ 177 Corey Dillon	.40	1.00
❑ 178 Bobby Engram	.25	.60
❑ 179 Curtis Conway	.25	.60
❑ 180 Curtis Enis	.15	.40
❑ 181 Muhsin Muhammad	.25	.60
❑ 182 Steve Beuerlein	.15	.40
❑ 183 Tim Biakabutuka	.25	.60
❑ 184 Bruce Smith	.25	.60
❑ 185 Andre Reed	.25	.60
❑ 186 Thurman Thomas	.25	.60
❑ 187 Eric Moulds	.40	1.00
❑ 188 Antowain Smith	.40	1.00
❑ 189 Doug Flutie	.40	1.00
❑ 190 Jermaine Lewis	.25	.60
❑ 191 Priest Holmes	.60	1.50
❑ 192 O.J. Santiago	.15	.40
❑ 193 Tim Dwight	.40	1.00
❑ 194 Terance Mathis	.25	.60
❑ 195 Chris Chandler	.25	.60
❑ 196 Jamal Anderson	.40	1.00
❑ 197 Rob Moore	.25	.60
❑ 198 Frank Sanders	.25	.60
❑ 199 Adrian Murrell	.25	.60
❑ 200 Jake Plummer	.25	.60
❑ RR1 Barry Sanders RFR	7.50	20.00

1999 Playoff Prestige SSD

Card		
❑ COMPLETE SET (200)	75.00	150.00
❑ COMP.SET w/o SP's (150)	25.00	50.00
❑ 1 Jake Plummer	.30	.75
❑ 2 Adrian Murrell	.30	.75
❑ 3 Frank Sanders	.30	.75
❑ 4 Rob Moore	.30	.75
❑ 5 Jamal Anderson	.50	1.25
❑ 6 Chris Chandler	.30	.75
❑ 7 Terance Mathis	.30	.75
❑ 8 Tim Dwight	.50	1.25
❑ 9 O.J. Santiago	.20	.50
❑ 10 Priest Holmes	.75	2.00
❑ 11 Jermaine Lewis	.30	.75
❑ 12 Doug Flutie	.50	1.25
❑ 13 Antowain Smith	.50	1.25
❑ 14 Eric Moulds	.50	1.25
❑ 15 Thurman Thomas	.30	.75
❑ 16 Andre Reed	.30	.75
❑ 17 Bruce Smith	.30	.75
❑ 18 Tim Biakabutuka	.30	.75
❑ 19 Steve Beuerlein	.20	.50
❑ 20 Muhsin Muhammad	.30	.75
❑ 21 Curtis Enis	.20	.50
❑ 22 Curtis Conway	.30	.75
❑ 23 Bobby Engram	.30	.75
❑ 24 Corey Dillon	.50	1.25
❑ 25 Carl Pickens	.30	.75
❑ 26 Jeff Blake	.30	.75
❑ 27 Darnay Scott	.20	.50
❑ 28 Leslie Shepherd	.20	.50
❑ 29 Ty Detmer	.30	.75
❑ 30 Terry Kirby	.20	.50
❑ 31 Chris Spielman	.20	.50
❑ 32 Troy Aikman	1.25	3.00
❑ 33 Emmitt Smith	1.25	3.00
❑ 34 Deion Sanders	.50	1.25
❑ 35 Michael Irvin	.30	.75
❑ 36 Ernie Mills	.20	.50
❑ 37 John Elway	2.00	5.00
❑ 38 Terrell Davis	.50	1.25
❑ 39 Ed McCaffrey	.30	.75
❑ 40 Rod Smith	.30	.75
❑ 41 Shannon Sharpe	.30	.75
❑ 42 Marcus Nash	.20	.50
❑ 43 Charlie Batch	.50	1.25
❑ 44 Herman Moore	.30	.75
❑ 45 Barry Sanders	2.00	5.00
❑ 46 Germane Crowell	.20	.50
❑ 47 Johnnie Morton	.30	.75
❑ 48 Brett Favre	2.00	5.00
❑ 49 Dorsey Levens	.50	1.25
❑ 50 Antonio Freeman	.50	1.25
❑ 51 Mark Chmura	.20	.50
❑ 52 Robert Brooks	.30	.75
❑ 53 Peyton Manning	2.00	5.00
❑ 54 Marvin Harrison	.50	1.25
❑ 55 Jerome Pathon	.20	.50
❑ 56 Mark Brunell	.50	1.25
❑ 57 Fred Taylor	.50	1.25
❑ 58 Jimmy Smith	.30	.75
❑ 59 Keenan McCardell	.30	.75
❑ 60 Tavian Banks	.20	.50
❑ 61 Elvis Grbac	.30	.75
❑ 62 Andre Rison	.30	.75
❑ 63 Byron Bam Morris	.20	.50
❑ 64 Derrick Alexander WR	.30	.75
❑ 65 Rashaan Shehee	.20	.50
❑ 66 Karim Abdul-Jabbar	.30	.75
❑ 67 Dan Marino	2.00	5.00
❑ 68 O.J. McDuffie	.30	.75
❑ 69 John Avery	.20	.50
❑ 70 Lamar Thomas	.20	.50
❑ 71 Randall Cunningham	.50	1.25
❑ 72 Robert Smith	.50	1.25
❑ 73 Cris Carter	.50	1.25
❑ 74 Randy Moss	1.50	4.00
❑ 75 Jake Reed	.30	.75
❑ 76 Leroy Hoard	.20	.50
❑ 77 Drew Bledsoe	.75	2.00
❑ 78 Terry Glenn	.50	1.25
❑ 79 Darick Holmes	.20	.50
❑ 80 Ben Coates	.30	.75
❑ 81 Tony Simmons	.20	.50
❑ 82 Cam Cleeland	.20	.50
❑ 83 Eddie Kennison	.30	.75
❑ 84 Lamar Smith	.30	.75
❑ 85 Gary Brown	.20	.50
❑ 86 Kent Graham	.20	.50
❑ 87 Ike Hilliard	.20	.50
❑ 88 Tiki Barber	.50	1.25
❑ 89 Joe Jurevicius	.30	.75
❑ 90 Curtis Martin	.50	1.25
❑ 91 Vinny Testaverde	.30	.75
❑ 92 Keyshawn Johnson	.50	1.25
❑ 93 Wayne Chrebet	.30	.75
❑ 94 Napoleon Kaufman	.50	1.25
❑ 95 Tim Brown	.50	1.25
❑ 96 Rickey Dudley	.20	.50
❑ 97 James Jett	.30	.75
❑ 98 Charles Woodson	.50	1.25
❑ 99 Duce Staley	.50	1.25
❑ 100 Charlie Garner	.30	.75
❑ 101 Bobby Hoying	.30	.75
❑ 102 Kordell Stewart	.30	.75
❑ 103 Jerome Bettis	.50	1.25
❑ 104 Chris Fuamatu-Ma'afala	.20	.50
❑ 105 Courtney Hawkins	.20	.50
❑ 106 Ryan Leaf	.50	1.25
❑ 107 Natrone Means	.30	.75
❑ 108 Mikhael Ricks	.20	.50
❑ 109 Junior Seau	.50	1.25
❑ 110 Steve Young	.75	2.00
❑ 111 Garrison Hearst	.30	.75
❑ 112 Jerry Rice	1.25	3.00
❑ 113 Terrell Owens	.50	1.25
❑ 114 J.J. Stokes	.30	.75
❑ 115 Trent Green	.50	1.25
❑ 116 Marshall Faulk	.60	1.50
❑ 117 Greg Hill	.20	.50
❑ 118 Robert Holcombe	.20	.50
❑ 119 Isaac Bruce	.50	1.25
❑ 120 Amp Lee	.20	.50
❑ 121 Jon Kitna	.50	1.25
❑ 122 Ricky Watters	.30	.75
❑ 123 Joey Galloway	.30	.75
❑ 124 Ahman Green	.50	1.25
❑ 125 Trent Dilfer	.30	.75
❑ 126 Warrick Dunn	.50	1.25
❑ 127 Mike Alstott	.50	1.25
❑ 128 Warren Sapp	.30	.75
❑ 129 Reidel Anthony	.30	.75
❑ 130 Jacquez Green	.20	.50
❑ 131 Eric Zeier	.20	.50
❑ 132 Eddie George	.50	1.25
❑ 133 Steve McNair	.50	1.25
❑ 134 Yancey Thigpen	.20	.50
❑ 135 Frank Wycheck	.20	.50
❑ 136 Kevin Dyson	.30	.75
❑ 137 Albert Connell	.20	.50
❑ 138 Terry Allen	.30	.75
❑ 139 Skip Hicks	.20	.50
❑ 140 Michael Westbrook	.30	.75
❑ 141 Tyrone Wheatley	.30	.75
❑ 142 Chris Calloway	.20	.50
❑ 143 Charles Johnson	.20	.50
❑ 144 Brad Johnson	.50	1.25
❑ 145 Kerry Collins	.30	.75
❑ 146 Scott Mitchell	.20	.50
❑ 147 Rich Gannon	.50	1.25
❑ 148 Jeff George	.30	.75
❑ 149 Warren Moon	.50	1.25
❑ 150 Jim Harbaugh	.30	.75
❑ 151 Randy Moss RP	2.50	6.00
❑ 152 Peyton Manning RP	3.00	8.00
❑ 153 Fred Taylor RP	1.00	2.50
❑ 154 Charlie Batch RP	1.00	2.50
❑ 155 Curtis Enis RP	.60	1.50
❑ 156 Ryan Leaf RP	.60	1.50
❑ 157 Tim Dwight RP	.60	1.50
❑ 158 Brian Griese RP	1.00	2.50
❑ 159 Skip Hicks RP	.60	1.50
❑ 160 Charles Woodson RP	1.00	2.50
❑ 161 Tim Couch RC	1.50	4.00
❑ 162 Ricky Williams RC	2.50	6.00
❑ 163 Donovan McNabb RC	6.00	15.00
❑ 164 Edgerrin James RC	5.00	12.00
❑ 165 Champ Bailey RC	2.00	5.00
❑ 166 Torry Holt RC	3.00	8.00
❑ 167 Chris Claiborne RC	.75	2.00
❑ 168 David Boston RC	1.50	4.00
❑ 169 Akili Smith RC	.60	1.50
❑ 170 Daunte Culpepper RC	5.00	12.00
❑ 171 Peerless Price RC	1.50	4.00
❑ 172 Troy Edwards RC	1.25	3.00
❑ 173 Rob Konrad RC	1.50	4.00
❑ 174 Kevin Johnson RC	1.50	4.00
❑ 175 D'Wayne Bates RC	1.25	3.00
❑ 176 Dameane Douglas RC	1.25	3.00
❑ 177 Amos Zereoue RC	1.50	4.00
❑ 178 Shaun King RC	1.25	3.00
❑ 179 Cade McNown RC	1.25	3.00
❑ 180 Brock Huard RC	1.50	4.00
❑ 181 Sedrick Irvin RC	.75	2.00
❑ 182 Chris McAlister RC	1.25	3.00
❑ 183 Kevin Faulk RC	1.50	4.00
❑ 184 Andy Katzenmoyer RC	1.25	3.00
❑ 185 Joe Germaine RC	1.25	3.00
❑ 186 Craig Yeast RC	1.25	3.00
❑ 187 Joe Montgomery RC	1.25	3.00
❑ 188 Ebenezer Ekuban RC	1.25	3.00
❑ 189 Jermaine Fazande RC	1.25	3.00
❑ 190 Tai Streets RC	1.50	4.00
❑ 191 James Johnson RC	1.25	3.00
❑ 192 Mike Cloud RC	1.25	3.00
❑ 193 Karsten Bailey RC	1.25	3.00
❑ 194 Shawn Bryson RC	1.50	4.00
❑ 195 Jeff Paulk RC	.75	2.00
❑ 196 Travis McGriff RC	.75	2.00
❑ 197 Aaron Brooks RC	2.50	6.00
❑ 198 Jevon Kearse RC	2.50	6.00
❑ 199 Al Wilson RC	1.25	3.00
❑ 200 Anthony McFarland RC	1.50	4.00

2000 Playoff Prestige

Card	Low	High
❑ COMPLETE SET (300)	175.00	350.00
❑ COMP.SET w/o SP's (200)	10.00	25.00
❑ 1 Frank Sanders	.15	.40
❑ 2 Rob Moore	.15	.40
❑ 3 Michael Pittman	.08	.25
❑ 4 Jake Plummer	.15	.40
❑ 5 David Boston	.25	.60
❑ 6 Chris Chandler	.15	.40
❑ 7 Tim Dwight	.25	.60
❑ 8 Shawn Jefferson	.08	.25
❑ 9 Terance Mathis	.15	.40
❑ 10 Jamal Anderson	.25	.60
❑ 11 Byron Hanspard	.08	.25
❑ 12 Ken Oxendine	.08	.25
❑ 13 Priest Holmes	.30	.75
❑ 14 Tony Banks	.15	.40
❑ 15 Shannon Sharpe	.15	.40
❑ 16 Rod Woodson	.15	.40
❑ 17 Jermaine Lewis	.15	.40
❑ 18 Qadry Ismail	.15	.40
❑ 19 Eric Moulds	.25	.60
❑ 20 Doug Flutie	.25	.60
❑ 21 Jay Riemersma	.08	.25
❑ 22 Antowain Smith	.15	.40
❑ 23 Jonathan Linton	.08	.25
❑ 24 Peerless Price	.15	.40
❑ 25 Rob Johnson	.15	.40
❑ 26 Muhsin Muhammad	.15	.40
❑ 27 Wesley Walls	.08	.25
❑ 28 Tim Biakabutuka	.15	.40
❑ 29 Steve Beuerlein	.15	.40
❑ 30 Patrick Jeffers	.25	.60
❑ 31 Natrone Means	.08	.25
❑ 32 Curtis Enis	.08	.25
❑ 33 Bobby Engram	.15	.40
❑ 34 Marcus Robinson	.25	.60
❑ 35 Marty Booker	.15	.40
❑ 36 Cade McNown	.08	.25
❑ 37 Damay Scott	.15	.40
❑ 38 Carl Pickens	.15	.40
❑ 39 Corey Dillon	.25	.60
❑ 40 Akili Smith	.08	.25
❑ 41 Michael Basnight	.08	.25
❑ 42 Karim Abdul-Jabbar	.15	.40
❑ 43 Tim Couch	.15	.40
❑ 44 Kevin Johnson	.25	.60
❑ 45 Darrin Chiaverini	.08	.25
❑ 46 Errict Rhett	.15	.40
❑ 47 Emmitt Smith	.50	1.25
❑ 48 Deion Sanders	.25	.60
❑ 49 Michael Irvin	.15	.40
❑ 50 Rocket Ismail	.15	.40
❑ 51 Troy Aikman	.50	1.25
❑ 52 Jason Tucker	.08	.25
❑ 53 Joey Galloway	.15	.40
❑ 54 David LaFleur	.08	.25
❑ 55 Wane McGarity	.08	.25
❑ 56 Ed McCaffrey	.25	.60
❑ 57 Rod Smith	.15	.40
❑ 58 Brian Griese	.25	.60
❑ 59 John Elway	.75	2.00
❑ 60 Gus Frerotte	.08	.25
❑ 61 Neil Smith	.08	.25
❑ 62 Terrell Davis	.25	.60
❑ 63 Olandis Gary	.25	.60
❑ 64 Johnnie Morton	.15	.40
❑ 65 Charlie Batch	.25	.60
❑ 66 Barry Sanders	.60	1.50
❑ 67 James Stewart	.15	.40
❑ 68 Germane Crowell	.08	.25
❑ 69 Sedrick Irvin	.08	.25
❑ 70 Herman Moore	.15	.40
❑ 71 Corey Bradford	.15	.40
❑ 72 Dorsey Levens	.15	.40
❑ 73 Antonio Freeman	.25	.60
❑ 74 Brett Favre	.75	2.00
❑ 75 De'Mond Parker	.08	.25
❑ 76 Bill Schroeder	.15	.40
❑ 77 Donald Driver	.25	.60
❑ 78 E.G. Green	.08	.25
❑ 79 Marvin Harrison	.25	.60
❑ 80 Peyton Manning	.60	1.50
❑ 81 Terrence Wilkins	.08	.25
❑ 82 Edgerrin James	.40	1.00
❑ 83 Keenan McCardell	.15	.40
❑ 84 Mark Brunell	.25	.60
❑ 85 Fred Taylor	.25	.60
❑ 86 Jimmy Smith	.15	.40
❑ 87 Derrick Alexander	.15	.40
❑ 88 Andre Rison	.15	.40
❑ 89 Elvis Grbac	.15	.40
❑ 90 Tony Gonzalez	.15	.40
❑ 91 Donnell Bennett	.08	.25
❑ 92 Warren Moon	.25	.60
❑ 93 Kimble Anders	.08	.25
❑ 94 Tony Richardson RC	.15	.40
❑ 95 Jay Fiedler	.25	.60
❑ 96 Zach Thomas	.25	.60
❑ 97 Oronde Gadsden	.15	.40
❑ 98 Dan Marino	.75	2.00
❑ 99 O.J. McDuffie	.15	.40
❑ 100 Tony Martin	.15	.40
❑ 101 James Johnson	.08	.25
❑ 102 Rob Konrad	.08	.25
❑ 103 Damon Huard	.25	.60
❑ 104 Thurman Thomas	.15	.40
❑ 105 Randy Moss	.50	1.25
❑ 106 Cris Carter	.25	.60
❑ 107 Robert Smith	.25	.60
❑ 108 Randall Cunningham	.25	.60
❑ 109 John Randle	.15	.40
❑ 110 Leroy Hoard	.08	.25
❑ 111 Daunte Culpepper	.30	.75
❑ 112 Matthew Hatchette	.08	.25
❑ 113 Troy Brown	.15	.40
❑ 114 Tony Simmons	.08	.25
❑ 115 Terry Glenn	.15	.40
❑ 116 Ben Coates	.08	.25
❑ 117 Drew Bledsoe	.30	.75
❑ 118 Terry Allen	.15	.40
❑ 119 Kevin Faulk	.08	.25
❑ 120 Ricky Williams	.25	.60
❑ 121 Jake Delhomme RC	1.25	3.00
❑ 122 Jake Reed	.15	.40
❑ 123 Jeff Blake	.15	.40
❑ 124 Amani Toomer	.15	.40
❑ 125 Kerry Collins	.15	.40
❑ 126 Tiki Barber	.25	.60
❑ 127 Ike Hilliard	.15	.40
❑ 128 Joe Montgomery	.08	.25
❑ 129 Sean Bennett	.08	.25
❑ 130 Curtis Martin	.25	.60
❑ 131 Vinny Testaverde	.15	.40
❑ 132 Wayne Chrebet	.15	.40
❑ 133 Ray Lucas	.15	.40
❑ 134 Tyrone Wheatley	.15	.40
❑ 135 Napoleon Kaufman	.15	.40
❑ 136 Tim Brown	.25	.60
❑ 137 Rickey Dudley	.08	.25
❑ 138 James Jett	.08	.25
❑ 139 Rich Gannon	.25	.60
❑ 140 Charles Woodson	.15	.40
❑ 141 Duce Staley	.25	.60
❑ 142 Donovan McNabb	.40	1.00
❑ 143 Na Brown	.08	.25
❑ 144 Kordell Stewart	.15	.40
❑ 145 Jerome Bettis	.25	.60
❑ 146 Hines Ward	.25	.60
❑ 147 Troy Edwards	.08	.25
❑ 148 Curtis Conway	.15	.40
❑ 149 Junior Seau	.25	.60
❑ 150 Jim Harbaugh	.15	.40
❑ 151 Jermaine Fazande	.08	.25
❑ 152 Terrell Owens	.25	.60
❑ 153 J.J. Stokes	.15	.40
❑ 154 Charlie Garner	.15	.40
❑ 155 Jerry Rice	.50	1.25
❑ 156 Garrison Hearst	.15	.40
❑ 157 Steve Young	.30	.75
❑ 158 Jeff Garcia	.25	.60
❑ 159 Derrick Mayes	.15	.40
❑ 160 Ahman Green	.25	.60
❑ 161 Ricky Watters	.15	.40
❑ 162 Jon Kitna	.25	.60
❑ 163 Karsten Bailey	.08	.25
❑ 164 Sean Dawkins	.08	.25
❑ 165 Az-Zahir Hakim	.15	.40
❑ 166 Isaac Bruce	.25	.60
❑ 167 Marshall Faulk	.30	.75
❑ 168 Trent Green	.25	.60
❑ 169 Kurt Warner	.50	1.25
❑ 170 Torry Holt	.25	.60
❑ 171 Robert Holcombe	.08	.25
❑ 172 Kevin Carter	.08	.25
❑ 173 Keyshawn Johnson	.25	.60
❑ 174 Jacquez Green	.08	.25
❑ 175 Reidel Anthony	.08	.25
❑ 176 Warren Sapp	.15	.40
❑ 177 Mike Alstott	.25	.60
❑ 178 Warrick Dunn	.25	.60
❑ 179 Trent Dilfer	.15	.40
❑ 180 Shaun King	.08	.25
❑ 181 Neil O'Donnell	.08	.25
❑ 182 Eddie George	.25	.60
❑ 183 Yancey Thigpen	.08	.25
❑ 184 Steve McNair	.25	.60
❑ 185 Kevin Dyson	.15	.40
❑ 186 Frank Wycheck	.08	.25
❑ 187 Jevon Kearse	.25	.60
❑ 188 Adrian Murrell	.08	.25
❑ 189 Jeff George	.15	.40
❑ 190 Stephen Davis	.25	.60
❑ 191 Stephen Alexander	.08	.25
❑ 192 Darrell Green	.08	.25
❑ 193 Skip Hicks	.08	.25
❑ 194 Brad Johnson	.25	.60
❑ 195 Michael Westbrook	.15	.40
❑ 196 Albert Connell	.08	.25
❑ 197 Irving Fryar	.15	.40
❑ 198 Bruce Smith	.15	.40
❑ 199 Champ Bailey	.15	.40
❑ 200 Larry Centers	.08	.25
❑ 201 Jake Plummer PP	.50	1.25
❑ 202 Doug Flutie PP	.50	1.25
❑ 203 Eric Moulds PP	.50	1.25
❑ 204 Muhsin Muhammad PP	.50	1.25
❑ 205 Marcus Robinson PP	.50	1.25
❑ 206 Cade McNown PP	.50	1.25
❑ 207 Corey Dillon PP	.50	1.25
❑ 208 Tim Couch PP	.50	1.25
❑ 209 Kevin Johnson PP	.50	1.25
❑ 210 Emmitt Smith PP	1.25	3.00
❑ 211 Troy Aikman PP	1.25	3.00
❑ 212 Brian Griese PP	.50	1.25
❑ 213 Olandis Gary PP	.50	1.25
❑ 214 Germane Crowell PP	.50	1.25
❑ 215 Brett Favre PP	2.00	5.00
❑ 216 Charlie Batch PP	.50	1.25
❑ 217 Antonio Freeman PP	.50	1.25
❑ 218 Dorsey Levens PP	.50	1.25
❑ 219 Peyton Manning PP	1.50	4.00
❑ 220 Edgerrin James PP	1.00	2.50
❑ 221 Marvin Harrison PP	.50	1.25
❑ 222 Fred Taylor PP	.50	1.25
❑ 223 Mark Brunell PP	.50	1.25
❑ 224 Jimmy Smith PP	.50	1.25
❑ 225 Dan Marino PP	2.00	5.00
❑ 226 Randy Moss PP	1.25	3.00
❑ 227 Cris Carter PP	.50	1.25
❑ 228 Robert Smith PP	.50	1.25
❑ 229 Drew Bledsoe PP	.75	2.00
❑ 230 Terry Glenn PP	.50	1.25
❑ 231 Ricky Williams PP	.50	1.25
❑ 232 Amani Toomer PP	.50	1.25
❑ 233 Keyshawn Johnson PP	.50	1.25
❑ 234 Curtis Martin PP	.50	1.25
❑ 235 Ray Lucas PP	.50	1.25
❑ 236 Tim Brown PP	.50	1.25
❑ 237 Duce Staley PP	.50	1.25
❑ 238 Donovan McNabb PP	1.00	2.50
❑ 239 Jerry Rice PP	1.25	3.00
❑ 240 Jon Kitna PP	.50	1.25
❑ 241 Isaac Bruce PP	.50	1.25
❑ 242 Kurt Warner PP	1.25	3.00
❑ 243 Torry Holt PP	.50	1.25
❑ 244 Mike Alstott PP	.50	1.25
❑ 245 Marshall Faulk PP	.75	2.00
❑ 246 Shaun King PP	.08	.25
❑ 247 Eddie George PP	.50	1.25
❑ 248 Steve McNair PP	.50	1.25
❑ 249 Stephen Davis PP	.50	1.25
❑ 250 Brad Johnson PP	.50	1.25

Card	Low	High
❑ 251 Rondell Mealey RC	1.00	2.50
❑ 252 Peter Warrick RC	1.50	4.00
❑ 253 Courtney Brown RC	.50	1.25
❑ 254 Plaxico Burress RC	3.00	8.00
❑ 255 Corey Simon RC	.50	1.25
❑ 256 Thomas Jones RC	2.50	6.00
❑ 257 Travis Taylor RC	.50	1.25
❑ 258 Shaun Alexander RC	5.00	12.00
❑ 259 Chris Redman RC	.50	1.25
❑ 260 Chad Pennington RC	4.00	10.00
❑ 261 Jamal Lewis RC	4.00	10.00
❑ 262 Bubba Franks RC	1.50	4.00
❑ 263 Dez White RC	1.50	4.00
❑ 264 Ron Dayne RC	1.50	4.00
❑ 265 Sylvester Morris RC	1.25	3.00
❑ 266 R.Jay Soward RC	1.25	3.00
❑ 267 Sherrod Gideon RC	1.00	2.50
❑ 268 Travis Prentice RC	1.25	3.00
❑ 269 Darrell Jackson RC	3.00	8.00
❑ 270 Giovanni Carmazzi RC	1.00	2.50
❑ 271 Anthony Lucas RC	1.00	2.50
❑ 272 Danny Farmer RC	1.25	3.00
❑ 273 Dennis Northcutt RC	1.50	4.00
❑ 274 Troy Walters RC	1.50	4.00
❑ 275 Laveranues Coles RC	2.00	5.00
❑ 276 Tee Martin RC	1.50	4.00
❑ 277 J.R. Redmond RC	1.25	3.00
❑ 278 Jerry Porter RC	2.00	5.00
❑ 279 Sebastian Janikowski RC	1.50	4.00
❑ 280 Michael Wiley RC	1.25	3.00
❑ 281 Reuben Droughns RC	2.00	5.00
❑ 282 Trung Canidate RC	1.25	3.00
❑ 283 Shyrone Stith RC	1.25	3.00
❑ 284 Trevor Gaylor RC	1.25	3.00
❑ 285 Marc Bulger RC	3.00	8.00
❑ 286 Tom Brady RC	50.00	100.00
❑ 287 Todd Husak RC	1.50	4.00
❑ 288 Jarious Jackson RC	1.25	3.00
❑ 289 Terrelle Smith RC	1.25	3.00
❑ 290 Chad Morton RC	1.50	4.00
❑ 291 Chris Cole RC	1.50	4.00
❑ 292 Kwame Cavil RC	1.00	2.50
❑ 293 JaJuan Dawson RC	1.00	2.50
❑ 294 Curtis Keaton RC	1.25	3.00
❑ 295 Tim Rattay RC	1.50	4.00
❑ 296 Joe Hamilton RC	1.25	3.00
❑ 297 Gari Scott RC	1.00	2.50
❑ 298 Mike Anderson RC	2.00	5.00
❑ 299 Ron Dugans RC	1.00	2.50
❑ 300 Todd Pinkston RC	1.50	4.00

2002 Playoff Prestige

Card	Low	High
❑ COMP.SET w/o SP's (150)	15.00	40.00
❑ 1 David Boston	.25	.60
❑ 2 MarTay Jenkins	.25	.60
❑ 3 Jake Plummer	.30	.75
❑ 4 Chris Chandler	.30	.75
❑ 5 Jamal Anderson	.30	.75
❑ 6 Michael Vick	.40	1.00
❑ 7 Maurice Smith	.25	.60
❑ 8 Elvis Grbac	.30	.75
❑ 9 Jamal Lewis	.30	.75
❑ 10 Todd Heap	.30	.75
❑ 11 Qadry Ismail	.30	.75
❑ 12 Shannon Sharpe	.40	1.00
❑ 13 Ray Lewis	.40	1.00
❑ 14 Rod Woodson	.40	1.00
❑ 15 Travis Henry	.30	.75
❑ 16 Rob Johnson	.30	.75
❑ 17 Eric Moulds	.30	.75
❑ 18 Nate Clements	.25	.60
❑ 19 Donald Hayes	.25	.60
❑ 20 Muhsin Muhammad	.30	.75
❑ 21 Steve Smith	.40	1.00
❑ 22 Wesley Walls	.30	.75
❑ 23 Chris Weinke	.25	.60
❑ 24 James Allen	.25	.60
❑ 25 David Terrell	.30	.75
❑ 26 Anthony Thomas	.30	.75
❑ 27 Dez White	.25	.60
❑ 28 Brian Urlacher	.50	1.25
❑ 29 Mike Brown	.30	.75
❑ 30 Corey Dillon	.30	.75
❑ 31 Chad Johnson	.40	1.00
❑ 32 Peter Warrick	.30	.75
❑ 33 Justin Smith	.25	.60
❑ 34 Tim Couch	.25	.60
❑ 35 James Jackson	.25	.60
❑ 36 Quincy Morgan	.25	.60
❑ 37 Kevin Johnson	.25	.60
❑ 38 Gerard Warren	.25	.60
❑ 39 Anthony Henry	.25	.60
❑ 40 Quincy Carter	.25	.60
❑ 41 Joey Galloway	.30	.75
❑ 42 Rocket Ismail	.30	.75
❑ 43 Ryan Leaf	.25	.60
❑ 44 Emmitt Smith	1.00	2.50
❑ 45 Troy Hambrick	.25	.60
❑ 46 Mike Anderson	.30	.75
❑ 47 Terrell Davis	.40	1.00
❑ 48 Brian Griese	.30	.75
❑ 49 Rod Smith	.30	.75
❑ 50 Ed McCaffrey	.30	.75
❑ 51 Charlie Batch	.30	.75
❑ 52 Johnnie Morton	.30	.75
❑ 53 Germane Crowell	.25	.60
❑ 54 James Stewart	.25	.60
❑ 55 Shaun Rogers	.25	.60
❑ 56 Brett Favre	1.00	2.50
❑ 57 Antonio Freeman	.40	1.00
❑ 58 Ahman Green	.30	.75
❑ 59 Bill Schroeder	.30	.75
❑ 60 Kabeer Gbaja-Biamila	.30	.75
❑ 61 Marvin Harrison	.40	1.00
❑ 62 Terrence Wilkins	.25	.60
❑ 63 Dominic Rhodes	.30	.75
❑ 64 Reggie Wayne	.40	1.00
❑ 65 Edgerrin James	.40	1.00
❑ 66 Mark Brunell	.30	.75
❑ 67 Keenan McCardell	.30	.75
❑ 68 Jimmy Smith	.30	.75
❑ 69 Fred Taylor	.40	1.00
❑ 70 Derrick Alexander	.30	.75
❑ 71 Tony Gonzalez	.30	.75
❑ 72 Trent Green	.30	.75
❑ 73 Priest Holmes	.40	1.00
❑ 74 Snoop Minnis	.25	.60
❑ 75 Chris Chambers	.40	1.00
❑ 76 Jay Fiedler	.30	.75
❑ 77 Travis Minor	.30	.75
❑ 78 Lamar Smith	.30	.75
❑ 79 Zach Thomas	.40	1.00
❑ 80 Michael Bennett	.30	.75
❑ 81 Cris Carter	.40	1.00
❑ 82 Daunte Culpepper	.30	.75
❑ 83 Randy Moss	.40	1.00
❑ 84 Drew Bledsoe	.40	1.00
❑ 85 Tom Brady	1.00	2.50
❑ 86 Troy Brown	.30	.75
❑ 87 Antowain Smith	.30	.75
❑ 88 Aaron Brooks	.30	.75
❑ 89 Joe Horn	.30	.75
❑ 90 Deuce McAllister	.40	1.00
❑ 91 Ricky Williams	.40	1.00
❑ 92 Kerry Collins	.30	.75
❑ 93 Ron Dayne	.30	.75
❑ 94 Michael Strahan	.40	1.00
❑ 95 Jason Sehorn	.30	.75
❑ 96 Wayne Chrebet	.30	.75
❑ 97 Laveranues Coles	.40	1.00
❑ 98 LaMont Jordan	.30	.75
❑ 99 Curtis Martin	.40	1.00
❑ 100 Santana Moss	.30	.75
❑ 101 Vinny Testaverde	.30	.75
❑ 102 Tim Brown	.40	1.00
❑ 103 Jerry Porter	.30	.75
❑ 104 Jerry Rice	.75	2.00
❑ 105 Charlie Garner	.30	.75
❑ 106 Tyrone Wheatley	.30	.75
❑ 107 Charles Woodson	.40	1.00
❑ 108 Correll Buckhalter	.30	.75
❑ 109 Todd Pinkston	.25	.60
❑ 110 Freddie Mitchell	.25	.60
❑ 111 James Thrash	.30	.75
❑ 112 Duce Staley	.30	.75
❑ 113 Jerome Bettis	.40	1.00
❑ 114 Plaxico Burress	.30	.75
❑ 115 Kordell Stewart	.30	.75
❑ 116 Hines Ward	.40	1.00
❑ 117 Kendrell Bell	.25	.60
❑ 118 Drew Brees	.60	1.50
❑ 119 Curtis Conway	.30	.75
❑ 120 Doug Flutie	.40	1.00
❑ 121 LaDainian Tomlinson	.60	1.50
❑ 122 Junior Seau	.40	1.00
❑ 123 Kevan Barlow	.25	.60
❑ 124 Jeff Garcia	.30	.75
❑ 125 Garrison Hearst	.30	.75
❑ 126 Terrell Owens	.40	1.00
❑ 127 Andre Carter	.25	.60
❑ 128 Shaun Alexander	.40	1.00
❑ 129 Matt Hasselbeck	.40	1.00
❑ 130 Koren Robinson	.25	.60
❑ 131 Ricky Watters	.30	.75
❑ 132 Isaac Bruce	.40	1.00
❑ 133 Trung Canidate	.25	.60
❑ 134 Marshall Faulk	.40	1.00
❑ 135 Torry Holt	.40	1.00
❑ 136 Kurt Warner	.40	1.00
❑ 137 Mike Alstott	.30	.75
❑ 138 Warrick Dunn	.30	.75
❑ 139 Brad Johnson	.30	.75
❑ 140 Keyshawn Johnson	.30	.75
❑ 141 Warren Sapp	.30	.75
❑ 142 Eddie George	.30	.75
❑ 143 Derrick Mason	.30	.75
❑ 144 Steve McNair	.40	1.00
❑ 145 Jevon Kearse	.30	.75
❑ 146 Stephen Davis	.30	.75
❑ 147 Rod Gardner	.25	.60
❑ 148 Champ Bailey	.40	1.00
❑ 149 Bruce Smith	.40	1.00
❑ 150 Houston Texans	.40	1.00
❑ 151 David Carr RC	1.25	3.00
❑ 152 Julius Peppers RC	2.00	5.00
❑ 153 Joey Harrington RC	1.25	3.00
❑ 154 Quentin Jammer RC	1.25	3.00
❑ 155 Ryan Sims RC	1.25	3.00
❑ 156 Bryant McKinnie RC	.75	2.00
❑ 157 Roy Williams RC	1.50	4.00
❑ 158 John Henderson RC	1.25	3.00
❑ 159 Dwight Freeney RC	2.00	5.00
❑ 160 Wendell Bryant RC	.75	2.00
❑ 161 Donte Stallworth RC	1.25	3.00
❑ 162 Jeremy Shockey RC	2.00	5.00
❑ 163 Albert Haynesworth RC	1.25	3.00
❑ 164 William Green RC	1.00	2.50
❑ 165 Phillip Buchanon RC	1.25	3.00
❑ 166 T.J. Duckett RC	1.25	3.00
❑ 167 Ashley Lelie RC	1.25	3.00
❑ 168 Javon Walker RC	1.25	3.00
❑ 169 Daniel Graham RC	1.00	2.50
❑ 170 Napoleon Harris RC	1.00	2.50
❑ 171 Lito Sheppard RC	1.25	3.00
❑ 172 Robert Thomas RC	.75	2.00
❑ 173 Patrick Ramsey RC	1.25	3.00
❑ 174 Jabar Gaffney RC	1.25	3.00
❑ 175 DeShaun Foster RC	1.25	3.00
❑ 176 Kalimba Edwards RC	1.00	2.50
❑ 177 Josh Reed RC	1.00	2.50
❑ 178 Larry Tripplett RC	.75	2.00
❑ 179 Andre Davis RC	1.00	2.50
❑ 180 Reche Caldwell RC	1.25	3.00
❑ 181 Levar Fisher RC	.75	2.00
❑ 182 Clinton Portis RC	3.00	8.00
❑ 183 Anthony Weaver RC	.75	2.00
❑ 184 Maurice Morris RC	1.25	3.00
❑ 185 Ladell Betts RC	1.25	3.00
❑ 186 Antwaan Randle El RC	1.25	3.00
❑ 187 Antonio Bryant RC	1.50	4.00
❑ 188 Rocky Calmus RC	1.00	2.50
❑ 189 Josh McCown RC	1.25	3.00
❑ 190 Lamar Gordon RC	1.25	3.00
❑ 191 Marquise Walker RC	.75	2.00
❑ 192 Cliff Russell RC	.75	2.00
❑ 193 Eric Crouch RC	1.25	3.00
❑ 194 Dennis Johnson RC	.75	2.00
❑ 195 Alex Brown RC	1.25	3.00
❑ 196 David Garrard RC	2.00	5.00
❑ 197 Rohan Davey RC	1.25	3.00
❑ 198 Alan Harper RC	.75	2.00
❑ 199 Ron Johnson RC	1.00	2.50
❑ 200 Andra Davis RC	.75	2.00
❑ 201 Kurt Kittner RC	.75	2.00

❑ 202 Freddie Milons RC	.75	2.00
❑ 203 Adrian Peterson RC	1.25	3.00
❑ 204 Luke Staley RC	.75	2.00
❑ 205 Tracey Wistrom RC	1.00	2.50
❑ 206 Woody Dantzler RC	1.00	2.50
❑ 207 Chad Hutchinson RC	.75	2.00
❑ 208 Zak Kustok RC	.75	2.00
❑ 209 Damien Anderson RC	1.00	2.50
❑ 210 James Mungro RC	1.25	3.00
❑ 211 Cortlen Johnson RC	.75	2.00
❑ 212 Demontray Carter RC	.75	2.00
❑ 213 Kelly Campbell RC	1.00	2.50
❑ 214 Brian Poli-Dixon RC	.75	2.00
❑ 215 Mike Rumph RC	.75	2.00
❑ 216 Najeh Davenport RC	1.25	3.00

2003 Playoff Prestige

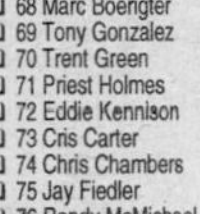
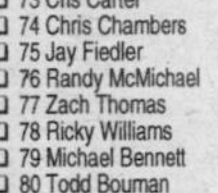
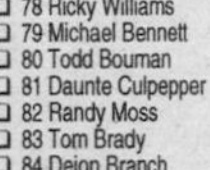

❑ COMP.SET w/o RC's (150)	12.50	30.00
❑ 1 David Boston	.25	.60
❑ 2 Thomas Jones	.30	.75
❑ 3 Jake Plummer	.30	.75
❑ 4 Marcel Shipp	.25	.60
❑ 5 T.J. Duckett	.30	.75
❑ 6 Warrick Dunn	.30	.75
❑ 7 Michael Vick	.40	1.00
❑ 8 Jeff Blake	.30	.75
❑ 9 Todd Heap	.30	.75
❑ 10 Jamal Lewis	.40	1.00
❑ 11 Ray Lewis	.40	1.00
❑ 12 Drew Bledsoe	.40	1.00
❑ 13 Travis Henry	.30	.75
❑ 14 Eric Moulds	.30	.75
❑ 15 Peerless Price	.25	.60
❑ 16 Josh Reed	.25	.60
❑ 17 DeShaun Foster	.30	.75
❑ 18 Muhsin Muhammad	.30	.75
❑ 19 Steve Smith	.40	1.00
❑ 20 Julius Peppers	.40	1.00
❑ 21 Marty Booker	.30	.75
❑ 22 David Terrell	.25	.60
❑ 23 Anthony Thomas	.30	.75
❑ 24 Brian Urlacher	.60	1.50
❑ 25 Corey Dillon	.30	.75
❑ 26 Chad Johnson	.40	1.00
❑ 27 Jon Kitna	.30	.75
❑ 28 Peter Warrick	.30	.75
❑ 29 Tim Couch	.25	.60
❑ 30 Andre Davis	.25	.60
❑ 31 William Green	.25	.60
❑ 32 Quincy Morgan	.25	.60
❑ 33 Dennis Northcutt	.25	.60
❑ 34 Antonio Bryant	.40	1.00
❑ 35 Quincy Carter	.25	.60
❑ 36 Troy Hambrick	.25	.60
❑ 37 Chad Hutchinson	.25	.60
❑ 38 Emmitt Smith	1.00	2.50
❑ 39 Roy Williams	.40	1.00
❑ 40 Brian Griese	.30	.75
❑ 41 Ashley Lelie	.25	.60
❑ 42 Ed McCaffrey	.30	.75
❑ 43 Clinton Portis	.50	1.25
❑ 44 Rod Smith	.30	.75
❑ 45 Germane Crowell	.25	.60
❑ 46 Az-Zahir Hakim	.25	.60
❑ 47 Joey Harrington	.30	.75
❑ 48 James Stewart	.30	.75
❑ 49 Donald Driver	.40	1.00
❑ 50 Brett Favre	1.00	2.50
❑ 51 Terry Glenn	.30	.75
❑ 52 Ahman Green	.40	1.00
❑ 53 Javon Walker	.30	.75
❑ 54 Corey Bradford	.25	.60
❑ 55 David Carr	.40	1.00
❑ 56 Jabar Gaffney	.25	.60
❑ 57 Jonathan Wells	.25	.60
❑ 58 Marvin Harrison	.40	1.00
❑ 59 Edgerrin James	.40	1.00
❑ 60 Peyton Manning	.75	2.00
❑ 61 James Mungro	.25	.60
❑ 62 Reggie Wayne	.30	.75
❑ 63 Mark Brunell	.30	.75
❑ 64 David Garrard	.40	1.00
❑ 65 Stacey Mack	.25	.60
❑ 66 Jimmy Smith	.30	.75
❑ 67 Fred Taylor	.40	1.00
❑ 68 Marc Boerigter	.25	.60
❑ 69 Tony Gonzalez	.30	.75
❑ 70 Trent Green	.30	.75
❑ 71 Priest Holmes	.40	1.00
❑ 72 Eddie Kennison	.25	.60
❑ 73 Cris Carter	.40	1.00
❑ 74 Chris Chambers	.30	.75
❑ 75 Jay Fiedler	.30	.75
❑ 76 Randy McMichael	.25	.60
❑ 77 Zach Thomas	.40	1.00
❑ 78 Ricky Williams	.30	.75
❑ 79 Michael Bennett	.30	.75
❑ 80 Todd Bouman	.25	.60
❑ 81 Daunte Culpepper	.40	1.00
❑ 82 Randy Moss	.40	1.00
❑ 83 Tom Brady	1.00	2.50
❑ 84 Deion Branch	.30	.75
❑ 85 Troy Brown	.30	.75
❑ 86 Kevin Faulk	.30	.75
❑ 87 Antowain Smith	.30	.75
❑ 88 Aaron Brooks	.30	.75
❑ 89 Joe Horn	.30	.75
❑ 90 Deuce McAllister	.40	1.00
❑ 91 Donte Stallworth	.30	.75
❑ 92 Tiki Barber	.40	1.00
❑ 93 Kerry Collins	.30	.75
❑ 94 Jeremy Shockey	.40	1.00
❑ 95 Michael Strahan	.30	.75
❑ 96 Amani Toomer	.30	.75
❑ 97 Laveranues Coles	.30	.75
❑ 98 LaMont Jordan	.30	.75
❑ 99 Curtis Martin	.40	1.00
❑ 100 Santana Moss	.30	.75
❑ 101 Chad Pennington	.40	1.00
❑ 102 Tim Brown	.40	1.00
❑ 103 Rich Gannon	.30	.75
❑ 104 Charlie Garner	.30	.75
❑ 105 Jerry Rice	.75	2.00
❑ 106 Charles Woodson	.30	.75
❑ 107 Antonio Freeman	.30	.75
❑ 108 Dorsey Levens	.30	.75
❑ 109 Donovan McNabb	.40	1.00
❑ 110 Duce Staley	.30	.75
❑ 111 James Thrash	.25	.60
❑ 112 Jerome Bettis	.40	1.00
❑ 113 Plaxico Burress	.40	1.00
❑ 114 Tommy Maddox	.30	.75
❑ 115 Antwaan Randle El	.30	.75
❑ 116 Kordell Stewart	.30	.75
❑ 117 Hines Ward	.40	1.00
❑ 118 Drew Brees	.40	1.00
❑ 119 Curtis Conway	.25	.60
❑ 120 Junior Seau	.40	1.00
❑ 121 LaDainian Tomlinson	.50	1.25
❑ 122 Kevan Barlow	.25	.60
❑ 123 Jeff Garcia	.40	1.00
❑ 124 Garrison Hearst	.30	.75
❑ 125 Terrell Owens	.40	1.00
❑ 126 Shaun Alexander	.40	1.00
❑ 127 Trent Dilfer	.30	.75
❑ 128 Darrell Jackson	.30	.75
❑ 129 Maurice Morris	.25	.60
❑ 130 Koren Robinson	.30	.75
❑ 131 Isaac Bruce	.40	1.00
❑ 132 Marc Bulger	.40	1.00
❑ 133 Marshall Faulk	.40	1.00
❑ 134 Torry Holt	.40	1.00
❑ 135 Kurt Warner	.40	1.00
❑ 136 Mike Alstott	.40	1.00
❑ 137 Brad Johnson	.30	.75
❑ 138 Keyshawn Johnson	.40	1.00
❑ 139 Dexter Jackson RC	.50	1.25
❑ 140 Warren Sapp	.30	.75
❑ 141 Kevin Dyson	.30	.75
❑ 142 Eddie George	.30	.75
❑ 143 Jevon Kearse	.30	.75
❑ 144 Derrick Mason	.30	.75
❑ 145 Steve McNair	.40	1.00
❑ 146 Stephen Davis	.30	.75
❑ 147 Rod Gardner	.25	.60
❑ 148 Shane Matthews	.25	.60
❑ 149 Patrick Ramsey	.30	.75
❑ 150 Derrius Thompson	.25	.60
❑ 151 Byron Leftwich RC	1.50	4.00
❑ 152 Carson Palmer RC	5.00	12.00
❑ 153 Chris Simms RC	1.25	3.00
❑ 154 Kliff Kingsbury RC	1.00	2.50
❑ 155 Dave Ragone RC	.75	2.00
❑ 156 Jason Gesser RC	1.00	2.50
❑ 157 Ken Dorsey RC	1.00	2.50
❑ 158 Kyle Boller RC	1.25	3.00
❑ 159 Brad Banks RC	1.00	2.50
❑ 160 Rex Grossman RC	1.25	3.00
❑ 161 Seneca Wallace RC	1.25	3.00
❑ 162 Brian St.Pierre RC	1.25	3.00
❑ 163 Larry Johnson RC	1.50	4.00
❑ 164 Earnest Graham RC	1.25	3.00
❑ 165 Musa Smith RC	1.00	2.50
❑ 166 Lee Suggs RC	1.00	2.50
❑ 167 Willis McGahee RC	2.50	6.00
❑ 168 Onterrio Smith RC	1.00	2.50
❑ 170 Sultan McCullough RC	.75	2.00
❑ 171 Chris Brown RC	1.25	3.00
❑ 172 Justin Fargas RC	1.25	3.00
❑ 173 Avon Cobourne RC	.75	2.00
❑ 174 Dahrran Diedrick RC	.75	2.00
❑ 175 LaBrandon Toefield RC	1.00	2.50
❑ 176 Artose Pinner RC	.75	2.00
❑ 177 Quentin Griffin RC	1.00	2.50
❑ 178 ReShard Lee RC	1.25	3.00
❑ 179 Andrew Pinnock RC	1.00	2.50
❑ 180 B.J. Askew RC	1.00	2.50
❑ 181 Andre Johnson RC	2.50	6.00
❑ 182 Brandon Lloyd RC	1.25	3.00
❑ 183 Bryant Johnson RC	1.25	3.00
❑ 184 Charles Rogers RC	1.00	2.50
❑ 185 Doug Gabriel RC	1.00	2.50
❑ 186 Justin Gage RC	1.25	3.00
❑ 187 Kareem Kelly RC	.75	2.00
❑ 188 Kelley Washington RC	1.00	2.50
❑ 189 Taylor Jacobs RC	1.00	2.50
❑ 190 Terrence Edwards RC	.75	2.00
❑ 191 Anquan Boldin RC	3.00	8.00
❑ 192 Billy McMullen RC	.75	2.00
❑ 193 Talman Gardner RC	.75	2.00
❑ 194 Arnaz Battle RC	1.25	3.00
❑ 195 Sam Aiken RC	1.25	3.00
❑ 196 Bobby Wade RC	1.00	2.50
❑ 197 Mike Bush RC	.75	2.00
❑ 198 Keenan Howry RC	.75	2.00
❑ 199 Jerel Myers RC	.75	2.00
❑ 200 Dallas Clark RC	2.50	6.00
❑ 201 Mike Pinkard RC	.75	2.00
❑ 202 Teyo Johnson RC	1.00	2.50
❑ 203 Trent Smith RC	1.00	2.50
❑ 204 George Wrighster RC	.75	2.00
❑ 205 Jason Witten RC	3.00	8.00
❑ 206 Cory Redding RC	1.00	2.50
❑ 207 DeWayne White RC	.75	2.00
❑ 208 Jerome McDougle RC	.75	2.00
❑ 209 Michael Haynes RC	.75	2.00
❑ 210 Chris Kelsay RC	1.00	2.50
❑ 211 Calvin Pace RC	1.00	2.50
❑ 212 Kenny King RC	1.00	2.50
❑ 213 Jimmy Kennedy RC	1.00	2.50
❑ 214 William Joseph RC	.75	2.00
❑ 215 DeWayne Robertson RC	1.00	2.50
❑ 216 Jarret Johnson RC	1.00	2.50
❑ 217 Rien Long RC	.75	2.00
❑ 218 Boss Bailey RC	1.00	2.50
❑ 219 Terrell Suggs RC	1.50	4.00
❑ 220 Terry Pierce RC	.75	2.00
❑ 221 Bradie James RC	1.25	3.00
❑ 222 Angelo Crowell RC	1.00	2.50
❑ 223 Andre Woolfolk RC	1.00	2.50
❑ 224 Dennis Weathersby RC	.75	2.00
❑ 225 Marcus Trufant RC	1.25	3.00
❑ 226 Terence Newman RC	1.25	3.00
❑ 227 Ricky Manning RC	1.00	2.50
❑ 228 Mike Doss RC	1.25	3.00
❑ 229 Julian Battle RC	1.00	2.50
❑ 230 Rashean Mathis RC	1.00	2.50

2004 Playoff Prestige

Card	Low	High
❑ COMP.SET w/o RC's (150)	10.00	25.00
❑ 1 Anquan Boldin	.40	1.00
❑ 2 Emmitt Smith	1.00	2.50
❑ 3 Jeff Blake	.30	.75
❑ 4 Marcel Shipp	.40	1.00
❑ 5 Michael Vick	.40	1.00
❑ 6 Peerless Price	.30	.75
❑ 7 T.J. Duckett	.30	.75
❑ 8 Warrick Dunn	.30	.75
❑ 9 Ed Reed	.30	.75
❑ 10 Jamal Lewis	.30	.75
❑ 11 Kyle Boller	.30	.75
❑ 12 Ray Lewis	.40	1.00
❑ 13 Todd Heap	.30	.75
❑ 14 Drew Bledsoe	.40	1.00
❑ 15 Eric Moulds	.30	.75
❑ 16 Josh Reed	.40	1.00
❑ 17 Travis Henry	.30	.75
❑ 18 DeShaun Foster	.30	.75
❑ 19 Stephen Davis	.30	.75
❑ 20 Jake Delhomme	.30	.75
❑ 21 Julius Peppers	.30	.75
❑ 22 Steve Smith	.40	1.00
❑ 23 Anthony Thomas	.30	.75
❑ 24 Brian Urlacher	.40	1.00
❑ 25 Marty Booker	.30	.75
❑ 26 Rex Grossman	.40	1.00
❑ 27 Chad Johnson	.30	.75
❑ 28 Corey Dillon	.30	.75
❑ 29 Carson Palmer	.50	1.25
❑ 30 Peter Warrick	.30	.75
❑ 31 Rudi Johnson	.30	.75
❑ 32 Andre Davis	.25	.60
❑ 33 Quincy Morgan	.25	.60
❑ 34 William Green	.25	.60
❑ 35 Kelly Holcomb	.30	.75
❑ 36 Antonio Bryant	.40	1.00
❑ 37 Quincy Carter	.25	.60
❑ 38 Roy Williams S	.30	.75
❑ 39 Terence Newman	.30	.75
❑ 40 Terry Glenn	.30	.75
❑ 41 Troy Hambrick	.25	.60
❑ 42 Ashley Lelie	.30	.75
❑ 43 Clinton Portis	.40	1.00
❑ 44 Rod Smith	.30	.75
❑ 45 Shannon Sharpe	.30	.75
❑ 46 Mike Anderson	.30	.75
❑ 47 Jake Plummer	.30	.75
❑ 48 Charles Rogers	.30	.75
❑ 49 Joey Harrington	.30	.75
❑ 50 Ahman Green	.40	1.00
❑ 51 Brett Favre	1.00	2.50
❑ 52 Donald Driver	.40	1.00
❑ 53 Javon Walker	.30	.75
❑ 54 Robert Ferguson	.25	.60
❑ 55 Andre Johnson	.40	1.00
❑ 56 David Carr	.30	.75
❑ 57 Domanick Davis	.30	.75
❑ 58 Jabar Gaffney	.30	.75
❑ 59 Dwight Freeney	.40	1.00
❑ 60 Dallas Clark	.40	1.00
❑ 61 Edgerrin James	.40	1.00
❑ 62 Marvin Harrison	.40	1.00
❑ 63 Peyton Manning	.75	2.00
❑ 64 Reggie Wayne	.30	.75
❑ 65 Byron Leftwich	.40	1.00
❑ 66 Fred Taylor	.30	.75
❑ 67 Jimmy Smith	.30	.75
❑ 68 Johnnie Morton	.30	.75
❑ 69 Priest Holmes	.40	1.00
❑ 70 Tony Gonzalez	.40	1.00
❑ 71 Trent Green	.30	.75
❑ 72 Chris Chambers	.30	.75
❑ 73 Jay Fiedler	.25	.60
❑ 74 Randy McMichael	.25	.60
❑ 75 Ricky Williams	.40	1.00
❑ 76 Zach Thomas	.40	1.00
❑ 77 Daunte Culpepper	.40	1.00
❑ 78 Kelly Campbell	.25	.60
❑ 79 Michael Bennett	.30	.75
❑ 80 Moe Williams	.25	.60
❑ 81 Nate Burleson	.30	.75
❑ 82 Randy Moss	.40	1.00
❑ 83 Deion Branch	.30	.75
❑ 84 Kevin Faulk	.30	.75
❑ 85 Tom Brady	1.00	2.50
❑ 86 Troy Brown	.30	.75
❑ 87 Tedy Bruschi	.40	1.00
❑ 88 Aaron Brooks	.30	.75
❑ 89 Deuce McAllister	.40	1.00
❑ 90 Donte Stallworth	.30	.75
❑ 91 Joe Horn	.30	.75
❑ 92 Amani Toomer	.30	.75
❑ 93 Ike Hilliard	.30	.75
❑ 94 Jeremy Shockey	.30	.75
❑ 95 Kerry Collins	.30	.75
❑ 96 Michael Strahan	.30	.75
❑ 97 Tiki Barber	.40	1.00
❑ 98 Chad Pennington	.40	1.00
❑ 99 Curtis Martin	.40	1.00
❑ 100 LaMont Jordan	.40	1.00
❑ 101 Santana Moss	.30	.75
❑ 102 Charlie Garner	.30	.75
❑ 103 Jerry Porter	.30	.75
❑ 104 Jerry Rice	.75	2.00
❑ 105 Justin Fargas	.30	.75
❑ 106 Rich Gannon	.30	.75
❑ 107 Rod Woodson	.30	.75
❑ 108 Tim Brown	.40	1.00
❑ 109 Brian Westbrook	.40	1.00
❑ 110 Correll Buckhalter	.30	.75
❑ 111 Donovan McNabb	.40	1.00
❑ 112 Freddie Mitchell	.25	.60
❑ 113 James Thrash	.25	.60
❑ 114 Amos Zereoue	.25	.60
❑ 115 Antwaan Randle El	.30	.75
❑ 116 Hines Ward	.40	1.00
❑ 117 Joey Porter	.30	.75
❑ 118 Kendrell Bell	.25	.60
❑ 119 Plaxico Burress	.30	.75
❑ 120 David Boston	.25	.60
❑ 121 Drew Brees	.40	1.00
❑ 122 LaDainian Tomlinson	.50	1.25
❑ 123 Jeff Garcia	.40	1.00
❑ 124 Kevan Barlow	.30	.75
❑ 125 Tai Streets	.25	.60
❑ 126 Terrell Owens	.40	1.00
❑ 127 Tim Rattay	.25	.60
❑ 128 Darrell Jackson	.30	.75
❑ 129 Koren Robinson	.40	1.00
❑ 130 Matt Hasselbeck	.40	1.00
❑ 131 Shaun Alexander	.40	1.00
❑ 132 Isaac Bruce	.30	.75
❑ 133 Marc Bulger	.30	.75
❑ 134 Marshall Faulk	.40	1.00
❑ 135 Torry Holt	.40	1.00
❑ 136 Brad Johnson	.30	.75
❑ 137 Derrick Brooks	.30	.75
❑ 138 Keenan McCardell	.25	.60
❑ 139 Keyshawn Johnson	.30	.75
❑ 140 Mike Alstott	.30	.75
❑ 141 Derrick Mason	.30	.75
❑ 142 Drew Bennett	.30	.75
❑ 143 Jevon Kearse	.30	.75
❑ 144 Justin McCareins	.25	.60
❑ 145 Steve McNair	.40	1.00
❑ 146 Tyrone Calico	.30	.75
❑ 147 Bruce Smith	.40	1.00
❑ 148 Laveranues Coles	.30	.75
❑ 149 Patrick Ramsey	.30	.75
❑ 150 LaVar Arrington	.30	.75
❑ 151 Eli Manning RC	6.00	15.00
❑ 152 Larry Fitzgerald RC	3.00	8.00
❑ 153 Philip Rivers RC	4.00	10.00
❑ 154 Sean Taylor RC	1.00	2.50
❑ 155 Kellen Winslow RC	1.25	3.00
❑ 156 Roy Williams RC	1.25	3.00
❑ 157 DeAngelo Hall RC	1.00	2.50
❑ 158 Reggie Williams RC	1.00	2.50
❑ 159 Ben Roethlisberger RC	8.00	20.00
❑ 160 Jonathan Vilma RC	1.00	2.50
❑ 161 Lee Evans RC	1.25	3.00
❑ 162 Tommie Harris RC	1.00	2.50
❑ 163 Michael Clayton RC	1.00	2.50
❑ 164 D.J. Williams SP RC	10.00	25.00
❑ 165 Will Smith RC	1.00	2.50
❑ 166 Kenechi Udeze RC	1.00	2.50
❑ 167 Vince Wilfork SP RC	10.00	25.00
❑ 168 J.P. Losman RC	1.00	2.50
❑ 169 Steven Jackson SP RC	20.00	50.00
❑ 170 Ahmad Carroll RC	1.00	2.50
❑ 171 Chris Perry RC	1.00	2.50
❑ 172 Jason Babin SP RC	8.00	20.00
❑ 173 Chris Gamble RC	.75	2.00
❑ 174 Michael Jenkins RC	1.00	2.50
❑ 175 Kevin Jones RC	1.00	2.50
❑ 176 Rashaun Woods RC	.60	1.50
❑ 177 Ben Watson RC	1.00	2.50
❑ 178 Karlos Dansby RC	1.00	2.50
❑ 179 Teddy Lehman RC	.75	2.00
❑ 180 Ricardo Colclough SP RC	10.00	25.00
❑ 181 Daryl Smith RC	.75	2.00
❑ 182 Ben Troupe RC	.75	2.00
❑ 183 Tatum Bell RC	1.00	2.50
❑ 184 Julius Jones RC	1.25	3.00
❑ 185 Bob Sanders RC	2.50	6.00
❑ 186 Devery Henderson RC	1.00	2.50
❑ 187 Dwan Edwards RC	.60	1.50
❑ 188 Michael Boulware RC	1.00	2.50
❑ 189 Darius Watts RC	.75	2.00
❑ 190 Greg Jones RC	1.00	2.50
❑ 191 Antwan Odom RC	1.00	2.50
❑ 192 Sean Jones SP RC	8.00	20.00
❑ 193 Courtney Watson RC	.75	2.00
❑ 194 Keary Colbert RC	.75	2.00
❑ 195 Keith Smith RC	.60	1.50
❑ 196 Derrick Strait RC	.75	2.00
❑ 197 Bernard Berrian RC	1.00	2.50
❑ 198 Devard Darling RC	.75	2.00
❑ 199 Matt Schaub RC	2.50	6.00
❑ 200 Will Poole RC	1.00	2.50
❑ 201 Samie Parker RC	.75	2.00
❑ 202 Luke McCown SP RC	10.00	25.00
❑ 203 Jerricho Cotchery RC	1.00	2.50
❑ 204 Mewelde Moore RC	1.00	2.50
❑ 205 Ernest Wilford RC	.75	2.00
❑ 206 Cedric Cobbs SP RC	8.00	20.00
❑ 207 Johnnie Morant RC	.75	2.00
❑ 208 Craig Krenzel RC	1.00	2.50
❑ 209 Michael Turner RC	2.50	6.00
❑ 210 D.J. Hackett RC	1.00	2.50
❑ 211 P.K. Sam RC	.60	1.50
❑ 212 Josh Harris RC	.60	1.50
❑ 213 Drew Henson RC	.60	1.50
❑ 214 Jeff Smoker RC	.75	2.00
❑ 215 John Navarre RC	.75	2.00
❑ 216 Cody Pickett RC	.75	2.00
❑ 217 Quincy Wilson RC	.75	2.00
❑ 218 Derek Abney RC	.60	1.50
❑ 219 Maurice Clarett SP RC	8.00	20.00
❑ 220 Mike Williams SP RC	8.00	20.00
❑ 221 B.J. Johnson RC	.60	1.50
❑ 222 Brandon Everage RC	.60	1.50
❑ 223 Derek McCoy RC	.60	1.50
❑ 224 Jared Lorenzen RC	.75	2.00
❑ 225 Jarrett Payton RC	.75	2.00
❑ 226 Jason Fife RC	.60	1.50
❑ 227 Robert Kent RC	.60	1.50

2005 Playoff Prestige

Card	Low	High
❑ COMP.SET w/o SP's (234)	50.00	100.00
❑ COMP.SET w/o RC's (150)	10.00	25.00
❑ ONE 151-244 DRAFT PICK PER PACK		
❑ 1 Anquan Boldin	.30	.75
❑ 2 Emmitt Smith	.75	2.00
❑ 3 Josh McCown	.30	.75
❑ 4 Larry Fitzgerald	.40	1.00
❑ 5 Michael Vick	.40	1.00
❑ 6 Peerless Price	.25	.60

Card	Low	High
❑ 7 Alge Crumpler	.30	.75
❑ 8 T.J. Duckett	.25	.60
❑ 9 Warrick Dunn	.30	.75
❑ 10 Ed Reed	.30	.75
❑ 11 Jamal Lewis	.30	.75
❑ 12 Kyle Boller	.30	.75
❑ 13 Ray Lewis	.40	1.00
❑ 14 Todd Heap	.30	.75
❑ 15 Drew Bledsoe	.40	1.00
❑ 16 Eric Moulds	.30	.75
❑ 17 Lee Evans	.30	.75
❑ 18 Travis Henry	.30	.75
❑ 19 Willis McGahee	.40	1.00
❑ 20 Anthony Thomas	.25	.60
❑ 21 Brian Urlacher	.40	1.00
❑ 22 Rex Grossman	.40	1.00
❑ 23 David Terrell	.25	.60
❑ 24 Thomas Jones	.30	.75
❑ 25 Carson Palmer	.40	1.00
❑ 26 Chad Johnson	.30	.75
❑ 27 Peter Warrick	.25	.60
❑ 28 Rudi Johnson	.30	.75
❑ 29 Antonio Bryant	.30	.75
❑ 30 William Green	.25	.60
❑ 31 Jeff Garcia	.30	.75
❑ 32 Kellen Winslow	.40	1.00
❑ 33 Lee Suggs	.30	.75
❑ 34 Drew Henson	.25	.60
❑ 35 Julius Jones	.40	1.00
❑ 36 Jason Witten	.40	1.00
❑ 37 Keyshawn Johnson	.30	.75
❑ 38 Roy Williams S	.30	.75
❑ 39 Ashley Lelie	.25	.60
❑ 40 Champ Bailey	.30	.75
❑ 41 Jake Plummer	.30	.75
❑ 42 Reuben Droughns	.25	.60
❑ 43 Rod Smith	.30	.75
❑ 44 Charles Rogers	.25	.60
❑ 45 Joey Harrington	.40	1.00
❑ 46 Kevin Jones	.30	.75
❑ 47 Roy Williams WR	.40	1.00
❑ 48 Ahman Green	.40	1.00
❑ 49 Donald Driver	.40	1.00
❑ 50 Javon Walker	.30	.75
❑ 51 Brett Favre	1.00	2.50
❑ 52 Andre Johnson	.30	.75
❑ 53 David Carr	.30	.75
❑ 54 Domanick Davis	.25	.60
❑ 55 Jabar Gaffney	.25	.60
❑ 56 Edgerrin James	.30	.75
❑ 57 Marvin Harrison	.40	1.00
❑ 58 Brandon Stokley	.25	.60
❑ 59 Peyton Manning	.60	1.50
❑ 60 Reggie Wayne	.30	.75
❑ 61 Byron Leftwich	.30	.75
❑ 62 Fred Taylor	.40	1.00
❑ 63 Jimmy Smith	.30	.75
❑ 64 Priest Holmes	.40	1.00
❑ 65 Tony Gonzalez	.30	.75
❑ 66 Johnnie Morton	.30	.75
❑ 67 Trent Green	.30	.75
❑ 68 Chris Chambers	.30	.75
❑ 69 Randy McMichael	.25	.60
❑ 70 A.J. Feeley	.25	.60
❑ 71 Zach Thomas	.40	1.00
❑ 72 Daunte Culpepper	.40	1.00
❑ 73 Marcus Robinson	.30	.75
❑ 74 Mewelde Moore	.25	.60
❑ 75 Nate Burleson	.30	.75
❑ 76 Onterrio Smith	.25	.60
❑ 77 Randy Moss	.40	1.00
❑ 78 Corey Dillon	.30	.75
❑ 79 Tom Brady	.75	2.00
❑ 80 Deion Branch	.30	.75
❑ 81 Tedy Bruschi	.40	1.00
❑ 82 David Givens	.30	.75
❑ 83 David Patten	.25	.60
❑ 84 Aaron Brooks	.25	.60
❑ 85 Deuce McAllister	.40	1.00
❑ 86 Donte Stallworth	.30	.75
❑ 87 Joe Horn	.30	.75
❑ 88 Eli Manning	.75	2.00
❑ 89 Jeremy Shockey	.40	1.00
❑ 90 Kurt Warner	.40	1.00
❑ 91 Michael Strahan	.30	.75
❑ 92 Tiki Barber	.40	1.00
❑ 93 Amani Toomer	.30	.75
❑ 94 Chad Pennington	.40	1.00
❑ 95 Curtis Martin	.40	1.00
❑ 96 Santana Moss	.30	.75
❑ 97 Justin McCareins	.25	.60
❑ 98 Charles Woodson	.30	.75
❑ 99 Kerry Collins	.30	.75
❑ 100 Warren Sapp	.30	.75
❑ 101 Jerry Porter	.30	.75
❑ 102 Donovan McNabb	.40	1.00
❑ 103 Jevon Kearse	.30	.75
❑ 104 Terrell Owens	.40	1.00
❑ 105 Brian Westbrook	.40	1.00
❑ 106 Todd Pinkston	.25	.60
❑ 107 Duce Staley	.30	.75
❑ 108 Hines Ward	.40	1.00
❑ 109 Jerome Bettis	.40	1.00
❑ 110 Joey Porter	.25	.60
❑ 111 Plaxico Burress	.30	.75
❑ 112 Ben Roethlisberger	1.00	2.50
❑ 113 Drew Brees	.40	1.00
❑ 114 LaDainian Tomlinson	.50	1.25
❑ 115 Keenan McCardell	.30	.75
❑ 116 Philip Rivers	.40	1.00
❑ 117 Antonio Gates	.40	1.00
❑ 118 Eric Johnson	.25	.60
❑ 119 Kevan Barlow	.25	.60
❑ 120 Brandon Lloyd	.25	.60
❑ 121 Tim Rattay	.25	.60
❑ 122 Darrell Jackson	.30	.75
❑ 123 Koren Robinson	.30	.75
❑ 124 Jerry Rice	.75	2.00
❑ 125 Matt Hasselbeck	.30	.75
❑ 126 Shaun Alexander	.40	1.00
❑ 127 Isaac Bruce	.30	.75
❑ 128 Marc Bulger	.30	.75
❑ 129 Marshall Faulk	.40	1.00
❑ 130 Steven Jackson	.50	1.25
❑ 131 Torry Holt	.30	.75
❑ 132 Derrick Brooks	.30	.75
❑ 133 Michael Clayton	.30	.75
❑ 134 Michael Pittman	.25	.60
❑ 135 Chris Simms	.30	.75
❑ 136 Chris Brown	.30	.75
❑ 137 Derrick Mason	.30	.75
❑ 138 Drew Bennett	.30	.75
❑ 139 Steve McNair	.40	1.00
❑ 140 Clinton Portis	.40	1.00
❑ 141 LaVar Arrington	.40	1.00
❑ 142 Laveranues Coles	.30	.75
❑ 143 Patrick Ramsey	.30	.75
❑ 144 Rod Gardner	.25	.60
❑ 145 DeShaun Foster	.30	.75
❑ 146 Stephen Davis	.30	.75
❑ 147 Jake Delhomme	.40	1.00
❑ 148 Muhsin Muhammad	.30	.75
❑ 149 Steve Smith	.40	1.00
❑ 150 Keary Colbert	.25	.60
❑ 151 Aaron Rodgers SP RC	20.00	50.00
❑ 152 Adrian McPherson SP RC	8.00	20.00
❑ 153 Alex Smith QB RC	1.00	2.50
❑ 154 Andrew Walter RC	.75	2.00
❑ 155 Brock Berlin RC	.75	2.00
❑ 156 Charlie Frye SP RC	10.00	25.00
❑ 157 Chris Rix RC	.75	2.00
❑ 158 Dan Orlovsky RC	1.00	2.50
❑ 159 Darian Durant RC	1.00	2.50
❑ 160 David Greene RC	.75	2.00
❑ 161 Derek Anderson RC	1.00	2.50
❑ 162 Gino Guidugli RC	.60	1.50
❑ 163 Jason Campbell RC	1.50	4.00
❑ 164 Jason White RC	1.00	2.50
❑ 165 Kyle Orton RC	1.50	4.00
❑ 166 Matt Jones SP RC	10.00	25.00
❑ 167 Ryan Fitzpatrick RC	1.00	2.50
❑ 168 Stefan LeFors RC	.75	2.00
❑ 169 Timmy Chang RC	.75	2.00
❑ 170 Alvin Pearman RC	.60	1.50
❑ 171 Anthony Davis RC	.75	2.00
❑ 172 Brandon Jacobs RC	1.25	3.00
❑ 173 Cadillac Williams RC	1.50	4.00
❑ 174 Cedric Benson RC	1.00	2.50
❑ 175 Cedric Houston RC	1.00	2.50
❑ 176 Ciatrick Fason RC	.75	2.00
❑ 177 Damien Nash RC	.75	2.00
❑ 178 Darren Sproles RC	1.25	3.00
❑ 179 Eric Shelton SP RC	8.00	20.00
❑ 180 Frank Gore SP RC	15.00	40.00
❑ 181 J.J. Arrington SP RC	10.00	25.00
❑ 182 Kay-Jay Harris RC	.75	2.00
❑ 183 Marion Barber RC	3.00	8.00
❑ 184 Ronnie Brown RC	3.00	8.00
❑ 185 Ryan Moats RC	.75	2.00
❑ 186 T.A. McLendon RC	.60	1.50
❑ 187 Vernand Morency RC	.75	2.00
❑ 188 Walter Reyes RC	.60	1.50
❑ 189 Braylon Edwards RC	2.50	6.00
❑ 190 Charles Frederick RC	.75	2.00
❑ 191 Chris Henry RC	1.00	2.50
❑ 192 Courtney Roby RC	.75	2.00
❑ 193 Craig Bragg RC	.60	1.50
❑ 194 Craphonso Thorpe SP RC	8.00	20.00
❑ 195 Dante Ridgeway RC	.60	1.50
❑ 196 Fred Amey RC	.75	2.00
❑ 197 Fred Gibson RC	.75	2.00
❑ 198 J.R. Russell RC	.60	1.50
❑ 199 Jerome Mathis SP RC	10.00	25.00
❑ 200 Josh Davis RC	.60	1.50
❑ 201 Larry Brackins RC	.60	1.50
❑ 202 Mark Bradley RC	.75	2.00
❑ 203 Mark Clayton SP RC	10.00	25.00
❑ 204 Mike Williams	.75	2.00
❑ 205 Reggie Brown RC	.75	2.00
❑ 206 Roddy White RC	1.25	3.00
❑ 207 Roscoe Parrish RC	.75	2.00
❑ 208 Roydell Williams RC	.75	2.00
❑ 209 Steve Savoy RC	.60	1.50
❑ 210 Tab Perry RC	1.00	2.50
❑ 211 Taylor Stubblefield RC	.60	1.50
❑ 212 Terrence Murphy RC	.60	1.50
❑ 213 Troy Williamson RC	1.00	2.50
❑ 214 Vincent Jackson RC	1.25	3.00
❑ 215 Alex Smith TE RC	1.00	2.50
❑ 216 Heath Miller RC	2.00	5.00
❑ 217 Dan Cody RC	1.00	2.50
❑ 218 David Pollack RC	.75	2.00
❑ 219 Erasmus James RC	.75	2.00
❑ 220 Justin Tuck RC	1.25	3.00
❑ 221 Marcus Spears RC	1.00	2.50
❑ 222 Matt Roth RC	1.00	2.50
❑ 223 Anttaj Hawthorne RC	.75	2.00
❑ 224 Mike Patterson RC	.75	2.00
❑ 225 Shaun Cody RC	.75	2.00
❑ 226 Travis Johnson RC	.60	1.50
❑ 227 Channing Crowder RC	.75	2.00
❑ 228 Darryl Blackstock RC	.60	1.50
❑ 229 DeMarcus Ware RC	1.50	4.00
❑ 230 Derrick Johnson RC	1.00	2.50
❑ 231 Kevin Burnett RC	.75	2.00
❑ 232 Shawne Merriman RC	1.00	2.50
❑ 233 Adam Jones RC	.75	2.00
❑ 234 Antrel Rolle RC	1.00	2.50
❑ 235 Brandon Browner RC	.60	1.50
❑ 236 Bryant McFadden RC	.75	2.00
❑ 237 Carlos Rogers RC	1.00	2.50
❑ 238 Corey Webster RC	1.00	2.50
❑ 239 Fabian Washington RC	1.00	2.50
❑ 240 Justin Miller RC	.75	2.00
❑ 241 Marlin Jackson RC	.75	2.00
❑ 242 Ernest Shazor RC	.75	2.00
❑ 243 Josh Bullocks RC	1.00	2.50
❑ 244 Thomas Davis RC	.75	2.00

2006 Playoff Prestige

Card	Low	High
❑ COMP.SET w/o SP's (239)	50.00	100.00
❑ COMP.SET w/o RC's (150)	10.00	25.00
❑ ONE ROOKIE PER HOBBY PACK		
❑ 1 Anquan Boldin	.30	.75
❑ 2 J.J. Arrington	.25	.60
❑ 3 Josh McCown	.30	.75
❑ 4 Larry Fitzgerald	.40	1.00
❑ 5 Marcel Shipp	.25	.60
❑ 6 Alge Crumpler	.30	.75
❑ 7 Michael Vick	.40	1.00
❑ 8 T.J. Duckett	.25	.60
❑ 9 Warrick Dunn	.30	.75
❑ 10 Michael Jenkins	.30	.75
❑ 11 Derrick Mason	.30	.75

Card	Lo	Hi
❑ 12 Jamal Lewis	.30	.75
❑ 13 Kyle Boller	.30	.75
❑ 14 Mark Clayton	.30	.75
❑ 15 Ray Lewis	.40	1.00
❑ 16 Eric Moulds	.30	.75
❑ 17 J.P. Losman	.30	.75
❑ 18 Lee Evans	.30	.75
❑ 19 Willis McGahee	.40	1.00
❑ 20 Jake Delhomme	.30	.75
❑ 21 Julius Peppers	.30	.75
❑ 22 Keary Colbert	.30	.75
❑ 23 Stephen Davis	.30	.75
❑ 24 Steve Smith	.40	1.00
❑ 25 Brian Urlacher	.40	1.00
❑ 26 Cedric Benson	.30	.75
❑ 27 Kyle Orton	.30	.75
❑ 28 Mark Bradley	.25	.60
❑ 29 Muhsin Muhammad	.30	.75
❑ 30 Thomas Jones	.30	.75
❑ 31 Carson Palmer	.40	1.00
❑ 32 Chad Johnson	.30	.75
❑ 33 Rudi Johnson	.30	.75
❑ 34 T.J. Houshmandzadeh	.30	.75
❑ 35 Braylon Edwards	.40	1.00
❑ 36 Dennis Northcutt	.25	.60
❑ 37 Antonio Bryant	.30	.75
❑ 38 Reuben Droughns	.30	.75
❑ 39 Trent Dilfer	.30	.75
❑ 40 Drew Bledsoe	.40	1.00
❑ 41 Jason Witten	.40	1.00
❑ 42 Julius Jones	.30	.75
❑ 43 Keyshawn Johnson	.30	.75
❑ 44 Roy Williams S	.30	.75
❑ 45 Terry Glenn	.30	.75
❑ 46 Ashley Lelie	.25	.60
❑ 47 Jake Plummer	.30	.75
❑ 48 Mike Anderson	.30	.75
❑ 49 Rod Smith	.30	.75
❑ 50 Tatum Bell	.25	.60
❑ 51 Joey Harrington	.25	.60
❑ 52 Kevin Jones	.30	.75
❑ 53 Mike Williams	.30	.75
❑ 54 Roy Williams WR	.40	1.00
❑ 55 Aaron Rodgers	.40	1.00
❑ 56 Brett Favre	.75	2.00
❑ 57 Donald Driver	.40	1.00
❑ 58 Javon Walker	.30	.75
❑ 59 Ahman Green	.30	.75
❑ 60 Andre Johnson	.30	.75
❑ 61 Corey Bradford	.25	.60
❑ 62 David Carr	.25	.60
❑ 63 Domanick Davis	.30	.75
❑ 64 Jabar Gaffney	.25	.60
❑ 65 Brandon Stokley	.30	.75
❑ 66 Dallas Clark	.30	.75
❑ 67 Edgerrin James	.30	.75
❑ 68 Marvin Harrison	.40	1.00
❑ 69 Peyton Manning	.60	1.50
❑ 70 Reggie Wayne	.30	.75
❑ 71 Byron Leftwich	.30	.75
❑ 72 Fred Taylor	.30	.75
❑ 73 Jimmy Smith	.30	.75
❑ 74 Matt Jones	.30	.75
❑ 75 Reggie Williams	.30	.75
❑ 76 Eddie Kennison	.25	.60
❑ 77 Larry Johnson	.30	.75
❑ 78 Priest Holmes	.30	.75
❑ 79 Tony Gonzalez	.30	.75
❑ 80 Trent Green	.30	.75
❑ 81 Chris Chambers	.30	.75
❑ 82 Marty Booker	.25	.60
❑ 83 Randy McMichael	.25	.60
❑ 84 Ricky Williams	.25	.60
❑ 85 Ronnie Brown	.40	1.00
❑ 86 Zach Thomas	.40	1.00
❑ 87 Daunte Culpepper	.40	1.00
❑ 88 Mewelde Moore	.25	.60
❑ 89 Nate Burleson	.30	.75
❑ 90 Jim Kleinsasser	.25	.60
❑ 91 Corey Dillon	.30	.75
❑ 92 David Givens	.30	.75
❑ 93 Deion Branch	.30	.75
❑ 94 Tedy Bruschi	.40	1.00
❑ 95 Tom Brady	.60	1.50
❑ 96 Aaron Brooks	.30	.75
❑ 97 Deuce McAllister	.30	.75
❑ 98 Donte Stallworth	.30	.75
❑ 99 Joe Horn	.30	.75
❑ 100 Amani Toomer	.30	.75
❑ 101 Eli Manning	.50	1.25
❑ 102 Jeremy Shockey	.40	1.00
❑ 103 Plaxico Burress	.30	.75
❑ 104 Tiki Barber	.40	1.00
❑ 105 Chad Pennington	.30	.75
❑ 106 Curtis Martin	.40	1.00
❑ 107 Justin McCareins	.25	.60
❑ 108 Laveranues Coles	.30	.75
❑ 109 Jerry Porter	.30	.75
❑ 110 Kerry Collins	.30	.75
❑ 111 LaMont Jordan	.30	.75
❑ 112 Randy Moss	.40	1.00
❑ 113 Brian Westbrook	.30	.75
❑ 114 Donovan McNabb	.40	1.00
❑ 115 Terrell Owens	.40	1.00
❑ 116 L.J. Smith	.25	.60
❑ 117 Ben Roethlisberger	.60	1.50
❑ 118 Hines Ward	.40	1.00
❑ 119 Heath Miller	.30	.75
❑ 120 Willie Parker	.50	1.25
❑ 121 Jerome Bettis	.40	1.00
❑ 122 Antonio Gates	.40	1.00
❑ 123 Drew Brees	.40	1.00
❑ 124 Keenan McCardell	.30	.75
❑ 125 LaDainian Tomlinson	.50	1.25
❑ 126 Alex Smith QB	.30	.75
❑ 127 Brandon Lloyd	.30	.75
❑ 128 Frank Gore	.40	1.00
❑ 129 Kevan Barlow	.30	.75
❑ 130 Darrell Jackson	.30	.75
❑ 131 Joe Jurevicius	.25	.60
❑ 132 Matt Hasselbeck	.30	.75
❑ 133 Shaun Alexander	.30	.75
❑ 134 Isaac Bruce	.30	.75
❑ 135 Marc Bulger	.30	.75
❑ 136 Marshall Faulk	.30	.75
❑ 137 Steven Jackson	.40	1.00
❑ 138 Torry Holt	.30	.75
❑ 139 Cadillac Williams	.40	1.00
❑ 140 Derrick Brooks	.30	.75
❑ 141 Joey Galloway	.30	.75
❑ 142 Michael Clayton	.30	.75
❑ 143 Brandon Jones	.25	.60
❑ 144 Chris Brown	.30	.75
❑ 145 Steve McNair	.30	.75
❑ 146 Tyrone Calico	.25	.60
❑ 147 Clinton Portis	.40	1.00
❑ 148 Mark Brunell	.30	.75
❑ 149 Santana Moss	.30	.75
❑ 150 David Patten	.25	.60
❑ 151 A.J. Hawk SP RC	15.00	40.00
❑ 152 Abdul Hodge RC	1.00	2.50
❑ 153 Alan Zemaitis RC	1.25	3.00
❑ 154 Andre Hall RC	1.00	2.50
❑ 155 Anthony Fasano RC	1.25	3.00
❑ 156 Ashton Youboty RC	1.00	2.50
❑ 157 Erik Meyer RC	1.00	2.50
❑ 158 Bobby Carpenter RC	1.00	2.50
❑ 159 Brad Smith RC	1.25	3.00
❑ 160 Brandon Kirsch RC	1.00	2.50
❑ 161 Brandon Marshall SP RC	8.00	20.00
❑ 162 Brandon Williams RC	1.00	2.50
❑ 163 Brian Calhoun SP RC	6.00	15.00
❑ 164 Brodie Croyle SP RC	10.00	25.00
❑ 165 Brodrick Bunkley RC	1.00	2.50
❑ 166 Bruce Gradkowski RC	1.25	3.00
❑ 167 Cedric Griffin RC	1.00	2.50
❑ 168 Cedric Humes RC	1.00	2.50
❑ 169 Chad Greenway RC	1.25	3.00
❑ 170 Chad Jackson RC	1.00	2.50
❑ 171 Charlie Whitehurst RC	1.25	3.00
❑ 172 Cory Rodgers RC	1.25	3.00
❑ 173 D.J. Shockley RC	1.00	2.50
❑ 174 Darnell Bing RC	1.00	2.50
❑ 175 Darrell Hackney RC	1.00	2.50
❑ 176 David Thomas SP RC	6.00	15.00
❑ 177 D'Brickashaw Ferguson RC	1.25	3.00
❑ 178 DeAngelo Williams RC	2.50	6.00
❑ 179 Dee Webb RC	1.00	2.50
❑ 180 Delanie Walker RC	1.00	2.50
❑ 181 DeMeco Ryans RC	1.50	4.00
❑ 182 Demetrius Williams RC	1.00	2.50
❑ 183 Derek Hagan RC	1.00	2.50
❑ 184 Devin Aromashodu RC	1.25	3.00
❑ 185 Dominique Byrd RC	1.00	2.50
❑ 186 DonTrell Moore RC	1.00	2.50
❑ 187 D'Qwell Jackson RC	1.00	2.50
❑ 188 Drew Olson RC	.75	2.00
❑ 189 Eric Winston RC	.75	2.00
❑ 190 Ernie Sims RC	1.00	2.50
❑ 191 Gerald Riggs RC	1.00	2.50
❑ 192 Greg Jennings RC	2.00	5.00
❑ 193 Greg Lee RC	.75	2.00
❑ 194 Haloti Ngata RC	1.25	3.00
❑ 195 Hank Baskett RC	1.25	3.00
❑ 196 Jason Avant RC	1.25	3.00
❑ 197 Jason Carter RC	1.00	2.50
❑ 198 Jay Cutler RC	3.00	8.00
❑ 199 Jeff Webb RC	1.00	2.50
❑ 200 Jeremy Bloom RC	1.00	2.50
❑ 201 Jerious Norwood RC	1.25	3.00
❑ 202 Jerome Harrison RC	1.25	3.00
❑ 203 Jimmy Williams RC	1.25	3.00
❑ 204 Joe Klopfenstein RC	1.00	2.50
❑ 205 Johnathan Joseph RC	1.00	2.50
❑ 206 Jonathan Orr RC	1.00	2.50
❑ 207 Joseph Addai RC	1.50	4.00
❑ 208 Kai Parham RC	1.25	3.00
❑ 209 Kamerion Wimbley RC	1.25	3.00
❑ 210 Kellen Clemens RC	1.25	3.00
❑ 211 Kelly Jennings RC	1.25	3.00
❑ 212 Ko Simpson RC	1.00	2.50
❑ 213 Laurence Maroney RC	1.50	4.00
❑ 214 Lawrence Vickers RC	1.00	2.50
❑ 215 LenDale White RC	1.50	4.00
❑ 216 Leon Washington RC	1.50	4.00
❑ 217 Leonard Pope RC	1.25	3.00
❑ 218 Marcedes Lewis RC	1.25	3.00
❑ 219 Marcus Vick SP RC	8.00	20.00
❑ 220 Mario Williams RC	1.50	4.00
❑ 221 Martin Nance RC	1.00	2.50
❑ 222 Mathias Kiwanuka RC	1.50	4.00
❑ 223 Matt Leinart RC	2.00	5.00
❑ 224 Maurice Drew SP RC	15.00	30.00
❑ 225 Maurice Stovall SP RC	6.00	15.00
❑ 226 Michael Huff RC	1.25	3.00
❑ 227 Michael Robinson SP RC	6.00	15.00
❑ 228 Mike Hass RC	1.25	3.00
❑ 229 Omar Jacobs RC	.75	2.00
❑ 230 Paul Pinegar RC	.75	2.00
❑ 231 Reggie Bush RC	3.00	8.00
❑ 232 Reggie McNeal RC	1.00	2.50
❑ 233 Rodrique Wright RC	.75	2.00
❑ 234 Santonio Holmes RC	3.00	8.00
❑ 235 Sinorice Moss RC	1.25	3.00
❑ 236 Skyler Green RC	.75	2.00
❑ 237 Tamba Hali RC	1.25	3.00
❑ 238 Tarvaris Jackson RC	1.25	3.00
❑ 239 Taurean Henderson RC	1.25	3.00
❑ 240 Terrence Whitehead RC	1.00	2.50
❑ 241 Tim Day SP RC	6.00	15.00
❑ 242 Todd Watkins RC	.75	2.00
❑ 243 Travis Wilson RC	.75	2.00
❑ 244 Tye Hill RC	1.00	2.50
❑ 245 Vernon Davis RC	1.25	3.00
❑ 246 Vince Young RC	3.00	8.00
❑ 247 Wali Lundy RC	1.25	3.00
❑ 248 Wendell Mathis RC	1.00	2.50
❑ 249 Willie Reid SP RC	6.00	15.00
❑ 250 Winston Justice RC	1.25	3.00

2007 Playoff Prestige

Card	Lo	Hi
❑ COMP.SET w/o SP's (240)	75.00	150.00
❑ COMP.SET w/o RC's (150)	10.00	25.00
❑ 1 Anquan Boldin	.30	.75
❑ 2 Edgerrin James	.30	.75
❑ 3 Larry Fitzgerald	.40	1.00
❑ 4 Matt Leinart	.40	1.00
❑ 5 Alge Crumpler	.30	.75
❑ 6 Michael Vick	.40	1.00
❑ 7 Jerious Norwood	.30	.75
❑ 8 Michael Jenkins	.30	.75
❑ 9 Warrick Dunn	.30	.75
❑ 10 Todd Heap	.25	.60
❑ 11 Jamal Lewis	.30	.75

❑ 12 Mark Clayton .30 .75
❑ 13 Demetrius Williams .25 .60
❑ 14 Steve McNair .30 .75
❑ 15 Ray Lewis .40 1.00
❑ 16 J.P. Losman .25 .60
❑ 17 Josh Reed .25 .60
❑ 18 Lee Evans .30 .75
❑ 19 Willis McGahee .30 .75
❑ 20 DeAngelo Williams .40 1.00
❑ 21 DeShaun Foster .30 .75
❑ 22 Jake Delhomme .30 .75
❑ 23 Keyshawn Johnson .30 .75
❑ 24 Steve Smith .30 .75
❑ 25 Bernard Berrian .25 .60
❑ 26 Brian Urlacher .40 1.00
❑ 27 Cedric Benson .30 .75
❑ 28 Muhsin Muhammad .30 .75
❑ 29 Rex Grossman .30 .75
❑ 30 Thomas Jones .30 .75
❑ 31 Carson Palmer .40 1.00
❑ 32 Chad Johnson .30 .75
❑ 33 Rudi Johnson .30 .75
❑ 34 T.J. Houshmandzadeh .30 .75
❑ 35 Braylon Edwards .30 .75
❑ 36 Kellen Winslow .30 .75
❑ 37 Charlie Frye .30 .75
❑ 38 Reuben Droughns .30 .75
❑ 39 Terry Glenn .30 .75
❑ 40 Julius Jones .30 .75
❑ 41 Roy Williams S .30 .75
❑ 42 Marion Barber .40 1.00
❑ 43 Terrell Owens .40 1.00
❑ 44 Tony Romo .60 1.50
❑ 45 Javon Walker .30 .75
❑ 46 Jay Cutler .40 1.00
❑ 47 Mike Bell .30 .75
❑ 48 Brandon Marshall .30 .75
❑ 49 Tatum Bell .25 .60
❑ 50 Jon Kitna .25 .60
❑ 51 Kevin Jones .25 .60
❑ 52 Roy Williams WR .30 .75
❑ 53 Mike Furrey .30 .75
❑ 54 A.J. Hawk .40 1.00
❑ 55 Brett Favre .75 2.00
❑ 56 Donald Driver .40 1.00
❑ 57 Greg Jennings .30 .75
❑ 58 Ahman Green .30 .75
❑ 59 Andre Johnson .30 .75
❑ 60 David Carr .30 .75
❑ 61 Eric Moulds .30 .75
❑ 62 Owen Daniels .25 .60
❑ 63 Wali Lundy .25 .60
❑ 64 Joseph Addai .40 1.00
❑ 65 Marvin Harrison .40 1.00
❑ 66 Peyton Manning .60 1.50
❑ 67 Reggie Wayne .30 .75
❑ 68 Dallas Clark .25 .60
❑ 69 Byron Leftwich .30 .75
❑ 70 Fred Taylor .30 .75
❑ 71 Marcedes Lewis .25 .60
❑ 72 Maurice Jones-Drew .40 1.00
❑ 73 Reggie Williams .30 .75
❑ 74 Eddie Kennison .25 .60
❑ 75 Larry Johnson .30 .75
❑ 76 Tony Gonzalez .30 .75
❑ 77 Trent Green .30 .75
❑ 78 Chris Chambers .30 .75
❑ 79 Daunte Culpepper .30 .75
❑ 80 Marty Booker .25 .60
❑ 81 Ronnie Brown .30 .75
❑ 82 Chester Taylor .25 .60
❑ 83 Tarvaris Jackson .30 .75
❑ 84 Troy Williamson .25 .60
❑ 85 Travis Taylor .25 .60
❑ 86 Ben Watson .25 .60
❑ 87 Tom Brady .75 2.00
❑ 88 Corey Dillon .30 .75
❑ 89 Laurence Maroney .40 1.00
❑ 90 Deuce McAllister .30 .75
❑ 91 Drew Brees .40 1.00
❑ 92 Marques Colston .40 1.00
❑ 93 Reggie Bush .50 1.25
❑ 94 Joe Horn .30 .75
❑ 95 Brandon Jacobs .30 .75
❑ 96 Eli Manning .40 1.00
❑ 97 Jeremy Shockey .30 .75
❑ 98 Plaxico Burress .30 .75
❑ 99 Chad Pennington .30 .75
❑ 100 Jerricho Cotchery .25 .60
❑ 101 Laveranues Coles .30 .75
❑ 102 Leon Washington .30 .75
❑ 103 Kevan Barlow .30 .75
❑ 104 Ronald Curry .30 .75
❑ 105 LaMont Jordan .30 .75
❑ 106 John Madsen .25 .60
❑ 107 Michael Huff .30 .75
❑ 108 Randy Moss .40 1.00
❑ 109 Brian Westbrook .30 .75
❑ 110 Donovan McNabb .40 1.00
❑ 111 Hank Baskett .30 .75
❑ 112 Donte Stallworth .30 .75
❑ 113 Reggie Brown .25 .60
❑ 114 Ben Roethlisberger .50 1.25
❑ 115 Hines Ward .40 1.00
❑ 116 Troy Polamalu .40 1.00
❑ 117 Willie Parker .30 .75
❑ 118 Santonio Holmes .30 .75
❑ 119 Antonio Gates .30 .75
❑ 120 LaDainian Tomlinson .50 1.25
❑ 121 Vincent Jackson .25 .60
❑ 122 Philip Rivers .40 1.00
❑ 123 Shawne Merriman .30 .75
❑ 124 Alex Smith QB .40 1.00
❑ 125 Antonio Bryant .30 .75
❑ 126 Frank Gore .40 1.00
❑ 127 Vernon Davis .30 .75
❑ 128 Darrell Jackson .30 .75
❑ 129 Deion Branch .30 .75
❑ 130 Matt Hasselbeck .30 .75
❑ 131 Shaun Alexander .30 .75
❑ 132 Isaac Bruce .30 .75
❑ 133 Marc Bulger .30 .75
❑ 134 Steven Jackson .40 1.00
❑ 135 Joe Klopfenstein .25 .60
❑ 136 Torry Holt .30 .75
❑ 137 Bruce Gradkowski .25 .60
❑ 138 Cadillac Williams .30 .75
❑ 139 Joey Galloway .30 .75
❑ 140 Mike Alstott .30 .75
❑ 141 Adam Jones .25 .60
❑ 142 Drew Bennett .25 .60
❑ 143 LenDale White .30 .75
❑ 144 Vince Young .40 1.00
❑ 145 Travis Henry .30 .75
❑ 146 Clinton Portis .30 .75
❑ 147 Jason Campbell .30 .75
❑ 148 Ladell Betts .25 .60
❑ 149 Santana Moss .30 .75
❑ 150 Chris Cooley .25 .60
❑ 151 Brady Quinn RC 2.50 6.00
❑ 152 JaMarcus Russell RC 1.50 4.00
❑ 153 Troy Smith RC 1.50 4.00
❑ 154 Drew Stanton RC 1.00 2.50
❑ 155 Adrian Peterson RC 10.00 25.00
❑ 156 Marshawn Lynch RC 2.00 5.00
❑ 157 Michael Bush RC 1.25 3.00
❑ 158 Kenny Irons SP RC 12.00 30.00
❑ 159 Antonio Pittman RC 1.25 3.00
❑ 160 Tony Hunt RC 1.25 3.00
❑ 161 Darius Walker SP RC 10.00 25.00
❑ 162 DeShawn Wynn RC 1.25 3.00
❑ 163 Calvin Johnson RC 3.00 8.00
❑ 164 Ted Ginn Jr. RC 2.00 5.00
❑ 165 Dwayne Jarrett RC 1.25 3.00
❑ 166 Sidney Rice RC 2.50 6.00
❑ 167 Dwayne Bowe RC 2.00 5.00
❑ 168 Robert Meachem RC 1.25 3.00
❑ 169 Anthony Gonzalez SP RC 15.00 40.00
❑ 170 Craig Buster Davis RC 1.25 3.00
❑ 171 Johnnie Lee Higgins RC 1.25 3.00
❑ 172 Steve Smith USC RC 2.00 5.00
❑ 173 Chansi Stuckey RC 1.25 3.00
❑ 174 David Clowney RC 1.25 3.00
❑ 175 Aundrae Allison RC 1.00 2.50
❑ 176 Jason Hill SP RC 12.00 30.00
❑ 177 Zach Miller RC 1.25 3.00
❑ 178 Greg Olsen RC 1.50 4.00
❑ 179 Gaines Adams RC 1.25 3.00
❑ 180 Jamaal Anderson RC 1.00 2.50
❑ 181 Victor Abiamiri RC 1.25 3.00
❑ 182 Adam Carriker RC 1.00 2.50
❑ 183 LaMarr Woodley RC 1.25 3.00
❑ 184 Quentin Moses RC 1.00 2.50
❑ 185 Charles Johnson RC .75 2.00
❑ 186 Alan Branch RC 1.00 2.50
❑ 187 Amobi Okoye RC 1.25 3.00
❑ 188 DeMarcus Tank Tyler RC 1.00 2.50
❑ 189 Patrick Willis SP RC 20.00 50.00
❑ 190 Paul Posluszny RC 1.50 4.00
❑ 191 Lawrence Timmons RC 1.25 3.00
❑ 192 Darrelle Revis RC 1.50 4.00
❑ 193 Leon Hall RC 1.25 3.00
❑ 194 Daymeion Hughes RC 1.00 2.50
❑ 195 Chris Houston RC 1.00 2.50
❑ 196 A.J. Davis RC .75 2.00
❑ 197 Aaron Ross RC 1.25 3.00
❑ 198 LaRon Landry RC 1.50 4.00
❑ 199 Reggie Nelson RC 1.00 2.50
❑ 200 Michael Griffin RC 1.25 3.00
❑ 201 Trent Edwards RC 2.00 5.00
❑ 202 Kevin Kolb RC 2.00 5.00
❑ 203 John Beck RC 1.25 3.00
❑ 204 Kenneth Darby RC 1.25 3.00
❑ 205 Lorenzo Booker RC 1.25 3.00
❑ 206 Jason Snelling RC 1.00 2.50
❑ 207 Selvin Young RC 1.25 3.00
❑ 208 Ahmad Bradshaw RC 1.50 4.00
❑ 209 Brandon Jackson RC 1.25 3.00
❑ 210 Courtney Taylor RC 1.00 2.50
❑ 211 Paul Williams SP RC 10.00 25.00
❑ 212 Rhema McKnight RC 1.00 2.50
❑ 213 David Ball RC .75 2.00
❑ 214 Syvelle Newton RC 1.00 2.50
❑ 215 Joel Filani RC 1.00 2.50
❑ 216 Chris Davis RC 1.00 2.50
❑ 217 Laurent Robinson RC 1.25 3.00
❑ 218 Jarrett Hicks RC 1.00 2.50
❑ 219 Dallas Baker RC 1.00 2.50
❑ 220 Matt Trannon RC 1.00 2.50
❑ 221 Mike Walker RC 1.25 3.00
❑ 222 Anthony Spencer RC 1.25 3.00
❑ 223 Jarvis Moss RC 1.25 3.00
❑ 224 Tim Crowder RC 1.25 3.00
❑ 225 Brandon Siler RC 1.00 2.50
❑ 226 David Harris RC 1.00 2.50
❑ 227 Buster Davis RC 1.00 2.50
❑ 228 Jon Abbate RC .75 2.00
❑ 229 Rufus Alexander RC 1.25 3.00
❑ 230 Jon Beason RC 1.25 3.00
❑ 231 Jonathan Wade RC 1.00 2.50
❑ 232 Marcus McCauley RC 1.00 2.50
❑ 233 Tanard Jackson RC .75 2.00
❑ 234 Kenny Scott RC .75 2.00
❑ 235 Brandon Meriweather RC 1.25 3.00
❑ 236 Aaron Rouse RC 1.25 3.00
❑ 237 Eric Weddle RC 1.00 2.50
❑ 238 Brian Leonard RC 1.00 2.50
❑ 239 Jared Zabransky SP RC 12.00 30.00
❑ 240 Chris Leak SP RC 10.00 25.00
❑ 241 Jordan Palmer SP RC 12.00 30.00
❑ 242 Garrett Wolfe SP RC 12.00 30.00
❑ 243 Gary Russell RC 1.00 2.50
❑ 244 Isaiah Stanback RC 1.25 3.00
❑ 245 Tyler Palko RC 1.00 2.50
❑ 246 Jeff Rowe RC 1.00 2.50
❑ 247 Kolby Smith RC 1.25 3.00
❑ 248 Dwayne Wright RC 1.00 2.50
❑ 249 Nate Ilaoa RC 1.25 3.00
❑ 250 Steve Breaston RC 1.25 3.00

2008 Playoff Prestige

❑ COMP.SET w/o SP's (190) 40.00 80.00
❑ COMP.SET w/o RC's (100) 8.00 20.00
❑ 1 Anquan Boldin .25 .60
❑ 2 Larry Fitzgerald .30 .75
❑ 3 Edgerrin James .25 .60
❑ 4 Matt Leinart .30 .75
❑ 5 Warrick Dunn .25 .60
❑ 6 Roddy White .25 .60
❑ 7 Derrick Mason .20 .50
❑ 8 Todd Heap .20 .50
❑ 9 Willis McGahee .25 .60
❑ 10 J.P. Losman .20 .50
❑ 11 Lee Evans .25 .60

Card	Low	High
❑ 12 Marshawn Lynch	.30	.75
❑ 13 Steve Smith	.25	.60
❑ 14 Keary Colbert	.20	.50
❑ 15 DeShaun Foster	.25	.60
❑ 16 Bernard Berrian	.25	.60
❑ 17 Cedric Benson	.25	.60
❑ 18 Devin Hester	.30	.75
❑ 19 Carson Palmer	.30	.75
❑ 20 Rudi Johnson	.25	.60
❑ 21 T.J. Houshmandzadeh	.25	.60
❑ 22 Chad Johnson	.25	.60
❑ 23 Derek Anderson	.25	.60
❑ 24 Kellen Winslow	.25	.60
❑ 25 Braylon Edwards	.25	.60
❑ 26 Tony Romo	.50	1.25
❑ 27 Terrell Owens	.30	.75
❑ 28 Marion Barber	.30	.75
❑ 29 Jay Cutler	.30	.75
❑ 30 Javon Walker	.25	.60
❑ 31 Brandon Marshall	.25	.60
❑ 32 Jon Kitna	.25	.60
❑ 33 Calvin Johnson	.30	.75
❑ 34 Roy Williams WR	.25	.60
❑ 35 Brett Favre	.75	2.00
❑ 36 Donald Driver	.25	.60
❑ 37 Greg Jennings	.25	.60
❑ 38 Matt Schaub	.25	.60
❑ 39 Andre Johnson	.25	.60
❑ 40 Ahman Green	.25	.60
❑ 41 Peyton Manning	.50	1.25
❑ 42 Joseph Addai	.30	.75
❑ 43 Reggie Wayne	.25	.60
❑ 44 Marvin Harrison	.30	.75
❑ 45 David Garrard	.25	.60
❑ 46 Fred Taylor	.25	.60
❑ 47 Maurice Jones-Drew	.25	.60
❑ 48 Tony Gonzalez	.25	.60
❑ 49 Dwayne Bowe	.25	.60
❑ 50 Larry Johnson	.25	.60
❑ 51 Ted Ginn Jr.	.25	.60
❑ 52 Ronnie Brown	.25	.60
❑ 53 Tarvaris Jackson	.25	.60
❑ 54 Adrian Peterson	.60	1.50
❑ 55 Chester Taylor	.20	.50
❑ 56 Tom Brady	.50	1.25
❑ 57 Randy Moss	.30	.75
❑ 58 Wes Welker	.30	.75
❑ 59 Laurence Maroney	.25	.60
❑ 60 Drew Brees	.30	.75
❑ 61 Reggie Bush	.30	.75
❑ 62 Deuce McAllister	.25	.60
❑ 63 Marques Colston	.25	.60
❑ 64 Eli Manning	.30	.75
❑ 65 Brandon Jacobs	.25	.60
❑ 66 Plaxico Burress	.25	.60
❑ 67 Jeremy Shockey	.25	.60
❑ 68 Jerricho Cotchery	.20	.50
❑ 69 Laveranues Coles	.25	.60
❑ 70 Thomas Jones	.25	.60
❑ 71 JaMarcus Russell	.30	.75
❑ 72 Jerry Porter	.25	.60
❑ 73 Ronald Curry	.25	.60
❑ 74 Donovan McNabb	.30	.75
❑ 75 Brian Westbrook	.25	.60
❑ 76 Kevin Curtis	.20	.50
❑ 77 Ben Roethlisberger	.40	1.00
❑ 78 Willie Parker	.25	.60
❑ 79 Hines Ward	.25	.60
❑ 80 Philip Rivers	.30	.75
❑ 81 Antonio Gates	.25	.60
❑ 82 LaDainian Tomlinson	.40	1.00
❑ 83 Alex Smith QB	.25	.60
❑ 84 Frank Gore	.25	.60
❑ 85 Vernon Davis	.20	.50
❑ 86 Matt Hasselbeck	.25	.60
❑ 87 Shaun Alexander	.25	.60
❑ 88 Deion Branch	.25	.60
❑ 89 Marc Bulger	.25	.60
❑ 90 Steven Jackson	.30	.75
❑ 91 Torry Holt	.25	.60
❑ 92 Jeff Garcia	.25	.60
❑ 93 Joey Galloway	.25	.60
❑ 94 Cadillac Williams	.25	.60
❑ 95 Vince Young	.25	.60
❑ 96 LenDale White	.25	.60
❑ 97 Brandon Jones	.20	.50
❑ 98 Jason Campbell	.25	.60
❑ 99 Clinton Portis	.25	.60
❑ 100 Chris Cooley	.25	.60

Card	Low	High
❑ 101 Adarius Bowman RC	.75	2.00
❑ 102 Adrian Arrington RC	.75	2.00
❑ 103 Ali Highsmith RC	.60	1.50
❑ 104 Allen Patrick RC	.75	2.00
❑ 105 Andre Caldwell RC	1.00	2.50
❑ 106 Andre Woodson RC	1.00	2.50
❑ 107 Anthony Alridge RC	.75	2.00
❑ 108 Antoine Cason RC	1.00	2.50
❑ 109 Aqib Talib RC	1.00	2.50
❑ 110 Chauncey Washington SP RC	10.00	25.00
❑ 111 Bernard Morris RC	.75	2.00
❑ 112 Brad Cottam RC	1.00	2.50
❑ 113 Brian Brohm RC	1.00	2.50
❑ 114 Chad Henne RC	1.50	4.00
❑ 115 Chris Johnson RC	3.00	8.00
❑ 116 Chris Long SP RC	10.00	25.00
❑ 117 Colt Brennan RC	1.50	4.00
❑ 118 Cory Boyd RC	.75	2.00
❑ 119 Curtis Lofton RC	1.00	2.50
❑ 120 DJ Hall RC	.75	2.00
❑ 121 Dan Connor SP RC	12.00	30.00
❑ 122 Dantrell Savage RC	1.00	2.50
❑ 123 Darius Reynaud RC	.75	2.00
❑ 124A Darren McFadden Red RC	2.00	5.00
❑ 124B Darren McFadden Wht RC	5.00	12.00
❑ 125 Davone Bess RC	1.25	3.00
❑ 126 Dennis Dixon RC	1.00	2.50
❑ 127 Derrick Harvey RC	.75	2.00
❑ 128 DeSean Jackson RC	2.00	5.00
❑ 129 Devin Thomas RC	1.00	2.50
❑ 130 Dexter Jackson RC	1.00	2.50
❑ 131 D.Rodgers-Cromartie RC	1.00	2.50
❑ 132 Donnie Avery RC	1.25	3.00
❑ 133 Dorien Bryant RC	.75	2.00
❑ 134 Earl Bennett RC	1.00	2.50
❑ 135 Early Doucet RC	1.00	2.50
❑ 136 Eddie Royal RC	1.50	4.00
❑ 137 Erik Ainge RC	1.00	2.50
❑ 138 Erin Henderson RC	.75	2.00
❑ 139 Felix Jones SP RC	15.00	40.00
❑ 140 Fred Davis RC	1.00	2.50
❑ 141 Glenn Dorsey RC	1.00	2.50
❑ 142 Harry Douglas SP RC	8.00	20.00
❑ 143 Jacob Hester RC	1.00	2.50
❑ 144 Jacob Tamme RC	1.00	2.50
❑ 145 Jamaal Charles RC	1.50	4.00
❑ 146 James Hardy RC	.75	2.00
❑ 147 Jason Rivers RC	1.00	2.50
❑ 148 Jed Collins SP RC	8.00	20.00
❑ 149 Jermichael Finley RC	1.00	2.50
❑ 150 Jerome Simpson RC	.75	2.00
❑ 151 Joe Flacco RC	3.00	8.00
❑ 152 John Carlson RC	1.00	2.50
❑ 153 John David Booty RC	1.00	2.50
❑ 154 Jonathan Stewart RC	2.00	5.00
❑ 155 Jordy Nelson SP RC	12.00	30.00
❑ 156 Josh Johnson RC	1.00	2.50
❑ 157 Josh Morgan RC	1.00	2.50
❑ 158 Justin Forsett RC	1.00	2.50
❑ 159 Kalvin McRae RC	.75	2.00
❑ 160 Keenan Burton RC	.75	2.00
❑ 161 Keith Rivers RC	1.00	2.50
❑ 162 Kellen Davis RC	.60	1.50
❑ 163 Kenny Phillips RC	1.00	2.50
❑ 164 Kevin O'Connell RC	1.00	2.50
❑ 165 Kevin Robinson RC	.75	2.00
❑ 166 Kevin Smith SP RC	15.00	40.00
❑ 167 Lavelle Hawkins RC	.75	2.00
❑ 168 Leodis McKelvin RC	1.00	2.50
❑ 169 Limas Sweed RC	1.00	2.50
❑ 170 Malcolm Kelly RC	1.00	2.50
❑ 171 Marcus Monk RC	1.00	2.50
❑ 172 Marcus Smith RC	.75	2.00
❑ 173 Mario Manningham RC	1.00	2.50
❑ 174 Mark Bradford RC	.75	2.00
❑ 175 Martellus Bennett RC	1.00	2.50
❑ 176 Martin Rucker RC	.75	2.00
❑ 177 Matt Flynn SP RC	10.00	25.00
❑ 178 Matt Forte RC	2.00	5.00
❑ 179 Matt Ryan RC	4.00	10.00
❑ 180 Mike Hart RC	1.00	2.50
❑ 181 Mike Jenkins RC	1.00	2.50
❑ 182 Owen Schmitt RC	1.00	2.50
❑ 183 Paul Hubbard RC	.75	2.00
❑ 184 Paul Smith RC	1.00	2.50
❑ 185 Peyton Hillis RC	1.00	2.50
❑ 186 Quentin Groves RC	.75	2.00
❑ 187 Rashard Mendenhall RC	2.00	5.00
❑ 188 Ray Rice RC	2.00	5.00
❑ 189 Reggie Smith SP RC	8.00	20.00
❑ 190 Ryan Grice-Mullen RC	1.00	2.50
❑ 191 Sam Keller RC	1.00	2.50
❑ 192 Sedrick Ellis RC	1.00	2.50
❑ 193 Steve Slaton RC	1.25	3.00
❑ 194 Tashard Choice RC	1.00	2.50
❑ 195 Terrell Thomas RC	.75	2.00
❑ 196 Thomas Brown RC	1.00	2.50
❑ 197 Tracy Porter RC	1.25	3.00
❑ 198 Vernon Gholston RC	1.00	2.50
❑ 199 Will Franklin RC	.75	2.00
❑ 200 Xavier Adibi RC	.75	2.00
❑ 201 Jake Long SP RC	75.00	150.00

2009 Playoff Prestige

Card	Low	High
❑ COMP.SET w/o RC's (100)	8.00	20.00
❑ 1 Kurt Warner	.30	.75
❑ 2 Larry Fitzgerald	.30	.75
❑ 3 Anquan Boldin	.25	.60
❑ 4 Tim Hightower	.25	.60
❑ 5 Roddy White	.25	.60
❑ 6 Michael Turner	.25	.60
❑ 7 Matt Ryan	.30	.75
❑ 8 Willis McGahee	.25	.60
❑ 9 Joe Flacco	.30	.75
❑ 10 Trent Edwards	.25	.60
❑ 11 Marshawn Lynch	.25	.60
❑ 12 Lee Evans	.25	.60
❑ 13 Steve Smith	.25	.60
❑ 14 DeAngelo Williams	.30	.75
❑ 15 Jake Delhomme	.25	.60
❑ 16 Jonathan Stewart	.25	.60
❑ 17 Greg Olsen	.20	.50
❑ 18 Kyle Orton	.25	.60
❑ 19 Matt Forte	.30	.75
❑ 20 Carson Palmer	.30	.75
❑ 21 Chad Ocho Cinco	.25	.60
❑ 22 T.J. Houshmandzadeh	.25	.60
❑ 23 Brady Quinn	.25	.60
❑ 24 Jamal Lewis	.25	.60
❑ 25 Kellen Winslow	.25	.60
❑ 26 Braylon Edwards	.25	.60
❑ 27 Tony Romo	.50	1.25
❑ 28 Terrell Owens	.30	.75
❑ 29 Marion Barber	.30	.75
❑ 30 Roy Williams WR	.25	.60
❑ 31 Jay Cutler	.30	.75
❑ 32 Brandon Marshall	.25	.60
❑ 33 Eddie Royal	.25	.60
❑ 34 Calvin Johnson	.30	.75
❑ 35 Kevin Smith	.25	.60
❑ 36 Aaron Rodgers	.30	.75
❑ 37 Ryan Grant	.25	.60
❑ 38 Greg Jennings	.30	.75
❑ 39 Matt Schaub	.25	.60
❑ 40 Andre Johnson	.25	.60
❑ 41 Steve Slaton	.25	.60
❑ 42 Peyton Manning	.50	1.25
❑ 43 Joseph Addai	.30	.75
❑ 44 Reggie Wayne	.25	.60
❑ 45 Anthony Gonzalez	.25	.60
❑ 46 David Garrard	.25	.60
❑ 47 Matt Jones	.25	.60
❑ 48 Maurice Jones-Drew	.25	.60
❑ 49 Larry Johnson	.25	.60
❑ 50 Dwayne Bowe	.25	.60
❑ 51 Chad Pennington	.25	.60
❑ 52 Ronnie Brown	.25	.60
❑ 53 Ted Ginn	.25	.60
❑ 54 Bernard Berrian	.25	.60
❑ 55 Adrian Peterson	.60	1.50
❑ 56 Chester Taylor	.20	.50
❑ 57 Tom Brady	.50	1.25
❑ 58 Randy Moss	.30	.75
❑ 59 Wes Welker	.30	.75
❑ 60 Drew Brees	.30	.75

- 61 Reggie Bush .30 .75
- 62 Marques Colston .25 .60
- 63 Eli Manning .30 .75
- 64 Steve Smith USC .25 .60
- 65 Brandon Jacobs .25 .60
- 66 Kellen Clemens .20 .50
- 67 Jerricho Cotchery .20 .50
- 68 Leon Washington .25 .60
- 69 Thomas Jones .25 .60
- 70 JaMarcus Russell .25 .60
- 71 Justin Fargas .20 .50
- 72 Darren McFadden .30 .75
- 73 Donovan McNabb .30 .75
- 74 Brian Westbrook .25 .60
- 75 DeSean Jackson .25 .60
- 76 Ben Roethlisberger .50 1.25
- 77 Willie Parker .25 .60
- 78 Hines Ward .25 .60
- 79 Santonio Holmes .25 .60
- 80 Philip Rivers .30 .75
- 81 LaDainian Tomlinson .30 .75
- 82 Antonio Gates .25 .60
- 83 Frank Gore .25 .60
- 84 Vernon Davis .20 .50
- 85 Matt Hasselbeck .25 .60
- 86 Deion Branch .25 .60
- 87 Julius Jones .25 .60
- 88 Marc Bulger .25 .60
- 89 Steven Jackson .25 .60
- 90 Torry Holt .25 .60
- 91 Antonio Bryant .25 .60
- 92 Earnest Graham .20 .50
- 93 Michael Clayton .20 .50
- 94 Kerry Collins .25 .60
- 95 LenDale White .25 .60
- 96 Chris Johnson .30 .75
- 97 Jason Campbell .25 .60
- 98 Clinton Portis .25 .60
- 99 Santana Moss .25 .60
- 100 Chris Cooley .25 .60
- 101A Aaron Curry RC 1.25 3.00
- 101B Aaron Curry SP Draft 6.00 15.00
- 102 Aaron Kelly RC .75 2.00
- 103 Aaron Maybin RC 1.00 2.50
- 104 Alphonso Smith RC .75 2.00
- 105 Andre Brown RC .75 2.00
- 106 Andre Smith RC 1.00 2.50
- 107 Arian Foster RC 1.00 2.50
- 108 Asher Allen RC .75 2.00
- 109 Austin Collie RC 2.00 5.00
- 110 B.J. Raji SP RC 15.00 30.00
- 111 Brandon Gibson RC 1.00 2.50
- 112A Brandon Pettigrew RC 1.25 3.00
- 112B B.Pettigrew SP Orng pants 5.00 12.00
- 113 Brandon Tate RC .75 2.00
- 114A Brian Cushing SP RC 10.00 25.00
- 114B Brian Cushing SP Draft 10.00 25.00
- 115A Brian Orakpo RC 1.25 3.00
- 115B Brian Orakpo SP Draft 8.00 20.00
- 116A Brian Robiskie RC 1.00 2.50
- 116B Brian Robiskie SP Red 6.00 15.00
- 117 Brooks Foster RC .75 2.00
- 118 Cedric Peerman RC .75 2.00
- 119A Chase Coffman RC .75 2.00
- 119B Chase Coffman SP Yellow 4.00 10.00
- 120 Chase Daniel SP RC 15.00 30.00
- 121 Chip Vaughn RC .60 1.50
- 122A Chris Wells RC 2.50 6.00
- 122B Chris Wells SP White 10.00 20.00
- 123 Clay Matthews RC 1.50 4.00
- 124A Clint Sintim RC 1.00 2.50
- 124B Clint Sintim SP White 4.00 10.00
- 125 Cornelius Ingram RC .60 1.50
- 126 Tony Fiammetta RC .75 2.00
- 127A D.J. Moore RC .75 2.00
- 127B D.J. Moore SP Gold 3.00 8.00
- 128 Darius Butler RC 1.00 2.50
- 129 Darius Passmore RC .75 2.00
- 130A Darrius Heyward-Bey RC 1.50 4.00
- 130B D.Heyward-Bey SP White 8.00 20.00
- 131 Travis Beckum RC .75 2.00
- 132 Deon Butler RC 1.00 2.50
- 133 Victor Harris RC 1.00 2.50
- 134A Derrick Williams RC 1.00 2.50
- 134B Derrick Williams SP Blue 5.00 12.00
- 135A Donald Brown RC 2.00 5.00
- 135B Donald Brown SP Blue 12.50 25.00
- 136 Eugene Monroe RC .75 2.00
- 137 Everette Brown RC 1.00 2.50
- 138 Duke Robinson RC .60 1.50
- 139 Glen Coffee RC 1.25 3.00
- 140A Graham Harrell SP RC 10.00 25.00
- 140B Graham Harrell SP Red 10.00 25.00
- 141 Demetrius Byrd RC .75 2.00
- 142A Hakeem Nicks SP RC 8.00 20.00
- 142B Hakeem Nicks SP 12.50 30.00
- 143 Hunter Cantwell RC 1.00 2.50
- 144 Ian Johnson SP RC 10.00 25.00
- 145 Jairus Byrd RC 1.25 3.00
- 146A James Casey RC .75 2.00
- 146B James Casey SP White 3.00 8.00
- 147 James Davis RC 1.00 2.50
- 148A James Laurinaitis RC 1.25 3.00
- 148B James Laurinaitis SP 5.00 12.00
- 149 Jared Cook SP RC 6.00 15.00
- 150 Jarett Dillard RC 1.00 2.50
- 151 Jason Smith RC .75 2.00
- 152A Javon Ringer RC 1.00 2.50
- 152B J.Ringer SP Ball in left arm 5.00 12.00
- 153A Jeremiah Johnson RC 1.00 2.50
- 153B Jeremiah Johnson SP Yellow 4.00 10.00
- 154 Vontae Davis RC 1.00 2.50
- 155A Jeremy Maclin RC 2.00 5.00
- 155B Jeremy Maclin SP Yellow 8.00 20.00
- 156 John Parker Wilson RC 1.00 2.50
- 157 John Phillips RC 1.00 2.50
- 158A Josh Freeman RC 2.00 5.00
- 158B Josh Freeman SP Draft 10.00 25.00
- 159A Juaquin Iglesias SP RC 12.00 30.00
- 159B Juaquin Iglesias SP White 10.00 25.00
- 160 Keenan Lewis RC 1.00 2.50
- 161A Kenny Britt RC 1.50 4.00
- 161B Kenny Britt SP Red 6.00 15.00
- 162 Kenny McKinley RC 1.00 2.50
- 163 Kevin Ogletree RC 1.00 2.50
- 164A Knowshon Moreno RC 2.50 6.00
- 164B K.Moreno SP White 10.00 20.00
- 165 Larry English RC 1.00 2.50
- 166A LeSean McCoy RC 2.00 5.00
- 166B LeSean McCoy SP Blue 8.00 20.00
- 167 William Moore RC .75 2.00
- 168 Louis Delmas RC 1.00 2.50
- 169A Louis Murphy RC 1.00 2.50
- 169B Louis Murphy SP White 4.00 10.00
- 170A Malcolm Jenkins RC 1.00 2.50
- 170B Malcolm Jenkins SP Red 4.00 10.00
- 171A Mark Sanchez RC 4.00 10.00
- 171B Mark Sanchez SP White 15.00 30.00
- 172A Matthew Stafford RC 3.00 8.00
- 172B Matthew Stafford SP Draft 15.00 30.00
- 173 Tom Brandstater RC 1.00 2.50
- 174A Michael Crabtree RC 2.50 6.00
- 174B Michael Crabtree SP Draft 12.50 25.00
- 175 Michael Hamlin RC .75 2.00
- 176 Michael Johnson RC .60 1.50
- 177 Michael Oher RC 2.00 5.00
- 178 Mike Mickens RC .75 2.00
- 179 Mike Thomas RC 1.00 2.50
- 180 Mohamed Massaquoi SP RC 6.00 15.00
- 181A Nate Davis RC 1.00 2.50
- 182 Nic Harris RC .75 2.00
- 183 P.J. Hill RC .75 2.00
- 184A Pat White RC 1.50 4.00
- 184B Pat White SP White 10.00 25.00
- 185 Patrick Chung RC 1.00 2.50
- 186 Patrick Turner RC .75 2.00
- 187A Percy Harvin RC 3.00 8.00
- 187B Percy Harvin SP White 10.00 25.00
- 188 Peria Jerry RC .75 2.00
- 189 Quan Cosby RC .75 2.00
- 190 Quinn Johnson RC .75 2.00
- 191A Ramses Barden RC .75 2.00
- 191B Ramses Barden SP w/o FB 5.00 12.00
- 192A Rashad Jennings RC 1.00 2.50
- 192B R.Jennings SP Bowl visible 4.00 10.00
- 193 Rashad Johnson RC .75 2.00
- 194A Rey Maualuga RC 1.50 4.00
- 194B Rey Maualuga SP White 8.00 20.00
- 195 Rhett Bomar RC .75 2.00
- 196 Sean Smith RC 1.00 2.50
- 197 Shawn Nelson RC .75 2.00
- 198 Sherrod Martin RC .75 2.00
- 199A Shonn Greene SP RC 10.00 25.00
- 199B Shonn Greene SP White 12.50 25.00
- 200 Stephen McGee RC 1.00 2.50

1989 Pro Set

- COMPLETE SET (561) 10.00 25.00
- COMP.SERIES 1 (440) 3.00 6.00
- COMP.SERIES 2 (100) 10.00 20.00
- COMP.FINAL FACT.SET (21) .75 2.00
- 1 Stacey Bailey .02 .10
- 2 Aundray Bruce RC .05 .15
- 3 Rick Bryan .02 .10
- 4 Bobby Butler .02 .10
- 5 Scott Case RC .02 .10
- 6 Tony Casillas .05 .15
- 7 Floyd Dixon .02 .10
- 8 Rick Donnelly .02 .10
- 9 Bill Fralic .05 .15
- 10 Mike Gann .02 .10
- 11 Mike Kenn .02 .10
- 12 Chris Miller RC .08 .25
- 13 John Rade .02 .10
- 14 Gerald Riggs UER .05 .15
- 15 John Settle RC .02 .10
- 16 Marion Campbell CO .02 .10
- 17 Cornelius Bennett .05 .15
- 18 Derrick Burroughs .02 .10
- 19 Shane Conlan .02 .10
- 20 Ronnie Harmon .05 .15
- 21 Kent Hull RC .05 .15
- 22 Jim Kelly .20 .50
- 23 Mark Kelso .05 .15
- 24 Pete Metzelaars .05 .15
- 25 Scott Norwood RC .05 .15
- 26 Andre Reed .08 .25
- 27 Fred Smerlas .02 .10
- 28 Bruce Smith .08 .25
- 29 Leonard Smith .02 .10
- 30 Art Still .02 .10
- 31 Darryl Talley .05 .15
- 32 Thurman Thomas RC .50 1.25
- 33 Will Wolford RC .05 .15
- 34 Marv Levy CO .05 .15
- 35 Neal Anderson .05 .15
- 36 Kevin Butler .02 .10
- 37 Jim Covert .05 .15
- 38 Richard Dent .05 .15
- 39 Dave Duerson .02 .10
- 40 Dennis Gentry .02 .10
- 41 Dan Hampton .05 .15
- 42 Jay Hilgenberg .02 .10
- 43 Dennis McKinnon UER .02 .10
- 44 Jim McMahon .05 .15
- 45 Steve McMichael .05 .15
- 46 Brad Muster RC .05 .15
- 47A William Perry SP 2.50 6.00
- 47B Ron Morris RC .02 .10
- 48 Ron Rivera .02 .10
- 49 Vestee Jackson RC .02 .10
- 50 Mike Singletary .05 .15
- 51 Mike Tomczak .05 .15
- 52 Keith Van Horne RC .02 .10
- 53A Mike Ditka CO .08 .25
- 53B Mike Ditka CO HOF .08 .25
- 54 Lewis Billups .02 .10
- 55 James Brooks .05 .15
- 56 Eddie Brown .02 .10
- 57 Jason Buck RC .02 .10
- 58 Boomer Esiason .05 .15
- 59 David Fulcher .05 .15
- 60A Rodney Holman ERR RC .05 .15
- 60B Rodney Holman COR RC .08 .25
- 61 Reggie Williams .05 .15
- 62 Joe Kelly RC .02 .10
- 63 Tim Krumrie .02 .10
- 64 Tim McGee .05 .15
- 65 Max Montoya .02 .10
- 66 Anthony Munoz .05 .15
- 67 Jim Skow .02 .10

Card	Low	High
68 Eric Thomas RC	.02	.10
69 Leon White	.02	.10
70 Ickey Woods RC	.05	.15
71 Carl Zander	.02	.10
72 Sam Wyche CO	.02	.10
73 Brian Brennan	.02	.10
74 Earnest Byner	.05	.15
75 Hanford Dixon	.02	.10
76 Mike Pagel	.02	.10
77 Bernie Kosar	.05	.15
78 Reggie Langhorne RC	.05	.15
79 Kevin Mack	.05	.15
80 Clay Matthews	.05	.15
81 Gerald McNeil	.02	.10
82 Frank Minnifield	.02	.10
83 Cody Risien	.02	.10
84 Webster Slaughter	.05	.15
85 Felix Wright	.02	.10
86 Bud Carson CO UER	.02	.10
87 Bill Bates	.05	.15
88 Kevin Brooks	.02	.10
89 Michael Irvin RC	.60	1.50
90 Jim Jeffcoat	.02	.10
91 Ed Too Tall Jones	.05	.15
92 Eugene Lockhart RC	.02	.10
93 Nate Newton RC	.05	.15
94 Danny Noonan	.02	.10
95 Steve Pelluer	.02	.10
96 Herschel Walker	.05	.15
97 Everson Walls	.02	.10
98 Jimmy Johnson CO RC	.08	.25
99 Keith Bishop	.02	.10
100A John Elway DRAFT	2.50	6.00
100B John Elway TRADE	.75	2.00
101 Simon Fletcher RC	.05	.15
102 Mike Harden	.02	.10
103 Mike Horan	.02	.10
104 Mark Jackson	.05	.15
105 Vance Johnson	.05	.15
106 Rulon Jones	.02	.10
107 Clarence Kay	.02	.10
108 Karl Mecklenburg	.05	.15
109 Ricky Nattiel	.02	.10
110 Steve Sewell RC	.02	.10
111 Dennis Smith	.05	.15
112 Gerald Willhite	.02	.10
113 Sammy Winder	.02	.10
114 Dan Reeves CO	.05	.15
115 Jim Arnold	.02	.10
116 Jerry Ball RC	.05	.15
117 Bennie Blades RC	.02	.10
118 Lomas Brown	.05	.15
119 Mike Cofer	.02	.10
120 Garry James	.02	.10
121 James Jones FB	.02	.10
122 Chuck Long	.02	.10
123 Pete Mandley	.02	.10
124 Eddie Murray	.02	.10
125 Chris Spielman RC	.08	.25
126 Dennis Gibson	.02	.10
127 Wayne Fontes CO	.02	.10
128 John Anderson	.02	.10
129 Brent Fullwood RC	.02	.10
130 Mark Cannon	.02	.10
131 Tim Harris	.02	.10
132 Mark Lee	.02	.10
133 Don Majkowski RC	.05	.15
134 Mark Murphy	.02	.10
135 Brian Noble	.02	.10
136 Ken Ruettgers RC	.02	.10
137 Johnny Holland	.02	.10
138 Randy Wright	.02	.10
139 Lindy Infante CO	.02	.10
140 Steve Brown	.02	.10
141 Ray Childress	.05	.15
142 Jeff Donaldson	.02	.10
143 Ernest Givins	.05	.15
144 John Grimsley	.02	.10
145 Alonzo Highsmith	.05	.15
146 Drew Hill	.05	.15
147 Robert Lyles	.02	.10
148 Bruce Matthews RC	.30	.75
149 Warren Moon	.08	.25
150 Mike Munchak	.05	.15
151 Allen Pinkett RC	.05	.15
152 Mike Rozier	.05	.15
153 Tony Zendejas	.02	.10
154 Jerry Glanville CO	.02	.10
155 Albert Bentley	.02	.10
156 Dean Biasucci	.02	.10
157 Duane Bickett	.02	.10
158 Bill Brooks	.05	.15
159 Chris Chandler RC	.40	1.00
160 Pat Beach	.02	.10
161 Ray Donaldson	.02	.10
162 Jon Hand	.02	.10
163 Chris Hinton	.02	.10
164 Rohn Stark	.02	.10
165 Fredd Young	.02	.10
166 Ron Meyer CO	.02	.10
167 Lloyd Burruss	.02	.10
168 Carlos Carson	.02	.10
169 Deron Cherry	.05	.15
170 Irv Eatman	.02	.10
171 Dino Hackett	.02	.10
172 Steve DeBerg	.05	.15
173 Albert Lewis	.02	.10
174 Nick Lowery	.02	.10
175 Bill Maas	.02	.10
176 Christian Okoye	.05	.15
177 Stephone Paige	.05	.15
178 Mark Adickes	.02	.10
179 Kevin Ross RC	.05	.15
180 Neil Smith RC	.20	.50
181 M. Schottenheimer CO	.02	.10
182 Marcus Allen	.08	.25
183 Tim Brown RC	.60	1.50
184 Willie Gault	.05	.15
185 Bo Jackson	.10	.30
186 Howie Long	.08	.25
187 Vann McElroy	.02	.10
188 Matt Millen	.05	.15
189 Don Mosebar RC	.02	.10
190 Bill Pickel	.02	.10
191 Jerry Robinson UER	.02	.10
192 Jay Schroeder	.02	.10
193A Stacey Toran	.02	.10
193B Stacey Toran	.20	.50
194 Mike Shanahan CO RC	.05	.15
195 Greg Bell	.02	.10
196 Ron Brown	.02	.10
197 Aaron Cox RC	.02	.10
198 Henry Ellard	.08	.25
199 Jim Everett	.05	.15
200 Jerry Gray	.02	.10
201 Kevin Greene	.08	.25
202 Pete Holohan	.02	.10
203 LeRoy Irvin	.05	.15
204 Mike Lansford	.02	.10
205 Tom Newberry RC	.02	.10
206 Mel Owens	.02	.10
207 Jackie Slater	.05	.15
208 Doug Smith	.02	.10
209 Mike Wilcher	.02	.10
210 John Robinson CO	.02	.10
211 John Bosa	.02	.10
212 Mark Brown	.02	.10
213 Mark Clayton	.05	.15
214A Ferrell Edmonds ERR RC	.20	.50
214B Ferrell Edmunds COR RC	.02	.10
215 Roy Foster	.02	.10
216 Lorenzo Hampton	.02	.10
217 Jim C.Jensen UER RC	.02	.10
218 William Judson	.02	.10
219 Eric Kumerow RC	.02	.10
220 Dan Marino	.75	2.00
221 John Offerdahl	.02	.10
222 Fuad Reveiz	.02	.10
223 Reggie Roby	.02	.10
224 Brian Sochia	.02	.10
225 Don Shula CO RC	.08	.25
226 Alfred Anderson	.02	.10
227 Joey Browner	.02	.10
228 Anthony Carter	.05	.15
229 Chris Doleman	.05	.15
230 Hassan Jones RC	.02	.10
231 Steve Jordan	.02	.10
232 Tommy Kramer	.05	.15
233 Carl Lee RC	.02	.10
234 Kirk Lowdermilk RC	.02	.10
235 Randall McDaniel RC	.50	1.25
236 Doug Martin	.02	.10
237 Keith Millard	.02	.10
238 Darrin Nelson	.02	.10
239 Jesse Solomon	.02	.10
240 Scott Studwell	.02	.10
241 Wade Wilson	.05	.15
242 Gary Zimmerman	.08	.25
243 Jerry Burns CO	.02	.10
244 Bruce Armstrong RC	.05	.15
245 Raymond Clayborn	.02	.10
246 Reggie Dupard	.02	.10
247 Tony Eason	.02	.10
248 Sean Farrell	.02	.10
249 Doug Flutie	.30	.75
250 Brent Williams RC	.02	.10
251 Roland James	.02	.10
252 Ronnie Lippett	.02	.10
253 Fred Marion	.02	.10
254 Larry McGrew	.02	.10
255 Stanley Morgan	.05	.15
256 Johnny Rembert RC	.02	.10
257 John Stephens RC	.02	.10
258 Andre Tippett	.08	.25
259 Garin Veris	.02	.10
260A Raymond Berry CO	.05	.15
260B Raymond Berry CO HOF	.05	.15
261 Morten Andersen	.05	.15
262 Hoby Brenner	.02	.10
263 Stan Brock	.02	.10
264 Brad Edelman	.02	.10
265 Jumpy Geathers	.02	.10
266A Bobby Hebert Passers	.20	.50
266B Bobby Hebert Passes	.05	.15
267 Craig Heyward RC	.08	.25
268 Lonzell Hill	.02	.10
269 Dalton Hilliard	.02	.10
270 Rickey Jackson	.05	.15
271 Steve Korte	.02	.10
272 Eric Martin	.02	.10
273 Rueben Mayes	.02	.10
274 Sam Mills	.05	.15
275 Brett Perriman RC	.08	.25
276 Pat Swilling	.05	.15
277 John Tice	.02	.10
278 Jim Mora CO	.02	.10
279 Eric Moore RC	.02	.10
280 Carl Banks	.05	.15
281 Mark Bavaro	.05	.15
282 Maurice Carthon	.02	.10
283 Mark Collins RC	.05	.15
284 Erik Howard	.02	.10
285 Terry Kinard	.02	.10
286 Sean Landeta	.02	.10
287 Lionel Manuel	.05	.15
288 Leonard Marshall	.05	.15
289 Joe Morris	.05	.15
290 Bart Oates	.02	.10
291 Phil Simms	.05	.15
292 Lawrence Taylor	.08	.25
293 Bill Parcells RC CO	.05	.15
294 Dave Cadigan	.02	.10
295 Kyle Clifton RC	.02	.10
296 Alex Gordon	.02	.10
297 James Hasty RC	.02	.10
298 Johnny Hector	.02	.10
299 Bobby Humphery	.05	.15
300 Pat Leahy	.02	.10
301 Marty Lyons	.02	.10
302 Reggie McElroy RC	.05	.15
303 Erik McMillan RC	.02	.10
304 Freeman McNeil	.05	.15
305 Ken O'Brien	.05	.15
306 Pat Ryan	.02	.10
307 Mickey Shuler	.02	.10
308 Al Toon	.05	.15
309 Jo Jo Townsell	.02	.10
310 Roger Vick	.02	.10
311 Joe Walton CO	.02	.10
312 Jerome Brown	.05	.15
313 Keith Byars	.05	.15
314 Cris Carter RC	.60	1.50
315 Randall Cunningham	.15	.40
316 Terry Hoage	.02	.10
317 Wes Hopkins	.02	.10
318 Keith Jackson RC	.08	.25
319 Mike Quick	.05	.15
320 Mike Reichenbach	.02	.10
321 Dave Rimington	.02	.10
322 John Teltschik	.02	.10
323 Anthony Toney	.02	.10
324 Andre Waters	.05	.15
325 Reggie White	.08	.25
326 Luis Zendejas	.02	.10
327 Buddy Ryan CO	.05	.15
328 Robert Awalt	.02	.10
329 Tim McDonald RC	.05	.15

❑ 330 Roy Green .05 .15
❑ 331 Neil Lomax .05 .15
❑ 332 Cedric Mack .02 .10
❑ 333 Stump Mitchell .02 .10
❑ 334 Niko Noga RC .02 .10
❑ 335 Jay Novacek RC .08 .25
❑ 336 Freddie Joe Nunn .02 .10
❑ 337 Luis Sharpe .02 .10
❑ 338 Vai Sikahema .02 .10
❑ 339 J.T. Smith .02 .10
❑ 340 Ron Wolfley .02 .10
❑ 341 Gene Stallings CO RC .05 .15
❑ 342 Gary Anderson K .02 .10
❑ 343 Bubby Brister RC .08 .25
❑ 344 Dermontti Dawson RC .05 .15
❑ 345 Thomas Everett RC .02 .10
❑ 346 Delton Hall RC .02 .10
❑ 347 Bryan Hinkle RC .02 .10
❑ 348 Merril Hoge RC .05 .15
❑ 349 Tunch Ilkin RC .02 .10
❑ 350 Aaron Jones RC .02 .10
❑ 351 Louis Lipps .05 .15
❑ 352 David Little .02 .10
❑ 353 Hardy Nickerson RC .08 .25
❑ 354 Rod Woodson RC .40 1.00
❑ 355A Chuck Noll CO RC .05 .15
❑ 355B Chuck Noll CO RC .05 .15
❑ 356 Gary Anderson RB .05 .15
❑ 357 Rod Bernstine RC .05 .15
❑ 358 Gill Byrd .02 .10
❑ 359 Vencie Glenn .02 .10
❑ 360 Dennis McKnight .02 .10
❑ 361 Lionel James .02 .10
❑ 362 Mark Malone .02 .10
❑ 363A Anthony Miller RC .08 .25
❑ 363B Anthony Miller RC .08 .25
❑ 364 Ralf Mojsiejenko .02 .10
❑ 365 Leslie O'Neal .05 .15
❑ 366 Jamie Holland RC .02 .10
❑ 367 Lee Williams .02 .10
❑ 368 Dan Henning CO .02 .10
❑ 369 Harris Barton RC .02 .10
❑ 370 Michael Carter .02 .10
❑ 371 Mike Cofer RC .02 .10
❑ 372 Roger Craig .08 .25
❑ 373 Riki Ellison RC .02 .10
❑ 374 Jim Fahnhorst .02 .10
❑ 375 John Frank .02 .10
❑ 376 Jeff Fuller .02 .10
❑ 377 Don Griffin .02 .10
❑ 378 Charles Haley .08 .25
❑ 379 Ronnie Lott .05 .15
❑ 380 Tim McKyer .02 .10
❑ 381 Joe Montana .75 2.00
❑ 382 Tom Rathman .05 .15
❑ 383 Jerry Rice .60 1.50
❑ 384 John Taylor RC .20 .50
❑ 385 Keena Turner .02 .10
❑ 386 Michael Walter .02 .10
❑ 387 Bubba Paris .02 .10
❑ 388 Steve Young 40 1.00
❑ 389 George Seifert CO RC .05 .15
❑ 390 Brian Blades RC .08 .25
❑ 391A B.Bosworth Seattle .10 .30
❑ 391B B.Bosworth Seahawks .05 .15
❑ 392 Jeff Bryant .02 .10
❑ 393 Jacob Green .05 .15
❑ 394 Norm Johnson .02 .10
❑ 395 Dave Krieg .05 .15
❑ 396 Steve Largent .08 .25
❑ 397 Bryan Millard RC .02 .10
❑ 398 Paul Moyer .02 .10
❑ 399 Joe Nash .02 .10
❑ 400 Rufus Porter RC .02 .10
❑ 401 Eugene Robinson RC .08 .25
❑ 402 Bruce Scholtz .02 .10
❑ 403 Kelly Stouffer RC .02 .10
❑ 404A Curt Warner 1455 .50 1.25
❑ 404B Curt Warner 6074 .05 .15
❑ 405 John L.Williams .02 .10
❑ 406 Tony Woods RC .05 .15
❑ 407 David Wyman .02 .10
❑ 408 Chuck Knox CO .05 .15
❑ 409 Mark Carrier RC .08 .25
❑ 410 Randy Grimes .02 .10
❑ 411 Paul Gruber RC .05 .15
❑ 412 Harry Hamilton .02 .10
❑ 413 Ron Holmes .02 .10
❑ 414 Donald Igwebuike .02 .10
❑ 415 Dan Turk .02 .10
❑ 416 Ricky Reynolds .02 .10
❑ 417 Bruce Hill RC .02 .10
❑ 418 Lars Tate .02 .10
❑ 419 Vinny Testaverde .10 .30
❑ 420 James Wilder .02 .10
❑ 421 Ray Perkins CO .02 .10
❑ 422 Jeff Bostic .02 .10
❑ 423 Kelvin Bryant .02 .10
❑ 424 Gary Clark .08 .25
❑ 425 Monte Coleman .02 .10
❑ 426 Darrell Green .05 .15
❑ 427 Joe Jacoby .05 .15
❑ 428 Jim Lachey .05 .15
❑ 429 Charles Mann .02 .10
❑ 430 Dexter Manley .05 .15
❑ 431 Darryl Grant .02 .10
❑ 432 Mark May RC .05 .15
❑ 433 Art Monk .05 .15
❑ 434 Mark Rypien RC .08 .25
❑ 435 Ricky Sanders .05 .15
❑ 436 Alvin Walton RC .02 .10
❑ 437 Don Warren .02 .10
❑ 438 Jamie Morris .02 .10
❑ 439 Doug Williams .05 .15
❑ 440 Joe Gibbs CO RC .08 .25
❑ 441 Marcus Cotton .02 .10
❑ 442 Joel Williams .02 .10
❑ 443 Joe Devlin .02 .10
❑ 444 Robb Riddick .02 .10
❑ 445 William Perry .05 .15
❑ 446 Thomas Sanders RC .02 .10
❑ 447 Brian Blados .02 .10
❑ 448 Cris Collinsworth .05 .15
❑ 449 Stanford Jennings .02 .10
❑ 450 Barry Krauss UER .02 .10
❑ 451 Ozzie Newsome .05 .15
❑ 452 Mike Oliphant RC .02 .10
❑ 453 Tony Dorsett .08 .25
❑ 454 Bruce McNorton .02 .10
❑ 455 Eric Dickerson .05 .15
❑ 456 Keith Bostic .02 .10
❑ 457 Sam Clancy RC .02 .10
❑ 458 Jack Del Rio RC .08 .25
❑ 459 Mike Webster .05 .15
❑ 460 Bob Golic .02 .10
❑ 461 Otis Wilson .02 .10
❑ 462 Mike Haynes .05 .15
❑ 463 Greg Townsend .05 .15
❑ 464 Mark Duper .05 .15
❑ 465 E.J. Junior .05 .15
❑ 466 Troy Stradford .02 .10
❑ 467 Mike Merriweather .05 .15
❑ 468 Irving Fryar .08 .25
❑ 469 Vaughan Johnson RC .05 .15
❑ 470 Pepper Johnson .05 .15
❑ 471 Gary Reasons RC .02 .10
❑ 472 Perry Williams RC .02 .10
❑ 473 Wesley Walker .05 .15
❑ 474 Anthony Bell RC .05 .15
❑ 475 Earl Ferrell .02 .10
❑ 476 Craig Wolfley .02 .10
❑ 477 Billy Ray Smith .02 .10
❑ 478A Jim McMahon NOTR .10 .30
❑ 478B Jim McMahon TR .05 .15
❑ 478C Jim McMahon 15.00 40.00
❑ 479 Eric Wright .02 .10
❑ 480A Earnest Byner NOTR .05 .15
❑ 480B Earnest Byner TR .10 .30
❑ 480C Earnest Byner TR 15.00 40.00
❑ 480D Earnest Byner NOTR 75.00 150.00
❑ 481 Russ Grimm .05 .15
❑ 482 Wilber Marshall .05 .15
❑ 483A Gerald Riggs NOTR .05 .15
❑ 483B Gerald Riggs TR .10 .30
❑ 483C Gerald Riggs TR 15.00 40.00
❑ 483D Gerald Riggs NOTR 75.00 150.00
❑ 484 Brian Davis RC .02 .10
❑ 485 Shawn Collins RC .02 .10
❑ 486 Deion Sanders RC .60 1.50
❑ 487 Trace Armstrong RC .05 .15
❑ 488 Donnell Woolford RC .05 .15
❑ 489 Eric Metcalf RC .08 .25
❑ 490 Troy Aikman RC 2.50 6.00
❑ 491 Steve Walsh RC .05 .15
❑ 492 Steve Atwater RC .08 .25
❑ 493 Bobby Humphrey RC .05 .15
❑ 494 Barry Sanders RC 2.50 6.00
❑ 495 Tony Mandarich RC .05 .15
❑ 496 David Williams RC .02 .10
❑ 497 Andre Rison UER RC .40 1.00
❑ 498 Derrick Thomas RC .60 1.50
❑ 499 Cleveland Gary RC .02 .10
❑ 500 Bill Hawkins RC .02 .10
❑ 501 Louis Oliver RC .05 .15
❑ 502 Sammie Smith RC .02 .10
❑ 503 Hart Lee Dykes RC .02 .10
❑ 504 Wayne Martin RC .02 .10
❑ 505 Brian Williams OL RC .02 .10
❑ 506 Jeff Lageman RC .05 .15
❑ 507 Eric Hill RC .05 .15
❑ 508 Joe Wolf RC .02 .10
❑ 509 Timm Rosenbach RC .05 .15
❑ 510 Tom Ricketts .02 .10
❑ 511 Tim Worley RC .02 .10
❑ 512 Burt Grossman RC .05 .15
❑ 513 Keith DeLong RC .02 .10
❑ 514 Andy Heck RC .02 .10
❑ 515 Broderick Thomas RC .08 .25
❑ 516 Don Beebe RC .08 .25
❑ 517 James Thornton RC .02 .10
❑ 518 Eric Kattus .02 .10
❑ 519 Bruce Kozerski RC .02 .10
❑ 520 Brian Washington RC .02 .10
❑ 521 Rodney Peete RC .20 .50
❑ 522 Erik Affholter RC .02 .10
❑ 523 Anthony Dilweg RC .02 .10
❑ 524 O'Brien Alston .02 .10
❑ 525 Mike Elkins .02 .10
❑ 526 Jonathan Hayes RC .02 .10
❑ 527 Terry McDaniel RC .02 .10
❑ 528 Frank Stams RC .02 .10
❑ 529 Darryl Ingram RC .02 .10
❑ 530 Henry Thomas .02 .10
❑ 531 Eric Coleman DB .02 .10
❑ 532 Sheldon White RC .02 .10
❑ 533 Eric Allen RC .08 .25
❑ 534 Robert Drummond .02 .10
❑ 535A Gizmo Williams RC bal 5.00 10.00
❑ 535B Gizmo Williams RC w/o scout .08 .25
❑ 535C Gizmo Williams RC w/scout .05 .15
❑ 536 Billy Joe Tolliver RC .05 .15
❑ 537 Daniel Stubbs RC .02 .10
❑ 538 Wesley Walls RC .15 .40
❑ 539A James Jefferson ERR RC .10 .30
❑ 539B James Jefferson COR RC .02 .10
❑ 540 Tracy Rocker .02 .10
❑ 541 Art Shell CO .05 .15
❑ 542 Lemuel Stinson RC .02 .10
❑ 543 Tyrone Braxton UER RC .02 .10
❑ 544 David Treadwell RC .02 .10
❑ 545 Flipper Anderson RC .08 .25
❑ 546 Dave Meggett RC .08 .25
❑ 547 Lewis Tillman RC .02 .10
❑ 548 Carnell Lake RC .08 .25
❑ 549 Marion Butts RC .05 .15
❑ 550 Sterling Sharpe RC .40 1.00
❑ 551 Ezra Johnson .02 .10
❑ 552 Clarence Verdin RC .02 .10
❑ 553 Mervyn Fernandez RC .02 .10
❑ 554 Ottis Anderson .05 .15
❑ 555 Gary Hogeboom .02 .10
❑ 556 Paul Palmer TR .02 .10
❑ 557 Jesse Solomon TR .02 .10
❑ 558 Chip Banks TR .05 .15
❑ 559 Steve Pelluer TR .02 .10
❑ 560 Darrin Nelson TR .02 .10
❑ 561 Herschel Walker TR .05 .15
❑ CC1 Pete Rozelle .20 .50

1990 Pro Set

❑ COMPLETE SET (801) 15.00 35.00
❑ COMP.SERIES 1 (377) 6.00 15.00
❑ COMP.SERIES 2 (392) 6.00 15.00
❑ COMP.FINAL SERIES (32) 2.00 5.00

❑ COMP.FINAL FACT. (32) 2.00 5.00
❑ 1A Ba.Sanders ROY Hawaii 30.00 80.00
❑ 1B Barry Sanders ROY .25 .60
❑ 2A Joe Montana POY 3521 ERR .20 .50
❑ 2B Joe Montana POY 3130 COR .20 .50
❑ 3 Lindy Infante COY UER .01 .05
❑ 4 Warren Moon MOY UER .08 .25
❑ 5 Keith Millard D-POY .01 .05
❑ 6 Derrick Thomas D-ROY .08 .25
❑ 7 Ottis Anderson CB POY .02 .10
❑ 8 Joe Montana LL UER .20 .50
❑ 9 Christian Okoye LL .01 .05
❑ 10 Thurman Thomas LL .08 .25
❑ 11 Mike Cofer LL .01 .05
❑ 12 Dalton Hilliard LL UER .01 .05
❑ 13 Sterling Sharpe LL .08 .25
❑ 14 Rich Camarillo LL .01 .05
❑ 15A Walter Stanley LL ERR 87/8 .20 .50
❑ 15B Walter Stanley LL COR .01 .05
❑ 16 Rod Woodson LL .08 .25
❑ 17 Felix Wright LL .01 .05
❑ 18A Chris Doleman LL ERR .20 .50
❑ 18B Chris Doleman LL COR .20 .50
❑ 19A Andre Ware RC no draft .02 .10
❑ 19B Andre Ware RC draft .02 .10
❑ 20A Mo Elewonibi RC .01 .05
❑ 20B Mo Elewonibi RC .01 .05
❑ 21A Percy Snow no draft .20 .50
❑ 21B Percy Snow draft .01 .05
❑ 22A Anthony Thompson RC .01 .05
❑ 22B A.Thompson RC draft .01 .05
❑ 23 Buck Buchanan HOF .01 .05
❑ 24 Bob Griese HOF .02 .10
❑ 25A Franco Harris HOF ERR .20 .50
❑ 25B Franco Harris HOF COR .02 .10
❑ 26 Ted Hendricks HOF .01 .05
❑ 27A Jack Lambert HOF ERR .20 .50
❑ 27B Jack Lambert HOF COR .20 .50
❑ 28 Tom Landry HOF .02 .10
❑ 29 Bob St.Clair HOF .01 .05
❑ 30 Aundray Bruce UER .01 .05
❑ 31 Tony Casillas UER .01 .05
❑ 32 Shawn Collins .01 .05
❑ 33 Marcus Cotton .01 .05
❑ 34 Bill Fralic .01 .05
❑ 35 Chris Miller .02 .10
❑ 36 Deion Sanders UER .20 .50
❑ 37 John Settle .01 .05
❑ 38 Jerry Glanville CO .01 .05
❑ 39 Cornelius Bennett .02 .10
❑ 40 Jim Kelly .08 .25
❑ 41 Mark Kelso UER .01 .05
❑ 42 Scott Norwood .01 .05
❑ 43 Nate Odomes RC .02 .10
❑ 44 Scott Radecic .01 .05
❑ 45 Jim Ritcher RC .01 .05
❑ 46 Leonard Smith .01 .05
❑ 47 Darryl Talley .01 .05
❑ 48 Marv Levy CO .01 .05
❑ 49 Neal Anderson .02 .10
❑ 50 Kevin Butler .01 .05
❑ 51 Jim Covert .01 .05
❑ 52 Richard Dent .02 .10
❑ 53 Jay Hilgenberg .01 .05
❑ 54 Steve McMichael .02 .10
❑ 55 Ron Morris .01 .05
❑ 56 John Roper .01 .05
❑ 57 Mike Singletary .02 .10
❑ 58 Keith Van Horne .01 .05
❑ 59A Mike Ditka CO LL .08 .25
❑ 59B Mike Ditka CO SL 2.00 5.00
❑ 60 Lewis Billups .01 .05
❑ 61 Eddie Brown .01 .05
❑ 62 Jason Buck .01 .05
❑ 63A Rickey Dixon ERR RC .20 .50
❑ 63B Rickey Dixon COR RC .20 .50
❑ 64 Tim McGee .01 .05
❑ 65 Eric Thomas .01 .05
❑ 66 Ickey Woods .01 .05
❑ 67 Carl Zander .01 .05
❑ 68A Sam Wyche CO ERR .20 .50
❑ 68B Sam Wyche CO COR .20 .50
❑ 69 Paul Farren .01 .05
❑ 70 Thane Gash RC .01 .05
❑ 71 David Grayson .01 .05
❑ 72 Bernie Kosar .02 .10
❑ 73 Reggie Langhorne .01 .05
❑ 74 Eric Metcalf .08 .25
❑ 75A Ozzie Newsome ERR .20 .50
❑ 75B Ozzie Newsome COR .20 .50
❑ 75C Cody Risien SP .20 .50
❑ 76 Felix Wright .01 .05
❑ 77 Bud Carson CO .01 .05
❑ 78 Troy Aikman .30 .75
❑ 79 Michael Irvin .08 .25
❑ 80 Jim Jeffcoat .01 .05
❑ 81 Crawford Ker .01 .05
❑ 82 Eugene Lockhart .01 .05
❑ 83 Kelvin Martin RC .01 .05
❑ 84 Ken Norton Jr. RC .08 .25
❑ 85 Jimmy Johnson CO .02 .10
❑ 86 Steve Atwater .01 .05
❑ 87 Tyrone Braxton .01 .05
❑ 88 John Elway .50 1.25
❑ 89 Simon Fletcher .01 .05
❑ 90 Ron Holmes .01 .05
❑ 91 Bobby Humphrey .01 .05
❑ 92 Vance Johnson .01 .05
❑ 93 Ricky Nattiel .01 .05
❑ 94 Dan Reeves CO .01 .05
❑ 95 Jim Arnold .01 .05
❑ 96 Jerry Ball .01 .05
❑ 97 Bennie Blades .01 .05
❑ 98 Lomas Brown .01 .05
❑ 99 Michael Cofer .01 .05
❑ 100 Richard Johnson .01 .05
❑ 101 Eddie Murray .01 .05
❑ 102 Barry Sanders .50 1.25
❑ 103 Chris Spielman .08 .25
❑ 104 William White RC .01 .05
❑ 105 Eric Williams RC .01 .05
❑ 106 Wayne Fontes CO UER .01 .05
❑ 107 Brent Fullwood .01 .05
❑ 108 Ron Hallstrom RC .01 .05
❑ 109 Tim Harris .01 .05
❑ 110A Johnny Holland ERR NN .20 .50
❑ 110B Johnny Holland COR .20 .50
❑ 111A Perry Kemp ERR .20 .50
❑ 111B Perry Kemp COR .20 .50
❑ 112 Don Majkowski .01 .05
❑ 113 Mark Murphy .01 .05
❑ 114A Sterling Sharpe ERR Gle .08 .25
❑ 114B Sterling Sharpe COR Chi .20 .50
❑ 115 Ed West RC .01 .05
❑ 116 Lindy Infante CO .01 .05
❑ 117 Steve Brown .01 .05
❑ 118 Ray Childress .01 .05
❑ 119 Ernest Givins .02 .10
❑ 120 John Grimsley .01 .05
❑ 121 Alonzo Highsmith .01 .05
❑ 122 Drew Hill .01 .05
❑ 123 Bubba McDowell .01 .05
❑ 124 Dean Steinkuhler .01 .05
❑ 125 Lorenzo White .02 .10
❑ 126 Tony Zendejas .01 .05
❑ 127 Jack Pardee CO .01 .05
❑ 128 Albert Bentley .01 .05
❑ 129 Dean Biasucci .01 .05
❑ 130 Duane Bickett .01 .05
❑ 131 Bill Brooks .01 .05
❑ 132 Jon Hand .01 .05
❑ 133 Mike Prior .01 .05
❑ 134A Andre Rison NOTR .08 .25
❑ 134B Andre Rison TR .08 .25
❑ 134C Andre Rison TR Lud/back .08 .25
❑ 135 Rohn Stark .01 .05
❑ 136 Donnell Thompson .01 .05
❑ 137 Clarence Verdin .01 .05
❑ 138 Fredd Young .01 .05
❑ 139 Ron Meyer CO .01 .05
❑ 140 John Alt RC .01 .05
❑ 141 Steve DeBerg .01 .05
❑ 142 Irv Eatman .01 .05
❑ 143 Dino Hackett .01 .05
❑ 144 Nick Lowery .01 .05
❑ 145 Bill Maas .01 .05
❑ 146 Stephone Paige .01 .05
❑ 147 Neil Smith .08 .25
❑ 148 M. Schottenheimer CO .01 .05
❑ 149 Steve Beuerlein .02 .10
❑ 150 Tim Brown .08 .25
❑ 151 Mike Dyal .01 .05
❑ 152A Mervyn Fernandez ERR .30 .75
❑ 152B Mervyn Fernandez COR .30 .75
❑ 153 Willie Gault .02 .10
❑ 154 Bob Golic .01 .05
❑ 155 Bo Jackson .10 .30
❑ 156 Don Mosebar .01 .05
❑ 157 Steve Smith .01 .05
❑ 158 Greg Townsend .01 .05
❑ 159 Bruce Wilkerson RC .01 .05
❑ 160 Steve Wisniewski .02 .10
❑ 161A Art Shell CO ERR .20 .50
❑ 161B Art Shell CO COR 3.00 8.00
❑ 161C Art Shell CO COR 4.00 10.00
❑ 162 Flipper Anderson .01 .05
❑ 163 Greg Bell UER .01 .05
❑ 164 Henry Ellard .02 .10
❑ 165 Jim Everett .02 .10
❑ 166 Jerry Gray .01 .05
❑ 167 Kevin Greene .02 .10
❑ 168 Pete Holohan .01 .05
❑ 169 Larry Kelm RC .01 .05
❑ 170 Tom Newberry .01 .05
❑ 171 Vince Newsome RC .01 .05
❑ 172 Irv Pankey .01 .05
❑ 173 Jackie Slater .01 .05
❑ 174 Fred Strickland RC .01 .05
❑ 175 Mike Wilcher UER .01 .05
❑ 176 John Robinson CO UER .01 .05
❑ 177 Mark Clayton .02 .10
❑ 178 Roy Foster .01 .05
❑ 179 Harry Galbreath RC .01 .05
❑ 180 Jim C. Jensen .01 .05
❑ 181 Dan Marino .50 1.25
❑ 182 Louis Oliver .01 .05
❑ 183 Sammie Smith .01 .05
❑ 184 Brian Sochia .01 .05
❑ 185 Don Shula CO .02 .10
❑ 186 Joey Browner .01 .05
❑ 187 Anthony Carter .02 .10
❑ 188 Chris Doleman .01 .05
❑ 189 Steve Jordan .01 .05
❑ 190 Carl Lee .01 .05
❑ 191 Randall McDaniel .05 .15
❑ 192 Mike Merriweather .01 .05
❑ 193 Keith Millard .01 .05
❑ 194 Al Noga .01 .05
❑ 195 Scott Studwell .01 .05
❑ 196 Henry Thomas .01 .05
❑ 197 Herschel Walker .02 .10
❑ 198 Wade Wilson .02 .10
❑ 199 Gary Zimmerman .02 .10
❑ 200 Jerry Burns CO .01 .05
❑ 201 Vincent Brown RC .01 .05
❑ 202 Hart Lee Dykes .01 .05
❑ 203 Sean Farrell .01 .05
❑ 204A Fred Marion belt 75.00 150.00
❑ 204B Fred Marion no belt .01 .05
❑ 205 Stanley Morgan UER .01 .05
❑ 206 Eric Sievers RC .01 .05
❑ 207 John Stephens .01 .05
❑ 208 Andre Tippett .01 .05
❑ 209 Rod Rust CO .01 .05
❑ 210A Morten Andersen wht .20 .50
❑ 210B Morten Andersen blk .20 .50
❑ 211 Brad Edelman .01 .05
❑ 212 John Fourcade .01 .05
❑ 213 Dalton Hilliard .01 .05
❑ 214 Rickey Jackson .02 .10
❑ 215 Vaughan Johnson .01 .05
❑ 216A Eric Martin wht .20 .50
❑ 216B Eric Martin blk .20 .50
❑ 217 Sam Mills .02 .10
❑ 218 Pat Swilling UER .02 .10
❑ 219 Frank Warren RC .01 .05
❑ 220 Jim Wilks .01 .05
❑ 221A Jim Mora CO wht .20 .50
❑ 221B Jim Mora CO blk .20 .50
❑ 222 Raul Allegre .01 .05
❑ 223 Carl Banks .01 .05
❑ 224 John Elliott .01 .05
❑ 225 Erik Howard .01 .05
❑ 226 Pepper Johnson .01 .05
❑ 227 Leonard Marshall UER .01 .05
❑ 228 Dave Meggett .02 .10
❑ 229 Bart Oates .01 .05
❑ 230 Phil Simms .02 .10
❑ 231 Lawrence Taylor .08 .25
❑ 232 Bill Parcells CO .02 .10
❑ 233 Troy Benson .01 .05
❑ 234 Kyle Clifton UER .01 .05
❑ 235 Johnny Hector .01 .05
❑ 236 Jeff Lageman .01 .05
❑ 237 Pat Leahy .01 .05
❑ 238 Freeman McNeil .01 .05
❑ 239 Ken O'Brien .01 .05

❑ 240 Al Toon .02 .10
❑ 241 Jo Jo Townsell .01 .05
❑ 242 Bruce Coslet CO .01 .05
❑ 243 Eric Allen .01 .05
❑ 244 Jerome Brown .01 .05
❑ 245 Keith Byars .01 .05
❑ 246 Cris Carter .20 .50
❑ 247 Randall Cunningham .08 .25
❑ 248 Keith Jackson .02 .10
❑ 249 Mike Quick .01 .05
❑ 250 Clyde Simmons .01 .05
❑ 251 Andre Waters .01 .05
❑ 252 Reggie White .08 .25
❑ 253 Buddy Ryan CO .01 .05
❑ 254 Rich Camarillo .01 .05
❑ 255 Earl Ferrell .01 .05
❑ 256 Roy Green .02 .10
❑ 257 Ken Harvey RC .08 .25
❑ 258 Ernie Jones RC .01 .05
❑ 259 Tim McDonald .01 .05
❑ 260 Timm Rosenbach UER .01 .05
❑ 261 Luis Sharpe .01 .05
❑ 262 Vai Sikahema .01 .05
❑ 263 J.T. Smith .01 .05
❑ 264 Ron Wolfley UER .01 .05
❑ 265 Joe Bugel CO .01 .05
❑ 266 Gary Anderson K .01 .05
❑ 267 Bubby Brister .01 .05
❑ 268 Merril Hoge .01 .05
❑ 269 Carnell Lake .01 .05
❑ 270 Louis Lipps .02 .10
❑ 271 David Little .01 .05
❑ 272 Greg Lloyd .08 .25
❑ 273 Keith Willis .01 .05
❑ 274 Tim Worley .01 .05
❑ 275 Chuck Noll CO .02 .10
❑ 276 Marion Butts .02 .10
❑ 277 Gill Byrd .01 .05
❑ 278 Vencie Glenn UER .01 .05
❑ 279 Burt Grossman .01 .05
❑ 280 Gary Plummer .01 .05
❑ 281 Billy Ray Smith .01 .05
❑ 282 Billy Joe Tolliver .01 .05
❑ 283 Dan Henning CO .01 .05
❑ 284 Harris Barton .01 .05
❑ 285 Michael Carter .01 .05
❑ 286 Mike Cofer .01 .05
❑ 287 Roger Craig .02 .10
❑ 288 Don Griffin .01 .05
❑ 289A Charles Haley ERR 4 fum 4.00 10.00
❑ 289B Charles Haley COR 5 fum .30 .75
❑ 290 Pierce Holt RC .01 .05
❑ 291 Ronnie Lott .02 .10
❑ 292 Guy McIntyre .01 .05
❑ 293 Joe Montana .50 1.25
❑ 294 Tom Rathman .01 .05
❑ 295 Jerry Rice .30 .75
❑ 296 Jesse Sapolu RC .01 .05
❑ 297 John Taylor .02 .10
❑ 298 Michael Walter .01 .05
❑ 299 George Seifert CO .02 .10
❑ 300 Jeff Bryant .01 .05
❑ 301 Jacob Green .01 .05
❑ 302 Norm Johnson UER .01 .05
❑ 303 Bryan Millard .01 .05
❑ 304 Joe Nash .01 .05
❑ 305 Eugene Robinson .01 .05
❑ 306 John L. Williams .01 .05
❑ 307 David Wyman .01 .05
❑ 308 Chuck Knox CO .01 .05
❑ 309 Mark Carrier WR .08 .25
❑ 310 Paul Gruber .01 .05
❑ 311 Harry Hamilton .01 .05
❑ 312 Bruce Hill .01 .05
❑ 313 Donald Igwebuike .01 .05
❑ 314 Kevin Murphy .01 .05
❑ 315 Ervin Randle .01 .05
❑ 316 Mark Robinson .01 .05
❑ 317 Lars Tate .01 .05
❑ 318 Vinny Testaverde .02 .10
❑ 319A Ray Perkins CO ERR NN .30 .75
❑ 319B Ray Perkins CO COR .01 .05
❑ 320 Earnest Byner .01 .05
❑ 321 Gary Clark .08 .25
❑ 322 Darryl Grant .01 .05
❑ 323 Darrell Green .02 .10
❑ 324 Jim Lachey .01 .05
❑ 325 Charles Mann .01 .05
❑ 326 Wilber Marshall .01 .05
❑ 327 Ralf Mojsiejenko .01 .05
❑ 328 Art Monk .02 .10
❑ 329 Gerald Riggs .02 .10
❑ 330 Mark Rypien .02 .10
❑ 331 Ricky Sanders .01 .05
❑ 332 Alvin Walton .01 .05
❑ 333 Joe Gibbs CO .02 .10
❑ 334 Aloha Stadium .01 .05
❑ 335 Brian Blades PB .01 .05
❑ 336 James Brooks PB .01 .05
❑ 337 Shane Conlan PB .01 .05
❑ 338A Eric Dickerson PB SP 1.25 3.00
❑ 338B Lud Denny Promo 75.00 200.00
❑ 339 Ray Donaldson PB .01 .05
❑ 340 Ferrell Edmunds PB .01 .05
❑ 341 Boomer Esiason PB .01 .05
❑ 342 David Fulcher PB .01 .05
❑ 343A Chris Hinton PB 3.00 8.00
❑ 343B Chris Hinton PB Trade .01 .05
❑ 344 Rodney Holman PB .01 .05
❑ 345 Kent Hull PB .01 .05
❑ 346 Tunch Ilkin PB .01 .05
❑ 347 Mike Johnson PB .01 .05
❑ 348 Greg Kragen PB .01 .05
❑ 349 Dave Krieg PB .02 .10
❑ 350 Albert Lewis PB .01 .05
❑ 351 Howie Long PB .02 .10
❑ 352 Bruce Matthews PB .01 .05
❑ 353 Clay Matthews PB .01 .05
❑ 354 Erik McMillan PB .01 .05
❑ 355 Karl Mecklenburg PB .01 .05
❑ 356 Anthony Miller PB .01 .05
❑ 357 Frank Minnifield PB .01 .05
❑ 358 Max Montoya PB .01 .05
❑ 359 Warren Moon PB .08 .25
❑ 360 Mike Munchak PB .01 .05
❑ 361 Anthony Munoz PB .01 .05
❑ 362 John Offerdahl PB .01 .05
❑ 363 Christian Okoye PB .01 .05
❑ 364 Leslie O'Neal PB .01 .05
❑ 365 Rufus Porter PB UER .01 .05
❑ 366 Andre Reed PB .02 .10
❑ 367 Johnny Rembert PB .01 .05
❑ 368 Reggie Roby PB .01 .05
❑ 369 Kevin Ross PB .01 .05
❑ 370 Webster Slaughter PB .01 .05
❑ 371 Bruce Smith PB .02 .10
❑ 372 Dennis Smith PB .01 .05
❑ 373 Derrick Thomas PB .02 .10
❑ 374 Thurman Thomas PB .08 .25
❑ 375 David Treadwell PB .01 .05
❑ 376 Lee Williams PB .01 .05
❑ 377 Rod Woodson PB .02 .10
❑ 378 Bud Carson CO PB .01 .05
❑ 379 Eric Allen PB .01 .05
❑ 380 Neal Anderson PB .02 .10
❑ 381 Jerry Ball PB .01 .05
❑ 382 Joey Browner PB .01 .05
❑ 383 Rich Camarillo PB .01 .05
❑ 384 Mark Carrier WR PB .01 .05
❑ 385 Roger Craig PB .02 .10
❑ 386A R.Cunningham PB small .20 .50
❑ 386B R.Cunningham PB large .20 .50
❑ 387 Chris Doleman PB .01 .05
❑ 388 Henry Ellard PB .01 .05
❑ 389 Bill Fralic PB .01 .05
❑ 390 Brent Fullwood PB .01 .05
❑ 391 Jerry Gray PB .01 .05
❑ 392 Kevin Greene PB .02 .10
❑ 393 Tim Harris PB .01 .05
❑ 394 Jay Hilgenberg PB .01 .05
❑ 395 Dalton Hilliard PB .01 .05
❑ 396 Keith Jackson PB .02 .10
❑ 397 Vaughan Johnson PB .01 .05
❑ 398 Steve Jordan PB .01 .05
❑ 399 Carl Lee PB .01 .05
❑ 400 Ronnie Lott PB .02 .10
❑ 401 Don Majkowski PB .01 .05
❑ 402 Charles Mann PB .01 .05
❑ 403 Randall McDaniel PB .02 .10
❑ 404 Tim McDonald PB .01 .05
❑ 405 Guy McIntyre PB .01 .05
❑ 406 Dave Meggett PB .01 .05
❑ 407 Keith Millard PB .01 .05
❑ 408 Joe Montana PB .20 .50
❑ 409 Eddie Murray PB .01 .05
❑ 410 Tom Newberry PB .01 .05
❑ 411 Jerry Rice PB .20 .50
❑ 412 Mark Rypien PB .01 .05
❑ 413 Barry Sanders PB .25 .60
❑ 414 Luis Sharpe PB .01 .05
❑ 415 Sterling Sharpe PB .01 .05
❑ 416 Mike Singletary PB .02 .10
❑ 417 Jackie Slater PB .01 .05
❑ 418 Doug Smith PB .01 .05
❑ 419 Chris Spielman PB .01 .05
❑ 420 Pat Swilling PB .01 .05
❑ 421 John Taylor PB .01 .05
❑ 422 Lawrence Taylor PB .02 .10
❑ 423 Reggie White PB .02 .10
❑ 424 Ron Wolfley PB .01 .05
❑ 425 Gary Zimmerman PB .02 .10
❑ 426 John Robinson CO PB .01 .05
❑ 427 Scott Case UER .01 .05
❑ 428 Mike Kenn .01 .05
❑ 429 Mike Gann .01 .05
❑ 430 Tim Green RC .01 .05
❑ 431 Michael Haynes RC .08 .25
❑ 432 Jessie Tuggle UER RC .01 .05
❑ 433 John Rade .01 .05
❑ 434 Andre Rison .08 .25
❑ 435 Don Beebe .02 .10
❑ 436 Ray Bentley .01 .05
❑ 437 Shane Conlan .01 .05
❑ 438 Kent Hull .01 .05
❑ 439 Pete Metzelaars .01 .05
❑ 440 Andre Reed UER .08 .25
❑ 441 Frank Reich .08 .25
❑ 442 Leon Seals RC .01 .05
❑ 443 Bruce Smith .08 .25
❑ 444 Thurman Thomas .08 .25
❑ 445 Will Wolford .01 .05
❑ 446 Trace Armstrong .01 .05
❑ 447 Mark Bortz RC .01 .05
❑ 448 Tom Thayer RC .01 .05
❑ 449A Dan Hampton DE .20 .50
❑ 449B Dan Hampton DT 4.00 10.00
❑ 450 Shaun Gayle RC .01 .05
❑ 451 Dennis Gentry .01 .05
❑ 452 Jim Harbaugh .08 .25
❑ 453 Vestee Jackson .01 .05
❑ 454 Brad Muster .01 .05
❑ 455 William Perry .02 .10
❑ 456 Ron Rivera .01 .05
❑ 457 James Thornton .01 .05
❑ 458 Mike Tomczak .02 .10
❑ 459 Donnell Woolford .01 .05
❑ 460 Eric Ball .01 .05
❑ 461 James Brooks .02 .10
❑ 462 David Fulcher .01 .05
❑ 463 Boomer Esiason .02 .10
❑ 464 Rodney Holman .01 .05
❑ 465 Bruce Kozerski .01 .05
❑ 466 Tim Krumrie .01 .05
❑ 467 Anthony Munoz .02 .10
❑ 468 Brian Blados .01 .05
❑ 469 Mike Baab .01 .05
❑ 470 Brian Brennan .01 .05
❑ 471 Raymond Clayborn .01 .05
❑ 472 Mike Johnson .01 .05
❑ 473 Kevin Mack .01 .05
❑ 474 Clay Matthews .02 .10
❑ 475 Frank Minnifield .01 .05
❑ 476 Gregg Rakoczy RC .01 .05
❑ 477 Webster Slaughter .02 .10
❑ 478 James Dixon .01 .05
❑ 479 Robert Awalt .01 .05
❑ 480 Dennis McKinnon UER .01 .05
❑ 481 Danny Noonan .01 .05
❑ 482 Jesse Solomon .01 .05
❑ 483 Daniel Stubbs UER .01 .05
❑ 484 Steve Walsh .02 .10
❑ 485 Michael Brooks RC .01 .05
❑ 486 Mark Jackson .01 .05
❑ 487 Greg Kragen .01 .05
❑ 488 Ken Lanier RC .01 .05
❑ 489 Karl Mecklenburg .01 .05
❑ 490 Steve Sewell .01 .05
❑ 491 Dennis Smith .01 .05
❑ 492 David Treadwell .01 .05
❑ 493 Michael Young RC .01 .05
❑ 494 Robert Clark RC .01 .05
❑ 495 Dennis Gibson .01 .05
❑ 496A Kevin Glover RC .20 .50
❑ 496B Kevin Glover RC .01 .05
❑ 497 Mel Gray .02 .10
❑ 498 Rodney Peete .02 .10
❑ 499 Dave Brown DB .01 .05

❑ 500 Jerry Holmes .01 .05
❑ 501 Chris Jacke .01 .05
❑ 502 Alan Veingrad .01 .05
❑ 503 Mark Lee .01 .05
❑ 504 Tony Mandarich .01 .05
❑ 505 Brian Noble .01 .05
❑ 506 Jeff Query .01 .05
❑ 507 Ken Ruettgers .01 .05
❑ 508 Patrick Allen .01 .05
❑ 509 Curtis Duncan .01 .05
❑ 510 William Fuller .02 .10
❑ 511 Haywood Jeffires RC .08 .25
❑ 512 Sean Jones .02 .10
❑ 513 Terry Kinard .01 .05
❑ 514 Bruce Matthews .02 .10
❑ 515 Gerald McNeil .01 .05
❑ 516 Greg Montgomery RC .01 .05
❑ 517 Warren Moon .08 .25
❑ 518 Mike Munchak .02 .10
❑ 519 Allen Pinkett .01 .05
❑ 520 Pat Beach .01 .05
❑ 521 Eugene Daniel .01 .05
❑ 522 Kevin Call .01 .05
❑ 523 Ray Donaldson .01 .05
❑ 524 Jeff Herrod RC .01 .05
❑ 525 Keith Taylor .01 .05
❑ 526 Jack Trudeau .01 .05
❑ 527 Deron Cherry .01 .05
❑ 528 Jeff Donaldson .01 .05
❑ 529 Albert Lewis .01 .05
❑ 530 Pete Mandley .01 .05
❑ 531 Chris Martin RC .01 .05
❑ 532 Christian Okoye .01 .05
❑ 533 Steve Pelluer .01 .05
❑ 534 Kevin Ross .01 .05
❑ 535 Dan Saleaumua .01 .05
❑ 536 Derrick Thomas .08 .25
❑ 537 Mike Webster .02 .10
❑ 538 Marcus Allen .08 .25
❑ 539 Greg Bell .01 .05
❑ 540 Thomas Benson .01 .05
❑ 541 Ron Brown .01 .05
❑ 542 Scott Davis .01 .05
❑ 543 Riki Ellison .01 .05
❑ 544 Jamie Holland .01 .05
❑ 545 Howie Long .08 .25
❑ 546 Terry McDaniel .01 .05
❑ 547 Max Montoya .01 .05
❑ 548 Jay Schroeder .01 .05
❑ 549 Lionel Washington .01 .05
❑ 550 Robert Delpino .01 .05
❑ 551 Bobby Humphery .01 .05
❑ 552 Mike Lansford .01 .05
❑ 553 Michael Stewart RC .01 .05
❑ 554 Doug Smith .01 .05
❑ 555 Curt Warner .01 .05
❑ 556 Alvin Wright RC .01 .05
❑ 557 Jeff Cross .01 .05
❑ 558 Jeff Dellenbach RC .01 .05
❑ 559 Mark Duper .02 .10
❑ 560 Ferrell Edmunds .01 .05
❑ 561 Tim McKyer .01 .05
❑ 562 John Offerdahl .01 .05
❑ 563 Reggie Roby .01 .05
❑ 564 Pete Stoyanovich .01 .05
❑ 565 Alfred Anderson .01 .05
❑ 566 Ray Berry .01 .05
❑ 567 Rick Fenney .01 .05
❑ 568 Rich Gannon RC .60 1.50
❑ 569 Tim Irwin .01 .05
❑ 570 Hassan Jones .01 .05
❑ 571 Cris Carter .20 .50
❑ 572 Kirk Lowdermilk .01 .05
❑ 573 Reggie Rutland RC .01 .05
❑ 574 Ken Stills .01 .05
❑ 575 Bruce Armstrong .01 .05
❑ 576 Irving Fryar .02 .10
❑ 577 Roland James .01 .05
❑ 578 Robert Perryman .01 .05
❑ 579 Cedric Jones .01 .05
❑ 580 Steve Grogan .02 .10
❑ 581 Johnny Rembert .01 .05
❑ 582 Ed Reynolds .01 .05
❑ 583 Brent Williams .01 .05
❑ 584 Marc Wilson .01 .05
❑ 585 Hoby Brenner .01 .05
❑ 586 Stan Brock .01 .05
❑ 587 Jim Dombrowski RC .01 .05
❑ 588 Joel Hilgenberg RC .01 .05
❑ 589 Robert Massey .01 .05
❑ 590 Floyd Turner .01 .05
❑ 591 Ottis Anderson .02 .10
❑ 592 Mark Bavaro .01 .05
❑ 593 Maurice Carthon .01 .05
❑ 594 Eric Dorsey RC .01 .05
❑ 595 Myron Guyton .01 .05
❑ 596 Jeff Hostetler RC .08 .25
❑ 597 Sean Landeta .01 .05
❑ 598 Lionel Manuel .01 .05
❑ 599 Odessa Turner RC .01 .05
❑ 600 Perry Williams .01 .05
❑ 601 James Hasty .01 .05
❑ 602 Erik McMillan .01 .05
❑ 603 Alex Gordon UER .01 .05
❑ 604 Ron Stallworth .01 .05
❑ 605 Byron Evans RC .01 .05
❑ 606 Ron Heller RC .01 .05
❑ 607 Wes Hopkins .01 .05
❑ 608 Mickey Shuler UER .01 .05
❑ 609 Seth Joyner .02 .10
❑ 610 Jim McMahon .02 .10
❑ 611 Mike Pitts .01 .05
❑ 612 Izel Jenkins RC .01 .05
❑ 613 Anthony Bell .01 .05
❑ 614 David Galloway .01 .05
❑ 615 Eric Hill .01 .05
❑ 616 Cedric Mack .01 .05
❑ 617 Freddie Joe Nunn .01 .05
❑ 618 Tootie Robbins .01 .05
❑ 619 Tom Tupa RC .01 .05
❑ 620 Joe Wolf .01 .05
❑ 621 Dermontti Dawson .02 .10
❑ 622 Thomas Everett .01 .05
❑ 623 Tunch Ilkin .01 .05
❑ 624 Hardy Nickerson .02 .10
❑ 625 Gerald Williams RC .01 .05
❑ 626 Rod Woodson .08 .25
❑ 627A Rod Bernstine TE .20 .50
❑ 627B Rod Bernstine RB .01 .05
❑ 628 Courtney Hall .01 .05
❑ 629 Ronnie Harmon .02 .10
❑ 630A Anthony Miller WR .08 .25
❑ 630B Anthony Miller WR-KR .02 .10
❑ 631 Joe Phillips .01 .05
❑ 632A Leslie O'Neal LB-DE .05 .15
❑ 632B Leslie O'Neal LB .02 .10
❑ 633A David Richards ERR RC .05 .15
❑ 633B David Richards G RC .05 .15
❑ 634 Mark Vlasic .01 .05
❑ 635 Lee Williams .01 .05
❑ 636 Chet Brooks .01 .05
❑ 637 Keena Turner .01 .05
❑ 638 Kevin Fagan RC .01 .05
❑ 639 Brent Jones RC .08 .25
❑ 640 Matt Millen .02 .10
❑ 641 Bubba Paris .01 .05
❑ 642 Bill Romanowski RC .40 1.00
❑ 643 Fred Smerlas UER .01 .05
❑ 644 Dave Waymer .01 .05
❑ 645 Steve Young .20 .50
❑ 646 Brian Blades .02 .10
❑ 647 Andy Heck .01 .05
❑ 648 Dave Krieg .02 .10
❑ 649 Rufus Porter .01 .05
❑ 650 Kelly Stouffer .01 .05
❑ 651 Tony Woods .01 .05
❑ 652 Gary Anderson RB .01 .05
❑ 653 Reuben Davis .01 .05
❑ 654 Randy Grimes .01 .05
❑ 655 Ron Hall .01 .05
❑ 656 Eugene Marve .01 .05
❑ 657A Curt Jarvis ERR .20 .50
❑ 657B Curt Jarvis COR 4.00 10.00
❑ 658 Ricky Reynolds .01 .05
❑ 659 Broderick Thomas .01 .05
❑ 660 Jeff Bostic .01 .05
❑ 661 Todd Bowles RC .01 .05
❑ 662 Ravin Caldwell .01 .05
❑ 663 Russ Grimm UER .01 .05
❑ 664 Joe Jacoby .01 .05
❑ 665 Mark May .01 .05
❑ 666 Walter Stanley .01 .05
❑ 667 Don Warren .01 .05
❑ 668 Stan Humphries RC .08 .25
❑ 669A Jeff George Illinois SP .40 1.00
❑ 669B Jeff George RC .20 .50
❑ 670 Blair Thomas RC .02 .10
❑ 671 Cortez Kennedy UER RC .08 .25
❑ 672 Keith McCants RC .01 .05
❑ 673 Junior Seau RC .50 1.25
❑ 674 Mark Carrier RC DB .08 .25
❑ 675 Andre Ware .02 .10
❑ 676 Chris Singleton UER RC .01 .05
❑ 677 Richmond Webb RC .01 .05
❑ 678 Ray Agnew RC .01 .05
❑ 679 Anthony Smith RC .01 .05
❑ 680 James Francis RC .01 .05
❑ 681 Percy Snow .01 .05
❑ 682 Renaldo Turnbull RC .01 .05
❑ 683 Lamar Lathon RC .02 .10
❑ 684 James Williams DB RC .01 .05
❑ 685 Emmitt Smith RC 2.00 5.00
❑ 686 Tony Bennett RC .08 .25
❑ 687 Darrell Thompson RC .01 .05
❑ 688 Steve Broussard RC .01 .05
❑ 689 Eric Green RC .02 .10
❑ 690 Ben Smith RC .01 .05
❑ 691 Bern Brostek UER RC .01 .05
❑ 692 Rodney Hampton RC .08 .25
❑ 693 Dexter Carter RC .01 .05
❑ 694 Rob Moore RC .20 .50
❑ 695 Alexander Wright RC .01 .05
❑ 696 Darion Conner RC .02 .10
❑ 697 Reggie Rembert UER RC .01 .05
❑ 698A Terry Wooden ERR RC .20 .50
❑ 698B Terry Wooden COR RC .01 .05
❑ 699 Reggie Cobb RC .01 .05
❑ 700 Anthony Thompson .01 .05
❑ 701 Fred Washington RC .01 .05
❑ 702 Ron Cox RC .01 .05
❑ 703 Robert Blackmon RC .01 .05
❑ 704 Dan Owens RC .01 .05
❑ 705 Anthony Johnson RC .08 .25
❑ 706 Aaron Wallace RC .01 .05
❑ 707 Harold Green RC .08 .25
❑ 708 Keith Sims RC .01 .05
❑ 709 Tim Grunhard RC .01 .05
❑ 710 Jeff Alm RC .01 .05
❑ 711 Carwell Gardner RC .01 .05
❑ 712 Kenny Davidson RC .01 .05
❑ 713 Vince Buck RC .01 .05
❑ 714 Leroy Hoard RC .08 .25
❑ 715 Andre Collins RC .01 .05
❑ 716 Dennis Brown RC .01 .05
❑ 717 LeRoy Butler RC .08 .25
❑ 718A Pat Terrell RC .20 .50
❑ 718B Pat Terrell RC .01 .05
❑ 719 Mike Bellamy RC .01 .05
❑ 720 Mike Fox RC .01 .05
❑ 721 Alton Montgomery RC .01 .05
❑ 722 Eric Davis RC .02 .10
❑ 723A Oliver Barnett RC .20 .50
❑ 723B Oliver Barnett RC NT .01 .05
❑ 724 Houston Hoover RC .01 .05
❑ 725 Howard Ballard RC .01 .05
❑ 726 Keith McKeller RC .01 .05
❑ 727 Wendell Davis RC .01 .05
❑ 728 Peter Tom Willis RC .01 .05
❑ 729 Bernard Clark .01 .05
❑ 730 Doug Widell RC .01 .05
❑ 731 Eric Andolsek .01 .05
❑ 732 Jeff Campbell RC .01 .05
❑ 733 Marc Spindler RC .01 .05
❑ 734 Keith Woodside .01 .05
❑ 735 Willis Peguese RC .01 .05
❑ 736 Frank Stams .01 .05
❑ 737 Jeff Uhlenhake .01 .05
❑ 738 Todd Kalis .01 .05
❑ 739 Tommy Hodson UER RC .01 .05
❑ 740 Greg McMurtry RC .01 .05
❑ 741 Mike Buck RC .01 .05
❑ 742 Kevin Haverdink UER .01 .05
❑ 743A Johnny Bailey RC .02 .10
❑ 743B Johnny Bailey RC .02 .10
❑ 744A Eric Moore NPSP .05 .15
❑ 744B Eric Moore PSP 4.00 10.00
❑ 745 Tony Stargell RC .01 .05
❑ 746 Fred Barnett RC .08 .25
❑ 747 Walter Reeves .01 .05
❑ 748 Derek Hill .01 .05
❑ 749 Quinn Early .08 .25
❑ 750 Ronald Lewis .01 .05
❑ 751 Ken Clark RC .01 .05
❑ 752 Garry Lewis RC .01 .05
❑ 753 James Lofton .02 .10
❑ 754 Steve Tasker UER .08 .25
❑ 755 Jim Shofner CO .01 .05

❑ 756 Jimmie Jones RC .01 .05
❑ 757 Jay Novacek .08 .25
❑ 758 Jessie Hester RC .01 .05
❑ 759 Barry Word RC .01 .05
❑ 760 Eddie Anderson RC .01 .05
❑ 761 Cleveland Gary .01 .05
❑ 762 Marcus Dupree RC .01 .05
❑ 763 David Griggs RC .01 .05
❑ 764 Rueben Mayes .01 .05
❑ 765 Stephen Baker .01 .05
❑ 766 Reyna Thompson UER RC .01 .05
❑ 767 Everson Walls .01 .05
❑ 768 Brad Baxter RC .01 .05
❑ 769 Steve Walsh .02 .10
❑ 770 Heath Sherman RC .01 .05
❑ 771 Johnny Johnson RC .02 .10
❑ 772A Dexter Manley Subst 150.00 300.00
❑ 772B Dexter Manley No Subst .01 .05
❑ 773 Ricky Proehl RC .08 .25
❑ 774 Frank Cornish .01 .05
❑ 775 Tommy Kane RC .01 .05
❑ 776 Derrick Fenner RC .01 .05
❑ 777 Steve Christie RC .01 .05
❑ 778 Wayne Haddix RC .01 .05
❑ 779 Richard Williamson UER .01 .05
❑ 780 Brian Mitchell RC .08 .25
❑ 781 American Bowl/London .01 .05
❑ 782 American Bowl/Berlin .01 .04
❑ 783 American Bowl/Tokyo .01 .04
❑ 784 American Bowl/Montreal .01 .04
❑ 785A Paul Tagliabue peered .30 .75
❑ 785B Paul Tagliabue poses .30 .75
❑ 786 Al Davis NEWS .01 .04
❑ 787 Jerry Glanville .01 .04
❑ 788 NFL Goes International .01 .04
❑ 789 Overseas Appeal .01 .04
❑ 790 Mike Mularkey PHOTO .01 .04
❑ 791 G.Reasons/Humphrey PHOTO .01 .04
❑ 792 M.Hurst/D.Hill PHOTO .01 .04
❑ 793 Ronnie Lott PHOTO .01 .04
❑ 794 Barry Sanders PHOTO .20 .50
❑ 795 George Seifert PHOTO .01 .04
❑ 796 Doug Smith PHOTO .01 .04
❑ 797 Doug Widell PHOTO .01 .04
❑ 798 Cris Carter PHOTO .01 .04
❑ 799 Ronnie Lott School .02 .10
❑ 800D Mark Carrier DB D-ROY .02 .10
❑ 800O Emmitt Smith O-ROY .60 1.50
❑ 1990 Santa Claus SP .20 .50
❑ CC2 Paul Tagliabue SP .15 .40
❑ CC3 Joe Robbie Mem SP .20 .50
❑ SC Super Pro SP .20 .50
❑ SC4 Fred Washington UER .01 .04
❑ SP1 Payne Stewart SP .40 1.00
❑ NNO Lombardi HOLO/10000 25.00 60.00
❑ NNO Super Bowl XXIV Logo .01 .05

1991 Pro Set

❑ COMPLETE SET (850) 15.00 35.00
❑ COMP.SERIES 1 (405) 6.00 15.00
❑ COMP.SERIES 2 (407) 6.00 15.00
❑ COMP.FINAL FACT. (38) 2.00 5.00
❑ 1D Mark Carrier DB D-ROY .02 .10
❑ 1O Emmitt Smith O-ROY .50 1.25
❑ 3 Joe Montana POY .20 .50
❑ 4 Art Shell .02 .10
❑ 5 Mike Singletary .02 .10
❑ 6 Bruce Smith .02 .10
❑ 7 Barry Word Comeback .01 .05
❑ 8A Jim Kelly LL w/LOGO .08 .25
❑ 8B Jim Kelly LL NO LOGO .08 .25
❑ 8C Jim Kelly LL Reg NO LOGO 3.00 6.00
❑ 9 Warren Moon LL .02 .10
❑ 10 Barry Sanders LL .20 .50
❑ 11 Jerry Rice LL .15 .40
❑ 12 Jay Novacek .02 .10
❑ 13 Thurman Thomas LL .02 .10
❑ 14 Nick Lowery .01 .05
❑ 15 Mike Horan .01 .05
❑ 16 Clarence Verdin .01 .05
❑ 17 Kevin Clark LL RC .01 .05
❑ 18 Mark Carrier DB LL .02 .10
❑ 19A Derrick Thomas LL Bills 7.50 20.00
❑ 19B Derrick Thomas LL COR .02 .10
❑ 20 Ottis Anderson ML .02 .10
❑ 21 Roger Craig ML .02 .10
❑ 22 Art Monk ML .02 .10
❑ 23 Chuck Noll ML .02 .10
❑ 24 Randall Cunningham ML .02 .10
❑ 25 Dan Marino ML .20 .50
❑ 26 49ers Road Record ML .01 .05
❑ 27 Earl Campbell HOF .01 .05
❑ 28 John Hannah HOF .01 .05
❑ 29 Stan Jones HOF .01 .05
❑ 30 Tex Schramm HOF .01 .05
❑ 31 Jan Stenerud HOF .01 .05
❑ 32 Russell Maryland RC .02 .10
❑ 33 Chris Zorich RC .02 .10
❑ 34 Darryll Lewis UER RC .02 .10
❑ 35 Alfred Williams RC .01 .05
❑ 36 Rocket Ismail TW RC .40 1.00
❑ 37 Ty Detmer HH RC .15 .40
❑ 38 Andre Ware Heisman .02 .10
❑ 39 Barry Sanders HH .20 .50
❑ 40 Tim Brown HH .02 .10
❑ 41 Vinny Testaverde HH .02 .10
❑ 42 Bo Jackson HH .10 .30
❑ 43 Mike Rozier HH .01 .05
❑ 44 Herschel Walker HH .02 .10
❑ 45 Marcus Allen HH .02 .10
❑ 46A James Lofton SB .02 .10
❑ 46B James Lofton SB .02 .10
❑ 47A Bruce Smith SB black ink .02 .10
❑ 47B Bruce Smith SB white ink .02 .10
❑ 48 Myron Guyton SB .01 .05
❑ 49 Stephen Baker SB .01 .05
❑ 50 Mark Ingram SB UER .01 .05
❑ 51 Ottis Anderson SB .02 .10
❑ 52 Thurman Thomas SB .08 .25
❑ 53 Matt Bahr SB .01 .05
❑ 54 Scott Norwood SB .01 .05
❑ 55 Stephen Baker .01 .05
❑ 56 Carl Banks .01 .05
❑ 57 Mark Collins .01 .05
❑ 58 Steve DeOssie .01 .05
❑ 59 Eric Dorsey .01 .05
❑ 60 John Elliott .01 .05
❑ 61 Myron Guyton .01 .05
❑ 62 Rodney Hampton .08 .25
❑ 63 Jeff Hostetler .02 .10
❑ 64 Erik Howard .01 .05
❑ 65 Mark Ingram .02 .10
❑ 66 Greg Jackson RC .01 .05
❑ 67 Leonard Marshall .01 .05
❑ 68 Dave Meggett .02 .10
❑ 69 Eric Moore .01 .05
❑ 70 Bart Oates .01 .05
❑ 71 Gary Reasons .01 .05
❑ 72 Bill Parcells CO .02 .10
❑ 73 Howard Ballard .01 .05
❑ 74A Corn.Bennett w/LOGO .08 .25
❑ 74B Corn.Bennett NO LOGO .01 .05
❑ 75 Shane Conlan .01 .05
❑ 76 Kent Hull .01 .05
❑ 77 Kirby Jackson RC .01 .05
❑ 78A Jim Kelly w/LOGO .25 .60
❑ 78B Jim Kelly NO LOGO .08 .25
❑ 79 Mark Kelso .01 .05
❑ 80 Nate Odomes .01 .05
❑ 81 Andre Reed .02 .10
❑ 82 Jim Ritcher .01 .05
❑ 83 Bruce Smith .08 .25
❑ 84 Darryl Talley .01 .05
❑ 85 Steve Tasker .02 .10
❑ 86 Thurman Thomas .08 .25
❑ 87 James Williams .01 .05
❑ 88 Will Wolford .01 .05
❑ 89 Jeff Wright UER RC .01 .05
❑ 90 Marv Levy CO .01 .05
❑ 91 Steve Broussard .01 .05
❑ 92A Darion Conner ERR '99 4.00 10.00
❑ 92B Darion Conner COR .08 .25
❑ 93 Bill Fralic .01 .05
❑ 94 Tim Green .01 .05
❑ 95 Michael Haynes .08 .25
❑ 96 Chris Hinton .01 .05
❑ 97 Chris Miller UER .02 .10
❑ 98 Deion Sanders UER .15 .40
❑ 99 Jerry Glanville CO .01 .05
❑ 100 Kevin Butler .01 .05
❑ 101 Mark Carrier DB .02 .10
❑ 102 Jim Covert .01 .05
❑ 103 Richard Dent .02 .10
❑ 104 Jim Harbaugh .08 .25
❑ 105 Brad Muster .01 .05
❑ 106 Lemuel Stinson .01 .05
❑ 107 Keith Van Horne .01 .05
❑ 108 Mike Ditka CO UER .08 .25
❑ 109 Lewis Billups .01 .05
❑ 110 James Brooks .02 .10
❑ 111 Boomer Esiason .02 .10
❑ 112 James Francis .01 .05
❑ 113 David Fulcher .01 .05
❑ 114 Rodney Holman .01 .05
❑ 115 Tim McGee .01 .05
❑ 116 Anthony Munoz .02 .10
❑ 117 Sam Wyche CO .01 .05
❑ 118 Paul Farren .01 .05
❑ 119 Thane Gash .01 .05
❑ 120 Mike Johnson .01 .05
❑ 121A Bernie Kosar w/LOGO .02 .10
❑ 121B Bernie Kosar NO LOGO .02 .10
❑ 122 Clay Matthews .02 .10
❑ 123 Eric Metcalf .02 .10
❑ 124 Frank Minnifield .01 .05
❑ 125A Webster Slaughter .02 .10
❑ 125B Webster Slaughter .02 .10
❑ 126 Bill Belichick CO RC .60 1.50
❑ 127 Tommie Agee .01 .05
❑ 128 Troy Aikman .30 .75
❑ 129 Jack Del Rio .02 .10
❑ 130 John Gesek RC .01 .05
❑ 131 Issiac Holt .01 .05
❑ 132 Michael Irvin .08 .25
❑ 133 Ken Norton .02 .10
❑ 134 Daniel Stubbs .01 .05
❑ 135 Jimmy Johnson CO .02 .10
❑ 136 Steve Atwater .01 .05
❑ 137 Michael Brooks .01 .05
❑ 138 John Elway .50 1.25
❑ 139 Wymon Henderson .01 .05
❑ 140 Bobby Humphrey .01 .05
❑ 141 Mark Jackson .01 .05
❑ 142 Karl Mecklenburg .01 .05
❑ 143 Doug Widell .01 .05
❑ 144 Dan Reeves CO .01 .05
❑ 145 Eric Andolsek .01 .05
❑ 146 Jerry Ball .01 .05
❑ 147 Bennie Blades .01 .05
❑ 148 Lomas Brown .01 .05
❑ 149 Robert Clark .01 .05
❑ 150 Michael Cofer .01 .05
❑ 151 Dan Owens .01 .05
❑ 152 Rodney Peete .02 .10
❑ 153 Wayne Fontes CO .01 .05
❑ 154 Tim Harris .01 .05
❑ 155 Johnny Holland .01 .05
❑ 156 Don Majkowski .01 .05
❑ 157 Tony Mandarich .01 .05
❑ 158 Mark Murphy .01 .05
❑ 159 Brian Noble .01 .05
❑ 160 Jeff Query .01 .05
❑ 161 Sterling Sharpe .08 .25
❑ 162 Lindy Infante CO .01 .05
❑ 163 Ray Childress .01 .05
❑ 164 Ernest Givins .02 .10
❑ 165 Richard Johnson CB .01 .05
❑ 166 Bruce Matthews .02 .10
❑ 167 Warren Moon .08 .25
❑ 168 Mike Munchak .02 .10
❑ 169 Al Smith .01 .05
❑ 170 Lorenzo White .01 .05
❑ 171 Jack Pardee CO .01 .05
❑ 172 Albert Bentley .01 .05
❑ 173 Duane Bickett .01 .05
❑ 174 Bill Brooks .01 .05
❑ 175A E.Dickerson w/LOGO .15 .40
❑ 175B E.Dickerson NO LOGO 667 .50 1.25
❑ 175C E.Dickerson NO LOGO 677 .08 .25
❑ 176 Ray Donaldson .01 .05
❑ 177 Jeff George .08 .25
❑ 178 Jeff Herrod .01 .05
❑ 179 Clarence Verdin .01 .05
❑ 180 Ron Meyer CO .01 .05

Card		
❑ 181 John Alt	.01	.05
❑ 182 Steve DeBerg	.01	.05
❑ 183 Albert Lewis	.01	.05
❑ 184 Nick Lowery UER	.01	.05
❑ 185 Christian Okoye	.01	.05
❑ 186 Stephone Paige	.01	.05
❑ 187 Kevin Porter	.01	.05
❑ 188 Derrick Thomas	.08	.25
❑ 189 Marty Schottenheimer CO	.01	.05
❑ 190 Willie Gault	.02	.10
❑ 191 Howie Long	.08	.25
❑ 192 Terry McDaniel	.01	.05
❑ 193 Jay Schroeder UER	.01	.05
❑ 194 Steve Smith	.01	.05
❑ 195 Greg Townsend	.01	.05
❑ 196 Lionel Washington	.01	.05
❑ 197 Steve Wisniewski UER	.01	.05
❑ 198 Art Shell CO	.02	.10
❑ 199 Henry Ellard	.02	.10
❑ 200 Jim Everett	.02	.10
❑ 201 Jerry Gray	.01	.05
❑ 202 Kevin Greene	.02	.10
❑ 203 Buford McGee	.01	.05
❑ 204 Tom Newberry	.01	.05
❑ 205 Frank Stams	.01	.05
❑ 206 Alvin Wright	.01	.05
❑ 207 John Robinson CO	.01	.05
❑ 208 Jeff Cross	.01	.05
❑ 209 Mark Duper	.02	.10
❑ 210 Dan Marino	.50	1.25
❑ 211A Tim McKyer	.02	.10
❑ 211B Tim McKyer TR	.08	.25
❑ 212 John Offerdahl	.01	.05
❑ 213 Sammie Smith	.01	.05
❑ 214 Richmond Webb	.01	.05
❑ 215 Jarvis Williams	.01	.05
❑ 216 Don Shula CO	.02	.10
❑ 217A D.Fullington ERR	.02	.10
❑ 217B D.Fullington COR	.02	.10
❑ 218 Tim Irwin	.01	.05
❑ 219 Mike Merriweather	.01	.05
❑ 220 Keith Millard	.01	.05
❑ 221 Al Noga	.01	.05
❑ 222 Henry Thomas	.01	.05
❑ 223 Wade Wilson	.02	.10
❑ 224 Gary Zimmerman	.02	.10
❑ 225 Jerry Burns CO	.01	.05
❑ 226 Bruce Armstrong	.01	.05
❑ 227 Marv Cook FPSC	.01	.05
❑ 228 Hart Lee Dykes	.01	.05
❑ 229 Tommy Hodson	.01	.05
❑ 230 Ronnie Lippett	.01	.05
❑ 231 Ed Reynolds	.01	.05
❑ 232 Chris Singleton	.01	.05
❑ 233 John Stephens	.01	.05
❑ 234 Dick MacPherson CO	.01	.05
❑ 235 Stan Brock	.01	.05
❑ 236 Craig Heyward	.02	.10
❑ 237 Vaughan Johnson	.01	.05
❑ 238 Robert Massey	.01	.05
❑ 239 Brett Maxie	.01	.05
❑ 240 Rueben Mayes	.01	.05
❑ 241 Pat Swilling	.02	.10
❑ 242 Renaldo Turnbull	.01	.05
❑ 243 Jim Mora CO	.01	.05
❑ 244 Kyle Clifton	.01	.05
❑ 245 Jeff Criswell	.01	.05
❑ 246 James Hasty	.01	.05
❑ 247 Erik McMillan	.01	.05
❑ 248 Scott Mersereau RC	.01	.05
❑ 249 Ken O'Brien	.01	.05
❑ 250A Blair Thomas w/LOGO	.08	.25
❑ 250B Blair Thomas NO LOGO	.02	.10
❑ 251 Al Toon	.02	.10
❑ 252 Bruce Coslet CO	.01	.05
❑ 253 Eric Allen	.01	.05
❑ 254 Fred Barnett	.08	.25
❑ 255 Keith Byars	.01	.05
❑ 256 Randall Cunningham	.08	.25
❑ 257 Seth Joyner	.02	.10
❑ 258 Clyde Simmons	.01	.05
❑ 259 Jessie Small	.01	.05
❑ 260 Andre Waters	.01	.05
❑ 261 Rich Kotite CO	.01	.05
❑ 262 Roy Green	.01	.05
❑ 263 Ernie Jones	.01	.05
❑ 264 Tim McDonald	.01	.05
❑ 265 Timm Rosenbach	.01	.05
❑ 266 Rod Saddler	.01	.05
❑ 267 Luis Sharpe	.01	.05
❑ 268 Anthony Thompson UER	.01	.05
❑ 269 Marcus Turner RC	.01	.05
❑ 270 Joe Bugel CO	.01	.05
❑ 271 Gary Anderson K	.01	.05
❑ 272 Dermontti Dawson	.01	.05
❑ 273 Eric Green	.01	.05
❑ 274 Merril Hoge	.01	.05
❑ 275 Tunch Ilkin	.01	.05
❑ 276 D.J. Johnson	.01	.05
❑ 277 Louis Lipps	.01	.05
❑ 278 Rod Woodson	.08	.25
❑ 279 Chuck Noll CO	.02	.10
❑ 280 Martin Bayless	.01	.05
❑ 281 Marion Butts UER	.02	.10
❑ 282 Gill Byrd	.01	.05
❑ 283 Burt Grossman	.01	.05
❑ 284 Courtney Hall	.01	.05
❑ 285 Anthony Miller	.02	.10
❑ 286 Leslie O'Neal	.02	.10
❑ 287 Billy Joe Tolliver	.01	.05
❑ 288 Dan Henning CO	.01	.05
❑ 289 Dexter Carter	.01	.05
❑ 290 Michael Carter	.01	.05
❑ 291 Kevin Fagan	.01	.05
❑ 292 Pierce Holt	.01	.05
❑ 293 Guy McIntyre	.01	.05
❑ 294 Tom Rathman	.01	.05
❑ 295 John Taylor	.02	.10
❑ 296 Steve Young	.30	.75
❑ 297 George Seifert CO	.02	.10
❑ 298 Brian Blades	.02	.10
❑ 299 Jeff Bryant	.01	.05
❑ 300 Norm Johnson	.01	.05
❑ 301 Tommy Kane	.01	.05
❑ 302 Cortez Kennedy UER	.08	.25
❑ 303 Bryan Millard	.01	.05
❑ 304 John L. Williams	.01	.05
❑ 305 David Wyman	.01	.05
❑ 306A Chuck Knox CO w/LOGO	.01	.05
❑ 306B Chuck Knox CO NO LOGO	.20	.50
❑ 307 Gary Anderson RB	.01	.05
❑ 308 Reggie Cobb	.01	.05
❑ 309 Randy Grimes	.01	.05
❑ 310 Harry Hamilton	.01	.05
❑ 311 Bruce Hill	.01	.05
❑ 312 Eugene Marve	.01	.05
❑ 313 Ervin Randle	.01	.05
❑ 314 Vinny Testaverde	.02	.10
❑ 315 Richard Williamson CO	.01	.05
❑ 316 Earnest Byner	.01	.05
❑ 317 Gary Clark	.08	.25
❑ 318A Andre Collins	.02	.10
❑ 318B Andre Collins	.02	.10
❑ 319 Darryl Grant	.01	.05
❑ 320 Chip Lohmiller	.01	.05
❑ 321 Martin Mayhew	.01	.05
❑ 322 Mark Rypien	.02	.10
❑ 323 Alvin Walton	.01	.05
❑ 324 Joe Gibbs CO UER	.02	.10
❑ 325 Jerry Glanville REP	.01	.05
❑ 326A J.Elway REP LOGO	2.00	4.00
❑ 326B J.Elway REP NO LOGO	.75	2.00
❑ 327 Boomer Esiason REP	.01	.05
❑ 328A Steve Tasker REP	2.00	4.00
❑ 328B Steve Tasker REP	.75	2.00
❑ 329 Jerry Rice REP	.15	.40
❑ 330 Jeff Rutledge REP	.01	.05
❑ 331 K.C. Defense REP	.01	.05
❑ 332 49ers Streak REP	.01	.05
❑ 333 Monday Meeting REP	.01	.05
❑ 334A R.Cunningham w/LOGO	.01	.05
❑ 334B R.Cunningham NO LOGO	.01	.05
❑ 335A Bo/Barry REP w/LOGO	.20	.50
❑ 335B Bo/Barry REP NO LOGO	.20	.50
❑ 336 Lawrence Taylor REP	.08	.25
❑ 337 Warren Moon REP	.08	.25
❑ 338 Alan Grant REP	.01	.05
❑ 339 Todd McNair REP	.01	.05
❑ 340A Miami Dolphins REP	.01	.05
❑ 340B Miami Dolphins REP	.01	.05
❑ 341A Highest Scoring REP	2.00	4.00
❑ 341B Highest Scoring REP	.75	2.00
❑ 342 Matt Bahr REP	.01	.05
❑ 343 Robert Tisch NEW	.01	.05
❑ 344 Sam Jankovich NEW	.01	.05
❑ 345 In-the-Grasp NEW	.01	.05
❑ 346 Bo Jackson NEW	.02	.10
❑ 347 NFL Teacher of the	.01	.05
❑ 348 Ronnie Lott NEW	.02	.10
❑ 349 Super Bowl XXV	.02	.10
❑ 350 Whitney Houston	.01	.05
❑ 351 U.S. Troops in	.01	.05
❑ 352 Art McNally OFF	.01	.05
❑ 353 Dick Jorgensen OFF	.01	.05
❑ 354 Jerry Seeman OFF	.01	.05
❑ 355 Jim Tunney OFF	.01	.05
❑ 356 Gerry Austin OFF	.01	.05
❑ 357 Gene Barth OFF	.01	.05
❑ 358 Red Cashion OFF	.01	.05
❑ 359 Tom Dooley OFF	.01	.05
❑ 360 Johnny Grier OFF	.01	.05
❑ 361 Pat Haggerty OFF	.01	.05
❑ 362 Dale Hamer OFF	.01	.05
❑ 363 Dick Hantak OFF	.01	.05
❑ 364 Jerry Markbreit OFF	.01	.05
❑ 365 Gordon McCarter OFF	.01	.05
❑ 366 Bob McElwee OFF	.01	.05
❑ 367 Howard Roe OFF	.01	.05
❑ 368 Tom White OFF	.01	.05
❑ 369 Norm Schachter OFF	.01	.05
❑ 370A Warren Moon Crack	.08	.25
❑ 370B Warren Moon Crack	.08	.25
❑ 371A Boomer Esiason	.20	.50
❑ 371B Boomer Esiason	.02	.10
❑ 372A Troy Aikman Str.ST	.15	.40
❑ 372B Troy Aikman Str.LT	.15	.40
❑ 373A Carl Banks	.20	.50
❑ 373B Carl Banks	.01	.05
❑ 374A Jim Everett	.20	.50
❑ 374B Jim Everett	.02	.10
❑ 375A Anth.Munoz dificul	.02	.10
❑ 375B Anth.Munoz dificil	.02	.10
❑ 375C Anth.Munoz large type	.02	.10
❑ 375D Anth.Munoz Quedate	.02	.10
❑ 376A Ray Childress	.50	1.25
❑ 376B Ray Childress	.01	.05
❑ 377A Charles Mann	.50	1.25
❑ 377B Charles Mann	.01	.05
❑ 378A Jackie Slater	.50	1.25
❑ 378B Jackie Slater	.01	.05
❑ 379 Jerry Rice PB	.15	.40
❑ 380 Andre Rison PB	.02	.10
❑ 381 Jim Lachey NFC	.01	.05
❑ 382 Jackie Slater NFC	.01	.05
❑ 383 Randall McDaniel NFC	.02	.10
❑ 384 Mark Bortz NFC	.01	.05
❑ 385 Jay Hilgenberg NFC	.01	.05
❑ 386 Keith Jackson NFC	.01	.05
❑ 387 Joe Montana PB	.20	.50
❑ 388 Barry Sanders PB	.20	.50
❑ 389 Neal Anderson NFC	.01	.05
❑ 390 Reggie White NFC	.08	.25
❑ 391 Chris Doleman NFC	.01	.05
❑ 392 Jerome Brown NFC	.01	.05
❑ 393 Charles Haley NFC	.01	.05
❑ 394 Lawrence Taylor PB	.08	.25
❑ 395 Pepper Johnson NFC	.01	.05
❑ 396 Mike Singletary NFC	.02	.10
❑ 397 Darrell Green NFC	.01	.05
❑ 398 Carl Lee NFC	.01	.05
❑ 399 Joey Browner NFC	.01	.05
❑ 400 Ronnie Lott NFC	.02	.10
❑ 401 Sean Landeta NFC	.01	.05
❑ 402 Morten Andersen NFC	.01	.05
❑ 403 Mel Gray NFC	.01	.05
❑ 404 Reyna Thompson NFC	.01	.05
❑ 405 Jimmy Johnson CO NFC	.02	.10
❑ 406 Andre Reed AFC	.02	.10
❑ 407 Anthony Miller AFC	.02	.10
❑ 408 Anthony Munoz AFC	.02	.10
❑ 409 Bruce Armstrong AFC	.01	.05
❑ 410 Bruce Matthews AFC	.01	.05
❑ 411 Mike Munchak AFC	.01	.05
❑ 412 Kent Hull AFC	.01	.05
❑ 413 Rodney Holman AFC	.01	.05
❑ 414 Warren Moon PB	.08	.25
❑ 415 Thurman Thomas PB	.08	.25
❑ 416 Marion Butts AFC	.02	.10
❑ 417 Bruce Smith AFC	.02	.10
❑ 418 Greg Townsend AFC	.01	.05
❑ 419 Ray Childress AFC	.01	.05
❑ 420 Derrick Thomas PB	.08	.25
❑ 421 Leslie O'Neal AFC	.02	.10
❑ 422 John Offerdahl AFC	.01	.05
❑ 423 Shane Conlan AFC	.01	.05
❑ 424 Rod Woodson PB	.08	.25
❑ 425 Albert Lewis AFC	.01	.05

❑ 426 Steve Atwater AFC .01 .05
❑ 427 David Fulcher AFC .01 .05
❑ 428 Rohn Stark AFC .01 .05
❑ 429 Nick Lowery AFC .01 .05
❑ 430 Clarence Verdin AFC .01 .05
❑ 431 Steve Tasker AFC .01 .05
❑ 432 Art Shell CO AFC .02 .10
❑ 433 Scott Case .01 .05
❑ 434 Tory Epps UER .01 .05
❑ 435 Mike Gann UER .01 .05
❑ 436 Brian Jordan FPSC UER .02 .10
❑ 437 Mike Kenn .01 .05
❑ 438 John Rade .01 .05
❑ 439 Andre Rison .02 .10
❑ 440 Mike Rozier .01 .05
❑ 441 Jessie Tuggle .01 .05
❑ 442 Don Beebe .01 .05
❑ 443 John Davis RC .01 .05
❑ 444 James Lofton .02 .10
❑ 445 Keith McKeller .01 .05
❑ 446 Jamie Mueller .01 .05
❑ 447 Scott Norwood .01 .05
❑ 448 Frank Reich .02 .10
❑ 449 Leon Seals .01 .05
❑ 450 Leonard Smith .01 .05
❑ 451 Neal Anderson .02 .10
❑ 452 Trace Armstrong .01 .05
❑ 453 Mark Bortz .01 .05
❑ 454 Wendell Davis .01 .05
❑ 455 Shaun Gayle .01 .05
❑ 456 Jay Hilgenberg .01 .05
❑ 457 Steve McMichael .02 .10
❑ 458 Mike Singletary .02 .10
❑ 459 Donnell Woolford .01 .05
❑ 460 Jim Breech .01 .05
❑ 461 Eddie Brown .01 .05
❑ 462 Barney Bussey RC .01 .05
❑ 463 Bruce Kozerski .01 .05
❑ 464 Tim Krumrie .01 .05
❑ 465 Bruce Reimers .01 .05
❑ 466 Kevin Walker RC .01 .05
❑ 467 Ickey Woods .01 .05
❑ 468 Carl Zander UER .01 .05
❑ 469 Mike Baab .01 .05
❑ 470 Brian Brennan .01 .05
❑ 471 Rob Burnett RC .02 .10
❑ 472 Raymond Clayborn .01 .05
❑ 473 Reggie Langhorne .01 .05
❑ 474 Kevin Mack .01 .05
❑ 475 Anthony Pleasant .01 .05
❑ 476 Joe Morris .01 .05
❑ 477 Dan Fike .01 .05
❑ 478 Ray Horton .01 .05
❑ 479 Jim Jeffcoat .01 .05
❑ 480 Jimmie Jones .01 .05
❑ 481 Kelvin Martin .01 .05
❑ 482 Nate Newton .02 .10
❑ 483 Danny Noonan .01 .05
❑ 484 Jay Novacek .08 .25
❑ 485 Emmitt Smith 1.00 2.50
❑ 486 James Washington RC .01 .05
❑ 487 Simon Fletcher .01 .05
❑ 488 Ron Holmes .01 .05
❑ 489 Mike Horan .01 .05
❑ 490 Vance Johnson .01 .05
❑ 491 Keith Kartz .01 .05
❑ 492 Greg Kragen .01 .05
❑ 493 Ken Lanier .01 .05
❑ 494 Warren Powers .01 .05
❑ 495 Dennis Smith .01 .05
❑ 496 Jeff Campbell .01 .05
❑ 497 Ken Dallafior .01 .05
❑ 498 Dennis Gibson .01 .05
❑ 499 Kevin Glover .01 .05
❑ 500 Mel Gray .02 .10
❑ 501 Eddie Murray .01 .05
❑ 502 Barry Sanders .50 1.25
❑ 503 Chris Spielman .02 .10
❑ 504 William White .01 .05
❑ 505 Matt Brock RC .01 .05
❑ 506 Robert Brown .01 .05
❑ 507 LeRoy Butler .02 .10
❑ 508 James Campen RC .01 .05
❑ 509 Jerry Holmes .01 .05
❑ 510 Perry Kemp .01 .05
❑ 511 Ken Ruettgers .01 .05
❑ 512 Scott Stephen RC .01 .05
❑ 513 Ed West .01 .05
❑ 514 Cris Dishman RC .01 .05
❑ 515 Curtis Duncan .01 .05
❑ 516 Drew Hill UER .01 .05
❑ 517 Haywood Jeffires .02 .10
❑ 518 Sean Jones .02 .10
❑ 519 Lamar Lathon .01 .05
❑ 520 Don Maggs .01 .05
❑ 521 Bubba McDowell .01 .05
❑ 522 Johnny Meads .01 .05
❑ 523A Chip Banks ERR No Text .20 .50
❑ 523B Chip Banks COR .01 .05
❑ 524 Pat Beach .01 .05
❑ 525 Sam Clancy .01 .05
❑ 526 Eugene Daniel .01 .05
❑ 527 Jon Hand .01 .05
❑ 528 Jessie Hester .01 .05
❑ 529A Mike Prior ERR No Text .20 .50
❑ 529B Mike Prior COR .01 .05
❑ 530 Keith Taylor .01 .05
❑ 531 Donnell Thompson .01 .05
❑ 532 Dino Hackett .01 .05
❑ 533 David Lutz RC .01 .05
❑ 534 Chris Martin .01 .05
❑ 535 Kevin Ross .01 .05
❑ 536 Dan Saleaumua .01 .05
❑ 537 Neil Smith .08 .25
❑ 538 Percy Snow .01 .05
❑ 539 Robb Thomas .01 .05
❑ 540 Barry Word .01 .05
❑ 541 Marcus Allen .08 .25
❑ 542 Eddie Anderson .01 .05
❑ 543 Scott Davis .01 .05
❑ 544 Mervyn Fernandez .01 .05
❑ 545 Ethan Horton .01 .05
❑ 546 Ronnie Lott .02 .10
❑ 547 Don Mosebar .01 .05
❑ 548 Jerry Robinson .01 .05
❑ 549 Aaron Wallace .01 .05
❑ 550 Flipper Anderson .01 .05
❑ 551 Cleveland Gary .01 .05
❑ 552 Damone Johnson RC .01 .05
❑ 553 Duval Love RC .01 .05
❑ 554 Irv Pankey .01 .05
❑ 555 Mike Piel .01 .05
❑ 556 Jackie Slater .01 .05
❑ 557 Michael Stewart .01 .05
❑ 558 Pat Terrell .01 .05
❑ 559 J.B. Brown .01 .05
❑ 560 Mark Clayton .02 .10
❑ 561 Ferrell Edmunds .01 .05
❑ 562 Harry Galbreath .01 .05
❑ 563 David Griggs .01 .05
❑ 564 Jim C. Jensen .01 .05
❑ 565 Louis Oliver .01 .05
❑ 566 Tony Paige .01 .05
❑ 567 Keith Sims .01 .05
❑ 568 Joey Browner .01 .05
❑ 569 Anthony Carter .02 .10
❑ 570 Chris Doleman .01 .05
❑ 571 Rich Gannon UER .08 .25
❑ 572 Hassan Jones .01 .05
❑ 573 Steve Jordan .01 .05
❑ 574 Carl Lee .01 .05
❑ 575 Randall McDaniel .02 .10
❑ 576 Herschel Walker .02 .10
❑ 577 Ray Agnew .01 .05
❑ 578 Vincent Brown .01 .05
❑ 579 Irving Fryar .02 .10
❑ 580 Tim Goad .01 .05
❑ 581 Maurice Hurst .01 .05
❑ 582 Fred Marion .01 .05
❑ 583 Johnny Rembert .01 .05
❑ 584 Andre Tippett .01 .05
❑ 585 Brent Williams .01 .05
❑ 586 Morten Andersen .01 .05
❑ 587 Toi Cook RC .01 .05
❑ 588 Jim Dombrowski .01 .05
❑ 589 Dalton Hilliard .01 .05
❑ 590 Rickey Jackson .01 .05
❑ 591 Eric Martin .01 .05
❑ 592 Sam Mills .01 .05
❑ 593 Bobby Hebert .01 .05
❑ 594 Steve Walsh .01 .05
❑ 595 Ottis Anderson .02 .10
❑ 596 Pepper Johnson .01 .05
❑ 597 Bob Kratch RC .01 .05
❑ 598 Sean Landeta .01 .05
❑ 599 Doug Riesenberg .01 .05
❑ 600 William Roberts .01 .05
❑ 601 Phil Simms .02 .10
❑ 602 Lawrence Taylor .08 .25
❑ 603 Everson Walls .01 .05
❑ 604 Brad Baxter .01 .05
❑ 605 Dennis Byrd .01 .05
❑ 606 Jeff Lageman .01 .05
❑ 607 Pat Leahy .01 .05
❑ 608 Rob Moore .08 .25
❑ 609 Joe Mott .01 .05
❑ 610 Tony Stargell .01 .05
❑ 611 Brian Washington .01 .05
❑ 612 Marvin Washington RC .01 .05
❑ 613 David Alexander .01 .05
❑ 614 Jerome Brown .01 .05
❑ 615 Byron Evans .01 .05
❑ 616 Ron Heller .01 .05
❑ 617 Wes Hopkins .01 .05
❑ 618 Keith Jackson .02 .10
❑ 619 Heath Sherman .01 .05
❑ 620 Reggie White .08 .25
❑ 621 Calvin Williams .02 .10
❑ 622 Ken Harvey .02 .10
❑ 623 Eric Hill .01 .05
❑ 624 Johnny Johnson .01 .05
❑ 625 Freddie Joe Nunn .01 .05
❑ 626 Ricky Proehl .01 .05
❑ 627 Tootie Robbins .01 .05
❑ 628 Jay Taylor .01 .05
❑ 629 Tom Tupa .01 .05
❑ 630 Jim Wahler RC .01 .05
❑ 631 Bubby Brister .01 .05
❑ 632 Thomas Everett .01 .05
❑ 633 Bryan Hinkle .01 .05
❑ 634 Carnell Lake .01 .05
❑ 635 David Little .01 .05
❑ 636 Hardy Nickerson .02 .10
❑ 637 Gerald Williams .01 .05
❑ 638 Keith Willis .01 .05
❑ 639 Tim Worley .01 .05
❑ 640 Rod Bernstine .01 .05
❑ 641 Frank Cornish .01 .05
❑ 642 Gary Plummer .01 .05
❑ 643 Henry Rolling RC .01 .05
❑ 644 Sam Seale .01 .05
❑ 645 Junior Seau .08 .25
❑ 646 Billy Ray Smith .01 .05
❑ 647 Broderick Thompson .01 .05
❑ 648 Derrick Walker RC .01 .05
❑ 649 Todd Bowles .01 .05
❑ 650 Don Griffin .01 .05
❑ 651 Charles Haley .02 .10
❑ 652 Brent Jones UER .02 .10
❑ 653 Joe Montana .50 1.25
❑ 654 Jerry Rice .30 .75
❑ 655 Bill Romanowski .01 .05
❑ 656 Michael Walter .01 .05
❑ 657 Dave Waymer .01 .05
❑ 658 Jeff Chadwick .01 .05
❑ 659 Derrick Fenner .01 .05
❑ 660 Nesby Glasgow .01 .05
❑ 661 Jacob Green .01 .05
❑ 662 Dwayne Harper RC .01 .05
❑ 663 Andy Heck .01 .05
❑ 664 Dave Krieg .02 .10
❑ 665 Rufus Porter .01 .05
❑ 666 Eugene Robinson .01 .05
❑ 667 Mark Carrier WR .08 .25
❑ 668 Steve Christie .01 .05
❑ 669 Reuben Davis .01 .05
❑ 670 Paul Gruber .01 .05
❑ 671 Wayne Haddix .01 .05
❑ 672 Ron Hall .01 .05
❑ 673 Keith McCants UER .01 .05
❑ 674 Ricky Reynolds .01 .05
❑ 675 Mark Robinson .01 .05
❑ 676 Jeff Bostic .01 .05
❑ 677 Darrell Green .01 .05
❑ 678 Markus Koch .01 .05
❑ 679 Jim Lachey .01 .05
❑ 680 Charles Mann .01 .05
❑ 681 Wilber Marshall .01 .05
❑ 682 Art Monk .02 .10
❑ 683 Gerald Riggs .01 .05
❑ 684 Ricky Sanders .01 .05
❑ 685 Ray Handley NEW .01 .05
❑ 686 NFL announces NEW .01 .05
❑ 687 Miami gets NEW .01 .05
❑ 688 Giants' George Young NEW .01 .05
❑ 689 Five-millionth fan NEW .01 .05
❑ 690 Sports Illustrated NEW .01 .05

❑ 691 American Bowl NEW	.01	.05
❑ 692 American Bowl NEW	.01	.05
❑ 693 American Bowl NEW	.01	.05
❑ 694A Russell Maryland	.08	.25
❑ 694B Joe Ferguson LEG	.01	.05
❑ 695 Carl Hairston LEG	.02	.10
❑ 696 Dan Hampton LEG	.02	.10
❑ 697 Mike Haynes LEG	.01	.05
❑ 698 Marty Lyons LEG	.01	.05
❑ 699 Ozzie Newsome LEGEND	.02	.10
❑ 700 Scott Studwell LEG	.01	.05
❑ 701 Mike Webster LEG	.01	.05
❑ 702 Dwayne Woodruff LEG	.01	.05
❑ 703 Larry Kennan CO	.01	.05
❑ 704 Stan Gelbaugh RC LL	.02	.10
❑ 705 John Brantley LL	.01	.05
❑ 706 Danny Lockett LL	.01	.05
❑ 707 Anthony Parker RC LL	.02	.10
❑ 708 Dan Crossman LL	.01	.05
❑ 709 Eric Wilkerson LL	.01	.05
❑ 710 Judd Garrett LL RC	.01	.05
❑ 711 Tony Baker LL	.01	.05
❑ 712 Ran.Cunningham PHOTO	.01	.05
❑ 713 2nd Place BW PHOTO	.01	.05
❑ 714 3rd Place BW PHOTO	.01	.05
❑ 715 1st Place Color PHOTO	.01	.05
❑ 716 2nd Place Color PHOTO	.01	.05
❑ 717 3rd Place Color PHOTO	.01	.05
❑ 718 1st Place Color PHOTO	.01	.05
❑ 719 2nd Place Color PHOTO	.01	.05
❑ 720 3rd Place Color PHOTO	.01	.05
❑ 721 Ray Bentley	.01	.05
❑ 722 Earnest Byner	.01	.05
❑ 723 Bill Fralic	.01	.05
❑ 724 Joe Jacoby	.01	.05
❑ 725 Howie Long	.08	.25
❑ 726 Dan Marino THINK	.20	.50
❑ 727 Ron Rivera	.01	.05
❑ 728 Mike Singletary	.02	.10
❑ 729 Cornelius Bennett	.02	.10
❑ 730 Russell Maryland	.08	.25
❑ 731 Eric Turner RC	.02	.10
❑ 732 Bruce Pickens UER RC	.01	.05
❑ 733 Mike Croel RC	.01	.05
❑ 734 Todd Lyght RC	.01	.05
❑ 735 Eric Swann RC	.08	.25
❑ 736 Charles McRae RC	.01	.05
❑ 737 Antone Davis RC	.01	.05
❑ 738 Stanley Richard RC	.01	.05
❑ 739 Herman Moore RC	.08	.25
❑ 740 Pat Harlow RC	.01	.05
❑ 741 Alvin Harper RC	.08	.25
❑ 742 Mike Pritchard RC	.08	.25
❑ 743 Leonard Russell RC	.08	.25
❑ 744 Huey Richardson RC	.01	.05
❑ 745 Dan McGwire RC	.01	.05
❑ 746 Bobby Wilson RC	.01	.05
❑ 747 Alfred Williams	.01	.05
❑ 748 Vinnie Clark RC	.01	.05
❑ 749 Kelvin Pritchett RC	.02	.10
❑ 750 Harvey Williams RC	.08	.25
❑ 751 Stan Thomas	.01	.05
❑ 752 Randal Hill RC	.02	.10
❑ 753 Todd Marinovich RC	.01	.05
❑ 754 Ted Washington RC	.01	.05
❑ 755 Henry Jones RC	.02	.10
❑ 756 Jarrod Bunch RC	.01	.05
❑ 757 Mike Dumas RC	.01	.05
❑ 758 Ed King RC	.01	.05
❑ 759 Reggie Johnson RC	.01	.05
❑ 760 Roman Phifer RC	.01	.05
❑ 761 Mike Jones DE RC	.01	.05
❑ 762 Brett Favre RC	3.00	8.00
❑ 763 Browning Nagle RC	.01	.05
❑ 764 Esera Tuaolo RC	.01	.05
❑ 765 George Thornton RC	.01	.05
❑ 766 Dixon Edwards RC	.01	.05
❑ 767 Darryll Lewis	.02	.10
❑ 768 Eric Bieniemy RC	.01	.05
❑ 769 Shane Curry	.01	.05
❑ 770 Jerome Henderson RC	.01	.05
❑ 771 Wesley Carroll RC	.01	.05
❑ 772 Nick Bell RC	.01	.05
❑ 773 John Flannery RC	.01	.05
❑ 774 Ricky Watters RC	.60	1.50
❑ 775 Jeff Graham RC	.08	.25
❑ 776 Eric Moten RC	.01	.05
❑ 777 Jesse Campbell RC	.01	.05
❑ 778 Chris Zorich	.02	.10
❑ 779 Joe Valerio	.01	.05
❑ 780 Doug Thomas RC	.01	.05
❑ 781 Lamar Rogers UER RC	.01	.05
❑ 782 John Johnson RC	.01	.05
❑ 783 Phil Hansen RC	.01	.05
❑ 784 Kanavis McGhee RC	.01	.05
❑ 785 Calvin Stephens UER RC	.01	.05
❑ 786 James Jones RC	.01	.05
❑ 787 Reggie Barrett	.01	.05
❑ 788 Aeneas Williams RC	.08	.25
❑ 789 Aaron Craver RC	.01	.05
❑ 790 Keith Traylor RC	.01	.05
❑ 791 Godfrey Myles RC	.01	.05
❑ 792 Mo Lewis RC	.02	.10
❑ 793 James Richard RC	.01	.05
❑ 794 Carlos Jenkins RC	.01	.05
❑ 795 Lawrence Dawsey RC	.02	.10
❑ 796 Don Davey	.01	.05
❑ 797 Jake Reed RC	.20	.50
❑ 798 Dave McCloughan	.01	.05
❑ 799 Erik Williams RC	.02	.10
❑ 800 Steve Jackson RC	.01	.05
❑ 801 Bob Dahl	.01	.05
❑ 802 Ernie Mills RC	.02	.10
❑ 803 David Daniels RC	.01	.05
❑ 804 Rob Selby RC	.01	.05
❑ 805 Ricky Ervins RC	.02	.10
❑ 806 Tim Barnett RC	.01	.05
❑ 807 Chris Gardocki RC	.08	.25
❑ 808 Kevin Donnalley RC	.01	.05
❑ 809 Robert Wilson RC	.01	.05
❑ 810 Chuck Webb RC	.01	.05
❑ 811 Darryl Wren RC	.01	.05
❑ 812 Ed McCaffrey RC	.75	2.00
❑ 813 Shula's 300th Victory	.01	.05
❑ 814 Raiders-49ers sell	.01	.05
❑ 815 NFL International NEWS	.01	.05
❑ 816 Moe Gardner RC	.01	.05
❑ 817 Tim McKyer	.01	.05
❑ 818 Tom Waddle RC	.01	.05
❑ 819 Michael Jackson WR RC	.08	.25
❑ 820 Tony Casillas	.01	.05
❑ 821 Gaston Green	.01	.05
❑ 822 Kenny Walker RC	.01	.05
❑ 823 Willie Green RC	.01	.05
❑ 824 Erik Kramer RC	.08	.25
❑ 825 William Fuller	.02	.10
❑ 826 Allen Pinkett	.01	.05
❑ 827 Rick Venturi CO	.01	.05
❑ 828 Bill Maas	.01	.05
❑ 829 Jeff Jaeger	.01	.05
❑ 830 Robert Delpino	.01	.05
❑ 831 Mark Higgs RC	.01	.05
❑ 832 Reggie Roby	.01	.05
❑ 833 Terry Allen RC	.60	1.50
❑ 834 Cris Carter	.20	.50
❑ 835 John Randle RC	.25	.60
❑ 836 Hugh Millen RC	.01	.05
❑ 837 Jon Vaughn RC	.01	.05
❑ 838 Gill Fenerty	.01	.05
❑ 839 Floyd Turner	.01	.05
❑ 840 Irv Eatman	.01	.05
❑ 841 Lonnie Young	.01	.05
❑ 842 Jim McMahon	.02	.10
❑ 843 Randal Hill	.01	.05
❑ 844 Barry Foster FPSC	.02	.10
❑ 845 Neil O'Donnell RC	.08	.25
❑ 846 John Friesz FPSC	.08	.25
❑ 847 Broderick Thomas	.01	.05
❑ 848 Brian Mitchell	.02	.10
❑ 849 Mike Utley RC	.02	.10
❑ 850 Mike Croel ROY	.01	.05
❑ SC1 SB XXVI Theme Art	.08	.25
❑ SC3 Jim Thorpe Pioneer	.30	.75
❑ SC4 Otto Graham Pioneer	.30	.75
❑ SC5 Paul Brown Pioneer	.30	.75
❑ PSS1 Walter Payton	.20	.50
❑ PSS2 Red Grange	.20	.50
❑ MVPC25 Ottis Anderson	.08	.25
❑ AU336 L.Taylor REP AU/500	100.00	175.00
❑ AU394 L.Taylor PB AU/500	100.00	175.00
❑ AU699 O.Newsome AU/500	25.00	50.00
❑ AU824 Erik Kramer AU	25.00	50.00
❑ NNO Mini Pro Set Gazette	.08	.25
❑ NNO Pro Set Gazette	.08	.25
❑ NNO Santa Claus	.20	.50
❑ NNO Super Bowl XXV Art	.08	.25
❑ NNO Super Bowl XXV Logo	.08	.25

1992 Pro Set

❑ COMPLETE SET (700)	8.00	20.00
❑ COMP.SERIES 1 (400)	4.00	10.00
❑ COMP.SERIES 2 (300)	4.00	10.00
❑ 1 Mike Croel LL	.01	.05
❑ 2 Thurman Thomas LL	.08	.25
❑ 3 Wayne Fontes CO LL	.01	.05
❑ 4 Anthony Munoz LL	.02	.10
❑ 5 Steve Young LL	.10	.30
❑ 6 Warren Moon LL	.02	.10
❑ 7 Emmitt Smith LL	.25	.60
❑ 8 Haywood Jeffires LL	.01	.05
❑ 9 Marv Cook LL	.01	.05
❑ 10 Michael Irvin LL	.08	.25
❑ 11 Thurman Thomas LL	.08	.25
❑ 12 Chip Lohmiller LL UER	.01	.05
❑ 13 Barry Sanders LL	.20	.50
❑ 14 Reggie Roby LL	.01	.05
❑ 15 Mel Gray LL	.01	.05
❑ 16 Ronnie Lott LL	.02	.10
❑ 17 Pat Swilling LL	.01	.05
❑ 18 Reggie White LL	.02	.10
❑ 19 Haywood Jeffires ML	.01	.05
❑ 20 Pat Leahy MILE	.01	.05
❑ 21 James Lofton MILE	.02	.10
❑ 22 Art Monk MILE	.02	.10
❑ 23 Don Shula MILE	.02	.10
❑ 24A Nick Lowery MILE ERR	.01	.05
❑ 24B Nick Lowery MILE COR	.01	.05
❑ 25 John Elway ML	.20	.50
❑ 26 Chicago Bears MILE	.01	.05
❑ 27 Marcus Allen MILE	.02	.10
❑ 28 Terrell Buckley RC	.01	.05
❑ 29 Amp Lee RC	.01	.05
❑ 30 Chris Mims RC	.01	.05
❑ 31 Leon Searcy RC	.01	.05
❑ 32 Jimmy Smith RC	1.25	3.00
❑ 33 Siran Stacy RC	.01	.05
❑ 34 Pete Gogolak INN	.01	.05
❑ 35 Cheerleaders INN	.01	.05
❑ 36 Houston Astrodome INN	.01	.05
❑ 37 Week 1 REPLAY	.01	.05
❑ 38 Week 2 REPLAY	.01	.05
❑ 39 Week 3 REPLAY	.01	.05
❑ 40 Week 4 REPLAY	.01	.05
❑ 41 Week 5 REPLAY	.01	.05
❑ 42 Week 6 REPLAY	.01	.05
❑ 43 Thurman Thomas REP	.02	.10
❑ 44 Week 8 REPLAY	.01	.05
❑ 45 Week 9 REPLAY UER	.01	.05
❑ 46 Week 10 REPLAY	.01	.05
❑ 47 Week 11 REPLAY	.01	.05
❑ 48 Week 12 REPLAY	.01	.05
❑ 49 M.Irvin/S.Beuerlein REP	.02	.10
❑ 50 Week 14 REPLAY	.01	.05
❑ 51 Week 15 REPLAY	.01	.05
❑ 52 Week 16 REPLAY	.01	.05
❑ 53 Week 17 REPLAY	.01	.05
❑ 54 AFC Wild Card REPLAY	.01	.05
❑ 55 AFC Wild Card REPLAY	.01	.05
❑ 56 NFC Wild Card REPLAY	.01	.05
❑ 57 NFC Wild Card REPLAY	.01	.05
❑ 58 AFC Divis. Playoff REPLAY	.01	.05
❑ 59 Thurman Thomas REP	.02	.10
❑ 60 Erik Kramer REP	.01	.05
❑ 61 NFC Divis. Playoff REPLAY	.01	.05
❑ 62 AFC Championship REPLAY	.01	.05
❑ 63 NFC Championship REPLAY	.01	.05
❑ 64 Super Bowl XXVI REPLAY	.01	.05
❑ 65 Super Bowl XXVI REPLAY	.01	.05
❑ 66 Super Bowl XXVI REPLAY	.01	.05
❑ 67 Super Bowl XXVI REPLAY	.01	.05
❑ 68 Super Bowl XXVI REPLAY	.01	.05
❑ 69 Thurman Thomas REP	.02	.10
❑ 70 Super Bowl XXVI REPLAY	.01	.05

❑ 71 Super Bowl XXVI REPLAY	.01	.05
❑ 72 Super Bowl XXVI REPLAY	.01	.05
❑ 73 Jeff Bostic	.01	.05
❑ 74 Earnest Byner	.01	.05
❑ 75 Gary Clark	.08	.25
❑ 76 Andre Collins	.01	.05
❑ 77 Darrell Green	.01	.05
❑ 78 Joe Jacoby	.01	.05
❑ 79 Jim Lachey	.01	.05
❑ 80 Chip Lohmiller	.01	.05
❑ 81 Charles Mann	.01	.05
❑ 82 Martin Mayhew	.01	.05
❑ 83 Matt Millen	.02	.10
❑ 84 Brian Mitchell	.02	.10
❑ 85 Art Monk	.02	.10
❑ 86 Gerald Riggs	.01	.05
❑ 87 Mark Rypien	.01	.05
❑ 88 Fred Stokes	.01	.05
❑ 89 Bobby Wilson	.01	.05
❑ 90 Joe Gibbs CO	.02	.10
❑ 91 Howard Ballard	.01	.05
❑ 92 Cornelius Bennett UER	.02	.10
❑ 93 Kenneth Davis	.01	.05
❑ 94 Al Edwards	.01	.05
❑ 95 Kent Hull	.01	.05
❑ 96 Kirby Jackson	.01	.05
❑ 97 Mark Kelso	.01	.05
❑ 98 James Lofton	.02	.10
❑ 99 Keith McKeller	.01	.05
❑ 100 Nate Odomes	.01	.05
❑ 101 Jim Ritcher	.01	.05
❑ 102 Leon Seals	.01	.05
❑ 103 Steve Tasker	.02	.10
❑ 104 Darryl Talley	.01	.05
❑ 105 Thurman Thomas	.08	.25
❑ 106 Will Wolford	.01	.05
❑ 107 Jeff Wright	.01	.05
❑ 108 Marv Levy CO	.01	.05
❑ 109 Darion Conner	.01	.05
❑ 110 Bill Fralic	.01	.05
❑ 111 Moe Gardner	.01	.05
❑ 112 Michael Haynes	.02	.10
❑ 113 Chris Miller	.02	.10
❑ 114 Erric Pegram	.02	.10
❑ 115 Bruce Pickens	.01	.05
❑ 116 Andre Rison	.02	.10
❑ 117 Jerry Glanville CO	.01	.05
❑ 118 Neal Anderson	.01	.05
❑ 119 Trace Armstrong	.01	.05
❑ 120 Wendell Davis	.01	.05
❑ 121 Richard Dent	.02	.10
❑ 122 Jay Hilgenberg	.01	.05
❑ 123 Lemuel Stinson	.01	.05
❑ 124 Stan Thomas	.01	.05
❑ 125 Tom Waddle	.01	.05
❑ 126 Mike Ditka CO	.08	.25
❑ 127 James Brooks	.02	.10
❑ 128 Eddie Brown	.01	.05
❑ 129 David Fulcher	.01	.05
❑ 130 Harold Green	.01	.05
❑ 131 Tim Krumrie UER	.01	.05
❑ 132 Anthony Munoz	.02	.10
❑ 133 Craig Taylor	.01	.05
❑ 134 Eric Thomas	.01	.05
❑ 135 David Shula CO RC	.01	.05
❑ 136 Mike Baab	.01	.05
❑ 137 Brian Brennan	.01	.05
❑ 138 Michael Jackson	.02	.10
❑ 139 James Jones DT UER	.01	.05
❑ 140 Ed King	.01	.05
❑ 141 Clay Matthews	.02	.10
❑ 142 Eric Metcalf	.02	.10
❑ 143 Joe Morris	.01	.05
❑ 144A Bill Belichick CO NPO	.08	.25
❑ 144B Bill Belichick CO	.08	.25
❑ 145 Steve Beuerlein	.02	.10
❑ 146 Larry Brown DB	.01	.05
❑ 147 Ray Horton	.01	.05
❑ 148 Ken Norton	.02	.10
❑ 149 Mike Saxon	.01	.05
❑ 150 Emmitt Smith	.60	1.50
❑ 151 Mark Stepnoski	.02	.10
❑ 152 Alexander Wright	.01	.05
❑ 153 Jimmy Johnson CO	.02	.10
❑ 154 Mike Croel	.01	.05
❑ 155 John Elway	.50	1.25
❑ 156 Gaston Green	.01	.05
❑ 157 Wymon Henderson	.01	.05
❑ 158 Karl Mecklenburg UER	.01	.05
❑ 159 Warren Powers	.01	.05
❑ 160 Steve Sewell UER	.01	.05
❑ 161 Doug Widell	.01	.05
❑ 162 Dan Reeves CO	.01	.05
❑ 163 Eric Andolsek	.01	.05
❑ 164 Jerry Ball	.01	.05
❑ 165 Bennie Blades	.01	.05
❑ 166 Ray Crockett	.01	.05
❑ 167 Willie Green	.01	.05
❑ 168 Erik Kramer	.02	.10
❑ 169 Barry Sanders	.50	1.25
❑ 170 Chris Spielman UER	.01	.05
❑ 171 Wayne Fontes CO	.01	.05
❑ 172 Vinnie Clark	.01	.05
❑ 173 Tony Mandarich	.01	.05
❑ 174 Brian Noble	.01	.05
❑ 175 Bryce Paup	.08	.25
❑ 176 Sterling Sharpe	.08	.25
❑ 177 Darrell Thompson	.01	.05
❑ 178 Esera Tuaolo UER	.01	.05
❑ 179 Ed West	.01	.05
❑ 180 Mike Holmgren CO RC	.08	.25
❑ 181 Ray Childress	.01	.05
❑ 182 Cris Dishman	.01	.05
❑ 183 Curtis Duncan	.01	.05
❑ 184 William Fuller	.01	.05
❑ 185 Lamar Lathon	.01	.05
❑ 186 Warren Moon	.08	.25
❑ 187 Bo Orlando RC	.01	.05
❑ 188 Lorenzo White	.01	.05
❑ 189 Jack Pardee CO	.01	.05
❑ 190 Chip Banks	.01	.05
❑ 191 Dean Biasucci UER	.01	.05
❑ 192 Bill Brooks	.01	.05
❑ 193 Ray Donaldson	.01	.05
❑ 194 Jeff Herrod	.01	.05
❑ 195 Mike Prior	.01	.05
❑ 196 Mark Vander Poel	.01	.05
❑ 197 Clarence Verdin	.01	.05
❑ 198 Ted Marchibroda CO	.01	.05
❑ 199 John Alt	.01	.05
❑ 200 Deron Cherry	.01	.05
❑ 201 Steve DeBerg	.01	.05
❑ 202 Nick Lowery	.01	.05
❑ 203 Neil Smith	.08	.25
❑ 204 Derrick Thomas	.08	.25
❑ 205 Joe Valerio	.01	.05
❑ 206 Barry Word	.01	.05
❑ 207 M. Schottenheimer CO	.01	.05
❑ 208 Marcus Allen	.08	.25
❑ 209 Nick Bell	.01	.05
❑ 210 Tim Brown	.08	.25
❑ 211 Howie Long	.08	.25
❑ 212 Ronnie Lott	.02	.10
❑ 213 Todd Marinovich	.01	.05
❑ 214 Greg Townsend	.01	.05
❑ 215 Steve Wright	.01	.05
❑ 216 Art Shell CO	.02	.10
❑ 217 Flipper Anderson	.01	.05
❑ 218 Robert Delpino	.01	.05
❑ 219 Henry Ellard	.02	.10
❑ 220 Kevin Greene	.02	.10
❑ 221 Todd Lyght	.01	.05
❑ 222 Tom Newberry	.01	.05
❑ 223 Roman Phifer	.01	.05
❑ 224 Michael Stewart	.01	.05
❑ 225 Chuck Knox CO	.01	.05
❑ 226 Aaron Craver	.01	.05
❑ 227 Jeff Cross	.01	.05
❑ 228 Mark Duper	.01	.05
❑ 229 Ferrell Edmunds	.01	.05
❑ 230 Jim C. Jensen	.01	.05
❑ 231 Louis Oliver UER	.01	.05
❑ 232 Reggie Roby	.01	.05
❑ 233 Sammie Smith	.01	.05
❑ 234 Don Shula CO	.02	.10
❑ 235 Joey Browner	.01	.05
❑ 236 Anthony Carter	.02	.10
❑ 237 Chris Doleman	.01	.05
❑ 238 Steve Jordan	.01	.05
❑ 239 Kirk Lowdermilk	.01	.05
❑ 240 Henry Thomas	.01	.05
❑ 241 Herschel Walker	.02	.10
❑ 242 Felix Wright	.01	.05
❑ 243 Dennis Green CO RC	.02	.10
❑ 244 Ray Agnew	.01	.05
❑ 245 Marv Cook	.01	.05
❑ 246 Irving Fryar UER	.02	.10
❑ 247 Pat Harlow	.01	.05
❑ 248 Hugh Millen	.01	.05
❑ 249 Leonard Russell	.02	.10
❑ 250 Andre Tippett	.01	.05
❑ 251 Jon Vaughn	.01	.05
❑ 252 Dick MacPherson CO	.01	.05
❑ 253 Morten Andersen	.01	.05
❑ 254 Bobby Hebert	.01	.05
❑ 255 Joel Hilgenberg	.01	.05
❑ 256 Vaughan Johnson	.01	.05
❑ 257 Sam Mills	.01	.05
❑ 258 Pat Swilling	.01	.05
❑ 259 Floyd Turner	.01	.05
❑ 260 Steve Walsh	.01	.05
❑ 261 Jim Mora CO UER	.01	.05
❑ 262 Stephen Baker	.01	.05
❑ 263 Mark Collins	.01	.05
❑ 264 Rodney Hampton	.02	.10
❑ 265 Jeff Hostetler	.02	.10
❑ 266 Erik Howard	.01	.05
❑ 267 Sean Landeta	.01	.05
❑ 268 Gary Reasons UER	.01	.05
❑ 269 Everson Walls	.01	.05
❑ 270 Ray Handley CO	.01	.05
❑ 271 Louie Aguiar RC	.01	.05
❑ 272 Brad Baxter	.01	.05
❑ 273 Chris Burkett	.01	.05
❑ 274 Irv Eatman	.01	.05
❑ 275 Jeff Lageman	.01	.05
❑ 276 Freeman McNeil	.01	.05
❑ 277 Rob Moore	.02	.10
❑ 278 Lonnie Young	.01	.05
❑ 279 Bruce Coslet CO	.01	.05
❑ 280 Jerome Brown	.01	.05
❑ 281 Keith Byars	.01	.05
❑ 282 Bruce Collie UER	.01	.05
❑ 283 Keith Jackson	.02	.10
❑ 284 James Joseph	.01	.05
❑ 285 Seth Joyner	.01	.05
❑ 286 Andre Waters	.01	.05
❑ 287 Reggie White	.08	.25
❑ 288 Rich Kotite CO	.01	.05
❑ 289 Rich Camarillo	.01	.05
❑ 290 Garth Jax	.01	.05
❑ 291 Ernie Jones	.01	.05
❑ 292 Tim McDonald	.01	.05
❑ 293 Rod Saddler	.01	.05
❑ 294 Anthony Thompson UER	.01	.05
❑ 295 Tom Tupa UER	.01	.05
❑ 296 Ron Wolfley	.01	.05
❑ 297 Joe Bugel CO	.01	.05
❑ 298 Gary Anderson K	.01	.05
❑ 299 Jeff Graham	.08	.25
❑ 300 Eric Green	.01	.05
❑ 301 Bryan Hinkle	.01	.05
❑ 302 Tunch Ilkin	.01	.05
❑ 303 Louis Lipps	.01	.05
❑ 304 Neil O'Donnell	.02	.10
❑ 305 Rod Woodson	.08	.25
❑ 306 Bill Cowher CO RC	.30	.75
❑ 307 Eric Bieniemy	.01	.05
❑ 308 Marion Butts	.01	.05
❑ 309 John Friesz	.02	.10
❑ 310 Courtney Hall	.01	.05
❑ 311 Ronnie Harmon	.01	.05
❑ 312 Henry Rolling	.01	.05
❑ 313 Billy Ray Smith	.01	.05
❑ 314 George Thornton	.01	.05
❑ 315 Bobby Ross CO RC	.01	.05
❑ 316 Todd Bowles	.01	.05
❑ 317 Michael Carter	.01	.05
❑ 318 Don Griffin	.01	.05
❑ 319 Charles Haley	.02	.10
❑ 320 Brent Jones	.02	.10
❑ 321 John Taylor	.02	.10
❑ 322 Ted Washington	.01	.05
❑ 323 Steve Young	.25	.60
❑ 324 George Seifert CO	.02	.10
❑ 325 Brian Blades	.02	.10
❑ 326 Jacob Green	.01	.05
❑ 327 Patrick Hunter	.01	.05
❑ 328 Tommy Kane	.01	.05
❑ 329 Cortez Kennedy	.02	.10
❑ 330 Dave Krieg	.02	.10
❑ 331 Rufus Porter	.01	.05
❑ 332 John L. Williams	.01	.05
❑ 333 Tom Flores CO	.01	.05
❑ 334 Gary Anderson RB	.01	.05
❑ 335 Mark Carrier WR	.02	.10
❑ 336 Reuben Davis	.01	.05

❑ 337 Lawrence Dawsey .02 .10
❑ 338 Keith McCants UER .01 .05
❑ 339 Vinny Testaverde .02 .10
❑ 340 Broderick Thomas .01 .05
❑ 341 Robert Wilson .01 .05
❑ 342 Sam Wyche CO .01 .05
❑ 343 1991 Teacher of .01 .05
❑ 344 Owners Reject Instant .01 .05
❑ 345 NFL Experience .01 .05
❑ 346 Chuck Noll Retires .02 .10
❑ 347 Isaac Curtis .01 .05
❑ 348 Michael Irvin/D.Pearson .02 .10
❑ 349 Barry Sanders/B.Sims .20 .50
❑ 350 Todd Marinovich/K.Stable .01 .05
❑ 351 Leonard Russell/C.James .02 .10
❑ 352 Bob Golic .01 .05
❑ 353 Pat Harlow .01 .05
❑ 354 Esera Tuaolo .01 .05
❑ 355 Mark Schlereth RC .01 .05
❑ 356 Trace Armstrong .01 .05
❑ 357 Eric Bieniemy .01 .05
❑ 358 Bill Romanowski .01 .05
❑ 359 Irv Eatman .01 .05
❑ 360 Jonathan Hayes .01 .05
❑ 361 Atlanta Falcons .01 .05
❑ 362 Chicago Bears .01 .05
❑ 363 Dallas Cowboys .01 .05
❑ 364 Detroit Lions .01 .05
❑ 365 Green Bay Packers .01 .05
❑ 366 Los Angeles Rams .01 .05
❑ 367 Minnesota Vikings .01 .05
❑ 368 New Orleans Saints UER .01 .05
❑ 369 New York Giants .01 .05
❑ 370 Philadelphia Eagles .01 .05
❑ 371 Phoenix Cardinals .01 .05
❑ 372 San Francisco 49ers .01 .05
❑ 373 Tampa Bay Buccaneers .01 .05
❑ 374 Washington Redskins .01 .05
❑ 375 Steve Atwater PB UER .01 .05
❑ 376 Cornelius Bennett PB .02 .10
❑ 377 Tim Brown PB .02 .10
❑ 378 Marion Butts PB .01 .05
❑ 379 Ray Childress PB .01 .05
❑ 380 Mark Clayton PB .01 .05
❑ 381 Marv Cook PB .01 .05
❑ 382 Cris Dishman PB .01 .05
❑ 383 William Fuller PB .01 .05
❑ 384 Gaston Green PB .01 .05
❑ 385 Jeff Jaeger PB .01 .05
❑ 386 Haywood Jeffires PB .02 .10
❑ 387 James Lofton PB .02 .10
❑ 388 Ronnie Lott PB .02 .10
❑ 389 Karl Mecklenburg PB UER .01 .05
❑ 390 Warren Moon PB .02 .10
❑ 391 Anthony Munoz PB .01 .05
❑ 392 Dennis Smith PB .01 .05
❑ 393 Neil Smith PB .02 .10
❑ 394 Darryl Talley PB .01 .05
❑ 395 Derrick Thomas PB .02 .10
❑ 396 Thurman Thomas PB .02 .10
❑ 397 Greg Townsend PB .01 .05
❑ 398 Richmond Webb PB .01 .05
❑ 399 Rod Woodson PB .02 .10
❑ 400 Dan Reeves CO PB .01 .05
❑ 401 Troy Aikman PB .15 .40
❑ 402 Eric Allen PB .01 .05
❑ 403 Bennie Blades PB .01 .05
❑ 404 Lomas Brown PB .01 .05
❑ 405 Mark Carrier DB PB .01 .05
❑ 406 Gary Clark PB .02 .10
❑ 407 Mel Gray PB .01 .05
❑ 408 Darrell Green PB .01 .05
❑ 409 Michael Irvin PB .08 .25
❑ 410 Vaughan Johnson PB .01 .05
❑ 411 Seth Joyner PB .01 .05
❑ 412 Jim Lachey PB .01 .05
❑ 413 Chip Lohmiller PB .01 .05
❑ 414 Charles Mann PB .01 .05
❑ 415 Chris Miller PB .02 .10
❑ 416 Sam Mills PB .01 .05
❑ 417 Bart Oates PB .01 .05
❑ 418 Jerry Rice PB .15 .40
❑ 419 Andre Rison PB .02 .10
❑ 420 Mark Rypien PB .01 .05
❑ 421 Barry Sanders PB .20 .50
❑ 422 Deion Sanders PB .08 .25
❑ 423 Mark Schlereth PB .01 .05
❑ 424 Mike Singletary PB .01 .05
❑ 425 Emmitt Smith PB .25 .60
❑ 426 Pat Swilling PB .01 .05
❑ 427 Reggie White PB .02 .10
❑ 428 Rick Bryan .01 .05
❑ 429 Tim Green .01 .05
❑ 430 Drew Hill .01 .05
❑ 431 Norm Johnson .01 .05
❑ 432 Keith Jones .01 .05
❑ 433 Mike Pritchard .02 .10
❑ 434 Deion Sanders .20 .50
❑ 435 Tony Smith RC .01 .05
❑ 436 Jessie Tuggle .01 .05
❑ 437 Steve Christie .01 .05
❑ 438 Shane Conlan .01 .05
❑ 439 Matt Darby RC .01 .05
❑ 440 John Fina RC .01 .05
❑ 441 Henry Jones .01 .05
❑ 442 Jim Kelly .08 .25
❑ 443 Pete Metzelaars .01 .05
❑ 444 Andre Reed .02 .10
❑ 445 Bruce Smith .08 .25
❑ 446 Troy Auzenne RC .01 .05
❑ 447 Mark Carrier DB .01 .05
❑ 448 Will Furrer RC .01 .05
❑ 449 Jim Harbaugh .08 .25
❑ 450 Brad Muster .01 .05
❑ 451 Darren Lewis .01 .05
❑ 452 Mike Singletary .02 .10
❑ 453 Alonzo Spellman RC .02 .10
❑ 454 Chris Zorich .02 .10
❑ 455 Jim Breech .01 .05
❑ 456 Boomer Esiason .02 .10
❑ 457 Derrick Fenner .01 .05
❑ 458 James Francis .01 .05
❑ 459 David Klingler RC .01 .05
❑ 460 Tim McGee .01 .05
❑ 461 Carl Pickens RC .08 .25
❑ 462 Alfred Williams .01 .05
❑ 463 Darryl Williams RC .01 .05
❑ 464 Mark Bavaro .01 .05
❑ 465 Jay Hilgenberg .01 .05
❑ 466 Leroy Hoard .02 .10
❑ 467 Bernie Kosar .02 .10
❑ 468 Michael Dean Perry .02 .10
❑ 469 Todd Philcox RC .01 .05
❑ 470 Patrick Rowe RC .01 .05
❑ 471 Tommy Vardell RC .01 .05
❑ 472 Everson Walls .01 .05
❑ 473 Troy Aikman .30 .75
❑ 474 Kenneth Gant RC .01 .05
❑ 475 Charles Haley .02 .10
❑ 476 Michael Irvin .08 .25
❑ 477 Robert Jones RC .01 .05
❑ 478 Russell Maryland .01 .05
❑ 479 Jay Novacek .02 .10
❑ 480 Kevin Smith RC .01 .05
❑ 481 Tony Tolbert .01 .05
❑ 482 Steve Atwater .01 .05
❑ 483 Shane Dronett RC .01 .05
❑ 484 Simon Fletcher .01 .05
❑ 485 Greg Lewis .01 .05
❑ 486 Tommy Maddox RC .75 2.00
❑ 487 Shannon Sharpe .08 .25
❑ 488 Dennis Smith .01 .05
❑ 489 Sammie Smith .01 .05
❑ 490 Kenny Walker .01 .05
❑ 491 Lomas Brown .01 .05
❑ 492 Mike Farr .01 .05
❑ 493 Mel Gray .02 .10
❑ 494 Jason Hanson RC .02 .10
❑ 495 Herman Moore .08 .25
❑ 496 Rodney Peete .02 .10
❑ 497 Robert Porcher RC .08 .25
❑ 498 Kelvin Pritchett .01 .05
❑ 499 Andre Ware .01 .05
❑ 500 Sanjay Beach RC .01 .05
❑ 501 Edgar Bennett RC .08 .25
❑ 502 Lewis Billups .01 .05
❑ 503 Terrell Buckley .01 .05
❑ 504 Ty Detmer .08 .25
❑ 505 Brett Favre 1.25 2.50
❑ 506 Johnny Holland .01 .05
❑ 507 Dexter McNabb RC .01 .05
❑ 508 Vince Workman .01 .05
❑ 509 Cody Carlson .01 .05
❑ 510 Ernest Givins .02 .10
❑ 511 Jerry Gray .01 .05
❑ 512 Haywood Jeffires .02 .10
❑ 513 Bruce Matthews .01 .05
❑ 514 Bubba McDowell .01 .05
❑ 515 Bucky Richardson RC .01 .05
❑ 516 Webster Slaughter .01 .05
❑ 517 Al Smith .01 .05
❑ 518 Mel Agee .01 .05
❑ 519 Ashley Ambrose RC .08 .25
❑ 520 Kevin Call .01 .05
❑ 521 Ken Clark .01 .05
❑ 522 Quentin Coryatt RC .01 .05
❑ 523 Steve Emtman RC .01 .05
❑ 524 Jeff George .08 .25
❑ 525 Jessie Hester .01 .05
❑ 526 Anthony Johnson .02 .10
❑ 527 Tim Barnett .01 .05
❑ 528 Martin Bayless .01 .05
❑ 529 J.J. Birden .01 .05
❑ 530 Dale Carter RC .02 .10
❑ 531 Dave Krieg .02 .10
❑ 532 Albert Lewis .01 .05
❑ 533 Nick Lowery .01 .05
❑ 534 Christian Okoye .01 .05
❑ 535 Harvey Williams .08 .25
❑ 536 Aundray Bruce .01 .05
❑ 537 Eric Dickerson .02 .10
❑ 538 Willie Gault .02 .10
❑ 539 Ethan Horton .01 .05
❑ 540 Jeff Jaeger .01 .05
❑ 541 Napoleon McCallum .01 .05
❑ 542 Chester McGlockton RC .02 .10
❑ 543 Steve Smith .01 .05
❑ 544 Steve Wisniewski .01 .05
❑ 545 Marc Boutte RC .01 .05
❑ 546 Pat Carter .01 .05
❑ 547 Jim Everett .02 .10
❑ 548 Cleveland Gary .01 .05
❑ 549 Sean Gilbert RC .02 .10
❑ 550 Steve Israel RC .01 .05
❑ 551 Todd Kinchen RC .01 .05
❑ 552 Jackie Slater .01 .05
❑ 553 Tony Zendejas .01 .05
❑ 554 Robert Clark .01 .05
❑ 555 Mark Clayton .02 .10
❑ 556 Marco Coleman RC .01 .05
❑ 557 Bryan Cox .02 .10
❑ 558 Keith Jackson .02 .10
❑ 559 Dan Marino .50 1.25
❑ 560 John Offerdahl .01 .05
❑ 561 Troy Vincent RC .01 .05
❑ 562 Richmond Webb .01 .05
❑ 563 Terry Allen .08 .25
❑ 564 Cris Carter .20 .50
❑ 565 Roger Craig .02 .10
❑ 566 Rich Gannon .08 .25
❑ 567 Hassan Jones .01 .05
❑ 568 Randall McDaniel .02 .10
❑ 569 Al Noga .01 .05
❑ 570 Todd Scott .01 .05
❑ 571 Van Waiters RC .01 .05
❑ 572 Bruce Armstrong .01 .05
❑ 573 Gene Chilton RC .01 .05
❑ 574 Eugene Chung RC .01 .05
❑ 575 Todd Collins RC .01 .05
❑ 576 Hart Lee Dykes .01 .05
❑ 577 David Howard RC .01 .05
❑ 578 Eugene Lockhart .01 .05
❑ 579 Greg McMurtry .01 .05
❑ 580 Rod Smith DB RC .01 .05
❑ 581 Gene Atkins .01 .05
❑ 582 Vince Buck .01 .05
❑ 583 Wesley Carroll .01 .05
❑ 584 Jim Dombrowski .01 .05
❑ 585 Vaughn Dunbar RC .01 .05
❑ 586 Craig Heyward .02 .10
❑ 587 Dalton Hilliard .01 .05
❑ 588 Wayne Martin .01 .05
❑ 589 Renaldo Turnbull .01 .05
❑ 590 Carl Banks .01 .05
❑ 591 Derek Brown TE RC .01 .05
❑ 592 Jarrod Bunch .01 .05
❑ 593 Mark Ingram .01 .05
❑ 594 Ed McCaffrey .10 .30
❑ 595 Phil Simms .02 .10
❑ 596 Phillippi Sparks RC .01 .05
❑ 597 Lawrence Taylor .08 .25
❑ 598 Lewis Tillman .01 .05
❑ 599 Kyle Clifton .01 .05
❑ 600 Mo Lewis .01 .05
❑ 601 Terance Mathis .02 .10
❑ 602 Scott Mersereau .01 .05
❑ 603 Johnny Mitchell RC .01 .05

❑ 604 Browning Nagle .01 .05
❑ 605 Ken O'Brien .01 .05
❑ 606 Al Toon .02 .10
❑ 607 Marvin Washington .01 .05
❑ 608 Eric Allen .01 .05
❑ 609 Fred Barnett .08 .25
❑ 610 John Booty .01 .05
❑ 611 Randall Cunningham .08 .25
❑ 612 Rich Miano .01 .05
❑ 613 Clyde Simmons .01 .05
❑ 614 Siran Stacy .01 .05
❑ 615 Herschel Walker .02 .10
❑ 616 Calvin Williams .02 .10
❑ 617 Chris Chandler .08 .25
❑ 618 Randal Hill .01 .05
❑ 619 Johnny Johnson .01 .05
❑ 620 Lorenzo Lynch .01 .05
❑ 621 Robert Massey .01 .05
❑ 622 Ricky Proehl .01 .05
❑ 623 Timm Rosenbach .01 .05
❑ 624 Tony Sacca RC .01 .05
❑ 625 Aeneas Williams UER .02 .10
❑ 626 Bubby Brister .01 .05
❑ 627 Barry Foster .02 .10
❑ 628 Merril Hoge .01 .05
❑ 629 D.J. Johnson .01 .05
❑ 630 David Little .01 .05
❑ 631 Greg Lloyd .02 .10
❑ 632 Ernie Mills .01 .05
❑ 633 Leon Searcy RC .01 .05
❑ 634 Dwight Stone .01 .05
❑ 635 Sam Anno RC .01 .05
❑ 636 Burt Grossman .01 .05
❑ 637 Stan Humphries .08 .25
❑ 638 Nate Lewis .01 .05
❑ 639 Anthony Miller .02 .10
❑ 640 Chris Mims .08 .25
❑ 641 Marquez Pope RC .01 .05
❑ 642 Stanley Richard .01 .05
❑ 643 Junior Seau .08 .25
❑ 644 Brian Bollinger RC .01 .05
❑ 645 Steve Bono RC .08 .25
❑ 646 Dexter Carter .01 .05
❑ 647 Dana Hall RC .01 .05
❑ 648 Amp Lee .01 .05
❑ 649 Joe Montana .50 1.25
❑ 650 Tom Rathman .01 .05
❑ 651 Jerry Rice .30 .75
❑ 652 Ricky Watters .08 .25
❑ 653 Robert Blackmon .01 .05
❑ 654 John Kasay .01 .05
❑ 655 Ronnie Lee RC .01 .05
❑ 656 Dan McGwire .01 .05
❑ 657 Ray Roberts RC .01 .05
❑ 658 Kelly Stouffer .01 .05
❑ 659 Chris Warren .08 .25
❑ 660 Tony Woods .01 .05
❑ 661 David Wyman .01 .05
❑ 662 Reggie Cobb .01 .05
❑ 663A Steve DeBerg ERR .02 .10
❑ 663B Steve DeBerg COR .02 .10
❑ 664 Santana Dotson RC .02 .10
❑ 665 Willie Drewery .01 .05
❑ 666 Paul Gruber .01 .05
❑ 667 Ron Hall .01 .05
❑ 668 Courtney Hawkins RC .02 .10
❑ 669 Charles McRae .01 .05
❑ 670 Ricky Reynolds .01 .05
❑ 671 Monte Coleman .01 .05
❑ 672 Brad Edwards .01 .05
❑ 673 Jumpy Geathers UER .01 .05
❑ 674 Kelly Goodburn .01 .05
❑ 675 Kurt Gouveia .01 .05
❑ 676 Chris Hakel RC .01 .05
❑ 677 Wilber Marshall .01 .05
❑ 678 Ricky Sanders .01 .05
❑ 679 Mark Schlereth .01 .05
❑ 680 Buffalo Bills .01 .05
❑ 681 Cincinnati Bengals .01 .05
❑ 682 Cleveland Browns .01 .05
❑ 683 Denver Broncos .01 .05
❑ 684 Houston Oilers .01 .05
❑ 685 Indianapolis Colts .01 .05
❑ 686 Tracy Simien SG .01 .05
❑ 687 Los Angeles Raiders .01 .05
❑ 688 Miami Dolphins .01 .05
❑ 689 New England Patriots .01 .05
❑ 690 New York Jets .01 .05
❑ 691 Pittsburgh Steelers .01 .05
❑ 692 San Diego Chargers .01 .05
❑ 693 Seattle Seahawks .01 .05
❑ 694 Play Smart .01 .05
❑ 695 Hank Williams Jr. NEW .01 .05
❑ 696 3 Brothers in NFL NEWS .01 .05
❑ 697 Japan Bowl NEWS .01 .05
❑ 698 Georgia Dome NEWS .01 .05
❑ 699 Theme Art NEWS .01 .05
❑ 700 Mark Rypien SB MVP NEW .01 .05
❑ AU150 Emmitt Smith AU/1000 60.00 120.00
❑ AU168 Erik Kramer AU/1000 12.50 30.00
❑ NNO E.Smith Power Preview .30 .75
❑ NNO Santa Claus .20 .50
❑ SC5 Super Bowl XXVI Logo .10 .30
❑ P1 Cover Card Promo .40 1.00

1993 Pro Set

❑ COMPLETE SET (449) 8.00 20.00
❑ 1 Marco Coleman .01 .05
❑ 2 Steve Young LL .10 .30
❑ 3 Mike Holmgren .02 .10
❑ 4 John Elway LL .30 .75
❑ 5 Steve Young LL .10 .30
❑ 6 Dan Marino LL .30 .75
❑ 7 Emmitt Smith LL .30 .75
❑ 8 Sterling Sharpe LL .02 .10
❑ 9 Jay Novacek .02 .10
❑ 10 Sterling Sharpe LL .02 .10
❑ 11 Thurman Thomas LL .02 .10
❑ 12 Pete Stoyanovich .01 .05
❑ 13 Greg Montgomery .01 .05
❑ 14 Johnny Bailey .01 .05
❑ 15 Jon Vaughn .01 .05
❑ 16 Audray McMillian .01 .05
❑ 17 Clyde Simmons .01 .05
❑ 18 Cortez Kennedy .01 .05
❑ 19 AFC Wildcard .01 .05
❑ 20 AFC Wildcard .01 .05
❑ 21 NFC Wildcard .01 .05
❑ 22 NFC Wildcard .01 .05
❑ 23 AFC Divisional .01 .05
❑ 24 Dan Marino REP .30 .75
❑ 25 Troy Aikman REP .20 .50
❑ 26 Ricky Watters REP .02 .10
❑ 27 AFC Championship .01 .05
❑ 28 NFC Championship .01 .05
❑ 29 Super Bowl XXVIII Logo .01 .05
❑ 30 Troy Aikman .30 .75
❑ 31 Thomas Everett .01 .05
❑ 32 Charles Haley .02 .10
❑ 33 Alvin Harper .02 .10
❑ 34 Michael Irvin .08 .25
❑ 35 Robert Jones .01 .05
❑ 36 Russell Maryland .01 .05
❑ 37 Ken Norton .02 .10
❑ 38 Jay Novacek .02 .10
❑ 39 Emmitt Smith .50 1.50
❑ 40 Darrin Smith RC .02 .10
❑ 41 Mark Stepnoski .01 .05
❑ 42 Kevin Williams RC WR .08 .25
❑ 43 Daryl Johnston .08 .25
❑ 44 Derrick Lassic RC .01 .05
❑ 45 Don Beebe .01 .05
❑ 46 Cornelius Bennett .02 .10
❑ 47 Bill Brooks .01 .05
❑ 48 Kenneth Davis .01 .05
❑ 49 Jim Kelly .08 .25
❑ 50 Andre Reed .02 .10
❑ 51 Bruce Smith .08 .25
❑ 52 Thomas Smith RC .02 .10
❑ 53 Darryl Talley .01 .05
❑ 54 Thurman Thomas .08 .25
❑ 55 Russell Copeland RC .02 .10
❑ 56 Steve Christie .01 .05
❑ 57 Pete Metzelaars .01 .05
❑ 58 Frank Reich .02 .10
❑ 59 Henry Jones .01 .05
❑ 60 Vinnie Clark .01 .05
❑ 61 Eric Dickerson .02 .10
❑ 62 Jumpy Geathers .01 .05
❑ 63 Roger Harper RC .01 .05
❑ 64 Michael Haynes .02 .10
❑ 65 Bobby Hebert .01 .05
❑ 66 Lincoln Kennedy RC .01 .05
❑ 67 Chris Miller .02 .10
❑ 68 Andre Rison .02 .10
❑ 69 Deion Sanders .20 .50
❑ 70 Jessie Tuggle .01 .05
❑ 71 Ron George .01 .05
❑ 72 Erric Pegram .02 .10
❑ 73 Melvin Jenkins .01 .05
❑ 74 Pierce Holt .01 .05
❑ 75 Neal Anderson .01 .05
❑ 76 Mark Carrier DB .01 .05
❑ 77 Curtis Conway RC .15 .40
❑ 78 Richard Dent .02 .10
❑ 79 Jim Harbaugh .08 .25
❑ 80 Craig Heyward .02 .10
❑ 81 Darren Lewis .01 .05
❑ 82 Alonzo Spellman .01 .05
❑ 83 Tom Waddle .01 .05
❑ 84 Wendell Davis .01 .05
❑ 85 Chris Zorich .01 .05
❑ 86 Carl Simpson RC .01 .05
❑ 87 Chris Gedney RC .01 .05
❑ 88 Trace Armstrong .01 .05
❑ 89 Peter Tom Willis .01 .05
❑ 90 John Copeland RC .02 .10
❑ 91 Derrick Fenner .01 .05
❑ 92 James Francis .01 .05
❑ 93 Harold Green .01 .05
❑ 94 David Klingler .01 .05
❑ 95 Tim Krumrie .01 .05
❑ 96 Tony McGee RC .02 .10
❑ 97 Carl Pickens .02 .10
❑ 98 Alfred Williams .01 .05
❑ 99 Doug Pelfrey RC .01 .05
❑ 100 Lance Gunn RC .01 .05
❑ 101 Jay Schroeder .01 .05
❑ 102 Steve Tovar RC .01 .05
❑ 103 Jeff Query .01 .05
❑ 104 Ty Parten RC .01 .05
❑ 105 Jerry Ball .01 .05
❑ 106 Mark Carrier WR .02 .10
❑ 107 Rob Burnett .01 .05
❑ 108 Michael Jackson .02 .10
❑ 109 Mike Johnson .01 .05
❑ 110 Bernie Kosar .02 .10
❑ 111 Clay Matthews .02 .10
❑ 112 Eric Metcalf .02 .10
❑ 113 Michael Dean Perry .02 .10
❑ 114 Vinny Testaverde .02 .10
❑ 115 Eric Turner .01 .05
❑ 116 Tommy Vardell .01 .05
❑ 117 Leroy Hoard .02 .10
❑ 118 Steve Everitt RC .01 .05
❑ 119 Everson Walls .01 .05
❑ 120 Steve Atwater .01 .05
❑ 121 Rod Bernstine .01 .05
❑ 122 Mike Croel .01 .05
❑ 123 John Elway .60 1.50
❑ 124 Simon Fletcher .01 .05
❑ 125 Glyn Milburn RC .08 .25
❑ 126 Reggie Rivers RC .01 .05
❑ 127 Shannon Sharpe .08 .25
❑ 128 Dennis Smith .01 .05
❑ 129 Dan Williams RC .01 .05
❑ 130 Rondell Jones RC .01 .05
❑ 131 Jason Elam RC .08 .25
❑ 132 Arthur Marshall RC .01 .05
❑ 133 Gary Zimmerman .01 .05
❑ 134 Karl Mecklenburg .01 .05
❑ 135 Bennie Blades .01 .05
❑ 136 Lomas Brown .01 .05
❑ 137 Bill Fralic .01 .05
❑ 138 Mel Gray .02 .10
❑ 139 Willie Green .01 .05
❑ 140 Ryan McNeil RC .08 .25
❑ 141 Rodney Peete .01 .05
❑ 142 Barry Sanders .50 1.25
❑ 143 Chris Spielman .02 .10
❑ 144 Pat Swilling .01 .05
❑ 145 Andre Ware .01 .05
❑ 146 Herman Moore .08 .25
❑ 147 Tim McKyer .01 .05

Card		
❑ 148 Brett Perriman	.08	.25
❑ 149 Antonio London RC	.01	.05
❑ 150 Edgar Bennett	.08	.25
❑ 151 Terrell Buckley	.01	.05
❑ 152 Brett Favre	.75	2.00
❑ 153 Jackie Harris	.01	.05
❑ 154 Johnny Holland	.01	.05
❑ 155 Sterling Sharpe	.08	.25
❑ 156 Tim Hauck	.01	.05
❑ 157 George Teague RC	.02	.10
❑ 158 Reggie White	.08	.25
❑ 159 Mark Clayton	.01	.05
❑ 160 Ty Detmer	.08	.25
❑ 161 Wayne Simmons RC	.01	.05
❑ 162 Mark Brunell RC	.60	1.50
❑ 163 Tony Bennett	.01	.05
❑ 164 Brian Noble	.01	.05
❑ 165 Cody Carlson	.01	.05
❑ 166 Ray Childress	.01	.05
❑ 167 Cris Dishman	.01	.05
❑ 168 Curtis Duncan	.01	.05
❑ 169 Brad Hopkins RC	.01	.05
❑ 170 Haywood Jeffires	.02	.10
❑ 171 Wilber Marshall	.01	.05
❑ 172 Micheal Barrow UER RC	.08	.25
❑ 173 Bubba McDowell	.01	.05
❑ 174 Warren Moon	.08	.25
❑ 175 Webster Slaughter	.01	.05
❑ 176 Travis Hannah RC	.01	.05
❑ 177 Lorenzo White	.01	.05
❑ 178 Ernest Givins UER	.02	.10
❑ 179 Keith McCants	.01	.05
❑ 180 Kerry Cash	.01	.05
❑ 181 Quentin Coryatt	.02	.10
❑ 182 Kirk Lowdermilk	.01	.05
❑ 183 Rodney Culver	.01	.05
❑ 184 Rohn Stark	.01	.05
❑ 185 Steve Emtman	.01	.05
❑ 186 Jeff George	.08	.25
❑ 187 Jeff Herrod	.01	.05
❑ 188 Reggie Langhorne	.01	.05
❑ 189 Roosevelt Potts RC	.01	.05
❑ 190 Jack Trudeau	.01	.05
❑ 191 Will Wolford	.01	.05
❑ 192 Jessie Hester	.01	.05
❑ 193 Anthony Johnson	.02	.10
❑ 194 Ray Buchanan RC	.08	.25
❑ 195 Dale Carter	.01	.05
❑ 196 Willie Davis	.08	.25
❑ 197 John Alt	.01	.05
❑ 198 Joe Montana	.60	1.50
❑ 199 Will Shields RC	.08	.25
❑ 200 Neil Smith	.08	.25
❑ 201 Derrick Thomas	.08	.25
❑ 202 Harvey Williams	.02	.10
❑ 203 Marcus Allen	.08	.25
❑ 204 J.J. Birden	.01	.05
❑ 205 Tim Barnett	.01	.05
❑ 206 Albert Lewis	.01	.05
❑ 207 Nick Lowery	.01	.05
❑ 208 Dave Krieg	.02	.10
❑ 209 Keith Cash	.01	.05
❑ 210 Patrick Bates RC	.01	.05
❑ 211 Nick Bell	.01	.05
❑ 212 Tim Brown	.08	.25
❑ 213 Willie Gault	.01	.05
❑ 214 Ethan Horton	.01	.05
❑ 215 Jeff Hostetler	.02	.10
❑ 216 Howie Long	.08	.25
❑ 217 Greg Townsend	.01	.05
❑ 218 Rocket Ismail	.02	.10
❑ 219 Alexander Wright	.01	.05
❑ 220 Greg Robinson RC	.01	.05
❑ 221 Billy Joe Hobert RC	.08	.25
❑ 222 Steve Wisniewski	.01	.05
❑ 223 Steve Smith	.01	.05
❑ 224 Vince Evans	.01	.05
❑ 225 Flipper Anderson	.01	.05
❑ 226 Jerome Bettis RC	1.50	4.00
❑ 227 Troy Drayton RC	.02	.10
❑ 228 Henry Ellard	.02	.10
❑ 229 Jim Everett	.02	.10
❑ 230 Tony Zendejas	.01	.05
❑ 231 Todd Lyght	.01	.05
❑ 232 Todd Kinchen	.01	.05
❑ 233 Jackie Slater	.01	.05
❑ 234 Fred Stokes	.01	.05
❑ 235 Russell White RC	.02	.10
❑ 236 Cleveland Gary	.01	.05
❑ 237 Sean LaChapelle RC	.01	.05
❑ 238 Steve Israel	.01	.05
❑ 239 Shane Conlan	.01	.05
❑ 240 Keith Byars	.01	.05
❑ 241 Marco Coleman	.01	.05
❑ 242 Bryan Cox	.01	.05
❑ 243 Irving Fryar	.02	.10
❑ 244 Richmond Webb	.01	.05
❑ 245 Mark Higgs	.01	.05
❑ 246 Terry Kirby RC	.08	.25
❑ 247 Mark Ingram	.01	.05
❑ 248 John Offerdahl	.01	.05
❑ 249 Keith Jackson	.02	.10
❑ 250 Dan Marino	.60	1.50
❑ 251 O.J.McDuffie RC	.08	.25
❑ 252 Louis Oliver	.01	.05
❑ 253 Pete Stoyanovich	.01	.05
❑ 254 Troy Vincent	.01	.05
❑ 255 Anthony Carter	.02	.10
❑ 256 Cris Carter	.08	.25
❑ 257 Roger Craig	.02	.10
❑ 258 Jack Del Rio	.01	.05
❑ 259 Chris Doleman	.01	.05
❑ 260 Barry Word	.01	.05
❑ 261 Qadry Ismail RC	.08	.25
❑ 262 Jim McMahon	.02	.10
❑ 263 Robert Smith RC	.50	1.25
❑ 264 Fred Strickland	.01	.05
❑ 265 Randall McDaniel	.02	.10
❑ 266 Carl Lee	.01	.05
❑ 267 Olanda Truitt UER RC	.01	.05
❑ 268 Terry Allen	.08	.25
❑ 269 Audray McMillian	.01	.05
❑ 270 Drew Bledsoe RC	1.00	2.50
❑ 271 Eugene Chung	.01	.05
❑ 272 Marv Cook	.01	.05
❑ 273 Pat Harlow	.01	.05
❑ 274 Greg McMurtry	.01	.05
❑ 275 Leonard Russell	.02	.10
❑ 276 Chris Slade RC	.02	.10
❑ 277 Andre Tippett	.01	.05
❑ 278 Vincent Brisby RC	.08	.25
❑ 279 Ben Coates	.20	.50
❑ 280 Sam Gash RC	.08	.25
❑ 281 Bruce Armstrong	.01	.05
❑ 282 Rod Smith DB	.01	.05
❑ 283 Michael Timpson	.01	.05
❑ 284 Scott Sisson RC	.01	.05
❑ 285 Morten Andersen	.01	.05
❑ 286 Reggie Freeman RC	.01	.05
❑ 287 Dalton Hilliard	.01	.05
❑ 288 Rickey Jackson	.01	.05
❑ 289 Vaughan Johnson	.01	.05
❑ 290 Eric Martin	.01	.05
❑ 291 Sam Mills	.01	.05
❑ 292 Brad Muster	.01	.05
❑ 293 Willie Roaf RC	.02	.10
❑ 294 Irv Smith RC	.01	.05
❑ 295 Wade Wilson	.01	.05
❑ 296 Derek Brown RBK RC	.02	.10
❑ 297 Quinn Early	.02	.10
❑ 298 Steve Walsh	.01	.05
❑ 299 Renaldo Turnbull	.01	.05
❑ 300 Jessie Armstead RC	.02	.10
❑ 301 Carlton Bailey	.01	.05
❑ 302 Michael Brooks	.01	.05
❑ 303 Rodney Hampton	.02	.10
❑ 304 Ed McCaffrey	.08	.25
❑ 305 Dave Meggett	.01	.05
❑ 306 Bart Oates	.01	.05
❑ 307 Mike Sherrard	.01	.05
❑ 308 Phil Simms	.02	.10
❑ 309 Lawrence Taylor	.08	.25
❑ 310 Mark Jackson	.01	.05
❑ 311 Jarrod Bunch	.01	.05
❑ 312 Howard Cross	.01	.05
❑ 313 Michael Strahan RC	.60	1.50
❑ 314 Marcus Buckley RC	.01	.05
❑ 315 Brad Baxter	.01	.05
❑ 316 Adrian Murrell RC	.08	.25
❑ 317 Boomer Esiason	.02	.10
❑ 318 Johnny Johnson	.01	.05
❑ 319 Marvin Jones RC	.01	.05
❑ 320 Jeff Lageman	.01	.05
❑ 321 Ronnie Lott	.02	.10
❑ 322 Leonard Marshall	.01	.05
❑ 323 Johnny Mitchell	.01	.05
❑ 324 Rob Moore	.02	.10
❑ 325 Browning Nagle	.01	.05
❑ 326 Blair Thomas	.01	.05
❑ 327 Brian Washington	.01	.05
❑ 328 Terance Mathis	.02	.10
❑ 329 Kyle Clifton	.01	.05
❑ 330 Eric Allen	.01	.05
❑ 331 Victor Bailey RC	.01	.05
❑ 332 Fred Barnett	.02	.10
❑ 333 Mark Bavaro	.01	.05
❑ 334 Randall Cunningham	.08	.25
❑ 335 Ken O'Brien	.01	.05
❑ 336 Seth Joyner	.01	.05
❑ 337 Leonard Renfro RC	.01	.05
❑ 338 Heath Sherman	.01	.05
❑ 339 Clyde Simmons	.01	.05
❑ 340 Herschel Walker	.02	.10
❑ 341 Calvin Williams	.02	.10
❑ 342 Bubby Brister	.01	.05
❑ 343 Vaughn Hebron RC	.01	.05
❑ 344 Keith Millard	.01	.05
❑ 345 Johnny Bailey	.01	.05
❑ 346 Steve Beuerlein	.02	.10
❑ 347 Chuck Cecil	.01	.05
❑ 348 Larry Centers RC	.08	.25
❑ 349 Chris Chandler	.02	.10
❑ 350 Ernest Dye RC	.01	.05
❑ 351 Garrison Hearst RC	.30	.75
❑ 352 Randal Hill	.01	.05
❑ 353 John Booty	.01	.05
❑ 354 Gary Clark	.02	.10
❑ 355 Ronald Moore RC	.02	.10
❑ 356 Ricky Proehl	.01	.05
❑ 357 Eric Swann	.02	.10
❑ 358 Ken Harvey	.01	.05
❑ 359 Ben Coleman RC	.01	.05
❑ 360 Deon Figures RC	.01	.05
❑ 361 Barry Foster	.02	.10
❑ 362 Jeff Graham	.02	.10
❑ 363 Eric Green	.01	.05
❑ 364 Kevin Greene	.02	.10
❑ 365 Andre Hastings RC	.02	.10
❑ 366 Greg Lloyd	.02	.10
❑ 367 Neil O'Donnell	.08	.25
❑ 368 Dwight Stone	.01	.05
❑ 369 Mike Tomczak	.01	.05
❑ 370 Rod Woodson	.08	.25
❑ 371 Chad Brown RC LB	.02	.10
❑ 372 Ernie Mills	.01	.05
❑ 373 Darren Perry	.01	.05
❑ 374 Leon Searcy	.01	.05
❑ 375 Marion Butts	.01	.05
❑ 376 John Carney	.01	.05
❑ 377 Ronnie Harmon	.01	.05
❑ 378 Stan Humphries	.02	.10
❑ 379 Nate Lewis	.01	.05
❑ 380 Natrone Means RC	.08	.25
❑ 381 Anthony Miller	.02	.10
❑ 382 Chris Mims	.01	.05
❑ 383 Leslie O'Neal	.02	.10
❑ 384 Joe Cocozzo RC	.01	.05
❑ 385 Junior Seau	.08	.25
❑ 386 Jerrol Williams	.01	.05
❑ 387 John Friesz	.02	.10
❑ 388 Darrien Gordon RC	.01	.05
❑ 389 Derrick Walker	.01	.05
❑ 390 Dana Hall	.01	.05
❑ 391 Brent Jones	.02	.10
❑ 392 Todd Kelly RC	.01	.05
❑ 393 Amp Lee	.01	.05
❑ 394 Tim McDonald	.01	.05
❑ 395 Jerry Rice	.40	1.00
❑ 396 Dana Stubblefield RC	.08	.25
❑ 397 John Taylor	.02	.10
❑ 398 Ricky Watters	.08	.25
❑ 399 Steve Young	.30	.75
❑ 400 Steve Bono	.02	.10
❑ 401 Adrian Hardy	.01	.05
❑ 402 Tom Rathman	.01	.05
❑ 403 Elvis Grbac RC	.60	1.50
❑ 404 Bill Romanowski	.01	.05
❑ 405 Brian Blades	.02	.10
❑ 406 Ferrell Edmunds	.01	.05
❑ 407 Carlton Gray RC	.01	.05
❑ 408 Cortez Kennedy	.02	.10
❑ 409 Kelvin Martin	.01	.05
❑ 410 Dan McGwire	.01	.05
❑ 411 Rick Mirer RC	.08	.25
❑ 412 Rufus Porter	.01	.05
❑ 413 Chris Warren	.02	.10
❑ 414 Jon Vaughn	.01	.05

❑ 415 John L. Williams	.01	.05
❑ 416 Eugene Robinson	.01	.05
❑ 417 Michael McCrary RC	.02	.10
❑ 418 Michael Bates RC	.01	.05
❑ 419 Stan Gelbaugh	.01	.05
❑ 420 Reggie Cobb	.01	.05
❑ 421 Eric Curry RC	.01	.05
❑ 422 Lawrence Dawsey	.01	.05
❑ 423 Santana Dotson	.02	.10
❑ 424 Craig Erickson	.02	.10
❑ 425 Ron Hall	.01	.05
❑ 426 Courtney Hawkins	.01	.05
❑ 427 Broderick Thomas	.01	.05
❑ 428 Vince Workman	.01	.05
❑ 429 Demetrius DuBose RC	.01	.05
❑ 430 Lamar Thomas RC	.01	.05
❑ 431 John Lynch RC	.25	.60
❑ 432 Hardy Nickerson	.02	.10
❑ 433 Horace Copeland RC	.02	.10
❑ 434 Steve DeBerg	.01	.05
❑ 435 Joe Jacoby	.01	.05
❑ 436 Tom Carter RC	.02	.10
❑ 437 Andre Collins	.01	.05
❑ 438 Darrell Green	.01	.05
❑ 439 Desmond Howard	.02	.10
❑ 440 Chip Lohmiller	.01	.05
❑ 441 Charles Mann	.01	.05
❑ 442 Tim McGee	.01	.05
❑ 443 Art Monk	.02	.10
❑ 444 Mark Rypien	.01	.05
❑ 445 Ricky Sanders	.01	.05
❑ 446 Brian Mitchell	.02	.10
❑ 447 Reggie Brooks RC	.02	.10
❑ 448 Carl Banks	.01	.05
❑ 449 Cary Conklin	.01	.05
❑ NNO Santa Claus	.60	1.50

1989 Score

❑ COMPLETE SET (330)	40.00	80.00
❑ COMP.FACT.SET (330)	40.00	80.00
❑ 1 Joe Montana	1.50	4.00
❑ 2 Bo Jackson	.25	.60
❑ 3 Boomer Esiason	.07	.20
❑ 4 Roger Craig	.20	.50
❑ 5 Ed Too Tall Jones	.07	.20
❑ 6 Phil Simms	.07	.20
❑ 7 Dan Hampton	.07	.20
❑ 8 John Settle RC	.02	.10
❑ 9 Bernie Kosar	.07	.20
❑ 10 Al Toon	.07	.20
❑ 11 Bubby Brister RC	.40	1.00
❑ 12 Mark Clayton	.07	.20
❑ 13 Dan Marino	1.50	4.00
❑ 14 Joe Morris	.02	.10
❑ 15 Warren Moon	.20	.50
❑ 16 Chuck Long	.02	.10
❑ 17 Mark Jackson	.02	.10
❑ 18 Michael Irvin RC	4.00	10.00
❑ 19 Bruce Smith	.20	.50
❑ 20 Anthony Carter	.07	.20
❑ 21 Charles Haley	.20	.50
❑ 22 Dave Duerson	.02	.10
❑ 23 Troy Stradford	.02	.10
❑ 24 Freeman McNeil	.02	.10
❑ 25 Jerry Gray	.02	.10
❑ 26 Bill Maas	.02	.10
❑ 27 Chris Chandler RC	1.25	3.00
❑ 28 Tom Newberry RC	.02	.10
❑ 29 Albert Lewis	.02	.10
❑ 30 Jay Schroeder	.02	.10
❑ 31 Dalton Hilliard	.02	.10
❑ 32 Tony Eason	.02	.10
❑ 33 Rick Donnelly UER	.02	.10
❑ 34 Herschel Walker	.07	.20
❑ 35 Wesley Walker	.02	.10
❑ 36 Chris Doleman	.07	.20

❑ 37 Pat Swilling	.07	.20
❑ 38 Joey Browner	.02	.10
❑ 39 Shane Conlan	.02	.10
❑ 40 Mike Tomczak	.07	.20
❑ 41 Webster Slaughter	.07	.20
❑ 42 Ray Donaldson	.02	.10
❑ 43 Christian Okoye	.02	.10
❑ 44 John Bosa	.02	.10
❑ 45 Aaron Cox RC	.02	.10
❑ 46 Bobby Hebert	.07	.20
❑ 47 Carl Banks	.02	.10
❑ 48 Jeff Fuller	.02	.10
❑ 49 Gerald Willhite	.02	.10
❑ 50 Mike Singletary	.07	.20
❑ 51 Stanley Morgan	.02	.10
❑ 52 Mark Bavaro	.07	.20
❑ 53 Mickey Shuler	.02	.10
❑ 54 Keith Millard	.02	.10
❑ 55 Andre Tippett	.02	.10
❑ 56 Vance Johnson	.07	.20
❑ 57 Bennie Blades RC	.07	.20
❑ 58 Tim Harris	.02	.10
❑ 59 Hanford Dixon	.02	.10
❑ 60 Chris Miller RC	.40	1.00
❑ 61 Cornelius Bennett	.20	.50
❑ 62 Neal Anderson	.07	.20
❑ 63 Ickey Woods UER RC	.20	.50
❑ 64 Gary Anderson RB	.02	.10
❑ 65 Vaughan Johnson RC	.02	.10
❑ 66 Ronnie Lippett	.02	.10
❑ 67 Mike Quick	.02	.10
❑ 68 Roy Green	.07	.20
❑ 69 Tim Krumrie	.02	.10
❑ 70 Mark Malone	.02	.10
❑ 71 James Jones FB	.02	.10
❑ 72 Cris Carter RC	4.00	10.00
❑ 73 Ricky Nattiel	.02	.10
❑ 74 Jim Arnold UER	.02	.10
❑ 75 Randall Cunningham	.40	1.00
❑ 76 John L.Williams	.02	.10
❑ 77 Paul Gruber RC	.02	.10
❑ 78 Rod Woodson RC	2.00	5.00
❑ 79 Ray Childress	.02	.10
❑ 80 Doug Williams	.07	.20
❑ 81 Deron Cherry	.07	.20
❑ 82 John Offerdahl	.02	.10
❑ 83 Louis Lipps	.07	.20
❑ 84 Neil Lomax	.02	.10
❑ 85 Wade Wilson	.07	.20
❑ 86 Tim Brown RC	4.00	10.00
❑ 87 Chris Hinton	.02	.10
❑ 88 Stump Mitchell	.02	.10
❑ 89 Tunch Ilkin RC	.02	.10
❑ 90 Steve Pelluer	.02	.10
❑ 91 Brian Noble	.02	.10
❑ 92 Reggie White	.20	.50
❑ 93 Aundray Bruce RC	.02	.10
❑ 94 Garry James	.02	.10
❑ 95 Drew Hill	.02	.10
❑ 96 Anthony Munoz	.07	.20
❑ 97 James Wilder	.02	.10
❑ 98 Dexter Manley	.02	.10
❑ 99 Lee Williams	.02	.10
❑ 100 Dave Krieg	.07	.20
❑ 101A Keith Jackson ERR RC	.20	.50
❑ 101B Keith Jackson COR RC	.20	.50
❑ 102 Luis Sharpe	.02	.10
❑ 103 Kevin Greene	.20	.50
❑ 104 Duane Bickett	.02	.10
❑ 105 Mark Rypien RC	.20	.50
❑ 106 Curt Warner	.02	.10
❑ 107 Jacob Green	.02	.10
❑ 108 Gary Clark	.20	.50
❑ 109 Bruce Matthews RC	1.25	3.00
❑ 110 Bill Fralic	.02	.10
❑ 111 Bill Bates	.07	.20
❑ 112 Jeff Bryant	.02	.10
❑ 113 Charles Mann	.02	.10
❑ 114 Richard Dent	.07	.20
❑ 115 Bruce Hill RC	.02	.10
❑ 116 Mark May RC	.02	.10
❑ 117 Mark Collins RC	.02	.10
❑ 118 Ron Holmes	.02	.10
❑ 119 Scott Case RC	.02	.10
❑ 120 Tom Rathman	.02	.10
❑ 121 Dennis McKinnon	.02	.10
❑ 122A Ricky Sanders ERR 46	.08	.25
❑ 122B Ricky Sanders COR 83	.20	.50
❑ 123 Michael Carter	.02	.10

❑ 124 Ozzie Newsome	.07	.20
❑ 125 Irving Fryar UER	.07	.20
❑ 126A Ron Hall ERR RC	.08	.25
❑ 126B Ron Hall COR RC	.20	.50
❑ 127 Clay Matthews	.07	.20
❑ 128 Leonard Marshall	.02	.10
❑ 129 Kevin Mack	.02	.10
❑ 130 Art Monk	.07	.20
❑ 131 Garin Veris	.02	.10
❑ 132 Steve Jordan	.02	.10
❑ 133 Frank Minnifield	.02	.10
❑ 134 Eddie Brown	.02	.10
❑ 135 Stacey Bailey	.02	.10
❑ 136 Rickey Jackson	.07	.20
❑ 137 Henry Ellard	.07	.20
❑ 138 Jim Burt	.02	.10
❑ 139 Jerome Brown	.07	.20
❑ 140 Rodney Holman RC	.02	.10
❑ 141 Sammy Winder	.02	.10
❑ 142 Marcus Cotton	.02	.10
❑ 143 Jim Jeffcoat	.02	.10
❑ 144 Rueben Mayes	.02	.10
❑ 145 Jim McMahon	.07	.20
❑ 146 Reggie Williams	.02	.10
❑ 147 John Anderson	.02	.10
❑ 148 Harris Barton RC	.02	.10
❑ 149 Phillip Epps	.02	.10
❑ 150 Jay Hilgenberg	.02	.10
❑ 151 Earl Ferrell	.02	.10
❑ 152 Andre Reed	.20	.50
❑ 153 Dennis Gentry	.02	.10
❑ 154 Max Montoya	.02	.10
❑ 155 Darrin Nelson	.02	.10
❑ 156 Jeff Chadwick	.02	.10
❑ 157 James Brooks	.07	.20
❑ 158 Keith Bishop	.02	.10
❑ 159 Robert Awalt	.02	.10
❑ 160 Marty Lyons	.02	.10
❑ 161 Johnny Hector	.02	.10
❑ 162 Tony Casillas	.02	.10
❑ 163 Kyle Clifton RC	.02	.10
❑ 164 Cody Risien	.02	.10
❑ 165 Jamie Holland RC	.02	.10
❑ 166 Merril Hoge RC	.02	.10
❑ 167 Chris Spielman RC	.40	1.00
❑ 168 Carlos Carson	.02	.10
❑ 169 Jerry Ball RC	.02	.10
❑ 170 Don Majkowski RC	.20	.50
❑ 171 Everson Walls	.02	.10
❑ 172 Mike Rozier	.02	.10
❑ 173 Matt Millen	.07	.20
❑ 174 Karl Mecklenburg	.02	.10
❑ 175 Paul Palmer	.02	.10
❑ 176 Brian Blades UER RC	.20	.50
❑ 177 Brent Fullwood RC	.02	.10
❑ 178 Anthony Miller RC	.20	.50
❑ 179 Brian Sochia	.02	.10
❑ 180 Stephen Baker RC	.02	.10
❑ 181 Jesse Solomon	.02	.10
❑ 182 John Grimsley	.02	.10
❑ 183 Timmy Newsome	.02	.10
❑ 184 Steve Sewell RC	.02	.10
❑ 185 Dean Biasucci	.02	.10
❑ 186 Alonzo Highsmith	.02	.10
❑ 187 Randy Grimes	.02	.10
❑ 188A Mark Carrier ERR RC	.40	1.00
❑ 188B Mark Carrier COR RC	.40	1.00
❑ 189 Vann McElroy	.02	.10
❑ 190 Greg Bell	.02	.10
❑ 191 Quinn Early RC	.40	1.00
❑ 192 Lawrence Taylor	.20	.50
❑ 193 Albert Bentley	.02	.10
❑ 194 Ernest Givins	.07	.20
❑ 195 Jackie Slater	.02	.10
❑ 196 Jim Sweeney	.02	.10
❑ 197 Freddie Joe Nunn	.02	.10
❑ 198 Keith Byars	.07	.20
❑ 199 Hardy Nickerson RC	.20	.50
❑ 200 Steve Beuerlein RC	1.25	3.00
❑ 201 Bruce Armstrong RC	.20	.50
❑ 202 Lionel Manuel	.02	.10
❑ 203 J.T. Smith	.02	.10
❑ 204 Mark Ingram RC	.20	.50
❑ 205 Fred Smerlas	.02	.10
❑ 206 Bryan Hinkle RC	.02	.10
❑ 207 Steve McMichael	.07	.20
❑ 208 Nick Lowery	.02	.10
❑ 209 Jack Trudeau	.02	.10
❑ 210 Lorenzo Hampton	.02	.10

❑ 211 Thurman Thomas RC 3.00 8.00
❑ 212 Steve Young .60 1.50
❑ 213 James Lofton .20 .50
❑ 214 Jim Covert .02 .10
❑ 215 Ronnie Lott .07 .20
❑ 216 Stephone Paige .02 .10
❑ 217 Mark Duper .07 .20
❑ 218A Willie Gault ERR 93 .08 .25
❑ 218B Willie Gault COR 83 .20 .50
❑ 219 Ken Ruettgers RC .02 .10
❑ 220 Kevin Ross RC .02 .10
❑ 221 Jerry Rice 1.50 3.00
❑ 222 Billy Ray Smith .02 .10
❑ 223 Jim Kelly .40 1.00
❑ 224 Vinny Testaverde .40 1.00
❑ 225 Steve Largent .20 .50
❑ 226 Warren Williams RC .02 .10
❑ 227 Morten Andersen .02 .10
❑ 228 Bill Brooks .07 .20
❑ 229 Reggie Langhorne RC .02 .10
❑ 230 Pepper Johnson .02 .10
❑ 231 Pat Leahy .02 .10
❑ 232 Fred Marion .02 .10
❑ 233 Gary Zimmerman .07 .20
❑ 234 Marcus Allen .20 .50
❑ 235 Gaston Green RC .02 .10
❑ 236 John Stephens RC .02 .10
❑ 237 Terry Kinard .02 .10
❑ 238 John Taylor RC .40 1.00
❑ 239 Brian Bosworth .07 .20
❑ 240 Anthony Toney .02 .10
❑ 241 Ken O'Brien .02 .10
❑ 242 Howie Long .20 .50
❑ 243 Doug Flutie 1.00 2.50
❑ 244 Jim Everett .20 .50
❑ 245 Broderick Thomas RC .02 .10
❑ 246 Deion Sanders RC 4.00 10.00
❑ 247 Donnell Woolford RC .02 .10
❑ 248 Wayne Martin RC .02 .10
❑ 249 David Williams RC .02 .10
❑ 250 Bill Hawkins RC .02 .10
❑ 251 Eric Hill RC .02 .10
❑ 252 Burt Grossman RC .02 .10
❑ 253 Tracy Rocker .02 .10
❑ 254 Steve Wisniewski RC .20 .50
❑ 255 Jessie Small RC .02 .10
❑ 256 David Braxton .02 .10
❑ 257 Barry Sanders RC 15.00 30.00
❑ 258 Derrick Thomas RC 3.00 8.00
❑ 259 Eric Metcalf RC .40 1.00
❑ 260 Keith DeLong RC .02 .10
❑ 261 Hart Lee Dykes RC .02 .10
❑ 262 Sammie Smith RC .02 .10
❑ 263 Steve Atwater RC .20 .50
❑ 264 Eric Ball RC .02 .10
❑ 265 Don Beebe RC .20 .50
❑ 266 Brian Williams OL RC .02 .10
❑ 267 Jeff Lageman RC .02 .10
❑ 268 Tim Worley RC .02 .10
❑ 269 Tony Mandarich RC .02 .10
❑ 270 Troy Aikman RC 12.50 30.00
❑ 271 Andy Heck RC .02 .10
❑ 272 Andre Rison RC 2.50 5.00
❑ 273 AFC Champ/Woods/Esiason .02 .10
❑ 274 NFC Champ/Joe Montana .40 1.00
❑ 275 Joe Montana/Jerry Rice .75 2.00
❑ 276 Rodney Carter .02 .10
❑ 277 Mark Jackson/V.Johnson/Nattiel .02 .10
❑ 278 John L. Williams .02 .10
❑ 279 Joe Montana/Jerry Rice .75 2.00
❑ 280 Roy Green/Lomax .02 .10
❑ 281 Ran.Cunningham/K.Jackson .02 .10
❑ 282 Chris Doleman and .02 .10
❑ 283 Mark Duper and .02 .10
❑ 284 Bo Jackson/Marcus Allen .25 .60
❑ 285 Frank Minnifield AP .02 .10
❑ 286 Bruce Matthews AP .15 .40
❑ 287 Joey Browner AP .02 .10
❑ 288 Jay Hilgenberg AP .02 .10
❑ 289 Carl Lee AP RC .02 .10
❑ 290 Scott Norwood RC .02 .10
❑ 291 John Taylor AP .20 .50
❑ 292 Jerry Rice AP .60 1.50
❑ 293A Keith Jackson AP 84 .20 .50
❑ 293B Keith Jackson AP 88 .20 .50
❑ 294 Gary Zimmerman AP .07 .20
❑ 295 Lawrence Taylor AP .20 .50
❑ 296 Reggie White AP .20 .50
❑ 297 Roger Craig AP .07 .20
❑ 298 Boomer Esiason AP .07 .20
❑ 299 Cornelius Bennett AP .07 .20
❑ 300 Mike Horan AP .02 .10
❑ 301 Deron Cherry AP .02 .10
❑ 302 Tom Newberry AP .02 .10
❑ 303 Mike Singletary AP .07 .20
❑ 304 Shane Conlan AP .02 .10
❑ 305A Tim Brown AP ERR 80 .75 2.00
❑ 305B Tim Brown AP COR 81 .75 2.00
❑ 306 Henry Ellard AP .07 .20
❑ 307 Bruce Smith AP .07 .20
❑ 308 Tim Krumrie AP .02 .10
❑ 309 Anthony Munoz AP .07 .20
❑ 310 Darrell Green SPD .02 .10
❑ 311 Anthony Miller SPD .20 .50
❑ 312 Wesley Walker SPEED .02 .10
❑ 313 Ron Brown SPEED .02 .10
❑ 314 Bo Jackson SPD .25 .60
❑ 315 Phillip Epps SPEED .02 .10
❑ 316A Eric Thomas RC .08 .25
❑ 316B Eric Thomas RC .20 .50
❑ 317 Herschel Walker SPD .07 .20
❑ 318 Jacob Green PRED .02 .10
❑ 319 Andre Tippett PRED .02 .10
❑ 320 Freddie Joe Nunn PRED .02 .10
❑ 321 Reggie White PRED .20 .50
❑ 322 Lawrence Taylor PRED .20 .50
❑ 323 Greg Townsend PRED .02 .10
❑ 324 Tim Harris PRED .02 .10
❑ 325 Bruce Smith PRED .07 .20
❑ 326 Tony Dorsett RB .20 .50
❑ 327 Steve Largent RB .20 .50
❑ 328 Tim Brown RB .75 2.00
❑ 329 Joe Montana RB .60 1.50
❑ 330 Tom Landry Tribute .40 1.00

1990 Score

❑ COMPLETE SET (660) 6.00 15.00
❑ COMP.FACT.SET (665) 7.50 20.00
❑ 1 Joe Montana .50 1.25
❑ 2 Christian Okoye .01 .04
❑ 3 Mike Singletary UER .02 .10
❑ 4 Jim Everett UER .02 .10
❑ 5 Phil Simms .02 .10
❑ 6 Brent Fullwood .01 .04
❑ 7 Bill Fralic .01 .04
❑ 8 Leslie O'Neal .02 .10
❑ 9 John Taylor .08 .25
❑ 10 Bo Jackson .10 .30
❑ 11 John Stephens .01 .04
❑ 12 Art Monk .02 .10
❑ 13 Dan Marino .50 1.25
❑ 14 John Settle .01 .04
❑ 15 Don Majkowski .01 .04
❑ 16 Bruce Smith .08 .25
❑ 17 Brad Muster .01 .04
❑ 18 Jason Buck .01 .04
❑ 19 James Brooks .02 .10
❑ 20 Barry Sanders .50 1.25
❑ 21 Troy Aikman .30 .75
❑ 22 Allen Pinkett .01 .04
❑ 23 Duane Bickett .01 .04
❑ 24 Kevin Ross .01 .04
❑ 25 John Elway .50 1.25
❑ 26 Jeff Query .01 .04
❑ 27 Eddie Murray .01 .04
❑ 28 Richard Dent .02 .10
❑ 29 Lorenzo White .01 .04
❑ 30 Eric Metcalf .08 .25
❑ 31 Jeff Dellenbach RC .01 .04
❑ 32 Leon White .01 .04
❑ 33 Jim Jeffcoat .01 .04
❑ 34 Herschel Walker .02 .10
❑ 35 Mike Johnson UER .01 .04
❑ 36 Joe Phillips .01 .04
❑ 37 Willie Gault .02 .10
❑ 38 Keith Millard .01 .04
❑ 39 Fred Marion .01 .04
❑ 40 Boomer Esiason .02 .10
❑ 41 Dermontti Dawson .02 .10
❑ 42 Dino Hackett .01 .04
❑ 43 Reggie Roby .01 .04
❑ 44 Roger Vick .01 .04
❑ 45 Bobby Hebert .01 .04
❑ 46 Don Beebe .02 .10
❑ 47 Neal Anderson .02 .10
❑ 48 Johnny Holland .01 .04
❑ 49 Bobby Humphery .01 .04
❑ 50 Lawrence Taylor .08 .25
❑ 51 Billy Ray Smith .01 .04
❑ 52 Robert Perryman .01 .04
❑ 53 Gary Anderson K .01 .04
❑ 54 Raul Allegre .01 .04
❑ 55 Pat Swilling .02 .10
❑ 56 Chris Doleman .01 .04
❑ 57 Andre Reed .08 .25
❑ 58 Seth Joyner .02 .10
❑ 59 Bart Oates .01 .04
❑ 60 Bernie Kosar .02 .10
❑ 61 Dave Krieg .02 .10
❑ 62 Lars Tate .01 .04
❑ 63 Scott Norwood .01 .04
❑ 64 Kyle Clifton .01 .04
❑ 65 Alan Veingrad .01 .04
❑ 66 Gerald Riggs UER .02 .10
❑ 67 Tim Worley .01 .04
❑ 68 Rodney Holman .01 .04
❑ 69 Tony Zendejas .01 .04
❑ 70 Chris Miller .08 .25
❑ 71 Wilber Marshall .01 .04
❑ 72 Skip McClendon RC .01 .04
❑ 73 Jim Covert .01 .04
❑ 74 Sam Mills .02 .10
❑ 75 Chris Hinton .01 .04
❑ 76 Irv Eatman .01 .04
❑ 77 Bubba Paris UER .01 .04
❑ 78 John Elliott UER .01 .04
❑ 79 Thomas Everett .01 .04
❑ 80 Steve Smith .01 .04
❑ 81 Jackie Slater .01 .04
❑ 82 Kelvin Martin RC .01 .04
❑ 83 Jo Jo Townsell .01 .04
❑ 84 Jim C. Jensen .01 .04
❑ 85 Bobby Humphrey .01 .04
❑ 86 Mike Dyal .01 .04
❑ 87 Andre Rison UER .08 .25
❑ 88 Brian Sochia .01 .04
❑ 89 Greg Bell .01 .04
❑ 90 Dalton Hilliard .01 .04
❑ 91 Carl Banks .01 .04
❑ 92 Dennis Smith .01 .04
❑ 93 Bruce Matthews .02 .10
❑ 94 Charles Haley .02 .10
❑ 95 Deion Sanders .20 .50
❑ 96 Stephone Paige .01 .04
❑ 97 Marion Butts FSC .02 .10
❑ 98 Howie Long .08 .25
❑ 99 Donald Igwebuike .01 .04
❑ 100 Roger Craig UER .02 .10
❑ 101 Charles Mann .01 .04
❑ 102 Fredd Young .01 .04
❑ 103 Chris Jacke .01 .04
❑ 104 Scott Case .01 .04
❑ 105 Warren Moon .08 .25
❑ 106 Clyde Simmons .01 .04
❑ 107 Steve Atwater .01 .04
❑ 108 Morten Andersen .01 .04
❑ 109 Eugene Marve .01 .04
❑ 110 Thurman Thomas .08 .25
❑ 111 Carnell Lake .01 .04
❑ 112 Jim Kelly .08 .25
❑ 113 Stanford Jennings .01 .04
❑ 114 Jacob Green .01 .04
❑ 115 Karl Mecklenburg .01 .04
❑ 116 Ray Childress .01 .04
❑ 117 Erik McMillan .01 .04
❑ 118 Harry Newsome .01 .04
❑ 119 James Dixon .01 .04
❑ 120 Hassan Jones .01 .04
❑ 121 Eric Allen .01 .04
❑ 122 Felix Wright .01 .04
❑ 123 Merril Hoge .01 .04
❑ 124 Eric Ball .01 .04
❑ 125 Flipper Anderson FSC .01 .04
❑ 126 James Jefferson .01 .04

❑ 127 Tim McDonald .01 .04
❑ 128 Larry Kinnebrew .01 .04
❑ 129 Mark Collins .01 .04
❑ 130 Ickey Woods .01 .04
❑ 131 Jeff Donaldson UER .01 .04
❑ 132 Rich Camarillo .01 .04
❑ 133 Melvin Bratton RC .01 .04
❑ 134A Kevin Butler .12 .35
❑ 134B Kevin Butler .20 .50
❑ 135 Albert Bentley .01 .04
❑ 136A Vai Sikahema .12 .35
❑ 136B Vai Sikahema .20 .50
❑ 137 Todd McNair RC .01 .04
❑ 138 Alonzo Highsmith .01 .04
❑ 139 Brian Blades .02 .10
❑ 140 Jeff Lageman .01 .04
❑ 141 Eric Thomas .01 .04
❑ 142 Derek Hill .01 .04
❑ 143 Rick Fenney .01 .04
❑ 144 Herman Heard .01 .04
❑ 145 Steve Young .20 .50
❑ 146 Kent Hull .01 .04
❑ 147A Joey Browner face left .12 .35
❑ 147B Joey Browner straight .20 .50
❑ 148 Frank Minnifield .01 .04
❑ 149 Robert Massey .01 .04
❑ 150 Dave Meggett .02 .10
❑ 151 Bubba McDowell .01 .04
❑ 152 Rickey Dixon RC .01 .04
❑ 153 Ray Donaldson .01 .04
❑ 154 Alvin Walton .01 .04
❑ 155 Mike Cofer .01 .04
❑ 156 Darryl Talley .01 .04
❑ 157 A.J. Johnson .01 .04
❑ 158 Jerry Gray .01 .04
❑ 159 Keith Byars .01 .04
❑ 160 Andy Heck .01 .04
❑ 161 Mike Munchak .02 .10
❑ 162 Dennis Gentry .01 .04
❑ 163 Timm Rosenbach UER .01 .04
❑ 164 Randall McDaniel .05 .15
❑ 165 Pat Leahy .01 .04
❑ 166 Bubby Brister .01 .04
❑ 167 Aundray Bruce .01 .04
❑ 168 Bill Brooks .01 .04
❑ 169 Eddie Anderson RC .01 .04
❑ 170 Ronnie Lott .02 .10
❑ 171 Jay Hilgenberg .01 .04
❑ 172 Joe Nash .01 .04
❑ 173 Simon Fletcher .01 .04
❑ 174 Shane Conlan .01 .04
❑ 175 Sean Landeta .01 .04
❑ 176 John Alt RC .01 .04
❑ 177 Clay Matthews .02 .10
❑ 178 Anthony Munoz .02 .10
❑ 179 Pete Holohan .01 .04
❑ 180 Robert Awalt .01 .04
❑ 181 Rohn Stark .01 .04
❑ 182 Vance Johnson .01 .04
❑ 183 David Fulcher .01 .04
❑ 184 Robert Delpino FSC .01 .04
❑ 185 Drew Hill .01 .04
❑ 186 Reggie Langhorne UER .01 .04
❑ 187 Lonzell Hill .01 .04
❑ 188 Tom Rathman UER .01 .04
❑ 189 Greg Montgomery RC .01 .04
❑ 190 Leonard Smith .01 .04
❑ 191 Chris Spielman .08 .25
❑ 192 Tom Newberry .01 .04
❑ 193 Cris Carter .20 .50
❑ 194 Kevin Porter RC .01 .04
❑ 195 Donnell Thompson .01 .04
❑ 196 Vaughan Johnson .01 .04
❑ 197 Steve McMichael .02 .10
❑ 198 Jim Sweeney .01 .04
❑ 199 Rich Karlis UER .01 .04
❑ 200 Jerry Rice .30 .75
❑ 201 Dan Hampton UER .02 .10
❑ 202 Jim Lachey .01 .04
❑ 203 Reggie White .08 .25
❑ 204 Jerry Ball .01 .04
❑ 205 Russ Grimm .01 .04
❑ 206 Tim Green RC .01 .04
❑ 207 Shawn Collins .01 .04
❑ 208A R.Mojsiejenko Chargers .05 .15
❑ 208B R.Mojsiejenko Redskins .20 .50
❑ 209 Trace Armstrong .01 .04
❑ 210 Keith Jackson .02 .10
❑ 211 Jamie Holland .01 .04
❑ 212 Mark Clayton .02 .10
❑ 213 Jeff Cross .01 .04
❑ 214 Bob Gagliano .01 .04
❑ 215 Louis Oliver UER .01 .04
❑ 216 Jim Arnold .01 .04
❑ 217 Robert Clark RC .01 .04
❑ 218 Gill Byrd .01 .04
❑ 219 Rodney Peete .02 .10
❑ 220 Anthony Miller .08 .25
❑ 221 Steve Grogan .02 .10
❑ 222 Vince Newsome RC .01 .04
❑ 223 Thomas Benson .01 .04
❑ 224 Kevin Murphy .01 .04
❑ 225 Henry Ellard .02 .10
❑ 226 Richard Johnson .01 .04
❑ 227 Jim Skow .01 .04
❑ 228 Keith Jones .01 .04
❑ 229 Dave Brown DB .01 .04
❑ 230 Marcus Allen .08 .25
❑ 231 Steve Walsh .02 .10
❑ 232 Jim Harbaugh .08 .25
❑ 233 Mel Gray .02 .10
❑ 234 David Treadwell .01 .04
❑ 235 John Offerdahl .01 .04
❑ 236 Gary Reasons .01 .04
❑ 237 Tim Krumrie .01 .04
❑ 238 Dave Duerson .01 .04
❑ 239 Gary Clark UER .08 .25
❑ 240 Mark Jackson .01 .04
❑ 241 Mark Murphy .01 .04
❑ 242 Jerry Holmes .01 .04
❑ 243 Tim McGee .01 .04
❑ 244 Mike Tomczak .02 .10
❑ 245 Sterling Sharpe UER .08 .25
❑ 246 Bennie Blades .01 .04
❑ 247 Ken Harvey UER RC .08 .25
❑ 248 Ron Heller .01 .04
❑ 249 Louis Lipps .02 .10
❑ 250 Wade Wilson .02 .10
❑ 251 Freddie Joe Nunn .01 .04
❑ 252 Jerome Brown UER .01 .04
❑ 253 Myron Guyton .01 .04
❑ 254 Nate Odomes RC .02 .10
❑ 255 Rod Woodson .08 .25
❑ 256 Cornelius Bennett .02 .10
❑ 257 Keith Woodside .01 .04
❑ 258 Jeff Uhlenhake UER .01 .04
❑ 259 Harry Hamilton .01 .04
❑ 260 Mark Bavaro .01 .04
❑ 261 Vinny Testaverde .02 .10
❑ 262 Steve DeBerg .01 .04
❑ 263 Steve Wisniewski UER .02 .10
❑ 264 Pete Mandley .01 .04
❑ 265 Tim Harris .01 .04
❑ 266 Jack Trudeau .01 .04
❑ 267 Mark Kelso .01 .04
❑ 268 Brian Noble .01 .04
❑ 269 Jessie Tuggle RC .01 .04
❑ 270 Ken O'Brien .01 .04
❑ 271 David Little .01 .04
❑ 272 Pete Stoyanovich .01 .04
❑ 273 Odessa Turner RC .01 .04
❑ 274 Anthony Toney .01 .04
❑ 275 Tunch Ilkin .01 .04
❑ 276 Carl Lee .01 .04
❑ 277 Hart Lee Dykes .01 .04
❑ 278 Al Noga .01 .04
❑ 279 Greg Lloyd .08 .25
❑ 280 Billy Joe Tolliver .01 .04
❑ 281 Kirk Lowdermilk .01 .04
❑ 282 Earl Ferrell .01 .04
❑ 283 Eric Sievers RC .01 .04
❑ 284 Steve Jordan .01 .04
❑ 285 Burt Grossman .01 .04
❑ 286 Johnny Rembert .01 .04
❑ 287 Jeff Jaeger RC .01 .04
❑ 288 James Hasty .01 .04
❑ 289 Tony Mandarich DP .01 .04
❑ 290 Chris Singleton RC .01 .04
❑ 291 Lynn James RC .01 .04
❑ 292 Andre Ware RC .08 .25
❑ 293 Ray Agnew RC .01 .04
❑ 294 Joel Smeenge RC .01 .04
❑ 295 Marc Spindler RC .01 .04
❑ 296 Renaldo Turnbull RC .01 .04
❑ 297 Reggie Rembert RC .01 .04
❑ 298 Jeff Alm RC .01 .04
❑ 299 Cortez Kennedy RC .08 .25
❑ 300 Blair Thomas RC .02 .10
❑ 301 Pat Terrell RC .01 .04
❑ 302 Junior Seau RC .50 1.25
❑ 303 Mo Elewonibi RC .01 .04
❑ 304 Tony Bennett RC .08 .25
❑ 305 Percy Snow RC .01 .04
❑ 306 Richmond Webb RC .01 .04
❑ 307 Rodney Hampton RC .08 .25
❑ 308 Barry Foster RC .08 .25
❑ 309 John Friesz RC .08 .25
❑ 310 Ben Smith RC .01 .04
❑ 311 Joe Montana HG .20 .50
❑ 312 Jim Everett HG .02 .10
❑ 313 Mark Rypien HG .02 .10
❑ 314 Phil Simms HG UER .02 .10
❑ 315 Don Majkowski HG .01 .04
❑ 316 Boomer Esiason HG .01 .04
❑ 317 Warren Moon HG Moon .08 .25
❑ 318 Jim Kelly HG .08 .25
❑ 319 Bernie Kosar HG UER .02 .10
❑ 320 Dan Marino HG UER .20 .50
❑ 321 Christian Okoye GF .01 .04
❑ 322 Thurman Thomas GF .08 .25
❑ 323 James Brooks GF .02 .10
❑ 324 Bobby Humphrey GF .01 .04
❑ 325 Barry Sanders GF .25 .60
❑ 326 Neal Anderson GF .01 .04
❑ 327 Dalton Hilliard GF .01 .04
❑ 328 Greg Bell GF .01 .04
❑ 329 Roger Craig GF UER .02 .10
❑ 330 Bo Jackson GF .10 .30
❑ 331 Don Warren .01 .04
❑ 332 Rufus Porter .01 .04
❑ 333 Sammie Smith .01 .04
❑ 334 Lewis Tillman .01 .04
❑ 335 Michael Walter .01 .04
❑ 336 Marc Logan .01 .04
❑ 337 Ron Hallstrom RC .01 .04
❑ 338 Stanley Morgan .01 .04
❑ 339 Mark Robinson .01 .04
❑ 340 Frank Reich .08 .25
❑ 341 Chip Lohmiller FSC .01 .04
❑ 342 Steve Beuerlein .02 .10
❑ 343 John L. Williams .01 .04
❑ 344 Irving Fryar .08 .25
❑ 345 Anthony Carter .02 .10
❑ 346 Al Toon .02 .10
❑ 347 J.T. Smith .01 .04
❑ 348 Pierce Holt RC .01 .04
❑ 349 Ferrell Edmunds .01 .04
❑ 350 Mark Rypien .02 .10
❑ 351 Paul Gruber .01 .04
❑ 352 Ernest Givins .02 .10
❑ 353 Ervin Randle .01 .04
❑ 354 Guy McIntyre .01 .04
❑ 355 Webster Slaughter .02 .10
❑ 356 Reuben Davis .01 .04
❑ 357 Rickey Jackson .02 .10
❑ 358 Earnest Byner .01 .04
❑ 359 Eddie Brown .01 .04
❑ 360 Troy Stradford .01 .04
❑ 361 Pepper Johnson .01 .04
❑ 362 Ravin Caldwell .01 .04
❑ 363 Chris Mohr RC .01 .04
❑ 364 Jeff Bryant .01 .04
❑ 365 Bruce Collie .01 .04
❑ 366 Courtney Hall .01 .04
❑ 367 Jerry Olsavsky .01 .04
❑ 368 David Galloway .01 .04
❑ 369 Wes Hopkins .01 .04
❑ 370 Johnny Hector .01 .04
❑ 371 Clarence Verdin .01 .04
❑ 372 Nick Lowery .01 .04
❑ 373 Tim Brown .08 .25
❑ 374 Kevin Greene .02 .10
❑ 375 Leonard Marshall .01 .04
❑ 376 Roland James .01 .04
❑ 377 Scott Studwell .01 .04
❑ 378 Jarvis Williams .01 .04
❑ 379 Mike Saxon .01 .04
❑ 380 Kevin Mack .01 .04
❑ 381 Joe Kelly .01 .04
❑ 382 Tom Thayer RC .01 .04
❑ 383 Roy Green .02 .10
❑ 384 Michael Brooks RC .01 .04
❑ 385 Michael Cofer .01 .04
❑ 386 Ken Ruettgers .01 .04
❑ 387 Dean Steinkuhler .01 .04
❑ 388 Maurice Carthon .01 .04
❑ 389 Ricky Sanders .01 .04

Card		
❑ 390 Winston Moss RC	.01	.04
❑ 391 Tony Woods	.01	.04
❑ 392 Keith DeLong	.01	.04
❑ 393 David Wyman	.01	.04
❑ 394 Vencie Glenn	.01	.04
❑ 395 Harris Barton	.01	.04
❑ 396 Bryan Hinkle	.01	.04
❑ 397 Derek Kennard	.01	.04
❑ 398 Heath Sherman RC	.01	.04
❑ 399 Troy Benson	.01	.04
❑ 400 Gary Zimmerman	.02	.10
❑ 401 Mark Duper	.02	.10
❑ 402 Eugene Lockhart	.01	.04
❑ 403 Tim Manoa	.01	.04
❑ 404 Reggie Williams	.01	.04
❑ 405 Mark Bortz RC	.01	.04
❑ 406 Mike Kenn	.01	.04
❑ 407 John Grimsley	.01	.04
❑ 408 Bill Romanowski RC	.40	1.00
❑ 409 Perry Kemp	.01	.04
❑ 410 Norm Johnson	.01	.04
❑ 411 Broderick Thomas	.01	.04
❑ 412 Joe Wolf	.01	.04
❑ 413 Andre Waters	.01	.04
❑ 414 Jason Staurovsky	.01	.04
❑ 415 Eric Martin	.01	.04
❑ 416 Joe Prokop	.01	.04
❑ 417 Steve Sewell	.01	.04
❑ 418 Cedric Jones	.01	.04
❑ 419 Alphonso Carreker	.01	.04
❑ 420 Keith Willis	.01	.04
❑ 421 Bobby Butler	.01	.04
❑ 422 John Roper	.01	.04
❑ 423 Tim Spencer	.01	.04
❑ 424 Jesse Sapolu RC	.01	.04
❑ 425 Ron Wolfley	.01	.04
❑ 426 Doug Smith	.01	.04
❑ 427 William Howard	.01	.04
❑ 428 Keith Van Horne	.01	.04
❑ 429 Tony Jordan	.01	.04
❑ 430 Mervyn Fernandez	.01	.04
❑ 431 Shaun Gayle RC	.01	.04
❑ 432 Ricky Nattiel	.01	.04
❑ 433 Albert Lewis	.01	.04
❑ 434 Fred Banks RC	.01	.04
❑ 435 Henry Thomas	.01	.04
❑ 436 Chet Brooks	.01	.04
❑ 437 Mark Ingram	.02	.10
❑ 438 Jeff Gossett	.01	.04
❑ 439 Mike Wilcher	.01	.04
❑ 440 Deron Cherry UER	.01	.04
❑ 441 Mike Rozier	.01	.04
❑ 442 Jon Hand	.01	.04
❑ 443 Ozzie Newsome	.02	.10
❑ 444 Sammy Martin	.01	.04
❑ 445 Luis Sharpe	.01	.04
❑ 446 Lee Williams	.01	.04
❑ 447 Chris Martin RC	.01	.04
❑ 448 Kevin Fagan RC	.01	.04
❑ 449 Gene Lang	.01	.04
❑ 450 Greg Townsend	.01	.04
❑ 451 Robert Lyles	.01	.04
❑ 452 Eric Hill	.01	.04
❑ 453 John Teltschik	.01	.04
❑ 454 Vestee Jackson	.01	.04
❑ 455 Bruce Reimers	.01	.04
❑ 456 Butch Rolle RC	.01	.04
❑ 457 Lawyer Tillman	.01	.04
❑ 458 Andre Tippett	.01	.04
❑ 459 James Thornton	.01	.04
❑ 460 Randy Grimes	.01	.04
❑ 461 Larry Roberts	.01	.04
❑ 462 Ron Holmes	.01	.04
❑ 463 Mike Wise DE	.01	.04
❑ 464 Danny Copeland RC	.01	.04
❑ 465 Bruce Wilkerson RC	.01	.04
❑ 466 Mike Quick	.01	.04
❑ 467 Mickey Shuler	.01	.04
❑ 468 Mike Prior	.01	.04
❑ 469 Ron Rivera	.01	.04
❑ 470 Dean Biasucci	.01	.04
❑ 471 Perry Williams	.01	.04
❑ 472 Darren Comeaux UER	.01	.04
❑ 473 Freeman McNeil	.01	.04
❑ 474 Tyrone Braxton	.01	.04
❑ 475 Jay Schroeder	.01	.04
❑ 476 Naz Worthen	.01	.04
❑ 477 Lionel Washington	.01	.04
❑ 478 Carl Zander	.01	.04
❑ 479 Al(Bubba) Baker	.02	.10
❑ 480 Mike Merriweather	.01	.04
❑ 481 Mike Gann	.01	.04
❑ 482 Brent Williams	.01	.04
❑ 483 Eugene Robinson	.01	.04
❑ 484 Ray Horton	.01	.04
❑ 485 Bruce Armstrong	.01	.04
❑ 486 John Fourcade	.01	.04
❑ 487 Lewis Billups	.01	.04
❑ 488 Scott Davis	.01	.04
❑ 489 Kenneth Sims	.01	.04
❑ 490 Chris Chandler	.08	.25
❑ 491 Mark Lee	.01	.04
❑ 492 Johnny Meads	.01	.04
❑ 493 Tim Irwin	.01	.04
❑ 494 E.J. Junior	.01	.04
❑ 495 Hardy Nickerson	.02	.10
❑ 496 Rob McGovern	.01	.04
❑ 497 Fred Strickland RC	.01	.04
❑ 498 Reggie Rutland RC	.01	.04
❑ 499 Mel Owens	.01	.04
❑ 500 Derrick Thomas	.08	.25
❑ 501 Jerrol Williams	.01	.04
❑ 502 Maurice Hurst RC	.01	.04
❑ 503 Larry Kelm RC	.01	.04
❑ 504 Herman Fontenot	.01	.04
❑ 505 Pat Beach	.01	.04
❑ 506 Haywood Jeffires RC	.08	.25
❑ 507 Neil Smith	.08	.25
❑ 508 Cleveland Gary FSC	.01	.04
❑ 509 William Perry	.02	.10
❑ 510 Michael Carter	.01	.04
❑ 511 Walker Lee Ashley	.01	.04
❑ 512 Bob Golic	.01	.04
❑ 513 Danny Villa RC	.01	.04
❑ 514 Matt Millen	.02	.10
❑ 515 Don Griffin	.01	.04
❑ 516 Jonathan Hayes	.01	.04
❑ 517 Gerald Williams RC	.01	.04
❑ 518 Scott Fulhage	.01	.04
❑ 519 Irv Pankey	.01	.04
❑ 520 Randy Dixon RC	.01	.04
❑ 521 Terry McDaniel	.01	.04
❑ 522 Dan Saleaumua	.01	.04
❑ 523 Darrin Nelson	.01	.04
❑ 524 Leonard Griffin	.01	.04
❑ 525 Michael Ball RC	.01	.04
❑ 526 Ernie Jones RC	.01	.04
❑ 527 Tony Eason UER	.01	.04
❑ 528 Ed Reynolds	.01	.04
❑ 529 Gary Hogeboom	.01	.04
❑ 530 Don Mosebar	.01	.04
❑ 531 Ottis Anderson	.02	.10
❑ 532 Bucky Scribner	.01	.04
❑ 533 Aaron Cox	.01	.04
❑ 534 Sean Jones	.02	.10
❑ 535 Doug Flutie	.20	.50
❑ 536 Leo Lewis	.01	.04
❑ 537 Art Still	.01	.04
❑ 538 Matt Bahr	.01	.04
❑ 539 Keena Turner	.01	.04
❑ 540 Sammy Winder	.01	.04
❑ 541 Mike Webster	.02	.10
❑ 542 Doug Riesenberg RC	.01	.04
❑ 543 Dan Fike	.01	.04
❑ 544 Clarence Kay	.01	.04
❑ 545 Jim Burt	.01	.04
❑ 546 Mike Horan	.01	.04
❑ 547 Al Harris	.01	.04
❑ 548 Maury Buford	.01	.04
❑ 549 Jerry Robinson	.01	.04
❑ 550 Tracy Rocker	.01	.04
❑ 551 Karl Mecklenburg CC	.01	.04
❑ 552 Lawrence Taylor CC	.08	.25
❑ 553 Derrick Thomas CC	.08	.25
❑ 554 Mike Singletary CC	.02	.10
❑ 555 Tim Harris CC	.01	.04
❑ 556 Jerry Rice RM	.20	.50
❑ 557 Art Monk RM	.02	.10
❑ 558 Mark Carrier WR RM	.02	.10
❑ 559 Andre Reed RM	.02	.10
❑ 560 Sterling Sharpe RM	.08	.25
❑ 561 Herschel Walker GF	.02	.10
❑ 562 Ottis Anderson GF	.02	.10
❑ 563 Randall Cunningham HG	.02	.10
❑ 564 John Elway HG	.20	.50
❑ 565 David Fulcher AP	.01	.04
❑ 566 Ronnie Lott AP	.02	.10
❑ 567 Jerry Gray AP	.01	.04
❑ 568 Albert Lewis AP	.01	.04
❑ 569 Karl Mecklenburg AP	.01	.04
❑ 570 Mike Singletary AP	.02	.10
❑ 571 Lawrence Taylor AP	.08	.25
❑ 572 Tim Harris AP	.01	.04
❑ 573 Keith Millard AP	.01	.04
❑ 574 Reggie White AP	.08	.25
❑ 575 Chris Doleman AP	.01	.04
❑ 576 Dave Meggett AP	.02	.10
❑ 577 Rod Woodson AP	.08	.25
❑ 578 Sean Landeta AP	.01	.04
❑ 579 Eddie Murray AP	.01	.04
❑ 580 Barry Sanders AP	.25	.60
❑ 581 Christian Okoye AP	.01	.04
❑ 582 Joe Montana AP	.20	.50
❑ 583 Jay Hilgenberg AP	.01	.04
❑ 584 Bruce Matthews AP	.02	.10
❑ 585 Tom Newberry AP	.01	.04
❑ 586 Gary Zimmerman AP	.02	.10
❑ 587 Anthony Munoz AP	.02	.10
❑ 588 Keith Jackson AP	.02	.10
❑ 589 Sterling Sharpe AP	.08	.25
❑ 590 Jerry Rice AP	.20	.50
❑ 591 Bo Jackson RB	.10	.30
❑ 592 Steve Largent RB	.08	.25
❑ 593 Flipper Anderson RB	.01	.04
❑ 594 Joe Montana RB	.20	.50
❑ 595 Franco Harris HOF	.02	.10
❑ 596 Bob St. Clair HOF	.01	.04
❑ 597 Tom Landry HOF	.02	.10
❑ 598 Jack Lambert HOF	.02	.10
❑ 599 Ted Hendricks HOF	.01	.04
❑ 600A Buck Buchanan HOF ERR 83	.02	.10
❑ 600B Buck Buchanan HOF COR 63	.02	.10
❑ 601 Bob Griese HOF	.02	.10
❑ 602 Super Bowl Wrap	.01	.04
❑ 603A Vince Lombardi w/o logo	.07	.20
❑ 603B Vince Lombardi Curt.logo	.07	.20
❑ 604 Mark Carrier WR UER	.02	.10
❑ 605 Randall Cunningham	.08	.25
❑ 606 Percy Snow C90	.01	.04
❑ 607 Andre Ware C90	.08	.25
❑ 608 Blair Thomas C90	.02	.10
❑ 609 Eric Green C90	.01	.04
❑ 610 Reggie Rembert C90	.01	.04
❑ 611 Richmond Webb C90	.01	.04
❑ 612 Bern Brostek C90	.01	.04
❑ 613 James Williams C90	.01	.04
❑ 614 Mark Carrier DB C90	.02	.10
❑ 615 Renaldo Turnbull C90	.01	.04
❑ 616 Cortez Kennedy C90	.02	.10
❑ 617 Keith McCants C90	.01	.04
❑ 618 Anthony Thompson RC	.01	.04
❑ 619 LeRoy Butler RC	.08	.25
❑ 620 Aaron Wallace RC	.01	.04
❑ 621 Alexander Wright RC	.01	.04
❑ 622 Keith McCants RC	.01	.04
❑ 623 Jimmie Jones RC	.01	.04
❑ 624 Anthony Johnson RC	.08	.25
❑ 625 Fred Washington RC	.01	.04
❑ 626 Mike Bellamy RC	.01	.04
❑ 627 Mark Carrier DB RC	.08	.25
❑ 628 Harold Green RC	.08	.25
❑ 629 Eric Green RC	.02	.10
❑ 630 Andre Collins RC	.01	.04
❑ 631 Lamar Lathon RC	.02	.10
❑ 632 Terry Wooden RC	.01	.04
❑ 633 Jesse Anderson RC	.01	.04
❑ 634 Jeff George RC	.20	.50
❑ 635 Carwell Gardner RC	.01	.04
❑ 636 Darrell Thompson RC	.01	.04
❑ 637 Vince Buck RC	.01	.04
❑ 638 Mike Jones TE RC	.01	.04
❑ 639 Charles Arbuckle RC	.01	.04
❑ 640 Dennis Brown RC	.01	.04
❑ 641 James Williams DB RC	.01	.04
❑ 642 Bern Brostek RC	.01	.04
❑ 643 Darion Conner RC	.02	.10
❑ 644 Mike Fox RC	.01	.04
❑ 645 Cary Conklin RC	.01	.04
❑ 646 Tim Grunhard RC	.01	.04
❑ 647 Ron Cox RC	.01	.04
❑ 648 Keith Sims RC	.01	.04
❑ 649 Alton Montgomery RC	.01	.04
❑ 650 Greg McMurtry RC	.01	.04
❑ 651 Scott Mitchell RC	.08	.25
❑ 652 Tim Ryan DE RC	.01	.04
❑ 653 Jeff Mills RC	.01	.04
❑ 654 Ricky Proehl RC	.08	.25

❑ 655 Steve Broussard RC .01 .04
❑ 656 Peter Tom Willis RC .01 .04
❑ 657 Dexter Carter RC .01 .04
❑ 658 Tony Casillas .01 .04
❑ 659 Joe Morris .01 .04
❑ 660 Greg Kragen .01 .04
❑ B1 Matt Stover FF .08 .25
❑ B2 Demetrius Davis .01 .04
❑ B3 Ken McMichel .01 .04
❑ B4 Judd Garrett FF .01 .04
❑ B5 Elliott Searcy .01 .04

1990 Score Supplemental

❑ COMP.FACT.SET (110) 30.00 80.00
❑ 1T Marcus Dupree RC .05 .15
❑ 2T Jerry Kauric .05 .15
❑ 3T Everson Walls .05 .15
❑ 4T Elliott Smith .05 .15
❑ 5T Donald Evans UER RC .10 .30
❑ 6T Jerry Holmes .05 .15
❑ 7T Dan Stryzinski RC .05 .15
❑ 8T Gerald McNeil .05 .15
❑ 9T Rick Tuten RC .05 .15
❑ 10T Mickey Shuler .05 .15
❑ 11T Jay Novacek .25 .60
❑ 12T Eric Williams RC .05 .15
❑ 13T Stanley Morgan .05 .15
❑ 14T Wayne Haddix RC .05 .15
❑ 15T Gary Anderson RB .05 .15
❑ 16T Stan Humphries RC .25 .60
❑ 17T Raymond Clayborn .05 .15
❑ 18T Mark Boyer RC .05 .15
❑ 19T Dave Waymer .05 .15
❑ 20T Andre Rison .25 .60
❑ 21T Daniel Stubbs .05 .15
❑ 22T Mike Rozier .05 .15
❑ 23T Damian Johnson .05 .15
❑ 24T Don Smith RBK RC .05 .15
❑ 25T Max Montoya .05 .15
❑ 26T Terry Kinard .05 .15
❑ 27T Herb Welch .05 .15
❑ 28T Cliff Odom .05 .15
❑ 29T John Kidd .05 .15
❑ 30T Barry Word RC .05 .15
❑ 31T Rich Karlis .05 .15
❑ 32T Mike Baab .05 .15
❑ 33T Ronnie Harmon .10 .30
❑ 34T Jeff Donaldson .05 .15
❑ 35T Riki Ellison .05 .15
❑ 36T Steve Walsh .10 .30
❑ 37T Bill Lewis RC .05 .15
❑ 38T Tim McKyer .05 .15
❑ 39T James Wilder .05 .15
❑ 40T Tony Paige .05 .15
❑ 41T Derrick Fenner RC .05 .15
❑ 42T Thane Gash RC .05 .15
❑ 43T Dave Duerson .05 .15
❑ 44T Clarence Weathers .05 .15
❑ 45T Matt Bahr .05 .15
❑ 46T Alonzo Highsmith .05 .15
❑ 47T Joe Kelly .05 .15
❑ 48T Chris Hinton .05 .15
❑ 49T Bobby Humphery .05 .15
❑ 50T Greg Bell .05 .15
❑ 51T Fred Smerlas .05 .15
❑ 52T Walter Stanley .05 .15
❑ 53T Jim Skow .05 .15
❑ 54T Renaldo Turnbull .05 .15
❑ 55T Bern Brostek .05 .15
❑ 56T Charles Wilson RC .05 .15
❑ 57T Keith McCants .05 .15
❑ 58T Alexander Wright .10 .30
❑ 59T Ian Beckles RC .05 .15
❑ 60T Eric Davis RC .10 .30
❑ 61T Chris Singleton .05 .15
❑ 62T Rob Moore RC 1.00 2.50
❑ 63T Darion Conner .10 .30
❑ 64T Tim Grunhard .05 .15
❑ 65T Junior Seau 2.50 6.00
❑ 66T Tony Stargell RC .05 .15
❑ 67T Anthony Thompson .05 .15
❑ 68T Cortez Kennedy .25 .60
❑ 69T Darrell Thompson .05 .15
❑ 70T Calvin Williams RC .25 .60
❑ 71T Rodney Hampton .25 .60
❑ 72T Terry Wooden .05 .15
❑ 73T Leo Goeas RC .05 .15
❑ 74T Ken Willis .05 .15
❑ 75T Ricky Proehl .25 .60
❑ 76T Steve Christie RC .05 .15
❑ 77T Andre Ware .25 .60
❑ 78T Jeff George 1.00 2.50
❑ 79T Walter Wilson .05 .15
❑ 80T Johnny Bailey RC .05 .15
❑ 81T Harold Green .10 .30
❑ 82T Mark Carrier DB .25 .60
❑ 83T Frank Cornish .05 .15
❑ 84T James Williams .05 .15
❑ 85T James Francis RC .05 .15
❑ 86T Percy Snow .05 .15
❑ 87T Anthony Johnson .25 .60
❑ 88T Tim Ryan DE .05 .15
❑ 89T Dan Owens RC .05 .15
❑ 90T Aaron Wallace RC .05 .15
❑ 91T Steve Broussard .05 .15
❑ 92T Eric Green .05 .15
❑ 93T Blair Thomas .10 .30
❑ 94T Robert Blackmon RC .05 .15
❑ 95T Alan Grant RC .05 .15
❑ 96T Andre Collins .05 .15
❑ 97T Dexter Carter .05 .15
❑ 98T Reggie Cobb RC .05 .15
❑ 99T Dennis Brown .05 .15
❑ 100T Kenny Davidson RC .05 .15
❑ 101T Emmitt Smith RC 25.00 50.00
❑ 102T Jeff Alm .05 .15
❑ 103T Alton Montgomery .05 .15
❑ 104T Tony Bennett .25 .60
❑ 105T Johnny Johnson RC .10 .30
❑ 106T Leroy Hoard RC .25 .60
❑ 107T Ray Agnew .05 .15
❑ 108T Richmond Webb .05 .15
❑ 109T Keith Sims .05 .15
❑ 110T Barry Foster .25 .60

1991 Score

❑ COMPLETE SET (686) 7.50 20.00
❑ COMP.FACT.SET (690) 12.50 25.00
❑ 1 Joe Montana .50 1.25
❑ 2 Eric Allen .01 .05
❑ 3 Rohn Stark .01 .05
❑ 4 Frank Reich .02 .10
❑ 5 Derrick Thomas .08 .25
❑ 6 Mike Singletary .02 .10
❑ 7 Boomer Esiason .02 .10
❑ 8 Matt Millen .02 .10
❑ 9 Chris Spielman .02 .10
❑ 10 Gerald McNeil .01 .05
❑ 11 Nick Lowery .01 .05
❑ 12 Randall Cunningham .08 .25
❑ 13 Marion Butts .02 .10
❑ 14 Tim Brown .08 .25
❑ 15 Emmitt Smith 1.00 2.50
❑ 16 Rich Camarillo .01 .05
❑ 17 Mike Merriweather .01 .05
❑ 18 Derrick Fenner .01 .05
❑ 19 Clay Matthews .02 .10
❑ 20 Barry Sanders .50 1.25
❑ 21 James Brooks .02 .10
❑ 22 Alton Montgomery .01 .05
❑ 23 Steve Atwater .01 .05
❑ 24 Ron Morris .01 .05
❑ 25 Brad Muster .01 .05
❑ 26 Andre Rison .02 .10
❑ 27 Brian Brennan .01 .05
❑ 28 Leonard Smith .01 .05
❑ 29 Kevin Butler .01 .05
❑ 30 Tim Harris .01 .05
❑ 31 Jay Novacek .08 .25
❑ 32 Eddie Murray .01 .05
❑ 33 Keith Woodside .01 .05
❑ 34 Ray Crockett RC .01 .05
❑ 35 Eugene Lockhart .01 .05
❑ 36 Bill Romanowski .01 .05
❑ 37 Eddie Brown .01 .05
❑ 38 Eugene Daniel .01 .05
❑ 39 Scott Fulhage .01 .05
❑ 40 Harold Green .02 .10
❑ 41 Mark Jackson .01 .05
❑ 42 Sterling Sharpe .08 .25
❑ 43 Mel Gray .02 .10
❑ 44 Jerry Holmes .01 .05
❑ 45 Allen Pinkett .01 .05
❑ 46 Warren Powers .01 .05
❑ 47 Rodney Peete .02 .10
❑ 48 Lorenzo White .01 .05
❑ 49 Dan Owens .01 .05
❑ 50 James Francis .01 .05
❑ 51 Ken Norton .02 .10
❑ 52 Ed West .01 .05
❑ 53 Andre Reed .02 .10
❑ 54 John Grimsley .01 .05
❑ 55 Michael Cofer .01 .05
❑ 56 Chris Doleman .01 .05
❑ 57 Pat Swilling .02 .10
❑ 58 Jessie Tuggle .01 .05
❑ 59 Mike Johnson .01 .05
❑ 60 Steve Walsh .01 .05
❑ 61 Sam Mills .01 .05
❑ 62 Don Mosebar .01 .05
❑ 63 Jay Hilgenberg .01 .05
❑ 64 Cleveland Gary .01 .05
❑ 65 Andre Tippett .01 .05
❑ 66 Tom Newberry .01 .05
❑ 67 Maurice Hurst .01 .05
❑ 68 Louis Oliver .01 .05
❑ 69 Fred Marion .01 .05
❑ 70 Christian Okoye .01 .05
❑ 71 Marv Cook FSC .01 .05
❑ 72 Darryl Talley .01 .05
❑ 73 Rick Fenney .01 .05
❑ 74 Kelvin Martin .01 .05
❑ 75 Howie Long .08 .25
❑ 76 Steve Wisniewski .01 .05
❑ 77 Karl Mecklenburg .01 .05
❑ 78 Dan Saleaumua .01 .05
❑ 79 Ray Childress .01 .05
❑ 80 Henry Ellard .02 .10
❑ 81 Ernest Givins UER .02 .10
❑ 82 Ferrell Edmunds .01 .05
❑ 83 Steve Jordan .01 .05
❑ 84 Tony Mandarich .01 .05
❑ 85 Eric Martin .01 .05
❑ 86 Rich Gannon FSC .08 .25
❑ 87 Irving Fryar .02 .10
❑ 88 Tom Rathman .01 .05
❑ 89 Dan Hampton .02 .10
❑ 90 Barry Word .01 .05
❑ 91 Kevin Greene .02 .10
❑ 92 Sean Landeta .01 .05
❑ 93 Trace Armstrong .01 .05
❑ 94 Dennis Byrd .01 .05
❑ 95 Timm Rosenbach .01 .05
❑ 96 Anthony Toney .01 .05
❑ 97 Tim Krumrie .01 .05
❑ 98 Jerry Ball .01 .05
❑ 99 Tim Green .01 .05
❑ 100 Bo Jackson .10 .30
❑ 101 Myron Guyton .01 .05
❑ 102 Mike Mularkey .01 .05
❑ 103 Jerry Gray .01 .05
❑ 104 Scott Stephen RC .01 .05
❑ 105 Anthony Bell .01 .05
❑ 106 Lomas Brown .01 .05
❑ 107 David Little .01 .05
❑ 108 Brad Baxter FSC .01 .05
❑ 109 Freddie Joe Nunn .01 .05
❑ 110 Dave Meggett .02 .10
❑ 111 Mark Rypien .02 .10
❑ 112 Warren Williams .01 .05
❑ 113 Ron Rivera .01 .05

- ❑ 114 Terance Mathis .02 .10
- ❑ 115 Anthony Munoz .02 .10
- ❑ 116 Jeff Bryant .01 .05
- ❑ 117 Issiac Holt .01 .05
- ❑ 118 Steve Sewell .01 .05
- ❑ 119 Tim Newton .01 .05
- ❑ 120 Emile Harry .01 .05
- ❑ 121 Gary Anderson K .01 .05
- ❑ 122 Mark Lee .01 .05
- ❑ 123 Alfred Anderson .01 .05
- ❑ 124 Anthony Blaylock .01 .05
- ❑ 125 Earnest Byner .01 .05
- ❑ 126 Bill Maas .01 .05
- ❑ 127 Keith Taylor .01 .05
- ❑ 128 Cliff Odom .01 .05
- ❑ 129 Bob Golic .01 .05
- ❑ 130 Bart Oates .01 .05
- ❑ 131 Jim Arnold .01 .05
- ❑ 132 Jeff Herrod .01 .05
- ❑ 133 Bruce Armstrong .01 .05
- ❑ 134 Craig Heyward .02 .10
- ❑ 135 Joey Browner .01 .05
- ❑ 136 Darren Comeaux .01 .05
- ❑ 137 Pat Beach .01 .05
- ❑ 138 Dalton Hilliard .01 .05
- ❑ 139 David Treadwell .01 .05
- ❑ 140 Gary Anderson RB .01 .05
- ❑ 141 Eugene Robinson .01 .05
- ❑ 142 Scott Case .01 .05
- ❑ 143 Paul Farren .01 .05
- ❑ 144 Gill Fenerty .01 .05
- ❑ 145 Tim Irwin .01 .05
- ❑ 146 Norm Johnson .01 .05
- ❑ 147 Willie Gault .02 .10
- ❑ 148 Clarence Verdin .01 .05
- ❑ 149 Jeff Uhlenhake .01 .05
- ❑ 150 Erik McMillan .01 .05
- ❑ 151 Kevin Ross .01 .05
- ❑ 152 Pepper Johnson .01 .05
- ❑ 153 Bryan Hinkle .01 .05
- ❑ 154 Gary Clark .08 .25
- ❑ 155 Robert Delpino .01 .05
- ❑ 156 Doug Smith .01 .05
- ❑ 157 Chris Martin .01 .05
- ❑ 158 Ray Berry .01 .05
- ❑ 159 Steve Christie .01 .05
- ❑ 160 Don Smith RB .01 .05
- ❑ 161 Greg McMurtry .01 .05
- ❑ 162 Jack Del Rio .02 .10
- ❑ 163 Floyd Dixon .01 .05
- ❑ 164 Buford McGee .01 .05
- ❑ 165 Brett Maxie .01 .05
- ❑ 166 Morten Andersen .01 .05
- ❑ 167 Kent Hull .01 .05
- ❑ 168 Skip McClendon .01 .05
- ❑ 169 Keith Sims .01 .05
- ❑ 170 Leonard Marshall .01 .05
- ❑ 171 Tony Woods .01 .05
- ❑ 172 Byron Evans .01 .05
- ❑ 173 Rob Burnett RC .02 .10
- ❑ 174 Tory Epps .01 .05
- ❑ 175 Toi Cook RC .01 .05
- ❑ 176 John Elliott .01 .05
- ❑ 177 Tommie Agee .01 .05
- ❑ 178 Keith Van Horne .01 .05
- ❑ 179 Dennis Smith .01 .05
- ❑ 180 James Lofton .02 .10
- ❑ 181 Art Monk .02 .10
- ❑ 182 Anthony Carter .02 .10
- ❑ 183 Louis Lipps .01 .05
- ❑ 184 Bruce Hill .01 .05
- ❑ 185 Michael Young .01 .05
- ❑ 186 Eric Green .01 .05
- ❑ 187 Barney Bussey RC .01 .05
- ❑ 188 Curtis Duncan .01 .05
- ❑ 189 Robert Awalt .01 .05
- ❑ 190 Johnny Johnson .01 .05
- ❑ 191 Jeff Cross .01 .05
- ❑ 192 Keith McKeller .01 .05
- ❑ 193 Robert Brown .01 .05
- ❑ 194 Vincent Brown .01 .05
- ❑ 195 Calvin Williams .02 .10
- ❑ 196 Sean Jones .02 .10
- ❑ 197 Willie Drewrey .01 .05
- ❑ 198 Bubba McDowell .01 .05
- ❑ 199 Al Noga .01 .05
- ❑ 200 Ronnie Lott .02 .10
- ❑ 201 Warren Moon .08 .25
- ❑ 202 Chris Hinton .01 .05
- ❑ 203 Jim Sweeney .01 .05
- ❑ 204 Wayne Haddix .01 .05
- ❑ 205 Tim Jorden RC .01 .05
- ❑ 206 Marvin Allen .01 .05
- ❑ 207 Jim Morrissey RC .01 .05
- ❑ 208 Ben Smith .01 .05
- ❑ 209 William White .01 .05
- ❑ 210 Jim C. Jensen .01 .05
- ❑ 211 Doug Reed .01 .05
- ❑ 212 Ethan Horton .01 .05
- ❑ 213 Chris Jacke .01 .05
- ❑ 214 Johnny Hector .01 .05
- ❑ 215 Drew Hill UER .01 .05
- ❑ 216 Roy Green .01 .05
- ❑ 217 Dean Steinkuhler .01 .05
- ❑ 218 Cedric Mack .01 .05
- ❑ 219 Chris Miller .02 .10
- ❑ 220 Keith Byars .01 .05
- ❑ 221 Lewis Billups .01 .05
- ❑ 222 Roger Craig .02 .10
- ❑ 223 Shaun Gayle .01 .05
- ❑ 224 Mike Rozier .01 .05
- ❑ 225 Troy Aikman .30 .75
- ❑ 226 Bobby Humphrey .01 .05
- ❑ 227 Eugene Marve .01 .05
- ❑ 228 Michael Carter .01 .05
- ❑ 229 Richard Johnson CB RC .01 .05
- ❑ 230 Billy Joe Tolliver .01 .05
- ❑ 231 Mark Murphy .01 .05
- ❑ 232 John L. Williams .01 .05
- ❑ 233 Ronnie Harmon .01 .05
- ❑ 234 Thurman Thomas .08 .25
- ❑ 235 Martin Mayhew .01 .05
- ❑ 236 Richmond Webb .01 .05
- ❑ 237 Gerald Riggs UER .02 .10
- ❑ 238 Mike Prior .01 .05
- ❑ 239 Mike Gann .01 .05
- ❑ 240 Alvin Walton .01 .05
- ❑ 241 Tim McGee .01 .05
- ❑ 242 Bruce Matthews .02 .10
- ❑ 243 Johnny Holland .01 .05
- ❑ 244 Martin Bayless .01 .05
- ❑ 245 Eric Metcalf .02 .10
- ❑ 246 John Alt .01 .05
- ❑ 247 Max Montoya .01 .05
- ❑ 248 Rod Bernstine .01 .05
- ❑ 249 Paul Gruber .01 .05
- ❑ 250 Charles Haley .02 .10
- ❑ 251 Scott Norwood .01 .05
- ❑ 252 Michael Haddix .01 .05
- ❑ 253 Ricky Sanders .01 .05
- ❑ 254 Ervin Randle .01 .05
- ❑ 255 Duane Bickett .01 .05
- ❑ 256 Mike Munchak .02 .10
- ❑ 257 Keith Jones .01 .05
- ❑ 258 Riki Ellison .01 .05
- ❑ 259 Vince Newsome .01 .05
- ❑ 260 Lee Williams .01 .05
- ❑ 261 Steve Smith .01 .05
- ❑ 262 Sam Clancy .01 .05
- ❑ 263 Pierce Holt .01 .05
- ❑ 264 Jim Harbaugh .08 .25
- ❑ 265 Dino Hackett .01 .05
- ❑ 266 Andy Heck .01 .05
- ❑ 267 Leo Goeas .01 .05
- ❑ 268 Russ Grimm .01 .05
- ❑ 269 Gill Byrd .01 .05
- ❑ 270 Neal Anderson .02 .10
- ❑ 271 Jackie Slater .01 .05
- ❑ 272 Joe Nash .01 .05
- ❑ 273 Todd Bowles .01 .05
- ❑ 274 D.J. Dozier .01 .05
- ❑ 275 Kevin Fagan .01 .05
- ❑ 276 Don Warren .01 .05
- ❑ 277 Jim Jeffcoat .01 .05
- ❑ 278 Bruce Smith .08 .25
- ❑ 279 Cortez Kennedy .08 .25
- ❑ 280 Thane Gash .01 .05
- ❑ 281 Perry Kemp .01 .05
- ❑ 282 John Taylor .02 .10
- ❑ 283 Stephone Paige .01 .05
- ❑ 284 Paul Skansi .01 .05
- ❑ 285 Shawn Collins .01 .05
- ❑ 286 Mervyn Fernandez .01 .05
- ❑ 287 Daniel Stubbs .01 .05
- ❑ 288 Chip Lohmiller .01 .05
- ❑ 289 Brian Blades .02 .10
- ❑ 290 Mark Carrier WR .08 .25
- ❑ 291 Carl Zander .01 .05
- ❑ 292 David Wyman .01 .05
- ❑ 293 Jeff Bostic .01 .05
- ❑ 294 Irv Pankey .01 .05
- ❑ 295 Keith Millard .01 .05
- ❑ 296 Jamie Mueller .01 .05
- ❑ 297 Bill Fralic .01 .05
- ❑ 298 Wendell Davis FSC .01 .05
- ❑ 299 Ken Clarke .01 .05
- ❑ 300 Wymon Henderson .01 .05
- ❑ 301 Jeff Campbell .01 .05
- ❑ 302 Cody Carlson RC .01 .05
- ❑ 303 Matt Brock RC .01 .05
- ❑ 304 Maurice Carthon .01 .05
- ❑ 305 Scott Mersereau RC .01 .05
- ❑ 306 Steve Wright RC .01 .05
- ❑ 307 J.B. Brown .01 .05
- ❑ 308 Ricky Reynolds .01 .05
- ❑ 309 Darryl Pollard .01 .05
- ❑ 310 Donald Evans .01 .05
- ❑ 311 Nick Bell RC .01 .05
- ❑ 312 Pat Harlow RC .01 .05
- ❑ 313 Dan McGwire RC .01 .05
- ❑ 314 Mike Dumas RC .01 .05
- ❑ 315 Mike Croel RC .01 .05
- ❑ 316 Chris Smith RC .01 .05
- ❑ 317 Kenny Walker RC .01 .05
- ❑ 318 Todd Lyght RC .01 .05
- ❑ 319 Mike Stonebreaker .01 .05
- ❑ 320 Randall Cunningham 90 .02 .10
- ❑ 321 Terance Mathis 90 .08 .25
- ❑ 322 Gaston Green 90 .01 .05
- ❑ 323 Johnny Bailey 90 .01 .05
- ❑ 324 Donnie Elder 90 .01 .05
- ❑ 325 Dwight Stone 90 UER .01 .05
- ❑ 326 J.J.Birden RC .02 .10
- ❑ 327 Alexander Wright 90 .01 .05
- ❑ 328 Eric Metcalf 90 .02 .10
- ❑ 329 Andre Rison TL .02 .10
- ❑ 330 Warren Moon TL UER .02 .10
- ❑ 331 Steve Tasker DT .01 .05
- ❑ 332 Mel Gray DT .02 .10
- ❑ 333 Nick Lowery DT .01 .05
- ❑ 334 Sean Landeta DT .01 .05
- ❑ 335 David Fulcher DT .01 .05
- ❑ 336 Joey Browner DT .01 .05
- ❑ 337 Albert Lewis DT .01 .05
- ❑ 338 Rod Woodson DT .02 .10
- ❑ 339 Shane Conlan DT .01 .05
- ❑ 340 Pepper Johnson DT .01 .05
- ❑ 341 Chris Spielman DT .01 .05
- ❑ 342 Derrick Thomas DT .02 .10
- ❑ 343 Ray Childress DT .01 .05
- ❑ 344 Reggie White DT .02 .10
- ❑ 345 Bruce Smith DT .02 .10
- ❑ 346 Darrell Green .01 .05
- ❑ 347 Ray Bentley .01 .05
- ❑ 348 Herschel Walker .02 .10
- ❑ 349 Rodney Holman .01 .05
- ❑ 350 Al Toon .02 .10
- ❑ 351 Harry Hamilton .01 .05
- ❑ 352 Albert Lewis .01 .05
- ❑ 353 Renaldo Turnbull .01 .05
- ❑ 354 Junior Seau .08 .25
- ❑ 355 Merril Hoge .01 .05
- ❑ 356 Shane Conlan .01 .05
- ❑ 357 Jay Schroeder .01 .05
- ❑ 358 Steve Broussard .01 .05
- ❑ 359 Mark Bavaro .01 .05
- ❑ 360 Jim Lachey .01 .05
- ❑ 361 Greg Townsend .01 .05
- ❑ 362 Dave Krieg .02 .10
- ❑ 363 Jessie Hester .01 .05
- ❑ 364 Steve Tasker .02 .10
- ❑ 365 Ron Hall .01 .05
- ❑ 366 Pat Leahy .01 .05
- ❑ 367 Jim Everett .02 .10
- ❑ 368 Felix Wright .01 .05
- ❑ 369 Ricky Proehl .01 .05
- ❑ 370 Anthony Miller .02 .10
- ❑ 371 Keith Jackson .02 .10
- ❑ 372 Pete Stoyanovich .01 .05
- ❑ 373 Tommy Kane .01 .05
- ❑ 374 Richard Johnson .01 .05
- ❑ 375 Randall McDaniel .02 .10
- ❑ 376 John Stephens .01 .05
- ❑ 377 Haywood Jeffires .02 .10
- ❑ 378 Rodney Hampton .08 .25
- ❑ 379 Tim Grunhard .01 .05
- ❑ 380 Jerry Rice .30 .75

Card		
❑ 381 Ken Harvey	.02	.10
❑ 382 Vaughan Johnson	.01	.05
❑ 383 J.T. Smith	.01	.05
❑ 384 Carnell Lake	.01	.05
❑ 385 Dan Marino	.50	1.25
❑ 386 Kyle Clifton	.01	.05
❑ 387 Wilber Marshall	.01	.05
❑ 388 Pete Holohan	.01	.05
❑ 389 Gary Plummer	.01	.05
❑ 390 William Perry	.02	.10
❑ 391 Mark Robinson	.01	.05
❑ 392 Nate Odomes	.01	.05
❑ 393 Ickey Woods	.01	.05
❑ 394 Reyna Thompson	.01	.05
❑ 395 Deion Sanders	.15	.40
❑ 396 Harris Barton	.01	.05
❑ 397 Sammie Smith	.01	.05
❑ 398 Vinny Testaverde	.02	.10
❑ 399 Ray Donaldson	.01	.05
❑ 400 Tim McKyer	.01	.05
❑ 401 Nesby Glasgow	.01	.05
❑ 402 Brent Williams	.01	.05
❑ 403 Rob Moore	.08	.25
❑ 404 Bubby Brister	.01	.05
❑ 405 David Fulcher	.01	.05
❑ 406 Reggie Cobb	.01	.05
❑ 407 Jerome Brown	.01	.05
❑ 408 Erik Howard	.01	.05
❑ 409 Tony Paige	.01	.05
❑ 410 John Elway	.50	1.25
❑ 411 Charles Mann	.01	.05
❑ 412 Luis Sharpe	.01	.05
❑ 413 Hassan Jones	.01	.05
❑ 414 Frank Minnifield	.01	.05
❑ 415 Steve DeBerg	.01	.05
❑ 416 Mark Carrier DB	.02	.10
❑ 417 Brian Jordan FSC	.02	.10
❑ 418 Reggie Langhorne	.01	.05
❑ 419 Don Majkowski	.01	.05
❑ 420 Marcus Allen	.08	.25
❑ 421 Michael Brooks	.01	.05
❑ 422 Vai Sikahema	.01	.05
❑ 423 Dermontti Dawson	.01	.05
❑ 424 Jacob Green	.01	.05
❑ 425 Flipper Anderson	.01	.05
❑ 426 Bill Brooks	.01	.05
❑ 427 Keith McCants	.01	.05
❑ 428 Ken O'Brien	.01	.05
❑ 429 Fred Barnett FSC	.08	.25
❑ 430 Mark Duper	.02	.10
❑ 431 Mark Kelso	.01	.05
❑ 432 Leslie O'Neal	.02	.10
❑ 433 Ottis Anderson	.02	.10
❑ 434 Jesse Sapolu	.01	.05
❑ 435 Gary Zimmerman	.02	.10
❑ 436 Kevin Porter	.01	.05
❑ 437 Anthony Thompson	.01	.05
❑ 438 Robert Clark	.01	.05
❑ 439 Chris Warren	.08	.25
❑ 440 Gerald Williams	.01	.05
❑ 441 Jim Skow	.01	.05
❑ 442 Rick Donnelly	.01	.05
❑ 443 Guy McIntyre	.01	.05
❑ 444 Jeff Lageman	.01	.05
❑ 445 John Offerdahl	.01	.05
❑ 446 Clyde Simmons	.01	.05
❑ 447 John Kidd	.01	.05
❑ 448 Chip Banks	.01	.05
❑ 449 Johnny Meads	.01	.05
❑ 450 Rickey Jackson	.01	.05
❑ 451 Lee Johnson	.01	.05
❑ 452 Michael Irvin	.08	.25
❑ 453 Leon Seals	.01	.05
❑ 454 Darrell Thompson	.01	.05
❑ 455 Everson Walls	.01	.05
❑ 456 LeRoy Butler	.02	.10
❑ 457 Marcus Dupree	.01	.05
❑ 458 Kirk Lowdermilk	.01	.05
❑ 459 Chris Singleton	.01	.05
❑ 460 Seth Joyner	.02	.10
❑ 461 Rueben Mayes UER	.01	.05
❑ 462 Ernie Jones	.01	.05
❑ 463 Greg Kragen	.01	.05
❑ 464 Bennie Blades	.01	.05
❑ 465 Mark Bortz	.01	.05
❑ 466 Tony Stargell	.01	.05
❑ 467 Mike Cofer	.01	.05
❑ 468 Randy Grimes	.01	.05
❑ 469 Tim Worley	.01	.05
❑ 470 Kevin Mack	.01	.05
❑ 471 Wes Hopkins	.01	.05
❑ 472 Will Wolford	.01	.05
❑ 473 Sam Seale	.01	.05
❑ 474 Jim Ritcher	.01	.05
❑ 475 Jeff Hostetler FSC	.08	.25
❑ 476 Mitchell Price RC	.01	.05
❑ 477 Ken Lanier	.01	.05
❑ 478 Naz Worthen	.01	.05
❑ 479 Ed Reynolds	.01	.05
❑ 480 Mark Clayton	.02	.10
❑ 481 Matt Bahr	.01	.05
❑ 482 Gary Reasons	.01	.05
❑ 483 David Szott	.01	.05
❑ 484 Barry Foster	.02	.10
❑ 485 Bruce Reimers	.01	.05
❑ 486 Dean Biasucci	.01	.05
❑ 487 Cris Carter	.20	.50
❑ 488 Albert Bentley	.01	.05
❑ 489 Robert Massey	.01	.05
❑ 490 Al Smith	.01	.05
❑ 491 Greg Lloyd	.08	.25
❑ 492 Steve McMichael UER	.02	.10
❑ 493 Jeff Wright RC	.01	.05
❑ 494 Scott Davis	.01	.05
❑ 495 Freeman McNeil	.01	.05
❑ 496 Simon Fletcher	.01	.05
❑ 497 Terry McDaniel	.01	.05
❑ 498 Heath Sherman	.01	.05
❑ 499 Jeff Jaeger	.01	.05
❑ 500 Mark Collins	.01	.05
❑ 501 Tim Goad	.01	.05
❑ 502 Jeff George	.08	.25
❑ 503 Jimmie Jones	.01	.05
❑ 504 Henry Thomas	.01	.05
❑ 505 Steve Young	.30	.75
❑ 506 William Roberts	.01	.05
❑ 507 Neil Smith	.08	.25
❑ 508 Mike Saxon	.01	.05
❑ 509 Johnny Bailey	.01	.05
❑ 510 Broderick Thomas	.01	.05
❑ 511 Wade Wilson	.02	.10
❑ 512 Hart Lee Dykes	.01	.05
❑ 513 Hardy Nickerson	.02	.10
❑ 514 Tim McDonald	.01	.05
❑ 515 Frank Cornish	.01	.05
❑ 516 Jarvis Williams	.01	.05
❑ 517 Carl Lee	.01	.05
❑ 518 Carl Banks	.01	.05
❑ 519 Mike Golic	.01	.05
❑ 520 Brian Noble	.01	.05
❑ 521 James Hasty	.01	.05
❑ 522 Bubba Paris	.01	.05
❑ 523 Kevin Walker RC	.01	.05
❑ 524 William Fuller	.02	.10
❑ 525 Eddie Anderson	.01	.05
❑ 526 Roger Ruzek	.01	.05
❑ 527 Robert Blackmon	.01	.05
❑ 528 Vince Buck	.01	.05
❑ 529 Lawrence Taylor	.08	.25
❑ 530 Reggie Roby	.01	.05
❑ 531 Doug Riesenberg	.01	.05
❑ 532 Joe Jacoby	.01	.05
❑ 533 Kirby Jackson RC	.01	.05
❑ 534 Robb Thomas	.01	.05
❑ 535 Don Griffin	.01	.05
❑ 536 Andre Waters	.01	.05
❑ 537 Marc Logan	.01	.05
❑ 538 James Thornton	.01	.05
❑ 539 Ray Agnew	.01	.05
❑ 540 Frank Stams	.01	.05
❑ 541 Brett Perriman	.08	.25
❑ 542 Andre Ware	.02	.10
❑ 543 Kevin Haverdink	.01	.05
❑ 544 Greg Jackson RC	.01	.05
❑ 545 Tunch Ilkin	.01	.05
❑ 546 Dexter Carter	.01	.05
❑ 547 Rod Woodson	.08	.25
❑ 548 Donnell Woolford	.01	.05
❑ 549 Mark Boyer	.01	.05
❑ 550 Jeff Query	.01	.05
❑ 551 Burt Grossman	.01	.05
❑ 552 Mike Kenn	.01	.05
❑ 553 Richard Dent	.02	.10
❑ 554 Gaston Green	.01	.05
❑ 555 Phil Simms	.02	.10
❑ 556 Brent Jones	.08	.25
❑ 557 Ronnie Lippett	.01	.05
❑ 558 Mike Horan	.01	.05
❑ 559 Danny Noonan	.01	.05
❑ 560 Reggie White	.08	.25
❑ 561 Rufus Porter	.01	.05
❑ 562 Aaron Wallace	.01	.05
❑ 563 Vance Johnson	.01	.05
❑ 564A Aaron Craver ERR RC	.01	.05
❑ 564B Aaron Craver COR RC	.01	.05
❑ 565A Russell Maryland ERR RC	.08	.25
❑ 565B Russell Maryland COR RC	.08	.25
❑ 566 Paul Justin RC	.01	.05
❑ 567 Walter Dean	.01	.05
❑ 568 Herman Moore RC	.08	.25
❑ 569 Bill Musgrave RC	.01	.05
❑ 570 Rob Carpenter RC	.01	.05
❑ 571 Greg Lewis RC	.01	.05
❑ 572 Ed King RC	.01	.05
❑ 573 Ernie Mills RC	.02	.10
❑ 574 Jake Reed RC	.20	.50
❑ 575 Ricky Watters RC	.60	1.50
❑ 576 Derek Russell RC	.01	.05
❑ 577 Shawn Moore RC	.01	.05
❑ 578 Eric Bieniemy RC	.01	.05
❑ 579 Chris Zorich RC	.08	.25
❑ 580 Scott Miller	.01	.05
❑ 581 Jarrod Bunch RC	.01	.05
❑ 582 Ricky Ervins RC	.02	.10
❑ 583 Browning Nagle RC	.01	.05
❑ 584 Eric Turner RC	.02	.10
❑ 585 William Thomas RC	.01	.05
❑ 586 Stanley Richard RC	.01	.05
❑ 587 Adrian Cooper RC	.01	.05
❑ 588 Harvey Williams RC	.08	.25
❑ 589 Alvin Harper RC	.08	.25
❑ 590 John Carney	.01	.05
❑ 591 Mark Vander Poel RC	.01	.05
❑ 592 Mike Pritchard RC	.08	.25
❑ 593 Eric Moten RC	.01	.05
❑ 594 Moe Gardner RC	.01	.05
❑ 595 Wesley Carroll RC	.01	.05
❑ 596 Eric Swann RC	.08	.25
❑ 597 Joe Kelly	.01	.05
❑ 598 Steve Jackson RC	.01	.05
❑ 599 Kelvin Pritchett RC	.02	.10
❑ 600 Jesse Campbell RC	.01	.05
❑ 601 Darryll Lewis UER RC	.02	.10
❑ 602 Howard Griffith	.01	.05
❑ 603 Blaise Bryant	.01	.05
❑ 604 Vinnie Clark RC	.01	.05
❑ 605 Mel Agee RC	.01	.05
❑ 606 Bobby Wilson RC	.01	.05
❑ 607 Kevin Donnalley RC	.01	.05
❑ 608 Randal Hill RC	.02	.10
❑ 609 Stan Thomas	.01	.05
❑ 610 Mike Heldt	.01	.05
❑ 611 Brett Favre RC	3.00	8.00
❑ 612 Lawrence Dawsey UER RC	.02	.10
❑ 613 Dennis Gibson	.01	.05
❑ 614 Dean Dingman	.01	.05
❑ 615 Bruce Pickens RC	.01	.05
❑ 616 Todd Marinovich RC	.01	.05
❑ 617 Gene Atkins	.01	.05
❑ 618 Marcus Dupree	.01	.05
❑ 619 Warren Moon Man of Year	.02	.10
❑ 620 Joe Montana TM	.20	.50
❑ 621 Neal Anderson MVP	.01	.05
❑ 622 James Brooks MVP	.02	.10
❑ 623 Thurman Thomas TM	.02	.10
❑ 624 Bobby Humphrey MVP	.01	.05
❑ 625 Kevin Mack MVP	.01	.05
❑ 626 Mark Carrier WR MVP	.01	.05
❑ 627 Johnny Johnson TM	.01	.05
❑ 628 Marion Butts MVP	.02	.10
❑ 629 Steve DeBerg MVP	.01	.05
❑ 630 Jeff George TM	.02	.10
❑ 631 Troy Aikman TM	.15	.40
❑ 632 Dan Marino TM	.20	.50
❑ 633 Randall Cunningham TM	.02	.10
❑ 634 Andre Rison TM	.02	.10
❑ 635 Pepper Johnson MVP	.01	.05
❑ 636 Pat Leahy MVP	.01	.05
❑ 637 Barry Sanders TM	.20	.50
❑ 638 Warren Moon TM	.02	.10
❑ 639 Sterling Sharpe TM	.01	.05
❑ 640 Bruce Armstrong MVP	.01	.05
❑ 641 Bo Jackson TM	.02	.10
❑ 642 Henry Ellard MVP	.02	.10
❑ 643 Earnest Byner MVP	.01	.05
❑ 644 Pat Swilling MVP	.01	.05
❑ 645 John L. Williams MVP	.01	.05

❑ 646 Rod Woodson TM .02 .10
❑ 647 Chris Doleman MVP .01 .05
❑ 648 Joey Browner CC .01 .05
❑ 649 Erik McMillan CC .01 .05
❑ 650 David Fulcher CC .01 .05
❑ 651A Ronnie Lott CC ERR .02 .10
❑ 651B Ronnie Lott CC COR .02 .10
❑ 652 Louis Oliver CC .01 .05
❑ 653 Mark Robinson CC .01 .05
❑ 654 Dennis Smith CC .01 .05
❑ 655 Reggie White SA ERR .02 .10
❑ 656 Charles Haley SA .01 .05
❑ 657 Leslie O'Neal SA .02 .10
❑ 658 Kevin Greene SA .02 .10
❑ 659 Dennis Byrd SA .01 .05
❑ 660 Bruce Smith SA .02 .10
❑ 661 Derrick Thomas SACK .02 .10
❑ 662 Steve DeBerg TL .01 .05
❑ 663 Barry Sanders TL .20 .50
❑ 664 Thurman Thomas TL .02 .10
❑ 665 Jerry Rice TL .15 .40
❑ 666 Derrick Thomas TL .02 .10
❑ 667 Bruce Smith TL .02 .10
❑ 668 Mark Carrier DB TL .01 .05
❑ 669 Richard Johnson CB TL .01 .05
❑ 670 Jan Stenerud HOF .01 .05
❑ 671 Stan Jones HOF .01 .05
❑ 672 John Hannah HOF .01 .05
❑ 673 Tex Schramm HOF .01 .05
❑ 674 Earl Campbell HOF .08 .25
❑ 675 Emmitt Smith/Carrier ROY .30 .75
❑ 676 Warren Moon DT .02 .10
❑ 677 Barry Sanders DT .20 .50
❑ 678 Thurman Thomas DT .08 .25
❑ 679 Andre Reed DT .02 .10
❑ 680 Andre Rison DT .02 .10
❑ 681 Keith Jackson DT .01 .05
❑ 682 Bruce Armstrong DT .01 .05
❑ 683 Jim Lachey DT .01 .05
❑ 684 Bruce Matthews DT .01 .05
❑ 685 Mike Munchak DT .01 .05
❑ 686 Don Mosebar DT .01 .05
❑ B1 Jeff Hostetler BONUS SB .08 .25
❑ B2 Matt Bahr SB .01 .05
❑ B3 Ottis Anderson SB .02 .10
❑ B4 Ottis Anderson SB .02 .10

1992 Score

❑ COMPLETE SET (550) 12.50 25.00
❑ 1 Barry Sanders .75 2.00
❑ 2 Pat Swilling .01 .05
❑ 3 Moe Gardner .01 .05
❑ 4 Steve Young .40 1.00
❑ 5 Chris Spielman .02 .10
❑ 6 Richard Dent .02 .10
❑ 7 Anthony Munoz .02 .10
❑ 8 Martin Mayhew .01 .05
❑ 9 Terry McDaniel .01 .05
❑ 10 Thurman Thomas .08 .25
❑ 11 Ricky Sanders .01 .05
❑ 12 Steve Atwater .01 .05
❑ 13 Tony Tolbert .01 .05
❑ 14 Vince Workman .01 .05
❑ 15 Haywood Jeffires .02 .10
❑ 16 Duane Bickett .01 .05
❑ 17 Jeff Uhlenhake .01 .05
❑ 18 Tim McDonald .01 .05
❑ 19 Cris Carter .20 .50
❑ 20 Derrick Thomas .08 .25
❑ 21 Hugh Millen .01 .05
❑ 22 Bart Oates .01 .05
❑ 23 Eugene Robinson .01 .05
❑ 24 Jerrol Williams .01 .05
❑ 25 Reggie White .08 .25
❑ 26 Marion Butts .01 .05
❑ 27 Jim Sweeney .01 .05
❑ 28 Tom Newberry .01 .05
❑ 29 Pete Stoyanovich .01 .05
❑ 30 Ronnie Lott .02 .10
❑ 31 Simon Fletcher .01 .05
❑ 32 Dino Hackett .01 .05
❑ 33 Morten Andersen .01 .05
❑ 34 Clyde Simmons .01 .05
❑ 35 Mark Rypien .01 .05
❑ 36 Greg Montgomery .01 .05
❑ 37 Nate Lewis .01 .05
❑ 38 Henry Ellard .02 .10
❑ 39 Luis Sharpe .01 .05
❑ 40 Michael Irvin .08 .25
❑ 41 Louis Lipps .01 .05
❑ 42 John L. Williams .01 .05
❑ 43 Broderick Thomas .01 .05
❑ 44 Michael Haynes .02 .10
❑ 45 Don Majkowski .01 .05
❑ 46 William Perry .02 .10
❑ 47 David Fulcher .01 .05
❑ 48 Tony Bennett .01 .05
❑ 49 Clay Matthews .02 .10
❑ 50 Warren Moon .08 .25
❑ 51 Bruce Armstrong .01 .05
❑ 52 Harry Newsome .01 .05
❑ 53 Bill Brooks .01 .05
❑ 54 Greg Townsend .01 .05
❑ 55 Tom Rathman .01 .05
❑ 56 Sean Landeta .01 .05
❑ 57 Kyle Clifton .01 .05
❑ 58 Steve Broussard .01 .05
❑ 59 Mark Carrier WR .02 .10
❑ 60 Mel Gray .02 .10
❑ 61 Tim Krumrie .01 .05
❑ 62 Rufus Porter .01 .05
❑ 63 Kevin Mack .01 .05
❑ 64 Todd Bowles .01 .05
❑ 65 Emmitt Smith 1.25 2.50
❑ 66 Mike Croel .01 .05
❑ 67 Brian Mitchell .02 .10
❑ 68 Bennie Blades .01 .05
❑ 69 Carnell Lake .01 .05
❑ 70 Cornelius Bennett .02 .10
❑ 71 Darrell Thompson .01 .05
❑ 72 Wes Hopkins .01 .05
❑ 73 Jessie Hester .01 .05
❑ 74 Irv Eatman .01 .05
❑ 75 Marv Cook .01 .05
❑ 76 Tim Brown .08 .25
❑ 77 Pepper Johnson .01 .05
❑ 78 Mark Duper .01 .05
❑ 79 Robert Delpino .01 .05
❑ 80 Charles Mann .01 .05
❑ 81 Brian Jordan .02 .10
❑ 82 Wendell Davis .01 .05
❑ 83 Lee Johnson .01 .05
❑ 84 Ricky Reynolds .01 .05
❑ 85 Vaughan Johnson .01 .05
❑ 86 Brian Blades .02 .10
❑ 87 Sam Seale .01 .05
❑ 88 Ed King .01 .05
❑ 89 Gaston Green .01 .05
❑ 90 Christian Okoye .01 .05
❑ 91 Chris Jacke .01 .05
❑ 92 Rohn Stark .01 .05
❑ 93 Kevin Greene .02 .10
❑ 94 Jay Novacek .02 .10
❑ 95 Chip Lohmiller .01 .05
❑ 96 Cris Dishman .01 .05
❑ 97 Ethan Horton .01 .05
❑ 98 Pat Harlow .01 .05
❑ 99 Mark Ingram .01 .05
❑ 100 Mark Carrier DB .01 .05
❑ 101 Deron Cherry .01 .05
❑ 102 Sam Mills .01 .05
❑ 103 Mark Higgs .01 .05
❑ 104 Keith Jackson .02 .10
❑ 105 Steve Tasker .02 .10
❑ 106 Ken Harvey .01 .05
❑ 107 Bryan Hinkle .01 .05
❑ 108 Anthony Carter .02 .10
❑ 109 Johnny Hector .01 .05
❑ 110 Randall McDaniel .02 .10
❑ 111 Johnny Johnson .01 .05
❑ 112 Shane Conlan .01 .05
❑ 113 Ray Horton .01 .05
❑ 114 Sterling Sharpe .08 .25
❑ 115 Guy McIntyre .01 .05
❑ 116 Tom Waddle .01 .05
❑ 117 Albert Lewis .01 .05
❑ 118 Riki Ellison .01 .05
❑ 119 Chris Doleman .01 .05
❑ 120 Andre Rison .02 .10
❑ 121 Bobby Hebert .01 .05
❑ 122 Dan Owens .01 .05
❑ 123 Rodney Hampton .02 .10
❑ 124 Ron Holmes .01 .05
❑ 125 Ernie Jones .01 .05
❑ 126 Michael Carter .01 .05
❑ 127 Reggie Cobb .01 .05
❑ 128 Esera Tuaolo .01 .05
❑ 129 Wilber Marshall .01 .05
❑ 130 Mike Munchak .02 .10
❑ 131 Cortez Kennedy .02 .10
❑ 132 Lamar Lathon .01 .05
❑ 133 Todd Lyght .01 .05
❑ 134 Jeff Feagles .01 .05
❑ 135 Burt Grossman .01 .05
❑ 136 Mike Cofer .01 .05
❑ 137 Frank Warren .01 .05
❑ 138 Jarvis Williams .01 .05
❑ 139 Eddie Brown .01 .05
❑ 140 John Elliott .01 .05
❑ 141 Jim Everett .02 .10
❑ 142 Hardy Nickerson .02 .10
❑ 143 Eddie Murray .01 .05
❑ 144 Andre Tippett .01 .05
❑ 145 Heath Sherman .01 .05
❑ 146 Ronnie Harmon .01 .05
❑ 147 Eric Metcalf .02 .10
❑ 148 Tony Martin .02 .10
❑ 149 Chris Burkett .01 .05
❑ 150 Andre Waters .01 .05
❑ 151 Ray Donaldson .01 .05
❑ 152 Paul Gruber .01 .05
❑ 153 Chris Singleton .01 .05
❑ 154 Clarence Kay .01 .05
❑ 155 Ernest Givins .02 .10
❑ 156 Eric Hill .01 .05
❑ 157 Jesse Sapolu .01 .05
❑ 158 Jack Del Rio .01 .05
❑ 159 Erric Pegram .02 .10
❑ 160 Joey Browner .01 .05
❑ 161 Marcus Allen .08 .25
❑ 162 Eric Moten .01 .05
❑ 163 Donnell Thompson .01 .05
❑ 164 Chuck Cecil .01 .05
❑ 165 Matt Millen .02 .10
❑ 166 Barry Foster .02 .10
❑ 167 Kent Hull .01 .05
❑ 168 Tony Jones WR .01 .05
❑ 169 Mike Prior .01 .05
❑ 170 Neal Anderson .01 .05
❑ 171 Roger Craig .02 .10
❑ 172 Felix Wright .01 .05
❑ 173 James Francis .01 .05
❑ 174 Eugene Lockhart .01 .05
❑ 175 Dalton Hilliard .01 .05
❑ 176 Nick Lowery .01 .05
❑ 177 Tim McKyer .01 .05
❑ 178 Lorenzo White .01 .05
❑ 179 Jeff Hostetler .02 .10
❑ 180 Jackie Harris RC .08 .25
❑ 181 Ken Norton .02 .10
❑ 182 Flipper Anderson .01 .05
❑ 183 Don Warren .01 .05
❑ 184 Brad Baxter .01 .05
❑ 185 John Taylor .02 .10
❑ 186 Harold Green .01 .05
❑ 187 James Washington .01 .05
❑ 188 Aaron Craver .01 .05
❑ 189 Mike Merriweather .01 .05
❑ 190 Gary Clark .08 .25
❑ 191 Vince Buck .01 .05
❑ 192 Cleveland Gary .01 .05
❑ 193 Dan Saleaumua .01 .05
❑ 194 Gary Zimmerman .01 .05
❑ 195 Richmond Webb .01 .05
❑ 196 Gary Plummer .01 .05
❑ 197 Willie Green .01 .05
❑ 198 Chris Warren .08 .25
❑ 199 Mike Pritchard .02 .10
❑ 200 Art Monk .02 .10
❑ 201 Matt Stover .01 .05
❑ 202 Tim Grunhard .01 .05
❑ 203 Mervyn Fernandez .01 .05
❑ 204 Mark Jackson .01 .05
❑ 205 Freddie Joe Nunn .01 .05

❑ 206 Stan Thomas	.01	.05
❑ 207 Keith McKeller	.01	.05
❑ 208 Jeff Lageman	.01	.05
❑ 209 Kenny Walker	.01	.05
❑ 210 Dave Krieg	.02	.10
❑ 211 Dean Biasucci	.01	.05
❑ 212 Herman Moore	.08	.25
❑ 213 Jon Vaughn	.01	.05
❑ 214 Howard Cross	.01	.05
❑ 215 Greg Davis	.01	.05
❑ 216 Bubby Brister	.01	.05
❑ 217 John Kasay	.01	.05
❑ 218 Ron Hall	.01	.05
❑ 219 Mo Lewis	.01	.05
❑ 220 Eric Green	.01	.05
❑ 221 Scott Case	.01	.05
❑ 222 Sean Jones	.01	.05
❑ 223 Winston Moss	.01	.05
❑ 224 Reggie Langhorne	.01	.05
❑ 225 Greg Lewis	.01	.05
❑ 226 Todd McNair	.01	.05
❑ 227 Rod Bernstine	.01	.05
❑ 228 Joe Jacoby	.01	.05
❑ 229 Brad Muster	.01	.05
❑ 230 Nick Bell	.01	.05
❑ 231 Terry Allen	.08	.25
❑ 232 Cliff Odom	.01	.05
❑ 233 Brian Hansen	.01	.05
❑ 234 William Fuller	.01	.05
❑ 235 Issiac Holt	.01	.05
❑ 236 Dexter Carter	.01	.05
❑ 237 Gene Atkins	.01	.05
❑ 238 Pat Beach	.01	.05
❑ 239 Tim McGee	.01	.05
❑ 240 Dermontti Dawson	.01	.05
❑ 241 Dan Fike	.01	.05
❑ 242 Don Beebe	.01	.05
❑ 243 Jeff Bostic	.01	.05
❑ 244 Mark Collins	.01	.05
❑ 245 Steve Sewell	.01	.05
❑ 246 Steve Walsh	.01	.05
❑ 247 Erik Kramer	.02	.10
❑ 248 Scott Norwood	.01	.05
❑ 249 Jesse Solomon	.01	.05
❑ 250 Jerry Ball	.01	.05
❑ 251 Eugene Daniel	.01	.05
❑ 252 Michael Stewart	.01	.05
❑ 253 Fred Barnett	.08	.25
❑ 254 Rodney Holman	.01	.05
❑ 255 Stephen Baker	.01	.05
❑ 256 Don Griffin	.01	.05
❑ 257 Will Wolford	.01	.05
❑ 258 Perry Kemp	.01	.05
❑ 259 Leonard Russell	.02	.10
❑ 260 Jeff Gossett	.01	.05
❑ 261 Dwayne Harper	.01	.05
❑ 262 Vinny Testaverde	.02	.10
❑ 263 Maurice Hurst	.01	.05
❑ 264 Tony Casillas	.01	.05
❑ 265 Louis Oliver	.01	.05
❑ 266 Jim Morrissey	.01	.05
❑ 267 Kenneth Davis	.01	.05
❑ 268 John Alt	.01	.05
❑ 269 Michael Zordich RC	.01	.05
❑ 270 Brian Brennan	.01	.05
❑ 271 Greg Kragen	.01	.05
❑ 272 Andre Collins	.01	.05
❑ 273 Dave Meggett	.02	.10
❑ 274 Scott Fulhage	.01	.05
❑ 275 Tony Zendejas	.01	.05
❑ 276 Herschel Walker	.02	.10
❑ 277 Keith Henderson	.01	.05
❑ 278 Johnny Bailey	.01	.05
❑ 279 Vince Newsome	.01	.05
❑ 280 Chris Hinton	.01	.05
❑ 281 Robert Blackmon	.01	.05
❑ 282 James Hasty	.01	.05
❑ 283 John Offerdahl	.01	.05
❑ 284 Wesley Carroll	.01	.05
❑ 285 Lomas Brown	.01	.05
❑ 286 Neil O'Donnell	.02	.10
❑ 287 Kevin Porter	.01	.05
❑ 288 Lionel Washington	.01	.05
❑ 289 Carlton Bailey RC	.01	.05
❑ 290 Leonard Marshall	.01	.05
❑ 291 John Carney	.01	.05
❑ 292 Bubba McDowell	.01	.05
❑ 293 Nate Newton	.01	.05
❑ 294 Dave Waymer	.01	.05
❑ 295 Rob Moore	.02	.10
❑ 296 Earnest Byner	.01	.05
❑ 297 Jason Staurovsky	.01	.05
❑ 298 Keith McCants	.01	.05
❑ 299 Floyd Turner	.01	.05
❑ 300 Steve Jordan	.01	.05
❑ 301 Nate Odomes	.01	.05
❑ 302 Gerald Riggs	.01	.05
❑ 303 Marvin Washington	.01	.05
❑ 304 Anthony Thompson	.01	.05
❑ 305 Steve DeBerg	.01	.05
❑ 306 Jim Harbaugh	.08	.25
❑ 307 Larry Brown DB	.01	.05
❑ 308 Roger Ruzek	.01	.05
❑ 309 Jessie Tuggle	.01	.05
❑ 310 Al Smith	.01	.05
❑ 311 Mark Kelso	.01	.05
❑ 312 Lawrence Dawsey	.02	.10
❑ 313 Steve Bono RC	.08	.25
❑ 314 Greg Lloyd	.02	.10
❑ 315 Steve Wisniewski	.01	.05
❑ 316 Gill Fenerty	.01	.05
❑ 317 Mark Stepnoski	.02	.10
❑ 318 Derek Russell	.01	.05
❑ 319 Chris Martin	.01	.05
❑ 320 Shaun Gayle	.01	.05
❑ 321 Bob Golic	.01	.05
❑ 322 Larry Kelm	.01	.05
❑ 323 Mike Brim RC	.01	.05
❑ 324 Tommy Kane	.01	.05
❑ 325 Mark Schlereth RC	.01	.05
❑ 326 Ray Childress	.01	.05
❑ 327 Richard Brown RC	.01	.05
❑ 328 Vincent Brown	.01	.05
❑ 329 Mike Farr UER	.01	.05
❑ 330 Eric Swann	.02	.10
❑ 331 Bill Fralic	.01	.05
❑ 332 Rodney Peete	.02	.10
❑ 333 Jerry Gray	.01	.05
❑ 334 Ray Berry	.01	.05
❑ 335 Dennis Smith	.01	.05
❑ 336 Jeff Herrod	.01	.05
❑ 337 Tony Mandarich	.01	.05
❑ 338 Matt Bahr	.01	.05
❑ 339 Mike Saxon	.01	.05
❑ 340 Bruce Matthews	.01	.05
❑ 341 Rickey Jackson	.01	.05
❑ 342 Eric Allen	.01	.05
❑ 343 Lonnie Young	.01	.05
❑ 344 Steve McMichael	.02	.10
❑ 345 Willie Gault	.02	.10
❑ 346 Barry Word	.01	.05
❑ 347 Rich Camarillo	.01	.05
❑ 348 Bill Romanowski	.01	.05
❑ 349 Jim Lachey	.01	.05
❑ 350 Jim Ritcher	.01	.05
❑ 351 Irving Fryar	.02	.10
❑ 352 Gary Anderson K	.01	.05
❑ 353 Henry Rolling	.01	.05
❑ 354 Mark Bortz	.01	.05
❑ 355 Mark Clayton	.02	.10
❑ 356 Keith Woodside	.01	.05
❑ 357 Jonathan Hayes	.01	.05
❑ 358 Derrick Fenner	.01	.05
❑ 359 Keith Byars	.01	.05
❑ 360 Drew Hill	.01	.05
❑ 361 Harris Barton	.01	.05
❑ 362 John Kidd	.01	.05
❑ 363 Aeneas Williams	.02	.10
❑ 364 Brian Washington	.01	.05
❑ 365 John Stephens	.01	.05
❑ 366 Norm Johnson	.01	.05
❑ 367 Darryl Henley	.01	.05
❑ 368 William White	.01	.05
❑ 369 Mark Murphy	.01	.05
❑ 370 Myron Guyton	.01	.05
❑ 371 Leon Seals	.01	.05
❑ 372 Rich Gannon	.08	.25
❑ 373 Toi Cook	.01	.05
❑ 374 Anthony Johnson	.02	.10
❑ 375 Rod Woodson	.08	.25
❑ 376 Alexander Wright	.01	.05
❑ 377 Kevin Butler	.01	.05
❑ 378 Neil Smith	.08	.25
❑ 379 Gary Anderson RB	.01	.05
❑ 380 Reggie Roby	.01	.05
❑ 381 Jeff Bryant	.01	.05
❑ 382 Ray Crockett	.01	.05
❑ 383 Richard Johnson CB	.01	.05
❑ 384 Hassan Jones	.01	.05
❑ 385 Karl Mecklenburg	.01	.05
❑ 386 Jeff Jaeger	.01	.05
❑ 387 Keith Willis	.01	.05
❑ 388 Phil Simms	.02	.10
❑ 389 Kevin Ross	.01	.05
❑ 390 Chris Miller	.02	.10
❑ 391 Brian Noble	.01	.05
❑ 392 Jamie Dukes RC	.01	.05
❑ 393 George Jamison	.01	.05
❑ 394 Rickey Dixon	.01	.05
❑ 395 Carl Lee	.01	.05
❑ 396 Jon Hand	.01	.05
❑ 397 Kirby Jackson	.01	.05
❑ 398 Pat Terrell	.01	.05
❑ 399 Howie Long	.08	.25
❑ 400 Michael Young	.01	.05
❑ 401 Keith Sims	.01	.05
❑ 402 Tommy Barnhardt	.01	.05
❑ 403 Greg McMurtry	.01	.05
❑ 404 Keith Van Horne	.01	.05
❑ 405 Seth Joyner	.01	.05
❑ 406 Jim Jeffcoat	.01	.05
❑ 407 Courtney Hall	.01	.05
❑ 408 Tony Covington	.01	.05
❑ 409 Jacob Green	.01	.05
❑ 410 Charles Haley	.02	.10
❑ 411 Darryl Talley	.01	.05
❑ 412 Jeff Cross	.01	.05
❑ 413 John Elway	.75	2.00
❑ 414 Donald Evans	.01	.05
❑ 415 Jackie Slater	.01	.05
❑ 416 John Friesz	.02	.10
❑ 417 Anthony Smith	.01	.05
❑ 418 Gill Byrd	.01	.05
❑ 419 Willie Drewrey	.01	.05
❑ 420 Jay Hilgenberg	.01	.05
❑ 421 David Treadwell	.01	.05
❑ 422 Curtis Duncan	.01	.05
❑ 423 Sammie Smith	.01	.05
❑ 424 Henry Thomas	.01	.05
❑ 425 James Lofton	.02	.10
❑ 426 Fred Marion	.01	.05
❑ 427 Bryce Paup	.08	.25
❑ 428 Michael Timpson RC	.01	.05
❑ 429 Reyna Thompson	.01	.05
❑ 430 Mike Kenn	.01	.05
❑ 431 Bill Maas	.01	.05
❑ 432 Quinn Early	.02	.10
❑ 433 Everson Walls	.01	.05
❑ 434 Jimmie Jones	.01	.05
❑ 435 Dwight Stone	.01	.05
❑ 436 Harry Colon	.01	.05
❑ 437 Don Mosebar	.01	.05
❑ 438 Calvin Williams	.02	.10
❑ 439 Tom Tupa	.01	.05
❑ 440 Darrell Green	.01	.05
❑ 441 Eric Thomas	.01	.05
❑ 442 Terry Wooden	.01	.05
❑ 443 Brett Perriman	.08	.25
❑ 444 Todd Marinovich	.01	.05
❑ 445 Jim Breech	.01	.05
❑ 446 Eddie Anderson	.01	.05
❑ 447 Jay Schroeder	.01	.05
❑ 448 William Roberts	.01	.05
❑ 449 Brad Edwards	.01	.05
❑ 450 Tunch Ilkin	.01	.05
❑ 451 Ivy Joe Hunter RC	.01	.05
❑ 452 Robert Clark	.01	.05
❑ 453 Tim Barnett	.01	.05
❑ 454 Jarrod Bunch	.01	.05
❑ 455 Tim Harris	.01	.05
❑ 456 James Brooks	.02	.10
❑ 457 Trace Armstrong	.01	.05
❑ 458 Michael Brooks	.01	.05
❑ 459 Andy Heck	.01	.05
❑ 460 Greg Jackson	.01	.05
❑ 461 Vance Johnson	.01	.05
❑ 462 Kirk Lowdermilk	.01	.05
❑ 463 Erik McMillan	.01	.05
❑ 464 Scott Mersereau	.01	.05
❑ 465 Jeff Wright	.01	.05
❑ 466 Mike Tomczak	.01	.05
❑ 467 David Alexander	.01	.05
❑ 468 Bryan Millard	.01	.05
❑ 469 John Randle	.02	.10
❑ 470 Joel Hilgenberg	.01	.05
❑ 471 Bennie Thompson RC	.01	.05
❑ 472 Freeman McNeil	.01	.05

Card		
❑ 473 Terry Orr RC	.01	.05
❑ 474 Mike Horan	.01	.05
❑ 475 Leroy Hoard	.02	.10
❑ 476 Patrick Rowe RC	.01	.05
❑ 477 Siran Stacy RC	.01	.05
❑ 478 Amp Lee RC	.01	.05
❑ 479 Eddie Blake RC	.01	.05
❑ 480 Joe Bowden RC	.01	.05
❑ 481 Rod Milstead RC	.01	.05
❑ 482 Keith Hamilton RC	.02	.10
❑ 483 Darryl Williams RC	.01	.05
❑ 484 Robert Porcher RC	.08	.25
❑ 485 Ed Cunningham RC	.01	.05
❑ 486 Chris Mims RC	.01	.05
❑ 487 Chris Hakel RC	.01	.05
❑ 488 Jimmy Smith RC	1.50	4.00
❑ 489 Todd Harrison RC	.01	.05
❑ 490 Edgar Bennett RC	.08	.25
❑ 491 Dexter McNabb RC	.01	.05
❑ 492 Leon Searcy RC	.01	.05
❑ 493 Tommy Vardell RC	.01	.05
❑ 494 Terrell Buckley RC	.01	.05
❑ 495 Kevin Turner RC	.01	.05
❑ 496 Russ Campbell RC	.01	.05
❑ 497 Torrance Small RC	.02	.10
❑ 498 Nate Turner RC	.01	.05
❑ 499 Cornelius Benton RC	.01	.05
❑ 500 Matt Elliott RC	.01	.05
❑ 501 Robert Stewart RC	.01	.05
❑ 502 Muhammad Shamsid-Deen RC	.01	.05
❑ 503 George Williams RC	.01	.05
❑ 504 Pumpy Tudors RC	.01	.05
❑ 505 Matt LaBounty RC	.01	.05
❑ 506 Darryl Hardy RC	.01	.05
❑ 507 Derrick Moore RC	.02	.10
❑ 508 Willie Clay RC	.01	.05
❑ 509 Bob Whitfield RC	.01	.05
❑ 510 Ricardo McDonald RC	.01	.05
❑ 511 Carlos Huerta RC	.01	.05
❑ 512 Selwyn Jones RC	.01	.05
❑ 513 Steve Gordon RC	.01	.05
❑ 514 Bob Meeks RC	.01	.05
❑ 515 Bennie Blades CC	.01	.05
❑ 516 Andre Waters CC	.01	.05
❑ 517 Bubba McDowell CC	.01	.05
❑ 518 Kevin Porter CC	.01	.05
❑ 519 Carnell Lake CC	.01	.05
❑ 520 Leonard Russell ROY	.02	.10
❑ 521 Mike Croel ROY	.01	.05
❑ 522 Lawrence Dawsey ROY	.01	.05
❑ 523 Moe Gardner ROY	.01	.05
❑ 524 Steve Broussard LBM	.01	.05
❑ 525 Dave Meggett LBM	.01	.05
❑ 526 Darrell Green LBM	.01	.05
❑ 527 Tony Jones WR LBM	.01	.05
❑ 528 Barry Sanders LBM	.40	1.00
❑ 529 Pat Swilling SA	.01	.05
❑ 530 Reggie White SA	.02	.10
❑ 531 William Fuller SA	.01	.05
❑ 532 Simon Fletcher SA	.01	.05
❑ 533 Derrick Thomas SA	.02	.10
❑ 534 Mark Rypien MOY	.01	.05
❑ 535 John Mackey HOF	.01	.05
❑ 536 John Riggins HOF	.02	.10
❑ 537 Lem Barney HOF	.01	.05
❑ 538 Shawn McCarthy RC 90	.01	.05
❑ 539 Al Edwards 90	.01	.05
❑ 540 Alexander Wright 90	.01	.05
❑ 541 Ray Crockett 90	.01	.05
❑ 542 Steve Young/J.Taylor 90	.08	.25
❑ 543 Nate Lewis 90	.01	.05
❑ 544 Dexter Carter 90	.01	.05
❑ 545 Reggie Rutland 90	.01	.05
❑ 546 Jon Vaughn 90	.01	.05
❑ 547 Chris Martin 90	.01	.05
❑ 548 Warren Moon HL	.02	.10
❑ 549 Super Bowl Highlights	.01	.05
❑ 550 Robb Thomas	.01	.05
❑ NNO Dick Butkus Promo	4.00	8.00

1993 Score

Card		
❑ COMPLETE SET (440)	6.00	15.00
❑ 1 Barry Sanders	.50	1.25
❑ 2 Moe Gardner	.01	.05
❑ 3 Ricky Watters	.08	.25
❑ 4 Todd Lyght	.01	.05
❑ 5 Rodney Hampton	.02	.10
❑ 6 Curtis Duncan	.01	.05
❑ 7 Barry Word	.01	.05
❑ 8 Reggie Cobb	.01	.05
❑ 9 Mike Kenn	.01	.05
❑ 10 Michael Irvin	.08	.25
❑ 11 Bryan Cox	.01	.05
❑ 12 Chris Doleman	.01	.05
❑ 13 Rod Woodson	.08	.25
❑ 14 Emmitt Smith	.60	1.50
❑ 15 Pete Stoyanovich	.01	.05
❑ 16 Steve Young	.30	.75
❑ 17 Randall McDaniel	.02	.10
❑ 18 Cortez Kennedy	.02	.10
❑ 19 Mel Gray	.02	.10
❑ 20 Barry Foster	.02	.10
❑ 21 Tim Brown	.08	.25
❑ 22 Todd McNair	.01	.05
❑ 23 Anthony Johnson	.02	.10
❑ 24 Nate Odomes	.01	.05
❑ 25 Brett Favre	.75	2.00
❑ 26 Jack Del Rio	.01	.05
❑ 27 Terry McDaniel	.01	.05
❑ 28 Haywood Jeffires	.02	.10
❑ 29 Jay Novacek	.02	.10
❑ 30 Wilber Marshall	.01	.05
❑ 31 Richmond Webb	.01	.05
❑ 32 Steve Atwater	.01	.05
❑ 33 James Lofton	.02	.10
❑ 34 Harold Green	.01	.05
❑ 35 Eric Metcalf	.02	.10
❑ 36 Bruce Matthews	.01	.05
❑ 37 Albert Lewis	.01	.05
❑ 38 Jeff Herrod	.01	.05
❑ 39 Vince Workman	.01	.05
❑ 40 John Elway	.60	1.50
❑ 41 Brett Perriman	.08	.25
❑ 42 Jon Vaughn	.01	.05
❑ 43 Terry Allen	.08	.25
❑ 44 Clyde Simmons	.01	.05
❑ 45 Bennie Thompson	.01	.05
❑ 46 Wendell Davis	.01	.05
❑ 47 Bobby Hebert	.01	.05
❑ 48 John Offerdahl	.01	.05
❑ 49 Jeff Graham	.02	.10
❑ 50 Steve Wisniewski	.01	.05
❑ 51 Louis Oliver	.01	.05
❑ 52 Rohn Stark	.01	.05
❑ 53 Cleveland Gary	.01	.05
❑ 54 John Randle	.02	.10
❑ 55 Jim Everett	.02	.10
❑ 56 Donnell Woolford	.01	.05
❑ 57 Pepper Johnson	.01	.05
❑ 58 Irving Fryar	.02	.10
❑ 59 Greg Townsend	.01	.05
❑ 60 Chris Burkett	.01	.05
❑ 61 Johnny Johnson	.01	.05
❑ 62 Ronnie Harmon	.01	.05
❑ 63 Don Griffin	.01	.05
❑ 64 Wayne Martin	.01	.05
❑ 65 John L. Williams	.01	.05
❑ 66 Brad Edwards	.01	.05
❑ 67 Toi Cook	.01	.05
❑ 68 Lawrence Dawsey	.01	.05
❑ 69 Johnny Bailey	.01	.05
❑ 70 Mike Brim	.01	.05
❑ 71 Andre Rison	.02	.10
❑ 72 Cornelius Bennett	.02	.10
❑ 73 Brad Muster	.01	.05

Card		
❑ 74 Broderick Thomas	.01	.05
❑ 75 Tom Waddle	.01	.05
❑ 76 Paul Gruber	.01	.05
❑ 77 Jackie Harris	.01	.05
❑ 78 Kenneth Davis	.01	.05
❑ 79 Norm Johnson	.01	.05
❑ 80 Jim Jeffcoat	.01	.05
❑ 81 Chris Warren	.02	.10
❑ 82 Greg Kragen	.01	.05
❑ 83 Ricky Reynolds	.01	.05
❑ 84 Hardy Nickerson	.02	.10
❑ 85 Brian Mitchell	.02	.10
❑ 86 Rufus Porter	.01	.05
❑ 87 Greg Jackson	.01	.05
❑ 88 Seth Joyner	.01	.05
❑ 89 Tim Grunhard	.01	.05
❑ 90 Tim Harris	.01	.05
❑ 91 Sterling Sharpe	.08	.25
❑ 92 Daniel Stubbs	.01	.05
❑ 93 Rob Burnett	.01	.05
❑ 94 Rich Camarillo	.01	.05
❑ 95 Al Smith	.01	.05
❑ 96 Thurman Thomas	.08	.25
❑ 97 Morten Andersen	.01	.05
❑ 98 Reggie White	.08	.25
❑ 99 Gill Byrd	.01	.05
❑ 100 Pierce Holt	.01	.05
❑ 101 Tim McGee	.01	.05
❑ 102 Rickey Jackson	.01	.05
❑ 103 Vince Newsome	.01	.05
❑ 104 Chris Spielman	.02	.10
❑ 105 Tim McDonald	.01	.05
❑ 106 James Francis	.01	.05
❑ 107 Andre Tippett	.01	.05
❑ 108 Sam Mills	.01	.05
❑ 109 Hugh Millen	.01	.05
❑ 110 Brad Baxter	.01	.05
❑ 111 Ricky Sanders	.01	.05
❑ 112 Marion Butts	.01	.05
❑ 113 Fred Barnett	.02	.10
❑ 114 Wade Wilson	.01	.05
❑ 115 Dave Meggett	.01	.05
❑ 116 Kevin Greene	.02	.10
❑ 117 Reggie Langhorne	.01	.05
❑ 118 Simon Fletcher	.01	.05
❑ 119 Tommy Vardell	.01	.05
❑ 120 Darion Conner	.01	.05
❑ 121 Darren Lewis	.01	.05
❑ 122 Charles Mann	.01	.05
❑ 123 David Fulcher	.01	.05
❑ 124 Tommy Kane	.01	.05
❑ 125 Richard Brown	.01	.05
❑ 126 Nate Lewis	.01	.05
❑ 127 Tony Tolbert	.01	.05
❑ 128 Greg Lloyd	.02	.10
❑ 129 Herman Moore	.08	.25
❑ 130 Robert Massey	.01	.05
❑ 131 Chris Jacke	.01	.05
❑ 132 Keith Byars	.01	.05
❑ 133 William Fuller	.01	.05
❑ 134 Rob Moore	.02	.10
❑ 135 Duane Bickett	.01	.05
❑ 136 Jarrod Bunch	.01	.05
❑ 137 Ethan Horton	.01	.05
❑ 138 Leonard Russell	.02	.10
❑ 139 Darryl Henley	.01	.05
❑ 140 Tony Bennett	.01	.05
❑ 141 Harry Newsome	.01	.05
❑ 142 Kelvin Martin	.01	.05
❑ 143 Audray McMillian	.01	.05
❑ 144 Chip Lohmiller	.01	.05
❑ 145 Henry Jones	.01	.05
❑ 146 Rod Bernstine	.01	.05
❑ 147 Darryl Talley	.01	.05
❑ 148 Clarence Verdin	.01	.05
❑ 149 Derrick Thomas	.08	.25
❑ 150 Raleigh McKenzie	.01	.05
❑ 151 Phil Hansen	.01	.05
❑ 152 Lin Elliott RC	.01	.05
❑ 153 Chip Banks	.01	.05
❑ 154 Shannon Sharpe	.08	.25
❑ 155 David Williams	.01	.05
❑ 156 Gaston Green	.01	.05
❑ 157 Trace Armstrong	.01	.05
❑ 158 Todd Scott	.01	.05
❑ 159 Stan Humphries	.02	.10
❑ 160 Christian Okoye	.01	.05
❑ 161 Dennis Smith	.01	.05
❑ 162 Derek Kennard	.01	.05

Card	Low	High
❑ 163 Melvin Jenkins	.01	.05
❑ 164 Tommy Barnhardt	.01	.05
❑ 165 Eugene Robinson	.01	.05
❑ 166 Tom Rathman	.01	.05
❑ 167 Chris Chandler	.02	.10
❑ 168 Steve Broussard	.01	.05
❑ 169 Wymon Henderson	.01	.05
❑ 170 Bryce Paup	.02	.10
❑ 171 Kent Hull	.01	.05
❑ 172 Willie Davis	.08	.25
❑ 173 Richard Dent	.02	.10
❑ 174 Rodney Peete	.01	.05
❑ 175 Clay Matthews	.02	.10
❑ 176 Erik Williams	.01	.05
❑ 177 Mike Cofer	.01	.05
❑ 178 Mark Kelso	.01	.05
❑ 179 Kurt Gouveia	.01	.05
❑ 180 Keith McCants	.01	.05
❑ 181 Jim Arnold	.01	.05
❑ 182 Sean Jones	.01	.05
❑ 183 Chuck Cecil	.01	.05
❑ 184 Mark Rypien	.01	.05
❑ 185 William Perry	.02	.10
❑ 186 Mark Jackson	.01	.05
❑ 187 Jim Dombrowski	.01	.05
❑ 188 Heath Sherman	.01	.05
❑ 189 Bubba McDowell	.01	.05
❑ 190 Fuad Reveiz	.01	.05
❑ 191 Darren Perry	.01	.05
❑ 192 Karl Mecklenburg	.01	.05
❑ 193 Frank Reich	.02	.10
❑ 194 Tony Casillas	.01	.05
❑ 195 Jerry Ball	.01	.05
❑ 196 Jessie Hester	.01	.05
❑ 197 David Lang	.01	.05
❑ 198 Sean Landeta	.01	.05
❑ 199 Jerry Gray	.01	.05
❑ 200 Mark Higgs	.01	.05
❑ 201 Bruce Armstrong	.01	.05
❑ 202 Vaughan Johnson	.01	.05
❑ 203 Calvin Williams	.02	.10
❑ 204 Leonard Marshall	.01	.05
❑ 205 Mike Munchak	.02	.10
❑ 206 Kevin Ross	.01	.05
❑ 207 Daryl Johnston	.08	.25
❑ 208 Jay Schroeder	.01	.05
❑ 209 Mo Lewis	.01	.05
❑ 210 Carlton Haselrig	.01	.05
❑ 211 Cris Carter	.08	.25
❑ 212 Marv Cook	.01	.05
❑ 213 Mark Duper	.01	.05
❑ 214 Jackie Slater	.01	.05
❑ 215 Mike Prior	.01	.05
❑ 216 Warren Moon	.08	.25
❑ 217 Mike Saxon	.01	.05
❑ 218 Derrick Fenner	.01	.05
❑ 219 Brian Washington	.01	.05
❑ 220 Jessie Tuggle	.01	.05
❑ 221 Jeff Hostetler	.02	.10
❑ 222 Deion Sanders	.20	.50
❑ 223 Neal Anderson	.01	.05
❑ 224 Kevin Mack	.01	.05
❑ 225 Tommy Maddox	.08	.25
❑ 226 Neil Smith	.08	.25
❑ 227 Ronnie Lott	.02	.10
❑ 228 Flipper Anderson	.01	.05
❑ 229 Keith Jackson	.02	.10
❑ 230 Pat Swilling	.01	.05
❑ 231 Carl Banks	.01	.05
❑ 232 Eric Allen	.01	.05
❑ 233 Randal Hill	.01	.05
❑ 234 Burt Grossman	.01	.05
❑ 235 Jerry Rice	.40	1.00
❑ 236 Santana Dotson	.02	.10
❑ 237 Andre Reed	.02	.10
❑ 238 Troy Aikman	.30	.75
❑ 239 Ray Childress	.01	.05
❑ 240 Phil Simms	.02	.10
❑ 241 Steve McMichael	.02	.10
❑ 242 Browning Nagle	.01	.05
❑ 243 Anthony Miller	.02	.10
❑ 244 Earnest Byner	.01	.05
❑ 245 Jay Hilgenberg	.01	.05
❑ 246 Jeff George	.08	.25
❑ 247 Marco Coleman	.01	.05
❑ 248 Mark Carrier DB	.01	.05
❑ 249 Howie Long	.08	.25
❑ 250 Ed McCaffrey	.08	.25
❑ 251 Jim Kelly	.08	.25
❑ 252 Henry Ellard	.02	.10
❑ 253 Joe Montana	.60	1.50
❑ 254 Dale Carter	.01	.05
❑ 255 Boomer Esiason	.02	.10
❑ 256 Gary Clark	.02	.10
❑ 257 Carl Pickens	.02	.10
❑ 258 Dave Krieg	.02	.10
❑ 259 Russell Maryland	.01	.05
❑ 260 Randall Cunningham	.08	.25
❑ 261 Leslie O'Neal	.02	.10
❑ 262 Vinny Testaverde	.02	.10
❑ 263 Ricky Ervins	.01	.05
❑ 264 Chris Mims	.01	.05
❑ 265 Dan Marino	.60	1.50
❑ 266 Eric Martin	.01	.05
❑ 267 Bruce Smith	.08	.25
❑ 268 Jim Harbaugh	.08	.25
❑ 269 Steve Emtman	.01	.05
❑ 270 Ricky Proehl	.01	.05
❑ 271 Vaughn Dunbar	.01	.05
❑ 272 Junior Seau	.08	.25
❑ 273 Sean Gilbert	.02	.10
❑ 274 Jim Lachey	.01	.05
❑ 275 Dalton Hilliard	.01	.05
❑ 276 David Klingler	.01	.05
❑ 277 Robert Jones	.01	.05
❑ 278 David Treadwell	.01	.05
❑ 279 Tracy Scroggins	.01	.05
❑ 280 Terrell Buckley	.01	.05
❑ 281 Quentin Coryatt	.02	.10
❑ 282 Jason Hanson	.01	.05
❑ 283 Shane Conlan	.01	.05
❑ 284 Guy McIntyre	.01	.05
❑ 285 Gary Zimmerman	.01	.05
❑ 286 Marty Carter	.01	.05
❑ 287 Jim Sweeney	.01	.05
❑ 288 Arthur Marshall RC	.01	.05
❑ 289 Eugene Chung	.01	.05
❑ 290 Mike Pritchard	.02	.10
❑ 291 Jim Ritcher	.01	.05
❑ 292 Todd Marinovich	.01	.05
❑ 293 Courtney Hall	.01	.05
❑ 294 Mark Collins	.01	.05
❑ 295 Troy Auzenne	.01	.05
❑ 296 Aeneas Williams	.01	.05
❑ 297 Andy Heck	.01	.05
❑ 298 Shaun Gayle	.01	.05
❑ 299 Kevin Fagan	.01	.05
❑ 300 Carnell Lake	.01	.05
❑ 301 Bernie Kosar	.02	.10
❑ 302 Maurice Hurst	.01	.05
❑ 303 Mike Merriweather	.01	.05
❑ 304 Reggie Roby	.01	.05
❑ 305 Darryl Williams	.01	.05
❑ 306 Jerome Bettis RC	2.50	5.00
❑ 307 Curtis Conway RC	.15	.40
❑ 308 Drew Bledsoe RC	1.00	2.50
❑ 309 John Copeland RC	.02	.10
❑ 310 Eric Curry RC	.01	.05
❑ 311 Lincoln Kennedy RC	.01	.05
❑ 312 Dan Williams RC	.01	.05
❑ 313 Patrick Bates RC	.01	.05
❑ 314 Tom Carter RC	.02	.10
❑ 315 Garrison Hearst RC	.30	.75
❑ 316 Joel Hilgenberg	.01	.05
❑ 317 Harris Barton	.01	.05
❑ 318 Jeff Lageman	.01	.05
❑ 319 Charles Mincy RC	.01	.05
❑ 320 Ricardo McDonald	.01	.05
❑ 321 Lorenzo White	.01	.05
❑ 322 Troy Vincent	.01	.05
❑ 323 Bennie Blades	.01	.05
❑ 324 Dana Hall	.01	.05
❑ 325 Ken Norton Jr.	.02	.10
❑ 326 Will Wolford	.01	.05
❑ 327 Neil O'Donnell	.08	.25
❑ 328 Tracy Simien	.01	.05
❑ 329 Darrell Green	.01	.05
❑ 330 Kyle Clifton	.01	.05
❑ 331 Elbert Shelley RC	.01	.05
❑ 332 Jeff Wright	.01	.05
❑ 333 Mike Johnson	.01	.05
❑ 334 John Gesek	.01	.05
❑ 335 Michael Brooks	.01	.05
❑ 336 George Jamison	.01	.05
❑ 337 Johnny Holland	.01	.05
❑ 338 Lamar Lathon	.01	.05
❑ 339 Bern Brostek	.01	.05
❑ 340 Steve Jordan	.01	.05
❑ 341 Gene Atkins	.01	.05
❑ 342 Aaron Wallace	.01	.05
❑ 343 Adrian Cooper	.01	.05
❑ 344 Amp Lee	.01	.05
❑ 345 Vincent Brown	.01	.05
❑ 346 James Hasty	.01	.05
❑ 347 Ron Hall	.01	.05
❑ 348 Matt Elliott	.01	.05
❑ 349 Tim Krumrie	.01	.05
❑ 350 Mark Stepnoski	.01	.05
❑ 351 Matt Stover	.01	.05
❑ 352 James Washington	.01	.05
❑ 353 Marc Spindler	.01	.05
❑ 354 Frank Warren	.01	.05
❑ 355 Vai Sikahema	.01	.05
❑ 356 Dan Saleaumua	.01	.05
❑ 357 Mark Clayton	.01	.05
❑ 358 Brent Jones	.02	.10
❑ 359 Andy Harmon RC	.02	.10
❑ 360 Anthony Parker	.01	.05
❑ 361 Chris Hinton	.01	.05
❑ 362 Greg Montgomery	.01	.05
❑ 363 Greg McMurtry	.01	.05
❑ 364 Craig Heyward	.02	.10
❑ 365 D.J. Johnson	.01	.05
❑ 366 Bill Romanowski	.01	.05
❑ 367 Steve Christie	.01	.05
❑ 368 Art Monk	.02	.10
❑ 369 Howard Ballard	.01	.05
❑ 370 Andre Collins	.01	.05
❑ 371 Alvin Harper	.02	.10
❑ 372 Blaise Winter RC	.01	.05
❑ 373 Al Del Greco	.01	.05
❑ 374 Eric Green	.01	.05
❑ 375 Chris Mohr	.01	.05
❑ 376 Tom Newberry	.01	.05
❑ 377 Cris Dishman	.01	.05
❑ 378 Jumpy Geathers	.01	.05
❑ 379 Don Mosebar	.01	.05
❑ 380 Andre Ware	.01	.05
❑ 381 Marvin Washington	.01	.05
❑ 382 Bobby Humphrey	.01	.05
❑ 383 Marc Logan	.01	.05
❑ 384 Lomas Brown	.01	.05
❑ 385 Steve Tasker	.02	.10
❑ 386 Chris Miller	.02	.10
❑ 387 Tony Paige	.01	.05
❑ 388 Charles Haley	.02	.10
❑ 389 Rich Moran	.01	.05
❑ 390 Mike Sherrard	.01	.05
❑ 391 Nick Lowery	.01	.05
❑ 392 Henry Thomas	.01	.05
❑ 393 Keith Sims	.01	.05
❑ 394 Thomas Everett	.01	.05
❑ 395 Steve Wallace	.01	.05
❑ 396 John Carney	.01	.05
❑ 397 Tim Johnson	.01	.05
❑ 398 Jeff Gossett	.01	.05
❑ 399 Anthony Smith	.01	.05
❑ 400 Kelvin Pritchett	.01	.05
❑ 401 Dermontti Dawson	.01	.05
❑ 402 Alfred Williams	.01	.05
❑ 403 Michael Haynes	.02	.10
❑ 404 Bart Oates	.01	.05
❑ 405 Ken Lanier	.01	.05
❑ 406 Vencie Glenn	.01	.05
❑ 407 John Taylor	.02	.10
❑ 408 Nate Newton	.02	.10
❑ 409 Mark Carrier WR	.02	.10
❑ 410 Ken Harvey	.01	.05
❑ 411 Troy Aikman SB	.15	.40
❑ 412 Charles Haley SB	.01	.05
❑ 413 Warren Moon/Jeffires DT	.02	.10
❑ 414 Henry Jones DT	.01	.05
❑ 415 Rickey Jackson DT	.01	.05
❑ 416 Clyde Simmons DT	.01	.05
❑ 417 Dale Carter ROY	.01	.05
❑ 418 Carl Pickens ROY	.02	.10
❑ 419 Vaughn Dunbar ROY	.01	.05
❑ 420 Santana Dotson ROY	.01	.05
❑ 421 Steve Emtman 90	.01	.05
❑ 422 Louis Oliver 90	.01	.05
❑ 423 Carl Pickens 90	.02	.10
❑ 424 Eddie Anderson 90	.01	.05
❑ 425 Deion Sanders 90	.08	.25
❑ 426 Jon Vaughn 90	.01	.05
❑ 427 Darren Lewis 90	.01	.05
❑ 428 Kevin Ross 90	.01	.05
❑ 429 David Brandon 90	.01	.05

Card		
❑ 430 Dave Meggett 90	.01	.05
❑ 431 Jerry Rice HL	.20	.50
❑ 432 Sterling Sharpe HL	.02	.10
❑ 433 Art Monk HL	.01	.05
❑ 434 James Lofton HL	.01	.05
❑ 435 Lawrence Taylor	.02	.10
❑ 436 Bill Walsh HOF RC	.02	.10
❑ 437 Chuck Noll HOF	.02	.10
❑ 438 Dan Fouts HOF	.01	.05
❑ 439 Larry Little HOF	.01	.05
❑ 440 Steve Young MOY	.15	.40
❑ NNO Dick Butkus AU/3000	25.00	40.00

1994 Score

Card		
❑ COMPLETE SET (330)	5.00	12.00
❑ 1 Barry Sanders	.50	1.25
❑ 2 Troy Aikman	.30	.75
❑ 3 Sterling Sharpe	.02	.10
❑ 4 Deion Sanders	.20	.50
❑ 5 Bruce Smith	.08	.25
❑ 6 Eric Metcalf	.02	.10
❑ 7 John Elway	.60	1.50
❑ 8 Bruce Matthews	.01	.05
❑ 9 Rickey Jackson	.01	.05
❑ 10 Cortez Kennedy	.02	.10
❑ 11 Jerry Rice	.30	.75
❑ 12 Stanley Richard	.01	.05
❑ 13 Rod Woodson	.02	.10
❑ 14 Eric Swann	.02	.10
❑ 15 Eric Allen	.01	.05
❑ 16 Richard Dent	.02	.10
❑ 17 Carl Pickens	.02	.10
❑ 18 Rohn Stark	.01	.05
❑ 19 Marcus Allen	.08	.25
❑ 20 Steve Wisniewski	.01	.05
❑ 21 Jerome Bettis	.20	.50
❑ 22 Darrell Green	.01	.05
❑ 23 Lawrence Dawsey	.01	.05
❑ 24 Larry Centers	.08	.25
❑ 25 Steve Jordan	.01	.05
❑ 26 Johnny Johnson	.01	.05
❑ 27 Phil Simms	.02	.10
❑ 28 Bruce Armstrong	.01	.05
❑ 29 Willie Roaf	.01	.05
❑ 30 Andre Rison	.02	.10
❑ 31 Henry Jones	.01	.05
❑ 32 Warren Moon	.08	.25
❑ 33 Sean Gilbert	.01	.05
❑ 34 Ben Coates	.02	.10
❑ 35 Seth Joyner	.01	.05
❑ 36 Ronnie Harmon	.01	.05
❑ 37 Quentin Coryatt	.01	.05
❑ 38 Ricky Sanders	.01	.05
❑ 39 Gerald Williams	.01	.05
❑ 40 Emmitt Smith	.40	1.00
❑ 41 Jason Hanson	.01	.05
❑ 42 Kevin Smith	.01	.05
❑ 43 Irving Fryar	.02	.10
❑ 44 Boomer Esiason	.02	.10
❑ 45 Darryl Talley	.01	.05
❑ 46 Paul Gruber	.01	.05
❑ 47 Anthony Smith	.01	.05
❑ 48 John Copeland	.01	.05
❑ 49 Michael Jackson	.02	.10
❑ 50 Shannon Sharpe	.02	.10
❑ 51 Reggie White	.08	.25
❑ 52 Andre Collins	.01	.05
❑ 53 Jack Del Rio	.01	.05
❑ 54 John Elliott	.01	.05
❑ 55 Kevin Greene	.02	.10
❑ 56 Steve Young	.25	.60
❑ 57 Erric Pegram	.01	.05
❑ 58 Donnell Woolford	.01	.05
❑ 59 Darryl Williams	.01	.05
❑ 60 Michael Irvin	.08	.25
❑ 61 Mel Gray	.01	.05
❑ 62 Greg Montgomery	.01	.05
❑ 63 Neil Smith	.02	.10
❑ 64 Andy Harmon	.01	.05
❑ 65 Dan Marino	.60	1.50
❑ 66 Leonard Russell	.01	.05
❑ 67 Joe Montana	.60	1.50
❑ 68 John Taylor	.02	.10
❑ 69 Cris Dishman	.01	.05
❑ 70 Cornelius Bennett	.02	.10
❑ 71 Harold Green	.01	.05
❑ 72 Anthony Pleasant	.01	.05
❑ 73 Dennis Smith	.01	.05
❑ 74 Bryce Paup	.02	.10
❑ 75 Jeff George	.08	.25
❑ 76 Henry Ellard	.02	.10
❑ 77 Randall McDaniel	.02	.10
❑ 78 Derek Brown RBK	.01	.05
❑ 79 Johnny Mitchell	.01	.05
❑ 80 Leroy Thompson	.01	.05
❑ 81 Junior Seau	.08	.25
❑ 82 Kelvin Martin	.01	.05
❑ 83 Guy McIntyre	.01	.05
❑ 84 Elbert Shelley	.01	.05
❑ 85 Louis Oliver	.01	.05
❑ 86 Tommy Vardell	.01	.05
❑ 87 Jeff Herrod	.01	.05
❑ 88 Edgar Bennett	.08	.25
❑ 89 Reggie Langhorne	.01	.05
❑ 90 Terry Kirby	.08	.25
❑ 91 Marcus Robertson	.01	.05
❑ 92 Mark Collins	.01	.05
❑ 93 Calvin Williams	.02	.10
❑ 94 Barry Foster	.01	.05
❑ 95 Brent Jones	.02	.10
❑ 96 Reggie Cobb	.01	.05
❑ 97 Ray Childress	.01	.05
❑ 98 Chris Miller	.01	.05
❑ 99 John Carney	.01	.05
❑ 100 Ricky Proehl	.01	.05
❑ 101 Renaldo Turnbull	.01	.05
❑ 102 John Randle	.02	.10
❑ 103 Flipper Anderson	.01	.05
❑ 104 Scottie Graham RC	.02	.10
❑ 105 Webster Slaughter	.01	.05
❑ 106 Tyrone Hughes	.02	.10
❑ 107 Ken Norton Jr.	.02	.10
❑ 108 Jim Kelly	.08	.25
❑ 109 Michael Haynes	.02	.10
❑ 110 Mark Carrier DB	.01	.05
❑ 111 Eddie Murray	.01	.05
❑ 112 Glyn Milburn	.02	.10
❑ 113 Jackie Harris	.01	.05
❑ 114 Dean Biasucci	.01	.05
❑ 115 Tim Brown	.08	.25
❑ 116 Mark Higgs	.01	.05
❑ 117 Steve Emtman	.01	.05
❑ 118 Clay Matthews	.01	.05
❑ 119 Clyde Simmons	.01	.05
❑ 120 Howard Ballard	.01	.05
❑ 121 Ricky Watters	.02	.10
❑ 122 William Fuller	.01	.05
❑ 123 Robert Brooks	.08	.25
❑ 124 Brian Blades	.02	.10
❑ 125 Leslie O'Neal	.01	.05
❑ 126 Gary Clark	.02	.10
❑ 127 Jim Sweeney	.01	.05
❑ 128 Vaughan Johnson	.01	.05
❑ 129 Gary Brown	.01	.05
❑ 130 Todd Lyght	.01	.05
❑ 131 Nick Lowery	.01	.05
❑ 132 Ernest Givins	.02	.10
❑ 133 Lomas Brown	.01	.05
❑ 134 Craig Erickson	.01	.05
❑ 135 James Francis	.01	.05
❑ 136 Andre Reed	.02	.10
❑ 137 Jim Everett	.02	.10
❑ 138 Nate Odomes	.01	.05
❑ 139 Tom Waddle	.01	.05
❑ 140 Stevon Moore	.01	.05
❑ 141 Rod Bernstine	.01	.05
❑ 142 Brett Favre	.60	1.50
❑ 143 Roosevelt Potts	.01	.05
❑ 144 Chester McGlockton	.01	.05
❑ 145 LeRoy Butler	.01	.05
❑ 146 Charles Haley	.02	.10
❑ 147 Rodney Hampton	.02	.10
❑ 148 George Teague	.01	.05
❑ 149 Gary Anderson K	.01	.05
❑ 150 Mark Stepnoski	.01	.05
❑ 151 Courtney Hawkins	.01	.05
❑ 152 Tim Grunhard	.01	.05
❑ 153 David Klingler	.01	.05
❑ 154 Erik Williams	.01	.05
❑ 155 Herman Moore	.08	.25
❑ 156 Daryl Johnston	.02	.10
❑ 157 Chris Zorich	.01	.05
❑ 158 Shane Conlan	.01	.05
❑ 159 Santana Dotson	.02	.10
❑ 160 Sam Mills	.01	.05
❑ 161 Ronnie Lott	.02	.10
❑ 162 Jesse Sapolu	.01	.05
❑ 163 Marion Butts	.01	.05
❑ 164 Eugene Robinson	.01	.05
❑ 165 Mark Schlereth	.01	.05
❑ 166 John L. Williams	.01	.05
❑ 167 Anthony Miller	.02	.10
❑ 168 Rich Camarillo	.01	.05
❑ 169 Jeff Lageman	.01	.05
❑ 170 Michael Brooks	.01	.05
❑ 171 Scott Mitchell	.02	.10
❑ 172 Duane Bickett	.01	.05
❑ 173 Willie Davis	.02	.10
❑ 174 Maurice Hurst	.01	.05
❑ 175 Brett Perriman	.02	.10
❑ 176 Jay Novacek	.02	.10
❑ 177 Terry Allen	.02	.10
❑ 178 Pete Metzelaars	.01	.05
❑ 179 Erik Kramer	.02	.10
❑ 180 Neal Anderson	.01	.05
❑ 181 Ethan Horton	.01	.05
❑ 182 Tony Bennett	.01	.05
❑ 183 Gary Zimmerman	.01	.05
❑ 184 Jeff Hostetler	.02	.10
❑ 185 Jeff Cross	.01	.05
❑ 186 Vincent Brown	.01	.05
❑ 187 Herschel Walker	.02	.10
❑ 188 Courtney Hall	.01	.05
❑ 189 Norm Johnson	.01	.05
❑ 190 Hardy Nickerson	.02	.10
❑ 191 Greg Townsend	.01	.05
❑ 192 Mike Munchak	.02	.10
❑ 193 Dante Jones	.01	.05
❑ 194 Vinny Testaverde	.02	.10
❑ 195 Vance Johnson	.01	.05
❑ 196 Chris Jacke	.01	.05
❑ 197 Will Wolford	.01	.05
❑ 198 Terry McDaniel	.01	.05
❑ 199 Bryan Cox	.01	.05
❑ 200 Nate Newton	.01	.05
❑ 201 Keith Byars	.01	.05
❑ 202 Neil O'Donnell	.08	.25
❑ 203 Harris Barton	.01	.05
❑ 204 Thurman Thomas	.08	.25
❑ 205 Jeff Query	.01	.05
❑ 206 Russell Maryland	.01	.05
❑ 207 Pat Swilling	.01	.05
❑ 208 Haywood Jeffires	.02	.10
❑ 209 John Alt	.01	.05
❑ 210 O.J.McDuffie	.08	.25
❑ 211 Keith Sims	.01	.05
❑ 212 Eric Martin	.01	.05
❑ 213 Kyle Clifton	.01	.05
❑ 214 Luis Sharpe	.01	.05
❑ 215 Thomas Everett	.01	.05
❑ 216 Chris Warren	.02	.10
❑ 217 Chris Doleman	.01	.05
❑ 218 Tony Jones T	.01	.05
❑ 219 Karl Mecklenburg	.01	.05
❑ 220 Rob Moore	.02	.10
❑ 221 Jessie Hester	.01	.05
❑ 222 Jeff Jaeger	.01	.05
❑ 223 Keith Jackson	.01	.05
❑ 224 Mo Lewis	.01	.05
❑ 225 Mike Horan	.01	.05
❑ 226 Eric Green	.01	.05
❑ 227 Jim Ritcher	.01	.05
❑ 228 Eric Curry	.01	.05
❑ 229 Stan Humphries	.02	.10
❑ 230 Mike Johnson	.01	.05
❑ 231 Alvin Harper	.02	.10
❑ 232 Bennie Blades	.01	.05
❑ 233 Cris Carter	.20	.50
❑ 234 Morten Andersen	.01	.05
❑ 235 Brian Washington	.01	.05
❑ 236 Eric Hill	.01	.05
❑ 237 Natrone Means	.08	.25
❑ 238 Carlton Bailey	.01	.05
❑ 239 Anthony Carter	.02	.10

Card		
❑ 240 Jessie Tuggle	.01	.05
❑ 241 Tim Irwin	.01	.05
❑ 242 Mark Carrier WR	.02	.10
❑ 243 Steve Atwater	.01	.05
❑ 244 Sean Jones	.01	.05
❑ 245 Bernie Kosar	.02	.10
❑ 246 Richmond Webb	.01	.05
❑ 247 Dave Meggett	.01	.05
❑ 248 Vincent Brisby	.02	.10
❑ 249 Fred Barnett	.02	.10
❑ 250 Greg Lloyd	.02	.10
❑ 251 Tim McDonald	.01	.05
❑ 252 Mike Pritchard	.01	.05
❑ 253 Greg Robinson	.01	.05
❑ 254 Tony McGee	.01	.05
❑ 255 Chris Spielman	.02	.10
❑ 256 Keith Loneker RC	.01	.05
❑ 257 Derrick Thomas	.08	.25
❑ 258 Wayne Martin	.01	.05
❑ 259 Art Monk	.02	.10
❑ 260 Andy Heck	.01	.05
❑ 261 Chip Lohmiller	.01	.05
❑ 262 Simon Fletcher	.01	.05
❑ 263 Ricky Reynolds	.01	.05
❑ 264 Chris Hinton	.01	.05
❑ 265 Ronald Moore	.01	.05
❑ 266 Rocket Ismail	.02	.10
❑ 267 Pete Stoyanovich	.01	.05
❑ 268 Mark Jackson	.01	.05
❑ 269 Randall Cunningham	.08	.25
❑ 270 Dermontti Dawson	.01	.05
❑ 271 Bill Romanowski	.01	.05
❑ 272 Tim Johnson	.01	.05
❑ 273 Steve Tasker	.02	.10
❑ 274 Keith Hamilton	.01	.05
❑ 275 Pierce Holt	.01	.05
❑ 276 Heath Shuler RC	.08	.25
❑ 277 Marshall Faulk RC	2.00	5.00
❑ 278 Charles Johnson RC	.08	.25
❑ 279 Sam Adams RC	.02	.10
❑ 280 Trev Alberts RC	.02	.10
❑ 281 Derrick Alexander WR RC	.08	.25
❑ 282 Bryant Young RC	.15	.40
❑ 283 Greg Hill RC	.08	.25
❑ 284 Darnay Scott RC	.20	.50
❑ 285 Willie McGinest RC	.08	.25
❑ 286 Thomas Randolph RC	.01	.05
❑ 287 Errict Rhett RC	.08	.25
❑ 288 Lamar Smith RC	.50	1.25
❑ 289 William Floyd RC	.08	.25
❑ 290 Johnnie Morton RC	.20	.50
❑ 291 Jamir Miller RC	.02	.10
❑ 292 David Palmer RC	.08	.25
❑ 293 Dan Wilkinson RC	.02	.10
❑ 294 Trent Dilfer RC	.50	1.25
❑ 295 Antonio Langham RC	.02	.10
❑ 296 Chuck Levy RC	.01	.05
❑ 297 John Thierry RC	.01	.05
❑ 298 Kevin Lee RC	.01	.05
❑ 299 Aaron Glenn RC	.08	.25
❑ 300 Charlie Garner RC	.50	1.25
❑ 301 Lonnie Johnson RC	.01	.05
❑ 302 LeShon Johnson RC	.02	.10
❑ 303 Thomas Lewis RC	.02	.10
❑ 304 Ryan Yarborough RC	.01	.05
❑ 305 Mario Bates RC	.08	.25
❑ 306 Buffalo Bills TC	.01	.05
❑ 307 Cincinnati Bengals TC	.01	.05
❑ 308 Cleveland Browns TC	.01	.05
❑ 309 Denver Broncos TC	.01	.05
❑ 310 Houston Oilers TC	.01	.05
❑ 311 Indianapolis Colts TC	.01	.05
❑ 312 Kansas City Chiefs TC	.01	.05
❑ 313 Los Angeles Raiders TC	.01	.05
❑ 314 Miami Dolphins TC	.01	.05
❑ 315 New England Patriots TC	.01	.05
❑ 316 New York Jets TC	.01	.05
❑ 317 Pittsburgh Steelers TC	.01	.05
❑ 318 San Diego Charges TC	.01	.05
❑ 319 Seattle Seahawks TC	.01	.05
❑ 320 Garrison Hearst FF	.08	.25
❑ 321 Drew Bledsoe FF	.30	.75
❑ 322 Tyrone Hughes FF	.02	.10
❑ 323 James Jett FF	.01	.05
❑ 324 Tom Carter FF	.01	.05
❑ 325 Reggie Brooks FF	.01	.05
❑ 326 Dana Stubblefield FF	.02	.10
❑ 327 Jerome Bettis FF	.08	.25
❑ 328 Chris Slade FF	.01	.05
❑ 329 Rick Mirer FF	.08	.25
❑ 330 Emmitt Smith MVP	.20	.50

1995 Score

Card		
❑ COMPLETE SET (275)	6.00	15.00
❑ 1 Steve Young	.25	.60
❑ 2 Barry Sanders	.50	1.25
❑ 3 Jerry Rice	.30	.75
❑ 4 Marshall Faulk	.40	1.00
❑ 5 Terance Mathis	.02	.10
❑ 6 Rod Woodson	.02	.10
❑ 7 Seth Joyner	.01	.05
❑ 8 Michael Timpson	.01	.05
❑ 9 Deion Sanders	.20	.50
❑ 10 Emmitt Smith	.50	1.25
❑ 11 Cris Carter	.08	.25
❑ 12 Jake Reed	.02	.10
❑ 13 Reggie White	.08	.25
❑ 14 Shannon Sharpe	.02	.10
❑ 15 Troy Aikman	.30	.75
❑ 16 Andre Reed	.02	.10
❑ 17 Tyrone Hughes	.02	.10
❑ 18 Sterling Sharpe	.02	.10
❑ 19 Jerome Bettis	.08	.25
❑ 20 Irving Fryar	.02	.10
❑ 21 Warren Moon	.02	.10
❑ 22 Ben Coates	.02	.10
❑ 23 Frank Reich	.01	.05
❑ 24 Henry Ellard	.02	.10
❑ 25 Steve Atwater	.01	.05
❑ 26 Willie Davis	.02	.10
❑ 27 Michael Irvin	.08	.25
❑ 28 Harvey Williams	.01	.05
❑ 29 Aeneas Williams	.01	.05
❑ 30 Errict Rhett	.02	.10
❑ 31 Lorenzo White	.01	.05
❑ 32 John Elway	.60	1.50
❑ 33 Rodney Hampton	.02	.10
❑ 34 Webster Slaughter	.01	.05
❑ 35 Eric Turner	.01	.05
❑ 36 Dan Marino	.60	1.50
❑ 37 Daryl Johnston	.02	.10
❑ 38 Bruce Smith	.08	.25
❑ 39 Ronald Moore	.01	.05
❑ 40 Larry Centers	.02	.10
❑ 41 Curtis Conway	.08	.25
❑ 42 Drew Bledsoe	.20	.50
❑ 43 Quinn Early	.02	.10
❑ 44 Marcus Allen	.08	.25
❑ 45 Andre Rison	.02	.10
❑ 46 Jeff Blake RC	.20	.50
❑ 47 Barry Foster	.02	.10
❑ 48 Antonio Langham	.01	.05
❑ 49 Herman Moore	.08	.25
❑ 50 Flipper Anderson	.01	.05
❑ 51 Rick Mirer	.02	.10
❑ 52 Jay Novacek	.02	.10
❑ 53 Tim Bowens	.01	.05
❑ 54 Carl Pickens	.02	.10
❑ 55 Lewis Tillman	.01	.05
❑ 56 Lawrence Dawsey	.01	.05
❑ 57 Leroy Hoard	.01	.05
❑ 58 Steve Broussard	.01	.05
❑ 59 Dave Krieg	.01	.05
❑ 60 John Taylor	.01	.05
❑ 61 Johnny Mitchell	.01	.05
❑ 62 Jessie Hester	.01	.05
❑ 63 Johnny Bailey	.01	.05
❑ 64 Brett Favre	.60	1.50
❑ 65 Bryce Paup	.02	.10
❑ 66 J.J. Birden	.01	.05
❑ 67 Steve Tasker	.02	.10
❑ 68 Edgar Bennett	.02	.10
❑ 69 Ray Buchanan	.01	.05
❑ 70 Brent Jones	.01	.05
❑ 71 Dave Meggett	.01	.05
❑ 72 Jeff Graham	.01	.05
❑ 73 Michael Brooks	.01	.05
❑ 74 Ricky Ervins	.01	.05
❑ 75 Chris Warren	.02	.10
❑ 76 Natrone Means	.02	.10
❑ 77 Tim Brown	.08	.25
❑ 78 Jim Everett	.01	.05
❑ 79 Chris Calloway	.01	.05
❑ 80 John L. Williams	.01	.05
❑ 81 Chris Chandler	.02	.10
❑ 82 Tim McDonald	.01	.05
❑ 83 Calvin Williams	.02	.10
❑ 84 Tony McGee	.01	.05
❑ 85 Erik Kramer	.01	.05
❑ 86 Eric Green	.01	.05
❑ 87 Nate Newton	.02	.10
❑ 88 Leonard Russell	.01	.05
❑ 89 Jeff George	.02	.10
❑ 90 Raymont Harris	.01	.05
❑ 91 Darnay Scott	.02	.10
❑ 92 Brian Mitchell	.01	.05
❑ 93 Craig Erickson	.01	.05
❑ 94 Cortez Kennedy	.02	.10
❑ 95 Derrick Alexander WR	.08	.25
❑ 96 Charles Haley	.02	.10
❑ 97 Randall Cunningham	.08	.25
❑ 98 Haywood Jeffires	.01	.05
❑ 99 Ronnie Harmon	.01	.05
❑ 100 Dale Carter	.02	.10
❑ 101 Dave Brown	.02	.10
❑ 102 Michael Haynes	.02	.10
❑ 103 Johnny Johnson	.01	.05
❑ 104 William Floyd	.02	.10
❑ 105 Jeff Hostetler	.02	.10
❑ 106 Bernie Parmalee	.02	.10
❑ 107 Mo Lewis	.01	.05
❑ 108 Byron Bam Morris	.01	.05
❑ 109 Vincent Brisby	.01	.05
❑ 110 John Randle	.02	.10
❑ 111 Steve Walsh	.01	.05
❑ 112 Terry Allen	.02	.10
❑ 113 Greg Lloyd	.02	.10
❑ 114 Merton Hanks	.01	.05
❑ 115 Mel Gray	.01	.05
❑ 116 Jim Kelly	.08	.25
❑ 117 Don Beebe	.01	.05
❑ 118 Floyd Turner	.01	.05
❑ 119 Neil Smith	.02	.10
❑ 120 Keith Byars	.01	.05
❑ 121 Rocket Ismail	.02	.10
❑ 122 Leslie O'Neal	.02	.10
❑ 123 Mike Sherrard	.01	.05
❑ 124 Marion Butts	.01	.05
❑ 125 Andre Coleman	.01	.05
❑ 126 Charles Johnson	.02	.10
❑ 127 Derrick Fenner	.01	.05
❑ 128 Vinny Testaverde	.02	.10
❑ 129 Chris Spielman	.02	.10
❑ 130 Bert Emanuel	.08	.25
❑ 131 Craig Heyward	.02	.10
❑ 132 Anthony Miller	.02	.10
❑ 133 Rob Moore	.02	.10
❑ 134 Gary Brown	.01	.05
❑ 135 David Klingler	.02	.10
❑ 136 Sean Dawkins	.02	.10
❑ 137 Terry McDaniel	.01	.05
❑ 138 Fred Barnett	.02	.10
❑ 139 Bryan Cox	.01	.05
❑ 140 Andrew Jordan	.01	.05
❑ 141 Leroy Thompson	.01	.05
❑ 142 Richmond Webb	.01	.05
❑ 143 Kimble Anders	.02	.10
❑ 144 Mario Bates	.02	.10
❑ 145 Irv Smith	.01	.05
❑ 146 Carnell Lake	.01	.05
❑ 147 Mark Seay	.02	.10
❑ 148 Dana Stubblefield	.02	.10
❑ 149 Kelvin Martin	.01	.05
❑ 150 Pete Metzelaars	.01	.05
❑ 151 Roosevelt Potts	.01	.05
❑ 152 Bubby Brister	.01	.05
❑ 153 Trent Dilfer	.08	.25
❑ 154 Ricky Proehl	.01	.05
❑ 155 Aaron Glenn	.01	.05
❑ 156 Eric Metcalf	.02	.10
❑ 157 Kevin Williams WR	.02	.10
❑ 158 Charlie Garner	.08	.25
❑ 159 Glyn Milburn	.01	.05
❑ 160 Fuad Reveiz	.01	.05

Card		
❑ 161 Brett Perriman	.02	.10
❑ 162 Neil O'Donnell	.02	.10
❑ 163 Tony Martin	.02	.10
❑ 164 Sam Adams	.01	.05
❑ 165 John Friesz	.02	.10
❑ 166 Bryant Young	.02	.10
❑ 167 Junior Seau	.08	.25
❑ 168 Ken Harvey	.01	.05
❑ 169 Bill Brooks	.01	.05
❑ 170 Eugene Robinson	.01	.05
❑ 171 Ricky Sanders	.02	.10
❑ 172 Rodney Peete	.01	.05
❑ 173 Boomer Esiason	.02	.10
❑ 174 Reggie Roby	.01	.05
❑ 175 Michael Jackson	.02	.10
❑ 176 Gus Frerotte	.02	.10
❑ 177 Terry Kirby	.02	.10
❑ 178 Jessie Tuggle	.01	.05
❑ 179 Courtney Hawkins	.01	.05
❑ 180 Heath Shuler	.02	.10
❑ 181 Jack Del Rio	.01	.05
❑ 182 O.J. McDuffie	.08	.25
❑ 183 Ricky Watters	.02	.10
❑ 184 Willie Roaf	.01	.05
❑ 185 Glenn Foley	.01	.05
❑ 186 Blair Thomas	.01	.05
❑ 187 Darren Woodson	.02	.10
❑ 188 Kevin Greene	.02	.10
❑ 189 Jeff Burris	.01	.05
❑ 190 Jay Schroeder	.01	.05
❑ 191 Stan Humphries	.02	.10
❑ 192 Irving Spikes	.02	.10
❑ 193 Jim Harbaugh	.02	.10
❑ 194 Robert Brooks	.08	.25
❑ 195 Greg Hill	.02	.10
❑ 196 Herschel Walker	.02	.10
❑ 197 Brian Blades	.02	.10
❑ 198 Mark Ingram	.01	.05
❑ 199 Kevin Turner	.01	.05
❑ 200 Lake Dawson	.02	.10
❑ 201 Alvin Harper	.01	.05
❑ 202 Derek Brown RBK	.01	.05
❑ 203 Qadry Ismail	.02	.10
❑ 204 Reggie Brooks	.02	.10
❑ 205 Steve Young SS	.10	.30
❑ 206 Emmitt Smith SS	.25	.60
❑ 207 Stan Humphries SS	.01	.05
❑ 208 Barry Sanders SS	.25	.60
❑ 209 Marshall Faulk SS	.15	.40
❑ 210 Drew Bledsoe SS	.08	.25
❑ 211 Jerry Rice SS	.15	.40
❑ 212 Tim Brown SS	.02	.10
❑ 213 Cris Carter SS	.08	.25
❑ 214 Dan Marino SS	.30	.75
❑ 215 Troy Aikman SS	.15	.40
❑ 216 Jerome Bettis SS	.02	.10
❑ 217 Deion Sanders SS	.08	.25
❑ 218 Junior Seau SS	.02	.10
❑ 219 John Elway SS	.30	.75
❑ 220 Warren Moon SS	.01	.05
❑ 221 Sterling Sharpe SS	.02	.10
❑ 222 Marcus Allen SS	.08	.25
❑ 223 Michael Irvin SS	.02	.10
❑ 224 Brett Favre SS	.30	.75
❑ 225 Rodney Hampton SS	.01	.05
❑ 226 Dave Brown SS	.02	.10
❑ 227 Ben Coates SS	.02	.10
❑ 228 Jim Kelly SS	.08	.25
❑ 229 Heath Shuler SS	.02	.10
❑ 230 Herman Moore SS	.08	.25
❑ 231 Jeff Hostetler SS	.02	.10
❑ 232 Rick Mirer SS	.02	.10
❑ 233 Byron Bam Morris SS	.01	.05
❑ 234 Terance Mathis SS	.01	.05
❑ 235 John Elway/B.Sanders CL	.15	.40
❑ 236 Troy Aikman CL	.08	.25
❑ 237 Jerry Rice CL	.08	.25
❑ 238 Emmitt Smith CL	.20	.50
❑ 239 Steve Young CL	.08	.25
❑ 240 Drew Bledsoe CL	.08	.25
❑ 241 Marshall Faulk CL	.08	.25
❑ 242 Dan Marino CL	.15	.40
❑ 243 Junior Seau CL	.02	.10
❑ 244 Ray Zellars RC	.02	.10
❑ 245 Rob Johnson RC	.30	.75
❑ 246 Tony Boselli RC	.08	.25
❑ 247 Kevin Carter RC	.08	.25
❑ 248 Steve McNair RC	1.00	2.50
❑ 249 Tyrone Wheatley RC	.30	.75
❑ 250 Steve Stenstrom RC	.01	.05
❑ 251 Stoney Case RC	.01	.05
❑ 252 Rodney Thomas RC	.02	.10
❑ 253 Michael Westbrook RC	.08	.25
❑ 254 Derrick Alexander DE RC	.01	.05
❑ 255 Kyle Brady RC	.08	.25
❑ 256 Kerry Collins RC	.75	2.00
❑ 257 Rashaan Salaam RC	.02	.10
❑ 258 Frank Sanders RC	.08	.25
❑ 259 John Walsh RC	.01	.05
❑ 260 Sherman Williams RC	.01	.05
❑ 261 Ki-Jana Carter RC	.08	.25
❑ 262 Jack Jackson RC	.01	.05
❑ 263 J.J. Stokes RC	.08	.25
❑ 264 Kordell Stewart RC	.50	1.25
❑ 265 Dave Barr RC	.01	.05
❑ 266 Eddie Goines RC	.01	.05
❑ 267 Warren Sapp RC	.50	1.25
❑ 268 James O. Stewart RC	.30	.75
❑ 269 Joey Galloway RC	.50	1.25
❑ 270 Tyrone Davis RC	.01	.05
❑ 271 Napoleon Kaufman RC	.40	1.00
❑ 272 Mark Bruener RC	.02	.10
❑ 273 Todd Collins RC	.30	.75
❑ 274 Billy Williams RC	.01	.05
❑ 275 James A.Stewart RC	.01	.05
❑ P264 Kordell Stewart PROMO	1.00	2.50
❑ AD3 Steve Young	1.25	3.00

1996 Score

Card		
❑ COMPLETE SET (275)	7.50	20.00
❑ 1 Emmitt Smith	.50	1.25
❑ 2 Flipper Anderson	.02	.10
❑ 3 Kordell Stewart	.15	.40
❑ 4 Bruce Smith	.07	.20
❑ 5 Marshall Faulk	.20	.50
❑ 6 William Floyd	.07	.20
❑ 7 Darren Woodson	.07	.20
❑ 8 Lake Dawson	.02	.10
❑ 9 Terry Allen	.07	.20
❑ 10 Ki-Jana Carter	.07	.20
❑ 11 Tony Boselli	.02	.10
❑ 12 Christian Fauria	.02	.10
❑ 13 Jeff George	.07	.20
❑ 14 Dan Marino	.60	1.50
❑ 15 Rodney Thomas	.02	.10
❑ 16 Anthony Miller	.07	.20
❑ 17 Chris Sanders	.07	.20
❑ 18 Natrone Means	.07	.20
❑ 19 Curtis Conway	.15	.40
❑ 20 Ben Coates	.07	.20
❑ 21 Alvin Harper	.02	.10
❑ 22 Frank Sanders	.07	.20
❑ 23 Boomer Esiason	.07	.20
❑ 24 Lovell Pinkney	.02	.10
❑ 25 Troy Aikman	.30	.75
❑ 26 Quinn Early	.02	.10
❑ 27 Adrian Murrell	.07	.20
❑ 28 Chris Spielman	.02	.10
❑ 29 Tyrone Wheatley	.07	.20
❑ 30 Tim Brown	.15	.40
❑ 31 Erik Kramer	.02	.10
❑ 32 Warren Moon	.07	.20
❑ 33 Jimmy Oliver	.02	.10
❑ 34 Herman Moore	.07	.20
❑ 35 Quentin Coryatt	.02	.10
❑ 36 Heath Shuler	.07	.20
❑ 37 Jim Kelly	.15	.40
❑ 38 Mike Morris	.02	.10
❑ 39 Harvey Williams	.02	.10
❑ 40 Vinny Testaverde	.07	.20
❑ 41 Steve McNair	.25	.60
❑ 42 Jerry Rice	.30	.75
❑ 43 Darick Holmes	.02	.10
❑ 44 Kyle Brady	.02	.10
❑ 45 Greg Lloyd	.07	.20
❑ 46 Kerry Collins	.15	.40
❑ 47 Willie McGinest	.02	.10
❑ 48 Isaac Bruce	.15	.40
❑ 49 Carnell Lake	.02	.10
❑ 50 Charles Haley	.07	.20
❑ 51 Troy Vincent	.02	.10
❑ 52 Randall Cunningham	.15	.40
❑ 53 Rashaan Salaam	.07	.20
❑ 54 Willie Jackson	.07	.20
❑ 55 Chris Warren	.07	.20
❑ 56 Michael Irvin	.15	.40
❑ 57 Mario Bates	.07	.20
❑ 58 Warren Sapp	.02	.10
❑ 59 John Elway	.60	1.50
❑ 60 Shannon Sharpe	.07	.20
❑ 61 Cornelius Bennett	.02	.10
❑ 62 Robert Brooks	.15	.40
❑ 63 Rodney Hampton	.07	.20
❑ 64 Ken Norton Jr.	.02	.10
❑ 65 Bryce Paup	.02	.10
❑ 66 Eric Swann	.02	.10
❑ 67 Rodney Peete	.02	.10
❑ 68 Larry Centers	.07	.20
❑ 69 Lamont Warren	.02	.10
❑ 70 Jay Novacek	.02	.10
❑ 71 Cris Carter	.15	.40
❑ 72 Terrell Fletcher	.02	.10
❑ 73 Andre Rison	.07	.20
❑ 74 Ricky Watters	.07	.20
❑ 75 Napoleon Kaufman	.15	.40
❑ 76 Reggie White	.15	.40
❑ 77 Yancey Thigpen	.07	.20
❑ 78 Terry Kirby	.07	.20
❑ 79 Deion Sanders	.15	.40
❑ 80 Irving Fryar	.07	.20
❑ 81 Marcus Allen	.15	.40
❑ 82 Carl Pickens	.07	.20
❑ 83 Drew Bledsoe	.20	.50
❑ 84 Eric Metcalf	.02	.10
❑ 85 Robert Smith	.07	.20
❑ 86 Tamarick Vanover	.07	.20
❑ 87 Henry Ellard	.02	.10
❑ 88 Kevin Greene	.07	.20
❑ 89 Mark Brunell	.20	.50
❑ 90 Terrell Davis	.25	.60
❑ 91 Brian Mitchell	.02	.10
❑ 92 Aaron Bailey	.02	.10
❑ 93 Rocket Ismail	.02	.10
❑ 94 Dave Brown	.02	.10
❑ 95 Rod Woodson	.07	.20
❑ 96 Sean Gilbert	.02	.10
❑ 97 Mark Seay	.02	.10
❑ 98 Zack Crockett	.02	.10
❑ 99 Scott Mitchell	.07	.20
❑ 100 Erric Pegram	.02	.10
❑ 101 David Palmer	.02	.10
❑ 102 Vincent Brisby	.02	.10
❑ 103 Brett Perriman	.02	.10
❑ 104 Jim Everett	.02	.10
❑ 105 Tony Martin	.07	.20
❑ 106 Desmond Howard	.07	.20
❑ 107 Stan Humphries	.07	.20
❑ 108 Bill Brooks	.02	.10
❑ 109 Neil Smith	.07	.20
❑ 110 Michael Westbrook	.15	.40
❑ 111 Herschel Walker	.07	.20
❑ 112 Andre Coleman	.02	.10
❑ 113 Derrick Alexander WR	.07	.20
❑ 114 Jeff Blake	.15	.40
❑ 115 Sherman Williams	.02	.10
❑ 116 James O.Stewart	.07	.20
❑ 117 Hardy Nickerson	.02	.10
❑ 118 Elvis Grbac	.07	.20
❑ 119 Brett Favre	.60	1.50
❑ 120 Mike Sherrard	.02	.10
❑ 121 Edgar Bennett	.07	.20
❑ 122 Calvin Williams	.02	.10
❑ 123 Brian Blades	.02	.10
❑ 124 Jeff Graham	.02	.10
❑ 125 Gary Brown	.02	.10
❑ 126 Bernie Parmalee	.02	.10
❑ 127 Kimble Anders	.07	.20
❑ 128 Hugh Douglas	.07	.20
❑ 129 James A.Stewart	.02	.10
❑ 130 Eric Bjornson	.02	.10
❑ 131 Ken Dilger	.07	.20
❑ 132 Jerome Bettis	.15	.40
❑ 133 Cortez Kennedy	.02	.10
❑ 134 Bryan Cox	.02	.10

Card		
❑ 135 Darnay Scott	.07	.20
❑ 136 Bert Emanuel	.07	.20
❑ 137 Steve Bono	.02	.10
❑ 138 Charles Johnson	.02	.10
❑ 139 Glyn Milburn	.02	.10
❑ 140 Derrick Alexander DE	.02	.10
❑ 141 Dave Meggett	.02	.10
❑ 142 Trent Dilfer	.15	.40
❑ 143 Eric Zeier	.02	.10
❑ 144 Jim Harbaugh	.07	.20
❑ 145 Antonio Freeman	.15	.40
❑ 146 Orlando Thomas	.02	.10
❑ 147 Russell Maryland	.02	.10
❑ 148 Chad May	.02	.10
❑ 149 Craig Heyward	.02	.10
❑ 150 Aeneas Williams	.02	.10
❑ 151 Kevin Williams WR	.02	.10
❑ 152 Charlie Garner	.07	.20
❑ 153 J.J. Stokes	.15	.40
❑ 154 Stoney Case	.02	.10
❑ 155 Mark Chmura	.07	.20
❑ 156 Mark Bruener	.02	.10
❑ 157 Derek Loville	.02	.10
❑ 158 Justin Armour	.02	.10
❑ 159 Brent Jones	.02	.10
❑ 160 Aaron Craver	.02	.10
❑ 161 Terance Mathis	.02	.10
❑ 162 Chris Zorich	.02	.10
❑ 163 Glenn Foley	.07	.20
❑ 164 Johnny Mitchell	.02	.10
❑ 165 Junior Seau	.15	.40
❑ 166 Willie Davis	.02	.10
❑ 167 Rick Mirer	.07	.20
❑ 168 Mike Jones LB	.02	.10
❑ 169 Greg Hill	.07	.20
❑ 170 Steve Tasker	.02	.10
❑ 171 Tony Bennett	.02	.10
❑ 172 Jeff Hostetler	.02	.10
❑ 173 Dave Krieg	.02	.10
❑ 174 Mark Carrier WR	.02	.10
❑ 175 Michael Haynes	.02	.10
❑ 176 Chris Chandler	.07	.20
❑ 177 Ernie Mills	.02	.10
❑ 178 Jake Reed	.07	.20
❑ 179 Errict Rhett	.07	.20
❑ 180 Garrison Hearst	.07	.20
❑ 181 Derrick Thomas	.15	.40
❑ 182 Aaron Hayden RC	.02	.10
❑ 183 Jackie Harris	.02	.10
❑ 184 Curtis Martin	.25	.60
❑ 185 Neil O'Donnell	.07	.20
❑ 186 Derrick Moore	.02	.10
❑ 187 Steve Young	.25	.60
❑ 188 Pat Swilling	.02	.10
❑ 189 Amp Lee	.02	.10
❑ 190 Rob Johnson	.15	.40
❑ 191 Todd Collins	.07	.20
❑ 192 J.J. Birden	.02	.10
❑ 193 O.J. McDuffie	.07	.20
❑ 194 Shawn Jefferson	.02	.10
❑ 195 Sean Dawkins	.02	.10
❑ 196 Fred Barnett	.02	.10
❑ 197 Roosevelt Potts	.02	.10
❑ 198 Rob Moore	.07	.20
❑ 199 Kevin Miniefield	.02	.10
❑ 200 Barry Sanders	.50	1.25
❑ 201 Floyd Turner	.02	.10
❑ 202 Wayne Chrebet	.25	.60
❑ 203 Andre Reed	.07	.20
❑ 204 Tyrone Hughes	.02	.10
❑ 205 Keenan McCardell	.15	.40
❑ 206 Gus Frerotte	.07	.20
❑ 207 Daryl Johnston	.07	.20
❑ 208 Steve Broussard	.02	.10
❑ 209 Steve Atwater	.02	.10
❑ 210 Thurman Thomas	.15	.40
❑ 211 Andre Hastings	.02	.10
❑ 212 Joey Galloway	.15	.40
❑ 213 Kevin Carter	.02	.10
❑ 214 Keyshawn Johnson RC	.40	1.00
❑ 215 Tony Brackens RC	.15	.40
❑ 216 Stepfret Williams RC	.07	.20
❑ 217 Mike Alstott RC	.40	1.00
❑ 218 Terry Glenn RC	.40	1.00
❑ 219 Tim Biakabutuka RC	.15	.40
❑ 220 Eric Moulds RC	.50	1.25
❑ 221 Jeff Lewis RC	.07	.20
❑ 222 Bobby Engram RC	.15	.40
❑ 223 Cedric Jones RC	.02	.10
❑ 224 Stanley Pritchett RC	.07	.20
❑ 225 Kevin Hardy RC	.15	.40
❑ 226 Alex Van Dyke RC	.07	.20
❑ 227 Willie Anderson RC	.02	.10
❑ 228 Regan Upshaw RC	.02	.10
❑ 229 Leeland McElroy RC	.07	.20
❑ 230 Marvin Harrison RC	1.00	2.50
❑ 231 Eddie George RC	.50	1.25
❑ 232 Lawrence Phillips RC	.15	.40
❑ 233 Daryl Gardener RC	.02	.10
❑ 234 Alex Molden RC	.02	.10
❑ 235 Derrick Mayes RC	.15	.40
❑ 236 John Mobley RC	.02	.10
❑ 237 Israel Ifeanyi RC	.02	.10
❑ 238 Pete Kendall RC	.02	.10
❑ 239 Danny Kanell RC	.15	.40
❑ 240 Jonathan Ogden RC	.15	.40
❑ 241 Reggie Brown LB RC	.02	.10
❑ 242 Marcus Jones RC	.02	.10
❑ 243 Jon Stark RC	.02	.10
❑ 244 Barry Sanders SE	.25	.60
❑ 245 Brett Favre SE	.30	.75
❑ 246 John Elway SE	.30	.75
❑ 247 Dan Marino SE	.30	.75
❑ 248 Drew Bledsoe SE	.15	.40
❑ 249 Michael Irvin SE	.07	.20
❑ 250 Troy Aikman SE	.15	.40
❑ 251 Emmitt Smith SE	.20	.50
❑ 252 Steve Young SE	.15	.40
❑ 253 Jerry Rice SE	.15	.40
❑ 254 Jeff Blake SE	.07	.20
❑ 255 Tim Brown SE	.07	.20
❑ 256 Eric Metcalf SE	.02	.10
❑ 257 Rodney Hampton SE	.02	.10
❑ 258 Scott Mitchell SE	.02	.10
❑ 259 Garrison Hearst SE	.07	.20
❑ 260 Larry Centers SE	.07	.20
❑ 261 Neil O'Donnell SE	.07	.20
❑ 262 Orlando Thomas SE	.02	.10
❑ 263 Hugh Douglas SE	.02	.10
❑ 264 Bill Brooks SE	.02	.10
❑ 265 Harvey Williams SE	.02	.10
❑ 266 Charles Haley SE	.07	.20
❑ 267 Greg Lloyd SE	.07	.20
❑ 268 Daryl Johnston SE	.07	.20
❑ 269 Dan Marino CL	.15	.40
❑ 270 Jeff Blake CL	.07	.20
❑ 271 John Elway CL	.15	.40
❑ 272 Emmitt Smith CL	.15	.40
❑ 273 Brett Favre CL	.15	.40
❑ 274 Jerry Rice CL	.15	.40
❑ 275 Five Star Players CL	.15	.40
❑ P1 Barry Sanders Promo	.75	2.00

1997 Score

Card		
❑ COMPLETE SET (330)	10.00	25.00
❑ 1 John Elway	.75	2.00
❑ 2 Drew Bledsoe	.25	.60
❑ 3 Brett Favre	.75	2.00
❑ 4 Emmitt Smith	.60	1.50
❑ 5 Kerry Collins	.20	.50
❑ 6 Jerry Rice	.40	1.00
❑ 7 Kordell Stewart	.20	.50
❑ 8 Barry Sanders	.60	1.50
❑ 9 Dan Marino	.75	2.00
❑ 10 Steve Young	.25	.60
❑ 11 Erik Kramer	.07	.20
❑ 12 Warren Moon	.20	.50
❑ 13 Chris Calloway	.07	.20
❑ 14 Doug Evans	.07	.20
❑ 15 Darren Woodson	.07	.20
❑ 16 Alonzo Spellman	.07	.20
❑ 17 Greg Hill	.07	.20
❑ 18 Aaron Craver	.07	.20
❑ 19 Jeff Hostetler	.07	.20
❑ 20 William Thomas	.07	.20
❑ 21 Marco Coleman	.07	.20
❑ 22 Wayne Simmons	.07	.20
❑ 23 Donnell Woolford	.07	.20
❑ 24 Vinny Testaverde	.10	.30
❑ 25 Ed McCaffrey	.10	.30
❑ 26 Jim Everett	.07	.20
❑ 27 Gilbert Brown	.10	.30
❑ 28 Jason Dunn	.07	.20
❑ 29 Stanley Pritchett	.07	.20
❑ 30 Joey Galloway	.10	.30
❑ 31 Amani Toomer	.10	.30
❑ 32 Chris Penn	.07	.20
❑ 33 Aeneas Williams	.07	.20
❑ 34 Bobby Taylor	.07	.20
❑ 35 Bryan Still	.07	.20
❑ 36 Ty Law	.10	.30
❑ 37 Shannon Sharpe	.10	.30
❑ 38 Marty Carter	.07	.20
❑ 39 Sam Mills	.07	.20
❑ 40 William Floyd	.10	.30
❑ 41 Brad Johnson	.20	.50
❑ 42 Sean Dawkins	.07	.20
❑ 43 Michael Irvin	.20	.50
❑ 44 Jeff George	.10	.30
❑ 45 Brent Jones	.10	.30
❑ 46 Mark Brunell	.25	.60
❑ 47 Rob Moore	.10	.30
❑ 48 Hardy Nickerson	.07	.20
❑ 49 Chris Chandler	.10	.30
❑ 50 Willie Anderson	.07	.20
❑ 51 Isaac Bruce	.20	.50
❑ 52 Natrone Means	.10	.30
❑ 53 Tony Banks	.10	.30
❑ 54 Marshall Faulk	.25	.60
❑ 55 Michael Westbrook	.10	.30
❑ 56 Bruce Smith	.10	.30
❑ 57 Jamal Anderson	.20	.50
❑ 58 Jackie Harris	.07	.20
❑ 59 Sean Gilbert	.07	.20
❑ 60 Ki-Jana Carter	.07	.20
❑ 61 Eric Moulds	.20	.50
❑ 62 James O.Stewart	.10	.30
❑ 63 Jeff Blake	.10	.30
❑ 64 O.J. McDuffie	.10	.30
❑ 65 Neil Smith	.10	.30
❑ 66 Kevin Smith	.07	.20
❑ 67 Terry Allen	.20	.50
❑ 68 Sean LaChapelle	.07	.20
❑ 69 Rashaan Salaam	.07	.20
❑ 70 Jeff Graham	.07	.20
❑ 71 Mark Carrier WR	.07	.20
❑ 72 Allen Aldridge	.07	.20
❑ 73 Keenan McCardell	.10	.30
❑ 74 Willie McGinest	.07	.20
❑ 75 Napoleon Kaufman	.20	.50
❑ 76 Jerris McPhail	.07	.20
❑ 77 Eric Swann	.07	.20
❑ 78 Kimble Anders	.10	.30
❑ 79 Charles Johnson	.10	.30
❑ 80 Bryan Cox	.07	.20
❑ 81 Johnnie Morton	.10	.30
❑ 82 Andre Rison	.10	.30
❑ 83 Corey Miller	.07	.20
❑ 84 Troy Drayton	.07	.20
❑ 85 Jim Harbaugh	.10	.30
❑ 86 Wesley Walls	.10	.30
❑ 87 Bryce Paup	.07	.20
❑ 88 Curtis Martin	.25	.60
❑ 89 Michael Sinclair	.07	.20
❑ 90 Chris T. Jones	.07	.20
❑ 91 Jake Reed	.10	.30
❑ 92 LeRoy Butler	.07	.20
❑ 93 Reggie Tongue	.07	.20
❑ 94 Bert Emanuel	.10	.30
❑ 95 Stan Humphries	.10	.30
❑ 96 Neil O'Donnell	.10	.30
❑ 97 Troy Vincent	.07	.20
❑ 98 Mike Alstott	.20	.50
❑ 99 Chad Cota	.07	.20
❑ 100 Marvin Harrison	.20	.50
❑ 101 Terrell Owens	.25	.60
❑ 102 Dave Brown	.07	.20
❑ 103 Harvey Williams	.07	.20
❑ 104 Desmond Howard	.10	.30
❑ 105 Carl Pickens	.10	.30
❑ 106 Kent Graham	.07	.20
❑ 107 Michael Bates	.07	.20
❑ 108 Terrell Davis	.25	.60
❑ 109 Marcus Allen	.20	.50

❑ 110 Ray Zellars	.07	.20
❑ 111 Chris Warren	.10	.30
❑ 112 Phillippi Sparks	.07	.20
❑ 113 Craig Erickson	.07	.20
❑ 114 Eddie George	.20	.50
❑ 115 Daryl Johnston	.10	.30
❑ 116 Ricky Watters	.10	.30
❑ 117 Tedy Bruschi	.40	1.00
❑ 118 Mike Mamula	.07	.20
❑ 119 Ken Harvey	.07	.20
❑ 120 John Randle	.10	.30
❑ 121 Mark Chmura	.10	.30
❑ 122 Sam Gash	.07	.20
❑ 123 John Kasay	.07	.20
❑ 124 Barry Minter	.07	.20
❑ 125 Raymont Harris	.07	.20
❑ 126 Derrick Thomas	.20	.50
❑ 127 Trent Dilfer	.20	.50
❑ 128 Carnell Lake	.07	.20
❑ 129 Brian Dawkins	.20	.50
❑ 130 Tyronne Drakeford	.07	.20
❑ 131 Daryl Gardener	.07	.20
❑ 132 Fred Strickland	.07	.20
❑ 133 Kevin Hardy	.07	.20
❑ 134 Winslow Oliver	.07	.20
❑ 135 Herman Moore	.10	.30
❑ 136 Keith Byars	.07	.20
❑ 137 Harold Green	.07	.20
❑ 138 Ty Detmer	.10	.30
❑ 139 Lamar Thomas	.07	.20
❑ 140 Elvis Grbac	.10	.30
❑ 141 Edgar Bennett	.10	.30
❑ 142 Cornelius Bennett	.07	.20
❑ 143 Tony Tolbert	.07	.20
❑ 144 James Hasty	.07	.20
❑ 145 Ben Coates	.10	.30
❑ 146 Errict Rhett	.07	.20
❑ 147 Jason Sehorn	.10	.30
❑ 148 Michael Jackson	.10	.30
❑ 149 John Mobley	.07	.20
❑ 150 Walt Harris	.07	.20
❑ 151 Terry Kirby	.10	.30
❑ 152 Devin Wyman	.07	.20
❑ 153 Ray Crockett	.07	.20
❑ 154 Quinn Early	.07	.20
❑ 155 Rodney Thomas	.07	.20
❑ 156 Mark Seay	.07	.20
❑ 157 Derrick Alexander WR	.10	.30
❑ 158 Lamar Lathon	.07	.20
❑ 159 Anthony Miller	.07	.20
❑ 160 Shawn Wooden RC	.07	.20
❑ 161 Antonio Freeman	.20	.50
❑ 162 Cortez Kennedy	.07	.20
❑ 163 Rickey Dudley	.10	.30
❑ 164 Tony Carter	.07	.20
❑ 165 Kevin Williams	.07	.20
❑ 166 Reggie White	.20	.50
❑ 167 Tim Bowens	.07	.20
❑ 168 Roy Barker	.07	.20
❑ 169 Adrian Murrell	.10	.30
❑ 170 Anthony Johnson	.07	.20
❑ 171 Terry Glenn	.20	.50
❑ 172 Jeff Lewis	.07	.20
❑ 173 Dorsey Levens	.20	.50
❑ 174 Willie Jackson	.07	.20
❑ 175 Willie Clay	.07	.20
❑ 176 Richmond Webb	.07	.20
❑ 177 Shawn Lee	.07	.20
❑ 178 Joe Aska	.07	.20
❑ 179 Rod Woodson	.10	.30
❑ 180 Jim Schwantz RC	.07	.20
❑ 181 Alfred Williams	.07	.20
❑ 182 Ferric Collons	.07	.20
❑ 183 Ken Norton Jr.	.07	.20
❑ 184 Rick Mirer	.07	.20
❑ 185 Leeland McElroy	.07	.20
❑ 186 Rodney Hampton	.10	.30
❑ 187 Ted Popson	.07	.20
❑ 188 Fred Barnett	.07	.20
❑ 189 Junior Seau	.20	.50
❑ 190 Micheal Barrow	.07	.20
❑ 191 Corey Widmer	.07	.20
❑ 192 Rodney Peete	.07	.20
❑ 193 Rod Smith WR	.20	.50
❑ 194 Muhsin Muhammad	.10	.30
❑ 195 Keith Jackson	.07	.20
❑ 196 Jimmy Smith	.10	.30
❑ 197 Dave Meggett	.07	.20
❑ 198 Lawrence Phillips	.07	.20
❑ 199 Chad Brown	.07	.20
❑ 200 Darrin Smith	.07	.20
❑ 201 Larry Centers	.10	.30
❑ 202 Kevin Greene	.10	.30
❑ 203 Sherman Williams	.07	.20
❑ 204 Chris Sanders	.07	.20
❑ 205 Shawn Jefferson	.07	.20
❑ 206 Thurman Thomas	.20	.50
❑ 207 Keyshawn Johnson	.20	.50
❑ 208 Bryant Young	.07	.20
❑ 209 Tim Biakabutuka	.10	.30
❑ 210 Troy Aikman	.40	1.00
❑ 211 Quentin Coryatt	.07	.20
❑ 212 Karim Abdul-Jabbar	.20	.50
❑ 213 Brian Blades	.07	.20
❑ 214 Ray Farmer	.07	.20
❑ 215 Simeon Rice	.10	.30
❑ 216 Tyrone Braxton	.07	.20
❑ 217 Jerome Woods	.07	.20
❑ 218 Charles Way	.10	.30
❑ 219 Garrison Hearst	.10	.30
❑ 220 Bobby Engram	.10	.30
❑ 221 Billy Davis RC	.07	.20
❑ 222 Ken Dilger	.07	.20
❑ 223 Robert Smith	.10	.30
❑ 224 John Friesz	.07	.20
❑ 225 Charlie Garner	.10	.30
❑ 226 Jerome Bettis	.20	.50
❑ 227 Darnay Scott	.10	.30
❑ 228 Terance Mathis	.10	.30
❑ 229 Brian Williams LB	.07	.20
❑ 230 Cris Carter	.20	.50
❑ 231 Michael Haynes	.07	.20
❑ 232 Cedric Jones	.07	.20
❑ 233 Danny Kanell	.10	.30
❑ 234 Deion Sanders	.20	.50
❑ 235 Steve Atwater	.07	.20
❑ 236 Jonathan Ogden	.07	.20
❑ 237 Lake Dawson	.07	.20
❑ 238 Eric Allen	.07	.20
❑ 239 Eddie Kennison	.10	.30
❑ 240 Irving Fryar	.10	.30
❑ 241 Michael Strahan	.10	.30
❑ 242 Steve McNair	.25	.60
❑ 243 Terrell Buckley	.07	.20
❑ 244 Merton Hanks	.07	.20
❑ 245 Jessie Armstead	.07	.20
❑ 246 Dana Stubblefield	.07	.20
❑ 247 Brett Perriman	.07	.20
❑ 248 Mark Collins	.07	.20
❑ 249 Willie Roaf	.07	.20
❑ 250 Gus Frerotte	.07	.20
❑ 251 William Fuller	.07	.20
❑ 252 Tamarick Vanover	.10	.30
❑ 253 Scott Mitchell	.10	.30
❑ 254 Eric Metcalf	.10	.30
❑ 255 Herschel Walker	.10	.30
❑ 256 Robert Brooks	.10	.30
❑ 257 Zach Thomas	.20	.50
❑ 258 Alvin Harper	.07	.20
❑ 259 Wayne Chrebet	.20	.50
❑ 260 Bill Romanowski	.07	.20
❑ 261 Willie Green	.07	.20
❑ 262 Dale Carter	.07	.20
❑ 263 Chris Slade	.07	.20
❑ 264 J.J. Stokes	.10	.30
❑ 265 Tim Brown	.20	.50
❑ 266 Eric Davis	.07	.20
❑ 267 Mark Carrier DB	.07	.20
❑ 268 Tony Martin	.10	.30
❑ 269 Tyrone Wheatley	.10	.30
❑ 270 Eugene Robinson	.07	.20
❑ 271 Curtis Conway	.10	.30
❑ 272 Michael Timpson	.07	.20
❑ 273 Orlando Pace RC	.20	.50
❑ 274 Tiki Barber RC	1.25	3.00
❑ 275 Byron Hanspard RC	.10	.30
❑ 276 Warrick Dunn RC	.60	1.50
❑ 277 Rae Carruth RC	.07	.20
❑ 278 Bryant Westbrook RC	.07	.20
❑ 279 Antowain Smith RC	.50	1.25
❑ 280 Peter Boulware RC	.20	.50
❑ 281 Reidel Anthony RC	.20	.50
❑ 282 Troy Davis RC	.10	.30
❑ 283 Jake Plummer RC	1.00	2.50
❑ 284 Chris Canty RC	.07	.20
❑ 285 Dwayne Rudd RC	.20	.50
❑ 286 Ike Hilliard RC	.30	.75
❑ 287 Reinard Wilson RC	.10	.30
❑ 288 Corey Dillon RC	1.25	3.00
❑ 289 Tony Gonzalez RC	.60	1.50
❑ 290 Darnell Autry RC	.10	.30
❑ 291 Kevin Lockett RC	.10	.30
❑ 292 Darrell Russell RC	.07	.20
❑ 293 Jim Druckenmiller RC	.10	.30
❑ 294 Shon Mitchell RC	.07	.20
❑ 295 Joey Kent RC	.20	.50
❑ 296 Shawn Springs RC	.10	.30
❑ 297 James Farrior RC	.20	.50
❑ 298 Sedrick Shaw RC	.10	.30
❑ 299 Marcus Harris RC	.07	.20
❑ 300 Danny Wuerffel RC	.20	.50
❑ 301 Marc Edwards RC	.07	.20
❑ 302 Michael Booker RC	.07	.20
❑ 303 David LaFleur RC	.07	.20
❑ 304 Mike Adams WR RC	.07	.20
❑ 305 Pat Barnes RC	.20	.50
❑ 306 George Jones RC	.10	.30
❑ 307 Yatil Green RC	.10	.30
❑ 308 Drew Bledsoe TBP	.20	.50
❑ 309 Troy Aikman TBP	.20	.50
❑ 310 Terrell Davis TBP	.10	.30
❑ 311 Jim Everett TBP	.07	.20
❑ 312 John Elway TBP	.40	1.00
❑ 313 Barry Sanders TBP	.30	.75
❑ 314 Jim Harbaugh TBP	.10	.30
❑ 315 Steve Young TBP	.20	.50
❑ 316 Dan Marino TBP	.40	1.00
❑ 317 Michael Irvin TBP	.20	.50
❑ 318 Emmitt Smith TBP	.30	.75
❑ 319 Jeff Hostetler TBP	.07	.20
❑ 320 Mark Brunell TBP	.20	.50
❑ 321 Jeff Blake TBP	.20	.50
❑ 322 Scott Mitchell TBP	.07	.20
❑ 323 Boomer Esiason TBP	.10	.30
❑ 324 Jerome Bettis TBP	.20	.50
❑ 325 Warren Moon TBP	.10	.30
❑ 326 Neil O'Donnell TBP	.10	.30
❑ 327 Jim Kelly TBP	.20	.50
❑ 328 Dan Marino CL	.20	.50
❑ 329 John Elway CL	.20	.50
❑ 330 Drew Bledsoe CL	.10	.30
❑ P1 Troy Aikman Promo	.40	1.00
❑ P2 Brett Favre Promo	.75	2.00
❑ P3 Dan Marino Promo	.75	2.00
❑ P4 Barry Sanders Promo	.60	1.50

1998 Score

❑ COMPLETE SET (270)	15.00	40.00
❑ 1 John Elway	.75	2.00
❑ 2 Kordell Stewart	.20	.50
❑ 3 Warrick Dunn	.20	.50
❑ 4 Brad Johnson	.20	.50
❑ 5 Kerry Collins	.10	.30
❑ 6 Danny Kanell	.10	.30
❑ 7 Emmitt Smith	.60	1.50
❑ 8 Jamal Anderson	.20	.50
❑ 9 Jim Harbaugh	.10	.30
❑ 10 Tony Martin	.10	.30
❑ 11 Rod Smith	.10	.30
❑ 12 Dorsey Levens	.20	.50
❑ 13 Steve McNair	.20	.50
❑ 14 Derrick Thomas	.20	.50
❑ 15 Rob Moore	.10	.30
❑ 16 Peter Boulware	.07	.20
❑ 17 Terry Allen	.20	.50
❑ 18 Joey Galloway	.10	.30
❑ 19 Jerome Bettis	.20	.50
❑ 20 Carl Pickens	.10	.30
❑ 21 Napoleon Kaufman	.20	.50
❑ 22 Troy Aikman	.40	1.00
❑ 23 Curtis Conway	.10	.30
❑ 24 Adrian Murrell	.10	.30
❑ 25 Elvis Grbac	.10	.30
❑ 26 Garrison Hearst	.20	.50

Card	Low	High
27 Chris Sanders	.07	.20
28 Scott Mitchell	.10	.30
29 Junior Seau	.20	.50
30 Chris Chandler	.10	.30
31 Kevin Hardy	.07	.20
32 Terrell Davis	.20	.50
33 Keyshawn Johnson	.20	.50
34 Natrone Means	.10	.30
35 Antowain Smith	.20	.50
36 Jake Plummer	.20	.50
37 Isaac Bruce	.20	.50
38 Tony Banks	.10	.30
39 Reidel Anthony	.10	.30
40 Darren Woodson	.07	.20
41 Corey Dillon	.20	.50
42 Antonio Freeman	.20	.50
43 Eddie George	.20	.50
44 Yancey Thigpen	.07	.20
45 Tim Brown	.20	.50
46 Wayne Chrebet	.20	.50
47 Andre Rison	.10	.30
48 Michael Strahan	.10	.30
49 Deion Sanders	.20	.50
50 Eric Moulds	.20	.50
51 Mark Brunell	.20	.50
52 Rae Carruth	.07	.20
53 Warren Sapp	.10	.30
54 Mark Chmura	.10	.30
55 Darrell Green	.10	.30
56 Quinn Early	.07	.20
57 Barry Sanders	.60	1.50
58 Neil O'Donnell	.10	.30
59 Tony Brackens	.07	.20
60 Willie Davis	.07	.20
61 Shannon Sharpe	.10	.30
62 Shawn Springs	.07	.20
63 Tony Gonzalez	.20	.50
64 Rodney Thomas	.07	.20
65 Terance Mathis	.10	.30
66 Brett Favre	.75	2.00
67 Eric Swann	.07	.20
68 Kevin Turner	.07	.20
69 Tyrone Wheatley	.10	.30
70 Trent Dilfer	.20	.50
71 Bryan Cox	.07	.20
72 Lake Dawson	.07	.20
73 Will Blackwell	.07	.20
74 Fred Lane	.07	.20
75 Ty Detmer	.10	.30
76 Eddie Kennison	.10	.30
77 Jimmy Smith	.10	.30
78 Chris Calloway	.07	.20
79 Shawn Jefferson	.07	.20
80 Dan Marino	.75	2.00
81 LeRoy Butler	.07	.20
82 William Roaf	.07	.20
83 Rick Mirer	.07	.20
84 Dermontti Dawson	.07	.20
85 Errict Rhett	.10	.30
86 Lamar Thomas	.07	.20
87 Lamar Lathon	.07	.20
88 John Randle	.10	.30
89 Darryl Williams	.07	.20
90 Keenan McCardell	.10	.30
91 Erik Kramer	.07	.20
92 Ken Dilger	.07	.20
93 Dave Meggett	.07	.20
94 Jeff Blake	.10	.30
95 Ed McCaffrey	.10	.30
96 Charles Johnson	.07	.20
97 Irving Spikes	.07	.20
98 Mike Alstott	.20	.50
99 Vincent Brisby	.07	.20
100 Michael Westbrook	.10	.30
101 Rickey Dudley	.07	.20
102 Bert Emanuel	.10	.30
103 Daryl Johnston	.10	.30
104 Lawrence Phillips	.07	.20
105 Eric Bieniemy	.07	.20
106 Bryant Westbrook	.07	.20
107 Rob Johnson	.10	.30
108 Ray Zellars	.07	.20
109 Anthony Johnson	.07	.20
110 Reggie White	.20	.50
111 Wesley Walls	.10	.30
112 Amani Toomer	.10	.30
113 Gary Brown	.07	.20
114 Brian Blades	.07	.20
115 Alex Van Dyke	.07	.20
116 Michael Haynes	.07	.20
117 Jessie Armstead	.07	.20
118 James Jett	.10	.30
119 Troy Drayton	.07	.20
120 Craig Heyward	.07	.20
121 Steve Atwater	.07	.20
122 Tiki Barber	.20	.50
123 Karim Abdul-Jabbar	.20	.50
124 Kimble Anders	.10	.30
125 Frank Sanders	.10	.30
126 David Sloan	.07	.20
127 Andre Hastings	.07	.20
128 Vinny Testaverde	.10	.30
129 Robert Smith	.20	.50
130 Horace Copeland	.07	.20
131 Larry Centers	.07	.20
132 J.J. Stokes	.10	.30
133 Ike Hilliard	.10	.30
134 Muhsin Muhammad	.10	.30
135 Sean Dawkins	.07	.20
136 Raymont Harris	.07	.20
137 Lamar Smith	.10	.30
138 David Palmer	.07	.20
139 Steve Young	.25	.60
140 Bryan Still	.07	.20
141 Keith Byars	.07	.20
142 Cris Carter	.20	.50
143 Charlie Garner	.10	.30
144 Drew Bledsoe	.30	.75
145 Simeon Rice	.10	.30
146 Merton Hanks	.07	.20
147 Aeneas Williams	.07	.20
148 Rodney Hampton	.10	.30
149 Zach Thomas	.20	.50
150 Mark Bruener	.07	.20
151 Jason Dunn	.07	.20
152 Danny Wuerffel	.10	.30
153 Jim Druckenmiller	.07	.20
154 Greg Hill	.07	.20
155 Earnest Byner	.07	.20
156 Greg Lloyd	.07	.20
157 John Mobley	.07	.20
158 Tim Biakabutuka	.10	.30
159 Terrell Owens	.20	.50
160 O.J. McDuffie	.10	.30
161 Glenn Foley	.10	.30
162 Derrick Brooks	.20	.50
163 Dave Brown	.07	.20
164 Ki-Jana Carter	.07	.20
165 Bobby Hoying	.10	.30
166 Randal Hill	.07	.20
167 Michael Irvin	.20	.50
168 Bruce Smith	.10	.30
169 Troy Davis	.07	.20
170 Derrick Mayes	.10	.30
171 Henry Ellard	.10	.30
172 Dana Stubblefield	.07	.20
173 Willie McGinest	.07	.20
174 Leeland McElroy	.07	.20
175 Edgar Bennett	.07	.20
176 Robert Porcher	.07	.20
177 Randall Cunningham	.20	.50
178 Jim Everett	.07	.20
179 Jake Reed	.10	.30
180 Quentin Coryatt	.07	.20
181 William Floyd	.07	.20
182 Jason Sehorn	.10	.30
183 Carnell Lake	.07	.20
184 Dexter Coakley	.07	.20
185 Derrick Alexander WR	.10	.30
186 Johnnie Morton	.10	.30
187 Irving Fryar	.10	.30
188 Warren Moon	.20	.50
189 Todd Collins	.07	.20
190 Ken Norton Jr.	.07	.20
191 Terry Glenn	.20	.50
192 Rashaan Salaam	.07	.20
193 Jerry Rice	.40	1.00
194 James O.Stewart	.10	.30
195 David LaFleur	.07	.20
196 Eric Green	.07	.20
197 Gus Frerotte	.07	.20
198 Willie Green	.07	.20
199 Marshall Faulk	.25	.60
200 Brett Perriman	.07	.20
201 Darnay Scott	.10	.30
202 Marvin Harrison	.20	.50
203 Joe Aska	.07	.20
204 Darrien Gordon	.07	.20
205 Herman Moore	.10	.30
206 Curtis Martin	.20	.50
207 Derek Loville	.07	.20
208 Dale Carter	.07	.20
209 Heath Shuler	.07	.20
210 Jonathan Ogden	.07	.20
211 Leslie Shepherd	.07	.20
212 Tony Boselli	.07	.20
213 Eric Metcalf	.07	.20
214 Neil Smith	.10	.30
215 Anthony Miller	.07	.20
216 Jeff George	.10	.30
217 Charles Way	.07	.20
218 Mario Bates	.10	.30
219 Ben Coates	.10	.30
220 Michael Jackson	.07	.20
221 Thurman Thomas	.20	.50
222 Kyle Brady	.07	.20
223 Marcus Allen	.20	.50
224 Robert Brooks	.10	.30
225 Yatil Green	.07	.20
226 Byron Hanspard	.07	.20
227 Andre Reed	.10	.30
228 Chris Warren	.10	.30
229 Jackie Harris	.07	.20
230 Ricky Watters	.10	.30
231 Bobby Engram	.10	.30
232 Tamarick Vanover	.07	.20
233 Peyton Manning RC	7.50	15.00
234 Curtis Enis RC	.30	.75
235 Randy Moss RC	4.00	10.00
236 Charles Woodson RC	.60	1.50
237 Robert Edwards RC	.40	1.00
238 Jacquez Green RC	.40	1.00
239 Keith Brooking RC	.60	1.50
240 Jerome Pathon RC	.60	1.50
241 Kevin Dyson RC	.60	1.50
242 Fred Taylor RC	.75	2.00
243 Tavian Banks RC	.40	1.00
244 Marcus Nash RC	.30	.75
245 Brian Griese RC	1.00	2.50
246 Andre Wadsworth RC	.40	1.00
247 Ahman Green RC	1.50	4.00
248 Joe Jurevicius RC	.60	1.50
249 Germane Crowell RC	.40	1.00
250 Skip Hicks RC	.40	1.00
251 Ryan Leaf RC	.60	1.50
252 Hines Ward RC	2.50	6.00
253 John Elway OS	.40	1.00
254 Mark Brunell OS	.20	.50
255 Brett Favre OS	.40	1.00
256 Troy Aikman OS	.20	.50
257 Warrick Dunn OS	.10	.30
258 Barry Sanders OS	.30	.75
259 Eddie George OS	.20	.50
260 Kordell Stewart OS	.20	.50
261 Emmitt Smith OS	.30	.75
262 Steve Young OS	.20	.50
263 Terrell Davis OS	.20	.50
264 Dorsey Levens OS	.10	.30
265 Dan Marino OS	.40	1.00
266 Jerry Rice OS	.20	.50
267 Drew Bledsoe OS	.20	.50
268 Brett Favre CL	.25	.60
269 Barry Sanders CL	.20	.50
270 Terrell Davis CL	.20	.50
251AU Ryan Leaf AUTO	15.00	40.00

1999 Score

Card	Low	High
COMPLETE SET (275)	25.00	60.00
COMP.SET w/o SP's (220)	6.00	15.00
1 Randy Moss	.60	1.50
2 Randall Cunningham	.25	.60
3 Cris Carter	.25	.60
4 Robert Smith	.25	.60
5 Jake Reed	.15	.40

❑ 6 Leroy Hoard	.08	.25
❑ 7 John Randle	.15	.40
❑ 8 Brett Favre	.75	2.00
❑ 9 Antonio Freeman	.25	.60
❑ 10 Dorsey Levens	.25	.60
❑ 11 Robert Brooks	.15	.40
❑ 12 Derrick Mayes	.15	.40
❑ 13 Mark Chmura	.15	.40
❑ 14 Darick Holmes	.08	.25
❑ 15 Vonnie Holliday	.08	.25
❑ 16 Mike Alstott	.25	.60
❑ 17 Warrick Dunn	.25	.60
❑ 18 Trent Dilfer	.15	.40
❑ 19 Jacquez Green	.08	.25
❑ 20 Reidel Anthony	.15	.40
❑ 21 Warren Sapp	.15	.40
❑ 22 Bert Emanuel	.15	.40
❑ 23 Curtis Enis	.08	.25
❑ 24 Curtis Conway	.15	.40
❑ 25 Bobby Engram	.15	.40
❑ 26 Erik Kramer	.15	.40
❑ 27 Moses Moreno	.08	.25
❑ 28 Edgar Bennett	.08	.25
❑ 29 Barry Sanders	.75	2.00
❑ 30 Charlie Batch	.25	.60
❑ 31 Herman Moore	.15	.40
❑ 32 Johnnie Morton	.15	.40
❑ 33 Germane Crowell	.08	.25
❑ 34 Terry Fair	.08	.25
❑ 35 Gary Brown	.08	.25
❑ 36 Kent Graham	.08	.25
❑ 37 Kerry Collins	.15	.40
❑ 38 Charles Way	.08	.25
❑ 39 Tiki Barber	.25	.60
❑ 40 Ike Hilliard	.08	.25
❑ 41 Joe Jurevicius	.15	.40
❑ 42 Michael Strahan	.15	.40
❑ 43 Jason Sehorn	.08	.25
❑ 44 Brad Johnson	.25	.60
❑ 45 Terry Allen	.15	.40
❑ 46 Skip Hicks	.08	.25
❑ 47 Michael Westbrook	.15	.40
❑ 48 Leslie Shepherd	.08	.25
❑ 49 Stephen Alexander	.08	.25
❑ 50 Albert Connell	.08	.25
❑ 51 Darrell Green	.15	.40
❑ 52 Jake Plummer	.15	.40
❑ 53 Adrian Murrell	.15	.40
❑ 54 Frank Sanders	.15	.40
❑ 55 Rob Moore	.15	.40
❑ 56 Larry Centers	.08	.25
❑ 57 Simeon Rice	.15	.40
❑ 58 Andre Wadsworth	.08	.25
❑ 59 Duce Staley	.25	.60
❑ 60 Charles Johnson	.08	.25
❑ 61 Charlie Garner	.15	.40
❑ 62 Bobby Hoying	.15	.40
❑ 63 Daryl Johnston	.15	.40
❑ 64 Emmitt Smith	.50	1.25
❑ 65 Troy Aikman	.50	1.25
❑ 66 Michael Irvin	.15	.40
❑ 67 Deion Sanders	.25	.60
❑ 68 Chris Warren	.08	.25
❑ 69 Darren Woodson	.08	.25
❑ 70 Rod Woodson	.15	.40
❑ 71 Travis Jervey	.08	.25
❑ 72 Jerry Rice	.50	1.25
❑ 73 Terrell Owens	.25	.60
❑ 74 Steve Young	.30	.75
❑ 75 Garrison Hearst	.15	.40
❑ 76 J.J. Stokes	.15	.40
❑ 77 Ken Norton	.08	.25
❑ 78 R.W. McQuarters	.08	.25
❑ 79 Bryant Young	.08	.25
❑ 80 Jamal Anderson	.25	.60
❑ 81 Chris Chandler	.15	.40
❑ 82 Terance Mathis	.15	.40
❑ 83 Tim Dwight	.25	.60
❑ 84 O.J. Santiago	.08	.25
❑ 85 Chris Calloway	.08	.25
❑ 86 Keith Brooking	.08	.25
❑ 87 Eddie Kennison	.15	.40
❑ 88 Willie Roaf	.08	.25
❑ 89 Cam Cleeland	.08	.25
❑ 90 Lamar Smith	.15	.40
❑ 91 Sean Dawkins	.08	.25
❑ 92 Tim Biakabutuka	.15	.40
❑ 93 Muhsin Muhammad	.15	.40
❑ 94 Steve Beuerlein	.08	.25
❑ 95 Rae Carruth	.08	.25
❑ 96 Wesley Walls	.15	.40
❑ 97 Kevin Greene	.15	.40
❑ 98 Trent Green	.25	.60
❑ 99 Tony Banks	.15	.40
❑ 100 Greg Hill	.08	.25
❑ 101 Robert Holcombe	.08	.25
❑ 102 Isaac Bruce	.25	.60
❑ 103 Amp Lee	.08	.25
❑ 104 Az-Zahir Hakim	.08	.25
❑ 105 Warren Moon	.25	.60
❑ 106 Jeff George	.15	.40
❑ 107 Rocket Ismail	.15	.40
❑ 108 Kordell Stewart	.15	.40
❑ 109 Jerome Bettis	.25	.60
❑ 110 Courtney Hawkins	.08	.25
❑ 111 Chris Fuamatu-Ma'afala	.08	.25
❑ 112 Levon Kirkland	.08	.25
❑ 113 Hines Ward	.25	.60
❑ 114 Will Blackwell	.08	.25
❑ 115 Corey Dillon	.25	.60
❑ 116 Carl Pickens	.15	.40
❑ 117 Neil O'Donnell	.15	.40
❑ 118 Jeff Blake	.15	.40
❑ 119 Darnay Scott	.08	.25
❑ 120 Takeo Spikes	.08	.25
❑ 121 Steve McNair	.25	.60
❑ 122 Frank Wycheck	.08	.25
❑ 123 Eddie George	.25	.60
❑ 124 Chris Sanders	.08	.25
❑ 125 Yancey Thigpen	.08	.25
❑ 126 Kevin Dyson	.15	.40
❑ 127 Blaine Bishop	.08	.25
❑ 128 Fred Taylor	.25	.60
❑ 129 Mark Brunell	.25	.60
❑ 130 Jimmy Smith	.15	.40
❑ 131 Keenan McCardell	.15	.40
❑ 132 Kyle Brady	.08	.25
❑ 133 Tavian Banks	.08	.25
❑ 134 James Stewart	.15	.40
❑ 135 Kevin Hardy	.08	.25
❑ 136 Jonathan Quinn	.08	.25
❑ 137 Jermaine Lewis	.15	.40
❑ 138 Priest Holmes	.40	1.00
❑ 139 Scott Mitchell	.15	.40
❑ 140 Eric Zeier	.15	.40
❑ 141 Patrick Johnson	.08	.25
❑ 142 Ray Lewis	.25	.60
❑ 143 Terry Kirby	.08	.25
❑ 144 Ty Detmer	.08	.25
❑ 145 Irv Smith	.08	.25
❑ 146 Chris Spielman	.08	.25
❑ 147 Antonio Langham	.08	.25
❑ 148 Dan Marino	.75	2.00
❑ 149 O.J. McDuffie	.15	.40
❑ 150 Oronde Gadsden	.15	.40
❑ 151 Karim Abdul-Jabbar	.15	.40
❑ 152 Yatil Green	.08	.25
❑ 153 Zach Thomas	.25	.60
❑ 154 John Avery	.08	.25
❑ 155 Lamar Thomas	.08	.25
❑ 156 Drew Bledsoe	.30	.75
❑ 157 Terry Glenn	.25	.60
❑ 158 Ben Coates	.15	.40
❑ 159 Shawn Jefferson	.08	.25
❑ 160 Sedrick Shaw	.08	.25
❑ 161 Tony Simmons	.08	.25
❑ 162 Ty Law	.15	.40
❑ 163 Robert Edwards	.08	.25
❑ 164 Curtis Martin	.25	.60
❑ 165 Keyshawn Johnson	.25	.60
❑ 166 Vinny Testaverde	.15	.40
❑ 167 Aaron Glenn	.08	.25
❑ 168 Wayne Chrebet	.15	.40
❑ 169 Dedric Ward	.08	.25
❑ 170 Peyton Manning	.75	2.00
❑ 171 Marshall Faulk	.30	.75
❑ 172 Marvin Harrison	.25	.60
❑ 173 Jerome Pathon	.08	.25
❑ 174 Ken Dilger	.08	.25
❑ 175 E.G. Green	.08	.25
❑ 176 Doug Flutie	.25	.60
❑ 177 Thurman Thomas	.15	.40
❑ 178 Andre Reed	.15	.40
❑ 179 Eric Moulds	.25	.60
❑ 180 Antowain Smith	.25	.60
❑ 181 Bruce Smith	.15	.40
❑ 182 Rob Johnson	.15	.40
❑ 183 Terrell Davis	.25	.60
❑ 184 John Elway	.75	2.00
❑ 185 Ed McCaffrey	.15	.40
❑ 186 Rod Smith	.15	.40
❑ 187 Shannon Sharpe	.15	.40
❑ 188 Marcus Nash	.08	.25
❑ 189 Brian Griese	.25	.60
❑ 190 Neil Smith	.15	.40
❑ 191 Bubby Brister	.08	.25
❑ 192 Ryan Leaf	.25	.60
❑ 193 Natrone Means	.15	.40
❑ 194 Mikhael Ricks	.08	.25
❑ 195 Junior Seau	.25	.60
❑ 196 Jim Harbaugh	.15	.40
❑ 197 Bryan Still	.08	.25
❑ 198 Freddie Jones	.08	.25
❑ 199 Andre Rison	.15	.40
❑ 200 Elvis Grbac	.15	.40
❑ 201 Byron Bam Morris	.08	.25
❑ 202 Rashaan Shehee	.08	.25
❑ 203 Kimble Anders	.15	.40
❑ 204 Donnell Bennett	.08	.25
❑ 205 Tony Gonzalez	.25	.60
❑ 206 Derrick Alexander WR	.15	.40
❑ 207 Jon Kitna	.25	.60
❑ 208 Ricky Watters	.15	.40
❑ 209 Joey Galloway	.15	.40
❑ 210 Ahman Green	.25	.60
❑ 211 Shawn Springs	.08	.25
❑ 212 Michael Sinclair	.08	.25
❑ 213 Napoleon Kaufman	.25	.60
❑ 214 Tim Brown	.25	.60
❑ 215 Charles Woodson	.25	.60
❑ 216 Harvey Williams	.08	.25
❑ 217 Jon Ritchie	.08	.25
❑ 218 Rich Gannon	.25	.60
❑ 219 Rickey Dudley	.08	.25
❑ 220 James Jett	.15	.40
❑ 221 Tim Couch RC	1.25	3.00
❑ 222 Ricky Williams RC	1.50	4.00
❑ 223 Donovan McNabb RC	4.00	10.00
❑ 224 Edgerrin James RC	3.00	8.00
❑ 225 Torry Holt RC	2.50	6.00
❑ 226 Daunte Culpepper RC	3.00	8.00
❑ 227 Akili Smith RC	.75	2.00
❑ 228 Champ Bailey RC	1.50	4.00
❑ 229 Chris Claiborne RC	.50	1.25
❑ 230 Chris McAlister RC	.75	2.00
❑ 231 Troy Edwards RC	.75	2.00
❑ 232 Jevon Kearse RC	2.00	5.00
❑ 233 Shaun King RC	.75	2.00
❑ 234 David Boston RC	1.25	3.00
❑ 235 Peerless Price RC	1.25	3.00
❑ 236 Cecil Collins RC	.50	1.25
❑ 237 Rob Konrad RC	.75	2.00
❑ 238 Cade McNown UER RC	.75	2.00
❑ 239 Shawn Bryson RC	1.25	3.00
❑ 240 Kevin Faulk RC	1.25	3.00
❑ 241 Scott Covington RC	1.25	3.00
❑ 242 James Johnson RC	.75	2.00
❑ 243 Mike Cloud RC	.75	2.00
❑ 244 Aaron Brooks RC	1.50	4.00
❑ 245 Sedrick Irvin RC	.50	1.25
❑ 246 Amos Zereoue RC	1.25	3.00
❑ 247 Jermaine Fazande RC	.75	2.00
❑ 248 Joe Germaine RC	.75	2.00
❑ 249 Brock Huard RC	1.25	3.00
❑ 250 Craig Yeast RC	.75	2.00
❑ 251 Travis McGriff RC	.50	1.25
❑ 252 D'Wayne Bates RC	.75	2.00
❑ 253 Na Brown RC	.75	2.00
❑ 254 Tai Streets RC	1.25	3.00
❑ 255 Andy Katzenmoyer RC	.75	2.00
❑ 256 Kevin Johnson RC	1.25	3.00
❑ 257 Joe Montgomery RC	.75	2.00
❑ 258 Karsten Bailey RC	.75	2.00
❑ 259 De'Mond Parker RC	.50	1.25
❑ 260 Reginald Kelly RC	.50	1.25
❑ 261 Eddie George AP	.60	1.50
❑ 262 Jamal Anderson AP	.60	1.50
❑ 263 Barry Sanders AP	2.50	6.00
❑ 264 Fred Taylor AP	.60	1.50
❑ 265 Keyshawn Johnson AP	.60	1.50
❑ 266 Jerry Rice AP	1.50	4.00
❑ 267 Doug Flutie AP	.60	1.50
❑ 268 Deion Sanders AP	.60	1.50
❑ 269 Randall Cunningham AP	.60	1.50
❑ 270 Steve Young AP	1.00	2.50
❑ 271 J.Elway/T.Davis GC	2.00	5.00
❑ 272 P.Manning/M.Faulk GC	2.00	5.00

Card	Low	High
❑ 273 B.Favre/A.Freeman GC	2.50	6.00
❑ 274 T.Aikman/E.Smith GC	1.50	4.00
❑ 275 C.Carter/R.Moss GC	1.50	4.00

1999 Score Supplemental

Card	Low	High
❑ COMPLETE SET (110)	10.00	25.00
❑ COMP.FACT.SET (110)	12.50	30.00
❑ S1 Chris Greisen RC	.40	1.00
❑ S2 Sherdrick Bonner RC	.25	.60
❑ S3 Joel Makovicka RC	.60	1.50
❑ S4 Andy McCullough RC	.25	.60
❑ S5 Jeff Paulk RC	.25	.60
❑ S6 Brandon Stokley RC	.75	2.00
❑ S7 Sheldon Jackson RC	.40	1.00
❑ S8 Bobby Collins RC	.25	.60
❑ S9 Kamil Loud RC	.25	.60
❑ S10 Antoine Winfield RC	.40	1.00
❑ S11 Jerry Azumah RC	.40	1.00
❑ S12 James Allen RC	.60	1.50
❑ S13 Nick Williams RC	.40	1.00
❑ S14 Michael Basnight RC	.25	.60
❑ S15 Damon Griffin RC	.40	1.00
❑ S16 Ronnie Powell RC	.25	.60
❑ S17 Darrin Chiaverini RC	.40	1.00
❑ S18 Mark Campbell RC	.40	1.00
❑ S19 Mike Lucky RC	.40	1.00
❑ S20 Wane McGarity RC	.25	.60
❑ S21 Jason Tucker RC	.40	1.00
❑ S22 Ebenezer Ekuban RC	.40	1.00
❑ S23 Robert Thomas RC	.40	1.00
❑ S24 Dat Nguyen RC	.40	1.00
❑ S25 Olandis Gary RC	.60	1.50
❑ S26 Desmond Clark RC	.60	1.50
❑ S27 Andre Cooper RC	.25	.60
❑ S28 Chris Watson RC	.25	.60
❑ S29 Al Wilson RC	.60	1.50
❑ S30 Cory Sauter RC	.25	.60
❑ S31 Brock Olivo RC	.25	.60
❑ S32 Basil Mitchell RC	.25	.60
❑ S33 Matt Snider RC	.25	.60
❑ S34 Antuan Edwards RC	.40	1.00
❑ S35 Mike McKenzie RC	.40	1.00
❑ S36 Terrence Wilkins RC	.40	1.00
❑ S37 Fernando Bryant RC	.40	1.00
❑ S38 Larry Parker RC	.60	1.50
❑ S39 Autry Denson RC	.40	1.00
❑ S40 Jim Kleinsasser RC	.60	1.50
❑ S41 Michael Bishop RC	.60	1.50
❑ S42 Andy Katzenmoyer	.08	.25
❑ S43 Brett Bech RC	.25	.60
❑ S44 Sean Bennett RC	.25	.60
❑ S45 Dan Campbell RC	.25	.60
❑ S46 Ray Lucas RC	.60	1.50
❑ S47 Scott Dreisbach RC	.40	1.00
❑ S48 Cecil Martin RC	.40	1.00
❑ S49 Dameane Douglas RC	.40	1.00
❑ S50 Jed Weaver RC	.40	1.00
❑ S51 Jerame Tuman RC	.60	1.50
❑ S52 Steve Heiden RC	.60	1.50
❑ S53 Jeff Garcia RC	1.50	4.00
❑ S54 Terry Jackson RC	.40	1.00
❑ S55 Charlie Rogers RC	.40	1.00
❑ S56 Lamar King RC	.40	1.00
❑ S57 Kurt Warner RC	3.00	8.00
❑ S58 Dre' Bly RC	.60	1.50
❑ S59 Justin Watson RC	.25	.60
❑ S60 Rabih Abdullah RC	.40	1.00
❑ S61 Martin Gramatica RC	.25	.60
❑ S62 Darnell McDonald RC	.40	1.00
❑ S63 Anthony McFarland RC	.40	1.00
❑ S64 Larry Brown TE RC	.25	.60
❑ S65 Kevin Daft RC	.40	1.00
❑ S66 Mike Sellers	.05	.15
❑ S67 Ken Oxendine	.05	.15
❑ S68 Errict Rhett	.08	.25
❑ S69 Stoney Case	.05	.15
❑ S70 Jonathan Linton	.05	.15
❑ S71 Marcus Robinson	.40	1.00
❑ S72 Shane Matthews	.08	.25
❑ S73 Cade McNown	.40	1.00
❑ S74 Akili Smith	.05	.15
❑ S75 Karim Abdul-Jabbar	.08	.25
❑ S76 Tim Couch	.60	1.50
❑ S77 Kevin Johnson	.15	.40
❑ S78 Ron Rivers	.05	.15
❑ S79 Bill Schroeder	.15	.40
❑ S80 Edgerrin James	1.00	2.50
❑ S81 Cecil Collins	.30	.75
❑ S82 Matthew Hatchette	.05	.15
❑ S83 Daunte Culpepper	1.00	2.50
❑ S84 Ricky Williams	.50	1.25
❑ S85 Tyrone Wheatley	.15	.40
❑ S86 Donovan McNabb	1.25	3.00
❑ S87 Marshall Faulk	.20	.50
❑ S88 Torry Holt	.75	2.00
❑ S89 Stephen Davis	.15	.40
❑ S90 Brad Johnson	.15	.40
❑ S91 Jake Plummer SS	.08	.25
❑ S92 Emmitt Smith SS	.30	.75
❑ S93 Troy Aikman SS	.30	.75
❑ S94 John Elway SS	.50	1.25
❑ S95 Terrell Davis SS	.15	.40
❑ S96 Barry Sanders SS	.50	1.25
❑ S97 Brett Favre SS	.50	1.25
❑ S98 Antonio Freeman SS	.15	.40
❑ S99 Peyton Manning SS	.50	1.25
❑ S100 Fred Taylor SS	.15	.40
❑ S101 Mark Brunell SS	.15	.40
❑ S102 Dan Marino SS	.50	1.25
❑ S103 Randy Moss SS	.40	1.00
❑ S104 Cris Carter SS	.15	.40
❑ S105 Drew Bledsoe SS	.20	.50
❑ S106 Terry Glenn SS	.15	.40
❑ S107 Keyshawn Johnson SS	.15	.40
❑ S108 Jerry Rice SS	.30	.75
❑ S109 Steve Young SS	.20	.50
❑ S110 Eddie George SS	.15	.40

2000 Score

Card	Low	High
❑ COMP.SET w/o SP's (220)	7.50	20.00
❑ 1 Michael Pittman	.08	.25
❑ 2 Jake Plummer	.15	.40
❑ 3 Rob Moore	.15	.40
❑ 4 David Boston	.25	.60
❑ 5 Frank Sanders	.15	.40
❑ 6 Jamal Anderson	.25	.60
❑ 7 Chris Chandler	.15	.40
❑ 8 Tim Dwight	.25	.60
❑ 9 Terance Mathis	.15	.40
❑ 10 Shawn Jefferson	.08	.25
❑ 11 Ashley Ambrose	.08	.25
❑ 12 Peter Boulware	.08	.25
❑ 13 Priest Holmes	.30	.75
❑ 14 Tony Banks	.15	.40
❑ 15 Qadry Ismail	.15	.40
❑ 16 Shannon Sharpe	.15	.40
❑ 17 Rod Woodson	.15	.40
❑ 18 Matt Stover	.08	.25
❑ 19 Michael McCrary	.08	.25
❑ 20 Doug Flutie	.25	.60
❑ 21 Rob Johnson	.15	.40
❑ 22 Eric Moulds	.25	.60
❑ 23 Peerless Price	.15	.40
❑ 24 Jonathan Linton	.08	.25
❑ 25 Antowain Smith	.15	.40
❑ 26 Jay Riemersma	.08	.25
❑ 27 Muhsin Muhammad	.15	.40
❑ 28 Tim Biakabutuka	.15	.40
❑ 29 Patrick Jeffers	.25	.60
❑ 30 Wesley Walls	.08	.25
❑ 31 Steve Beuerlein	.15	.40
❑ 32 John Kasay	.08	.25
❑ 33 Curtis Enis	.08	.25
❑ 34 Cade McNown	.08	.25
❑ 35 Marcus Robinson	.25	.60
❑ 36 Bobby Engram	.08	.25
❑ 37 Eddie Kennison	.08	.25
❑ 38 Akili Smith	.08	.25
❑ 39 Carl Pickens	.15	.40
❑ 40 Corey Dillon	.25	.60
❑ 41 Darnay Scott	.15	.40
❑ 42 Errict Rhett	.15	.40
❑ 43 Karim Abdul-Jabbar	.15	.40
❑ 44 Tim Couch	.15	.40
❑ 45 Kevin Johnson	.25	.60
❑ 46 Darrin Chiaverini	.08	.25
❑ 47 Terry Kirby	.08	.25
❑ 48 Jason Tucker	.08	.25
❑ 49 Rocket Ismail	.15	.40
❑ 50 Joey Galloway	.15	.40
❑ 51 Michael Irvin	.15	.40
❑ 52 Troy Aikman	.50	1.25
❑ 53 Emmitt Smith	.50	1.25
❑ 54 David LaFleur	.08	.25
❑ 55 Trevor Pryce	.08	.25
❑ 56 Brian Griese	.25	.60
❑ 57 Olandis Gary	.25	.60
❑ 58 Terrell Davis	.25	.60
❑ 59 Rod Smith	.15	.40
❑ 60 Ed McCaffrey	.25	.60
❑ 61 Gus Frerotte	.08	.25
❑ 62 Jason Elam	.08	.25
❑ 63 Kavika Pittman	.08	.25
❑ 64 James Stewart	.15	.40
❑ 65 Charlie Batch	.25	.60
❑ 66 Johnnie Morton	.15	.40
❑ 67 Herman Moore	.15	.40
❑ 68 Germane Crowell	.08	.25
❑ 69 Barry Sanders	.60	1.50
❑ 70 Chris Claiborne	.08	.25
❑ 71 Brett Favre	.75	2.00
❑ 72 Antonio Freeman	.25	.60
❑ 73 Dorsey Levens	.15	.40
❑ 74 De'Mond Parker	.08	.25
❑ 75 Corey Bradford	.15	.40
❑ 76 Basil Mitchell	.08	.25
❑ 77 Bill Schroeder	.15	.40
❑ 78 Peyton Manning	.60	1.50
❑ 79 Marvin Harrison	.25	.60
❑ 80 Terrence Wilkins	.08	.25
❑ 81 Edgerrin James	.40	1.00
❑ 82 E.G. Green	.08	.25
❑ 83 Chad Bratzke	.08	.25
❑ 84 Mark Brunell	.25	.60
❑ 85 Fred Taylor	.25	.60
❑ 86 Jimmy Smith	.15	.40
❑ 87 Keenan McCardell	.15	.40
❑ 88 Kevin Hardy	.08	.25
❑ 89 Aaron Beasley	.08	.25
❑ 90 Elvis Grbac	.15	.40
❑ 91 Derrick Alexander	.15	.40
❑ 92 Tony Gonzalez	.15	.40
❑ 93 Donnell Bennett	.08	.25
❑ 94 Warren Moon	.25	.60
❑ 95 Andre Rison	.15	.40
❑ 96 James Hasty	.08	.25
❑ 97 Dan Marino	.75	2.00
❑ 98 Thurman Thomas	.15	.40
❑ 99 James Johnson	.08	.25
❑ 100 O.J. McDuffie	.15	.40
❑ 101 Tony Martin	.15	.40
❑ 102 Oronde Gadsden	.15	.40
❑ 103 Zach Thomas	.25	.60
❑ 104 Sam Madison	.08	.25
❑ 105 Jay Fiedler	.25	.60
❑ 106 Damon Huard	.25	.60
❑ 107 Robert Smith	.25	.60
❑ 108 Leroy Hoard	.08	.25
❑ 109 Randy Moss	.50	1.25
❑ 110 Cris Carter	.25	.60
❑ 111 Daunte Culpepper	.30	.75
❑ 112 John Randle	.15	.40
❑ 113 Randall Cunningham	.25	.60
❑ 114 Gary Anderson	.08	.25
❑ 115 Drew Bledsoe DP	.30	.75
❑ 116 Terry Glenn	.15	.40
❑ 117 Kevin Faulk	.15	.40
❑ 118 Terry Allen SP	7.50	15.00
❑ 119 Adam Vinatieri	.25	.60
❑ 120 Ty Law	.15	.40
❑ 121 Lawyer Milloy	.15	.40

Card		
❑ 122 Troy Brown	.15	.40
❑ 123 Ben Coates	.08	.25
❑ 124 Cam Cleeland	.08	.25
❑ 125 Jeff Blake	.15	.40
❑ 126 Ricky Williams	.25	.60
❑ 127 Jake Reed	.15	.40
❑ 128 Jake Delhomme RC	1.00	2.50
❑ 129 Andrew Glover	.08	.25
❑ 130 Keith Poole	.08	.25
❑ 131 Joe Horn	.15	.40
❑ 132 Kerry Collins	.15	.40
❑ 133 Joe Montgomery	.08	.25
❑ 134 Sean Bennett	.08	.25
❑ 135 Amani Toomer	.08	.25
❑ 136 Ike Hilliard	.15	.40
❑ 137 Joe Jurevicius	.08	.25
❑ 138 Tiki Barber	.25	.60
❑ 139 Victor Green	.08	.25
❑ 140 Ray Lucas	.15	.40
❑ 141 Vinny Testaverde	.15	.40
❑ 142 Curtis Martin	.25	.60
❑ 143 Wayne Chrebet	.15	.40
❑ 144 Tyrone Wheatley	.15	.40
❑ 145 Rich Gannon	.25	.60
❑ 146 Napoleon Kaufman	.15	.40
❑ 147 Tim Brown	.08	.25
❑ 148 Rickey Dudley	.08	.25
❑ 149 Charles Woodson	.25	.60
❑ 150 James Jett	.08	.25
❑ 151 Duce Staley	.25	.60
❑ 152 Charles Johnson	.15	.40
❑ 153 Donovan McNabb	.40	1.00
❑ 154 Troy Vincent	.08	.25
❑ 155 Troy Edwards	.08	.25
❑ 156 Jerome Bettis	.25	.60
❑ 157 Kordell Stewart	.15	.40
❑ 158 Richard Huntley	.08	.25
❑ 159 Hines Ward	.25	.60
❑ 160 Levon Kirkland	.08	.25
❑ 161 Ryan Leaf	.15	.40
❑ 162 Jim Harbaugh	.15	.40
❑ 163 Jermaine Fazande	.08	.25
❑ 164 Natrone Means	.08	.25
❑ 165 Junior Seau	.25	.60
❑ 166 Curtis Conway	.15	.40
❑ 167 Freddie Jones	.08	.25
❑ 168 Jeff Graham	.08	.25
❑ 169 Terrell Owens	.25	.60
❑ 170 Jeff Garcia	.25	.60
❑ 171 Jerry Rice	.50	1.25
❑ 172 Steve Young	.30	.75
❑ 173 Garrison Hearst	.15	.40
❑ 174 Charlie Garner	.15	.40
❑ 175 Fred Beasley	.08	.25
❑ 176 Bryant Young	.08	.25
❑ 177 Derrick Mayes	.15	.40
❑ 178 Sean Dawkins	.08	.25
❑ 179 Jon Kitna	.25	.60
❑ 180 Ricky Watters	.15	.40
❑ 181 Charlie Rogers	.08	.25
❑ 182 Kurt Warner	.50	1.25
❑ 183 Marshall Faulk	.30	.75
❑ 184 Isaac Bruce	.25	.60
❑ 185 Az-Zahir Hakim	.15	.40
❑ 186 Trent Green	.25	.60
❑ 187 Jeff Wilkins	.08	.25
❑ 188 Torry Holt	.25	.60
❑ 189 London Fletcher RC	.15	.40
❑ 190 Robert Holcombe	.08	.25
❑ 191 Todd Lyght	.08	.25
❑ 192 Keyshawn Johnson	.25	.60
❑ 193 Derrick Brooks	.25	.60
❑ 194 Warren Sapp	.15	.40
❑ 195 Shaun King	.08	.25
❑ 196 Warrick Dunn	.25	.60
❑ 197 Mike Alstott	.25	.60
❑ 198 Jacquez Green	.08	.25
❑ 199 Reidel Anthony	.08	.25
❑ 200 Martin Gramatica	.08	.25
❑ 201 Donnie Abraham	.08	.25
❑ 202 Steve McNair	.25	.60
❑ 203 Eddie George	.25	.60
❑ 204 Jevon Kearse	.25	.60
❑ 205 Frank Wycheck	.08	.25
❑ 206 Kevin Dyson	.15	.40
❑ 207 Yancey Thigpen	.08	.25
❑ 208 Al Del Greco	.08	.25
❑ 209 Jeff George	.15	.40
❑ 210 Adrian Murrell	.15	.40
❑ 211 Brad Johnson	.25	.60
❑ 212 Stephen Davis	.25	.60
❑ 213 Stephen Alexander	.08	.25
❑ 214 Michael Westbrook	.15	.40
❑ 215 Darrell Green	.08	.25
❑ 216 Champ Bailey	.25	.60
❑ 217 Albert Connell	.08	.25
❑ 218 Larry Centers	.08	.25
❑ 219 Bruce Smith	.15	.40
❑ 220 Deion Sanders	.25	.60
❑ 221 Ricky Williams SS	.25	.60
❑ 222 Edgerrin James SS	.40	1.00
❑ 223 Tim Couch SS	.15	.40
❑ 224 Cade McNown SS	.10	.30
❑ 225 Olandis Gary SS	.30	.75
❑ 226 Torry Holt SS	.30	.75
❑ 227 Donovan McNabb SS	.40	1.00
❑ 228 Shaun King SS	.08	.25
❑ 229 Kevin Johnson SS	.30	.75
❑ 230 Kurt Warner SS	.60	1.50
❑ 231 Tony Gonzalez AP	.20	.50
❑ 232 Frank Wycheck AP	.10	.30
❑ 233 Eddie George AP	.30	.75
❑ 234 Mark Brunell AP	.30	.75
❑ 235 Corey Dillon AP	.30	.75
❑ 236 Peyton Manning AP	.75	2.00
❑ 237 Keyshawn Johnson AP	.30	.75
❑ 238 Rich Gannon AP	.30	.75
❑ 239 Terry Glenn AP	.20	.50
❑ 240 Tony Brackens AP	.10	.30
❑ 241 Edgerrin James AP	.40	1.00
❑ 242 Tim Brown AP	.30	.75
❑ 243 Michael Strahan AP	.20	.50
❑ 244 Kurt Warner AP	.60	1.50
❑ 245 Brad Johnson AP	.30	.75
❑ 246 Aeneas Williams AP	.10	.30
❑ 247 Marshall Faulk AP	.40	1.00
❑ 248 Dexter Coakley AP	.10	.30
❑ 249 Warren Sapp AP	.20	.50
❑ 250 Mike Alstott AP	.30	.75
❑ 251 David Sloan AP	.10	.30
❑ 252 Cris Carter AP	.30	.75
❑ 253 Muhsin Muhammad AP	.10	.30
❑ 254 Isaac Bruce AP	.30	.75
❑ 255 Wesley Walls AP	.10	.30
❑ 256 Steve Beuerlein LL	.20	.50
❑ 257 Kurt Warner LL	.60	1.50
❑ 258 Peyton Manning LL	.75	2.00
❑ 259 Brad Johnson LL	.30	.75
❑ 260 Edgerrin James LL	.40	1.00
❑ 261 Curtis Martin LL	.30	.75
❑ 262 Stephen Davis LL	.30	.75
❑ 263 Emmitt Smith LL	.60	1.50
❑ 264 Marvin Harrison LL	.30	.75
❑ 265 Jimmy Smith LL	.20	.50
❑ 266 Randy Moss LL	.60	1.50
❑ 267 Marcus Robinson LL	.30	.75
❑ 268 Kevin Carter LL	.10	.30
❑ 269 Simeon Rice LL	.20	.50
❑ 270 Robert Porcher LL	.10	.30
❑ 271 Jevon Kearse LL	.30	.75
❑ 272 Mike Vanderjagt LL	.10	.30
❑ 273 Olindo Mare LL	.10	.30
❑ 274 Todd Peterson LL	.10	.30
❑ 275 Mike Hollis LL	.10	.30
❑ 276 Mike Anderson RC/500	8.00	20.00
❑ 277 Peter Warrick RC	.75	2.00
❑ 278 Courtney Brown RC	.30	.75
❑ 279 Plaxico Burress RC	1.50	4.00
❑ 280 Corey Simon RC	.30	.75
❑ 281 Thomas Jones RC	1.25	3.00
❑ 282 Travis Taylor RC	.30	.75
❑ 283 Shaun Alexander RC	2.50	6.00
❑ 284 Patrick Pass RC/500	6.00	15.00
❑ 285 Chris Redman RC	.20	.50
❑ 286 Chad Pennington RC	2.00	5.00
❑ 287 Jamal Lewis RC	2.00	5.00
❑ 288 Brian Urlacher RC	3.00	8.00
❑ 289 Bubba Franks RC	.75	2.00
❑ 290 Dez White RC	.75	2.00
❑ 291 Frank Moreau RC/500	6.00	15.00
❑ 292 Ron Dayne RC	.75	2.00
❑ 293 Sylvester Morris RC	.20	.50
❑ 294 R.Jay Soward RC	.60	1.50
❑ 295 Curtis Keaton RC	.60	1.50
❑ 296 Spergon Wynn RC/500	6.00	15.00
❑ 297 Rondell Mealey RC	.60	1.50
❑ 298 Travis Prentice RC	.60	1.50
❑ 299 Darrell Jackson RC	1.50	4.00
❑ 300 Giovanni Carmazzi RC	.60	1.50
❑ 301 Anthony Lucas RC	.60	1.50
❑ 302 Danny Farmer RC	.60	1.50
❑ 303 Dennis Northcutt RC	.75	2.00
❑ 304 Troy Walters RC	.75	2.00
❑ 305 Laveranues Coles RC	1.00	2.50
❑ 306 Kwame Cavil RC	.60	1.50
❑ 307 Tee Martin RC	.75	2.00
❑ 308 J.R. Redmond RC	.60	1.50
❑ 309 Tim Rattay RC	.75	2.00
❑ 310 Jerry Porter RC	1.00	2.50
❑ 311 Michael Wiley RC	.60	1.50
❑ 312 Reuben Droughns RC	1.00	2.50
❑ 313 Trung Canidate RC	.60	1.50
❑ 314 Shyrone Stith RC	.60	1.50
❑ 315 Marc Bulger RC	1.50	4.00
❑ 316 Tom Brady RC	20.00	40.00
❑ 317 Doug Johnson RC	.75	2.00
❑ 318 Todd Husak RC	.75	2.00
❑ 319 Gari Scott RC	.60	1.50
❑ 320 Windrell Hayes RC/500	6.00	15.00
❑ 321 Chris Cole RC	.60	1.50
❑ 322 Sammy Morris RC	.75	2.00
❑ 323 Trevor Gaylor RC	.60	1.50
❑ 324 Jarious Jackson RC	.60	1.50
❑ 325 Doug Chapman RC/500	6.00	15.00
❑ 326 Ron Dugans RC	.60	1.50
❑ 327 Ron Dixon RC/500	6.00	15.00
❑ 328 Joe Hamilton RC	.60	1.50
❑ 329 Todd Pinkston RC	.75	2.00
❑ 330 Chad Morton RC	.75	2.00

2001 Score

Card		
❑ COMPLETE SET (330)	40.00	80.00
❑ COMP.SET w/o SP's (220)	10.00	25.00
❑ 1 David Boston	.10	.25
❑ 2 Frank Sanders	.10	.25
❑ 3 Jake Plummer	.12	.30
❑ 4 Michael Pittman	.12	.30
❑ 5 Rob Moore	.10	.25
❑ 6 Thomas Jones	.12	.30
❑ 7 Chris Chandler	.12	.30
❑ 8 Doug Johnson	.10	.25
❑ 9 Jamal Anderson	.12	.30
❑ 10 Tim Dwight	.12	.30
❑ 11 Brandon Stokley	.12	.30
❑ 12 Chris Redman	.15	.40
❑ 13 Jamal Lewis	.15	.40
❑ 14 Qadry Ismail	.12	.30
❑ 15 Ray Lewis	.15	.40
❑ 16 Rod Woodson	.15	.40
❑ 17 Shannon Sharpe	.15	.40
❑ 18 Travis Taylor	.10	.25
❑ 19 Trent Dilfer	.12	.30
❑ 20 Elvis Grbac	.12	.30
❑ 21 Eric Moulds	.12	.30
❑ 22 Jay Riemersma	.10	.25
❑ 23 Peerless Price	.10	.25
❑ 24 Rob Johnson	.12	.30
❑ 25 Sam Cowart	.10	.25
❑ 26 Sammy Morris	.12	.30
❑ 27 Shawn Bryson	.10	.25
❑ 28 Donald Hayes	.10	.25
❑ 29 Muhsin Muhammad	.12	.30
❑ 30 Patrick Jeffers	.10	.25
❑ 31 Reggie White DE	.15	.40
❑ 32 Steve Beuerlein	.12	.30
❑ 33 Tim Biakabutuka	.10	.25
❑ 34 Wesley Walls	.10	.25
❑ 35 Brian Urlacher	.20	.50
❑ 36 Cade McNown	.12	.30
❑ 37 Dez White	.12	.30
❑ 38 James Allen	.10	.25
❑ 39 Marcus Robinson	.12	.30
❑ 40 Marty Booker	.12	.30
❑ 41 Akili Smith	.10	.25

Card		
42 Corey Dillon	.12	.30
43 Danny Farmer	.10	.25
44 Peter Warrick	.12	.30
45 Ron Dugans	.10	.25
46 Takeo Spikes	.10	.25
47 Courtney Brown	.10	.25
48 Dennis Northcutt	.10	.25
49 JaJuan Dawson	.10	.25
50 Kevin Johnson	.10	.25
51 Tim Couch	.10	.25
52 Travis Prentice	.10	.25
53 Anthony Wright	.10	.25
54 Emmitt Smith	.40	1.00
55 James McKnight	.10	.25
56 Joey Galloway	.12	.30
57 Rocket Ismail	.12	.30
58 Randall Cunningham	.15	.40
59 Troy Aikman	.25	.60
60 Brian Griese	.12	.30
61 Ed McCaffrey	.12	.30
62 Gus Frerotte	.12	.30
63 John Elway	.40	1.00
64 Mike Anderson	.12	.30
65 Olandis Gary	.10	.25
66 Rod Smith	.12	.30
67 Terrell Davis	.15	.40
68 Barry Sanders	.40	1.00
69 Charlie Batch	.12	.30
70 Germane Crowell	.10	.25
71 Herman Moore	.12	.30
72 James Stewart	.10	.25
73 Johnnie Morton	.12	.30
74 Robert Porcher	.10	.25
75 Jim Harbaugh	.12	.30
76 Ahman Green	.15	.40
77 Antonio Freeman	.15	.40
78 Bill Schroeder	.12	.30
79 Brett Favre	.50	1.25
80 Bubba Franks	.12	.30
81 Dorsey Levens	.12	.30
82 E.G. Green	.10	.25
83 Edgerrin James	.15	.40
84 Jerome Pathon	.10	.25
85 Ken Dilger	.10	.25
86 Marcus Pollard	.10	.25
87 Marvin Harrison	.15	.40
88 Peyton Manning	.40	1.00
89 Terrence Wilkins	.10	.25
90 Fred Taylor	.15	.40
91 Hardy Nickerson	.10	.25
92 Jimmy Smith	.12	.30
93 Keenan McCardell	.12	.30
94 Kyle Brady	.10	.25
95 Mark Brunell	.15	.40
96 Tony Brackens	.10	.25
97 Derrick Alexander	.10	.25
98 Sylvester Morris	.10	.25
99 Tony Gonzalez	.12	.30
100 Tony Richardson	.10	.25
101 Kimble Anders	.10	.25
102 Warren Moon	.15	.40
103 Dan Marino	.50	1.25
104 Jay Fiedler	.12	.30
105 Lamar Smith	.12	.30
106 O.J. McDuffie	.10	.25
107 Oronde Gadsden	.10	.25
108 Sam Madison	.10	.25
109 Thurman Thomas	.15	.40
110 Tony Martin	.12	.30
111 Zach Thomas	.15	.40
112 Cris Carter	.15	.40
113 Daunte Culpepper	.15	.40
114 Matthew Hatchette	.10	.25
115 Randy Moss	.20	.50
116 Robert Smith	.12	.30
117 Drew Bledsoe	.15	.40
118 J.R. Redmond	.10	.25
119 Kevin Faulk	.12	.30
120 Michael Bishop	.12	.30
121 Terry Glenn	.12	.30
122 Troy Brown	.12	.30
123 Ty Law	.12	.30
124 Aaron Brooks	.12	.30
125 Darren Howard	.10	.25
126 Jake Reed	.12	.30
127 Jeff Blake	.12	.30
128 Joe Horn	.12	.30
129 La'Roi Glover	.10	.25
130 Ricky Williams	.15	.40
131 Willie Jackson	.10	.25
132 Albert Connell	.10	.25
133 Amani Toomer	.12	.30
134 Ike Hilliard	.12	.30
135 Jason Sehorn	.12	.30
136 Jessie Armstead	.10	.25
137 Kerry Collins	.12	.30
138 Michael Strahan	.15	.40
139 Ron Dayne	.12	.30
140 Ron Dixon	.10	.25
141 Tiki Barber	.15	.40
142 Anthony Becht	.10	.25
143 Chad Pennington	.15	.40
144 Curtis Martin	.15	.40
145 Dedric Ward	.10	.25
146 Laveranues Coles	.15	.40
147 Vinny Testaverde	.12	.30
148 Wayne Chrebet	.12	.30
149 Andre Rison	.12	.30
150 Charles Woodson	.15	.40
151 Darrell Russell	.10	.25
152 Napoleon Kaufman	.10	.25
153 Rich Gannon	.12	.30
154 Tim Brown	.15	.40
155 Tyrone Wheatley	.12	.30
156 Chad Lewis	.10	.25
157 Charles Johnson	.10	.25
158 Donovan McNabb	.20	.50
159 Duce Staley	.12	.30
160 Hugh Douglas	.10	.25
161 Na Brown	.10	.25
162 Todd Pinkston	.10	.25
163 James Thrash	.12	.30
164 Bobby Shaw	.10	.25
165 Hines Ward	.15	.40
166 Jerome Bettis	.15	.40
167 Kordell Stewart	.12	.30
168 Levon Kirkland	.10	.25
169 Plaxico Burress	.12	.30
170 Richard Huntley	.10	.25
171 Troy Edwards	.10	.25
172 Jeff Graham	.10	.25
173 Junior Seau	.15	.40
174 Doug Flutie	.15	.40
175 Charlie Garner	.12	.30
176 Jeff Garcia	.12	.30
177 Jerry Rice	.30	.75
178 Steve Young	.20	.50
179 Terrell Owens	.15	.40
180 Brock Huard	.10	.25
181 Darrell Jackson	.12	.30
182 Derrick Mayes	.10	.25
183 Ricky Watters	.12	.30
184 Shaun Alexander	.15	.40
185 Matt Hasselbeck	.15	.40
186 John Randle	.12	.30
187 Az-Zahir Hakim	.10	.25
188 Isaac Bruce	.15	.40
189 Kurt Warner	.20	.50
190 Marshall Faulk	.15	.40
191 Torry Holt	.12	.30
192 Trent Green	.15	.40
193 Derrick Brooks	.15	.40
194 Jacquez Green	.10	.25
195 John Lynch	.12	.30
196 Keyshawn Johnson	.12	.30
197 Mike Alstott	.12	.30
198 Reidel Anthony	.10	.25
199 Shaun King	.10	.25
200 Warren Sapp	.12	.30
201 Warrick Dunn	.15	.40
202 Ryan Leaf	.10	.25
203 Carl Pickens	.12	.30
204 Derrick Mason	.12	.30
205 Eddie George	.15	.40
206 Frank Wycheck	.10	.25
207 Jevon Kearse	.12	.30
208 Neil O'Donnell	.12	.30
209 Steve McNair	.15	.40
210 Yancey Thigpen	.10	.25
211 Andre Reed	.15	.40
212 Brad Johnson	.12	.30
213 Bruce Smith	.15	.40
214 Champ Bailey	.15	.40
215 Darrell Green	.15	.40
216 Deion Sanders	.15	.40
217 Irving Fryar	.12	.30
218 Jeff George	.12	.30
219 Michael Westbrook	.10	.25
220 Stephen Davis	.12	.30
221 Terrell Owens AP	.25	.60
222 Peyton Manning AP	.60	1.50
223 Stephen Davis AP	.20	.50
224 Marvin Harrison AP	.25	.60
225 Donovan McNabb AP	.30	.75
226 Edgerrin James AP	.25	.60
227 Eric Moulds AP	.20	.50
228 Daunte Culpepper AP	.25	.60
229 Eddie George AP	.25	.60
230 Cris Carter AP	.25	.60
231 Rich Gannon AP	.20	.50
232 Jeff Garcia AP	.20	.50
233 Jimmy Smith AP	.20	.50
234 Tony Gonzalez AP	.20	.50
235 Torry Holt AP	.20	.50
236 Jevon Kearse AP	.20	.50
237 Ray Lewis AP	.25	.60
238 Warren Sapp AP	.20	.50
239 Brian Urlacher AP	.30	.75
240 Champ Bailey AP	.25	.60
241 Peyton Manning LL	.60	1.50
242 Jeff Garcia LL	.20	.50
243 Elvis Grbac LL	.20	.50
244 Daunte Culpepper LL	.25	.60
245 Brett Favre LL	.75	2.00
246 Edgerrin James LL	.25	.60
247 Robert Smith LL	.20	.50
248 Eddie George LL	.25	.60
249 Mike Anderson LL	.20	.50
250 Corey Dillon LL	.20	.50
251 Torry Holt LL	.20	.50
252 Rod Smith LL	.20	.50
253 Isaac Bruce LL	.25	.60
254 Terrell Owens LL	.25	.60
255 Randy Moss LL	.30	.75
256 La'Roi Glover LL	.15	.40
257 Trace Armstrong LL	.15	.40
258 Warren Sapp LL	.20	.50
259 Hugh Douglas LL	.15	.40
260 Jason Taylor LL	.25	.60
261 Mike Anderson SS	.20	.50
262 Jamal Lewis SS	.25	.60
263 Sylvester Morris SS	.15	.40
264 Darrell Jackson SS	.20	.50
265 Peter Warrick SS	.20	.50
266 Ron Dayne SS	.20	.50
267 Shaun Alexander SS	.25	.60
268 Plaxico Burress SS	.20	.50
269 Brian Urlacher SS	.30	.75
270 Courtney Brown SS	.15	.40
271 Michael Vick RC	1.50	4.00
272 Drew Brees RC	4.00	10.00
273 Chris Weinke RC	.60	1.50
274 Quincy Carter RC	.60	1.50
275 Sage Rosenfels RC	.75	2.00
276 Josh Heupel RC	.75	2.00
277 David Rivers RC	.50	1.25
278 Ben Leard RC	.50	1.25
279 Marques Tuiasosopo RC	.60	1.50
280 Mike McMahon RC	.60	1.50
281 Deuce McAllister RC	1.00	2.50
282 LaMont Jordan RC	.75	2.00
283 LaDainian Tomlinson RC	5.00	12.00
284 James Jackson RC	.60	1.50
285 Anthony Thomas RC	.75	2.00
286 Travis Henry RC	.75	2.00
287 Travis Minor RC	.60	1.50
288 Rudi Johnson RC	.75	2.00
289 Michael Bennett RC	.75	2.00
290 Kevan Barlow RC	.60	1.50
291 Reggie White RC	.50	1.25
292 Moran Norris RC	.50	1.25
293 Ja'Mar Toombs RC	.50	1.25
294 Heath Evans RC	.60	1.50
295 David Terrell RC	.60	1.50
296 Santana Moss RC	1.25	3.00
297 Rod Gardner RC	.60	1.50
298 Quincy Morgan RC	.60	1.50
299 Freddie Mitchell RC	.50	1.25
300 Boo Williams RC	.60	1.50
301 Reggie Wayne RC	2.00	5.00
302 Ronney Daniels RC	.50	1.25
303 Bobby Newcombe RC	.60	1.50
304 Vinny Sutherland RC	.50	1.25
305 Cedrick Wilson RC	.75	2.00
306 Robert Ferguson RC	.75	2.00
307 Ken-Yon Rambo RC	.50	1.25
308 Alex Bannister RC	.50	1.25

❑ 309 Koren Robinson RC .75 2.00
❑ 310 Chad Johnson RC 2.00 5.00
❑ 311 Chris Chambers RC 1.25 3.00
❑ 312 Javon Green RC .50 1.25
❑ 313 Snoop Minnis RC .60 1.50
❑ 314 Scotty Anderson RC .60 1.50
❑ 315 Todd Heap RC .75 2.00
❑ 316 Alge Crumpler RC .75 2.00
❑ 317 Marcellus Rivers RC .50 1.25
❑ 318 Rashon Burns RC .50 1.25
❑ 319 Jamal Reynolds RC .60 1.50
❑ 320 Andre Carter RC .75 2.00
❑ 321 Justin Smith RC .75 2.00
❑ 322 Gerard Warren RC .60 1.50
❑ 323 Tommy Polley RC .60 1.50
❑ 324 Dan Morgan RC .75 2.00
❑ 325 Torrance Marshall RC .60 1.50
❑ 326 Correll Buckhalter RC .75 2.00
❑ 327 Derrick Gibson RC .50 1.25
❑ 328 Adam Archuleta RC .60 1.50
❑ 329 Jamar Fletcher RC .50 1.25
❑ 330 Nate Clements RC .75 2.00

2002 Score

❑ COMPLETE SET (330) 20.00 50.00
❑ 1 David Boston .12 .30
❑ 2 Arnold Jackson .12 .30
❑ 3 MarTay Jenkins .12 .30
❑ 4 Thomas Jones .15 .40
❑ 5 Kwamie Lassiter .12 .30
❑ 6 Michael Pittman .15 .40
❑ 7 Jake Plummer .15 .40
❑ 8 Chris Chandler .15 .40
❑ 9 Alge Crumpler .15 .40
❑ 10 Terance Mathis .12 .30
❑ 11 Maurice Smith .12 .30
❑ 12 Ray Buchanan .12 .30
❑ 13 Jamal Anderson .15 .40
❑ 14 Keith Brooking .12 .30
❑ 15 Michael Vick .20 .50
❑ 16 Obafemi Ayanbadejo .12 .30
❑ 17 Jason Brookins .12 .30
❑ 18 Randall Cunningham .15 .40
❑ 19 Elvis Grbac .15 .40
❑ 20 Todd Heap .15 .40
❑ 21 Qadry Ismail .15 .40
❑ 22 Shannon Sharpe .20 .50
❑ 23 Travis Taylor .12 .30
❑ 24 Ray Lewis .20 .50
❑ 25 Jamal Lewis .15 .40
❑ 26 Larry Centers .15 .40
❑ 27 Rob Johnson .15 .40
❑ 28 Shawn Bryson .12 .30
❑ 29 Eric Moulds .15 .40
❑ 30 Peerless Price .12 .30
❑ 31 Nate Clements .12 .30
❑ 32 Travis Henry .15 .40
❑ 33 Isaac Byrd .12 .30
❑ 34 Nick Goings .12 .30
❑ 35 Donald Hayes .12 .30
❑ 36 Richard Huntley .12 .30
❑ 37 Muhsin Muhammad .15 .40
❑ 38 Steve Smith .20 .50
❑ 39 Wesley Walls .15 .40
❑ 40 Chris Weinke .12 .30
❑ 41 James Allen .12 .30
❑ 42 Marty Booker .15 .40
❑ 43 Jim Miller .15 .40
❑ 44 David Terrell .15 .40
❑ 45 Dez White .12 .30
❑ 46 Brian Urlacher .25 .60
❑ 47 Mike Brown .15 .40
❑ 48 Anthony Thomas .15 .40
❑ 49 T.J. Houshmandzadeh .20 .50
❑ 50 Chad Johnson .20 .50
❑ 51 Darnay Scott .15 .40
❑ 52 Peter Warrick .15 .40
❑ 53 Akili Smith .15 .40
❑ 54 Jon Kitna .15 .40
❑ 55 Justin Smith .12 .30
❑ 56 Corey Dillon .15 .40
❑ 57 Benjamin Gay .12 .30
❑ 58 Kevin Johnson .12 .30
❑ 59 Quincy Morgan .12 .30
❑ 60 James Jackson .12 .30
❑ 61 Anthony Henry .12 .30
❑ 62 Gerard Warren .12 .30
❑ 63 Jamir Miller .12 .30
❑ 64 Tim Couch .12 .30
❑ 65 Quincy Carter .12 .30
❑ 66 Joey Galloway .15 .40
❑ 67 Troy Hambrick .12 .30
❑ 68 Rocket Ismail .15 .40
❑ 69 Dexter Coakley .12 .30
❑ 70 Darren Woodson .15 .40
❑ 71 Emmitt Smith .50 1.25
❑ 72 Mike Anderson .15 .40
❑ 73 Terrell Davis .20 .50
❑ 74 Kevin Kasper .12 .30
❑ 75 Rod Smith .15 .40
❑ 76 Ed McCaffrey .15 .40
❑ 77 Olandis Gary .15 .40
❑ 78 Dwayne Carswell .12 .30
❑ 79 Deltha O'Neal .12 .30
❑ 80 Brian Griese .15 .40
❑ 81 Scotty Anderson .12 .30
❑ 82 Johnnie Morton .15 .40
❑ 83 Cory Schlesinger .12 .30
❑ 84 James Stewart .12 .30
❑ 85 Shaun Rogers .12 .30
❑ 86 Mike McMahon .12 .30
❑ 87 Charlie Batch .15 .40
❑ 88 Robert Porcher .12 .30
❑ 89 Bubba Franks .15 .40
❑ 90 Robert Ferguson .15 .40
❑ 91 Antonio Freeman .20 .50
❑ 92 Ahman Green .15 .40
❑ 93 Bill Schroeder .15 .40
❑ 94 Kabeer Gbaja-Biamila .15 .40
❑ 95 Jamal Reynolds .12 .30
❑ 96 Darren Sharper .15 .40
❑ 97 Brett Favre .50 1.25
❑ 98 Marvin Harrison .20 .50
❑ 99 Dominic Rhodes .15 .40
❑ 100 Edgerrin James .20 .50
❑ 101 Reggie Wayne .20 .50
❑ 102 Terrence Wilkins .12 .30
❑ 103 Ken Dilger .15 .40
❑ 104 Peyton Manning .40 1.00
❑ 105 Elvis Joseph .12 .30
❑ 106 Stacey Mack .12 .30
❑ 107 Fred Taylor .20 .50
❑ 108 Keenan McCardell .15 .40
❑ 109 Jimmy Smith .15 .40
❑ 110 Mark Brunell .15 .40
❑ 111 Derrick Alexander .15 .40
❑ 112 Tony Gonzalez .15 .40
❑ 113 Trent Green .15 .40
❑ 114 Snoop Minnis .12 .30
❑ 115 Priest Holmes .20 .50
❑ 116 Chris Chambers .20 .50
❑ 117 Jay Fiedler .15 .40
❑ 118 Oronde Gadsden .12 .30
❑ 119 Travis Minor .15 .40
❑ 120 Lamar Smith .15 .40
❑ 121 Zach Thomas .20 .50
❑ 122 Michael Bennett .15 .40
❑ 123 Todd Bouman .12 .30
❑ 124 Cris Carter .20 .50
❑ 125 Byron Chamberlain .12 .30
❑ 126 Randy Moss .20 .50
❑ 127 Jake Reed .15 .40
❑ 128 Daunte Culpepper .15 .40
❑ 129 Drew Bledsoe .20 .50
❑ 130 Troy Brown .15 .40
❑ 131 David Patten .12 .30
❑ 132 J.R. Redmond .12 .30
❑ 133 Antowain Smith .15 .40
❑ 134 Ty Law .15 .40
❑ 135 Richard Seymour .15 .40
❑ 136 Adam Vinatieri .20 .50
❑ 137 Tom Brady .50 1.25
❑ 138 Joe Horn .15 .40
❑ 139 Willie Jackson .12 .30
❑ 140 Deuce McAllister .20 .50
❑ 141 Boo Williams .12 .30
❑ 142 Ricky Williams .20 .50
❑ 143 La'Roi Glover .12 .30
❑ 144 Sammy Knight .12 .30
❑ 145 Aaron Brooks .15 .40
❑ 146 Tiki Barber .20 .50
❑ 147 Ron Dayne .15 .40
❑ 148 Ike Hilliard .15 .40
❑ 149 Amani Toomer .15 .40
❑ 150 Will Allen .12 .30
❑ 151 Michael Strahan .20 .50
❑ 152 Jason Sehorn .15 .40
❑ 153 Kerry Collins .15 .40
❑ 154 Anthony Becht .12 .30
❑ 155 Wayne Chrebet .15 .40
❑ 156 Laveranues Coles .20 .50
❑ 157 LaMont Jordan .15 .40
❑ 158 Santana Moss .15 .40
❑ 159 Chad Pennington .20 .50
❑ 160 John Abraham .15 .40
❑ 161 Vinny Testaverde .15 .40
❑ 162 Curtis Martin .20 .50
❑ 163 Tim Brown .20 .50
❑ 164 Rich Gannon .15 .40
❑ 165 Charlie Garner .15 .40
❑ 166 Jerry Porter .15 .40
❑ 167 Marques Tuiasosopo .12 .30
❑ 168 Tyrone Wheatley .15 .40
❑ 169 Charles Woodson .20 .50
❑ 170 Jerry Rice .40 1.00
❑ 171 Correll Buckhalter .15 .40
❑ 172 Chad Lewis .12 .30
❑ 173 Brian Mitchell .15 .40
❑ 174 Freddie Mitchell .12 .30
❑ 175 Todd Pinkston .12 .30
❑ 176 Duce Staley .15 .40
❑ 177 Tony Stewart .12 .30
❑ 178 James Thrash .15 .40
❑ 179 Hugh Douglas .12 .30
❑ 180 Donovan McNabb .25 .60
❑ 181 Plaxico Burress .15 .40
❑ 182 Chris Fuamatu-Ma'afala .12 .30
❑ 183 Kordell Stewart .15 .40
❑ 184 Hines Ward .20 .50
❑ 185 Amos Zereoue .12 .30
❑ 186 Kendrell Bell .12 .30
❑ 187 Casey Hampton .12 .30
❑ 188 Jerome Bettis .20 .50
❑ 189 Drew Brees .30 .75
❑ 190 Curtis Conway .15 .40
❑ 191 Tim Dwight .15 .40
❑ 192 Doug Flutie .20 .50
❑ 193 Junior Seau .20 .50
❑ 194 Marcellus Wiley .12 .30
❑ 195 Ryan McNeil .12 .30
❑ 196 Jeff Graham .12 .30
❑ 197 LaDainian Tomlinson .30 .75
❑ 198 Kevan Barlow .12 .30
❑ 199 Garrison Hearst .15 .40
❑ 200 Eric Johnson .12 .30
❑ 201 Terrell Owens .20 .50
❑ 202 J.J. Stokes .12 .30
❑ 203 Andre Carter .12 .30
❑ 204 Jeff Garcia .15 .40
❑ 205 Trent Dilfer .15 .40
❑ 206 Matt Hasselbeck .20 .50
❑ 207 Darrell Jackson .15 .40
❑ 208 Koren Robinson .12 .30
❑ 209 Ricky Watters .15 .40
❑ 210 John Randle .15 .40
❑ 211 Shaun Alexander .20 .50
❑ 212 Isaac Bruce .20 .50
❑ 213 Trung Canidate .12 .30
❑ 214 Marshall Faulk .20 .50
❑ 215 Az-Zahir Hakim .12 .30
❑ 216 Torry Holt .20 .50
❑ 217 Yo Murphy .12 .30
❑ 218 Ricky Proehl .15 .40
❑ 219 Adam Archuleta .12 .30
❑ 220 Dre Bly .12 .30
❑ 221 London Fletcher .12 .30
❑ 222 Tommy Polley .12 .30
❑ 223 Aeneas Williams .15 .40
❑ 224 Kurt Warner .20 .50
❑ 225 Mike Alstott .15 .40
❑ 226 Warrick Dunn .15 .40
❑ 227 Jacquez Green .12 .30
❑ 228 Derrick Brooks .20 .50
❑ 229 John Lynch .15 .40

Card		
❑ 230 Warren Sapp	.15	.40
❑ 231 Ronde Barber	.15	.40
❑ 232 Brad Johnson	.15	.40
❑ 233 Keyshawn Johnson	.15	.40
❑ 234 Drew Bennett	.15	.40
❑ 235 Kevin Dyson	.15	.40
❑ 236 Eddie George	.15	.40
❑ 237 Derrick Mason	.15	.40
❑ 238 Justin McCareins	.15	.40
❑ 239 Frank Wycheck	.12	.30
❑ 240 Jevon Kearse	.15	.40
❑ 241 Samari Rolle	.12	.30
❑ 242 Steve McNair	.20	.50
❑ 243 Tony Banks	.12	.30
❑ 244 Stephen Davis	.15	.40
❑ 245 Michael Westbrook	.12	.30
❑ 246 Champ Bailey	.20	.50
❑ 247 Darrell Green	.20	.50
❑ 248 Bruce Smith	.20	.50
❑ 249 Fred Smoot	.15	.40
❑ 250 Rod Gardner	.12	.30
❑ 251 David Carr RC	.40	1.00
❑ 252 Joey Harrington RC	.40	1.00
❑ 253 Patrick Ramsey RC	.40	1.00
❑ 254 Kurt Kittner RC	.25	.60
❑ 255 Eric Crouch RC	.40	1.00
❑ 256 Josh McCown RC	.40	1.00
❑ 257 David Garrard RC	.60	1.50
❑ 258 Rohan Davey RC	.40	1.00
❑ 259 Ronald Curry RC	.40	1.00
❑ 260 Chad Hutchinson RC	.25	.60
❑ 261 William Green RC	.30	.75
❑ 262 T.J. Duckett RC	.40	1.00
❑ 263 Clinton Portis RC	1.00	2.50
❑ 264 DeShaun Foster RC	.40	1.00
❑ 265 Luke Staley RC	.25	.60
❑ 266 Wes Pate RC	.25	.60
❑ 267 Travis Stephens RC	.25	.60
❑ 268 Adrian Peterson RC	.40	1.00
❑ 269 Zak Kustok RC	.25	.60
❑ 270 Maurice Morris RC	.40	1.00
❑ 271 Lamar Gordon RC	.40	1.00
❑ 272 Chester Taylor RC	.60	1.50
❑ 273 Najeh Davenport RC	.40	1.00
❑ 274 Ladell Betts RC	.40	1.00
❑ 275 Ashley Lelie RC	.40	1.00
❑ 276 Josh Reed RC	.30	.75
❑ 277 Cliff Russell RC	.25	.60
❑ 278 Javon Walker RC	.40	1.00
❑ 279 Ron Johnson RC	.30	.75
❑ 280 Antwaan Randle El RC	.40	1.00
❑ 281 Andre Davis RC	.30	.75
❑ 282 Marquise Walker RC	.25	.60
❑ 283 Kelly Campbell RC	.30	.75
❑ 284 Tavon Mason RC	.25	.60
❑ 285 Antonio Bryant RC	.50	1.25
❑ 286 Jabar Gaffney RC	.40	1.00
❑ 287 Donte Stallworth RC	.40	1.00
❑ 288 Tim Carter RC	.30	.75
❑ 289 Reche Caldwell RC	.40	1.00
❑ 290 Freddie Milons RC	.25	.60
❑ 291 Brian Poli-Dixon RC	.25	.60
❑ 292 Brian Westbrook RC	1.25	3.00
❑ 293 Josh Scobey RC	.30	.75
❑ 294 Jeremy Shockey RC	.60	1.50
❑ 295 Daniel Graham RC	.30	.75
❑ 296 Deion Branch RC	.40	1.00
❑ 297 Julius Peppers RC	.60	1.50
❑ 298 Kalimba Edwards RC	.30	.75
❑ 299 Dwight Freeney RC	.60	1.50
❑ 300 Terry Charles RC	.25	.60
❑ 301 Alex Brown RC	.40	1.00
❑ 302 Jason McAddley RC	.30	.75
❑ 303 Michael Lewis RC	.40	1.00
❑ 304 Dennis Johnson RC	.25	.60
❑ 305 Albert Haynesworth RC	.40	1.00
❑ 306 Ryan Sims RC	.40	1.00
❑ 307 Larry Tripplett RC	.25	.60
❑ 308 Anthony Weaver RC	.25	.60
❑ 309 Wendell Bryant RC	.25	.60
❑ 310 John Henderson RC	.40	1.00
❑ 311 Alan Harper RC	.25	.60
❑ 312 Napoleon Harris RC	.30	.75
❑ 313 Bryan Thomas RC	.25	.60
❑ 314 Andra Davis RC	.25	.60
❑ 315 Levar Fisher RC	.25	.60
❑ 316 Woody Dantzler RC	.30	.75
❑ 317 Robert Thomas RC	.25	.60
❑ 318 Quentin Jammer RC	.40	1.00
❑ 319 Lito Sheppard RC	.40	1.00
❑ 320 Travis Fisher RC	.30	.75
❑ 321 Roy Williams RC	.50	1.25
❑ 322 Phillip Buchanon RC	.40	1.00
❑ 323 Joseph Jefferson RC	.25	.60
❑ 324 Ed Reed RC	1.25	3.00
❑ 325 Lamont Thompson RC	.30	.75
❑ 326 Raonall Smith RC	.25	.60
❑ 327 Mike Rumph RC	.25	.60
❑ 328 Rocky Calmus RC	.30	.75
❑ 329 Bryant McKinnie RC	.25	.60
❑ 330 Mike Williams RC	.25	.60

2003 Score

Card		
❑ COMPLETE SET (327)	20.00	50.00
❑ 1 Jeff Blake	.15	.40
❑ 2 Todd Heap	.15	.40
❑ 3 Ron Johnson	.12	.30
❑ 4 Jamal Lewis	.20	.50
❑ 5 Ray Lewis	.20	.50
❑ 6 Chris Redman	.12	.30
❑ 7 Ed Reed	.20	.50
❑ 8 Travis Taylor	.12	.30
❑ 9 Anthony Weaver	.12	.30
❑ 10 Drew Bledsoe	.20	.50
❑ 11 Larry Centers	.15	.40
❑ 12 Nate Clements	.15	.40
❑ 13 Travis Henry	.15	.40
❑ 14 Eric Moulds	.15	.40
❑ 15 Peerless Price	.12	.30
❑ 16 Josh Reed	.12	.30
❑ 17 Coy Wire	.12	.30
❑ 18 Corey Dillon	.15	.40
❑ 19 T.J. Houshmandzadeh	.20	.50
❑ 20 Chad Johnson	.20	.50
❑ 21 Jon Kitna	.15	.40
❑ 22 Lorenzo Neal	.15	.40
❑ 23 Peter Warrick	.15	.40
❑ 24 Nicolas Luchey RC	.12	.30
❑ 25 Tim Couch	.12	.30
❑ 26 Andre Davis	.12	.30
❑ 27 William Green	.12	.30
❑ 28 Kevin Johnson	.12	.30
❑ 29 Quincy Morgan	.12	.30
❑ 30 Dennis Northcutt	.12	.30
❑ 31 Jamel White	.12	.30
❑ 32 Mike Anderson	.15	.40
❑ 33 Steve Beuerlein	.15	.40
❑ 34 Jason Elam	.15	.40
❑ 35 Olandis Gary	.15	.40
❑ 36 Brian Griese	.15	.40
❑ 37 Ashley Lelie	.12	.30
❑ 38 Ed McCaffrey	.15	.40
❑ 39 Clinton Portis	.25	.60
❑ 40 Shannon Sharpe	.15	.40
❑ 41 Rod Smith	.15	.40
❑ 42 James Allen	.12	.30
❑ 43 Corey Bradford	.12	.30
❑ 44 David Carr	.20	.50
❑ 45 JaJuan Dawson	.12	.30
❑ 46 Jabar Gaffney	.12	.30
❑ 47 Aaron Glenn	.12	.30
❑ 48 Billy Miller	.12	.30
❑ 49 Jonathan Wells	.12	.30
❑ 50 Dwight Freeney	.15	.40
❑ 51 Marvin Harrison	.20	.50
❑ 52 Qadry Ismail	.15	.40
❑ 53 Edgerrin James	.20	.50
❑ 54 Peyton Manning	.40	1.00
❑ 55 James Mungro	.12	.30
❑ 56 Marcus Pollard	.12	.30
❑ 57 Reggie Wayne	.15	.40
❑ 58 Kyle Brady	.12	.30
❑ 59 Mark Brunell	.15	.40
❑ 60 David Garrard	.20	.50
❑ 61 John Henderson	.15	.40
❑ 62 Stacey Mack	.12	.30
❑ 63 Jimmy Smith	.15	.40
❑ 64 Fred Taylor	.20	.50
❑ 65 Marc Boerigter	.12	.30
❑ 66 Tony Gonzalez	.15	.40
❑ 67 Trent Green	.15	.40
❑ 68 Priest Holmes	.20	.50
❑ 69 Eddie Kennison	.12	.30
❑ 70 Snoop Minnis	.12	.30
❑ 71 Johnnie Morton	.15	.40
❑ 72 Cris Carter	.20	.50
❑ 73 Chris Chambers	.15	.40
❑ 74 Robert Edwards	.15	.40
❑ 75 Jay Fiedler	.15	.40
❑ 76 Ray Lucas	.12	.30
❑ 77 Randy McMichael	.12	.30
❑ 78 Travis Minor	.12	.30
❑ 79 Zach Thomas	.20	.50
❑ 80 Ricky Williams	.15	.40
❑ 81 Tom Brady	.50	1.25
❑ 82 Deion Branch	.15	.40
❑ 83 Troy Brown	.15	.40
❑ 84 Tedy Bruschi	.20	.50
❑ 85 Kevin Faulk	.15	.40
❑ 86 Daniel Graham	.12	.30
❑ 87 David Patten	.12	.30
❑ 88 Antowain Smith	.15	.40
❑ 89 Adam Vinatieri	.20	.50
❑ 90 Donnie Abraham	.15	.40
❑ 91 Anthony Becht	.15	.40
❑ 92 Wayne Chrebet	.15	.40
❑ 93 Laveranues Coles	.15	.40
❑ 94 LaMont Jordan	.15	.40
❑ 95 Curtis Martin	.20	.50
❑ 96 Chad Morton	.12	.30
❑ 97 Santana Moss	.15	.40
❑ 98 Chad Pennington	.20	.50
❑ 99 Vinny Testaverde	.15	.40
❑ 100 Tim Brown	.20	.50
❑ 101 Phillip Buchanon	.12	.30
❑ 102 Rich Gannon	.15	.40
❑ 103 Charlie Garner	.15	.40
❑ 104 Doug Jolley	.12	.30
❑ 105 Jerry Porter	.15	.40
❑ 106 Jerry Rice	.40	1.00
❑ 107 Marques Tuiasosopo	.12	.30
❑ 108 Charles Woodson	.15	.40
❑ 109 Rod Woodson	.20	.50
❑ 110 Kendrell Bell	.12	.30
❑ 111 Jerome Bettis	.20	.50
❑ 112 Plaxico Burress	.20	.50
❑ 113 Tommy Maddox	.15	.40
❑ 114 Joey Porter	.20	.50
❑ 115 Antwaan Randle El	.15	.40
❑ 116 Kordell Stewart	.15	.40
❑ 117 Hines Ward	.20	.50
❑ 118 Amos Zereoue	.12	.30
❑ 119 Drew Brees	.20	.50
❑ 120 Reche Caldwell	.12	.30
❑ 121 Curtis Conway	.12	.30
❑ 122 Tim Dwight	.12	.30
❑ 123 Doug Flutie	.20	.50
❑ 124 Quentin Jammer	.12	.30
❑ 125 Ben Leber	.12	.30
❑ 126 Josh Norman	.12	.30
❑ 127 Junior Seau	.20	.50
❑ 128 LaDainian Tomlinson	.25	.60
❑ 129 Keith Bulluck	.12	.30
❑ 130 Rocky Calmus	.12	.30
❑ 131 Kevin Carter	.15	.40
❑ 132 Kevin Dyson	.15	.40
❑ 133 Eddie George	.15	.40
❑ 134 Albert Haynesworth	.20	.50
❑ 135 Jevon Kearse	.15	.40
❑ 136 Derrick Mason	.15	.40
❑ 137 Justin McCareins	.15	.40
❑ 138 Steve McNair	.20	.50
❑ 139 Frank Wycheck	.12	.30
❑ 140 David Boston	.12	.30
❑ 141 MarTay Jenkins	.12	.30
❑ 142 Freddie Jones	.12	.30
❑ 143 Thomas Jones	.15	.40
❑ 144 Jason McAddley	.12	.30
❑ 145 Josh McCown	.15	.40
❑ 146 Jake Plummer	.15	.40
❑ 147 Marcel Shipp	.12	.30
❑ 148 Alge Crumpler	.15	.40
❑ 149 T.J. Duckett	.15	.40
❑ 150 Warrick Dunn	.15	.40

Card	Low	High
❑ 151 Brian Finneran	.12	.30
❑ 152 Trevor Gaylor	.12	.30
❑ 153 Shawn Jefferson	.12	.30
❑ 154 Michael Vick	.20	.50
❑ 155 Randy Fasani	.12	.30
❑ 156 DeShaun Foster	.15	.40
❑ 157 Muhsin Muhammad	.15	.40
❑ 158 Rodney Peete	.12	.30
❑ 159 Julius Peppers	.20	.50
❑ 160 Lamar Smith	.15	.40
❑ 161 Steve Smith	.20	.50
❑ 162 Chris Weinke	.15	.40
❑ 163 Wesley Walls	.15	.40
❑ 164 Marty Booker	.15	.40
❑ 165 Mike Brown	.15	.40
❑ 166 Chris Chandler	.15	.40
❑ 167 Jim Miller	.15	.40
❑ 168 Marcus Robinson	.15	.40
❑ 169 David Terrell	.12	.30
❑ 170 Anthony Thomas	.15	.40
❑ 171 Brian Urlacher	.30	.75
❑ 172 Dez White	.12	.30
❑ 173 Antonio Bryant	.20	.50
❑ 174 Quincy Carter	.12	.30
❑ 175 Dexter Coakley	.15	.40
❑ 176 Joey Galloway	.15	.40
❑ 177 La'Roi Glover	.12	.30
❑ 178 Troy Hambrick	.12	.30
❑ 179 Chad Hutchinson	.12	.30
❑ 180 Rocket Ismail	.15	.40
❑ 181 Emmitt Smith	.50	1.25
❑ 182 Roy Williams	.20	.50
❑ 183 Scotty Anderson	.15	.40
❑ 184 Germane Crowell	.12	.30
❑ 185 Az-Zahir Hakim	.12	.30
❑ 186 Joey Harrington	.15	.40
❑ 187 Cory Schlesinger	.12	.30
❑ 188 Bill Schroeder	.12	.30
❑ 189 James Stewart	.15	.40
❑ 190 Marques Anderson	.12	.30
❑ 191 Najeh Davenport	.15	.40
❑ 192 Donald Driver	.20	.50
❑ 193 Brett Favre	.50	1.25
❑ 194 Bubba Franks	.15	.40
❑ 195 Terry Glenn	.15	.40
❑ 196 Ahman Green	.20	.50
❑ 197 Darren Sharper	.15	.40
❑ 198 Javon Walker	.15	.40
❑ 199 D'Wayne Bates	.12	.30
❑ 200 Michael Bennett	.15	.40
❑ 201 Todd Bouman	.12	.30
❑ 202 Byron Chamberlain	.12	.30
❑ 203 Daunte Culpepper	.20	.50
❑ 204 Randy Moss	.20	.50
❑ 205 Kelly Campbell	.12	.30
❑ 206 Aaron Brooks	.15	.40
❑ 207 Charles Grant	.15	.40
❑ 208 Joe Horn	.15	.40
❑ 209 Michael Lewis	.12	.30
❑ 210 Deuce McAllister	.20	.50
❑ 211 Jerome Pathon	.12	.30
❑ 212 Donte Stallworth	.15	.40
❑ 213 Boo Williams	.12	.30
❑ 214 Tiki Barber	.20	.50
❑ 215 Tim Carter	.12	.30
❑ 216 Kerry Collins	.15	.40
❑ 217 Ron Dayne	.15	.40
❑ 218 Jesse Palmer	.12	.30
❑ 219 Will Peterson	.15	.40
❑ 220 Jason Sehorn	.15	.40
❑ 221 Jeremy Shockey	.20	.50
❑ 222 Michael Strahan	.15	.40
❑ 223 Amani Toomer	.15	.40
❑ 224 Koy Detmer	.12	.30
❑ 225 Antonio Freeman	.15	.40
❑ 226 Dorsey Levens	.15	.40
❑ 227 Chad Lewis	.15	.40
❑ 228 Donovan McNabb	.20	.50
❑ 229 Freddie Mitchell	.15	.40
❑ 230 Duce Staley	.15	.40
❑ 231 James Thrash	.12	.30
❑ 232 Brian Westbrook	.20	.50
❑ 233 Kevan Barlow	.12	.30
❑ 234 Andre Carter	.12	.30
❑ 235 Jeff Garcia	.20	.50
❑ 236 Garrison Hearst	.15	.40
❑ 237 Eric Johnson	.15	.40
❑ 238 Terrell Owens	.20	.50
❑ 239 Jamal Robertson	.12	.30
❑ 240 Tai Streets	.12	.30
❑ 241 Shaun Alexander	.20	.50
❑ 242 Trent Dilfer	.15	.40
❑ 243 Bobby Engram	.12	.30
❑ 244 Matt Hasselbeck	.15	.40
❑ 245 Darrell Jackson	.15	.40
❑ 246 Maurice Morris	.12	.30
❑ 247 Koren Robinson	.15	.40
❑ 248 Jerramy Stevens	.15	.40
❑ 249 Isaac Bruce	.20	.50
❑ 250 Marc Bulger	.20	.50
❑ 251 Marshall Faulk	.20	.50
❑ 252 Lamar Gordon	.12	.30
❑ 253 Torry Holt	.20	.50
❑ 254 Ricky Proehl	.15	.40
❑ 255 Kurt Warner	.20	.50
❑ 256 Aeneas Williams	.15	.40
❑ 257 Mike Alstott	.20	.50
❑ 258 Ken Dilger	.15	.40
❑ 259 Brad Johnson	.15	.40
❑ 260 Keyshawn Johnson	.20	.50
❑ 261 Rob Johnson	.15	.40
❑ 262 John Lynch	.15	.40
❑ 263 Keenan McCardell	.15	.40
❑ 264 Michael Pittman	.12	.30
❑ 265 Warren Sapp	.15	.40
❑ 266 Marquise Walker	.12	.30
❑ 267 Champ Bailey	.15	.40
❑ 268 Stephen Davis	.15	.40
❑ 269 Rod Gardner	.12	.30
❑ 270 Darrell Green	.20	.50
❑ 271 Shane Matthews	.12	.30
❑ 272 Damerien McCants	.12	.30
❑ 273 Patrick Ramsey	.15	.40
❑ 274 Bruce Smith	.15	.40
❑ 275 Kenny Watson	.12	.30
❑ 276 Carson Palmer RC	2.00	5.00
❑ 277 Byron Leftwich RC	.60	1.50
❑ 278 Kyle Boller RC	.50	1.25
❑ 279 Chris Simms RC	.50	1.25
❑ 280 Dave Ragone RC	.30	.75
❑ 281 Rex Grossman RC	.50	1.25
❑ 282 Brian St.Pierre RC	.50	1.25
❑ 283 Larry Johnson RC	.60	1.50
❑ 284 Lee Suggs RC	.40	1.00
❑ 285 Justin Fargas RC	.50	1.25
❑ 286 Onterrio Smith RC	.40	1.00
❑ 287 Willis McGahee RC	1.00	2.50
❑ 288 Chris Brown RC	.50	1.25
❑ 289 Musa Smith RC	.40	1.00
❑ 290 Artose Pinner RC	.30	.75
❑ 291 Cecil Sapp RC	.30	.75
❑ 292 Derek Watson SP RC	15.00	40.00
❑ 293 LaBrandon Toefield RC	.40	1.00
❑ 294 Charles Rogers RC	.40	1.00
❑ 295 Andre Johnson RC	1.00	2.50
❑ 296 Taylor Jacobs RC	.40	1.00
❑ 297 Bryant Johnson RC	.50	1.25
❑ 298 Kelley Washington RC	.40	1.00
❑ 299 Brandon Lloyd RC	.50	1.25
❑ 300 Justin Gage RC	.50	1.25
❑ 301 Tyrone Calico RC	.40	1.00
❑ 302 Kevin Curtis RC	.50	1.25
❑ 303 Sam Aiken RC	.50	1.25
❑ 304 Doug Gabriel RC	.40	1.00
❑ 305 Talman Gardner RC	.30	.75
❑ 306 Jason Witten RC	1.25	3.00
❑ 307 Mike Pinkard RC	.30	.75
❑ 308 Teyo Johnson RC	.40	1.00
❑ 309 Bennie Joppru RC	.30	.75
❑ 310 Dallas Clark RC	1.00	2.50
❑ 311 Terrell Suggs RC	.60	1.50
❑ 312 Chris Kelsay RC	.40	1.00
❑ 313 Jerome McDougle RC	.30	.75
❑ 314 Andrew Williams RC	.30	.75
❑ 315 Michael Haynes RC	.30	.75
❑ 316 Jimmy Kennedy RC	.40	1.00
❑ 317 Kevin Williams RC	.50	1.25
❑ 318 Ken Dorsey RC	.40	1.00
❑ 319 William Joseph RC	.30	.75
❑ 320 Kenny Peterson RC	.40	1.00
❑ 321 Rien Long RC	.30	.75
❑ 322 Boss Bailey RC	.40	1.00
❑ 323 E.J. Henderson SP RC	15.00	40.00
❑ 324 Terence Newman RC	.50	1.25
❑ 325 Marcus Trufant RC	.50	1.25
❑ 326 Andre Woolfolk RC	.40	1.00
❑ 327 Dennis Weathersby RC	.30	.75
❑ 328 Eugene Wilson SP RC	15.00	40.00
❑ 329 Mike Doss RC	.50	1.25
❑ 330 Rashean Mathis RC	.40	1.00

2004 Score

Card	Low	High
❑ COMPLETE SET (440)	40.00	80.00
❑ 1 Emmitt Smith	.50	1.25
❑ 2 Anquan Boldin	.20	.50
❑ 3 Bryant Johnson	.15	.40
❑ 4 Marcel Shipp	.20	.50
❑ 5 Josh McCown	.15	.40
❑ 6 Dexter Jackson	.12	.30
❑ 7 Bertrand Berry	.15	.40
❑ 8 Freddie Jones	.12	.30
❑ 9 Duane Starks	.12	.30
❑ 10 Michael Vick	.20	.50
❑ 11 T.J. Duckett	.15	.40
❑ 12 Warrick Dunn	.15	.40
❑ 13 Peerless Price	.15	.40
❑ 14 Alge Crumpler	.15	.40
❑ 15 Brian Finneran	.12	.30
❑ 16 Jason Webster	.12	.30
❑ 17 Dez White	.15	.40
❑ 18 Keith Brooking	.12	.30
❑ 19 Rod Coleman	.12	.30
❑ 20 Jamal Lewis	.15	.40
❑ 21 Kyle Boller	.15	.40
❑ 22 Todd Heap	.15	.40
❑ 23 Jonathan Ogden	.15	.40
❑ 24 Travis Taylor	.12	.30
❑ 25 Ray Lewis	.20	.50
❑ 26 Peter Boulware	.15	.40
❑ 27 Terrell Suggs	.12	.30
❑ 28 Chris McAlister	.12	.30
❑ 29 Ed Reed	.15	.40
❑ 30 Drew Bledsoe	.20	.50
❑ 31 Travis Henry	.15	.40
❑ 32 Eric Moulds	.15	.40
❑ 33 Josh Reed	.20	.50
❑ 34 Willis McGahee	.20	.50
❑ 35 Takeo Spikes	.12	.30
❑ 36 Lawyer Milloy	.12	.30
❑ 37 Troy Vincent	.15	.40
❑ 38 Sam Adams	.12	.30
❑ 39 Nate Clements	.15	.40
❑ 40 Jake Delhomme	.15	.40
❑ 41 Stephen Davis	.15	.40
❑ 42 DeShaun Foster	.15	.40
❑ 43 Muhsin Muhammad	.15	.40
❑ 44 Steve Smith	.20	.50
❑ 45 Ricky Proehl	.15	.40
❑ 46 Julius Peppers	.15	.40
❑ 47 Kris Jenkins	.15	.40
❑ 48 Dan Morgan	.15	.40
❑ 49 Ricky Manning	.12	.30
❑ 50 Brad Hoover	.15	.40
❑ 51 Carson Palmer	.25	.60
❑ 52 Rudi Johnson	.15	.40
❑ 53 Corey Dillon	.15	.40
❑ 54 Chad Johnson	.15	.40
❑ 55 Peter Warrick	.15	.40
❑ 56 Kelley Washington	.12	.30
❑ 57 Kevin Hardy	.15	.40
❑ 58 Tory James	.12	.30
❑ 59 Ickey Woods	.20	.50
❑ 60 Anthony Thomas	.15	.40
❑ 61 Thomas Jones	.15	.40
❑ 62 Rex Grossman	.20	.50
❑ 63 Marty Booker	.15	.40
❑ 64 Justin Gage	.15	.40
❑ 65 David Terrell	.12	.30
❑ 66 Brian Urlacher	.20	.50
❑ 67 Mike Brown	.15	.40
❑ 68 Charles Tillman	.15	.40
❑ 69 Jeff Garcia	.20	.50
❑ 70 Lee Suggs	.20	.50
❑ 71 William Green	.12	.30

Card		
❑ 72 Kelly Holcomb	.15	.40
❑ 73 Quincy Morgan	.12	.30
❑ 74 Andre Davis	.12	.30
❑ 75 Dennis Northcutt	.12	.30
❑ 76 Gerard Warren	.12	.30
❑ 77 Courtney Brown	.15	.40
❑ 78 Joey Harrington	.15	.40
❑ 79 Shawn Bryson	.12	.30
❑ 80 Charles Rogers	.15	.40
❑ 81 Mikhael Ricks	.12	.30
❑ 82 Artose Pinner	.12	.30
❑ 83 Az-Zahir Hakim	.12	.30
❑ 84 Dre Bly	.12	.30
❑ 85 Fernando Bryant	.12	.30
❑ 86 Boss Bailey	.12	.30
❑ 87 Tai Streets	.12	.30
❑ 88 Jake Plummer	.15	.40
❑ 89 Quentin Griffin	.15	.40
❑ 90 Mike Anderson	.15	.40
❑ 91 Garrison Hearst	.15	.40
❑ 92 Rod Smith	.15	.40
❑ 93 Ashley Lelie	.15	.40
❑ 94 Shannon Sharpe	.15	.40
❑ 95 Al Wilson	.12	.30
❑ 96 Champ Bailey	.15	.40
❑ 97 Jason Elam	.15	.40
❑ 98 John Lynch	.15	.40
❑ 99 Quincy Carter	.12	.30
❑ 100 Antonio Bryant	.20	.50
❑ 101 Terry Glenn	.15	.40
❑ 102 Keyshawn Johnson	.15	.40
❑ 103 Jason Witten	.20	.50
❑ 104 La'Roi Glover	.15	.40
❑ 105 Dat Nguyen	.12	.30
❑ 106 Dexter Coakley	.12	.30
❑ 107 Terence Newman	.15	.40
❑ 108 Darren Woodson	.15	.40
❑ 109 Roy Williams S	.15	.40
❑ 110 Brett Favre	.50	1.25
❑ 111 Ahman Green	.20	.50
❑ 112 Najeh Davenport	.15	.40
❑ 113 Donald Driver	.20	.50
❑ 114 Robert Ferguson	.12	.30
❑ 115 Javon Walker	.15	.40
❑ 116 Bubba Franks	.15	.40
❑ 117 Kabeer Gbaja-Biamila	.15	.40
❑ 118 Darren Sharper	.15	.40
❑ 119 Mike McKenzie	.15	.40
❑ 120 Nick Barnett	.15	.40
❑ 121 David Carr	.15	.40
❑ 122 Domanick Davis	.15	.40
❑ 123 Andre Johnson	.20	.50
❑ 124 Corey Bradford	.15	.40
❑ 125 Jabar Gaffney	.15	.40
❑ 126 Billy Miller	.12	.30
❑ 127 Gary Walker	.12	.30
❑ 128 Jamie Sharper	.12	.30
❑ 129 Aaron Glenn	.15	.40
❑ 130 Robaire Smith	.12	.30
❑ 131 Peyton Manning	.40	1.00
❑ 132 Edgerrin James	.20	.50
❑ 133 Dominic Rhodes	.15	.40
❑ 134 Marvin Harrison	.20	.50
❑ 135 Reggie Wayne	.15	.40
❑ 136 Brandon Stokley	.15	.40
❑ 137 Marcus Pollard	.12	.30
❑ 138 Dallas Clark	.20	.50
❑ 139 Mike Vanderjagt	.12	.30
❑ 140 Dwight Freeney	.20	.50
❑ 141 Mike Doss	.15	.40
❑ 142 Byron Leftwich	.20	.50
❑ 143 Fred Taylor	.15	.40
❑ 144 LaBrandon Toefield	.12	.30
❑ 145 Jimmy Smith	.15	.40
❑ 146 Kevin Johnson	.12	.30
❑ 147 Marcus Stroud	.12	.30
❑ 148 John Henderson	.12	.30
❑ 149 Donovin Darius	.12	.30
❑ 150 Deon Grant	.12	.30
❑ 151 Rashean Mathis	.12	.30
❑ 152 Trent Green	.15	.40
❑ 153 Priest Holmes	.20	.50
❑ 154 Johnnie Morton	.15	.40
❑ 155 Eddie Kennison	.15	.40
❑ 156 Marc Boerigter	.15	.40
❑ 157 Tony Gonzalez	.20	.50
❑ 158 Dante Hall	.15	.40
❑ 159 Tony Richardson	.12	.30
❑ 160 Gary Stills	.12	.30
❑ 161 Daunte Culpepper	.20	.50
❑ 162 Michael Bennett	.15	.40
❑ 163 Moe Williams	.12	.30
❑ 164 Onterrio Smith	.12	.30
❑ 165 Jim Kleinsasser	.12	.30
❑ 166 Antoine Winfield	.15	.40
❑ 167 Nate Burleson	.15	.40
❑ 168 Randy Moss	.20	.50
❑ 169 Marcus Robinson	.15	.40
❑ 170 Chris Hovan	.12	.30
❑ 171 Brian Russell RC	.12	.30
❑ 172 A.J. Feeley	.15	.40
❑ 173 Jay Fiedler	.12	.30
❑ 174 Ricky Williams	.20	.50
❑ 175 Chris Chambers	.15	.40
❑ 176 David Boston	.12	.30
❑ 177 Randy McMichael	.12	.30
❑ 178 Jason Taylor	.20	.50
❑ 179 Adewale Ogunleye	.15	.40
❑ 180 Zach Thomas	.20	.50
❑ 181 Junior Seau	.20	.50
❑ 182 Patrick Surtain	.12	.30
❑ 183 Tom Brady	.50	1.25
❑ 184 Kevin Faulk	.15	.40
❑ 185 Troy Brown	.15	.40
❑ 186 Deion Branch	.15	.40
❑ 187 David Givens	.15	.40
❑ 188 Bethel Johnson	.12	.30
❑ 189 Richard Seymour	.12	.30
❑ 190 Tedy Bruschi	.20	.50
❑ 191 Ty Law	.15	.40
❑ 192 Rodney Harrison	.15	.40
❑ 193 Willie McGinest	.15	.40
❑ 194 Adam Vinatieri	.20	.50
❑ 195 Aaron Brooks	.15	.40
❑ 196 Deuce McAllister	.20	.50
❑ 197 Joe Horn	.15	.40
❑ 198 Donte Stallworth	.15	.40
❑ 199 Jerome Pathon	.12	.30
❑ 200 Boo Williams	.12	.30
❑ 201 Charles Grant	.12	.30
❑ 202 Darren Howard	.12	.30
❑ 203 Michael Lewis	.15	.40
❑ 204 Johnathan Sullivan	.12	.30
❑ 205 LeCharles Bentley RC	.12	.30
❑ 206 Kerry Collins	.15	.40
❑ 207 Tiki Barber	.20	.50
❑ 208 Amani Toomer	.15	.40
❑ 209 Ike Hilliard	.15	.40
❑ 210 Tim Carter	.12	.30
❑ 211 Jeremy Shockey	.15	.40
❑ 212 Michael Strahan	.15	.40
❑ 213 Will Allen	.12	.30
❑ 214 Will Peterson	.12	.30
❑ 215 William Joseph	.12	.30
❑ 216 Chad Pennington	.20	.50
❑ 217 Curtis Martin	.20	.50
❑ 218 LaMont Jordan	.20	.50
❑ 219 Santana Moss	.15	.40
❑ 220 Justin McCareins	.12	.30
❑ 221 Wayne Chrebet	.15	.40
❑ 222 Anthony Becht	.12	.30
❑ 223 Shaun Ellis	.12	.30
❑ 224 John Abraham	.12	.30
❑ 225 DeWayne Robertson	.12	.30
❑ 226 Rich Gannon	.15	.40
❑ 227 Justin Fargas	.15	.40
❑ 228 Tyrone Wheatley	.15	.40
❑ 229 Jerry Rice	.40	1.00
❑ 230 Tim Brown	.20	.50
❑ 231 Jerry Porter	.15	.40
❑ 232 Teyo Johnson	.15	.40
❑ 233 Charles Woodson	.20	.50
❑ 234 Phillip Buchanon	.15	.40
❑ 235 Rod Woodson	.15	.40
❑ 236 Warren Sapp	.15	.40
❑ 237 Donovan McNabb	.20	.50
❑ 238 Brian Westbrook	.20	.50
❑ 239 Correll Buckhalter	.15	.40
❑ 240 Chad Lewis	.15	.40
❑ 241 L.J. Smith	.15	.40
❑ 242 Terrell Owens	.20	.50
❑ 243 Todd Pinkston	.12	.30
❑ 244 Freddie Mitchell	.12	.30
❑ 245 Jevon Kearse	.15	.40
❑ 246 Brian Dawkins	.15	.40
❑ 247 Corey Simon	.15	.40
❑ 248 Tommy Maddox	.15	.40
❑ 249 Duce Staley	.15	.40
❑ 250 Jerome Bettis	.20	.50
❑ 251 Hines Ward	.20	.50
❑ 252 Plaxico Burress	.15	.40
❑ 253 Antwaan Randle El	.15	.40
❑ 254 Kendrell Bell	.12	.30
❑ 255 Joey Porter	.15	.40
❑ 256 Alan Faneca	.20	.50
❑ 257 Casey Hampton	.12	.30
❑ 258 Drew Brees	.20	.50
❑ 259 Doug Flutie	.20	.50
❑ 260 LaDainian Tomlinson	.25	.60
❑ 261 Reche Caldwell	.15	.40
❑ 262 Tim Dwight	.15	.40
❑ 263 Eric Parker	.15	.40
❑ 264 Kevin Dyson	.12	.30
❑ 265 Antonio Gates	.20	.50
❑ 266 Quentin Jammer	.12	.30
❑ 267 Zeke Moreno	.12	.30
❑ 268 Tim Rattay	.12	.30
❑ 269 Kevan Barlow	.15	.40
❑ 270 Cedrick Wilson	.12	.30
❑ 271 Brandon Lloyd	.12	.30
❑ 272 Fred Beasley	.12	.30
❑ 273 Andre Carter	.12	.30
❑ 274 Julian Peterson	.15	.40
❑ 275 Ahmed Plummer	.12	.30
❑ 276 Tony Parrish	.12	.30
❑ 277 Bryant Young	.15	.40
❑ 278 Matt Hasselbeck	.20	.50
❑ 279 Shaun Alexander	.20	.50
❑ 280 Maurice Morris	.15	.40
❑ 281 Koren Robinson	.20	.50
❑ 282 Darrell Jackson	.15	.40
❑ 283 Bobby Engram	.15	.40
❑ 284 Grant Wistrom	.15	.40
❑ 285 Chad Brown	.12	.30
❑ 286 Marcus Trufant	.12	.30
❑ 287 Bobby Taylor	.15	.40
❑ 288 Marc Bulger	.15	.40
❑ 289 Kurt Warner	.20	.50
❑ 290 Marshall Faulk	.20	.50
❑ 291 Lamar Gordon	.12	.30
❑ 292 Torry Holt	.20	.50
❑ 293 Isaac Bruce	.15	.40
❑ 294 Leonard Little	.12	.30
❑ 295 Aeneas Williams	.12	.30
❑ 296 Orlando Pace	.15	.40
❑ 297 Tommy Polley	.12	.30
❑ 298 Pisa Tinoisamoa	.12	.30
❑ 299 Brad Johnson	.15	.40
❑ 300 Michael Pittman	.15	.40
❑ 301 Charlie Garner	.15	.40
❑ 302 Mike Alstott	.15	.40
❑ 303 Keenan McCardell	.12	.30
❑ 304 Joey Galloway	.15	.40
❑ 305 Joe Jurevicius	.12	.30
❑ 306 Anthony McFarland	.12	.30
❑ 307 Derrick Brooks	.15	.40
❑ 308 Ronde Barber	.15	.40
❑ 309 Shelton Quarles	.12	.30
❑ 310 Steve McNair	.20	.50
❑ 311 Eddie George	.15	.40
❑ 312 Chris Brown	.15	.40
❑ 313 Derrick Mason	.15	.40
❑ 314 Tyrone Calico	.15	.40
❑ 315 Drew Bennett	.15	.40
❑ 316 Kevin Carter	.15	.40
❑ 317 Keith Bulluck	.12	.30
❑ 318 Samari Rolle	.12	.30
❑ 319 Albert Haynesworth	.12	.30
❑ 320 Erron Kinney	.12	.30
❑ 321 Mark Brunell	.15	.40
❑ 322 Patrick Ramsey	.15	.40
❑ 323 Laveranues Coles	.15	.40
❑ 324 Rod Gardner	.12	.30
❑ 325 Darnerien McCants	.12	.30
❑ 326 Clinton Portis	.20	.50
❑ 327 LaVar Arrington	.15	.40
❑ 328 Shawn Springs	.12	.30
❑ 329 Fred Smoot	.12	.30
❑ 330 James Thrash	.12	.30
❑ 331 Marvin Harrison PB	.12	.30
❑ 332 Steve McNair PB	.12	.30
❑ 333 Ray Lewis PB	.12	.30
❑ 334 Trent Green PB	.10	.25
❑ 335 Peyton Manning PB	.25	.60
❑ 336 Priest Holmes PB	.12	.30
❑ 337 Clinton Portis PB	.12	.30
❑ 338 Torry Holt PB	.12	.30

Card	Low	High
❑ 339 Anquan Boldin PB	.12	.30
❑ 340 Daunte Culpepper PB	.12	.30
❑ 341 Ahman Green PB	.12	.30
❑ 342 Brian Urlacher PB	.12	.30
❑ 343 Donovan McNabb PB	.12	.30
❑ 344 Marc Bulger PB	.10	.25
❑ 345 Shaun Alexander PB	.12	.30
❑ 346 Peyton Manning LL	.25	.60
❑ 347 Daunte Culpepper LL	.12	.30
❑ 348 Brett Favre LL	.30	.75
❑ 349 Steve McNair LL	.12	.30
❑ 350 Tom Brady LL	.30	.75
❑ 351 Jamal Lewis LL	.10	.25
❑ 352 Deuce McAllister LL	.12	.30
❑ 353 Clinton Portis LL	.12	.30
❑ 354 Ahman Green LL	.12	.30
❑ 355 LaDainian Tomlinson LL	.15	.40
❑ 356 Torry Holt LL	.12	.30
❑ 357 Anquan Boldin LL	.12	.30
❑ 358 Randy Moss LL	.12	.30
❑ 359 Chad Johnson LL	.10	.25
❑ 360 Marvin Harrison LL	.12	.30
❑ 361 Peyton Manning HL	.25	.60
❑ 362 Jamal Lewis HL	.10	.25
❑ 363 Ray Lewis HL	.12	.30
❑ 364 Anquan Boldin HL	.12	.30
❑ 365 Terrell Suggs HL	.07	.20
❑ 366 Jamal Lewis HL	.10	.25
❑ 367 Priest Holmes HL	.12	.30
❑ 368 Tom Brady HL	.30	.75
❑ 369 Marc Bulger HL	.10	.25
❑ 370 Steve McNair HL	.12	.30
❑ 371 Eli Manning RC	3.00	8.00
❑ 372 Robert Gallery RC	.50	1.25
❑ 373 Larry Fitzgerald RC	1.50	4.00
❑ 374 Philip Rivers RC	2.00	5.00
❑ 375 Sean Taylor RC	.50	1.25
❑ 376 Kellen Winslow RC	.60	1.50
❑ 377 Roy Williams RC	.60	1.50
❑ 378 DeAngelo Hall RC	.50	1.25
❑ 379 Reggie Williams RC	.50	1.25
❑ 380 Dunta Robinson RC	.40	1.00
❑ 381 Ben Roethlisberger RC	4.00	10.00
❑ 382 Jonathan Vilma RC	.50	1.25
❑ 383 Lee Evans RC	.60	1.50
❑ 384 Tommie Harris RC	.50	1.25
❑ 385 Michael Clayton RC	.50	1.25
❑ 386 D.J. Williams RC	.50	1.25
❑ 387 Will Smith RC	.50	1.25
❑ 388 Kenechi Udeze RC	.50	1.25
❑ 389 Vince Wilfork RC	.50	1.25
❑ 390 J.P. Losman RC	.50	1.25
❑ 391 Marcus Tubbs RC	.30	.75
❑ 392 Steven Jackson RC	1.25	3.00
❑ 393 Ahmad Carroll RC	.50	1.25
❑ 394 Chris Perry RC	.50	1.25
❑ 395 Jason Babin RC	.40	1.00
❑ 396 Chris Gamble RC	.40	1.00
❑ 397 Michael Jenkins RC	.50	1.25
❑ 398 Kevin Jones RC	.50	1.25
❑ 399 Rashaun Woods RC	.30	.75
❑ 400 Ben Watson RC	.50	1.25
❑ 401 Karlos Dansby RC	.50	1.25
❑ 402 Igor Olshansky RC	.50	1.25
❑ 403 Junior Siavii RC	.30	.75
❑ 404 Teddy Lehman RC	.40	1.00
❑ 405 Ricardo Colclough RC	.50	1.25
❑ 406 Daryl Smith RC	.40	1.00
❑ 407 Ben Troupe RC	.40	1.00
❑ 408 Tatum Bell RC	.50	1.25
❑ 409 Travis LaBoy RC	.40	1.00
❑ 410 Julius Jones RC	.60	1.50
❑ 411 Mewelde Moore RC	.50	1.25
❑ 412 Drew Henson RC	.30	.75
❑ 413 Dontarrious Thomas RC	.40	1.00
❑ 414 Keiwan Ratliff RC	.30	.75
❑ 415 Devery Henderson RC	.50	1.25
❑ 416 Dwan Edwards RC	.30	.75
❑ 417 Michael Boulware RC	.50	1.25
❑ 418 Darius Watts RC	.40	1.00
❑ 419 Greg Jones RC	.50	1.25
❑ 420 Madieu Williams RC	.30	.75
❑ 421 Antwan Odom RC	.50	1.25
❑ 422 Shawntae Spencer RC	.30	.75
❑ 423 Sean Jones RC	.40	1.00
❑ 424 Courtney Watson RC	.40	1.00
❑ 425 Kris Wilson RC	.40	1.00
❑ 426 Keary Colbert RC	.40	1.00
❑ 427 Marquise Hill RC	.30	.75
❑ 428 Darnell Dockett RC	.30	.75
❑ 429 Stuart Schweigert RC	.40	1.00
❑ 430 Ben Hartsock RC	.40	1.00
❑ 431 Joey Thomas RC	.30	.75
❑ 432 Randy Starks RC	.30	.75
❑ 433 Keith Smith RC	.30	.75
❑ 434 Derrick Hamilton RC	.30	.75
❑ 435 Bernard Berrian RC	.50	1.25
❑ 436 Chris Cooley RC	.50	1.25
❑ 437 Devard Darling RC	.40	1.00
❑ 438 Matt Schaub RC	1.25	3.00
❑ 439 Luke McCown RC	.50	1.25
❑ 440 Cedric Cobbs RC	.40	1.00

2005 Score

Card	Low	High
❑ COMPLETE SET (385)	40.00	80.00
❑ ONE ROOKIE PER PACK		
❑ 1 Anquan Boldin	.15	.40
❑ 2 Bertrand Berry	.12	.30
❑ 3 Bryant Johnson	.15	.40
❑ 4 Darnell Dockett	.12	.30
❑ 5 Freddie Jones	.12	.30
❑ 6 Josh McCown	.15	.40
❑ 7 Karlos Dansby	.12	.30
❑ 8 Larry Fitzgerald	.20	.50
❑ 9 Alge Crumpler	.15	.40
❑ 10 DeAngelo Hall	.15	.40
❑ 11 Keith Brooking	.12	.30
❑ 12 Michael Jenkins	.15	.40
❑ 13 Michael Vick	.20	.50
❑ 14 Peerless Price	.12	.30
❑ 15 Rod Coleman	.12	.30
❑ 16 T.J. Duckett	.12	.30
❑ 17 Warrick Dunn	.15	.40
❑ 18 Chris McAlister	.12	.30
❑ 19 Clarence Moore	.12	.30
❑ 20 Ed Reed	.15	.40
❑ 21 Jamal Lewis	.15	.40
❑ 22 Jonathan Ogden	.12	.30
❑ 23 Kyle Boller	.15	.40
❑ 24 Peter Boulware	.12	.30
❑ 25 Ray Lewis	.20	.50
❑ 26 Terrell Suggs	.15	.40
❑ 27 Todd Heap	.15	.40
❑ 28 Drew Bledsoe	.20	.50
❑ 29 Eric Moulds	.15	.40
❑ 30 Josh Reed	.12	.30
❑ 31 Lee Evans	.15	.40
❑ 32 Nate Clements	.15	.40
❑ 33 Takeo Spikes	.12	.30
❑ 34 Travis Henry	.15	.40
❑ 35 Willis McGahee	.20	.50
❑ 36 Dan Morgan	.12	.30
❑ 37 DeShaun Foster	.15	.40
❑ 38 Jake Delhomme	.20	.50
❑ 39 Julius Peppers	.15	.40
❑ 40 Keary Colbert	.12	.30
❑ 41 Kris Jenkins	.12	.30
❑ 42 Muhsin Muhammad	.15	.40
❑ 43 Nick Goings	.12	.30
❑ 44 Stephen Davis	.15	.40
❑ 45 Steve Smith	.20	.50
❑ 46 Anthony Thomas	.12	.30
❑ 47 Adewale Ogunleye	.12	.30
❑ 48 Bernard Berrian	.15	.40
❑ 49 Brian Urlacher	.20	.50
❑ 50 David Terrell	.12	.30
❑ 51 Mike Brown	.12	.30
❑ 52 Rex Grossman	.20	.50
❑ 53 Thomas Jones	.15	.40
❑ 54 Tommie Harris	.12	.30
❑ 55 Carson Palmer	.20	.50
❑ 56 Chad Johnson	.15	.40
❑ 57 Chris Perry	.12	.30
❑ 58 Kelley Washington	.12	.30
❑ 59 Madieu Williams	.12	.30
❑ 60 Peter Warrick	.12	.30
❑ 61 Rudi Johnson	.15	.40
❑ 62 T.J. Houshmandzadeh	.15	.40
❑ 63 Tory James	.12	.30
❑ 64 Andre Davis	.12	.30
❑ 65 Antonio Bryant	.15	.40
❑ 66 Dennis Northcutt	.12	.30
❑ 67 Gerard Warren	.12	.30
❑ 68 Jeff Garcia	.15	.40
❑ 69 Kellen Winslow Jr.	.20	.50
❑ 70 Lee Suggs	.15	.40
❑ 71 William Green	.12	.30
❑ 72 Drew Henson	.12	.30
❑ 73 Jason Witten	.20	.50
❑ 74 Julius Jones	.20	.50
❑ 75 Keyshawn Johnson	.15	.40
❑ 76 La'Roi Glover	.15	.40
❑ 77 J.P. Losman	.15	.40
❑ 78 Roy Williams S	.15	.40
❑ 79 Terence Newman	.12	.30
❑ 80 Terry Glenn	.12	.30
❑ 81 Al Wilson	.12	.30
❑ 82 Ashley Lelie	.12	.30
❑ 83 Champ Bailey	.15	.40
❑ 84 D.J. Williams	.12	.30
❑ 85 Jake Plummer	.15	.40
❑ 86 Jason Elam	.12	.30
❑ 87 John Lynch	.15	.40
❑ 88 Reuben Droughns	.12	.30
❑ 89 Rod Smith	.15	.40
❑ 90 Tatum Bell	.15	.40
❑ 91 Trent Dilfer	.15	.40
❑ 92 Charles Rogers	.12	.30
❑ 93 Dre' Bly	.12	.30
❑ 94 Joey Harrington	.20	.50
❑ 95 Kevin Jones	.15	.40
❑ 96 Roy Williams WR	.20	.50
❑ 97 Shawn Bryson	.12	.30
❑ 98 Tai Streets	.12	.30
❑ 99 Teddy Lehman	.12	.30
❑ 100 Ahman Green	.20	.50
❑ 101 Brett Favre	.50	1.25
❑ 102 Bubba Franks	.15	.40
❑ 103 Darren Sharper	.15	.40
❑ 104 Donald Driver	.20	.50
❑ 105 Javon Walker	.15	.40
❑ 106 Najeh Davenport	.15	.40
❑ 107 Nick Barnett	.15	.40
❑ 108 Robert Ferguson	.15	.40
❑ 109 Aaron Glenn	.12	.30
❑ 110 Andre Johnson	.15	.40
❑ 111 Corey Bradford	.15	.40
❑ 112 David Carr	.15	.40
❑ 113 Domanick Davis	.12	.30
❑ 114 Dunta Robinson	.12	.30
❑ 115 Jabar Gaffney	.12	.30
❑ 116 Jamie Sharper	.12	.30
❑ 117 Jason Babin	.12	.30
❑ 118 Brandon Stokley	.12	.30
❑ 119 Dallas Clark	.15	.40
❑ 120 Dwight Freeney	.15	.40
❑ 121 Edgerrin James	.15	.40
❑ 122 Marcus Pollard	.12	.30
❑ 123 Marvin Harrison	.20	.50
❑ 124 Peyton Manning	.30	.75
❑ 125 Reggie Wayne	.15	.40
❑ 126 Robert Mathis RC	.60	1.50
❑ 127 Byron Leftwich	.15	.40
❑ 128 Daryl Smith	.12	.30
❑ 129 Donovan Darius	.12	.30
❑ 130 Ernest Wilford	.15	.40
❑ 131 Fred Taylor	.20	.50
❑ 132 Jimmy Smith	.15	.40
❑ 133 John Henderson	.12	.30
❑ 134 Marcus Stroud	.12	.30
❑ 135 Reggie Williams	.15	.40
❑ 136 Dante Hall	.15	.40
❑ 137 Eddie Kennison	.12	.30
❑ 138 Jared Allen	.20	.50
❑ 139 Johnnie Morton	.15	.40
❑ 140 Larry Johnson	.20	.50
❑ 141 Priest Holmes	.20	.50
❑ 142 Samie Parker	.12	.30
❑ 143 Tony Gonzalez	.15	.40
❑ 144 Trent Green	.15	.40
❑ 145 A.J. Feeley	.12	.30
❑ 146 Chris Chambers	.15	.40
❑ 147 Jason Taylor	.15	.40
❑ 148 Junior Seau	.20	.50

❑ 149 Marty Booker .12 .30
❑ 150 Patrick Surtain .12 .30
❑ 151 Randy McMichael .12 .30
❑ 152 Sammy Morris .12 .30
❑ 153 Zach Thomas .20 .50
❑ 154 Daunte Culpepper .20 .50
❑ 155 Jim Kleinsasser .12 .30
❑ 156 Kelly Campbell .15 .40
❑ 157 Kevin Williams .12 .30
❑ 158 Marcus Robinson .15 .40
❑ 159 Mewelde Moore .12 .30
❑ 160 Michael Bennett .15 .40
❑ 161 Nate Burleson .15 .40
❑ 162 Ontorrio Smith .12 .30
❑ 163 Randy Moss .20 .50
❑ 164 Adam Vinatieri .20 .50
❑ 165 Corey Dillon .15 .40
❑ 166 David Givens .15 .40
❑ 167 David Patten .12 .30
❑ 168 Deion Branch .15 .40
❑ 169 Mike Vrabel .20 .50
❑ 170 Richard Seymour .12 .30
❑ 171 Tedy Bruschi .20 .50
❑ 172 Tom Brady .40 1.00
❑ 173 Troy Brown .12 .30
❑ 174 Ty Law .15 .40
❑ 175 Aaron Brooks .12 .30
❑ 176 Charles Grant .12 .30
❑ 177 Deuce McAllister .20 .50
❑ 178 Devery Henderson .12 .30
❑ 179 Donte Stallworth .15 .40
❑ 180 Jerome Pathon .12 .30
❑ 181 Joe Horn .15 .40
❑ 182 Will Smith .12 .30
❑ 183 Amani Toomer .15 .40
❑ 184 Eli Manning .40 1.00
❑ 185 Gibril Wilson .12 .30
❑ 186 Ike Hilliard .12 .30
❑ 187 Jeremy Shockey .20 .50
❑ 188 Michael Strahan .15 .40
❑ 189 Tiki Barber .20 .50
❑ 190 Jamaar Taylor .12 .30
❑ 191 Tim Carter .12 .30
❑ 192 Chad Pennington .20 .50
❑ 193 DeWayne Robertson .12 .30
❑ 194 Curtis Martin .20 .50
❑ 195 John Abraham .12 .30
❑ 196 Jonathan Vilma .15 .40
❑ 197 Justin McCareins .12 .30
❑ 198 LaMont Jordan .15 .40
❑ 199 Santana Moss .15 .40
❑ 200 Shaun Ellis .12 .30
❑ 201 Wayne Chrebet .15 .40
❑ 202 Charles Woodson .15 .40
❑ 203 Doug Jolley .12 .30
❑ 204 Jerry Porter .15 .40
❑ 205 Justin Fargas .15 .40
❑ 206 Kerry Collins .15 .40
❑ 207 Robert Gallery .12 .30
❑ 208 Ronald Curry .15 .40
❑ 209 Sebastian Janikowski .12 .30
❑ 210 Tyrone Wheatley .12 .30
❑ 211 Warren Sapp .15 .40
❑ 212 Brian Dawkins .15 .40
❑ 213 Brian Westbrook .20 .50
❑ 214 Chad Lewis .12 .30
❑ 215 Corey Simon .12 .30
❑ 216 Donovan McNabb .20 .50
❑ 217 Freddie Mitchell .12 .30
❑ 218 Jevon Kearse .15 .40
❑ 219 L.J. Smith .15 .40
❑ 220 Lito Sheppard .15 .40
❑ 221 Terrell Owens .20 .50
❑ 222 Todd Pinkston .12 .30
❑ 223 Alan Faneca .30 .75
❑ 224 Antwaan Randle El .15 .40
❑ 225 Ben Roethlisberger .50 1.25
❑ 226 Duce Staley .15 .40
❑ 227 Hines Ward .20 .50
❑ 228 James Farrior .12 .30
❑ 229 Jerome Bettis .20 .50
❑ 230 Joey Porter .12 .30
❑ 231 Kendrell Bell .12 .30
❑ 232 Plaxico Burress .15 .40
❑ 233 Troy Polamalu .25 .60
❑ 234 Antonio Gates .20 .50
❑ 235 Reche Caldwell .12 .30
❑ 236 Doug Flutie .20 .50
❑ 237 Drew Brees .20 .50
❑ 238 Eric Parker .12 .30
❑ 239 Keenan McCardell .15 .40
❑ 240 LaDainian Tomlinson .25 .60
❑ 241 Philip Rivers .20 .50
❑ 242 Quentin Jammer .12 .30
❑ 243 Tim Dwight .12 .30
❑ 244 Brandon Lloyd .12 .30
❑ 245 Bryant Young .12 .30
❑ 246 Cedrick Wilson .12 .30
❑ 247 Eric Johnson .12 .30
❑ 248 Julian Peterson .12 .30
❑ 249 Kevan Barlow .12 .30
❑ 250 Rashaun Woods .12 .30
❑ 251 Maurice Hicks RC .12 .30
❑ 252 Tim Rattay .12 .30
❑ 253 Bobby Engram .15 .40
❑ 254 Chad Brown .12 .30
❑ 255 Darrell Jackson .15 .40
❑ 256 Grant Wistrom .12 .30
❑ 257 Jerramy Stevens .15 .40
❑ 258 Koren Robinson .15 .40
❑ 259 Marcus Trufant .15 .40
❑ 260 Matt Hasselbeck .15 .40
❑ 261 Michael Boulware .12 .30
❑ 262 Shaun Alexander .20 .50
❑ 263 Isaac Bruce .15 .40
❑ 264 Leonard Little .12 .30
❑ 265 Marc Bulger .15 .40
❑ 266 Marshall Faulk .20 .50
❑ 267 Orlando Pace .12 .30
❑ 268 Pisa Tinoisamoa .12 .30
❑ 269 Shaun McDonald .12 .30
❑ 270 Steven Jackson .25 .60
❑ 271 Torry Holt .15 .40
❑ 272 Anthony McFarland .12 .30
❑ 273 Brian Griese .15 .40
❑ 274 Charlie Garner .15 .40
❑ 275 Derrick Brooks .15 .40
❑ 276 Joe Jurevicius .15 .40
❑ 277 Joey Galloway .15 .40
❑ 278 Michael Clayton .15 .40
❑ 279 Michael Pittman .12 .30
❑ 280 Mike Alstott .15 .40
❑ 281 Ronde Barber .15 .40
❑ 282 Albert Haynesworth .12 .30
❑ 283 Ben Troupe .12 .30
❑ 284 Billy Volek .15 .40
❑ 285 Chris Brown .15 .40
❑ 286 Derrick Mason .15 .40
❑ 287 Drew Bennett .15 .40
❑ 288 Keith Bulluck .12 .30
❑ 289 Kevin Carter .12 .30
❑ 290 Samari Rolle .12 .30
❑ 291 Steve McNair .20 .50
❑ 292 Tyrone Calico .15 .40
❑ 293 Chris Cooley .15 .40
❑ 294 Clinton Portis .20 .50
❑ 295 Fred Smoot .12 .30
❑ 296 LaVar Arrington .20 .50
❑ 297 Laveranues Coles .15 .40
❑ 298 Patrick Ramsey .15 .40
❑ 299 Rod Gardner .12 .30
❑ 300 Sean Taylor .15 .40
❑ 301 Michael Vick PB .15 .40
❑ 302 Daunte Culpepper PB .15 .40
❑ 303 Donovan McNabb PB .15 .40
❑ 304 Brian Westbrook PB .15 .40
❑ 305 Tiki Barber PB .15 .40
❑ 306 Ahman Green PB .15 .40
❑ 307 Joe Horn PB .12 .30
❑ 308 Javon Walker PB .12 .30
❑ 309 Torry Holt PB .12 .30
❑ 310 Muhsin Muhammad PB .12 .30
❑ 311 Jason Witten PB .15 .40
❑ 312 Alge Crumpler PB .12 .30
❑ 313 Peyton Manning PB .25 .60
❑ 314 Tom Brady PB .30 .75
❑ 315 Drew Brees PB .15 .40
❑ 316 LaDainian Tomlinson PB .20 .50
❑ 317 Rudi Johnson PB .12 .30
❑ 318 Jerome Bettis PB .15 .40
❑ 319 Marvin Harrison PB .15 .40
❑ 320 Hines Ward PB .15 .40
❑ 321 Andre Johnson PB .12 .30
❑ 322 Chad Johnson PB .12 .30
❑ 323 Tony Gonzalez PB .12 .30
❑ 324 Adam Vinatieri PB .15 .40
❑ 325 David Akers PB .10 .25
❑ 326 Takeo Spikes PB .10 .25
❑ 327 Joey Porter PB .10 .25
❑ 328 Tedy Bruschi PB .15 .40
❑ 329 Ed Reed PB .12 .30
❑ 330 Terrell Owens PB .15 .40
❑ 331 Alex Smith QB RC .40 1.00
❑ 332 Ronnie Brown RC 1.25 3.00
❑ 333 Braylon Edwards RC 1.00 2.50
❑ 334 Cedric Benson RC .40 1.00
❑ 335 Cadillac Williams RC .60 1.50
❑ 336 Adam Jones RC .30 .75
❑ 337 Troy Williamson RC .40 1.00
❑ 338 Antrel Rolle RC .40 1.00
❑ 339 Carlos Rogers RC .40 1.00
❑ 340 Mike Williams .30 .75
❑ 341 DeMarcus Ware RC .60 1.50
❑ 342 Shawne Merriman RC .40 1.00
❑ 343 Thomas Davis RC .30 .75
❑ 344 Derrick Johnson RC .40 1.00
❑ 345 Travis Johnson RC .25 .60
❑ 346 David Pollack RC .30 .75
❑ 347 Erasmus James RC .30 .75
❑ 348 Marcus Spears RC .40 1.00
❑ 349 Matt Jones RC .40 1.00
❑ 350 Mark Clayton RC .40 1.00
❑ 351 Fabian Washington RC .40 1.00
❑ 352 Aaron Rodgers RC 1.25 3.00
❑ 353 Jason Campbell RC .60 1.50
❑ 354 Roddy White RC .50 1.25
❑ 355 Marlin Jackson RC .30 .75
❑ 356 Heath Miller RC .75 2.00
❑ 357 Mike Patterson RC .30 .75
❑ 358 Reggie Brown RC .30 .75
❑ 359 Shaun Cody RC .30 .75
❑ 360 Mark Bradley RC .30 .75
❑ 361 J.J. Arrington RC .40 1.00
❑ 362 Dan Cody RC .40 1.00
❑ 363 Eric Shelton RC .30 .75
❑ 364 Roscoe Parrish RC .30 .75
❑ 365 Terrence Murphy RC .25 .60
❑ 366 Vincent Jackson RC .50 1.25
❑ 367 Frank Gore RC .75 2.00
❑ 368 Charlie Frye RC .40 1.00
❑ 369 Courtney Roby RC .30 .75
❑ 370 Andrew Walter RC .30 .75
❑ 371 Vernand Morency RC .30 .75
❑ 372 Ryan Moats RC .30 .75
❑ 373 Chris Henry RC .40 1.00
❑ 374 David Greene RC .30 .75
❑ 375 Brandon Jones RC .40 1.00
❑ 376 Maurice Clarett .30 .75
❑ 377 Kyle Orton RC .60 1.50
❑ 378 Marion Barber RC 1.25 3.00
❑ 379 Brandon Jacobs RC .50 1.25
❑ 380 Ciatrick Fason RC .30 .75
❑ 381 Jerome Mathis RC .40 1.00
❑ 382 Craphonso Thorpe RC .30 .75
❑ 383 Stefan LeFors RC .30 .75
❑ 384 Darren Sproles RC .50 1.25
❑ 385 Fred Gibson RC .30 .75

2006 Score

❑ COMP.FACT.SET (440) 25.00 50.00
❑ COMPLETE SET (385) 25.00 50.00
❑ 1 Kurt Warner .20 .50
❑ 2 J.J. Arrington .12 .30
❑ 3 Anquan Boldin .15 .40
❑ 4 Larry Fitzgerald .20 .50
❑ 5 Marcel Shipp .12 .30
❑ 6 Bryant Johnson .12 .30
❑ 7 Bertrand Berry .12 .30
❑ 8 John Navarre .12 .30
❑ 9A Michael Vick .20 .50
❑ 9B Michael Vick Falcons .20 .50
❑ 10 Warrick Dunn .15 .40
❑ 11 Roddy White .15 .40
❑ 12 Alge Crumpler .15 .40

Card		
❑ 13A T.J. Duckett	.12	.30
❑ 13B T.J. Duckett Redskins	.12	.30
❑ 14 Michael Jenkins	.15	.40
❑ 15 DeAngelo Hall	.15	.40
❑ 16 Brian Finneran	.12	.30
❑ 17 Kyle Boller	.15	.40
❑ 18 Jamal Lewis	.15	.40
❑ 19A Chester Taylor	.15	.40
❑ 19B Chester Taylor Vikings	.15	.40
❑ 20 Derrick Mason	.15	.40
❑ 21 Mark Clayton	.15	.40
❑ 22 Todd Heap	.15	.40
❑ 23 Ray Lewis	.20	.50
❑ 24 Devard Darling	.12	.30
❑ 25 J.P. Losman	.15	.40
❑ 26 Willis McGahee	.20	.50
❑ 27 Lee Evans	.15	.40
❑ 28A Eric Moulds	.15	.40
❑ 28B Eric Moulds Texans	.15	.40
❑ 29A Lawyer Milloy	.12	.30
❑ 29B Lawyer Milloy Falcons	.12	.30
❑ 30 Josh Reed	.12	.30
❑ 31 Kelly Holcomb	.12	.30
❑ 32 Jake Delhomme	.15	.40
❑ 33 DeShaun Foster	.15	.40
❑ 34 Steve Smith	.20	.50
❑ 35 Julius Peppers	.15	.40
❑ 36 Drew Carter	.12	.30
❑ 37 Chris Gamble	.12	.30
❑ 38 Stephen Davis	.15	.40
❑ 39 Keary Colbert	.15	.40
❑ 40 Nick Goings	.12	.30
❑ 41 Eric Shelton	.12	.30
❑ 42 Rex Grossman	.20	.50
❑ 43 Thomas Jones	.15	.40
❑ 44 Cedric Benson	.15	.40
❑ 45 Muhsin Muhammad	.15	.40
❑ 46 Brian Urlacher	.20	.50
❑ 47 Mark Bradley	.12	.30
❑ 48 Kyle Orton	.15	.40
❑ 49 Tommie Harris	.12	.30
❑ 50 Adrian Peterson	.15	.40
❑ 51 Bernard Berrian	.15	.40
❑ 52 Justin Gage	.12	.30
❑ 53 Carson Palmer	.20	.50
❑ 54 Rudi Johnson	.15	.40
❑ 55 Chad Johnson	.15	.40
❑ 56 T.J. Houshmandzadeh	.15	.40
❑ 57 Chris Henry	.12	.30
❑ 58 Chris Perry	.15	.40
❑ 59A Jon Kitna	.15	.40
❑ 59B Jon Kitna Lions	.15	.40
❑ 60 Deltha O'Neal	.12	.30
❑ 61 Charlie Frye	.15	.40
❑ 62 Reuben Droughns	.15	.40
❑ 63 Braylon Edwards	.20	.50
❑ 64 Kellen Winslow	.20	.50
❑ 65A Antonio Bryant	.15	.40
❑ 65B Antonio Bryant 49ers	.15	.40
❑ 66A Trent Dilfer	.15	.40
❑ 66B Trent Dilfer 49ers	.15	.40
❑ 67 Dennis Northcutt	.12	.30
❑ 68 Drew Bledsoe	.20	.50
❑ 69 Julius Jones	.15	.40
❑ 70 Marion Barber	.20	.50
❑ 71 Terry Glenn	.15	.40
❑ 72A Keyshawn Johnson	.15	.40
❑ 72B Keyshawn Johnson Panthers	.15	.40
❑ 73 Roy Williams S	.15	.40
❑ 74 Jason Witten	.20	.50
❑ 75 Terence Newman	.12	.30
❑ 76 Drew Henson	.12	.30
❑ 77 Patrick Crayton	.12	.30
❑ 78 Jake Plummer	.15	.40
❑ 79A Mike Anderson	.15	.40
❑ 79B Mike Anderson Ravens	.15	.40
❑ 80 Tatum Bell	.12	.30
❑ 81A Ashley Lelie	.12	.30
❑ 81B Ashley Lelie Falcons	.12	.30
❑ 82 Rod Smith	.15	.40
❑ 83 D.J. Williams	.12	.30
❑ 84 Darius Watts	.12	.30
❑ 85 Ron Dayne	.15	.40
❑ 86A Jeb Putzier	.12	.30
❑ 86B Jeb Putzier Texans	.12	.30
❑ 87A Joey Harrington	.12	.30
❑ 87B Joey Harrington Dolphins	.12	.30
❑ 88 Kevin Jones	.15	.40
❑ 89 Roy Williams WR	.20	.50
❑ 90 Mike Williams	.15	.40
❑ 91 Charles Rogers	.15	.40
❑ 92 Teddy Lehman	.12	.30
❑ 93 Marcus Pollard	.12	.30
❑ 94 Artose Pinner	.12	.30
❑ 95 Brett Favre	.40	1.00
❑ 96 Ahman Green	.15	.40
❑ 97 Najeh Davenport	.15	.40
❑ 98 Samkon Gado	.20	.50
❑ 99A Javon Walker	.15	.40
❑ 99B Javon Walker Broncos	.15	.40
❑ 100 Donald Driver	.20	.50
❑ 101 Aaron Rodgers	.20	.50
❑ 102 Robert Ferguson	.12	.30
❑ 103 David Carr	.12	.30
❑ 104 Domanick Davis	.15	.40
❑ 105 Andre Johnson	.15	.40
❑ 106A Jabar Gaffney	.12	.30
❑ 106B Jabar Gaffney Eagles	.12	.30
❑ 107 Jonathan Wells	.12	.30
❑ 108 Vernand Morency	.12	.30
❑ 109A Corey Bradford	.12	.30
❑ 109B Corey Bradford Lions	.12	.30
❑ 110 Jerome Mathis	.12	.30
❑ 111A Peyton Manning	.30	.75
❑ 111B Peyton Manning Colts	.30	.75
❑ 112A Edgerrin James	.15	.40
❑ 112B Edgerrin James Cardinals	.15	.40
❑ 113 Marvin Harrison	.20	.50
❑ 114 Reggie Wayne	.15	.40
❑ 115 Dwight Freeney	.15	.40
❑ 116 Dallas Clark	.15	.40
❑ 117 Dominic Rhodes	.15	.40
❑ 118 Jim Sorgi	.12	.30
❑ 119 Brandon Stokley	.15	.40
❑ 120 Bob Sanders	.15	.40
❑ 121 Mike Doss	.12	.30
❑ 122 Marlin Jackson	.12	.30
❑ 123 Byron Leftwich	.15	.40
❑ 124 Fred Taylor	.15	.40
❑ 125 Jimmy Smith	.15	.40
❑ 126 Matt Jones	.15	.40
❑ 127 Ernest Wilford	.12	.30
❑ 128 Greg Jones	.12	.30
❑ 129 Mike Peterson	.12	.30
❑ 130 Reggie Williams	.15	.40
❑ 131 Rashean Mathis	.12	.30
❑ 132 Trent Green	.15	.40
❑ 133 Larry Johnson	.15	.40
❑ 134 Priest Holmes	.15	.40
❑ 135 Eddie Kennison	.12	.30
❑ 136 Tony Gonzalez	.15	.40
❑ 137 Kendrell Bell	.12	.30
❑ 138 Samie Parker	.12	.30
❑ 139 Dante Hall	.15	.40
❑ 140A Tony Richardson	.12	.30
❑ 140B Tony Richardson Vikings	.12	.30
❑ 141A Gus Frerotte	.12	.30
❑ 141B Gus Frerotte Rams	.12	.30
❑ 142 Ronnie Brown	.20	.50
❑ 143A Neil Rackers	.12	.30
❑ 143B Neil Rackers Cardinals	.12	.30
❑ 144 Chris Chambers	.15	.40
❑ 145 Zach Thomas	.20	.50
❑ 146 Cliff Russell	.12	.30
❑ 147A David Boston	.12	.30
❑ 147B David Boston Bucs	.12	.30
❑ 148 Wes Welker	.20	.50
❑ 149 Marty Booker	.12	.30
❑ 150 Randy McMichael	.12	.30
❑ 151A Daunte Culpepper	.20	.50
❑ 151B Daunte Culpepper Dolphins	.20	.50
❑ 152 Mewelde Moore	.12	.30
❑ 153A Nate Burleson	.15	.40
❑ 153B Nate Burleson Seahawks	.15	.40
❑ 154 Troy Williamson	.15	.40
❑ 155 Koren Robinson	.12	.30
❑ 156 Erasmus James	.12	.30
❑ 157 Marcus Robinson	.15	.40
❑ 158 E.J. Henderson	.12	.30
❑ 159 Brad Johnson	.15	.40
❑ 160A Michael Bennett	.12	.30
❑ 160B Michael Bennett Chiefs	.12	.30
❑ 161 Travis Taylor	.12	.30
❑ 162 Tom Brady	.30	.75
❑ 163 Corey Dillon	.15	.40
❑ 164 Deion Branch	.15	.40
❑ 165 Tedy Bruschi	.20	.50
❑ 166 Ben Watson	.12	.30
❑ 167 Daniel Graham	.12	.30
❑ 168A Bethel Johnson	.12	.30
❑ 168B Bethel Johnson Saints	.12	.30
❑ 169 Kevin Faulk	.15	.40
❑ 170A David Givens	.15	.40
❑ 170B David Givens Titans	.15	.40
❑ 171 Troy Brown	.12	.30
❑ 172A Aaron Brooks	.15	.40
❑ 172B Aaron Brooks Raiders	.15	.40
❑ 173 Deuce McAllister	.15	.40
❑ 174 Joe Horn	.15	.40
❑ 175A Donte Stallworth	.15	.40
❑ 175B Donte Stallworth Eagles	.15	.40
❑ 176A Antowain Smith	.12	.30
❑ 176B Antowain Smith Texans	.12	.30
❑ 177 Devery Henderson	.12	.30
❑ 178 Eli Manning	.25	.60
❑ 179 Tiki Barber	.20	.50
❑ 180 Plaxico Burress	.15	.40
❑ 181 Jeremy Shockey	.20	.50
❑ 182A Osi Umenyiora	.15	.40
❑ 182B Osi Umenyiora Giants	.15	.40
❑ 183 Gibril Wilson	.12	.30
❑ 184 Brandon Jacobs	.20	.50
❑ 185 Michael Strahan	.15	.40
❑ 186A Will Allen	.12	.30
❑ 186B Will Allen Dolphins	.12	.30
❑ 187 Amani Toomer	.15	.40
❑ 188 Chad Pennington	.15	.40
❑ 189 Curtis Martin	.20	.50
❑ 190 Laveranues Coles	.15	.40
❑ 191 Jonathan Vilma	.15	.40
❑ 192A Ty Law	.12	.30
❑ 192B Ty Law Chiefs	.12	.30
❑ 193 Cedric Houston	.12	.30
❑ 194 Justin McCareins	.12	.30
❑ 195 Jerald Sowell	.12	.30
❑ 196 Josh Brown	.12	.30
❑ 197 LaMont Jordan	.15	.40
❑ 198 Randy Moss	.20	.50
❑ 199 Jerry Porter	.15	.40
❑ 200 Doug Gabriel	.12	.30
❑ 201 Johnnie Morant	.12	.30
❑ 202 Zack Crockett	.12	.30
❑ 203A Derrick Burgess	.12	.30
❑ 203B Derrick Burgess Raiders	.12	.30
❑ 204 Donovan McNabb	.20	.50
❑ 205 Brian Westbrook	.15	.40
❑ 206 Reggie Brown	.12	.30
❑ 207A Terrell Owens	.20	.50
❑ 207B Terrell Owens Cowboys	.20	.50
❑ 208 Ryan Moats	.15	.40
❑ 209 Correll Buckhalter	.12	.30
❑ 210 Jevon Kearse	.15	.40
❑ 211 L.J. Smith	.12	.30
❑ 212 Lamar Gordon	.12	.30
❑ 213 Greg Lewis	.12	.30
❑ 214 Ben Roethlisberger	.30	.75
❑ 215 Willie Parker	.25	.60
❑ 216 Jerome Bettis	.20	.50
❑ 217 Hines Ward	.20	.50
❑ 218 Troy Polamalu	.25	.60
❑ 219 Heath Miller	.15	.40
❑ 220A Antwaan Randle El	.15	.40
❑ 220B Antwaan Randle El Redskins	.15	.40
❑ 221 Duce Staley	.12	.30
❑ 222 Cedrick Wilson	.12	.30
❑ 223 James Farrior	.12	.30
❑ 224A Drew Brees	.20	.50
❑ 224B Drew Brees Saints	.20	.50
❑ 225 LaDainian Tomlinson	.25	.60
❑ 226 Keenan McCardell	.15	.40
❑ 227 Antonio Gates	.20	.50
❑ 228 Shawne Merriman	.15	.40
❑ 229 Philip Rivers	.20	.50
❑ 230 Vincent Jackson	.15	.40
❑ 231 Donnie Edwards	.12	.30
❑ 232 Eric Parker	.12	.30
❑ 233A Reche Caldwell	.12	.30
❑ 233B Reche Caldwell Patriots	.12	.30
❑ 234 Alex Smith QB	.15	.40
❑ 235 Frank Gore	.20	.50
❑ 236A Brandon Lloyd	.15	.40
❑ 236B Brandon Lloyd Redskins	.15	.40
❑ 237A Kevan Barlow	.15	.40
❑ 237B Kevan Barlow Jets	.15	.40
❑ 238A Rashaun Woods	.12	.30
❑ 238B Lorenzo Neal	.12	.30
❑ 239 Arnaz Battle	.12	.30

Card	Low	High
❑ 240 Matt Hasselbeck	.15	.40
❑ 241 Shaun Alexander	.15	.40
❑ 242 Darrell Jackson	.15	.40
❑ 243 Jerramy Stevens	.15	.40
❑ 244 Lofa Tatupu	.15	.40
❑ 245 D.J. Hackett	.15	.40
❑ 246 Bobby Engram	.12	.30
❑ 247A Joe Jurevicius	.12	.30
❑ 247B Joe Jurevicius Browns	.12	.30
❑ 248 Maurice Morris	.12	.30
❑ 249 Marc Bulger	.15	.40
❑ 250 Steven Jackson	.20	.50
❑ 251 Torry Holt	.15	.40
❑ 252 Isaac Bruce	.15	.40
❑ 253 Kevin Curtis	.15	.40
❑ 254 Marshall Faulk	.15	.40
❑ 255 Shaun McDonald	.12	.30
❑ 256 Chris Simms	.15	.40
❑ 257 Cadillac Williams	.20	.50
❑ 258 Joey Galloway	.15	.40
❑ 259 Michael Clayton	.15	.40
❑ 260 Derrick Brooks	.15	.40
❑ 261 Ronde Barber	.15	.40
❑ 262 Michael Pittman	.12	.30
❑ 263 Alex Smith TE	.12	.30
❑ 264 Simeon Rice	.12	.30
❑ 265A Steve McNair	.15	.40
❑ 265B Steve McNair Ravens	.15	.40
❑ 266 Chris Brown	.15	.40
❑ 267 Drew Bennett	.15	.40
❑ 268 Brandon Jones	.12	.30
❑ 269 Adam Jones	.12	.30
❑ 270 Keith Bulluck	.12	.30
❑ 271 Ben Troupe	.12	.30
❑ 272 Jarrett Payton	.12	.30
❑ 273 Tyrone Calico	.12	.30
❑ 274 Bobby Wade	.12	.30
❑ 275 Troy Fleming	.12	.30
❑ 276 Mark Brunell	.15	.40
❑ 277 Clinton Portis	.20	.50
❑ 278 Santana Moss	.15	.40
❑ 279 Jason Campbell	.15	.40
❑ 280 Chris Cooley	.15	.40
❑ 281 Carlos Rogers	.12	.30
❑ 282 Ladell Betts	.15	.40
❑ 283A Patrick Ramsey	.15	.40
❑ 283B Patrick Ramsey Jets	.15	.40
❑ 284 Taylor Jacobs	.12	.30
❑ 285 James Thrash	.12	.30
❑ 286 Adrian Wilson	.12	.30
❑ 287 London Fletcher	.12	.30
❑ 288 Lance Briggs	.15	.40
❑ 289 Robert Mathis	.12	.30
❑ 290 Rod Coleman	.12	.30
❑ 291 Bart Scott RC	.60	1.50
❑ 292 Brian Moorman RC	.20	.50
❑ 293 Shayne Graham RC	.20	.50
❑ 294 Kevin Kaesviharn RC	.20	.50
❑ 295 Leigh Bodden RC	.25	.60
❑ 296 Lousaka Polite RC	.20	.50
❑ 297 Todd Devoe RC	.30	.75
❑ 298 Scottie Vines	.20	.50
❑ 299 Cullen Jenkins RC	.20	.50
❑ 300 Donovan Morgan RC	.20	.50
❑ 301 C.C. Brown	.20	.50
❑ 302 Demarcus Faggins RC	.20	.50
❑ 303 Shantee Orr RC	.20	.50
❑ 304 Vashon Pearson RC	.20	.50
❑ 305 Reggie Hayward RC	.20	.50
❑ 306 Paul Spicer RC	.20	.50
❑ 307A Kenny Wright Jaguars RC	.20	.50
❑ 307B Kenny Wright Redskins	.20	.50
❑ 308 Rich Alexis RC	.20	.50
❑ 309 Terrence Melton RC	.20	.50
❑ 310 Willie Whitehead RC	.20	.50
❑ 311A Kendrick Clancy Giants RC	.20	.50
❑ 311B Kendrick Clancy Cardinals	.20	.50
❑ 312 Mark Brown RC	.20	.50
❑ 313 Tommy Kelly RC	.20	.50
❑ 314 Josh Parry RC	.20	.50
❑ 315 Malcom Floyd RC	.40	1.00
❑ 316 Mike Adams RC	.20	.50
❑ 317 Ben Emanuel RC	.20	.50
❑ 318 Brandon Moore RC	.20	.50
❑ 319 Chartric Darby RC	.20	.50
❑ 320 Bryce Fisher RC	.20	.50
❑ 321 D.D. Lewis RC	.20	.50
❑ 322 Jimmy Williams DB RC	.20	.50
❑ 323A Robert Pollard portrait RC	.20	.50
❑ 323B Robert Pollard action	.20	.50
❑ 324A Chris Johnson Rams RC	.30	.75
❑ 324B Chris Johnson Chiefs	.30	.75
❑ 325 Edell Shepherd RC	.20	.50
❑ 326 O.J. Small RC	.20	.50
❑ 327A Brad Kassell Titans RC	.20	.50
❑ 327B Brad Kassell Jets	.20	.50
❑ 328 M.Leinart/R.Bush	.75	2.00
❑ 329 M.Leinart/V.Young	.75	2.00
❑ 330 White/Leinart/Bush	.75	2.00
❑ 331 Matt Leinart RC	.75	2.00
❑ 332A Chad Greenway RC	.50	1.25
❑ 332B Chad Greenway	.50	1.25
❑ 333A Devin Aromashodu RC	.50	1.25
❑ 333B Devin Aromashodu	.50	1.25
❑ 334 DeAngelo Williams RC	1.00	2.50
❑ 335 Travis Wilson RC	.30	.75
❑ 336 Leon Washington RC	.60	1.50
❑ 337 Maurice Stovall RC	.40	1.00
❑ 338 Michael Huff SP RC	.50	1.25
❑ 339 Charlie Whitehurst RC	.50	1.25
❑ 340 Vince Young RC	1.25	3.00
❑ 341 Jerious Norwood RC	.50	1.25
❑ 342A D'Brickashaw Ferguson RC	.50	1.25
❑ 342B D'Brickashaw Ferguson	.50	1.25
❑ 343A Taurean Henderson RC	.50	1.25
❑ 343B Sam Hurd RC	.75	2.00
❑ 344A Dominique Byrd RC	.40	1.00
❑ 344B Dominique Byrd	.40	1.00
❑ 345 Sinorice Moss SP RC	.50	1.25
❑ 346A Martin Nance RC	.40	1.00
❑ 346B Martin Nance	.40	1.00
❑ 347 Vernon Davis RC	.50	1.25
❑ 348 Ko Simpson RC	.40	1.00
❑ 349A Jerome Harrison RC	.50	1.25
❑ 349B Jerome Harrison	.50	1.25
❑ 350A Jay Cutler RC	1.25	3.00
❑ 350B Jay Cutler	1.25	3.00
❑ 351A Alan Zemaitis RC	.50	1.25
❑ 351B Alan Zemaitis	.50	1.25
❑ 352A Haloti Ngata SP RC	.50	1.25
❑ 352B Haloti Ngata	.50	1.25
❑ 353A Greg Lee RC	.30	.75
❑ 353B Greg Lee	.30	.75
❑ 354 Laurence Maroney RC	.60	1.50
❑ 355A Bobby Carpenter SP RC	.40	1.00
❑ 355B Bobby Carpenter	.40	1.00
❑ 356A Jonathan Orr RC	.40	1.00
❑ 356B Jonathan Orr	.40	1.00
❑ 357 Marcedes Lewis RC	.50	1.25
❑ 358A Brodrick Bunkley SP RC	.40	1.00
❑ 358B Brodrick Bunkley	.40	1.00
❑ 359A Todd Watkins RC	.30	.75
❑ 359B Todd Watkins	.30	.75
❑ 360 Reggie Bush RC	1.25	3.00
❑ 361A Jimmy Williams RC	.50	1.25
❑ 361B Jimmy Williams	.50	1.25
❑ 362 Maurice Drew RC	1.00	2.50
❑ 363 Mario Williams RC	.60	1.50
❑ 364 Derek Hagan RC	.40	1.00
❑ 365 Santonio Holmes RC	1.25	3.00
❑ 366A Tye Hill RC	.40	1.00
❑ 366B Tye Hill	.40	1.00
❑ 367 Jason Avant RC	.50	1.25
❑ 368A Tamba Hali SP RC	.50	1.25
❑ 368B Tamba Hali	.50	1.25
❑ 369 Joe Klopfenstein RC	.40	1.00
❑ 370 LenDale White RC	.60	1.50
❑ 371A DeMeco Ryans RC	.60	1.50
❑ 371B DeMeco Ryans	.60	1.50
❑ 372A Bruce Gradkowski SP RC	.50	1.25
❑ 372B Bruce Gradkowski	.50	1.25
❑ 373 A.J. Hawk RC	.75	2.00
❑ 374A Gabe Watson RC	.30	.75
❑ 374B Gabe Watson	.30	.75
❑ 375A Devin Hester SP RC	1.00	2.50
❑ 375B Devin Hester	1.00	2.50
❑ 376 Demetrius Williams SP RC	.40	1.00
❑ 377A Joseph Addai RC	.60	1.50
❑ 377B Joseph Addai	.60	1.50
❑ 378A Leonard Pope RC	.50	1.25
❑ 378B Leonard Pope	.50	1.25
❑ 379 Omar Jacobs RC	.30	.75
❑ 380A Brad Smith SP RC	.50	1.25
❑ 380B Brad Smith	.50	1.25
❑ 381 Michael Robinson RC	.40	1.00
❑ 382A Brodie Croyle RC	.50	1.25
❑ 382B Brodie Croyle	.50	1.25
❑ 383A Anthony Fasano RC	.50	1.25
❑ 383B Anthony Fasano	.50	1.25
❑ 384 Brian Calhoun RC	.40	1.00
❑ 385 Chad Jackson RC	.40	1.00
❑ 386 Drew Olson RC	.30	.75
❑ 387 Greg Jennings RC	.75	2.00
❑ 388 Andre Hall RC	.40	1.00
❑ 389 Mike Espy RC	.50	1.25
❑ 390 Tim Day RC	.40	1.00
❑ 391 Brandon Williams RC	.40	1.00
❑ 392 Mark Anderson RC	1.25	3.00
❑ 393 DonTrell Moore RC	.50	1.25
❑ 394 Kellen Clemens RC	.50	1.25
❑ 395 Ernie Sims RC	.40	1.00
❑ 396 Cedric Humes RC	.40	1.00
❑ 397 Brandon Kirsch RC	.50	1.25
❑ 398 Tony Scheffler RC	.50	1.25
❑ 399 Kelly Jennings RC	.50	1.25
❑ 400 Manny Lawson RC	.50	1.25
❑ 401 Terrence Whitehead RC	.40	1.00
❑ 402 Marcus Vick RC	.30	.75
❑ 403 De'Arrius Howard RC	.50	1.25
❑ 404 Wendell Mathis RC	.40	1.00
❑ 405 Abdul Hodge RC	.40	1.00
❑ 406 Owen Daniels RC	.50	1.25
❑ 407 Mike Hass RC	.50	1.25
❑ 408 Brett Elliott RC	.50	1.25
❑ 409 Kamerion Wimbley RC	.50	1.25
❑ 410 Jeremy Bloom RC	.40	1.00
❑ 411 D.J. Shockley RC	.40	1.00
❑ 412 Darnell Bing RC	.40	1.00
❑ 413 Miles Austin RC	1.25	3.00
❑ 414 D'Qwell Jackson RC	.40	1.00
❑ 415 Tarvaris Jackson RC	.50	1.25
❑ 416 Mathias Kiwanuka RC	.60	1.50
❑ 417 Mike Bell RC	.50	1.25
❑ 418 Paul Pinegar RC	.30	.75
❑ 419 David Thomas RC	.50	1.25
❑ 420 Hank Baskett RC	.50	1.25
❑ 421 P.J. Daniels RC	.30	.75
❑ 422 Jon Alston RC	.30	.75
❑ 423 Reggie McNeal RC	.40	1.00
❑ 424 Brandon Marshall RC	.50	1.25
❑ 425 Gerald Riggs RC	.40	1.00
❑ 426 Delanie Walker RC	.40	1.00
❑ 427 Erik Meyer RC	.40	1.00
❑ 428 Jeff Webb RC	.40	1.00
❑ 429 Skyler Green RC	.30	.75
❑ 430 Thomas Howard RC	.40	1.00
❑ 431 Ashton Youboty RC	.40	1.00
❑ 432 Cedric Griffin RC	.40	1.00
❑ 433 Donte Whitner RC	.50	1.25
❑ 434 Jason Allen RC	.40	1.00
❑ 435 Pat Watkins RC	.50	1.25
❑ 436 Rocky McIntosh RC	.50	1.25
❑ 437 Ingle Martin RC	.40	1.00
❑ 438 John David Washington RC	.40	1.00
❑ 439 Cory Rodgers RC	.50	1.25
❑ 440 Willie Reid RC	.40	1.00

2007 Score

Card	Low	High
❑ COMPLETE SET (385)	25.00	50.00
❑ COMP.FACT.SET (440)	30.00	50.00
❑ 1 Tony Romo	.30	.75
❑ 2 Julius Jones	.15	.40
❑ 3 Terry Glenn	.15	.40
❑ 4 Terrell Owens	.20	.50
❑ 5 Jason Witten	.20	.50
❑ 6 Marion Barber	.20	.50
❑ 7 Patrick Crayton	.12	.30
❑ 8 Bradie James	.12	.30
❑ 9 DeMarcus Ware	.15	.40
❑ 10 Roy Williams S	.15	.40
❑ 11 Eli Manning	.20	.50
❑ 12 Plaxico Burress	.15	.40
❑ 13 Jeremy Shockey	.15	.40
❑ 14 Brandon Jacobs	.15	.40

❑ 15 Sinorice Moss .15 .40
❑ 16 Antonio Pierce .12 .30
❑ 17 David Tyree .12 .30
❑ 18 Donovan McNabb .20 .50
❑ 19 Brian Westbrook .15 .40
❑ 20 Reggie Brown .12 .30
❑ 21 L.J. Smith .12 .30
❑ 22 Hank Baskett .15 .40
❑ 23 Jeremiah Trotter .12 .30
❑ 24 Trent Cole .12 .30
❑ 25 Lito Sheppard .12 .30
❑ 26 Jason Campbell .15 .40
❑ 27 Clinton Portis .15 .40
❑ 28 Santana Moss .15 .40
❑ 29 Brandon Lloyd .15 .40
❑ 30 Chris Cooley .15 .40
❑ 31 Sean Taylor .12 .30
❑ 32 Lemar Marshall .12 .30
❑ 33 Ladell Betts .12 .30
❑ 34 London Fletcher .12 .30
❑ 35 Rex Grossman .15 .40
❑ 36 Cedric Benson .15 .40
❑ 37 Muhsin Muhammad .15 .40
❑ 38 Bernard Berrian .12 .30
❑ 39 Desmond Clark .12 .30
❑ 40 Lance Briggs .12 .30
❑ 41 Robbie Gould .12 .30
❑ 42 Devin Hester .20 .50
❑ 43 Mark Anderson .15 .40
❑ 44 Brian Urlacher .20 .50
❑ 45 Jon Kitna .12 .30
❑ 46 Kevin Jones .12 .30
❑ 47 Roy Williams WR .15 .40
❑ 48 Mike Furrey .15 .40
❑ 49 Cory Redding .12 .30
❑ 50 Ernie Sims .12 .30
❑ 51 Tatum Bell .12 .30
❑ 52 Brian Calhoun .12 .30
❑ 53 Brett Favre .40 1.00
❑ 54 Vernand Morency .15 .40
❑ 55 Donald Driver .20 .50
❑ 56 Greg Jennings .15 .40
❑ 57 Aaron Kampman .15 .40
❑ 58 Charles Woodson .15 .40
❑ 59 A.J. Hawk .20 .50
❑ 60 Nick Barnett .12 .30
❑ 61 Aaron Rodgers .20 .50
❑ 62 Tarvaris Jackson .15 .40
❑ 63 Chester Taylor .12 .30
❑ 64 Troy Williamson .12 .30
❑ 65 Jim Kleinsasser .12 .30
❑ 66 Dwight Smith .12 .30
❑ 67 Antoine Winfield .12 .30
❑ 68 E.J. Henderson .12 .30
❑ 69 Mewelde Moore .12 .30
❑ 70 Michael Vick .20 .50
❑ 71 Warrick Dunn .15 .40
❑ 72 Joe Horn .15 .40
❑ 73 Michael Jenkins .15 .40
❑ 74 Alge Crumpler .15 .40
❑ 75 DeAngelo Hall .15 .40
❑ 76 Keith Brooking .12 .30
❑ 77 Lawyer Milloy .12 .30
❑ 78 Jerious Norwood .15 .40
❑ 79 Matt Schaub .15 .40
❑ 80 Jake Delhomme .15 .40
❑ 81 DeShaun Foster .15 .40
❑ 82 Steve Smith .15 .40
❑ 83 Keyshawn Johnson .15 .40
❑ 84 Julius Peppers .15 .40
❑ 85 DeAngelo Williams .20 .50
❑ 86 Chris Draft .12 .30
❑ 87 Drew Brees .20 .50
❑ 88 Deuce McAllister .15 .40
❑ 89 Scott Fujita .12 .30
❑ 90 Marques Colston .20 .50
❑ 91 Terrance Copper .15 .40
❑ 92 Will Smith .12 .30
❑ 93 Charles Grant .12 .30
❑ 94 Devery Henderson .12 .30
❑ 95 Reggie Bush .25 .60
❑ 96 Jeff Garcia .15 .40
❑ 97 Cadillac Williams .15 .40
❑ 98 Joey Galloway .15 .40
❑ 99 Michael Clayton .15 .40
❑ 100 Alex Smith TE .12 .30
❑ 101 Ronde Barber .12 .30
❑ 102 Jermaine Phillips .12 .30
❑ 103 Derrick Brooks .15 .40
❑ 104 Matt Leinart .20 .50
❑ 105 Edgerrin James .15 .40
❑ 106 Anquan Boldin .15 .40
❑ 107 Larry Fitzgerald .20 .50
❑ 108 Neil Rackers .12 .30
❑ 109 Adrian Wilson .12 .30
❑ 110 Karlos Dansby .12 .30
❑ 111 Chike Okeafor .12 .30
❑ 112 Marc Bulger .15 .40
❑ 113 Steven Jackson .20 .50
❑ 114 Torry Holt .15 .40
❑ 115 Isaac Bruce .15 .40
❑ 116 Joe Klopfenstein .12 .30
❑ 117 Randy McMichael .12 .30
❑ 118 Will Witherspoon .12 .30
❑ 119 Drew Bennett .12 .30
❑ 120 Alex Smith QB .20 .50
❑ 121 Frank Gore .20 .50
❑ 122 Arnaz Battle .12 .30
❑ 123 Ashley Lelie .15 .40
❑ 124 Vernon Davis .15 .40
❑ 125 Walt Harris .12 .30
❑ 126 Brandon Moore .12 .30
❑ 127 Nate Clements .12 .30
❑ 128 Matt Hasselbeck .15 .40
❑ 129 Shaun Alexander .15 .40
❑ 130 Deion Branch .15 .40
❑ 131 Darrell Jackson .15 .40
❑ 132 Nate Burleson .12 .30
❑ 133 Julian Peterson .12 .30
❑ 134 Lofa Tatupu .15 .40
❑ 135 Mack Strong .12 .30
❑ 136 Josh Brown .12 .30
❑ 137 J.P. Losman .12 .30
❑ 138 Anthony Thomas .12 .30
❑ 139 Lee Evans .15 .40
❑ 140 Josh Reed .12 .30
❑ 141 Roscoe Parrish .12 .30
❑ 142 Aaron Schobel .12 .30
❑ 143 Donte Whitner .12 .30
❑ 144 Shaud Williams .12 .30
❑ 145 Daunte Culpepper .15 .40
❑ 146 Ronnie Brown .15 .40
❑ 147 Chris Chambers .15 .40
❑ 148 Marty Booker .12 .30
❑ 149 Derek Hagan .12 .30
❑ 150 Jason Taylor .12 .30
❑ 151 Vonnie Holliday .12 .30
❑ 152 Zach Thomas .15 .40
❑ 153 Channing Crowder .12 .30
❑ 154 Joey Porter .12 .30
❑ 155 Tom Brady .40 1.00
❑ 156 Laurence Maroney .20 .50
❑ 157 Chad Jackson .12 .30
❑ 158 Wes Welker .20 .50
❑ 159 Ben Watson .12 .30
❑ 160 Donte Stallworth .15 .40
❑ 161 Rosevelt Colvin .12 .30
❑ 162 Ty Warren .12 .30
❑ 163 Asante Samuel .12 .30
❑ 164 Adalius Thomas .12 .30
❑ 165 Tedy Bruschi .20 .50
❑ 166 Chad Pennington .15 .40
❑ 167 Thomas Jones .15 .40
❑ 168 Laveranues Coles .15 .40
❑ 169 Jerricho Cotchery .12 .30
❑ 170 Chris Baker .12 .30
❑ 171 Bryan Thomas .12 .30
❑ 172 Leon Washington .15 .40
❑ 173 Jonathan Vilma .15 .40
❑ 174 Eric Barton .12 .30
❑ 175 Erik Coleman .12 .30
❑ 176 Steve McNair .15 .40
❑ 177 Willis McGahee .15 .40
❑ 178 Derrick Mason .12 .30
❑ 179 Demetrius Williams .12 .30
❑ 180 Todd Heap .12 .30
❑ 181 Ray Lewis .20 .50
❑ 182 Trevor Pryce .12 .30
❑ 183 Bart Scott .15 .40
❑ 184 Terrell Suggs .12 .30
❑ 185 Mark Clayton .15 .40
❑ 186 Carson Palmer .20 .50
❑ 187 Rudi Johnson .15 .40
❑ 188 Chad Johnson .15 .40
❑ 189 T.J. Houshmandzadeh .15 .40
❑ 190 Robert Geathers .12 .30
❑ 191 Justin Smith .12 .30
❑ 192 Tory James .12 .30
❑ 193 Landon Johnson .12 .30
❑ 194 Shayne Graham .12 .30
❑ 195 Charlie Frye .15 .40
❑ 196 Reuben Droughns .15 .40
❑ 197 Braylon Edwards .15 .40
❑ 198 Travis Wilson .12 .30
❑ 199 Kellen Winslow .15 .40
❑ 200 Kamerion Wimbley .12 .30
❑ 201 Sean Jones
❑ 202 Andra Davis .12 .30
❑ 203 Jamal Lewis .15 .40
❑ 204 Ben Roethlisberger .30 .75
❑ 205 Willie Parker .15 .40
❑ 206 Hines Ward .20 .50
❑ 207 Santonio Holmes .15 .40
❑ 208 Heath Miller .12 .30
❑ 209 Troy Polamalu .20 .50
❑ 210 James Farrior .12 .30
❑ 211 Cedrick Wilson .12 .30
❑ 212 Dunta Robinson .12 .30
❑ 213 Ahman Green .15 .40
❑ 214 Andre Johnson .15 .40
❑ 215 Jerome Mathis .12 .30
❑ 216 Owen Daniels .12 .30
❑ 217 DeMeco Ryans .15 .40
❑ 218 Wali Lundy .12 .30
❑ 219 Mario Williams .15 .40
❑ 220 Peyton Manning .30 .75
❑ 221 Joseph Addai .20 .50
❑ 222 Marvin Harrison .20 .50
❑ 223 Reggie Wayne .15 .40
❑ 224 Dallas Clark .12 .30
❑ 225 Robert Mathis .12 .30
❑ 226 Cato June .12 .30
❑ 227 Adam Vinatieri .15 .40
❑ 228 Bob Sanders .15 .40
❑ 229 Dwight Freeney .15 .40
❑ 230 Byron Leftwich .15 .40
❑ 231 Fred Taylor .15 .40
❑ 232 Matt Jones .15 .40
❑ 233 Reggie Williams .15 .40
❑ 234 Marcedes Lewis .12 .30
❑ 235 Bobby McCray .12 .30
❑ 236 Rashean Mathis .12 .30
❑ 237 Maurice Jones-Drew .20 .50
❑ 238 Ernest Wilford .12 .30
❑ 239 Daryl Smith .12 .30
❑ 240 Vince Young .20 .50
❑ 241 LenDale White .15 .40
❑ 242 Brandon Jones .12 .30
❑ 243 Bo Scaife .12 .30
❑ 244 Keith Bulluck .12 .30
❑ 245 Chris Hope .12 .30
❑ 246 Kyle Vanden Bosch .12 .30
❑ 247 Roydell Williams .12 .30
❑ 248 Jay Cutler .20 .50
❑ 249 Travis Henry .15 .40
❑ 250 Javon Walker .15 .40
❑ 251 Rod Smith .15 .40
❑ 252 Tony Scheffler .15 .40
❑ 253 Elvis Dumervil .12 .30
❑ 254 Champ Bailey .15 .40
❑ 255 Mike Bell .15 .40
❑ 256 Brandon Marshall .15 .40
❑ 257 Al Wilson .12 .30
❑ 258 Trent Green .15 .40
❑ 259 Larry Johnson .15 .40
❑ 260 Eddie Kennison .12 .30
❑ 261 Samie Parker .12 .30
❑ 262 Tony Gonzalez .15 .40
❑ 263 Jared Allen .20 .50
❑ 264 Kawika Mitchell .12 .30
❑ 265 Tamba Hali .12 .30
❑ 266 Dante Hall .15 .40
❑ 267 Brodie Croyle .15 .40
❑ 268 Andrew Walter .12 .30
❑ 269 LaMont Jordan .15 .40
❑ 270 Dominic Rhodes .15 .40
❑ 271 Randy Moss .20 .50
❑ 272 Ronald Curry .15 .40
❑ 273 Courtney Anderson .12 .30
❑ 274 Derrick Burgess .12 .30
❑ 275 Warren Sapp .15 .40
❑ 276 Michael Huff .15 .40
❑ 277 Thomas Howard .12 .30
❑ 278 Kirk Morrison .12 .30
❑ 279 Philip Rivers .20 .50
❑ 280 LaDainian Tomlinson .25 .60
❑ 281 Vincent Jackson .12 .30

- ❑ 282 Lorenzo Neal .12 .30
- ❑ 283 Antonio Gates .15 .40
- ❑ 284 Shawne Merriman .15 .40
- ❑ 285 Shaun Phillips .12 .30
- ❑ 286 Michael Turner .20 .50
- ❑ 287 Jamal Williams .12 .30
- ❑ 288 Nate Kaeding .12 .30
- ❑ 289 Michael Okwo RC .40 1.00
- ❑ 290 Gary Russell RC .40 1.00
- ❑ 291 Josh Wilson RC .40 1.00
- ❑ 292 Thomas Clayton RC .40 1.00
- ❑ 293 Jerard Rabb RC .40 1.00
- ❑ 294 Roy Hall RC .50 1.25
- ❑ 295 LaMarr Woodley RC .50 1.25
- ❑ 296 Eric Wright RC .50 1.25
- ❑ 297 Dan Bazuin RC .40 1.00
- ❑ 298 A.J. Davis RC .30 .75
- ❑ 299 Buster Davis RC .40 1.00
- ❑ 300 Stewart Bradley RC .50 1.25
- ❑ 301 Toby Korrodi RC .40 1.00
- ❑ 302 Marcus McCauley RC .40 1.00
- ❑ 303 Demarcus Tank Tyler RC .40 1.00
- ❑ 304 Jon Abbate RC .30 .75
- ❑ 305 Ikaika Alama-Francis RC .50 1.25
- ❑ 306 Tim Crowder RC .50 1.25
- ❑ 307 D'Juan Woods RC .40 1.00
- ❑ 308 Tim Shaw RC .40 1.00
- ❑ 309 Fred Bennett RC .30 .75
- ❑ 310 Victor Abiamiri RC .50 1.25
- ❑ 311 Eric Weddle RC .40 1.00
- ❑ 312 Danny Ware RC .50 1.25
- ❑ 313 Quentin Moses RC .40 1.00
- ❑ 314 Ryan McBean RC .50 1.25
- ❑ 315 David Harris RC .40 1.00
- ❑ 316 David Irons RC .30 .75
- ❑ 317 Syndric Steptoe RC .40 1.00
- ❑ 318 Eric Frampton RC .40 1.00
- ❑ 319 Jemalle Cornelius RC .40 1.00
- ❑ 320 Earl Everett RC .40 1.00
- ❑ 321 Alonzo Coleman RC .40 1.00
- ❑ 322 Josh Gattis RC .30 .75
- ❑ 323 Zak DeOssie RC .40 1.00
- ❑ 324 Jon Beason RC .50 1.25
- ❑ 325 Joe Staley RC .40 1.00
- ❑ 326 Aaron Rouse RC .50 1.25
- ❑ 327 Reggie Ball RC .40 1.00
- ❑ 328 Rufus Alexander RC .50 1.25
- ❑ 329 Daymeion Hughes RC .40 1.00
- ❑ 330 Justin Durant RC .40 1.00
- ❑ 331 JaMarcus Russell RC .60 1.50
- ❑ 332 Paul Williams RC .40 1.00
- ❑ 333 Kenny Irons RC .50 1.25
- ❑ 334 Chris Davis RC .40 1.00
- ❑ 335 Darius Walker RC .40 1.00
- ❑ 336 Dwayne Bowe RC .75 2.00
- ❑ 337 Isaiah Stanback RC .50 1.25
- ❑ 338 Leon Hall RC .50 1.25
- ❑ 339 Sidney Rice RC 1.00 2.50
- ❑ 340 Amobi Okoye RC .50 1.25
- ❑ 341 Adrian Peterson RC 4.00 10.00
- ❑ 342 LaRon Landry RC .00 1.50
- ❑ 343 Lorenzo Booker RC .50 1.25
- ❑ 344 Craig Buster Davis RC .50 1.25
- ❑ 345 Mike Walker RC .50 1.25
- ❑ 346 Zach Miller RC .50 1.25
- ❑ 347 Levi Brown RC .50 1.25
- ❑ 348 Brian Leonard RC .40 1.00
- ❑ 349 Aundrae Allison RC .40 1.00
- ❑ 350 Brandon Siler RC .40 1.00
- ❑ 351 Calvin Johnson RC 1.25 3.00
- ❑ 352 Gaines Adams RC .50 1.25
- ❑ 353 Anthony Gonzalez RC .60 1.50
- ❑ 354 John Beck RC .50 1.25
- ❑ 355 Joe Thomas RC .50 1.25
- ❑ 356 Michael Bush RC .50 1.25
- ❑ 357 Courtney Taylor RC .40 1.00
- ❑ 358 Lawrence Timmons RC .50 1.25
- ❑ 359 Drew Stanton RC .40 1.00
- ❑ 360 Chansi Stuckey RC .50 1.25
- ❑ 361 Greg Olsen RC .60 1.50
- ❑ 362 Rhema McKnight RC .40 1.00
- ❑ 363 Antonio Pittman RC .50 1.25
- ❑ 364 Kevin Kolb RC .75 2.00
- ❑ 365 Alan Branch RC .40 1.00
- ❑ 366 Robert Meachem RC .50 1.25
- ❑ 367 Troy Smith RC .60 1.50
- ❑ 368 Jamaal Anderson RC .40 1.00
- ❑ 369 Tony Hunt RC .50 1.25
- ❑ 370 David Clowney RC .50 1.25
- ❑ 371 Brady Quinn RC 1.00 2.50
- ❑ 372 Michael Griffin RC .50 1.25
- ❑ 373 Jared Zabransky RC .50 1.25
- ❑ 374 Jason Hill RC .50 1.25
- ❑ 375 Trent Edwards RC .75 2.00
- ❑ 376 Dwayne Jarrett RC .50 1.25
- ❑ 377 DeShawn Wynn RC .50 1.25
- ❑ 378 Patrick Willis RC .75 2.00
- ❑ 379 Steve Smith USC RC .75 2.00
- ❑ 380 David Ball RC .30 .75
- ❑ 381 Marshawn Lynch RC .75 2.00
- ❑ 382 Paul Posluszny RC .60 1.50
- ❑ 383 Johnnie Lee Higgins RC .50 1.25
- ❑ 384 Kolby Smith RC .50 1.25
- ❑ 385 Ted Ginn Jr. RC .75 2.00
- ❑ 386 Adam Carriker RC .40 1.00
- ❑ 387 Tyler Palko RC .40 1.00
- ❑ 388 Joel Filani RC .40 1.00
- ❑ 389 Garrett Wolfe RC .50 1.25
- ❑ 390 Ryne Robinson RC .40 1.00
- ❑ 391 Reggie Nelson RC .40 1.00
- ❑ 392 Dallas Baker RC .40 1.00
- ❑ 393 Dwayne Wright RC .40 1.00
- ❑ 394 Scott Chandler RC .40 1.00
- ❑ 395 Jordan Kent RC .40 1.00
- ❑ 396 Jarvis Moss RC .50 1.25
- ❑ 397 Jonathan Wade RC .40 1.00
- ❑ 398 Ben Grubbs RC .40 1.00
- ❑ 399 Jason Snelling RC .40 1.00
- ❑ 400 Jeff Rowe RC .40 1.00
- ❑ 401 Aaron Ross RC .50 1.25
- ❑ 402 Daniel Sepulveda RC .50 1.25
- ❑ 403 Chris Henry RC .40 1.00
- ❑ 404 James Jones RC .50 1.25
- ❑ 405 Matt Spaeth RC .50 1.25
- ❑ 406 Brandon Meriweather RC .50 1.25
- ❑ 407 Nate Ilaoa RC .50 1.25
- ❑ 408 Mason Crosby RC .50 1.25
- ❑ 409 Ray McDonald RC .40 1.00
- ❑ 410 Chris Leak RC .40 1.00
- ❑ 411 Darrelle Revis RC .60 1.50
- ❑ 412 Ahmad Bradshaw RC .60 1.50
- ❑ 413 Tyler Thigpen RC .50 1.25
- ❑ 414 Justise Hairston RC .40 1.00
- ❑ 415 Charles Johnson RC .30 .75
- ❑ 416 Anthony Spencer RC .50 1.25
- ❑ 417 Legedu Naanee RC .50 1.25
- ❑ 418 Kenneth Darby RC .50 1.25
- ❑ 419 Steve Breaston RC .50 1.25
- ❑ 420 Ben Patrick RC .40 1.00
- ❑ 421 Chris Houston RC .40 1.00
- ❑ 422 Jordan Palmer RC .50 1.25
- ❑ 423 Laurent Robinson RC .50 1.25
- ❑ 424 Selvin Young RC .50 1.25
- ❑ 425 Justin Harrell RC .50 1.25
- ❑ 426 Sabby Piscitelli RC .50 1.25
- ❑ 427 Yamon Figurs RC .30 .75
- ❑ 428 Brandon Jackson RC .50 1.25
- ❑ 429 Jacoby Jones RC .50 1.25
- ❑ 430 H.B. Blades RC .40 1.00
- ❑ 431 Tanard Jackson RC .30 .75
- ❑ 432 Matt Gutierrez RC .50 1.25
- ❑ 433 Matt Moore RC .60 1.50
- ❑ 434 Clifton Dawson RC .50 1.25
- ❑ 435 Marcus Mason RC .50 1.25
- ❑ 436 Pierre Thomas RC 2.00 5.00
- ❑ 437 Dante Rosario RC .50 1.25
- ❑ 438 Biren Ealy RC .40 1.00
- ❑ 439 John Broussard RC .40 1.00
- ❑ 440 Kenton Keith RC .50 1.25

2008 Score

- ❑ COMPLETE SET (440) 30.00 60.00
- ❑ COMP.FACT. SET (440) 30.00 50.00
- ❑ COMP.SET w/o RC's (330) 15.00 30.00
- ❑ 1 Matt Leinart .20 .50
- ❑ 2 Kurt Warner .20 .50
- ❑ 3 Larry Fitzgerald .20 .50
- ❑ 4 Anquan Boldin .15 .40
- ❑ 5 Edgerrin James .15 .40
- ❑ 6 Neil Rackers .12 .30
- ❑ 7 Steve Breaston .12 .30
- ❑ 8 Antrel Rolle .12 .30
- ❑ 9 Karlos Dansby .12 .30
- ❑ 10 Joey Harrington .15 .40
- ❑ 11 Jerious Norwood .15 .40
- ❑ 12 Roddy White .15 .40
- ❑ 13 Michael Jenkins .12 .30
- ❑ 14 Joe Horn .15 .40
- ❑ 15 Keith Brooking .12 .30
- ❑ 16 Lawyer Milloy .12 .30
- ❑ 17 John Abraham .12 .30
- ❑ 18 Michael Turner .20 .50
- ❑ 19 Troy Smith .15 .40
- ❑ 20 Willis McGahee .15 .40
- ❑ 21 Musa Smith .12 .30
- ❑ 22 Derrick Mason .12 .30
- ❑ 23 Mark Clayton .15 .40
- ❑ 24 Bart Scott .12 .30
- ❑ 25 Demetrius Williams .12 .30
- ❑ 26 Yamon Figurs .12 .30
- ❑ 27 Ray Lewis .20 .50
- ❑ 28 Terrell Suggs .12 .30
- ❑ 29 Ed Reed .15 .40
- ❑ 30 Trent Edwards .20 .50
- ❑ 31 Marshawn Lynch .20 .50
- ❑ 32 Lee Evans .15 .40
- ❑ 33 Roscoe Parrish .12 .30
- ❑ 34 Paul Posluszny .15 .40
- ❑ 35 John DiGiorgio RC .15 .40
- ❑ 36 Angelo Crowell .12 .30
- ❑ 37 Jabari Greer RC .12 .30
- ❑ 38 Chris Kelsay .12 .30
- ❑ 39 Fred Jackson RC .25 .60
- ❑ 40 Matt Moore .15 .40
- ❑ 41 Steve Smith .15 .40
- ❑ 42 DeAngelo Williams .15 .40
- ❑ 43 Brad Hoover .12 .30
- ❑ 44 Dante Rosario .12 .30
- ❑ 45 Julius Peppers .15 .40
- ❑ 46 Jon Beason .12 .30
- ❑ 47 Chris Harris .12 .30
- ❑ 48 D.J. Hackett .12 .30
- ❑ 49 Jake Delhomme .15 .40
- ❑ 50 Adrian Peterson .12 .30
- ❑ 51 Mark Anderson .12 .30
- ❑ 52 Desmond Clark .12 .30
- ❑ 53 Greg Olsen .15 .40
- ❑ 54 Devin Hester .20 .50
- ❑ 55 Brian Urlacher .20 .50
- ❑ 56 Jason McKie RC .15 .40
- ❑ 57 Lance Briggs .12 .30
- ❑ 58 Rex Grossman .15 .40
- ❑ 59 Carson Palmer .20 .50
- ❑ 60 Chad Johnson .15 .40
- ❑ 61 T.J. Houshmandzadeh .15 .40
- ❑ 62 Rudi Johnson .15 .40
- ❑ 63 Kenny Watson .12 .30
- ❑ 64 Dhani Jones .12 .30
- ❑ 65 Leon Hall .12 .30
- ❑ 66 Johnathan Joseph .12 .30
- ❑ 67 Derek Anderson .15 .40
- ❑ 68 Brady Quinn .20 .50
- ❑ 69 Jamal Lewis .15 .40
- ❑ 70 Josh Cribbs .20 .50
- ❑ 71 Kellen Winslow .15 .40
- ❑ 72 Braylon Edwards .15 .40
- ❑ 73 Joe Jurevicius .12 .30
- ❑ 74 D'Qwell Jackson .12 .30
- ❑ 75 Leigh Bodden .12 .30
- ❑ 76 Sean Jones .12 .30
- ❑ 77 Tony Romo .30 .75
- ❑ 78 Terrell Owens .20 .50
- ❑ 79 Marion Barber .20 .50
- ❑ 80 Jason Witten .20 .50
- ❑ 81 Patrick Crayton .15 .40
- ❑ 82 Anthony Henry .12 .30
- ❑ 83 DeMarcus Ware .15 .40
- ❑ 84 Terence Newman .12 .30
- ❑ 85 Greg Ellis .12 .30
- ❑ 86 Zach Thomas .15 .40
- ❑ 87 Keary Colbert .12 .30
- ❑ 88 Jay Cutler .20 .50
- ❑ 89 Tony Scheffler .12 .30
- ❑ 90 Selvin Young .12 .30

Card	Low	High
91 Brandon Marshall	.15	.40
92 Brandon Stokley	.15	.40
93 Champ Bailey	.12	.30
94 John Lynch	.15	.40
95 Dre Bly	.12	.30
96 Elvis Dumervil	.12	.30
97 Jon Kitna	.15	.40
98 Tatum Bell	.12	.30
99 Shaun McDonald	.12	.30
100 Roy Williams WR	.15	.40
101 Calvin Johnson	.20	.50
102 Mike Furrey	.15	.40
103 Ernie Sims	.12	.30
104 Aveion Cason	.12	.30
105 Aaron Rodgers	.20	.50
106 Brett Favre	.50	1.25
107 Ryan Grant	.20	.50
108 Greg Jennings	.15	.40
109 Donald Driver	.15	.40
110 Donald Lee	.15	.40
111 James Jones	.12	.30
112 Al Harris	.12	.30
113 Nick Barnett	.12	.30
114 Charles Woodson	.15	.40
115 Aaron Kampman	.15	.40
116 Mason Crosby	.12	.30
117 Matt Schaub	.15	.40
118 Ahman Green	.15	.40
119 Andre Johnson	.15	.40
120 Kevin Walter	.15	.40
121 Owen Daniels	.12	.30
122 Andre Davis	.12	.30
123 DeMeco Ryans	.15	.40
124 Mario Williams	.15	.40
125 Dunta Robinson	.12	.30
126 Chris Brown	.12	.30
127 Peyton Manning	.30	.75
128 Joseph Addai	.20	.50
129 Marvin Harrison	.20	.50
130 Reggie Wayne	.15	.40
131 Dallas Clark	.15	.40
132 Anthony Gonzalez	.15	.40
133 Kenton Keith	.12	.30
134 Adam Vinatieri	.20	.50
135 Bob Sanders	.15	.40
136 Kelvin Hayden	.12	.30
137 Freddie Keiaho	.12	.30
138 David Garrard	.15	.40
139 Fred Taylor	.15	.40
140 Maurice Jones-Drew	.15	.40
141 Greg Jones	.12	.30
142 Dennis Northcutt	.12	.30
143 Reggie Williams	.15	.40
144 Marcedes Lewis	.12	.30
145 Matt Jones	.15	.40
146 Reggie Nelson	.12	.30
147 Cleo Lemon	.12	.30
148 Jerry Porter	.15	.40
149 Damon Huard	.12	.30
150 Brodie Croyle	.15	.40
151 Larry Johnson	.15	.40
152 Kolby Smith	.12	.30
153 Tony Gonzalez	.15	.40
154 Dwayne Bowe	.15	.40
155 Donnie Edwards	.12	.30
156 Jared Allen	.20	.50
157 Patrick Surtain	.12	.30
158 Derrick Johnson	.12	.30
159 Ernest Wilford	.12	.30
160 John Beck	.12	.30
161 Ronnie Brown	.15	.40
162 Greg Camarillo RC	.40	1.00
163 Ted Ginn Jr.	.15	.40
164 Derek Hagan	.12	.30
165 Channing Crowder	.12	.30
166 Joey Porter	.12	.30
167 Jason Taylor	.15	.40
168 Josh McCown	.12	.30
169 Bernard Berrian	.15	.40
170 Maurice Hicks	.12	.30
171 Tarvaris Jackson	.15	.40
172 Adrian Peterson	.40	1.00
173 Chester Taylor	.12	.30
174 Bobby Wade	.12	.30
175 Sidney Rice	.20	.50
176 Robert Ferguson	.12	.30
177 Darren Sharper	.15	.40
178 Visanthe Shiancoe	.12	.30
179 E.J. Henderson	.12	.30
180 Cedric Griffin	.12	.30
181 Chad Greenway	.12	.30
182 Tom Brady	.30	.75
183 Randy Moss	.20	.50
184 Laurence Maroney	.15	.40
185 Wes Welker	.20	.50
186 Sammy Morris	.12	.30
187 Kevin Faulk	.15	.40
188 Ben Watson	.12	.30
189 Tedy Bruschi	.20	.50
190 Rodney Harrison	.12	.30
191 Mike Vrabel	.12	.30
192 Drew Brees	.20	.50
193 Reggie Bush	.20	.50
194 Deuce McAllister	.15	.40
195 Marques Colston	.15	.40
196 David Patten	.12	.30
197 Devery Henderson	.12	.30
198 Scott Fujita	.12	.30
199 Roman Harper	.12	.30
200 Mike McKenzie	.12	.30
201 Will Smith	.12	.30
202 Billy Miller	.12	.30
203 Sammy Knight	.12	.30
204 Eli Manning	.20	.50
205 Plaxico Burress	.15	.40
206 Brandon Jacobs	.15	.40
207 Ahmad Bradshaw	.15	.40
208 David Tyree	.15	.40
209 Amani Toomer	.15	.40
210 Jeremy Shockey	.15	.40
211 Steve Smith USC	.15	.40
212 Aaron Ross	.12	.30
213 Antonio Pierce	.12	.30
214 Michael Strahan	.15	.40
215 Jesse Chatman	.12	.30
216 Calvin Pace	.12	.30
217 Kellen Clemens	.15	.40
218 Leon Washington	.15	.40
219 Jerricho Cotchery	.12	.30
220 Laveranues Coles	.15	.40
221 Chris Baker	.12	.30
222 Brad Smith	.12	.30
223 Thomas Jones	.15	.40
224 Darrelle Revis	.15	.40
225 David Harris	.12	.30
226 DeAngelo Hall	.12	.30
227 Drew Carter	.12	.30
228 Javon Walker	.15	.40
229 JaMarcus Russell	.20	.50
230 Justin Fargas	.12	.30
231 Michael Bush	.15	.40
232 Ronald Curry	.15	.40
233 Zach Miller	.15	.40
234 Thomas Howard	.12	.30
235 Johnnie Lee Higgins	.12	.30
236 Kirk Morrison	.12	.30
237 Michael Huff	.12	.30
238 Asante Samuel	.12	.30
239 Donovan McNabb	.20	.50
240 Brian Westbrook	.15	.40
241 Correll Buckhalter	.15	.40
242 Kevin Curtis	.12	.30
243 Reggie Brown	.12	.30
244 L.J. Smith	.12	.30
245 Greg Lewis	.12	.30
246 Lito Sheppard	.12	.30
247 Omar Gaither	.12	.30
248 Ben Roethlisberger	.30	.75
249 Willie Parker	.15	.40
250 Najeh Davenport	.12	.30
251 Hines Ward	.15	.40
252 Santonio Holmes	.15	.40
253 Heath Miller	.12	.30
254 Cedrick Wilson	.12	.30
255 James Harrison RC	1.00	2.50
256 Ike Taylor	.12	.30
257 James Farrior	.12	.30
258 Troy Polamalu	.20	.50
259 Philip Rivers	.20	.50
260 LaDainian Tomlinson	.25	.60
261 Darren Sproles	.12	.30
262 Vincent Jackson	.12	.30
263 Chris Chambers	.15	.40
264 Antonio Gates	.15	.40
265 Craig Buster Davis	.12	.30
266 Malcom Floyd	.12	.30
267 Antonio Cromartie	.12	.30
268 Shawne Merriman	.15	.40
269 DeShaun Foster	.15	.40
270 Alex Smith QB	.15	.40
271 Frank Gore	.15	.40
272 Michael Robinson	.12	.30
273 Vernon Davis	.12	.30
274 Arnaz Battle	.12	.30
275 Isaac Bruce	.15	.40
276 Patrick Willis	.15	.40
277 Nate Clements	.12	.30
278 Jason Hill	.12	.30
279 T.J. Duckett	.12	.30
280 Matt Hasselbeck	.15	.40
281 Julian Peterson	.12	.30
282 Maurice Morris	.12	.30
283 Bobby Engram	.12	.30
284 Nate Burleson	.12	.30
285 Deion Branch	.15	.40
286 Lofa Tatupu	.15	.40
287 Marcus Trufant	.12	.30
288 Darryl Tapp	.12	.30
289 Julius Jones	.15	.40
290 Marc Bulger	.15	.40
291 Steven Jackson	.20	.50
292 Brian Leonard	.12	.30
293 Torry Holt	.15	.40
294 Dante Hall	.12	.30
295 Randy McMichael	.12	.30
296 Drew Bennett	.12	.30
297 Will Witherspoon	.12	.30
298 Tye Hill	.12	.30
299 Corey Chavous	.12	.30
300 Warrick Dunn	.15	.40
301 Brian Griese	.12	.30
302 Jeff Garcia	.15	.40
303 Cadillac Williams	.15	.40
304 Earnest Graham	.12	.30
305 Joey Galloway	.15	.40
306 Ike Hilliard	.12	.30
307 Michael Clayton	.15	.40
308 Derrick Brooks	.15	.40
309 Phillip Buchanon	.12	.30
310 Alex Smith TE	.12	.30
311 Ronde Barber	.12	.30
312 Justin McCareins	.12	.30
313 Jevon Kearse	.15	.40
314 Vince Young	.15	.40
315 LenDale White	.15	.40
316 Justin Gage	.12	.30
317 Roydell Williams	.12	.30
318 Alge Crumpler	.15	.40
319 Brandon Jones	.12	.30
320 Michael Griffin	.12	.30
321 Keith Bulluck	.12	.30
322 Jason Campbell	.15	.40
323 Clinton Portis	.15	.40
324 Ladell Betts	.12	.30
325 Santana Moss	.12	.30
326 Chris Cooley	.15	.40
327 Antwaan Randle El	.12	.30
328 London Fletcher	.12	.30
329 Shawn Springs	.12	.30
330 LaRon Landry	.15	.40
331 Jake Long RC	.50	1.25
332 Chris Long RC	.50	1.25
333 Matt Ryan RC	2.00	5.00
334 Darren McFadden RC	1.00	2.50
335 Glenn Dorsey RC	.50	1.25
336 Vernon Gholston RC	.50	1.25
337 Sedrick Ellis RC	.50	1.25
338 Derrick Harvey RC	.40	1.00
339 Keith Rivers RC	.50	1.25
340 Jerod Mayo RC	.60	1.50
341 Leodis McKelvin RC	.50	1.25
342 Jonathan Stewart RC	1.00	2.50
343 D.Rodgers-Cromartie RC	.50	1.25
344 Joe Flacco RC	1.50	4.00
345 Aqib Talib RC	.50	1.25
346 Felix Jones RC	1.00	2.50
347 Rashard Mendenhall RC	1.00	2.50
348 Chris Johnson RC	1.50	4.00
349 Mike Jenkins RC	.50	1.25
350 Antoine Cason RC	.50	1.25
351 Lawrence Jackson RC	.40	1.00
352 Kentwan Balmer RC	.40	1.00
353 Dustin Keller RC	.50	1.25
354 Kenny Phillips RC	.50	1.25
355 Phillip Merling RC	.40	1.00
356 Donnie Avery RC	.60	1.50
357 Devin Thomas RC	.50	1.25

❑ 358 Brandon Flowers RC	.50	1.25
❑ 359 Jordy Nelson RC	.60	1.50
❑ 360 Curtis Lofton RC	.50	1.25
❑ 361 John Carlson RC	.50	1.25
❑ 362 Tracy Porter RC	.60	1.50
❑ 363 James Hardy RC	.40	1.00
❑ 364 Eddie Royal RC	.75	2.00
❑ 365 Matt Forte RC	1.00	2.50
❑ 366 Jordon Dizon RC	.50	1.25
❑ 367 Jerome Simpson RC	.40	1.00
❑ 368 Fred Davis RC	.50	1.25
❑ 369 DeSean Jackson RC	1.00	2.50
❑ 370 Calais Campbell RC	.40	1.00
❑ 371 Malcolm Kelly RC	.50	1.25
❑ 372 Quentin Groves RC	.40	1.00
❑ 373 Limas Sweed RC	.50	1.25
❑ 374 Ray Rice RC	1.00	2.50
❑ 375 Brian Brohm RC	.50	1.25
❑ 376 Chad Henne RC	.75	2.00
❑ 377 Dexter Jackson RC	.50	1.25
❑ 378 Martellus Bennett RC	.50	1.25
❑ 379 Terrell Thomas RC	.40	1.00
❑ 380 Kevin Smith RC	.75	2.00
❑ 381 Anthony Alridge RC	.40	1.00
❑ 382 Jacob Hester RC	.50	1.25
❑ 383 Earl Bennett RC	.50	1.25
❑ 384 Jamaal Charles RC	.75	2.00
❑ 385 Dan Connor RC	.50	1.25
❑ 386 Reggie Smith RC	.40	1.00
❑ 387 Brad Cottam RC	.50	1.25
❑ 388 Pat Sims RC	.40	1.00
❑ 389 Dantrell Savage RC	.50	1.25
❑ 390 Early Doucet RC	.50	1.25
❑ 391 Harry Douglas RC	.40	1.00
❑ 392 Steve Slaton RC	.60	1.50
❑ 393 Jermichael Finley RC	.50	1.25
❑ 394 Kevin O'Connell RC	.50	1.25
❑ 395 Mario Manningham RC	.50	1.25
❑ 396 Andre Caldwell RC	.50	1.25
❑ 397 Will Franklin RC	.40	1.00
❑ 398 Marcus Smith RC	.40	1.00
❑ 399 Martin Rucker RC	.40	1.00
❑ 400 Xavier Adibi RC	.40	1.00
❑ 401 Craig Steltz RC	.40	1.00
❑ 402 Tashard Choice RC	.50	1.25
❑ 403 Lavelle Hawkins RC	.40	1.00
❑ 404 Jacob Tamme RC	.50	1.25
❑ 405 Keenan Burton RC	.40	1.00
❑ 406 John David Booty RC	.50	1.25
❑ 407 Ryan Torain RC	.50	1.25
❑ 408 Tim Hightower RC	.60	1.50
❑ 409 Dennis Dixon RC	.50	1.25
❑ 410 Kellen Davis RC	.30	.75
❑ 411 Josh Johnson RC	.50	1.25
❑ 412 Erik Ainge RC	.50	1.25
❑ 413 Owen Schmitt RC	.50	1.25
❑ 414 Marcus Thomas RC	.40	1.00
❑ 415 Thomas Brown RC	.50	1.25
❑ 416 Josh Morgan RC	.50	1.25
❑ 417 Kevin Robinson RC	.40	1.00
❑ 418 Colt Brennan RC	.75	2.00
❑ 419 Paul Hubbard RC	.40	1.00
❑ 420 Andre Woodson RC	.50	1.25
❑ 421 Mike Hart RC	.50	1.25
❑ 422 Matt Flynn RC	.50	1.25
❑ 423 Chauncey Washington RC	.40	1.00
❑ 424 Caleb Campbell RC	.50	1.25
❑ 425 Peyton Hillis RC	.50	1.25
❑ 426 Justin Forsett RC	.50	1.25
❑ 427 Adrian Arrington RC	.40	1.00
❑ 428 Cory Boyd RC	.40	1.00
❑ 429 Allen Patrick RC	.40	1.00
❑ 430 Marcus Monk RC	.50	1.25
❑ 431 DJ Hall RC	.40	1.00
❑ 432 Darrell Strong RC	.40	1.00
❑ 433 Jason Rivers RC	.50	1.25
❑ 434 Jed Collins RC	.40	1.00
❑ 435 Paul Smith RC	.50	1.25
❑ 436 Darius Reynaud RC	.40	1.00
❑ 437 Ali Highsmith RC	.30	.75
❑ 438 Davone Bess RC	.60	1.50
❑ 439 Erin Henderson RC	.40	1.00
❑ 440 Kalvin McRae RC	.40	1.00

2009 Score

❑ COMPLETE SET (400)	30.00	60.00
❑ 1 Adrian Wilson	.12	.30
❑ 2 Anquan Boldin	.15	.40
❑ 3 Dominique Rodgers-Cromartie	.12	.30
❑ 4 Edgerrin James	.15	.40
❑ 5 Kurt Warner	.20	.50
❑ 6 Larry Fitzgerald	.20	.50
❑ 7 Matt Leinart	.15	.40
❑ 8 Steve Breaston	.15	.40
❑ 9 Tim Hightower	.15	.40
❑ 10 Chris Houston	.12	.30
❑ 11 Curtis Lofton	.12	.30
❑ 12 Harry Douglas	.12	.30
❑ 13 Jerious Norwood	.15	.40
❑ 14 John Abraham	.12	.30
❑ 15 Matt Ryan	.20	.50
❑ 16 Michael Jenkins	.12	.30
❑ 17 Michael Turner	.15	.40
❑ 18 Roddy White	.15	.40
❑ 19 Demetrius Williams	.12	.30
❑ 20 Derrick Mason	.12	.30
❑ 21 Joe Flacco	.20	.50
❑ 22 Le'Ron McClain	.15	.40
❑ 23 Mark Clayton	.12	.30
❑ 24 Ray Lewis	.20	.50
❑ 25 Ray Rice	.20	.50
❑ 26 Terrell Suggs	.12	.30
❑ 27 Todd Heap	.12	.30
❑ 28 Willis McGahee	.15	.40
❑ 29 Derek Fine	.12	.30
❑ 30 Fred Jackson	.15	.40
❑ 31 James Hardy	.15	.40
❑ 32 Lee Evans	.15	.40
❑ 33 Leodis McKelvin	.12	.30
❑ 34 Marshawn Lynch	.15	.40
❑ 35 Paul Posluszny	.15	.40
❑ 36 Steve Johnson	.12	.30
❑ 37 Trent Edwards	.15	.40
❑ 38 Charles Godfrey	.12	.30
❑ 39 Chris Gamble	.12	.30
❑ 40 Dante Rosario	.12	.30
❑ 41 DeAngelo Williams	.20	.50
❑ 42 Jake Delhomme	.15	.40
❑ 43 Jon Beason	.12	.30
❑ 44 Jonathan Stewart	.15	.40
❑ 45 Muhsin Muhammad	.15	.40
❑ 46 Steve Smith	.15	.40
❑ 47 Alex Brown	.12	.30
❑ 48 Brian Urlacher	.20	.50
❑ 49 Desmond Clark	.12	.30
❑ 50 Devin Hester	.20	.50
❑ 51 Earl Bennett	.15	.40
❑ 52 Greg Olsen	.12	.30
❑ 53 Kyle Orton	.15	.40
❑ 54 Lance Briggs	.15	.40
❑ 55 Matt Forte	.20	.50
❑ 56 Andre Caldwell	.12	.30
❑ 57 Carson Palmer	.20	.50
❑ 58 Cedric Benson	.15	.40
❑ 59 Chad Ochocinco	.15	.40
❑ 60 Dhani Jones	.12	.30
❑ 61 Jerome Simpson	.12	.30
❑ 62 Keith Rivers	.12	.30
❑ 63 Reggie Kelly	.12	.30
❑ 64 T.J. Houshmandzadeh	.15	.40
❑ 65 Brady Quinn	.15	.40
❑ 66 Braylon Edwards	.15	.40
❑ 67 D'Qwell Jackson	.12	.30
❑ 68 Jamal Lewis	.15	.40
❑ 69 Jerome Harrison	.15	.40
❑ 70 Josh Cribbs	.20	.50
❑ 71 Kellen Winslow	.15	.40
❑ 72 Shaun Rogers	.12	.30
❑ 73 Steve Heiden	.12	.30
❑ 74 DeMarcus Ware	.15	.40
❑ 75 Felix Jones	.20	.50
❑ 76 Jason Witten	.20	.50
❑ 77 Marion Barber	.20	.50
❑ 78 Patrick Crayton	.12	.30
❑ 79 Roy Williams WR	.15	.40
❑ 80 Tashard Choice	.15	.40
❑ 81 Terrell Owens	.20	.50
❑ 82 Terence Newman	.12	.30
❑ 83 Tony Romo	.30	.75
❑ 84 Brandon Marshall	.15	.40
❑ 85 Brandon Stokley	.15	.40
❑ 86 Champ Bailey	.15	.40
❑ 87 Daniel Graham	.12	.30
❑ 88 Eddie Royal	.15	.40
❑ 89 Jay Cutler	.20	.50
❑ 90 Peyton Hillis	.12	.30
❑ 91 D.J. Williams	.12	.30
❑ 92 Tony Scheffler	.12	.30
❑ 93 Calvin Johnson	.20	.50
❑ 94 Daunte Culpepper	.15	.40
❑ 95 Ernie Sims	.12	.30
❑ 96 Jerome Felton	.12	.30
❑ 97 Jordon Dizon	.12	.30
❑ 98 Kevin Smith	.15	.40
❑ 99 Paris Lenon	.12	.30
❑ 100 Rudi Johnson	.12	.30
❑ 101 Shaun McDonald	.12	.30
❑ 102 Aaron Rodgers	.20	.50
❑ 103 A.J. Hawk	.15	.40
❑ 104 Brandon Jackson	.15	.40
❑ 105 Donald Driver	.15	.40
❑ 106 Donald Lee	.12	.30
❑ 107 Greg Jennings	.20	.50
❑ 108 James Jones	.12	.30
❑ 109 Jermichael Finley	.12	.30
❑ 110 Jordy Nelson	.15	.40
❑ 111 Ryan Grant	.15	.40
❑ 112 Amobi Okoye	.12	.30
❑ 113 Andre Johnson	.15	.40
❑ 114 Chester Pitts	.12	.30
❑ 115 DeMeco Ryans	.15	.40
❑ 116 Kevin Walter	.15	.40
❑ 117 Kris Brown	.12	.30
❑ 118 Mario Williams	.15	.40
❑ 119 Matt Schaub	.15	.40
❑ 120 Owen Daniels	.12	.30
❑ 121 Steve Slaton	.15	.40
❑ 122 Adam Vinatieri	.15	.40
❑ 123 Anthony Gonzalez	.15	.40
❑ 124 Dallas Clark	.15	.40
❑ 125 Dominic Rhodes	.12	.30
❑ 126 Dwight Freeney	.15	.40
❑ 127 Joseph Addai	.20	.50
❑ 128 Freddie Keiaho	.12	.30
❑ 129 Mike Hart	.15	.40
❑ 130 Peyton Manning	.30	.75
❑ 131 Reggie Wayne	.15	.40
❑ 132 David Garrard	.15	.40
❑ 133 Dennis Northcutt	.12	.30
❑ 134 Derrick Harvey	.12	.30
❑ 135 Josh Scobee	.12	.30
❑ 136 Marcedes Lewis	.12	.30
❑ 137 Mike Peterson	.12	.30
❑ 138 Maurice Jones-Drew	.15	.40
❑ 139 Quentin Groves	.12	.30
❑ 140 Reggie Nelson	.12	.30
❑ 141 Brian Williams	.12	.30
❑ 142 Derrick Johnson	.12	.30
❑ 143 Matt Cassel	.15	.40
❑ 144 Dwayne Bowe	.15	.40
❑ 145 Jamaal Charles	.15	.40
❑ 146 Kolby Smith	.12	.30
❑ 147 Larry Johnson	.15	.40
❑ 148 Mark Bradley	.12	.30
❑ 149 Tony Gonzalez	.15	.40
❑ 150 Tyler Thigpen	.12	.30
❑ 151 Anthony Fasano	.12	.30
❑ 152 Chad Henne	.20	.50
❑ 153 Chad Pennington	.15	.40
❑ 154 Davone Bess	.15	.40
❑ 155 Joey Porter	.15	.40
❑ 156 Greg Camarillo	.15	.40
❑ 157 Jake Long	.12	.30
❑ 158 Ricky Williams	.15	.40
❑ 159 Ronnie Brown	.15	.40
❑ 160 Ted Ginn	.15	.40
❑ 161 Adrian Peterson	.40	1.00
❑ 162 Bernard Berrian	.15	.40

❑ 163 Chad Greenway .12 .30
❑ 164 Chester Taylor .12 .30
❑ 165 Erin Henderson .12 .30
❑ 166 Jared Allen .20 .50
❑ 167 John David Booty .15 .40
❑ 168 Sidney Rice .15 .40
❑ 169 Tarvaris Jackson .15 .40
❑ 170 Visanthe Shiancoe .12 .30
❑ 171 Brandon Meriweather .12 .30
❑ 172 Jerod Mayo .15 .40
❑ 173 Kevin Faulk .12 .30
❑ 174 LaMont Jordan .12 .30
❑ 175 Laurence Maroney .15 .40
❑ 176 Randy Moss .20 .50
❑ 177 Tedy Bruschi .15 .40
❑ 178 Terrence Wheatley .12 .30
❑ 179 Tom Brady .30 .75
❑ 180 Wes Welker .20 .50
❑ 181 Adrian Arrington .12 .30
❑ 182 Devery Henderson .12 .30
❑ 183 Drew Brees .20 .50
❑ 184 Jeremy Shockey .12 .30
❑ 185 Jonathan Vilma .12 .30
❑ 186 Lance Moore .15 .40
❑ 187 Marques Colston .15 .40
❑ 188 Pierre Thomas .15 .40
❑ 189 Reggie Bush .20 .50
❑ 190 Scott Shanle .12 .30
❑ 191 Ahmad Bradshaw .15 .40
❑ 192 Antonio Pierce .12 .30
❑ 193 Brandon Jacobs .15 .40
❑ 194 Derrick Ward .15 .40
❑ 195 Domenik Hixon .12 .30
❑ 196 Eli Manning .20 .50
❑ 197 Justin Tuck .15 .40
❑ 198 Kenny Phillips .12 .30
❑ 199 Kevin Boss .12 .30
❑ 200 Steve Smith USC .15 .40
❑ 201 Calvin Pace .12 .30
❑ 202 Chansi Stuckey .12 .30
❑ 203 Dustin Keller .12 .30
❑ 204 Jerricho Cotchery .12 .30
❑ 205 Kellen Clemens .12 .30
❑ 206 Laveranues Coles .15 .40
❑ 207 Leon Washington .15 .40
❑ 208 Thomas Jones .15 .40
❑ 209 Vernon Gholston .12 .30
❑ 210 Chaz Schilens .12 .30
❑ 211 Darren McFadden .20 .50
❑ 212 JaMarcus Russell .15 .40
❑ 213 Johnnie Lee Higgins .12 .30
❑ 214 Justin Fargas .12 .30
❑ 215 Michael Bush .15 .40
❑ 216 Nnamdi Asomugha .12 .30
❑ 217 Sebastian Janikowski .12 .30
❑ 218 Zach Miller .12 .30
❑ 219 Brian Westbrook .15 .40
❑ 220 Correll Buckhalter .12 .30
❑ 221 DeSean Jackson .15 .40
❑ 222 Donovan McNabb .20 .50
❑ 223 Greg Lewis .12 .30
❑ 224 Hank Baskett .12 .30
❑ 225 Kevin Curtis .12 .30
❑ 226 Reggie Brown .12 .30
❑ 227 Stewart Bradley .12 .30
❑ 228 Ben Roethlisberger .30 .75
❑ 229 Heath Miller .15 .40
❑ 230 Hines Ward .15 .40
❑ 231 James Harrison .20 .50
❑ 232 Troy Polamalu .20 .50
❑ 233 Nate Washington .12 .30
❑ 234 Rashard Mendenhall .15 .40
❑ 235 Santonio Holmes .15 .40
❑ 236 Willie Parker .15 .40
❑ 237 Antonio Gates .15 .40
❑ 238 Chris Chambers .15 .40
❑ 239 Darren Sproles .15 .40
❑ 240 Eric Weddle .12 .30
❑ 241 Jacob Hester .12 .30
❑ 242 LaDainian Tomlinson .20 .50
❑ 243 Philip Rivers .20 .50
❑ 244 Shawne Merriman .15 .40
❑ 245 Vincent Jackson .15 .40
❑ 246 Brandon Jones .12 .30
❑ 247 Frank Gore .15 .40
❑ 248 Isaac Bruce .15 .40
❑ 249 Josh Morgan .12 .30
❑ 250 Michael Robinson .12 .30
❑ 251 Patrick Willis .15 .40
❑ 252 Reggie Smith .12 .30
❑ 253 Shaun Hill .12 .30
❑ 254 Vernon Davis .12 .30
❑ 255 Deion Branch .15 .40
❑ 256 John Carlson .15 .40
❑ 257 Julian Peterson .12 .30
❑ 258 Julius Jones .15 .40
❑ 259 Lofa Tatupu .15 .40
❑ 260 Matt Hasselbeck .15 .40
❑ 261 Nate Burleson .12 .30
❑ 262 Owen Schmitt .12 .30
❑ 263 T.J. Duckett .12 .30
❑ 264 Antonio Pittman .12 .30
❑ 265 Chris Long .15 .40
❑ 266 Donnie Avery .15 .40
❑ 267 Keenan Burton .12 .30
❑ 268 Marc Bulger .15 .40
❑ 269 Pisa Tinoisamoa .12 .30
❑ 270 Steven Jackson .15 .40
❑ 271 Torry Holt .15 .40
❑ 272 Antonio Bryant .15 .40
❑ 273 Aqib Talib .12 .30
❑ 274 Cadillac Williams .15 .40
❑ 275 Dexter Jackson .12 .30
❑ 276 Earnest Graham .12 .30
❑ 277 Gaines Adams .12 .30
❑ 278 Michael Clayton .12 .30
❑ 279 Ronde Barber .12 .30
❑ 280 Barrett Ruud .12 .30
❑ 281 Albert Haynesworth .12 .30
❑ 282 Bo Scaife .12 .30
❑ 283 Chris Johnson .20 .50
❑ 284 Justin Gage .12 .30
❑ 285 Keith Bulluck .12 .30
❑ 286 Kerry Collins .15 .40
❑ 287 LenDale White .15 .40
❑ 288 Rob Bironas .12 .30
❑ 289 Roydell Williams .12 .30
❑ 290 Vince Young .15 .40
❑ 291 Chris Cooley .12 .30
❑ 292 Chris Horton .15 .40
❑ 293 Clinton Portis .15 .40
❑ 294 Colt Brennan .15 .40
❑ 295 Devin Thomas .12 .30
❑ 296 Jason Campbell .15 .40
❑ 297 Kedric Golston .20 .50
❑ 298 Ladell Betts .12 .30
❑ 299 Malcolm Kelly .12 .30
❑ 300 Santana Moss .15 .40
❑ 301 Aaron Brown RC .50 1.25
❑ 302 Aaron Curry RC .60 1.50
❑ 303 Aaron Kelly RC .40 1.00
❑ 304 Aaron Maybin RC .50 1.25
❑ 305 Alphonso Smith RC .40 1.00
❑ 306 Andre Brown RC .40 1.00
❑ 307 Andre Smith RC .50 1.25
❑ 308 Anthony Hill RC .30 .75
❑ 309 Arian Foster RC .50 1.25
❑ 310 Austin Collie RC 1.00 2.50
❑ 311 B.J. Raji RC .60 1.50
❑ 312 Brandon Gibson RC .50 1.25
❑ 313 Brandon Pettigrew RC .60 1.50
❑ 314 Brandon Tate RC .40 1.00
❑ 315 Brian Cushing RC .60 1.50
❑ 316 Brian Hartline RC .50 1.25
❑ 317 Brian Orakpo RC .60 1.50
❑ 318 Brian Robiskie RC .50 1.25
❑ 319 Brooks Foster RC .40 1.00
❑ 320 Cameron Morrah RC .30 .75
❑ 321 Cedric Peerman RC .40 1.00
❑ 322 Chase Coffman RC .40 1.00
❑ 323 Chris Wells RC 1.25 3.00
❑ 324 Clay Matthews RC .75 2.00
❑ 325 Clint Sintim RC .50 1.25
❑ 326 Cornelius Ingram RC .30 .75
❑ 327 Curtis Painter RC .50 1.25
❑ 328 Darius Butler RC .50 1.25
❑ 329 Darius Passmore RC .40 1.00
❑ 330 Darrius Heyward-Bey RC .75 2.00
❑ 331 Davon Drew RC .40 1.00
❑ 332 Demetrius Byrd RC .40 1.00
❑ 333 Deon Butler RC .50 1.25
❑ 334 Derrick Williams RC .50 1.25
❑ 335 Devin Moore RC .40 1.00
❑ 336 Dominique Edison RC .30 .75
❑ 337 Donald Brown RC 1.00 2.50
❑ 338 Eugene Monroe RC .40 1.00
❑ 339 Everette Brown RC .50 1.25
❑ 340 Gartrell Johnson RC .40 1.00
❑ 341 Glen Coffee RC .60 1.50
❑ 342 Graham Harrell RC .50 1.25
❑ 343 Hakeem Nicks RC 1.00 2.50
❑ 344 Hunter Cantwell RC .50 1.25
❑ 345 Jairus Byrd RC .60 1.50
❑ 346 James Casey RC .40 1.00
❑ 347 James Davis RC .50 1.25
❑ 348 James Laurinaitis RC .60 1.50
❑ 349 Jared Cook RC .40 1.00
❑ 350 Jarett Dillard RC .50 1.25
❑ 351 Jason Smith RC .40 1.00
❑ 352 Javon Ringer RC .50 1.25
❑ 353 Jeremiah Johnson RC .50 1.25
❑ 354 Jeremy Childs RC .40 1.00
❑ 355 Jeremy Maclin RC 1.00 2.50
❑ 356 John Parker Wilson RC .50 1.25
❑ 357 Johnny Knox RC .75 2.00
❑ 358 Josh Freeman RC 1.00 2.50
❑ 359 Juaquin Iglesias RC .50 1.25
❑ 360 Keith Null RC .50 1.25
❑ 361 Kenny Britt RC .75 2.00
❑ 362 Kenny McKinley RC .50 1.25
❑ 363 Kevin Ogletree RC .50 1.25
❑ 364 Knowshon Moreno RC 1.25 3.00
❑ 365 Kory Sheets RC .40 1.00
❑ 366 Larry English RC .50 1.25
❑ 367 LeSean McCoy RC 1.00 2.50
❑ 368 Louis Murphy RC .50 1.25
❑ 369 Malcolm Jenkins RC .50 1.25
❑ 370 Mark Sanchez RC 2.00 5.00
❑ 371 Matthew Stafford RC 1.50 4.00
❑ 372 Michael Crabtree RC 1.25 3.00
❑ 373 Mike Goodson RC .50 1.25
❑ 374 Mike Thomas RC .50 1.25
❑ 375 Mike Wallace RC 1.00 2.50
❑ 376 Mohamed Massaquoi RC .50 1.25
❑ 377 Nate Davis RC .50 1.25
❑ 378 Nathan Brown RC .40 1.00
❑ 379 P.J. Hill RC .40 1.00
❑ 380 Pat White RC .75 2.00
❑ 381 Patrick Chung RC .50 1.25
❑ 382 Patrick Turner RC .40 1.00
❑ 383 Percy Harvin RC 1.50 4.00
❑ 384 Quan Cosby RC .40 1.00
❑ 385 Quinn Johnson RC .40 1.00
❑ 386 Quinten Lawrence RC .40 1.00
❑ 387 Ramses Barden RC .40 1.00
❑ 388 Rashad Jennings RC .50 1.25
❑ 389 Rey Maualuga RC .75 2.00
❑ 390 Rhett Bomar RC .40 1.00
❑ 391 Richard Quinn RC .40 1.00
❑ 392 Shawn Nelson RC .40 1.00
❑ 393 Shonn Greene RC 1.00 2.50
❑ 394 Stephen McGee RC .50 1.25
❑ 395 Tom Brandstater RC .50 1.25
❑ 396 Tony Fiammetta RC .40 1.00
❑ 397 Travis Beckum RC .40 1.00
❑ 398 Tyrell Sutton RC .40 1.00
❑ 399 Tyson Jackson RC .50 1.25
❑ 400 Vontae Davis RC .50 1.25

2009 Score Inscriptions

❑ COMP.SET w/o RC's (300) 20.00 40.00
❑ 1 Adrian Wilson .20 .50
❑ 2 Anquan Boldin .25 .60
❑ 3 Dominique Rodgers-Cromartie .20 .50
❑ 4 Edgerrin James .25 .60
❑ 5 Kurt Warner .30 .75
❑ 6 Larry Fitzgerald .30 .75
❑ 7 Matt Leinart .25 .60
❑ 8 Steve Breaston .25 .60
❑ 9 Tim Hightower .25 .60
❑ 10 Chris Houston .20 .50
❑ 11 Curtis Lofton .20 .50
❑ 12 Harry Douglas .20 .50
❑ 13 Jerious Norwood .25 .60

❑ 14 John Abraham .20 .50
❑ 15 Matt Ryan .30 .75
❑ 16 Michael Jenkins .20 .50
❑ 17 Michael Turner .25 .60
❑ 18 Roddy White .25 .60
❑ 19 Demetrius Williams .20 .50
❑ 20 Derrick Mason .20 .50
❑ 21 Joe Flacco .30 .75
❑ 22 Le'Ron McClain .25 .60
❑ 23 Mark Clayton .20 .50
❑ 24 Ray Lewis .30 .75
❑ 25 Ray Rice .30 .75
❑ 26 Terrell Suggs .20 .50
❑ 27 Todd Heap .20 .50
❑ 28 Willis McGahee .25 .60
❑ 29 Derek Fine .20 .50
❑ 30 Fred Jackson .25 .60
❑ 31 James Hardy .25 .60
❑ 32 Lee Evans .25 .60
❑ 33 Leodis McKelvin .20 .50
❑ 34 Marshawn Lynch .25 .60
❑ 35 Paul Posluszny .25 .60
❑ 36 Steve Johnson .20 .50
❑ 37 Trent Edwards .25 .60
❑ 38 Charles Godfrey .20 .50
❑ 39 Chris Gamble .20 .50
❑ 40 Dante Rosario .20 .50
❑ 41 DeAngelo Williams .30 .75
❑ 42 Jake Delhomme .25 .60
❑ 43 Jon Beason .20 .50
❑ 44 Jonathan Stewart .25 .60
❑ 45 Muhsin Muhammad .25 .60
❑ 46 Steve Smith .25 .60
❑ 47 Alex Brown .20 .50
❑ 48 Brian Urlacher .30 .75
❑ 49 Desmond Clark .20 .50
❑ 50 Devin Hester .30 .75
❑ 51 Earl Bennett .25 .60
❑ 52 Greg Olsen .20 .50
❑ 53 Kyle Orton .25 .60
❑ 54 Lance Briggs .25 .60
❑ 55 Matt Forte .30 .75
❑ 56 Andre Caldwell .20 .50
❑ 57 Carson Palmer .30 .75
❑ 58 Cedric Benson .25 .60
❑ 59 Chad Ochocinco .25 .60
❑ 60 Dhani Jones .20 .50
❑ 61 Jerome Simpson .20 .50
❑ 62 Keith Rivers .20 .50
❑ 63 Reggie Kelly .20 .50
❑ 64 T.J. Houshmandzadeh .25 .60
❑ 65 Brady Quinn .25 .60
❑ 66 Braylon Edwards .25 .60
❑ 67 D'Qwell Jackson .20 .50
❑ 68 Jamal Lewis .25 .60
❑ 69 Jerome Harrison .25 .60
❑ 70 Josh Cribbs .30 .75
❑ 71 Kellen Winslow .25 .60
❑ 72 Shaun Rogers .20 .50
❑ 73 Steve Heiden .20 .50
❑ 74 DeMarcus Ware .25 .60
❑ 75 Felix Jones .30 .75
❑ 76 Jason Witten .30 .75
❑ 77 Marion Barber .30 .75
❑ 78 Patrick Crayton .20 .50
❑ 79 Roy Williams WR .25 .60
❑ 80 Tashard Choice .25 .60
❑ 81 Terrell Owens .30 .75
❑ 82 Terence Newman .20 .50
❑ 83 Tony Romo .50 1.25
❑ 84 Brandon Marshall .25 .60
❑ 85 Brandon Stokley .25 .60
❑ 86 Champ Bailey .25 .60
❑ 87 Daniel Graham .20 .50
❑ 88 Eddie Royal .25 .60
❑ 89 Jay Cutler .30 .75
❑ 90 Peyton Hillis .20 .50
❑ 91 D.J. Williams .20 .50
❑ 92 Tony Scheffler .20 .50
❑ 93 Calvin Johnson .30 .75
❑ 94 Daunte Culpepper .25 .60
❑ 95 Ernie Sims .20 .50
❑ 96 Jerome Felton .20 .50
❑ 97 Jordon Dizon .20 .50
❑ 98 Kevin Smith .25 .60
❑ 99 Paris Lenon .20 .50
❑ 100 Rudi Johnson .20 .50
❑ 101 Shaun McDonald .20 .50
❑ 102 Aaron Rodgers .30 .75
❑ 103 A.J. Hawk .25 .60
❑ 104 Brandon Jackson .25 .60
❑ 105 Donald Driver .25 .60
❑ 106 Donald Lee .20 .50
❑ 107 Greg Jennings .30 .75
❑ 108 James Jones .20 .50
❑ 109 Jermichael Finley .20 .50
❑ 110 Jordy Nelson .25 .60
❑ 111 Ryan Grant .25 .60
❑ 112 Amobi Okoye .20 .50
❑ 113 Andre Johnson .25 .60
❑ 114 Chester Pitts .20 .50
❑ 115 DeMeco Ryans .25 .60
❑ 116 Kevin Walter .25 .60
❑ 117 Kris Brown .20 .50
❑ 118 Mario Williams .25 .60
❑ 119 Matt Schaub .25 .60
❑ 120 Owen Daniels .20 .50
❑ 121 Steve Slaton .25 .60
❑ 122 Adam Vinatieri .25 .60
❑ 123 Anthony Gonzalez .25 .60
❑ 124 Dallas Clark .25 .60
❑ 125 Dominic Rhodes .20 .50
❑ 126 Dwight Freeney .25 .60
❑ 127 Joseph Addai .30 .75
❑ 128 Freddie Keiaho .20 .50
❑ 129 Mike Hart .25 .60
❑ 130 Peyton Manning .50 1.25
❑ 131 Reggie Wayne .25 .60
❑ 132 David Garrard .25 .60
❑ 133 Dennis Northcutt .20 .50
❑ 134 Derrick Harvey .20 .50
❑ 135 Josh Scobee .20 .50
❑ 136 Marcedes Lewis .20 .50
❑ 137 Mike Peterson .20 .50
❑ 138 Maurice Jones-Drew .25 .60
❑ 139 Quentin Groves .20 .50
❑ 140 Reggie Nelson .20 .50
❑ 141 Brian Williams .20 .50
❑ 142 Derrick Johnson .20 .50
❑ 143 Matt Cassel .25 .60
❑ 144 Dwayne Bowe .25 .60
❑ 145 Jamaal Charles .25 .60
❑ 146 Kolby Smith .20 .50
❑ 147 Larry Johnson .25 .60
❑ 148 Mark Bradley .20 .50
❑ 149 Tony Gonzalez .25 .60
❑ 150 Tyler Thigpen .20 .50
❑ 151 Anthony Fasano .20 .50
❑ 152 Chad Henne .30 .75
❑ 153 Chad Pennington .25 .60
❑ 154 Davone Bess .25 .60
❑ 155 Joey Porter .25 .60
❑ 156 Greg Camarillo .25 .60
❑ 157 Jake Long .20 .50
❑ 158 Ricky Williams .25 .60
❑ 159 Ronnie Brown .25 .60
❑ 160 Ted Ginn .25 .60
❑ 161 Adrian Peterson .60 1.50
❑ 162 Bernard Berrian .25 .60
❑ 163 Chad Greenway .20 .50
❑ 164 Chester Taylor .20 .50
❑ 165 Erin Henderson .20 .50
❑ 166 Jared Allen .30 .75
❑ 167 John David Booty .25 .60
❑ 168 Sidney Rice .25 .60
❑ 169 Tarvaris Jackson .25 .60
❑ 170 Visanthe Shiancoe .20 .50
❑ 171 Brandon Meriweather .20 .50
❑ 172 Jerod Mayo .25 .60
❑ 173 Kevin Faulk .20 .50
❑ 174 LaMont Jordan .20 .50
❑ 175 Laurence Maroney .25 .60
❑ 176 Randy Moss .30 .75
❑ 177 Tedy Bruschi .25 .60
❑ 178 Terrence Wheatley .20 .50
❑ 179 Tom Brady .50 1.25
❑ 180 Wes Welker .30 .75
❑ 181 Adrian Arrington .20 .50
❑ 182 Devery Henderson .20 .50
❑ 183 Drew Brees .30 .75
❑ 184 Jeremy Shockey .20 .50
❑ 185 Jonathan Vilma .20 .50
❑ 186 Lance Moore .25 .60
❑ 187 Marques Colston .25 .60
❑ 188 Pierre Thomas .25 .60
❑ 189 Reggie Bush .30 .75
❑ 190 Scott Shanle .20 .50
❑ 191 Ahmad Bradshaw .25 .60
❑ 192 Antonio Pierce .20 .50
❑ 193 Brandon Jacobs .25 .60
❑ 194 Derrick Ward .25 .60
❑ 195 Domenik Hixon .20 .50
❑ 196 Eli Manning .30 .75
❑ 197 Justin Tuck .25 .60
❑ 198 Kenny Phillips .20 .50
❑ 199 Kevin Boss .20 .50
❑ 200 Steve Smith USC .25 .60
❑ 201 Calvin Pace .20 .50
❑ 202 Chansi Stuckey .20 .50
❑ 203 Dustin Keller .20 .50
❑ 204 Jerricho Cotchery .20 .50
❑ 205 Kellen Clemens .20 .50
❑ 206 Laveranues Coles .25 .60
❑ 207 Leon Washington .25 .60
❑ 208 Thomas Jones .25 .60
❑ 209 Vernon Gholston .20 .50
❑ 210 Chaz Schilens .20 .50
❑ 211 Darren McFadden .30 .75
❑ 212 JaMarcus Russell .25 .60
❑ 213 Johnnie Lee Higgins .20 .50
❑ 214 Justin Fargas .20 .50
❑ 215 Michael Bush .25 .60
❑ 216 Nnamdi Asomugha .20 .50
❑ 217 Sebastian Janikowski .20 .50
❑ 218 Zach Miller .20 .50
❑ 219 Brian Westbrook .25 .60
❑ 220 Correll Buckhalter .20 .50
❑ 221 DeSean Jackson .25 .60
❑ 222 Donovan McNabb .30 .75
❑ 223 Greg Lewis .20 .50
❑ 224 Hank Baskett .20 .50
❑ 225 Kevin Curtis .20 .50
❑ 226 Reggie Brown .20 .50
❑ 227 Stewart Bradley .20 .50
❑ 228 Ben Roethlisberger .50 1.25
❑ 229 Heath Miller .25 .60
❑ 230 Hines Ward .25 .60
❑ 231 James Harrison .30 .75
❑ 232 Troy Polamalu .30 .75
❑ 233 Nate Washington .20 .50
❑ 234 Rashard Mendenhall .25 .60
❑ 235 Santonio Holmes .25 .60
❑ 236 Willie Parker .25 .60
❑ 237 Antonio Gates .25 .60
❑ 238 Chris Chambers .25 .60
❑ 239 Darren Sproles .25 .60
❑ 240 Eric Weddle .20 .50
❑ 241 Jacob Hester .20 .50
❑ 242 LaDainian Tomlinson .30 .75
❑ 243 Philip Rivers .30 .75
❑ 244 Shawne Merriman .25 .60
❑ 245 Vincent Jackson .25 .60
❑ 246 Brandon Jones .20 .50
❑ 247 Frank Gore .25 .60
❑ 248 Isaac Bruce .25 .60
❑ 249 Josh Morgan .20 .50
❑ 250 Michael Robinson .20 .50
❑ 251 Patrick Willis .25 .60
❑ 252 Reggie Smith .20 .50
❑ 253 Shaun Hill .20 .50
❑ 254 Vernon Davis .20 .50
❑ 255 Deion Branch .25 .60
❑ 256 John Carlson .25 .60
❑ 257 Julian Peterson .20 .50
❑ 258 Julius Jones .25 .60
❑ 259 Lofa Tatupu .25 .60
❑ 260 Matt Hasselbeck .25 .60
❑ 261 Nate Burleson .20 .50
❑ 262 Owen Schmitt .20 .50
❑ 263 T.J. Duckett .20 .50
❑ 264 Antonio Pittman .20 .50
❑ 265 Chris Long .25 .60
❑ 266 Donnie Avery .25 .60
❑ 267 Keenan Burton .20 .50
❑ 268 Marc Bulger .25 .60
❑ 269 Pisa Tinoisamoa .20 .50
❑ 270 Steven Jackson .25 .60
❑ 271 Torry Holt .25 .60
❑ 272 Antonio Bryant .25 .60
❑ 273 Aqib Talib .20 .50
❑ 274 Cadillac Williams .25 .60
❑ 275 Dexter Jackson .20 .50
❑ 276 Earnest Graham .20 .50
❑ 277 Gaines Adams .20 .50
❑ 278 Michael Clayton .20 .50
❑ 279 Ronde Barber .20 .50
❑ 280 Barrett Ruud .20 .50

❑ 281 Albert Haynesworth	.20	.50
❑ 282 Bo Scaife	.20	.50
❑ 283 Chris Johnson	.30	.75
❑ 284 Justin Gage	.20	.50
❑ 285 Keith Bulluck	.20	.50
❑ 286 Kerry Collins	.25	.60
❑ 287 LenDale White	.25	.60
❑ 288 Rob Bironas	.20	.50
❑ 289 Roydell Williams	.20	.50
❑ 290 Vince Young	.25	.60
❑ 291 Chris Cooley	.20	.50
❑ 292 Chris Horton	.25	.60
❑ 293 Clinton Portis	.25	.60
❑ 294 Colt Brennan	.25	.60
❑ 295 Devin Thomas	.20	.50
❑ 296 Jason Campbell	.25	.60
❑ 297 Kedric Golston	.30	.75
❑ 298 Ladell Betts	.20	.50
❑ 299 Malcolm Kelly	.20	.50
❑ 300 Santana Moss	.25	.60
❑ 301 Aaron Brown RC	1.25	3.00
❑ 302 Aaron Curry RC	1.50	4.00
❑ 303 Aaron Kelly RC	1.00	2.50
❑ 304 Aaron Maybin RC	1.25	3.00
❑ 305 Alphonso Smith RC	1.00	2.50
❑ 306 Andre Brown RC	1.00	2.50
❑ 307 Andre Smith RC	1.25	3.00
❑ 308 Anthony Hill RC	.75	2.00
❑ 309 Arian Foster RC	1.25	3.00
❑ 310 Austin Collie RC	2.50	6.00
❑ 311 B.J. Raji RC	1.50	4.00
❑ 312 Brandon Gibson RC	1.25	3.00
❑ 313 Brandon Pettigrew RC	1.50	4.00
❑ 314 Brandon Tate RC	1.00	2.50
❑ 315 Brian Cushing RC	1.50	4.00
❑ 316 Brian Hartline RC	1.25	3.00
❑ 317 Brian Orakpo RC	1.50	4.00
❑ 318 Brian Robiskie RC	1.25	3.00
❑ 319 Brooks Foster RC	1.00	2.50
❑ 320 Cameron Morrah RC	.75	2.00
❑ 321 Cedric Peerman RC	1.00	2.50
❑ 322 Chase Coffman RC	1.00	2.50
❑ 323 Chris Wells RC	3.00	8.00
❑ 324 Clay Matthews RC	2.00	5.00
❑ 325 Clint Sintim RC	1.25	3.00
❑ 326 Cornelius Ingram RC	.75	2.00
❑ 327 Curtis Painter RC	1.25	3.00
❑ 328 Darius Butler RC	1.25	3.00
❑ 329 Darius Passmore RC	1.00	2.50
❑ 330 Darrius Heyward-Bey RC	2.00	5.00
❑ 331 Davon Drew RC	1.00	2.50
❑ 332 Demetrius Byrd RC	1.00	2.50
❑ 333 Deon Butler RC	1.25	3.00
❑ 334 Derrick Williams RC	1.25	3.00
❑ 335 Devin Moore RC	1.00	2.50
❑ 336 Dominique Edison RC	.75	2.00
❑ 337 Donald Brown RC	2.50	6.00
❑ 338 Eugene Monroe RC	1.00	2.50
❑ 339 Everette Brown RC	1.25	3.00
❑ 340 Gartrell Johnson RC	1.00	2.50
❑ 341 Glen Coffee RC	1.50	4.00
❑ 342 Graham Harrell RC	1.25	3.00
❑ 343 Hakeem Nicks RC	2.50	6.00
❑ 344 Hunter Cantwell RC	1.25	3.00
❑ 345 Jairus Byrd RC	1.50	4.00
❑ 346 James Casey RC	1.00	2.50
❑ 347 James Davis RC	1.25	3.00
❑ 348 James Laurinaitis RC	1.50	4.00
❑ 349 Jared Cook RC	1.00	2.50
❑ 350 Jarett Dillard RC	1.25	3.00
❑ 351 Jason Smith RC	1.00	2.50
❑ 352 Javon Ringer RC	1.25	3.00
❑ 353 Jeremiah Johnson RC	1.25	3.00
❑ 354 Jeremy Childs RC	1.00	2.50
❑ 355 Jeremy Maclin RC	2.50	6.00
❑ 356 John Parker Wilson RC	1.25	3.00
❑ 357 Johnny Knox RC	2.00	5.00
❑ 358 Josh Freeman RC	2.50	6.00
❑ 359 Juaquin Iglesias RC	1.25	3.00
❑ 360 Keith Null RC	1.25	3.00
❑ 361 Kenny Britt RC	2.00	5.00
❑ 362 Kenny McKinley RC	1.25	3.00
❑ 363 Kevin Ogletree RC	1.25	3.00
❑ 364 Knowshon Moreno RC	3.00	8.00
❑ 365 Kory Sheets RC	1.00	2.50
❑ 366 Larry English RC	1.25	3.00
❑ 367 LeSean McCoy RC	2.50	6.00
❑ 368 Louis Murphy RC	1.25	3.00
❑ 369 Malcolm Jenkins RC	1.25	3.00
❑ 370 Mark Sanchez RC	5.00	12.00
❑ 371 Matthew Stafford RC	4.00	10.00
❑ 372 Michael Crabtree RC	3.00	8.00
❑ 373 Mike Goodson RC	1.25	3.00
❑ 374 Mike Thomas RC	1.25	3.00
❑ 375 Mike Wallace RC	2.50	6.00
❑ 376 Mohamed Massaquoi RC	1.25	3.00
❑ 377 Nate Davis RC	1.25	3.00
❑ 378 Nathan Brown RC	1.00	2.50
❑ 379 P.J. Hill RC	1.00	2.50
❑ 380 Pat White RC	2.00	5.00
❑ 381 Patrick Chung RC	1.25	3.00
❑ 382 Patrick Turner RC	1.00	2.50
❑ 383 Percy Harvin RC	4.00	10.00
❑ 384 Quan Cosby RC	1.00	2.50
❑ 385 Quinn Johnson RC	1.00	2.50
❑ 386 Quinten Lawrence RC	1.00	2.50
❑ 387 Ramses Barden RC	1.00	2.50
❑ 388 Rashad Jennings RC	1.25	3.00
❑ 389 Rey Maualuga RC	2.00	5.00
❑ 390 Rhett Bomar RC	1.00	2.50
❑ 391 Richard Quinn RC	1.00	2.50
❑ 392 Shawn Nelson RC	1.00	2.50
❑ 393 Shonn Greene RC	2.50	6.00
❑ 394 Stephen McGee RC	1.25	3.00
❑ 395 Tom Brandstater RC	1.25	3.00
❑ 396 Tony Fiammetta RC	1.00	2.50
❑ 397 Travis Beckum RC	1.00	2.50
❑ 398 Tyrell Sutton RC	1.00	2.50
❑ 399 Tyson Jackson RC	1.25	3.00
❑ 400 Vontae Davis RC	1.25	3.00

2006 Select

❑ COMP.SET w/o RC's (330)	25.00	50.00
❑ 331-430 RC PRINT RUN 599 SETS		
❑ 1 Kurt Warner	.30	.75
❑ 2 J.J. Arrington	.20	.50
❑ 3 Anquan Boldin	.25	.60
❑ 4 Larry Fitzgerald	.30	.75
❑ 5 Marcel Shipp	.20	.50
❑ 6 Bryant Johnson	.20	.50
❑ 7 Bertrand Berry	.20	.50
❑ 8 John Navarre	.20	.50
❑ 9 Michael Vick	.30	.75
❑ 10 Warrick Dunn	.25	.60
❑ 11 Roddy White	.25	.60
❑ 12 Alge Crumpler	.25	.60
❑ 13 T.J. Duckett	.20	.50
❑ 14 Michael Jenkins	.25	.60
❑ 15 DeAngelo Hall	.25	.60
❑ 16 Brian Finneran	.20	.50
❑ 17 Kyle Boller	.25	.60
❑ 18 Jamal Lewis	.25	.60
❑ 19 Chester Taylor	.25	.60
❑ 20 Derrick Mason	.25	.60
❑ 21 Mark Clayton	.25	.60
❑ 22 Todd Heap	.25	.60
❑ 23 Ray Lewis	.30	.75
❑ 24 Devard Darling	.20	.50
❑ 25 J.P. Losman	.25	.60
❑ 26 Willis McGahee	.30	.75
❑ 27 Lee Evans	.25	.60
❑ 28 Eric Moulds	.25	.60
❑ 29 Lawyer Milloy	.20	.50
❑ 30 Josh Reed	.20	.50
❑ 31 Kelly Holcomb	.20	.50
❑ 32 Jake Delhomme	.25	.60
❑ 33 DeShaun Foster	.25	.60
❑ 34 Steve Smith	.30	.75
❑ 35 Julius Peppers	.25	.60
❑ 36 Drew Carter	.20	.50
❑ 37 Chris Gamble	.20	.50
❑ 38 Stephen Davis	.25	.60
❑ 39 Keary Colbert	.25	.60
❑ 40 Nick Goings	.20	.50
❑ 41 Eric Shelton	.20	.50
❑ 42 Rex Grossman	.30	.75
❑ 43 Thomas Jones	.25	.60
❑ 44 Cedric Benson	.25	.60
❑ 45 Muhsin Muhammad	.25	.60
❑ 46 Brian Urlacher	.30	.75
❑ 47 Mark Bradley	.20	.50
❑ 48 Kyle Orton	.25	.60
❑ 49 Tommie Harris	.20	.50
❑ 50 Adrian Peterson	.25	.60
❑ 51 Bernard Berrian	.25	.60
❑ 52 Justin Gage	.20	.50
❑ 53 Carson Palmer	.30	.75
❑ 54 Rudi Johnson	.25	.60
❑ 55 Chad Johnson	.25	.60
❑ 56 T.J. Houshmandzadeh	.25	.60
❑ 57 Chris Henry	.20	.50
❑ 58 Chris Perry	.25	.60
❑ 59 Jon Kitna	.25	.60
❑ 60 Deltha O'Neal	.20	.50
❑ 61 Charlie Frye	.25	.60
❑ 62 Reuben Droughns	.25	.60
❑ 63 Braylon Edwards	.30	.75
❑ 64 Kellen Winslow	.30	.75
❑ 65 Antonio Bryant	.25	.60
❑ 66 Trent Dilfer	.25	.00
❑ 67 Dennis Northcutt	.20	.50
❑ 68 Drew Bledsoe	.30	.75
❑ 69 Julius Jones	.25	.60
❑ 70 Marion Barber	.30	.75
❑ 71 Terry Glenn	.25	.60
❑ 72 Keyshawn Johnson	.25	.60
❑ 73 Roy Williams S	.25	.60
❑ 74 Jason Witten	.30	.75
❑ 75 Terence Newman	.20	.50
❑ 76 Drew Henson	.20	.50
❑ 77 Patrick Crayton	.20	.50
❑ 78 Jake Plummer	.25	.60
❑ 79 Mike Anderson	.25	.60
❑ 80 Tatum Bell	.20	.50
❑ 81 Ashley Lelie	.20	.50
❑ 82 Rod Smith	.25	.60
❑ 83 D.J. Williams	.20	.50
❑ 84 Darius Watts	.20	.50
❑ 85 Ron Dayne	.25	.60
❑ 86 Jeb Putzier	.20	.50
❑ 87 Joey Harrington	.20	.50
❑ 88 Kevin Jones	.25	.60
❑ 89 Roy Williams WR	.30	.75
❑ 90 Mike Williams	.25	.60
❑ 91 Charles Rogers	.25	.60
❑ 92 Teddy Lehman	.20	.50
❑ 93 Marcus Pollard	.20	.50
❑ 94 Artose Pinner	.20	.50
❑ 95 Brett Favre	.60	1.50
❑ 96 Ahman Green	.25	.60
❑ 97 Najeh Davenport	.25	.60
❑ 98 Samkon Gado	.30	.75
❑ 99 Javon Walker	.25	.60
❑ 100 Donald Driver	.30	.75
❑ 101 Aaron Rodgers	.30	.75
❑ 102 Robert Ferguson	.20	.50
❑ 103 David Carr	.20	.50
❑ 104 Domanick Davis	.25	.60
❑ 105 Andre Johnson	.25	.60
❑ 106 Jabar Gaffney	.20	.50
❑ 107 Jonathan Wells	.20	.50
❑ 108 Vernand Morency	.20	.50
❑ 109 Corey Bradford	.20	.50
❑ 110 Jerome Mathis	.20	.50
❑ 111 Peyton Manning	.50	1.25
❑ 112 Edgerrin James	.25	.60
❑ 113 Marvin Harrison	.30	.75
❑ 114 Reggie Wayne	.25	.60
❑ 115 Dwight Freeney	.25	.60
❑ 116 Dallas Clark	.25	.60
❑ 117 Dominic Rhodes	.25	.60
❑ 118 Jim Sorgi	.20	.50
❑ 119 Brandon Stokley	.25	.60
❑ 120 Bob Sanders	.25	.60
❑ 121 Mike Doss	.20	.50
❑ 122 Marlin Jackson	.20	.50
❑ 123 Byron Leftwich	.25	.60
❑ 124 Fred Taylor	.25	.60
❑ 125 Jimmy Smith	.25	.60
❑ 126 Matt Jones	.25	.60
❑ 127 Ernest Wilford	.20	.50
❑ 128 Greg Jones	.20	.50
❑ 129 Mike Peterson	.20	.50
❑ 130 Reggie Williams	.25	.60

Card	Low	High
❑ 131 Rashean Mathis	.20	.50
❑ 132 Trent Green	.25	.60
❑ 133 Larry Johnson	.25	.60
❑ 134 Priest Holmes	.25	.60
❑ 135 Eddie Kennison	.20	.50
❑ 136 Tony Gonzalez	.25	.60
❑ 137 Kendrell Bell	.20	.50
❑ 138 Samie Parker	.20	.50
❑ 139 Dante Hall	.25	.60
❑ 140 Tony Richardson	.20	.50
❑ 141 Gus Frerotte	.20	.50
❑ 142 Ronnie Brown	.30	.75
❑ 143 Neil Rackers	.20	.50
❑ 144 Chris Chambers	.25	.60
❑ 145 Zach Thomas	.30	.75
❑ 146 Cliff Russell	.20	.50
❑ 147 David Boston	.20	.50
❑ 148 Wes Welker	.30	.75
❑ 149 Marty Booker	.20	.50
❑ 150 Randy McMichael	.20	.50
❑ 151 Daunte Culpepper	.30	.75
❑ 152 Mewelde Moore	.20	.50
❑ 153 Nate Burleson	.25	.60
❑ 154 Troy Williamson	.25	.60
❑ 155 Koren Robinson	.20	.50
❑ 156 Erasmus James	.20	.50
❑ 157 Marcus Robinson	.25	.60
❑ 158 E.J. Henderson	.20	.50
❑ 159 Brad Johnson	.25	.60
❑ 160 Michael Bennett	.20	.50
❑ 161 Travis Taylor	.20	.50
❑ 162 Tom Brady	.50	1.25
❑ 163 Corey Dillon	.25	.60
❑ 164 Deion Branch	.25	.60
❑ 165 Tedy Bruschi	.30	.75
❑ 166 Ben Watson	.20	.50
❑ 167 Daniel Graham	.20	.50
❑ 168 Bethel Johnson	.20	.50
❑ 169 Kevin Faulk	.25	.60
❑ 170 David Givens	.25	.60
❑ 171 Troy Brown	.20	.50
❑ 172 Aaron Brooks	.25	.60
❑ 173 Deuce McAllister	.25	.60
❑ 174 Joe Horn	.25	.60
❑ 175 Donte Stallworth	.25	.60
❑ 176 Antowain Smith	.20	.50
❑ 177 Devery Henderson	.20	.50
❑ 178 Eli Manning	.40	1.00
❑ 179 Tiki Barber	.30	.75
❑ 180 Plaxico Burress	.25	.60
❑ 181 Jeremy Shockey	.30	.75
❑ 182 Osi Umenyiora	.25	.60
❑ 183 Gibril Wilson	.20	.50
❑ 184 Brandon Jacobs	.30	.75
❑ 185 Michael Strahan	.25	.60
❑ 186 Will Allen	.20	.50
❑ 187 Amani Toomer	.25	.60
❑ 188 Chad Pennington	.25	.60
❑ 189 Curtis Martin	.30	.75
❑ 190 Laveranues Coles	.25	.60
❑ 191 Jonathan Vilma	.25	.60
❑ 192 Ty Law	.20	.50
❑ 193 Cedric Houston	.20	.50
❑ 194 Justin McCareins	.20	.50
❑ 195 Jerald Sowell	.20	.50
❑ 196 Josh Brown	.20	.50
❑ 197 LaMont Jordan	.25	.60
❑ 198 Randy Moss	.30	.75
❑ 199 Jerry Porter	.25	.60
❑ 200 Doug Gabriel	.20	.50
❑ 201 Johnnie Morant	.20	.50
❑ 202 Zack Crockett	.20	.50
❑ 203 Derrick Burgess	.20	.50
❑ 204 Donovan McNabb	.30	.75
❑ 205 Brian Westbrook	.25	.60
❑ 206 Reggie Brown	.20	.50
❑ 207 Terrell Owens	.30	.75
❑ 208 Ryan Moats	.25	.60
❑ 209 Correll Buckhalter	.20	.50
❑ 210 Jevon Kearse	.25	.60
❑ 211 L.J. Smith	.20	.50
❑ 212 Lamar Gordon	.20	.50
❑ 213 Greg Lewis	.20	.50
❑ 214 Ben Roethlisberger	.50	1.25
❑ 215 Willie Parker	.40	1.00
❑ 216 Jerome Bettis	.30	.75
❑ 217 Hines Ward	.30	.75
❑ 218 Troy Polamalu	.40	1.00
❑ 219 Heath Miller	.25	.60
❑ 220 Antwaan Randle El	.25	.60
❑ 221 Duce Staley	.20	.50
❑ 222 Cedrick Wilson	.20	.50
❑ 223 James Farrior	.20	.50
❑ 224 Drew Brees	.30	.75
❑ 225 LaDainian Tomlinson	.40	1.00
❑ 226 Keenan McCardell	.25	.60
❑ 227 Antonio Gates	.30	.75
❑ 228 Shawne Merriman	.25	.60
❑ 229 Philip Rivers	.30	.75
❑ 230 Vincent Jackson	.25	.60
❑ 231 Donnie Edwards	.20	.50
❑ 232 Eric Parker	.20	.50
❑ 233 Reche Caldwell	.20	.50
❑ 234 Alex Smith QB	.25	.60
❑ 235 Frank Gore	.30	.75
❑ 236 Brandon Lloyd	.25	.60
❑ 237 Kevan Barlow	.25	.60
❑ 238 Rashaun Woods	.20	.50
❑ 239 Arnaz Battle	.20	.50
❑ 240 Matt Hasselbeck	.25	.60
❑ 241 Shaun Alexander	.25	.60
❑ 242 Darrell Jackson	.25	.60
❑ 243 Jerramy Stevens	.25	.60
❑ 244 Lofa Tatupu	.25	.60
❑ 245 D.J. Hackett	.25	.60
❑ 246 Bobby Engram	.20	.50
❑ 247 Joe Jurevicius	.20	.50
❑ 248 Maurice Morris	.20	.50
❑ 249 Marc Bulger	.25	.60
❑ 250 Steven Jackson	.30	.75
❑ 251 Torry Holt	.25	.60
❑ 252 Isaac Bruce	.25	.60
❑ 253 Kevin Curtis	.25	.60
❑ 254 Marshall Faulk	.25	.60
❑ 255 Shaun McDonald	.20	.50
❑ 256 Chris Simms	.25	.60
❑ 257 Cadillac Williams	.30	.75
❑ 258 Joey Galloway	.25	.60
❑ 259 Michael Clayton	.25	.60
❑ 260 Derrick Brooks	.25	.60
❑ 261 Ronde Barber	.25	.60
❑ 262 Michael Pittman	.20	.50
❑ 263 Alex Smith TE	.20	.50
❑ 264 Simeon Rice	.20	.50
❑ 265 Steve McNair	.25	.60
❑ 266 Chris Brown	.25	.60
❑ 267 Drew Bennett	.25	.60
❑ 268 Brandon Jones	.20	.50
❑ 269 Adam Jones	.20	.50
❑ 270 Keith Bulluck	.20	.50
❑ 271 Ben Troupe	.20	.50
❑ 272 Jarrett Payton	.20	.50
❑ 273 Tyrone Calico	.20	.50
❑ 274 Bobby Wade	.20	.50
❑ 275 Troy Fleming	.20	.50
❑ 276 Mark Brunell	.25	.60
❑ 277 Clinton Portis	.30	.75
❑ 278 Santana Moss	.25	.60
❑ 279 Jason Campbell	.25	.60
❑ 280 Chris Cooley	.25	.60
❑ 281 Carlos Rogers	.20	.50
❑ 282 Ladell Betts	.25	.60
❑ 283 Patrick Ramsey	.25	.60
❑ 284 Taylor Jacobs	.20	.50
❑ 285 James Thrash	.20	.50
❑ 286 Adrian Wilson	.20	.50
❑ 287 London Fletcher	.20	.50
❑ 288 Lance Briggs	.25	.60
❑ 289 Robert Mathis	.20	.50
❑ 290 Rod Coleman	.20	.50
❑ 291 Bart Scott RC	1.00	2.50
❑ 292 Brian Moorman RC	.30	.75
❑ 293 Shayne Graham RC	.30	.75
❑ 294 Kevin Kaesviharn RC	.30	.75
❑ 295 Leigh Bodden RC	.40	1.00
❑ 296 Lousaka Polite RC	.30	.75
❑ 297 Todd Devoe RC	.50	1.25
❑ 298 Scottie Vines	.30	.75
❑ 299 Cullen Jenkins RC	.30	.75
❑ 300 Donovan Morgan RC	.30	.75
❑ 301 C.C. Brown	.30	.75
❑ 302 Demarcus Faggins RC	.30	.75
❑ 303 Shantee Orr RC	.30	.75
❑ 304 Vashon Pearson RC	.30	.75
❑ 305 Reggie Hayward RC	.30	.75
❑ 306 Paul Spicer RC	.30	.75
❑ 307 Kenny Wright RC	.30	.75
❑ 308 Rich Alexis RC	.30	.75
❑ 309 Terrence Melton RC	.30	.75
❑ 310 Willie Whitehead RC	.30	.75
❑ 311 Kendrick Clancy RC	.30	.75
❑ 312 Mark Brown RC	.30	.75
❑ 313 Tommy Kelly	.30	.75
❑ 314 Josh Parry RC	.30	.75
❑ 315 Malcom Floyd RC	.60	1.50
❑ 316 Mike Adams RC	.30	.75
❑ 317 Ben Emanuel RC	.30	.75
❑ 318 Brandon Moore RC	.30	.75
❑ 319 Chartric Darby RC	.30	.75
❑ 320 Bryce Fisher RC	.30	.75
❑ 321 D.D. Lewis RC	.30	.75
❑ 322 Jimmy Williams DB RC	.30	.75
❑ 323 Robert Pollard RC	.30	.75
❑ 324 Chris Johnson RC	.50	1.25
❑ 325 Edell Shepherd RC	.30	.75
❑ 326 O.J. Small RC	.30	.75
❑ 327 Brad Kassell RC	.30	.75
❑ 328 M.Leinart/R.Bush	1.25	3.00
❑ 329 M.Leinart/V.Young	1.25	3.00
❑ 330 White/Leinart/Bush	1.25	3.00
❑ 331 Matt Leinart RC	4.00	10.00
❑ 332 Chad Greenway RC	2.50	6.00
❑ 333 Devin Aromashodu RC	2.50	6.00
❑ 334 DeAngelo Williams RC	5.00	12.00
❑ 335 Travis Wilson RC	1.50	4.00
❑ 336 Leon Washington RC	3.00	8.00
❑ 337 Maurice Stovall RC	2.00	5.00
❑ 338 Michael Huff RC	2.50	6.00
❑ 339 Charlie Whitehurst RC	2.50	6.00
❑ 340 Vince Young RC	6.00	15.00
❑ 341 Jerious Norwood RC	2.50	6.00
❑ 342 D'Brickashaw Ferguson RC	2.50	6.00
❑ 343 Taurean Henderson RC	2.50	6.00
❑ 344 Dominique Byrd RC	2.00	5.00
❑ 345 Sinorice Moss RC	2.50	6.00
❑ 346 Martin Nance RC	2.00	5.00
❑ 347 Vernon Davis RC	2.50	6.00
❑ 348 Ko Simpson RC	2.00	5.00
❑ 349 Jerome Harrison RC	2.50	6.00
❑ 350 Jay Cutler RC	6.00	15.00
❑ 351 Alan Zemaitis RC	2.50	6.00
❑ 352 Haloti Ngata RC	2.50	6.00
❑ 353 Greg Lee RC	1.50	4.00
❑ 354 Laurence Maroney RC	3.00	8.00
❑ 355 Bobby Carpenter RC	2.00	5.00
❑ 356 Jonathan Orr RC	2.00	5.00
❑ 357 Marcedes Lewis RC	2.50	6.00
❑ 358 Brodrick Bunkley RC	2.00	5.00
❑ 359 Todd Watkins RC	1.50	4.00
❑ 360 Reggie Bush RC	6.00	15.00
❑ 361 Jimmy Williams RC	2.50	6.00
❑ 362 Maurice Drew RC	5.00	12.00
❑ 363 Mario Williams RC	3.00	8.00
❑ 364 Derek Hagan RC	2.00	5.00
❑ 365 Santonio Holmes RC	6.00	15.00
❑ 366 Tye Hill RC	2.00	5.00
❑ 367 Jason Avant RC	2.50	6.00
❑ 368 Tamba Hali RC	2.50	6.00
❑ 369 Joe Klopfenstein RC	2.00	5.00
❑ 370 LenDale White RC	3.00	8.00
❑ 371 DeMeco Ryans RC	3.00	8.00
❑ 372 Bruce Gradkowski RC	2.50	6.00
❑ 373 A.J. Hawk RC	4.00	10.00
❑ 374 Gabe Watson RC	1.50	4.00
❑ 375 Devin Hester RC	5.00	12.00
❑ 376 Demetrius Williams RC	2.00	5.00
❑ 377 Joseph Addai RC	3.00	8.00
❑ 378 Leonard Pope RC	2.50	6.00
❑ 379 Omar Jacobs RC	1.50	4.00
❑ 380 Brad Smith RC	2.50	6.00
❑ 381 Michael Robinson RC	2.00	5.00
❑ 382 Brodie Croyle RC	2.50	6.00
❑ 383 Anthony Fasano RC	2.50	6.00
❑ 384 Brian Calhoun RC	2.00	5.00
❑ 385 Chad Jackson RC	2.00	5.00
❑ 386 Drew Olson RC	1.50	4.00
❑ 387 Greg Jennings RC	4.00	10.00
❑ 388 Andre Hall RC	2.00	5.00
❑ 389 Ryan Gilbert RC	2.00	5.00
❑ 390 Tim Day RC	2.00	5.00
❑ 391 Brandon Williams RC	2.00	5.00
❑ 392 Mark Anderson RC	6.00	15.00
❑ 393 DonTrell Moore RC	2.00	5.00
❑ 394 Kellen Clemens RC	2.50	6.00
❑ 395 Ernie Sims RC	2.00	5.00
❑ 396 Cedric Humes RC	2.00	5.00
❑ 397 Brandon Kirsch RC	2.00	5.00

Card	Low	High
❑ 398 Tony Scheffler RC	2.50	6.00
❑ 399 Kelly Jennings RC	2.50	6.00
❑ 400 Manny Lawson RC	2.50	6.00
❑ 401 Terrence Whitehead RC	2.00	5.00
❑ 402 Marcus Vick RC	1.50	4.00
❑ 403 De'Arrius Howard RC	2.50	6.00
❑ 404 Wendell Mathis RC	2.00	5.00
❑ 405 Abdul Hodge RC	2.00	5.00
❑ 406 Owen Daniels RC	2.50	6.00
❑ 407 Mike Hass RC	2.50	6.00
❑ 408 Brett Elliott RC	2.50	6.00
❑ 409 Kamerion Wimbley RC	2.50	6.00
❑ 410 Jeremy Bloom RC	2.00	5.00
❑ 411 D.J. Shockley RC	2.00	5.00
❑ 412 Darnell Bing RC	2.00	5.00
❑ 413 Miles Austin RC	6.00	15.00
❑ 414 D'Qwell Jackson RC	2.00	5.00
❑ 415 Tarvaris Jackson RC	2.50	6.00
❑ 416 Mathias Kiwanuka RC	3.00	8.00
❑ 417 Mike Bell RC	2.50	6.00
❑ 418 Paul Pinegar RC	1.50	4.00
❑ 419 David Thomas RC	2.50	6.00
❑ 420 Hank Baskett RC	2.50	6.00
❑ 421 P.J. Daniels RC	1.50	4.00
❑ 422 Jon Alston RC	1.50	4.00
❑ 423 Reggie McNeal RC	2.00	5.00
❑ 424 Brandon Marshall RC	2.50	6.00
❑ 425 Gerald Riggs RC	2.00	5.00
❑ 426 Delanie Walker RC	2.00	5.00
❑ 427 Erik Meyer RC	2.00	5.00
❑ 428 Jeff Webb RC	2.00	5.00
❑ 429 Skyler Green RC	1.50	4.00
❑ 430 Thomas Howard RC	2.00	5.00

2007 Select

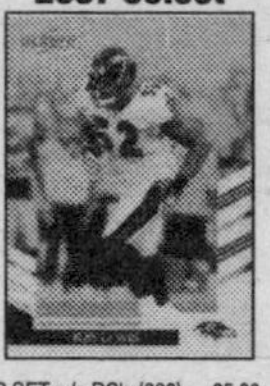

Card	Low	High
❑ COMP.SET w/o RC's (288)	25.00	50.00
❑ 1 Tony Romo	.50	1.25
❑ 2 Julius Jones	.25	.60
❑ 3 Terry Glenn	.25	.60
❑ 4 Terrell Owens	.30	.75
❑ 5 Jason Witten	.30	.75
❑ 6 Marion Barber	.30	.75
❑ 7 Patrick Crayton	.20	.50
❑ 8 Bradie James	.20	.50
❑ 9 DeMarcus Ware	.25	.60
❑ 10 Roy Williams S	.25	.60
❑ 11 Eli Manning	.30	.75
❑ 12 Plaxico Burress	.25	.60
❑ 13 Jeremy Shockey	.25	.60
❑ 14 Brandon Jacobs	.25	.60
❑ 15 Sinorice Moss	.25	.60
❑ 16 Antonio Pierce	.20	.50
❑ 17 David Tyree	.20	.50
❑ 18 Donovan McNabb	.30	.75
❑ 19 Brian Westbrook	.25	.60
❑ 20 Reggie Brown	.20	.50
❑ 21 L.J. Smith	.20	.50
❑ 22 Hank Baskett	.25	.60
❑ 23 Jeremiah Trotter	.20	.50
❑ 24 Trent Cole	.20	.50
❑ 25 Lito Sheppard	.20	.50
❑ 26 Jason Campbell	.25	.60
❑ 27 Clinton Portis	.25	.60
❑ 28 Santana Moss	.25	.60
❑ 29 Brandon Lloyd	.25	.60
❑ 30 Chris Cooley	.25	.60
❑ 31 Sean Taylor	.20	.50
❑ 32 Lemar Marshall	.20	.50
❑ 33 Ladell Betts	.20	.50
❑ 34 London Fletcher	.20	.50
❑ 35 Rex Grossman	.25	.60
❑ 36 Cedric Benson	.25	.60
❑ 37 Muhsin Muhammad	.25	.60
❑ 38 Bernard Berrian	.20	.50
❑ 39 Desmond Clark	.20	.50
❑ 40 Lance Briggs	.20	.50

Card	Low	High
❑ 41 Robbie Gould	.20	.50
❑ 42 Devin Hester	.30	.75
❑ 43 Mark Anderson	.25	.60
❑ 44 Brian Urlacher	.30	.75
❑ 45 Jon Kitna	.20	.50
❑ 46 Kevin Jones	.20	.50
❑ 47 Roy Williams WR	.25	.60
❑ 48 Mike Furrey	.25	.60
❑ 49 Cory Redding	.20	.50
❑ 50 Ernie Sims	.20	.50
❑ 51 Tatum Bell	.20	.50
❑ 52 Brian Calhoun	.20	.50
❑ 53 Brett Favre	.60	1.50
❑ 54 Vernand Morency	.25	.60
❑ 55 Donald Driver	.30	.75
❑ 56 Greg Jennings	.25	.60
❑ 57 Aaron Kampman	.25	.60
❑ 58 Charles Woodson	.25	.60
❑ 59 A.J. Hawk	.30	.75
❑ 60 Nick Barnett	.20	.50
❑ 61 Aaron Rodgers	.30	.75
❑ 62 Tarvaris Jackson	.25	.60
❑ 63 Chester Taylor	.20	.50
❑ 64 Troy Williamson	.20	.50
❑ 65 Jim Kleinsasser	.20	.50
❑ 66 Dwight Smith	.20	.50
❑ 67 Antoine Winfield	.20	.50
❑ 68 E.J. Henderson	.20	.50
❑ 69 Mewelde Moore	.20	.50
❑ 70 Michael Vick	.30	.75
❑ 71 Warrick Dunn	.25	.60
❑ 72 Joe Horn	.25	.60
❑ 73 Michael Jenkins	.25	.60
❑ 74 Alge Crumpler	.25	.60
❑ 75 DeAngelo Hall	.25	.60
❑ 76 Keith Brooking	.20	.50
❑ 77 Lawyer Milloy	.20	.50
❑ 78 Jerious Norwood	.25	.60
❑ 79 Matt Schaub	.25	.60
❑ 80 Jake Delhomme	.25	.60
❑ 81 DeShaun Foster	.25	.60
❑ 82 Steve Smith	.25	.60
❑ 83 Keyshawn Johnson	.25	.60
❑ 84 Julius Peppers	.25	.60
❑ 85 DeAngelo Williams	.30	.75
❑ 86 Chris Draft	.20	.50
❑ 87 Drew Brees	.30	.75
❑ 88 Deuce McAllister	.25	.60
❑ 89 Scott Fujita	.20	.50
❑ 90 Marques Colston	.30	.75
❑ 91 Terrance Copper	.25	.60
❑ 92 Will Smith	.20	.50
❑ 93 Charles Grant	.20	.50
❑ 94 Devery Henderson	.20	.50
❑ 95 Reggie Bush	.40	1.00
❑ 96 Jeff Garcia	.25	.60
❑ 97 Cadillac Williams	.25	.60
❑ 98 Joey Galloway	.25	.60
❑ 99 Michael Clayton	.25	.60
❑ 100 Alex Smith TE	.20	.50
❑ 101 Ronde Barber	.20	.50
❑ 102 Jermaine Phillips	.20	.50
❑ 103 Derrick Brooks	.25	.60
❑ 104 Matt Leinart	.30	.75
❑ 105 Edgerrin James	.25	.60
❑ 106 Anquan Boldin	.25	.60
❑ 107 Larry Fitzgerald	.30	.75
❑ 108 Neil Rackers	.20	.50
❑ 109 Adrian Wilson	.20	.50
❑ 110 Karlos Dansby	.20	.50
❑ 111 Chike Okeafor	.20	.50
❑ 112 Marc Bulger	.25	.60
❑ 113 Steven Jackson	.30	.75
❑ 114 Torry Holt	.25	.60
❑ 115 Isaac Bruce	.25	.60
❑ 116 Joe Klopfenstein	.20	.50
❑ 117 Randy McMichael	.20	.50
❑ 118 Will Witherspoon	.20	.50
❑ 119 Drew Bennett	.20	.50
❑ 120 Alex Smith QB	.30	.75
❑ 121 Frank Gore	.30	.75
❑ 122 Arnaz Battle	.20	.50
❑ 123 Ashley Lelie	.25	.60
❑ 124 Vernon Davis	.25	.60
❑ 125 Walt Harris	.20	.50
❑ 126 Brandon Moore	.20	.50
❑ 127 Nate Clements	.20	.50
❑ 128 Matt Hasselbeck	.25	.60
❑ 129 Shaun Alexander	.25	.60

Card	Low	High
❑ 130 Deion Branch	.25	.60
❑ 131 Darrell Jackson	.25	.60
❑ 132 Nate Burleson	.20	.50
❑ 133 Julian Peterson	.20	.50
❑ 134 Lofa Tatupu	.25	.60
❑ 135 Mack Strong	.20	.50
❑ 136 Josh Brown	.20	.50
❑ 137 J.P. Losman	.20	.50
❑ 138 Anthony Thomas	.20	.50
❑ 139 Lee Evans	.25	.60
❑ 140 Josh Reed	.20	.50
❑ 141 Roscoe Parrish	.20	.50
❑ 142 Aaron Schobel	.20	.50
❑ 143 Donte Whitner	.20	.50
❑ 144 Shaud Williams	.20	.50
❑ 145 Daunte Culpepper	.25	.60
❑ 146 Ronnie Brown	.25	.60
❑ 147 Chris Chambers	.25	.60
❑ 148 Marty Booker	.20	.50
❑ 149 Derek Hagan	.20	.50
❑ 150 Jason Taylor	.20	.50
❑ 151 Vonnie Holliday	.20	.50
❑ 152 Zach Thomas	.25	.60
❑ 153 Channing Crowder	.20	.50
❑ 154 Joey Porter	.20	.50
❑ 155 Tom Brady	.60	1.50
❑ 156 Laurence Maroney	.30	.75
❑ 157 Chad Jackson	.20	.50
❑ 158 Wes Welker	.30	.75
❑ 159 Ben Watson	.20	.50
❑ 160 Donte Stallworth	.25	.60
❑ 161 Rosevelt Colvin	.20	.50
❑ 162 Ty Warren	.20	.50
❑ 163 Asante Samuel	.20	.50
❑ 164 Adalius Thomas	.20	.50
❑ 165 Tedy Bruschi	.30	.75
❑ 166 Chad Pennington	.25	.60
❑ 167 Thomas Jones	.25	.60
❑ 168 Laveranues Coles	.25	.60
❑ 169 Jerricho Cotchery	.20	.50
❑ 170 Chris Baker	.20	.50
❑ 171 Bryan Thomas	.20	.50
❑ 172 Leon Washington	.25	.60
❑ 173 Jonathan Vilma	.25	.60
❑ 174 Eric Barton	.20	.50
❑ 175 Erik Coleman	.20	.50
❑ 176 Steve McNair	.25	.60
❑ 177 Willis McGahee	.25	.60
❑ 178 Derrick Mason	.20	.50
❑ 179 Demetrius Williams	.20	.50
❑ 180 Todd Heap	.20	.50
❑ 181 Ray Lewis	.30	.75
❑ 182 Trevor Pryce	.20	.50
❑ 183 Bart Scott	.25	.60
❑ 184 Terrell Suggs	.20	.50
❑ 185 Mark Clayton	.25	.60
❑ 186 Carson Palmer	.30	.75
❑ 187 Rudi Johnson	.25	.60
❑ 188 Chad Johnson	.25	.60
❑ 189 T.J. Houshmandzadeh	.25	.60
❑ 190 Robert Geathers	.20	.50
❑ 191 Justin Smith	.20	.50
❑ 192 Tory James	.20	.50
❑ 193 Landon Johnson	.20	.50
❑ 194 Shayne Graham	.20	.50
❑ 195 Charlie Frye	.25	.60
❑ 196 Reuben Droughns	.25	.60
❑ 197 Braylon Edwards	.25	.60
❑ 198 Travis Wilson	.20	.50
❑ 199 Kellen Winslow	.25	.60
❑ 200 Kamerion Wimbley	.20	.50
❑ 201 Sean Jones		
❑ 202 Andra Davis	.20	.50
❑ 203 Jamal Lewis	.25	.60
❑ 204 Ben Roethlisberger	.40	1.00
❑ 205 Willie Parker	.25	.60
❑ 206 Hines Ward	.30	.75
❑ 207 Santonio Holmes	.25	.60
❑ 208 Heath Miller	.20	.50
❑ 209 Troy Polamalu	.30	.75
❑ 210 James Farrior	.20	.50
❑ 211 Cedrick Wilson	.20	.50
❑ 212 Dunta Robinson	.20	.50
❑ 213 Ahman Green	.25	.60
❑ 214 Andre Johnson	.25	.60
❑ 215 Jerome Mathis	.20	.50
❑ 216 Owen Daniels	.20	.50
❑ 217 DeMeco Ryans	.25	.60
❑ 218 Wali Lundy	.20	.50

Card	Low	High
❑ 219 Mario Williams	.25	.60
❑ 220 Peyton Manning	.50	1.25
❑ 221 Joseph Addai	.30	.75
❑ 222 Marvin Harrison	.30	.75
❑ 223 Reggie Wayne	.25	.60
❑ 224 Dallas Clark	.20	.50
❑ 225 Robert Mathis	.20	.50
❑ 226 Cato June	.20	.50
❑ 227 Adam Vinatieri	.25	.60
❑ 228 Bob Sanders	.25	.60
❑ 229 Dwight Freeney	.25	.60
❑ 230 Byron Leftwich	.25	.60
❑ 231 Fred Taylor	.25	.60
❑ 232 Matt Jones	.25	.60
❑ 233 Reggie Williams	.25	.60
❑ 234 Marcedes Lewis	.20	.50
❑ 235 Bobby McCray	.20	.50
❑ 236 Rashean Mathis	.20	.50
❑ 237 Maurice Jones-Drew	.30	.75
❑ 238 Ernest Wilford	.20	.50
❑ 239 Daryl Smith	.20	.50
❑ 240 Vince Young	.30	.75
❑ 241 LenDale White	.25	.60
❑ 242 Brandon Jones	.20	.50
❑ 243 Bo Scaife	.20	.50
❑ 244 Keith Bulluck	.20	.50
❑ 245 Chris Hope	.20	.50
❑ 246 Kyle Vanden Bosch	.20	.50
❑ 247 Roydell Williams	.20	.50
❑ 248 Jay Cutler	.30	.75
❑ 249 Travis Henry	.25	.60
❑ 250 Javon Walker	.25	.60
❑ 251 Rod Smith	.25	.60
❑ 252 Tony Scheffler	.25	.60
❑ 253 Elvis Dumervil	.20	.50
❑ 254 Champ Bailey	.25	.60
❑ 255 Mike Bell	.25	.60
❑ 256 Brandon Marshall	.25	.60
❑ 257 Al Wilson	.20	.50
❑ 258 Trent Green	.25	.60
❑ 259 Larry Johnson	.25	.60
❑ 260 Eddie Kennison	.20	.50
❑ 261 Samie Parker	.20	.50
❑ 262 Tony Gonzalez	.25	.60
❑ 263 Jared Allen	.30	.75
❑ 264 Kawika Mitchell	.20	.50
❑ 265 Tamba Hali	.20	.50
❑ 266 Dante Hall	.25	.60
❑ 267 Brodie Croyle	.25	.60
❑ 268 Andrew Walter	.20	.50
❑ 269 LaMont Jordan	.25	.60
❑ 270 Dominic Rhodes	.25	.60
❑ 271 Randy Moss	.30	.75
❑ 272 Ronald Curry	.25	.60
❑ 273 Courtney Anderson	.20	.50
❑ 274 Derrick Burgess	.20	.50
❑ 275 Warren Sapp	.25	.60
❑ 276 Michael Huff	.25	.60
❑ 277 Thomas Howard	.20	.50
❑ 278 Kirk Morrison	.20	.50
❑ 279 Philip Rivers	.30	.75
❑ 280 LaDainian Tomlinson	.40	1.00
❑ 281 Vincent Jackson	.20	.50
❑ 282 Lorenzo Neal	.20	.50
❑ 283 Antonio Gates	.25	.60
❑ 284 Shawne Merriman	.25	.60
❑ 285 Shaun Phillips	.20	.50
❑ 286 Michael Turner	.30	.75
❑ 287 Jamal Williams	.20	.50
❑ 288 Nate Kaeding	.20	.50
❑ 289 Michael Okwo RC	.60	1.50
❑ 290 Gary Russell RC	.60	1.50
❑ 291 Josh Wilson RC	.60	1.50
❑ 292 Thomas Clayton RC	.60	1.50
❑ 293 Jerard Rabb RC	.60	1.50
❑ 294 Roy Hall RC	.75	2.00
❑ 295 LaMarr Woodley RC	.75	2.00
❑ 296 Eric Wright RC	.75	2.00
❑ 297 Dan Bazuin RC	.60	1.50
❑ 298 A.J. Davis RC	.50	1.25
❑ 299 Buster Davis RC	.60	1.50
❑ 300 Stewart Bradley RC	.75	2.00
❑ 301 Toby Korrodi RC	.60	1.50
❑ 302 Marcus McCauley RC	.60	1.50
❑ 303 DeMarcus Tank Tyler RC	.60	1.50
❑ 304 Jon Abbate RC	.50	1.25
❑ 305 Ikaika Alama-Francis RC	.75	2.00
❑ 306 Tim Crowder RC	.75	2.00
❑ 307 D'Juan Woods RC	.60	1.50
❑ 308 Tim Shaw RC	.60	1.50
❑ 309 Fred Bennett RC	.50	1.25
❑ 310 Victor Abiamiri RC	.75	2.00
❑ 311 Eric Weddle RC	.60	1.50
❑ 312 Danny Ware RC	.75	2.00
❑ 313 Quentin Moses RC	.60	1.50
❑ 314 Ryan McBean RC	.75	2.00
❑ 315 David Harris RC	.60	1.50
❑ 316 David Irons RC	.50	1.25
❑ 317 Syndric Steptoe RC	.60	1.50
❑ 318 Eric Frampton RC	.60	1.50
❑ 319 Jemalle Cornelius RC	.60	1.50
❑ 320 Earl Everett RC	.60	1.50
❑ 321 Alonzo Coleman RC	.60	1.50
❑ 322 Josh Gattis RC	.50	1.25
❑ 323 Zak DeOssie RC	.60	1.50
❑ 324 Jon Beason RC	.75	2.00
❑ 325 Joe Staley RC	.60	1.50
❑ 326 Aaron Rouse RC	.75	2.00
❑ 327 Reggie Ball RC	.60	1.50
❑ 328 Rufus Alexander RC	.75	2.00
❑ 329 Daymeion Hughes RC	.60	1.50
❑ 330 Justin Durant RC	.60	1.50
❑ 331 JaMarcus Russell RC	3.00	8.00
❑ 332 Paul Williams RC	2.00	5.00
❑ 333 Kenny Irons RC	2.50	6.00
❑ 334 Chris Davis RC	2.00	5.00
❑ 335 Darius Walker RC	2.00	5.00
❑ 336 Dwayne Bowe RC	4.00	10.00
❑ 337 Isaiah Stanback RC	2.50	6.00
❑ 338 Leon Hall RC	2.50	6.00
❑ 339 Sidney Rice RC	5.00	12.00
❑ 340 Amobi Okoye RC	2.50	6.00
❑ 341 Adrian Peterson RC	20.00	50.00
❑ 342 LaRon Landry RC	3.00	8.00
❑ 343 Lorenzo Booker RC	2.50	6.00
❑ 344 Craig Buster Davis RC	2.50	6.00
❑ 345 Mike Walker RC	2.50	6.00
❑ 346 Zach Miller RC	2.50	6.00
❑ 347 Levi Brown RC	2.50	6.00
❑ 348 Brian Leonard RC	2.00	5.00
❑ 349 Aundrae Allison RC	2.00	5.00
❑ 350 Brandon Siler RC	2.00	5.00
❑ 351 Calvin Johnson RC	6.00	15.00
❑ 352 Gaines Adams RC	2.50	6.00
❑ 353 Anthony Gonzalez RC	3.00	8.00
❑ 354 John Beck RC	2.50	6.00
❑ 355 Joe Thomas RC	2.50	6.00
❑ 356 Michael Bush RC	2.50	6.00
❑ 357 Courtney Taylor RC	2.00	5.00
❑ 358 Lawrence Timmons RC	2.50	6.00
❑ 359 Drew Stanton RC	2.00	5.00
❑ 360 Chansi Stuckey RC	2.50	6.00
❑ 361 Greg Olsen RC	3.00	8.00
❑ 362 Rhema McKnight RC	2.00	5.00
❑ 363 Antonio Pittman RC	2.50	6.00
❑ 364 Kevin Kolb RC	4.00	10.00
❑ 365 Alan Branch RC	2.00	5.00
❑ 366 Robert Meachem RC	2.50	6.00
❑ 367 Troy Smith RC	3.00	8.00
❑ 368 Jamaal Anderson RC	2.00	5.00
❑ 369 Tony Hunt RC	2.50	6.00
❑ 370 David Clowney RC	2.50	6.00
❑ 371 Brady Quinn RC	5.00	12.00
❑ 372 Michael Griffin RC	2.50	6.00
❑ 373 Jared Zabransky RC	2.50	6.00
❑ 374 Jason Hill RC	2.50	6.00
❑ 375 Trent Edwards RC	4.00	10.00
❑ 376 Dwayne Jarrett RC	2.50	6.00
❑ 377 DeShawn Wynn RC	2.50	6.00
❑ 378 Patrick Willis RC	4.00	10.00
❑ 379 Steve Smith USC RC	4.00	10.00
❑ 380 David Ball RC	1.50	4.00
❑ 381 Marshawn Lynch RC	4.00	10.00
❑ 382 Paul Posluszny RC	3.00	8.00
❑ 383 Johnnie Lee Higgins RC	2.50	6.00
❑ 384 Kolby Smith RC	2.50	6.00
❑ 385 Ted Ginn Jr. RC	4.00	10.00
❑ 386 Adam Carriker RC	2.00	5.00
❑ 387 Tyler Palko RC	2.00	5.00
❑ 388 Joel Filani RC	2.00	5.00
❑ 389 Garrett Wolfe RC	2.50	6.00
❑ 390 Ryne Robinson RC	2.00	5.00
❑ 391 Reggie Nelson RC	2.00	5.00
❑ 392 Dallas Baker RC	2.00	5.00
❑ 393 Dwayne Wright RC	2.00	5.00
❑ 394 Scott Chandler RC	2.00	5.00
❑ 395 Jordan Kent RC	2.00	5.00
❑ 396 Jarvis Moss RC	2.50	6.00
❑ 397 Jonathan Wade RC	2.00	5.00
❑ 398 Ben Grubbs RC	2.00	5.00
❑ 399 Jason Snelling RC	2.00	5.00
❑ 400 Jeff Rowe RC	2.00	5.00
❑ 401 Aaron Ross RC	2.50	6.00
❑ 402 Jarrett Hicks RC	2.00	5.00
❑ 403 Chris Henry RC	2.00	5.00
❑ 404 James Jones RC	2.50	6.00
❑ 405 Matt Spaeth RC	2.50	6.00
❑ 406 Brandon Meriweather RC	2.50	6.00
❑ 407 Nate Ilaoa RC	2.50	6.00
❑ 408 Brandon Myles RC	2.00	5.00
❑ 409 Ray McDonald RC	2.00	5.00
❑ 410 Chris Leak RC	2.00	5.00
❑ 411 Darrelle Revis RC	3.00	8.00
❑ 412 Ahmad Bradshaw RC	3.00	8.00
❑ 413 Tyler Thigpen RC	2.50	6.00
❑ 414 Justise Hairston RC	2.00	5.00
❑ 415 Charles Johnson RC	1.50	4.00
❑ 416 Anthony Spencer RC	2.50	6.00
❑ 417 Legedu Naanee RC	2.50	6.00
❑ 418 Kenneth Darby RC	2.50	6.00
❑ 419 Steve Breaston RC	2.50	6.00
❑ 420 Ben Patrick RC	2.00	5.00
❑ 421 Chris Houston RC	2.00	5.00
❑ 422 Jordan Palmer RC	2.50	6.00
❑ 423 Laurent Robinson RC	2.50	6.00
❑ 424 Selvin Young RC	2.50	6.00
❑ 425 Justin Harrell RC	2.50	6.00
❑ 426 Sabby Piscitelli RC	2.50	6.00
❑ 427 Yamon Figurs RC	1.50	4.00
❑ 428 Brandon Jackson RC	2.50	6.00
❑ 429 Jacoby Jones RC	2.50	6.00
❑ 430 H.B. Blades RC	2.00	5.00

2008 Select

Card	Low	High
❑ COMP.SET w/o RC's (330)	25.00	50.00
❑ 1 Matt Leinart	.30	.75
❑ 2 Kurt Warner	.30	.75
❑ 3 Larry Fitzgerald	.30	.75
❑ 4 Anquan Boldin	.25	.60
❑ 5 Edgerrin James	.25	.60
❑ 6 Neil Rackers	.20	.50
❑ 7 Steve Breaston	.20	.50
❑ 8 Antrel Rolle	.20	.50
❑ 9 Karlos Dansby	.20	.50
❑ 10 Joey Harrington	.25	.60
❑ 11 Jerious Norwood	.25	.60
❑ 12 Roddy White	.25	.60
❑ 13 Michael Jenkins	.20	.50
❑ 14 Joe Horn	.25	.60
❑ 15 Keith Brooking	.20	.50
❑ 16 Lawyer Milloy	.20	.50
❑ 17 John Abraham	.20	.50
❑ 18 Michael Turner	.30	.75
❑ 19 Troy Smith	.25	.60
❑ 20 Willis McGahee	.25	.60
❑ 21 Musa Smith	.20	.50
❑ 22 Derrick Mason	.20	.50
❑ 23 Mark Clayton	.25	.60
❑ 24 Bart Scott	.20	.50
❑ 25 Demetrius Williams	.20	.50
❑ 26 Yamon Figurs	.20	.50
❑ 27 Ray Lewis	.30	.75
❑ 28 Terrell Suggs	.20	.50
❑ 29 Ed Reed	.25	.60
❑ 30 Trent Edwards	.30	.75
❑ 31 Marshawn Lynch	.30	.75
❑ 32 Lee Evans	.25	.60
❑ 33 Roscoe Parrish	.20	.50
❑ 34 Paul Posluszny	.25	.60
❑ 35 John DiGiorgio RC	.25	.60
❑ 36 Angelo Crowell	.20	.50
❑ 37 Jabari Greer RC	.20	.50
❑ 38 Chris Kelsay	.20	.50
❑ 39 Fred Jackson RC	.40	1.00

❑ 40 Matt Moore .25 .60
❑ 41 Steve Smith .25 .60
❑ 42 DeAngelo Williams .25 .60
❑ 43 Brad Hoover .20 .50
❑ 44 Dante Rosario .20 .50
❑ 45 Julius Peppers .25 .60
❑ 46 Jon Beason .20 .50
❑ 47 Chris Harris .20 .50
❑ 48 D.J. Hackett .20 .50
❑ 49 Jake Delhomme .25 .60
❑ 50 Adrian Peterson .20 .50
❑ 51 Mark Anderson .20 .50
❑ 52 Desmond Clark .20 .50
❑ 53 Greg Olsen .25 .60
❑ 54 Devin Hester .30 .75
❑ 55 Brian Urlacher .30 .75
❑ 56 Jason McKie RC .25 .60
❑ 57 Lance Briggs .20 .50
❑ 58 Rex Grossman .25 .60
❑ 59 Carson Palmer .30 .75
❑ 60 Chad Johnson .25 .60
❑ 61 T.J. Houshmandzadeh .25 .60
❑ 62 Rudi Johnson .25 .60
❑ 63 Kenny Watson .20 .50
❑ 64 Dhani Jones .20 .50
❑ 65 Leon Hall .20 .50
❑ 66 Johnathan Joseph .20 .50
❑ 67 Derek Anderson .25 .60
❑ 68 Brady Quinn .30 .75
❑ 69 Jamal Lewis .25 .60
❑ 70 Josh Cribbs .30 .75
❑ 71 Kellen Winslow .25 .60
❑ 72 Braylon Edwards .25 .60
❑ 73 Joe Jurevicius .20 .50
❑ 74 D'Qwell Jackson .20 .50
❑ 75 Leigh Bodden .20 .50
❑ 76 Sean Jones .20 .50
❑ 77 Tony Romo .50 1.25
❑ 78 Terrell Owens .30 .75
❑ 79 Marion Barber .30 .75
❑ 80 Jason Witten .30 .75
❑ 81 Patrick Crayton .25 .60
❑ 82 Anthony Henry .20 .50
❑ 83 DeMarcus Ware .25 .60
❑ 84 Terence Newman .20 .50
❑ 85 Greg Ellis .20 .50
❑ 86 Zach Thomas .25 .60
❑ 87 Keary Colbert .20 .50
❑ 88 Jay Cutler .30 .75
❑ 89 Tony Scheffler .20 .50
❑ 90 Selvin Young .20 .50
❑ 91 Brandon Marshall .25 .60
❑ 92 Brandon Stokley .25 .60
❑ 93 Champ Bailey .20 .50
❑ 94 John Lynch .25 .60
❑ 95 Dre Bly .20 .50
❑ 96 Elvis Dumervil .20 .50
❑ 97 Jon Kitna .25 .60
❑ 98 Tatum Bell .20 .50
❑ 99 Shaun McDonald .20 .50
❑ 100 Roy Williams WR .25 .60
❑ 101 Calvin Johnson .30 .75
❑ 102 Mike Furrey .25 .60
❑ 103 Ernie Sims .20 .50
❑ 104 Aveion Cason .20 .50
❑ 105 Aaron Rodgers .30 .75
❑ 106 Brett Favre .75 2.00
❑ 107 Ryan Grant .30 .75
❑ 108 Greg Jennings .25 .60
❑ 109 Donald Driver .25 .60
❑ 110 Donald Lee .25 .60
❑ 111 James Jones .20 .50
❑ 112 Al Harris .20 .50
❑ 113 Nick Barnett .20 .50
❑ 114 Charles Woodson .25 .60
❑ 115 Aaron Kampman .25 .60
❑ 116 Mason Crosby .20 .50
❑ 117 Matt Schaub .25 .60
❑ 118 Ahman Green .25 .60
❑ 119 Andre Johnson .25 .60
❑ 120 Kevin Walter .25 .60
❑ 121 Owen Daniels .20 .50
❑ 122 Andre Davis .20 .50
❑ 123 DeMeco Ryans .25 .60
❑ 124 Mario Williams .25 .60
❑ 125 Dunta Robinson .20 .50
❑ 126 Chris Brown .20 .50
❑ 127 Peyton Manning .50 1.25
❑ 128 Joseph Addai .30 .75
❑ 129 Marvin Harrison .30 .75
❑ 130 Reggie Wayne .25 .60
❑ 131 Dallas Clark .25 .60
❑ 132 Anthony Gonzalez .25 .60
❑ 133 Kenton Keith .20 .50
❑ 134 Adam Vinatieri .30 .75
❑ 135 Bob Sanders .25 .60
❑ 136 Kelvin Hayden .20 .50
❑ 137 Freddie Keiaho .20 .50
❑ 138 David Garrard .25 .60
❑ 139 Fred Taylor .25 .60
❑ 140 Maurice Jones-Drew .25 .60
❑ 141 Greg Jones .20 .50
❑ 142 Dennis Northcutt .20 .50
❑ 143 Reggie Williams .25 .60
❑ 144 Marcedes Lewis .20 .50
❑ 145 Matt Jones .25 .60
❑ 146 Reggie Nelson .20 .50
❑ 147 Cleo Lemon .20 .50
❑ 148 Jerry Porter .25 .60
❑ 149 Damon Huard .20 .50
❑ 150 Brodie Croyle .25 .60
❑ 151 Larry Johnson .25 .60
❑ 152 Kolby Smith .20 .50
❑ 153 Tony Gonzalez .25 .60
❑ 154 Dwayne Bowe .25 .80
❑ 155 Donnie Edwards .20 .50
❑ 156 Jared Allen .30 .75
❑ 157 Patrick Surtain .20 .50
❑ 158 Derrick Johnson .20 .50
❑ 159 Ernest Wilford .20 .50
❑ 160 John Beck .20 .50
❑ 161 Ronnie Brown .25 .60
❑ 162 Greg Camarillo RC .60 1.50
❑ 163 Ted Ginn Jr. .25 .60
❑ 164 Derek Hagan .20 .50
❑ 165 Channing Crowder .20 .50
❑ 166 Joey Porter .20 .50
❑ 167 Jason Taylor .25 .60
❑ 168 Josh McCown .20 .50
❑ 169 Bernard Berrian .25 .60
❑ 170 Maurice Hicks .20 .50
❑ 171 Tarvaris Jackson .25 .60
❑ 172 Adrian Peterson .60 1.50
❑ 173 Chester Taylor .20 .50
❑ 174 Bobby Wade .20 .50
❑ 175 Sidney Rice .30 .75
❑ 176 Robert Ferguson .20 .50
❑ 177 Darren Sharper .25 .60
❑ 178 Visanthe Shiancoe .20 .50
❑ 179 E.J. Henderson .20 .50
❑ 180 Cedric Griffin .20 .50
❑ 181 Chad Greenway .20 .50
❑ 182 Tom Brady .50 1.25
❑ 183 Randy Moss .30 .75
❑ 184 Laurence Maroney .25 .60
❑ 185 Wes Welker .30 .75
❑ 186 Sammy Morris .20 .50
❑ 187 Kevin Faulk .25 .60
❑ 188 Ben Watson .20 .50
❑ 189 Tedy Bruschi .30 .75
❑ 190 Rodney Harrison .20 .50
❑ 191 Mike Vrabel .20 .50
❑ 192 Drew Brees .30 .75
❑ 193 Reggie Bush .30 .75
❑ 194 Deuce McAllister .25 .60
❑ 195 Marques Colston .25 .60
❑ 196 David Patten .20 .50
❑ 197 Devery Henderson .20 .50
❑ 198 Scott Fujita .20 .50
❑ 199 Roman Harper .20 .50
❑ 200 Mike McKenzie .20 .50
❑ 201 Will Smith .20 .50
❑ 202 Billy Miller .20 .50
❑ 203 Sammy Knight .20 .50
❑ 204 Eli Manning .30 .75
❑ 205 Plaxico Burress .25 .60
❑ 206 Brandon Jacobs .25 .60
❑ 207 Ahmad Bradshaw .25 .60
❑ 208 David Tyree .25 .60
❑ 209 Amani Toomer .25 .60
❑ 210 Jeremy Shockey .25 .60
❑ 211 Steve Smith USC .25 .60
❑ 212 Aaron Ross .20 .50
❑ 213 Antonio Pierce .20 .50
❑ 214 Michael Strahan .25 .60
❑ 215 Jesse Chatman .20 .50
❑ 216 Calvin Pace .20 .50
❑ 217 Kellen Clemens .25 .60
❑ 218 Leon Washington .25 .60
❑ 219 Jerricho Cotchery .20 .50
❑ 220 Laveranues Coles .25 .60
❑ 221 Chris Baker .20 .50
❑ 222 Brad Smith .20 .50
❑ 223 Thomas Jones .25 .60
❑ 224 Darrelle Revis .25 .60
❑ 225 David Harris .20 .50
❑ 226 DeAngelo Hall .20 .50
❑ 227 Drew Carter .20 .50
❑ 228 Javon Walker .25 .60
❑ 229 JaMarcus Russell .30 .75
❑ 230 Justin Fargas .20 .50
❑ 231 Michael Bush .25 .60
❑ 232 Ronald Curry .25 .60
❑ 233 Zach Miller .25 .60
❑ 234 Thomas Howard .20 .50
❑ 235 Johnnie Lee Higgins .20 .50
❑ 236 Kirk Morrison .20 .50
❑ 237 Michael Huff .20 .50
❑ 238 Asante Samuel .20 .50
❑ 239 Donovan McNabb .30 .75
❑ 240 Brian Westbrook .25 .60
❑ 241 Correll Buckhalter .25 .60
❑ 242 Kevin Curtis .20 .50
❑ 243 Reggie Brown .20 .50
❑ 244 L.J. Smith .20 .50
❑ 245 Greg Lewis .20 .50
❑ 246 Lito Sheppard .20 .50
❑ 247 Omar Gaither .20 .50
❑ 248 Ben Roethlisberger .40 1.00
❑ 249 Willie Parker .25 .60
❑ 250 Najeh Davenport .20 .50
❑ 251 Hines Ward .25 .60
❑ 252 Santonio Holmes .25 .60
❑ 253 Heath Miller .20 .50
❑ 254 Cedrick Wilson .20 .50
❑ 255 James Harrison RC 1.25 3.00
❑ 256 Ike Taylor .20 .50
❑ 257 James Farrior .20 .50
❑ 258 Troy Polamalu .30 .75
❑ 259 Philip Rivers .30 .75
❑ 260 LaDainian Tomlinson .40 1.00
❑ 261 Darren Sproles .20 .50
❑ 262 Vincent Jackson .20 .50
❑ 263 Chris Chambers .25 .60
❑ 264 Antonio Gates .25 .60
❑ 265 Craig Buster Davis .20 .50
❑ 266 Malcom Floyd .20 .50
❑ 267 Antonio Cromartie .20 .50
❑ 268 Shawne Merriman .25 .60
❑ 269 DeShaun Foster .25 .60
❑ 270 Alex Smith QB .25 .60
❑ 271 Frank Gore .25 .60
❑ 272 Michael Robinson .20 .50
❑ 273 Vernon Davis .20 .50
❑ 274 Arnaz Battle .20 .50
❑ 275 Isaac Bruce .25 .60
❑ 276 Patrick Willis .25 .60
❑ 277 Nate Clements .20 .50
❑ 278 Jason Hill .20 .50
❑ 279 T.J. Duckett .20 .50
❑ 280 Matt Hasselbeck .25 .60
❑ 281 Julian Peterson .20 .50
❑ 282 Maurice Morris .20 .50
❑ 283 Bobby Engram .20 .50
❑ 284 Nate Burleson .20 .50
❑ 285 Deion Branch .25 .60
❑ 286 Lofa Tatupu .25 .60
❑ 287 Marcus Trufant .20 .50
❑ 288 Darryl Tapp .20 .50
❑ 289 Julius Jones .25 .60
❑ 290 Marc Bulger .25 .60
❑ 291 Steven Jackson .30 .75
❑ 292 Brian Leonard .20 .50
❑ 293 Torry Holt .25 .60
❑ 294 Dante Hall .20 .50
❑ 295 Randy McMichael .20 .50
❑ 296 Drew Bennett .20 .50
❑ 297 Will Witherspoon .20 .50
❑ 298 Tye Hill .20 .50
❑ 299 Corey Chavous .20 .50
❑ 300 Warrick Dunn .25 .60
❑ 301 Brian Griese .20 .50
❑ 302 Jeff Garcia .25 .60
❑ 303 Cadillac Williams .25 .60
❑ 304 Earnest Graham .20 .50
❑ 305 Joey Galloway .25 .60
❑ 306 Ike Hilliard .20 .50

Card		
❑ 307 Michael Clayton	.25	.60
❑ 308 Derrick Brooks	.25	.60
❑ 309 Phillip Buchanon	.20	.50
❑ 310 Alex Smith TE	.20	.50
❑ 311 Ronde Barber	.20	.50
❑ 312 Justin McCareins	.20	.50
❑ 313 Jevon Kearse	.25	.60
❑ 314 Vince Young	.25	.60
❑ 315 LenDale White	.25	.60
❑ 316 Justin Gage	.20	.50
❑ 317 Roydell Williams	.20	.50
❑ 318 Alge Crumpler	.25	.60
❑ 319 Brandon Jones	.20	.50
❑ 320 Michael Griffin	.20	.50
❑ 321 Keith Bulluck	.20	.50
❑ 322 Jason Campbell	.25	.60
❑ 323 Clinton Portis	.25	.60
❑ 324 Ladell Betts	.20	.50
❑ 325 Santana Moss	.20	.50
❑ 326 Chris Cooley	.25	.60
❑ 327 Antwaan Randle El	.20	.50
❑ 328 London Fletcher	.20	.50
❑ 329 Shawn Springs	.20	.50
❑ 330 LaRon Landry	.25	.60
❑ 331 Jake Long RC	1.50	4.00
❑ 332 Chris Long RC	1.50	4.00
❑ 333 Matt Ryan RC	6.00	15.00
❑ 334 Darren McFadden RC	3.00	8.00
❑ 335 Glenn Dorsey RC	1.50	4.00
❑ 336 Vernon Gholston RC	1.50	4.00
❑ 337 Sedrick Ellis RC	1.50	4.00
❑ 338 Derrick Harvey RC	1.25	3.00
❑ 339 Keith Rivers RC	1.50	4.00
❑ 340 Jerod Mayo RC	2.00	5.00
❑ 341 Leodis McKelvin RC	1.50	4.00
❑ 342 Jonathan Stewart RC	3.00	8.00
❑ 343 D.Rodgers-Cromartie RC	1.50	4.00
❑ 344 Joe Flacco RC	5.00	12.00
❑ 345 Aqib Talib RC	1.50	4.00
❑ 346 Felix Jones RC	3.00	8.00
❑ 347 Rashard Mendenhall RC	3.00	8.00
❑ 348 Chris Johnson RC	5.00	12.00
❑ 349 Mike Jenkins RC	1.50	4.00
❑ 350 Antoine Cason RC	1.50	4.00
❑ 351 Lawrence Jackson RC	1.25	3.00
❑ 352 Kentwan Balmer RC	1.25	3.00
❑ 353 Dustin Keller RC	1.50	4.00
❑ 354 Kenny Phillips RC	1.50	4.00
❑ 355 Phillip Merling RC	1.25	3.00
❑ 356 Donnie Avery RC	2.00	5.00
❑ 357 Devin Thomas RC	1.50	4.00
❑ 358 Brandon Flowers RC	1.50	4.00
❑ 359 Jordy Nelson RC	2.00	5.00
❑ 360 Curtis Lofton RC	1.50	4.00
❑ 361 John Carlson RC	1.50	4.00
❑ 362 Tracy Porter RC	2.00	5.00
❑ 363 James Hardy RC	1.25	3.00
❑ 364 Eddie Royal RC	2.50	6.00
❑ 365 Matt Forte RC	3.00	8.00
❑ 366 Jordon Dizon RC	1.50	4.00
❑ 367 Jerome Simpson RC	1.25	3.00
❑ 368 Fred Davis RC	1.50	4.00
❑ 369 DeSean Jackson RC	3.00	8.00
❑ 370 Calais Campbell RC	1.25	3.00
❑ 371 Malcolm Kelly RC	1.50	4.00
❑ 372 Quentin Groves RC	1.25	3.00
❑ 373 Limas Sweed RC	1.50	4.00
❑ 374 Ray Rice RC	3.00	8.00
❑ 375 Brian Brohm RC	1.50	4.00
❑ 376 Chad Henne RC	2.50	6.00
❑ 377 Dexter Jackson RC	1.50	4.00
❑ 378 Martellus Bennett RC	1.50	4.00
❑ 379 Terrell Thomas RC	1.25	3.00
❑ 380 Kevin Smith RC	2.50	6.00
❑ 381 Anthony Alridge RC	1.25	3.00
❑ 382 Jacob Hester RC	1.50	4.00
❑ 383 Earl Bennett RC	1.50	4.00
❑ 384 Jamaal Charles RC	2.50	6.00
❑ 385 Dan Connor RC	1.50	4.00
❑ 386 Reggie Smith RC	1.25	3.00
❑ 387 Brad Cottam RC	1.50	4.00
❑ 388 Pat Sims RC	1.25	3.00
❑ 389 Dantrell Savage RC	1.50	4.00
❑ 390 Early Doucet RC	1.50	4.00
❑ 391 Harry Douglas RC	1.25	3.00
❑ 392 Steve Slaton RC	2.00	5.00
❑ 393 Jermichael Finley RC	1.50	4.00
❑ 394 Kevin O'Connell RC	1.50	4.00
❑ 395 Mario Manningham RC	1.50	4.00
❑ 396 Andre Caldwell RC	1.50	4.00
❑ 397 Will Franklin RC	1.25	3.00
❑ 398 Marcus Smith RC	1.25	3.00
❑ 399 Martin Rucker RC	1.25	3.00
❑ 400 Xavier Adibi RC	1.25	3.00
❑ 401 Craig Steltz RC	1.25	3.00
❑ 402 Tashard Choice RC	1.50	4.00
❑ 403 Lavelle Hawkins RC	1.25	3.00
❑ 404 Jacob Tamme RC	1.50	4.00
❑ 405 Keenan Burton RC	1.25	3.00
❑ 406 John David Booty RC	1.50	4.00
❑ 407 Ryan Torain RC	1.50	4.00
❑ 408 Tim Hightower RC	2.00	5.00
❑ 409 Dennis Dixon RC	1.50	4.00
❑ 410 Kellen Davis RC	1.00	2.50
❑ 411 Josh Johnson RC	1.50	4.00
❑ 412 Erik Ainge RC	1.50	4.00
❑ 413 Owen Schmitt RC	1.50	4.00
❑ 414 Marcus Thomas RC	1.25	3.00
❑ 415 Thomas Brown RC	1.50	4.00
❑ 416 Josh Morgan RC	1.50	4.00
❑ 417 Kevin Robinson RC	1.25	3.00
❑ 418 Colt Brennan RC	2.50	6.00
❑ 419 Paul Hubbard RC	1.25	3.00
❑ 420 Andre Woodson RC	1.50	4.00
❑ 421 Mike Hart RC	1.50	4.00
❑ 422 Matt Flynn RC	1.50	4.00
❑ 423 Chauncey Washington RC	1.25	3.00
❑ 424 Caleb Campbell RC	1.50	4.00
❑ 425 Peyton Hillis RC	1.50	4.00
❑ 426 Justin Forsett RC	1.50	4.00
❑ 427 Adrian Arrington RC	1.25	3.00
❑ 428 Cory Boyd RC	1.25	3.00
❑ 429 Allen Patrick RC	1.25	3.00
❑ 430 Marcus Monk RC	1.50	4.00
❑ 431 DJ Hall RC	1.25	3.00
❑ 432 Darrell Strong RC	1.25	3.00
❑ 433 Jason Rivers RC	1.50	4.00
❑ 434 Jed Collins RC	1.25	3.00
❑ 435 Paul Smith RC	1.50	4.00
❑ 436 Darius Reynaud RC	1.25	3.00
❑ 437 Ali Highsmith RC	1.00	2.50
❑ 438 Davone Bess RC	2.00	5.00
❑ 439 Erin Henderson RC	1.25	3.00
❑ 440 Kalvin McRae RC	1.25	3.00

1993 SP

Card		
❑ COMPLETE SET (270)	25.00	60.00
❑ 1 Curtis Conway RC	1.50	4.00
❑ 2 John Copeland RC	.30	.75
❑ 3 Kevin Williams RC	.60	1.50
❑ 4 Dan Williams RC	.30	.75
❑ 5 Patrick Bates RC	.30	.75
❑ 6 Jerome Bettis RC	15.00	25.00
❑ 7 O.J.McDuffie RC	1.25	3.00
❑ 8 Robert Smith RC	3.00	8.00
❑ 9 Drew Bledsoe RC	12.50	30.00
❑ 10 Irv Smith RC	.30	.75
❑ 11 Marvin Jones RC	.30	.75
❑ 12 Victor Bailey RC	.30	.75
❑ 13 Garrison Hearst RC	3.00	8.00
❑ 14 Natrone Means RC	1.25	3.00
❑ 15 Todd Kelly RC	.30	.75
❑ 16 Rick Mirer RC	1.25	3.00
❑ 17 Eric Curry RC	.30	.75
❑ 18 Reggie Brooks RC	.60	1.50
❑ 19 Eric Dickerson	.20	.50
❑ 20 Roger Harper RC	.10	.30
❑ 21 Michael Haynes	.20	.50
❑ 22 Bobby Hebert	.10	.30
❑ 23 Lincoln Kennedy RC	.10	.30
❑ 24 Chris Miller	.20	.50
❑ 25 Mike Pritchard	.20	.50
❑ 26 Andre Rison	.20	.50
❑ 27 Deion Sanders	.60	1.50
❑ 28 Cornelius Bennett	.20	.50
❑ 29 Kenneth Davis	.10	.30
❑ 30 Henry Jones	.10	.30
❑ 31 Jim Kelly	.40	1.00
❑ 32 John Parrella RC	.10	.30
❑ 33 Andre Reed	.20	.50
❑ 34 Bruce Smith	.40	1.00
❑ 35 Thomas Smith RC	.20	.50
❑ 36 Thurman Thomas	.40	1.00
❑ 37 Neal Anderson	.10	.30
❑ 38 Myron Baker RC	.10	.30
❑ 39 Mark Carrier DB	.10	.30
❑ 40 Richard Dent	.20	.50
❑ 41 Chris Gedney RC	.10	.30
❑ 42 Jim Harbaugh	.40	1.00
❑ 43 Craig Heyward	.20	.50
❑ 44 Carl Simpson RC	.10	.30
❑ 45 Alonzo Spellman	.10	.30
❑ 46 Derrick Fenner	.10	.30
❑ 47 Harold Green	.10	.30
❑ 48 David Klingler	.10	.30
❑ 49 Ricardo McDonald	.10	.30
❑ 50 Tony McGee RC	.20	.50
❑ 51 Carl Pickens	.20	.50
❑ 52 Steve Tovar RC	.10	.30
❑ 53 Alfred Williams	.10	.30
❑ 54 Darryl Williams	.10	.30
❑ 55 Jerry Ball	.10	.30
❑ 56 Mike Caldwell RC	.10	.30
❑ 57 Mark Carrier WR	.20	.50
❑ 58 Steve Everitt RC	.10	.30
❑ 59 Dan Footman RC	.10	.30
❑ 60 Pepper Johnson	.10	.30
❑ 61 Bernie Kosar	.20	.50
❑ 62 Eric Metcalf	.20	.50
❑ 63 Michael Dean Perry	.20	.50
❑ 64 Troy Aikman	1.25	2.50
❑ 65 Charles Haley	.20	.50
❑ 66 Michael Irvin	.40	1.00
❑ 67 Robert Jones	.10	.30
❑ 68 Derrick Lassic RC	.10	.30
❑ 69 Russell Maryland	.10	.30
❑ 70 Ken Norton Jr.	.20	.50
❑ 71 Darrin Smith RC	.20	.50
❑ 72 Emmitt Smith	2.50	5.00
❑ 73 Steve Atwater	.10	.30
❑ 74 Rod Bernstine	.10	.30
❑ 75 Jason Elam RC	.40	1.00
❑ 76 John Elway	2.00	5.00
❑ 77 Simon Fletcher	.10	.30
❑ 78 Tommy Maddox	.40	1.00
❑ 79 Glyn Milburn RC	.40	1.00
❑ 80 Derek Russell	.10	.30
❑ 81 Shannon Sharpe	.40	1.00
❑ 82 Bennie Blades	.10	.30
❑ 83 Willie Green	.10	.30
❑ 84 Antonio London RC	.10	.30
❑ 85 Ryan McNeil RC	.40	1.00
❑ 86 Herman Moore	.40	1.00
❑ 87 Rodney Peete	.10	.30
❑ 88 Barry Sanders	1.50	4.00
❑ 89 Chris Spielman	.20	.50
❑ 90 Pat Swilling	.10	.30
❑ 91 Mark Brunell RC	6.00	15.00
❑ 92 Terrell Buckley	.10	.30
❑ 93 Brett Favre	3.00	6.00
❑ 94 Jackie Harris	.10	.30
❑ 95 Sterling Sharpe	.40	1.00
❑ 96 John Stephens	.10	.30
❑ 97 Wayne Simmons RC	.10	.30
❑ 98 George Teague RC	.20	.50
❑ 99 Reggie White	.40	1.00
❑ 100 Micheal Barrow RC	.40	1.00
❑ 101 Cody Carlson	.10	.30
❑ 102 Ray Childress	.10	.30
❑ 103 Brad Hopkins RC	.10	.30
❑ 104 Haywood Jeffires	.20	.50
❑ 105 Wilber Marshall	.10	.30
❑ 106 Warren Moon	.40	1.00
❑ 107 Webster Slaughter	.10	.30
❑ 108 Lorenzo White	.10	.30
❑ 109 John Baylor	.10	.30
❑ 110 Duane Bickett	.10	.30
❑ 111 Quentin Coryatt	.20	.50
❑ 112 Steve Emtman	.10	.30
❑ 113 Jeff George	.40	1.00
❑ 114 Jessie Hester	.10	.30
❑ 115 Anthony Johnson	.20	.50
❑ 116 Reggie Langhorne	.10	.30
❑ 117 Roosevelt Potts RC	.10	.30

Card		
❑ 118 Marcus Allen	.40	1.00
❑ 119 J.J. Birden	.10	.30
❑ 120 Willie Davis	.40	1.00
❑ 121 Jaime Fields RC	.10	.30
❑ 122 Joe Montana	2.00	5.00
❑ 123 Will Shields RC	.40	1.00
❑ 124 Neil Smith	.40	1.00
❑ 125 Derrick Thomas	.40	1.00
❑ 126 Harvey Williams	.20	.50
❑ 127 Tim Brown	.40	1.00
❑ 128 Billy Joe Hobert RC	.40	1.00
❑ 129 Jeff Hostetler	.20	.50
❑ 130 Ethan Horton	.10	.30
❑ 131 Rocket Ismail	.20	.50
❑ 132 Howie Long	.40	1.00
❑ 133 Terry McDaniel	.10	.30
❑ 134 Greg Robinson RC	.10	.30
❑ 135 Anthony Smith	.10	.30
❑ 136 Flipper Anderson	.10	.30
❑ 137 Marc Boutte	.10	.30
❑ 138 Shane Conlan	.10	.30
❑ 139 Troy Drayton RC	.20	.50
❑ 140 Henry Ellard	.20	.50
❑ 141 Jim Everett	.20	.50
❑ 142 Cleveland Gary	.10	.30
❑ 143 Sean Gilbert	.20	.50
❑ 144 Robert Young	.10	.30
❑ 145 Marco Coleman	.10	.30
❑ 146 Bryan Cox	.10	.30
❑ 147 Irving Fryar	.20	.50
❑ 148 Keith Jackson	.20	.50
❑ 149 Terry Kirby RC	.40	1.00
❑ 150 Dan Marino	2.00	5.00
❑ 151 Scott Mitchell	.40	1.00
❑ 152 Louis Oliver	.10	.30
❑ 153 Troy Vincent	.10	.30
❑ 154 Anthony Carter	.20	.50
❑ 155 Cris Carter	.40	1.00
❑ 156 Roger Craig	.20	.50
❑ 157 Chris Doleman	.10	.30
❑ 158 Qadry Ismail RC	.75	2.00
❑ 159 Steve Jordan	.10	.30
❑ 160 Randall McDaniel	.10	.30
❑ 161 Audray McMillian	.10	.30
❑ 162 Barry Word	.10	.30
❑ 163 Vincent Brown	.10	.30
❑ 164 Marv Cook	.10	.30
❑ 165 Sam Gash RC	.40	1.00
❑ 166 Pat Harlow	.10	.30
❑ 167 Greg McMurtry	.10	.30
❑ 168 Todd Rucci RC	.10	.30
❑ 169 Leonard Russell	.20	.50
❑ 170 Scott Sisson RC	.10	.30
❑ 171 Chris Slade RC	.20	.50
❑ 172 Morten Andersen	.10	.30
❑ 173 Derek Brown RBK RC	.20	.50
❑ 174 Reggie Freeman RC	.10	.30
❑ 175 Rickey Jackson	.10	.30
❑ 176 Eric Martin	.10	.30
❑ 177 Wayne Martin	.10	.30
❑ 178 Brad Muster	.10	.30
❑ 179 Willie Roaf RC	.20	.50
❑ 180 Renaldo Turnbull	.10	.30
❑ 181 Derek Brown TE	.10	.30
❑ 182 Marcus Buckley RC	.10	.30
❑ 183 Jarrod Bunch	.10	.30
❑ 184 Rodney Hampton	.20	.50
❑ 185 Ed McCaffrey	.40	1.00
❑ 186 Kanavis McGhee	.10	.30
❑ 187 Mike Sherrard	.10	.30
❑ 188 Phil Simms	.20	.50
❑ 189 Lawrence Taylor	.40	1.00
❑ 190 Kurt Barber	.10	.30
❑ 191 Boomer Esiason	.20	.50
❑ 192 Johnny Johnson	.10	.30
❑ 193 Ronnie Lott	.20	.50
❑ 194 Johnny Mitchell	.10	.30
❑ 195 Rob Moore	.20	.50
❑ 196 Adrian Murrell RC	.40	1.00
❑ 197 Browning Nagle	.10	.30
❑ 198 Marvin Washington	.10	.30
❑ 199 Eric Allen	.10	.30
❑ 200 Fred Barnett	.20	.50
❑ 201 Randall Cunningham	.40	1.00
❑ 202 Byron Evans	.10	.30
❑ 203 Tim Harris	.10	.30
❑ 204 Seth Joyner	.10	.30
❑ 205 Leonard Renfro RC	.10	.30
❑ 206 Heath Sherman	.10	.30
❑ 207 Clyde Simmons	.10	.30
❑ 208 Johnny Bailey	.10	.30
❑ 209 Steve Beuerlein	.20	.50
❑ 210 Chuck Cecil	.10	.30
❑ 211 Larry Centers RC	.40	1.00
❑ 212 Gary Clark	.20	.50
❑ 213 Ernest Dye RC	.10	.30
❑ 214 Ken Harvey	.10	.30
❑ 215 Randal Hill	.10	.30
❑ 216 Ricky Proehl	.10	.30
❑ 217 Deon Figures RC	.10	.30
❑ 218 Barry Foster	.20	.50
❑ 219 Eric Green	.10	.30
❑ 220 Kevin Greene	.20	.50
❑ 221 Carlton Haselrig	.10	.30
❑ 222 Andre Hastings RC	.20	.50
❑ 223 Greg Lloyd	.20	.50
❑ 224 Neil O'Donnell	.40	1.00
❑ 225 Rod Woodson	.40	1.00
❑ 226 Marion Butts	.10	.30
❑ 227 Darren Carrington RC	.10	.30
❑ 228 Darrien Gordon RC	.10	.30
❑ 229 Ronnie Harmon	.10	.30
❑ 230 Stan Humphries	.20	.50
❑ 231 Anthony Miller	.20	.50
❑ 232 Chris Mims	.10	.30
❑ 233 Leslie O'Neal	.20	.50
❑ 234 Junior Seau	.40	1.00
❑ 235 Dana Hall	.10	.30
❑ 236 Adrian Hardy	.10	.30
❑ 237 Brent Jones	.20	.50
❑ 238 Tim McDonald	.10	.30
❑ 239 Tom Rathman	.10	.30
❑ 240 Jerry Rice	1.50	3.00
❑ 241 Dana Stubblefield RC	.40	1.00
❑ 242 Ricky Watters	.40	1.00
❑ 243 Steve Young	1.25	2.50
❑ 244 Brian Blades	.20	.50
❑ 245 Ferrell Edmunds	.10	.30
❑ 246 Carlton Gray RC	.10	.30
❑ 247 Cortez Kennedy	.20	.50
❑ 248 Kelvin Martin	.10	.30
❑ 249 Dan McGwire	.10	.30
❑ 250 Jon Vaughn	.10	.30
❑ 251 Chris Warren	.20	.50
❑ 252 John L. Williams	.10	.30
❑ 253 Reggie Cobb	.10	.30
❑ 254 Horace Copeland RC	.20	.50
❑ 255 Lawrence Dawsey	.10	.30
❑ 256 Demetrius DuBose RC	.10	.30
❑ 257 Craig Erickson	.20	.50
❑ 258 Courtney Hawkins	.10	.30
❑ 259 John Lynch RC	3.00	8.00
❑ 260 Hardy Nickerson	.20	.50
❑ 261 Lamar Thomas RC	.10	.30
❑ 262 Carl Banks	.10	.30
❑ 263 Tom Carter RC	.20	.50
❑ 264 Brad Edwards	.10	.30
❑ 265 Kurt Gouveia	.10	.30
❑ 266 Desmond Howard	.20	.50
❑ 267 Charles Mann	.10	.30
❑ 268 Art Monk	.20	.50
❑ 269 Mark Rypien	.10	.30
❑ 270 Ricky Sanders	.10	.30
❑ P1 Joe Montana Promo	2.00	5.00

1994 SP

Card		
❑ COMPLETE SET (200)	25.00	50.00
❑ 1 Dan Wilkinson RC	.50	1.25
❑ 2 Heath Shuler RC	.30	.75
❑ 3 Marshall Faulk RC	6.00	15.00
❑ 4 Willie McGinest RC	.75	2.00
❑ 5 Trent Dilfer RC	2.00	5.00
❑ 6 Bryant Young RC	.75	2.00
❑ 7 Antonio Langham RC	.15	.40
❑ 8 John Thierry RC	.15	.40
❑ 9 Aaron Glenn RC	.50	1.25
❑ 10 Charles Johnson RC	.50	1.25
❑ 11 Dewayne Washington RC	.15	.40
❑ 12 Johnnie Morton RC	1.25	3.00
❑ 13 Greg Hill RC	.30	.75
❑ 14 William Floyd RC	.30	.75
❑ 15 Derrick Alexander WR RC	.50	1.25
❑ 16 Darnay Scott RC	.50	1.25
❑ 17 Errict Rhett RC	.50	1.25
❑ 18 Charlie Garner RC	1.25	3.00
❑ 19 Thomas Lewis RC	.15	.40
❑ 20 David Palmer FOIL RC	.50	1.25
❑ 21 Andre Reed	.10	.30
❑ 22 Thurman Thomas	.20	.50
❑ 23 Bruce Smith	.20	.50
❑ 24 Jim Kelly	.20	.50
❑ 25 Cornelius Bennett	.10	.30
❑ 26 Bucky Brooks RC	.05	.15
❑ 27 Jeff Burris RC	.10	.30
❑ 28 Jim Harbaugh	.20	.50
❑ 29 Tony Bennett	.05	.15
❑ 30 Quentin Coryatt	.05	.15
❑ 31 Floyd Turner	.05	.15
❑ 32 Roosevelt Potts	.05	.15
❑ 33 Jeff Herrod	.05	.15
❑ 34 Irving Fryar	.10	.30
❑ 35 Bryan Cox	.05	.15
❑ 36 Dan Marino	1.50	4.00
❑ 37 Terry Kirby	.20	.50
❑ 38 Michael Stewart	.05	.15
❑ 39 Bernie Kosar	.10	.30
❑ 40 Aubrey Beavers RC	.05	.15
❑ 41 Vincent Brisby	.10	.30
❑ 42 Ben Coates	.10	.30
❑ 43 Drew Bledsoe	.75	2.00
❑ 44 Marion Butts	.05	.15
❑ 45 Chris Slade	.05	.15
❑ 46 Michael Timpson	.05	.15
❑ 47 Ray Crittenden RC	.05	.15
❑ 48 Rob Moore	.10	.30
❑ 49 Johnny Mitchell	.05	.15
❑ 50 Art Monk	.10	.30
❑ 51 Boomer Esiason	.10	.30
❑ 52 Ronnie Lott	.10	.30
❑ 53 Ryan Yarborough RC	.05	.15
❑ 54 Carl Pickens	.10	.30
❑ 55 David Klingler	.05	.15
❑ 56 Harold Green	.05	.15
❑ 57 John Copeland	.05	.15
❑ 58 Louis Oliver	.05	.15
❑ 59 Corey Sawyer	.10	.30
❑ 60 Michael Jackson	.10	.30
❑ 61 Mark Rypien	.05	.15
❑ 62 Vinny Testaverde	.10	.30
❑ 63 Eric Metcalf	.10	.30
❑ 64 Eric Turner	.05	.15
❑ 65 Haywood Jeffires	.10	.30
❑ 66 Micheal Barrow	.05	.15
❑ 67 Cody Carlson	.05	.15
❑ 68 Gary Brown	.05	.15
❑ 69 Bucky Richardson	.05	.15
❑ 70 Al Smith	.05	.15
❑ 71 Eric Green	.05	.15
❑ 72 Neil O'Donnell	.20	.50
❑ 73 Barry Foster	.05	.15
❑ 74 Greg Lloyd	.10	.30
❑ 75 Rod Woodson	.10	.30
❑ 76 Byron Bam Morris RC	.10	.30
❑ 77 John L. Williams	.05	.15
❑ 78 Anthony Miller	.10	.30
❑ 79 Mike Pritchard	.05	.15
❑ 80 John Elway	1.50	4.00
❑ 81 Shannon Sharpe	.10	.30
❑ 82 Steve Atwater	.05	.15
❑ 83 Simon Fletcher	.05	.15
❑ 84 Glyn Milburn	.10	.30
❑ 85 Mark Collins	.05	.15
❑ 86 Keith Cash	.05	.15
❑ 87 Willie Davis	.10	.30
❑ 88 Joe Montana	1.50	4.00
❑ 89 Marcus Allen	.20	.50
❑ 90 Neil Smith	.10	.30
❑ 91 Derrick Thomas	.20	.50
❑ 92 Tim Brown	.20	.50
❑ 93 Jeff Hostetler	.10	.30
❑ 94 Terry McDaniel	.05	.15
❑ 95 Rocket Ismail	.10	.30
❑ 96 Rob Fredrickson RC	.10	.30
❑ 97 Harvey Williams	.10	.30

Card		
❑ 98 Steve Wisniewski	.05	.15
❑ 99 Stan Humphries	.10	.30
❑ 100 Natrone Means	.20	.50
❑ 101 Leslie O'Neal	.05	.15
❑ 102 Junior Seau	.20	.50
❑ 103 Ronnie Harmon	.05	.15
❑ 104 Shawn Jefferson	.05	.15
❑ 105 Howard Ballard	.05	.15
❑ 106 Rick Mirer	.20	.50
❑ 107 Cortez Kennedy	.10	.30
❑ 108 Chris Warren	.10	.30
❑ 109 Brian Blades	.10	.30
❑ 110 Sam Adams RC	.10	.30
❑ 111 Gary Clark	.10	.30
❑ 112 Steve Beuerlein	.10	.30
❑ 113 Ronald Moore	.05	.15
❑ 114 Eric Swann	.10	.30
❑ 115 Clyde Simmons	.05	.15
❑ 116 Seth Joyner	.05	.15
❑ 117 Troy Aikman	.75	2.00
❑ 118 Charles Haley	.10	.30
❑ 119 Alvin Harper	.10	.30
❑ 120 Michael Irvin	.20	.50
❑ 121 Daryl Johnston	.10	.30
❑ 122 Emmitt Smith	1.25	3.00
❑ 123 Shante Carver RC	.05	.15
❑ 124 Dave Brown	.10	.30
❑ 125 Rodney Hampton	.10	.30
❑ 126 Dave Meggett	.05	.15
❑ 127 Chris Calloway	.05	.15
❑ 128 Mike Sherrard	.05	.15
❑ 129 Carlton Bailey	.05	.15
❑ 130 Randall Cunningham	.20	.50
❑ 131 William Fuller	.05	.15
❑ 132 Eric Allen	.05	.15
❑ 133 Calvin Williams	.10	.30
❑ 134 Herschel Walker	.10	.30
❑ 135 Bernard Williams RC	.05	.15
❑ 136 Henry Ellard	.10	.30
❑ 137 Ethan Horton	.05	.15
❑ 138 Desmond Howard	.10	.30
❑ 139 Reggie Brooks	.10	.30
❑ 140 John Friesz	.10	.30
❑ 141 Tom Carter	.05	.15
❑ 142 Terry Allen	.10	.30
❑ 143 Adrian Cooper	.05	.15
❑ 144 Qadry Ismail	.20	.50
❑ 145 Warren Moon	.20	.50
❑ 146 Henry Thomas	.05	.15
❑ 147 Todd Steussie RC	.10	.30
❑ 148 Cris Carter	.30	.75
❑ 149 Andy Heck	.05	.15
❑ 150 Curtis Conway	.20	.50
❑ 151 Erik Kramer	.10	.30
❑ 152 Lewis Tillman	.05	.15
❑ 153 Dante Jones	.05	.15
❑ 154 Alonzo Spellman	.05	.15
❑ 155 Herman Moore	.20	.50
❑ 156 Broderick Thomas	.05	.15
❑ 157 Scott Mitchell	.10	.30
❑ 158 Barry Sanders	1.25	3.00
❑ 159 Chris Spielman	.10	.30
❑ 160 Pat Swilling	.05	.15
❑ 161 Bennie Blades	.05	.15
❑ 162 Sterling Sharpe	.10	.30
❑ 163 Brett Favre	1.50	4.00
❑ 164 Reggie Cobb	.05	.15
❑ 165 Reggie White	.20	.50
❑ 166 Sean Jones	.05	.15
❑ 167 George Teague	.05	.15
❑ 168 LeShon Johnson RC	.10	.30
❑ 169 Courtney Hawkins	.05	.15
❑ 170 Jackie Harris	.05	.15
❑ 171 Craig Erickson	.05	.15
❑ 172 Santana Dotson	.10	.30
❑ 173 Eric Curry	.05	.15
❑ 174 Hardy Nickerson	.10	.30
❑ 175 Derek Brown RBK	.05	.15
❑ 176 Jim Everett	.10	.30
❑ 177 Michael Haynes	.10	.30
❑ 178 Tyrone Hughes	.10	.30
❑ 179 Wayne Martin	.05	.15
❑ 180 Willie Roaf	.05	.15
❑ 181 Irv Smith	.05	.15
❑ 182 Jeff George	.20	.50
❑ 183 Andre Rison	.10	.30
❑ 184 Erric Pegram	.05	.15
❑ 185 Bert Emanuel RC	.40	1.00
❑ 186 Chris Doleman	.05	.15
❑ 187 Ron George	.05	.15
❑ 188 Chris Miller	.05	.15
❑ 189 Troy Drayton	.05	.15
❑ 190 Chris Chandler	.10	.30
❑ 191 Jerome Bettis	.40	1.00
❑ 192 Jimmie Jones	.05	.15
❑ 193 Sean Gilbert	.05	.15
❑ 194 Jerry Rice	.75	2.00
❑ 195 Brent Jones	.10	.30
❑ 196 Deion Sanders	.40	1.00
❑ 197 Steve Young	.60	1.50
❑ 198 Ricky Watters	.10	.30
❑ 199 Dana Stubblefield	.10	.30
❑ 200 Ken Norton Jr.	.10	.30
❑ RB1 Dan Marino RB	10.00	25.00
❑ RB2 Jerry Rice RB	12.50	25.00
❑ P16 Joe Montana Promo	1.50	4.00

1995 SP

Card		
❑ COMPLETE SET (200)	20.00	50.00
❑ 1 Ki-Jana Carter RC	.75	2.00
❑ 2 Eric Zeier RC	.75	2.00
❑ 3 Steve McNair RC	4.00	10.00
❑ 4 Michael Westbrook RC	.75	2.00
❑ 5 Kerry Collins RC	2.50	6.00
❑ 6 Joey Galloway RC	2.00	5.00
❑ 7 Kevin Carter RC	.75	2.00
❑ 8 Mike Mamula RC	.20	.50
❑ 9 Kyle Brady RC	.75	2.00
❑ 10 J.J. Stokes RC	.75	2.00
❑ 11 Tyrone Poole RC	.75	2.00
❑ 12 Rashaan Salaam RC	.40	1.00
❑ 13 Sherman Williams RC	.20	.50
❑ 14 Luther Elliss RC	.20	.50
❑ 15 James O. Stewart RC	1.25	3.00
❑ 16 Tamarick Vanover RC	.75	2.00
❑ 17 Napoleon Kaufman RC	1.25	3.00
❑ 18 Curtis Martin RC	6.00	12.00
❑ 19 Tyrone Wheatley RC	1.25	3.00
❑ 20 Frank Sanders RC	.75	2.00
❑ 21 Devin Bush	.07	.20
❑ 22 Terance Mathis	.15	.40
❑ 23 Bert Emanuel	.30	.75
❑ 24 Eric Metcalf	.15	.40
❑ 25 Craig Heyward	.15	.40
❑ 26 Jeff George	.15	.40
❑ 27 Mark Carrier WR	.15	.40
❑ 28 Pete Metzelaars	.07	.20
❑ 29 Frank Reich	.07	.20
❑ 30 Sam Mills	.15	.40
❑ 31 John Kasay	.07	.20
❑ 32 Willie Green	.15	.40
❑ 33 Jeff Graham	.07	.20
❑ 34 Curtis Conway	.30	.75
❑ 35 Steve Walsh	.07	.20
❑ 36 Erik Kramer	.07	.20
❑ 37 Michael Timpson	.07	.20
❑ 38 Mark Carrier DB	.07	.20
❑ 39 Troy Aikman	.75	2.00
❑ 40 Michael Irvin	.30	.75
❑ 41 Charles Haley	.15	.40
❑ 42 Deion Sanders	.50	1.25
❑ 43 Jay Novacek	.15	.40
❑ 44 Emmitt Smith	1.25	3.00
❑ 45 Herman Moore	.30	.75
❑ 46 Scott Mitchell UER	.15	.40
❑ 47 Bennie Blades	.07	.20
❑ 48 Johnnie Morton	.15	.40
❑ 49 Chris Spielman	.15	.40
❑ 50 Barry Sanders	1.25	3.00
❑ 51 Edgar Bennett	.15	.40
❑ 52 Reggie White	.30	.75
❑ 53 Sean Jones	.07	.20
❑ 54 Mark Ingram	.07	.20
❑ 55 Robert Brooks	.30	.75
❑ 56 Brett Favre	1.50	4.00
❑ 57 Lovell Pinkney RC	.20	.50
❑ 58 Chris Miller	.07	.20
❑ 59 Isaac Bruce	.50	1.25
❑ 60 Roman Phifer	.07	.20
❑ 61 Sean Gilbert	.15	.40
❑ 62 Jerome Bettis	.30	.75
❑ 63 Derrick Alexander DE RC	.20	.50
❑ 64 Cris Carter	.30	.75
❑ 65 Jake Reed	.15	.40
❑ 66 Robert Smith	.30	.75
❑ 67 David Palmer	.15	.40
❑ 68 Warren Moon	.15	.40
❑ 69 Ray Zellars RC	.40	1.00
❑ 70 Jim Everett	.07	.20
❑ 71 Michael Haynes	.15	.40
❑ 72 Quinn Early	.15	.40
❑ 73 Willie Roaf	.07	.20
❑ 74 Mario Bates	.15	.40
❑ 75 Mike Sherrard	.07	.20
❑ 76 Chris Calloway	.07	.20
❑ 77 Dave Brown	.15	.40
❑ 78 Thomas Lewis	.15	.40
❑ 79 Herschel Walker	.15	.40
❑ 80 Rodney Hampton	.15	.40
❑ 81 Fred Barnett	.15	.40
❑ 82 Calvin Williams	.15	.40
❑ 83 Randall Cunningham	.30	.75
❑ 84 Charlie Garner	.30	.75
❑ 85 Bobby Taylor RC	1.25	3.00
❑ 86 Ricky Watters	.15	.40
❑ 87 Dave Krieg	.07	.20
❑ 88 Rob Moore	.15	.40
❑ 89 Eric Swann	.15	.40
❑ 90 Clyde Simmons	.07	.20
❑ 91 Seth Joyner	.07	.20
❑ 92 Garrison Hearst	.30	.75
❑ 93 Jerry Rice	.75	2.00
❑ 94 Bryant Young	.15	.40
❑ 95 Brent Jones	.07	.20
❑ 96 Ken Norton	.15	.40
❑ 97 William Floyd	.15	.40
❑ 98 Steve Young	.60	1.50
❑ 99 Warren Sapp RC	2.00	5.00
❑ 100 Trent Dilfer	.30	.75
❑ 101 Alvin Harper	.07	.20
❑ 102 Hardy Nickerson	.07	.20
❑ 103 Derrick Brooks RC	2.00	5.00
❑ 104 Errict Rhett	.15	.40
❑ 105 Henry Ellard	.15	.40
❑ 106 Ken Harvey	.07	.20
❑ 107 Gus Frerotte	.15	.40
❑ 108 Brian Mitchell	.07	.20
❑ 109 Terry Allen	.15	.40
❑ 110 Heath Shuler	.15	.40
❑ 111 Jim Kelly	.30	.75
❑ 112 Andre Reed	.15	.40
❑ 113 Bruce Smith	.30	.75
❑ 114 Darick Holmes RC	.40	1.00
❑ 115 Bryce Paup	.15	.40
❑ 116 Cornelius Bennett	.15	.40
❑ 117 Carl Pickens	.15	.40
❑ 118 Darnay Scott	.15	.40
❑ 119 Jeff Blake RC	.75	2.00
❑ 120 Steve Tovar	.07	.20
❑ 121 Tony McGee	.07	.20
❑ 122 Dan Wilkinson	.15	.40
❑ 123 Craig Powell RC	.07	.20
❑ 124 Vinny Testaverde	.15	.40
❑ 125 Eric Turner	.07	.20
❑ 126 Leroy Hoard	.07	.20
❑ 127 Lorenzo White	.07	.20
❑ 128 Andre Rison	.15	.40
❑ 129 Shannon Sharpe	.15	.40
❑ 130 Terrell Davis RC	3.00	8.00
❑ 131 Anthony Miller	.15	.40
❑ 132 Mike Pritchard	.07	.20
❑ 133 Steve Atwater	.07	.20
❑ 134 John Elway	1.50	4.00
❑ 135 Haywood Jeffires	.07	.20
❑ 136 Gary Brown	.07	.20
❑ 137 Al Smith	.07	.20
❑ 138 Rodney Thomas RC	.40	1.00
❑ 139 Chris Chandler	.15	.40
❑ 140 Mel Gray	.07	.20
❑ 141 Craig Erickson	.07	.20
❑ 142 Sean Dawkins	.15	.40
❑ 143 Ken Dilger RC	.75	2.00
❑ 144 Ellis Johnson RC	.20	.50
❑ 145 Quentin Coryatt	.15	.40

Card	Low	High
❑ 146 Marshall Faulk	1.00	2.50
❑ 147 Tony Boselli RC	.75	2.00
❑ 148 Rob Johnson RC	1.25	3.00
❑ 149 Desmond Howard	.15	.40
❑ 150 Steve Beuerlein	.15	.40
❑ 151 Reggie Cobb	.07	.20
❑ 152 Jeff Lageman	.07	.20
❑ 153 Willie Davis	.15	.40
❑ 154 Marcus Allen	.30	.75
❑ 155 Neil Smith	.15	.40
❑ 156 Greg Hill	.15	.40
❑ 157 Steve Bono	.15	.40
❑ 158 Derrick Thomas	.30	.75
❑ 159 Jeff Hostetler	.15	.40
❑ 160 Harvey Williams	.07	.20
❑ 161 Rocket Ismail	.15	.40
❑ 162 Chester McGlockton	.15	.40
❑ 163 Terry McDaniel	.07	.20
❑ 164 Tim Brown	.30	.75
❑ 165 Terry Kirby	.15	.40
❑ 166 Irving Fryar	.15	.40
❑ 167 O.J. McDuffie	.30	.75
❑ 168 Bryan Cox	.07	.20
❑ 169 Eric Green	.07	.20
❑ 170 Dan Marino	1.50	4.00
❑ 171 Ben Coates	.15	.40
❑ 172 Vincent Brisby	.07	.20
❑ 173 Chris Slade	.07	.20
❑ 174 Ty Law RC	1.50	4.00
❑ 175 Vincent Brown	.07	.20
❑ 176 Drew Bledsoe	.50	1.25
❑ 177 Johnny Mitchell	.07	.20
❑ 178 Boomer Esiason	.15	.40
❑ 179 Wayne Chrebet RC	2.00	5.00
❑ 180 Mo Lewis	.07	.20
❑ 181 Ronald Moore	.07	.20
❑ 182 Aaron Glenn	.07	.20
❑ 183 Mark Bruener RC	.40	1.00
❑ 184 Neil O'Donnell	.15	.40
❑ 185 Charles Johnson	.15	.40
❑ 186 Greg Lloyd	.15	.40
❑ 187 Rod Woodson	.15	.40
❑ 188 Byron Bam Morris	.07	.20
❑ 189 Terrell Fletcher RC	.20	.50
❑ 190 Terrance Shaw UER RC	.20	.50
❑ 191 Stan Humphries	.15	.40
❑ 192 Junior Seau	.30	.75
❑ 193 Leslie O'Neal	.15	.40
❑ 194 Natrone Means	.15	.40
❑ 195 Christian Fauria RC	.40	1.00
❑ 196 Rick Mirer	.15	.40
❑ 197 Sam Adams	.07	.20
❑ 198 Cortez Kennedy	.15	.40
❑ 199 Eugene Robinson	.07	.20
❑ 200 Chris Warren	.15	.40
❑ DM1 Dan Marino Tribute	7.50	20.00
❑ JM1 Joe Montana Salute	7.50	20.00
❑ JMAP Joe Montana Promo	1.50	4.00
❑ NNO Dan Marino TRI Jumbo	10.00	25.00
❑ NNO Joe Montana SAL Jumbo	10.00	25.00
❑ P113 Dan Marino Promo	1.25	3.00

1996 SP

Card	Low	High
❑ COMPLETE SET (188)	40.00	100.00
❑ 1 Keyshawn Johnson RC	4.00	8.00
❑ 2 Kevin Hardy RC	.30	.75
❑ 3 Simeon Rice RC	1.25	3.00
❑ 4 Jonathan Ogden RC	.50	1.25
❑ 5 Eddie George RC	4.00	10.00
❑ 6 Terry Glenn RC	2.50	6.00
❑ 7 Terrell Owens RC	12.50	25.00
❑ 8 Tim Biakabutuka RC	.75	2.00
❑ 9 Lawrence Phillips RC	.30	.75
❑ 10 Alex Molden RC	.15	.40
❑ 11 Regan Upshaw RC	.15	.40
❑ 12 Rickey Dudley RC	.50	1.25
❑ 13 Duane Clemons RC	.15	.40
❑ 14 John Mobley RC	.30	.75
❑ 15 Eddie Kennison RC	.75	2.00
❑ 16 Karim Abdul-Jabbar RC	.50	1.25
❑ 17 Eric Moulds RC	2.50	6.00
❑ 18 Marvin Harrison RC	6.00	15.00
❑ 19 Stepfret Williams RC	.15	.40
❑ 20 Stephen Davis RC	4.00	10.00
❑ 21 Deion Sanders	.50	1.25
❑ 22 Emmitt Smith	1.25	3.00
❑ 23 Troy Aikman	.75	2.00
❑ 24 Michael Irvin	.30	.75
❑ 25 Herschel Walker	.15	.40
❑ 26 Kavika Pittman RC	.07	.20
❑ 27 Andre Hastings	.07	.20
❑ 28 Jerome Bettis	.30	.75
❑ 29 Mike Tomczak	.07	.20
❑ 30 Kordell Stewart	.30	.75
❑ 31 Charles Johnson	.07	.20
❑ 32 Greg Lloyd	.15	.40
❑ 33 Brett Favre	1.50	4.00
❑ 34 Mark Chmura	.15	.40
❑ 35 Edgar Bennett	.15	.40
❑ 36 Robert Brooks	.15	.40
❑ 37 Craig Newsome	.07	.20
❑ 38 Reggie White	.30	.75
❑ 39 Jim Harbaugh	.15	.40
❑ 40 Marshall Faulk	.40	1.00
❑ 41 Sean Dawkins	.07	.20
❑ 42 Quentin Coryatt	.07	.20
❑ 43 Ray Buchanan	.07	.20
❑ 44 Ken Dilger	.15	.40
❑ 45 Jerry Rice	.75	2.00
❑ 46 J.J. Stokes	.30	.75
❑ 47 Steve Young	.60	1.50
❑ 48 Derek Loville	.07	.20
❑ 49 Terry Kirby	.15	.40
❑ 50 Ken Norton	.07	.20
❑ 51 Tamarick Vanover	.15	.40
❑ 52 Marcus Allen	.30	.75
❑ 53 Steve Bono	.07	.20
❑ 54 Neil Smith	.15	.40
❑ 55 Derrick Thomas	.30	.75
❑ 56 Dale Carter	.07	.20
❑ 57 Terance Mathis	.07	.20
❑ 58 Eric Metcalf	.07	.20
❑ 59 Jamal Anderson RC	.60	1.50
❑ 60 Bert Emanuel	.15	.40
❑ 61 Craig Heyward	.07	.20
❑ 62 Cornelius Bennett	.07	.20
❑ 63 Tony Martin	.15	.40
❑ 64 Stan Humphries	.15	.40
❑ 65 Andre Coleman	.07	.20
❑ 66 Junior Seau	.30	.75
❑ 67 Terrell Fletcher	.07	.20
❑ 68 John Carney	.07	.20
❑ 69 Charlie Jones RC	.15	.40
❑ 70 Ricky Watters	.15	.40
❑ 71 Charlie Garner	.15	.40
❑ 72 Bobby Hoying RC	.30	.75
❑ 73 Jason Dunn RC	.15	.40
❑ 74 Bobby Taylor	.07	.20
❑ 75 Irving Fryar	.15	.40
❑ 76 Jim Kelly	.30	.75
❑ 77 Thurman Thomas	.30	.75
❑ 78 Bruce Smith	.15	.40
❑ 79 Bryce Paup	.07	.20
❑ 80 Darick Holmes	.07	.20
❑ 81 Andre Reed	.15	.40
❑ 82 Glyn Milburn	.07	.20
❑ 83 Brett Perriman	.07	.20
❑ 84 Herman Moore	.15	.40
❑ 85 Scott Mitchell	.15	.40
❑ 86 Barry Sanders	1.25	3.00
❑ 87 Johnnie Morton	.15	.40
❑ 88 Dan Marino	1.50	4.00
❑ 89 O.J. McDuffie	.15	.40
❑ 90 Stanley Pritchett RC	.07	.20
❑ 91 Zach Thomas RC	2.00	5.00
❑ 92 Daryl Gardener RC	.07	.20
❑ 93 Rashaan Salaam	.15	.40
❑ 94 Erik Kramer	.07	.20
❑ 95 Curtis Conway	.30	.75
❑ 96 Bobby Engram RC	.30	.75
❑ 97 Walt Harris RC	.07	.20
❑ 98 Bryan Cox	.07	.20
❑ 99 John Elway	1.50	4.00
❑ 100 Terrell Davis	.60	1.50
❑ 101 Anthony Miller	.15	.40
❑ 102 Shannon Sharpe	.15	.40
❑ 103 Tory James RC	.30	.75
❑ 104 Jeff Lewis RC	.15	.40
❑ 105 Joey Galloway	.30	.75
❑ 106 Chris Warren	.15	.40
❑ 107 Rick Mirer	.15	.40
❑ 108 Cortez Kennedy	.07	.20
❑ 109 Michael Sinclair	.07	.20
❑ 110 John Friesz	.07	.20
❑ 111 Warren Moon	.15	.40
❑ 112 Cris Carter	.30	.75
❑ 113 Jake Reed	.15	.40
❑ 114 Robert Smith	.15	.40
❑ 115 John Randle	.15	.40
❑ 116 Orlando Thomas	.07	.20
❑ 117 Jeff Hostetler	.07	.20
❑ 118 Tim Brown	.30	.75
❑ 119 Joe Aska	.07	.20
❑ 120 Napoleon Kaufman	.30	.75
❑ 121 Terry McDaniel	.07	.20
❑ 122 Harvey Williams	.07	.20
❑ 123 Trent Dilfer	.30	.75
❑ 124 Reggie Brooks	.07	.20
❑ 125 Alvin Harper	.07	.20
❑ 126 Mike Alstott RC	2.00	5.00
❑ 127 Hardy Nickerson	.07	.20
❑ 128 Mario Bates	.15	.40
❑ 129 Jim Everett	.07	.20
❑ 130 Tyrone Hughes	.07	.20
❑ 131 Michael Haynes	.07	.20
❑ 132 Eric Allen	.07	.20
❑ 133 Isaac Bruce	.30	.75
❑ 134 Kevin Carter	.07	.20
❑ 135 Leslie O'Neal	.07	.20
❑ 136 Tony Banks RC	.30	.75
❑ 137 Chris Chandler	.15	.40
❑ 138 Steve McNair	.60	1.50
❑ 139 Chris Sanders	.15	.40
❑ 140 Ronnie Harmon	.07	.20
❑ 141 Willie Davis	.07	.20
❑ 142 Michael Westbrook	.30	.75
❑ 143 Terry Allen	.15	.40
❑ 144 Brian Mitchell	.07	.20
❑ 145 Henry Ellard	.07	.20
❑ 146 Gus Frerotte	.15	.40
❑ 147 Kerry Collins	.30	.75
❑ 148 Sam Mills	.07	.20
❑ 149 Wesley Walls	.15	.40
❑ 150 Kevin Greene	.15	.40
❑ 151 Muhsin Muhammad RC	2.00	5.00
❑ 152 Winslow Oliver	.07	.20
❑ 153 Jeff Blake	.30	.75
❑ 154 Carl Pickens	.15	.40
❑ 155 Darnay Scott	.15	.40
❑ 156 Garrison Hearst	.15	.40
❑ 157 Marco Battaglia RC	.07	.20
❑ 158 Drew Bledsoe	.50	1.25
❑ 159 Curtis Martin	.60	1.50
❑ 160 Shawn Jefferson	.07	.20
❑ 161 Ben Coates	.15	.40
❑ 162 Lawyer Milloy RC	1.00	2.50
❑ 163 Tyrone Wheatley	.15	.40
❑ 164 Rodney Hampton	.15	.40
❑ 165 Chris Calloway	.07	.20
❑ 166 Dave Brown	.07	.20
❑ 167 Amani Toomer RC	2.00	5.00
❑ 168 Vinny Testaverde	.15	.40
❑ 169 Michael Jackson	.15	.40
❑ 170 Eric Turner	.07	.20
❑ 171 DeRon Jenkins	.07	.20
❑ 172 Jermaine Lewis RC	.30	.75
❑ 173 Frank Sanders	.15	.40
❑ 174 Rob Moore	.15	.40
❑ 175 Kent Graham	.07	.20
❑ 176 Leeland McElroy RC	.15	.40
❑ 177 Larry Centers	.15	.40
❑ 178 Eric Swann	.07	.20
❑ 179 Mark Brunell	.50	1.25
❑ 180 Willie Jackson	.15	.40
❑ 181 James O. Stewart	.15	.40
❑ 182 Natrone Means	.15	.40
❑ 183 Tony Brackens RC	.30	.75
❑ 184 Adrian Murrell	.15	.40
❑ 185 Neil O'Donnell	.15	.40
❑ 186 Hugh Douglas	.15	.40
❑ 187 Wayne Chrebet	.40	1.00
❑ 188 Alex Van Dyke RC	.15	.40
❑ SP13 Dan Marino Promo	1.25	3.00

1997 SP Authentic

❑ COMPLETE SET (198)	50.00	100.00
❑ 1 Orlando Pace RC	.75	2.00
❑ 2 Darrell Russell RC	.20	.50
❑ 3 Shawn Springs RC	.40	1.00
❑ 4 Peter Boulware RC	1.50	4.00
❑ 5 Bryant Westbrook RC	.40	1.00
❑ 6 Walter Jones RC	.75	2.00
❑ 7 Ike Hilliard RC	1.50	4.00
❑ 8 James Farrior RC	1.25	3.00
❑ 9 Tom Knight RC	.20	.50
❑ 10 Warrick Dunn RC	6.00	15.00
❑ 11 Tony Gonzalez RC	6.00	15.00
❑ 12 Reinard Wilson RC	.40	1.00
❑ 13 Yatil Green RC	.40	1.00
❑ 14 Reidel Anthony RC	.75	2.00
❑ 15 Kenny Holmes RC	.20	.50
❑ 16 Dwayne Rudd RC	.20	.50
❑ 17 Renaldo Wynn RC	.20	.50
❑ 18 David LaFleur RC	.20	.50
❑ 19 Antowain Smith RC	2.50	6.00
❑ 20 Jim Druckenmiller RC	.40	1.00
❑ 21 Rae Carruth RC	.20	.50
❑ 22 Byron Hanspard RC	.40	1.00
❑ 23 Jake Plummer RC	5.00	12.00
❑ 24 Joey Kent RC	.40	1.00
❑ 25 Corey Dillon RC	4.00	10.00
❑ 26 Danny Wuerffel RC	2.00	5.00
❑ 27 Will Blackwell RC	.20	.50
❑ 28 Troy Davis RC	.40	1.00
❑ 29 Darnell Autry RC	.40	1.00
❑ 30 Pat Barnes RC	.40	1.00
❑ 31 Kent Graham	.20	.50
❑ 32 Simeon Rice	.30	.75
❑ 33 Frank Sanders	.30	.75
❑ 34 Rob Moore	.30	.75
❑ 35 Eric Swann	.20	.50
❑ 36 Chris Chandler	.30	.75
❑ 37 Jamal Anderson	.50	1.25
❑ 38 Terance Mathis	.30	.75
❑ 39 Bert Emanuel	.30	.75
❑ 40 Michael Booker	.20	.50
❑ 41 Vinny Testaverde	.30	.75
❑ 42 Byron Bam Morris	.20	.50
❑ 43 Michael Jackson	.30	.75
❑ 44 Derrick Alexander WR	.30	.75
❑ 45 Jamie Sharper RC	.75	2.00
❑ 46 Kim Herring RC	.20	.50
❑ 47 Todd Collins	.20	.50
❑ 48 Thurman Thomas	.50	1.25
❑ 49 Andre Reed	.30	.75
❑ 50 Quinn Early	.20	.50
❑ 51 Bryce Paup	.20	.50
❑ 52 Lonnie Johnson	.20	.50
❑ 53 Kerry Collins	.50	1.25
❑ 54 Anthony Johnson	.20	.50
❑ 55 Tim Biakabutuka	.30	.75
❑ 56 Muhsin Muhammad	.30	.75
❑ 57 Sam Mills	.20	.50
❑ 58 Wesley Walls	.30	.75
❑ 59 Rick Mirer	.20	.50
❑ 60 Raymont Harris	.20	.50
❑ 61 Curtis Conway	.30	.75
❑ 62 Bobby Engram	.30	.75
❑ 63 Bryan Cox	.20	.50
❑ 64 John Allred RC	.20	.50
❑ 65 Jeff Blake	.30	.75
❑ 66 Ki-Jana Carter	.20	.50
❑ 67 Darnay Scott	.30	.75
❑ 68 Carl Pickens	.30	.75
❑ 69 Dan Wilkinson	.20	.50
❑ 70 Troy Aikman	1.25	2.50
❑ 71 Emmitt Smith	2.00	4.00
❑ 72 Michael Irvin	.50	1.25
❑ 73 Deion Sanders	.50	1.25
❑ 74 Anthony Miller	.20	.50
❑ 75 Antonio Anderson RC	.20	.50
❑ 76 John Elway	2.00	5.00
❑ 77 Terrell Davis	.60	1.50
❑ 78 Rod Smith WR	.50	1.25
❑ 79 Shannon Sharpe	.30	.75
❑ 80 Neil Smith	.30	.75
❑ 81 Trevor Pryce RC	.75	2.00
❑ 82 Scott Mitchell	.30	.75
❑ 83 Barry Sanders	1.50	4.00
❑ 84 Herman Moore	.30	.75
❑ 85 Johnnie Morton	.30	.75
❑ 86 Matt Russell RC	.20	.50
❑ 87 Brett Favre	2.50	5.00
❑ 88 Edgar Bennett	.30	.75
❑ 89 Robert Brooks	.30	.75
❑ 90 Antonio Freeman	.50	1.25
❑ 91 Reggie White	.50	1.25
❑ 92 Craig Newsome	.20	.50
❑ 93 Jim Harbaugh	.30	.75
❑ 94 Marshall Faulk	.60	1.50
❑ 95 Sean Dawkins	.20	.50
❑ 96 Marvin Harrison	.50	1.25
❑ 97 Quentin Coryatt	.20	.50
❑ 98 Tarik Glenn RC	.40	1.00
❑ 99 Mark Brunell	.60	1.50
❑ 100 Natrone Means	.30	.75
❑ 101 Keenan McCardell	.30	.75
❑ 102 Jimmy Smith	.30	.75
❑ 103 Tony Brackens	.20	.50
❑ 104 Kevin Hardy	.20	.50
❑ 105 Elvis Grbac	.30	.75
❑ 106 Marcus Allen	.50	1.25
❑ 107 Greg Hill	.20	.50
❑ 108 Derrick Thomas	.50	1.25
❑ 109 Dale Carter	.20	.50
❑ 110 Dan Marino	2.00	5.00
❑ 111 Karim Abdul-Jabbar	.30	.75
❑ 112 Brian Manning RC	.20	.50
❑ 113 Daryl Gardener	.20	.50
❑ 114 Troy Drayton	.20	.50
❑ 115 Zach Thomas	.50	1.25
❑ 116 Jason Taylor RC	6.00	15.00
❑ 117 Brad Johnson	.50	1.25
❑ 118 Robert Smith	.30	.75
❑ 119 John Randle	.30	.75
❑ 120 Cris Carter	.50	1.25
❑ 121 Jake Reed	.30	.75
❑ 122 Randall Cunningham	.50	1.25
❑ 123 Drew Bledsoe	.60	1.50
❑ 124 Curtis Martin	.60	1.50
❑ 125 Terry Glenn	.50	1.25
❑ 126 Willie McGinest	.20	.50
❑ 127 Chris Canty RC	.20	.50
❑ 128 Sedrick Shaw RC	.40	1.00
❑ 129 Heath Shuler	.20	.50
❑ 130 Mario Bates	.20	.50
❑ 131 Ray Zellars	.20	.50
❑ 132 Andre Hastings	.20	.50
❑ 133 Dave Brown	.20	.50
❑ 134 Tyrone Wheatley	.30	.75
❑ 135 Rodney Hampton	.30	.75
❑ 136 Chris Calloway	.20	.50
❑ 137 Tiki Barber RC	10.00	25.00
❑ 138 Neil O'Donnell	.30	.75
❑ 139 Adrian Murrell	.30	.75
❑ 140 Wayne Chrebet	.50	1.25
❑ 141 Keyshawn Johnson	.50	1.25
❑ 142 Hugh Douglas	.20	.50
❑ 143 Jeff George	.30	.75
❑ 144 Napoleon Kaufman	.50	1.25
❑ 145 Tim Brown	.50	1.25
❑ 146 Desmond Howard	.30	.75
❑ 147 Rickey Dudley	.30	.75
❑ 148 Terry McDaniel	.20	.50
❑ 149 Ty Detmer	.30	.75
❑ 150 Ricky Watters	.30	.75
❑ 151 Chris T. Jones	.20	.50
❑ 152 Irving Fryar	.30	.75
❑ 153 Mike Mamula	.20	.50
❑ 154 Jon Harris RC	.20	.50
❑ 155 Kordell Stewart	.50	1.25
❑ 156 Jerome Bettis	.50	1.25
❑ 157 Charles Johnson	.30	.75
❑ 158 Greg Lloyd	.20	.50
❑ 159 George Jones RC	.20	.50
❑ 160 Terrell Fletcher	.20	.50
❑ 161 Stan Humphries	.30	.75
❑ 162 Tony Martin	.30	.75
❑ 163 Eric Metcalf	.30	.75
❑ 164 Junior Seau	.50	1.25
❑ 165 Rod Woodson	.30	.75
❑ 166 Steve Young	.60	1.50
❑ 167 Terry Kirby	.30	.75
❑ 168 Garrison Hearst	.30	.75
❑ 169 Jerry Rice	1.25	2.50
❑ 170 Ken Norton	.20	.50
❑ 171 Kevin Greene	.30	.75
❑ 172 Lamar Smith	.50	1.25
❑ 173 Warren Moon	.50	1.25
❑ 174 Chris Warren	.30	.75
❑ 175 Cortez Kennedy	.20	.50
❑ 176 Joey Galloway	.30	.75
❑ 177 Tony Banks	.30	.75
❑ 178 Isaac Bruce	.50	1.25
❑ 179 Eddie Kennison	.30	.75
❑ 180 Kevin Carter	.20	.50
❑ 181 Craig Heyward	.20	.50
❑ 182 Trent Dilfer	.50	1.25
❑ 183 Errict Rhett	.20	.50
❑ 184 Mike Alstott	.50	1.25
❑ 185 Hardy Nickerson	.20	.50
❑ 186 Ronde Barber RC	4.00	10.00
❑ 187 Steve McNair	.60	1.50
❑ 188 Eddie George	.50	1.25
❑ 189 Chris Sanders	.20	.50
❑ 190 Blaine Bishop	.20	.50
❑ 191 Derrick Mason RC	5.00	12.00
❑ 192 Gus Frerotte	.20	.50
❑ 193 Terry Allen	.50	1.25
❑ 194 Brian Mitchell	.20	.50
❑ 195 Alvin Harper	.20	.50
❑ 196 Jeff Hostetler	.20	.50
❑ 197 Leslie Shepherd	.20	.50
❑ 198 Stephen Davis	.50	1.25
❑ A1 Aikman Audio Blue	1.50	4.00
❑ A2 Aikman Audio Pro Bowl	4.00	10.00
❑ A3 Aikman Audio White/500	15.00	30.00

1998 SP Authentic

❑ COMP.SET w/o SP's (84)	20.00	40.00
❑ *HAND NUMBERED RCs: .3X TO .8X		
❑ 1 Andre Wadsworth RC	8.00	20.00
❑ 2 Corey Chavous RC	8.00	20.00
❑ 3 Keith Brooking RC	12.00	30.00
❑ 4 Duane Starks RC	5.00	12.00
❑ 5 Pat Johnson RC	5.00	12.00
❑ 6 Jason Peter RC	5.00	12.00
❑ 7 Curtis Enis RC	6.00	15.00
❑ 8 Takeo Spikes RC	8.00	20.00
❑ 9 Greg Ellis RC	6.00	15.00
❑ 10 Marcus Nash RC	5.00	12.00
❑ 11 Brian Griese RC	12.00	30.00
❑ 12 Germane Crowell RC	6.00	15.00
❑ 13 Vonnie Holliday RC	8.00	20.00
❑ 14 Peyton Manning RC	550.00	800.00
❑ 15 Jerome Pathon RC	5.00	12.00
❑ 16 Fred Taylor RC	20.00	50.00
❑ 17 John Avery RC	5.00	12.00
❑ 18 Randy Moss RC	75.00	150.00
❑ 19 Robert Edwards RC	5.00	12.00
❑ 20 Tony Simmons RC	5.00	12.00
❑ 21 Shaun Williams RC	5.00	12.00
❑ 22 Joe Jurevicius RC	8.00	20.00
❑ 23 Charles Woodson RC	25.00	50.00
❑ 24 Tra Thomas RC	5.00	12.00
❑ 25 Grant Wistrom RC	6.00	15.00
❑ 26 Ryan Leaf RC	8.00	20.00
❑ 27 Ahman Green RC	15.00	40.00
❑ 28 Jacquez Green RC	5.00	12.00
❑ 29 Kevin Dyson RC	8.00	20.00
❑ 30 Stephen Alexander RC	6.00	15.00
❑ 31 John Elway TW	6.00	15.00
❑ 32 Jerry Rice TW	5.00	12.00
❑ 33 Emmitt Smith TW	6.00	15.00

- ❑ 34 Steve Young TW 3.00 8.00
- ❑ 35 Jerome Bettis TW 2.50 6.00
- ❑ 36 Deion Sanders TW 2.50 6.00
- ❑ 37 Andre Rison TW 1.50 4.00
- ❑ 38 Warren Moon TW 2.50 6.00
- ❑ 39 Mark Brunell TW 2.00 5.00
- ❑ 40 Ricky Watters TW 1.50 4.00
- ❑ 41 Dan Marino TW 8.00 20.00
- ❑ 42 Brett Favre TW 10.00 25.00
- ❑ 43 Jake Plummer .40 1.00
- ❑ 44 Adrian Murrell .25 .60
- ❑ 45 Eric Swann .15 .40
- ❑ 46 Jamal Anderson .40 1.00
- ❑ 47 Chris Chandler .25 .60
- ❑ 48 Jim Harbaugh .25 .60
- ❑ 49 Michael Jackson .15 .40
- ❑ 50 Jermaine Lewis .25 .60
- ❑ 51 Rob Johnson .25 .60
- ❑ 52 Antowain Smith .40 1.00
- ❑ 53 Thurman Thomas .40 1.00
- ❑ 54 Kerry Collins .25 .60
- ❑ 55 Fred Lane .15 .40
- ❑ 56 Rae Carruth .15 .40
- ❑ 57 Erik Kramer .15 .40
- ❑ 58 Curtis Conway .25 .60
- ❑ 59 Corey Dillon .40 1.00
- ❑ 60 Neil O'Donnell .25 .60
- ❑ 61 Carl Pickens .25 .60
- ❑ 62 Troy Aikman .75 2.00
- ❑ 63 Emmitt Smith 1.25 3.00
- ❑ 64 Deion Sanders .40 1.00
- ❑ 65 Terrell Davis .40 1.00
- ❑ 66 John Elway 1.50 4.00
- ❑ 67 Rod Smith .25 .60
- ❑ 68 Scott Mitchell .25 .60
- ❑ 69 Barry Sanders 1.25 3.00
- ❑ 70 Herman Moore .25 .60
- ❑ 71 Brett Favre 1.50 4.00
- ❑ 72 Dorsey Levens .40 1.00
- ❑ 73 Antonio Freeman .40 1.00
- ❑ 74 Marshall Faulk .50 1.25
- ❑ 75 Marvin Harrison .40 1.00
- ❑ 76 Mark Brunell .40 1.00
- ❑ 77 Keenan McCardell .25 .60
- ❑ 78 Jimmy Smith .25 .60
- ❑ 79 Andre Rison .25 .60
- ❑ 80 Elvis Grbac .25 .60
- ❑ 81 Derrick Alexander .25 .60
- ❑ 82 Dan Marino 1.50 4.00
- ❑ 83 Karim Abdul-Jabbar .40 1.00
- ❑ 84 O.J. McDuffie .25 .60
- ❑ 85 Brad Johnson .40 1.00
- ❑ 86 Cris Carter .40 1.00
- ❑ 87 Robert Smith .40 1.00
- ❑ 88 Drew Bledsoe .60 1.50
- ❑ 89 Terry Glenn .40 1.00
- ❑ 90 Ben Coates .25 .60
- ❑ 91 Lamar Smith .25 .60
- ❑ 92 Danny Wuerffel .25 .60
- ❑ 93 Tiki Barber .40 1.00
- ❑ 94 Danny Kanell .25 .60
- ❑ 95 Ike Hilliard .25 .60
- ❑ 96 Curtis Martin .40 1.00
- ❑ 97 Keyshawn Johnson .40 1.00
- ❑ 98 Glenn Foley .25 .60
- ❑ 99 Jeff George .25 .60
- ❑ 100 Tim Brown .40 1.00
- ❑ 101 Napoleon Kaufman .40 1.00
- ❑ 102 Bobby Hoying .25 .60
- ❑ 103 Charlie Garner .25 .60
- ❑ 104 Irving Fryar .25 .60
- ❑ 105 Kordell Stewart .40 1.00
- ❑ 106 Jerome Bettis .40 1.00
- ❑ 107 Charles Johnson .15 .40
- ❑ 108 Tony Banks .25 .60
- ❑ 109 Isaac Bruce .40 1.00
- ❑ 110 Natrone Means .25 .60
- ❑ 111 Junior Seau .40 1.00
- ❑ 112 Steve Young .50 1.25
- ❑ 113 Jerry Rice .75 2.00
- ❑ 114 Garrison Hearst .40 1.00
- ❑ 115 Ricky Watters .25 .60
- ❑ 116 Warren Moon .40 1.00
- ❑ 117 Joey Galloway .25 .60
- ❑ 118 Trent Dilfer .40 1.00
- ❑ 119 Warrick Dunn .50 1.25
- ❑ 120 Mike Alstott .40 1.00
- ❑ 121 Steve McNair .40 1.00
- ❑ 122 Eddie George .40 1.00
- ❑ 123 Yancey Thigpen .15 .40
- ❑ 124 Gus Frerotte .15 .40
- ❑ 125 Terry Allen .40 1.00
- ❑ 126 Michael Westbrook .25 .60
- ❑ AE13 Dan Marino SAMPLE .75 2.00

1999 SP Authentic

- ❑ COMP.SET w/o SPs (90) 15.00 35.00
- ❑ *HAND NUMBERED RCs: .3X TO .8X
- ❑ 1 Jake Plummer .25 .60
- ❑ 2 Adrian Murrell .25 .60
- ❑ 3 Frank Sanders .25 .60
- ❑ 4 Jamal Anderson .40 1.00
- ❑ 5 Chris Chandler .25 .60
- ❑ 6 Terance Mathis .25 .60
- ❑ 7 Priest Holmes .60 1.50
- ❑ 8 Jermaine Lewis .25 .60
- ❑ 9 Antowain Smith .40 1.00
- ❑ 10 Doug Flutie .40 1.00
- ❑ 11 Eric Moulds .40 1.00
- ❑ 12 Muhsin Muhammad .25 .60
- ❑ 13 Tim Biakabutuka .25 .60
- ❑ 14 Wesley Walls .25 .60
- ❑ 15 Curtis Enis .15 .40
- ❑ 16 Bobby Engram .25 .60
- ❑ 17 Corey Dillon .40 1.00
- ❑ 18 Darnay Scott .25 .60
- ❑ 19 Terry Kirby .15 .40
- ❑ 20 Ty Detmer .25 .60
- ❑ 21 Troy Aikman .75 2.00
- ❑ 22 Michael Irvin .25 .60
- ❑ 23 Emmitt Smith .75 2.00
- ❑ 24 Terrell Davis .40 1.00
- ❑ 25 Brian Griese .40 1.00
- ❑ 26 Rod Smith .25 .60
- ❑ 27 Shannon Sharpe .25 .60
- ❑ 28 Barry Sanders 1.25 3.00
- ❑ 29 Charlie Batch .40 1.00
- ❑ 30 Herman Moore .25 .60
- ❑ 31 Johnnie Morton .25 .60
- ❑ 32 Brett Favre 1.25 3.00
- ❑ 33 Antonio Freeman .40 1.00
- ❑ 34 Dorsey Levens .40 1.00
- ❑ 35 Mark Chmura .25 .60
- ❑ 36 Peyton Manning 1.25 3.00
- ❑ 37 Marvin Harrison .40 1.00
- ❑ 38 Mark Brunell .40 1.00
- ❑ 39 Fred Taylor .40 1.00
- ❑ 40 Jimmy Smith .25 .60
- ❑ 41 Elvis Grbac .25 .60
- ❑ 42 Andre Rison .25 .60
- ❑ 43 Dan Marino 1.25 3.00
- ❑ 44 O.J. McDuffie .25 .60
- ❑ 45 Yatil Green .15 .40
- ❑ 46 Randall Cunningham .40 1.00
- ❑ 47 Randy Moss 1.25 3.00
- ❑ 48 Robert Smith .40 1.00
- ❑ 49 Cris Carter .40 1.00
- ❑ 50 Drew Bledsoe .50 1.25
- ❑ 51 Ben Coates .15 .40
- ❑ 52 Terry Glenn .40 1.00
- ❑ 53 Eddie Kennison .25 .60
- ❑ 54 Cam Cleeland .15 .40
- ❑ 55 Ike Hilliard .25 .60
- ❑ 56 Gary Brown .15 .40
- ❑ 57 Kerry Collins .25 .60
- ❑ 58 Vinny Testaverde .25 .60
- ❑ 59 Keyshawn Johnson .40 1.00
- ❑ 60 Wayne Chrebet .40 1.00
- ❑ 61 Curtis Martin .40 1.00
- ❑ 62 Tim Brown .40 1.00
- ❑ 63 Napoleon Kaufman .40 1.00
- ❑ 64 Charles Woodson .40 1.00
- ❑ 65 Duce Staley .40 1.00
- ❑ 66 Charles Johnson .25 .60
- ❑ 67 Kordell Stewart .25 .60
- ❑ 68 Jerome Bettis .40 1.00
- ❑ 69 Marshall Faulk .50 1.25
- ❑ 70 Isaac Bruce .40 1.00
- ❑ 71 Trent Green .40 1.00
- ❑ 72 Jim Harbaugh .25 .60
- ❑ 73 Junior Seau .40 1.00
- ❑ 74 Natrone Means .25 .60
- ❑ 75 Steve Young .50 1.25
- ❑ 76 Jerry Rice .75 2.00
- ❑ 77 Terrell Owens .40 1.00
- ❑ 78 Lawrence Phillips .25 .60
- ❑ 79 Joey Galloway .25 .60
- ❑ 80 Ricky Watters .25 .60
- ❑ 81 Jon Kitna .40 1.00
- ❑ 82 Warrick Dunn .40 1.00
- ❑ 83 Trent Dilfer .25 .60
- ❑ 84 Mike Alstott .40 1.00
- ❑ 85 Eddie George .40 1.00
- ❑ 86 Steve McNair .40 1.00
- ❑ 87 Yancey Thigpen .15 .40
- ❑ 88 Brad Johnson .40 1.00
- ❑ 89 Skip Hicks .15 .40
- ❑ 90 Michael Westbrook .25 .60
- ❑ 91 Ricky Williams RC 10.00 25.00
- ❑ 92 Tim Couch RC 5.00 12.00
- ❑ 93 Akili Smith RC 5.00 12.00
- ❑ 94 Edgerrin James RC 10.00 25.00
- ❑ 95 Donovan McNabb RC 20.00 50.00
- ❑ 96 Torry Holt RC 15.00 40.00
- ❑ 97 Cade McNown RC 5.00 12.00
- ❑ 98 Shaun King RC 4.00 10.00
- ❑ 99 Daunte Culpepper RC 10.00 25.00
- ❑ 100 Brock Huard RC 4.00 10.00
- ❑ 101 Chris Claiborne RC 3.00 8.00
- ❑ 102 James Johnson RC 3.00 8.00
- ❑ 103 Rob Konrad RC 4.00 10.00
- ❑ 104 Peerless Price RC 5.00 12.00
- ❑ 105 Kevin Faulk RC 6.00 15.00
- ❑ 106 Andy Katzenmoyer RC 4.00 10.00
- ❑ 107 Troy Edwards RC 4.00 10.00
- ❑ 108 Kevin Johnson RC 4.00 10.00
- ❑ 109 Mike Cloud RC 3.00 8.00
- ❑ 110 David Boston RC 4.00 10.00
- ❑ 111 Champ Bailey RC 10.00 25.00
- ❑ 112 D'Wayne Bates RC 3.00 8.00
- ❑ 113 Joe Germaine RC 4.00 10.00
- ❑ 114 Antoine Winfield RC 5.00 10.00
- ❑ 115 Fernando Bryant RC 3.00 8.00
- ❑ 116 Jevon Kearse RC 8.00 20.00
- ❑ 117 Chris McAlister RC 4.00 10.00
- ❑ 118 Brandon Stokley RC 5.00 12.00
- ❑ 119 Karsten Bailey RC 3.00 8.00
- ❑ 120 Daylon McCutcheon RC 3.00 8.00
- ❑ 121 Jermaine Fazande RC 3.00 8.00
- ❑ 122 Joel Makovicka RC 3.00 8.00
- ❑ 123 Ebenezer Ekuban RC 3.00 8.00
- ❑ 124 Joe Montgomery RC 3.00 8.00
- ❑ 125 Sean Bennett RC 3.00 8.00
- ❑ 126 Na Brown RC 3.00 8.00
- ❑ 127 De'Mond Parker RC 3.00 8.00
- ❑ 128 Sedrick Irvin RC 3.00 8.00
- ❑ 129 Terry Jackson RC 3.00 8.00
- ❑ 130 Jeff Paulk RC 3.00 8.00
- ❑ 131 Cecil Collins RC 3.00 8.00
- ❑ 132 Bobby Collins RC 3.00 8.00
- ❑ 133 Amos Zereoue RC 4.00 10.00
- ❑ 134 Travis McGriff RC 3.00 8.00
- ❑ 135 Larry Parker RC 3.00 8.00
- ❑ 136 Wane McGarity RC 3.00 8.00
- ❑ 137 Cecil Martin RC 3.00 8.00
- ❑ 138 Al Wilson RC 5.00 12.00
- ❑ 139 Jim Kleinsasser RC 5.00 12.00
- ❑ 140 Dat Nguyen RC 4.00 10.00
- ❑ 141 Marty Booker RC 4.00 10.00
- ❑ 142 Reginald Kelly RC 3.00 8.00
- ❑ 143 Scott Covington RC 3.00 8.00
- ❑ 144 Antuan Edwards RC 3.00 8.00
- ❑ 145 Craig Yeast RC 3.00 8.00
- ❑ WPA W.Payton AU/100 400.00 600.00
- ❑ WPSP W.Payton Jsy AU/34 1000.00 1500.00

2000 SP Authentic

Card		
❑ COMP.SET w/o SP's (90)	6.00	15.00
❑ 1 Jake Plummer	.25	.60
❑ 2 David Boston	.40	1.00
❑ 3 Frank Sanders	.25	.60
❑ 4 Chris Chandler	.25	.60
❑ 5 Jamal Anderson	.40	1.00
❑ 6 Shawn Jefferson	.15	.40
❑ 7 Tony Banks	.25	.60
❑ 8 Shannon Sharpe	.25	.60
❑ 9 Rob Johnson	.25	.60
❑ 10 Antowain Smith	.25	.60
❑ 11 Muhsin Muhammad	.25	.60
❑ 12 Steve Beuerlein	.25	.60
❑ 13 Cade McNown	.15	.40
❑ 14 Curtis Enis	.15	.40
❑ 15 Marcus Robinson	.40	1.00
❑ 16 Akili Smith	.15	.40
❑ 17 Corey Dillon	.40	1.00
❑ 18 Tim Couch	.25	.60
❑ 19 Kevin Johnson	.40	1.00
❑ 20 Errict Rhett	.15	.40
❑ 21 Troy Aikman	.75	2.00
❑ 22 Emmitt Smith	1.00	2.50
❑ 23 Rocket Ismail	.25	.60
❑ 24 Joey Galloway	.25	.60
❑ 25 Terrell Davis	.40	1.00
❑ 26 Olandis Gary	.40	1.00
❑ 27 Ed McCaffrey	.40	1.00
❑ 28 Brian Griese	.40	1.00
❑ 29 Charlie Batch	.40	1.00
❑ 30 Germane Crowell	.15	.40
❑ 31 James O. Stewart	.25	.60
❑ 32 Brett Favre	1.25	3.00
❑ 33 Antonio Freeman	.40	1.00
❑ 34 Dorsey Levens	.25	.60
❑ 35 Peyton Manning	1.00	2.50
❑ 36 Edgerrin James	.60	1.50
❑ 37 Marvin Harrison	.40	1.00
❑ 38 Mark Brunell	.40	1.00
❑ 39 Fred Taylor	.40	1.00
❑ 40 Jimmy Smith	.25	.60
❑ 41 Elvis Grbac	.25	.60
❑ 42 Tony Gonzalez	.25	.60
❑ 43 James Johnson	.15	.40
❑ 44 Oronde Gadsden	.25	.60
❑ 45 Damon Huard	.40	1.00
❑ 46 Randy Moss	.75	2.00
❑ 47 Cris Carter	.40	1.00
❑ 48 Daunte Culpepper	.50	1.25
❑ 49 Drew Bledsoe	.50	1.25
❑ 50 Terry Glenn	.25	.60
❑ 51 Ricky Williams	.40	1.00
❑ 52 Jeff Blake	.25	.60
❑ 53 Keith Poole	.15	.40
❑ 54 Kerry Collins	.25	.60
❑ 55 Amani Toomer	.25	.60
❑ 56 Ike Hilliard	.25	.60
❑ 57 Wayne Chrebet	.25	.60
❑ 58 Curtis Martin	.40	1.00
❑ 59 Vinny Testaverde	.25	.60
❑ 60 Tim Brown	.40	1.00
❑ 61 Rich Gannon	.40	1.00
❑ 62 Tyrone Wheatley	.25	.60
❑ 63 Duce Staley	.40	1.00
❑ 64 Donovan McNabb	.60	1.50
❑ 65 Troy Edwards	.15	.40
❑ 66 Jerome Bettis	.40	1.00
❑ 67 Kordell Stewart	.25	.60
❑ 68 Marshall Faulk	.50	1.25
❑ 69 Kurt Warner	.60	1.50
❑ 70 Isaac Bruce	.40	1.00
❑ 71 Torry Holt	.40	1.00
❑ 72 Ryan Leaf	.25	.60
❑ 73 Jim Harbaugh	.25	.60
❑ 74 Jermaine Fazande	.15	.40
❑ 75 Jerry Rice	.75	2.00
❑ 76 Terrell Owens	.40	1.00
❑ 77 Jeff Garcia	.40	1.00
❑ 78 Ricky Watters	.25	.60
❑ 79 Jon Kitna	.40	1.00
❑ 80 Derrick Mayes	.25	.60
❑ 81 Shaun King	.15	.40
❑ 82 Mike Alstott	.40	1.00
❑ 83 Keyshawn Johnson	.40	1.00
❑ 84 Warrick Dunn	.40	1.00
❑ 85 Eddie George	.40	1.00
❑ 86 Steve McNair	.40	1.00
❑ 87 Jevon Kearse	.40	1.00
❑ 88 Brad Johnson	.40	1.00
❑ 89 Stephen Davis	.40	1.00
❑ 90 Michael Westbrook	.25	.60
❑ 91 Anthony Lucas RC	3.00	8.00
❑ 92 Avion Black RC	4.00	10.00
❑ 93 Dante Hall RC	5.00	12.00
❑ 94 Darrell Jackson RC	5.00	12.00
❑ 95 Deltha O'Neal RC	5.00	12.00
❑ 96 Erron Kinney RC	5.00	12.00
❑ 97 Doug Chapman RC	4.00	10.00
❑ 98 Frank Murphy RC	3.00	8.00
❑ 99 Gari Scott RC	3.00	8.00
❑ 100 Giovanni Carmazzi RC	3.00	8.00
❑ 101 JaJuan Dawson RC	3.00	8.00
❑ 102 Jarious Jackson RC	4.00	10.00
❑ 103 Rashard Anderson RC	4.00	10.00
❑ 104 Michael Wiley RC	4.00	10.00
❑ 105 Spergon Wynn RC	4.00	10.00
❑ 106 Muneer Moore RC	3.00	8.00
❑ 107 Ahmed Plummer RC	5.00	12.00
❑ 108 Chad Morton RC	5.00	12.00
❑ 109 Rob Morris RC	4.00	10.00
❑ 110 Ron Dixon RC	4.00	10.00
❑ 111 Rondell Mealey RC	3.00	8.00
❑ 112 Sebastian Janikowski RC	5.00	12.00
❑ 113 Shaun Ellis RC	5.00	12.00
❑ 114 Rogers Beckett RC	4.00	10.00
❑ 115 Shyrone Stith RC	4.00	10.00
❑ 116 Tim Rattay RC	5.00	12.00
❑ 117 Todd Husak RC	5.00	12.00
❑ 118 Tom Brady RC	600.00	1200.00
❑ 119 Trevor Gaylor RC	4.00	10.00
❑ 120 Windrell Hayes RC	4.00	10.00
❑ 121 Anthony Becht RC	5.00	12.00
❑ 122 Brian Urlacher RC	25.00	60.00
❑ 123 Bubba Franks RC	5.00	12.00
❑ 124 Chad Pennington RC	10.00	25.00
❑ 125 Chris Redman RC	4.00	10.00
❑ 126 Corey Simon RC	5.00	12.00
❑ 127 Curtis Keaton RC	4.00	10.00
❑ 128 Danny Farmer RC	4.00	10.00
❑ 129 Dennis Northcutt RC	5.00	12.00
❑ 130 Dez White RC	5.00	12.00
❑ 131 J.R. Redmond RC	4.00	10.00
❑ 132 Jamal Lewis RC	8.00	20.00
❑ 133 Jerry Porter RC	5.00	12.00
❑ 134 Joe Hamilton RC	4.00	10.00
❑ 135 Laveranues Coles RC	6.00	15.00
❑ 136 R.Jay Soward RC	4.00	10.00
❑ 137 Reuben Droughns RC	5.00	12.00
❑ 138 Ron Dayne RC	5.00	12.00
❑ 139 Ron Dugans RC	3.00	8.00
❑ 140 Shaun Alexander RC	8.00	20.00
❑ 141 Sylvester Morris RC	4.00	10.00
❑ 142 Tee Martin RC	5.00	12.00
❑ 143 Thomas Jones RC	8.00	20.00
❑ 144 Todd Pinkston RC	5.00	12.00
❑ 145 Travis Prentice RC	4.00	10.00
❑ 146 Travis Taylor RC	5.00	12.00
❑ 147 Trung Canidate RC	4.00	10.00
❑ 148 Courtney Brown RC	5.00	12.00
❑ 149 Plaxico Burress RC	6.00	15.00
❑ 150 Peter Warrick RC	5.00	12.00
❑ 151 Billy Volek RC	5.00	12.00
❑ 152 Bobby Shaw RC	3.00	8.00
❑ 153 Brad Hoover RC	4.00	10.00
❑ 154 Brian Finneran RC	5.00	12.00
❑ 155 Charles Lee RC	3.00	8.00
❑ 156 Chris Cole RC	3.00	8.00
❑ 157 Clint Stoerner RC	4.00	10.00
❑ 158 Doug Johnson RC	5.00	12.00
❑ 159 Frank Moreau RC	4.00	10.00
❑ 160 Jake Delhomme RC	12.00	30.00
❑ 161 KaRon Coleman RC	3.00	8.00
❑ 162 Kevin McDougal RC	3.00	8.00
❑ 163 Larry Foster RC	3.00	8.00
❑ 164 Mike Anderson RC	5.00	12.00
❑ 165 Patrick Pass RC	3.00	8.00
❑ 166 Reggie Jones RC	3.00	8.00
❑ 167 Sammy Morris RC	5.00	12.00
❑ 168 Shockmain Davis RC	3.00	8.00
❑ 169 Terrelle Smith RC	3.00	8.00
❑ 170 Ronney Jenkins RC	3.00	8.00
❑ 171 Troy Walters RC	4.00	10.00

2001 SP Authentic

Card		
❑ COMP.SET w/o SP's (90)	7.50	20.00
❑ 1 Jake Plummer	.25	.60
❑ 2 Thomas Jones	.25	.60
❑ 3 Frank Sanders	.20	.50
❑ 4 Jamal Anderson	.25	.60
❑ 5 Chris Chandler	.25	.60
❑ 6 Tony Martin	.25	.60
❑ 7 Jamal Lewis	.30	.75
❑ 8 Elvis Grbac	.25	.60
❑ 9 Travis Taylor	.20	.50
❑ 10 Peerless Price	.20	.50
❑ 11 Rob Johnson	.25	.60
❑ 12 Eric Moulds	.25	.60
❑ 13 Muhsin Muhammad	.25	.60
❑ 14 Isaac Byrd	.20	.50
❑ 15 Wesley Walls	.20	.50
❑ 16 James Allen	.20	.50
❑ 17 Marcus Robinson	.25	.60
❑ 18 Brian Urlacher	.40	1.00
❑ 19 Jon Kitna	.25	.60
❑ 20 Peter Warrick	.25	.60
❑ 21 Corey Dillon	.25	.60
❑ 22 Kevin Johnson	.20	.50
❑ 23 JaJuan Dawson	.20	.50
❑ 24 Tim Couch	.20	.50
❑ 25 Rocket Ismail	.25	.60
❑ 26 Emmitt Smith	.75	2.00
❑ 27 Joey Galloway	.25	.60
❑ 28 Terrell Davis	.30	.75
❑ 29 Mike Anderson	.25	.60
❑ 30 Brian Griese	.25	.60
❑ 31 Ed McCaffrey	.25	.60
❑ 32 Charlie Batch	.25	.60
❑ 33 James O. Stewart	.20	.50
❑ 34 Johnnie Morton	.25	.60
❑ 35 Brett Favre	1.00	2.50
❑ 36 Antonio Freeman	.30	.75
❑ 37 Bill Schroeder	.25	.60
❑ 38 Ahman Green	.30	.75
❑ 39 Peyton Manning	.75	2.00
❑ 40 Edgerrin James	.30	.75
❑ 41 Marvin Harrison	.30	.75
❑ 42 Mark Brunell	.30	.75
❑ 43 Fred Taylor	.30	.75
❑ 44 Jimmy Smith	.25	.60
❑ 45 Tony Gonzalez	.25	.60
❑ 46 Trent Green	.30	.75
❑ 47 Oronde Gadsden	.20	.50
❑ 48 Jay Fiedler	.25	.60
❑ 49 Lamar Smith	.25	.60
❑ 50 Randy Moss	.40	1.00
❑ 51 Cris Carter	.30	.75
❑ 52 Daunte Culpepper	.30	.75
❑ 53 Drew Bledsoe	.30	.75
❑ 54 Terry Glenn	.25	.60
❑ 55 Antowain Smith	.25	.60
❑ 56 Ricky Williams	.30	.75
❑ 57 Joe Horn	.25	.60
❑ 58 Aaron Brooks	.25	.60
❑ 59 Kerry Collins	.25	.60
❑ 60 Tiki Barber	.30	.75
❑ 61 Ron Dayne	.25	.60
❑ 62 Vinny Testaverde	.25	.60
❑ 63 Wayne Chrebet	.25	.60
❑ 64 Curtis Martin	.30	.75

❑ 65 Tim Brown .30 .75
❑ 66 Rich Gannon .25 .60
❑ 67 Jerry Rice .60 1.50
❑ 68 Duce Staley .25 .60
❑ 69 Donovan McNabb .40 1.00
❑ 70 Kordell Stewart .25 .60
❑ 71 Jerome Bettis .30 .75
❑ 72 Marshall Faulk .30 .75
❑ 73 Kurt Warner .40 1.00
❑ 74 Isaac Bruce .30 .75
❑ 75 Doug Flutie .30 .75
❑ 76 Junior Seau .30 .75
❑ 77 Jeff Garcia .25 .60
❑ 78 Garrison Hearst .25 .60
❑ 79 Terrell Owens .30 .75
❑ 80 Ricky Watters .25 .60
❑ 81 Matt Hasselbeck .30 .75
❑ 82 Brad Johnson .25 .60
❑ 83 Warrick Dunn .30 .75
❑ 84 Mike Alstott .25 .60
❑ 85 Kevin Dyson .25 .60
❑ 86 Eddie George .30 .75
❑ 87 Steve McNair .30 .75
❑ 88 Champ Bailey .30 .75
❑ 89 Michael Westbrook .20 .50
❑ 90 Stephen Davis .25 .60
❑ 91 Michael Vick JSY AU RC 250.00 500.00
❑ 92 Rod Gardner JSY AU RC 10.00 25.00
❑ 93 Freddie Mitchell JSY AU RC 8.00 20.00
❑ 94 Koren Robinson JSY/500 RC 10.00 25.00
❑ 95 David Terrell JSY/500 RC 8.00 20.00
❑ 96 Michael Bennett JSY RC 10.00 25.00
❑ 97 Robert Ferguson JSY RC 10.00 25.00
❑ 98 Deuce McAllister JSY RC 12.00 30.00
❑ 99 Travis Henry JSY RC 10.00 25.00
❑ 100 Andre Carter JSY RC 10.00 25.00
❑ 101 Drew Brees JSY RC 125.00 250.00
❑ 102 Santana Moss JSY/500 RC 15.00 40.00
❑ 103 Chris Weinke JSY/390 RC 8.00 20.00
❑ 104 Chad Johnson JSY/160 RC 150.00 300.00
❑ 105 Reggie Wayne JSY RC 40.00 80.00
❑ 106 Kevan Barlow JSY/500 RC 8.00 20.00
❑ 107 C.Chambers JSY/500 RC 15.00 40.00
❑ 108 Todd Heap JSY/500 RC 12.00 30.00
❑ 109 A.Thomas JSY/500 RC 10.00 25.00
❑ 110 James Jackson JSY/500 RC 8.00 20.00
❑ 111 Rudi Johnson JSY/500 RC 10.00 25.00
❑ 112 Mike McMahon JSY RC 8.00 20.00
❑ 113 Josh Heupel JSY RC 10.00 25.00
❑ 114 Travis Minor JSY/500 RC 8.00 20.00
❑ 115 Quincy Morgan JSY/500 RC 8.00 20.00
❑ 116 Dan Morgan JSY/500 RC 10.00 25.00
❑ 117 Jesse Palmer JSY/500 RC 10.00 25.00
❑ 118 Sage Rosenfels JSY/300 RC 12.00 30.00
❑ 119 M.Tuiasosopo JSY RC 8.00 20.00
❑ 120 L.Tomlinson JSY/500 RC 200.00 400.00
❑ 123 Alge Crumpler AU RC 8.00 20.00
❑ 124 Arnold Jackson AU RC 5.00 12.00
❑ 125 Bobby Newcombe AU RC 6.00 15.00
❑ 126 Brand Manumaleuna AU RC 6.00 15.00
❑ 127 Cedrick Wilson AU RC 8.00 20.00
❑ 128 Brian Allen AU RC 5.00 12.00
❑ 129 Dee Brown AU RC 5.00 12.00
❑ 130 Damerien McCants AU RC 6.00 15.00
❑ 131 Dave Dickenson AU RC 6.00 15.00
❑ 132 Derrick Blaylock AU RC 6.00 15.00
❑ 133 Eddie Berlin AU RC 5.00 12.00
❑ 134 Francis St.Paul AU RC 5.00 12.00
❑ 135 Jamar Fletcher AU RC 5.00 12.00
❑ 136 Josh Booty AU RC 6.00 15.00
❑ 137 Scotty Anderson AU RC 6.00 15.00
❑ 138 Ken-Yon Rambo AU RC 5.00 12.00
❑ 139 Kenyatta Walker AU RC 5.00 12.00
❑ 140 Kevin Kasper AU RC 6.00 15.00
❑ 141 Snoop Minnis AU RC 6.00 15.00
❑ 142 Houshmandzadeh AU RC 15.00 40.00
❑ 143 Quincy Carter AU RC 6.00 15.00
❑ 144 Ronney Daniels AU RC 5.00 12.00
❑ 145 Sedrick Hodge AU RC 5.00 12.00
❑ 146 Steve Smith AU RC 75.00 135.00
❑ 147 Tim Hasselbeck AU RC 6.00 15.00
❑ 148 Vinny Sutherland AU RC 5.00 12.00
❑ 149 Richard Seymour AU RC 8.00 20.00
❑ 150 Jamie Winborn AU 6.00 15.00
❑ 151 Gerard Warren RC 2.50 6.00
❑ 152 Justin Smith RC 3.00 8.00
❑ 153 David Martin RC 2.00 5.00
❑ 154 Jamal Reynolds RC 2.50 6.00
❑ 155 Dominic Rhodes RC 3.00 8.00
❑ 156 Nate Clements RC 3.00 8.00
❑ 157 Michael Lewis RC 3.00 8.00
❑ 158 Andre King RC 2.00 5.00
❑ 159 Benjamin Gay RC 2.50 6.00
❑ 160 Correll Buckhalter RC 3.00 8.00
❑ 161 Roderick Robinson RC 2.00 5.00
❑ 162 Moran Norris RC 2.00 5.00
❑ 163 Onome Ojo RC 2.00 5.00
❑ 164 Will Allen RC 3.00 8.00
❑ 165 Jonathan Carter RC 2.00 5.00
❑ 166 LaMont Jordan RC 3.00 8.00
❑ 167 DeLawrence Grant RC 2.00 5.00
❑ 168 Derrick Gibson RC 2.00 5.00
❑ 169 A.J. Feeley RC 2.50 6.00
❑ 170 Tim Baker RC 2.00 5.00
❑ 171 Kendrell Bell RC 3.00 8.00
❑ 172 Zeke Moreno RC 2.50 6.00
❑ 173 Carlos Polk RC 2.00 5.00
❑ 174 Ken Lucas RC 2.50 6.00
❑ 175 Heath Evans RC 2.50 6.00
❑ 176 Elvis Joseph RC 2.00 5.00
❑ 177 Damione Lewis RC 2.50 6.00
❑ 178 Tommy Polley RC 2.50 6.00
❑ 179 Fred Smoot RC 3.00 8.00
❑ 180 Jason Brookins RC 3.00 8.00
❑ 181 Nick Goings RC 3.00 8.00
❑ 182 Drew Bennett RC 3.00 8.00
❑ 183 Justin McCareins RC 2.50 6.00
❑ 184 Kabeer Gbaja-Biamila RC 3.00 8.00
❑ 185 Edgerton Hartwell RC 2.00 5.00
❑ 186 Robert Carswell RC 2.00 5.00
❑ 187 Aaron Schobel RC 3.00 8.00
❑ 188 Dan Alexander RC 2.50 6.00
❑ 189 Jamie Winborn RC 2.50 6.00
❑ 190 Karon Riley RC 2.00 5.00
❑ EG Eddie George SAMPLE 1.50 3.00

2002 SP Authentic

❑ COMP.SET w/o SP's (90) 10.00 25.00
❑ 1 Tom Brady 1.00 2.50
❑ 2 Antowain Smith .30 .75
❑ 3 Troy Brown .30 .75
❑ 4 Kurt Warner .40 1.00
❑ 5 Marshall Faulk .40 1.00
❑ 6 Isaac Bruce .40 1.00
❑ 7 Kordell Stewart .30 .75
❑ 8 Jerome Bettis .40 1.00
❑ 9 Plaxico Burress .30 .75
❑ 10 Hines Ward .40 1.00
❑ 11 Donovan McNabb .50 1.25
❑ 12 Duce Staley .30 .75
❑ 13 Dorsey Levens .30 .75
❑ 14 Antonio Freeman .40 1.00
❑ 15 Jerry Rice .75 2.00
❑ 16 Rich Gannon .30 .75
❑ 17 Tim Brown .40 1.00
❑ 18 Jim Miller .30 .75
❑ 19 Marty Booker .30 .75
❑ 20 Brian Urlacher .50 1.25
❑ 21 Jamal Lewis .30 .75
❑ 22 Chris Redman .25 .60
❑ 23 Ray Lewis .40 1.00
❑ 24 Brett Favre 1.00 2.50
❑ 25 Ahman Green .30 .75
❑ 26 Terry Glenn .30 .75
❑ 27 Keyshawn Johnson .30 .75
❑ 28 Keenan McCardell .30 .75
❑ 29 Michael Pittman .30 .75
❑ 30 Curtis Martin .40 1.00
❑ 31 Vinny Testaverde .30 .75
❑ 32 Chad Pennington .40 1.00
❑ 33 Wayne Chrebet .30 .75
❑ 34 Terrell Owens .40 1.00
❑ 35 Garrison Hearst .30 .75
❑ 36 Jay Fiedler .30 .75
❑ 37 Ricky Williams .40 1.00
❑ 38 Chris Chambers .40 1.00
❑ 39 Shaun Alexander .40 1.00
❑ 40 Darrell Jackson .30 .75
❑ 41 Drew Bledsoe .40 1.00
❑ 42 Travis Henry .30 .75
❑ 43 Eric Moulds .30 .75
❑ 44 Stephen Davis .30 .75
❑ 45 Rod Gardner .25 .60
❑ 46 Brian Griese .30 .75
❑ 47 Olandis Gary .30 .75
❑ 48 Shannon Sharpe .40 1.00
❑ 49 Tim Couch .25 .60
❑ 50 Kevin Johnson .25 .60
❑ 51 Steve McNair .40 1.00
❑ 52 Eddie George .30 .75
❑ 53 Aaron Brooks .30 .75
❑ 54 Deuce McAllister .40 1.00
❑ 55 Joe Horn .30 .75
❑ 56 Michael Vick .40 1.00
❑ 57 Warrick Dunn .30 .75
❑ 58 Kerry Collins .30 .75
❑ 59 Tiki Barber .40 1.00
❑ 60 Amani Toomer .30 .75
❑ 61 Jake Plummer .30 .75
❑ 62 David Boston .25 .60
❑ 63 Thomas Jones .30 .75
❑ 64 Edgerrin James .40 1.00
❑ 65 Marvin Harrison .40 1.00
❑ 66 Mark Brunell .30 .75
❑ 67 Jimmy Smith .30 .75
❑ 68 Fred Taylor .40 1.00
❑ 69 Corey Dillon .30 .75
❑ 70 Jon Kitna .30 .75
❑ 71 Michael Westbrook .25 .60
❑ 72 Trent Green .30 .75
❑ 73 Priest Holmes .40 1.00
❑ 74 Tony Gonzalez .30 .75
❑ 75 Daunte Culpepper .30 .75
❑ 76 Michael Bennett .30 .75
❑ 77 Randy Moss .40 1.00
❑ 78 Drew Brees .60 1.50
❑ 79 Curtis Conway .30 .75
❑ 80 Junior Seau .40 1.00
❑ 81 Quincy Carter .25 .60
❑ 82 Emmitt Smith 1.00 2.50
❑ 83 Joey Galloway .30 .75
❑ 84 Cory Schlesinger .25 .60
❑ 85 James Stewart .25 .60
❑ 86 Az-Zahir Hakim .25 .60
❑ 87 Rodney Peete .30 .75
❑ 88 Lamar Smith .30 .75
❑ 89 Corey Bradford .25 .60
❑ 90 Jermaine Lewis .25 .60
❑ 91 Peyton Manning AU 60.00 120.00
❑ 92 Anthony Thomas AU 10.00 25.00
❑ 93 LaDainian Tomlinson AU 40.00 80.00
❑ 94 Jeff Garcia AU 10.00 25.00
❑ 95 Kurt Warner SC 1.25 3.00
❑ 96 Brett Favre SC 3.00 8.00
❑ 97 Michael Vick SC 1.25 3.00
❑ 98 Donovan McNabb SC 1.50 4.00
❑ 99 Daunte Culpepper SC 1.00 2.50
❑ 100 Tom Brady SC 3.00 8.00
❑ 101 Drew Brees SC 2.00 5.00
❑ 102 Kordell Stewart SC 1.00 2.50
❑ 103 Steve McNair SC 1.25 3.00
❑ 104 Peyton Manning SC 2.50 6.00
❑ 105 Mark Brunell SC 1.00 2.50
❑ 106 Jeff Garcia SC 1.00 2.50
❑ 107 Aaron Brooks SC 1.00 2.50
❑ 108 Rich Gannon SC 1.00 2.50
❑ 109 Tim Couch SC .75 2.00
❑ 110 Jake Plummer SC 1.00 2.50
❑ 111 Drew Bledsoe SC 1.25 3.00
❑ 112 Brian Griese SC 1.00 2.50
❑ 113 Quincy Carter SC .75 2.00
❑ 114 Vinny Testaverde SC 1.00 2.50
❑ 115 Chad Pennington SC 1.25 3.00
❑ 116 Brad Johnson SC 1.00 2.50
❑ 117 Trent Dilfer SC 1.00 2.50
❑ 118 Jim Miller SC 1.00 2.50
❑ 119 Tommy Maddox SC 1.00 2.50
❑ 120 Trent Green SC 1.00 2.50
❑ 121 Rodney Peete SC 1.00 2.50
❑ 122 Jay Fiedler SC 1.00 2.50
❑ 123 Kerry Collins SC 1.00 2.50
❑ 124 Chris Redman SC .75 2.00
❑ 125 Marshall Faulk SS 1.50 4.00
❑ 126 Donovan McNabb SS 2.00 5.00

Card	Low	High
❑ 127 Michael Vick SS	1.50	4.00
❑ 128 Brett Favre SS	4.00	10.00
❑ 129 Peyton Manning SS	3.00	8.00
❑ 130 Kurt Warner SS	1.50	4.00
❑ 131 Curtis Martin SS	1.50	4.00
❑ 132 Randy Moss SS	1.50	4.00
❑ 133 Edgerrin James SS	1.50	4.00
❑ 134 Jerome Bettis SS	1.50	4.00
❑ 135 Emmitt Smith SS	4.00	10.00
❑ 136 LaDainian Tomlinson SS	2.50	6.00
❑ 137 Jeff Garcia SS	1.25	3.00
❑ 138 Kordell Stewart SS	1.25	3.00
❑ 139 Anthony Thomas SS	1.25	3.00
❑ 140 Tom Brady SS	4.00	10.00
❑ 141 Daunte Culpepper SS	1.25	3.00
❑ 142 Drew Bledsoe SS	1.50	4.00
❑ 143 Ricky Williams SS	1.50	4.00
❑ 144 Warrick Dunn SS	1.25	3.00
❑ 145 Steve McNair SS	1.50	4.00
❑ 146 Rich Gannon SS	1.25	3.00
❑ 147 Jake Plummer SS	1.25	3.00
❑ 148 Jerry Rice SS	3.00	8.00
❑ 149 Mark Brunell SS	1.25	3.00
❑ 150 Brian Griese SS	1.25	3.00
❑ 151 Eddie George SS	1.25	3.00
❑ 152 Tim Couch SS	1.00	2.50
❑ 153 Keyshawn Johnson SS	1.25	3.00
❑ 154 Shannon Sharpe SS	1.50	4.00
❑ 155 Phillip Buchanon RC	2.50	6.00
❑ 156 Brian Allen RC	2.00	5.00
❑ 157 Brian Westbrook RC	20.00	40.00
❑ 158 Lito Sheppard RC	2.50	6.00
❑ 159 Daryl Jones RC	1.50	4.00
❑ 160 Javin Hunter RC	1.50	4.00
❑ 161 Derrick Lewis RC	1.50	4.00
❑ 162 Javon Walker RC	2.50	6.00
❑ 163 Tank Williams RC	2.00	5.00
❑ 164 Shaun Hill RC	8.00	20.00
❑ 165 Napoleon Harris RC	2.00	5.00
❑ 166 Herb Haygood RC	1.50	4.00
❑ 167 Jake Schifino RC	1.50	4.00
❑ 168 Quentin Jammer RC	2.50	6.00
❑ 169 Jason McAddley RC	2.00	5.00
❑ 170 Jerramy Stevens RC	2.50	6.00
❑ 171 Jesse Chatman RC	1.50	4.00
❑ 172 Larry Ned RC	1.50	4.00
❑ 173 Najeh Davenport RC	2.50	6.00
❑ 174 Lamont Thompson RC	2.00	5.00
❑ 175 Darrell Hill RC	1.50	4.00
❑ 176 Ryan Sims RC	2.50	6.00
❑ 177 Ryan Denney RC	1.50	4.00
❑ 178 Jamin Elliott RC	1.50	4.00
❑ 179 Sam Simmons RC	1.50	4.00
❑ 180 Seth Burford RC	1.50	4.00
❑ 181 Tellis Redmon RC	1.50	4.00
❑ 182 Ben Leber RC	1.50	4.00
❑ 183 Kendall Newson RC	1.50	4.00
❑ 184 Marques Anderson RC	2.00	5.00
❑ 185 Adrian Peterson AU RC	8.00	20.00
❑ 187 Antwoine Womack AU RC	5.00	12.00
❑ 188 Brandon Doman AU RC	5.00	12.00
❑ 189 Craig Nall AU RC	6.00	15.00
❑ 190 Chad Hutchinson AU RC	5.00	12.00
❑ 191 Chester Taylor AU RC	12.00	30.00
❑ 192 Damien Anderson AU RC	6.00	15.00
❑ 193 Deion Branch AU RC	8.00	20.00
❑ 194 Dusty Bonner AU RC	5.00	12.00
❑ 195 Ed Reed AU RC	30.00	60.00
❑ 196 Eric McCoo AU RC	5.00	12.00
❑ 197 J.T. O'Sullivan AU RC	8.00	20.00
❑ 198 Kalimba Edwards AU RC	6.00	15.00
❑ 199 Jonathan Wells AU RC	8.00	20.00
❑ 200 Josh Scobey AU RC	6.00	15.00
❑ 201 Kelly Campbell AU RC	6.00	15.00
❑ 202 Kurt Kittner AU RC	5.00	12.00
❑ 203 Lamar Gordon AU RC	8.00	20.00
❑ 204 Lee Mays AU RC	5.00	12.00
❑ 205 Leonard Henry AU RC	5.00	12.00
❑ 206 Luke Staley AU RC	5.00	12.00
❑ 207 Justin Peelle AU RC	5.00	12.00
❑ 208 Randy Fasani AU RC	6.00	15.00
❑ 209 Ricky Williams AU RC	6.00	15.00
❑ 210 Ronald Curry AU RC	8.00	20.00
❑ 211 Travis Stephens AU RC	5.00	12.00
❑ 212 Wendell Bryant AU RC	5.00	12.00
❑ 213 Woody Dantzler AU RC	6.00	15.00
❑ 214 Kahlil Hill AU RC	5.00	12.00
❑ 215 Donte Stallworth JSY RC	6.00	15.00
❑ 216 Joey Harrington AU/280 RC	12.00	30.00
❑ 217 Cliff Russell JSY RC	4.00	10.00
❑ 218 Clinton Portis JSY RC	15.00	40.00
❑ 219 Daniel Graham JSY RC	5.00	12.00
❑ 220 David Garrard JSY RC	10.00	25.00
❑ 221 DeShaun Foster JSY RC	6.00	15.00
❑ 222 Julius Peppers JSY RC	10.00	25.00
❑ 223 Jeremy Shockey JSY RC	15.00	30.00
❑ 224 Patrick Ramsey JSY RC	6.00	15.00
❑ 225 Josh Reed JSY RC	5.00	12.00
❑ 226 LaDell Betts JSY RC	6.00	15.00
❑ 227 Mike Williams JSY/350 RC	4.00	10.00
❑ 228 Reche Caldwell JSY RC	6.00	15.00
❑ 229 Rohan Davey JSY RC	6.00	15.00
❑ 230 Ron Johnson JSY RC	5.00	12.00
❑ 231 Roy Williams JSY/350 RC	10.00	25.00
❑ 232 T.J. Duckett JSY RC	6.00	15.00
❑ 233 Tim Carter JSY RC	5.00	12.00
❑ 234 William Green JSY RC	5.00	12.00
❑ 235 Randle El JSY AU RC	15.00	40.00
❑ 237 David Carr JSY AU RC	15.00	40.00
❑ 238 Andre Davis JSY AU RC	12.00	30.00
❑ 239 Eric Crouch JSY AU RC	15.00	40.00
❑ 240 Antonio Bryant JSY AU RC	20.00	50.00
❑ 241 Jabar Gaffney JSY AU RC	15.00	40.00
❑ 242 Marquise Walker JSY AU RC	10.00	25.00
❑ 243 Maurice Morris JSY AU RC	15.00	40.00
❑ 244 Josh McCown JSY AU RC	15.00	40.00
❑ AP1 Walter Payton AU/34	500.00	750.00
❑ SW1 Walter Payton JSY/150	50.00	120.00
❑ SW1 W.Payton Gold JSY/34	100.00	200.00
❑ SCPS Payt/Smith JSY/250	60.00	120.00
❑ SCPSG Payt/Smith Gld JSY/34	175.00	300.00

2003 SP Authentic

Card	Low	High
❑ COMP.SET w/o SP's (90)	7.50	20.00
❑ 1 Donovan McNabb	.40	1.00
❑ 2 Tim Couch	.25	.60
❑ 3 Joey Harrington	.30	.75
❑ 4 Brett Favre	1.00	2.50
❑ 5 Jeff Garcia	.40	1.00
❑ 6 Kerry Collins	.30	.75
❑ 7 Michael Vick	.40	1.00
❑ 8 David Carr	.40	1.00
❑ 9 Steve McNair	.40	1.00
❑ 10 Chad Pennington	.40	1.00
❑ 11 Patrick Ramsey	.30	.75
❑ 12 Rich Gannon	.30	.75
❑ 13 Kurt Warner	.40	1.00
❑ 14 Brad Johnson	.30	.75
❑ 15 Jay Fiedler	.30	.75
❑ 16 Jake Plummer	.30	.75
❑ 17 Mark Brunell	.30	.75
❑ 18 Peyton Manning	.75	2.00
❑ 19 Brian Griese	.30	.75
❑ 20 Kordell Stewart	.30	.75
❑ 21 Kelly Holcomb	.25	.60
❑ 22 Josh McCown	.30	.75
❑ 23 Matt Hasselbeck	.30	.75
❑ 24 Marc Bulger	.40	1.00
❑ 25 Chris Redman	.25	.60
❑ 26 Rodney Peete	.25	.60
❑ 27 Jake Delhomme	.40	1.00
❑ 28 Jon Kitna	.30	.75
❑ 29 Trent Green	.30	.75
❑ 30 Quincy Carter	.25	.60
❑ 31 Chad Hutchinson	.25	.60
❑ 32 Edgerrin James	.40	1.00
❑ 33 Deuce McAllister	.40	1.00
❑ 34 Ricky Williams	.30	.75
❑ 35 Priest Holmes	.40	1.00
❑ 36 Curtis Martin	.40	1.00
❑ 37 Shaun Alexander	.40	1.00
❑ 38 Eddie George	.30	.75
❑ 39 Marshall Faulk	.40	1.00
❑ 40 Garrison Hearst	.30	.75
❑ 41 Ahman Green	.40	1.00
❑ 42 Corey Dillon	.30	.75
❑ 43 Jamal Lewis	.40	1.00
❑ 44 William Green	.25	.60
❑ 45 Travis Henry	.30	.75
❑ 46 Mike Alstott	.40	1.00
❑ 47 Amos Zereoue	.25	.60
❑ 48 Stephen Davis	.30	.75
❑ 49 Duce Staley	.30	.75
❑ 50 Fred Taylor	.40	1.00
❑ 51 Anthony Thomas	.30	.75
❑ 52 Charlie Garner	.30	.75
❑ 53 Kevan Barlow	.25	.60
❑ 54 Brian Urlacher	.60	1.50
❑ 55 Junior Seau	.40	1.00
❑ 56 Zach Thomas	.40	1.00
❑ 57 Ray Lewis	.40	1.00
❑ 58 Jerry Porter	.30	.75
❑ 59 Marty Booker	.30	.75
❑ 60 Javon Walker	.30	.75
❑ 61 Donald Driver	.40	1.00
❑ 62 Amani Toomer	.30	.75
❑ 63 Peerless Price	.25	.60
❑ 64 Santana Moss	.30	.75
❑ 65 Laveranues Coles	.30	.75
❑ 66 Troy Brown	.30	.75
❑ 67 Chris Chambers	.30	.75
❑ 68 Rod Smith	.30	.75
❑ 69 Ashley Lelie	.25	.60
❑ 70 Plaxico Burress	.40	1.00
❑ 71 Keyshawn Johnson	.40	1.00
❑ 72 Isaac Bruce	.40	1.00
❑ 73 Torry Holt	.40	1.00
❑ 74 Koren Robinson	.30	.75
❑ 75 Derrick Mason	.30	.75
❑ 76 Kevin Johnson	.25	.60
❑ 77 Andre' Davis	.25	.60
❑ 78 Antonio Bryant	.40	1.00
❑ 79 Eric Moulds	.30	.75
❑ 80 Jerry Rice	.75	2.00
❑ 81 Tim Brown	.40	1.00
❑ 82 Antwaan Randle El	.30	.75
❑ 83 Donte Stallworth	.30	.75
❑ 84 Randy Moss	.40	1.00
❑ 85 Chad Johnson	.40	1.00
❑ 86 Hines Ward	.40	1.00
❑ 87 Rod Gardner	.25	.60
❑ 88 Marvin Harrison	.40	1.00
❑ 89 David Boston	.25	.60
❑ 90 Julius Peppers	.40	1.00
❑ 91 Dewayne White RC	1.00	2.50
❑ 92 Casey Fitzsimmons RC	1.25	3.00
❑ 93 Aaron Moorehead RC	1.25	3.00
❑ 94 Jimmy Farris RC	1.00	2.50
❑ 95 Eric Parker RC	1.50	4.00
❑ 96 Michael Haynes RC	1.00	2.50
❑ 97 J.J. Moses RC	1.00	2.50
❑ 98 Ken Hamlin RC	1.50	4.00
❑ 99 William Joseph RC	1.00	2.50
❑ 100 Alonzo Jackson RC	1.00	2.50
❑ 101 Tyler Brayton RC	1.25	3.00
❑ 102 Eddie Moore RC	1.00	2.50
❑ 103 Cleo Lemon RC	1.50	4.00
❑ 104 Arlen Harris RC	1.00	2.50
❑ 105 Cortez Hankton RC	1.25	3.00
❑ 106 Angelo Crowell RC	1.25	3.00
❑ 107 Johnathan Sullivan RC	1.00	2.50
❑ 108 Pisa Tinoisamoa RC	1.50	4.00
❑ 109 Boss Bailey RC	1.25	3.00
❑ 110 Tommy Jones RC	1.00	2.50
❑ 111 E.J. Henderson RC	1.25	3.00
❑ 112 Jimmy Kennedy RC	1.25	3.00
❑ 113 Nnamdi Asomugha RC	2.50	6.00
❑ 114 Hanik Milligan RC	1.00	2.50
❑ 115 Sammy Davis RC	1.25	3.00
❑ 116 Drayton Florence RC	1.25	3.00
❑ 117 Andre Woolfolk RC	1.25	3.00
❑ 118 Dennis Weathersby RC	1.00	2.50
❑ 119 Mike Doss RC	1.50	4.00
❑ 120 Troy Polamalu RC	20.00	40.00
❑ 121 Clinton Portis SS	2.00	5.00
❑ 122 Daunte Culpepper SS	1.50	4.00
❑ 123 Jeremy Shockey SS	1.50	4.00
❑ 124 Drew Brees SS	1.50	4.00
❑ 125 Marshall Faulk SS	1.50	4.00
❑ 126 Emmitt Smith SS	4.00	10.00
❑ 127 Terrell Owens SS	1.50	4.00
❑ 128 Ricky Williams SS	1.25	3.00
❑ 129 Deuce McAllister SS	1.50	4.00
❑ 130 Ahman Green SS	1.50	4.00

❑ 131 Chad Pennington SS 1.50 4.00
❑ 132 Plaxico Burress SS 1.50 4.00
❑ 133 Steve McNair SS 1.50 4.00
❑ 134 Keyshawn Johnson SS 1.50 4.00
❑ 135 Jeff Garcia SS 1.50 4.00
❑ 136 Drew Bledsoe SS 1.50 4.00
❑ 137 Jerry Rice SS 3.00 8.00
❑ 138 Randy Moss SS 1.50 4.00
❑ 139 David Carr SS 1.50 4.00
❑ 140 Joey Harrington SS 1.25 3.00
❑ 141 Michael Vick SS 1.50 4.00
❑ 142 Tom Brady SS 4.00 10.00
❑ 143 Brian Urlacher SS 2.50 6.00
❑ 144 Brett Favre SS 4.00 10.00
❑ 145 Kurt Warner SS 1.50 4.00
❑ 146 LaDainian Tomlinson SS 2.00 5.00
❑ 147 Aaron Brooks SS 1.25 3.00
❑ 148 Edgerrin James SS 1.50 4.00
❑ 149 Peyton Manning SS 3.00 8.00
❑ 150 Donovan McNabb SS 1.50 4.00
❑ 151 Jason Gesser RC 1.50 4.00
❑ 152 Ken Dorsey RC 1.50 4.00
❑ 153 Jason Johnson RC 1.25 3.00
❑ 154 Avon Cobourne RC 1.25 3.00
❑ 155 Andrew Pinnock RC 1.50 4.00
❑ 156 Kirk Farmer RC 1.50 4.00
❑ 157 Reno Mahe RC 1.50 4.00
❑ 158 Lon Sheriff RC 1.25 3.00
❑ 159 Marquel Blackwell RC 1.25 3.00
❑ 160 Quentin Griffin RC 1.50 4.00
❑ 161 Rashean Mathis RC 1.50 4.00
❑ 162 Lee Suggs RC 1.50 4.00
❑ 163 Jeremi Johnson RC 1.25 3.00
❑ 164 Ovie Mughelli RC 1.25 3.00
❑ 165 Nick Barnett RC 2.00 5.00
❑ 166 Brock Forsey RC 1.50 4.00
❑ 167 Malaefou MacKenzie RC 1.25 3.00
❑ 168 Ahmaad Galloway RC 1.50 4.00
❑ 169 Cecil Sapp RC 1.25 3.00
❑ 170 Kerry Carter RC 1.25 3.00
❑ 171 Dahrran Diedrick RC 1.25 3.00
❑ 171A Terrence Edwards RC 1.25 3.00
❑ 172 Joffrey Reynolds RC 1.25 3.00
❑ 173 Sultan McCullough RC 1.25 3.00
❑ 174 Brandon Drumm RC 1.25 3.00
❑ 175 Casey Moore RC 1.25 3.00
❑ 176 Gerald Hayes RC 1.50 4.00
❑ 178 Jamal Burke RC 1.25 3.00
❑ 179 Antonio Chatman RC 2.00 5.00
❑ 180 Reggie Newhouse RC 1.25 3.00
❑ 181 Chris Horn RC 1.50 4.00
❑ 182 Denero Marriott RC 1.25 3.00
❑ 183 DeAndrew Rubin RC 1.25 3.00
❑ 184 Taco Wallace RC 1.25 3.00
❑ 185 Doug Gabriel RC 1.50 4.00
❑ 186 Willie Ponder RC 1.25 3.00
❑ 187 David Tyree RC 2.00 5.00
❑ 188 Kevin Walter RC 2.00 5.00
❑ 189 Zuriel Smith RC 1.25 3.00
❑ 190 Keenan Howry RC 1.25 3.00
❑ 191 C.J. Jones RC 1.25 3.00
❑ 192 Arnaz Battle RC 2.00 5.00
❑ 193 Walter Young RC 1.25 3.00
❑ 194 Anthony Adams RC 1.50 4.00
❑ 195 Jerome McDougle RC 1.25 3.00
❑ 196 Will Heller RC 1.50 4.00
❑ 197 Cecil Moore RC 1.25 3.00
❑ 198 Mike Seidman RC 1.25 3.00
❑ 199 Jason Witten RC 15.00 30.00
❑ 200 L.J. Smith RC 2.00 5.00
❑ 201 Bennie Joppru RC 1.25 3.00
❑ 202 Donald Lee RC 1.50 4.00
❑ 203 Aaron Walker RC 1.50 4.00
❑ 204 Antonio Brown RC 1.25 3.00
❑ 205 George Wrighster RC 1.25 3.00
❑ 206 Danny Curley RC 1.25 3.00
❑ 207 Mike Banks RC 1.25 3.00
❑ 208 Mike Pinkard RC 1.25 3.00
❑ 209 Ryan Hoag RC 1.25 3.00
❑ 210 Brad Pyatt RC 1.25 3.00
❑ 211 Charles Rogers RC 1.50 4.00
❑ 212 Chris Simms AU/250 RC 15.00 40.00
❑ 213 Nate Hybl AU RC 4.00 10.00
❑ 214 Brandon Lloyd AU RC 5.00 12.00
❑ 215 ReShard Lee AU RC 5.00 12.00
❑ 216 Dwone Hicks AU RC 3.00 8.00
❑ 217 Tony Romo AU RC 250.00 400.00
❑ 218 Brett Engemann AU RC 3.00 8.00
❑ 219 Nick Maddox AU RC 3.00 8.00
❑ 220 James MacPherson AU RC 4.00 10.00
❑ 221 Juston Wood AU RC 3.00 8.00
❑ 222 Adrian Madise AU RC 3.00 8.00
❑ 223 Shaun McDonald AU RC 5.00 12.00
❑ 224 Carl Ford AU RC 3.00 8.00
❑ 225 Vishante Shiancoe AU RC 12.50 25.00
❑ 226 Gibran Hamdan AU RC 3.00 8.00
❑ 227 Brooks Bollinger AU RC 5.00 12.00
❑ 228 B.J. Askew AU RC 4.00 10.00
❑ 229 Domanick Davis AU RC 5.00 12.00
❑ 230 LaBrandon Toefield AU RC 4.00 10.00
❑ 231 Bobby Wade AU RC 4.00 10.00
❑ 232 Justin Gage AU RC 5.00 12.00
❑ 233 Billy McMullen AU RC 3.00 8.00
❑ 234 David Kircus AU RC 5.00 12.00
❑ 235 J.R. Tolver AU RC 4.00 10.00
❑ 236 Sam Aiken AU RC 5.00 12.00
❑ 237 LaTarence Dunbar AU RC 3.00 8.00
❑ 238 Kassim Osgood AU RC 5.00 12.00
❑ 239 Tony Hollings AU RC 4.00 10.00
❑ 240 Justin Griffith AU RC 4.00 10.00
❑ 241 Brian St.Pierre JSY RC 6.00 15.00
❑ 242 Kevin Curtis JSY RC 6.00 15.00
❑ 243 Dallas Clark JSY RC 15.00 30.00
❑ 244 Willis McGahee JSY RC 12.00 30.00
❑ 245 Terence Newman JSY RC 8.00 15.00
❑ 246 Justin Fargas JSY AU RC 12.00 30.00
❑ 247 Artose Pinner JSY RC 4.00 10.00
❑ 248 Kelley Washington JSY RC 5.00 12.00
❑ 249 DeWayne Robertson JSY RC 5.00 12.00
❑ 250 Nate Burleson JSY RC 5.00 12.00
❑ 251 Kliff Kingsbury JSY RC 5.00 12.00
❑ 252 Bethel Johnson JSY RC 5.00 12.00
❑ 253 Anquan Boldin JSY RC 15.00 40.00
❑ 254 Bryant Johnson JSY AU RC 12.00 30.00
❑ 255 Terrell Suggs JSY AU RC 15.00 40.00
❑ 256 Musa Smith JSY RC 5.00 12.00
❑ 257 Chris Brown JSY RC 6.00 15.00
❑ 258 Marcus Trufant JSY RC 6.00 15.00
❑ 259 Teyo Johnson JSY RC 5.00 12.00
❑ 260 Tyrone Calico JSY RC 5.00 12.00
❑ 261 Dave Ragone JSY AU RC 8.00 20.00
❑ 262 Kyle Boller JSY AU RC 12.00 30.00
❑ 263 Onterrio Smith JSY AU RC 10.00 25.00
❑ 264 Rex Grossman JSY RC 6.00 15.00
❑ 265 Larry Johnson JSY RC 8.00 20.00
❑ 266 Seneca Wallace JSY AU RC 12.00 30.00
❑ 268 Taylor Jacobs JSY AU RC 10.00 25.00
❑ 269 Byron Leftwich JSY AU RC 15.00 40.00
❑ 270 Carson Palmer JSY AU RC 150.00 300.00

2004 SP Authentic

❑ COMP.SET w/o SP's (90) 10.00 25.00
❑ 151-185 AU RC PRINT RUN 990 SER.#'d SETS
❑ 186-200 JSY AU RC PRINT RUN 799
❑ 201-206 JSY AU RC PRINT RUN 499
❑ 207-216 JSY AU RC PRINT RUN 299
❑ 1 Josh McCown .30 .75
❑ 2 Anquan Boldin .40 1.00
❑ 3 Michael Vick .40 1.00
❑ 4 Peerless Price .30 .75
❑ 5 Todd Heap .30 .75
❑ 6 Kyle Boller .30 .75
❑ 7 Jamal Lewis .30 .75
❑ 8 Drew Bledsoe .40 1.00
❑ 9 Travis Henry .30 .75
❑ 10 Eric Moulds .30 .75
❑ 11 Steve Smith .40 1.00
❑ 12 Stephen Davis .30 .75
❑ 13 Jake Delhomme .30 .75
❑ 14 Rex Grossman .40 1.00
❑ 15 Brian Urlacher .40 1.00
❑ 16 Thomas Jones .30 .75
❑ 17 Chad Johnson .30 .75
❑ 18 Rudi Johnson .30 .75
❑ 19 Carson Palmer .50 1.25
❑ 20 William Green .25 .60
❑ 21 Andre Davis .25 .60
❑ 22 Jeff Garcia .40 1.00
❑ 23 Roy Williams S .30 .75
❑ 24 Eddie George .30 .75
❑ 25 Keyshawn Johnson .30 .75
❑ 26 Ashley Lelie .30 .75
❑ 27 Jake Plummer .30 .75
❑ 28 Champ Bailey .30 .75
❑ 29 Charles Rogers .30 .75
❑ 30 Joey Harrington .30 .75
❑ 31 Ahman Green .40 1.00
❑ 32 Brett Favre 1.00 2.50
❑ 33 Javon Walker .30 .75
❑ 34 David Carr .30 .75
❑ 35 Domanick Davis .30 .75
❑ 36 Andre Johnson .40 1.00
❑ 37 Marvin Harrison .40 1.00
❑ 38 Edgerrin James .40 1.00
❑ 39 Peyton Manning .75 2.00
❑ 40 Byron Leftwich .40 1.00
❑ 41 Fred Taylor .30 .75
❑ 42 Trent Green .30 .75
❑ 43 Tony Gonzalez .40 1.00
❑ 44 Priest Holmes .40 1.00
❑ 45 Ricky Williams .40 1.00
❑ 46 Chris Chambers .30 .75
❑ 47 Jay Fiedler .25 .60
❑ 48 Daunte Culpepper .40 1.00
❑ 49 Randy Moss .40 1.00
❑ 50 Onterrio Smith .25 .60
❑ 51 Tom Brady 1.00 2.50
❑ 52 Troy Brown .30 .75
❑ 53 Corey Dillon .30 .75
❑ 54 Deuce McAllister .40 1.00
❑ 55 Aaron Brooks .30 .75
❑ 56 Joe Horn .30 .75
❑ 57 Amani Toomer .30 .75
❑ 58 Kurt Warner .40 1.00
❑ 59 Jeremy Shockey .30 .75
❑ 60 Chad Pennington .40 1.00
❑ 61 Santana Moss .30 .75
❑ 62 Curtis Martin .40 1.00
❑ 63 Rich Gannon .30 .75
❑ 64 Jerry Rice .75 2.00
❑ 65 Jerry Porter .30 .75
❑ 66 Terrell Owens .40 1.00
❑ 67 Jevon Kearse .30 .75
❑ 68 Donovan McNabb .40 1.00
❑ 69 Hines Ward .40 1.00
❑ 70 Plaxico Burress .30 .75
❑ 71 Tommy Maddox .30 .75
❑ 72 Drew Brees .40 1.00
❑ 73 LaDainian Tomlinson .50 1.25
❑ 74 Tim Rattay .25 .60
❑ 75 Brandon Lloyd .25 .60
❑ 76 Kevan Barlow .30 .75
❑ 77 Shaun Alexander .40 1.00
❑ 78 Koren Robinson .40 1.00
❑ 79 Matt Hasselbeck .40 1.00
❑ 80 Marshall Faulk .40 1.00
❑ 81 Torry Holt .40 1.00
❑ 82 Marc Bulger .30 .75
❑ 83 Brad Johnson .30 .75
❑ 84 Joey Galloway .30 .75
❑ 85 Steve McNair .40 1.00
❑ 86 Derrick Mason .30 .75
❑ 87 Chris Brown .30 .75
❑ 88 Mark Brunell .30 .75
❑ 89 Laveranues Coles .30 .75
❑ 90 Clinton Portis .40 1.00
❑ 91 Triandos Luke RC 1.50 4.00
❑ 92 Keith Smith RC 1.50 4.00
❑ 93 Shaun Phillips RC 2.00 5.00
❑ 94 D.J. Williams RC 2.50 6.00
❑ 95 Keiwan Ratliff RC 1.50 4.00
❑ 96 Madieu Williams RC 1.50 4.00
❑ 97 Chris Cooley RC 2.50 6.00
❑ 98 Stuart Schweigert RC 2.00 5.00
❑ 99 Sloan Thomas RC 2.00 5.00
❑ 100 Chad Lavalais RC 1.50 4.00
❑ 101 Jared Allen RC 15.00 30.00
❑ 102 Brian Jones RC 1.50 4.00
❑ 103 Matt Ware RC 2.50 6.00
❑ 104 Daryl Smith RC 2.00 5.00
❑ 105 J.R. Reed RC 1.50 4.00
❑ 106 D.J. Hackett RC 2.50 6.00
❑ 107 Jeris McIntyre RC 1.50 4.00
❑ 108 Dexter Reid RC 1.50 4.00

❑ 109 Courtney Anderson RC 1.50 4.00
❑ 110 Courtney Watson RC 2.00 5.00
❑ 111 Larry Croom RC 1.50 4.00
❑ 112 Jonathan Smith RC 1.50 4.00
❑ 113 Vernon Carey RC 1.50 4.00
❑ 114 Michael Gaines RC 1.50 4.00
❑ 115 Chris Snee RC 2.00 5.00
❑ 116 Nathan Vasher RC 2.50 6.00
❑ 117 Teddy Lehman RC 2.00 5.00
❑ 118 Marcus Tubbs RC 1.50 4.00
❑ 119 Ben Utecht RC 2.00 5.00
❑ 120 Maurice Mann RC 1.50 4.00
❑ 121 Thomas Tapeh RC 2.00 5.00
❑ 122 Will Allen RC 2.00 5.00
❑ 123 Demorrio Williams RC 2.50 6.00
❑ 124 Ran Carthon RC 1.50 4.00
❑ 125 Tim Euhus RC 1.50 4.00
❑ 126 Bradlee Van Pelt RC 2.00 5.00
❑ 127 Patrick Crayton RC 3.00 8.00
❑ 128 Ryan Krause RC 1.50 4.00
❑ 129 Joey Thomas RC 1.50 4.00
❑ 130 Antwan Odom RC 2.50 6.00
❑ 131 Karlos Dansby RC 2.50 6.00
❑ 132 Junior Siavii RC 1.50 4.00
❑ 133 Jamaar Taylor RC 1.50 4.00
❑ 134 Kendrick Starling RC 1.50 4.00
❑ 135 Wes Welker RC 10.00 20.00
❑ 136 Igor Olshansky RC 2.50 6.00
❑ 137 Mark Jones RC 1.50 4.00
❑ 138 Bruce Thornton RC 1.50 4.00
❑ 139 Michael Boulware RC 2.50 6.00
❑ 140 Matt Mauck RC 2.00 5.00
❑ 141 Clarence Moore RC 2.00 5.00
❑ 142 Derrick Strait RC 2.00 5.00
❑ 143 Jarrett Payton RC 2.00 5.00
❑ 144 Dontarrious Thomas RC 2.00 5.00
❑ 145 Shawntae Spencer RC 1.50 4.00
❑ 146 Bob Sanders RC 12.50 25.00
❑ 147 Darnell Dockett RC 1.50 4.00
❑ 148 Sean Taylor RC 2.50 6.00
❑ 149 Jason Babin RC 2.00 5.00
❑ 150 Ricardo Colclough RC 2.50 6.00
❑ 151 Brandon Chillar AU RC 4.00 10.00
❑ 152 Clarence Farmer AU RC 3.00 8.00
❑ 153 B.J. Symons AU RC 3.00 8.00
❑ 154 John Navarre AU RC 4.00 10.00
❑ 155 P.K. Sam AU RC 3.00 8.00
❑ 156 Casey Clausen AU RC 4.00 10.00
❑ 157 Drew Henson AU RC 3.00 8.00
❑ 158 Kris Wilson AU RC 4.00 10.00
❑ 159 Vince Wilfork AU RC 5.00 12.00
❑ 160 Michael Turner AU RC 25.00 50.00
❑ 161 Jonathan Vilma AU RC 5.00 12.00
❑ 162 Samie Parker AU RC 4.00 10.00
❑ 163 B.J. Sams AU RC 4.00 10.00
❑ 164 A.Echemandu AU RC 4.00 10.00
❑ 165 Ernest Wilford AU RC 4.00 10.00
❑ 166 Troy Fleming AU RC 3.00 8.00
❑ 167 Tommie Harris AU RC 5.00 12.00
❑ 168 Jammal Lord AU RC 3.00 8.00
❑ 169 Kenechi Udeze AU RC 5.00 12.00
❑ 170 Chris Gamble AU RC 4.00 10.00
❑ 171 Carlos Francis AU RC 3.00 8.00
❑ 172 Mewelde Moore AU RC 5.00 12.00
❑ 173 Jared Lorenzen AU RC 4.00 10.00
❑ 174 Jeff Smoker AU RC 4.00 10.00
❑ 175 Ben Hartsock AU RC 4.00 10.00
❑ 176 Jerricho Cotchery AU RC 5.00 12.00
❑ 177 Josh Harris AU RC 3.00 8.00
❑ 178 Cody Pickett AU RC 4.00 10.00
❑ 179 Quincy Wilson AU RC 4.00 10.00
❑ 180 Will Smith AU RC 5.00 12.00
❑ 181 Ahmad Carroll AU RC 5.00 12.00
❑ 182 B.J. Johnson AU RC 3.00 8.00
❑ 183 Dunta Robinson AU RC 4.00 10.00
❑ 184 Craig Krenzel AU RC 5.00 12.00
❑ 185 Johnnie Morant AU RC 4.00 10.00
❑ 186 Cedric Cobbs JSY AU RC 10.00 25.00
❑ 187 Matt Schaub JSY AU RC 40.00 100.00
❑ 188 Bernard Berrian JSY AU RC 12.00 30.00
❑ 189 Devard Darling JSY AU RC 10.00 25.00
❑ 190 Ben Watson JSY AU RC 12.00 30.00
❑ 191 Darius Watts JSY AU RC 10.00 25.00
❑ 192 DeAngelo Hall JSY AU RC 12.00 30.00
❑ 193 Ben Troupe JSY AU RC 10.00 25.00
❑ 194 Mich Jenkins JSY AU RC 12.00 30.00
❑ 195 Keary Colbert JSY AU RC 10.00 25.00
❑ 196 Robert Gallery JSY AU RC 12.00 30.00
❑ 197 Greg Jones JSY AU RC 12.00 30.00
❑ 198 Mich.Clayton JSY AU RC 12.00 30.00
❑ 199 Luke McCown JSY AU RC 12.00 30.00
❑ 200 Derrick Hamilton JSY AU RC 8.0020.00
❑ 201 Ras.Woods JSY AU RC 10.00 25.00
❑ 202 Chris Perry JSY AU RC 15.00 40.00
❑ 203 D.Henderson JSY AU RC 15.00 40.00
❑ 204 Tatum Bell JSY AU RC 15.00 40.00
❑ 205 Lee Evans JSY AU RC 20.00 50.00
❑ 206 J.P. Losman JSY AU RC 15.00 40.00
❑ 207 Kel.Winslow JSY AU RC 25.00 60.00
❑ 208 Reg.Williams JSY AU RC 20.00 50.00
❑ 209 Julius Jones JSY AU RC 25.00 60.00
❑ 210 S.Jackson JSY AU RC 100.00 200.00
❑ 211 Kevin Jones JSY AU RC 20.00 50.00
❑ 212 Roy Williams JSY AU RC 25.00 60.00
❑ 213 Roethlisberger JSY AU RC 350.00 600.00
❑ 214 Philip Rivers JSY AU RC 250.00 400.00
❑ 215 L.Fitzgerald JSY AU RC 200.00 350.00
❑ 216 Eli Manning JSY AU RC 250.00 500.00

2005 SP Authentic

❑ COMP.SET w/o RC's (90) 10.00 25.00
❑ 91-180 PRINT RUN 750 SER.#'d SETS
❑ 181-220/254-257 PRINT RUN 850 SETS
❑ 221-253 PRINT RUN 99-899 SER.#'d SETS
❑ UNPRICED NFL LOGO PATCHES #'d TO 1
❑ 1 Kurt Warner .40 1.00
❑ 2 Larry Fitzgerald .40 1.00
❑ 3 Anquan Boldin .30 .75
❑ 4 Michael Vick .40 1.00
❑ 5 Alge Crumpler .30 .75
❑ 6 Warrick Dunn .30 .75
❑ 7 Kyle Boller .30 .75
❑ 8 Jamal Lewis .30 .75
❑ 9 J.P. Losman .30 .75
❑ 10 Willis McGahee .40 1.00
❑ 11 Lee Evans .30 .75
❑ 12 Jake Delhomme .40 1.00
❑ 13 DeShaun Foster .30 .75
❑ 14 Muhsin Muhammad .30 .75
❑ 15 Walter Payton 1.00 2.50
❑ 16 Brian Urlacher .40 1.00
❑ 17 Carson Palmer .40 1.00
❑ 18 Rudi Johnson .30 .75
❑ 19 Chad Johnson .30 .75
❑ 20 Lee Suggs .30 .75
❑ 21 Antonio Bryant .30 .75
❑ 22 Julius Jones .40 1.00
❑ 23 Drew Bledsoe .40 1.00
❑ 24 Keyshawn Johnson .30 .75
❑ 25 Tatum Bell .30 .75
❑ 26 Jake Plummer .30 .75
❑ 27 Roy Williams WR .40 1.00
❑ 28 Kevin Jones .30 .75
❑ 29 Jeff Garcia .30 .75
❑ 30 Brett Favre 1.00 2.50
❑ 31 Ahman Green .40 1.00
❑ 32 Javon Walker .30 .75
❑ 33 David Carr .30 .75
❑ 34 Andre Johnson .30 .75
❑ 35 Domanick Davis .25 .60
❑ 36 Peyton Manning .60 1.50
❑ 37 Edgerrin James .30 .75
❑ 38 Reggie Wayne .30 .75
❑ 39 Byron Leftwich .30 .75
❑ 40 Fred Taylor .40 1.00
❑ 41 Jimmy Smith .30 .75
❑ 42 Priest Holmes .40 1.00
❑ 43 Larry Johnson .40 1.00
❑ 44 Trent Green .30 .75
❑ 45 Randy McMichael .25 .60
❑ 46 Chris Chambers .30 .75
❑ 47 Ricky Williams .30 .75
❑ 48 Daunte Culpepper .40 1.00
❑ 49 Nate Burleson .30 .75
❑ 50 Tom Brady .75 2.00
❑ 51 Corey Dillon .30 .75
❑ 52 David Givens .30 .75
❑ 53 Aaron Brooks .25 .60
❑ 54 Deuce McAllister .40 1.00
❑ 55 Joe Horn .30 .75
❑ 56 Eli Manning .75 2.00
❑ 57 Jeremy Shockey .40 1.00
❑ 58 Tiki Barber .40 1.00
❑ 59 Chad Pennington .40 1.00
❑ 60 Santana Moss .30 .75
❑ 61 Curtis Martin .40 1.00
❑ 62 Randy Moss .40 1.00
❑ 63 LaMont Jordan .30 .75
❑ 64 Kerry Collins .30 .75
❑ 65 Donovan McNabb .40 1.00
❑ 66 Brian Westbrook .40 1.00
❑ 67 Terrell Owens .40 1.00
❑ 68 Ben Roethlisberger 1.00 2.50
❑ 69 Hines Ward .40 1.00
❑ 70 Jerome Bettis .40 1.00
❑ 71 Drew Brees .40 1.00
❑ 72 Antonio Gates .40 1.00
❑ 73 LaDainian Tomlinson .50 1.25
❑ 74 Kevan Barlow .25 .60
❑ 75 Brandon Lloyd .25 .60
❑ 76 Matt Hasselbeck .30 .75
❑ 77 Shaun Alexander .40 1.00
❑ 78 Darrell Jackson .30 .75
❑ 79 Marc Bulger .30 .75
❑ 80 Steven Jackson .50 1.25
❑ 81 Torry Holt .30 .75
❑ 82 Brian Griese .30 .75
❑ 83 Michael Clayton .30 .75
❑ 84 Michael Pittman .25 .60
❑ 85 Steve McNair .40 1.00
❑ 86 Drew Bennett .30 .75
❑ 87 Chris Brown .30 .75
❑ 88 Clinton Portis .40 1.00
❑ 89 Patrick Ramsey .30 .75
❑ 90 Laveranues Coles .30 .75
❑ 91 Nehemiah Broughton RC 2.00 5.00
❑ 92 Madison Hedgecock RC 2.50 6.00
❑ 93 Damien Nash RC 2.00 5.00
❑ 94 Michael Boley RC 1.50 4.00
❑ 95 Lionel Gates RC 1.50 4.00
❑ 96 Noah Herron RC 2.50 6.00
❑ 97 Bo Scaife RC 2.00 5.00
❑ 98 Joel Dreessen RC 2.00 5.00
❑ 99 Rasheed Marshall RC 2.00 5.00
❑ 100 Andre Maddox RC 1.50 4.00
❑ 101 Tab Perry RC 2.50 6.00
❑ 102 Dante Ridgeway RC 1.50 4.00
❑ 103 Patrick Estes RC 1.50 4.00
❑ 104 Billy Bajema RC 1.50 4.00
❑ 105 Paris Warren RC 2.00 5.00
❑ 106 LeRon McCoy RC 1.50 4.00
❑ 107 Adam Bergen RC 1.50 4.00
❑ 108 Manuel White RC 2.00 5.00
❑ 109 Stephen Spach RC 1.50 4.00
❑ 110 Donte Nicholson RC 2.00 5.00
❑ 111 Brodney Pool RC 2.00 5.00
❑ 112 Stanford Routt RC 2.00 5.00
❑ 113 Josh Bullocks RC 2.50 6.00
❑ 114 Ronald Bartell RC 2.00 5.00
❑ 115 Nick Collins RC 2.50 6.00
❑ 116 Darrent Williams RC 2.50 6.00
❑ 117 Justin Miller RC 2.00 5.00
❑ 118 Kelvin Hayden RC 2.00 5.00
❑ 119 Bryant McFadden RC 2.00 5.00
❑ 120 Oshiomogho Atogwe RC 1.50 4.00
❑ 121 Stanley Wilson RC 2.00 5.00
❑ 122 Eric Green RC 1.50 4.00
❑ 123 Michael Hawkins RC 1.50 4.00
❑ 124 Marcus Spears RC 2.50 6.00
❑ 125 Ellis Hobbs RC 2.50 6.00
❑ 126 Scott Starks RC 2.00 5.00
❑ 127 Domonique Foxworth RC 2.00 5.00
❑ 128 Sean Considine RC 1.50 4.00
❑ 129 James Sanders RC 1.50 4.00
❑ 130 Travis Daniels RC 2.00 5.00
❑ 131 Vincent Fuller RC 2.00 5.00
❑ 132 Marviel Underwood RC 2.00 5.00
❑ 133 Jerome Carter RC 1.50 4.00
❑ 134 Kerry Rhodes RC 2.50 6.00
❑ 135 Fred Amey RC 2.00 5.00
❑ 136 Eric King RC 1.50 4.00
❑ 137 Derrick Johnson CB RC 1.50 4.00
❑ 138 Luis Castillo RC 2.50 6.00
❑ 139 Shaun Cody RC 2.00 5.00

Card	Low	High
❑ 140 Matt Roth RC	2.50	6.00
❑ 141 Jonathan Babineaux RC	2.00	5.00
❑ 142 Justin Tuck RC	6.00	15.00
❑ 143 Sione Pouha RC	1.50	4.00
❑ 144 Daven Holly RC	1.50	4.00
❑ 145 Vincent Burns RC	1.50	4.00
❑ 146 Derrick Johnson RC	2.50	6.00
❑ 147 Lofa Tatupu RC	2.50	6.00
❑ 148 Odell Thurman RC	2.50	6.00
❑ 149 Rick Razzano RC	1.50	4.00
❑ 150 Channing Crowder RC	2.00	5.00
❑ 151 Kirk Morrison RC	2.50	6.00
❑ 152 Alfred Fincher RC	2.00	5.00
❑ 153 Jordan Beck RC	2.00	5.00
❑ 154 Darryl Blackstock RC	1.50	4.00
❑ 155 Leroy Hill RC	2.50	6.00
❑ 156 Jammal Brown RC	2.50	6.00
❑ 157 Alex Barron RC	1.50	4.00
❑ 158 Chris Spencer RC	2.50	6.00
❑ 159 Logan Mankins RC	2.50	6.00
❑ 160 David Baas RC	1.50	4.00
❑ 161 Michael Roos RC	1.50	4.00
❑ 162 Kurt Campbell RC	1.50	4.00
❑ 163 Khalif Barnes RC	1.50	4.00
❑ 164 Antonio Perkins RC	2.00	5.00
❑ 165 Vonta Leach RC	1.50	4.00
❑ 166 Brady Poppinga RC	2.50	6.00
❑ 167 Trent Cole RC	2.50	6.00
❑ 168 Dave Rayner RC	1.50	4.00
❑ 169 Bill Swancutt RC	1.50	4.00
❑ 170 Eric Moore RC	1.50	4.00
❑ 171 Justin Green RC	2.50	6.00
❑ 172 Shaun Suisham RC	1.50	4.00
❑ 173 C.J. Mosley RC	1.50	4.00
❑ 174 Ryan Riddle RC	1.50	4.00
❑ 175 Darrell Shropshire RC	1.50	4.00
❑ 176 Boomer Grigsby RC	2.50	6.00
❑ 177 Rian Wallace RC	2.00	5.00
❑ 178 Lance Mitchell RC	2.00	5.00
❑ 179 Nick Speegle RC	1.50	4.00
❑ 180 Tyson Thompson RC	2.50	6.00
❑ 181 Dan Orlovsky AU RC	6.00	15.00
❑ 182 Anthony Davis AU RC	5.00	12.00
❑ 183 Kay-Jay Harris AU RC	5.00	12.00
❑ 184 Walter Reyes AU RC	4.00	10.00
❑ 185 Darren Sproles AU RC	20.00	50.00
❑ 186 Marlin Jackson AU RC	5.00	12.00
❑ 187 Corey Webster AU RC	8.00	20.00
❑ 188 Marion Barber AU RC	40.00	80.00
❑ 189 Chris Henry AU RC	6.00	15.00
❑ 190 Derek Anderson AU RC	10.00	25.00
❑ 191 David Pollack AU RC	5.00	12.00
❑ 192 Anttaj Hawthorne AU RC	5.00	12.00
❑ 193 David Greene AU RC	5.00	12.00
❑ 194 Erasmus James AU RC	5.00	12.00
❑ 195 Ryan Fitzpatrick AU RC	6.00	15.00
❑ 196 Derrick Johnson AU	6.00	15.00
❑ 197 Barrett Ruud AU RC	6.00	15.00
❑ 198 Kevin Burnett AU RC	5.00	12.00
❑ 200 J.R. Russell AU RC	4.00	10.00
❑ 201 Larry Brackins AU RC	4.00	10.00
❑ 202 Thomas Davis AU RC	5.00	12.00
❑ 203 Fred Gibson AU RC	5.00	12.00
❑ 204 Craphonso Thorpe AU RC	5.00	12.00
❑ 205 Brandon Jacobs AU RC	15.00	40.00
❑ 206 Taylor Stubblefield AU RC	4.00	10.00
❑ 207 Shawne Merriman AU RC	12.00	30.00
❑ 208 Travis Johnson AU RC	4.00	10.00
❑ 209 Adrian McPherson AU RC	5.00	12.00
❑ 210 Brandon Jones AU RC	6.00	15.00
❑ 211 Jerome Mathis AU RC	6.00	15.00
❑ 212 Alex Smith TE AU RC	6.00	15.00
❑ 213 Fabian Washington AU RC	6.00	15.00
❑ 214 Mike Nugent AU RC	5.00	12.00
❑ 215 Chase Lyman AU RC	4.00	10.00
❑ 216 Roydell Williams AU RC	5.00	12.00
❑ 217 Matt Cassel AU RC	30.00	60.00
❑ 218 Alvin Pearman AU RC	4.00	10.00
❑ 219 DeMarcus Ware AU RC	20.00	40.00
❑ 220 Mike Patterson AU RC	5.00	12.00
❑ 221 C.Roby JSY/899 AU RC	10.00	25.00
❑ 222 E.Shelton JSY/899 AU RC	10.00	25.00
❑ 223 S.LeFors JSY/899 AU RC	10.00	25.00
❑ 224 Frank Gore JSY/899 AU RC	25.00	60.00
❑ 225 Ryan Moats JSY/899 AU RC	10.00	25.00
❑ 226 A.Walter JSY/899 AU RC	10.00	25.00
❑ 227 A.Jones JSY/899 AU RC	10.00	25.00
❑ 228 C.Rogers JSY/699 AU RC	12.00	30.00
❑ 229 T.Murphy JSY/899 AU RC	8.00	20.00
❑ 230 Kyle Orton JSY/699 AU RC	20.00	50.00
❑ 231 C.Fason JSY/699 AU RC	10.00	25.00
❑ 232 V.Morency JSY/699 AU RC	10.00	25.00
❑ 233 R.Parrish JSY/699 AU RC	10.00	25.00
❑ 234 V.Jackson JSY/699 AU RC	30.00	60.00
❑ 235 M.Bradley JSY/699 AU RC	10.00	25.00
❑ 236 Re.Brown JSY/599 AU RC	10.00	25.00
❑ 237 Ro.White JSY/499 AU RC	30.00	60.00
❑ 238 M.Clayton JSY/499 AU RC	15.00	40.00
❑ 239 Antrel Rolle JSY/499 AU RC	15.00	40.00
❑ 240 Maurice Clarett JSY/499 AU	12.00	30.00
❑ 241 J.Arrington JSY/699 AU RC	12.00	30.00
❑ 242 Matt Jones JSY/399 AU RC	15.00	40.00
❑ 243 Ro.Brown JSY/299 AU RC	75.00	150.00
❑ 244 C.Frye JSY/499 AU RC	15.00	40.00
❑ 245 J.Campbell JSY/299 AU RC	30.00	60.00
❑ 246 T.Willmsn JSY/299 AU RC	15.00	40.00
❑ 247 B.Edwrd JSY/299 AU RC	40.00	80.00
❑ 248 A.Smith QB JSY/299 AU RC	40.00	100.00
❑ 249 C.Willms JSY/299 AU RC	30.00	80.00
❑ 250 H.Miller JSY/299 AU RC	30.00	60.00
❑ 251 C.Benson JSY/99 AU RC	90.00	150.00
❑ 252 A.Rodgers JSY/99 AU RC	350.00	550.00
❑ 253 M.Williams JSY/99 AU	20.00	50.00
❑ 254 Chris Carr AU RC	5.00	12.00
❑ 255 Deandra Cobb AU RC	5.00	12.00
❑ 256 James Kilian AU RC	4.00	10.00
❑ 257 Airese Currie AU RC	5.00	12.00

2006 SP Authentic

Card	Low	High
❑ COMP.SET w/o RC's (90)	8.00	20.00
❑ 1 Edgerrin James	.30	.75
❑ 2 Larry Fitzgerald	.40	1.00
❑ 3 Anquan Boldin	.30	.75
❑ 4 Michael Vick	.40	1.00
❑ 5 Warrick Dunn	.30	.75
❑ 6 Alge Crumpler	.30	.75
❑ 7 Steve McNair	.30	.75
❑ 8 Jamal Lewis	.30	.75
❑ 9 Derrick Mason	.30	.75
❑ 10 Willis McGahee	.40	1.00
❑ 11 Lee Evans	.30	.75
❑ 12 Jake Delhomme	.30	.75
❑ 13 Steve Smith	.40	1.00
❑ 14 DeShaun Foster	.30	.75
❑ 15 Rex Grossman	.40	1.00
❑ 16 Thomas Jones	.30	.75
❑ 17 Brian Urlacher	.40	1.00
❑ 18 Carson Palmer	.40	1.00
❑ 19 Chad Johnson	.30	.75
❑ 20 Rudi Johnson	.30	.75
❑ 21 Charlie Frye	.30	.75
❑ 22 Braylon Edwards	.40	1.00
❑ 23 Reuben Droughns	.30	.75
❑ 24 Drew Bledsoe	.40	1.00
❑ 25 Terrell Owens	.40	1.00
❑ 26 Julius Jones	.30	.75
❑ 27 Jake Plummer	.30	.75
❑ 28 Tatum Bell	.25	.60
❑ 29 Javon Walker	.30	.75
❑ 30 Kevin Jones	.30	.75
❑ 31 Roy Williams WR	.40	1.00
❑ 32 Brett Favre	.75	2.00
❑ 33 Donald Driver	.40	1.00
❑ 34 David Carr	.25	.60
❑ 35 Ron Dayne	.30	.75
❑ 36 Andre Johnson	.30	.75
❑ 37 Peyton Manning	.60	1.50
❑ 38 Marvin Harrison	.40	1.00
❑ 39 Reggie Wayne	.30	.75
❑ 40 Byron Leftwich	.30	.75
❑ 41 Fred Taylor	.30	.75
❑ 42 Matt Jones	.30	.75
❑ 43 Trent Green	.30	.75
❑ 44 Larry Johnson	.30	.75
❑ 45 Tony Gonzalez	.30	.75
❑ 46 Daunte Culpepper	.40	1.00
❑ 47 Ronnie Brown	.40	1.00
❑ 48 Chris Chambers	.30	.75
❑ 49 Chester Taylor	.30	.75
❑ 50 Troy Williamson	.30	.75
❑ 51 Tom Brady	.60	1.50
❑ 52 Corey Dillon	.30	.75
❑ 53 Troy Brown	.25	.60
❑ 54 Drew Brees	.40	1.00
❑ 55 Deuce McAllister	.30	.75
❑ 56 Joe Horn	.30	.75
❑ 57 Eli Manning	.50	1.25
❑ 58 Tiki Barber	.40	1.00
❑ 59 Plaxico Burress	.30	.75
❑ 60 Laveranues Coles	.30	.75
❑ 61 Chad Pennington	.30	.75
❑ 62 Aaron Brooks	.30	.75
❑ 63 Randy Moss	.40	1.00
❑ 64 LaMont Jordan	.30	.75
❑ 65 Donovan McNabb	.40	1.00
❑ 66 Brian Westbrook	.30	.75
❑ 67 Ben Roethlisberger	.60	1.50
❑ 68 Willie Parker	.50	1.25
❑ 69 Hines Ward	.40	1.00
❑ 70 Philip Rivers	.40	1.00
❑ 71 LaDainian Tomlinson	.50	1.25
❑ 72 Antonio Gates	.40	1.00
❑ 73 Alex Smith QB	.30	.75
❑ 74 Frank Gore	.40	1.00
❑ 75 Antonio Bryant	.30	.75
❑ 76 Matt Hasselbeck	.30	.75
❑ 77 Shaun Alexander	.30	.75
❑ 78 Darrell Jackson	.30	.75
❑ 79 Marc Bulger	.30	.75
❑ 80 Steven Jackson	.40	1.00
❑ 81 Torry Holt	.30	.75
❑ 82 Chris Simms	.30	.75
❑ 83 Cadillac Williams	.40	1.00
❑ 84 Joey Galloway	.30	.75
❑ 85 Travis Henry	.30	.75
❑ 86 Drew Bennett	.30	.75
❑ 87 David Givens	.30	.75
❑ 88 Mark Brunell	.30	.75
❑ 89 Clinton Portis	.40	1.00
❑ 90 Santana Moss	.30	.75
❑ 91 Bernard Pollard RC	4.00	10.00
❑ 92 Brodie Croyle RC	5.00	12.00
❑ 93 Cedric Griffin RC	4.00	10.00
❑ 94 Marques Colston RC	12.00	30.00
❑ 95 Daniel Bullocks RC	5.00	12.00
❑ 96 Darryl Tapp RC	4.00	10.00
❑ 97 David Thomas RC	5.00	12.00
❑ 98 Montell Owens RC	4.00	10.00
❑ 99 DeMeco Ryans RC	6.00	15.00
❑ 100 Devin Hester RC	10.00	25.00
❑ 101 Donte Whitner RC	5.00	12.00
❑ 102 D'Qwell Jackson RC	4.00	10.00
❑ 103 Patrick Cobbs RC	4.00	10.00
❑ 104 Haloti Ngata RC	5.00	12.00
❑ 105 Lawrence Vickers RC	4.00	10.00
❑ 106 Jeff King RC	4.00	10.00
❑ 107 Jeremy Bloom RC	4.00	10.00
❑ 108 Johnathan Joseph RC	4.00	10.00
❑ 109 DeDe Dorsey RC	4.00	10.00
❑ 110 Marcus Vick RC	3.00	8.00
❑ 111 Bobby Carpenter RC	4.00	10.00
❑ 112 Manny Lawson RC	5.00	12.00
❑ 113 Nick Mangold RC	4.00	10.00
❑ 114 Quinn Sypniewski RC	4.00	10.00
❑ 115 Richard Marshall RC	4.00	10.00
❑ 116 Rocky McIntosh RC	5.00	12.00
❑ 117 Roman Harper RC	4.00	10.00
❑ 118 Tamba Hali RC	5.00	12.00
❑ 119 Tony Scheffler RC	5.00	12.00
❑ 120 Wali Lundy RC	5.00	12.00
❑ 121 A.J. Nicholson RC	2.50	6.00
❑ 122 Abdul Hodge RC	3.00	8.00
❑ 123 Adam Jennings RC	3.00	8.00
❑ 124 Alan Zemaitis RC	4.00	10.00
❑ 125 Andrew Whitworth RC	2.50	6.00
❑ 126 Anthony Schlegel RC	3.00	8.00
❑ 127 Anthony Smith RC	4.00	10.00
❑ 128 Antoine Bethea RC	5.00	12.00
❑ 129 Barry Cofield RC	4.00	10.00
❑ 130 Brandon Johnson RC	3.00	8.00
❑ 131 Calvin Lowry RC	4.00	10.00
❑ 132 Shaun Bodiford RC	3.00	8.00
❑ 133 Charlie Peprah RC	3.00	8.00
❑ 134 Claude Wroten RC	2.50	6.00

❑ 135 Clint Ingram RC 4.00 10.00
❑ 136 Cortland Finnegan RC 4.00 10.00
❑ 137 Daryn Colledge RC 4.00 10.00
❑ 138 David Anderson RC 3.00 8.00
❑ 139 David Kirtman RC 3.00 8.00
❑ 140 Boone Stutz RC 3.00 8.00
❑ 141 Delanie Walker RC 3.00 8.00
❑ 142 Sam Hurd RC 6.00 15.00
❑ 143 Derrick Martin RC 3.00 8.00
❑ 144 Willie Andrews RC 3.00 8.00
❑ 145 Dusty Dvoracek RC 4.00 10.00
❑ 146 Elvis Dumervil RC 4.00 10.00
❑ 147 Eric Smith RC 3.00 8.00
❑ 148 Freddie Keiaho RC 3.00 8.00
❑ 149 Gabe Watson RC 2.50 6.00
❑ 150 Gerris Wilkinson RC 2.50 6.00
❑ 151 Greg Blue RC 3.00 8.00
❑ 152 Guy Whimper RC 2.50 6.00
❑ 153 Jamar Williams RC 3.00 8.00
❑ 154 James Anderson RC 2.50 6.00
❑ 155 Jason Spitz RC 4.00 10.00
❑ 156 Jeff Webb RC 3.00 8.00
❑ 157 Jeremy Mincey RC 3.00 8.00
❑ 158 Jeremy Trueblood RC 3.00 8.00
❑ 159 Omar Gaither RC 3.00 8.00
❑ 160 Jon Alston RC 2.50 6.00
❑ 161 Julian Jenkins RC 3.00 8.00
❑ 162 Keith Ellison RC 3.00 8.00
❑ 163 Kevin McMahan RC 3.00 8.00
❑ 164 Kyle Williams RC 4.00 10.00
❑ 165 Leon Williams RC 3.00 8.00
❑ 166 Mark Anderson RC 6.00 15.00
❑ 167 LaJuan Ramsey RC 4.00 10.00
❑ 168 Nate Salley RC 3.00 8.00
❑ 169 Rob Ninkovich RC 3.00 8.00
❑ 170 Parys Haralson RC 3.00 8.00
❑ 171 Pat Watkins RC 4.00 10.00
❑ 172 Paul McQuistan RC 2.50 6.00
❑ 173 Rashad Butler RC 2.50 6.00
❑ 174 Ray Edwards RC 4.00 10.00
❑ 175 Reed Doughty RC 3.00 8.00
❑ 176 Ronnie Prude RC 3.00 8.00
❑ 177 Stephen Tulloch RC 3.00 8.00
❑ 178 Tim Jennings RC 3.00 8.00
❑ 179 Jarrad Page RC 4.00 10.00
❑ 180 Victor Adeyanju RC 3.00 8.00
❑ 181 Andre Hall AU RC 5.00 12.00
❑ 182 Anthony Fasano AU RC 6.00 15.00
❑ 183 Antonio Cromartie AU RC 10.00 20.00
❑ 184 Ashton Youboty AU RC 5.00 12.00
❑ 185 Kamerion Wimbley AU RC 6.00 15.00
❑ 186 Brad Smith AU RC 6.00 15.00
❑ 187 Brodrick Bunkley AU RC 5.00 12.00
❑ 188 Bruce Gradkowski AU RC 8.00 20.00
❑ 189 Chad Greenway AU RC 6.00 15.00
❑ 190 Cory Rodgers AU RC 6.00 15.00
❑ 191 D.J. Shockley AU RC 5.00 12.00
❑ 192 Danieal Manning AU RC 6.00 15.00
❑ 193 Darnell Bing AU RC 5.00 12.00
❑ 194 Darrell Hackney AU RC 5.00 12.00
❑ 195 D'Brickashaw Ferguson AU RC 6.00 15.00
❑ 196 Dominique Byrd AU RC 5.00 12.00
❑ 197 Drew Olson AU RC 4.00 10.00
❑ 198 Ernie Sims AU RC 5.00 12.00
❑ 199 Garrett Mills AU/99 RC 30.00 60.00
❑ 200 Gerald Riggs AU RC 5.00 12.00
❑ 201 Greg Jennings AU RC 20.00 35.00
❑ 202 Greg Lee AU RC 4.00 10.00
❑ 203 Hank Baskett AU RC 6.00 15.00
❑ 204 Ingle Martin AU RC 5.00 12.00
❑ 205 Jason Allen AU RC 5.00 12.00
❑ 206 Jerome Harrison AU RC 20.00 35.00
❑ 207 Jimmy Williams AU RC 6.00 15.00
❑ 208 John McCargo AU RC 5.00 12.00
❑ 209 Josh Betts AU RC 5.00 12.00
❑ 210 Leonard Pope AU RC 6.00 15.00
❑ 211 Marques Hagans AU RC 5.00 12.00
❑ 212 Martin Nance AU RC 5.00 12.00
❑ 213 Mathias Kiwanuka AU RC 8.00 20.00
❑ 214 Mike Bell AU RC 10.00 20.00
❑ 215 Mike Hass AU RC 6.00 15.00
❑ 216 Owen Daniels AU RC 6.00 15.00
❑ 217 P.J. Daniels AU RC 4.00 10.00
❑ 218 Reggie McNeal AU RC 5.00 12.00
❑ 219 Skyler Green AU RC 4.00 10.00
❑ 220 Terrence Whitehead AU RC 5.00 12.00
❑ 221 Thomas Howard AU RC 5.00 12.00
❑ 222 Tye Hill AU RC 5.00 12.00
❑ 223 Will Blackmon AU RC 6.00 15.00
❑ 224 Willie Reid AU RC 5.00 12.00
❑ 225 Winston Justice AU RC 6.00 15.00
❑ 226 Jay Cutler AU/99 RC 600.00 1000.00
❑ 227 Joseph Addai AU/99 RC 100.00 200.00
❑ 228 Br.Williams JSY/999 AU RC 8.00 20.00
❑ 229 B.Calhoun JSY/999 AU RC 8.00 20.00
❑ 230 Ch.Jackson JSY/699 AU RC 10.00 25.00
❑ 231 C.Whitehurst JSY/999 AU RC 10.00 25.00
❑ 232 DeA.Wilms JSY/175 AU RC 100.00 200.00
❑ 233 Dem.Williams JSY/999 AU RC 8.00 20.00
❑ 234 Derek Hagan JSY/999 AU RC 8.00 20.00
❑ 235 Jason Avant JSY/999 AU RC 10.00 25.00
❑ 236 J.Norwood JSY/999 AU RC 15.00 40.00
❑ 237 J.Klopfenstein JSY/999 AU RC 8.00 20.00
❑ 238 K.Clemens JSY/999 AU RC 10.00 25.00
❑ 239 K.Jennings JSY/199 AU RC 15.00 40.00
❑ 240 L.Maroney JSY/999 AU RC 30.00 60.00
❑ 241 L.White JSY/999 AU RC 40.00 80.00
❑ 242 L.Washington JSY/999 AU RC 15.00 40.00
❑ 243 M.Lewis JSY/999 AU RC 10.00 25.00
❑ 244 M.McNeill JSY/260 AU RC 15.00 40.00
❑ 245 Ma.Williams JSY/699 AU RC 20.00 50.00
❑ 246 Matt Leinart JSY/299 AU RC 125.00 200.00
❑ 247 M.Drew JSY/999 AU RC 60.00 120.00
❑ 248 M.Stovall JSY/999 AU RC 8.00 20.00
❑ 249 Michael Huff JSY/999 AU RC 10.00 25.00
❑ 250 M.Robinson JSY/999 AU RC 8.00 20.00
❑ 251 Omar Jacobs/750 RC 3.00 8.00
❑ 252 R.Bush JSY/299 AU RC 150.00 300.00
❑ 253 S.Holmes JSY/399 AU RC 60.00 120.00
❑ 254 Sinorice Moss JSY/99 AU RC 30.00 60.00
❑ 255 T.Jackson JSY/999 AU RC 10.00 25.00
❑ 256 Travis Wilson JSY/999 AU RC 6.00 15.00
❑ 257 V.Davis JSY/699 AU RC 25.00 60.00
❑ 258 V.Young JSY/270 AU RC 150.00 250.00
❑ 259 A.J. Hawk JSY/399 AU RC 25.00 60.00
❑ 260 B.Marshall JSY/999 AU RC 25.00 50.00

2007 SP Authentic

❑ COMP.SET w/o RC's (100) 8.00 20.00
❑ 1 Ahman Green .25 .60
❑ 2 A.J. Hawk .30 .75
❑ 3 Alex Smith QB .30 .75
❑ 4 Andre Johnson .25 .60
❑ 5 Antonio Gates .25 .60
❑ 6 Ben Roethlisberger .50 1.25
❑ 7 Bernard Berrian .20 .50
❑ 8 Brandon Jacobs .25 .60
❑ 9 Braylon Edwards .25 .60
❑ 10 Brett Favre .60 1.50
❑ 11 Brian Urlacher .30 .75
❑ 12 Brian Westbrook .25 .60
❑ 13 Brodie Croyle .25 .60
❑ 14 Byron Leftwich .25 .60
❑ 15 Cadillac Williams .25 .60
❑ 16 Carson Palmer .30 .75
❑ 17 Cedric Benson .25 .60
❑ 18 Chad Johnson .25 .60
❑ 19 Chad Pennington .25 .60
❑ 20 Champ Bailey .25 .60
❑ 21 Derek Anderson .25 .60
❑ 22 Chester Taylor .20 .50
❑ 23 Chris Brown .20 .50
❑ 24 Chris Chambers .25 .60
❑ 25 Clinton Portis .25 .60
❑ 26 Darrell Jackson .25 .60
❑ 27 Deuce McAllister .25 .60
❑ 28 Dominic Rhodes .25 .60
❑ 29 Donald Driver .30 .75
❑ 30 Donovan McNabb .30 .75
❑ 31 Donte Stallworth .25 .60
❑ 32 Drew Brees .30 .75
❑ 33 Edgerrin James .25 .60
❑ 34 Eli Manning .30 .75
❑ 35 Frank Gore .30 .75
❑ 36 Fred Taylor .25 .60
❑ 37 Greg Jennings .25 .60
❑ 38 Hines Ward .30 .75
❑ 39 Jake Delhomme .25 .60
❑ 40 Jamal Lewis .25 .60
❑ 41 Jason Campbell .25 .60
❑ 42 Jason Taylor .20 .50
❑ 43 Jason Witten .30 .75
❑ 44 Javon Walker .25 .60
❑ 45 Jay Cutler .30 .75
❑ 46 Jerious Norwood .25 .60
❑ 47 Jerry Porter .25 .60
❑ 48 Jon Kitna .20 .50
❑ 49 Joseph Addai .30 .75
❑ 50 Julius Jones .25 .60
❑ 51 LaDainian Tomlinson .40 1.00
❑ 52 Larry Johnson .25 .60
❑ 53 Larry Fitzgerald .30 .75
❑ 54 Laurence Maroney .30 .75
❑ 55 Marc Bulger .25 .60
❑ 56 Marion Barber .30 .75
❑ 57 Mark Clayton .25 .60
❑ 58 Marques Colston .30 .75
❑ 59 Marvin Harrison .30 .75
❑ 60 Matt Hasselbeck .25 .60
❑ 61 Matt Jones .25 .60
❑ 62 Matt Leinart .30 .75
❑ 63 Matt Schaub .25 .60
❑ 64 Maurice Jones-Drew .30 .75
❑ 65 Jeff Garcia .25 .60
❑ 66 Mike Alstott .25 .60
❑ 67 David Garrard .25 .60
❑ 68 Peyton Manning .50 1.25
❑ 69 Philip Rivers .30 .75
❑ 70 Plaxico Burress .25 .60
❑ 71 Randy Moss .30 .75
❑ 72 Reggie Brown .20 .50
❑ 73 Reggie Bush .40 1.00
❑ 74 Reggie Wayne .25 .60
❑ 75 Rex Grossman .25 .60
❑ 76 Ronnie Brown .25 .60
❑ 77 Roy Williams S .25 .60
❑ 78 Roy Williams WR .25 .60
❑ 79 Rudi Johnson .25 .60
❑ 80 Shaun Alexander .25 .60
❑ 81 Shawne Merriman .25 .60
❑ 82 Steven Jackson .30 .75
❑ 83 Steve McNair .25 .60
❑ 84 Steve Smith .25 .60
❑ 85 T.J. Houshmandzadeh .25 .60
❑ 86 Tarvaris Jackson .25 .60
❑ 87 Tedy Bruschi .30 .75
❑ 88 Terrell Owens .30 .75
❑ 89 Thomas Jones .25 .60
❑ 90 Tom Brady .60 1.50
❑ 91 Torry Holt .25 .60
❑ 92 Travis Henry .25 .60
❑ 93 Trent Green .25 .60
❑ 94 Vince Young .30 .75
❑ 95 Vincent Jackson .20 .50
❑ 96 Walter Jones .20 .50
❑ 97 Warrick Dunn .25 .60
❑ 98 Willie Parker .25 .60
❑ 99 Willis McGahee .25 .60
❑ 100 Tony Romo .50 1.25
❑ 101 Deon Anderson RC 3.00 8.00
❑ 102 Ben Patrick RC 3.00 8.00
❑ 103 Reagan Mauia RC 2.50 6.00
❑ 104 Derek Schouman RC 3.00 8.00
❑ 105 Keyunta Dawson RC 3.00 8.00
❑ 106 Usama Young RC 3.00 8.00
❑ 107 Syndric Steptoe RC 3.00 8.00
❑ 108 Martrez Milner RC 3.00 8.00
❑ 109 Brandon McDonald RC 2.50 6.00
❑ 110 Jason Snelling RC 3.00 8.00
❑ 111 Derek Stanley RC 3.00 8.00
❑ 112 Ed Johnson RC 3.00 8.00
❑ 113 Jacob Bender RC 2.50 6.00
❑ 114 Charles Ali RC 3.00 8.00
❑ 115 Tanard Jackson RC 2.50 6.00
❑ 116 Paul Soliai RC 2.50 6.00
❑ 117 Marvin White RC 2.50 6.00
❑ 118 Jared Gaither RC 2.50 6.00
❑ 119 Baraka Atkins RC 2.50 6.00
❑ 120 Marcus Thomas RC 3.00 8.00
❑ 121 Fred Bennett RC 2.50 6.00
❑ 122 Dashon Goldson RC 2.50 6.00
❑ 123 Kareem Brown RC 3.00 8.00
❑ 124 Courtney Bryan RC 2.50 6.00
❑ 125 Joe Cohen RC 2.50 6.00

❑ 126 Jay Richardson RC 3.00 8.00
❑ 127 Greg Peterson RC 3.00 8.00
❑ 128 Dallas Sartz RC 3.00 8.00
❑ 129 Brandon Harrison RC 2.50 6.00
❑ 130 Tarell Brown RC 2.50 6.00
❑ 131 Matt Gutierrez RC 4.00 10.00
❑ 132 Edmond Miles RC 3.00 8.00
❑ 133 Clifton Ryan RC 3.00 8.00
❑ 134 Antwan Barnes RC 3.00 8.00
❑ 135 Tim Shaw RC 3.00 8.00
❑ 136 Eric Frampton RC 3.00 8.00
❑ 137 William Gay RC 3.00 8.00
❑ 138 Nick Graham RC 3.00 8.00
❑ 139 Matt Toeaina RC 3.00 8.00
❑ 140 John Wendling RC 3.00 8.00
❑ 141 Mason Crosby RC 4.00 10.00
❑ 142 C.J. Wallace RC 3.00 8.00
❑ 143 Prescott Burgess RC 3.00 8.00
❑ 144 Oscar Lua RC 3.00 8.00
❑ 145 Chase Pittman RC 3.00 8.00
❑ 146 Zachary Diles RC 3.00 8.00
❑ 147 Kelvin Smith RC 3.00 8.00
❑ 148 Marvin Mitchell RC 3.00 8.00
❑ 149 Trumaine McBride RC 3.00 8.00
❑ 150 Edgar Jones RC 3.00 8.00
❑ 151 Abraham Wright RC 2.50 6.00
❑ 152 Nick Folk RC 4.00 10.00
❑ 153 Brandon Siler RC 3.00 8.00
❑ 154 Clint Session RC 3.00 8.00
❑ 155 Nedu Ndukwe RC 4.00 10.00
❑ 156 C.J. Wilson RC 3.00 8.00
❑ 157 Desmond Bishop RC 3.00 8.00
❑ 158 Melvin Bullitt RC 3.00 8.00
❑ 159 Courtney Brown RC 3.00 8.00
❑ 160 Troy Smith RC 5.00 12.00
❑ 161 Levi Brown RC 4.00 10.00
❑ 162 Justin Harrell RC 4.00 10.00
❑ 163 Jarvis Moss RC 4.00 10.00
❑ 164 Aaron Ross RC 4.00 10.00
❑ 165 Jon Beason RC 4.00 10.00
❑ 166 Anthony Spencer RC 4.00 10.00
❑ 167 Joe Staley RC 3.00 8.00
❑ 168 Ben Grubbs RC 3.00 8.00
❑ 169 Arron Sears RC 3.00 8.00
❑ 170 Eric Weddle RC 3.00 8.00
❑ 171 Justin Blalock RC 2.50 6.00
❑ 172 Chris Houston RC 3.00 8.00
❑ 173 David Harris RC 3.00 8.00
❑ 174 Justin Durant RC 3.00 8.00
❑ 175 Turk McBride RC 3.00 8.00
❑ 176 Josh Wilson RC 3.00 8.00
❑ 177 Tim Crowder RC 4.00 10.00
❑ 178 Victor Abiamiri RC 4.00 10.00
❑ 179 Ikaika Alama-Francis RC 4.00 10.00
❑ 180 Ryan Kalil RC 3.00 8.00
❑ 181 Samson Satele RC 3.00 8.00
❑ 182 Gerald Alexander RC 2.50 6.00
❑ 183 Corey Graham RC 2.50 6.00
❑ 184 Sabby Piscitelli RC 4.00 10.00
❑ 185 Quincy Black RC 4.00 10.00
❑ 186 Daniel Coats RC 3.00 8.00
❑ 187 Tony Ugoh RC 3.00 8.00
❑ 188 David Jones RC 2.50 6.00
❑ 189 DeMarcus Tank Tyler RC 3.00 8.00
❑ 190 Chad Nkang RC 2.50 6.00
❑ 191 Jonathan Wade RC 3.00 8.00
❑ 192 Brandon Mebane RC 3.00 8.00
❑ 193 Stewart Bradley RC 4.00 10.00
❑ 194 Aaron Rouse RC 4.00 10.00
❑ 195 Michael Okwo RC 3.00 8.00
❑ 196 Anthony Waters RC 3.00 8.00
❑ 197 Ray McDonald RC 3.00 8.00
❑ 198 Clifton Dawson RC 4.00 10.00
❑ 199 Brian Robison RC 4.00 10.00
❑ 200 Jay Moore RC 3.00 8.00
❑ 201 Dante Rosario AU RC 6.00 15.00
❑ 202 Ahmad Bradshaw AU RC 15.00 40.00
❑ 203 Roy Hall AU RC 6.00 15.00
❑ 204 Aundrae Allison AU RC 5.00 12.00
❑ 205 Brent Celek AU RC 12.50 25.00
❑ 206 Chansi Stuckey AU RC 6.00 15.00
❑ 207 Courtney Taylor AU RC 5.00 12.00
❑ 208 Dallas Baker AU RC 5.00 12.00
❑ 209 Darius Walker AU RC 5.00 12.00
❑ 210 David Ball AU RC 4.00 10.00
❑ 211 David Clowney AU RC 6.00 15.00
❑ 212 David Irons AU RC 4.00 10.00
❑ 213 Daymeion Hughes AU RC 5.00 12.00
❑ 214 DeShawn Wynn AU RC 6.00 15.00
❑ 215 Jordan Kent AU RC 5.00 12.00
❑ 216 Dwayne Wright AU RC 5.00 12.00
❑ 217 Eric Wright AU RC 6.00 15.00
❑ 218 Gary Russell AU RC EXCH 5.00 12.00
❑ 219 Mike Walker AU RC 10.00 20.00
❑ 220 Isaiah Stanback AU RC 6.00 15.00
❑ 221 Jamaal Anderson AU RC 5.00 12.00
❑ 222 Jared Zabransky AU RC 6.00 15.00
❑ 223 Jeff Rowe AU RC 5.00 12.00
❑ 224 Joel Filani AU RC 5.00 12.00
❑ 225 Jordan Palmer AU RC 6.00 15.00
❑ 226 Kenneth Darby AU RC 6.00 15.00
❑ 227 Kolby Smith AU RC 6.00 15.00
❑ 228 Thomas Clayton AU RC 5.00 12.00
❑ 229 Steve Breaston AU RC 15.00 30.00
❑ 230 James Jones AU RC 6.00 15.00
❑ 231 Marcus McCauley AU RC 5.00 12.00
❑ 232 Alan Branch AU RC 5.00 12.00
❑ 233 Michael Griffin AU RC 6.00 15.00
❑ 234 Paul Posluszny AU RC 8.00 20.00
❑ 235 Quentin Moses AU RC 5.00 12.00
❑ 236 Lawrence Timmons AU RC 6.00 15.00
❑ 237 Scott Chandler AU RC 5.00 12.00
❑ 238 Jacoby Jones AU RC 6.00 15.00
❑ 239 Tyler Thigpen AU RC 6.00 15.00
❑ 240 Laurent Robinson AU RC 6.00 15.00
❑ 241 John Broussard AU RC 5.00 12.00
❑ 242 Zach Miller AU RC 6.00 15.00
❑ 243 Matt Spaeth AU RC 6.00 15.00
❑ 244 Ryne Robinson AU RC EXCH 5.00 12.00
❑ 245 Danny Ware AU RC 6.00 15.00
❑ 246 Legedu Naanee AU RC 6.00 15.00
❑ 247 Le'Ron McClain AU RC 6.00 15.00
❑ 248 Kevin Boss AU RC 15.00 30.00
❑ 249 Orenthal O'Neal AU RC 4.00 10.00
❑ 250 Amobi Okoye AU RC 6.00 15.00
❑ 251 Darrelle Revis AU RC 30.00 50.00
❑ 252 LaRon Landry AU RC 12.00 30.00
❑ 253 Chris Leak AU RC 8.00 20.00
❑ 254 Craig Davis AU RC 10.00 25.00
❑ 255 Leon Hall AU RC 10.00 25.00
❑ 256 Reggie Nelson AU RC 8.00 20.00
❑ 257 Adam Carriker AU RC 8.00 20.00
❑ 258 H.B. Blades AU RC 8.00 20.00
❑ 259 LaMarr Woodley AU RC 20.00 40.00
❑ 260 Korey Hall AU RC 8.00 20.00
❑ 261 Rhema McKnight AU RC 8.00 20.00
❑ 262 B.Meriweather AU RC 10.00 25.00
❑ 263 Matt Moore AU RC 50.00 80.00
❑ 264 Selvin Young AU RC 10.00 25.00
❑ 265 Tyler Palko AU RC 8.00 20.00
❑ 266 A.Gonzalez JSY AU RC 25.00 50.00
❑ 267 A.Pittman JSY AU RC 15.00 40.00
❑ 268 Br.Jackson JSY AU RC 15.00 40.00
❑ 269 Brian Leonard JSY AU RC 12.00 30.00
❑ 270 Chris Henry JSY AU RC 12.00 30.00
❑ 271 Drew Stanton JSY AU RC 12.00 30.00
❑ 273 Garrett Wolfe JSY AU RC 15.00 40.00
❑ 274 Greg Olsen JSY AU RC 20.00 50.00
❑ 275 Jason Hill JSY AU RC 15.00 40.00
❑ 276 Joe Thomas JSY AU RC 15.00 40.00
❑ 277 John Beck JSY AU RC 15.00 40.00
❑ 278 J.Lee Higgins JSY AU RC 15.00 40.00
❑ 279 Kenny Irons JSY AU RC 15.00 40.00
❑ 280 Kevin Kolb JSY AU RC 60.00 100.00
❑ 281 Lorenzo Booker JSY AU RC 15.00 40.00
❑ 282 Michael Bush JSY AU RC 15.00 40.00
❑ 283 Patrick Willis JSY AU RC 30.00 60.00
❑ 284 Paul Williams JSY AU RC 12.00 30.00
❑ 285 Steve Smith JSY AU RC 30.00 60.00
❑ 286 Tony Hunt JSY AU RC 15.00 40.00
❑ 287 Trent Edwards JSY AU RC 25.00 60.00
❑ 288 Yamon Figurs JSY AU RC 10.00 25.00
❑ 289 A.Peterson JSY AU RC 400.00 600.00
❑ 290 Brady Quinn JSY AU RC 60.00 120.00
❑ 291 C.Johnson JSY AU RC 75.00 150.00
❑ 292 J.Russell JSY AU RC 25.00 60.00
❑ 293 M.Lynch JSY AU RC 30.00 80.00
❑ 294 Dwayne Bowe JSY AU RC 25.00 60.00
❑ 295 Sidney Rice JSY AU RC 60.00 100.00
❑ 296 R.Meachem JSY AU RC 30.00 60.00
❑ 297 Dwayne Jarrett JSY AU RC 20.00 50.00
❑ 298 Ted Ginn JSY AU RC 25.00 60.00

2008 SP Authentic

❑ COMP.SET w/o RC's (100) 8.00 20.00
❑ 1 Marshawn Lynch .30 .75
❑ 2 Trent Edwards .30 .75
❑ 3 Roscoe Parrish .20 .50
❑ 4 Jason Taylor .25 .60
❑ 5 Ronnie Brown .25 .60
❑ 6 Chad Pennington .25 .60
❑ 7 Tom Brady .50 1.25
❑ 8 Laurence Maroney .25 .60
❑ 9 Randy Moss .30 .75
❑ 10 Darrelle Revis .25 .60
❑ 11 Jerricho Cotchery .20 .50
❑ 12 Thomas Jones .25 .60
❑ 13 Ray Lewis .30 .75
❑ 14 Ed Reed .25 .60
❑ 15 Willis McGahee .25 .60
❑ 16 Carson Palmer .30 .75
❑ 17 T.J. Houshmandzadeh .25 .60
❑ 18 Chad Johnson .25 .60
❑ 19 Kellen Winslow .25 .60
❑ 20 Derek Anderson .25 .60
❑ 21 Braylon Edwards .25 .60
❑ 22 Ben Roethlisberger .50 1.25
❑ 23 Willie Parker .25 .60
❑ 24 Matt Schaub .25 .60
❑ 25 DeMeco Ryans .25 .60
❑ 26 Andre Johnson .25 .60
❑ 27 Darius Walker .20 .50
❑ 28 Peyton Manning .50 1.25
❑ 29 Reggie Wayne .25 .60
❑ 30 Joseph Addai .30 .75
❑ 31 David Garrard .25 .60
❑ 32 Maurice Jones-Drew .25 .60
❑ 33 Fred Taylor .25 .60
❑ 34 Vince Young .25 .60
❑ 35 LenDale White .25 .60
❑ 36 Alge Crumpler .25 .60
❑ 37 Jay Cutler .30 .75
❑ 38 Brandon Marshall .25 .60
❑ 39 Jason Witten .30 .75
❑ 40 Brodie Croyle .25 .60
❑ 41 Larry Johnson .25 .60
❑ 42 Derrick Johnson .20 .50
❑ 43 JaMarcus Russell .30 .75
❑ 44 Ronald Curry .25 .60
❑ 45 Jeremy Shockey .25 .60
❑ 46 Antonio Gates .25 .60
❑ 47 LaDainian Tomlinson .40 1.00
❑ 48 Antonio Cromartie .20 .50
❑ 49 Philip Rivers .30 .75
❑ 50 Tony Romo .50 1.25
❑ 51 Terrell Owens .30 .75
❑ 52 DeMarcus Ware .25 .60
❑ 53 Marion Barber .30 .75
❑ 54 Eli Manning .30 .75
❑ 55 Brandon Jacobs .25 .60
❑ 56 Plaxico Burress .25 .60
❑ 57 Antonio Pierce .20 .50
❑ 58 Donovan McNabb .30 .75
❑ 59 Brian Dawkins .25 .60
❑ 60 Brian Westbrook .25 .60
❑ 61 Chris Cooley .25 .60
❑ 62 Jason Campbell .25 .60
❑ 63 Clinton Portis .25 .60
❑ 64 Brian Urlacher .30 .75
❑ 65 Lance Briggs .20 .50
❑ 66 Devin Hester .30 .75
❑ 67 Roy Williams WR .25 .60
❑ 68 Calvin Johnson .30 .75
❑ 69 Brett Favre .75 2.00
❑ 70 Aaron Rodgers .30 .75
❑ 71 Ryan Grant .30 .75
❑ 72 Greg Jennings .25 .60
❑ 73 Tarvaris Jackson .25 .60

❑ 74 Adrian Peterson .60 1.50
❑ 75 Sidney Rice .30 .75
❑ 76 Michael Turner .30 .75
❑ 77 Jerious Norwood .25 .60
❑ 78 Jake Delhomme .25 .60
❑ 79 DeAngelo Williams .25 .60
❑ 80 Steve Smith .25 .60
❑ 81 Julius Peppers .25 .60
❑ 82 Drew Brees .30 .75
❑ 83 Reggie Bush .30 .75
❑ 84 Marques Colston .25 .60
❑ 85 Jonathan Vilma .25 .60
❑ 86 Joey Galloway .25 .60
❑ 87 Jeff Garcia .25 .60
❑ 88 Earnest Graham .20 .50
❑ 89 Kurt Warner .30 .75
❑ 90 Edgerrin James .25 .60
❑ 91 Larry Fitzgerald .30 .75
❑ 92 Anquan Boldin .25 .60
❑ 93 Marc Bulger .25 .60
❑ 94 Steven Jackson .30 .75
❑ 95 Torry Holt .25 .60
❑ 96 J.T. O'Sullivan .20 .50
❑ 97 Frank Gore .25 .60
❑ 98 Nate Clements .20 .50
❑ 99 Matt Hasselbeck .25 .60
❑ 100 Deion Branch .25 .60
❑ 101 Kregg Lumpkin RC 2.50 6.00
❑ 102 Donovan Woods RC 2.50 6.00
❑ 103 Joe Mays RC 2.00 5.00
❑ 104 Anthony Alridge RC 2.50 6.00
❑ 105 Beau Bell RC 2.50 6.00
❑ 106 Brad Cottam RC 3.00 8.00
❑ 107 Brandon Flowers RC 3.00 8.00
❑ 108 Darrell Strong RC 2.50 6.00
❑ 109 Mike Tolbert RC 3.00 8.00
❑ 110 Bryan Kehl RC 2.50 6.00
❑ 111 Andy Studebaker RC 2.50 6.00
❑ 112 Duane Brown RC 2.50 6.00
❑ 113 Mike Humpal RC 3.00 8.00
❑ 114 Corey Clark RC 2.00 5.00
❑ 115 Josh Sitton RC 2.50 6.00
❑ 116 Curtis Lofton RC 3.00 8.00
❑ 117 Lance Leggett RC 3.00 8.00
❑ 118 Gary Barnidge RC 2.50 6.00
❑ 119 Marcus Dixon RC 2.00 5.00
❑ 120 Dominique Barber RC 2.00 5.00
❑ 121 Reggie Smith RC 2.50 6.00
❑ 122 John Sullivan RC 2.50 6.00
❑ 123 Jabari Arthur RC 2.50 6.00
❑ 124 Maurice Leggett RC 2.50 6.00
❑ 125 Jehuu Caulcrick RC 2.50 6.00
❑ 126 Philip Wheeler RC 3.00 8.00
❑ 127 Jo-Lonn Dunbar RC 2.50 6.00
❑ 128 Josh Barrett RC 2.00 5.00
❑ 129 Danny Amendola RC 2.00 5.00
❑ 130 Kenny Iwebema RC 2.00 5.00
❑ 131 Lance Ball RC 2.00 5.00
❑ 132 Caleb Hanie RC 2.50 6.00
❑ 133 Chris Chamberlain RC 2.00 5.00
❑ 134 Marcus Howard RC 3.00 8.00
❑ 135 Shaheer McBride RC 2.00 5.00
❑ 136 Orlando Scandrick RC 3.00 8.00
❑ 137 Quentin Groves RC 2.50 6.00
❑ 138 Quintin Demps RC 3.00 8.00
❑ 139 John Greco RC 2.50 6.00
❑ 140 Jamey Richard RC 2.00 5.00
❑ 141 Corey Lynch RC 2.00 5.00
❑ 142 Orlando Scandrick RC 3.00 8.00
❑ 143 Lex Hilliard RC 3.00 8.00
❑ 144 Tyrell Johnson RC 3.00 8.00
❑ 145 Martellus Bennett RC 3.00 8.00
❑ 146 Simeon Castille RC 2.50 6.00
❑ 147 Steve Johnson RC 3.00 8.00
❑ 148 Steven Justice RC 2.00 5.00
❑ 149 Terrell Thomas RC 2.50 6.00
❑ 150 Thomas Brown RC 3.00 8.00
❑ 151 Thomas DeCoud RC 2.00 5.00
❑ 152 Matt Slater RC 3.00 8.00
❑ 153 Tom Zbikowski RC 3.00 8.00
❑ 154 Jaymar Johnson RC 2.50 6.00
❑ 155 Brian Johnston RC 2.00 5.00
❑ 156 Trevor Laws RC 3.00 8.00
❑ 157 Will Franklin RC 2.50 6.00
❑ 158 Xavier Adibi RC 2.50 6.00
❑ 159 Chaz Schilens RC 3.00 8.00
❑ 160 Zack Bowman RC 2.50 6.00
❑ 161 Tim Hightower RC 4.00 10.00
❑ 162 Barry Richardson RC 2.00 5.00
❑ 163 Pierre Garcon RC 10.00 25.00
❑ 164 Tyvon Branch RC 2.50 6.00
❑ 165 Marcus Henry RC 2.50 6.00
❑ 166 Carl Nicks RC 2.50 6.00
❑ 167 Chauncey Washington RC 2.50 6.00
❑ 168 Chilo Rachal RC 2.00 5.00
❑ 169 Chris Williams RC 2.50 6.00
❑ 170 Craig Stevens RC 2.50 6.00
❑ 171 Jordan Dizon RC 3.00 8.00
❑ 172 Dantrell Savage RC 3.00 8.00
❑ 173 Clifton Smith RC 3.00 8.00
❑ 174 Drew Radovich RC 2.50 6.00
❑ 175 Jerome Felton RC 2.00 5.00
❑ 176 Haruki Nakamura RC 2.00 5.00
❑ 177 Olaniyi Sobomehin RC 2.00 5.00
❑ 178 Jamie Silva RC 2.50 6.00
❑ 179 Brandon Carr RC 2.50 6.00
❑ 180 Jeff Otah RC 2.50 6.00
❑ 181 William Hayes RC 2.00 5.00
❑ 182 Jerome Simpson RC 2.50 6.00
❑ 183 Anthony Collins RC 2.00 5.00
❑ 184 Alex Hall RC 2.50 6.00
❑ 185 Branden Albert RC 3.00 8.00
❑ 186 Jalen Parmele RC 2.50 6.00
❑ 187 Stanford Keglar RC 2.00 5.00
❑ 188 Louis Rankin RC 2.50 6.00
❑ 189 Maurice Purify RC 3.00 8.00
❑ 190 Darnell Jenkins RC 2.50 6.00
❑ 191 Pat Sims RC 2.50 6.00
❑ 192 Patrick Lee RC 3.00 8.00
❑ 193 Roy Schuening RC 2.00 5.00
❑ 194 Lynell Hamilton RC 5.00 12.00
❑ 195 Joey LaRocque RC 2.00 5.00
❑ 196 Terrence Wheatley RC 2.50 6.00
❑ 197 Tracy Porter RC 4.00 10.00
❑ 198 Brett Swain RC 2.50 6.00
❑ 199 Wesley Woodyard RC 2.50 6.00
❑ 200 Xavier Omon RC 3.00 8.00
❑ 201 Allen Patrick AU RC 4.00 10.00
❑ 202 Marcus Monk AU RC 5.00 12.00
❑ 203 Anthony Morelli AU RC 5.00 12.00
❑ 204 Antoine Cason AU RC 5.00 12.00
❑ 205 Aqib Talib AU RC 5.00 12.00
❑ 206 Ben Moffitt AU RC 3.00 8.00
❑ 207 Chris Long AU RC 5.00 12.00
❑ 208 Bruce Davis AU RC 5.00 12.00
❑ 209 Calais Campbell AU RC 4.00 10.00
❑ 210 Mario Urrutia AU RC 4.00 10.00
❑ 211 Chevis Jackson AU RC 4.00 10.00
❑ 212 Chris Ellis AU RC 4.00 10.00
❑ 213 Josh Morgan AU RC 5.00 12.00
❑ 214 Craig Steltz AU RC 4.00 10.00
❑ 215 DJ Hall AU RC 4.00 10.00
❑ 216 Dan Connor AU RC 5.00 12.00
❑ 217 Darius Reynaud AU RC 4.00 10.00
❑ 218 DeJuan Tribble AU RC 3.00 8.00
❑ 219 DeMario Pressley AU RC 4.00 10.00
❑ 220 Dennis Keyes AU RC 3.00 8.00
❑ 221 Derrick Harvey AU RC 4.00 10.00
❑ 222 Owen Schmitt AU RC 5.00 12.00
❑ 223 Dwight Lowery AU RC 4.00 10.00
❑ 224 Erik Ainge AU RC 5.00 12.00
❑ 225 Erin Henderson AU RC 4.00 10.00
❑ 226 DaJuan Morgan AU RC 4.00 10.00
❑ 227 Frank Okam AU RC 3.00 8.00
❑ 228 Matt Flynn AU RC 5.00 12.00
❑ 229 Phillip Merling AU RC 4.00 10.00
❑ 230 Ryan Clady AU RC 5.00 12.00
❑ 231 Davone Bess AU RC 8.00 20.00
❑ 232 Fred Davis AU RC 5.00 12.00
❑ 234 Gosder Cherilus AU RC 4.00 10.00
❑ 235 Tashard Choice AU RC 15.00 30.00
❑ 236 J Leman AU RC 4.00 10.00
❑ 237 Jack Ikegwuonu AU RC 4.00 10.00
❑ 238 Jacob Hester AU RC 5.00 12.00
❑ 239 Jacob Tamme AU RC 5.00 12.00
❑ 240 Sedrick Ellis AU RC 5.00 12.00
❑ 241 Jermichael Finley AU RC 15.00 30.00
❑ 242 John Carlson AU RC 8.00 20.00
❑ 243 Jonathan Goff AU RC 4.00 10.00
❑ 245 Shawn Crable AU RC 5.00 12.00
❑ 246 Josh Johnson AU RC 5.00 12.00
❑ 247 Justin Forsett AU RC 7.50 15.00
❑ 248 Justin King AU RC 4.00 10.00
❑ 249 Keenan Burton AU RC 4.00 10.00
❑ 250 Sam Baker AU RC 3.00 8.00
❑ 251 Colt Brennan AU/399 RC 25.00 50.00
❑ 252 Adrian Arrington AU/399 RC 6.00 15.00
❑ 253 Alex Brink AU/399 RC 8.00 20.00
❑ 254 Ali Highsmith AU/399 RC 5.00 12.00
❑ 255 Keith Rivers AU/499 RC 8.00 20.00
❑ 256 Kellen Davis AU/399 RC 5.00 12.00
❑ 257 Kenny Phillips AU/399 RC 8.00 20.00
❑ 258 Geno Hayes AU/399 RC 5.00 12.00
❑ 259 Paul Smith AU/399 RC 8.00 20.00
❑ 260 Lavelle Hawkins AU/499 RC 6.00 15.00
❑ 261 L.Jackson AU/399 RC 6.00 15.00
❑ 262 Leodis McKelvin AU/399 RC 8.00 20.00
❑ 263 Andre Woodson AU/399 RC 8.00 20.00
❑ 264 Mike Hart AU/499 RC 8.00 20.00
❑ 265 Martin Rucker AU/399 RC 6.00 15.00
❑ 266 Dennis Dixon AU/399 RC 8.00 20.00
❑ 267 Paul Hubbard AU/399 RC 6.00 15.00
❑ 268 Peyton Hillis AU/399 RC 8.00 20.00
❑ 269 R.Grice-Mullins AU/399 RC 8.00 20.00
❑ 270 V.Gholston AU/399 RC 8.00 20.00
❑ 271 Jerome Simpson JSY AU RC 10.00 25.00
❑ 272 Dexter Jackson JSY AU RC 12.00 30.00
❑ 273 Donnie Avery JSY AU RC 15.00 40.00
❑ 275 Jake Long JSY AU RC 12.00 30.00
❑ 276 D.Keller JSY AU RC EXCH 12.00 30.00
❑ 277 James Hardy JSY AU RC 10.00 25.00
❑ 278 Andre Caldwell JSY AU RC 12.00 30.00
❑ 279 J.Nelson JSY AU RC EXCH 15.00 40.00
❑ 280 Kevin Smith JSY AU RC 20.00 50.00
❑ 281 Eddie Royal JSY AU RC 20.00 50.00
❑ 282 M.Manningham JSY AU RC 20.00 40.00
❑ 283 Earl Bennett JSY AU RC 12.00 30.00
❑ 284 H.Douglas JSY AU RC EXCH 10.00 25.00
❑ 285 Ray Rice JSY AU RC 60.00 120.00
❑ 286 Steve Slaton JSY AU RC 25.00 50.00
❑ 288 C.Johnson JSY AU RC EXCH 100.00 200.00
❑ 289 Kevin O'Connell JSY AU RC 12.00 30.00
❑ 290 DeSean Jackson JSY AU RC 60.00 100.00
❑ 291 Early Doucet JSY AU RC 12.00 30.00
❑ 292 Felix Jones JSY AU RC 50.00 100.00
❑ 293 Jamaal Charles JSY AU RC 30.00 60.00
❑ 294 J.David Booty JSY AU RC 12.00 30.00
❑ 295 J.Flacco JSY AU RC EXCH 100.00 200.00
❑ 297 M.Kelly JSY AU RC EXCH 12.00 30.00
❑ 298 Matt Forte JSY AU RC 40.00 80.00
❑ 299 McFadden JSY AU/499 RC 50.00 100.00
❑ 300 Matt Ryan JSY AU/499 RC 175.00 350.00
❑ 301 Brian Brohm JSY AU/499 RC 15.00 40.00
❑ 302 C.Henne JSY AU/499 RC 60.00 120.00
❑ 303 D.Thomas JSY AU/499 RC 15.00 40.00
❑ 304 Mendenhall JSY AU/499 RC 75.00 150.00
❑ 305 J.Stewart JSY AU/499 RC 50.00 100.00

2008 SP Rookie Edition

❑ COMP.SET w/o SP's (150) 25.00 50.00
❑ 1 Marshawn Lynch .30 .75
❑ 2 Trent Edwards .30 .75
❑ 3 Roscoe Parrish .20 .50
❑ 4 Jason Taylor .25 .60
❑ 5 Ronnie Brown .25 .60
❑ 6 Hines Ward .25 .60
❑ 7 Tom Brady .50 1.25
❑ 8 Laurence Maroney .25 .60
❑ 9 Randy Moss .30 .75
❑ 10 Thomas Jones .25 .60
❑ 11 Jerricho Cotchery .20 .50
❑ 12 Brett Favre 1.50 4.00
❑ 13 Ray Lewis .30 .75
❑ 14 Ed Reed .25 .60
❑ 15 Willis McGahee .25 .60
❑ 16 Carson Palmer .30 .75
❑ 17 T.J. Houshmandzadeh .25 .60
❑ 18 Dwayne Bowe .25 .60
❑ 19 Kellen Winslow .25 .60
❑ 20 Derek Anderson .25 .60
❑ 21 Braylon Edwards .25 .60
❑ 22 Ben Roethlisberger .50 1.25
❑ 23 Willie Parker .25 .60
❑ 24 Wes Welker .30 .75

Card		
❑ 25 DeMeco Ryans	.25	.60
❑ 26 Andre Johnson	.25	.60
❑ 27 Darius Walker	.20	.50
❑ 28 Peyton Manning	.50	1.25
❑ 29 Reggie Wayne	.25	.60
❑ 30 Joseph Addai	.30	.75
❑ 31 David Garrard	.25	.60
❑ 32 Maurice Jones-Drew	.25	.60
❑ 33 Fred Taylor	.25	.60
❑ 34 Vince Young	.25	.60
❑ 35 LenDale White	.25	.60
❑ 36 Alge Crumpler	.25	.60
❑ 37 Jay Cutler	.30	.75
❑ 38 Brandon Marshall	.25	.60
❑ 39 John Lynch	.25	.60
❑ 40 Brodie Croyle	.25	.60
❑ 41 Larry Johnson	.25	.60
❑ 42 Derrick Johnson	.20	.50
❑ 43 JaMarcus Russell	.30	.75
❑ 44 Ronald Curry	.25	.60
❑ 45 Jake Delhomme	.25	.60
❑ 46 Antonio Gates	.25	.60
❑ 47 LaDainian Tomlinson	.40	1.00
❑ 48 Antonio Cromartie	.20	.50
❑ 49 Philip Rivers	.30	.75
❑ 50 Tony Romo	.50	1.25
❑ 51 Terrell Owens	.30	.75
❑ 52 DeMarcus Ware	.25	.60
❑ 53 Marion Barber	.30	.75
❑ 54 Eli Manning	.30	.75
❑ 55 Brandon Jacobs	.25	.60
❑ 56 Plaxico Burress	.25	.60
❑ 57 Antonio Pierce	.20	.50
❑ 58 Donovan McNabb	.30	.75
❑ 59 Brian Dawkins	.25	.60
❑ 60 Brian Westbrook	.25	.60
❑ 61 Chris Cooley	.25	.60
❑ 62 Jason Campbell	.25	.60
❑ 63 Clinton Portis	.25	.60
❑ 64 Brian Urlacher	.30	.75
❑ 65 Lance Briggs	.20	.50
❑ 66 Devin Hester	.30	.75
❑ 67 Roy Williams WR	.25	.60
❑ 68 Calvin Johnson	.30	.75
❑ 69 Ernie Sims	.20	.50
❑ 70 Aaron Rodgers	.30	.75
❑ 71 Ryan Grant	.30	.75
❑ 72 Greg Jennings	.25	.60
❑ 73 Tarvaris Jackson	.25	.60
❑ 74 Adrian Peterson	.60	1.50
❑ 75 Sidney Rice	.30	.75
❑ 76 Michael Turner	.30	.75
❑ 77 Roddy White	.25	.60
❑ 78 Jason Witten	.30	.75
❑ 79 DeAngelo Williams	.25	.60
❑ 80 Steve Smith	.25	.60
❑ 81 Julius Peppers	.25	.60
❑ 82 Drew Brees	.30	.75
❑ 83 Reggie Bush	.30	.75
❑ 84 Marques Colston	.25	.60
❑ 85 Jonathan Vilma	.25	.60
❑ 86 Joey Galloway	.25	.60
❑ 87 Jeff Garcia	.25	.60
❑ 88 Cadillac Williams	.25	.60
❑ 89 Kurt Warner	.30	.75
❑ 90 Edgerrin James	.25	.60
❑ 91 Larry Fitzgerald	.30	.75
❑ 92 Anquan Boldin	.25	.60
❑ 93 Marc Bulger	.25	.60
❑ 94 Steven Jackson	.30	.75
❑ 95 Torry Holt	.25	.60
❑ 96 J.T. O'Sullivan	.20	.50
❑ 97 Frank Gore	.25	.60
❑ 98 Nate Clements	.20	.50
❑ 99 Matt Hasselbeck	.25	.60
❑ 100 Deion Branch	.25	.60
❑ 101 Alex Brink RC	.60	1.50
❑ 102 Andre Woodson RC	.60	1.50
❑ 103 Brian Brohm RC	.60	1.50
❑ 104 Dorien Bryant RC	.50	1.25
❑ 105 Colt Brennan RC	1.00	2.50
❑ 106 Calais Campbell RC	.50	1.25
❑ 107 Chad Henne RC	1.00	2.50
❑ 108 Chris Johnson RC	2.00	5.00
❑ 109 Chris Long RC	.60	1.50
❑ 110 Jacob Tamme RC	.60	1.50
❑ 111 Dan Connor RC	.60	1.50
❑ 112 Dennis Dixon RC	.60	1.50
❑ 113 DeSean Jackson RC	1.25	3.00
❑ 114 Dennis Keyes RC	.40	1.00
❑ 115 Darren McFadden RC	1.25	3.00
❑ 116 D.Rodgers-Cromartie RC	.60	1.50
❑ 117 Devin Thomas RC	.60	1.50
❑ 118 Erik Ainge RC	.60	1.50
❑ 119 Early Doucet RC	.60	1.50
❑ 120 Erin Henderson RC	.50	1.25
❑ 121 Fred Davis RC	.60	1.50
❑ 122 Felix Jones RC	1.25	3.00
❑ 123 Matt Forte RC	1.25	3.00
❑ 124 Glenn Dorsey RC	.60	1.50
❑ 125 John David Booty RC	.60	1.50
❑ 126 Jamaal Charles RC	1.00	2.50
❑ 127 Joe Flacco RC	2.00	5.00
❑ 128 Jonathan Goff RC	.50	1.25
❑ 129 Jake Long RC	.60	1.50
❑ 130 Jordy Nelson RC	.75	2.00
❑ 131 Jonathan Stewart RC	1.25	3.00
❑ 132 Davone Bess RC	.75	2.00
❑ 133 Kalvin McRae RC	.50	1.25
❑ 134 Kenny Phillips RC	.60	1.50
❑ 135 Kevin Smith RC	1.00	2.50
❑ 136 Leodis McKelvin RC	.60	1.50
❑ 137 Limas Sweed RC	.60	1.50
❑ 138 Matt Flynn RC	.60	1.50
❑ 139 Mike Hart RC	.60	1.50
❑ 140 Aqib Talib RC	.60	1.50
❑ 141 Malcolm Kelly RC	.60	1.50
❑ 142 Mario Manningham RC	.60	1.50
❑ 143 Matt Ryan RC	2.50	6.00
❑ 144 Paul Smith RC	.60	1.50
❑ 145 Rashard Mendenhall RC	1.25	3.00
❑ 146 Ray Rice RC	1.25	3.00
❑ 147 Sedrick Ellis RC	.60	1.50
❑ 148 Donnie Avery RC	.75	2.00
❑ 149 Tashard Choice RC	.60	1.50
❑ 150 Vernon Gholston RC	.60	1.50
❑ 151 Alex Brink 93	1.00	2.50
❑ 152 Andre Caldwell 93	1.00	2.50
❑ 153 Allen Patrick 93	.75	2.00
❑ 154 Andre Woodson 93	1.00	2.50
❑ 155 Brian Brohm 93	1.00	2.50
❑ 156 Dorien Bryant 93	.75	2.00
❑ 157 Colt Brennan 93	1.50	4.00
❑ 158 Chris Ellis 93	.75	2.00
❑ 159 Chad Henne 93	1.50	4.00
❑ 160 Chris Johnson 93	3.00	8.00
❑ 161 Chris Long 93	1.00	2.50
❑ 162 Donnie Avery 93	1.25	3.00
❑ 163 Davone Bess 93	1.25	3.00
❑ 164 Dan Connor 93	1.00	2.50
❑ 165 Dennis Dixon 93	1.00	2.50
❑ 166 DeSean Jackson 93	2.00	5.00
❑ 167 Darren McFadden 93	2.00	5.00
❑ 168 Erik Ainge 93	1.00	2.50
❑ 169 Early Doucet 93	1.00	2.50
❑ 170 Fred Davis 93	1.00	2.50
❑ 171 Felix Jones 93	2.00	5.00
❑ 172 Matt Forte 93	2.00	5.00
❑ 173 Geno Hayes 93	.60	1.50
❑ 174 Chevis Jackson 93	.75	2.00
❑ 175 John David Booty 93	1.00	2.50
❑ 176 Jamaal Charles 93	1.50	4.00
❑ 177 Joe Flacco 93	3.00	8.00
❑ 178 Peyton Hillis 93	1.00	2.50
❑ 179 Jake Long 93	1.00	2.50
❑ 180 Jordy Nelson 93	1.25	3.00
❑ 181 Jonathan Stewart 93	2.00	5.00
❑ 182 Justin Forsett 93	1.00	2.50
❑ 183 Kevin O'Connell 93	1.00	2.50
❑ 184 Kenny Phillips 93	1.00	2.50
❑ 185 Kevin Smith 93	1.50	4.00
❑ 186 Lance Ball 93	.60	1.50
❑ 187 Leodis McKelvin 93	1.00	2.50
❑ 188 Limas Sweed 93	1.00	2.50
❑ 189 Marcus Monk 93	1.00	2.50
❑ 190 Matt Flynn 93	1.00	2.50
❑ 191 Mike Hart 93	1.00	2.50
❑ 192 Mike Jenkins 93	1.00	2.50
❑ 193 Malcolm Kelly 93	1.00	2.50
❑ 194 Mario Manningham 93	1.00	2.50
❑ 195 Dre Moore 93	.75	2.00
❑ 196 Matt Ryan 93	4.00	10.00
❑ 197 Ryan Clady 93	1.00	2.50
❑ 198 Rashard Mendenhall 93	2.00	5.00
❑ 199 Ray Rice 93	2.00	5.00
❑ 200 Tashard Choice 93	1.00	2.50
❑ 201 Alex Brink 94	1.25	3.00
❑ 202 Aqib Talib 94	1.25	3.00
❑ 203 Andre Woodson 94	1.25	3.00
❑ 204 Brian Brohm 94	1.25	3.00
❑ 205 Dorien Bryant 94	1.00	2.50
❑ 206 Colt Brennan 94	2.00	5.00
❑ 207 Calais Campbell 94	1.00	2.50
❑ 208 Chad Henne 94	2.00	5.00
❑ 209 Chris Johnson 94	4.00	10.00
❑ 210 Chris Long 94	1.25	3.00
❑ 211 Donnie Avery 94	1.50	4.00
❑ 212 Davone Bess 94	1.50	4.00
❑ 213 Dennis Dixon 94	1.25	3.00
❑ 214 DeSean Jackson 94	2.50	6.00
❑ 215 Darren McFadden 94	2.50	6.00
❑ 216 D.Rodgers-Cromartie 94	1.25	3.00
❑ 217 Erik Ainge 94	1.25	3.00
❑ 218 Early Doucet 94	1.25	3.00
❑ 219 Fred Davis 94	1.25	3.00
❑ 220 Felix Jones 94	2.50	6.00
❑ 221 Matt Forte 94	2.50	6.00
❑ 222 Harry Douglas 94	1.00	2.50
❑ 223 John David Booty 94	1.25	3.00
❑ 224 Jamaal Charles 94	2.00	5.00
❑ 225 Joe Flacco 94	4.00	10.00
❑ 226 James Hardy 94	1.00	2.50
❑ 227 Josh Johnson 94	1.25	3.00
❑ 228 Jordy Nelson 94	1.50	4.00
❑ 229 Jonathan Stewart 94	2.50	6.00
❑ 230 Keenan Burton 94	1.00	2.50
❑ 231 Kenny Phillips 94	1.25	3.00
❑ 232 Keith Rivers 94	1.25	3.00
❑ 233 Kevin Smith 94	2.00	5.00
❑ 234 Lavelle Hawkins 94	1.00	2.50
❑ 235 Leodis McKelvin 94	1.25	3.00
❑ 236 Limas Sweed 94	1.25	3.00
❑ 237 Matt Flynn 94	1.25	3.00
❑ 238 Mike Hart 94	1.25	3.00
❑ 239 Adrian Arrington 94	1.00	2.50
❑ 240 Malcolm Kelly 94	1.25	3.00
❑ 241 Mario Manningham 94	1.25	3.00
❑ 242 Matt Ryan 94	5.00	12.00
❑ 243 Phillip Merling 94	1.00	2.50
❑ 244 Darius Reynaud 94	1.00	2.50
❑ 245 Rashard Mendenhall 94	2.50	6.00
❑ 246 Ray Rice 94	2.50	6.00
❑ 247 Ryan Torain 94	1.25	3.00
❑ 248 Thomas Brown 94	1.25	3.00
❑ 249 Tashard Choice 94	1.25	3.00
❑ 250 Vernon Gholston 94	1.25	3.00
❑ 251 Alex Brink 95	1.50	4.00
❑ 252 Allen Patrick 95	1.25	3.00
❑ 253 Aqib Talib 95	1.50	4.00
❑ 254 Andre Woodson 95	1.50	4.00
❑ 255 Brian Brohm 95	1.50	4.00
❑ 256 Dorien Bryant 95	1.25	3.00
❑ 257 Colt Brennan 95	2.50	6.00
❑ 258 Chad Henne 95	2.50	6.00
❑ 259 Chris Johnson 95	5.00	12.00
❑ 260 Chris Long 95	1.50	4.00
❑ 261 Davone Bess 95	2.00	5.00
❑ 262 Dennis Dixon 95	1.50	4.00
❑ 263 DeSean Jackson 95	3.00	8.00
❑ 264 Darren McFadden 95	3.00	8.00
❑ 265 Erik Ainge 95	1.50	4.00
❑ 266 Early Doucet 95	1.50	4.00
❑ 267 Fred Davis 95	1.50	4.00
❑ 268 Felix Jones 95	3.00	8.00
❑ 269 Matt Forte 95	3.00	8.00
❑ 270 Geno Hayes 95	1.00	2.50
❑ 271 Harry Douglas 95	1.25	3.00
❑ 272 John David Booty 95	1.50	4.00
❑ 273 Jamaal Charles 95	2.50	6.00
❑ 274 Joe Flacco 95	5.00	12.00
❑ 275 Peyton Hillis 95	1.50	4.00
❑ 276 Jacob Hester 95	1.50	4.00
❑ 277 Josh Johnson 95	1.50	4.00
❑ 278 Jordy Nelson 95	2.00	5.00
❑ 279 Jonathan Stewart 95	3.00	8.00
❑ 280 Keenan Burton 95	1.25	3.00
❑ 281 Kenny Phillips 95	1.50	4.00
❑ 282 Kevin Smith 95	2.50	6.00
❑ 283 Lance Ball 95	1.00	2.50
❑ 284 Lavelle Hawkins 95	1.25	3.00
❑ 285 Limas Sweed 95	1.50	4.00
❑ 286 Matt Flynn 95	1.50	4.00
❑ 287 Mike Hart 95	1.50	4.00
❑ 288 Adrian Arrington 95	1.25	3.00
❑ 289 Malcolm Kelly 95	1.50	4.00
❑ 290 Mario Manningham 95	1.50	4.00
❑ 291 Marcus Monk 95	1.50	4.00

Card		
292 Matt Ryan 95	6.00	15.00
293 Mario Urrutia 95	1.25	3.00
294 Paul Hubbard 95	1.25	3.00
295 Rashard Mendenhall 95	3.00	8.00
296 Ray Rice 95	3.00	8.00
297 Ryan Torain 95	1.50	4.00
298 Thomas Brown 95	1.50	4.00
299 Tashard Choice 95	1.50	4.00
300 Yvenson Bernard 95	1.50	4.00
301 Alex Brink 96	1.50	4.00
302 Chevis Jackson 96	1.25	3.00
303 Andre Caldwell 96	1.50	4.00
304 Allen Patrick 96	1.25	3.00
305 Kevin O'Connell 96	1.50	4.00
306 Andre Woodson 96	1.50	4.00
307 Brian Brohm 96	1.50	4.00
308 Mike Jenkins 96	1.50	4.00
309 Tom Zbikowski 96	1.50	4.00
310 Dorien Bryant 96	1.25	3.00
311 Colt Brennan 96	2.50	6.00
312 Chad Henne 96	2.50	6.00
313 Chris Johnson 96	5.00	12.00
314 Chris Long 96	1.50	4.00
315 Donnie Avery 96	2.00	5.00
316 Davone Bess 96	2.00	5.00
317 Dennis Dixon 96	1.50	4.00
318 DeSean Jackson 96	3.00	8.00
319 Darren McFadden 96	3.00	8.00
320 DeMario Pressley 96	1.25	3.00
321 Dre Moore 96	1.25	3.00
322 Erik Ainge 96	1.50	4.00
323 Early Doucet 96	1.50	4.00
324 Fred Davis 96	1.50	4.00
325 Felix Jones 96	3.00	8.00
326 Matt Forte 96	3.00	8.00
327 Harry Douglas 96	1.25	3.00
328 John David Booty 96	1.50	4.00
329 Jamaal Charles 96	2.50	6.00
330 Joe Flacco 96	5.00	12.00
331 Jordy Nelson 96	2.00	5.00
332 Jonathan Stewart 96	3.00	8.00
333 Kalvin McRae 96	1.25	3.00
334 Kenny Phillips 96	1.50	4.00
335 Kevin Smith 96	2.50	6.00
336 Lavelle Hawkins 96	1.25	3.00
337 Limas Sweed 96	1.50	4.00
338 Marcus Monk 96	1.50	4.00
339 Matt Flynn 96	1.50	4.00
340 Mike Hart 96	1.50	4.00
341 Adrian Arrington 96	1.25	3.00
342 Malcolm Kelly 96	1.50	4.00
343 Mario Manningham 96	1.50	4.00
344 Ben Moffitt 96	1.00	2.50
345 Matt Ryan 96	6.00	15.00
346 Mario Urrutia 96	1.25	3.00
347 Rashard Mendenhall 96	3.00	8.00
348 Ray Rice 96	3.00	8.00
349 Ryan Torain 96	1.50	4.00
350 Tashard Choice 96	1.50	4.00
352 Bob Griese 96	1.25	3.00
353 Bert Jones 96	.75	2.00
354 Bruce Smith 96	.75	2.00
355 Barry Sanders 96	2.00	5.00
356 Dick Butkus 96	1.50	4.00
357 Daryl Johnston 96	1.25	3.00
359 Franco Harris 96	1.25	3.00
360 Fran Tarkenton 96	1.25	3.00
363 Bo Jackson 96	1.50	4.00
365 John Elway 96	2.00	5.00
366 Joe Greene 96	1.25	3.00
367 Jack Ham 96	1.00	2.50
368 Jerry Kramer 96	1.00	2.50
369 Jim Kelly 96	1.25	3.00
372 Joe Theismann 96	1.25	3.00
373 Ken Anderson 96	1.00	2.50
376 Jerry Rice 96	2.00	5.00
377 Emmitt Smith 96	2.50	6.00
379 Ottis Anderson 96	.75	2.00
380 Paul Hornung 96	1.25	3.00
381 Roger Craig 96	1.00	2.50
382 Roman Gabriel 96	1.00	2.50
383 Chuck Bednarik 96	1.00	2.50
384 Rod Woodson 96	1.25	3.00
385 Billy Sims 96	1.00	2.50
386 Archie Manning 96	1.25	3.00
387 Bart Starr 96	2.00	5.00
388 Steve Young 96	1.50	4.00
389 Troy Aikman 96	1.50	4.00
391 Tom Rathman 96	1.00	2.50
392 Y.A. Tittle 96	1.25	3.00
394 Bob Griese 93	1.25	3.00
395 Bert Jones 93	.75	2.00
396 Bruce Smith 93	.75	2.00
397 Barry Sanders 93	2.00	5.00
398 Dick Butkus 93	1.50	4.00
399 Daryl Johnston 93	1.25	3.00
401 Franco Harris 93	1.25	3.00
402 Fran Tarkenton 93	1.25	3.00
405 Bo Jackson 93	1.50	4.00
407 John Elway 93	2.00	5.00
408 Joe Greene 93	1.25	3.00
409 Jack Ham 93	1.00	2.50
410 Jim Kelly 93	1.25	3.00
411 Jerry Kramer 93	1.00	2.50
414 Joe Theismann 93	1.25	3.00
415 Ken Anderson 93	1.00	2.50
418 Roger Staubach 93	1.50	4.00
419 Chuck Bednarik 93	1.00	2.50
421 Ottis Anderson 93	.75	2.00
422 Paul Hornung 93	1.25	3.00
423 Roger Craig 93	1.00	2.50
424 Roman Gabriel 93	1.00	2.50
426 Rod Woodson 93	1.25	3.00
427 Billy Sims 93	1.00	2.50
428 Archie Manning 93	1.25	3.00
429 Bart Starr 93	2.00	5.00
430 Steve Young 93	1.50	4.00
431 Troy Aikman 93	1.50	4.00
433 Tom Rathman 93	1.00	2.50
434 Y.A. Tittle 93	1.25	3.00

1999 SPx

Card		
COMPLETE SET (135)	1000.00	2000.00
COMP.SET w/o SP's (90)	12.50	25.00
*HAND NUMBERED RCs: .5X TO .8X		
1 Jake Plummer	.40	1.00
2 Adrian Murrell	.40	1.00
3 Frank Sanders	.40	1.00
4 Jamal Anderson	.60	1.50
5 Chris Chandler	.40	1.00
6 Terance Mathis	.40	1.00
7 Tony Banks	.40	1.00
8 Priest Holmes	1.00	2.50
9 Jermaine Lewis	.40	1.00
10 Antowain Smith	.60	1.50
11 Doug Flutie	.60	1.50
12 Eric Moulds	.60	1.50
13 Tim Biakabutuka	.40	1.00
14 Steve Beuerlein	.40	1.00
15 Muhsin Muhammad	.40	1.00
16 Bobby Engram	.40	1.00
17 Curtis Conway	.40	1.00
18 Curtis Enis	.25	.60
19 Corey Dillon	.60	1.50
20 Jeff Blake	.40	1.00
21 Carl Pickens	.40	1.00
22 Ty Detmer	.40	1.00
23 Terry Kirby	.25	.60
24 Leslie Shepherd	.25	.60
25 Troy Aikman	1.25	3.00
26 Emmitt Smith	1.25	3.00
27 Deion Sanders	.60	1.50
28 Terrell Davis	.60	1.50
29 Rod Smith	.40	1.00
30 Bubby Brister	.40	1.00
31 Barry Sanders	2.00	5.00
32 Herman Moore	.40	1.00
33 Charlie Batch	.60	1.50
34 Brett Favre	2.00	5.00
35 Antonio Freeman	.60	1.50
36 Dorsey Levens	.60	1.50
37 Peyton Manning	2.00	5.00
38 Marvin Harrison	.60	1.50
39 Jerome Pathon	.25	.60
40 Mark Brunell	.60	1.50
41 Jimmy Smith	.40	1.00
42 Fred Taylor	.60	1.50
43 Elvis Grbac	.40	1.00
44 Andre Rison	.40	1.00
45 Warren Moon	.60	1.50
46 Dan Marino	2.00	5.00
47 Karim Abdul-Jabbar	.40	1.00
48 O.J. McDuffie	.40	1.00
49 Randall Cunningham	.60	1.50
50 Robert Smith	.60	1.50
51 Randy Moss	1.50	4.00
52 Drew Bledsoe	.75	2.00
53 Terry Glenn	.60	1.50
54 Tony Simmons	.25	.60
55 Danny Wuerffel	.25	.60
56 Cam Cleeland	.25	.60
57 Kerry Collins	.40	1.00
58 Gary Brown	.25	.60
59 Ike Hilliard	.25	.60
60 Vinny Testaverde	.40	1.00
61 Curtis Martin	.60	1.50
62 Keyshawn Johnson	.60	1.50
63 Rich Gannon	.60	1.50
64 Napoleon Kaufman	.60	1.50
65 Tim Brown	.60	1.50
66 Duce Staley	.60	1.50
67 Doug Pederson	.25	.60
68 Charles Johnson	.25	.60
69 Kordell Stewart	.40	1.00
70 Jerome Bettis	.60	1.50
71 Trent Green	.60	1.50
72 Marshall Faulk	.75	2.00
73 Ryan Leaf	.60	1.50
74 Natrone Means	.40	1.00
75 Jim Harbaugh	.40	1.00
76 Steve Young	.75	2.00
77 Garrison Hearst	.40	1.00
78 Jerry Rice	1.25	3.00
79 Terrell Owens	.60	1.50
80 Ricky Watters	.40	1.00
81 Joey Galloway	.40	1.00
82 Jon Kitna	.60	1.50
83 Warrick Dunn	.60	1.50
84 Trent Dilfer	.40	1.00
85 Mike Alstott	.60	1.50
86 Steve McNair	.60	1.50
87 Eddie George	.60	1.50
88 Yancey Thigpen	.25	.60
89 Skip Hicks	.25	.60
90 Michael Westbrook	.40	1.00
91 Amos Zereoue RC	6.00	15.00
92 Chris Claiborne AU RC	10.00	25.00
93 Scott Covington RC	6.00	15.00
94 Jeff Paulk RC	4.00	10.00
95 Brandon Stokley AU RC	12.50	30.00
96 Antoine Winfield RC	5.00	12.00
97 Reginald Kelly RC	4.00	10.00
98 Jermaine Fazande AU RC	6.00	15.00
99 Andy Katzenmoyer RC	5.00	12.00
100 Craig Yeast RC	5.00	12.00
101 Joe Montgomery RC	5.00	12.00
102 Darrin Chiaverini RC	5.00	12.00
103 Travis McGriff RC	4.00	10.00
104 Jevon Kearse RC	12.50	30.00
105 Joel Makovicka AU RC	6.00	15.00
106 Aaron Brooks RC	8.00	20.00
107 Chris McAlister RC	5.00	12.00
108 Jim Kleinsasser RC	6.00	15.00
109 Ebenezer Ekuban RC	5.00	12.00
110 Karsten Bailey RC	5.00	12.00
111 Sedrick Irvin AU RC	5.00	12.00
112 D'Wayne Bates AU RC	5.00	12.00
113 Joe Germaine AU RC	6.00	15.00
114 Cecil Collins AU RC	6.00	15.00
115 Mike Cloud RC	5.00	12.00
116 James Johnson RC	5.00	12.00
117 Champ Bailey AU RC	15.00	40.00
118 Rob Konrad RC	6.00	15.00
119 Peerless Price AU RC	10.00	25.00
120 Kevin Faulk AU RC	10.00	25.00
121 Dameane Douglas RC	4.00	10.00
122 Kevin Johnson AU RC	6.00	15.00
123 Troy Edwards AU RC	10.00	25.00
124 Edgerrin James AU RC	20.00	50.00
125 David Boston AU RC	10.00	25.00
126 Michael Bishop AU RC	10.00	25.00
127 Shaun King AU SP RC	20.00	50.00
127X Shaun King EXCH	4.00	10.00
128 Brock Huard AU RC	6.00	15.00

- ❑ 129 Torry Holt AU RC 30.00 60.00
- ❑ 130 Cade McNown AU/500 RC 15.00 40.00
- ❑ 131 Tim Couch AU/500 RC 15.00 40.00
- ❑ 132 Donovan McNabb AU RC 50.00 100.00
- ❑ 132X Donovan McNabb EXCH 2.00 5.00
- ❑ 133 Akili Smith AU/500 RC 15.00 40.00
- ❑ 134 D.Culpepper AU/500 RC 40.00 80.00
- ❑ 135 Ricky Williams AU/500 RC 30.00 60.00
- ❑ S8 Troy Aikman Sample .75 2.00

2000 SPx

- ❑ COMP.SET w/o SP's (90) 7.50 20.00
- ❑ 1 Jake Plummer .25 .60
- ❑ 2 David Boston .40 1.00
- ❑ 3 Frank Sanders .25 .60
- ❑ 4 Chris Chandler .25 .60
- ❑ 5 Jamal Anderson .40 1.00
- ❑ 6 Shawn Jefferson .15 .40
- ❑ 7 Qadry Ismail .25 .60
- ❑ 8 Tony Banks .25 .60
- ❑ 9 Shannon Sharpe .25 .60
- ❑ 10 Rob Johnson .25 .60
- ❑ 11 Eric Moulds .40 1.00
- ❑ 12 Muhsin Muhammad .25 .60
- ❑ 13 Steve Beuerlein .15 .40
- ❑ 14 Cade McNown .15 .40
- ❑ 15 Marcus Robinson .40 1.00
- ❑ 16 Akili Smith .15 .40
- ❑ 17 Corey Dillon .40 1.00
- ❑ 18 Darnay Scott .25 .60
- ❑ 19 Tim Couch .25 .60
- ❑ 20 Kevin Johnson .40 1.00
- ❑ 21 Errict Rhett .15 .40
- ❑ 22 Troy Aikman .75 2.00
- ❑ 23 Emmitt Smith .75 2.00
- ❑ 24 Joey Galloway .25 .60
- ❑ 25 Terrell Davis .40 1.00
- ❑ 26 Olandis Gary .40 1.00
- ❑ 27 Brian Griese .40 1.00
- ❑ 28 Charlie Batch .40 1.00
- ❑ 29 Germane Crowell .15 .40
- ❑ 30 James Stewart .25 .60
- ❑ 31 Brett Favre 1.25 3.00
- ❑ 32 Antonio Freeman .40 1.00
- ❑ 33 Dorsey Levens .25 .60
- ❑ 34 Peyton Manning 1.00 2.50
- ❑ 35 Edgerrin James .60 1.50
- ❑ 36 Marvin Harrison .40 1.00
- ❑ 37 Mark Brunell .40 1.00
- ❑ 38 Fred Taylor .40 1.00
- ❑ 39 Jimmy Smith .25 .60
- ❑ 40 Keenan McCardell .25 .60
- ❑ 41 Elvis Grbac .25 .60
- ❑ 42 Tony Gonzalez .25 .60
- ❑ 43 Tony Martin .25 .60
- ❑ 44 Jay Fiedler .40 1.00
- ❑ 45 Damon Huard .40 1.00
- ❑ 46 Randy Moss .75 2.00
- ❑ 47 Robert Smith .40 1.00
- ❑ 48 Cris Carter .40 1.00
- ❑ 49 Daunte Culpepper .50 1.25
- ❑ 50 Drew Bledsoe .50 1.25
- ❑ 51 Terry Glenn .25 .60
- ❑ 52 Ricky Williams .40 1.00
- ❑ 53 Jeff Blake .25 .60
- ❑ 54 Keith Poole .15 .40
- ❑ 55 Kerry Collins .25 .60
- ❑ 56 Amani Toomer .25 .60
- ❑ 57 Ike Hilliard .25 .60
- ❑ 58 Ray Lucas .25 .60
- ❑ 59 Curtis Martin .40 1.00
- ❑ 60 Vinny Testaverde .25 .60
- ❑ 61 Tim Brown .40 1.00
- ❑ 62 Rich Gannon .40 1.00
- ❑ 63 Tyrone Wheatley .25 .60
- ❑ 64 Napoleon Kaufman .25 .60
- ❑ 65 Duce Staley .40 1.00
- ❑ 66 Donovan McNabb .60 1.50
- ❑ 67 Troy Edwards .15 .40
- ❑ 68 Jerome Bettis .40 1.00
- ❑ 69 Kordell Stewart .25 .60
- ❑ 70 Marshall Faulk .50 1.25
- ❑ 71 Kurt Warner .60 1.50
- ❑ 72 Isaac Bruce .40 1.00
- ❑ 73 Torry Holt .40 1.00
- ❑ 74 Ryan Leaf .25 .60
- ❑ 75 Jim Harbaugh .25 .60
- ❑ 76 Jerry Rice .75 2.00
- ❑ 77 Terrell Owens .40 1.00
- ❑ 78 Jeff Garcia .40 1.00
- ❑ 79 Ricky Watters .25 .60
- ❑ 80 Jon Kitna .40 1.00
- ❑ 81 Derrick Mayes .25 .60
- ❑ 82 Shaun King .15 .40
- ❑ 83 Mike Alstott .40 1.00
- ❑ 84 Keyshawn Johnson .40 1.00
- ❑ 85 Eddie George .40 1.00
- ❑ 86 Steve McNair .40 1.00
- ❑ 87 Jevon Kearse .40 1.00
- ❑ 88 Brad Johnson .40 1.00
- ❑ 89 Stephen Davis .40 1.00
- ❑ 90 Michael Westbrook .25 .60
- ❑ 91 Anthony Lucas RC 2.50 6.00
- ❑ 92 Avion Black RC 3.00 8.00
- ❑ 93 Corey Moore RC 2.50 6.00
- ❑ 94 Chris Cole RC 3.00 8.00
- ❑ 95 Chris Hovan RC 3.00 8.00
- ❑ 96 Dante Hall RC 5.00 12.00
- ❑ 97 Darrell Jackson RC 5.00 12.00
- ❑ 98 Deltha O'Neal RC 4.00 10.00
- ❑ 99 Doug Chapman RC 3.00 8.00
- ❑ 100 Doug Johnson RC 4.00 10.00
- ❑ 101 Erron Kinney RC 4.00 10.00
- ❑ 102 Frank Moreau RC 3.00 8.00
- ❑ 103 Patrick Pass RC 3.00 8.00
- ❑ 104 Gari Scott RC 2.50 6.00
- ❑ 105 Giovanni Carmazzi RC 2.50 6.00
- ❑ 106 JaJuan Dawson RC 2.50 6.00
- ❑ 107 James Williams RC 3.00 8.00
- ❑ 108 Jarious Jackson RC 3.00 8.00
- ❑ 109 John Abraham RC 5.00 12.00
- ❑ 110 Keith Bulluck RC 4.00 10.00
- ❑ 111 Jonas Lewis RC 2.50 6.00
- ❑ 112 Mike Green RC 3.00 8.00
- ❑ 113 Ronney Jenkins RC 3.00 8.00
- ❑ 114 Michael Wiley RC 3.00 8.00
- ❑ 115 Mike Anderson RC 4.00 10.00
- ❑ 116 Mareno Philyaw RC 2.50 6.00
- ❑ 117 Muneer Moore RC 2.50 6.00
- ❑ 118 Paul Smith RC 3.00 8.00
- ❑ 119 Raynoch Thompson RC 3.00 8.00
- ❑ 120 Rob Morris RC 3.00 8.00
- ❑ 121 Ron Dixon RC 3.00 8.00
- ❑ 122 Rondell Mealey RC 2.50 6.00
- ❑ 123 Sebastian Janikowski RC 4.00 10.00
- ❑ 124 Shaun Ellis RC 4.00 10.00
- ❑ 125 Charles Lee RC 3.00 8.00
- ❑ 126 Shyrone Stith RC 3.00 8.00
- ❑ 127 Thomas Hamner RC 2.50 6.00
- ❑ 128 Tim Rattay RC 4.00 10.00
- ❑ 129 Todd Husak RC 4.00 10.00
- ❑ 130 Tom Brady RC 225.00 400.00
- ❑ 131 Trevor Gaylor RC 3.00 8.00
- ❑ 132 Windrell Hayes RC 3.00 8.00
- ❑ 133 Anthony Becht JSY AU RC 10.00 25.00
- ❑ 134 Brian Urlacher JSY AU RC 75.00 135.00
- ❑ 135 Bubba Franks JSY AU RC 10.00 25.00
- ❑ 136 C Pennington JSY AU RC 20.00 50.00
- ❑ 137 Chr Redman JSY AU RC 8.00 20.00
- ❑ 138 Corey Simon JSY AU RC 10.00 25.00
- ❑ 139 Curtis Keaton JSY AU RC 6.00 15.00
- ❑ 140 Danny Farmer JSY AU RC 6.00 15.00
- ❑ 141 Den Northcutt JSY AU RC 10.00 25.00
- ❑ 142 Dez White JSY AU RC 10.00 25.00
- ❑ 143 J.R. Redmond JSY AU SP RC 8.00 20.00
- ❑ 144 Jamal Lewis JSY AU RC 20.00 50.00
- ❑ 145 Jerry Porter JSY AU RC 12.50 30.00
- ❑ 146 Joe Hamilton EXCH 1.25 3.00
- ❑ 147 Laver Coles JSY AU RC 15.00 40.00
- ❑ 148 R.Jay Soward JSY AU RC 8.00 20.00
- ❑ 149 Reu Droughns JSY AU RC 10.00 25.00
- ❑ 150 Ron Dayne JSY AU RC 12.50 30.00
- ❑ 151 Ron Dugans JSY AU RC 6.00 15.00
- ❑ 152 Sha Alexander JSY AU RC 20.00 50.00
- ❑ 153 Sylvester Morris JSY AU RC 8.00 20.00
- ❑ 154 Tee Martin JSY AU RC 10.00 25.00
- ❑ 155 Th.Jones JSY AU RC SP 75.00 150.00
- ❑ 156 Todd Pinkston JSY AU RC 10.00 25.00
- ❑ 157 Travis Prentice JSY AU RC 8.00 20.00
- ❑ 158 Travis Taylor JSY AU SP RC 10.00 25.00
- ❑ 159 Trung Canidate JSY AU RC 8.00 20.00
- ❑ 160 Courtney Brown JSY AU RC 12.50 30.00
- ❑ 161 Peter Warrick JSY AU RC 12.50 30.00
- ❑ 162 Plaxico Burress JSY AU RC 40.00 100.00
- ❑ S1 Peyton Manning Sample 1.50 4.00

2001 SPx

- ❑ COMP.SET w/o SP's (90) 7.50 20.00
- ❑ 1 Jake Plummer .25 .60
- ❑ 2 David Boston .20 .50
- ❑ 3 Jamal Anderson .25 .60
- ❑ 4 Chris Chandler .25 .60
- ❑ 5 Tony Martin .25 .60
- ❑ 6 Elvis Grbac .25 .60
- ❑ 7 Qadry Ismail .25 .60
- ❑ 8 Ray Lewis .30 .75
- ❑ 9 Rob Johnson .25 .60
- ❑ 10 Shawn Bryson .20 .50
- ❑ 11 Eric Moulds .25 .60
- ❑ 12 Tim Biakabutuka .20 .50
- ❑ 13 Jeff Lewis .20 .50
- ❑ 14 Muhsin Muhammad .25 .60
- ❑ 15 Shane Matthews .20 .50
- ❑ 16 Marcus Robinson .25 .60
- ❑ 17 Brian Urlacher .40 1.00
- ❑ 18 Jon Kitna .25 .60
- ❑ 19 Peter Warrick .25 .60
- ❑ 20 Corey Dillon .25 .60
- ❑ 21 Tim Couch .20 .50
- ❑ 22 Travis Prentice .20 .50
- ❑ 23 Kevin Johnson .20 .50
- ❑ 24 Rocket Ismail .25 .60
- ❑ 25 Emmitt Smith .75 2.00
- ❑ 26 Joey Galloway .25 .60
- ❑ 27 Terrell Davis .30 .75
- ❑ 28 Brian Griese .25 .60
- ❑ 29 Rod Smith .25 .60
- ❑ 30 Ed McCaffrey .25 .60
- ❑ 31 Charlie Batch .25 .60
- ❑ 32 Germane Crowell .20 .50
- ❑ 33 James O. Stewart .20 .50
- ❑ 34 Brett Favre 1.00 2.50
- ❑ 35 Antonio Freeman .30 .75
- ❑ 36 Ahman Green .30 .75
- ❑ 37 Peyton Manning .75 2.00
- ❑ 38 Edgerrin James .30 .75
- ❑ 39 Marvin Harrison .30 .75
- ❑ 40 Mark Brunell .30 .75
- ❑ 41 Fred Taylor .30 .75
- ❑ 42 Jimmy Smith .25 .60
- ❑ 43 Tony Gonzalez .25 .60
- ❑ 44 Trent Green .30 .75
- ❑ 45 Priest Holmes .30 .75
- ❑ 46 Lamar Smith .25 .60
- ❑ 47 Jay Fiedler .25 .60
- ❑ 48 Oronde Gadsden .20 .50
- ❑ 49 Daunte Culpepper .30 .75
- ❑ 50 Randy Moss .40 1.00
- ❑ 51 Cris Carter .30 .75
- ❑ 52 Drew Bledsoe .30 .75
- ❑ 53 Troy Brown .25 .60
- ❑ 54 Ricky Williams .30 .75
- ❑ 55 Joe Horn .25 .60
- ❑ 56 Aaron Brooks .25 .60
- ❑ 57 Albert Connell .20 .50
- ❑ 58 Kerry Collins .25 .60
- ❑ 59 Tiki Barber .30 .75
- ❑ 60 Ron Dayne .25 .60
- ❑ 61 Vinny Testaverde .25 .60
- ❑ 62 Wayne Chrebet .25 .60
- ❑ 63 Curtis Martin .30 .75

❑ 64 Tim Brown .30 .75
❑ 65 Jerry Rice .60 1.50
❑ 66 Rich Gannon .25 .60
❑ 67 Duce Staley .25 .60
❑ 68 Donovan McNabb .40 1.00
❑ 69 Kordell Stewart .25 .60
❑ 70 Jerome Bettis .30 .75
❑ 71 Marshall Faulk .30 .75
❑ 72 Kurt Warner .40 1.00
❑ 73 Isaac Bruce .30 .75
❑ 74 Torry Holt .25 .60
❑ 75 Doug Flutie .30 .75
❑ 76 Junior Seau .30 .75
❑ 77 Jeff Garcia .25 .60
❑ 78 Garrison Hearst .25 .60
❑ 79 Terrell Owens .30 .75
❑ 80 Ricky Watters .25 .60
❑ 81 Matt Hasselbeck .30 .75
❑ 82 Brad Johnson .25 .60
❑ 83 Keyshawn Johnson .25 .60
❑ 84 Warrick Dunn .30 .75
❑ 85 Mike Alstott .25 .60
❑ 86 Kevin Dyson .25 .60
❑ 87 Eddie George .30 .75
❑ 88 Steve McNair .30 .75
❑ 89 Michael Westbrook .20 .50
❑ 90 Stephen Davis .25 .60
❑ 91B D.McAllister JSY AU/250 RC 20.00 50.00
❑ 91G D.McAllister JSY AU/250 RC 20.00 50.00
❑ 92B F.Mitchell JSY AU/250 RC 10.00 25.00
❑ 92G F.Mitchell JSY AU/250 RC 10.00 25.00
❑ 93B Koren Robinson/999 RC 2.50 6.00
❑ 93G Koren Robinson/999 RC 2.50 6.00
❑ 94B David Terrell/999 RC 2.00 5.00
❑ 94G David Terrell/999 RC 2.00 5.00
❑ 95B M.Vick JSY AU/250 RC 50.00 100.00
❑ 95G M.Vick JSY AU/250 RC 50.00 100.00
❑ 96B M.Bennett JSY AU/550 RC 10.00 25.00
❑ 96G M.Bennett JSY AU/550 RC 10.00 25.00
❑ 97B Robert Ferguson/999 RC 2.50 6.00
❑ 97G Robert Ferguson/999 RC 2.50 6.00
❑ 98B Rod Gardner/999 RC 2.00 5.00
❑ 98G Rod Gardner/999 RC 2.00 5.00
❑ 99B Travis Henry JSY AU/550 RC 10.00 25.00
❑ 99G Travis Henry JSY AU/550 RC 10.00 25.00
❑ 100B C.Johnson JSY AU/550 RC 25.00 60.00
❑ 100G C.Johnson JSY AU/550 RC 25.00 60.00
❑ 101B D.Brees JSY AU/250 RC 150.00 250.00
❑ 101G D.Brees JSY AU/250 RC 150.00 250.00
❑ 102B S Moss JSY AU/550 RC 15.00 40.00
❑ 102G S Moss JSY AU/550 RC 15.00 40.00
❑ 103B C Weinke JSY AU/550 RC 8.00 20.00
❑ 103G C Weinke JSY AU/550 RC 8.00 20.00
❑ 104B R Seymour JSY AU/900 RC 10.00 25.00
❑ 104G R Seymour JSY AU/900 RC 10.00 25.00
❑ 105B Reggie Wayne/999 RC 6.00 15.00
❑ 105G Reggie Wayne/999 RC 6.00 15.00
❑ 106B K.Barlow JSY AU/550 RC 8.00 20.00
❑ 106G K.Barlow JSY AU/550 RC 8.00 20.00
❑ 107B Chambers JSY AU/900 RC 15.00 40.00
❑ 107G Chambers JSY AU/900 RC 15.00 40.00
❑ 108B Todd Heap JSY AU/900 RC 10.00 25.00
❑ 108G Todd Heap JSY AU/900 RC 10.00 25.00
❑ 109B A.Thomas JSY AU/550 RC 10.00 25.00
❑ 109G A.Thomas JSY AU/550 RC 10.00 25.00
❑ 110B J.Jackson JSY AU/550 RC 8.00 20.00
❑ 110G J.Jackson JSY AU/550 RC 8.00 20.00
❑ 111B R.Johnson JSY AU/900 RC 10.00 25.00
❑ 111G R.Johnson JSY AU/900 RC 10.00 25.00
❑ 112B M.McMahon JSY AU/900 RC 8.00 20.00
❑ 112G M.McMahon JSY AU/900 RC 8.00 20.00
❑ 113B J.Heupel JSY AU/900 RC 10.00 25.00
❑ 113G J.Heupel JSY AU/900 RC 10.00 25.00
❑ 114B T.Minor JSY AU/900 RC 8.00 20.00
❑ 114G T.Minor JSY AU/900 RC 8.00 20.00
❑ 115B Quincy Morgan/999 RC 2.00 5.00
❑ 115G Quincy Morgan/999 RC 2.00 5.00
❑ 116B D.Morgan JSY AU/900 RC 10.00 25.00
❑ 116G D.Morgan JSY AU/900 RC 10.00 25.00
❑ 117B J.Palmer JSY AU/900 RC 10.00 25.00
❑ 117G J.Palmer JSY AU/900 RC 10.00 25.00
❑ 118B S.Rosenfels JSY AU/900 RC 10.00 25.00
❑ 118G S.Rosenfels JSY AU/900 RC 10.00 25.00
❑ 119B Tuiasosopo JSY AU/900 RC 8.00 20.00
❑ 119G Tuiasosopo JSY AU/900 RC 8.00 20.00
❑ 120B Damerien McCants/999 RC 2.00 5.00
❑ 120G Damerien McCants/999 RC 2.00 5.00
❑ 121B Snoop Minnis/999 RC 2.00 5.00
❑ 121G Snoop Minnis/999 RC 2.00 5.00
❑ 122B L.Tomlinson JSY/250 RC 60.00 120.00
❑ 122G L.Tomlinson JSY/250 RC 60.00 120.00
❑ 123B Quincy Carter/999 RC 2.00 5.00
❑ 123G Quincy Carter/999 RC 2.00 5.00
❑ 124B Arnold Jackson/999 RC 1.50 4.00
❑ 124G Arnold Jackson/999 RC 1.50 4.00
❑ 125B Justin McCareins/999 RC 2.00 5.00
❑ 125G Justin McCareins/999 RC 2.00 5.00
❑ 126B Eddie Berlin/999 RC 1.50 4.00
❑ 126G Eddie Berlin/999 RC 1.50 4.00
❑ 127B Quentin McCord/999 RC 2.00 5.00
❑ 127G Quentin McCord/999 RC 2.00 5.00
❑ 128B Vinny Sutherland/999 RC 1.50 4.00
❑ 128G Vinny Sutherland/999 RC 1.50 4.00
❑ 129B Willie Middlebrooks/999 RC 2.00 5.00
❑ 129G Willie Middlebrooks/999 RC 2.00 5.00
❑ 130B Dan Alexander/999 RC 2.00 5.00
❑ 130G Dan Alexander/999 RC 2.00 5.00
❑ 131B Dee Brown/999 RC 1.50 4.00
❑ 131G Dee Brown/999 RC 1.50 4.00
❑ 132B Andre Carter/999 RC 2.50 6.00
❑ 132G Andre Carter/999 RC 2.50 6.00
❑ 133B Justin Smith/999 RC 2.50 6.00
❑ 133G Justin Smith/999 RC 2.50 6.00
❑ 134B Houshmandzadeh/999 RC 4.00 10.00
❑ 134G Houshmandzadeh/999 RC 4.00 10.00
❑ 135B Andre King/999 RC 1.50 4.00
❑ 135G Andre King/999 RC 1.50 4.00
❑ 136B Nick Goings/999 RC 2.50 6.00
❑ 136G Nick Goings/999 RC 2.50 6.00
❑ 137B Scotty Anderson/999 RC 2.00 5.00
❑ 137G Scotty Anderson/999 RC 2.00 5.00
❑ 138B David Martin/999 RC 1.50 4.00
❑ 138G David Martin/999 RC 1.50 4.00
❑ 139B Derrick Blaylock/999 RC 2.00 5.00
❑ 139G Derrick Blaylock/999 RC 2.00 5.00
❑ 140B Onome Ojo/999 RC 1.50 4.00
❑ 140G Onome Ojo/999 RC 1.50 4.00
❑ 141B Jonathan Carter/999 RC 1.50 4.00
❑ 141G Jonathan Carter/999 RC 1.50 4.00
❑ 142B LaMont Jordan/999 RC 2.50 6.00
❑ 142G LaMont Jordan/999 RC 2.50 6.00
❑ 143B Dominic Rhodes/999 RC 2.50 6.00
❑ 143G Dominic Rhodes/999 RC 2.50 6.00
❑ 145B A.J. Feeley/999 RC 2.00 5.00
❑ 145G A.J. Feeley/999 RC 2.00 5.00
❑ 146B Correll Buckhalter/999 RC 2.50 6.00
❑ 146G Correll Buckhalter/999 RC 2.50 6.00
❑ 147B Steve Smith/999 RC 6.00 15.00
❑ 147G Steve Smith/999 RC 6.00 15.00
❑ 148B Dave Dickenson/999 RC 2.00 5.00
❑ 148G Dave Dickenson/999 RC 2.00 5.00
❑ 149B Cedrick Wilson/999 RC 2.50 6.00
❑ 149G Cedrick Wilson/999 RC 2.50 6.00
❑ 150B Jamie Winborn/999 RC 2.00 5.00
❑ 150G Jamie Winborn/999 RC 2.00 5.00
❑ 151B Alex Bannister/999 RC 1.50 4.00
❑ 151G Alex Bannister/999 RC 1.50 4.00
❑ 152B Heath Evans/999 RC 2.00 5.00
❑ 152G Heath Evans/999 RC 2.00 5.00
❑ 153B Josh Booty/999 RC 2.00 5.00
❑ 153G Josh Booty/999 RC 2.00 5.00
❑ 154B Adam Archuleta/999 RC 2.00 5.00
❑ 154G Adam Archuleta/999 RC 2.00 5.00
❑ 155B Francis St.Paul/999 RC 1.50 4.00
❑ 155G Francis St.Paul/999 RC 1.50 4.00
❑ 156B Andre Dyson/999 RC 1.50 4.00
❑ 156G Andre Dyson/999 RC 1.50 4.00
❑ RM Randy Moss SAMPLE .75 2.00

2002 SPx

❑ COMP.SET w/o SP's (90) 7.50 20.00
❑ 1 Drew Bledsoe .30 .75
❑ 2 Peerless Price .20 .50
❑ 3 Travis Henry .25 .60
❑ 4 Ricky Williams .30 .75
❑ 5 Jay Fiedler .25 .60
❑ 6 Tom Brady .75 2.00
❑ 7 Troy Brown .25 .60
❑ 8 Antowain Smith .25 .60
❑ 9 Santana Moss .25 .60
❑ 10 Curtis Martin .30 .75
❑ 11 Vinny Testaverde .25 .60
❑ 12 Jamal Lewis .25 .60
❑ 13 Chris Redman .20 .50
❑ 14 Travis Taylor .20 .50
❑ 15 Corey Dillon .25 .60
❑ 16 T.J. Houshmandzadeh .30 .75
❑ 17 Peter Warrick .25 .60
❑ 18 Courtney Brown .20 .50
❑ 19 Kevin Johnson .20 .50
❑ 20 Tim Couch .20 .50
❑ 21 Hines Ward .30 .75
❑ 22 Jerome Bettis .30 .75
❑ 23 Kordell Stewart .25 .60
❑ 24 Corey Bradford .20 .50
❑ 25 Jermaine Lewis .20 .50
❑ 26 Edgerrin James .30 .75
❑ 27 Marvin Harrison .30 .75
❑ 28 Peyton Manning .60 1.50
❑ 29 Jimmy Smith .25 .60
❑ 30 Mark Brunell .25 .60
❑ 31 Fred Taylor .30 .75
❑ 32 Eddie George .25 .60
❑ 33 Steve McNair .30 .75
❑ 34 Brian Griese .25 .60
❑ 35 Shannon Sharpe .30 .75
❑ 36 Rod Smith .25 .60
❑ 37 Trent Green .25 .60
❑ 38 Johnnie Morton .25 .60
❑ 39 Priest Holmes .30 .75
❑ 40 Jerry Rice .60 1.50
❑ 41 Rich Gannon .25 .60
❑ 42 Tim Brown .30 .75
❑ 43 Drew Brees .50 1.25
❑ 44 Junior Seau .30 .75
❑ 45 LaDainian Tomlinson .50 1.25
❑ 46 Emmitt Smith .75 2.00
❑ 47 Quincy Carter .20 .50
❑ 48 Rocket Ismail .25 .60
❑ 49 Amani Toomer .25 .60
❑ 50 Kerry Collins .25 .60
❑ 51 Ron Dayne .25 .60
❑ 52 Donovan McNabb .40 1.00
❑ 53 Duce Staley .25 .60
❑ 54 Antonio Freeman .30 .75
❑ 55 Rod Gardner .20 .50
❑ 56 Stephen Davis .25 .60
❑ 57 Brian Urlacher .40 1.00
❑ 58 Anthony Thomas .25 .60
❑ 59 Jim Miller .25 .60
❑ 60 Marty Booker .25 .60
❑ 61 Az-Zahir Hakim .20 .50
❑ 62 James Stewart .20 .50
❑ 63 Ahman Green .25 .60
❑ 64 Brett Favre .75 2.00
❑ 65 Robert Ferguson .25 .60
❑ 66 Terry Glenn .25 .60
❑ 67 Randy Moss .30 .75
❑ 68 Daunte Culpepper .25 .60
❑ 69 Michael Bennett .25 .60
❑ 70 Michael Vick .30 .75
❑ 71 Warrick Dunn .25 .60
❑ 72 Rodney Peete .25 .60
❑ 73 Muhsin Muhammad .25 .60
❑ 74 Aaron Brooks .25 .60
❑ 75 Deuce McAllister .30 .75
❑ 76 Keyshawn Johnson .25 .60
❑ 77 Michael Pittman .25 .60
❑ 78 Brad Johnson .25 .60
❑ 79 Thomas Jones .25 .60
❑ 80 David Boston .20 .50
❑ 81 Jake Plummer .25 .60
❑ 82 Terrell Owens .30 .75
❑ 83 Garrison Hearst .25 .60
❑ 84 Jeff Garcia .25 .60
❑ 85 Darrell Jackson .25 .60
❑ 86 Shaun Alexander .30 .75
❑ 87 Trent Dilfer .25 .60
❑ 88 Isaac Bruce .30 .75
❑ 89 Kurt Warner .30 .75
❑ 90 Marshall Faulk .30 .75
❑ 91 Saleem Rasheed RC 1.50 4.00
❑ 92 Jason McAddley RC 2.00 5.00
❑ 93 Brandon Doman RC 1.50 4.00

Card	Low	High
❑ 94 Mike Rumph RC	1.50	4.00
❑ 95 Wendell Bryant RC	1.50	4.00
❑ 96 Bryan Thomas RC	1.50	4.00
❑ 97 Anthony Weaver RC	1.50	4.00
❑ 98 Chester Taylor RC	4.00	10.00
❑ 99 Ed Reed RC	8.00	20.00
❑ 100 Lamar Gordon RC	2.50	6.00
❑ 101 Tellis Redmon RC	1.50	4.00
❑ 102 Ben Leber RC	1.50	4.00
❑ 103 Javin Hunter RC	1.50	4.00
❑ 104 Javon Walker RC	2.50	6.00
❑ 105 Shaun Hill RC	3.00	8.00
❑ 106 Raonall Smith RC	1.50	4.00
❑ 107 Darrell Hill RC	1.50	4.00
❑ 108 Kalimba Edwards RC	2.00	5.00
❑ 109 Robert Thomas RC	1.50	4.00
❑ 110 Craig Nall RC	2.00	5.00
❑ 111 Marques Anderson RC	2.00	5.00
❑ 112 Najeh Davenport RC	2.50	6.00
❑ 113 Jonathan Wells RC	2.50	6.00
❑ 114 Dwight Freeney RC	4.00	10.00
❑ 115 Larry Tripplett RC	1.50	4.00
❑ 116 T.J. Duckett RC	2.50	6.00
❑ 117 John Henderson RC	2.50	6.00
❑ 118 Albert Haynesworth RC	2.50	6.00
❑ 119 Tank Williams RC	2.00	5.00
❑ 120 Ryan Sims RC	2.50	6.00
❑ 121 Leonard Henry RC	1.50	4.00
❑ 122 Clinton Portis RC	6.00	15.00
❑ 123 Josh Reed RC	2.00	5.00
❑ 124 Chad Hutchinson RC	1.50	4.00
❑ 125 Deion Branch RC	2.50	6.00
❑ 126 Rocky Calmus RC	2.00	5.00
❑ 127 Donte Stallworth RC	2.50	6.00
❑ 128 Daryl Jones RC	1.50	4.00
❑ 129 Joey Harrington RC	2.50	6.00
❑ 130 Napoleon Harris RC	2.00	5.00
❑ 131 Phillip Buchanon RC	2.50	6.00
❑ 132 Patrick Ramsey RC	2.50	6.00
❑ 133 Brian Westbrook RC	8.00	20.00
❑ 134 Freddie Milons RC	1.50	4.00
❑ 135 Lito Sheppard RC	2.50	6.00
❑ 136 Michael Lewis RC	2.50	6.00
❑ 137 Jamin Elliott RC	1.50	4.00
❑ 138 Lee Mays RC	1.50	4.00
❑ 139 Verron Haynes RC	2.00	5.00
❑ 140 Jesse Chatman RC	1.50	4.00
❑ 141 Quentin Jammer RC	2.50	6.00
❑ 142 Seth Burford RC	1.50	4.00
❑ 143 Julius Peppers RC	4.00	10.00
❑ 144 William Green RC	2.00	5.00
❑ 145 DeShaun Foster RC	2.50	6.00
❑ 146 Daniel Graham RC	2.00	5.00
❑ 147 David Garrard RC	4.00	10.00
❑ 148 Reche Caldwell RC	2.50	6.00
❑ 149 Randy Fasani RC	2.00	5.00
❑ 150 J.T. O'Sullivan RC	2.50	6.00
❑ 151 Josh McCown JSY AU RC	8.00	20.00
❑ 152 Kurt Kittner JSY AU RC	5.00	12.00
❑ 153 Kahlil Hill JSY AU RC	5.00	12.00
❑ 154 Ladell Betts JSY AU RC	8.00	20.00
❑ 155 Ron Johnson JSY AU RC	6.00	15.00
❑ 156 Maurice Morris JSY AU RC	8.00	20.00
❑ 157 Andre Davis JSY AU RC	6.00	15.00
❑ 158 Antonio Bryant JSY AU RC	10.00	25.00
❑ 159 Roy Williams JSY AU RC	10.00	25.00
❑ 160 Lam Thompson JSY AU RC	6.00	15.00
❑ 161 Cliff Russell JSY AU RC	5.00	12.00
❑ 162 Woody Dantzler JSY AU RC	6.00	15.00
❑ 163 Travis Stephens JSY AU RC	5.00	12.00
❑ 164 Tony Fisher JSY AU RC	6.00	15.00
❑ 165 Eric McCoo JSY AU RC	5.00	12.00
❑ 166 Eric Crouch JSY AU RC	8.00	20.00
❑ 167 Rohan Davey JSY AU RC	8.00	20.00
❑ 168 Marquise Walker JSY AU RC	5.00	12.00
❑ 169 Jeremy Shockey JSY RC	8.00	20.00
❑ 170 Tim Carter JSY AU RC	6.00	15.00
❑ 171 Atrews Bell JSY AU RC	5.00	12.00
❑ 172 Ant Randle El JSY AU RC	8.00	20.00
❑ 173 Ricky Williams JSY AU RC	6.00	15.00
❑ 174 Mike Williams JSY AU	5.00	12.00
❑ 175 Adrian Peterson JSY AU RC	8.00	20.00
❑ 176 Jab Gaffney JSY AU/650 RC	8.00	20.00
❑ 177 Ashley Lelie JSY AU/250 RC	12.00	30.00
❑ 178 David Carr JSY AU/250 RC	12.00	30.00

2003 SPx

Card	Low	High
❑ COMP.SET w/o SP's (110)	10.00	25.00
❑ 1 Peyton Manning	.75	2.00
❑ 2 Aaron Brooks	.30	.75
❑ 3 Joey Harrington	.30	.75
❑ 4 Tim Couch	.25	.60
❑ 5 Jeff Garcia	.40	1.00
❑ 6 Jay Fiedler	.30	.75
❑ 7 Chad Hutchinson	.25	.60
❑ 8 Tommy Maddox	.30	.75
❑ 9 Drew Brees		
❑ 10 Trent Green	.30	.75
❑ 11 Patrick Ramsey	.30	.75
❑ 12 Daunte Culpepper	.40	1.00
❑ 13 Kurt Warner	.40	1.00
❑ 14 Brad Johnson	.30	.75
❑ 15 Rich Gannon	.30	.75
❑ 16 Jake Plummer	.30	.75
❑ 17 Steve McNair	.40	1.00
❑ 18 Mark Brunell	.30	.75
❑ 19 Drew Bledsoe	.40	1.00
❑ 20 Kordell Stewart	.30	.75
❑ 21 Kelly Holcomb	.25	.60
❑ 22 Josh McCown	.30	.75
❑ 23 Matt Hasselbeck	.30	.75
❑ 24 Marc Bulger	.40	1.00
❑ 25 Chris Redman	.25	.60
❑ 26 Rodney Peete	.25	.60
❑ 27 Jake Delhomme	.40	1.00
❑ 28 Jon Kitna	.30	.75
❑ 29 Kerry Collins	.30	.75
❑ 30 Quincy Carter	.25	.60
❑ 31 Ricky Williams	.30	.75
❑ 32 Clinton Portis	.50	1.25
❑ 33 Deuce McAllister	.40	1.00
❑ 34 Ahman Green	.40	1.00
❑ 35 Priest Holmes	.40	1.00
❑ 36 Curtis Martin	.40	1.00
❑ 37 Michael Bennett	.30	.75
❑ 38 Eddie George	.30	.75
❑ 39 Marshall Faulk	.40	1.00
❑ 40 Garrison Hearst	.30	.75
❑ 41 Shaun Alexander	.40	1.00
❑ 42 Corey Dillon	.30	.75
❑ 43 Jamal Lewis	.40	1.00
❑ 44 William Green	.25	.60
❑ 45 Travis Henry	.30	.75
❑ 46 Randy Moss	.40	1.00
❑ 47 Terrell Owens	.40	1.00
❑ 48 Peerless Price	.25	.60
❑ 49 David Boston	.25	.60
❑ 50 Eric Moulds	.30	.75
❑ 51 Marvin Harrison	.40	1.00
❑ 52 Laveranues Coles	.30	.75
❑ 53 Santana Moss	.30	.75
❑ 54 Troy Brown	.30	.75
❑ 55 Chris Chambers	.30	.75
❑ 56 Tim Brown	.40	1.00
❑ 57 Rod Smith	.30	.75
❑ 58 Hines Ward	.40	1.00
❑ 59 Keyshawn Johnson	.40	1.00
❑ 60 Isaac Bruce	.40	1.00
❑ 61 Torry Holt	.40	1.00
❑ 62 Koren Robinson	.30	.75
❑ 63 Chad Johnson	.40	1.00
❑ 64 Derrick Mason	.30	.75
❑ 65 Antonio Bryant	.40	1.00
❑ 66 Kevin Johnson	.25	.60
❑ 67 Todd Heap	.30	.75
❑ 68 Tony Gonzalez	.30	.75
❑ 69 Jeremy Shockey	.40	1.00
❑ 70 Brian Urlacher	.60	1.50
❑ 71 Emmitt Smith/500	6.00	15.00
❑ 72 Edgerrin James/500	2.50	6.00
❑ 73 LaDainian Tomlinson/500	3.00	8.00

Card	Low	High
❑ 74 Brett Favre/500	6.00	15.00
❑ 75 Donovan McNabb/500	2.50	6.00
❑ 76 Tom Brady/500	6.00	15.00
❑ 77 Michael Vick/500	2.50	6.00
❑ 78 David Carr/500	2.50	6.00
❑ 79 Jerry Rice/500	5.00	12.00
❑ 80 Chad Pennington/500	2.50	6.00
❑ 81 Joey Harrington XCT	.30	.75
❑ 82 Clinton Portis XCT	.50	1.25
❑ 83 Jeremy Shockey XCT	.40	1.00
❑ 84 David Boston XCT	.25	.60
❑ 85 Marshall Faulk XCT	.40	1.00
❑ 86 Emmitt Smith XCT	1.00	2.50
❑ 87 Terrell Owens XCT	.40	1.00
❑ 88 Randy Moss XCT	.40	1.00
❑ 89 Deuce McAllister XCT	.40	1.00
❑ 90 Ahman Green XCT	.40	1.00
❑ 91 Peerless Price XCT	.25	.60
❑ 92 Plaxico Burress XCT	.40	1.00
❑ 93 Marvin Harrison XCT	.40	1.00
❑ 94 Keyshawn Johnson XCT	.40	1.00
❑ 95 Laveranues Coles XCT	.30	.75
❑ 96 Drew Bledsoe XCT	.40	1.00
❑ 97 Eric Moulds XCT	.30	.75
❑ 98 Chad Pennington XCT	.40	1.00
❑ 99 Jerry Rice XCT	.75	2.00
❑ 100 David Carr XCT	.40	1.00
❑ 101 Michael Vick XCT	.40	1.00
❑ 102 Tom Brady XCT	1.00	2.50
❑ 103 Donovan McNabb XCT	.40	1.00
❑ 104 Brett Favre XCT	1.00	2.50
❑ 105 Kurt Warner XCT	.40	1.00
❑ 106 LaDainian Tomlinson XCT	.50	1.25
❑ 107 Drew Brees XCT	.40	1.00
❑ 108 Edgerrin James XCT	.40	1.00
❑ 109 Peyton Manning XCT	.75	2.00
❑ 110 Ricky Williams XCT	.30	.75
❑ 111 Brooks Bollinger RC	2.50	6.00
❑ 112 Gibran Hamden RC	1.50	4.00
❑ 113 Jason Johnson RC	1.50	4.00
❑ 114 Tony Romo RC	25.00	50.00
❑ 115 Juston Wood RC	1.50	4.00
❑ 116 Kirk Farmer RC	2.00	5.00
❑ 117 Kliff Kingsbury RC	2.00	5.00
❑ 118 Jason Gesser RC	2.00	5.00
❑ 119 Brad Banks RC	2.00	5.00
❑ 120 Rob Adamson RC	1.50	4.00
❑ 121 Ken Dorsey RC	2.00	5.00
❑ 122 Curt Anes RC	1.50	4.00
❑ 123 George Wrighster RC	1.50	4.00
❑ 124 Brett Engemann RC	1.50	4.00
❑ 125 Aaron Walker RC	2.00	5.00
❑ 126 Nate Hybl RC	2.00	5.00
❑ 127 Chris Simms RC	2.50	6.00
❑ 128 Marquel Blackwell RC	1.50	4.00
❑ 129 Domanick Davis RC	2.50	6.00
❑ 130 Quentin Griffin RC	2.00	5.00
❑ 131 B.J. Askew RC	2.00	5.00
❑ 132 Earnest Graham RC	2.50	6.00
❑ 133 Sultan McCullough RC	1.50	4.00
❑ 134 Dahrran Diedrick RC	1.50	4.00
❑ 135 Cecil Sapp RC	1.50	4.00
❑ 136 LaBrandon Toefield RC	2.00	5.00
❑ 137 ReShard Lee RC	2.50	6.00
❑ 138 Dwone Hicks RC	1.50	4.00
❑ 139 Brock Forsey RC	2.00	5.00
❑ 140 Bethel Johnson RC	2.00	5.00
❑ 141 Andrew Pinnock RC	2.00	5.00
❑ 142 Ahmaad Galloway RC	2.00	5.00
❑ 143 J.T. Wall RC	1.50	4.00
❑ 144 Tom Lopienski RC	1.50	4.00
❑ 145 Justin Griffith RC	2.00	5.00
❑ 146 Lee Suggs RC	2.00	5.00
❑ 147 Nick Maddox RC	1.50	4.00
❑ 148 Jeremi Johnson RC	1.50	4.00
❑ 149 Doug Gabriel RC	2.00	5.00
❑ 150 Bobby Wade RC	2.00	5.00
❑ 151 Justin Gage RC	2.50	6.00
❑ 152 Arnaz Battle RC	2.50	6.00
❑ 153 Brandon Lloyd RC	2.50	6.00
❑ 154 Talman Gardner RC	1.50	4.00
❑ 155 Kareem Kelly RC	1.50	4.00
❑ 156 Billy McMullen RC	1.50	4.00
❑ 157 Antwone Savage RC	1.50	4.00
❑ 158 J.R. Tolver RC	2.00	5.00
❑ 159 Kassim Osgood RC	2.50	6.00
❑ 160 Shaun McDonald RC	2.50	6.00
❑ 161 Sam Aiken RC	2.50	6.00
❑ 162 Adrian Madise RC	1.50	4.00

Card	Low	High
163 Charles Rogers RC	2.00	5.00
164 David Kircus RC	2.50	6.00
165 Zuriel Smith RC	1.50	4.00
166 LaTarence Dunbar RC	1.50	4.00
167 Willie Ponder RC	1.50	4.00
168 David Tyree RC	2.50	6.00
169 Kevin Walter RC	2.50	6.00
170 Keenan Howry RC	1.50	4.00
171 Walter Young RC	1.50	4.00
172 DeAndrew Rubin RC	1.50	4.00
173 Carl Ford RC	1.50	4.00
174 Taco Wallace RC	1.50	4.00
175 Travis Anglin RC	1.50	4.00
176 Ryan Hoag RC	1.50	4.00
177 Ronald Bellamy RC	2.00	5.00
178 Terrence Edwards RC	1.50	4.00
179 Jerel Myers RC	1.50	4.00
180 Mike Bush RC	1.50	4.00
181 Dan Curley RC	1.50	4.00
182 Carl Morris RC	1.50	4.00
183 Reggie Newhouse RC	1.50	4.00
184 Troy Polamalu RC	20.00	35.00
185 Cecil Moore RC	1.50	4.00
186 Bennie Joppru RC	1.50	4.00
187 Donald Lee RC	2.00	5.00
188 Jason Witten RC	6.00	15.00
189 Mike Seidman RC	1.50	4.00
190 Vishante Shiancoe RC	2.50	6.00
191 Anquan Boldin JSY AU RC	20.00	50.00
192 Kyle Boller JSY AU/450 RC	15.00	40.00
193 Chris Brown JSY AU RC	12.00	30.00
194 Nate Burleson JSY AU RC	10.00	25.00
195 Tyro Calico JSY AU/450 RC	12.00	30.00
196 Dallas Clark JSY AU RC	25.00	40.00
197 Kevin Curtis JSY AU RC	12.00	30.00
198 Kliff Kingsbury JSY AU RC	10.00	25.00
199 Justin Fargas JSY AU RC	12.00	30.00
200 Grossman JSY AU/450 RC	15.00	40.00
201 Taylor Jacobs JSY AU RC	10.00	25.00
202 An.Johnson JSY AU/250 RC	75.00	150.00
203 Malae MacKenzie JSY AU RC	8.00	20.00
204 Bryant Johnson JSY AU RC	12.00	30.00
205 Larry Johnson JSY AU RC	20.00	50.00
206 T.Johnson JSY AU/450 RC	12.00	30.00
207 Leftwich JSY AU/250 RC	20.00	50.00
208 McGahee JSY AU/450 RC	40.00	80.00
210 C.Palmer JSY AU/250 RC	75.00	150.00
211 Artose Pinner JSY AU RC	8.00	20.00
212 Dave Ragone JSY AU RC	8.00	20.00
213 Terrell Suggs JSY AU RC	15.00	40.00
215 Onterio Smith JSY AU RC	10.00	25.00
216 Musa Smith JSY AU RC	10.00	25.00
217 Brian St.Pierre JSY AU RC	12.00	30.00
218 Marcus Trufant JSY AU RC	12.00	30.00
219 Seneca Wallace JSY AU RC	12.00	30.00
220 Kell Washington JSY AU RC	10.00	25.00

2004 SPx

Card	Low	High
COMP.SET w/o SP's (100)	15.00	30.00
191-221 JSY AU RC #'d TO 1499 UNLESS NOTED		
1 Anquan Boldin	.40	1.00
2 Marcel Shipp	.40	1.00
3 Josh McCown	.30	.75
4 Peerless Price	.30	.75
5 Michael Vick	.40	1.00
6 T.J. Duckett	.30	.75
7 Kyle Boller	.30	.75
8 Todd Heap	.30	.75
9 Jamal Lewis	.30	.75
10 Travis Henry	.30	.75
11 Drew Bledsoe	.40	1.00
12 Eric Moulds	.30	.75
13 Jake Delhomme	.30	.75
14 Steve Smith	.40	1.00
15 Stephen Davis	.30	.75
16 Brian Urlacher	.40	1.00
17 Rex Grossman	.40	1.00
18 Thomas Jones	.30	.75
19 Chad Johnson	.30	.75
20 Carson Palmer	.50	1.25
21 Rudi Johnson	.30	.75
22 William Green	.25	.60
23 Jeff Garcia	.40	1.00
24 Andre Davis	.25	.60
25 Roy Williams S	.30	.75
26 Eddie George	.30	.75
27 Keyshawn Johnson	.30	.75
28 Jake Plummer	.30	.75
29 Ashley Lelie	.30	.75
30 Quentin Griffin	.30	.75
31 Charles Rogers	.30	.75
32 Olandis Gary	.30	.75
33 Joey Harrington	.30	.75
34 Brett Favre	1.00	2.50
35 Javon Walker	.30	.75
36 Ahman Green	.40	1.00
37 Andre Johnson	.40	1.00
38 Domanick Davis	.30	.75
39 David Carr	.30	.75
40 Peyton Manning	.75	2.00
41 Edgerrin James	.40	1.00
42 Marvin Harrison	.40	1.00
43 Byron Leftwich	.40	1.00
44 Jimmy Smith	.30	.75
45 Fred Taylor	.30	.75
46 Trent Green	.30	.75
47 Priest Holmes	.40	1.00
48 Dante Hall	.30	.75
49 Tony Gonzalez	.40	1.00
50 A.J. Feeley	.30	.75
51 Marty Booker	.30	.75
52 Chris Chambers	.30	.75
53 Zach Thomas	.40	1.00
54 Randy Moss	.40	1.00
55 Daunte Culpepper	.40	1.00
56 Onterrio Smith	.25	.60
57 Troy Brown	.30	.75
58 Corey Dillon	.30	.75
59 Tom Brady	1.00	2.50
60 Deuce McAllister	.40	1.00
61 Joe Horn	.30	.75
62 Aaron Brooks	.30	.75
63 Jeremy Shockey	.30	.75
64 Kurt Warner	.40	1.00
65 Tiki Barber	.40	1.00
66 Chad Pennington	.40	1.00
67 Curtis Martin	.40	1.00
68 Santana Moss	.30	.75
69 Rich Gannon	.30	.75
70 Jerry Rice	.75	2.00
71 Warren Sapp	.30	.75
72 Donovan McNabb	.40	1.00
73 Terrell Owens	.40	1.00
74 Jevon Kearse	.30	.75
75 Brian Westbrook	.40	1.00
76 Hines Ward	.40	1.00
77 Duce Staley	.30	.75
78 Tommy Maddox	.30	.75
79 LaDainian Tomlinson	.50	1.25
80 Drew Brees	.40	1.00
81 Tim Rattay	.25	.60
82 Kevan Barlow	.30	.75
83 Brandon Lloyd	.25	.60
84 Shaun Alexander	.40	1.00
85 Matt Hasselbeck	.40	1.00
86 Koren Robinson	.40	1.00
87 Marc Bulger	.30	.75
88 Marshall Faulk	.40	1.00
89 Torry Holt	.40	1.00
90 Isaac Bruce	.30	.75
91 Brad Johnson	.30	.75
92 Keenan McCardell	.25	.60
93 Derrick Brooks	.30	.75
94 Steve McNair	.40	1.00
95 Chris Brown	.30	.75
96 Derrick Mason	.30	.75
97 Clinton Portis	.40	1.00
98 Mark Brunell	.30	.75
99 Laveranues Coles	.30	.75
100 LaVar Arrington	.30	.75
101 B.J. Johnson RC	1.25	3.00
102 Craig Krenzel RC	2.00	5.00
103 Will Smith RC	2.00	5.00
104 Jamaar Taylor RC	1.25	3.00
105 Tommie Harris RC	2.00	5.00
106 Shawn Andrews RC	1.50	4.00
107 Kendrick Starling RC	1.25	3.00
108 Jeris McIntyre RC	1.25	3.00
109 Jason Babin RC	1.50	4.00
110 Marcus Tubbs RC	1.25	3.00
111 Triandos Luke RC	1.25	3.00
112 Karlos Dansby RC	2.00	5.00
113 Vernon Carey RC	1.25	3.00
114 Ryan Krause RC	1.25	3.00
115 Daryl Smith RC	1.50	4.00
116 Ricardo Colclough RC	2.00	5.00
117 Michael Boulware RC	2.00	5.00
118 Chris Cooley RC	2.00	5.00
119 Tank Johnson RC	1.50	4.00
120 Marquise Hill RC	1.25	3.00
121 Teddy Lehman RC	1.50	4.00
122 Antwan Odom RC	2.00	5.00
123 Sean Jones RC	1.50	4.00
124 Junior Siavii RC	1.25	3.00
125 Joey Thomas RC	1.25	3.00
126 Shawntae Spencer RC	1.25	3.00
127 Dontarrious Thomas RC	1.50	4.00
128 Travis LaBoy RC	1.50	4.00
129 Justin Jenkins RC	1.25	3.00
130 Dwan Edwards RC	1.25	3.00
131 Derrick Strait RC	1.50	4.00
132 Matt Ware RC	2.00	5.00
133 Jared Lorenzen RC	1.50	4.00
134 Demorrio Williams RC	2.00	5.00
135 Bob Sanders RC	6.00	15.00
136 Justin Smiley RC	1.50	4.00
137 Casey Bramlet RC	1.25	3.00
138 Jake Grove RC	1.25	3.00
139 Thomas Tapeh RC	1.50	4.00
140 Igor Olshansky RC	2.00	5.00
141 Stuart Schweigert RC	1.50	4.00
142 Cody Pickett RC	1.50	4.00
143 Derrick Ward RC	2.00	5.00
144 Gilbert Gardner RC	1.25	3.00
145 D.J. Hackett RC	2.00	5.00
146 Marquis Cooper RC	2.00	5.00
147 Courtney Watson RC	1.50	4.00
148 Jim Sorgi RC	2.00	5.00
149 Caleb Miller RC	1.25	3.00
150 Casey Clausen RC	1.50	4.00
151 Jammal Lord RC	1.25	3.00
152 Sloan Thomas RC	1.50	4.00
153 Keyaron Fox RC	1.50	4.00
154 Adimchinobe Echemandu RC	1.50	4.00
155 Ryan Dinwiddie RC	1.25	3.00
156 Kris Wilson RC	1.50	4.00
157 D.J. Williams RC	2.00	5.00
158 Tim Euhus RC	1.25	3.00
159 Bradlee Van Pelt RC	1.50	4.00
160 Keiwan Ratliff RC	1.25	3.00
161 Darnell Dockett RC	1.25	3.00
162 Troy Fleming RC	1.25	3.00
163 Tramon Douglas RC	1.25	3.00
164 Jeremy LeSueur RC	1.25	3.00
165 Matt Mauck RC	1.50	4.00
166 Sean Taylor RC	4.00	10.00
167 B.J. Symons RC	2.50	6.00
168 Quincy Wilson RC	3.00	8.00
169 Ernest Wilford RC	3.00	8.00
170 Jerricho Cotchery RC	4.00	10.00
171 Michael Turner RC	10.00	25.00
172 Samie Parker RC	3.00	8.00
173 Andy Hall RC	3.00	8.00
174 Keith Smith RC	2.50	6.00
175 Josh Harris RC	2.50	6.00
176 Maurice Mann RC	2.50	6.00
177 Jonathan Vilma RC	4.00	10.00
178 Jeff Smoker RC	3.00	8.00
179 Ben Hartsock RC	3.00	8.00
180 Chris Gamble RC	3.00	8.00
181 Derrick Hamilton RC	2.50	6.00
182 John Navarre RC	3.00	8.00
183 P.K. Sam RC	2.50	6.00
184 Kenechi Udeze RC	4.00	10.00
185 Mewelde Moore RC	4.00	10.00
186 Carlos Francis RC	2.50	6.00
187 Dunta Robinson RC	3.00	8.00
188 Johnnie Morant RC	3.00	8.00
189 Ahmad Carroll RC	4.00	10.00
190 Vince Wilfork RC	4.00	10.00
191 Tatum Bell JSY AU RC	8.00	20.00
192 Cedric Cobbs JSY AU RC	6.00	15.00
193 Darius Watts JSY AU RC	6.00	15.00
194 Jul.Jones JSY AU/375 RC	15.00	40.00

❑ 195 Robert Gallery JSY AU RC 8.00 20.00
❑ 196 DeAngelo Hall JSY AU RC 8.00 20.00
❑ 197 Ben Watson JSY AU RC 8.00 20.00
❑ 198 Ben Troupe JSY AU RC 6.00 15.00
❑ 199 Matt Schaub JSY AU RC 15.00 40.00
❑ 200 Michael Jenkins JSY AU RC 8.00 20.00
❑ 201 Luke McCown JSY AU RC 8.00 20.00
❑ 202 Devery Henderson JSY AU RC 8.00 20.00
❑ 203 Bernard Berrian JSY AU RC 8.00 20.00
❑ 204 Keary Colbert JSY AU RC 6.00 15.00
❑ 205 Devard Darling JSY AU RC 6.00 15.00
❑ 206 Lee Evans JSY AU RC 10.00 25.00
❑ 207 Greg Jones JSY AU RC 8.00 20.00
❑ 208 Mich.Clayton JSY AU RC 8.00 20.00
❑ 209 Re.Williams JSY AU RC 8.00 20.00
❑ 210 C.Perry JSY AU/799 RC 8.00 20.00
❑ 211 Rash.Woods JSY AU RC 5.00 12.00
❑ 212 J.P. Losman JSY AU RC 8.00 20.00
❑ 213 Kevin Jones JSY AU RC 8.00 20.00
❑ 214 K.Winslow JSY AU/375 RC 15.00 40.00
❑ 215 S.Jackson JSY AU/375 RC 30.00 80.00
❑ 216 Hamilton JSY AU RC 5.00 12.00
❑ 217 Ro.Will.JSY AU/375 RC 15.00 40.00
❑ 218 P.Rivers JSY AU/375 RC 60.00 120.00
❑ 219 Fitzgerald JSY AU/100 RC 150.00 250.00
❑ 220 Roethlis.JSY AU/375 RC 125.00 250.00
❑ 221 Manning JSY AU/375 RC 75.00 150.00

2005 SPx

❑ COMP.SET w/o SP's (100) 15.00 30.00
❑ 101-170 RC PRINT RUN 1199 SER.#'d SETS
❑ 171-200 RC PRINT RUN 499 SER.#'d SETS
❑ JSY AU RC PRINT RUN 150-1275
❑ UNPRICED NFL LOGO AUTOS #'d OF 1
❑ 1 Larry Fitzgerald .40 1.00
❑ 2 Anquan Boldin .30 .75
❑ 3 Josh McCown .30 .75
❑ 4 Michael Vick .40 1.00
❑ 5 Alge Crumpler .30 .75
❑ 6 Peerless Price .25 .60
❑ 7 Ray Lewis .40 1.00
❑ 8 Jamal Lewis .30 .75
❑ 9 Kyle Boller .30 .75
❑ 10 J.P. Losman .30 .75
❑ 11 Willis McGahee .40 1.00
❑ 12 Eric Moulds .30 .75
❑ 13 Jake Delhomme .40 1.00
❑ 14 DeShaun Foster .30 .75
❑ 15 Steve Smith .40 1.00
❑ 16 Brian Urlacher .40 1.00
❑ 17 Rex Grossman .40 1.00
❑ 18 Muhsin Muhammad .30 .75
❑ 19 Carson Palmer .40 1.00
❑ 20 Rudi Johnson .30 .75
❑ 21 Chad Johnson .30 .75
❑ 22 Julius Jones .40 1.00
❑ 23 Keyshawn Johnson .30 .75
❑ 24 Roy Williams S .30 .75
❑ 25 Tatum Bell .30 .75
❑ 26 Jake Plummer .30 .75
❑ 27 Ashley Lelie .25 .60
❑ 28 Roy Williams WR .40 1.00
❑ 29 Kevin Jones .30 .75
❑ 30 Joey Harrington .40 1.00
❑ 31 Brett Favre 1.00 2.50
❑ 32 Ahman Green .40 1.00
❑ 33 Javon Walker .30 .75
❑ 34 David Carr .30 .75
❑ 35 Andre Johnson .30 .75
❑ 36 Domanick Davis .25 .60
❑ 37 Peyton Manning .60 1.50
❑ 38 Reggie Wayne .30 .75
❑ 39 Edgerrin James .30 .75
❑ 40 Marvin Harrison .40 1.00
❑ 41 Byron Leftwich .30 .75
❑ 42 Fred Taylor .40 1.00
❑ 43 Jimmy Smith .30 .75
❑ 44 Priest Holmes .40 1.00
❑ 45 Larry Johnson .40 1.00
❑ 46 Trent Green .30 .75
❑ 47 A.J. Feeley .25 .60
❑ 48 Chris Chambers .30 .75
❑ 49 Randy McMichael .25 .60
❑ 50 Daunte Culpepper .40 1.00
❑ 51 Nate Burleson .30 .75
❑ 52 Michael Bennett .30 .75
❑ 53 Tom Brady .75 2.00
❑ 54 Corey Dillon .30 .75
❑ 55 Deion Branch .30 .75
❑ 56 David Givens .30 .75
❑ 57 Aaron Brooks .25 .60
❑ 58 Deuce McAllister .40 1.00
❑ 59 Joe Horn .30 .75
❑ 60 Eli Manning .75 2.00
❑ 61 Jeremy Shockey .40 1.00
❑ 62 Tiki Barber .40 1.00
❑ 63 Chad Pennington .40 1.00
❑ 64 Curtis Martin .40 1.00
❑ 65 Laveranues Coles .30 .75
❑ 66 Kerry Collins .30 .75
❑ 67 Jerry Porter .30 .75
❑ 68 Randy Moss .40 1.00
❑ 69 Donovan McNabb .40 1.00
❑ 70 Terrell Owens .40 1.00
❑ 71 Brian Dawkins .30 .75
❑ 72 Brian Westbrook .40 1.00
❑ 73 Ben Roethlisberger 1.00 2.50
❑ 74 Jerome Bettis .40 1.00
❑ 75 Hines Ward .40 1.00
❑ 76 Duce Staley .30 .75
❑ 77 Drew Brees .40 1.00
❑ 78 LaDainian Tomlinson .50 1.25
❑ 79 Antonio Gates .40 1.00
❑ 80 Eric Parker .25 .60
❑ 81 Tim Rattay .25 .60
❑ 82 Kevan Barlow .25 .60
❑ 83 Eric Johnson .25 .60
❑ 84 Shaun Alexander .40 1.00
❑ 85 Darrell Jackson .30 .75
❑ 86 Matt Hasselbeck .30 .75
❑ 87 Marc Bulger .30 .75
❑ 88 Steven Jackson .50 1.25
❑ 89 Marshall Faulk .40 1.00
❑ 90 Torry Holt .30 .75
❑ 91 Michael Pittman .25 .60
❑ 92 Brian Griese .30 .75
❑ 93 Michael Clayton .30 .75
❑ 94 Steve McNair .40 1.00
❑ 95 Drew Bennett .30 .75
❑ 96 Billy Volek .30 .75
❑ 97 Chris Brown .30 .75
❑ 98 Clinton Portis .40 1.00
❑ 99 Patrick Ramsey .30 .75
❑ 100 Santana Moss .30 .75
❑ 101 Matt Jones RC 2.00 5.00
❑ 102 Jonathan Babineaux RC 1.50 4.00
❑ 103 Darrent Williams RC 2.00 5.00
❑ 104 Timmy Chang RC 1.50 4.00
❑ 105 Kelvin Hayden RC 1.50 4.00
❑ 106 Paris Warren RC 1.50 4.00
❑ 107 Stanley Wilson RC 1.50 4.00
❑ 108 Walter Reyes RC 1.25 3.00
❑ 109 Roydell Williams RC 1.50 4.00
❑ 110 Chase Lyman RC 1.25 3.00
❑ 111 Anthony Davis RC 1.50 4.00
❑ 112 Rasheed Marshall RC 1.50 4.00
❑ 113 Jerome Carter RC 1.25 3.00
❑ 114 Mike Nugent RC 1.50 4.00
❑ 115 Brodney Pool RC 1.50 4.00
❑ 116 Sean Considine RC 1.25 3.00
❑ 117 Chris Rix RC 1.50 4.00
❑ 118 Donte Nicholson RC 1.50 4.00
❑ 119 Dustin Fox RC 2.00 5.00
❑ 120 Oshiomogho Atogwe RC 1.25 3.00
❑ 121 Vincent Fuller RC 1.50 4.00
❑ 122 Josh Bullocks RC 2.00 5.00
❑ 123 Ronald Bartell RC 1.50 4.00
❑ 124 Brock Berlin RC 1.50 4.00
❑ 125 Fabian Washington RC 2.00 5.00
❑ 126 Domonique Foxworth RC 1.50 4.00
❑ 127 Bryant McFadden RC 1.50 4.00
❑ 128 Marlin Jackson RC 1.50 4.00
❑ 129 Eric Green RC 1.25 3.00
❑ 130 Justin Miller RC 1.50 4.00
❑ 131 Lofa Tatupu RC 2.00 5.00
❑ 132 Justin Tuck RC 2.50 6.00
❑ 133 Kurt Campbell RC 1.25 3.00
❑ 134 Darryl Blackstock RC 1.25 3.00
❑ 135 Kevin Burnett RC 1.50 4.00
❑ 136 Marviel Underwood RC 1.50 4.00
❑ 137 Kirk Morrison RC 2.00 5.00
❑ 138 Alfred Fincher RC 1.50 4.00
❑ 139 Lance Mitchell RC 1.50 4.00
❑ 140 Barrett Ruud RC 2.00 5.00
❑ 141 David Pollack RC 1.50 4.00
❑ 142 Bill Swancutt RC 1.25 3.00
❑ 143 DeMarcus Ware RC 3.00 8.00
❑ 144 Steve Savoy RC 1.25 3.00
❑ 145 Matt Roth RC 2.00 5.00
❑ 146 Shaun Cody RC 1.50 4.00
❑ 147 Dan Cody RC 2.00 5.00
❑ 148 Jordan Beck RC 1.50 4.00
❑ 149 Kevin Everett RC 2.00 5.00
❑ 150 Anttaj Hawthorne RC 1.50 4.00
❑ 151 Mike Patterson RC 1.50 4.00
❑ 152 Jerome Collins RC 1.50 4.00
❑ 153 Dante Ridgeway RC 1.25 3.00
❑ 154 Bryan Randall RC 1.50 4.00
❑ 155 Marcus Maxwell RC 1.25 3.00
❑ 156 Airese Currie RC 1.50 4.00
❑ 157 Chad Owens RC 2.00 5.00
❑ 158 Brandon Jacobs RC 2.50 6.00
❑ 159 Manuel White RC 1.50 4.00
❑ 160 Ellis Hobbs RC 2.00 5.00
❑ 161 Lionel Gates RC 1.25 3.00
❑ 162 Ryan Fitzpatrick RC 2.00 5.00
❑ 163 Noah Herron RC 2.00 5.00
❑ 164 Kay-Jay Harris RC 1.50 4.00
❑ 165 T.A. McLendon RC 1.25 3.00
❑ 166 Kerry Rhodes RC 2.00 5.00
❑ 167 Nick Collins RC 2.00 5.00
❑ 168 Eric Moore RC 1.25 3.00
❑ 169 Harry Williams RC 1.50 4.00
❑ 170 Luis Castillo RC 2.00 5.00
❑ 171 James Kilian RC 2.00 5.00
❑ 172 Matt Cassel RC 6.00 15.00
❑ 173 Alvin Pearman RC 2.00 5.00
❑ 174 Dan Orlovsky RC 3.00 8.00
❑ 175 Damien Nash RC 2.50 6.00
❑ 176 Jason White RC 3.00 8.00
❑ 177 Craig Bragg RC 2.00 5.00
❑ 178 Craphonso Thorpe RC 2.50 6.00
❑ 179 Derrick Johnson RC 3.00 8.00
❑ 180 Derek Anderson RC 3.00 8.00
❑ 181 Darren Sproles RC 4.00 10.00
❑ 182 Cedric Houston RC 3.00 8.00
❑ 183 Jerome Mathis RC 3.00 8.00
❑ 184 Larry Brackins RC 2.00 5.00
❑ 185 Fred Gibson RC 2.50 6.00
❑ 186 J.R. Russell RC 2.00 5.00
❑ 187 Alex Smith TE RC 3.00 8.00
❑ 188 Deandra Cobb RC 2.50 6.00
❑ 189 Tab Perry RC 3.00 8.00
❑ 190 Travis Johnson RC 2.00 5.00
❑ 191A Marion Barber RC 10.00 25.00
❑ 191B Andrew Walter JSY AU RC 10.00 25.00
❑ 192A Erasmus James RC 2.50 6.00
❑ 192B V.Morency JSY AU RC 10.00 25.00
❑ 193A Marcus Spears RC 3.00 8.00
❑ 193B Antrel Rolle JSY AU RC 12.00 30.00
❑ 194A Channing Crowder RC 2.50 6.00
❑ 194B Adam Jones JSY AU RC 10.00 25.00
❑ 195A Odell Thurman RC 3.00 8.00
❑ 195B M.Clarett JSY AU/250 12.00 30.00
❑ 196A Shawne Merriman RC 3.00 8.00
❑ 196B Mark Bradley JSY AU RC 10.00 25.00
❑ 197A Adrian McPherson RC 2.50 6.00
❑ 197B Eric Shelton JSY AU RC 10.00 25.00
❑ 198A Chris Henry RC 3.00 8.00
❑ 198B Kyle Orton JSY AU RC 15.00 40.00
❑ 199A Thomas Davis RC 2.50 6.00
❑ 199B Ryan Moats JSY AU RC 10.00 25.00
❑ 200A Corey Webster RC 3.00 8.00
❑ 200B Frank Gore JSY AU RC 20.00 50.00
❑ 201 J.J. Arrington JSY AU RC 10.00 25.00
❑ 202 M.Williams JSY AU/250 12.00 30.00
❑ 203 V.Jackson JSY AU RC 15.00 30.00
❑ 204 Stefan LeFors JSY AU RC 8.00 20.00
❑ 206 T.Murphy JSY AU RC 6.00 15.00
❑ 207 Courtney Roby JSY AU RC 8.00 20.00
❑ 208 Carlos Rogers JSY AU RC 10.00 25.00
❑ 209 Charlie Frye JSY AU RC 10.00 25.00
❑ 210 Mark Clayton JSY AU RC 10.00 25.00
❑ 211 Roddy White JSY AU RC 15.00 30.00

Card	Low	High
❑ 212 Jason Campbell JSY AU RC	15.00	40.00
❑ 213 Roscoe Parrish JSY AU RC	8.00	20.00
❑ 214 Reggie Brown JSY AU RC	8.00	20.00
❑ 215 Heath Miller JSY AU RC	20.00	50.00
❑ 216 Williamson JSY AU/250 RC	15.00	40.00
❑ 217 Ciatrick Fason JSY AU RC	8.00	20.00
❑ 218 C.Benson JSY AU/150 RC	30.00	60.00
❑ 219 B.Edwards JSY AU/250 RC	40.00	100.00
❑ 220 Ro.Brown JSY AU/250 RC	50.00	120.00
❑ 221 C.Williams JSY AU/250 RC	40.00	100.00
❑ 222 A.Smith QB JSY AU/250 RC	30.00	60.00
❑ 223 A.Rodgers JSY AU/250 RC	90.00	150.00

2006 SPx

Card	Low	High
❑ COMP.SET w/o RC's (90)	12.50	30.00
❑ 1 Edgerrin James	.30	.75
❑ 2 Kurt Warner	.40	1.00
❑ 3 Larry Fitzgerald	.40	1.00
❑ 4 Michael Vick	.40	1.00
❑ 5 Warrick Dunn	.30	.75
❑ 6 Michael Jenkins	.30	.75
❑ 7 Jamal Lewis	.30	.75
❑ 8 Kyle Boller	.30	.75
❑ 9 Derrick Mason	.30	.75
❑ 10 Willis McGahee	.40	1.00
❑ 11 Lee Evans	.30	.75
❑ 12 Jake Delhomme	.30	.75
❑ 13 Steve Smith	.40	1.00
❑ 14 DeShaun Foster	.30	.75
❑ 15 Rex Grossman	.40	1.00
❑ 16 Muhsin Muhammad	.30	.75
❑ 17 Thomas Jones	.30	.75
❑ 18 Carson Palmer	.40	1.00
❑ 19 Chad Johnson	.30	.75
❑ 20 Rudi Johnson	.30	.75
❑ 21 Charlie Frye	.30	.75
❑ 22 Reuben Droughns	.30	.75
❑ 23 Braylon Edwards	.40	1.00
❑ 24 Drew Bledsoe	.40	1.00
❑ 25 Terrell Owens	.40	1.00
❑ 26 Julius Jones	.30	.75
❑ 27 Jake Plummer	.30	.75
❑ 28 Tatum Bell	.25	.60
❑ 29 Rod Smith	.30	.75
❑ 30 Kevin Jones	.30	.75
❑ 31 Roy Williams WR	.40	1.00
❑ 32 Brett Favre	.75	2.00
❑ 33 Ahman Green	.00	.75
❑ 34 Donald Driver	.40	1.00
❑ 35 David Carr	.25	.60
❑ 36 Andre Johnson	.30	.75
❑ 37 Peyton Manning	.60	1.50
❑ 38 Marvin Harrison	.40	1.00
❑ 39 Reggie Wayne	.30	.75
❑ 40 Byron Leftwich	.30	.75
❑ 41 Fred Taylor	.30	.75
❑ 42 Ernest Wilford	.25	.60
❑ 43 Larry Johnson	.30	.75
❑ 44 Trent Green	.30	.75
❑ 45 Tony Gonzalez	.30	.75
❑ 46 Daunte Culpepper	.40	1.00
❑ 47 Ronnie Brown	.40	1.00
❑ 48 Chris Chambers	.30	.75
❑ 49 Troy Williamson	.30	.75
❑ 50 Chester Taylor	.30	.75
❑ 51 Brad Johnson	.30	.75
❑ 52 Tom Brady	.60	1.50
❑ 53 Deion Branch	.30	.75
❑ 54 Corey Dillon	.30	.75
❑ 55 Drew Brees	.40	1.00
❑ 56 Deuce McAllister	.30	.75
❑ 57 Donte Stallworth	.30	.75
❑ 58 Eli Manning	.50	1.25
❑ 59 Tiki Barber	.40	1.00
❑ 60 Plaxico Burress	.30	.75
❑ 61 Chad Pennington	.30	.75
❑ 62 Curtis Martin	.40	1.00
❑ 63 Randy Moss	.40	1.00
❑ 64 LaMont Jordan	.30	.75
❑ 65 Aaron Brooks	.30	.75
❑ 66 Donovan McNabb	.40	1.00
❑ 67 Brian Westbrook	.30	.75
❑ 68 Ben Roethlisberger	.60	1.50
❑ 69 Hines Ward	.40	1.00
❑ 70 Willie Parker	.50	1.25
❑ 71 LaDainian Tomlinson	.50	1.25
❑ 72 Philip Rivers	.40	1.00
❑ 73 Antonio Gates	.40	1.00
❑ 74 Alex Smith QB	.30	.75
❑ 75 Antonio Bryant	.30	.75
❑ 76 Frank Gore	.40	1.00
❑ 77 Shaun Alexander	.30	.75
❑ 78 Matt Hasselbeck	.30	.75
❑ 79 Nate Burleson	.30	.75
❑ 80 Marc Bulger	.30	.75
❑ 81 Steven Jackson	.40	1.00
❑ 82 Torry Holt	.30	.75
❑ 83 Cadillac Williams	.40	1.00
❑ 84 Joey Galloway	.30	.75
❑ 85 Chris Simms	.30	.75
❑ 86 Billy Volek	.25	.60
❑ 87 Drew Bennett	.30	.75
❑ 88 Clinton Portis	.40	1.00
❑ 89 Santana Moss	.30	.75
❑ 90 Mark Brunell	.30	.75
❑ 91 Haloti Ngata RC	4.00	10.00
❑ 92 Willie Reid RC	3.00	8.00
❑ 93 Kamerion Wimbley RC	4.00	10.00
❑ 94 Donte Whitner RC	4.00	10.00
❑ 95 Ethan Kilmer RC	4.00	10.00
❑ 96 Johnathan Joseph RC	3.00	8.00
❑ 97 Brodie Croyle RC	4.00	10.00
❑ 98 Bobby Carpenter RC	3.00	8.00
❑ 99 Antonio Cromartie RC	4.00	10.00
❑ 100 Eric Winston RC	2.50	6.00
❑ 101 Nick Mangold RC	3.00	8.00
❑ 102 Manny Lawson RC	4.00	10.00
❑ 103 Claude Wroten RC	2.50	6.00
❑ 104 D'Qwell Jackson RC	3.00	8.00
❑ 105 Richard Marshall RC	3.00	8.00
❑ 106 Tamba Hali RC	4.00	10.00
❑ 107 Ko Simpson RC	3.00	8.00
❑ 108 Danieal Manning RC	4.00	10.00
❑ 109 Gabe Watson RC	2.50	6.00
❑ 110 Kevin McMahan RC	3.00	8.00
❑ 111 Jai Lewis RC	3.00	8.00
❑ 112 Darryl Tapp RC	3.00	8.00
❑ 113 John McCargo RC	3.00	8.00
❑ 114 Jeff King RC	3.00	8.00
❑ 115 Charles Davis RC	3.00	8.00
❑ 116 Calvin Lowry RC	4.00	10.00
❑ 117 Delanie Walker RC	3.00	8.00
❑ 118 Roman Harper RC	3.00	8.00
❑ 119 Nate Salley RC	3.00	8.00
❑ 120 Cooper Wallace RC	3.00	8.00
❑ 121 Bernard Pollard RC	3.00	8.00
❑ 122 Derrick Ross RC	3.00	8.00
❑ 123 Ingle Martin RC	3.00	8.00
❑ 124 Wali Lundy RC	4.00	10.00
❑ 125 Marcus Vick RC	2.50	6.00
❑ 126 Cedric Humes RC	3.00	8.00
❑ 127 Marques Hagans RC	3.00	8.00
❑ 128 Taurean Henderson RC	4.00	10.00
❑ 129 Marques Colston RC	10.00	25.00
❑ 130 Devin Aromashodu RC	4.00	10.00
❑ 131 Jonathan Orr RC	3.00	8.00
❑ 132 Skyler Green RC	2.50	6.00
❑ 133 Jeff Webb RC	3.00	8.00
❑ 134 Jon Alston RC	2.50	6.00
❑ 135 Daniel Bullocks RC	4.00	10.00
❑ 136 Anthony Schlegel RC	3.00	8.00
❑ 137 Adam Jennings RC	3.00	8.00
❑ 138 Gerris Wilkinson RC	2.50	6.00
❑ 139 James Anderson RC	2.50	6.00
❑ 140 Owen Daniels RC	4.00	10.00
❑ 141 Ray Edwards RC	4.00	10.00
❑ 142 Chris Gocong RC	3.00	8.00
❑ 143 Babatunde Oshinowo RC	3.00	8.00
❑ 144 Marvin Philip RC	4.00	10.00
❑ 145 Stanley McClover RC	3.00	8.00
❑ 146 DeMeco Ryans RC	5.00	12.00
❑ 147 Tony Scheffler RC	4.00	10.00
❑ 148 T.J. Williams RC	4.00	10.00
❑ 149 P.J. Daniels RC	2.50	6.00
❑ 150 Bennie Brazell RC	3.00	8.00
❑ 151 Will Blackmon RC	4.00	10.00
❑ 152 Bruce Gradkowski RC	4.00	10.00
❑ 153 Drew Olson RC	2.50	6.00
❑ 154 Darnell Bing RC	3.00	8.00
❑ 155 Darrell Hackney RC	3.00	8.00
❑ 156 Cory Rodgers RC	4.00	10.00
❑ 157 DonTrell Moore RC	3.00	8.00
❑ 158 Ernie Sims RC	3.00	8.00
❑ 159 Jay Cutler RC	10.00	25.00
❑ 160 D.J. Shockley RC	3.00	8.00
❑ 161 Martin Nance RC	3.00	8.00
❑ 162 Joseph Addai RC	5.00	12.00
❑ 163 Leonard Pope RC	4.00	10.00
❑ 164 Anthony Fasano RC	4.00	10.00
❑ 165 Mathias Kiwanuka RC	5.00	12.00
❑ 166 Greg Jennings RC	6.00	15.00
❑ 167 Greg Lee RC	2.50	6.00
❑ 168 Jerome Harrison RC	4.00	10.00
❑ 169 Jimmy Williams RC	4.00	10.00
❑ 170 Josh Betts RC	3.00	8.00
❑ 171 Ashton Youboty RC	3.00	8.00
❑ 172 Terrence Whitehead RC	3.00	8.00
❑ 173 Brad Smith RC	4.00	10.00
❑ 174 D'Brickashaw Ferguson RC	4.00	10.00
❑ 175 Mike Hass RC	4.00	10.00
❑ 176 Reggie McNeal RC	3.00	8.00
❑ 177 Dominique Byrd RC	3.00	8.00
❑ 178 Winston Justice RC	4.00	10.00
❑ 179 Chad Greenway RC	4.00	10.00
❑ 180 Tye Hill RC	3.00	8.00
❑ 181 Chad Jackson JSY AU RC	10.00	25.00
❑ 182 DeA.Williams JSY AU RC	30.00	60.00
❑ 183 Vince Young JSY AU RC	40.00	80.00
❑ 184 S.Holmes JSY AU RC	30.00	60.00
❑ 185 Sinorice Moss JSY AU RC	10.00	25.00
❑ 186 Matt Leinart JSY AU RC	40.00	80.00
❑ 187 Reggie Bush JSY AU RC	60.00	100.00
❑ 188 LenDale White JSY AU RC	15.00	40.00
❑ 189 Vernon Davis JSY AU RC	8.00	20.00
❑ 190 L.Maroney JSY AU RC	20.00	50.00
❑ 191 A.J. Hawk JSY AU RC	20.00	50.00
❑ 192 Marcus McNeill JSY AU RC	6.00	15.00
❑ 193 Kelly Jennings JSY AU RC	8.00	20.00
❑ 194 B.Williams JSY AU RC	6.00	15.00
❑ 195 Brian Calhoun JSY AU RC	6.00	15.00
❑ 196 Travis Wilson JSY AU RC	5.00	12.00
❑ 197 C.Whitehurst JSY AU RC	8.00	20.00
❑ 198 Omar Jacobs JSY AU RC	5.00	12.00
❑ 199 J.Klopfenstein JSY AU RC	6.00	15.00
❑ 200 Derek Hagan JSY AU RC	6.00	15.00
❑ 201 Michael Huff JSY AU RC	8.00	20.00
❑ 202 Maurice Stovall JSY AU RC	6.00	15.00
❑ 203 Maurice Drew JSY AU RC	25.00	50.00
❑ 204 Jason Avant JSY AU RC	8.00	20.00
❑ 205 K.Clemens JSY AU RC	10.00	25.00
❑ 206 J.Norwood JSY AU RC	10.00	25.00
❑ 207 T.Jackson JSY AU RC	10.00	25.00
❑ 208 B.Marshall JSY AU RC	12.50	25.00
❑ 209 Dem.Williams JSY AU RC	6.00	15.00
❑ 210 L.Washington JSY AU RC	15.00	30.00
❑ 211 M.Robinson JSY AU RC	6.00	15.00
❑ 212 Marcedes Lewis JSY AU RC	8.00	20.00
❑ 213 Mario Williams JSY AU RC	10.00	25.00

2007 SPx

Card	Low	High
❑ COMP.SET w/o RC's (100)	20.00	40.00
❑ 1 Matt Leinart	.50	1.25
❑ 2 Anquan Boldin	.40	1.00
❑ 3 Larry Fitzgerald	.50	1.25
❑ 4 Edgerrin James	.40	1.00
❑ 5 Michael Vick	.50	1.25
❑ 6 Warrick Dunn	.40	1.00
❑ 7 DeAngelo Hall	.40	1.00
❑ 8 Steve McNair	.40	1.00
❑ 9 Willis McGahee	.40	1.00
❑ 10 Ray Lewis	.50	1.25

Card		
❑ 11 J.P. Losman	.30	.75
❑ 12 Lee Evans	.40	1.00
❑ 13 Anthony Thomas	.30	.75
❑ 14 Jake Delhomme	.40	1.00
❑ 15 Steve Smith	.40	1.00
❑ 16 DeAngelo Williams	.50	1.25
❑ 17 Brian Urlacher	.50	1.25
❑ 18 Cedric Benson	.40	1.00
❑ 19 Rex Grossman	.40	1.00
❑ 20 Carson Palmer	.50	1.25
❑ 21 Chad Johnson	.40	1.00
❑ 22 Rudi Johnson	.40	1.00
❑ 23 Charlie Frye	.40	1.00
❑ 24 Braylon Edwards	.40	1.00
❑ 25 Jamal Lewis	.40	1.00
❑ 26 Tony Romo	.75	2.00
❑ 27 Terrell Owens	.50	1.25
❑ 28 Julius Jones	.40	1.00
❑ 29 Marion Barber	.50	1.25
❑ 30 Jay Cutler	.50	1.25
❑ 31 Javon Walker	.40	1.00
❑ 32 Travis Henry	.40	1.00
❑ 33 Roy Williams WR	.40	1.00
❑ 34 Mike Furrey	.40	1.00
❑ 35 Tatum Bell	.30	.75
❑ 36 Greg Jennings	.40	1.00
❑ 37 Brett Favre	1.00	2.50
❑ 38 A.J. Hawk	.50	1.25
❑ 39 Matt Schaub	.40	1.00
❑ 40 Andre Johnson	.40	1.00
❑ 41 Ahman Green	.40	1.00
❑ 42 Peyton Manning	.75	2.00
❑ 43 Marvin Harrison	.50	1.25
❑ 44 Reggie Wayne	.40	1.00
❑ 45 Joseph Addai	.50	1.25
❑ 46 Fred Taylor	.40	1.00
❑ 47 Maurice Jones-Drew	.50	1.25
❑ 48 Byron Leftwich	.40	1.00
❑ 49 Damon Huard	.40	1.00
❑ 50 Larry Johnson	.40	1.00
❑ 51 Tony Gonzalez	.40	1.00
❑ 52 Zach Thomas	.40	1.00
❑ 53 Ronnie Brown	.40	1.00
❑ 54 Chris Chambers	.40	1.00
❑ 55 Tarvaris Jackson	.40	1.00
❑ 56 Chester Taylor	.30	.75
❑ 57 Troy Williamson	.30	.75
❑ 58 Tom Brady	1.00	2.50
❑ 59 Donte Stallworth	.40	1.00
❑ 60 Laurence Maroney	.50	1.25
❑ 61 Reggie Bush	.60	1.50
❑ 62 Deuce McAllister	.40	1.00
❑ 63 Drew Brees	.50	1.25
❑ 64 Marques Colston	.50	1.25
❑ 65 Eli Manning	.50	1.25
❑ 66 Plaxico Burress	.40	1.00
❑ 67 Brandon Jacobs	.40	1.00
❑ 68 Chad Pennington	.40	1.00
❑ 69 Thomas Jones	.40	1.00
❑ 70 Laveranues Coles	.40	1.00
❑ 71 LaMont Jordan	.40	1.00
❑ 72 Randy Moss	.50	1.25
❑ 73 Nnamdi Asomugha	.30	.75
❑ 74 Donovan McNabb	.50	1.25
❑ 75 Brian Westbrook	.40	1.00
❑ 76 Reggie Brown	.30	.75
❑ 77 Ben Roethlisberger	.75	2.00
❑ 78 Hines Ward	.50	1.25
❑ 79 Willie Parker	.40	1.00
❑ 80 LaDainian Tomlinson	.60	1.50
❑ 81 Philip Rivers	.50	1.25
❑ 82 Antonio Gates	.40	1.00
❑ 83 Frank Gore	.50	1.25
❑ 84 Alex Smith QB	.50	1.25
❑ 85 Ashley Lelie	.40	1.00
❑ 86 Matt Hasselbeck	.40	1.00
❑ 87 Shaun Alexander	.40	1.00
❑ 88 Deion Branch	.40	1.00
❑ 89 Marc Bulger	.40	1.00
❑ 90 Torry Holt	.40	1.00
❑ 91 Steven Jackson	.50	1.25
❑ 92 Cadillac Williams	.40	1.00
❑ 93 Chris Simms	.30	.75
❑ 94 Joey Galloway	.40	1.00
❑ 95 Vince Young	.50	1.25
❑ 96 David Givens	.30	.75
❑ 97 LenDale White	.40	1.00
❑ 98 Jason Campbell	.40	1.00
❑ 99 Santana Moss	.40	1.00
❑ 100 Clinton Portis	.40	1.00
❑ 101 Levi Brown RC	4.00	10.00
❑ 102 Adam Carriker RC	3.00	8.00
❑ 103 Jarvis Moss RC	4.00	10.00
❑ 104 Aaron Ross RC	4.00	10.00
❑ 105 Chris Houston RC	3.00	8.00
❑ 106 Michael Griffin RC	4.00	10.00
❑ 107 Justin Harrell RC	4.00	10.00
❑ 108 Joe Staley RC	3.00	8.00
❑ 109 Jon Beason RC	4.00	10.00
❑ 110 Anthony Spencer RC	4.00	10.00
❑ 111 Ben Grubbs RC	3.00	8.00
❑ 112 Charles Johnson RC	2.50	6.00
❑ 113 Marcus McCauley RC	3.00	8.00
❑ 114 Justin Blalock RC	2.50	6.00
❑ 115 Tim Crowder RC	4.00	10.00
❑ 116 Brandon Meriweather RC	4.00	10.00
❑ 117 Arron Sears RC	3.00	8.00
❑ 118 Zach Miller RC	4.00	10.00
❑ 119 Turk McBride RC	3.00	8.00
❑ 120 Ryan Kalil RC	3.00	8.00
❑ 121 Tony Ugoh RC	3.00	8.00
❑ 122 David Harris RC	3.00	8.00
❑ 123 Jonathan Wade RC	3.00	8.00
❑ 124 Josh Wilson RC	3.00	8.00
❑ 125 Demarcus Tank Tyler RC	3.00	8.00
❑ 126 Tanard Jackson RC	2.50	6.00
❑ 127 Jordan Kent RC	3.00	8.00
❑ 128 Ray McDonald RC	3.00	8.00
❑ 129 Quentin Moses RC	3.00	8.00
❑ 130 Eric Weddle RC	3.00	8.00
❑ 131 Victor Abiamiri RC	4.00	10.00
❑ 132 Josh Beekman RC	2.50	6.00
❑ 133 Brandon Siler RC	3.00	8.00
❑ 134 Aundrae Allison RC	3.00	8.00
❑ 135 Ben Patrick RC	3.00	8.00
❑ 136 Chris Davis RC	3.00	8.00
❑ 137 A.J. Davis RC	2.50	6.00
❑ 138 Scott Chandler RC	3.00	8.00
❑ 139 Mason Crosby RC	4.00	10.00
❑ 140 Zak DeOssie RC	3.00	8.00
❑ 141 Matt Spaeth RC	4.00	10.00
❑ 142 James Jones RC	4.00	10.00
❑ 143 Mike Walker RC	4.00	10.00
❑ 144 Martrez Milner RC	3.00	8.00
❑ 145 Michael Okwo RC	3.00	8.00
❑ 146 Steve Breaston RC	4.00	10.00
❑ 147 Isaiah Stanback RC	4.00	10.00
❑ 148 Laurent Robinson RC	4.00	10.00
❑ 149 Brandon Mebane RC	3.00	8.00
❑ 150 Quinn Pitcock RC	3.00	8.00
❑ 151 Roy Hall RC	4.00	10.00
❑ 152 Buster Davis RC	3.00	8.00
❑ 153 Alan Branch RC	3.00	8.00
❑ 154 Josh Gattis RC	2.50	6.00
❑ 155 Aaron Rouse RC	4.00	10.00
❑ 156 Tim Shaw RC	3.00	8.00
❑ 157 Sabby Piscitelli RC	4.00	10.00
❑ 158 Rufus Alexander RC	4.00	10.00
❑ 159 Marcus Thomas RC	3.00	8.00
❑ 160 Tarell Brown RC	2.50	6.00
❑ 161 Chris Leak AU RC	6.00	15.00
❑ 162 Amobi Okoye AU RC	8.00	20.00
❑ 163 Tyler Palko AU RC	6.00	15.00
❑ 164 Craig Buster Davis AU RC	8.00	20.00
❑ 165 Courtney Taylor AU RC	6.00	15.00
❑ 166 Tyrone Moss AU RC	5.00	12.00
❑ 167 Darrelle Revis AU RC	10.00	25.00
❑ 168 David Ball AU RC	5.00	12.00
❑ 169 David Clowney AU RC	8.00	20.00
❑ 170 Daymeion Hughes AU RC	6.00	15.00
❑ 171 DeShawn Wynn AU RC	8.00	20.00
❑ 172 Drew Tate AU RC	6.00	15.00
❑ 173 Dwayne Wright AU RC	6.00	15.00
❑ 174 Eric Wright AU RC	8.00	20.00
❑ 175 Kenneth Darby AU RC	8.00	20.00
❑ 176 H.B. Blades AU RC	6.00	15.00
❑ 177 Jamaal Anderson AU RC	6.00	15.00
❑ 178 Jared Zabransky AU RC	8.00	20.00
❑ 179 Rhema McKnight AU RC	6.00	15.00
❑ 180 Jeff Rowe AU RC	6.00	15.00
❑ 181 LaRon Landry AU RC	10.00	25.00
❑ 182 Jordan Palmer AU RC	8.00	20.00
❑ 183 Kolby Smith AU RC	8.00	20.00
❑ 184 LaMarr Woodley AU RC	12.50	25.00
❑ 185 Lawrence Timmons AU RC	8.00	20.00
❑ 186 Leon Hall AU RC	8.00	20.00
❑ 187 Matt Moore AU RC	15.00	30.00
❑ 188 Gary Russell AU RC	6.00	15.00
❑ 189 Paul Posluszny AU RC	10.00	25.00
❑ 190 Reggie Nelson AU RC	6.00	15.00
❑ 191 Antonio Pittman JSY AU RC	10.00	25.00
❑ 192 A.Gonzalez JSY AU/399 RC	15.00	40.00
❑ 193 Gaines Adams JSY AU RC	10.00	25.00
❑ 194 Brandon Jackson JSY AU RC	10.00	25.00
❑ 195 Brian Leonard JSY AU RC	8.00	20.00
❑ 196 J.Higgins JSY AU RC	10.00	25.00
❑ 197 Chris Henry RB JSY AU RC	8.00	20.00
❑ 198 Patrick Willis JSY AU RC	15.00	40.00
❑ 199 Drew Stanton JSY AU RC	8.00	20.00
❑ 200 D.Bowe JSY AU/399 RC	20.00	50.00
❑ 201 Greg Olsen JSY AU RC	15.00	40.00
❑ 202 John Beck JSY AU RC	10.00	25.00
❑ 203 Jason Hill JSY AU RC	10.00	25.00
❑ 204 Paul Williams JSY AU RC	8.00	20.00
❑ 205 Joe Thomas JSY AU RC	10.00	25.00
❑ 206 Lorenzo Booker JSY AU RC	10.00	25.00
❑ 207 Yamon Figurs JSY AU RC	6.00	15.00
❑ 208 Kenny Irons JSY AU RC	10.00	25.00
❑ 209 Kevin Kolb JSY AU/399 RC	20.00	50.00
❑ 210 Garrett Wolfe JSY AU RC	10.00	25.00
❑ 211 Michael Bush JSY AU RC	10.00	25.00
❑ 212 R.Meachem JSY AU/399 RC	15.00	40.00
❑ 213 Sidney Rice JSY AU/399 RC	25.00	60.00
❑ 214 Stovo Smith JSY AU RC	15.00	30.00
❑ 215 Tony Hunt JSY AU RC	10.00	25.00
❑ 217 T.Edwards JSY AU/399 RC	20.00	50.00
❑ 218 A.Peterson JSY AU/299 RC	200.00	400.00
❑ 219 B.Quinn JSY AU/299 RC	40.00	100.00
❑ 220 Ca.Johnson JSY AU/299 RC	50.00	120.00
❑ 221 D.Jarrett JSY AU/299 RC	15.00	40.00
❑ 222 J.Russell JSY AU/299 RC	20.00	50.00
❑ 223 M.Lynch JSY AU/299 RC	25.00	60.00
❑ 224 Ted Ginn Jr. JSY AU/299 RC	25.00	60.00

2009 SPx

Card		
❑ COMP.SET w/o RC's (90)	15.00	40.00
❑ 1 Aaron Rodgers	.50	1.25
❑ 2 Adrian Peterson	1.00	2.50
❑ 3 Adrian Wilson	.30	.75
❑ 4 Albert Haynesworth	.30	.75
❑ 5 Andre Johnson	.40	1.00
❑ 6 Anquan Boldin	.40	1.00
❑ 7 Antonio Bryant	.40	1.00
❑ 8 Antonio Gates	.40	1.00
❑ 9 Ben Roethlisberger	.75	2.00
❑ 10 Bob Sanders	.40	1.00
❑ 11 Brady Quinn	.40	1.00
❑ 12 Brandon Jacobs	.40	1.00
❑ 13 Brandon Marshall	.40	1.00
❑ 14 Braylon Edwards	.40	1.00
❑ 15 Brian Westbrook	.40	1.00
❑ 16 Calvin Johnson	.50	1.25
❑ 17 Carson Palmer	.50	1.25
❑ 18 Chad Pennington	.40	1.00
❑ 19 Charles Woodson	.40	1.00
❑ 20 Chris Johnson	.50	1.25
❑ 21 Clinton Portis	.40	1.00
❑ 22 Darren McFadden	.50	1.25
❑ 23 Darren Sproles	.40	1.00
❑ 24 David Garrard	.40	1.00
❑ 25 DeAngelo Williams	.50	1.25
❑ 26 DeMarcus Ware	.40	1.00
❑ 27 DeSean Jackson	.40	1.00
❑ 28 Donnie Avery	.40	1.00
❑ 29 Donovan McNabb	.50	1.25
❑ 30 Drew Brees	.50	1.25
❑ 31 Dwayne Bowe	.40	1.00
❑ 32 Ed Reed	.40	1.00
❑ 33 Eddie Royal	.40	1.00
❑ 34 Eli Manning	.50	1.25
❑ 35 Frank Gore	.40	1.00
❑ 36 Greg Jennings	.50	1.25
❑ 37 Hines Ward	.40	1.00
❑ 38 Jake Delhomme	.40	1.00

Card	Low	High
❑ 39 Jamal Lewis	.40	1.00
❑ 40 James Farrior	.30	.75
❑ 41 James Harrison	.50	1.25
❑ 42 Jason Witten	.50	1.25
❑ 43 Jay Cutler	.50	1.25
❑ 44 Joe Flacco	.50	1.25
❑ 45 Joey Porter	.40	1.00
❑ 46 Jonathan Stewart	.40	1.00
❑ 47 Julius Peppers	.40	1.00
❑ 48 Justin Tuck	.40	1.00
❑ 49 Kevin Smith	.40	1.00
❑ 50 Kevin Williams	.30	.75
❑ 51 Kurt Warner	.50	1.25
❑ 52 LaDainian Tomlinson	.50	1.25
❑ 53 Lance Briggs	.40	1.00
❑ 54 Lance Moore	.40	1.00
❑ 55 Larry Fitzgerald	.50	1.25
❑ 56 Lee Evans	.40	1.00
❑ 57 Le'Ron McClain	.40	1.00
❑ 58 Mario Williams	.40	1.00
❑ 59 Marion Barber	.50	1.25
❑ 60 Marshawn Lynch	.40	1.00
❑ 61 Matt Cassel	.40	1.00
❑ 62 Matt Forte	.50	1.25
❑ 63 Matt Ryan	.50	1.25
❑ 64 Matt Schaub	.40	1.00
❑ 65 Maurice Jones-Drew	.40	1.00
❑ 66 Michael Turner	.40	1.00
❑ 67 Nnamdi Asomugha	.30	.75
❑ 68 Patrick Willis	.40	1.00
❑ 69 Peyton Manning	.75	2.00
❑ 70 Philip Rivers	.50	1.25
❑ 71 Randy Moss	.50	1.25
❑ 72 Ray Lewis	.50	1.25
❑ 73 Reggie Wayne	.40	1.00
❑ 74 Roddy White	.40	1.00
❑ 75 Ronde Barber	.30	.75
❑ 76 Ronnie Brown	.40	1.00
❑ 77 Ryan Grant	.40	1.00
❑ 78 Santana Moss	.40	1.00
❑ 79 Steve Slaton	.40	1.00
❑ 80 Steve Smith	.40	1.00
❑ 81 Steven Jackson	.40	1.00
❑ 82 T.J. Houshmandzadeh	.40	1.00
❑ 83 Terrell Owens	.50	1.25
❑ 84 Thomas Jones	.40	1.00
❑ 85 Tom Brady	.75	2.00
❑ 86 Tony Gonzalez	.40	1.00
❑ 87 Tony Romo	.75	2.00
❑ 88 Troy Polamalu	.50	1.25
❑ 89 Walter Jones	.30	.75
❑ 90 Wes Welker	.50	1.25
❑ 91 M.Stafford JSY AU/275 RC	60.00	120.00
❑ 92 M.Crabtree JSY AU/275 RC	50.00	100.00
❑ 93 M.Sanchez JSY AU/275 RC	75.00	150.00
❑ 94 C.Wells JSY AU/275 RC	25.00	60.00
❑ 95 K.Moreno JSY AU/275 RC	40.00	80.00
❑ 96 D.Brown JSY AU/275 RC	25.00	60.00
❑ 97 J.Freeman JSY AU/275 RC	20.00	50.00
❑ 98 D.Hey-Bey JSY AU/275 RC	15.00	40.00
❑ 99 J.Maclin JSY AU/275 RC	20.00	50.00
❑ 100 Pat White JSY AU/275 RC	15.00	40.00
❑ 101 Brian Robiskie JSY AU RC	8.00	20.00
❑ 102 Aaron Curry JSY AU/546 RC	10.00	25.00
❑ 103 Derrick Williams JSY AU RC	8.00	20.00
❑ 104 LeSean McCoy JSY AU RC	15.00	40.00
❑ 105 Stephen McGee JSY AU RC	8.00	20.00
❑ 106 Rhett Bomar JSY AU RC	6.00	15.00
❑ 107 Ramses Barden JSY AU RC	6.00	15.00
❑ 108 Javon Ringer JSY AU RC	8.00	20.00
❑ 109 Andre Brown JSY AU RC	6.00	15.00
❑ 110 Juaquin Iglesias JSY AU RC	8.00	20.00
❑ 111 Patrick Turner JSY AU RC	6.00	15.00
❑ 112 Tyson Jackson JSY AU RC	8.00	20.00
❑ 113 Nate Davis JSY AU RC	8.00	20.00
❑ 114 Glen Coffee JSY AU RC	10.00	25.00
❑ 115 Percy Harvin JSY AU RC	40.00	80.00
❑ 116 M.Massaquoi JSY AU RC	8.00	20.00
❑ 117 Shonn Greene JSY AU RC	15.00	40.00
❑ 118 Mike Thomas JSY AU RC	8.00	20.00
❑ 119 Kenny Britt JSY AU RC	12.00	30.00
❑ 120 Mike Wallace JSY AU RC	20.00	40.00
❑ 121 B.Pettigrew JSY AU RC	10.00	25.00
❑ 122 Hakeem Nicks JSY AU RC	15.00	40.00
❑ 123 Jason Smith JSY AU RC	6.00	15.00
❑ 124 Brian Orakpo AU RC	8.00	20.00
❑ 125 Frank Summers AU RC	6.00	15.00
❑ 126 Tom Brandstater AU RC	6.00	15.00
❑ 127 Gartrell Johnson AU RC	5.00	12.00
❑ 128 Eugene Monroe AU RC	5.00	12.00
❑ 129 B.J. Raji AU RC	8.00	20.00
❑ 130 Vontae Davis AU RC	6.00	15.00
❑ 131 Mike Goodson AU RC	6.00	15.00
❑ 132 Clay Matthews AU RC	10.00	25.00
❑ 133 Michael Johnson AU RC	4.00	10.00
❑ 134 Peria Jerry AU RC	5.00	12.00
❑ 135 Brian Cushing AU RC	8.00	20.00
❑ 136 Brandon Tate AU RC	5.00	12.00
❑ 137 Louis Delmas AU RC	6.00	15.00
❑ 138 Malcolm Jenkins AU RC	6.00	15.00
❑ 139 Cedric Peerman AU RC	5.00	12.00
❑ 140 Bear Pascoe AU RC	6.00	15.00
❑ 141 Curtis Painter AU RC	6.00	15.00
❑ 142 James Laurinaitis AU RC	8.00	20.00
❑ 143 Travis Beckum AU RC	5.00	12.00
❑ 144 Clint Sintim AU RC	6.00	15.00
❑ 145 Patrick Chung AU RC	6.00	15.00
❑ 146 Marko Mitchell AU RC	5.00	12.00
❑ 147 Austin Collie AU RC	15.00	30.00
❑ 148 Chase Coffman AU RC	5.00	12.00
❑ 149 Andre Smith AU RC	6.00	15.00
❑ 150 Demetrius Byrd AU RC	5.00	12.00
❑ 151 Deon Butler AU RC	6.00	15.00
❑ 152 Alphonso Smith AU RC	5.00	12.00
❑ 153 Brandon Gibson AU RC	6.00	15.00
❑ 154 Brian Hartline AU RC	10.00	20.00
❑ 155 James Davis AU RC	6.00	15.00
❑ 156 Alex Mack AU RC	5.00	12.00
❑ 157 Rey Maualuga AU RC	10.00	25.00
❑ 158 Jarett Dillard AU RC	6.00	15.00
❑ 159 Robert Ayers AU RC	8.00	20.00
❑ 160 Jared Cook AU RC	5.00	12.00
❑ 161 Brooks Foster AU RC	5.00	12.00
❑ 162 Larry English AU RC	6.00	15.00
❑ 163 Rashad Jennings AU RC	6.00	15.00
❑ 164 Aaron Brown RC	2.50	6.00
❑ 165 Connor Barwin RC	2.00	5.00
❑ 166 Evander Hood RC	4.00	10.00
❑ 167 David Veikune RC	2.00	5.00
❑ 168 Bernard Scott RC	2.50	6.00
❑ 169 Darcel McBath RC	2.50	6.00
❑ 170 Keith Null RC	2.50	6.00
❑ 171 Andy Levitre RC	2.00	5.00
❑ 172 Louis Murphy RC	2.50	6.00
❑ 173 Eric Wood RC	2.00	5.00
❑ 174 Freddie Brown RC	2.00	5.00
❑ 175 Cody Brown RC	2.00	5.00
❑ 176 Kenny McKinley RC	2.50	6.00
❑ 177 Paul Kruger RC	2.00	5.00
❑ 178 Johnny Knox RC	4.00	10.00
❑ 179 Sebastian Vollmer RC	1.50	4.00
❑ 180 Shawn Nelson RC	2.00	5.00
❑ 181 Jairus Byrd RC	3.00	8.00
❑ 182 Anthony Hill RC	1.50	4.00
❑ 183 Eben Britton RC	2.00	5.00
❑ 184 Max Unger RC	2.00	5.00
❑ 185 Ron Brace RC	2.00	5.00
❑ 186 Mike Teel RC	2.50	6.00
❑ 187 Sherrod Martin RC	2.00	5.00
❑ 188 Fili Moala RC	2.00	5.00
❑ 189 Aaron Maybin RC	2.50	6.00
❑ 190 Chris Ogbonnaya RC	2.50	6.00
❑ 191 Louis Vasquez RC	2.00	5.00
❑ 192 Javarris Williams RC	2.00	5.00
❑ 193 D.J. Moore RC	2.00	5.00
❑ 194 Sean Smith RC	2.50	6.00
❑ 195 Brandon Williams RC	2.50	6.00
❑ 196 William Beatty RC	1.50	4.00
❑ 197 Fui Vakapuna RC	2.00	5.00
❑ 198 David Bruton RC	2.00	5.00
❑ 199 Quinn Johnson RC	2.00	5.00
❑ 200 Kraig Urbik RC	2.00	5.00
❑ 201 LaRod Stephens-Howling RC	6.00	12.00
❑ 202 Tony Fiammetta RC	2.00	5.00
❑ 203 William Moore RC	2.00	5.00
❑ 204 Eddie Williams RC	2.00	5.00
❑ 205 Manuel Johnson RC	2.00	5.00
❑ 206 Tiquan Underwood RC	2.00	5.00
❑ 207 Marlon Lucky RC	2.00	5.00
❑ 208 Julian Edelman RC	6.00	15.00
❑ 209 Dominique Edison RC	1.50	4.00
❑ 210 Michael Oher RC	5.00	12.00
❑ 211 Sen'Derrick Marks RC	1.50	4.00
❑ 212 Mike Mitchell RC	2.50	6.00
❑ 213 DeAndre Levy RC	2.50	6.00
❑ 214 Sammie Stroughter RC	2.50	6.00
❑ 215 Derek Kinder RC	1.50	4.00
❑ 216 Richard Quinn RC	2.00	5.00
❑ 217 Kaluka Maiava RC	2.50	6.00
❑ 218 Keenan Lewis RC	2.50	6.00
❑ 219 Kyle Moore RC	2.00	5.00
❑ 220 Victor Butler RC	2.00	5.00
❑ 221 Everette Brown RC	2.50	6.00
❑ 222 Phil Loadholt RC	2.00	5.00
❑ 223 Darius Butler RC	2.50	6.00

1991 Stadium Club

Card	Low	High
❑ COMPLETE SET (500)	30.00	60.00
❑ 1 Pepper Johnson	.07	.20
❑ 2 Emmitt Smith	2.00	5.00
❑ 3 Deion Sanders	.60	1.50
❑ 4 Andre Collins	.07	.20
❑ 5 Eric Metcalf	.15	.40
❑ 6 Richard Dent	.15	.40
❑ 7 Eric Martin	.07	.20
❑ 8 Marcus Allen	.30	.75
❑ 9 Gary Anderson K	.07	.20
❑ 10 Joey Browner	.07	.20
❑ 11 Lorenzo White	.07	.20
❑ 12 Bruce Smith	.30	.75
❑ 13 Mark Boyer	.07	.20
❑ 14 Mike Piel	.07	.20
❑ 15 Albert Bentley	.07	.20
❑ 16 Bennie Blades	.07	.20
❑ 17 Jason Staurovsky	.07	.20
❑ 18 Anthony Toney	.07	.20
❑ 19 Dave Krieg	.15	.40
❑ 20 Harvey Williams RC	.30	.75
❑ 21 Bubba Paris	.07	.20
❑ 22 Tim McGee	.07	.20
❑ 23 Brian Noble	.07	.20
❑ 24 Vinny Testaverde	.15	.40
❑ 25 Doug Widell	.07	.20
❑ 26 John Jackson WR RC	.07	.20
❑ 27 Marion Butts	.15	.40
❑ 28 Deron Cherry	.07	.20
❑ 29 Don Warren	.07	.20
❑ 30 Rod Woodson	.30	.75
❑ 31 Mike Baab	.07	.20
❑ 32 Greg Jackson RC	.07	.20
❑ 33 Jerry Robinson	.07	.20
❑ 34 Dalton Hilliard	.07	.20
❑ 35 Brian Jordan	.15	.40
❑ 36 James Thornton UER	.07	.20
❑ 37 Michael Irvin	.30	.75
❑ 38 Billy Joe Tolliver	.07	.20
❑ 39 Jeff Herrod	.07	.20
❑ 40 Scott Norwood	.07	.20
❑ 41 Ferrell Edmunds	.07	.20
❑ 42 Andre Waters	.07	.20
❑ 43 Kevin Glover	.07	.20
❑ 44 Ray Berry	.07	.20
❑ 45 Timm Rosenbach	.07	.20
❑ 46 Reuben Davis	.07	.20
❑ 47 Charles Wilson	.07	.20
❑ 48 Todd Marinovich RC	.07	.20
❑ 49 Harris Barton	.07	.20
❑ 50 Jim Breech	.07	.20
❑ 51 Ron Holmes	.07	.20
❑ 52 Chris Singleton	.07	.20
❑ 53 Pat Leahy	.07	.20
❑ 54 Tom Newberry	.07	.20
❑ 55 Greg Montgomery	.07	.20
❑ 56 Robert Blackmon	.07	.20
❑ 57 Jay Hilgenberg	.07	.20
❑ 58 Rodney Hampton	.30	.75
❑ 59 Brett Perriman	.30	.75
❑ 60 Ricky Watters RC	2.50	6.00
❑ 61 Howie Long	.30	.75
❑ 62 Frank Cornish	.07	.20
❑ 63 Chris Miller	.15	.40
❑ 64 Keith Taylor	.07	.20
❑ 65 Tony Paige	.07	.20
❑ 66 Gary Zimmerman	.07	.20

Card		
❑ 67 Mark Royals RC	.07	.20
❑ 68 Ernie Jones	.07	.20
❑ 69 David Grant	.07	.20
❑ 70 Shane Conlan	.07	.20
❑ 71 Jerry Rice	1.00	2.50
❑ 72 Christian Okoye	.07	.20
❑ 73 Eddie Murray	.07	.20
❑ 74 Reggie White	.30	.75
❑ 75 Jeff Graham RC	.40	1.00
❑ 76 Mark Jackson	.07	.20
❑ 77 David Grayson	.07	.20
❑ 78 Dan Stryzinski	.07	.20
❑ 79 Sterling Sharpe	.30	.75
❑ 80 Cleveland Gary	.07	.20
❑ 81 Johnny Meads	.07	.20
❑ 82 Howard Cross	.07	.20
❑ 83 Ken O'Brien	.07	.20
❑ 84 Brian Blades	.15	.40
❑ 85 Ethan Horton	.07	.20
❑ 86 Bruce Armstrong	.07	.20
❑ 87 James Washington RC	.07	.20
❑ 88 Eugene Daniel	.07	.20
❑ 89 James Lofton	.15	.40
❑ 90 Louis Oliver	.07	.20
❑ 91 Boomer Esiason	.15	.40
❑ 92 Seth Joyner	.15	.40
❑ 93 Mark Carrier WR	.30	.75
❑ 94 Brett Favre UER RC	25.00	50.00
❑ 95 Lee Williams	.07	.20
❑ 96 Neal Anderson	.15	.40
❑ 97 Brent Jones	.30	.75
❑ 98 John Alt	.07	.20
❑ 99 Rodney Peete	.15	.40
❑ 100 Steve Broussard	.07	.20
❑ 101 Cedric Mack	.07	.20
❑ 102 Pat Swilling	.15	.40
❑ 103 Stan Humphries	.30	.75
❑ 104 Darrell Thompson	.07	.20
❑ 105 Reggie Langhorne	.07	.20
❑ 106 Kenny Davidson	.07	.20
❑ 107 Jim Everett	.15	.40
❑ 108 Keith Millard	.07	.20
❑ 109 Garry Lewis	.07	.20
❑ 110 Jeff Hostetler	.15	.40
❑ 111 Lamar Lathon	.07	.20
❑ 112 Johnny Bailey	.07	.20
❑ 113 Cornelius Bennett	.15	.40
❑ 114 Travis McNeal	.07	.20
❑ 115 Jeff Lageman	.07	.20
❑ 116 Nick Bell RC	.07	.20
❑ 117 Calvin Williams	.15	.40
❑ 118 Shawn Lee RC	.07	.20
❑ 119 Anthony Munoz	.15	.40
❑ 120 Jay Novacek	.30	.75
❑ 121 Kevin Fagan	.07	.20
❑ 122 Leo Goeas	.07	.20
❑ 123 Vance Johnson	.07	.20
❑ 124 Brent Williams	.07	.20
❑ 125 Clarence Verdin	.07	.20
❑ 126 Luis Sharpe	.07	.20
❑ 127 Darrell Green	.07	.20
❑ 128 Barry Word	.07	.20
❑ 129 Steve Walsh	.07	.20
❑ 130 Bryan Hinkle	.07	.20
❑ 131 Ed West	.07	.20
❑ 132 Jeff Campbell	.07	.20
❑ 133 Dennis Byrd	.07	.20
❑ 134 Nate Odomes	.07	.20
❑ 135 Trace Armstrong	.07	.20
❑ 136 Jarvis Williams	.07	.20
❑ 137 Warren Moon	.30	.75
❑ 138 Eric Moten RC	.07	.20
❑ 139 Tony Woods	.07	.20
❑ 140 Phil Simms	.15	.40
❑ 141 Ricky Reynolds	.07	.20
❑ 142 Frank Stams	.07	.20
❑ 143 Kevin Mack	.07	.20
❑ 144 Wade Wilson	.15	.40
❑ 145 Shawn Collins	.07	.20
❑ 146 Roger Craig	.15	.40
❑ 147 Jeff Feagles RC	.07	.20
❑ 148 Norm Johnson	.07	.20
❑ 149 Terance Mathis	.15	.40
❑ 150 Reggie Cobb	.07	.20
❑ 151 Chip Banks	.07	.20
❑ 152 Darryl Pollard	.07	.20
❑ 153 Karl Mecklenburg	.07	.20
❑ 154 Ricky Proehl	.07	.20
❑ 155 Pete Stoyanovich	.07	.20
❑ 156 John Stephens	.07	.20
❑ 157 Ron Morris	.07	.20
❑ 158 Steve DeBerg	.07	.20
❑ 159 Mike Munchak	.15	.40
❑ 160 Brett Maxie	.07	.20
❑ 161 Don Beebe	.07	.20
❑ 162 Martin Mayhew	.07	.20
❑ 163 Merril Hoge	.07	.20
❑ 164 Kelvin Pritchett RC	.15	.40
❑ 165 Jim Jeffcoat	.07	.20
❑ 166 Myron Guyton	.07	.20
❑ 167 Ickey Woods	.07	.20
❑ 168 Andre Ware	.15	.40
❑ 169 Gary Plummer	.07	.20
❑ 170 Henry Ellard	.15	.40
❑ 171 Scott Davis	.07	.20
❑ 172 Randall McDaniel	.07	.20
❑ 173 Randal Hill RC	.15	.40
❑ 174 Anthony Bell	.07	.20
❑ 175 Gary Anderson RB	.07	.20
❑ 176 Byron Evans	.07	.20
❑ 177 Tony Mandarich	.07	.20
❑ 178 Jeff George	.40	1.00
❑ 179 Art Monk	.15	.40
❑ 180 Mike Kenn	.07	.20
❑ 181 Sean Landeta	.07	.20
❑ 182 Shaun Gayle	.07	.20
❑ 183 Michael Carter	.07	.20
❑ 184 Robb Thomas	.07	.20
❑ 185 Richmond Webb	.07	.20
❑ 186 Carnell Lake	.07	.20
❑ 187 Rueben Mayes	.07	.20
❑ 188 Issiac Holt	.07	.20
❑ 189 Leon Seals	.07	.20
❑ 190 Al Smith	.07	.20
❑ 191 Steve Atwater	.07	.20
❑ 192 Greg McMurtry	.07	.20
❑ 193 Al Toon	.15	.40
❑ 194 Cortez Kennedy	.30	.75
❑ 195 Gill Byrd	.07	.20
❑ 196 Carl Zander	.07	.20
❑ 197 Robert Brown	.07	.20
❑ 198 Buford McGee	.07	.20
❑ 199 Mervyn Fernandez	.07	.20
❑ 200 Mike Dumas RC	.07	.20
❑ 201 Rob Burnett RC	.15	.40
❑ 202 Brian Mitchell	.15	.40
❑ 203 Randall Cunningham	.30	.75
❑ 204 Sammie Smith	.07	.20
❑ 205 Ken Clarke	.07	.20
❑ 206 Floyd Dixon	.07	.20
❑ 207 Ken Norton	.15	.40
❑ 208 Tony Siragusa RC	.15	.40
❑ 209 Louis Lipps	.07	.20
❑ 210 Chris Martin	.07	.20
❑ 211 Jamie Mueller	.07	.20
❑ 212 Dave Waymer	.07	.20
❑ 213 Donnell Woolford	.07	.20
❑ 214 Paul Gruber	.07	.20
❑ 215 Ken Harvey	.15	.40
❑ 216 Henry Jones RC	.15	.40
❑ 217 Tommy Barnhardt RC	.07	.20
❑ 218 Arthur Cox	.07	.20
❑ 219 Pat Terrell	.07	.20
❑ 220 Curtis Duncan	.07	.20
❑ 221 Jeff Jaeger	.07	.20
❑ 222 Scott Stephen RC	.07	.20
❑ 223 Rob Moore	.40	1.00
❑ 224 Chris Hinton	.07	.20
❑ 225 Marv Cook	.07	.20
❑ 226 Patrick Hunter RC	.07	.20
❑ 227 Earnest Byner	.07	.20
❑ 228 Troy Aikman	1.25	3.00
❑ 229 Kevin Walker RC	.07	.20
❑ 230 Keith Jackson	.15	.40
❑ 231 Russell Maryland RC	.30	.75
❑ 232 Charles Haley	.15	.40
❑ 233 Nick Lowery	.07	.20
❑ 234 Erik Howard	.07	.20
❑ 235 Leonard Smith	.07	.20
❑ 236 Tim Irwin	.07	.20
❑ 237 Simon Fletcher	.07	.20
❑ 238 Thomas Everett	.07	.20
❑ 239 Reggie Roby	.07	.20
❑ 240 Leroy Hoard	.15	.40
❑ 241 Wayne Haddix	.07	.20
❑ 242 Gary Clark	.30	.75
❑ 243 Eric Andolsek	.07	.20
❑ 244 Jim Wahler RC	.07	.20
❑ 245 Vaughan Johnson	.07	.20
❑ 246 Kevin Butler	.07	.20
❑ 247 Steve Tasker	.15	.40
❑ 248 LeRoy Butler	.15	.40
❑ 249 Darion Conner	.07	.20
❑ 250 Eric Turner RC	.15	.40
❑ 251 Kevin Ross	.07	.20
❑ 252 Stephen Baker	.07	.20
❑ 253 Harold Green	.15	.40
❑ 254 Rohn Stark	.07	.20
❑ 255 Joe Nash	.07	.20
❑ 256 Jesse Sapolu	.07	.20
❑ 257 Willie Gault	.15	.40
❑ 258 Jerome Brown	.07	.20
❑ 259 Ken Willis	.07	.20
❑ 260 Courtney Hall	.07	.20
❑ 261 Hart Lee Dykes	.07	.20
❑ 262 William Fuller	.15	.40
❑ 263 Stan Thomas	.07	.20
❑ 264 Dan Marino	1.50	4.00
❑ 265 Ron Cox	.07	.20
❑ 266 Eric Green	.07	.20
❑ 267 Anthony Carter	.15	.40
❑ 268 Jerry Ball	.07	.20
❑ 269 Ron Hall	.07	.20
❑ 270 Dennis Smith	.07	.20
❑ 271 Eric Hill	.07	.20
❑ 272 Dan McGwire RC	.07	.20
❑ 273 Lewis Billups UER	.07	.20
❑ 274 Rickey Jackson	.07	.20
❑ 275 Jim Sweeney	.07	.20
❑ 276 Pat Beach	.07	.20
❑ 277 Kevin Porter	.07	.20
❑ 278 Mike Sherrard	.07	.20
❑ 279 Andy Heck	.07	.20
❑ 280 Ron Brown	.07	.20
❑ 281 Lawrence Taylor	.30	.75
❑ 282 Anthony Pleasant	.07	.20
❑ 283 Wes Hopkins	.07	.20
❑ 284 Jim Lachey	.07	.20
❑ 285 Tim Harris	.07	.20
❑ 286 Tory Epps	.07	.20
❑ 287 Wendell Davis	.07	.20
❑ 288 Bubba McDowell	.07	.20
❑ 289 Bubby Brister	.07	.20
❑ 290 Chris Zorich RC	.30	.75
❑ 291 Mike Merriweather	.07	.20
❑ 292 Burt Grossman	.07	.20
❑ 293 Erik McMillan	.07	.20
❑ 294 John Elway	1.50	4.00
❑ 295 Toi Cook RC	.07	.20
❑ 296 Tom Rathman	.07	.20
❑ 297 Matt Bahr	.07	.20
❑ 298 Chris Spielman	.15	.40
❑ 299 F.J.Nunn w/Aikman/Emmitt	.15	.40
❑ 300 Jim C. Jensen	.07	.20
❑ 301 David Fulcher UER	.07	.20
❑ 302 Tommy Hodson	.07	.20
❑ 303 Stephone Paige	.07	.20
❑ 304 Greg Townsend	.07	.20
❑ 305 Dean Biasucci	.07	.20
❑ 306 Jimmie Jones	.07	.20
❑ 307 Eugene Marve	.07	.20
❑ 308 Flipper Anderson	.07	.20
❑ 309 Darryl Talley	.07	.20
❑ 310 Mike Croel RC	.07	.20
❑ 311 Thane Gash	.07	.20
❑ 312 Perry Kemp	.07	.20
❑ 313 Heath Sherman	.07	.20
❑ 314 Mike Singletary	.15	.40
❑ 315 Chip Lohmiller	.07	.20
❑ 316 Tunch Ilkin	.07	.20
❑ 317 Junior Seau	.50	1.25
❑ 318 Mike Gann	.07	.20
❑ 319 Tim McDonald	.07	.20
❑ 320 Kyle Clifton	.07	.20
❑ 321 Dan Owens	.07	.20
❑ 322 Tim Grunhard	.07	.20
❑ 323 Stan Brock	.07	.20
❑ 324 Rodney Holman	.07	.20
❑ 325 Mark Ingram	.15	.40
❑ 326 Browning Nagle RC	.07	.20
❑ 327 Joe Montana	2.00	5.00
❑ 328 Carl Lee	.07	.20
❑ 329 John L. Williams	.07	.20
❑ 330 David Griggs	.07	.20
❑ 331 Clarence Kay	.07	.20
❑ 332 Irving Fryar	.15	.40
❑ 333 Doug Smith DT RC	.15	.40

Card		
❑ 334 Kent Hull	.07	.20
❑ 335 Mike Wilcher	.07	.20
❑ 336 Ray Donaldson	.07	.20
❑ 337 Mark Carrier DB UER	.07	.20
❑ 338 Kelvin Martin	.07	.20
❑ 339 Keith Byars	.07	.20
❑ 340 Wilber Marshall	.07	.20
❑ 341 Ronnie Lott	.15	.40
❑ 342 Blair Thomas	.07	.20
❑ 343 Ronnie Harmon	.07	.20
❑ 344 Brian Brennan	.07	.20
❑ 345 Charles McRae RC	.07	.20
❑ 346 Michael Cofer	.07	.20
❑ 347 Keith Willis	.07	.20
❑ 348 Bruce Kozerski	.07	.20
❑ 349 Dave Meggett	.15	.40
❑ 350 John Taylor	.15	.40
❑ 351 Johnny Holland	.07	.20
❑ 352 Steve Christie	.07	.20
❑ 353 Ricky Ervins RC	.15	.40
❑ 354 Robert Massey	.07	.20
❑ 355 Derrick Thomas	.30	.75
❑ 356 Tommy Kane	.07	.20
❑ 357 Melvin Bratton	.07	.20
❑ 358 Bruce Matthews	.15	.40
❑ 359 Mark Duper	.15	.40
❑ 360 Jeff Wright RC	.07	.20
❑ 361 Barry Sanders	1.50	4.00
❑ 362 Chuck Webb RC	.07	.20
❑ 363 Darryl Grant	.07	.20
❑ 364 William Roberts	.07	.20
❑ 365 Reggie Rutland	.07	.20
❑ 366 Clay Matthews	.15	.40
❑ 367 Anthony Miller	.15	.40
❑ 368 Mike Prior	.07	.20
❑ 369 Jessie Tuggle	.07	.20
❑ 370 Brad Muster	.07	.20
❑ 371 Jay Schroeder	.07	.20
❑ 372 Greg Lloyd	.30	.75
❑ 373 Mike Cofer	.07	.20
❑ 374 James Brooks	.15	.40
❑ 375 Danny Noonan UER	.07	.20
❑ 376 Latin Berry RC	.07	.20
❑ 377 Brad Baxter	.07	.20
❑ 378 Godfrey Myles RC	.07	.20
❑ 379 Morten Andersen	.07	.20
❑ 380 Keith Woodside	.07	.20
❑ 381 Bobby Humphrey	.07	.20
❑ 382 Mike Golic	.07	.20
❑ 383 Keith McCants	.07	.20
❑ 384 Anthony Thompson	.07	.20
❑ 385 Mark Clayton	.15	.40
❑ 386 Neil Smith	.30	.75
❑ 387 Bryan Millard	.07	.20
❑ 388 Mel Gray UER	.15	.40
❑ 389 Ernest Givins	.15	.40
❑ 390 Reyna Thompson	.07	.20
❑ 391 Eric Bieniemy RC	.07	.20
❑ 392 Jon Hand	.07	.20
❑ 393 Mark Rypien	.15	.40
❑ 394 Bill Romanowski	.07	.20
❑ 395 Thurman Thomas	.30	.75
❑ 396 Jim Harbaugh	.30	.75
❑ 397 Don Mosebar	.07	.20
❑ 398 Andre Rison	.15	.40
❑ 399 Mike Johnson	.07	.20
❑ 400 Dermontti Dawson	.07	.20
❑ 401 Herschel Walker	.15	.40
❑ 402 Joe Prokop	.07	.20
❑ 403 Eddie Brown	.07	.20
❑ 404 Nate Newton	.15	.40
❑ 405 Damone Johnson RC	.07	.20
❑ 406 Jessie Hester	.07	.20
❑ 407 Jim Arnold	.07	.20
❑ 408 Ray Agnew	.07	.20
❑ 409 Michael Brooks	.07	.20
❑ 410 Keith Sims	.07	.20
❑ 411 Carl Banks	.07	.20
❑ 412 Jonathan Hayes	.07	.20
❑ 413 Richard Johnson CB RC	.07	.20
❑ 414 Darryll Lewis RC	.15	.40
❑ 415 Jeff Bryant	.07	.20
❑ 416 Leslie O'Neal	.15	.40
❑ 417 Andre Reed	.15	.40
❑ 418 Charles Mann	.07	.20
❑ 419 Keith DeLong	.07	.20
❑ 420 Bruce Hill	.07	.20
❑ 421 Matt Brock RC	.07	.20
❑ 422 Johnny Johnson	.07	.20

Card		
❑ 423 Mark Bortz	.07	.20
❑ 424 Ben Smith	.07	.20
❑ 425 Jeff Cross	.07	.20
❑ 426 Irv Pankey	.07	.20
❑ 427 Hassan Jones	.07	.20
❑ 428 Andre Tippett	.07	.20
❑ 429 Tim Worley	.07	.20
❑ 430 Daniel Stubbs	.07	.20
❑ 431 Max Montoya	.07	.20
❑ 432 Jumbo Elliott	.07	.20
❑ 433 Duane Bickett	.07	.20
❑ 434 Nate Lewis RC	.07	.20
❑ 435 Leonard Russell RC	.30	.75
❑ 436 Hoby Brenner	.07	.20
❑ 437 Ricky Sanders	.07	.20
❑ 438 Pierce Holt	.07	.20
❑ 439 Derrick Fenner	.07	.20
❑ 440 Drew Hill	.07	.20
❑ 441 Will Wolford	.07	.20
❑ 442 Albert Lewis	.07	.20
❑ 443 James Francis	.07	.20
❑ 444 Chris Jacke	.07	.20
❑ 445 Mike Farr	.07	.20
❑ 446 Stephen Braggs	.07	.20
❑ 447 Michael Haynes	.30	.75
❑ 448 Freeman McNeil UER	.07	.20
❑ 449 Kevin Donnalley RC	.07	.20
❑ 450 John Offerdahl	.07	.20
❑ 451 Eric Allen	.07	.20
❑ 452 Keith McKeller	.07	.20
❑ 453 Kevin Greene	.15	.40
❑ 454 Ronnie Lippett	.07	.20
❑ 455 Ray Childress	.07	.20
❑ 456 Mike Saxon	.07	.20
❑ 457 Mark Robinson	.07	.20
❑ 458 Greg Kragen	.07	.20
❑ 459 Steve Jordan	.07	.20
❑ 460 John Johnson RC	.07	.20
❑ 461 Sam Mills	.07	.20
❑ 462 Bo Jackson	.40	1.00
❑ 463 Mark Collins	.07	.20
❑ 464 Percy Snow	.07	.20
❑ 465 Jeff Bostic	.07	.20
❑ 466 Jacob Green	.07	.20
❑ 467 Dexter Carter	.07	.20
❑ 468 Rich Camarillo	.07	.20
❑ 469 Bill Brooks	.07	.20
❑ 470 John Carney	.07	.20
❑ 471 Don Majkowski	.07	.20
❑ 472 Ralph Tamm RC	.07	.20
❑ 473 Fred Barnett	.30	.75
❑ 474 Jim Covert	.07	.20
❑ 475 Kenneth Davis	.07	.20
❑ 476 Jerry Gray	.07	.20
❑ 477 Broderick Thomas	.07	.20
❑ 478 Chris Doleman	.07	.20
❑ 479 Haywood Jeffires	.15	.40
❑ 480 Craig Heyward	.15	.40
❑ 481 Markus Koch	.07	.20
❑ 482 Tim Krumrie	.07	.20
❑ 483 Robert Clark	.07	.20
❑ 484 Mike Rozier	.07	.20
❑ 485 Danny Villa	.07	.20
❑ 486 Gerald Williams	.07	.20
❑ 487 Steve Wisniewski	.07	.20
❑ 488 J.B. Brown	.07	.20
❑ 489 Eugene Robinson	.07	.20
❑ 490 Ottis Anderson	.15	.40
❑ 491 Tony Stargell	.07	.20
❑ 492 Jack Del Rio	.15	.40
❑ 493 Lamar Rogers RC	.07	.20
❑ 494 Ricky Nattiel	.07	.20
❑ 495 Dan Saleaumua	.07	.20
❑ 496 Checklist 1-100	.07	.20
❑ 497 Checklist 101-200	.07	.20
❑ 498 Checklist 201-300	.07	.20
❑ 499 Checklist 301-400	.07	.20
❑ 500 Checklist 401-500	.07	.20

1992 Stadium Club

Card		
❑ COMPLETE SET (700)	100.00	200.00
❑ COMP.SERIES 1 (300)	6.00	15.00
❑ COMP.SERIES 2 (300)	6.00	15.00
❑ COMP.HIGH SER.(100)	100.00	175.00
❑ 1 Mark Rypien	.02	.10
❑ 2 Carlton Bailey RC	.02	.10
❑ 3 Kevin Glover	.02	.10
❑ 4 Vance Johnson	.02	.10
❑ 5 Jim Jeffcoat	.02	.10
❑ 6 Dan Saleaumua	.02	.10
❑ 7 Darion Conner	.02	.10
❑ 8 Don Maggs	.02	.10
❑ 9 Richard Dent	.05	.15
❑ 10 Mark Murphy	.02	.10
❑ 11 Wesley Carroll	.02	.10
❑ 12 Chris Burkett	.02	.10
❑ 13 Steve Wallace	.02	.10
❑ 14 Jacob Green	.02	.10
❑ 15 Roger Ruzek	.02	.10
❑ 16 J.B. Brown	.02	.10
❑ 17 Dave Meggett	.05	.15
❑ 18 D.J. Johnson	.02	.10
❑ 19 Rich Gannon	.10	.30
❑ 20 Kevin Mack	.02	.10
❑ 21A Reggie Cobb ERR	.02	.10
❑ 21B Reggie Cobb COR	.02	.10
❑ 22 Nate Lewis	.02	.10
❑ 23 Doug Smith	.02	.10
❑ 24 Irving Fryar	.05	.15
❑ 25 Anthony Thompson	.02	.10
❑ 26 Duane Bickett	.02	.10
❑ 27 Don Majkowski	.02	.10
❑ 28 Mark Schlereth RC	.02	.10
❑ 29 Melvin Jenkins	.02	.10
❑ 30 Michael Haynes	.05	.15
❑ 31 Greg Lewis	.02	.10
❑ 32 Kenneth Davis	.02	.10
❑ 33 Derrick Thomas	.10	.30
❑ 34 David Williams	.02	.10
❑ 35 Neal Anderson	.02	.10
❑ 36 Andre Collins	.02	.10
❑ 37 Jesse Solomon	.02	.10
❑ 38 Barry Sanders	1.00	2.50
❑ 39 Jeff Gossett	.02	.10
❑ 40 Rickey Jackson	.02	.10
❑ 41 Ray Berry	.02	.10
❑ 42 Leroy Hoard	.05	.15
❑ 43 Eric Thomas	.02	.10
❑ 44 Brian Washington	.02	.10
❑ 45 Pat Terrell	.02	.10
❑ 46 Eugene Robinson	.02	.10
❑ 47 Luis Sharpe	.02	.10
❑ 48 Jerome Brown	.02	.10
❑ 49 Mark Collins	.02	.10
❑ 50 Johnny Holland	.02	.10
❑ 51 Tony Paige	.02	.10
❑ 52 Willie Green	.02	.10
❑ 53 Steve Atwater	.02	.10
❑ 54 Brad Muster	.02	.10
❑ 55 Cris Dishman	.02	.10
❑ 56 Eddie Anderson	.02	.10
❑ 57 Sam Mills	.02	.10
❑ 58 Donald Evans	.02	.10
❑ 59 Jon Vaughn	.02	.10
❑ 60 Marion Butts	.02	.10
❑ 61 Rodney Holman	.02	.10
❑ 62 Dwayne White RC	.02	.10
❑ 63 Martin Mayhew	.02	.10
❑ 64 Jonathan Hayes	.02	.10
❑ 65 Andre Rison	.05	.15
❑ 66 Calvin Williams	.05	.15
❑ 67 James Washington	.02	.10
❑ 68 Tim Harris	.02	.10
❑ 69 Jim Ritcher	.02	.10

❑ 70 Johnny Johnson	.02	.10
❑ 71 John Offerdahl	.02	.10
❑ 72 Herschel Walker	.05	.15
❑ 73 Perry Kemp	.02	.10
❑ 74 Erik Howard	.02	.10
❑ 75 Lamar Lathon	.02	.10
❑ 76 Greg Kragen	.02	.10
❑ 77 Jay Schroeder	.02	.10
❑ 78 Jim Arnold	.02	.10
❑ 79 Chris Miller	.05	.15
❑ 80 Deron Cherry	.02	.10
❑ 81 Jim Harbaugh	.10	.30
❑ 82 Gill Fenerty	.02	.10
❑ 83 Fred Stokes	.02	.10
❑ 84 Roman Phifer	.02	.10
❑ 85 Clyde Simmons	.02	.10
❑ 86 Vince Newsome	.02	.10
❑ 87 Lawrence Dawsey	.05	.15
❑ 88 Eddie Brown	.02	.10
❑ 89 Greg Montgomery	.02	.10
❑ 90 Jeff Lageman	.02	.10
❑ 91 Terry Wooden	.02	.10
❑ 92 Nate Newton	.02	.10
❑ 93 David Richards	.02	.10
❑ 94 Derek Russell	.02	.10
❑ 95 Steve Jordan	.02	.10
❑ 96 Hugh Millen	.02	.10
❑ 97 Mark Duper	.02	.10
❑ 98 Sean Landeta	.02	.10
❑ 99 James Thornton	.02	.10
❑ 100 Darrell Green	.02	.10
❑ 101 Harris Barton	.02	.10
❑ 102 John Alt	.02	.10
❑ 103 Mike Farr	.02	.10
❑ 104 Bob Golic	.02	.10
❑ 105 Gene Atkins	.02	.10
❑ 106 Gary Anderson K	.02	.10
❑ 107 Norm Johnson	.02	.10
❑ 108 Eugene Daniel	.02	.10
❑ 109 Kent Hull	.02	.10
❑ 110 John Elway	1.00	2.50
❑ 111 Rich Camarillo	.02	.10
❑ 112 Charles Wilson	.02	.10
❑ 113 Matt Bahr	.02	.10
❑ 114 Mark Carrier WR	.05	.15
❑ 115 Richmond Webb	.02	.10
❑ 116 Charles Mann	.02	.10
❑ 117 Tim McGee	.02	.10
❑ 118 Wes Hopkins	.02	.10
❑ 119 Mo Lewis	.02	.10
❑ 120 Warren Moon	.10	.30
❑ 121 Damone Johnson	.02	.10
❑ 122 Kevin Gogan	.02	.10
❑ 123 Joey Browner	.02	.10
❑ 124 Tommy Kane	.02	.10
❑ 125 Vincent Brown	.02	.10
❑ 126 Barry Word	.02	.10
❑ 127 Michael Brooks	.02	.10
❑ 128 Jumbo Elliott	.02	.10
❑ 129 Marcus Allen	.10	.30
❑ 130 Tom Waddle	.02	.10
❑ 131 Jim Dombrowski	.02	.10
❑ 132 Aeneas Williams	.05	.15
❑ 133 Clay Matthews	.05	.15
❑ 134 Thurman Thomas	.10	.30
❑ 135 Dean Biasucci	.02	.10
❑ 136 Moe Gardner	.02	.10
❑ 137 James Campen	.02	.10
❑ 138 Tim Johnson	.02	.10
❑ 139 Erik Kramer	.05	.15
❑ 140 Keith McCants	.02	.10
❑ 141 John Carney	.02	.10
❑ 142 Tunch Ilkin	.02	.10
❑ 143 Louis Oliver	.02	.10
❑ 144 Bill Maas	.02	.10
❑ 145 Wendell Davis	.02	.10
❑ 146 Pepper Johnson	.02	.10
❑ 147 Howie Long	.10	.30
❑ 148 Brett Maxie	.02	.10
❑ 149 Tony Casillas	.02	.10
❑ 150 Michael Carter	.02	.10
❑ 151 Byron Evans	.02	.10
❑ 152 Lorenzo White	.02	.10
❑ 153 Larry Kelm	.02	.10
❑ 154 Andy Heck	.02	.10
❑ 155 Harry Newsome	.02	.10
❑ 156 Chris Singleton	.02	.10
❑ 157 Mike Kenn	.02	.10
❑ 158 Jeff Faulkner	.02	.10
❑ 159 Ken Lanier	.02	.10
❑ 160 Darryl Talley	.02	.10
❑ 161 Louie Aguiar RC	.02	.10
❑ 162 Danny Copeland	.02	.10
❑ 163 Kevin Porter	.02	.10
❑ 164 Trace Armstrong	.02	.10
❑ 165 Dermontti Dawson	.02	.10
❑ 166 Fred McAfee RC	.02	.10
❑ 167 Ronnie Lott	.05	.15
❑ 168 Tony Mandarich	.02	.10
❑ 169 Howard Cross	.02	.10
❑ 170 Vestee Jackson	.02	.10
❑ 171 Jeff Herrod	.02	.10
❑ 172 Randy Hilliard RC	.02	.10
❑ 173 Robert Wilson	.02	.10
❑ 174 Joe Walter RC	.02	.10
❑ 175 Chris Spielman	.05	.15
❑ 176 Darryl Henley	.02	.10
❑ 177 Jay Hilgenberg	.02	.10
❑ 178 John Kidd	.02	.10
❑ 179 Doug Widell	.02	.10
❑ 180 Seth Joyner	.02	.10
❑ 181 Nick Bell	.02	.10
❑ 182 Don Griffin	.02	.10
❑ 183 Johnny Meads	.02	.10
❑ 184 Jeff Bostic	.02	.10
❑ 185 Johnny Hector	.02	.10
❑ 186 Jessie Tuggle	.02	.10
❑ 187 Robb Thomas	.02	.10
❑ 188 Shane Conlan	.02	.10
❑ 189 Michael Zordich RC	.02	.10
❑ 190 Emmitt Smith	1.50	3.00
❑ 191 Robert Blackmon	.02	.10
❑ 192 Carl Lee	.02	.10
❑ 193 Harry Galbreath	.02	.10
❑ 194 Ed King	.02	.10
❑ 195 Stan Thomas	.02	.10
❑ 196 Andre Waters	.02	.10
❑ 197 Pat Harlow	.02	.10
❑ 198 Zefross Moss	.02	.10
❑ 199 Bobby Hebert	.02	.10
❑ 200 Doug Riesenberg	.02	.10
❑ 201 Mike Croel	.02	.10
❑ 202 Jeff Jaeger	.02	.10
❑ 203 Gary Plummer	.02	.10
❑ 204 Chris Jacke	.02	.10
❑ 205 Neil O'Donnell	.05	.15
❑ 206 Mark Bortz	.02	.10
❑ 207 Tim Barnett	.02	.10
❑ 208 Jerry Ball	.02	.10
❑ 209 Chip Lohmiller	.02	.10
❑ 210 Jim Everett	.05	.15
❑ 211 Tim McKyer	.02	.10
❑ 212 Aaron Craver	.02	.10
❑ 213 John L. Williams	.02	.10
❑ 214 Simon Fletcher	.02	.10
❑ 215 Walter Reeves	.02	.10
❑ 216 Terance Mathis	.05	.15
❑ 217 Mike Pitts	.02	.10
❑ 218 Bruce Matthews	.02	.10
❑ 219 Howard Ballard	.02	.10
❑ 220 Leonard Russell	.05	.15
❑ 221 Michael Stewart	.02	.10
❑ 222 Mike Merriweather	.02	.10
❑ 223 Ricky Sanders	.02	.10
❑ 224 Ray Horton	.02	.10
❑ 225 Michael Jackson	.05	.15
❑ 226 Bill Romanowski	.02	.10
❑ 227 Steve McMichael UER	.05	.15
❑ 228 Chris Martin	.02	.10
❑ 229 Tim Green	.02	.10
❑ 230 Karl Mecklenburg	.02	.10
❑ 231 Felix Wright	.02	.10
❑ 232 Charles McRae	.02	.10
❑ 233 Pete Stoyanovich	.02	.10
❑ 234 Stephen Baker	.02	.10
❑ 235 Herman Moore	.10	.30
❑ 236 Terry McDaniel	.02	.10
❑ 237 Dalton Hilliard	.02	.10
❑ 238 Gill Byrd	.02	.10
❑ 239 Leon Seals	.02	.10
❑ 240 Rod Woodson	.10	.30
❑ 241 Curtis Duncan	.02	.10
❑ 242 Keith Jackson	.05	.15
❑ 243 Mark Stepnoski	.05	.15
❑ 244 Art Monk	.05	.15
❑ 245 Matt Stover	.02	.10
❑ 246 John Roper	.02	.10
❑ 247 Rodney Hampton	.05	.15
❑ 248 Steve Wisniewski	.02	.10
❑ 249 Bryan Millard	.02	.10
❑ 250 Todd Lyght	.02	.10
❑ 251 Marvin Washington	.02	.10
❑ 252 Eric Swann	.05	.15
❑ 253 Bruce Kozerski	.02	.10
❑ 254 Jon Hand	.02	.10
❑ 255 Scott Fulhage	.02	.10
❑ 256 Chuck Cecil	.02	.10
❑ 257 Eric Martin	.02	.10
❑ 258 Eric Metcalf	.05	.15
❑ 259 T.J. Turner	.02	.10
❑ 260 Kirk Lowdermilk	.02	.10
❑ 261 Keith McKeller	.02	.10
❑ 262 Wymon Henderson	.02	.10
❑ 263 David Alexander	.02	.10
❑ 264 George Jamison	.02	.10
❑ 265 Ken Norton Jr.	.05	.15
❑ 266 Jim Lachey	.02	.10
❑ 267 Bo Orlando RC	.02	.10
❑ 268 Nick Lowery	.02	.10
❑ 269 Keith Van Horne	.02	.10
❑ 270 Dwight Stone	.02	.10
❑ 271 Keith DeLong	.02	.10
❑ 272 James Francis	.02	.10
❑ 273 Greg McMurtry	.02	.10
❑ 274 Ethan Horton	.02	.10
❑ 275 Stan Brock	.02	.10
❑ 276 Ken Harvey	.02	.10
❑ 277 Ronnie Harmon	.02	.10
❑ 278 Mike Pritchard	.05	.15
❑ 279 Kyle Clifton	.02	.10
❑ 280 Anthony Johnson	.05	.15
❑ 281 Esera Tuaolo	.02	.10
❑ 282 Vernon Turner	.02	.10
❑ 283 David Griggs	.02	.10
❑ 284 Dino Hackett	.02	.10
❑ 285 Carwell Gardner	.02	.10
❑ 286 Ron Hall	.02	.10
❑ 287 Reggie White	.10	.30
❑ 288 Checklist 1-100	.02	.10
❑ 289 Checklist 101-200	.02	.10
❑ 290 Checklist 201-300	.02	.10
❑ 291 Mark Clayton MC	.02	.10
❑ 292 Pat Swilling MC	.02	.10
❑ 293 Ernest Givins MC	.02	.10
❑ 294 Broderick Thomas MC	.02	.10
❑ 295 John Friesz MC	.02	.10
❑ 296 Cornelius Bennett MC	.02	.10
❑ 297 Anthony Carter MC	.05	.15
❑ 298 Earnest Byner MC	.02	.10
❑ 299 Michael Irvin MC	.10	.30
❑ 300 Cortez Kennedy MC	.02	.10
❑ 301 Barry Sanders MC	.60	1.50
❑ 302 Mike Croel MC	.02	.10
❑ 303 Emmitt Smith MC	.75	2.00
❑ 304 Leonard Russell MC	.02	.10
❑ 305 Neal Anderson MC	.02	.10
❑ 306 Derrick Thomas MC	.05	.15
❑ 307 Mark Rypien MC	.02	.10
❑ 308 Reggie White MC	.05	.15
❑ 309 Rod Woodson MC	.05	.15
❑ 310 Rodney Hampton MC	.05	.15
❑ 311 Carnell Lake	.02	.10
❑ 312 Robert Delpino	.02	.10
❑ 313 Brian Blades	.05	.15
❑ 314 Marc Spindler	.02	.10
❑ 315 Scott Norwood	.02	.10
❑ 316 Frank Warren	.02	.10
❑ 317 David Treadwell	.02	.10
❑ 318 Steve Broussard	.02	.10
❑ 319 Lorenzo Lynch	.02	.10
❑ 320 Ray Agnew	.02	.10
❑ 321 Derrick Walker	.02	.10
❑ 322 Vinson Smith RC	.02	.10
❑ 323 Gary Clark	.10	.30
❑ 324 Charles Haley	.05	.15
❑ 325 Keith Byars	.02	.10
❑ 326 Winston Moss	.02	.10
❑ 327 Paul McJulien UER RC	.02	.10
❑ 328 Tony Covington	.02	.10
❑ 329 Mark Carrier DB	.02	.10
❑ 330 Mark Tuinei	.02	.10
❑ 331 Tracy Simien RC	.02	.10
❑ 332 Jeff Wright	.02	.10
❑ 333 Bryan Cox	.05	.15
❑ 334 Lonnie Young	.02	.10
❑ 335 Clarence Verdin	.02	.10
❑ 336 Dan Fike	.02	.10

Card	Low	High
❑ 337 Steve Sewell	.02	.10
❑ 338 Gary Zimmerman	.02	.10
❑ 339 Barney Bussey	.02	.10
❑ 340 William Perry	.05	.15
❑ 341 Jeff Hostetler	.05	.15
❑ 342 Doug Smith	.02	.10
❑ 343 Cleveland Gary	.02	.10
❑ 344 Todd Marinovich	.02	.10
❑ 345 Rich Moran	.02	.10
❑ 346 Tony Woods	.02	.10
❑ 347 Vaughan Johnson	.02	.10
❑ 348 Marv Cook	.02	.10
❑ 349 Pierce Holt	.02	.10
❑ 350 Gerald Williams	.02	.10
❑ 351 Kevin Butler	.02	.10
❑ 352 William White	.02	.10
❑ 353 Henry Rolling	.02	.10
❑ 354 James Joseph	.02	.10
❑ 355 Vinny Testaverde	.05	.15
❑ 356 Scott Radecic	.02	.10
❑ 357 Lee Johnson	.02	.10
❑ 358 Steve Tasker	.05	.15
❑ 359 David Lutz	.02	.10
❑ 360 Audray McMillian UER	.02	.10
❑ 361 Brad Baxter	.02	.10
❑ 362 Mark Dennis	.02	.10
❑ 363 Erric Pegram	.05	.15
❑ 364 Sean Jones	.02	.10
❑ 365 William Roberts	.02	.10
❑ 366 Steve Young	.40	1.00
❑ 367 Joe Jacoby	.02	.10
❑ 368 Richard Brown RC	.02	.10
❑ 369 Keith Kartz	.02	.10
❑ 370 Freddie Joe Nunn	.02	.10
❑ 371 Darren Comeaux	.02	.10
❑ 372 Larry Brown DB	.02	.10
❑ 373 Haywood Jeffires	.05	.15
❑ 374 Tom Newberry	.02	.10
❑ 375 Steve Bono RC	.10	.30
❑ 376 Kevin Ross	.02	.10
❑ 377 Kelvin Pritchett	.02	.10
❑ 378 Jessie Hester	.02	.10
❑ 379 Mitchell Price	.02	.10
❑ 380 Barry Foster	.05	.15
❑ 381 Reyna Thompson	.02	.10
❑ 382 Cris Carter	.30	.75
❑ 383 Lemuel Stinson	.02	.10
❑ 384 Rod Bernstine	.02	.10
❑ 385 James Lofton	.05	.15
❑ 386 Kevin Murphy	.02	.10
❑ 387 Greg Townsend	.02	.10
❑ 388 Edgar Bennett RC	.10	.30
❑ 389 Rob Moore	.05	.15
❑ 390 Eugene Lockhart	.02	.10
❑ 391 Bern Brostek	.02	.10
❑ 392 Craig Heyward	.05	.15
❑ 393 Ferrell Edmunds	.02	.10
❑ 394 John Kasay	.02	.10
❑ 395 Jesse Sapolu	.02	.10
❑ 396 Jim Breech	.02	.10
❑ 397 Neil Smith	.10	.30
❑ 398 Bryce Paup	.10	.30
❑ 399 Tony Tolbert	.02	.10
❑ 400 Bubby Brister	.02	.10
❑ 401 Dennis Smith	.02	.10
❑ 402 Dan Owens	.02	.10
❑ 403 Steve Beuerlein	.05	.15
❑ 404 Rick Tuten	.02	.10
❑ 405 Eric Allen	.02	.10
❑ 406 Eric Hill	.02	.10
❑ 407 Don Warren	.02	.10
❑ 408 Greg Jackson	.02	.10
❑ 409 Chris Doleman	.02	.10
❑ 410 Anthony Munoz	.05	.15
❑ 411 Michael Young	.02	.10
❑ 412 Cornelius Bennett	.05	.15
❑ 413 Ray Childress	.02	.10
❑ 414 Kevin Call	.02	.10
❑ 415 Burt Grossman	.02	.10
❑ 416 Scott Miller	.02	.10
❑ 417 Tim Newton	.02	.10
❑ 418 Robert Young	.02	.10
❑ 419 Tommy Vardell RC	.02	.10
❑ 420 Michael Walter	.02	.10
❑ 421 Chris Port RC	.02	.10
❑ 422 Carlton Haselrig RC	.02	.10
❑ 423 Rodney Peete	.05	.15
❑ 424 Scott Stephen	.02	.10
❑ 425 Chris Warren	.10	.30
❑ 426 Scott Galbraith RC	.02	.10
❑ 427 Fuad Reveiz UER	.02	.10
❑ 428 Irv Eatman	.02	.10
❑ 429 David Szott	.02	.10
❑ 430 Brent Williams	.02	.10
❑ 431 Mike Horan	.02	.10
❑ 432 Brent Jones	.05	.15
❑ 433 Paul Gruber	.02	.10
❑ 434 Carlos Huerta	.02	.10
❑ 435 Scott Case	.02	.10
❑ 436 Greg Davis	.02	.10
❑ 437 Ken Clarke	.02	.10
❑ 438 Alfred Williams	.02	.10
❑ 439 Jim C. Jensen	.02	.10
❑ 440 Louis Lipps	.02	.10
❑ 441 Larry Roberts	.02	.10
❑ 442 James Jones DT	.02	.10
❑ 443 Don Mosebar	.02	.10
❑ 444 Quinn Early	.05	.15
❑ 445 Robert Brown	.02	.10
❑ 446 Tom Thayer	.02	.10
❑ 447 Michael Irvin	.10	.30
❑ 448 Jarrod Bunch	.02	.10
❑ 449 Riki Ellison	.02	.10
❑ 450 Joe Phillips	.02	.10
❑ 451 Ernest Givins	.05	.15
❑ 452 Glenn Parker	.02	.10
❑ 453 Brett Perriman UER	.10	.30
❑ 454 Jayice Pearson RC	.02	.10
❑ 455 Mark Jackson	.02	.10
❑ 456 Siran Stacy RC	.02	.10
❑ 457 Rufus Porter	.02	.10
❑ 458 Michael Ball	.02	.10
❑ 459 Craig Taylor	.02	.10
❑ 460 George Thomas RC	.02	.10
❑ 461 Alvin Wright	.02	.10
❑ 462 Ron Hallstrom	.02	.10
❑ 463 Mike Mooney RC	.02	.10
❑ 464 Dexter Carter	.02	.10
❑ 465 Marty Carter RC	.02	.10
❑ 466 Pat Swilling	.02	.10
❑ 467 Mike Golic	.02	.10
❑ 468 Reggie Roby	.02	.10
❑ 469 Randall McDaniel	.05	.15
❑ 470 John Stephens	.02	.10
❑ 471 Ricardo McDonald RC	.02	.10
❑ 472 Wilber Marshall	.02	.10
❑ 473 Jim Sweeney	.02	.10
❑ 474 Ernie Jones	.02	.10
❑ 475 Bennie Blades	.02	.10
❑ 476 Don Beebe	.02	.10
❑ 477 Grant Feasel	.02	.10
❑ 478 Ernie Mills	.02	.10
❑ 479 Tony Jones T	.02	.10
❑ 480 Jeff Uhlenhake	.02	.10
❑ 481 Gaston Green	.02	.10
❑ 482 John Taylor	.05	.15
❑ 483 Anthony Smith	.02	.10
❑ 484 Tony Bennett	.02	.10
❑ 485 David Brandon RC	.02	.10
❑ 486 Shawn Jefferson	.02	.10
❑ 487 Christian Okoye	.02	.10
❑ 488 Leonard Marshall	.02	.10
❑ 489 Jay Novacek	.05	.15
❑ 490 Harold Green	.02	.10
❑ 491 Bubba McDowell	.02	.10
❑ 492 Gary Anderson RB	.02	.10
❑ 493 Terrell Buckley RC	.02	.10
❑ 494 Jamie Dukes RC	.02	.10
❑ 495 Morten Andersen	.02	.10
❑ 496 Henry Thomas	.02	.10
❑ 497 Bill Lewis	.02	.10
❑ 498 Jeff Cross	.02	.10
❑ 499 Hardy Nickerson	.05	.15
❑ 500 Henry Ellard	.05	.15
❑ 501 Joe Bowden RC	.02	.10
❑ 502 Brian Noble	.02	.10
❑ 503 Mike Cofer	.02	.10
❑ 504 Jeff Bryant	.02	.10
❑ 505 Lomas Brown	.02	.10
❑ 506 Chip Banks	.02	.10
❑ 507 Keith Traylor	.02	.10
❑ 508 Mark Kelso	.02	.10
❑ 509 Dexter McNabb RC	.02	.10
❑ 510 Gene Chilton RC	.02	.10
❑ 511 George Thornton	.02	.10
❑ 512 Jeff Criswell	.02	.10
❑ 513 Brad Edwards	.02	.10
❑ 514 Ron Heller	.02	.10
❑ 515 Tim Brown	.10	.30
❑ 516 Keith Hamilton RC	.05	.15
❑ 517 Mark Higgs	.02	.10
❑ 518 Tommy Barnhardt	.02	.10
❑ 519 Brian Jordan	.05	.15
❑ 520 Ray Crockett	.02	.10
❑ 521 Karl Wilson	.02	.10
❑ 522 Ricky Reynolds	.02	.10
❑ 523 Max Montoya	.02	.10
❑ 524 David Little	.02	.10
❑ 525 Alonzo Mitz RC	.02	.10
❑ 526 Darryll Lewis	.02	.10
❑ 527 Keith Henderson	.02	.10
❑ 528 LeRoy Butler	.02	.10
❑ 529 Rob Burnett	.02	.10
❑ 530 Chris Chandler	.10	.30
❑ 531 Maury Buford	.02	.10
❑ 532 Mark Ingram	.02	.10
❑ 533 Mike Saxon	.02	.10
❑ 534 Bill Fralic	.02	.10
❑ 535 Craig Patterson RC	.02	.10
❑ 536 John Randle	.05	.15
❑ 537 Dwayne Harper	.02	.10
❑ 538 Chris Hakel RC	.02	.10
❑ 539 Maurice Hurst	.02	.10
❑ 540 Warren Powers UER	.02	.10
❑ 541 Will Wolford	.02	.10
❑ 542 Dennis Gibson	.02	.10
❑ 543 Jackie Slater	.02	.10
❑ 544 Floyd Turner	.02	.10
❑ 545 Guy McIntyre	.02	.10
❑ 546 Eric Green	.02	.10
❑ 547 Rohn Stark	.02	.10
❑ 548 William Fuller	.02	.10
❑ 549 Alvin Harper	.05	.15
❑ 550 Mark Clayton	.05	.15
❑ 551 Natu Tuatagaloa RC	.02	.10
❑ 552 Fred Barnett	.10	.30
❑ 553 Bob Whitfield RC	.02	.10
❑ 554 Courtney Hall	.02	.10
❑ 555 Brian Mitchell	.05	.15
❑ 556 Patrick Hunter	.02	.10
❑ 557 Rick Bryan	.02	.10
❑ 558 Anthony Carter	.05	.15
❑ 559 Jim Wahler	.02	.10
❑ 560 Joe Morris	.02	.10
❑ 561 Tony Zendejas	.02	.10
❑ 562 Mervyn Fernandez	.02	.10
❑ 563 Jamie Williams	.02	.10
❑ 564 Darrell Thompson	.02	.10
❑ 565 Adrian Cooper	.02	.10
❑ 566 Chris Goode	.02	.10
❑ 567 Jeff Davidson RC	.02	.10
❑ 568 James Hasty	.02	.10
❑ 569 Chris Mims RC	.02	.10
❑ 570 Ray Seals RC	.02	.10
❑ 571 Myron Guyton	.02	.10
❑ 572 Todd McNair	.02	.10
❑ 573 Andre Tippett	.02	.10
❑ 574 Kirby Jackson	.02	.10
❑ 575 Mel Gray	.05	.15
❑ 576 Stephone Paige	.02	.10
❑ 577 Scott Davis	.02	.10
❑ 578 John Gesek	.02	.10
❑ 579 Earnest Byner	.02	.10
❑ 580 John Friesz	.05	.15
❑ 581 Al Smith	.02	.10
❑ 582 Flipper Anderson	.02	.10
❑ 583 Amp Lee RC	.02	.10
❑ 584 Greg Lloyd	.05	.15
❑ 585 Cortez Kennedy	.05	.15
❑ 586 Keith Sims	.02	.10
❑ 587 Terry Allen	.10	.30
❑ 588 David Fulcher	.02	.10
❑ 589 Chris Hinton	.02	.10
❑ 590 Tim McDonald	.02	.10
❑ 591 Bruce Armstrong	.02	.10
❑ 592 Sterling Sharpe	.10	.30
❑ 593 Tom Rathman	.02	.10
❑ 594 Bill Brooks	.02	.10
❑ 595 Broderick Thomas	.02	.10
❑ 596 Jim Wilks	.02	.10
❑ 597 Tyrone Braxton UER	.02	.10
❑ 598 Checklist 301-400 UER	.02	.10
❑ 599 Checklist 401-500	.02	.10
❑ 600 Checklist 501-600	.02	.10
❑ 601 Andre Reed MC	.30	.75
❑ 602 Troy Aikman MC	2.00	4.00
❑ 603 Dan Marino MC	2.50	6.00

❑ 604 Randall Cunningham MC .30 .75
❑ 605 Jim Kelly MC .60 1.50
❑ 606 Deion Sanders MC .75 2.00
❑ 607 Junior Seau MC .60 1.50
❑ 608 Jerry Rice MC 2.00 4.00
❑ 609 Bruce Smith MC .30 .75
❑ 610 Lawrence Taylor MC .60 1.50
❑ 611 Todd Collins RC .20 .50
❑ 612 Ty Detmer .60 1.50
❑ 613 Browning Nagle .20 .50
❑ 614 Tony Sacca UER RC .20 .50
❑ 615 Boomer Esiason .30 .75
❑ 616 Billy Joe Tolliver .20 .50
❑ 617 Leslie O'Neal .30 .75
❑ 618 Mark Wheeler RC .20 .50
❑ 619 Eric Dickerson .30 .75
❑ 620 Phil Simms .30 .75
❑ 621 Troy Vincent RC .20 .50
❑ 622 Jason Hanson RC .30 .75
❑ 623 Andre Reed .30 .75
❑ 624 Russell Maryland .20 .50
❑ 625 Steve Emtman RC .20 .50
❑ 626 Sean Gilbert RC .30 .75
❑ 627 Dana Hall RC .20 .50
❑ 628 Dan McGwire .20 .50
❑ 629 Lewis Billups .20 .50
❑ 630 Darryl Williams RC .20 .50
❑ 631 Dwayne Sabb RC .20 .50
❑ 632 Mark Royals .20 .50
❑ 633 Cary Conklin .20 .50
❑ 634 Al Toon .30 .75
❑ 635 Junior Seau .60 1.50
❑ 636 Greg Skrepenak UER RC .20 .50
❑ 637 Deion Sanders 1.50 3.00
❑ 638 Steve DeOssie .20 .50
❑ 639 Randall Cunningham .60 1.50
❑ 640 Jim Kelly .60 1.50
❑ 641 Michael Brandon RC .20 .50
❑ 642 Clayton Holmes RC .20 .50
❑ 643 Webster Slaughter .20 .50
❑ 644 Ricky Proehl .20 .50
❑ 645 Jerry Rice 2.50 5.00
❑ 646 Carl Banks .20 .50
❑ 647 J.J.Birden .20 .50
❑ 648 Tracy Scroggins RC .20 .50
❑ 649 Alonzo Spellman RC .30 .75
❑ 650 Joe Montana 3.00 8.00
❑ 651 Courtney Hawkins RC .30 .75
❑ 652 Corey Widmer RC .20 .50
❑ 653 Robert Brooks RC 1.50 4.00
❑ 654 Darren Woodson RC .60 1.50
❑ 655 Derrick Fenner .20 .50
❑ 656 Steve Christie .20 .50
❑ 657 Chester McGlockton RC .30 .75
❑ 658 Steve Israel RC .20 .50
❑ 659 Robert Harris RC .20 .50
❑ 660 Dan Marino 3.00 8.00
❑ 661 Ed McCaffrey 2.00 5.00
❑ 662 Johnny Mitchell RC .20 .50
❑ 663 Timm Rosenbach .20 .50
❑ 664 Anthony Miller .30 .75
❑ 665 Merril Hoge .20 .50
❑ 666 Eugene Chung RC .20 .50
❑ 667 Rueben Mayes .20 .50
❑ 668 Martin Bayless .20 .50
❑ 669 Ashley Ambrose RC .60 1.50
❑ 670 Michael Cofer UER .20 .50
❑ 671 Shane Dronett RC .20 .50
❑ 672 Bernie Kosar .30 .75
❑ 673 Mike Singletary .30 .75
❑ 674 Mike Lodish RC .20 .50
❑ 675 Phillippi Sparks RC .20 .50
❑ 676 Joel Steed RC .20 .50
❑ 677 Kevin Fagan .20 .50
❑ 678 Randal Hill .20 .50
❑ 679 Ken O'Brien .20 .50
❑ 680 Lawrence Taylor .60 1.50
❑ 681 Harvey Williams .60 1.50
❑ 682 Quentin Coryatt RC .20 .50
❑ 683 Brett Favre 60.00 120.00
❑ 684 Robert Jones RC .20 .50
❑ 685 Michael Dean Perry .30 .75
❑ 686 Bruce Smith .60 1.50
❑ 687 Troy Auzenne RC .20 .50
❑ 688 Thomas McLemore RC .20 .50
❑ 689 Dale Carter RC .30 .75
❑ 690 Marc Boutte RC .20 .50
❑ 691 Jeff George .60 1.50
❑ 692 Dion Lambert RC .20 .50
❑ 693 Vaughn Dunbar RC .20 .50
❑ 694 Derek Brown TE RC .20 .50
❑ 695 Troy Aikman 2.50 5.00
❑ 696 John Fina RC .20 .50
❑ 697 Kevin Smith RC .20 .50
❑ 698 Corey Miller RC .20 .50
❑ 699 Lance Olberding RC .20 .50
❑ 700 Checklist 601-700 UER .20 .50
❑ P1 Promo Sheet Natl. 4.00 10.00
❑ P2 Promo Sheet Diam.Day 5.00 12.00

1993 Stadium Club

❑ COMPLETE SET (550) 15.00 40.00
❑ COMP.SERIES 1 (250) 10.00 25.00
❑ COMP.SERIES 2 (250) 6.00 15.00
❑ COMP.HIGH SERIES (50) 4.00 8.00
❑ COMP.HIGH FACT.SET (51) 5.00 12.00
❑ 1 Sterling Sharpe .07 .20
❑ 2 Chris Burkett .02 .10
❑ 3 Santana Dotson .07 .20
❑ 4 Michael Jackson .07 .20
❑ 5 Neal Anderson .02 .10
❑ 6 Bryan Cox .02 .10
❑ 7 Dennis Gibson .02 .10
❑ 8 Jeff Graham .07 .20
❑ 9 Roger Ruzek .02 .10
❑ 10 Duane Bickett .02 .10
❑ 11 Charles Mann .02 .10
❑ 12 Tommy Maddox .15 .40
❑ 13 Vaughn Dunbar .02 .10
❑ 14 Gary Plummer .02 .10
❑ 15 Chris Miller .07 .20
❑ 16 Chris Warren .07 .20
❑ 17 Alvin Harper .07 .20
❑ 18 Eric Dickerson .07 .20
❑ 19 Mike Jones .02 .10
❑ 20 Ernest Givins .07 .20
❑ 21 Natrone Means RC .15 .40
❑ 22 Doug Riesenberg .02 .10
❑ 23 Barry Word .02 .10
❑ 24 Sean Salisbury .02 .10
❑ 25 Derrick Fenner .02 .10
❑ 26 David Howard .02 .10
❑ 27 Mark Kelso .02 .10
❑ 28 Todd Lyght .02 .10
❑ 29 Dana Hall .02 .10
❑ 30 Eric Metcalf .07 .20
❑ 31 Jason Hanson .02 .10
❑ 32 Dwight Stone .02 .10
❑ 33 Johnny Mitchell .02 .10
❑ 34 Reggie Roby .02 .10
❑ 35 Terrell Buckley .02 .10
❑ 36 Steve McMichael .07 .20
❑ 37 Marty Carter .02 .10
❑ 38 Seth Joyner .02 .10
❑ 39 Rohn Stark .02 .10
❑ 40 Eric Curry RC .02 .10
❑ 41 Tommy Barnhardt .02 .10
❑ 42 Karl Mecklenburg .02 .10
❑ 43 Darion Conner .02 .10
❑ 44 Ronnie Harmon .02 .10
❑ 45 Cortez Kennedy .07 .20
❑ 46 Tim Brown .15 .40
❑ 47 Bill Lewis .02 .10
❑ 48 Randall McDaniel .05 .15
❑ 49 Curtis Duncan .02 .10
❑ 50 Troy Aikman .60 1.50
❑ 51 David Klingler .02 .10
❑ 52 Brent Jones .07 .20
❑ 53 Dave Krieg .07 .20
❑ 54 Bruce Smith .15 .40
❑ 55 Vincent Brown .02 .10
❑ 56 O.J.McDuffie RC .15 .40
❑ 57 Cleveland Gary .02 .10
❑ 58 Larry Centers RC .15 .40
❑ 59 Pepper Johnson .02 .10
❑ 60 Dan Marino 1.25 3.00
❑ 61 Robert Porcher .02 .10
❑ 62 Jim Harbaugh .15 .40
❑ 63 Sam Mills .02 .10
❑ 64 Gary Anderson RB .02 .10
❑ 65 Neil O'Donnell .07 .20
❑ 66 Keith Byars .02 .10
❑ 67 Jeff Herrod .02 .10
❑ 68 Marion Butts .02 .10
❑ 69 Terry McDaniel .02 .10
❑ 70 John Elway 1.25 3.00
❑ 71 Steve Broussard .02 .10
❑ 72 Kelvin Martin .02 .10
❑ 73 Tom Carter RC .07 .20
❑ 74 Bryce Paup .07 .20
❑ 75 Jim Kelly UER .07 .20
❑ 76 Bill Romanowski .02 .10
❑ 77 Andre Collins .02 .10
❑ 78 Mike Farr .02 .10
❑ 79 Henry Ellard .07 .20
❑ 80 Dale Carter .02 .10
❑ 81 Johnny Bailey .02 .10
❑ 82 Garrison Hearst RC .60 1.50
❑ 83 Brent Williams .02 .10
❑ 84 Ricardo McDonald .02 .10
❑ 85 Emmitt Smith 1.50 3.00
❑ 86 Vai Sikahema .02 .10
❑ 87 Jackie Harris .02 .10
❑ 88 Alonzo Spellman .02 .10
❑ 89 Mark Wheeler .02 .10
❑ 90 Dalton Hilliard .02 .10
❑ 91 Mark Higgs .02 .10
❑ 92 Aaron Wallace .02 .10
❑ 93 Earnest Byner .02 .10
❑ 94 Stanley Richard .02 .10
❑ 95 Cris Carter .15 .40
❑ 96 Bobby Houston RC .02 .10
❑ 97 Craig Heyward .07 .20
❑ 98 Bernie Kosar .07 .20
❑ 99 Mike Croel .02 .10
❑ 100 Deion Sanders .40 1.00
❑ 101 Warren Moon .07 .20
❑ 102 Christian Okoye .02 .10
❑ 103 Ricky Watters .15 .40
❑ 104 Eric Swann .07 .20
❑ 105 Rodney Hampton .07 .20
❑ 106 Daryl Johnston .07 .20
❑ 107 Andre Reed .07 .20
❑ 108 Jerome Bettis RC 4.00 8.00
❑ 109 Eugene Daniel .02 .10
❑ 110 Leonard Russell .07 .20
❑ 111 Darryl Williams .02 .10
❑ 112 Rod Woodson .15 .40
❑ 113 Boomer Esiason .07 .20
❑ 114 James Hasty .02 .10
❑ 115 Marc Boutte .02 .10
❑ 116 Tom Waddle .02 .10
❑ 117 Lawrence Dawsey .02 .10
❑ 118 Mark Collins .02 .10
❑ 119 Willie Gault .02 .10
❑ 120 Barry Sanders 1.00 2.50
❑ 121 Leroy Hoard .07 .20
❑ 122 Anthony Munoz .07 .20
❑ 123 Jesse Sapolu .02 .10
❑ 124 Art Monk .07 .20
❑ 125 Randal Hill .02 .10
❑ 126 John Offerdahl .02 .10
❑ 127 Carlos Jenkins .02 .10
❑ 128 Al Smith .02 .10
❑ 129 Michael Irvin .15 .40
❑ 130 Kenneth Davis .02 .10
❑ 131 Curtis Conway RC .30 .75
❑ 132 Steve Atwater .02 .10
❑ 133 Neil Smith .15 .40
❑ 134 Steve Everitt RC .02 .10
❑ 135 Chris Mims .02 .10
❑ 136 Rickey Jackson .02 .10
❑ 137 Edgar Bennett .15 .40
❑ 138 Mike Pritchard .07 .20
❑ 139 Richard Dent .07 .20
❑ 140 Barry Foster .07 .20
❑ 141 Eugene Robinson .02 .10
❑ 142 Jackie Slater .02 .10
❑ 143 Paul Gruber .02 .10
❑ 144 Rob Moore .07 .20
❑ 145 Robert Smith RC 1.00 2.50
❑ 146 Lorenzo White .02 .10
❑ 147 Tommy Vardell .02 .10
❑ 148 Dave Meggett .02 .10

Card	Low	High
❑ 149 Vince Workman	.02	.10
❑ 150 Terry Allen	.15	.40
❑ 151 Howie Long	.15	.40
❑ 152 Charles Haley	.07	.20
❑ 153 Pete Metzelaars	.02	.10
❑ 154 John Copeland RC	.07	.20
❑ 155 Aeneas Williams	.02	.10
❑ 156 Ricky Sanders	.02	.10
❑ 157 Andre Ware	.02	.10
❑ 158 Tony Paige	.02	.10
❑ 159 Jerome Henderson	.02	.10
❑ 160 Harold Green	.02	.10
❑ 161 Wymon Henderson	.02	.10
❑ 162 Andre Rison	.07	.20
❑ 163 Donald Evans	.02	.10
❑ 164 Todd Scott	.02	.10
❑ 165 Steve Emtman	.02	.10
❑ 166 William Fuller	.02	.10
❑ 167 Michael Dean Perry	.07	.20
❑ 168 Randall Cunningham	.15	.40
❑ 169 Toi Cook	.02	.10
❑ 170 Browning Nagle	.02	.10
❑ 171 Darryl Henley	.02	.10
❑ 172 George Teague RC	.07	.20
❑ 173 Derrick Thomas	.15	.40
❑ 174 Jay Novacek	.07	.20
❑ 175 Mark Carrier DB	.02	.10
❑ 176 Kevin Fagan	.02	.10
❑ 177 Nate Lewis	.02	.10
❑ 178 Courtney Hawkins	.02	.10
❑ 179 Robert Blackmon	.02	.10
❑ 180 Rick Mirer RC	.15	.40
❑ 181 Mike Lodish	.02	.10
❑ 182 Jarrod Bunch	.02	.10
❑ 183 Anthony Smith	.02	.10
❑ 184 Brian Noble	.02	.10
❑ 185 Eric Bieniemy	.02	.10
❑ 186 Keith Jackson	.07	.20
❑ 187 Eric Martin	.02	.10
❑ 188 Vance Johnson	.02	.10
❑ 189 Kevin Mack	.02	.10
❑ 190 Rich Camarillo	.02	.10
❑ 191 Ashley Ambrose	.02	.10
❑ 192 Ray Childress	.02	.10
❑ 193 Jim Arnold	.02	.10
❑ 194 Ricky Ervins	.02	.10
❑ 195 Gary Anderson K	.02	.10
❑ 196 Eric Allen	.02	.10
❑ 197 Roger Craig	.07	.20
❑ 198 Jon Vaughn	.02	.10
❑ 199 Tim McDonald	.02	.10
❑ 200 Broderick Thomas	.02	.10
❑ 201 Jessie Tuggle	.02	.10
❑ 202 Alonzo Mitz	.02	.10
❑ 203 Harvey Williams	.07	.20
❑ 204 Russell Maryland	.02	.10
❑ 205 Marvin Washington	.02	.10
❑ 206 Jim Everett	.07	.20
❑ 207 Trace Armstrong	.02	.10
❑ 208 Steve Young	.60	1.50
❑ 209 Tony Woods	.02	.10
❑ 210 Brett Favre	2.00	4.00
❑ 211 Nate Odomes	.02	.10
❑ 212 Ricky Proehl	.02	.10
❑ 213 Jim Dombrowski	.02	.10
❑ 214 Anthony Carter	.07	.20
❑ 215 Tracy Simien	.02	.10
❑ 216 Clay Matthews	.07	.20
❑ 217 Patrick Bates RC	.02	.10
❑ 218 Jeff George	.15	.40
❑ 219 David Fulcher	.02	.10
❑ 220 Phil Simms	.07	.20
❑ 221 Eugene Chung	.02	.10
❑ 222 Reggie Cobb	.02	.10
❑ 223 Jim Sweeney	.02	.10
❑ 224 Greg Lloyd	.07	.20
❑ 225 Sean Jones	.02	.10
❑ 226 Marvin Jones RC	.02	.10
❑ 227 Bill Brooks	.02	.10
❑ 228 Moe Gardner	.02	.10
❑ 229 Louis Oliver	.02	.10
❑ 230 Flipper Anderson	.02	.10
❑ 231 Marc Spindler	.02	.10
❑ 232 Jerry Rice	.75	2.00
❑ 233 Chip Lohmiller	.02	.10
❑ 234 Nolan Harrison	.02	.10
❑ 235 Heath Sherman	.02	.10
❑ 236 Reyna Thompson	.02	.10
❑ 237 Derrick Walker	.02	.10
❑ 238 Rufus Porter	.02	.10
❑ 239 Checklist 1-125	.02	.10
❑ 240 Checklist 126-250	.02	.10
❑ 241 John Elway MC	.60	1.50
❑ 242 Troy Aikman MC	.30	.75
❑ 243 Steve Emtman MC	.02	.10
❑ 244 Ricky Watters MC	.07	.20
❑ 245 Barry Foster MC	.02	.10
❑ 246 Dan Marino MC	.60	1.50
❑ 247 Reggie White MC	.07	.20
❑ 248 Thurman Thomas MC	.07	.20
❑ 249 Broderick Thomas MC	.02	.10
❑ 250 Joe Montana MC	.60	1.50
❑ 251 Tim Goad	.02	.10
❑ 252 Joe Nash	.02	.10
❑ 253 Anthony Johnson	.07	.20
❑ 254 Carl Pickens	.07	.20
❑ 255 Steve Beuerlein	.07	.20
❑ 256 Anthony Newman	.02	.10
❑ 257 Corey Miller	.02	.10
❑ 258 Steve DeBerg	.02	.10
❑ 259 Johnny Holland	.02	.10
❑ 260 Jerry Ball	.02	.10
❑ 261 Siupeli Malamala RC	.02	.10
❑ 262 Steve Wisniewski	.02	.10
❑ 263 Kelvin Pritchett	.02	.10
❑ 264 Chris Gardocki	.02	.10
❑ 265 Henry Thomas	.02	.10
❑ 266 Arthur Marshall RC	.02	.10
❑ 267 Quinn Early	.07	.20
❑ 268 Jonathan Hayes	.02	.10
❑ 269 Erric Pegram	.07	.20
❑ 270 Clyde Simmons	.02	.10
❑ 271 Eric Moten	.02	.10
❑ 272 Brian Mitchell	.07	.20
❑ 273 Adrian Cooper	.02	.10
❑ 274 Gaston Green	.02	.10
❑ 275 John Taylor	.07	.20
❑ 276 Jeff Uhlenhake	.02	.10
❑ 277 Phil Hansen	.02	.10
❑ 278A Kevin Williams ERR RC	.15	.40
❑ 278B Kevin Williams COR RC	.15	.40
❑ 279 Robert Massey	.02	.10
❑ 280A Drew Bledsoe ERR RC	3.00	8.00
❑ 280B Drew Bledsoe COR RC	2.00	5.00
❑ 281 Walter Reeves	.02	.10
❑ 282A Carlton Gray ERR RC	.08	.25
❑ 282B Carlton Gray COR RC	.05	.15
❑ 283 Derek Brown TE	.02	.10
❑ 284 Martin Mayhew	.02	.10
❑ 285 Sean Gilbert	.07	.20
❑ 286 Jessie Hester	.02	.10
❑ 287 Mark Clayton	.02	.10
❑ 288 Blair Thomas	.02	.10
❑ 289 J.J. Birden	.02	.10
❑ 290 Shannon Sharpe	.15	.40
❑ 291 Richard Fain RC	.02	.10
❑ 292 Gene Atkins	.02	.10
❑ 293 Burt Grossman	.02	.10
❑ 294 Chris Doleman	.02	.10
❑ 295 Pat Swilling	.02	.10
❑ 296 Mike Kenn	.02	.10
❑ 297 Merril Hoge	.02	.10
❑ 298 Don Mosebar	.02	.10
❑ 299 Kevin Smith	.07	.20
❑ 300 Darrell Green	.02	.10
❑ 301A Dan Footman ERR RC	.08	.25
❑ 301B Dan Footman COR RC	.05	.15
❑ 302 Vestee Jackson	.02	.10
❑ 303 Carwell Gardner	.02	.10
❑ 304 Amp Lee	.02	.10
❑ 305 Bruce Matthews	.02	.10
❑ 306 Antone Davis	.02	.10
❑ 307 Dean Biasucci	.02	.10
❑ 308 Maurice Hurst	.02	.10
❑ 309 John Kasay	.02	.10
❑ 310 Lawrence Taylor	.07	.20
❑ 311 Ken Harvey	.02	.10
❑ 312 Willie Davis	.07	.20
❑ 313 Tony Bennett	.02	.10
❑ 314 Jay Schroeder	.02	.10
❑ 315 Darren Perry	.02	.10
❑ 316A Troy Drayton ERR RC	.08	.25
❑ 316B Troy Drayton COR RC	.05	.15
❑ 317A Dan Williams ERR RC	.08	.25
❑ 317B Dan Williams COR RC	.05	.15
❑ 318 Michael Haynes	.07	.20
❑ 319 Renaldo Turnbull	.02	.10
❑ 320 Junior Seau	.15	.40
❑ 321 Ray Crockett	.02	.10
❑ 322 Will Furrer	.02	.10
❑ 323 Byron Evans	.02	.10
❑ 324 Jim McMahon	.07	.20
❑ 325 Robert Jones	.02	.10
❑ 326 Eric Davis	.02	.10
❑ 327 Jeff Cross	.02	.10
❑ 328 Kyle Clifton	.02	.10
❑ 329 Haywood Jeffires	.07	.20
❑ 330 Jeff Hostetler	.07	.20
❑ 331 Darryl Talley	.02	.10
❑ 332 Keith McCants	.02	.10
❑ 333 Mo Lewis	.02	.10
❑ 334 Matt Stover	.02	.10
❑ 335 Ferrell Edmunds	.02	.10
❑ 336 Matt Brock	.02	.10
❑ 337 Ernie Mills	.02	.10
❑ 338 Shane Dronett	.02	.10
❑ 339 Brad Muster	.02	.10
❑ 340 Jesse Solomon	.02	.10
❑ 341 John Randle	.07	.20
❑ 342 Chris Spielman	.07	.20
❑ 343 David Whitmore	.02	.10
❑ 344 Glenn Parker	.02	.10
❑ 345 Marco Coleman	.02	.10
❑ 346 Kenneth Gant	.02	.10
❑ 347 Cris Dishman	.02	.10
❑ 348 Kenny Walker	.02	.10
❑ 349A Roosevelt Potts ERR RC	.08	.25
❑ 349B Roosevelt Potts COR RC	.05	.15
❑ 350 Reggie White	.15	.40
❑ 351 Gerald Robinson	.02	.10
❑ 352 Mark Rypien	.02	.10
❑ 353 Stan Humphries	.07	.20
❑ 354 Chris Singleton	.02	.10
❑ 355 Herschel Walker	.07	.20
❑ 356 Ron Hall	.02	.10
❑ 357 Ethan Horton	.02	.10
❑ 358 Anthony Pleasant	.02	.10
❑ 359A Thomas Smith ERR RC	.08	.25
❑ 359B Thomas Smith COR RC	.05	.15
❑ 360 Audray McMillian	.02	.10
❑ 361 D.J. Johnson	.02	.10
❑ 362 Ron Heller	.02	.10
❑ 363 Bern Brostek	.02	.10
❑ 364 Ronnie Lott	.07	.20
❑ 365 Reggie Johnson	.02	.10
❑ 366 Lin Elliott	.02	.10
❑ 367 Lemuel Stinson	.02	.10
❑ 368 William White	.02	.10
❑ 369 Ernie Jones	.02	.10
❑ 370 Tom Rathman	.02	.10
❑ 371 Tommy Kane	.02	.10
❑ 372 David Brandon	.02	.10
❑ 373 Lee Johnson	.02	.10
❑ 374 Wade Wilson	.02	.10
❑ 375 Nick Lowery	.02	.10
❑ 376 Bubba McDowell	.02	.10
❑ 377A Wayne Simmons ERR RC	.08	.25
❑ 377B Wayne Simmons COR RC	.05	.15
❑ 378 Calvin Williams	.07	.20
❑ 379 Courtney Hall	.02	.10
❑ 380 Troy Vincent	.02	.10
❑ 381 Tim McGee	.02	.10
❑ 382 Russell Freeman RC	.02	.10
❑ 383 Steve Tasker	.07	.20
❑ 384A Michael Strahan ERR RC	1.25	3.00
❑ 384B Michael Strahan COR RC	1.00	2.50
❑ 385 Greg Skrepenak	.02	.10
❑ 386 Jake Reed	.07	.20
❑ 387 Pete Stoyanovich	.02	.10
❑ 388 Levon Kirkland	.02	.10
❑ 389 Mel Gray	.07	.20
❑ 390 Brian Washington	.02	.10
❑ 391 Don Griffin	.02	.10
❑ 392 Desmond Howard	.07	.20
❑ 393 Luis Sharpe	.02	.10
❑ 394 Mike Johnson	.02	.10
❑ 395 Andre Tippett	.02	.10
❑ 396 Donnell Woolford	.02	.10
❑ 397A Demetrius DuBose ERR RC	.08	.25
❑ 397B Demetrius DuBose COR RC	.05	.15
❑ 398 Pat Terrell	.02	.10
❑ 399 Todd McNair	.02	.10
❑ 400 Ken Norton	.07	.20
❑ 401 Keith Hamilton	.02	.10
❑ 402 Andy Heck	.02	.10
❑ 403 Jeff Gossett	.02	.10
❑ 404 Dexter McNabb	.02	.10

Card		
❑ 405 Richmond Webb	.02	.10
❑ 406 Irving Fryar	.07	.20
❑ 407 Brian Hansen	.02	.10
❑ 408 David Little	.02	.10
❑ 409A Glyn Milburn ERR RC	.15	.40
❑ 409B Glyn Milburn COR RC	.07	.20
❑ 410 Doug Dawson	.02	.10
❑ 411 Scott Mersereau	.02	.10
❑ 412 Don Beebe	.02	.10
❑ 413 Vaughan Johnson	.02	.10
❑ 414 Jack Del Rio	.02	.10
❑ 415A Darrien Gordon ERR RC	.08	.25
❑ 415B Darrien Gordon COR RC	.05	.15
❑ 416 Mark Schlereth	.02	.10
❑ 417 Lomas Brown	.02	.10
❑ 418 William Thomas	.02	.10
❑ 419 James Francis	.02	.10
❑ 420 Quentin Coryatt	.07	.20
❑ 421 Tyji Armstrong	.02	.10
❑ 422 Hugh Millen	.02	.10
❑ 423 Adrian White RC	.02	.10
❑ 424 Eddie Anderson	.02	.10
❑ 425 Mark Ingram	.02	.10
❑ 426 Ken O'Brien	.02	.10
❑ 427 Simon Fletcher	.02	.10
❑ 428 Tim McKyer	.02	.10
❑ 429 Leonard Marshall	.02	.10
❑ 430 Eric Green	.02	.10
❑ 431 Leonard Harris	.02	.10
❑ 432 Darin Jordan RC	.02	.10
❑ 433 Erik Howard	.02	.10
❑ 434 David Lang	.02	.10
❑ 435 Eric Turner	.02	.10
❑ 436 Michael Cofer	.02	.10
❑ 437 Jeff Bryant	.02	.10
❑ 438 Charles McRae	.02	.10
❑ 439 Henry Jones	.02	.10
❑ 440 Joe Montana	1.25	3.00
❑ 441 Morten Andersen	.02	.10
❑ 442 Jeff Jaeger	.02	.10
❑ 443 Leslie O'Neal	.07	.20
❑ 444 LeRoy Butler	.02	.10
❑ 445 Steve Jordan	.02	.10
❑ 446 Brad Edwards	.02	.10
❑ 447 J.B. Brown	.02	.10
❑ 448 Kerry Cash	.02	.10
❑ 449 Mark Tuinei	.02	.10
❑ 450 Rodney Peete	.02	.10
❑ 451 Sheldon White	.02	.10
❑ 452 Wesley Carroll	.02	.10
❑ 453 Brad Baxter	.02	.10
❑ 454 Mike Pitts	.02	.10
❑ 455 Greg Montgomery	.02	.10
❑ 456 Kenny Davidson	.02	.10
❑ 457 Scott Fulhage	.02	.10
❑ 458 Greg Townsend	.02	.10
❑ 459 Rod Bernstine	.02	.10
❑ 460 Gary Clark	.07	.20
❑ 461 Hardy Nickerson	.07	.20
❑ 462 Sean Landeta	.02	.10
❑ 463 Rob Burnett	.02	.10
❑ 464 Fred Barnett	.07	.20
❑ 465 John L. Williams	.02	.10
❑ 466 Anthony Miller	.07	.20
❑ 467 Roman Phifer	.02	.10
❑ 468 Rich Moran	.02	.10
❑ 469A Willie Roaf ERR RC	.08	.25
❑ 469B Willie Roaf COR RC	.05	.15
❑ 470 William Perry	.07	.20
❑ 471 Marcus Allen	.15	.40
❑ 472 Carl Lee	.02	.10
❑ 473 Kurt Gouveia	.02	.10
❑ 474 Jarvis Williams	.02	.10
❑ 475 Alfred Williams	.02	.10
❑ 476 Mark Stepnoski	.02	.10
❑ 477 Steve Wallace	.02	.10
❑ 478 Pat Harlow	.02	.10
❑ 479 Chip Banks	.02	.10
❑ 480 Cornelius Bennett	.07	.20
❑ 481A Ryan McNeil RC ERR	.05	.15
❑ 481B Ryan McNeil RC COR	.15	.40
❑ 482 Norm Johnson	.02	.10
❑ 483 Dermontti Dawson	.02	.10
❑ 484 Dwayne White	.02	.10
❑ 485 Derek Russell	.02	.10
❑ 486 Lionel Washington	.02	.10
❑ 487 Eric Hill	.02	.10
❑ 488 Micheal Barrow RC	.15	.40
❑ 489 Checklist 251-375 UER	.02	.10
❑ 490 Checklist 376-500 UER	.02	.10
❑ 491 Emmitt Smith MC	.60	1.50
❑ 492 Derrick Thomas MC	.07	.20
❑ 493 Deion Sanders MC	.15	.40
❑ 494 Randall Cunningham MC	.07	.20
❑ 495 Sterling Sharpe MC	.07	.20
❑ 496 Barry Sanders MC	.50	1.25
❑ 497 Thurman Thomas MC	.07	.20
❑ 498 Brett Favre MC	.75	2.00
❑ 499 Vaughan Johnson MC	.02	.10
❑ 500 Steve Young MC	.30	.75
❑ 501 Marvin Jones MC	.02	.10
❑ 502 Reggie Brooks MC RC	.07	.20
❑ 503 Eric Curry MC	.02	.10
❑ 504 Drew Bledsoe MC	.75	2.00
❑ 505 Glyn Milburn MC	.07	.20
❑ 506 Jerome Bettis MC	1.50	4.00
❑ 507 Robert Smith MC	.40	1.00
❑ 508 Dana Stubblefield MC RC	.15	.40
❑ 509 Tom Carter MC	.07	.20
❑ 510 Rick Mirer MC	.15	.40
❑ 511 Russell Copeland RC	.07	.20
❑ 512 Deon Figures RC	.02	.10
❑ 513 Tony McGee RC	.07	.20
❑ 514 Derrick Lassic RC	.02	.10
❑ 515 Everett Lindsay RC	.02	.10
❑ 516 Derek Brown RBK RC	.02	.10
❑ 517 Harold Alexander RC	.02	.10
❑ 518 Tom Scott RC	.02	.10
❑ 519 Elvis Grbac RC	1.25	3.00
❑ 520 Terry Kirby RC	.15	.40
❑ 521 Doug Pelfrey RC	.02	.10
❑ 522 Horace Copeland RC	.07	.20
❑ 523 Irv Smith RC	.02	.10
❑ 524 Lincoln Kennedy RC	.02	.10
❑ 525 Jason Elam RC	.15	.40
❑ 526 Qadry Ismail RC	.15	.40
❑ 527 Artie Smith RC	.02	.10
❑ 528 Tyrone Hughes RC	.07	.20
❑ 529 Lance Gunn RC	.02	.10
❑ 530 Vincent Brisby RC	.15	.40
❑ 531 Patrick Robinson RC	.02	.10
❑ 532 Rocket Ismail	.07	.20
❑ 533 Willie Beamon RC	.02	.10
❑ 534 Vaughn Hebron RC	.02	.10
❑ 535 Darren Drozdov RC	.15	.40
❑ 536 James Jett RC	.15	.40
❑ 537 Michael Bates RC	.02	.10
❑ 538 Tom Rouen RC	.02	.10
❑ 539 Michael Husted RC	.02	.10
❑ 540 Greg Robinson RC	.02	.10
❑ 541 Carl Banks	.02	.10
❑ 542 Kevin Greene	.07	.20
❑ 543 Scott Mitchell	.15	.40
❑ 544 Michael Brooks	.02	.10
❑ 545 Shane Conlan	.02	.10
❑ 546 Vinny Testaverde	.07	.20
❑ 547 Robert Delpino	.02	.10
❑ 548 Bill Fralic	.02	.10
❑ 549 Carlton Bailey	.02	.10
❑ 550 Johnny Johnson	.02	.10
❑ NNO Jerry Rice RB	4.00	10.00
❑ P1 Promo Sheet	2.00	5.00

1994 Stadium Club

Card		
❑ COMPLETE SET (630)	25.00	60.00
❑ COMP.SERIES 1 (270)	10.00	25.00
❑ COMP.SERIES 2 (270)	10.00	25.00
❑ COMP.HIGH SERIES (90)	5.00	10.00
❑ 1 Dan Wilkinson RC	.07	.20
❑ 2 Chip Lohmiller	.02	.10
❑ 3 Roosevelt Potts	.02	.10
❑ 4 Martin Mayhew	.02	.10
❑ 5 Shane Conlan	.02	.10
❑ 6 Sam Adams RC	.07	.20
❑ 7 Mike Kenn	.02	.10
❑ 8 Tim Goad	.02	.10
❑ 9 Tony Jones T	.02	.10
❑ 10 Ronald Moore	.02	.10
❑ 11 Mark Bortz	.02	.10
❑ 12 Darren Carrington	.02	.10
❑ 13 Eric Martin	.02	.10
❑ 14 Eric Allen	.02	.10
❑ 15 Aaron Glenn RC	.15	.40
❑ 16 Bryan Cox	.02	.10
❑ 17 Levon Kirkland	.02	.10
❑ 18 Qadry Ismail	.15	.40
❑ 19 Shane Dronett	.02	.10
❑ 20 Chris Spielman	.07	.20
❑ 21 Rob Fredrickson RC	.07	.20
❑ 22 Wayne Simmons	.02	.10
❑ 23 Glenn Montgomery	.02	.10
❑ 24 Jason Sehorn RC	.25	.60
❑ 25 Nick Lowery	.02	.10
❑ 26 Dennis Brown	.02	.10
❑ 27 Kenneth Davis	.02	.10
❑ 28 Shante Carver RC	.02	.10
❑ 29 Ryan Yarborough RC	.02	.10
❑ 30 Cortez Kennedy	.07	.20
❑ 31 Anthony Pleasant	.02	.10
❑ 32 Jessie Tuggle	.02	.10
❑ 33 Herschel Walker	.07	.20
❑ 34 Andre Collins	.02	.10
❑ 35 William Floyd RC	.15	.40
❑ 36 Harold Green	.02	.10
❑ 37 Courtney Hawkins	.02	.10
❑ 38 Curtis Conway	.15	.40
❑ 39 Ben Coates	.07	.20
❑ 40 Natrone Means	.15	.40
❑ 41 Eric Hill	.02	.10
❑ 42 Keith Kartz	.02	.10
❑ 43 Alexander Wright	.02	.10
❑ 44 Willie Roaf	.02	.10
❑ 45 Vencie Glenn	.02	.10
❑ 46 Ronnie Lott	.07	.20
❑ 47 George Koonce	.02	.10
❑ 48 Rod Woodson	.07	.20
❑ 49 Tim Grunhard	.02	.10
❑ 50 Cody Carlson	.02	.10
❑ 51 Bryant Young RC	.25	.60
❑ 52 Jay Novacek	.07	.20
❑ 53 Darryl Talley	.02	.10
❑ 54 Harry Colon	.02	.10
❑ 55 Dave Meggett	.02	.10
❑ 56 Aubrey Beavers RC	.02	.10
❑ 57 James Folston	.02	.10
❑ 58 Willie Davis	.07	.20
❑ 59 Jason Elam	.07	.20
❑ 60 Eric Metcalf	.07	.20
❑ 61 Bruce Armstrong	.02	.10
❑ 62 Ron Heller	.02	.10
❑ 63 LeRoy Butler	.02	.10
❑ 64 Terry Obee	.02	.10
❑ 65 Kurt Gouveia	.02	.10
❑ 66 Pierce Holt	.02	.10
❑ 67 David Alexander	.02	.10
❑ 68 Deral Boykin	.02	.10
❑ 69 Carl Pickens	.07	.20
❑ 70 Broderick Thomas	.02	.10
❑ 71 Barry Sanders CT	.50	1.25
❑ 72 Qadry Ismail CT	.15	.40
❑ 73 Thurman Thomas CT	.15	.40
❑ 74 Junior Seau	.15	.40
❑ 75 Vinny Testaverde	.07	.20
❑ 76 Tyrone Hughes	.07	.20
❑ 77 Nate Newton	.02	.10
❑ 78 Eric Swann	.07	.20
❑ 79 Brad Baxter	.02	.10
❑ 80 Dana Stubblefield	.07	.20
❑ 81 Jumbo Elliott	.02	.10
❑ 82 Steve Wisniewski	.02	.10
❑ 83 Eddie Robinson	.02	.10
❑ 84 Isaac Davis	.02	.10
❑ 85 Cris Carter	.25	.60
❑ 86 Mel Gray	.02	.10
❑ 87 Cornelius Bennett	.07	.20
❑ 88 Neil O'Donnell	.15	.40
❑ 89 Jon Hand	.02	.10
❑ 90 John Elway	1.25	3.00
❑ 91 Bill Hitchcock	.02	.10
❑ 92 Neil Smith	.07	.20
❑ 93 Joe Johnson RC	.02	.10
❑ 94 Edgar Bennett	.15	.40
❑ 95 Vincent Brown	.02	.10
❑ 96 Tommy Vardell	.02	.10

❑ 97 Donnell Woolford .02 .10
❑ 98 Lincoln Kennedy .02 .10
❑ 99 O.J.McDuffie .15 .40
❑ 100 Heath Shuler RC .15 .40
❑ 101 Jerry Rice BO .30 .75
❑ 102 Erik Williams BO .02 .10
❑ 103 Randall McDaniel BO .05 .15
❑ 104 Dermontti Dawson BO .02 .10
❑ 105 Nate Newton BO .02 .10
❑ 106 Harris Barton BO .02 .10
❑ 107 Shannon Sharpe BO .07 .20
❑ 108 Sterling Sharpe BO .07 .20
❑ 109 Steve Young BO .25 .60
❑ 110 Emmitt Smith BO .50 1.25
❑ 111 Thurman Thomas BO .15 .40
❑ 112 Kyle Clifton .02 .10
❑ 113 Desmond Howard .07 .20
❑ 114 Quinn Early .07 .20
❑ 115 David Klingler .02 .10
❑ 116 Bern Brostek .02 .10
❑ 117 Gary Clark .07 .20
❑ 118 Courtney Hall .02 .10
❑ 119 Joe King .02 .10
❑ 120 Quentin Coryatt .02 .10
❑ 121 Johnnie Morton RC .75 2.00
❑ 122 Andre Reed .07 .20
❑ 123 Eric Davis .02 .10
❑ 124 Jack Del Rio .02 .10
❑ 125 Greg Lloyd .07 .20
❑ 126 Bubba McDowell .02 .10
❑ 127 Mark Jackson .02 .10
❑ 128 Jeff Jaeger .02 .10
❑ 129 Chris Warren .07 .20
❑ 130 Tom Waddle .02 .10
❑ 131 Tony Smith RB .02 .10
❑ 132 Todd Collins .02 .10
❑ 133 Mark Bavaro .02 .10
❑ 134 Joe Phillips .02 .10
❑ 135 Chris Jacke .02 .10
❑ 136 Glyn Milburn .07 .20
❑ 137 Keith Jackson .02 .10
❑ 138 Steve Tovar .02 .10
❑ 139 Tim Johnson .02 .10
❑ 140 Brian Washington .02 .10
❑ 141 Troy Drayton .02 .10
❑ 142 Dewayne Washington RC .07 .20
❑ 143 Erik Williams .02 .10
❑ 144 Eric Turner .02 .10
❑ 145 John Taylor .07 .20
❑ 146 Richard Cooper .02 .10
❑ 147 Van Malone .02 .10
❑ 148 Tim Ruddy RC .02 .10
❑ 149 Henry Jones .02 .10
❑ 150 Tim Brown .15 .40
❑ 151 Stan Humphries .07 .20
❑ 152 Harry Newsome .02 .10
❑ 153 Craig Erickson .02 .10
❑ 154 Gary Anderson K .02 .10
❑ 155 Ray Childress .02 .10
❑ 156 Howard Cross .02 .10
❑ 157 Heath Sherman .02 .10
❑ 158 Terrell Buckley .02 .10
❑ 159 J.B. Brown .02 .10
❑ 160 Joe Montana 1.25 3.00
❑ 161 David Wyman .02 .10
❑ 162 Norm Johnson .02 .10
❑ 163 Rod Stephens .02 .10
❑ 164 Willie McGinest RC .15 .40
❑ 165 Barry Sanders 1.00 2.50
❑ 166 Marc Logan .02 .10
❑ 167 Anthony Newman .02 .10
❑ 168 Russell Maryland .02 .10
❑ 169 Luis Sharpe .02 .10
❑ 170 Jim Kelly .15 .40
❑ 171 Tre Johnson RC .02 .10
❑ 172 Johnny Mitchell .02 .10
❑ 173 David Palmer RC .15 .40
❑ 174 Bob Dahl .02 .10
❑ 175 Aaron Wallace .02 .10
❑ 176 Chris Gardocki .02 .10
❑ 177 Hardy Nickerson .07 .20
❑ 178 Jeff Query .02 .10
❑ 179 Leslie O'Neal .02 .10
❑ 180 Kevin Greene .07 .20
❑ 181 Alonzo Spellman .02 .10
❑ 182 Reggie Brooks .07 .20
❑ 183 Dana Stubblefield .07 .20
❑ 184 Tyrone Hughes .07 .20
❑ 185 Drew Bledsoe GE .15 .40
❑ 186 Ronald Moore GE .02 .10
❑ 187 Jason Elam GE .02 .10
❑ 188 Rick Mirer GE .15 .40
❑ 189 Willie Roaf GE .02 .10
❑ 190 Jerome Bettis GE .15 .40
❑ 191 Brad Hopkins .02 .10
❑ 192 Derek Brown RBK .02 .10
❑ 193 Nolan Harrison .02 .10
❑ 194 John Randle .07 .20
❑ 195 Carlton Bailey .02 .10
❑ 196 Kevin Williams WR .07 .20
❑ 197 Greg Hill RC .15 .40
❑ 198 Mark McMillian .02 .10
❑ 199 Brad Edwards .02 .10
❑ 200 Dan Marino 1.25 3.00
❑ 201 Ricky Watters .07 .20
❑ 202 George Teague .02 .10
❑ 203 Steve Beuerlein .07 .20
❑ 204 Jeff Burris RC .07 .20
❑ 205 Steve Atwater .02 .10
❑ 206 John Thierry RC .02 .10
❑ 207 Patrick Hunter .02 .10
❑ 208 Wayne Gandy .02 .10
❑ 209 Derrick Moore .02 .10
❑ 210 Phil Simms .07 .20
❑ 211 Kirk Lowdermilk .02 .10
❑ 212 Patrick Robinson .02 .10
❑ 213 Kevin Mitchell .02 .10
❑ 214 Jonathan Hayes .02 .10
❑ 215 Michael Dean Perry .07 .20
❑ 216 John Fina .02 .10
❑ 217 Anthony Smith .02 .10
❑ 218 Paul Gruber .02 .10
❑ 219 Carnell Lake .02 .10
❑ 220 Carl Lee .02 .10
❑ 221 Steve Christie .02 .10
❑ 222 Greg Montgomery .02 .10
❑ 223 Reggie Brooks .07 .20
❑ 224 Derrick Thomas .15 .40
❑ 225 Eric Metcalf .07 .20
❑ 226 Michael Haynes .07 .20
❑ 227 Bobby Hebert .02 .10
❑ 228 Tyrone Hughes .07 .20
❑ 229 Donald Frank .02 .10
❑ 230 Vaughan Johnson .02 .10
❑ 231 Eric Thomas .02 .10
❑ 232 Ernest Givins .07 .20
❑ 233 Charles Haley .07 .20
❑ 234 Darrell Green .02 .10
❑ 235 Harold Alexander .02 .10
❑ 236 Dwayne Sabb .02 .10
❑ 237 Harris Barton .02 .10
❑ 238 Randall Cunningham .15 .40
❑ 239 Ray Buchanan .02 .10
❑ 240 Sterling Sharpe .07 .20
❑ 241 Chris Mims .02 .10
❑ 242 Mark Carrier DB .02 .10
❑ 243 Ricky Proehl .02 .10
❑ 244 Michael Brooks .02 .10
❑ 245 Sean Gilbert .02 .10
❑ 246 David Lutz .02 .10
❑ 247 Kelvin Martin .02 .10
❑ 248 Scottie Graham RC .07 .20
❑ 249 Irving Fryar .07 .20
❑ 250 Ricardo McDonald .02 .10
❑ 251 Marvcus Patton .02 .10
❑ 252 Errict Rhett RC .15 .40
❑ 253 Winston Moss .02 .10
❑ 254 Rod Bernstine .02 .10
❑ 255 Terry Wooden .02 .10
❑ 256 Antonio Langham RC .07 .20
❑ 257 Tommy Barnhardt .02 .10
❑ 258 Marvin Washington .02 .10
❑ 259 Bo Orlando .02 .10
❑ 260 Marcus Allen .15 .40
❑ 261 Mario Bates RC .15 .40
❑ 262 Marco Coleman .02 .10
❑ 263 Doug Riesenberg .02 .10
❑ 264 Jesse Sapolu .02 .10
❑ 265 Dermontti Dawson .02 .10
❑ 266 Fernando Smith RC .02 .10
❑ 267 David Szott .02 .10
❑ 268 Steve Christie .02 .10
❑ 269 Bruce Matthews .02 .10
❑ 270 Michael Irvin .15 .40
❑ 271 Seth Joyner .02 .10
❑ 272 Santana Dotson .07 .20
❑ 273 Vincent Brisby .07 .20
❑ 274 Rohn Stark .02 .10
❑ 275 John Copeland .02 .10
❑ 276 Toby Wright .02 .10
❑ 277 David Griggs .02 .10
❑ 278 Aaron Taylor .02 .10
❑ 279 Chris Doleman .02 .10
❑ 280 Reggie Brooks .07 .20
❑ 281 Flipper Anderson .02 .10
❑ 282 Alvin Harper .07 .20
❑ 283 Chris Hinton .02 .10
❑ 284 Kelvin Pritchett .02 .10
❑ 285 Russell Copeland .02 .10
❑ 286 Dwight Stone .02 .10
❑ 287 Jeff Gossett .02 .10
❑ 288 Larry Allen RC .15 .40
❑ 289 Kevin Mawae RC .15 .40
❑ 290 Mark Collins .02 .10
❑ 291 Chris Zorich .02 .10
❑ 292 Vince Buck .02 .10
❑ 293 Gene Atkins .02 .10
❑ 294 Webster Slaughter .02 .10
❑ 295 Steve Young .50 1.25
❑ 296 Dan Williams .02 .10
❑ 297 Jessie Armstead .02 .10
❑ 298 Victor Bailey .02 .10
❑ 299 John Carney .02 .10
❑ 300 Emmitt Smith 1.00 2.50
❑ 301 Bucky Brooks RC .02 .10
❑ 302 Mo Lewis .02 .10
❑ 303 Eugene Daniel .02 .10
❑ 304 Tyji Armstrong .02 .10
❑ 305 Eugene Chung .02 .10
❑ 306 Rocket Ismail .07 .20
❑ 307 Sean Jones .02 .10
❑ 308 Rick Cunningham .02 .10
❑ 309 Ken Harvey .02 .10
❑ 310 Jeff George .15 .40
❑ 311 Jon Vaughn .02 .10
❑ 312 Roy Barker RC .02 .10
❑ 313 Micheal Barrow .02 .10
❑ 314 Ryan McNeil .02 .10
❑ 315 Pete Stoyanovich .02 .10
❑ 316 Darryl Williams .02 .10
❑ 317 Renaldo Turnbull .02 .10
❑ 318 Eric Green .02 .10
❑ 319 Nate Lewis .02 .10
❑ 320 Mike Flores .02 .10
❑ 321 Derek Russell .02 .10
❑ 322 Marcus Spears RC .02 .10
❑ 323 Corey Miller .02 .10
❑ 324 Derrick Thomas .15 .40
❑ 325 Steve Everitt .02 .10
❑ 326 Brent Jones .07 .20
❑ 327 Marshall Faulk RC 2.50 6.00
❑ 328 Don Beebe .02 .10
❑ 329 Harry Swayne .02 .10
❑ 330 Boomer Esiason .07 .20
❑ 331 Don Mosebar .02 .10
❑ 332 Isaac Bruce RC 2.00 5.00
❑ 333 Rickey Jackson .02 .10
❑ 334 Daryl Johnston .07 .20
❑ 335 Lorenzo Lynch .02 .10
❑ 336 Brian Blades .07 .20
❑ 337 Michael Timpson .02 .10
❑ 338 Reggie Cobb .02 .10
❑ 339 Joe Walter .02 .10
❑ 340 Barry Foster .02 .10
❑ 341 Richmond Webb .02 .10
❑ 342 Pat Swilling .02 .10
❑ 343 Shaun Gayle .02 .10
❑ 344 Reggie Roby .02 .10
❑ 345 Chris Calloway .02 .10
❑ 346 Doug Dawson .02 .10
❑ 347 Rob Burnett .02 .10
❑ 348 Dana Hall .02 .10
❑ 349 Horace Copeland .02 .10
❑ 350 Shannon Sharpe .07 .20
❑ 351 Rich Miano .02 .10
❑ 352 Henry Thomas .02 .10
❑ 353 Dan Saleaumua .02 .10
❑ 354 Kevin Ross .02 .10
❑ 355 Morten Andersen .02 .10
❑ 356 Anthony Blaylock .02 .10
❑ 357 Stanley Richard .02 .10
❑ 358 Albert Lewis .02 .10
❑ 359 Darren Woodson .07 .20
❑ 360 Drew Bledsoe .40 1.00
❑ 361 Eric Mahlum .02 .10
❑ 362 Trent Dilfer RC .60 1.50
❑ 363 William Roberts .02 .10

❑ 364 Robert Brooks .15 .40
❑ 365 Jason Hanson .02 .10
❑ 366 Troy Vincent .02 .10
❑ 367 William Thomas .02 .10
❑ 368 Lonnie Johnson RC .02 .10
❑ 369 Jamir Miller RC .07 .20
❑ 370 Michael Jackson .07 .20
❑ 371 Charlie Ward CT RC .15 .40
❑ 372 Shannon Sharpe CT .07 .20
❑ 373 Jackie Slater CT .02 .10
❑ 374 Steve Young CT .25 .60
❑ 375 Bobby Wilson .02 .10
❑ 376 Paul Frase .02 .10
❑ 377 Dale Carter .02 .10
❑ 378 Robert Delpino .02 .10
❑ 379 Bert Emanuel RC .15 .40
❑ 380 Rick Mirer .15 .40
❑ 381 Carlos Jenkins .02 .10
❑ 382 Gary Brown .02 .10
❑ 383 Doug Pelfrey .02 .10
❑ 384 Dexter Carter .02 .10
❑ 385 Chris Miller .02 .10
❑ 386 Charles Johnson RC .15 .40
❑ 387 James Joseph .02 .10
❑ 388 Darrin Smith .02 .10
❑ 389 James Jett .02 .10
❑ 390 Junior Seau .15 .40
❑ 391 Chris Slade .02 .10
❑ 392 Jim Harbaugh .15 .40
❑ 393 Herman Moore .15 .40
❑ 394 Thomas Randolph RC .02 .10
❑ 395 Lamar Thomas .02 .10
❑ 396 Reggie Rivers .02 .10
❑ 397 Larry Centers .15 .40
❑ 398 Chad Brown .02 .10
❑ 399 Terry Kirby .15 .40
❑ 400 Bruce Smith .15 .40
❑ 401 Keenan McCardell RC .75 2.00
❑ 402 Tim McDonald .02 .10
❑ 403 Robert Smith .15 .40
❑ 404 Matt Brock .02 .10
❑ 405 Tony McGee .02 .10
❑ 406 Ethan Horton .02 .10
❑ 407 Michael Haynes .07 .20
❑ 408 Steve Jackson .02 .10
❑ 409 Erik Kramer .07 .20
❑ 410 Jerome Bettis .25 .60
❑ 411 D.J. Johnson .02 .10
❑ 412 John Alt .02 .10
❑ 413 Jeff Lageman .02 .10
❑ 414 Rick Tuten .02 .10
❑ 415 Jeff Robinson .02 .10
❑ 416 Kevin Lee RC .02 .10
❑ 417 Thomas Lewis RC .07 .20
❑ 418 Kerry Cash .02 .10
❑ 419 Chuck Levy RC .02 .10
❑ 420 Mark Ingram .02 .10
❑ 421 Dennis Gibson .02 .10
❑ 422 Tyronne Drakeford .02 .10
❑ 423 James Washington .02 .10
❑ 424 Dante Jones .02 .10
❑ 425 Eugene Robinson .02 .10
❑ 426 Johnny Johnson .02 .10
❑ 427 Brian Mitchell .02 .10
❑ 428 Charles Mincy .02 .10
❑ 429 Mark Carrier WR .07 .20
❑ 430 Vince Workman .02 .10
❑ 431 James Francis .02 .10
❑ 432 Clay Matthews .02 .10
❑ 433 Randall McDaniel .05 .15
❑ 434 Brad Ottis .02 .10
❑ 435 Bruce Smith .15 .40
❑ 436 Cortez Kennedy BD .02 .10
❑ 437 John Randle BD .07 .20
❑ 438 Neil Smith BD .07 .20
❑ 439 Cornelius Bennett BD .07 .20
❑ 440 Junior Seau BD .07 .20
❑ 441 Derrick Thomas BD .07 .20
❑ 442 Rod Woodson BD .07 .20
❑ 443 Terry McDaniel BD .02 .10
❑ 444 Tim McDonald BD .02 .10
❑ 445 Mark Carrier DB BD .02 .10
❑ 446 Irv Smith .02 .10
❑ 447 Steve Wallace .02 .10
❑ 448 Cris Dishman .02 .10
❑ 449 Bill Brooks .02 .10
❑ 450 Jeff Hostetler .07 .20
❑ 451 Brentson Buckner RC .02 .10
❑ 452 Ken Ruettgers .02 .10
❑ 453 Marc Boutte .02 .10
❑ 454 John Offerdahl .02 .10
❑ 455 Allen Aldridge .02 .10
❑ 456 Steve Emtman .02 .10
❑ 457 Andre Rison .07 .20
❑ 458 Shawn Jefferson .02 .10
❑ 459 Todd Steussie RC .07 .20
❑ 460 Scott Mitchell .07 .20
❑ 461 Tom Carter .02 .10
❑ 462 Donnell Bennett RC .15 .40
❑ 463 James Jones DT .02 .10
❑ 464 Antone Davis .02 .10
❑ 465 Jim Everett .07 .20
❑ 466 Tony Tolbert .02 .10
❑ 467 Merril Hoge .02 .10
❑ 468 Michael Bates .02 .10
❑ 469 Phil Hansen .02 .10
❑ 470 Rodney Hampton .07 .20
❑ 471 Aeneas Williams .02 .10
❑ 472 Al Del Greco .02 .10
❑ 473 Todd Lyght .02 .10
❑ 474 Joel Steed .02 .10
❑ 475 Merton Hanks .07 .20
❑ 476 Tony Stargell .02 .10
❑ 477 Greg Robinson .02 .10
❑ 478 Roger Duffy .02 .10
❑ 479 Simon Fletcher .02 .10
❑ 480 Reggie White .15 .40
❑ 481 Lee Johnson .02 .10
❑ 482 Wayne Martin .02 .10
❑ 483 Thurman Thomas .15 .40
❑ 484 Warren Moon .15 .40
❑ 485 Sam Rogers RC .02 .10
❑ 486 Erric Pegram .02 .10
❑ 487 Will Wolford .02 .10
❑ 488 Duane Young .02 .10
❑ 489 Keith Hamilton .02 .10
❑ 490 Haywood Jeffires .07 .20
❑ 491 Trace Armstrong .02 .10
❑ 492 J.J. Birden .02 .10
❑ 493 Ricky Ervins .02 .10
❑ 494 Robert Blackmon .02 .10
❑ 495 William Perry .07 .20
❑ 496 Robert Massey .02 .10
❑ 497 Jim Jeffcoat .02 .10
❑ 498 Pat Harlow .02 .10
❑ 499 Jeff Cross .02 .10
❑ 500 Jerry Rice .60 1.50
❑ 501 Darnay Scott RC .40 1.00
❑ 502 Clyde Simmons .02 .10
❑ 503 Henry Rolling .02 .10
❑ 504 James Hasty .02 .10
❑ 505 Leroy Thompson .02 .10
❑ 506 Darrell Thompson .02 .10
❑ 507 Tim Bowens RC .07 .20
❑ 508 Gerald Perry .02 .10
❑ 509 Mike Croel .02 .10
❑ 510 Sam Mills .02 .10
❑ 511 Steve Young RZ .25 .60
❑ 512 Hardy Nickerson RZ .07 .20
❑ 513 Cris Carter RZ .07 .20
❑ 514 Boomer Esiason RZ .02 .10
❑ 515 Bruce Smith RZ .07 .20
❑ 516 Emmitt Smith RZ .50 1.25
❑ 517 Eugene Robinson RZ .02 .10
❑ 518 Gary Brown RZ .02 .10
❑ 519 Jerry Rice RZ .30 .75
❑ 520 Troy Aikman RZ .30 .75
❑ 521 Marcus Allen RZ .07 .20
❑ 522 Junior Seau RZ .07 .20
❑ 523 Sterling Sharpe RZ .07 .20
❑ 524 Dana Stubblefield RZ .07 .20
❑ 525 Tom Carter RZ .02 .10
❑ 526 Pete Metzelaars .02 .10
❑ 527 Russell Freeman .02 .10
❑ 528 Keith Cash .02 .10
❑ 529 Willie Drewrey .02 .10
❑ 530 Randal Hill .02 .10
❑ 531 Pepper Johnson .02 .10
❑ 532 Rob Moore .07 .20
❑ 533 Todd Kelly .02 .10
❑ 534 Keith Byars .02 .10
❑ 535 Mike Fox .02 .10
❑ 536 Brett Favre 1.25 3.00
❑ 537 Terry McDaniel .02 .10
❑ 538 Darren Perry .02 .10
❑ 539 Maurice Hurst .02 .10
❑ 540 Troy Aikman .60 1.50
❑ 541 Junior Seau .15 .40
❑ 542 Steve Broussard .02 .10
❑ 543 Lorenzo White .02 .10
❑ 544 Terry McDaniel .02 .10
❑ 545 Henry Thomas .02 .10
❑ 546 Tyrone Hughes .07 .20
❑ 547 Mark Collins .02 .10
❑ 548 Gary Anderson K .02 .10
❑ 549 Darrell Green .02 .10
❑ 550 Jerry Rice .50 1.25
❑ 551 Cornelius Bennett .07 .20
❑ 552 Aeneas Williams .02 .10
❑ 553 Eric Metcalf .07 .20
❑ 554 Jumbo Elliott .02 .10
❑ 555 Mo Lewis .02 .10
❑ 556 Darren Carrington .02 .10
❑ 557 Kevin Greene .07 .20
❑ 558 John Elway 1.00 2.50
❑ 559 Eugene Robinson .02 .10
❑ 560 Drew Bledsoe .30 .75
❑ 561 Fred Barnett .07 .20
❑ 562 Bernie Parmalee RC .15 .40
❑ 563 Bryce Paup .07 .20
❑ 564 Donnell Woolford .02 .10
❑ 565 Terance Mathis .07 .20
❑ 566 Santana Dotson .07 .20
❑ 567 Randall McDaniel .05 .15
❑ 568 Stanley Richard .02 .10
❑ 569 Brian Blades .07 .20
❑ 570 Jerome Bettis .20 .50
❑ 571 Neil Smith .07 .20
❑ 572 Andre Reed .07 .20
❑ 573 Michael Bankston .02 .10
❑ 574 Dana Stubblefield .07 .20
❑ 575 Rod Woodson .07 .20
❑ 576 Ken Harvey .02 .10
❑ 577 Andre Rison .07 .20
❑ 578 Darion Conner .02 .10
❑ 579 Michael Strahan .15 .40
❑ 580 Barry Sanders .75 2.00
❑ 581 Pepper Johnson .02 .10
❑ 582 Lewis Tillman .02 .10
❑ 583 Jeff George .15 .40
❑ 584 Michael Haynes .07 .20
❑ 585 Herschel Walker .07 .20
❑ 586 Tim Brown .15 .40
❑ 587 Jim Kelly .15 .40
❑ 588 Ricky Watters .07 .20
❑ 589 Randall Cunningham .15 .40
❑ 590 Troy Aikman .50 1.25
❑ 591 Ken Norton Jr. .07 .20
❑ 592 Cortez Kennedy .07 .20
❑ 593 Ricky Ervins .02 .10
❑ 594 Cris Carter .20 .50
❑ 595 Sterling Sharpe .07 .20
❑ 596 John Randle .07 .20
❑ 597 Shannon Sharpe .07 .20
❑ 598 Ray Crittenden RC .02 .10
❑ 599 Barry Foster .02 .10
❑ 600 Deion Sanders .25 .60
❑ 601 Seth Joyner .02 .10
❑ 602 Chris Warren .07 .20
❑ 603 Tom Rathman .02 .10
❑ 604 Brett Favre 1.00 2.50
❑ 605 Marshall Faulk .75 2.00
❑ 606 Terry Allen .07 .20
❑ 607 Ben Coates .07 .20
❑ 608 Brian Washington .02 .10
❑ 609 Henry Ellard .07 .20
❑ 610 Dave Meggett .02 .10
❑ 611 Stan Humphries .07 .20
❑ 612 Warren Moon .15 .40
❑ 613 Marcus Allen .15 .40
❑ 614 Ed McDaniel .02 .10
❑ 615 Joe Montana 1.00 2.50
❑ 616 Jeff Hostetler .07 .20
❑ 617 Johnny Johnson .02 .10
❑ 618 Andre Coleman RC .02 .10
❑ 619 Willie Davis .07 .20
❑ 620 Rick Mirer .15 .40
❑ 621 Dan Marino 1.00 2.50
❑ 622 Rob Moore .07 .20
❑ 623 Byron Bam Morris RC .07 .20
❑ 624 Natrone Means .15 .40
❑ 625 Steve Young .30 .75
❑ 626 Jim Everett .07 .20
❑ 627 Michael Brooks .02 .10
❑ 628 Dermontti Dawson .02 .10
❑ 629 Reggie White .15 .40
❑ 630 Emmitt Smith .60 1.50

Card	Low	High
❑ O Micheal Barrow TSC	2.00	4.00
❑ NNO Checklist Card 1	.02	.10
❑ NNO Checklist Card 2	.02	.10
❑ NNO Checklist Card 3	.02	.10

1995 Stadium Club

Card	Low	High
❑ COMPLETE SET (450)	25.00	60.00
❑ COMP.SERIES 1 (225)	12.50	30.00
❑ COMP.SERIES 2 (225)	12.50	30.00
❑ 1 Steve Young	.50	1.25
❑ 2 Stan Humphries	.07	.20
❑ 3 Chris Boniol RC	.02	.10
❑ 4 Darren Perry	.02	.10
❑ 5 Vinny Testaverde	.07	.20
❑ 6 Aubrey Beavers	.02	.10
❑ 7 Dewayne Washington	.07	.20
❑ 8 Marion Butts	.02	.10
❑ 9 George Koonce	.02	.10
❑ 10 Joe Cain	.02	.10
❑ 11 Mike Johnson	.02	.10
❑ 12 Dale Carter	.07	.20
❑ 13 Greg Biekert	.02	.10
❑ 14 Aaron Pierce	.02	.10
❑ 15 Aeneas Williams	.02	.10
❑ 16 Stephen Grant RC	.02	.10
❑ 17 Henry Jones	.02	.10
❑ 18 James Williams LB	.02	.10
❑ 19 Andy Harmon	.02	.10
❑ 20 Anthony Miller	.07	.20
❑ 21 Kevin Ross	.02	.10
❑ 22 Erik Howard	.02	.10
❑ 23 Brian Blades	.07	.20
❑ 24 Trent Dilfer	.15	.40
❑ 25 Roman Phifer	.02	.10
❑ 26 Bruce Kozerski	.02	.10
❑ 27 Henry Ellard	.07	.20
❑ 28 Rich Camarillo	.02	.10
❑ 29 Richmond Webb	.02	.10
❑ 30 George Teague	.02	.10
❑ 31 Antonio Langham	.02	.10
❑ 32 Barry Foster	.07	.20
❑ 33 Bruce Armstrong	.02	.10
❑ 34 Tim McDonald	.02	.10
❑ 35 James Harris DE	.02	.10
❑ 36 Lomas Brown	.02	.10
❑ 37 Jay Novacek	.07	.20
❑ 38 John Thierry	.02	.10
❑ 39 John Elliott	.02	.10
❑ 40 Terry McDaniel	.02	.10
❑ 41 Shawn Lee	.02	.10
❑ 42 Shane Dronett	.02	.10
❑ 43 Cornelius Bennett	.07	.20
❑ 44 Steve Bono	.07	.20
❑ 45 Byron Evans	.02	.10
❑ 46 Eugene Robinson	.02	.10
❑ 47 Tony Bennett	.02	.10
❑ 48 Michael Bankston	.02	.10
❑ 49 Willie Roaf	.02	.10
❑ 50 Bobby Houston	.02	.10
❑ 51 Ken Harvey	.02	.10
❑ 52 Bruce Matthews	.02	.10
❑ 53 Lincoln Kennedy	.02	.10
❑ 54 Todd Lyght	.02	.10
❑ 55 Paul Gruber	.02	.10
❑ 56 Corey Sawyer	.02	.10
❑ 57 Myron Guyton	.02	.10
❑ 58 John Jackson T	.02	.10
❑ 59 Sean Jones	.02	.10
❑ 60 Pepper Johnson	.02	.10
❑ 61 Steve Walsh	.02	.10
❑ 62 Corey Miller	.02	.10
❑ 63 Fuad Reveiz	.02	.10
❑ 64 Rickey Jackson	.02	.10
❑ 65 Scott Mitchell	.07	.20
❑ 66 Michael Irvin	.15	.40
❑ 67 Andre Reed	.07	.20
❑ 68 Mark Seay	.07	.20
❑ 69 Keith Byars	.02	.10
❑ 70 Marcus Allen	.15	.40
❑ 71 Shannon Sharpe	.07	.20
❑ 72 Eric Hill	.02	.10
❑ 73 James Washington	.02	.10
❑ 74 Greg Jackson	.02	.10
❑ 75 Chris Warren	.07	.20
❑ 76 Will Wolford	.02	.10
❑ 77 Anthony Smith	.02	.10
❑ 78 Cris Dishman	.02	.10
❑ 79 Carl Pickens	.07	.20
❑ 80 Tyrone Hughes	.07	.20
❑ 81 Chris Miller	.02	.10
❑ 82 Clay Matthews	.07	.20
❑ 83 Lonnie Marts	.02	.10
❑ 84 Jerome Henderson	.02	.10
❑ 85 Ben Coates	.07	.20
❑ 86 Deon Figures	.02	.10
❑ 87 Anthony Pleasant	.02	.10
❑ 88 Guy McIntyre	.02	.10
❑ 89 Jake Reed	.07	.20
❑ 90 Rodney Hampton	.07	.20
❑ 91 Santana Dotson	.02	.10
❑ 92 Jeff Blackshear	.02	.10
❑ 93 Willie Clay	.02	.10
❑ 94 Nate Newton	.07	.20
❑ 95 Bucky Brooks	.02	.10
❑ 96 Lamar Lathon	.02	.10
❑ 97 Tim Grunhard	.02	.10
❑ 98 Harris Barton	.02	.10
❑ 99 Brian Mitchell	.02	.10
❑ 100 Natrone Means	.07	.20
❑ 101 Sean Dawkins	.07	.20
❑ 102 Chris Slade	.02	.10
❑ 103 Tom Rathman	.02	.10
❑ 104 Fred Barnett	.07	.20
❑ 105 Gary Brown	.02	.10
❑ 106 Leonard Russell	.02	.10
❑ 107 Alfred Williams	.02	.10
❑ 108 Kelvin Martin	.02	.10
❑ 109 Alexander Wright	.02	.10
❑ 110 O.J. McDuffie	.15	.40
❑ 111 Mario Bates	.07	.20
❑ 112 Tony Casillas	.02	.10
❑ 113 Michael Timpson	.02	.10
❑ 114 Robert Brooks	.15	.40
❑ 115 Rob Burnett	.02	.10
❑ 116 Mark Collins	.02	.10
❑ 117 Chris Calloway	.02	.10
❑ 118 Courtney Hawkins	.02	.10
❑ 119 Marvcus Patton	.02	.10
❑ 120 Greg Lloyd	.07	.20
❑ 121 Ryan McNeil	.02	.10
❑ 122 Gary Plummer	.02	.10
❑ 123 Dwayne Sabb	.02	.10
❑ 124 Jessie Hester	.02	.10
❑ 125 Terance Mathis	.07	.20
❑ 126 Steve Atwater	.02	.10
❑ 127 Lorenzo Lynch	.02	.10
❑ 128 James Francis	.02	.10
❑ 129 John Fina	.02	.10
❑ 130 Emmitt Smith	1.25	2.50
❑ 131 Bryan Cox	.02	.10
❑ 132 Robert Blackmon	.02	.10
❑ 133 Kenny Davidson	.02	.10
❑ 134 Eugene Daniel	.02	.10
❑ 135 Vince Buck	.02	.10
❑ 136 Leslie O'Neal	.07	.20
❑ 137 James Jett	.07	.20
❑ 138 Johnny Johnson	.02	.10
❑ 139 Michael Zordich	.02	.10
❑ 140 Warren Moon	.07	.20
❑ 141 William White	.02	.10
❑ 142 Carl Banks	.02	.10
❑ 143 Marty Carter	.02	.10
❑ 144 Keith Hamilton	.02	.10
❑ 145 Alvin Harper	.02	.10
❑ 146 Corey Harris	.02	.10
❑ 147 Elijah Alexander RC	.02	.10
❑ 148 Darrell Green	.02	.10
❑ 149 Yancey Thigpen RC	.07	.20
❑ 150 Deion Sanders	.40	1.00
❑ 151 Burt Grossman	.02	.10
❑ 152 J.B. Brown	.02	.10
❑ 153 Johnny Bailey	.02	.10
❑ 154 Harvey Williams	.02	.10
❑ 155 Jeff Blake RC	.40	1.00
❑ 156 Al Smith	.02	.10
❑ 157 Chris Doleman	.02	.10
❑ 158 Garrison Hearst	.15	.40
❑ 159 Bryce Paup	.07	.20
❑ 160 Herman Moore	.15	.40
❑ 161 Cortez Kennedy	.07	.20
❑ 162 Marquez Pope	.02	.10
❑ 163 Quinn Early	.07	.20
❑ 164 Broderick Thomas	.02	.10
❑ 165 Jeff Herrod	.02	.10
❑ 166 Robert Jones	.02	.10
❑ 167 Mo Lewis	.02	.10
❑ 168 Ray Crittenden	.02	.10
❑ 169 Raymont Harris	.02	.10
❑ 170 Bruce Smith	.15	.40
❑ 171 Dana Stubblefield	.07	.20
❑ 172 Charles Haley	.07	.20
❑ 173 Charles Johnson	.07	.20
❑ 174 Shawn Jefferson	.02	.10
❑ 175 Leroy Hoard	.02	.10
❑ 176 Bernie Parmalee	.07	.20
❑ 177 Scottie Graham	.07	.20
❑ 178 Edgar Bennett	.07	.20
❑ 179 Aubrey Matthews	.02	.10
❑ 180 Don Beebe	.02	.10
❑ 181 Eric Swann EC SP	.10	.30
❑ 182 Jeff George EC SP	.10	.30
❑ 183 Jim Kelly EC SP	.25	.60
❑ 184 Sam Mills EC SP	.10	.30
❑ 185 Mark Carrier DB EC SP	.07	.20
❑ 186 Dan Wilkinson EC SP	.10	.30
❑ 187 Eric Turner EC SP	.07	.20
❑ 188 Troy Aikman EC SP	.75	2.00
❑ 189 John Elway EC SP	1.50	4.00
❑ 190 Barry Sanders EC SP	1.25	3.00
❑ 191 Brett Favre EC SP	2.00	4.00
❑ 192 Micheal Barrow EC SP	.07	.20
❑ 193 Marshall Faulk EC SP	1.00	2.50
❑ 194 Steve Beuerlein EC SP	.10	.30
❑ 195 Neil Smith EC SP	.10	.30
❑ 196 Jeff Hostetler EC SP	.10	.30
❑ 197 Jerome Bettis EC SP	.25	.60
❑ 198 Dan Marino EC SP	1.50	4.00
❑ 199 Cris Carter EC SP	.25	.60
❑ 200 Drew Bledsoe EC SP	.40	1.00
❑ 201 Jim Everett EC SP	.07	.20
❑ 202 Dave Brown EC SP	.10	.30
❑ 203 Boomer Esiason EC SP	.10	.30
❑ 204 Randall Cunningham EC SP	.10	.30
❑ 205 Rod Woodson EC SP	.10	.30
❑ 206 Junior Seau EC SP	.25	.60
❑ 207 Jerry Rice EC SP	.75	2.00
❑ 208 Rick Mirer EC SP	.10	.30
❑ 209 Errict Rhett EC SP	.10	.30
❑ 210 Heath Shuler EC SP	.10	.30
❑ 211 Bobby Taylor SP RC	.25	.60
❑ 212 Jesse James SP RC	.07	.20
❑ 213 Devin Bush SP RC	.07	.20
❑ 214 Luther Elliss SP RC	.07	.20
❑ 215 Kerry Collins SP RC	1.00	2.50
❑ 216 Derrick Alexander SP RC	.07	.20
❑ 217 Rashaan Salaam SP RC	.10	.30
❑ 218 J.J. Stokes SP RC	.25	.60
❑ 219 Todd Collins SP RC	.75	2.00
❑ 220 Ki-Jana Carter SP RC	.25	.60
❑ 221 Kyle Brady SP RC	.25	.60
❑ 222 Kevin Carter SP RC	.25	.60
❑ 223 Tony Boselli SP RC	.25	.60
❑ 224 Scott Gragg SP RC	.07	.20
❑ 225 Warren Sapp SP RC	.75	2.00
❑ 226 Ricky Reynolds	.02	.10
❑ 227 Roosevelt Potts	.02	.10
❑ 228 Jessie Tuggle	.02	.10
❑ 229 Anthony Newman	.02	.10
❑ 230 Randall Cunningham	.15	.40
❑ 231 Jason Elam	.07	.20
❑ 232 Darnay Scott	.07	.20
❑ 233 Tom Carter	.02	.10
❑ 234 Micheal Barrow	.02	.10
❑ 235 Steve Tasker	.07	.20
❑ 236 Howard Cross	.02	.10
❑ 237 Charles Wilson	.02	.10
❑ 238 Rob Fredrickson	.02	.10
❑ 239 Russell Maryland	.02	.10
❑ 240 Dan Marino	1.25	3.00
❑ 241 Rafael Robinson	.02	.10
❑ 242 Ed McDaniel	.02	.10
❑ 243 Brett Perriman	.07	.20
❑ 244 Chuck Levy	.02	.10
❑ 245 Errict Rhett	.07	.20

Card		
❑ 246 Tracy Simien	.02	.10
❑ 247 Steve Everitt	.02	.10
❑ 248 John Jurkovic	.02	.10
❑ 249 Johnny Mitchell	.02	.10
❑ 250 Mark Carrier DB	.02	.10
❑ 251 Merton Hanks	.02	.10
❑ 252 Joe Johnson	.02	.10
❑ 253 Andre Coleman	.02	.10
❑ 254 Ray Buchanan	.02	.10
❑ 255 Jeff George	.07	.20
❑ 256 Shane Conlan	.02	.10
❑ 257 Gus Frerotte	.07	.20
❑ 258 Doug Pelfrey	.02	.10
❑ 259 Glenn Montgomery	.02	.10
❑ 260 John Elway	1.25	3.00
❑ 261 Larry Centers	.07	.20
❑ 262 Calvin Williams	.07	.20
❑ 263 Gene Atkins	.02	.10
❑ 264 Tim Brown	.15	.40
❑ 265 Leon Lett	.02	.10
❑ 266 Martin Mayhew	.02	.10
❑ 267 Arthur Marshall	.02	.10
❑ 268 Maurice Hurst	.02	.10
❑ 269 Greg Hill	.07	.20
❑ 270 Junior Seau	.15	.40
❑ 271 Rick Mirer	.07	.20
❑ 272 Jack Del Rio	.02	.10
❑ 273 Lewis Tillman	.02	.10
❑ 274 Renaldo Turnbull	.02	.10
❑ 275 Dan Footman	.02	.10
❑ 276 John Taylor	.02	.10
❑ 277 Russell Copeland	.02	.10
❑ 278 Tracy Scroggins	.02	.10
❑ 279 Lou Benfatti	.02	.10
❑ 280 Rod Woodson	.07	.20
❑ 281 Troy Drayton	.02	.10
❑ 282 Quentin Coryatt	.07	.20
❑ 283 Craig Heyward	.07	.20
❑ 284 Jeff Cross	.02	.10
❑ 285 Hardy Nickerson	.02	.10
❑ 286 Dorsey Levens	.30	.75
❑ 287 Derek Russell	.02	.10
❑ 288 Seth Joyner	.02	.10
❑ 289 Kimble Anders	.07	.20
❑ 290 Drew Bledsoe	.30	.75
❑ 291 Bryant Young	.07	.20
❑ 292 Chris Zorich	.02	.10
❑ 293 Michael Strahan	.15	.40
❑ 294 Kevin Greene	.07	.20
❑ 295 Aaron Glenn	.02	.10
❑ 296 Jimmy Spencer RC	.02	.10
❑ 297 Eric Turner	.02	.10
❑ 298 William Thomas	.02	.10
❑ 299 Dan Wilkinson	.07	.20
❑ 300 Troy Aikman	.60	1.50
❑ 301 Terry Wooden	.02	.10
❑ 302 Heath Shuler	.07	.20
❑ 303 Jeff Burris	.02	.10
❑ 304 Mark Stepnoski	.02	.10
❑ 305 Chris Mims	.02	.10
❑ 306 Todd Steussie	.02	.10
❑ 307 Johnnie Morton	.07	.20
❑ 308 Darryl Talley	.02	.10
❑ 309 Nolan Harrison	.02	.10
❑ 310 Dave Brown	.07	.20
❑ 311 Brent Jones	.02	.10
❑ 312 Curtis Conway	.15	.40
❑ 313 Ronald Humphrey	.02	.10
❑ 314 Richie Anderson RC	.20	.50
❑ 315 Jim Everett	.02	.10
❑ 316 Willie Davis	.07	.20
❑ 317 Ed Cunningham	.02	.10
❑ 318 Willie McGinest	.07	.20
❑ 319 Sean Gilbert	.07	.20
❑ 320 Brett Favre	1.50	3.00
❑ 321 Bennie Thompson	.02	.10
❑ 322 Neil O'Donnell	.07	.20
❑ 323 Vince Workman	.02	.10
❑ 324 Terry Kirby	.07	.20
❑ 325 Simon Fletcher	.02	.10
❑ 326 Ricardo McDonald	.02	.10
❑ 327 Duane Young	.02	.10
❑ 328 Jim Harbaugh	.07	.20
❑ 329 D.J. Johnson	.02	.10
❑ 330 Boomer Esiason	.07	.20
❑ 331 Donnell Woolford	.02	.10
❑ 332 Mike Sherrard	.02	.10
❑ 333 Tyrone Legette	.02	.10
❑ 334 Larry Brown DB	.02	.10
❑ 335 William Floyd	.07	.20
❑ 336 Reggie Brooks	.07	.20
❑ 337 Patrick Bates	.02	.10
❑ 338 Jim Jeffcoat	.02	.10
❑ 339 Ray Childress	.02	.10
❑ 340 Cris Carter	.15	.40
❑ 341 Charlie Garner	.15	.40
❑ 342 Bill Hitchcock	.02	.10
❑ 343 Levon Kirkland	.02	.10
❑ 344 Robert Porcher	.02	.10
❑ 345 Darryl Williams	.02	.10
❑ 346 Vincent Brisby	.02	.10
❑ 347 Kenyon Rasheed	.02	.10
❑ 348 Floyd Turner	.02	.10
❑ 349 Bob Whitfield	.02	.10
❑ 350 Jerome Bettis	.15	.40
❑ 351 Brad Baxter	.02	.10
❑ 352 Darrin Smith	.02	.10
❑ 353 Lamar Thomas	.02	.10
❑ 354 Lorenzo Neal	.02	.10
❑ 355 Erik Kramer	.02	.10
❑ 356 Dwayne Harper	.02	.10
❑ 357 Doug Evans RC	.15	.40
❑ 358 Jeff Feagles	.02	.10
❑ 359 Ray Crockett	.02	.10
❑ 360 Neil Smith	.07	.20
❑ 361 Troy Vincent	.02	.10
❑ 362 Don Griffin	.02	.10
❑ 363 Michael Brooks	.02	.10
❑ 364 Carlton Gray	.02	.10
❑ 365 Thomas Smith	.02	.10
❑ 366 Ken Norton	.07	.20
❑ 367 Tony McGee	.02	.10
❑ 368 Eric Metcalf	.07	.20
❑ 369 Mel Gray	.02	.10
❑ 370 Barry Sanders	1.00	2.50
❑ 371 Rocket Ismail	.07	.20
❑ 372 Chad Brown	.07	.20
❑ 373 Qadry Ismail	.07	.20
❑ 374 Anthony Prior	.02	.10
❑ 375 Kevin Lee	.02	.10
❑ 376 Robert Young	.02	.10
❑ 377 Kevin Williams WR	.07	.20
❑ 378 Tydus Winans	.02	.10
❑ 379 Ricky Watters	.07	.20
❑ 380 Jim Kelly	.15	.40
❑ 381 Eric Swann	.07	.20
❑ 382 Mike Pritchard	.02	.10
❑ 383 Derek Brown RBK	.02	.10
❑ 384 Dennis Gibson	.02	.10
❑ 385 Byron Bam Morris	.02	.10
❑ 386 Reggie White	.15	.40
❑ 387 Jeff Graham	.02	.10
❑ 388 Marshall Faulk	.75	2.00
❑ 389 Joe Phillips	.02	.10
❑ 390 Jeff Hostetler	.07	.20
❑ 391 Irving Fryar	.07	.20
❑ 392 Stevon Moore	.02	.10
❑ 393 Bert Emanuel	.15	.40
❑ 394 Leon Searcy	.02	.10
❑ 395 Robert Smith	.15	.40
❑ 396 Michael Bates	.02	.10
❑ 397 Thomas Lewis	.07	.20
❑ 398 Joe Bowden	.02	.10
❑ 399 Steve Tovar	.02	.10
❑ 400 Jerry Rice	.60	1.50
❑ 401 Toby Wright	.02	.10
❑ 402 Daryl Johnston	.07	.20
❑ 403 Vincent Brown	.02	.10
❑ 404 Marvin Washington	.02	.10
❑ 405 Chris Spielman	.07	.20
❑ 406 Willie Jackson ET SP	.10	.30
❑ 407 Harry Boatswain ET SP	.07	.20
❑ 408 Kelvin Pritchett ET SP	.07	.20
❑ 409 Dave Widell ET SP	.07	.20
❑ 410 Frank Reich ET SP	.07	.20
❑ 411 Corey Mayfield ET SP RC	.07	.20
❑ 412 Pete Metzelaars ET SP	.07	.20
❑ 413 Keith Goganious ET SP	.07	.20
❑ 414 John Kasay ET SP	.07	.20
❑ 415 Ernest Givins ET SP	.07	.20
❑ 416 Randy Baldwin ET SP	.07	.20
❑ 417 Shawn Bouwens ET SP	.07	.20
❑ 418 Mike Fox ET SP	.07	.20
❑ 419 Mark Carrier WR ET SP	.10	.30
❑ 420 Steve Beuerlein ET SP	.10	.30
❑ 421 Steve Lofton ET SP	.07	.20
❑ 422 Jeff Lageman ET SP	.07	.20
❑ 423 Paul Butcher ET SP	.07	.20
❑ 424 Mark Brunell ET SP	.40	1.00
❑ 425 Vernon Turner ET SP	.07	.20
❑ 426 Tim McKyer ET SP	.07	.20
❑ 427 James Williams ET SP	.07	.20
❑ 428 Tommy Barnhardt ET SP	.07	.20
❑ 429 Rogerick Green ET SP	.07	.20
❑ 430 Desmond Howard ET SP	.10	.30
❑ 431 Darion Conner ET SP	.07	.20
❑ 432 Reggie Clark ET SP	.07	.20
❑ 433 Eric Guliford ET SP	.07	.20
❑ 434 Rob Johnson SP RC	.50	1.25
❑ 435 Sam Mills ET SP	.10	.30
❑ 436 Kordell Stewart SP RC	.75	2.00
❑ 437 James O. Stewart SP RC	.60	1.50
❑ 438 Zach Wiegert SP	.07	.20
❑ 439 Ellis Johnson SP RC	.07	.20
❑ 440 Matt O'Dwyer SP RC	.07	.20
❑ 441 Anthony Cook SP RC	.07	.20
❑ 442 Ron Davis SP RC	.07	.20
❑ 443 Chris Hudson SP RC	.07	.20
❑ 444 Hugh Douglas SP RC	.25	.60
❑ 445 Tyrone Poole RC SP	.25	.60
❑ 446 Korey Stringer SP RC	.20	.50
❑ 447 Ruben Brown SP RC	.25	.60
❑ 448 Brian DeMarco SP RC	.07	.20
❑ 449 Michael Westbrook SP RC	.25	.60
❑ 450 Steve McNair SP RC	1.50	4.00

1996 Stadium Club

Card		
❑ COMPLETE SET (360)	30.00	60.00
❑ COMP.SERIES 1 (180)	15.00	30.00
❑ COMP.SERIES 2 (180)	15.00	30.00
❑ 1 Kyle Brady	.02	.10
❑ 2 Mickey Washington	.02	.10
❑ 3 Seth Joyner	.02	.10
❑ 4 Vinny Testaverde	.08	.25
❑ 5 Thomas Randolph	.02	.10
❑ 6 Heath Shuler	.08	.25
❑ 7 Ty Law	.20	.50
❑ 8 Blake Brockermeyer	.02	.10
❑ 9 Darryll Lewis	.02	.10
❑ 10 Jeff Blake	.20	.50
❑ 11 Tyrone Hughes	.02	.10
❑ 12 Horace Copeland	.02	.10
❑ 13 Roman Phifer	.02	.10
❑ 14 Eugene Robinson	.02	.10
❑ 15 Anthony Miller	.08	.25
❑ 16 Robert Smith	.08	.25
❑ 17 Chester McGlockton	.02	.10
❑ 18 Marty Carter	.02	.10
❑ 19 Scott Mitchell	.08	.25
❑ 20 O.J. McDuffie	.08	.25
❑ 21 Stan Humphries	.08	.25
❑ 22 Eugene Daniel	.02	.10
❑ 23 Devin Bush	.02	.10
❑ 24 Darick Holmes	.02	.10
❑ 25 Ricky Watters	.08	.25
❑ 26 J.J. Stokes	.20	.50
❑ 27 George Koonce	.02	.10
❑ 28 Tamarick Vanover	.08	.25
❑ 29 Yancey Thigpen	.08	.25
❑ 30 Troy Aikman	.50	1.25
❑ 31 Rashaan Salaam	.08	.25
❑ 32 Anthony Cook	.02	.10
❑ 33 Tim McKyer	.02	.10
❑ 34 Dale Carter	.02	.10
❑ 35 Marvin Washington	.02	.10
❑ 36 Terry Allen	.08	.25
❑ 37 Keith Goganious	.02	.10
❑ 38 Pepper Johnson	.02	.10
❑ 39 Dave Brown	.02	.10
❑ 40 Levon Kirkland	.02	.10
❑ 41 Ken Dilger	.08	.25
❑ 42 Harvey Williams	.02	.10
❑ 43 Robert Blackmon	.02	.10
❑ 44 Kevin Carter	.02	.10

Card	Lo	Hi
❑ 45 Warren Moon	.08	.25
❑ 46 Allen Aldridge	.02	.10
❑ 47 Terance Mathis	.02	.10
❑ 48 Junior Seau	.20	.50
❑ 49 William Fuller	.02	.10
❑ 50 Lee Woodall	.02	.10
❑ 51 Aeneas Williams	.02	.10
❑ 52 Thomas Smith	.02	.10
❑ 53 Chris Slade	.02	.10
❑ 54 Eric Allen	.02	.10
❑ 55 David Sloan	.02	.10
❑ 56 Hardy Nickerson	.02	.10
❑ 57 Michael Irvin	.20	.50
❑ 58 Corey Sawyer	.02	.10
❑ 59 Eric Green	.02	.10
❑ 60 Reggie White	.20	.50
❑ 61 Isaac Bruce	.20	.50
❑ 62 Darrell Green	.02	.10
❑ 63 Aaron Glenn	.02	.10
❑ 64 Mark Brunell	.30	.75
❑ 65 Mark Carrier WR	.02	.10
❑ 66 Mel Gray	.02	.10
❑ 67 Phillippi Sparks	.02	.10
❑ 68 Ernie Mills	.02	.10
❑ 69 Rick Mirer	.08	.25
❑ 70 Neil Smith	.08	.25
❑ 71 Terry McDaniel	.02	.10
❑ 72 Terrell Davis	.40	1.00
❑ 73 Alonzo Spellman	.02	.10
❑ 74 Jessie Tuggle	.02	.10
❑ 75 Terry Kirby	.08	.25
❑ 76 David Palmer	.02	.10
❑ 77 Calvin Williams	.02	.10
❑ 78 Shaun Gayle	.02	.10
❑ 79 Bryant Young	.08	.25
❑ 80 Jim Harbaugh	.08	.25
❑ 81 Michael Jackson	.08	.25
❑ 82 Dave Meggett	.02	.10
❑ 83 Henry Thomas	.02	.10
❑ 84 Jim Kelly	.20	.50
❑ 85 Frank Sanders	.08	.25
❑ 86 Daryl Johnston	.08	.25
❑ 87 Alvin Harper	.02	.10
❑ 88 John Copeland	.02	.10
❑ 89 Mark Chmura	.08	.25
❑ 90 Jim Everett	.02	.10
❑ 91 Bobby Houston	.02	.10
❑ 92 Willie Jackson	.08	.25
❑ 93 Carlton Bailey	.02	.10
❑ 94 Todd Lyght	.02	.10
❑ 95 Ken Harvey	.02	.10
❑ 96 Erric Pegram	.02	.10
❑ 97 Anthony Smith	.02	.10
❑ 98 Kimble Anders	.08	.25
❑ 99 Steve McNair	.40	1.00
❑ 100 Jeff George	.08	.25
❑ 101 Michael Timpson	.02	.10
❑ 102 Brent Jones	.02	.10
❑ 103 Mike Mamula	.02	.10
❑ 104 Jeff Cross	.02	.10
❑ 105 Craig Newsome	.02	.10
❑ 106 Howard Cross	.02	.10
❑ 107 Terry Wooden	.02	.10
❑ 108 Randall McDaniel	.05	.15
❑ 109 Andre Reed	.08	.25
❑ 110 Steve Atwater	.02	.10
❑ 111 Larry Centers	.08	.25
❑ 112 Tony Bennett	.02	.10
❑ 113 Drew Bledsoe	.30	.75
❑ 114 Terrell Fletcher	.02	.10
❑ 115 Warren Sapp	.02	.10
❑ 116 Deion Sanders	.30	.75
❑ 117 Bryce Paup	.02	.10
❑ 118 Mario Bates	.08	.25
❑ 119 Steve Tovar	.02	.10
❑ 120 Barry Sanders	.75	2.00
❑ 121 Tony Boselli	.02	.10
❑ 122 Micheal Barrow	.02	.10
❑ 123 Sam Mills	.02	.10
❑ 124 Tim Brown	.20	.50
❑ 125 Darren Perry	.02	.10
❑ 126 Brian Blades	.02	.10
❑ 127 Tyrone Wheatley	.08	.25
❑ 128 Derrick Thomas	.20	.50
❑ 129 Edgar Bennett	.08	.25
❑ 130 Cris Carter	.20	.50
❑ 131 Stephen Grant	.02	.10
❑ 132 Kevin Williams	.02	.10
❑ 133 Darnay Scott	.08	.25
❑ 134 Rod Stephens	.02	.10
❑ 135 Ken Norton	.02	.10
❑ 136 Tim Biakabutuka SP RC	.20	.50
❑ 137 Willie Anderson SP RC	.02	.10
❑ 138 Lawrence Phillips SP RC	.20	.50
❑ 139 Jonathan Ogden SP RC	.20	.50
❑ 140 Simeon Rice SP RC	.50	1.25
❑ 141 Alex Van Dyke SP RC	.08	.25
❑ 142 Jerome Woods SP RC	.02	.10
❑ 143 Eric Moulds RC	.75	2.00
❑ 144 Mike Alstott SP RC	.60	1.50
❑ 145 Marvin Harrison SP RC	1.50	4.00
❑ 146 Duane Clemons SP RC	.02	.10
❑ 147 Regan Upshaw SP RC	.02	.10
❑ 148 Eddie Kennison SP RC	.20	.50
❑ 149 John Mobley SP RC	.02	.10
❑ 150 Keyshawn Johnson SP RC	.60	1.50
❑ 151 Marco Battaglia SP RC	.02	.10
❑ 152 Rickey Dudley SP RC	.20	.50
❑ 153 Kevin Hardy SP RC	.20	.50
❑ 154 Curtis Martin SM SP	.40	1.00
❑ 155 Dan Marino SM SP	1.00	2.50
❑ 156 Rashaan Salaam SM SP	.08	.25
❑ 157 Joey Galloway SM SP	.20	.50
❑ 158 John Elway SM SP	1.00	2.50
❑ 159 Marshall Faulk SM SP	.25	.60
❑ 160 Jerry Rice SM SP	.50	1.25
❑ 161 Darren Bennett SM SP	.02	.10
❑ 162 Tamarick Vanover SM SP	.08	.25
❑ 163 Orlando Thomas SM SP	.02	.10
❑ 164 Jim Kelly SM SP	.20	.50
❑ 165 Larry Brown SM SP	.02	.10
❑ 166 Errict Rhett SM SP	.08	.25
❑ 167 Warren Moon SM SP	.02	.10
❑ 168 Hugh Douglas SM SP	.02	.10
❑ 169 Jim Everett SM SP	.02	.10
❑ 170 AFC Championship Game SP	.02	.10
❑ 171 Larry Centers SM SP	.08	.25
❑ 172 Marcus Allen GM SP	.20	.50
❑ 173 Morten Andersen GM SP	.02	.10
❑ 174 Brett Favre GM SP	1.00	2.50
❑ 175 Jerry Rice GM SP	.50	1.25
❑ 176 Glyn Milburn GM SP	.02	.10
❑ 177 Thurman Thomas GM SP	.08	.25
❑ 178 Michael Irvin GM SP	.08	.25
❑ 179 Barry Sanders GM SP	.75	2.00
❑ 180 Dan Marino GM SP	1.00	2.50
❑ 181 Joey Galloway	.20	.50
❑ 182 Dwayne Harper	.02	.10
❑ 183 Antonio Langham	.02	.10
❑ 184 Chris Zorich	.02	.10
❑ 185 Willie McGinest	.02	.10
❑ 186 Wayne Chrebet	.30	.75
❑ 187 Dermontti Dawson	.02	.10
❑ 188 Charlie Garner	.08	.25
❑ 189 Quentin Coryatt	.02	.10
❑ 190 Rodney Hampton	.08	.25
❑ 191 Kelvin Pritchett	.02	.10
❑ 192 Willie Green	.02	.10
❑ 193 Garrison Hearst	.08	.25
❑ 194 Tracy Scroggins	.02	.10
❑ 195 Rocket Ismail	.02	.10
❑ 196 Michael Westbrook	.20	.50
❑ 197 Troy Drayton	.02	.10
❑ 198 Rob Fredrickson	.02	.10
❑ 199 Sean Lumpkin	.02	.10
❑ 200 John Elway	1.00	2.50
❑ 201 Bernie Parmalee	.02	.10
❑ 202 Chris Chandler	.08	.25
❑ 203 Lake Dawson	.02	.10
❑ 204 Orlando Thomas	.02	.10
❑ 205 Carl Pickens	.08	.25
❑ 206 Kurt Schulz	.02	.10
❑ 207 Clay Matthews	.02	.10
❑ 208 Winston Moss	.02	.10
❑ 209 Sean Dawkins	.02	.10
❑ 210 Emmitt Smith	.75	2.00
❑ 211 Mark Carrier DB	.02	.10
❑ 212 Clyde Simmons	.02	.10
❑ 213 Derrick Brooks	.20	.50
❑ 214 William Floyd	.08	.25
❑ 215 Aaron Hayden	.02	.10
❑ 216 Brian DeMarco	.02	.10
❑ 217 Ben Coates	.08	.25
❑ 218 Renaldo Turnbull	.02	.10
❑ 219 Adrian Murrell	.08	.25
❑ 220 Marcus Allen	.20	.50
❑ 221 Brett Maxie	.02	.10
❑ 222 Trev Alberts	.02	.10
❑ 223 Darren Woodson	.08	.25
❑ 224 Brian Mitchell	.02	.10
❑ 225 Michael Haynes	.02	.10
❑ 226 Sean Jones	.02	.10
❑ 227 Eric Zeier	.02	.10
❑ 228 Herman Moore	.08	.25
❑ 229 Shane Conlan	.02	.10
❑ 230 Chris Warren	.08	.25
❑ 231 Dana Stubblefield	.08	.25
❑ 232 Andre Coleman	.02	.10
❑ 233 Kordell Stewart UER	.20	.50
❑ 234 Ray Crockett	.02	.10
❑ 235 Craig Heyward	.02	.10
❑ 236 Mike Fox	.02	.10
❑ 237 Derek Brown RBK	.02	.10
❑ 238 Thomas Lewis	.02	.10
❑ 239 Hugh Douglas	.08	.25
❑ 240 Tom Carter	.02	.10
❑ 241 Toby Wright	.02	.10
❑ 242 Jason Belser	.02	.10
❑ 243 Rodney Peete	.02	.10
❑ 244 Napoleon Kaufman	.20	.50
❑ 245 Merton Hanks	.02	.10
❑ 246 Harry Colon	.02	.10
❑ 247 Greg Hill	.08	.25
❑ 248 Vincent Brisby	.02	.10
❑ 249 Eric Hill	.02	.10
❑ 250 Brett Favre	1.00	2.50
❑ 251 Leroy Hoard	.02	.10
❑ 252 Eric Guliford	.02	.10
❑ 253 Stanley Richard	.08	.25
❑ 254 Carlos Jenkins	.02	.10
❑ 255 D'Marco Farr	.02	.10
❑ 256 Carlton Gray	.02	.10
❑ 257 Derek Loville	.02	.10
❑ 258 Ray Buchanan	.02	.10
❑ 259 Jake Reed	.08	.25
❑ 260 Dan Marino	1.00	2.50
❑ 261 Brad Baxter	.02	.10
❑ 262 Pat Swilling	.02	.10
❑ 263 Andy Harmon	.02	.10
❑ 264 Harold Green	.02	.10
❑ 265 Shannon Sharpe	.08	.25
❑ 266 Erik Kramer	.02	.10
❑ 267 Lamar Lathon	.02	.10
❑ 268 Stevon Moore	.02	.10
❑ 269 Tony Martin	.08	.25
❑ 270 Bruce Smith	.08	.25
❑ 271 James Washington	.02	.10
❑ 272 Tyrone Poole	.02	.10
❑ 273 Eric Swann	.02	.10
❑ 274 Dexter Carter	.02	.10
❑ 275 Greg Lloyd	.08	.25
❑ 276 Michael Zordich	.02	.10
❑ 277 Steve Wisniewski	.02	.10
❑ 278 Chris Calloway	.02	.10
❑ 279 Irv Smith	.02	.10
❑ 280 Steve Young	.40	1.00
❑ 281 James O.Stewart	.08	.25
❑ 282 Blaine Bishop	.02	.10
❑ 283 Rob Moore	.08	.25
❑ 284 Eric Metcalf	.02	.10
❑ 285 Kerry Collins	.20	.50
❑ 286 Dan Wilkinson	.02	.10
❑ 287 Curtis Conway	.20	.50
❑ 288 Jay Novacek	.02	.10
❑ 289 Henry Ellard	.02	.10
❑ 290 Curtis Martin	.40	1.00
❑ 291 Brett Perriman	.02	.10
❑ 292 Jeff Lageman	.02	.10
❑ 293 Trent Dilfer	.20	.50
❑ 294 Cortez Kennedy	.02	.10
❑ 295 Jeff Hostetler	.02	.10
❑ 296 Mark Fields	.02	.10
❑ 297 Qadry Ismail	.08	.25
❑ 298 Steve Bono	.02	.10
❑ 299 Tony Tolbert	.02	.10
❑ 300 Jerry Rice	.50	1.25
❑ 301 Marvcus Patton	.02	.10
❑ 302 Robert Brooks	.20	.50
❑ 303 Terry Ray RC	.02	.10
❑ 304 John Thierry	.02	.10
❑ 305 Errict Rhett	.08	.25
❑ 306 Ricardo McDonald	.02	.10
❑ 307 Antonio London	.02	.10
❑ 308 Lonnie Johnson	.02	.10
❑ 309 Mark Collins	.02	.10
❑ 310 Marshall Faulk	.25	.60
❑ 311 Anthony Pleasant	.02	.10

Card		
❑ 312 Howard Griffith	.02	.10
❑ 313 Roosevelt Potts	.02	.10
❑ 314 Jim Flanigan	.02	.10
❑ 315 Omar Ellison RC	.02	.10
❑ 316 Boomer Esiason SP	.08	.25
❑ 317 Leslie O'Neal SP	.02	.10
❑ 318 Jerome Bettis SP	.20	.50
❑ 319 Larry Brown SP	.02	.10
❑ 320 Neil O'Donnell SP	.08	.25
❑ 321 Andre Rison SP	.08	.25
❑ 322 Cornelius Bennett SP	.02	.10
❑ 323 Quinn Early SP	.02	.10
❑ 324 Bryan Cox SP	.02	.10
❑ 325 Irving Fryar SP	.08	.25
❑ 326 Eddie Robinson SP	.02	.10
❑ 327 Chris Doleman SP	.02	.10
❑ 328 Sean Gilbert SP	.02	.10
❑ 329 Steve Walsh SP	.02	.10
❑ 330 Kevin Greene SP	.08	.25
❑ 331 Chris Spielman SP	.02	.10
❑ 332 Jeff Graham SP	.02	.10
❑ 333 Anthony Dorsett SP RC	.02	.10
❑ 334 Amani Toomer SP RC	.60	1.50
❑ 335 Walt Harris SP RC	.02	.10
❑ 336 Ray Mickens SP RC	.02	.10
❑ 337 Danny Kanell SP RC	.20	.50
❑ 338 Daryl Gardener SP RC	.02	.10
❑ 339 Jonathan Ogden SP	.08	.25
❑ 340 Eddie George SP RC	.75	2.00
❑ 341 Jeff Lewis SP RC	.08	.25
❑ 342 Terrell Owens SP RC	1.50	4.00
❑ 343 Brian Dawkins SP RC	.75	2.00
❑ 344 Tim Biakabutuka SP	.20	.50
❑ 345 Marvin Harrison SP	.60	1.50
❑ 346 Lawyer Milloy SP RC	.25	.60
❑ 347 Eric Moulds SP	.30	.75
❑ 348 Alex Van Dyke SP	.08	.25
❑ 349 John Mobley SP	.02	.10
❑ 350 Kevin Hardy SP	.20	.50
❑ 351 Ray Lewis SP RC	2.00	5.00
❑ 352 Lawrence Phillips SP	.20	.50
❑ 353 Stepfret Williams SP RC	.08	.25
❑ 354 Bobby Engram SP RC	.20	.50
❑ 355 Leeland McElroy SP RC	.08	.25
❑ 356 Marco Battaglia SP	.02	.10
❑ 357 Rickey Dudley SP	.20	.50
❑ 358 Bobby Hoying SP RC	.20	.50
❑ 359 Cedric Jones SP RC	.02	.10
❑ 360 Keyshawn Johnson SP	.20	.50
❑ P19 Scott Mitchell Prototype	.20	.50
❑ P31 Rashaan Salaam Prototype	.30	.75
❑ P56 Hardy Nickerson Prototype	.20	.50
❑ NNO Checklist Card	.02	.10

1997 Stadium Club

Card		
❑ COMPLETE SET (340)	25.00	60.00
❑ COMP.SERIES 1 (170)	15.00	30.00
❑ COMP.SERIES 2 (170)	15.00	30.00
❑ 1 Junior Seau	.30	.75
❑ 2 Michael Irvin	.30	.75
❑ 3 Marcus Allen	.30	.75
❑ 4 Dale Carter	.10	.30
❑ 5 Darnell Autry RC	.20	.50
❑ 6 Isaac Bruce	.30	.75
❑ 7 Darrell Green	.20	.50
❑ 8 Joey Galloway	.20	.50
❑ 9 Steve Atwater	.10	.30
❑ 10 Kordell Stewart	.30	.75
❑ 11 Tony Brackens	.10	.30
❑ 12 Gus Frerotte	.10	.30
❑ 13 Henry Ellard	.10	.30
❑ 14 Charles Way	.20	.50
❑ 15 Jim Druckenmiller RC	.20	.50
❑ 16 Orlando Thomas	.10	.30
❑ 17 Terrell Davis	.40	1.00
❑ 18 Jim Schwantz	.10	.30
❑ 19 Derrick Thomas	.30	.75
❑ 20 Curtis Martin	.40	1.00
❑ 21 Deion Sanders	.30	.75
❑ 22 Bruce Smith	.20	.50
❑ 23 Jake Reed	.20	.50
❑ 24 Leeland McElroy	.10	.30
❑ 25 Jerome Bettis	.30	.75
❑ 26 Neil Smith	.20	.50
❑ 27 Terry Allen	.30	.75
❑ 28 Gilbert Brown	.20	.50
❑ 29 Steve McNair	.40	1.00
❑ 30 Kerry Collins	.30	.75
❑ 31 Thurman Thomas	.30	.75
❑ 32 Kenny Holmes RC	.30	.75
❑ 33 Karim Abdul-Jabbar	.30	.75
❑ 34 Steve Young	.40	1.00
❑ 35 Jerry Rice	.60	1.50
❑ 36 Jeff George	.20	.50
❑ 37 Errict Rhett	.10	.30
❑ 38 Mike Alstott	.30	.75
❑ 39 Tim Brown	.30	.75
❑ 40 Keyshawn Johnson	.30	.75
❑ 41 Jim Harbaugh	.20	.50
❑ 42 Kevin Hardy	.10	.30
❑ 43 Kevin Greene	.20	.50
❑ 44 Eric Metcalf	.20	.50
❑ 45 Troy Aikman	.60	1.50
❑ 46 Marshall Faulk	.40	1.00
❑ 47 Shannon Sharpe	.20	.50
❑ 48 Warren Moon	.30	.75
❑ 49 Mark Brunell	.40	1.00
❑ 50 Dan Marino	1.25	3.00
❑ 51 Byron Hanspard RC	.20	.50
❑ 52 Chris Chandler	.20	.50
❑ 53 Wayne Chrebet	.30	.75
❑ 54 Antonio Langham	.10	.30
❑ 55 Barry Sanders	1.00	2.50
❑ 56 Curtis Conway	.20	.50
❑ 57 Ricky Watters	.20	.50
❑ 58 William Thomas	.10	.30
❑ 59 Chris Warren	.20	.50
❑ 60 Terry Glenn	.30	.75
❑ 61 Peter Boulware RC	.30	.75
❑ 62 Chad Cota	.10	.30
❑ 63 Eddie Kennison	.20	.50
❑ 64 Lamar Smith	.30	.75
❑ 65 Brett Favre	1.50	3.00
❑ 66 Michael Westbrook	.20	.50
❑ 67 Larry Centers	.20	.50
❑ 68 Trent Dilfer	.30	.75
❑ 69 Stevon Moore	.10	.30
❑ 70 John Elway	1.25	3.00
❑ 71 Bryce Paup	.10	.30
❑ 72 Quentin Coryatt	.10	.30
❑ 73 Rashaan Salaam	.10	.30
❑ 74 Thomas Lewis	.10	.30
❑ 75 Drew Bledsoe	.40	1.00
❑ 76 Cris Carter	.30	.75
❑ 77 Joe Bowden	.10	.30
❑ 78 Allen Aldridge	.10	.30
❑ 79 Zach Thomas	.30	.75
❑ 80 Emmitt Smith	1.00	2.50
❑ 81 Daryl Johnston	.20	.50
❑ 82 Vinny Testaverde	.20	.50
❑ 83 James O.Stewart	.20	.50
❑ 84 Edgar Bennett	.20	.50
❑ 85 Shawn Springs RC	.20	.50
❑ 86 Elvis Grbac	.20	.50
❑ 87 Levon Kirkland	.10	.30
❑ 88 Jeff Graham	.10	.30
❑ 89 Terrell Fletcher	.10	.30
❑ 90 Eddie George	.30	.75
❑ 91 Jessie Tuggle	.10	.30
❑ 92 Terrell Owens	.40	1.00
❑ 93 Wayne Martin	.10	.30
❑ 94 Dwayne Harper	.10	.30
❑ 95 Mark Collins	.10	.30
❑ 96 Marvcus Patton	.10	.30
❑ 97 Napoleon Kaufman	.30	.75
❑ 98 Keenan McCardell	.20	.50
❑ 99 Ty Detmer	.20	.50
❑ 100 Reggie White	.30	.75
❑ 101 William Floyd	.20	.50
❑ 102 Scott Mitchell	.20	.50
❑ 103 Robert Blackmon	.10	.30
❑ 104 Dan Wilkinson	.10	.30
❑ 105 Warren Sapp	.20	.50
❑ 106 Dave Meggett	.10	.30
❑ 107 Brian Mitchell	.10	.30
❑ 108 Tyrone Poole	.10	.30
❑ 109 Derrick Alexander WR	.20	.50
❑ 110 David Palmer	.10	.30
❑ 111 James Farrior RC	.30	.75
❑ 112 Chad Brown	.10	.30
❑ 113 Marty Carter	.10	.30
❑ 114 Lawrence Phillips	.10	.30
❑ 115 Wesley Walls	.20	.50
❑ 116 John Friesz	.10	.30
❑ 117 Roman Phifer	.10	.30
❑ 118 Jason Sehorn	.20	.50
❑ 119 Henry Thomas	.10	.30
❑ 120 Natrone Means	.20	.50
❑ 121 Ty Law	.20	.50
❑ 122 Tony Gonzalez RC	1.25	3.00
❑ 123 Kevin Williams	.10	.30
❑ 124 Regan Upshaw	.10	.30
❑ 125 Antonio Freeman	.30	.75
❑ 126 Jessie Armstead	.10	.30
❑ 127 Pat Barnes RC	.30	.75
❑ 128 Charlie Garner	.20	.50
❑ 129 Irving Fryar	.20	.50
❑ 130 Rickey Dudley	.20	.50
❑ 131 Rodney Harrison RC	.60	1.50
❑ 132 Brent Jones	.20	.50
❑ 133 Neil O'Donnell	.20	.50
❑ 134 Darryll Lewis	.10	.30
❑ 135 Jason Belser	.10	.30
❑ 136 Mark Chmura	.20	.50
❑ 137 Seth Joyner	.10	.30
❑ 138 Herschel Walker	.20	.50
❑ 139 Santana Dotson	.10	.30
❑ 140 Carl Pickens	.20	.50
❑ 141 Terance Mathis	.20	.50
❑ 142 Walt Harris	.10	.30
❑ 143 John Mobley	.10	.30
❑ 144 Gabe Northern	.10	.30
❑ 145 Herman Moore	.20	.50
❑ 146 Michael Jackson	.20	.50
❑ 147 Chris Sanders	.10	.30
❑ 148 LeShon Johnson	.10	.30
❑ 149 Darrell Russell RC	.10	.30
❑ 150 Winslow Oliver	.10	.30
❑ 151 Tamarick Vanover	.20	.50
❑ 152 Tony Martin	.20	.50
❑ 153 Lamar Lathon	.10	.30
❑ 154 Ray Mickens	.10	.30
❑ 155 Derrick Brooks	.30	.75
❑ 156 Warrick Dunn RC	1.25	3.00
❑ 157 Tim McDonald	.10	.30
❑ 158 Keith Lyle	.10	.30
❑ 159 Terry McDaniel	.10	.30
❑ 160 Andre Hastings	.10	.30
❑ 161 Phillippi Sparks	.10	.30
❑ 162 Tedy Bruschi	.60	1.50
❑ 163 Bryant Westbrook RC	.10	.30
❑ 164 Victor Green	.10	.30
❑ 165 Jimmy Smith	.20	.50
❑ 166 Greg Biekert	.10	.30
❑ 167 Frank Sanders	.20	.50
❑ 168 Chris Doleman	.10	.30
❑ 169 Phil Hansen	.10	.30
❑ 170 Walter Jones RC	.30	.75
❑ 171 Mark Carrier WR	.10	.30
❑ 172 Greg Hill	.10	.30
❑ 173 Erik Kramer	.10	.30
❑ 174 Chris Spielman	.10	.30
❑ 175 Tom Knight RC	.10	.30
❑ 176 Sam Mills	.10	.30
❑ 177 Robert Smith	.20	.50
❑ 178 Dorsey Levens	.30	.75
❑ 179 Chris Slade	.10	.30
❑ 180 Troy Vincent	.10	.30
❑ 181 Mario Bates	.10	.30
❑ 182 Ed McCaffrey	.20	.50
❑ 183 Mike Mamula	.10	.30
❑ 184 Chad Hennings	.10	.30
❑ 185 Stan Humphries	.20	.50
❑ 186 Reinard Wilson RC	.20	.50
❑ 187 Kevin Carter	.10	.30
❑ 188 Qadry Ismail	.20	.50
❑ 189 Cortez Kennedy	.10	.30
❑ 190 Eric Swann	.10	.30
❑ 191 Corey Dillon RC	2.50	6.00
❑ 192 Renaldo Wynn	.10	.30
❑ 193 Bobby Hebert	.10	.30
❑ 194 Fred Barnett	.10	.30
❑ 195 Ray Lewis	.50	1.25
❑ 196 Robert Jones	.10	.30

❑ 197 Brian Williams .10 .30
❑ 198 Willie McGinest .10 .30
❑ 199 Jake Plummer RC 2.00 5.00
❑ 200 Aeneas Williams .10 .30
❑ 201 Ashley Ambrose .10 .30
❑ 202 Cornelius Bennett .10 .30
❑ 203 Mo Lewis .10 .30
❑ 204 James Hasty .10 .30
❑ 205 Carnell Lake .10 .30
❑ 206 Heath Shuler .10 .30
❑ 207 Dana Stubblefield .10 .30
❑ 208 Corey Miller .10 .30
❑ 209 Ike Hilliard RC .50 1.25
❑ 210 Bryant Young .10 .30
❑ 211 Hardy Nickerson .10 .30
❑ 212 Blaine Bishop .10 .30
❑ 213 Marcus Robertson .10 .30
❑ 214 Tony Bennett .10 .30
❑ 215 Kent Graham .10 .30
❑ 216 Steve Bono .20 .50
❑ 217 Will Blackwell RC .20 .50
❑ 218 Tyrone Braxton .10 .30
❑ 219 Eric Moulds .30 .75
❑ 220 Rod Woodson .20 .50
❑ 221 Anthony Johnson .10 .30
❑ 222 Willie Davis .10 .30
❑ 223 Darrin Smith .10 .30
❑ 224 Rick Mirer .10 .30
❑ 225 Marvin Harrison .30 .75
❑ 226 Terrell Buckley .10 .30
❑ 227 Joe Aska .10 .30
❑ 228 Yatil Green RC .20 .50
❑ 229 William Fuller .10 .30
❑ 230 Eddie Robinson .10 .30
❑ 231 Brian Blades .10 .30
❑ 232 Michael Sinclair .10 .30
❑ 233 Ken Harvey .10 .30
❑ 234 Harvey Williams .10 .30
❑ 235 Simeon Rice .20 .50
❑ 236 Chris T. Jones .10 .30
❑ 237 Bert Emanuel .20 .50
❑ 238 Corey Sawyer .10 .30
❑ 239 Chris Calloway .10 .30
❑ 240 Jeff Blake .20 .50
❑ 241 Alonzo Spellman .10 .30
❑ 242 Bryan Cox .10 .30
❑ 243 Antowain Smith RC 1.00 2.50
❑ 244 Tim Biakabutuka .20 .50
❑ 245 Ray Crockett .10 .30
❑ 246 Dwayne Rudd .10 .30
❑ 247 Glyn Milburn .10 .30
❑ 248 Gary Plummer .10 .30
❑ 249 O.J. McDuffie .20 .50
❑ 250 Willie Clay .10 .30
❑ 251 Jim Everett .10 .30
❑ 252 Eugene Daniel .10 .30
❑ 253 Corey Widmer .10 .30
❑ 254 Mel Gray .10 .30
❑ 255 Ken Norton .10 .30
❑ 256 Johnnie Morton .20 .50
❑ 257 Courtney Hawkins .10 .30
❑ 258 Ricardo McDonald .10 .30
❑ 259 Todd Lyght .10 .30
❑ 260 Micheal Barrow .10 .30
❑ 261 Aaron Glenn .10 .30
❑ 262 Jeff Herrod .10 .30
❑ 263 Troy Davis RC .20 .50
❑ 264 Eric Hill .10 .30
❑ 265 Darrien Gordon .10 .30
❑ 266 Lake Dawson .10 .30
❑ 267 John Randle .20 .50
❑ 268 Henry Jones .10 .30
❑ 269 Mickey Washington .10 .30
❑ 270 Amani Toomer .20 .50
❑ 271 Steve Grant .10 .30
❑ 272 Adrian Murrell .20 .50
❑ 273 Derrick Witherspoon .10 .30
❑ 274 Albert Lewis .10 .30
❑ 275 Ben Coates .20 .50
❑ 276 Reidel Anthony RC .30 .75
❑ 277 Jim Schwantz .10 .30
❑ 278 Aaron Hayden .10 .30
❑ 279 Ryan McNeil .10 .30
❑ 280 LeRoy Butler .10 .30
❑ 281 Craig Newsome .10 .30
❑ 282 Bill Romanowski .10 .30
❑ 283 Michael Bankston .10 .30
❑ 284 Kevin Smith .10 .30
❑ 285 Byron Bam Morris .10 .30
❑ 286 Darnay Scott .20 .50
❑ 287 David LaFleur RC .10 .30
❑ 288 Randall Cunningham .30 .75
❑ 289 Eric Davis .10 .30
❑ 290 Todd Collins .10 .30
❑ 291 Steve Tovar .10 .30
❑ 292 Jermaine Lewis .30 .75
❑ 293 Alfred Williams .10 .30
❑ 294 Brad Johnson .30 .75
❑ 295 Charles Johnson .20 .50
❑ 296 Ted Johnson .10 .30
❑ 297 Merton Hanks .10 .30
❑ 298 Andre Coleman .10 .30
❑ 299 Keith Jackson .10 .30
❑ 300 Terry Kirby .20 .50
❑ 301 Tony Banks .20 .50
❑ 302 Terrance Shaw .10 .30
❑ 303 Bobby Engram .20 .50
❑ 304 Hugh Douglas .10 .30
❑ 305 Lawyer Milloy .20 .50
❑ 306 James Jett .20 .50
❑ 307 Joey Kent RC .30 .75
❑ 308 Rodney Hampton .20 .50
❑ 309 Dewayne Washington .10 .30
❑ 310 Kevin Lockett RC .20 .50
❑ 311 Ki-Jana Carter .10 .30
❑ 312 Jeff Lageman .10 .30
❑ 313 Don Beebe .10 .30
❑ 314 Willie Williams .10 .30
❑ 315 Tyrone Wheatley .20 .50
❑ 316 Leslie O'Neal .10 .30
❑ 317 Quinn Early .10 .30
❑ 318 Sean Gilbert .10 .30
❑ 319 Tim Bowens .10 .30
❑ 320 Sean Dawkins .10 .30
❑ 321 Ken Dilger .10 .30
❑ 322 George Koonce .10 .30
❑ 323 Jevon Langford .10 .30
❑ 324 Mike Caldwell .10 .30
❑ 325 Orlando Pace RC .30 .75
❑ 326 Garrison Hearst .20 .50
❑ 327 Mike Tomczak .10 .30
❑ 328 Rob Moore .20 .50
❑ 329 Andre Reed .20 .50
❑ 330 Kimble Anders .20 .50
❑ 331 Qadry Ismail .20 .50
❑ 332 Eric Allen .10 .30
❑ 333 Dave Brown .10 .30
❑ 334 Bennie Blades .10 .30
❑ 335 Jamal Anderson .30 .75
❑ 336 John Lynch .20 .50
❑ 337 Tyrone Hughes .10 .30
❑ 338 Ronnie Harmon .10 .30
❑ 339 Rae Carruth RC .10 .30
❑ 340 Robert Brooks .20 .50
❑ P1 Junior Seau Prototype .20 .50
❑ P20 Curtis Martin Prototype .40 1.00
❑ P21 Deion Sanders Prototype .20 .50
❑ P30 Kerry Collins Prototype .30 .75
❑ P47 Shannon Sharpe Prototype .20 .50
❑ P84 Edgar Bennett Prototype .20 .50

1998 Stadium Club

❑ COMPLETE SET (195) 25.00 60.00
❑ 1 Barry Sanders 1.00 2.50
❑ 2 Tony Martin .20 .50
❑ 3 Fred Lane .10 .30
❑ 4 Darren Woodson .10 .30
❑ 5 Andre Reed .20 .50
❑ 6 Blaine Bishop .10 .30
❑ 7 Robert Brooks .20 .50
❑ 8 Tony Banks .20 .50
❑ 9 Charles Way .10 .30
❑ 10 Mark Brunell .30 .75
❑ 11 Darrell Green .20 .50
❑ 12 Aeneas Williams .10 .30
❑ 13 Rob Johnson .20 .50
❑ 14 Deion Sanders .30 .75
❑ 15 Marshall Faulk .40 1.00
❑ 16 Stephen Boyd .10 .30
❑ 17 Adrian Murrell .20 .50
❑ 18 Wayne Chrebet .30 .75
❑ 19 Michael Sinclair .10 .30
❑ 20 Dan Marino 1.25 3.00
❑ 21 Willie Davis .10 .30
❑ 22 Chris Warren .20 .50
❑ 23 John Mobley .10 .30
❑ 24 Shannon Sharpe .20 .50
❑ 25 Thurman Thomas .30 .75
❑ 26 Corey Dillon .30 .75
❑ 27 Zach Thomas .30 .75
❑ 28 James Jett .20 .50
❑ 29 Eric Metcalf .10 .30
❑ 30 Drew Bledsoe .50 1.25
❑ 31 Scott Greene .10 .30
❑ 32 Simeon Rice .20 .50
❑ 33 Robert Smith .30 .75
❑ 34 Keenan McCardell .20 .50
❑ 35 Jessie Armstead .10 .30
❑ 36 Jerry Rice .60 1.50
❑ 37 Eric Green .10 .30
❑ 38 Terrell Owens .30 .75
❑ 39 Tim Brown .30 .75
❑ 40 Vinny Testaverde .20 .50
❑ 41 Brian Stablein .10 .30
❑ 42 Bert Emanuel .20 .50
❑ 43 Terry Glenn .30 .75
❑ 44 Chad Cota .10 .30
❑ 45 Jermaine Lewis .20 .50
❑ 46 Derrick Thomas .30 .75
❑ 47 O.J. McDuffie .20 .50
❑ 48 Frank Wycheck .10 .30
❑ 49 Steve Broussard .10 .30
❑ 50 Terrell Davis .30 .75
❑ 51 Eric Allen .10 .30
❑ 52 Napoleon Kaufman .30 .75
❑ 53 Dan Wilkinson .10 .30
❑ 54 Kerry Collins .20 .50
❑ 55 Frank Sanders .20 .50
❑ 56 Jeff Burris .10 .30
❑ 57 Michael Westbrook .20 .50
❑ 58 Michael McCrary .10 .30
❑ 59 Bobby Hoying .20 .50
❑ 60 Jerome Bettis .30 .75
❑ 61 Amp Lee .10 .30
❑ 62 Levon Kirkland .10 .30
❑ 63 Dana Stubblefield .10 .30
❑ 64 Terance Mathis .20 .50
❑ 65 Mark Chmura .20 .50
❑ 66 Bryant Westbrook .10 .30
❑ 67 Rod Smith .20 .50
❑ 68 Derrick Alexander .20 .50
❑ 69 Jason Taylor .20 .50
❑ 70 Eddie George .30 .75
❑ 71 Elvis Grbac .20 .50
❑ 72 Junior Seau .30 .75
❑ 73 Marvin Harrison .30 .75
❑ 74 Neil O'Donnell .20 .50
❑ 75 Johnnie Morton .20 .50
❑ 76 John Randle .20 .50
❑ 77 Danny Kanell .20 .50
❑ 78 Charlie Garner .20 .50
❑ 79 J.J. Stokes .20 .50
❑ 80 Troy Aikman .60 1.50
❑ 81 Gus Frerotte .10 .30
❑ 82 Jake Plummer .30 .75
❑ 83 Andre Hastings .10 .30
❑ 84 Steve Atwater .10 .30
❑ 85 Larry Centers .10 .30
❑ 86 Kevin Hardy .10 .30
❑ 87 Willie McGinest .10 .30
❑ 88 Joey Galloway .20 .50
❑ 89 Charles Johnson .10 .30
❑ 90 Warrick Dunn .30 .75
❑ 91 Derrick Rodgers .10 .30
❑ 92 Aaron Glenn .10 .30
❑ 93 Shawn Jefferson .10 .30
❑ 94 Antonio Freeman .30 .75
❑ 95 Jake Reed .20 .50
❑ 96 Reidel Anthony .20 .50
❑ 97 Cris Dishman .10 .30
❑ 98 Jason Sehorn .20 .50
❑ 99 Herman Moore .20 .50
❑ 100 John Elway 1.25 3.00
❑ 101 Brad Johnson .30 .75

❑ 102 Jeff George .20 .50
❑ 103 Emmitt Smith 1.00 2.50
❑ 104 Steve McNair .30 .75
❑ 105 Ed McCaffrey .20 .50
❑ 106 Errict Rhett .20 .50
❑ 107 Dorsey Levens .30 .75
❑ 108 Michael Jackson .10 .30
❑ 109 Carl Pickens .20 .50
❑ 110 James Stewart .20 .50
❑ 111 Karim Abdul-Jabbar .30 .75
❑ 112 Jim Harbaugh .20 .50
❑ 113 Yancey Thigpen .10 .30
❑ 114 Chad Brown .10 .30
❑ 115 Chris Sanders .10 .30
❑ 116 Cris Carter .30 .75
❑ 117 Glenn Foley .20 .50
❑ 118 Ben Coates .20 .50
❑ 119 Jamal Anderson .30 .75
❑ 120 Steve Young .40 1.00
❑ 121 Scott Mitchell .20 .50
❑ 122 Rob Moore .20 .50
❑ 123 Bobby Engram .20 .50
❑ 124 Rod Woodson .20 .50
❑ 125 Terry Allen .30 .75
❑ 126 Warren Sapp .20 .50
❑ 127 Irving Fryar .20 .50
❑ 128 Isaac Bruce .30 .75
❑ 129 Rae Carruth .10 .30
❑ 130 Sean Dawkins .10 .30
❑ 131 Andre Rison .20 .50
❑ 132 Kevin Greene .20 .50
❑ 133 Warren Moon .30 .75
❑ 134 Keyshawn Johnson .30 .75
❑ 135 Jay Graham .10 .30
❑ 136 Mike Alstott .30 .75
❑ 137 Peter Boulware .10 .30
❑ 138 Doug Evans .10 .30
❑ 139 Jimmy Smith .20 .50
❑ 140 Kordell Stewart .30 .75
❑ 141 Tamarick Vanover .10 .30
❑ 142 Chris Slade .10 .30
❑ 143 Freddie Jones .10 .30
❑ 144 Erik Kramer .10 .30
❑ 145 Ricky Watters .20 .50
❑ 146 Chris Chandler .20 .50
❑ 147 Garrison Hearst .30 .75
❑ 148 Trent Dilfer .30 .75
❑ 149 Bruce Smith .20 .50
❑ 150 Brett Favre 1.25 3.00
❑ 151 Will Blackwell .10 .30
❑ 152 Rickey Dudley .10 .30
❑ 153 Natrone Means .20 .50
❑ 154 Curtis Conway .20 .50
❑ 155 Tony Gonzalez .30 .75
❑ 156 Jeff Blake .20 .50
❑ 157 Michael Irvin .30 .75
❑ 158 Curtis Martin .30 .75
❑ 159 Tim McDonald .10 .30
❑ 160 Wesley Walls .20 .50
❑ 161 Michael Strahan .20 .50
❑ 162 Reggie White .30 .75
❑ 163 Jeff Graham .10 .30
❑ 164 Ray Lewis .30 .75
❑ 165 Antowain Smith .30 .75
❑ 166 Ryan Leaf RC 1.00 2.50
❑ 167 Jerome Pathon RC 1.00 2.50
❑ 168 Duane Starks RC .50 1.25
❑ 169 Brian Simmons RC .75 2.00
❑ 170 Pat Johnson RC .75 2.00
❑ 171 Keith Brooking RC 1.00 2.50
❑ 172 Kevin Dyson RC 1.00 2.50
❑ 173 Robert Edwards RC .75 2.00
❑ 174 Grant Wistrom RC .75 2.00
❑ 175 Curtis Enis RC .50 1.25
❑ 176 John Avery RC .75 2.00
❑ 177 Jason Peter RC .50 1.25
❑ 178 Brian Griese RC 2.00 5.00
❑ 179 Tavian Banks RC .75 2.00
❑ 180 Andre Wadsworth RC .75 2.00
❑ 181 Skip Hicks RC .75 2.00
❑ 182 Hines Ward RC 5.00 10.00
❑ 183 Greg Ellis RC .50 1.25
❑ 184 Robert Holcombe RC .75 2.00
❑ 185 Joe Jurevicius RC 1.00 2.50
❑ 186 Takeo Spikes RC 1.00 2.50
❑ 187 Ahman Green RC 2.50 6.00
❑ 188 Jacquez Green RC .75 2.00
❑ 189 Randy Moss RC 6.00 15.00
❑ 190 Charles Woodson RC 1.25 3.00
❑ 191 Fred Taylor RC 1.50 4.00
❑ 192 Marcus Nash RC .50 1.25
❑ 193 Germane Crowell RC .75 2.00
❑ 194 Tim Dwight RC 1.00 2.50
❑ 195 Peyton Manning RC 12.50 25.00

1999 Stadium Club

❑ COMPLETE SET (200) 25.00 60.00
❑ COMP.SET w/o SP's (175) 7.50 20.00
❑ UNPRICED 1/1 PRESS PLATES EXIST
❑ FOUR DIFF.PP's PRODUCED PER CARD
❑ 1 Dan Marino 1.00 2.50
❑ 2 Andre Reed .20 .50
❑ 3 Michael Westbrook .20 .50
❑ 4 Isaac Bruce .30 .75
❑ 5 Curtis Martin .30 .75
❑ 6 Courtney Hawkins .10 .30
❑ 7 Charles Way .10 .30
❑ 8 Terrell Owens .30 .75
❑ 9 Warrick Dunn .30 .75
❑ 10 Jake Plummer .20 .50
❑ 11 Chad Brown .10 .30
❑ 12 Yancey Thigpen .10 .30
❑ 13 Lamar Thomas .10 .30
❑ 14 Keenan McCardell .20 .50
❑ 15 Shannon Sharpe .20 .50
❑ 16 Robert Brooks .20 .50
❑ 17 Cameron Cleeland .10 .30
❑ 18 Derrick Thomas .30 .75
❑ 19 Mark Brunell .30 .75
❑ 20 Jamal Anderson .30 .75
❑ 21 Germane Crowell .10 .30
❑ 22 Rod Smith .20 .50
❑ 23 Ty Law .20 .50
❑ 24 Cris Carter .30 .75
❑ 25 Terrell Davis .30 .75
❑ 26 Takeo Spikes .10 .30
❑ 27 Tim Biakabutuka .20 .50
❑ 28 Jermaine Lewis .20 .50
❑ 29 Adrian Murrell .20 .50
❑ 30 Doug Flutie .30 .75
❑ 31 Curtis Enis .10 .30
❑ 32 Skip Hicks .10 .30
❑ 33 Steve McNair .30 .75
❑ 34 Charles Woodson .30 .75
❑ 35 Jessie Armstead .10 .30
❑ 36 Shawn Springs .10 .30
❑ 37 Levon Kirkland .10 .30
❑ 38 Freddie Jones .10 .30
❑ 39 Warren Sapp .10 .30
❑ 40 Emmitt Smith .60 1.50
❑ 41 Reidel Anthony .20 .50
❑ 42 Tony Simmons .10 .30
❑ 43 Andre Hastings .10 .30
❑ 44 Byron Bam Morris .10 .30
❑ 45 Jimmy Smith .20 .50
❑ 46 Antonio Freeman .30 .75
❑ 47 Herman Moore .20 .50
❑ 48 Muhsin Muhammad .20 .50
❑ 49 Chris Chandler .20 .50
❑ 50 John Elway 1.00 2.50
❑ 51 Aeneas Williams .10 .30
❑ 52 Bobby Engram .20 .50
❑ 53 Keith Poole .10 .30
❑ 54 Zach Thomas .30 .75
❑ 55 Mike Alstott .30 .75
❑ 56 Junior Seau .30 .75
❑ 57 Aaron Glenn .10 .30
❑ 58 Darrell Green .10 .30
❑ 59 Thurman Thomas .20 .50
❑ 60 Troy Aikman .60 1.50
❑ 61 Bill Romanowski .10 .30
❑ 62 Wesley Walls .20 .50
❑ 63 Andre Wadsworth .10 .30
❑ 64 Robert Smith .30 .75
❑ 65 Elvis Grbac .20 .50
❑ 66 Terry Fair .10 .30
❑ 67 Ben Coates .20 .50
❑ 68 Bert Emanuel .20 .50
❑ 69 Jacquez Green .10 .30
❑ 70 Barry Sanders 1.00 2.50
❑ 71 James Jett .20 .50
❑ 72 Gary Brown .10 .30
❑ 73 Stephen Alexander .10 .30
❑ 74 Wayne Chrebet .20 .50
❑ 75 Drew Bledsoe .40 1.00
❑ 76 John Lynch .20 .50
❑ 77 Jake Reed .20 .50
❑ 78 Marvin Harrison .30 .75
❑ 79 Johnnie Morton .20 .50
❑ 80 Brett Favre 1.00 2.50
❑ 81 Charlie Batch .30 .75
❑ 82 Antowain Smith .30 .75
❑ 83 Mikhael Ricks .10 .30
❑ 84 Derrick Mayes .10 .30
❑ 85 John Mobley .10 .30
❑ 86 Ernie Mills .10 .30
❑ 87 Jeff Blake .20 .50
❑ 88 Curtis Conway .20 .50
❑ 89 Bruce Smith .20 .50
❑ 90 Peyton Manning 1.00 2.50
❑ 91 Tyrone Davis .10 .30
❑ 92 Ray Buchanan .10 .30
❑ 93 Tim Dwight .30 .75
❑ 94 O.J. McDuffie .20 .50
❑ 95 Vonnie Holliday .10 .30
❑ 96 Jon Kitna .30 .75
❑ 97 Trent Dilfer .20 .50
❑ 98 Jerome Bettis .30 .75
❑ 99 Dedric Ward .10 .30
❑ 100 Fred Taylor .30 .75
❑ 101 Ike Hilliard .10 .30
❑ 102 Frank Wycheck .10 .30
❑ 103 Eric Moulds .30 .75
❑ 104 Rob Moore .20 .50
❑ 105 Ed McCaffrey .20 .50
❑ 106 Carl Pickens .20 .50
❑ 107 Priest Holmes .50 1.25
❑ 108 Kevin Hardy .10 .30
❑ 109 Terry Glenn .30 .75
❑ 110 Keyshawn Johnson .30 .75
❑ 111 Karim Abdul-Jabbar .20 .50
❑ 112 Stephen Boyd .10 .30
❑ 113 Ahman Green .30 .75
❑ 114 Duce Staley .30 .75
❑ 115 Vinny Testaverde .20 .50
❑ 116 Napoleon Kaufman .30 .75
❑ 117 Frank Sanders .20 .50
❑ 118 Peter Boulware .10 .30
❑ 119 Kevin Greene .10 .30
❑ 120 Steve Young .40 1.00
❑ 121 Damay Scott .10 .30
❑ 122 Deion Sanders .30 .75
❑ 123 Corey Dillon .30 .75
❑ 124 Randall Cunningham .30 .75
❑ 125 Eddie George .30 .75
❑ 126 Derrick Alexander .10 .30
❑ 127 Mark Chmura .10 .30
❑ 128 Michael Sinclair .10 .30
❑ 129 Rickey Dudley .10 .30
❑ 130 Joey Galloway .20 .50
❑ 131 Michael Strahan .20 .50
❑ 132 Ricky Proehl .10 .30
❑ 133 Natrone Means .20 .50
❑ 134 Dorsey Levens .30 .75
❑ 135 Andre Rison .20 .50
❑ 136 Alonzo Mayes .10 .30
❑ 137 John Randle .20 .50
❑ 138 Terance Mathis .20 .50
❑ 139 Rae Carruth .10 .30
❑ 140 Jerry Rice .60 1.50
❑ 141 Michael Irvin .20 .50
❑ 142 Oronde Gadsden .20 .50
❑ 143 Jerome Pathon .10 .30
❑ 144 Ricky Watters .20 .50
❑ 145 J.J. Stokes .20 .50
❑ 146 Kordell Stewart .20 .50
❑ 147 Tim Brown .30 .75
❑ 148 Garrison Hearst .20 .50
❑ 149 Tony Gonzalez .30 .75
❑ 150 Randy Moss .75 2.00
❑ 151 Daunte Culpepper RC 2.50 6.00
❑ 152 Amos Zereoue RC .75 2.00
❑ 153 Champ Bailey RC 1.00 2.50
❑ 154 Peerless Price RC .75 2.00

Card		
❑ 155 Edgerrin James RC	2.50	6.00
❑ 156 Joe Germaine RC	.60	1.50
❑ 157 David Boston RC	.75	2.00
❑ 158 Kevin Faulk RC	.75	2.00
❑ 159 Troy Edwards RC	.60	1.50
❑ 160 Akili Smith RC	.60	1.50
❑ 161 Kevin Johnson RC	.75	2.00
❑ 162 Rob Konrad RC	.60	1.50
❑ 163 Shaun King RC	.60	1.50
❑ 164 James Johnson RC	.60	1.50
❑ 165 Donovan McNabb RC	3.00	8.00
❑ 166 Torry Holt RC	1.50	4.00
❑ 167 Mike Cloud RC	.60	1.50
❑ 168 Sodrick Irvin RC	.40	1.00
❑ 169 Cade McNown RC	.60	1.50
❑ 170 Ricky Williams RC	1.25	3.00
❑ 171 Karsten Bailey RC	.60	1.50
❑ 172 Cecil Collins RC	.40	1.00
❑ 173 Brock Huard RC	.75	2.00
❑ 174 D'Wayne Bates RC	.60	1.50
❑ 175 Tim Couch RC	.75	2.00
❑ 176 Torrance Small	.10	.30
❑ 177 Warren Moon	.30	.75
❑ 178 Rocket Ismail	.20	.50
❑ 179 Marshall Faulk	.40	1.00
❑ 180 Trent Green	.30	.75
❑ 181 Sean Dawkins	.10	.30
❑ 182 Pete Mitchell	.10	.30
❑ 183 Jeff Graham	.10	.30
❑ 184 Eddie Kennison	.20	.50
❑ 185 Kerry Collins	.20	.50
❑ 186 Eric Green	.10	.30
❑ 187 Kyle Brady	.10	.30
❑ 188 Tony Martin	.20	.50
❑ 189 Jim Harbaugh	.20	.50
❑ 190 Erik Kramer	.10	.30
❑ 191 Steve Atwater	.10	.30
❑ 192 Chad Bratzke	.10	.30
❑ 193 Charles Johnson	.10	.30
❑ 194 Damon Gibson	.10	.30
❑ 195 Jeff George	.20	.50
❑ 196 Scott Mitchell	.10	.30
❑ 197 Terry Kirby	.10	.30
❑ 198 Rich Gannon	.30	.75
❑ 199 Chris Spielman	.10	.30
❑ 200 Brad Johnson	.30	.75

2000 Stadium Club

Card		
❑ COMPLETE SET (175)	20.00	50.00
❑ COMP.SET w/o SP's (150)	7.50	20.00
❑ 1 Peyton Manning	.60	1.50
❑ 2 Pete Mitchell	.08	.25
❑ 3 Napoleon Kaufman	.15	.40
❑ 4 Mikhael Ricks	.08	.25
❑ 5 Mike Alstott	.25	.60
❑ 6 Brad Johnson	.25	.60
❑ 7 Tony Gonzalez	.15	.40
❑ 8 Germane Crowell	.08	.25
❑ 9 Marcus Robinson	.25	.60
❑ 10 Stephen Davis	.25	.60
❑ 11 Terance Mathis	.15	.40
❑ 12 Jake Plummer	.15	.40
❑ 13 Qadry Ismail	.15	.40
❑ 14 Cade McNown	.08	.25
❑ 15 Zach Thomas	.25	.60
❑ 16 Curtis Martin	.25	.60
❑ 17 Torrance Small	.08	.25
❑ 18 Steve McNair	.25	.60
❑ 19 Jim Harbaugh	.15	.40
❑ 20 Keyshawn Johnson	.25	.60
❑ 21 Antonio Freeman	.25	.60
❑ 22 Ed McCaffrey	.25	.60
❑ 23 Elvis Grbac	.15	.40
❑ 24 Peerless Price	.15	.40
❑ 25 Jerome Bettis	.25	.60
❑ 26 Yancey Thigpen	.08	.25
❑ 27 Jake Delhomme RC	1.25	3.00
❑ 28 Keith Poole	.08	.25
❑ 29 Carl Pickens	.15	.40
❑ 30 Jerry Rice	.50	1.25
❑ 31 Rob Moore	.15	.40
❑ 32 Reidel Anthony	.08	.25
❑ 33 Jimmy Smith	.15	.40
❑ 34 Ray Lucas	.15	.40
❑ 35 Troy Aikman	.50	1.25
❑ 36 Steve Beuerlein	.15	.40
❑ 37 Charlie Batch	.25	.60
❑ 38 Derrick Mayes	.15	.40
❑ 39 Tim Brown	.25	.60
❑ 40 Eddie George	.25	.60
❑ 41 O.J. McDuffie	.15	.40
❑ 42 Ike Hilliard	.15	.40
❑ 43 Bill Schroeder	.15	.40
❑ 44 Jim Miller	.08	.25
❑ 45 Chris Chandler	.15	.40
❑ 46 Fred Taylor	.25	.60
❑ 47 Ricky Watters	.15	.40
❑ 48 Tyrone Wheatley	.15	.40
❑ 49 Bruce Smith	.15	.40
❑ 50 Marshall Faulk	.30	.75
❑ 51 Kevin Carter	.08	.25
❑ 52 Champ Bailey	.15	.40
❑ 53 Troy Edwards	.08	.25
❑ 54 Doug Flutie	.25	.60
❑ 55 Charles Johnson	.15	.40
❑ 56 Michael Westbrook	.15	.40
❑ 57 Frank Wycheck	.08	.25
❑ 58 Drew Bledsoe	.30	.75
❑ 59 Terrence Wilkins	.08	.25
❑ 60 Ricky Williams	.25	.60
❑ 61 Rod Smith	.15	.40
❑ 62 Errict Rhett	.15	.40
❑ 63 Vinny Testaverde	.15	.40
❑ 64 Jacquez Green	.08	.25
❑ 65 Curtis Conway	.15	.40
❑ 66 Wayne Chrebet	.15	.40
❑ 67 Albert Connell	.08	.25
❑ 68 Kordell Stewart	.15	.40
❑ 69 Bert Emanuel	.08	.25
❑ 70 Randy Moss	.50	1.25
❑ 71 Akili Smith	.08	.25
❑ 72 Brian Griese	.25	.60
❑ 73 Frank Sanders	.15	.40
❑ 74 Wesley Walls	.08	.25
❑ 75 Michael Pittman	.08	.25
❑ 76 Steve Young	.30	.75
❑ 77 Jevon Kearse	.25	.60
❑ 78 Az-Zahir Hakim	.15	.40
❑ 79 James Stewart	.15	.40
❑ 80 Brett Favre	.75	2.00
❑ 81 Dan Marino	.75	2.00
❑ 82 Joe Horn	.15	.40
❑ 83 Mark Brunell	.25	.60
❑ 84 Eddie Kennison	.15	.40
❑ 85 Deion Sanders	.25	.60
❑ 86 Priest Holmes	.30	.75
❑ 87 Torry Glenn	.15	.40
❑ 88 Olandis Gary	.25	.60
❑ 89 Patrick Jeffers	.25	.60
❑ 90 Emmitt Smith	.50	1.25
❑ 91 J.J. Stokes	.15	.40
❑ 92 Warrick Dunn	.25	.60
❑ 93 Damon Huard	.25	.60
❑ 94 Herman Moore	.15	.40
❑ 95 Corey Dillon	.25	.60
❑ 96 Joey Galloway	.15	.40
❑ 97 Jamal Anderson	.25	.60
❑ 98 Junior Seau	.25	.60
❑ 99 Robert Smith	.25	.60
❑ 100 Edgerrin James	.40	1.00
❑ 101 Derrick Alexander	.15	.40
❑ 102 Johnnie Morton	.15	.40
❑ 103 Sean Dawkins	.08	.25
❑ 104 Derrick Brooks	.25	.60
❑ 105 Rickey Dudley	.08	.25
❑ 106 Keenan McCardell	.15	.40
❑ 107 Kerry Collins	.15	.40
❑ 108 Kevin Johnson	.25	.60
❑ 109 Eric Moulds	.25	.60
❑ 110 Terrell Davis	.25	.60
❑ 111 Shawn Jefferson	.08	.25
❑ 112 Donovan McNabb	.40	1.00
❑ 113 Torry Holt	.25	.60
❑ 114 Marvin Harrison	.25	.60
❑ 115 Amani Toomer	.15	.40
❑ 116 Tony Martin	.15	.40
❑ 117 Curtis Enis	.08	.25
❑ 118 Tiki Barber	.25	.60
❑ 119 Freddie Jones	.08	.25
❑ 120 Muhsin Muhammad	.15	.40
❑ 121 Shaun King	.08	.25
❑ 122 Isaac Bruce	.25	.60
❑ 123 Duce Staley	.25	.60
❑ 124 Hardy Nickerson	.08	.25
❑ 125 Corey Bradford	.15	.40
❑ 126 Kevin Hardy	.08	.25
❑ 127 Hines Ward	.25	.60
❑ 128 Charlie Garner	.15	.40
❑ 129 Warren Sapp	.15	.40
❑ 130 Tim Couch	.15	.40
❑ 131 Kevin Dyson	.15	.40
❑ 132 Rocket Ismail	.15	.40
❑ 133 Tim Dwight	.25	.60
❑ 134 Darnay Scott	.15	.40
❑ 135 Jeff George	.15	.40
❑ 136 Dorsey Levens	.15	.40
❑ 137 Jeff Blake	.15	.40
❑ 138 Jon Kitna	.25	.60
❑ 139 Rich Gannon	.25	.60
❑ 140 Cris Carter	.25	.60
❑ 141 Jeff Graham	.08	.25
❑ 142 James Johnson	.08	.25
❑ 143 Tim Biakabutuka	.15	.40
❑ 144 Bobby Engram	.15	.40
❑ 145 Tony Banks	.15	.40
❑ 146 Shannon Sharpe	.15	.40
❑ 147 Antowain Smith	.15	.40
❑ 148 Terrell Owens	.25	.60
❑ 149 Rob Johnson	.15	.40
❑ 150 Kurt Warner	.50	1.25
❑ 151 Thomas Jones RC	1.50	4.00
❑ 152 Chad Pennington RC	2.50	6.00
❑ 153 Ron Dayne RC	1.00	2.50
❑ 154 Tee Martin RC	1.00	2.50
❑ 155 Reuben Droughns RC	1.25	3.00
❑ 156 Jerry Porter RC	1.25	3.00
❑ 157 R.Jay Soward RC	.75	2.00
❑ 158 Sylvester Morris RC	.75	2.00
❑ 159 Todd Pinkston RC	1.00	2.50
❑ 160 Courtney Brown RC	1.00	2.50
❑ 161 Travis Taylor RC	1.00	2.50
❑ 162 Ron Dugans RC	.75	2.00
❑ 163 Laveranues Coles RC	1.25	3.00
❑ 164 Joe Hamilton RC	.75	2.00
❑ 165 Curtis Keaton RC	.75	2.00
❑ 166 Bubba Franks RC	1.00	2.50
❑ 167 Dennis Northcutt RC	1.00	2.50
❑ 168 Chris Redman RC	.75	2.00
❑ 169 Travis Prentice RC	.75	2.00
❑ 170 Shaun Alexander RC	3.00	8.00
❑ 171 Jamal Lewis RC	2.50	6.00
❑ 172 Peter Warrick RC	1.00	2.50
❑ 173 J.R. Redmond RC	.75	2.00
❑ 174 Trung Canidate RC	.75	2.00
❑ 175 Plaxico Burress RC	2.00	5.00

2001 Stadium Club

Card		
❑ COMPLETE SET (175)	60.00	120.00
❑ COMP.SET w/o SPs (125)	7.50	20.00
❑ 1 Peyton Manning	.60	1.50
❑ 2 Akili Smith	.15	.40
❑ 3 Brian Griese	.20	.50
❑ 4 Wayne Chrebet	.20	.50
❑ 5 Oronde Gadsden	.15	.40
❑ 6 Marvin Harrison	.25	.60
❑ 7 Charles Johnson	.15	.40
❑ 8 Jay Fiedler	.20	.50
❑ 9 Kerry Collins	.20	.50
❑ 10 Troy Aikman	.40	1.00
❑ 11 Donovan McNabb	.30	.75
❑ 12 Ike Hilliard	.20	.50

Card	Low	High
❑ 13 Warrick Dunn	.25	.60
❑ 14 Derrick Alexander	.15	.40
❑ 15 Jake Plummer	.20	.50
❑ 16 Corey Dillon	.20	.50
❑ 17 Ahman Green	.25	.60
❑ 18 Keenan McCardell	.20	.50
❑ 19 Derrick Mason	.20	.50
❑ 20 Jerry Rice	.50	1.25
❑ 21 Emmitt Smith	.60	1.50
❑ 22 Dedric Ward	.15	.40
❑ 23 Jamal Anderson	.20	.50
❑ 24 Charlie Garner	.20	.50
❑ 25 Vinny Testaverde	.20	.50
❑ 26 Shaun Alexander	.25	.60
❑ 27 Terry Glenn	.20	.50
❑ 28 Cade McNown	.20	.50
❑ 29 Germane Crowell	.15	.40
❑ 30 Jeff Graham	.15	.40
❑ 31 Rich Gannon	.20	.50
❑ 32 Jevon Kearse	.20	.50
❑ 33 Shannon Sharpe	.25	.60
❑ 34 Marcus Robinson	.20	.50
❑ 35 Rod Smith	.20	.50
❑ 36 Curtis Martin	.25	.60
❑ 37 Robert Smith	.20	.50
❑ 38 Marshall Faulk	.25	.60
❑ 39 Tony Richardson	.15	.40
❑ 40 Travis Prentice	.15	.40
❑ 41 Edgerrin James	.25	.60
❑ 42 Duce Staley	.20	.50
❑ 43 Keyshawn Johnson	.20	.50
❑ 44 Joe Horn	.20	.50
❑ 45 Shawn Bryson	.15	.40
❑ 46 Ray Lewis	.25	.60
❑ 47 Fred Taylor	.25	.60
❑ 48 Jeff George	.20	.50
❑ 49 Sean Dawkins	.15	.40
❑ 50 Daunte Culpepper	.25	.60
❑ 51 Chris Chandler	.20	.50
❑ 52 Tim Couch	.15	.40
❑ 53 Trent Dilfer	.20	.50
❑ 54 Steve McNair	.25	.60
❑ 55 Kordell Stewart	.20	.50
❑ 56 Aaron Brooks	.20	.50
❑ 57 Michael Pittman	.20	.50
❑ 58 Bill Schroeder	.20	.50
❑ 59 Junior Seau	.25	.60
❑ 60 Kurt Warner	.30	.75
❑ 61 Drew Bledsoe	.25	.60
❑ 62 Steve Beuerlein	.20	.50
❑ 63 Mike Anderson	.20	.50
❑ 64 Brad Johnson	.20	.50
❑ 65 Tim Brown	.25	.60
❑ 66 Qadry Ismail	.20	.50
❑ 67 Doug Flutie	.25	.60
❑ 68 Terrell Owens	.25	.60
❑ 69 Rocket Ismail	.20	.50
❑ 70 Charlie Batch	.20	.50
❑ 71 Jerome Pathon	.15	.40
❑ 72 Peter Warrick	.20	.50
❑ 73 Hines Ward	.25	.60
❑ 74 Ron Dayne	.20	.50
❑ 75 Lamar Smith	.20	.50
❑ 76 Amani Toomer	.20	.50
❑ 77 Joey Galloway	.20	.50
❑ 78 James Allen	.15	.40
❑ 79 Isaac Bruce	.25	.60
❑ 80 David Boston	.15	.40
❑ 81 James Thrash	.20	.50
❑ 82 Tony Gonzalez	.20	.50
❑ 83 Jason Taylor	.25	.60
❑ 84 Ricky Watters	.20	.50
❑ 85 Terance Mathis	.15	.40
❑ 86 Troy Brown	.20	.50
❑ 87 Mark Brunell	.25	.60
❑ 88 Rob Johnson	.20	.50
❑ 89 Freddie Jones	.15	.40
❑ 90 Eddie George	.25	.60
❑ 91 Tiki Barber	.25	.60
❑ 92 Donald Hayes	.15	.40
❑ 93 Muhsin Muhammad	.20	.50
❑ 94 Johnnie Morton	.20	.50
❑ 95 Warren Sapp	.20	.50
❑ 96 Bobby Shaw	.15	.40
❑ 97 Randy Moss	.30	.75
❑ 98 Jerome Bettis	.25	.60
❑ 99 Antonio Freeman	.25	.60
❑ 100 Jamal Lewis	.25	.60
❑ 101 Andre Rison	.20	.50
❑ 102 Kevin Faulk	.20	.50
❑ 103 Jon Kitna	.20	.50
❑ 104 Shawn Jefferson	.15	.40
❑ 105 Kevin Johnson	.15	.40
❑ 106 Torry Holt	.20	.50
❑ 107 Cris Carter	.25	.60
❑ 108 Chad Lewis	.15	.40
❑ 109 Stephen Davis	.20	.50
❑ 110 Jeff Blake	.20	.50
❑ 111 Elvis Grbac	.20	.50
❑ 112 Ed McCaffrey	.20	.50
❑ 113 Tim Biakabutuka	.15	.40
❑ 114 Trent Green	.25	.60
❑ 115 Jeff Garcia	.20	.50
❑ 116 Jacquez Green	.15	.40
❑ 117 Shaun King	.15	.40
❑ 118 Jimmy Smith	.20	.50
❑ 119 James Stewart	.15	.40
❑ 120 Brian Urlacher	.30	.75
❑ 121 Tyrone Wheatley	.20	.50
❑ 122 J.R. Redmond	.15	.40
❑ 123 Eric Moulds	.20	.50
❑ 124 Ricky Williams	.25	.60
❑ 125 Brett Favre	.75	2.00
❑ 126 Koren Robinson RC	.75	2.00
❑ 127 Richard Seymour RC	.75	2.00
❑ 128 Jamal Reynolds RC	.60	1.50
❑ 129 Kevin Kasper RC	.60	1.50
❑ 130 LaMont Jordan RC	.75	2.00
❑ 131 Reggie Wayne RC	2.00	5.00
❑ 132 Travis Henry RC	.75	2.00
❑ 133 Alge Crumpler RC	.75	2.00
❑ 134 Quincy Carter RC	.60	1.50
❑ 135 Michael Bennett RC	.75	2.00
❑ 136 Jamie Winborn RC	.60	1.50
❑ 137 Josh Heupel RC	.75	2.00
❑ 138 Will Allen RC	.75	2.00
❑ 139 Scotty Anderson RC	.60	1.50
❑ 140 LaDainian Tomlinson RC	5.00	12.00
❑ 141 Freddie Mitchell RC	.50	1.25
❑ 142 Gerard Warren RC	.60	1.50
❑ 143 Chad Johnson RC	2.00	5.00
❑ 144 Todd Heap RC	.75	2.00
❑ 145 Leonard Davis RC	.60	1.50
❑ 146 Kevan Barlow RC	.60	1.50
❑ 147 Correll Buckhalter RC	.75	2.00
❑ 148 Fred Smoot RC	.75	2.00
❑ 149 Steve Smith RC	2.00	5.00
❑ 150 David Terrell RC	.60	1.50
❑ 151 Chris Chambers RC	1.25	3.00
❑ 152 Mike McMahon RC	.60	1.50
❑ 153 Rudi Johnson RC	.75	2.00
❑ 154 Marques Tuiasosopo RC	.60	1.50
❑ 155 Deuce McAllister RC	1.00	2.50
❑ 156 Marcus Stroud RC	.60	1.50
❑ 157 Bobby Newcombe RC	.60	1.50
❑ 158 Rod Gardner RC	.60	1.50
❑ 159 Drew Brees RC	4.00	10.00
❑ 160 Jesse Palmer RC	.75	2.00
❑ 161 Derrick Gibson RC	.50	1.25
❑ 162 James Jackson RC	.60	1.50
❑ 163 Dan Morgan RC	.75	2.00
❑ 164 Michael Vick RC	1.50	4.00
❑ 165 Snoop Minnis RC	.60	1.50
❑ 166 Anthony Thomas RC	.75	2.00
❑ 167 Andre Carter RC	.75	2.00
❑ 168 Travis Minor RC	.60	1.50
❑ 169 Quincy Morgan RC	.60	1.50
❑ 170 Justin Smith RC	.75	2.00
❑ 171 Tay Cody RC	.50	1.25
❑ 172 Santana Moss RC	1.25	3.00
❑ 173 Sage Rosenfels RC	.75	2.00
❑ 174 Robert Ferguson RC	.75	2.00
❑ 175 Chris Weinke RC	.60	1.50

2002 Stadium Club

Card	Low	High
❑ COMPLETE SET (200)	40.00	80.00
❑ COMP.SET w/o SP's (125)	10.00	25.00
❑ 1 Randy Moss	.25	.60
❑ 2 Kordell Stewart	.20	.50
❑ 3 Marvin Harrison	.25	.60
❑ 4 Chris Weinke	.15	.40
❑ 5 James Allen	.15	.40
❑ 6 Michael Pittman	.20	.50
❑ 7 Quincy Carter	.15	.40
❑ 8 Mike Anderson	.20	.50
❑ 9 Mike McMahon	.15	.40
❑ 10 Chris Chambers	.25	.60
❑ 11 Laveranues Coles	.25	.60
❑ 12 Curtis Conway	.20	.50
❑ 13 Brad Johnson	.20	.50
❑ 14 Shaun Alexander	.25	.60
❑ 15 Jerry Rice	.50	1.25
❑ 16 Rod Gardner	.15	.40
❑ 17 Derrick Mason	.20	.50
❑ 18 Tom Brady	.60	1.50
❑ 19 Jimmy Smith	.20	.50
❑ 20 Tim Couch	.15	.40
❑ 21 Jim Miller	.20	.50
❑ 22 Eric Moulds	.20	.50
❑ 23 Michael Vick	.25	.60
❑ 24 Jon Kitna	.20	.50
❑ 25 Johnnie Morton	.20	.50
❑ 26 Priest Holmes	.25	.60
❑ 27 Aaron Brooks	.20	.50
❑ 28 Duce Staley	.20	.50
❑ 29 LaDainian Tomlinson	.40	1.00
❑ 30 Lamar Smith	.20	.50
❑ 31 Rod Smith	.20	.50
❑ 32 Richard Huntley	.15	.40
❑ 33 Antonio Freeman	.25	.60
❑ 34 Amani Toomer	.20	.50
❑ 35 Hines Ward	.25	.60
❑ 36 Marshall Faulk	.25	.60
❑ 37 Steve McNair	.25	.60
❑ 38 Tim Brown	.25	.60
❑ 39 Curtis Martin	.25	.60
❑ 40 Kevin Johnson	.15	.40
❑ 41 Rob Johnson	.20	.50
❑ 42 Qadry Ismail	.20	.50
❑ 43 Daunte Culpepper	.20	.50
❑ 44 Willie Jackson	.15	.40
❑ 45 Jeff Garcia	.20	.50
❑ 46 Matt Hasselbeck	.25	.60
❑ 47 Corey Bradford	.15	.40
❑ 48 Snoop Minnis	.15	.40
❑ 49 Ron Dayne	.20	.50
❑ 50 Peyton Manning	.50	1.25
❑ 51 Drew Bledsoe	.25	.60
❑ 52 Terry Glenn	.20	.50
❑ 53 Warrick Dunn	.20	.50
❑ 54 Mark Brunell	.20	.50
❑ 55 James Stewart	.15	.40
❑ 56 Muhsin Muhammad	.20	.50
❑ 57 Jake Plummer	.20	.50
❑ 58 Terance Mathis	.15	.40
❑ 59 Rocket Ismail	.20	.50
❑ 60 Joe Horn	.20	.50
❑ 61 Wayne Chrebet	.20	.50
❑ 62 James Thrash	.20	.50
❑ 63 Stephen Davis	.20	.50
❑ 64 Isaac Bruce	.25	.60
❑ 65 Peter Warrick	.20	.50
❑ 66 Anthony Thomas	.20	.50
❑ 67 Maurice Smith	.15	.40
❑ 68 Tony Gonzalez	.20	.50
❑ 69 Michael Bennett	.20	.50
❑ 70 Ike Hilliard	.20	.50
❑ 71 Plaxico Burress	.20	.50
❑ 72 Darrell Jackson	.20	.50
❑ 73 Kevan Barlow	.15	.40
❑ 74 Ray Lewis	.25	.60
❑ 75 Emmitt Smith	.60	1.50
❑ 76 Bill Schroeder	.20	.50
❑ 77 Az-Zahir Hakim	.15	.40
❑ 78 Troy Brown	.20	.50
❑ 79 Keyshawn Johnson	.20	.50
❑ 80 Tim Dwight	.20	.50
❑ 81 Peerless Price	.15	.40
❑ 82 Marty Booker	.20	.50
❑ 83 Terrell Davis	.25	.60
❑ 84 Dominic Rhodes	.20	.50
❑ 85 Jay Fiedler	.20	.50
❑ 86 Rich Gannon	.20	.50
❑ 87 Terrell Owens	.25	.60

❑ 88 Donald Hayes	.15	.40
❑ 89 Thomas Jones	.20	.50
❑ 90 Ricky Williams	.25	.60
❑ 91 Donovan McNabb	.30	.75
❑ 92 Eddie George	.20	.50
❑ 93 Germane Crowell	.15	.40
❑ 94 David Terrell	.20	.50
❑ 95 Alex Van Pelt	.15	.40
❑ 96 Antowain Smith	.20	.50
❑ 97 Jerome Bettis	.25	.60
❑ 98 Mike Alstott	.20	.50
❑ 99 Doug Flutie	.25	.60
❑ 100 Kurt Warner	.25	.60
❑ 101 Cris Carter	.25	.60
❑ 102 Oronde Gadsden	.15	.40
❑ 103 Ahman Green	.20	.50
❑ 104 Corey Dillon	.20	.50
❑ 105 Marcus Robinson	.20	.50
❑ 106 Shannon Sharpe	.25	.60
❑ 107 Kerry Collins	.20	.50
❑ 108 Garrison Hearst	.20	.50
❑ 109 David Boston	.15	.40
❑ 110 Travis Henry	.20	.50
❑ 111 James Jackson	.15	.40
❑ 112 Fred Taylor	.25	.60
❑ 113 Edgerrin James	.25	.60
❑ 114 Vinny Testaverde	.20	.50
❑ 115 Todd Pinkston	.15	.40
❑ 116 Koren Robinson	.15	.40
❑ 117 Torry Holt	.25	.60
❑ 118 Brian Griese	.20	.50
❑ 119 Trent Green	.20	.50
❑ 120 James McKnight	.15	.40
❑ 121 Charlie Garner	.20	.50
❑ 122 Tiki Barber	.25	.60
❑ 123 Joey Galloway	.20	.50
❑ 124 Quincy Morgan	.15	.40
❑ 125 Brett Favre	.60	1.50
❑ 126 Joey Harrington RC	1.00	2.50
❑ 127 Ashley Lelie RC	1.00	2.50
❑ 128 Terry Charles RC	.60	1.50
❑ 129 Charles Grant RC	1.00	2.50
❑ 130 Levar Fisher RC	.60	1.50
❑ 131 Larry Tripplett RC	.60	1.50
❑ 132 Quentin Jammer RC	1.00	2.50
❑ 133 Ron Johnson RC	.75	2.00
❑ 134 Maurice Morris RC	1.00	2.50
❑ 135 Roy Williams RC	1.25	3.00
❑ 136 Kurt Kittner RC	.60	1.50
❑ 137 Dennis Johnson RC	.60	1.50
❑ 138 Seth Burford RC	.60	1.50
❑ 139 Michael Lewis RC	1.00	2.50
❑ 140 William Green RC	.75	2.00
❑ 141 Rohan Davey RC	1.00	2.50
❑ 142 Rocky Calmus RC	.75	2.00
❑ 143 Robert Thomas RC	.60	1.50
❑ 144 Travis Stephens RC	.60	1.50
❑ 145 Ladell Betts RC	1.00	2.50
❑ 146 Daniel Graham RC	.75	2.00
❑ 147 Chester Taylor RC	1.50	4.00
❑ 148 Tim Carter RC	.75	2.00
❑ 149 Lito Sheppard RC	1.00	2.50
❑ 150 David Carr RC	1.00	2.50
❑ 151 Alex Brown RC	1.00	2.50
❑ 152 John Henderson RC	1.00	2.50
❑ 153 Jamar Martin RC	.75	2.00
❑ 154 Raonall Smith RC	.60	1.50
❑ 155 Leonard Henry RC	.60	1.50
❑ 156 T.J. Duckett RC	1.00	2.50
❑ 157 Patrick Ramsey RC	1.00	2.50
❑ 158 Antwaan Randle El RC	1.00	2.50
❑ 159 Luke Staley RC	.60	1.50
❑ 160 Jon McGraw RC	.60	1.50
❑ 161 Phillip Buchanon RC	1.00	2.50
❑ 162 Dwight Freeney RC	1.50	4.00
❑ 163 Mike Rumph RC	.60	1.50
❑ 164 Albert Haynesworth RC	1.00	2.50
❑ 165 Antonio Bryant RC	1.25	3.00
❑ 166 Josh Reed RC	.75	2.00
❑ 167 Eric Crouch RC	1.00	2.50
❑ 168 Reche Caldwell RC	1.00	2.50
❑ 169 Adrian Peterson RC	1.00	2.50
❑ 170 Jonathan Wells RC	1.00	2.50
❑ 171 Wendell Bryant RC	.60	1.50
❑ 172 Tellis Redmon RC	.60	1.50
❑ 173 Josh McCown RC	1.00	2.50
❑ 174 DeShaun Foster RC	1.00	2.50
❑ 175 Cliff Russell RC	.60	1.50
❑ 176 David Garrard RC	1.50	4.00
❑ 177 Brian Westbrook RC	3.00	8.00
❑ 178 Anthony Weaver RC	.60	1.50
❑ 179 Bryan Thomas RC	.60	1.50
❑ 180 Kalimba Edwards RC	.75	2.00
❑ 181 Javon Walker RC	1.00	2.50
❑ 182 Marquise Walker RC	.60	1.50
❑ 183 Deion Branch RC	1.00	2.50
❑ 184 Lamar Gordon RC	1.00	2.50
❑ 185 Jeremy Shockey RC	1.50	4.00
❑ 186 Clinton Portis RC	2.50	6.00
❑ 187 Napoleon Harris RC	.75	2.00
❑ 188 Freddie Milons RC	.60	1.50
❑ 189 Julius Peppers RC	1.50	4.00
❑ 190 Andre Davis RC	.75	2.00
❑ 191 Travis Fisher RC	.75	2.00
❑ 192 Chad Hutchinson RC	.60	1.50
❑ 193 Najeh Davenport RC	1.00	2.50
❑ 194 Ed Reed RC	3.00	8.00
❑ 195 Donte Stallworth RC	1.00	2.50
❑ 196 Brandon Doman RC	.60	1.50
❑ 197 Zak Kustok RC	.60	1.50
❑ 198 Randy Fasani RC	.75	2.00
❑ 199 J.T. O'Sullivan RC	1.00	2.50
❑ 200 Jabar Gaffney RC	1.00	2.50

2008 Stadium Club

❑ COMP.SET w/o RC's (100)	25.00	50.00
❑ 1 Drew Brees	.50	1.25
❑ 2 Tom Brady	.75	2.00
❑ 3 Peyton Manning	.75	2.00
❑ 4 Carson Palmer	.50	1.25
❑ 5 Ben Roethlisberger	.60	1.50
❑ 6 Eli Manning	.50	1.25
❑ 7 Tony Romo	.75	2.00
❑ 8 Tarvaris Jackson	.40	1.00
❑ 9 Vince Young	.40	1.00
❑ 10 Steven Jackson	.50	1.25
❑ 11 Willie Parker	.40	1.00
❑ 12 Clinton Portis	.40	1.00
❑ 13 Adrian Peterson	1.00	2.50
❑ 14 LaDainian Tomlinson	.60	1.50
❑ 15 Marion Barber	.50	1.25
❑ 16 Brian Westbrook	.40	1.00
❑ 17 Fred Taylor	.40	1.00
❑ 18 Marshawn Lynch	.50	1.25
❑ 19 Joseph Addai	.50	1.25
❑ 20 Willis McGahee	.40	1.00
❑ 21 Frank Gore	.40	1.00
❑ 22 Reggie Wayne	.40	1.00
❑ 23 Anquan Boldin	.40	1.00
❑ 24 Randy Moss	.50	1.25
❑ 25 Plaxico Burress	.40	1.00
❑ 26 Terrell Owens	.50	1.25
❑ 27 Andre Johnson	.40	1.00
❑ 28 Larry Fitzgerald	.50	1.25
❑ 29 Braylon Edwards	.40	1.00
❑ 30 Steve Smith	.40	1.00
❑ 31 Jon Kitna	.40	1.00
❑ 32 Matt Hasselbeck	.40	1.00
❑ 33 Derek Anderson	.40	1.00
❑ 34 Jay Cutler	.50	1.25
❑ 35 Kurt Warner	.50	1.25
❑ 36 Donovan McNabb	.50	1.25
❑ 37 Philip Rivers	.50	1.25
❑ 38 Jason Campbell	.40	1.00
❑ 39 David Garrard	.40	1.00
❑ 40 Jeff Garcia	.40	1.00
❑ 41 Marc Bulger	.40	1.00
❑ 42 Jamal Lewis	.40	1.00
❑ 43 Edgerrin James	.40	1.00
❑ 44 Thomas Jones	.40	1.00
❑ 45 Lendale White	.40	1.00
❑ 46 Justin Fargas	.30	.75
❑ 47 Brandon Jacobs	.40	1.00
❑ 48 Ryan Grant	.50	1.25
❑ 49 Earnest Graham	.30	.75
❑ 50 Chad Johnson	.40	1.00
❑ 51 Brandon Marshall	.40	1.00
❑ 52 Roddy White	.40	1.00
❑ 53 Marques Colston	.40	1.00
❑ 54 Torry Holt	.40	1.00
❑ 55 Wes Welker	.50	1.25
❑ 56 Bobby Engram	.30	.75
❑ 57 T.J. Houshmandzadeh	.40	1.00
❑ 58 Jerricho Cotchery	.30	.75
❑ 59 Kevin Curtis	.30	.75
❑ 60 Derrick Mason	.30	.75
❑ 61 Donald Driver	.40	1.00
❑ 62 Jason Witten	.50	1.25
❑ 63 Tony Gonzalez	.40	1.00
❑ 64 Kellen Winslow	.40	1.00
❑ 65 Antonio Gates	.40	1.00
❑ 66 Chris Cooley	.40	1.00
❑ 67 Matt Schaub	.40	1.00
❑ 68 Laurence Maroney	.40	1.00
❑ 69 Joey Galloway	.40	1.00
❑ 70 Jeremy Shockey	.40	1.00
❑ 71 Dwayne Bowe	.40	1.00
❑ 72 Dallas Clark	.40	1.00
❑ 73 Maurice Jones-Drew	.40	1.00
❑ 74 Ray Lewis	.50	1.25
❑ 75 Michael Strahan	.40	1.00
❑ 76 Derrick Brooks	.40	1.00
❑ 77 Ed Reed	.40	1.00
❑ 78 Brian Urlacher	.50	1.25
❑ 79 Jason Taylor	.40	1.00
❑ 80 Bob Sanders	.40	1.00
❑ 81 Patrick Kerney	.30	.75
❑ 82 Albert Haynesworth	.30	.75
❑ 83 Antonio Cromartie	.30	.75
❑ 84 Mike Vrabel	.30	.75
❑ 85 DeMarcus Ware	.40	1.00
❑ 86 Ronde Barber	.30	.75
❑ 87 James Harrison RC	3.00	8.00
❑ 88 Patrick Willis	.40	1.00
❑ 89 Mario Williams	.40	1.00
❑ 90 Osi Umenyiora	.30	.75
❑ 91 Damon Huard	.30	.75
❑ 92 Joey Harrington	.40	1.00
❑ 93 Roy Williams WR	.40	1.00
❑ 94 Champ Bailey	.30	.75
❑ 95 Shawne Merriman	.40	1.00
❑ 96 Chester Taylor	.30	.75
❑ 97 Ron Dayne	.40	1.00
❑ 98 Santonio Holmes	.40	1.00
❑ 99 Lee Evans	.40	1.00
❑ 100 Chris Chambers	.40	1.00
❑ 101 Matt Ryan RC	6.00	15.00
❑ 102 Brian Brohm RC	1.50	4.00
❑ 103 Chad Henne RC	2.50	6.00
❑ 104 Joe Flacco RC	5.00	12.00
❑ 105 Andre Woodson RC	1.50	4.00
❑ 106 John David Booty RC	1.50	4.00
❑ 107 Josh Johnson RC	1.50	4.00
❑ 108 Colt Brennan RC	2.50	6.00
❑ 109 Dennis Dixon RC	1.50	4.00
❑ 110 Erik Ainge RC	1.50	4.00
❑ 111 Darren McFadden RC	3.00	8.00
❑ 112 Rashard Mendenhall RC	3.00	8.00
❑ 113 Jonathan Stewart RC	3.00	8.00
❑ 114 Felix Jones RC	3.00	8.00
❑ 115 Jamaal Charles RC	2.50	6.00
❑ 116 Ray Rice RC	3.00	8.00
❑ 117 Chris Johnson RC	5.00	12.00
❑ 118 Mike Hart RC	1.50	4.00
❑ 119 Matt Forte RC	3.00	8.00
❑ 120 Kevin Smith RC	2.50	6.00
❑ 121 Steve Slaton RC	2.00	5.00
❑ 122 Malcolm Kelly RC	1.50	4.00
❑ 123 Limas Sweed RC	1.50	4.00
❑ 124 DeSean Jackson RC	3.00	8.00
❑ 125 James Hardy RC	1.25	3.00
❑ 126 Mario Manningham RC	1.50	4.00
❑ 127 Devin Thomas RC	1.50	4.00
❑ 128 Early Doucet RC	1.50	4.00
❑ 129 Andre Caldwell RC	1.50	4.00
❑ 130 Jordy Nelson RC	2.00	5.00
❑ 131 Eddie Royal RC	2.50	6.00
❑ 132 Earl Bennett RC	1.50	4.00
❑ 133 Fred Davis RC	1.50	4.00
❑ 134 Dustin Keller RC	1.50	4.00
❑ 135 John Carlson RC	1.50	4.00
❑ 136 Chris Long RC	1.50	4.00
❑ 137 Jake Long RC	1.50	4.00
❑ 138 Glenn Dorsey RC	1.50	4.00

Card		
❑ 139 Sedrick Ellis RC	1.50	4.00
❑ 140 Vernon Gholston RC	1.50	4.00
❑ 141 Kevin O'Connell RC	1.50	4.00
❑ 142 Leodis McKelvin RC	1.50	4.00
❑ 143 Keith Rivers RC	1.50	4.00
❑ 144 Mike Jenkins RC	1.50	4.00
❑ 145 Derrick Harvey RC	1.25	3.00
❑ 146 Phillip Merling RC	1.25	3.00
❑ 147 Kentwan Balmer RC	1.25	3.00
❑ 148 Dan Connor RC	1.50	4.00
❑ 149 D.Rodgers-Cromartie RC	1.50	4.00
❑ 150 Aqib Talib RC	1.50	4.00
❑ 151 Sam Baker RC	1.00	2.50
❑ 152 Adrian Arrington RC	1.25	3.00
❑ 153 Donnie Avery RC	2.00	5.00
❑ 154 Marcus Henry RC	1.25	3.00
❑ 155 Dexter Jackson RC	1.50	4.00
❑ 156 Jerome Simpson RC	1.25	3.00
❑ 157 Keenan Burton RC	1.25	3.00
❑ 158 Tashard Choice RC	1.50	4.00
❑ 159 Harry Douglas RC	1.25	3.00
❑ 160 Marcus Griffin RC	1.00	2.50
❑ 161 DJ Hall RC	1.25	3.00
❑ 162 Justin Forsett RC	1.50	4.00
❑ 163 Jaymar Johnson RC	1.25	3.00
❑ 164 Jacob Hester RC	1.50	4.00
❑ 165 Ali Highsmith RC	1.00	2.50
❑ 166 Sam Keller RC	1.50	4.00
❑ 167 Lance Leggett RC	1.50	4.00
❑ 168 Xavier Omon RC	1.50	4.00
❑ 169 Marcus Monk RC	1.50	4.00
❑ 170 Anthony Morelli RC	1.50	4.00
❑ 171 Marcus Smith RC	1.25	3.00
❑ 172 Allen Patrick RC	1.25	3.00
❑ 173 Kenny Phillips RC	1.50	4.00
❑ 174 Tyrell Johnson RC	1.50	4.00
❑ 175 Matt Flynn RC	1.50	4.00
❑ 176 Martin Rucker RC	1.25	3.00
❑ 177 Jordon Dizon RC	1.50	4.00
❑ 178 Owen Schmitt RC	1.50	4.00
❑ 179 Martellus Bennett RC	1.50	4.00
❑ 180 Terrence Wheatley RC	1.25	3.00
❑ 181 Terrell Thomas RC	1.25	3.00
❑ 182 Kyle Wright RC	1.25	3.00
❑ 183 Darius Reynaud RC	1.25	3.00
❑ 184 Chris Williams RC	1.25	3.00
❑ 185 Jeff Otah RC	1.25	3.00
❑ 186 Xavier Adibi RC	1.25	3.00
❑ 187 Jerod Mayo RC	2.00	5.00
❑ 188 Calais Campbell RC	1.25	3.00
❑ 189 Charles Godfrey RC	1.25	3.00
❑ 190 Reggie Smith RC	1.25	3.00
❑ 191 Pat Sims RC	1.25	3.00
❑ 192 Curtis Lofton RC	1.50	4.00
❑ 193 Tracy Porter RC	2.00	5.00
❑ 194 Patrick Lee RC	1.50	4.00
❑ 195 Cliff Avril RC	1.25	3.00
❑ 196 Trevor Laws RC	1.50	4.00
❑ 197 Lawrence Jackson RC	1.25	3.00
❑ 198 Antoine Cason RC	1.50	4.00
❑ 199 Chevis Jackson RC	1.25	3.00
❑ 200 Justin King RC	1.25	3.00

1955 Topps All American

Card		
❑ COMPLETE SET (100)	2800.00	3800.00
❑ WRAPPER (1-CENT)	250.00	300.00
❑ WRAPPER (5-CENT)	200.00	250.00
❑ 1 Herman Hickman RC	65.00	125.00
❑ 2 John Kimbrough RC	10.00	18.00
❑ 3 Ed Weir RC	10.00	18.00
❑ 4 Erny Pinckert RC	10.00	18.00
❑ 5 Bobby Grayson RC	10.00	18.00
❑ 6 Nile Kinnick UER RC	75.00	135.00
❑ 7 Andy Bershak RC	10.00	18.00
❑ 8 George Cafego RC	10.00	18.00
❑ 9 Tom Hamilton SP	20.00	30.00
❑ 10 Bill Dudley	25.00	40.00
❑ 11 Bobby Dodd SP RC	20.00	30.00
❑ 12 Otto Graham	100.00	200.00
❑ 13 Aaron Rosenberg	10.00	18.00
❑ 14A Gaynell Tinsley ERR RC	50.00	100.00
❑ 14B Gaynell Tinsley COR RC	15.00	25.00
❑ 15 Ed Kaw SP	20.00	30.00
❑ 16 Knute Rockne	175.00	275.00
❑ 17 Bob Reynolds	10.00	18.00
❑ 18 Pudg.Heffelfinger SP RC	25.00	40.00
❑ 19 Bruce Smith	25.00	40.00
❑ 20 Sammy Baugh	125.00	200.00
❑ 21A W.White RC SP ERR	150.00	250.00
❑ 21B W.White RC SP COR	60.00	100.00
❑ 22 Brick Muller RC	10.00	18.00
❑ 23 Dick Kazmaier RC	15.00	25.00
❑ 24 Ken Strong	30.00	50.00
❑ 25 Casimir Myslinski SP RC	20.00	30.00
❑ 26 Larry Kelley SP RC	25.00	40.00
❑ 27 Red Grange UER	200.00	300.00
❑ 28 Mel Hein SP RC	60.00	100.00
❑ 29 Leo Nomellini SP	50.00	80.00
❑ 30 Wes Fesler RC	10.00	18.00
❑ 31 George Sauer Sr. RC	15.00	25.00
❑ 32 Hank Foldberg RC	10.00	18.00
❑ 33 Bob Higgins RC	10.00	18.00
❑ 34 Davey O'Brien RC	30.00	50.00
❑ 35 Tom Harmon SP RC	60.00	100.00
❑ 36 Turk Edwards SP	35.00	60.00
❑ 37 Jim Thorpe	275.00	400.00
❑ 38 Amos A. Stagg RC	40.00	75.00
❑ 39 Jerome Holland RC	15.00	25.00
❑ 40 Donn Moomaw RC	10.00	18.00
❑ 41 Joseph Alexander SP RC	20.00	30.00
❑ 42 Eddie Tryon SP RC	25.00	40.00
❑ 43 George Savitsky RC	10.00	18.00
❑ 44 Ed Garbisch RC	10.00	18.00
❑ 45 Elmer Oliphant RC	10.00	18.00
❑ 46 Arnold Lassman	10.00	18.00
❑ 47 Bo McMillin RC	15.00	25.00
❑ 48 Ed Widseth RC	10.00	18.00
❑ 49 Don Gordon Zimmerman RC	10.00	18.00
❑ 50 Ken Kavanaugh	15.00	25.00
❑ 51 Duane Purvis SP RC	20.00	30.00
❑ 52 Johnny Lujack	50.00	90.00
❑ 53 John F. Green RC	10.00	18.00
❑ 54 Edwin Dooley SP RC	20.00	30.00
❑ 55 Frank Merritt SP RC	20.00	30.00
❑ 56 Ernie Nevers RC	75.00	125.00
❑ 57 Vic Hanson SP RC	20.00	30.00
❑ 58 Ed Franco RC	10.00	18.00
❑ 59 Doc Blanchard RC	30.00	50.00
❑ 60 Dan Hill RC	10.00	18.00
❑ 61 Charles Brickley SP RC	20.00	30.00
❑ 62 Harry Newman RC	10.00	18.00
❑ 63 Charlie Justice	20.00	35.00
❑ 64 Benny Friedman RC	18.00	30.00
❑ 65 Joe Donchess SP RC	20.00	30.00
❑ 66 Bruiser Kinard RC	20.00	35.00
❑ 67 Frankie Albert	15.00	25.00
❑ 68 Four Horsemen SP RC	325.00	500.00
❑ 69 Frank Sinkwich RC	15.00	25.00
❑ 70 Bill Daddio RC	10.00	18.00
❑ 71 Bobby Wilson	10.00	18.00
❑ 72 Chub Peabody RC	10.00	18.00
❑ 73 Paul Governali RC	15.00	25.00
❑ 74 Gene McEver RC	10.00	18.00
❑ 75 Hugh Gallarneau RC	10.00	18.00
❑ 76 Angelo Bertelli RC	15.00	25.00
❑ 77 Bowden Wyatt SP RC	20.00	30.00
❑ 78 Jay Berwanger RC	20.00	35.00
❑ 79 Pug Lund RC	10.00	18.00
❑ 80 Bennie Oosterbaan RC	10.00	18.00
❑ 81 Cotton Warburton RC	10.00	18.00
❑ 82 Alex Wojciechowicz	20.00	35.00
❑ 83 Ted Coy SP RC	20.00	30.00
❑ 84 Ace Parker SP RC	30.00	50.00
❑ 85 Sid Luckman	60.00	120.00
❑ 86 Albie Booth SP RC	20.00	30.00
❑ 87 Adolph Schultz SP	20.00	30.00
❑ 88 Ralph Kercheval RC	10.00	18.00
❑ 89 Marshall Goldberg	15.00	25.00
❑ 90 Charlie O'Rourke RC	10.00	18.00
❑ 91 Bob Odell UER RC	10.00	18.00
❑ 92 Biggie Munn RC	10.00	18.00
❑ 93 Willie Heston SP RC	25.00	40.00
❑ 94 Joe Bernard SP RC	25.00	40.00
❑ 95 Chris Cagle SP RC	25.00	40.00
❑ 96 Bill Hollenback SP	25.00	40.00
❑ 97 Don Hutson SP RC	150.00	225.00
❑ 98 Beattie Feathers SP RC	60.00	100.00
❑ 99 Don Whitmire SP RC	25.00	40.00
❑ 100 Fats Henry SP RC	100.00	200.00

1956 Topps

Card		
❑ COMPLETE SET (120)	1200.00	1800.00
❑ WRAPPER (1-CENT)	200.00	250.00
❑ WRAPPER (5-CENT)	40.00	50.00
❑ 1 Johnny Carson SP	40.00	80.00
❑ 2 Gordy Soltau	3.50	6.00
❑ 3 Frank Varrichione	3.50	6.00
❑ 4 Eddie Bell	3.50	6.00
❑ 5 Alex Webster RC	7.50	15.00
❑ 6 Norm Van Brocklin	18.00	30.00
❑ 7 Green Bay Packers	15.00	25.00
❑ 8 Lou Creekmur	7.50	15.00
❑ 9 Lou Groza	15.00	25.00
❑ 10 Tom Bienemann SP RC	15.00	25.00
❑ 11 George Blanda	30.00	50.00
❑ 12 Alan Ameche	6.00	12.00
❑ 13 Vic Janowicz SP	25.00	45.00
❑ 14 Dick Moegle	4.00	8.00
❑ 15 Fran Rogel	3.50	6.00
❑ 16 Harold Giancanelli	3.50	6.00
❑ 17 Emlen Tunnell	7.50	15.00
❑ 18 Tank Younger	6.00	12.00
❑ 19 Billy Howton	4.00	8.00
❑ 20 Jack Christiansen	7.50	15.00
❑ 21 Darrel Brewster	3.50	6.00
❑ 22 Chicago Cardinals SP	60.00	100.00
❑ 23 Ed Brown	4.00	8.00
❑ 24 Joe Campanella	3.50	6.00
❑ 25 Leon Heath SP	15.00	25.00
❑ 26 San Francisco 49ers	10.00	18.00
❑ 27 Dick Flanagan RC	3.50	6.00
❑ 28 Chuck Bednarik	15.00	25.00
❑ 29 Kyle Rote	6.00	12.00
❑ 30 Les Richter	4.00	8.00
❑ 31 Howard Ferguson	3.50	6.00
❑ 32 Dorne Dibble	3.50	6.00
❑ 33 Kenny Konz	3.50	6.00
❑ 34 Dave Mann SP RC	15.00	25.00
❑ 35 Rick Casares	6.00	12.00
❑ 36 Art Donovan	18.00	30.00
❑ 37 Chuck Drazenovich SP	15.00	25.00
❑ 38 Joe Arenas	3.50	6.00
❑ 39 Lynn Chandnois	3.50	6.00
❑ 40 Philadelphia Eagles	10.00	18.00
❑ 41 Roosevelt Brown RC	25.00	40.00
❑ 42 Tom Fears	15.00	25.00
❑ 43 Gary Knafelc RC	3.50	6.00
❑ 44 Joe Schmidt RC	30.00	50.00
❑ 45 Cleveland Browns	10.00	18.00
❑ 46 Len Teeuws SP RC	15.00	25.00
❑ 47 Bill George RC	20.00	35.00
❑ 48 Baltimore Colts	10.00	18.00
❑ 49 Eddie LeBaron SP	25.00	45.00
❑ 50 Hugh McElhenny	18.00	30.00
❑ 51 Ted Marchibroda	6.00	12.00
❑ 52 Adrian Burk	3.50	6.00
❑ 53 Frank Gifford	35.00	60.00
❑ 54 Charley Toogood	3.50	6.00
❑ 55 Tobin Rote	4.00	8.00
❑ 56 Bill Stits	3.50	6.00
❑ 57 Don Colo	3.50	6.00
❑ 58 Ollie Matson SP	40.00	75.00
❑ 59 Harlon Hill	4.00	8.00
❑ 60 Lenny Moore RC	50.00	90.00
❑ 61 Wash.Redskins SP	50.00	90.00
❑ 62 Billy Wilson	3.50	6.00
❑ 63 Pittsburgh Steelers	10.00	18.00
❑ 64 Bob Pellegrini RC	3.50	6.00
❑ 65 Ken MacAfee E	3.50	6.00
❑ 66 Willard Sherman RC	3.50	6.00
❑ 67 Roger Zatkoff	3.50	6.00

❑ 68 Dave Middleton RC 3.50 6.00
❑ 69 Ray Renfro 4.00 8.00
❑ 70 Don Stonesifer SP 15.00 25.00
❑ 71 Stan Jones RC 25.00 40.00
❑ 72 Jim Mutscheller RC 3.50 6.00
❑ 73 Volney Peters SP 15.00 25.00
❑ 74 Leo Nomellini 12.00 20.00
❑ 75 Ray Mathews 3.50 6.00
❑ 76 Dick Bielski 3.50 6.00
❑ 77 Charley Conerly 15.00 25.00
❑ 78 Elroy Hirsch 18.00 30.00
❑ 79 Bill Forester RC 4.00 8.00
❑ 80 Jim Doran RC 3.50 6.00
❑ 81 Fred Morrison 3.50 6.00
❑ 82 Jack Simmons SP 15.00 25.00
❑ 83 Bill McColl 3.50 6.00
❑ 84 Bert Rechichar 3.50 6.00
❑ 85 Joe Scudero SP RC 15.00 25.00
❑ 86 Y.A.Tittle 30.00 50.00
❑ 87 Ernie Stautner 12.00 20.00
❑ 88 Norm Willey 3.50 6.00
❑ 89 Bob Schnelker RC 3.50 6.00
❑ 90 Dan Towler 6.00 12.00
❑ 91 John Martinkovic 3.50 6.00
❑ 92 Detroit Lions 10.00 18.00
❑ 93 George Ratterman 4.00 8.00
❑ 94 Chuck Ulrich SP 15.00 25.00
❑ 95 Bobby Watkins 3.50 6.00
❑ 96 Buddy Young 6.00 12.00
❑ 97 Billy Wells SP RC 15.00 25.00
❑ 98 Bob Toneff 3.50 6.00
❑ 99 Bill McPeak 3.50 6.00
❑ 100 Bobby Thomason 3.50 6.00
❑ 101 Roosevelt Grier RC 30.00 50.00
❑ 102 Ron Waller RC 3.50 6.00
❑ 103 Bobby Dillon 3.50 6.00
❑ 104 Leon Hart 6.00 12.00
❑ 105 Mike McCormack 7.50 15.00
❑ 106 John Olszewski SP 15.00 25.00
❑ 107 Bill Wightkin 3.50 6.00
❑ 108 George Shaw RC 4.00 8.00
❑ 109 Dale Atkeson SP 15.00 25.00
❑ 110 Joe Perry 15.00 25.00
❑ 111 Dale Dodrill 3.50 6.00
❑ 112 Tom Scott 3.50 6.00
❑ 113 New York Giants 10.00 18.00
❑ 114 Los Angeles Rams 10.00 18.00
❑ 115 Al Carmichael 3.50 6.00
❑ 116 Bobby Layne 30.00 50.00
❑ 117 Ed Modzelewski 3.50 6.00
❑ 118 Lamar McHan RC SP 15.00 25.00
❑ 119 Chicago Bears 10.00 18.00
❑ 120 Billy Vessels RC 20.00 40.00

1957 Topps

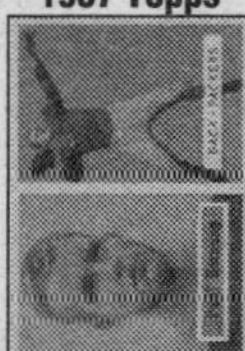

❑ COMPLETE SET (154) 1600.00 2200.00
❑ COMMON CARD (1-88) 2.50 4.00
❑ COMMON CARD (89-154) 5.00 10.00
❑ WRAPPER (1-CENT) 30.00 50.00
❑ WRAPPER (5-CENT) 50.00 75.00
❑ 1 Eddie LeBaron 30.00 50.00
❑ 2 Pete Retzlaff RC 7.50 15.00
❑ 3 Mike McCormack 6.00 12.00
❑ 4 Lou Baldacci RC 2.50 4.00
❑ 5 Gino Marchetti 10.00 20.00
❑ 6 Leo Nomellini 10.00 20.00
❑ 7 Bobby Watkins 2.50 4.00
❑ 8 Dave Middleton 2.50 4.00
❑ 9 Bobby Dillon 2.50 4.00
❑ 10 Les Richter 3.50 6.00
❑ 11 Roosevelt Brown 10.00 20.00
❑ 12 Lavern Torgeson RC 2.50 4.00
❑ 13 Dick Bielski 2.50 4.00
❑ 14 Pat Summerall 10.00 20.00
❑ 15 Jack Butler RC 5.00 10.00
❑ 16 John Henry Johnson 7.50 15.00
❑ 17 Art Spinney 2.50 4.00
❑ 18 Bob St. Clair 6.00 12.00
❑ 19 Perry Jeter RC 2.50 4.00
❑ 20 Lou Creekmur 6.00 12.00
❑ 21 Dave Hanner 3.50 6.00
❑ 22 Norm Van Brocklin 18.00 30.00
❑ 23 Don Chandler RC 5.00 10.00
❑ 24 Al Dorow 2.50 4.00
❑ 25 Tom Scott 2.50 4.00
❑ 26 Ollie Matson 12.00 20.00
❑ 27 Fran Rogel 2.50 4.00
❑ 28 Lou Groza 15.00 25.00
❑ 29 Billy Vessels 3.50 6.00
❑ 30 Y.A.Tittle 25.00 40.00
❑ 31 George Blanda 25.00 40.00
❑ 32 Bobby Layne 25.00 40.00
❑ 33 Billy Howton 3.50 6.00
❑ 34 Bill Wade 5.00 10.00
❑ 35 Emlen Tunnell 7.50 15.00
❑ 36 Leo Elter RC 2.50 4.00
❑ 37 Clarence Peaks RC 3.50 6.00
❑ 38 Don Stonesifer 2.50 4.00
❑ 39 George Tarasovic 2.50 4.00
❑ 40 Darrel Brewster 2.50 4.00
❑ 41 Bert Rechichar 2.50 4.00
❑ 42 Billy Wilson 2.50 4.00
❑ 43 Ed Brown 3.50 6.00
❑ 44 Gene Gedman RC 2.50 4.00
❑ 45 Gary Knafelc 2.50 4.00
❑ 46 Elroy Hirsch 18.00 30.00
❑ 47 Don Heinrich 3.50 6.00
❑ 48 Gene Brito 2.50 4.00
❑ 49 Chuck Bednarik 15.00 25.00
❑ 50 Dave Mann 2.50 4.00
❑ 51 Bill McPeak 2.50 4.00
❑ 52 Kenny Konz 2.50 4.00
❑ 53 Alan Ameche 5.00 10.00
❑ 54 Gordy Soltau 2.50 4.00
❑ 55 Rick Casares 3.50 6.00
❑ 56 Charlie Ane 2.50 4.00
❑ 57 Al Carmichael 2.50 4.00
❑ 58A Willard Sherman ERR 175.00 300.00
❑ 58B Willard Sherman COR 2.50 4.00
❑ 59 Kyle Rote 5.00 10.00
❑ 60 Chuck Drazenovich 2.50 4.00
❑ 61 Bobby Walston 2.50 4.00
❑ 62 John Olszewski 2.50 4.00
❑ 63 Ray Mathews 2.50 4.00
❑ 64 Maurice Bassett 2.50 4.00
❑ 65 Art Donovan 15.00 25.00
❑ 66 Joe Arenas 2.50 4.00
❑ 67 Harlon Hill 3.50 6.00
❑ 68 Yale Lary 6.00 12.00
❑ 69 Bill Forester 3.50 6.00
❑ 70 Bob Boyd 2.50 4.00
❑ 71 Andy Robustelli 12.00 20.00
❑ 72 Sam Baker RC 3.50 6.00
❑ 73 Bob Pellegrini 2.50 4.00
❑ 74 Leo Sanford 2.50 4.00
❑ 75 Sid Watson RC 2.50 4.00
❑ 76 Ray Renfro 3.50 6.00
❑ 77 Carl Taseff 2.50 4.00
❑ 78 Clyde Conner RC 2.50 4.00
❑ 79 J.C. Caroline RC 2.50 4.00
❑ 80 Howard Cassady RC 7.50 15.00
❑ 81 Tobin Rote 3.50 6.00
❑ 82 Ron Waller 2.50 4.00
❑ 83 Jim Patton RC 3.50 6.00
❑ 84 Volney Peters 2.50 4.00
❑ 85 Dick Lane RC 30.00 50.00
❑ 86 Royce Womble 2.50 4.00
❑ 87 Duane Putnam RC 3.50 6.00
❑ 88 Frank Gifford 30.00 60.00
❑ 89 Steve Meilinger 5.00 10.00
❑ 90 Buck Lansford 5.00 10.00
❑ 91 Lindon Crow DP 4.00 8.00
❑ 92 Ernie Stautner DP 12.50 25.00
❑ 93 Preston Carpenter DP RC 4.00 8.00
❑ 94 Raymond Berry RC 75.00 135.00
❑ 95 Hugh McElhenny 18.00 30.00
❑ 96 Stan Jones 15.00 25.00
❑ 97 Dorne Dibble 5.00 10.00
❑ 98 Joe Scudero DP 4.00 8.00
❑ 99 Eddie Bell 5.00 10.00
❑ 100 Joe Childress DP RC 4.00 8.00
❑ 101 Elbert Nickel 6.00 12.00
❑ 102 Walt Michaels 6.00 12.00
❑ 103 Jim Mutscheller DP 4.00 8.00
❑ 104 Earl Morrall RC 30.00 50.00
❑ 105 Larry Strickland RC 5.00 10.00
❑ 106 Jack Christiansen 7.50 15.00
❑ 107 Fred Cone DP 4.00 8.00
❑ 108 Bud McFadin RC 6.00 12.00
❑ 109 Charley Conerly 18.00 30.00
❑ 110 Tom Runnels DP RC 4.00 8.00
❑ 111 Ken Keller DP RC 4.00 8.00
❑ 112 James Root RC 5.00 10.00
❑ 113 Ted Marchibroda DP 5.00 10.00
❑ 114 Don Paul DB 5.00 10.00
❑ 115 George Shaw 6.00 12.00
❑ 116 Dick Moegle 6.00 12.00
❑ 117 Don Bingham 5.00 10.00
❑ 118 Leon Hart 7.50 15.00
❑ 119 Bart Starr RC 350.00 500.00
❑ 120 Paul Miller DP RC 4.00 8.00
❑ 121 Alex Webster 6.00 12.00
❑ 122 Ray Wietecha DP 4.00 8.00
❑ 123 Johnny Carson 5.00 10.00
❑ 124 Tom. McDonald DP RC 18.00 30.00
❑ 125 Jerry Tubbs RC 6.00 12.00
❑ 126 Jack Scarbath 5.00 10.00
❑ 127 Ed Modzelewski DP 4.00 8.00
❑ 128 Lenny Moore 30.00 50.00
❑ 129 Joe Perry DP 15.00 25.00
❑ 130 Bill Wightkin 5.00 10.00
❑ 131 Jim Doran 5.00 10.00
❑ 132 Howard Ferguson UER 5.00 10.00
❑ 133 Tom Wilson RC 5.00 10.00
❑ 134 Dick James RC 5.00 10.00
❑ 135 Jimmy Harris RC 5.00 10.00
❑ 136 Chuck Ulrich 5.00 10.00
❑ 137 Lynn Chandnois 5.00 10.00
❑ 138 Johnny Unitas DP RC 300.00 450.00
❑ 139 Jim Ridlon DP RC 4.00 8.00
❑ 140 Zeke Bratkowski DP 5.00 10.00
❑ 141 Ray Krouse 5.00 10.00
❑ 142 John Martinkovic 5.00 10.00
❑ 143 Jim Cason DP RC 4.00 8.00
❑ 144 Ken MacAfee E 5.00 10.00
❑ 145 Sid Youngelman RC 6.00 12.00
❑ 146 Paul Larson RC 5.00 10.00
❑ 147 Len Ford 18.00 30.00
❑ 148 Bob Toneff DP 4.00 8.00
❑ 149 Ronnie Knox DP RC 4.00 8.00
❑ 150 Jim David RC 6.00 12.00
❑ 151 Paul Hornung RC 250.00 400.00
❑ 152 Tank Younger 7.00 14.00
❑ 153 Bill Svoboda DP RC 4.00 8.00
❑ 154 Fred Morrison 35.00 70.00
❑ CL1 Checklist Bazooka SP 500.00 750.00
❑ CL2 Checklist Blony SP 500.00 750.00

1958 Topps

❑ COMPLETE SET (132) 850.00 1250.00
❑ WRAPPER (1-CENT) 35.00 60.00
❑ WRAPPER (5-CENT) 75.00 125.00
❑ 1 Gene Filipski RC 7.50 15.00
❑ 2 Bobby Layne 20.00 35.00
❑ 3 Joe Schmidt 6.00 12.00
❑ 4 Bill Barnes RC 2.00 4.00
❑ 5 Milt Plum RC 5.00 10.00
❑ 6 Billy Howton UER 2.50 5.00
❑ 7 Howard Cassady 2.50 5.00
❑ 8 Jim Dooley 2.00 4.00
❑ 9 Cleveland Browns 3.00 6.00
❑ 10 Lenny Moore 15.00 30.00
❑ 11 Darrel Brewster 2.00 4.00
❑ 12 Alan Ameche 4.00 8.00
❑ 13 Jim David 2.00 4.00
❑ 14 Jim Mutscheller 2.00 4.00
❑ 15 Andy Robustelli 5.00 10.00
❑ 16 Gino Marchetti 6.00 12.00
❑ 17 Ray Renfro 2.50 5.00
❑ 18 Yale Lary 4.00 8.00
❑ 19 Gary Glick RC 2.00 4.00

Card		
20 Jon Arnett RC	4.00	8.00
21 Bob Boyd	2.00	4.00
22 Johnny Unitas UER	75.00	135.00
23 Zeke Bratkowski	2.50	5.00
24 Sid Youngelman UER	2.00	4.00
25 Leo Elter	2.00	4.00
26 Kenny Konz	2.00	4.00
27 Washington Redskins	3.00	6.00
28 Carl Brettschneider RC	2.00	4.00
29 Chicago Bears	3.00	6.00
30 Alex Webster	2.50	5.00
31 Al Carmichael	2.00	4.00
32 Bobby Dillon	2.00	4.00
33 Steve Meilinger	2.00	4.00
34 Sam Baker	2.00	4.00
35 Chuck Bednarik	7.50	15.00
36 Bert Vic Zucco RC	2.00	4.00
37 George Tarasovic	2.00	4.00
38 Bill Wade	4.00	8.00
39 Dick Stanfel	2.50	5.00
40 Jerry Norton	2.00	4.00
41 San Francisco 49ers	3.00	6.00
42 Emlen Tunnell	5.00	10.00
43 Jim Doran	2.00	4.00
44 Ted Marchibroda	4.00	8.00
45 Chet Hanulak	2.00	4.00
46 Dale Dodrill	2.00	4.00
47 Johnny Carson	2.00	4.00
48 Dick Deschaine RC	2.00	4.00
49 Billy Wells UER	2.00	4.00
50 Larry Morris RC	2.00	4.00
51 Jack McClairen RC	2.00	4.00
52 Lou Groza	7.50	15.00
53 Rick Casares	2.50	5.00
54 Don Chandler	2.50	5.00
55 Duane Putnam	2.00	4.00
56 Gary Knafelc	2.00	4.00
57 Earl Morrall	5.00	10.00
58 Ron Kramer RC	2.50	5.00
59 Mike McCormack	4.00	8.00
60 Gern Nagler	2.00	4.00
61 New York Giants	3.00	6.00
62 Jim Brown RC	350.00	500.00
63 Joe Marconi RC	2.00	4.00
64 R.C. Owens UER RC	2.50	5.00
65 Jimmy Carr RC	2.50	5.00
66 Bart Starr UER	90.00	150.00
67 Tom Wilson	2.00	4.00
68 Lamar McHan	2.00	4.00
69 Chicago Cardinals	3.00	6.00
70 Jack Christiansen	4.00	8.00
71 Don McIlhenny RC	2.00	4.00
72 Ron Waller	2.00	4.00
73 Frank Gifford	25.00	50.00
74 Bert Rechichar	2.00	4.00
75 John Henry Johnson	5.00	10.00
76 Jack Butler	2.50	5.00
77 Frank Varrichione	2.00	4.00
78 Ray Mathews	2.00	4.00
79 Marv Matuszak UER RC	2.00	4.00
80 Harlon Hill UER	2.00	4.00
81 Lou Creekmur	4.00	8.00
82 Woodley Lewis UER	2.00	4.00
83 Don Heinrich	2.00	4.00
84 Charley Conerly	7.50	15.00
85 Los Angeles Rams	3.00	6.00
86 Y.A.Tittle	18.00	30.00
87 Bobby Walston	2.00	4.00
88 Earl Putman RC	2.00	4.00
89 Leo Nomellini	7.50	15.00
90 Sonny Jurgensen RC	60.00	100.00
91 Don Paul DB	2.00	4.00
92 Paige Cothren RC	2.00	4.00
93 Joe Perry	7.50	15.00
94 Tobin Rote	2.50	5.00
95 Billy Wilson	2.00	4.00
96 Green Bay Packers	7.50	15.00
97 Lavern Torgeson	2.00	4.00
98 Milt Davis RC	2.00	4.00
99 Larry Strickland	2.00	4.00
100 Matt Hazeltine RC	2.50	5.00
101 Walt Yowarsky RC	2.00	4.00
102 Roosevelt Brown	4.00	8.00
103 Jim Ringo	5.00	10.00
104 Joe Krupa RC	2.00	4.00
105 Les Richter	2.50	5.00
106 Art Donovan	12.00	20.00
107 John Olszewski	2.00	4.00
108 Ken Keller	2.00	4.00
109 Philadelphia Eagles	3.00	6.00
110 Baltimore Colts	3.00	6.00
111 Dick Bielski	2.00	4.00
112 Eddie LeBaron	4.00	8.00
113 Gene Brito	2.00	4.00
114 Willie Galimore RC	4.00	8.00
115 Detroit Lions	3.00	6.00
116 Pittsburgh Steelers	3.00	6.00
117 L.G. Dupre	2.50	5.00
118 Babe Parilli	2.50	5.00
119 Bill George	5.00	10.00
120 Raymond Berry	25.00	40.00
121 Jim Podoley UER RC	2.00	4.00
122 Hugh McElhenny	7.50	15.00
123 Ed Brown	2.50	5.00
124 Dick Moegle	2.50	5.00
125 Tom Scott	2.00	4.00
126 Tommy McDonald	6.00	12.00
127 Ollie Matson	10.00	20.00
128 Preston Carpenter	2.00	4.00
129 George Blanda	18.00	30.00
130 Gordy Soltau	2.00	4.00
131 Dick Nolan RC	2.50	5.00
132 Don Bosseler RC	10.00	20.00

1959 Topps

Card		
COMPLETE SET (176)	600.00	900.00
COMMON CARD (1-88)	1.50	3.00
COMMON CARD (89-176)	1.00	2.00
WRAPPER (1-CENT)	50.00	90.00
WRAPPER (1-CENT, REP)	50.00	80.00
WRAPPER (5-CENT)	50.00	80.00
1 Johnny Unitas	90.00	150.00
2 Gene Brito	1.50	3.00
3 Detroit Lions CL	3.00	6.00
4 Max McGee RC	12.50	25.00
5 Hugh McElhenny	7.50	15.00
6 Joe Schmidt	4.00	8.00
7 Kyle Rote	3.00	6.00
8 Clarence Peaks	1.50	3.00
9 Steelers Pennant	1.75	3.50
10 Jim Brown	90.00	150.00
11 Ray Mathews	1.50	3.00
12 Bobby Dillon	1.50	3.00
13 Joe Childress	1.50	3.00
14 Terry Barr RC	1.50	3.00
15 Del Shofner RC	2.00	4.00
16 Bob Pellegrini UER	1.50	3.00
17 Baltimore Colts CL	3.00	6.00
18 Preston Carpenter	1.50	3.00
19 Leo Nomellini	5.00	10.00
20 Frank Gifford	25.00	40.00
21 Charlie Ane	1.50	3.00
22 Jack Butler	1.50	3.00
23 Bart Starr	35.00	60.00
24 Cardinals Pennant	1.75	3.50
25 Bill Barnes	1.50	3.00
26 Walt Michaels	2.00	4.00
27 Clyde Conner UER	1.50	3.00
28 Paige Cothren	1.50	3.00
29 Roosevelt Grier	3.00	6.00
30 Alan Ameche	3.00	6.00
31 Philadelphia Eagles CL	3.00	6.00
32 Dick Nolan	2.00	4.00
33 R.C. Owens	2.00	4.00
34 Dale Dodrill	1.50	3.00
35 Gene Gedman	1.50	3.00
36 Gene Lipscomb RC	5.00	10.00
37 Ray Renfro	2.00	4.00
38 Browns Pennant	1.75	3.50
39 Bill Forester	2.00	4.00
40 Bobby Layne	15.00	25.00
41 Pat Summerall	5.00	10.00
42 Jerry Mertens RC	1.50	3.00
43 Steve Myhra RC	1.50	3.00
44 John Henry Johnson	4.00	8.00
45 Woodley Lewis UER	1.50	3.00
46 Green Bay Packers CL	5.00	10.00
47 Don Owens UER RC	1.50	3.00
48 Ed Beatty RC	1.50	3.00
49 Don Chandler	1.50	3.00
50 Ollie Matson	6.00	12.00
51 Sam Huff RC	30.00	50.00
52 Tom Miner RC	1.50	3.00
53 Giants Pennant	1.75	3.50
54 Kenny Konz	1.50	3.00
55 Raymond Berry	10.00	20.00
56 Howard Ferguson UER	1.50	3.00
57 Chuck Ulrich	1.50	3.00
58 Bob St.Clair	3.00	6.00
59 Don Burroughs RC	1.50	3.00
60 Lou Groza	7.50	15.00
61 San Francisco 49ers CL	3.00	6.00
62 Andy Nelson RC	1.50	3.00
63 Harold Bradley RC	1.50	3.00
64 Dave Hanner	2.00	4.00
65 Charley Conerly	6.00	12.00
66 Gene Cronin RC	1.50	3.00
67 Duane Putnam	1.50	3.00
68 Colts Pennant	1.75	3.50
69 Ernie Stautner	4.00	8.00
70 Jon Arnett	2.00	4.00
71 Ken Panfil RC	1.50	3.00
72 Matt Hazeltine	1.50	3.00
73 Harley Sewell	1.50	3.00
74 Mike McCormack	3.00	6.00
75 Jim Ringo	4.00	8.00
76 Los Angeles Rams CL	3.00	6.00
77 Bob Gain RC	1.50	3.00
78 Buzz Nutter RC	1.50	3.00
79 Jerry Norton	1.50	3.00
80 Joe Perry	6.00	12.00
81 Carl Brettschneider	1.50	3.00
82 Paul Hornung	30.00	60.00
83 Eagles Pennant	1.75	3.50
84 Les Richter	2.00	4.00
85 Howard Cassady	2.00	4.00
86 Art Donovan	7.50	15.00
87 Jim Patton	2.00	4.00
88 Pete Retzlaff	2.00	4.00
89 Jim Mutscheller	1.00	2.00
90 Zeke Bratkowski	1.50	3.00
91 Washington Redskins CL	2.00	4.00
92 Art Hunter	1.00	2.00
93 Gern Nagler	1.00	2.00
94 Chuck Weber RC	1.00	2.00
95 Lew Carpenter RC	1.50	3.00
96 Stan Jones	2.50	5.00
97 Ralph Guglielmi UER	1.50	3.00
98 Packers Pennant	2.00	4.00
99 Ray Wietecha	1.00	2.00
100 Lenny Moore	6.00	12.00
101 Jim Ray Smith UER RC	1.50	3.00
102 Abe Woodson RC	1.50	3.00
103 Alex Karras RC	25.00	40.00
104 Chicago Bears CL	2.00	4.00
105 John David Crow RC	6.00	12.00
106 Joe Fortunato RC	1.00	2.00
107 Babe Parilli	1.50	3.00
108 Proverb Jacobs RC	1.00	2.00
109 Gino Marchetti	4.00	8.00
110 Bill Wade	1.50	3.00
111 49ers Pennant	1.50	3.00
112 Karl Rubke RC	1.00	2.00
113 Dave Middleton UER	1.00	2.00
114 Roosevelt Brown	2.50	5.00
115 John Olszewski	1.00	2.00
116 Jerry Kramer RC	18.00	30.00
117 King Hill RC	1.50	3.00
118 Chicago Cardinals CL	2.00	4.00
119 Frank Varrichione	1.00	2.00
120 Rick Casares	1.50	3.00
121 George Strugar RC	1.00	2.00
122 Bill Glass RC	1.50	3.00
123 Don Bosseler	1.00	2.00
124 John Reger RC	1.00	2.00
125 Jim Ninowski RC	1.00	2.00
126 Rams Pennant	1.50	3.00
127 Willard Sherman	1.00	2.00
128 Bob Schnelker	1.00	2.00
129 Ollie Spencer RC	1.00	2.00
130 Y.A.Tittle	15.00	25.00
131 Yale Lary	2.50	5.00
132 Jim Parker RC	15.00	30.00
133 New York Giants CL	2.00	4.00

❑ 134 Jim Schrader RC 1.00 2.00
❑ 135 M.C. Reynolds RC 1.00 2.00
❑ 136 Mike Sandusky RC 1.00 2.00
❑ 137 Ed Brown 1.50 3.00
❑ 138 Al Barry RC 1.00 2.00
❑ 139 Lions Pennant 1.50 3.00
❑ 140 Bobby Mitchell RC 20.00 35.00
❑ 141 Larry Morris 1.00 2.00
❑ 142 Jim Phillips RC 1.50 3.00
❑ 143 Jim David 1.00 2.00
❑ 144 Joe Krupa 1.00 2.00
❑ 145 Willie Galimore 1.50 3.00
❑ 146 Pittsburgh Steelers CL 2.00 4.00
❑ 147 Andy Robustelli 4.00 8.00
❑ 148 Billy Wilson 1.00 2.00
❑ 149 Leo Sanford 1.00 2.00
❑ 150 Eddie LeBaron 2.50 5.00
❑ 151 Bill McColl 1.00 2.00
❑ 152 Buck Lansford UER 1.00 2.00
❑ 153 Bears Pennant 1.50 3.00
❑ 154 Leo Sugar RC 1.00 2.00
❑ 155 Jim Taylor UER RC 20.00 35.00
❑ 156 Lindon Crow 1.00 2.00
❑ 157 Jack McClairen 1.00 2.00
❑ 158 Vince Costello RC UER 1.00 2.00
❑ 159 Stan Wallace RC 1.00 2.00
❑ 160 Mel Triplett RC 1.00 2.00
❑ 161 Cleveland Browns CL 2.00 4.00
❑ 162 Dan Currie RC 2.00 4.00
❑ 163 L.G. Dupre UER 1.50 3.00
❑ 164 John Morrow UER RC 1.00 2.00
❑ 165 Jim Podoley 1.00 2.00
❑ 166 Bruce Bosley RC 1.00 2.00
❑ 167 Harlon Hill 1.00 2.00
❑ 168 Redskins Pennant 1.50 3.00
❑ 169 Junior Wren RC 1.00 2.00
❑ 170 Tobin Rote 1.50 3.00
❑ 171 Art Spinney 1.00 2.00
❑ 172 Chuck Drazenovich UER 1.00 2.00
❑ 173 Bobby Joe Conrad RC 1.50 3.00
❑ 174 Jesse Richardson RC 1.00 2.00
❑ 175 Sam Baker 1.00 2.00
❑ 176 Tom Tracy RC 4.00 8.00

1960 Topps

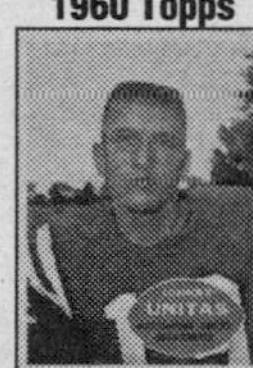

❑ COMPLETE SET (132) 400.00 600.00
❑ WRAPPER (1-CENT) 50.00 80.00
❑ WRAPPER (1-CENT, REP) 150.00 300.00
❑ WRAPPER (5-CENT) 50.00 80.00
❑ 1 Johnny Unitas ! 40.00 80.00
❑ 2 Alan Ameche 2.00 4.00
❑ 3 Lenny Moore 5.00 10.00
❑ 4 Raymond Berry 6.00 12.00
❑ 5 Jim Parker 4.00 8.00
❑ 6 George Preas RC 1.25 2.50
❑ 7 Art Spinney 1.25 2.50
❑ 8 Bill Pellington RC 1.50 3.00
❑ 9 Johnny Sample RC 1.50 3.00
❑ 10 Gene Lipscomb 1.50 3.00
❑ 11 Baltimore Colts 1.50 3.00
❑ 12 Ed Brown 1.50 3.00
❑ 13 Rick Casares 1.50 3.00
❑ 14 Willie Galimore 1.50 3.00
❑ 15 Jim Dooley 1.25 2.50
❑ 16 Harlon Hill UER 1.25 2.50
❑ 17 Stan Jones 2.00 4.00
❑ 18 Bill George 2.00 4.00
❑ 19 Erich Barnes RC 1.50 3.00
❑ 20 Doug Atkins 3.00 6.00
❑ 21 Chicago Bears 1.50 3.00
❑ 22 Milt Plum 1.50 3.00
❑ 23 Jim Brown 60.00 100.00
❑ 24 Sam Baker 1.25 2.50
❑ 25 Bobby Mitchell 5.00 10.00
❑ 26 Ray Renfro 1.50 3.00
❑ 27 Billy Howton 1.50 3.00
❑ 28 Jim Ray Smith 1.25 2.50
❑ 29 Jim Shofner RC 1.50 3.00
❑ 30 Bob Gain 1.25 2.50
❑ 31 Cleveland Browns 1.50 3.00
❑ 32 Don Heinrich 1.25 2.50
❑ 33 Ed Modzelewski UER 1.25 2.50
❑ 34 Fred Cone 1.25 2.50
❑ 35 L.G. Dupre 1.50 3.00
❑ 36 Dick Bielski 1.25 2.50
❑ 37 Charlie Ane UER 1.25 2.50
❑ 38 Jerry Tubbs 1.50 3.00
❑ 39 Doyle Nix RC 1.25 2.50
❑ 40 Ray Krouse 1.25 2.50
❑ 41 Earl Morrall 2.00 4.00
❑ 42 Howard Cassady 1.50 3.00
❑ 43 Dave Middleton 1.25 2.50
❑ 44 Jim Gibbons RC 1.50 3.00
❑ 45 Darris McCord RC 1.25 2.50
❑ 46 Joe Schmidt 3.00 6.00
❑ 47 Terry Barr 1.25 2.50
❑ 48 Yale Lary 2.00 4.00
❑ 49 Gil Mains RC 1.25 2.50
❑ 50 Detroit Lions 1.50 3.00
❑ 51 Bart Starr 30.00 50.00
❑ 52 Jim Taylor UER 4.00 8.00
❑ 53 Lew Carpenter 1.50 3.00
❑ 54 Paul Hornung 30.00 45.00
❑ 55 Max McGee 2.00 4.00
❑ 56 Forrest Gregg RC 25.00 40.00
❑ 57 Jim Ringo 2.50 5.00
❑ 58 Bill Forester 1.50 3.00
❑ 59 Dave Hanner 1.50 3.00
❑ 60 Green Bay Packers 4.00 8.00
❑ 61 Bill Wade 1.50 3.00
❑ 62 Frank Ryan RC 2.50 5.00
❑ 63 Ollie Matson 5.00 10.00
❑ 64 Jon Arnett 1.50 3.00
❑ 65 Del Shofner 1.50 3.00
❑ 66 Jim Phillips 1.25 2.50
❑ 67 Art Hunter 1.25 2.50
❑ 68 Les Richter 1.50 3.00
❑ 69 Lou Michaels RC 1.50 3.00
❑ 70 John Baker RC 1.25 2.50
❑ 71 Los Angeles Rams 1.50 3.00
❑ 72 Charley Conerly 4.00 8.00
❑ 73 Mel Triplett 1.25 2.50
❑ 74 Frank Gifford 20.00 35.00
❑ 75 Alex Webster 1.50 3.00
❑ 76 Bob Schnelker 1.25 2.50
❑ 77 Pat Summerall 4.00 8.00
❑ 78 Roosevelt Brown 2.00 4.00
❑ 79 Jim Patton 1.25 2.50
❑ 80 Sam Huff 10.00 20.00
❑ 81 Andy Robustelli 3.00 6.00
❑ 82 New York Giants 1.50 3.00
❑ 83 Clarence Peaks 1.25 2.50
❑ 84 Bill Barnes 1.25 2.50
❑ 85 Pete Retzlaff 1.50 3.00
❑ 86 Bobby Walston 1.25 2.50
❑ 87 Chuck Bednarik UER 4.00 8.00
❑ 88 Bob Pellegrini 1.25 2.50
❑ 89 Tom Brookshier RC 1.50 3.00
❑ 90 Marion Campbell 1.50 3.00
❑ 91 Jesse Richardson 1.25 2.50
❑ 92 Philadelphia Eagles 1.50 3.00
❑ 93 Bobby Layne 18.00 30.00
❑ 94 John Henry Johnson 3.00 6.00
❑ 95 Tom Tracy UER 1.50 3.00
❑ 96 Preston Carpenter 1.25 2.50
❑ 97 Frank Varrichione UER 1.25 2.50
❑ 98 John Nisby RC 1.25 2.50
❑ 99 Dean Derby RC 1.25 2.50
❑ 100 George Tarasovic 1.25 2.50
❑ 101 Ernie Stautner 2.50 5.00
❑ 102 Pittsburgh Steelers 1.50 3.00
❑ 103 King Hill 1.25 2.50
❑ 104 Mal Hammack RC 1.25 2.50
❑ 105 John David Crow 1.50 3.00
❑ 106 Bobby Joe Conrad 1.50 3.00
❑ 107 Woodley Lewis 1.25 2.50
❑ 108 Don Gillis RC 1.25 2.50
❑ 109 Carl Brettschneider 1.25 2.50
❑ 110 Leo Sugar 1.25 2.50
❑ 111 Frank Fuller RC 1.25 2.50
❑ 112 St. Louis Cardinals 1.50 3.00
❑ 113 Y.A.Tittle 18.00 30.00
❑ 114 Joe Perry 4.00 8.00
❑ 115 J.D.Smith RC 1.50 3.00
❑ 116 Hugh McElhenny 4.00 8.00
❑ 117 Billy Wilson 1.25 2.50
❑ 118 Bob St.Clair 2.00 4.00
❑ 119 Matt Hazeltine 1.25 2.50
❑ 120 Abe Woodson 1.25 2.50
❑ 121 Leo Nomellini 2.50 5.00
❑ 122 San Francisco 49ers 1.50 3.00
❑ 123 Ralph Guglielmi UER 1.25 2.50
❑ 124 Don Bosseler 1.25 2.50
❑ 125 John Olszewski 1.25 2.50
❑ 126 Bill Anderson UER RC 1.25 2.50
❑ 127 Joe Walton RC 1.50 3.00
❑ 128 Jim Schrader 1.25 2.50
❑ 129 Ralph Felton RC 1.25 2.50
❑ 130 Gary Glick 1.25 2.50
❑ 131 Bob Toneff 1.25 2.50
❑ 132 Redskins Team ! 18.00 30.00

1961 Topps

❑ COMPLETE SET (198) 650.00 1000.00
❑ COMMON CARD (1-132) 1.25 2.50
❑ COMMON CARD (133-198) 1.50 3.00
❑ WRAPPER (1-CENT) 200.00 350.00
❑ WRAPPER (1-CENT, REP) 125.00 200.00
❑ WRAPPER (5-CENT) 60.00 100.00
❑ 1 Johnny Unitas 50.00 100.00
❑ 2 Lenny Moore 6.00 12.00
❑ 3 Alan Ameche 2.00 4.00
❑ 4 Raymond Berry 6.00 12.00
❑ 5 Jim Mutscheller 1.25 2.50
❑ 6 Jim Parker 2.50 5.00
❑ 7 Gino Marchetti 3.00 6.00
❑ 8 Gene Lipscomb 2.00 4.00
❑ 9 Baltimore Colts 1.50 3.00
❑ 10 Bill Wade 1.50 3.00
❑ 11 Johnny Morris RC 3.00 6.00
❑ 12 Rick Casares 1.50 3.00
❑ 13 Harlon Hill 1.25 2.50
❑ 14 Stan Jones 2.00 4.00
❑ 15 Doug Atkins 2.50 5.00
❑ 16 Bill George 2.00 4.00
❑ 17 J.C. Caroline 1.25 2.50
❑ 18 Chicago Bears 1.50 3.00
❑ 19 Eddie LeBaron IA 1.50 3.00
❑ 20 Eddie LeBaron 1.50 3.00
❑ 21 Don McIlhenny 1.25 2.50
❑ 22 L.G. Dupre 1.50 3.00
❑ 23 Jim Doran 1.25 2.50
❑ 24 Billy Howton 1.50 3.00
❑ 25 Buzz Guy RC 1.25 2.50
❑ 26 Jack Patera RC 1.25 2.50
❑ 27 Tom Franckhauser RC 1.25 2.50
❑ 28 Cowboys Team 7.50 15.00
❑ 29 Jim Ninowski 1.25 2.50
❑ 30 Dan Lewis RC 1.25 2.50
❑ 31 Nick Pietrosante RC 1.50 3.00
❑ 32 Gail Cogdill RC 1.50 3.00
❑ 33 Jim Gibbons 1.25 2.50
❑ 34 Jim Martin 1.25 2.50
❑ 35 Alex Karras 7.50 15.00
❑ 36 Joe Schmidt 2.50 5.00
❑ 37 Detroit Lions 1.50 3.00
❑ 38 Paul Hornung IA 9.00 18.00
❑ 39 Bart Starr 25.00 40.00
❑ 40 Paul Hornung 25.00 40.00
❑ 41 Jim Taylor 20.00 35.00
❑ 42 Max McGee 2.00 4.00
❑ 43 Boyd Dowler RC 4.00 8.00
❑ 44 Jim Ringo 2.50 5.00
❑ 45 Hank Jordan RC 18.00 30.00
❑ 46 Bill Forester 1.50 3.00
❑ 47 Green Bay Packers 7.50 15.00
❑ 48 Frank Ryan 1.50 3.00
❑ 49 Jon Arnett 1.50 3.00
❑ 50 Ollie Matson 4.00 8.00
❑ 51 Jim Phillips 1.25 2.50
❑ 52 Del Shofner 1.50 3.00

Card		
❑ 53 Art Hunter	1.25	2.50
❑ 54 Gene Brito	1.25	2.50
❑ 55 Lindon Crow	1.25	2.50
❑ 56 Los Angeles Rams	1.50	3.00
❑ 57 Johnny Unitas IA	15.00	25.00
❑ 58 Y.A.Tittle	18.00	30.00
❑ 59 John Brodie RC	25.00	40.00
❑ 60 J.D. Smith	1.25	2.50
❑ 61 R.C. Owens	1.50	3.00
❑ 62 Clyde Conner	1.25	2.50
❑ 63 Bob St.Clair	2.00	4.00
❑ 64 Leo Nomellini	3.00	6.00
❑ 65 Abe Woodson	1.25	2.50
❑ 66 San Francisco 49ers	1.50	3.00
❑ 67 Checklist Card	25.00	40.00
❑ 68 Milt Plum	1.50	3.00
❑ 69 Ray Renfro	1.50	3.00
❑ 70 Bobby Mitchell	4.00	8.00
❑ 71 Jim Brown	75.00	125.00
❑ 72 Mike McCormack	2.00	4.00
❑ 73 Jim Ray Smith	1.25	2.50
❑ 74 Sam Baker	1.25	2.50
❑ 75 Walt Michaels	1.50	3.00
❑ 76 Cleveland Browns	1.50	3.00
❑ 77 Jim Brown IA	20.00	35.00
❑ 78 George Shaw	1.25	2.50
❑ 79 Hugh McElhenny	4.00	8.00
❑ 80 Clancy Osborne RC	1.25	2.50
❑ 81 Dave Middleton	1.25	2.50
❑ 82 Frank Youso RC	1.25	2.50
❑ 83 Don Joyce RC	1.25	2.50
❑ 84 Ed Culpepper RC	1.25	2.50
❑ 85 Charley Conerly	4.00	8.00
❑ 86 Mel Triplett	1.25	2.50
❑ 87 Kyle Rote	1.50	3.00
❑ 88 Roosevelt Brown	2.00	4.00
❑ 89 Ray Wietecha	1.25	2.50
❑ 90 Andy Robustelli	2.50	5.00
❑ 91 Sam Huff	4.00	8.00
❑ 92 Jim Patton	1.25	2.50
❑ 93 New York Giants	1.50	3.00
❑ 94 Charley Conerly IA	3.00	6.00
❑ 95 Sonny Jurgensen	15.00	25.00
❑ 96 Tommy McDonald	2.50	5.00
❑ 97 Bill Barnes	1.25	2.50
❑ 98 Bobby Walston	1.25	2.50
❑ 99 Pete Retzlaff	1.50	3.00
❑ 100 Jim McCusker RC	1.25	2.50
❑ 101 Chuck Bednarik	4.00	8.00
❑ 102 Tom Brookshier	1.50	3.00
❑ 103 Philadelphia Eagles	1.50	3.00
❑ 104 Bobby Layne	18.00	30.00
❑ 105 John Henry Johnson	2.00	4.00
❑ 106 Tom Tracy	1.50	3.00
❑ 107 Buddy Dial RC	1.25	2.50
❑ 108 Jimmy Orr RC	2.00	4.00
❑ 109 Mike Sandusky	1.25	2.50
❑ 110 John Reger	1.25	2.50
❑ 111 Junior Wren	1.25	2.50
❑ 112 Pittsburgh Steelers	1.50	3.00
❑ 113 Bobby Layne IA	5.00	10.00
❑ 114 John Roach RC	1.25	2.50
❑ 115 Sam Etcheverry RC	1.50	3.00
❑ 116 John David Crow	1.50	3.00
❑ 117 Mal Hammack	1.25	2.50
❑ 118 Sonny Randle RC	1.50	3.00
❑ 119 Leo Sugar	1.25	2.50
❑ 120 Jerry Norton	1.25	2.50
❑ 121 St. Louis Cardinals	1.50	3.00
❑ 122 Checklist Card	30.00	50.00
❑ 123 Ralph Guglielmi	1.25	2.50
❑ 124 Dick James	1.25	2.50
❑ 125 Don Bosseler	1.25	2.50
❑ 126 Joe Walton	1.25	2.50
❑ 127 Bill Anderson	1.25	2.50
❑ 128 Vince Promuto RC	1.25	2.50
❑ 129 Bob Toneff	1.25	2.50
❑ 130 John Paluck RC	1.25	2.50
❑ 131 Washington Redskins	1.50	3.00
❑ 132 Milt Plum IA !	1.25	2.50
❑ 133 Abner Haynes !	4.00	8.00
❑ 134 Mel Branch UER	2.00	4.00
❑ 135 Jerry Cornelison UER	1.50	3.00
❑ 136 Bill Krisher	1.50	3.00
❑ 137 Paul Miller	1.50	3.00
❑ 138 Jack Spikes	2.00	4.00
❑ 139 Johnny Robinson RC	4.00	8.00
❑ 140 Cotton Davidson RC	2.00	4.00
❑ 141 Dave Smith RB	1.50	3.00
❑ 142 Bill Groman	1.50	3.00
❑ 143 Rich Michael RC	1.50	3.00
❑ 144 Mike Dukes RC	1.50	3.00
❑ 145 George Blanda	15.00	25.00
❑ 146 Billy Cannon	3.00	6.00
❑ 147 Dennit Morris RC	1.50	3.00
❑ 148 Jacky Lee UER	2.00	4.00
❑ 149 Al Dorow	1.50	3.00
❑ 150 Don Maynard RC	25.00	50.00
❑ 151 Art Powell RC	4.00	8.00
❑ 152 Sid Youngelman	1.50	3.00
❑ 153 Bob Mischak RC	1.50	3.00
❑ 154 Larry Grantham	1.50	3.00
❑ 155 Tom Saidock	1.50	3.00
❑ 156 Roger Donnahoo RC	1.50	3.00
❑ 157 Laverne Torczon RC	1.50	3.00
❑ 158 Archie Matsos RC	2.00	4.00
❑ 159 Elbert Dubenion	2.00	4.00
❑ 160 Wray Carlton RC	2.00	4.00
❑ 161 Rich McCabe RC	1.50	3.00
❑ 162 Ken Rice RC	1.50	3.00
❑ 163 Art Baker RC	1.50	3.00
❑ 164 Tom Rychlec	1.50	3.00
❑ 165 Mack Yoho	1.50	3.00
❑ 166 Jack Kemp	50.00	80.00
❑ 167 Paul Lowe	3.00	6.00
❑ 168 Ron Mix	5.00	10.00
❑ 169 Paul Maguire UER	3.00	6.00
❑ 170 Volney Peters	1.50	3.00
❑ 171 Ernie Wright RC	2.00	4.00
❑ 172 Ron Nery RC	1.50	3.00
❑ 173 Dave Kocourek RC	2.00	4.00
❑ 174 Jim Colclough RC	1.50	3.00
❑ 175 Babe Parilli	2.00	4.00
❑ 176 Billy Lott	1.50	3.00
❑ 177 Fred Bruney	1.50	3.00
❑ 178 Ross O'Hanley RC	1.50	3.00
❑ 179 Walt Cudzik RC	1.50	3.00
❑ 180 Charley Leo	1.50	3.00
❑ 181 Bob Dee	1.50	3.00
❑ 182 Jim Otto RC	25.00	40.00
❑ 183 Eddie Macon RC	1.50	3.00
❑ 184 Dick Christy RC	1.50	3.00
❑ 185 Alan Miller RC	1.50	3.00
❑ 186 Tom Flores RC	10.00	20.00
❑ 187 Joe Cannavino RC	1.50	3.00
❑ 188 Don Manoukian	1.50	3.00
❑ 189 Bob Coolbaugh RC	1.50	3.00
❑ 190 Lionel Taylor RC	4.00	8.00
❑ 191 Bud McFadin	1.50	3.00
❑ 192 Goose Gonsoulin RC	3.00	6.00
❑ 193 Frank Tripucka	2.00	4.00
❑ 194 Gene Mingo RC	2.00	4.00
❑ 195 Eldon Danenhauer RC	1.50	3.00
❑ 196 Bob McNamara	1.50	3.00
❑ 197 Dave Rolle UER RC	1.50	3.00
❑ 198 Checklist UER !	60.00	100.00

1962 Topps

Card		
❑ COMPLETE SET (176)	1200.00	2000.00
❑ WRAPPER (1-CENT)	175.00	250.00
❑ WRAPPER (5-CENT,STARS)	25.00	50.00
❑ WRAPPER (5-CENT,BUCKS)	25.00	40.00
❑ 1 Johnny Unitas	125.00	200.00
❑ 2 Lenny Moore	6.00	12.00
❑ 3 Alex Hawkins SP RC	5.00	10.00
❑ 4 Joe Perry	4.00	8.00
❑ 5 Raymond Berry SP	25.00	40.00
❑ 6 Steve Myhra	2.00	4.00
❑ 7 Tom Gilburg SP RC	4.00	8.00
❑ 8 Gino Marchetti	4.00	8.00
❑ 9 Bill Pellington	2.00	4.00
❑ 10 Andy Nelson	2.00	4.00
❑ 11 Wendell Harris SP RC	4.00	8.00
❑ 12 Baltimore Colts	3.00	6.00
❑ 13 Bill Wade SP	5.00	10.00
❑ 14 Willie Galimore	2.50	5.00
❑ 15 Johnny Morris SP	4.00	8.00
❑ 16 Rick Casares	2.50	5.00
❑ 17 Mike Ditka RC	175.00	300.00
❑ 18 Stan Jones	3.00	6.00
❑ 19 Roger LeClerc RC	2.00	4.00
❑ 20 Angelo Coia RC	2.00	4.00
❑ 21 Doug Atkins	3.50	7.00
❑ 22 Bill George	3.00	6.00
❑ 23 Richie Petitbon RC	2.50	5.00
❑ 24 Ronnie Bull SP RC	4.00	8.00
❑ 25 Chicago Bears	3.00	6.00
❑ 26 Howard Cassady	2.50	5.00
❑ 27 Ray Renfro SP	5.00	10.00
❑ 28 Jim Brown	100.00	175.00
❑ 29 Rich Kreitling RC	2.00	4.00
❑ 30 Jim Ray Smith	2.00	4.00
❑ 31 John Morrow	2.00	4.00
❑ 32 Lou Groza	7.50	15.00
❑ 33 Bob Gain	2.00	4.00
❑ 34 Bernie Parrish RC	2.00	4.00
❑ 35 Jim Shofner	2.00	4.00
❑ 36 Ernie Davis SP RC	90.00	150.00
❑ 37 Cleveland Browns	3.00	6.00
❑ 38 Eddie LeBaron	2.50	5.00
❑ 39 Don Meredith SP	60.00	100.00
❑ 40 J.W. Lockett SP RC	4.00	8.00
❑ 41 Don Perkins RC	5.00	10.00
❑ 42 Billy Howton	2.50	5.00
❑ 43 Dick Bielski	2.00	4.00
❑ 44 Mike Connelly RC	2.00	4.00
❑ 45 Jerry Tubbs SP	4.00	8.00
❑ 46 Don Bishop SP RC	4.00	8.00
❑ 47 Dick Moegle	2.00	4.00
❑ 48 Bobby Plummer SP RC	4.00	8.00
❑ 49 Cowboys Team	12.00	20.00
❑ 50 Milt Plum	2.50	5.00
❑ 51 Dan Lewis	2.00	4.00
❑ 52 Nick Pietrosante SP	4.00	8.00
❑ 53 Gail Cogdill	2.00	4.00
❑ 54 Jim Gibbons	2.00	4.00
❑ 55 Jim Martin	2.00	4.00
❑ 56 Yale Lary	3.00	6.00
❑ 57 Darris McCord	2.00	4.00
❑ 58 Alex Karras	15.00	25.00
❑ 59 Joe Schmidt	3.50	7.00
❑ 60 Dick Lane	3.00	6.00
❑ 61 John Lomakoski SP RC	4.00	8.00
❑ 62 Detroit Lions SP	10.00	18.00
❑ 63 Bart Starr SP	75.00	125.00
❑ 64 Paul Hornung SP	60.00	100.00
❑ 65 Tom Moore SP	6.00	12.00
❑ 66 Jim Taylor SP	30.00	50.00
❑ 67 Max McGee SP	6.00	12.00
❑ 68 Jim Ringo SP	7.50	15.00
❑ 69 Fuzzy Thurston RC SP	15.00	25.00
❑ 70 Forrest Gregg	3.50	7.00
❑ 71 Boyd Dowler	3.00	6.00
❑ 72 Hank Jordan SP	7.50	15.00
❑ 73 Bill Forester SP	5.00	10.00
❑ 74 Earl Gros SP RC	4.00	8.00
❑ 75 Packers Team SP	25.00	40.00
❑ 76 Checklist SP	50.00	80.00
❑ 77 Zeke Bratkowski SP	5.00	10.00
❑ 78 Jon Arnett SP	5.00	10.00
❑ 79 Ollie Matson SP	20.00	35.00
❑ 80 Dick Bass SP	5.00	10.00
❑ 81 Jim Phillips	2.00	4.00
❑ 82 Carroll Dale RC	2.50	5.00
❑ 83 Frank Varrichione	2.00	4.00
❑ 84 Art Hunter	2.00	4.00
❑ 85 Danny Villanueva RC	2.00	4.00
❑ 86 Les Richter SP	4.00	8.00
❑ 87 Lindon Crow	2.00	4.00
❑ 88 Roman Gabriel SP RC	35.00	60.00
❑ 89 Los Angeles Rams SP	10.00	18.00
❑ 90 Fran Tarkenton SP RC	125.00	225.00
❑ 91 Jerry Reichow SP RC	4.00	8.00
❑ 92 Hugh McElhenny SP	18.00	30.00
❑ 93 Mel Triplett SP	4.00	8.00
❑ 94 Tommy Mason SP RC	6.00	12.00
❑ 95 Dave Middleton SP	4.00	8.00
❑ 96 Frank Youso SP	4.00	8.00
❑ 97 Mike Mercer SP RC	4.00	8.00
❑ 98 Rip Hawkins SP	4.00	8.00
❑ 99 Cliff Livingston SP RC	4.00	8.00
❑ 100 Roy Winston SP RC	4.00	8.00
❑ 101 Vikings Team SP	15.00	25.00
❑ 102 Y.A.Tittle	25.00	40.00

Card		
❑ 103 Joe Walton	2.00	4.00
❑ 104 Frank Gifford	30.00	50.00
❑ 105 Alex Webster	2.50	5.00
❑ 106 Del Shofner	2.50	5.00
❑ 107 Don Chandler	2.00	4.00
❑ 108 Andy Robustelli	3.50	7.00
❑ 109 Jim Katcavage RC	2.50	5.00
❑ 110 Sam Huff SP	25.00	40.00
❑ 111 Erich Barnes	2.00	4.00
❑ 112 Jim Patton	2.00	4.00
❑ 113 Jerry Hillebrand SP	4.00	8.00
❑ 114 New York Giants	3.00	6.00
❑ 115 Sonny Jurgensen	25.00	40.00
❑ 116 Tommy McDonald	4.00	8.00
❑ 117 Ted Dean SP	4.00	8.00
❑ 118 Clarence Peaks	2.00	4.00
❑ 119 Bobby Walston	2.00	4.00
❑ 120 Pete Retzlaff SP	5.00	10.00
❑ 121 Jim Schrader SP	4.00	8.00
❑ 122 J.D. Smith T RC	2.00	4.00
❑ 123 King Hill	2.00	4.00
❑ 124 Maxie Baughan	2.50	5.00
❑ 125 Pete Case SP RC	4.00	8.00
❑ 126 Philadelphia Eagles	3.00	6.00
❑ 127 Bobby Layne	25.00	40.00
❑ 128 Tom Tracy	2.50	5.00
❑ 129 John Henry Johnson	3.00	6.00
❑ 130 Buddy Dial SP	5.00	10.00
❑ 131 Preston Carpenter	2.00	4.00
❑ 132 Lou Michaels SP	4.00	8.00
❑ 133 Gene Lipscomb SP	5.00	10.00
❑ 134 Ernie Stautner SP	12.00	20.00
❑ 135 John Reger SP	4.00	8.00
❑ 136 Myron Pottios RC	2.00	4.00
❑ 137 Bob Ferguson SP RC	4.00	8.00
❑ 138 Pittsburgh Steelers SP	10.00	18.00
❑ 139 Sam Etcheverry	2.50	5.00
❑ 140 John David Crow SP	5.00	10.00
❑ 141 Bobby Joe Conrad SP	5.00	10.00
❑ 142 Prentice Gautt SP RC	4.00	8.00
❑ 143 Frank Mestnik	2.00	4.00
❑ 144 Sonny Randle	2.50	5.00
❑ 145 Gerry Perry UER RC	2.00	4.00
❑ 146 Jerry Norton	2.00	4.00
❑ 147 Jimmy Hill RC	2.00	4.00
❑ 148 Bill Stacy	2.00	4.00
❑ 149 Fate Echols SP RC	4.00	8.00
❑ 150 St. Louis Cardinals	3.00	6.00
❑ 151 Billy Kilmer RC	25.00	40.00
❑ 152 John Brodie	10.00	18.00
❑ 153 J.D. Smith RB	2.50	5.00
❑ 154 C.R. Roberts SP RC	4.00	8.00
❑ 155 Monty Stickles	2.00	4.00
❑ 156 Clyde Conner UER	2.00	4.00
❑ 157 Bob St.Clair	3.00	6.00
❑ 158 Tommy Davis RC	2.00	4.00
❑ 159 Leo Nomellini	4.00	8.00
❑ 160 Matt Hazeltine	2.00	4.00
❑ 161 Abe Woodson	2.00	4.00
❑ 162 Dave Baker	2.00	4.00
❑ 163 San Francisco 49ers	3.00	6.00
❑ 164 Norm Snead SP RC	18.00	30.00
❑ 165 Dick James RC	2.50	5.00
❑ 166 Bobby Mitchell	4.00	8.00
❑ 167 Sam Horner RC	2.00	4.00
❑ 168 Bill Barnes	2.00	4.00
❑ 169 Bill Anderson	2.00	4.00
❑ 170 Fred Dugan	2.00	4.00
❑ 171 John Aveni SP RC	4.00	8.00
❑ 172 Bob Toneff	2.00	4.00
❑ 173 Jim Kerr RC	2.00	4.00
❑ 174 Leroy Jackson SP RC	4.00	8.00
❑ 175 Washington Redskins	3.00	6.00
❑ 176 Checklist !	60.00	100.00

1963 Topps

Card		
❑ COMPLETE SET (170)	850.00	1350.00
❑ WRAPPER (1-CENT)	500.00	800.00
❑ WRAPPER (5-CENT)	50.00	80.00
❑ 1 Johnny Unitas !	75.00	135.00
❑ 2 Lenny Moore	4.00	8.00
❑ 3 Jimmy Orr	1.50	3.00
❑ 4 Raymond Berry	4.00	8.00
❑ 5 Jim Parker	2.50	5.00
❑ 6 Alex Sandusky	1.25	2.50
❑ 7 Dick Szymanski RC	1.25	2.50
❑ 8 Gino Marchetti	3.00	6.00
❑ 9 Billy Ray Smith RC	1.50	3.00
❑ 10 Bill Pellington	1.25	2.50
❑ 11 Bob Boyd DB RC	1.25	2.50
❑ 12 Baltimore Colts SP	5.00	10.00
❑ 13 Frank Ryan SP	4.00	8.00
❑ 14 Jim Brown SP	100.00	200.00
❑ 15 Ray Renfro SP	4.00	8.00
❑ 16 Rich Kreitling SP	3.50	6.00
❑ 17 Mike McCormack SP	5.00	10.00
❑ 18 Jim Ray Smith SP	3.50	6.00
❑ 19 Lou Groza SP	15.00	25.00
❑ 20 Bill Glass SP	3.50	6.00
❑ 21 Galen Fiss SP	3.50	6.00
❑ 22 Don Fleming SP RC	4.00	8.00
❑ 23 Bob Gain SP	3.50	6.00
❑ 24 Cleveland Browns SP	5.00	10.00
❑ 25 Milt Plum	1.50	3.00
❑ 26 Dan Lewis	1.25	2.50
❑ 27 Nick Pietrosante	1.25	2.50
❑ 28 Gail Cogdill	1.25	2.50
❑ 29 Harley Sewell	1.25	2.50
❑ 30 Jim Gibbons	1.25	2.50
❑ 31 Carl Brettschneider	1.25	2.50
❑ 32 Dick Lane	2.50	5.00
❑ 33 Yale Lary	2.50	5.00
❑ 34 Roger Brown RC	1.50	3.00
❑ 35 Joe Schmidt	3.00	6.00
❑ 36 Detroit Lions SP	5.00	10.00
❑ 37 Roman Gabriel	4.00	8.00
❑ 38 Zeke Bratkowski	1.50	3.00
❑ 39 Dick Bass	1.50	3.00
❑ 40 Jon Arnett	1.50	3.00
❑ 41 Jim Phillips	1.25	2.50
❑ 42 Frank Varrichione	1.25	2.50
❑ 43 Danny Villanueva	1.25	2.50
❑ 44 Deacon Jones RC	30.00	50.00
❑ 45 Lindon Crow	1.25	2.50
❑ 46 Marlin McKeever RC	1.25	2.50
❑ 47 Ed Meador RC	1.25	2.50
❑ 48 Los Angeles Rams	2.00	4.00
❑ 49 Y.A.Tittle SP	30.00	50.00
❑ 50 Del Shofner SP	3.50	6.00
❑ 51 Alex Webster SP	4.00	8.00
❑ 52 Phil King SP RC	3.50	6.00
❑ 53 Jack Stroud SP	3.50	6.00
❑ 54 Darrell Dess SP	3.50	6.00
❑ 55 Jim Katcavage SP	3.50	6.00
❑ 56 Roosevelt Grier SP	5.00	10.00
❑ 57 Erich Barnes SP	3.50	6.00
❑ 58 Jim Patton SP	3.50	6.00
❑ 59 Sam Huff SP	12.00	20.00
❑ 60 New York Giants	2.00	4.00
❑ 61 Bill Wade	1.50	3.00
❑ 62 Mike Ditka	35.00	60.00
❑ 63 Johnny Morris	1.25	2.50
❑ 64 Roger LeClerc	1.25	2.50
❑ 65 Roger Davis RC	1.25	2.50
❑ 66 Joe Marconi	1.25	2.50
❑ 67 Herman Lee RC	1.25	2.50
❑ 68 Doug Atkins	3.00	6.00
❑ 69 Joe Fortunato	1.25	2.50
❑ 70 Bill George	2.50	5.00
❑ 71 Richie Petitbon	1.50	3.00
❑ 72 Bears Team SP	5.00	10.00
❑ 73 Eddie LeBaron SP	5.00	10.00
❑ 74 Don Meredith SP	35.00	60.00
❑ 75 Don Perkins SP	5.00	10.00
❑ 76 Amos Marsh SP RC	3.50	6.00
❑ 77 Billy Howton SP	4.00	8.00
❑ 78 Andy Cvercko SP RC	3.50	6.00
❑ 79 Sam Baker SP	3.50	6.00
❑ 80 Jerry Tubbs SP	3.50	6.00
❑ 81 Don Bishop SP	3.50	6.00
❑ 82 Bob Lilly SP RC	100.00	175.00
❑ 83 Jerry Norton SP	3.50	6.00
❑ 84 Cowboys Team SP	12.00	20.00
❑ 85 Checklist	15.00	25.00
❑ 86 Bart Starr	40.00	75.00

Card		
❑ 87 Jim Taylor	18.00	30.00
❑ 88 Boyd Dowler	2.50	5.00
❑ 89 Forrest Gregg	3.00	6.00
❑ 90 Fuzzy Thurston	3.00	6.00
❑ 91 Jim Ringo	3.00	6.00
❑ 92 Ron Kramer	1.50	3.00
❑ 93 Hank Jordan	3.00	6.00
❑ 94 Bill Forester	1.50	3.00
❑ 95 Willie Wood RC	25.00	40.00
❑ 96 Ray Nitschke RC	90.00	150.00
❑ 97 Green Bay Packers	7.50	15.00
❑ 98 Fran Tarkenton	35.00	60.00
❑ 99 Tommy Mason	1.50	3.00
❑ 100 Mel Triplett	1.25	2.50
❑ 101 Jerry Reichow	1.25	2.50
❑ 102 Frank Youso	1.25	2.50
❑ 103 Hugh McElhenny	4.00	8.00
❑ 104 Gerald Huth RC	1.25	2.50
❑ 105 Ed Sharockman RC	1.25	2.50
❑ 106 Rip Hawkins	1.25	2.50
❑ 107 Jim Marshall RC	20.00	35.00
❑ 108 Jim Prestel RC	1.25	2.50
❑ 109 Minnesota Vikings	2.00	4.00
❑ 110 Sonny Jurgensen SP	15.00	25.00
❑ 111 Timmy Brown SP RC	5.00	10.00
❑ 112 Tommy McDonald SP	7.50	15.00
❑ 113 Clarence Peaks SP	3.50	6.00
❑ 114 Pete Retzlaff SP	4.00	8.00
❑ 115 Jim Schrader SP	3.50	6.00
❑ 116 Jim McCusker SP	3.50	6.00
❑ 117 Don Burroughs SP	3.50	6.00
❑ 118 Maxie Baughan SP	3.50	6.00
❑ 119 Riley Gunnels SP RC	3.50	6.00
❑ 120 Jimmy Carr SP	3.50	6.00
❑ 121 Philadelphia Eagles SP	5.00	10.00
❑ 122 Ed Brown SP	4.00	8.00
❑ 123 John H.Johnson SP	7.50	15.00
❑ 124 Buddy Dial SP	3.50	6.00
❑ 125 Bill Red Mack SP RC	3.50	6.00
❑ 126 Preston Carpenter SP	3.50	6.00
❑ 127 Ray Lemek SP RC	3.50	6.00
❑ 128 Buzz Nutter SP	3.50	6.00
❑ 129 Ernie Stautner SP	7.50	15.00
❑ 130 Lou Michaels SP	3.50	6.00
❑ 131 Clendon Thomas SP RC	3.50	6.00
❑ 132 Tom Bettis SP	3.50	6.00
❑ 133 Pittsburgh Steelers SP	5.00	10.00
❑ 134 John Brodie	4.00	8.00
❑ 135 J.D. Smith	1.25	2.50
❑ 136 Billy Kilmer	2.50	5.00
❑ 137 Bernie Casey RC	1.50	3.00
❑ 138 Tommy Davis	1.25	2.50
❑ 139 Ted Connolly RC	1.25	2.50
❑ 140 Bob St.Clair	2.50	5.00
❑ 141 Abe Woodson	1.25	2.50
❑ 142 Matt Hazeltine	1.25	2.50
❑ 143 Leo Nomellini	3.00	6.00
❑ 144 Dan Colchico RC	1.25	2.50
❑ 145 San Francisco 49ers SP	5.00	10.00
❑ 146 Charlie Johnson RC	4.00	8.00
❑ 147 John David Crow	1.50	3.00
❑ 148 Bobby Joe Conrad	1.50	3.00
❑ 149 Sonny Randle	1.25	2.50
❑ 150 Prentice Gautt	1.25	2.50
❑ 151 Taz Anderson RC	1.25	2.50
❑ 152 Ernie McMillan RC	1.50	3.00
❑ 153 Jimmy Hill	1.25	2.50
❑ 154 Bill Koman RC	1.25	2.50
❑ 155 Larry Wilson RC	12.00	20.00
❑ 156 Don Owens	1.25	2.50
❑ 157 St. Louis Cardinals SP	5.00	10.00
❑ 158 Norm Snead SP	5.00	10.00
❑ 159 Bobby Mitchell SP	7.50	15.00
❑ 160 Bill Barnes SP	3.50	6.00
❑ 161 Fred Dugan SP	3.50	6.00
❑ 162 Don Bosseler SP	3.50	6.00
❑ 163 John Nisby SP	3.50	6.00
❑ 164 Riley Mattson SP RC	3.50	6.00
❑ 165 Bob Toneff SP	3.50	6.00
❑ 166 Rod Breedlove SP RC	3.50	6.00
❑ 167 Dick James SP	3.50	6.00
❑ 168 Claude Crabb SP RC	3.50	6.00
❑ 169 Washington Redskins SP	5.00	10.00
❑ 170 Checklist UER !	30.00	50.00

1964 Topps

❑ COMPLETE SET (176)	1000.00	1500.00
❑ WRAPPER (1-CENT)	30.00	40.00
❑ WRAPPER (5-CENT, PENN)	75.00	125.00
❑ WRAP. (5-CENT, 8-CARD)	90.00	150.00
❑ 1 Tommy Addison SP	15.00	40.00
❑ 2 Houston Antwine RC	2.00	4.00
❑ 3 Nick Buoniconti	15.00	25.00
❑ 4 Ron Burton SP	5.00	10.00
❑ 5 Gino Cappelletti	2.50	5.00
❑ 6 Jim Colclough SP	3.00	6.00
❑ 7 Bob Dee SP	3.00	6.00
❑ 8 Larry Eisenhauer	2.00	4.00
❑ 9 Dick Felt SP	3.00	6.00
❑ 10 Larry Garron	2.00	4.00
❑ 11 Art Graham RC	2.00	4.00
❑ 12 Ron Hall DB RC	2.00	4.00
❑ 13 Charles Long	2.00	4.00
❑ 14 Don McKinnon RC	2.00	4.00
❑ 15 Don Oakes SP RC	3.00	6.00
❑ 16 Ross O'Hanley SP	3.00	6.00
❑ 17 Babe Parilli SP	5.00	10.00
❑ 18 Jesse Richardson SP	3.00	6.00
❑ 19 Jack Rudolph SP RC	3.00	6.00
❑ 20 Don Webb RC	2.00	4.00
❑ 21 Boston Patriots	3.00	6.00
❑ 22 Ray Abruzzese UER	2.00	4.00
❑ 23 Stew Barber RC	2.00	4.00
❑ 24 Dave Behrman RC	2.00	4.00
❑ 25 Al Bemiller RC	2.00	4.00
❑ 26 Elbert Dubenion SP	5.00	10.00
❑ 27 Jim Dunaway SP RC	3.00	6.00
❑ 28 Booker Edgerson SP	3.00	6.00
❑ 29 Cookie Gilchrist SP	15.00	25.00
❑ 30 Jack Kemp SP	60.00	120.00
❑ 31 Daryle Lamonica RC	40.00	75.00
❑ 32 Bill Miller	2.00	4.00
❑ 33 Herb Paterra RC	2.00	4.00
❑ 34 Ken Rice SP	3.00	6.00
❑ 35 Ed Rutkowski UER RC	2.00	4.00
❑ 36 George Saimes RC	2.00	4.00
❑ 37 Tom Sestak	2.00	4.00
❑ 38 Billy Shaw SP	7.50	15.00
❑ 39 Mike Stratton	2.50	5.00
❑ 40 Gene Sykes RC	2.00	4.00
❑ 41 John Tracey SP RC	3.00	6.00
❑ 42 Sid Youngelman SP	3.00	6.00
❑ 43 Buffalo Bills	3.00	6.00
❑ 44 Eldon Danenhauer SP	3.00	6.00
❑ 45 Jim Fraser SP	3.00	6.00
❑ 46 Chuck Gavin SP	3.00	6.00
❑ 47 Goose Gonsoulin SP	5.00	10.00
❑ 48 Ernie Barnes RC	2.00	4.00
❑ 49 Tom Janik RC	2.00	4.00
❑ 50 Billy Joe RC	2.50	5.00
❑ 51 Ike Lassiter RC	2.00	4.00
❑ 52 John McCormick SP RC	3.00	6.00
❑ 53 Bud McFadin SP	3.00	6.00
❑ 54 Gene Mingo SP	3.00	6.00
❑ 55 Charlie Mitchell RC	2.00	4.00
❑ 56 John Nocera SP RC	3.00	6.00
❑ 57 Tom Nomina RC	2.00	4.00
❑ 58 Harold Olson SP RC	3.00	6.00
❑ 59 Bob Scarpitto	2.00	4.00
❑ 60 John Sklopan RC	2.00	4.00
❑ 61 Mickey Slaughter RC	2.00	4.00
❑ 62 Don Stone	2.00	4.00
❑ 63 Jerry Sturm RC	2.00	4.00
❑ 64 Lionel Taylor SP	6.00	12.00
❑ 65 Broncos Team SP	10.00	20.00
❑ 66 Scott Appleton RC	2.00	4.00
❑ 67 Tony Banfield SP	3.00	6.00
❑ 68 George Blanda SP	40.00	75.00
❑ 69 Billy Cannon	3.00	6.00
❑ 70 Doug Cline SP	3.00	6.00
❑ 71 Gary Cutsinger SP RC	3.00	6.00
❑ 72 Willard Dewveall SP RC	3.00	6.00
❑ 73 Don Floyd SP	3.00	6.00
❑ 74 Freddy Glick SP RC	3.00	6.00
❑ 75 Charlie Hennigan SP	5.00	10.00
❑ 76 Ed Husmann SP	3.00	6.00
❑ 77 Bobby Jancik SP RC	3.00	6.00
❑ 78 Jacky Lee SP	5.00	10.00
❑ 79 Bob McLeod SP RC	3.00	6.00
❑ 80 Rich Michael SP	3.00	6.00
❑ 81 Larry Onesti RC	2.00	4.00
❑ 82 Checklist Card UER	30.00	60.00
❑ 83 Bob Schmidt SP RC	3.00	6.00
❑ 84 Walt Suggs SP RC	3.00	6.00
❑ 85 Bob Talamini SP	3.00	6.00
❑ 86 Charley Tolar SP	3.00	6.00
❑ 87 Don Trull RC	2.00	4.00
❑ 88 Houston Oilers	3.00	6.00
❑ 89 Fred Arbanas	2.00	4.00
❑ 90 Bobby Bell RC	25.00	40.00
❑ 91 Mel Branch SP	5.00	10.00
❑ 92 Buck Buchanan RC	25.00	40.00
❑ 93 Ed Budde RC	2.00	4.00
❑ 94 Chris Burford SP	5.00	10.00
❑ 95 Walt Corey RC	2.50	5.00
❑ 96 Len Dawson SP	40.00	75.00
❑ 97 Dave Grayson RC	2.00	4.00
❑ 98 Abner Haynes	3.00	6.00
❑ 99 Sherrill Headrick SP	5.00	10.00
❑ 100 E.J. Holub	2.00	4.00
❑ 101 Bobby Hunt RC	2.00	4.00
❑ 102 Frank Jackson SP	3.00	6.00
❑ 103 Curtis McClinton	2.50	5.00
❑ 104 Jerry Mays SP	5.00	10.00
❑ 105 Johnny Robinson SP	6.00	12.00
❑ 106 Jack Spikes SP	3.00	6.00
❑ 107 Smokey Stover SP RC	3.00	6.00
❑ 108 Jim Tyrer RC	5.00	10.00
❑ 109 Duane Wood SP RC	3.00	6.00
❑ 110 Kansas City Chiefs	3.00	6.00
❑ 111 Dick Christy SP	3.00	6.00
❑ 112 Dan Ficca SP RC	3.00	6.00
❑ 113 Larry Grantham	2.00	4.00
❑ 114 Curley Johnson SP	3.00	6.00
❑ 115 Gene Heeter RC	2.00	4.00
❑ 116 Jack Klotz RC	2.00	4.00
❑ 117 Pete Liske RC	2.50	5.00
❑ 118 Bob McAdam RC	2.00	4.00
❑ 119 Dee Mackey SP RC	3.00	6.00
❑ 120 Bill Mathis SP	5.00	10.00
❑ 121 Don Maynard	20.00	35.00
❑ 122 Dainard Paulson SP	3.00	6.00
❑ 123 Gerry Philbin RC	2.50	5.00
❑ 124 Mark Smolinski SP RC	3.00	6.00
❑ 125 Matt Snell RC	10.00	20.00
❑ 126 Mike Taliaferro RC	2.00	4.00
❑ 127 Bake Turner SP RC	5.00	10.00
❑ 128 Jeff Ware RC	2.00	4.00
❑ 129 Clyde Washington RC	2.00	4.00
❑ 130 Dick Wood RC	2.00	4.00
❑ 131 New York Jets	3.00	6.00
❑ 132 Dalva Allen SP	3.00	6.00
❑ 133 Dan Birdwell RC	2.00	4.00
❑ 134 Dave Costa RC	2.00	4.00
❑ 135 Dobie Craig RC	2.00	4.00
❑ 136 Clem Daniels	2.50	5.00
❑ 137 Cotton Davidson SP	5.00	10.00
❑ 138 Claude Gibson RC	2.00	4.00
❑ 139 Tom Flores SP	7.50	15.00
❑ 140 Wayne Hawkins SP	3.00	6.00
❑ 141 Ken Herock RC	2.00	4.00
❑ 142 Jon Jelacic SP RC	3.00	6.00
❑ 143 Joe Krakoski RC	2.00	4.00
❑ 144 Archie Matsos SP	3.00	6.00
❑ 145 Mike Mercer	2.00	4.00
❑ 146 Alan Miller SP	3.00	6.00
❑ 147 Bob Mischak SP	3.00	6.00
❑ 148 Jim Otto SP	18.00	30.00
❑ 149 Clancy Osborne SP	3.00	6.00
❑ 150 Art Powell SP	6.00	12.00
❑ 151 Bo Roberson	2.00	4.00
❑ 152 Fred Williamson SP	18.00	30.00
❑ 153 Oakland Raiders	3.00	6.00
❑ 154 Chuck Allen RC SP	5.00	10.00
❑ 155 Lance Alworth	30.00	50.00
❑ 156 George Blair RC	2.00	4.00
❑ 157 Earl Faison	2.00	4.00
❑ 158 Sam Gruneisen RC	2.00	4.00
❑ 159 John Hadl RC	25.00	40.00
❑ 160 Dick Harris SP	3.00	6.00
❑ 161 Emil Karas SP RC	3.00	6.00
❑ 162 Dave Kocourek SP	3.00	6.00
❑ 163 Ernie Ladd	4.00	8.00
❑ 164 Keith Lincoln	3.00	6.00
❑ 165 Paul Lowe SP	6.00	12.00
❑ 166 Charley McNeil	2.00	4.00
❑ 167 Jacque MacKinnon SP RC	3.00	6.00
❑ 168 Ron Mix SP	10.00	20.00
❑ 169 Don Norton SP	3.00	6.00
❑ 170 Don Rogers SP RC	3.00	6.00
❑ 171 Tobin Rote SP	5.00	10.00
❑ 172 Henry Schmidt SP RC	3.00	6.00
❑ 173 Bud Whitehead RC	2.00	4.00
❑ 174 Ernie Wright SP	5.00	10.00
❑ 175 San Diego Chargers	3.00	6.00
❑ 176 Checklist SP UER	80.00	160.00

1965 Topps

❑ COMPLETE SET (176)	2500.00	4000.00
❑ WRAPPER (5-CENT)	90.00	150.00
❑ 1 Tommy Addison SP !	20.00	35.00
❑ 2 Houston Antwine SP	7.00	12.00
❑ 3 Nick Buoniconti SP	18.00	30.00
❑ 4 Ron Burton SP	10.00	20.00
❑ 5 Gino Cappelletti SP	10.00	20.00
❑ 6 Jim Colclough	3.50	7.00
❑ 7 Bob Dee SP	7.00	12.00
❑ 8 Larry Eisenhauer	3.50	7.00
❑ 9 J.D. Garrett RC	3.50	7.00
❑ 10 Larry Garron	3.50	7.00
❑ 11 Art Graham SP	7.00	12.00
❑ 12 Ron Hall DB	3.50	7.00
❑ 13 Charles Long	3.50	7.00
❑ 14 Jon Morris RC	5.00	10.00
❑ 15 Billy Neighbors SP	7.00	12.00
❑ 16 Ross O'Hanley	3.50	7.00
❑ 17 Babe Parilli SP	10.00	20.00
❑ 18 Tony Romeo SP RC	7.00	12.00
❑ 19 Jack Rudolph SP	7.00	12.00
❑ 20 Bob Schmidt	3.50	7.00
❑ 21 Don Webb SP	7.00	12.00
❑ 22 Jim Whalen SP RC	7.00	12.00
❑ 23 Stew Barber	3.50	7.00
❑ 24 Glenn Bass SP RC	7.00	12.00
❑ 25 Al Bemiller SP	7.00	12.00
❑ 26 Wray Carlton SP	7.00	12.00
❑ 27 Tom Day RC	3.50	7.00
❑ 28 Elbert Dubenion SP	7.50	15.00
❑ 29 Jim Dunaway	3.50	7.00
❑ 30 Pete Gogolak SP RC	10.00	20.00
❑ 31 Dick Hudson SP	7.00	12.00
❑ 32 Harry Jacobs SP	7.00	12.00
❑ 33 Billy Joe SP	7.50	15.00
❑ 34 Tom Keating SP RC	7.00	12.00
❑ 35 Jack Kemp SP !	75.00	150.00
❑ 36 Daryle Lamonica SP	30.00	50.00
❑ 37 Paul Maguire SP	10.00	20.00
❑ 38 Ron McDole SP RC	7.00	12.00
❑ 39 George Saimes SP	7.00	12.00
❑ 40 Tom Sestak SP	7.00	12.00
❑ 41 Billy Shaw SP	10.00	20.00
❑ 42 Mike Stratton SP	7.00	12.00
❑ 43 John Tracey SP	7.00	12.00
❑ 44 Ernie Warlick	3.50	7.00
❑ 45 Odell Barry RC	3.50	7.00
❑ 46 Willie Brown SP RC	75.00	135.00
❑ 47 Gerry Bussell SP RC	7.00	12.00
❑ 48 Eldon Danenhauer SP	7.00	12.00
❑ 49 Al Denson SP RC	7.00	12.00
❑ 50 Hewritt Dixon SP RC	7.50	15.00
❑ 51 Cookie Gilchrist SP	18.00	30.00
❑ 52 Goose Gonsoulin SP	7.50	15.00
❑ 53 Abner Haynes SP	10.00	20.00
❑ 54 Jerry Hopkins RC	3.50	7.00
❑ 55 Ray Jacobs SP	7.00	12.00

❑ 56 Jacky Lee SP 7.50 15.00
❑ 57 John McCormick QB 3.50 7.00
❑ 58 Bob McCullough SP 7.00 12.00
❑ 59 John McGeever RC 3.50 7.00
❑ 60 Charlie Mitchell SP 7.00 12.00
❑ 61 Jim Perkins SP RC 7.00 12.00
❑ 62 Bob Scarpitto SP 7.00 12.00
❑ 63 Mickey Slaughter SP 7.00 12.00
❑ 64 Jerry Sturm SP 7.00 12.00
❑ 65 Lionel Taylor SP 10.00 20.00
❑ 66 Scott Appleton SP 7.00 12.00
❑ 67 Johnny Baker SP RC 7.00 12.00
❑ 68 Sonny Bishop SP RC 7.00 12.00
❑ 69 George Blanda SP 75.00 125.00
❑ 70 Sid Blanks SP RC 7.00 12.00
❑ 71 Ode Burrell SP RC 7.00 12.00
❑ 72 Doug Cline SP 7.00 12.00
❑ 73 Willard Dewveall 3.50 7.00
❑ 74 Larry Elkins RC 3.50 7.00
❑ 75 Don Floyd SP 7.00 12.00
❑ 76 Freddy Glick 3.50 7.00
❑ 77 Tom Goode SP RC 7.00 12.00
❑ 78 Charlie Hennigan SP 10.00 20.00
❑ 79 Ed Husmann 3.50 7.00
❑ 80 Bobby Jancik SP 7.00 12.00
❑ 81 Bud McFadin SP 7.00 12.00
❑ 82 Bob McLeod SP 7.00 12.00
❑ 83 Jim Norton SP 7.00 12.00
❑ 84 Walt Suggs 3.50 7.00
❑ 85 Bob Talamini 3.50 7.00
❑ 86 Charley Tolar SP 7.00 12.00
❑ 87 Checklist SP ! 100.00 175.00
❑ 88 Don Trull SP 7.00 12.00
❑ 89 Fred Arbanas SP 7.00 12.00
❑ 90 Pete Beathard SP RC 7.00 12.00
❑ 91 Bobby Bell SP 25.00 40.00
❑ 92 Mel Branch SP 7.00 12.00
❑ 93 Tommy Brooker SP RC 7.00 12.00
❑ 94 Buck Buchanan SP 20.00 35.00
❑ 95 Ed Budde SP 7.00 12.00
❑ 96 Chris Burford SP 7.00 12.00
❑ 97 Walt Corey 3.50 7.00
❑ 98 Jerry Cornelison 3.50 7.00
❑ 99 Len Dawson SP 60.00 100.00
❑ 100 Jon Gilliam SP RC 7.00 12.00
❑ 101 Sherrill Headrick SP UER 7.00 12.00
❑ 102 Dave Hill SP RC 7.00 12.00
❑ 103 E.J. Holub SP 7.00 12.00
❑ 104 Bobby Hunt SP 7.00 12.00
❑ 105 Frank Jackson SP 7.00 12.00
❑ 106 Jerry Mays 5.00 10.00
❑ 107 Curtis McClinton SP 7.50 15.00
❑ 108 Bobby Ply SP RC 7.00 12.00
❑ 109 Johnny Robinson SP 7.50 15.00
❑ 110 Jim Tyrer SP 7.00 12.00
❑ 111 Bill Baird SP RC 7.00 12.00
❑ 112 Ralph Baker SP RC 7.00 12.00
❑ 113 Sam DeLuca SP 7.00 12.00
❑ 114 Larry Grantham SP 7.50 15.00
❑ 115 Gene Heeter SP 7.00 12.00
❑ 116 Winston Hill SP RC 10.00 20.00
❑ 117 John Huarte SP RC 18.00 30.00
❑ 118 Cosmo Iacavazzi SP RC 7.00 12.00
❑ 119 Curley Johnson SP 7.00 12.00
❑ 120 Dee Mackey UER 3.50 7.00
❑ 121 Don Maynard 30.00 50.00
❑ 122 Joe Namath SP RC 1200.00 1800.00
❑ 123 Dainard Paulson 3.50 7.00
❑ 124 Gerry Philbin SP 7.00 12.00
❑ 125 Sherman Plunkett SP RC 7.50 15.00
❑ 126 Mark Smolinski 3.50 7.00
❑ 127 Matt Snell SP 18.00 30.00
❑ 128 Mike Taliaferro SP 7.00 12.00
❑ 129 Bake Turner SP 7.00 12.00
❑ 130 Clyde Washington SP 7.00 12.00
❑ 131 Verlon Biggs SP RC 7.00 12.00
❑ 132 Dalva Allen 3.50 7.00
❑ 133 Fred Biletnikoff SP RC 150.00 250.00
❑ 134 Billy Cannon SP 10.00 20.00
❑ 135 Dave Costa SP 7.00 12.00
❑ 136 Clem Daniels SP 7.50 15.00
❑ 137 Ben Davidson SP RC 35.00 60.00
❑ 138 Cotton Davidson SP 7.50 15.00
❑ 139 Tom Flores SP 10.00 20.00
❑ 140 Claude Gibson 3.50 7.00
❑ 141 Wayne Hawkins 3.50 7.00
❑ 142 Archie Matsos SP 7.00 12.00
❑ 143 Mike Mercer SP 7.00 12.00
❑ 144 Bob Mischak SP 7.00 12.00
❑ 145 Jim Otto 18.00 30.00
❑ 146 Art Powell UER 5.00 10.00
❑ 147 Warren Powers SP RC 7.00 12.00
❑ 148 Ken Rice SP 7.00 12.00
❑ 149 Bo Roberson SP 7.00 12.00
❑ 150 Harry Schuh RC 3.50 7.00
❑ 151 Larry Todd SP RC 7.00 12.00
❑ 152 Fred Williamson SP 15.00 30.00
❑ 153 J.R. Williamson RC 3.50 7.00
❑ 154 Chuck Allen 5.00 10.00
❑ 155 Lance Alworth 50.00 75.00
❑ 156 Frank Buncom RC 3.50 7.00
❑ 157 Steve DeLong SP RC 7.00 12.00
❑ 158 Earl Faison SP 7.50 15.00
❑ 159 Kenny Graham SP RC 7.00 12.00
❑ 160 George Gross SP RC 7.00 12.00
❑ 161 John Hadl SP 20.00 35.00
❑ 162 Emil Karas SP 7.00 12.00
❑ 163 Dave Kocourek SP 7.00 12.00
❑ 164 Ernie Ladd SP 10.00 20.00
❑ 165 Keith Lincoln SP 10.00 20.00
❑ 166 Paul Lowe SP 10.00 20.00
❑ 167 Jacque MacKinnon 3.50 7.00
❑ 168 Ron Mix 12.00 20.00
❑ 169 Don Norton SP 7.00 12.00
❑ 170 Bob Petrich RC 3.50 7.00
❑ 171 Rick Redman SP RC 7.00 12.00
❑ 172 Pat Shea RC 3.50 7.00
❑ 173 Walt Sweeney SP RC 7.50 15.00
❑ 174 Dick Westmoreland RC 3.50 7.00
❑ 175 Ernie Wright SP 10.00 20.00
❑ 176 Checklist SP ! 125.00 225.00

1966 Topps

❑ COMPLETE SET (132) 950.00 1500.00
❑ WRAPPER (5-CENT) 30.00 60.00
❑ 1 Tommy Addison 10.00 20.00
❑ 2 Houston Antwine 3.00 5.00
❑ 3 Nick Buoniconti 5.00 10.00
❑ 4 Gino Cappelletti 3.50 7.00
❑ 5 Bob Dee 3.00 5.00
❑ 6 Larry Garron 3.00 5.00
❑ 7 Art Graham 3.00 5.00
❑ 8 Ron Hall DB 3.00 5.00
❑ 9 Charles Long 3.00 5.00
❑ 10 Jon Morris 3.00 5.00
❑ 11 Don Oakes 3.00 5.00
❑ 12 Babe Parilli 3.50 7.00
❑ 13 Don Webb 3.00 5.00
❑ 14 Jim Whalen 3.00 5.00
❑ 15 Funny Ring Checklist ! 200.00 300.00
❑ 16 Stew Barber 3.00 5.00
❑ 17 Glenn Bass 3.00 5.00
❑ 18 Dave Behrman 3.00 5.00
❑ 19 Al Bemiller 3.00 5.00
❑ 20 Butch Byrd RC 3.50 7.00
❑ 21 Wray Carlton 3.00 5.00
❑ 22 Tom Day 3.00 5.00
❑ 23 Elbert Dubenion 3.50 7.00
❑ 24 Jim Dunaway 3.00 5.00
❑ 25 Dick Hudson 3.00 5.00
❑ 26 Jack Kemp 60.00 120.00
❑ 27 Daryle Lamonica 12.00 20.00
❑ 28 Tom Sestak 3.00 5.00
❑ 29 Billy Shaw 5.00 10.00
❑ 30 Mike Stratton 3.00 5.00
❑ 31 Eldon Danenhauer 3.00 5.00
❑ 32 Cookie Gilchrist 5.00 10.00
❑ 33 Goose Gonsoulin 3.50 7.00
❑ 34 Wendell Hayes RC 5.00 10.00
❑ 35 Abner Haynes 5.00 10.00
❑ 36 Jerry Hopkins 3.00 5.00
❑ 37 Ray Jacobs 3.00 5.00
❑ 38 Charlie Janerette RC 3.00 5.00
❑ 39 Ray Kubala RC 3.00 5.00
❑ 40 John McCormick QB 3.00 5.00
❑ 41 Leroy Moore RC 3.00 5.00
❑ 42 Bob Scarpitto 3.00 5.00
❑ 43 Mickey Slaughter 3.00 5.00
❑ 44 Jerry Sturm 3.00 5.00
❑ 45 Lionel Taylor 5.00 10.00
❑ 46 Scott Appleton 3.00 5.00
❑ 47 Johnny Baker 3.00 5.00
❑ 48 George Blanda 20.00 35.00
❑ 49 Sid Blanks 3.00 5.00
❑ 50 Danny Brabham RC 3.00 5.00
❑ 51 Ode Burrell 3.00 5.00
❑ 52 Gary Cutsinger 3.00 5.00
❑ 53 Larry Elkins 3.00 5.00
❑ 54 Don Floyd 3.00 5.00
❑ 55 Willie Frazier RC 3.50 7.00
❑ 56 Freddy Glick 3.00 5.00
❑ 57 Charlie Hennigan 3.50 7.00
❑ 58 Bobby Jancik 3.00 5.00
❑ 59 Rich Michael 3.00 5.00
❑ 60 Don Trull 3.00 5.00
❑ 61 Checklist 30.00 55.00
❑ 62 Fred Arbanas 3.00 5.00
❑ 63 Pete Beathard 3.00 5.00
❑ 64 Bobby Bell 5.00 10.00
❑ 65 Ed Budde 3.00 5.00
❑ 66 Chris Burford 3.00 5.00
❑ 67 Len Dawson 25.00 40.00
❑ 68 Jon Gilliam 3.00 5.00
❑ 69 Sherrill Headrick 3.00 5.00
❑ 70 E.J. Holub UER 3.00 5.00
❑ 71 Bobby Hunt 3.00 5.00
❑ 72 Curtis McClinton 3.50 7.00
❑ 73 Jerry Mays 3.00 5.00
❑ 74 Johnny Robinson 3.50 7.00
❑ 75 Otis Taylor RC 15.00 25.00
❑ 76 Tom Erlandson RC 3.50 7.00
❑ 77 Norm Evans RC 5.00 10.00
❑ 78 Tom Goode 3.50 7.00
❑ 79 Mike Hudock 3.50 7.00
❑ 80 Frank Jackson 3.50 7.00
❑ 81 Billy Joe 3.50 7.00
❑ 82 Dave Kocourek 3.50 7.00
❑ 83 Bo Roberson 3.50 7.00
❑ 84 Jack Spikes 3.50 7.00
❑ 85 Jim Warren RC 3.50 7.00
❑ 86 Willie West RC 3.50 7.00
❑ 87 Dick Westmoreland 3.50 7.00
❑ 88 Eddie Wilson RC 3.50 7.00
❑ 89 Dick Wood 3.50 7.00
❑ 90 Verlon Biggs 3.50 7.00
❑ 91 Sam DeLuca 3.00 5.00
❑ 92 Winston Hill 3.00 5.00
❑ 93 Dee Mackey 3.00 5.00
❑ 94 Bill Mathis 3.00 5.00
❑ 95 Don Maynard 18.00 30.00
❑ 96 Joe Namath 150.00 250.00
❑ 97 Dainard Paulson 3.00 5.00
❑ 98 Gerry Philbin 3.50 7.00
❑ 99 Sherman Plunkett 3.00 5.00
❑ 100 Paul Rochester 3.00 5.00
❑ 101 George Sauer Jr. RC 7.50 15.00
❑ 102 Matt Snell 5.00 10.00
❑ 103 Jim Turner RC 3.50 7.00
❑ 104 Fred Biletnikoff UER 30.00 50.00
❑ 105 Bill Budness RC 3.00 5.00
❑ 106 Billy Cannon 5.00 10.00
❑ 107 Clem Daniels 3.50 7.00
❑ 108 Ben Davidson 7.50 15.00
❑ 109 Cotton Davidson 3.50 7.00
❑ 110 Claude Gibson 3.00 5.00
❑ 111 Wayne Hawkins 3.00 5.00
❑ 112 Ken Herock 3.00 5.00
❑ 113 Bob Mischak 3.00 5.00
❑ 114 Gus Otto RC 3.00 5.00
❑ 115 Jim Otto 12.00 20.00
❑ 116 Art Powell 5.00 10.00
❑ 117 Harry Schuh 3.00 5.00
❑ 118 Chuck Allen 3.00 5.00
❑ 119 Lance Alworth 25.00 40.00
❑ 120 Frank Buncom 3.00 5.00
❑ 121 Steve DeLong 3.00 5.00
❑ 122 John Farris RC 3.00 5.00
❑ 123 Kenny Graham 3.00 5.00
❑ 124 Sam Gruneisen 3.00 5.00
❑ 125 John Hadl 5.00 10.00
❑ 126 Walt Sweeney 3.00 5.00
❑ 127 Keith Lincoln 5.00 10.00
❑ 128 Ron Mix 5.00 10.00
❑ 129 Don Norton 3.00 5.00

❑ 130 Pat Shea	3.00	5.00
❑ 131 Ernie Wright	5.00	10.00
❑ 132 Checklist	50.00	100.00

1967 Topps

❑ COMPLETE SET (132)	400.00	700.00
❑ WRAPPER (5-CENT)	30.00	60.00
❑ 1 John Huarte	10.00	18.00
❑ 2 Babe Parilli	2.00	4.00
❑ 3 Gino Cappelletti	2.00	4.00
❑ 4 Larry Garron	1.50	3.00
❑ 5 Tommy Addison	1.50	3.00
❑ 6 Jon Morris	1.50	3.00
❑ 7 Houston Antwine	1.50	3.00
❑ 8 Don Oakes	1.50	3.00
❑ 9 Larry Eisenhauer	1.50	3.00
❑ 10 Jim Hunt RC	1.50	3.00
❑ 11 Jim Whalen	1.50	3.00
❑ 12 Art Graham	1.50	3.00
❑ 13 Nick Buoniconti	3.00	6.00
❑ 14 Bob Dee	1.50	3.00
❑ 15 Keith Lincoln	3.00	6.00
❑ 16 Tom Flores	2.00	4.00
❑ 17 Art Powell	2.00	4.00
❑ 18 Stew Barber	1.50	3.00
❑ 19 Wray Carlton	1.50	3.00
❑ 20 Elbert Dubenion	2.00	4.00
❑ 21 Jim Dunaway	1.50	3.00
❑ 22 Dick Hudson	1.50	3.00
❑ 23 Harry Jacobs	1.50	3.00
❑ 24 Jack Kemp	40.00	80.00
❑ 25 Ron McDole	1.50	3.00
❑ 26 George Saimes	1.50	3.00
❑ 27 Tom Sestak	1.50	3.00
❑ 28 Billy Shaw	3.00	6.00
❑ 29 Mike Stratton	1.50	3.00
❑ 30 Nemiah Wilson RC	1.50	3.00
❑ 31 John McCormick QB	1.50	3.00
❑ 32 Rex Mirich RC	1.50	3.00
❑ 33 Dave Costa	1.50	3.00
❑ 34 Goose Gonsoulin	2.00	4.00
❑ 35 Abner Haynes	3.00	6.00
❑ 36 Wendell Hayes	2.00	4.00
❑ 37 Archie Matsos	1.50	3.00
❑ 38 John Bramlett RC	1.50	3.00
❑ 39 Jerry Sturm	1.50	3.00
❑ 40 Max Leetzow RC	1.50	3.00
❑ 41 Bob Scarpitto	1.50	3.00
❑ 42 Lionel Taylor	3.00	6.00
❑ 43 Al Denson	1.50	3.00
❑ 44 Miller Farr RC	1.50	3.00
❑ 45 Don Trull	1.50	3.00
❑ 46 Jacky Lee	2.00	4.00
❑ 47 Bobby Jancik	1.50	3.00
❑ 48 Ode Burrell	1.50	3.00
❑ 49 Larry Elkins	1.50	3.00
❑ 50 W.K. Hicks RC	1.50	3.00
❑ 51 Sid Blanks	1.50	3.00
❑ 52 Jim Norton	1.50	3.00
❑ 53 Bobby Maples RC	1.50	3.00
❑ 54 Bob Talamini	1.50	3.00
❑ 55 Walt Suggs	1.50	3.00
❑ 56 Gary Cutsinger	1.50	3.00
❑ 57 Danny Brabham	1.50	3.00
❑ 58 Ernie Ladd	3.00	6.00
❑ 59 Checklist	25.00	50.00
❑ 60 Pete Beathard	1.50	3.00
❑ 61 Len Dawson	18.00	30.00
❑ 62 Bobby Hunt	1.50	3.00
❑ 63 Bert Coan RC	1.50	3.00
❑ 64 Curtis McClinton	2.00	4.00
❑ 65 Johnny Robinson	2.00	4.00
❑ 66 E.J. Holub	1.50	3.00
❑ 67 Jerry Mays	1.50	3.00
❑ 68 Jim Tyrer	2.00	4.00
❑ 69 Bobby Bell	3.00	6.00
❑ 70 Fred Arbanas	1.50	3.00
❑ 71 Buck Buchanan	3.00	6.00
❑ 72 Chris Burford	1.50	3.00
❑ 73 Otis Taylor	3.00	6.00
❑ 74 Cookie Gilchrist	4.00	8.00
❑ 75 Earl Faison	1.50	3.00
❑ 76 George Wilson Jr. RC	2.00	4.00
❑ 77 Rick Norton RC	1.50	3.00
❑ 78 Frank Jackson	2.00	4.00
❑ 79 Joe Auer RC	1.50	3.00
❑ 80 Willie West	1.50	3.00
❑ 81 Jim Warren	1.50	3.00
❑ 82 Wahoo McDaniel RC	30.00	50.00
❑ 83 Ernie Park RC	1.50	3.00
❑ 84 Billy Neighbors	1.50	3.00
❑ 85 Norm Evans	2.00	4.00
❑ 86 Tom Nomina	1.50	3.00
❑ 87 Rich Zecher RC	1.50	3.00
❑ 88 Dave Kocourek	1.50	3.00
❑ 89 Bill Baird	1.50	3.00
❑ 90 Ralph Baker	1.50	3.00
❑ 91 Verlon Biggs	1.50	3.00
❑ 92 Sam DeLuca	1.50	3.00
❑ 93 Larry Grantham	2.00	4.00
❑ 94 Jim Harris RC	1.50	3.00
❑ 95 Winston Hill	1.50	3.00
❑ 96 Bill Mathis	1.50	3.00
❑ 97 Don Maynard	12.00	20.00
❑ 98 Joe Namath	75.00	150.00
❑ 99 Gerry Philbin	2.00	4.00
❑ 100 Paul Rochester	1.50	3.00
❑ 101 George Sauer Jr.	2.00	4.00
❑ 102 Matt Snell	3.00	6.00
❑ 103 Daryle Lamonica	5.00	10.00
❑ 104 Glenn Bass	1.50	3.00
❑ 105 Jim Otto	3.00	6.00
❑ 106 Fred Biletnikoff	18.00	30.00
❑ 107 Cotton Davidson	2.00	4.00
❑ 108 Larry Todd	1.50	3.00
❑ 109 Billy Cannon	3.00	6.00
❑ 110 Clem Daniels	2.00	4.00
❑ 111 Dave Grayson	1.50	3.00
❑ 112 Kent McCloughan RC	1.50	3.00
❑ 113 Bob Svihus RC	1.50	3.00
❑ 114 Ike Lassiter	1.50	3.00
❑ 115 Harry Schuh	1.50	3.00
❑ 116 Ben Davidson	4.00	8.00
❑ 117 Tom Day	1.50	3.00
❑ 118 Scott Appleton	1.50	3.00
❑ 119 Steve Tensi RC	1.50	3.00
❑ 120 John Hadl	3.00	6.00
❑ 121 Paul Lowe	2.00	4.00
❑ 122 Jim Allison RC	1.50	3.00
❑ 123 Lance Alworth	20.00	35.00
❑ 124 Jacque MacKinnon	1.50	3.00
❑ 125 Ron Mix	3.00	6.00
❑ 126 Bob Petrich	1.50	3.00
❑ 127 Howard Kindig RC	1.50	3.00
❑ 128 Steve DeLong	1.50	3.00
❑ 129 Chuck Allen	1.50	3.00
❑ 130 Frank Buncom	1.50	3.00
❑ 131 Speedy Duncan RC	2.50	5.00
❑ 132 Checklist	35.00	70.00

1968 Topps

❑ COMPLETE SET (219)	350.00	550.00
❑ WRAPPER (5-CENT, SER.1)	10.00	20.00
❑ WRAPPER (5-CENT, SER.2)	20.00	30.00
❑ 1 Bart Starr	25.00	40.00
❑ 2 Dick Bass	1.00	2.00
❑ 3 Grady Alderman	.75	1.50
❑ 4 Obert Logan	.75	1.50
❑ 5 Ernie Koy RC	1.00	2.00
❑ 6 Don Hultz RC	.75	1.50
❑ 7 Earl Gros	.75	1.50
❑ 8 Jim Bakken	.75	1.50
❑ 9 George Mira	1.00	2.00
❑ 10 Carl Kammerer RC	.75	1.50
❑ 11 Willie Frazier	.75	1.50
❑ 12 Kent McCloughan UER	.75	1.50
❑ 13 George Sauer Jr.	1.00	2.00
❑ 14 Jack Clancy RC	.75	1.50
❑ 15 Jim Tyrer	1.00	2.00
❑ 16 Bobby Maples	.75	1.50
❑ 17 Bo Hickey RC	.75	1.50
❑ 18 Frank Buncom	.75	1.50
❑ 19 Keith Lincoln	1.00	2.00
❑ 20 Jim Whalen	.75	1.50
❑ 21 Junior Coffey	.75	1.50
❑ 22 Billy Ray Smith	.75	1.50
❑ 23 Johnny Morris	.75	1.50
❑ 24 Ernie Green	.75	1.50
❑ 25 Don Meredith	15.00	25.00
❑ 26 Wayne Walker	.75	1.50
❑ 27 Carroll Dale	1.00	2.00
❑ 28 Bernie Casey	1.00	2.00
❑ 29 Dave Osborn RC	1.00	2.00
❑ 30 Ray Poage	.75	1.50
❑ 31 Homer Jones	.75	1.50
❑ 32 Sam Baker	.75	1.50
❑ 33 Bill Saul RC	.75	1.50
❑ 34 Ken Willard	1.00	2.00
❑ 35 Bobby Mitchell	2.00	4.00
❑ 36 Gary Garrison RC	1.00	2.00
❑ 37 Billy Cannon	1.00	2.00
❑ 38 Ralph Baker	.75	1.50
❑ 39 Howard Twilley RC	2.00	4.00
❑ 40 Wendell Hayes	1.00	2.00
❑ 41 Jim Norton	.75	1.50
❑ 42 Tom Beer RC	.75	1.50
❑ 43 Chris Burford	.75	1.50
❑ 44 Stew Barber	.75	1.50
❑ 45 Leroy Mitchell UER RC	.75	1.50
❑ 46 Dan Grimm	.75	1.50
❑ 47 Jerry Logan	.75	1.50
❑ 48 Andy Livingston RC	.75	1.50
❑ 49 Paul Warfield	7.50	15.00
❑ 50 Don Perkins	1.50	3.00
❑ 51 Ron Kramer	.75	1.50
❑ 52 Bob Jeter RC	1.00	2.00
❑ 53 Les Josephson RC	1.00	2.00
❑ 54 Bobby Walden	.75	1.50
❑ 55 Checklist	7.50	15.00
❑ 56 Walter Roberts	.75	1.50
❑ 57 Henry Carr	.75	1.50
❑ 58 Gary Ballman	.75	1.50
❑ 59 J.R. Wilburn RC	.75	1.50
❑ 60 Jim Hart RC	5.00	10.00
❑ 61 Jim Johnson	1.50	3.00
❑ 62 Chris Hanburger	1.00	2.00
❑ 63 John Hadl	1.50	3.00
❑ 64 Hewritt Dixon	1.00	2.00
❑ 65 Joe Namath	50.00	80.00
❑ 66 Jim Warren	.75	1.50
❑ 67 Curtis McClinton	1.00	2.00
❑ 68 Bob Talamini	.75	1.50
❑ 69 Steve Tensi	.75	1.50
❑ 70 Dick Van Raaphorst UER RC	.75	1.50
❑ 71 Art Powell	1.00	2.00
❑ 72 Jim Nance RC	2.00	4.00
❑ 73 Bob Riggle RC	.75	1.50
❑ 74 John Mackey	2.50	5.00
❑ 75 Gale Sayers	25.00	40.00
❑ 76 Gene Hickerson	1.25	2.50
❑ 77 Dan Reeves	5.00	10.00
❑ 78 Tom Nowatzke	.75	1.50
❑ 79 Elijah Pitts	1.50	3.00
❑ 80 Lamar Lundy	1.00	2.00
❑ 81 Paul Flatley	.75	1.50
❑ 82 Dave Whitsell	.75	1.50
❑ 83 Spider Lockhart	1.00	2.00
❑ 84 Dave Lloyd	.75	1.50
❑ 85 Roy Jefferson	1.00	2.00
❑ 86 Jackie Smith	3.00	6.00
❑ 87 John David Crow	1.00	2.00
❑ 88 Sonny Jurgensen	3.00	6.00
❑ 89 Ron Mix	1.50	3.00
❑ 90 Clem Daniels	1.00	2.00
❑ 91 Cornell Gordon RC	.75	1.50
❑ 92 Tom Goode	.75	1.50
❑ 93 Bobby Bell	1.50	3.00
❑ 94 Walt Suggs	.75	1.50
❑ 95 Eric Crabtree RC	.75	1.50
❑ 96 Sherrill Headrick	.75	1.50
❑ 97 Wray Carlton	.75	1.50

Card		
❑ 98 Gino Cappelletti	1.00	2.00
❑ 99 Tommy McDonald	2.00	4.00
❑ 100 Johnny Unitas	25.00	40.00
❑ 101 Richie Petitbon	.75	1.50
❑ 102 Erich Barnes	.75	1.50
❑ 103 Bob Hayes	5.00	10.00
❑ 104 Milt Plum	1.00	2.00
❑ 105 Boyd Dowler	1.00	2.00
❑ 106 Ed Meador	.75	1.50
❑ 107 Fred Cox	.75	1.50
❑ 108 Steve Stonebreaker RC	.75	1.50
❑ 109 Aaron Thomas	.75	1.50
❑ 110 Norm Snead	1.00	2.00
❑ 111 Paul Martha RC	.75	1.50
❑ 112 Jerry Stovall	.75	1.50
❑ 113 Kay McFarland RC	.75	1.50
❑ 114 Pat Richter	.75	1.50
❑ 115 Rick Redman	.75	1.50
❑ 116 Tom Keating	.75	1.50
❑ 117 Matt Snell	1.00	2.00
❑ 118 Dick Westmoreland	.75	1.50
❑ 119 Jerry Mays	.75	1.50
❑ 120 Sid Blanks	.75	1.50
❑ 121 Al Denson	.75	1.50
❑ 122 Bobby Hunt	.75	1.50
❑ 123 Mike Mercer	.75	1.50
❑ 124 Nick Buoniconti	1.50	3.00
❑ 125 Ron Vanderkelen RC	.75	1.50
❑ 126 Ordell Braase	.75	1.50
❑ 127 Dick Butkus	30.00	50.00
❑ 128 Gary Collins	1.00	2.00
❑ 129 Mel Renfro	3.00	6.00
❑ 130 Alex Karras	2.50	5.00
❑ 131 Herb Adderley !	2.50	5.00
❑ 132 Roman Gabriel !	2.00	4.00
❑ 133 Bill Brown	1.25	2.50
❑ 134 Kent Kramer RC	1.00	2.00
❑ 135 Tucker Frederickson	1.25	2.50
❑ 136 Nate Ramsey	1.00	2.00
❑ 137 Marv Woodson RC	1.00	2.00
❑ 138 Ken Gray	1.00	2.00
❑ 139 John Brodie	2.50	5.00
❑ 140 Jerry Smith	1.00	2.00
❑ 141 Brad Hubbert RC	1.00	2.00
❑ 142 George Blanda	10.00	20.00
❑ 143 Pete Lammons RC	1.00	2.00
❑ 144 Doug Moreau RC	1.00	2.00
❑ 145 E.J. Holub	1.00	2.00
❑ 146 Ode Burrell	1.00	2.00
❑ 147 Bob Scarpitto	1.00	2.00
❑ 148 Andre White RC	1.00	2.00
❑ 149 Jack Kemp	30.00	50.00
❑ 150 Art Graham	1.00	2.00
❑ 151 Tommy Nobis	3.00	6.00
❑ 152 Willie Richardson RC	1.25	2.50
❑ 153 Jack Concannon	1.00	2.00
❑ 154 Bill Glass	1.00	2.00
❑ 155 Craig Morton RC	5.00	10.00
❑ 156 Pat Studstill	1.00	2.00
❑ 157 Ray Nitschke	5.00	10.00
❑ 158 Rogor Brown	1.00	2.00
❑ 159 Joe Kapp RC	2.50	5.00
❑ 160 Jim Taylor	7.50	15.00
❑ 161 Fran Tarkenton	10.00	20.00
❑ 162 Mike Ditka	18.00	30.00
❑ 163 Andy Russell RC	4.00	8.00
❑ 164 Larry Wilson	2.00	4.00
❑ 165 Tommy Davis	1.00	2.00
❑ 166 Paul Krause	2.00	4.00
❑ 167 Speedy Duncan	1.00	2.00
❑ 168 Fred Biletnikoff	7.50	15.00
❑ 169 Don Maynard	5.00	10.00
❑ 170 Frank Emanuel RC	1.00	2.00
❑ 171 Len Dawson	7.50	15.00
❑ 172 Miller Farr	1.00	2.00
❑ 173 Floyd Little RC	10.00	20.00
❑ 174 Lonnie Wright RC	1.00	2.00
❑ 175 Paul Costa RC	1.00	2.00
❑ 176 Don Trull	1.00	2.00
❑ 177 Jerry Simmons RC	1.00	2.00
❑ 178 Tom Matte	1.25	2.50
❑ 179 Bennie McRae	1.00	2.00
❑ 180 Jim Kanicki RC	1.00	2.00
❑ 181 Bob Lilly	7.50	15.00
❑ 182 Tom Watkins	1.00	2.00
❑ 183 Jim Grabowski RC	3.00	6.00
❑ 184 Jack Snow RC	2.00	4.00
❑ 185 Gary Cuozzo RC	1.25	2.50
❑ 186 Billy Kilmer	2.00	4.00
❑ 187 Jim Katcavage	1.00	2.00
❑ 188 Floyd Peters	1.00	2.00
❑ 189 Bill Nelsen	1.25	2.50
❑ 190 Bobby Joe Conrad	1.25	2.50
❑ 191 Kermit Alexander	1.00	2.00
❑ 192 Charley Taylor UER	3.00	6.00
❑ 193 Lance Alworth	10.00	20.00
❑ 194 Daryle Lamonica	2.50	5.00
❑ 195 Al Atkinson RC	1.00	2.00
❑ 196 Bob Griese RC	50.00	90.00
❑ 197 Buck Buchanan	2.00	4.00
❑ 198 Pete Beathard	1.00	2.00
❑ 199 Nemiah Wilson	1.00	2.00
❑ 200 Ernie Wright	1.00	2.00
❑ 201 George Saimes	1.00	2.00
❑ 202 John Charles RC	1.00	2.00
❑ 203 Randy Johnson	1.00	2.00
❑ 204 Tony Lorick	1.00	2.00
❑ 205 Dick Evey	1.00	2.00
❑ 206 Leroy Kelly	5.00	10.00
❑ 207 Lee Roy Jordan	3.00	6.00
❑ 208 Jim Gibbons	1.00	2.00
❑ 209 Donny Anderson RC	2.00	4.00
❑ 210 Maxie Baughan	1.00	2.00
❑ 211 Joe Morrison	1.00	2.00
❑ 212 Jim Snowden RC	1.00	2.00
❑ 213 Lenny Lyles	1.00	2.00
❑ 214 Bobby Joe Green	1.00	2.00
❑ 215 Frank Ryan	1.25	2.50
❑ 216 Cornell Green	1.25	2.50
❑ 217 Karl Sweetan	1.00	2.00
❑ 218 Dave Williams RC	1.00	2.00
❑ 219A Checklist Green !	10.00	18.00
❑ 219B Checklist Blue !	12.00	20.00

1969 Topps

Card		
❑ COMPLETE SET (263)	350.00	550.00
❑ WRAPPER (5-CENT)	15.00	30.00
❑ 1 Leroy Kelly	10.00	20.00
❑ 2 Paul Flatley	.75	1.50
❑ 3 Jim Cadile RC	.75	1.50
❑ 4 Erich Barnes	.75	1.50
❑ 5 Willie Richardson	.75	1.50
❑ 6 Bob Hayes	4.00	8.00
❑ 7 Bob Jeter	.75	1.50
❑ 8 Jim Colclough	.75	1.50
❑ 9 Sherrill Headrick	.75	1.50
❑ 10 Jim Dunaway	.75	1.50
❑ 11 Bill Munson	1.00	2.00
❑ 12 Jack Pardee	1.00	2.00
❑ 13 Jim Lindsey RC	.75	1.50
❑ 14 Dave Whitsell	.75	1.50
❑ 15 Tucker Frederickson	.75	1.50
❑ 16 Alvin Haymond	1.00	2.00
❑ 17 Andy Russell	1.00	2.00
❑ 18 Tom Beer	.75	1.50
❑ 19 Bobby Maples	.75	1.50
❑ 20 Len Dawson	4.00	8.00
❑ 21 Willis Crenshaw	.75	1.50
❑ 22 Tommy Davis	.75	1.50
❑ 23 Rickie Harris	.75	1.50
❑ 24 Jerry Simmons	.75	1.50
❑ 25 Johnny Unitas	25.00	40.00
❑ 26 Brian Piccolo UER RC	50.00	80.00
❑ 27 Bob Matheson RC	.75	1.50
❑ 28 Howard Twilley	1.00	2.00
❑ 29 Jim Turner	1.00	2.00
❑ 30 Pete Banaszak RC	1.00	2.00
❑ 31 Lance Rentzel RC	1.00	2.00
❑ 32 Bill Triplett	.75	1.50
❑ 33 Boyd Dowler	1.00	2.00
❑ 34 Merlin Olsen	2.50	5.00
❑ 35 Joe Kapp	1.50	3.00
❑ 36 Dan Abramowicz RC	2.00	4.00
❑ 37 Spider Lockhart	1.00	2.00
❑ 38 Tom Day	.75	1.50

Card		
❑ 39 Art Graham	.75	1.50
❑ 40 Bob Cappadona RC	.75	1.50
❑ 41 Gary Ballman	.75	1.50
❑ 42 Clendon Thomas	.75	1.50
❑ 43 Jackie Smith	2.00	4.00
❑ 44 Dave Wilcox	1.50	3.00
❑ 45 Jerry Smith	.75	1.50
❑ 46 Dan Grimm	.75	1.50
❑ 47 Tom Matte	1.00	2.00
❑ 48 John Stofa RC	.75	1.50
❑ 49 Rex Mirich	.75	1.50
❑ 50 Miller Farr	.75	1.50
❑ 51 Gale Sayers	25.00	40.00
❑ 52 Bill Nelsen	1.00	2.00
❑ 53 Bob Lilly	3.00	6.00
❑ 54 Wayne Walker	.75	1.50
❑ 55 Ray Nitschke	2.50	5.00
❑ 56 Ed Meador	.75	1.50
❑ 57 Lonnie Warwick RC	.75	1.50
❑ 58 Wendell Hayes	.75	1.50
❑ 59 Dick Anderson RC	2.50	5.00
❑ 60 Don Maynard	3.00	6.00
❑ 61 Tony Lorick	.75	1.50
❑ 62 Pete Gogolak	.75	1.50
❑ 63 Nate Ramsey	.75	1.50
❑ 64 Dick Shiner RC	.75	1.50
❑ 65 Larry Wilson UER	1.50	3.00
❑ 66 Ken Willard	1.00	2.00
❑ 67 Charley Taylor	2.50	5.00
❑ 68 Billy Cannon	1.00	2.00
❑ 69 Lance Alworth	4.00	8.00
❑ 70 Jim Nance	1.00	2.00
❑ 71 Nick Rassas RC	.75	1.50
❑ 72 Lenny Lyles	.75	1.50
❑ 73 Bennie McRae	.75	1.50
❑ 74 Bill Glass	.75	1.50
❑ 75 Don Meredith	15.00	25.00
❑ 76 Dick LeBeau	.75	1.50
❑ 77 Carroll Dale	1.00	2.00
❑ 78 Ron McDole	.75	1.50
❑ 79 Charley King RC	.75	1.50
❑ 80 Checklist UER	7.50	15.00
❑ 81 Dick Bass	1.00	2.00
❑ 82 Roy Winston	.75	1.50
❑ 83 Don McCall RC	.75	1.50
❑ 84 Jim Katcavage	1.00	2.00
❑ 85 Norm Snead	1.00	2.00
❑ 86 Earl Gros	.75	1.50
❑ 87 Don Brumm RC	.75	1.50
❑ 88 Sonny Bishop	.75	1.50
❑ 89 Fred Arbanas	.75	1.50
❑ 90 Karl Noonan RC	.75	1.50
❑ 91 Dick Witcher RC	.75	1.50
❑ 92 Vince Promuto	.75	1.50
❑ 93 Tommy Nobis	2.00	4.00
❑ 94 Jerry Hill RC	.75	1.50
❑ 95 Ed O'Bradovich RC	.75	1.50
❑ 96 Ernie Kellerman RC	.75	1.50
❑ 97 Chuck Howley	1.00	2.00
❑ 98 Hewritt Dixon	.75	1.50
❑ 00 Ron Mix	1.50	3.00
❑ 100 Joe Namath	40.00	75.00
❑ 101 Billy Gambrell RC	.75	1.50
❑ 102 Elijah Pitts	1.00	2.00
❑ 103 Billy Truax RC	1.00	2.00
❑ 104 Ed Sharockman	.75	1.50
❑ 105 Doug Atkins	1.50	3.00
❑ 106 Greg Larson	.75	1.50
❑ 107 Israel Lang RC	.75	1.50
❑ 108 Houston Antwine	.75	1.50
❑ 109 Paul Guidry RC	.75	1.50
❑ 110 Al Denson	.75	1.50
❑ 111 Roy Jefferson	1.00	2.00
❑ 112 Chuck Latourette RC	.75	1.50
❑ 113 Jim Johnson	1.50	3.00
❑ 114 Bobby Mitchell	2.00	4.00
❑ 115 Randy Johnson	.75	1.50
❑ 116 Lou Michaels	.75	1.50
❑ 117 Rudy Kuechenberg RC	.75	1.50
❑ 118 Walt Suggs	.75	1.50
❑ 119 Goldie Sellers RC	.75	1.50
❑ 120 Larry Csonka RC	40.00	75.00
❑ 121 Jim Houston	.75	1.50
❑ 122 Craig Baynham RC	.75	1.50
❑ 123 Alex Karras	2.50	5.00
❑ 124 Jim Grabowski	1.00	2.00
❑ 125 Roman Gabriel	1.50	3.00
❑ 126 Larry Bowie	.75	1.50
❑ 127 Dave Parks	1.00	2.00

Card	Low	High
❑ 128 Ben Davidson	1.50	3.00
❑ 129 Steve DeLong	.75	1.50
❑ 130 Fred Hill RC	.75	1.50
❑ 131 Ernie Koy	1.00	2.00
❑ 132A Checklist no border	7.50	15.00
❑ 132B Checklist bordered	10.00	20.00
❑ 133 Dick Hoak	1.00	2.00
❑ 134 Larry Stallings RC	1.00	2.00
❑ 135 Clifton McNeil RC	1.00	2.00
❑ 136 Walter Rock	1.00	2.00
❑ 137 Billy Lothridge RC	1.00	2.00
❑ 138 Bob Vogel	1.00	2.00
❑ 139 Dick Butkus	25.00	40.00
❑ 140 Frank Ryan	1.25	2.50
❑ 141 Larry Garron	1.00	2.00
❑ 142 George Saimes	1.00	2.00
❑ 143 Frank Buncom	1.00	2.00
❑ 144 Don Perkins	1.25	2.50
❑ 145 Johnnie Robinson UER RC	1.00	2.00
❑ 146 Lee Roy Caffey	1.25	2.50
❑ 147 Bernie Casey	1.25	2.50
❑ 148 Billy Martin E	1.00	2.00
❑ 149 Gene Howard RC	1.00	2.00
❑ 150 Fran Tarkenton	10.00	20.00
❑ 151 Eric Crabtree	1.00	2.00
❑ 152 W.K. Hicks	1.00	2.00
❑ 153 Bobby Bell	2.00	4.00
❑ 154 Sam Baker	1.00	2.00
❑ 155 Marv Woodson	1.00	2.00
❑ 156 Dave Williams	1.00	2.00
❑ 157 Bruce Bosley UER	1.00	2.00
❑ 158 Carl Kammerer	1.00	2.00
❑ 159 Jim Burson RC	1.00	2.00
❑ 160 Roy Hilton RC	1.00	2.00
❑ 161 Bob Griese	15.00	25.00
❑ 162 Bob Talamini	1.00	2.00
❑ 163 Jim Otto	2.00	4.00
❑ 164 Ronnie Bull	1.00	2.00
❑ 165 Walter Johnson RC	1.00	2.00
❑ 166 Lee Roy Jordan	2.00	4.00
❑ 167 Mike Lucci	1.25	2.50
❑ 168 Willie Wood	2.00	4.00
❑ 169 Maxie Baughan	1.00	2.00
❑ 170 Bill Brown	1.25	2.50
❑ 171 John Hadl	2.00	4.00
❑ 172 Gino Cappelletti	1.25	2.50
❑ 173 George Butch Byrd	1.25	2.50
❑ 174 Steve Stonebreaker	1.00	2.00
❑ 175 Joe Morrison	1.00	2.00
❑ 176 Joe Scarpati	1.00	2.00
❑ 177 Bobby Walden	1.00	2.00
❑ 178 Roy Shivers	1.00	2.00
❑ 179 Kermit Alexander	1.00	2.00
❑ 180 Pat Richter	1.00	2.00
❑ 181 Pete Perreault RC	1.00	2.00
❑ 182 Pete Duranko RC	1.00	2.00
❑ 183 Leroy Mitchell	1.00	2.00
❑ 184 Jim Simon RC	1.00	2.00
❑ 185 Billy Ray Smith	1.00	2.00
❑ 186 Jack Concannon	1.00	2.00
❑ 187 Ben Davis RC	1.00	2.00
❑ 188 Mike Clark	1.00	2.00
❑ 189 Jim Gibbons	1.00	2.00
❑ 190 Dave Robinson	1.25	2.50
❑ 191 Otis Taylor	1.25	2.50
❑ 192 Nick Buoniconti	2.00	4.00
❑ 193 Matt Snell	1.25	2.50
❑ 194 Bruce Gossett	1.00	2.00
❑ 195 Mick Tingelhoff	1.25	2.50
❑ 196 Earl Leggett	1.00	2.00
❑ 197 Pete Case	1.00	2.00
❑ 198 Tom Woodeshick RC	1.00	2.00
❑ 199 Ken Kortas RC	1.00	2.00
❑ 200 Jim Hart	2.00	4.00
❑ 201 Fred Biletnikoff	5.00	10.00
❑ 202 Jacque MacKinnon	1.00	2.00
❑ 203 Jim Whalen	1.00	2.00
❑ 204 Matt Hazeltine	1.00	2.00
❑ 205 Charlie Gogolak	1.00	2.00
❑ 206 Ray Ogden RC	1.00	2.00
❑ 207 John Mackey	2.00	4.00
❑ 208 Roosevelt Taylor	1.00	2.00
❑ 209 Gene Hickerson	1.25	2.50
❑ 210 Dave Edwards RC	1.25	2.50
❑ 211 Tom Sestak	1.00	2.00
❑ 212 Ernie Wright	1.00	2.00
❑ 213 Dave Costa	1.00	2.00
❑ 214 Tom Vaughn RC	1.00	2.00
❑ 215 Bart Starr	25.00	40.00
❑ 216 Les Josephson	1.00	2.00
❑ 217 Fred Cox	1.00	2.00
❑ 218 Mike Tilleman RC	1.00	2.00
❑ 219 Darrell Dess	1.00	2.00
❑ 220 Dave Lloyd	1.00	2.00
❑ 221 Pete Beathard	1.00	2.00
❑ 222 Buck Buchanan	2.00	4.00
❑ 223 Frank Emanuel	1.00	2.00
❑ 224 Paul Martha	1.00	2.00
❑ 225 Johnny Roland	1.00	2.00
❑ 226 Gary Lewis	1.00	2.00
❑ 227 Sonny Jurgensen UER	3.00	6.00
❑ 228 Jim Butler	1.00	2.00
❑ 229 Mike Curtis RC	4.00	8.00
❑ 230 Richie Petitbon	1.00	2.00
❑ 231 George Sauer Jr.	1.25	2.50
❑ 232 George Blanda	10.00	20.00
❑ 233 Gary Garrison	1.00	2.00
❑ 234 Gary Collins	1.25	2.50
❑ 235 Craig Morton	2.00	4.00
❑ 236 Tom Nowatzke	1.00	2.00
❑ 237 Donny Anderson	1.25	2.50
❑ 238 Deacon Jones	2.00	4.00
❑ 239 Grady Alderman	1.00	2.00
❑ 240 Billy Kilmer	2.00	4.00
❑ 241 Mike Taliaferro	1.00	2.00
❑ 242 Stew Barber	1.00	2.00
❑ 243 Bobby Hunt	1.00	2.00
❑ 244 Homer Jones	1.00	2.00
❑ 245 Bob Brown OT	2.00	4.00
❑ 246 Bill Asbury	1.00	2.00
❑ 247 Charlie Johnson	1.25	2.50
❑ 248 Chris Hanburger	1.25	2.50
❑ 249 John Brodie	3.00	6.00
❑ 250 Earl Morrall	1.25	2.50
❑ 251 Floyd Little	2.50	5.00
❑ 252 Jerrel Wilson RC	1.00	2.00
❑ 253 Jim Keyes RC	1.00	2.00
❑ 254 Mel Renfro	2.00	4.00
❑ 255 Herb Adderley	2.00	4.00
❑ 256 Jack Snow	1.25	2.50
❑ 257 Charlie Durkee RC	1.00	2.00
❑ 258 Charlie Harper RC	1.00	2.00
❑ 259 J.R. Wilburn	1.00	2.00
❑ 260 Charlie Krueger	1.00	2.00
❑ 261 Pete Jacques RC	1.00	2.00
❑ 262 Gerry Philbin	1.00	2.00
❑ 263 Daryle Lamonica	5.00	10.00

1970 Topps

Card	Low	High
❑ COMPLETE SET (263)	300.00	475.00
❑ WRAPPER (10-CENT)	8.00	12.00
❑ 1 Len Dawson UER	12.00	20.00
❑ 2 Doug Hart RC	.40	1.00
❑ 3 Verlon Biggs	.40	1.00
❑ 4 Ralph Neely RC	.60	1.50
❑ 5 Harmon Wages RC	.40	1.00
❑ 6 Dan Conners RC	.40	1.00
❑ 7 Gino Cappelletti	.60	1.50
❑ 8 Erich Barnes	.40	1.00
❑ 9 Checklist	5.00	10.00
❑ 10 Bob Griese	7.50	15.00
❑ 11 Ed Flanagan RC	.40	1.00
❑ 12 George Seals RC	.40	1.00
❑ 13 Harry Jacobs	.40	1.00
❑ 14 Mike Haffner RC	.40	1.00
❑ 15 Bob Vogel	.40	1.00
❑ 16 Bill Peterson RC	.40	1.00
❑ 17 Spider Lockhart	.40	1.00
❑ 18 Billy Truax	.40	1.00
❑ 19 Jim Beirne RC	.40	1.00
❑ 20 Leroy Kelly	3.00	6.00
❑ 21 Dave Lloyd	.40	1.00
❑ 22 Mike Tilleman	.40	1.00
❑ 23 Gary Garrison	.40	1.00
❑ 24 Larry Brown RC	4.00	8.00
❑ 25 Jan Stenerud RC	6.00	12.00
❑ 26 Rolf Krueger RC	.40	1.00
❑ 27 Roland Lakes	.40	1.00
❑ 28 Dick Hoak	.40	1.00
❑ 29 Gene Washington Vik RC	1.25	2.50
❑ 30 Bart Starr	12.50	25.00
❑ 31 Dave Grayson	.40	1.00
❑ 32 Jerry Rush RC	.40	1.00
❑ 33 Len St. Jean RC	.40	1.00
❑ 34 Randy Edmunds RC	.40	1.00
❑ 35 Matt Snell	.60	1.50
❑ 36 Paul Costa	.40	1.00
❑ 37 Mike Pyle	.40	1.00
❑ 38 Roy Hilton	.40	1.00
❑ 39 Steve Tensi	.40	1.00
❑ 40 Tommy Nobis	1.25	2.50
❑ 41 Pete Case	.40	1.00
❑ 42 Andy Rice RC	.40	1.00
❑ 43 Elvin Bethea RC	4.00	8.00
❑ 44 Jack Snow	.60	1.50
❑ 45 Mel Renfro	1.25	2.50
❑ 46 Andy Livingston	.40	1.00
❑ 47 Gary Ballman	.40	1.00
❑ 48 Bob DeMarco	.40	1.00
❑ 49 Steve DeLong	.40	1.00
❑ 50 Daryle Lamonica	2.00	4.00
❑ 51 Jim Lynch RC	.40	1.00
❑ 52 Mel Farr RC	.40	1.00
❑ 53 Bob Long RC	.40	1.00
❑ 54 John Elliott RC	.40	1.00
❑ 55 Ray Nitschke	2.50	5.00
❑ 56 Jim Shorter	.40	1.00
❑ 57 Dave Wilcox	1.25	2.50
❑ 58 Eric Crabtree	.40	1.00
❑ 59 Alan Page RC	15.00	30.00
❑ 60 Jim Nance	.60	1.50
❑ 61 Glen Ray Hines RC	.40	1.00
❑ 62 John Mackey	1.25	2.50
❑ 63 Ron McDole	.40	1.00
❑ 64 Tom Beier RC	.40	1.00
❑ 65 Bill Nelsen	.60	1.50
❑ 66 Paul Flatley	.40	1.00
❑ 67 Sam Brunelli RC	.40	1.00
❑ 68 Jack Pardee	.60	1.50
❑ 69 Brig Owens	.40	1.00
❑ 70 Gale Sayers	12.50	25.00
❑ 71 Lee Roy Jordan	1.25	2.50
❑ 72 Harold Jackson RC	2.50	5.00
❑ 73 John Hadl	1.25	2.50
❑ 74 Dave Parks	.40	1.00
❑ 75 Lem Barney RC	7.00	14.00
❑ 76 Johnny Roland	.40	1.00
❑ 77 Ed Budde	.40	1.00
❑ 78 Ben McGee	.40	1.00
❑ 79 Ken Bowman RC	.40	1.00
❑ 80 Fran Tarkenton	7.50	15.00
❑ 81 Gene Washington 49er RC	2.50	5.00
❑ 82 Larry Grantham	.40	1.00
❑ 83 Bill Brown	.60	1.50
❑ 84 John Charles	.40	1.00
❑ 85 Fred Biletnikoff	3.50	7.00
❑ 86 Royce Berry RC	.40	1.00
❑ 87 Bob Lilly	2.50	5.00
❑ 88 Earl Morrall	.60	1.50
❑ 89 Jerry LeVias RC	.60	1.50
❑ 90 O.J. Simpson RC	40.00	80.00
❑ 91 Mike Howell RC	.40	1.00
❑ 92 Ken Gray	.40	1.00
❑ 93 Chris Hanburger	.40	1.00
❑ 94 Larry Seiple RC	.40	1.00
❑ 95 Rich Jackson RC	.40	1.00
❑ 96 Rockne Freitas RC	.40	1.00
❑ 97 Dick Post RC	.60	1.50
❑ 98 Ben Hawkins RC	.40	1.00
❑ 99 Ken Reaves RC	.40	1.00
❑ 100 Roman Gabriel	1.25	2.50
❑ 101 Dave Rowe RC	.40	1.00
❑ 102 Dave Robinson	.40	1.00
❑ 103 Otis Taylor	.60	1.50
❑ 104 Jim Turner	.40	1.00
❑ 105 Joe Morrison	.40	1.00
❑ 106 Dick Evey	.40	1.00
❑ 107 Ray Mansfield RC	.40	1.00
❑ 108 Grady Alderman	.40	1.00
❑ 109 Bruce Gossett	.40	1.00
❑ 110 Bob Trumpy RC	2.00	4.00
❑ 111 Jim Hunt	.40	1.00
❑ 112 Larry Stallings	.40	1.00
❑ 113A Lance Rentzel Red	.60	1.50

Card		
❑ 113B Lance Rentzel Black	.60	1.50
❑ 114 Bubba Smith RC	12.50	25.00
❑ 115 Norm Snead	.60	1.50
❑ 116 Jim Otto	1.25	2.50
❑ 117 Bo Scott RC	.40	1.00
❑ 118 Rick Redman	.40	1.00
❑ 119 George Butch Byrd	.40	1.00
❑ 120 George Webster RC	.60	1.50
❑ 121 Chuck Walton RC	.40	1.00
❑ 122 Dave Costa	.40	1.00
❑ 123 Al Dodd RC	.40	1.00
❑ 124 Len Hauss	.40	1.00
❑ 125 Deacon Jones	1.25	2.50
❑ 126 Randy Johnson	.40	1.00
❑ 127 Ralph Heck	.40	1.00
❑ 128 Emerson Boozer RC	.60	1.50
❑ 129 Johnny Robinson	.60	1.50
❑ 130 John Brodie	2.50	5.00
❑ 131 Gale Gillingham RC	.40	1.00
❑ 132 Checklist DP	3.00	6.00
❑ 133 Chuck Walker RC	.50	1.25
❑ 134 Bennie McRae	.50	1.25
❑ 135 Paul Warfield	3.50	7.00
❑ 136 Dan Darragh RC	.50	1.25
❑ 137 Paul Robinson RC	.50	1.25
❑ 138 Ed Philpott RC	.50	1.25
❑ 139 Craig Morton	1.50	3.00
❑ 140 Tom Dempsey RC	.75	2.00
❑ 141 Al Nelson RC	.50	1.25
❑ 142 Tom Matte	.75	2.00
❑ 143 Dick Schafrath	.50	1.25
❑ 144 Willie Brown	2.00	4.00
❑ 145 Charley Taylor UER	2.50	5.00
❑ 146 John Huard RC	.50	1.25
❑ 147 Dave Osborn	.50	1.25
❑ 148 Gene Mingo	.50	1.25
❑ 149 Larry Hand RC	.50	1.25
❑ 150 Joe Namath	25.00	50.00
❑ 151 Tom Mack RC	5.00	10.00
❑ 152 Kenny Graham	.50	1.25
❑ 153 Don Herrmann RC	.50	1.25
❑ 154 Bobby Bell	1.50	3.00
❑ 155 Hoyle Granger RC	.50	1.25
❑ 156 Claude Humphrey RC	4.00	8.00
❑ 157 Clifton McNeil	.50	1.25
❑ 158 Mick Tingelhoff	.75	2.00
❑ 159 Don Horn RC	.50	1.25
❑ 160 Larry Wilson	1.50	3.00
❑ 161 Tom Neville RC	.50	1.25
❑ 162 Larry Csonka	10.00	20.00
❑ 163 Doug Buffone RC	.50	1.25
❑ 164 Cornell Green	.75	2.00
❑ 165 Haven Moses RC	.75	2.00
❑ 166 Billy Kilmer	1.50	3.00
❑ 167 Tim Rossovich RC	.50	1.25
❑ 168 Bill Bergey RC	2.00	4.00
❑ 169 Gary Collins	.75	2.00
❑ 170 Floyd Little	1.50	3.00
❑ 171 Tom Keating	.50	1.25
❑ 172 Pat Fischer	.50	1.25
❑ 173 Walt Sweeney	.50	1.25
❑ 174 Greg Larson	.50	1.25
❑ 175 Carl Eller	1.50	3.00
❑ 176 George Sauer Jr.	.75	2.00
❑ 177 Jim Hart	1.50	3.00
❑ 178 Bob Brown OT	1.50	3.00
❑ 179 Mike Garrett RC	.75	2.00
❑ 180 Johnny Unitas	15.00	25.00
❑ 181 Tom Regner RC	.50	1.25
❑ 182 Bob Jeter	.50	1.25
❑ 183 Gail Cogdill	.50	1.25
❑ 184 Earl Gros	.50	1.25
❑ 185 Dennis Partee RC	.50	1.25
❑ 186 Charlie Krueger	.50	1.25
❑ 187 Martin Baccaglio RC	.50	1.25
❑ 188 Charles Long	.50	1.25
❑ 189 Bob Hayes	3.00	6.00
❑ 190 Dick Butkus	12.50	25.00
❑ 191 Al Bemiller	.50	1.25
❑ 192 Dick Westmoreland	.50	1.25
❑ 193 Joe Scarpati	.50	1.25
❑ 194 Ron Snidow RC	.50	1.25
❑ 195 Earl McCullouch RC	.50	1.25
❑ 196 Jake Kupp RC	.50	1.25
❑ 197 Bob Lurtsema RC	.50	1.25
❑ 198 Mike Current RC	.50	1.25
❑ 199 Charlie Smith RB RC	.50	1.25
❑ 200 Sonny Jurgensen	3.00	6.00
❑ 201 Mike Curtis	.75	2.00
❑ 202 Aaron Brown RC	.50	1.25
❑ 203 Richie Petitbon	.50	1.25
❑ 204 Walt Suggs	.50	1.25
❑ 205 Roy Jefferson	.50	1.25
❑ 206 Russ Washington RC	.50	1.25
❑ 207 Woody Peoples RC	.50	1.25
❑ 208 Dave Williams	.50	1.25
❑ 209 John Zook RC	.50	1.25
❑ 210 Tom Woodeshick	.50	1.25
❑ 211 Howard Fest RC	.50	1.25
❑ 212 Jack Concannon	.50	1.25
❑ 213 Jim Marshall	1.50	3.00
❑ 214 Jon Morris	.50	1.25
❑ 215 Dan Abramowicz	.75	2.00
❑ 216 Paul Martha	.50	1.25
❑ 217 Ken Willard	.50	1.25
❑ 218 Walter Rock	.50	1.25
❑ 219 Garland Boyette	.50	1.25
❑ 220 Buck Buchanan	1.50	3.00
❑ 221 Bill Munson	.75	2.00
❑ 222 David Lee RC	.50	1.25
❑ 223 Karl Noonan	.50	1.25
❑ 224 Harry Schuh	.50	1.25
❑ 225 Jackie Smith	1.50	3.00
❑ 226 Gerry Philbin	.50	1.25
❑ 227 Ernie Koy	.50	1.25
❑ 228 Chuck Howley	.75	2.00
❑ 229 Billy Shaw	1.50	3.00
❑ 230 Jerry Hillebrand	.50	1.25
❑ 231 Bill Thompson RC	.75	2.00
❑ 232 Carroll Dale	.75	2.00
❑ 233 Gene Hickerson	1.00	2.50
❑ 234 Jim Butler	.50	1.25
❑ 235 Greg Cook RC	.50	1.25
❑ 236 Lee Roy Caffey	.50	1.25
❑ 237 Merlin Olsen	2.00	4.00
❑ 238 Fred Cox	.50	1.25
❑ 239 Nate Ramsey	.50	1.25
❑ 240 Lance Alworth	3.50	7.00
❑ 241 Chuck Hinton RC	.50	1.25
❑ 242 Jerry Smith	.50	1.25
❑ 243 Tony Baker FB RC	.50	1.25
❑ 244 Nick Buoniconti	1.50	3.00
❑ 245 Jim Johnson	1.50	3.00
❑ 246 Willie Richardson	.50	1.25
❑ 247 Fred Dryer RC	5.00	10.00
❑ 248 Bobby Maples	.50	1.25
❑ 249 Alex Karras	2.00	4.00
❑ 250 Joe Kapp	.75	2.00
❑ 251 Ben Davidson	1.50	3.00
❑ 252 Mike Stratton	.50	1.25
❑ 253 Les Josephson	.50	1.25
❑ 254 Don Maynard	3.00	6.00
❑ 255 Houston Antwine	.50	1.25
❑ 256 Mac Percival RC	.50	1.25
❑ 257 George Goeddeke RC	.50	1.25
❑ 258 Homer Jones	.50	1.25
❑ 259 Bob Berry RC	.50	1.25
❑ 260A Calvin Hill RC Red RC	7.50	15.00
❑ 260B Calvin Hill Black RC	10.00	20.00
❑ 261 Willie Wood	1.50	3.00
❑ 262 Ed Weisacosky RC	.50	1.25
❑ 263 Jim Tyrer	1.50	3.00

1971 Topps

Card		
❑ COMPLETE SET (263)	300.00	500.00
❑ 1 Johnny Unitas	15.00	30.00
❑ 2 Jim Butler	.40	1.00
❑ 3 Marty Schottenheimer RC	6.00	12.00
❑ 4 Joe O'Donnell RC	.40	1.00
❑ 5 Tom Dempsey	.50	1.25
❑ 6 Chuck Allen	.40	1.00
❑ 7 Ernie Kellerman	.40	1.00
❑ 8 Walt Garrison RC	.75	2.00
❑ 9 Bill Van Heusen RC	.40	1.00
❑ 10 Lance Alworth	4.00	8.00
❑ 11 Greg Landry RC	.75	2.00
❑ 12 Larry Krause RC	.40	1.00
❑ 13 Buck Buchanan	.75	2.00
❑ 14 Roy Gerela RC	.50	1.25
❑ 15 Clifton McNeil	.40	1.00
❑ 16 Bob Brown OT	.75	2.00
❑ 17 Lloyd Mumphord RC	.40	1.00
❑ 18 Gary Cuozzo	.40	1.00
❑ 19 Don Maynard	2.50	5.00
❑ 20 Larry Wilson	.75	2.00
❑ 21 Charlie Smith RB	.40	1.00
❑ 22 Ken Avery RC	.40	1.00
❑ 23 Billy Walik RC	.40	1.00
❑ 24 Jim Johnson	.75	2.00
❑ 25 Dick Butkus	12.50	25.00
❑ 26 Charley Taylor UER	2.00	4.00
❑ 27 Checklist UER	4.00	8.00
❑ 28 Lionel Aldridge RC	.40	1.00
❑ 29 Billy Lothridge	.40	1.00
❑ 30 Terry Hanratty RC	.50	1.25
❑ 31 Lee Roy Jordan	.75	2.00
❑ 32 Rick Volk RC	.40	1.00
❑ 33 Howard Kindig	.40	1.00
❑ 34 Carl Garrett RC	.40	1.00
❑ 35 Bobby Bell	.75	2.00
❑ 36 Gene Hickerson	.60	1.50
❑ 37 Dave Parks	.40	1.00
❑ 38 Paul Martha	.40	1.00
❑ 39 George Blanda	7.50	15.00
❑ 40 Tom Woodeshick	.40	1.00
❑ 41 Alex Karras	1.50	3.00
❑ 42 Rick Redman	.40	1.00
❑ 43 Zeke Moore RC	.40	1.00
❑ 44 Jack Snow	.50	1.25
❑ 45 Larry Csonka	7.50	15.00
❑ 46 Karl Kassulke RC	.40	1.00
❑ 47 Jim Hart	.75	2.00
❑ 48 Al Atkinson	.40	1.00
❑ 49 Horst Muhlmann RC	.40	1.00
❑ 50 Sonny Jurgensen	2.50	5.00
❑ 51 Ron Johnson RC	.50	1.25
❑ 52 Cas Banaszek RC	.40	1.00
❑ 53 Bubba Smith	4.00	8.00
❑ 54 Bobby Douglass RC	.50	1.25
❑ 55 Willie Wood	.75	2.00
❑ 56 Bake Turner	.40	1.00
❑ 57 Mike Morgan LB RC	.40	1.00
❑ 58 George Butch Byrd	.50	1.25
❑ 59 Don Horn	.40	1.00
❑ 60 Tommy Nobis	.75	2.00
❑ 61 Jan Stenerud	2.00	4.00
❑ 62 Altie Taylor RC	.40	1.00
❑ 63 Gary Pettigrew RC	.40	1.00
❑ 64 Spike Jones RC	.40	1.00
❑ 65 Duane Thomas RC	.75	2.00
❑ 66 Marty Domres RC	.40	1.00
❑ 67 Dick Anderson	.50	1.25
❑ 68 Ken Iman RC	.40	1.00
❑ 69 Miller Farr	.40	1.00
❑ 70 Daryle Lamonica	1.50	3.00
❑ 71 Alan Page	6.00	12.00
❑ 72 Pat Matson RC	.40	1.00
❑ 73 Emerson Boozer	.40	1.00
❑ 74 Pat Fischer	.40	1.00
❑ 75 Gary Collins	.50	1.25
❑ 76 John Fuqua RC	.50	1.25
❑ 77 Bruce Gossett	.40	1.00
❑ 78 Ed O'Bradovich	.40	1.00
❑ 79 Bob Tucker RC	.50	1.25
❑ 80 Mike Curtis	.50	1.25
❑ 81 Rich Jackson	.40	1.00
❑ 82 Tom Janik	.40	1.00
❑ 83 Gale Gillingham	.40	1.00
❑ 84 Jim Mitchell TE RC	.40	1.00
❑ 85 Charlie Johnson	.50	1.25
❑ 86 Edgar Chandler RC	.40	1.00
❑ 87 Cyril Pinder RC	.40	1.00
❑ 88 Johnny Robinson	.50	1.25
❑ 89 Ralph Neely	.40	1.00
❑ 90 Dan Abramowicz	.40	1.00
❑ 91 Mercury Morris RC	2.50	5.00
❑ 92 Steve DeLong	.40	1.00
❑ 93 Larry Stallings	.40	1.00
❑ 94 Tom Mack	.75	2.00
❑ 95 Hewritt Dixon	.40	1.00
❑ 96 Fred Cox	.40	1.00
❑ 97 Chris Hanburger	.40	1.00
❑ 98 Gerry Philbin	.40	1.00
❑ 99 Ernie Wright	.40	1.00

Card		
❑ 100 John Brodie	2.00	4.00
❑ 101 Tucker Frederickson	.40	1.00
❑ 102 Bobby Walden	.40	1.00
❑ 103 Dick Gordon	.40	1.00
❑ 104 Walter Johnson	.40	1.00
❑ 105 Mike Lucci	.50	1.25
❑ 106 Checklist DP	3.00	6.00
❑ 107 Ron Berger RC	.40	1.00
❑ 108 Dan Sullivan RC	.40	1.00
❑ 109 George Kunz RC	.40	1.00
❑ 110 Floyd Little	.75	2.00
❑ 111 Zeke Bratkowski	.50	1.25
❑ 112 Haven Moses	.50	1.25
❑ 113 Ken Houston RC	7.50	15.00
❑ 114 Willie Lanier RC	7.50	15.00
❑ 115 Larry Brown	.75	2.00
❑ 116 Tim Rossovich	.40	1.00
❑ 117 Errol Linden RC	.40	1.00
❑ 118 Mel Renfro	.75	2.00
❑ 119 Mike Garrett	.40	1.00
❑ 120 Fran Tarkenton	7.50	15.00
❑ 121 Garo Yepremian RC	.75	2.00
❑ 122 Glen Condren RC	.40	1.00
❑ 123 Johnny Roland	.40	1.00
❑ 124 Dave Herman	.40	1.00
❑ 125 Merlin Olsen	1.50	3.00
❑ 126 Doug Buffone	.40	1.00
❑ 127 Earl McCullouch	.40	1.00
❑ 128 Spider Lockhart	.40	1.00
❑ 129 Ken Willard	.40	1.00
❑ 130 Gene Washington Vik	.40	1.00
❑ 131 Mike Phipps RC	.50	1.25
❑ 132 Andy Russell	.50	1.25
❑ 133 Ray Nitschke	2.00	4.00
❑ 134 Jerry Logan	.50	1.25
❑ 135 MacArthur Lane RC	.60	1.50
❑ 136 Jim Turner	.50	1.25
❑ 137 Kent McCloughan	.50	1.25
❑ 138 Paul Guidry	.50	1.25
❑ 139 Otis Taylor	.60	1.50
❑ 140 Virgil Carter RC	.50	1.25
❑ 141 Joe Dawkins RC	.50	1.25
❑ 142 Steve Preece RC	.50	1.25
❑ 143 Mike Bragg RC	.50	1.25
❑ 144 Bob Lilly	2.50	5.00
❑ 145 Joe Kapp	.60	1.50
❑ 146 Al Dodd	.50	1.25
❑ 147 Nick Buoniconti	1.25	2.50
❑ 148 Speedy Duncan	.50	1.25
❑ 149 Cedrick Hardman RC	.50	1.25
❑ 150 Gale Sayers	12.50	25.00
❑ 151 Jim Otto	1.25	2.50
❑ 152 Billy Truax	.50	1.25
❑ 153 John Elliott	.50	1.25
❑ 154 Dick LeBeau	.50	1.25
❑ 155 Bill Bergey	.60	1.50
❑ 156 Terry Bradshaw RC !	125.00	200.00
❑ 157 Leroy Kelly	3.00	6.00
❑ 158 Paul Krause	1.25	2.50
❑ 159 Ted Vactor RC	.50	1.25
❑ 160 Bob Griese	7.50	15.00
❑ 161 Ernie McMillan	.50	1.25
❑ 162 Donny Anderson	.60	1.50
❑ 163 John Pitts RC	.50	1.25
❑ 164 Dave Costa	.50	1.25
❑ 165 Gene Washington 49er	.60	1.50
❑ 166 John Zook	.50	1.25
❑ 167 Pete Gogolak	.50	1.25
❑ 168 Erich Barnes	.50	1.25
❑ 169 Alvin Reed RC	.50	1.25
❑ 170 Jim Nance	.60	1.50
❑ 171 Craig Morton	1.25	2.50
❑ 172 Gary Garrison	.50	1.25
❑ 173 Joe Scarpati	.50	1.25
❑ 174 Adrian Young UER RC	.50	1.25
❑ 175 John Mackey	1.25	2.50
❑ 176 Mac Percival	.50	1.25
❑ 177 Preston Pearson RC	2.00	4.00
❑ 178 Fred Biletnikoff	4.00	8.00
❑ 179 Mike Battle RC	.50	1.25
❑ 180 Len Dawson	4.00	8.00
❑ 181 Les Josephson	.50	1.25
❑ 182 Royce Berry	.50	1.25
❑ 183 Herman Weaver RC	.50	1.25
❑ 184 Norm Snead	.60	1.50
❑ 185 Sam Brunelli	.50	1.25
❑ 186 Jim Kiick RC	2.50	5.00
❑ 187 Austin Denney RC	.50	1.25
❑ 188 Roger Wehrli RC	6.00	12.00
❑ 189 Dave Wilcox	1.25	2.50
❑ 190 Bob Hayes	2.00	4.00
❑ 191 Joe Morrison	.50	1.25
❑ 192 Manny Sistrunk RC	.50	1.25
❑ 193 Don Cockroft RC	.50	1.25
❑ 194 Lee Bouggess RC	.50	1.25
❑ 195 Bob Berry	.50	1.25
❑ 196 Ron Sellers RC	.50	1.25
❑ 197 George Webster	.50	1.25
❑ 198 Hoyle Granger	.50	1.25
❑ 199 Bob Vogel	.50	1.25
❑ 200 Bart Starr	10.00	20.00
❑ 201 Mike Mercer	.50	1.25
❑ 202 Dave Smith WR	.50	1.25
❑ 203 Lee Roy Caffey	.50	1.25
❑ 204 Mick Tingelhoff	.60	1.50
❑ 205 Matt Snell	.60	1.50
❑ 206 Jim Tyrer	.50	1.25
❑ 207 Willie Brown	1.25	2.50
❑ 208 Bob Johnson RC	.50	1.25
❑ 209 Deacon Jones	1.25	2.50
❑ 210 Charlie Sanders RC	4.00	8.00
❑ 211 Jake Scott RC	3.00	6.00
❑ 212 Bob Anderson RC	.50	1.25
❑ 213 Charlie Krueger	.50	1.25
❑ 214 Jim Bakken	.50	1.25
❑ 215 Harold Jackson	.60	1.50
❑ 216 Bill Brundige RC	.50	1.25
❑ 217 Calvin Hill	2.50	5.00
❑ 218 Claude Humphrey	.50	1.25
❑ 219 Glen Ray Hines	.50	1.25
❑ 220 Bill Nelsen	.60	1.50
❑ 221 Roy Hilton	.50	1.25
❑ 222 Don Herrmann	.50	1.25
❑ 223 John Bramlett	.50	1.25
❑ 224 Ken Ellis RC	.50	1.25
❑ 225 Dave Osborn	.60	1.50
❑ 226 Edd Hargett RC	.50	1.25
❑ 227 Gene Mingo	.50	1.25
❑ 228 Larry Grantham	.50	1.25
❑ 229 Dick Post	.50	1.25
❑ 230 Roman Gabriel	1.25	2.50
❑ 231 Mike Eischeid RC	.50	1.25
❑ 232 Jim Lynch	.50	1.25
❑ 233 Lemar Parrish RC	.60	1.50
❑ 234 Cecil Turner RC	.50	1.25
❑ 235 Dennis Shaw RC	.50	1.25
❑ 236 Mel Farr	.50	1.25
❑ 237 Curt Knight RC	.50	1.25
❑ 238 Chuck Howley	.60	1.50
❑ 239 Bruce Taylor RC	.50	1.25
❑ 240 Jerry LeVias	.50	1.25
❑ 241 Bob Lurtsema	.50	1.25
❑ 242 Earl Morrall	.60	1.50
❑ 243 Kermit Alexander	.50	1.25
❑ 244 Jackie Smith	1.25	2.50
❑ 245 Joe Greene RC	30.00	50.00
❑ 246 Harmon Wages	.50	1.25
❑ 247 Errol Mann	.50	1.25
❑ 248 Mike McCoy DT RC	.50	1.25
❑ 249 Milt Morin RC	.50	1.25
❑ 250 Joe Namath	35.00	60.00
❑ 251 Jackie Burkett	.50	1.25
❑ 252 Steve Chomyszak RC	.50	1.25
❑ 253 Ed Sharockman	.50	1.25
❑ 254 Robert Holmes RC	.50	1.25
❑ 255 John Hadl	1.25	2.50
❑ 256 Cornell Gordon	.50	1.25
❑ 257 Mark Moseley RC	.60	1.50
❑ 258 Gus Otto	.50	1.25
❑ 259 Mike Taliaferro	.50	1.25
❑ 260 O.J.Simpson	12.50	25.00
❑ 261 Paul Warfield	4.00	8.00
❑ 262 Jack Concannon	.50	1.25
❑ 263 Tom Matte	1.25	2.50

1972 Topps

Card		
❑ COMPLETE SET (351)	1500.00	2500.00
❑ COMMON CARD (1-132)	.25	.60
❑ COMMON CARD (264-351)	10.00	18.00
❑ WRAPPER (10-CENT)	6.00	10.00
❑ WRAPPER SER.3 (10-CENT)	15.00	20.00
❑ 1 L.Csonka/Litt/Hubb LL	2.00	4.00
❑ 2 NFC Rushing Leaders	.25	.60
❑ 3 B.Griese/Dawson/Cart LL	.75	2.00
❑ 4 R.Staubach/Lan/Kil LL	2.50	5.00
❑ 5 AFC Receiving Leaders	.40	1.00
❑ 6 NFC Receiving Leaders	.25	.60
❑ 7 Yepre/Stener/O'Brien LL	.25	.60
❑ 8 NFC Scoring Leaders	.25	.60
❑ 9 Jim Kiick	.75	2.00
❑ 10 Otis Taylor	.40	1.00
❑ 11 Bobby Joe Green	.25	.60
❑ 12 Ken Ellis	.25	.60
❑ 13 John Riggins RC	10.00	20.00
❑ 14 Dave Parks	.25	.60
❑ 15 John Hadl	.75	2.00
❑ 16 Ron Hornsby RC	.25	.60
❑ 17 Chip Myers RC	.25	.60
❑ 18 Billy Kilmer	.75	2.00
❑ 19 Fred Hoaglin RC	.25	.60
❑ 20 Carl Eller	.75	2.00
❑ 21 Steve Zabel RC	.25	.60
❑ 22 Vic Washington RC	.25	.60
❑ 23 Len St. Jean	.25	.60
❑ 24 Bill Thompson	.25	.60
❑ 25 Steve Owens RC	1.25	3.00
❑ 26 Ken Burrough RC	.40	1.00
❑ 27 Mike Clark	.25	.60
❑ 28 Willie Brown	.75	2.00
❑ 29 Checklist	3.00	6.00
❑ 30 Marlin Briscoe RC	.25	.60
❑ 31 Jerry Logan	.25	.60
❑ 32 Donny Anderson	.40	1.00
❑ 33 Rich McGeorge RC	.25	.60
❑ 34 Charlie Durkee	.25	.60
❑ 35 Willie Lanier	2.00	4.00
❑ 36 Chris Farasopoulos RC	.25	.60
❑ 37 Ron Shanklin RC	.25	.60
❑ 38 Forrest Blue RC	.25	.60
❑ 39 Ken Reaves	.25	.60
❑ 40 Roman Gabriel	.75	2.00
❑ 41 Mac Percival	.25	.60
❑ 42 Lem Barney	1.50	3.00
❑ 43 Nick Buoniconti	.75	2.00
❑ 44 Charlie Gogolak	.25	.60
❑ 45 Bill Bradley RC	.40	1.00
❑ 46 Joe Jones DE RC	.25	.60
❑ 47 Dave Williams	.25	.60
❑ 48 Pete Athas RC	.25	.60
❑ 49 Virgil Carter	.25	.60
❑ 50 Floyd Little	.75	2.00
❑ 51 Curt Knight	.25	.60
❑ 52 Bobby Maples	.25	.60
❑ 53 Charlie West RC	.25	.60
❑ 54 Marv Hubbard RC	.40	1.00
❑ 55 Archie Manning RC	10.00	20.00
❑ 56 Jim O'Brien RC	.40	1.00
❑ 57 Wayne Patrick RC	.25	.60
❑ 58 Ken Bowman	.25	.60
❑ 59 Roger Wehrli	.50	1.25
❑ 60 Charlie Sanders	.50	1.25
❑ 61 Jan Stenerud	.75	2.00
❑ 62 Willie Ellison RC	.25	.60
❑ 63 Walt Sweeney	.25	.60
❑ 64 Ron Smith	.25	.60
❑ 65 Jim Plunkett RC	10.00	20.00
❑ 66 Herb Adderley UER	.75	2.00
❑ 67 Mike Reid RC	.75	2.00
❑ 68 Richard Caster RC	.40	1.00
❑ 69 Dave Wilcox	.75	2.00

❑ 70 Leroy Kelly 1.50 3.00
❑ 71 Bob Lee RC .25 .60
❑ 72 Verlon Biggs .25 .60
❑ 73 Henry Allison RC .25 .60
❑ 74 Steve Ramsey RC .25 .60
❑ 75 Claude Humphrey .40 1.00
❑ 76 Bob Grim RC .25 .60
❑ 77 John Fuqua .40 1.00
❑ 78 Ken Houston 2.00 4.00
❑ 79 Checklist DP 2.50 5.00
❑ 80 Bob Griese 4.00 8.00
❑ 81 Lance Rentzel .40 1.00
❑ 82 Ed Podolak RC .40 1.00
❑ 83 Ike Hill RC .25 .60
❑ 84 George Farmer RC .25 .60
❑ 85 John Brockington RC .75 2.00
❑ 86 Jim Otto .75 2.00
❑ 87 Richard Neal RC .25 .60
❑ 88 Jim Hart .75 2.00
❑ 89 Bob Babich RC .25 .60
❑ 90 Gene Washington 49er .40 1.00
❑ 91 John Zook .25 .60
❑ 92 Bobby Duhon RC .25 .60
❑ 93 Ted Hendricks RC 7.50 15.00
❑ 94 Rockne Freitas .25 .60
❑ 95 Larry Brown .75 2.00
❑ 96 Mike Phipps .40 1.00
❑ 97 Julius Adams RC .25 .60
❑ 98 Dick Anderson .40 1.00
❑ 99 Fred Willis RC .25 .60
❑ 100 Joe Namath 20.00 35.00
❑ 101 L.C.Greenwood RC 7.50 15.00
❑ 102 Mark Nordquist RC .25 .60
❑ 103 Robert Holmes .25 .60
❑ 104 Ron Yary RC 2.00 5.00
❑ 105 Bob Hayes 1.00 2.50
❑ 106 Lyle Alzado RC 7.50 15.00
❑ 107 Bob Berry .25 .60
❑ 108 Phil Villapiano RC .40 1.00
❑ 109 Dave Elmendorf RC .25 .60
❑ 110 Gale Sayers 10.00 20.00
❑ 111 Jim Tyrer .25 .60
❑ 112 Mel Gray RC .75 2.00
❑ 113 Gerry Philbin .25 .60
❑ 114 Bob James RC .25 .60
❑ 115 Garo Yepremian .40 1.00
❑ 116 Dave Robinson .40 1.00
❑ 117 Jeff Queen RC .25 .60
❑ 118 Norm Snead .40 1.00
❑ 119 Jim Nance IA .40 1.00
❑ 120 Terry Bradshaw IA 7.50 15.00
❑ 121 Jim Kiick IA .40 1.00
❑ 122 Roger Staubach IA 12.00 20.00
❑ 123 Bo Scott IA .25 .60
❑ 124 John Brodie IA .75 2.00
❑ 125 Rick Volk IA .25 .60
❑ 126 John Riggins IA 3.00 6.00
❑ 127 Bubba Smith IA .75 2.00
❑ 128 Roman Gabriel IA .40 1.00
❑ 129 Calvin Hill IA .40 1.00
❑ 130 Bill Nelsen IA .25 .60
❑ 131 Tom Matte IA .40 1.00
❑ 132 Bob Griese IA 2.00 4.00
❑ 133 AFC Semi-Final .40 1.00
❑ 134 NFC Semi-Final .40 1.00
❑ 135 AFC Semi-Final .40 1.00
❑ 136 NFC Semi-Final .40 1.00
❑ 137 AFC Title Game/Unitas 1.50 3.00
❑ 138 NFC Title Game/Bob Lilly .75 2.00
❑ 139 Super Bowl VI/Staubach 2.50 5.00
❑ 140 Larry Csonka 4.00 8.00
❑ 141 Rick Volk .30 .75
❑ 142 Roy Jefferson .40 1.00
❑ 143 Raymond Chester RC .40 1.00
❑ 144 Bobby Douglass .30 .75
❑ 145 Bob Lilly 2.50 5.00
❑ 146 Harold Jackson .40 1.00
❑ 147 Pete Gogolak .30 .75
❑ 148 Art Malone RC .30 .75
❑ 149 Ed Flanagan .30 .75
❑ 150 Terry Bradshaw 25.00 40.00
❑ 151 MacArthur Lane .40 1.00
❑ 152 Jack Snow .40 1.00
❑ 153 Al Beauchamp RC .30 .75
❑ 154 Bob Anderson .30 .75
❑ 155 Ted Kwalick RC .30 .75
❑ 156 Dan Pastorini RC .75 2.00
❑ 157 Emmitt Thomas RC 10.00 20.00
❑ 158 Randy Vataha RC .30 .75
❑ 159 Al Atkinson .30 .75
❑ 160 O.J.Simpson 7.50 15.00
❑ 161 Jackie Smith .75 2.00
❑ 162 Ernie Kellerman .30 .75
❑ 163 Dennis Partee .30 .75
❑ 164 Jake Kupp .30 .75
❑ 165 Johnny Unitas 10.00 20.00
❑ 166 Clint Jones RC .30 .75
❑ 167 Paul Warfield 3.00 6.00
❑ 168 Roland McDole RC .30 .75
❑ 169 Daryle Lamonica .75 2.00
❑ 170 Dick Butkus 7.50 15.00
❑ 171 Jim Butler .30 .75
❑ 172 Mike McCoy DT .30 .75
❑ 173 Dave Smith WR .30 .75
❑ 174 Greg Landry .40 1.00
❑ 175 Tom Dempsey .40 1.00
❑ 176 John Charles .30 .75
❑ 177 Bobby Bell .75 2.00
❑ 178 Don Horn .30 .75
❑ 179 Bob Trumpy .75 2.00
❑ 180 Duane Thomas .40 1.00
❑ 181 Merlin Olsen 1.50 3.00
❑ 182 Dave Herman .30 .75
❑ 183 Jim Nance .40 1.00
❑ 184 Pete Beathard .30 .75
❑ 185 Bob Tucker .30 .75
❑ 186 Gene Upshaw RC 7.50 15.00
❑ 187 Bo Scott .30 .75
❑ 188 J.D.Hill RC .30 .75
❑ 189 Bruce Gossett .30 .75
❑ 190 Bubba Smith 2.00 4.00
❑ 191 Edd Hargett .30 .75
❑ 192 Gary Garrison .30 .75
❑ 193 Jake Scott .40 1.00
❑ 194 Fred Cox .30 .75
❑ 195 Sonny Jurgensen 2.00 4.00
❑ 196 Greg Brezina RC .30 .75
❑ 197 Ed O'Bradovich .30 .75
❑ 198 John Rowser RC .30 .75
❑ 199 Altie Taylor UER .30 .75
❑ 200 Roger Staubach RC 100.00 175.00
❑ 201 Leroy Keyes RC .30 .75
❑ 202 Garland Boyette .30 .75
❑ 203 Tom Beer .30 .75
❑ 204 Buck Buchanan .75 2.00
❑ 205 Larry Wilson .75 2.00
❑ 206 Scott Hunter RC .30 .75
❑ 207 Ron Johnson .30 .75
❑ 208 Sam Brunelli .30 .75
❑ 209 Deacon Jones .75 2.00
❑ 210 Fred Biletnikoff 3.00 6.00
❑ 211 Bill Nelsen .40 1.00
❑ 212 George Nock RC .30 .75
❑ 213 Dan Abramowicz .40 1.00
❑ 214 Irv Goode .30 .75
❑ 215 Isiah Robertson RC .40 1.00
❑ 216 Tom Matte .40 1.00
❑ 217 Pat Fischer .30 .75
❑ 218 Gene Washington Vik .30 .75
❑ 219 Paul Robinson .30 .75
❑ 220 John Brodie 2.00 4.00
❑ 221 Manny Fernandez RC .40 1.00
❑ 222 Errol Mann .30 .75
❑ 223 Dick Gordon .30 .75
❑ 224 Calvin Hill .75 2.00
❑ 225 Fran Tarkenton 6.00 12.00
❑ 226 Jim Turner .30 .75
❑ 227 Jim Mitchell TE .30 .75
❑ 228 Pete Liske .30 .75
❑ 229 Carl Garrett .30 .75
❑ 230 Joe Greene 10.00 20.00
❑ 231 Gale Gillingham .30 .75
❑ 232 Norm Bulaich RC .40 1.00
❑ 233 Spider Lockhart .30 .75
❑ 234 Ken Willard .30 .75
❑ 235 George Blanda 6.00 12.00
❑ 236 Wayne Mulligan RC .30 .75
❑ 237 Dave Lewis RC .30 .75
❑ 238 Dennis Shaw .30 .75
❑ 239 Fair Hooker RC .30 .75
❑ 240 Larry Little RC 7.50 15.00
❑ 241 Mike Garrett .30 .75
❑ 242 Glen Ray Hines .30 .75
❑ 243 Myron Pottios .30 .75
❑ 244 Charlie Joiner RC 10.00 20.00
❑ 245 Len Dawson 3.00 6.00
❑ 246 W.K. Hicks .30 .75
❑ 247 Les Josephson .30 .75
❑ 248 Lance Alworth UER 3.00 6.00
❑ 249 Frank Nunley RC .30 .75
❑ 250 Mel Farr IA .30 .75
❑ 251 Johnny Unitas IA 4.00 8.00
❑ 252 George Farmer IA .30 .75
❑ 253 Duane Thomas IA .40 1.00
❑ 254 John Hadl IA .75 2.00
❑ 255 Vic Washington IA .30 .75
❑ 256 Don Horn IA .30 .75
❑ 257 L.C.Greenwood IA .75 2.00
❑ 258 Bob Lee IA .30 .75
❑ 259 Larry Csonka IA 2.00 4.00
❑ 260 Mike McCoy DT IA .30 .75
❑ 261 Greg Landry IA .40 1.00
❑ 262 Ray May IA .30 .75
❑ 263 Bobby Douglass IA .30 .75
❑ 264 Charlie Sanders AP 15.00 30.00
❑ 265 Ron Yary AP 15.00 30.00
❑ 266 Rayfield Wright AP 20.00 40.00
❑ 267 Larry Little AP 20.00 35.00
❑ 268 John Niland AP 15.00 30.00
❑ 269 Forrest Blue AP 15.00 30.00
❑ 270 Otis Taylor AP 15.00 30.00
❑ 271 Paul Warfield AP 30.00 50.00
❑ 272 Bob Griese AP 40.00 70.00
❑ 273 John Brockington AP 15.00 30.00
❑ 274 Floyd Little AP 15.00 30.00
❑ 275 Garo Yepremian AP 15.00 30.00
❑ 276 Jerrel Wilson AP 10.00 18.00
❑ 277 Carl Eller AP 15.00 30.00
❑ 278 Bubba Smith AP 25.00 40.00
❑ 279 Alan Page AP 25.00 40.00
❑ 280 Bob Lilly AP 30.00 60.00
❑ 281 Ted Hendricks AP 30.00 50.00
❑ 282 Dave Wilcox AP 15.00 30.00
❑ 283 Willie Lanier AP 20.00 35.00
❑ 284 Jim Johnson AP 15.00 30.00
❑ 285 Willie Brown AP 20.00 35.00
❑ 286 Bill Bradley AP 15.00 30.00
❑ 287 Ken Houston AP 20.00 35.00
❑ 288 Mel Farr 10.00 18.00
❑ 289 Kermit Alexander 10.00 18.00
❑ 290 John Gilliam RC 12.50 25.00
❑ 291 Steve Spurrier RC 50.00 100.00
❑ 292 Walter Johnson 10.00 18.00
❑ 293 Jack Pardee 12.50 25.00
❑ 294 Checklist UER 50.00 80.00
❑ 295 Winston Hill 10.00 18.00
❑ 296 Hugo Hollas RC 10.00 18.00
❑ 297 Ray May RC 10.00 18.00
❑ 298 Jim Bakken 10.00 18.00
❑ 299 Larry Carwell RC 10.00 18.00
❑ 300 Alan Page 30.00 50.00
❑ 301 Walt Garrison 12.50 25.00
❑ 302 Mike Lucci 12.50 25.00
❑ 303 Nemiah Wilson 10.00 18.00
❑ 304 Carroll Dale 12.50 25.00
❑ 305 Jim Kanicki 10.00 18.00
❑ 306 Preston Pearson 15.00 30.00
❑ 307 Lemar Parrish 12.50 25.00
❑ 308 Earl Morrall 12.50 25.00
❑ 309 Tommy Nobis 12.50 25.00
❑ 310 Rich Jackson 10.00 18.00
❑ 311 Doug Cunningham RC 10.00 18.00
❑ 312 Jim Marsalis RC 10.00 18.00
❑ 313 Jim Beirne 10.00 18.00
❑ 314 Tom McNeill RC 10.00 18.00
❑ 315 Milt Morin 10.00 18.00
❑ 316 Rayfield Wright RC 25.00 40.00
❑ 317 Jerry LeVias 12.50 25.00
❑ 318 Travis Williams RC 12.50 25.00
❑ 319 Edgar Chandler 10.00 18.00
❑ 320 Bob Wallace RC 10.00 18.00
❑ 321 Delles Howell RC 10.00 18.00
❑ 322 Emerson Boozer 12.50 25.00
❑ 323 George Atkinson RC 12.50 25.00
❑ 324 Mike Montler RC 10.00 18.00
❑ 325 Randy Johnson 10.00 18.00
❑ 326 Mike Curtis UER 12.50 25.00
❑ 327 Miller Farr 10.00 18.00
❑ 328 Horst Muhlmann 10.00 18.00
❑ 329 John Niland RC 12.50 25.00
❑ 330 Andy Russell 15.00 30.00
❑ 331 Mercury Morris 25.00 40.00
❑ 332 Jim Johnson 15.00 30.00
❑ 333 Jerrel Wilson 10.00 18.00
❑ 334 Charley Taylor 25.00 40.00
❑ 335 Dick LeBeau 10.00 18.00
❑ 336 Jim Marshall 15.00 30.00

Card		
❑ 337 Tom Mack	15.00	30.00
❑ 338 Steve Spurrier IA	30.00	60.00
❑ 339 Floyd Little IA	12.50	25.00
❑ 340 Len Dawson IA	25.00	40.00
❑ 341 Dick Butkus IA	40.00	70.00
❑ 342 Larry Brown IA	12.50	25.00
❑ 343 Joe Namath IA	75.00	150.00
❑ 344 Jim Turner IA	10.00	18.00
❑ 345 Doug Cunningham IA	10.00	18.00
❑ 346 Edd Hargett IA	10.00	18.00
❑ 347 Steve Owens IA	10.00	18.00
❑ 348 George Blanda IA	30.00	50.00
❑ 349 Ed Podolak IA	10.00	18.00
❑ 350 Rich Jackson IA	10.00	18.00
❑ 351 Ken Willard IA	25.00	40.00

1973 Topps

Card		
❑ COMPLETE SET (528)	200.00	400.00
❑ 1 Simpson/L.Brown LL	3.00	8.00
❑ 2 Passing Leaders	.40	1.00
❑ 3 Jackson/Biletnikoff LL	.60	1.50
❑ 4 Scoring Leaders	.25	.60
❑ 5 Interception Leaders	.25	.60
❑ 6 Punting Leaders	.25	.60
❑ 7 Bob Trumpy	.60	1.50
❑ 8 Mel Tom RC	.25	.60
❑ 9 Clarence Ellis RC	.25	.60
❑ 10 John Niland	.25	.60
❑ 11 Randy Jackson RC	.25	.60
❑ 12 Greg Landry	.60	1.50
❑ 13 Cid Edwards RC	.25	.60
❑ 14 Phil Olsen RC	.25	.60
❑ 15 Terry Bradshaw	15.00	25.00
❑ 16 Al Cowlings RC	.60	1.50
❑ 17 Walker Gillette RC	.25	.60
❑ 18 Bob Atkins RC	.25	.60
❑ 19 Diron Talbert RC	.25	.60
❑ 20 Jim Johnson	.60	1.50
❑ 21 Howard Twilley	.40	1.00
❑ 22 Dick Enderle RC	.25	.60
❑ 23 Wayne Colman RC	.25	.60
❑ 24 John Schmitt RC	.25	.60
❑ 25 George Blanda	5.00	10.00
❑ 26 Milt Morin	.25	.60
❑ 27 Mike Current	.25	.60
❑ 28 Rex Kern RC	.25	.60
❑ 29 MacArthur Lane	.40	1.00
❑ 30 Alan Page	1.50	3.00
❑ 31 Randy Vataha	.25	.60
❑ 32 Jim Kearney RC	.25	.60
❑ 33 Steve Smith T RC	.25	.60
❑ 34 Ken Anderson RC	7.50	15.00
❑ 35 Calvin Hill	.60	1.50
❑ 36 Andy Maurer RC	.25	.60
❑ 37 Joe Taylor RC	.25	.60
❑ 38 Deacon Jones	.60	1.50
❑ 39 Mike Weger RC	.25	.60
❑ 40 Roy Gerela	.40	1.00
❑ 41 Les Josephson	.25	.60
❑ 42 Dave Washington RC	.25	.60
❑ 43 Bill Curry RC	.40	1.00
❑ 44 Fred Heron RC	.25	.60
❑ 45 John Brodie	1.50	3.00
❑ 46 Roy Winston	.25	.60
❑ 47 Mike Bragg	.25	.60
❑ 48 Mercury Morris	.60	1.50
❑ 49 Jim Files RC	.25	.60
❑ 50 Gene Upshaw	1.50	3.00
❑ 51 Hugo Hollas	.25	.60
❑ 52 Rod Sherman RC	.25	.60
❑ 53 Ron Snidow	.25	.60
❑ 54 Steve Tannen RC	.25	.60
❑ 55 Jim Carter RC	.25	.60
❑ 56 Lydell Mitchell RC	.60	1.50
❑ 57 Jack Rudnay RC	.25	.60
❑ 58 Halvor Hagen RC	.25	.60
❑ 59 Tom Dempsey	.40	1.00
❑ 60 Fran Tarkenton	5.00	10.00
❑ 61 Lance Alworth	2.50	5.00
❑ 62 Vern Holland RC	.25	.60
❑ 63 Steve DeLong	.25	.60
❑ 64 Art Malone	.25	.60
❑ 65 Isiah Robertson	.40	1.00
❑ 66 Jerry Rush	.25	.60
❑ 67 Bryant Salter RC	.25	.60
❑ 68 Checklist 1-132	2.50	5.00
❑ 69 J.D. Hill	.25	.60
❑ 70 Forrest Blue	.25	.60
❑ 71 Myron Pottios	.25	.60
❑ 72 Norm Thompson RC	.25	.60
❑ 73 Paul Robinson	.25	.60
❑ 74 Larry Grantham	.25	.60
❑ 75 Manny Fernandez	.40	1.00
❑ 76 Kent Nix RC	.25	.60
❑ 77 Art Shell RC	7.50	15.00
❑ 78 George Saimes	.25	.60
❑ 79 Don Cockroft	.25	.60
❑ 80 Bob Tucker	.40	1.00
❑ 81 Don McCauley RC	.25	.60
❑ 82 Bob Brown DT RC	.25	.60
❑ 83 Larry Carwell	.25	.60
❑ 84 Mo Moorman RC	.25	.60
❑ 85 John Gilliam	.40	1.00
❑ 86 Wade Key RC	.25	.60
❑ 87 Ross Brupbacher RC	.25	.60
❑ 88 Dave Lewis	.25	.60
❑ 89 Franco Harris RC	25.00	50.00
❑ 90 Tom Mack	.60	1.50
❑ 91 Mike Tilleman	.25	.60
❑ 92 Carl Mauck RC	.25	.60
❑ 93 Larry Hand	.25	.60
❑ 94 Dave Foley RC	.25	.60
❑ 95 Frank Nunley	.25	.60
❑ 96 John Charles	.25	.60
❑ 97 Jim Bakken	.25	.60
❑ 98 Pat Fischer	.40	1.00
❑ 99 Randy Rasmussen RC	.25	.60
❑ 100 Larry Csonka	3.00	6.00
❑ 101 Mike Siani RC	.25	.60
❑ 102 Tom Roussel RC	.25	.60
❑ 103 Clarence Scott RC	.40	1.00
❑ 104 Charlie Johnson	.40	1.00
❑ 105 Rick Volk	.25	.60
❑ 106 Willie Young RC	.25	.60
❑ 107 Emmitt Thomas	.60	1.50
❑ 108 Jon Morris	.25	.60
❑ 109 Clarence Williams RC	.25	.60
❑ 110 Rayfield Wright	.40	1.00
❑ 111 Norm Bulaich	.25	.60
❑ 112 Mike Eischeid	.25	.60
❑ 113 Speedy Thomas RC	.25	.60
❑ 114 Glen Holloway RC	.25	.60
❑ 115 Jack Ham RC	15.00	30.00
❑ 116 Jim Nettles RC	.25	.60
❑ 117 Errol Mann	.25	.60
❑ 118 John Mackey	.60	1.50
❑ 119 George Kunz	.25	.60
❑ 120 Bob James	.25	.60
❑ 121 Garland Boyette	.25	.60
❑ 122 Mel Phillips RC	.25	.60
❑ 123 Johnny Roland	.25	.60
❑ 124 Doug Swift RC	.25	.60
❑ 125 Archie Manning	2.00	4.00
❑ 126 Dave Herman	.25	.60
❑ 127 Carleton Oats RC	.25	.60
❑ 128 Bill Van Heusen	.25	.60
❑ 129 Rich Jackson	.25	.60
❑ 130 Len Hauss	.40	1.00
❑ 131 Billy Parks RC	.25	.60
❑ 132 Ray May	.25	.60
❑ 133 NFC Semi/Staubach	2.00	5.00
❑ 134 AFC Semi/Immac.Rec.	1.00	2.50
❑ 135 NFC Semi-Final	.40	1.00
❑ 136 AFC Semi/L.Csonka	.75	2.00
❑ 137 NFC Title Game/Kilmer	.60	1.50
❑ 138 AFC Title Game	.40	1.00
❑ 139 Super Bowl VII	.60	1.50
❑ 140 Dwight White RC	2.00	5.00
❑ 141 Jim Marsalis	.25	.60
❑ 142 Doug Van Horn RC	.25	.60
❑ 143 Al Matthews RC	.25	.60
❑ 144 Bob Windsor RC	.25	.60
❑ 145 Dave Hampton RC	.25	.60
❑ 146 Horst Muhlmann	.25	.60
❑ 147 Wally Hilgenberg RC	.25	.60
❑ 148 Ron Smith	.25	.60
❑ 149 Coy Bacon RC	.40	1.00
❑ 150 Winston Hill	.25	.60
❑ 151 Ron Jessie RC	.40	1.00
❑ 152 Ken Iman	.25	.60
❑ 153 Ron Saul RC	.25	.60
❑ 154 Jim Braxton RC	.40	1.00
❑ 155 Bubba Smith	1.25	2.50
❑ 156 Gary Cuozzo	.40	1.00
❑ 157 Charlie Krueger	.40	1.00
❑ 158 Tim Foley RC	.40	1.00
❑ 159 Lee Roy Jordan	.60	1.50
❑ 160 Bob Brown OT	.60	1.50
❑ 161 Margene Adkins RC	.25	.60
❑ 162 Ron Widby RC	.25	.60
❑ 163 Jim Houston	.25	.60
❑ 164 Joe Dawkins	.25	.60
❑ 165 L.C.Greenwood	2.00	4.00
❑ 166 Richmond Flowers RC	.25	.60
❑ 167 Curley Culp RC	.60	1.50
❑ 168 Len St. Jean	.25	.60
❑ 169 Walter Rock	.25	.60
❑ 170 Bill Bradley	.40	1.00
❑ 171 Ken Riley RC	.60	1.50
❑ 172 Rich Coady RC	.25	.60
❑ 173 Don Hansen RC	.25	.60
❑ 174 Lionel Aldridge	.25	.60
❑ 175 Don Maynard	2.00	4.00
❑ 176 Dave Osborn	.40	1.00
❑ 177 Jim Bailey	.25	.60
❑ 178 John Pitts	.25	.60
❑ 179 Dave Parks	.25	.60
❑ 180 Chester Marcol RC	.25	.60
❑ 181 Len Rohde RC	.25	.60
❑ 182 Jeff Staggs RC	.25	.60
❑ 183 Gene Hickerson	.60	1.25
❑ 184 Charlie Evans RC	.25	.60
❑ 185 Mel Renfro	.60	1.50
❑ 186 Marvin Upshaw RC	.25	.60
❑ 187 George Atkinson	.40	1.00
❑ 188 Norm Evans	.40	1.00
❑ 189 Steve Ramsey	.25	.60
❑ 190 Dave Chapple RC	.25	.60
❑ 191 Gerry Mullins RC	.25	.60
❑ 192 John Didion RC	.25	.60
❑ 193 Bob Gladieux RC	.25	.60
❑ 194 Don Hultz	.25	.60
❑ 195 Mike Lucci	.25	.60
❑ 196 John Wilbur RC	.25	.60
❑ 197 George Farmer	.25	.60
❑ 198 Tommy Casanova RC	.40	1.00
❑ 199 Russ Washington	.25	.60
❑ 200 Claude Humphrey	.60	1.50
❑ 201 Pat Hughes RC	.25	.60
❑ 202 Zeke Moore	.25	.60
❑ 203 Chip Glass RC	.25	.60
❑ 204 Glenn Ressler RC	.25	.60
❑ 205 Willie Ellison	.40	1.00
❑ 206 John Leypoldt RC	.25	.60
❑ 207 Johnny Fuller RC	.25	.60
❑ 208 Bill Hayhoe RC	.25	.60
❑ 209 Ed Bell RC	.25	.60
❑ 210 Willie Brown	.60	1.50
❑ 211 Carl Eller	.60	1.50
❑ 212 Mark Nordquist	.25	.60
❑ 213 Larry Willingham RC	.25	.60
❑ 214 Nick Buoniconti	.60	1.50
❑ 215 John Hadl	.60	1.50
❑ 216 Jethro Pugh RC	.60	1.50
❑ 217 Leroy Mitchell	.25	.60
❑ 218 Billy Newsome RC	.25	.60
❑ 219 John McMakin RC	.25	.60
❑ 220 Larry Brown	.60	1.50
❑ 221 Clarence Scott RC	.25	.60
❑ 222 Paul Naumoff RC	.25	.60
❑ 223 Ted Fritsch Jr. RC	.25	.60
❑ 224 Checklist 133-264	2.50	5.00
❑ 225 Dan Pastorini	.60	1.50
❑ 226 Joe Beauchamp UER RC	.25	.60
❑ 227 Pat Matson	.25	.60
❑ 228 Tony McGee DT RC	.25	.60
❑ 229 Mike Phipps	.40	1.00
❑ 230 Harold Jackson	.60	1.50
❑ 231 Willie Williams RC	.25	.60
❑ 232 Spike Jones	.25	.60
❑ 233 Jim Tyrer	.25	.60
❑ 234 Roy Hilton	.25	.60
❑ 235 Phil Villapiano	.40	1.00
❑ 236 Charley Taylor UER	1.50	3.00

Card		
❑ 237 Malcolm Snider RC	.25	.60
❑ 238 Vic Washington	.25	.60
❑ 239 Grady Alderman	.25	.60
❑ 240 Dick Anderson	.40	1.00
❑ 241 Ron Yankowski RC	.25	.60
❑ 242 Billy Masters RC	.25	.60
❑ 243 Herb Adderley	.60	1.50
❑ 244 David Ray RC	.25	.60
❑ 245 John Riggins	4.00	8.00
❑ 246 Mike Wagner RC	1.25	3.00
❑ 247 Don Morrison RC	.25	.60
❑ 248 Earl McCullouch	.25	.60
❑ 249 Dennis Wirgowski RC	.25	.60
❑ 250 Chris Hanburger	.40	1.00
❑ 251 Pat Sullivan RC	.60	1.50
❑ 252 Walt Sweeney	.25	.60
❑ 253 Willie Alexander RC	.25	.60
❑ 254 Doug Dressler RC	.25	.60
❑ 255 Walter Johnson	.25	.60
❑ 256 Ron Hornsby	.25	.60
❑ 257 Ben Hawkins	.25	.60
❑ 258 Donnie Green RC	.25	.60
❑ 259 Fred Hoaglin	.25	.60
❑ 260 Jerrel Wilson	.25	.60
❑ 261 Horace Jones	.25	.60
❑ 262 Woody Peoples	.25	.60
❑ 263 Jim Hill RC	.25	.60
❑ 264 John Fuqua	.25	.60
❑ 265 Donny Anderson KP	.40	1.00
❑ 266 Roman Gabriel KP	.60	1.50
❑ 267 Mike Garrett KP	.40	1.00
❑ 268 Rufus Mayes RC	.25	.60
❑ 269 Chip Myrtle RC	.25	.60
❑ 270 Bill Stanfill RC	.40	1.00
❑ 271 Clint Jones	.25	.60
❑ 272 Miller Farr	.25	.60
❑ 273 Harry Schuh	.25	.60
❑ 274 Bob Hayes	.75	2.00
❑ 275 Bobby Douglass	.40	1.00
❑ 276 Gus Hollomon RC	.25	.60
❑ 277 Del Williams RC	.25	.60
❑ 278 Julius Adams	.25	.60
❑ 279 Herman Weaver	.25	.60
❑ 280 Joe Greene	4.00	8.00
❑ 281 Wes Chesson RC	.25	.60
❑ 282 Charlie Harraway RC	.25	.60
❑ 283 Paul Guidry	.25	.60
❑ 284 Terry Owens RC	.25	.60
❑ 285 Jan Stenerud	.60	1.50
❑ 286 Pete Athas	.25	.60
❑ 287 Dale Lindsey RC	.25	.60
❑ 288 Jack Tatum RC	6.00	15.00
❑ 289 Floyd Little	.60	1.50
❑ 290 Bob Johnson	.25	.60
❑ 291 Tommy Hart RC	.25	.60
❑ 292 Tom Mitchell RC	.25	.60
❑ 293 Walt Patulski RC	.25	.60
❑ 294 Jim Skaggs	.25	.60
❑ 295 Bob Griese	3.00	6.00
❑ 296 Mike McCoy DT	.25	.60
❑ 297 Mel Gray	.40	1.00
❑ 298 Bobby Bryant RC	.25	.60
❑ 299 Blaine Nye RC	.25	.60
❑ 300 Dick Butkus	6.00	12.00
❑ 301 Charlie Cowan RC	.25	.60
❑ 302 Mark Lomas RC	.25	.60
❑ 303 Josh Ashton RC	.25	.60
❑ 304 Happy Feller RC	.25	.60
❑ 305 Ron Shanklin	.25	.60
❑ 306 Wayne Rasmussen	.25	.60
❑ 307 Jerry Smith	.25	.60
❑ 308 Ken Reaves	.25	.60
❑ 309 Ron East RC	.25	.60
❑ 310 Otis Taylor	.60	1.50
❑ 311 John Garlington RC	.25	.60
❑ 312 Lyle Alzado	2.00	4.00
❑ 313 Remi Prudhomme RC	.25	.60
❑ 314 Cornelius Johnson RC	.25	.60
❑ 315 Lemar Parrish	.40	1.00
❑ 316 Jim Kiick	.60	1.50
❑ 317 Steve Zabel	.25	.60
❑ 318 Alden Roche RC	.25	.60
❑ 319 Tom Blanchard RC	.25	.60
❑ 320 Fred Biletnikoff	2.00	4.00
❑ 321 Ralph Neely	.40	1.00
❑ 322 Dan Dierdorf RC	7.50	20.00
❑ 323 Richard Caster	.40	1.00
❑ 324 Gene Howard	.25	.60
❑ 325 Elvin Bethea	.60	1.50
❑ 326 Carl Garrett	.40	1.00
❑ 327 Ron Billingsley RC	.25	.60
❑ 328 Charlie West	.25	.60
❑ 329 Tom Neville	.25	.60
❑ 330 Ted Kwalick	.40	1.00
❑ 331 Rudy Redmond RC	.25	.60
❑ 332 Henry Davis RC	.25	.60
❑ 333 John Zook	.25	.60
❑ 334 Jim Turner	.25	.60
❑ 335 Len Dawson	2.50	5.00
❑ 336 Bob Chandler RC	.40	1.00
❑ 337 Al Beauchamp	.25	.60
❑ 338 Tom Matte	.40	1.00
❑ 339 Paul Laaveg RC	.25	.60
❑ 340 Ken Ellis	.25	.60
❑ 341 Jim Langer RC	6.00	12.00
❑ 342 Ron Porter	.25	.60
❑ 343 Jack Youngblood RC	7.50	15.00
❑ 344 Cornell Green	.60	1.50
❑ 345 Marv Hubbard	.40	1.00
❑ 346 Bruce Taylor	.25	.60
❑ 347 Sam Havrilak RC	.25	.60
❑ 348 Walt Sumner RC	.25	.60
❑ 349 Steve O'Neal RC	.25	.60
❑ 350 Ron Johnson	.40	1.00
❑ 351 Rockne Freitas	.25	.60
❑ 352 Larry Stallings	.25	.60
❑ 353 Jim Cadile	.25	.60
❑ 354 Ken Burrough	.40	1.00
❑ 355 Jim Plunkett	2.00	4.00
❑ 356 Dave Long RC	.25	.60
❑ 357 Ralph Anderson RC	.25	.60
❑ 358 Checklist 265-396	2.50	5.00
❑ 359 Gene Washington Vik	.40	1.00
❑ 360 Dave Wilcox	.60	1.50
❑ 361 Paul Smith RC	.25	.60
❑ 362 Alvin Wyatt RC	.25	.60
❑ 363 Charlie Smith RB	.25	.60
❑ 364 Royce Berry	.25	.60
❑ 365 Dave Elmendorf	.25	.60
❑ 366 Scott Hunter	.40	1.00
❑ 367 Bob Kuechenberg RC	1.25	3.00
❑ 368 Pete Gogolak	.25	.60
❑ 369 Dave Edwards	.25	.60
❑ 370 Lem Barney	1.25	2.50
❑ 371 Verlon Biggs	.25	.60
❑ 372 John Reaves RC	.25	.60
❑ 373 Ed Podolak	.40	1.00
❑ 374 Chris Farasopoulos	.25	.60
❑ 375 Gary Garrison	.25	.60
❑ 376 Tom Funchess RC	.25	.60
❑ 377 Bobby Joe Green	.25	.60
❑ 378 Don Brumm	.25	.60
❑ 379 Jim O'Brien	.25	.60
❑ 380 Paul Krause	.60	1.50
❑ 381 Leroy Kelly	1.25	2.50
❑ 382 Ray Mansfield	.25	.60
❑ 383 Dan Abramowicz	.40	1.00
❑ 384 John Outlaw RC	.25	.60
❑ 385 Tommy Nobis	.60	1.50
❑ 386 Tom Domres RC	.25	.60
❑ 387 Ken Willard	.25	.60
❑ 388 Mike Stratton	.25	.60
❑ 389 Fred Dryer	1.25	2.50
❑ 390 Jake Scott	.60	1.50
❑ 391 Rich Houston RC	.25	.60
❑ 392 Virgil Carter	.25	.60
❑ 393 Tody Smith RC	.25	.60
❑ 394 Ernie Calloway RC	.25	.60
❑ 395 Charlie Sanders	.60	1.50
❑ 396 Fred Willis	.25	.60
❑ 397 Curt Knight	.25	.60
❑ 398 Nemiah Wilson	.25	.60
❑ 399 Carroll Dale	.40	1.00
❑ 400 Joe Namath	15.00	30.00
❑ 401 Wayne Mulligan	.25	.60
❑ 402 Jim Harrison RC	.25	.60
❑ 403 Tim Rossovich	.25	.60
❑ 404 David Lee	.25	.60
❑ 405 Frank Pitts RC	.25	.60
❑ 406 Jim Marshall	.60	1.50
❑ 407 Bob Brown TE	.25	.60
❑ 408 John Rowser	.25	.60
❑ 409 Mike Montler	.25	.60
❑ 410 Willie Lanier	.60	1.50
❑ 411 Bill Bell K RC	.25	.60
❑ 412 Cedrick Hardman	.25	.60
❑ 413 Bob Anderson	.25	.60
❑ 414 Earl Morrall	.60	1.50
❑ 415 Ken Houston	.60	1.50
❑ 416 Jack Snow	.40	1.00
❑ 417 Dick Cunningham RC	.25	.60
❑ 418 Greg Larson	.25	.60
❑ 419 Mike Bass RC	.40	1.00
❑ 420 Mike Reid	.60	1.50
❑ 421 Walt Garrison	.60	1.50
❑ 422 Pete Liske	.25	.60
❑ 423 Jim Yarbrough RC	.25	.60
❑ 424 Rich McGeorge	.25	.60
❑ 425 Bobby Howfield RC	.25	.60
❑ 426 Pete Banaszak	.25	.60
❑ 427 Willie Holman RC	.25	.60
❑ 428 Dale Hackbart	.25	.60
❑ 429 Fair Hooker	.25	.60
❑ 430 Ted Hendricks	2.50	5.00
❑ 431 Mike Garrett	.40	1.00
❑ 432 Glen Ray Hines	.25	.60
❑ 433 Fred Cox	.25	.60
❑ 434 Bobby Walden	.25	.60
❑ 435 Bobby Bell	.60	1.50
❑ 436 Dave Rowe	.25	.60
❑ 437 Bob Berry	.25	.60
❑ 438 Bill Thompson	.25	.60
❑ 439 Jim Beirne	.25	.60
❑ 440 Larry Little	1.50	3.00
❑ 441 Rocky Thompson RC	.25	.60
❑ 442 Brig Owens	.25	.60
❑ 443 Richard Neal	.25	.60
❑ 444 Al Nelson	.25	.60
❑ 445 Chip Myers	.25	.60
❑ 446 Ken Bowman	.25	.60
❑ 447 Jim Purnell RC	.25	.60
❑ 448 Altie Taylor	.25	.60
❑ 449 Linzy Cole	.25	.60
❑ 450 Bob Lilly	2.50	5.00
❑ 451 Charlie Ford RC	.25	.60
❑ 452 Milt Sunde	.25	.60
❑ 453 Doug Wyatt RC	.25	.60
❑ 454 Don Nottingham RC	.40	1.00
❑ 455 Johnny Unitas	7.50	15.00
❑ 456 Frank Lewis RC	.40	1.00
❑ 457 Roger Wehrli	.40	1.00
❑ 458 Jim Cheyunski RC	.25	.60
❑ 459 Jerry Sherk RC	.40	1.00
❑ 460 Gene Washington 49er	.40	1.00
❑ 461 Jim Otto	.60	1.50
❑ 462 Ed Budde	.25	.60
❑ 463 Jim Mitchell TE	.40	1.00
❑ 464 Emerson Boozer	.40	1.00
❑ 465 Garo Yepremian	.60	1.50
❑ 466 Pete Duranko	.25	.60
❑ 467 Charlie Joiner	4.00	8.00
❑ 468 Spider Lockhart	.40	1.00
❑ 469 Marty Domres	.25	.60
❑ 470 John Brockington	.60	1.50
❑ 471 Ed Flanagan	.25	.60
❑ 472 Roy Jefferson	.40	1.00
❑ 473 Julian Fagan RC	.25	.60
❑ 474 Bill Brown	.40	1.00
❑ 475 Roger Staubach	15.00	30.00
❑ 476 Jan White RC	.25	.60
❑ 477 Pat Holmes RC	.25	.60
❑ 478 Bob DeMarco	.25	.60
❑ 479 Merlin Olsen	1.25	2.50
❑ 480 Andy Russell	.60	1.50
❑ 481 Steve Spurrier	10.00	20.00
❑ 482 Nate Ramsey	.25	.60
❑ 483 Dennis Partee	.25	.60
❑ 484 Jerry Simmons	.25	.60
❑ 485 Donny Anderson	.60	1.50
❑ 486 Ralph Baker	.25	.60
❑ 487 Ken Stabler RC	35.00	60.00
❑ 488 Ernie McMillan	.25	.60
❑ 489 Ken Burrow RC	.25	.60
❑ 490 Jack Gregory RC	.25	.60
❑ 491 Larry Seiple	.40	1.00
❑ 492 Mick Tingelhoff	.40	1.00
❑ 493 Craig Morton	.60	1.50
❑ 494 Cecil Turner	.25	.60
❑ 495 Steve Owens	.60	1.50
❑ 496 Rickie Harris	.25	.60
❑ 497 Buck Buchanan	.60	1.50
❑ 498 Checklist 397-528	2.50	5.00
❑ 499 Billy Kilmer	.60	1.50
❑ 500 O.J.Simpson	7.50	15.00
❑ 501 Bruce Gossett	.25	.60
❑ 502 Art Thoms RC	.25	.60
❑ 503 Larry Kaminski RC	.25	.60

Card	Low	High
504 Larry Smith RB RC	.25	.60
505 Bruce Van Dyke RC	.25	.60
506 Alvin Reed	.25	.60
507 Delles Howell	.25	.60
508 Leroy Keyes	.25	.60
509 Bo Scott	.40	1.00
510 Ron Yary	.60	1.50
511 Paul Warfield	2.50	5.00
512 Mac Percival	.25	.60
513 Essex Johnson RC	.25	.60
514 Jackie Smith	.60	1.50
515 Norm Snead	.60	1.50
516 Charlie Stukes RC	.25	.60
517 Reggie Rucker RC	.40	1.00
518 Bill Sandeman UER RC	.25	.60
519 Mel Farr	.40	1.00
520 Raymond Chester	.40	1.00
521 Fred Carr RC	.40	1.00
522 Jerry LeVias	.40	1.00
523 Jim Strong RC	.25	.60
524 Roland McDole	.25	.60
525 Dennis Shaw	.25	.60
526 Dave Manders	.25	.60
527 Skip Vanderbundt RC	.25	.60
528 Mike Sensibaugh RC	.60	1.50

1974 Topps

Card	Low	High
COMPLETE SET (528)	175.00	300.00
1 O.J.Simpson RB UER	10.00	20.00
2 Blaine Nye	.25	.60
3 Don Hansen	.25	.60
4 Ken Bowman	.25	.60
5 Carl Eller	.60	1.50
6 Jerry Smith	.25	.60
7 Ed Podolak	.25	.60
8 Mel Gray	.60	1.50
9 Pat Matson	.25	.60
10 Floyd Little	.60	1.50
11 Frank Pitts	.25	.60
12 Vern Den Herder RC	.40	1.00
13 John Fuqua	.40	1.00
14 Jack Tatum	.75	2.00
15 Winston Hill	.25	.60
16 John Beasley RC	.25	.60
17 David Lee	.25	.60
18 Rich Coady	.25	.60
19 Ken Willard	.25	.60
20 Coy Bacon	.40	1.00
21 Ben Hawkins	.25	.60
22 Paul Guidry	.25	.60
23 Norm Snead HOR	.40	1.00
24 Jim Yarbrough	.25	.60
25 Jack Reynolds RC	1.25	3.00
26 Josh Ashton	.25	.60
27 Donnie Green	.25	.60
28 Bob Hayes	.75	2.00
29 John Zook	.25	.60
30 Bobby Bryant	.25	.60
31 Scott Hunter	.40	1.00
32 Dan Dierdorf	3.00	6.00
33 Curt Knight	.25	.60
34 Elmo Wright RC	.25	.60
35 Essex Johnson	.25	.60
36 Walt Sumner	.25	.60
37 Marv Montgomery RC	.25	.60
38 Tim Foley	.40	1.00
39 Mike Siani	.25	.60
40 Joe Greene	3.00	6.00
41 Bobby Howfield	.25	.60
42 Del Williams	.25	.60
43 Don McCauley	.25	.60
44 Randy Jackson	.25	.60
45 Ron Smith	.25	.60
46 Gene Washington 49er	.40	1.00
47 Po James RC	.25	.60
48 Solomon Freelon RC	.25	.60
49 Bob Windsor HOR	.25	.60
50 John Hadl	.60	1.50
51 Greg Larson	.25	.60
52 Steve Owens	.40	1.00
53 Jim Cheyunski	.25	.60
54 Rayfield Wright	.40	1.00
55 Dave Hampton	.25	.60
56 Ron Widby	.25	.60
57 Milt Sunde	.25	.60
58 Billy Kilmer	.60	1.50
59 Bobby Bell	.60	1.50
60 Jim Bakken	.25	.60
61 Rufus Mayes	.25	.60
62 Vic Washington	.25	.60
63 Gene Washington Vik	.40	1.00
64 Clarence Scott	.25	.60
65 Gene Upshaw	.75	2.00
66 Larry Seiple	.40	1.00
67 John McMakin	.25	.60
68 Ralph Baker	.25	.60
69 Lydell Mitchell	.40	1.00
70 Archie Manning	1.25	2.50
71 George Farmer	.25	.60
72 Ron East	.25	.60
73 Al Nelson	.25	.60
74 Pat Hughes	.25	.60
75 Fred Willis	.25	.60
76 Larry Walton RC	.25	.60
77 Tom Neville	.25	.60
78 Ted Kwalick	.25	.60
79 Walt Patulski	.25	.60
80 John Niland	.25	.60
81 Ted Fritsch Jr.	.25	.60
82 Paul Krause	.60	1.50
83 Jack Snow	.40	1.00
84 Mike Bass	.25	.60
85 Jim Tyrer	.25	.60
86 Ron Yankowski	.25	.60
87 Mike Phipps	.40	1.00
88 Al Beauchamp	.25	.60
89 Riley Odoms RC	.60	1.50
90 MacArthur Lane	.25	.60
91 Art Thoms	.25	.60
92 Marlin Briscoe	.25	.60
93 Bruce Van Dyke	.25	.60
94 Tom Myers RC	.25	.60
95 Calvin Hill	.60	1.50
96 Bruce Laird RC	.25	.60
97 Tony McGee DT	.25	.60
98 Len Rohde	.25	.60
99 Tom McNeill	.25	.60
100 Delles Howell	.25	.60
101 Gary Garrison	.25	.60
102 Dan Goich RC	.25	.60
103 Len St. Jean	.25	.60
104 Zeke Moore	.25	.60
105 Ahmad Rashad RC	10.00	20.00
106 Mel Renfro	.60	1.50
107 Jim Mitchell TE	.25	.60
108 Ed Budde	.25	.60
109 Harry Schuh	.25	.60
110 Greg Pruitt RC	2.00	4.00
111 Ed Flanagan	.25	.60
112 Larry Stallings	.25	.60
113 Chuck Foreman RC	2.50	5.00
114 Royce Berry	.25	.60
115 Gale Gillingham	.25	.60
116 Charlie Johnson HOR	.60	1.50
117 Checklist 1-132 UER	2.00	4.00
118 Bill Butler RC	.25	.60
119 Roy Jefferson	.40	1.00
120 Bobby Douglass	.40	1.00
121 Harold Carmichael RC	6.00	12.00
122 George Kunz AP	.25	.60
123 Larry Little	.75	2.00
124 Forrest Blue AP	.25	.60
125 Ron Yary	.60	1.50
126 Tom Mack AP	.60	1.50
127 Bob Tucker AP	.40	1.00
128 Paul Warfield	2.00	4.00
129 Fran Tarkenton	5.00	10.00
130 O.J.Simpson	6.00	12.00
131 Larry Csonka	3.00	6.00
132 Bruce Gossett AP	.25	.60
133 Bill Stanfill AP	.40	1.00
134 Alan Page	1.25	2.50
135 Paul Smith AP	.25	.60
136 Claude Humphrey AP	.40	1.00
137 Jack Ham	5.00	10.00
138 Lee Roy Jordan	.60	1.50
139 Phil Villapiano AP	.40	1.00
140 Ken Ellis AP	.25	.60
141 Willie Brown	.60	1.50
142 Dick Anderson AP	.40	1.00
143 Bill Bradley AP	.40	1.00
144 Jerrel Wilson AP	.25	.60
145 Reggie Rucker	.40	1.00
146 Marty Domres	.25	.60
147 Bob Kowalkowski RC	.25	.60
148 John Matuszak RC	2.50	6.00
149 Mike Adamle RC	.40	1.00
150 Johnny Unitas	7.50	15.00
151 Charlie Ford	.25	.60
152 Bob Klein RC	.25	.60
153 Jim Merlo RC	.25	.60
154 Willie Young	.25	.60
155 Donny Anderson	.40	1.00
156 Brig Owens	.25	.60
157 Bruce Jarvis RC	.25	.60
158 Ron Carpenter RC	.25	.60
159 Don Cockroft	.25	.60
160 Tommy Nobis	.60	1.50
161 Craig Morton	.60	1.50
162 Jon Staggers RC	.25	.60
163 Mike Eischeid	.25	.60
164 Jerry Sisemore RC	.25	.60
165 Cedrick Hardman	.25	.60
166 Bill Thompson	.40	1.00
167 Jim Lynch	.40	1.00
168 Bob Moore RC	.25	.60
169 Glen Edwards RC	.25	.60
170 Mercury Morris	.60	1.50
171 Julius Adams	.25	.60
172 Cotton Speyrer RC	.25	.60
173 Bill Munson	.40	1.00
174 Benny Johnson	.25	.60
175 Burgess Owens RC	.25	.60
176 Cid Edwards	.25	.60
177 Doug Buffone	.25	.60
178 Charlie Cowan	.25	.60
179 Bob Newland RC	.25	.60
180 Ron Johnson	.40	1.00
181 Bob Rowe RC	.25	.60
182 Len Hauss	.25	.60
183 Joe DeLamielleure RC	6.00	12.00
184 Sherman White RC	.25	.60
185 Fair Hooker	.25	.60
186 Nick Mike-Mayer RC	.25	.60
187 Ralph Neely	.25	.60
188 Rich McGeorge	.25	.60
189 Ed Marinaro RC	1.50	4.00
190 Dave Wilcox	.60	1.50
191 Joe Owens RC	.25	.60
192 Bill Van Heusen	.25	.60
193 Jim Kearney	.25	.60
194 Otis Sistrunk RC	.60	1.50
195 Ron Shanklin	.25	.60
196 Bill Lenkaitis RC	.25	.60
197 Tom Drougas RC	.25	.60
198 Larry Hand	.25	.60
199 Mack Alston RC	.25	.60
200 Bob Griese	3.00	6.00
201 Earlie Thomas RC	.25	.60
202 Carl Gersbach RC	.25	.60
203 Jim Harrison	.25	.60
204 Jake Kupp	.25	.60
205 Merlin Olsen	.75	2.00
206 Spider Lockhart	.40	1.00
207 Walker Gillette	.25	.60
208 Verlon Biggs	.25	.60
209 Bob James	.25	.60
210 Bob Trumpy	.60	1.50
211 Jerry Sherk	.25	.60
212 Andy Maurer	.25	.60
213 Fred Carr	.25	.60
214 Mick Tingelhoff	.40	1.00
215 Steve Spurrier	7.50	15.00
216 Richard Harris RC	.25	.60
217 Charlie Greer RC	.25	.60
218 Buck Buchanan	.60	1.50
219 Ray Guy RC	6.00	12.00
220 Franco Harris	6.00	12.00
221 Darryl Stingley RC	.60	1.50
222 Rex Kern	.25	.60
223 Toni Fritsch RC	.40	1.00
224 Levi Johnson RC	.25	.60
225 Bob Kuechenberg	.40	1.00
226 Elvin Bethea	.60	1.50

Card		
227 Al Woodall RC	.40	1.00
228 Terry Owens	.25	.60
229 Bivian Lee RC	.25	.60
230 Dick Butkus	5.00	10.00
231 Jim Bertelsen RC	.40	1.00
232 John Mendenhall RC	.25	.60
233 Conrad Dobler RC	.60	1.50
234 J.D. Hill	.40	1.00
235 Ken Houston	.60	1.50
236 Dave Lewis	.25	.60
237 John Garlington	.25	.60
238 Bill Sandeman	.25	.60
239 Alden Roche	.25	.60
240 John Gilliam	.40	1.00
241 Bruce Taylor	.25	.60
242 Vern Winfield RC	.25	.60
243 Bobby Maples	.25	.60
244 Wendell Hayes	.25	.60
245 George Blanda	4.00	8.00
246 Dwight White	.40	1.00
247 Sandy Durko RC	.25	.60
248 Tom Mitchell	.25	.60
249 Chuck Walton	.25	.60
250 Bob Lilly	2.00	4.00
251 Doug Swift	.25	.60
252 Lynn Dickey RC	.60	1.50
253 Jerome Barkum RC	.25	.60
254 Clint Jones	.25	.60
255 Billy Newsome	.25	.60
256 Bob Asher RC	.25	.60
257 Joe Scibelli RC	.25	.60
258 Tom Blanchard	.25	.60
259 Norm Thompson	.25	.60
260 Larry Brown	.60	1.50
261 Paul Seymour RC	.25	.60
262 Checklist 133-264	2.00	4.00
263 Doug Dieken RC	.25	.60
264 Lemar Parrish	.40	1.00
265 Bob Lee UER	.25	.60
266 Bob Brown DT	.25	.60
267 Roy Winston	.25	.60
268 Randy Beisler RC	.25	.60
269 Joe Dawkins	.25	.60
270 Tom Dempsey	.40	1.00
271 Jack Rudnay	.25	.60
272 Art Shell	2.50	5.00
273 Mike Wagner	.40	1.00
274 Rick Cash RC	.25	.60
275 Greg Landry	.60	1.50
276 Glenn Ressler	.25	.60
277 Billy Joe DuPree RC	1.25	3.00
278 Norm Evans	.25	.60
279 Billy Parks	.25	.60
280 John Riggins	3.00	6.00
281 Lionel Aldridge	.25	.60
282 Steve O'Neal	.25	.60
283 Craig Clemons RC	.25	.60
284 Willie Williams	.25	.60
285 Isiah Robertson	.40	1.00
286 Dennis Shaw	.25	.60
287 Bill Brundige	.25	.60
288 John Leypoldt	.25	.60
289 John DeMarie RC	.25	.60
290 Mike Reid	.60	1.50
291 Greg Brezina	.25	.60
292 Willie Buchanon RC	.25	.60
293 Dave Osborn	.40	1.00
294 Mel Phillips	.25	.60
295 Haven Moses	.40	1.00
296 Wade Key	.25	.60
297 Marvin Upshaw	.25	.60
298 Ray Mansfield	.25	.60
299 Edgar Chandler	.25	.60
300 Marv Hubbard	.40	1.00
301 Herman Weaver	.25	.60
302 Jim Bailey	.25	.60
303 D.D.Lewis RC	.60	1.50
304 Ken Burrough	.40	1.00
305 Jake Scott	.60	1.50
306 Randy Rasmussen	.25	.60
307 Pettis Norman	.25	.60
308 Carl Johnson RC	.25	.60
309 Joe Taylor	.25	.60
310 Pete Gogolak	.25	.60
311 Tony Baker FB	.25	.60
312 John Richardson RC	.25	.60
313 Dave Robinson	.40	1.00
314 Reggie McKenzie RC	.60	1.50
315 Isaac Curtis RC	.60	1.50
316 Thom Darden RC	.25	.60
317 Ken Reaves	.25	.60
318 Malcolm Snider	.25	.60
319 Jeff Siemon RC	.40	1.00
320 Dan Abramowicz	.40	1.00
321 Lyle Alzado	.75	2.00
322 John Reaves	.25	.60
323 Morris Stroud RC	.25	.60
324 Bobby Walden	.25	.60
325 Randy Vataha	.25	.60
326 Nemiah Wilson	.25	.60
327 Paul Naumoff	.25	.60
328 O.J.Simpson/Brock LL	1.50	3.00
329 R.Staubach/Stabler LL	2.50	5.00
330 Harold Carmichael/Wil LL	.60	1.50
331 Scoring Leaders	.40	1.00
332 Interception Leaders	.40	1.00
333 Punting Leaders	.40	1.00
334 Dennis Nelson RC	.25	.60
335 Walt Garrison	.40	1.00
336 Tody Smith	.25	.60
337 Ed Bell	.25	.60
338 Bryant Salter	.25	.60
339 Wayne Colman	.25	.60
340 Garo Yepremian	.40	1.00
341 Bob Newton RC	.25	.60
342 Vince Clements RC	.25	.60
343 Ken Iman	.25	.60
344 Jim Tolbert RC	.25	.60
345 Chris Hanburger	.40	1.00
346 Dave Foley	.25	.60
347 Tommy Casanova	.40	1.00
348 John James RC	.25	.60
349 Clarence Williams	.25	.60
350 Leroy Kelly	.60	1.50
351 Stu Voigt RC	.40	1.00
352 Skip Vanderbundt	.25	.60
353 Pete Duranko	.25	.60
354 John Outlaw	.25	.60
355 Jan Stenerud	.60	1.50
356 Barry Pearson RC	.25	.60
357 Brian Dowling RC	.25	.60
358 Dan Conners	.25	.60
359 Bob Bell RC	.25	.60
360 Rick Volk	.25	.60
361 Pat Toomay RC	.40	1.00
362 Bob Gresham RC	.25	.60
363 John Schmitt	.25	.60
364 Mel Rogers RC	.25	.60
365 Manny Fernandez	.40	1.00
366 Ernie Jackson RC	.25	.60
367 Gary Huff RC	.40	1.00
368 Bob Grim	.25	.60
369 Ernie McMillan	.25	.60
370 Dave Elmendorf	.25	.60
371 Mike Bragg	.25	.60
372 John Skorupan RC	.25	.60
373 Howard Fest	.25	.60
374 Jerry Tagge RC	.40	1.00
375 Art Malone	.25	.60
376 Bob Babich	.25	.60
377 Jim Marshall	.60	1.50
378 Bob Hoskins RC	.25	.60
379 Don Zimmerman RC	.25	.60
380 Ray May	.25	.60
381 Emmitt Thomas	.40	1.00
382 Terry Hanratty	.40	1.00
383 John Hannah RC	7.50	15.00
384 George Atkinson	.25	.60
385 Ted Hendricks	1.50	3.00
386 Jim O'Brien	.25	.60
387 Jethro Pugh	.40	1.00
388 Elbert Drungo RC	.25	.60
389 Richard Caster	.40	1.00
390 Deacon Jones	.60	1.50
391 Checklist 265-396	2.00	4.00
392 Jess Phillips RC	.25	.60
393 Garry Lyle UER RC	.25	.60
394 Jim Files	.25	.60
395 Jim Hart	.60	1.50
396 Dave Chapple	.25	.60
397 Jim Langer	.75	2.00
398 John Wilbur	.25	.60
399 Dwight Harrison RC	.25	.60
400 John Brockington	.40	1.00
401 Ken Anderson	3.00	6.00
402 Mike Tilleman	.25	.60
403 Charlie Hall RC	.25	.60
404 Tommy Hart	.25	.60
405 Norm Bulaich	.40	1.00
406 Jim Turner	.25	.60
407 Mo Moorman	.25	.60
408 Ralph Anderson	.25	.60
409 Jim Otto	.60	1.50
410 Andy Russell	.60	1.50
411 Glenn Doughty RC	.25	.60
412 Altie Taylor	.25	.60
413 Marv Bateman RC	.25	.60
414 Willie Alexander	.25	.60
415 Bill Zapalac RC	.25	.60
416 Russ Washington	.25	.60
417 Joe Federspiel RC	.25	.60
418 Craig Cotton RC	.25	.60
419 Randy Johnson	.25	.60
420 Harold Jackson	.60	1.50
421 Roger Wehrli	.40	1.00
422 Charlie Harraway	.25	.60
423 Spike Jones	.25	.60
424 Bob Johnson	.25	.60
425 Mike McCoy DT	.25	.60
426 Dennis Havig RC	.25	.60
427 Bob McKay RC	.25	.60
428 Steve Zabel	.25	.60
429 Horace Jones	.25	.60
430 Jim Johnson	.60	1.50
431 Roy Gerela	.40	1.00
432 Tom Graham RC	.25	.60
433 Curley Culp	.40	1.00
434 Ken Mendenhall RC	.25	.60
435 Jim Plunkett	1.25	2.50
436 Julian Fagan	.25	.60
437 Mike Garrett	.40	1.00
438 Bobby Joe Green	.25	.60
439 Jack Gregory	.25	.60
440 Charlie Sanders	.40	1.00
441 Bill Curry	.40	1.00
442 Bob Pollard RC	.25	.60
443 David Ray	.25	.60
444 Terry Metcalf RC	1.50	3.00
445 Pat Fischer	.40	1.00
446 Bob Chandler	.40	1.00
447 Bill Bergey	.40	1.00
448 Walter Johnson	.25	.60
449 Charle Young RC	.60	1.50
450 Chester Marcol	.25	.60
451 Ken Stabler	10.00	20.00
452 Preston Pearson	.60	1.50
453 Mike Current	.25	.60
454 Ron Bolton RC	.25	.60
455 Mark Lomas	.25	.60
456 Raymond Chester	.40	1.00
457 Jerry LeVias	.40	1.00
458 Skip Butler RC	.25	.60
459 Mike Livingston RC	.25	.60
460 AFC Semi-Final	.40	1.00
461 NFC Semi/Staubach	2.00	4.00
462 Playoff Champs/Stabler	1.50	3.00
463 SB VIII/L.Csonka	.75	2.00
464 Wayne Mulligan	.25	.60
465 Horst Muhlmann	.25	.60
466 Milt Morin	.25	.60
467 Don Parish RC	.25	.60
468 Richard Neal	.25	.60
469 Ron Jessie	.40	1.00
470 Terry Bradshaw	12.50	25.00
471 Fred Dryer	.60	1.50
472 Jim Carter	.25	.60
473 Ken Burrow	.25	.60
474 Wally Chambers RC	.40	1.00
475 Dan Pastorini	.60	1.50
476 Don Morrison	.25	.60
477 Carl Mauck	.25	.60
478 Larry Cole RC	.40	1.00
479 Jim Kiick	.60	1.50
480 Willie Lanier	.60	1.50
481 Don Herrmann	.40	1.00
482 George Hunt RC	.25	.60
483 Bob Howard RC	.25	.60
484 Myron Pottios	.25	.60
485 Jackie Smith	.60	1.50
486 Vern Holland	.25	.60
487 Jim Braxton	.25	.60
488 Joe Reed RC	.25	.60
489 Wally Hilgenberg	.25	.60
490 Fred Biletnikoff	2.00	4.00
491 Bob DeMarco	.25	.60
492 Mark Nordquist	.25	.60
493 Larry Brooks RC	.25	.60

❑ 494 Pete Athas .25 .60
❑ 495 Emerson Boozer .40 1.00
❑ 496 L.C.Greenwood .75 2.00
❑ 497 Rockne Freitas .25 .60
❑ 498 Checklist 397-528 UER 2.00 4.00
❑ 499 Joe Schmiesing RC .25 .60
❑ 500 Roger Staubach 12.50 25.00
❑ 501 Al Cowlings UER .40 1.00
❑ 502 Sam Cunningham RC .60 1.50
❑ 503 Dennis Partee .25 .60
❑ 504 John Didion .25 .60
❑ 505 Nick Buoniconti .60 1.50
❑ 506 Carl Garrett .40 1.00
❑ 507 Doug Van Horn .25 .60
❑ 508 Jamie Rivers RC .25 .60
❑ 509 Jack Youngblood 2.00 4.00
❑ 510 Charley Taylor UER 1.25 2.50
❑ 511 Ken Riley .60 1.50
❑ 512 Joe Ferguson RC 1.25 3.00
❑ 513 Bill Lueck RC .25 .60
❑ 514 Ray Brown DB RC .25 .60
❑ 515 Fred Cox .25 .60
❑ 516 Joe Jones DE .25 .60
❑ 517 Larry Schreiber RC .25 .60
❑ 518 Dennis Wirgowski .25 .60
❑ 519 Leroy Mitchell .25 .60
❑ 520 Otis Taylor .60 1.50
❑ 521 Henry Davis .25 .60
❑ 522 Bruce Barnes RC .25 .60
❑ 523 Charlie Smith RB .25 .60
❑ 524 Bert Jones RC 2.00 5.00
❑ 525 Lem Barney .75 2.00
❑ 526 John Fitzgerald RC .25 .60
❑ 527 Tom Funchess .25 .60
❑ 528 Steve Tannen .60 1.50

1975 Topps

❑ COMPLETE SET (528) 175.00 300.00
❑ 1 McCutcheon/Armstrong LL .60 1.50
❑ 2 Jurgensen/K.Anderson LL .60 1.50
❑ 3 Receiving Leaders .60 1.50
❑ 4 Scoring Leaders .30 .75
❑ 5 Interception Leaders .30 .75
❑ 6 Punting Leaders .60 1.50
❑ 7 George Blanda HL 2.50 5.00
❑ 8 George Blanda 2.50 5.00
❑ 9 Ralph Baker .20 .50
❑ 10 Don Woods RC .20 .50
❑ 11 Bob Asher .20 .50
❑ 12 Mel Blount RC 10.00 20.00
❑ 13 Sam Cunningham .30 .75
❑ 14 Jackie Smith .60 1.50
❑ 15 Greg Landry .30 .75
❑ 16 Buck Buchanan .60 1.50
❑ 17 Haven Moses .30 .75
❑ 18 Clarence Ellis .20 .50
❑ 19 Jim Carter .20 .50
❑ 20 Charley Taylor UER .75 2.00
❑ 21 Jess Phillips .20 .50
❑ 22 Larry Seiple .20 .50
❑ 23 Doug Dieken .20 .50
❑ 24 Ron Saul .20 .50
❑ 25 Isaac Curtis .60 1.50
❑ 26 Gary Larsen RC .20 .50
❑ 27 Bruce Jarvis .20 .50
❑ 28 Steve Zabel .20 .50
❑ 29 John Mendenhall .20 .50
❑ 30 Rick Volk .20 .50
❑ 31 Checklist 1-132 2.00 4.00
❑ 32 Dan Abramowicz .30 .75
❑ 33 Bubba Smith .60 1.50
❑ 34 David Ray .20 .50
❑ 35 Dan Dierdorf 2.00 4.00
❑ 36 Randy Rasmussen .20 .50
❑ 37 Bob Howard .20 .50
❑ 38 Gary Huff .30 .75
❑ 39 Rocky Bleier RC 10.00 20.00
❑ 40 Mel Gray .30 .75
❑ 41 Tony McGee DT .20 .50
❑ 42 Larry Hand .20 .50
❑ 43 Wendell Hayes .20 .50
❑ 44 Doug Wilkerson RC .20 .50
❑ 45 Paul Smith .20 .50
❑ 46 Dave Robinson .30 .75
❑ 47 Bivian Lee .20 .50
❑ 48 Jim Mandich RC .30 .75
❑ 49 Greg Pruitt .60 1.50
❑ 50 Dan Pastorini .60 1.50
❑ 51 Ron Pritchard RC .20 .50
❑ 52 Dan Conners .20 .50
❑ 53 Fred Cox .20 .50
❑ 54 Tony Greene RC .20 .50
❑ 55 Craig Morton .60 1.50
❑ 56 Jerry Sisemore .20 .50
❑ 57 Glenn Doughty .20 .50
❑ 58 Larry Schreiber .20 .50
❑ 59 Charlie Waters RC 2.00 4.00
❑ 60 Jack Youngblood .60 1.50
❑ 61 Bill Lenkaitis .20 .50
❑ 62 Greg Brezina .20 .50
❑ 63 Bob Pollard .20 .50
❑ 64 Mack Alston .20 .50
❑ 65 Drew Pearson RC 10.00 20.00
❑ 66 Charlie Stukes .20 .50
❑ 67 Emerson Boozer .30 .75
❑ 68 Dennis Partee .20 .50
❑ 69 Bob Newton .20 .50
❑ 70 Jack Tatum .60 1.50
❑ 71 Frank Lewis .20 .50
❑ 72 Bob Young RC .20 .50
❑ 73 Julius Adams .20 .50
❑ 74 Paul Naumoff .20 .50
❑ 75 Otis Taylor .60 1.50
❑ 76 Dave Hampton .20 .50
❑ 77 Mike Current .20 .50
❑ 78 Brig Owens .20 .50
❑ 79 Bobby Scott RC .20 .50
❑ 80 Harold Carmichael 1.50 3.00
❑ 81 Bill Stanfill .20 .50
❑ 82 Bob Babich .20 .50
❑ 83 Vic Washington .20 .50
❑ 84 Mick Tingelhoff .30 .75
❑ 85 Bob Trumpy .60 1.50
❑ 86 Earl Edwards RC .20 .50
❑ 87 Ron Hornsby .20 .50
❑ 88 Don McCauley .20 .50
❑ 89 Jim Johnson .60 1.50
❑ 90 Andy Russell .30 .75
❑ 91 Cornell Green .60 1.50
❑ 92 Charlie Cowan .20 .50
❑ 93 Jon Staggers .20 .50
❑ 94 Billy Newsome .20 .50
❑ 95 Willie Brown .60 1.50
❑ 96 Carl Mauck .20 .50
❑ 97 Doug Buffone .20 .50
❑ 98 Preston Pearson .30 .75
❑ 99 Jim Bakken .20 .50
❑ 100 Bob Griese 2.50 5.00
❑ 101 Bob Windsor .20 .50
❑ 102 Rockne Freitas .20 .50
❑ 103 Jim Marsalis .20 .50
❑ 104 Bill Thompson .30 .75
❑ 105 Ken Burrow .20 .50
❑ 106 Diron Talbert .20 .50
❑ 107 Joe Federspiel .20 .50
❑ 108 Norm Bulaich .30 .75
❑ 109 Bob DeMarco .20 .50
❑ 110 Tom Wittum RC .20 .50
❑ 111 Larry Hefner RC .20 .50
❑ 112 Tody Smith .20 .50
❑ 113 Stu Voigt .20 .50
❑ 114 Horst Muhlmann .20 .50
❑ 115 Ahmad Rashad 3.00 6.00
❑ 116 Joe Dawkins .20 .50
❑ 117 George Kunz .20 .50
❑ 118 D.D.Lewis .30 .75
❑ 119 Levi Johnson .20 .50
❑ 120 Len Dawson 2.00 4.00
❑ 121 Jim Bertelsen .20 .50
❑ 122 Ed Bell .20 .50
❑ 123 Art Thoms .20 .50
❑ 124 Joe Beauchamp .20 .50
❑ 125 Jack Ham 3.00 6.00
❑ 126 Carl Garrett .20 .50
❑ 127 Roger Finnie RC .20 .50
❑ 128 Howard Twilley .30 .75
❑ 129 Bruce Barnes .20 .50
❑ 130 Nate Wright RC .20 .50
❑ 131 Jerry Tagge .20 .50
❑ 132 Floyd Little .60 1.50
❑ 133 John Zook .20 .50
❑ 134 Len Hauss .20 .50
❑ 135 Archie Manning .60 1.50
❑ 136 Po James .20 .50
❑ 137 Walt Sumner .20 .50
❑ 138 Randy Beisler .20 .50
❑ 139 Willie Alexander .20 .50
❑ 140 Garo Yepremian .30 .75
❑ 141 Chip Myers .20 .50
❑ 142 Jim Braxton .20 .50
❑ 143 Doug Van Horn .20 .50
❑ 144 Stan White RC .20 .50
❑ 145 Roger Staubach 10.00 20.00
❑ 146 Herman Weaver .20 .50
❑ 147 Marvin Upshaw .20 .50
❑ 148 Bob Klein .20 .50
❑ 149 Earlie Thomas .20 .50
❑ 150 John Brockington .30 .75
❑ 151 Mike Siani .20 .50
❑ 152 Sam Davis RC .20 .50
❑ 153 Mike Wagner .30 .75
❑ 154 Larry Stallings .20 .50
❑ 155 Wally Chambers .20 .50
❑ 156 Randy Vataha .20 .50
❑ 157 Jim Marshall .60 1.50
❑ 158 Jim Turner .20 .50
❑ 159 Walt Sweeney .20 .50
❑ 160 Ken Anderson 2.00 4.00
❑ 161 Ray Brown DB .20 .50
❑ 162 John Didion .20 .50
❑ 163 Tom Dempsey .20 .50
❑ 164 Clarence Scott .20 .50
❑ 165 Gene Washington 49er .30 .75
❑ 166 Willie Rodgers RC .20 .50
❑ 167 Doug Swift .20 .50
❑ 168 Rufus Mayes .20 .50
❑ 169 Marv Bateman .20 .50
❑ 170 Lydell Mitchell .30 .75
❑ 171 Ron Smith .20 .50
❑ 172 Bill Munson .30 .75
❑ 173 Bob Grim .20 .50
❑ 174 Ed Budde .20 .50
❑ 175 Bob Lilly UER 2.00 4.00
❑ 176 Jim Youngblood RC .60 1.50
❑ 177 Steve Tannen .20 .50
❑ 178 Rich McGeorge .20 .50
❑ 179 Jim Tyrer .20 .50
❑ 180 Forrest Blue .20 .50
❑ 181 Jerry LeVias .30 .75
❑ 182 Joe Gilliam RC .60 1.50
❑ 183 Jim Otis RC .30 .75
❑ 184 Mel Tom .20 .50
❑ 185 Paul Seymour .20 .50
❑ 186 George Webster .20 .50
❑ 187 Pete Duranko .20 .50
❑ 188 Essex Johnson .20 .50
❑ 189 Bob Lee .30 .75
❑ 190 Gene Upshaw .60 1.50
❑ 191 Tom Myers .20 .50
❑ 192 Don Zimmerman .20 .50
❑ 193 John Garlington .20 .50
❑ 194 Skip Butler .20 .50
❑ 195 Tom Mitchell .20 .50
❑ 196 Jim Langer .60 1.50
❑ 197 Ron Carpenter .20 .50
❑ 198 Dave Foley .20 .50
❑ 199 Bert Jones .60 1.50
❑ 200 Larry Brown .30 .75
❑ 201 Biletnikoff/C.Taylor AP .75 2.00
❑ 202 All Pro Tackles .20 .50
❑ 203 L.Little/T.Mack AP .60 1.50
❑ 204 All Pro Centers .20 .50
❑ 205 Hannah/Gillingham AP .60 1.50
❑ 206 Dan Dierdorf/W.Hill AP .60 1.50
❑ 207 All Pro Tight Ends .30 .75
❑ 208 F.Tarkenton/Stabler AP 2.00 4.00
❑ 209 Simpson/McCutch. AP 1.50 3.00
❑ 210 All Pro Backs .30 .75
❑ 211 All Pro Receivers .30 .75
❑ 212 All Pro Kickers .20 .50
❑ 213 Youngblood/Bethea AP .60 1.50
❑ 214 All Pro Tackles .30 .75
❑ 215 M.Olsen/M.Reid AP .60 1.50
❑ 216 Carl Eller/L.Alzado AP .60 1.50

❑ 217 Hendricks/Villapiano AP .60 1.50
❑ 218 Willie Lanier/Jordan AP .60 1.50
❑ 219 All Pro Linebackers .30 .75
❑ 220 All Pro Cornerbacks .20 .50
❑ 221 All Pro Cornerbacks .20 .50
❑ 222 K.Houston/D.Anderson AP .30 .75
❑ 223 Cliff Harris/J.Tatum AP .60 1.50
❑ 224 All Pro Punters .30 .75
❑ 225 All Pro Returners .30 .75
❑ 226 Ted Kwalick .20 .50
❑ 227 Spider Lockhart .30 .75
❑ 228 Mike Livingston .20 .50
❑ 229 Larry Cole .20 .50
❑ 230 Gary Garrison .20 .50
❑ 231 Larry Brooks .20 .50
❑ 232 Bobby Howfield .20 .50
❑ 233 Fred Carr .20 .50
❑ 234 Norm Evans .20 .50
❑ 235 Dwight White .30 .75
❑ 236 Conrad Dobler .30 .75
❑ 237 Garry Lyle .20 .50
❑ 238 Darryl Stingley .60 1.50
❑ 239 Tom Graham .20 .50
❑ 240 Chuck Foreman .60 1.50
❑ 241 Ken Riley .30 .75
❑ 242 Don Morrison .20 .50
❑ 243 Lynn Dickey .30 .75
❑ 244 Don Cockroft .20 .50
❑ 245 Claude Humphrey .30 .75
❑ 246 John Skorupan .20 .50
❑ 247 Raymond Chester .30 .75
❑ 248 Cas Banaszek .20 .50
❑ 249 Art Malone .20 .50
❑ 250 Ed Flanagan .20 .50
❑ 251 Checklist 133-264 2.00 4.00
❑ 252 Nemiah Wilson .20 .50
❑ 253 Ron Jessie .20 .50
❑ 254 Jim Lynch .20 .50
❑ 255 Bob Tucker .30 .75
❑ 256 Terry Owens .20 .50
❑ 257 John Fitzgerald .20 .50
❑ 258 Jack Snow .30 .75
❑ 259 Garry Puetz RC .20 .50
❑ 260 Mike Phipps .30 .75
❑ 261 Al Matthews .20 .50
❑ 262 Bob Kuechenberg .20 .50
❑ 263 Ron Yankowski .20 .50
❑ 264 Ron Shanklin .20 .50
❑ 265 Bobby Douglass .30 .75
❑ 266 Josh Ashton .20 .50
❑ 267 Bill Van Heusen .20 .50
❑ 268 Jeff Siemon .20 .50
❑ 269 Bob Newland .20 .50
❑ 270 Gale Gillingham .20 .50
❑ 271 Zeke Moore .20 .50
❑ 272 Mike Tilleman .20 .50
❑ 273 John Leypoldt .20 .50
❑ 274 Ken Mendenhall .20 .50
❑ 275 Norm Snead .30 .75
❑ 276 Bill Bradley .30 .75
❑ 277 Jerry Smith .20 .50
❑ 278 Clarence Davis RC .20 .50
❑ 279 Jim Yarbrough .20 .50
❑ 280 Lemar Parrish .20 .50
❑ 281 Bobby Bell .60 1.50
❑ 282 Lynn Swann UER RC 30.00 60.00
❑ 283 John Hicks RC .20 .50
❑ 284 Coy Bacon .30 .75
❑ 285 Lee Roy Jordan .60 1.50
❑ 286 Willie Buchanon .20 .50
❑ 287 Al Woodall .20 .50
❑ 288 Reggie Rucker .30 .75
❑ 289 John Schmitt .20 .50
❑ 290 Carl Eller .60 1.50
❑ 291 Jake Scott .30 .75
❑ 292 Donny Anderson .30 .75
❑ 293 Charley Wade RC .20 .50
❑ 294 John Tanner RC .20 .50
❑ 295 Charlie Johnson .30 .75
❑ 296 Tom Blanchard .20 .50
❑ 297 Curley Culp .30 .75
❑ 298 Jeff Van Note RC .30 .75
❑ 299 Bob James .20 .50
❑ 300 Franco Harris 4.00 8.00
❑ 301 Tim Berra RC .30 .75
❑ 302 Bruce Gossett .20 .50
❑ 303 Verlon Biggs .20 .50
❑ 304 Bob Kowalkowski .20 .50
❑ 305 Marv Hubbard .20 .50
❑ 306 Ken Avery .20 .50
❑ 307 Mike Adamle .20 .50
❑ 308 Don Herrmann .20 .50
❑ 309 Chris Fletcherv RC .20 .50
❑ 310 Roman Gabriel .60 1.50
❑ 311 Billy Joe DuPree .60 1.50
❑ 312 Fred Dryer .60 1.50
❑ 313 John Riggins 2.50 5.00
❑ 314 Bob McKay .20 .50
❑ 315 Ted Hendricks .60 1.50
❑ 316 Bobby Bryant .20 .50
❑ 317 Don Nottingham .20 .50
❑ 318 John Hannah 2.00 4.00
❑ 319 Rich Coady .20 .50
❑ 320 Phil Villapiano .30 .75
❑ 321 Jim Plunkett .60 1.50
❑ 322 Lyle Alzado .60 1.50
❑ 323 Ernie Jackson .20 .50
❑ 324 Billy Parks .20 .50
❑ 325 Willie Lanier .60 1.50
❑ 326 John James .20 .50
❑ 327 Joe Ferguson .30 .75
❑ 328 Ernie Holmes RC .60 1.50
❑ 329 Bruce Laird .20 .50
❑ 330 Chester Marcol .20 .50
❑ 331 Dave Wilcox .60 1.50
❑ 332 Pat Fischer .30 .75
❑ 333 Steve Owens .30 .75
❑ 334 Royce Berry .20 .50
❑ 335 Russ Washington .20 .50
❑ 336 Walker Gillette .20 .50
❑ 337 Mark Nordquist .20 .50
❑ 338 James Harris RC 1.00 2.50
❑ 339 Warren Koegel RC .20 .50
❑ 340 Emmitt Thomas .30 .75
❑ 341 Walt Garrison .30 .75
❑ 342 Thom Darden .20 .50
❑ 343 Mike Eischeid .20 .50
❑ 344 Ernie McMillan .20 .50
❑ 345 Nick Buoniconti .60 1.50
❑ 346 George Farmer .20 .50
❑ 347 Sam Adams OL .20 .50
❑ 348 Larry Cipa RC .20 .50
❑ 349 Bob Moore .20 .50
❑ 350 Otis Armstrong RC .60 1.50
❑ 351 George Blanda RB 1.50 3.00
❑ 352 Fred Cox RB .30 .75
❑ 353 Tom Dempsey RB .30 .75
❑ 354 Ken Houston RB .60 1.50
❑ 355 O.J.Simpson RB 2.50 5.00
❑ 356 Ron Smith RB .30 .75
❑ 357 Bob Atkins .20 .50
❑ 358 Pat Sullivan .30 .75
❑ 359 Joe DeLamielleure 1.00 2.50
❑ 360 Lawrence McCutcheon RC .60 1.50
❑ 361 David Lee .20 .50
❑ 362 Mike McCoy DT .20 .50
❑ 363 Skip Vanderbundt .20 .50
❑ 364 Mark Moseley .30 .75
❑ 365 Lem Barney .60 1.50
❑ 366 Doug Dressler .20 .50
❑ 367 Dan Fouts RC 20.00 40.00
❑ 368 Bob Hyland RC .20 .50
❑ 369 John Outlaw .20 .50
❑ 370 Roy Gerela .20 .50
❑ 371 Isiah Robertson .30 .75
❑ 372 Jerome Barkum .20 .50
❑ 373 Ed Podolak .20 .50
❑ 374 Milt Morin .20 .50
❑ 375 John Niland .20 .50
❑ 376 Checklist 265-396 UER 2.00 4.00
❑ 377 Ken Iman .20 .50
❑ 378 Manny Fernandez .30 .75
❑ 379 Dave Gallagher RC .20 .50
❑ 380 Ken Stabler 7.50 15.00
❑ 381 Mack Herron RC .20 .50
❑ 382 Bill McClard RC .20 .50
❑ 383 Ray May .20 .50
❑ 384 Don Hansen .20 .50
❑ 385 Elvin Bethea .60 1.50
❑ 386 Joe Scibelli .20 .50
❑ 387 Neal Craig RC .20 .50
❑ 388 Marty Domres .20 .50
❑ 389 Ken Ellis .20 .50
❑ 390 Charle Young .30 .75
❑ 391 Tommy Hart .20 .50
❑ 392 Moses Denson RC .20 .50
❑ 393 Larry Walton .20 .50
❑ 394 Dave Green RC .20 .50
❑ 395 Ron Johnson .30 .75
❑ 396 Ed Bradley RC .20 .50
❑ 397 J.T. Thomas RC .20 .50
❑ 398 Jim Bailey .20 .50
❑ 399 Barry Pearson .20 .50
❑ 400 Fran Tarkenton 4.00 8.00
❑ 401 Jack Rudnay .20 .50
❑ 402 Rayfield Wright .30 .75
❑ 403 Roger Wehrli .40 1.00
❑ 404 Vern Den Herder .20 .50
❑ 405 Fred Biletnikoff 1.50 3.00
❑ 406 Ken Grandberry RC .20 .50
❑ 407 Bob Adams RC .20 .50
❑ 408 Jim Merlo .20 .50
❑ 409 John Pitts .20 .50
❑ 410 Dave Osborn .30 .75
❑ 411 Dennis Havig .20 .50
❑ 412 Bob Johnson .20 .50
❑ 413 Ken Burrough UER .30 .75
❑ 414 Jim Cheyunski .20 .50
❑ 415 MacArthur Lane .20 .50
❑ 416 Joe Theismann RC 12.50 25.00
❑ 417 Mike Boryla RC .20 .50
❑ 418 Bruce Taylor .20 .50
❑ 419 Chris Hanburger .30 .75
❑ 420 Tom Mack .60 1.50
❑ 421 Errol Mann .20 .50
❑ 422 Jack Gregory .20 .50
❑ 423 Harrison Davis RC .20 .50
❑ 424 Burgess Owens .20 .50
❑ 425 Joe Greene 2.50 5.00
❑ 426 Morris Stroud .20 .50
❑ 427 John DeMarie .20 .50
❑ 428 Mel Renfro .60 1.50
❑ 429 Cid Edwards .20 .50
❑ 430 Mike Reid .60 1.50
❑ 431 Jack Mildren RC .20 .50
❑ 432 Jerry Simmons .20 .50
❑ 433 Ron Yary .60 1.50
❑ 434 Howard Stevens RC .20 .50
❑ 435 Ray Guy .75 2.00
❑ 436 Tommy Nobis .60 1.50
❑ 437 Solomon Freelon .20 .50
❑ 438 J.D. Hill .30 .75
❑ 439 Toni Linhart RC .20 .50
❑ 440 Dick Anderson .30 .75
❑ 441 Guy Morriss RC .20 .50
❑ 442 Bob Hoskins .20 .50
❑ 443 John Hadl .60 1.50
❑ 444 Roy Jefferson .20 .50
❑ 445 Charlie Sanders .40 1.00
❑ 446 Pat Curran RC .20 .50
❑ 447 David Knight RC .20 .50
❑ 448 Bob Brown DT .20 .50
❑ 449 Pete Gogolak .20 .50
❑ 450 Terry Metcalf .60 1.50
❑ 451 Bill Bergey .60 1.50
❑ 452 Dan Abramowicz HL .30 .75
❑ 453 Otis Armstrong HL .30 .75
❑ 454 Cliff Branch HL .60 1.50
❑ 455 John James HL .20 .50
❑ 456 Lydell Mitchell HL .30 .75
❑ 457 Lemar Parrish HL .30 .75
❑ 458 Ken Stabler HL 2.50 5.00
❑ 459 Lynn Swann HL 4.00 8.00
❑ 460 Emmitt Thomas HL .20 .50
❑ 461 Terry Bradshaw 10.00 20.00
❑ 462 Jerrel Wilson .20 .50
❑ 463 Walter Johnson .20 .50
❑ 464 Golden Richards RC .30 .75
❑ 465 Tommy Casanova .30 .75
❑ 466 Randy Jackson .20 .50
❑ 467 Ron Bolton .20 .50
❑ 468 Joe Owens .20 .50
❑ 469 Wally Hilgenberg .20 .50
❑ 470 Riley Odoms .30 .75
❑ 471 Otis Sistrunk .30 .75
❑ 472 Eddie Ray RC .20 .50
❑ 473 Reggie McKenzie .30 .75
❑ 474 Elbert Drungo .20 .50
❑ 475 Mercury Morris .60 1.50
❑ 476 Dan Dickel RC .20 .50
❑ 477 Merritt Kersey RC .20 .50
❑ 478 Mike Holmes RC .20 .50
❑ 479 Clarence Williams .20 .50
❑ 480 Billy Kilmer .60 1.50
❑ 481 Altie Taylor .20 .50
❑ 482 Dave Elmendorf .20 .50
❑ 483 Bob Rowe .20 .50

Card		
❑ 484 Pete Athas	.20	.50
❑ 485 Winston Hill	.20	.50
❑ 486 Bo Matthews RC	.20	.50
❑ 487 Earl Thomas RC	.20	.50
❑ 488 Jan Stenerud	.60	1.50
❑ 489 Steve Holden RC	.20	.50
❑ 490 Cliff Harris RC	3.00	6.00
❑ 491 Boobie Clark RC	.30	.75
❑ 492 Joe Taylor	.20	.50
❑ 493 Tom Neville	.20	.50
❑ 494 Wayne Colman	.20	.50
❑ 495 Jim Mitchell TE	.20	.50
❑ 496 Paul Krause	.60	1.50
❑ 497 Jim Otto	.60	1.50
❑ 498 John Rowser	.20	.50
❑ 499 Larry Little	.60	1.50
❑ 500 O.J.Simpson	5.00	10.00
❑ 501 John Dutton RC	.60	1.50
❑ 502 Pat Hughes	.20	.50
❑ 503 Malcolm Snider	.20	.50
❑ 504 Fred Willis	.20	.50
❑ 505 Harold Jackson	.60	1.50
❑ 506 Mike Bragg	.20	.50
❑ 507 Jerry Sherk	.30	.75
❑ 508 Mirro Roder RC	.20	.50
❑ 509 Tom Sullivan RC	.20	.60
❑ 510 Jim Hart	.60	1.50
❑ 511 Cedrick Hardman	.20	.50
❑ 512 Blaine Nye	.20	.50
❑ 513 Elmo Wright	.20	.50
❑ 514 Herb Orvis RC	.20	.50
❑ 515 Richard Caster	.30	.75
❑ 516 Doug Kotar RC	.20	.50
❑ 517 Checklist 397-528	2.00	4.00
❑ 518 Jesse Freitas RC	.20	.50
❑ 519 Ken Houston	.60	1.50
❑ 520 Alan Page	.60	1.50
❑ 521 Tim Foley	.30	.75
❑ 522 Bill Olds RC	.20	.50
❑ 523 Bobby Maples	.20	.50
❑ 524 Cliff Branch RC	7.50	15.00
❑ 525 Merlin Olsen	.60	1.50
❑ 526 AFC Champs/Brad./Harris	2.00	4.00
❑ 527 NFC Champs/Foreman	.60	1.50
❑ 528 Super Bowl IX/Bradshaw	2.50	5.00

1976 Topps

Card		
❑ COMPLETE SET (528)	200.00	350.00
❑ 1 George Blanda RB !	2.50	5.00
❑ 2 Neal Colzie RB	.30	.75
❑ 3 Chuck Foreman RB	.30	.75
❑ 4 Jim Marshall RB	.30	.75
❑ 5 Terry Metcalf RB	.30	.75
❑ 6 O.J.Simpson RB	1.50	3.00
❑ 7 Fran Tarkenton RB	1.50	3.00
❑ 8 Charley Taylor RB	.60	1.50
❑ 9 Ernie Holmes	.30	.75
❑ 10 Ken Anderson	.60	1.50
❑ 11 Bobby Bryant	.20	.50
❑ 12 Jerry Smith	.30	.75
❑ 13 David Lee	.20	.50
❑ 14 Robert Newhouse RC	.60	1.50
❑ 15 Vern Den Herder	.20	.50
❑ 16 John Hannah	.60	1.50
❑ 17 J.D. Hill	.30	.75
❑ 18 James Harris	.30	.75
❑ 19 Willie Buchanon	.20	.50
❑ 20 Charlie Young	.30	.75
❑ 21 Jim Yarbrough	.20	.50
❑ 22 Ronnie Coleman RC	.20	.50
❑ 23 Don Cockroft	.20	.50
❑ 24 Willie Lanier	.60	1.50
❑ 25 Fred Biletnikoff	1.50	3.00
❑ 26 Ron Yankowski	.20	.50
❑ 27 Spider Lockhart	.20	.50
❑ 28 Bob Johnson	.20	.50
❑ 29 J.T. Thomas	.20	.50
❑ 30 Ron Yary	.60	1.50
❑ 31 Brad Dusek RC	.20	.50
❑ 32 Raymond Chester	.30	.75
❑ 33 Larry Little	.60	1.50
❑ 34 Pat Leahy RC	.60	1.50
❑ 35 Steve Bartkowski RC	2.00	4.00
❑ 36 Tom Myers	.20	.50
❑ 37 Bill Van Heusen	.20	.50
❑ 38 Russ Washington	.20	.50
❑ 39 Tom Sullivan	.20	.50
❑ 40 Curley Culp	.30	.75
❑ 41 Johnnie Gray RC	.20	.50
❑ 42 Bob Klein	.20	.50
❑ 43 Lem Barney	.60	1.50
❑ 44 Harvey Martin RC	3.00	6.00
❑ 45 Reggie Rucker	.30	.75
❑ 46 Neil Clabo RC	.20	.50
❑ 47 Ray Hamilton RC	.20	.50
❑ 48 Joe Ferguson	.30	.75
❑ 49 Ed Podolak	.20	.50
❑ 50 Ray Guy	.60	1.50
❑ 51 Glen Edwards	.20	.50
❑ 52 Jim LeClair RC	.20	.50
❑ 53 Mike Barnes RC	.20	.50
❑ 54 Nat Moore RC	.60	1.50
❑ 55 Billy Kilmer	.60	1.50
❑ 56 Larry Stallings	.20	.50
❑ 57 Jack Gregory	.20	.50
❑ 58 Steve Mike-Mayer RC	.20	.50
❑ 59 Virgil Livers RC	.20	.50
❑ 60 Jerry Sherk	.30	.75
❑ 61 Guy Morriss	.20	.50
❑ 62 Barty Smith	.20	.50
❑ 63 Jerome Barkum	.20	.50
❑ 64 Ira Gordon RC	.20	.50
❑ 65 Paul Krause	.60	1.50
❑ 66 John McMakin	.20	.50
❑ 67 Checklist 1-132	1.50	3.00
❑ 68 Charlie Johnson UER	.30	.75
❑ 69 Tommy Nobis	.60	1.50
❑ 70 Lydell Mitchell	.30	.75
❑ 71 Vern Holland	.20	.50
❑ 72 Tim Foley	.30	.75
❑ 73 Golden Richards	.30	.75
❑ 74 Bryant Salter	.20	.50
❑ 75 Terry Bradshaw	10.00	20.00
❑ 76 Ted Hendricks	.60	1.50
❑ 77 Rich Saul RC	.20	.50
❑ 78 John Smith RC	.20	.50
❑ 79 Altie Taylor	.20	.50
❑ 80 Cedrick Hardman	.20	.50
❑ 81 Ken Payne RC	.20	.50
❑ 82 Zeke Moore	.20	.50
❑ 83 Alvin Maxson RC	.20	.50
❑ 84 Wally Hilgenberg	.20	.50
❑ 85 John Niland	.20	.50
❑ 86 Mike Sensibaugh	.20	.50
❑ 87 Ron Johnson	.30	.75
❑ 88 Winston Hill	.20	.50
❑ 89 Charlie Joiner	2.00	4.00
❑ 90 Roger Wehrli	.30	.75
❑ 91 Mike Bragg	.20	.50
❑ 92 Dan Dickel	.20	.50
❑ 93 Earl Morrall	.30	.75
❑ 94 Pat Toomay	.20	.50
❑ 95 Gary Garrison	.20	.50
❑ 96 Ken Geddes RC	.20	.50
❑ 97 Mike Current	.20	.50
❑ 98 Bob Avellini RC	.30	.75
❑ 99 Dave Pureifory RC	.20	.50
❑ 100 Franco Harris	4.00	8.00
❑ 101 Randy Logan RC	.20	.50
❑ 102 John Fitzgerald	.20	.50
❑ 103 Gregg Bingham RC	.30	.75
❑ 104 Jim Plunkett	.60	1.50
❑ 105 Carl Eller	.60	1.50
❑ 106 Larry Walton	.20	.50
❑ 107 Clarence Scott	.20	.50
❑ 108 Skip Vanderbundt	.20	.50
❑ 109 Boobie Clark	.30	.75
❑ 110 Tom Mack	.60	1.50
❑ 111 Bruce Laird	.20	.50
❑ 112 Dave Dalby RC	.20	.50
❑ 113 John Leypoldt	.20	.50
❑ 114 Barry Pearson	.20	.50
❑ 115 Larry Brown	.30	.75
❑ 116 Jackie Smith	.60	1.50
❑ 117 Pat Hughes	.20	.50
❑ 118 Al Woodall	.20	.50
❑ 119 John Zook	.20	.50
❑ 120 Jake Scott	.30	.75
❑ 121 Rich Glover RC	.20	.50
❑ 122 Ernie Jackson	.20	.50
❑ 123 Otis Armstrong	.60	1.50
❑ 124 Bob Grim	.20	.50
❑ 125 Jeff Siemon	.30	.75
❑ 126 Harold Hart RC	.20	.50
❑ 127 John DeMarie	.20	.50
❑ 128 Dan Fouts	6.00	12.00
❑ 129 Jim Kearney	.20	.50
❑ 130 John Dutton	.30	.75
❑ 131 Calvin Hill	.60	1.50
❑ 132 Toni Fritsch	.20	.50
❑ 133 Ron Jessie	.20	.50
❑ 134 Don Nottingham	.20	.50
❑ 135 Lemar Parrish	.20	.50
❑ 136 Russ Francis RC	.60	1.50
❑ 137 Joe Reed	.20	.50
❑ 138 C.L. Whittington RC	.20	.50
❑ 139 Otis Sistrunk	.30	.75
❑ 140 Lynn Swann	10.00	20.00
❑ 141 Jim Carter	.20	.50
❑ 142 Mike Montler	.20	.50
❑ 143 Walter Johnson	.20	.50
❑ 144 Doug Kotar	.20	.50
❑ 145 Roman Gabriel	.60	1.50
❑ 146 Billy Newsome	.20	.50
❑ 147 Ed Bradley	.20	.50
❑ 148 Walter Payton RC	125.00	250.00
❑ 149 Johnny Fuller	.20	.50
❑ 150 Alan Page	.60	1.50
❑ 151 Frank Grant RC	.20	.50
❑ 152 Dave Green	.20	.50
❑ 153 Nelson Munsey RC	.20	.50
❑ 154 Jim Mandich	.20	.50
❑ 155 Lawrence McCutcheon	.60	1.50
❑ 156 Steve Ramsey	.20	.50
❑ 157 Ed Flanagan	.20	.50
❑ 158 Randy White RC	10.00	20.00
❑ 159 Gerry Mullins	.20	.50
❑ 160 Jan Stenerud	.60	1.50
❑ 161 Steve Odom RC	.20	.50
❑ 162 Roger Finnie	.20	.50
❑ 163 Norm Snead	.30	.75
❑ 164 Jeff Van Note	.30	.75
❑ 165 Bill Bergey	.60	1.50
❑ 166 Allen Carter RC	.20	.50
❑ 167 Steve Holden	.20	.50
❑ 168 Sherman White	.20	.50
❑ 169 Bob Berry	.20	.50
❑ 170 Ken Houston	.60	1.50
❑ 171 Bill Olds	.20	.50
❑ 172 Larry Seiple	.20	.50
❑ 173 Cliff Branch	2.00	4.00
❑ 174 Reggie McKenzie	.30	.75
❑ 175 Dan Pastorini	.60	1.50
❑ 176 Paul Naumoff	.20	.50
❑ 177 Checklist 133-264	1.50	3.00
❑ 178 Durwood Keeton RC	.20	.50
❑ 179 Earl Thomas	.20	.50
❑ 180 L.C.Greenwood	.60	1.50
❑ 181 John Outlaw	.20	.50
❑ 182 Frank Nunley	.20	.50
❑ 183 Dave Jennings RC	.30	.75
❑ 184 MacArthur Lane	.20	.50
❑ 185 Chester Marcol	.20	.50
❑ 186 J.J. Jones RC	.20	.50
❑ 187 Tom DeLeone RC	.20	.50
❑ 188 Steve Zabel	.20	.50
❑ 189 Ken Johnson DT RC	.20	.50
❑ 190 Rayfield Wright	.30	.75
❑ 191 Brent McClanahan RC	.20	.50
❑ 192 Pat Fischer	.30	.75
❑ 193 Roger Carr RC	.30	.75
❑ 194 Manny Fernandez	.30	.75
❑ 195 Roy Gerela	.20	.50
❑ 196 Dave Elmendorf	.20	.50
❑ 197 Bob Kowalkowski	.20	.50
❑ 198 Phil Villapiano	.30	.75
❑ 199 Will Wynn RC	.20	.50
❑ 200 Terry Metcalf	.60	1.50
❑ 201 Tarkenton/Anderson LL	.75	2.00
❑ 202 Receiving Leaders	.30	.75
❑ 203 O.J.Simpson/J.Otis LL	1.25	2.50
❑ 204 Simpson/Foreman LL	1.25	2.50
❑ 205 M.Blount/P.Krause LL	.60	1.50
❑ 206 Punting Leaders	.30	.75

Card		
❑ 207 Ken Ellis	.20	.50
❑ 208 Ron Saul	.20	.50
❑ 209 Toni Linhart	.20	.50
❑ 210 Jim Langer	.60	1.50
❑ 211 Jeff Wright S RC	.20	.50
❑ 212 Moses Denson	.20	.50
❑ 213 Earl Edwards	.20	.50
❑ 214 Walker Gillette	.20	.50
❑ 215 Bob Trumpy	.30	.75
❑ 216 Emmitt Thomas	.30	.75
❑ 217 Lyle Alzado	.60	1.50
❑ 218 Carl Garrett	.30	.75
❑ 219 Van Green RC	.20	.50
❑ 220 Jack Lambert RC	20.00	35.00
❑ 221 Spike Jones	.20	.50
❑ 222 John Hadl	.60	1.50
❑ 223 Billy Johnson RC	.60	1.50
❑ 224 Tony McGee DT	.20	.50
❑ 225 Preston Pearson	.30	.75
❑ 226 Isiah Robertson	.30	.75
❑ 227 Errol Mann	.20	.50
❑ 228 Paul Seal RC	.20	.50
❑ 229 Roland Harper RC	.20	.50
❑ 230 Ed White RC	.30	.75
❑ 231 Joe Theismann	3.00	6.00
❑ 232 Jim Cheyunski	.20	.50
❑ 233 Bill Stanfill	.30	.75
❑ 234 Marv Hubbard	.20	.50
❑ 235 Tommy Casanova	.30	.75
❑ 236 Bob Hyland	.20	.50
❑ 237 Jesse Freitas	.20	.50
❑ 238 Norm Thompson	.20	.50
❑ 239 Charlie Smith WR	.20	.50
❑ 240 John James	.20	.50
❑ 241 Alden Roche	.20	.50
❑ 242 Gordon Jolley RC	.20	.50
❑ 243 Larry Ely RC	.20	.50
❑ 244 Richard Caster	.20	.50
❑ 245 Joe Greene	2.00	5.00
❑ 246 Larry Schreiber	.20	.50
❑ 247 Terry Schmidt RC	.20	.50
❑ 248 Jerrel Wilson	.20	.50
❑ 249 Marty Domres	.20	.50
❑ 250 Isaac Curtis	.30	.75
❑ 251 Harold McLinton RC	.20	.50
❑ 252 Fred Dryer	.60	1.50
❑ 253 Bill Lenkaitis	.20	.50
❑ 254 Don Hardeman RC	.20	.50
❑ 255 Bob Griese	2.00	4.00
❑ 256 Oscar Roan RC	.20	.50
❑ 257 Randy Gradishar RC	1.50	4.00
❑ 258 Bob Thomas RC	.20	.50
❑ 259 Joe Owens	.20	.50
❑ 260 Cliff Harris	.60	1.50
❑ 261 Frank Lewis	.20	.50
❑ 262 Mike McCoy DT	.20	.50
❑ 263 Rickey Young RC	.20	.50
❑ 264 Brian Kelley RC	.20	.50
❑ 265 Charlie Sanders	.30	.75
❑ 266 Jim Hart	.60	1.50
❑ 267 Greg Gantt RC	.20	.50
❑ 268 John Ward RC	.20	.50
❑ 269 Al Beauchamp	.20	.50
❑ 270 Jack Tatum	.60	1.50
❑ 271 Jim Lash RC	.20	.50
❑ 272 Diron Talbert	.20	.50
❑ 273 Checklist 265-396	1.50	3.00
❑ 274 Steve Spurrier	3.00	8.00
❑ 275 Greg Pruitt	.60	1.50
❑ 276 Jim Mitchell TE	.20	.50
❑ 277 Jack Rudnay	.20	.50
❑ 278 Freddie Solomon RC	.30	.75
❑ 279 Frank LeMaster RC	.20	.50
❑ 280 Wally Chambers	.20	.50
❑ 281 Mike Collier RC	.20	.50
❑ 282 Clarence Williams	.20	.50
❑ 283 Mitch Hoopes RC	.20	.50
❑ 284 Ron Bolton	.20	.50
❑ 285 Harold Jackson	.60	1.50
❑ 286 Greg Landry	.30	.75
❑ 287 Tony Greene	.20	.50
❑ 288 Howard Stevens	.20	.50
❑ 289 Roy Jefferson	.20	.50
❑ 290 Jim Bakken	.20	.50
❑ 291 Doug Sutherland RC	.20	.50
❑ 292 Marvin Cobb RC	.20	.50
❑ 293 Mack Alston	.20	.50
❑ 294 Rod McNeill RC	.20	.50
❑ 295 Gene Upshaw	.60	1.50
❑ 296 Dave Gallagher	.20	.50
❑ 297 Larry Ball RC	.20	.50
❑ 298 Ron Howard RC	.20	.50
❑ 299 Don Strock RC	.60	1.50
❑ 300 O.J.Simpson	4.00	8.00
❑ 301 Ray Mansfield	.20	.50
❑ 302 Larry Marshall RC	.20	.50
❑ 303 Dick Himes RC	.20	.50
❑ 304 Ray Wersching RC	.20	.50
❑ 305 John Riggins	2.00	4.00
❑ 306 Bob Parsons RC	.20	.50
❑ 307 Ray Brown DB	.20	.50
❑ 308 Len Dawson	1.50	3.00
❑ 309 Andy Maurer	.20	.50
❑ 310 Jack Youngblood	.60	1.50
❑ 311 Essex Johnson	.20	.50
❑ 312 Stan White	.20	.50
❑ 313 Drew Pearson	2.00	5.00
❑ 314 Rockne Freitas	.20	.50
❑ 315 Mercury Morris	.60	1.50
❑ 316 Willie Alexander	.20	.50
❑ 317 Paul Warfield	1.50	3.00
❑ 318 Bob Chandler	.30	.75
❑ 319 Bobby Walden	.20	.50
❑ 320 Riley Odoms	.30	.75
❑ 321 Mike Boryla	.20	.50
❑ 322 Bruce Van Dyke	.20	.50
❑ 323 Pete Banaszak	.20	.50
❑ 324 Darryl Stingley	.60	1.50
❑ 325 John Mendenhall	.20	.50
❑ 326 Dan Dierdorf	.75	2.00
❑ 327 Bruce Taylor	.20	.50
❑ 328 Don McCauley	.20	.50
❑ 329 John Reaves UER	.20	.50
❑ 330 Chris Hanburger	.30	.75
❑ 331 NFC Champs/Staubach	1.50	3.00
❑ 332 AFC Champs/F.Harris	.75	2.00
❑ 333 Super Bowl X/Bradshaw	1.25	2.50
❑ 334 Godwin Turk RC	.20	.50
❑ 335 Dick Anderson	.30	.75
❑ 336 Woody Green RC	.20	.50
❑ 337 Pat Curran	.20	.50
❑ 338 Council Rudolph RC	.20	.50
❑ 339 Joe Lavender RC	.20	.50
❑ 340 John Gilliam	.30	.75
❑ 341 Steve Furness RC	.30	.75
❑ 342 D.D. Lewis	.30	.75
❑ 343 Duane Carrell RC	.20	.50
❑ 344 Jon Morris	.20	.50
❑ 345 John Brockington	.30	.75
❑ 346 Mike Phipps	.30	.75
❑ 347 Lyle Blackwood RC	.20	.50
❑ 348 Julius Adams	.20	.50
❑ 349 Terry Hermeling RC	.20	.50
❑ 350 Rolland Lawrence RC	.20	.50
❑ 351 Glenn Doughty	.20	.50
❑ 352 Doug Swift	.20	.50
❑ 353 Mike Strachan RC	.20	.50
❑ 354 Craig Morton	.60	1.50
❑ 355 George Blanda	2.50	5.00
❑ 356 Garry Puetz	.20	.50
❑ 357 Carl Mauck	.20	.50
❑ 358 Walt Patulski	.20	.50
❑ 359 Stu Voigt	.20	.50
❑ 360 Fred Carr	.20	.50
❑ 361 Po James	.20	.50
❑ 362 Otis Taylor	.60	1.50
❑ 363 Jeff West RC	.20	.50
❑ 364 Gary Huff	.30	.75
❑ 365 Dwight White	.30	.75
❑ 366 Dan Ryczek RC	.20	.50
❑ 367 Jon Keyworth RC	.20	.50
❑ 368 Mel Renfro	.60	1.50
❑ 369 Bruce Coslet RC	.60	1.50
❑ 370 Len Hauss	.20	.50
❑ 371 Rick Volk	.20	.50
❑ 372 Howard Twilley	.30	.75
❑ 373 Cullen Bryant RC	.30	.75
❑ 374 Bob Babich	.20	.50
❑ 375 Herman Weaver	.20	.50
❑ 376 Steve Grogan RC	1.25	3.00
❑ 377 Bubba Smith	.60	1.50
❑ 378 Burgess Owens	.20	.50
❑ 379 Al Matthews	.20	.50
❑ 380 Art Shell	.60	1.50
❑ 381 Larry Brown	.20	.50
❑ 382 Horst Muhlmann	.20	.50
❑ 383 Ahmad Rashad	1.25	2.50
❑ 384 Bobby Maples	.20	.50
❑ 385 Jim Marshall	.60	1.50
❑ 386 Joe Dawkins	.20	.50
❑ 387 Dennis Partee	.20	.50
❑ 388 Eddie McMillan RC	.20	.50
❑ 389 Randy Johnson	.20	.50
❑ 390 Bob Kuechenberg	.20	.50
❑ 391 Rufus Mayes	.20	.50
❑ 392 Lloyd Mumphord	.20	.50
❑ 393 Ike Harris RC	.20	.50
❑ 394 Dave Hampton	.20	.50
❑ 395 Roger Staubach	10.00	20.00
❑ 396 Doug Buffone	.20	.50
❑ 397 Howard Fest	.20	.50
❑ 398 Wayne Mulligan	.20	.50
❑ 399 Bill Bradley	.30	.75
❑ 400 Chuck Foreman	.60	1.50
❑ 401 Jack Snow	.30	.75
❑ 402 Bob Howard	.20	.50
❑ 403 John Matuszak	.60	1.50
❑ 404 Bill Munson	.30	.75
❑ 405 Andy Russell	.30	.75
❑ 406 Skip Butler	.20	.50
❑ 407 Hugh McKinnis RC	.20	.50
❑ 408 Bob Penchion RC	.20	.50
❑ 409 Mike Bass	.20	.50
❑ 410 George Kunz	.20	.50
❑ 411 Ron Pritchard	.20	.50
❑ 412 Barry Smith RC	.20	.50
❑ 413 Norm Bulaich	.20	.50
❑ 414 Marv Bateman	.20	.50
❑ 415 Ken Stabler	6.00	12.00
❑ 416 Conrad Dobler	.30	.75
❑ 417 Bob Tucker	.30	.75
❑ 418 Gene Washington 49er	.30	.75
❑ 419 Ed Marinaro	.60	1.50
❑ 420 Jack Ham	2.00	4.00
❑ 421 Jim Turner	.20	.50
❑ 422 Chris Fletcher	.20	.50
❑ 423 Carl Barzilauskas RC	.20	.50
❑ 424 Robert Brazile RC	.60	1.50
❑ 425 Harold Carmichael	.75	2.00
❑ 426 Ron Jaworski RC	2.00	5.00
❑ 427 Ed Too Tall Jones RC	10.00	20.00
❑ 428 Larry McCarren RC	.20	.50
❑ 429 Mike Thomas RC	.20	.50
❑ 430 Joe DeLamielleure	.60	1.50
❑ 431 Tom Blanchard	.20	.50
❑ 432 Ron Carpenter	.20	.50
❑ 433 Levi Johnson	.20	.50
❑ 434 Sam Cunningham	.30	.75
❑ 435 Garo Yepremian	.30	.75
❑ 436 Mike Livingston	.20	.50
❑ 437 Larry Csonka	2.00	4.00
❑ 438 Doug Dieken	.30	.75
❑ 439 Bill Lueck	.20	.50
❑ 440 Tom MacLeod RC	.20	.50
❑ 441 Mick Tingelhoff	.30	.75
❑ 442 Terry Hanratty	.30	.75
❑ 443 Mike Siani	.20	.50
❑ 444 Dwight Harrison	.20	.50
❑ 445 Jim Otis	.30	.75
❑ 446 Jack Reynolds	.30	.75
❑ 447 Jean Fugett RC	.30	.75
❑ 448 Dave Beverly RC	.20	.50
❑ 449 Bernard Jackson RC	.20	.50
❑ 450 Charley Taylor	.75	2.00
❑ 451 Atlanta Falcons CL	.75	2.00
❑ 452 Baltimore Colts CL	.75	2.00
❑ 453 Buffalo Bills CL	.75	2.00
❑ 454 Chicago Bears CL	.75	2.00
❑ 455 Cincinnati Bengals CL	.75	2.00
❑ 456 Cleveland Browns CL	.75	2.00
❑ 457 Dallas Cowboys CL	.75	2.00
❑ 458 Denver Broncos CL UER	.75	2.00
❑ 459 Detroit Lions CL	.75	2.00
❑ 460 Green Bay Packers CL	.75	2.00
❑ 461 Houston Oilers CL	.75	2.00
❑ 462 Kansas City Chiefs CL	.75	2.00
❑ 463 Los Angeles Rams CL	.75	2.00
❑ 464 Miami Dolphins CL	.75	2.00
❑ 465 Minnesota Vikings CL	.75	2.00
❑ 466 New England Patriots CL	.75	2.00
❑ 467 New Orleans Saints CL	.75	2.00
❑ 468 New York Giants CL	.75	2.00
❑ 469 New York Jets CL	.75	2.00
❑ 470 Oakland Raiders CL	.75	2.00
❑ 471 Philadelphia Eagles CL	.75	2.00
❑ 472 Pittsburgh Steelers CL	.75	2.00
❑ 473 St. Louis Cardinals CL	.75	2.00

Card		
❑ 474 San Diego Chargers CL	.75	2.00
❑ 475 San Francisco 49ers CL	.75	2.00
❑ 476 Seattle Seahawks CL	.75	2.00
❑ 477 Tampa Bay Buccaneers CL	.75	2.00
❑ 478 Washington Redskins CL	.75	2.00
❑ 479 Fred Cox	.20	.50
❑ 480 Mel Blount	3.00	6.00
❑ 481 John Bunting RC	.30	.75
❑ 482 Ken Mendenhall	.20	.50
❑ 483 Will Harrell RC	.20	.50
❑ 484 Marlin Briscoe	.20	.50
❑ 485 Archie Manning	.60	1.50
❑ 486 Tody Smith	.20	.50
❑ 487 George Hunt	.20	.50
❑ 488 Roscoe Word RC	.20	.50
❑ 489 Paul Seymour	.20	.50
❑ 490 Lee Roy Jordan	.60	1.50
❑ 491 Chip Myers	.20	.50
❑ 492 Norm Evans	.20	.50
❑ 493 Jim Bertelsen	.20	.50
❑ 494 Mark Moseley	.30	.75
❑ 495 George Buehler RC	.20	.50
❑ 496 Charlie Hall	.20	.50
❑ 497 Marvin Upshaw	.20	.50
❑ 498 Tom Banks RC	.20	.50
❑ 499 Randy Vataha	.20	.50
❑ 500 Fran Tarkenton	3.00	6.00
❑ 501 Mike Wagner	.30	.75
❑ 502 Art Malone	.20	.50
❑ 503 Fred Cook RC	.20	.50
❑ 504 Rich McGeorge	.20	.50
❑ 505 Ken Burrough	.30	.75
❑ 506 Nick Mike-Mayer	.20	.50
❑ 507 Checklist 397-528	1.50	3.00
❑ 508 Steve Owens	.30	.75
❑ 509 Brad Van Pelt RC	.20	.50
❑ 510 Ken Riley	.30	.75
❑ 511 Art Thoms	.20	.50
❑ 512 Ed Bell	.20	.50
❑ 513 Tom Wittum	.20	.50
❑ 514 Jim Braxton	.20	.50
❑ 515 Nick Buoniconti	.60	1.50
❑ 516 Brian Sipe RC	2.50	6.00
❑ 517 Jim Lynch	.20	.50
❑ 518 Prentice McCray RC	.20	.50
❑ 519 Tom Dempsey	.20	.50
❑ 520 Mel Gray	.30	.75
❑ 521 Nate Wright	.20	.50
❑ 522 Rocky Bleier	3.00	6.00
❑ 523 Dennis Johnson RC	.20	.50
❑ 524 Jerry Sisemore	.20	.50
❑ 525 Bert Jones	.20	.50
❑ 526 Perry Smith RC	.20	.50
❑ 527 Blaine Nye	.20	.50
❑ 528 Bob Moore !	.60	1.50

1977 Topps

Card		
❑ COMPLETE SET (528)	125.00	250.00
❑ 1 K.Stabler/J.Harris LL !	1.25	2.50
❑ 2 Drew Pearson/M.Lane LL	.40	1.00
❑ 3 W.Payton/Simpson LL	5.00	10.00
❑ 4 Scoring Leaders	.25	.60
❑ 5 Interception Leaders	.25	.60
❑ 6 Punting Leaders	.15	.40
❑ 7 Mike Phipps	.25	.60
❑ 8 Rick Volk	.15	.40
❑ 9 Steve Furness	.25	.60
❑ 10 Isaac Curtis	.25	.60
❑ 11 Nate Wright	.25	.60
❑ 12 Jean Fugett	.15	.40
❑ 13 Ken Mendenhall	.15	.40
❑ 14 Sam Adams OL	.15	.40
❑ 15 Charlie Waters	.40	1.00
❑ 16 Bill Stanfill	.15	.40
❑ 17 John Holland RC	.15	.40
❑ 18 Pat Haden RC	.75	2.00
❑ 19 Bob Young	.15	.40
❑ 20 Wally Chambers	.15	.40
❑ 21 Lawrence Gaines RC	.15	.40
❑ 22 Larry McCarren	.15	.40
❑ 23 Horst Muhlmann	.15	.40
❑ 24 Phil Villapiano	.25	.60
❑ 25 Greg Pruitt	.25	.60
❑ 26 Ron Howard	.15	.40
❑ 27 Craig Morton	.40	1.00
❑ 28 Rufus Mayes	.15	.40
❑ 29 Lee Roy Selmon UER RC	6.00	12.00
❑ 30 Ed White	.25	.60
❑ 31 Harold McLinton	.15	.40
❑ 32 Glenn Doughty	.15	.40
❑ 33 Bob Kuechenberg	.40	1.00
❑ 34 Duane Carrell	.15	.40
❑ 35 Riley Odoms	.15	.40
❑ 36 Bobby Scott	.15	.40
❑ 37 Nick Mike-Mayer	.15	.40
❑ 38 Bill Lenkaitis	.15	.40
❑ 39 Roland Harper	.25	.60
❑ 40 Tommy Hart	.15	.40
❑ 41 Mike Sensibaugh	.15	.40
❑ 42 Rusty Jackson RC	.15	.40
❑ 43 Levi Johnson	.15	.40
❑ 44 Mike McCoy DT	.15	.40
❑ 45 Roger Staubach	10.00	20.00
❑ 46 Fred Cox	.15	.40
❑ 47 Bob Babich	.15	.40
❑ 48 Reggie McKenzie	.25	.60
❑ 49 Dave Jennings	.15	.40
❑ 50 Mike Haynes RC	4.00	10.00
❑ 51 Larry Brown	.25	.60
❑ 52 Marvin Cobb	.15	.40
❑ 53 Fred Cook	.15	.40
❑ 54 Freddie Solomon	.25	.60
❑ 55 John Riggins	1.25	2.50
❑ 56 John Bunting	.25	.60
❑ 57 Ray Wersching	.25	.60
❑ 58 Mike Livingston	.15	.40
❑ 59 Billy Johnson	.25	.60
❑ 60 Mike Wagner	.15	.40
❑ 61 Waymond Bryant RC	.15	.40
❑ 62 Jim Otis	.25	.60
❑ 63 Ed Galigher RC	.15	.40
❑ 64 Randy Vataha	.15	.40
❑ 65 Jim Zorn RC	2.00	5.00
❑ 66 Jon Keyworth	.15	.40
❑ 67 Checklist 1-132	.75	2.00
❑ 68 Henry Childs RC	.15	.40
❑ 69 Thom Darden	.15	.40
❑ 70 George Kunz	.15	.40
❑ 71 Lenvil Elliott RC	.15	.40
❑ 72 Curtis Johnson RC	.15	.40
❑ 73 Doug Van Horn	.15	.40
❑ 74 Joe Theismann	2.00	4.00
❑ 75 Dwight White	.25	.60
❑ 76 Scott Laidlaw RC	.15	.40
❑ 77 Monte Johnson RC	.15	.40
❑ 78 Dave Beverly	.15	.40
❑ 79 Jim Mitchell TE	.15	.40
❑ 80 Jack Youngblood	.40	1.00
❑ 81 Mel Gray	.25	.60
❑ 82 Dwight Harrison	.15	.40
❑ 83 John Hadl	.25	.60
❑ 84 Matt Blair RC	.40	1.00
❑ 85 Charlie Sanders	.25	.60
❑ 86 Noah Jackson RC	.15	.40
❑ 87 Ed Marinaro	.25	.60
❑ 88 Bob Howard	.15	.40
❑ 89 John McDaniel RC	.15	.40
❑ 90 Dan Dierdorf	.60	1.50
❑ 91 Mark Moseley	.25	.60
❑ 92 Cleo Miller RC	.15	.40
❑ 93 Andre Tillman RC	.15	.40
❑ 94 Bruce Taylor	.15	.40
❑ 95 Bert Jones	.40	1.00
❑ 96 Anthony Davis RC	.40	1.00
❑ 97 Don Goode RC	.15	.40
❑ 98 Ray Rhodes RC	3.00	6.00
❑ 99 Mike Webster RC	6.00	12.00
❑ 100 O.J.Simpson	3.00	6.00
❑ 101 Doug Plank RC	.15	.40
❑ 102 Efren Herrera RC	.25	.60
❑ 103 Charlie Smith WR	.15	.40
❑ 104 Carlos Brown RC	.40	1.00
❑ 105 Jim Marshall	.40	1.00
❑ 106 Paul Naumoff	.15	.40
❑ 107 Walter White RC	.15	.40
❑ 108 John Cappelletti RC	1.25	3.00
❑ 109 Chip Myers	.15	.40
❑ 110 Ken Stabler	5.00	10.00
❑ 111 Joe Ehrmann RC	.15	.40
❑ 112 Rick Engles RC	.15	.40
❑ 113 Jack Dolbin RC	.15	.40
❑ 114 Ron Bolton	.15	.40
❑ 115 Mike Thomas	.15	.40
❑ 116 Mike Fuller RC	.15	.40
❑ 117 John Hill RC	.15	.40
❑ 118 Richard Todd RC	.40	1.00
❑ 119 Duriel Harris RC	.40	1.00
❑ 120 John James	.15	.40
❑ 121 Lionel Antoine RC	.15	.40
❑ 122 John Skorupan	.15	.40
❑ 123 Skip Butler	.15	.40
❑ 124 Bob Tucker	.15	.40
❑ 125 Paul Krause	.40	1.00
❑ 126 Dave Hampton	.15	.40
❑ 127 Tom Wittum	.15	.40
❑ 128 Gary Huff	.25	.60
❑ 129 Emmitt Thomas	.25	.60
❑ 130 Drew Pearson	.75	2.00
❑ 131 Ron Saul	.15	.40
❑ 132 Steve Niehaus RC	.15	.40
❑ 133 Fred Carr	.40	1.00
❑ 134 Norm Bulaich	.15	.40
❑ 135 Bob Trumpy	.25	.60
❑ 136 Greg Landry	.25	.60
❑ 137 George Buehler	.15	.40
❑ 138 Reggie Rucker	.25	.60
❑ 139 Julius Adams	.15	.40
❑ 140 Jack Ham	1.25	2.50
❑ 141 Wayne Morris RC	.15	.40
❑ 142 Marv Bateman	.15	.40
❑ 143 Bobby Maples	.15	.40
❑ 144 Harold Carmichael	.40	1.00
❑ 145 Bob Avellini	.25	.60
❑ 146 Harry Carson RC	1.50	3.00
❑ 147 Lawrence Pillers RC	.15	.40
❑ 148 Ed Williams RC	.15	.40
❑ 149 Dan Pastorini	.25	.60
❑ 150 Ron Yary	.40	1.00
❑ 151 Joe Lavender	.15	.40
❑ 152 Pat McInally RC	.25	.60
❑ 153 Lloyd Mumphord	.15	.40
❑ 154 Cullen Bryant	.25	.60
❑ 155 Willie Lanier	.40	1.00
❑ 156 Gene Washington 49er	.25	.60
❑ 157 Scott Hunter	.15	.40
❑ 158 Jim Merlo	.15	.40
❑ 159 Randy Grossman RC	.25	.60
❑ 160 Blaine Nye	.15	.40
❑ 161 Ike Harris	.15	.40
❑ 162 Doug Dieken	.15	.40
❑ 163 Guy Morriss	.15	.40
❑ 164 Bob Parsons	.15	.40
❑ 165 Steve Grogan	.40	1.00
❑ 166 John Brockington	.25	.60
❑ 167 Charlie Joiner	1.25	2.50
❑ 168 Ron Carpenter	.15	.40
❑ 169 Jeff Wright S	.15	.40
❑ 170 Chris Hanburger	.15	.40
❑ 171 Roosevelt Leaks RC	.25	.60
❑ 172 Larry Little	.40	1.00
❑ 173 John Matuszak	.25	.60
❑ 174 Joe Ferguson	.25	.60
❑ 175 Brad Van Pelt	.25	.60
❑ 176 Dexter Bussey RC	.25	.60
❑ 177 Steve Largent RC	20.00	40.00
❑ 178 Dewey Selmon RC	.25	.60
❑ 179 Randy Gradishar	.40	1.00
❑ 180 Mel Blount	1.50	3.00
❑ 181 Dan Neal RC	.15	.40
❑ 182 Rich Szaro RC	.15	.40
❑ 183 Mike Boryla	.15	.40
❑ 184 Steve Jones RC	.15	.40
❑ 185 Paul Warfield	1.25	2.50
❑ 186 Greg Buttle RC	.15	.40
❑ 187 Rich McGeorge	.15	.40
❑ 188 Leon Gray RC	.25	.60
❑ 189 John Shinners RC	.15	.40
❑ 190 Toni Linhart	.15	.40
❑ 191 Robert Miller RC	.15	.40
❑ 192 Jake Scott	.15	.40
❑ 193 Jon Morris	.15	.40
❑ 194 Randy Crowder RC	.15	.40
❑ 195 Lynn Swann UER	10.00	18.00
❑ 196 Marsh White RC	.15	.40

Card	Low	High
❑ 197 Rod Perry RC	.40	1.00
❑ 198 Willie Hall RC	.15	.40
❑ 199 Mike Hartenstine RC	.15	.40
❑ 200 Jim Bakken	.15	.40
❑ 201 Atlanta Falcons CL UER	.50	1.25
❑ 202 Baltimore Colts CL	.50	1.25
❑ 203 Buffalo Bills CL	.50	1.25
❑ 204 Chicago Bears CL	.50	1.25
❑ 205 Cincinnati Bengals CL	.50	1.25
❑ 206 Cleveland Browns CL	.50	1.25
❑ 207 Dallas Cowboys CL	.50	1.25
❑ 208 Denver Broncos CL	.50	1.25
❑ 209 Detroit Lions CL	.50	1.25
❑ 210 Green Bay Packers CL	.50	1.25
❑ 211 Houston Oilers CL	.50	1.25
❑ 212 Kansas City Chiefs CL	.50	1.25
❑ 213 Los Angeles Rams CL	.50	1.25
❑ 214 Miami Dolphins CL	.50	1.25
❑ 215 Minnesota Vikings CL	.50	1.25
❑ 216 New England Patriots CL	.50	1.25
❑ 217 New Orleans Saints CL	.50	1.25
❑ 218 New York Giants CL	.50	1.25
❑ 219 New York Jets CL	.50	1.25
❑ 220 Oakland Raiders CL	.50	1.25
❑ 221 Philadelphia Eagles CL	.50	1.25
❑ 222 Pittsburgh Steelers CL	.50	1.25
❑ 223 St. Louis Cardinals CL	.50	1.25
❑ 224 San Diego Chargers CL	.50	1.25
❑ 225 San Francisco 49ers CL	.50	1.25
❑ 226 Seattle Seahawks CL	.50	1.25
❑ 227 Tampa Bay Buccaneers CL	.50	1.25
❑ 228 Washington Redskins CL	.50	1.25
❑ 229 Sam Cunningham	.25	.60
❑ 230 Alan Page	.40	1.00
❑ 231 Eddie Brown S RC	.15	.40
❑ 232 Stan White	.15	.40
❑ 233 Vern Den Herder	.15	.40
❑ 234 Clarence Davis	.15	.40
❑ 235 Ken Anderson	.40	1.00
❑ 236 Karl Chandler RC	.15	.40
❑ 237 Will Harrell	.15	.40
❑ 238 Clarence Scott	.15	.40
❑ 239 Bo Rather RC	.15	.40
❑ 240 Robert Brazile	.25	.60
❑ 241 Bob Bell	.15	.40
❑ 242 Rolland Lawrence	.15	.40
❑ 243 Tom Sullivan	.15	.40
❑ 244 Larry Brunson RC	.15	.40
❑ 245 Terry Bradshaw	10.00	20.00
❑ 246 Rich Saul	.15	.40
❑ 247 Cleveland Elam RC	.15	.40
❑ 248 Don Woods	.15	.40
❑ 249 Bruce Laird	.15	.40
❑ 250 Coy Bacon	.25	.60
❑ 251 Russ Francis	.40	1.00
❑ 252 Jim Braxton	.15	.40
❑ 253 Perry Smith	.15	.40
❑ 254 Jerome Barkum	.15	.40
❑ 255 Garo Yepremian	.25	.60
❑ 256 Checklist 133-264	.75	2.00
❑ 257 Tony Galbreath RC	.25	.60
❑ 258 Troy Archer RC	.15	.40
❑ 259 Brian Sipe	.40	1.00
❑ 260 Billy Joe DuPree	.25	.60
❑ 261 Bobby Walden	.15	.40
❑ 262 Larry Marshall	.15	.40
❑ 263 Ted Fritsch Jr.	.15	.40
❑ 264 Larry Hand	.15	.40
❑ 265 Tom Mack	.40	1.00
❑ 266 Ed Bradley	.15	.40
❑ 267 Pat Leahy	.25	.60
❑ 268 Louis Carter RC	.15	.40
❑ 269 Archie Griffin RC	3.00	6.00
❑ 270 Art Shell	.40	1.00
❑ 271 Stu Voigt	.15	.40
❑ 272 Prentice McCray	.15	.40
❑ 273 MacArthur Lane	.15	.40
❑ 274 Dan Fouts	3.00	6.00
❑ 275 Charle Young	.25	.60
❑ 276 Wilbur Jackson RC	.15	.40
❑ 277 John Hicks	.15	.40
❑ 278 Nat Moore	.40	1.00
❑ 279 Virgil Livers	.15	.40
❑ 280 Curley Culp	.25	.60
❑ 281 Rocky Bleier	1.25	2.50
❑ 282 John Zook	.15	.40
❑ 283 Tom DeLeone	.15	.40
❑ 284 Danny White RC	5.00	10.00
❑ 285 Otis Armstrong	.25	.60
❑ 286 Larry Walton	.15	.40
❑ 287 Jim Carter	.15	.40
❑ 288 Don McCauley	.15	.40
❑ 289 Frank Grant	.15	.40
❑ 290 Roger Wehrli	.25	.60
❑ 291 Mick Tingelhoff	.25	.60
❑ 292 Bernard Jackson	.15	.40
❑ 293 Tom Owen RC	.15	.40
❑ 294 Mike Esposito RC	.15	.40
❑ 295 Fred Biletnikoff	1.25	2.50
❑ 296 Revie Sorey RC	.15	.40
❑ 297 John McMakin	.15	.40
❑ 298 Dan Ryczek	.15	.40
❑ 299 Wayne Moore RC	.15	.40
❑ 300 Franco Harris	2.00	4.00
❑ 301 Rick Upchurch RC	.40	1.00
❑ 302 Jim Stienke RC	.15	.40
❑ 303 Charlie Davis RC	.15	.40
❑ 304 Don Cockroft	.15	.40
❑ 305 Ken Burrough	.25	.60
❑ 306 Clark Gaines RC	.15	.40
❑ 307 Bobby Douglass	.15	.40
❑ 308 Ralph Perretta RC	.15	.40
❑ 309 Wally Hilgenberg	.15	.40
❑ 310 Monte Jackson RC	.25	.60
❑ 311 Chris Bahr RC	.25	.60
❑ 312 Jim Cheyunski	.15	.40
❑ 313 Mike Patrick RC	.15	.40
❑ 314 Ed Too Tall Jones	2.50	5.00
❑ 315 Bill Bradley	.15	.40
❑ 316 Benny Malone RC	.15	.40
❑ 317 Paul Seymour	.15	.40
❑ 318 Jim Laslavic RC	.15	.40
❑ 319 Frank Lewis	.25	.60
❑ 320 Ray Guy	.40	1.00
❑ 321 Allan Ellis RC	.15	.40
❑ 322 Conrad Dobler	.25	.60
❑ 323 Chester Marcol	.15	.40
❑ 324 Doug Kotar	.15	.40
❑ 325 Lemar Parrish	.25	.60
❑ 326 Steve Holden	.15	.40
❑ 327 Jeff Van Note	.25	.60
❑ 328 Howard Stevens	.15	.40
❑ 329 Brad Dusek	.25	.60
❑ 330 Joe DeLamielleure	.40	1.00
❑ 331 Jim Plunkett	.40	1.00
❑ 332 Checklist 265-396	.75	2.00
❑ 333 Lou Piccone RC	.15	.40
❑ 334 Ray Hamilton	.15	.40
❑ 335 Jan Stenerud	.40	1.00
❑ 336 Jeris White RC	.15	.40
❑ 337 Sherman Smith RC	.15	.40
❑ 338 Dave Green	.15	.40
❑ 339 Terry Schmidt	.15	.40
❑ 340 Sammie White RC	.40	1.00
❑ 341 Jon Kolb RC	.15	.40
❑ 342 Randy White	4.00	8.00
❑ 343 Bob Klein	.15	.40
❑ 344 Bob Kowalkowski	.15	.40
❑ 345 Terry Metcalf	.25	.60
❑ 346 Joe Danelo RC	.15	.40
❑ 347 Ken Payne	.15	.40
❑ 348 Neal Craig	.15	.40
❑ 349 Dennis Johnson	.15	.40
❑ 350 Bill Bergey	.25	.60
❑ 351 Raymond Chester	.15	.40
❑ 352 Bob Matheson	.15	.40
❑ 353 Mike Kadish RC	.15	.40
❑ 354 Mark Van Eeghen RC	.60	1.50
❑ 355 L.C.Greenwood	.40	1.00
❑ 356 Sam Hunt RC	.15	.40
❑ 357 Darrell Austin RC	.15	.40
❑ 358 Jim Turner	.15	.40
❑ 359 Ahmad Rashad	.75	2.00
❑ 360 Walter Payton	15.00	40.00
❑ 361 Mark Arneson RC	.15	.40
❑ 362 Jerrel Wilson	.15	.40
❑ 363 Steve Bartkowski	.40	1.00
❑ 364 John Watson RC	.15	.40
❑ 365 Ken Riley	.25	.60
❑ 366 Gregg Bingham	.15	.40
❑ 367 Golden Richards	.25	.60
❑ 368 Clyde Powers RC	.15	.40
❑ 369 Diron Talbert	.15	.40
❑ 370 Lydell Mitchell	.25	.60
❑ 371 Bob Jackson RC	.15	.40
❑ 372 Jim Mandich	.15	.40
❑ 373 Frank LeMaster	.15	.40
❑ 374 Ronny Ricardo RC	.15	.40
❑ 375 Lawrence McCutcheon	.25	.60
❑ 376 Lynn Dickey	.25	.60
❑ 377 Phil Wise RC	.15	.40
❑ 378 Tony McGee DT	.15	.40
❑ 379 Norm Thompson	.15	.40
❑ 380 Dave Casper RC	1.50	4.00
❑ 381 Glen Edwards	.15	.40
❑ 382 Bob Thomas	.15	.40
❑ 383 Bob Chandler	.25	.60
❑ 384 Rickey Young	.25	.60
❑ 385 Carl Eller	.40	1.00
❑ 386 Lyle Alzado	.40	1.00
❑ 387 John Leypoldt	.15	.40
❑ 388 Gordon Bell RC	.15	.40
❑ 389 Mike Bragg	.15	.40
❑ 390 Jim Langer	.40	1.00
❑ 391 Vern Holland	.15	.40
❑ 392 Nelson Munsey	.15	.40
❑ 393 Mack Mitchell RC	.15	.40
❑ 394 Tony Adams RC	.15	.40
❑ 395 Preston Pearson	.25	.60
❑ 396 Emanuel Zanders RC	.15	.40
❑ 397 Vince Papale RC	8.00	20.00
❑ 398 Joe Fields RC	.25	.60
❑ 399 Craig Clemons	.15	.40
❑ 400 Fran Tarkenton	2.50	5.00
❑ 401 Andy Johnson RC	.15	.40
❑ 402 Willie Buchanon	.15	.40
❑ 403 Pat Curran	.15	.40
❑ 404 Ray Jarvis RC	.15	.40
❑ 405 Joe Greene	1.25	2.50
❑ 406 Bill Simpson RC	.15	.40
❑ 407 Ronnie Coleman	.15	.40
❑ 408 J.K. McKay RC	.25	.60
❑ 409 Pat Fischer	.25	.60
❑ 410 John Dutton	.25	.60
❑ 411 Boobie Clark	.15	.40
❑ 412 Pat Tilley RC	.40	1.00
❑ 413 Don Strock	.25	.60
❑ 414 Brian Kelley	.15	.40
❑ 415 Gene Upshaw	.40	1.00
❑ 416 Mike Montler	.15	.40
❑ 417 Checklist 397-528	.75	2.00
❑ 418 John Gilliam	.15	.40
❑ 419 Brent McClanahan	.15	.40
❑ 420 Jerry Sherk	.15	.40
❑ 421 Roy Gerela	.15	.40
❑ 422 Tim Fox RC	.25	.60
❑ 423 John Ebersole RC	.15	.40
❑ 424 James Scott RC	.15	.40
❑ 425 Delvin Williams RC	.25	.60
❑ 426 Spike Jones	.15	.40
❑ 427 Harvey Martin	.40	1.00
❑ 428 Don Herrmann	.15	.40
❑ 429 Calvin Hill	.25	.60
❑ 430 Isiah Robertson	.15	.40
❑ 431 Tony Greene	.15	.40
❑ 432 Bob Johnson	.15	.40
❑ 433 Lem Barney	.40	1.00
❑ 434 Eric Torkelson RC	.15	.40
❑ 435 John Mendenhall	.15	.40
❑ 436 Larry Seiple	.25	.60
❑ 437 Art Kuehn RC	.15	.40
❑ 438 John Vella RC	.15	.40
❑ 439 Greg Latta RC	.15	.40
❑ 440 Roger Carr	.25	.60
❑ 441 Doug Sutherland	.15	.40
❑ 442 Mike Kruczek RC	.15	.40
❑ 443 Steve Zabel	.15	.40
❑ 444 Mike Pruitt RC	.40	1.00
❑ 445 Harold Jackson	.25	.60
❑ 446 George Jakowenko RC	.15	.40
❑ 447 John Fitzgerald	.15	.40
❑ 448 Carey Joyce RC	.15	.40
❑ 449 Jim LeClair	.15	.40
❑ 450 Ken Houston	.40	1.00
❑ 451 Steve Grogan RB	.25	.60
❑ 452 Jim Marshall RB	.25	.60
❑ 453 O.J.Simpson RB	1.25	2.50
❑ 454 Fran Tarkenton RB	1.50	3.00
❑ 455 Jim Zorn RB	.40	1.00
❑ 456 Robert Pratt RC	.15	.40
❑ 457 Walker Gillette	.15	.40
❑ 458 Charlie Hall	.15	.40
❑ 459 Robert Newhouse	.25	.60
❑ 460 John Hannah	.40	1.00
❑ 461 Ken Reaves	.15	.40
❑ 462 Herman Weaver	.15	.40
❑ 463 James Harris	.25	.60

❑ 464 Howard Twilley	.25	.60
❑ 465 Jeff Siemon	.25	.60
❑ 466 John Outlaw	.15	.40
❑ 467 Chuck Muncie RC	.40	1.00
❑ 468 Bob Moore	.15	.40
❑ 469 Robert Woods RC	.15	.40
❑ 470 Cliff Branch	.75	2.00
❑ 471 Johnnie Gray	.15	.40
❑ 472 Don Hardeman	.15	.40
❑ 473 Steve Ramsey	.15	.40
❑ 474 Steve Mike-Mayer	.15	.40
❑ 475 Gary Garrison	.15	.40
❑ 476 Walter Johnson	.15	.40
❑ 477 Neil Clabo	.15	.40
❑ 478 Len Hauss	.15	.40
❑ 479 Darryl Stingley	.25	.60
❑ 480 Jack Lambert	4.00	8.00
❑ 481 Mike Adamle	.25	.60
❑ 482 David Lee	.15	.40
❑ 483 Tom Mullen RC	.15	.40
❑ 484 Claude Humphrey	.15	.40
❑ 485 Jim Hart	.40	1.00
❑ 486 Bobby Thompson RC	.15	.40
❑ 487 Jack Rudnay	.15	.40
❑ 488 Rich Sowells RC	.15	.40
❑ 489 Reuben Gant RC	.15	.40
❑ 490 Cliff Harris	.40	1.00
❑ 491 Bob Brown DT	.15	.40
❑ 492 Don Nottingham	.15	.40
❑ 493 Ron Jessie	.15	.40
❑ 494 Otis Sistrunk	.25	.60
❑ 495 Billy Kilmer	.25	.60
❑ 496 Oscar Roan	.15	.40
❑ 497 Bill Van Heusen	.15	.40
❑ 498 Randy Logan	.15	.40
❑ 499 John Smith	.15	.40
❑ 500 Chuck Foreman	.25	.60
❑ 501 J.T. Thomas	.15	.40
❑ 502 Steve Schubert RC	.15	.40
❑ 503 Mike Barnes	.15	.40
❑ 504 J.V. Cain RC	.15	.40
❑ 505 Larry Csonka	1.50	3.00
❑ 506 Elvin Bethea	.40	1.00
❑ 507 Ray Easterling RC	.15	.40
❑ 508 Joe Reed	.15	.40
❑ 509 Steve Odom	.15	.40
❑ 510 Tommy Casanova	.15	.40
❑ 511 Dave Dalby	.15	.40
❑ 512 Richard Caster	.15	.40
❑ 513 Fred Dryer	.40	1.00
❑ 514 Jeff Kinney RC	.15	.40
❑ 515 Bob Griese	1.50	3.00
❑ 516 Butch Johnson RC	.40	1.00
❑ 517 Gerald Irons RC	.15	.40
❑ 518 Don Calhoun RC	.15	.40
❑ 519 Jack Gregory	.15	.40
❑ 520 Tom Banks	.15	.40
❑ 521 Bobby Bryant	.15	.40
❑ 522 Reggie Harrison RC	.15	.40
❑ 523 Terry Hermeling	.15	.40
❑ 524 David Taylor RC	.15	.40
❑ 525 Brian Baschnagel RC	.25	.60
❑ 526 AFC Champ/Stabler	.40	1.00
❑ 527 NFC Championship	.25	.60
❑ 528 Super Bowl XI	.60	1.50

1978 Topps

❑ COMPLETE SET (528)	80.00	150.00
❑ 1 Gary Huff HL	.40	1.00
❑ 2 Craig Morton HL	.40	1.00
❑ 3 Walter Payton HL	3.00	8.00
❑ 4 O.J.Simpson HL	.75	2.00
❑ 5 Fran Tarkenton HL	.75	2.00
❑ 6 Bob Thomas HL	.10	.30
❑ 7 Joe Pisarcik RC	.20	.50
❑ 8 Skip Thomas RC	.10	.30
❑ 9 Roosevelt Leaks	.10	.30
❑ 10 Ken Houston	.40	1.00
❑ 11 Tom Blanchard	.10	.30
❑ 12 Jim Turner	.10	.30
❑ 13 Tom DeLeone	.10	.30
❑ 14 Jim LeClair	.10	.30
❑ 15 Bob Avellini	.20	.50
❑ 16 Tony McGee DT	.10	.30
❑ 17 James Harris	.20	.50
❑ 18 Terry Nelson RC	.10	.30
❑ 19 Rocky Bleier	.75	2.00
❑ 20 Joe DeLamielleure	.40	1.00
❑ 21 Richard Caster	.10	.30
❑ 22 A.J.Duhe RC	.40	1.00
❑ 23 John Outlaw	.10	.30
❑ 24 Danny White	.50	1.25
❑ 25 Larry Csonka	1.00	2.50
❑ 26 David Hill RC	.20	.50
❑ 27 Mark Arneson	.10	.30
❑ 28 Jack Tatum	.20	.50
❑ 29 Norm Thompson	.10	.30
❑ 30 Sammie White	.20	.50
❑ 31 Dennis Johnson	.10	.30
❑ 32 Robin Earl RC	.10	.30
❑ 33 Don Cockroft	.10	.30
❑ 34 Bob Johnson	.10	.30
❑ 35 John Hannah	.40	1.00
❑ 36 Scott Hunter	.10	.30
❑ 37 Ken Burrough	.20	.50
❑ 38 Wilbur Jackson	.20	.50
❑ 39 Rich McGeorge	.10	.30
❑ 40 Lyle Alzado	.40	1.00
❑ 41 John Ebersole	.10	.30
❑ 42 Gary Green RC	.10	.30
❑ 43 Art Kuehn	.10	.30
❑ 44 Glen Edwards	.20	.50
❑ 45 Lawrence McCutcheon	.20	.50
❑ 46 Duriel Harris	.10	.30
❑ 47 Rich Szaro	.10	.30
❑ 48 Mike Washington RC	.10	.30
❑ 49 Stan White	.10	.30
❑ 50 Dave Casper	.40	1.00
❑ 51 Len Hauss	.10	.30
❑ 52 James Scott	.10	.30
❑ 53 Brian Sipe	.40	1.00
❑ 54 Gary Shirk RC	.10	.30
❑ 55 Archie Griffin	.40	1.00
❑ 56 Mike Patrick	.10	.30
❑ 57 Mario Clark RC	.10	.30
❑ 58 Jeff Siemon	.10	.30
❑ 59 Steve Mike-Mayer	.10	.30
❑ 60 Randy White	2.00	4.00
❑ 61 Darrell Austin	.10	.30
❑ 62 Tom Sullivan	.10	.30
❑ 63 Johnny Rodgers RC	.40	1.00
❑ 64 Ken Reaves	.10	.30
❑ 65 Terry Bradshaw	6.00	12.00
❑ 66 Fred Steinfort RC	.10	.30
❑ 67 Curley Culp	.20	.50
❑ 68 Ted Hendricks	.40	1.00
❑ 69 Raymond Chester	.10	.30
❑ 70 Jim Langer	.40	1.00
❑ 71 Calvin Hill	.20	.50
❑ 72 Mike Hartenstine	.10	.30
❑ 73 Gerald Irons	.10	.30
❑ 74 Billy Brooks RC	.20	.50
❑ 75 John Mendenhall	.10	.30
❑ 76 Andy Johnson	.10	.30
❑ 77 Tom Wittum	.10	.30
❑ 78 Lynn Dickey	.20	.50
❑ 79 Carl Eller	.40	1.00
❑ 80 Tom Mack	.40	1.00
❑ 81 Clark Gaines	.10	.30
❑ 82 Lem Barney	.40	1.00
❑ 83 Mike Montler	.10	.30
❑ 84 Jon Kolb	.10	.30
❑ 85 Bob Chandler	.20	.50
❑ 86 Robert Newhouse	.20	.50
❑ 87 Frank LeMaster	.10	.30
❑ 88 Jeff West	.10	.30
❑ 89 Lyle Blackwood	.20	.50
❑ 90 Gene Upshaw	.40	1.00
❑ 91 Frank Grant	.10	.30
❑ 92 Tom Hicks RC	.10	.30
❑ 93 Mike Pruitt	.20	.50
❑ 94 Chris Bahr	.10	.30
❑ 95 Russ Francis	.20	.50
❑ 96 Norris Thomas RC	.10	.30
❑ 97 Gary Barbaro RC	.20	.50
❑ 98 Jim Merlo	.10	.30
❑ 99 Karl Chandler	.10	.30
❑ 100 Fran Tarkenton	1.50	4.00
❑ 101 Abdul Salaam RC	.10	.30
❑ 102 Marv Kellum RC	.10	.30
❑ 103 Herman Weaver	.10	.30
❑ 104 Roy Gerela	.10	.30
❑ 105 Harold Jackson	.20	.50
❑ 106 Dewey Selmon	.20	.50
❑ 107 Checklist 1-132	.40	1.00
❑ 108 Clarence Davis	.10	.30
❑ 109 Robert Pratt	.10	.30
❑ 110 Harvey Martin	.40	1.00
❑ 111 Brad Dusek	.10	.30
❑ 112 Greg Latta	.10	.30
❑ 113 Tony Peters RC	.10	.30
❑ 114 Jim Braxton	.10	.30
❑ 115 Ken Riley	.20	.50
❑ 116 Steve Nelson RC	.10	.30
❑ 117 Rick Upchurch	.20	.50
❑ 118 Spike Jones	.10	.30
❑ 119 Doug Kotar	.10	.30
❑ 120 Bob Griese	1.00	2.50
❑ 121 Burgess Owens	.10	.30
❑ 122 Rolf Benirschke RC	.20	.50
❑ 123 Haskel Stanback RC	.10	.30
❑ 124 J.T. Thomas	.10	.30
❑ 125 Ahmad Rashad	.60	1.50
❑ 126 Rick Kane RC	.10	.30
❑ 127 Elvin Bethea	.40	1.00
❑ 128 Dave Dalby	.10	.30
❑ 129 Mike Barnes	.10	.30
❑ 130 Isiah Robertson	.10	.30
❑ 131 Jim Plunkett	.40	1.00
❑ 132 Allan Ellis	.10	.30
❑ 133 Mike Bragg	.10	.30
❑ 134 Bob Jackson	.10	.30
❑ 135 Coy Bacon	.10	.30
❑ 136 John Smith	.10	.30
❑ 137 Chuck Muncie	.20	.50
❑ 138 Johnnie Gray	.10	.30
❑ 139 Jimmy Robinson RC	.10	.30
❑ 140 Tom Banks	.10	.30
❑ 141 Marvin Powell RC	.10	.30
❑ 142 Jerrel Wilson	.10	.30
❑ 143 Ron Howard	.10	.30
❑ 144 Rob Lytle RC	.20	.50
❑ 145 L.C.Greenwood	.40	1.00
❑ 146 Morris Owens RC	.10	.30
❑ 147 Joe Reed	.10	.30
❑ 148 Mike Kadish	.10	.30
❑ 149 Phil Villapiano	.20	.50
❑ 150 Lydell Mitchell	.20	.50
❑ 151 Randy Logan	.10	.30
❑ 152 Mike Williams RC	.10	.30
❑ 153 Jeff Van Note	.20	.50
❑ 154 Steve Schubert	.10	.30
❑ 155 Billy Kilmer	.20	.50
❑ 156 Boobie Clark	.10	.30
❑ 157 Charlie Hall	.10	.30
❑ 158 Raymond Clayborn RC	.40	1.00
❑ 159 Jack Gregory	.10	.30
❑ 160 Cliff Harris	.40	1.00
❑ 161 Joe Fields	.10	.30
❑ 162 Don Nottingham	.10	.30
❑ 163 Ed White	.20	.50
❑ 164 Toni Fritsch	.10	.30
❑ 165 Jack Lambert	2.00	4.00
❑ 166 NFC Champs/Staubach	.60	1.50
❑ 167 AFC Champs/Lytle	.20	.50
❑ 168 Super Bowl XII/Dorsett	1.50	3.00
❑ 169 Neal Colzie RC	.10	.30
❑ 170 Cleveland Elam	.10	.30
❑ 171 David Lee	.10	.30
❑ 172 Jim Otis	.10	.30
❑ 173 Archie Manning	.40	1.00
❑ 174 Jim Carter	.10	.30
❑ 175 Jean Fugett	.10	.30
❑ 176 Willie Parker RC	.10	.30
❑ 177 Haven Moses	.20	.50
❑ 178 Horace King RC	.10	.30
❑ 179 Bob Thomas	.10	.30
❑ 180 Monte Jackson	.10	.30
❑ 181 Steve Zabel	.10	.30
❑ 182 John Fitzgerald	.10	.30
❑ 183 Mike Livingston	.10	.30
❑ 184 Larry Poole RC	.10	.30
❑ 185 Isaac Curtis	.20	.50
❑ 186 Chuck Ramsey RC	.10	.30

❑ 187 Bob Klein .10 .30
❑ 188 Ray Rhodes .40 1.00
❑ 189 Otis Sistrunk .20 .50
❑ 190 Bill Bergey .20 .50
❑ 191 Sherman Smith .20 .50
❑ 192 Dave Green .10 .30
❑ 193 Carl Mauck .10 .30
❑ 194 Reggie Harrison .10 .30
❑ 195 Roger Carr .20 .50
❑ 196 Steve Bartkowski .40 1.00
❑ 197 Ray Wersching .10 .30
❑ 198 Willie Buchanon .10 .30
❑ 199 Neil Clabo .10 .30
❑ 200 Walter Payton UER 12.50 25.00
❑ 201 Sam Adams OL .10 .30
❑ 202 Larry Gordon RC .10 .30
❑ 203 Pat Tilley .20 .50
❑ 204 Mack Mitchell .10 .30
❑ 205 Ken Anderson .40 1.00
❑ 206 Scott Dierking RC .10 .30
❑ 207 Jack Rudnay .10 .30
❑ 208 Jim Stienke .10 .30
❑ 209 Bill Simpson .10 .30
❑ 210 Errol Mann .10 .30
❑ 211 Bucky Dilts RC .10 .30
❑ 212 Reuben Gant .10 .30
❑ 213 Thomas Henderson RC .60 1.50
❑ 214 Steve Furness .20 .50
❑ 215 John Riggins .75 2.00
❑ 216 Keith Krepfle RC .10 .30
❑ 217 Fred Dean RC 6.00 12.00
❑ 218 Emanuel Zanders .10 .30
❑ 219 Don Testerman RC .10 .30
❑ 220 George Kunz .10 .30
❑ 221 Darryl Stingley .20 .50
❑ 222 Ken Sanders RC .10 .30
❑ 223 Gary Huff .10 .30
❑ 224 Gregg Bingham .10 .30
❑ 225 Jerry Sherk .10 .30
❑ 226 Doug Plank .10 .30
❑ 227 Ed Taylor RC .10 .30
❑ 228 Emery Moorehead RC .10 .30
❑ 229 Reggie Williams RC .40 1.00
❑ 230 Claude Humphrey .10 .30
❑ 231 Randy Cross RC .75 2.00
❑ 232 Jim Hart .40 1.00
❑ 233 Bobby Bryant .10 .30
❑ 234 Larry Brown .10 .30
❑ 235 Mark Van Eeghen .20 .50
❑ 236 Terry Hermeling .10 .30
❑ 237 Steve Odom .10 .30
❑ 238 Jan Stenerud .40 1.00
❑ 239 Andre Tillman .10 .30
❑ 240 Tom Jackson RC 2.00 5.00
❑ 241 Ken Mendenhall .10 .30
❑ 242 Tim Fox .10 .30
❑ 243 Don Herrmann .10 .30
❑ 244 Eddie McMillan .10 .30
❑ 245 Greg Pruitt .20 .50
❑ 246 J.K. McKay .10 .30
❑ 247 Larry Kollor RC .10 .30
❑ 248 Dave Jennings .20 .50
❑ 249 Bo Harris RC .10 .30
❑ 250 Revie Sorey .10 .30
❑ 251 Tony Greene .10 .30
❑ 252 Butch Johnson .20 .50
❑ 253 Paul Naumoff .10 .30
❑ 254 Rickey Young .20 .50
❑ 255 Dwight White .20 .50
❑ 256 Joe Lavender .10 .30
❑ 257 Checklist 133-264 .40 1.00
❑ 258 Ronnie Coleman .10 .30
❑ 259 Charlie Smith WR .10 .30
❑ 260 Ray Guy .40 1.00
❑ 261 David Taylor .10 .30
❑ 262 Bill Lenkaitis .10 .30
❑ 263 Jim Mitchell TE .10 .30
❑ 264 Delvin Williams .10 .30
❑ 265 Jack Youngblood .40 1.00
❑ 266 Chuck Crist RC .10 .30
❑ 267 Richard Todd .20 .50
❑ 268 Dave Logan RC .40 1.00
❑ 269 Rufus Mayes .10 .30
❑ 270 Brad Van Pelt .10 .30
❑ 271 Chester Marcol .10 .30
❑ 272 J.V. Cain .10 .30
❑ 273 Larry Seiple .10 .30
❑ 274 Brent McClanahan .10 .30
❑ 275 Mike Wagner .10 .30
❑ 276 Diron Talbert .10 .30
❑ 277 Brian Baschnagel .10 .30
❑ 278 Ed Podolak .10 .30
❑ 279 Don Goode .10 .30
❑ 280 John Dutton .20 .50
❑ 281 Don Calhoun .10 .30
❑ 282 Monte Johnson .10 .30
❑ 283 Ron Jessie .10 .30
❑ 284 Jon Morris .10 .30
❑ 285 Riley Odoms .10 .30
❑ 286 Marv Bateman .10 .30
❑ 287 Joe Klecko RC .40 1.00
❑ 288 Oliver Davis RC .10 .30
❑ 289 John McDaniel .10 .30
❑ 290 Roger Staubach 6.00 12.00
❑ 291 Brian Kelley .10 .30
❑ 292 Mike Hogan RC .10 .30
❑ 293 John Leypoldt .10 .30
❑ 294 Jack Novak RC .10 .30
❑ 295 Joe Greene .75 2.00
❑ 296 John Hill .10 .30
❑ 297 Danny Buggs RC .10 .30
❑ 298 Ted Albrecht RC .10 .30
❑ 299 Nelson Munsey .10 .30
❑ 300 Chuck Foreman .20 .50
❑ 301 Dan Pastorini .20 .50
❑ 302 Tommy Hart .10 .30
❑ 303 Dave Beverly .10 .30
❑ 304 Tony Reed RC .20 .50
❑ 305 Cliff Branch .60 1.50
❑ 306 Clarence Duren RC .10 .30
❑ 307 Randy Rasmussen .10 .30
❑ 308 Oscar Roan .10 .30
❑ 309 Lenvil Elliott .10 .30
❑ 310 Dan Dierdorf .40 1.00
❑ 311 Johnny Perkins RC .10 .30
❑ 312 Rafael Septien RC .20 .50
❑ 313 Terry Beeson RC .10 .30
❑ 314 Lee Roy Selmon .75 2.00
❑ 315 Tony Dorsett RC 25.00 40.00
❑ 316 Greg Landry .20 .50
❑ 317 Jake Scott .10 .30
❑ 318 Dan Peiffer RC .10 .30
❑ 319 John Bunting .20 .50
❑ 320 John Stallworth RC 10.00 20.00
❑ 321 Bob Howard .10 .30
❑ 322 Larry Little .40 1.00
❑ 323 Reggie McKenzie .20 .50
❑ 324 Duane Carrell .10 .30
❑ 325 Ed Simonini RC .10 .30
❑ 326 John Vella .10 .30
❑ 327 Wesley Walker RC 1.50 3.00
❑ 328 Jon Keyworth .10 .30
❑ 329 Ron Bolton .10 .30
❑ 330 Tommy Casanova .10 .30
❑ 331 R.Staubach/B.Griese LL 2.00 4.00
❑ 332 A.Rashad/Mitchell LL .40 1.00
❑ 333 W.Payton/VanEeghenLL 1.25 3.00
❑ 334 W.Payton/E.Mann LL 1.25 3.00
❑ 335 Interception Leaders .10 .30
❑ 336 Punting Leaders .20 .50
❑ 337 Robert Brazile .20 .50
❑ 338 Charlie Joiner .60 1.50
❑ 339 Joe Ferguson .20 .50
❑ 340 Bill Thompson .10 .30
❑ 341 Sam Cunningham .20 .50
❑ 342 Curtis Johnson .10 .30
❑ 343 Jim Marshall .40 1.00
❑ 344 Charlie Sanders .20 .50
❑ 345 Willie Hall .10 .30
❑ 346 Pat Haden .40 1.00
❑ 347 Jim Bakken .10 .30
❑ 348 Bruce Taylor .10 .30
❑ 349 Barty Smith .10 .30
❑ 350 Drew Pearson .60 1.50
❑ 351 Mike Webster 1.00 2.50
❑ 352 Bobby Hammond RC .10 .30
❑ 353 Dave Mays RC .10 .30
❑ 354 Pat McInally .10 .30
❑ 355 Toni Linhart .10 .30
❑ 356 Larry Hand .10 .30
❑ 357 Ted Fritsch Jr. .10 .30
❑ 358 Larry Marshall .10 .30
❑ 359 Waymond Bryant .10 .30
❑ 360 Louie Kelcher RC .20 .50
❑ 361 Stanley Morgan RC .75 2.00
❑ 362 Bruce Harper RC .20 .50
❑ 363 Bernard Jackson .10 .30
❑ 364 Walter White .10 .30
❑ 365 Ken Stabler 4.00 8.00
❑ 366 Fred Dryer .40 1.00
❑ 367 Ike Harris .10 .30
❑ 368 Norm Bulaich .10 .30
❑ 369 Merv Krakau RC .10 .30
❑ 370 John James .10 .30
❑ 371 Bennie Cunningham RC .10 .30
❑ 372 Doug Van Horn .10 .30
❑ 373 Thom Darden .10 .30
❑ 374 Eddie Edwards RC .10 .30
❑ 375 Mike Thomas .10 .30
❑ 376 Fred Cook .10 .30
❑ 377 Mike Phipps .20 .50
❑ 378 Paul Krause .40 1.00
❑ 379 Harold Carmichael .40 1.00
❑ 380 Mike Haynes .40 1.00
❑ 381 Wayne Morris .10 .30
❑ 382 Greg Buttle .10 .30
❑ 383 Jim Zorn .40 1.00
❑ 384 Jack Dolbin .10 .30
❑ 385 Charlie Waters .20 .50
❑ 386 Dan Ryczek .10 .30
❑ 387 Joe Washington RC .40 1.00
❑ 388 Checklist 265-396 .40 1.00
❑ 389 James Hunter RC .10 .30
❑ 390 Billy Johnson .20 .50
❑ 391 Jim Allen RC .10 .30
❑ 392 George Buehler .10 .30
❑ 393 Harry Carson .40 1.00
❑ 394 Cleo Miller .10 .30
❑ 395 Gary Burley RC .10 .30
❑ 396 Mark Moseley .20 .50
❑ 397 Virgil Livers .10 .30
❑ 398 Joe Ehrmann .10 .30
❑ 399 Freddie Solomon .10 .30
❑ 400 O.J.Simpson 2.00 4.00
❑ 401 Julius Adams .10 .30
❑ 402 Artimus Parker RC .10 .30
❑ 403 Gene Washington 49er .20 .50
❑ 404 Herman Edwards RC .20 .50
❑ 405 Craig Morton .40 1.00
❑ 406 Alan Page .40 1.00
❑ 407 Larry McCarren .10 .30
❑ 408 Tony Galbreath .20 .50
❑ 409 Roman Gabriel .40 1.00
❑ 410 Efren Herrera .10 .30
❑ 411 Jim Smith RC .40 1.00
❑ 412 Bill Bryant RC .10 .30
❑ 413 Doug Dieken .10 .30
❑ 414 Marvin Cobb .10 .30
❑ 415 Fred Biletnikoff .75 2.00
❑ 416 Joe Theismann 1.00 2.50
❑ 417 Roland Harper .10 .30
❑ 418 Derrel Luce RC .10 .30
❑ 419 Ralph Perretta .10 .30
❑ 420 Louis Wright RC .40 1.00
❑ 421 Prentice McCray .10 .30
❑ 422 Garry Puetz .10 .30
❑ 423 Alfred Jenkins RC .40 1.00
❑ 424 Paul Seymour .10 .30
❑ 425 Garo Yepremian .20 .50
❑ 426 Emmitt Thomas .20 .50
❑ 427 Dexter Bussey .10 .30
❑ 428 John Sanders RC .10 .30
❑ 429 Ed Too Tall Jones .75 2.00
❑ 430 Ron Yary .40 1.00
❑ 431 Frank Lewis .20 .50
❑ 432 Jerry Golsteyn RC .10 .30
❑ 433 Clarence Scott .10 .30
❑ 434 Pete Johnson RC .40 1.00
❑ 435 Charle Young .20 .50
❑ 436 Harold McLinton .10 .30
❑ 437 Noah Jackson .10 .30
❑ 438 Bruce Laird .10 .30
❑ 439 John Matuszak .20 .50
❑ 440 Nat Moore .20 .50
❑ 441 Leon Gray .10 .30
❑ 442 Jerome Barkum .10 .30
❑ 443 Steve Largent 6.00 12.00
❑ 444 John Zook .10 .30
❑ 445 Preston Pearson .20 .50
❑ 446 Conrad Dobler .20 .50
❑ 447 Wilbur Summers RC .10 .30
❑ 448 Lou Piccone .10 .30
❑ 449 Ron Jaworski .40 1.00
❑ 450 Jack Ham .60 1.50
❑ 451 Mick Tingelhoff .20 .50
❑ 452 Clyde Powers .10 .30
❑ 453 John Cappelletti .40 1.00

Card	Low	High
❑ 454 Dick Ambrose RC	.10	.30
❑ 455 Lemar Parrish	.10	.30
❑ 456 Ron Saul	.10	.30
❑ 457 Bob Parsons	.10	.30
❑ 458 Glenn Doughty	.10	.30
❑ 459 Don Woods	.10	.30
❑ 460 Art Shell	.40	1.00
❑ 461 Sam Hunt	.10	.30
❑ 462 Lawrence Pillers	.10	.30
❑ 463 Henry Childs	.10	.30
❑ 464 Roger Wehrli	.20	.50
❑ 465 Otis Armstrong	.20	.50
❑ 466 Bob Baumhower RC	.75	2.00
❑ 467 Ray Jarvis	.10	.30
❑ 468 Guy Morriss	.10	.30
❑ 469 Matt Blair	.20	.50
❑ 470 Billy Joe DuPree	.20	.50
❑ 471 Roland Hooks RC	.10	.30
❑ 472 Joe Danelo	.10	.30
❑ 473 Reggie Rucker	.20	.50
❑ 474 Vern Holland	.10	.30
❑ 475 Mel Blount	.60	1.50
❑ 476 Eddie Brown S	.10	.30
❑ 477 Bo Rather	.10	.30
❑ 478 Don McCauley	.10	.30
❑ 479 Glen Walker RC	.10	.30
❑ 480 Randy Gradishar	.40	1.00
❑ 481 Dave Rowe	.10	.30
❑ 482 Pat Leahy	.20	.50
❑ 483 Mike Fuller	.10	.30
❑ 484 David Lewis RC	.10	.30
❑ 485 Steve Grogan	.40	1.00
❑ 486 Mel Gray	.20	.50
❑ 487 Eddie Payton RC	.20	.50
❑ 488 Checklist 397-528	.40	1.00
❑ 489 Stu Voigt	.10	.30
❑ 490 Rolland Lawrence	.10	.30
❑ 491 Nick Mike-Mayer	.10	.30
❑ 492 Troy Archer	.10	.30
❑ 493 Benny Malone	.10	.30
❑ 494 Golden Richards	.20	.50
❑ 495 Chris Hanburger	.10	.30
❑ 496 Dwight Harrison	.10	.30
❑ 497 Gary Fencik RC	.40	1.00
❑ 498 Rich Saul	.10	.30
❑ 499 Dan Fouts	2.00	4.00
❑ 500 Franco Harris	2.00	4.00
❑ 501 Atlanta Falcons TL	.30	.75
❑ 502 Baltimore Colts TL	.30	.75
❑ 503 Bills TL/O.J.Simpson	.60	1.50
❑ 504 Bears TL/Walter Payton	.75	2.00
❑ 505 Bengals TL/Reg.Williams	.30	.75
❑ 506 Cleveland Browns TL	.30	.75
❑ 507 Cowboys TL/T.Dorsett	1.00	2.50
❑ 508 Denver Broncos TL	.40	1.00
❑ 509 Detroit Lions TL	.30	.75
❑ 510 Green Bay Packers TL	.40	1.00
❑ 511 Houston Oilers TL	.30	.75
❑ 512 Kansas City Chiefs TL	.30	.75
❑ 513 Los Angeles Rams TL	.30	.75
❑ 514 Miami Dolphins TL	.40	1.00
❑ 515 Minnesota Vikings TL	.30	.75
❑ 516 New England Patriots TL	.30	.75
❑ 517 New Orleans Saints TL	.30	.75
❑ 518 New York Giants TL	.30	.75
❑ 519 Jets TL/Wesley Walker	.30	.75
❑ 520 Oakland Raiders TL	.40	1.00
❑ 521 Philadelphia Eagles TL	.30	.75
❑ 522 Steelers TL/Harris/Blount	.40	1.00
❑ 523 St.Louis Cardinals TL	.30	.75
❑ 524 San Diego Chargers TL	.40	1.00
❑ 525 San Francisco 49ers TL	.30	.75
❑ 526 Seahawks TL/S.Largent	.60	1.50
❑ 527 Tampa Bay Bucs TL	.30	.75
❑ 528 Redskins TL/Ken Houston	.40	1.00

1979 Topps

Card	Low	High
❑ COMPLETE SET (528)	75.00	150.00
❑ 1 Staubach/Bradshaw LL	4.00	8.00
❑ 2 S.Largent/R.Young LL	.40	1.00
❑ 3 E.Campbell/W.Payton LL	4.00	8.00
❑ 4 Scoring Leaders	.10	.30
❑ 5 Interception Leaders	.10	.30
❑ 6 Punting Leaders	.10	.30
❑ 7 Johnny Perkins	.10	.30
❑ 8 Charles Phillips RC	.10	.30
❑ 9 Derrel Luce	.10	.30
❑ 10 John Riggins	.50	1.25
❑ 11 Chester Marcol	.10	.30
❑ 12 Bernard Jackson	.10	.30
❑ 13 Dave Logan	.10	.30
❑ 14 Bo Harris	.10	.30
❑ 15 Alan Page	.40	1.00
❑ 16 John Smith	.10	.30
❑ 17 Dwight McDonald RC	.10	.30
❑ 18 John Cappelletti	.20	.50
❑ 19 Steelers TL/Harris/Dungy	5.00	12.00
❑ 20 Bill Bergey	.20	.50
❑ 21 Jerome Barkum	.10	.30
❑ 22 Larry Csonka	1.00	2.50
❑ 23 Joe Ferguson	.20	.50
❑ 24 Ed Too Tall Jones	.50	1.25
❑ 25 Dave Jennings	.20	.50
❑ 26 Horace King	.10	.30
❑ 27 Steve Little RC	.20	.50
❑ 28 Morris Bradshaw RC	.10	.30
❑ 29 Joe Ehrmann	.10	.30
❑ 30 Ahmad Rashad	.40	1.00
❑ 31 Joe Lavender	.10	.30
❑ 32 Dan Neal	.10	.30
❑ 33 Johnny Evans RC	.10	.30
❑ 34 Pete Johnson	.20	.50
❑ 35 Mike Haynes	.40	1.00
❑ 36 Tim Mazzetti RC	.10	.30
❑ 37 Mike Barber RC	.10	.30
❑ 38 49ers TL/O.J.Simpson	.60	1.50
❑ 39 Bill Gregory RC	.10	.30
❑ 40 Randy Gradishar	.40	1.00
❑ 41 Richard Todd	.20	.50
❑ 42 Henry Marshall	.10	.30
❑ 43 John Hill	.10	.30
❑ 44 Sidney Thornton RC	.10	.30
❑ 45 Ron Jessie	.10	.30
❑ 46 Bob Baumhower	.20	.50
❑ 47 Johnnie Gray	.10	.30
❑ 48 Doug Williams RC	3.00	6.00
❑ 49 Don McCauley	.10	.30
❑ 50 Ray Guy	.20	.50
❑ 51 Bob Klein	.10	.30
❑ 52 Golden Richards	.10	.30
❑ 53 Mark Miller QB RC	.10	.30
❑ 54 John Sanders	.10	.30
❑ 55 Gary Burley	.10	.30
❑ 56 Steve Nelson	.10	.30
❑ 57 Buffalo Bills TL	.30	.75
❑ 58 Bobby Bryant	.10	.30
❑ 59 Rick Kane	.10	.30
❑ 60 Larry Little	.40	1.00
❑ 61 Ted Fritsch Jr.	.10	.30
❑ 62 Larry Mallory RC	.10	.30
❑ 63 Marvin Powell	.10	.30
❑ 64 Jim Hart	.40	1.00
❑ 65 Joe Greene	.60	1.50
❑ 66 Walter White	.10	.30
❑ 67 Gregg Bingham	.10	.30
❑ 68 Errol Mann	.10	.30
❑ 69 Bruce Laird	.10	.30
❑ 70 Drew Pearson	.40	1.00
❑ 71 Steve Bartkowski	.40	1.00
❑ 72 Ted Albrecht	.10	.30
❑ 73 Charlie Hall	.10	.30
❑ 74 Pat McInally	.10	.30
❑ 75 Bubba Baker RC	.40	1.00
❑ 76 New England Pats TL	.30	.75
❑ 77 Steve DeBerg RC	.75	2.00
❑ 78 John Yarno RC	.10	.30
❑ 79 Stu Voigt	.10	.30
❑ 80 Frank Corral AP RC	.10	.30
❑ 81 Troy Archer	.10	.30
❑ 82 Bruce Harper	.10	.30
❑ 83 Tom Jackson	.60	1.50
❑ 84 Larry Brown	.20	.50
❑ 85 Wilbert Montgomery RC	.40	1.00
❑ 86 Butch Johnson	.20	.50
❑ 87 Mike Kadish	.10	.30
❑ 88 Ralph Perretta	.10	.30
❑ 89 David Lee	.10	.30
❑ 90 Mark Van Eeghen	.20	.50
❑ 91 John McDaniel	.10	.30
❑ 92 Gary Fencik	.20	.50
❑ 93 Mack Mitchell	.10	.30
❑ 94 Cincinnati Bengals TL/Jauron	.40	1.00
❑ 95 Steve Grogan	.40	1.00
❑ 96 Garo Yepremian	.20	.50
❑ 97 Barty Smith	.10	.30
❑ 98 Frank Reed RC	.10	.30
❑ 99 Jim Clack RC	.10	.30
❑ 100 Chuck Foreman	.20	.50
❑ 101 Joe Klecko	.40	1.00
❑ 102 Pat Tilley	.20	.50
❑ 103 Conrad Dobler	.20	.50
❑ 104 Craig Colquitt RC	.10	.30
❑ 105 Dan Pastorini	.20	.50
❑ 106 Rod Perry AP	.10	.30
❑ 107 Nick Mike-Mayer	.10	.30
❑ 108 John Matuszak	.20	.50
❑ 109 David Taylor	.10	.30
❑ 110 Billy Joe DuPree	.20	.50
❑ 111 Harold McLinton	.10	.30
❑ 112 Virgil Livers	.10	.30
❑ 113 Cleveland Browns TL	.30	.75
❑ 114 Checklist 1-132	.40	1.00
❑ 115 Ken Anderson	.40	1.00
❑ 116 Bill Lenkaitis	.10	.30
❑ 117 Bucky Dilts	.10	.30
❑ 118 Tony Greene	.10	.30
❑ 119 Bobby Hammond	.10	.30
❑ 120 Nat Moore	.20	.50
❑ 121 Pat Leahy	.20	.50
❑ 122 James Harris	.20	.50
❑ 123 Lee Roy Selmon	.50	1.25
❑ 124 Bennie Cunningham	.20	.50
❑ 125 Matt Blair AP	.20	.50
❑ 126 Jim Allen	.10	.30
❑ 127 Alfred Jenkins	.20	.50
❑ 128 Arthur Whittington RC	.10	.30
❑ 129 Norm Thompson	.10	.30
❑ 130 Pat Haden	.40	1.00
❑ 131 Freddie Solomon	.10	.30
❑ 132 Bears TL/W.Payton	.75	2.00
❑ 133 Mark Moseley	.10	.30
❑ 134 Cleo Miller	.10	.30
❑ 135 Ross Browner RC	.20	.50
❑ 136 Don Calhoun	.10	.30
❑ 137 David Whitehurst RC	.10	.30
❑ 138 Terry Beeson	.10	.30
❑ 139 Ken Stone RC	.10	.30
❑ 140 Brad Van Pelt AP	.10	.30
❑ 141 Wesley Walker	.40	1.00
❑ 142 Jan Stenerud	.40	1.00
❑ 143 Henry Childs	.10	.30
❑ 144 Otis Armstrong	.40	1.00
❑ 145 Dwight White	.20	.50
❑ 146 Steve Wilson RC	.10	.30
❑ 147 Tom Skladany RC	.10	.30
❑ 148 Lou Piccone	.10	.30
❑ 149 Monte Johnson	.10	.30
❑ 150 Joe Washington	.20	.50
❑ 151 Eagles TL/W.Montgomery	.30	.75
❑ 152 Fred Dean	.40	1.00
❑ 153 Rolland Lawrence	.10	.30
❑ 154 Brian Baschnagel	.10	.30
❑ 155 Joe Theismann	.75	2.00
❑ 156 Marvin Cobb	.10	.30
❑ 157 Dick Ambrose	.10	.30
❑ 158 Mike Patrick	.10	.30
❑ 159 Gary Shirk	.10	.30
❑ 160 Tony Dorsett	6.00	12.00
❑ 161 Greg Buttle	.10	.30
❑ 162 A.J. Duhe	.20	.50

Card		
❑ 163 Mick Tingelhoff	.20	.50
❑ 164 Ken Burrough	.20	.50
❑ 165 Mike Wagner	.10	.30
❑ 166 AFC Champs/F.Harris	.40	1.00
❑ 167 NFC Championship	.20	.50
❑ 168 Super Bowl XIII/Harris	.50	1.25
❑ 169 Raiders TL/Ted Hendricks	.40	1.00
❑ 170 O.J.Simpson	1.50	4.00
❑ 171 Doug Nettles RC	.10	.30
❑ 172 Dan Dierdorf	.40	1.00
❑ 173 Dave Beverly	.10	.30
❑ 174 Jim Zorn	.40	1.00
❑ 175 Mike Thomas	.10	.30
❑ 176 John Outlaw	.10	.30
❑ 177 Jim Turner	.10	.30
❑ 178 Freddie Scott RC	.10	.30
❑ 179 Mike Phipps	.20	.50
❑ 180 Jack Youngblood	.40	1.00
❑ 181 Sam Hunt	.10	.30
❑ 182 Tony Hill RC	.40	1.00
❑ 183 Gary Barbaro	.10	.30
❑ 184 Archie Griffin	.20	.50
❑ 185 Jerry Sherk	.10	.30
❑ 186 Bobby Jackson RC	.10	.30
❑ 187 Don Woods	.10	.30
❑ 188 New York Giants TL	.30	.75
❑ 189 Raymond Chester	.10	.30
❑ 190 Joe DeLamielleure AP	.40	1.00
❑ 191 Tony Galbreath	.20	.50
❑ 192 Robert Brazile AP	.20	.50
❑ 193 Neil O'Donoghue RC	.10	.30
❑ 194 Mike Webster	.40	1.00
❑ 195 Ed Simonini	.10	.30
❑ 196 Benny Malone	.10	.30
❑ 197 Tom Wittum	.10	.30
❑ 198 Steve Largent	4.00	8.00
❑ 199 Tommy Hart	.10	.30
❑ 200 Fran Tarkenton	1.50	3.00
❑ 201 Leon Gray AP	.10	.30
❑ 202 Leroy Harris RC	.10	.30
❑ 203 Eric Williams LB RC	.10	.30
❑ 204 Thom Darden AP	.10	.30
❑ 205 Ken Riley	.20	.50
❑ 206 Clark Gaines	.10	.30
❑ 207 Kansas City Chiefs TL	.30	.75
❑ 208 Joe Danelo	.10	.30
❑ 209 Glen Walker	.10	.30
❑ 210 Art Shell	.40	1.00
❑ 211 Jon Keyworth	.10	.30
❑ 212 Herman Edwards	.10	.30
❑ 213 John Fitzgerald	.10	.30
❑ 214 Jim Smith	.20	.50
❑ 215 Coy Bacon	.20	.50
❑ 216 Dennis Johnson RBK RC	.10	.30
❑ 217 John Jefferson RC	1.50	3.00
❑ 218 Gary Weaver RC	.10	.30
❑ 219 Tom Blanchard	.10	.30
❑ 220 Bert Jones	.40	1.00
❑ 221 Stanley Morgan	.40	1.00
❑ 222 James Hunter	.10	.30
❑ 223 Jim O'Bradovich	.10	.30
❑ 224 Carl Mauck	.10	.30
❑ 225 Chris Bahr	.10	.30
❑ 226 Jets TL/Wesley Walker	.30	.75
❑ 227 Roland Harper	.10	.30
❑ 228 Randy Dean RC	.10	.30
❑ 229 Bob Jackson	.10	.30
❑ 230 Sammie White	.20	.50
❑ 231 Mike Dawson RC	.10	.30
❑ 232 Checklist 133-264	.40	1.00
❑ 233 Ken MacAfee RC	.10	.30
❑ 234 Jon Kolb AP	.10	.30
❑ 235 Willie Hall	.10	.30
❑ 236 Ron Saul AP	.10	.30
❑ 237 Haskel Stanback	.10	.30
❑ 238 Zenon Andrusyshyn RC	.10	.30
❑ 239 Norris Thomas	.10	.30
❑ 240 Rick Upchurch	.20	.50
❑ 241 Robert Pratt	.10	.30
❑ 242 Julius Adams	.10	.30
❑ 243 Rich McGeorge	.10	.30
❑ 244 Seahawks TL/S.Largent	.50	1.25
❑ 245 Blair Bush RC	.10	.30
❑ 246 Billy Johnson	.20	.50
❑ 247 Randy Rasmussen	.10	.30
❑ 248 Brian Kelley	.10	.30
❑ 249 Mike Pruitt	.20	.50
❑ 250 Harold Carmichael	.40	1.00
❑ 251 Mike Hartenstine	.10	.30
❑ 252 Robert Newhouse	.20	.50
❑ 253 Gary Danielson RC	.40	1.00
❑ 254 Mike Fuller	.10	.30
❑ 255 L.C.Greenwood	.40	1.00
❑ 256 Lemar Parrish	.10	.30
❑ 257 Ike Harris	.10	.30
❑ 258 Ricky Bell RC	.40	1.00
❑ 259 Willie Parker C	.10	.30
❑ 260 Gene Upshaw	.40	1.00
❑ 261 Glenn Doughty	.10	.30
❑ 262 Steve Zabel	.10	.30
❑ 263 Atlanta Falcons TL	.30	.75
❑ 264 Ray Wersching	.10	.30
❑ 265 Lawrence McCutcheon	.20	.50
❑ 266 Willie Buchanon AP	.10	.30
❑ 267 Matt Robinson RC	.10	.30
❑ 268 Reggie Rucker	.20	.50
❑ 269 Doug Van Horn	.10	.30
❑ 270 Lydell Mitchell	.20	.50
❑ 271 Vern Holland	.10	.30
❑ 272 Eason Ramson RC	.10	.30
❑ 273 Steve Towle RC	.10	.30
❑ 274 Jim Marshall	.40	1.00
❑ 275 Mel Blount	.50	1.25
❑ 276 Bob Kuziel RC	.10	.30
❑ 277 James Scott	.10	.30
❑ 278 Tony Reed	.10	.30
❑ 279 Dave Green	.10	.30
❑ 280 Toni Linhart	.10	.30
❑ 281 Andy Johnson	.10	.30
❑ 282 Los Angeles Rams TL	.30	.75
❑ 283 Phil Villapiano	.20	.50
❑ 284 Dexter Bussey	.10	.30
❑ 285 Craig Morton	.40	1.00
❑ 286 Guy Morriss	.10	.30
❑ 287 Lawrence Pillers	.10	.30
❑ 288 Gerald Irons	.10	.30
❑ 289 Scott Perry RC	.10	.30
❑ 290 Randy White	.75	2.00
❑ 291 Jack Gregory	.10	.30
❑ 292 Bob Chandler	.10	.30
❑ 293 Rich Szaro	.10	.30
❑ 294 Sherman Smith	.10	.30
❑ 295 Tom Banks AP	.10	.30
❑ 296 Revie Sorey AP	.10	.30
❑ 297 Ricky Thompson RC	.10	.30
❑ 298 Ron Yary	.40	1.00
❑ 299 Lyle Blackwood	.10	.30
❑ 300 Franco Harris	1.25	2.50
❑ 301 Oilers TL/E.Campbell	1.50	3.00
❑ 302 Scott Bull RC	.10	.30
❑ 303 Dewey Selmon	.20	.50
❑ 304 Jack Rudnay	.10	.30
❑ 305 Fred Biletnikoff	.75	2.00
❑ 306 Jeff West	.10	.30
❑ 307 Shafer Suggs RC	.10	.30
❑ 308 Ozzie Newsome RC	6.00	12.00
❑ 309 Boobie Clark	.10	.30
❑ 310 James Lofton RC	6.00	12.00
❑ 311 Joe Pisarcik	.10	.30
❑ 312 Bill Simpson AP	.10	.30
❑ 313 Haven Moses	.20	.50
❑ 314 Jim Merlo	.10	.30
❑ 315 Preston Pearson	.20	.50
❑ 316 Larry Tearry RC	.10	.30
❑ 317 Tom Dempsey	.10	.30
❑ 318 Greg Latta	.10	.30
❑ 319 Redskins TL/John Riggins	.60	1.50
❑ 320 Jack Ham	.50	1.25
❑ 321 Harold Jackson	.20	.50
❑ 322 George Roberts RC	.10	.30
❑ 323 Ron Jaworski	.40	1.00
❑ 324 Jim Otis	.10	.30
❑ 325 Roger Carr	.20	.50
❑ 326 Jack Tatum	.20	.50
❑ 327 Derrick Gaffney RC	.10	.30
❑ 328 Reggie Williams	.40	1.00
❑ 329 Doug Dieken	.10	.30
❑ 330 Efren Herrera	.10	.30
❑ 331 Earl Campbell RB	3.00	6.00
❑ 332 Tony Galbreath RB	.10	.30
❑ 333 Bruce Harper RB	.10	.30
❑ 334 John James RB	.10	.30
❑ 335 Walter Payton RB	1.50	4.00
❑ 336 Rickey Young RB	.10	.30
❑ 337 Jeff Van Note	.20	.50
❑ 338 Chargers TL/J.Jefferson	.40	1.00
❑ 339 Stan Walters RC	.10	.30
❑ 340 Louis Wright	.20	.50
❑ 341 Horace Ivory RC	.10	.30
❑ 342 Andre Tillman	.10	.30
❑ 343 Greg Coleman RC	.10	.30
❑ 344 Doug English RC	.40	1.00
❑ 345 Ted Hendricks	.40	1.00
❑ 346 Rich Saul	.10	.30
❑ 347 Mel Gray	.20	.50
❑ 348 Toni Fritsch	.10	.30
❑ 349 Cornell Webster RC	.10	.30
❑ 350 Ken Houston	.40	1.00
❑ 351 Ron Johnson DB RC	.20	.50
❑ 352 Doug Kotar	.10	.30
❑ 353 Brian Sipe	.40	1.00
❑ 354 Billy Brooks	.10	.30
❑ 355 John Dutton	.20	.50
❑ 356 Don Goode	.10	.30
❑ 357 Detroit Lions TL	.30	.75
❑ 358 Reuben Gant	.10	.30
❑ 359 Bob Parsons	.10	.30
❑ 360 Cliff Harris	.40	1.00
❑ 361 Raymond Clayborn	.20	.50
❑ 362 Scott Dierking	.10	.30
❑ 363 Bill Bryan RC	.10	.30
❑ 364 Mike Livingston	.10	.30
❑ 365 Otis Sistrunk	.20	.50
❑ 366 Charle Young	.20	.50
❑ 367 Keith Wortman RC	.10	.30
❑ 368 Checklist 265-396	.40	1.00
❑ 369 Mike Michel RC	.10	.30
❑ 370 Delvin Williams AP	.10	.30
❑ 371 Steve Furness	.20	.50
❑ 372 Emery Moorehead	.10	.30
❑ 373 Clarence Scott	.10	.30
❑ 374 Rufus Mayes	.10	.30
❑ 375 Chris Hanburger	.10	.30
❑ 376 Baltimore Colts TL	.30	.75
❑ 377 Bob Avellini	.20	.50
❑ 378 Jeff Siemon	.10	.30
❑ 379 Roland Hooks	.10	.30
❑ 380 Russ Francis	.20	.50
❑ 381 Roger Wehrli	.20	.50
❑ 382 Joe Fields	.10	.30
❑ 383 Archie Manning	.40	1.00
❑ 384 Rob Lytle	.10	.30
❑ 385 Thomas Henderson	.20	.50
❑ 386 Morris Owens	.10	.30
❑ 387 Dan Fouts	1.50	3.00
❑ 388 Chuck Crist	.10	.30
❑ 389 Ed O'Neil RC	.10	.30
❑ 390 Earl Campbell RC	15.00	30.00
❑ 391 Randy Grossman	.10	.30
❑ 392 Monte Jackson	.10	.30
❑ 393 John Mendenhall	.10	.30
❑ 394 Miami Dolphins TL	.40	1.00
❑ 395 Isaac Curtis	.20	.50
❑ 396 Mike Bragg	.10	.30
❑ 397 Doug Plank	.10	.30
❑ 398 Mike Barnes	.10	.30
❑ 399 Calvin Hill	.20	.50
❑ 400 Roger Staubach	5.00	10.00
❑ 401 Doug Beaudoin RC	.10	.30
❑ 402 Chuck Ramsey	.10	.30
❑ 403 Mike Hogan	.10	.30
❑ 404 Mario Clark	.10	.30
❑ 405 Riley Odoms	.10	.30
❑ 406 Carl Eller	.40	1.00
❑ 407 Packers TL/J.Lofton	.60	1.50
❑ 408 Mark Arneson	.10	.30
❑ 409 Vince Ferragamo RC	.40	1.00
❑ 410 Cleveland Elam	.10	.30
❑ 411 Donnie Shell RC	1.50	4.00
❑ 412 Ray Rhodes	.40	1.00
❑ 413 Don Cockroft	.10	.30
❑ 414 Don Bass RC	.20	.50
❑ 415 Cliff Branch	.40	1.00
❑ 416 Diron Talbert	.10	.30
❑ 417 Tom Hicks	.10	.30
❑ 418 Roosevelt Leaks	.10	.30
❑ 419 Charlie Joiner	.40	1.00
❑ 420 Lyle Alzado	.40	1.00
❑ 421 Sam Cunningham	.20	.50
❑ 422 Larry Keller	.10	.30
❑ 423 Jim Mitchell TE	.10	.30
❑ 424 Randy Logan	.10	.30
❑ 425 Jim Langer	.40	1.00
❑ 426 Gary Green	.10	.30
❑ 427 Luther Blue RC	.10	.30
❑ 428 Dennis Johnson	.10	.30
❑ 429 Danny White	.40	1.00

❑ 430 Roy Gerela	.10	.30
❑ 431 Jimmy Robinson	.10	.30
❑ 432 Minnesota Vikings TL	.30	.75
❑ 433 Oliver Davis	.10	.30
❑ 434 Lenvil Elliott	.10	.30
❑ 435 Willie Miller RC	.10	.30
❑ 436 Brad Dusek	.10	.30
❑ 437 Bob Thomas	.10	.30
❑ 438 Ken Mendenhall	.10	.30
❑ 439 Clarence Davis	.10	.30
❑ 440 Bob Griese	1.00	2.50
❑ 441 Tony McGee DT	.10	.30
❑ 442 Ed Taylor	.10	.30
❑ 443 Ron Howard	.10	.30
❑ 444 Wayne Morris	.10	.30
❑ 445 Charlie Waters	.20	.50
❑ 446 Rick Danmeier RC	.10	.30
❑ 447 Paul Naumoff	.10	.30
❑ 448 Keith Krepfle	.10	.30
❑ 449 Rusty Jackson	.10	.30
❑ 450 John Stallworth	2.00	4.00
❑ 451 New Orleans Saints TL	.30	.75
❑ 452 Ron Mikolajczyk RC	.10	.30
❑ 453 Fred Dryer	.40	1.00
❑ 454 Jim LeClair	.10	.30
❑ 455 Greg Pruitt	.20	.50
❑ 456 Jake Scott	.10	.30
❑ 457 Steve Schubert	.10	.30
❑ 458 George Kunz	.10	.30
❑ 459 Mike Williams	.10	.30
❑ 460 Dave Casper AP	.40	1.00
❑ 461 Sam Adams OL	.10	.30
❑ 462 Abdul Salaam	.10	.30
❑ 463 Terdell Middleton RC	.20	.50
❑ 464 Mike Wood RC	.10	.30
❑ 465 Bill Thompson AP	.10	.30
❑ 466 Larry Gordon	.10	.30
❑ 467 Benny Ricardo	.10	.30
❑ 468 Reggie McKenzie	.20	.50
❑ 469 Cowboys TL/T.Dorsett	.60	1.50
❑ 470 Rickey Young	.20	.50
❑ 471 Charlie Smith WR	.10	.30
❑ 472 Al Dixon RC	.10	.30
❑ 473 Tom DeLeone	.10	.30
❑ 474 Louis Breeden RC	.20	.50
❑ 475 Jack Lambert	.75	2.00
❑ 476 Terry Hermeling	.10	.30
❑ 477 J.K. McKay	.10	.30
❑ 478 Stan White	.10	.30
❑ 479 Terry Nelson	.10	.30
❑ 480 Walter Payton	10.00	20.00
❑ 481 Dave Dalby	.10	.30
❑ 482 Burgess Owens	.10	.30
❑ 483 Rolf Benirschke	.10	.30
❑ 484 Jack Dolbin	.10	.30
❑ 485 John Hannah	.40	1.00
❑ 486 Checklist 397-528	.40	1.00
❑ 487 Greg Landry	.20	.50
❑ 488 St. Louis Cardinals TL	.30	.75
❑ 489 Paul Krause	.40	1.00
❑ 490 John James	.10	.30
❑ 491 Merv Krakau	.10	.30
❑ 492 Dan Doornink RC	.10	.30
❑ 493 Curtis Johnson	.10	.30
❑ 494 Rafael Septien	.10	.30
❑ 495 Jean Fugett	.10	.30
❑ 496 Frank LeMaster	.10	.30
❑ 497 Allan Ellis	.10	.30
❑ 498 Billy Waddy RC	.20	.50
❑ 499 Hank Bauer RC	.10	.30
❑ 500 Terry Bradshaw UER	5.00	10.00
❑ 501 Larry McCarren	.10	.30
❑ 502 Fred Cook	.10	.30
❑ 503 Chuck Muncie	.20	.50
❑ 504 Herman Weaver	.10	.30
❑ 505 Eddie Edwards	.10	.30
❑ 506 Tony Peters	.10	.30
❑ 507 Denver Broncos TL	.30	.75
❑ 508 Jimbo Elrod RC	.10	.30
❑ 509 David Hill	.10	.30
❑ 510 Harvey Martin	.20	.50
❑ 511 Terry Miller RC	.20	.50
❑ 512 June Jones RC	.20	.50
❑ 513 Randy Cross	.40	1.00
❑ 514 Duriel Harris	.10	.30
❑ 515 Harry Carson	.40	1.00
❑ 516 Tim Fox	.10	.30
❑ 517 John Zook	.10	.30
❑ 518 Bob Tucker	.10	.30
❑ 519 Kevin Long RC	.10	.30
❑ 520 Ken Stabler	3.00	6.00
❑ 521 John Bunting	.20	.50
❑ 522 Rocky Bleier	.50	1.25
❑ 523 Noah Jackson	.10	.30
❑ 524 Cliff Parsley RC	.10	.30
❑ 525 Louie Kelcher AP	.20	.50
❑ 526 Bucs TL/Ricky Bell	.30	.75
❑ 527 Bob Brudzinski RC	.10	.30
❑ 528 Danny Buggs	.10	.30

1980 Topps

❑ COMPLETE SET (528)	40.00	75.00
❑ 1 Ottis Anderson RB	.40	1.00
❑ 2 Harold Carmichael RB	.40	1.00
❑ 3 Dan Fouts RB	.40	1.00
❑ 4 Paul Krause RB	.20	.50
❑ 5 Rick Upchurch RB	.20	.50
❑ 6 Garo Yepremian RB	.08	.25
❑ 7 Harold Jackson	.20	.50
❑ 8 Mike Williams	.08	.25
❑ 9 Calvin Hill	.20	.50
❑ 10 Jack Ham	.40	1.00
❑ 11 Dan Melville	.08	.25
❑ 12 Matt Robinson	.08	.25
❑ 13 Billy Campfield	.08	.25
❑ 14 Phil Tabor	.08	.25
❑ 15 Randy Hughes UER	.08	.25
❑ 16 Andre Tillman	.08	.25
❑ 17 Isaac Curtis	.20	.50
❑ 18 Charley Hannah	.08	.25
❑ 19 Redskins TL/J.Riggins	.40	1.00
❑ 20 Jim Zorn	.20	.50
❑ 21 Brian Baschnagel	.08	.25
❑ 22 Jon Keyworth	.08	.25
❑ 23 Phil Villapiano	.08	.25
❑ 24 Richard Osborne	.08	.25
❑ 25 Rich Saul AP	.08	.25
❑ 26 Doug Beaudoin	.08	.25
❑ 27 Cleveland Elam	.08	.25
❑ 28 Charlie Joiner	.40	1.00
❑ 29 Dick Ambrose	.08	.25
❑ 30 Mike Reinfeldt RC	.08	.25
❑ 31 Matt Bahr RC	.40	1.00
❑ 32 Keith Krepfle	.08	.25
❑ 33 Herb Scott	.08	.25
❑ 34 Doug Kotar	.08	.25
❑ 35 Bob Griese	.60	1.50
❑ 36 Jerry Butler RC	.40	1.00
❑ 37 Rolland Lawrence	.08	.25
❑ 38 Gary Weaver	.08	.25
❑ 39 Chiefs TL/J.T.Smith	.20	.50
❑ 40 Chuck Muncie	.20	.50
❑ 41 Mike Hartenstine	.08	.25
❑ 42 Sammie White	.20	.50
❑ 43 Ken Clark	.08	.25
❑ 44 Clarence Harmon	.08	.25
❑ 45 Bert Jones	.40	1.00
❑ 46 Mike Washington	.08	.25
❑ 47 Joe Fields	.08	.25
❑ 48 Mike Wood	.08	.25
❑ 49 Oliver Davis	.08	.25
❑ 50 Stan Walters AP	.08	.25
❑ 51 Riley Odoms	.08	.25
❑ 52 Steve Pisarkiewicz	.08	.25
❑ 53 Tony Hill	.40	1.00
❑ 54 Scott Perry	.08	.25
❑ 55 George Martin RC	.08	.25
❑ 56 George Roberts	.08	.25
❑ 57 Seahawks TL/S. Largent	.40	1.00
❑ 58 Billy Johnson	.20	.50
❑ 59 Reuben Gant	.08	.25
❑ 60 Dennis Harrah RC	.08	.25
❑ 61 Rocky Bleier	.40	1.00
❑ 62 Sam Hunt	.08	.25
❑ 63 Allan Ellis	.08	.25
❑ 64 Ricky Thompson	.08	.25
❑ 65 Ken Stabler	2.00	4.00
❑ 66 Dexter Bussey	.08	.25
❑ 67 Ken Mendenhall	.08	.25
❑ 68 Woodrow Lowe	.08	.25
❑ 69 Thom Darden	.08	.25
❑ 70 Randy White	.60	1.50
❑ 71 Ken MacAfee	.08	.25
❑ 72 Ron Jaworski	.40	1.00
❑ 73 William Andrews RC	.40	1.00
❑ 74 Jimmy Robinson	.08	.25
❑ 75 Roger Wehrli AP	.20	.50
❑ 76 Dolphins TL/L.Csonka	.40	1.00
❑ 77 Jack Rudnay	.08	.25
❑ 78 James Lofton	.75	2.00
❑ 79 Robert Brazile	.20	.50
❑ 80 Russ Francis	.20	.50
❑ 81 Ricky Bell	.40	1.00
❑ 82 Bob Avellini	.20	.50
❑ 83 Bobby Jackson	.08	.25
❑ 84 Mike Bragg	.08	.25
❑ 85 Cliff Branch	.40	1.00
❑ 86 Blair Bush	.08	.25
❑ 87 Sherman Smith	.08	.25
❑ 88 Glen Edwards	.08	.25
❑ 89 Don Cockroft	.08	.25
❑ 90 Louis Wright	.20	.50
❑ 91 Randy Grossman	.08	.25
❑ 92 Carl Hairston RC	.40	1.00
❑ 93 Archie Manning	.40	1.00
❑ 94 New York Giants TL	.20	.50
❑ 95 Preston Pearson	.20	.50
❑ 96 Rusty Chambers	.08	.25
❑ 97 Greg Coleman	.08	.25
❑ 98 Charle Young	.08	.25
❑ 99 Matt Cavanaugh RC	.20	.50
❑ 100 Jesse Baker	.08	.25
❑ 101 Doug Plank	.08	.25
❑ 102 Checklist 1-132	.30	.75
❑ 103 Luther Bradley RC	.08	.25
❑ 104 Bob Kuziel	.08	.25
❑ 105 Craig Morton	.20	.50
❑ 106 Sherman White	.08	.25
❑ 107 Jim Breech RC	.20	.50
❑ 108 Hank Bauer	.08	.25
❑ 109 Tom Blanchard	.08	.25
❑ 110 Ozzie Newsome	.75	2.00
❑ 111 Steve Furness	.08	.25
❑ 112 Frank LeMaster	.08	.25
❑ 113 Cowboys TL/T.Dorsett	.40	1.00
❑ 114 Doug Van Horn	.08	.25
❑ 115 Delvin Williams	.08	.25
❑ 116 Lyle Blackwood	.08	.25
❑ 117 Derrick Gaffney	.08	.25
❑ 118 Cornell Webster	.08	.25
❑ 119 Sam Cunningham	.20	.50
❑ 120 Jim Youngblood AP	.20	.50
❑ 121 Bob Thomas	.08	.25
❑ 122 Jack Thompson RC	.20	.50
❑ 123 Randy Cross	.40	1.00
❑ 124 Karl Lorch RC	.08	.25
❑ 125 Mel Gray	.08	.25
❑ 126 John James	.08	.25
❑ 127 Terdell Middleton	.08	.25
❑ 128 Leroy Jones	.08	.25
❑ 129 Tom DeLeone	.08	.25
❑ 130 John Stallworth	.60	1.50
❑ 131 Jimmie Giles RC	.20	.50
❑ 132 Philadelphia Eagles TL	.40	1.00
❑ 133 Gary Green	.08	.25
❑ 134 John Dutton	.20	.50
❑ 135 Harry Carson	.40	1.00
❑ 136 Bob Kuechenberg	.20	.50
❑ 137 Ike Harris	.08	.25
❑ 138 Tommy Kramer RC	.40	1.00
❑ 139 Sam Adams OL	.08	.25
❑ 140 Doug English	.20	.50
❑ 141 Steve Schubert	.08	.25
❑ 142 Rusty Jackson	.08	.25
❑ 143 Reese McCall	.08	.25
❑ 144 Scott Dierking	.08	.25
❑ 145 Ken Houston	.40	1.00
❑ 146 Bob Martin	.08	.25
❑ 147 Sam McCullum	.08	.25
❑ 148 Tom Banks	.08	.25
❑ 149 Willie Buchanon	.08	.25
❑ 150 Greg Pruitt	.20	.50
❑ 151 Denver Broncos TL	.40	1.00
❑ 152 Don Smith RC	.08	.25

❑ 153 Pete Johnson	.20	.50
❑ 154 Charlie Smith WR	.08	.25
❑ 155 Mel Blount	.40	1.00
❑ 156 John Mendenhall	.08	.25
❑ 157 Danny White	.40	1.00
❑ 158 Jimmy Cefalo RC	.20	.50
❑ 159 Richard Bishop AP	.08	.25
❑ 160 Walter Payton	6.00	12.00
❑ 161 Dave Dalby	.08	.25
❑ 162 Preston Dennard	.08	.25
❑ 163 Johnnie Gray	.08	.25
❑ 164 Russell Erxleben	.08	.25
❑ 165 Toni Fritsch AP	.08	.25
❑ 166 Terry Hermeling	.08	.25
❑ 167 Roland Hooks	.08	.25
❑ 168 Roger Carr	.08	.25
❑ 169 San Diego Chargers TL	.40	1.00
❑ 170 Ottis Anderson RC	1.50	4.00
❑ 171 Brian Sipe	.40	1.00
❑ 172 Leonard Thompson	.08	.25
❑ 173 Tony Reed	.08	.25
❑ 174 Bob Tucker	.08	.25
❑ 175 Joe Greene	.40	1.00
❑ 176 Jack Dolbin	.08	.25
❑ 177 Chuck Ramsey	.08	.25
❑ 178 Paul Hofer	.08	.25
❑ 179 Randy Logan	.08	.25
❑ 180 David Lewis AP	.08	.25
❑ 181 Duriel Harris	.08	.25
❑ 182 June Jones	.20	.50
❑ 183 Larry McCarren	.08	.25
❑ 184 Ken Johnson RB	.08	.25
❑ 185 Charlie Waters	.20	.50
❑ 186 Noah Jackson	.08	.25
❑ 187 Reggie Williams	.20	.50
❑ 188 New England Patriots TL	.20	.50
❑ 189 Carl Eller	.40	1.00
❑ 190 Ed White AP	.08	.25
❑ 191 Mario Clark	.08	.25
❑ 192 Roosevelt Leaks	.08	.25
❑ 193 Ted McKnight	.08	.25
❑ 194 Danny Buggs	.08	.25
❑ 195 Lester Hayes RC	1.50	4.00
❑ 196 Clarence Scott	.08	.25
❑ 197 Saints TL/Wes Chandler	.20	.50
❑ 198 Richard Caster	.08	.25
❑ 199 Louie Giammona	.08	.25
❑ 200 Terry Bradshaw	3.00	8.00
❑ 201 Ed Newman	.08	.25
❑ 202 Fred Dryer	.40	1.00
❑ 203 Dennis Franks	.08	.25
❑ 204 Bob Breunig RC	.20	.50
❑ 205 Alan Page	.40	1.00
❑ 206 Earnest Gray RC	.08	.25
❑ 207 Vikings TL/A.Rashad	.40	1.00
❑ 208 Horace Ivory	.08	.25
❑ 209 Isaac Hagins	.08	.25
❑ 210 Gary Johnson AP	.08	.25
❑ 211 Kevin Long	.08	.25
❑ 212 Bill Thompson	.08	.25
❑ 213 Don Bass	.08	.25
❑ 214 George Starke RC	.08	.25
❑ 215 Efren Herrera	.08	.25
❑ 216 Theo Bell	.08	.25
❑ 217 Monte Jackson	.08	.25
❑ 218 Reggie McKenzie	.08	.25
❑ 219 Bucky Dilts	.08	.25
❑ 220 Lyle Alzado	.40	1.00
❑ 221 Tim Foley	.08	.25
❑ 222 Mark Arneson	.08	.25
❑ 223 Fred Quillan	.08	.25
❑ 224 Benny Ricardo	.08	.25
❑ 225 Phil Simms RC	4.00	10.00
❑ 226 Bears TL/Walter Payton	.50	1.25
❑ 227 Max Runager	.08	.25
❑ 228 Barty Smith	.08	.25
❑ 229 Jay Saldi	.20	.50
❑ 230 John Hannah	.40	1.00
❑ 231 Tim Wilson	.08	.25
❑ 232 Jeff Van Note	.08	.25
❑ 233 Henry Marshall	.08	.25
❑ 234 Diron Talbert	.08	.25
❑ 235 Garo Yepremian	.20	.50
❑ 236 Larry Brown	.08	.25
❑ 237 Clarence Williams RB	.08	.25
❑ 238 Burgess Owens	.08	.25
❑ 239 Vince Ferragamo	.20	.50
❑ 240 Rickey Young	.08	.25
❑ 241 Dave Logan	.08	.25
❑ 242 Larry Gordon	.08	.25
❑ 243 Terry Miller	.08	.25
❑ 244 Baltimore Colts TL	.40	1.00
❑ 245 Steve DeBerg	.40	1.00
❑ 246 Checklist 133-264	.30	.75
❑ 247 Greg Latta	.08	.25
❑ 248 Raymond Clayborn	.20	.50
❑ 249 Jim Clack	.08	.25
❑ 250 Drew Pearson	.40	1.00
❑ 251 John Bunting	.20	.50
❑ 252 Rob Lytle	.08	.25
❑ 253 Jim Hart	.40	1.00
❑ 254 John McDaniel	.08	.25
❑ 255 Dave Pear AP	.08	.25
❑ 256 Donnie Shell	.40	1.00
❑ 257 Dan Doornink	.08	.25
❑ 258 Wallace Francis RC	.40	1.00
❑ 259 Dave Beverly	.08	.25
❑ 260 Lee Roy Selmon	.40	1.00
❑ 261 Doug Dieken	.08	.25
❑ 262 Gary Davis	.08	.25
❑ 263 Bob Rush	.08	.25
❑ 264 Buffalo Bills TL	.20	.50
❑ 265 Greg Landry	.20	.50
❑ 266 Jan Stenerud	.40	1.00
❑ 267 Tom Hicks	.08	.25
❑ 268 Pat McInally	.08	.25
❑ 269 Tim Fox	.08	.25
❑ 270 Harvey Martin	.20	.50
❑ 271 Dan Lloyd	.08	.25
❑ 272 Mike Barber	.08	.25
❑ 273 Wendell Tyler RC	.40	1.00
❑ 274 Jeff Komlo	.08	.25
❑ 275 Wes Chandler RC	.40	1.00
❑ 276 Brad Dusek	.08	.25
❑ 277 Charlie Johnson NT	.08	.25
❑ 278 Dennis Swilley	.08	.25
❑ 279 Johnny Evans	.08	.25
❑ 280 Jack Lambert	.60	1.50
❑ 281 Vern Den Herder	.08	.25
❑ 282 Tampa Bay Bucs TL	.40	1.00
❑ 283 Bob Klein	.08	.25
❑ 284 Jim Turner	.08	.25
❑ 285 Marvin Powell AP	.20	.50
❑ 286 Aaron Kyle	.08	.25
❑ 287 Dan Neal	.08	.25
❑ 288 Wayne Morris	.08	.25
❑ 289 Steve Bartkowski	.20	.50
❑ 290 Dave Jennings AP	.20	.50
❑ 291 John Smith	.08	.25
❑ 292 Bill Gregory	.08	.25
❑ 293 Frank Lewis	.08	.25
❑ 294 Fred Cook	.08	.25
❑ 295 David Hill AP	.08	.25
❑ 296 Wade Key	.08	.25
❑ 297 Sidney Thornton	.08	.25
❑ 298 Charlie Hall	.08	.25
❑ 299 Joe Lavender	.08	.25
❑ 300 Tom Rafferty RC	.08	.25
❑ 301 Mike Renfro RC	.20	.50
❑ 302 Wilbur Jackson	.20	.50
❑ 303 Packers TL/J.Lofton	.40	1.00
❑ 304 Henry Childs	.08	.25
❑ 305 Russ Washington AP	.08	.25
❑ 306 Jim LeClair	.08	.25
❑ 307 Tommy Hart	.08	.25
❑ 308 Gary Barbaro	.08	.25
❑ 309 Billy Taylor	.08	.25
❑ 310 Ray Guy	.20	.50
❑ 311 Don Hasselbeck RC	.20	.50
❑ 312 Doug Williams	.40	1.00
❑ 313 Nick Mike-Mayer	.08	.25
❑ 314 Don McCauley	.08	.25
❑ 315 Wesley Walker	.40	1.00
❑ 316 Dan Dierdorf	.40	1.00
❑ 317 Dave Brown DB RC	.20	.50
❑ 318 Leroy Harris	.08	.25
❑ 319 Steelers TL/Harris/Lambrt	.40	1.00
❑ 320 Mark Moseley AP UER	.08	.25
❑ 321 Mark Dennard	.08	.25
❑ 322 Terry Nelson	.08	.25
❑ 323 Tom Jackson	.40	1.00
❑ 324 Rick Kane	.08	.25
❑ 325 Jerry Sherk	.08	.25
❑ 326 Ray Preston	.08	.25
❑ 327 Golden Richards	.08	.25
❑ 328 Randy Dean	.08	.25
❑ 329 Rick Danmeier	.08	.25
❑ 330 Tony Dorsett	3.00	6.00
❑ 331 R.Staubach/Fouts LL	1.50	3.00
❑ 332 Receiving Leaders	.20	.50
❑ 333 Sacks Leaders	.40	1.00
❑ 334 Scoring Leaders	.40	1.00
❑ 335 Interception Leaders	.40	1.00
❑ 336 Punting Leaders	.40	1.00
❑ 337 Freddie Solomon	.08	.25
❑ 338 Cincinnati Bengals TL/Jauron	.40	1.00
❑ 339 Ken Stone	.08	.25
❑ 340 Greg Buttle AP	.08	.25
❑ 341 Bob Baumhower	.20	.50
❑ 342 Billy Waddy	.08	.25
❑ 343 Cliff Parsley	.08	.25
❑ 344 Walter White	.08	.25
❑ 345 Mike Thomas	.08	.25
❑ 346 Neil O'Donoghue	.08	.25
❑ 347 Freddie Scott	.08	.25
❑ 348 Joe Ferguson	.20	.50
❑ 349 Doug Nettles	.08	.25
❑ 350 Mike Webster	.40	1.00
❑ 351 Ron Saul	.08	.25
❑ 352 Julius Adams	.08	.25
❑ 353 Rafael Septien	.08	.25
❑ 354 Cleo Miller	.08	.25
❑ 355 Keith Simpson AP	.08	.25
❑ 356 Johnny Perkins	.08	.25
❑ 357 Jerry Sisemore	.08	.25
❑ 358 Arthur Whittington	.08	.25
❑ 359 Cardinals TL/Anderson	.40	1.00
❑ 360 Rick Upchurch	.20	.50
❑ 361 Kim Bokamper RC	.08	.25
❑ 362 Roland Harper	.08	.25
❑ 363 Pat Leahy	.08	.25
❑ 364 Louis Breeden	.08	.25
❑ 365 John Jefferson	.40	1.00
❑ 366 Jerry Eckwood	.08	.25
❑ 367 David Whitehurst	.08	.25
❑ 368 Willie Parker C	.08	.25
❑ 369 Ed Simonini	.08	.25
❑ 370 Jack Youngblood	.40	1.00
❑ 371 Don Warren RC	.40	1.00
❑ 372 Andy Johnson	.08	.25
❑ 373 D.D. Lewis	.20	.50
❑ 374A Beasley Reece ERR RC	.40	1.00
❑ 374B Beasley Reece COR RC	.20	.50
❑ 375 L.C.Greenwood	.40	1.00
❑ 376 Cleveland Browns TL	.20	.50
❑ 377 Herman Edwards	.08	.25
❑ 378 Rob Carpenter RC	.08	.25
❑ 379 Herman Weaver	.08	.25
❑ 380 Gary Fencik	.08	.25
❑ 381 Don Strock	.20	.50
❑ 382 Art Shell	.40	1.00
❑ 383 Tim Mazzetti	.08	.25
❑ 384 Bruce Harper	.08	.25
❑ 385 Al (Bubba) Baker	.20	.50
❑ 386 Conrad Dobler	.08	.25
❑ 387 Stu Voigt	.08	.25
❑ 388 Ken Anderson	.40	1.00
❑ 389 Pat Tilley	.08	.25
❑ 390 John Riggins	.40	1.00
❑ 391 Checklist 265-396	.30	.75
❑ 392 Fred Dean	.20	.50
❑ 393 Benny Barnes RC	.08	.25
❑ 394 Los Angeles Rams TL	.20	.50
❑ 395 Brad Van Pelt	.08	.25
❑ 396 Eddie Hare	.08	.25
❑ 397 John Sciarra RC	.08	.25
❑ 398 Bob Jackson	.08	.25
❑ 399 John Yarno	.08	.25
❑ 400 Franco Harris	.75	2.00
❑ 401 Ray Wersching	.08	.25
❑ 402 Virgil Livers	.08	.25
❑ 403 Raymond Chester	.08	.25
❑ 404 Leon Gray	.08	.25
❑ 405 Richard Todd	.20	.50
❑ 406 Larry Little	.40	1.00
❑ 407 Ted Fritsch Jr.	.08	.25
❑ 408 Larry Mucker	.08	.25
❑ 409 Jim Allen	.08	.25
❑ 410 Randy Gradishar	.40	1.00
❑ 411 Atlanta Falcons TL	.40	1.00
❑ 412 Louie Kelcher	.20	.50
❑ 413 Robert Newhouse	.20	.50
❑ 414 Gary Shirk	.08	.25
❑ 415 Mike Haynes	.40	1.00
❑ 416 Craig Colquitt	.08	.25
❑ 417 Lou Piccone	.08	.25
❑ 418 Clay Matthews RC	1.00	2.50

Card		
❑ 419 Marvin Cobb	.08	.25
❑ 420 Harold Carmichael	.40	1.00
❑ 421 Uwe Von Schamann	.20	.50
❑ 422 Mike Phipps	.20	.50
❑ 423 Nolan Cromwell RC	.40	1.00
❑ 424 Glenn Doughty	.08	.25
❑ 425 Bob Young AP	.08	.25
❑ 426 Tony Galbreath	.08	.25
❑ 427 Luke Prestridge RC	.08	.25
❑ 428 Terry Beeson	.08	.25
❑ 429 Jack Tatum	.20	.50
❑ 430 Lemar Parrish AP	.08	.25
❑ 431 Chester Marcol	.08	.25
❑ 432 Houston Oilers TL	.40	1.00
❑ 433 John Fitzgerald	.08	.25
❑ 434 Gary Jeter RC	.20	.50
❑ 435 Steve Grogan	.40	1.00
❑ 436 Jon Kolb UER	.08	.25
❑ 437 Jim O'Bradovich UER	.08	.25
❑ 438 Gerald Irons	.08	.25
❑ 439 Jeff West	.08	.25
❑ 440 Wilbert Montgomery	.20	.50
❑ 441 Norris Thomas	.08	.25
❑ 442 James Scott	.08	.25
❑ 443 Curtis Brown	.08	.25
❑ 444 Ken Fantetti	.08	.25
❑ 445 Pat Haden	.40	1.00
❑ 446 Carl Mauck	.08	.25
❑ 447 Bruce Laird	.08	.25
❑ 448 Otis Armstrong	.08	.25
❑ 449 Gene Upshaw	.40	1.00
❑ 450 Steve Largent	3.00	6.00
❑ 451 Benny Malone	.08	.25
❑ 452 Steve Nelson	.08	.25
❑ 453 Mark Cotney	.08	.25
❑ 454 Joe Danelo	.08	.25
❑ 455 Billy Joe DuPree	.20	.50
❑ 456 Ron Johnson DB	.08	.25
❑ 457 Archie Griffin	.20	.50
❑ 458 Reggie Rucker	.08	.25
❑ 459 Claude Humphrey	.08	.25
❑ 460 Lydell Mitchell	.20	.50
❑ 461 Steve Towle	.08	.25
❑ 462 Revie Sorey	.08	.25
❑ 463 Tom Skladany	.08	.25
❑ 464 Clark Gaines	.08	.25
❑ 465 Frank Corral	.08	.25
❑ 466 Steve Fuller RC	.20	.50
❑ 467 Ahmad Rashad	.40	1.00
❑ 468 Oakland Raiders TL	.40	1.00
❑ 469 Brian Peets	.08	.25
❑ 470 Pat Donovan RC	.20	.50
❑ 471 Ken Burrough	.08	.25
❑ 472 Don Calhoun	.08	.25
❑ 473 Bill Bryan	.08	.25
❑ 474 Terry Jackson	.08	.25
❑ 475 Joe Theismann	.50	1.25
❑ 476 Jim Smith	.20	.50
❑ 477 Joe DeLamielleure	.40	1.00
❑ 478 Mike Pruitt AP	.20	.50
❑ 479 Steve Mike-Mayer	.08	.25
❑ 480 Bill Bergey	.20	.50
❑ 481 Mike Fuller	.08	.25
❑ 482 Bob Parsons	.08	.25
❑ 483 Billy Brooks	.08	.25
❑ 484 Jerome Barkum	.08	.25
❑ 485 Larry Csonka	.60	1.50
❑ 486 John Hill	.08	.25
❑ 487 Mike Dawson	.08	.25
❑ 488 Detroit Lions TL	.20	.50
❑ 489 Ted Hendricks	.40	1.00
❑ 490 Dan Pastorini	.20	.50
❑ 491 Stanley Morgan	.40	1.00
❑ 492 AFC Champs/Bleier	.40	1.00
❑ 493 NFC Champs/Ferragamo	.20	.50
❑ 494 Super Bowl XIV	.40	1.00
❑ 495 Dwight White	.20	.50
❑ 496 Haven Moses	.08	.25
❑ 497 Guy Morriss	.08	.25
❑ 498 Dewey Selmon	.20	.50
❑ 499 Dave Butz RC	.40	1.00
❑ 500 Chuck Foreman	.20	.50
❑ 501 Chris Bahr	.08	.25
❑ 502 Mark Miller QB	.08	.25
❑ 503 Tony Greene	.08	.25
❑ 504 Brian Kelley	.08	.25
❑ 505 Joe Washington	.20	.50
❑ 506 Butch Johnson	.20	.50
❑ 507 New York Jets TL	.20	.50
❑ 508 Steve Little	.08	.25
❑ 509 Checklist 397-528	.30	.75
❑ 510 Mark Van Eeghen	.08	.25
❑ 511 Gary Danielson	.20	.50
❑ 512 Manu Tuiasosopo	.08	.25
❑ 513 Paul Coffman RC	.20	.50
❑ 514 Cullen Bryant	.08	.25
❑ 515 Nat Moore	.20	.50
❑ 516 Bill Lenkaitis	.08	.25
❑ 517 Lynn Cain RC	.08	.25
❑ 518 Gregg Bingham	.08	.25
❑ 519 Ted Albrecht	.08	.25
❑ 520 Dan Fouts	.75	2.00
❑ 521 Bernard Jackson	.08	.25
❑ 522 Coy Bacon	.08	.25
❑ 523 Tony Franklin RC	.20	.50
❑ 524 Bo Harris	.08	.25
❑ 525 Bob Grupp AP	.08	.25
❑ 526 San Francisco 49ers TL	.40	1.00
❑ 527 Steve Wilson	.08	.25
❑ 528 Bennie Cunningham	.20	.50

1981 Topps

Card		
❑ COMPLETE SET (528)	100.00	200.00
❑ 1 Ron Jaworski/B.Sipe LL	.40	1.00
❑ 2 K.Winslow/Cooper LL	.40	1.00
❑ 3 Sack Leaders	.20	.50
❑ 4 Scoring Leaders	.08	.25
❑ 5 Interception Leaders	.20	.50
❑ 6 Punting Leaders	.08	.25
❑ 7 Don Calhoun	.08	.25
❑ 8 Jack Tatum	.20	.50
❑ 9 Reggie Rucker	.08	.25
❑ 10 Mike Webster	.40	1.00
❑ 11 Vince Evans RC	.40	1.00
❑ 12 Ottis Anderson SA	.40	1.00
❑ 13 Leroy Harris	.08	.25
❑ 14 Gordon King	.08	.25
❑ 15 Harvey Martin	.20	.50
❑ 16 Johnny Lam Jones RC	.20	.50
❑ 17 Ken Greene	.08	.25
❑ 18 Frank Lewis	.08	.25
❑ 19 Seahawks TL/Largent	.40	1.00
❑ 20 Lester Hayes	.40	1.00
❑ 21 Uwe Von Schamann	.08	.25
❑ 22 Joe Washington	.08	.25
❑ 23 Louie Kelcher	.08	.25
❑ 24 Willie Miller	.08	.25
❑ 25 Steve Grogan	.40	1.00
❑ 26 John Hill	.08	.25
❑ 27 Stan White	.08	.25
❑ 28 William Andrews SA	.20	.50
❑ 29 Clarence Scott	.08	.25
❑ 30 Leon Gray AP	.08	.25
❑ 31 Craig Colquitt	.08	.25
❑ 32 Doug Williams	.40	1.00
❑ 33 Bob Breunig	.20	.50
❑ 34 Billy Taylor	.08	.25
❑ 35 Harold Carmichael	.40	1.00
❑ 36 Ray Wersching	.08	.25
❑ 37 Dennis Johnson LB RC	.08	.25
❑ 38 Archie Griffin	.20	.50
❑ 39 Los Angeles Rams TL	.20	.50
❑ 40 Gary Fencik	.20	.50
❑ 41 Lynn Dickey	.08	.25
❑ 42 Steve Bartkowski SA	.20	.50
❑ 43 Art Shell	.40	1.00
❑ 44 Wilbur Jackson	.08	.25
❑ 45 Frank Corral	.08	.25
❑ 46 Ted McKnight	.08	.25
❑ 47 Joe Klecko	.20	.50
❑ 48 Dan Doornink	.08	.25
❑ 49 Doug Dieken	.08	.25
❑ 50 Jerry Robinson RC	.20	.50
❑ 51 Wallace Francis	.08	.25
❑ 52 Dave Preston RC	.08	.25
❑ 53 Jay Saldi	.08	.25
❑ 54 Rush Brown	.08	.25
❑ 55 Phil Simms	1.00	2.50
❑ 56 Nick Mike-Mayer	.08	.25
❑ 57 Redskins TL/A.Monk	.75	2.00
❑ 58 Mike Renfro	.08	.25
❑ 59 Ted Brown SA	.08	.25
❑ 60 Steve Nelson	.08	.25
❑ 61 Sidney Thornton	.08	.25
❑ 62 Kent Hill	.08	.25
❑ 63 Don Bessillieu	.08	.25
❑ 64 Fred Cook	.08	.25
❑ 65 Raymond Chester	.08	.25
❑ 66 Rick Kane	.08	.25
❑ 67 Mike Fuller	.08	.25
❑ 68 Dewey Selmon	.20	.50
❑ 69 Charles White RC	.40	1.00
❑ 70 Jeff Van Note	.08	.25
❑ 71 Robert Newhouse	.20	.50
❑ 72 Roynell Young RC	.08	.25
❑ 73 Lynn Cain SA	.08	.25
❑ 74 Mike Friede	.08	.25
❑ 75 Earl Cooper RC	.08	.25
❑ 76 New Orleans Saints TL	.20	.50
❑ 77 Rick Danmeier	.08	.25
❑ 78 Darrol Ray	.08	.25
❑ 79 Gregg Bingham	.08	.25
❑ 80 John Hannah	.40	1.00
❑ 81 Jack Thompson	.20	.50
❑ 82 Rick Upchurch	.20	.50
❑ 83 Mike Butler	.08	.25
❑ 84 Don Warren	.08	.25
❑ 85 Mark Van Eeghen	.08	.25
❑ 86 J.T.Smith RC	.40	1.00
❑ 87 Herman Weaver	.08	.25
❑ 88 Terry Bradshaw SA	1.00	2.50
❑ 89 Charlie Hall	.08	.25
❑ 90 Donnie Shell	.40	1.00
❑ 91 Ike Harris	.08	.25
❑ 92 Charlie Johnson NT	.08	.25
❑ 93 Rickey Watts	.08	.25
❑ 94 New England Patriots TL	.40	1.00
❑ 95 Drew Pearson	.40	1.00
❑ 96 Neil O'Donoghue	.08	.25
❑ 97 Conrad Dobler	.08	.25
❑ 98 Jewerl Thomas RC	.08	.25
❑ 99 Mike Barber	.08	.25
❑ 100 Billy Sims RC	1.25	3.00
❑ 101 Vern Den Herder	.08	.25
❑ 102 Greg Landry	.20	.50
❑ 103 Joe Cribbs SA	.20	.50
❑ 104 Mark Murphy RC	.08	.25
❑ 105 Chuck Muncie	.20	.50
❑ 106 Alfred Jackson	.20	.50
❑ 107 Chris Bahr	.08	.25
❑ 108 Gordon Jones	.08	.25
❑ 109 Willie Harper RC	.08	.25
❑ 110 Dave Jennings	.08	.25
❑ 111 Bennie Cunningham	.08	.25
❑ 112 Jerry Sisemore	.08	.25
❑ 113 Cleveland Browns TL	.40	1.00
❑ 114 Rickey Young	.08	.25
❑ 115 Ken Anderson	.40	1.00
❑ 116 Randy Gradishar	.40	1.00
❑ 117 Eddie Lee Ivery RC	.08	.25
❑ 118 Wesley Walker	.40	1.00
❑ 119 Chuck Foreman	.20	.50
❑ 120 Nolan Cromwell UER	.20	.50
❑ 121 Curtis Dickey SA	.08	.25
❑ 122 Wayne Morris	.08	.25
❑ 123 Greg Stemrick	.08	.25
❑ 124 Coy Bacon	.08	.25
❑ 125 Jim Zorn	.20	.50
❑ 126 Henry Childs	.08	.25
❑ 127 Checklist 1-132	.40	1.00
❑ 128 Len Walterscheid	.08	.25
❑ 129 Johnny Evans	.08	.25
❑ 130 Gary Barbaro	.08	.25
❑ 131 Jim Smith	.08	.25
❑ 132 New York Jets TL	.20	.50
❑ 133 Curtis Brown	.08	.25
❑ 134 D.D. Lewis	.08	.25
❑ 135 Jim Plunkett	.40	1.00
❑ 136 Nat Moore	.20	.50
❑ 137 Don McCauley	.08	.25
❑ 138 Tony Dorsett SA	.40	1.00
❑ 139 Julius Adams	.08	.25
❑ 140 Ahmad Rashad	.40	1.00
❑ 141 Rich Saul	.08	.25

❑ 142 Ken Fantetti .08 .25
❑ 143 Kenny Johnson .08 .25
❑ 144 Clark Gaines .08 .25
❑ 145 Mark Moseley .08 .25
❑ 146 Vernon Perry RC .08 .25
❑ 147 Jerry Eckwood .08 .25
❑ 148 Freddie Solomon .08 .25
❑ 149 Jerry Sherk .08 .25
❑ 150 Kellen Winslow RC 4.00 8.00
❑ 151 Packers TL/Lofton .40 1.00
❑ 152 Ross Browner .08 .25
❑ 153 Dan Fouts SA .40 1.00
❑ 154 Woody Peoples .08 .25
❑ 155 Jack Lambert .50 1.25
❑ 156 Mike Dennis .08 .25
❑ 157 Rafael Septien .08 .25
❑ 158 Archie Manning .40 1.00
❑ 159 Don Hasselbeck .08 .25
❑ 160 Alan Page .40 1.00
❑ 161 Arthur Whittington .08 .25
❑ 162 Billy Waddy .08 .25
❑ 163 Horace Belton .08 .25
❑ 164 Luke Prestridge .08 .25
❑ 165 Joe Theismann .50 1.25
❑ 166 Morris Towns .08 .25
❑ 167 Dave Brown DB .08 .25
❑ 168 Ezra Johnson .08 .25
❑ 169 Tampa Bay Bucs TL .08 .25
❑ 170 Joe DeLamielleure .40 1.00
❑ 171 Earnest Gray SA .08 .25
❑ 172 Mike Thomas .08 .25
❑ 173 Jim Haslett RC .75 2.00
❑ 174 David Woodley RC .20 .50
❑ 175 Al(Bubba) Baker .20 .50
❑ 176 Nesby Glasgow RC .08 .25
❑ 177 Pat Leahy .08 .25
❑ 178 Tom Brahaney .08 .25
❑ 179 Herman Edwards .08 .25
❑ 180 Junior Miller RC .08 .25
❑ 181 Richard Wood RC .08 .25
❑ 182 Lenvil Elliott .08 .25
❑ 183 Sammie White .20 .50
❑ 184 Russell Erxleben .08 .25
❑ 185 Ed Too Tall Jones .50 1.25
❑ 186 Ray Guy SA .20 .50
❑ 187 Haven Moses .08 .25
❑ 188 New York Giants TL .20 .50
❑ 189 David Whitehurst .08 .25
❑ 190 John Jefferson .40 1.00
❑ 191 Terry Beeson .08 .25
❑ 192 Dan Ross RC .20 .50
❑ 193 Dave Williams RB RC .08 .25
❑ 194 Art Monk RC 7.50 15.00
❑ 195 Roger Wehrli .20 .50
❑ 196 Ricky Feacher .08 .25
❑ 197 Miami Dolphins TL .40 1.00
❑ 198 Carl Roaches RC .08 .25
❑ 199 Billy Campfield .08 .25
❑ 200 Ted Hendricks .40 1.00
❑ 201 Fred Smerlas RC .40 1.00
❑ 202 Walter Payton SA 1.25 3.00
❑ 203 Luther Bradley .08 .25
❑ 204 Herb Scott .08 .25
❑ 205 Jack Youngblood .40 1.00
❑ 206 Danny Pittman .08 .25
❑ 207 Houston Oilers TL .20 .50
❑ 208 Vagas Ferguson RC .20 .50
❑ 209 Mark Dennard .08 .25
❑ 210 Lemar Parrish .08 .25
❑ 211 Bruce Harper .08 .25
❑ 212 Ed Simonini .08 .25
❑ 213 Nick Lowery RC .40 1.00
❑ 214 Kevin House RC .20 .50
❑ 215 Mike Kenn RC .40 1.00
❑ 216 Joe Montana RC 75.00 150.00
❑ 217 Joe Senser .08 .25
❑ 218 Lester Hayes SA .20 .50
❑ 219 Gene Upshaw .40 1.00
❑ 220 Franco Harris .60 1.50
❑ 221 Ron Bolton .08 .25
❑ 222 Charles Alexander RC .20 .50
❑ 223 Matt Robinson .08 .25
❑ 224 Ray Oldham .08 .25
❑ 225 George Martin .08 .25
❑ 226 Buffalo Bills TL .40 1.00
❑ 227 Tony Franklin .08 .25
❑ 228 George Cumby .08 .25
❑ 229 Butch Johnson .20 .50
❑ 230 Mike Haynes .40 1.00
❑ 231 Rob Carpenter .20 .50
❑ 232 Steve Fuller .20 .50
❑ 233 John Sawyer .08 .25
❑ 234 Kenny King SA .08 .25
❑ 235 Jack Ham .50 1.25
❑ 236 Jimmy Rogers .08 .25
❑ 237 Bob Parsons .08 .25
❑ 238 Marty Lyons RC .40 1.00
❑ 239 Pat Tilley .08 .25
❑ 240 Dennis Harrah .08 .25
❑ 241 Thom Darden .08 .25
❑ 242 Rolf Benirschke .08 .25
❑ 243 Gerald Small .08 .25
❑ 244 Atlanta Falcons TL .40 1.00
❑ 245 Roger Carr .08 .25
❑ 246 Sherman White .08 .25
❑ 247 Ted Brown .08 .25
❑ 248 Matt Cavanaugh .20 .50
❑ 249 John Dutton .08 .25
❑ 250 Bill Bergey .20 .50
❑ 251 Jim Allen .08 .25
❑ 252 Mike Nelms SA .08 .25
❑ 253 Tom Blanchard .08 .25
❑ 254 Ricky Thompson .08 .25
❑ 255 John Matuszak .20 .50
❑ 256 Randy Grossman .08 .25
❑ 257 Ray Griffin RC .08 .25
❑ 258 Lynn Cain .08 .25
❑ 259 Checklist 133-264 .40 1.00
❑ 260 Mike Pruitt .20 .50
❑ 261 Chris Ward RC .08 .25
❑ 262 Fred Steinfort .08 .25
❑ 263 James Owens .08 .25
❑ 264 Bears TL/Payton/Hampton .60 1.50
❑ 265 Dan Fouts .60 1.50
❑ 266 Arnold Morgado .08 .25
❑ 267 John Jefferson SA .40 1.00
❑ 268 Bill Lenkaitis .08 .25
❑ 269 James Jones COW .08 .25
❑ 270 Brad Van Pelt .08 .25
❑ 271 Steve Largent 1.25 2.50
❑ 272 Elvin Bethea .40 1.00
❑ 273 Cullen Bryant .08 .25
❑ 274 Gary Danielson .20 .50
❑ 275 Tony Galbreath .08 .25
❑ 276 Dave Butz .08 .25
❑ 277 Steve Mike-Mayer .08 .25
❑ 278 Ron Johnson DB .08 .25
❑ 279 Tom DeLeone .08 .25
❑ 280 Ron Jaworski .40 1.00
❑ 281 Mel Gray .08 .25
❑ 282 San Diego Chargers TL .40 1.00
❑ 283 Mark Brammer RC .08 .25
❑ 284 Alfred Jenkins SA .20 .50
❑ 285 Greg Buttle .08 .25
❑ 286 Randy Hughes .08 .25
❑ 287 Delvin Williams .08 .25
❑ 288 Brian Baschnagel .08 .25
❑ 289 Gary Jeter .08 .25
❑ 290 Stanley Morgan .40 1.00
❑ 291 Gerry Ellis .08 .25
❑ 292 Al Richardson .08 .25
❑ 293 Jimmie Giles .20 .50
❑ 294 Dave Jennings SA .08 .25
❑ 295 Wilbert Montgomery .20 .50
❑ 296 Dave Pureifory .08 .25
❑ 297 Greg Hawthorne .08 .25
❑ 298 Dick Ambrose .08 .25
❑ 299 Terry Hermeling .08 .25
❑ 300 Danny White .40 1.00
❑ 301 Ken Burrough .08 .25
❑ 302 Paul Hofer .08 .25
❑ 303 Denver Broncos TL .40 1.00
❑ 304 Eddie Payton .20 .50
❑ 305 Isaac Curtis .20 .50
❑ 306 Benny Ricardo .08 .25
❑ 307 Riley Odoms .08 .25
❑ 308 Bob Chandler .08 .25
❑ 309 Larry Heater .08 .25
❑ 310 Art Still RC .40 1.00
❑ 311 Harold Jackson .20 .50
❑ 312 Charlie Joiner SA .40 1.00
❑ 313 Jeff Nixon .08 .25
❑ 314 Aundra Thompson .08 .25
❑ 315 Richard Todd .20 .50
❑ 316 Dan Hampton RC 1.25 3.00
❑ 317 Doug Marsh .08 .25
❑ 318 Louie Giammona .08 .25
❑ 319 49ers TL/Dwight Clark .40 1.00
❑ 320 Manu Tuiasosopo .08 .25
❑ 321 Rich Milot .08 .25
❑ 322 Mike Guman RC .08 .25
❑ 323 Bob Kuechenberg .20 .50
❑ 324 Tom Skladany .08 .25
❑ 325 Dave Logan .08 .25
❑ 326 Bruce Laird .08 .25
❑ 327 James Jones COW SA .08 .25
❑ 328 Joe Danelo .08 .25
❑ 329 Kenny King RC .20 .50
❑ 330 Pat Donovan .08 .25
❑ 331 Earl Cooper RB .20 .50
❑ 332 John Jefferson RB .40 1.00
❑ 333 Kenny King RB .20 .50
❑ 334 Rod Martin RB .20 .50
❑ 335 Jim Plunkett RB .40 1.00
❑ 336 Bill Thompson RB .20 .50
❑ 337 John Cappelletti .20 .50
❑ 338 Lions TL/Billy Sims .40 1.00
❑ 339 Don Smith .08 .25
❑ 340 Rod Perry .08 .25
❑ 341 David Lewis .08 .25
❑ 342 Mark Gastineau RC .50 1.25
❑ 343 Steve Largent SA .40 1.00
❑ 344 Charle Young .08 .25
❑ 345 Toni Fritsch .08 .25
❑ 346 Matt Blair .20 .50
❑ 347 Don Bass .08 .25
❑ 348 Jim Jensen RC .20 .50
❑ 349 Karl Lorch .08 .25
❑ 350 Brian Sipe .20 .50
❑ 351 Theo Bell .08 .25
❑ 352 Sam Adams OL .08 .25
❑ 353 Paul Coffman .08 .25
❑ 354 Eric Harris .08 .25
❑ 355 Tony Hill .20 .50
❑ 356 J.T. Turner .08 .25
❑ 357 Frank LeMaster .08 .25
❑ 358 Jim Jodat .08 .25
❑ 359 Raiders TL/Hendricks .40 1.00
❑ 360 Joe Cribbs RC .40 1.00
❑ 361 James Lofton SA .40 1.00
❑ 362 Dexter Bussey .08 .25
❑ 363 Bobby Jackson .08 .25
❑ 364 Steve DeBerg .40 1.00
❑ 365 Ottis Anderson .40 1.00
❑ 366 Tom Myers .08 .25
❑ 367 John James .08 .25
❑ 368 Reese McCall .08 .25
❑ 369 Jack Reynolds .20 .50
❑ 370 Gary Johnson .08 .25
❑ 371 Jimmy Cefalo .08 .25
❑ 372 Horace Ivory .08 .25
❑ 373 Garo Yepremian .08 .25
❑ 374 Brian Kelley .08 .25
❑ 375 Terry Bradshaw 3.00 8.00
❑ 376 Cowboys TL/Tony Dorsett .40 1.00
❑ 377 Randy Logan .08 .25
❑ 378 Tim Wilson .08 .25
❑ 379 Archie Manning SA .40 1.00
❑ 380 Revie Sorey .08 .25
❑ 381 Randy Holloway .08 .25
❑ 382 Henry Lawrence .08 .25
❑ 383 Pat McInally .08 .25
❑ 384 Kevin Long .08 .25
❑ 385 Louis Wright .20 .50
❑ 386 Leonard Thompson .08 .25
❑ 387 Jan Stenerud .20 .50
❑ 388 Raymond Butler RC .08 .25
❑ 389 Checklist 265-396 .40 1.00
❑ 390 Steve Bartkowski .20 .50
❑ 391 Clarence Harmon .08 .25
❑ 392 Wilbert Montgomery SA .20 .50
❑ 393 Billy Joe DuPree .20 .50
❑ 394 Kansas City Chiefs TL .20 .50
❑ 395 Earnest Gray .08 .25
❑ 396 Ray Hamilton .08 .25
❑ 397 Brenard Wilson .08 .25
❑ 398 Calvin Hill .20 .50
❑ 399 Robin Cole .08 .25
❑ 400 Walter Payton 6.00 12.00
❑ 401 Jim Hart .40 1.00
❑ 402 Ron Yary .20 .50
❑ 403 Cliff Branch .40 1.00
❑ 404 Roland Hooks .08 .25
❑ 405 Ken Stabler 1.50 3.00
❑ 406 Chuck Ramsey .08 .25
❑ 407 Mike Nelms RC .08 .25
❑ 408 Ron Jaworski SA .20 .50

Card	Low	High
❑ 409 James Hunter	.08	.25
❑ 410 Lee Roy Selmon	.40	1.00
❑ 411 Baltimore Colts TL	.20	.50
❑ 412 Henry Marshall	.08	.25
❑ 413 Preston Pearson	.20	.50
❑ 414 Richard Bishop	.08	.25
❑ 415 Greg Pruitt	.20	.50
❑ 416 Matt Bahr	.20	.50
❑ 417 Tom Mullady	.08	.25
❑ 418 Glen Edwards	.08	.25
❑ 419 Sam McCullum	.08	.25
❑ 420 Stan Walters	.08	.25
❑ 421 George Roberts	.08	.25
❑ 422 Dwight Clark RC	2.00	5.00
❑ 423 Pat Thomas RC	.08	.25
❑ 424 Bruce Harper SA	.08	.25
❑ 425 Craig Morton	.20	.50
❑ 426 Derrick Gaffney	.08	.25
❑ 427 Pete Johnson	.08	.25
❑ 428 Wes Chandler	.40	1.00
❑ 429 Burgess Owens	.08	.25
❑ 430 James Lofton	.75	2.00
❑ 431 Tony Reed	.08	.25
❑ 432 Vikings TL/A.Rashad	.40	1.00
❑ 433 Ron Springs RC	.20	.50
❑ 434 Tim Fox	.08	.25
❑ 435 Ozzie Newsome	.75	2.00
❑ 436 Steve Furness	.08	.25
❑ 437 Will Lewis	.08	.25
❑ 438 Mike Hartenstine	.08	.25
❑ 439 John Bunting	.08	.25
❑ 440 Eddie Murray RC	.40	1.00
❑ 441 Mike Pruitt SA	.20	.50
❑ 442 Larry Swider	.08	.25
❑ 443 Steve Freeman	.08	.25
❑ 444 Bruce Hardy RC	.08	.25
❑ 445 Pat Haden	.20	.50
❑ 446 Curtis Dickey RC	.08	.25
❑ 447 Doug Wilkerson	.08	.25
❑ 448 Alfred Jenkins	.20	.50
❑ 449 Dave Dalby	.08	.25
❑ 450 Robert Brazile	.08	.25
❑ 451 Bobby Hammond	.08	.25
❑ 452 Raymond Clayborn	.08	.25
❑ 453 Jim Miller P RC	.08	.25
❑ 454 Roy Simmons	.08	.25
❑ 455 Charlie Waters	.20	.50
❑ 456 Ricky Bell	.40	1.00
❑ 457 Ahmad Rashad SA	.40	1.00
❑ 458 Don Cockroft	.08	.25
❑ 459 Keith Krepfle	.08	.25
❑ 460 Marvin Powell	.08	.25
❑ 461 Tommy Kramer	.40	1.00
❑ 462 Jim LeClair	.08	.25
❑ 463 Freddie Scott	.08	.25
❑ 464 Rob Lytle	.08	.25
❑ 465 Johnnie Gray	.08	.25
❑ 466 Doug France RC	.08	.25
❑ 467 Carlos Carson RC	.20	.50
❑ 468 Cardinals TL/O.Anderson	.40	1.00
❑ 469 Efren Herrera	.08	.25
❑ 470 Randy White	.50	1.25
❑ 471 Richard Caster	.08	.25
❑ 472 Andy Johnson	.08	.25
❑ 473 Billy Sims SA	.40	1.00
❑ 474 Joe Lavender	.08	.25
❑ 475 Harry Carson	.20	.50
❑ 476 John Stallworth	.50	1.25
❑ 477 Bob Thomas	.08	.25
❑ 478 Keith Wright RC	.08	.25
❑ 479 Ken Stone	.08	.25
❑ 480 Carl Hairston	.20	.50
❑ 481 Reggie McKenzie	.08	.25
❑ 482 Bob Griese	.60	1.50
❑ 483 Mike Bragg	.08	.25
❑ 484 Scott Dierking	.08	.25
❑ 485 David Hill	.08	.25
❑ 486 Brian Sipe SA	.20	.50
❑ 487 Rod Martin RC	.20	.50
❑ 488 Cincinnati Bengals TL	.20	.50
❑ 489 Preston Dennard	.08	.25
❑ 490 John Smith	.08	.25
❑ 491 Mike Reinfeldt	.08	.25
❑ 492 NFC Champs/Jaworski	.40	1.00
❑ 493 AFC Champs/Plunkett	.40	1.00
❑ 494 Super Bowl XV/J.Plunkett	.40	1.00
❑ 495 Joe Greene	.50	1.25
❑ 496 Charlie Joiner	.40	1.00
❑ 497 Rolland Lawrence	.08	.25
❑ 498 Al(Bubba) Baker SA	.20	.50
❑ 499 Brad Dusek	.08	.25
❑ 500 Tony Dorsett	2.00	4.00
❑ 501 Robin Earl	.08	.25
❑ 502 Theotis Brown RC	.08	.25
❑ 503 Joe Ferguson	.20	.50
❑ 504 Beasley Reece	.08	.25
❑ 505 Lyle Alzado	.40	1.00
❑ 506 Tony Nathan RC	.40	1.00
❑ 507 Philadelphia Eagles TL	.20	.50
❑ 508 Herb Orvis	.08	.25
❑ 509 Clarence Williams RB	.08	.25
❑ 510 Ray Guy	.20	.50
❑ 511 Jeff Komlo	.08	.25
❑ 512 Freddie Solomon SA	.08	.25
❑ 513 Tim Mazzetti	.08	.25
❑ 514 Elvis Peacock RC	.08	.25
❑ 515 Russ Francis	.20	.50
❑ 516 Roland Harper	.08	.25
❑ 517 Checklist 397-528	.40	1.00
❑ 518 Billy Johnson	.20	.50
❑ 519 Dan Dierdorf	.40	1.00
❑ 520 Fred Dean	.20	.50
❑ 521 Jerry Butler	.08	.25
❑ 522 Ron Saul	.08	.25
❑ 523 Charlie Smith WR	.08	.25
❑ 524 Kellen Winslow SA	1.50	3.00
❑ 525 Bert Jones	.40	1.00
❑ 526 Steelers TL/Fr.Harris	.40	1.00
❑ 527 Duriel Harris	.08	.25
❑ 528 William Andrews	.40	1.00

1982 Topps

Card	Low	High
❑ COMPLETE SET (528)	40.00	80.00
❑ 1 Ken Anderson RB	.40	1.00
❑ 2 Dan Fouts RB	.40	1.00
❑ 3 LeRoy Irvin RB	.08	.25
❑ 4 Stump Mitchell RB	.08	.25
❑ 5 George Rogers RB	.40	1.00
❑ 6 Dan Ross RB	.08	.25
❑ 7 AFC Champs/K.Anderson	.40	1.00
❑ 8 NFC Champs/E.Cooper	.40	1.00
❑ 9 Super Bowl XVI/A.Munoz	.40	1.00
❑ 10 Baltimore Colts TL	.08	.25
❑ 11 Raymond Butler	.08	.25
❑ 12 Roger Carr	.08	.25
❑ 13 Curtis Dickey	.20	.50
❑ 14 Zachary Dixon	.08	.25
❑ 15 Nesby Glasgow	.08	.25
❑ 16 Bert Jones	.40	1.00
❑ 17 Bruce Laird	.08	.25
❑ 18 Reese McCall	.08	.25
❑ 19 Randy McMillan	.08	.25
❑ 20 Ed Simonini	.08	.25
❑ 21 Buffalo Bills TL	.20	.50
❑ 22 Mark Brammer	.08	.25
❑ 23 Curtis Brown	.08	.25
❑ 24 Jerry Butler	.08	.25
❑ 25 Mario Clark	.08	.25
❑ 26 Joe Cribbs	.20	.50
❑ 27 Joe Cribbs IA	.20	.50
❑ 28 Joe Ferguson	.20	.50
❑ 29 Jim Haslett	.40	1.00
❑ 30 Frank Lewis	.08	.25
❑ 31 Frank Lewis IA	.08	.25
❑ 32 Shane Nelson	.08	.25
❑ 33 Charles Romes	.08	.25
❑ 34 Bill Simpson	.08	.25
❑ 35 Fred Smerlas	.08	.25
❑ 36 Bengals TL/C.Collinswort	.20	.50
❑ 37 Charles Alexander	.08	.25
❑ 38 Ken Anderson	.40	1.00
❑ 39 Ken Anderson IA	.40	1.00
❑ 40 Jim Breech	.08	.25
❑ 41 Jim Breech IA	.08	.25
❑ 42 Louis Breeden	.08	.25
❑ 43 Ross Browner	.08	.25
❑ 44 Cris Collinsworth RC	.75	2.00
❑ 45 Cris Collinsworth IA	.40	1.00
❑ 46 Isaac Curtis	.08	.25
❑ 47 Pete Johnson	.08	.25
❑ 48 Pete Johnson IA	.08	.25
❑ 49 Steve Kreider	.08	.25
❑ 50 Pat McInally	.08	.25
❑ 51 Anthony Munoz RC	4.00	8.00
❑ 52 Dan Ross	.08	.25
❑ 53 David Verser RC	.08	.25
❑ 54 Reggie Williams	.20	.50
❑ 55 Browns TL/O.Newsome	.20	.50
❑ 56 Lyle Alzado	.40	1.00
❑ 57 Dick Ambrose	.08	.25
❑ 58 Ron Bolton	.08	.25
❑ 59 Steve Cox	.08	.25
❑ 60 Joe DeLamielleure	.40	1.00
❑ 61 Tom DeLeone	.08	.25
❑ 62 Doug Dieken	.08	.25
❑ 63 Ricky Feacher	.08	.25
❑ 64 Don Goode	.08	.25
❑ 65 Robert L.Jackson RC	.08	.25
❑ 66 Dave Logan	.08	.25
❑ 67 Ozzie Newsome	.50	1.25
❑ 68 Ozzie Newsome IA	.40	1.00
❑ 69 Greg Pruitt	.20	.50
❑ 70 Mike Pruitt	.20	.50
❑ 71 Mike Pruitt IA	.20	.50
❑ 72 Reggie Rucker	.08	.25
❑ 73 Clarence Scott	.08	.25
❑ 74 Brian Sipe	.20	.50
❑ 75 Charles White	.20	.50
❑ 76 Denver Broncos TL	.20	.50
❑ 77 Rubin Carter	.08	.25
❑ 78 Steve Foley	.08	.25
❑ 79 Randy Gradishar	.20	.50
❑ 80 Tom Jackson	.40	1.00
❑ 81 Craig Morton	.20	.50
❑ 82 Craig Morton IA	.20	.50
❑ 83 Riley Odoms	.08	.25
❑ 84 Rick Parros	.08	.25
❑ 85 Dave Preston	.08	.25
❑ 86 Tony Reed	.08	.25
❑ 87 Bob Swenson RC	.08	.25
❑ 88 Bill Thompson	.08	.25
❑ 89 Rick Upchurch	.20	.50
❑ 90 Steve Watson RC	.20	.50
❑ 91 Steve Watson IA	.08	.25
❑ 92 Houston Oilers TL	.08	.25
❑ 93 Mike Barber	.08	.25
❑ 94 Elvin Bethea	.40	1.00
❑ 95 Gregg Bingham	.08	.25
❑ 96 Robert Brazile	.08	.25
❑ 97 Ken Burrough	.08	.25
❑ 98 Toni Fritsch	.08	.25
❑ 99 Leon Gray	.08	.25
❑ 100 Gifford Nielsen RC	.20	.50
❑ 101 Vernon Perry	.08	.25
❑ 102 Mike Reinfeldt	.08	.25
❑ 103 Mike Renfro	.08	.25
❑ 104 Carl Roaches	.08	.25
❑ 105 Ken Stabler	.75	2.00
❑ 106 Greg Stemrick	.08	.25
❑ 107 J.C. Wilson	.08	.25
❑ 108 Tim Wilson	.08	.25
❑ 109 Kansas City Chiefs TL	.08	.25
❑ 110 Gary Barbaro	.08	.25
❑ 111 Brad Budde RC	.08	.25
❑ 112 Joe Delaney RC	.40	1.00
❑ 113 Joe Delaney IA	.20	.50
❑ 114 Steve Fuller	.08	.25
❑ 115 Gary Green	.08	.25
❑ 116 James Hadnot	.08	.25
❑ 117 Eric Harris	.08	.25
❑ 118 Billy Jackson	.08	.25
❑ 119 Bill Kenney RC	.08	.25
❑ 120 Nick Lowery	.40	1.00
❑ 121 Nick Lowery IA	.20	.50
❑ 122 Henry Marshall	.08	.25
❑ 123 J.T.Smith	.20	.50
❑ 124 Art Still	.08	.25
❑ 125 Miami Dolphins TL	.20	.50
❑ 126 Bob Baumhower	.20	.50
❑ 127 Glenn Blackwood RC	.08	.25
❑ 128 Jimmy Cefalo	.08	.25
❑ 129 A.J. Duhe	.20	.50
❑ 130 Andra Franklin RC	.08	.25
❑ 131 Duriel Harris	.08	.25

Card		
❑ 132 Nat Moore	.20	.50
❑ 133 Tony Nathan	.20	.50
❑ 134 Ed Newman	.08	.25
❑ 135 Earnie Rhone	.08	.25
❑ 136 Don Strock	.08	.25
❑ 137 Tommy Vigorito	.08	.25
❑ 138 Uwe Von Schamann	.08	.25
❑ 139 Uwe Von Schamann IA	.08	.25
❑ 140 David Woodley	.20	.50
❑ 141 New England Pats TL	.20	.50
❑ 142 Julius Adams	.08	.25
❑ 143 Richard Bishop	.08	.25
❑ 144 Matt Cavanaugh	.08	.25
❑ 145 Raymond Clayborn	.08	.25
❑ 146 Tony Collins RC	.08	.25
❑ 147 Vagas Ferguson	.08	.25
❑ 148 Tim Fox	.08	.25
❑ 149 Steve Grogan	.20	.50
❑ 150 John Hannah	.40	1.00
❑ 151 John Hannah IA	.20	.50
❑ 152 Don Hasselbeck	.08	.25
❑ 153 Mike Haynes	.20	.50
❑ 154 Harold Jackson	.20	.50
❑ 155 Andy Johnson	.08	.25
❑ 156 Stanley Morgan	.20	.50
❑ 157 Stanley Morgan IA	.20	.50
❑ 158 Steve Nelson	.08	.25
❑ 159 Rod Shoate	.08	.25
❑ 160 Jets TL/F.McNeil	.20	.50
❑ 161 Dan Alexander RC	.08	.25
❑ 162 Mike Augustyniak	.08	.25
❑ 163 Jerome Barkum	.08	.25
❑ 164 Greg Buttle	.08	.25
❑ 165 Scott Dierking	.08	.25
❑ 166 Joe Fields	.08	.25
❑ 167 Mark Gastineau	.20	.50
❑ 168 Mark Gastineau IA	.20	.50
❑ 169 Bruce Harper	.08	.25
❑ 170 Johnny Lam Jones	.08	.25
❑ 171 Joe Klecko	.20	.50
❑ 172 Joe Klecko IA	.20	.50
❑ 173 Pat Leahy	.20	.50
❑ 174 Pat Leahy IA	.08	.25
❑ 175 Marty Lyons	.20	.50
❑ 176 Freeman McNeil RC	.40	1.00
❑ 177 Marvin Powell	.08	.25
❑ 178 Chuck Ramsey	.08	.25
❑ 179 Darrol Ray	.08	.25
❑ 180 Abdul Salaam	.08	.25
❑ 181 Richard Todd	.20	.50
❑ 182 Richard Todd IA	.20	.50
❑ 183 Wesley Walker	.20	.50
❑ 184 Chris Ward	.08	.25
❑ 185 Oakland Raiders TL	.20	.50
❑ 186 Cliff Branch	.40	1.00
❑ 187 Bob Chandler	.08	.25
❑ 188 Ray Guy	.20	.50
❑ 189 Lester Hayes	.20	.50
❑ 190 Ted Hendricks	.40	1.00
❑ 191 Monte Jackson	.08	.25
❑ 192 Derrick Jensen	.08	.25
❑ 193 Kenny King	.08	.25
❑ 194 Rod Martin	.08	.25
❑ 195 John Matuszak	.20	.50
❑ 196 Matt Millen RC	.60	1.50
❑ 197 Derrick Ramsey	.08	.25
❑ 198 Art Shell	.40	1.00
❑ 199 Mark Van Eeghen	.08	.25
❑ 200 Arthur Whittington	.08	.25
❑ 201 Marc Wilson RC	.20	.50
❑ 202 Steelers TL/Fr.Harris	.40	1.00
❑ 203 Mel Blount	.40	1.00
❑ 204 Terry Bradshaw	2.00	5.00
❑ 205 Terry Bradshaw IA	.75	2.00
❑ 206 Craig Colquitt	.08	.25
❑ 207 Bennie Cunningham	.08	.25
❑ 208 Russell Davis RC	.08	.25
❑ 209 Gary Dunn	.08	.25
❑ 210 Jack Ham	.40	1.00
❑ 211 Franco Harris	.50	1.25
❑ 212 Franco Harris IA	.40	1.00
❑ 213 Jack Lambert	.40	1.00
❑ 214 Jack Lambert IA	.40	1.00
❑ 215 Mark Malone RC	.40	1.00
❑ 216 Frank Pollard RC	.08	.25
❑ 217 Donnie Shell	.40	1.00
❑ 218 Jim Smith	.08	.25
❑ 219 John Stallworth	.40	1.00
❑ 220 John Stallworth IA	.40	1.00
❑ 221 David Trout	.08	.25
❑ 222 Mike Webster	.40	1.00
❑ 223 San Diego Chargers TL	.40	1.00
❑ 224 Rolf Benirschke	.08	.25
❑ 225 Rolf Benirschke IA	.08	.25
❑ 226 James Brooks RC	.40	1.00
❑ 227 Willie Buchanon	.08	.25
❑ 228 Wes Chandler	.40	1.00
❑ 229 Wes Chandler IA	.20	.50
❑ 230 Dan Fouts	.50	1.25
❑ 231 Dan Fouts IA	.40	1.00
❑ 232 Gary Johnson	.08	.25
❑ 233 Charlie Joiner	.40	1.00
❑ 234 Charlie Joiner IA	.40	1.00
❑ 235 Louie Kelcher	.08	.25
❑ 236 Chuck Muncie	.20	.50
❑ 237 Chuck Muncie IA	.08	.25
❑ 238 George Roberts	.08	.25
❑ 239 Ed White	.08	.25
❑ 240 Doug Wilkerson	.08	.25
❑ 241 Kellen Winslow	.75	2.00
❑ 242 Kellen Winslow IA	.40	1.00
❑ 243 Seahawks TL/S.Largent	.40	1.00
❑ 244 Theotis Brown	.08	.25
❑ 245 Dan Doornink	.08	.25
❑ 246 John Harris	.08	.25
❑ 247 Efren Herrera	.08	.25
❑ 248 David Hughes	.08	.25
❑ 249 Steve Largent	.75	2.00
❑ 250 Steve Largent IA	.40	1.00
❑ 251 Sam McCullum	.08	.25
❑ 252 Sherman Smith	.08	.25
❑ 253 Manu Tuiasosopo	.08	.25
❑ 254 John Yarno	.08	.25
❑ 255 Jim Zorn	.20	.50
❑ 256 Jim Zorn IA	.20	.50
❑ 257 J.Montana/Anderson LL	2.00	4.00
❑ 258 Kellen Winslow/Clark LL	.40	1.00
❑ 259 QB Sack Leaders	.08	.25
❑ 260 Scoring Leaders	.20	.50
❑ 261 Interception Leaders	.20	.50
❑ 262 Punting Leaders	.08	.25
❑ 263 Brothers: Bahr	.08	.25
❑ 264 Brothers: Blackwood	.20	.50
❑ 265 Brothers: Brock	.08	.25
❑ 266 Brothers: Griffin	.20	.50
❑ 267 Brothers: Hannah	.40	1.00
❑ 268 Brothers: Jackson	.08	.25
❑ 269 Walter/Eddie Payton	.50	1.25
❑ 270 Brothers: Selmon	.40	1.00
❑ 271 Atlanta Falcons TL	.20	.50
❑ 272 William Andrews	.20	.50
❑ 273 William Andrews IA	.20	.50
❑ 274 Steve Bartkowski	.20	.50
❑ 275 Steve Bartkowski IA	.20	.50
❑ 276 Bobby Butler RC	.08	.25
❑ 277 Lynn Cain	.08	.25
❑ 278 Wallace Francis	.08	.25
❑ 279 Alfred Jackson	.08	.25
❑ 280 John James	.08	.25
❑ 281 Alfred Jenkins	.08	.25
❑ 282 Alfred Jenkins IA	.08	.25
❑ 283 Kenny Johnson	.08	.25
❑ 284 Mike Kenn	.40	1.00
❑ 285 Fulton Kuykendall	.08	.25
❑ 286 Mick Luckhurst RC	.08	.25
❑ 287 Mick Luckhurst IA	.08	.25
❑ 288 Junior Miller	.08	.25
❑ 289 Al Richardson	.08	.25
❑ 290 R.C.Thielemann RC	.08	.25
❑ 291 Jeff Van Note	.08	.25
❑ 292 Bears TL/Walter Payton	.40	1.00
❑ 293 Brian Baschnagel	.08	.25
❑ 294 Robin Earl	.08	.25
❑ 295 Vince Evans	.20	.50
❑ 296 Gary Fencik	.08	.25
❑ 297 Dan Hampton	.40	1.00
❑ 298 Noah Jackson	.08	.25
❑ 299 Ken Margerum	.08	.25
❑ 300 Jim Osborne	.08	.25
❑ 301 Bob Parsons	.08	.25
❑ 302 Walter Payton	4.00	10.00
❑ 303 Walter Payton IA	1.50	4.00
❑ 304 Revie Sorey	.08	.25
❑ 305 Matt Suhey RC	.40	1.00
❑ 306 Rickey Watts	.08	.25
❑ 307 Cowboys TL/Dorsett	.40	1.00
❑ 308 Bob Breunig	.08	.25
❑ 309 Doug Cosbie RC	.08	.25
❑ 310 Pat Donovan	.08	.25
❑ 311 Tony Dorsett	.75	2.00
❑ 312 Tony Dorsett IA	.40	1.00
❑ 313 Michael Downs RC	.08	.25
❑ 314 Billy Joe DuPree	.20	.50
❑ 315 John Dutton	.08	.25
❑ 316 Tony Hill	.20	.50
❑ 317 Butch Johnson	.20	.50
❑ 318 Ed Too Tall Jones	.40	1.00
❑ 319 James Jones COW	.08	.25
❑ 320 Harvey Martin	.20	.50
❑ 321 Drew Pearson	.40	1.00
❑ 322 Herb Scott	.08	.25
❑ 323 Rafael Septien	.08	.25
❑ 324 Rafael Septien IA	.08	.25
❑ 325 Ron Springs	.20	.50
❑ 326 Dennis Thurman RC	.08	.25
❑ 327 Everson Walls RC	.40	1.00
❑ 328 Everson Walls IA	.40	1.00
❑ 329 Danny White	.40	1.00
❑ 330 Danny White IA	.20	.50
❑ 331 Randy White	.40	1.00
❑ 332 Randy White IA	.40	1.00
❑ 333 Detroit Lions TL	.20	.50
❑ 334 Jim Allen	.08	.25
❑ 335 Al(Bubba) Baker	.20	.50
❑ 336 Dexter Bussey	.08	.25
❑ 337 Doug English	.20	.50
❑ 338 Ken Fantetti	.08	.25
❑ 339 William Gay	.08	.25
❑ 340 David Hill	.08	.25
❑ 341 Eric Hipple RC	.08	.25
❑ 342 Rick Kane	.08	.25
❑ 343 Eddie Murray	.40	1.00
❑ 344 Eddie Murray IA	.20	.50
❑ 345 Ray Oldham	.08	.25
❑ 346 Dave Pureifory	.08	.25
❑ 347 Freddie Scott	.08	.25
❑ 348 Freddie Scott IA	.08	.25
❑ 349 Billy Sims	.40	1.00
❑ 350 Billy Sims IA	.40	1.00
❑ 351 Tom Skladany	.08	.25
❑ 352 Leonard Thompson	.08	.25
❑ 353 Stan White	.08	.25
❑ 354 Packers TL/Lofton	.40	1.00
❑ 355 Paul Coffman	.08	.25
❑ 356 George Cumby	.08	.25
❑ 357 Lynn Dickey	.08	.25
❑ 358 Lynn Dickey IA	.08	.25
❑ 359 Gerry Ellis	.08	.25
❑ 360 Maurice Harvey	.08	.25
❑ 361 Harlan Huckleby	.08	.25
❑ 362 John Jefferson	.40	1.00
❑ 363 Mark Lee RC	.08	.25
❑ 364 James Lofton	.50	1.25
❑ 365 James Lofton IA	.40	1.00
❑ 366 Jan Stenerud	.20	.50
❑ 367 Jan Stenerud IA	.20	.50
❑ 368 Rich Wingo	.08	.25
❑ 369 Los Angeles Rams TL	.20	.50
❑ 370 Frank Corral	.08	.25
❑ 371 Nolan Cromwell	.20	.50
❑ 372 Nolan Cromwell IA	.20	.50
❑ 373 Preston Dennard	.08	.25
❑ 374 Mike Fanning	.08	.25
❑ 375 Doug France	.08	.25
❑ 376 Mike Guman	.08	.25
❑ 377 Pat Haden	.20	.50
❑ 378 Dennis Harrah	.08	.25
❑ 379 Drew Hill RC	.40	1.00
❑ 380 LeRoy Irvin RC	.08	.25
❑ 381 Cody Jones	.08	.25
❑ 382 Rod Perry	.08	.25
❑ 383 Rich Saul	.08	.25
❑ 384 Pat Thomas	.08	.25
❑ 385 Wendell Tyler	.20	.50
❑ 386 Wendell Tyler IA	.20	.50
❑ 387 Billy Waddy	.08	.25
❑ 388 Jack Youngblood	.40	1.00
❑ 389 Minnesota Vikings TL	.08	.25
❑ 390 Matt Blair	.08	.25
❑ 391 Ted Brown	.08	.25
❑ 392 Ted Brown IA	.08	.25
❑ 393 Rick Danmeier	.08	.25
❑ 394 Tommy Kramer	.20	.50
❑ 395 Mark Mullaney	.08	.25
❑ 396 Eddie Payton	.08	.25
❑ 397 Ahmad Rashad	.40	1.00
❑ 398 Joe Senser	.08	.25

❑ 399 Joe Senser IA .08 .25
❑ 400 Sammie White .20 .50
❑ 401 Sammie White IA .08 .25
❑ 402 Ron Yary .40 1.00
❑ 403 Rickey Young .08 .25
❑ 404 Saints TL/Ric.Jackson .20 .50
❑ 405 Russell Erxleben .08 .25
❑ 406 Elois Grooms .08 .25
❑ 407 Jack Holmes .08 .25
❑ 408 Archie Manning .40 1.00
❑ 409 Derland Moore .08 .25
❑ 410 George Rogers RC .40 1.00
❑ 411 George Rogers IA .40 1.00
❑ 412 Toussaint Tyler .08 .25
❑ 413 Dave Waymer RC .08 .25
❑ 414 Wayne Wilson .08 .25
❑ 415 New York Giants TL .08 .25
❑ 416 Scott Brunner RC .08 .25
❑ 417 Rob Carpenter .08 .25
❑ 418 Harry Carson .20 .50
❑ 419 Bill Currier .08 .25
❑ 420 Joe Danelo .08 .25
❑ 421 Joe Danelo IA .08 .25
❑ 422 Mark Haynes RC .08 .25
❑ 423 Terry Jackson .08 .25
❑ 424 Dave Jennings .08 .25
❑ 425 Gary Jeter .08 .25
❑ 426 Brian Kelley .08 .25
❑ 427 George Martin .08 .25
❑ 428 Curtis McGriff .08 .25
❑ 429 Bill Neill .08 .25
❑ 430 Johnny Perkins .08 .25
❑ 431 Beasley Reece .08 .25
❑ 432 Gary Shirk .08 .25
❑ 433 Phil Simms 1.00 1.50
❑ 434 Lawrence Taylor RC 7.50 20.00
❑ 435 Lawrence Taylor IA 4.00 10.00
❑ 436 Brad Van Pelt .08 .25
❑ 437 Philadelphia Eagles TL .20 .50
❑ 438 John Bunting .08 .25
❑ 439 Billy Campfield .08 .25
❑ 440 Harold Carmichael .40 1.00
❑ 441 Harold Carmichael IA .40 1.00
❑ 442 Herman Edwards .08 .25
❑ 443 Tony Franklin .08 .25
❑ 444 Tony Franklin IA .08 .25
❑ 445 Carl Hairston .08 .25
❑ 446 Dennis Harrison .08 .25
❑ 447 Ron Jaworski .40 1.00
❑ 448 Charlie Johnson NT .08 .25
❑ 449 Keith Krepfle .08 .25
❑ 450 Frank LeMaster .08 .25
❑ 451 Randy Logan .08 .25
❑ 452 Wilbert Montgomery .20 .50
❑ 453 Wilbert Montgomery IA .20 .50
❑ 454 Hubie Oliver .08 .25
❑ 455 Jerry Robinson .08 .25
❑ 456 Jerry Robinson IA .08 .25
❑ 457 Jerry Sisemore .08 .25
❑ 458 Charlie Smith WR .08 .25
❑ 459 Stan Walters .08 .25
❑ 460 Brenard Wilson .08 .25
❑ 461 Roynell Young .08 .25
❑ 462 Cardinals TL/O.Anderson .20 .50
❑ 463 Ottis Anderson .40 1.00
❑ 464 Ottis Anderson IA .40 1.00
❑ 465 Carl Birdsong .08 .25
❑ 466 Rush Brown .08 .25
❑ 467 Mel Gray .20 .50
❑ 468 Ken Greene .08 .25
❑ 469 Jim Hart .40 1.00
❑ 470 E.J.Junior RC .20 .50
❑ 471 Neil Lomax RC .40 1.00
❑ 472 Stump Mitchell RC .40 1.00
❑ 473 Wayne Morris .08 .25
❑ 474 Neil O'Donoghue .08 .25
❑ 475 Pat Tilley .08 .25
❑ 476 Pat Tilley IA .08 .25
❑ 477 49ers TL/Dwight Clark .20 .50
❑ 478 Dwight Clark .40 1.00
❑ 479 Dwight Clark IA .40 1.00
❑ 480 Earl Cooper .08 .25
❑ 481 Randy Cross .20 .50
❑ 482 Johnny Davis RC .08 .25
❑ 483 Fred Dean .20 .50
❑ 484 Fred Dean IA .08 .25
❑ 485 Dwight Hicks RC .40 1.00
❑ 486 Ronnie Lott RC 7.50 20.00
❑ 487 Ronnie Lott IA 3.00 6.00
❑ 488 Joe Montana 7.50 20.00
❑ 489 Joe Montana IA 5.00 12.00
❑ 490 Ricky Patton .08 .25
❑ 491 Jack Reynolds .20 .50
❑ 492 Freddie Solomon .08 .25
❑ 493 Ray Wersching .08 .25
❑ 494 Charle Young .08 .25
❑ 495 Tampa Bay Bucs TL .20 .50
❑ 496 Cedric Brown .08 .25
❑ 497 Neal Colzie .08 .25
❑ 498 Jerry Eckwood .08 .25
❑ 499 Jimmie Giles .20 .50
❑ 500 Hugh Green RC .40 1.00
❑ 501 Kevin House .08 .25
❑ 502 Kevin House IA .08 .25
❑ 503 Cecil Johnson .08 .25
❑ 504 James Owens .08 .25
❑ 505 Lee Roy Selmon .40 1.00
❑ 506 Mike Washington .08 .25
❑ 507 James Wilder RC .20 .50
❑ 508 Doug Williams .20 .50
❑ 509 Redskins TL/Monk .40 1.00
❑ 510 Perry Brooks .08 .25
❑ 511 Dave Butz .20 .50
❑ 512 Wilbur Jackson .08 .25
❑ 513 Joe Lavender .08 .25
❑ 514 Terry Metcalf .20 .50
❑ 515 Art Monk 1.25 3.00
❑ 516 Mark Moseley .08 .25
❑ 517 Mark Murphy .08 .25
❑ 518 Mike Nelms .08 .25
❑ 519 Lemar Parrish .08 .25
❑ 520 John Riggins .40 1.00
❑ 521 Joe Theismann .40 1.00
❑ 522 Ricky Thompson .08 .25
❑ 523 Don Warren UER .08 .25
❑ 524 Joe Washington .20 .50
❑ 525 Checklist 1-132 .40 1.00
❑ 526 Checklist 133-264 .40 1.00
❑ 527 Checklist 265-396 .40 1.00
❑ 528 Checklist 397-528 .40 1.00

1983 Topps

❑ COMPLETE SET (396) 30.00 60.00
❑ 1 Ken Anderson RB .25 .60
❑ 2 Tony Dorsett RB .25 .60
❑ 3 Dan Fouts RB .25 .60
❑ 4 Joe Montana RB 1.50 3.00
❑ 5 Mark Moseley RB .15 .40
❑ 6 Mike Nelms RB .08 .25
❑ 7 Darrol Ray RB .08 .25
❑ 8 John Riggins RB .25 .60
❑ 9 Fulton Walker RB .08 .25
❑ 10 NFC Champs/Riggins .25 .60
❑ 11 AFC Championship .15 .40
❑ 12 Super Bowl XVII/J.Riggins .08 .25
❑ 13 Atlanta Falcons TL .15 .40
❑ 14 William Andrews DP .15 .40
❑ 15 Steve Bartkowski .15 .40
❑ 16 Bobby Butler .08 .25
❑ 17 Buddy Curry .08 .25
❑ 18 Alfred Jackson DP .08 .25
❑ 19 Alfred Jenkins .08 .25
❑ 20 Kenny Johnson .08 .25
❑ 21 Mike Kenn .08 .25
❑ 22 Mick Luckhurst .08 .25
❑ 23 Junior Miller .08 .25
❑ 24 Al Richardson .08 .25
❑ 25 Gerald Riggs DP RC .15 .40
❑ 26 R.C. Thielemann .08 .25
❑ 27 Jeff Van Note .08 .25
❑ 28 Bears TL/W.Payton .40 1.00
❑ 29 Brian Baschnagel .08 .25
❑ 30 Dan Hampton .25 .60
❑ 31 Mike Hartenstine .08 .25
❑ 32 Noah Jackson .08 .25
❑ 33 Jim McMahon RC 4.00 8.00
❑ 34 Emery Moorehead DP .08 .25
❑ 35 Bob Parsons .08 .25
❑ 36 Walter Payton 3.00 6.00
❑ 37 Terry Schmidt .08 .25
❑ 38 Mike Singletary RC 4.00 8.00
❑ 39 Matt Suhey DP .15 .40
❑ 40 Rickey Watts DP .08 .25
❑ 41 Otis Wilson RC DP .15 .40
❑ 42 Cowboys TL/Tony Dorsett .25 .60
❑ 43 Bob Breunig .15 .40
❑ 44 Doug Cosbie .08 .25
❑ 45 Pat Donovan .08 .25
❑ 46 Tony Dorsett DP .40 1.00
❑ 47 Tony Hill .15 .40
❑ 48 Butch Johnson DP .15 .40
❑ 49 Ed Too Tall Jones DP .25 .60
❑ 50 Harvey Martin DP .15 .40
❑ 51 Drew Pearson .25 .60
❑ 52 Rafael Septien .08 .25
❑ 53 Ron Springs DP .08 .25
❑ 54 Dennis Thurman .08 .25
❑ 55 Everson Walls .15 .40
❑ 56 Danny White DP .25 .60
❑ 57 Handy White .25 .60
❑ 58 Detroit Lions TL .15 .40
❑ 59 Al(Bubba) Baker DP .15 .40
❑ 60 Dexter Bussey DP .08 .25
❑ 61 Gary Danielson DP .08 .25
❑ 62 Keith Dorney DP .08 .25
❑ 63 Doug English .08 .25
❑ 64 Ken Fantetti DP .08 .25
❑ 65 Alvin Hall DP .08 .25
❑ 66 David Hill DP .08 .25
❑ 67 Eric Hipple .08 .25
❑ 68 Eddie Murray DP .15 .40
❑ 69 Freddie Scott .08 .25
❑ 70 Billy Sims DP .15 .40
❑ 71 Tom Skladany DP .08 .25
❑ 72 Leonard Thompson DP .08 .25
❑ 73 Bobby Watkins .08 .25
❑ 74 Green Bay Packers TL .08 .25
❑ 75 John Anderson .08 .25
❑ 76 Paul Coffman .08 .25
❑ 77 Lynn Dickey .08 .25
❑ 78 Mike Douglass DP .08 .25
❑ 79 Eddie Lee Ivery .08 .25
❑ 80 John Jefferson DP .25 .60
❑ 81 Ezra Johnson .08 .25
❑ 82 Mark Lee .08 .25
❑ 83 James Lofton .25 .60
❑ 84 Larry McCarren .08 .25
❑ 85 Jan Stenerud DP .15 .40
❑ 86 Los Angeles Rams TL .08 .25
❑ 87 Bill Bain DP .08 .25
❑ 88 Nolan Cromwell .15 .40
❑ 89 Preston Dennard .08 .25
❑ 90 Vince Ferragamo DP .15 .40
❑ 91 Mike Guman .08 .25
❑ 92 Kent Hill .08 .25
❑ 93 Mike Lansford DP RC .08 .25
❑ 94 Rod Perry .08 .25
❑ 95 Pat Thomas DP .08 .25
❑ 96 Jack Youngblood .25 .60
❑ 97 Minnesota Vikings TL .08 .25
❑ 98 Matt Blair .08 .25
❑ 99 Ted Brown .08 .25
❑ 100 Greg Coleman .08 .25
❑ 101 Randy Holloway .08 .25
❑ 102 Tommy Kramer .15 .40
❑ 103 Doug Martin DP .08 .25
❑ 104 Mark Mullaney .08 .25
❑ 105 Joe Senser .08 .25
❑ 106 Willie Teal DP .08 .25
❑ 107 Sammie White .15 .40
❑ 108 Rickey Young .08 .25
❑ 109 New Orleans Saints TL .15 .40
❑ 110 Stan Brock RC .08 .25
❑ 111 Bruce Clark RC .08 .25
❑ 112 Russell Erxleben DP .08 .25
❑ 113 Russell Gary .08 .25
❑ 114 Jeff Groth DP .08 .25
❑ 115 John Hill DP .08 .25
❑ 116 Derland Moore .08 .25
❑ 117 George Rogers .15 .40
❑ 118 Ken Stabler .60 1.50
❑ 119 Wayne Wilson .08 .25
❑ 120 New York Giants TL .08 .25
❑ 121 Scott Brunner .08 .25

❑ 122 Rob Carpenter	.08	.25
❑ 123 Harry Carson	.15	.40
❑ 124 Joe Danelo DP	.08	.25
❑ 125 Earnest Gray	.08	.25
❑ 126 Mark Haynes DP	.15	.40
❑ 127 Terry Jackson	.08	.25
❑ 128 Dave Jennings	.08	.25
❑ 129 Brian Kelley	.08	.25
❑ 130 George Martin	.08	.25
❑ 131 Tom Mullady	.08	.25
❑ 132 Johnny Perkins	.08	.25
❑ 133 Lawrence Taylor	2.00	5.00
❑ 134 Brad Van Pelt	.08	.25
❑ 135 Butch Woolfolk DP RC	.08	.25
❑ 136 Philadelphia Eagles TL	.15	.40
❑ 137 Harold Carmichael	.25	.60
❑ 138 Herman Edwards	.08	.25
❑ 139 Tony Franklin DP	.08	.25
❑ 140 Carl Hairston DP	.08	.25
❑ 141 Dennis Harrison DP	.08	.25
❑ 142 Ron Jaworski DP	.15	.40
❑ 143 Frank LeMaster	.08	.25
❑ 144 Wilbert Montgomery DP	.15	.40
❑ 145 Guy Morriss	.08	.25
❑ 146 Jerry Robinson	.08	.25
❑ 147 Max Runager	.08	.25
❑ 148 Ron Smith DP RC	.08	.25
❑ 149 John Spagnola	.08	.25
❑ 150 Stan Walters DP	.08	.25
❑ 151 Roynell Young DP	.08	.25
❑ 152 Cardinals TL/O.Anderson	.15	.40
❑ 153 Ottis Anderson	.25	.60
❑ 154 Carl Birdsong	.08	.25
❑ 155 Dan Dierdorf DP	.25	.60
❑ 156 Roy Green RC	.25	.60
❑ 157 Elois Grooms	.08	.25
❑ 158 Neil Lomax DP	.15	.40
❑ 159 Wayne Morris	.08	.25
❑ 160 Tootie Robbins RC	.08	.25
❑ 161 Luis Sharpe RC	.08	.25
❑ 162 Pat Tilley	.08	.25
❑ 163 San Francisco 49ers TL	.08	.25
❑ 164 Dwight Clark	.25	.60
❑ 165 Randy Cross	.15	.40
❑ 166 Russ Francis	.15	.40
❑ 167 Dwight Hicks	.08	.25
❑ 168 Ronnie Lott	1.25	2.50
❑ 169 Joe Montana DP	4.00	10.00
❑ 170 Jeff Moore	.08	.25
❑ 171 R.Nehemiah DP RC	.25	.60
❑ 172 Freddie Solomon	.08	.25
❑ 173 Ray Wersching DP	.08	.25
❑ 174 Tampa Bay Bucs TL	.08	.25
❑ 175 Cedric Brown	.08	.25
❑ 176 Bill Capece	.08	.25
❑ 177 Neal Colzie	.08	.25
❑ 178 Jimmie Giles	.08	.25
❑ 179 Hugh Green	.15	.40
❑ 180 Kevin House DP	.08	.25
❑ 181 James Owens	.08	.25
❑ 182 Lee Roy Selmon	.25	.60
❑ 183 Mike Washington	.08	.25
❑ 184 James Wilder	.08	.25
❑ 185 Doug Williams DP	.15	.40
❑ 186 Redskins TL/John Riggins	.25	.60
❑ 187 Jeff Bostic DP RC	.40	1.00
❑ 188 Charlie Brown RC	.15	.40
❑ 189 Vernon Dean DP RC	.08	.25
❑ 190 Joe Jacoby RC	1.25	3.00
❑ 191 Dexter Manley RC	.15	.40
❑ 192 Rich Milot	.08	.25
❑ 193 Art Monk DP	.40	1.00
❑ 194 Mark Moseley DP	.08	.25
❑ 195 Mike Nelms	.08	.25
❑ 196 Neal Olkewicz DP	.08	.25
❑ 197 Tony Peters	.08	.25
❑ 198 John Riggins DP	.25	.60
❑ 199 Joe Theismann	.25	.60
❑ 200 Don Warren	.08	.25
❑ 201 Jeris White DP	.08	.25
❑ 202 J.Theismann/K.Anderson LL	.25	.60
❑ 203 Receiving Leaders	.15	.40
❑ 204 Tony Dorsett/F.McNeil LL	.25	.60
❑ 205 M.Allen/W.Tyler LL	.50	1.25
❑ 206 Interception Leaders	.15	.40
❑ 207 Punting Leaders	.08	.25
❑ 208 Baltimore Colts TL	.08	.25
❑ 209 Matt Bouza	.08	.25
❑ 210 Johnie Cooks DP RC	.08	.25
❑ 211 Curtis Dickey	.08	.25
❑ 212 Nesby Glasgow DP	.08	.25
❑ 213 Derrick Hatchett	.08	.25
❑ 214 Randy McMillan	.08	.25
❑ 215 Mike Pagel RC	.15	.40
❑ 216 Rohn Stark DP RC	.15	.40
❑ 217 Donnell Thompson DP RC	.08	.25
❑ 218 Leo Wisniewski DP	.08	.25
❑ 219 Buffalo Bills TL	.15	.40
❑ 220 Curtis Brown	.08	.25
❑ 221 Jerry Butler	.08	.25
❑ 222 Greg Cater DP	.08	.25
❑ 223 Joe Cribbs	.15	.40
❑ 224 Joe Ferguson	.15	.40
❑ 225 Roosevelt Leaks	.08	.25
❑ 226 Frank Lewis	.08	.25
❑ 227 Eugene Marve RC	.08	.25
❑ 228 Fred Smerlas DP	.08	.25
❑ 229 Ben Williams DP	.08	.25
❑ 230 Cincinnati Bengals TL	.08	.25
❑ 231 Charles Alexander	.08	.25
❑ 232 Ken Anderson DP	.25	.60
❑ 233 Jim Breech DP	.08	.25
❑ 234 Ross Browner	.08	.25
❑ 235 Cris Collinsworth DP	.25	.60
❑ 236 Isaac Curtis	.08	.25
❑ 237 Pete Johnson	.08	.25
❑ 238 Steve Kreider DP	.08	.25
❑ 239 Max Montoya DP RC	.08	.25
❑ 240 Anthony Munoz	.40	1.00
❑ 241 Ken Riley	.08	.25
❑ 242 Dan Ross	.08	.25
❑ 243 Reggie Williams	.15	.40
❑ 244 Cleveland Browns TL	.15	.40
❑ 245 Chip Banks DP RC	.15	.40
❑ 246 Tom Cousineau DP RC	.15	.40
❑ 247 Joe DeLamielleure DP	.15	.40
❑ 248 Doug Dieken DP	.08	.25
❑ 249 Hanford Dixon RC	.08	.25
❑ 250 Ricky Feacher DP	.08	.25
❑ 251 Lawrence Johnson DP	.08	.25
❑ 252 Dave Logan DP	.08	.25
❑ 253 Paul McDonald DP	.08	.25
❑ 254 Ozzie Newsome DP	.25	.60
❑ 255 Mike Pruitt	.15	.40
❑ 256 Clarence Scott DP	.08	.25
❑ 257 Brian Sipe DP	.15	.40
❑ 258 Dwight Walker DP	.08	.25
❑ 259 Charles White	.15	.40
❑ 260 Denver Broncos TL	.08	.25
❑ 261 Steve DeBerg DP	.15	.40
❑ 262 Randy Gradishar DP	.15	.40
❑ 263 Rulon Jones DP RC	.08	.25
❑ 264 Rich Karlis DP	.08	.25
❑ 265 Don Latimer	.08	.25
❑ 266 Rick Parros DP	.08	.25
❑ 267 Luke Prestridge	.08	.25
❑ 268 Rick Upchurch	.15	.40
❑ 269 Steve Watson DP	.08	.25
❑ 270 Gerald Willhite DP	.08	.25
❑ 271 Houston Oilers TL	.08	.25
❑ 272 Harold Bailey	.08	.25
❑ 273 Jesse Baker DP	.08	.25
❑ 274 Gregg Bingham DP	.08	.25
❑ 275 Robert Brazile DP	.08	.25
❑ 276 Donnie Craft	.08	.25
❑ 277 Daryl Hunt	.08	.25
❑ 278 Archie Manning DP	.15	.40
❑ 279 Gifford Nielsen	.08	.25
❑ 280 Mike Renfro	.08	.25
❑ 281 Carl Roaches DP	.08	.25
❑ 282 Kansas City Chiefs TL	.15	.40
❑ 283 Gary Barbaro	.08	.25
❑ 284 Joe Delaney	.08	.25
❑ 285 Jeff Gossett RC	.25	.60
❑ 286 Gary Green DP	.08	.25
❑ 287 Eric Harris DP	.08	.25
❑ 288 Billy Jackson DP	.08	.25
❑ 289 Bill Kenney DP	.08	.25
❑ 290 Nick Lowery	.25	.60
❑ 291 Henry Marshall	.08	.25
❑ 292 Art Still DP	.08	.25
❑ 293 Raiders TL/M.Allen	.75	2.00
❑ 294 Marcus Allen DP RC	6.00	15.00
❑ 295 Lyle Alzado	.25	.60
❑ 296 Chris Bahr DP	.08	.25
❑ 297 Cliff Branch	.25	.60
❑ 298 Todd Christensen RC	.30	.75
❑ 299 Ray Guy	.15	.40
❑ 300 Frank Hawkins DP	.08	.25
❑ 301 Lester Hayes DP	.08	.25
❑ 302 Ted Hendricks DP	.25	.60
❑ 303 Kenny King DP	.08	.25
❑ 304 Rod Martin	.08	.25
❑ 305 Matt Millen DP	.25	.60
❑ 306 Burgess Owens	.08	.25
❑ 307 Jim Plunkett	.25	.60
❑ 308 Miami Dolphins TL	.15	.40
❑ 309 Bob Baumhower	.08	.25
❑ 310 Glenn Blackwood	.08	.25
❑ 311 Lyle Blackwood DP	.08	.25
❑ 312 A.J. Duhe	.08	.25
❑ 313 Andra Franklin	.08	.25
❑ 314 Duriel Harris	.08	.25
❑ 315 Bob Kuechenberg DP	.15	.40
❑ 316 Don McNeal	.08	.25
❑ 317 Tony Nathan	.15	.40
❑ 318 Ed Newman	.08	.25
❑ 319 Earnie Rhone DP	.08	.25
❑ 320 Joe Rose DP	.08	.25
❑ 321 Don Strock DP	.08	.25
❑ 322 Uwe Von Schamann	.08	.25
❑ 323 David Woodley DP	.15	.40
❑ 324 New England Pats TL	.08	.25
❑ 325 Julius Adams	.08	.25
❑ 326 Pete Brock	.08	.25
❑ 327 Rich Camarillo DP RC	.08	.25
❑ 328 Tony Collins DP	.08	.25
❑ 329 Steve Grogan	.15	.40
❑ 330 John Hannah	.25	.60
❑ 331 Don Hasselbeck	.08	.25
❑ 332 Mike Haynes	.15	.40
❑ 333 Roland James RC	.08	.25
❑ 334A Stanley Morgan ERR IL	.25	.60
❑ 334B Stanley Morgan COR	.15	.40
❑ 335 Steve Nelson	.08	.25
❑ 336 Kenneth Sims DP	.08	.25
❑ 337 Mark Van Eeghen	.15	.40
❑ 338 New York Jets TL	.15	.40
❑ 339 Greg Buttle	.08	.25
❑ 340 Joe Fields	.08	.25
❑ 341 Mark Gastineau DP	.15	.40
❑ 342 Bruce Harper	.08	.25
❑ 343 Bobby Jackson	.08	.25
❑ 344 Bobby Jones	.08	.25
❑ 345 Johnny Lam Jones DP	.08	.25
❑ 346 Joe Klecko	.15	.40
❑ 347 Marty Lyons	.08	.25
❑ 348 Freeman McNeil	.25	.60
❑ 349 Lance Mehl RC	.08	.25
❑ 350 Marvin Powell DP	.08	.25
❑ 351 Darrol Ray DP	.08	.25
❑ 352 Abdul Salaam	.08	.25
❑ 353 Richard Todd	.15	.40
❑ 354 Wesley Walker	.15	.40
❑ 355 Steelers TL/Franco Harris	.25	.60
❑ 356 Gary Anderson DP RC	3.00	6.00
❑ 357 Mel Blount DP	.25	.60
❑ 358 Terry Bradshaw DP	.60	1.50
❑ 359 Larry Brown	.08	.25
❑ 360 Bennie Cunningham	.08	.25
❑ 361 Gary Dunn	.08	.25
❑ 362 Franco Harris	.30	.75
❑ 363 Jack Lambert	.25	.60
❑ 364 Frank Pollard	.08	.25
❑ 365 Donnie Shell	.15	.40
❑ 366 John Stallworth	.25	.60
❑ 367 Loren Toews	.08	.25
❑ 368 Mike Webster DP	.25	.60
❑ 369 Dwayne Woodruff RC	.08	.25
❑ 370 San Diego Chargers TL	.15	.40
❑ 371 Rolf Benirschke DP	.08	.25
❑ 372 James Brooks	.25	.60
❑ 373 Wes Chandler	.15	.40
❑ 374 Dan Fouts DP	.25	.60
❑ 375 Tim Fox	.08	.25
❑ 376 Gary Johnson	.08	.25
❑ 377 Charlie Joiner DP	.25	.60
❑ 378 Louie Kelcher	.08	.25
❑ 379 Chuck Muncie	.08	.25
❑ 380 Cliff Thrift	.08	.25
❑ 381 Doug Wilkerson	.08	.25
❑ 382 Kellen Winslow	.30	.75
❑ 383 Seattle Seahawks TL	.08	.25
❑ 384 Kenny Easley RC	.25	.60
❑ 385 Jacob Green RC	.15	.40
❑ 386 John Harris	.08	.25
❑ 387 Michael Jackson	.08	.25

❑ 388 Norm Johnson RC	.08	.25
❑ 389 Steve Largent	.50	1.25
❑ 390 Keith Simpson	.08	.25
❑ 391 Sherman Smith	.08	.25
❑ 392 Jeff West DP	.08	.25
❑ 393 Jim Zorn DP	.15	.40
❑ 394 Checklist 1-132	.25	.60
❑ 395 Checklist 133-264	.25	.60
❑ 396 Checklist 265-396	.25	.60

1984 Topps

❑ COMPLETE SET (396)	100.00	200.00
❑ COMP.FACT.SET (396)	200.00	350.00
❑ 1 Eric Dickerson RB	.25	.60
❑ 2 Ali Haji-Sheikh RB	.15	.40
❑ 3 Franco Harris RB	.25	.60
❑ 4 Mark Moseley RB	.15	.40
❑ 5 John Riggins RB	.25	.60
❑ 6 Jan Stenerud RB	.15	.40
❑ 7 AFC Champs/M.Allen	.25	.60
❑ 8 NFC Champs/Riggins	.15	.40
❑ 9 Super Bowl XVIII/Allen UER	.25	.60
❑ 10 Indianapolis Colts TL	.08	.25
❑ 11 Raul Allegre RC	.08	.25
❑ 12 Curtis Dickey	.15	.40
❑ 13 Ray Donaldson RC	.15	.40
❑ 14 Nesby Glasgow	.08	.25
❑ 15 Chris Hinton RC	.25	.60
❑ 16 Vernon Maxwell RC	.08	.25
❑ 17 Randy McMillan	.08	.25
❑ 18 Mike Pagel	.15	.40
❑ 19 Rohn Stark	.15	.40
❑ 20 Leo Wisniewski	.08	.25
❑ 21 Buffalo Bills TL	.15	.40
❑ 22 Jerry Butler	.08	.25
❑ 23 Joe Danelo	.08	.25
❑ 24 Joe Ferguson	.15	.40
❑ 25 Steve Freeman	.08	.25
❑ 26 Roosevelt Leaks	.15	.40
❑ 27 Frank Lewis	.08	.25
❑ 28 Eugene Marve	.08	.25
❑ 29 Booker Moore	.08	.25
❑ 30 Fred Smerlas	.08	.25
❑ 31 Ben Williams	.15	.40
❑ 32 Cincinnati Bengals TL	.15	.40
❑ 33 Charles Alexander	.08	.25
❑ 34 Ken Anderson	.25	.60
❑ 35 Ken Anderson IR	.25	.60
❑ 36 Jim Breech	.08	.25
❑ 37 Cris Collinsworth	.25	.60
❑ 38 Cris Collinsworth IR	.25	.60
❑ 39 Isaac Curtis	.15	.40
❑ 40 Eddie Edwards	.08	.25
❑ 41 Ray Horton RC	.08	.25
❑ 42 Pete Johnson	.15	.40
❑ 43 Steve Kreider	.08	.25
❑ 44 Max Montoya	.08	.25
❑ 45 Anthony Munoz	.25	.60
❑ 46 Reggie Williams	.15	.40
❑ 47 Cleveland Browns TL	.15	.40
❑ 48 Matt Bahr	.15	.40
❑ 49 Chip Banks	.08	.25
❑ 50 Tom Cousineau	.08	.25
❑ 51 Joe DeLamielleure	.25	.60
❑ 52 Doug Dieken	.08	.25
❑ 53 Bob Golic RC	.25	.60
❑ 54 Bobby Jones	.08	.25
❑ 55 Dave Logan	.08	.25
❑ 56 Clay Matthews	.25	.60
❑ 57 Paul McDonald	.08	.25
❑ 58 Ozzie Newsome	.25	.60
❑ 59 Ozzie Newsome IR	.25	.60
❑ 60 Mike Pruitt	.15	.40
❑ 61 Denver Broncos TL	.15	.40
❑ 62 Barney Chavous RC	.08	.25
❑ 63 John Elway RC	30.00	60.00
❑ 64 Steve Foley	.08	.25
❑ 65 Tom Jackson	.25	.60
❑ 66 Rich Karlis	.08	.25
❑ 67 Luke Prestridge	.08	.25
❑ 68 Zach Thomas WR	.08	.25
❑ 69 Rick Upchurch	.15	.40
❑ 70 Steve Watson	.15	.40
❑ 71 Sammy Winder RC	.15	.40
❑ 72 Louis Wright	.15	.40
❑ 73 Houston Oilers TL	.08	.25
❑ 74 Jesse Baker	.08	.25
❑ 75 Gregg Bingham	.08	.25
❑ 76 Robert Brazile	.15	.40
❑ 77 Steve Brown RC	.08	.25
❑ 78 Chris Dressel	.08	.25
❑ 79 Doug France	.08	.25
❑ 80 Florian Kempf	.08	.25
❑ 81 Carl Roaches	.15	.40
❑ 82 Tim Smith WR RC	.15	.40
❑ 83 Willie Tullis	.08	.25
❑ 84 Kansas City Chiefs TL	.08	.25
❑ 85 Mike Bell RC	.08	.25
❑ 86 Theotis Brown	.08	.25
❑ 87 Carlos Carson	.25	.60
❑ 88 Carlos Carson IR	.15	.40
❑ 89 Deron Cherry RC	.15	.40
❑ 90 Gary Green	.08	.25
❑ 91 Billy Jackson	.08	.25
❑ 92 Bill Kenney	.15	.40
❑ 93 Bill Kenney IR	.15	.40
❑ 94 Nick Lowery	.25	.60
❑ 95 Henry Marshall	.08	.25
❑ 96 Art Still	.08	.25
❑ 97 Los Angeles Raiders TL	.15	.40
❑ 98 Marcus Allen	2.50	5.00
❑ 99 Marcus Allen IR	1.00	2.50
❑ 100 Lyle Alzado	.15	.40
❑ 101 Lyle Alzado IR	.15	.40
❑ 102 Chris Bahr	.08	.25
❑ 103 Malcolm Barnwell RC	.08	.25
❑ 104 Cliff Branch	.25	.60
❑ 105 Todd Christensen	.25	.60
❑ 106 Todd Christensen IR	.25	.60
❑ 107 Ray Guy	.25	.60
❑ 108 Frank Hawkins	.08	.25
❑ 109 Lester Hayes	.15	.40
❑ 110 Ted Hendricks	.25	.60
❑ 111 Howie Long RC	6.00	15.00
❑ 112 Rod Martin	.15	.40
❑ 113 Vann McElroy RC	.08	.25
❑ 114 Jim Plunkett	.25	.60
❑ 115 Greg Pruitt	.15	.40
❑ 116 Dolphins TL/M.Duper	.25	.60
❑ 117 Bob Baumhower	.08	.25
❑ 118 Doug Betters RC	.08	.25
❑ 119 A.J. Duhe	.08	.25
❑ 120 Mark Duper RC	.25	.60
❑ 121 Andra Franklin	.08	.25
❑ 122 William Judson	.08	.25
❑ 123 Dan Marino RC	30.00	60.00
❑ 124 Dan Marino IR	5.00	12.00
❑ 125 Nat Moore	.15	.40
❑ 126 Ed Newman	.08	.25
❑ 127 Reggie Roby RC	.15	.40
❑ 128 Gerald Small	.08	.25
❑ 129 Dwight Stephenson RC	2.00	5.00
❑ 130 Uwe Von Schamann	.08	.25
❑ 131 New England Pats TL	.08	.25
❑ 132 Rich Camarillo	.15	.40
❑ 133 Tony Collins	.15	.40
❑ 134 Tony Collins IR	.08	.25
❑ 135 Bob Cryder	.08	.25
❑ 136 Steve Grogan	.15	.40
❑ 137 John Hannah	.25	.60
❑ 138 Brian Holloway RC	.08	.25
❑ 139 Roland James	.08	.25
❑ 140 Stanley Morgan	.15	.40
❑ 141 Rick Sanford	.08	.25
❑ 142 Mosi Tatupu RC	.08	.25
❑ 143 Andre Tippett RC	2.00	5.00
❑ 144 New York Jets TL	.15	.40
❑ 145 Jerome Barkum	.08	.25
❑ 146 Mark Gastineau	.15	.40
❑ 147 Mark Gastineau IR	.15	.40
❑ 148 Bruce Harper	.08	.25
❑ 149 Johnny Lam Jones	.08	.25
❑ 150 Joe Klecko	.15	.40
❑ 151 Pat Leahy	.08	.25
❑ 152 Freeman McNeil	.15	.40
❑ 153 Lance Mehl	.08	.25
❑ 154 Marvin Powell	.15	.40
❑ 155 Darrol Ray UER	.08	.25
❑ 156 Pat Ryan RC	.08	.25
❑ 157 Kirk Springs	.08	.25
❑ 158 Wesley Walker	.15	.40
❑ 159 Steelers TL/F.Harris	.25	.60
❑ 160 Walter Abercrombie RC	.15	.40
❑ 161 Gary Anderson K	.25	.60
❑ 162 Terry Bradshaw	.75	2.00
❑ 163 Craig Colquitt	.08	.25
❑ 164 Bennie Cunningham	.08	.25
❑ 165 Franco Harris	.25	.60
❑ 166 Franco Harris IR	.25	.60
❑ 167 Jack Lambert	.25	.60
❑ 168 Jack Lambert IR	.25	.60
❑ 169 Frank Pollard	.08	.25
❑ 170 Donnie Shell	.15	.40
❑ 171 Mike Webster	.15	.40
❑ 172 Keith Willis RC	.08	.25
❑ 173 Rick Woods	.08	.25
❑ 174 Chargers TL/K.Winslow	.25	.60
❑ 175 Rolf Benirschke	.08	.25
❑ 176 James Brooks	.15	.40
❑ 177 Maury Buford	.08	.25
❑ 178 Wes Chandler	.15	.40
❑ 179 Dan Fouts	.30	.75
❑ 180 Dan Fouts IR	.25	.60
❑ 181 Charlie Joiner	.25	.60
❑ 182 Linden King	.08	.25
❑ 183 Chuck Muncie	.15	.40
❑ 184 Billy Ray Smith RC	.25	.60
❑ 185 Danny Walters RC	.08	.25
❑ 186 Kellen Winslow	.30	.75
❑ 187 Kellen Winslow IR	.25	.60
❑ 188 Seahawks TL/C.Warner	.25	.60
❑ 189 Steve August	.08	.25
❑ 190 Dave Brown DB	.08	.25
❑ 191 Zachary Dixon	.08	.25
❑ 192 Kenny Easley	.15	.40
❑ 193 Jacob Green	.08	.25
❑ 194 Norm Johnson	.15	.40
❑ 195 Dave Krieg RC	.60	1.50
❑ 196 Steve Largent	.40	1.00
❑ 197 Steve Largent IR	.25	.60
❑ 198 Curt Warner RC	.25	.60
❑ 199 Curt Warner IR	.25	.60
❑ 200 Jeff West	.08	.25
❑ 201 Charlie Young	.08	.25
❑ 202 D.Marino/Bartkow. LL	2.50	6.00
❑ 203 Receiving Leaders	.15	.40
❑ 204 Eric Dickerson/Warner LL	.25	.60
❑ 205 Scoring Leaders	.08	.25
❑ 206 Interception Leaders	.08	.25
❑ 207 Punting Leaders	.08	.25
❑ 208 Atlanta Falcons TL	.15	.40
❑ 209 William Andrews	.15	.40
❑ 210 William Andrews IR	.15	.40
❑ 211 Stacey Bailey RC	.08	.25
❑ 212 Steve Bartkowski	.25	.60
❑ 213 Steve Bartkowski IR	.15	.40
❑ 214 Ralph Giacomarro	.08	.25
❑ 215 Billy Johnson	.15	.40
❑ 216 Mike Kenn	.15	.40
❑ 217 Mick Luckhurst	.08	.25
❑ 218 Gerald Riggs	.25	.60
❑ 219 R.C. Thielemann	.08	.25
❑ 220 Jeff Van Note	.15	.40
❑ 221 Bears TL/W.Payton	.30	.75
❑ 222 Jim Covert RC	.25	.60
❑ 223 Leslie Frazier	.08	.25
❑ 224 Willie Gault RC	.25	.60
❑ 225 Mike Hartenstine	.08	.25
❑ 226 Noah Jackson UER	.08	.25
❑ 227 Jim McMahon	.50	1.25
❑ 228 Walter Payton	2.50	6.00
❑ 229 Walter Payton IR	.50	1.25
❑ 230 Mike Richardson RC	.08	.25
❑ 231 Terry Schmidt	.08	.25
❑ 232 Mike Singletary	.50	1.25
❑ 233 Matt Suhey	.15	.40
❑ 234 Bob Thomas	.08	.25
❑ 235 Cowboys TL/T.Dorsett	.25	.60
❑ 236 Bob Breunig	.08	.25
❑ 237 Doug Cosbie	.15	.40
❑ 238 Tony Dorsett	.40	1.00
❑ 239 Tony Dorsett IR	.25	.60
❑ 240 John Dutton	.08	.25
❑ 241 Tony Hill	.15	.40

- ❑ 242 Ed Too Tall Jones .25 .60
- ❑ 243 Drew Pearson .25 .60
- ❑ 244 Rafael Septien .08 .25
- ❑ 245 Ron Springs .15 .40
- ❑ 246 Dennis Thurman .08 .25
- ❑ 247 Everson Walls .08 .25
- ❑ 248 Danny White .25 .60
- ❑ 249 Randy White .25 .60
- ❑ 250 Detroit Lions TL .15 .40
- ❑ 251 Jeff Chadwick RC .15 .40
- ❑ 252 Garry Cobb .08 .25
- ❑ 253 Doug English .15 .40
- ❑ 254 William Gay .08 .25
- ❑ 255 Eric Hipple .15 .40
- ❑ 256 James Jones FB RC .15 .40
- ❑ 257 Bruce McNorton .08 .25
- ❑ 258 Eddie Murray .15 .40
- ❑ 259 Ulysses Norris .08 .25
- ❑ 260 Billy Sims .25 .60
- ❑ 261 Billy Sims IR .15 .40
- ❑ 262 Leonard Thompson .08 .25
- ❑ 263 Packers TL/J.Lofton .25 .60
- ❑ 264 John Anderson .08 .25
- ❑ 265 Paul Coffman .15 .40
- ❑ 266 Lynn Dickey .15 .40
- ❑ 267 Gerry Ellis .08 .25
- ❑ 268 John Jefferson .25 .60
- ❑ 269 John Jefferson IR .25 .60
- ❑ 270 Ezra Johnson .08 .25
- ❑ 271 Tim Lewis RC .08 .25
- ❑ 272 James Lofton .25 .60
- ❑ 273 James Lofton IR .25 .60
- ❑ 274 Larry McCarren .08 .25
- ❑ 275 Jan Stenerud .15 .40
- ❑ 276 Rams TL/E.Dickerson .25 .60
- ❑ 277 Mike Barber .08 .25
- ❑ 278 Jim Collins .08 .25
- ❑ 279 Nolan Cromwell .15 .40
- ❑ 280 Eric Dickerson RC 4.00 10.00
- ❑ 281 Eric Dickerson IR .75 2.00
- ❑ 282 George Farmer South. .08 .25
- ❑ 283 Vince Ferragamo .15 .40
- ❑ 284 Kent Hill .08 .25
- ❑ 285 John Misko .08 .25
- ❑ 286 Jackie Slater RC 1.50 4.00
- ❑ 287 Jack Youngblood .15 .40
- ❑ 288 Minnesota Vikings TL .08 .25
- ❑ 289 Ted Brown .15 .40
- ❑ 290 Greg Coleman .08 .25
- ❑ 291 Steve Dils .08 .25
- ❑ 292 Tony Galbreath .08 .25
- ❑ 293 Tommy Kramer .15 .40
- ❑ 294 Doug Martin .08 .25
- ❑ 295 Darrin Nelson RC .15 .40
- ❑ 296 Benny Ricardo .08 .25
- ❑ 297 John Swain .08 .25
- ❑ 298 John Turner .08 .25
- ❑ 299 New Orleans Saints TL .15 .40
- ❑ 300 Morten Andersen RC .60 1.50
- ❑ 301 Russell Erxleben .08 .25
- ❑ 302 Jeff Groth .08 .25
- ❑ 303 Rickey Jackson RC .25 .60
- ❑ 304 Johnnie Poe RC .08 .25
- ❑ 305 George Rogers .15 .40
- ❑ 306 Richard Todd .15 .40
- ❑ 307 Jim Wilks RC .08 .25
- ❑ 308 Dave Wilson RC .08 .25
- ❑ 309 Wayne Wilson .08 .25
- ❑ 310 New York Giants TL .08 .25
- ❑ 311 Leon Bright .08 .25
- ❑ 312 Scott Brunner .08 .25
- ❑ 313 Rob Carpenter .08 .25
- ❑ 314 Harry Carson .15 .40
- ❑ 315 Earnest Gray .08 .25
- ❑ 316 Ali Haji-Sheikh RC .08 .25
- ❑ 317 Mark Haynes .15 .40
- ❑ 318 Dave Jennings .08 .25
- ❑ 319 Brian Kelley .08 .25
- ❑ 320 Phil Simms .30 .75
- ❑ 321 Lawrence Taylor 1.50 3.00
- ❑ 322 Lawrence Taylor IR .60 1.50
- ❑ 323 Brad Van Pelt .08 .25
- ❑ 324 Butch Woolfolk .08 .25
- ❑ 325 Eagles TL/M.Quick .15 .40
- ❑ 326 Harold Carmichael .15 .40
- ❑ 327 Herman Edwards .08 .25
- ❑ 328 Michael Haddix RC .08 .25
- ❑ 329 Dennis Harrison .08 .25
- ❑ 330 Ron Jaworski .15 .40
- ❑ 331 Wilbert Montgomery .15 .40
- ❑ 332 Hubie Oliver .08 .25
- ❑ 333 Mike Quick RC .25 .60
- ❑ 334 Jerry Robinson .08 .25
- ❑ 335 Max Runager .08 .25
- ❑ 336 Michael Williams .08 .25
- ❑ 337 Cardinals TL/O.Anderson .15 .40
- ❑ 338 Ottis Anderson .25 .60
- ❑ 339 Al(Bubba) Baker .15 .40
- ❑ 340 Carl Birdsong .08 .25
- ❑ 341 David Galloway .08 .25
- ❑ 342 Roy Green .15 .40
- ❑ 343 Roy Green IR .15 .40
- ❑ 344 Curtis Greer RC .08 .25
- ❑ 345 Neil Lomax .15 .40
- ❑ 346 Doug Marsh .08 .25
- ❑ 347 Stump Mitchell .15 .40
- ❑ 348 Lionel Washington RC .15 .40
- ❑ 349 49ers TL/D.Clark .15 .40
- ❑ 350 Dwaine Board .08 .25
- ❑ 351 Dwight Clark .25 .60
- ❑ 352 Dwight Clark IR .15 .40
- ❑ 353 Roger Craig RC ! 1.25 3.00
- ❑ 354 Fred Dean .15 .40
- ❑ 355 Fred Dean IR w/Marino .25 .60
- ❑ 356 Dwight Hicks .15 .40
- ❑ 357 Ronnie Lott .60 1.50
- ❑ 358 Joe Montana 4.00 10.00
- ❑ 359 Joe Montana IR 1.50 3.00
- ❑ 360 Freddie Solomon .08 .25
- ❑ 361 Wendell Tyler .08 .25
- ❑ 362 Ray Wersching .08 .25
- ❑ 363 Eric Wright RC .15 .40
- ❑ 364 Tampa Bay Bucs TL .08 .25
- ❑ 365 Gerald Carter .08 .25
- ❑ 366 Hugh Green .15 .40
- ❑ 367 Kevin House .15 .40
- ❑ 368 Michael Morton RC .08 .25
- ❑ 369 James Owens .08 .25
- ❑ 370 Booker Reese .08 .25
- ❑ 371 Lee Roy Selmon .25 .60
- ❑ 372 Jack Thompson .15 .40
- ❑ 373 James Wilder .15 .40
- ❑ 374 Steve Wilson .08 .25
- ❑ 375 Redskins TL/J.Riggins .25 .60
- ❑ 376 Jeff Bostic .08 .25
- ❑ 377 Charlie Brown .25 .60
- ❑ 378 Charlie Brown IR .15 .40
- ❑ 379 Dave Butz .15 .40
- ❑ 380 Darrell Green RC 6.00 12.00
- ❑ 381 Russ Grimm RC 1.25 3.00
- ❑ 382 Joe Jacoby .15 .40
- ❑ 383 Dexter Manley .15 .40
- ❑ 384 Art Monk .40 1.00
- ❑ 385 Mark Moseley .15 .40
- ❑ 386 Mark Murphy .08 .25
- ❑ 387 Mike Nelms .08 .25
- ❑ 388 John Riggins .25 .60
- ❑ 389 John Riggins IR .25 .60
- ❑ 390 Joe Theismann .25 .60
- ❑ 391 Joe Theismann IR .25 .60
- ❑ 392 Don Warren .15 .40
- ❑ 393 Joe Washington .15 .40
- ❑ 394 Checklist 1-132 .10 .60
- ❑ 395 Checklist 133-264 .10 .60
- ❑ 396 Checklist 265-396 .10 .60

1984 Topps USFL

- ❑ COMP.FACT.SET (132) 150.00 300.00
- ❑ COMPLETE SET (132) 150.00 300.00
- ❑ 1 Luther Bradley .75 2.00
- ❑ 2 Frank Corral .75 2.00
- ❑ 3 Trumaine Johnson .75 2.00
- ❑ 4 Greg Landry 1.25 2.50
- ❑ 5 Kit Lathrop .75 2.00
- ❑ 6 Kevin Long .75 2.00
- ❑ 7 Tim Spencer .75 2.00
- ❑ 8 Stan White .75 2.00
- ❑ 9 Buddy Aydelette .75 2.00
- ❑ 10 Tom Banks .75 2.00
- ❑ 11 Fred Bohannon .75 2.00
- ❑ 12 Joe Cribbs 2.00 4.00
- ❑ 13 Joey Jones .75 2.00
- ❑ 14 Scott Norwood XRC 1.25 2.50
- ❑ 15 Jim Smith 1.25 2.50
- ❑ 16 Cliff Stoudt 2.00 4.00
- ❑ 17 Vince Evans 2.00 4.00
- ❑ 18 Vagas Ferguson .75 2.00
- ❑ 19 John Gillen .75 2.00
- ❑ 20 Kris Haines .75 2.00
- ❑ 21 Glenn Hyde .75 2.00
- ❑ 22 Mark Keel .75 2.00
- ❑ 23 Gary Lewis XRC .75 2.00
- ❑ 24 Doug Plank .75 2.00
- ❑ 25 Neil Balholm .75 2.00
- ❑ 26 David Dumars .75 2.00
- ❑ 27 David Martin XRC .75 2.00
- ❑ 28 Craig Penrose .75 2.00
- ❑ 29 Dave Stalls .75 2.00
- ❑ 30 Harry Sydney XRC .75 2.00
- ❑ 31 Vincent White .75 2.00
- ❑ 32 George Yarno .75 2.00
- ❑ 33 Kiki DeAyala .75 2.00
- ❑ 34 Sam Harrell .75 2.00
- ❑ 35 Mike Hawkins .75 2.00
- ❑ 36 Jim Kelly XRC 30.00 60.00
- ❑ 37 Mark Rush .75 2.00
- ❑ 38 Ricky Sanders XRC 3.00 6.00
- ❑ 39 Paul Bergmann .75 2.00
- ❑ 40 Tom Dinkel .75 2.00
- ❑ 41 Wyatt Henderson .75 2.00
- ❑ 42 Vaughan Johnson XRC 1.25 2.50
- ❑ 43 Willie McClendon Geor. .75 2.00
- ❑ 44 Matt Robinson .75 2.00
- ❑ 45 George Achica .75 2.00
- ❑ 46 Mark Adickes .75 2.00
- ❑ 47 Howard Carson .75 2.00
- ❑ 48 Kevin Nelson .75 2.00
- ❑ 49 Jeff Partridge .75 2.00
- ❑ 50 Jo Jo Townsell 1.25 2.50
- ❑ 51 Eddie Weaver .75 2.00
- ❑ 52 Steve Young XRC 50.00 100.00
- ❑ 53 Derrick Crawford .75 2.00
- ❑ 54 Walter Lewis .75 2.00
- ❑ 55 Phil McKinnely .75 2.00
- ❑ 56 Vic Minore .75 2.00
- ❑ 57 Gary Shirk .75 2.00
- ❑ 58 Reggie White XRC 30.00 60.00
- ❑ 59 Anthony Carter XRC 5.00 12.00
- ❑ 60 John Corker .75 2.00
- ❑ 61 David Greenwood .75 2.00
- ❑ 62 Bobby Hebert XRC 2.00 4.00
- ❑ 63 Derek Holloway .75 2.00
- ❑ 64 Ken Lacy .75 2.00
- ❑ 65 Tyrone McGriff .75 2.00
- ❑ 66 Ray Pinney .75 2.00
- ❑ 67 Gary Barbaro .75 2.00
- ❑ 68 Sam Bowers .75 2.00
- ❑ 69 Clarence Collins .75 2.00
- ❑ 70 Willie Harper .75 2.00
- ❑ 71 Jim LeClair .75 2.00
- ❑ 72 Bobby Leopold XRC .75 2.00
- ❑ 73 Brian Sipe 2.00 4.00
- ❑ 74 Herschel Walker XRC 12.50 25.00
- ❑ 75 Junior Ah You XRC .75 2.00
- ❑ 76 Marcus Dupree XRC 2.50 6.00
- ❑ 77 Marcus Marek .75 2.00
- ❑ 78 Tim Mazzetti .75 2.00
- ❑ 79 Mike Robinson XRC .75 2.00
- ❑ 80 Dan Ross 2.00 4.00
- ❑ 81 Mark Schellen .75 2.00
- ❑ 82 Johnnie Walton .75 2.00
- ❑ 83 Gordon Banks .75 2.00
- ❑ 84 Fred Besana .75 2.00
- ❑ 85 Dave Browning .75 2.00
- ❑ 86 Eric Jordan .75 2.00
- ❑ 87 Frank Manumaleuga .75 2.00
- ❑ 88 Gary Plummer XRC 2.00 4.00
- ❑ 89 Stan Talley .75 2.00
- ❑ 90 Arthur Whittington .75 2.00
- ❑ 91 Terry Beeson .75 2.00
- ❑ 92 Mel Gray 2.00 4.00
- ❑ 93 Mike Katolin .75 2.00
- ❑ 94 Dewey McClain .75 2.00
- ❑ 95 Sidney Thornton .75 2.00

❑ 96 Doug Williams	2.00	4.00
❑ 97 Kelvin Bryant XRC	2.00	4.00
❑ 98 John Bunting	.75	2.00
❑ 99 Irv Eatman XRC	1.25	2.50
❑ 100 Scott Fitzkee	.75	2.00
❑ 101 Chuck Fusina	.75	2.00
❑ 102 Sean Landeta XRC	1.25	2.50
❑ 103 David Trout	.75	2.00
❑ 104 Scott Woerner	.75	2.00
❑ 105 Glenn Carano	.75	2.00
❑ 106 Ron Crosby	.75	2.00
❑ 107 Jerry Holmes	.75	2.00
❑ 108 Bruce Huther	.75	2.00
❑ 109 Mike Rozier XRC	2.00	4.00
❑ 110 Larry Swider	.75	2.00
❑ 111 Danny Buggs	.75	2.00
❑ 112 Putt Choate	.75	2.00
❑ 113 Rich Garza	.75	2.00
❑ 114 Joey Hackett	.75	2.00
❑ 115 Rick Neuheisel XRC	2.00	4.00
❑ 116 Mike St. Clair	.75	2.00
❑ 117 Gary Anderson XRC RB	2.00	4.00
❑ 118 Zenon Andrusyshyn	.75	2.00
❑ 119 Doug Beaudoin	.75	2.00
❑ 120 Mike Butler	.75	2.00
❑ 121 Willie Gillespie	.75	2.00
❑ 122 Fred Nordgren	.75	2.00
❑ 123 John Reaves	.75	2.00
❑ 124 Eric Truvillion	.75	2.00
❑ 125 Reggie Collier	.75	2.00
❑ 126 Mike Guess	.75	2.00
❑ 127 Mike Hohensee	.75	2.00
❑ 128 Craig James XRC	3.00	8.00
❑ 129 Eric Robinson	.75	2.00
❑ 130 Billy Taylor	.75	2.00
❑ 131 Joey Walters	.75	2.00
❑ 132 Checklist 1-132	1.25	2.50

1985 Topps

❑ COMPLETE SET (396)	35.00	60.00
❑ COMP.FACT.SET (396)	40.00	75.00
❑ 1 Mark Clayton RB	.20	.50
❑ 2 Eric Dickerson RB	.20	.50
❑ 3 Charlie Joiner RB	.20	.50
❑ 4 Dan Marino RB	3.00	6.00
❑ 5 Art Monk RB	.20	.50
❑ 6 Walter Payton RB	.40	1.00
❑ 7 NFC Champs/Suhey	.10	.30
❑ 8 AFC Championship	.10	.30
❑ 9 Super Bowl XIX	.10	.30
❑ 10 Atlanta Falcons TL	.07	.20
❑ 11 William Andrews	.10	.30
❑ 12 Stacey Bailey	.07	.20
❑ 13 Steve Bartkowski	.20	.50
❑ 14 Rick Bryan RC	.07	.20
❑ 15 Alfred Jackson	.07	.20
❑ 16 Kenny Johnson	.07	.20
❑ 17 Mike Kenn	.07	.20
❑ 18 Mike Pitts RC	.07	.20
❑ 19 Gerald Riggs	.10	.30
❑ 20 Sylvester Stamps	.07	.20
❑ 21 R.C. Thielemann	.07	.20
❑ 22 Bears TL/W.Payton	.30	.75
❑ 23 Todd Bell RC	.07	.20
❑ 24 Richard Dent RC	1.50	4.00
❑ 25 Gary Fencik	.10	.30
❑ 26 Dave Finzer	.07	.20
❑ 27 Leslie Frazier	.07	.20
❑ 28 Steve Fuller	.10	.30
❑ 29 Willie Gault	.20	.50
❑ 30 Dan Hampton	.20	.50
❑ 31 Jim McMahon	.30	.75
❑ 32 Steve McMichael RC	.20	.50
❑ 33 Walter Payton	2.50	6.00
❑ 34 Mike Singletary	.30	.75
❑ 35 Matt Suhey	.07	.20
❑ 36 Bob Thomas	.07	.20
❑ 37 Cowboys TL/Dorsett	.20	.50
❑ 38 Bill Bates RC	.40	1.00
❑ 39 Doug Cosbie	.10	.30
❑ 40 Tony Dorsett	.30	.75
❑ 41 Michael Downs	.07	.20
❑ 42 Mike Hegman UER RC	.07	.20
❑ 43 Tony Hill	.10	.30
❑ 44 Gary Hogeboom RC	.07	.20
❑ 45 Jim Jeffcoat RC	.20	.50
❑ 46 Ed Too Tall Jones	.20	.50
❑ 47 Mike Renfro	.07	.20
❑ 48 Rafael Septien	.07	.20
❑ 49 Dennis Thurman	.07	.20
❑ 50 Everson Walls	.10	.30
❑ 51 Danny White	.20	.50
❑ 52 Randy White	.20	.50
❑ 53 Detroit Lions TL	.07	.20
❑ 54 Jeff Chadwick	.07	.20
❑ 55 Michael Cofer RC	.07	.20
❑ 56 Gary Danielson	.07	.20
❑ 57 Keith Dorney	.07	.20
❑ 58 Doug English	.10	.30
❑ 59 William Gay	.07	.20
❑ 60 Ken Jenkins	.07	.20
❑ 61 James Jones FB	.10	.30
❑ 62 Eddie Murray	.10	.30
❑ 63 Billy Sims	.20	.50
❑ 64 Leonard Thompson	.07	.20
❑ 65 Bobby Watkins	.07	.20
❑ 66 Green Bay Packers TL	.10	.30
❑ 67 Paul Coffman	.07	.20
❑ 68 Lynn Dickey	.10	.30
❑ 69 Mike Douglass	.07	.20
❑ 70 Tom Flynn RC	.07	.20
❑ 71 Eddie Lee Ivery	.07	.20
❑ 72 Ezra Johnson	.07	.20
❑ 73 Mark Lee	.07	.20
❑ 74 Tim Lewis	.07	.20
❑ 75 James Lofton	.20	.50
❑ 76 Bucky Scribner	.07	.20
❑ 77 Rams TL/Dickerson	.20	.50
❑ 78 Nolan Cromwell	.10	.30
❑ 79 Eric Dickerson	.50	1.25
❑ 80 Henry Ellard RC	1.00	2.50
❑ 81 Kent Hill	.07	.20
❑ 82 LeRoy Irvin	.10	.30
❑ 83 Jeff Kemp RC	.10	.30
❑ 84 Mike Lansford	.07	.20
❑ 85 Barry Redden	.07	.20
❑ 86 Jackie Slater	.20	.50
❑ 87 Doug Smith C RC	.10	.30
❑ 88 Jack Youngblood	.10	.30
❑ 89 Minnesota Vikings TL	.07	.20
❑ 90 Alfred Anderson RC	.07	.20
❑ 91 Ted Brown	.10	.30
❑ 92 Greg Coleman	.07	.20
❑ 93 Tommy Hannon	.07	.20
❑ 94 Tommy Kramer	.10	.30
❑ 95 Leo Lewis RC	.10	.30
❑ 96 Doug Martin	.07	.20
❑ 97 Darrin Nelson	.10	.30
❑ 98 Jan Stenerud	.10	.30
❑ 99 Sammie White	.10	.30
❑ 100 New Orleans Saints TL	.07	.20
❑ 101 Morten Andersen	.20	.50
❑ 102 Hoby Brenner RC	.10	.30
❑ 103 Bruce Clark	.07	.20
❑ 104 Hokie Gajan	.07	.20
❑ 105 Brian Hansen RC	.07	.20
❑ 106 Rickey Jackson	.20	.50
❑ 107 George Rogers	.10	.30
❑ 108 Dave Wilson	.07	.20
❑ 109 Tyrone Young	.07	.20
❑ 110 New York Giants TL	.07	.20
❑ 111 Carl Banks RC	.40	1.00
❑ 112 Jim Burt RC	.20	.50
❑ 113 Rob Carpenter	.07	.20
❑ 114 Harry Carson	.10	.30
❑ 115 Earnest Gray	.07	.20
❑ 116 Ali Haji-Sheikh	.07	.20
❑ 117 Mark Haynes	.10	.30
❑ 118 Bobby Johnson	.07	.20
❑ 119 Lionel Manuel RC	.10	.30
❑ 120 Joe Morris RC	.20	.50
❑ 121 Zeke Mowatt RC	.10	.30
❑ 122 Jeff Rutledge RC	.07	.20
❑ 123 Phil Simms	.20	.50
❑ 124 Lawrence Taylor	.60	1.50
❑ 125 Philadelphia Eagles TL	.07	.20
❑ 126 Greg Brown	.07	.20
❑ 127 Ray Ellis	.07	.20
❑ 128 Dennis Harrison	.07	.20
❑ 129 Wes Hopkins RC	.10	.30
❑ 130 Mike Horan RC	.07	.20
❑ 131 Kenny Jackson RC	.07	.20
❑ 132 Ron Jaworski	.10	.30
❑ 133 Paul McFadden	.07	.20
❑ 134 Wilbert Montgomery	.10	.30
❑ 135 Mike Quick	.20	.50
❑ 136 John Spagnola	.07	.20
❑ 137 St.Louis Cardinals TL	.07	.20
❑ 138 Ottis Anderson	.20	.50
❑ 139 Al(Bubba) Baker	.10	.30
❑ 140 Roy Green	.10	.30
❑ 141 Curtis Greer	.07	.20
❑ 142 E.J.Junior	.07	.20
❑ 143 Neil Lomax	.10	.30
❑ 144 Stump Mitchell	.10	.30
❑ 145 Neil O'Donoghue	.07	.20
❑ 146 Pat Tilley	.07	.20
❑ 147 Lionel Washington	.07	.20
❑ 148 49ers TL/J.Montana	.50	1.25
❑ 149 Dwaine Board	.07	.20
❑ 150 Dwight Clark	.20	.50
❑ 151 Roger Craig	.40	1.00
❑ 152 Randy Cross	.10	.30
❑ 153 Fred Dean	.10	.30
❑ 154 Keith Fahnhorst RC	.07	.20
❑ 155 Dwight Hicks	.07	.20
❑ 156 Ronnie Lott	.20	.50
❑ 157 Joe Montana	4.00	10.00
❑ 158 Renaldo Nehemiah	.10	.30
❑ 159 Fred Quillan	.07	.20
❑ 160 Jack Reynolds	.07	.20
❑ 161 Freddie Solomon	.07	.20
❑ 162 Keena Turner RC	.07	.20
❑ 163 Wendell Tyler	.07	.20
❑ 164 Ray Wersching	.07	.20
❑ 165 Carlton Williamson	.07	.20
❑ 166 Tampa Bay Bucs TL	.10	.30
❑ 167 Gerald Carter	.07	.20
❑ 168 Mark Cotney	.07	.20
❑ 169 Steve DeBerg	.20	.50
❑ 170 Sean Farrell RC	.07	.20
❑ 171 Hugh Green	.10	.30
❑ 172 Kevin House	.10	.30
❑ 173 David Logan	.07	.20
❑ 174 Michael Morton	.07	.20
❑ 175 Lee Roy Selmon	.20	.50
❑ 176 James Wilder	.07	.20
❑ 177 Redskins TL/J.Riggins	.20	.50
❑ 178 Charlie Brown	.07	.20
❑ 179 Monte Coleman RC	.10	.30
❑ 180 Vernon Dean	.07	.20
❑ 181 Darrell Green	.20	.50
❑ 182 Russ Grimm	.10	.30
❑ 183 Joe Jacoby	.10	.30
❑ 184 Dexter Manley	.10	.30
❑ 185 Art Monk	.20	.50
❑ 186 Mark Moseley	.10	.30
❑ 187 Calvin Muhammad	.07	.20
❑ 188 Mike Nelms	.07	.20
❑ 189 John Riggins	.20	.50
❑ 190 Joe Theismann	.20	.50
❑ 191 Joe Washington	.10	.30
❑ 192 D.Marino/Montana LL	4.00	10.00
❑ 193 Art Monk/O.Newsome LL	.10	.30
❑ 194 E.Dickerson/Jackson LL	.20	.50
❑ 195 Scoring Leaders	.07	.20
❑ 196 Interception Leaders	.07	.20
❑ 197 Punting Leaders	.07	.20
❑ 198 Bills TL/Greg Bell	.07	.20
❑ 199 Greg Bell RC	.10	.30
❑ 200 Preston Dennard	.07	.20
❑ 201 Joe Ferguson	.10	.30
❑ 202 Byron Franklin	.07	.20
❑ 203 Steve Freeman	.07	.20
❑ 204 Jim Haslett	.10	.30
❑ 205 Charles Romes	.07	.20
❑ 206 Fred Smerlas	.07	.20
❑ 207 Darryl Talley RC	.20	.50
❑ 208 Van Williams	.07	.20
❑ 209 Cincinnati Bengals TL	.10	.30
❑ 210 Ken Anderson	.20	.50
❑ 211 Jim Breech	.07	.20
❑ 212 Louis Breeden	.07	.20
❑ 213 James Brooks	.10	.30

❑ 214 Ross Browner .10 .30
❑ 215 Eddie Edwards .07 .20
❑ 216 M.L. Harris .07 .20
❑ 217 Bobby Kemp .07 .20
❑ 218 Larry Kinnebrew RC .07 .20
❑ 219 Anthony Munoz .20 .50
❑ 220 Reggie Williams .10 .30
❑ 221 Cleveland Browns TL .07 .20
❑ 222 Matt Bahr .10 .30
❑ 223 Chip Banks .07 .20
❑ 224 Reggie Camp .07 .20
❑ 225 Tom Cousineau .07 .20
❑ 226 Joe DeLamielleure .20 .50
❑ 227 Ricky Feacher .07 .20
❑ 228 Boyce Green RC .07 .20
❑ 229 Al Gross .07 .20
❑ 230 Clay Matthews .20 .50
❑ 231 Paul McDonald .07 .20
❑ 232 Ozzie Newsome .20 .50
❑ 233 Mike Pruitt .10 .30
❑ 234 Don Rogers DB .07 .20
❑ 235 Broncos TL/J.Elway 1.00 2.50
❑ 236 Rubin Carter .07 .20
❑ 237 Barney Chavous .07 .20
❑ 238 John Elway 5.00 12.00
❑ 239 Steve Foley .07 .20
❑ 240 Mike Harden RC .07 .20
❑ 241 Tom Jackson .20 .50
❑ 242 Butch Johnson .07 .20
❑ 243 Rulon Jones .07 .20
❑ 244 Rich Karlis .07 .20
❑ 245 Steve Watson .10 .30
❑ 246 Gerald Willhite .07 .20
❑ 247 Sammy Winder .10 .30
❑ 248 Houston Oilers TL .07 .20
❑ 249 Jesse Baker .07 .20
❑ 250 Carter Hartwig .07 .20
❑ 251 Warren Moon RC 6.00 15.00
❑ 252 Larry Moriarty RC .07 .20
❑ 253 Mike Munchak RC 1.25 3.00
❑ 254 Carl Roaches .07 .20
❑ 255 Tim Smith .10 .30
❑ 256 Willie Tullis .07 .20
❑ 257 Jamie Williams RC .07 .20
❑ 258 Indianapolis Colts TL .07 .20
❑ 259 Raymond Butler .07 .20
❑ 260 Johnie Cooks .07 .20
❑ 261 Eugene Daniel RC .07 .20
❑ 262 Curtis Dickey .10 .30
❑ 263 Chris Hinton .10 .30
❑ 264 Vernon Maxwell .07 .20
❑ 265 Randy McMillan .07 .20
❑ 266 Art Schlichter RC .20 .50
❑ 267 Rohn Stark .10 .30
❑ 268 Leo Wisniewski .07 .20
❑ 269 Kansas City Chiefs TL .07 .20
❑ 270 Jim Arnold .07 .20
❑ 271 Mike Bell .07 .20
❑ 272 Todd Blackledge RC .10 .30
❑ 273 Carlos Carson .10 .30
❑ 274 Deron Cherry .10 .30
❑ 275 Herman Heard RC .07 .20
❑ 276 Bill Kenney .10 .30
❑ 277 Nick Lowery .20 .50
❑ 278 Bill Maas RC .07 .20
❑ 279 Henry Marshall .07 .20
❑ 280 Art Still .07 .20
❑ 281 Raiders TL/M.Allen .20 .50
❑ 282 Marcus Allen 1.00 2.50
❑ 283 Lyle Alzado .10 .30
❑ 284 Chris Bahr .07 .20
❑ 285 Malcolm Barnwell .07 .20
❑ 286 Cliff Branch .20 .50
❑ 287 Todd Christensen .20 .50
❑ 288 Ray Guy .20 .50
❑ 289 Lester Hayes .10 .30
❑ 290 Mike Haynes .10 .30
❑ 291 Henry Lawrence .07 .20
❑ 292 Howie Long .75 2.00
❑ 293 Rod Martin .10 .30
❑ 294 Vann McElroy .07 .20
❑ 295 Matt Millen .10 .30
❑ 296 Bill Pickel RC .07 .20
❑ 297 Jim Plunkett .20 .50
❑ 298 Dokie Williams RC .07 .20
❑ 299 Marc Wilson .10 .30
❑ 300 Dolphins TL/Duper .10 .30
❑ 301 Bob Baumhower .07 .20
❑ 302 Doug Betters .07 .20

❑ 303 Glenn Blackwood .10 .30
❑ 304 Lyle Blackwood .10 .30
❑ 305 Kim Bokamper .07 .20
❑ 306 Charles Bowser RC .07 .20
❑ 307 Jimmy Cefalo .07 .20
❑ 308 Mark Clayton RC .50 1.25
❑ 309 A.J. Duhe .07 .20
❑ 310 Mark Duper .20 .50
❑ 311 Andra Franklin .07 .20
❑ 312 Bruce Hardy .07 .20
❑ 313 Pete Johnson .10 .30
❑ 314 Dan Marino 5.00 12.00
❑ 315 Tony Nathan .10 .30
❑ 316 Ed Newman .07 .20
❑ 317 Reggie Roby .20 .50
❑ 318 Dwight Stephenson .40 1.00
❑ 319 Uwe Von Schamann .07 .20
❑ 320 New England Pats TL .07 .20
❑ 321 Raymond Clayborn .10 .30
❑ 322 Tony Collins .10 .30
❑ 323 Tony Eason RC .20 .50
❑ 324 Tony Franklin .07 .20
❑ 325 Irving Fryar RC 2.00 5.00
❑ 326 John Hannah .20 .50
❑ 327 Brian Holloway .07 .20
❑ 328 Craig James RC .50 1.25
❑ 329 Stanley Morgan .10 .30
❑ 330 Steve Nelson .07 .20
❑ 331 Derrick Ramsey .07 .20
❑ 332 Stephen Starring RC .10 .30
❑ 333 Mosi Tatupu .07 .20
❑ 334 Andre Tippett .20 .50
❑ 335 New York Jets TL .10 .30
❑ 336 Russell Carter RC .07 .20
❑ 337 Mark Gastineau .10 .30
❑ 338 Bruce Harper .07 .20
❑ 339 Bobby Humphery RC .07 .20
❑ 340 Johnny Lam Jones .07 .20
❑ 341 Joe Klecko .10 .30
❑ 342 Pat Leahy .07 .20
❑ 343 Marty Lyons .10 .30
❑ 344 Freeman McNeil .10 .30
❑ 345 Lance Mehl .07 .20
❑ 346 Ken O'Brien RC .20 .50
❑ 347 Marvin Powell .07 .20
❑ 348 Pat Ryan .07 .20
❑ 349 Mickey Shuler RC .07 .20
❑ 350 Wesley Walker .10 .30
❑ 351 Pittsburgh Steelers TL .10 .30
❑ 352 Walter Abercrombie .07 .20
❑ 353 Gary Anderson K .10 .30
❑ 354 Robin Cole .07 .20
❑ 355 Bennie Cunningham .07 .20
❑ 356 Rich Erenberg .07 .20
❑ 357 Jack Lambert .20 .50
❑ 358 Louis Lipps RC .20 .50
❑ 359 Mark Malone .10 .30
❑ 360 Mike Merriweather RC .07 .20
❑ 361 Frank Pollard .07 .20
❑ 362 Donnie Shell .10 .30
❑ 363 John Stallworth .20 .50
❑ 364 Sam Washington .07 .20
❑ 365 Mike Webster .10 .30
❑ 366 Dwayne Woodruff .07 .20
❑ 367 San Diego Chargers TL .07 .20
❑ 368 Rolf Benirschke .07 .20
❑ 369 Gill Byrd RC .20 .50
❑ 370 Wes Chandler .10 .30
❑ 371 Bobby Duckworth .07 .20
❑ 372 Dan Fouts .20 .50
❑ 373 Mike Green .07 .20
❑ 374 Pete Holohan RC .07 .20
❑ 375 Earnest Jackson RC .10 .30
❑ 376 Lionel James RC .10 .30
❑ 377 Charlie Joiner .20 .50
❑ 378 Billy Ray Smith .10 .30
❑ 379 Kellen Winslow .20 .50
❑ 380 Seattle Seahawks TL .10 .30
❑ 381 Dave Brown DB .07 .20
❑ 382 Jeff Bryant .07 .20
❑ 383 Dan Doornink .07 .20
❑ 384 Kenny Easley .10 .30
❑ 385 Jacob Green .10 .30
❑ 386 David Hughes .07 .20
❑ 387 Norm Johnson .07 .20
❑ 388 Dave Krieg .20 .50
❑ 389 Steve Largent .40 1.00
❑ 390 Joe Nash RC .07 .20
❑ 391 Daryl Turner RC .07 .20

❑ 392 Curt Warner .20 .50
❑ 393 Fredd Young RC .10 .30
❑ 394 Checklist 1-132 .20 .50
❑ 395 Checklist 133-264 .20 .50
❑ 396 Checklist 265-396 .20 .50

1985 Topps USFL

❑ COMP.FACT.SET (132) 60.00 120.00
❑ COMPLETE SET (132) 60.00 120.00
❑ 1 Case DeBruijn .20 .50
❑ 2 Mike Katolin .20 .50
❑ 3 Bruce Laird .20 .50
❑ 4 Kit Lathrop .20 .50
❑ 5 Kevin Long .20 .50
❑ 6 Karl Lorch .20 .50
❑ 7 Dave Tipton DT .20 .50
❑ 8 Doug Williams .75 2.00
❑ 9 Luis Zendejas XRC .20 .50
❑ 10 Kelvin Bryant .40 1.00
❑ 11 Willie Collier .20 .50
❑ 12 Irv Eatman .20 .50
❑ 13 Scott Fitzkee .20 .50
❑ 14 William Fuller XRC 1.25 3.00
❑ 15 Chuck Fusina .20 .50
❑ 16 Pete Kugler .20 .50
❑ 17 Garcia Lane .20 .50
❑ 18 Mike Lush .20 .50
❑ 19 Sam Mills XRC 2.00 5.00
❑ 20 Buddy Aydelette .20 .50
❑ 21 Joe Cribbs .75 2.00
❑ 22 David Dumars .20 .50
❑ 23 Robin Earl .20 .50
❑ 24 Joey Jones .20 .50
❑ 25 Leon Perry RB .20 .50
❑ 26 Dave Pureifory .20 .50
❑ 27 Bill Roe .20 .50
❑ 28 Doug Smith DT XRC .75 2.00
❑ 29 Cliff Stoudt .40 1.00
❑ 30 Jeff Delaney .20 .50
❑ 31 Vince Evans .40 1.00
❑ 32 Leonard Harris XRC .20 .50
❑ 33 Bill Johnson RB .20 .50
❑ 34 Marc Lewis XRC .20 .50
❑ 35 David Martin .20 .50
❑ 36 Bruce Thornton .20 .50
❑ 37 Craig Walls .20 .50
❑ 38 Vincent White .20 .50
❑ 39 Luther Bradley .20 .50
❑ 40 Pete Catan .20 .50
❑ 41 Kiki DeAyala .20 .50
❑ 42 Toni Fritsch .20 .50
❑ 43 Sam Harrell .20 .50
❑ 44 Richard Johnson WR XRC .40 1.00
❑ 45 Jim Kelly 10.00 20.00
❑ 46 Gerald McNeil XRC .20 .50
❑ 47 Clarence Verdin XRC .75 2.00
❑ 48 Dale Walters .20 .50
❑ 49 Gary Clark XRC 2.50 6.00
❑ 50 Tom Dinkel .20 .50
❑ 51 Mike Edwards LB .20 .50
❑ 52 Brian Franco .20 .50
❑ 53 Bob Gruber .20 .50
❑ 54 Robbie Mahfouz .20 .50
❑ 55 Mike Rozier .75 2.00
❑ 56 Brian Sipe .40 1.00
❑ 57 J.T. Turner .20 .50
❑ 58 Howard Carson .20 .50
❑ 59 Wymon Henderson XRC .20 .50
❑ 60 Kevin Nelson .20 .50
❑ 61 Jeff Partridge .20 .50
❑ 62 Ben Rudolph .20 .50
❑ 63 Jo Jo Townsell .40 1.00
❑ 64 Eddie Weaver .20 .50
❑ 65 Steve Young 15.00 30.00
❑ 66 Tony Zendejas XRC .40 1.00
❑ 67 Mossy Cade .20 .50

Card		
❑ 68 Leonard Coleman XRC	.20	.50
❑ 69 John Corker	.20	.50
❑ 70 Derrick Crawford	.20	.50
❑ 71 Art Kuehn	.20	.50
❑ 72 Walter Lewis	.20	.50
❑ 73 Tyrone McGriff	.20	.50
❑ 74 Tim Spencer	.40	1.00
❑ 75 Reggie White	12.50	25.00
❑ 76 Gizmo Williams XRC	.75	2.00
❑ 77 Sam Bowers	.20	.50
❑ 78 Maurice Carthon XRC	.75	2.00
❑ 79 Clarence Collins	.20	.50
❑ 80 Doug Flutie XRC	10.00	25.00
❑ 81 Freddie Gilbert DE	.20	.50
❑ 82 Kerry Justin	.20	.50
❑ 83 Dave Lapham	.20	.50
❑ 84 Rick Partridge	.20	.50
❑ 85 Roger Ruzek XRC	.40	1.00
❑ 86 Herschel Walker	3.00	8.00
❑ 87 Gordon Banks	.20	.50
❑ 88 Monte Bennett	.20	.50
❑ 89 Albert Bentley XRC	.40	1.00
❑ 90 Novo Bojovic	.20	.50
❑ 91 Dave Browning	.20	.50
❑ 92 Anthony Carter	.75	2.00
❑ 93 Bobby Hebert	.75	2.00
❑ 94 Ray Pinney	.20	.50
❑ 95 Stan Talley	.20	.50
❑ 96 Ruben Vaughan	.20	.50
❑ 97 Curtis Bledsoe	.20	.50
❑ 98 Reggie Collier	.20	.50
❑ 99 Jerry Doerger	.20	.50
❑ 100 Jerry Golsteyn	.20	.50
❑ 101 Bob Niziolek	.20	.50
❑ 102 Joel Patten	.20	.50
❑ 103 Ricky Simmons	.20	.50
❑ 104 Joey Walters	.20	.50
❑ 105 Marcus Dupree	.40	1.00
❑ 106 Jeff Gossett	.40	1.00
❑ 107 Frank Lockett	.20	.50
❑ 108 Marcus Marek	.20	.50
❑ 109 Kenny Neil	.20	.50
❑ 110 Robert Pennywell	.20	.50
❑ 111 Matt Robinson	.20	.50
❑ 112 Dan Ross	.40	1.00
❑ 113 Doug Woodward	.20	.50
❑ 114 Danny Buggs	.20	.50
❑ 115 Putt Choate	.20	.50
❑ 116 Greg Fields	.20	.50
❑ 117 Ken Hartley	.20	.50
❑ 118 Nick Mike-Mayer	.20	.50
❑ 119 Rick Neuheisel	.75	2.00
❑ 120 Peter Raeford	.20	.50
❑ 121 Gary Worthy	.20	.50
❑ 122 Gary Anderson RB	.40	1.00
❑ 123 Zenon Andrusyshyn	.20	.50
❑ 124 Greg Boone	.20	.50
❑ 125 Mike Butler	.20	.50
❑ 126 Mike Clark	.20	.50
❑ 127 Willie Gillespie	.20	.50
❑ 128 James Harrell	.20	.50
❑ 129 Marvin Harvey	.20	.50
❑ 130 John Reaves	.40	1.00
❑ 131 Eric Truvillion	.20	.50
❑ 132 Checklist 1-132	.40	1.00

1986 Topps

Card		
❑ COMPLETE SET (396)	60.00	120.00
❑ COMP.FACT.SET (396)	150.00	225.00
❑ 1 Marcus Allen RB	.30	.75
❑ 2 Eric Dickerson RB	.20	.50
❑ 3 Lionel James RB	.07	.20
❑ 4 Steve Largent RB	.20	.50
❑ 5 George Martin RB	.07	.20
❑ 6 Stephone Paige RB	.07	.20
❑ 7 Walter Payton RB	.30	.75
❑ 8 Super Bowl XX	.10	.30
❑ 9 Bears TL/W.Payton	.25	.60
❑ 10 Jim McMahon	.20	.50
❑ 11 Walter Payton	2.50	6.00
❑ 12 Matt Suhey	.07	.20
❑ 13 Willie Gault	.10	.30
❑ 14 Dennis McKinnon RC	.07	.20
❑ 15 Emery Moorehead	.07	.20
❑ 16 Jim Covert	.10	.30
❑ 17 Jay Hilgenberg RC	.20	.50
❑ 18 Kevin Butler RC	.10	.30
❑ 19 Richard Dent	.30	.75
❑ 20 William Perry RC	.40	.50
❑ 21 Steve McMichael	.20	.50
❑ 22 Dan Hampton	.20	.50
❑ 23 Otis Wilson	.07	.20
❑ 24 Mike Singletary	.25	.60
❑ 25 Wilber Marshall RC	.20	.50
❑ 26 Leslie Frazier	.07	.20
❑ 27 Dave Duerson RC	.07	.20
❑ 28 Gary Fencik	.07	.20
❑ 29 Patriots TL	.20	.50
❑ 30 Tony Eason	.07	.20
❑ 31 Steve Grogan	.10	.30
❑ 32 Craig James	.20	.50
❑ 33 Tony Collins	.07	.20
❑ 34 Irving Fryar	.50	1.25
❑ 35 Brian Holloway	.07	.20
❑ 36 John Hannah	.20	.50
❑ 37 Tony Franklin	.07	.20
❑ 38 Garin Veris RC	.07	.20
❑ 39 Andre Tippett	.20	.50
❑ 40 Steve Nelson	.07	.20
❑ 41 Raymond Clayborn	.07	.20
❑ 42 Fred Marion RC	.07	.20
❑ 43 Rich Camarillo	.07	.20
❑ 44 Dolphins TL/D.Marino	.75	2.00
❑ 45 Dan Marino	4.00	8.00
❑ 46 Tony Nathan	.10	.30
❑ 47 Ron Davenport RC	.07	.20
❑ 48 Mark Duper	.20	.50
❑ 49 Mark Clayton	.20	.50
❑ 50 Nat Moore	.10	.30
❑ 51 Bruce Hardy	.07	.20
❑ 52 Roy Foster	.07	.20
❑ 53 Dwight Stephenson	.30	.75
❑ 54 Fuad Reveiz RC	.10	.30
❑ 55 Bob Baumhower	.07	.20
❑ 56 Mike Charles	.07	.20
❑ 57 Hugh Green	.10	.30
❑ 58 Glenn Blackwood	.07	.20
❑ 59 Reggie Roby	.10	.30
❑ 60 Raiders TL/M.Allen	.20	.50
❑ 61 Marc Wilson	.07	.20
❑ 62 Marcus Allen	.60	1.50
❑ 63 Dokie Williams	.07	.20
❑ 64 Todd Christensen	.20	.50
❑ 65 Chris Bahr	.07	.20
❑ 66 Fulton Walker	.07	.20
❑ 67 Howie Long	.50	1.25
❑ 68 Bill Pickel	.07	.20
❑ 69 Ray Guy	.20	.50
❑ 70 Greg Townsend RC	.20	.50
❑ 71 Rod Martin	.10	.30
❑ 72 Matt Millen	.10	.30
❑ 73 Mike Haynes	.10	.30
❑ 74 Lester Hayes	.10	.30
❑ 75 Vann McElroy	.07	.20
❑ 76 Rams TL/ Dickerson	.20	.50
❑ 77 Dieter Brock RC	.10	.30
❑ 78 Eric Dickerson	.30	.75
❑ 79 Henry Ellard	.40	1.00
❑ 80 Ron Brown RC	.10	.30
❑ 81 Tony Hunter RC	.07	.20
❑ 82 Kent Hill AP	.07	.20
❑ 83 Doug Smith	.07	.20
❑ 84 Dennis Harrah	.07	.20
❑ 85 Jackie Slater	.20	.50
❑ 86 Mike Lansford	.07	.20
❑ 87 Gary Jeter	.07	.20
❑ 88 Mike Wilcher	.07	.20
❑ 89 Jim Collins	.07	.20
❑ 90 LeRoy Irvin	.10	.30
❑ 91 Gary Green	.07	.20
❑ 92 Nolan Cromwell	.10	.30
❑ 93 Dale Hatcher RC	.07	.20
❑ 94 Jets TL	.10	.30
❑ 95 Ken O'Brien	.20	.50
❑ 96 Freeman McNeil	.10	.30
❑ 97 Tony Paige RC	.07	.20
❑ 98 Johnny Lam Jones	.07	.20
❑ 99 Wesley Walker	.10	.30
❑ 100 Kurt Sohn	.07	.20
❑ 101 Al Toon RC	.20	.50
❑ 102 Mickey Shuler	.07	.20
❑ 103 Marvin Powell	.07	.20
❑ 104 Pat Leahy	.07	.20
❑ 105 Mark Gastineau	.10	.30
❑ 106 Joe Klecko	.10	.30
❑ 107 Marty Lyons	.07	.20
❑ 108 Lance Mehl	.07	.20
❑ 109 Bobby Jackson	.07	.20
❑ 110 Dave Jennings	.07	.20
❑ 111 Broncos TL	.10	.30
❑ 112 John Elway	4.00	8.00
❑ 113 Sammy Winder	.10	.30
❑ 114 Gerald Willhite	.07	.20
❑ 115 Steve Watson	.07	.20
❑ 116 Vance Johnson RC	.20	.50
❑ 117 Rich Karlis	.07	.20
❑ 118 Rulon Jones	.07	.20
❑ 119 Karl Mecklenburg RC	.20	.50
❑ 120 Louis Wright	.07	.20
❑ 121 Mike Harden	.07	.20
❑ 122 Dennis Smith RC	.20	.50
❑ 123 Steve Foley	.07	.20
❑ 124 Cowboys TL	.10	.30
❑ 125 Danny White	.20	.50
❑ 126 Tony Dorsett	.25	.60
❑ 127 Timmy Newsome	.07	.20
❑ 128 Mike Renfro	.07	.20
❑ 129 Tony Hill	.10	.30
❑ 130 Doug Cosbie	.10	.30
❑ 131 Rafael Septien	.07	.20
❑ 132 Ed Too Tall Jones	.20	.50
❑ 133 Randy White	.20	.50
❑ 134 Jim Jeffcoat	.20	.50
❑ 135 Everson Walls	.10	.30
❑ 136 Dennis Thurman	.07	.20
❑ 137 Giants TL	.10	.30
❑ 138 Phil Simms	.20	.50
❑ 139 Joe Morris	.20	.50
❑ 140 George Adams RC	.07	.20
❑ 141 Lionel Manuel	.10	.30
❑ 142 Bobby Johnson	.07	.20
❑ 143 Phil McConkey RC	.10	.30
❑ 144 Mark Bavaro RC	.20	.50
❑ 145 Zeke Mowatt	.07	.20
❑ 146 Brad Benson RC	.07	.20
❑ 147 Bart Oates RC	.10	.30
❑ 148 Leonard Marshall RC	.20	.50
❑ 149 Jim Burt	.10	.30
❑ 150 George Martin	.07	.20
❑ 151 Lawrence Taylor	.50	1.25
❑ 152 Harry Carson	.10	.30
❑ 153 Elvis Patterson RC	.07	.20
❑ 154 Sean Landeta RC	.10	.30
❑ 155 49ers TL/Roger Craig	.20	.50
❑ 156 Joe Montana	4.00	8.00
❑ 157 Roger Craig	.20	.50
❑ 158 Wendell Tyler	.07	.20
❑ 159 Carl Monroe	.07	.20
❑ 160 Dwight Clark	.10	.30
❑ 161 Jerry Rice RC	40.00	80.00
❑ 162 Randy Cross	.10	.30
❑ 163 Keith Fahnhorst	.07	.20
❑ 164 Jeff Stover	.07	.20
❑ 165 Michael Carter RC	.07	.20
❑ 166 Dwaine Board	.07	.20
❑ 167 Eric Wright	.10	.30
❑ 168 Ronnie Lott	.30	.75
❑ 169 Carlton Williamson	.07	.20
❑ 170 Redskins TL	.10	.30
❑ 171 Joe Theismann	.20	.50
❑ 172 Jay Schroeder RC	.20	.50
❑ 173 George Rogers	.10	.30
❑ 174 Ken Jenkins	.07	.20
❑ 175 Art Monk	.20	.50
❑ 176 Gary Clark RC	.75	2.00
❑ 177 Joe Jacoby	.10	.30
❑ 178 Russ Grimm	.10	.30
❑ 179 Mark Moseley	.07	.20
❑ 180 Dexter Manley	.10	.30
❑ 181 Charles Mann RC	.20	.50
❑ 182 Vernon Dean	.07	.20
❑ 183 Raphel Cherry RC	.07	.20
❑ 184 Curtis Jordan	.07	.20
❑ 185 Browns TL/Kosar	.20	.50

Card		
❑ 186 Gary Danielson	.10	.30
❑ 187 Bernie Kosar RC	1.25	3.00
❑ 188 Kevin Mack RC	.20	.50
❑ 189 Earnest Byner RC	.30	.75
❑ 190 Glen Young	.07	.20
❑ 191 Ozzie Newsome	.20	.50
❑ 192 Mike Baab	.07	.20
❑ 193 Cody Risien	.10	.30
❑ 194 Bob Golic	.10	.30
❑ 195 Reggie Camp	.07	.20
❑ 196 Chip Banks	.10	.30
❑ 197 Tom Cousineau	.07	.20
❑ 198 Frank Minnifield RC	.07	.20
❑ 199 Al Gross	.07	.20
❑ 200 Seahawks TL	.10	.30
❑ 201 Dave Krieg	.20	.50
❑ 202 Curt Warner	.10	.30
❑ 203 Steve Largent	.25	.60
❑ 204 Norm Johnson	.07	.20
❑ 205 Daryl Turner	.07	.20
❑ 206 Jacob Green	.07	.20
❑ 207 Joe Nash	.07	.20
❑ 208 Jeff Bryant	.07	.20
❑ 209 Randy Edwards	.07	.20
❑ 210 Fredd Young	.07	.20
❑ 211 Kenny Easley	.07	.20
❑ 212 John Harris	.07	.20
❑ 213 Packers TL	.07	.20
❑ 214 Lynn Dickey	.10	.30
❑ 215 Gerry Ellis	.07	.20
❑ 216 Eddie Lee Ivery	.07	.20
❑ 217 Jessie Clark	.07	.20
❑ 218 James Lofton	.20	.50
❑ 219 Paul Coffman	.07	.20
❑ 220 Alphonso Carreker	.07	.20
❑ 221 Ezra Johnson	.07	.20
❑ 222 Mike Douglass	.07	.20
❑ 223 Tim Lewis	.07	.20
❑ 224 Mark Murphy RC	.07	.20
❑ 225 Joe Montana/K.O'Brien LL	.40	1.00
❑ 226 Receiving Leaders	.10	.30
❑ 227 Marcus Allen/G.Riggs LL	.20	.50
❑ 228 Scoring Leaders	.10	.30
❑ 229 Interception Leaders	.07	.20
❑ 230 Chargers TL/Dan Fouts	.20	.50
❑ 231 Dan Fouts	.20	.50
❑ 232 Lionel James	.07	.20
❑ 233 Gary Anderson RB RC	.20	.50
❑ 234 Tim Spencer RC	.10	.30
❑ 235 Wes Chandler	.10	.30
❑ 236 Charlie Joiner	.20	.50
❑ 237 Kellen Winslow	.20	.50
❑ 238 Jim Lachey RC	.20	.50
❑ 239 Bob Thomas	.07	.20
❑ 240 Jeffery Dale	.07	.20
❑ 241 Ralf Mojsiejenko	.07	.20
❑ 242 Lions TL	.07	.20
❑ 243 Eric Hipple	.07	.20
❑ 244 Billy Sims	.10	.30
❑ 245 James Jones FB	.07	.20
❑ 246 Pete Mandley RC	.07	.20
❑ 247 Leonard Thompson	.07	.20
❑ 248 Lomas Brown RC	.10	.30
❑ 249 Eddie Murray	.10	.30
❑ 250 Curtis Green	.07	.20
❑ 251 William Gay	.07	.20
❑ 252 Jimmy Williams	.07	.20
❑ 253 Bobby Watkins	.07	.20
❑ 254 Bengals TL/B.Esiason	.20	.50
❑ 255 Boomer Esiason RC	2.50	6.00
❑ 256 James Brooks	.10	.30
❑ 257 Larry Kinnebrew	.07	.20
❑ 258 Cris Collinsworth	.10	.30
❑ 259 Mike Martin	.07	.20
❑ 260 Eddie Brown RC	.20	.50
❑ 261 Anthony Munoz	.20	.50
❑ 262 Jim Breech	.07	.20
❑ 263 Ross Browner	.10	.30
❑ 264 Carl Zander	.07	.20
❑ 265 James Griffin	.07	.20
❑ 266 Robert Jackson	.07	.20
❑ 267 Pat McInally	.07	.20
❑ 268 Eagles TL	.20	.50
❑ 269 Ron Jaworski	.10	.30
❑ 270 Earnest Jackson	.10	.30
❑ 271 Mike Quick	.10	.30
❑ 272 John Spagnola	.07	.20
❑ 273 Mark Dennard	.07	.20
❑ 274 Paul McFadden	.07	.20
❑ 275 Reggie White RC	7.50	15.00
❑ 276 Greg Brown	.07	.20
❑ 277 Herman Edwards	.07	.20
❑ 278 Roynell Young	.07	.20
❑ 279 Wes Hopkins	.07	.20
❑ 280 Steelers TL	.10	.30
❑ 281 Mark Malone	.10	.30
❑ 282 Frank Pollard	.07	.20
❑ 283 Walter Abercrombie	.07	.20
❑ 284 Louis Lipps	.20	.50
❑ 285 John Stallworth	.20	.50
❑ 286 Mike Webster	.10	.30
❑ 287 Gary Anderson K	.10	.30
❑ 288 Keith Willis	.07	.20
❑ 289 Mike Merriweather	.07	.20
❑ 290 Dwayne Woodruff	.07	.20
❑ 291 Donnie Shell	.10	.30
❑ 292 Vikings TL	.10	.30
❑ 293 Tommy Kramer	.10	.30
❑ 294 Darrin Nelson	.07	.20
❑ 295 Ted Brown	.10	.30
❑ 296 Buster Rhymes	.07	.20
❑ 297 Anthony Carter RC	.40	1.00
❑ 298 Steve Jordan RC	.20	.50
❑ 299 Keith Millard RC	.20	.50
❑ 300 Joey Browner RC	.20	.50
❑ 301 John Turner	.07	.20
❑ 302 Greg Coleman	.07	.20
❑ 303 Chiefs TL	.07	.20
❑ 304 Bill Kenney	.07	.20
❑ 305 Herman Heard	.07	.20
❑ 306 Stephone Paige RC	.20	.50
❑ 307 Carlos Carson	.10	.30
❑ 308 Nick Lowery	.10	.30
❑ 309 Mike Bell	.07	.20
❑ 310 Bill Maas	.07	.20
❑ 311 Art Still	.07	.20
❑ 312 Albert Lewis RC	.20	.50
❑ 313 Deron Cherry	.10	.30
❑ 314 Colts TL	.07	.20
❑ 315 Mike Pagel	.07	.20
❑ 316 Randy McMillan	.07	.20
❑ 317 Albert Bentley RC	.10	.30
❑ 318 George Wonsley RC	.07	.20
❑ 319 Robbie Martin	.07	.20
❑ 320 Pat Beach	.07	.20
❑ 321 Chris Hinton	.10	.30
❑ 322 Duane Bickett RC	.20	.50
❑ 323 Eugene Daniel	.07	.20
❑ 324 Cliff Odom RC	.07	.20
❑ 325 Rohn Stark	.10	.30
❑ 326 Cardinals TL	.07	.20
❑ 327 Neil Lomax	.10	.30
❑ 328 Stump Mitchell	.10	.30
❑ 329 Ottis Anderson	.20	.50
❑ 330 J.T.Smith	.10	.30
❑ 331 Pat Tilley	.07	.20
❑ 332 Roy Green	.10	.30
❑ 333 Lance Smith RC	.07	.20
❑ 334 Curtis Greer	.07	.20
❑ 335 Freddie Joe Nunn RC	.10	.30
❑ 336 E.J. Junior	.10	.30
❑ 337 Lonnie Young RC	.07	.20
❑ 338 Saints TL	.07	.20
❑ 339 Bobby Hebert RC	.20	.50
❑ 340 Dave Wilson	.07	.20
❑ 341 Wayne Wilson	.07	.20
❑ 342 Hoby Brenner	.07	.20
❑ 343 Stan Brock	.10	.30
❑ 344 Morten Andersen	.20	.50
❑ 345 Bruce Clark	.07	.20
❑ 346 Rickey Jackson	.20	.50
❑ 347 Dave Waymer	.07	.20
❑ 348 Brian Hansen	.07	.20
❑ 349 Oilers TL/W.Moon	.20	.50
❑ 350 Warren Moon	1.50	3.00
❑ 351 Mike Rozier RC	.20	.50
❑ 352 Butch Woolfolk	.07	.20
❑ 353 Drew Hill	.20	.50
❑ 354 Willie Drewrey RC	.07	.20
❑ 355 Tim Smith	.10	.30
❑ 356 Mike Munchak	.20	.50
❑ 357 Ray Childress RC	.20	.50
❑ 358 Frank Bush	.07	.20
❑ 359 Steve Brown	.07	.20
❑ 360 Falcons TL	.07	.20
❑ 361 David Archer RC	.20	.50
❑ 362 Gerald Riggs	.10	.30
❑ 363 William Andrews	.10	.30
❑ 364 Billy Johnson	.10	.30
❑ 365 Arthur Cox	.07	.20
❑ 366 Mike Kenn	.07	.20
❑ 367 Bill Fralic RC	.10	.30
❑ 368 Mick Luckhurst	.07	.20
❑ 369 Rick Bryan	.07	.20
❑ 370 Bobby Butler	.07	.20
❑ 371 Rick Donnelly RC	.07	.20
❑ 372 Buccaneers TL	.07	.20
❑ 373 Steve DeBerg	.20	.50
❑ 374 Steve Young RC	10.00	20.00
❑ 375 James Wilder	.07	.20
❑ 376 Kevin House	.07	.20
❑ 377 Gerald Carter	.07	.20
❑ 378 Jimmie Giles	.10	.30
❑ 379 Sean Farrell	.07	.20
❑ 380 Donald Igwebuike	.07	.20
❑ 381 David Logan	.07	.20
❑ 382 Jeremiah Castille RC	.07	.20
❑ 383 Bills TL	.07	.20
❑ 384 Bruce Mathison RC	.07	.20
❑ 385 Joe Cribbs	.10	.30
❑ 386 Greg Bell	.10	.30
❑ 387 Jerry Butler	.07	.20
❑ 388 Andre Reed RC	3.00	8.00
❑ 389 Bruce Smith RC	4.00	8.00
❑ 390 Fred Smerlas	.07	.20
❑ 391 Darryl Talley	.20	.50
❑ 392 Jim Haslett	.10	.30
❑ 393 Charles Romes	.07	.20
❑ 394 Checklist 1-132	.10	.30
❑ 395 Checklist 133-264	.10	.30
❑ 396 Checklist 265-396	.10	.30

1987 Topps

Card		
❑ COMPLETE SET (396)	15.00	30.00
❑ COMP.FACT.SET (396)	50.00	80.00
❑ 1 Super Bowl XXI	.20	.50
❑ 2 Todd Christensen RB	.08	.25
❑ 3 Dave Jennings RB	.05	.15
❑ 4 Charlie Joiner RB	.20	.50
❑ 5 Steve Largent RB	.20	.50
❑ 6 Dan Marino RB	.75	2.00
❑ 7 Donnie Shell RB	.08	.25
❑ 8 Phil Simms RB	.20	.50
❑ 9 New York Giants TL	.08	.25
❑ 10 Phil Simms	.20	.50
❑ 11 Joe Morris	.08	.25
❑ 12 Maurice Carthon RC	.20	.50
❑ 13 Lee Rouson	.05	.15
❑ 14 Bobby Johnson	.05	.15
❑ 15 Lionel Manuel	.05	.15
❑ 16 Phil McConkey	.05	.15
❑ 17 Mark Bavaro	.20	.50
❑ 18 Zeke Mowatt	.05	.15
❑ 19 Raul Allegre	.05	.15
❑ 20 Sean Landeta	.05	.15
❑ 21 Brad Benson	.05	.15
❑ 22 Jim Burt	.05	.15
❑ 23 Leonard Marshall	.20	.50
❑ 24 Carl Banks	.20	.50
❑ 25 Harry Carson	.05	.15
❑ 26 Lawrence Taylor	.30	.75
❑ 27 Terry Kinard RC	.05	.15
❑ 28 Pepper Johnson RC	.20	.50
❑ 29 Erik Howard RC	.05	.15
❑ 30 Broncos TL	.05	.15
❑ 31 John Elway	2.50	6.00
❑ 32 Gerald Willhite	.05	.15
❑ 33 Sammy Winder	.08	.25
❑ 34 Ken Bell	.05	.15
❑ 35 Steve Watson	.05	.15
❑ 36 Rich Karlis	.05	.15
❑ 37 Keith Bishop	.05	.15
❑ 38 Rulon Jones	.05	.15
❑ 39 Karl Mecklenburg	.20	.50

❑ 40 Louis Wright .05 .15
❑ 41 Mike Harden .05 .15
❑ 42 Dennis Smith .08 .25
❑ 43 Bears TL/W.Payton .20 .50
❑ 44 Jim McMahon .20 .50
❑ 45 Doug Flutie RC 3.00 8.00
❑ 46 Walter Payton 2.00 5.00
❑ 47 Matt Suhey .05 .15
❑ 48 Willie Gault .08 .25
❑ 49 Dennis Gentry RC .05 .15
❑ 50 Kevin Butler .05 .15
❑ 51 Jim Covert .05 .15
❑ 52 Jay Hilgenberg .08 .25
❑ 53 Dan Hampton .20 .50
❑ 54 Steve McMichael .20 .50
❑ 55 William Perry .20 .50
❑ 56 Richard Dent .20 .50
❑ 57 Otis Wilson .05 .15
❑ 58 Mike Singletary .20 .50
❑ 59 Wilber Marshall .20 .50
❑ 60 Mike Richardson .05 .15
❑ 61 Dave Duerson .05 .15
❑ 62 Gary Fencik .05 .15
❑ 63 Redskins TL .08 .25
❑ 64 Jay Schroeder .08 .25
❑ 65 George Rogers .08 .25
❑ 66 Kelvin Bryant RC .08 .25
❑ 67 Ken Jenkins .05 .15
❑ 68 Gary Clark .20 .50
❑ 69 Art Monk .20 .50
❑ 70 Clint Didier RC .05 .15
❑ 71 Steve Cox .05 .15
❑ 72 Joe Jacoby .05 .15
❑ 73 Russ Grimm .05 .15
❑ 74 Charles Mann .08 .25
❑ 75 Dave Butz .05 .15
❑ 76 Dexter Manley .08 .25
❑ 77 Darrell Green .20 .50
❑ 78 Curtis Jordan .05 .15
❑ 79 Browns TL .05 .15
❑ 80 Bernie Kosar .20 .50
❑ 81 Curtis Dickey .05 .15
❑ 82 Kevin Mack .08 .25
❑ 83 Herman Fontenot .05 .15
❑ 84 Brian Brennan RC .05 .15
❑ 85 Ozzie Newsome .20 .50
❑ 86 Jeff Gossett .08 .25
❑ 87 Cody Risien .05 .15
❑ 88 Reggie Camp .05 .15
❑ 89 Bob Golic .05 .15
❑ 90 Carl Hairston .05 .15
❑ 91 Chip Banks .05 .15
❑ 92 Frank Minnifield .05 .15
❑ 93 Hanford Dixon .05 .15
❑ 94 Gerald McNeil RC .05 .15
❑ 95 Dave Puzzuoli .05 .15
❑ 96 Patriots TL .05 .15
❑ 97 Tony Eason .08 .25
❑ 98 Craig James .08 .25
❑ 99 Tony Collins .08 .25
❑ 100 Mosi Tatupu .05 .15
❑ 101 Stanley Morgan .08 .25
❑ 102 Irving Fryar .20 .50
❑ 103 Stephen Starring .05 .15
❑ 104 Tony Franklin .05 .15
❑ 105 Rich Camarillo .05 .15
❑ 106 Garin Veris .05 .15
❑ 107 Andre Tippett .08 .25
❑ 108 Don Blackmon .05 .15
❑ 109 Ronnie Lippett RC .05 .15
❑ 110 Raymond Clayborn .05 .15
❑ 111 49ers TL/R.Craig .08 .25
❑ 112 Joe Montana 2.50 6.00
❑ 113 Roger Craig .20 .50
❑ 114 Joe Cribbs .08 .25
❑ 115 Jerry Rice 2.50 6.00
❑ 116 Dwight Clark .08 .25
❑ 117 Ray Wersching .05 .15
❑ 118 Max Runager .05 .15
❑ 119 Jeff Stover .05 .15
❑ 120 Dwaine Board .05 .15
❑ 121 Tim McKyer RC .08 .25
❑ 122 Don Griffin RC .08 .25
❑ 123 Ronnie Lott .20 .50
❑ 124 Tom Holmoe .05 .15
❑ 125 Charles Haley RC .75 2.00
❑ 126 Jets TL .05 .15
❑ 127 Ken O'Brien .08 .25
❑ 128 Pat Ryan .05 .15
❑ 129 Freeman McNeil .08 .25
❑ 130 Johnny Hector RC .05 .15
❑ 131 Al Toon .20 .50
❑ 132 Wesley Walker .08 .25
❑ 133 Mickey Shuler .05 .15
❑ 134 Pat Leahy .05 .15
❑ 135 Mark Gastineau .08 .25
❑ 136 Joe Klecko .08 .25
❑ 137 Marty Lyons .05 .15
❑ 138 Bob Crable .05 .15
❑ 139 Lance Mehl .05 .15
❑ 140 Dave Jennings .05 .15
❑ 141 Harry Hamilton RC .05 .15
❑ 142 Lester Lyles .05 .15
❑ 143 Bobby Humphery UER .05 .15
❑ 144 Rams TL/E.Dickerson .20 .50
❑ 145 Jim Everett RC .50 1.25
❑ 146 Eric Dickerson .20 .50
❑ 147 Barry Redden .05 .15
❑ 148 Ron Brown .08 .25
❑ 149 Kevin House .05 .15
❑ 150 Henry Ellard .20 .50
❑ 151 Doug Smith .05 .15
❑ 152 Dennis Harrah .05 .15
❑ 153 Jackie Slater .08 .25
❑ 154 Gary Jeter .05 .15
❑ 155 Carl Ekern .05 .15
❑ 156 Mike Wilcher .05 .15
❑ 157 Jerry Gray RC .05 .15
❑ 158 LeRoy Irvin .05 .15
❑ 159 Nolan Cromwell .08 .25
❑ 160 Chiefs TL .05 .15
❑ 161 Bill Kenney .05 .15
❑ 162 Stephone Paige .08 .25
❑ 163 Henry Marshall .05 .15
❑ 164 Carlos Carson .05 .15
❑ 165 Nick Lowery .08 .25
❑ 166 Irv Eatman RC .05 .15
❑ 167 Brad Budde .05 .15
❑ 168 Art Still .05 .15
❑ 169 Bill Maas .05 .15
❑ 170 Lloyd Burruss RC .05 .15
❑ 171 Deron Cherry .05 .15
❑ 172 Seahawks TL .08 .25
❑ 173 Dave Krieg .20 .50
❑ 174 Curt Warner .08 .25
❑ 175 John L.Williams RC .20 .50
❑ 176 Bobby Joe Edmonds RC .08 .25
❑ 177 Steve Largent .25 .60
❑ 178 Bruce Scholtz .05 .15
❑ 179 Norm Johnson .05 .15
❑ 180 Jacob Green .05 .15
❑ 181 Fredd Young .05 .15
❑ 182 Dave Brown DB .05 .15
❑ 183 Kenny Easley .05 .15
❑ 184 Bengals TL .08 .25
❑ 185 Boomer Esiason .20 .50
❑ 186 James Brooks .08 .25
❑ 187 Larry Kinnebrew .05 .15
❑ 188 Cris Collinsworth .08 .25
❑ 189 Eddie Brown .20 .50
❑ 190 Tim McGee RC .20 .50
❑ 191 Jim Breech .05 .15
❑ 192 Anthony Munoz .20 .50
❑ 193 Max Montoya .05 .15
❑ 194 Eddie Edwards .05 .15
❑ 195 Ross Browner .08 .25
❑ 196 Emanuel King .05 .15
❑ 197 Louis Breeden .05 .15
❑ 198 Vikings TL .05 .15
❑ 199 Tommy Kramer .08 .25
❑ 200 Darrin Nelson .05 .15
❑ 201 Allen Rice .05 .15
❑ 202 Anthony Carter .20 .50
❑ 203 Leo Lewis .05 .15
❑ 204 Steve Jordan .20 .50
❑ 205 Chuck Nelson RC .05 .15
❑ 206 Greg Coleman .05 .15
❑ 207 Gary Zimmerman RC 1.00 2.50
❑ 208 Doug Martin .05 .15
❑ 209 Keith Millard .05 .15
❑ 210 Issiac Holt RC .05 .15
❑ 211 Joey Browner .08 .25
❑ 212 Rufus Bess .05 .15
❑ 213 Raiders TL/M.Allen .20 .50
❑ 214 Jim Plunkett .20 .50
❑ 215 Marcus Allen .40 1.00
❑ 216 Napoleon McCallum RC .08 .25
❑ 217 Dokie Williams .05 .15
❑ 218 Todd Christensen .20 .50
❑ 219 Chris Bahr .05 .15
❑ 220 Howie Long .25 .60
❑ 221 Bill Pickel .05 .15
❑ 222 Sean Jones RC .20 .50
❑ 223 Lester Hayes .08 .25
❑ 224 Mike Haynes .08 .25
❑ 225 Vann McElroy .05 .15
❑ 226 Fulton Walker .05 .15
❑ 227 Dan Marino/T.Kramer LL .50 1.25
❑ 228 J.Rice/Christensen LL .50 1.25
❑ 229 Eric Dickerson/Warner LL .20 .50
❑ 230 Scoring Leaders .05 .15
❑ 231 Interception Leaders .20 .50
❑ 232 Dolphins TL .08 .25
❑ 233 Dan Marino 2.50 6.00
❑ 234 Lorenzo Hampton RC .05 .15
❑ 235 Tony Nathan .08 .25
❑ 236 Mark Duper .20 .50
❑ 237 Mark Clayton .20 .50
❑ 238 Nat Moore .08 .25
❑ 239 Bruce Hardy .05 .15
❑ 240 Reggie Roby .08 .25
❑ 241 Roy Foster .05 .15
❑ 242 Dwight Stephenson .20 .50
❑ 243 Hugh Green .05 .15
❑ 244 John Offerdahl RC .20 .50
❑ 245 Mark Brown .05 .15
❑ 246 Doug Betters .05 .15
❑ 247 Bob Baumhower .05 .15
❑ 248 Falcons TL .05 .15
❑ 249 David Archer .20 .50
❑ 250 Gerald Riggs .08 .25
❑ 251 William Andrews .08 .25
❑ 252 Charlie Brown .05 .15
❑ 253 Arthur Cox .05 .15
❑ 254 Rick Donnelly .05 .15
❑ 255 Bill Fralic .05 .15
❑ 256 Mike Gann RC .05 .15
❑ 257 Rick Bryan .05 .15
❑ 258 Bret Clark .05 .15
❑ 259 Mike Pitts .05 .15
❑ 260 Cowboys TL/T.Dorsett .20 .50
❑ 261 Danny White .20 .50
❑ 262 Steve Pelluer RC .05 .15
❑ 263 Tony Dorsett UER .20 .50
❑ 264 Herschel Walker RC 1.00 2.50
❑ 265 Timmy Newsome .05 .15
❑ 266 Tony Hill .08 .25
❑ 267 Mike Sherrard RC .20 .50
❑ 268 Jim Jeffcoat .20 .50
❑ 269 Ron Fellows .05 .15
❑ 270 Bill Bates .20 .50
❑ 271 Michael Downs .05 .15
❑ 272 Saints TL/B.Hebert .08 .25
❑ 273 Dave Wilson .05 .15
❑ 274 Rueben Mayes UER RC .05 .15
❑ 275 Hoby Brenner .05 .15
❑ 276 Eric Martin RC .20 .50
❑ 277 Morten Andersen .08 .25
❑ 278 Brian Hansen .05 .15
❑ 279 Rickey Jackson .20 .50
❑ 280 Dave Waymer .05 .15
❑ 281 Bruce Clark .05 .15
❑ 282 Jumpy Geathers RC .08 .25
❑ 283 Steelers TL .08 .25
❑ 284 Mark Malone .08 .25
❑ 285 Earnest Jackson .05 .15
❑ 286 Walter Abercrombie .05 .15
❑ 287 Louis Lipps .08 .25
❑ 288 John Stallworth UER .20 .50
❑ 289 Gary Anderson K .05 .15
❑ 290 Keith Willis .05 .15
❑ 291 Mike Merriweather .05 .15
❑ 292 Lupe Sanchez .05 .15
❑ 293 Donnie Shell .08 .25
❑ 294 Eagles TL/K.Byars .20 .50
❑ 295 Mike Reichenbach .05 .15
❑ 296 Randall Cunningham RC 3.00 6.00
❑ 297 Keith Byars RC .30 .75
❑ 298 Mike Quick .08 .25
❑ 299 Kenny Jackson .05 .15
❑ 300 John Teltschik RC .05 .15
❑ 301 Reggie White 1.50 3.00
❑ 302 Ken Clarke .05 .15
❑ 303 Greg Brown .05 .15
❑ 304 Roynell Young .05 .15
❑ 305 Andre Waters RC .20 .50
❑ 306 Oilers TL/W.Moon .20 .50

❑ 307 Warren Moon .60 1.50
❑ 308 Mike Rozier .08 .25
❑ 309 Drew Hill .08 .25
❑ 310 Ernest Givins RC .20 .50
❑ 311 Lee Johnson RC .05 .15
❑ 312 Kent Hill .05 .15
❑ 313 Dean Steinkuhler RC .08 .25
❑ 314 Ray Childress .20 .50
❑ 315 John Grimsley RC .05 .15
❑ 316 Jesse Baker .05 .15
❑ 317 Lions TL .05 .15
❑ 318 Chuck Long RC .08 .25
❑ 319 James Jones FB .05 .15
❑ 320 Garry James .05 .15
❑ 321 Jeff Chadwick .05 .15
❑ 322 Leonard Thompson .05 .15
❑ 323 Pete Mandley .05 .15
❑ 324 Jimmie Giles .08 .25
❑ 325 Herman Hunter .05 .15
❑ 326 Keith Ferguson .05 .15
❑ 327 Devon Mitchell .05 .15
❑ 328 Cardinals TL .05 .15
❑ 329 Neil Lomax .08 .25
❑ 330 Stump Mitchell .05 .15
❑ 331 Earl Ferrell .05 .15
❑ 332 Vai Sikahema RC .08 .25
❑ 333 Ron Wolfley RC .05 .15
❑ 334 J.T.Smith .08 .25
❑ 335 Roy Green .08 .25
❑ 336 Al(Bubba) Baker .05 .15
❑ 337 Freddie Joe Nunn .05 .15
❑ 338 Cedric Mack .05 .15
❑ 339 Chargers TL .08 .25
❑ 340 Dan Fouts .20 .50
❑ 341 Gary Anderson RB UER .20 .50
❑ 342 Wes Chandler .08 .25
❑ 343 Kellen Winslow .20 .50
❑ 344 Ralf Mojsiejenko .05 .15
❑ 345 Rolf Benirschke .05 .15
❑ 346 Lee Williams RC .08 .25
❑ 347 Leslie O'Neal RC .40 1.00
❑ 348 Billy Ray Smith .08 .25
❑ 349 Gill Byrd .08 .25
❑ 350 Packers TL .05 .15
❑ 351 Randy Wright .05 .15
❑ 352 Kenneth Davis RC .20 .50
❑ 353 Gerry Ellis .05 .15
❑ 354 James Lofton .20 .50
❑ 355 Phillip Epps RC .05 .15
❑ 356 Walter Stanley RC .05 .15
❑ 357 Eddie Lee Ivery .05 .15
❑ 358 Tim Harris RC .20 .50
❑ 359 Mark Lee UER .05 .15
❑ 360 Mossy Cade .05 .15
❑ 361 Bills TL/J.Kelly .40 1.00
❑ 362 Jim Kelly RC 4.00 10.00
❑ 363 Robb Riddick RC .05 .15
❑ 364 Greg Bell .05 .15
❑ 365 Andre Reed .50 1.25
❑ 366 Pete Metzelaars RC .20 .50
❑ 367 Sean McNanie .05 .15
❑ 368 Fred Smerlas .05 .15
❑ 369 Bruce Smith .75 2.00
❑ 370 Darryl Talley .08 .25
❑ 371 Charles Romes .05 .15
❑ 372 Colts TL .05 .15
❑ 373 Jack Trudeau RC .08 .25
❑ 374 Gary Hogeboom .05 .15
❑ 375 Randy McMillan .05 .15
❑ 376 Albert Bentley .05 .15
❑ 377 Matt Bouza .05 .15
❑ 378 Bill Brooks RC .30 .75
❑ 379 Rohn Stark .05 .15
❑ 380 Chris Hinton .05 .15
❑ 381 Ray Donaldson .05 .15
❑ 382 Jon Hand RC .05 .15
❑ 383 Buccaneers TL .05 .15
❑ 384 Steve Young 2.00 5.00
❑ 385 James Wilder .05 .15
❑ 386 Frank Garcia .05 .15
❑ 387 Gerald Carter .05 .15
❑ 388 Phil Freeman .05 .15
❑ 389 Calvin Magee .05 .15
❑ 390 Donald Igwebuike .05 .15
❑ 391 David Logan .05 .15
❑ 392 Jeff Davis .05 .15
❑ 393 Chris Washington .05 .15
❑ 394 Checklist 1-132 .08 .25
❑ 395 Checklist 133-264 .08 .25
❑ 396 Checklist 265-396 .08 .25

1988 Topps

❑ COMPLETE SET (396) 7.50 20.00
❑ COMP.FACT.SET (396) 15.00 30.00
❑ 1 Super Bowl XXII .07 .20
❑ 2 Vencie Glenn RB .05 .15
❑ 3 Steve Largent RB .15 .40
❑ 4 Joe Montana RB .30 .75
❑ 5 Walter Payton RB .15 .40
❑ 6 Jerry Rice RB .30 .75
❑ 7 Redskins TL .07 .20
❑ 8 Doug Williams .07 .20
❑ 9 George Rogers .07 .20
❑ 10 Kelvin Bryant .07 .20
❑ 11 Timmy Smith SR .07 .20
❑ 12 Art Monk .15 .40
❑ 13 Gary Clark .15 .40
❑ 14 Ricky Sanders RC .15 .40
❑ 15 Steve Cox .05 .15
❑ 16 Joe Jacoby .05 .15
❑ 17 Charles Mann .07 .20
❑ 18 Dave Butz .05 .15
❑ 19 Darrell Green .07 .20
❑ 20 Dexter Manley .05 .15
❑ 21 Barry Wilburn .05 .15
❑ 22 Broncos TL .05 .15
❑ 23 John Elway .75 2.00
❑ 24 Sammy Winder .05 .15
❑ 25 Vance Johnson .07 .20
❑ 26 Mark Jackson RC .15 .40
❑ 27 Ricky Nattiel RC .05 .15
❑ 28 Clarence Kay .05 .15
❑ 29 Rich Karlis .05 .15
❑ 30 Keith Bishop .05 .15
❑ 31 Mike Horan .05 .15
❑ 32 Rulon Jones .05 .15
❑ 33 Karl Mecklenburg .07 .20
❑ 34 Jim Ryan .05 .15
❑ 35 Mark Haynes .07 .20
❑ 36 Mike Harden .05 .15
❑ 37 49ers TL .15 .40
❑ 38 Joe Montana .75 2.00
❑ 39 Steve Young .40 1.00
❑ 40 Roger Craig .07 .20
❑ 41 Tom Rathman RC .15 .40
❑ 42 Joe Cribbs .07 .20
❑ 43 Jerry Rice .75 2.00
❑ 44 Mike Wilson RC .05 .15
❑ 45 Ron Heller TE RC .05 .15
❑ 46 Ray Wersching .05 .15
❑ 47 Michael Carter .05 .15
❑ 48 Dwaine Board .05 .15
❑ 49 Michael Walter .05 .15
❑ 50 Don Griffin .05 .15
❑ 51 Ronnie Lott .15 .40
❑ 52 Charles Haley .15 .40
❑ 53 Dana McLemore .05 .15
❑ 54 Saints TL .07 .20
❑ 55 Bobby Hebert .07 .20
❑ 56 Rueben Mayes .05 .15
❑ 57 Dalton Hilliard RC .05 .15
❑ 58 Eric Martin .07 .20
❑ 59 John Tice RC .05 .15
❑ 60 Brad Edelman .05 .15
❑ 61 Morten Andersen .07 .20
❑ 62 Brian Hansen .05 .15
❑ 63 Mel Gray RC .15 .40
❑ 64 Rickey Jackson .07 .20
❑ 65 Sam Mills RC .30 .75
❑ 66 Pat Swilling RC .15 .40
❑ 67 Dave Waymer .05 .15
❑ 68 Bears TL .07 .20
❑ 69 Jim McMahon .15 .40
❑ 70 Mike Tomczak RC .05 .15
❑ 71 Neal Anderson RC .15 .40
❑ 72 Willie Gault .07 .20
❑ 73 Dennis Gentry .05 .15
❑ 74 Dennis McKinnon .05 .15
❑ 75 Kevin Butler .05 .15
❑ 76 Jim Covert .05 .15
❑ 77 Jay Hilgenberg .05 .15
❑ 78 Steve McMichael .07 .20
❑ 79 William Perry .07 .20
❑ 80 Richard Dent .15 .40
❑ 81 Ron Rivera RC .05 .15
❑ 82 Mike Singletary .15 .40
❑ 83 Dan Hampton .15 .40
❑ 84 Dave Duerson .05 .15
❑ 85 Browns TL .07 .20
❑ 86 Bernie Kosar .15 .40
❑ 87 Earnest Byner .15 .40
❑ 88 Kevin Mack .07 .20
❑ 89 Webster Slaughter RC .15 .40
❑ 90 Gerald McNeil .05 .15
❑ 91 Brian Brennan .05 .15
❑ 92 Ozzie Newsome .15 .40
❑ 93 Cody Risien .05 .15
❑ 94 Bob Golic .05 .15
❑ 95 Carl Hairston .05 .15
❑ 96 Mike Johnson RC .05 .15
❑ 97 Clay Matthews .07 .20
❑ 98 Frank Minnifield .05 .15
❑ 99 Hanford Dixon .05 .15
❑ 100 Dave Puzzuoli .05 .15
❑ 101 Felix Wright RC .05 .15
❑ 102 Oilers TL/Moon .15 .40
❑ 103 Warren Moon .20 .50
❑ 104 Mike Rozier .05 .15
❑ 105 Alonzo Highsmith RC .07 .20
❑ 106 Drew Hill .07 .20
❑ 107 Ernest Givins .15 .40
❑ 108 Curtis Duncan RC .15 .40
❑ 109 Tony Zendejas RC .05 .15
❑ 110 Mike Munchak .15 .40
❑ 111 Kent Hill .05 .15
❑ 112 Ray Childress .07 .20
❑ 113 Al Smith RC .07 .20
❑ 114 Keith Bostic RC .05 .15
❑ 115 Jeff Donaldson .05 .15
❑ 116 Colts TL/Dickerson .15 .40
❑ 117 Jack Trudeau .05 .15
❑ 118 Eric Dickerson .15 .40
❑ 119 Albert Bentley .05 .15
❑ 120 Matt Bouza .05 .15
❑ 121 Bill Brooks .15 .40
❑ 122 Dean Biasucci RC .05 .15
❑ 123 Chris Hinton .05 .15
❑ 124 Ray Donaldson .05 .15
❑ 125 Ron Solt RC .05 .15
❑ 126 Donnell Thompson .05 .15
❑ 127 Barry Krauss RC .05 .15
❑ 128 Duane Bickett .05 .15
❑ 129 Mike Prior RC .05 .15
❑ 130 Seahawks TL .07 .20
❑ 131 Dave Kiley .07 .20
❑ 132 Curt Warner .07 .20
❑ 133 John L.Williams .15 .40
❑ 134 Bobby Joe Edmonds .05 .15
❑ 135 Steve Largent .15 .40
❑ 136 Raymond Butler .05 .15
❑ 137 Norm Johnson .05 .15
❑ 138 Ruben Rodriguez .05 .15
❑ 139 Blair Bush .05 .15
❑ 140 Jacob Green .05 .15
❑ 141 Joe Nash .05 .15
❑ 142 Jeff Bryant .05 .15
❑ 143 Fredd Young .05 .15
❑ 144 Brian Bosworth RC .60 1.50
❑ 145 Kenny Easley .05 .15
❑ 146 Vikings TL .07 .20
❑ 147 Wade Wilson RC .15 .40
❑ 148 Tommy Kramer .07 .20
❑ 149 Darrin Nelson .05 .15
❑ 150 D.J.Dozier RC .07 .20
❑ 151 Anthony Carter .07 .20
❑ 152 Leo Lewis .05 .15
❑ 153 Steve Jordan .07 .20
❑ 154 Gary Zimmerman .10 .30
❑ 155 Chuck Nelson .05 .15
❑ 156 Henry Thomas RC .15 .40
❑ 157 Chris Doleman RC .15 .40
❑ 158 Scott Studwell RC .05 .15
❑ 159 Jesse Solomon RC .05 .15

❑ 160 Joey Browner	.05	.15
❑ 161 Neal Guggemos	.05	.15
❑ 162 Steelers TL	.07	.20
❑ 163 Mark Malone	.05	.15
❑ 164 Walter Abercrombie	.05	.15
❑ 165 Earnest Jackson	.05	.15
❑ 166 Frank Pollard	.05	.15
❑ 167 Dwight Stone RC	.07	.20
❑ 168 Gary Anderson K	.05	.15
❑ 169 Harry Newsome RC	.05	.15
❑ 170 Keith Willis	.05	.15
❑ 171 Keith Gary	.05	.15
❑ 172 David Little RC	.07	.20
❑ 173 Mike Merriweather	.05	.15
❑ 174 Dwayne Woodruff	.05	.15
❑ 175 Patriots TL	.15	.40
❑ 176 Steve Grogan	.07	.20
❑ 177 Tony Eason	.07	.20
❑ 178 Tony Collins	.07	.20
❑ 179 Mosi Tatupu	.05	.15
❑ 180 Stanley Morgan	.07	.20
❑ 181 Irving Fryar	.15	.40
❑ 182 Stephen Starring	.05	.15
❑ 183 Tony Franklin	.05	.15
❑ 184 Rich Camarillo	.05	.15
❑ 185 Garin Veris	.05	.15
❑ 186 Andre Tippett	.07	.20
❑ 187 Ronnie Lippett	.05	.15
❑ 188 Fred Marion	.05	.15
❑ 189 Dolphins TL/D.Marino	.30	.75
❑ 190 Dan Marino	.75	2.00
❑ 191 Troy Stradford RC	.07	.20
❑ 192 Lorenzo Hampton	.05	.15
❑ 193 Mark Duper	.07	.20
❑ 194 Mark Clayton	.07	.20
❑ 195 Reggie Roby	.07	.20
❑ 196 Dwight Stephenson	.15	.40
❑ 197 T.J. Turner RC	.05	.15
❑ 198 John Bosa RC	.05	.15
❑ 199 Jackie Shipp	.05	.15
❑ 200 John Offerdahl	.07	.20
❑ 201 Mark Brown	.05	.15
❑ 202 Paul Lankford	.05	.15
❑ 203 Chargers TL	.15	.40
❑ 204 Tim Spencer	.05	.15
❑ 205 Gary Anderson RB	.07	.20
❑ 206 Curtis Adams	.05	.15
❑ 207 Lionel James	.05	.15
❑ 208 Chip Banks	.05	.15
❑ 209 Kellen Winslow	.15	.40
❑ 210 Ralf Mojsiejenko	.05	.15
❑ 211 Jim Lachey	.07	.20
❑ 212 Lee Williams	.05	.15
❑ 213 Billy Ray Smith	.05	.15
❑ 214 Vencie Glenn RC	.07	.20
❑ 215 J.Montana/B.Kosar LL	.20	.50
❑ 216 Receiving Leaders	.07	.20
❑ 217 Eric Dickerson/C.White L	.07	.20
❑ 218 Jerry Rice/J.Breech LL	.15	.40
❑ 219 Interception Leaders	.05	.15
❑ 220 Bills TL/Jim Kelly	.15	.40
❑ 221 Jim Kelly	.30	.75
❑ 222 Ronnie Harmon RC	.15	.40
❑ 223 Robb Riddick	.05	.15
❑ 224 Andre Reed	.15	.40
❑ 225 Chris Burkett RC	.05	.15
❑ 226 Pete Metzelaars	.15	.40
❑ 227 Bruce Smith	.20	.50
❑ 228 Darryl Talley	.07	.20
❑ 229 Eugene Marve	.05	.15
❑ 230 Cornelius Bennett RC	.30	.75
❑ 231 Mark Kelso RC	.05	.15
❑ 232 Shane Conlan RC	.15	.40
❑ 233 Eagles TL/R.Cunningham	.15	.40
❑ 234 Randall Cunningham	.40	1.00
❑ 235 Keith Byars	.15	.40
❑ 236 Anthony Toney RC	.05	.15
❑ 237 Mike Quick	.07	.20
❑ 238 Kenny Jackson	.05	.15
❑ 239 John Spagnola	.05	.15
❑ 240 Paul McFadden	.05	.15
❑ 241 Reggie White	.25	.60
❑ 242 Ken Clarke	.05	.15
❑ 243 Mike Pitts	.05	.15
❑ 244 Clyde Simmons RC	.15	.40
❑ 245 Seth Joyner RC	.15	.40
❑ 246 Andre Waters	.15	.40
❑ 247 Jerome Brown RC	.15	.40
❑ 248 Cardinals TL	.05	.15
❑ 249 Neil Lomax	.07	.20
❑ 250 Stump Mitchell	.05	.15
❑ 251 Earl Ferrell	.05	.15
❑ 252 Vai Sikahema	.05	.15
❑ 253 J.T. Smith	.07	.20
❑ 254 Roy Green	.07	.20
❑ 255 Robert Awalt RC	.07	.20
❑ 256 Freddie Joe Nunn	.05	.15
❑ 257 Leonard Smith RC	.05	.15
❑ 258 Travis Curtis	.05	.15
❑ 259 Cowboys TL/H.Walker	.15	.40
❑ 260 Danny White	.15	.40
❑ 261 Herschel Walker	.15	.40
❑ 262 Tony Dorsett	.15	.40
❑ 263 Doug Cosbie	.05	.15
❑ 264 Roger Ruzek RC	.07	.20
❑ 265 Darryl Clack	.05	.15
❑ 266 Ed Too Tall Jones	.15	.40
❑ 267 Jim Jeffcoat	.05	.15
❑ 268 Everson Walls	.05	.15
❑ 269 Bill Bates	.07	.20
❑ 270 Michael Downs	.05	.15
❑ 271 Giants TL	.07	.20
❑ 272 Phil Simms	.15	.40
❑ 273 Joe Morris	.07	.20
❑ 274 Lee Rouson	.05	.15
❑ 275 George Adams	.05	.15
❑ 276 Lionel Manuel	.05	.15
❑ 277 Mark Bavaro	.07	.20
❑ 278 Raul Allegre	.05	.15
❑ 279 Sean Landeta	.05	.15
❑ 280 Erik Howard	.05	.15
❑ 281 Leonard Marshall	.07	.20
❑ 282 Carl Banks	.07	.20
❑ 283 Pepper Johnson	.07	.20
❑ 284 Harry Carson	.07	.20
❑ 285 Lawrence Taylor	.15	.40
❑ 286 Terry Kinard	.05	.15
❑ 287 Rams TL/Everett	.15	.40
❑ 288 Jim Everett	.15	.40
❑ 289 Charles White	.07	.20
❑ 290 Ron Brown	.07	.20
❑ 291 Henry Ellard	.15	.40
❑ 292 Mike Lansford	.05	.15
❑ 293 Dale Hatcher	.05	.15
❑ 294 Doug Smith	.05	.15
❑ 295 Jackie Slater	.07	.20
❑ 296 Jim Collins	.05	.15
❑ 297 Jerry Gray	.05	.15
❑ 298 LeRoy Irvin	.05	.15
❑ 299 Nolan Cromwell	.07	.20
❑ 300 Kevin Greene RC	.50	1.25
❑ 301 Jets TL	.07	.20
❑ 302 Ken O'Brien	.07	.20
❑ 303 Freeman McNeil	.07	.20
❑ 304 Johnny Hector	.05	.15
❑ 305 Al Toon	.07	.20
❑ 306 JoJo Townsell RC	.07	.20
❑ 307 Mickey Shuler	.05	.15
❑ 308 Pat Leahy	.05	.15
❑ 309 Roger Vick	.05	.15
❑ 310 Alex Gordon RC	.05	.15
❑ 311 Troy Benson	.05	.15
❑ 312 Bob Crable	.05	.15
❑ 313 Harry Hamilton	.05	.15
❑ 314 Packers TL	.05	.15
❑ 315 Randy Wright	.05	.15
❑ 316 Kenneth Davis	.07	.20
❑ 317 Phillip Epps	.05	.15
❑ 318 Walter Stanley	.05	.15
❑ 319 Frankie Neal	.05	.15
❑ 320 Don Bracken	.05	.15
❑ 321 Brian Noble RC	.07	.20
❑ 322 Johnny Holland RC	.07	.20
❑ 323 Tim Harris	.07	.20
❑ 324 Mark Murphy	.05	.15
❑ 325 Raiders TL/B.Jackson	.20	.50
❑ 326 Marc Wilson	.05	.15
❑ 327 Bo Jackson RC	2.00	5.00
❑ 328 Marcus Allen	.15	.40
❑ 329 James Lofton	.15	.40
❑ 330 Todd Christensen	.07	.20
❑ 331 Chris Bahr	.05	.15
❑ 332 Stan Talley	.05	.15
❑ 333 Howie Long	.15	.40
❑ 334 Sean Jones	.15	.40
❑ 335 Matt Millen	.07	.20
❑ 336 Stacey Toran	.05	.15
❑ 337 Vann McElroy	.05	.15
❑ 338 Greg Townsend	.07	.20
❑ 339 Bengals TL/Esiason	.15	.40
❑ 340 Boomer Esiason	.15	.40
❑ 341 Larry Kinnebrew	.05	.15
❑ 342 Stanford Jennings RC	.05	.15
❑ 343 Eddie Brown	.07	.20
❑ 344 Jim Breech	.05	.15
❑ 345 Anthony Munoz	.15	.40
❑ 346 Scott Fulhage RC	.05	.15
❑ 347 Tim Krumrie RC	.05	.15
❑ 348 Reggie Williams	.07	.20
❑ 349 David Fulcher RC	.05	.15
❑ 350 Buccaneers TL	.05	.15
❑ 351 Frank Garcia	.05	.15
❑ 352 Vinny Testaverde RC	1.50	4.00
❑ 353 James Wilder	.05	.15
❑ 354 Jeff Smith RBK	.05	.15
❑ 355 Gerald Carter	.05	.15
❑ 356 Calvin Magee	.05	.15
❑ 357 Donald Igwebuike	.05	.15
❑ 358 Ron Holmes RC	.05	.15
❑ 359 Chris Washington	.05	.15
❑ 360 Ervin Randle	.05	.15
❑ 361 Chiefs TL	.05	.15
❑ 362 Bill Kenney	.05	.15
❑ 363 Christian Okoye RC	.15	.40
❑ 364 Paul Palmer	.05	.15
❑ 365 Stephone Paige	.07	.20
❑ 366 Carlos Carson	.05	.15
❑ 367 Kelly Goodburn RC	.05	.15
❑ 368 Bill Maas	.05	.15
❑ 369 Mike Bell	.05	.15
❑ 370 Dino Hackett RC	.05	.15
❑ 371 Deron Cherry	.05	.15
❑ 372 Lions TL	.05	.15
❑ 373 Chuck Long	.07	.20
❑ 374 Garry James	.05	.15
❑ 375 James Jones FB	.05	.15
❑ 376 Pete Mandley	.05	.15
❑ 377 Gary Lee RC	.05	.15
❑ 378 Eddie Murray	.05	.15
❑ 379 Jim Arnold	.05	.15
❑ 380 Dennis Gibson RC	.05	.15
❑ 381 Michael Cofer LB	.05	.15
❑ 382 James Griffin	.05	.15
❑ 383 Falcons TL	.05	.15
❑ 384 Scott Campbell	.05	.15
❑ 385 Gerald Riggs	.07	.20
❑ 386 Floyd Dixon RC	.05	.15
❑ 387 Rick Donnelly	.05	.15
❑ 388 Bill Fralic	.07	.20
❑ 389 Major Everett	.05	.15
❑ 390 Mike Gann	.05	.15
❑ 391 Tony Casillas RC	.07	.20
❑ 392 Rick Bryan	.05	.15
❑ 393 John Rade RC	.05	.15
❑ 394 Checklist 1-132	.05	.15
❑ 395 Checklist 133-264	.05	.15
❑ 396 Checklist 265-396	.05	.15

1989 Topps

❑ COMPLETE SET (396)	7.50	20.00
❑ COMP.FACT.SET (396)	10.00	25.00
❑ 1 Super Bowl XXIII/Montana	.20	.50
❑ 2 Tim Brown RB	.20	.50
❑ 3 Eric Dickerson RB	.05	.15
❑ 4 Steve Largent RB	.08	.25
❑ 5 Dan Marino RB	.30	.75
❑ 6 49ers TL/Montana	.20	.50
❑ 7 Jerry Rice	.60	1.50
❑ 8 Roger Craig	.08	.25
❑ 9 Ronnie Lott	.08	.25
❑ 10 Michael Carter	.02	.10
❑ 11 Charles Haley	.08	.25
❑ 12 Joe Montana	.75	2.00
❑ 13 John Taylor RC	.20	.50

❑ 14 Michael Walter .02 .10
❑ 15 Mike Cofer RC .02 .10
❑ 16 Tom Rathman .05 .15
❑ 17 Daniel Stubbs RC .02 .10
❑ 18 Keena Turner .02 .10
❑ 19 Tim McKyer .02 .10
❑ 20 Larry Roberts .02 .10
❑ 21 Jeff Fuller .02 .10
❑ 22 Bubba Paris .02 .10
❑ 23 Bengals Team UER .02 .10
❑ 24 Eddie Brown .02 .10
❑ 25 Boomer Esiason .08 .25
❑ 26 Tim Krumrie .02 .10
❑ 27 Ickey Woods RC .15 .40
❑ 28 Anthony Munoz .08 .25
❑ 29 Tim McGee .02 .10
❑ 30 Max Montoya .02 .10
❑ 31 David Grant .02 .10
❑ 32 Rodney Holman RC .02 .10
❑ 33 David Fulcher .02 .10
❑ 34 Jim Skow .02 .10
❑ 35 James Brooks .05 .15
❑ 36 Reggie Williams .02 .10
❑ 37 Eric Thomas RC .02 .10
❑ 38 Stanford Jennings .02 .10
❑ 39 Jim Breech .02 .10
❑ 40 Bills TL/Jim Kelly .08 .25
❑ 41 Shane Conlan .02 .10
❑ 42 Scott Norwood RC .02 .10
❑ 43 Cornelius Bennett .08 .25
❑ 44 Bruce Smith .08 .25
❑ 45 Thurman Thomas RC .50 1.25
❑ 46 Jim Kelly .20 .50
❑ 47 John Kidd .02 .10
❑ 48 Kent Hull RC .02 .10
❑ 49 Art Still .02 .10
❑ 50 Fred Smerlas .02 .10
❑ 51A Derrick Burroughs .02 .10
❑ 51B Derrick Burroughs .02 .10
❑ 52 Andre Reed .08 .25
❑ 53 Robb Riddick .02 .10
❑ 54 Chris Burkett .02 .10
❑ 55 Ronnie Harmon .02 .10
❑ 56 Mark Kelso UER .02 .10
❑ 57 Bears Team .02 .10
❑ 58 Mike Singletary .08 .25
❑ 59 Jay Hilgenberg UER .02 .10
❑ 60 Richard Dent .08 .25
❑ 61 Ron Rivera .02 .10
❑ 62 Jim McMahon .08 .25
❑ 63 Mike Tomczak .05 .15
❑ 64 Neal Anderson .08 .25
❑ 65 Dennis Gentry .02 .10
❑ 66 Dan Hampton .08 .25
❑ 67 David Tate .02 .10
❑ 68 Thomas Sanders RC .02 .10
❑ 69 Steve McMichael .05 .15
❑ 70 Dennis McKinnon .02 .10
❑ 71 Brad Muster RC .08 .25
❑ 72 Vestee Jackson RC .02 .10
❑ 73 Dave Duerson .02 .10
❑ 74 Vikings Team .02 .10
❑ 75 Joey Browner .05 .15
❑ 76 Carl Lee RC .02 .10
❑ 77 Gary Zimmerman .08 .25
❑ 78 Hassan Jones RC .02 .10
❑ 79 Anthony Carter .08 .25
❑ 80 Ray Berry .02 .10
❑ 81 Steve Jordan .02 .10
❑ 82 Issiac Holt .02 .10
❑ 83 Wade Wilson .05 .15
❑ 84 Chris Doleman .05 .15
❑ 85 Alfred Anderson .02 .10
❑ 86 Keith Millard .02 .10
❑ 87 Darrin Nelson .02 .10
❑ 88 D.J. Dozier .02 .10
❑ 89 Scott Studwell .02 .10
❑ 90 Oilers Team .02 .10
❑ 91 Bruce Matthews RC .30 .75
❑ 92 Curtis Duncan .02 .10
❑ 93 Warren Moon .08 .25
❑ 94 Johnny Meads RC .02 .10
❑ 95 Drew Hill .05 .15
❑ 96 Alonzo Highsmith .05 .15
❑ 97 Mike Munchak .08 .25
❑ 98 Mike Rozier .05 .15
❑ 99 Tony Zendejas .02 .10
❑ 100 Jeff Donaldson .02 .10
❑ 101 Ray Childress .05 .15
❑ 102 Sean Jones .02 .10
❑ 103 Ernest Givins .05 .15
❑ 104 William Fuller RC .08 .25
❑ 105 Allen Pinkett RC .02 .10
❑ 106 Eagles TL/R.Cunningham .02 .10
❑ 107 Keith Jackson RC .08 .25
❑ 108 Reggie White .08 .25
❑ 109 Clyde Simmons .05 .15
❑ 110 John Teltschik .02 .10
❑ 111 Wes Hopkins .05 .15
❑ 112 Keith Byars .05 .15
❑ 113 Jerome Brown .05 .15
❑ 114 Mike Quick .05 .15
❑ 115 Randall Cunningham .15 .40
❑ 116 Anthony Toney .02 .10
❑ 117 Ron Johnson WR .02 .10
❑ 118 Terry Hoage .02 .10
❑ 119 Seth Joyner .05 .15
❑ 120 Eric Allen RC .08 .25
❑ 121 Cris Carter RC .60 1.50
❑ 122 Rams Team .02 .10
❑ 123 Tom Newberry RC .02 .10
❑ 124 Pete Holohan .02 .10
❑ 125 Robert Delpino UER RC .02 .10
❑ 126 Carl Ekern .02 .10
❑ 127 Greg Bell .02 .10
❑ 128 Mike Lansford .02 .10
❑ 129 Jim Everett .08 .25
❑ 130 Mike Wilcher .02 .10
❑ 131 Jerry Gray .02 .10
❑ 132 Dale Hatcher .02 .10
❑ 133 Doug Smith .02 .10
❑ 134 Kevin Greene .08 .25
❑ 135 Jackie Slater .08 .25
❑ 136 Aaron Cox RC .02 .10
❑ 137 Henry Ellard .08 .25
❑ 138 Browns Team .02 .10
❑ 139 Frank Minnifield .02 .10
❑ 140 Webster Slaughter .05 .15
❑ 141 Bernie Kosar .08 .25
❑ 142 Charles Buchanan .02 .10
❑ 143 Clay Matthews .05 .15
❑ 144 Reggie Langhorne RC .08 .25
❑ 145 Hanford Dixon .02 .10
❑ 146 Brian Brennan .02 .10
❑ 147 Earnest Byner .05 .15
❑ 148 Michael Dean Perry RC .05 .15
❑ 149 Kevin Mack .05 .15
❑ 150 Matt Bahr .02 .10
❑ 151 Ozzie Newsome .08 .25
❑ 152 Saints Team .02 .10
❑ 153 Morten Andersen .05 .15
❑ 154 Pat Swilling .05 .15
❑ 155 Sam Mills .05 .15
❑ 156 Lonzell Hill .02 .10
❑ 157 Dalton Hilliard .02 .10
❑ 158 Craig Heyward RC .08 .25
❑ 159 Vaughan Johnson RC .05 .15
❑ 160 Rueben Mayes .02 .10
❑ 161 Gene Atkins RC .02 .10
❑ 162 Bobby Hebert .05 .15
❑ 163 Rickey Jackson .05 .15
❑ 164 Eric Martin .02 .10
❑ 165 Giants Team .02 .10
❑ 166 Lawrence Taylor .08 .25
❑ 167 Bart Oates .05 .15
❑ 168 Carl Banks .05 .15
❑ 169 Eric Moore RC .02 .10
❑ 170 Sheldon White RC .02 .10
❑ 171 Mark Collins RC .08 .25
❑ 172 Phil Simms .08 .25
❑ 173 Jim Burt .05 .15
❑ 174 Stephen Baker RC .08 .25
❑ 175 Mark Bavaro .05 .15
❑ 176 Pepper Johnson .05 .15
❑ 177 Lionel Manuel .05 .15
❑ 178 Joe Morris .05 .15
❑ 179 Jumbo Elliott RC .05 .15
❑ 180 Gary Reasons RC .02 .10
❑ 181 Seahawks Team .02 .10
❑ 182 Brian Blades RC .08 .25
❑ 183 Steve Largent .08 .25
❑ 184 Rufus Porter RC .02 .10
❑ 185 Ruben Rodriguez .02 .10
❑ 186 Curt Warner .05 .15
❑ 187 Paul Moyer .02 .10
❑ 188 Dave Krieg .05 .15
❑ 189 Jacob Green .05 .15
❑ 190 John L.Williams .05 .15
❑ 191 Eugene Robinson RC .08 .25
❑ 192 Brian Bosworth .08 .25
❑ 193 Patriots Team .02 .10
❑ 194 John Stephens RC .02 .10
❑ 195 Robert Perryman RC .02 .10
❑ 196 Andre Tippett .08 .25
❑ 197 Fred Marion .02 .10
❑ 198 Doug Flutie .40 1.00
❑ 199 Stanley Morgan .05 .15
❑ 200 Johnny Rembert RC .02 .10
❑ 201 Tony Eason .05 .15
❑ 202 Marvin Allen .02 .10
❑ 203 Raymond Clayborn .02 .10
❑ 204 Irving Fryar .08 .25
❑ 205 Colts Team .02 .10
❑ 206 Eric Dickerson .08 .25
❑ 207 Chris Hinton .02 .10
❑ 208 Duane Bickett .02 .10
❑ 209 Chris Chandler RC .40 1.00
❑ 210 Jon Hand .02 .10
❑ 211 Ray Donaldson .02 .10
❑ 212 Dean Biasucci .02 .10
❑ 213 Bill Brooks .05 .15
❑ 214 Chris Goode RC .02 .10
❑ 215 Clarence Verdin RC .02 .10
❑ 216 Albert Bentley .02 .10
❑ 217 Passing Leaders .05 .15
❑ 218 Receiving Leaders .05 .15
❑ 219 Eric Dickerson/Walker LL .05 .15
❑ 220 Scoring Leaders .02 .10
❑ 221 Interception Leaders .02 .10
❑ 222 Jets Team .02 .10
❑ 223 Erik McMillan RC .02 .10
❑ 224 James Hasty RC .02 .10
❑ 225 Al Toon .05 .15
❑ 226 John Booty RC .02 .10
❑ 227 Johnny Hector .02 .10
❑ 228 Ken O'Brien .05 .15
❑ 229 Marty Lyons .02 .10
❑ 230 Mickey Shuler .02 .10
❑ 231 Robin Cole .02 .10
❑ 232 Freeman McNeil .05 .15
❑ 233 Marion Barber RC .08 .25
❑ 234 Jo Jo Townsell .02 .10
❑ 235 Wesley Walker .05 .15
❑ 236 Roger Vick .02 .10
❑ 237 Pat Leahy .02 .10
❑ 238 Broncos TL/Elway .20 .50
❑ 239 Mike Horan .02 .10
❑ 240 Tony Dorsett .08 .25
❑ 241 John Elway .75 2.00
❑ 242 Mark Jackson .02 .10
❑ 243 Sammy Winder .02 .10
❑ 244 Rich Karlis .02 .10
❑ 245 Vance Johnson .02 .10
❑ 246 Steve Sewell RC .02 .10
❑ 247 Karl Mecklenburg UER .05 .15
❑ 248 Rulon Jones .02 .10
❑ 249 Simon Fletcher RC .02 .10
❑ 250 Redskins Team .05 .15
❑ 251 Chip Lohmiller RC .02 .10
❑ 252 Jamie Morris .05 .15
❑ 253 Mark Rypien UER RC .08 .25
❑ 254 Barry Wilburn .02 .10
❑ 255 Mark May RC .05 .15
❑ 256 Wilber Marshall .05 .15
❑ 257 Charles Mann .02 .10
❑ 258 Gary Clark .08 .25
❑ 259 Doug Williams .08 .25
❑ 260 Art Monk .08 .25
❑ 261 Kelvin Bryant .02 .10
❑ 262 Dexter Manley .05 .15
❑ 263 Ricky Sanders .05 .15
❑ 264 Raiders Team .08 .25
❑ 265 Tim Brown RC .60 1.50
❑ 266 Jay Schroeder .02 .10
❑ 267 Marcus Allen .08 .25
❑ 268 Mike Haynes .05 .15
❑ 269 Bo Jackson .10 .30
❑ 270 Steve Beuerlein RC .25 .60
❑ 271 Vann McElroy .02 .10
❑ 272 Willie Gault .05 .15
❑ 273 Howie Long .08 .25
❑ 274 Greg Townsend .02 .10
❑ 275 Mike Wise DE .02 .10
❑ 276 Cardinals Team .02 .10
❑ 277 Luis Sharpe .02 .10
❑ 278 Scott Dill .02 .10
❑ 279 Vai Sikahema .02 .10

Card	Low	High
❑ 280 Ron Wolfley	.02	.10
❑ 281 David Galloway	.02	.10
❑ 282 Jay Novacek RC	.20	.50
❑ 283 Neil Lomax	.05	.15
❑ 284 Robert Awalt	.02	.10
❑ 285 Cedric Mack	.02	.10
❑ 286 Freddie Joe Nunn	.02	.10
❑ 287 J.T. Smith	.05	.15
❑ 288 Stump Mitchell	.05	.15
❑ 289 Roy Green	.05	.15
❑ 290 Dolphins TL/Marino	.20	.50
❑ 291 Jarvis Williams RC	.02	.10
❑ 292 Troy Stradford	.02	.10
❑ 293 Dan Marino	.75	2.00
❑ 294 T.J. Turner	.02	.10
❑ 295 John Offerdahl	.02	.10
❑ 296 Ferrell Edmunds RC	.02	.10
❑ 297 Scott Schwedes	.02	.10
❑ 298 Lorenzo Hampton	.02	.10
❑ 299 Jim C.Jensen RC	.02	.10
❑ 300 Brian Sochia	.02	.10
❑ 301 Reggie Roby	.02	.10
❑ 302 Mark Clayton	.05	.15
❑ 303 Chargers Team	.02	.10
❑ 304 Lee Williams	.02	.10
❑ 305 Gary Plummer RC	.05	.15
❑ 306 Gary Anderson RB	.02	.10
❑ 307 Gill Byrd	.02	.10
❑ 308 Jamie Holland RC	.02	.10
❑ 309 Billy Ray Smith	.05	.15
❑ 310 Lionel James	.02	.10
❑ 311 Mark Vlasic RC	.02	.10
❑ 312 Curtis Adams	.02	.10
❑ 313 Anthony Miller RC	.08	.25
❑ 314 Steelers Team	.02	.10
❑ 315 Bubby Brister RC	.08	.25
❑ 316 David Little	.02	.10
❑ 317 Tunch Ilkin RC	.02	.10
❑ 318 Louis Lipps	.05	.15
❑ 319 Warren Williams RC	.02	.10
❑ 320 Dwight Stone	.02	.10
❑ 321 Merril Hoge RC	.08	.25
❑ 322 Thomas Everett RC	.02	.10
❑ 323 Rod Woodson RC	.40	1.00
❑ 324 Gary Anderson K	.02	.10
❑ 325 Buccaneers Team	.02	.10
❑ 326 Donnie Elder	.02	.10
❑ 327 Vinny Testaverde	.10	.30
❑ 328 Harry Hamilton	.02	.10
❑ 329 James Wilder	.02	.10
❑ 330 Lars Tate	.02	.10
❑ 331 Mark Carrier RC	.08	.25
❑ 332 Bruce Hill RC	.02	.10
❑ 333 Paul Gruber RC	.05	.15
❑ 334 Ricky Reynolds	.02	.10
❑ 335 Eugene Marve	.02	.10
❑ 336 Falcons Team	.02	.10
❑ 337 Aundray Bruce RC	.02	.10
❑ 338 John Rade	.02	.10
❑ 339 Scott Case RC	.02	.10
❑ 340 Robert Moore	.02	.10
❑ 341 Chris Miller RC	.08	.25
❑ 342 Gerald Riggs	.05	.15
❑ 343 Gene Lang	.02	.10
❑ 344 Marcus Cotton	.02	.10
❑ 345 Rick Donnelly	.02	.10
❑ 346 John Settle RC	.02	.10
❑ 347 Bill Fralic	.05	.15
❑ 348 Chiefs Team	.02	.10
❑ 349 Steve DeBerg	.05	.15
❑ 350 Mike Stensrud	.02	.10
❑ 351 Dino Hackett	.02	.10
❑ 352 Deron Cherry	.02	.10
❑ 353 Christian Okoye	.05	.15
❑ 354 Bill Maas	.02	.10
❑ 355 Carlos Carson	.05	.15
❑ 356 Albert Lewis	.05	.15
❑ 357 Paul Palmer	.02	.10
❑ 358 Nick Lowery	.02	.10
❑ 359 Stephone Paige	.05	.15
❑ 360 Lions Team	.02	.10
❑ 361 Chris Spielman RC	.08	.25
❑ 362 Jim Arnold	.02	.10
❑ 363 Devon Mitchell	.02	.10
❑ 364 Mike Cofer	.02	.10
❑ 365 Bennie Blades RC	.02	.10
❑ 366 James Jones FB	.02	.10
❑ 367 Garry James	.02	.10
❑ 368 Pete Mandley	.02	.10
❑ 369 Keith Ferguson	.02	.10
❑ 370 Dennis Gibson	.02	.10
❑ 371 Packers Team UER	.02	.10
❑ 372 Brent Fullwood RC	.02	.10
❑ 373 Don Majkowski RC	.08	.25
❑ 374 Tim Harris	.02	.10
❑ 375 Keith Woodside RC	.02	.10
❑ 376 Mark Murphy	.02	.10
❑ 377 Dave Brown DB	.02	.10
❑ 378 Perry Kemp RC	.02	.10
❑ 379 Sterling Sharpe RC	.30	.75
❑ 380 Chuck Cecil RC	.05	.15
❑ 381 Walter Stanley	.02	.10
❑ 382 Cowboys Team	.02	.10
❑ 383 Michael Irvin RC	.60	1.50
❑ 384 Bill Bates	.05	.15
❑ 385 Herschel Walker	.08	.25
❑ 386 Darryl Clack	.02	.10
❑ 387 Danny Noonan	.02	.10
❑ 388 Eugene Lockhart RC	.02	.10
❑ 389 Ed Too Tall Jones	.05	.15
❑ 390 Steve Pelluer	.02	.10
❑ 391 Ray Alexander	.02	.10
❑ 392 Nate Newton RC	.08	.25
❑ 393 Garry Cobb	.02	.10
❑ 394 Checklist 1-132	.02	.10
❑ 395 Checklist 133-264	.02	.10
❑ 396 Checklist 265-396	.02	.10

1989 Topps Traded

Card	Low	High
❑ COMP.FACT.SET (132)	6.00	15.00
❑ 1T Eric Ball RC	.05	.15
❑ 2T Tony Mandarich RC	.05	.15
❑ 3T Shawn Collins RC	.05	.15
❑ 4T Ray Bentley RC	.02	.10
❑ 5T Tony Casillas	.05	.15
❑ 6T Al Del Greco RC	.05	.15
❑ 7T Dan Saleaumua RC	.05	.15
❑ 8T Keith Bishop	.02	.10
❑ 9T Rodney Peete RC	.20	.50
❑ 10T Lorenzo White RC	.08	.25
❑ 11T Steve Smith RC	.02	.10
❑ 12T Pete Mandley	.02	.10
❑ 13T Mervyn Fernandez RC	.02	.10
❑ 14T Flipper Anderson RC	.08	.25
❑ 15T Louis Oliver RC	.05	.15
❑ 16T Rick Fenney	.02	.10
❑ 17T Gary Jeter	.02	.10
❑ 18T Greg Cox	.02	.10
❑ 19T Bubba McDowell RC	.02	.10
❑ 20T Ron Heller	.02	.10
❑ 21T Tim McDonald RC	.05	.15
❑ 22T Jerrol Williams RC	.02	.10
❑ 23T Marion Butts RC	.08	.25
❑ 24T Steve Young	.30	.75
❑ 25T Mike Merriweather	.05	.15
❑ 26T Richard Johnson	.02	.10
❑ 27T Gerald Riggs	.05	.15
❑ 28T Dave Waymer	.02	.10
❑ 29T Issiac Holt	.02	.10
❑ 30T Deion Sanders RC	.60	1.50
❑ 31T Todd Blackledge	.05	.15
❑ 32T Jeff Cross RC	.05	.15
❑ 33T Steve Wisniewski RC	.08	.25
❑ 34T Ron Brown	.02	.10
❑ 35T Rod Bernstine RC	.05	.15
❑ 36T Jeff Uhlenhake RC	.02	.10
❑ 37T Donnell Woolford RC	.08	.25
❑ 38T Bob Gagliano RC	.02	.10
❑ 39T Ezra Johnson	.02	.10
❑ 40T Ron Jaworski	.08	.25
❑ 41T Lawyer Tillman RC	.05	.15
❑ 42T Lorenzo Lynch RC	.02	.10
❑ 43T Mike Alexander	.02	.10
❑ 44T Tim Worley RC	.05	.15
❑ 45T Guy Bingham	.02	.10
❑ 46T Cleveland Gary RC	.05	.15
❑ 47T Danny Peebles	.02	.10
❑ 48T Clarence Weathers RC	.08	.25
❑ 49T Jeff Lageman RC	.08	.25
❑ 50T Eric Metcalf RC	.08	.25
❑ 51T Myron Guyton RC	.05	.15
❑ 52T Steve Atwater RC	.08	.25
❑ 53T John Fourcade RC	.05	.15
❑ 54T Randall McDaniel RC	.40	1.00
❑ 55T Al Noga RC	.02	.10
❑ 56T Sammie Smith RC	.05	.15
❑ 57T Jesse Solomon	.02	.10
❑ 58T Greg Kragen RC	.02	.10
❑ 59T Don Beebe RC	.08	.25
❑ 60T Hart Lee Dykes RC	.02	.10
❑ 61T Trace Armstrong RC	.05	.15
❑ 62T Steve Pelluer	.02	.10
❑ 63T Barry Krauss	.02	.10
❑ 64T Kevin Murphy RC	.02	.10
❑ 65T Steve Tasker RC	.08	.25
❑ 66T Jessie Small RC	.05	.15
❑ 67T Dave Meggett RC	.08	.25
❑ 68T Dean Hamel	.02	.10
❑ 69T Jim Covert	.05	.15
❑ 70T Troy Aikman RC	2.00	5.00
❑ 71T Raul Allegre	.02	.10
❑ 72T Chris Jacke RC	.02	.10
❑ 73T Leslie O'Neal	.05	.15
❑ 74T Keith Taylor RC	.02	.10
❑ 75T Steve Walsh RC	.08	.25
❑ 76T Tracy Rocker	.02	.10
❑ 77T Robert Massey RC	.02	.10
❑ 78T Bryan Wagner	.02	.10
❑ 79T Steve DeOssie	.05	.15
❑ 80T Carnell Lake RC	.08	.25
❑ 81T Frank Reich RC	.08	.25
❑ 82T Tyrone Braxton RC	.05	.15
❑ 83T Barry Sanders RC	2.50	6.00
❑ 84T Pete Stoyanovich RC	.05	.15
❑ 85T Paul Palmer	.02	.10
❑ 86T Billy Joe Tolliver RC	.05	.15
❑ 87T Eric Hill RC	.02	.10
❑ 88T Gerald McNeil	.02	.10
❑ 89T Bill Hawkins RC	.02	.10
❑ 90T Derrick Thomas RC	.50	1.25
❑ 91T Jim Harbaugh RC	.30	.75
❑ 92T Brian Williams OL RC	.02	.10
❑ 93T Jack Trudeau	.02	.10
❑ 94T Leonard Smith	.02	.10
❑ 95T Gary Hogeboom	.02	.10
❑ 96T A.J.Johnson RC	.02	.10
❑ 97T Jim McMahon	.05	.15
❑ 98T David Williams RC	.02	.10
❑ 99T Rohn Stark	.02	.10
❑ 100T Sean Landeta	.05	.15
❑ 101T Tim Johnson RC	.05	.15
❑ 102T Andre Rison RC	.30	.75
❑ 103T Earnest Byner	.05	.15
❑ 104T Don McPherson RC	.02	.10
❑ 105T Zefross Moss RC	.02	.10
❑ 106T Frank Stams RC	.02	.10
❑ 107T Courtney Hall RC	.02	.10
❑ 108T Marc Logan RC	.02	.10
❑ 109T James Lofton	.08	.25
❑ 110T Lewis Tillman RC	.05	.15
❑ 111T Irv Pankey RC	.02	.10
❑ 112T Ralf Mojsiejenko	.02	.10
❑ 113T Bobby Humphrey RC	.05	.15
❑ 114T Chris Burkett	.02	.10
❑ 115T Greg Lloyd RC	.08	.25
❑ 116T Matt Millen	.05	.15
❑ 117T Carl Zander	.02	.10
❑ 118T Wayne Martin RC	.08	.25
❑ 119T Mike Saxon	.02	.10
❑ 120T Herschel Walker	.08	.25
❑ 121T Andy Heck RC	.02	.10
❑ 122T Mark Robinson	.02	.10
❑ 123T Keith Van Horne RC	.02	.10
❑ 124T Ricky Hunley	.02	.10
❑ 125T Timm Rosenbach RC	.05	.15
❑ 126T Steve Grogan	.08	.25
❑ 127T Stephen Braggs RC	.02	.10
❑ 128T Terry Long	.02	.10
❑ 129T Evan Cooper	.02	.10
❑ 130T Robert Lyles	.02	.10
❑ 131T Mike Webster	.08	.25
❑ 132T Checklist 1-132	.02	.10

1990 Topps

Card		
❑ COMPLETE SET (528)	10.00	25.00
❑ COMP.FACT.SET (528)	12.50	30.00
❑ 1 Joe Montana RB	.20	.50
❑ 2 Flipper Anderson RB	.01	.05
❑ 3 Troy Aikman RB	.15	.40
❑ 4 Kevin Butler RB	.01	.05
❑ 5 Super Bowl XXIV	.01	.05
❑ 6 Dexter Carter RC	.01	.05
❑ 7 Matt Millen	.02	.10
❑ 8 Jerry Rice	.30	.75
❑ 9 Ronnie Lott	.02	.10
❑ 10 John Taylor	.02	.10
❑ 11 Guy McIntyre	.01	.05
❑ 12 Roger Craig	.02	.10
❑ 13 Joe Montana	.50	1.25
❑ 14 Brent Jones RC	.08	.25
❑ 15 Tom Rathman	.01	.05
❑ 16 Harris Barton	.01	.05
❑ 17 Charles Haley	.02	.10
❑ 18 Pierce Holt RC	.01	.05
❑ 19 Michael Carter	.01	.05
❑ 20 Chet Brooks	.01	.05
❑ 21 Eric Wright	.01	.05
❑ 22 Mike Cofer	.01	.05
❑ 23 Jim Fahnhorst	.01	.05
❑ 24 Keena Turner	.01	.05
❑ 25 Don Griffin	.01	.05
❑ 26 Kevin Fagan RC	.01	.05
❑ 27 Bubba Paris	.01	.05
❑ 28 Barry Sanders/C.Okoye LL	.20	.50
❑ 29 Steve Atwater	.01	.05
❑ 30 Tyrone Braxton	.01	.05
❑ 31 Ron Holmes	.01	.05
❑ 32 Bobby Humphrey	.01	.05
❑ 33 Greg Kragen	.01	.05
❑ 34 David Treadwell	.01	.05
❑ 35 Karl Mecklenburg	.01	.05
❑ 36 Dennis Smith	.01	.05
❑ 37 John Elway	.50	1.25
❑ 38 Vance Johnson	.01	.05
❑ 39 Simon Fletcher UER	.01	.05
❑ 40 Jim Juriga	.01	.05
❑ 41 Mark Jackson	.01	.05
❑ 42 Melvin Bratton RC	.01	.05
❑ 43 Wymon Henderson RC	.01	.05
❑ 44 Ken Bell	.01	.05
❑ 45 Sammy Winder	.01	.05
❑ 46 Alphonso Carreker	.01	.05
❑ 47 Orson Mobley RC	.01	.05
❑ 48 Rodney Hampton RC	.08	.25
❑ 49 Dave Meggett	.02	.10
❑ 50 Myron Guyton	.01	.05
❑ 51 Phil Simms	.02	.10
❑ 52 Lawrence Taylor	.08	.25
❑ 53 Carl Banks	.01	.05
❑ 54 Pepper Johnson	.01	.05
❑ 55 Leonard Marshall	.01	.05
❑ 56 Mark Collins	.01	.05
❑ 57 Erik Howard	.01	.05
❑ 58 Eric Dorsey RC	.01	.05
❑ 59 Ottis Anderson	.02	.10
❑ 60 Mark Bavaro	.01	.05
❑ 61 Odessa Turner RC	.01	.05
❑ 62 Gary Reasons	.01	.05
❑ 63 Maurice Carthon	.01	.05
❑ 64 Lionel Manuel	.01	.05
❑ 65 Sean Landeta	.01	.05
❑ 66 Perry Williams	.01	.05
❑ 67 Pat Terrell RC	.01	.05
❑ 68 Flipper Anderson	.01	.05
❑ 69 Jackie Slater	.01	.05
❑ 70 Tom Newberry	.01	.05
❑ 71 Jerry Gray	.01	.05
❑ 72 Henry Ellard	.02	.10
❑ 73 Doug Smith	.01	.05
❑ 74 Kevin Greene	.02	.10
❑ 75 Jim Everett	.02	.10
❑ 76 Mike Lansford	.01	.05
❑ 77 Greg Bell	.01	.05
❑ 78 Pete Holohan	.01	.05
❑ 79 Robert Delpino	.01	.05
❑ 80 Mike Wilcher	.01	.05
❑ 81 Mike Piel	.01	.05
❑ 82 Mel Owens	.01	.05
❑ 83 Michael Stewart RC	.01	.05
❑ 84 Ben Smith RC	.01	.05
❑ 85 Keith Jackson	.02	.10
❑ 86 Reggie White	.08	.25
❑ 87 Eric Allen	.01	.05
❑ 88 Jerome Brown	.01	.05
❑ 89 Robert Drummond	.01	.05
❑ 90 Anthony Toney	.01	.05
❑ 91 Keith Byars	.01	.05
❑ 92 Cris Carter	.20	.50
❑ 93 Randall Cunningham	.08	.25
❑ 94 Ron Johnson WR	.01	.05
❑ 95 Mike Quick	.01	.05
❑ 96 Clyde Simmons	.01	.05
❑ 97 Mike Pitts	.01	.05
❑ 98 Izel Jenkins RC	.01	.05
❑ 99 Seth Joyner	.02	.10
❑ 100 Mike Schad	.01	.05
❑ 101 Wes Hopkins	.01	.05
❑ 102 Kirk Lowdermilk	.01	.05
❑ 103 Rick Fenney	.01	.05
❑ 104 Randall McDaniel	.08	.25
❑ 105 Herschel Walker	.02	.10
❑ 106 Al Noga	.01	.05
❑ 107 Gary Zimmerman	.02	.10
❑ 108 Chris Doleman	.01	.05
❑ 109 Keith Millard	.01	.05
❑ 110 Carl Lee	.01	.05
❑ 111 Joey Browner	.01	.05
❑ 112 Steve Jordan	.01	.05
❑ 113 Reggie Rutland RC	.01	.05
❑ 114 Wade Wilson	.02	.10
❑ 115 Anthony Carter	.02	.10
❑ 116 Rich Karlis	.01	.05
❑ 117 Hassan Jones	.01	.05
❑ 118 Henry Thomas	.01	.05
❑ 119 Scott Studwell	.01	.05
❑ 120 Ralf Mojsiejenko	.01	.05
❑ 121 Earnest Byner	.01	.05
❑ 122 Gerald Riggs	.02	.10
❑ 123 Tracy Rocker	.01	.05
❑ 124 A.J. Johnson	.01	.05
❑ 125 Charles Mann	.01	.05
❑ 126 Art Monk	.02	.10
❑ 127 Ricky Sanders	.01	.05
❑ 128 Gary Clark	.08	.25
❑ 129 Jim Lachey	.01	.05
❑ 130 Martin Mayhew RC	.01	.05
❑ 131 Ravin Caldwell	.01	.05
❑ 132 Don Warren	.01	.05
❑ 133 Mark Hypien	.02	.10
❑ 134 Ed Simmons RC	.01	.05
❑ 135 Darryl Grant	.01	.05
❑ 136 Darrell Green	.02	.10
❑ 137 Chip Lohmiller	.01	.05
❑ 138 Tony Bennett RC	.08	.25
❑ 139 Tony Mandarich	.01	.05
❑ 140 Sterling Sharpe	.08	.25
❑ 141 Tim Harris	.01	.05
❑ 142 Don Majkowski	.01	.05
❑ 143 Rich Moran RC	.01	.05
❑ 144 Jeff Query	.01	.05
❑ 145 Brent Fullwood	.01	.05
❑ 146 Chris Jacke	.01	.05
❑ 147 Keith Woodside	.01	.05
❑ 148 Perry Kemp	.01	.05
❑ 149 Herman Fontenot	.01	.05
❑ 150 Dave Brown DB	.01	.05
❑ 151 Brian Noble	.01	.05
❑ 152 Johnny Holland	.01	.05
❑ 153 Mark Murphy	.01	.05
❑ 154 Bob Nelson NT	.01	.05
❑ 155 Darrell Thompson RC	.01	.05
❑ 156 Lawyer Tillman	.01	.05
❑ 157 Eric Metcalf	.08	.25
❑ 158 Webster Slaughter	.02	.10
❑ 159 Frank Minnifield	.01	.05
❑ 160 Brian Brennan	.01	.05
❑ 161 Thane Gash RC	.01	.05
❑ 162 Robert Banks DE	.01	.05
❑ 163 Bernie Kosar	.02	.10
❑ 164 David Grayson	.01	.05
❑ 165 Kevin Mack	.01	.05
❑ 166 Mike Johnson	.01	.05
❑ 167 Tim Manoa	.01	.05
❑ 168 Ozzie Newsome	.02	.10
❑ 169 Felix Wright	.01	.05
❑ 170A Al Baker Orng.	.02	.10
❑ 170B Al Baker Wht.	.02	.10
❑ 171 Reggie Langhorne	.01	.05
❑ 172 Clay Matthews	.02	.10
❑ 173 Andrew Stewart	.01	.05
❑ 174 Barry Foster RC	.08	.25
❑ 175 Tim Worley	.01	.05
❑ 176 Tim Johnson	.01	.05
❑ 177 Carnell Lake	.01	.05
❑ 178 Greg Lloyd	.08	.25
❑ 179 Rod Woodson	.08	.25
❑ 180 Tunch Ilkin	.01	.05
❑ 181 Dermontti Dawson	.02	.10
❑ 182 Gary Anderson K	.01	.05
❑ 183 Bubby Brister	.01	.05
❑ 184 Louis Lipps	.02	.10
❑ 185 Merril Hoge	.01	.05
❑ 186 Mike Mularkey	.01	.05
❑ 187 Derek Hill	.01	.05
❑ 188 Rodney Carter	.01	.05
❑ 189 Dwayne Woodruff	.01	.05
❑ 190 Keith Willis	.01	.05
❑ 191 Jerry Olsavsky	.01	.05
❑ 192 Mark Stock	.01	.05
❑ 193 Sacks Leaders	.01	.05
❑ 194 Leonard Smith	.01	.05
❑ 195 Darryl Talley	.01	.05
❑ 196 Mark Kelso	.01	.05
❑ 197 Kent Hull	.01	.05
❑ 198 Nate Odomes RC	.02	.10
❑ 199 Pete Metzelaars	.01	.05
❑ 200 Don Beebe	.02	.10
❑ 201 Ray Bentley	.01	.05
❑ 202 Steve Tasker	.02	.10
❑ 203 Scott Norwood	.01	.05
❑ 204 Andre Reed	.08	.25
❑ 205 Bruce Smith	.08	.25
❑ 206 Thurman Thomas	.08	.25
❑ 207 Jim Kelly	.08	.25
❑ 208 Cornelius Bennett	.02	.10
❑ 209 Shane Conlan	.01	.05
❑ 210 Larry Kinnebrew	.01	.05
❑ 211 Jeff Alm RC	.01	.05
❑ 212 Robert Lyles	.01	.05
❑ 213 Bubba McDowell	.01	.05
❑ 214 Mike Munchak	.02	.10
❑ 215 Bruce Matthews	.02	.10
❑ 216 Warren Moon	.08	.25
❑ 217 Drew Hill	.01	.05
❑ 218 Ray Childress	.01	.05
❑ 219 Steve Brown	.01	.05
❑ 220 Alonzo Highsmith	.01	.05
❑ 221 Allen Pinkett	.01	.05
❑ 222 Sean Jones	.02	.10
❑ 223 Johnny Meads	.01	.05
❑ 224 John Grimsley	.01	.05
❑ 225 Haywood Jeffires RC	.08	.25
❑ 226 Curtis Duncan	.01	.05
❑ 227 Greg Montgomery RC	.01	.05
❑ 228 Ernest Givins	.02	.10
❑ 229 Joe Montana/B.Esiason LL	.10	.30
❑ 230 Robert Massey	.01	.05
❑ 231 John Fourcade	.01	.05
❑ 232 Dalton Hilliard	.01	.05
❑ 233 Vaughan Johnson	.01	.05
❑ 234 Hoby Brenner	.01	.05
❑ 235 Pat Swilling	.02	.10
❑ 236 Kevin Haverdink	.01	.05
❑ 237 Bobby Hebert	.01	.05
❑ 238 Sam Mills	.02	.10
❑ 239 Eric Martin	.01	.05
❑ 240 Lonzell Hill	.01	.05
❑ 241 Steve Trapilo	.01	.05
❑ 242 Rickey Jackson	.02	.10
❑ 243 Craig Heyward	.02	.10
❑ 244 Rueben Mayes	.01	.05
❑ 245 Morten Andersen	.01	.05
❑ 246 Percy Snow RC	.01	.05
❑ 247 Pete Mandley	.01	.05
❑ 248 Derrick Thomas	.08	.25
❑ 249 Dan Saleaumua	.01	.05

❑ 250 Todd McNair RC	.01	.05
❑ 251 Leonard Griffin	.01	.05
❑ 252 Jonathan Hayes	.01	.05
❑ 253 Christian Okoye	.01	.05
❑ 254 Albert Lewis	.01	.05
❑ 255 Nick Lowery	.01	.05
❑ 256 Kevin Ross	.01	.05
❑ 257 Steve DeBerg UER	.01	.05
❑ 258 Stephone Paige	.01	.05
❑ 259 James Saxon RC	.01	.05
❑ 260 Herman Heard	.01	.05
❑ 261 Deron Cherry	.01	.05
❑ 262 Dino Hackett	.01	.05
❑ 263 Neil Smith	.08	.25
❑ 264 Steve Pelluer	.01	.05
❑ 265 Eric Thomas	.01	.05
❑ 266 Eric Ball	.01	.05
❑ 267 Leon White	.01	.05
❑ 268 Tim Krumrie	.01	.05
❑ 269 Jason Buck	.01	.05
❑ 270 Boomer Esiason	.02	.10
❑ 271 Carl Zander	.01	.05
❑ 272 Eddie Brown	.01	.05
❑ 273 David Fulcher	.01	.05
❑ 274 Tim McGee	.01	.05
❑ 275 James Brooks	.02	.10
❑ 276 Rickey Dixon RC	.01	.05
❑ 277 Ickey Woods	.01	.05
❑ 278 Anthony Munoz	.02	.10
❑ 279 Rodney Holman	.01	.05
❑ 280 Mike Alexander	.01	.05
❑ 281 Mervyn Fernandez	.01	.05
❑ 282 Steve Wisniewski	.02	.10
❑ 283 Steve Smith	.01	.05
❑ 284 Howie Long	.08	.25
❑ 285 Bo Jackson	.10	.30
❑ 286 Mike Dyal	.01	.05
❑ 287 Thomas Benson	.01	.05
❑ 288 Willie Gault	.02	.10
❑ 289 Marcus Allen	.08	.25
❑ 290 Greg Townsend	.01	.05
❑ 291 Steve Beuerlein	.02	.10
❑ 292 Scott Davis	.01	.05
❑ 293 Eddie Anderson RC	.01	.05
❑ 294 Terry McDaniel	.01	.05
❑ 295 Tim Brown	.08	.25
❑ 296 Bob Golic	.01	.05
❑ 297 Jeff Jaeger RC	.01	.05
❑ 298 Jeff George RC	.20	.50
❑ 299 Chip Banks	.01	.05
❑ 300 Andre Rison UER	.08	.25
❑ 301 Rohn Stark	.01	.05
❑ 302 Keith Taylor	.01	.05
❑ 303 Jack Trudeau	.01	.05
❑ 304 Chris Hinton	.01	.05
❑ 305 Ray Donaldson	.01	.05
❑ 306 Jeff Herrod RC	.01	.05
❑ 307 Clarence Verdin	.01	.05
❑ 308 Jon Hand	.01	.05
❑ 309 Bill Brooks	.01	.05
❑ 310 Albert Bentley	.01	.05
❑ 311 Mike Prior	.01	.05
❑ 312 Pat Beach	.01	.05
❑ 313 Eugene Daniel	.01	.05
❑ 314 Duane Bickett	.01	.05
❑ 315 Dean Biasucci	.01	.05
❑ 316 Richmond Webb RC	.01	.05
❑ 317 Jeff Cross	.01	.05
❑ 318 Louis Oliver	.01	.05
❑ 319 Sammie Smith	.01	.05
❑ 320 Pete Stoyanovich	.01	.05
❑ 321 John Offerdahl	.01	.05
❑ 322 Ferrell Edmunds	.01	.05
❑ 323 Dan Marino	.50	1.25
❑ 324 Andre Brown	.01	.05
❑ 325 Reggie Roby	.01	.05
❑ 326 Jarvis Williams	.01	.05
❑ 327 Roy Foster	.01	.05
❑ 328 Mark Clayton	.02	.10
❑ 329 Brian Sochia	.01	.05
❑ 330 Mark Duper	.02	.10
❑ 331 T.J. Turner	.01	.05
❑ 332 Jeff Uhlenhake	.01	.05
❑ 333 Jim C.Jensen	.01	.05
❑ 334 Cortez Kennedy RC	.08	.25
❑ 335 Andy Heck	.01	.05
❑ 336 Rufus Porter	.01	.05
❑ 337 Brian Blades	.02	.10
❑ 338 Dave Krieg	.02	.10
❑ 339 John L. Williams	.01	.05
❑ 340 David Wyman	.01	.05
❑ 341 Paul Skansi RC	.01	.05
❑ 342 Eugene Robinson	.01	.05
❑ 343 Joe Nash	.01	.05
❑ 344 Jacob Green	.01	.05
❑ 345 Jeff Bryant	.01	.05
❑ 346 Ruben Rodriguez	.01	.05
❑ 347 Norm Johnson	.01	.05
❑ 348 Darren Comeaux	.01	.05
❑ 349 Andre Ware RC	.02	.10
❑ 350 Richard Johnson	.01	.05
❑ 351 Rodney Peete	.02	.10
❑ 352 Barry Sanders	.50	1.25
❑ 353 Chris Spielman	.08	.25
❑ 354 Eddie Murray	.01	.05
❑ 355 Jerry Ball	.01	.05
❑ 356 Mel Gray	.02	.10
❑ 357 Eric Williams RC	.01	.05
❑ 358 Robert Clark RC	.01	.05
❑ 359 Jason Phillips	.01	.05
❑ 360 Terry Taylor RC	.01	.05
❑ 361 Bennie Blades	.01	.05
❑ 362 Michael Cofer	.01	.05
❑ 363 Jim Arnold	.01	.05
❑ 364 Marc Spindler RC	.01	.05
❑ 365 Jim Covert	.01	.05
❑ 366 Jim Harbaugh	.08	.25
❑ 367 Neal Anderson	.02	.10
❑ 368 Mike Singletary	.02	.10
❑ 369 John Roper	.01	.05
❑ 370 Steve McMichael	.02	.10
❑ 371 Dennis Gentry	.01	.05
❑ 372 Brad Muster	.01	.05
❑ 373 Ron Morris	.01	.05
❑ 374 James Thornton	.01	.05
❑ 375 Kevin Butler	.01	.05
❑ 376 Richard Dent	.02	.10
❑ 377 Dan Hampton	.02	.10
❑ 378 Jay Hilgenberg	.01	.05
❑ 379 Donnell Woolford	.01	.05
❑ 380 Trace Armstrong	.01	.05
❑ 381 Junior Seau RC	.50	1.25
❑ 382 Rod Bernstine	.01	.05
❑ 383 Marion Butts	.02	.10
❑ 384 Burt Grossman	.01	.05
❑ 385 Darrin Nelson	.01	.05
❑ 386 Leslie O'Neal	.02	.10
❑ 387 Billy Joe Tolliver	.01	.05
❑ 388 Courtney Hall	.01	.05
❑ 389 Lee Williams	.01	.05
❑ 390 Anthony Miller	.08	.25
❑ 391 Gill Byrd	.01	.05
❑ 392 Wayne Walker WR	.01	.05
❑ 393 Billy Ray Smith	.01	.05
❑ 394 Vencie Glenn	.01	.05
❑ 395 Tim Spencer	.01	.05
❑ 396 Gary Plummer	.01	.05
❑ 397 Arthur Cox	.01	.05
❑ 398 Jamie Holland	.01	.05
❑ 399 Keith McCants RC	.01	.05
❑ 400 Kevin Murphy	.01	.05
❑ 401 Danny Peebles	.01	.05
❑ 402 Mark Robinson	.01	.05
❑ 403 Broderick Thomas	.01	.05
❑ 404 Ron Hall	.01	.05
❑ 405 Mark Carrier WR	.08	.25
❑ 406 Paul Gruber	.01	.05
❑ 407 Vinny Testaverde	.02	.10
❑ 408 Bruce Hill	.01	.05
❑ 409 Lars Tate	.01	.05
❑ 410 Harry Hamilton	.01	.05
❑ 411 Ricky Reynolds	.01	.05
❑ 412 Donald Igwebuike	.01	.05
❑ 413 Reuben Davis	.01	.05
❑ 414 William Howard	.01	.05
❑ 415 Winston Moss RC	.01	.05
❑ 416 Chris Singleton RC	.01	.05
❑ 417 Hart Lee Dykes	.01	.05
❑ 418 Steve Grogan	.02	.10
❑ 419 Bruce Armstrong	.01	.05
❑ 420 Robert Perryman	.01	.05
❑ 421 Andre Tippett	.01	.05
❑ 422 Sammy Martin	.01	.05
❑ 423 Stanley Morgan	.01	.05
❑ 424 Cedric Jones	.01	.05
❑ 425 Sean Farrell	.01	.05
❑ 426 Marc Wilson	.01	.05
❑ 427 John Stephens	.01	.05
❑ 428 Eric Sievers RC	.01	.05
❑ 429 Maurice Hurst RC	.01	.05
❑ 430 Johnny Rembert	.01	.05
❑ 431 Jerry Rice/Andre Reed LL	.10	.30
❑ 432 Eric Hill	.01	.05
❑ 433 Gary Hogeboom	.01	.05
❑ 434 Timm Rosenbach UER	.01	.05
❑ 435 Tim McDonald	.01	.05
❑ 436 Rich Camarillo	.01	.05
❑ 437 Luis Sharpe	.01	.05
❑ 438 J.T. Smith	.01	.05
❑ 439 Roy Green	.02	.10
❑ 440 Ernie Jones RC	.01	.05
❑ 441 Robert Awalt	.01	.05
❑ 442 Vai Sikahema	.01	.05
❑ 443 Joe Wolf	.01	.05
❑ 444 Stump Mitchell	.01	.05
❑ 445 David Galloway	.01	.05
❑ 446 Ron Wolfley	.01	.05
❑ 447 Freddie Joe Nunn	.01	.05
❑ 448 Blair Thomas RC	.02	.10
❑ 449 Jeff Lageman	.01	.05
❑ 450 Tony Eason	.01	.05
❑ 451 Erik McMillan	.01	.05
❑ 452 Jim Sweeney	.01	.05
❑ 453 Ken O'Brien	.01	.05
❑ 454 Johnny Hector	.01	.05
❑ 455 Jo Jo Townsell	.01	.05
❑ 456 Roger Vick	.01	.05
❑ 457 James Hasty	.01	.05
❑ 458 Dennis Byrd RC	.02	.10
❑ 459 Ron Stallworth	.01	.05
❑ 460 Mickey Shuler	.01	.05
❑ 461 Bobby Humphery	.01	.05
❑ 462 Kyle Clifton	.01	.05
❑ 463 Al Toon	.02	.10
❑ 464 Freeman McNeil	.01	.05
❑ 465 Pat Leahy	.01	.05
❑ 466 Scott Case	.01	.05
❑ 467 Shawn Collins	.01	.05
❑ 468 Floyd Dixon	.01	.05
❑ 469 Deion Sanders	.20	.50
❑ 470 Tony Casillas	.01	.05
❑ 471 Michael Haynes RC	.08	.25
❑ 472 Chris Miller	.08	.25
❑ 473 John Settle	.01	.05
❑ 474 Aundray Bruce	.01	.05
❑ 475 Gene Lang	.01	.05
❑ 476 Tim Gordon RC	.01	.05
❑ 477 Scott Fulhage	.01	.05
❑ 478 Bill Fralic	.01	.05
❑ 479 Jessie Tuggle RC	.01	.05
❑ 480 Marcus Cotton	.01	.05
❑ 481 Steve Walsh	.02	.10
❑ 482 Troy Aikman	.30	.75
❑ 483 Ray Horton	.01	.05
❑ 484 Tony Tolbert RC	.02	.10
❑ 485 Steve Folsom	.01	.05
❑ 486 Ken Norton Jr. RC	.08	.25
❑ 487 Kelvin Martin RC	.01	.05
❑ 488 Jack Del Rio	.02	.10
❑ 489 Daryl Johnston RC	.40	1.00
❑ 490 Bill Bates	.02	.10
❑ 491 Jim Jeffcoat	.01	.05
❑ 492 Vince Albritton	.01	.05
❑ 493 Eugene Lockhart	.01	.05
❑ 494 Mike Saxon	.01	.05
❑ 495 James Dixon	.01	.05
❑ 496 Willie Broughton	.01	.05
❑ 497 Checklist 1-132	.01	.05
❑ 498 Checklist 133-264	.01	.05
❑ 499 Checklist 265-396	.01	.05
❑ 500 Checklist 397-528	.01	.05
❑ 501 Bears Team	.02	.10
❑ 502 Bengals Team	.01	.05
❑ 503 Bills Team	.01	.05
❑ 504 Broncos Team	.01	.05
❑ 505 Browns Team	.01	.05
❑ 506 Buccaneers Team	.01	.05
❑ 507 Cardinals Team	.01	.05
❑ 508 Chargers Team	.01	.05
❑ 509 Chiefs Team	.01	.05
❑ 510 Colts Team	.01	.05
❑ 511 Cowboys TL/Aikman	.10	.30
❑ 512 Dolphins Team	.01	.05
❑ 513 Eagles Team	.01	.05
❑ 514 Falcons Team	.01	.05
❑ 515 49ers TL/Montana/Craig	.10	.30
❑ 516 Giants Team	.01	.05

Card		
517 Jets Team	.01	.05
518 Lions Team	.01	.05
519 Oilers TL/Moon	.02	.10
520 Packers Team	.01	.05
521 Patriots Team	.01	.05
522 Raiders TL/Bo Jackson	.02	.10
523 Rams Team	.01	.05
524 Redskins Team	.01	.05
525 Saints Team	.01	.05
526 Seahawks Team	.01	.05
527 Steelers Team	.01	.05
528 Vikings Team	.01	.05

1990 Topps Traded

Card		
COMP.FACT.SET (132)	6.00	15.00
1T Gerald McNeil	.01	.05
2T Andre Rison	.08	.25
3T Steve Walsh	.08	.25
4T Lorenzo White	.02	.10
5T Max Montoya	.01	.05
6T William Roberts RC	.01	.05
7T Alonzo Highsmith	.01	.05
8T Chris Hinton	.02	.10
9T Stanley Morgan	.02	.10
10T Mickey Shuler	.01	.05
11T Bobby Humphery	.01	.05
12T Gary Anderson RB	.01	.05
13T Mike Tomczak	.02	.10
14T Anthony Pleasant RC	.02	.10
15T Walter Stanley	.01	.05
16T Greg Bell	.01	.05
17T Tony Martin RC	.30	.75
18T Terry Kinard	.01	.05
19T Cris Carter	.20	.50
20T James Wilder	.01	.05
21T Jerry Kauric	.01	.05
22T Irving Fryar	.08	.25
23T Ken Harvey RC	.08	.25
24T James Williams DB RC	.01	.05
25T Ron Cox RC	.01	.05
26T Andre Ware	.08	.25
27T Emmitt Smith RC	5.00	12.00
28T Junior Seau	.30	.75
29T Mark Carrier RC DB	.08	.25
30T Rodney Hampton	.08	.25
31T Rob Moore RC	.20	.50
32T Bern Brostek RC	.01	.05
33T Dexter Carter	.02	.10
34T Blair Thomas	.02	.10
35T Harold Green RC	.08	.25
36T Darrell Thompson	.01	.05
37T Eric Green RC	.08	.25
38T Renaldo Turnbull RC	.08	.25
39T Leroy Hoard RC	.08	.25
40T Anthony Thompson RC	.02	.10
41T Jeff George	.08	.25
42T Alexander Wright RC	.01	.05
43T Richmond Webb	.01	.05
44T Cortez Kennedy	.08	.25
45T Ray Agnew RC	.01	.05
46T Percy Snow	.01	.05
47T Chris Singleton	.01	.05
48T James Francis RC	.02	.10
49T Tony Bennett	.02	.10
50T Reggie Cobb RC	.02	.10
51T Barry Foster	.08	.25
52T Ben Smith	.01	.05
53T Anthony Smith RC	.08	.25
54T Steve Christie RC	.01	.05
55T Johnny Bailey RC	.02	.10
56T Alan Grant RC	.01	.05
57T Eric Floyd RC	.01	.05
58T Robert Blackmon RC	.01	.05
59T Brent Williams	.01	.05
60T Raymond Clayborn	.01	.05
61T Dave Duerson	.01	.05
62T Derrick Fenner RC	.02	.10
63T Ken Willis	.01	.05
64T Brad Baxter RC	.02	.10
65T Tony Paige	.01	.05
66T Jay Schroeder	.01	.05
67T Jim Breech	.01	.05
68T Barry Word RC	.02	.10
69T Anthony Dilweg FTC	.01	.05
70T Rich Gannon RC	.75	2.00
71T Stan Humphries RC	.08	.25
72T Jay Novacek	.08	.25
73T Tommy Kane RC	.01	.05
74T Everson Walls	.01	.05
75T Mike Rozier	.02	.10
76T Robb Thomas	.01	.05
77T Terance Mathis RC	.30	.75
78T LeRoy Irvin	.01	.05
79T Jeff Donaldson	.01	.05
80T Ethan Horton RC	.02	.10
81T J.B.Brown RC	.01	.05
82T Joe Kelly	.01	.05
83T John Carney RC	.01	.05
84T Dan Stryzinski RC	.01	.05
85T John Kidd	.01	.05
86T Al Smith	.02	.10
87T Travis McNeal	.01	.05
88T Reyna Thompson RC	.01	.05
89T Rick Donnelly	.01	.05
90T Marv Cook RC	.02	.10
91T Mike Farr RC	.01	.05
92T Daniel Stubbs	.01	.05
93T Jeff Campbell RC	.01	.05
94T Tim McKyer	.01	.05
95T Ian Beckles RC	.01	.05
96T Lemuel Stinson	.01	.05
97T Frank Cornish	.01	.05
98T Riki Ellison	.01	.05
99T Jamie Mueller RC	.01	.05
100T Brian Hansen	.01	.05
101T Warren Powers RC	.01	.05
102T Howard Cross RC	.01	.05
103T Tim Grunhard RC	.01	.05
104T Johnny Johnson RC	.08	.25
105T Calvin Williams RC	.08	.25
106T Keith McCants	.01	.05
107T Lamar Lathon RC	.02	.10
108T Steve Broussard RC	.02	.10
109T Glenn Parker RC	.01	.05
110T Alton Montgomery RC	.01	.05
111T Jim McMahon	.02	.10
112T Aaron Wallace RC	.01	.05
113T Keith Sims RC	.01	.05
114T Ervin Randle	.01	.05
115T Walter Wilson	.01	.05
116T Terry Wooden RC	.01	.05
117T Bernard Clark	.01	.05
118T Tony Stargell RC	.01	.05
119T Jimmie Jones RC	.01	.05
120T Andre Collins RC	.02	.10
121T Ricky Proehl RC	.08	.25
122T Darion Conner RC	.02	.10
123T Jeff Rutledge	.01	.05
124T Heath Sherman RC	.02	.10
125T Tommie Agee RC	.01	.05
126T Tory Epps RC	.01	.05
127T Tommy Hodson RC	.01	.05
128T Jessie Hester RC	.01	.05
129T Alfred Oglesby RC	.01	.05
130T Chris Chandler	.08	.25
131T Fred Barnett RC	.08	.25
132T Checklist 1-132	.01	.05

1991 Topps

Card		
COMPLETE SET (660)	10.00	20.00
COMP.FACT.SET (660)	15.00	30.00
1 Super Bowl XXV	.01	.05
2 Roger Craig HL	.02	.10
3 Derrick Thomas HL	.02	.10
4 Pete Stoyanovich HL	.01	.05
5 Ottis Anderson HL	.02	.10
6 Jerry Rice HL	.20	.50
7 Warren Moon HL	.02	.10
8 Warren Moon/J.Everett LL	.02	.10
9 B.Sanders/T.Thomas LL	.15	.40
10 J.Rice/H.Jeffires LL	.10	.30
11 M.Carrier DB/R.Johnson DB LL	.01	.05
12 Derrick Thomas/C.Haley L	.02	.10
13 Jumbo Elliott	.01	.05
14 Leonard Marshall	.01	.05
15 William Roberts	.01	.05
16 Lawrence Taylor	.08	.25
17 Mark Ingram	.02	.10
18 Rodney Hampton	.08	.25
19 Carl Banks	.01	.05
20 Ottis Anderson	.02	.10
21 Mark Collins	.01	.05
22 Pepper Johnson	.01	.05
23 Dave Meggett	.02	.10
24 Reyna Thompson	.01	.05
25 Stephen Baker	.01	.05
26 Mike Fox	.01	.05
27 Maurice Carthon UER	.01	.05
28 Jeff Hostetler	.08	.25
29 Greg Jackson RC	.01	.05
30 Sean Landeta	.01	.05
31 Bart Oates	.01	.05
32 Phil Simms	.02	.10
33 Erik Howard	.01	.05
34 Myron Guyton	.01	.05
35 Mark Bavaro	.01	.05
36 Jarrod Bunch RC	.01	.05
37 Will Wolford	.01	.05
38 Ray Bentley	.01	.05
39 Nate Odomes	.01	.05
40 Scott Norwood	.01	.05
41 Darryl Talley	.01	.05
42 Carwell Gardner	.01	.05
43 James Lofton	.02	.10
44 Shane Conlan	.01	.05
45 Steve Tasker	.02	.10
46 James Williams	.01	.05
47 Kent Hull	.01	.05
48 Al Edwards	.01	.05
49 Frank Reich	.02	.10
50 Leon Seals	.01	.05
51 Keith McKeller	.01	.05
52 Thurman Thomas	.08	.25
53 Leonard Smith	.01	.05
54 Andre Reed	.02	.10
55 Kenneth Davis	.01	.05
56 Jeff Wright RC	.01	.05
57 Jamie Mueller	.01	.05
58 Jim Ritcher	.01	.05
59 Bruce Smith	.08	.25
60 Ted Washington RC	.01	.05
61 Guy McIntyre	.01	.05
62 Michael Carter	.01	.05
63 Pierce Holt	.01	.05
64 Darryl Pollard	.01	.05
65 Mike Sherrard	.01	.05
66 Dexter Carter	.01	.05
67 Bubba Paris	.01	.05
68 Harry Sydney	.01	.05
69 Tom Rathman	.01	.05
70 Jesse Sapolu	.01	.05
71 Mike Cofer	.01	.05
72 Keith DeLong	.01	.05
73 Joe Montana	.50	1.25
74 Bill Romanowski	.01	.05
75 John Taylor	.02	.10
76 Brent Jones	.08	.25
77 Harris Barton	.01	.05
78 Charles Haley	.02	.10
79 Eric Davis	.01	.05
80 Kevin Fagan	.01	.05
81 Jerry Rice	.30	.75
82 Dave Waymer	.01	.05
83 Todd Marinovich RC	.01	.05
84 Steve Smith	.01	.05
85 Tim Brown	.08	.25
86 Ethan Horton	.01	.05
87 Marcus Allen	.08	.25
88 Terry McDaniel	.01	.05
89 Thomas Benson	.01	.05
90 Roger Craig	.02	.10

Card		
❏ 91 Don Mosebar	.01	.05
❏ 92 Aaron Wallace	.01	.05
❏ 93 Eddie Anderson	.01	.05
❏ 94 Willie Gault	.02	.10
❏ 95 Howie Long	.08	.25
❏ 96 Jay Schroeder	.01	.05
❏ 97 Ronnie Lott	.02	.10
❏ 98 Bob Golic	.01	.05
❏ 99 Bo Jackson	.10	.30
❏ 100 Max Montoya	.01	.05
❏ 101 Scott Davis	.01	.05
❏ 102 Greg Townsend	.01	.05
❏ 103 Garry Lewis	.01	.05
❏ 104 Mervyn Fernandez	.01	.05
❏ 105 Steve Wisniewski UER	.01	.05
❏ 106 Jeff Jaeger	.01	.05
❏ 107 Nick Bell RC	.01	.05
❏ 108 Mark Dennis RC	.01	.05
❏ 109 Jarvis Williams	.01	.05
❏ 110 Mark Clayton	.02	.10
❏ 111 Harry Galbreath	.01	.05
❏ 112 Dan Marino	.50	1.25
❏ 113 Louis Oliver	.01	.05
❏ 114 Pete Stoyanovich	.01	.05
❏ 115 Ferrell Edmunds	.01	.05
❏ 116 Jeff Cross	.01	.05
❏ 117 Richmond Webb	.01	.05
❏ 118 Jim C. Jensen	.01	.05
❏ 119 Keith Sims	.01	.05
❏ 120 Mark Duper	.02	.10
❏ 121 Shawn Lee RC	.01	.05
❏ 122 Reggie Roby	.01	.05
❏ 123 Jeff Uhlenhake	.01	.05
❏ 124 Sammie Smith	.01	.05
❏ 125 John Offerdahl	.01	.05
❏ 126 Hugh Green	.01	.05
❏ 127 Tony Paige	.01	.05
❏ 128 David Griggs	.01	.05
❏ 129 J.B. Brown	.01	.05
❏ 130 Harvey Williams RC	.08	.25
❏ 131 John Alt	.01	.05
❏ 132 Albert Lewis	.01	.05
❏ 133 Robb Thomas	.01	.05
❏ 134 Neil Smith	.08	.25
❏ 135 Stephone Paige	.01	.05
❏ 136 Nick Lowery	.01	.05
❏ 137 Steve DeBerg	.01	.05
❏ 138 Rich Baldinger RC	.01	.05
❏ 139 Percy Snow	.01	.05
❏ 140 Kevin Porter	.01	.05
❏ 141 Chris Martin	.01	.05
❏ 142 Deron Cherry	.01	.05
❏ 143 Derrick Thomas	.08	.25
❏ 144 Tim Grunhard	.01	.05
❏ 145 Todd McNair	.01	.05
❏ 146 David Szott	.01	.05
❏ 147 Dan Saleaumua	.01	.05
❏ 148 Jonathan Hayes	.01	.05
❏ 149 Christian Okoye	.01	.05
❏ 150 Dino Hackett	.01	.05
❏ 151 Bryan Barker RC	.01	.05
❏ 152 Kevin Ross	.01	.05
❏ 153 Barry Word	.01	.05
❏ 154 Stan Thomas	.01	.05
❏ 155 Brad Muster	.01	.05
❏ 156 Donnell Woolford	.01	.05
❏ 157 Neal Anderson	.02	.10
❏ 158 Jim Covert	.01	.05
❏ 159 Jim Harbaugh	.08	.25
❏ 160 Shaun Gayle	.01	.05
❏ 161 William Perry	.02	.10
❏ 162 Ron Morris	.01	.05
❏ 163 Mark Bortz	.01	.05
❏ 164 James Thornton	.01	.05
❏ 165 Ron Rivera	.01	.05
❏ 166 Kevin Butler	.01	.05
❏ 167 Jay Hilgenberg	.01	.05
❏ 168 Peter Tom Willis	.01	.05
❏ 169 Johnny Bailey	.01	.05
❏ 170 Ron Cox	.01	.05
❏ 171 Keith Van Horne	.01	.05
❏ 172 Mark Carrier DB	.02	.10
❏ 173 Richard Dent	.02	.10
❏ 174 Wendell Davis	.01	.05
❏ 175 Trace Armstrong	.01	.05
❏ 176 Mike Singletary	.02	.10
❏ 177 Chris Zorich RC	.08	.25
❏ 178 Gerald Riggs	.01	.05
❏ 179 Jeff Bostic	.01	.05
❏ 180 Kurt Gouveia RC	.01	.05
❏ 181 Stan Humphries	.08	.25
❏ 182 Chip Lohmiller	.01	.05
❏ 183 Raleigh McKenzie RC	.01	.05
❏ 184 Alvin Walton	.01	.05
❏ 185 Earnest Byner	.01	.05
❏ 186 Markus Koch	.01	.05
❏ 187 Art Monk	.02	.10
❏ 188 Ed Simmons	.01	.05
❏ 189 Bobby Wilson RC	.01	.05
❏ 190 Charles Mann	.01	.05
❏ 191 Darrell Green	.01	.05
❏ 192 Mark Rypien	.02	.10
❏ 193 Ricky Sanders	.01	.05
❏ 194 Jim Lachey	.01	.05
❏ 195 Martin Mayhew	.01	.05
❏ 196 Gary Clark	.08	.25
❏ 197 Wilber Marshall	.01	.05
❏ 198 Darryl Grant	.01	.05
❏ 199 Don Warren	.01	.05
❏ 200 Ricky Ervins UER RC	.02	.10
❏ 201 Eric Allen	.01	.05
❏ 202 Anthony Toney	.01	.05
❏ 203 Ben Smith UER	.01	.05
❏ 204 David Alexander	.01	.05
❏ 205 Jerome Brown	.01	.05
❏ 206 Mike Golic	.01	.05
❏ 207 Roger Ruzek	.01	.05
❏ 208 Andre Waters	.01	.05
❏ 209 Fred Barnett	.08	.25
❏ 210 Randall Cunningham	.08	.25
❏ 211 Mike Schad	.01	.05
❏ 212 Reggie White	.08	.25
❏ 213 Mike Bellamy	.01	.05
❏ 214 Jeff Feagles RC	.01	.05
❏ 215 Wes Hopkins	.01	.05
❏ 216 Clyde Simmons	.01	.05
❏ 217 Keith Byars	.01	.05
❏ 218 Seth Joyner	.02	.10
❏ 219 Byron Evans	.01	.05
❏ 220 Keith Jackson	.02	.10
❏ 221 Calvin Williams	.02	.10
❏ 222 Mike Dumas RC	.01	.05
❏ 223 Ray Childress	.01	.05
❏ 224 Ernest Givins	.02	.10
❏ 225 Lamar Lathon	.01	.05
❏ 226 Greg Montgomery	.01	.05
❏ 227 Mike Munchak	.02	.10
❏ 228 Al Smith	.01	.05
❏ 229 Bubba McDowell	.01	.05
❏ 230 Haywood Jeffires	.02	.10
❏ 231 Drew Hill	.01	.05
❏ 232 William Fuller	.02	.10
❏ 233 Warren Moon	.08	.25
❏ 234 Doug Smith DT RC	.02	.10
❏ 235 Cris Dishman RC	.01	.05
❏ 236 Teddy Garcia RC	.01	.05
❏ 237 Richard Johnson CB RC	.01	.05
❏ 238 Bruce Matthews	.02	.10
❏ 239 Gerald McNeil	.01	.05
❏ 240 Johnny Meads	.01	.05
❏ 241 Curtis Duncan	.01	.05
❏ 242 Sean Jones	.02	.10
❏ 243 Lorenzo White	.01	.05
❏ 244 Rob Carpenter RC	.01	.05
❏ 245 Bruce Reimers	.01	.05
❏ 246 Ickey Woods	.01	.05
❏ 247 Lewis Billups	.01	.05
❏ 248 Boomer Esiason	.02	.10
❏ 249 Tim Krumrie	.01	.05
❏ 250 David Fulcher	.01	.05
❏ 251 Jim Breech	.01	.05
❏ 252 Mitchell Price RC	.01	.05
❏ 253 Carl Zander	.01	.05
❏ 254 Barney Bussey RC	.01	.05
❏ 255 Leon White	.01	.05
❏ 256 Eddie Brown	.01	.05
❏ 257 James Francis	.01	.05
❏ 258 Harold Green	.02	.10
❏ 259 Anthony Munoz	.02	.10
❏ 260 James Brooks	.02	.10
❏ 261 Kevin Walker UER RC	.01	.05
❏ 262 Bruce Kozerski	.01	.05
❏ 263 David Grant	.01	.05
❏ 264 Tim McGee	.01	.05
❏ 265 Rodney Holman	.01	.05
❏ 266 Dan McGwire RC	.01	.05
❏ 267 Andy Heck	.01	.05
❏ 268 Dave Krieg	.02	.10
❏ 269 David Wyman	.01	.05
❏ 270 Robert Blackmon	.01	.05
❏ 271 Grant Feasel	.01	.05
❏ 272 Patrick Hunter RC	.01	.05
❏ 273 Travis McNeal	.01	.05
❏ 274 John L. Williams	.01	.05
❏ 275 Tony Woods	.01	.05
❏ 276 Derrick Fenner	.01	.05
❏ 277 Jacob Green	.01	.05
❏ 278 Brian Blades	.02	.10
❏ 279 Eugene Robinson	.01	.05
❏ 280 Terry Wooden	.01	.05
❏ 281 Jeff Bryant	.01	.05
❏ 282 Norm Johnson	.01	.05
❏ 283 Joe Nash UER	.01	.05
❏ 284 Rick Donnelly	.01	.05
❏ 285 Chris Warren	.08	.25
❏ 286 Tommy Kane	.01	.05
❏ 287 Cortez Kennedy	.08	.25
❏ 288 Ernie Mills RC	.02	.10
❏ 289 Dermontti Dawson	.01	.05
❏ 290 Tunch Ilkin	.01	.05
❏ 291 Tim Worley	.01	.05
❏ 292 David Little	.01	.05
❏ 293 Gary Anderson K	.01	.05
❏ 294 Chris Calloway	.01	.05
❏ 295 Carnell Lake	.01	.05
❏ 296 Dan Stryzinski	.01	.05
❏ 297 Rod Woodson	.08	.25
❏ 298 John Jackson T RC	.01	.05
❏ 299 Bubby Brister	.01	.05
❏ 300 Thomas Everett	.01	.05
❏ 301 Merril Hoge	.01	.05
❏ 302 Eric Green	.01	.05
❏ 303 Greg Lloyd	.08	.25
❏ 304 Gerald Williams	.01	.05
❏ 305 Bryan Hinkle	.01	.05
❏ 306 Keith Willis	.01	.05
❏ 307 Louis Lipps	.01	.05
❏ 308 Donald Evans	.01	.05
❏ 309 D.J. Johnson	.01	.05
❏ 310 Wesley Carroll RC	.01	.05
❏ 311 Eric Martin	.01	.05
❏ 312 Brett Maxie	.01	.05
❏ 313 Rickey Jackson	.01	.05
❏ 314 Robert Massey	.01	.05
❏ 315 Pat Swilling	.02	.10
❏ 316 Morten Andersen	.01	.05
❏ 317 Toi Cook RC	.01	.05
❏ 318 Sam Mills	.01	.05
❏ 319 Steve Walsh	.01	.05
❏ 320 Tommy Barnhardt RC	.01	.05
❏ 321 Vince Buck	.01	.05
❏ 322 Joel Hilgenberg	.01	.05
❏ 323 Rueben Mayes	.01	.05
❏ 324 Renaldo Turnbull	.01	.05
❏ 325 Brett Perriman	.08	.25
❏ 326 Vaughan Johnson	.01	.05
❏ 327 Gill Fenerty	.01	.05
❏ 328 Stan Brock	.01	.05
❏ 329 Dalton Hilliard	.01	.05
❏ 330 Hoby Brenner	.01	.05
❏ 331 Craig Heyward	.02	.10
❏ 332 Jon Hand	.01	.05
❏ 333 Duane Bickett	.01	.05
❏ 334 Jessie Hester	.01	.05
❏ 335 Rohn Stark	.01	.05
❏ 336 Zefross Moss	.01	.05
❏ 337 Bill Brooks	.01	.05
❏ 338 Clarence Verdin	.01	.05
❏ 339 Mike Prior	.01	.05
❏ 340 Chip Banks	.01	.05
❏ 341 Dean Biasucci	.01	.05
❏ 342 Ray Donaldson	.01	.05
❏ 343 Jeff Herrod	.01	.05
❏ 344 Donnell Thompson	.01	.05
❏ 345 Chris Goode	.01	.05
❏ 346 Eugene Daniel	.01	.05
❏ 347 Pat Beach	.01	.05
❏ 348 Keith Taylor	.01	.05
❏ 349 Jeff George	.08	.25
❏ 350 Tony Siragusa RC	.02	.10
❏ 351 Randy Dixon	.01	.05
❏ 352 Albert Bentley	.01	.05
❏ 353 Russell Maryland RC	.08	.25
❏ 354 Mike Saxon	.01	.05
❏ 355 Godfrey Myles UER RC	.01	.05
❏ 356 Mark Stepnoski RC	.02	.10
❏ 357 James Washington RC	.01	.05

❑ 358 Jay Novacek .08 .25
❑ 359 Kelvin Martin .01 .05
❑ 360 Emmitt Smith UER 1.00 2.50
❑ 361 Jim Jeffcoat .01 .05
❑ 362 Alexander Wright .01 .05
❑ 363 James Dixon UER .01 .05
❑ 364 Alonzo Highsmith .01 .05
❑ 365 Daniel Stubbs .01 .05
❑ 366 Jack Del Rio .02 .10
❑ 367 Mark Tuinei RC .01 .05
❑ 368 Michael Irvin .08 .25
❑ 369 John Gesek RC .01 .05
❑ 370 Ken Willis .01 .05
❑ 371 Troy Aikman .30 .75
❑ 372 Jimmie Jones .01 .05
❑ 373 Nate Newton .02 .10
❑ 374 Issiac Holt .01 .05
❑ 375 Alvin Harper RC .08 .25
❑ 376 Todd Kalis .01 .05
❑ 377 Wade Wilson .02 .10
❑ 378 Joey Browner .01 .05
❑ 379 Chris Doleman .01 .05
❑ 380 Hassan Jones .01 .05
❑ 381 Henry Thomas .01 .05
❑ 382 Darrell Fullington .01 .05
❑ 383 Steve Jordan .01 .05
❑ 384 Gary Zimmerman .02 .10
❑ 385 Ray Berry .01 .05
❑ 386 Cris Carter .20 .50
❑ 387 Mike Merriweather .01 .05
❑ 388 Carl Lee .01 .05
❑ 389 Keith Millard .01 .05
❑ 390 Reggie Rutland .01 .05
❑ 391 Anthony Carter .02 .10
❑ 392 Mark Dusbabek .01 .05
❑ 393 Kirk Lowdermilk .01 .05
❑ 394 Al Noga UER .01 .05
❑ 395 Herschel Walker .02 .10
❑ 396 Randall McDaniel .02 .10
❑ 397 Herman Moore RC .08 .25
❑ 398 Eddie Murray .01 .05
❑ 399 Lomas Brown .01 .05
❑ 400 Marc Spindler .01 .05
❑ 401 Bennie Blades .01 .05
❑ 402 Kevin Glover .01 .05
❑ 403 Aubrey Matthews RC .01 .05
❑ 404 Michael Cofer .01 .05
❑ 405 Robert Clark .01 .05
❑ 406 Eric Andolsek .01 .05
❑ 407 William White .01 .05
❑ 408 Rodney Peete .02 .10
❑ 409 Mel Gray .02 .10
❑ 410 Jim Arnold .01 .05
❑ 411 Jeff Campbell .01 .05
❑ 412 Chris Spielman .02 .10
❑ 413 Jerry Ball .01 .05
❑ 414 Dan Owens .01 .05
❑ 415 Barry Sanders .50 1.25
❑ 416 Andre Ware .02 .10
❑ 417 Stanley Richard RC .01 .05
❑ 418 Gill Byrd .01 .05
❑ 419 John Kidd .01 .05
❑ 420 Sam Seale .01 .05
❑ 421 Gary Plummer .01 .05
❑ 422 Anthony Miller .02 .10
❑ 423 Ronnie Harmon .01 .05
❑ 424 Frank Cornish .01 .05
❑ 425 Marion Butts .02 .10
❑ 426 Leo Goeas .01 .05
❑ 427 Junior Seau .08 .25
❑ 428 Courtney Hall .01 .05
❑ 429 Leslie O'Neal .02 .10
❑ 430 Martin Bayless .01 .05
❑ 431 John Carney .01 .05
❑ 432 Lee Williams .01 .05
❑ 433 Arthur Cox .01 .05
❑ 434 Burt Grossman .01 .05
❑ 435 Nate Lewis RC .01 .05
❑ 436 Rod Bernstine .01 .05
❑ 437 Henry Rolling RC .01 .05
❑ 438 Billy Joe Tolliver .01 .05
❑ 439 Vinnie Clark RC .01 .05
❑ 440 Brian Noble .01 .05
❑ 441 Charles Wilson .01 .05
❑ 442 Don Majkowski .01 .05
❑ 443 Tim Harris .01 .05
❑ 444 Scott Stephen RC .01 .05
❑ 445 Perry Kemp .01 .05
❑ 446 Darrell Thompson .01 .05
❑ 447 Chris Jacke .01 .05
❑ 448 Mark Murphy .01 .05
❑ 449 Ed West .01 .05
❑ 450 LeRoy Butler .02 .10
❑ 451 Keith Woodside .01 .05
❑ 452 Tony Bennett .02 .10
❑ 453 Mark Lee .01 .05
❑ 454 James Campen RC .01 .05
❑ 455 Robert Brown .01 .05
❑ 456 Sterling Sharpe .08 .25
❑ 457A T.Mandarich ERR Bronc. 1.25 2.50
❑ 457B T.Mandarich COR Packers .01 .05
❑ 458 Johnny Holland .01 .05
❑ 459 Matt Brock RC .01 .05
❑ 460A Esera Tuaolo ERR RC .01 .05
❑ 460B Esera Tuaolo COR RC .01 .05
❑ 461 Freeman McNeil .01 .05
❑ 462 Terance Mathis UER 460 .08 .25
❑ 463 Rob Moore .08 .25
❑ 464 Darrell Davis RC .01 .05
❑ 465 Chris Burkett .01 .05
❑ 466 Jeff Criswell .01 .05
❑ 467 Tony Stargell .01 .05
❑ 468 Ken O'Brien .01 .05
❑ 469 Erik McMillan .01 .05
❑ 470 Jeff Lageman UER .01 .05
❑ 471 Pat Leahy .01 .05
❑ 472 Dennis Byrd .01 .05
❑ 473 Jim Sweeney .01 .05
❑ 474 Brad Baxter .01 .05
❑ 475 Joe Kelly .01 .05
❑ 476 Al Toon .02 .10
❑ 477 Joe Prokop .01 .05
❑ 478 Mark Boyer .01 .05
❑ 479 Kyle Clifton .01 .05
❑ 480 James Hasty .01 .05
❑ 481 Browning Nagle RC .01 .05
❑ 482 Gary Anderson RB .01 .05
❑ 483 Mark Carrier WR .08 .25
❑ 484 Ricky Reynolds .01 .05
❑ 485 Bruce Hill .01 .05
❑ 486 Steve Christie .01 .05
❑ 487 Paul Gruber .01 .05
❑ 488 Jesse Anderson .01 .05
❑ 489 Reggie Cobb .01 .05
❑ 490 Harry Hamilton .01 .05
❑ 491 Vinny Testaverde .02 .10
❑ 492 Mark Royals RC .01 .05
❑ 493 Keith McCants .01 .05
❑ 494 Ron Hall .01 .05
❑ 495 Ian Beckles .01 .05
❑ 496 Mark Robinson .01 .05
❑ 497 Reuben Davis .01 .05
❑ 498 Wayne Haddix .01 .05
❑ 499 Kevin Murphy .01 .05
❑ 500 Eugene Marve .01 .05
❑ 501 Broderick Thomas .01 .05
❑ 502 Eric Swann UER RC .08 .25
❑ 503 Ernie Jones .01 .05
❑ 504 Rich Camarillo .01 .05
❑ 505 Tim McDonald .01 .05
❑ 506 Freddie Joe Nunn .01 .05
❑ 507 Tim Jorden RC .01 .05
❑ 508 Johnny Johnson .01 .05
❑ 509 Eric Hill .01 .05
❑ 510 Derek Kennard .01 .05
❑ 511 Ricky Proehl .01 .05
❑ 512 Bill Lewis .01 .05
❑ 513 Roy Green .01 .05
❑ 514 Anthony Bell .01 .05
❑ 515 Timm Rosenbach .01 .05
❑ 516 Jim Wahler RC .01 .05
❑ 517 Anthony Thompson .01 .05
❑ 518 Ken Harvey .02 .10
❑ 519 Luis Sharpe .01 .05
❑ 520 Walter Reeves .01 .05
❑ 521 Lonnie Young .01 .05
❑ 522 Rod Saddler .01 .05
❑ 523 Todd Lyght RC .01 .05
❑ 524 Alvin Wright .01 .05
❑ 525 Flipper Anderson .01 .05
❑ 526 Jackie Slater .01 .05
❑ 527 Damone Johnson RC .01 .05
❑ 528 Cleveland Gary .01 .05
❑ 529 Mike Piel .01 .05
❑ 530 Buford McGee .01 .05
❑ 531 Michael Stewart .01 .05
❑ 532 Jim Everett .02 .10
❑ 533 Mike Wilcher .01 .05
❑ 534 Irv Pankey .01 .05
❑ 535 Bern Brostek .01 .05
❑ 536 Henry Ellard .02 .10
❑ 537 Doug Smith .01 .05
❑ 538 Larry Kelm .01 .05
❑ 539 Pat Terrell .01 .05
❑ 540 Tom Newberry .01 .05
❑ 541 Jerry Gray .01 .05
❑ 542 Kevin Greene .02 .10
❑ 543 Duval Love RC .01 .05
❑ 544 Frank Stams .01 .05
❑ 545 Mike Croel RC .01 .05
❑ 546 Mark Jackson .01 .05
❑ 547 Greg Kragen .01 .05
❑ 548 Karl Mecklenburg .01 .05
❑ 549 Simon Fletcher .01 .05
❑ 550 Bobby Humphrey .01 .05
❑ 551 Ken Lanier .01 .05
❑ 552 Vance Johnson .01 .05
❑ 553 Ron Holmes .01 .05
❑ 554 John Elway .50 1.25
❑ 555 Melvin Bratton .01 .05
❑ 556 Dennis Smith .01 .05
❑ 557 Ricky Nattiel .01 .05
❑ 558 Clarence Kay .01 .05
❑ 559 Michael Brooks .01 .05
❑ 560 Mike Horan .01 .05
❑ 561 Warren Powers .01 .05
❑ 562 Keith Kartz .01 .05
❑ 563 Shannon Sharpe .20 .50
❑ 564 Wymon Henderson .01 .05
❑ 565 Steve Atwater .01 .05
❑ 566 David Treadwell .01 .05
❑ 567 Bruce Pickens RC .01 .05
❑ 568 Jessie Tuggle .01 .05
❑ 569 Chris Hinton .01 .05
❑ 570 Keith Jones .01 .05
❑ 571 Bill Fralic .01 .05
❑ 572 Mike Rozier .01 .05
❑ 573 Scott Fulhage .01 .05
❑ 574 Floyd Dixon .01 .05
❑ 575 Andre Rison .02 .10
❑ 576 Darion Conner .01 .05
❑ 577 Brian Jordan .02 .10
❑ 578 Michael Haynes .08 .25
❑ 579 Oliver Barnett .01 .05
❑ 580 Shawn Collins .01 .05
❑ 581 Tim Green .01 .05
❑ 582 Deion Sanders .15 .40
❑ 583 Mike Kenn .01 .05
❑ 584 Mike Gann .01 .05
❑ 585 Chris Miller .02 .10
❑ 586 Tory Epps .01 .05
❑ 587 Steve Broussard .01 .05
❑ 588 Gary Wilkins .01 .05
❑ 589 Eric Turner RC .02 .10
❑ 590 Thane Gash .01 .05
❑ 591 Clay Matthews .02 .10
❑ 592 Mike Johnson .01 .05
❑ 593 Raymond Clayborn .01 .05
❑ 594 Leroy Hoard .02 .10
❑ 595 Reggie Langhorne .01 .05
❑ 596 Mike Baab .01 .05
❑ 597 Anthony Pleasant .01 .05
❑ 598 David Grayson .01 .05
❑ 599 Rob Burnett RC .02 .10
❑ 600 Frank Minnifield .01 .05
❑ 601 Gregg Rakoczy .01 .05
❑ 602 Eric Metcalf UER .08 .25
❑ 603 Paul Farren .01 .05
❑ 604 Brian Brennan .01 .05
❑ 605 Tony Jones T RC .01 .05
❑ 606 Stephen Braggs .01 .05
❑ 607 Kevin Mack .01 .05
❑ 608 Pat Harlow RC .01 .05
❑ 609 Marv Cook .01 .05
❑ 610 John Stephens .01 .05
❑ 611 Ed Reynolds .01 .05
❑ 612 Tim Goad .01 .05
❑ 613 Chris Singleton .01 .05
❑ 614 Bruce Armstrong .01 .05
❑ 615 Tommy Hodson .01 .05
❑ 616 Sammy Martin .01 .05
❑ 617 Andre Tippett .01 .05
❑ 618 Johnny Rembert .01 .05
❑ 619 Maurice Hurst .01 .05
❑ 620 Vincent Brown .01 .05
❑ 621 Ray Agnew .01 .05
❑ 622 Ronnie Lippett .01 .05

Card		
623 Greg McMurtry	.01	.05
624 Brent Williams	.01	.05
625 Jason Staurovsky	.01	.05
626 Marvin Allen	.01	.05
627 Hart Lee Dykes	.01	.05
628 Atlanta Falcons	.01	.05
629 Buffalo Bills	.01	.05
630 Chicago Bears	.02	.10
631 Cincinnati Bengals	.01	.05
632 Cleveland Browns	.01	.05
633 Dallas Cowboys	.01	.05
634 Denver Broncos	.01	.05
635 Detroit Lions	.01	.05
636 Green Bay Packers	.01	.05
637 Oilers TL/Warren Moon	.02	.10
638 Colts TL/Jeff George	.01	.05
639 Kansas City Chiefs	.01	.05
640 Los Angeles Raiders	.02	.10
641 Los Angeles Rams	.01	.05
642 Miami Dolphins	.01	.05
643 Minnesota Vikings	.02	.10
644 New Eng. Patriots	.01	.05
645 New Orleans Saints	.01	.05
646 New York Giants	.01	.05
647 New York Jets	.01	.05
648 Eagles TL/R.Cunningham	.01	.05
649 Phoenix Cardinals	.01	.05
650 Pittsburgh Steelers	.01	.05
651 San Diego Chargers	.01	.05
652 San Francisco 49ers	.01	.05
653 Seattle Seahawks	.01	.05
654 Tampa Bay Buccaneers	.01	.05
655 Washington Redskins	.01	.05
656 Checklist 1-132	.01	.05
657 Checklist 132-264	.01	.05
658 Checklist 265-396	.01	.05
659 Checklist 397-528	.01	.05
660 Checklist 529-660	.01	.05

1992 Topps

Card		
COMPLETE SET (759)	25.00	50.00
COMP.FACT.SET (680)	40.00	80.00
COMP.SERIES 1 (330)	10.00	20.00
COMP.SERIES 2 (330)	10.00	20.00
COMP.HIGH SER.(99)	5.00	10.00
COMP.FACT.HIGH SET (113)	5.00	12.00
1 Tim McGee	.01	.05
2 Rich Camarillo	.01	.05
3 Anthony Johnson	.02	.10
4 Larry Kelm	.01	.05
5 Irving Fryar	.02	.10
6 Joey Browner	.01	.05
7 Michael Walter	.01	.05
8 Cortez Kennedy	.02	.10
9 Reyna Thompson	.01	.05
10 John Friesz	.02	.10
11 Leroy Hoard	.02	.10
12 Steve McMichael	.02	.10
13 Marvin Washington	.01	.05
14 Clyde Simmons	.01	.05
15 Stephone Paige	.01	.05
16 Mike Utley	.02	.10
17 Tunch Ilkin	.01	.05
18 Lawrence Dawsey	.02	.10
19 Vance Johnson	.01	.05
20 Bryce Paup	.08	.25
21 Jeff Wright	.01	.05
22 Gill Fenerty	.01	.05
23 Lamar Lathon	.01	.05
24 Danny Copeland	.01	.05
25 Marcus Allen	.08	.25
26 Tim Green	.01	.05
27 Pete Stoyanovich	.01	.05
28 Alvin Harper	.02	.10
29 Roy Foster	.01	.05
30 Eugene Daniel	.01	.05
31 Luis Sharpe	.01	.05
32 Terry Wooden	.01	.05
33 Jim Breech	.01	.05
34 Randy Hilliard RC	.01	.05
35 Roman Phifer	.01	.05
36 Erik Howard	.01	.05
37 Chris Singleton	.01	.05
38 Matt Stover	.01	.05
39 Tim Irwin	.01	.05
40 Karl Mecklenburg	.01	.05
41 Joe Phillips	.01	.05
42 Bill Jones RC	.01	.05
43 Mark Carrier DB	.01	.05
44 George Jamison	.01	.05
45 Rob Taylor	.01	.05
46 Jeff Jaeger	.01	.05
47 Don Majkowski	.01	.05
48 Al Edwards	.01	.05
49 Curtis Duncan	.01	.05
50 Sam Mills	.01	.05
51 Terance Mathis	.02	.10
52 Brian Mitchell	.02	.10
53 Mike Pritchard	.02	.10
54 Calvin Williams	.02	.10
55 Hardy Nickerson	.02	.10
56 Nate Newton	.01	.05
57 Steve Wallace	.01	.05
58 John Offerdahl	.01	.05
59 Aeneas Williams	.02	.10
60 Lee Johnson	.01	.05
61 Ricardo McDonald RC	.01	.05
62 David Richards	.01	.05
63 Paul Gruber	.01	.05
64 Greg McMurtry	.01	.05
65 Jay Hilgenberg	.01	.05
66 Tim Grunhard	.01	.05
67 Dwayne White RC	.01	.05
68 Don Beebe	.01	.05
69 Simon Fletcher	.01	.05
70 Warren Moon	.08	.25
71 Chris Jacke	.01	.05
72 Steve Wisniewski UER	.01	.05
73 Mike Cofer	.01	.05
74 Tim Johnson UER	.01	.05
75 T.J. Turner	.01	.05
76 Scott Case	.01	.05
77 Michael Jackson	.02	.10
78 Jon Hand	.01	.05
79 Stan Brock	.01	.05
80 Robert Blackmon	.01	.05
81 D.J. Johnson	.01	.05
82 Damone Johnson	.01	.05
83 Marc Spindler	.01	.05
84 Larry Brown DB	.01	.05
85 Ray Berry	.01	.05
86 Andre Waters	.01	.05
87 Carlos Huerta	.01	.05
88 Brad Muster	.01	.05
89 Chuck Cecil	.01	.05
90 Nick Lowery	.01	.05
91 Cornelius Bennett	.02	.10
92 Jessie Tuggle	.01	.05
93 Mark Schlereth RC	.01	.05
94 Vestee Jackson	.01	.05
95 Eric Bieniemy	.01	.05
96 Jeff Hostetler	.02	.10
97 Ken Lanier	.01	.05
98 Wayne Haddix	.01	.05
99 Lorenzo White	.01	.05
100 Mervyn Fernandez	.01	.05
101 Brent Williams	.01	.05
102 Ian Beckles	.01	.05
103 Harris Barton	.01	.05
104 Edgar Bennett RC	.08	.25
105 Mike Pitts	.01	.05
106 Fuad Reveiz	.01	.05
107 Vernon Turner	.01	.05
108 Tracy Hayworth RC	.01	.05
109 Checklist 1-110	.01	.05
110 Tom Waddle	.01	.05
111 Fred Stokes	.01	.05
112 Howard Ballard	.01	.05
113 David Szott	.01	.05
114 Tim McKyer	.01	.05
115 Kyle Clifton	.01	.05
116 Tony Bennett	.01	.05
117 Joel Hilgenberg	.01	.05
118 Dwayne Harper	.01	.05
119 Mike Baab	.01	.05
120 Mark Clayton	.02	.10
121 Eric Swann	.02	.10
122 Neil O'Donnell	.02	.10
123 Mike Munchak	.02	.10
124 Howie Long	.08	.25
125 John Elway	.50	1.25
126 Joe Prokop	.01	.05
127 Pepper Johnson	.01	.05
128 Richard Dent	.02	.10
129 Robert Porcher RC	.08	.25
130 Earnest Byner	.01	.05
131 Kent Hull	.01	.05
132 Mike Merriweather	.01	.05
133 Scott Fulhage	.01	.05
134 Kevin Porter	.01	.05
135 Tony Casillas	.01	.05
136 Dean Biasucci	.01	.05
137 Ben Smith	.01	.05
138 Bruce Kozerski	.01	.05
139 Jeff Campbell	.01	.05
140 Kevin Greene	.02	.10
141 Gary Plummer	.01	.05
142 Vincent Brown	.01	.05
143 Ron Hall	.01	.05
144 Louie Aguiar RC	.01	.05
145 Mark Duper	.01	.05
146 Jesse Sapolu	.01	.05
147 Jeff Gossett	.01	.05
148 Brian Noble	.01	.05
149 Derek Russell	.01	.05
150 Carlton Bailey RC	.01	.05
151 Kelly Goodburn	.01	.05
152 Audray McMillian UER	.01	.05
153 Neal Anderson	.01	.05
154 Bill Maas	.01	.05
155 Rickey Jackson	.01	.05
156 Chris Miller	.02	.10
157 Darren Comeaux	.01	.05
158 David Williams	.01	.05
159 Rich Gannon	.08	.25
160 Kevin Mack	.01	.05
161 Jim Arnold	.01	.05
162 Reggie White	.08	.25
163 Leonard Russell	.02	.10
164 Doug Smith	.01	.05
165 Tony Mandarich	.01	.05
166 Greg Lloyd	.02	.10
167 Jumbo Elliott	.01	.05
168 Jonathan Hayes	.01	.05
169 Jim Ritcher	.01	.05
170 Mike Kenn	.01	.05
171 James Washington	.01	.05
172 Tim Harris	.01	.05
173 James Thornton	.01	.05
174 John Brandes RC	.01	.05
175 Fred McAfee RC	.01	.05
176 Henry Rolling	.01	.05
177 Tony Paige	.01	.05
178 Jay Schroeder	.01	.05
179 Jeff Herrod	.01	.05
180 Emmitt Smith	.60	1.50
181 Wymon Henderson	.01	.05
182 Rob Moore	.02	.10
183 Robert Wilson	.01	.05
184 Michael Zordich RC	.01	.05
185 Jim Harbaugh	.08	.25
186 Vince Workman	.01	.05
187 Ernest Givins	.02	.10
188 Herschel Walker	.02	.10
189 Dan Fike	.01	.05
190 Seth Joyner	.01	.05
191 Steve Young	.25	.60
192 Dennis Gibson	.01	.05
193 Darryl Talley	.01	.05
194 Emile Harry	.01	.05
195 Bill Fralic	.01	.05
196 Michael Stewart	.01	.05
197 James Francis	.01	.05
198 Jerome Henderson	.01	.05
199 John L. Williams	.01	.05
200 Rod Woodson	.08	.25
201 Mike Farr	.01	.05
202 Greg Montgomery	.01	.05
203 Andre Collins	.01	.05
204 Scott Miller	.01	.05
205 Clay Matthews	.02	.10
206 Ethan Horton	.01	.05
207 Rich Miano	.01	.05
208 Chris Mims RC	.01	.05

❑ 209 Anthony Morgan	.01	.05
❑ 210 Rodney Hampton	.02	.10
❑ 211 Chris Hinton	.01	.05
❑ 212 Esera Tuaolo	.01	.05
❑ 213 Shane Conlan	.01	.05
❑ 214 John Carney	.01	.05
❑ 215 Kenny Walker	.01	.05
❑ 216 Scott Radecic	.01	.05
❑ 217 Chris Martin	.01	.05
❑ 218 Checklist 111-220 UER	.01	.05
❑ 219 Wesley Carroll	.01	.05
❑ 220 Bill Romanowski	.01	.05
❑ 221 Reggie Cobb	.01	.05
❑ 222 Alfred Anderson	.01	.05
❑ 223 Cleveland Gary	.01	.05
❑ 224 Eddie Blake RC	.01	.05
❑ 225 Chris Spielman	.02	.10
❑ 226 John Roper	.01	.05
❑ 227 George Thomas RC	.01	.05
❑ 228 Jeff Faulkner	.01	.05
❑ 229 Chip Lohmiller UER	.01	.05
❑ 230 Hugh Millen	.01	.05
❑ 231 Ray Horton	.01	.05
❑ 232 James Campen	.01	.05
❑ 233 Howard Cross	.01	.05
❑ 234 Keith McKeller	.01	.05
❑ 235 Dino Hackett	.01	.05
❑ 236 Jerome Brown	.01	.05
❑ 237 Andy Heck	.01	.05
❑ 238 Rodney Holman	.01	.05
❑ 239 Bruce Matthews	.01	.05
❑ 240 Jeff Lageman	.01	.05
❑ 241 Bobby Hebert	.01	.05
❑ 242 Gary Anderson K	.01	.05
❑ 243 Mark Bortz	.01	.05
❑ 244 Rich Moran	.01	.05
❑ 245 Jeff Uhlenhake	.01	.05
❑ 246 Ricky Sanders	.01	.05
❑ 247 Clarence Kay	.01	.05
❑ 248 Ed King	.01	.05
❑ 249 Eddie Anderson	.01	.05
❑ 250 Amp Lee RC	.01	.05
❑ 251 Norm Johnson	.01	.05
❑ 252 Michael Carter	.01	.05
❑ 253 Felix Wright	.01	.05
❑ 254 Leon Seals	.01	.05
❑ 255 Nate Lewis	.01	.05
❑ 256 Kevin Call	.01	.05
❑ 257 Darryl Henley	.01	.05
❑ 258 Jon Vaughn	.01	.05
❑ 259 Matt Bahr	.01	.05
❑ 260 Johnny Johnson	.01	.05
❑ 261 Ken Norton	.02	.10
❑ 262 Wendell Davis	.01	.05
❑ 263 Eugene Robinson	.01	.05
❑ 264 David Treadwell	.01	.05
❑ 265 Michael Haynes	.02	.10
❑ 266 Robb Thomas	.01	.05
❑ 267 Nate Odomes	.01	.05
❑ 268 Martin Mayhew	.01	.05
❑ 269 Perry Kemp	.01	.05
❑ 270 Jerry Ball	.01	.05
❑ 271 Tommy Vardell RC	.01	.05
❑ 272 Ernie Mills	.01	.05
❑ 273 Mo Lewis	.01	.05
❑ 274 Roger Ruzek	.01	.05
❑ 275 Steve Smith	.01	.05
❑ 276 Bo Orlando RC	.01	.05
❑ 277 Louis Oliver	.01	.05
❑ 278 Toi Cook	.01	.05
❑ 279 Eddie Brown	.01	.05
❑ 280 Keith McCants	.01	.05
❑ 281 Rob Burnett	.01	.05
❑ 282 Keith DeLong	.01	.05
❑ 283 Stan Thomas UER	.01	.05
❑ 284 Robert Brown	.01	.05
❑ 285 John Alt	.01	.05
❑ 286 Randy Dixon	.01	.05
❑ 287 Siran Stacy RC	.01	.05
❑ 288 Ray Agnew	.01	.05
❑ 289 Darion Conner	.01	.05
❑ 290 Kirk Lowdermilk	.01	.05
❑ 291 Greg Jackson	.01	.05
❑ 292 Ken Harvey	.01	.05
❑ 293 Jacob Green	.01	.05
❑ 294 Mark Tuinei	.01	.05
❑ 295 Mark Rypien	.01	.05
❑ 296 Gerald Robinson RC	.01	.05
❑ 297 Broderick Thompson	.01	.05
❑ 298 Doug Widell	.01	.05
❑ 299 Carwell Gardner	.01	.05
❑ 300 Barry Sanders	.50	1.25
❑ 301 Eric Metcalf	.02	.10
❑ 302 Eric Thomas	.01	.05
❑ 303 Terrell Buckley RC	.01	.05
❑ 304 Byron Evans	.01	.05
❑ 305 Johnny Hector	.01	.05
❑ 306 Steve Broussard	.01	.05
❑ 307 Gene Atkins	.01	.05
❑ 308 Terry McDaniel	.01	.05
❑ 309 Charles McRae	.01	.05
❑ 310 Jim Lachey	.01	.05
❑ 311 Pat Harlow	.01	.05
❑ 312 Kevin Butler	.01	.05
❑ 313 Scott Stephen	.01	.05
❑ 314 Dermontti Dawson	.01	.05
❑ 315 Johnny Meads	.01	.05
❑ 316 Checklist 221-330	.01	.05
❑ 317 Aaron Craver	.01	.05
❑ 318 Michael Brooks	.01	.05
❑ 319 Guy McIntyre	.01	.05
❑ 320 Thurman Thomas	.08	.25
❑ 321 Courtney Hall	.01	.05
❑ 322 Dan Saleaumua	.01	.05
❑ 323 Vinson Smith RC	.01	.05
❑ 324 Steve Jordan	.01	.05
❑ 325 Walter Reeves	.01	.05
❑ 326 Erik Kramer	.02	.10
❑ 327 Duane Bickett	.01	.05
❑ 328 Tom Newberry	.01	.05
❑ 329 John Kasay	.01	.05
❑ 330 Dave Meggett	.02	.10
❑ 331 Kevin Ross	.01	.05
❑ 332 Keith Hamilton RC	.02	.10
❑ 333 Dwight Stone	.01	.05
❑ 334 Mel Gray	.02	.10
❑ 335 Harry Galbreath	.01	.05
❑ 336 William Perry	.02	.10
❑ 337 Brian Blades	.02	.10
❑ 338 Randall McDaniel	.02	.10
❑ 339 Pat Coleman RC	.01	.05
❑ 340 Michael Irvin	.08	.25
❑ 341 Checklist 331-440	.01	.05
❑ 342 Chris Mohr	.01	.05
❑ 343 Greg Davis	.01	.05
❑ 344 Dave Cadigan	.01	.05
❑ 345 Art Monk	.02	.10
❑ 346 Tim Goad	.01	.05
❑ 347 Vinnie Clark	.01	.05
❑ 348 David Fulcher	.01	.05
❑ 349 Craig Heyward	.02	.10
❑ 350 Ronnie Lott	.02	.10
❑ 351 Dexter Carter	.01	.05
❑ 352 Mark Jackson	.01	.05
❑ 353 Brian Jordan	.02	.10
❑ 354 Ray Donaldson	.01	.05
❑ 355 Jim Price	.01	.05
❑ 356 Rod Bernstine	.01	.05
❑ 357 Tony Mayberry RC	.01	.05
❑ 358 Richard Brown RC	.01	.05
❑ 359 David Alexander	.01	.05
❑ 360 Haywood Jeffires	.02	.10
❑ 361 Henry Thomas	.01	.05
❑ 362 Jeff Graham	.08	.25
❑ 363 Don Warren	.01	.05
❑ 364 Scott Davis	.01	.05
❑ 365 Harlon Barnett	.01	.05
❑ 366 Mark Collins	.01	.05
❑ 367 Rick Tuten	.01	.05
❑ 368 Lonnie Marts RC	.01	.05
❑ 369 Dennis Smith	.01	.05
❑ 370 Steve Tasker	.02	.10
❑ 371 Robert Massey	.01	.05
❑ 372 Ricky Reynolds	.01	.05
❑ 373 Alvin Wright	.01	.05
❑ 374 Kelvin Martin	.01	.05
❑ 375 Vince Buck	.01	.05
❑ 376 John Kidd	.01	.05
❑ 377 William White	.01	.05
❑ 378 Bryan Cox	.02	.10
❑ 379 Jamie Dukes RC	.01	.05
❑ 380 Anthony Munoz	.02	.10
❑ 381 Mark Gunn RC	.01	.05
❑ 382 Keith Henderson	.01	.05
❑ 383 Charles Wilson	.01	.05
❑ 384 Shawn McCarthy RC	.01	.05
❑ 385 Ernie Jones	.01	.05
❑ 386 Nick Bell	.01	.05
❑ 387 Derrick Walker	.01	.05
❑ 388 Mark Stepnoski	.02	.10
❑ 389 Broderick Thomas	.01	.05
❑ 390 Reggie Roby	.01	.05
❑ 391 Bubba McDowell	.01	.05
❑ 392 Eric Martin	.01	.05
❑ 393 Toby Caston RC	.01	.05
❑ 394 Bern Brostek	.01	.05
❑ 395 Christian Okoye	.01	.05
❑ 396 Frank Minnifield	.01	.05
❑ 397 Mike Golic	.01	.05
❑ 398 Grant Feasel	.01	.05
❑ 399 Michael Ball	.01	.05
❑ 400 Mike Croel	.01	.05
❑ 401 Maury Buford	.01	.05
❑ 402 Jeff Bostic UER	.01	.05
❑ 403 Sean Landeta	.01	.05
❑ 404 Terry Allen	.08	.25
❑ 405 Donald Evans	.01	.05
❑ 406 Don Mosebar	.01	.05
❑ 407 D.J. Dozier	.01	.05
❑ 408 Bruce Pickens	.01	.05
❑ 409 Jim Dombrowski	.01	.05
❑ 410 Deron Cherry	.01	.05
❑ 411 Richard Johnson CB	.01	.05
❑ 412 Alexander Wright	.01	.05
❑ 413 Tom Rathman	.01	.05
❑ 414 Mark Dennis	.01	.05
❑ 415 Phil Hansen	.01	.05
❑ 416 Lonnie Young	.01	.05
❑ 417 Burt Grossman	.01	.05
❑ 418 Tony Covington	.01	.05
❑ 419 John Stephens	.01	.05
❑ 420 Jim Everett	.02	.10
❑ 421 Johnny Holland	.01	.05
❑ 422 Mike Barber RC	.01	.05
❑ 423 Carl Lee	.01	.05
❑ 424 Craig Patterson RC	.01	.05
❑ 425 Greg Townsend	.01	.05
❑ 426 Brett Perriman	.08	.25
❑ 427 Morten Andersen	.01	.05
❑ 428 John Gesek	.01	.05
❑ 429 Bryan Barker	.01	.05
❑ 430 John Taylor	.02	.10
❑ 431 Donnell Woolford	.01	.05
❑ 432 Ron Holmes	.01	.05
❑ 433 Lee Williams	.01	.05
❑ 434 Alfred Oglesby	.01	.05
❑ 435 Jarrod Bunch	.01	.05
❑ 436 Carlton Haselrig RC	.01	.05
❑ 437 Rufus Porter	.01	.05
❑ 438 Rohn Stark	.01	.05
❑ 439 Tony Jones T	.01	.05
❑ 440 Andre Rison	.02	.10
❑ 441 Eric Hill	.01	.05
❑ 442 Jesse Solomon	.01	.05
❑ 443 Jackie Slater	.01	.05
❑ 444 Donnie Elder	.01	.05
❑ 445 Brett Maxie	.01	.05
❑ 446 Max Montoya	.01	.05
❑ 447 Will Wolford	.01	.05
❑ 448 Craig Taylor	.01	.05
❑ 449 Jimmie Jones	.01	.05
❑ 450 Anthony Carter	.02	.10
❑ 451 Brian Bollinger RC	.01	.05
❑ 452 Checklist 441-550	.01	.05
❑ 453 Brad Edwards	.01	.05
❑ 454 Gene Chilton RC	.01	.05
❑ 455 Eric Allen	.01	.05
❑ 456 William Roberts	.01	.05
❑ 457 Eric Green	.01	.05
❑ 458 Irv Eatman	.01	.05
❑ 459 Derrick Thomas	.08	.25
❑ 460 Tommy Kane	.01	.05
❑ 461 LeRoy Butler	.01	.05
❑ 462 Oliver Barnett	.01	.05
❑ 463 Anthony Smith	.01	.05
❑ 464 Cris Dishman	.01	.05
❑ 465 Pat Terrell	.01	.05
❑ 466 Greg Kragen	.01	.05
❑ 467 Rodney Peete	.02	.10
❑ 468 Willie Drewrey	.01	.05
❑ 469 Jim Wilks	.01	.05
❑ 470 Vince Newsome	.01	.05
❑ 471 Chris Gardocki	.01	.05
❑ 472 Chris Chandler	.08	.25
❑ 473 George Thornton	.01	.05
❑ 474 Albert Lewis	.01	.05
❑ 475 Kevin Glover	.01	.05

Card		
❑ 476 Joe Bowden RC	.01	.05
❑ 477 Harry Sydney	.01	.05
❑ 478 Bob Golic	.01	.05
❑ 479 Tony Zendejas	.01	.05
❑ 480 Brad Baxter	.01	.05
❑ 481 Steve Beuerlein	.02	.10
❑ 482 Mark Higgs	.01	.05
❑ 483 Drew Hill	.01	.05
❑ 484 Bryan Millard	.01	.05
❑ 485 Mark Kelso	.01	.05
❑ 486 David Grant	.01	.05
❑ 487 Gary Zimmerman	.01	.05
❑ 488 Leonard Marshall	.01	.05
❑ 489 Keith Jackson	.02	.10
❑ 490 Sterling Sharpe	.08	.25
❑ 491 Ferrell Edmunds	.01	.05
❑ 492 Wilber Marshall	.01	.05
❑ 493 Charles Haley	.02	.10
❑ 494 Riki Ellison	.01	.05
❑ 495 Bill Brooks	.01	.05
❑ 496 Bill Hawkins	.01	.05
❑ 497 Erik Williams	.01	.05
❑ 498 Leon Searcy RC	.01	.05
❑ 499 Mike Horan	.01	.05
❑ 500 Pat Swilling	.01	.05
❑ 501 Maurice Hurst	.01	.05
❑ 502 William Fuller	.01	.05
❑ 503 Tim Newton	.01	.05
❑ 504 Lorenzo Lynch	.01	.05
❑ 505 Tim Barnett	.01	.05
❑ 506 Tom Thayer	.01	.05
❑ 507 Chris Burkett	.01	.05
❑ 508 Ronnie Harmon	.01	.05
❑ 509 James Brooks	.02	.10
❑ 510 Bennie Blades	.01	.05
❑ 511 Roger Craig	.02	.10
❑ 512 Tony Woods	.01	.05
❑ 513 Greg Lewis	.01	.05
❑ 514 Erric Pegram	.02	.10
❑ 515 Elvis Patterson	.01	.05
❑ 516 Jeff Cross	.01	.05
❑ 517 Myron Guyton	.01	.05
❑ 518 Jay Novacek	.02	.10
❑ 519 Leo Barker RC	.01	.05
❑ 520 Keith Byars	.01	.05
❑ 521 Dalton Hilliard	.01	.05
❑ 522 Ted Washington	.01	.05
❑ 523 Dexter McNabb RC	.01	.05
❑ 524 Frank Reich	.02	.10
❑ 525 Henry Ellard	.02	.10
❑ 526 Barry Foster	.02	.10
❑ 527 Barry Word	.01	.05
❑ 528 Gary Anderson RB	.01	.05
❑ 529 Reggie Rutland	.01	.05
❑ 530 Stephen Baker	.01	.05
❑ 531 John Flannery	.01	.05
❑ 532 Steve Wright	.01	.05
❑ 533 Eric Sanders	.01	.05
❑ 534 Bob Whitfield RC	.01	.05
❑ 535 Gaston Green	.01	.05
❑ 536 Anthony Pleasant	.01	.05
❑ 537 Jeff Bryant	.01	.05
❑ 538 Jarvis Williams	.01	.05
❑ 539 Jim Morrissey	.01	.05
❑ 540 Andre Tippett	.01	.05
❑ 541 Gill Byrd	.01	.05
❑ 542 Raleigh McKenzie	.01	.05
❑ 543 Jim Sweeney	.01	.05
❑ 544 David Lutz	.01	.05
❑ 545 Wayne Martin	.01	.05
❑ 546 Karl Wilson	.01	.05
❑ 547 Pierce Holt	.01	.05
❑ 548 Doug Smith	.01	.05
❑ 549 Nolan Harrison RC	.01	.05
❑ 550 Freddie Joe Nunn	.01	.05
❑ 551 Eric Moore	.01	.05
❑ 552 Cris Carter	.20	.50
❑ 553 Kevin Gogan	.01	.05
❑ 554 Harold Green	.01	.05
❑ 555 Kenneth Davis	.01	.05
❑ 556 Travis McNeal	.01	.05
❑ 557 Jim C. Jensen	.01	.05
❑ 558 Willie Green	.01	.05
❑ 559 Scott Galbraith RC	.01	.05
❑ 560 Louis Lipps	.01	.05
❑ 561 Matt Brock	.01	.05
❑ 562 Mike Prior	.01	.05
❑ 563 Checklist 551-660	.01	.05
❑ 564 Robert Delpino	.01	.05
❑ 565 Vinny Testaverde	.02	.10
❑ 566 Willie Gault	.02	.10
❑ 567 Quinn Early	.02	.10
❑ 568 Eric Moten	.01	.05
❑ 569 Lance Smith	.01	.05
❑ 570 Darrell Green	.01	.05
❑ 571 Moe Gardner	.01	.05
❑ 572 Steve Atwater	.01	.05
❑ 573 Ray Childress	.01	.05
❑ 574 Dave Krieg	.02	.10
❑ 575 Bruce Armstrong	.01	.05
❑ 576 Fred Barnett	.08	.25
❑ 577 Don Griffin	.01	.05
❑ 578 David Brandon RC	.01	.05
❑ 579 Robert Young	.01	.05
❑ 580 Keith Van Horne	.01	.05
❑ 581 Jeff Criswell	.01	.05
❑ 582 Lewis Tillman	.01	.05
❑ 583 Bubby Brister	.01	.05
❑ 584 Aaron Wallace	.01	.05
❑ 585 Chris Doleman	.01	.05
❑ 586 Marty Carter RC	.01	.05
❑ 587 Chris Warren	.08	.25
❑ 588 David Griggs	.01	.05
❑ 589 Darrell Thompson	.01	.05
❑ 590 Marion Butts	.01	.05
❑ 591 Scott Norwood	.01	.05
❑ 592 Lomas Brown	.01	.05
❑ 593 Daryl Johnston	.08	.25
❑ 594 Alonzo Mitz RC	.01	.05
❑ 595 Tommy Barnhardt	.01	.05
❑ 596 Tim Jorden	.01	.05
❑ 597 Neil Smith	.08	.25
❑ 598 Todd Marinovich	.01	.05
❑ 599 Sean Jones	.01	.05
❑ 600 Clarence Verdin	.01	.05
❑ 601 Trace Armstrong	.01	.05
❑ 602 Steve Bono RC	.08	.25
❑ 603 Mark Ingram	.01	.05
❑ 604 Flipper Anderson	.01	.05
❑ 605 James Jones DT	.01	.05
❑ 606 Al Noga	.01	.05
❑ 607 Rick Bryan	.01	.05
❑ 608 Eugene Lockhart	.01	.05
❑ 609 Charles Mann	.01	.05
❑ 610 James Hasty	.01	.05
❑ 611 Jeff Feagles	.01	.05
❑ 612 Tim Brown	.08	.25
❑ 613 David Little	.01	.05
❑ 614 Keith Sims	.01	.05
❑ 615 Kevin Murphy	.01	.05
❑ 616 Ray Crockett	.01	.05
❑ 617 Jim Jeffcoat	.01	.05
❑ 618 Patrick Hunter	.01	.05
❑ 619 Keith Kartz	.01	.05
❑ 620 Peter Tom Willis	.01	.05
❑ 621 Vaughan Johnson	.01	.05
❑ 622 Shawn Jefferson	.01	.05
❑ 623 Anthony Thompson	.01	.05
❑ 624 John Rienstra	.01	.05
❑ 625 Don Maggs	.01	.05
❑ 626 Todd Lyght	.01	.05
❑ 627 Brent Jones	.02	.10
❑ 628 Todd McNair	.01	.05
❑ 629 Winston Moss	.01	.05
❑ 630 Mark Carrier WR	.02	.10
❑ 631 Dan Owens	.01	.05
❑ 632 Sammie Smith UER	.01	.05
❑ 633 James Lofton	.02	.10
❑ 634 Paul McJulien RC	.01	.05
❑ 635 Tony Tolbert	.01	.05
❑ 636 Carnell Lake	.01	.05
❑ 637 Gary Clark	.08	.25
❑ 638 Brian Washington	.01	.05
❑ 639 Jessie Hester	.01	.05
❑ 640 Doug Riesenberg	.01	.05
❑ 641 Joe Walter RC	.01	.05
❑ 642 John Rade	.01	.05
❑ 643 Wes Hopkins	.01	.05
❑ 644 Kelly Stouffer	.01	.05
❑ 645 Marv Cook	.01	.05
❑ 646 Ken Clarke	.01	.05
❑ 647 Bobby Humphrey UER	.01	.05
❑ 648 Tim McDonald	.01	.05
❑ 649 Donald Frank RC	.01	.05
❑ 650 Richmond Webb	.01	.05
❑ 651 Lemuel Stinson	.01	.05
❑ 652 Merton Hanks	.02	.10
❑ 653 Frank Warren	.01	.05
❑ 654 Thomas Benson	.01	.05
❑ 655 Al Smith	.01	.05
❑ 656 Steve DeBerg	.01	.05
❑ 657 Jayice Pearson RC	.01	.05
❑ 658 Joe Morris	.01	.05
❑ 659 Fred Strickland	.01	.05
❑ 660 Kelvin Pritchett	.01	.05
❑ 661 Lewis Billups	.01	.05
❑ 662 Todd Collins RC	.01	.05
❑ 663 Corey Miller RC	.01	.05
❑ 664 Levon Kirkland RC	.01	.05
❑ 665 Jerry Rice	.30	.75
❑ 666 Mike Lodish RC	.01	.05
❑ 667 Chuck Smith RC	.01	.05
❑ 668 Lance Olberding RC	.01	.05
❑ 669 Kevin Smith RC	.01	.05
❑ 670 Dale Carter RC	.02	.10
❑ 671 Sean Gilbert RC	.02	.10
❑ 672 Ken O'Brien	.01	.05
❑ 673 Ricky Proehl	.01	.05
❑ 674 Junior Seau	.08	.25
❑ 675 Courtney Hawkins RC	.02	.10
❑ 676 Eddie Robinson RC	.01	.05
❑ 677 Tommy Jeter RC	.01	.05
❑ 678 Jeff George	.08	.25
❑ 679 Cary Conklin	.01	.05
❑ 680 Rueben Mayes	.01	.05
❑ 681 Sean Lumpkin RC	.01	.05
❑ 682 Dan Marino	.50	1.25
❑ 683 Ed McDaniel RC	.01	.05
❑ 684 Greg Skrepenak RC	.01	.05
❑ 685 Tracy Scroggins RC	.01	.05
❑ 686 Tommy Maddox RC	.75	2.00
❑ 687 Mike Singletary	.02	.10
❑ 688 Patrick Rowe RC	.01	.05
❑ 689 Phillippi Sparks RC	.01	.05
❑ 690 Joel Steed RC	.01	.05
❑ 691 Kevin Fagan	.01	.05
❑ 692 Deion Sanders	.20	.50
❑ 693 Bruce Smith	.08	.25
❑ 694 David Klingler RC	.01	.05
❑ 695 Clayton Holmes RC	.01	.05
❑ 696 Brett Favre	2.50	6.00
❑ 697 Marc Boutte RC	.01	.05
❑ 698 Dwayne Sabb RC	.01	.05
❑ 699 Ed McCaffrey	.10	.30
❑ 700 Randall Cunningham	.08	.25
❑ 701 Quentin Coryatt RC	.01	.05
❑ 702 Bernie Kosar	.02	.10
❑ 703 Vaughn Dunbar RC	.01	.05
❑ 704 Browning Nagle	.01	.05
❑ 705 Mark Wheeler RC	.01	.05
❑ 706 Paul Siever RC	.01	.05
❑ 707 Anthony Miller	.02	.10
❑ 708 Corey Widmer RC	.01	.05
❑ 709 Eric Dickerson	.02	.10
❑ 710 Martin Bayless	.01	.05
❑ 711 Jason Hanson RC	.02	.10
❑ 712 Michael Dean Perry	.02	.10
❑ 713 Billy Joe Tolliver UER	.01	.05
❑ 714 Chad Hennings RC	.02	.10
❑ 715 Bucky Richardson RC	.01	.05
❑ 716 Steve Israel RC	.01	.05
❑ 717 Robert Harris RC	.01	.05
❑ 718 Timm Rosenbach	.01	.05
❑ 719 Joe Montana	.50	1.25
❑ 720 Derek Brown TE RC	.01	.05
❑ 721 Robert Brooks RC	.30	.75
❑ 722 Boomer Esiason	.02	.10
❑ 723 Troy Auzenne RC	.01	.05
❑ 724 John Fina RC	.01	.05
❑ 725 Chris Crooms RC	.01	.05
❑ 726 Eugene Chung RC	.01	.05
❑ 727 Darren Woodson RC	.08	.25
❑ 728 Leslie O'Neal	.02	.10
❑ 729 Dan McGwire	.01	.05
❑ 730 Al Toon	.02	.10
❑ 731 Michael Brandon RC	.01	.05
❑ 732 Steve DeOssie	.01	.05
❑ 733 Jim Kelly	.08	.25
❑ 734 Webster Slaughter	.01	.05
❑ 735 Tony Smith RC	.01	.05
❑ 736 Shane Collins RC	.01	.05
❑ 737 Randal Hill	.01	.05
❑ 738 Chris Holder RC	.01	.05
❑ 739 Russell Maryland	.01	.05
❑ 740 Carl Pickens RC	.08	.25
❑ 741 Andre Reed	.02	.10
❑ 742 Steve Emtman RC	.01	.05

Card		
❑ 743 Carl Banks	.01	.05
❑ 744 Troy Aikman	.30	.75
❑ 745 Mark Royals	.01	.05
❑ 746 J.J.Birden	.01	.05
❑ 747 Michael Cofer	.01	.05
❑ 748 Darryl Ashmore RC	.01	.05
❑ 749 Dion Lambert RC	.01	.05
❑ 750 Phil Simms	.02	.10
❑ 751 Reggie E.White RC	.01	.05
❑ 752 Harvey Williams	.08	.25
❑ 753 Ty Detmer	.08	.25
❑ 754 Tony Brooks RC	.01	.05
❑ 755 Steve Christie	.01	.05
❑ 756 Lawrence Taylor	.08	.25
❑ 757 Merril Hoge	.01	.05
❑ 758 Robert Jones RC	.01	.05
❑ 759 Checklist 661-759	.01	.05

1993 Topps

Card		
❑ COMPLETE SET (660)	12.00	30.00
❑ COMP.FACT.SET (673)	75.00	125.00
❑ COMP.SERIES 1 (330)	6.00	15.00
❑ COMP.SERIES 2 (330)	6.00	15.00
❑ 1 Art Monk RB	.02	.10
❑ 2 Jerry Rice RB	.20	.50
❑ 3 Stanley Richard	.01	.05
❑ 4 Ron Hall	.01	.05
❑ 5 Daryl Johnston	.08	.25
❑ 6 Wendell Davis	.01	.05
❑ 7 Vaughn Dunbar	.01	.05
❑ 8 Mike Jones	.01	.05
❑ 9 Anthony Johnson	.02	.10
❑ 10 Chris Miller	.02	.10
❑ 11 Kyle Clifton	.01	.05
❑ 12 Curtis Conway RC	.15	.40
❑ 13 Lionel Washington	.01	.05
❑ 14 Reggie Johnson	.01	.05
❑ 15 David Little	.01	.05
❑ 16 Nick Lowery	.01	.05
❑ 17 Darryl Williams	.01	.05
❑ 18 Brent Jones	.02	.10
❑ 19 Bruce Matthews	.02	.10
❑ 20 Heath Sherman	.01	.05
❑ 21 John Kasay UER	.01	.05
❑ 22 Troy Drayton RC	.02	.10
❑ 23 Eric Metcalf	.02	.10
❑ 24 Andre Tippett	.02	.10
❑ 25 Rodney Hampton	.02	.10
❑ 26 Henry Jones	.01	.05
❑ 27 Jim Everett	.02	.10
❑ 28 Steve Jordan	.01	.05
❑ 29 LeRoy Butler	.01	.05
❑ 30 Troy Vincent	.01	.05
❑ 31 Nate Lewis	.01	.05
❑ 32 Rickey Jackson	.02	.10
❑ 33 Darion Conner	.01	.05
❑ 34 Tom Carter RC	.02	.10
❑ 35 Jeff George	.08	.25
❑ 36 Larry Centers RC	.08	.25
❑ 37 Reggie Cobb	.01	.05
❑ 38 Mike Saxon	.01	.05
❑ 39 Brad Baxter	.01	.05
❑ 40 Reggie White	.08	.25
❑ 41 Haywood Jeffires	.02	.10
❑ 42 Alfred Williams	.01	.05
❑ 43 Aaron Wallace	.01	.05
❑ 44 Tracy Simien	.01	.05
❑ 45 Pat Harlow	.01	.05
❑ 46 D.J. Johnson	.01	.05
❑ 47 Don Griffin	.01	.05
❑ 48 Flipper Anderson	.02	.10
❑ 49 Keith Kartz	.01	.05
❑ 50 Bernie Kosar	.02	.10
❑ 51 Kent Hull	.01	.05
❑ 52 Erik Howard	.01	.05
❑ 53 Pierce Holt	.01	.05
❑ 54 Dwayne Harper	.01	.05
❑ 55 Bennie Blades	.01	.05
❑ 56 Mark Duper	.01	.05
❑ 57 Brian Noble	.01	.05
❑ 58 Jeff Feagles	.01	.05
❑ 59 Michael Haynes	.02	.10
❑ 60 Junior Seau	.08	.25
❑ 61 Gary Anderson RB	.02	.10
❑ 62 Jon Hand	.01	.05
❑ 63 Lin Elliott RC	.01	.05
❑ 64 Dana Stubblefield RC	.08	.25
❑ 65 Vaughan Johnson	.01	.05
❑ 66 Mo Lewis	.01	.05
❑ 67 Aeneas Williams	.02	.10
❑ 68 David Fulcher	.01	.05
❑ 69 Chip Lohmiller	.01	.05
❑ 70 Greg Townsend	.02	.10
❑ 71 Simon Fletcher	.01	.05
❑ 72 Sean Salisbury	.02	.10
❑ 73 Christian Okoye	.02	.10
❑ 74 Jim Arnold	.01	.05
❑ 75 Bruce Smith	.08	.25
❑ 76 Fred Barnett	.02	.10
❑ 77 Bill Romanowski	.02	.10
❑ 78 Dermontti Dawson	.01	.05
❑ 79 Bern Brostek	.01	.05
❑ 80 Warren Moon	.08	.25
❑ 81 Bill Fralic	.01	.05
❑ 82 Lomas Brown FP	.01	.05
❑ 83 Duane Bickett FP	.01	.05
❑ 84 Neil Smith FP	.02	.10
❑ 85 Reggie White FP	.02	.10
❑ 86 Tim McDonald FP	.01	.05
❑ 87 Leslie O'Neal FP	.01	.05
❑ 88 Steve Young FP	.15	.40
❑ 89 Paul Gruber FP	.01	.05
❑ 90 Wilber Marshall FP	.01	.05
❑ 91 Trace Armstrong	.01	.05
❑ 92 Bobby Houston RC	.01	.05
❑ 93 George Thornton	.01	.05
❑ 94 Keith McCants	.01	.05
❑ 95 Ricky Sanders	.01	.05
❑ 96 Jackie Harris	.01	.05
❑ 97 Todd Marinovich	.01	.05
❑ 98 Henry Thomas	.01	.05
❑ 99 Jeff Wright	.01	.05
❑ 100 John Elway	.60	1.50
❑ 101 Garrison Hearst RC	.30	.75
❑ 102 Roy Foster	.01	.05
❑ 103 David Lang	.01	.05
❑ 104 Matt Stover	.01	.05
❑ 105 Lawrence Taylor	.08	.25
❑ 106 Pete Stoyanovich	.01	.05
❑ 107 Jessie Tuggle	.01	.05
❑ 108 William White	.01	.05
❑ 109 Andy Harmon RC	.02	.10
❑ 110 John L. Williams	.01	.05
❑ 111 Jon Vaughn	.01	.05
❑ 112 John Alt	.01	.05
❑ 113 Chris Jacke	.01	.05
❑ 114 Jim Breech	.01	.05
❑ 115 Eric Martin	.01	.05
❑ 116 Derrick Walker	.01	.05
❑ 117 Ricky Ervins	.01	.05
❑ 118 Roger Craig	.02	.10
❑ 119 Jeff Gossett	.01	.05
❑ 120 Emmitt Smith	.60	1.50
❑ 121 Bob Whitfield	.01	.05
❑ 122 Alonzo Spellman	.01	.05
❑ 123 David Klingler	.01	.05
❑ 124 Tommy Maddox	.08	.25
❑ 125 Robert Porcher	.01	.05
❑ 126 Edgar Bennett	.08	.25
❑ 127 Harvey Williams	.02	.10
❑ 128 Dave Brown RC	.08	.25
❑ 129 Johnny Mitchell	.01	.05
❑ 130 Drew Bledsoe RC	1.00	2.50
❑ 131 Zefross Moss	.01	.05
❑ 132 Nate Odomes	.01	.05
❑ 133 Rufus Porter	.01	.05
❑ 134 Jackie Slater	.02	.10
❑ 135 Steve Young	.30	.75
❑ 136 Chris Calloway	.02	.10
❑ 137 Steve Atwater	.02	.10
❑ 138 Mark Carrier DB	.01	.05
❑ 139 Marvin Washington	.01	.05
❑ 140 Barry Foster	.02	.10
❑ 141 Ricky Reynolds	.01	.05
❑ 142 Bubba McDowell	.01	.05
❑ 143 Dan Footman RC	.01	.05
❑ 144 Richmond Webb	.01	.05
❑ 145 Mike Pritchard	.02	.10
❑ 146 Chris Spielman	.02	.10
❑ 147 Dave Krieg	.02	.10
❑ 148 Nick Bell	.01	.05
❑ 149 Vincent Brown	.01	.05
❑ 150 Seth Joyner	.01	.05
❑ 151 Tommy Kane	.01	.05
❑ 152 Carlton Gray RC	.01	.05
❑ 153 Harry Newsome	.01	.05
❑ 154 Rohn Stark	.01	.05
❑ 155 Shannon Sharpe	.08	.25
❑ 156 Charles Haley	.02	.10
❑ 157 Cornelius Bennett	.02	.10
❑ 158 Doug Riesenberg	.01	.05
❑ 159 Amp Lee	.01	.05
❑ 160 Sterling Sharpe UER	.08	.25
❑ 161 Alonzo Mitz	.01	.05
❑ 162 Pat Terrell	.01	.05
❑ 163 Mark Schlereth	.01	.05
❑ 164 Gary Anderson K	.01	.05
❑ 165 Quinn Early	.02	.10
❑ 166 Jerome Bettis RC	2.50	5.00
❑ 167 Lawrence Dawsey	.01	.05
❑ 168 Derrick Thomas	.08	.25
❑ 169 Rodney Peete	.01	.05
❑ 170 Jim Kelly	.08	.25
❑ 171 Deion Sanders TL	.08	.25
❑ 172 Richard Dent TL	.01	.05
❑ 173 Emmitt Smith TL	.30	.75
❑ 174 Barry Sanders TL	.25	.60
❑ 175 Sterling Sharpe TL	.02	.10
❑ 176 Cleveland Gary TL	.01	.05
❑ 177 Terry Allen TL	.02	.10
❑ 178 Vaughan Johnson TL	.01	.05
❑ 179 Rodney Hampton TL	.01	.05
❑ 180 Randall Cunningham TL	.02	.10
❑ 181 Ricky Proehl TL	.01	.05
❑ 182 Jerry Rice TL	.20	.50
❑ 183 Reggie Cobb TL	.01	.05
❑ 184 Earnest Byner TL	.01	.05
❑ 185 Jeff Lageman	.01	.05
❑ 186 Carlos Jenkins	.01	.05
❑ 187 G.Hearst/Dye/Moore/Cole.	.15	.40
❑ 188 Todd Lyght	.01	.05
❑ 189 Carl Simpson RC	.01	.05
❑ 190 Barry Sanders	.50	1.25
❑ 191 Jim Harbaugh	.08	.25
❑ 192 Roger Ruzek	.01	.05
❑ 193 Brent Williams	.01	.05
❑ 194 Chip Banks	.01	.05
❑ 195 Mike Croel	.01	.05
❑ 196 Marion Butts	.02	.10
❑ 197 James Washington	.01	.05
❑ 198 John Offerdahl	.01	.05
❑ 199 Tom Rathman	.02	.10
❑ 200 Joe Montana	.60	1.50
❑ 201 Pepper Johnson	.02	.10
❑ 202 Cris Dishman	.01	.05
❑ 203 Adrian White RC	.01	.05
❑ 204 Reggie Brooks RC	.02	.10
❑ 205 Cortez Kennedy	.02	.10
❑ 206 Robert Massey	.01	.05
❑ 207 Toi Cook	.01	.05
❑ 208 Harry Sydney	.01	.05
❑ 209 Lincoln Kennedy RC	.01	.05
❑ 210 Randall McDaniel	.05	.15
❑ 211 Eugene Daniel	.01	.05
❑ 212 Rob Burnett	.01	.05
❑ 213 Steve Broussard	.01	.05
❑ 214 Brian Washington	.01	.05
❑ 215 Leonard Renfro RC	.01	.05
❑ 216 Audray McMillian LL	.01	.05
❑ 217 Sterling Sharpe/Miller L	.01	.05
❑ 218 Clyde Simmons LL	.01	.05
❑ 219 Emmitt Smith/B.Foster LL	.15	.40
❑ 220 Steve Young/W.Moon LL	.08	.25
❑ 221 Mel Gray	.02	.10
❑ 222 Luis Sharpe	.01	.05
❑ 223 Eric Moten	.01	.05
❑ 224 Albert Lewis	.01	.05
❑ 225 Alvin Harper	.02	.10
❑ 226 Steve Wallace	.01	.05
❑ 227 Mark Higgs	.01	.05
❑ 228 Eugene Lockhart	.01	.05
❑ 229 Sean Jones	.01	.05
❑ 230 J.Lynch RC/Thom/DuBose	.25	.60
❑ 231 Jimmy Williams	.01	.05

❑ 232 Demetrius DuBose RC	.01	.05
❑ 233 John Roper	.01	.05
❑ 234 Keith Hamilton	.01	.05
❑ 235 Donald Evans	.01	.05
❑ 236 Kenneth Davis	.02	.10
❑ 237 John Copeland RC	.02	.10
❑ 238 Leonard Russell	.02	.10
❑ 239 Ken Harvey	.01	.05
❑ 240 Dale Carter	.01	.05
❑ 241 Anthony Pleasant	.01	.05
❑ 242 Darrell Green	.02	.10
❑ 243 Natrone Means RC	.08	.25
❑ 244 Rob Moore	.02	.10
❑ 245 Chris Doleman	.01	.05
❑ 246 J.B. Brown	.01	.05
❑ 247 Ray Crockett	.01	.05
❑ 248 John Taylor	.02	.10
❑ 249 Russell Maryland	.01	.05
❑ 250 Brett Favre	.75	2.00
❑ 251 Carl Pickens	.02	.10
❑ 252 Andy Heck	.01	.05
❑ 253 Jerome Henderson	.01	.05
❑ 254 Deion Sanders	.20	.50
❑ 255 Steve Emtman	.01	.05
❑ 256 Calvin Williams	.02	.10
❑ 257 Sean Gilbert	.02	.10
❑ 258 Don Beebe	.01	.05
❑ 259 Robert Smith RC	.50	1.25
❑ 260 Robert Blackmon	.01	.05
❑ 261 Jim Kelly TL	.02	.10
❑ 262 Harold Green TL UER	.01	.05
❑ 263 Clay Matthews TL	.01	.05
❑ 264 John Elway TL	.30	.75
❑ 265 Warren Moon TL	.02	.10
❑ 266 Jeff George TL	.02	.10
❑ 267 Derrick Thomas TL	.02	.10
❑ 268 Howie Long TL	.01	.05
❑ 269 Dan Marino TL	.30	.75
❑ 270 Jon Vaughn TL	.01	.05
❑ 271 Chris Burkett TL	.01	.05
❑ 272 Barry Foster TL	.01	.05
❑ 273 Marion Butts TL	.01	.05
❑ 274 Chris Warren TL	.01	.05
❑ 275 M.Strahan RC/M.Buck.	.75	2.00
❑ 276 Tony Casillas	.01	.05
❑ 277 Jarrod Bunch	.01	.05
❑ 278 Eric Green	.01	.05
❑ 279 Stan Brock	.01	.05
❑ 280 Chester McGlockton	.02	.10
❑ 281 Ricky Watters	.08	.25
❑ 282 Dan Saleaumua	.01	.05
❑ 283 Rich Camarillo	.01	.05
❑ 284 Cris Carter	.08	.25
❑ 285 Rick Mirer RC	.08	.25
❑ 286 Matt Brock	.01	.05
❑ 287 Burt Grossman	.01	.05
❑ 288 Andre Collins	.01	.05
❑ 289 Mark Jackson	.01	.05
❑ 290 Dan Marino	.60	1.50
❑ 291 Cornelius Bennett FG	.01	.05
❑ 292 Steve Atwater FG	.01	.05
❑ 293 Bryan Cox FG	.01	.05
❑ 294 Sam Mills FG	.01	.05
❑ 295 Pepper Johnson FG	.01	.05
❑ 296 Seth Joyner FG	.01	.05
❑ 297 Chris Spielman FG	.01	.05
❑ 298 Junior Seau FG	.02	.10
❑ 299 Cortez Kennedy FG	.01	.05
❑ 300 Broderick Thomas FG	.01	.05
❑ 301 Todd McNair	.01	.05
❑ 302 Nate Newton	.02	.10
❑ 303 Michael Walter	.01	.05
❑ 304 Clyde Simmons	.01	.05
❑ 305 Ernie Mills	.01	.05
❑ 306 Steve Wisniewski	.01	.05
❑ 307 Coleman Rudolph RC	.01	.05
❑ 308 Thurman Thomas	.08	.25
❑ 309 Reggie Roby	.01	.05
❑ 310 Eric Swann	.02	.10
❑ 311 Mark Wheeler	.01	.05
❑ 312 Jeff Herrod	.01	.05
❑ 313 Leroy Hoard	.02	.10
❑ 314 Patrick Bates RC	.01	.05
❑ 315 Earnest Byner	.01	.05
❑ 316 Dave Meggett	.01	.05
❑ 317 George Teague RC	.02	.10
❑ 318 Ray Childress	.02	.10
❑ 319 Mike Kenn	.01	.05
❑ 320 Jason Hanson	.01	.05
❑ 321 Gary Clark	.02	.10
❑ 322 Chris Gardocki	.01	.05
❑ 323 Ken Norton	.02	.10
❑ 324 Eric Curry RC	.01	.05
❑ 325 Byron Evans	.01	.05
❑ 326 O.J.McDuffie RC	.08	.25
❑ 327 Dwight Stone	.01	.05
❑ 328 Tommy Barnhardt	.01	.05
❑ 329 Checklist 1-165	.01	.05
❑ 330 Checklist 166-329	.01	.05
❑ 331 Erik Williams	.01	.05
❑ 332 Phil Hansen	.01	.05
❑ 333 Martin Harrison RC	.01	.05
❑ 334 Mark Ingram	.01	.05
❑ 335 Mark Rypien	.02	.10
❑ 336 Anthony Miller	.02	.10
❑ 337 Antone Davis	.01	.05
❑ 338 Mike Munchak	.02	.10
❑ 339 Wayne Martin	.01	.05
❑ 340 Joe Montana	.60	1.50
❑ 341 Deon Figures RC	.01	.05
❑ 342 Ed McDaniel	.01	.05
❑ 343 Chris Burkett	.01	.05
❑ 344 Tony Smith RB	.01	.05
❑ 345 James Lofton	.02	.10
❑ 346 Courtney Hawkins	.01	.05
❑ 347 Dennis Smith	.01	.05
❑ 348 Anthony Morgan	.01	.05
❑ 349 Chris Goode	.01	.05
❑ 350 Phil Simms	.02	.10
❑ 351 Patrick Hunter	.01	.05
❑ 352 Brett Perriman	.08	.25
❑ 353 Corey Miller	.01	.05
❑ 354 Harry Galbreath	.01	.05
❑ 355 Mark Carrier WR	.02	.10
❑ 356 Troy Drayton	.02	.10
❑ 357 Greg Davis	.01	.05
❑ 358 Tim Krumrie	.01	.05
❑ 359 Tim McDonald	.01	.05
❑ 360 Webster Slaughter	.01	.05
❑ 361 Steve Christie	.01	.05
❑ 362 Courtney Hall	.01	.05
❑ 363 Charles Mann	.01	.05
❑ 364 Vestee Jackson	.01	.05
❑ 365 Robert Jones	.01	.05
❑ 366 Rich Miano	.01	.05
❑ 367 Morten Andersen	.02	.10
❑ 368 Jeff Graham	.02	.10
❑ 369 Martin Mayhew	.01	.05
❑ 370 Anthony Carter	.02	.10
❑ 371 Greg Kragen	.01	.05
❑ 372 Ron Cox	.01	.05
❑ 373 Perry Williams	.01	.05
❑ 374 Willie Gault	.02	.10
❑ 375 Chris Warren	.02	.10
❑ 376 Reyna Thompson	.01	.05
❑ 377 Bennie Thompson	.01	.05
❑ 378 Kevin Mack	.01	.05
❑ 379 Clarence Verdin	.01	.05
❑ 380 Marc Boutte	.01	.05
❑ 381 Marvin Jones RC	.01	.05
❑ 382 Greg Jackson	.01	.05
❑ 383 Steve Bono	.02	.10
❑ 384 Terrell Buckley	.01	.05
❑ 385 Garrison Hearst	.08	.25
❑ 386 Mike Brim	.01	.05
❑ 387 Jesse Sapolu	.01	.05
❑ 388 Carl Lee	.01	.05
❑ 389 Jeff Cross	.01	.05
❑ 390 Karl Mecklenburg	.02	.10
❑ 391 Chad Hennings	.01	.05
❑ 392 Oliver Barnett	.01	.05
❑ 393 Dalton Hilliard	.01	.05
❑ 394 Broderick Thompson	.01	.05
❑ 395 Rocket Ismail	.02	.10
❑ 396 John Kidd	.01	.05
❑ 397 Eddie Anderson	.01	.05
❑ 398 Lamar Lathon	.01	.05
❑ 399 Darren Perry	.01	.05
❑ 400 Drew Bledsoe	.50	1.25
❑ 401 Ferrell Edmunds	.01	.05
❑ 402 Lomas Brown	.01	.05
❑ 403 Drew Hill	.02	.10
❑ 404 David Whitmore	.01	.05
❑ 405 Mike Johnson	.01	.05
❑ 406 Paul Gruber	.01	.05
❑ 407 Kirk Lowdermilk	.01	.05
❑ 408 Curtis Conway	.08	.25
❑ 409 Bryce Paup	.02	.10
❑ 410 Boomer Esiason	.02	.10
❑ 411 Jay Schroeder	.01	.05
❑ 412 Anthony Newman	.01	.05
❑ 413 Ernie Jones	.01	.05
❑ 414 Carlton Bailey	.01	.05
❑ 415 Kenneth Gant	.01	.05
❑ 416 Todd Scott	.01	.05
❑ 417 Anthony Smith	.01	.05
❑ 418 Erik McMillan	.01	.05
❑ 419 Ronnie Harmon	.01	.05
❑ 420 Andre Reed	.02	.10
❑ 421 Wymon Henderson	.01	.05
❑ 422 Carnell Lake	.01	.05
❑ 423 Al Noga	.01	.05
❑ 424 Curtis Duncan	.01	.05
❑ 425 Mike Gann	.01	.05
❑ 426 Eugene Robinson	.02	.10
❑ 427 Scott Mersereau	.01	.05
❑ 428 Chris Singleton	.01	.05
❑ 429 Gerald Robinson	.01	.05
❑ 430 Pat Swilling	.02	.10
❑ 431 Ed McCaffrey	.08	.25
❑ 432 Neal Anderson	.02	.10
❑ 433 Joe Phillips	.01	.05
❑ 434 Jerry Ball	.01	.05
❑ 435 Tyronne Stowe	.01	.05
❑ 436 Dana Stubblefield	.08	.25
❑ 437 Eric Curry	.01	.05
❑ 438 Derrick Fenner	.01	.05
❑ 439 Mark Clayton	.02	.10
❑ 440 Quentin Coryatt	.02	.10
❑ 441 Willie Roaf RC	.02	.10
❑ 442 Ernest Dye	.01	.05
❑ 443 Jeff Jaeger	.01	.05
❑ 444 Stan Humphries	.02	.10
❑ 445 Johnny Johnson	.01	.05
❑ 446 Larry Brown DB	.01	.05
❑ 447 Kurt Gouveia	.01	.05
❑ 448 Qadry Ismail RC	.08	.25
❑ 449 Dan Footman	.01	.05
❑ 450 Tom Waddle	.01	.05
❑ 451 Kelvin Martin	.01	.05
❑ 452 Kanavis McGhee	.01	.05
❑ 453 Herman Moore	.08	.25
❑ 454 Jesse Solomon	.01	.05
❑ 455 Shane Conlan	.01	.05
❑ 456 Joel Steed	.01	.05
❑ 457 Charles Arbuckle	.01	.05
❑ 458 Shane Dronett	.01	.05
❑ 459 Steve Tasker	.02	.10
❑ 460 Herschel Walker	.02	.10
❑ 461 Willie Davis	.08	.25
❑ 462 Al Smith	.01	.05
❑ 463 O.J.McDuffie	.08	.25
❑ 464 Kevin Fagan	.01	.05
❑ 465 Hardy Nickerson	.02	.10
❑ 466 Leonard Marshall	.02	.10
❑ 467 John Baylor	.01	.05
❑ 468 Jay Novacek	.02	.10
❑ 469 Wayne Simmons RC	.01	.05
❑ 470 Tommy Vardell	.01	.05
❑ 471 Cleveland Gary	.01	.05
❑ 472 Mark Collins	.02	.10
❑ 473 Craig Heyward	.02	.10
❑ 474 John Copeland UER	.02	.10
❑ 475 Jeff Hostetler	.02	.10
❑ 476 Brian Mitchell	.02	.10
❑ 477 Natrone Means	.08	.25
❑ 478 Brad Muster	.01	.05
❑ 479 David Lutz	.01	.05
❑ 480 Andre Rison	.02	.10
❑ 481 Michael Zordich	.01	.05
❑ 482 Jim McMahon	.02	.10
❑ 483 Carlton Gray	.01	.05
❑ 484 Chris Mohr	.01	.05
❑ 485 Ernest Givins	.02	.10
❑ 486 Tony Tolbert	.01	.05
❑ 487 Vai Sikahema	.01	.05
❑ 488 Larry Webster	.01	.05
❑ 489 James Hasty	.01	.05
❑ 490 Reggie White	.08	.25
❑ 491 Reggie Rivers RC	.01	.05
❑ 492 Roman Phifer	.01	.05
❑ 493 Levon Kirkland	.01	.05
❑ 494 Demetrius DuBose	.01	.05
❑ 495 William Perry	.02	.10
❑ 496 Clay Matthews	.02	.10
❑ 497 Aaron Jones	.01	.05
❑ 498 Jack Trudeau	.01	.05

Card	Low	High
❑ 499 Michael Brooks	.01	.05
❑ 500 Jerry Rice	.40	1.00
❑ 501 Lonnie Marts	.01	.05
❑ 502 Tim McGee	.02	.10
❑ 503 Kelvin Pritchett	.01	.05
❑ 504 Bobby Hebert	.02	.10
❑ 505 Audray McMillian	.01	.05
❑ 506 Chuck Cecil	.01	.05
❑ 507 Leonard Renfro	.01	.05
❑ 508 Ethan Horton	.01	.05
❑ 509 Kevin Smith	.02	.10
❑ 510 Louis Oliver	.01	.05
❑ 511 John Stephens	.01	.05
❑ 512 Browning Nagle	.01	.05
❑ 513 Ricardo McDonald	.01	.05
❑ 514 Leslie O'Neal	.02	.10
❑ 515 Lorenzo White	.01	.05
❑ 516 Thomas Smith RC	.02	.10
❑ 517 Tony Woods	.01	.05
❑ 518 Darryl Henley	.01	.05
❑ 519 Robert Delpino	.01	.05
❑ 520 Rod Woodson	.08	.25
❑ 521 Phillippi Sparks	.01	.05
❑ 522 Jessie Hester	.01	.05
❑ 523 Shaun Gayle	.01	.05
❑ 524 Brad Edwards	.01	.05
❑ 525 Randall Cunningham	.08	.25
❑ 526 Marv Cook	.01	.05
❑ 527 Dennis Gibson	.01	.05
❑ 528 Eric Pegram	.02	.10
❑ 529 Terry McDaniel	.01	.05
❑ 530 Troy Aikman	.30	.75
❑ 531 Irving Fryar	.02	.10
❑ 532 Blair Thomas	.01	.05
❑ 533 Jim Wilks	.01	.05
❑ 534 Michael Jackson	.02	.10
❑ 535 Eric Davis	.01	.05
❑ 536 James Campen	.01	.05
❑ 537 Steve Beuerlein	.02	.10
❑ 538 Robert Smith	.20	.50
❑ 539 J.J. Birden	.01	.05
❑ 540 Broderick Thomas	.01	.05
❑ 541 Darryl Talley	.01	.05
❑ 542 Russell Freeman RC	.01	.05
❑ 543 David Alexander	.01	.05
❑ 544 Chris Mims	.01	.05
❑ 545 Coleman Rudolph	.01	.05
❑ 546 Steve McMichael	.02	.10
❑ 547 David Williams	.01	.05
❑ 548 Chris Hinton	.01	.05
❑ 549 Jim Jeffcoat	.01	.05
❑ 550 Howie Long	.08	.25
❑ 551 Roosevelt Potts RC	.01	.05
❑ 552 Bryan Cox	.01	.05
❑ 553 David Richards UER	.01	.05
❑ 554 Reggie Brooks	.02	.10
❑ 555 Neil O'Donnell	.08	.25
❑ 556 Irv Smith RC	.01	.05
❑ 557 Henry Ellard	.02	.10
❑ 558 Steve DeBerg	.02	.10
❑ 559 Jim Sweeney	.01	.05
❑ 560 Harold Green	.01	.05
❑ 561 Darrell Thompson	.01	.05
❑ 562 Vinny Testaverde	.02	.10
❑ 563 Bubby Brister	.01	.05
❑ 564 Sean Landeta	.02	.10
❑ 565 Neil Smith	.08	.25
❑ 566 Craig Erickson	.02	.10
❑ 567 Jim Ritcher	.01	.05
❑ 568 Don Mosebar	.01	.05
❑ 569 John Gesek	.01	.05
❑ 570 Gary Plummer	.01	.05
❑ 571 Norm Johnson	.01	.05
❑ 572 Ron Heller	.01	.05
❑ 573 Carl Simpson	.01	.05
❑ 574 Greg Montgomery	.01	.05
❑ 575 Dana Hall	.01	.05
❑ 576 Vencie Glenn	.01	.05
❑ 577 Dean Biasucci	.01	.05
❑ 578 Rod Bernstine UER	.01	.05
❑ 579 Randal Hill	.01	.05
❑ 580 Sam Mills	.02	.10
❑ 581 Santana Dotson	.02	.10
❑ 582 Greg Lloyd	.02	.10
❑ 583 Eric Thomas	.01	.05
❑ 584 Henry Rolling	.01	.05
❑ 585 Tony Bennett	.01	.05
❑ 586 Sheldon White	.01	.05
❑ 587 Mark Kelso	.02	.10
❑ 588 Marc Spindler	.01	.05
❑ 589 Greg McMurtry	.01	.05
❑ 590 Art Monk	.02	.10
❑ 591 Marco Coleman	.01	.05
❑ 592 Tony Jones T	.01	.05
❑ 593 Melvin Jenkins	.01	.05
❑ 594 Kevin Ross	.01	.05
❑ 595 William Fuller	.01	.05
❑ 596 James Joseph	.01	.05
❑ 597 Lamar McGriggs RC	.01	.05
❑ 598 Gill Byrd	.01	.05
❑ 599 Alexander Wright	.01	.05
❑ 600 Rick Mirer	.08	.25
❑ 601 Richard Dent	.02	.10
❑ 602 Thomas Everett	.01	.05
❑ 603 Jack Del Rio	.02	.10
❑ 604 Jerome Bettis	1.00	2.50
❑ 605 Ronnie Lott	.02	.10
❑ 606 Marty Carter	.01	.05
❑ 607 Arthur Marshall RC	.01	.05
❑ 608 Lee Johnson	.01	.05
❑ 609 Bruce Armstrong	.01	.05
❑ 610 Ricky Proehl	.02	.10
❑ 611 Will Wolford	.01	.05
❑ 612 Mike Prior	.01	.05
❑ 613 George Jamison	.01	.05
❑ 614 Gene Atkins	.01	.05
❑ 615 Merril Hoge	.02	.10
❑ 616 Desmond Howard	.02	.10
❑ 617 Jarvis Williams	.01	.05
❑ 618 Marcus Allen	.08	.25
❑ 619 Gary Brown	.01	.05
❑ 620 Bill Brooks	.01	.05
❑ 621 Eric Allen	.01	.05
❑ 622 Todd Kelly	.01	.05
❑ 623 Michael Dean Perry	.02	.10
❑ 624 David Braxton	.01	.05
❑ 625 Mike Sherrard	.01	.05
❑ 626 Jeff Bryant	.01	.05
❑ 627 Eric Bieniemy	.01	.05
❑ 628 Tim Brown	.08	.25
❑ 629 Troy Auzenne	.01	.05
❑ 630 Michael Irvin	.08	.25
❑ 631 Maurice Hurst	.01	.05
❑ 632 Duane Bickett	.01	.05
❑ 633 George Teague	.02	.10
❑ 634 Vince Workman	.01	.05
❑ 635 Renaldo Turnbull	.01	.05
❑ 636 Johnny Bailey	.01	.05
❑ 637 Dan Williams RC	.01	.05
❑ 638 James Thornton	.01	.05
❑ 639 Terry Allen	.08	.25
❑ 640 Kevin Greene	.02	.10
❑ 641 Tony Zendejas	.01	.05
❑ 642 Scott Kowalkowski RC	.01	.05
❑ 643 Jeff Query UER	.01	.05
❑ 644 Brian Blades	.02	.10
❑ 645 Keith Jackson	.02	.10
❑ 646 Monte Coleman	.01	.05
❑ 647 Guy McIntyre	.01	.05
❑ 648 Barry Word	.01	.05
❑ 649 Steve Everitt RC	.01	.05
❑ 650 Patrick Bates	.01	.05
❑ 651 Marcus Robertson RC	.01	.05
❑ 652 John Carney	.01	.05
❑ 653 Derek Brown TE	.01	.05
❑ 654 Carwell Gardner	.01	.05
❑ 655 Moe Gardner	.01	.05
❑ 656 Andre Ware	.02	.10
❑ 657 Keith Van Horne	.01	.05
❑ 658 Hugh Millen	.01	.05
❑ 659 Checklist 330-495	.01	.05
❑ 660 Checklist 496-660	.01	.05

1994 Topps

Card	Low	High
❑ COMPLETE SET (660)	40.00	80.00
❑ COMP.FACT.SET	45.00	80.00
❑ COMP.SERIES 1 (330)	12.50	25.00
❑ COMP.SERIES 2 (330)	12.50	25.00
❑ 1 Emmitt Smith	.60	1.50
❑ 2 Russell Copeland	.01	.05
❑ 3 Jesse Sapolu	.01	.05
❑ 4 David Szott	.01	.05
❑ 5 Rodney Hampton	.02	.10
❑ 6 Bubba McDowell	.01	.05
❑ 7 Bryce Paup	.02	.10
❑ 8 Winston Moss	.01	.05
❑ 9 Brett Perriman	.02	.10
❑ 10 Rod Woodson	.02	.10
❑ 11 John Randle	.02	.10
❑ 12 David Wyman	.01	.05
❑ 13 Jeff Cross	.01	.05
❑ 14 Richard Cooper	.01	.05
❑ 15 Johnny Mitchell	.01	.05
❑ 16 David Alexander	.01	.05
❑ 17 Ronnie Harmon	.01	.05
❑ 18 Tyronne Stowe UER	.01	.05
❑ 19 Chris Zorich	.01	.05
❑ 20 Rob Burnett	.01	.05
❑ 21 Harold Alexander	.01	.05
❑ 22 Rod Stephens	.01	.05
❑ 23 Mark Wheeler	.01	.05
❑ 24 Dwayne Sabb	.01	.05
❑ 25 Troy Drayton	.01	.05
❑ 26 Kurt Gouveia	.01	.05
❑ 27 Warren Moon	.08	.25
❑ 28 Jeff Query	.01	.05
❑ 29 Chuck Levy RC	.01	.05
❑ 30 Bruce Smith	.08	.25
❑ 31 Doug Riesenberg	.01	.05
❑ 32 Willie Drewrey	.01	.05
❑ 33 Nate Newton UER	.01	.05
❑ 34 James Jett	.01	.05
❑ 35 George Teague	.01	.05
❑ 36 Marc Spindler	.01	.05
❑ 37 Jack Del Rio	.01	.05
❑ 38 Dale Carter	.01	.05
❑ 39 Steve Atwater	.01	.05
❑ 40 Herschel Walker	.02	.10
❑ 41 James Hasty	.01	.05
❑ 42 Seth Joyner	.01	.05
❑ 43 Keith Jackson	.01	.05
❑ 44 Tommy Vardell	.01	.05
❑ 45 Antonio Langham RC	.02	.10
❑ 46 Derek Brown RBK	.01	.05
❑ 47 John Wojciechowski	.01	.05
❑ 48 Horace Copeland	.01	.05
❑ 49 Luis Sharpe	.01	.05
❑ 50 Pat Harlow	.01	.05
❑ 51 David Palmer RC	.08	.25
❑ 52 Tony Smith RB	.01	.05
❑ 53 Tim Johnson	.01	.05
❑ 54 Anthony Newman	.01	.05
❑ 55 Terry Wooden	.01	.05
❑ 56 Derrick Fenner	.01	.05
❑ 57 Mike Fox	.01	.05
❑ 58 Brad Hopkins	.01	.05
❑ 59 Daryl Johnston UER	.02	.10
❑ 60 Steve Young	.30	.75
❑ 61 Scottie Graham RC	.02	.10
❑ 62 Nolan Harrison	.01	.05
❑ 63 David Richards	.01	.05
❑ 64 Chris Mohr	.01	.05
❑ 65 Hardy Nickerson	.02	.10
❑ 66 Heath Sherman	.01	.05
❑ 67 Irving Fryar	.02	.10
❑ 68 Ray Buchanan UER	.01	.05
❑ 69 Jay Taylor	.01	.05
❑ 70 Shannon Sharpe	.02	.10
❑ 71 Vinny Testaverde	.02	.10
❑ 72 Renaldo Turnbull	.01	.05
❑ 73 Dwight Stone	.01	.05
❑ 74 Willie McGinest RC	.08	.25
❑ 75 Darrell Green	.01	.05
❑ 76 Kyle Clifton	.01	.05
❑ 77 Leo Goeas	.01	.05
❑ 78 Ken Ruettgers	.01	.05
❑ 79 Craig Heyward	.02	.10
❑ 80 Andre Rison	.02	.10
❑ 81 Chris Mims	.01	.05
❑ 82 Gary Clark	.02	.10
❑ 83 Ricardo McDonald	.01	.05
❑ 84 Patrick Hunter	.01	.05
❑ 85 Bruce Matthews	.01	.05

- ❑ 86 Russell Maryland .01 .05
- ❑ 87 Gary Anderson K .01 .05
- ❑ 88 Brad Edwards .01 .05
- ❑ 89 Carlton Bailey .01 .05
- ❑ 90 Qadry Ismail .08 .25
- ❑ 91 Terry McDaniel .01 .05
- ❑ 92 Willie Green .01 .05
- ❑ 93 Cornelius Bennett .02 .10
- ❑ 94 Paul Gruber .01 .05
- ❑ 95 Pete Stoyanovich .01 .05
- ❑ 96 Merton Hanks .02 .10
- ❑ 97 Tre Johnson RC .01 .05
- ❑ 98 Jonathan Hayes .01 .05
- ❑ 99 Jason Elam .02 .10
- ❑ 100 Jerome Bettis .20 .50
- ❑ 101 Ronnie Lott .02 .10
- ❑ 102 Maurice Hurst .01 .05
- ❑ 103 Kirk Lowdermilk .01 .05
- ❑ 104 Tony Jones T .01 .05
- ❑ 105 Steve Beuerlein .02 .10
- ❑ 106 Isaac Davis RC .01 .05
- ❑ 107 Vaughan Johnson .01 .05
- ❑ 108 Terrell Buckley .01 .05
- ❑ 109 Pierce Holt .01 .05
- ❑ 110 Alonzo Spellman .01 .05
- ❑ 111 Patrick Robinson .01 .05
- ❑ 112 Cortez Kennedy .02 .10
- ❑ 113 Kevin Williams WR .02 .10
- ❑ 114 Danny Copeland .01 .05
- ❑ 115 Chris Doleman .01 .05
- ❑ 116 Jerry Rice LL .20 .50
- ❑ 117 Neil Smith LL .02 .10
- ❑ 118 Emmitt Smith LL .30 .75
- ❑ 119 E.Robinson/Odomes LL .01 .05
- ❑ 120 Steve Young LL .08 .25
- ❑ 121 Carnell Lake .01 .05
- ❑ 122 Ernest Givins UER .02 .10
- ❑ 123 Henry Jones .01 .05
- ❑ 124 Michael Brooks .01 .05
- ❑ 125 Jason Hanson .01 .05
- ❑ 126 Andy Harmon .01 .05
- ❑ 127 Errict Rhett RC .08 .25
- ❑ 128 Harris Barton .01 .05
- ❑ 129 Greg Robinson .01 .05
- ❑ 130 Derrick Thomas .08 .25
- ❑ 131 Keith Kartz .01 .05
- ❑ 132 Lincoln Kennedy .01 .05
- ❑ 133 Leslie O'Neal .01 .05
- ❑ 134 Tim Goad .01 .05
- ❑ 135 Rohn Stark .01 .05
- ❑ 136 O.J.McDuffie .08 .25
- ❑ 137 Donnell Woolford .01 .05
- ❑ 138 Jamir Miller RC .02 .10
- ❑ 139 Eric Thomas UER .01 .05
- ❑ 140 Willie Roaf .01 .05
- ❑ 141 Wayne Gandy RC .01 .05
- ❑ 142 Mike Brim .01 .05
- ❑ 143 Kelvin Martin .01 .05
- ❑ 144 Edgar Bennett .08 .25
- ❑ 145 Michael Dean Perry .02 .10
- ❑ 146 Shante Carver RC .01 .05
- ❑ 147 Jessie Armstead UER .01 .05
- ❑ 148 Mo Elewonibi .01 .05
- ❑ 149 Dana Stubblefield .02 .10
- ❑ 150 Cody Carlson .01 .05
- ❑ 151 Vencie Glenn .01 .05
- ❑ 152 Levon Kirkland .01 .05
- ❑ 153 Derrick Moore .01 .05
- ❑ 154 John Fina .01 .05
- ❑ 155 Jeff Hostetler .02 .10
- ❑ 156 Courtney Hawkins .01 .05
- ❑ 157 Todd Collins .01 .05
- ❑ 158 Neil Smith .02 .10
- ❑ 159 Simon Fletcher .01 .05
- ❑ 160 Dan Marino .75 2.00
- ❑ 161 Sam Adams RC .02 .10
- ❑ 162 Marvin Washington .01 .05
- ❑ 163 John Copeland .01 .05
- ❑ 164 Eugene Robinson .01 .05
- ❑ 165 Mark Carrier DB .01 .05
- ❑ 166 Mike Kenn .01 .05
- ❑ 167 Tyrone Hughes .02 .10
- ❑ 168 Darren Carrington .01 .05
- ❑ 169 Shane Conlan .01 .05
- ❑ 170 Ricky Proehl .01 .05
- ❑ 171 Jeff Herrod .01 .05
- ❑ 172 Mark Carrier WR .02 .10
- ❑ 173 George Koonce .01 .05
- ❑ 174 Desmond Howard .02 .10
- ❑ 175 Dave Meggett .01 .05
- ❑ 176 Charles Haley .02 .10
- ❑ 177 Steve Wisniewski .01 .05
- ❑ 178 Dermontti Dawson .01 .05
- ❑ 179 Tim McDonald .01 .05
- ❑ 180 Broderick Thomas .01 .05
- ❑ 181 Bernard Dafney .01 .05
- ❑ 182 Bo Orlando .01 .05
- ❑ 183 Andre Reed .02 .10
- ❑ 184 Randall Cunningham .08 .25
- ❑ 185 Chris Spielman .02 .10
- ❑ 186 Keith Byars .01 .05
- ❑ 187 Ben Coates .02 .10
- ❑ 188 Tracy Simien .01 .05
- ❑ 189 Carl Pickens .02 .10
- ❑ 190 Reggie White .08 .25
- ❑ 191 Norm Johnson .01 .05
- ❑ 192 Brian Washington .01 .05
- ❑ 193 Stan Humphries .02 .10
- ❑ 194 Fred Stokes .01 .05
- ❑ 195 Dan Williams .01 .05
- ❑ 196 John Elway TOG .30 .75
- ❑ 197 Eric Allen TOG .01 .05
- ❑ 198 Hardy Nickerson TOG .02 .10
- ❑ 199 Jerome Bettis TOG .08 .25
- ❑ 200 Troy Aikman TOG .20 .50
- ❑ 201 Thurman Thomas TOG .02 .10
- ❑ 202 Cornelius Bennett TOG UER .02 .10
- ❑ 203 Michael Irvin TOG .02 .10
- ❑ 204 Jim Kelly TOG .02 .10
- ❑ 205 Junior Seau TOG .02 .10
- ❑ 206 Heath Shuler UER RC .08 .25
- ❑ 207 Howard Cross UER .01 .05
- ❑ 208 Pat Swilling .01 .05
- ❑ 209 Pete Metzelaars .01 .05
- ❑ 210 Tony McGee .01 .05
- ❑ 211 Neil O'Donnell .08 .25
- ❑ 212 Eugene Chung .01 .05
- ❑ 213 J.B. Brown .01 .05
- ❑ 214 Marcus Allen .08 .25
- ❑ 215 Harry Newsome .01 .05
- ❑ 216 Greg Hill RC .08 .25
- ❑ 217 Ryan Yarborough .01 .05
- ❑ 218 Marty Carter .01 .05
- ❑ 219 Bern Brostek .01 .05
- ❑ 220 Boomer Esiason .02 .10
- ❑ 221 Vince Buck .01 .05
- ❑ 222 Jim Jeffcoat .01 .05
- ❑ 223 Bob Dahl .01 .05
- ❑ 224 Marion Butts .01 .05
- ❑ 225 Ronald Moore .01 .05
- ❑ 226 Robert Blackmon .01 .05
- ❑ 227 Curtis Conway .08 .25
- ❑ 228 Jon Hand .01 .05
- ❑ 229 Shane Dronett .01 .05
- ❑ 230 Erik Williams UER .01 .05
- ❑ 231 Dennis Brown .01 .05
- ❑ 232 Ray Childress .01 .05
- ❑ 233 Johnnie Morton RC .20 .50
- ❑ 234 Kent Hull .01 .05
- ❑ 235 John Elliott .01 .05
- ❑ 236 Ron Heller .01 .05
- ❑ 237 J.J. Birden .01 .05
- ❑ 238 Thomas Randolph RC .01 .05
- ❑ 239 Chip Lohmiller .01 .05
- ❑ 240 Tim Brown .08 .25
- ❑ 241 Steve Tovar .01 .05
- ❑ 242 Moe Gardner .01 .05
- ❑ 243 Vincent Brown .01 .05
- ❑ 244 Tony Zendejas .01 .05
- ❑ 245 Eric Allen .01 .05
- ❑ 246 Joe King RC .01 .05
- ❑ 247 Mo Lewis .01 .05
- ❑ 248 Rod Bernstine .01 .05
- ❑ 249 Tom Waddle .01 .05
- ❑ 250 Junior Seau .08 .25
- ❑ 251 Eric Metcalf .02 .10
- ❑ 252 Cris Carter .20 .50
- ❑ 253 Bill Hitchcock .01 .05
- ❑ 254 Zefross Moss .01 .05
- ❑ 255 Morten Andersen .01 .05
- ❑ 256 Keith Rucker RC .01 .05
- ❑ 257 Chris Jacke .01 .05
- ❑ 258 Richmond Webb .01 .05
- ❑ 259 Herman Moore .08 .25
- ❑ 260 Phil Simms .02 .10
- ❑ 261 Mark Tuinei .01 .05
- ❑ 262 Don Beebe .01 .05
- ❑ 263 Marc Logan .01 .05
- ❑ 264 Willie Davis .02 .10
- ❑ 265 David Klingler .01 .05
- ❑ 266 Martin Mayhew UER .01 .05
- ❑ 267 Mark Bavaro .01 .05
- ❑ 268 Greg Lloyd .02 .10
- ❑ 269 Al Del Greco .01 .05
- ❑ 270 Reggie Brooks .02 .10
- ❑ 271 Greg Townsend .01 .05
- ❑ 272 Rohn Stark CAL .01 .05
- ❑ 273 Marcus Allen CAL .02 .10
- ❑ 274 Ronnie Lott CAL .02 .10
- ❑ 275 Dan Marino CAL .30 .75
- ❑ 276 Sean Gilbert .01 .05
- ❑ 277 LeRoy Butler .01 .05
- ❑ 278 Troy Auzenne .01 .05
- ❑ 279 Eric Swann .02 .10
- ❑ 280 Quentin Coryatt .01 .05
- ❑ 281 Anthony Pleasant .01 .05
- ❑ 282 Brad Baxter .01 .05
- ❑ 283 Carl Lee .01 .05
- ❑ 284 Courtney Hall .01 .05
- ❑ 285 Quinn Early .02 .10
- ❑ 286 Eddie Robinson .01 .05
- ❑ 287 Marco Coleman .01 .05
- ❑ 288 Harold Green .01 .05
- ❑ 289 Santana Dotson .02 .10
- ❑ 290 Robert Porcher .01 .05
- ❑ 291 Joe Phillips .01 .05
- ❑ 292 Mark McMillian .01 .05
- ❑ 293 Eric Davis .01 .05
- ❑ 294 Mark Jackson .01 .05
- ❑ 295 Darryl Talley .01 .05
- ❑ 296 Curtis Duncan .01 .05
- ❑ 297 Bruce Armstrong .01 .05
- ❑ 298 Eric Hill .01 .05
- ❑ 299 Andre Collins .01 .05
- ❑ 300 Jay Novacek .02 .10
- ❑ 301 Roosevelt Potts .01 .05
- ❑ 302 Eric Martin .01 .05
- ❑ 303 Chris Warren .02 .10
- ❑ 304 Deral Boykin RC .01 .05
- ❑ 305 Jessie Tuggle .01 .05
- ❑ 306 Glyn Milburn .02 .10
- ❑ 307 Terry Obee .01 .05
- ❑ 308 Eric Turner .01 .05
- ❑ 309 Dewayne Washington RC .02 .10
- ❑ 310 Sterling Sharpe .02 .10
- ❑ 311 Jeff Gossett .01 .05
- ❑ 312 John Carney .01 .05
- ❑ 313 Aaron Glenn RC .08 .25
- ❑ 314 Nick Lowery .01 .05
- ❑ 315 Thurman Thomas .08 .25
- ❑ 316 Troy Aikman MG .20 .50
- ❑ 317 Thurman Thomas MG .02 .10
- ❑ 318 Michael Irvin MG .02 .10
- ❑ 319 Steve Beuerlein MG .02 .10
- ❑ 320 Jerry Rice .40 1.00
- ❑ 321 Alexander Wright .01 .05
- ❑ 322 Michael Bates .01 .05
- ❑ 323 Greg Davis .01 .05
- ❑ 324 Mark Bortz .01 .05
- ❑ 325 Kevin Greene .02 .10
- ❑ 326 Wayne Simmons .01 .05
- ❑ 327 Wayne Martin .01 .05
- ❑ 328 Michael Irvin UER .08 .25
- ❑ 329 Checklist Card .01 .05
- ❑ 330 Checklist Card .01 .05
- ❑ 331 Doug Pelfrey .01 .05
- ❑ 332 Myron Guyton .01 .05
- ❑ 333 Howard Ballard .01 .05
- ❑ 334 Ricky Ervins .01 .05
- ❑ 335 Steve Emtman .01 .05
- ❑ 336 Eric Curry .01 .05
- ❑ 337 Bert Emanuel RC .08 .25
- ❑ 338 Darryl Ashmore .01 .05
- ❑ 339 Stevon Moore .01 .05
- ❑ 340 Garrison Hearst .08 .25
- ❑ 341 Vance Johnson .01 .05
- ❑ 342 Anthony Johnson .02 .10
- ❑ 343 Merril Hoge .01 .05
- ❑ 344 William Thomas .01 .05
- ❑ 345 Scott Mitchell .02 .10
- ❑ 346 Jim Everett .02 .10
- ❑ 347 Ray Crockett .01 .05
- ❑ 348 Bryan Cox .01 .05
- ❑ 349 Charles Johnson RC .08 .25
- ❑ 350 Randall McDaniel .02 .10
- ❑ 351 Micheal Barrow .01 .05
- ❑ 352 Darrell Thompson .01 .05

❑ 353 Kevin Gogan .01 .05
❑ 354 Brad Daluiso .01 .05
❑ 355 Mark Collins .01 .05
❑ 356 Bryant Young RC .15 .40
❑ 357 Steve Christie .01 .05
❑ 358 Derek Kennard .01 .05
❑ 359 Jon Vaughn .01 .05
❑ 360 Drew Bledsoe 3X .30 .75
❑ 361 Randy Baldwin .01 .05
❑ 362 Kevin Ross .01 .05
❑ 363 Reuben Davis .01 .05
❑ 364 Chris Miller .01 .05
❑ 365 Tim McGee .01 .05
❑ 366 Tony Woods .01 .05
❑ 367 Dean Biasucci .01 .05
❑ 368 George Jamison .01 .05
❑ 369 Lorenzo Lynch .01 .05
❑ 370 Johnny Johnson .01 .05
❑ 371 Greg Kragen .01 .05
❑ 372 Vinson Smith .01 .05
❑ 373 Vince Workman .01 .05
❑ 374 Allen Aldridge .01 .05
❑ 375 Terry Kirby .08 .25
❑ 376 Mario Bates RC .08 .25
❑ 377 Dixon Edwards .01 .05
❑ 378 Leon Searcy .01 .05
❑ 379 Eric Guliford RC .01 .05
❑ 380 Gary Brown .01 .05
❑ 381 Phil Hansen .01 .05
❑ 382 Keith Hamilton .01 .05
❑ 383 John Alt .01 .05
❑ 384 John Taylor .02 .10
❑ 385 Reggie Cobb .01 .05
❑ 386 Rob Fredrickson RC .02 .10
❑ 387 Pepper Johnson .01 .05
❑ 388 Kevin Lee RC .01 .05
❑ 389 Stanley Richard .01 .05
❑ 390 Jackie Slater .01 .05
❑ 391 Darrick Brilz .01 .05
❑ 392 John Gesek .01 .05
❑ 393 Kelvin Pritchett .01 .05
❑ 394 Aeneas Williams .01 .05
❑ 395 Henry Ford .01 .05
❑ 396 Eric Mahlum .01 .05
❑ 397 Tom Rouen .01 .05
❑ 398 Vinnie Clark .01 .05
❑ 399 Jim Sweeney .01 .05
❑ 400 Troy Aikman .40 1.00
❑ 401 Toi Cook .01 .05
❑ 402 Dan Saleaumua .01 .05
❑ 403 Andy Heck .01 .05
❑ 404 Deon Figures .01 .05
❑ 405 Henry Thomas .01 .05
❑ 406 Glenn Montgomery .01 .05
❑ 407 Trent Dilfer RC .40 1.00
❑ 408 Eddie Murray .01 .05
❑ 409 Gene Atkins .01 .05
❑ 410 Mike Sherrard .01 .05
❑ 411 Don Mosebar .01 .05
❑ 412 Thomas Smith .01 .05
❑ 413 Ken Norton Jr. .02 .10
❑ 414 Robert Brooks .08 .25
❑ 415 Jeff Lageman .01 .05
❑ 416 Tony Siragusa .01 .05
❑ 417 Brian Blades .02 .10
❑ 418 Matt Stover .01 .05
❑ 419 Jesse Solomon .01 .05
❑ 420 Reggie Roby .01 .05
❑ 421 Shawn Jefferson .01 .05
❑ 422 Marc Boutte .01 .05
❑ 423 William White .01 .05
❑ 424 Clyde Simmons .01 .05
❑ 425 Anthony Miller .02 .10
❑ 426 Brent Jones .02 .10
❑ 427 Tim Grunhard .01 .05
❑ 428 Alfred Williams .01 .05
❑ 429 Roy Barker RC .01 .05
❑ 430 Dante Jones .01 .05
❑ 431 Leroy Thompson .01 .05
❑ 432 Marcus Robertson .01 .05
❑ 433 Thomas Lewis RC .02 .10
❑ 434 Sean Jones .01 .05
❑ 435 Michael Haynes .02 .10
❑ 436 Albert Lewis .01 .05
❑ 437 Tim Bowens RC .02 .10
❑ 438 Marvcus Patton .01 .05
❑ 439 Rich Miano .01 .05
❑ 440 Craig Erickson .01 .05
❑ 441 Larry Allen RC .08 .25
❑ 442 Fernando Smith .01 .05
❑ 443 D.J. Johnson .01 .05
❑ 444 Leonard Russell .01 .05
❑ 445 Marshall Faulk RC 2.00 5.00
❑ 446 Najee Mustafaa .01 .05
❑ 447 Brian Hansen .01 .05
❑ 448 Isaac Bruce RC 2.00 4.00
❑ 449 Kevin Scott .01 .05
❑ 450 Natrone Means UER .08 .25
❑ 451 Tracy Rogers RC .01 .05
❑ 452 Mike Croel .01 .05
❑ 453 Anthony Edwards .01 .05
❑ 454 Brentson Buckner RC .01 .05
❑ 455 Tom Carter .01 .05
❑ 456 Burt Grossman .01 .05
❑ 457 Jimmy Spencer RC .01 .05
❑ 458 Rocket Ismail .02 .10
❑ 459 Fred Strickland .01 .05
❑ 460 Jeff Burris RC .02 .10
❑ 461 Adrian Hardy .01 .05
❑ 462 Lamar McGriggs .01 .05
❑ 463 Webster Slaughter .01 .05
❑ 464 Demetrius DuBose .01 .05
❑ 465 Dave Brown .02 .10
❑ 466 Kenneth Gant .01 .05
❑ 467 Erik Kramer .02 .10
❑ 468 Mark Ingram .01 .05
❑ 469 Roman Phifer .01 .05
❑ 470 Steve Young .20 .50
❑ 471 Nick Lowery .01 .05
❑ 472 Irving Fryar .02 .10
❑ 473 Art Monk .02 .10
❑ 474 Mel Gray .01 .05
❑ 475 Reggie White .08 .25
❑ 476 Eric Ball .01 .05
❑ 477 Dwayne Harper .01 .05
❑ 478 Will Shields .01 .05
❑ 479 Roger Harper .01 .05
❑ 480 Rick Mirer .08 .25
❑ 481 Vincent Brisby .02 .10
❑ 482 John Jurkovic RC .02 .10
❑ 483 Michael Jackson .02 .10
❑ 484 Ed Cunningham .01 .05
❑ 485 Brad Ottis .01 .05
❑ 486 Sterling Palmer RC .01 .05
❑ 487 Tony Bennett .01 .05
❑ 488 Mike Pritchard .01 .05
❑ 489 Bucky Brooks RC .01 .05
❑ 490 Troy Vincent .01 .05
❑ 491 Eric Green .01 .05
❑ 492 Van Malone .01 .05
❑ 493 Marcus Spears RC .01 .05
❑ 494 Brian Williams OL .01 .05
❑ 495 Robert Smith .08 .25
❑ 496 Haywood Jeffires .02 .10
❑ 497 Darrin Smith .01 .05
❑ 498 Tommy Barnhardt .01 .05
❑ 499 Anthony Smith .01 .05
❑ 500 Ricky Watters .02 .10
❑ 501 Antonio Davis .01 .05
❑ 502 David Braxton .01 .05
❑ 503 Donnell Bennett RC .08 .25
❑ 504 Donald Evans .01 .05
❑ 505 Lewis Tillman .01 .05
❑ 506 Lance Smith .01 .05
❑ 507 Aaron Taylor .01 .05
❑ 508 Ricky Sanders .01 .05
❑ 509 Dennis Smith .01 .05
❑ 510 Barry Foster .01 .05
❑ 511 Stan Brock .01 .05
❑ 512 Henry Rolling .01 .05
❑ 513 Walter Reeves .01 .05
❑ 514 John Booty .01 .05
❑ 515 Kenneth Davis .01 .05
❑ 516 Cris Dishman .01 .05
❑ 517 Bill Lewis .01 .05
❑ 518 Jeff Bryant .01 .05
❑ 519 Brian Mitchell .01 .05
❑ 520 Joe Montana .75 2.00
❑ 521 Keith Sims .01 .05
❑ 522 Harry Colon .01 .05
❑ 523 Leon Lett .01 .05
❑ 524 Carlos Jenkins .01 .05
❑ 525 Victor Bailey .01 .05
❑ 526 Harvey Williams .02 .10
❑ 527 Irv Smith .01 .05
❑ 528 Jason Sehorn RC .15 .40
❑ 529 John Thierry RC .01 .05
❑ 530 Brett Favre .75 2.00
❑ 531 Sean Dawkins RC .08 .25
❑ 532 Erric Pegram .01 .05
❑ 533 Jimmy Williams .01 .05
❑ 534 Michael Timpson .01 .05
❑ 535 Flipper Anderson .01 .05
❑ 536 John Parrella .01 .05
❑ 537 Freddie Joe Nunn .01 .05
❑ 538 Doug Dawson .01 .05
❑ 539 Michael Stewart .01 .05
❑ 540 John Elway .75 2.00
❑ 541 Ronnie Lott .02 .10
❑ 542 Barry Sanders TOG .30 .75
❑ 543 Andre Reed TOG .02 .10
❑ 544 Deion Sanders TOG .08 .25
❑ 545 Dan Marino TOG .30 .75
❑ 546 Carlton Bailey TOG .01 .05
❑ 547 Emmitt Smith TOG .30 .75
❑ 548 Alvin Harper TOG .02 .10
❑ 549 Eric Metcalf TOG .02 .10
❑ 550 Jerry Rice TOG .20 .50
❑ 551 Derrick Thomas TOG .08 .25
❑ 552 Mark Collins TOG .01 .05
❑ 553 Eric Turner TOG .01 .05
❑ 554 Sterling Sharpe TOG .02 .10
❑ 555 Steve Young TOG .08 .25
❑ 556 Darnay Scott RC .20 .50
❑ 557 Joel Steed .01 .05
❑ 558 Dennis Gibson .01 .05
❑ 559 Charles Mincy .01 .05
❑ 560 Rickey Jackson .01 .05
❑ 561 Dave Cadigan .01 .05
❑ 562 Rick Tuten .01 .05
❑ 563 Mike Caldwell .01 .05
❑ 564 Todd Steussie RC .02 .10
❑ 565 Kevin Smith .01 .05
❑ 566 Arthur Marshall .01 .05
❑ 567 Aaron Wallace .01 .05
❑ 568 Calvin Williams .02 .10
❑ 569 Todd Kelly .01 .05
❑ 570 Barry Sanders .60 1.50
❑ 571 Shaun Gayle .01 .05
❑ 572 Will Wolford .01 .05
❑ 573 Ethan Horton .01 .05
❑ 574 Chris Slade .01 .05
❑ 575 Jeff Wright .01 .05
❑ 576 Toby Wright .01 .05
❑ 577 Lamar Thomas .01 .05
❑ 578 Chris Singleton .01 .05
❑ 579 Ed West .01 .05
❑ 580 Jeff George .08 .25
❑ 581 Kevin Mitchell .01 .05
❑ 582 Chad Brown .01 .05
❑ 583 Rich Camarillo .01 .05
❑ 584 Gary Zimmerman .01 .05
❑ 585 Randal Hill .01 .05
❑ 586 Keith Cash .01 .05
❑ 587 Sam Mills .01 .05
❑ 588 Shawn Lee .01 .05
❑ 589 Kent Graham .02 .10
❑ 590 Steve Everitt .01 .05
❑ 591 Rob Moore .02 .10
❑ 592 Kevin Mawae RC .08 .25
❑ 593 Jerry Ball .01 .05
❑ 594 Larry Brown DB .01 .05
❑ 595 Tim Krumrie .01 .05
❑ 596 Aubrey Beavers RC .01 .05
❑ 597 Chris Hinton .01 .05
❑ 598 Greg Montgomery .01 .05
❑ 599 Jimmie Jones .01 .05
❑ 600 Jim Kelly .08 .25
❑ 601 Joe Johnson RC .01 .05
❑ 602 Tim Irwin .01 .05
❑ 603 Steve Jackson .01 .05
❑ 604 James Williams RC .01 .05
❑ 605 Blair Thomas .01 .05
❑ 606 Danan Hughes .01 .05
❑ 607 Russell Freeman .01 .05
❑ 608 Andre Hastings .02 .10
❑ 609 Ken Harvey .01 .05
❑ 610 Jim Harbaugh .08 .25
❑ 611 Emmitt Smith MG .30 .75
❑ 612 Andre Rison MG .02 .10
❑ 613 Steve Young MG .08 .25
❑ 614 Anthony Miller MG .01 .05
❑ 615 Barry Sanders MG .30 .75
❑ 616 Bernie Kosar .02 .10
❑ 617 Chris Gardocki .01 .05
❑ 618 William Floyd RC .08 .25
❑ 619 Matt Brock .01 .05

Card		
620 Dan Wilkinson RC	.02	.10
621 Tony Meola RC	.02	.10
622 Tony Tolbert	.01	.05
623 Mike Zandofsky	.01	.05
624 William Fuller	.01	.05
625 Steve Jordan	.01	.05
626 Mike Johnson	.01	.05
627 Ferrell Edmunds	.01	.05
628 Gene Williams	.01	.05
629 Willie Beamon	.01	.05
630 Gerald Perry	.01	.05
631 John Baylor	.01	.05
632 Carwell Gardner	.01	.05
633 Thomas Everett	.01	.05
634 Lamar Lathon	.01	.05
635 Michael Bankston	.01	.05
636 Ray Crittenden RC	.01	.05
637 Kimble Anders	.02	.10
638 Robert Delpino	.01	.05
639 Darren Perry	.01	.05
640 Byron Evans	.01	.05
641 Mark Higgs	.01	.05
642 Lorenzo Neal	.01	.05
643 Henry Ellard	.02	.10
644 Trace Armstrong	.01	.05
645 Greg McMurtry	.01	.05
646 Steve McMichael	.02	.10
647 Terance Mathis	.02	.10
648 Eric Bieniemy	.01	.05
649 Bobby Houston	.01	.05
650 Alvin Harper	.02	.10
651 James Folston RC	.01	.05
652 Mel Gray	.01	.05
653 Adrian Cooper	.01	.05
654 Dexter Carter	.01	.05
655 Don Griffin	.01	.05
656 Corey Widmer	.01	.05
657 Lee Johnson	.01	.05
658 Nate Odomes	.01	.05
659 Checklist Card	.01	.05
660 Checklist Card	.01	.05
P1 Promo Sheet	1.50	4.00
P2 Promo Sheet Special Effects	1.50	4.00

1995 Topps

Card		
COMPLETE SET (468)	15.00	40.00
COMP.FACT.SET (478)	30.00	60.00
COMP.SERIES 1 (248)	8.00	20.00
COMP.SERIES 2 (220)	8.00	20.00
1 Barry Sanders TYC	.30	.75
2 Chris Warren TYC	.07	.20
3 Jerry Rice TYC	.20	.50
4 Emmitt Smith TYC	.30	.75
5 Henry Ellard TYC	.07	.20
6 Natrone Means TYC	.07	.20
7 Terance Mathis TYC	.07	.20
8 Tim Brown TYC	.07	.20
9 Andre Reed TYC	.07	.20
10 Marshall Faulk TYC	.25	.60
11 Irving Fryar TYC	.07	.20
12 Cris Carter TYC	.10	.30
13 Michael Irvin TYC	.10	.30
14 Jake Reed TYC	.07	.20
15 Ben Coates TYC	.07	.20
16 Herman Moore TYC	.10	.30
17 Carl Pickens TYC	.07	.20
18 Fred Barnett TYC	.07	.20
19 Sterling Sharpe TYC	.07	.20
20 Anthony Miller TYC	.07	.20
21 Thurman Thomas TYC	.10	.30
22 Andre Rison TYC	.07	.20
23 Brian Blades TYC	.07	.20
24 Rodney Hampton TYC	.07	.20
25 Terry Allen TYC	.07	.20
26 Jerome Bettis TYC	.10	.30
27 Errict Rhett TYC	.07	.20
28 Rob Moore TYC	.07	.20
29 Shannon Sharpe TYC	.07	.20
30 Drew Bledsoe TYC	.10	.30
31 Dan Marino TYC	.40	1.00
32 Warren Moon TYC	.07	.20
33 Steve Young TYC	.15	.40
34 Brett Favre TYC	.40	1.00
35 Jim Everett TYC	.02	.10
36 Jeff George TYC	.07	.20
37 John Elway TYC	.40	1.00
38 Jeff Hostetler TYC	.07	.20
39 Randall Cunningham TYC	.10	.30
40 Stan Humphries TYC	.07	.20
41 Jim Kelly TYC	.10	.30
42 Tommy Barnhardt	.02	.10
43 Bob Whitfield	.02	.10
44 William Thomas	.02	.10
45 Glyn Milburn	.02	.10
46 Steve Christie	.02	.10
47 Kevin Mawae	.02	.10
48 Vencie Glenn	.02	.10
49 Eric Curry	.02	.10
50 Jeff Hostetler	.07	.20
51 Tyronne Stowe	.02	.10
52 Steve Jackson	.02	.10
53 Ben Coleman	.02	.10
54 Brad Baxter	.02	.10
55 Darryl Williams	.02	.10
56 Troy Drayton	.02	.10
57 George Teague	.02	.10
58 Calvin Williams	.07	.20
59 Jeff Cross	.02	.10
60 Leroy Hoard	.02	.10
61 John Carney	.02	.10
62 Daryl Johnston	.07	.20
63 Jim Jeffcoat	.02	.10
64 Matt Stover	.02	.10
65 LeRoy Butler	.02	.10
66 Curtis Conway	.10	.30
67 O.J. McDuffie	.10	.30
68 Robert Massey	.02	.10
69 Ed McDaniel	.02	.10
70 William Floyd	.07	.20
71 Willie Davis	.07	.20
72 William Roberts	.02	.10
73 Chester McGlockton	.07	.20
74 D.J. Johnson	.02	.10
75 Rondell Jones	.02	.10
76 Morten Andersen	.02	.10
77 Glenn Parker	.02	.10
78 William Fuller	.02	.10
79 Ray Buchanan	.02	.10
80 Maurice Hurst	.02	.10
81 Wayne Gandy	.02	.10
82 Marcus Turner	.02	.10
83 Greg Davis	.02	.10
84 Terry Wooden	.02	.10
85 Thomas Everett	.02	.10
86 Steve Broussard	.02	.10
87 Tom Carter	.02	.10
88 Glenn Montgomery	.02	.10
89 Larry Allen	.07	.20
90 Donnell Woolford	.02	.10
91 John Alt	.02	.10
92 Phil Hansen	.02	.10
93 Seth Joyner	.02	.10
94 Michael Brooks	.02	.10
95 Randall McDaniel	.05	.15
96 Tydus Winans	.02	.10
97 Rob Fredrickson	.02	.10
98 Ray Crockett	.02	.10
99 Courtney Hall	.02	.10
100 Merton Hanks	.02	.10
101 Aaron Glenn	.02	.10
102 Roosevelt Potts	.02	.10
103 Leon Lett	.02	.10
104 Jessie Tuggle	.02	.10
105 Martin Mayhew	.02	.10
106 Willie Roaf	.02	.10
107 Todd Lyght	.02	.10
108 Ernest Givins	.02	.10
109 Tony McGee	.02	.10
110 Barry Sanders	.60	1.50
111 Dermontti Dawson	.07	.20
112 Rick Tuten	.02	.10
113 Vincent Brisby	.02	.10
114 Charlie Garner	.10	.30
115 Irving Fryar	.07	.20
116 Stevon Moore	.02	.10
117 Matt Darby	.02	.10
118 Howard Cross	.02	.10
119 John Gesek	.02	.10
120 Jack Del Rio	.02	.10
121 Marcus Allen	.10	.30
122 Torrance Small	.02	.10
123 Chris Mims	.02	.10
124 Don Mosebar	.02	.10
125 Carl Pickens	.07	.20
126 Tom Rouen	.02	.10
127 Garrison Hearst	.10	.30
128 Charles Johnson	.07	.20
129 Derek Brown RBK	.02	.10
130 Troy Aikman	.40	1.00
131 Troy Vincent	.02	.10
132 Ken Ruettgers	.02	.10
133 Michael Jackson	.07	.20
134 Dennis Gibson	.02	.10
135 Brett Perriman	.07	.20
136 Jeff Graham	.02	.10
137 Chad Brown	.07	.20
138 Ken Norton Jr.	.07	.20
139 Chris Slade	.02	.10
140 Dave Brown	.07	.20
141 Bert Emanuel	.10	.30
142 Renaldo Turnbull	.02	.10
143 Jim Harbaugh	.07	.20
144 Micheal Barrow	.02	.10
145 Vincent Brown	.02	.10
146 Bryant Young	.07	.20
147 Boomer Esiason	.07	.20
148 Sean Gilbert	.07	.20
149 Greg Truitt	.02	.10
150 Rod Woodson	.07	.20
151 Robert Porcher	.02	.10
152 Joe Phillips	.02	.10
153 Gary Zimmerman	.02	.10
154 Bruce Smith	.10	.30
155 Randall Cunningham	.10	.30
156 Fred Strickland	.02	.10
157 Derrick Alexander WR	.10	.30
158 James Williams LB	.02	.10
159 Scott Dill	.02	.10
160 Tim Bowens	.02	.10
161 Floyd Turner	.02	.10
162 Ronnie Harmon	.02	.10
163 Wayne Martin	.02	.10
164 John Randle	.07	.20
165 Larry Centers	.07	.20
166 Larry Brown DB	.02	.10
167 Albert Lewis	.02	.10
168 Michael Strahan	.10	.30
169 Reggie Brooks	.07	.20
170 Craig Heyward	.07	.20
171 Pat Harlow	.02	.10
172 Eugene Robinson	.02	.10
173 Shane Conlan	.02	.10
174 Bennie Blades	.02	.10
175 Neil O'Donnell	.07	.20
176 Steve Tovar	.02	.10
177 Donald Evans	.02	.10
178 Brent Jones	.02	.10
179 Ray Childress	.02	.10
180 Reggie White	.10	.30
181 David Alexander	.02	.10
182 Greg Hill	.07	.20
183 Vinny Testaverde	.07	.20
184 Jeff Burris	.02	.10
185 Hardy Nickerson	.02	.10
186 Terry Kirby	.07	.20
187 Kirk Lowdermilk	.02	.10
188 Eric Swann	.07	.20
189 Chris Zorich	.02	.10
190 Simon Fletcher	.02	.10
191 Qadry Ismail	.07	.20
192 Heath Shuler	.07	.20
193 Michael Haynes	.07	.20
194 Mike Sherrard	.02	.10
195 Nolan Harrison	.02	.10
196 Marcus Robertson	.02	.10
197 Kevin Williams WR	.07	.20
198 Moe Gardner	.02	.10
199 Rick Mirer	.07	.20
200 Junior Seau	.10	.30
201 Byron Bam Morris	.02	.10
202 Willie McGinest	.07	.20
203 Chris Spielman	.07	.20
204 Darnay Scott	.07	.20
205 Jesse Sapolu	.02	.10

Card	Low	High
❑ 206 Marvin Washington	.02	.10
❑ 207 Anthony Newman	.02	.10
❑ 208 Cortez Kennedy	.07	.20
❑ 209 Quentin Coryatt	.07	.20
❑ 210 Neil Smith	.07	.20
❑ 211 Keith Sims	.02	.10
❑ 212 Sean Jones	.02	.10
❑ 213 Tony Jones T	.02	.10
❑ 214 Lewis Tillman	.02	.10
❑ 215 Darren Woodson	.07	.20
❑ 216 Jason Hanson	.02	.10
❑ 217 John Taylor	.02	.10
❑ 218 Shawn Lee	.02	.10
❑ 219 Kevin Greene	.07	.20
❑ 220 Jerry Rice	.40	1.00
❑ 221 Ki-Jana Carter RC	.10	.30
❑ 222 Tony Boselli RC	.10	.30
❑ 223 Michael Westbrook RC	.10	.30
❑ 224 Kerry Collins RC	.75	2.00
❑ 225 Kevin Carter RC	.10	.30
❑ 226 Kyle Brady RC	.10	.30
❑ 227 J.J. Stokes RC	.10	.30
❑ 228 Derrick Alexander DE RC	.02	.10
❑ 229 Warren Sapp RC	.60	1.50
❑ 230 Ruben Brown RC	.10	.30
❑ 231 Hugh Douglas RC	.10	.30
❑ 232 Luther Elliss RC	.02	.10
❑ 233 Rashaan Salaam RC	.07	.20
❑ 234 Tyrone Poole RC	.10	.30
❑ 235 Korey Stringer RC	.10	.30
❑ 236 Devin Bush RC	.02	.10
❑ 237 Cory Raymer RC	.02	.10
❑ 238 Zach Wiegert RC	.02	.10
❑ 239 Ron Davis RC	.02	.10
❑ 240 Todd Collins RC	.50	1.25
❑ 241 Bobby Taylor RC	.10	.30
❑ 242 Patrick Riley RC	.02	.10
❑ 243 Scott Gragg	.02	.10
❑ 244 Marvcus Patton	.02	.10
❑ 245 Alvin Harper	.02	.10
❑ 246 Ricky Watters	.07	.20
❑ 247 Checklist 1	.02	.10
❑ 248 Checklist 2	.02	.10
❑ 249 Terance Mathis	.07	.20
❑ 250 Mark Carrier DB	.02	.10
❑ 251 Elijah Alexander	.02	.10
❑ 252 George Koonce	.02	.10
❑ 253 Tony Bennett	.02	.10
❑ 254 Steve Wisniewski	.02	.10
❑ 255 Bernie Parmalee	.07	.20
❑ 256 Dwayne Sabb	.02	.10
❑ 257 Lorenzo Neal	.02	.10
❑ 258 Corey Miller	.02	.10
❑ 259 Fred Barnett	.07	.20
❑ 260 Greg Lloyd	.07	.20
❑ 261 Robert Blackmon	.02	.10
❑ 262 Ken Harvey	.02	.10
❑ 263 Eric Hill	.02	.10
❑ 264 Russell Copeland	.02	.10
❑ 265 Jeff Blake RC	.30	.75
❑ 266 Carl Banks	.02	.10
❑ 267 Jay Novacek	.07	.20
❑ 268 Mel Gray	.02	.10
❑ 269 Kimble Anders	.07	.20
❑ 270 Cris Carter	.10	.30
❑ 271 Johnny Mitchell	.02	.10
❑ 272 Shawn Jefferson	.02	.10
❑ 273 Doug Brien	.02	.10
❑ 274 Sean Landeta	.02	.10
❑ 275 Scott Mitchell	.07	.20
❑ 276 Charles Wilson	.02	.10
❑ 277 Anthony Smith	.02	.10
❑ 278 Anthony Miller	.07	.20
❑ 279 Steve Walsh	.02	.10
❑ 280 Drew Bledsoe	.25	.60
❑ 281 Jamir Miller	.02	.10
❑ 282 Robert Brooks	.10	.30
❑ 283 Sean Lumpkin	.02	.10
❑ 284 Bryan Cox	.02	.10
❑ 285 Byron Evans	.02	.10
❑ 286 Chris Doleman	.02	.10
❑ 287 Anthony Pleasant	.02	.10
❑ 288 Stephen Grant RC	.02	.10
❑ 289 Doug Riesenberg	.02	.10
❑ 290 Natrone Means	.07	.20
❑ 291 Henry Thomas	.02	.10
❑ 292 Mike Pritchard	.02	.10
❑ 293 Courtney Hawkins	.02	.10
❑ 294 Bill Bates	.07	.20
❑ 295 Jerome Bettis	.10	.30
❑ 296 Russell Maryland	.02	.10
❑ 297 Stanley Richard	.02	.10
❑ 298 William White	.02	.10
❑ 299 Dan Wilkinson	.07	.20
❑ 300 Steve Young	.30	.75
❑ 301 Gary Brown	.02	.10
❑ 302 Jake Reed	.07	.20
❑ 303 Carlton Gray	.02	.10
❑ 304 Levon Kirkland	.02	.10
❑ 305 Shannon Sharpe	.07	.20
❑ 306 Luis Sharpe	.02	.10
❑ 307 Marshall Faulk	.50	1.25
❑ 308 Stan Humphries	.07	.20
❑ 309 Chris Calloway	.02	.10
❑ 310 Tim Brown	.10	.30
❑ 311 Steve Everitt	.02	.10
❑ 312 Raymont Harris	.02	.10
❑ 313 Tim McDonald	.02	.10
❑ 314 Trent Dilfer	.10	.30
❑ 315 Jim Everett	.02	.10
❑ 316 Ray Crittenden	.02	.10
❑ 317 Jim Kelly	.10	.30
❑ 318 Andre Reed	.07	.20
❑ 319 Chris Miller	.02	.10
❑ 320 Bobby Houston	.02	.10
❑ 321 Charles Haley	.07	.20
❑ 322 James Francis	.02	.10
❑ 323 Bernard Williams	.02	.10
❑ 324 Michael Bates	.02	.10
❑ 325 Brian Mitchell	.02	.10
❑ 326 Mike Johnson	.02	.10
❑ 327 Eric Bieniemy	.02	.10
❑ 328 Aubrey Beavers	.02	.10
❑ 329 Dale Carter	.07	.20
❑ 330 Emmitt Smith	.60	1.50
❑ 331 Darren Perry	.02	.10
❑ 332 Marquez Pope	.02	.10
❑ 333 Clyde Simmons	.02	.10
❑ 334 Corey Croom	.02	.10
❑ 335 Thomas Randolph	.02	.10
❑ 336 Harvey Williams	.02	.10
❑ 337 Michael Timpson	.02	.10
❑ 338 Eugene Daniel	.02	.10
❑ 339 Shane Dronett	.02	.10
❑ 340 Eric Turner	.02	.10
❑ 341 Eric Metcalf	.07	.20
❑ 342 Leslie O'Neal	.07	.20
❑ 343 Mark Wheeler	.02	.10
❑ 344 Mark Pike	.02	.10
❑ 345 Brett Favre	.75	2.00
❑ 346 Johnny Bailey	.02	.10
❑ 347 Henry Ellard	.07	.20
❑ 348 Chris Gardocki	.02	.10
❑ 349 Henry Jones	.02	.10
❑ 350 Dan Marino	.75	2.00
❑ 351 Lake Dawson	.07	.20
❑ 352 Mark McMillian	.02	.10
❑ 353 Deion Sanders	.25	.60
❑ 354 Antonio London	.02	.10
❑ 355 Cris Dishman	.02	.10
❑ 356 Ricardo McDonald	.02	.10
❑ 357 Dexter Carter	.02	.10
❑ 358 Kevin Smith	.02	.10
❑ 359 Yancey Thigpen RC	.07	.20
❑ 360 Chris Warren	.07	.20
❑ 361 Quinn Early	.07	.20
❑ 362 John Mangum	.02	.10
❑ 363 Santana Dotson	.02	.10
❑ 364 Rocket Ismail	.07	.20
❑ 365 Aeneas Williams	.02	.10
❑ 366 Dan Williams	.02	.10
❑ 367 Sean Dawkins	.07	.20
❑ 368 Pepper Johnson	.02	.10
❑ 369 Roman Phifer	.02	.10
❑ 370 Rodney Hampton	.07	.20
❑ 371 Darrell Green	.02	.10
❑ 372 Michael Zordich	.02	.10
❑ 373 Andre Coleman	.02	.10
❑ 374 Wayne Simmons	.02	.10
❑ 375 Michael Irvin	.10	.30
❑ 376 Clay Matthews	.07	.20
❑ 377 Dewayne Washington	.07	.20
❑ 378 Keith Byars	.02	.10
❑ 379 Todd Collins LB	.10	.30
❑ 380 Mark Collins	.02	.10
❑ 381 Joel Steed	.02	.10
❑ 382 Bart Oates	.02	.10
❑ 383 Al Smith	.02	.10
❑ 384 Rafael Robinson	.02	.10
❑ 385 Mo Lewis	.02	.10
❑ 386 Aubrey Matthews	.02	.10
❑ 387 Corey Sawyer	.02	.10
❑ 388 Bucky Brooks	.02	.10
❑ 389 Erik Kramer	.02	.10
❑ 390 Tyrone Hughes	.07	.20
❑ 391 Terry McDaniel	.02	.10
❑ 392 Craig Erickson	.02	.10
❑ 393 Mike Flores	.02	.10
❑ 394 Harry Swayne	.02	.10
❑ 395 Irving Spikes	.07	.20
❑ 396 Lorenzo Lynch	.02	.10
❑ 397 Antonio Langham	.02	.10
❑ 398 Edgar Bennett	.07	.20
❑ 399 Thomas Lewis	.07	.20
❑ 400 John Elway	.75	2.00
❑ 401 Jeff George	.07	.20
❑ 402 Errict Rhett	.07	.20
❑ 403 Bill Romanowski	.02	.10
❑ 404 Alexander Wright	.02	.10
❑ 405 Warren Moon	.07	.20
❑ 406 Eddie Robinson	.02	.10
❑ 407 John Copeland	.02	.10
❑ 408 Robert Jones	.02	.10
❑ 409 Steve Bono	.07	.20
❑ 410 Cornelius Bennett	.07	.20
❑ 411 Ben Coates	.07	.20
❑ 412 Dana Stubblefield	.07	.20
❑ 413 Darryl Talley	.02	.10
❑ 414 Brian Blades	.07	.20
❑ 415 Herman Moore	.10	.30
❑ 416 Nick Lowery	.02	.10
❑ 417 Donnell Bennett	.07	.20
❑ 418 Van Malone	.02	.10
❑ 419 Pete Stoyanovich	.02	.10
❑ 420 Joe Montana	.75	2.00
❑ 421 Steve Young	.20	.50
❑ 422 Steve Young	.20	.50
❑ 423 Steve Young	.20	.50
❑ 424 Steve Young	.20	.50
❑ 425 Steve Young	.20	.50
❑ 426 Rod Stephens	.02	.10
❑ 427 Ellis Johnson UER RC	.02	.10
❑ 428 Kordell Stewart RC	.50	1.25
❑ 429 James O. Stewart RC	.40	1.00
❑ 430 Steve McNair RC	1.00	2.50
❑ 431 Brian DeMarco	.07	.20
❑ 432 Matt O'Dwyer	.02	.10
❑ 433 Lorenzo Styles RC	.02	.10
❑ 434 Anthony Cook RC	.02	.10
❑ 435 Jesse James	.02	.10
❑ 436 Darryl Pounds RC	.02	.10
❑ 437 Derrick Graham	.02	.10
❑ 438 Vernon Turner	.02	.10
❑ 439 Carlton Bailey	.02	.10
❑ 440 Darion Conner	.02	.10
❑ 441 Randy Baldwin	.02	.10
❑ 442 Tim McKyer	.02	.10
❑ 443 Sam Mills	.07	.20
❑ 444 Bob Christian	.02	.10
❑ 445 Steve Lofton	.02	.10
❑ 446 Lamar Lathon	.02	.10
❑ 447 Tony Smith RB	.02	.10
❑ 448 Don Beebe	.02	.10
❑ 449 Barry Foster	.07	.20
❑ 450 Frank Reich	.02	.10
❑ 451 Pete Metzelaars	.02	.10
❑ 452 Reggie Cobb	.02	.10
❑ 453 Jeff Lageman	.02	.10
❑ 454 Derek Brown TE	.02	.10
❑ 455 Desmond Howard	.07	.20
❑ 456 Vinnie Clark	.02	.10
❑ 457 Keith Goganious	.02	.10
❑ 458 Shawn Bouwens	.02	.10
❑ 459 Rob Johnson RC	.30	.75
❑ 460 Steve Beuerlein	.07	.20
❑ 461 Mark Brunell	.25	.60
❑ 462 Harry Colon	.02	.10
❑ 463 Chris Hudson	.02	.10
❑ 464 Darren Carrington	.02	.10
❑ 465 Ernest Givins	.02	.10
❑ 466 Kelvin Pritchett	.02	.10
❑ 467 Checklist (249-358)	.02	.10
❑ 468 Checklist ([illegible])	.02	.10

1996 Topps

Card		
❑ COMPLETE SET (440)	20.00	40.00
❑ COMP.FACT.SET (448)	35.00	60.00
❑ COMP.CER.FACT.SET (445)	20.00	40.00
❑ 1 Troy Aikman	.40	1.00
❑ 2 Kevin Greene	.07	.20
❑ 3 Robert Brooks	.10	.30
❑ 4 Eugene Daniel	.02	.10
❑ 5 Rodney Peete	.02	.10
❑ 6 James Hasty	.02	.10
❑ 7 Tim McDonald	.02	.10
❑ 8 Darick Holmes	.02	.10
❑ 9 Morten Andersen	.02	.10
❑ 10 Junior Seau	.10	.30
❑ 11 Brett Perriman	.02	.10
❑ 12 Eric Green	.02	.10
❑ 13 Jim Flanigan	.02	.10
❑ 14 Cortez Kennedy	.02	.10
❑ 15 Orlando Thomas	.02	.10
❑ 16 Anthony Miller	.07	.20
❑ 17 Sean Gilbert	.02	.10
❑ 18 Rob Fredrickson	.02	.10
❑ 19 Willie Green	.02	.10
❑ 20 Jeff Blake	.10	.30
❑ 21 Trent Dilfer	.10	.30
❑ 22 Chris Chandler	.07	.20
❑ 23 Renaldo Turnbull	.02	.10
❑ 24 Dave Meggett	.02	.10
❑ 25 Heath Shuler	.07	.20
❑ 26 Michael Jackson	.07	.20
❑ 27 Thomas Randolph	.02	.10
❑ 28 Keith Goganious	.02	.10
❑ 29 Seth Joyner	.02	.10
❑ 30 Wayne Chrebet	.25	.60
❑ 31 Craig Newsome	.02	.10
❑ 32 William Fuller	.02	.10
❑ 33 Merton Hanks	.02	.10
❑ 34 Dale Carter	.02	.10
❑ 35 Quentin Coryatt	.02	.10
❑ 36 Robert Jones	.02	.10
❑ 37 Eric Metcalf	.02	.10
❑ 38 Byron Bam Morris	.02	.10
❑ 39 Bill Brooks	.02	.10
❑ 40 Barry Sanders	.60	1.50
❑ 41 Michael Haynes	.02	.10
❑ 42 Joey Galloway	.10	.30
❑ 43 Robert Smith	.07	.20
❑ 44 John Thierry	.02	.10
❑ 45 Bryan Cox	.02	.10
❑ 46 Anthony Parker	.02	.10
❑ 47 Harvey Williams	.02	.10
❑ 48 Terrell Davis	.30	.75
❑ 49 Darnay Scott	.07	.20
❑ 50 Kerry Collins	.10	.30
❑ 51 Cris Dishman	.02	.10
❑ 52 Dwayne Harper	.02	.10
❑ 53 Warren Sapp	.02	.10
❑ 54 Will Moore	.02	.10
❑ 55 Earnest Byner	.02	.10
❑ 56 Aaron Glenn	.02	.10
❑ 57 Michael Westbrook	.10	.30
❑ 58 Vencie Glenn	.02	.10
❑ 59 Rob Moore	.07	.20
❑ 60 Mark Brunell	.25	.60
❑ 61 Craig Heyward	.02	.10
❑ 62 Eric Allen	.02	.10
❑ 63 Bill Romanowski	.02	.10
❑ 64 Dana Stubblefield	.07	.20
❑ 65 Steve Bono	.02	.10
❑ 66 George Koonce	.02	.10
❑ 67 Larry Brown	.02	.10
❑ 68 Warren Moon	.07	.20
❑ 69 Erric Pegram	.02	.10
❑ 70 Jim Kelly	.10	.30
❑ 71 Jason Belser	.02	.10
❑ 72 Henry Thomas	.02	.10
❑ 73 Mark Carrier DB	.02	.10
❑ 74 Terry Wooden	.02	.10
❑ 75 Terry McDaniel	.02	.10
❑ 76 O.J. McDuffie	.07	.20
❑ 77 Dan Wilkinson	.02	.10
❑ 78 Blake Brockermeyer	.02	.10
❑ 79 Micheal Barrow	.02	.10
❑ 80 Dave Brown	.02	.10
❑ 81 Todd Lyght	.02	.10
❑ 82 Henry Ellard	.02	.10
❑ 83 Jeff Lageman	.02	.10
❑ 84 Anthony Pleasant	.02	.10
❑ 85 Aeneas Williams	.02	.10
❑ 86 Vincent Brisby	.02	.10
❑ 87 Terrell Fletcher	.02	.10
❑ 88 Brad Baxter	.02	.10
❑ 89 Shannon Sharpe	.07	.20
❑ 90 Erric Rhett	.07	.20
❑ 91 Michael Zordich	.02	.10
❑ 92 Dan Saleaumua	.02	.10
❑ 93 Devin Bush	.02	.10
❑ 94 Wayne Simmons	.02	.10
❑ 95 Tyrone Hughes	.02	.10
❑ 96 John Randle	.07	.20
❑ 97 Tony Tolbert	.02	.10
❑ 98 Yancey Thigpen	.07	.20
❑ 99 J.J. Stokes	.10	.30
❑ 100 Marshall Faulk	.15	.40
❑ 101 Barry Minter	.02	.10
❑ 102 Glenn Foley	.07	.20
❑ 103 Chester McGlockton	.02	.10
❑ 104 Carlton Gray	.02	.10
❑ 105 Terry Kirby	.07	.20
❑ 106 Darryll Lewis	.02	.10
❑ 107 Thomas Smith	.02	.10
❑ 108 Mike Fox	.02	.10
❑ 109 Antonio Langham	.02	.10
❑ 110 Drew Bledsoe	.25	.60
❑ 111 Troy Drayton	.02	.10
❑ 112 Marvcus Patton	.02	.10
❑ 113 Tyrone Wheatley	.07	.20
❑ 114 Desmond Howard	.07	.20
❑ 115 Johnny Mitchell	.02	.10
❑ 116 Dave Krieg	.02	.10
❑ 117 Natrone Means	.07	.20
❑ 118 Herman Moore	.07	.20
❑ 119 Darren Woodson	.07	.20
❑ 120 Ricky Watters	.07	.20
❑ 121 Emmitt Smith TYC	.30	.75
❑ 122 Barry Sanders TYC	.30	.75
❑ 123 Curtis Martin TYC	.10	.30
❑ 124 Chris Warren TYC	.07	.20
❑ 125 Terry Allen TYC	.07	.20
❑ 126 Ricky Watters TYC	.07	.20
❑ 127 Errict Rhett TYC	.07	.20
❑ 128 Rodney Hampton TYC	.02	.10
❑ 129 Terrell Davis TYC	.10	.30
❑ 130 Harvey Williams TYC	.02	.10
❑ 131 Craig Heyward TYC	.02	.10
❑ 132 Marshall Faulk TYC	.10	.30
❑ 133 Rashaan Salaam TYC	.07	.20
❑ 134 Garrison Hearst TYC	.07	.20
❑ 135 Edgar Bennett TYC	.07	.20
❑ 136 Thurman Thomas TYC	.07	.20
❑ 137 Brian Washington	.02	.10
❑ 138 Derek Loville	.02	.10
❑ 139 Curtis Conway	.10	.30
❑ 140 Isaac Bruce	.10	.30
❑ 141 Ricardo McDonald	.02	.10
❑ 142 Bruce Armstrong	.02	.10
❑ 143 Will Wolford	.02	.10
❑ 144 Thurman Thomas	.10	.30
❑ 145 Mel Gray	.02	.10
❑ 146 Napoleon Kaufman	.10	.30
❑ 147 Terry Allen	.07	.20
❑ 148 Chris Calloway	.02	.10
❑ 149 Harry Colon	.02	.10
❑ 150 Pepper Johnson	.02	.10
❑ 151 Marco Coleman	.02	.10
❑ 152 Shawn Jefferson	.02	.10
❑ 153 Larry Centers	.07	.20
❑ 154 Lamar Lathon	.02	.10
❑ 155 Mark Chmura	.07	.20
❑ 156 Dermontti Dawson	.02	.10
❑ 157 Alvin Harper	.02	.10
❑ 158 Randall McDaniel	.05	.15
❑ 159 Allen Aldridge	.02	.10
❑ 160 Chris Warren	.07	.20
❑ 161 Jessie Tuggle	.02	.10
❑ 162 Sean Lumpkin	.02	.10
❑ 163 Bobby Houston	.02	.10
❑ 164 Dexter Carter	.02	.10
❑ 165 Erik Kramer	.02	.10
❑ 166 Brock Marion	.02	.10
❑ 167 Toby Wright	.02	.10
❑ 168 John Copeland	.02	.10
❑ 169 Sean Dawkins	.02	.10
❑ 170 Tim Brown	.10	.30
❑ 171 Darion Conner	.02	.10
❑ 172 Aaron Hayden RC	.02	.10
❑ 173 Charlie Garner	.07	.20
❑ 174 Anthony Cook	.02	.10
❑ 175 Derrick Thomas	.10	.30
❑ 176 Willie McGinest	.02	.10
❑ 177 Thomas Lewis	.02	.10
❑ 178 Sherman Williams	.02	.10
❑ 179 Cornelius Bennett	.02	.10
❑ 180 Frank Sanders	.10	.30
❑ 181 Leroy Hoard	.02	.10
❑ 182 Bernie Parmalee	.02	.10
❑ 183 Sterling Palmer	.02	.10
❑ 184 Kelvin Pritchett	.02	.10
❑ 185 Kordell Stewart	.10	.30
❑ 186 Brent Jones	.02	.10
❑ 187 Robert Blackmon	.02	.10
❑ 188 Adrian Murrell	.07	.20
❑ 189 Edgar Bennett	.07	.20
❑ 190 Rashaan Salaam	.07	.20
❑ 191 Ellis Johnson	.02	.10
❑ 192 Andre Coleman	.02	.10
❑ 193 Will Shields	.02	.10
❑ 194 Derrick Brooks	.10	.30
❑ 195 Carl Pickens	.07	.20
❑ 196 Carlton Bailey	.02	.10
❑ 197 Terance Mathis	.07	.20
❑ 198 Carlos Jenkins	.02	.10
❑ 199 Derrick Alexander	.02	.10
❑ 200 Deion Sanders	.25	.60
❑ 201 Glyn Milburn	.02	.10
❑ 202 Chris Sanders	.07	.20
❑ 203 Rocket Ismail	.02	.10
❑ 204 Fred Barnett	.02	.10
❑ 205 Quinn Early	.02	.10
❑ 206 Henry Jones	.02	.10
❑ 207 Herschel Walker	.07	.20
❑ 208 James Washington	.02	.10
❑ 209 Lee Woodall	.02	.10
❑ 210 Neil Smith	.07	.20
❑ 211 Tony Bennett	.02	.10
❑ 212 Ernie Mills	.02	.10
❑ 213 Clyde Simmons	.02	.10
❑ 214 Chris Slade	.02	.10
❑ 215 Tony Boselli	.02	.10
❑ 216 Ryan McNeil	.02	.10
❑ 217 Rob Burnett	.02	.10
❑ 218 Stan Humphries	.07	.20
❑ 219 Rick Mirer	.07	.20
❑ 220 Troy Vincent	.02	.10
❑ 221 Sean Jones	.02	.10
❑ 222 Marty Carter	.02	.10
❑ 223 Boomer Esiason	.07	.20
❑ 224 Charles Haley	.07	.20
❑ 225 Sam Mills	.02	.10
❑ 226 Greg Biekert	.02	.10
❑ 227 Bryant Young	.07	.20
❑ 228 Ken Dilger	.07	.20
❑ 229 Levon Kirkland	.02	.10
❑ 230 Brian Mitchell	.02	.10
❑ 231 Hardy Nickerson	.02	.10
❑ 232 Elvis Grbac	.07	.20
❑ 233 Kurt Schulz	.02	.10
❑ 234 Chris Doleman	.02	.10
❑ 235 Tamarick Vanover	.07	.20
❑ 236 Jesse Campbell	.02	.10
❑ 237 William Thomas	.02	.10
❑ 238 Shane Conlan	.02	.10
❑ 239 Jason Elam	.07	.20
❑ 240 Steve McNair	.30	.75
❑ 241 Jerry Rice TYC	.20	.50
❑ 242 Isaac Bruce TYC	.10	.30
❑ 243 Herman Moore TYC	.07	.20
❑ 244 Michael Irvin TYC	.07	.20
❑ 245 Robert Brooks TYC	.10	.30
❑ 246 Brett Perriman TYC	.02	.10
❑ 247 Cris Carter TYC	.10	.30
❑ 248 Tim Brown TYC	.07	.20
❑ 249 Yancey Thigpen TYC	.07	.20

❑ 250 Jeff Graham TYC .02 .10
❑ 251 Carl Pickens TYC .07 .20
❑ 252 Tony Martin TYC .02 .10
❑ 253 Eric Metcalf TYC .02 .10
❑ 254 Jake Reed TYC .07 .20
❑ 255 Quinn Early TYC .02 .10
❑ 256 Anthony Miller TYC .07 .20
❑ 257 Joey Galloway TYC .10 .30
❑ 258 Bert Emanuel TYC .07 .20
❑ 259 Terance Mathis TYC .02 .10
❑ 260 Curtis Conway TYC .07 .20
❑ 261 Henry Ellard TYC .02 .10
❑ 262 Mark Carrier TYC .02 .10
❑ 263 Brian Blades TYC .02 .10
❑ 264 William Roaf .02 .10
❑ 265 Ed McDaniel .02 .10
❑ 266 Nate Newton .02 .10
❑ 267 Brett Maxie .02 .10
❑ 268 Anthony Smith .02 .10
❑ 269 Mickey Washington .02 .10
❑ 270 Jerry Rice .40 1.00
❑ 271 Shaun Gayle .02 .10
❑ 272 Gilbert Brown RC .10 .30
❑ 273 Mark Bruener .02 .10
❑ 274 Eugene Robinson .02 .10
❑ 275 Marvin Washington .02 .10
❑ 276 Keith Sims .02 .10
❑ 277 Ashley Ambrose .02 .10
❑ 278 Garrison Hearst .07 .20
❑ 279 Donnell Woolford .02 .10
❑ 280 Cris Carter .10 .30
❑ 281 Curtis Martin .30 .75
❑ 282 Scott Mitchell .07 .20
❑ 283 Stevon Moore .02 .10
❑ 284 Roman Phifer .02 .10
❑ 285 Ken Harvey .02 .10
❑ 286 Rodney Hampton .07 .20
❑ 287 Willie Davis .02 .10
❑ 288 Yonel Jourdain .02 .10
❑ 289 Brian DeMarco .02 .10
❑ 290 Reggie White .10 .30
❑ 291 Kevin Williams .02 .10
❑ 292 Gary Plummer .02 .10
❑ 293 Terrance Shaw .02 .10
❑ 294 Calvin Williams .02 .10
❑ 295 Eddie Robinson .02 .10
❑ 296 Tony McGee .02 .10
❑ 297 Clay Matthews .02 .10
❑ 298 Joe Cain .02 .10
❑ 299 Tim McKyer .02 .10
❑ 300 Greg Lloyd .07 .20
❑ 301 Steve Wisniewski .02 .10
❑ 302 Ray Buchanan .02 .10
❑ 303 Lake Dawson .02 .10
❑ 304 Kevin Carter .02 .10
❑ 305 Phillippi Sparks .02 .10
❑ 306 Emmitt Smith .60 1.50
❑ 307 Ruben Brown .02 .10
❑ 308 Tom Carter .02 .10
❑ 309 William Floyd .07 .20
❑ 310 Jim Everett .02 .10
❑ 311 Vincent Brown .02 .10
❑ 312 Dennis Gibson .02 .10
❑ 313 Lorenzo Lynch .02 .10
❑ 314 Corey Harris .02 .10
❑ 315 James O.Stewart .07 .20
❑ 316 Kyle Brady .02 .10
❑ 317 Irving Fryar .07 .20
❑ 318 Jake Reed .07 .20
❑ 319 Vinny Testaverde .07 .20
❑ 320 John Elway .75 2.00
❑ 321 Tracy Scroggins .02 .10
❑ 322 Chris Spielman .02 .10
❑ 323 Horace Copeland .02 .10
❑ 324 Chris Zorich .02 .10
❑ 325 Mike Mamula .02 .10
❑ 326 Henry Ford .02 .10
❑ 327 Steve Walsh .02 .10
❑ 328 Stanley Richard .07 .20
❑ 329 Mike Jones .02 .10
❑ 330 Jim Harbaugh .07 .20
❑ 331 Darren Perry .02 .10
❑ 332 Ken Norton .02 .10
❑ 333 Kimble Anders .07 .20
❑ 334 Harold Green .02 .10
❑ 335 Tyrone Poole .02 .10
❑ 336 Mark Fields .02 .10
❑ 337 Darren Bennett .02 .10
❑ 338 Mike Sherrard .02 .10
❑ 339 Terry Ray RC .02 .10
❑ 340 Bruce Smith .07 .20
❑ 341 Daryl Johnston .07 .20
❑ 342 Vinnie Clark .02 .10
❑ 343 Mike Caldwell .02 .10
❑ 344 Vinson Smith .02 .10
❑ 345 Mo Lewis .02 .10
❑ 346 Brian Blades .02 .10
❑ 347 Rod Stephens .02 .10
❑ 348 David Palmer .02 .10
❑ 349 Blaine Bishop .02 .10
❑ 350 Jeff George .07 .20
❑ 351 George Teague .02 .10
❑ 352 Jeff Hostetler .02 .10
❑ 353 Michael Strahan .07 .20
❑ 354 Eric Davis .02 .10
❑ 355 Jerome Bettis .10 .30
❑ 356 Irv Smith .02 .10
❑ 357 Jeff Herrod .02 .10
❑ 358 Jay Novacek .02 .10
❑ 359 Bryce Paup .02 .10
❑ 360 Neil O'Donnell .07 .20
❑ 361 Eric Swann .02 .10
❑ 362 Corey Sawyer .02 .10
❑ 363 Ty Law .10 .30
❑ 364 Bo Orlando .02 .10
❑ 365 Marcus Allen .10 .30
❑ 366 Mark McMillian .02 .10
❑ 367 Mark Carrier WR .02 .10
❑ 368 Jackie Harris .02 .10
❑ 369 Steve Atwater .02 .10
❑ 370 Steve Young .30 .75
❑ 371 Brett Favre TYC .40 1.00
❑ 372 Scott Mitchell TYC .02 .10
❑ 373 Warren Moon TYC .02 .10
❑ 374 Jeff George TYC .07 .20
❑ 375 Jim Everett TYC .02 .10
❑ 376 John Elway TYC .40 1.00
❑ 377 Erik Kramer TYC .02 .10
❑ 378 Jeff Blake TYC .07 .20
❑ 379 Dan Marino TYC .40 1.00
❑ 380 Dave Krieg TYC .02 .10
❑ 381 Drew Bledsoe TYC .10 .30
❑ 382 Stan Humphries TYC .02 .10
❑ 383 Troy Aikman TYC .20 .50
❑ 384 Steve Young TYC .10 .30
❑ 385 Jim Kelly TYC .10 .30
❑ 386 Steve Bono TYC .02 .10
❑ 387 David Sloan .02 .10
❑ 388 Jeff Graham .02 .10
❑ 389 Hugh Douglas .07 .20
❑ 390 Dan Marino .75 2.00
❑ 391 Winston Moss .02 .10
❑ 392 Darrell Green .02 .10
❑ 393 Mark Stepnoski .02 .10
❑ 394 Bert Emanuel .07 .20
❑ 395 Eric Zeier .02 .10
❑ 396 Willie Jackson .07 .20
❑ 397 Qadry Ismail .07 .20
❑ 398 Michael Brooks .02 .10
❑ 399 D'Marco Farr .02 .10
❑ 400 Brett Favre .75 2.00
❑ 401 Carnell Lake .02 .10
❑ 402 Pat Swilling .02 .10
❑ 403 Stephen Grant .02 .10
❑ 404 Steve Tasker .02 .10
❑ 405 Ben Coates .07 .20
❑ 406 Steve Tovar .02 .10
❑ 407 Tony Martin .07 .20
❑ 408 Greg Hill .07 .20
❑ 409 Eric Guliford .02 .10
❑ 410 Michael Irvin .10 .30
❑ 411 Eric Hill .02 .10
❑ 412 Mario Bates .07 .20
❑ 413 Brian Stablein RC .02 .10
❑ 414 Marcus Jones RC .02 .10
❑ 415 Reggie Brown LB RC .02 .10
❑ 416 Lawrence Phillips RC .10 .30
❑ 417 Alex Van Dyke RC .07 .20
❑ 418 Daryl Gardener RC .02 .10
❑ 419 Mike Alstott RC .40 1.00
❑ 420 Kevin Hardy RC .10 .30
❑ 421 Rickey Dudley RC .10 .30
❑ 422 Jerome Woods RC .02 .10
❑ 423 Eric Moulds RC .50 1.25
❑ 424 Cedric Jones RC .02 .10
❑ 425 Simeon Rice RC .30 .75
❑ 426 Marvin Harrison RC 1.00 2.50
❑ 427 Tim Biakabutuka RC .10 .30
❑ 428 Duane Clemons RC .02 .10
❑ 429 Alex Molden RC .02 .10
❑ 430 Keyshawn Johnson RC .40 1.00
❑ 431 Willie Anderson RC .02 .10
❑ 432 John Mobley RC .02 .10
❑ 433 Leeland McElroy RC .07 .20
❑ 434 Regan Upshaw RC .02 .10
❑ 435 Eddie George RC .50 1.25
❑ 436 Jonathan Ogden RC .10 .30
❑ 437 Eddie Kennison RC .10 .30
❑ 438 Jermane Mayberry RC .02 .10
❑ 439 Checklist 1 of 2 .02 .10
❑ 440 Checklist 2 of 2 .02 .10
❑ P1 J.Namath/Steve Young Promo 7.50 15.00
❑ P1R Joe Namath Promo
Steve Young 10.00 20.00

1997 Topps

❑ COMPLETE SET (415) 20.00 40.00
❑ COMP.FACT.SET (424) 40.00 70.00
❑ 1 Brett Favre .75 2.00
❑ 2 Lawyer Milloy .10 .30
❑ 3 Tim Biakabutuka .10 .30
❑ 4 Clyde Simmons .07 .20
❑ 5 Deion Sanders .20 .50
❑ 6 Anthony Miller .07 .20
❑ 7 Marquez Pope .07 .20
❑ 8 Mike Tomczak .07 .20
❑ 9 William Thomas .07 .20
❑ 10 Marshall Faulk .25 .60
❑ 11 John Randle .10 .30
❑ 12 Jim Kelly .20 .50
❑ 13 Steve Bono .10 .30
❑ 14 Rod Stephens .07 .20
❑ 15 Stan Humphries .07 .20
❑ 16 Terrell Buckley .07 .20
❑ 17 Ki-Jana Carter .07 .20
❑ 18 Marcus Robertson .07 .20
❑ 19 Corey Harris .07 .20
❑ 20 Rashaan Salaam .07 .20
❑ 21 Rickey Dudley .10 .30
❑ 22 Jamir Miller .07 .20
❑ 23 Martin Mayhew .07 .20
❑ 24 Jason Sehorn .10 .30
❑ 25 Isaac Bruce .20 .50
❑ 26 Johnnie Morton .10 .30
❑ 27 Antonio Langham .07 .20
❑ 28 Cornelius Bennett .07 .20
❑ 29 Joe Johnson .07 .20
❑ 30 Keyshawn Johnson .20 .50
❑ 31 Willie Green .07 .20
❑ 32 Craig Newsome .07 .20
❑ 33 Brock Marion .07 .20
❑ 34 Corey Fuller .07 .20
❑ 35 Ben Coates .10 .30
❑ 36 Ty Detmer .10 .30
❑ 37 Charles Johnson .10 .30
❑ 38 Willie Jackson .07 .20
❑ 39 Tyronne Drakeford .07 .20
❑ 40 Gus Frerotte .07 .20
❑ 41 Robert Blackmon .07 .20
❑ 42 Andre Coleman .07 .20
❑ 43 Mario Bates .07 .20
❑ 44 Chris Calloway .07 .20
❑ 45 Terry McDaniel .07 .20
❑ 46 Anthony Davis .07 .20
❑ 47 Stanley Pritchett .07 .20
❑ 48 Ray Buchanan .07 .20
❑ 49 Chris Chandler .10 .30
❑ 50 Ashley Ambrose .07 .20
❑ 51 Tyrone Braxton .07 .20
❑ 52 Pepper Johnson .07 .20
❑ 53 Frank Sanders .10 .30
❑ 54 Clay Matthews .07 .20
❑ 55 Bruce Smith .10 .30
❑ 56 Jermaine Lewis .20 .60

❑ 57 Mark Carrier WR UER .07 .20
❑ 58 Jeff Graham .07 .20
❑ 59 Keith Lyle .07 .20
❑ 60 Trent Dilfer .20 .50
❑ 61 Trace Armstrong .07 .20
❑ 62 Jeff Herrod .07 .20
❑ 63 Tyrone Wheatley .10 .30
❑ 64 Torrance Small .07 .20
❑ 65 Chris Warren .10 .30
❑ 66 Terry Kirby .10 .30
❑ 67 Erric Pegram .07 .20
❑ 68 Sean Gilbert .07 .20
❑ 69 Greg Biekert .07 .20
❑ 70 Ricky Watters .10 .30
❑ 71 Chris Hudson .07 .20
❑ 72 Tamarick Vanover .10 .30
❑ 73 Orlando Thomas .07 .20
❑ 74 Jimmy Spencer .07 .20
❑ 75 John Mobley .07 .20
❑ 76 Henry Thomas .07 .20
❑ 77 Santana Dotson .07 .20
❑ 78 Boomer Esiason .10 .30
❑ 79 Bobby Hebert .07 .20
❑ 80 Kerry Collins .20 .50
❑ 81 Bobby Engram .10 .30
❑ 82 Kevin Smith .07 .20
❑ 83 Rick Mirer .07 .20
❑ 84 Ted Johnson .07 .20
❑ 85 Derrick Alexander WR .10 .30
❑ 86 Hugh Douglas .07 .20
❑ 87 Rodney Harrison RC .40 1.00
❑ 88 Roman Phifer .07 .20
❑ 89 Warren Moon .20 .50
❑ 90 Thurman Thomas .20 .50
❑ 91 Michael McCrary .07 .20
❑ 92 Dana Stubblefield .07 .20
❑ 93 Andre Hastings UER .07 .20
❑ 94 William Fuller .07 .20
❑ 95 Jeff Hostetler .07 .20
❑ 96 Danny Kanell .07 .20
❑ 97 Mark Fields .07 .20
❑ 98 Eddie Robinson .07 .20
❑ 99 Daryl Gardener .07 .20
❑ 100 Drew Bledsoe .25 .60
❑ 101 Winslow Oliver .07 .20
❑ 102 Raymont Harris .07 .20
❑ 103 LeShon Johnson .07 .20
❑ 104 Byron Bam Morris .07 .20
❑ 105 Herman Moore .10 .30
❑ 106 Keith Jackson .07 .20
❑ 107 Chris Penn .07 .20
❑ 108 Robert Griffith RC .07 .20
❑ 109 Jeff Burris .07 .20
❑ 110 Troy Aikman .40 1.00
❑ 111 Allen Aldridge .07 .20
❑ 112 Mel Gray .07 .20
❑ 113 Aaron Bailey .07 .20
❑ 114 Michael Strahan .10 .30
❑ 115 Adrian Murrell .10 .30
❑ 116 Chris Mims .07 .20
❑ 117 Robert Jones .07 .20
❑ 118 Derrick Brooks .20 .50
❑ 119 Tom Carter .07 .20
❑ 120 Carl Pickens .10 .30
❑ 121 Tony Brackens .07 .20
❑ 122 O.J. McDuffie .10 .30
❑ 123 Napoleon Kaufman .20 .50
❑ 124 Chris T. Jones .07 .20
❑ 125 Kordell Stewart .20 .50
❑ 126 Ray Zellars .07 .20
❑ 127 Jessie Tuggle .07 .20
❑ 128 Greg Kragen .07 .20
❑ 129 Brett Perriman .07 .20
❑ 130 Steve Young .25 .60
❑ 131 Willie Clay .07 .20
❑ 132 Kimble Anders .10 .30
❑ 133 Eugene Daniel .07 .20
❑ 134 Jevon Langford .07 .20
❑ 135 Shannon Sharpe .10 .30
❑ 136 Wayne Simmons .07 .20
❑ 137 Leeland McElroy .07 .20
❑ 138 Mike Caldwell .07 .20
❑ 139 Eric Moulds .20 .50
❑ 140 Eddie George .20 .50
❑ 141 Jamal Anderson .20 .50
❑ 142 Michael Timpson .07 .20
❑ 143 Tony Tolbert .07 .20
❑ 144 Robert Smith .10 .30
❑ 145 Mike Alstott .20 .50
❑ 146 Gary Jones .07 .20
❑ 147 Terrance Shaw .07 .20
❑ 148 Carlton Gray .07 .20
❑ 149 Kevin Carter .07 .20
❑ 150 Darrell Green .10 .30
❑ 151 David Dunn .07 .20
❑ 152 Ken Norton .07 .20
❑ 153 Chad Brown .07 .20
❑ 154 Pat Swilling .07 .20
❑ 155 Irving Fryar .10 .30
❑ 156 Michael Haynes .07 .20
❑ 157 Shawn Jefferson .07 .20
❑ 158 Stephen Grant .07 .20
❑ 159 James O.Stewart .10 .30
❑ 160 Derrick Thomas .20 .50
❑ 161 Tim Bowens .07 .20
❑ 162 Dixon Edwards .07 .20
❑ 163 Micheal Barrow .07 .20
❑ 164 Antonio Freeman .20 .50
❑ 165 Terrell Davis .25 .60
❑ 166 Henry Ellard .10 .30
❑ 167 Daryl Johnston .10 .30
❑ 168 Bryan Cox .07 .20
❑ 169 Chad Cota .07 .20
❑ 170 Vinny Testaverde .10 .30
❑ 171 Andre Reed .10 .30
❑ 172 Larry Centers .10 .30
❑ 173 Craig Heyward .07 .20
❑ 174 Glyn Milburn .07 .20
❑ 175 Hardy Nickerson .07 .20
❑ 176 Corey Miller .07 .20
❑ 177 Bobby Houston .07 .20
❑ 178 Marco Coleman .07 .20
❑ 179 Winston Moss .07 .20
❑ 180 Tony Banks .10 .30
❑ 181 Jeff Lageman .07 .20
❑ 182 Jason Belser .07 .20
❑ 183 James Jett .10 .30
❑ 184 Wayne Martin .07 .20
❑ 185 Dave Meggett .07 .20
❑ 186 Terrell Owens .25 .60
❑ 187 Willie Williams .07 .20
❑ 188 Eric Turner .07 .20
❑ 189 Chuck Smith .07 .20
❑ 190 Simeon Rice .10 .30
❑ 191 Kevin Greene .10 .30
❑ 192 Lance Johnstone .07 .20
❑ 193 Marty Carter .07 .20
❑ 194 Ricardo McDonald .07 .20
❑ 195 Michael Irvin .20 .50
❑ 196 George Koonce .07 .20
❑ 197 Robert Porcher .07 .20
❑ 198 Mark Collins .07 .20
❑ 199 Louis Oliver .07 .20
❑ 200 John Elway .75 2.00
❑ 201 Jake Reed .10 .30
❑ 202 Rodney Hampton .10 .30
❑ 203 Aaron Glenn .07 .20
❑ 204 Mike Mamula .07 .20
❑ 205 Terry Allen .20 .50
❑ 206 John Lynch .10 .30
❑ 207 Todd Lyght .07 .20
❑ 208 Dean Wells .07 .20
❑ 209 Aaron Hayden .07 .20
❑ 210 Blaine Bishop .07 .20
❑ 211 Bert Emanuel .10 .30
❑ 212 Mark Carrier DB UER .07 .20
❑ 213 Dale Carter .07 .20
❑ 214 Jimmy Smith .10 .30
❑ 215 Jim Harbaugh .10 .30
❑ 216 Jeff George .10 .30
❑ 217 Anthony Newman .07 .20
❑ 218 Ty Law .10 .30
❑ 219 Brent Jones .07 .20
❑ 220 Emmitt Smith .60 1.50
❑ 221 Bennie Blades .07 .20
❑ 222 Alfred Williams .07 .20
❑ 223 Eugene Robinson .07 .20
❑ 224 Fred Barnett .07 .20
❑ 225 Errict Rhett .07 .20
❑ 226 Leslie O'Neal .07 .20
❑ 227 Michael Sinclair .07 .20
❑ 228 Marvcus Patton .07 .20
❑ 229 Darrien Gordon .07 .20
❑ 230 Jerome Bettis .20 .50
❑ 231 Troy Vincent .07 .20
❑ 232 Ray Mickens .07 .20
❑ 233 Lonnie Johnson .07 .20
❑ 234 Charles Way .07 .20
❑ 235 Chris Sanders .07 .20
❑ 236 Bracy Walker .07 .20
❑ 237 Dave Krieg UER .07 .20
❑ 238 Kent Graham .07 .20
❑ 239 Ray Lewis .30 .75
❑ 240 Cris Carter .20 .50
❑ 241 Elvis Grbac .10 .30
❑ 242 Eric Davis .07 .20
❑ 243 Harvey Williams .07 .20
❑ 244 Eric Allen .07 .20
❑ 245 Bryant Young .07 .20
❑ 246 Terrell Fletcher .07 .20
❑ 247 Darren Perry .07 .20
❑ 248 Ken Harvey .07 .20
❑ 249 Marvin Washington .07 .20
❑ 250 Marcus Allen .20 .50
❑ 251 Darrin Smith .07 .20
❑ 252 James Francis .07 .20
❑ 253 Michael Jackson .10 .30
❑ 254 Ryan McNeil .07 .20
❑ 255 Mark Chmura .10 .30
❑ 256 Keenan McCardell .10 .30
❑ 257 Tony Bennett .07 .20
❑ 258 Irving Spikes .07 .20
❑ 259 Jason Dunn .07 .20
❑ 260 Joey Galloway .10 .30
❑ 261 Eddie Kennison .10 .30
❑ 262 Lonnie Marts .07 .20
❑ 263 Thomas Lewis .07 .20
❑ 264 Tedy Bruschi .40 1.00
❑ 265 Steve Atwater .07 .20
❑ 266 Dorsey Levens .20 .50
❑ 267 Kurt Schulz .07 .20
❑ 268 Rob Moore .10 .30
❑ 269 Walt Harris .07 .20
❑ 270 Steve McNair .25 .60
❑ 271 Bill Romanowski .07 .20
❑ 272 Sean Dawkins .07 .20
❑ 273 Don Beebe .07 .20
❑ 274 Fernando Smith .07 .20
❑ 275 Willie McGinest .07 .20
❑ 276 Levon Kirkland .07 .20
❑ 277 Tony Martin .10 .30
❑ 278 Warren Sapp .10 .30
❑ 279 Lamar Smith .20 .50
❑ 280 Mark Brunell .25 .60
❑ 281 Jim Everett .07 .20
❑ 282 Victor Green .07 .20
❑ 283 Mike Jones .07 .20
❑ 284 Charlie Garner .10 .30
❑ 285 Karim Abdul-Jabbar .10 .30
❑ 286 Michael Westbrook .10 .30
❑ 287 Lawrence Phillips .07 .20
❑ 288 Amani Toomer .10 .30
❑ 289 Neil Smith .10 .30
❑ 290 Barry Sanders .60 1.50
❑ 291 Willie Davis .07 .20
❑ 292 Bo Orlando .07 .20
❑ 293 Alonzo Spellman .07 .20
❑ 294 Eric Hill .07 .20
❑ 295 Wesley Walls .10 .30
❑ 296 Todd Collins .07 .20
❑ 297 Stevon Moore .07 .20
❑ 298 Eric Metcalf .10 .30
❑ 299 Darren Woodson .07 .20
❑ 300 Jerry Rice .40 1.00
❑ 301 Scott Mitchell .10 .30
❑ 302 Ray Crockett .07 .20
❑ 303 Jim Schwantz UER RC .07 .20
❑ 304 Steve Tovar .07 .20
❑ 305 Terance Mathis .10 .30
❑ 306 Earnest Byner .07 .20
❑ 307 Chris Spielman .07 .20
❑ 308 Curtis Conway .10 .30
❑ 309 Cris Dishman .07 .20
❑ 310 Marvin Harrison .20 .50
❑ 311 Sam Mills .07 .20
❑ 312 Brent Alexander RC .07 .20
❑ 313 Shawn Wooden RC .07 .20
❑ 314 Dewayne Washington .07 .20
❑ 315 Terry Glenn .20 .50
❑ 316 Winfred Tubbs .07 .20
❑ 317 Dave Brown .07 .20
❑ 318 Neil O'Donnell .10 .30
❑ 319 Anthony Parker .07 .20
❑ 320 Junior Seau .20 .50
❑ 321 Brian Mitchell .07 .20
❑ 322 Regan Upshaw .07 .20
❑ 323 Darryl Williams .07 .20

Card		
❑ 324 Chris Doleman	.07	.20
❑ 325 Rod Woodson	.10	.30
❑ 326 Derrick Witherspoon	.07	.20
❑ 327 Chester McGlockton	.07	.20
❑ 328 Mickey Washington	.07	.20
❑ 329 Greg Hill	.07	.20
❑ 330 Reggie White	.20	.50
❑ 331 John Copeland	.07	.20
❑ 332 Doug Evans	.07	.20
❑ 333 Lamar Lathon	.07	.20
❑ 334 Mark Maddox	.07	.20
❑ 335 Natrone Means	.10	.30
❑ 336 Corey Widmer	.07	.20
❑ 337 Terry Wooden	.07	.20
❑ 338 Merton Hanks	.07	.20
❑ 339 Cortez Kennedy	.07	.20
❑ 340 Tyrone Hughes	.07	.20
❑ 341 Tim Brown	.20	.50
❑ 342 John Jurkovic	.07	.20
❑ 343 Carnell Lake	.07	.20
❑ 344 Stanley Richard	.07	.20
❑ 345 Darryll Lewis	.07	.20
❑ 346 Dan Wilkinson	.07	.20
❑ 347 Broderick Thomas	.07	.20
❑ 348 Brian Williams	.07	.20
❑ 349 Eric Swann	.07	.20
❑ 350 Dan Marino	.75	2.00
❑ 351 Anthony Johnson	.07	.20
❑ 352 Joe Cain	.07	.20
❑ 353 Quinn Early	.07	.20
❑ 354 Seth Joyner	.07	.20
❑ 355 Garrison Hearst	.10	.30
❑ 356 Edgar Bennett	.10	.30
❑ 357 Brian Washington	.07	.20
❑ 358 Kevin Hardy	.07	.20
❑ 359 Quentin Coryatt	.07	.20
❑ 360 Tim McDonald	.07	.20
❑ 361 Brian Blades	.07	.20
❑ 362 Courtney Hawkins	.07	.20
❑ 363 Ray Farmer	.07	.20
❑ 364 Jessie Armstead	.07	.20
❑ 365 Curtis Martin	.25	.60
❑ 366 Zach Thomas	.20	.50
❑ 367 Frank Wycheck	.10	.30
❑ 368 Darnay Scott	.10	.30
❑ 369 Percy Ellsworth RC	.07	.20
❑ 370 Desmond Howard	.10	.30
❑ 371 Aeneas Williams	.07	.20
❑ 372 Bryce Paup	.07	.20
❑ 373 Michael Bates	.07	.20
❑ 374 Brad Johnson	.20	.50
❑ 375 Jeff Blake	.10	.30
❑ 376 Donnell Woolford UER	.07	.20
❑ 377 Mo Lewis	.07	.20
❑ 378 Phillippi Sparks	.07	.20
❑ 379 Michael Bankston	.07	.20
❑ 380 LeRoy Butler	.07	.20
❑ 381 Tyrone Poole	.07	.20
❑ 382 Wayne Chrebet	.20	.50
❑ 383 Chris Slade	.07	.20
❑ 384 Checklist 1 (1-208)	.07	.20
❑ 385 Checklist 2 (209-415)	.07	.20
❑ 386 Will Blackwell SP RC	.10	.30
❑ 387 Tom Knight SP RC	.07	.20
❑ 388 Darnell Autry SP RC	.20	.50
❑ 389 Bryant Westbrook SP RC	.07	.20
❑ 390 David LaFleur RC SP	.10	.30
❑ 391 Antowain Smith SP RC	1.00	2.50
❑ 392 Kevin Lockett SP RC	.20	.50
❑ 393 Rae Carruth SP RC	.10	.30
❑ 394 Renaldo Wynn SP RC	.10	.30
❑ 395 Jim Druckenmiller SP RC	.20	.50
❑ 396 Kenny Holmes SP RC	.30	.75
❑ 397 Shawn Springs SP RC	.20	.50
❑ 398 Troy Davis SP RC	.20	.50
❑ 399 Dwayne Rudd SP RC	.30	.75
❑ 400 Orlando Pace SP RC	.30	.75
❑ 401 Byron Hanspard SP RC	.20	.50
❑ 402 Corey Dillon SP RC	2.50	6.00
❑ 403 Walter Jones SP RC	.30	.75
❑ 404 Reidel Anthony SP RC	.30	.75
❑ 405 Peter Boulware SP RC	.30	.75
❑ 406 Reinard Wilson SP RC	.20	.50
❑ 407 Pat Barnes SP RC	.30	.75
❑ 408 Yatil Green SP RC	.30	.75
❑ 409 Joey Kent SP RC	.30	.75
❑ 410 Ike Hilliard SP RC	.60	1.50
❑ 411 Jake Plummer SP RC	2.00	5.00
❑ 412 Darrell Russell SP RC	.10	.30
❑ 413 James Farrior SP RC	.30	.75
❑ 414 Tony Gonzalez SP RC	1.25	3.00
❑ 415 Warrick Dunn SP RC	1.25	3.00
❑ P40 Gus Frerotte PROMO	.08	.25
❑ P170 Vinny Testaverde PROMO	.08	.25
❑ P240 Cris Carter PROMO	.15	.40
❑ P250 Marcus Allen PROMO	.15	.40
❑ P285 Karim Abdul-Jabbar PROMO	.08	.25
❑ P356 Edgar Bennett PROMO	.08	.25

1998 Topps

Card		
❑ COMPLETE SET (360)	30.00	60.00
❑ COMP.FACT.SET (365)	40.00	80.00
❑ 1 Barry Sanders	.60	1.50
❑ 2 Derrick Rodgers	.07	.20
❑ 3 Chris Calloway	.07	.20
❑ 4 Bruce Armstrong	.07	.20
❑ 5 Horace Copeland	.07	.20
❑ 6 Chad Brown	.07	.20
❑ 7 Ken Harvey	.07	.20
❑ 8 Levon Kirkland	.07	.20
❑ 9 Glenn Foley	.10	.30
❑ 10 Corey Dillon	.20	.50
❑ 11 Sean Dawkins	.07	.20
❑ 12 Curtis Conway	.10	.30
❑ 13 Chris Chandler	.10	.30
❑ 14 Kerry Collins	.10	.30
❑ 15 Jonathan Ogden	.07	.20
❑ 16 Sam Shade	.07	.20
❑ 17 Vaughn Hebron	.07	.20
❑ 18 Quentin Coryatt	.07	.20
❑ 19 Jerris McPhail	.07	.20
❑ 20 Warrick Dunn	.20	.50
❑ 21 Wayne Martin	.07	.20
❑ 22 Chad Lewis	.10	.30
❑ 23 Danny Kanell	.10	.30
❑ 24 Shawn Springs	.07	.20
❑ 25 Emmitt Smith	.60	1.50
❑ 26 Todd Lyght	.07	.20
❑ 27 Donnie Edwards	.07	.20
❑ 28 Charlie Jones	.07	.20
❑ 29 Willie McGinest	.07	.20
❑ 30 Steve Young	.25	.60
❑ 31 Darrell Russell	.07	.20
❑ 32 Gary Anderson	.07	.20
❑ 33 Stanley Richard	.07	.20
❑ 34 Leslie O'Neal	.07	.20
❑ 35 Dermontti Dawson	.07	.20
❑ 36 Jeff Brady	.07	.20
❑ 37 Kimble Anders	.10	.30
❑ 38 Glyn Milburn	.07	.20
❑ 39 Greg Hill	.07	.20
❑ 40 Freddie Jones	.07	.20
❑ 41 Bobby Engram	.10	.30
❑ 42 Aeneas Williams	.07	.20
❑ 43 Antowain Smith	.20	.50
❑ 44 Reggie White	.20	.50
❑ 45 Rae Carruth	.07	.20
❑ 46 Leon Johnson	.07	.20
❑ 47 Bryant Young	.07	.20
❑ 48 Jamie Asher	.07	.20
❑ 49 Hardy Nickerson	.07	.20
❑ 50 Jerome Bettis	.20	.50
❑ 51 Michael Strahan	.10	.30
❑ 52 John Randle	.10	.30
❑ 53 Kevin Hardy	.07	.20
❑ 54 Eric Bjornson	.07	.20
❑ 55 Morten Andersen UER	.07	.20
❑ 56 Larry Centers	.07	.20
❑ 57 Bryce Paup	.07	.20
❑ 58 John Mobley	.07	.20
❑ 59 Michael Bates	.07	.20
❑ 60 Tim Brown	.20	.50
❑ 61 Doug Evans	.07	.20
❑ 62 Will Shields	.07	.20
❑ 63 Jeff Graham	.07	.20
❑ 64 Tony Martin	.07	.20
❑ 65 Steve Broussard	.07	.20
❑ 66 Blaine Bishop	.07	.20
❑ 67 Ernie Conwell	.07	.20
❑ 68 Heath Shuler	.07	.20
❑ 69 Eric Metcalf	.07	.20
❑ 70 Terry Glenn	.20	.50
❑ 71 James Hasty	.07	.20
❑ 72 Robert Porcher	.07	.20
❑ 73 Keenan McCardell	.10	.30
❑ 74 Tyrone Hughes	.07	.20
❑ 75 Troy Aikman	.40	1.00
❑ 76 Peter Boulware	.07	.20
❑ 77 Rob Johnson	.10	.30
❑ 78 Erik Kramer	.07	.20
❑ 79 Kevin Smith	.07	.20
❑ 80 Andre Rison	.10	.30
❑ 81 Jim Harbaugh	.10	.30
❑ 82 Chris Hudson	.07	.20
❑ 83 Ray Zellars	.07	.20
❑ 84 Jeff George	.10	.30
❑ 85 Willie Davis	.07	.20
❑ 86 Jason Gildon	.07	.20
❑ 87 Robert Brooks	.10	.30
❑ 88 Chad Cota	.07	.20
❑ 89 Simeon Rice	.10	.30
❑ 90 Mark Brunell	.20	.50
❑ 91 Jay Graham	.07	.20
❑ 92 Scott Greene	.07	.20
❑ 93 Jeff Blake	.10	.30
❑ 94 Jason Belser	.07	.20
❑ 95 Derrick Alexander DE	.07	.20
❑ 96 Ty Law	.10	.30
❑ 97 Charles Johnson	.07	.20
❑ 98 James Jett	.10	.30
❑ 99 Darrell Green	.10	.30
❑ 100 Brett Favre	.75	2.00
❑ 101 George Jones	.07	.20
❑ 102 Derrick Mason	.10	.30
❑ 103 Sam Adams	.07	.20
❑ 104 Lawrence Phillips	.07	.20
❑ 105 Randal Hill	.07	.20
❑ 106 John Mangum	.07	.20
❑ 107 Natrone Means	.10	.30
❑ 108 Bill Romanowski	.07	.20
❑ 109 Terance Mathis	.10	.30
❑ 110 Bruce Smith	.10	.30
❑ 111 Pete Mitchell	.07	.20
❑ 112 Duane Clemons	.07	.20
❑ 113 Willie Clay	.07	.20
❑ 114 Eric Allen	.07	.20
❑ 115 Troy Drayton	.07	.20
❑ 116 Derrick Thomas	.20	.50
❑ 117 Charles Way	.07	.20
❑ 118 Wayne Chrebet	.20	.50
❑ 119 Bobby Hoying	.10	.30
❑ 120 Michael Jackson	.07	.20
❑ 121 Gary Zimmerman	.07	.20
❑ 122 Yancey Thigpen	.07	.20
❑ 123 Dana Stubblefield	.07	.20
❑ 124 Keith Lyle	.07	.20
❑ 125 Marco Coleman	.07	.20
❑ 126 Karl Williams	.07	.20
❑ 127 Stephen Davis	.07	.20
❑ 128 Chris Sanders	.07	.20
❑ 129 Cris Dishman	.07	.20
❑ 130 Jake Plummer	.20	.50
❑ 131 Darryl Williams	.07	.20
❑ 132 Merton Hanks	.07	.20
❑ 133 Torrance Small	.07	.20
❑ 134 Aaron Glenn	.07	.20
❑ 135 Chester McGlockton	.07	.20
❑ 136 William Thomas	.07	.20
❑ 137 Kordell Stewart	.20	.50
❑ 138 Jason Taylor	.10	.30
❑ 139 Lake Dawson	.07	.20
❑ 140 Carl Pickens	.10	.30
❑ 141 Eugene Robinson	.07	.20
❑ 142 Ed McCaffrey	.10	.30
❑ 143 Lamar Lathon	.07	.20
❑ 144 Ray Buchanan	.07	.20
❑ 145 Thurman Thomas	.20	.50
❑ 146 Andre Reed	.10	.30
❑ 147 Wesley Walls	.10	.30
❑ 148 Rob Moore	.10	.30
❑ 149 Darren Woodson	.07	.20
❑ 150 Eddie George	.20	.50
❑ 151 Michael Irvin	.20	.50
❑ 152 Johnnie Morton	.10	.00

Card	Low	High
❑ 153 Ken Dilger	.07	.20
❑ 154 Tony Boselli	.07	.20
❑ 155 Randall McDaniel	.07	.20
❑ 156 Mark Fields	.07	.20
❑ 157 Phillippi Sparks	.07	.20
❑ 158 Troy Davis	.07	.20
❑ 159 Troy Vincent	.07	.20
❑ 160 Cris Carter	.20	.50
❑ 161 Amp Lee	.07	.20
❑ 162 Will Blackwell	.07	.20
❑ 163 Chad Scott	.07	.20
❑ 164 Henry Ellard	.10	.30
❑ 165 Robert Jones	.07	.20
❑ 166 Garrison Hearst	.20	.50
❑ 167 James McKnight	.20	.50
❑ 168 Rodney Harrison	.10	.30
❑ 169 Adrian Murrell	.10	.30
❑ 170 Rod Smith WR	.10	.30
❑ 171 Desmond Howard	.10	.30
❑ 172 Ben Coates	.10	.30
❑ 173 David Palmer	.07	.20
❑ 174 Zach Thomas	.20	.50
❑ 175 Dale Carter	.07	.20
❑ 176 Mark Chmura	.10	.30
❑ 177 Elvis Grbac	.10	.30
❑ 178 Jason Hanson	.07	.20
❑ 179 Walt Harris	.07	.20
❑ 180 Ricky Watters	.10	.30
❑ 181 Ray Lewis	.20	.50
❑ 182 Lonnie Johnson	.07	.20
❑ 183 Marvin Harrison	.20	.50
❑ 184 Dorsey Levens	.20	.50
❑ 185 Tony Gonzalez	.20	.50
❑ 186 Andre Hastings	.07	.20
❑ 187 Kevin Turner	.07	.20
❑ 188 Mo Lewis	.07	.20
❑ 189 Jason Sehorn	.10	.30
❑ 190 Drew Bledsoe	.30	.75
❑ 191 Michael Sinclair	.07	.20
❑ 192 William Floyd	.07	.20
❑ 193 Kenny Holmes	.07	.20
❑ 194 Marvcus Patton	.07	.20
❑ 195 Warren Sapp	.10	.30
❑ 196 Junior Seau	.20	.50
❑ 197 Ryan McNeil	.07	.20
❑ 198 Tyrone Wheatley	.10	.30
❑ 199 Robert Smith	.20	.50
❑ 200 Terrell Davis	.20	.50
❑ 201 Brett Perriman	.07	.20
❑ 202 Tamarick Vanover	.07	.20
❑ 203 Stephen Boyd	.07	.20
❑ 204 Zack Crockett	.07	.20
❑ 205 Sherman Williams	.07	.20
❑ 206 Neil Smith	.10	.30
❑ 207 Jermaine Lewis	.10	.30
❑ 208 Kevin Williams	.07	.20
❑ 209 Byron Hanspard	.07	.20
❑ 210 Warren Moon	.20	.50
❑ 211 Tony McGee	.07	.20
❑ 212 Raymont Harris	.07	.20
❑ 213 Eric Davis	.07	.20
❑ 214 Darrien Gordon	.07	.20
❑ 215 James Stewart	.10	.30
❑ 216 Derrick Mayes	.10	.30
❑ 217 Brad Johnson	.20	.50
❑ 218 Karim Abdul-Jabbar UER	.20	.50
❑ 219 Hugh Douglas	.07	.20
❑ 220 Terry Allen	.20	.50
❑ 221 Rhett Hall	.07	.20
❑ 222 Terrell Fletcher	.07	.20
❑ 223 Carnell Lake	.07	.20
❑ 224 Darryll Lewis	.07	.20
❑ 225 Chris Slade	.07	.20
❑ 226 Michael Westbrook	.10	.30
❑ 227 Willie Williams	.07	.20
❑ 228 Tony Banks	.10	.30
❑ 229 Keyshawn Johnson	.20	.50
❑ 230 Mike Alstott	.20	.50
❑ 231 Tiki Barber	.20	.50
❑ 232 Jake Reed	.10	.30
❑ 233 Eric Swann	.07	.20
❑ 234 Eric Moulds	.20	.50
❑ 235 Vinny Testaverde	.10	.30
❑ 236 Jessie Tuggle	.07	.20
❑ 237 Ryan Wetnight RC	.07	.20
❑ 238 Tyrone Poole	.07	.20
❑ 239 Bryant Westbrook	.07	.20
❑ 240 Steve McNair	.20	.50
❑ 241 Jimmy Smith	.10	.30
❑ 242 Dewayne Washington	.07	.20
❑ 243 Robert Harris	.07	.20
❑ 244 Rod Woodson	.10	.30
❑ 245 Reidel Anthony	.10	.30
❑ 246 Jessie Armstead	.07	.20
❑ 247 O.J. McDuffie	.10	.30
❑ 248 Carlton Gray	.07	.20
❑ 249 LeRoy Butler	.07	.20
❑ 250 Jerry Rice	.40	1.00
❑ 251 Frank Sanders	.10	.30
❑ 252 Todd Collins	.07	.20
❑ 253 Fred Lane	.07	.20
❑ 254 David Dunn	.07	.20
❑ 255 Micheal Barrow	.07	.20
❑ 256 Luther Elliss	.07	.20
❑ 257 Scott Mitchell	.10	.30
❑ 258 Dave Meggett	.07	.20
❑ 259 Rickey Dudley	.07	.20
❑ 260 Isaac Bruce	.20	.50
❑ 261 Henry Jones	.10	.30
❑ 262 Leslie Shepherd	.07	.20
❑ 263 Derrick Brooks	.20	.50
❑ 264 Greg Lloyd	.07	.20
❑ 265 Terrell Buckley	.07	.20
❑ 266 Antonio Freeman	.20	.50
❑ 267 Tony Brackens	.07	.20
❑ 268 Mark McMillian	.07	.20
❑ 269 Dexter Coakley	.07	.20
❑ 270 Dan Marino	.75	2.00
❑ 271 Bryan Cox	.07	.20
❑ 272 Leeland McElroy	.07	.20
❑ 273 Jeff Burris	.07	.20
❑ 274 Eric Green	.07	.20
❑ 275 Darnay Scott	.10	.30
❑ 276 Greg Clark	.07	.20
❑ 277 Mario Bates	.10	.30
❑ 278 Eric Turner	.07	.20
❑ 279 Neil O'Donnell	.10	.30
❑ 280 Herman Moore	.10	.30
❑ 281 Gary Brown	.07	.20
❑ 282 Terrell Owens	.20	.50
❑ 283 Frank Wycheck	.07	.20
❑ 284 Trent Dilfer	.20	.50
❑ 285 Curtis Martin	.20	.50
❑ 286 Ricky Proehl	.07	.20
❑ 287 Steve Atwater	.07	.20
❑ 288 Aaron Bailey	.07	.20
❑ 289 William Henderson	.10	.30
❑ 290 Marcus Allen	.20	.50
❑ 291 Tom Knight	.07	.20
❑ 292 Quinn Early	.07	.20
❑ 293 Michael McCrary	.07	.20
❑ 294 Bert Emanuel	.10	.30
❑ 295 Tom Carter	.07	.20
❑ 296 Kevin Glover	.07	.20
❑ 297 Marshall Faulk	.25	.60
❑ 298 Harvey Williams	.07	.20
❑ 299 Chris Warren	.10	.30
❑ 300 John Elway	.75	2.00
❑ 301 Eddie Kennison	.10	.30
❑ 302 Gus Frerotte	.07	.20
❑ 303 Regan Upshaw	.07	.20
❑ 304 Kevin Gogan	.07	.20
❑ 305 Napoleon Kaufman	.20	.50
❑ 306 Charlie Garner	.10	.30
❑ 307 Shawn Jefferson	.07	.20
❑ 308 Tommy Vardell	.07	.20
❑ 309 Mike Hollis	.07	.20
❑ 310 Irving Fryar	.10	.30
❑ 311 Shannon Sharpe	.10	.30
❑ 312 Byron Bam Morris	.07	.20
❑ 313 Jamal Anderson	.20	.50
❑ 314 Chris Gedney	.07	.20
❑ 315 Chris Spielman	.07	.20
❑ 316 Derrick Alexander WR	.10	.30
❑ 317 O.J. Santiago	.07	.20
❑ 318 Anthony Miller	.07	.20
❑ 319 Ki-Jana Carter	.07	.20
❑ 320 Deion Sanders	.20	.50
❑ 321 Joey Galloway	.10	.30
❑ 322 J.J. Stokes	.10	.30
❑ 323 Rodney Thomas	.07	.20
❑ 324 John Lynch	.10	.30
❑ 325 Mike Pritchard	.07	.20
❑ 326 Terrance Shaw	.07	.20
❑ 327 Ted Johnson	.07	.20
❑ 328 Ashley Ambrose	.07	.20
❑ 329 Checklist 1	.07	.20
❑ 330 Checklist 2	.07	.20
❑ 331 Jerome Pathon RC	1.00	2.50
❑ 332 Ryan Leaf RC	1.00	2.50
❑ 333 Duane Starks RC	.50	1.25
❑ 334 Brian Simmons RC	.75	2.00
❑ 335 Keith Brooking RC	1.00	2.50
❑ 336 Robert Edwards RC	.75	2.00
❑ 337 Curtis Enis RC	.50	1.25
❑ 338 John Avery RC	.75	2.00
❑ 339 Fred Taylor RC	1.50	4.00
❑ 340 Germane Crowell RC	.75	2.00
❑ 341 Hines Ward RC	4.00	10.00
❑ 342 Marcus Nash RC	.50	1.25
❑ 343 Jacquez Green RC	.75	2.00
❑ 344 Joe Jurevicius RC	1.00	2.50
❑ 345 Greg Ellis RC	.50	1.25
❑ 346 Brian Griese RC	2.00	5.00
❑ 347 Tavian Banks RC	.75	2.00
❑ 348 Robert Holcombe RC	.75	2.00
❑ 349 Skip Hicks RC	.75	2.00
❑ 350 Ahman Green RC	2.50	6.00
❑ 351 Takeo Spikes RC	1.00	2.50
❑ 352 Randy Moss RC	5.00	12.00
❑ 353 Andre Wadsworth RC	.75	2.00
❑ 354 Jason Peter RC	.50	1.25
❑ 355 Grant Wistrom RC	.75	2.00
❑ 356 Charles Woodson RC	1.25	3.00
❑ 357 Kevin Dyson RC	1.00	2.50
❑ 358 Pat Johnson RC	.75	2.00
❑ 359 Tim Dwight RC	1.00	2.50
❑ 360 Peyton Manning RC	8.00	20.00

1999 Topps

Card	Low	High
❑ COMPLETE SET (357)	20.00	50.00
❑ COMP.SET w/o SP's (330)	10.00	20.00
❑ 1 Terrell Davis	.25	.60
❑ 2 Adrian Murrell	.15	.40
❑ 3 Ernie Mills	.08	.25
❑ 4 Jimmy Hitchcock	.08	.25
❑ 5 Charlie Garner	.15	.40
❑ 6 Blaine Bishop	.08	.25
❑ 7 Junior Seau	.25	.60
❑ 8 Andre Rison	.15	.40
❑ 9 Jake Reed	.15	.40
❑ 10 Cris Carter	.25	.60
❑ 11 Torrance Small	.08	.25
❑ 12 Ronald McKinnon	.08	.25
❑ 13 Tyrone Davis	.08	.25
❑ 14 Warren Moon	.25	.60
❑ 15 Joe Johnson	.08	.25
❑ 16 Bert Emanuel	.15	.40
❑ 17 Brad Culpepper	.08	.25
❑ 18 Henry Jones	.08	.25
❑ 19 Jonathan Ogden	.08	.25
❑ 20 Terrell Owens	.25	.60
❑ 21 Derrick Mason	.15	.40
❑ 22 Jon Ritchie	.08	.25
❑ 23 Eric Metcalf	.08	.25
❑ 24 Kevin Carter	.08	.25
❑ 25 Fred Taylor	.25	.60
❑ 26 DeWayne Washington	.08	.25
❑ 27 William Thomas	.08	.25
❑ 28 Rocket Ismail	.15	.40
❑ 29 Jason Taylor	.08	.25
❑ 30 Doug Flutie	.25	.60
❑ 31 Michael Sinclair	.08	.25
❑ 32 Yancey Thigpen	.08	.25
❑ 33 Darnay Scott	.08	.25
❑ 34 Amani Toomer	.08	.25
❑ 35 Edgar Bennett	.08	.25
❑ 36 LeRoy Butler	.08	.25
❑ 37 Jessie Tuggle	.08	.25
❑ 38 Andrew Glover	.08	.25
❑ 39 Tim McDonald	.08	.25
❑ 40 Marshall Faulk	.30	.75
❑ 41 Ray Mickens	.08	.25
❑ 42 Kimble Anders	.15	.40

Card	Low	High
❑ 43 Trent Green	.25	.60
❑ 44 Dermontti Dawson	.08	.25
❑ 45 Greg Ellis	.08	.25
❑ 46 Hugh Douglas	.08	.25
❑ 47 Amp Lee	.08	.25
❑ 48 Lamar Thomas	.08	.25
❑ 49 Curtis Conway	.15	.40
❑ 50 Emmitt Smith	.50	1.25
❑ 51 Elvis Grbac	.15	.40
❑ 52 Tony Simmons	.08	.25
❑ 53 Darrin Smith	.08	.25
❑ 54 Donovin Darius	.08	.25
❑ 55 Corey Chavous	.08	.25
❑ 56 Phillippi Sparks	.08	.25
❑ 57 Luther Elliss	.08	.25
❑ 58 Tim Dwight	.25	.60
❑ 59 Andre Hastings	.08	.25
❑ 60 Dan Marino	.75	2.00
❑ 61 Micheal Barrow	.08	.25
❑ 62 Corey Fuller	.08	.25
❑ 63 Bill Romanowski	.08	.25
❑ 64 Derrick Rodgers	.15	.40
❑ 65 Natrone Means	.15	.40
❑ 66 Peter Boulware	.08	.25
❑ 67 Brian Mitchell	.08	.25
❑ 68 Cornelius Bennett	.08	.25
❑ 69 Dedric Ward	.08	.25
❑ 70 Drew Bledsoe	.30	.75
❑ 71 Freddie Jones	.08	.25
❑ 72 Derrick Thomas	.25	.60
❑ 73 Willie Davis	.08	.25
❑ 74 Larry Centers	.08	.25
❑ 75 Mark Brunell	.25	.60
❑ 76 Chuck Smith	.08	.25
❑ 77 Desmond Howard	.15	.40
❑ 78 Sedrick Shaw	.08	.25
❑ 79 Tiki Barber	.25	.60
❑ 80 Curtis Martin	.25	.60
❑ 81 Barry Minter	.08	.25
❑ 82 Skip Hicks	.08	.25
❑ 83 O.J. Santiago	.08	.25
❑ 84 Ed McCaffrey	.15	.40
❑ 85 Terrell Buckley	.08	.25
❑ 86 Charlie Jones	.08	.25
❑ 87 Pete Mitchell	.08	.25
❑ 88 La'Roi Glover RC	.25	.60
❑ 89 Eric Davis	.08	.25
❑ 90 John Elway	.75	2.00
❑ 91 Kavika Pittman	.08	.25
❑ 92 Fred Lane	.08	.25
❑ 93 Warren Sapp	.08	.25
❑ 94 Lorenzo Bromell RC	.25	.60
❑ 95 Lawyer Milloy	.15	.40
❑ 96 Aeneas Williams	.08	.25
❑ 97 Michael McCrary	.08	.25
❑ 98 Rickey Dudley	.08	.25
❑ 99 Bryce Paup	.08	.25
❑ 100 Jamal Anderson	.25	.60
❑ 101 D'Marco Farr	.08	.25
❑ 102 Johnnie Morton	.15	.40
❑ 103 Jeff Graham	.08	.25
❑ 104 Sam Cowart	.08	.25
❑ 105 Bryant Young	.08	.25
❑ 106 Jermaine Lewis	.15	.40
❑ 107 Chad Bratzke	.08	.25
❑ 108 Jeff Burris	.08	.25
❑ 109 Roell Preston	.08	.25
❑ 110 Vinny Testaverde	.15	.40
❑ 111 Ruben Brown	.08	.25
❑ 112 Darryll Lewis	.08	.25
❑ 113 Billy Davis	.08	.25
❑ 114 Bryant Westbrook	.08	.25
❑ 115 Stephen Alexander	.08	.25
❑ 116 Terrell Fletcher	.08	.25
❑ 117 Terry Glenn	.25	.60
❑ 118 Rod Smith	.15	.40
❑ 119 Carl Pickens	.15	.40
❑ 120 Tim Brown	.25	.60
❑ 121 Mikhael Ricks	.08	.25
❑ 122 Jason Gildon	.08	.25
❑ 123 Charles Way	.08	.25
❑ 124 Rob Moore	.15	.40
❑ 125 Jerome Bettis	.25	.60
❑ 126 Kerry Collins	.15	.40
❑ 127 Bruce Smith	.15	.40
❑ 128 James Hasty	.08	.25
❑ 129 Ken Norton Jr.	.08	.25
❑ 130 Charles Woodson	.25	.60
❑ 131 Tony McGee	.08	.25
❑ 132 Kevin Turner	.08	.25
❑ 133 Jerome Pathon	.08	.25
❑ 134 Garrison Hearst	.15	.40
❑ 135 Craig Newsome	.08	.25
❑ 136 Hardy Nickerson	.08	.25
❑ 137 Ray Lewis	.25	.60
❑ 138 Derrick Alexander	.08	.25
❑ 139 Phil Hansen	.08	.25
❑ 140 Joey Galloway	.15	.40
❑ 141 Oronde Gadsden	.15	.40
❑ 142 Herman Moore	.15	.40
❑ 143 Bobby Taylor	.08	.25
❑ 144 Mario Bates	.08	.25
❑ 145 Kevin Dyson	.15	.40
❑ 146 Aaron Glenn	.08	.25
❑ 147 Ed McDaniel	.08	.25
❑ 148 Terry Allen	.15	.40
❑ 149 Ike Hilliard	.08	.25
❑ 150 Steve Young	.30	.75
❑ 151 Eugene Robinson	.08	.25
❑ 152 John Mobley	.08	.25
❑ 153 Kevin Hardy	.08	.25
❑ 154 Lance Johnstone	.08	.25
❑ 155 Willie McGinest	.08	.25
❑ 156 Gary Anderson	.08	.25
❑ 157 Dexter Coakley	.08	.25
❑ 158 Mark Fields	.08	.25
❑ 159 Steve McNair	.25	.60
❑ 160 Corey Dillon	.25	.60
❑ 161 Zach Thomas	.25	.60
❑ 162 Kent Graham	.08	.25
❑ 163 Tony Parrish	.08	.25
❑ 164 Sam Gash	.08	.25
❑ 165 Kyle Brady	.08	.25
❑ 166 Donnell Bennett	.08	.25
❑ 167 Tony Martin	.15	.40
❑ 168 Michael Bates	.08	.25
❑ 169 Bobby Engram	.15	.40
❑ 170 Jimmy Smith	.15	.40
❑ 171 Vonnie Holliday	.08	.25
❑ 172 Simeon Rice	.15	.40
❑ 173 Kevin Greene	.08	.25
❑ 174 Mike Alstott	.25	.60
❑ 175 Eddie George	.25	.60
❑ 176 Michael Jackson	.08	.25
❑ 177 Neil O'Donnell	.15	.40
❑ 178 Sean Dawkins	.08	.25
❑ 179 Courtney Hawkins	.08	.25
❑ 180 Michael Irvin	.15	.40
❑ 181 Thurman Thomas	.15	.40
❑ 182 Cam Cleeland	.08	.25
❑ 183 Ellis Johnson	.08	.25
❑ 184 Will Blackwell	.08	.25
❑ 185 Ty Law	.15	.40
❑ 186 Merton Hanks	.08	.25
❑ 187 Dan Wilkinson	.08	.25
❑ 188 Andre Wadsworth	.08	.25
❑ 189 Troy Vincent	.08	.25
❑ 190 Frank Sanders	.15	.40
❑ 191 Stephen Boyd	.08	.25
❑ 192 Jason Elam	.08	.25
❑ 193 Kordell Stewart	.15	.40
❑ 194 Ted Johnson	.08	.25
❑ 195 Glyn Milburn	.08	.25
❑ 196 Gary Brown	.08	.25
❑ 197 Travis Hall	.08	.25
❑ 198 John Randle	.15	.40
❑ 199 Jay Riemersma	.08	.25
❑ 200 Barry Sanders	.75	2.00
❑ 201 Chris Spielman	.08	.25
❑ 202 Rod Woodson	.15	.40
❑ 203 Darrell Russell	.08	.25
❑ 204 Tony Boselli	.08	.25
❑ 205 Darren Woodson	.08	.25
❑ 206 Muhsin Muhammad	.15	.40
❑ 207 Jim Harbaugh	.15	.40
❑ 208 Isaac Bruce	.25	.60
❑ 209 Mo Lewis	.08	.25
❑ 210 Dorsey Levens	.25	.60
❑ 211 Frank Wycheck	.08	.25
❑ 212 Napoleon Kaufman	.25	.60
❑ 213 Walt Harris	.08	.25
❑ 214 Leon Lett	.08	.25
❑ 215 Karim Abdul-Jabbar	.15	.40
❑ 216 Carnell Lake	.08	.25
❑ 217 Byron Bam Morris	.08	.25
❑ 218 John Avery	.08	.25
❑ 219 Chris Slade	.08	.25
❑ 220 Robert Smith	.25	.60
❑ 221 Mike Pritchard	.08	.25
❑ 222 Ty Detmer	.15	.40
❑ 223 Randall Cunningham	.25	.60
❑ 224 Alonzo Mayes	.08	.25
❑ 225 Jake Plummer	.15	.40
❑ 226 Derrick Mayes	.08	.25
❑ 227 Jeff Brady	.08	.25
❑ 228 John Lynch	.15	.40
❑ 229 Steve Atwater	.08	.25
❑ 230 Warrick Dunn	.25	.60
❑ 231 Shawn Jefferson	.08	.25
❑ 232 Erik Kramer	.08	.25
❑ 233 Ken Dilger	.08	.25
❑ 234 Ryan Leaf	.25	.60
❑ 235 Ray Buchanan	.08	.25
❑ 236 Kevin Williams	.08	.25
❑ 237 Ricky Watters	.15	.40
❑ 238 Dwayne Rudd	.08	.25
❑ 239 Duce Staley	.25	.60
❑ 240 Charlie Batch	.25	.60
❑ 241 Tim Biakabutuka	.15	.40
❑ 242 Tony Gonzalez	.25	.60
❑ 243 Bryan Still	.08	.25
❑ 244 Donnie Edwards	.08	.25
❑ 245 Troy Aikman	.50	1.25
❑ 246 Tony Banks	.15	.40
❑ 247 Curtis Enis	.08	.25
❑ 248 Chris Chandler	.15	.40
❑ 249 James Jett	.15	.40
❑ 250 Brett Favre	.75	2.00
❑ 251 Keith Poole	.08	.25
❑ 252 Ricky Proehl	.08	.25
❑ 253 Shannon Sharpe	.15	.40
❑ 254 Robert Jones	.08	.25
❑ 255 Chad Brown	.08	.25
❑ 256 Ben Coates	.15	.40
❑ 257 Jacquez Green	.08	.25
❑ 258 Jessie Armstead	.08	.25
❑ 259 Dale Carter	.08	.25
❑ 260 Antowain Smith	.25	.60
❑ 261 Mark Chmura	.08	.25
❑ 262 Michael Westbrook	.15	.40
❑ 263 Marvin Harrison	.25	.60
❑ 264 Darrien Gordon	.08	.25
❑ 265 Rodney Harrison	.08	.25
❑ 266 Charles Johnson	.08	.25
❑ 267 Roman Phifer	.08	.25
❑ 268 Reidel Anthony	.15	.40
❑ 269 Jerry Rice	.50	1.25
❑ 270 Eric Moulds	.25	.60
❑ 271 Robert Porcher	.08	.25
❑ 272 Deion Sanders	.25	.60
❑ 273 Germane Crowell	.08	.25
❑ 274 Randy Moss	.60	1.50
❑ 275 Antonio Freeman	.25	.60
❑ 276 Trent Dilfer	.15	.40
❑ 277 Eric Turner	.08	.25
❑ 278 Jeff George	.15	.40
❑ 279 Levon Kirkland	.08	.25
❑ 280 O.J. McDuffie	.15	.40
❑ 281 Takeo Spikes	.08	.25
❑ 282 Jim Flanigan	.08	.25
❑ 283 Chris Warren	.08	.25
❑ 284 J.J. Stokes	.15	.40
❑ 285 Bryan Cox	.08	.25
❑ 286 Sam Madison	.08	.25
❑ 287 Priest Holmes	.40	1.00
❑ 288 Keenan McCardell	.15	.40
❑ 289 Michael Strahan	.15	.40
❑ 290 Robert Edwards	.08	.25
❑ 291 Tommy Vardell	.08	.25
❑ 292 Wayne Chrebet	.15	.40
❑ 293 Chris Calloway	.08	.25
❑ 294 Wesley Walls	.15	.40
❑ 295 Derrick Brooks	.25	.60
❑ 296 Trace Armstrong	.08	.25
❑ 297 Brian Simmons	.08	.25
❑ 298 Darrell Green	.08	.25
❑ 299 Robert Brooks	.15	.40
❑ 300 Peyton Manning	.75	2.00
❑ 301 Dana Stubblefield	.08	.25
❑ 302 Shawn Springs	.08	.25
❑ 303 Leslie Shepherd	.08	.25
❑ 304 Ken Harvey	.08	.25
❑ 305 Jon Kitna	.25	.60
❑ 306 Terance Mathis	.15	.40
❑ 307 Andre Reed	.15	.40
❑ 308 Jackie Harris	.08	.25
❑ 309 Rich Gannon	.25	.60

❑ 010 Keyshawn Johnson .25 .60
❑ 311 Victor Green .08 .25
❑ 312 Eric Allen .08 .25
❑ 313 Terry Fair .08 .25
❑ 314 Jason Elam SH .08 .25
❑ 315 Garrison Hearst SH .15 .40
❑ 316 Jake Plummer SH .15 .40
❑ 317 Randall Cunningham SH .25 .60
❑ 318 Randy Moss SH .30 .75
❑ 319 Jamal Anderson SH .25 .60
❑ 320 John Elway SH .40 1.00
❑ 321 Doug Flutie SH .15 .40
❑ 322 Emmitt Smith SH .30 .75
❑ 323 Terrell Davis SH .25 .60
❑ 324 Jerris McPhail .08 .25
❑ 325 Damon Gibson .08 .25
❑ 326 Jim Pyne .08 .25
❑ 327 Antonio Langham .08 .25
❑ 328 Freddie Solomon .08 .25
❑ 329 Ricky Williams RC 1.50 4.00
❑ 330 Daunte Culpepper RC 3.00 8.00
❑ 331 Chris Claiborne RC .50 1.25
❑ 332 Amos Zereoue RC 1.00 2.50
❑ 333 Chris McAlister RC .75 2.00
❑ 334 Kevin Faulk RC 1.00 2.50
❑ 335 James Johnson RC .75 2.00
❑ 336 Mike Cloud RC .75 2.00
❑ 337 Jevon Kearse RC 1.50 4.00
❑ 338 Akili Smith RC .75 2.00
❑ 339 Edgerrin James RC 3.00 8.00
❑ 340 Cecil Collins RC .50 1.25
❑ 341 Donovan McNabb RC 4.00 10.00
❑ 342 Kevin Johnson RC 1.00 2.50
❑ 343 Torry Holt RC 2.00 5.00
❑ 344 Rob Konrad RC .50 1.25
❑ 345 Tim Couch RC 1.00 2.50
❑ 346 David Boston RC 1.00 2.50
❑ 347 Karsten Bailey RC .75 2.00
❑ 348 Troy Edwards RC .75 2.00
❑ 349 Sedrick Irvin RC .50 1.25
❑ 350 Shaun King RC .75 2.00
❑ 351 Peerless Price RC 1.00 2.50
❑ 352 Brock Huard RC 1.00 2.50
❑ 353 Cade McNown RC .75 2.00
❑ 354 Champ Bailey RC 1.25 3.00
❑ 355 D'Wayne Bates RC .75 2.00
❑ 356 Checklist Card .08 .25
❑ 357 Checklist Card .08 .25

2000 Topps

❑ COMPLETE SET (400) 25.00 60.00
❑ COMP.SET w/o SP's (360) 7.50 20.00
❑ SBMVP STATED ODDS 1:1287 HTA
❑ 1 Kurt Warner .50 1.25
❑ 2 Darrell Russell .08 .25
❑ 3 Tai Streets .08 .25
❑ 4 Bryant Young .08 .25
❑ 5 Kent Graham .08 .25
❑ 6 Shawn Jefferson .08 .25
❑ 7 Wesley Walls .08 .25
❑ 8 Jessie Armstead .08 .25
❑ 9 Dedric Ward .08 .25
❑ 10 Emmitt Smith .50 1.25
❑ 11 James Stewart .15 .40
❑ 12 Frank Sanders .08 .25
❑ 13 Ray Buchanan .08 .25
❑ 14 Olindo Mare .08 .25
❑ 15 Andre Reed .15 .40
❑ 16 Curtis Conway .15 .40
❑ 17 Patrick Jeffers .25 .60
❑ 18 Greg Hill .08 .25
❑ 19 John Unitas .25 .60
❑ 20 Brett Favre .75 2.00
❑ 21 Jerome Pathon .15 .40
❑ 22 Jason Tucker .08 .25
❑ 23 Charles Johnson .15 .40
❑ 24 Brian Mitchell .08 .25
❑ 25 Billy Miller .08 .25
❑ 26 Jay Fiedler .25 .60
❑ 27 Marcus Pollard .08 .25
❑ 28 De'Mond Parker .08 .25
❑ 29 Leslie Shepherd .08 .25
❑ 30 Fred Taylor .25 .60
❑ 31 Michael Pittman .08 .25
❑ 32 Ricky Watters .15 .40
❑ 33 Derrick Brooks .25 .60
❑ 34 Junior Seau .25 .60
❑ 35 Troy Vincent .08 .25
❑ 36 Eric Allen .08 .25
❑ 37 Pete Mitchell .08 .25
❑ 38 Tony Simmons .08 .25
❑ 39 Az-Zahir Hakim .15 .40
❑ 40 Dan Marino .75 2.00
❑ 41 Mac Cody .08 .25
❑ 42 Scott Dreisbach .08 .25
❑ 43 Al Wilson .08 .25
❑ 44 Luther Broughton RC .15 .40
❑ 45 Wane McGarity .08 .25
❑ 46 Stephen Boyd .08 .25
❑ 47 Michael Strahan .15 .40
❑ 48 Chris Chandler .15 .40
❑ 49 Tony Martin .15 .40
❑ 50 Edgerrin James .40 1.00
❑ 51 John Randle .15 .40
❑ 52 Warrick Dunn .25 .60
❑ 53 Elvis Grbac .15 .40
❑ 54 Champ Bailey .15 .40
❑ 55 Kyle Brady .08 .25
❑ 56 John Lynch .15 .40
❑ 57 Kevin Carter .08 .25
❑ 58 Mike Pritchard .08 .25
❑ 59 Deon Mitchell RC .15 .40
❑ 60 Randy Moss .50 1.25
❑ 61 Jermaine Fazande .08 .25
❑ 62 Donovan McNabb .40 1.00
❑ 63 Richard Huntley .08 .25
❑ 64 Rich Gannon .25 .60
❑ 65 Aaron Glenn .08 .25
❑ 66 Amani Toomer .08 .25
❑ 67 Andre Hastings .08 .25
❑ 68 Ricky Williams .25 .60
❑ 69 Sam Madison .08 .25
❑ 70 Drew Bledsoe .30 .75
❑ 71 Eric Moulds .25 .60
❑ 72 Justin Armour .08 .25
❑ 73 Jamal Anderson .25 .60
❑ 74 Mario Bates .08 .25
❑ 75 Sam Gash .08 .25
❑ 76 Macey Brooks .08 .25
❑ 77 Tremain Mack .08 .25
❑ 78 David LaFleur .08 .25
❑ 79 Dexter Coakley .08 .25
❑ 80 Cris Carter .25 .60
❑ 81 Byron Chamberlain .08 .25
❑ 82 David Sloan .08 .25
❑ 83 Mike Devlin RC .08 .25
❑ 84 Jimmy Smith .15 .40
❑ 85 Derrick Alexander .15 .40
❑ 86 Damon Huard .25 .60
❑ 87 Jake Reed .15 .40
❑ 88 Darrell Green .08 .25
❑ 89 Derrick Mason .15 .40
❑ 90 Curtis Martin .25 .60
❑ 91 Donnie Abraham .08 .25
❑ 92 D'Marco Farr .08 .25
❑ 93 Ahman Green .25 .60
❑ 94 Shane Matthews .15 .40
❑ 95 Torrance Small .08 .25
❑ 96 Duce Staley .25 .60
❑ 97 Jon Ritchie .08 .25
❑ 98 Victor Green .08 .25
❑ 99 Kerry Collins .15 .40
❑ 100 Peyton Manning .60 1.50
❑ 101 Ben Coates .08 .25
❑ 102 Thurman Thomas .15 .40
❑ 103 Cornelius Bennett .08 .25
❑ 104 Terance Mathis .15 .40
❑ 105 Adrian Murrell .15 .40
❑ 106 Donald Hayes .08 .25
❑ 107 Terry Kirby .08 .25
❑ 108 James Allen .15 .40
❑ 109 Ty Law .15 .40
❑ 110 Tim Brown .25 .60
❑ 111 Chad Bratzke .08 .25
❑ 112 Deion Sanders .25 .60
❑ 113 James Johnson .08 .25
❑ 114 Tony Richardson RC .15 .40
❑ 115 Tony Brackens .08 .25
❑ 116 Ken Dilger .08 .25
❑ 117 Albert Connell .08 .25
❑ 118 Neil O'Donnell .08 .25
❑ 119 Selucio Sanford EP RC .25 .60
❑ 120 Steve Young .30 .75
❑ 121 Tony Horne .08 .25
❑ 122 Charlie Rogers .08 .25
❑ 123 J.J. Stokes .15 .40
❑ 124 Kenny Bynum .08 .25
❑ 125 Jeff Graham .08 .25
❑ 126 Ike Hilliard .15 .40
❑ 127 Ray Lucas .15 .40
❑ 128 Terry Glenn .15 .40
❑ 129 Rickey Dudley .08 .25
❑ 130 Joey Galloway .15 .40
❑ 131 Brian Dawkins .25 .60
❑ 132 Rob Moore .15 .40
❑ 133 Bob Christian .08 .25
❑ 134 Anthony Wright RC .75 2.00
❑ 135 Antowain Smith .15 .40
❑ 136 Kevin Johnson .25 .60
❑ 137 Scott Covington .08 .25
❑ 138 D'Wayne Bates .08 .25
❑ 139 Sam Cowart .08 .25
❑ 140 Isaac Bruce .25 .60
❑ 141 Tony McGee .08 .25
❑ 142 Dale Carter .08 .25
❑ 143 Matt Hasselbeck .15 .40
❑ 144 Torry Holt .25 .60
❑ 145 Daunte Culpepper .30 .75
❑ 146 Yatil Green .08 .25
❑ 147 Chris Howard .08 .25
❑ 148 Irving Fryar .15 .40
❑ 149 Derrick Mayes .15 .40
❑ 150 Warren Sapp .15 .40
❑ 151 Ricky Proehl .08 .25
❑ 152 Eric Kresser EP .20 .50
❑ 153 Jeff Garcia .25 .60
❑ 154 Freddie Jones .08 .25
❑ 155 Mike Cloud .08 .25
❑ 156 Wayne Chrebet .15 .40
❑ 157 Joe Montgomery .08 .25
❑ 158 Shannon Sharpe .15 .40
❑ 159 Eddie Kennison .08 .25
❑ 160 Eddie George .25 .60
❑ 161 Jay Riemersma .08 .25
❑ 162 Peter Boulware .08 .25
❑ 163 Aeneas Williams .08 .25
❑ 164 Jim Miller .08 .25
❑ 165 Jamir Miller .08 .25
❑ 166 Tim Biakabutuka .15 .40
❑ 167 Kordell Stewart .15 .40
❑ 168 Charlie Garner .15 .40
❑ 169 Germane Crowell .08 .25
❑ 170 Stephen Davis .25 .60
❑ 171 Jeff George .15 .40
❑ 172 Mark Brunell .25 .60
❑ 173 Stephen Alexander .08 .25
❑ 174 Mike Alstott .25 .60
❑ 175 Terry Allen .15 .40
❑ 176 Ed McCaffrey .25 .60
❑ 177 Bobby Engram .08 .25
❑ 178 Andre Cooper .08 .25
❑ 179 Kevin Faulk .08 .25
❑ 180 Errict Rhett .15 .40
❑ 181 Jammi German .08 .25
❑ 182 Oronde Gadsden .15 .40
❑ 183 Jevon Kearse .25 .60
❑ 184 Herman Moore .15 .40
❑ 185 Terrence Wilkins .08 .25
❑ 186 Rocket Ismail .15 .40
❑ 187 Patrick Johnson .08 .25
❑ 188 Simeon Rice .15 .40
❑ 189 Mo Lewis .08 .25
❑ 190 Qadry Ismail .15 .40
❑ 191 Terry Jackson .08 .25
❑ 192 Rashaan Shehee .08 .25
❑ 193 Charles Woodson .15 .40
❑ 194 Akili Smith .08 .25
❑ 195 Yancey Thigpen .08 .25
❑ 196 Michael Westbrook .15 .40
❑ 197 Donnell Bennett .08 .25
❑ 198 Sedrick Irvin .08 .25
❑ 199 Keenan McCardell .15 .40
❑ 200 Marshall Faulk .30 .75
❑ 201 Jeff Blake .15 .40

Card		
❑ 202 Rob Johnson	.15	.40
❑ 203 Vinny Testaverde	.15	.40
❑ 204 Andy Katzenmoyer	.08	.25
❑ 205 Michael Basnight	.08	.25
❑ 206 Lance Schulters	.08	.25
❑ 207 Shaun King	.08	.25
❑ 208 Bill Schroeder	.15	.40
❑ 209 Skip Hicks	.08	.25
❑ 210 Jake Plummer	.15	.40
❑ 211 Leroy Hoard	.08	.25
❑ 212 Reggie Barlow	.08	.25
❑ 213 E.G. Green	.08	.25
❑ 214 Fred Lane	.08	.25
❑ 215 Antonio Freeman	.25	.60
❑ 216 Grant Wistrom	.08	.25
❑ 217 Kevin Dyson	.15	.40
❑ 218 Mikhael Ricks	.08	.25
❑ 219 Rod Woodson	.15	.40
❑ 220 Tim Dwight	.25	.60
❑ 221 Darnay Scott	.15	.40
❑ 222 Curtis Enis	.08	.25
❑ 223 Sean Bennett	.08	.25
❑ 224 Napoleon Kaufman	.15	.40
❑ 225 Jonathan Linton	.08	.25
❑ 226 Jim Harbaugh	.15	.40
❑ 227 Hardy Nickerson	.08	.25
❑ 228 Todd Lyght	.08	.25
❑ 229 Dorsey Levens	.15	.40
❑ 230 Steve Beuerlein	.15	.40
❑ 231 Marty Booker	.15	.40
❑ 232 Andre Wadsworth	.08	.25
❑ 233 James Hasty	.08	.25
❑ 234 Shawn Bryson	.08	.25
❑ 235 Larry Centers	.08	.25
❑ 236 Charlie Batch	.25	.60
❑ 237 Steve McNair	.25	.60
❑ 238 Darrin Chiaverini	.08	.25
❑ 239 Jerome Bettis	.25	.60
❑ 240 Muhsin Muhammad	.15	.40
❑ 241 Terrell Fletcher	.08	.25
❑ 242 Jon Kitna	.25	.60
❑ 243 Frank Wycheck	.08	.25
❑ 244 Tony Gonzalez	.15	.40
❑ 245 Ron Rivers	.08	.25
❑ 246 Olandis Gary	.25	.60
❑ 247 Jermaine Lewis	.08	.25
❑ 248 Joe Jurevicius	.08	.25
❑ 249 Richie Anderson	.15	.40
❑ 250 Marcus Robinson	.25	.60
❑ 251 Shawn Springs	.08	.25
❑ 252 William Floyd	.08	.25
❑ 253 Bobby Shaw RC	.25	.60
❑ 254 Glyn Milburn	.08	.25
❑ 255 Brian Griese	.25	.60
❑ 256 Donnie Edwards	.08	.25
❑ 257 Joe Horn	.15	.40
❑ 258 Cameron Cleeland	.08	.25
❑ 259 Glenn Foley	.08	.25
❑ 260 Corey Dillon	.25	.60
❑ 261 Troy Brown	.15	.40
❑ 262 Stoney Case	.08	.25
❑ 263 Kevin Williams	.08	.25
❑ 264 London Fletcher RC	.15	.40
❑ 265 O.J. McDuffie	.15	.40
❑ 266 Jonathan Quinn	.08	.25
❑ 267 Trent Dilfer	.15	.40
❑ 268 Dameyune Craig	.08	.25
❑ 269 Terrell Owens	.25	.60
❑ 270 Tim Couch	.15	.40
❑ 271 Dameane Douglas	.08	.25
❑ 272 Moses Moreno	.08	.25
❑ 273 Bruce Smith	.15	.40
❑ 274 Peerless Price	.15	.40
❑ 275 Sam Gardes	.08	.25
❑ 276 Natrone Means	.08	.25
❑ 277 Na Brown	.08	.25
❑ 278 Dave Moore	.08	.25
❑ 279 Chris Sanders	.08	.25
❑ 280 Troy Aikman	.50	1.25
❑ 281 Cecil Collins	.08	.25
❑ 282 Matthew Hatchette	.08	.25
❑ 283 Bill Romanowski	.08	.25
❑ 284 Basil Mitchell	.08	.25
❑ 285 Tony Banks	.15	.40
❑ 286 Jake Delhomme RC	1.25	3.00
❑ 287 Keyshawn Johnson	.25	.60
❑ 288 Dexter McCleon RC	.25	.60
❑ 289 Corey Bradford	.15	.40
❑ 290 Terrell Davis	.25	.60
❑ 291 Johnnie Morton	.15	.40
❑ 292 Kevin Lockett	.08	.25
❑ 293 Robert Smith	.25	.60
❑ 294 Jeff Lewis	.08	.25
❑ 295 Wali Rainer	.08	.25
❑ 296 Troy Edwards	.08	.25
❑ 297 Keith Poole	.08	.25
❑ 298 Priest Holmes	.30	.75
❑ 299 David Boston	.25	.60
❑ 300 Marvin Harrison	.25	.60
❑ 301 Levon Kirkland	.08	.25
❑ 302 Robert Holcombe	.08	.25
❑ 303 Autry Denson	.08	.25
❑ 304 Kevin Hardy	.08	.25
❑ 305 Rod Smith	.15	.40
❑ 306 Robert Porcher	.08	.25
❑ 307 Cade McNown	.08	.25
❑ 308 Craig Yeast	.08	.25
❑ 309 Doug Flutie	.25	.60
❑ 310 Jerry Rice	.50	1.25
❑ 311 Brad Johnson	.25	.60
❑ 312 Tiki Barber	.25	.60
❑ 313 Will Blackwell	.08	.25
❑ 314 Sean Dawkins	.08	.25
❑ 315 Jacquez Green	.08	.25
❑ 316 Zach Thomas	.25	.60
❑ 317 Gus Frerotte	.08	.25
❑ 318 Chris Warren	.08	.25
❑ 319 Carl Pickens	.15	.40
❑ 320 Tyrone Wheatley HL	.08	.25
❑ 321 Kurt Warner HL	.25	.60
❑ 322 Dan Marino HL	.40	1.00
❑ 323 Cris Carter HL	.15	.40
❑ 324 Brett Favre HL	.40	1.00
❑ 325 Marshall Faulk HL	.25	.60
❑ 326 Jevon Kearse HL	.15	.40
❑ 327 Edgerrin James HL	.25	.60
❑ 328 Emmitt Smith HL	.25	.60
❑ 329 Andre Reed HL	.08	.25
❑ 330 K.Dyson/F.Wycheck HL	.08	.25
❑ 331 Olindo Mare MM	.08	.25
❑ 332 Marcus Coleman MM	.08	.25
❑ 333 James Johnson MM	.08	.25
❑ 334 Ray Lucas MM	.15	.40
❑ 335 Dedric Ward MM	.08	.25
❑ 336 Richie Cunningham MM	.08	.25
❑ 337 James Hasty MM	.08	.25
❑ 338 Sedrick Shaw MM	.08	.25
❑ 339 Kurt Warner MM	.25	.60
❑ 340 Marshall Faulk MM	.25	.60
❑ 341 Brian Shay EP	.20	.50
❑ 342 L.C. Stevens EP	.20	.50
❑ 343 Corey Thomas EP	.20	.50
❑ 344 Scott Milanovich EP	.25	.60
❑ 345 Pat Barnes EP	.25	.60
❑ 346 Danny Wuerffel EP	.25	.60
❑ 347 Kevin Daft EP	.20	.50
❑ 348 Ron Powlus EP RC	.40	1.00
❑ 349 Tony Graziani EP	.25	.60
❑ 350 Norman Miller EP RC	.20	.50
❑ 351 Cory Sauter EP	.20	.50
❑ 352 Marcus Crandell EP RC	.25	.60
❑ 353 Sean Morey EP RC	.25	.60
❑ 354 Jeff Ogden EP	.25	.60
❑ 355 Ted White EP	.20	.50
❑ 356 Jim Kubiak EP RC	.25	.60
❑ 357 Aaron Stecker EP RC	.40	1.00
❑ 358 Ronnie Powell EP	.20	.50
❑ 359 Matt Lytle EP RC	.25	.60
❑ 360 Kendrick Nord EP RC	.20	.50
❑ 361 Tim Rattay RC	1.00	2.50
❑ 362 Rob Morris RC	1.00	2.50
❑ 363 Chris Samuels RC	.75	2.00
❑ 364 Todd Husak RC	1.00	2.50
❑ 365 Ahmed Plummer RC	1.00	2.50
❑ 366 Frank Murphy RC	.75	2.00
❑ 367 Michael Wiley RC	1.00	2.50
❑ 368 Giovanni Carmazzi RC	.75	2.00
❑ 369 Anthony Becht RC	1.00	2.50
❑ 370 John Abraham RC	1.00	2.50
❑ 371 Shaun Alexander RC	3.00	8.00
❑ 372 Thomas Jones RC	1.50	4.00
❑ 373 Courtney Brown RC	.40	1.00
❑ 374 Curtis Keaton RC	.75	2.00
❑ 375 Jerry Porter RC	1.25	3.00
❑ 376 Corey Simon RC	.40	1.00
❑ 377 Dez White RC	1.00	2.50
❑ 378 Jamal Lewis RC	2.50	6.00
❑ 379 Ron Dayne RC	1.00	2.50
❑ 380 R.Jay Soward RC	1.00	2.50
❑ 381 Tee Martin RC	1.00	2.50
❑ 382 Shaun Ellis RC	1.00	2.50
❑ 383 Brian Urlacher RC	4.00	10.00
❑ 384 Reuben Droughns RC	1.50	4.00
❑ 385 Travis Taylor RC	.40	1.00
❑ 386 Plaxico Burress RC	2.00	5.00
❑ 387 Chad Pennington RC	2.50	6.00
❑ 388 Sylvester Morris RC	1.00	2.50
❑ 389 Ron Dugans RC	.75	2.00
❑ 390 Joe Hamilton RC	1.00	2.50
❑ 391 Chris Redman RC	.25	.60
❑ 392 Trung Canidate RC	1.00	2.50
❑ 393 J.R. Redmond RC	1.00	2.50
❑ 394 Danny Farmer RC	1.00	2.50
❑ 395 Todd Pinkston RC	1.00	2.50
❑ 396 Dennis Northcutt RC	1.00	2.50
❑ 397 Laveranues Coles RC	1.25	3.00
❑ 398 Bubba Franks RC	1.00	2.50
❑ 399 Travis Prentice RC	1.00	2.50
❑ 400 Peter Warrick RC	1.00	2.50
❑ SBMVP Kurt Warner FB AU	50.00	120.00

2001 Topps

Card		
❑ COMPLETE SET (385)	45.00	75.00
❑ 1 Marshall Faulk	.25	.60
❑ 2 Lawyer Milloy	.20	.50
❑ 3 Rich Gannon	.20	.50
❑ 4 Rod Smith	.20	.50
❑ 5 David Boston	.15	.40
❑ 6 Jeremy McDaniel	.15	.40
❑ 7 Joey Galloway	.20	.50
❑ 8 Ron Dixon	.15	.40
❑ 9 Terrell Fletcher	.15	.40
❑ 10 Deion Sanders	.25	.60
❑ 11 Jevon Kearse	.20	.50
❑ 12 Charles Woodson	.25	.60
❑ 13 Brian Walker	.15	.40
❑ 14 Mike Peterson	.15	.40
❑ 15 Marcus Robinson	.20	.50
❑ 16 Duane Starks	.15	.40
❑ 17 KaRon Coleman	.15	.40
❑ 18 Randy Moss	.30	.75
❑ 19 Reggie Jones	.15	.40
❑ 20 Derrick Brooks	.25	.60
❑ 21 Eddie George	.25	.60
❑ 22 Wayne Chrebet	.20	.50
❑ 23 Kevin Hardy	.15	.40
❑ 24 Bill Schroeder	.20	.50
❑ 25 Doug Flutie	.25	.60
❑ 26 Tim Dwight	.20	.50
❑ 27 Eddie Kennison	.20	.50
❑ 28 Reggie Kelly	.15	.40
❑ 29 Ricky Watters	.20	.50
❑ 30 Stephen Alexander	.15	.40
❑ 31 Az-Zahir Hakim	.15	.40
❑ 32 Henri Crockett	.15	.40
❑ 33 Joe Horn	.20	.50
❑ 34 Danny Farmer	.15	.40
❑ 35 Shannon Sharpe	.25	.60
❑ 36 Brad Hoover	.20	.50
❑ 37 David Patten	.15	.40
❑ 38 Kevin Faulk	.20	.50
❑ 39 Freddie Jones	.15	.40
❑ 40 Michael Westbrook	.15	.40
❑ 41 Jacquez Green	.15	.40
❑ 42 Torrance Small	.15	.40
❑ 43 Terrence Wilkins	.15	.40
❑ 44 Brett Favre	.75	2.00
❑ 45 Tony Banks	.15	.40
❑ 46 Johnnie Morton	.20	.50
❑ 47 Jimmy Smith	.20	.50
❑ 48 Jerry Rice	.50	1.25
❑ 49 Jeff George	.20	.50
❑ 50 Ray Lewis	.25	.60
❑ 51 Joe Johnson	.15	.40

Card		
❑ 52 Rocket Ismail	.20	.50
❑ 53 Muhsin Muhammad	.20	.50
❑ 54 Ken Dilger	.15	.40
❑ 55 Ike Hilliard	.20	.50
❑ 56 Joey Porter RC	1.25	3.00
❑ 57 Shaun Alexander	.25	.60
❑ 58 Jeff Garcia	.20	.50
❑ 59 Jay Fiedler	.20	.50
❑ 60 Wane McGarity	.15	.40
❑ 61 Steve Beuerlein	.20	.50
❑ 62 Tywan Mitchell	.15	.40
❑ 63 Travis Prentice	.15	.40
❑ 64 Robert Griffith	.15	.40
❑ 65 Napoleon Kaufman	.15	.40
❑ 66 Randall Godfrey	.15	.40
❑ 67 Junior Seau	.25	.60
❑ 68 Willie Jackson	.15	.40
❑ 69 Larry Foster	.15	.40
❑ 70 Brandon Stokley	.20	.50
❑ 71 Hugh Douglas	.15	.40
❑ 72 James Thrash	.20	.50
❑ 73 Vinny Testaverde	.20	.50
❑ 74 Leslie Shepherd	.15	.40
❑ 75 Terrell Davis	.25	.60
❑ 76 Jake Plummer	.20	.50
❑ 77 Corey Dillon	.20	.50
❑ 78 Ron Dayne	.20	.50
❑ 79 Brock Huard	.15	.40
❑ 80 Todd Husak	.15	.40
❑ 81 Richard Huntley	.15	.40
❑ 82 Shaun Ellis	.15	.40
❑ 83 Kyle Brady	.15	.40
❑ 84 Corey Bradford	.15	.40
❑ 85 Eric Moulds	.20	.50
❑ 86 Brian Finneran	.20	.50
❑ 87 Antonio Freeman	.25	.60
❑ 88 Terry Glenn	.20	.50
❑ 89 Tai Streets	.15	.40
❑ 90 Chris Sanders	.15	.40
❑ 91 Sylvester Morris	.15	.40
❑ 92 Peter Warrick	.20	.50
❑ 93 Chris Greisen	.15	.40
❑ 94 Cade McNown	.20	.50
❑ 95 Jerome Pathon	.15	.40
❑ 96 John Randle	.20	.50
❑ 97 Curtis Conway	.20	.50
❑ 98 Keyshawn Johnson	.20	.50
❑ 99 Trent Green	.25	.60
❑ 100 Mike Anderson	.20	.50
❑ 101 Jeff Blake	.20	.50
❑ 102 Tee Martin	.20	.50
❑ 103 Darrell Jackson	.20	.50
❑ 104 Mark Brunell	.25	.60
❑ 105 Charlie Batch	.20	.50
❑ 106 Wesley Walls	.15	.40
❑ 107 Edgerrin James	.25	.60
❑ 108 Robert Wilson	.15	.40
❑ 109 Donovan McNabb	.30	.75
❑ 110 Champ Bailey	.25	.60
❑ 111 Isaac Bruce	.25	.60
❑ 112 Michael Strahan	.25	.60
❑ 113 Donnie Edwards	.15	.40
❑ 114 Randall Cunningham	.25	.60
❑ 115 Germane Crowell	.15	.40
❑ 116 Jermaine Lewis	.15	.40
❑ 117 Dennis McKinley	.15	.40
❑ 118 Ryan Leaf	.15	.40
❑ 119 Samari Rolle	.15	.40
❑ 120 Daunte Culpepper	.25	.60
❑ 121 Tim Couch	.15	.40
❑ 122 Greg Biekert	.15	.40
❑ 123 Warrick Dunn	.25	.60
❑ 124 Richie Anderson	.15	.40
❑ 125 Trace Armstrong	.15	.40
❑ 126 Bernardo Harris	.15	.40
❑ 127 Kwame Cavil	.15	.40
❑ 128 James Allen	.15	.40
❑ 129 Anthony Becht	.15	.40
❑ 130 Tiki Barber	.25	.60
❑ 131 Brad Johnson	.20	.50
❑ 132 Tyrone Wheatley	.20	.50
❑ 133 Kurt Warner	.30	.75
❑ 134 Desmond Howard	.20	.50
❑ 135 Thomas Jones	.20	.50
❑ 136 Peyton Manning	.60	1.50
❑ 137 Tony Richardson	.15	.40
❑ 138 Chris Chandler	.20	.50
❑ 139 Plaxico Burress	.20	.50
❑ 140 J.R. Redmond	.15	.40
❑ 141 Fred Taylor	.25	.60
❑ 142 Akili Smith	.15	.40
❑ 143 Sammy Morris	.20	.50
❑ 144 Jessie Armstead	.15	.40
❑ 145 Charlie Garner	.20	.50
❑ 146 Steve McNair	.25	.60
❑ 147 Charles Johnson	.15	.40
❑ 148 Troy Aikman	.40	1.00
❑ 149 Kevin Johnson	.15	.40
❑ 150 Brian Urlacher	.30	.75
❑ 151 Travis Taylor	.15	.40
❑ 152 Aaron Shea	.15	.40
❑ 153 Mike Cloud	.15	.40
❑ 154 Donald Driver	.25	.60
❑ 155 Chad Pennington	.25	.60
❑ 156 Troy Edwards	.15	.40
❑ 157 Reidel Anthony	.15	.40
❑ 158 Michael Bishop	.20	.50
❑ 159 Mo Lewis	.15	.40
❑ 160 Damon Huard	.20	.50
❑ 161 James McKnight	.15	.40
❑ 162 Craig Yeast	.15	.40
❑ 163 Michael Pittman	.20	.50
❑ 164 Robert Smith	.20	.50
❑ 165 Terrelle Smith	.15	.40
❑ 166 Jeremiah Trotter	.15	.40
❑ 167 Amani Toomer	.20	.50
❑ 168 JaJuan Dawson	.15	.40
❑ 169 Tim Biakabutuka	.15	.40
❑ 170 Oronde Gadsden	.15	.40
❑ 171 Ray Lucas	.15	.40
❑ 172 Jermaine Fazande	.15	.40
❑ 173 Todd Bouman	.15	.40
❑ 174 Frank Wycheck	.15	.40
❑ 175 Hines Ward	.25	.60
❑ 176 Ahman Green	.25	.60
❑ 177 Kaseem Sinceno	.15	.40
❑ 178 Jamal Anderson	.20	.50
❑ 179 Jay Riemersma	.15	.40
❑ 180 Jarious Jackson	.15	.40
❑ 181 Andre Rison	.20	.50
❑ 182 Jerome Bettis	.25	.60
❑ 183 Blaine Bishop	.15	.40
❑ 184 Dorsey Levens	.20	.50
❑ 185 James Stewart	.15	.40
❑ 186 Chad Lewis	.15	.40
❑ 187 Justin Watson	.15	.40
❑ 188 Warren Sapp	.20	.50
❑ 189 Rod Woodson	.25	.60
❑ 190 Ricky Williams	.25	.60
❑ 191 Marty Booker	.20	.50
❑ 192 MarTay Jenkins	.15	.40
❑ 193 Peerless Price	.15	.40
❑ 194 Tony Gonzalez	.20	.50
❑ 195 Jon Kitna	.20	.50
❑ 196 Stephen Davis	.20	.50
❑ 197 Curtis Martin	.25	.60
❑ 198 Matt Hasselbeck	.25	.60
❑ 199 Pat Johnson	.15	.40
❑ 200 Emmitt Smith	.60	1.50
❑ 201 Doug Johnson	.15	.40
❑ 202 Autry Denson	.15	.40
❑ 203 Troy Brown	.20	.50
❑ 204 Jeff Graham	.15	.40
❑ 205 Corey Simon	.15	.40
❑ 206 Jamel White	.15	.40
❑ 207 Jeff Lewis	.15	.40
❑ 208 Frank Sanders	.15	.40
❑ 209 Al Wilson	.15	.40
❑ 210 Jason Sehorn	.20	.50
❑ 211 Shaun King	.15	.40
❑ 212 Torry Holt	.20	.50
❑ 213 Kordell Stewart	.20	.50
❑ 214 Keenan McCardell	.20	.50
❑ 215 Dedric Ward	.15	.40
❑ 216 Michael Wiley	.15	.40
❑ 217 Rob Johnson	.20	.50
❑ 218 Jamal Lewis	.25	.60
❑ 219 Herman Moore	.20	.50
❑ 220 Ron Dugans	.15	.40
❑ 221 Jason Taylor	.25	.60
❑ 222 Charles Lee	.15	.40
❑ 223 J.J. Stokes	.15	.40
❑ 224 Albert Connell	.15	.40
❑ 225 Keith Poole	.15	.40
❑ 226 Elvis Grbac	.20	.50
❑ 227 Shawn Jefferson	.15	.40
❑ 228 Jackie Harris	.20	.50
❑ 229 Derrick Alexander	.15	.40
❑ 230 Darnell Autry	.15	.40
❑ 231 Bobby Shaw	.15	.40
❑ 232 Aaron Brooks	.20	.50
❑ 233 Cris Carter	.25	.60
❑ 234 Desmond Clark	.20	.50
❑ 235 Spergon Wynn	.15	.40
❑ 236 Qadry Ismail	.20	.50
❑ 237 Sam Cowart	.15	.40
❑ 238 Zach Thomas	.25	.60
❑ 239 Drew Bledsoe	.25	.60
❑ 240 Ronney Jenkins	.15	.40
❑ 241 Keith Mitchell RC	.15	.40
❑ 242 Laveranues Coles	.25	.60
❑ 243 Marcus Pollard	.15	.40
❑ 244 Darren Sharper	.20	.50
❑ 245 Donald Hayes	.15	.40
❑ 246 Brian Griese	.20	.50
❑ 247 Frank Moreau	.15	.40
❑ 248 Bruce Smith	.25	.60
❑ 249 Fred Beasley	.15	.40
❑ 250 Mike Alstott	.20	.50
❑ 251 Trent Dilfer	.20	.50
❑ 252 Terance Mathis	.15	.40
❑ 253 Shawn Bryson	.15	.40
❑ 254 Dennis Northcutt	.15	.40
❑ 255 Brandon Bennett	.15	.40
❑ 256 Stacey Mack	.15	.40
❑ 257 Tim Brown	.25	.60
❑ 258 Duce Staley	.20	.50
❑ 259 Sean Dawkins	.15	.40
❑ 260 Ricky Proehl	.15	.40
❑ 261 Chris Fuamatu-ma'afala	.15	.40
❑ 262 La'Roi Glover	.15	.40
❑ 263 Bubba Franks	.20	.50
❑ 264 Kevin Lockett	.15	.40
❑ 265 Lamar Smith	.20	.50
❑ 266 Priest Holmes	.25	.60
❑ 267 Macey Brooks	.15	.40
❑ 268 Anthony Wright	.15	.40
❑ 269 Ed McCaffrey	.20	.50
❑ 270 Joe Jurevicius	.15	.40
❑ 271 Terrell Owens	.25	.60
❑ 272 Tony Simmons	.15	.40
❑ 273 Itula Mili	.15	.40
❑ 274 Chad Morton	.15	.40
❑ 275 Marvin Harrison	.25	.60
❑ 276 Jason Gildon	.20	.50
❑ 277 Derrick Mason	.20	.50
❑ 278 Greg Clark	.15	.40
❑ 279 Casey Crawford	.15	.40
❑ 280 Kerry Collins	.20	.50
❑ 281 Terrell Owens	.20	.50
❑ 282 Marshall Faulk	.20	.50
❑ 283 Mike Anderson	.15	.40
❑ 284 Cris Carter	.20	.50
❑ 285 Corey Dillon	.15	.40
❑ 286 Daunte Culpepper	.20	.50
❑ 287 Peyton Manning	.50	1.25
❑ 288 Torry Holt	.15	.40
❑ 289 Marvin Harrison	.20	.50
❑ 290 Edgerrin James	.20	.50
❑ 291 Takeo Spikes	.15	.40
❑ 292 John Lynch	.20	.50
❑ 293 Sam Madison	.15	.40
❑ 294 Stephen Boyd	.15	.40
❑ 295 Tony Siragusa	.20	.50
❑ 296 Robert Porcher	.15	.40
❑ 297 Donnell Bennett	.15	.40
❑ 298 Hardy Nickerson	.15	.40
❑ 299 Jonathan Quinn	.15	.40
❑ 300 Rob Morris	.15	.40
❑ 301 E.G. Green	.15	.40
❑ 302 David Sloan	.15	.40
❑ 303 Jason Tucker	.15	.40
❑ 304 Darrin Chiaverini	.15	.40
❑ 305 Wali Rainer	.15	.40
❑ 306 Jerry Azumah	.15	.40
❑ 307 Jonathan Linton	.15	.40
❑ 308 Dameyune Craig	.15	.40
❑ 309 Courtney Brown	.15	.40
❑ 310 Jammi German	.15	.40
❑ 311 Michael Vick RC	1.00	2.50
❑ 312 Jamar Fletcher RC	.30	.75
❑ 313 Will Allen RC	.50	1.25
❑ 314 Jamal Reynolds RC	.40	1.00
❑ 315 Quincy Morgan RC	.40	1.00
❑ 316 Eric Kelly RC	.30	.75
❑ 317 Michael Stone RC	.30	.75
❑ 318 Rod Gardner RC	.40	1.00

Card		
❑ 319 Ken-Yon Rambo RC	.30	.75
❑ 320 Eric Westmoreland RC	.30	.75
❑ 321 Steve Smith RC	1.25	3.00
❑ 322 George Layne RC	.30	.75
❑ 323 Justin McCareins RC	.40	1.00
❑ 324 Adam Archuleta RC	.40	1.00
❑ 325 Justin Smith RC	.50	1.25
❑ 326 David Terrell RC	.40	1.00
❑ 327 Correll Buckhalter RC	.50	1.25
❑ 328 Drew Brees RC	5.00	12.00
❑ 329 Chris Barnes RC	.30	.75
❑ 330 Santana Moss RC	.75	2.00
❑ 331 Josh Heupel RC	.50	1.25
❑ 332 Cedrick Wilson RC	.50	1.25
❑ 333 Gerard Warren RC	.40	1.00
❑ 334 Jamie Henderson RC	.40	1.00
❑ 335 Onomo Ojo RC	.30	.75
❑ 336 Marcus Stroud RC	.40	1.00
❑ 337 Quincy Carter RC	.40	1.00
❑ 338 Koren Robinson RC	.50	1.25
❑ 339 Ryan Pickett RC	.30	.75
❑ 340 Chad Johnson RC	1.25	3.00
❑ 341 Nate Clements RC	.50	1.25
❑ 342 Jesse Palmer RC	.50	1.25
❑ 343 Snoop Minnis RC	.40	1.00
❑ 344 Reggie Wayne RC	1.25	3.00
❑ 345 Kevin Kasper RC	.40	1.00
❑ 346 Will Peterson RC	.40	1.00
❑ 347 Marques Tuiasosopo RC	.40	1.00
❑ 348 Sage Rosenfels RC	.50	1.25
❑ 349 Dan Alexander RC	.40	1.00
❑ 350 LaDainian Tomlinson RC	6.00	15.00
❑ 351 Dan Morgan RC	.50	1.25
❑ 352 Scotty Anderson RC	.40	1.00
❑ 353 Deuce McAllister RC	.60	1.50
❑ 354 Todd Heap RC	.50	1.25
❑ 355 Tony Dixon RC	.40	1.00
❑ 356 Chris Chambers RC	.75	2.00
❑ 357 Eddie Berlin RC	.30	.75
❑ 358 Anthony Thomas RC	.50	1.25
❑ 359 James Jackson RC	.40	1.00
❑ 360 Richard Seymour RC	.50	1.25
❑ 361 Andre Carter RC	.50	1.25
❑ 362 Bobby Newcombe RC	.40	1.00
❑ 363 Robert Ferguson RC	.50	1.25
❑ 364 Jonathan Carter RC	.30	.75
❑ 365 Damione Lewis RC	.40	1.00
❑ 366 Damerien McCants RC	.40	1.00
❑ 367 Tim Hasselbeck RC	.40	1.00
❑ 368 Derrick Gibson RC	.30	.75
❑ 369 Rudi Johnson RC	.50	1.25
❑ 370 Alge Crumpler RC	.50	1.25
❑ 371 Derrick Blaylock RC	.40	1.00
❑ 372 Moran Norris RC	.30	.75
❑ 373 Travis Minor RC	.40	1.00
❑ 374 LaMont Jordan RC	.50	1.25
❑ 375 Kevan Barlow RC	.40	1.00
❑ 376 Freddie Mitchell RC	.30	.75
❑ 377 Shaun Rogers RC	.50	1.25
❑ 378 Tay Cody RC	.30	.75
❑ 379 Travis Henry RC	.50	1.25
❑ 380 Chris Weinke RC	.40	1.00
❑ 381 Willie Middlebrooks RC	.40	1.00
❑ 382 Rashard Casey RC	.30	.75
❑ 383 Mike McMahon RC	.40	1.00
❑ 384 Michael Bennett RC	.50	1.25
❑ 385 Jabari Holloway RC	.40	1.00
❑ SBMVP Ray Lewis FB AU	150.00	300.00

2002 Topps

Card		
❑ COMPLETE SET (385)	20.00	50.00
❑ 1 Kurt Warner	.25	.60
❑ 2 Jeff Graham	.15	.40
❑ 3 Todd Bouman	.15	.40
❑ 4 Duce Staley	.20	.50
❑ 5 Jon Kitna	.20	.50
❑ 6 Shannon Sharpe	.25	.60
❑ 7 Darrell Jackson	.20	.50
❑ 8 Michael Pittman	.20	.50
❑ 9 Tony Gonzalez	.20	.50
❑ 10 Wayne Chrebet	.20	.50
❑ 11 Jevon Kearse	.20	.50
❑ 12 Bill Schroeder	.20	.50
❑ 13 Jeremy McDaniel	.15	.40
❑ 14 Todd Pinkston	.15	.40
❑ 15 Maurice Smith	.15	.40
❑ 16 Charlie Batch	.20	.50
❑ 17 Olandis Gary	.20	.50
❑ 18 Ron Dugans	.15	.40
❑ 19 Brian Urlacher	.30	.75
❑ 20 Amani Toomer	.20	.50
❑ 21 Tim Couch	.15	.40
❑ 22 Derrick Brooks	.25	.60
❑ 23 Frank Sanders	.15	.40
❑ 24 James Williams	.15	.40
❑ 25 Lamar Smith	.20	.50
❑ 26 Darrick Vaughn	.15	.40
❑ 27 Cris Carter	.25	.60
❑ 28 Roland Williams	.15	.40
❑ 29 Bobby Shaw	.15	.40
❑ 30 Jerome Pathon	.15	.40
❑ 31 Rod Woodson	.25	.60
❑ 32 Ronney Jenkins	.15	.40
❑ 33 Chris Chandler	.20	.50
❑ 34 Dez White	.15	.40
❑ 35 Rod Smith	.20	.50
❑ 36 Troy Brown	.20	.50
❑ 37 JaJuan Dawson	.15	.40
❑ 38 Reidel Anthony	.15	.40
❑ 39 Mike Green	.15	.40
❑ 40 Steve Smith	.25	.60
❑ 41 Willie Jackson	.15	.40
❑ 42 MarTay Jenkins	.15	.40
❑ 43 Reggie Germany	.15	.40
❑ 44 Desmond Howard	.20	.50
❑ 45 Fred Taylor	.25	.60
❑ 46 Scotty Anderson	.15	.40
❑ 47 John Lynch	.20	.50
❑ 48 Amos Zereoue	.15	.40
❑ 49 Darnay Scott	.20	.50
❑ 50 Anthony Thomas	.20	.50
❑ 51 Jeff Garcia	.20	.50
❑ 52 Charlie Garner	.20	.50
❑ 53 Drew Bledsoe	.25	.60
❑ 54 Donnie Edwards	.15	.40
❑ 55 Corey Bradford	.15	.40
❑ 56 Desmond Clark	.20	.50
❑ 57 Courtney Brown	.15	.40
❑ 58 Wesley Walls	.20	.50
❑ 59 Chad Brown	.15	.40
❑ 60 Shawn Jefferson	.15	.40
❑ 61 Corey Dillon	.20	.50
❑ 62 Johnnie Morton	.20	.50
❑ 63 Marcus Pollard	.15	.40
❑ 64 Jason Taylor	.25	.60
❑ 65 Kevin Faulk	.20	.50
❑ 66 Shane Matthews	.15	.40
❑ 67 Hines Ward	.25	.60
❑ 68 Garrison Hearst	.20	.50
❑ 69 Trung Canidate	.15	.40
❑ 70 Tony Banks	.15	.40
❑ 71 Matt Hasselbeck	.25	.60
❑ 72 Correll Buckhalter	.20	.50
❑ 73 Ron Dayne	.20	.50
❑ 74 Zach Thomas	.25	.60
❑ 75 Emmitt Smith	.60	1.50
❑ 76 Peter Warrick	.20	.50
❑ 77 Rob Johnson	.20	.50
❑ 78 Michael Strahan	.25	.60
❑ 79 Ray Lewis	.25	.60
❑ 80 Jamir Miller	.15	.40
❑ 81 Brian Griese	.20	.50
❑ 82 Stacey Mack	.15	.40
❑ 83 Michael Bennett	.20	.50
❑ 84 Ricky Williams	.25	.60
❑ 85 Jamal Lewis	.20	.50
❑ 86 Doug Flutie	.25	.60
❑ 87 Jonathan Quinn	.15	.40
❑ 88 Mike Alstott	.20	.50
❑ 89 Samari Rolle	.15	.40
❑ 90 LaMont Jordan	.20	.50
❑ 91 Dominic Rhodes	.20	.50
❑ 92 Quincy Carter	.15	.40
❑ 93 Marcus Robinson	.20	.50
❑ 94 Travis Henry	.20	.50
❑ 95 Jason Brookins	.15	.40
❑ 96 Nick Goings	.15	.40
❑ 97 Brian Finneran	.20	.50
❑ 98 Dorsey Levens	.20	.50
❑ 99 Reggie Swinton	.15	.40
❑ 100 Chris Chambers	.25	.60
❑ 101 Kordell Stewart	.20	.50
❑ 102 Tai Streets	.15	.40
❑ 103 Chris Redman	.15	.40
❑ 104 Jacquez Green	.15	.40
❑ 105 Rod Gardner	.15	.40
❑ 106 Kevin Kasper	.15	.40
❑ 107 Anthony Henry	.15	.40
❑ 108 Dan Morgan	.15	.40
❑ 109 Ronald McKinnon	.15	.40
❑ 110 Qadry Ismail	.20	.50
❑ 111 Chad Johnson	.25	.60
❑ 112 James Stewart	.15	.40
❑ 113 Terrence Wilkins	.15	.40
❑ 114 Joey Galloway	.20	.50
❑ 115 Deuce McAllister	.25	.60
❑ 116 Joe Jurevicius	.20	.50
❑ 117 Tyrone Wheatley	.20	.50
❑ 118 Jason Gildon	.20	.50
❑ 119 LaDainian Tomlinson	.40	1.00
❑ 120 Grant Wistrom	.20	.50
❑ 121 Eddie George	.20	.50
❑ 122 Laveranues Coles	.25	.60
❑ 123 Antowain Smith	.20	.50
❑ 124 Larry Parker	.15	.40
❑ 125 Bubba Franks	.20	.50
❑ 126 Troy Hambrick	.15	.40
❑ 127 Jamal Reynolds	.15	.40
❑ 128 Doug Chapman	.15	.40
❑ 129 Freddie Mitchell	.15	.40
❑ 130 Tim Dwight	.20	.50
❑ 131 Erron Kinney	.15	.40
❑ 132 James Allen	.15	.40
❑ 133 Eric Moulds	.20	.50
❑ 134 Keenan McCardell	.20	.50
❑ 135 David Sloan	.15	.40
❑ 136 Dennis Northcutt	.15	.40
❑ 137 Kevan Barlow	.15	.40
❑ 138 Bobby Engram	.20	.50
❑ 139 Champ Bailey	.25	.60
❑ 140 Donald Hayes	.15	.40
❑ 141 Brandon Bennett	.15	.40
❑ 142 Deltha O'Neal	.15	.40
❑ 143 James Jackson	.15	.40
❑ 144 Shaun Rogers	.15	.40
❑ 145 Joe Johnson	.15	.40
❑ 146 Ricky Watters	.20	.50
❑ 147 Warrick Dunn	.20	.50
❑ 148 Steve McNair	.25	.60
❑ 149 Marvin Harrison	.25	.60
❑ 150 Kendrell Bell	.15	.40
❑ 151 Jim Miller	.20	.50
❑ 152 Terry Allen	.20	.50
❑ 153 Jake Plummer	.20	.50
❑ 154 James McKnight	.15	.40
❑ 155 Curtis Martin	.25	.60
❑ 156 Keyshawn Johnson	.20	.50
❑ 157 Kevin Lockett	.15	.40
❑ 158 Jeremiah Trotter	.15	.40
❑ 159 Derrick Alexander	.20	.50
❑ 160 Brandon Stokley	.20	.50
❑ 161 J.J. Stokes	.15	.40
❑ 162 Drew Bennett	.20	.50
❑ 163 Drew Brees	.40	1.00
❑ 164 Tim Brown	.25	.60
❑ 165 Daunte Culpepper	.20	.50
❑ 166 Rocket Ismail	.20	.50
❑ 167 Alex Van Pelt	.15	.40
❑ 168 Arnold Jackson	.15	.40
❑ 169 Oronde Gadsden	.15	.40
❑ 170 Isaac Bruce	.25	.60
❑ 171 Warren Sapp	.20	.50
❑ 172 Michael Westbrook	.15	.40
❑ 173 John Abraham	.20	.50
❑ 174 Jessie Armstead	.15	.40
❑ 175 Brock Marion	.15	.40
❑ 176 Brett Favre	.60	1.50
❑ 177 Benjamin Gay	.15	.40
❑ 178 Muhsin Muhammad	.20	.50
❑ 179 Reggie Wayne	.25	.60
❑ 180 Kailee Wong	.15	.40
❑ 181 Rich Gannon	.20	.50
❑ 182 Chris Fuamatu-Ma'afala	.15	.40
❑ 183 Shaun Alexander	.25	.60

❑ 184 Kevin Dyson .20 .50
❑ 185 Kwamie Lassiter .15 .40
❑ 186 Elvis Joseph .15 .40
❑ 187 Trent Dilfer .20 .50
❑ 188 Marty Booker .20 .50
❑ 189 Travis Taylor .15 .40
❑ 190 Michael Vick .25 .60
❑ 191 Mike McMahon .15 .40
❑ 192 Jay Fiedler .20 .50
❑ 193 Zack Bronson .15 .40
❑ 194 Derrick Mason .20 .50
❑ 195 Anthony Becht .15 .40
❑ 196 Ahman Green .20 .50
❑ 197 Alge Crumpler .20 .50
❑ 198 Thomas Jones .20 .50
❑ 199 Tiki Barber .25 .60
❑ 200 Donovan McNabb .30 .75
❑ 201 Andre Carter .15 .40
❑ 202 Stephen Davis .20 .50
❑ 203 Troy Edwards .15 .40
❑ 204 Lawyer Milloy .20 .50
❑ 205 Peyton Manning .50 1.25
❑ 206 James Farrior .20 .50
❑ 207 Gerard Warren .15 .40
❑ 208 Peerless Price .15 .40
❑ 209 Avion Black .15 .40
❑ 210 Marcellus Wiley .15 .40
❑ 211 Torry Holt .25 .60
❑ 212 A.J. Feeley .20 .50
❑ 213 Travis Minor .20 .50
❑ 214 Darren Sharper .20 .50
❑ 215 Jerry Porter .20 .50
❑ 216 Randall Cunningham .20 .50
❑ 217 Chris Weinke .15 .40
❑ 218 Mike Anderson .20 .50
❑ 219 Snoop Minnis .15 .40
❑ 220 David Martin .15 .40
❑ 221 Vinny Sutherland .15 .40
❑ 222 Ki-Jana Carter .20 .50
❑ 223 Kevin Swayne .15 .40
❑ 224 Mark Brunell .20 .50
❑ 225 Quincy Morgan .15 .40
❑ 226 David Terrell .20 .50
❑ 227 Terance Mathis .15 .40
❑ 228 Frank Wycheck .15 .40
❑ 229 Az-Zahir Hakim .15 .40
❑ 230 Freddie Jones .15 .40
❑ 231 Jerry Rice .50 1.25
❑ 232 Ike Hilliard .20 .50
❑ 233 Terrell Davis .25 .60
❑ 234 Shawn Bryson .15 .40
❑ 235 David Boston .15 .40
❑ 236 Edgerrin James .25 .60
❑ 237 Trent Green .20 .50
❑ 238 Charlie Rogers .15 .40
❑ 239 Vinny Testaverde .20 .50
❑ 240 Koren Robinson .15 .40
❑ 241 Ronde Barber .20 .50
❑ 242 Dwayne Carswell .15 .40
❑ 243 Dedric Ward .15 .40
❑ 244 Richard Huntley .15 .40
❑ 245 Jamal Anderson .20 .50
❑ 246 Ryan Leaf .15 .40
❑ 247 Priest Holmes .25 .60
❑ 248 Tom Brady .60 1.50
❑ 249 Charles Woodson .25 .60
❑ 250 Jerome Bettis .25 .60
❑ 251 Tommy Polley .15 .40
❑ 252 Anthony Wright .15 .40
❑ 253 Chad Pennington .25 .60
❑ 254 David Patten .15 .40
❑ 255 Antonio Freeman .25 .60
❑ 256 Jamel White .15 .40
❑ 257 Jermaine Lewis .15 .40
❑ 258 Aaron Brooks .20 .50
❑ 259 Ron Dixon .15 .40
❑ 260 James Thrash .20 .50
❑ 261 Junior Seau .25 .60
❑ 262 Byron Chamberlain .15 .40
❑ 263 Ed McCaffrey .20 .50
❑ 264 Nate Clements .15 .40
❑ 265 Tony Martin .20 .50
❑ 266 Germane Crowell .15 .40
❑ 267 Terrell Owens .25 .60
❑ 268 Marshall Faulk .25 .60
❑ 269 Dat Nguyen .15 .40
❑ 270 Elvis Grbac .20 .50
❑ 271 Dante Hall .20 .50
❑ 272 Sylvester Morris .15 .40
❑ 273 Mike Brown .20 .50
❑ 274 Kevin Johnson .15 .40
❑ 275 Jimmy Smith .20 .50
❑ 276 Randy Moss .25 .60
❑ 277 Kerry Collins .20 .50
❑ 278 Santana Moss .20 .50
❑ 279 Plaxico Burress .20 .50
❑ 280 Brad Johnson .20 .50
❑ 281 Curtis Conway .20 .50
❑ 282 Eric Johnson .15 .40
❑ 283 Joe Horn .20 .50
❑ 284 Peter Boulware .20 .50
❑ 285 Larry Foster .15 .40
❑ 286 Nate Jacquet .15 .40
❑ 287 Terry Glenn .20 .50
❑ 288 Jarious Jackson .15 .40
❑ 289 Hugh Douglas .15 .40
❑ 290 Chad Lewis .15 .40
❑ 291 Ahman Green WW .15 .40
❑ 292 Peyton Manning WW .40 1.00
❑ 293 Kurt Warner WW .20 .50
❑ 294 Daunte Culpepper WW .15 .40
❑ 295 Tom Brady WW .50 1.25
❑ 296 Rod Gardner WW .12 .30
❑ 297 Corey Dillon WW .15 .40
❑ 298 Priest Holmes WW .20 .50
❑ 299 Shaun Alexander WW .20 .50
❑ 300 Randy Moss WW .20 .50
❑ 301 Eric Moulds WW .15 .40
❑ 302 Brett Favre WW .50 1.25
❑ 303 Todd Bouman WW .12 .30
❑ 304 Dominic Rhodes WW .15 .40
❑ 305 Marvin Harrison WW .20 .50
❑ 306 Torry Holt WW .20 .50
❑ 307 Derrick Mason WW .15 .40
❑ 308 Jerry Rice WW .40 1.00
❑ 309 Donovan McNabb WW .25 .60
❑ 310 Marshall Faulk WW .20 .50
❑ 311 David Carr RC .50 1.25
❑ 312 Quentin Jammer RC .50 1.25
❑ 313 Mike Williams RC .30 .75
❑ 314 Rocky Calmus RC .40 1.00
❑ 315 Travis Fisher RC .40 1.00
❑ 316 Dwight Freeney RC .75 2.00
❑ 317 Jeremy Shockey RC .75 2.00
❑ 318 Marquise Walker RC .30 .75
❑ 319 Eric Crouch RC .50 1.25
❑ 320 DeShaun Foster RC .50 1.25
❑ 321 Roy Williams RC .60 1.50
❑ 322 Andre Davis RC .40 1.00
❑ 323 Alex Brown RC .50 1.25
❑ 324 Michael Lewis RC .50 1.25
❑ 325 Terry Charles RC .30 .75
❑ 326 Clinton Portis RC 1.25 3.00
❑ 327 Dennis Johnson RC .30 .75
❑ 328 Lito Sheppard RC .50 1.25
❑ 329 Ryan Sims RC .50 1.25
❑ 330 Raonall Smith RC .30 .75
❑ 331 Albert Haynesworth RC .50 1.25
❑ 332 Eddie Freeman RC .30 .75
❑ 333 Levi Jones RC .30 .75
❑ 334 Josh McCown RC .50 1.25
❑ 335 Cliff Russell RC .30 .75
❑ 336 Maurice Morris RC .50 1.25
❑ 337 Antwaan Randle El RC .50 1.25
❑ 338 Ladell Betts RC .50 1.25
❑ 339 Daniel Graham RC .40 1.00
❑ 340 David Garrard RC .75 2.00
❑ 341 Antonio Bryant RC .60 1.50
❑ 342 Patrick Ramsey RC .50 1.25
❑ 343 Kelly Campbell RC .40 1.00
❑ 344 Will Overstreet RC .30 .75
❑ 345 Ryan Denney RC .30 .75
❑ 346 John Henderson RC .50 1.25
❑ 347 Freddie Milons RC .30 .75
❑ 348 Tim Carter RC .40 1.00
❑ 349 Kurt Kittner RC .30 .75
❑ 350 Joey Harrington RC .50 1.25
❑ 351 Ricky Williams RC .40 1.00
❑ 352 Bryant McKinnie RC .30 .75
❑ 353 Ed Reed RC 1.50 4.00
❑ 354 Josh Reed RC .40 1.00
❑ 355 Seth Burford RC .30 .75
❑ 356 Javon Walker RC .50 1.25
❑ 357 Jamar Martin RC .40 1.00
❑ 358 Leonard Henry RC .30 .75
❑ 359 Julius Peppers RC .75 2.00
❑ 360 Jabar Gaffney RC .50 1.25
❑ 361 Kalimba Edwards RC .40 1.00
❑ 362 Napoleon Harris RC .40 1.00
❑ 363 Ashley Lelie RC .50 1.25
❑ 364 Anthony Weaver RC .30 .75
❑ 365 Bryan Thomas RC .30 .75
❑ 366 Wendell Bryant RC .30 .75
❑ 367 Damien Anderson RC .40 1.00
❑ 368 Travis Stephens RC .30 .75
❑ 369 Rohan Davey RC .50 1.25
❑ 370 Mike Pearson RC .30 .75
❑ 371 Marc Colombo RC .30 .75
❑ 372 Phillip Buchanon RC .50 1.25
❑ 373 T.J. Duckett RC .50 1.25
❑ 374 Ron Johnson RC .40 1.00
❑ 375 Larry Tripplett RC .30 .75
❑ 376 Randy Fasani RC .40 1.00
❑ 377 Keyuo Craver RC .30 .75
❑ 378 Marquand Manuel RC .30 .75
❑ 379 Jonathan Wells RC .50 1.25
❑ 380 Reche Caldwell RC .50 1.25
❑ 381 Luke Staley RC .30 .75
❑ 382 Donte Stallworth RC .50 1.25
❑ 383 Levar Fisher RC .30 .75
❑ 384 Lamar Gordon RC .50 1.25
❑ 385 William Green RC .40 1.00
❑ SBMVP Tom Brady FB AU/150 350.00 600.00

2003 Topps

❑ COMPLETE SET (385) 25.00 60.00
❑ 1 Michael Vick .25 .60
❑ 2 Wesley Walls .20 .50
❑ 3 Josh Reed .15 .40
❑ 4 Josh McCown .20 .50
❑ 5 James Stewart .20 .50
❑ 6 Deltha O'Neal .15 .40
❑ 7 Quincy Morgan .15 .40
❑ 8 Tony Fisher .15 .40
❑ 9 Corey Bradford .15 .40
❑ 10 Byron Chamberlain .15 .40
❑ 11 James McKnight .15 .40
❑ 12 Fred Taylor .25 .60
❑ 13 David Patten .15 .40
❑ 14 Jerome Bettis .25 .60
❑ 15 Jerry Porter .20 .50
❑ 16 Anthony Becht .20 .50
❑ 17 Steve McNair .25 .60
❑ 18 Stephen Davis .20 .50
❑ 19 Terrence Wilkins .15 .40
❑ 20 Jamie Martin .20 .50
❑ 21 Tai Streets .15 .40
❑ 22 Frank Wycheck .15 .40
❑ 23 Sammy Knight .15 .40
❑ 24 Marcus Pollard .15 .40
❑ 25 Jamie Sharper .15 .40
❑ 26 T.J. Houshmandzadeh .25 .60
❑ 27 Javin Hunter .15 .40
❑ 28 Alge Crumpler .20 .50
❑ 29 Chris Weinke .20 .50
❑ 30 David Terrell .15 .40
❑ 31 Troy Hambrick .15 .40
❑ 32 Bubba Franks .20 .50
❑ 33 Todd Bouman .15 .40
❑ 34 Trent Green .20 .50
❑ 35 Mark Brunell .20 .50
❑ 36 James Thrash .15 .40
❑ 37 Donnie Edwards .15 .40
❑ 38 Mike Alstott .25 .60
❑ 39 Bobby Engram .15 .40
❑ 40 Deuce McAllister .25 .60
❑ 41 Santana Moss .20 .50
❑ 42 Kordell Stewart .20 .50
❑ 43 Jason Taylor .20 .50
❑ 44 Corey Dillon .20 .50
❑ 45 Damien Anderson .15 .40
❑ 46 Rodney Peete .15 .40
❑ 47 Jeff Blake .20 .50

Card		
❑ 48 Mike McMahon	.15	.40
❑ 49 Ed McCaffrey	.20	.50
❑ 50 Priest Holmes	.25	.60
❑ 51 Moe Williams	.15	.40
❑ 52 Brian Dawkins	.20	.50
❑ 53 Tim Brown	.25	.60
❑ 54 Curtis Martin	.25	.60
❑ 55 Charles Stackhouse	.15	.40
❑ 56 Derrius Thompson	.15	.40
❑ 57 John Simon	.15	.40
❑ 58 Joe Jurevicius	.20	.50
❑ 59 Jonathan Wells	.15	.40
❑ 60 William Green	.15	.40
❑ 61 Ken-Yon Rambo	.15	.40
❑ 62 Frank Sanders	.15	.40
❑ 63 Chester Taylor	.20	.50
❑ 64 Keith Brooking	.20	.50
❑ 65 Bill Schroeder	.15	.40
❑ 66 Travis Minor	.15	.40
❑ 67 Eric Parker RC	.30	.75
❑ 68 Phillip Buchanon	.15	.40
❑ 69 Amos Zereoue	.15	.40
❑ 70 Warren Sapp	.20	.50
❑ 71 Ladell Betts	.20	.50
❑ 72 Lamar Gordon	.15	.40
❑ 73 Koren Robinson	.20	.50
❑ 74 Ron Dayne	.20	.50
❑ 75 Donovan McNabb	.25	.60
❑ 76 Edgerrin James	.25	.60
❑ 77 Stacey Mack	.15	.40
❑ 78 Justin Smith	.20	.50
❑ 79 Kelly Holcomb	.15	.40
❑ 80 Thomas Jones	.20	.50
❑ 81 Randy McMichael	.15	.40
❑ 82 Daunte Culpepper	.25	.60
❑ 83 Tommy Maddox	.20	.50
❑ 84 Tyrone Wheatley	.20	.50
❑ 85 Kevin Dyson	.20	.50
❑ 86 Rod Gardner	.15	.40
❑ 87 Wayne Chrebet	.20	.50
❑ 88 Marc Boerigter	.15	.40
❑ 89 Darnay Scott	.20	.50
❑ 90 T.J. Duckett	.20	.50
❑ 91 Marcel Shipp	.15	.40
❑ 92 Ross Tucker	.15	.40
❑ 93 Drew Bledsoe	.25	.60
❑ 94 Scotty Anderson	.20	.50
❑ 95 Rod Smith	.20	.50
❑ 96 Jim Kleinsasser	.15	.40
❑ 97 Peyton Manning	.50	1.25
❑ 98 Junior Seau	.25	.60
❑ 99 Darrell Jackson	.20	.50
❑ 100 Brett Favre	.60	1.50
❑ 101 Ashley Lelie	.15	.40
❑ 102 Jajuan Dawson	.15	.40
❑ 103 Kyle Brady	.15	.40
❑ 104 Kevin Faulk	.20	.50
❑ 105 Jeremy Shockey	.25	.60
❑ 106 Hines Ward	.25	.60
❑ 107 Jeff Garcia	.25	.60
❑ 108 Shane Matthews	.15	.40
❑ 109 Jevon Kearse	.20	.50
❑ 110 Eddie Kennison	.15	.40
❑ 111 Quincy Carter	.15	.40
❑ 112 Brian Urlacher	.40	1.00
❑ 113 Charlie Rogers	.15	.40
❑ 114 Robert Ferguson	.15	.40
❑ 115 Christian Fauria	.15	.40
❑ 116 Brian Westbrook	.25	.60
❑ 117 Antwaan Randle El	.20	.50
❑ 118 Eddie George	.20	.50
❑ 119 Derrick Brooks	.20	.50
❑ 120 Isaac Bruce	.25	.60
❑ 121 Joe Horn	.20	.50
❑ 122 Jermaine Lewis	.15	.40
❑ 123 Jon Kitna	.20	.50
❑ 124 David Boston	.15	.40
❑ 125 Todd Heap	.20	.50
❑ 126 Lamar Smith	.20	.50
❑ 127 Marcus Robinson	.20	.50
❑ 128 Germane Crowell	.15	.40
❑ 129 Kevin Johnson	.15	.40
❑ 130 Cris Carter	.25	.60
❑ 131 Drew Brees	.25	.60
❑ 132 Champ Bailey	.20	.50
❑ 133 Brian Finneran	.15	.40
❑ 134 Mike Anderson	.20	.50
❑ 135 Derek Ross	.15	.40
❑ 136 Javon Walker	.20	.50
❑ 137 D'Wayne Bates	.15	.40
❑ 138 Chad Lewis	.20	.50
❑ 139 Charlie Garner	.20	.50
❑ 140 Laveranues Coles	.20	.50
❑ 141 Ron Dixon	.15	.40
❑ 142 Rob Johnson	.20	.50
❑ 143 Shaun Alexander	.25	.60
❑ 144 Kevan Barlow	.15	.40
❑ 145 Aaron Brooks	.20	.50
❑ 146 Jay Foreman	.15	.40
❑ 147 Mike Peterson	.15	.40
❑ 148 Brandon Bennett	.15	.40
❑ 149 Jake Plummer	.20	.50
❑ 150 Emmitt Smith	.60	1.50
❑ 151 Mikhael Ricks	.15	.40
❑ 152 Terry Glenn	.20	.50
❑ 153 Michael Bennett	.20	.50
❑ 154 Deion Branch	.20	.50
❑ 155 Justin McCareins	.20	.50
❑ 156 Keyshawn Johnson	.25	.60
❑ 157 Marc Bulger	.25	.60
❑ 158 Matt Hasselbeck	.20	.50
❑ 159 Garrison Hearst	.20	.50
❑ 160 Jamel White	.15	.40
❑ 161 Doug Johnson	.15	.40
❑ 162 Larry Centers	.20	.50
❑ 163 Dee Brown	.15	.40
❑ 164 Dez White	.15	.40
❑ 165 Brian Griese	.20	.50
❑ 166 Johnnie Morton	.20	.50
❑ 167 Oronde Gadsden	.15	.40
❑ 168 Chad Morton	.15	.40
❑ 169 Rod Woodson	.25	.60
❑ 170 Ricky Proehl	.20	.50
❑ 171 Tim Dwight	.15	.40
❑ 172 Patrick Ramsey	.20	.50
❑ 173 Donald Driver	.25	.60
❑ 174 Joey Harrington	.20	.50
❑ 175 Ricky Williams	.20	.50
❑ 176 David Givens	.20	.50
❑ 177 Antonio Freeman	.20	.50
❑ 178 Dwight Freeney	.20	.50
❑ 179 Jabar Gaffney	.15	.40
❑ 180 Leon Johnson	.15	.40
❑ 181 Freddie Jones	.15	.40
❑ 182 Ron Johnson	.15	.40
❑ 183 Duce Staley	.20	.50
❑ 184 Charles Woodson	.20	.50
❑ 185 Trung Canidate	.15	.40
❑ 186 Jerome Pathon	.15	.40
❑ 187 Jimmy Smith	.20	.50
❑ 188 Reggie Wayne	.20	.50
❑ 189 Chad Johnson	.25	.60
❑ 190 Steve Beuerlein	.20	.50
❑ 191 Joey Galloway	.20	.50
❑ 192 Chris Walsh	.15	.40
❑ 193 Ty Law	.20	.50
❑ 194 Ike Hilliard	.20	.50
❑ 195 Curtis Conway	.15	.40
❑ 196 Kenny Watson	.15	.40
❑ 197 Brad Johnson	.20	.50
❑ 198 Shawn Jefferson	.15	.40
❑ 199 Jamal Lewis	.25	.60
❑ 200 Terrell Owens	.25	.60
❑ 201 Todd Pinkston	.15	.40
❑ 202 Maurice Morris	.15	.40
❑ 203 Dante Hall	.20	.50
❑ 204 Jeremiah Trotter UER	.20	.50
❑ 205 Keenan McCardell	.20	.50
❑ 206 Antonio Bryant	.25	.60
❑ 207 Trevor Gaylor	.15	.40
❑ 208 Eric Moulds	.20	.50
❑ 209 Jim Miller	.20	.50
❑ 210 Kabeer Gbaja-Biamila	.20	.50
❑ 211 James Mungro	.15	.40
❑ 212 Troy Brown	.20	.50
❑ 213 J.J. Stokes	.20	.50
❑ 214 Rich Gannon	.20	.50
❑ 215 Chad Pennington	.25	.60
❑ 216 Michael Strahan	.20	.50
❑ 217 David Garrard	.25	.60
❑ 218 Chris Chambers	.20	.50
❑ 219 Antowain Smith	.20	.50
❑ 220 Olandis Gary	.20	.50
❑ 221 Jason McAddley	.15	.40
❑ 222 Brandon Stokley	.20	.50
❑ 223 Derrick Alexander	.15	.40
❑ 224 Hugh Douglas	.20	.50
❑ 225 Danny Wuerffel	.20	.50
❑ 226 Derrick Mason	.20	.50
❑ 227 Michael Pittman	.15	.40
❑ 228 Torry Holt	.25	.60
❑ 229 Bobby Shaw	.15	.40
❑ 230 Tony Gonzalez	.20	.50
❑ 231 Ed Hartwell	.15	.40
❑ 232 Kris Mangum RC	.15	.40
❑ 233 Martay Jenkins	.15	.40
❑ 234 Marty Booker	.20	.50
❑ 235 London Fletcher	.15	.40
❑ 236 Shannon Sharpe	.20	.50
❑ 237 Zach Thomas	.25	.60
❑ 238 Plaxico Burress	.25	.60
❑ 239 Trent Dilfer	.20	.50
❑ 240 Kurt Warner	.25	.60
❑ 241 Vinny Testaverde	.20	.50
❑ 242 Al Wilson	.20	.50
❑ 243 Chris Redman	.15	.40
❑ 244 Warrick Dunn	.20	.50
❑ 245 Jay Fiedler	.20	.50
❑ 246 A.J. Feeley	.15	.40
❑ 247 LaMont Jordan	.20	.50
❑ 248 Kerry Collins	.20	.50
❑ 249 Michael Lewis	.15	.40
❑ 250 Jerry Rice	.50	1.25
❑ 251 Simeon Rice	.20	.50
❑ 252 Reche Caldwell	.15	.40
❑ 253 Randy Moss	.25	.60
❑ 254 Az-Zahir Hakim	.15	.40
❑ 255 Nate Wayne	.15	.40
❑ 256 James Allen	.15	.40
❑ 257 Qadry Ismail	.20	.50
❑ 258 Tom Brady	.60	1.50
❑ 259 Brian Kelly	.15	.40
❑ 260 Ray Lucas	.15	.40
❑ 261 Amani Toomer	.20	.50
❑ 262 Travis Henry	.20	.50
❑ 263 Chris Chandler	.20	.50
❑ 264 Peter Warrick	.20	.50
❑ 265 Ray Lewis	.25	.60
❑ 266 Sam Cowart	.15	.40
❑ 267 Donte Stallworth	.20	.50
❑ 268 David Carr	.25	.60
❑ 269 Andre Davis	.15	.40
❑ 270 Jake Delhomme	.25	.60
❑ 271 Travis Taylor	.15	.40
❑ 272 Steve Smith	.25	.60
❑ 273 Tiki Barber	.25	.60
❑ 274 Chad Hutchinson	.15	.40
❑ 275 Marshall Faulk	.25	.60
❑ 276 Chris Claiborne	.15	.40
❑ 277 Billy Miller	.15	.40
❑ 278 Peerless Price	.15	.40
❑ 279 Ed Reed	.25	.60
❑ 280 Ahman Green	.25	.60
❑ 281 Roy Williams	.25	.60
❑ 282 Dennis Northcutt	.15	.40
❑ 283 Julius Peppers	.25	.60
❑ 284 John Davis	.15	.40
❑ 285 LaDainian Tomlinson	.30	.75
❑ 286 Muhsin Muhammad	.20	.50
❑ 287 Tim Couch	.15	.40
❑ 288 Clinton Portis	.30	.75
❑ 289 Anthony Thomas	.20	.50
❑ 290 Marvin Harrison	.25	.60
❑ 291 Priest Holmes WW	.20	.50
❑ 292 Drew Bledsoe WW	.20	.50
❑ 293 Tom Brady WW	.50	1.25
❑ 294 Shaun Alexander WW	.20	.50
❑ 295 Brett Favre WW	.50	1.25
❑ 296 Travis Henry WW	.15	.40
❑ 297 Marshall Faulk WW	.20	.50
❑ 298 Terrell Owens WW	.20	.50
❑ 299 Jeff Garcia WW	.20	.50
❑ 300 Plaxico Burress WW	.20	.50
❑ 301 Donovan McNabb WW	.20	.50
❑ 302 Ricky Williams WW	.15	.40
❑ 303 Michael Vick WW	.20	.50
❑ 304 Steve Smith WW	.20	.50
❑ 305 Marvin Harrison WW	.20	.50
❑ 306 Chad Pennington WW	.20	.50
❑ 307 Jeremy Shockey WW	.20	.50
❑ 308 Tommy Maddox WW	.15	.40
❑ 309 Steve McNair WW	.20	.50
❑ 310 Rich Gannon WW	.15	.40
❑ 311 Carson Palmer RC	2.00	5.00
❑ 312 Keenan Howry RC	.30	.75
❑ 313 Michael Haynes RC	.30	.75
❑ 314 Terrell Suggs RC	.60	1.50

Card	Low	High
❑ 315 Rashean Mathis RC	.40	1.00
❑ 316 Chris Kelsay RC	.40	1.00
❑ 317 Brad Banks RC	.40	1.00
❑ 318 Jordan Gross RC	.30	.75
❑ 319 Lee Suggs RC	.40	1.00
❑ 320 Kliff Kingsbury RC	.40	1.00
❑ 321 William Joseph RC	.30	.75
❑ 322 Kelley Washington RC	.40	1.00
❑ 323 Jerome McDougle RC	.30	.75
❑ 324 Osi Umenyiora RC	.75	2.00
❑ 325 Chris Simms RC	.50	1.25
❑ 326 Alonzo Jackson RC	.30	.75
❑ 327 L.J. Smith RC	.50	1.25
❑ 328 Mike Doss RC	.50	1.25
❑ 329 Bobby Wade RC	.40	1.00
❑ 330 Ken Hamlin RC	.50	1.25
❑ 331 Brandon Lloyd RC	.50	1.25
❑ 332 Justin Fargas RC	.50	1.25
❑ 333 DeWayne Robertson RC	.40	1.00
❑ 334 Bryant Johnson RC	.50	1.25
❑ 335 Boss Bailey RC	.40	1.00
❑ 336 Onterrio Smith RC	.40	1.00
❑ 337 Doug Gabriel RC	.40	1.00
❑ 338 Jimmy Kennedy RC	.40	1.00
❑ 339 B.J. Askew RC	.40	1.00
❑ 340 Taylor Jacobs RC	.40	1.00
❑ 341 Dallas Clark RC	1.00	2.50
❑ 342 DeWayne White RC	.30	.75
❑ 343 Arnaz Battle RC	.50	1.25
❑ 344 Kareem Kelly RC	.30	.75
❑ 345 Terry Pierce RC	.30	.75
❑ 346 Billy McMullen RC	.30	.75
❑ 347 Talman Gardner RC	.30	.75
❑ 348 Anquan Boldin RC	1.25	3.00
❑ 349 Travis Anglin RC	.30	.75
❑ 350 Byron Leftwich RC	.60	1.50
❑ 351 Marcus Trufant RC	.50	1.25
❑ 352 Sam Aiken RC	.50	1.25
❑ 353 LaBrandon Toefield RC	.40	1.00
❑ 354 J.R. Tolver RC	.40	1.00
❑ 355 Charles Rogers RC	.40	1.00
❑ 356 Chaun Thompson RC	.30	.75
❑ 357 Chris Brown RC	.50	1.25
❑ 358 Justin Gage RC	.50	1.25
❑ 359 Kevin Williams RC	.50	1.25
❑ 360 Willis McGahee RC	1.00	2.50
❑ 361 Victor Hobson RC	.30	.75
❑ 362 Brian St.Pierre RC	.50	1.25
❑ 363 Nate Burleson RC	.40	1.00
❑ 364 Calvin Pace RC	.40	1.00
❑ 365 Larry Johnson RC	.60	1.50
❑ 366 Andre Woolfolk RC	.40	1.00
❑ 367 Tyrone Calico RC	.40	1.00
❑ 368 Seneca Wallace RC	.50	1.25
❑ 369 Domanick Davis RC	.50	1.25
❑ 370 Rex Grossman RC	.60	1.50
❑ 371 Artose Pinner RC	.30	.75
❑ 372 Jason Witten RC	1.25	3.00
❑ 373 Bennie Joppru RC	.30	.75
❑ 374 Bethel Johnson RC	.40	1.00
❑ 375 Kyle Boller RC	.50	1.25
❑ 376 Shaun McDonald RC	.50	1.25
❑ 377 Musa Smith RC	.40	1.00
❑ 378 Ken Dorsey RC	.40	1.00
❑ 379 Johnathan Sullivan RC	.30	.75
❑ 380 Andre Johnson RC	1.00	2.50
❑ 381 Nick Barnett RC	.50	1.25
❑ 382 Teyo Johnson RC	.40	1.00
❑ 383 Terence Newman RC	.50	1.25
❑ 384 Kevin Curtis RC	.50	1.25
❑ 385 Dave Ragone RC	.30	.75
❑ MVP Dex.Jackson FB AU/250	50.00	120.00
❑ RH Dexter Jackson RH	.75	2.00
❑ RHA Dexter Jackson RH AU	75.00	150.00

2004 Topps

Card	Low	High
❑ COMPLETE SET (385)	30.00	60.00
❑ RH38 STATED ODDS 1:36 H/HTA/R		
❑ RH38A ODDS 1:13,494H, 1:3895HTA		
❑ SBMVP ODDS 1:35,787H,1:10,710HTA ,1:33,984R		
❑ 1 Peyton Manning	.50	1.25
❑ 2 Curtis Conway	.20	.50
❑ 3 Tim Brown	.25	.60
❑ 4 David Givens	.20	.50
❑ 5 Dorsey Levens	.20	.50
❑ 6 Jamal Robertson	.15	.40
❑ 7 Doug Flutie	.25	.60
❑ 8 Lamar Gordon	.15	.40
❑ 9 Leonard Little	.15	.40
❑ 10 Patrick Ramsey	.20	.50
❑ 11 Justin McCareins	.15	.40
❑ 12 Charles Lee	.15	.40
❑ 13 Matt Hasselbeck	.25	.60
❑ 14 Chris Chambers	.20	.50
❑ 15 Derrick Blaylock	.15	.40
❑ 16 Shannon Sharpe	.20	.50
❑ 17 Bubba Franks	.20	.50
❑ 18 London Fletcher	.15	.40
❑ 19 Eric Moulds	.20	.50
❑ 20 Anquan Boldin	.25	.60
❑ 21 Brian Urlacher	.25	.60
❑ 22 Stephen Davis	.20	.50
❑ 23 Mikhael Ricks	.15	.40
❑ 24 Jason Taylor	.25	.60
❑ 25 Michael Vick	.25	.60
❑ 26 Dante Hall	.20	.50
❑ 27 Marcus Pollard	.15	.40
❑ 28 Rick Mirer	.20	.50
❑ 29 David Tyree	.25	.60
❑ 30 Chad Pennington	.25	.60
❑ 31 Kevan Barlow	.20	.50
❑ 32 James Farrior	.15	.40
❑ 33 James Thrash	.15	.40
❑ 34 Darnerien McCants	.15	.40
❑ 35 L.J. Smith	.20	.50
❑ 36 Tommy Maddox	.20	.50
❑ 37 Tedy Bruschi	.25	.60
❑ 38 Moe Williams	.15	.40
❑ 39 Todd Bouman	.15	.40
❑ 40 Domanick Davis	.20	.50
❑ 41 Dwight Freeney	.25	.60
❑ 42 Kyle Brady	.20	.50
❑ 43 LaVar Arrington	.20	.50
❑ 44 Troy Hambrick	.15	.40
❑ 45 Jake Plummer	.20	.50
❑ 46 Freddie Jones	.15	.40
❑ 47 Chester Taylor	.25	.60
❑ 48 Willis McGahee	.25	.60
❑ 49 Bobby Wade	.20	.50
❑ 50 Steve McNair	.25	.60
❑ 51 Joe Jurevicius	.15	.40
❑ 52 Ladell Betts	.20	.50
❑ 53 LaMont Jordan	.25	.60
❑ 54 Kerry Collins	.20	.50
❑ 55 Hines Ward	.25	.60
❑ 56 Scott Fujita	.15	.40
❑ 57 Kevin Johnson	.15	.40
❑ 58 Troy Brown	.20	.50
❑ 59 Jerome Pathon	.15	.40
❑ 60 Andre Johnson	.25	.60
❑ 61 DeShaun Foster	.20	.50
❑ 62 Terrell Suggs	.15	.40
❑ 63 Marcel Shipp	.25	.60
❑ 64 Allen Rossum	.15	.40
❑ 65 Kyle Boller	.20	.50
❑ 66 Terence Newman	.20	.50
❑ 67 Javon Walker	.20	.50
❑ 68 Shawn Bryson	.15	.40
❑ 69 Travis Minor	.15	.40
❑ 70 Terrell Owens	.25	.60
❑ 71 Kassim Osgood	.15	.40
❑ 72 Bobby Engram	.20	.50
❑ 73 Drew Bennett	.20	.50
❑ 74 Rock Cartwright	.15	.40
❑ 75 Ahman Green	.25	.60
❑ 76 Steve Beuerlein	.20	.50
❑ 77 Takeo Spikes	.15	.40
❑ 78 Dez White	.20	.50
❑ 79 Tim Couch	.20	.50
❑ 80 Travis Henry	.20	.50
❑ 81 T.J. Duckett	.20	.50
❑ 82 LaBrandon Toefield	.15	.40
❑ 83 Randy McMichael	.15	.40
❑ 84 Jonathan Carter	.15	.40
❑ 85 Jerry Rice	.50	1.25
❑ 86 Maurice Morris	.20	.50
❑ 87 Kurt Warner	.25	.60
❑ 88 Josh Scobey	.15	.40
❑ 89 Travis Taylor	.15	.40
❑ 90 Fred Taylor	.20	.50
❑ 91 Zach Thomas	.25	.60
❑ 92 Kelly Campbell	.15	.40
❑ 93 Tim Carter	.15	.40
❑ 94 Marques Tuiasosopo	.15	.40
❑ 95 Laveranues Coles	.20	.50
❑ 96 Chris Brown	.20	.50
❑ 97 Thomas Jones	.20	.50
❑ 98 Dane Looker	.20	.50
❑ 99 Ross Tucker	.15	.40
❑ 100 Priest Holmes	.25	.60
❑ 101 Troy Walters	.15	.40
❑ 102 Jamie Sharper	.15	.40
❑ 103 Quincy Morgan	.15	.40
❑ 104 Aveion Cason	.15	.40
❑ 105 Joey Galloway	.20	.50
❑ 106 Bill Schroeder	.20	.50
❑ 107 Tony Fisher	.15	.40
❑ 108 Adewale Ogunleye	.20	.50
❑ 109 Justin Fargas	.20	.50
❑ 110 Daunte Culpepper	.25	.60
❑ 111 Donnie Edwards	.20	.50
❑ 112 Jed Weaver	.15	.40
❑ 113 Arlen Harris	.15	.40
❑ 114 Keenan McCardell	.15	.40
❑ 115 Chad Johnson	.20	.50
❑ 116 Marty Booker	.20	.50
❑ 117 Anthony Wright	.20	.50
❑ 118 Brian Finneran	.15	.40
❑ 119 Robert Ferguson	.15	.40
❑ 120 Ricky Williams	.25	.60
❑ 121 Shaun Ellis	.15	.40
❑ 122 Brian Westbrook	.25	.60
❑ 123 Sam Cowart	.15	.40
❑ 124 Tim Rattay	.15	.40
❑ 125 LaDainian Tomlinson	.30	.75
❑ 126 Simeon Rice	.20	.50
❑ 127 Jason Witten	.25	.60
❑ 128 Lee Suggs	.25	.60
❑ 129 Keith Brooking	.15	.40
❑ 130 Rex Grossman	.25	.60
❑ 131 Kelley Washington	.15	.40
❑ 132 Antonio Bryant	.25	.60
❑ 133 Dallas Clark	.25	.60
❑ 134 Stacey Mack	.15	.40
❑ 135 Charles Rogers	.20	.50
❑ 136 Donte' Stallworth	.20	.50
❑ 137 Deion Branch	.20	.50
❑ 138 Nate Burleson	.20	.50
❑ 139 Ike Hilliard	.20	.50
❑ 140 Randy Moss	.25	.60
❑ 141 Michael Strahan	.20	.50
❑ 142 John Abraham	.15	.40
❑ 143 Tim Dwight	.20	.50
❑ 144 Isaac Bruce	.20	.50
❑ 145 Brad Johnson	.20	.50
❑ 146 Trung Canidate	.15	.40
❑ 147 Warrick Dunn	.20	.50
❑ 148 Josh McCown	.20	.50
❑ 149 Muhsin Muhammad	.20	.50
❑ 150 Donovan McNabb	.25	.60
❑ 151 Tai Streets	.15	.40
❑ 152 Antonio Gates	.25	.60
❑ 153 Antwaan Randle El	.20	.50
❑ 154 Doug Jolley	.15	.40
❑ 155 Shaun Alexander	.25	.60
❑ 156 William Green	.15	.40
❑ 157 Carson Palmer	.30	.75
❑ 158 Quentin Griffin	.20	.50
❑ 159 Az-Zahir Hakim	.15	.40
❑ 160 Edgerrin James	.25	.60
❑ 161 Gus Frerotte	.20	.50
❑ 162 Brandon Lloyd	.15	.40
❑ 163 Brian Griese	.20	.50
❑ 164 Boo Williams	.15	.40
❑ 165 Santana Moss	.20	.50
❑ 166 Tyrone Wheatley	.20	.50
❑ 167 Eric Parker	.20	.50
❑ 168 Amos Zereoue	.15	.40
❑ 169 Itula Mili	.15	.40
❑ 170 Marshall Faulk	.25	.60
❑ 171 Tyrone Calico	.20	.50
❑ 172 Tim Hasselbeck	.20	.50
❑ 173 Anthony Becht	.15	.40

Card		
❑ 174 Larry Johnson	.40	1.00
❑ 175 Marvin Harrison	.25	.60
❑ 176 Tony Gonzalez	.25	.60
❑ 177 Wayne Chrebet	.20	.50
❑ 178 Mike Barrow	.15	.40
❑ 179 Bethel Johnson	.15	.40
❑ 180 Deuce McAllister	.25	.60
❑ 181 Drew Brees	.25	.60
❑ 182 Teyo Johnson	.20	.50
❑ 183 Garrison Hearst	.20	.50
❑ 184 Todd Pinkston	.15	.40
❑ 185 Jeff Garcia	.25	.60
❑ 186 Darrell Jackson	.20	.50
❑ 187 Billy Volek	.20	.50
❑ 188 Ray Lewis	.25	.60
❑ 189 Ricky Proehl	.20	.50
❑ 190 Rudi Johnson	.20	.50
❑ 191 Emmitt Smith	.60	1.50
❑ 192 Cedrick Wilson	.15	.40
❑ 193 Julius Peppers	.20	.50
❑ 194 Peter Warrick	.20	.50
❑ 195 Trent Green	.20	.50
❑ 196 Derrius Thompson	.15	.40
❑ 197 Onterrio Smith	.15	.40
❑ 198 Jerome Bettis	.25	.60
❑ 199 Keyshawn Johnson	.20	.50
❑ 200 Jamal Lewis	.20	.50
❑ 201 Alge Crumpler	.20	.50
❑ 202 Justin Gage	.20	.50
❑ 203 Mike Rucker	.15	.40
❑ 204 Michael Bennett	.20	.50
❑ 205 Jimmy Smith	.20	.50
❑ 206 Ricky Williams TT	.15	.40
❑ 207 Corey Bradford	.20	.50
❑ 208 Jerry Porter	.20	.50
❑ 209 Erron Kinney	.15	.40
❑ 210 Marc Bulger	.20	.50
❑ 211 Jeff Blake	.20	.50
❑ 212 Terry Jones	.15	.40
❑ 213 Kordell Stewart	.20	.50
❑ 214 Andra Davis	.15	.40
❑ 215 David Carr	.20	.50
❑ 216 Nick Barnett	.20	.50
❑ 217 Mark Brunell	.20	.50
❑ 218 Daniel Graham	.15	.40
❑ 219 Jim Kleinsasser	.15	.40
❑ 220 Aaron Brooks	.20	.50
❑ 221 Plaxico Burress	.20	.50
❑ 222 Correll Buckhalter	.20	.50
❑ 223 Jevon Kearse	.20	.50
❑ 224 Michael Pittman	.20	.50
❑ 225 Clinton Portis	.25	.60
❑ 226 Corey Dillon	.20	.50
❑ 227 Steve Smith	.25	.60
❑ 228 David Thornton	.15	.40
❑ 229 Eddie Kennison	.20	.50
❑ 230 Amani Toomer	.20	.50
❑ 231 Artose Pinner	.15	.40
❑ 232 Kelly Holcomb	.20	.50
❑ 233 Jay Fiedler	.15	.40
❑ 234 Ernie Conwell	.15	.40
❑ 235 Torry Holt	.25	.60
❑ 236 Eddie George	.20	.50
❑ 237 Jeremy Shockey	.20	.50
❑ 238 Troy Edwards	.15	.40
❑ 239 Antowain Smith	.20	.50
❑ 240 Jon Kitna	.20	.50
❑ 241 Bryant Johnson	.20	.50
❑ 242 Todd Heap	.20	.50
❑ 243 Doug Johnson	.15	.40
❑ 244 Ashley Lelie	.20	.50
❑ 245 Byron Leftwich	.25	.60
❑ 246 Shawn Barber	.15	.40
❑ 247 Duce Staley	.20	.50
❑ 248 Rod Gardner	.15	.40
❑ 249 Warren Sapp	.20	.50
❑ 250 Brett Favre	.60	1.50
❑ 251 Olandis Gary	.20	.50
❑ 252 Reggie Wayne	.20	.50
❑ 253 Billy Miller	.15	.40
❑ 254 Johnnie Morton	.20	.50
❑ 255 Joe Horn	.20	.50
❑ 256 Curtis Martin	.25	.60
❑ 257 Freddie Mitchell	.15	.40
❑ 258 Charlie Garner	.20	.50
❑ 259 Marcus Robinson	.20	.50
❑ 260 Derrick Mason	.20	.50
❑ 261 Bobby Shaw	.15	.40
❑ 262 Desmond Clark	.20	.50

Card		
❑ 263 James Jackson	.15	.40
❑ 264 Josh Reed	.25	.60
❑ 265 David Boston	.15	.40
❑ 266 Drew Bledsoe	.25	.60
❑ 267 Brock Forsey	.15	.40
❑ 268 Dat Nguyen	.15	.40
❑ 269 Mike Anderson	.20	.50
❑ 270 Anthony Thomas	.20	.50
❑ 271 Najeh Davenport	.20	.50
❑ 272 Jabar Gaffney	.20	.50
❑ 273 Tiki Barber	.25	.60
❑ 274 Rich Gannon	.20	.50
❑ 275 Tom Brady	.60	1.50
❑ 276 Terry Glenn	.20	.50
❑ 277 Dennis Northcutt	.15	.40
❑ 278 A.J. Feeley	.20	.50
❑ 279 Peerless Price	.20	.50
❑ 280 Jake Delhomme	.20	.50
❑ 281 Kevin Faulk	.20	.50
❑ 282 Quincy Carter	.15	.40
❑ 283 Andre' Davis	.15	.40
❑ 284 Tony Hollings	.15	.40
❑ 285 Joey Harrington	.20	.50
❑ 286 Richie Anderson	.15	.40
❑ 287 Donald Driver	.25	.60
❑ 288 Koren Robinson	.25	.60
❑ 289 Tony Banks	.20	.50
❑ 290 Rod Smith	.20	.50
❑ 291 Anquan Boldin WW	.15	.40
❑ 292 Jamal Lewis WW	.12	.30
❑ 293 Priest Holmes WW	.15	.40
❑ 294 Peyton Manning WW	.30	.75
❑ 295 Marvin Harrison WW	.15	.40
❑ 296 Steve McNair WW	.15	.40
❑ 297 Travis Henry WW	.12	.30
❑ 298 Torry Holt WW	.15	.40
❑ 299 Tom Brady WW	.40	1.00
❑ 300 Ahman Green WW	.15	.40
❑ 301 Donovan McNabb WW	.15	.40
❑ 302 Deuce McAllister WW	.15	.40
❑ 303 Domanick Davis WW	.12	.30
❑ 304 Clinton Portis WW	.15	.40
❑ 305 Rudi Johnson WW	.12	.30
❑ 306 Brett Favre WW	.40	1.00
❑ 307 LaDainian Tomlinson WW	.20	.50
❑ 308 Steve Smith WW	.15	.40
❑ 309 Edgerrin James WW	.15	.40
❑ 310 Ty Law WW	.12	.30
❑ 311 Ben Roethlisberger RC	6.00	15.00
❑ 312 Ahmad Carroll RC	.60	1.50
❑ 313 Johnnie Morant RC	.50	1.25
❑ 314 Greg Jones RC	.60	1.50
❑ 315 Michael Clayton RC	.60	1.50
❑ 316 Josh Harris RC	.40	1.00
❑ 317 Tatum Bell RC	.60	1.50
❑ 318 Robert Gallery RC	.60	1.50
❑ 319 B.J. Symons RC	.40	1.00
❑ 320 Roy Williams RC	.75	2.00
❑ 321 DeAngelo Hall RC	.60	1.50
❑ 322 Jeff Smoker RC	.50	1.25
❑ 323 Lee Evans RC	.75	2.00
❑ 324 Michael Jenkins RC	.60	1.50
❑ 325 Steven Jackson RC	1.50	4.00
❑ 326 Will Smith RC	.60	1.50
❑ 327 Vince Wilfork RC	.60	1.50
❑ 328 Ben Troupe RC	.50	1.25
❑ 329 Chris Gamble RC	.50	1.25
❑ 330 Kevin Jones RC	.60	1.50
❑ 331 Jonathan Vilma RC	.60	1.50
❑ 332 Dontarrious Thomas RC	.50	1.25
❑ 333 Michael Boulware RC	.60	1.50
❑ 334 Mewelde Moore RC	.60	1.50
❑ 335 Drew Henson RC	.40	1.00
❑ 336 D.J. Williams RC	.60	1.50
❑ 337 Ernest Wilford RC	.50	1.25
❑ 338 John Navarre RC	.50	1.25
❑ 339 Jerricho Cotchery RC	.60	1.50
❑ 340 Derrick Hamilton RC	.40	1.00
❑ 341 Carlos Francis RC	.40	1.00
❑ 342 Ben Watson RC	.60	1.50
❑ 343 Reggie Williams RC	.60	1.50
❑ 344 Devard Darling RC	.50	1.25
❑ 345 Chris Perry RC	.60	1.50
❑ 346 Derrick Strait RC	.50	1.25
❑ 347 Sean Taylor RC	.60	1.50
❑ 348 Michael Turner RC	1.50	4.00
❑ 349 Keary Colbert RC	.50	1.25
❑ 350 Eli Manning RC	5.00	12.00
❑ 351 Julius Jones RC	.75	2.00

Card		
❑ 352 Jason Babin RC	.50	1.25
❑ 353 Cody Pickett RC	.50	1.25
❑ 354 Kenechi Udeze RC	.60	1.50
❑ 355 Rashaun Woods RC	.40	1.00
❑ 356 Matt Schaub RC	1.50	4.00
❑ 357 Tommie Harris RC	.60	1.50
❑ 358 Dwan Edwards RC	.40	1.00
❑ 359 Shawn Andrews RC	.50	1.25
❑ 360 Larry Fitzgerald RC	2.00	5.00
❑ 361 P.K. Sam RC	.40	1.00
❑ 362 Teddy Lehman RC	.50	1.25
❑ 363 Darius Watts RC	.50	1.25
❑ 364 D.J. Hackett RC	.60	1.50
❑ 365 Cedric Cobbs RC	.50	1.25
❑ 366 Antwan Odom RC	.60	1.50
❑ 367 Marquise Hill RC	.40	1.00
❑ 368 Luke McCown RC	.60	1.50
❑ 369 Triandos Luke RC	.40	1.00
❑ 370 Kellen Winslow RC	.75	2.00
❑ 371 Derek Abney RC	.40	1.00
❑ 372 Chris Cooley RC	.60	1.50
❑ 373 Dunta Robinson RC	.50	1.25
❑ 374 Sean Jones RC	.50	1.25
❑ 375 Philip Rivers RC	2.50	6.00
❑ 376 Craig Krenzel RC	.60	1.50
❑ 377 Daryl Smith RC	.50	1.25
❑ 378 Samie Parker RC	.50	1.25
❑ 379 Ben Hartsock RC	.50	1.25
❑ 380 J.P. Losman RC	.60	1.50
❑ 381 Karlos Dansby RC	.60	1.50
❑ 382 Ricardo Colclough RC	.60	1.50
❑ 383 Bernard Berrian RC	.60	1.50
❑ 384 Junior Siavii RC	.40	1.00
❑ 385 Devery Henderson RC	.60	1.50
❑ TB38 Tom Brady RH	2.50	6.00
❑ RHTBR2 Tom Brady RH AU	350.00	550.00
❑ SBMVP Tom Brady FB AU/99	350.00	500.00

2005 Topps

Card		
❑ COMP.COWBOYS SET (445)	25.00	50.00
❑ COMP.EAGLES SET (445)	25.00	50.00
❑ COMP.FACT.SET (445)	25.00	50.00
❑ COMP.PACKERS SET (445)	25.00	50.00
❑ COMP.RAIDERS SET (445)	25.00	50.00
❑ COMP.SB XL SET (445)	50.00	80.00
❑ COMPLETE SET (440)	25.00	50.00
❑ 1 Brian Westbrook	.25	.60
❑ 2 Tim Rattay	.15	.40
❑ 3 Domanick Davis	.15	.40
❑ 4 Lee Suggs	.20	.50
❑ 5 Keith Brooking	.15	.40
❑ 6 Rex Grossman	.25	.60
❑ 7 Chad Johnson	.20	.50
❑ 8 Willis McGahee	.25	.60
❑ 9 Eli Manning	.50	1.25
❑ 10 Tom Brady	.50	1.25
❑ 11 Ray Lewis	.25	.60
❑ 12 Terence Newman	.15	.40
❑ 13 Daunte Culpepper	.25	.60
❑ 14 Marvin Harrison	.25	.60
❑ 15 Greg Jones	.15	.40
❑ 16 Anquan Boldin	.20	.50
❑ 17 Julius Peppers	.20	.50
❑ 18 Kevin Jones	.20	.50
❑ 19 Javon Walker	.20	.50
❑ 20 Michael Lewis	.15	.40
❑ 21 Jamaar Taylor	.15	.40
❑ 22 Hines Ward	.25	.60
❑ 23 Drew Brees	.25	.60
❑ 24 Marcus Trufant	.20	.50
❑ 25 Derrick Brooks	.20	.50
❑ 26 Sean Taylor	.20	.50
❑ 27 Derrius Thompson	.15	.40
❑ 28 Nick Barnett	.20	.50
❑ 29 Dante Hall	.20	.50
❑ 30 Mike Cloud	.15	.40

❑ 31 Jake Plummer .20 .50
❑ 32 Donte Stallworth .20 .50
❑ 33 Shaun Ellis .15 .40
❑ 34 Jeremy Shockey .25 .60
❑ 35 Teyo Johnson .15 .40
❑ 36 Adam Archuleta .15 .40
❑ 37 Darius Watts .15 .40
❑ 38 Michael Pittman .15 .40
❑ 39 Drew Bennett .20 .50
❑ 40 Aaron Stecker .15 .40
❑ 41 Artose Pinner .15 .40
❑ 42 Dane Looker .15 .40
❑ 43 Jeff Garcia .20 .50
❑ 44 Travis Taylor .15 .40
❑ 45 Najeh Davenport .20 .50
❑ 46 Walter Jones .15 .40
❑ 47 Donnie Edwards .15 .40
❑ 48 Terrell Owens .25 .60
❑ 49 Matt Birk .15 .40
❑ 50 Chris Baker .15 .40
❑ 51 Brandon Lloyd .15 .40
❑ 52 Marshall Faulk .25 .60
❑ 53 Jonathan Vilma .20 .50
❑ 54 Dallas Clark .20 .50
❑ 55 David Carr .20 .50
❑ 56 Jerricho Cotchery .20 .50
❑ 57 Deuce McAllister .25 .60
❑ 58 Donald Driver .25 .60
❑ 59 Jeff Smoker .15 .40
❑ 60 Champ Bailey .20 .50
❑ 61 Jason Witten .25 .60
❑ 62 T.J. Houshmandzadeh .20 .50
❑ 63 Jay Fiedler .15 .40
❑ 64 Philip Rivers .25 .60
❑ 65 Jake Delhomme .25 .60
❑ 66 Terrence McGee RC .20 .50
❑ 67 Chester Taylor .20 .50
❑ 68 Tommy Maddox .20 .50
❑ 69 Bryant Johnson .20 .50
❑ 70 Justin Gage .20 .50
❑ 71 Troy Hambrick .15 .40
❑ 72 Kerry Collins .20 .50
❑ 73 Jeb Putzier .15 .40
❑ 74 Keary Colbert .15 .40
❑ 75 Jason Elam .15 .40
❑ 76 Jerramy Stevens .20 .50
❑ 77 Clinton Portis .25 .60
❑ 78 Sam Aiken .15 .40
❑ 79 Trent Green .20 .50
❑ 80 Dat Nguyen .15 .40
❑ 81 Ladell Betts .20 .50
❑ 82 Peter Warrick .15 .40
❑ 83 Dominic Rhodes .20 .50
❑ 84 Jason Taylor .20 .50
❑ 85 Antwaan Randle El .20 .50
❑ 86 Michael Jenkins .20 .50
❑ 87 Adam Vinatieri .25 .60
❑ 88 Mark Brunell .20 .50
❑ 89 Brian Finneran .15 .40
❑ 90 Ernie Conwell .15 .40
❑ 91 Chad Pennington .25 .60
❑ 92 Dan Morgan .15 .40
❑ 93 Kelly Holcomb .15 .40
❑ 94 Ronde Barber .20 .50
❑ 95 Torry Holt .20 .50
❑ 96 Bubba Franks .20 .50
❑ 97 Keyshawn Johnson .20 .50
❑ 98 J.P. Losman .20 .50
❑ 99 Ed Reed .20 .50
❑ 100 Chris McAlister .15 .40
❑ 101 Jamie Sharper .15 .40
❑ 102 Chad Lewis .15 .40
❑ 103 Chris Brown .20 .50
❑ 104 Marc Boerigter .15 .40
❑ 105 Zach Thomas .25 .60
❑ 106 Byron Leftwich .20 .50
❑ 107 Tatum Bell .20 .50
❑ 108 Tai Streets .15 .40
❑ 109 Tory James .15 .40
❑ 110 Cedrick Wilson .15 .40
❑ 111 Darrell Jackson .20 .50
❑ 112 Ben Roethlisberger .60 1.50
❑ 113 Quentin Jammer .15 .40
❑ 114 Maurice Morris .15 .40
❑ 115 Simeon Rice .15 .40
❑ 116 Tyrone Calico .20 .50
❑ 117 Patrick Ramsey .20 .50
❑ 118 Marcus Robinson .20 .50
❑ 119 Reggie Wayne .20 .50
❑ 120 Kevin Faulk .20 .50
❑ 121 Nate Burleson .20 .50
❑ 122 Aaron Brooks .15 .40
❑ 123 Willie Roaf .15 .40
❑ 124 Fred Taylor .25 .60
❑ 125 Dwight Freeney .20 .50
❑ 126 Olin Kreutz .20 .50
❑ 127 Dunta Robinson .15 .40
❑ 128 Warren Sapp .20 .50
❑ 129 Chris Perry .15 .40
❑ 130 Desmond Clark .15 .40
❑ 131 Takeo Spikes .15 .40
❑ 132 B.J. Sams .15 .40
❑ 133 Bertrand Berry .15 .40
❑ 134 Drew Henson .15 .40
❑ 135 Robert Ferguson .20 .50
❑ 136 Julius Jones .25 .60
❑ 137 Jeremiah Trotter .15 .40
❑ 138 Chris Simms .20 .50
❑ 139 Damerien McCants .15 .40
❑ 140 Robert Gallery .15 .40
❑ 141 Michael Strahan .20 .50
❑ 142 Reggie Williams .20 .50
❑ 143 Tony Gonzalez .20 .50
❑ 144 Priest Holmes .25 .60
❑ 145 Luke McCown .15 .40
❑ 146 Allen Rossum .15 .40
❑ 147 Eric Moulds .20 .50
❑ 148 Jonathan Wells .15 .40
❑ 149 Randy McMichael .15 .40
❑ 150 John Abraham .15 .40
❑ 151 Doug Gabriel .15 .40
❑ 152 Tiki Barber .25 .60
❑ 153 Marcel Shipp .15 .40
❑ 154 LaDainian Tomlinson .30 .75
❑ 155 Richard Seymour .15 .40
❑ 156 Mike Vanderjagt .15 .40
❑ 157 Roy Williams WR .25 .60
❑ 158 William Green .15 .40
❑ 159 DeAngelo Hall .20 .50
❑ 160 Josh McCown .20 .50
❑ 161 Terrell Suggs .20 .50
❑ 162 Brian Dawkins .20 .50
❑ 163 Lee Evans .20 .50
❑ 164 Nick Goings .15 .40
❑ 165 Carson Palmer .25 .60
❑ 166 Charles Woodson .20 .50
❑ 167 Keenan McCardell .20 .50
❑ 168 Kevan Barlow .15 .40
❑ 169 Matt Hasselbeck .20 .50
❑ 170 Steven Jackson .30 .75
❑ 171 Ben Troupe .15 .40
❑ 172 Jamal Lewis .20 .50
❑ 173 Sammy Morris .15 .40
❑ 174 Troy Polamalu .30 .75
❑ 175 Donovan McNabb .25 .60
❑ 176 Curtis Martin .25 .60
❑ 177 David Givens .20 .50
❑ 178 Kenechi Udeze .15 .40
❑ 179 A.J. Feeley .15 .40
❑ 180 Eddie Kennison .15 .40
❑ 181 LaBrandon Toefield .15 .40
❑ 182 Jabar Gaffney .15 .40
❑ 183 Bethel Johnson .15 .40
❑ 184 Eddie Drummond .15 .40
❑ 185 Rod Smith .20 .50
❑ 186 La'Roi Glover .20 .50
❑ 187 Onterrio Smith .15 .40
❑ 188 Antonio Bryant .20 .50
❑ 189 Lee Mays .15 .40
❑ 190 Michael Vick .25 .60
❑ 191 Samie Parker .15 .40
❑ 192 London Fletcher .15 .40
❑ 193 DeShaun Foster .20 .50
❑ 194 Rashaun Woods .15 .40
❑ 195 Marc Bulger .20 .50
❑ 196 Adrian Peterson .20 .50
❑ 197 Justin McCareins .15 .40
❑ 198 Corey Dillon .20 .50
❑ 199 James Farrior .15 .40
❑ 200 Antonio Gates .25 .60
❑ 201 Todd Pinkston .15 .40
❑ 202 Randy Hymes .15 .40
❑ 203 Peyton Manning .40 1.00
❑ 204 Ahman Green .25 .60
❑ 205 Charles Rogers .15 .40
❑ 206 John Lynch .20 .50
❑ 207 Larry Fitzgerald .25 .60
❑ 208 Jonathan Ogden .15 .40
❑ 209 Michael Bennett .20 .50
❑ 210 DeWayne Robertson .15 .40
❑ 211 Justin Fargas .20 .50
❑ 212 Duce Staley .20 .50
❑ 213 Koren Robinson .20 .50
❑ 214 Billy Volek .20 .50
❑ 215 Laveranues Coles .20 .50
❑ 216 Michael Clayton .20 .50
❑ 217 Amani Toomer .20 .50
❑ 218 Thomas Jones .20 .50
❑ 219 Todd Heap .20 .50
❑ 220 Ken Lucas .15 .40
❑ 221 Donovin Darius .15 .40
❑ 222 Ashley Lelie .15 .40
❑ 223 Warrick Dunn .20 .50
❑ 224 Doug Jolley .15 .40
❑ 225 Jimmy Smith .20 .50
❑ 226 Quentin Griffin .20 .50
❑ 227 Isaac Bruce .20 .50
❑ 228 Ronald Curry .20 .50
❑ 229 Corey Bradford .20 .50
❑ 230 LaVar Arrington .25 .60
❑ 231 William Henderson .20 .50
❑ 232 Brandon Stokley .15 .40
❑ 233 Alge Crumpler .20 .50
❑ 234 Joe Horn .20 .50
❑ 235 Bernard Berrian .20 .50
❑ 236 Michael Boulware .15 .40
❑ 237 Brett Favre .60 1.50
❑ 238 Dennis Northcutt .15 .40
❑ 239 Muhsin Muhammad .20 .50
❑ 240 Shawn Springs .15 .40
❑ 241 Kelly Campbell .20 .50
❑ 242 Johnnie Morton .20 .50
❑ 243 Derrick Blaylock .15 .40
❑ 244 Chris Chambers .20 .50
❑ 245 Joey Harrington .25 .60
❑ 246 Brian Urlacher .25 .60
❑ 247 T.J. Duckett .15 .40
❑ 248 Quincy Morgan .15 .40
❑ 249 Darren Sharper .20 .50
❑ 250 L.J. Smith .20 .50
❑ 251 Steve McNair .25 .60
❑ 252 Eric Parker .15 .40
❑ 253 Jerome Bettis .25 .60
❑ 254 LaMont Jordan .20 .50
❑ 255 Tedy Bruschi .25 .60
❑ 256 Ernest Wilford .20 .50
❑ 257 Reuben Droughns .15 .40
❑ 258 Lito Sheppard .20 .50
❑ 259 Steve Smith .25 .60
❑ 260 Shaun Alexander .25 .60
❑ 261 Kevin Curtis .20 .50
❑ 262 Drew Bledsoe .25 .60
❑ 263 Derrick Mason .20 .50
❑ 264 Jevon Kearse .20 .50
❑ 265 Jerry Porter .20 .50
❑ 266 Edgerrin James .20 .50
❑ 267 Santana Moss .20 .50
❑ 268 Kyle Boller .20 .50
❑ 269 Travis Henry .20 .50
❑ 270 Stephen Davis .20 .50
❑ 271 Gibril Wilson .15 .40
❑ 272 Plaxico Burress .20 .50
❑ 273 Deion Branch .20 .50
❑ 274 Larry Johnson .25 .60
❑ 275 Rudi Johnson .20 .50
❑ 276 Andre Johnson .20 .50
❑ 277 David Akers .15 .40
❑ 278 Randy Moss .25 .60
❑ 279 Roy Williams S .20 .50
❑ 280 Antoine Winfield .20 .50
❑ 281 Antonio Pierce .15 .40
❑ 282 Keith Bulluck .15 .40
❑ 283 Correll Buckhalter .20 .50
❑ 284 Troy Vincent .20 .50
❑ 285 D.J. Williams .15 .40
❑ 286 Matt Schaub .25 .60
❑ 287 Clarence Moore .15 .40
❑ 288 Billy Miller .15 .40
❑ 289 Terrence Holt .15 .40
❑ 290 Tony Hollings .15 .40
❑ 291 E.J. Henderson .15 .40
❑ 292 Fred Smoot .15 .40
❑ 293 Patrick Crayton .25 .60
❑ 294 Mike Alstott .20 .50
❑ 295 Mewelde Moore .15 .40
❑ 296 Shawn Bryson .15 .40
❑ 297 David Garrard .25 .60

Card	Low	High
❑ 298 Kurt Warner	.25	.60
❑ 299 Nate Clements	.20	.50
❑ 300 Kellen Winslow	.25	.60
❑ 301 Eric Johnson	.15	.40
❑ 302 Peerless Price	.15	.40
❑ 303 Joey Galloway	.20	.50
❑ 304 Sebastian Janikowski	.15	.40
❑ 305 Jason McAddley	.15	.40
❑ 306 Chris Gamble	.15	.40
❑ 307 Brian Griese	.20	.50
❑ 308 Greg Lewis	.20	.50
❑ 309 Wes Welker	.25	.60
❑ 310 Jesse Chatman	.15	.40
❑ 311 Curtis Martin LL	.20	.50
❑ 312 Daunte Culpepper LL	.20	.50
❑ 313 Muhsin Muhammad LL	.15	.40
❑ 314 Shaun Alexander LL	.20	.50
❑ 315 Trent Green LL	.15	.40
❑ 316 Joe Horn LL	.15	.40
❑ 317 Corey Dillon LL	.15	.40
❑ 318 Peyton Manning LL	.30	.75
❑ 319 Javon Walker LL	.15	.40
❑ 320 Edgerrin James LL	.15	.40
❑ 321 Jake Scott GM	.15	.40
❑ 322 John Elway GM	.50	1.25
❑ 323 Dwight Clark GM	.20	.50
❑ 324 Lawrence Taylor GM	.25	.60
❑ 325 Joe Namath GM	.40	1.00
❑ 326 Richard Dent GM	.20	.50
❑ 327 Peyton Manning GM	.40	1.00
❑ 328 Don Maynard GM	.20	.50
❑ 329 Joe Greene GM	.25	.60
❑ 330 Roger Staubach GM	.40	1.00
❑ 331 Daunte Culpepper AP	.20	.50
❑ 332 Peyton Manning AP	.30	.75
❑ 333 Tiki Barber AP	.20	.50
❑ 334 Antonio Gates AP	.20	.50
❑ 335 Marvin Harrison AP	.20	.50
❑ 336 Lito Sheppard AP	.15	.40
❑ 337 LaDainian Tomlinson AP	.25	.60
❑ 338 Muhsin Muhammad AP	.15	.40
❑ 339 Allen Rossum AP	.12	.30
❑ 340 Dwight Freeney AP	.15	.40
❑ 341 Jerome Bettis AP	.20	.50
❑ 342 Alge Crumpler AP	.15	.40
❑ 343 Ed Reed AP	.15	.40
❑ 344 Ronde Barber AP	.15	.40
❑ 345 Takeo Spikes AP	.12	.30
❑ 346 Rudi Johnson AP	.15	.40
❑ 347 Adam Vinatieri AP	.20	.50
❑ 348 Torry Holt AP	.15	.40
❑ 349 Chad Johnson AP	.15	.40
❑ 350 Brian Westbrook AP	.20	.50
❑ 351 Michael Vick AP	.20	.50
❑ 352 Tom Brady AP	.40	1.00
❑ 353 Donovan McNabb AP	.20	.50
❑ 354 Ahman Green AP	.20	.50
❑ 355 Andre Johnson AP	.15	.40
❑ 356 Drew Brees AP	.20	.50
❑ 357 Hines Ward AP	.20	.50
❑ 358 Deion Branch PH	.15	.40
❑ 359 Philadelphia Eagles PH	.20	.50
❑ 360 Tom Brady PH	.40	1.00
❑ 361 Taylor Stubblefield RC	.40	1.00
❑ 362 Dan Cody RC	.60	1.50
❑ 363 Ryan Claridge RC	.40	1.00
❑ 364 David Pollack RC	.50	1.25
❑ 365 Craig Bragg RC	.40	1.00
❑ 366 Alvin Pearman RC	.40	1.00
❑ 367 Marcus Maxwell RC	.40	1.00
❑ 368 Brock Berlin RC	.50	1.25
❑ 369 Khalif Barnes RC	.40	1.00
❑ 370 Eric King RC	.40	1.00
❑ 371 Alex Smith TE RC	.60	1.50
❑ 372 Dante Ridgeway RC	.40	1.00
❑ 373 Shaun Cody RC	.50	1.25
❑ 374 Donte Nicholson RC	.50	1.25
❑ 375 DeMarcus Ware RC	1.00	2.50
❑ 376 Lionel Gates RC	.40	1.00
❑ 377 Fabian Washington RC	.60	1.50
❑ 378 Brandon Jacobs RC	.75	2.00
❑ 379 Noah Herron RC	.60	1.50
❑ 380 Derrick Johnson RC	.60	1.50
❑ 381 J.R. Russell RC	.40	1.00
❑ 382 Adrian McPherson RC	.50	1.25
❑ 383 Marcus Spears RC	.60	1.50
❑ 384 Justin Miller RC	.50	1.25
❑ 385 Marion Barber RC	2.00	5.00
❑ 386 Anthony Davis RC	.50	1.25
❑ 387 Chad Owens RC	.60	1.50
❑ 388 Craphonso Thorpe RC	.50	1.25
❑ 389 Travis Johnson RC	.40	1.00
❑ 390 Erasmus James RC	.50	1.25
❑ 391 Mike Patterson RC	.50	1.25
❑ 392 Alphonso Hodge RC	.40	1.00
❑ 393 Airese Currie RC	.50	1.25
❑ 394 Justin Tuck RC	.75	2.00
❑ 395 Dan Orlovsky RC	.60	1.50
❑ 396 Thomas Davis RC	.50	1.25
❑ 397 Derek Anderson RC	.60	1.50
❑ 398 Matt Roth RC	.60	1.50
❑ 399 Darryl Blackstock RC	.40	1.00
❑ 400 Chris Henry RC	.60	1.50
❑ 401 Rasheed Marshall RC	.50	1.25
❑ 402 Anttaj Hawthorne RC	.50	1.25
❑ 403 Bryant McFadden RC	.50	1.25
❑ 404 Darren Sproles RC	.75	2.00
❑ 405 Oshiomogho Atogwe RC	.40	1.00
❑ 406 Fred Gibson RC	.50	1.25
❑ 407 J.J. Arrington RC	.60	1.50
❑ 408 Cedric Benson RC	.60	1.50
❑ 409 Mark Bradley RC	.50	1.25
❑ 410 Reggie Brown RC	.50	1.25
❑ 411 Ronnie Brown RC	2.00	5.00
❑ 412 Jason Campbell RC	1.00	2.50
❑ 413 Maurice Clarett	.50	1.25
❑ 414 Mark Clayton RC	.60	1.50
❑ 415 Braylon Edwards RC	1.50	4.00
❑ 416 Ciatrick Fason RC	.50	1.25
❑ 417 Charlie Frye RC	.60	1.50
❑ 418 Frank Gore RC	1.25	3.00
❑ 419 David Greene RC	.50	1.25
❑ 420 Vincent Jackson RC	.75	2.00
❑ 421 Adam Jones RC	.50	1.25
❑ 422 Matt Jones RC	.60	1.50
❑ 423 Stefan LeFors RC	.50	1.25
❑ 424 Heath Miller RC	1.25	3.00
❑ 425 Ryan Moats RC	.50	1.25
❑ 426 Vernand Morency RC	.50	1.25
❑ 427 Terrence Murphy RC	.40	1.00
❑ 428 Kyle Orton RC	1.00	2.50
❑ 429 Roscoe Parrish RC	.50	1.25
❑ 430 Courtney Roby RC	.50	1.25
❑ 431 Aaron Rodgers RC	2.00	5.00
❑ 432 Carlos Rogers RC	.60	1.50
❑ 433 Antrel Rolle RC	.60	1.50
❑ 434 Eric Shelton RC	.50	1.25
❑ 435 Alex Smith QB RC	.60	1.50
❑ 436 Andrew Walter RC	.50	1.25
❑ 437 Roddy White RC	.75	2.00
❑ 438 Cadillac Williams RC	1.00	2.50
❑ 439 Mike Williams	.50	1.25
❑ 440 Troy Williamson RC	.60	1.50
❑ RHDB Deion Branch RH	2.00	5.00
❑ RHDBA Deion Branch RH AU	200.00	350.00
❑ SBMVP D.Branch FB AU/200	60.00	150.00

2006 Topps

Card	Low	High
❑ COMP.FACT.SET (390)	25.00	50.00
❑ COMP.GIANTS SET (390)	25.00	50.00
❑ COMP.PACKERS SET (390)	25.00	50.00
❑ COMP.PATRIOTS SET (390)	25.00	50.00
❑ COMP.STEELERS SET (390)	25.00	50.00
❑ COMP.TARGET FACT.(391)	30.00	50.00
❑ COMPLETE SET (385)	25.00	50.00
❑ 1 Jonathan Vilma	.20	.50
❑ 2 Mewelde Moore	.15	.40
❑ 3 Shaun McDonald	.15	.40
❑ 4 Marcus Pollard	.15	.40
❑ 5 Marcus Robinson	.20	.50
❑ 6 David Garrard	.25	.60
❑ 7 Chris Gamble	.15	.40
❑ 8 Rex Grossman	.25	.60
❑ 9 Lee Suggs	.20	.50
❑ 10 Steve McNair	.20	.50
❑ 11 Chester Taylor	.20	.50
❑ 12 Randy Moss	.25	.60
❑ 13 Jeremy Shockey	.25	.60
❑ 14 Tedy Bruschi	.25	.60
❑ 15 Walter Jones	.15	.40
❑ 16 Troy Polamalu	.30	.75
❑ 17 Ladell Betts	.20	.50
❑ 18 DeMarcus Ware	.20	.50
❑ 19 Erron Kinney	.15	.40
❑ 20 Trent Cole	.15	.40
❑ 21 Charlie Adams	.15	.40
❑ 22 Brandon Jacobs	.25	.60
❑ 23 Nathan Vasher	.15	.40
❑ 24 Shawne Merriman	.20	.50
❑ 25 Drew Carter	.15	.40
❑ 26 Clinton Portis	.25	.60
❑ 27 Alex Brown	.15	.40
❑ 28 Osi Umenyiora	.20	.50
❑ 29 Willie Parker	.30	.75
❑ 30 Lofa Tatupu	.20	.50
❑ 31 Odell Thurman	.15	.40
❑ 32 Scottie Vines	.15	.40
❑ 33 Sam Gado	.25	.60
❑ 34 Todd DeVoe	.25	.60
❑ 35 Keith Brooking	.15	.40
❑ 36 Eddie Kennison	.15	.40
❑ 37 Mike Williams	.20	.50
❑ 38 Adam Jones	.15	.40
❑ 39 Charlie Frye	.20	.50
❑ 40 Reggie Wayne	.20	.50
❑ 41 Donte Stallworth	.20	.50
❑ 42 Vincent Jackson	.20	.50
❑ 43 Alex Smith QB	.20	.50
❑ 44 Greg Lewis	.15	.40
❑ 45 Billy Volek	.15	.40
❑ 46 Domonique Foxworth	.15	.40
❑ 47 Terrell Owens	.25	.60
❑ 48 Josh McCown	.20	.50
❑ 49 Simeon Rice	.15	.40
❑ 50 Curtis Martin	.25	.60
❑ 51 Peyton Manning	.40	1.00
❑ 52 Nick Barnett	.20	.50
❑ 53 Marion Barber	.25	.60
❑ 54 Chris McAlister	.15	.40
❑ 55 Jerramy Stevens	.20	.50
❑ 56 Jerome Bettis	.25	.60
❑ 57 Chris Brown	.20	.50
❑ 58 LeRon McCoy	.15	.40
❑ 59 John Abraham	.15	.40
❑ 60 LaMont Jordan	.20	.50
❑ 61 Jason Taylor	.20	.50
❑ 62 Michael Clayton	.20	.50
❑ 63 Jake Plummer	.20	.50
❑ 64 Travis Taylor	.15	.40
❑ 65 Samie Parker	.15	.40
❑ 66 Carlos Rogers	.15	.40
❑ 67 Kevin Faulk	.20	.50
❑ 68 Alvin Pearman	.15	.40
❑ 69 Derrick Johnson	.20	.50
❑ 70 Cedric Benson	.20	.50
❑ 71 J.P. Losman	.20	.50
❑ 72 Julius Peppers	.20	.50
❑ 73 DeAngelo Hall	.20	.50
❑ 74 Joey Galloway	.20	.50
❑ 75 Marcus Trufant	.15	.40
❑ 76 Frisman Jackson	.15	.40
❑ 77 Jason Campbell	.20	.50
❑ 78 Ron Dayne	.20	.50
❑ 79 Ashley Lelie	.15	.40
❑ 80 Drew Bennett	.20	.50
❑ 81 Brandon Lloyd	.20	.50
❑ 82 Trent Dilfer	.20	.50
❑ 83 Marty Booker	.15	.40
❑ 84 Aaron O'Rodgers	.25	.60
❑ 85 Deltha O'Neal	.15	.40
❑ 86 Jon Kitna	.20	.50
❑ 87 Doug Gabriel	.15	.40
❑ 88 Keenan McCardell	.20	.50
❑ 89 Brian Griese	.20	.50
❑ 90 Michael Jenkins	.20	.50
❑ 91 Brian Westbrook	.20	.50
❑ 92 Terrence Holt	.15	.40
❑ 93 Justin Gage	.15	.40
❑ 94 Shayne Graham	.15	.40
❑ 95 D.J. Hackett	.20	.50
❑ 96 Kevan Barlow	.20	.50
❑ 97 Bob Sanders	.20	.50
❑ 98 Charles Rogers	.20	.50
❑ 99 Kevin Curtis	.20	.50

❑ 100 LaDainian Tomlinson .30 .75
❑ 101 Plaxico Burress .20 .50
❑ 102 Kyle Boller .20 .50
❑ 103 Donald Driver .25 .60
❑ 104 Jerome Mathis .15 .40
❑ 105 Takeo Spikes .15 .40
❑ 106 Tony Gonzalez .20 .50
❑ 107 Keary Colbert .20 .50
❑ 108 Derrick Burgess .15 .40
❑ 109 T.J. Duckett .15 .40
❑ 110 Chris Chambers .20 .50
❑ 111 Cadillac Williams .25 .60
❑ 112 Jerricho Cotchery .15 .40
❑ 113 Ernest Wilford .15 .40
❑ 114 Torry Holt .20 .50
❑ 115 Corey Dillon .20 .50
❑ 116 Chris Simms .20 .50
❑ 117 Philip Rivers .25 .60
❑ 118 LaVar Arrington .25 .60
❑ 119 Andrew Walter .20 .50
❑ 120 Joe Jurevicius .15 .40
❑ 121 Kyle Vanden Bosch .15 .40
❑ 122 London Fletcher .15 .40
❑ 123 Deuce McAllister .20 .50
❑ 124 Cedrick Wilson .15 .40
❑ 125 Jason Witten .25 .60
❑ 126 Troy Williamson .20 .50
❑ 127 Dominic Rhodes .20 .50
❑ 128 Koren Robinson .15 .40
❑ 129 Eli Manning .30 .75
❑ 130 Brian Finneran .15 .40
❑ 131 Fabian Washington .15 .40
❑ 132 Michael Boulware .15 .40
❑ 133 Bernard Berrian .20 .50
❑ 134 Stephen Davis .20 .50
❑ 135 Reggie Brown .15 .40
❑ 136 Chad Johnson .20 .50
❑ 137 Ronnie Brown .25 .60
❑ 138 Amani Toomer .20 .50
❑ 139 Deion Branch .20 .50
❑ 140 Darren Sproles .25 .60
❑ 141 L.J. Smith .15 .40
❑ 142 Arnaz Battle .15 .40
❑ 143 Jerry Porter .20 .50
❑ 144 Terry Glenn .20 .50
❑ 145 Mike Vrabel .20 .50
❑ 146 Chad Pennington .20 .50
❑ 147 Allen Rossum .15 .40
❑ 148 Greg Jones .15 .40
❑ 149 Jake Delhomme .20 .50
❑ 150 Tom Brady .40 1.00
❑ 151 Neil Rackers .15 .40
❑ 152 Charles Woodson .20 .50
❑ 153 Carson Palmer .25 .60
❑ 154 Kerry Collins .20 .50
❑ 155 Brian Urlacher .25 .60
❑ 156 Kevin Jones .20 .50
❑ 157 Eric Parker .15 .40
❑ 158 Daniel Graham .15 .40
❑ 159 Dallas Clark .20 .50
❑ 160 Matt Schaub .20 .50
❑ 161 Drew Brees .25 .60
❑ 162 Andre Johnson .20 .50
❑ 163 Ray Lewis .25 .60
❑ 164 Cato June .20 .50
❑ 165 J.J. Arrington .15 .40
❑ 166 Warren Sapp .20 .50
❑ 167 T.J. Houshmandzadeh .20 .50
❑ 168 Donnie Edwards .15 .40
❑ 169 Thomas Jones .20 .50
❑ 170 Mark Clayton .20 .50
❑ 171 Kyle Orton .20 .50
❑ 172 Najeh Davenport .20 .50
❑ 173 Dan Morgan .15 .40
❑ 174 David Pollack .15 .40
❑ 175 D.J. Williams .15 .40
❑ 176 Julius Jones .20 .50
❑ 177 Roy Williams WR .25 .60
❑ 178 Willis McGahee .25 .60
❑ 179 Keyshawn Johnson .20 .50
❑ 180 Dennis Northcutt .15 .40
❑ 181 Courtney Roby .15 .40
❑ 182 Jonathan Ogden .15 .40
❑ 183 Kellen Winslow .25 .60
❑ 184 Matt Jones .20 .50
❑ 185 Robert Gallery .15 .40
❑ 186 Mike Anderson .20 .50
❑ 187 Frank Gore .25 .60
❑ 188 Jimmy Smith .20 .50
❑ 189 Antonio Pierce .15 .40
❑ 190 Todd Heap .20 .50
❑ 191 Champ Bailey .20 .50
❑ 192 Roddy White .20 .50
❑ 193 Rod Smith .20 .50
❑ 194 Brian Dawkins .20 .50
❑ 195 Larry Johnson .20 .50
❑ 196 Ed Reed .20 .50
❑ 197 Marc Bulger .20 .50
❑ 198 Zach Thomas .25 .60
❑ 199 Cedric Houston .15 .40
❑ 200 Brett Favre .50 1.25
❑ 201 Mark Brunell .20 .50
❑ 202 Edgerrin James .20 .50
❑ 203 Ronald Curry .20 .50
❑ 204 Antonio Gates .25 .60
❑ 205 Roscoe Parrish .15 .40
❑ 206 Steve Smith .25 .60
❑ 207 Reuben Droughns .20 .50
❑ 208 Michael Vick .25 .60
❑ 209 Chris Cooley .20 .50
❑ 210 Chris Perry .20 .50
❑ 211 Muhsin Muhammad .20 .50
❑ 212 Trent Green .20 .50
❑ 213 Matt Hasselbeck .20 .50
❑ 214 Ben Roethlisberger .40 1.00
❑ 215 Tyrone Calico .15 .40
❑ 216 Jamal Lewis .20 .50
❑ 217 Antwaan Randle El .20 .50
❑ 218 Byron Leftwich .20 .50
❑ 219 Priest Holmes .20 .50
❑ 220 Anquan Boldin .20 .50
❑ 221 Drew Bledsoe .25 .60
❑ 222 Randy McMichael .15 .40
❑ 223 Tatum Bell .15 .40
❑ 224 Daunte Culpepper .25 .60
❑ 225 David Carr .15 .40
❑ 226 Mark Bradley .15 .40
❑ 227 Lee Evans .20 .50
❑ 228 Domanick Davis .20 .50
❑ 229 Robert Ferguson .15 .40
❑ 230 Peter Warrick .20 .50
❑ 231 Heath Miller .20 .50
❑ 232 Derrick Brooks .20 .50
❑ 233 Isaac Bruce .20 .50
❑ 234 Aaron Brooks .20 .50
❑ 235 Nate Burleson .20 .50
❑ 236 Braylon Edwards .25 .60
❑ 237 Ben Watson .15 .40
❑ 238 Hines Ward .25 .60
❑ 239 Shaun Alexander .20 .50
❑ 240 Kurt Warner .25 .60
❑ 241 Warrick Dunn .20 .50
❑ 242 Rodney Harrison .15 .40
❑ 243 Dante Hall .20 .50
❑ 244 Tiki Barber .25 .60
❑ 245 Santana Moss .20 .50
❑ 246 Fred Taylor .20 .50
❑ 247 Laveranues Coles .20 .50
❑ 248 Darren Sharper .20 .50
❑ 249 Brandon Stokley .20 .50
❑ 250 Alge Crumpler .20 .50
❑ 251 Derrick Mason .20 .50
❑ 252 Antonio Bryant .20 .50
❑ 253 Antrel Rolle .15 .40
❑ 254 Eric Moulds .20 .50
❑ 255 Bubba Franks .15 .40
❑ 256 Joe Horn .20 .50
❑ 257 Dunta Robinson .15 .40
❑ 258 Larry Fitzgerald .25 .60
❑ 259 Roy Williams S .20 .50
❑ 260 Javon Walker .20 .50
❑ 261 Alex Smith TE .15 .40
❑ 262 Travis Henry .20 .50
❑ 263 Luke McCown .15 .40
❑ 264 James Farrior .15 .40
❑ 265 Darrell Jackson .20 .50
❑ 266 Marvin Harrison .25 .60
❑ 267 Patrick Ramsey .20 .50
❑ 268 Ernie Conwell .15 .40
❑ 269 Ahman Green .20 .50
❑ 270 Ryan Moats .20 .50
❑ 271 Donovan McNabb .25 .60
❑ 272 Steven Jackson .25 .60
❑ 273 Ronde Barber .20 .50
❑ 274 Michael Strahan .20 .50
❑ 275 Dwight Freeney .20 .50
❑ 276 DeShaun Foster .20 .50
❑ 277 Terence Newman .15 .40
❑ 278 Rudi Johnson .20 .50
❑ 279 Shaun Alexander LL .12 .30
❑ 280 Tom Brady LL .25 .60
❑ 281 Steve Smith LL .15 .40
❑ 282 Tiki Barber LL .15 .40
❑ 283 Trent Green LL .12 .30
❑ 284 Santana Moss LL .12 .30
❑ 285 Larry Johnson LL .12 .30
❑ 286 Brett Favre LL .30 .75
❑ 287 Chad Johnson AP .12 .30
❑ 288 Peyton Manning AP .25 .60
❑ 289 Matt Hasselbeck AP .12 .30
❑ 290 Edgerrin James AP .12 .30
❑ 291 Shaun Alexander AP .12 .30
❑ 292 Larry Johnson AP .12 .30
❑ 293 Tiki Barber AP .15 .40
❑ 294 Marvin Harrison AP .15 .40
❑ 295 Santana Moss AP .12 .30
❑ 296 Chad Johnson AP .12 .30
❑ 297 Alge Crumpler AP .12 .30
❑ 298 LaDainian Tomlinson AP .20 .50
❑ 299 Derrick Brooks AP .12 .30
❑ 300 Antonio Gates AP .15 .40
❑ 301 Steve Smith AP .15 .40
❑ 302 Shawne Merriman AP .12 .30
❑ 303 Michael Vick AP .15 .40
❑ 304 Tony Gonzalez AP .12 .30
❑ 305 Jake Delhomme AP .12 .30
❑ 306 Steve McNair AP .12 .30
❑ 307 Larry Fitzgerald AP .15 .40
❑ 308 Ben Roethlisberger HL .25 .60
❑ 309 Seattle Seahawks HL .25 .60
❑ 310 Pittsburgh Steelers HL .25 .60
❑ 311 Tamba Hali RC .60 1.50
❑ 312 Haloti Ngata RC .60 1.50
❑ 313 Mike Hass RC .60 1.50
❑ 314 Manny Lawson RC .60 1.50
❑ 315 Reggie McNeal RC .50 1.25
❑ 316 Kelly Jennings RC .60 1.50
❑ 317 Jason Allen RC .50 1.25
❑ 318 Joe Klopfenstein RC .50 1.25
❑ 319 Willie Reid RC .50 1.25
❑ 320 Brad Smith RC .60 1.50
❑ 321 Bruce Gradkowski RC .60 1.50
❑ 322 Ashton Youboty RC .50 1.25
❑ 323 Abdul Hodge RC .50 1.25
❑ 324 P.J. Daniels RC .40 1.00
❑ 325 D'Qwell Jackson RC .50 1.25
❑ 326 Johnathan Joseph RC .50 1.25
❑ 327 Antonio Cromartie RC .60 1.50
❑ 328 Elvis Dumervil RC .60 1.50
❑ 329 Tye Hill RC .50 1.25
❑ 330 Mathias Kiwanuka RC .75 2.00
❑ 331 Leonard Pope RC .60 1.50
❑ 332 DeMeco Ryans RC .75 2.00
❑ 333 Brodrick Bunkley RC .50 1.25
❑ 334 Devin Hester RC 1.25 3.00
❑ 335 Thomas Howard RC .50 1.25
❑ 336 Cory Rodgers RC .60 1.50
❑ 337 Ernie Sims RC .50 1.25
❑ 338 Todd Watkins RC .40 1.00
❑ 339 Rocky McIntosh RC .60 1.50
❑ 340 Donte Whitner RC .60 1.50
❑ 341 Anthony Schlegel RC .50 1.25
❑ 342 Kamerion Wimbley RC .60 1.50
❑ 343 Wali Lundy RC .60 1.50
❑ 344 Bobby Carpenter RC .50 1.25
❑ 345 Jimmy Williams RC .60 1.50
❑ 346 Michael Robinson RC .50 1.25
❑ 347 Brandon Williams RC .50 1.25
❑ 348 Skyler Green RC .40 1.00
❑ 349 Jerious Norwood RC .60 1.50
❑ 350 Travis Wilson RC .40 1.00
❑ 351 Mario Williams RC .75 2.00
❑ 352 Santonio Holmes RC 1.50 4.00
❑ 353 Vince Young RC 1.50 4.00
❑ 354 Matt Leinart RC 1.00 2.50
❑ 355 D'Brickashaw Ferguson RC .60 1.50
❑ 356 Michael Huff RC .60 1.50
❑ 357 Chad Greenway RC .60 1.50
❑ 358 Chad Jackson RC .50 1.25
❑ 359A Reggie Bush RC 1.50 4.00
❑ 359B Reggie Bush RC 1.50 4.00
❑ 360 A.J. Hawk RC 1.00 2.50
❑ 361 DeAngelo Williams RC 1.25 3.00
❑ 362 Derek Hagan RC .50 1.25
❑ 363 Vernon Davis RC .60 1.50
❑ 364 Joseph Addai RC .75 2.00
❑ 365 Jay Cutler RC 1.50 4.00

Card		
❑ 366 Jason Avant RC	.60	1.50
❑ 367 Brian Calhoun RC	.50	1.25
❑ 368 LenDale White RC	.75	2.00
❑ 369 Greg Jennings RC	1.00	2.50
❑ 370 Charlie Whitehurst RC	.60	1.50
❑ 371 Sinorice Moss RC	.60	1.50
❑ 372 Maurice Stovall RC	.50	1.25
❑ 373 Laurence Maroney RC	.75	2.00
❑ 374 Brodie Croyle RC	.60	1.50
❑ 375 Demetrius Williams RC	.50	1.25
❑ 376 Jerome Harrison RC	.60	1.50
❑ 377 Maurice Drew RC	1.25	3.00
❑ 378 Kellen Clemens RC	.60	1.50
❑ 379 Marcedes Lewis RC	.60	1.50
❑ 380 Leon Washington RC	.75	2.00
❑ 381 Anthony Fasano RC	.60	1.50
❑ 382 Jeremy Bloom RC	.50	1.25
❑ 383 Omar Jacobs RC	.40	1.00
❑ 384 Tarvaris Jackson RC	.60	1.50
❑ 385 Brandon Marshall RC	.60	1.50

2007 Topps

Card		
❑ COMP.FACT.SET (445)	30.00	50.00
❑ COMP.BEARS SET (445)	30.00	50.00
❑ COMP.CHARGER SET (445)	30.00	50.00
❑ COMP.COLTS SET (445)	30.00	50.00
❑ COMP.JETS SET (445)	30.00	50.00
❑ COMPLETE SET (440)	25.00	50.00
❑ 1 Matt Leinart	.25	.60
❑ 2 Kurt Warner	.20	.50
❑ 3 Matt Schaub	.20	.50
❑ 4 Michael Vick	.25	.60
❑ 5 Kyle Boller	.15	.40
❑ 6 Steve McNair	.20	.50
❑ 7 J.P. Losman	.15	.40
❑ 8 Jake Delhomme	.20	.50
❑ 9 Rex Grossman	.20	.50
❑ 10 Brian Griese	.20	.50
❑ 11 Carson Palmer	.25	.60
❑ 12 Charlie Frye	.20	.50
❑ 13 Drew Bledsoe	.25	.60
❑ 14 Tony Romo	.40	1.00
❑ 15 Joey Harrington	.20	.50
❑ 16 Jay Cutler	.25	.60
❑ 17 Jon Kitna	.15	.40
❑ 18 Aaron Rodgers	.25	.60
❑ 19 Brett Favre	.50	1.25
❑ 20 David Carr	.20	.50
❑ 21 Peyton Manning	.40	1.00
❑ 22 David Garrard	.20	.50
❑ 23 Byron Leftwich	.20	.50
❑ 24 Trent Green	.20	.50
❑ 25 Damon Huard	.20	.50
❑ 26 Daunte Culpepper	.20	.50
❑ 27 Tarvaris Jackson	.20	.50
❑ 28 Tom Brady	.50	1.25
❑ 29 Drew Brees	.25	.60
❑ 30 Eli Manning	.25	.60
❑ 31 Chad Pennington	.20	.50
❑ 32 Andrew Walter	.15	.40
❑ 33 Aaron Brooks	.15	.40
❑ 34 Donovan McNabb	.25	.60
❑ 35 Jeff Garcia	.20	.50
❑ 36 Ben Roethlisberger	.40	1.00
❑ 37 Philip Rivers	.25	.60
❑ 38 Alex Smith QB	.25	.60
❑ 39 Matt Hasselbeck	.20	.50
❑ 40 Seneca Wallace	.15	.40
❑ 41 Marc Bulger	.20	.50
❑ 42 Chris Simms	.15	.40
❑ 43 Bruce Gradkowski	.15	.40
❑ 44 Vince Young	.25	.60
❑ 45 Jason Campbell	.20	.50
❑ 46 Jared Lorenzen	.15	.40
❑ 47 Mark Brunell	.20	.50
❑ 48 J.J. Arrington	.20	.50
❑ 49 Edgerrin James	.20	.50
❑ 50 Jerious Norwood	.20	.50
❑ 51 Warrick Dunn	.20	.50
❑ 52 Mike Anderson	.20	.50
❑ 53 Jamal Lewis	.20	.50
❑ 54 Willis McGahee	.20	.50
❑ 55 DeShaun Foster	.20	.50
❑ 56 DeAngelo Williams	.25	.60
❑ 57 Cedric Benson	.20	.50
❑ 58 Thomas Jones	.20	.50
❑ 59 Chris Perry	.15	.40
❑ 60 Rudi Johnson	.20	.50
❑ 61 Reuben Droughns	.20	.50
❑ 62 Jerome Harrison	.15	.40
❑ 63 Marion Barber	.25	.60
❑ 64 Julius Jones	.20	.50
❑ 65 Tatum Bell	.15	.40
❑ 66 Mike Bell	.20	.50
❑ 67 Kevin Jones	.15	.40
❑ 68 Brian Calhoun	.15	.40
❑ 69 Ahman Green	.20	.50
❑ 70 Vernand Morency	.20	.50
❑ 71 Ron Dayne	.20	.50
❑ 72 Wali Lundy	.15	.40
❑ 73 Dominic Rhodes	.20	.50
❑ 74 Joseph Addai	.25	.60
❑ 75 Fred Taylor	.20	.50
❑ 76 Maurice Jones-Drew	.25	.60
❑ 77 Larry Johnson	.20	.50
❑ 78 Sammy Morris	.15	.40
❑ 79 Ronnie Brown	.20	.50
❑ 80 Mewelde Moore	.15	.40
❑ 81 Chester Taylor	.15	.40
❑ 82 Kevin Faulk	.15	.40
❑ 83 Corey Dillon	.20	.50
❑ 84 Laurence Maroney	.25	.60
❑ 85 Deuce McAllister	.20	.50
❑ 86 Reggie Bush	.30	.75
❑ 87 Brandon Jacobs	.20	.50
❑ 88 Anthony Thomas	.15	.40
❑ 89 Cedric Houston	.15	.40
❑ 90 Leon Washington	.20	.50
❑ 91 Kevan Barlow	.20	.50
❑ 92 LaMont Jordan	.20	.50
❑ 93 Justin Fargas	.15	.40
❑ 94 Brian Westbrook	.20	.50
❑ 95 Correll Buckhalter	.20	.50
❑ 96 Willie Parker	.20	.50
❑ 97 Najeh Davenport	.15	.40
❑ 98 LaDainian Tomlinson	.30	.75
❑ 99 Darren Sproles	.15	.40
❑ 100 Frank Gore	.25	.60
❑ 101 Michael Robinson	.20	.50
❑ 102 Shaun Alexander	.20	.50
❑ 103 Maurice Morris	.15	.40
❑ 104 Steven Jackson	.25	.60
❑ 105 Stephen Davis	.20	.50
❑ 106 Cadillac Williams	.20	.50
❑ 107 Travis Henry	.20	.50
❑ 108 LenDale White	.20	.50
❑ 109 Ladell Betts	.15	.40
❑ 110 Clinton Portis	.20	.50
❑ 111 Michael Turner	.25	.60
❑ 112 T.J. Duckett	.15	.40
❑ 113 Anquan Boldin	.20	.50
❑ 114 Larry Fitzgerald	.25	.60
❑ 115 Bryant Johnson	.15	.40
❑ 116 Michael Jenkins	.20	.50
❑ 117 Ashley Lelie	.20	.50
❑ 118 Roddy White	.20	.50
❑ 119 Mark Clayton	.20	.50
❑ 120 Derrick Mason	.15	.40
❑ 121 Demetrius Williams	.15	.40
❑ 122 Peerless Price	.15	.40
❑ 123 Lee Evans	.20	.50
❑ 124 Drew Carter	.15	.40
❑ 125 Keyshawn Johnson	.20	.50
❑ 126 Steve Smith	.20	.50
❑ 127 Bernard Berrian	.15	.40
❑ 128 Mark Bradley	.15	.40
❑ 129 Muhsin Muhammad	.20	.50
❑ 130 Chad Johnson	.20	.50
❑ 131 T.J. Houshmandzadeh	.20	.50
❑ 132 Chris Henry	.15	.40
❑ 133 Joe Jurevicius	.15	.40
❑ 134 Braylon Edwards	.20	.50
❑ 135 Terrell Owens	.25	.60
❑ 136 Terry Glenn	.20	.50
❑ 137 Skyler Green	.15	.40
❑ 138 Rod Smith	.20	.50
❑ 139 Javon Walker	.20	.50
❑ 140 Brandon Marshall	.20	.50
❑ 141 Mike Furrey	.20	.50
❑ 142 Mike Williams	.15	.40
❑ 143 Roy Williams WR	.20	.50
❑ 144 Donald Driver	.25	.60
❑ 145 Greg Jennings	.20	.50
❑ 146 Andre Johnson	.20	.50
❑ 147 Eric Moulds	.20	.50
❑ 148 Reggie Wayne	.20	.50
❑ 149 Marvin Harrison	.25	.60
❑ 150 Ernest Wilford	.15	.40
❑ 151 Matt Jones	.20	.50
❑ 152 Reggie Williams	.20	.50
❑ 153 Eddie Kennison	.15	.40
❑ 154 Samie Parker	.15	.40
❑ 155 Marty Booker	.15	.40
❑ 156 Chris Chambers	.20	.50
❑ 157 Wes Welker	.25	.60
❑ 158 Travis Taylor	.15	.40
❑ 159 Troy Williamson	.15	.40
❑ 160 Reche Caldwell	.15	.40
❑ 161 Chad Jackson	.15	.40
❑ 162 Devery Henderson	.15	.40
❑ 163 Joe Horn	.20	.50
❑ 164 Marques Colston	.25	.60
❑ 165 Plaxico Burress	.20	.50
❑ 166 Amani Toomer	.20	.50
❑ 167 Sinorice Moss	.20	.50
❑ 168 Jerricho Cotchery	.15	.40
❑ 169 Laveranues Coles	.20	.50
❑ 170 Randy Moss	.25	.60
❑ 171 Ronald Curry	.20	.50
❑ 172 Donte Stallworth	.20	.50
❑ 173 Reggie Brown	.15	.40
❑ 174 Hines Ward	.25	.60
❑ 175 Nate Washington	.15	.40
❑ 176 Santonio Holmes	.20	.50
❑ 177 Keenan McCardell	.15	.40
❑ 178 Eric Parker	.15	.40
❑ 179 Arnaz Battle	.15	.40
❑ 180 Antonio Bryant	.20	.50
❑ 181 D.J. Hackett	.15	.40
❑ 182 Deion Branch	.20	.50
❑ 183 Darrell Jackson	.20	.50
❑ 184 Kevin Curtis	.15	.40
❑ 185 Torry Holt	.20	.50
❑ 186 Isaac Bruce	.20	.50
❑ 187 Michael Clayton	.20	.50
❑ 188 Joey Galloway	.20	.50
❑ 189 Drew Bennett	.15	.40
❑ 190 Bobby Wade	.15	.40
❑ 191 Antwaan Randle El	.15	.40
❑ 192 Santana Moss	.20	.50
❑ 193 Roscoe Parrish	.15	.40
❑ 194 Leonard Pope	.15	.40
❑ 195 Alge Crumpler	.20	.50
❑ 196 Todd Heap	.15	.40
❑ 197 Desmond Clark	.15	.40
❑ 198 Kellen Winslow	.20	.50
❑ 199 Jason Witten	.25	.60
❑ 200 Marcus Pollard	.15	.40
❑ 201 Bubba Franks	.15	.40
❑ 202 Dallas Clark	.15	.40
❑ 203 George Wrighster	.15	.40
❑ 204 Tony Gonzalez	.20	.50
❑ 205 Randy McMichael	.15	.40
❑ 206 Jermaine Wiggins	.15	.40
❑ 207 Ben Watson	.15	.40
❑ 208 Ernie Conwell	.15	.40
❑ 209 Jeremy Shockey	.20	.50
❑ 210 L.J. Smith	.15	.40
❑ 211 Heath Miller	.15	.40
❑ 212 Antonio Gates	.20	.50
❑ 213 Vernon Davis	.20	.50
❑ 214 Jerramy Stevens	.15	.40
❑ 215 Joe Klopfenstein	.15	.40
❑ 216 Alex Smith TE	.15	.40
❑ 217 Bo Scaife	.15	.40
❑ 218 Anthony Fasano	.15	.40
❑ 219 Chris Cooley	.20	.50
❑ 220 Robbie Gould	.15	.40
❑ 221 Adam Vinatieri	.20	.50
❑ 222 Devin Hester	.25	.60
❑ 223 Justin Miller	.15	.40
❑ 224 Sean Taylor	.15	.40
❑ 225 DeAngelo Hall	.20	.50
❑ 226 Chris McAlister	.15	.40

Card	Low	High
❑ 227 Nate Clements	.15	.40
❑ 228 Chris Gamble	.15	.40
❑ 229 Ricky Manning	.15	.40
❑ 230 Charles Tillman	.15	.40
❑ 231 Deltha O'Neal	.15	.40
❑ 232 Terence Newman	.15	.40
❑ 233 Champ Bailey	.20	.50
❑ 234 Charles Woodson	.20	.50
❑ 235 Dunta Robinson	.15	.40
❑ 236 Rashean Mathis	.15	.40
❑ 237 Antoine Winfield	.15	.40
❑ 238 Asante Samuel	.15	.40
❑ 239 Nnamdi Asomugha	.15	.40
❑ 240 Lito Sheppard	.15	.40
❑ 241 Walt Harris	.15	.40
❑ 242 Tye Hill	.15	.40
❑ 243 Ronde Barber	.15	.40
❑ 244 Quentin Jammer	.15	.40
❑ 245 Ed Reed	.20	.50
❑ 246 Roy Williams S	.20	.50
❑ 247 Troy Polamalu	.25	.60
❑ 248 Brian Dawkins	.20	.50
❑ 249 Terrell Suggs	.15	.40
❑ 250 Aaron Schobel	.15	.40
❑ 251 Julius Peppers	.20	.50
❑ 252 Alex Brown	.15	.40
❑ 253 Kamerion Wimbley	.15	.40
❑ 254 DeMarcus Ware	.20	.50
❑ 255 Elvis Dumervil	.15	.40
❑ 256 Mario Williams	.20	.50
❑ 257 Dwight Freeney	.20	.50
❑ 258 Tamba Hali	.15	.40
❑ 259 Jason Taylor	.15	.40
❑ 260 Michael Strahan	.20	.50
❑ 261 Aaron Kampman	.20	.50
❑ 262 Derrick Burgess	.15	.40
❑ 263 Leonard Little	.15	.40
❑ 264 Ty Warren	.15	.40
❑ 265 Warren Sapp	.20	.50
❑ 266 Luis Castillo	.15	.40
❑ 267 Keith Brooking	.15	.40
❑ 268 Ray Lewis	.25	.60
❑ 269 London Fletcher	.15	.40
❑ 270 Brian Urlacher	.25	.60
❑ 271 Ernie Sims	.15	.40
❑ 272 A.J. Hawk	.25	.60
❑ 273 DeMeco Ryans	.20	.50
❑ 274 Cato June	.15	.40
❑ 275 Derrick Johnson LB	.15	.40
❑ 276 Zach Thomas	.20	.50
❑ 277 Antonio Pierce	.15	.40
❑ 278 Jonathan Vilma	.20	.50
❑ 279 James Farrior	.15	.40
❑ 280 Shawne Merriman	.20	.50
❑ 281 Lofa Tatupu	.20	.50
❑ 282 Derrick Brooks	.20	.50
❑ 283 Jonathan Ogden	.15	.40
❑ 284 Steve Hutchinson	.15	.40
❑ 285 Walter Jones	.15	.40
❑ 286 JaMarcus Russell RC	.75	2.00
❑ 287 Brady Quinn RC	1.25	3.00
❑ 288 Drew Stanton RC	.50	1.25
❑ 289 Troy Smith RC	.75	2.00
❑ 290 Kevin Kolb RC	1.00	2.50
❑ 291 Trent Edwards RC	1.00	2.50
❑ 292 John Beck RC	.60	1.50
❑ 293 Jordan Palmer RC	.60	1.50
❑ 294 Chris Leak RC	.50	1.25
❑ 295 Isaiah Stanback RC	.60	1.50
❑ 296 Tyler Palko RC	.50	1.25
❑ 297 Jared Zabransky RC	.60	1.50
❑ 298 Jeff Rowe RC	.50	1.25
❑ 299 Zac Taylor RC	.60	1.50
❑ 300 Lester Ricard RC	.60	1.50
❑ 301 Adrian Peterson RC	5.00	12.00
❑ 302 Marshawn Lynch RC	1.00	2.50
❑ 303 Brandon Jackson RC	.60	1.50
❑ 304 Michael Bush RC	.60	1.50
❑ 305 Kenny Irons RC	.60	1.50
❑ 306 Antonio Pittman RC	.60	1.50
❑ 307 Tony Hunt RC	.60	1.50
❑ 308 Darius Walker RC	.50	1.25
❑ 309 Dwayne Wright RC	.50	1.25
❑ 310 Lorenzo Booker RC	.60	1.50
❑ 311 Kenneth Darby RC	.60	1.50
❑ 312 Chris Henry RC	.50	1.25
❑ 313 Selvin Young RC	.60	1.50
❑ 314 Brian Leonard RC	.50	1.25
❑ 315 Ahmad Bradshaw RC	.75	2.00
❑ 316 Gary Russell RC	.50	1.25
❑ 317 Kolby Smith RC	.60	1.50
❑ 318 Thomas Clayton RC	.50	1.25
❑ 319 Garrett Wolfe RC	.60	1.50
❑ 320 Calvin Johnson RC	1.50	4.00
❑ 321 Ted Ginn Jr. RC	1.00	2.50
❑ 322 Dwayne Jarrett RC	.60	1.50
❑ 323 Dwayne Bowe RC	1.00	2.50
❑ 324 Sidney Rice RC	1.25	3.00
❑ 325 Robert Meachem RC	.60	1.50
❑ 326 Anthony Gonzalez RC	.75	2.00
❑ 327 Craig Buster Davis RC	.60	1.50
❑ 328 Aundrae Allison RC	.50	1.25
❑ 329 Chansi Stuckey RC	.60	1.50
❑ 330 David Clowney RC	.60	1.50
❑ 331 Steve Smith USC RC	1.00	2.50
❑ 332 Courtney Taylor RC	.50	1.25
❑ 333 Paul Williams RC	.50	1.25
❑ 334 Johnnie Lee Higgins RC	.60	1.50
❑ 335 Rhema McKnight RC	.50	1.25
❑ 336 Jason Hill RC	.60	1.50
❑ 337 Dallas Baker RC	.50	1.25
❑ 338 Greg Olsen RC	.75	2.00
❑ 339 Yamon Figurs RC	.40	1.00
❑ 340 Scott Chandler RC	.50	1.25
❑ 341 Matt Spaeth RC	.60	1.50
❑ 342 Ben Patrick RC	.50	1.25
❑ 343 Clark Harris RC	.60	1.50
❑ 344 Martrez Milner RC	.50	1.25
❑ 345 Joe Newton RC	.50	1.25
❑ 346 Alan Branch RC	.50	1.25
❑ 347 Amobi Okoye RC	.60	1.50
❑ 348 DeMarcus Tank Tyler RC	.50	1.25
❑ 349 Justin Harrell RC	.60	1.50
❑ 350 Brandon Mebane RC	.50	1.25
❑ 351 Gaines Adams RC	.60	1.50
❑ 352 Jamaal Anderson RC	.50	1.25
❑ 353 Adam Carriker RC	.50	1.25
❑ 354 Jarvis Moss RC	.60	1.50
❑ 355 Charles Johnson RC	.40	1.00
❑ 356 Anthony Spencer RC	.60	1.50
❑ 357 Quentin Moses RC	.50	1.25
❑ 358 LaMarr Woodley RC	.60	1.50
❑ 359 Victor Abiamiri RC	.60	1.50
❑ 360 Ray McDonald RC	.50	1.25
❑ 361 Tim Crowder RC	.60	1.50
❑ 362 Patrick Willis RC	1.00	2.50
❑ 363 Brandon Siler RC	.50	1.25
❑ 364 David Harris RC	.50	1.25
❑ 365 Buster Davis RC	.50	1.25
❑ 366 Lawrence Timmons RC	.60	1.50
❑ 367 Paul Posluszny RC	.75	2.00
❑ 368 Jon Beason RC	.60	1.50
❑ 369 Rufus Alexander RC	.60	1.50
❑ 370 Earl Everett RC	.50	1.25
❑ 371 Stewart Bradley RC	.60	1.50
❑ 372 Prescott Burgess RC	.50	1.25
❑ 373 Leon Hall RC	.60	1.50
❑ 374 Darrelle Revis RC	.75	2.00
❑ 375 Aaron Ross RC	.60	1.50
❑ 376 Daymeion Hughes RC	.50	1.25
❑ 377 Marcus McCauley RC	.50	1.25
❑ 378 Chris Houston RC	.50	1.25
❑ 379 Tanard Jackson RC	.40	1.00
❑ 380 Jonathan Wade RC	.50	1.25
❑ 381 Josh Wilson RC	.50	1.25
❑ 382 Eric Wright RC	.60	1.50
❑ 383 A.J. Davis RC	.40	1.00
❑ 384 David Irons RC	.40	1.00
❑ 385 LaRon Landry RC	.75	2.00
❑ 386 Reggie Nelson RC	.50	1.25
❑ 387 Michael Griffin RC	.60	1.50
❑ 388 Brandon Meriweather RC	.60	1.50
❑ 389 Eric Weddle RC	.50	1.25
❑ 390 Aaron Rouse RC	.60	1.50
❑ 391 Josh Gattis RC	.40	1.00
❑ 392 Joe Thomas RC	.60	1.50
❑ 393 Levi Brown RC	.60	1.50
❑ 394 Tony Ugoh RC	.50	1.25
❑ 395 Ryan Kalil RC	.50	1.25
❑ 396 Peyton Manning LL	.30	.75
❑ 397 Marc Bulger LL	.15	.40
❑ 398 LaDainian Tomlinson LL	.25	.60
❑ 399 Larry Johnson LL	.15	.40
❑ 400 Frank Gore LL	.20	.50
❑ 401 Chad Johnson LL	.15	.40
❑ 402 Marvin Harrison LL	.20	.50
❑ 403 Reggie Wayne LL	.15	.40
❑ 404 LaDainian Tomlinson LL	.25	.60
❑ 405 Peyton Manning PB	.30	.75
❑ 406 Marvin Harrison PB	.20	.50
❑ 407 LaDainian Tomlinson PB	.25	.60
❑ 408 Reggie Wayne PB	.15	.40
❑ 409 Antonio Gates PB	.15	.40
❑ 410 Jeff Saturday PB	.12	.30
❑ 411 Jason Taylor PB	.12	.30
❑ 412 Shawne Merriman PB	.15	.40
❑ 413 Champ Bailey PB	.15	.40
❑ 414 Troy Polamalu PB	.20	.50
❑ 415 Drew Brees PB	.20	.50
❑ 416 Frank Gore PB	.20	.50
❑ 417 Tony Gonzalez PB	.15	.40
❑ 418 Steve Smith PB	.15	.40
❑ 419 Walter Jones PB	.12	.30
❑ 420 Devin Hester PB	.20	.50
❑ 421 Julius Peppers PB	.15	.40
❑ 422 Tony Romo PB	.30	.75
❑ 423 Ronde Barber PB	.12	.30
❑ 424 Larry Johnson PB	.15	.40
❑ 425 LaDainian Tomlinson MVP	.25	.60
❑ 426 Vince Young OROY	.20	.50
❑ 427 DeMeco Ryans DROY	.15	.40
❑ 428 P.Manning/R.Wayne PSH	.30	.75
❑ 429 Drew Brees LL	.20	.50
❑ 430 Asante Samuel PSH	.12	.30
❑ 431 New Orleans Saints PSH	.20	.50
❑ 432 Reggie Bush PSH	.25	.60
❑ 433 Peyton Manning PSH	.30	.75
❑ 434 Robbie Gould PSH	.12	.30
❑ 435 T.Jones/C.Benson PSH	.15	.40
❑ 436 Joseph Addai PSH	.20	.50
❑ 437 Tom Brady PSH	.40	1.00
❑ 438 Colts Defense PSH	.15	.40
❑ 439 Adam Vinatieri PSH	.15	.40
❑ 440 Devin Hester PSH	.20	.50
❑ RH41 Peyton Manning RH	2.50	6.00
❑ RH41A Peyton Manning RH AU	250.00	350.00
❑ SBMVP P.Manning MVP FB/25	125.00	200.00

2008 Topps

Card	Low	High
❑ COMP.FACT.SET (445)	30.00	50.00
❑ COMP.COWBOY SET (445)	30.00	50.00
❑ COMP.GIANTS SET (445)	30.00	50.00
❑ COMP.PACKER SET (445)	30.00	50.00
❑ COMP.PATRIOT SET (445)	30.00	50.00
❑ COMPLETE SET (440)	25.00	50.00
❑ 1 Drew Brees	.25	.60
❑ 2 Jon Kitna	.20	.50
❑ 3 Tom Brady	.40	1.00
❑ 4 Chad Pennington	.20	.50
❑ 5 Steve McNair	.20	.50
❑ 6 Josh McCown	.15	.40
❑ 7 Matt Hasselbeck	.20	.50
❑ 8 David Garrard	.20	.50
❑ 9 Jay Cutler	.25	.60
❑ 10 Matt Schaub	.20	.50
❑ 11 Daunte Culpepper	.20	.50
❑ 12 Kellen Clemens	.20	.50
❑ 13 John Beck	.15	.40
❑ 14 Trent Edwards	.25	.60
❑ 15 Brodie Croyle	.20	.50
❑ 16 Trent Dilfer	.20	.50
❑ 17 Chris Redman	.15	.40
❑ 18 Peyton Manning	.40	1.00
❑ 19 Carson Palmer	.25	.60
❑ 20 Ben Roethlisberger	.40	1.00
❑ 21 Eli Manning	.25	.60
❑ 22 Tony Romo	.40	1.00
❑ 23 Donovan McNabb	.25	.60
❑ 24 Joey Harrington	.20	.50
❑ 25 Jeff Garcia	.20	.50
❑ 26 Derek Anderson	.20	.50
❑ 27 Rex Grossman	.20	.50
❑ 28 Kyle Boller	.15	.40
❑ 29 Sage Rosenfels	.15	.40

Card	Low	High
❑ 30 JaMarcus Russell	.25	.60
❑ 31 Gus Frerotte	.15	.40
❑ 32 Luke McCown	.15	.40
❑ 33 Marc Bulger	.20	.50
❑ 34A Brett Favre	.60	1.50
❑ 34B Brett Favre Lombardi	150.00	300.00
❑ 34C B.Favre Tractor Packers	175.00	300.00
❑ 34D Brett Favre Jets	5.00	12.00
❑ 34E B.Favre Tractor Jets/500	50.00	100.00
❑ 35 Philip Rivers	.25	.60
❑ 36 Vince Young	.20	.50
❑ 37 Kurt Warner	.25	.60
❑ 38 Cleo Lemon	.15	.40
❑ 39 Damon Huard	.15	.40
❑ 40 Jason Campbell	.20	.50
❑ 41 Brian Griese	.15	.40
❑ 42 Tarvaris Jackson	.20	.50
❑ 43 J.P. Losman	.15	.40
❑ 44 Troy Smith	.20	.50
❑ 45 Brady Quinn	.25	.60
❑ 46 Trent Green	.20	.50
❑ 47 Quinn Gray	.15	.40
❑ 48 Alex Smith QB	.20	.50
❑ 49 Todd Collins	.20	.50
❑ 50 Matt Moore	.20	.50
❑ 51 A.J. Feeley	.15	.40
❑ 52 Matt Leinart	.25	.60
❑ 53 Jake Delhomme	.20	.50
❑ 54 Steven Jackson	.25	.60
❑ 55 Willie Parker	.20	.50
❑ 56 Derrick Ward	.20	.50
❑ 57 Julius Jones	.20	.50
❑ 58 DeShaun Foster	.20	.50
❑ 59 Shaun Alexander	.20	.50
❑ 60 Reggie Bush	.25	.60
❑ 61 Clinton Portis	.20	.50
❑ 62 Ron Dayne	.20	.50
❑ 63 Maurice Jones-Drew	.20	.50
❑ 64 Warrick Dunn	.20	.50
❑ 65 Adrian Peterson	.50	1.25
❑ 66 Brian Leonard	.15	.40
❑ 67 Jerious Norwood	.20	.50
❑ 68 Thomas Jones	.20	.50
❑ 69 LaDainian Tomlinson	.30	.75
❑ 70 Cedric Benson	.20	.50
❑ 71 Marion Barber	.25	.60
❑ 72 Brian Westbrook	.20	.50
❑ 73 LenDale White	.20	.50
❑ 74 Ronnie Brown	.20	.50
❑ 75 Travis Henry	.20	.50
❑ 76 Kenny Watson	.15	.40
❑ 77 Fred Taylor	.20	.50
❑ 78 Ryan Grant	.25	.60
❑ 79 Marshawn Lynch	.25	.60
❑ 80 Selvin Young	.15	.40
❑ 81 Joseph Addai	.25	.60
❑ 82 Laurence Maroney	.20	.50
❑ 83 Brandon Jacobs	.20	.50
❑ 84 Willis McGahee	.20	.50
❑ 85 Frank Gore	.20	.50
❑ 86 Edgerrin James	.20	.50
❑ 87 Kevin Jones	.15	.40
❑ 88 DeAngelo Williams	.20	.50
❑ 89 Jamal Lewis	.20	.50
❑ 90 Chester Taylor	.15	.40
❑ 91 Earnest Graham	.15	.40
❑ 92 Justin Fargas	.15	.40
❑ 93 Kolby Smith	.15	.40
❑ 94 Maurice Morris	.15	.40
❑ 95 Larry Johnson	.20	.50
❑ 96 LaMont Jordan	.20	.50
❑ 97 Kenton Keith	.15	.40
❑ 98 Jesse Chatman	.15	.40
❑ 99 Adrian Peterson Bears	.15	.40
❑ 100 Najeh Davenport	.15	.40
❑ 101 Rudi Johnson	.20	.50
❑ 102 Chris Brown	.15	.40
❑ 103 Aaron Stecker	.15	.40
❑ 104 Sammy Morris	.15	.40
❑ 105 Leon Washington	.20	.50
❑ 106 T.J. Duckett	.15	.40
❑ 107 Ladell Betts	.15	.40
❑ 108 Michael Turner	.25	.60
❑ 109 Correll Buckhalter	.20	.50
❑ 110 Ahmad Bradshaw	.20	.50
❑ 111 Greg Jennings	.20	.50
❑ 112 Torry Holt	.20	.50
❑ 113 T.J. Houshmandzadeh	.20	.50
❑ 114 Jerricho Cotchery	.15	.40
❑ 115 Derrick Mason	.15	.40
❑ 116 Kevin Curtis	.15	.40
❑ 117 Kevin Walter	.20	.50
❑ 118 Joey Galloway	.20	.50
❑ 119 Anquan Boldin	.20	.50
❑ 120 Santonio Holmes	.20	.50
❑ 121 Lee Evans	.20	.50
❑ 122 Dwayne Bowe	.20	.50
❑ 123 Laurent Robinson	.15	.40
❑ 124 Wes Welker	.25	.60
❑ 125 Roy Williams WR	.20	.50
❑ 126 Randy Moss	.25	.60
❑ 127 Plaxico Burress	.20	.50
❑ 128 Terrell Owens	.25	.60
❑ 129 Andre Johnson	.20	.50
❑ 130 Roddy White	.20	.50
❑ 131 Brandon Marshall	.20	.50
❑ 132 Donald Driver	.20	.50
❑ 133 Hines Ward	.20	.50
❑ 134 Ike Hilliard	.15	.40
❑ 135 James Jones	.15	.40
❑ 136 Calvin Johnson	.25	.60
❑ 137 Marques Colston	.20	.50
❑ 138 Reggie Wayne	.20	.50
❑ 139 Chad Johnson	.20	.50
❑ 140 Amani Toomer	.20	.50
❑ 141 Bernard Berrian	.20	.50
❑ 142 Steve Smith	.20	.50
❑ 143 Larry Fitzgerald	.25	.60
❑ 144 Chris Chambers	.20	.50
❑ 145 Braylon Edwards	.20	.50
❑ 146 David Patten	.15	.40
❑ 147 Bobby Engram	.15	.40
❑ 148 Shaun McDonald	.15	.40
❑ 149 Anthony Gonzalez	.20	.50
❑ 150 Sidney Rice	.25	.60
❑ 151 Santana Moss	.15	.40
❑ 152 Reggie Brown	.15	.40
❑ 153 Justin Gage	.15	.40
❑ 154 Isaac Bruce	.20	.50
❑ 155 Antwaan Randle El	.15	.40
❑ 156 Roydell Williams	.15	.40
❑ 157 Ronald Curry	.20	.50
❑ 158 Jerry Porter	.20	.50
❑ 159 Patrick Crayton	.20	.50
❑ 160 Donte Stallworth	.20	.50
❑ 161 Nate Burleson	.15	.40
❑ 162 Mike Furrey	.20	.50
❑ 163 Deion Branch	.20	.50
❑ 164 Bobby Wade	.15	.40
❑ 165 Laveranues Coles	.20	.50
❑ 166 Brandon Stokley	.20	.50
❑ 167 Reggie Williams	.20	.50
❑ 168 Vincent Jackson	.15	.40
❑ 169 Joe Jurevicius	.15	.40
❑ 170 Dennis Northcutt	.15	.40
❑ 171 Arnaz Battle	.15	.40
❑ 172 Steve Smith USC	.20	.50
❑ 173 Ted Ginn Jr.	.20	.50
❑ 174 Antonio Gates	.20	.50
❑ 175 Chris Cooley	.20	.50
❑ 176 Owen Daniels	.15	.40
❑ 177 Kellen Winslow	.20	.50
❑ 178 Tony Gonzalez	.20	.50
❑ 179 Jason Witten	.25	.60
❑ 180 Greg Olsen	.20	.50
❑ 181 Jeremy Shockey	.20	.50
❑ 182 Dallas Clark	.20	.50
❑ 183 Donald Lee	.20	.50
❑ 184 Heath Miller	.15	.40
❑ 185 Tony Scheffler	.15	.40
❑ 186 Desmond Clark	.15	.40
❑ 187 Vernon Davis	.15	.40
❑ 188 Alge Crumpler	.20	.50
❑ 189 Zach Miller	.20	.50
❑ 190 Randy McMichael	.15	.40
❑ 191 Bo Scaife	.15	.40
❑ 192 Chris Baker	.15	.40
❑ 193 Jeff King	.15	.40
❑ 194 Marcedes Lewis	.15	.40
❑ 195 Ben Watson	.15	.40
❑ 196 Albert Haynesworth	.15	.40
❑ 197 Kevin Williams	.15	.40
❑ 198 Pat Williams	.15	.40
❑ 199 Tommie Harris	.15	.40
❑ 200 Darnell Dockett	.15	.40
❑ 201 Vince Wilfork	.15	.40
❑ 202 Jamal Williams	.15	.40
❑ 203 Casey Hampton	.15	.40
❑ 204 Amobi Okoye	.15	.40
❑ 205 Patrick Kerney	.15	.40
❑ 206 Gaines Adams	.15	.40
❑ 207 Osi Umenyiora	.15	.40
❑ 208 Mario Williams	.20	.50
❑ 209 Jared Allen	.25	.60
❑ 210 Trent Cole	.15	.40
❑ 211 Aaron Kampman	.20	.50
❑ 212 Kyle Vanden Bosch	.15	.40
❑ 213 Elvis Dumervil	.15	.40
❑ 214 Jason Taylor	.20	.50
❑ 215 Aaron Schobel	.15	.40
❑ 216 Andre Carter	.15	.40
❑ 217 John Abraham	.15	.40
❑ 218 Justin Tuck	.20	.50
❑ 219 Michael Strahan	.20	.50
❑ 220 Kabeer Gbaja-Biamila	.15	.40
❑ 221 Adewale Ogunleye	.15	.40
❑ 222 Julius Peppers	.20	.50
❑ 223 Tamba Hali	.15	.40
❑ 224 Luis Castillo	.15	.40
❑ 225 Jon Beason	.15	.40
❑ 226 D.J. Williams	.15	.40
❑ 227 Ernie Sims	.15	.40
❑ 228 DeMarcus Ware	.20	.50
❑ 229 Nick Barnett	.15	.40
❑ 230 Patrick Willis	.20	.50
❑ 231 Mike Vrabel	.15	.40
❑ 232 Shawne Merriman	.20	.50
❑ 233 Greg Ellis	.15	.40
❑ 234 Thomas Howard	.15	.40
❑ 235 Brian Urlacher	.25	.60
❑ 236 Keith Bulluck	.15	.40
❑ 237 London Fletcher	.15	.40
❑ 238 DeMeco Ryans	.20	.50
❑ 239 David Harris	.15	.40
❑ 240 Angelo Crowell	.15	.40
❑ 241 James Harrison RC	1.50	4.00
❑ 242 Julian Peterson	.15	.40
❑ 243 Lance Briggs	.15	.40
❑ 244 Lofa Tatupu	.20	.50
❑ 245 Ray Lewis	.25	.60
❑ 246 Shaun Phillips	.15	.40
❑ 247 Antonio Pierce	.15	.40
❑ 248 Antonio Cromartie	.15	.40
❑ 249 Marcus Trufant	.15	.40
❑ 250 Asante Samuel	.15	.40
❑ 251 Anthony Henry	.15	.40
❑ 252 Leigh Bodden	.15	.40
❑ 253 Antrel Rolle	.15	.40
❑ 254 Roderick Hood	.15	.40
❑ 255 DeAngelo Hall	.15	.40
❑ 256 Dre Bly	.15	.40
❑ 257 Leon Hall	.15	.40
❑ 258 Ronde Barber	.15	.40
❑ 259 Al Harris	.15	.40
❑ 260 Terence Newman	.15	.40
❑ 261 Champ Bailey	.15	.40
❑ 262 Aaron Ross	.15	.40
❑ 263 Bob Sanders	.20	.50
❑ 264 Reggie Nelson	.15	.40
❑ 265 Marvin Harrison	.25	.60
❑ 266 Ed Reed	.20	.50
❑ 267 O.J. Atogwe	.15	.40
❑ 268 Ken Hamlin	.15	.40
❑ 269 Kerry Rhodes	.15	.40
❑ 270 Clinton Hart	.15	.40
❑ 271 Atari Bigby	.15	.40
❑ 272 Sean Jones	.15	.40
❑ 273 Darren Sharper	.20	.50
❑ 274 Roy Williams S	.20	.50
❑ 275 Troy Polamalu	.25	.60
❑ 276 John Lynch	.20	.50
❑ 277 Antoine Bethea	.15	.40
❑ 278 LaRon Landry	.20	.50
❑ 279 Walter Jones	.15	.40
❑ 280 Jonathan Ogden	.15	.40
❑ 281 Joe Thomas	.20	.50
❑ 282 Nick Folk	.15	.40
❑ 283 Rob Bironas	.15	.40
❑ 284 Devin Hester	.25	.60
❑ 285 Josh Cribbs	.25	.60
❑ 286 Tom Brady LL	.30	.75
❑ 287 Drew Brees LL	.20	.50
❑ 288 Tony Romo LL	.30	.75
❑ 289 LaDainian Tomlinson LL	.25	.60
❑ 290 Adrian Peterson LL	.40	1.00
❑ 291 Brian Westbrook LL	.15	.40
❑ 292 Reggie Wayne LL	.15	.40

Card		
❑ 293 Randy Moss LL	.20	.50
❑ 294 Chad Johnson LL	.15	.40
❑ 295 Randy Moss LL	.20	.50
❑ 296 Matt Hasselbeck PB	.15	.40
❑ 297 Tony Romo PB	.30	.75
❑ 298 Adrian Peterson PB	.40	1.00
❑ 299 Marion Barber PB	.20	.50
❑ 300 Brian Westbrook PB	.15	.40
❑ 301 Larry Fitzgerald PB	.20	.50
❑ 302 Terrell Owens PB	.20	.50
❑ 303 Osi Umenyiora PB	.15	.40
❑ 304 Lofa Tatupu PB	.15	.40
❑ 305 Jason Witten PB	.20	.50
❑ 306 Torry Holt PB	.15	.40
❑ 307 Donald Driver PB	.15	.40
❑ 308 Peyton Manning PB	.30	.75
❑ 309 Ben Roethlisberger PB	.30	.75
❑ 310 Joseph Addai PB	.20	.50
❑ 311 Reggie Wayne PB	.15	.40
❑ 312 Braylon Edwards PB	.15	.40
❑ 313 Devin Hester PB	.20	.50
❑ 314 Champ Bailey PB	.12	.30
❑ 315 Ed Reed PB	.15	.40
❑ 316 Eli Manning PSH	.20	.50
❑ 317 David Tyree PSH	.15	.40
❑ 318 Plaxico Burress PSH	.15	.40
❑ 319 Lawrence Tynes PSH	.15	.40
❑ 320 Patriots Defense PSH	.20	.50
❑ 321 R.W. McQuarters PSH	.15	.40
❑ 322 Ryan Grant PSH	.20	.50
❑ 323 Philip Rivers PSH	.20	.50
❑ 324 David Garrard PSH	.15	.40
❑ 325 Laurence Maroney PSH	.15	.40
❑ 326 Seattle Seahawks PSH	.15	.40
❑ 327 San Diego Chargers PSH	.15	.40
❑ 328 Tom Brady MVP	.30	.75
❑ 329 Adrian Peterson OROY	.40	1.00
❑ 330 Patrick Willis DROY	.15	.40
❑ 331 Matt Ryan RC	2.50	6.00
❑ 331B Matt Ryan No Helm	60.00	100.00
❑ 332 Brian Brohm RC	.60	1.50
❑ 332B Brian Brohm No Helm	15.00	40.00
❑ 333 Andre Woodson RC	.60	1.50
❑ 334 Chad Henne RC	1.00	2.50
❑ 335 Joe Flacco RC	2.00	5.00
❑ 336 John David Booty RC	.60	1.50
❑ 337 Colt Brennan RC	1.00	2.50
❑ 338 Dennis Dixon RC	.60	1.50
❑ 339 Erik Ainge RC	.60	1.50
❑ 340 Josh Johnson RC	.60	1.50
❑ 341 Kevin O'Connell RC	.60	1.50
❑ 342 Matt Flynn RC	.60	1.50
❑ 343 Sam Keller RC	.60	1.50
❑ 344 Harry Douglas RC	.50	1.25
❑ 345 Anthony Morelli RC	.60	1.50
❑ 346 Darren McFadden RC	1.25	3.00
❑ 346B Darren McFadden FB	20.00	50.00
❑ 347 Rashard Mendenhall RC	1.25	3.00
❑ 347B Rashard Mendenhall FB	20.00	50.00
❑ 348 Jonathan Stewart RC	1.25	3.00
❑ 348B Jonathan Stewart No Helm	25.00	50.00
❑ 349 Felix Jones RC	1.25	3.00
❑ 350 Jamaal Charles RC	1.00	2.50
❑ 351 Chris Johnson RC	2.00	5.00
❑ 352 Ray Rice RC	1.25	3.00
❑ 353 Mike Hart RC	.60	1.50
❑ 354 Kevin Smith RC	1.00	2.50
❑ 355 Steve Slaton RC	.75	2.00
❑ 356 Matt Forte RC	1.25	3.00
❑ 357 Tashard Choice RC	.60	1.50
❑ 358 D.Rodgers-Cromartie RC	.60	1.50
❑ 359 Cory Boyd RC	.50	1.25
❑ 360 Allen Patrick RC	.50	1.25
❑ 361 Thomas Brown RC	.60	1.50
❑ 362 Justin Forsett RC	.60	1.50
❑ 363 DeSean Jackson RC	1.25	3.00
❑ 364 Malcolm Kelly RC	.60	1.50
❑ 365 Limas Sweed RC UER 362	.60	1.50
❑ 366 Mario Manningham RC	.60	1.50
❑ 367 James Hardy RC	.50	1.25
❑ 368 Early Doucet RC	.60	1.50
❑ 369 Donnie Avery RC	.75	2.00
❑ 370 Dexter Jackson RC	.60	1.50
❑ 371 Devin Thomas RC	.60	1.50
❑ 372 Jordy Nelson RC	.75	2.00
❑ 373 Keenan Burton RC	.50	1.25
❑ 374 Chris Williams RC	.50	1.25
❑ 375 Earl Bennett RC	.60	1.50
❑ 376 Jerome Simpson RC	.50	1.25
❑ 377 Andre Caldwell RC	.60	1.50
❑ 378 Josh Morgan RC	.60	1.50
❑ 379 Fred Davis RC	.60	1.50
❑ 380 John Carlson RC	.60	1.50
❑ 381 Martellus Bennett RC	.60	1.50
❑ 382 Martin Rucker RC	.50	1.25
❑ 383 Jermichael Finley RC	.60	1.50
❑ 384 Dustin Keller RC	.60	1.50
❑ 385 Jacob Tamme RC	.60	1.50
❑ 386 Kellen Davis RC	.40	1.00
❑ 387 Jake Long RC	.60	1.50
❑ 388 Sam Baker RC	.40	1.00
❑ 389 Jeff Otah RC	.50	1.25
❑ 390 Owen Schmitt RC	.60	1.50
❑ 391 Chevis Jackson RC	.50	1.25
❑ 392 Jacob Hester RC	.60	1.50
❑ 393 Glenn Dorsey RC	.60	1.50
❑ 394 Sedrick Ellis RC	.60	1.50
❑ 395 Kentwan Balmer RC	.50	1.25
❑ 396 Pat Sims RC	.50	1.25
❑ 397 Marcus Harrison RC	.60	1.50
❑ 398 Dre Moore RC	.50	1.25
❑ 399 Red Bryant RC	.40	1.00
❑ 400 Trevor Laws RC	.60	1.50
❑ 401 Chris Long RC	.60	1.50
❑ 402 Vernon Gholston RC	.60	1.50
❑ 403 Derrick Harvey RC	.50	1.25
❑ 404 Calais Campbell RC	.50	1.25
❑ 405 Terrence Wheatley RC	.50	1.25
❑ 406 Phillip Merling RC	.50	1.25
❑ 407 Chris Ellis RC	.50	1.25
❑ 408 Lawrence Jackson RC	.50	1.25
❑ 409 Dan Connor RC	.60	1.50
❑ 410 Curtis Lofton RC	.60	1.50
❑ 411 Jerod Mayo RC	.75	2.00
❑ 412 Tavares Gooden RC	.50	1.25
❑ 413 Beau Bell RC	.50	1.25
❑ 414 Philip Wheeler RC	.60	1.50
❑ 415 Vince Hall RC	.40	1.00
❑ 416 Jonathan Goff RC	.50	1.25
❑ 417 Keith Rivers RC	.60	1.50
❑ 418 Ali Highsmith RC	.40	1.00
❑ 419 Xavier Adibi RC	.50	1.25
❑ 420 Erin Henderson RC	.50	1.25
❑ 421 Bruce Davis RC	.60	1.50
❑ 422 Jordon Dizon RC	.60	1.50
❑ 423 Shawn Crable RC	.60	1.50
❑ 424 Geno Hayes RC	.40	1.00
❑ 425 Mike Jenkins RC	.60	1.50
❑ 426 Aqib Talib RC	.60	1.50
❑ 427 Leodis McKelvin RC	.60	1.50
❑ 428 Terrell Thomas RC	.50	1.25
❑ 429 Reggie Smith RC	.50	1.25
❑ 430 Antoine Cason RC	.60	1.50
❑ 431 Patrick Lee RC	.60	1.50
❑ 432 Tracy Porter RC	.75	2.00
❑ 433 Kenny Phillips RC	.60	1.50
❑ 434 Simeon Castille RC	.50	1.25
❑ 435 Eddie Royal RC	1.00	2.50
❑ 436 Thomas DeCoud RC	.40	1.00
❑ 437 Marcus Griffin RC	.40	1.00
❑ 438 Charles Godfrey RC	.50	1.25
❑ 439 Tyrell Johnson RC	.60	1.50
❑ 440 Jamar Adams RC	.50	1.25
❑ RH42 Eli Manning RH	2.50	6.00
❑ RHA42 Eli Manning RH AU	250.00	400.00
❑ SBAEM Eli Manning FB AU/50	200.00	350.00
❑ SBEM Eli Manning FB/99	50.00	100.00

2009 Topps

Card		
❑ COMPLETE SET (440)	25.00	50.00
❑ COMP.FACT.SET (445)	30.00	50.00
❑ 1 Hines Ward	.20	.50
❑ 2 Ryan Torain	.15	.40
❑ 3 Harry Douglas	.15	.40
❑ 4 James Jones	.15	.40
❑ 5 Willis McGahee	.20	.50
❑ 6 Owen Daniels	.15	.40
❑ 7 Peyton Hillis	.15	.40
❑ 8 Hank Baskett	.15	.40
❑ 9 Leonard Davis	.15	.40
❑ 10 Peyton Manning	.40	1.00
❑ 11 Shawne Merriman	.20	.50
❑ 12 Laurence Maroney	.20	.50
❑ 13 Chris Hope	.15	.40
❑ 14 Joe Thomas	.20	.50
❑ 15 Marshawn Lynch	.20	.50
❑ 16 Kevin Williams	.15	.40
❑ 17 London Fletcher	.15	.40
❑ 18 Jason Campbell	.20	.50
❑ 19 Antonio Bryant	.20	.50
❑ 20 LaDainian Tomlinson	.25	.60
❑ 21 Marc Bulger	.20	.50
❑ 22 Vernon Davis	.15	.40
❑ 23 Justin Tuck	.20	.50
❑ 24 Deuce McAllister	.20	.50
❑ 25 T.J. Houshmandzadeh	.20	.50
❑ 26 Bernard Berrian	.20	.50
❑ 27 Ryan Grant	.20	.50
❑ 28 Tashard Choice	.20	.50
❑ 29 Michael Jenkins	.15	.40
❑ 30 Brian Dawkins	.20	.50
❑ 31 Michael Turner	.20	.50
❑ 32 Anquan Boldin	.20	.50
❑ 33 Justin Gage	.15	.40
❑ 34 Michael Bush	.20	.50
❑ 35 Braylon Edwards	.20	.50
❑ 36 Rashard Mendenhall	.20	.50
❑ 37 Leon Washington	.20	.50
❑ 38 Ricky Williams	.20	.50
❑ 39 Rashean Mathis	.15	.40
❑ 40 Ray Lewis	.25	.60
❑ 41 Josh Cribbs	.25	.60
❑ 42 James Hardy	.20	.50
❑ 43 Joe Flacco	.25	.60
❑ 44 Terrell Suggs	.15	.40
❑ 45 Jay Cutler	.25	.60
❑ 46 Glenn Holt	.15	.40
❑ 47 D.J. Williams	.15	.40
❑ 48 Andre Davis	.15	.40
❑ 49 Dwayne Bowe	.20	.50
❑ 50 DeAngelo Williams	.25	.60
❑ 51 Wes Welker	.25	.60
❑ 52 Willie Parker	.20	.50
❑ 53 Dominique Rodgers-Cromartie	.15	.40
❑ 54A Tony Romo	.40	1.00
❑ 54B Tony Romo SP Golf	25.00	50.00
❑ 55 Steve Slaton	.20	.50
❑ 56 Jason Witten	.25	.60
❑ 57 Terence Newman	.15	.40
❑ 58 Jeff Garcia	.20	.50
❑ 59 Barrett Ruud	.15	.40
❑ 60 Andre Johnson	.20	.50
❑ 61 Jordy Nelson	.20	.50
❑ 62 Davone Bess	.20	.50
❑ 63 Jacob Hester	.15	.40
❑ 64 Jason Avant	.15	.40
❑ 65 Joseph Addai	.25	.60
❑ 66 Dennis Northcutt	.15	.40
❑ 67 Maurice Morris	.15	.40
❑ 68 Shaun Hill	.20	.50
❑ 69 Dustin Keller	.15	.40
❑ 70 Antonio Gates	.20	.50
❑ 71 BenJarvus Green-Ellis RC	.40	1.00
❑ 72 Brent Celek	.20	.50
❑ 73 Ray Rice	.25	.60
❑ 74 Vince Young	.20	.50
❑ 75 Maurice Jones-Drew	.20	.50
❑ 76 Devery Henderson	.15	.40
❑ 77 Domenik Hixon	.15	.40
❑ 78 Mike Walker	.20	.50
❑ 79 Miles Austin	.25	.60
❑ 80 DeMarcus Ware	.20	.50
❑ 81 Jordan Gross	.15	.40
❑ 82 Chris Samuels	.15	.40
❑ 83 Jay Ratliff	.25	.60
❑ 84 Pat Williams	.15	.40
❑ 85 Tony Gonzalez	.20	.50
❑ 86 Andre Gurode	.15	.40
❑ 87 Nick Mangold	.15	.40
❑ 88 Bobby Engram	.15	.40
❑ 89 Osi Umenyiora	.20	.50
❑ 90 Brian Westbrook	.20	.50
❑ 91 Jason Peters	.15	.40
❑ 92 Shaun Rogers	.15	.40

Card	Low	High
❑ 93 Kris Jenkins	.15	.40
❑ 94 Kevin Mawae	.15	.40
❑ 95 Ronnie Brown	.20	.50
❑ 96 Joey Galloway	.20	.50
❑ 97 Chris Snee	.15	.40
❑ 98 Nick Collins	.15	.40
❑ 99 Adrian Wilson	.15	.40
❑ 100 Reggie Wayne	.20	.50
❑ 101 Kellen Clemens	.15	.40
❑ 102 LaRon Landry	.15	.40
❑ 103 Walter Jones	.15	.40
❑ 104 Josh Morgan	.15	.40
❑ 105 Joey Porter	.20	.50
❑ 106 Martellus Bennett	.15	.40
❑ 107 Kirk Morrison	.15	.40
❑ 108 Bradie James	.15	.40
❑ 109 Le'Ron McClain	.20	.50
❑ 110A Adrian Peterson	.50	1.25
❑ 110B A.Peterson SP Red Shirt	25.00	50.00
❑ 111 Trent Edwards	.20	.50
❑ 112 Carson Palmer	.25	.60
❑ 113 Jamal Lewis	.20	.50
❑ 114 Champ Bailey	.20	.50
❑ 115A Tom Brady	.40	1.00
❑ 115B T.Brady SP No helm	40.00	80.00
❑ 116 Dominic Rhodes	.15	.40
❑ 117 David Garrard	.20	.50
❑ 118 Jamaal Charles	.20	.50
❑ 119 Fred Taylor	.20	.50
❑ 120 Matt Leinart	.20	.50
❑ 121 Ted Ginn	.20	.50
❑ 122 Sammy Morris	.15	.40
❑ 123 Jerricho Cotchery	.15	.40
❑ 124 JaMarcus Russell	.20	.50
❑ 125 Thomas Jones	.20	.50
❑ 126 Mewelde Moore	.15	.40
❑ 127 Philip Rivers	.25	.60
❑ 128 Antonio Cromartie	.15	.40
❑ 129 Bo Scaife	.15	.40
❑ 130 Jonathan Vilma	.15	.40
❑ 131 Kurt Warner	.25	.60
❑ 132 Steve Breaston	.20	.50
❑ 133 Roddy White	.20	.50
❑ 134 Jake Delhomme	.20	.50
❑ 135 Darren McFadden	.25	.60
❑ 136 Muhsin Muhammad	.20	.50
❑ 137 Greg Olsen	.15	.40
❑ 138 Felix Jones	.25	.60
❑ 139 Ernie Sims	.15	.40
❑ 140 Ed Reed	.20	.50
❑ 141 Aaron Rodgers	.25	.60
❑ 142 Donald Lee	.15	.40
❑ 143 Visanthe Shiancoe	.15	.40
❑ 144 Drew Brees	.25	.60
❑ 145A Ben Roethlisberger	.40	1.00
❑ 145B Roethlisbrgr SP Trophy	30.00	60.00
❑ 146 Jason David	.15	.40
❑ 147 Samari Rolle	.15	.40
❑ 148 Brandon Jacobs	.20	.50
❑ 149 DeSean Jackson	.20	.50
❑ 150 Brady Quinn	.20	.50
❑ 151 Isaac Bruce	.20	.50
❑ 152 Matt Hasselbeck	.20	.50
❑ 153 Lofa Tatupu	.20	.50
❑ 154 Oshiomogho Atogwe	.15	.40
❑ 155 Troy Polamalu	.25	.60
❑ 156 Marvin Harrison	.25	.60
❑ 157 Roscoe Parrish	.15	.40
❑ 158 Paul Posluszny	.20	.50
❑ 159 Eli Manning	.25	.60
❑ 160 Randy Moss	.25	.60
❑ 161 Earnest Graham	.15	.40
❑ 162 Derrick Brooks	.20	.50
❑ 163 Chris Cooley	.20	.50
❑ 164 Antwaan Randle El	.15	.40
❑ 165 Santonio Holmes	.20	.50
❑ 166 Ronde Barber	.15	.40
❑ 167 Donnie Avery	.20	.50
❑ 168 Nate Clements	.15	.40
❑ 169 Kevin Boss	.15	.40
❑ 170 Jon Beason	.15	.40
❑ 171 Jeremy Shockey	.15	.40
❑ 172 Antoine Winfield	.15	.40
❑ 173 Charles Woodson	.20	.50
❑ 174 Terrell Owens	.25	.60
❑ 175 Chris Johnson	.25	.60
❑ 176 Charles Tillman	.15	.40
❑ 177 Julius Peppers	.20	.50
❑ 178 John Abraham	.15	.40
❑ 179 Karlos Dansby	.15	.40
❑ 180 Steve Smith USC	.20	.50
❑ 181 Edgerrin James	.20	.50
❑ 182 Cortland Finnegan	.15	.40
❑ 183 Keith Bulluck	.15	.40
❑ 184 Stephen Cooper RC	.20	.50
❑ 185 LenDale White	.20	.50
❑ 186 Vincent Jackson	.20	.50
❑ 187 LaMarr Woodley	.15	.40
❑ 188 Nnamdi Asomugha	.15	.40
❑ 189 Calvin Pace	.15	.40
❑ 190 Kellen Winslow Jr.	.20	.50
❑ 191 Brandon Meriweather	.15	.40
❑ 192 Matt Cassel	.20	.50
❑ 193 Greg Camarillo	.20	.50
❑ 194 Jarrad Page	.15	.40
❑ 195 Tim Hightower	.20	.50
❑ 196 Larry Johnson	.20	.50
❑ 197 Matt Jones	.20	.50
❑ 198 Bob Sanders	.20	.50
❑ 199 Dwight Freeney	.20	.50
❑ 200 Brandon Marshall	.20	.50
❑ 201 Mario Williams	.20	.50
❑ 202 Tony Scheffler	.15	.40
❑ 203 D'Qwell Jackson	.15	.40
❑ 204 Keith Rivers	.15	.40
❑ 205 Larry Fitzgerald	.25	.60
❑ 206 Chad Ochocinco	.20	.50
❑ 207 Fred Jackson	.20	.50
❑ 208 Bart Scott	.15	.40
❑ 209 Todd Heap	.15	.40
❑ 210 Clinton Portis	.20	.50
❑ 211 Santana Moss	.20	.50
❑ 212 Aqib Talib	.15	.40
❑ 213 Warrick Dunn	.20	.50
❑ 214 Torry Holt	.20	.50
❑ 215 Matt Ryan	.25	.60
❑ 216 Julius Jones	.20	.50
❑ 217 Patrick Willis	.20	.50
❑ 218 Correll Buckhalter	.15	.40
❑ 219 Derrick Ward	.20	.50
❑ 220 Steven Jackson	.20	.50
❑ 221 Pierre Thomas	.20	.50
❑ 222 Tarvaris Jackson	.20	.50
❑ 223 Donald Driver	.20	.50
❑ 224 Devin Hester	.25	.60
❑ 225 Jonathan Stewart	.20	.50
❑ 226 Steve Smith	.20	.50
❑ 227 Jerious Norwood	.20	.50
❑ 228 Albert Haynesworth	.15	.40
❑ 229 Darren Sproles	.20	.50
❑ 230 Frank Gore	.20	.50
❑ 231 James Harrison	.25	.60
❑ 232 Zach Miller	.15	.40
❑ 233 Darrelle Revis	.20	.50
❑ 234 Richard Seymour	.15	.40
❑ 235 Matt Forte	.25	.60
❑ 236 Ellis Hobbs	.15	.40
❑ 237 Anthony Fasano	.15	.40
❑ 238 Chad Pennington	.20	.50
❑ 239 Tyler Thigpen	.15	.40
❑ 240 Donovan McNabb	.25	.60
❑ 241 Robert Mathis	.15	.40
❑ 242 Kevin Walter	.20	.50
❑ 243 Matt Schaub	.20	.50
❑ 244 Brandon McDonald	.15	.40
❑ 245 Marion Barber	.25	.60
❑ 246 Cedric Benson	.20	.50
❑ 247 Lee Evans	.20	.50
❑ 248 Derrick Mason	.15	.40
❑ 249 Eddie Royal	.20	.50
❑ 250 Reggie Bush	.25	.60
❑ 251 Dallas Clark	.20	.50
❑ 252 Anthony Gonzalez	.20	.50
❑ 253 Derrick Johnson	.15	.40
❑ 254 Jerod Mayo	.20	.50
❑ 255 Kevin Smith	.20	.50
❑ 256 Laveranues Coles	.20	.50
❑ 257 Gibril Wilson	.15	.40
❑ 258 Justin Fargas	.15	.40
❑ 259 Lance Briggs	.20	.50
❑ 260 Greg Jennings	.25	.60
❑ 261 Kyle Orton	.20	.50
❑ 262 Michael Griffin	.15	.40
❑ 263 Kerry Collins	.20	.50
❑ 264 Chris Chambers	.20	.50
❑ 265 Jared Allen	.25	.60
❑ 266 Heath Miller	.20	.50
❑ 267 James Farrior	.15	.40
❑ 268 John Carlson	.20	.50
❑ 269 J.T. O'Sullivan	.15	.40
❑ 270 Calvin Johnson	.25	.60
❑ 271 Asante Samuel	.15	.40
❑ 272 Ahmad Bradshaw	.20	.50
❑ 273 Trent Cole	.15	.40
❑ 274 Lance Moore	.20	.50
❑ 275 Marques Colston	.20	.50
❑ 276 Chester Taylor	.15	.40
❑ 277 Aaron Kampman	.20	.50
❑ 278 Derrick Harvey	.15	.40
❑ 279 Brian Urlacher	.25	.60
❑ 280 Roy Williams WR	.20	.50
❑ 281 Drew Brees LL	.20	.50
❑ 282 Kurt Warner LL	.20	.50
❑ 283 Jay Cutler LL	.20	.50
❑ 284 Adrian Peterson LL	.40	1.00
❑ 285 Michael Turner LL	.15	.40
❑ 286 DeAngelo Williams LL	.20	.50
❑ 287 Andre Johnson LL	.15	.40
❑ 288 Larry Fitzgerald LL	.20	.50
❑ 289 Steve Smith LL	.15	.40
❑ 290 Drew Brees PB	.20	.50
❑ 291 Adrian Peterson PB	.40	1.00
❑ 292 Larry Fitzgerald PB	.20	.50
❑ 293 Anquan Boldin PB	.15	.40
❑ 294 Steve Smith PB	.15	.40
❑ 295 Jason Witten PB	.20	.50
❑ 296 DeMarcus Ware PB	.15	.40
❑ 297 Jon Beason PB	.12	.30
❑ 298 James Harrison PB	.20	.50
❑ 299 Michael Turner PB	.15	.40
❑ 300 Peyton Manning PB	.30	.75
❑ 301 Eli Manning PB	.20	.50
❑ 302 Thomas Jones PB	.15	.40
❑ 303 Andre Johnson PB	.15	.40
❑ 304 Brandon Marshall PB	.15	.40
❑ 305 Reggie Wayne PB	.15	.40
❑ 306 Tony Gonzalez PB	.15	.40
❑ 307 Ray Lewis PB	.20	.50
❑ 308 Darrelle Revis PB	.15	.40
❑ 309 Joey Porter PB	.15	.40
❑ 310 Donovan McNabb PH	.20	.50
❑ 311 Joe Flacco PH	.20	.50
❑ 312 Larry Fitzgerald PH	.20	.50
❑ 313 Darren Sproles PH	.15	.40
❑ 314 Ed Reed PH	.15	.40
❑ 315 Kurt Warner PH	.20	.50
❑ 316 Willie Parker PH	.15	.40
❑ 317 Asante Samuel PH	.12	.30
❑ 318 Troy Polamalu PH	.20	.50
❑ 319 Larry Fitzgerald PH	.20	.50
❑ 320 Santonio Holmes PH	.15	.40
❑ 321 Peyton Manning MVP	.30	.75
❑ 322 James Harrison D-POY	.20	.50
❑ 323 Matt Ryan O-ROY	.20	.50
❑ 324 Jerod Mayo D-ROY	.15	.40
❑ 325 Jonathan Stewart CC DeAngelo Williams	.20	.50
❑ 326 Ed Reed CC Ray Lewis	.20	.50
❑ 327 LenDale White CC Chris Johnson	.20	.50
❑ 328 Thomas Jones CC Leon Washington	.15	.40
❑ 329 Ben Roethlisberger CC Willie Parker	.30	.75
❑ 330 DeAngelo Williams LL	.20	.50
❑ 331 Aaron Brown RC	.60	1.50
❑ 332 B.J. Raji RC	.75	2.00
❑ 333 Aaron Maybin RC	.60	1.50
❑ 334 Alphonso Smith RC	.50	1.25
❑ 335 Hakeem Nicks RC	1.25	3.00
❑ 336 Andre Smith RC	.60	1.50
❑ 337 Andy Levitre RC	.50	1.25
❑ 338 Asher Allen RC	.50	1.25
❑ 339 Austin Collie RC	1.25	3.00
❑ 340A Aaron Curry RC	.75	2.00
❑ 340B A.Curry SP FB in hand	15.00	30.00
❑ 341 Brandon Gibson RC	.60	1.50
❑ 342 Michael Oher RC	1.25	3.00
❑ 343 Brandon Tate RC	.50	1.25
❑ 344 Brandon Underwood RC	.60	1.50
❑ 345 Javon Ringer RC	.60	1.50
❑ 346 Brian Hartline RC	.60	1.50
❑ 347 Brian Orakpo RC	.75	2.00
❑ 348 Mike Wallace RC	1.25	3.00
❑ 349 Brooks Foster RC	.50	1.25
❑ 350 Brian Cushing RC	.75	2.00

Card	Low	High
❑ 351 Chase Coffman RC	.50	1.25
❑ 352 Darius Butler RC	.60	1.50
❑ 353 Clay Matthews RC	1.00	2.50
❑ 354 Clint Sintim RC	.60	1.50
❑ 355 Kenny Britt RC	1.00	2.50
❑ 356 Patrick Turner RC	.50	1.25
❑ 357 Courtney Greene RC	.40	1.00
❑ 358 Curtis Painter RC	.60	1.50
❑ 359 D.J. Moore RC	.50	1.25
❑ 360 Chris Wells RC	1.50	4.00
❑ 361A Darrius Heyward-Bey RC	1.00	2.50
❑ 361B Heywrd-By SP FB in hands	20.00	40.00
❑ 362 Demetrius Byrd RC	.50	1.25
❑ 363 Deon Butler RC	.60	1.50
❑ 364 Derrick Williams RC	.60	1.50
❑ 365 Pat White RC	1.00	2.50
❑ 366 Duke Robinson RC	.40	1.00
❑ 367 Eben Britton RC	.50	1.25
❑ 368 Eugene Monroe RC	.50	1.25
❑ 369 Everette Brown RC	.60	1.50
❑ 370A Donald Brown RC	1.25	3.00
❑ 370B D.Brown SP No helm	20.00	40.00
❑ 371 Gartrell Johnson RC	.50	1.25
❑ 372 Glen Coffee RC	.75	2.00
❑ 373 Andre Brown RC	.50	1.25
❑ 374 James Casey RC	.50	1.25
❑ 375A Percy Harvin RC	2.00	5.00
❑ 375B P.Harvin SP No helm	25.00	50.00
❑ 376 Roy Miller RC	.60	1.50
❑ 377 Jamon Meredith RC	.50	1.25
❑ 378 Jared Cook RC	.50	1.25
❑ 379 Jarett Dillard RC	.60	1.50
❑ 380A Jeremy Maclin RC	1.25	3.00
❑ 380B J.Maclin SP FB in hand	25.00	50.00
❑ 381 Jason Williams RC	.60	1.50
❑ 382 Javarris Williams RC	.50	1.25
❑ 383 Cedric Peerman RC	.50	1.25
❑ 384 Jason Smith RC	.50	1.25
❑ 385 Fili Moala RC	.50	1.25
❑ 386 Rey Maualuga RC	1.00	2.50
❑ 387 Travis Beckum RC	.50	1.25
❑ 388 Juaquin Iglesias RC	.60	1.50
❑ 389 Connor Barwin RC	.50	1.25
❑ 390A Knowshon Moreno RC	1.50	4.00
❑ 390B K.Moreno SP Cutting	20.00	40.00
❑ 391 Kenny McKinley RC	.60	1.50
❑ 392 Kevin Ellison RC	.50	1.25
❑ 393 Larry English RC	.60	1.50
❑ 394 Marko Mitchell RC	.50	1.25
❑ 395 Louis Delmas RC	.60	1.50
❑ 396 Shonn Greene RC	1.25	3.00
❑ 397 Malcolm Jenkins RC	.60	1.50
❑ 398 Manuel Johnson RC	.50	1.25
❑ 399 Marcus Freeman RC	.60	1.50
❑ 400 LeSean McCoy RC	1.25	3.00
❑ 401 Zack Follett RC	.40	1.00
❑ 402 Shawn Nelson RC	.50	1.25
❑ 403 Rashad Jennings RC	.60	1.50
❑ 404 Michael Hamlin RC	.50	1.25
❑ 405 Michael Johnson RC	.40	1.00
❑ 406 Brandon Pettigrew RC	.75	2.00
❑ 407 Mike Goodson RC	.60	1.50
❑ 408 Mike Mickens RC	.50	1.25
❑ 409 Mike Teel RC	.60	1.50
❑ 410 Mike Thomas RC	.60	1.50
❑ 411 Brian Robiskie RC	.60	1.50
❑ 412 Mohamed Massaquoi RC	.60	1.50
❑ 413 Nate Davis RC	.60	1.50
❑ 414 Patrick Chung RC	.60	1.50
❑ 415 Cornelius Ingram RC	.40	1.00
❑ 416 James Davis RC	.60	1.50
❑ 417 Peria Jerry RC	.50	1.25
❑ 418 Phil Loadholt RC	.50	1.25
❑ 419 Ramses Barden RC	.50	1.25
❑ 420A Michael Crabtree RC	1.50	4.00
❑ 420B M.Crabtree SP No helm	25.00	50.00
❑ 421 Rashad Johnson RC	.50	1.25
❑ 422 Johnny Knox RC	1.00	2.50
❑ 423 Rhett Bomar RC	.50	1.25
❑ 424 Robert Ayers RC	.60	1.50
❑ 425 James Laurinaitis RC	.75	2.00
❑ 426 Sammie Stroughter RC	.60	1.50
❑ 427 Scott McKillop RC	.50	1.25
❑ 428 Sean Smith RC	.60	1.50
❑ 429 Sen'Derrick Marks RC	.40	1.00
❑ 430A Matthew Stafford RC	2.00	5.00
❑ 430B M.Stafford SP No helm	20.00	50.00
❑ 431 Louis Murphy RC	.60	1.50
❑ 432 Stephen McGee RC	.60	1.50
❑ 433 Tiquan Underwood RC	.50	1.25
❑ 434 Tom Brandstater RC	.60	1.50
❑ 435A Josh Freeman RC	1.25	3.00
❑ 435B J.Freeman SP No helm	20.00	40.00
❑ 436 Tyson Jackson RC	.60	1.50
❑ 437 Victor Harris RC	.60	1.50
❑ 438 Vontae Davis RC	.60	1.50
❑ 439 William Moore RC	.50	1.25
❑ 440A Mark Sanchez RC	2.50	6.00
❑ 440B M.Sanchez SP w/helmet	40.00	80.00
❑ 441 Barack Obama SP	30.00	80.00
❑ RH43 Santonio Holmes RH	1.00	2.50
❑ RH43A Santonio Holmes RH AU	125.00	250.00

1996 Topps Chrome

Card	Low	High
❑ COMPLETE SET (165)	40.00	100.00
❑ 1 Troy Aikman	1.00	2.50
❑ 2 Kevin Greene	.20	.50
❑ 3 Robert Brooks	.40	1.00
❑ 4 Junior Seau	.40	1.00
❑ 5 Brett Perriman	.07	.20
❑ 6 Cortez Kennedy	.07	.20
❑ 7 Orlando Thomas	.07	.20
❑ 8 Anthony Miller	.20	.50
❑ 9 Jeff Blake	.40	1.00
❑ 10 Trent Dilfer	.40	1.00
❑ 11 Heath Shuler	.20	.50
❑ 12 Michael Jackson	.20	.50
❑ 13 Merton Hanks	.07	.20
❑ 14 Dale Carter	.07	.20
❑ 15 Eric Metcalf	.07	.20
❑ 16 Barry Sanders	1.50	4.00
❑ 17 Joey Galloway	.40	1.00
❑ 18 Bryan Cox	.07	.20
❑ 19 Harvey Williams	.07	.20
❑ 20 Terrell Davis	.60	1.50
❑ 21 Darnay Scott	.20	.50
❑ 22 Kerry Collins	.40	1.00
❑ 23 Warren Sapp	.07	.20
❑ 24 Michael Westbrook	.40	1.00
❑ 25 Mark Brunell	.60	1.50
❑ 26 Craig Heyward	.07	.20
❑ 27 Eric Allen	.07	.20
❑ 28 Dana Stubblefield	.20	.50
❑ 29 Steve Bono	.07	.20
❑ 30 Larry Brown	.07	.20
❑ 31 Warren Moon	.20	.50
❑ 32 Jim Kelly	.40	1.00
❑ 33 Terry McDaniel	.07	.20
❑ 34 Dan Wilkinson	.07	.20
❑ 35 Dave Brown	.07	.20
❑ 36 Todd Lyght	.07	.20
❑ 37 Aeneas Williams	.07	.20
❑ 38 Shannon Sharpe	.20	.50
❑ 39 Errict Rhett	.20	.50
❑ 40 Yancey Thigpen	.20	.50
❑ 41 J.J. Stokes	.40	1.00
❑ 42 Marshall Faulk	.50	1.25
❑ 43 Chester McGlockton	.07	.20
❑ 44 Darryll Lewis	.07	.20
❑ 45 Drew Bledsoe	.60	1.50
❑ 46 Tyrone Wheatley	.20	.50
❑ 47 Herman Moore	.20	.50
❑ 48 Darren Woodson	.20	.50
❑ 49 Ricky Watters	.20	.50
❑ 50 Emmitt Smith TYC	.60	1.50
❑ 51 Barry Sanders TYC	.60	1.50
❑ 52 Curtis Martin TYC	.40	1.00
❑ 53 Chris Warren TYC	.20	.50
❑ 54 Errict Rhett TYC	.20	.50
❑ 55 Rodney Hampton TYC	.07	.20
❑ 56 Terrell Davis TYC	.40	1.00
❑ 57 Marshall Faulk TYC	.40	1.00
❑ 58 Rashaan Salaam TYC	.20	.50
❑ 59 Curtis Conway	.40	1.00
❑ 60 Isaac Bruce	.40	1.00
❑ 61 Thurman Thomas	.40	1.00
❑ 62 Terry Allen	.20	.50
❑ 63 Lamar Lathon	.07	.20
❑ 64 Mark Chmura	.20	.50
❑ 65 Chris Warren	.20	.50
❑ 66 Jessie Tuggle	.07	.20
❑ 67 Erik Kramer	.07	.20
❑ 68 Tim Brown	.40	1.00
❑ 69 Derrick Thomas	.40	1.00
❑ 70 Willie McGinest	.07	.20
❑ 71 Frank Sanders	.20	.50
❑ 72 Bernie Parmalee	.07	.20
❑ 73 Kordell Stewart	.40	1.00
❑ 74 Brent Jones	.07	.20
❑ 75 Edgar Bennett	.20	.50
❑ 76 Rashaan Salaam	.20	.50
❑ 77 Carl Pickens	.20	.50
❑ 78 Terance Mathis	.07	.20
❑ 79 Deion Sanders	.50	1.25
❑ 80 Glyn Milburn	.07	.20
❑ 81 Lee Woodall	.07	.20
❑ 82 Neil Smith	.20	.50
❑ 83 Stan Humphries	.20	.50
❑ 84 Rick Mirer	.20	.50
❑ 85 Troy Vincent	.07	.20
❑ 86 Sam Mills	.07	.20
❑ 87 Brian Mitchell	.07	.20
❑ 88 Hardy Nickerson	.07	.20
❑ 89 Tamarick Vanover	.20	.50
❑ 90 Steve McNair	.60	1.50
❑ 91 Jerry Rice TYC	.40	1.00
❑ 92 Isaac Bruce TYC	.40	1.00
❑ 93 Herman Moore TYC	.20	.50
❑ 94 Cris Carter TYC	.40	1.00
❑ 95 Tim Brown TYC	.20	.50
❑ 96 Carl Pickens TYC	.20	.50
❑ 97 Joey Galloway TYC	.40	1.00
❑ 98 Jerry Rice	1.00	2.50
❑ 99 Cris Carter	.40	1.00
❑ 100 Curtis Martin	.60	1.50
❑ 101 Scott Mitchell	.20	.50
❑ 102 Ken Harvey	.07	.20
❑ 103 Rodney Hampton	.20	.50
❑ 104 Reggie White	.40	1.00
❑ 105 Eddie Robinson	.07	.20
❑ 106 Greg Lloyd	.20	.50
❑ 107 Phillippi Sparks	.07	.20
❑ 108 Emmitt Smith	1.50	4.00
❑ 109 Tom Carter	.07	.20
❑ 110 Jim Everett	.07	.20
❑ 111 James O.Stewart	.20	.50
❑ 112 Kyle Brady	.07	.20
❑ 113 Irving Fryar	.20	.50
❑ 114 Vinny Testaverde	.20	.50
❑ 115 John Elway	2.00	5.00
❑ 116 Chris Spielman	.07	.20
❑ 117 Mike Mamula	.07	.20
❑ 118 Jim Harbaugh	.20	.50
❑ 119 Ken Norton	.07	.20
❑ 120 Bruce Smith	.20	.50
❑ 121 Daryl Johnston	.20	.50
❑ 122 Blaine Bishop	.07	.20
❑ 123 Jeff George	.20	.50
❑ 124 Jeff Hostetler	.07	.20
❑ 125 Jerome Bettis	.40	1.00
❑ 126 Jay Novacek	.07	.20
❑ 127 Bryce Paup	.07	.20
❑ 128 Neil O'Donnell	.20	.50
❑ 129 Marcus Allen	.40	1.00
❑ 130 Steve Young	.60	1.50
❑ 131 Brett Favre TYC	.75	2.00
❑ 132 Scott Mitchell TYC	.07	.20
❑ 133 John Elway TYC	.75	2.00
❑ 134 Jeff Blake TYC	.20	.50
❑ 135 Dan Marino TYC	.75	2.00
❑ 136 Drew Bledsoe TYC	.40	1.00
❑ 137 Troy Aikman TYC	.40	1.00
❑ 138 Steve Young TYC	.40	1.00
❑ 139 Jim Kelly TYC	.40	1.00
❑ 140 Jeff Graham	.07	.20
❑ 141 Hugh Douglas	.20	.50
❑ 142 Dan Marino	2.00	5.00
❑ 143 Darrell Green	.07	.20
❑ 144 Eric Zeier	.07	.20
❑ 145 Brett Favre	2.00	5.00

Card		
❑ 146 Carnell Lake	.07	.20
❑ 147 Ben Coates	.20	.50
❑ 148 Tony Martin	.20	.50
❑ 149 Michael Irvin	.40	1.00
❑ 150 Lawrence Phillips RC	.40	1.00
❑ 151 Alex Van Dyke RC	.60	1.50
❑ 152 Kevin Hardy RC	.60	1.50
❑ 153 Rickey Dudley RC	2.00	5.00
❑ 154 Eric Moulds RC	4.00	10.00
❑ 155 Simeon Rice RC	1.50	4.00
❑ 156 Marvin Harrison RC	12.50	25.00
❑ 157 Tim Biakabutuka RC	1.50	4.00
❑ 158 Duane Clemons RC	.40	1.00
❑ 159 Keyshawn Johnson RC	5.00	12.00
❑ 160 John Mobley RC	.60	1.50
❑ 161 Leeland McElroy RC	.60	1.50
❑ 162 Eddie George RC	6.00	12.00
❑ 163 Jonathan Ogden RC	.75	2.00
❑ 164 Eddie Kennison RC	2.00	5.00
❑ 165 Checklist	.07	.20

1997 Topps Chrome

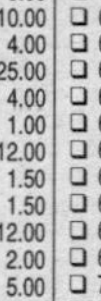
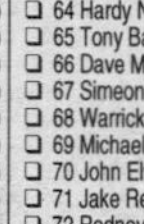
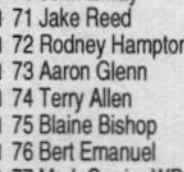

Card		
❑ COMPLETE SET (165)	30.00	60.00
❑ 1 Brett Favre	2.50	6.00
❑ 2 Tim Biakabutuka	.40	1.00
❑ 3 Deion Sanders	.60	1.50
❑ 4 Marshall Faulk	.75	2.00
❑ 5 John Randle	.40	1.00
❑ 6 Stan Humphries	.40	1.00
❑ 7 Ki-Jana Carter	.25	.60
❑ 8 Rashaan Salaam	.25	.60
❑ 9 Rickey Dudley	.40	1.00
❑ 10 Isaac Bruce	.60	1.50
❑ 11 Keyshawn Johnson	.60	1.50
❑ 12 Ben Coates	.40	1.00
❑ 13 Ty Detmer	.40	1.00
❑ 14 Gus Frerotte	.25	.60
❑ 15 Mario Bates	.25	.60
❑ 16 Chris Calloway	.25	.60
❑ 17 Frank Sanders	.40	1.00
❑ 18 Bruce Smith	.40	1.00
❑ 19 Jeff Graham	.25	.60
❑ 20 Trent Dilfer	.60	1.50
❑ 21 Tyrone Wheatley	.40	1.00
❑ 22 Chris Warren	.40	1.00
❑ 23 Terry Kirby	.40	1.00
❑ 24 Tony Gonzalez RC	3.00	8.00
❑ 25 Ricky Watters	.40	1.00
❑ 26 Tamarick Vanover	.40	1.00
❑ 27 Kerry Collins	.60	1.50
❑ 28 Bobby Engram	.40	1.00
❑ 29 Derrick Alexander WR	.40	1.00
❑ 30 Hugh Douglas	.25	.60
❑ 31 Thurman Thomas	.60	1.50
❑ 32 Drew Bledsoe	.75	2.00
❑ 33 LeShon Johnson	.25	.60
❑ 34 Byron Bam Morris	.25	.60
❑ 35 Herman Moore	.40	1.00
❑ 36 Troy Aikman	1.25	3.00
❑ 37 Mel Gray	.25	.60
❑ 38 Adrian Murrell	.40	1.00
❑ 39 Carl Pickens	.40	1.00
❑ 40 Tony Brackens	.25	.60
❑ 41 O.J. McDuffie	.40	1.00
❑ 42 Napoleon Kaufman	.60	1.50
❑ 43 Chris T. Jones	.25	.60
❑ 44 Kordell Stewart	.60	1.50
❑ 45 Steve Young	.75	2.00
❑ 46 Shannon Sharpe	.40	1.00
❑ 47 Leeland McElroy	.25	.60
❑ 48 Eric Moulds	.60	1.50
❑ 49 Eddie George	.60	1.50
❑ 50 Jamal Anderson	.60	1.50
❑ 51 Robert Smith	.40	1.00
❑ 52 Mike Alstott	.60	1.50
❑ 53 Darrell Green	.40	1.00
❑ 54 Irving Fryar	.40	1.00
❑ 55 Derrick Thomas	.60	1.50
❑ 56 Antonio Freeman	.60	1.50
❑ 57 Terrell Davis	.75	2.00
❑ 58 Henry Ellard	.25	.60
❑ 59 Daryl Johnston	.40	1.00
❑ 60 Bryan Cox	.25	.60
❑ 61 Vinny Testaverde	.40	1.00
❑ 62 Andre Reed	.40	1.00
❑ 63 Larry Centers	.40	1.00
❑ 64 Hardy Nickerson	.25	.60
❑ 65 Tony Banks	.40	1.00
❑ 66 Dave Meggett	.25	.60
❑ 67 Simeon Rice	.40	1.00
❑ 68 Warrick Dunn RC	4.00	10.00
❑ 69 Michael Irvin	.60	1.50
❑ 70 John Elway	2.50	6.00
❑ 71 Jake Reed	.40	1.00
❑ 72 Rodney Hampton	.40	1.00
❑ 73 Aaron Glenn	.25	.60
❑ 74 Terry Allen	.60	1.50
❑ 75 Blaine Bishop	.25	.60
❑ 76 Bert Emanuel	.40	1.00
❑ 77 Mark Carrier WR	.25	.60
❑ 78 Jimmy Smith	.40	1.00
❑ 79 Jim Harbaugh	.40	1.00
❑ 80 Brent Jones	.40	1.00
❑ 81 Emmitt Smith	2.00	5.00
❑ 82 Fred Barnett	.25	.60
❑ 83 Errict Rhett	.25	.60
❑ 84 Michael Sinclair	.25	.60
❑ 85 Jerome Bettis	.60	1.50
❑ 86 Chris Sanders	.25	.60
❑ 87 Kent Graham	.25	.60
❑ 88 Cris Carter	.60	1.50
❑ 89 Harvey Williams	.25	.60
❑ 90 Eric Allen	.25	.60
❑ 91 Bryant Young	.25	.60
❑ 92 Marcus Allen	.60	1.50
❑ 93 Michael Jackson	.40	1.00
❑ 94 Mark Chmura	.40	1.00
❑ 95 Keenan McCardell	.40	1.00
❑ 96 Joey Galloway	.40	1.00
❑ 97 Eddie Kennison	.40	1.00
❑ 98 Steve Atwater	.25	.60
❑ 99 Dorsey Levens	.60	1.50
❑ 100 Rob Moore	.40	1.00
❑ 101 Steve McNair	.75	2.00
❑ 102 Sean Dawkins	.25	.60
❑ 103 Don Beebe	.25	.60
❑ 104 Willie McGinest	.25	.60
❑ 105 Tony Martin	.40	1.00
❑ 106 Mark Brunell	.75	2.00
❑ 107 Karim Abdul-Jabbar	.60	1.50
❑ 108 Michael Westbrook	.40	1.00
❑ 109 Lawrence Phillips	.25	.60
❑ 110 Barry Sanders	2.00	5.00
❑ 111 Willie Davis	.25	.60
❑ 112 Wesley Walls	.40	1.00
❑ 113 Todd Collins	.25	.60
❑ 114 Jerry Rice	1.25	3.00
❑ 115 Scott Mitchell	.40	1.00
❑ 116 Terance Mathis	.40	1.00
❑ 117 Chris Spielman	.25	.60
❑ 118 Curtis Conway	.40	1.00
❑ 119 Marvin Harrison	.60	1.50
❑ 120 Terry Glenn	.60	1.50
❑ 121 Dave Brown	.25	.60
❑ 122 Neil O'Donnell	.40	1.00
❑ 123 Junior Seau	.60	1.50
❑ 124 Reggie White	.60	1.50
❑ 125 Lamar Lathon	.25	.60
❑ 126 Natrone Means	.40	1.00
❑ 127 Tim Brown	.60	1.50
❑ 128 Eric Swann	.25	.60
❑ 129 Dan Marino	2.50	6.00
❑ 130 Anthony Johnson	.25	.60
❑ 131 Edgar Bennett	.40	1.00
❑ 132 Kevin Hardy	.25	.60
❑ 133 Brian Blades	.25	.60
❑ 134 Curtis Martin	.75	2.00
❑ 135 Zach Thomas	.60	1.50
❑ 136 Darnay Scott	.40	1.00
❑ 137 Desmond Howard	.40	1.00
❑ 138 Aeneas Williams	.25	.60
❑ 139 Bryce Paup	.25	.60
❑ 140 Brad Johnson	.60	1.50
❑ 141 Jeff Blake	.40	1.00
❑ 142 Wayne Chrebet	.60	1.50
❑ 143 Will Blackwell RC	.50	1.25
❑ 144 Tom Knight RC	.25	.60
❑ 145 Darnell Autry RC	.40	1.00
❑ 146 Bryant Westbrook RC	.25	.60
❑ 147 David LaFleur RC	.30	.75
❑ 148 Antowain Smith RC	3.00	8.00
❑ 149 Rae Carruth RC	.30	.75
❑ 150 Jim Druckenmiller RC	.40	1.00
❑ 151 Shawn Springs RC	.30	.75
❑ 152 Troy Davis RC	.50	1.25
❑ 153 Orlando Pace RC	.75	2.00
❑ 154 Byron Hanspard RC	.50	1.25
❑ 155 Corey Dillon RC	4.00	10.00
❑ 156 Reidel Anthony RC	.75	2.00
❑ 157 Peter Boulware RC	.75	2.00
❑ 158 Reinard Wilson RC	.50	1.25
❑ 159 Pat Barnes RC	.75	2.00
❑ 160 Joey Kent RC	.75	2.00
❑ 161 Ike Hilliard RC	1.25	3.00
❑ 162 Jake Plummer RC	3.00	8.00
❑ 163 Darrell Russell RC	.30	.75
❑ 164 Checklist Card	.25	.60
❑ 165 Checklist Card	.25	.60

1998 Topps Chrome

Card		
❑ COMPLETE SET (165)	50.00	120.00
❑ 1 Barry Sanders	1.50	4.00
❑ 2 Duane Starks RC	.75	2.00
❑ 3 J.J. Stokes	.30	.75
❑ 4 Joey Galloway	.30	.75
❑ 5 Deion Sanders	.50	1.25
❑ 6 Anthony Miller	.20	.50
❑ 7 Jamal Anderson	.50	1.25
❑ 8 Shannon Sharpe	.30	.75
❑ 9 Irving Fryar	.30	.75
❑ 10 Curtis Martin	.50	1.25
❑ 11 Shawn Jefferson	.20	.50
❑ 12 Charlie Garner	.30	.75
❑ 13 Robert Edwards RC	1.25	3.00
❑ 14 Napoleon Kaufman	.50	1.25
❑ 15 Gus Frerotte	.20	.50
❑ 16 John Elway	2.00	5.00
❑ 17 Jerome Pathon RC	1.50	4.00
❑ 18 Marshall Faulk	.60	1.50
❑ 19 Michael McCrary	.20	.50
❑ 20 Marcus Allen	.50	1.25
❑ 21 Trent Dilfer	.50	1.25
❑ 22 Frank Wycheck	.20	.50
❑ 23 Terrell Owens	.50	1.25
❑ 24 Herman Moore	.30	.75
❑ 25 Neil O'Donnell	.30	.75
❑ 26 Darnay Scott	.30	.75
❑ 27 Keith Brooking RC	1.50	4.00
❑ 28 Eric Green	.20	.50
❑ 29 Dan Marino	2.00	5.00
❑ 30 Antonio Freeman	.50	1.25
❑ 31 Tony Martin	.30	.75
❑ 32 Isaac Bruce	.50	1.25
❑ 33 Rickey Dudley	.20	.50
❑ 34 Scott Mitchell	.30	.75
❑ 35 Randy Moss RC	10.00	25.00
❑ 36 Fred Lane	.20	.50
❑ 37 Frank Sanders	.30	.75
❑ 38 Jerry Rice	1.00	2.50
❑ 39 O.J. McDuffie	.30	.75
❑ 40 Jessie Armstead	.20	.50
❑ 41 Reidel Anthony	.30	.75
❑ 42 Steve McNair	.50	1.25
❑ 43 Jake Reed	.30	.75
❑ 44 Charles Woodson RC	2.00	5.00
❑ 45 Tiki Barber	.50	1.25

Card		
❑ 46 Mike Alstott	.50	1.25
❑ 47 Keyshawn Johnson	.50	1.25
❑ 48 Tony Banks	.30	.75
❑ 49 Michael Westbrook	.30	.75
❑ 50 Chris Slade	.20	.50
❑ 51 Terry Allen	.50	1.25
❑ 52 Karim Abdul-Jabbar	.50	1.25
❑ 53 Brad Johnson	.50	1.25
❑ 54 Tony McGee	.20	.50
❑ 55 Kevin Dyson RC	1.50	4.00
❑ 56 Warren Moon	.50	1.25
❑ 57 Byron Hanspard	.20	.50
❑ 58 Jermaine Lewis	.30	.75
❑ 59 Neil Smith	.30	.75
❑ 60 Tamarick Vanover	.20	.50
❑ 61 Terrell Davis	.50	1.25
❑ 62 Robert Smith	.50	1.25
❑ 63 Junior Seau	.50	1.25
❑ 64 Warren Sapp	.30	.75
❑ 65 Michael Sinclair	.20	.50
❑ 66 Ryan Leaf RC	1.50	4.00
❑ 67 Drew Bledsoe	.75	2.00
❑ 68 Jason Sehorn	.30	.75
❑ 69 Andre Hastings	.20	.50
❑ 70 Tony Gonzalez	.50	1.25
❑ 71 Dorsey Levens	.50	1.25
❑ 72 Ray Lewis	.50	1.25
❑ 73 Grant Wistrom RC	1.25	3.00
❑ 74 Elvis Grbac	.30	.75
❑ 75 Mark Chmura	.30	.75
❑ 76 Zach Thomas	.50	1.25
❑ 77 Ben Coates	.30	.75
❑ 78 Rod Smith WR	.30	.75
❑ 79 Andre Wadsworth RC	1.25	3.00
❑ 80 Garrison Hearst	.50	1.25
❑ 81 Will Blackwell	.20	.50
❑ 82 Cris Carter	.50	1.25
❑ 83 Mark Fields	.20	.50
❑ 84 Ken Dilger	.20	.50
❑ 85 Johnnie Morton	.30	.75
❑ 86 Michael Irvin	.50	1.25
❑ 87 Eddie George	.50	1.25
❑ 88 Rob Moore	.30	.75
❑ 89 Takeo Spikes RC	1.50	4.00
❑ 90 Wesley Walls	.30	.75
❑ 91 Andre Reed	.30	.75
❑ 92 Thurman Thomas	.50	1.25
❑ 93 Ed McCaffrey	.30	.75
❑ 94 Carl Pickens	.30	.75
❑ 95 Jason Taylor	.30	.75
❑ 96 Kordell Stewart	.50	1.25
❑ 97 Greg Ellis RC	.75	2.00
❑ 98 Aaron Glenn	.20	.50
❑ 99 Jake Plummer	.50	1.25
❑ 100 Checklist	.20	.50
❑ 101 Chris Sanders	.20	.50
❑ 102 Michael Jackson	.20	.50
❑ 103 Bobby Hoying	.30	.75
❑ 104 Wayne Chrebet	.50	1.25
❑ 105 Charles Way	.20	.50
❑ 106 Derrick Thomas	.50	1.25
❑ 107 Troy Drayton	.20	.50
❑ 108 Robert Holcombe RC	1.25	3.00
❑ 109 Pete Mitchell	.20	.50
❑ 110 Bruce Smith	.30	.75
❑ 111 Terance Mathis	.30	.75
❑ 112 Lawrence Phillips	.20	.50
❑ 113 Brett Favre	2.00	5.00
❑ 114 Darrell Green	.30	.75
❑ 115 Charles Johnson	.20	.50
❑ 116 Jeff Blake	.30	.75
❑ 117 Mark Brunell	.50	1.25
❑ 118 Simeon Rice	.30	.75
❑ 119 Robert Brooks	.30	.75
❑ 120 Jacquez Green RC	1.25	3.00
❑ 121 Willie Davis	.20	.50
❑ 122 Jeff George	.30	.75
❑ 123 Andre Rison	.30	.75
❑ 124 Erik Kramer	.20	.50
❑ 125 Peter Boulware	.20	.50
❑ 126 Marcus Nash RC	.75	2.00
❑ 127 Troy Aikman	1.00	2.50
❑ 128 Keenan McCardell	.30	.75
❑ 129 Bryant Westbrook	.20	.50
❑ 130 Terry Glenn	.50	1.25
❑ 131 Blaine Bishop	.20	.50
❑ 132 Tim Brown	.50	1.25
❑ 133 Brian Griese RC	2.50	6.00
❑ 134 John Mobley	.20	.50
❑ 135 Larry Centers	.20	.50
❑ 136 Eric Bjornson	.20	.50
❑ 137 Kevin Hardy	.20	.50
❑ 138 John Randle	.30	.75
❑ 139 Michael Strahan	.30	.75
❑ 140 Jerome Bettis	.50	1.25
❑ 141 Rae Carruth	.20	.50
❑ 142 Reggie White	.50	1.25
❑ 143 Antowain Smith	.50	1.25
❑ 144 Aeneas Williams	.20	.50
❑ 145 Bobby Engram	.30	.75
❑ 146 Germane Crowell RC	1.25	3.00
❑ 147 Freddie Jones	.20	.50
❑ 148 Kimble Anders	.30	.75
❑ 149 Steve Young	.60	1.50
❑ 150 Willie McGinest	.20	.50
❑ 151 Emmitt Smith	1.50	4.00
❑ 152 Fred Taylor RC	2.50	6.00
❑ 153 Danny Kanell	.30	.75
❑ 154 Warrick Dunn	.50	1.25
❑ 155 Kerry Collins	.30	.75
❑ 156 Chris Chandler	.30	.75
❑ 157 Curtis Conway	.30	.75
❑ 158 Curtis Enis RC	.75	2.00
❑ 159 Corey Dillon	.50	1.25
❑ 160 Glenn Foley	.30	.75
❑ 161 Marvin Harrison	.50	1.25
❑ 162 Chad Brown	.20	.50
❑ 163 Derrick Rodgers	.20	.50
❑ 164 Levon Kirkland	.20	.50
❑ 165 Peyton Manning RC	20.00	50.00

1999 Topps Chrome

Card		
❑ COMPLETE SET (165)	60.00	150.00
❑ COMP.SET w/o SP's (135)	25.00	50.00
❑ 1 Randy Moss	1.25	3.00
❑ 2 Keyshawn Johnson	.50	1.25
❑ 3 Priest Holmes	.75	2.00
❑ 4 Warren Moon	.50	1.25
❑ 5 Joey Galloway	.30	.75
❑ 6 Zach Thomas	.50	1.25
❑ 7 Cam Cleeland	.20	.50
❑ 8 Jim Harbaugh	.30	.75
❑ 9 Napoleon Kaufman	.50	1.25
❑ 10 Fred Taylor	.50	1.25
❑ 11 Mark Brunell	.50	1.25
❑ 12 Shannon Sharpe	.30	.75
❑ 13 Jacquez Green	.20	.50
❑ 14 Adrian Murrell	.30	.75
❑ 15 Cris Carter	.50	1.25
❑ 16 Jerome Pathon	.20	.50
❑ 17 Drew Bledsoe	.60	1.50
❑ 18 Curtis Martin	.50	1.25
❑ 19 Johnnie Morton	.30	.75
❑ 20 Doug Flutie	.50	1.25
❑ 21 Carl Pickens	.30	.75
❑ 22 Jerome Bettis	.50	1.25
❑ 23 Derrick Alexander	.20	.50
❑ 24 Antowain Smith	.50	1.25
❑ 25 Barry Sanders	1.50	4.00
❑ 26 Reidel Anthony	.30	.75
❑ 27 Wayne Chrebet	.30	.75
❑ 28 Terance Mathis	.30	.75
❑ 29 Shawn Springs	.20	.50
❑ 30 Emmitt Smith	1.00	2.50
❑ 31 Robert Smith	.50	1.25
❑ 32 Charles Johnson	.20	.50
❑ 33 Mike Alstott	.50	1.25
❑ 34 Ike Hilliard	.20	.50
❑ 35 Ricky Watters	.30	.75
❑ 36 Charles Woodson	.50	1.25
❑ 37 Rod Smith	.30	.75
❑ 38 Pete Mitchell	.20	.50
❑ 39 Derrick Thomas	.50	1.25
❑ 40 Dan Marino	1.50	4.00
❑ 41 Darnay Scott	.20	.50
❑ 42 Jake Reed	.30	.75
❑ 43 Chris Chandler	.30	.75
❑ 44 Dorsey Levens	.50	1.25
❑ 45 Kordell Stewart	.30	.75
❑ 46 Eddie George	.50	1.25
❑ 47 Corey Dillon	.50	1.25
❑ 48 Rich Gannon	.50	1.25
❑ 49 Chris Spielman	.20	.50
❑ 50 Jerry Rice	1.00	2.50
❑ 51 Trent Dilfer	.30	.75
❑ 52 Mark Chmura	.20	.50
❑ 53 Jimmy Smith	.30	.75
❑ 54 Isaac Bruce	.50	1.25
❑ 55 Karim Abdul-Jabbar	.30	.75
❑ 56 Sedrick Shaw	.20	.50
❑ 57 Jake Plummer	.30	.75
❑ 58 Tony Gonzalez	.50	1.25
❑ 59 Ben Coates	.30	.75
❑ 60 John Elway	1.50	4.00
❑ 61 Bruce Smith	.30	.75
❑ 62 Tim Brown	.50	1.25
❑ 63 Tim Dwight	.50	1.25
❑ 64 Yancey Thigpen	.20	.50
❑ 65 Terrell Owens	.50	1.25
❑ 66 Kyle Brady	.20	.50
❑ 67 Tony Martin	.30	.75
❑ 68 Michael Strahan	.30	.75
❑ 69 Deion Sanders	.50	1.25
❑ 70 Steve Young	.60	1.50
❑ 71 Dale Carter	.20	.50
❑ 72 Ty Law	.30	.75
❑ 73 Frank Wycheck	.20	.50
❑ 74 Marshall Faulk	.60	1.50
❑ 75 Vinny Testaverde	.30	.75
❑ 76 Chad Brown	.20	.50
❑ 77 Natrone Means	.30	.75
❑ 78 Bert Emanuel	.30	.75
❑ 79 Kerry Collins	.30	.75
❑ 80 Randall Cunningham	.50	1.25
❑ 81 Garrison Hearst	.30	.75
❑ 82 Curtis Enis	.20	.50
❑ 83 Steve Atwater	.20	.50
❑ 84 Kevin Greene	.20	.50
❑ 85 Steve McNair	.50	1.25
❑ 86 Andre Reed	.30	.75
❑ 87 J.J. Stokes	.30	.75
❑ 88 Eric Moulds	.50	1.25
❑ 89 Marvin Harrison	.50	1.25
❑ 90 Troy Aikman	1.00	2.50
❑ 91 Herman Moore	.30	.75
❑ 92 Michael Irvin	.30	.75
❑ 93 Frank Sanders	.30	.75
❑ 94 Duce Staley	.50	1.25
❑ 95 James Jett	.30	.75
❑ 96 Ricky Proehl	.20	.50
❑ 97 Andre Rison	.30	.75
❑ 98 Leslie Shepherd	.20	.50
❑ 99 Trent Green	.50	1.25
❑ 100 Terrell Davis	.50	1.25
❑ 101 Freddie Jones	.20	.50
❑ 102 Skip Hicks	.20	.50
❑ 103 Jeff Graham	.20	.50
❑ 104 Rob Moore	.30	.75
❑ 105 Torrance Small	.20	.50
❑ 106 Antonio Freeman	.50	1.25
❑ 107 Robert Brooks	.30	.75
❑ 108 Jon Kitna	.50	1.25
❑ 109 Curtis Conway	.30	.75
❑ 110 Brett Favre	1.50	4.00
❑ 111 Warrick Dunn	.50	1.25
❑ 112 Elvis Grbac	.30	.75
❑ 113 Corey Fuller	.20	.50
❑ 114 Rickey Dudley	.20	.50
❑ 115 Jamal Anderson	.50	1.25
❑ 116 Terry Glenn	.50	1.25
❑ 117 Rocket Ismail	.30	.75
❑ 118 John Randle	.30	.75
❑ 119 Chris Calloway	.20	.50
❑ 120 Peyton Manning	1.50	4.00
❑ 121 Keenan McCardell	.30	.75
❑ 122 O.J. McDuffie	.30	.75
❑ 123 Ed McCaffrey	.30	.75
❑ 124 Charlie Batch	.50	1.25
❑ 125 Jason Elam SH	.20	.50
❑ 126 Randy Moss SH	.60	1.50

❑ 127 John Elway SH .75 2.00
❑ 128 Emmitt Smith SH .50 1.25
❑ 129 Terrell Davis SH .50 1.25
❑ 130 Jerris McPhail .20 .50
❑ 131 Damon Gibson .20 .50
❑ 132 Jim Pyne .20 .50
❑ 133 Antonio Langham .20 .50
❑ 134 Freddie Solomon .20 .50
❑ 135 Ricky Williams RC 4.00 10.00
❑ 136 Daunte Culpepper RC 10.00 20.00
❑ 137 Chris Claiborne RC .75 2.00
❑ 138 Amos Zereoue RC 2.00 5.00
❑ 139 Chris McAlister RC 1.50 4.00
❑ 140 Kevin Faulk RC 2.00 5.00
❑ 141 James Johnson RC 1.50 4.00
❑ 142 Mike Cloud RC 1.50 4.00
❑ 143 Jevon Kearse RC 4.00 10.00
❑ 144 Akili Smith RC 1.50 4.00
❑ 145 Edgerrin James RC 10.00 20.00
❑ 146 Cecil Collins RC .75 2.00
❑ 147 Donovan McNabb RC 12.50 25.00
❑ 148 Kevin Johnson RC 2.00 5.00
❑ 149 Torry Holt RC 6.00 15.00
❑ 150 Rob Konrad RC 2.00 5.00
❑ 151 Tim Couch RC 2.00 5.00
❑ 152 David Boston RC 2.00 5.00
❑ 153 Karsten Bailey RC 1.50 4.00
❑ 154 Troy Edwards RC 1.50 4.00
❑ 155 Sedrick Irvin RC .75 2.00
❑ 156 Shaun King RC 1.50 4.00
❑ 157 Peerless Price RC 2.00 5.00
❑ 158 Brock Huard RC 2.00 5.00
❑ 159 Cade McNown RC 1.50 4.00
❑ 160 Champ Bailey RC 3.00 8.00
❑ 161 D'Wayne Bates RC 1.50 4.00
❑ 162 Joe Germaine RC 1.50 4.00
❑ 163 Andy Katzenmoyer RC 1.50 4.00
❑ 164 Antoine Winfield RC 1.50 4.00
❑ 165 Checklist Card .20 .50

2000 Topps Chrome

❑ COMPLETE SET (270) 400.00 800.00
❑ COMP.SET w/o SPs (180) 25.00 50.00
❑ 1 Daunte Culpepper .60 1.50
❑ 2 Troy Edwards .15 .40
❑ 3 Terrell Owens .50 1.25
❑ 4 Ricky Proehl .15 .40
❑ 5 Shaun King .15 .40
❑ 6 Jeff George .25 .60
❑ 7 Champ Bailey .25 .60
❑ 8 Amani Toomer .15 .40
❑ 9 Stephen Boyd .15 .40
❑ 10 Thurman Thomas .25 .60
❑ 11 Patrick Jeffers .50 1.25
❑ 12 Jake Plummer .25 .60
❑ 13 Peter Boulware .15 .40
❑ 14 Darrin Chiaverini .15 .40
❑ 15 Olandis Gary .50 1.25
❑ 16 Peyton Manning 1.25 3.00
❑ 17 Joe Horn .25 .60
❑ 18 Wayne Chrebet .25 .60
❑ 19 Freddie Jones .15 .40
❑ 20 Kurt Warner 1.00 2.50
❑ 21 Mike Alstott .50 1.25
❑ 22 Stephen Davis .50 1.25
❑ 23 Tim Brown .50 1.25
❑ 24 Damon Huard .50 1.25
❑ 25 Terry Glenn .25 .60
❑ 26 Ricky Williams .50 1.25
❑ 27 Tim Dwight .50 1.25
❑ 28 Jay Riemersma .15 .40
❑ 29 Carl Pickens .25 .60
❑ 30 Brett Favre 1.50 4.00
❑ 31 Oronde Gadsden .25 .60
❑ 32 Steve McNair .50 1.25
❑ 33 Michael Pittman .15 .40
❑ 34 Emmitt Smith 1.00 2.50
❑ 35 Mark Brunell .50 1.25
❑ 36 Ed McCaffrey .50 1.25
❑ 37 Tyrone Wheatley .25 .60
❑ 38 Sean Dawkins .15 .40
❑ 39 Jevon Kearse .50 1.25
❑ 40 Tai Streets .15 .40
❑ 41 Keyshawn Johnson .50 1.25
❑ 42 Germane Crowell .15 .40
❑ 43 Yatil Green .15 .40
❑ 44 Anthony Wright RC 1.50 4.00
❑ 45 Jerry Rice 1.00 2.50
❑ 46 Az-Zahir Hakim .25 .60
❑ 47 Stephen Alexander .15 .40
❑ 48 Zach Thomas .50 1.25
❑ 49 Tony Simmons .15 .40
❑ 50 Jessie Armstead .15 .40
❑ 51 Kordell Stewart .25 .60
❑ 52 Cade McNown .15 .40
❑ 53 Tony Gonzalez .25 .60
❑ 54 John Randle .25 .60
❑ 55 Donovan McNabb .75 2.00
❑ 56 Warrick Dunn .50 1.25
❑ 57 Dorsey Levens .25 .60
❑ 58 Errict Rhett .25 .60
❑ 59 Priest Holmes .60 1.50
❑ 60 Terrell Davis .50 1.25
❑ 61 Natrone Means .15 .40
❑ 62 Brad Johnson .50 1.25
❑ 63 Rickey Dudley .15 .40
❑ 64 Billy Miller .15 .40
❑ 65 Randy Moss 1.00 2.50
❑ 66 Joe Montgomery .15 .40
❑ 67 Johnnie Morton .25 .60
❑ 68 Peerless Price .25 .60
❑ 69 Rocket Ismail .25 .60
❑ 70 David Boston .50 1.25
❑ 71 Fred Taylor .50 1.25
❑ 72 Jermaine Fazande .15 .40
❑ 73 Elvis Grbac .25 .60
❑ 74 Derrick Mayes .25 .60
❑ 75 Yancey Thigpen .15 .40
❑ 76 Ike Hilliard .25 .60
❑ 77 Muhsin Muhammad .25 .60
❑ 78 Shawn Jefferson .15 .40
❑ 79 Rod Smith .25 .60
❑ 80 Darnay Scott .25 .60
❑ 81 Cam Cleeland .15 .40
❑ 82 Steve Young .60 1.50
❑ 83 E.G. Green .15 .40
❑ 84 Robert Smith .50 1.25
❑ 85 Jermaine Lewis .25 .60
❑ 86 Tim Biakabutuka .25 .60
❑ 87 Jerome Pathon .25 .60
❑ 88 Kent Graham .15 .40
❑ 89 Bruce Smith .25 .60
❑ 90 Isaac Bruce .50 1.25
❑ 91 Curtis Enis .15 .40
❑ 92 D'Marco Farr .15 .40
❑ 93 Keith Poole .15 .40
❑ 94 Troy Aikman 1.00 2.50
❑ 95 Rich Gannon .50 1.25
❑ 96 Michael Westbrook .25 .60
❑ 97 Albert Connell .15 .40
❑ 98 James Johnson .15 .40
❑ 99 Jeff Blake .25 .60
❑ 100 Joey Galloway .25 .60
❑ 101 Rob Moore .25 .60
❑ 102 Chris Chandler .25 .60
❑ 103 Fred Lane .15 .40
❑ 104 Eddie Kennison .25 .60
❑ 105 Kevin Hardy .15 .40
❑ 106 Napoleon Kaufman .25 .60
❑ 107 Kevin Dyson .25 .60
❑ 108 Keenan McCardell .25 .60
❑ 109 Drew Bledsoe .60 1.50
❑ 110 Kevin Johnson .50 1.25
❑ 111 Terance Mathis .25 .60
❑ 112 Gus Frerotte .15 .40
❑ 113 Matthew Hatchette .15 .40
❑ 114 Herman Moore .25 .60
❑ 115 Curtis Martin .50 1.25
❑ 116 Jacquez Green .15 .40
❑ 117 Jake Reed .25 .60
❑ 118 Antonio Freeman .50 1.25
❑ 119 Jim Miller .15 .40
❑ 120 Frank Sanders .25 .60
❑ 121 Brian Griese .50 1.25
❑ 122 Troy Brown .25 .60
❑ 123 Jeff Graham .15 .40
❑ 124 Marshall Faulk .60 1.50
❑ 125 Vinny Testaverde .25 .60
❑ 126 Frank Wycheck .15 .40
❑ 127 Kerry Collins .25 .60
❑ 128 Jay Fiedler .50 1.25
❑ 129 Cris Carter .50 1.25
❑ 130 Jason Tucker .15 .40
❑ 131 Antowain Smith .25 .60
❑ 132 Tony Banks .25 .60
❑ 133 Terrence Wilkins .15 .40
❑ 134 Tony Martin .25 .60
❑ 135 Richard Huntley .15 .40
❑ 136 J.J. Stokes .25 .60
❑ 137 Ricky Watters .25 .60
❑ 138 Pete Mitchell .15 .40
❑ 139 Jimmy Smith .25 .60
❑ 140 Doug Flutie .50 1.25
❑ 141 Corey Bradford .25 .60
❑ 142 Curtis Conway .25 .60
❑ 143 Moses Moreno .15 .40
❑ 144 Torry Holt .50 1.25
❑ 145 Warren Sapp .25 .60
❑ 146 Duce Staley .50 1.25
❑ 147 Mikhael Ricks .15 .40
❑ 148 Edgerrin James .75 2.00
❑ 149 Charlie Batch .50 1.25
❑ 150 Rob Johnson .25 .60
❑ 151 Jamal Anderson .50 1.25
❑ 152 Tim Couch .25 .60
❑ 153 O.J. McDuffie .25 .60
❑ 154 Charles Woodson .25 .60
❑ 155 Jake Delhomme RC 5.00 12.00
❑ 156 Eddie George .50 1.25
❑ 157 Jim Harbaugh .25 .60
❑ 158 Jon Kitna .50 1.25
❑ 159 Derrick Alexander .25 .60
❑ 160 Marvin Harrison .50 1.25
❑ 161 James Stewart .25 .60
❑ 162 Qadry Ismail .25 .60
❑ 163 Wesley Walls .15 .40
❑ 164 Steve Beuerlein .25 .60
❑ 165 Marcus Robinson .50 1.25
❑ 166 Bill Schroeder .25 .60
❑ 167 Charles Johnson .25 .60
❑ 168 Charlie Garner .25 .60
❑ 169 Eric Moulds .50 1.25
❑ 170 Jerome Bettis .50 1.25
❑ 171 Tai Streets .15 .40
❑ 172 Akili Smith .15 .40
❑ 173 Jonathan Linton .15 .40
❑ 174 Corey Dillon .50 1.25
❑ 175 Junior Seau .50 1.25
❑ 176 Jonathan Quinn .15 .40
❑ 177 Bobby Engram .15 .40
❑ 178 Shannon Sharpe .25 .60
❑ 179 Michael Basnight .15 .40
❑ 180 Sedrick Irvin .15 .40
❑ 181 Sammy Morris RC 5.00 12.00
❑ 182 Ron Dixon RC 4.00 10.00
❑ 183 Trevor Gaylor RC 4.00 10.00
❑ 184 Chris Cole RC 3.00 8.00
❑ 185 Deltha O'Neal RC 6.00 15.00
❑ 186 Sebastian Janikowski RC 6.00 15.00
❑ 187 Kwame Cavil RC 3.00 8.00
❑ 188 Chad Morton RC 6.00 15.00
❑ 189 Terrelle Smith RC 4.00 10.00
❑ 190 Frank Moreau RC 4.00 10.00
❑ 191 Kurt Warner HL .60 1.50
❑ 192 Dan Marino HL 1.00 2.50
❑ 193 Cris Carter HL .25 .60
❑ 194 Brett Favre HL 1.00 2.50
❑ 195 Marshall Faulk HL .50 1.25
❑ 196 Jevon Kearse HL .25 .60
❑ 197 Edgerrin James HL .60 1.50
❑ 198 Emmitt Smith HL .60 1.50
❑ 199 Andre Reed HL .15 .40
❑ 200 K.Dyson/F.Wycheck HL .15 .40
❑ 201 Olindo Mare MM .15 .40
❑ 202 Marcus Coleman MM .15 .40
❑ 203 James Johnson MM .15 .40
❑ 204 Ray Lucas MM .25 .60
❑ 205 Dedric Ward MM .15 .40
❑ 206 Richie Cunningham MM .15 .40
❑ 207 James Hasty MM .15 .40

Card		
❑ 208 Sedrick Shaw MM	.15	.40
❑ 209 Kurt Warner MM	.60	1.50
❑ 210 Marshall Faulk MM	.50	1.25
❑ 211 Brian Shay EP	.40	1.00
❑ 212 L.C. Stevens EP	.40	1.00
❑ 213 Corey Thomas EP	.40	1.00
❑ 214 Scott Milanovich EP	.60	1.50
❑ 215 Pat Barnes EP	.60	1.50
❑ 216 Danny Wuerffel EP	.60	1.50
❑ 217 Kevin Daft EP	.40	1.00
❑ 218 Ron Powlus EP RC	.75	2.00
❑ 219 Eric Kresser EP	.40	1.00
❑ 220 Norman Miller EP RC	.40	1.00
❑ 221 Cory Sauter EP	.40	1.00
❑ 222 Marcus Crandell EP RC	.60	1.50
❑ 223 Sean Morey EP RC	.60	1.50
❑ 224 Jeff Ogden EP	.60	1.50
❑ 225 Ted White EP	.40	1.00
❑ 226 Jim Kubiak EP RC	.60	1.50
❑ 227 Aaron Stecker EP RC	.75	2.00
❑ 228 Ronnie Powell EP	.40	1.00
❑ 229 Matt Lytle EP RC	.60	1.50
❑ 230 Kendrick Nord EP RC	.40	1.00
❑ 231 Tim Rattay RC	6.00	15.00
❑ 232 Rob Morris RC	4.00	10.00
❑ 233 Chris Samuels RC	4.00	10.00
❑ 234 Todd Husak RC	6.00	15.00
❑ 235 Ahmed Plummer RC	6.00	15.00
❑ 236 Frank Murphy RC	3.00	8.00
❑ 237 Michael Wiley RC	4.00	10.00
❑ 238 Giovanni Carmazzi RC	3.00	8.00
❑ 239 Anthony Becht RC	6.00	15.00
❑ 240 John Abraham RC	7.50	20.00
❑ 241 Shaun Alexander RC	12.50	30.00
❑ 242 Thomas Jones RC	12.50	30.00
❑ 243 Courtney Brown RC	6.00	15.00
❑ 244 Curtis Keaton RC	4.00	10.00
❑ 245 Jerry Porter RC	10.00	25.00
❑ 246 Corey Simon RC	6.00	15.00
❑ 247 Dez White RC	6.00	15.00
❑ 248 Jamal Lewis RC	12.50	30.00
❑ 249 Ron Dayne RC	6.00	15.00
❑ 250 R.Jay Soward RC	4.00	10.00
❑ 251 Tee Martin RC	6.00	15.00
❑ 252 Shaun Ellis RC	6.00	15.00
❑ 253 Brian Urlacher RC	20.00	50.00
❑ 254 Reuben Droughns RC	6.00	15.00
❑ 255 Travis Taylor RC	6.00	15.00
❑ 256 Plaxico Burress RC	12.50	30.00
❑ 257 Chad Pennington RC	12.50	30.00
❑ 258 Sylvester Morris RC	4.00	10.00
❑ 259 Ron Dugans RC	3.00	8.00
❑ 260 Joe Hamilton RC	4.00	10.00
❑ 261 Chris Redman RC	4.00	10.00
❑ 262 Trung Canidate RC	4.00	10.00
❑ 263 J.R. Redmond RC	4.00	10.00
❑ 264 Danny Farmer RC	4.00	10.00
❑ 265 Todd Pinkston RC	6.00	15.00
❑ 266 Dennis Northcutt RC	6.00	15.00
❑ 267 Laveranues Coles RC	7.50	20.00
❑ 268 Bubba Franks RC	6.00	15.00
❑ 269 Travis Prentice RC	4.00	10.00
❑ 270 Peter Warrick RC	6.00	15.00

2001 Topps Chrome

Card		
❑ COMP.SET w/o SP's (210)	20.00	50.00
❑ 1 Randy Moss	1.00	2.50
❑ 2 Desmond Howard	.20	.50
❑ 3 Shawn Bryson	.20	.50
❑ 4 Lamar Smith	.30	.75
❑ 5 Peter Warrick	.50	1.25
❑ 6 Hines Ward	.50	1.25
❑ 7 J.R. Redmond	.20	.50
❑ 8 Reidel Anthony	.20	.50
❑ 9 Rich Gannon	.50	1.25
❑ 10 Ed McCaffrey	.50	1.25
❑ 11 Jamel White	.20	.50
❑ 12 Michael Pittman	.20	.50
❑ 13 Rob Johnson	.30	.75
❑ 14 Tim Couch	.30	.75
❑ 15 Stephen Alexander	.20	.50
❑ 16 Ricky Watters	.30	.75
❑ 17 Kerry Collins	.30	.75
❑ 18 Ricky Williams	.50	1.25
❑ 19 Joey Galloway	.30	.75
❑ 20 Chris Chandler	.30	.75
❑ 21 Marty Booker	.20	.50
❑ 22 Mark Brunell	.50	1.25
❑ 23 Antonio Freeman	.50	1.25
❑ 24 Richie Anderson	.20	.50
❑ 25 Amani Toomer	.30	.75
❑ 26 Trent Green	.50	1.25
❑ 27 Terrell Fletcher	.20	.50
❑ 28 Kevin Lockett	.20	.50
❑ 29 Ron Dixon	.20	.50
❑ 30 Charlie Batch	.50	1.25
❑ 31 Oronde Gadsden	.30	.75
❑ 32 Dorsey Levens	.30	.75
❑ 33 Jamal Lewis	.75	2.00
❑ 34 Craig Yeast	.20	.50
❑ 35 Muhsin Muhammad	.30	.75
❑ 36 Willie Jackson	.20	.50
❑ 37 Isaac Bruce	.50	1.25
❑ 38 Frank Wycheck	.20	.50
❑ 39 Troy Brown	.30	.75
❑ 40 Anthony Wright	.20	.50
❑ 41 Zach Thomas	.50	1.25
❑ 42 Qadry Ismail	.30	.75
❑ 43 Jake Plummer	.30	.75
❑ 44 Keenan McCardell	.20	.50
❑ 45 Charles Johnson	.20	.50
❑ 46 Brett Favre	1.50	4.00
❑ 47 Jacquez Green	.20	.50
❑ 48 Matt Hasselbeck	.30	.75
❑ 49 Tiki Barber	.50	1.25
❑ 50 Jeff Garcia	.50	1.25
❑ 51 Shawn Jefferson	.20	.50
❑ 52 Kevin Johnson	.30	.75
❑ 53 Terrence Wilkins	.20	.50
❑ 54 Mike Anderson	.50	1.25
❑ 55 Tim Brown	.50	1.25
❑ 56 Champ Bailey	.50	1.25
❑ 57 Jimmy Smith	.30	.75
❑ 58 Trent Dilfer	.30	.75
❑ 59 James Allen	.30	.75
❑ 60 David Boston	.50	1.25
❑ 61 Jeremiah Trotter	.30	.75
❑ 62 Freddie Jones	.20	.50
❑ 63 Deion Sanders	.50	1.25
❑ 64 Darrell Jackson	.50	1.25
❑ 65 David Patten	.20	.50
❑ 66 Jeremy McDaniel	.20	.50
❑ 67 Jay Fiedler	.50	1.25
❑ 68 Chad Lewis	.20	.50
❑ 69 Rocket Ismail	.30	.75
❑ 70 Cade McNown	.20	.50
❑ 71 Jevon Kearse	.30	.75
❑ 72 Jermaine Fazande	.20	.50
❑ 73 Junior Seau	.50	1.25
❑ 74 Rod Smith	.30	.75
❑ 75 Jermaine Lewis	.20	.50
❑ 76 Dennis Northcutt	.30	.75
❑ 77 Charlie Garner	.30	.75
❑ 78 Charles Woodson	.30	.75
❑ 79 Wayne Chrebet	.30	.75
❑ 80 Ahman Green	.50	1.25
❑ 81 Donald Hayes	.20	.50
❑ 82 Terance Mathis	.20	.50
❑ 83 Warrick Dunn	.50	1.25
❑ 84 Chris Sanders	.20	.50
❑ 85 Albert Connell	.20	.50
❑ 86 Robert Griffith	.20	.50
❑ 87 Germane Crowell	.20	.50
❑ 88 Tony Banks	.30	.75
❑ 89 Travis Taylor	.30	.75
❑ 90 Akili Smith	.20	.50
❑ 91 Michael Westbrook	.30	.75
❑ 92 Doug Flutie	.50	1.25
❑ 93 Ike Hilliard	.30	.75
❑ 94 Terry Glenn	.20	.50
❑ 95 Leslie Shepherd	.20	.50
❑ 96 Az-Zahir Hakim	.20	.50
❑ 97 La'Roi Glover	.20	.50
❑ 98 Peyton Manning	1.25	3.00
❑ 99 Jackie Harris	.20	.50
❑ 100 Edgerrin James	.60	1.50
❑ 101 Peerless Price	.30	.75
❑ 102 Jamal Anderson	.50	1.25
❑ 103 Keyshawn Johnson	.50	1.25
❑ 104 Derrick Mason	.30	.75
❑ 105 J.J. Stokes	.30	.75
❑ 106 Kevin Faulk	.30	.75
❑ 107 Tony Richardson	.20	.50
❑ 108 James Stewart	.30	.75
❑ 109 Tim Biakabutuka	.30	.75
❑ 110 Jon Kitna	.50	1.25
❑ 111 Thomas Jones	.30	.75
❑ 112 Steve McNair	.50	1.25
❑ 113 Sean Dawkins	.20	.50
❑ 114 Jerome Bettis	.50	1.25
❑ 115 Donovan McNabb	.60	1.50
❑ 116 Bill Schroeder	.30	.75
❑ 117 Rod Woodson	.30	.75
❑ 118 James McKnight	.30	.75
❑ 119 Daunte Culpepper	.50	1.25
❑ 120 Todd Husak	.20	.50
❑ 121 Shaun King	.20	.50
❑ 122 Tyrone Wheatley	.30	.75
❑ 123 Curtis Martin	.50	1.25
❑ 124 Terrell Davis	.50	1.25
❑ 125 Steve Beuerlein	.30	.75
❑ 126 Brad Johnson	.50	1.25
❑ 127 Joe Horn	.30	.75
❑ 128 Fred Taylor	.50	1.25
❑ 129 Brian Urlacher	.75	2.00
❑ 130 Ray Lewis	.50	1.25
❑ 131 Marshall Faulk	.60	1.50
❑ 132 Curtis Conway	.30	.75
❑ 133 Jason Sehorn	.20	.50
❑ 134 Jerome Pathon	.30	.75
❑ 135 Derrick Alexander	.30	.75
❑ 136 Jerry Rice	1.00	2.50
❑ 137 Jeff George	.30	.75
❑ 138 Johnnie Morton	.30	.75
❑ 139 Eric Moulds	.30	.75
❑ 140 Duce Staley	.50	1.25
❑ 141 Vinny Testaverde	.30	.75
❑ 142 Eddie George	.50	1.25
❑ 143 Shaun Alexander	.60	1.50
❑ 144 Drew Bledsoe	.60	1.50
❑ 145 Emmitt Smith	1.00	2.50
❑ 146 Marvin Harrison	.50	1.25
❑ 147 Frank Sanders	.20	.50
❑ 148 Aaron Shea	.20	.50
❑ 149 Cris Carter	.50	1.25
❑ 150 Tony Gonzalez	.30	.75
❑ 151 Marcus Robinson	.50	1.25
❑ 152 Danny Farmer	.20	.50
❑ 153 Warren Sapp	.30	.75
❑ 154 Kurt Warner	1.00	2.50
❑ 155 Jessie Armstead	.20	.50
❑ 156 Lawyer Milloy	.30	.75
❑ 157 Brian Griese	.50	1.25
❑ 158 Jason Taylor	.20	.50
❑ 159 Jeff Lewis	.20	.50
❑ 160 Travis Prentice	.20	.50
❑ 161 Tim Dwight	.50	1.25
❑ 162 Kyle Brady	.20	.50
❑ 163 Bubba Franks	.30	.75
❑ 164 James Thrash	.30	.75
❑ 165 Bobby Shaw	.20	.50
❑ 166 Ron Dayne	.50	1.25
❑ 167 Mike Alstott	.50	1.25
❑ 168 Bruce Smith	.20	.50
❑ 169 Jeff Graham	.20	.50
❑ 170 Jeff Blake	.30	.75
❑ 171 Laveranues Coles	.50	1.25
❑ 172 Herman Moore	.30	.75
❑ 173 Shannon Sharpe	.30	.75
❑ 174 Corey Dillon	.50	1.25
❑ 175 Ken Dilger	.20	.50
❑ 176 Eddie Kennison	.20	.50
❑ 177 Andre Rison	.30	.75
❑ 178 Stephen Davis	.50	1.25
❑ 179 Torry Holt	.50	1.25
❑ 180 Samari Rolle	.20	.50
❑ 181 Michael Strahan	.30	.75
❑ 182 Plaxico Burress	.50	1.25
❑ 183 Darnell Autry	.20	.50
❑ 184 Wesley Walls	.20	.50

Card	Low	High
❑ 185 Elvis Grbac	.30	.75
❑ 186 Marcus Pollard	.20	.50
❑ 187 Keith Poole	.20	.50
❑ 188 Ryan Leaf	.30	.75
❑ 189 Terrell Owens	.50	1.25
❑ 190 Dedric Ward	.20	.50
❑ 191 Donald Driver	.30	.75
❑ 192 Larry Foster	.20	.50
❑ 193 Priest Holmes	.60	1.50
❑ 194 Sammy Morris	.20	.50
❑ 195 Reggie Jones	.20	.50
❑ 196 Kordell Stewart	.30	.75
❑ 197 Sylvester Morris	.20	.50
❑ 198 Aaron Brooks	.50	1.25
❑ 199 Tai Streets	.20	.50
❑ 200 Chad Pennington	.75	2.00
❑ 201 Terrell Owens SH	.50	1.25
❑ 202 Marshall Faulk SH	.50	1.25
❑ 203 Mike Anderson SH	.30	.75
❑ 204 Cris Carter SH	.50	1.25
❑ 205 Corey Dillon SH	.50	1.25
❑ 206 Daunte Culpepper SH	.50	1.25
❑ 207 Peyton Manning SH	.60	1.50
❑ 208 Torry Holt SH	.50	1.25
❑ 209 Marvin Harrison SH	.50	1.25
❑ 210 Edgerrin James SH	.50	1.25
❑ 211 Sam Madison	.20	.50
❑ 212 Jonathan Quinn	.20	.50
❑ 213 Rob Morris	.20	.50
❑ 214 E.G. Green	.20	.50
❑ 215 David Sloan	.20	.50
❑ 216 Jason Tucker	.20	.50
❑ 217 Wali Rainer	.20	.50
❑ 218 Jerry Azumah	.20	.50
❑ 219 Dameyune Craig	.20	.50
❑ 220 Jammi German	.20	.50
❑ 221 LaDainian Tomlinson RC	75.00	150.00
❑ 222 Quincy Morgan RC	7.50	20.00
❑ 223 Steve Smith RC	20.00	40.00
❑ 224 Santana Moss RC	12.50	30.00
❑ 225 Koren Robinson RC	7.50	20.00
❑ 226 Kevin Kasper RC	7.50	20.00
❑ 227 Jamie Henderson RC	5.00	12.00
❑ 228 Adam Archuleta RC	7.50	20.00
❑ 229 Drew Brees RC	60.00	120.00
❑ 230 Michael Stone RC	3.00	8.00
❑ 231 Jamar Fletcher RC	5.00	12.00
❑ 232 Eric Westmoreland RC	5.00	12.00
❑ 233 Chris Barnes RC	5.00	12.00
❑ 234 Gerard Warren RC	7.50	20.00
❑ 235 Snoop Minnis RC	5.00	12.00
❑ 236 Chris Chambers RC	12.50	25.00
❑ 237 Damerien McCants RC	5.00	12.00
❑ 238 Kevan Barlow RC	7.50	20.00
❑ 239 Mike McMahon RC	7.50	20.00
❑ 240 Jabari Holloway RC	5.00	12.00
❑ 241 Travis Henry RC	7.50	20.00
❑ 242 Derrick Blaylock RC	7.50	20.00
❑ 243 Tim Hasselbeck RC	7.50	20.00
❑ 244 Andre Carter RC	7.50	20.00
❑ 245 Sage Rosenfels RC	7.50	20.00
❑ 246 Cedrick Wilson RC	7.50	20.00
❑ 247 Scotty Anderson RC	5.00	12.00
❑ 248 Ken-Yon Rambo RC	5.00	12.00
❑ 249 Marques Tuiasosopo RC	7.50	20.00
❑ 250 Reggie Wayne RC	15.00	30.00
❑ 251 Onomo Ojo RC	5.00	12.00
❑ 252 James Jackson RC	7.50	20.00
❑ 253 Moran Norris RC	3.00	8.00
❑ 254 Rashard Casey RC	5.00	12.00
❑ 255 Rudi Johnson RC	15.00	40.00
❑ 256 Willie Middlebrooks RC	5.00	12.00
❑ 257 Freddie Mitchell RC	7.50	20.00
❑ 258 Deuce McAllister RC	12.00	30.00
❑ 259 Chad Johnson RC	20.00	50.00
❑ 260 David Terrell RC	7.50	20.00
❑ 261 Jamal Reynolds RC	7.50	20.00
❑ 262 Michael Vick RC	30.00	60.00
❑ 263 Marcus Stroud RC	7.50	20.00
❑ 264 Dan Alexander RC	7.50	20.00
❑ 265 Jonathan Carter RC	5.00	12.00
❑ 266 Bobby Newcombe RC	5.00	12.00
❑ 267 Eddie Berlin RC	5.00	12.00
❑ 268 LaMont Jordan RC	15.00	40.00
❑ 269 Michael Bennett RC	7.50	20.00
❑ 270 Shaun Rogers RC	7.50	20.00
❑ 271 Travis Minor RC	5.00	12.00
❑ 272 Jesse Palmer RC	7.50	20.00
❑ 273 Derrick Gibson RC	5.00	12.00
❑ 274 Chris Weinke RC	7.50	20.00
❑ 275 Nate Clements RC	7.50	20.00
❑ 276 Eric Kelly RC	3.00	8.00
❑ 277 Justin Smith RC	7.50	20.00
❑ 278 Ryan Pickett RC	3.00	8.00
❑ 279 Anthony Thomas RC	7.50	20.00
❑ 280 Will Allen RC	5.00	12.00
❑ 281 Quincy Carter RC	7.50	20.00
❑ 282 Richard Seymour RC	7.50	20.00
❑ 283 Dan Morgan RC	7.50	20.00
❑ 284 Tay Cody RC	3.00	8.00
❑ 285 Alge Crumpler RC	10.00	25.00
❑ 286 Robert Ferguson RC	7.50	20.00
❑ 287 Will Peterson RC	5.00	12.00
❑ 288 Tony Dixon RC	5.00	12.00
❑ 289 Correll Buckhalter RC	7.50	20.00
❑ 290 Rod Gardner RC	7.50	20.00
❑ 291 Justin McCareins RC	7.50	20.00
❑ 292 Josh Heupel RC	7.50	20.00
❑ 293 Todd Heap RC	7.50	20.00
❑ 294 Damione Lewis RC	5.00	12.00
❑ 295 George Layne RC	5.00	12.00
❑ 296 Jamie Winborn RC	5.00	12.00
❑ 297 Billy Baber RC	3.00	8.00
❑ 298 T.J. Houshmandzadeh RC	10.00	25.00
❑ 299 Aaron Schobel RC	7.50	20.00
❑ 300 Gary Baxter RC	5.00	12.00
❑ 301 DeLawrence Grant RC	3.00	8.00
❑ 302 Morlon Greenwood RC	5.00	12.00
❑ 303 Shad Meier RC	5.00	12.00
❑ 304 Torrance Marshall RC	7.50	20.00
❑ 305 David Martin RC	5.00	12.00
❑ 306 Anthony Henry RC	7.50	20.00
❑ 307 Derrick Burgess RC	7.50	20.00
❑ 308 Andre Dyson RC	3.00	8.00
❑ 309 Ryan Helming RC	3.00	8.00
❑ 310 Fred Smoot RC	7.50	20.00
❑ 311 Arther Love RC	3.00	8.00
❑ 312 John Capel RC	5.00	12.00
❑ 313 Brandon Spoon RC	5.00	12.00
❑ 314 Karon Riley RC	3.00	8.00
❑ 315 Andre King RC	5.00	12.00
❑ 316 Quentin McCord RC	5.00	12.00
❑ 317 Zeke Moreno RC	7.50	20.00
❑ 318 Francis St. Paul RC	5.00	12.00
❑ 319 Richmond Flowers RC	5.00	12.00
❑ 320 Derek Combs RC	5.00	12.00

2002 Topps Chrome

Card	Low	High
❑ COMP.SET w/o SP's (165)	20.00	50.00
❑ 1 Anthony Thomas	.40	1.00
❑ 2 Jake Plummer	.40	1.00
❑ 3 Maurice Smith	.30	.75
❑ 4 Jamal Lewis	.40	1.00
❑ 5 Ray Lewis	.50	1.25
❑ 6 Alex Van Pelt	.30	.75
❑ 7 Chris Weinke	.30	.75
❑ 8 Corey Dillon	.40	1.00
❑ 9 Quincy Morgan	.30	.75
❑ 10 Rocket Ismail	.40	1.00
❑ 11 Brian Griese	.40	1.00
❑ 12 Johnnie Morton	.40	1.00
❑ 13 Edgerrin James	.50	1.25
❑ 14 Keenan McCardell	.40	1.00
❑ 15 Travis Minor	.40	1.00
❑ 16 Sylvester Morris	.30	.75
❑ 17 Randy Moss	.50	1.25
❑ 18 Drew Bledsoe	.50	1.25
❑ 19 Willie Jackson	.30	.75
❑ 20 Michael Strahan	.50	1.25
❑ 21 Santana Moss	.40	1.00
❑ 22 Duce Staley	.40	1.00
❑ 23 Kendrell Bell	.30	.75
❑ 24 LaDainian Tomlinson	.75	2.00
❑ 25 Terrell Owens	.50	1.25
❑ 26 Shaun Alexander	.50	1.25
❑ 27 Trung Canidate	.30	.75
❑ 28 Mike Alstott	.40	1.00
❑ 29 Kevin Dyson	.40	1.00
❑ 30 Rod Gardner	.30	.75
❑ 31 David Boston	.30	.75
❑ 32 Michael Vick	.50	1.25
❑ 33 Qadry Ismail	.40	1.00
❑ 34 Peerless Price	.30	.75
❑ 35 Rob Johnson	.40	1.00
❑ 36 Marcus Robinson	.40	1.00
❑ 37 Peter Warrick	.40	1.00
❑ 38 Kevin Johnson	.30	.75
❑ 39 Ed McCaffrey	.40	1.00
❑ 40 Shaun Rogers	.30	.75
❑ 41 Marvin Harrison	.50	1.25
❑ 42 Priest Holmes	.50	1.25
❑ 43 Oronde Gadsden	.30	.75
❑ 44 Terry Glenn	.40	1.00
❑ 45 Ike Hilliard	.40	1.00
❑ 46 Charles Woodson	.50	1.25
❑ 47 Freddie Mitchell	.30	.75
❑ 48 Drew Brees	.75	2.00
❑ 49 Jeff Garcia	.40	1.00
❑ 50 Kurt Warner	.50	1.25
❑ 51 Keyshawn Johnson	.40	1.00
❑ 52 Jevon Kearse	.40	1.00
❑ 53 Stephen Davis	.40	1.00
❑ 54 Shannon Sharpe	.50	1.25
❑ 55 Eric Moulds	.40	1.00
❑ 56 Muhsin Muhammad	.40	1.00
❑ 57 Brian Urlacher	.60	1.50
❑ 58 Chad Johnson	.50	1.25
❑ 59 Tim Couch	.30	.75
❑ 60 Mike Anderson	.40	1.00
❑ 61 James Stewart	.30	.75
❑ 62 Corey Bradford	.30	.75
❑ 63 Reggie Wayne	.50	1.25
❑ 64 Mark Brunell	.40	1.00
❑ 65 Trent Green	.40	1.00
❑ 66 Zach Thomas	.50	1.25
❑ 67 Michael Bennett	.40	1.00
❑ 68 Troy Brown	.40	1.00
❑ 69 Amani Toomer	.40	1.00
❑ 70 Curtis Martin	.50	1.25
❑ 71 Tim Brown	.50	1.25
❑ 72 Correll Buckhalter	.40	1.00
❑ 73 Kordell Stewart	.40	1.00
❑ 74 Junior Seau	.50	1.25
❑ 75 Kevan Barlow	.30	.75
❑ 76 Matt Hasselbeck	.50	1.25
❑ 77 Marshall Faulk	.50	1.25
❑ 78 Warren Sapp	.40	1.00
❑ 79 Frank Wycheck	.30	.75
❑ 80 Michael Westbrook	.30	.75
❑ 81 Travis Henry	.40	1.00
❑ 82 David Terrell	.40	1.00
❑ 83 Jon Kitna	.40	1.00
❑ 84 James Jackson	.30	.75
❑ 85 Joey Galloway	.40	1.00
❑ 86 Rod Smith	.40	1.00
❑ 87 Gormano Crowell	.30	.75
❑ 88 Bill Schroeder	.40	1.00
❑ 89 Dominic Rhodes	.40	1.00
❑ 90 Fred Taylor	.50	1.25
❑ 91 Snoop Minnis	.30	.75
❑ 92 Chris Chambers	.50	1.25
❑ 93 Daunte Culpepper	.40	1.00
❑ 94 Deuce McAllister	.50	1.25
❑ 95 Kerry Collins	.40	1.00
❑ 96 John Abraham	.40	1.00
❑ 97 Rich Gannon	.40	1.00
❑ 98 Tiki Barber	.50	1.25
❑ 99 Hines Ward	.50	1.25
❑ 100 Tom Brady	1.25	3.00
❑ 101 Tim Dwight	.40	1.00
❑ 102 Garrison Hearst	.40	1.00
❑ 103 Darrell Jackson	.40	1.00
❑ 104 Isaac Bruce	.50	1.25
❑ 105 Brad Johnson	.40	1.00
❑ 106 Steve McNair	.50	1.25
❑ 107 Champ Bailey	.50	1.25
❑ 108 Emmitt Smith	1.25	3.00
❑ 109 Mike McMahon	.30	.75
❑ 110 Terrell Davis	.50	1.25
❑ 111 Antonio Freeman	.50	1.25

Card		
112 Jimmy Smith	.40	1.00
113 Tony Gonzalez	.40	1.00
114 Jay Fiedler	.40	1.00
115 Cris Carter	.50	1.25
116 David Patten	.30	.75
117 Joe Horn	.40	1.00
118 Laveranues Coles	.50	1.25
119 Charlie Garner	.40	1.00
120 Donovan McNabb	.60	1.50
121 Jerome Bettis	.50	1.25
122 Curtis Conway	.40	1.00
123 Az-Zahir Hakim	.30	.75
124 Warrick Dunn	.40	1.00
125 Eddie George	.40	1.00
126 Quincy Carter	.30	.75
127 Ahman Green	.40	1.00
128 Peyton Manning	1.00	2.50
129 James McKnight	.30	.75
130 Antowain Smith	.40	1.00
131 Ricky Williams	.50	1.25
132 Chad Pennington	.50	1.25
133 Jerry Rice	1.00	2.50
134 Todd Pinkston	.30	.75
135 Plaxico Burress	.40	1.00
136 Doug Flutie	.50	1.25
137 Koren Robinson	.30	.75
138 Torry Holt	.50	1.25
139 Aaron Brooks	.40	1.00
140 Ron Dayne	.40	1.00
141 Vinny Testaverde	.40	1.00
142 Brett Favre	1.25	3.00
143 James Thrash	.40	1.00
144 Wayne Chrebet	.40	1.00
145 Derrick Mason	.40	1.00
146 Ahman Green WW	.30	.75
147 Peyton Manning WW	.75	2.00
148 Kurt Warner WW	.40	1.00
149 Daunte Culpepper WW	.30	.75
150 Tom Brady WW	1.00	2.50
151 Rod Gardner WW	.25	.60
152 Corey Dillon WW	.30	.75
153 Priest Holmes WW	.40	1.00
154 Shaun Alexander WW	.40	1.00
155 Randy Moss WW	.40	1.00
156 Eric Moulds WW	.30	.75
157 Brett Favre WW	1.00	2.50
158 Todd Bouman WW	.25	.60
159 Dominic Rhodes WW	.30	.75
160 Marvin Harrison WW	.40	1.00
161 Torry Holt WW	.40	1.00
162 Derrick Mason WW	.30	.75
163 Jerry Rice WW	.75	2.00
164 Donovan McNabb WW	.50	1.25
165 Marshall Faulk WW	.40	1.00
166 David Carr RC	4.00	10.00
167 Quentin Jammer RC	4.00	10.00
168 Mike Williams RC	2.50	6.00
169 Rocky Calmus RC	3.00	8.00
170 Travis Fisher RC	3.00	8.00
171 Dwight Freeney RC	6.00	15.00
172 Jeremy Shockey RC	6.00	15.00
173 Marquise Walker RC	2.50	6.00
174 Eric Crouch RC	4.00	10.00
175 DeShaun Foster RC	4.00	10.00
176 Roy Williams RC	5.00	12.00
177 Andre Davis RC	3.00	8.00
178 Alex Brown RC	4.00	10.00
179 Michael Lewis RC	4.00	10.00
180 Terry Charles RC	2.50	6.00
181 Clinton Portis RC	10.00	25.00
182 Dennis Johnson RC	2.50	6.00
183 Lito Sheppard RC	4.00	10.00
184 Ryan Sims RC	4.00	10.00
185 Raonall Smith RC	2.50	6.00
186 Albert Haynesworth RC	4.00	10.00
187 Eddie Freeman RC	2.50	6.00
188 Levi Jones RC	2.50	6.00
189 Josh McCown RC	4.00	10.00
190 Cliff Russell RC	2.50	6.00
191 Maurice Morris RC	4.00	10.00
192 Antwaan Randle El RC	4.00	10.00
193 Ladell Betts RC	4.00	10.00
194 Daniel Graham RC	3.00	8.00
195 David Garrard RC	6.00	15.00
196 Antonio Bryant RC	5.00	12.00
197 Patrick Ramsey RC	4.00	10.00
198 Kelly Campbell RC	3.00	8.00
199 Will Overstreet RC	2.50	6.00
200 Ryan Denney RC	2.50	6.00
201 John Henderson RC	4.00	10.00
202 Freddie Milons RC	2.50	6.00
203 Tim Carter RC	3.00	8.00
204 Kurt Kittner RC	2.50	6.00
205 Joey Harrington RC	4.00	10.00
206 Ricky Williams RC	3.00	8.00
207 Bryant McKinnie RC	2.50	6.00
208 Ed Reed RC	12.00	30.00
209 Josh Reed RC	3.00	8.00
210 Seth Burford RC	2.50	6.00
211 Javon Walker RC	4.00	10.00
212 Jamar Martin RC	3.00	8.00
213 Leonard Henry RC	2.50	6.00
214 Julius Peppers RC	6.00	15.00
215 Jabar Gaffney RC	4.00	10.00
216 Kalimba Edwards RC	3.00	8.00
217 Napoleon Harris RC	3.00	8.00
218 Ashley Lelie RC	4.00	10.00
219 Anthony Weaver RC	2.50	6.00
220 Bryan Thomas RC	2.50	6.00
221 Wendell Bryant RC	2.50	6.00
222 Damien Anderson RC	3.00	8.00
223 Travis Stephens RC	2.50	6.00
224 Rohan Davey RC	4.00	10.00
225 Mike Pearson RC	2.50	6.00
226 Marc Colombo RC	2.50	6.00
227 Phillip Buchanon RC	4.00	10.00
228 T.J. Duckett RC	4.00	10.00
229 Ron Johnson RC	3.00	8.00
230 Larry Tripplett RC	2.50	6.00
231 Randy Fasani RC	3.00	8.00
232 Keyuo Craver RC	2.50	6.00
233 Marquand Manuel RC	2.50	6.00
234 Jonathan Wells RC	4.00	10.00
235 Reche Caldwell RC	4.00	10.00
236 Luke Staley RC	2.50	6.00
237 Donte Stallworth RC	4.00	10.00
238 Levar Fisher RC	2.50	6.00
239 Lamar Gordon RC	4.00	10.00
240 William Green RC	3.00	8.00
241 Dusty Bonner RC	2.50	6.00
242 Craig Nall RC	3.00	8.00
243 Eric McCoo RC	2.50	6.00
244 David Thornton RC	2.50	6.00
245 Terry Jones RC	2.50	6.00
246 Lee Mays RC	2.50	6.00
247 Bryan Fletcher RC	2.50	6.00
248 Verron Haynes RC	3.00	8.00
249 Zak Kustok RC	2.50	6.00
250 Chad Hutchinson RC	2.50	6.00
251 Andra Davis RC	2.50	6.00
252 Wes Pate RC	2.50	6.00
253 Jon McGraw RC	2.50	6.00
254 Howard Green RC	2.50	6.00
255 Daryl Jones RC	2.50	6.00
256 David Priestley RC	2.50	6.00
257 Marques Anderson RC	3.00	8.00
258 Roosevelt Williams RC	2.50	6.00
259 Major Applewhite RC	4.00	10.00
260 Ronald Curry RC	4.00	10.00
261 Adrian Peterson RC	4.00	10.00
262 Tellis Redmon RC	2.50	6.00
263 Chester Taylor RC	6.00	15.00
264 Deion Branch RC	4.00	10.00
265 Tank Williams RC	3.00	8.00

2003 Topps Chrome

Card		
COMP.SET w/o SP's (165)	15.00	40.00
1 Michael Vick	.50	1.25
2 Josh Reed	.30	.75
3 James Stewart	.40	1.00
4 Quincy Morgan	.30	.75
5 Corey Bradford	.30	.75
6 Fred Taylor	.50	1.25
7 David Patten	.30	.75
8 Jerome Bettis	.50	1.25
9 Jerry Porter	.40	1.00
10 Steve McNair	.50	1.25
11 Stephen Davis	.40	1.00
12 Frank Wycheck	.30	.75
13 Marcus Pollard	.30	.75
14 David Terrell	.30	.75
15 Bubba Franks	.40	1.00
16 Trent Green	.40	1.00
17 Mark Brunell	.40	1.00
18 James Thrash	.30	.75
19 Mike Alstott	.50	1.25
20 Deuce McAllister	.50	1.25
21 Santana Moss	.40	1.00
22 Jason Taylor	.40	1.00
23 Corey Dillon	.40	1.00
24 Jeff Blake	.40	1.00
25 Ed McCaffrey	.40	1.00
26 Priest Holmes	.50	1.25
27 Tim Brown	.50	1.25
28 Curtis Martin	.50	1.25
29 Derrius Thompson	.30	.75
30 Jonathan Wells	.30	.75
31 William Green	.30	.75
32 Bill Schroeder	.30	.75
33 Amos Zereoue	.30	.75
34 Warren Sapp	.40	1.00
35 Koren Robinson	.40	1.00
36 Donovan McNabb	.50	1.25
37 Edgerrin James	.50	1.25
38 Kelly Holcomb	.30	.75
39 Daunte Culpepper	.50	1.25
40 Tommy Maddox	.40	1.00
41 Rod Gardner	.30	.75
42 T.J. Duckett	.40	1.00
43 Drew Bledsoe	.50	1.25
44 Rod Smith	.40	1.00
45 Peyton Manning	1.00	2.50
46 Darrell Jackson	.40	1.00
47 Brett Favre	1.25	3.00
48 Ashley Lelie	.30	.75
49 Jeremy Shockey	.50	1.25
50 Hines Ward	.50	1.25
51 Jeff Garcia	.50	1.25
52 Eddie Kennison	.30	.75
53 Brian Urlacher	.75	2.00
54 Antwaan Randle El	.40	1.00
55 Eddie George	.40	1.00
56 Derrick Brooks	.40	1.00
57 Isaac Bruce	.50	1.25
58 Joe Horn	.40	1.00
59 Jon Kitna	.40	1.00
60 David Boston	.30	.75
61 Todd Heap	.40	1.00
62 Lamar Smith	.40	1.00
63 Germane Crowell	.30	.75
64 Kevin Johnson	.30	.75
65 Drew Brees	.50	1.25
66 Chad Lewis	.40	1.00
67 Charlie Garner	.40	1.00
68 Laveranues Coles	.40	1.00
69 Shaun Alexander	.50	1.25
70 Kevan Barlow	.30	.75
71 Aaron Brooks	.40	1.00
72 Jake Plummer	.40	1.00
73 Emmitt Smith	1.25	3.00
74 Terry Glenn	.40	1.00
75 Michael Bennett	.40	1.00
76 Deion Branch	.40	1.00
77 Keyshawn Johnson	.50	1.25
78 Marc Bulger	.50	1.25
79 Matt Hasselbeck	.40	1.00
80 Garrison Hearst	.40	1.00
81 Brian Griese	.40	1.00
82 Johnnie Morton	.40	1.00
83 Patrick Ramsey	.40	1.00
84 Donald Driver	.50	1.25
85 Joey Harrington	.40	1.00
86 Ricky Williams	.40	1.00
87 Jabar Gaffney	.30	.75
88 Duce Staley	.40	1.00
89 Jimmy Smith	.40	1.00
90 Reggie Wayne	.40	1.00
91 Chad Johnson	.50	1.25
92 Steve Beuerlein	.40	1.00
93 Joey Galloway	.40	1.00

Card	Low	High
❑ 94 Curtis Conway	.30	.75
❑ 95 Brad Johnson	.40	1.00
❑ 96 Jamal Lewis	.50	1.25
❑ 97 Terrell Owens	.50	1.25
❑ 98 Todd Pinkston	.30	.75
❑ 99 Keenan McCardell	.40	1.00
❑ 100 Antonio Bryant	.50	1.25
❑ 101 Eric Moulds	.40	1.00
❑ 102 Jim Miller	.40	1.00
❑ 103 Troy Brown	.40	1.00
❑ 104 Rich Gannon	.40	1.00
❑ 105 Chad Pennington	.50	1.25
❑ 106 Michael Strahan	.40	1.00
❑ 107 Chris Chambers	.40	1.00
❑ 108 Antowain Smith	.40	1.00
❑ 109 Derrick Mason	.40	1.00
❑ 110 Michael Pittman	.30	.75
❑ 111 Torry Holt	.50	1.25
❑ 112 Tony Gonzalez	.40	1.00
❑ 113 Marty Booker	.40	1.00
❑ 114 Shannon Sharpe	.40	1.00
❑ 115 Zach Thomas	.50	1.25
❑ 116 Plaxico Burress	.50	1.25
❑ 117 Kurt Warner	.50	1.25
❑ 118 Warrick Dunn	.40	1.00
❑ 119 Jay Fiedler	.40	1.00
❑ 120 LaMont Jordan	.40	1.00
❑ 121 Kerry Collins	.40	1.00
❑ 122 Jerry Rice	1.00	2.50
❑ 123 Randy Moss	.50	1.25
❑ 124 Tom Brady	1.25	3.00
❑ 125 Amani Toomer	.40	1.00
❑ 126 Travis Henry	.40	1.00
❑ 127 Chris Chandler	.40	1.00
❑ 128 Ray Lewis	.50	1.25
❑ 129 Donte Stallworth	.40	1.00
❑ 130 David Carr	.50	1.25
❑ 131 Andre Davis	.30	.75
❑ 132 Travis Taylor	.30	.75
❑ 133 Steve Smith	.50	1.25
❑ 134 Tiki Barber	.50	1.25
❑ 135 Chad Hutchinson	.30	.75
❑ 136 Marshall Faulk	.50	1.25
❑ 137 Peerless Price	.30	.75
❑ 138 Ahman Green	.50	1.25
❑ 139 Julius Peppers	.50	1.25
❑ 140 LaDainian Tomlinson	.60	1.50
❑ 141 Muhsin Muhammad	.40	1.00
❑ 142 Tim Couch	.30	.75
❑ 143 Clinton Portis	.60	1.50
❑ 144 Anthony Thomas	.40	1.00
❑ 145 Marvin Harrison	.50	1.25
❑ 146 Priest Holmes WW	.40	1.00
❑ 147 Drew Bledsoe WW	.40	1.00
❑ 148 Tom Brady WW	1.00	2.50
❑ 149 Shaun Alexander WW	.40	1.00
❑ 150 Brett Favre WW	1.00	2.50
❑ 151 Travis Henry WW	.30	.75
❑ 152 Marshall Faulk WW	.40	1.00
❑ 153 Terrell Owens WW	.40	1.00
❑ 154 Jeff Garcia WW	.40	1.00
❑ 155 Plaxico Burress WW	.40	1.00
❑ 156 Donovan McNabb WW	.40	1.00
❑ 157 Ricky Williams WW	.30	.75
❑ 158 Michael Vick WW	.40	1.00
❑ 159 Steve Smith WW	.40	1.00
❑ 160 Marvin Harrison WW	.40	1.00
❑ 161 Chad Pennington WW	.40	1.00
❑ 162 Jeremy Shockey WW	.40	1.00
❑ 163 Tommy Maddox WW	.30	.75
❑ 164 Steve McNair WW	.40	1.00
❑ 165 Rich Gannon WW	.30	.75
❑ 166 Carson Palmer RC	8.00	20.00
❑ 167 J.R. Tolver RC	1.50	4.00
❑ 168 Michael Haynes RC	1.25	3.00
❑ 169 Terrell Suggs RC	2.50	6.00
❑ 170 Rashean Mathis RC	1.50	4.00
❑ 171 Chris Kelsay RC	1.50	4.00
❑ 172 Brad Banks RC	1.50	4.00
❑ 173 Jordan Gross RC	1.25	3.00
❑ 174 Lee Suggs RC	1.50	4.00
❑ 175 Kliff Kingsbury RC	1.50	4.00
❑ 176 William Joseph RC	1.25	3.00
❑ 177 Kelley Washington RC	1.50	4.00
❑ 178 Jerome McDougle RC	1.25	3.00
❑ 179 Keenan Howry RC	1.25	3.00
❑ 180 Chris Simms RC	2.00	5.00
❑ 181 Alonzo Jackson RC	1.25	3.00
❑ 182 L.J. Smith RC	2.00	5.00
❑ 183 Mike Doss RC	2.00	5.00
❑ 184 Bobby Wade RC	1.50	4.00
❑ 185 Ken Hamlin RC	2.00	5.00
❑ 186 Brandon Lloyd RC	2.00	5.00
❑ 187 Justin Fargas RC	2.00	5.00
❑ 188 DeWayne Robertson RC	1.50	4.00
❑ 189 Bryant Johnson RC	2.00	5.00
❑ 190 Boss Bailey RC	1.50	4.00
❑ 191 Onterrio Smith RC	1.50	4.00
❑ 192 Doug Gabriel RC	1.50	4.00
❑ 193 Jimmy Kennedy RC	1.50	4.00
❑ 194 B.J. Askew RC	1.50	4.00
❑ 195 Taylor Jacobs RC	1.50	4.00
❑ 196 Dallas Clark RC	4.00	10.00
❑ 197 DeWayne White RC	1.25	3.00
❑ 198 Arnaz Battle RC	2.00	5.00
❑ 199 Kareem Kelly RC	1.25	3.00
❑ 200 Talman Gardner RC	1.25	3.00
❑ 201 Billy McMullen RC	1.25	3.00
❑ 202 Travis Anglin RC	1.25	3.00
❑ 203 Anquan Boldin RC	5.00	12.00
❑ 204 Osi Umenyiora RC	3.00	8.00
❑ 205 Byron Leftwich RC	2.50	6.00
❑ 206 Marcus Trufant RC	2.00	5.00
❑ 207 Sam Aiken RC	2.00	5.00
❑ 208 LaBrandon Toefield RC	1.50	4.00
❑ 209 Terry Pierce RC	1.25	3.00
❑ 210 Charles Rogers RC	1.50	4.00
❑ 211 Chaun Thompson RC	1.25	3.00
❑ 212 Chris Brown RC	2.00	5.00
❑ 213 Justin Gage RC	2.00	5.00
❑ 214 Kevin Williams RC	2.00	5.00
❑ 215 Willis McGahee RC	4.00	10.00
❑ 216 Victor Hobson RC	1.25	3.00
❑ 217 Brian St.Pierre RC	2.00	5.00
❑ 218 Nate Burleson RC	1.50	4.00
❑ 219 Calvin Pace RC	1.50	4.00
❑ 220 Larry Johnson RC	2.50	6.00
❑ 221 Andre Woolfolk RC	1.50	4.00
❑ 222 Tyrone Calico RC	1.50	4.00
❑ 223 Seneca Wallace RC	2.00	5.00
❑ 224 Domanick Davis RC	2.00	5.00
❑ 225 Rex Grossman RC	2.00	5.00
❑ 226 Artose Pinner RC	1.25	3.00
❑ 227 Jason Witten RC	5.00	12.00
❑ 228 Bennie Joppru RC	1.25	3.00
❑ 229 Bethel Johnson RC	1.50	4.00
❑ 230 Kyle Boller RC	2.00	5.00
❑ 231 Shaun McDonald RC	2.00	5.00
❑ 232 Musa Smith RC	1.50	4.00
❑ 233 Ken Dorsey RC	1.50	4.00
❑ 234 Johnathan Sullivan RC	1.25	3.00
❑ 235 Andre Johnson RC	4.00	10.00
❑ 236 Nick Barnett RC	2.00	5.00
❑ 237 Teyo Johnson RC	1.50	4.00
❑ 238 Terence Newman RC	2.00	5.00
❑ 239 Kevin Curtis RC	2.00	5.00
❑ 240 Dave Ragone RC	1.25	3.00
❑ 241 Ty Warren RC	2.00	5.00
❑ 242 Walter Young RC	1.25	3.00
❑ 243 Kevin Walter RC	2.00	5.00
❑ 244 Carl Ford RC	1.25	3.00
❑ 245 Cecil Sapp RC	1.25	3.00
❑ 246 Sultan McCullough RC	1.25	3.00
❑ 247 Eugene Wilson RC	2.00	5.00
❑ 248 Ricky Manning RC	1.50	4.00
❑ 249 Andrew Williams RC	1.25	3.00
❑ 250 Juston Wood RC	1.25	3.00
❑ 251 Cory Redding RC	1.50	4.00
❑ 252 Charles Tillman RC	2.50	6.00
❑ 253 Terrence Edwards RC	1.25	3.00
❑ 254 Adrian Madise RC	1.25	3.00
❑ 255 David Kircus RC	2.00	5.00
❑ 256 Zuriel Smith RC	1.25	3.00
❑ 257 Earnest Graham RC	2.00	5.00
❑ 258 Ronald Bellamy RC	1.50	4.00
❑ 259 John Anderson RC	1.25	3.00
❑ 260 David Tyree RC	2.00	5.00
❑ 261 Malaefou MacKenzie RC	1.25	3.00
❑ 262 Ahmaad Galloway RC	1.50	4.00
❑ 263 Brooks Bollinger RC	2.00	5.00
❑ 264 Gibran Hamdan RC	1.25	3.00
❑ 265 Taco Wallace RC	1.25	3.00
❑ 266 LaTarence Dunbar RC	1.25	3.00
❑ 267 Justin Griffith RC	1.50	4.00
❑ 268 Bradie James RC	2.00	5.00
❑ 269 Danny Curley RC	1.25	3.00
❑ 270 Kenny Peterson RC	1.50	4.00
❑ 271 DeAndrew Rubin RC	1.25	3.00
❑ 272 Ryan Hoag RC	1.25	3.00
❑ 273 Rien Long RC	1.25	3.00
❑ 274 Troy Polamalu RC	15.00	30.00
❑ 275 Terrence Holt RC	1.50	4.00

2004 Topps Chrome

Card	Low	High
❑ COMP.SET w/o SP's (165)	12.50	30.00
❑ 1 Peyton Manning	.75	2.00
❑ 2 Patrick Ramsey	.30	.75
❑ 3 Justin McCareins	.25	.60
❑ 4 Matt Hasselbeck	.40	1.00
❑ 5 Chris Chambers	.30	.75
❑ 6 Bubba Franks	.30	.75
❑ 7 Eric Moulds	.30	.75
❑ 8 Anquan Boldin	.40	1.00
❑ 9 Brian Urlacher	.40	1.00
❑ 10 Stephen Davis	.30	.75
❑ 11 Michael Vick	.40	1.00
❑ 12 Dante Hall	.30	.75
❑ 13 Chad Pennington	.40	1.00
❑ 14 Kevan Barlow	.30	.75
❑ 15 Tommy Maddox	.30	.75
❑ 16 Domanick Davis	.30	.75
❑ 17 Dwight Freeney	.40	1.00
❑ 18 LaVar Arrington	.30	.75
❑ 19 Troy Hambrick	.25	.60
❑ 20 Jake Plummer	.30	.75
❑ 21 Willis McGahee	.40	1.00
❑ 22 Steve McNair	.40	1.00
❑ 23 Kerry Collins	.30	.75
❑ 24 Hines Ward	.40	1.00
❑ 25 Terrell Owens	.40	1.00
❑ 26 Jerome Pathon	.25	.60
❑ 27 Andre Johnson	.40	1.00
❑ 28 DeShaun Foster	.30	.75
❑ 29 Terrell Suggs	.25	.60
❑ 30 Marcel Shipp	.40	1.00
❑ 31 Kyle Boller	.30	.75
❑ 32 Javon Walker	.30	.75
❑ 33 Ahman Green	.40	1.00
❑ 34 Travis Henry	.30	.75
❑ 35 Randy McMichael	.25	.60
❑ 36 Jerry Rice	.75	2.00
❑ 37 Travis Taylor	.25	.60
❑ 38 Fred Taylor	.30	.75
❑ 39 Zach Thomas	.40	1.00
❑ 40 Marques Tuiasosopo	.25	.60
❑ 41 Laveranues Coles	.30	.75
❑ 42 Thomas Jones	.30	.75
❑ 43 Jamie Sharper	.25	.60
❑ 44 Quincy Morgan	.25	.60
❑ 45 Troy Brown	.30	.75
❑ 46 Joey Galloway	.30	.75
❑ 47 Justin Fargas	.30	.75
❑ 48 Daunte Culpepper	.40	1.00
❑ 49 Keenan McCardell	.25	.60
❑ 50 Priest Holmes	.40	1.00
❑ 51 Chad Johnson	.30	.75
❑ 52 Marty Booker	.30	.75
❑ 53 Tim Rattay	.25	.60
❑ 54 Brian Westbrook	.40	1.00
❑ 55 Ricky Williams	.40	1.00
❑ 56 Lee Suggs	.40	1.00
❑ 57 Keith Brooking	.25	.60
❑ 58 Rex Grossman	.40	1.00
❑ 59 Dallas Clark	.40	1.00
❑ 60 Charles Rogers	.30	.75
❑ 61 Donte' Stallworth	.30	.75
❑ 62 Deion Branch	.30	.75
❑ 63 Ike Hilliard	.30	.75
❑ 64 Michael Strahan	.30	.75
❑ 65 Randy Moss	.40	1.00

Card	Low	High
❑ 66 Isaac Bruce	.30	.75
❑ 67 Brad Johnson	.30	.75
❑ 68 Warrick Dunn	.30	.75
❑ 69 Josh McCown	.30	.75
❑ 70 Donovan McNabb	.40	1.00
❑ 71 Shaun Alexander	.40	1.00
❑ 72 William Green	.25	.60
❑ 73 Carson Palmer	.50	1.25
❑ 74 Quentin Griffin	.30	.75
❑ 75 LaDainian Tomlinson	.50	1.25
❑ 76 Edgerrin James	.40	1.00
❑ 77 Santana Moss	.30	.75
❑ 78 Marshall Faulk	.40	1.00
❑ 79 Tyrone Calico	.30	.75
❑ 80 Marvin Harrison	.40	1.00
❑ 81 Tony Gonzalez	.40	1.00
❑ 82 Deuce McAllister	.40	1.00
❑ 83 Drew Brees	.40	1.00
❑ 84 Todd Pinkston	.25	.60
❑ 85 Jeff Garcia	.40	1.00
❑ 86 Darrell Jackson	.30	.75
❑ 87 Ray Lewis	.40	1.00
❑ 88 Billy Volek	.30	.75
❑ 89 Rudi Johnson	.30	.75
❑ 90 Julius Peppers	.30	.75
❑ 91 Peter Warrick	.30	.75
❑ 92 Trent Green	.30	.75
❑ 93 Onterrio Smith	.25	.60
❑ 94 Jerome Bettis	.40	1.00
❑ 95 Keyshawn Johnson	.30	.75
❑ 96 Jamal Lewis	.30	.75
❑ 97 Alge Crumpler	.30	.75
❑ 98 Michael Bennett	.30	.75
❑ 99 Jimmy Smith	.30	.75
❑ 100 Brett Favre	1.00	2.50
❑ 101 Jerry Porter	.30	.75
❑ 102 Marc Bulger	.30	.75
❑ 103 David Carr	.30	.75
❑ 104 Mark Brunell	.30	.75
❑ 105 Aaron Brooks	.30	.75
❑ 106 Plaxico Burress	.30	.75
❑ 107 Correll Buckhalter	.30	.75
❑ 108 Jevon Kearse	.30	.75
❑ 109 Michael Pittman	.30	.75
❑ 110 Clinton Portis	.40	1.00
❑ 111 Corey Dillon	.30	.75
❑ 112 Steve Smith	.40	1.00
❑ 113 Eddie Kennison	.30	.75
❑ 114 Amani Toomer	.30	.75
❑ 115 Kelly Holcomb	.30	.75
❑ 116 Torry Holt	.40	1.00
❑ 117 Eddie George	.30	.75
❑ 118 Jeremy Shockey	.30	.75
❑ 119 Jon Kitna	.30	.75
❑ 120 Todd Heap	.30	.75
❑ 121 Ashley Lelie	.30	.75
❑ 122 Byron Leftwich	.40	1.00
❑ 123 Duce Staley	.30	.75
❑ 124 Rod Gardner	.25	.60
❑ 125 Tom Brady	1.00	2.50
❑ 126 Reggie Wayne	.30	.75
❑ 127 Joe Horn	.30	.75
❑ 128 Curtis Martin	.40	1.00
❑ 129 Charlie Garner	.30	.75
❑ 130 Derrick Mason	.30	.75
❑ 131 Marcus Robinson	.30	.75
❑ 132 David Boston	.25	.60
❑ 133 Drew Bledsoe	.40	1.00
❑ 134 Anthony Thomas	.30	.75
❑ 135 Tiki Barber	.40	1.00
❑ 136 Terry Glenn	.30	.75
❑ 137 A.J. Feeley	.30	.75
❑ 138 Peerless Price	.30	.75
❑ 139 Jake Delhomme	.30	.75
❑ 140 Kevin Faulk	.30	.75
❑ 141 Quincy Carter	.25	.60
❑ 142 Joey Harrington	.30	.75
❑ 143 Donald Driver	.40	1.00
❑ 144 Koren Robinson	.40	1.00
❑ 145 Rod Smith	.30	.75
❑ 146 Anquan Boldin WW	.25	.60
❑ 147 Jamal Lewis WW	.20	.50
❑ 148 Priest Holmes WW	.25	.60
❑ 149 Peyton Manning WW	.50	1.25
❑ 150 Marvin Harrison WW	.25	.60
❑ 151 Steve McNair WW	.25	.60
❑ 152 Travis Henry WW	.20	.50
❑ 153 Torry Holt WW	.25	.60
❑ 154 Tom Brady WW	.60	1.50
❑ 155 Ahman Green WW	.25	.60
❑ 156 Donovan McNabb WW	.25	.60
❑ 157 Deuce McAllister WW	.25	.60
❑ 158 Domanick Davis WW	.20	.50
❑ 159 Clinton Portis WW	.25	.60
❑ 160 Rudi Johnson WW	.20	.50
❑ 161 Brett Favre WW	.60	1.50
❑ 162 LaDainian Tomlinson WW	.30	.75
❑ 163 Steve Smith WW	.25	.60
❑ 164 Edgerrin James WW	.25	.60
❑ 165 Ty Law WW	.20	.50
❑ 166 Ben Roethlisberger RC	15.00	40.00
❑ 167 Ahmad Carroll RC	2.00	5.00
❑ 168 Johnnie Morant RC	1.50	4.00
❑ 169 Greg Jones RC	2.00	5.00
❑ 170 Michael Clayton RC	2.00	5.00
❑ 171 Josh Harris RC	1.25	3.00
❑ 172 Tatum Bell RC	2.00	5.00
❑ 173 Robert Gallery RC	2.00	5.00
❑ 174 B.J. Symons RC	1.25	3.00
❑ 175 Roy Williams RC	2.50	6.00
❑ 176 DeAngelo Hall RC	2.00	5.00
❑ 177 Jeff Smoker RC	1.50	4.00
❑ 178 Lee Evans RC	2.50	6.00
❑ 179 Michael Jenkins RC	2.00	5.00
❑ 180 Steven Jackson RC	5.00	12.00
❑ 181 Will Smith RC	2.00	5.00
❑ 182 Vince Wilfork RC	2.00	5.00
❑ 183 Ben Troupe RC	1.50	4.00
❑ 184 Chris Gamble RC	1.50	4.00
❑ 185 Kevin Jones RC	2.00	5.00
❑ 186 Jonathan Vilma RC	2.00	5.00
❑ 187 Dontarrious Thomas RC	1.50	4.00
❑ 188 Michael Boulware RC	2.00	5.00
❑ 189 Mewelde Moore RC	2.00	5.00
❑ 190 Drew Henson RC	1.25	3.00
❑ 191 D.J. Williams RC	2.00	5.00
❑ 192 Ernest Wilford RC	1.50	4.00
❑ 193 John Navarre RC	1.50	4.00
❑ 194 Jerricho Cotchery RC	2.00	5.00
❑ 195 Derrick Hamilton RC	1.25	3.00
❑ 196 Carlos Francis RC	1.25	3.00
❑ 197 Ben Watson RC	2.00	5.00
❑ 198 Reggie Williams RC	2.00	5.00
❑ 199 Devard Darling RC	1.50	4.00
❑ 200 Chris Perry RC	2.00	5.00
❑ 201 Derrick Strait RC	1.50	4.00
❑ 202 Sean Taylor RC	2.00	5.00
❑ 203 Michael Turner RC	5.00	12.00
❑ 204 Keary Colbert RC	1.50	4.00
❑ 205 Eli Manning RC	12.00	30.00
❑ 206 Julius Jones RC	2.50	6.00
❑ 207 Jason Babin RC	1.50	4.00
❑ 208 Cody Pickett RC	1.50	4.00
❑ 209 Kenechi Udeze RC	2.00	5.00
❑ 210 Rashaun Woods RC	1.25	3.00
❑ 211 Matt Schaub RC	5.00	12.00
❑ 212 Tommie Harris RC	2.00	5.00
❑ 213 Dwan Edwards RC	1.25	3.00
❑ 214 Shawn Andrews RC	1.50	4.00
❑ 215 Larry Fitzgerald RC	6.00	15.00
❑ 216 P.K. Sam RC	1.25	3.00
❑ 217 Teddy Lehman RC	1.50	4.00
❑ 218 Darius Watts RC	1.50	4.00
❑ 219 D.J. Hackett RC	2.00	5.00
❑ 220 Cedric Cobbs RC	1.50	4.00
❑ 221 Antwan Odom RC	2.00	5.00
❑ 222 Marquise Hill RC	1.25	3.00
❑ 223 Luke McCown RC	2.00	5.00
❑ 224 Triandos Luke RC	1.25	3.00
❑ 225 Kellen Winslow RC	2.50	6.00
❑ 226 Derek Abney RC	1.25	3.00
❑ 227 Chris Cooley RC	2.00	5.00
❑ 228 Dunta Robinson RC	1.50	4.00
❑ 229 Sean Jones RC	1.50	4.00
❑ 230 Philip Rivers RC	8.00	20.00
❑ 231 Craig Krenzel RC	2.00	5.00
❑ 232 Daryl Smith RC	1.50	4.00
❑ 233 Samie Parker RC	1.50	4.00
❑ 234 Ben Hartsock RC	1.50	4.00
❑ 235 J.P. Losman RC	2.00	5.00
❑ 236 Karlos Dansby RC	2.00	5.00
❑ 237 Ricardo Colclough RC	2.00	5.00
❑ 238 Bernard Berrian RC	2.00	5.00
❑ 239 Junior Siavii RC	1.25	3.00
❑ 240 Devery Henderson RC	2.00	5.00
❑ 241 Adimchinobe Echemandu RC	1.50	4.00
❑ 242 Patrick Crayton RC	2.50	6.00
❑ 243 Marcus Tubbs RC	1.25	3.00
❑ 244 Jamaar Taylor RC	1.25	3.00
❑ 245 Andy Hall RC	1.50	4.00
❑ 246 Darnell Dockett RC	1.25	3.00
❑ 247 Darrion Scott RC	1.50	4.00
❑ 248 Jim Sorgi RC	2.00	5.00
❑ 249 Jeff Dugan RC	1.25	3.00
❑ 250 Ryan Krause RC	1.25	3.00
❑ 251 Nate Lawrie RC	1.25	3.00
❑ 252 Casey Bramlet RC	1.25	3.00
❑ 253 Donnell Washington RC	1.50	4.00
❑ 254 Jonathan Smith RC	1.25	3.00
❑ 255 Tank Johnson RC	1.50	4.00
❑ 256 Keith Smith RC	1.25	3.00
❑ 257 Brandon Miree RC	1.25	3.00
❑ 258 Michael Gaines RC	1.25	3.00
❑ 259 Keiwan Ratliff RC	1.25	3.00
❑ 260 Stuart Schweigert RC	1.50	4.00
❑ 261 Derrick Ward RC	2.00	5.00
❑ 262 Matt Ware RC	2.00	5.00
❑ 263 Tim Anderson RC	1.50	4.00
❑ 264 Bradlee Van Pelt RC	1.50	4.00
❑ 265 Shawntae Spencer RC	1.25	3.00
❑ 266 Joey Thomas RC	1.25	3.00
❑ 267 Maurice Mann RC	1.25	3.00
❑ 268 Tim Euhus RC	1.25	3.00
❑ 269 Matt Mauck RC	1.50	4.00
❑ 270 Sloan Thomas RC	1.50	4.00
❑ 271 Jeris McIntyre RC	1.25	3.00
❑ 272 Randy Starks RC	1.25	3.00
❑ 273 Clarence Moore RC	1.50	4.00
❑ 274 Drew Carter RC	2.00	5.00
❑ 275 Sean Ryan RC	1.25	3.00
❑ RH38 Tom Brady RH	2.00	5.00

2005 Topps Chrome

Card	Low	High
❑ COMPLETE SET (275)	75.00	150.00
❑ COMP.SET w/o RC's (165)	12.50	30.00
❑ 1 Deuce McAllister	.40	1.00
❑ 2 Sean Taylor	.30	.75
❑ 3 Koren Robinson	.30	.75
❑ 4 Tiki Barber	.40	1.00
❑ 5 LaDainian Tomlinson	.50	1.25
❑ 6 Lee Evans	.30	.75
❑ 7 Aaron Brooks	.25	.60
❑ 8 LaMont Jordan	.30	.75
❑ 9 Dante Hall	.30	.75
❑ 10 Daunte Culpepper	.40	1.00
❑ 11 Thomas Jones	.30	.75
❑ 12 Warrick Dunn	.30	.75
❑ 13 Willis McGahee	.40	1.00
❑ 14 Ed Reed	.30	.75
❑ 15 Derrick Mason	.30	.75
❑ 16 Jason Witten	.40	1.00
❑ 17 Chad Johnson	.30	.75
❑ 18 Amani Toomer	.30	.75
❑ 19 Joey Harrington	.40	1.00
❑ 20 Brian Urlacher	.40	1.00
❑ 21 Brian Westbrook	.40	1.00
❑ 22 Matt Hasselbeck	.30	.75
❑ 23 Michael Vick	.40	1.00
❑ 24 Kevin Jones	.30	.75
❑ 25 Julius Peppers	.30	.75
❑ 26 Michael Clayton	.30	.75
❑ 27 Javon Walker	.30	.75
❑ 28 Santana Moss	.30	.75
❑ 29 Travis Henry	.30	.75
❑ 30 Stephen Davis	.30	.75
❑ 31 Larry Johnson	.40	1.00
❑ 32 Terrell Owens	.40	1.00
❑ 33 Ray Lewis	.40	1.00
❑ 34 Jake Plummer	.30	.75
❑ 35 Philip Rivers	.40	1.00

Card	Low	High
❑ 36 Eli Manning	.75	2.00
❑ 37 Tedy Bruschi	.40	1.00
❑ 38 Adam Vinatieri	.40	1.00
❑ 39 J.P. Losman	.30	.75
❑ 40 Zach Thomas	.40	1.00
❑ 41 Deion Branch	.30	.75
❑ 42 Andre Johnson	.30	.75
❑ 43 Marshall Faulk	.40	1.00
❑ 44 Bertrand Berry	.25	.60
❑ 45 Terrell Suggs	.30	.75
❑ 46 Tom Brady	.75	2.00
❑ 47 Ashley Lelie	.25	.60
❑ 48 Jonathan Wells	.25	.60
❑ 49 Randy McMichael	.25	.60
❑ 50 Charles Rogers	.25	.60
❑ 51 Larry Fitzgerald	.40	1.00
❑ 52 Hines Ward	.40	1.00
❑ 53 Jason Taylor	.30	.75
❑ 54 Ronde Barber	.30	.75
❑ 55 T.J. Houshmandzadeh	.30	.75
❑ 56 Keary Colbert	.25	.60
❑ 57 DeAngelo Hall	.30	.75
❑ 58 Chris Brown	.30	.75
❑ 59 Chris Perry	.25	.60
❑ 60 Steven Jackson	.50	1.25
❑ 61 Kyle Boller	.30	.75
❑ 62 Rudi Johnson	.30	.75
❑ 63 Roy Williams S	.30	.75
❑ 64 Onterrio Smith	.25	.60
❑ 65 Roy Williams WR	.40	1.00
❑ 66 Jerry Porter	.30	.75
❑ 67 Edgerrin James	.30	.75
❑ 68 Randy Moss	.40	1.00
❑ 69 Brian Griese	.30	.75
❑ 70 Donovan McNabb	.40	1.00
❑ 71 Joe Horn	.30	.75
❑ 72 Muhsin Muhammad	.30	.75
❑ 73 Johnnie Morton	.30	.75
❑ 74 Chad Pennington	.40	1.00
❑ 75 Torry Holt	.30	.75
❑ 76 Marc Bulger	.30	.75
❑ 77 Duce Staley	.30	.75
❑ 78 Todd Heap	.30	.75
❑ 79 Lee Suggs	.30	.75
❑ 80 Patrick Ramsey	.30	.75
❑ 81 Drew Bennett	.30	.75
❑ 82 Michael Strahan	.30	.75
❑ 83 Priest Holmes	.40	1.00
❑ 84 DeShaun Foster	.30	.75
❑ 85 Corey Dillon	.30	.75
❑ 86 Antonio Gates	.40	1.00
❑ 87 Trent Green	.30	.75
❑ 88 Brandon Stokley	.25	.60
❑ 89 Alge Crumpler	.30	.75
❑ 90 Keyshawn Johnson	.30	.75
❑ 91 Byron Leftwich	.30	.75
❑ 92 Dunta Robinson	.25	.60
❑ 93 Ben Roethlisberger	1.00	2.50
❑ 94 Rod Smith	.30	.75
❑ 95 Robert Gallery	.25	.60
❑ 96 Tony Gonzalez	.30	.75
❑ 97 Steve McNair	.40	1.00
❑ 98 Jeremy Shockey	.40	1.00
❑ 99 Dominic Rhodes	.30	.75
❑ 100 Michael Jenkins	.30	.75
❑ 101 Jake Delhomme	.40	1.00
❑ 102 Jerome Bettis	.40	1.00
❑ 103 Jevon Kearse	.30	.75
❑ 104 Plaxico Burress	.30	.75
❑ 105 Dwight Freeney	.30	.75
❑ 106 Marcus Robinson	.30	.75
❑ 107 Rex Grossman	.40	1.00
❑ 108 Drew Henson	.25	.60
❑ 109 Julius Jones	.40	1.00
❑ 110 Jamal Lewis	.30	.75
❑ 111 Justin McCareins	.25	.60
❑ 112 Billy Volek	.30	.75
❑ 113 Curtis Martin	.40	1.00
❑ 114 Tatum Bell	.30	.75
❑ 115 Domanick Davis	.25	.60
❑ 116 Marvin Harrison	.40	1.00
❑ 117 Anquan Boldin	.30	.75
❑ 118 Jimmy Smith	.30	.75
❑ 119 Drew Brees	.40	1.00
❑ 120 Donte Stallworth	.30	.75
❑ 121 Nate Burleson	.30	.75
❑ 122 Fred Taylor	.40	1.00
❑ 123 Takeo Spikes	.25	.60
❑ 124 Jonathan Ogden	.25	.60
❑ 125 Michael Bennett	.30	.75
❑ 126 Clinton Portis	.40	1.00
❑ 127 Ahman Green	.40	1.00
❑ 128 Drew Bledsoe	.40	1.00
❑ 129 Darrell Jackson	.30	.75
❑ 130 Jonathan Vilma	.30	.75
❑ 131 David Carr	.30	.75
❑ 132 Champ Bailey	.30	.75
❑ 133 Derrick Blaylock	.25	.60
❑ 134 T.J. Duckett	.25	.60
❑ 135 Shaun Alexander	.40	1.00
❑ 136 Peyton Manning	.60	1.50
❑ 137 Isaac Bruce	.30	.75
❑ 138 LaVar Arrington	.40	1.00
❑ 139 Brett Favre	1.00	2.50
❑ 140 Allen Rossum	.25	.60
❑ 141 Eric Moulds	.30	.75
❑ 142 Carson Palmer	.40	1.00
❑ 143 Laveranues Coles	.30	.75
❑ 144 Chester Taylor	.30	.75
❑ 145 Reggie Wayne	.30	.75
❑ 146 Curtis Martin LL	.30	.75
❑ 147 Daunte Culpepper LL	.30	.75
❑ 148 Muhsin Muhammad LL	.25	.60
❑ 149 Shaun Alexander LL	.30	.75
❑ 150 Trent Green LL	.25	.60
❑ 151 Joe Horn LL	.25	.60
❑ 152 Corey Dillon LL	.25	.60
❑ 153 Peyton Manning LL	.50	1.25
❑ 154 Javon Walker LL	.25	.60
❑ 155 Edgerrin James LL	.25	.60
❑ 156 Jake Scott GM	.20	.50
❑ 157 John Elway GM	.60	1.50
❑ 158 Dwight Clark GM	.25	.60
❑ 159 Lawrence Taylor GM	.30	.75
❑ 160 Joe Namath GM	.50	1.25
❑ 161 Richard Dent GM	.25	.60
❑ 162 Peyton Manning GM	.50	1.25
❑ 163 Don Maynard GM	.25	.60
❑ 164 Joe Greene GM	.30	.75
❑ 165 Roger Staubach GM	.50	1.25
❑ 166 J.J. Arrington RC	2.00	5.00
❑ 167 Cedric Benson RC	2.00	5.00
❑ 168 Mark Bradley RC	1.50	4.00
❑ 169 Reggie Brown RC	1.50	4.00
❑ 170 Ronnie Brown RC	6.00	15.00
❑ 171 Jason Campbell RC	3.00	8.00
❑ 172 Maurice Clarett	1.50	4.00
❑ 173 Mark Clayton RC	2.00	5.00
❑ 174 Braylon Edwards RC	5.00	12.00
❑ 175 Ciatrick Fason RC	1.50	4.00
❑ 176 Charlie Frye RC	2.00	5.00
❑ 177 Frank Gore RC	4.00	10.00
❑ 178 David Greene RC	1.50	4.00
❑ 179 Vincent Jackson RC	2.50	6.00
❑ 180 Adam Jones RC	1.50	4.00
❑ 181 Matt Jones RC	2.00	5.00
❑ 182 Stefan LeFors RC	1.50	4.00
❑ 183 Heath Miller RC	4.00	10.00
❑ 184 Ryan Moats RC	1.50	4.00
❑ 185 Vernand Morency RC	1.50	4.00
❑ 186 Terrence Murphy RC	1.25	3.00
❑ 187 Kyle Orton RC	3.00	8.00
❑ 188 Roscoe Parrish RC	1.50	4.00
❑ 189 Courtney Roby RC	1.50	4.00
❑ 190 Aaron Rodgers RC	6.00	15.00
❑ 191 Carlos Rogers RC	2.00	5.00
❑ 192 Antrel Rolle RC	2.00	5.00
❑ 193 Eric Shelton RC	1.50	4.00
❑ 194 Alex Smith QB RC	2.00	5.00
❑ 195 Andrew Walter RC	1.50	4.00
❑ 196 Roddy White RC	2.50	6.00
❑ 197 Cadillac Williams RC	3.00	8.00
❑ 198 Mike Williams	1.50	4.00
❑ 199 Troy Williamson RC	2.00	5.00
❑ 200 Taylor Stubblefield RC	1.25	3.00
❑ 201 Dan Cody RC	2.00	5.00
❑ 202 David Pollack RC	1.50	4.00
❑ 203 Craig Bragg RC	1.25	3.00
❑ 204 Alvin Pearman RC	1.25	3.00
❑ 205 Marcus Maxwell RC	1.25	3.00
❑ 206 Brock Berlin RC	1.50	4.00
❑ 207 Khalif Barnes RC	1.25	3.00
❑ 208 Eric King RC	1.25	3.00
❑ 209 Alex Smith TE RC	2.00	5.00
❑ 210 Dante Ridgeway RC	1.25	3.00
❑ 211 Shaun Cody RC	1.50	4.00
❑ 212 Donte Nicholson RC	1.50	4.00
❑ 213 DeMarcus Ware RC	3.00	8.00
❑ 214 Lionel Gates RC	1.25	3.00
❑ 215 Fabian Washington RC	2.00	5.00
❑ 216 Brandon Jacobs RC	2.50	6.00
❑ 217 Noah Herron RC	2.00	5.00
❑ 218 Derrick Johnson RC	2.00	5.00
❑ 219 J.R. Russell RC	1.25	3.00
❑ 220 Adrian McPherson RC	1.50	4.00
❑ 221 Marcus Spears RC	2.00	5.00
❑ 222 Justin Miller RC	1.50	4.00
❑ 223 Marion Barber RC	6.00	15.00
❑ 224 Anthony Davis RC	1.50	4.00
❑ 225 Chad Owens RC	2.00	5.00
❑ 226 Craphonso Thorpe RC	1.50	4.00
❑ 227 Travis Johnson RC	1.25	3.00
❑ 228 Erasmus James RC	1.50	4.00
❑ 229 Mike Patterson RC	1.50	4.00
❑ 230 Airese Currie RC	1.50	4.00
❑ 231 Justin Tuck RC	2.50	6.00
❑ 232 Dan Orlovsky RC	2.00	5.00
❑ 233 Thomas Davis RC	1.50	4.00
❑ 234 Derek Anderson RC	2.00	5.00
❑ 235 Matt Roth RC	2.00	5.00
❑ 236 Chris Henry RC	2.00	5.00
❑ 237 Rasheed Marshall RC	1.50	4.00
❑ 238 Bryant McFadden RC	1.50	4.00
❑ 239 Darren Sproles RC	2.50	6.00
❑ 240 Fred Gibson RC	1.50	4.00
❑ 241 Barrett Ruud RC	2.00	5.00
❑ 242 Kelvin Hayden RC	1.50	4.00
❑ 243 Ryan Fitzpatrick RC	2.00	5.00
❑ 244 Patrick Estes RC	1.25	3.00
❑ 245 Zach Tuiasosopo RC	1.25	3.00
❑ 246 Luis Castillo RC	2.00	5.00
❑ 247 Lance Mitchell RC	1.50	4.00
❑ 248 Ronald Bartell RC	1.50	4.00
❑ 249 Jerome Mathis RC	2.00	5.00
❑ 250 Marlin Jackson RC	1.50	4.00
❑ 251 James Kilian RC	1.25	3.00
❑ 252 Roydell Williams RC	1.50	4.00
❑ 253 Joel Dreessen RC	1.50	4.00
❑ 254 Paris Warren RC	1.50	4.00
❑ 255 Dustin Fox RC	2.00	5.00
❑ 256 Ellis Hobbs RC	2.00	5.00
❑ 257 Mike Nugent RC	1.50	4.00
❑ 258 Channing Crowder RC	1.50	4.00
❑ 259 Kerry Rhodes RC	2.00	5.00
❑ 260 Jerome Collins RC	1.50	4.00
❑ 261 Stanford Routt RC	1.50	4.00
❑ 262 Madison Hedgecock RC	2.00	5.00
❑ 263 Rian Wallace RC	1.50	4.00
❑ 264 Larry Brackins RC	1.25	3.00
❑ 265 Manuel White RC	1.50	4.00
❑ 266 Corey Webster RC	2.00	5.00
❑ 267 Eric Moore RC	1.25	3.00
❑ 268 Kirk Morrison RC	2.00	5.00
❑ 269 Atiyyah Ellison RC	1.25	3.00
❑ 270 Travis Daniels RC	1.50	4.00
❑ 271 Boomer Grigsby RC	2.00	5.00
❑ 272 Alex Barron RC	1.25	3.00
❑ 273 Tab Perry RC	2.00	5.00
❑ 274 Cedric Houston RC	2.00	5.00
❑ 275 Kevin Burnett RC	1.50	4.00
❑ RH39 Deion Branch RH	2.00	5.00
❑ RH39R Deion Branch RHR/100	6.00	15.00

2006 Topps Chrome

Card	Low	High
❑ COMPLETE SET (270)	125.00	250.00
❑ COMP.SET w/o RC's (165)	12.50	30.00
❑ 1 Jonathan Vilma	.30	.75
❑ 2 Chester Taylor	.30	.75
❑ 3 Troy Polamalu	.50	1.25
❑ 4 Nathan Vasher	.25	.60

Card		
❑ 5 Clinton Portis	.40	1.00
❑ 6 Willie Parker	.50	1.25
❑ 7 Lofa Tatupu	.30	.75
❑ 8 Peyton Manning	.60	1.50
❑ 9 LaMont Jordan	.30	.75
❑ 10 Jason Taylor	.30	.75
❑ 11 Travis Taylor	.25	.60
❑ 12 Derrick Johnson	.30	.75
❑ 13 Jason Campbell	.30	.75
❑ 14 Aaron Rodgers	.40	1.00
❑ 15 Deltha O'Neal	.25	.60
❑ 16 LaDainian Tomlinson	.50	1.25
❑ 17 Keary Colbert	.30	.75
❑ 18 Chris Chambers	.30	.75
❑ 19 Chris Simms	.30	.75
❑ 20 Troy Williamson	.30	.75
❑ 21 Chad Johnson	.30	.75
❑ 22 Jake Delhomme	.30	.75
❑ 23 Willis McGahee	.40	1.00
❑ 24 Roddy White	.30	.75
❑ 25 Rod Smith	.30	.75
❑ 26 Zach Thomas	.40	1.00
❑ 27 Antonio Gates	.40	1.00
❑ 28 Michael Vick	.40	1.00
❑ 29 Antwaan Randle El	.30	.75
❑ 30 Drew Bledsoe	.40	1.00
❑ 31 Randy McMichael	.25	.60
❑ 32 Heath Miller	.30	.75
❑ 33 Fred Taylor	.30	.75
❑ 34 Alge Crumpler	.30	.75
❑ 35 Roy Williams S	.30	.75
❑ 36 Ryan Moats	.30	.75
❑ 37 Dwight Freeney	.30	.75
❑ 38 Jeremy Shockey	.40	1.00
❑ 39 Shawne Merriman	.30	.75
❑ 40 Charlie Frye	.30	.75
❑ 41 Reggie Wayne	.30	.75
❑ 42 Alex Smith QB	.30	.75
❑ 43 Jerome Bettis	.40	1.00
❑ 44 Chris Brown	.30	.75
❑ 45 Michael Clayton	.30	.75
❑ 46 Carlos Rogers	.25	.60
❑ 47 DeAngelo Hall	.30	.75
❑ 48 Drew Bennett	.30	.75
❑ 49 Brandon Lloyd	.30	.75
❑ 50 Corey Dillon	.30	.75
❑ 51 Eli Manning	.50	1.25
❑ 52 Jerry Porter	.30	.75
❑ 53 Carson Palmer	.40	1.00
❑ 54 Kevin Jones	.30	.75
❑ 55 Andre Johnson	.30	.75
❑ 56 Ray Lewis	.40	1.00
❑ 57 Kyle Orton	.30	.75
❑ 58 Julius Jones	.30	.75
❑ 59 Roy Williams WR	.40	1.00
❑ 60 Jonathan Ogden	.25	.60
❑ 61 Antonio Pierce	.25	.60
❑ 62 Larry Johnson	.30	.75
❑ 63 Muhsin Muhammad	.30	.75
❑ 64 Trent Green	.30	.75
❑ 65 Tatum Bell	.25	.60
❑ 66 Lee Evans	.30	.75
❑ 67 Braylon Edwards	.40	1.00
❑ 68 Hines Ward	.40	1.00
❑ 69 Warrick Dunn	.30	.75
❑ 70 Antonio Bryant	.30	.75
❑ 71 Meweide Moore	.25	.60
❑ 72 Samkon Gado	.40	1.00
❑ 73 Mike Williams	.30	.75
❑ 74 Marion Barber	.40	1.00
❑ 75 Samie Parker	.25	.60
❑ 76 Julius Peppers	.30	.75
❑ 77 Brian Westbrook	.30	.75
❑ 78 Kevan Barlow	.30	.75
❑ 79 Kyle Boller	.30	.75
❑ 80 Donnie Edwards	.25	.60
❑ 81 Courtney Roby	.25	.60
❑ 82 Marc Bulger	.30	.75
❑ 83 Steve Smith	.40	1.00
❑ 84 Ben Roethlisberger	.60	1.50
❑ 85 Byron Leftwich	.30	.75
❑ 86 Isaac Bruce	.30	.75
❑ 87 Kurt Warner	.40	1.00
❑ 88 Tiki Barber	.40	1.00
❑ 89 Derrick Mason	.30	.75
❑ 90 Joe Horn	.30	.75
❑ 91 Donovan McNabb	.40	1.00
❑ 92 DeShaun Foster	.30	.75
❑ 93 Rex Grossman	.40	1.00
❑ 94 Randy Moss	.40	1.00
❑ 95 Tedy Bruschi	.40	1.00
❑ 96 Tony Gonzalez	.30	.75
❑ 97 Cadillac Williams	.40	1.00
❑ 98 Torry Holt	.30	.75
❑ 99 Philip Rivers	.40	1.00
❑ 100 Deuce McAllister	.30	.75
❑ 101 Jason Witten	.40	1.00
❑ 102 Reggie Brown	.25	.60
❑ 103 Ronnie Brown	.40	1.00
❑ 104 Deion Branch	.30	.75
❑ 105 Terry Glenn	.30	.75
❑ 106 Tom Brady	.60	1.50
❑ 107 Dallas Clark	.30	.75
❑ 108 Mark Clayton	.30	.75
❑ 109 D.J. Williams	.25	.60
❑ 110 Matt Jones	.30	.75
❑ 111 Ed Reed	.30	.75
❑ 112 Reuben Droughns	.30	.75
❑ 113 Matt Hasselbeck	.30	.75
❑ 114 Anquan Boldin	.30	.75
❑ 115 David Carr	.25	.60
❑ 116 Domanick Davis	.30	.75
❑ 117 Nate Burleson	.30	.75
❑ 118 Shaun Alexander	.30	.75
❑ 119 Dante Hall	.30	.75
❑ 120 Santana Moss	.30	.75
❑ 121 Brandon Stokley	.30	.75
❑ 122 Larry Fitzgerald	.40	1.00
❑ 123 Marvin Harrison	.40	1.00
❑ 124 Steve McNair	.30	.75
❑ 125 Osi Umenyiora	.30	.75
❑ 126 Odell Thurman	.25	.60
❑ 127 Josh McCown	.30	.75
❑ 128 Curtis Martin	.40	1.00
❑ 129 Jake Plummer	.30	.75
❑ 130 Cedric Benson	.30	.75
❑ 131 J.P. Losman	.30	.75
❑ 132 Joey Galloway	.30	.75
❑ 133 Brian Griese	.30	.75
❑ 134 Plaxico Burress	.30	.75
❑ 135 Brian Urlacher	.40	1.00
❑ 136 T.J. Houshmandzadeh	.30	.75
❑ 137 Todd Heap	.30	.75
❑ 138 Champ Bailey	.30	.75
❑ 139 Mark Brunell	.30	.75
❑ 140 Chris Cooley	.30	.75
❑ 141 Priest Holmes	.30	.75
❑ 142 Aaron Brooks	.30	.75
❑ 143 Steven Jackson	.40	1.00
❑ 144 Michael Strahan	.30	.75
❑ 145 Rudi Johnson	.30	.75
❑ 146 Terrell Owens	.40	1.00
❑ 147 John Abraham	.25	.60
❑ 148 Jon Kitna	.30	.75
❑ 149 LaVar Arrington	.40	1.00
❑ 150 Joe Jurevicius	.25	.60
❑ 151 Dominic Rhodes	.30	.75
❑ 152 Chad Pennington	.30	.75
❑ 153 Charles Woodson	.30	.75
❑ 154 Kerry Collins	.30	.75
❑ 155 Drew Brees	.40	1.00
❑ 156 Keyshawn Johnson	.30	.75
❑ 157 Mike Anderson	.30	.75
❑ 158 Jimmy Smith	.30	.75
❑ 159 Brett Favre	.75	2.00
❑ 160 Edgerrin James	.30	.75
❑ 161 Jamal Lewis	.30	.75
❑ 162 Daunte Culpepper	.40	1.00
❑ 163 Eric Moulds	.30	.75
❑ 164 Patrick Ramsey	.30	.75
❑ 165 Ahman Green	.30	.75
❑ 166 Kamerion Wimbley RC	2.00	5.00
❑ 167 Bobby Carpenter RC	1.50	4.00
❑ 168 Abdul Hodge RC	1.50	4.00
❑ 169 P.J. Daniels RC	1.25	3.00
❑ 170 D'Qwell Jackson RC	1.50	4.00
❑ 171 Johnathan Joseph RC	1.50	4.00
❑ 172 Antonio Cromartie RC	2.00	5.00
❑ 173 Elvis Dumervil RC	2.00	5.00
❑ 174 Tamba Hali RC	2.00	5.00
❑ 175 Derek Hagan RC	1.50	4.00
❑ 176 Haloti Ngata RC	2.00	5.00
❑ 177 Manny Lawson RC	2.00	5.00
❑ 178 Kelly Jennings RC	2.00	5.00
❑ 179 Jason Allen RC	1.50	4.00
❑ 180 Mathias Kiwanuka RC	2.50	6.00
❑ 181 Marques Hagans RC	1.50	4.00
❑ 182 Devin Aromashodu RC	2.00	5.00
❑ 183 Brandon Johnson RC	1.50	4.00
❑ 184 Ingle Martin RC	1.50	4.00
❑ 185 Claude Wroten RC	1.25	3.00
❑ 186 Tye Hill RC	1.50	4.00
❑ 187 Ashton Youboty RC	1.50	4.00
❑ 188 DeMeco Ryans RC	2.50	6.00
❑ 189 Brodrick Bunkley RC	1.50	4.00
❑ 190 Thomas Howard RC	1.50	4.00
❑ 191 Ernie Sims RC	1.50	4.00
❑ 192 Rocky McIntosh RC	2.00	5.00
❑ 193 Donte Whitner RC	2.00	5.00
❑ 194 Anthony Schlegel RC	1.50	4.00
❑ 195 Jimmy Williams RC	2.00	5.00
❑ 196 Brett Basanez RC	2.00	5.00
❑ 197 Ben Obomanu RC	1.50	4.00
❑ 198 Jonathan Orr RC	1.50	4.00
❑ 199 Andre Hall RC	1.50	4.00
❑ 200 James Anderson RC	1.25	3.00
❑ 201 Darnell Bing RC	1.50	4.00
❑ 202 Jovon Bouknight RC	1.50	4.00
❑ 203 Gabe Watson RC	1.25	3.00
❑ 204 Garrett Mills RC	1.50	4.00
❑ 205 Jeff Webb RC	1.50	4.00
❑ 206 Kevin McMahan RC	1.50	4.00
❑ 207 D.J. Shockley RC	1.50	4.00
❑ 208 A.J. Nicholson RC	1.25	3.00
❑ 209 Cedric Humes RC	1.50	4.00
❑ 210 Winston Justice RC	2.00	5.00
❑ 211 Lawrence Vickers RC	1.50	4.00
❑ 212 Daniel Bullocks RC	2.00	5.00
❑ 213 Tim Day RC	1.50	4.00
❑ 214 Ko Simpson RC	1.50	4.00
❑ 215 Dusty Dvoracek RC	2.00	5.00
❑ 216 Davin Joseph RC	1.50	4.00
❑ 217 Dominique Byrd RC	1.50	4.00
❑ 218 Marcus Vick RC	1.25	3.00
❑ 219 John McCargo RC	1.50	4.00
❑ 220 Danieal Manning RC	2.00	5.00
❑ 221 Reggie Bush RC	5.00	12.00
❑ 222 A.J. Hawk RC	3.00	8.00
❑ 223 Vince Young RC	5.00	12.00
❑ 224 Matt Leinart RC	3.00	8.00
❑ 225 Kellen Clemens RC	2.00	5.00
❑ 226 Sinorice Moss RC	2.00	5.00
❑ 227 Laurence Maroney RC	2.50	6.00
❑ 228 DeAngelo Williams RC	4.00	10.00
❑ 229 Jay Cutler RC	5.00	12.00
❑ 230 LenDale White RC	2.50	6.00
❑ 231 Leonard Pope RC	2.00	5.00
❑ 232 Chad Greenway RC	2.00	5.00
❑ 233 Chad Jackson RC	1.50	4.00
❑ 234 Vernon Davis RC	2.00	5.00
❑ 235 Todd Watkins RC	1.25	3.00
❑ 236 David Thomas RC	2.00	5.00
❑ 237 Marcedes Lewis RC	2.00	5.00
❑ 238 Leon Washington RC	2.50	6.00
❑ 239 Will Blackmon RC	2.00	5.00
❑ 240 Michael Huff RC	2.00	5.00
❑ 241 Jerious Norwood RC	2.00	5.00
❑ 242 Reggie McNeal RC	1.50	4.00
❑ 243 Wali Lundy RC	2.00	5.00
❑ 244 Santonio Holmes RC	5.00	12.00
❑ 245 Jerome Harrison RC	2.00	5.00
❑ 246 Bruce Gradkowski RC	2.00	5.00
❑ 247 Maurice Drew RC	4.00	10.00
❑ 248 Brandon Williams RC	1.50	4.00
❑ 249 Anthony Fasano RC	2.00	5.00
❑ 250 Omar Jacobs RC	1.25	3.00
❑ 251 Domenik Hixon RC	2.00	5.00
❑ 252 Devin Hester RC	4.00	10.00
❑ 253 Maurice Stovall RC	1.50	4.00
❑ 254 Tarvaris Jackson RC	2.00	5.00
❑ 255 Michael Robinson RC	1.50	4.00
❑ 256 Mario Williams RC	2.50	6.00
❑ 257 Jason Avant RC	2.00	5.00
❑ 258 Brian Calhoun RC	1.50	4.00
❑ 259 Skyler Green RC	1.25	3.00
❑ 260 Greg Jennings RC	3.00	8.00
❑ 261 Charlie Whitehurst RC	2.00	5.00
❑ 262 Mike Hass RC	2.00	5.00
❑ 263 Brandon Marshall RC	2.00	5.00
❑ 264 Drew Olson RC	1.25	3.00
❑ 265 Demetrius Williams RC	1.50	4.00
❑ 266 Travis Wilson RC	1.25	3.00
❑ 267 Joe Klopfenstein RC	1.50	4.00
❑ 268 Joseph Addai RC	2.50	6.00

❑ 269 Brad Smith RC 2.00 5.00
❑ 270 Willie Reid RC 1.50 4.00
❑ RH40 Hines Ward RH 2.50 6.00

2007 Topps Chrome

❑ COMPLETE SET (265) 60.00 150.00
❑ COMP.SET w/o RC's (165) 12.50 30.00
❑ TC1 Matt Leinart .40 1.00
❑ TC2 J.P. Losman .25 .60
❑ TC3 Carson Palmer .40 1.00
❑ TC4 Jay Cutler .40 1.00
❑ TC5 Peyton Manning .60 1.50
❑ TC6 Tom Brady .75 2.00
❑ TC7 Chad Pennington .30 .75
❑ TC8 Philip Rivers .40 1.00
❑ TC9 Marc Bulger .30 .75
❑ TC10 Edgerrin James .30 .75
❑ TC11 Willis McGahee .30 .75
❑ TC12 Thomas Jones .30 .75
❑ TC13 Marion Barber .40 1.00
❑ TC14 Fred Taylor .30 .75
❑ TC15 Chester Taylor .25 .60
❑ TC16 Reggie Bush .50 1.25
❑ TC17 Willie Parker .30 .75
❑ TC18 Shaun Alexander .30 .75
❑ TC19 LenDale White .30 .75
❑ TC20 Larry Fitzgerald .40 1.00
❑ TC21 Lee Evans .30 .75
❑ TC22 Muhsin Muhammad .30 .75
❑ TC23 Rod Smith .30 .75
❑ TC24 Andre Johnson .30 .75
❑ TC25 Matt Jones .30 .75
❑ TC26 Devery Henderson .25 .60
❑ TC27 Plaxico Burress .30 .75
❑ TC28 Randy Moss .40 1.00
❑ TC29 Santonio Holmes .30 .75
❑ TC30 Torry Holt .30 .75
❑ TC31 Antwaan Randle El .25 .60
❑ TC32 Todd Heap .25 .60
❑ TC33 Tony Gonzalez .30 .75
❑ TC34 Heath Miller .25 .60
❑ TC35 Alex Smith TE .25 .60
❑ TC36 Champ Bailey .30 .75
❑ TC37 Roy Williams S .00 .75
❑ TC38 Julius Peppers .30 .75
❑ TC39 Jason Taylor .25 .60
❑ TC40 Brian Urlacher .40 1.00
❑ TC41 Marc Bulger LL .25 .60
❑ TC42 Frank Gore LL .30 .75
❑ TC43 Reggie Wayne LL .25 .60
❑ TC44 Peyton Manning PB .50 1.25
❑ TC45 Reggie Wayne PB .25 .60
❑ TC46 Jason Taylor PB .20 .50
❑ TC47 Troy Polamalu PB .30 .75
❑ TC48 Tony Gonzalez PB .25 .60
❑ TC49 Devin Hester PB .30 .75
❑ TC50 LaDainian Tomlinson MVP .40 1.00
❑ TC51 P.Manning/R.Wayne PSH .50 1.25
❑ TC52 New Orleans Saints PSH .30 .75
❑ TC53 Peyton Manning PSH .50 1.25
❑ TC54 T.Jones/C.Benson PSH .25 .60
❑ TC55 Colts Defense PSH .25 .60
❑ TC56 Steve McNair .30 .75
❑ TC57 Rex Grossman .30 .75
❑ TC58 Tony Romo .60 1.50
❑ TC59 David Carr .30 .75
❑ TC60 Tarvaris Jackson .30 .75
❑ TC61 Eli Manning .40 1.00
❑ TC62 Ben Roethlisberger .50 1.25
❑ TC63 Matt Hasselbeck .30 .75
❑ TC64 Jason Campbell .30 .75
❑ TC65 Warrick Dunn .30 .75
❑ TC66 Jamal Lewis .30 .75
❑ TC67 Cedric Benson .30 .75
❑ TC68 Reuben Droughns .30 .75
❑ TC69 Joseph Addai .40 1.00
❑ TC70 Ronnie Brown .30 .75
❑ TC71 Deuce McAllister .30 .75
❑ TC72 Brian Westbrook .30 .75
❑ TC73 Frank Gore .40 1.00
❑ TC74 Cadillac Williams .30 .75
❑ TC75 Anquan Boldin .30 .75
❑ TC76 Mark Clayton .30 .75
❑ TC77 Bernard Berrian .25 .60
❑ TC78 Braylon Edwards .30 .75
❑ TC79 Donald Driver .40 1.00
❑ TC80 Marvin Harrison .40 1.00
❑ TC81 Troy Williamson .25 .60
❑ TC82 Marques Colston .40 1.00
❑ TC83 Laveranues Coles .30 .75
❑ TC84 Hines Ward .40 1.00
❑ TC85 Deion Branch .30 .75
❑ TC86 Alge Crumpler .30 .75
❑ TC87 Kellen Winslow .30 .75
❑ TC88 Dallas Clark .25 .60
❑ TC89 L.J. Smith .25 .60
❑ TC90 Vernon Davis .30 .75
❑ TC91 Sean Taylor .25 .60
❑ TC92 Ronde Barber .25 .60
❑ TC93 Brian Dawkins .30 .75
❑ TC94 Dwight Freeney .30 .75
❑ TC95 Ray Lewis .40 1.00
❑ TC96 Peyton Manning LL .50 1.25
❑ TC97 Larry Johnson LL .25 .60
❑ TC98 Marvin Harrison LL .30 .75
❑ TC99 LaDainian Tomlinson PB .40 1.00
❑ TC100 Jeff Saturday PB .20 .50
❑ TC101 Champ Bailey PB .25 .60
❑ TC102 Frank Gore PB .30 .75
❑ TC103 Walter Jones PB .20 .50
❑ TC104 Tony Romo PB .50 1.25
❑ TC105 Ronde Barber PB .20 .50
❑ TC106 Larry Johnson PB .25 .60
❑ TC107 Vince Young OROY .30 .75
❑ TC108 Asante Samuel PSH .20 .50
❑ TC109 Tom Brady PSH .60 1.50
❑ TC110 Devin Hester PSH .30 .75
❑ TC111 Michael Vick SP 60.00 100.00
❑ TC112 Jake Delhomme .30 .75
❑ TC113 Charlie Frye .30 .75
❑ TC114 Brett Favre .75 2.00
❑ TC115 Trent Green .30 .75
❑ TC116 Drew Brees .40 1.00
❑ TC117 Donovan McNabb .40 1.00
❑ TC118 Alex Smith QB .40 1.00
❑ TC119 Vince Young .40 1.00
❑ TC120 DeAngelo Williams .40 1.00
❑ TC121 Rudi Johnson .30 .75
❑ TC122 Julius Jones .30 .75
❑ TC123 Larry Johnson .30 .75
❑ TC124 Laurence Maroney .40 1.00
❑ TC125 Brandon Jacobs .30 .75
❑ TC126 LaDainian Tomlinson .50 1.25
❑ TC127 Steven Jackson .40 1.00
❑ TC128 Clinton Portis .30 .75
❑ TC129 Michael Jenkins .30 .75
❑ TC130 Steve Smith .30 .75
❑ TC131 Chad Johnson .30 .75
❑ TC132 Roy Williams WR .30 .75
❑ TC133 Reggie Wayne .30 .75
❑ TC134 Reggie Williams .30 .75
❑ TC135 Chris Chambers .30 .75
❑ TC136 Sinorice Moss .30 .75
❑ TC137 Reggie Brown .25 .60
❑ TC138 Arnaz Battle .25 .60
❑ TC139 Michael Clayton .30 .75
❑ TC140 Santana Moss .30 .75
❑ TC141 Desmond Clark .25 .60
❑ TC142 Jeremy Shockey .30 .75
❑ TC143 Antonio Gates .30 .75
❑ TC144 Chris Cooley .30 .75
❑ TC145 Devin Hester .40 1.00
❑ TC146 Asante Samuel .25 .60
❑ TC147 Troy Polamalu .40 1.00
❑ TC148 DeMarcus Ware .30 .75
❑ TC149 Michael Strahan .30 .75
❑ TC150 A.J. Hawk .40 1.00
❑ TC151 LaDainian Tomlinson LL .40 1.00
❑ TC152 Chad Johnson LL .25 .60
❑ TC153 LaDainian Tomlinson LL .40 1.00
❑ TC154 Marvin Harrison PB .30 .75
❑ TC155 Antonio Gates PB .25 .60
❑ TC156 Shawne Merriman PB .25 .60
❑ TC157 Drew Brees PB .30 .75
❑ TC158 Steve Smith PB .25 .60
❑ TC159 Julius Peppers PB .25 .60
❑ TC160 DeMeco Ryans DROY .25 .60
❑ TC161 Drew Brees PSH .30 .75
❑ TC162 Reggie Bush PSH .40 1.00
❑ TC163 Robbie Gould PSH .20 .50
❑ TC164 Joseph Addai PSH .30 .75
❑ TC165 Adam Vinatieri PSH .25 .60
❑ TC166 JaMarcus Russell RC 2.00 5.00
❑ TC167 Brady Quinn RC 3.00 8.00
❑ TC168 Drew Stanton RC 1.25 3.00
❑ TC169 Troy Smith RC 2.00 5.00
❑ TC170 Kevin Kolb RC 2.50 6.00
❑ TC171 Trent Edwards RC 2.50 6.00
❑ TC172 John Beck RC 1.50 4.00
❑ TC173 Jordan Palmer RC 1.50 4.00
❑ TC174 Chris Leak RC 1.25 3.00
❑ TC175 Isaiah Stanback RC 1.50 4.00
❑ TC176 Tyler Palko RC 1.25 3.00
❑ TC177 Jared Zabransky RC 1.50 4.00
❑ TC178 Jeff Rowe RC 1.25 3.00
❑ TC179 Zac Taylor RC 1.50 4.00
❑ TC180 Lester Ricard RC 1.50 4.00
❑ TC181 Adrian Peterson RC 15.00 40.00
❑ TC182 Marshawn Lynch RC 3.00 8.00
❑ TC183 Brandon Jackson RC 1.50 4.00
❑ TC184 Michael Bush RC 1.50 4.00
❑ TC185 Kenny Irons RC 1.50 4.00
❑ TC186 Antonio Pittman RC 1.50 4.00
❑ TC187 Tony Hunt RC 1.50 4.00
❑ TC188 Darius Walker RC 1.25 3.00
❑ TC189 Dwayne Wright RC 1.25 3.00
❑ TC190 Lorenzo Booker RC 1.50 4.00
❑ TC191 Kenneth Darby RC 1.50 4.00
❑ TC192 Chris Henry RB RC 1.25 3.00
❑ TC193 Selvin Young RC 1.50 4.00
❑ TC194 Brian Leonard RC 1.25 3.00
❑ TC195 Ahmad Bradshaw RC 2.00 5.00
❑ TC196 Gary Russell RC 1.25 3.00
❑ TC197 Kolby Smith RC 1.50 4.00
❑ TC198 Thomas Clayton RC 1.25 3.00
❑ TC199 Garrett Wolfe RC 1.50 4.00
❑ TC200 Calvin Johnson RC 4.00 10.00
❑ TC201 Ted Ginn Jr. RC 2.50 6.00
❑ TC202 Dwayne Jarrett RC 1.50 4.00
❑ TC203 Dwayne Bowe RC 2.50 6.00
❑ TC204 Sidney Rice RC 3.00 8.00
❑ TC205 Robert Meachem RC 1.50 4.00
❑ TC206 Anthony Gonzalez RC 2.00 5.00
❑ TC207 Craig Buster Davis RC 1.50 4.00
❑ TC208 Aundrae Allison RC 1.25 3.00
❑ TC209 Chansi Stuckey RC 1.50 4.00
❑ TC210 David Clowney RC 1.50 4.00
❑ TC211 Steve Smith USC RC 2.50 6.00
❑ TC212 Courtney Taylor RC 1.25 3.00
❑ TC213 Paul Williams RC 1.25 3.00
❑ TC214 Johnnie Lee Higgins RC 1.50 4.00
❑ TC215 Rhema McKnight RC 1.25 3.00
❑ TC216 Jason Hill RC 1.50 4.00
❑ TC217 Dallas Baker RC 1.25 3.00
❑ TC218 Greg Olsen RC 2.00 5.00
❑ TC219 Yamon Figurs RC 1.00 2.50
❑ TC220 Scott Chandler RC 1.25 3.00
❑ TC221 Matt Spaeth RC 1.50 4.00
❑ TC222 Ben Patrick RC 1.25 3.00
❑ TC223 Clark Harris RC 1.50 4.00
❑ TC224 Martrez Milner RC 1.25 3.00
❑ TC225 Alan Branch RC 1.25 3.00
❑ TC226 Amobi Okoye RC 1.50 4.00
❑ TC227 DeMarcus Tank Tyler RC 1.25 3.00
❑ TC228 Justin Harrell RC 1.50 4.00
❑ TC229 Gaines Adams RC 1.50 4.00
❑ TC230 Jamaal Anderson RC 1.25 3.00
❑ TC231 Adam Carriker RC 1.25 3.00
❑ TC232 Jarvis Moss RC 1.50 4.00
❑ TC233 Charles Johnson RC 1.00 2.50
❑ TC234 Anthony Spencer RC 1.50 4.00
❑ TC235 Quentin Moses RC 1.25 3.00
❑ TC236 LaMarr Woodley RC 1.50 4.00
❑ TC237 Victor Abiamiri RC 1.50 4.00
❑ TC238 Ray McDonald RC 1.25 3.00
❑ TC239 Tim Crowder RC 1.50 4.00
❑ TC240 Patrick Willis RC 2.50 6.00
❑ TC241 David Harris RC 1.25 3.00
❑ TC242 Buster Davis RC 1.25 3.00
❑ TC243 Lawrence Timmons RC 1.50 4.00

Card		
❑ TC244 Paul Posluszny RC	2.00	5.00
❑ TC245 Jon Beason RC	1.50	4.00
❑ TC246 Rufus Alexander RC	1.50	4.00
❑ TC247 Prescott Burgess RC	1.25	3.00
❑ TC248 Leon Hall RC	1.50	4.00
❑ TC249 Darrelle Revis RC	2.00	5.00
❑ TC250 Aaron Ross RC	1.50	4.00
❑ TC251 Daymeion Hughes RC	1.25	3.00
❑ TC252 Marcus McCauley RC	1.25	3.00
❑ TC253 Chris Houston RC	1.25	3.00
❑ TC254 Tanard Jackson RC	1.00	2.50
❑ TC255 Jonathan Wade RC	1.25	3.00
❑ TC256 Josh Wilson RC	1.25	3.00
❑ TC257 Eric Wright RC	1.50	4.00
❑ TC258 David Irons RC	1.00	2.50
❑ TC259 Laron Landry RC	2.00	5.00
❑ TC260 Reggie Nelson RC	1.25	3.00
❑ TC261 Michael Griffin RC	1.50	4.00
❑ TC262 Brandon Meriweather RC	1.50	4.00
❑ TC263 Eric Weddle RC	1.25	3.00
❑ TC264 Joe Thomas RC	1.50	4.00
❑ TC265 Levi Brown RC	1.50	4.00
❑ RH41 Peyton Manning RH	2.00	5.00

2008 Topps Chrome

Card		
❑ COMPLETE SET (275)	40.00	80.00
❑ COMP.SET w/o RC's (165)	12.50	30.00
❑ TC1 Drew Brees	.40	1.00
❑ TC2 Jon Kitna	.30	.75
❑ TC3 Tom Brady	.60	1.50
❑ TC4 Chad Pennington	.30	.75
❑ TC5 Matt Hasselbeck	.30	.75
❑ TC6 David Garrard	.30	.75
❑ TC7 Jay Cutler	.40	1.00
❑ TC8 Matt Schaub	.30	.75
❑ TC9 Trent Edwards	.40	1.00
❑ TC10 Peyton Manning	.60	1.50
❑ TC11 Carson Palmer	.40	1.00
❑ TC12 Ben Roethlisberger	.60	1.50
❑ TC13 Eli Manning	.40	1.00
❑ TC14 Tony Romo	.60	1.50
❑ TC15 Donovan McNabb	.40	1.00
❑ TC16 Joey Harrington	.30	.75
❑ TC17 Jeff Garcia	.30	.75
❑ TC18 Derek Anderson	.30	.75
❑ TC19 Kyle Boller	.25	.60
❑ TC20 Sage Rosenfels	.25	.60
❑ TC21 Marc Bulger	.30	.75
❑ TC22 Brett Favre	1.00	2.50
❑ TC23 Philip Rivers	.40	1.00
❑ TC24 Vince Young	.30	.75
❑ TC25 Kurt Warner	.40	1.00
❑ TC26 Cleo Lemon	.25	.60
❑ TC27 Damon Huard	.25	.60
❑ TC28 Jason Campbell	.30	.75
❑ TC29 Brian Griese	.25	.60
❑ TC30 Tarvaris Jackson	.30	.75
❑ TC31 Steven Jackson	.40	1.00
❑ TC32 Willie Parker	.30	.75
❑ TC33 DeShaun Foster	.30	.75
❑ TC34 Shaun Alexander	.30	.75
❑ TC35 Clinton Portis	.30	.75
❑ TC36 Ron Dayne	.30	.75
❑ TC37 Maurice Jones-Drew	.30	.75
❑ TC38 Warrick Dunn	.30	.75
❑ TC39 Adrian Peterson	.75	2.00
❑ TC40 Thomas Jones	.30	.75
❑ TC41 LaDainian Tomlinson	.50	1.25
❑ TC42 Marion Barber	.40	1.00
❑ TC43 Brian Westbrook	.30	.75
❑ TC44 LenDale White	.30	.75
❑ TC45 Kenny Watson	.25	.60
❑ TC46 Fred Taylor	.30	.75
❑ TC47 Ryan Grant	.40	1.00
❑ TC48 Marshawn Lynch	.40	1.00
❑ TC49 Selvin Young	.25	.60
❑ TC50 Joseph Addai	.40	1.00
❑ TC51 Laurence Maroney	.30	.75
❑ TC52 Brandon Jacobs	.30	.75
❑ TC53 Willis McGahee	.30	.75
❑ TC54 Frank Gore	.30	.75
❑ TC55 Edgerrin James	.30	.75
❑ TC56 DeAngelo Williams	.30	.75
❑ TC57 Jamal Lewis	.30	.75
❑ TC58 Chester Taylor	.25	.60
❑ TC59 Earnest Graham	.25	.60
❑ TC60 Justin Fargas	.25	.60
❑ TC61 Greg Jennings	.30	.75
❑ TC62 Torry Holt	.30	.75
❑ TC63 T.J. Houshmandzadeh	.30	.75
❑ TC64 Jerricho Cotchery	.25	.60
❑ TC65 Derrick Mason	.25	.60
❑ TC66 Kevin Curtis	.25	.60
❑ TC67 Joey Galloway	.30	.75
❑ TC68 Anquan Boldin	.30	.75
❑ TC69 Santonio Holmes	.30	.75
❑ TC70 Lee Evans	.30	.75
❑ TC71 Dwayne Bowe	.30	.75
❑ TC72 Wes Welker	.40	1.00
❑ TC73 Roy Williams WR	.30	.75
❑ TC74 Randy Moss	.40	1.00
❑ TC75 Plaxico Burress	.30	.75
❑ TC76 Terrell Owens	.40	1.00
❑ TC77 Andre Johnson	.30	.75
❑ TC78 Roddy White	.30	.75
❑ TC79 Brandon Marshall	.30	.75
❑ TC80 Donald Driver	.30	.75
❑ TC81 Marques Colston	.30	.75
❑ TC82 Reggie Wayne	.30	.75
❑ TC83 Chad Johnson	.30	.75
❑ TC84 Bernard Berrian	.30	.75
❑ TC85 Steve Smith	.30	.75
❑ TC86 Larry Fitzgerald	.40	1.00
❑ TC87 Braylon Edwards	.30	.75
❑ TC88 Bobby Engram	.25	.60
❑ TC89 Shaun McDonald	.25	.60
❑ TC90 Santana Moss	.25	.60
❑ TC91 Antonio Gates	.30	.75
❑ TC92 Chris Cooley	.30	.75
❑ TC93 Owen Daniels	.25	.60
❑ TC94 Kellen Winslow	.30	.75
❑ TC95 Tony Gonzalez	.30	.75
❑ TC96 Jason Witten	.40	1.00
❑ TC97 Jeremy Shockey	.30	.75
❑ TC98 Dallas Clark	.30	.75
❑ TC99 Donald Lee	.30	.75
❑ TC100 Heath Miller	.25	.60
❑ TC101 Tony Scheffler	.25	.60
❑ TC102 Desmond Clark	.25	.60
❑ TC103 Vernon Davis	.25	.60
❑ TC104 Alge Crumpler	.30	.75
❑ TC105 Zach Miller	.30	.75
❑ TC106 Patrick Kerney	.25	.60
❑ TC107 Osi Umenyiora	.25	.60
❑ TC108 Mario Williams	.30	.75
❑ TC109 Jared Allen	.40	1.00
❑ TC110 Michael Strahan	.30	.75
❑ TC111 Ernie Sims	.25	.60
❑ TC112 DeMarcus Ware	.30	.75
❑ TC113 Patrick Willis	.30	.75
❑ TC114 Shawne Merriman	.30	.75
❑ TC115 Brian Urlacher	.40	1.00
❑ TC116 Ray Lewis	.40	1.00
❑ TC117 Antonio Cromartie	.25	.60
❑ TC118 Champ Bailey	.25	.60
❑ TC119 Bob Sanders	.30	.75
❑ TC120 Ed Reed	.30	.75
❑ TC121 Tom Brady LL	.50	1.25
❑ TC122 Drew Brees LL	.30	.75
❑ TC123 Tony Romo LL	.50	1.25
❑ TC124 LaDainian Tomlinson LL	.40	1.00
❑ TC125 Adrian Peterson LL	.60	1.50
❑ TC126 Brian Westbrook LL	.25	.60
❑ TC127 Reggie Wayne LL	.25	.60
❑ TC128 Randy Moss LL	.30	.75
❑ TC129 Chad Johnson LL	.25	.60
❑ TC130 Randy Moss LL	.30	.75
❑ TC131 Matt Hasselbeck AP	.25	.60
❑ TC132 Tony Romo AP	.50	1.25
❑ TC133 Adrian Peterson AP	.60	1.50
❑ TC134 Marion Barber AP	.30	.75
❑ TC135 Brian Westbrook AP	.25	.60
❑ TC136 Larry Fitzgerald AP	.30	.75
❑ TC137 Terrell Owens AP	.30	.75
❑ TC138 Osi Umenyiora AP	.20	.50
❑ TC139 Lofa Tatupu AP	.25	.60
❑ TC140 Jason Witten AP	.30	.75
❑ TC141 Torry Holt AP	.25	.60
❑ TC142 Donald Driver AP	.25	.60
❑ TC143 Peyton Manning AP	.50	1.25
❑ TC144 Ben Roethlisberger AP	.50	1.25
❑ TC145 Joseph Addai AP	.30	.75
❑ TC146 Reggie Wayne AP	.25	.60
❑ TC147 Braylon Edwards AP	.25	.60
❑ TC148 Devin Hester AP	.30	.75
❑ TC149 Champ Bailey AP	.20	.50
❑ TC150 Ed Reed AP	.25	.60
❑ TC151 Eli Manning PSH	.30	.75
❑ TC152 David Tyree PSH	.25	.60
❑ TC153 Plaxico Burress PSH	.25	.60
❑ TC154 Lawrence Tynes PSH	.20	.50
❑ TC155 Patriots defense PSH	.30	.75
❑ TC156 R.W. McQuarters PSH	.20	.50
❑ TC157 Ryan Grant PSH	.30	.75
❑ TC158 Philip Rivers PSH	.30	.75
❑ TC159 David Garrard PSH	.25	.60
❑ TC160 Laurence Maroney PSH	.25	.60
❑ TC161 Seahawks PSH	.25	.60
❑ TC162 Chargers defense PSH	.20	.50
❑ TC163 Tom Brady MVP	.50	1.25
❑ TC164 Adrian Peterson OROY	.60	1.50
❑ TC165 Patrick Willis DROY	.25	.60
❑ TC166 Matt Ryan RC	5.00	12.00
❑ TC167 Brian Brohm RC	1.25	3.00
❑ TC168 Andre Woodson RC	1.25	3.00
❑ TC169 Chad Henne RC	2.00	5.00
❑ TC170 Joe Flacco RC	4.00	10.00
❑ TC171 John David Booty RC	1.25	3.00
❑ TC172 Colt Brennan RC	2.00	5.00
❑ TC173 Dennis Dixon RC	1.25	3.00
❑ TC174 Erik Ainge RC	1.25	3.00
❑ TC175 Josh Johnson RC	1.25	3.00
❑ TC176 Kevin O'Connell RC	1.25	3.00
❑ TC177 Matt Flynn RC	1.25	3.00
❑ TC178 Sam Keller RC	1.25	3.00
❑ TC179 Harry Douglas RC	1.00	2.50
❑ TC180 Anthony Morelli RC	1.25	3.00
❑ TC181 Darren McFadden RC	2.50	6.00
❑ TC182 Rashard Mendenhall RC	2.50	6.00
❑ TC183 Jonathan Stewart RC	2.50	6.00
❑ TC184 Felix Jones RC	2.50	6.00
❑ TC185 Jamaal Charles RC	2.00	5.00
❑ TC186 Chris Johnson RC	4.00	10.00
❑ TC187 Ray Rice RC	2.50	6.00
❑ TC188 Mike Hart RC	1.25	3.00
❑ TC189 Kevin Smith RC	2.00	5.00
❑ TC190 Steve Slaton RC	1.50	4.00
❑ TC191 Matt Forte RC	2.50	6.00
❑ TC192 Tashard Choice RC	1.25	3.00
❑ TC193 D.Rodgers-Cromartie RC	1.25	3.00
❑ TC194 Cory Boyd RC	1.00	2.50
❑ TC195 Allen Patrick RC	1.00	2.50
❑ TC196 Thomas Brown RC	1.25	3.00
❑ TC197 Justin Forsett RC	1.25	3.00
❑ TC198 DeSean Jackson RC	2.50	6.00
❑ TC199 Malcolm Kelly RC	1.25	3.00
❑ TC200 Limas Sweed RC	1.25	3.00
❑ TC201 Mario Manningham RC	1.25	3.00
❑ TC202 James Hardy RC	1.00	2.50
❑ TC203 Early Doucet RC	1.25	3.00
❑ TC204 Donnie Avery RC	1.50	4.00
❑ TC205 Dexter Jackson RC	1.25	3.00
❑ TC206 Devin Thomas RC	1.25	3.00
❑ TC207 Jordy Nelson RC	1.50	4.00
❑ TC208 Keenan Burton RC	1.00	2.50
❑ TC209 Chris Williams RC	1.00	2.50
❑ TC210 Earl Bennett RC	1.25	3.00
❑ TC211 Jerome Simpson RC	1.00	2.50
❑ TC212 Andre Caldwell RC	1.25	3.00
❑ TC213 Josh Morgan RC	1.25	3.00
❑ TC214 Fred Davis RC	1.25	3.00
❑ TC215 John Carlson RC	1.25	3.00
❑ TC216 Martellus Bennett RC	1.25	3.00
❑ TC217 Martin Rucker RC	1.00	2.50
❑ TC218 Jermichael Finley RC	1.25	3.00
❑ TC219 Dustin Keller RC	1.25	3.00
❑ TC220 Jacob Tamme RC	1.25	3.00
❑ TC221 Kellen Davis RC	.75	2.00
❑ TC222 Jake Long RC	1.25	3.00
❑ TC223 Sam Baker RC	.75	2.00

Card		
TC224 Jeff Otah RC	1.00	2.50
TC225 Owen Schmitt RC	1.25	3.00
TC226 Chevis Jackson RC	1.00	2.50
TC227 Jacob Hester RC	1.25	3.00
TC228 Glenn Dorsey RC	1.25	3.00
TC229 Sedrick Ellis RC	1.25	3.00
TC230 Kentwan Balmer RC	1.00	2.50
TC231 Pat Sims RC	1.00	2.50
TC232 Marcus Harrison RC	1.25	3.00
TC233 Dre Moore RC	1.00	2.50
TC234 Red Bryant RC	.75	2.00
TC235 Trevor Laws RC	1.25	3.00
TC236 Chris Long RC	1.25	3.00
TC237 Vernon Gholston RC	1.25	3.00
TC238 Derrick Harvey RC	1.00	2.50
TC239 Calais Campbell RC	1.00	2.50
TC240 Terrence Wheatley RC	1.00	2.50
TC241 Phillip Merling RC	1.00	2.50
TC242 Chris Ellis RC	1.00	2.50
TC243 Lawrence Jackson RC	1.00	2.50
TC244 Dan Connor RC	1.25	3.00
TC245 Curtis Lofton RC	1.25	3.00
TC246 Jerod Mayo RC	1.50	4.00
TC247 Tavares Gooden RC	1.00	2.50
TC248 Beau Bell RC	1.00	2.50
TC249 Philip Wheeler RC	1.25	3.00
TC250 Vince Hall RC	.75	2.00
TC251 Jonathan Goff RC	1.00	2.50
TC252 Keith Rivers RC	1.25	3.00
TC253 Ali Highsmith RC	.75	2.00
TC254 Xavier Adibi RC	1.00	2.50
TC255 Erin Henderson RC	1.00	2.50
TC256 Bruce Davis RC	1.25	3.00
TC257 Jordon Dizon RC	1.25	3.00
TC258 Shawn Crable RC	1.25	3.00
TC259 Geno Hayes RC	.75	2.00
TC260 Mike Jenkins RC	1.25	3.00
TC261 Aqib Talib RC	1.25	3.00
TC262 Leodis McKelvin RC	1.25	3.00
TC263 Terrell Thomas RC	1.00	2.50
TC264 Reggie Smith RC	1.00	2.50
TC265 Antoine Cason RC	1.25	3.00
TC266 Patrick Lee RC	1.25	3.00
TC267 Tracy Porter RC	1.50	4.00
TC268 Kenny Phillips RC	1.25	3.00
TC269 Simeon Castille RC	1.00	2.50
TC270 Eddie Royal RC	2.00	5.00
TC271 Thomas DeCoud RC	.75	2.00
TC272 Marcus Griffin RC	.75	2.00
TC273 Charles Godfrey RC	1.00	2.50
TC274 Tyrell Johnson RC	1.25	3.00
TC275 Jamar Adams RC	1.00	2.50
RH42 Eli Manning RH	1.00	2.50

2009 Topps Chrome

Card		
COMPLETE SET (220)	75.00	150.00
COMP.SET w/o RC's (110)	8.00	20.00
TC1 Santana Moss	.25	.60
TC2 Vernon Davis	.20	.50
TC3 Philip Rivers	.30	.75
TC4 Santonio Holmes	.25	.60
TC5 Jamarcus Russell	.25	.60
TC6 Thomas Jones	.25	.60
TC7 Randy Moss	.30	.75
TC8 Tyler Thigpen	.20	.50
TC9 Maurice Jones-Drew	.25	.60
TC10 Calvin Johnson	.30	.75
TC11 Champ Bailey	.25	.60
TC12 Felix Jones	.30	.75
TC13 Brady Quinn	.25	.60
TC14 Carson Palmer	.30	.75
TC15 Marshawn Lynch	.25	.60
TC16 Ed Reed	.25	.60
TC17 Tim Hightower	.25	.60
TC18 Karlos Dansby	.20	.50
TC19 Chris Cooley	.25	.60
TC20 Donnie Avery	.25	.60
TC21 John Carlson	.25	.60
TC22 Hines Ward	.25	.60
TC23 DeSean Jackson	.25	.60
TC24 Justin Tuck	.25	.60
TC25 Marques Colston	.25	.60
TC26A D.Brees back in view	.30	.75
TC26B D.Brees facing SP	10.00	25.00
TC27 Wes Welker	.30	.75
TC28A Adrian Peterson wht	.60	1.50
TC28B Adrian Peterson prple SP	25.00	50.00
TC29 David Garrard	.25	.60
TC30 Greg Jennings	.30	.75
TC31 Kevin Smith	.25	.60
TC32 Marion Barber	.30	.75
TC33 Keith Rivers	.20	.50
TC34 Devin Hester	.30	.75
TC35 Trent Edwards	.25	.60
TC36 Kurt Warner	.30	.75
TC37 Clinton Portis	.25	.60
TC38 LenDale White	.25	.60
TC39 Chris Johnson	.30	.75
TC40 Antonio Bryant	.25	.60
TC41 Matt Hasselbeck	.25	.60
TC42 Frank Gore	.25	.60
TC43 Antonio Gates	.25	.60
TC44 Troy Polamalu	.30	.75
TC45 Brian Westbrook	.25	.60
TC46 Steve Smith	.25	.60
TC47 Darrelle Revis	.25	.60
TC48 Kevin Boss	.20	.50
TC49 Jeremy Shockey	.20	.50
TC50 Tarvaris Jackson	.25	.60
TC51 Ted Ginn Jr.	.25	.60
TC52 Dwayne Bowe	.25	.60
TC53 Bob Sanders	.25	.60
TC54 Reggie Wayne	.25	.60
TC55 DeMarcus Ware	.25	.60
TC56A T.Romo in tunnel	.50	1.25
TC56B T.Romo passing SP	12.00	30.00
TC57 Matt Forte	.30	.75
TC58 Jonathan Stewart	.25	.60
TC59 Roddy White	.25	.60
TC60 Anquan Boldin	.25	.60
TC61 Kerry Collins	.25	.60
TC62 Steven Jackson	.25	.60
TC63 Darren Sproles	.25	.60
TC64 Willie Parker	.25	.60
TC65 Asante Samuel	.20	.50
TC66 Donovan McNabb	.30	.75
TC67 Jerricho Cotchery	.20	.50
TC68 Brandon Jacobs	.25	.60
TC69 Jerod Mayo	.25	.60
TC70A T.Brady passing	.50	1.25
TC70B T.Brady drop back SP	20.00	40.00
TC71 Jared Allen	.30	.75
TC72 Ronnie Brown	.25	.60
TC73 Tony Gonzalez	.25	.60
TC74A Andre Johnson wht	.25	.60
TC74B Andre Johnson blu SP	8.00	20.00
TC75A A.Rodgers passing	.30	.75
TC75B A.Rodgers jogging SP	15.00	30.00
TC76 Eddie Royal	.25	.60
TC77 Terrell Owens	.30	.75
TC78 Kellen Winslow Jr.	.25	.60
TC79 Chad Ochocinco	.25	.60
TC80 DeAngelo Williams	.30	.75
TC81 Joe Flacco	.30	.75
TC82 Michael Turner	.25	.60
TC83 Larry Fitzgerald	.30	.75
TC84 Keith Bulluck	.20	.50
TC85 Aqib Talib	.20	.50
TC86 Patrick Willis	.25	.60
TC87 LaDainian Tomlinson	.30	.75
TC88 Ben Roethlisberger	.50	1.25
TC89 Darren McFadden	.30	.75
TC90 Leon Washington	.25	.60
TC91 Eli Manning	.30	.75
TC92 Reggie Bush	.30	.75
TC93 Chad Pennington	.25	.60
TC94 Joey Porter	.25	.60
TC95 Anthony Gonzalez	.25	.60
TC96A Peyton Manning blu	.50	1.25
TC96B Peyton Manning wht SP	20.00	40.00
TC97 Matt Schaub	.25	.60
TC98 Steve Slaton	.25	.60
TC99 Aaron Kampman	.25	.60
TC100 Ernie Sims	.20	.50
TC101 Brandon Marshall	.25	.60
TC102 Jay Cutler	.30	.75
TC103 Jason Witten	.30	.75
TC104 Braylon Edwards	.25	.60
TC105 T.J. Houshmandzadeh	.25	.60
TC106 Brian Urlacher	.30	.75
TC107 Julius Peppers	.25	.60
TC108 Willis McGahee	.25	.60
TC109 Ray Lewis	.30	.75
TC110 Matt Ryan	.30	.75
TC111 Aaron Brown RC	1.25	3.00
TC112 B.J. Raji RC	1.50	4.00
TC113 Aaron Maybin RC	1.25	3.00
TC114 Alphonso Smith RC	1.00	2.50
TC115 Hakeem Nicks RC	2.50	6.00
TC116 Andre Smith RC	1.25	3.00
TC117 Andy Levitre RC	1.00	2.50
TC118 Asher Allen RC	1.00	2.50
TC119 Austin Collie RC	2.50	6.00
TC120 Aaron Curry RC	1.50	4.00
TC121 Brandon Gibson RC	1.25	3.00
TC122 Michael Oher RC	2.50	6.00
TC123 Brandon Tate RC	1.00	2.50
TC124 Brandon Underwood RC	1.25	3.00
TC125 Javon Ringer RC	1.25	3.00
TC126 Brian Hartline RC	1.25	3.00
TC127 Brian Orakpo RC	1.50	4.00
TC128 Mike Wallace RC	2.50	6.00
TC129 Brooks Foster RC	1.00	2.50
TC130 Brian Cushing RC	1.50	4.00
TC131 Chase Coffman RC	1.00	2.50
TC132 Darius Butler RC	1.25	3.00
TC133 Clay Matthews RC	2.00	5.00
TC134 Clint Sintim RC	1.25	3.00
TC135 Kenny Britt RC	2.00	5.00
TC136 Patrick Turner RC	1.00	2.50
TC137 Courtney Greene RC	.75	2.00
TC138 Curtis Painter RC	1.25	3.00
TC139 D.J. Moore RC	1.00	2.50
TC140 Chris Wells RC	3.00	8.00
TC141 Darrius Heyward-Bey RC	2.00	5.00
TC142 Demetrius Byrd RC	1.00	2.50
TC143 Deon Butler RC	1.25	3.00
TC144 Derrick Williams RC	1.25	3.00
TC145A Pat White scrmblng RC	2.00	5.00
TC145B Pat White passing SP	15.00	30.00
TC146 Duke Robinson RC	.75	2.00
TC147 Eben Britton RC	1.00	2.50
TC148 Eugene Monroe RC	1.00	2.50
TC149 Everette Brown RC	1.25	3.00
TC150 Donald Brown RC	2.50	6.00
TC151 Gartrell Johnson RC	1.00	2.50
TC152 Glen Coffee RC	1.50	4.00
TC153 Andre Brown RC	1.00	2.50
TC154 James Casey RC	1.00	2.50
TC155 Percy Harvin RC	4.00	10.00
TC156 Roy Miller RC	1.25	3.00
TC157 Jamon Meredith RC	1.00	2.50
TC158 Jared Cook RC	1.00	2.50
TC159 Jarett Dillard RC	1.25	3.00
TC160 Jeremy Maclin RC	2.50	6.00
TC161 Jason Williams RC	1.25	3.00
TC162 Javarris Williams RC	1.00	2.50
TC163 Cedric Peerman RC	1.00	2.50
TC164 Jason Smith RC	1.00	2.50
TC165 Fili Moala RC	1.00	2.50
TC166 Rey Maualuga RC	2.00	5.00
TC167 Travis Beckum RC	1.00	2.50
TC168 Juaquin Iglesias RC	1.25	3.00
TC169 Connor Barwin RC	1.00	2.50
TC170 Knowshon Moreno RC	3.00	8.00
TC171 Kenny McKinley RC	1.25	3.00
TC172 Kevin Ellison RC	1.00	2.50
TC173 Larry English RC	1.25	3.00
TC174 Marko Mitchell RC	1.00	2.50
TC175 Louis Delmas RC	1.25	3.00
TC176 Shonn Greene RC	2.50	6.00
TC177 Malcolm Jenkins RC	1.25	3.00
TC178 Manuel Johnson RC	1.00	2.50
TC179 Marcus Freeman RC	1.25	3.00
TC180 LeSean McCoy RC	2.50	6.00
TC181 Zack Follett RC	.75	2.00
TC182 Shawn Nelson RC	1.00	2.50
TC183 Rashad Jennings RC	1.25	3.00
TC184 Michael Hamlin RC	1.00	2.50
TC185 Michael Johnson RC	.75	2.00

Card		
❑ TC186 Brandon Pettigrew RC	1.50	4.00
❑ TC187 Mike Goodson RC	1.25	3.00
❑ TC188 Mike Mickens RC	1.00	2.50
❑ TC189 Mike Teel RC	1.25	3.00
❑ TC190 Mike Thomas RC	1.25	3.00
❑ TC191 Brian Robiskie RC	1.25	3.00
❑ TC192 Mohamed Massaquoi RC	1.25	3.00
❑ TC193 Nate Davis RC	1.25	3.00
❑ TC194 Patrick Chung RC	1.25	3.00
❑ TC195 Cornelius Ingram RC	.75	2.00
❑ TC196 James Davis RC	1.25	3.00
❑ TC197 Peria Jerry RC	1.00	2.50
❑ TC198 Phil Loadholt RC	1.00	2.50
❑ TC199 Ramses Barden RC	1.00	2.50
❑ TC200A Michael Crabtree RC	3.00	8.00
❑ TC200B M.Crabtree ball in air SP	15.00	30.00
❑ TC201 Rashad Johnson RC	1.00	2.50
❑ TC202 Johnny Knox RC	2.00	5.00
❑ TC203 Rhett Bomar RC	1.00	2.50
❑ TC204 Robert Ayers RC	1.25	3.00
❑ TC205 James Laurinaitis RC	1.50	4.00
❑ TC206 Sammie Stroughter RC	1.25	3.00
❑ TC207 Scott McKillop RC	1.00	2.50
❑ TC208 Sean Smith RC	1.25	3.00
❑ TC209 Sen'Derrick Marks RC	.75	2.00
❑ TC210 Matthew Stafford RC	6.00	15.00
❑ TC211 Louis Murphy RC	1.25	3.00
❑ TC212 Stephen McGee RC	1.25	3.00
❑ TC213 Tiquan Underwood RC	1.00	2.50
❑ TC214 Tom Brandstater RC	1.25	3.00
❑ TC215 Josh Freeman RC	2.50	6.00
❑ TC216 Tyson Jackson RC	1.25	3.00
❑ TC217 Victor Harris RC	1.25	3.00
❑ TC218 Vontae Davis RC	1.25	3.00
❑ TC219 William Moore RC	1.00	2.50
❑ TC220A Mark Sanchez RC	12.50	25.00
❑ TC220B Mark Sanchez w/hlmt SP	40.00	80.00
❑ RHC43 Santonio Holmes RH	.75	2.00

2003 Topps Draft Picks and Prospects

Card		
❑ COMPLETE SET (165)	25.00	50.00
❑ 1 Priest Holmes	.30	.75
❑ 2 Tommy Maddox	.25	.60
❑ 3 Donald Driver	.30	.75
❑ 4 Drew Bledsoe	.30	.75
❑ 5 Tiki Barber	.30	.75
❑ 6 Terrell Owens	.30	.75
❑ 7 Rich Gannon	.25	.60
❑ 8 Isaac Bruce	.30	.75
❑ 9 Stephen Davis	.25	.60
❑ 10 Peyton Manning	.60	1.50
❑ 11 Tony Gonzalez	.25	.60
❑ 12 Marty Booker	.25	.60
❑ 13 Warrick Dunn	.25	.60
❑ 14 Jimmy Smith	.25	.60
❑ 15 Troy Brown	.25	.60
❑ 16 Jerry Rice	.60	1.50
❑ 17 Curtis Conway	.20	.50
❑ 18 Kurt Warner	.30	.75
❑ 19 Steve McNair	.30	.75
❑ 20 Edgerrin James	.30	.75
❑ 21 Aaron Brooks	.25	.60
❑ 22 Joey Galloway	.25	.60
❑ 23 Peerless Price	.20	.50
❑ 24 Torry Holt	.30	.75
❑ 25 Derrick Mason	.25	.60
❑ 26 Curtis Martin	.30	.75
❑ 27 Daunte Culpepper	.30	.75
❑ 28 Ahman Green	.30	.75
❑ 29 Tim Couch	.20	.50
❑ 30 Ricky Williams	.25	.60
❑ 31 Darrell Jackson	.25	.60
❑ 32 Keyshawn Johnson	.30	.75
❑ 33 Jeff Garcia	.30	.75
❑ 34 Charlie Garner	.25	.60
❑ 35 Randy Moss	.30	.75
❑ 36 Rod Smith	.25	.60
❑ 37 Jamal Lewis	.30	.75
❑ 38 Corey Dillon	.25	.60
❑ 39 Marvin Harrison	.30	.75
❑ 40 Joe Horn	.25	.60
❑ 41 Laveranues Coles	.25	.60
❑ 42 Hines Ward	.30	.75
❑ 43 Brad Johnson	.25	.60
❑ 44 Eddie George	.25	.60
❑ 45 Donovan McNabb	.30	.75
❑ 46 Marshall Faulk	.30	.75
❑ 47 Amani Toomer	.25	.60
❑ 48 Trent Green	.25	.60
❑ 49 Emmitt Smith	.75	2.00
❑ 50 Brett Favre	.75	2.00
❑ 51 Brian Griese	.25	.60
❑ 52 Eric Moulds	.25	.60
❑ 53 Plaxico Burress	.30	.75
❑ 54 Fred Taylor	.30	.75
❑ 55 Tom Brady	.75	2.00
❑ 56 Michael Vick	.30	.75
❑ 57 Andre Davis	.20	.50
❑ 58 Chris Chambers	.25	.60
❑ 59 Javon Walker	.25	.60
❑ 60 Marc Bulger	.30	.75
❑ 61 LaDainian Tomlinson	.40	1.00
❑ 62 Chad Pennington	.30	.75
❑ 63 Marc Boerigter	.20	.50
❑ 64 Rod Gardner	.20	.50
❑ 65 DeShaun Foster	.25	.60
❑ 66 Chris Redman	.20	.50
❑ 67 Chad Hutchinson	.20	.50
❑ 68 Deion Branch	.25	.60
❑ 69 Jeremy Shockey	.30	.75
❑ 70 Shaun Alexander	.30	.75
❑ 71 Derrius Thompson	.20	.50
❑ 72 A.J. Feeley	.20	.50
❑ 73 Reggie Wayne	.25	.60
❑ 74 William Green	.20	.50
❑ 75 Julius Peppers	.30	.75
❑ 76 Travis Henry	.25	.60
❑ 77 Marcel Shipp	.20	.50
❑ 78 Michael Bennett	.25	.60
❑ 79 Maurice Morris	.20	.50
❑ 80 Josh Reed	.20	.50
❑ 81 David Terrell	.20	.50
❑ 82 Drew Brees	.30	.75
❑ 83 Jonathan Wells	.20	.50
❑ 84 Anthony Thomas	.25	.60
❑ 85 Quincy Morgan	.20	.50
❑ 86 Jerry Porter	.25	.60
❑ 87 Ron Johnson	.20	.50
❑ 88 Najeh Davenport	.25	.60
❑ 89 Lamar Gordon	.20	.50
❑ 90 Joey Harrington	.25	.60
❑ 91 Donte Stallworth	.25	.60
❑ 92 Kenny Watson	.20	.50
❑ 93 LaMont Jordan	.25	.60
❑ 94 Antonio Bryant	.30	.75
❑ 95 Steve Smith	.30	.75
❑ 96 T.J. Duckett	.25	.60
❑ 97 Patrick Ramsey	.25	.60
❑ 98 Santana Moss	.25	.60
❑ 99 Chad Johnson	.30	.75
❑ 100 Clinton Portis	.40	1.00
❑ 101 Reche Caldwell	.20	.50
❑ 102 Kevan Barlow	.20	.50
❑ 103 Deuce McAllister	.30	.75
❑ 104 Koren Robinson	.25	.60
❑ 105 Todd Heap	.25	.60
❑ 106 Jabar Gaffney	.20	.50
❑ 107 Randy McMichael	.20	.50
❑ 108 Dwight Freeney	.25	.60
❑ 109 Antwaan Randle El	.25	.60
❑ 110 David Carr	.30	.75
❑ 111 Carson Palmer RC	2.50	6.00
❑ 112 Dahrran Diedrick RC	.40	1.00
❑ 113 Kyle Boller RC	.60	1.50
❑ 114 Terrell Suggs RC	.75	2.00
❑ 115 Rien Long RC	.40	1.00
❑ 116 Justin Gage RC	.60	1.50
❑ 117 William Joseph RC	.40	1.00
❑ 118 Chris Simms RC	.60	1.50
❑ 119 Avon Cobourne RC	.40	1.00
❑ 120 Victor Hobson RC	.40	1.00
❑ 121 Jason Gesser RC	.50	1.25
❑ 122 Ronald Bellamy RC	.50	1.25
❑ 123 Terence Newman RC	.60	1.50
❑ 124 Terrence Edwards RC	.40	1.00
❑ 125 Sultan McCullough RC	.40	1.00
❑ 126 Kareem Kelly RC	.40	1.00
❑ 127 Jason Witten RC	1.50	4.00
❑ 128 Mike Doss RC	.60	1.50
❑ 129 Seneca Wallace RC	.60	1.50
❑ 130 Chris Brown RC	.60	1.50
❑ 131 Larry Johnson RC	.75	2.00
❑ 132 Taylor Jacobs RC	.50	1.25
❑ 133 Jerome McDougle RC	.40	1.00
❑ 134 Kelley Washington RC	.50	1.25
❑ 135 Brad Banks RC	.50	1.25
❑ 136 DeWayne White RC	.40	1.00
❑ 137 LaBrandon Toefield RC	.50	1.25
❑ 138 Brian St.Pierre RC	.60	1.50
❑ 139 Kindal Moorehead RC	.50	1.25
❑ 140 Willis McGahee RC	1.25	3.00
❑ 141 Jimmy Kennedy RC	.50	1.25
❑ 142 Talman Gardner RC	.40	1.00
❑ 143 Chris Kelsay RC	.50	1.25
❑ 144 Cory Redding RC	.50	1.25
❑ 145 Dave Ragone RC	.40	1.00
❑ 146 Earnest Graham RC	.60	1.50
❑ 147 Andre Johnson RC	1.25	3.00
❑ 148 Boss Bailey RC	.50	1.25
❑ 149 Sam Aiken RC	.60	1.50
❑ 150 Byron Leftwich RC	.75	2.00
❑ 151 Teyo Johnson RC	.50	1.25
❑ 152 Quentin Griffin RC	.50	1.25
❑ 153 Justin Fargas RC	.60	1.50
❑ 154 Bradie James RC	.60	1.50
❑ 155 Andre Woolfolk RC	.50	1.25
❑ 156 Marcus Trufant RC	.60	1.50
❑ 157 Ken Dorsey RC	.50	1.25
❑ 158 Onterrio Smith RC	.50	1.25
❑ 159 Bryant Johnson RC	.60	1.50
❑ 160 Charles Rogers RC	.50	1.25
❑ 161 Kliff Kingsbury RC	.50	1.25
❑ 162 Michael Haynes RC	.40	1.00
❑ 163 Bennie Joppru RC	.40	1.00
❑ 164 Brandon Lloyd RC	.60	1.50
❑ 165 Jarret Johnson RC	.50	1.25

2004 Topps Draft Picks and Prospects

Card		
❑ COMPLETE SET (165)	40.00	80.00
❑ 1 Steve McNair	.40	1.00
❑ 2 Stephen Davis	.30	.75
❑ 3 Chris Chambers	.30	.75
❑ 4 Curtis Martin	.40	1.00
❑ 5 Shaun Alexander	.40	1.00
❑ 6 Jon Kitna	.30	.75
❑ 7 Jimmy Smith	.30	.75
❑ 8 Travis Henry	.30	.75
❑ 9 Torry Holt	.40	1.00
❑ 10 Jamal Lewis	.30	.75
❑ 11 Clinton Portis	.40	1.00
❑ 12 Aaron Brooks	.30	.75
❑ 13 Plaxico Burress	.30	.75
❑ 14 Trent Green	.30	.75
❑ 15 Chad Johnson	.30	.75
❑ 16 Jake Delhomme	.30	.75
❑ 17 David Boston	.25	.60
❑ 18 Joe Horn	.30	.75
❑ 19 Ahman Green	.40	1.00
❑ 20 Fred Taylor	.30	.75
❑ 21 Terrell Owens	.40	1.00
❑ 22 Brad Johnson	.30	.75
❑ 23 Laveranues Coles	.30	.75
❑ 24 Ricky Williams	.40	1.00
❑ 25 Peyton Manning	.75	2.00

❑ 26 Hines Ward	.40	1.00
❑ 27 Matt Hasselbeck	.40	1.00
❑ 28 Marshall Faulk	.40	1.00
❑ 29 Tony Gonzalez	.40	1.00
❑ 30 Marvin Harrison	.40	1.00
❑ 31 Eric Moulds	.30	.75
❑ 32 Chad Pennington	.40	1.00
❑ 33 Jerry Porter	.30	.75
❑ 34 Jeff Garcia	.40	1.00
❑ 35 Derrick Mason	.30	.75
❑ 36 Anthony Thomas	.30	.75
❑ 37 Drew Bledsoe	.40	1.00
❑ 38 Jake Plummer	.30	.75
❑ 39 Tiki Barber	.40	1.00
❑ 40 Brett Favre	1.00	2.50
❑ 41 Joey Harrington	.30	.75
❑ 42 Daunte Culpepper	.40	1.00
❑ 43 LaVar Arrington	.30	.75
❑ 44 Santana Moss	.30	.75
❑ 45 David Carr	.30	.75
❑ 46 Randy Moss	.40	1.00
❑ 47 LaDainian Tomlinson	.50	1.25
❑ 48 Deuce McAllister	.40	1.00
❑ 49 Amani Toomer	.30	.75
❑ 50 Donovan McNabb	.40	1.00
❑ 51 Priest Holmes	.40	1.00
❑ 52 Corey Dillon	.30	.75
❑ 53 Tom Brady	1.00	2.50
❑ 54 Edgerrin James	.40	1.00
❑ 55 Michael Vick	.40	1.00
❑ 56 Anquan Boldin	.40	1.00
❑ 57 Robert Ferguson	.25	.60
❑ 58 Onterrio Smith	.25	.60
❑ 59 Marques Tuiasosopo	.25	.60
❑ 60 Rudi Johnson	.30	.75
❑ 61 Alge Crumpler	.30	.75
❑ 62 Antonio Bryant	.40	1.00
❑ 63 LaMont Jordan	.40	1.00
❑ 64 Lamar Gordon	.25	.60
❑ 65 Tim Rattay	.25	.60
❑ 66 Antwaan Randle El	.30	.75
❑ 67 Ladell Betts	.30	.75
❑ 68 LaBrandon Toefield	.25	.60
❑ 69 Ashley Lelie	.30	.75
❑ 70 Marc Bulger	.30	.75
❑ 71 Reggie Wayne	.30	.75
❑ 72 William Green	.25	.60
❑ 73 Josh Reed	.40	1.00
❑ 74 T.J. Duckett	.30	.75
❑ 75 Andre Johnson	.40	1.00
❑ 76 Deion Branch	.30	.75
❑ 77 Tyrone Calico	.30	.75
❑ 78 Jeremy Shockey	.30	.75
❑ 79 Najeh Davenport	.30	.75
❑ 80 Byron Leftwich	.40	1.00
❑ 81 Correll Buckhalter	.30	.75
❑ 82 Justin McCareins	.25	.60
❑ 83 Carson Palmer	.50	1.25
❑ 84 Bryant Johnson	.30	.75
❑ 85 Patrick Ramsey	.30	.75
❑ 86 Justin Fargas	.30	.75
❑ 87 Dallas Clark	.40	1.00
❑ 88 Kelly Campbell	.25	.60
❑ 89 DeShaun Foster	.30	.75
❑ 90 Charles Rogers	.30	.75
❑ 91 Donte' Stallworth	.30	.75
❑ 92 Dante Hall	.30	.75
❑ 93 Randy McMichael	.25	.60
❑ 94 Marcel Shipp	.40	1.00
❑ 95 Kyle Boller	.30	.75
❑ 96 Steve Smith	.40	1.00
❑ 97 Brian Westbrook	.40	1.00
❑ 98 Kevan Barlow	.30	.75
❑ 99 Damerien McCants	.25	.60
❑ 100 Domanick Davis	.30	.75
❑ 101 Andre' Davis	.25	.60
❑ 102 Nate Burleson	.30	.75
❑ 103 Larry Johnson	.60	1.50
❑ 104 Drew Brees	.40	1.00
❑ 105 Koren Robinson	.40	1.00
❑ 106 Quincy Carter	.25	.60
❑ 107 Javon Walker	.30	.75
❑ 108 Willis McGahee	.40	1.00
❑ 109 Chris Simms	.30	.75
❑ 110 Rex Grossman	.40	1.00
❑ 111 Steven Jackson RC	2.00	5.00
❑ 112 Greg Jones RC	.75	2.00
❑ 113 Brandon Everage RC	.50	1.25
❑ 114 DeAngelo Hall RC	.75	2.00
❑ 115 Tatum Bell RC	.75	2.00
❑ 116 B.J. Symons RC	.50	1.25
❑ 117 Michael Clayton RC	.75	2.00
❑ 118 Jared Lorenzen RC	.60	1.50
❑ 119 Josh Harris RC	.50	1.25
❑ 120 Roy Williams RC	1.00	2.50
❑ 121 Mewelde Moore RC	.75	2.00
❑ 122 Jeff Smoker RC	.60	1.50
❑ 123 Lee Evans RC	1.00	2.50
❑ 124 Michael Jenkins RC	.75	2.00
❑ 125 Drew Henson RC	.50	1.25
❑ 126 Ben Watson RC	.75	2.00
❑ 127 Jerricho Cotchery RC	.75	2.00
❑ 128 Ben Troupe RC	.60	1.50
❑ 129 Chris Gamble RC	.60	1.50
❑ 130 Kevin Jones RC	.75	2.00
❑ 131 Cody Pickett RC	.60	1.50
❑ 132 J.P. Losman RC	.75	2.00
❑ 133 Michael Boulware RC	.75	2.00
❑ 134 Julius Jones RC	1.00	2.50
❑ 135 Keary Colbert RC	.60	1.50
❑ 136 Vince Wilfork RC	.75	2.00
❑ 137 Ernest Wilford RC	.60	1.50
❑ 138 John Navarre RC	.60	1.50
❑ 139 D.J. Williams RC	.75	2.00
❑ 140 Larry Fitzgerald RC	2.50	6.00
❑ 141 Quincy Wilson RC	.60	1.50
❑ 142 James Newson RC	.75	2.00
❑ 143 Reggie Williams RC	.75	2.00
❑ 144 Devard Darling RC	.60	1.50
❑ 145 Chris Perry RC	.75	2.00
❑ 146 Derrick Strait RC	.60	1.50
❑ 147 Teddy Lehman RC	.60	1.50
❑ 148 Michael Turner RC	2.00	5.00
❑ 149 Will Smith RC	.75	2.00
❑ 150 Eli Manning RC	6.00	15.00
❑ 151 Cedric Cobbs RC	.60	1.50
❑ 152 Ell Roberson UER RC	.75	2.00
❑ 153 Matt Schaub RC	2.00	5.00
❑ 154 Derrick Knight RC	.50	1.25
❑ 155 Rashaun Woods RC	.50	1.25
❑ 156 Jonathan Vilma RC	.75	2.00
❑ 157 Tommie Harris RC	.75	2.00
❑ 158 Dwan Edwards RC	.50	1.25
❑ 159 Will Poole RC	.75	2.00
❑ 160 Mike Williams RC	.60	1.50
❑ 161 Philip Rivers RC	3.00	8.00
❑ 162 Sean Taylor RC	.75	2.00
❑ 163 Darius Watts RC	.60	1.50
❑ 164 Casey Clausen RC	.60	1.50
❑ 165 Ben Roethlisberger RC	8.00	20.00

2005 Topps Draft Picks and Prospects

❑ COMP.SET w/o AU's (165)	15.00	40.00
❑ COMP.SET w/o RC's (110)	10.00	25.00
❑ 1 Marvin Harrison	.40	1.00
❑ 2 Rudi Johnson	.30	.75
❑ 3 Matt Hasselbeck	.30	.75
❑ 4 Plaxico Burress	.30	.75
❑ 5 Chad Pennington	.40	1.00
❑ 6 Jamal Lewis	.30	.75
❑ 7 Terrell Owens	.40	1.00
❑ 8 LaDainian Tomlinson	.50	1.25
❑ 9 Tiki Barber	.40	1.00
❑ 10 Dante Hall	.30	.75
❑ 11 Peyton Manning	.60	1.50
❑ 12 Marshall Faulk	.40	1.00
❑ 13 Donovan McNabb	.40	1.00
❑ 14 Randy Moss	.40	1.00
❑ 15 Muhsin Muhammad	.30	.75
❑ 16 Deuce McAllister	.40	1.00
❑ 17 Fred Taylor	.40	1.00
❑ 18 Jake Plummer	.30	.75
❑ 19 Javon Walker	.30	.75
❑ 20 Tony Gonzalez	.30	.75
❑ 21 Michael Vick	.40	1.00
❑ 22 Brett Favre	1.00	2.50
❑ 23 Joe Horn	.30	.75
❑ 24 Jeremy Shockey	.40	1.00
❑ 25 Laveranues Coles	.30	.75
❑ 26 Trent Green	.30	.75
❑ 27 Alge Crumpler	.30	.75
❑ 28 Curtis Martin	.40	1.00
❑ 29 Torry Holt	.30	.75
❑ 30 Daunte Culpepper	.40	1.00
❑ 31 Aaron Brooks	.25	.60
❑ 32 Priest Holmes	.40	1.00
❑ 33 Eric Moulds	.30	.75
❑ 34 Jerome Bettis	.40	1.00
❑ 35 David Carr	.30	.75
❑ 36 Chad Johnson	.30	.75
❑ 37 Ahman Green	.40	1.00
❑ 38 Clinton Portis	.40	1.00
❑ 39 Drew Brees	.40	1.00
❑ 40 Darrell Jackson	.30	.75
❑ 41 Corey Dillon	.30	.75
❑ 42 Reggie Wayne	.30	.75
❑ 43 Shaun Alexander	.40	1.00
❑ 44 Hines Ward	.40	1.00
❑ 45 Tom Brady	.75	2.00
❑ 46 Isaac Bruce	.30	.75
❑ 47 Byron Leftwich	.30	.75
❑ 48 Chris Chambers	.30	.75
❑ 49 Marc Bulger	.30	.75
❑ 50 Edgerrin James	.30	.75
❑ 51 Jake Delhomme	.40	1.00
❑ 52 Koren Robinson	.30	.75
❑ 53 Brian Westbrook	.40	1.00
❑ 54 Reuben Droughns	.25	.60
❑ 55 Joey Harrington	.40	1.00
❑ 56 Eli Manning	.75	2.00
❑ 57 Julius Jones	.40	1.00
❑ 58 Nick Goings	.25	.60
❑ 59 T.J. Houshmandzadeh	.30	.75
❑ 60 Ben Roethlisberger	1.00	2.50
❑ 61 Charles Rogers	.25	.60
❑ 62 Billy Volek	.30	.75
❑ 63 Drew Henson	.25	.60
❑ 64 Andre Johnson	.30	.75
❑ 65 Carson Palmer	.40	1.00
❑ 66 Anquan Boldin	.30	.75
❑ 67 Lee Suggs	.30	.75
❑ 68 Jerry Porter	.30	.75
❑ 69 J.P. Losman	.30	.75
❑ 70 Nate Burleson	.30	.75
❑ 71 Lee Evans	.30	.75
❑ 72 Tatum Bell	.30	.75
❑ 73 Chester Taylor	.30	.75
❑ 74 Philip Rivers	.40	1.00
❑ 75 Rex Grossman	.40	1.00
❑ 76 Willis McGahee	.40	1.00
❑ 77 Antonio Gates	.40	1.00
❑ 78 Steven Jackson	.50	1.25
❑ 79 Roy Williams WR	.40	1.00
❑ 80 Chris Simms	.30	.75
❑ 81 Najeh Davenport	.30	.75
❑ 82 Kevin Jones	.30	.75
❑ 83 Jason Witten	.40	1.00
❑ 84 Brandon Lloyd	.25	.60
❑ 85 Larry Johnson	.40	1.00
❑ 86 Ronald Curry	.30	.75
❑ 87 Chris Brown	.30	.75
❑ 88 Kyle Boller	.30	.75
❑ 89 Chris Perry	.25	.60
❑ 90 Keary Colbert	.25	.60
❑ 91 Sean Taylor	.30	.75
❑ 92 Greg Jones	.25	.60
❑ 93 Larry Fitzgerald	.40	1.00
❑ 94 Michael Clayton	.30	.75
❑ 95 Mewelde Moore	.25	.60
❑ 96 Drew Bennett	.30	.75
❑ 97 Reggie Williams	.30	.75
❑ 98 Quentin Griffin	.30	.75
❑ 99 Josh McCown	.30	.75
❑ 100 Santana Moss	.30	.75
❑ 101 Kellen Winslow	.40	1.00
❑ 102 Michael Jenkins	.30	.75
❑ 103 Dunta Robinson	.25	.60
❑ 104 Luke McCown	.25	.60
❑ 105 Brandon Stokley	.25	.60

❑ 106 Derrick Blaylock .25 .60
❑ 107 Ernest Wilford .30 .75
❑ 108 Domanick Davis .25 .60
❑ 109 Jonathan Vilma .30 .75
❑ 110 Dwight Freeney .30 .75
❑ 111 Alex Smith QB AU RC 60.00 120.00
❑ 112 Derrick Johnson AU RC 25.00 60.00
❑ 113 Charlie Frye AU RC 20.00 50.00
❑ 114 Ronnie Brown AU RC 60.00 120.00
❑ 115 Mike Williams AU 20.00 50.00
❑ 116 Erasmus James RC .60 1.50
❑ 117 Alex Smith TE RC .75 2.00
❑ 118 Dan Orlovsky RC .75 2.00
❑ 119 Eric Shelton RC .60 1.50
❑ 120 Reggie Brown RC .60 1.50
❑ 121 Carlos Rogers RC .75 2.00
❑ 122 Dan Cody RC .75 2.00
❑ 123 J.J. Arrington RC .75 2.00
❑ 124 Travis Johnson RC .50 1.25
❑ 125 Antrel Rolle RC .75 2.00
❑ 126 Andrew Walter RC .60 1.50
❑ 127 Craphonso Thorpe RC .60 1.50
❑ 128 Bryan Randall RC .60 1.50
❑ 129 Anttaj Hawthorne RC .60 1.50
❑ 130 David Pollack RC .60 1.50
❑ 131 Heath Miller RC 1.50 4.00
❑ 132 Charles Frederick RC .60 1.50
❑ 133 Anthony Davis RC .60 1.50
❑ 134 Chris Rix RC .60 1.50
❑ 135 T.A. McLendon RC .50 1.25
❑ 136 David Greene RC .60 1.50
❑ 137 Timmy Chang RC .60 1.50
❑ 138 Marcus Spears RC .75 2.00
❑ 139 Airese Currie RC .60 1.50
❑ 140 Chris Henry RC .75 2.00
❑ 141 Josh Davis RC .50 1.25
❑ 142 Jason Campbell RC 1.25 3.00
❑ 143 Barrett Ruud RC .75 2.00
❑ 144 Courtney Roby RC .60 1.50
❑ 145 Mike Patterson RC .60 1.50
❑ 146 Jason White RC .75 2.00
❑ 147 Fred Gibson RC .60 1.50
❑ 148 Marion Barber RC 2.50 6.00
❑ 149 Braylon Edwards RC 2.00 5.00
❑ 150 Cadillac Williams RC 1.25 3.00
❑ 151 Kyle Orton RC 1.25 3.00
❑ 152 Aaron Rodgers RC 2.50 6.00
❑ 153 Alvin Pearman RC .50 1.25
❑ 154 Stefan LeFors RC .60 1.50
❑ 155 Marlin Jackson RC .60 1.50
❑ 156 Taylor Stubblefield RC .50 1.25
❑ 157 Ciatrick Fason RC .60 1.50
❑ 158 Kay-Jay Harris RC .60 1.50
❑ 159 Frank Gore RC 1.50 4.00
❑ 160 Vernand Morency RC .60 1.50
❑ 161 Adam Jones RC .60 1.50
❑ 162 Troy Williamson RC .75 2.00
❑ 163 Roddy White RC 1.00 2.50
❑ 164 Thomas Davis RC .60 1.50
❑ 165 Mark Clayton RC .75 2.00
❑ 166 Craig Bragg RC .50 1.25
❑ 167 Noah Herron RC .75 2.00
❑ 168 Darren Sproles RC 1.00 2.50
❑ 169 Terrence Murphy RC .50 1.25
❑ 170 Walter Reyes RC .50 1.25

2006 Topps Draft Picks and Prospects

❑ COMP.SET w/o SP's (165) 12.50 30.00
❑ COMP.SET w/o RC's (110) 6.00 15.00
❑ ONE ROOKIE CARD PER PACK
❑ 166-175 ROOKIE AU/199 ODDS 1:1282
❑ 1 Plaxico Burress .30 .75
❑ 2 Ahman Green .30 .75
❑ 3 Domanick Davis .30 .75
❑ 4 Andre Johnson .30 .75
❑ 5 Donovan McNabb .40 1.00
❑ 6 Marvin Harrison .40 1.00
❑ 7 Michael Vick .40 1.00
❑ 8 Priest Holmes .30 .75
❑ 9 Torry Holt .30 .75
❑ 10 Marc Bulger .30 .75
❑ 11 Ben Roethlisberger .60 1.50
❑ 12 Larry Fitzgerald .40 1.00
❑ 13 Peyton Manning .60 1.50
❑ 14 Chris Perry .30 .75
❑ 15 Antonio Gates .40 1.00
❑ 16 Eli Manning .50 1.25
❑ 17 Brett Favre .75 2.00
❑ 18 Reggie Brown .25 .60
❑ 19 Curtis Martin .40 1.00
❑ 20 Charlie Frye .30 .75
❑ 21 Tom Brady .60 1.50
❑ 22 Cadillac Williams .40 1.00
❑ 23 Trent Green .30 .75
❑ 24 Matt Jones .30 .75
❑ 25 Anquan Boldin .30 .75
❑ 26 Larry Johnson .30 .75
❑ 27 Rudi Johnson .30 .75
❑ 28 Marion Barber .40 1.00
❑ 29 Jake Delhomme .30 .75
❑ 30 Philip Rivers .40 1.00
❑ 31 Fred Taylor .30 .75
❑ 32 Frank Gore .40 1.00
❑ 33 Shaun Alexander .30 .75
❑ 34 Chris Simms .30 .75
❑ 35 LaDainian Tomlinson .50 1.25
❑ 36 Troy Williamson .30 .75
❑ 37 Clinton Portis .40 1.00
❑ 38 Kyle Orton .30 .75
❑ 39 Tony Gonzalez .30 .75
❑ 40 Mark Clayton .30 .75
❑ 41 Steve Smith .40 1.00
❑ 42 Heath Miller .30 .75
❑ 43 Warrick Dunn .30 .75
❑ 44 Alex Smith TE .25 .60
❑ 45 Chris Brown .30 .75
❑ 46 Billy Volek .25 .60
❑ 47 Tiki Barber .40 1.00
❑ 48 Julius Jones .30 .75
❑ 49 Drew Bledsoe .40 1.00
❑ 50 Charles Rogers .30 .75
❑ 51 Jake Plummer .30 .75
❑ 52 Greg Jones .25 .60
❑ 53 Chad Johnson .30 .75
❑ 54 Braylon Edwards .40 1.00
❑ 55 Carson Palmer .40 1.00
❑ 56 Scottie Vines .25 .60
❑ 57 Keary Colbert .30 .75
❑ 58 Alex Smith QB .30 .75
❑ 59 Roy Williams WR .40 1.00
❑ 60 Roddy White .30 .75
❑ 61 Willis McGahee .40 1.00
❑ 62 Michael Clayton .30 .75
❑ 63 Edgerrin James .30 .75
❑ 64 Aaron Rodgers .40 1.00
❑ 65 Byron Leftwich .30 .75
❑ 66 Tatum Bell .25 .60
❑ 67 Daunte Culpepper .40 1.00
❑ 68 Chris Henry .25 .60
❑ 69 Corey Dillon .30 .75
❑ 70 Ronnie Brown .40 1.00
❑ 71 Kevin Jones .30 .75
❑ 72 J.P. Losman .30 .75
❑ 73 Steven Jackson .40 1.00
❑ 74 Mike Williams .30 .75
❑ 75 Jeremy Shockey .40 1.00
❑ 76 DeMarcus Ware .30 .75
❑ 77 LaMont Jordan .30 .75
❑ 78 Cedric Benson .30 .75
❑ 79 Ricky Williams .25 .60
❑ 80 Brandon Jones .25 .60
❑ 81 Brian Westbrook .30 .75
❑ 82 Willie Parker .50 1.25
❑ 83 Hines Ward .40 1.00
❑ 84 Ernest Wilford .25 .60
❑ 85 Matt Hasselbeck .30 .75
❑ 86 Jason Campbell .30 .75
❑ 87 Joey Galloway .30 .75
❑ 88 Odell Thurman .25 .60
❑ 89 Santana Moss .30 .75
❑ 90 Courtney Roby .25 .60
❑ 91 Deuce McAllister .30 .75
❑ 92 Derrick Johnson .30 .75
❑ 93 Drew Brees .40 1.00
❑ 94 Michael Jenkins .30 .75
❑ 95 Jerome Bettis .40 1.00
❑ 96 Osi Umenyiora .30 .75
❑ 97 Reggie Wayne .30 .75
❑ 98 Ryan Moats .30 .75
❑ 99 Randy Moss .40 1.00
❑ 100 Samie Parker .25 .60
❑ 101 Mark Bradley .25 .60
❑ 102 Samkon Gado .40 1.00
❑ 103 Matt Schaub .30 .75
❑ 104 Shaun McDonald .25 .60
❑ 105 D.J. Hackett .30 .75
❑ 106 Mewelde Moore .25 .60
❑ 107 Chester Taylor .30 .75
❑ 108 Greg Lewis .25 .60
❑ 109 Chris Cooley .30 .75
❑ 110 Todd DeVoe RC .40 1.00
❑ 111 Joel Klopfenstein RC .75 2.00
❑ 112 Devin Hester RC 2.00 5.00
❑ 113 Brad Smith RC 1.00 2.50
❑ 114 Jason Avant RC 1.00 2.50
❑ 115 Michael Robinson RC .75 2.00
❑ 116 Kellen Clemens RC 1.00 2.50
❑ 117 Anthony Fasano RC 1.00 2.50
❑ 118 Leon Washington RC 1.25 3.00
❑ 119 Laurence Maroney RC 1.25 3.00
❑ 120 Martin Nance RC .75 2.00
❑ 121 Demetrius Williams RC .75 2.00
❑ 122 A.J. Nicholson RC .60 1.50
❑ 123 Jimmy Williams RC 1.00 2.50
❑ 124 Michael Huff RC 1.00 2.50
❑ 125 Chad Jackson RC .75 2.00
❑ 126 Mike Hass RC 1.00 2.50
❑ 127 Brodie Croyle RC 1.00 2.50
❑ 128 Jerome Harrison RC 1.00 2.50
❑ 129 Hank Baskett RC 1.00 2.50
❑ 130 Santonio Holmes RC 2.50 6.00
❑ 131 Chad Greenway RC 1.00 2.50
❑ 132 Mario Williams RC 1.25 3.00
❑ 133 Charlie Whitehurst RC 1.00 2.50
❑ 134 Darrell Hackney RC .75 2.00
❑ 135 DeMeco Ryans RC 1.25 3.00
❑ 136 Mathias Kiwanuka RC 1.25 3.00
❑ 137 Omar Jacobs RC .60 1.50
❑ 138 Bruce Gradkowski RC 1.00 2.50
❑ 139 Drew Olson RC .60 1.50
❑ 140 Maurice Stovall RC .75 2.00
❑ 141 Greg Jennings RC 1.50 4.00
❑ 142 D'Brickashaw Ferguson RC 1.00 2.50
❑ 143 Manny Lawson RC 1.00 2.50
❑ 144 Tamba Hali RC 1.00 2.50
❑ 145 Vernon Davis RC 1.00 2.50
❑ 146 Greg Lee RC .60 1.50
❑ 147 Dominique Byrd RC .75 2.00
❑ 148 Leonard Pope RC 1.00 2.50
❑ 149 Bobby Carpenter RC .75 2.00
❑ 150 Haloti Ngata RC 1.00 2.50
❑ 151 Marcedes Lewis RC 1.00 2.50
❑ 152 Ernie Sims RC .75 2.00
❑ 153 Ashton Youboty RC .75 2.00
❑ 154 D.J. Shockley RC .75 2.00
❑ 155 Paul Pinegar RC .60 1.50
❑ 156 Maurice Drew RC 2.00 5.00
❑ 157 Jeremy Bloom RC .75 2.00
❑ 158 Cory Rodgers RC 1.00 2.50
❑ 159 Abdul Hodge RC .75 2.00
❑ 160 Tye Hill RC .75 2.00
❑ 161 D'Qwell Jackson RC .75 2.00
❑ 162 Jonathan Orr RC .75 2.00
❑ 163 Antonio Cromartie RC 1.00 2.50
❑ 164 Todd Watkins RC .60 1.50
❑ 165 Gerald Riggs RC .75 2.00
❑ 166 Matt Leinart AU RC 50.00 100.00
❑ 167 Reggie Bush AU RC 60.00 150.00
❑ 168 DeAngelo Williams AU RC 40.00 80.00
❑ 169 A.J. Hawk AU RC 40.00 80.00
❑ 170 Vince Young AU RC 40.00 100.00
❑ 171 Derek Hagan AU RC 10.00 25.00
❑ 172 Joseph Addai AU RC 40.00 80.00
❑ 173 Jay Cutler AU RC 60.00 120.00
❑ 174 Sinorice Moss AU RC 15.00 40.00
❑ 175 LenDale White AU RC 30.00 60.00
❑ RBML R.Bush/Leinart AU/25 125.00 250.00

2007 Topps Draft Picks and Prospects

Card		
❑ COMPLETE SET (155)	20.00	50.00
❑ 1 Donovan McNabb	.40	1.00
❑ 2 Larry Johnson	.30	.75
❑ 3 Willis McGahee	.30	.75
❑ 4 Tom Brady	.75	2.00
❑ 5 Anquan Boldin	.30	.75
❑ 6 Steve Smith	.30	.75
❑ 7 Philip Rivers	.40	1.00
❑ 8 LaDainian Tomlinson	.50	1.25
❑ 9 Reuben Droughns	.30	.75
❑ 10 Julius Jones	.30	.75
❑ 11 Drew Brees	.40	1.00
❑ 12 Chad Johnson	.30	.75
❑ 13 Ronnie Brown	.30	.75
❑ 14 Brett Favre	.75	2.00
❑ 15 J.P. Losman	.25	.60
❑ 16 Clinton Portis	.30	.75
❑ 17 Edgerrin James	.30	.75
❑ 18 Andre Johnson	.30	.75
❑ 19 Fred Taylor	.30	.75
❑ 20 Marc Bulger	.30	.75
❑ 21 Peyton Manning	.60	1.50
❑ 22 Reggie Wayne	.30	.75
❑ 23 Hines Ward	.40	1.00
❑ 24 Michael Vick	.40	1.00
❑ 25 Santana Moss	.30	.75
❑ 26 Torry Holt	.30	.75
❑ 27 Jake Delhomme	.30	.75
❑ 28 Brian Westbrook	.30	.75
❑ 29 Tony Gonzalez	.30	.75
❑ 30 Larry Fitzgerald	.40	1.00
❑ 31 Matt Hasselbeck	.30	.75
❑ 32 Kevin Jones	.25	.60
❑ 33 Willie Parker	.30	.75
❑ 34 Jeremy Shockey	.30	.75
❑ 35 Marvin Harrison	.40	1.00
❑ 36 Warrick Dunn	.30	.75
❑ 37 Ahman Green	.30	.75
❑ 38 Ben Roethlisberger	.50	1.25
❑ 39 Randy Moss	.40	1.00
❑ 40 Rudi Johnson	.30	.75
❑ 41 Carson Palmer	.40	1.00
❑ 42 Trent Green	.30	.75
❑ 43 Plaxico Burress	.30	.75
❑ 44 Steven Jackson	.40	1.00
❑ 45 Deuce McAllister	.30	.75
❑ 46 Antonio Gates	.30	.75
❑ 47 Cadillac Williams	.30	.75
❑ 48 Eli Manning	.40	1.00
❑ 49 Rex Grossman	.30	.75
❑ 50 Shaun Alexander	.30	.75
❑ 51 DeAngelo Williams	.40	1.00
❑ 52 Joseph Addai	.40	1.00
❑ 53 Vince Young	.40	1.00
❑ 54 Matt Leinart	.40	1.00
❑ 55 Sinorice Moss	.30	.75
❑ 56 Matt Jones	.30	.75
❑ 57 Tony Romo	.60	1.50
❑ 58 Jay Cutler	.40	1.00
❑ 59 Marques Colston	.40	1.00
❑ 60 Vernon Davis	.30	.75
❑ 61 Cedric Benson	.30	.75
❑ 62 Mario Williams	.30	.75
❑ 63 Hank Baskett	.30	.75
❑ 64 Alex Smith QB	.40	1.00
❑ 65 Jason Campbell	.30	.75
❑ 66 Mike Furrey	.30	.75
❑ 67 Greg Jennings	.30	.75
❑ 68 Laurence Maroney	.40	1.00
❑ 69 Charlie Frye	.30	.75
❑ 70 Michael Robinson	.30	.75
❑ 71 Michael Huff	.30	.75
❑ 72 A.J. Hawk	.40	1.00
❑ 73 Marion Barber	.40	1.00
❑ 74 Santonio Holmes	.30	.75
❑ 75 Kellen Winslow	.30	.75
❑ 76 Reggie Bush	.50	1.25
❑ 77 Charlie Whitehurst	.25	.60
❑ 78 Brad Smith	.25	.60
❑ 79 Leon Washington	.30	.75
❑ 80 Wali Lundy	.25	.60
❑ 81 Owen Daniels	.25	.60
❑ 82 Devin Hester	.40	1.00
❑ 83 Chad Jackson	.25	.60
❑ 84 Braylon Edwards	.30	.75
❑ 85 Bruce Gradkowski	.25	.60
❑ 86 Tarvaris Jackson	.30	.75
❑ 87 Derek Hagan	.25	.60
❑ 88 Mike Bell	.30	.75
❑ 89 Frank Gore	.40	1.00
❑ 90 LenDale White	.30	.75
❑ 91 Chris Henry	.25	.60
❑ 92 Kellen Clemens	.30	.75
❑ 93 Nate Washington	.25	.60
❑ 94 Jerious Norwood	.30	.75
❑ 95 Maurice Jones-Drew	.40	1.00
❑ 96 Mark Clayton	.30	.75
❑ 97 Jason Avant	.25	.60
❑ 98 Mathias Kiwanuka	.25	.60
❑ 99 Brandon Jacobs	.30	.75
❑ 100 Chris Cooley	.30	.75
❑ 101 Brady Quinn RC	2.00	5.00
❑ 102 Michael Bush RC	1.00	2.50
❑ 103 Leon Hall RC	1.00	2.50
❑ 104 Jason Hill RC	1.00	2.50
❑ 105 Patrick Willis RC	1.50	4.00
❑ 106 Brian Leonard RC	.75	2.00
❑ 107 Gaines Adams RC	1.00	2.50
❑ 108 Kenneth Darby RC	1.00	2.50
❑ 109 Marcus McCauley RC	.75	2.00
❑ 110 Paul Posluszny RC	1.25	3.00
❑ 111 Drew Stanton RC	.75	2.00
❑ 112 Troy Smith RC	1.25	3.00
❑ 113 Garrett Wolfe RC	1.00	2.50
❑ 114 Chris Leak RC	.75	2.00
❑ 115 Joe Thomas RC	1.00	2.50
❑ 116 Paul Williams RC	.75	2.00
❑ 117 LaRon Landry RC	1.25	3.00
❑ 118 Aundrae Allison RC	.75	2.00
❑ 119 Kenny Irons RC	1.00	2.50
❑ 120 Kevin Kolb RC	1.50	4.00
❑ 121 Tyler Palko RC	.75	2.00
❑ 122 Steve Smith USC RC	1.50	4.00
❑ 123 Steve Breaston RC	1.00	2.50
❑ 124 Tyrone Moss RC	.60	1.50
❑ 125 LaMarr Woodley RC	1.00	2.50
❑ 126 Brandon Meriweather RC	1.00	2.50
❑ 127 Rhema McKnight RC	.75	2.00
❑ 128 Daymeion Hughes RC	.75	2.00
❑ 129 Jared Zabransky RC	1.00	2.50
❑ 130 Chansi Stuckey RC	1.00	2.50
❑ 131 Amobi Okoye RC	1.00	2.50
❑ 132 Calvin Johnson RC	2.50	6.00
❑ 133 Marshawn Lynch RC	1.50	4.00
❑ 134 Ted Ginn Jr. RC	1.50	4.00
❑ 135 Adrian Peterson RC	8.00	20.00
❑ 136 Dwayne Jarrett RC	1.00	2.50
❑ 137 Greg Olsen RC	1.25	3.00
❑ 138 Adam Carriker RC	.75	2.00
❑ 139 Darius Walker RC	.75	2.00
❑ 140 Robert Meachem RC	1.00	2.50
❑ 141 Jordan Palmer RC	1.00	2.50
❑ 142 JaMarcus Russell RC	1.25	3.00
❑ 143 DeShawn Wynn RC	1.00	2.50
❑ 144 Zach Miller RC	1.00	2.50
❑ 145 Lorenzo Booker RC	1.00	2.50
❑ 146 Selvin Young RC	1.00	2.50
❑ 147 Courtney Lewis RC	.75	2.00
❑ 148 Tony Hunt RC	1.00	2.50
❑ 149 Dwayne Bowe RC	1.50	4.00
❑ 150 Aaron Ross RC	1.00	2.50
❑ 151 Antonio Pittman RC	1.00	2.50
❑ 152 Anthony Gonzalez RC	1.25	3.00
❑ 153 John Beck RC	1.00	2.50
❑ 154 Sidney Rice RC	2.00	5.00
❑ 155 Lawrence Timmons RC	1.00	2.50

2009 Topps Kickoff

Card		
❑ COMPLETE SET (165)	15.00	40.00
❑ 1 Larry Fitzgerald	.20	.50
❑ 2 Anquan Boldin	.15	.40
❑ 3 Roddy White	.15	.40
❑ 4 Terrell Owens	.20	.50
❑ 5 Steve Smith	.15	.40
❑ 6 Chad Ochocinco	.15	.40
❑ 7 Laveranues Coles	.15	.40
❑ 8 Braylon Edwards	.15	.40
❑ 9 Brandon Marshall	.15	.40
❑ 10 Eddie Royal	.15	.40
❑ 11 Calvin Johnson	.20	.50
❑ 12 Greg Jennings	.20	.50
❑ 13 Andre Johnson	.15	.40
❑ 14 Anthony Gonzalez	.15	.40
❑ 15 Reggie Wayne	.15	.40
❑ 16 Dwayne Bowe	.15	.40
❑ 17 Randy Moss	.20	.50
❑ 18 Marques Colston	.15	.40
❑ 19 Steve Smith	.15	.40
❑ 20 Jerricho Cotchery	.12	.30
❑ 21 DeSean Jackson	.15	.40
❑ 22 Hines Ward	.15	.40
❑ 23 Santonio Holmes	.15	.40
❑ 24 Chris Chambers	.15	.40
❑ 25 T.J. Houshmandzadeh	.15	.40
❑ 26 Donnie Avery	.15	.40
❑ 27 Antonio Bryant	.15	.40
❑ 28 Santana Moss	.15	.40
❑ 29 Jason Witten	.20	.50
❑ 30 Dallas Clark	.15	.40
❑ 31 Tony Gonzalez	.15	.40
❑ 32 Jeremy Shockey	.12	.30
❑ 33 Heath Miller	.15	.40
❑ 34 Antonio Gates	.15	.40
❑ 35 Vernon Davis	.12	.30
❑ 36 John Carlson	.15	.40
❑ 37 Kellen Winslow Jr.	.15	.40
❑ 38 Chris Cooley	.15	.40
❑ 39 Ed Reed	.15	.40
❑ 40 Troy Polamalu	.20	.50
❑ 41 Michael Turner	.15	.40
❑ 42 Willis McGahee	.15	.40
❑ 43 Marshawn Lynch	.15	.40
❑ 44 DeAngelo Williams	.20	.50
❑ 45 Jonathan Stewart	.15	.40
❑ 46 Matt Forte	.20	.50
❑ 47 Jamal Lewis	.15	.40
❑ 48 Marion Barber	.20	.50
❑ 49 Kevin Smith	.15	.40
❑ 50 Steve Slaton	.15	.40
❑ 51 Joseph Addai	.20	.50
❑ 52 Maurice Jones-Drew	.15	.40
❑ 53 Larry Johnson	.15	.40
❑ 54 Jamaal Charles	.15	.40
❑ 55 Ronnie Brown	.15	.40
❑ 56 Adrian Peterson	.40	1.00
❑ 57 Chester Taylor	.12	.30
❑ 58 Wes Welker	.20	.50
❑ 59 Reggie Bush	.20	.50
❑ 60 Brandon Jacobs	.15	.40
❑ 61 Leon Washington	.15	.40
❑ 62 Thomas Jones	.15	.40
❑ 63 Darren McFadden	.20	.50
❑ 64 Justin Fargas	.12	.30
❑ 65 Brian Westbrook	.15	.40
❑ 66 Willie Parker	.15	.40
❑ 67 LaDainian Tomlinson	.20	.50
❑ 68 Darren Sproles	.15	.40
❑ 69 Frank Gore	.15	.40
❑ 70 Steven Jackson	.15	.40
❑ 71 Warrick Dunn	.15	.40

	Card	Low	High
❑	72 Earnest Graham	.12	.30
❑	73 Chris Johnson	.20	.50
❑	74 LenDale White	.15	.40
❑	75 Clinton Portis	.15	.40
❑	76 Kurt Warner	.20	.50
❑	77 Matt Ryan	.20	.50
❑	78 Joe Flacco	.20	.50
❑	79 Trent Edwards	.15	.40
❑	80 Kyle Orton	.15	.40
❑	81 Carson Palmer	.20	.50
❑	82 Brady Quinn	.15	.40
❑	83 Tony Romo	.30	.75
❑	84 Jay Cutler	.20	.50
❑	85 Aaron Rodgers	.20	.50
❑	86 Matt Schaub	.15	.40
❑	87 Peyton Manning	.30	.75
❑	88 David Garrard	.15	.40
❑	89 Matt Cassel	.15	.40
❑	90 Chad Pennington	.15	.40
❑	91 Tarvaris Jackson	.15	.40
❑	92 Tom Brady	.30	.75
❑	93 Drew Brees	.20	.50
❑	94 Eli Manning	.20	.50
❑	95 JaMarcus Russell	.15	.40
❑	96 Donovan McNabb	.20	.50
❑	97 Ben Roethlisberger	.30	.75
❑	98 Philip Rivers	.20	.50
❑	99 Matt Hasselbeck	.15	.40
❑	100 Marc Bulger	.15	.40
❑	101 Jason Campbell	.15	.40
❑	102 Ray Lewis	.20	.50
❑	103 Brian Urlacher	.20	.50
❑	104 Ernie Sims	.12	.30
❑	105 Joey Porter	.15	.40
❑	106 Jerod Mayo	.15	.40
❑	107 James Harrison	.20	.50
❑	108 Patrick Willis	.15	.40
❑	109 Julius Peppers	.15	.40
❑	110 DeMarcus Ware	.15	.40
❑	111 Brian Orakpo RC	.50	1.25
❑	112 Pat White RC	.60	1.50
❑	113 Malcolm Jenkins RC	.40	1.00
❑	114 Nate Davis RC	.40	1.00
❑	115 Rhett Bomar RC	.30	.75
❑	116 Matthew Stafford RC	1.25	3.00
❑	117 Stephen McGee RC	.40	1.00
❑	118 Aaron Maybin RC	.40	1.00
❑	119 Josh Freeman RC	.75	2.00
❑	120 Mark Sanchez RC	1.50	4.00
❑	121 B.J. Raji RC	.50	1.25
❑	122 Javon Ringer RC	.40	1.00
❑	123 Chris Wells RC	1.00	2.50
❑	124 Donald Brown RC	.75	2.00
❑	125 Gartrell Johnson RC	.30	.75
❑	126 Glen Coffee RC	.50	1.25
❑	127 Andre Brown RC	.40	1.00
❑	128 Aaron Curry RC	.50	1.25
❑	129 Cedric Peerman RC	.30	.75
❑	130 Knowshon Moreno RC	1.00	2.50
❑	131 Shonn Greene RC	.75	2.00
❑	132 LeSean McCoy RC	.75	2.00
❑	133 Rashad Jennings RC	.40	1.00
❑	134 Brian Cushing RC	.50	1.25
❑	135 James Davis RC	.40	1.00
❑	136 Hakeem Nicks RC	.75	2.00
❑	137 Austin Collie RC	.75	2.00
❑	138 Eugene Monroe RC	.30	.75
❑	139 Brandon Tate RC	.30	.75
❑	140 Clay Matthews RC	.60	1.50
❑	141 Chase Coffman RC	.30	.75
❑	142 Brooks Foster RC	.30	.75
❑	143 Kenny Britt RC	.60	1.50
❑	144 Patrick Turner RC	.30	.75
❑	145 Darrius Heyward-Bey RC	.60	1.50
❑	146 Rey Maualuga RC	.60	1.50
❑	147 Deon Butler RC	.40	1.00
❑	148 Derrick Williams RC	.40	1.00
❑	149 Percy Harvin RC	1.25	3.00
❑	150 Jarett Dillard RC	.40	1.00
❑	151 Jeremy Maclin RC	.75	2.00
❑	152 Juaquin Iglesias RC	.40	1.00
❑	153 Jared Cook RC	.30	.75
❑	154 James Laurinaitis RC	.50	1.25
❑	155 Brandon Pettigrew RC	.50	1.25
❑	156 Andre Smith RC	.40	1.00
❑	157 Brian Robiskie RC	.40	1.00
❑	158 Mohamed Massaquoi RC	.40	1.00
❑	159 Ramses Barden RC	.30	.75
❑	160 Michael Crabtree RC	1.00	2.50
❑	161 Michael Oher RC	.75	2.00
❑	162 Patrick Chung RC	.40	1.00
❑	163 Louis Murphy RC	.40	1.00
❑	164 William Moore RC	.30	.75
❑	165 Victor Harris RC	.40	1.00

2008 Topps Letterman

	Card	Low	High
❑	1 Drew Brees	1.00	2.50
❑	2 Tom Brady	1.50	4.00
❑	3 Peyton Manning	1.50	4.00
❑	4 Carson Palmer	1.00	2.50
❑	5 Ben Roethlisberger	1.25	3.00
❑	6 Eli Manning	1.00	2.50
❑	7 Tony Romo	1.50	4.00
❑	8 Vince Young	.75	2.00
❑	9 Matt Hasselbeck	.75	2.00
❑	10 Derek Anderson	.75	2.00
❑	11 Jay Cutler	1.00	2.50
❑	12 Philip Rivers	1.00	2.50
❑	13 Steven Jackson	1.00	2.50
❑	14 Willie Parker	.75	2.00
❑	15 Clinton Portis	.75	2.00
❑	16 Adrian Peterson	2.00	5.00
❑	17 LaDainian Tomlinson	1.25	3.00
❑	18 Marion Barber	1.00	2.50
❑	19 Brian Westbrook	.75	2.00
❑	20 Fred Taylor	.75	2.00
❑	21 Marshawn Lynch	1.00	2.50
❑	22 Joseph Addai	1.00	2.50
❑	23 Willis McGahee	.75	2.00
❑	24 Frank Gore	.75	2.00
❑	25 Larry Johnson	.75	2.00
❑	26 Brandon Jacobs	.75	2.00
❑	27 Ryan Grant	1.00	2.50
❑	28 Chester Taylor	.60	1.50
❑	29 Laurence Maroney	.75	2.00
❑	30 Thomas Jones	.75	2.00
❑	31 Chad Johnson	.75	2.00
❑	32 Reggie Wayne	.75	2.00
❑	33 Anquan Boldin	.75	2.00
❑	34 Randy Moss	1.00	2.50
❑	35 Plaxico Burress	.75	2.00
❑	36 Terrell Owens	1.00	2.50
❑	37 Andre Johnson	.75	2.00
❑	38 Larry Fitzgerald	1.00	2.50
❑	39 Braylon Edwards	.75	2.00
❑	40 Steve Smith	.75	2.00
❑	41 T.J. Houshmandzadeh	.75	2.00
❑	42 Torry Holt	.75	2.00
❑	43 Brandon Marshall	.75	2.00
❑	44 Wes Welker	1.00	2.50
❑	45 Dwayne Bowe	.75	2.00
❑	46 Terry Bradshaw	2.00	5.00
❑	47 Brett Favre	6.00	15.00
❑	48 John Elway	2.00	5.00
❑	49 Lawrence Taylor	1.25	3.00
❑	50 Joe Namath	1.50	4.00
❑	51 Matt Ryan RC	6.00	15.00
❑	52 Brian Brohm RC	1.50	4.00
❑	53 Chad Henne RC	2.50	6.00
❑	54 Joe Flacco RC	5.00	12.00
❑	55 Andre Woodson RC	1.50	4.00
❑	56 John David Booty RC	1.50	4.00
❑	57 Josh Johnson RC	1.50	4.00
❑	58 Colt Brennan RC	2.50	6.00
❑	59 Dennis Dixon RC	1.50	4.00
❑	60 Erik Ainge RC	1.50	4.00
❑	61 Kevin O'Connell RC	1.50	4.00
❑	62 Darren McFadden RC	3.00	8.00
❑	63 Rashard Mendenhall RC	3.00	8.00
❑	64 Jonathan Stewart RC	3.00	8.00
❑	65 Felix Jones RC	3.00	8.00
❑	66 Jamaal Charles RC	2.50	6.00
❑	67 Ray Rice RC	3.00	8.00
❑	68 Chris Johnson RC	5.00	12.00
❑	70 Matt Forte RC	3.00	8.00
❑	71 Kevin Smith RC	2.50	6.00
❑	72 Steve Slaton RC	2.00	5.00
❑	73 Malcolm Kelly RC	1.50	4.00
❑	74 Limas Sweed RC	1.50	4.00
❑	75 DeSean Jackson RC	3.00	8.00
❑	76 James Hardy RC	1.25	3.00
❑	77 Mario Manningham RC	1.50	4.00
❑	78 Devin Thomas RC	1.50	4.00
❑	79 Early Doucet RC	1.50	4.00
❑	80 Andre Caldwell RC	1.50	4.00
❑	81 Jordy Nelson RC	2.00	5.00
❑	82 Eddie Royal RC	2.50	6.00
❑	83 Earl Bennett RC	1.50	4.00
❑	84 Donnie Avery RC	2.00	5.00
❑	85 Dexter Jackson RC	1.50	4.00
❑	86 Jerome Simpson RC	1.25	3.00
❑	87 Harry Douglas RC	1.25	3.00
❑	88 Keenan Burton RC	1.25	3.00
❑	89 Marcus Smith RC	1.25	3.00
❑	90 Dustin Keller RC	1.50	4.00
❑	91 John Carlson RC	1.50	4.00
❑	92 Jake Long RC	1.50	4.00
❑	93 Chris Long RC	1.50	4.00
❑	94 Vernon Gholston RC	1.50	4.00
❑	95 Glenn Dorsey RC	1.50	4.00
❑	96 Sedrick Ellis RC	1.50	4.00
❑	97 Keith Rivers RC	1.50	4.00
❑	98 Leodis McKelvin RC	1.50	4.00
❑	99 D.Rodgers-Cromartie RC	1.50	4.00
❑	100 Aqib Talib RC	1.50	4.00

2009 Topps Magic

	Card	Low	High
❑	COMPLETE SET (250)	75.00	150.00
❑	COMP.SET w/o SP's (200)	15.00	40.00
❑	1 Domenik Hixon	.20	.50
❑	2 Brodie Croyle SP	1.50	4.00
❑	3 LaDainian Tomlinson	.30	.75
❑	4 Glen Coffee RC	.75	2.00
❑	5 Cullen Harper RC	.60	1.50
❑	6 DeMeco Ryans SP	2.00	5.00
❑	7 Roddy White	.25	.60
❑	8 Dexter Jackson	.20	.50
❑	9 Derek Hagan	.20	.50
❑	10 Zach Miller	.20	.50
❑	11 Ryan Torain	.20	.50
❑	12 Andrew Walter	.20	.50
❑	13 Tarvaris Jackson	.25	.60
❑	14 Felix Jones	.30	.75
❑	15 Darren McFadden	.30	.75
❑	16 Jason Campbell	.25	.60
❑	17 Peyton Manning	.75	2.00
❑	18 Kenny Irons SP	1.50	4.00
❑	19 Bo Jackson	.60	1.50
❑	20 Gartrell Johnson RC	.50	1.25
❑	21 Ben Obomanu SP	1.50	4.00
❑	22 Jerod Mayo	.25	.60
❑	23 Courtney Taylor	.20	.50
❑	24 Cadillac Williams	.25	.60
❑	25 Nate Davis RC	.60	1.50
❑	26 Robert Meachem SP	2.00	5.00
❑	27 Isaiah Stanback SP	1.50	4.00
❑	28 Earl Campbell	.50	1.25
❑	29 Mathias Kiwanuka	.20	.50
❑	30 Rashad Jennings RC	.60	1.50
❑	31 Matt Ryan	.30	.75
❑	32 Jamaal Charles	.25	.60
❑	33 Marcus Griffin	.20	.50
❑	34 John Beck SP	1.50	4.00
❑	35 Justin Forsett SP	1.50	4.00
❑	36 Lavelle Hawkins SP	1.50	4.00
❑	37 DeSean Jackson	.25	.60

Card	Low	High
❑ 38 Marshawn Lynch	.25	.60
❑ 39 Brandon Marshall	.25	.60
❑ 40 Chase Coffman RC	.50	1.25
❑ 41 Kevin Smith	.25	.60
❑ 42 Aaron Ross	.20	.50
❑ 43 Gaines Adams	.20	.50
❑ 44 Tye Hill SP	1.50	4.00
❑ 45 Winston Justice	.20	.50
❑ 46 Chris Simms SP	1.50	4.00
❑ 47 Chris Brown SP	1.50	4.00
❑ 48 Limas Sweed	.25	.60
❑ 49 David Anderson	.20	.50
❑ 50 Donald Brown RC	1.25	3.00
❑ 51 Joe Flacco	.30	.75
❑ 52 Dave Thomas SP	1.50	4.00
❑ 53 Dallas Baker	.20	.50
❑ 54 Andre Caldwell	.20	.50
❑ 55 Derrick Harvey SP	1.50	4.00
❑ 56 David Clowney	.20	.50
❑ 57 Percy Harvin RC	2.00	5.00
❑ 58 Fred Taylor SP	2.00	5.00
❑ 59 DeShawn Wynn	.20	.50
❑ 60 Lorenzo Booker SP	1.50	4.00
❑ 61 Roy Williams WR	.25	.60
❑ 62 Chris Davis	.20	.50
❑ 63 Sebastian Janikowski SP	1.50	4.00
❑ 64 Greg Jones	.20	.50
❑ 65 James Laurinaitis RC	.75	2.00
❑ 66 Ernie Sims SP	1.50	4.00
❑ 67 Lawrence Timmons	.20	.50
❑ 68 Leon Washington	.25	.60
❑ 69 Kamerion Wimbley	.20	.50
❑ 70 Bernard Berrian	.25	.60
❑ 71 Selvin Young	.20	.50
❑ 72 Vince Young	.25	.60
❑ 73 Paul Williams	.20	.50
❑ 74 Reggie Brown	.20	.50
❑ 75 Sean Jones SP	1.50	4.00
❑ 76 Knowshon Moreno RC	1.50	4.00
❑ 77 Matthew Stafford RC	2.00	5.00
❑ 78 Mohamed Massaquoi RC	.60	1.50
❑ 79 Leonard Pope SP	1.50	4.00
❑ 80 D.J. Shockley	.20	.50
❑ 81 Tashard Choice	.25	.60
❑ 82 P.J. Daniels SP	1.50	4.00
❑ 83 Colt Brennan	.25	.60
❑ 84 John Parker Wilson RC	.60	1.50
❑ 85 Donnie Avery	.25	.60
❑ 86 Kevin Kolb SP	1.50	4.00
❑ 87 Graham Harrell RC	.60	1.50
❑ 88 Rashard Mendenhall	.25	.60
❑ 89 Laurent Robinson	.20	.50
❑ 90 James Hardy	.25	.60
❑ 91 Antwaan Randle El	.20	.50
❑ 92 Scott Chandler	.20	.50
❑ 93 Chad Greenway	.20	.50
❑ 94 Ramses Barden RC	.50	1.25
❑ 95 Shonn Greene RC	1.25	3.00
❑ 96 Aqib Talib	.20	.50
❑ 97 Michael Crabtree RC	1.50	4.00
❑ 98 Yamon Figurs SP	1.50	4.00
❑ 99 Josh Freeman RC	1.25	3.00
❑ 100 Jordy Nelson	.25	.60
❑ 101 Zach Thomas	.25	.60
❑ 102 Antonio Gates	.25	.60
❑ 103 Keenan Burton	.20	.50
❑ 104 Matt Forte	.30	.75
❑ 105 Terry Bradshaw SP	4.00	10.00
❑ 106 Ryan Moats	.20	.50
❑ 107 John David Booty	.25	.60
❑ 108 Brian Brohm	.25	.60
❑ 109 Michael Bush	.25	.60
❑ 110 Amobi Okoye	.20	.50
❑ 111 Kolby Smith SP	1.50	4.00
❑ 112 Joseph Addai	.30	.75
❑ 113 Dwayne Bowe	.25	.60
❑ 114 Michael Clayton	.20	.50
❑ 115 Craig Buster Davis	.20	.50
❑ 116 Early Doucet	.25	.60
❑ 117 Reggie Bush	.30	.75
❑ 118 Matt Flynn	.20	.50
❑ 119 Fred Davis	.20	.50
❑ 120 Kory Sheets RC	.50	1.25
❑ 121 Jacob Hester	.20	.50
❑ 122 LaRon Landry	.20	.50
❑ 123 Justin Fargas	.20	.50
❑ 124 Dwayne Jarrett	.20	.50
❑ 125 Ahmad Bradshaw SP	2.00	5.00

Card	Low	High
❑ 126 Randy Moss	.30	.75
❑ 127 Chad Pennington	.25	.60
❑ 128 Darrius Heyward-Bey RC	1.00	2.50
❑ 129 Matt Leinart	.25	.60
❑ 130 Shawne Merriman SP	2.00	5.00
❑ 131 DeAngelo Williams SP	2.50	6.00
❑ 132 Frank Gore	.25	.60
❑ 133 Devin Hester	.30	.75
❑ 134 Ray Lewis	.30	.75
❑ 135 Willis McGahee	.25	.60
❑ 136 Greg Olsen SP	1.50	4.00
❑ 137 Roscoe Parrish	.20	.50
❑ 138 Antrel Rolle SP	1.50	4.00
❑ 139 Reggie Wayne	.25	.60
❑ 140 Kellen Winslow	.25	.60
❑ 141 Adrian Arrington	.20	.50
❑ 142 B.J. Askew	.20	.50
❑ 143 Jason Avant	.20	.50
❑ 144 Mark Sanchez RC	2.50	6.00
❑ 145 Tom Brady	.75	2.00
❑ 146 Steve Breaston	.25	.60
❑ 147 Braylon Edwards	.25	.60
❑ 148 Leon Hall	.20	.50
❑ 149 Steve Smith USC	.25	.60
❑ 150 Mike Hart	.25	.60
❑ 151 Chad Henne	.30	.75
❑ 152 Drew Henson	.20	.50
❑ 153 Steve Hutchinson	.20	.50
❑ 154 Marlin Jackson SP	1.50	4.00
❑ 155 Ty Law	.20	.50
❑ 156 Mario Manningham	.25	.60
❑ 157 LaMarr Woodley	.20	.50
❑ 158 Javon Ringer RC	.60	1.50
❑ 159 LenDale White	.25	.60
❑ 160 Drew Stanton	.20	.50
❑ 161 Devin Thomas	.20	.50
❑ 162 Laurence Maroney	.25	.60
❑ 163 Alex Smith QB	.20	.50
❑ 164 Eli Manning	.40	1.00
❑ 165 Deuce McAllister SP	2.00	5.00
❑ 166 Patrick Willis	.25	.60
❑ 167 Jerious Norwood	.25	.60
❑ 168 Jordan Palmer	.20	.50
❑ 169 Chase Daniel RC	.75	2.00
❑ 170 Jeremy Maclin RC	1.25	3.00
❑ 171 Jay Cutler	.30	.75
❑ 172 Brad Smith SP	1.50	4.00
❑ 173 Thomas Jones	.25	.60
❑ 174 Brandon Jackson SP	2.00	5.00
❑ 175 Nate Burleson	.20	.50
❑ 176 Alvin Pearman SP	1.50	4.00
❑ 177 Marcus Smith	.20	.50
❑ 178 Matt Schaub SP	2.00	5.00
❑ 179 DeAngelo Hall	.25	.60
❑ 180 Ronald Curry SP	1.50	4.00
❑ 181 Hakeem Nicks RC	1.25	3.00
❑ 182 Kevin Jones	.20	.50
❑ 183 Willie Parker	.25	.60
❑ 184 Andre Brown RC	.50	1.25
❑ 185 DaJuan Morgan SP	1.50	4.00
❑ 186 Philip Rivers	.30	.75
❑ 187 Mario Williams	.25	.60
❑ 188 Vincent Jackson	.25	.60
❑ 189 Garrett Wolfe	.20	.50
❑ 190 Xavier Omon	.20	.50
❑ 191 John Carlson	.25	.60
❑ 192 Anthony Fasano	.20	.50
❑ 193 Julius Jones SP	2.00	5.00
❑ 194 Brady Quinn	.25	.60
❑ 195 Maurice Stovall SP	1.50	4.00
❑ 196 Bobby Carpenter	.20	.50
❑ 197 Chris Wells RC	1.50	4.00
❑ 198 Joey Galloway	.25	.60
❑ 199 Vernon Gholston SP	1.50	4.00
❑ 200 Ted Ginn	.25	.60
❑ 201 Anthony Gonzalez	.25	.60
❑ 202 Eddie Royal	.25	.60
❑ 203 Michael Jenkins	.20	.50
❑ 204 Jason Hill	.20	.50
❑ 205 Troy Smith	.25	.60
❑ 206 Marc Bulger SP	2.00	5.00
❑ 207 Mark Bradley SP	1.50	4.00
❑ 208 Owen Schmitt SP	1.50	4.00
❑ 209 Juaquin Iglesias RC	.60	1.50
❑ 210 Malcolm Kelly	.20	.50
❑ 211 Allen Patrick SP	1.50	4.00
❑ 212 Adrian Peterson	.60	1.50
❑ 213 Tatum Bell	.20	.50

Card	Low	High
❑ 214 Brandon Pettigrew RC	.75	2.00
❑ 215 Kellen Clemens	.20	.50
❑ 216 Dennis Dixon	.25	.60
❑ 217 Jonathan Stewart	.25	.60
❑ 218 Demetrius Williams	.20	.50
❑ 219 Derek Anderson	.25	.60
❑ 220 Steven Jackson	.25	.60
❑ 221 Chad Johnson	.25	.60
❑ 222 Reggie Williams SP	1.50	4.00
❑ 223 Dan Connor	.20	.50
❑ 224 Derrick Williams SP RC	2.00	5.00
❑ 225 Larry Johnson	.25	.60
❑ 226 Pat White RC	1.00	2.50
❑ 227 Paul Posluszny	.25	.60
❑ 228 Tony Dorsett	.50	1.25
❑ 229 LeSean McCoy RC	1.25	3.00
❑ 230 Dan Marino	1.25	3.00
❑ 231 Drew Brees	.30	.75
❑ 232 Dustin Keller	.20	.50
❑ 233 Kyle Orton SP	2.00	5.00
❑ 234 Steve Slaton	.25	.60
❑ 235 Kenny Britt RC	1.00	2.50
❑ 236 Brian Leonard SP	1.50	4.00
❑ 237 Ray Rice	.30	.75
❑ 238 Kevin O'Connell	.20	.50
❑ 239 Lee Evans SP	2.00	5.00
❑ 240 James Jones	.20	.50
❑ 241 Eric Dickerson	.40	1.00
❑ 242 Jared Cook RC	.50	1.25
❑ 243 P.J. Hill RC	.50	1.25
❑ 244 Andre Hall	.20	.50
❑ 245 Rhett Bomar RC	.50	1.25
❑ 246 Trent Edwards	.25	.60
❑ 247 John Elway	1.00	2.50
❑ 248 Jim Brown	.60	1.50
❑ 249 Dwight Freeney	.25	.60
❑ 250 Joe Thomas	.25	.60
❑ TMJR Jackie Robinson	8.00	20.00

2008 Topps Mayo

Card	Low	High
❑ COMPLETE SET (330)	60.00	120.00
❑ COMP.SET w/o SP's (275)	20.00	40.00
❑ 1 Drew Brees	.30	.75
❑ 2 Kyle Orton SP	1.25	3.00
❑ 3 LenDale White SP	1.25	3.00
❑ 4 Shaun McDonald	.20	.50
❑ 5 Bobby Wade	.20	.50
❑ 6 Javon Walker	.25	.60
❑ 7 Owen Daniels	.20	.50
❑ 8 Justin Tuck SP	1.25	3.00
❑ 9 Amobi Okoye	.20	.50
❑ 10 Rich Eisen	.20	.50
❑ 11 Fred Taylor SP	1.25	3.00
❑ 12 Ryan Torain SP RC	1.25	3.00
❑ 13 Steve Slaton RC	1.25	3.00
❑ 14 Jake Long SP RC	1.25	3.00
❑ 15 Peyton Manning	.50	1.25
❑ 16 Jon Kitna	.25	.60
❑ 17 Ryan Grant	.30	.75
❑ 18 Brandon Stokley	.25	.60
❑ 19 Troy Williamson SP	1.00	2.50
❑ 20 Reggie Brown	.20	.50
❑ 21 Zach Miller	.25	.60
❑ 22 Aaron Kampman SP	1.25	3.00
❑ 23 Albert Haynesworth	.20	.50
❑ 24 Matt Cassel	.30	.75
❑ 25 Selvin Young SP	1.00	2.50
❑ 26 Will Franklin SP RC	1.00	2.50
❑ 27 Matt Forte RC	2.00	5.00
❑ 28 Glenn Dorsey RC	1.00	2.50
❑ 29 Marc Bulger	.25	.60
❑ 30 Jeff Garcia	.25	.60
❑ 31 DeAngelo Williams	.25	.60
❑ 32 Roydell Williams	.20	.50

☐ 33 Sidney Rice .30 .75
☐ 34 James Jones SP 1.00 2.50
☐ 35 L.J. Smith .20 .50
☐ 36 Aaron Schobel .20 .50
☐ 37 Tommie Harris .20 .50
☐ 38 Tyler Thigpen .25 .60
☐ 39 LaDainian Tomlinson SP 2.00 5.00
☐ 40 Marcus Smith SP RC 1.00 2.50
☐ 41 Tashard Choice RC 1.00 2.50
☐ 42 Chris Long RC 1.00 2.50
☐ 43 Matt Moore SP 1.25 3.00
☐ 44 Chris Redman .20 .50
☐ 45 Laurence Maroney .25 .60
☐ 46 Larry Fitzgerald .30 .75
☐ 47 Donte Stallworth .25 .60
☐ 48 Marty Booker .20 .50
☐ 49 Greg Olsen .25 .60
☐ 50 Terrell Suggs .20 .50
☐ 51 Kevin Williams .20 .50
☐ 52 Derrick Ward .25 .60
☐ 53 Steven Jackson SP 1.50 4.00
☐ 54 Adrian Arrington SP RC 1.00 2.50
☐ 55 Tim Hightower RC 1.25 3.00
☐ 56 Chauncey Washington RC .75 2.00
☐ 57 Joe Thomas .25 .60
☐ 58 Matt Leinart SP 1.50 4.00
☐ 59 Jamal Lewis .25 .60
☐ 60 Braylon Edwards .25 .60
☐ 61 Steve Smith USC .25 .60
☐ 62 Mark Bradley .20 .50
☐ 63 Leonard Pope .20 .50
☐ 64 Dwight Freeney .25 .60
☐ 65 Adam Carriker .20 .50
☐ 66 Devery Henderson .20 .50
☐ 67 Willis McGahee SP 1.25 3.00
☐ 68 Fred Davis SP RC 1.25 3.00
☐ 69 Harry Douglas RC .75 2.00
☐ 70 Anthony Alridge SP RC 1.00 2.50
☐ 71 Rex Grossman .25 .60
☐ 72 Kellen Clemens .25 .60
☐ 73 Justin Fargas .20 .50
☐ 74 Steve Smith .25 .60
☐ 75 Hines Ward .25 .60
☐ 76 Muhsin Muhammad .25 .60
☐ 77 Randy McMichael .20 .50
☐ 78 Tamba Hali .20 .50
☐ 79 Archie Manning .30 .75
☐ 80 Orville Wright .20 .50
☐ 81 Michael Turner SP 1.50 4.00
☐ 82 Paul Smith RC 1.00 2.50
☐ 83 DeSean Jackson RC 2.00 5.00
☐ 84 Josh McCown .20 .50
☐ 85 John Beck .20 .50
☐ 86 LaMont Jordan SP 1.25 3.00
☐ 87 Greg Jennings .25 .60
☐ 88 Deion Branch .25 .60
☐ 89 David Patten .20 .50
☐ 90 Bob Sanders .25 .60
☐ 91 Luis Castillo .20 .50
☐ 92 Troy Aikman .40 1.00
☐ 93 Le'Ron McClain .30 .75
☐ 94 Todd Heap SP 1.00 2.50
☐ 95 Kyle Wright RC .75 2.00
☐ 96 Malcolm Kelly RC 1.00 2.50
☐ 97 Vince Young .25 .60
☐ 98 Troy Smith .25 .60
☐ 99 Reggie Bush .30 .75
☐ 100 Jerricho Cotchery .20 .50
☐ 101 Jerry Porter .25 .60
☐ 102 Ike Hilliard .20 .50
☐ 103 Ed Reed .25 .60
☐ 104 John Abraham .20 .50
☐ 105 Sterling Sharpe .25 .60
☐ 106 Brodie Croyle .25 .60
☐ 107 Jeremy Shockey SP 1.25 3.00
☐ 108 Andre Woodson RC 1.00 2.50
☐ 109 Limas Sweed RC 1.00 2.50
☐ 110 Jay Cutler .30 .75
☐ 111 Adrian Peterson .60 1.50
☐ 112 Larry Johnson .25 .60
☐ 113 Joey Galloway .25 .60
☐ 114 Reggie Williams .25 .60
☐ 115 Justin McCareins .20 .50
☐ 116 Roy Williams S .25 .60
☐ 117 Julius Peppers .25 .60
☐ 118 Terry Bradshaw .50 1.25
☐ 119 James Harrison RC 5.00 12.00
☐ 120 Heath Miller SP 1.00 2.50
☐ 121 Chad Henne RC 1.50 4.00
☐ 122 Mario Manningham RC 1.00 2.50
☐ 123 J.P. Losman .20 .50
☐ 124 Willie Parker .25 .60
☐ 125 Rudi Johnson .25 .60
☐ 126 Lee Evans .25 .60
☐ 127 Marvin Harrison .30 .75
☐ 128 Isaac Bruce .25 .60
☐ 129 Kerry Rhodes .20 .50
☐ 130 Brian Urlacher SP 1.50 4.00
☐ 131 John Elway .50 1.25
☐ 132 LaMarr Woodley .25 .60
☐ 133 Calvin Johnson SP 1.50 4.00
☐ 134 Joe Flacco RC 3.00 8.00
☐ 135 James Hardy SP RC 1.00 2.50
☐ 136 Jason Campbell .25 .60
☐ 137 DeShaun Foster .25 .60
☐ 138 Ahmad Bradshaw .25 .60
☐ 139 Roy Williams WR .25 .60
☐ 140 Amani Toomer .25 .60
☐ 141 Bryant Johnson .20 .50
☐ 142 Troy Polamalu .30 .75
☐ 143 DeMarcus Ware .25 .60
☐ 144 Dan Marino .60 1.50
☐ 145 Grover Cleveland .20 .50
☐ 146 Plaxico Burress SP 1.25 3.00
☐ 147 Colt Brennan RC 1.50 4.00
☐ 148 Early Doucet RC 1.00 2.50
☐ 149 Matt Hasselbeck .25 .60
☐ 150 Jerious Norwood .25 .60
☐ 151 Leon Washington .25 .60
☐ 152 Arnaz Battle .20 .50
☐ 153 Ted Ginn Jr. .25 .60
☐ 154 Drew Bennett .20 .50
☐ 155 Brian Dawkins .25 .60
☐ 156 Patrick Willis .25 .60
☐ 157 Sonny Jurgensen .25 .60
☐ 158 Susan B. Anthony .20 .50
☐ 159 Terrell Owens SP 1.50 4.00
☐ 160 Dennis Dixon RC 1.00 2.50
☐ 161 Donnie Avery RC 1.25 3.00
☐ 162 Matt Schaub .25 .60
☐ 163 Kerry Collins .25 .60
☐ 164 Ronnie Brown .25 .60
☐ 165 Bobby Engram .20 .50
☐ 166 Laveranues Coles .25 .60
☐ 167 Antonio Gates .25 .60
☐ 168 LaRon Landry .25 .60
☐ 169 Ray Lewis .30 .75
☐ 170 Joe Namath .40 1.00
☐ 171 William Cody .20 .50
☐ 172 Andre Johnson SP 1.25 3.00
☐ 173 Erik Ainge RC 1.00 2.50
☐ 174 Dexter Jackson RC 1.00 2.50
☐ 175 Philip Rivers .30 .75
☐ 176 Marion Barber .30 .75
☐ 177 Chris Perry .20 .50
☐ 178 Torry Holt .25 .60
☐ 179 Anthony Gonzalez .25 .60
☐ 180 Kellen Winslow .25 .60
☐ 181 Adrian Wilson .20 .50
☐ 182 Shawne Merriman .25 .60
☐ 183 Lawrence Taylor .30 .75
☐ 184 William Rockefeller .20 .50
☐ 185 Brandon Marshall SP 1.25 3.00
☐ 186 Josh Johnson RC 1.00 2.50
☐ 187 Devin Thomas RC 1.00 2.50
☐ 188 Chad Pennington .25 .60
☐ 189 Brian Westbrook .25 .60
☐ 190 Ahman Green .25 .60
☐ 191 Derrick Mason .20 .50
☐ 192 Ernest Wilford .20 .50
☐ 193 Tony Scheffler .20 .50
☐ 194 Champ Bailey .20 .50
☐ 195 DeMeco Ryans .25 .60
☐ 196 Gale Sayers .40 1.00
☐ 197 Gus Frerotte .20 .50
☐ 198 Dwayne Bowe SP 1.25 3.00
☐ 199 Kevin O'Connell RC 1.00 2.50
☐ 200 Jordy Nelson RC 1.25 3.00
☐ 201 Trent Edwards .30 .75
☐ 202 Kolby Smith .20 .50
☐ 203 Brian Leonard .20 .50
☐ 204 Mike Furrey .25 .60
☐ 205 Jabar Gaffney .20 .50
☐ 206 Donald Lee .25 .60
☐ 207 Antonio Cromartie .20 .50
☐ 208 Joey Porter .20 .50
☐ 209 Norman Rockwell .20 .50
☐ 210 Tom Brady SP 2.50 6.00
☐ 211 Nate Burleson SP 1.00 2.50
☐ 212 Funkmaster Flex SP 1.00 2.50
☐ 213 Keenan Burton RC .75 2.00
☐ 214 Donovan McNabb .30 .75
☐ 215 Marshawn Lynch .30 .75
☐ 216 Earnest Graham .20 .50
☐ 217 Donald Driver .25 .60
☐ 218 Mark Clayton .25 .60
☐ 219 Vernon Davis .20 .50
☐ 220 Asante Samuel .20 .50
☐ 221 Mike Vrabel .20 .50
☐ 222 King Edward VIII .20 .50
☐ 223 Warren Haynes SP 1.00 2.50
☐ 224 Antwaan Randle El SP 1.00 2.50
☐ 225 Darren McFadden RC 2.00 5.00
☐ 226 Earl Bennett RC 1.00 2.50
☐ 227 Derek Anderson .25 .60
☐ 228 Joseph Addai .30 .75
☐ 229 Julius Jones .25 .60
☐ 230 T.J. Houshmandzadeh .25 .60
☐ 231 Kevin Walter .25 .60
☐ 232 Chris Cooley .25 .60
☐ 233 Leon Hall .20 .50
☐ 234 D.J. Williams .20 .50
☐ 235 Guglielmo Marconi .20 .50
☐ 236 David Garrard SP 1.25 3.00
☐ 237 Vincent Jackson SP 1.00 2.50
☐ 238 Jonathan Stewart RC 2.00 5.00
☐ 239 Jerome Simpson RC .75 2.00
☐ 240 Kyle Boller .20 .50
☐ 241 Warrick Dunn .25 .60
☐ 242 Ricky Williams .25 .60
☐ 243 Kevin Curtis .20 .50
☐ 244 Justin Gage .20 .50
☐ 245 Tony Gonzalez .25 .60
☐ 246 DeAngelo Hall .20 .50
☐ 247 Antonio Pierce .20 .50
☐ 248 Claude Monet .20 .50
☐ 249 Carson Palmer SP 1.50 4.00
☐ 250 Laurent Robinson SP 1.00 2.50
☐ 251 Felix Jones RC 2.00 5.00
☐ 252 Andre Caldwell RC 1.00 2.50
☐ 253 JaMarcus Russell .30 .75
☐ 254 Frank Gore .25 .60
☐ 255 Dominic Rhodes .20 .50
☐ 256 Santonio Holmes .25 .60
☐ 257 J.T. O'Sullivan .20 .50
☐ 258 Dallas Clark .25 .60
☐ 259 Terence Newman .20 .50
☐ 260 Ernie Sims .20 .50
☐ 261 Paul Gauguin .20 .50
☐ 262 Ben Roethlisberger SP 2.50 6.00
☐ 263 Chris Chambers SP 1.25 3.00
☐ 264 John David Booty RC 1.00 2.50
☐ 265 Eddie Royal RC 1.50 4.00
☐ 266 Brady Quinn .30 .75
☐ 267 Maurice Jones-Drew .25 .60
☐ 268 Deuce McAllister .25 .60
☐ 269 Wes Welker .30 .75
☐ 270 Darrell Jackson .20 .50
☐ 271 Jason Witten .30 .75
☐ 272 Nate Clements .20 .50
☐ 273 A.J. Hawk .25 .60
☐ 274 Dr. John Harvey Kellogg .20 .50
☐ 275 Eli Manning SP 1.50 4.00
☐ 276 Matt Ryan SP RC 5.00 12.00
☐ 277 Jamaal Charles RC 1.50 4.00
☐ 278 Lavelle Hawkins RC .75 2.00
☐ 279 Jake Delhomme .25 .60
☐ 280 Thomas Jones .25 .60
☐ 281 Chad Johnson .25 .60
☐ 282 Roddy White .25 .60
☐ 283 Devard Darling .20 .50
☐ 284 Alge Crumpler .25 .60
☐ 285 Jared Allen .30 .75
☐ 286 Jonathan Vilma .25 .60
☐ 287 Milton Hershey .20 .50
☐ 288 Tony Romo SP 2.50 6.00
☐ 289 Brian Brohm SP RC 1.25 3.00
☐ 290 Chris Johnson RC 3.00 8.00
☐ 291 Vernon Gholston RC 1.00 2.50
☐ 292 Alex Smith QB .25 .60
☐ 293 Brandon Jacobs .25 .60
☐ 294 Reggie Wayne .25 .60
☐ 295 Marques Colston .25 .60
☐ 296 Ronald Curry .25 .60

Card	Low	High
❑ 297 Ben Watson	.20	.50
❑ 298 Mario Williams	.25	.60
❑ 299 Derrick Brooks	.25	.60
❑ 300 Thomas Edison	.20	.50
❑ 301 Brett Favre SP	4.00	10.00
❑ 302 Anthony Morelli SP RC	1.25	3.00
❑ 303 Ray Rice RC	2.00	5.00
❑ 304 Dustin Keller RC	1.00	2.50
❑ 305 Aaron Rodgers	.30	.75
❑ 306 Edgerrin James	.25	.60
❑ 307 Anquan Boldin	.25	.60
❑ 308 Bernard Berrian	.25	.60
❑ 309 Dennis Northcutt	.20	.50
❑ 310 Marcedes Lewis	.20	.50
❑ 311 Jason Taylor	.25	.60
❑ 312 Lofa Tatupu	.25	.60
❑ 313 Arthur Conan Doyle	.20	.50
❑ 314 Kurt Warner SP	1.50	4.00
❑ 315 Rashard Mendenhall SP RC	2.50	6.00
❑ 316 Mike Hart SP RC	1.25	3.00
❑ 317 Owen Schmitt RC	1.00	2.50
❑ 318 Tarvaris Jackson	.25	.60
❑ 319 Chester Taylor	.20	.50
❑ 320 Randy Moss	.30	.75
❑ 321 Santana Moss	.20	.50
❑ 322 Patrick Crayton	.25	.60
❑ 323 Chris Baker	.20	.50
❑ 324 Osi Umenyiora	.20	.50
❑ 325 Shaun Rogers	.20	.50
❑ 326 Rudyard Kipling	.20	.50
❑ 327 Clinton Portis SP	1.25	3.00
❑ 328 Xavier Omon SP RC	1.25	3.00
❑ 329 Kevin Smith RC	1.50	4.00
❑ 330 Jacob Hester RC	1.00	2.50

2009 Topps Mayo

Card	Low	High
❑ COMPLETE SET (330)	60.00	120.00
❑ COMP.SET w/o SP's (275)	20.00	40.00
❑ 1 Benjamin Harrison Pres.	.20	.50
❑ 2 Aaron Curry RC	.75	2.00
❑ 3 Aaron Kampman	.25	.60
❑ 4 Aaron Maybin RC	.60	1.50
❑ 5 Aaron Rodgers	.30	.75
❑ 6 Adrian Peterson	.60	1.50
❑ 7 Adrian Wilson	.20	.50
❑ 8 Ahmad Bradshaw	.25	.60
❑ 9 Al Harris	.20	.50
❑ 10 Albert Haynesworth	.20	.50
❑ 11 Alex Smith QB	.20	.50
❑ 12 Andre Brown RC	.50	1.25
❑ 13 Andre Caldwell	.20	.50
❑ 14 Andre Johnson	.25	.60
❑ 15 Anquan Boldin	.25	.60
❑ 16 Anthony Gonzalez	.25	.60
❑ 17 Antoine Winfield	.20	.50
❑ 18 Antonio Gates	.25	.60
❑ 19 Antonio Pierce	.20	.50
❑ 20 Antwaan Randle El	.20	.50
❑ 21 Asante Samuel	.20	.50
❑ 22 Austin Collie RC	1.25	3.00
❑ 23 B.J. Raji RC	.75	2.00
❑ 24 Barry Sanders	.60	1.50
❑ 25 Ben Roethlisberger	.50	1.25
❑ 26 Bernard Berrian	.25	.60
❑ 27 Bo Scaife	.20	.50
❑ 28 Bobby Engram	.20	.50
❑ 29 Bobby Wade	.20	.50
❑ 30 Bradie James	.20	.50
❑ 31 Brady Quinn	.25	.60
❑ 32 Brandon Marshall	.25	.60
❑ 33 Brandon Pettigrew RC	.75	2.00
❑ 34 Brandon Tate RC	.50	1.25
❑ 35 Brian Cushing RC	.75	2.00
❑ 36 Brian Dawkins	.25	.60
❑ 37 Brian Hartline RC	.60	1.50
❑ 38 Brian Orakpo RC	.75	2.00
❑ 39 Brian Robiskie RC	.60	1.50
❑ 40 Brian Urlacher	.30	.75
❑ 41 Brian Westbrook	.25	.60
❑ 42 Brooks Foster RC	.50	1.25
❑ 43 Buffalo Bill	.20	.50
❑ 44 Carson Palmer	.30	.75
❑ 45 Cedric Benson	.25	.60
❑ 46 Chad Ochocinco	.25	.60
❑ 47 Champ Bailey	.25	.60
❑ 48 Charles Woodson	.25	.60
❑ 49 Chester Taylor	.20	.50
❑ 50 Chris Chambers	.25	.60
❑ 51 Chris Cooley	.25	.60
❑ 52 Chris Johnson	.30	.75
❑ 53 Chris Wells RC	1.50	4.00
❑ 54 Clay Matthews RC	1.00	2.50
❑ 55 Clinton Portis	.25	.60
❑ 56 Grover Cleveland Pres.	.20	.50
❑ 57 D'Qwell Jackson	.20	.50
❑ 58 Dallas Clark	.25	.60
❑ 59 Dan Marino	.75	2.00
❑ 60 Darrelle Revis	.25	.60
❑ 61 Darren McFadden	.30	.75
❑ 62 Darrius Heyward-Bey RC	1.00	2.50
❑ 63 Daunte Culpepper	.25	.60
❑ 64 DeAngelo Hall	.25	.60
❑ 65 DeAngelo Williams	.30	.75
❑ 66 Deion Branch	.25	.60
❑ 67 DeMarcus Ware	.25	.60
❑ 68 Derek Anderson	.25	.60
❑ 69 Derrick Mason	.20	.50
❑ 70 Derrick Ward	.25	.60
❑ 71 Derrick Williams RC	.60	1.50
❑ 72 DeSean Jackson	.25	.60
❑ 73 Devery Henderson	.20	.50
❑ 74 Devin Hester	.30	.75
❑ 75 Domenik Hixon	.20	.50
❑ 76 Donald Brown RC	1.25	3.00
❑ 77 Donald Driver	.25	.60
❑ 78 Donnie Avery	.25	.60
❑ 79 Donovan McNabb	.30	.75
❑ 80 Drew Brees	.30	.75
❑ 81 Dustin Keller	.20	.50
❑ 82 Dwayne Bowe	.25	.60
❑ 83 Dwight Freeney	.25	.60
❑ 84 Orville Wright inventor	.20	.50
❑ 85 Ed Reed	.25	.60
❑ 86 Eddie Royal	.25	.60
❑ 87 Eli Manning	.30	.75
❑ 88 Ernie Sims	.20	.50
❑ 89 Evander Hood RC	1.00	2.50
❑ 90 Annie Oakley	.20	.50
❑ 91 Felix Jones	.30	.75
❑ 92 Frank Gore	.25	.60
❑ 93 Fred Jackson	.25	.60
❑ 94 Fred Taylor	.25	.60
❑ 95 Nikola Tesla engineer	.20	.50
❑ 96 Gaines Adams	.20	.50
❑ 97 Glen Coffee RC	.75	2.00
❑ 98 Greg Camarillo	.25	.60
❑ 99 Greg Jennings	.30	.75
❑ 100 Greg Olsen	.20	.50
❑ 101 William McKinley Pres.	.20	.50
❑ 102 Heath Miller	.25	.60
❑ 103 Hines Ward	.25	.60
❑ 104 George Westinghouse entrepren.	.20	.50
❑ 105 Isaac Bruce	.25	.60
❑ 106 Theodore Roosevelt Pres.	.20	.50
❑ 107 Jake Delhomme	.25	.60
❑ 108 Jamaal Charles	.25	.60
❑ 109 Jamal Lewis	.25	.60
❑ 110 JaMarcus Russell	.25	.60
❑ 111 James Farrior	.20	.50
❑ 112 James Harrison	.30	.75
❑ 113 Jared Allen	.30	.75
❑ 114 Jared Cook RC	.50	1.25
❑ 115 Jason Witten	.30	.75
❑ 116 Jay Cutler	.30	.75
❑ 117 Jeremy Maclin RC	1.25	3.00
❑ 118 Jeremy Shockey	.20	.50
❑ 119 Jerious Norwood	.25	.60
❑ 120 Jerod Mayo	.25	.60
❑ 121 Jerricho Cotchery	.20	.50
❑ 122 Jerry Rice	.60	1.50
❑ 123 Jim Brown	.60	1.25
❑ 124 Joe Flacco	.30	.75
❑ 125 Joe Montana	.75	2.00
❑ 126 Joey Galloway	.25	.60
❑ 127 Joey Porter	.25	.60
❑ 128 John Abraham	.20	.50
❑ 129 John Carlson	.25	.60
❑ 130 John Elway	.60	1.50
❑ 131 Johnny Knox RC	1.00	2.50
❑ 132 Jon Beason	.20	.50
❑ 133 Jonathan Stewart	.25	.60
❑ 134 Jonathan Vilma	.20	.50
❑ 135 Joseph Addai	.30	.75
❑ 136 Josh Freeman RC	1.25	3.00
❑ 137 Josh Reed	.20	.50
❑ 138 Juaquin Iglesias RC	.60	1.50
❑ 139 Julian Peterson	.20	.50
❑ 140 Julius Peppers	.25	.60
❑ 141 Justin Fargas	.20	.50
❑ 142 Justin Gage	.20	.50
❑ 143 Justin Tuck	.25	.60
❑ 144 Clara Barton nurse	.20	.50
❑ 145 Kellen Winslow Jr.	.25	.60
❑ 146 Kenny Britt RC	1.00	2.50
❑ 147 Kenny McKinley RC	.60	1.50
❑ 148 Kerry Collins	.25	.60
❑ 149 Kevin Faulk	.20	.50
❑ 150 Kevin Smith	.25	.60
❑ 151 Kevin Walter	.25	.60
❑ 152 Kevin Williams	.20	.50
❑ 153 Knowshon Moreno RC	1.50	4.00
❑ 154 Kris Jenkins	.20	.50
❑ 155 Kurt Warner	.30	.75
❑ 156 Kyle Orton	.25	.60
❑ 157 LaDainian Tomlinson	.30	.75
❑ 158 LaMarr Woodley	.20	.50
❑ 159 Lance Briggs	.25	.60
❑ 160 Lance Moore	.25	.60
❑ 161 Larry English RC	.60	1.50
❑ 162 Larry Fitzgerald	.30	.75
❑ 163 Larry Johnson	.25	.60
❑ 164 Laurence Maroney	.25	.60
❑ 165 Laveranues Coles	.25	.60
❑ 166 Le'Ron McClain	.25	.60
❑ 167 Lee Evans	.25	.60
❑ 168 LenDale White	.25	.60
❑ 169 Leon Washington	.25	.60
❑ 170 LeSean McCoy RC	1.25	3.00
❑ 171 London Fletcher	.20	.50
❑ 172 Thomas Edison inventor	.20	.50
❑ 173 Malcolm Jenkins RC	.60	1.50
❑ 174 Marc Bulger	.25	.60
❑ 175 Mario Williams	.25	.60
❑ 176 Marion Barber	.30	.75
❑ 177 Mark Clayton	.20	.50
❑ 178 Mark Sanchez RC	2.50	6.00
❑ 179 Marques Colston	.25	.60
❑ 180 Marshawn Lynch	.25	.60
❑ 181 Mathias Kiwanuka	.20	.50
❑ 182 Matt Cassel	.25	.60
❑ 183 Matt Forte	.30	.75
❑ 184 Matt Hasselbeck	.25	.60
❑ 185 Matt Ryan	.30	.75
❑ 186 Matt Schaub	.25	.60
❑ 187 Matthew Stafford RC	2.00	5.00
❑ 188 Maurice Jones-Drew	.25	.60
❑ 189 Mewelde Moore	.20	.50
❑ 190 Michael Bush	.25	.60
❑ 191 Michael Crabtree RC	1.50	4.00
❑ 192 Michael Jenkins	.20	.50
❑ 193 Michael Turner	.25	.60
❑ 194 Mike Goodson RC	.60	1.50
❑ 195 Mike Thomas RC	.60	1.50
❑ 196 Mike Wallace RC	1.25	3.00
❑ 197 Mohamed Massaquoi RC	.60	1.50
❑ 198 Muhsin Muhammad	.25	.60
❑ 199 Andrew Mellon banker	.20	.50
❑ 200 Nate Davis RC	.60	1.50
❑ 201 Nate Washington	.20	.50
❑ 202 Nnamdi Asomugha	.20	.50
❑ 203 Fred Grandy Congress	.20	.50
❑ 204 Owen Daniels	.20	.50
❑ 205 Barack Obama	.30	.75
❑ 206 Pat White RC	1.00	2.50
❑ 207 Patrick Turner RC	.50	1.25
❑ 208 Patrick Willis	.25	.60
❑ 209 Percy Harvin RC	2.00	5.00
❑ 210 Peria Jerry RC	.50	1.25
❑ 211 Peyton Manning	.50	1.25
❑ 212 Philip Rivers	.30	.75

❑ 213 Pierre Thomas .25 .60
❑ 214 Jay Ratliff .30 .75
❑ 215 Robert Jarvik inventor .20 .50
❑ 216 Ramses Barden RC .50 1.25
❑ 217 Randy Moss .30 .75
❑ 218 Rashard Mendenhall .25 .60
❑ 219 Ray Lewis .30 .75
❑ 220 Ray Rice .30 .75
❑ 221 Reggie Bush .30 .75
❑ 222 Reggie Wayne .25 .60
❑ 223 Rhett Bomar RC .50 1.25
❑ 224 Richard Seymour .20 .50
❑ 225 Ricky Williams .25 .60
❑ 226 Robert Ayers RC .60 1.50
❑ 227 Roddy White .25 .60
❑ 228 Ronde Barber .20 .50
❑ 229 Ronnie Brown .25 .60
❑ 230 Roscoe Parrish .20 .50
❑ 231 Roy Williams WR .25 .60
❑ 232 Ryan Grant .25 .60
❑ 233 Pawnee Bill .20 .50
❑ 234 Sage Rosenfels .20 .50
❑ 235 Santana Moss .25 .60
❑ 236 Shaun Hill .25 .60
❑ 237 Shaun Rogers .20 .50
❑ 238 Shonn Greene RC 1.25 3.00
❑ 239 Stephen McGee RC .60 1.50
❑ 240 Steve Slaton .25 .60
❑ 241 Steve Smith .25 .60
❑ 242 Steve Smith USC .25 .60
❑ 243 Steven Jackson .25 .60
❑ 244 Richmond Hobson Admiral .20 .50
❑ 245 T.J. Houshmandzadeh .25 .60
❑ 246 Tarvaris Jackson .25 .60
❑ 247 Tashard Choice .25 .60
❑ 248 Ted Ginn Jr. .25 .60
❑ 249 Terence Newman .20 .50
❑ 250 Terrell Owens .30 .75
❑ 251 Terrell Suggs .20 .50
❑ 252 Terry Bradshaw .60 1.50
❑ 253 Thomas Jones .25 .60
❑ 254 Tim Hightower .25 .60
❑ 255 Tom Brady .50 1.25
❑ 256 Tony Dorsett .40 1.00
❑ 257 Tony Gonzalez .25 .60
❑ 258 Tony Romo .50 1.25
❑ 259 Torry Holt .25 .60
❑ 260 Edgerrin James .25 .60
❑ 261 Travis Beckum RC .50 1.25
❑ 262 Troy Aikman .50 1.25
❑ 263 Troy Polamalu .30 .75
❑ 264 Tyson Jackson RC .60 1.50
❑ 265 Paddy Doyle athlete .20 .50
❑ 266 John D. Rockefeller tycoon .20 .50
❑ 267 Vince Young .25 .60
❑ 268 Vincent Jackson .25 .60
❑ 269 Vontae Davis RC .60 1.50
❑ 270 Kevin Young track .20 .50
❑ 271 Wes Welker .30 .75
❑ 272 Willie Parker .25 .60
❑ 273 Willis McGahee .25 .60
❑ 274 Booker T. Washington .20 .50
❑ 275 Zach Miller .20 .50
❑ 276 Anthony Fasano 1.00 2.50
❑ 277 Antonio Bryant 1.25 3.00
❑ 278 Mike Powell track 1.00 2.50
❑ 279 Barrett Ruud 1.00 2.50
❑ 280 Brandon Jacobs 1.25 3.00
❑ 281 Braylon Edwards 1.25 3.00
❑ 282 Calvin Johnson 1.50 4.00
❑ 283 Chad Pennington 1.25 3.00
❑ 284 Chase Coffman RC 1.00 2.50
❑ 285 Chris Hope 1.00 2.50
❑ 286 Cortland Finnegan 1.00 2.50
❑ 287 Brett Favre 6.00 15.00
❑ 288 Darren Howard 1.00 2.50
❑ 289 Darren Sproles 1.25 3.00
❑ 290 David Garrard 1.25 3.00
❑ 291 Deon Butler RC 1.25 3.00
❑ 292 Dominic Rhodes 1.00 2.50
❑ 293 Earnest Graham 1.00 2.50
❑ 294 Gartrell Johnson RC 1.00 2.50
❑ 295 Gibril Wilson 1.00 2.50
❑ 296 Hakeem Nicks RC 2.50 6.00
❑ 297 J.T. O'Sullivan 1.00 2.50
❑ 298 James Casey RC 1.00 2.50
❑ 299 Jarett Dillard RC 1.25 3.00
❑ 300 Jason Campbell 1.25 3.00
❑ 301 Jason Smith RC 1.00 2.50
❑ 302 Michael Vick 1.50 4.00
❑ 303 Jeff Garcia 1.25 3.00
❑ 304 Joe Namath 2.00 5.00
❑ 305 Jon Kitna 1.00 2.50
❑ 306 Josh Cribbs 1.50 4.00
❑ 307 Julius Jones 1.25 3.00
❑ 308 Kenny Phillips 1.00 2.50
❑ 309 Kirk Morrison 1.00 2.50
❑ 310 Maurice Greene track 1.00 2.50
❑ 311 Louis Murphy RC 1.25 3.00
❑ 312 Manuel Johnson RC 1.00 2.50
❑ 313 Matt Leinart 1.25 3.00
❑ 314 Maurice Morris 1.00 2.50
❑ 315 Michael Griffin 1.00 2.50
❑ 316 Nick Collins 1.00 2.50
❑ 317 Pat Williams 1.00 2.50
❑ 318 Robert Mathis 1.00 2.50
❑ 319 Ryan Fitzpatrick 1.00 2.50
❑ 320 Sammy Morris 1.00 2.50
❑ 321 Santonio Holmes 1.25 3.00
❑ 322 Seneca Wallace 1.00 2.50
❑ 323 Ted Kennedy 1.25 3.00
❑ 324 Shawn Nelson RC 1.00 2.50
❑ 325 Steve Breaston 1.25 3.00
❑ 326 Tony Scheffler 1.00 2.50
❑ 327 Trent Cole 1.00 2.50
❑ 328 Trent Edwards 1.25 3.00
❑ 329 Tyler Thigpen 1.00 2.50
❑ 330 Jackie Joyner-Kersee track 1.00 2.50

2009 Topps Platinum

❑ COMPLETE SET (165) 25.00 50.00
❑ 1 Drew Brees .25 .60
❑ 2 Kurt Warner .25 .60
❑ 3 Jay Cutler .25 .60
❑ 4 Aaron Rodgers .25 .60
❑ 5 Philip Rivers .25 .60
❑ 6 Peyton Manning .40 1.00
❑ 7 Donovan McNabb .25 .60
❑ 8 Matt Cassel .20 .50
❑ 9 David Garrard .20 .50
❑ 10 Brett Favre 4.00 10.00
❑ 11 Tony Romo .40 1.00
❑ 12 Matt Ryan .25 .60
❑ 13 Ben Roethlisberger .40 1.00
❑ 14 Eli Manning .25 .60
❑ 15 Matt Schaub .20 .50
❑ 16 Joe Flacco .25 .60
❑ 17 Carson Palmer .25 .60
❑ 18 Tom Brady .40 1.00
❑ 19 Adrian Peterson .50 1.25
❑ 20 Michael Turner .20 .50
❑ 21 DeAngelo Williams .25 .60
❑ 22 Clinton Portis .20 .50
❑ 23 Thomas Jones .20 .50
❑ 24 Steve Slaton .20 .50
❑ 25 Matt Forte .25 .60
❑ 26 Chris Johnson .25 .60
❑ 27 Ryan Grant .20 .50
❑ 28 LaDainian Tomlinson .25 .60
❑ 29 Brandon Jacobs .20 .50
❑ 30 Steven Jackson .20 .50
❑ 31 Marshawn Lynch .20 .50
❑ 32 Frank Gore .20 .50
❑ 33 Kevin Smith .20 .50
❑ 34 Brian Westbrook .20 .50
❑ 35 Ronnie Brown .20 .50
❑ 36 Marion Barber .25 .60
❑ 37 Jonathan Stewart .20 .50
❑ 38 Maurice Jones-Drew .20 .50
❑ 39 Willie Parker .20 .50
❑ 40 Darren McFadden .25 .60
❑ 41 Reggie Bush .25 .60
❑ 42 Joseph Addai .25 .60
❑ 43 LenDale White .20 .50
❑ 44 Felix Jones .25 .60
❑ 45 Ray Rice .25 .60
❑ 46 Fred Jackson .20 .50
❑ 47 Leon Washington .20 .50
❑ 48 Andre Johnson .20 .50
❑ 49 Larry Fitzgerald .25 .60
❑ 50 Steve Smith .20 .50
❑ 51 Roddy White .20 .50
❑ 52 Calvin Johnson .25 .60
❑ 53 Greg Jennings .25 .60
❑ 54 Brandon Marshall .20 .50
❑ 55 Antonio Bryant .20 .50
❑ 56 Wes Welker .25 .60
❑ 57 Reggie Wayne .20 .50
❑ 58 Marques Colston .20 .50
❑ 59 Terrell Owens .25 .60
❑ 60 Santana Moss .20 .50
❑ 61 Hines Ward .20 .50
❑ 62 Anquan Boldin .20 .50
❑ 63 Dwayne Bowe .20 .50
❑ 64 Roy Williams WR .20 .50
❑ 65 Donald Driver .20 .50
❑ 66 Randy Moss .25 .60
❑ 67 Eddie Royal .20 .50
❑ 68 DeSean Jackson .20 .50
❑ 69 T.J. Houshmandzadeh .20 .50
❑ 70 Jerricho Cotchery .15 .40
❑ 71 Santonio Holmes .20 .50
❑ 72 Chad Ochocinco .20 .50
❑ 73 Vincent Jackson .20 .50
❑ 74 Lee Evans .20 .50
❑ 75 Devin Hester .25 .60
❑ 76 Anthony Gonzalez .20 .50
❑ 77 Tony Gonzalez .20 .50
❑ 78 Jason Witten .25 .60
❑ 79 Dallas Clark .20 .50
❑ 80 Antonio Gates .20 .50
❑ 81 Chris Cooley .20 .50
❑ 82 Zach Miller .15 .40
❑ 83 Greg Olsen .15 .40
❑ 84 John Carlson .20 .50
❑ 85 Willis McGahee .20 .50
❑ 86 Fred Taylor .20 .50
❑ 87 John Abraham .15 .40
❑ 88 Jared Allen .25 .60
❑ 89 Julius Peppers .20 .50
❑ 90 Mario Williams .20 .50
❑ 91 Dwight Freeney .20 .50
❑ 92 DeMarcus Ware .20 .50
❑ 93 Joey Porter .20 .50
❑ 94 James Harrison .25 .60
❑ 95 LaMarr Woodley .15 .40
❑ 96 Patrick Willis .20 .50
❑ 97 Brian Urlacher .25 .60
❑ 98 Terrell Suggs .15 .40
❑ 99 Jerod Mayo .20 .50
❑ 100 Ray Lewis .25 .60
❑ 101 Charles Woodson .20 .50
❑ 102 Darrelle Revis .20 .50
❑ 103 Antoine Winfield .15 .40
❑ 104 Asante Samuel .15 .40
❑ 105 Chris Johnson CB .15 .40
❑ 106 Nnamdi Asomugha .15 .40
❑ 107 Champ Bailey .20 .50
❑ 108 Ed Reed .20 .50
❑ 109 Troy Polamalu .25 .60
❑ 110 Adrian Wilson .15 .40
❑ 111 Andre Brown RC .75 2.00
❑ 112 Aaron Curry RC 1.25 3.00
❑ 113 Brandon Pettigrew RC 1.25 3.00
❑ 114 Brian Robiskie RC 1.00 2.50
❑ 115 Chris Wells RC 2.50 6.00
❑ 116 Deon Butler RC 1.00 2.50
❑ 117 Donald Brown RC 2.00 5.00
❑ 118 Darrius Heyward-Bey RC 1.50 4.00
❑ 119 Derrick Williams RC 1.00 2.50
❑ 120 Glen Coffee RC 1.25 3.00
❑ 121 Hakeem Nicks RC 2.00 5.00
❑ 122 Josh Freeman RC 2.00 5.00
❑ 123 Juaquin Iglesias RC 1.00 2.50
❑ 124 Jeremy Maclin RC 2.00 5.00
❑ 125 Matthew Stafford RC 3.00 8.00
❑ 126 Javon Ringer RC 1.00 2.50
❑ 127 Jason Smith RC .75 2.00
❑ 128 Kenny Britt RC 1.50 4.00
❑ 129 Knowshon Moreno RC 2.50 6.00

Card		
❑ 130 LeSean McCoy RC	2.00	5.00
❑ 131 Michael Crabtree RC	2.50	6.00
❑ 132 Mohamed Massaquoi RC	1.00	2.50
❑ 133 Mark Sanchez RC	4.00	10.00
❑ 134 Mike Thomas RC	1.00	2.50
❑ 135 Mike Wallace RC	2.00	5.00
❑ 136 Nate Davis RC	1.00	2.50
❑ 137 Percy Harvin RC	3.00	8.00
❑ 138 Patrick Turner RC	.75	2.00
❑ 139 Pat White RC	1.50	4.00
❑ 140 Ramses Barden RC	.75	2.00
❑ 141 Rhett Bomar RC	.75	2.00
❑ 142 Shonn Greene RC	2.00	5.00
❑ 143 Stephen McGee RC	1.00	2.50
❑ 144 Tyson Jackson RC	1.00	2.50
❑ 145 Chase Coffman RC	.75	2.00
❑ 146 Tom Brandstater RC	1.00	2.50
❑ 147 Brian Orakpo RC	1.25	3.00
❑ 148 Malcolm Jenkins RC	1.00	2.50
❑ 149 Brian Cushing RC	1.25	3.00
❑ 150 Brian Hartline RC	1.00	2.50
❑ 151 Mike Goodson RC	1.00	2.50
❑ 152 Shawn Nelson RC	.75	2.00
❑ 153 Austin Collie RC	2.00	5.00
❑ 154 Louis Murphy RC	1.00	2.50
❑ 155 Johnny Knox RC	1.50	4.00
❑ 156 Rashad Jennings RC	1.00	2.50
❑ 157 Jarett Dillard RC	1.00	2.50
❑ 158 Quan Cosby RC	.75	2.00
❑ 159 Julian Edelman RC	2.00	5.00
❑ 160 James Laurinaitis RC	1.25	3.00
❑ 161 Gartrell Johnson RC	.75	2.00
❑ 162 Brandon Gibson RC	1.00	2.50
❑ 163 James Davis RC	1.00	2.50
❑ 164 Rey Maualuga RC	1.50	4.00
❑ 165 Sammie Stroughter RC	1.00	2.50

2008 Topps Rookie Progression

Card		
❑ COMPLETE SET (220)	30.00	60.00
❑ 1 Drew Brees	.40	1.00
❑ 2 Jon Kitna	.30	.75
❑ 3 Tom Brady	.60	1.50
❑ 4 Chad Pennington	.30	.75
❑ 5 Steve McNair	.30	.75
❑ 6 Josh McCown	.25	.60
❑ 7 Matt Hasselbeck	.30	.75
❑ 8 David Garrard	.30	.75
❑ 9 Jay Cutler	.40	1.00
❑ 10 Matt Schaub	.30	.75
❑ 11 Daunte Culpepper	.30	.75
❑ 12 Kellen Clemens	.30	.75
❑ 13 John Beck	.25	.60
❑ 14 Trent Edwards	.40	1.00
❑ 15 Steven Jackson	.40	1.00
❑ 16 Willie Parker	.30	.75
❑ 17 Derrick Ward	.30	.75
❑ 18 Julius Jones	.30	.75
❑ 19 DeShaun Foster	.30	.75
❑ 20 Shaun Alexander	.30	.75
❑ 21 Reggie Bush	.40	1.00
❑ 22 Clinton Portis	.30	.75
❑ 23 Ron Dayne	.30	.75
❑ 24 Maurice Jones-Drew	.30	.75
❑ 25 Warrick Dunn	.30	.75
❑ 26 Adrian Peterson	.75	2.00
❑ 27 Brian Leonard	.25	.60
❑ 28 Greg Jennings	.30	.75
❑ 29 Torry Holt	.30	.75
❑ 30 T.J. Houshmandzadeh	.30	.75
❑ 31 Jerricho Cotchery	.25	.60
❑ 32 Derrick Mason	.25	.60
❑ 33 Kevin Curtis	.25	.60
❑ 34 Kevin Walter	.30	.75
❑ 35 Joey Galloway	.30	.75
❑ 36 Anquan Boldin	.30	.75
❑ 37 Santonio Holmes	.30	.75
❑ 38 Lee Evans	.30	.75
❑ 39 Dwayne Bowe	.30	.75
❑ 40 Laurent Robinson	.25	.60
❑ 41 Antonio Gates	.30	.75
❑ 42 Chris Cooley	.30	.75
❑ 43 Owen Daniels	.25	.60
❑ 44 Patrick Kerney	.25	.60
❑ 45 Gaines Adams	.25	.60
❑ 46 Jon Beason	.25	.60
❑ 47 Antonio Cromartie	.25	.60
❑ 48 Bob Sanders	.30	.75
❑ 49 Reggie Nelson	.25	.60
❑ 50 John Elway	.75	2.00
❑ 51 Allen Patrick RC	.60	1.50
❑ 52 Steve Young	.60	1.50
❑ 53 Bruce Davis RC	.75	2.00
❑ 54 Cliff Avril RC	.60	1.50
❑ 55 Chevis Jackson RC	.60	1.50
❑ 56 Peyton Manning	.60	1.50
❑ 57 Carson Palmer	.40	1.00
❑ 58 Ben Roethlisberger	.50	1.25
❑ 59 Eli Manning	.40	1.00
❑ 60 Tony Romo	.60	1.50
❑ 61 Donovan McNabb	.40	1.00
❑ 62 Joey Harrington	.30	.75
❑ 63 Jeff Garcia	.30	.75
❑ 64 Derek Anderson	.30	.75
❑ 65 Rex Grossman	.30	.75
❑ 66 Kyle Boller	.25	.60
❑ 67 Sage Rosenfels	.25	.60
❑ 68 JaMarcus Russell	.40	1.00
❑ 69 Jerious Norwood	.30	.75
❑ 70 Thomas Jones	.30	.75
❑ 71 LaDainian Tomlinson	.50	1.25
❑ 72 Cedric Benson	.30	.75
❑ 73 Marion Barber	.40	1.00
❑ 74 Brian Westbrook	.30	.75
❑ 75 LenDale White	.30	.75
❑ 76 Ronnie Brown	.30	.75
❑ 77 Travis Henry	.30	.75
❑ 78 Kenny Watson	.25	.60
❑ 79 Fred Taylor	.30	.75
❑ 80 Ryan Grant	.40	1.00
❑ 81 Marshawn Lynch	.40	1.00
❑ 82 Selvin Young	.25	.60
❑ 83 Wes Welker	.40	1.00
❑ 84 Roy Williams WR	.30	.75
❑ 85 Randy Moss	.40	1.00
❑ 86 Plaxico Burress	.30	.75
❑ 87 Terrell Owens	.40	1.00
❑ 88 Andre Johnson	.30	.75
❑ 89 Roddy White	.30	.75
❑ 90 Brandon Marshall	.30	.75
❑ 91 Donald Driver	.30	.75
❑ 92 Hines Ward	.30	.75
❑ 93 Ike Hilliard	.25	.60
❑ 94 James Jones	.25	.60
❑ 95 Calvin Johnson	.40	1.00
❑ 96 Kellen Winslow	.30	.75
❑ 97 Tony Gonzalez	.30	.75
❑ 98 Osi Umenyiora	.25	.60
❑ 99 Mario Williams	.30	.75
❑ 100 D.J. Williams	.25	.60
❑ 101 Ernie Sims	.25	.60
❑ 102 Marcus Trufant	.25	.60
❑ 103 Sean Taylor	.30	.75
❑ 104 Troy Aikman	.60	1.50
❑ 105 Dan Marino	1.00	2.50
❑ 106 Dantrell Savage RC	.75	2.00
❑ 107 DJ Hall RC	.60	1.50
❑ 108 Eddie Royal RC	1.25	3.00
❑ 109 Harry Douglas RC	.60	1.50
❑ 110 Marcus Griffin RC	.50	1.25
❑ 111 Marc Bulger	.30	.75
❑ 112 Peyton Hillis RC	.75	2.00
❑ 113 Philip Rivers	.40	1.00
❑ 114 Vince Young	.30	.75
❑ 115 Kurt Warner	.40	1.00
❑ 116 Cleo Lemon	.25	.60
❑ 117 Damon Huard	.25	.60
❑ 118 Jason Campbell	.30	.75
❑ 119 Brian Griese	.25	.60
❑ 120 Tarvaris Jackson	.30	.75
❑ 121 J.P. Losman	.25	.60
❑ 122 Troy Smith	.30	.75
❑ 123 Brady Quinn	.40	1.00
❑ 124 Joseph Addai	.40	1.00
❑ 125 Laurence Maroney	.30	.75
❑ 126 Brandon Jacobs	.30	.75
❑ 127 Willis McGahee	.30	.75
❑ 128 Frank Gore	.30	.75
❑ 129 Edgerrin James	.30	.75
❑ 130 Kevin Jones	.25	.60
❑ 131 DeAngelo Williams	.30	.75
❑ 132 Jamal Lewis	.30	.75
❑ 133 Chester Taylor	.25	.60
❑ 134 Earnest Graham	.25	.60
❑ 135 Justin Fargas	.25	.60
❑ 136 Kolby Smith	.25	.60
❑ 137 Marques Colston	.30	.75
❑ 138 Reggie Wayne	.30	.75
❑ 139 Chad Johnson	.30	.75
❑ 140 Amani Toomer	.30	.75
❑ 141 Bernard Berrian	.30	.75
❑ 142 Steve Smith	.30	.75
❑ 143 Larry Fitzgerald	.40	1.00
❑ 144 Chris Chambers	.30	.75
❑ 145 Braylon Edwards	.30	.75
❑ 146 David Patten	.25	.60
❑ 147 Bobby Engram	.25	.60
❑ 148 Shaun McDonald	.25	.60
❑ 149 Anthony Gonzalez	.30	.75
❑ 150 Sidney Rice	.40	1.00
❑ 151 Jason Witten	.40	1.00
❑ 152 Greg Olsen	.30	.75
❑ 153 Jared Allen	.40	1.00
❑ 154 DeMarcus Ware	.30	.75
❑ 155 Nick Barnett	.25	.60
❑ 156 Patrick Willis	.30	.75
❑ 157 Ed Reed	.30	.75
❑ 158 Asante Samuel	.25	.60
❑ 159 Rafael Little RC	.60	1.50
❑ 160 Joe Montana	1.00	2.50
❑ 161 Lawrence Jackson RC	.60	1.50
❑ 162 Chauncey Washington RC	.60	1.50
❑ 163 Keenan Burton RC	.60	1.50
❑ 164 John Carlson RC	.75	2.00
❑ 165 Dorien Bryant RC	.60	1.50
❑ 166 Adarius Bowman RC	.60	1.50
❑ 167 Ali Highsmith RC	.50	1.25
❑ 168 Andre Woodson RC	.75	2.00
❑ 169 Darren McFadden RC	1.50	4.00
❑ 170 Brian Brohm RC	.75	2.00
❑ 171 Brandon Flowers RC	.75	2.00
❑ 172 Matt Ryan RC	3.00	8.00
❑ 173 Calais Campbell RC	.60	1.50
❑ 174 Quentin Groves RC	.60	1.50
❑ 175 Curtis Lofton RC	.75	2.00
❑ 176 Justin Forsett RC	.75	2.00
❑ 177 Lavelle Hawkins RC	.60	1.50
❑ 178 DeSean Jackson RC	1.50	4.00
❑ 179 Dan Connor RC	.75	2.00
❑ 180 Dennis Dixon RC	.75	2.00
❑ 181 Derrick Harvey RC	.60	1.50
❑ 182 Erik Ainge RC	.75	2.00
❑ 183 Earl Bennett RC	.75	2.00
❑ 184 Early Doucet RC	.75	2.00
❑ 185 Erin Henderson RC	.60	1.50
❑ 186 Felix Jones RC	1.50	4.00
❑ 187 James Hardy RC	.60	1.50
❑ 188 Jonathan Stewart RC	1.50	4.00
❑ 189 Kenny Phillips RC	.75	2.00
❑ 190 Keith Rivers RC	.75	2.00
❑ 191 Kevin Smith RC	1.25	3.00
❑ 192 Mike Jenkins RC	.75	2.00
❑ 193 Malcom Kelly RC	.75	2.00
❑ 195 Chad Henne RC	1.25	3.00
❑ 196 Jake Long RC	.75	2.00
❑ 197 Mario Manningham RC	.75	2.00
❑ 198 Rashard Mendenhall RC	1.50	4.00
❑ 199 Reggie Smith RC	.60	1.50
❑ 200 Ray Rice RC	1.50	4.00
❑ 201 Steve Slaton RC	1.00	2.50
❑ 202 Tracy Porter RC	1.00	2.50
❑ 203 Jerod Mayo RC	1.00	2.50
❑ 204 John David Booty RC	.75	2.00
❑ 205 Fred Davis RC	.75	2.00
❑ 206 Sedrick Ellis RC	.75	2.00
❑ 207 Chris Johnson RC	2.50	6.00
❑ 208 Andre Caldwell RC	.75	2.00
❑ 209 Tashard Choice RC	.75	2.00
❑ 210 Glenn Dorsey RC	.75	2.00
❑ 211 Vernon Gholston RC	.75	2.00

Card	Low	High
❑ 212 Chris Long RC	.75	2.00
❑ 213 Xavier Adibi RC	.60	1.50
❑ 214 Donnie Avery RC	1.00	2.50
❑ 215 Colt Brennan RC	1.25	3.00
❑ 216 Kentwan Balmer RC	.60	1.50
❑ 217 Jamaal Charles RC	1.25	3.00
❑ 218 Limas Sweed RC	.75	2.00
❑ 219 Matt Forte RC	1.50	4.00
❑ 220 Owen Schmitt RC	.75	2.00

2003 Topps Total

Card	Low	High
❑ COMPLETE SET (550)	40.00	80.00
❑ 1 Rich Gannon	.20	.50
❑ 2 Travis Henry	.20	.50
❑ 3 Brian Finneran	.15	.40
❑ 4 Ed Hartwell	.15	.40
❑ 5 Az-Zahir Hakim	.15	.40
❑ 6 Rodney Peete	.15	.40
❑ 7 David Terrell	.15	.40
❑ 8 Matt Schobel	.20	.50
❑ 9 Andre Davis	.15	.40
❑ 10 Dexter Coakley	.20	.50
❑ 11 Rod Smith	.20	.50
❑ 12 Damerien McCants	.15	.40
❑ 13 Robert Ferguson	.15	.40
❑ 14 Kailee Wong	.15	.40
❑ 15 James Mungro	.15	.40
❑ 16 Fred Taylor	.25	.60
❑ 17 Tony Gonzalez	.20	.50
❑ 18 Randall Godfrey	.15	.40
❑ 19 Robert Thomas	.15	.40
❑ 20 Rohan Davey	.15	.40
❑ 21 Terrell Owens	.25	.60
❑ 22 Ron Dayne	.20	.50
❑ 23 Charlie Batch	.15	.40
❑ 24 Brian Westbrook	.25	.60
❑ 25 Plaxico Burress	.25	.60
❑ 26 Reche Caldwell	.15	.40
❑ 27 Fred Beasley	.15	.40
❑ 28 Anthony Simmons	.15	.40
❑ 29 Rod Woodson	.25	.60
❑ 30 Derrick Brooks	.20	.50
❑ 31 Shaun Ellis	.15	.40
❑ 32 Ladell Betts	.20	.50
❑ 33 Russell Davis	.15	.40
❑ 34 Warrick Dunn	.20	.50
❑ 35 Jeremy Shockey	.25	.60
❑ 36 Alex Van Pelt	.15	.40
❑ 37 Todd Bouman	.15	.40
❑ 38 Kelly Campbell	.15	.40
❑ 39 Justin Smith	.20	.50
❑ 40 Jamel White	.15	.40
❑ 41 La'Roi Glover	.15	.40
❑ 42 Ian Gold	.15	.40
❑ 43 Robert Porcher	.15	.40
❑ 44 Jermaine Lewis	.15	.40
❑ 45 Marvin Harrison	.25	.60
❑ 46 Darren Sharper	.20	.50
❑ 47 Jamie Sharper	.15	.40
❑ 48 Tony Richardson	.15	.40
❑ 49 Moe Williams	.15	.40
❑ 50 Ricky Williams	.20	.50
❑ 51 Ty Law	.20	.50
❑ 52 Donte Stallworth	.20	.50
❑ 53 Shannon Sharpe	.20	.50
❑ 54 Santana Moss	.20	.50
❑ 55 Charlie Garner	.20	.50
❑ 56 Brian Dawkins	.20	.50
❑ 57 Dan Campbell	.15	.40
❑ 58 William Green	.15	.40
❑ 59 Ron Dugans	.15	.40
❑ 60 Darrell Jackson	.20	.50
❑ 61 Marc Bulger	.25	.60
❑ 62 Joe Jurevicius	.20	.50
❑ 63 Erron Kinney	.15	.40
❑ 64 Champ Bailey	.20	.50
❑ 65 Peerless Price	.15	.40
❑ 66 Gary Baxter	.15	.40
❑ 67 Chris Redman	.15	.40
❑ 68 London Fletcher	.15	.40
❑ 69 Dee Brown	.15	.40
❑ 70 Anthony Thomas	.20	.50
❑ 71 Jake Delhomme	.25	.60
❑ 72 Dorsey Levens	.20	.50
❑ 73 Roy Williams	.25	.60
❑ 74 Ashley Lelie	.15	.40
❑ 75 Joey Harrington	.20	.50
❑ 76 William Henderson	.20	.50
❑ 77 Corey Bradford	.15	.40
❑ 78 Reggie Wayne	.20	.50
❑ 79 Kyle Brady	.15	.40
❑ 80 Trent Green	.20	.50
❑ 81 Bill Romanowski	.20	.50
❑ 82 Chike Okeafor RC	.30	.75
❑ 83 David Patten	.15	.40
❑ 84 Terrelle Smith	.15	.40
❑ 85 Kerry Collins	.20	.50
❑ 86 Derrick Mason	.20	.50
❑ 87 Trung Canidate	.15	.40
❑ 88 A.J. Feeley	.15	.40
❑ 89 Jason Gildon	.20	.50
❑ 90 Doug Flutie	.25	.60
❑ 91 Tai Streets	.15	.40
❑ 92 Keith Newman	.15	.40
❑ 93 Adam Archuleta	.15	.40
❑ 94 Simeon Rice	.20	.50
❑ 95 Eddie George	.20	.50
❑ 96 Frank Sanders	.15	.40
❑ 97 Freddie Jones	.15	.40
❑ 98 Charles Johnson	.15	.40
❑ 99 Keith Traylor	.20	.50
❑ 100 Drew Bledsoe	.25	.60
❑ 101 Muhsin Muhammad	.20	.50
❑ 102 Marques Anderson	.15	.40
❑ 103 Donald Hayes	.15	.40
❑ 104 Quincy Morgan	.15	.40
❑ 105 Chad Hutchinson	.15	.40
❑ 106 Mike Anderson	.20	.50
❑ 107 Randy McMichael	.15	.40
❑ 108 Vonnie Holliday	.15	.40
❑ 109 Marcus Coleman	.15	.40
❑ 110 Edgerrin James	.25	.60
❑ 111 Michael Lewis	.15	.40
❑ 112 Wayne Chrebet	.20	.50
❑ 113 Antwaan Randle El	.20	.50
❑ 114 Byron Chamberlain	.15	.40
❑ 115 Jeff Garcia	.25	.60
❑ 116 Kim Herring	.15	.40
❑ 117 Kenny Holmes	.15	.40
❑ 118 John Lynch	.20	.50
❑ 119 Doug Jolley	.15	.40
❑ 120 Duce Staley	.20	.50
❑ 121 Kordell Stewart	.20	.50
❑ 122 Stephen Alexander	.15	.40
❑ 123 Andre Carter	.15	.40
❑ 124 Bobby Engram	.15	.40
❑ 125 Marshall Faulk	.25	.60
❑ 126 Peter Simon RC	.15	.40
❑ 127 Alge Crumpler	.20	.50
❑ 128 Kenny Watson	.15	.40
❑ 129 Duane Starks	.15	.40
❑ 130 Jeff Blake	.20	.50
❑ 131 Todd Heap	.20	.50
❑ 132 Bobby Shaw	.15	.40
❑ 133 Ricky Proehl	.20	.50
❑ 134 John Abraham	.20	.50
❑ 135 T.J. Houshmandzadeh	.25	.60
❑ 136 Brian Urlacher	.40	1.00
❑ 137 Darren Woodson	.20	.50
❑ 138 Steve Beuerlein	.20	.50
❑ 139 Cory Schlesinger	.15	.40
❑ 140 Ahman Green	.25	.60
❑ 141 Jabar Gaffney	.15	.40
❑ 142 Eddie Drummond	.15	.40
❑ 143 Stacey Mack	.15	.40
❑ 144 Johnnie Morton	.20	.50
❑ 145 Chris Chambers	.20	.50
❑ 146 Jim Kleinsasser	.15	.40
❑ 147 Tebucky Jones	.15	.40
❑ 148 Marcus Pollard	.15	.40
❑ 149 Tony Brackens	.15	.40
❑ 150 Chad Pennington	.25	.60
❑ 151 Kevin Faulk	.20	.50
❑ 152 Michael Lewis	.15	.40
❑ 153 Mark Bruener	.15	.40
❑ 154 Tim Dwight	.15	.40
❑ 155 Jerry Rice	.50	1.25
❑ 156 Trent Dilfer	.20	.50
❑ 157 Jon Ritchie	.15	.40
❑ 158 Michael Pittman	.15	.40
❑ 159 Lamar Gordon	.15	.40
❑ 160 Rod Gardner	.15	.40
❑ 161 Ken Dilger	.20	.50
❑ 162 Doug Johnson	.15	.40
❑ 163 Peter Boulware	.20	.50
❑ 164 Jevon Kearse	.20	.50
❑ 165 Julius Peppers	.25	.60
❑ 166 Chris Chandler	.20	.50
❑ 167 Lorenzo Neal	.20	.50
❑ 168 Kevin Johnson	.15	.40
❑ 169 Kevin Hardy	.15	.40
❑ 170 KaRon Coleman	.15	.40
❑ 171 James Stewart	.20	.50
❑ 172 Tony Fisher	.15	.40
❑ 173 Billy Miller	.15	.40
❑ 174 Phillip Crosby	.15	.40
❑ 175 Priest Holmes	.25	.60
❑ 176 Elvis Joseph	.15	.40
❑ 177 Bryan Gilmore	.15	.40
❑ 178 D'Wayne Bates	.15	.40
❑ 179 Quincy Carter	.15	.40
❑ 180 Joe Horn	.20	.50
❑ 181 Anthony Henry	.15	.40
❑ 182 Anthony Becht	.20	.50
❑ 183 Mike Peterson	.15	.40
❑ 184 James Thrash	.15	.40
❑ 185 Jerome Bettis	.25	.60
❑ 186 Marcellus Wiley	.15	.40
❑ 187 Tim Rattay	.15	.40
❑ 188 Maurice Morris	.15	.40
❑ 189 Jason Taylor	.20	.50
❑ 190 Keyshawn Johnson	.25	.60
❑ 191 John Simon	.15	.40
❑ 192 Fred Smoot	.15	.40
❑ 193 Wendell Bryant	.15	.40
❑ 194 Brandon Stokley	.20	.50
❑ 195 Kurt Warner	.25	.60
❑ 196 Steve Smith	.25	.60
❑ 197 Dez White	.15	.40
❑ 198 Jim Miller	.20	.50
❑ 199 Robert Griffith	.15	.40
❑ 200 Michael Vick	.25	.60
❑ 201 Antonio Bryant	.25	.60
❑ 202 Laveranues Coles	.20	.50
❑ 203 Kalimba Edwards	.15	.40
❑ 204 Bubba Franks	.20	.50
❑ 205 David Carr	.25	.60
❑ 206 Dwight Freeney	.20	.50
❑ 207 Eric Johnson	.20	.50
❑ 208 Reggie Tongue	.15	.40
❑ 209 Cam Cleeland	.15	.40
❑ 210 Michael Bennett	.20	.50
❑ 211 Antowain Smith	.20	.50
❑ 212 Warren Sapp	.20	.50
❑ 213 Ike Hilliard	.20	.50
❑ 214 Olandis Gary	.20	.50
❑ 215 Tim Brown	.25	.60
❑ 216 Kevin Dyson	.20	.50
❑ 217 Eddie Kennison	.15	.40
❑ 218 Junior Seau	.25	.60
❑ 219 Donnie Edwards	.15	.40
❑ 220 Shaun Alexander	.25	.60
❑ 221 Terrence Wilkins	.15	.40
❑ 222 Garrison Hearst	.20	.50
❑ 223 Keith Bulluck	.15	.40
❑ 224 Zeron Flemister	.15	.40
❑ 225 Jake Plummer	.20	.50
❑ 226 Chad Johnson	.25	.60
❑ 227 Travis Taylor	.15	.40
❑ 228 Josh Reed	.15	.40
❑ 229 James Farrior	.20	.50
❑ 230 Marty Booker	.20	.50
❑ 231 Todd Pinkston	.15	.40
❑ 232 Dennis Northcutt	.15	.40
❑ 233 Troy Hambrick	.15	.40
❑ 234 Roland Williams	.15	.40
❑ 235 Bill Schroeder	.15	.40
❑ 236 Javon Walker	.20	.50
❑ 237 Kevin Swayne	.15	.40
❑ 238 Dominic Rhodes	.20	.50

Card	Low	High
239 David Garrard	.25	.60
240 Mike Maslowski RC	.15	.40
241 Travis Minor	.15	.40
242 Terry Glenn	.20	.50
243 Deion Branch	.20	.50
244 Adrian Peterson	.15	.40
245 Tiki Barber	.25	.60
246 Ray Lewis	.25	.60
247 Marques Tuiasosopo	.15	.40
248 Chad Lewis	.20	.50
249 Takeo Spikes	.15	.40
250 LaDainian Tomlinson	.30	.75
251 Stephen Davis	.20	.50
252 Koren Robinson	.20	.50
253 Daylon McCutcheon	.15	.40
254 Rob Johnson	.20	.50
255 Donovan McNabb	.25	.60
256 Derrius Thompson	.15	.40
257 Marcel Shipp	.15	.40
258 Keith Brooking	.20	.50
259 Chris McAlister	.20	.50
260 Eric Moulds	.20	.50
261 Amos Zereoue	.15	.40
262 Drew Brees	.25	.60
263 Jon Kitna	.20	.50
264 Brad Johnson	.20	.50
265 Emmitt Smith	.60	1.50
266 Trevor Pryce	.20	.50
267 Mike McMahon	.15	.40
268 Patrick Ramsey	.20	.50
269 Jonathan Wells	.15	.40
270 Mark Brunell	.20	.50
271 Marc Boerigter	.15	.40
272 Rob Konrad	.15	.40
273 Derrick Alexander	.15	.40
274 Joey Galloway	.20	.50
275 Peyton Manning	.50	1.25
276 Najeh Davenport	.20	.50
277 Jesse Palmer	.15	.40
278 LaMont Jordan	.20	.50
279 Ernie Conwell	.15	.40
280 Hines Ward	.25	.60
281 Freddie Mitchell	.20	.50
282 Curtis Conway	.15	.40
283 Cedrick Wilson	.15	.40
284 Troy Brown	.20	.50
285 Torry Holt	.25	.60
286 Mike Alstott	.25	.60
287 Frank Wycheck	.15	.40
288 Jeremiah Trotter	.20	.50
289 Tyrone Wheatley	.20	.50
290 David Boston	.15	.40
291 Jay Fiedler	.20	.50
292 Troy Walters	.15	.40
293 Warrick Holdman	.15	.40
294 Peter Warrick	.20	.50
295 Tim Couch	.15	.40
296 Aaron Glenn	.15	.40
297 Deuce McAllister	.25	.60
298 Michael Strahan	.20	.50
299 Tom Brady	.60	1.50
300 Brett Favre	.60	1.50
301 Isaac Bruce	.25	.60
302 Jimmy Smith	.20	.50
303 Dante Hall	.20	.50
304 James McKnight	.15	.40
305 Daunte Culpepper	.25	.60
306 Lawyer Milloy	.20	.50
307 Jerome Pathon	.15	.40
308 Steve McNair	.25	.60
309 Vinny Testaverde	.20	.50
310 Tommy Maddox	.20	.50
311 Amani Toomer	.20	.50
312 Aaron Brooks	.20	.50
313 Gus Frerotte	.20	.50
314 Kevan Barlow	.15	.40
315 Matt Hasselbeck	.20	.50
316 Clinton Portis	.30	.75
317 Keenan McCardell	.20	.50
318 Zach Thomas	.25	.60
319 Curtis Martin	.25	.60
320 Jamal Lewis	.25	.60
321 T.J. Duckett	.20	.50
322 Jerry Porter	.20	.50
323 Randy Moss	.25	.60
324 Rosevelt Colvin	.20	.50
325 Corey Dillon	.20	.50
326 Kelly Holcomb	.15	.40
327 Josh McCown	.20	.50
328 Ed McCaffrey	.20	.50
329 Mikhael Ricks	.15	.40
330 Donald Driver	.25	.60
331 Darling/Thompson/McKinnon	.15	.40
332 Hall/Carpenter/Buchanon	.15	.40
333 Thomas/Weaver/Gregg RC	.15	.40
334 Winfield/Wire/Clements	.20	.50
335 Morgan/Fields/Witherspoon	.20	.50
336 Brown/Robinson RC/Daniels	.15	.40
337 Powell RC/Thornton/Williams RC	.15	.40
338 Taylor RC/Little/Bentley	.15	.40
339 Ekuban/Ellis/Myers	.25	.60
340 Gard/Dalton RC/Berry RC	.30	.75
341 Green/Curry RC/Holmes	.15	.40
342 Hunt RC/KGB/Walker RC	.20	.50
343 Walker/Deloach RC/Payne	.15	.40
344 Bratzke/Washington/Morris	.15	.40
345 Henderson/Coleman/Stroud	.15	.40
346 Hicks/Browning RC/Sims	.15	.40
347 A.Ogunleye RC/Chester RC	.75	2.00
348 Robbins/Mixon/Johnstone	.15	.40
349 Phifer/Johnson/Bruschi	.25	.60
350 Grant/Chase RC/Howard	.20	.50
351 Short/Jones RC/Barrow	.15	.40
352 Jones/Lewis/Cowart	.15	.40
353 Barton/Parrella/Harris	.15	.40
354 Whiting/Simon/Walker	.20	.50
355 Smith/Hamp/von Oel	.40	1.00
356 Williams RC/Fisk/Johnson	.15	.40
357 Smith/Ulbrich/Peterson	.15	.40
358 Cochran RC/Eaton/Randle	.20	.50
359 Lewis/Wistrom/Little	.15	.40
360 Rudd/Spires/Quarles RC	.15	.40
361 Haynesworth/Carter/Smith	.25	.60
362 Smith/Armstead/Upshaw	.15	.40
363 Ad.Wilson/Dex.Jackson RC	.30	.75
364 F.Wakefield/K.Vanden	.15	.40
365 K.Kasper/J.McAddley	.15	.40
366 B.Smith/P.Kerney	.20	.50
367 M.Jenkins/T.Gaylor	.15	.40
368 C.Draft/M.Stewart	.15	.40
369 J.Hunter/R.Johnson	.15	.40
370 C.Fuller/E.Reed	.25	.60
371 A.Schobel/J.Posey RC	.20	.50
372 P.Williams/S.Adams	.20	.50
373 D.Grant/M.Minter	.15	.40
374 B.Buckner/K.Jenkins	.15	.40
375 R.Howard RC/T.Cousin RC	.15	.40
376 M.Brown/M.Green	.20	.50
377 J.Azumah/R.W.McQuarters	.15	.40
378 B.Simmons/S.Foley	.15	.40
379 A.Hawkins/J.Burris	.15	.40
380 Jo.Armour RC/M.Manuel	.15	.40
381 G.Warren/O.Roye	.15	.40
382 C.Brown/K.Lang	.15	.40
383 D.Ross/M.Edwards	.15	.40
384 A.Singleton RC/D.Nguyen	.15	.40
385 A.Wilson/J.Mobley	.15	.40
386 D.O'Neal/K.Kennedy	.15	.40
387 L.Elliss/S.Rogers	.15	.40
388 C.Cash/D.Bly	.15	.40
389 B.Walker/C.Harris	.15	.40
390 H.Navies RC/N.Diggs	.15	.40
391 A.Harris/M.McKenzie	.20	.50
392 C.Clemons/J.Foreman	.15	.40
393 E.Brown/M.Stevens	.15	.40
394 B.Scioli/L.Tripplett	.15	.40
395 D.Macklin/W.Harris	.15	.40
396 A.Ayodele/H.Douglas	.20	.50
397 F.Bryant/J.Craft RC	.15	.40
398 D.Darius/M.McCree	.15	.40
399 S.Fujita/S.Barber	.15	.40
400 E.Warfield RC/W.Bartee	.20	.50
401 G.Wesley/J.Woods	.15	.40
402 P.Surtain/S.Madison	.20	.50
403 B.Marion/S.Knight	.15	.40
404 G.Biekert/H.Crockett	.15	.40
405 C.Claiborne/C.Hovan	.20	.50
406 C.Chavous/K.Irvin	.15	.40
407 C.Fauria/D.Graham	.15	.40
408 O.Smith/R.Harrison	.20	.50
409 A.Pleasant/R.Seymour	.20	.50
410 D.Smith/S.Hodge	.15	.40
411 A.Ambrose/D.Carter	.15	.40
412 M.Mitchell/D.Rodgers	.15	.40
413 W.Allen/W.Peterson	.20	.50
414 C.Griffin/K.Hamilton	.15	.40
415 O.Stoutmire/S.Williams	.15	.40
416 A.Beasley/D.Abraham	.20	.50
417 J.McGraw/S.Games	.15	.40
418 C.Woodson/P.Buchanon	.20	.50
419 T.Bryant/T.Armstrong	.15	.40
420 B.Taylor/T.Vincent	.20	.50
421 C.Emmons/N.Wayne	.15	.40
422 B.Alexander/C.Hope	.15	.40
423 J.Porter/K.Bell	.25	.60
424 C.Scott/D.Washington	.15	.40
425 B.Leber/R.McNeil	.15	.40
426 Q.Jammer/T.Cody	.15	.40
427 A.Plummer/J.Webster	.15	.40
428 T.Parrish/Z.Bronson	.15	.40
429 I.Mili/J.Stevens	.20	.50
430 K.Lucas/S.Springs	.15	.40
431 C.Brown/O.Huff	.15	.40
432 J.Duncan/T.Polley	.15	.40
433 A.Williams/T.Fisher	.20	.50
434 B.Kelly/R.Barber	.20	.50
435 A.Stecker/K.Williams	.15	.40
436 D.Bennett/J.McCareins	.20	.50
437 L.Schulters/T.Williams	.15	.40
438 A.Dyson/S.Rolle	.20	.50
439 I.Ohalete/M.Bowen	.15	.40
440 B.Noble/D.Wilkinson	.20	.50
441 Charles Rogers RC	.40	1.00
442 Jimmy Kennedy RC	.40	1.00
443 Kelley Washington RC	.40	1.00
444 Trent Smith RC	.40	1.00
445 Rashean Mathis RC	.40	1.00
446 Brian St.Pierre RC	.50	1.25
447 Bethel Johnson RC	.40	1.00
448 Alonzo Jackson RC	.30	.75
449 Arnaz Battle RC	.50	1.25
450 Carson Palmer RC	2.00	5.00
451 Michael Haynes RC	.30	.75
452 LaBrandon Toefield RC	.40	1.00
453 Earnest Graham RC	.50	1.25
454 Walter Young RC	.30	.75
455 Terry Pierce RC	.30	.75
456 Talman Gardner RC	.30	.75
457 J.T. Wall RC	.30	.75
458 DeWayne Robertson RC	.40	1.00
459 Bradie James RC	.50	1.25
460 Andre Johnson RC	1.00	2.50
461 Bobby Wade RC	.40	1.00
462 Chris Davis RC	.40	1.00
463 Kliff Kingsbury RC	.40	1.00
464 Osi Umenyiora RC	.75	2.00
465 Domanick Davis RC	.50	1.25
466 Sam Aiken RC	.50	1.25
467 Ty Warren RC	.50	1.25
468 Terence Newman RC	.60	1.50
469 Zuriel Smith RC	.30	.75
470 Willis McGahee RC	1.00	2.50
471 David Kircus RC	.50	1.25
472 Billy McMullen RC	.30	.75
473 Antwoine Sanders RC	.30	.75
474 Adrian Madise RC	.30	.75
475 Byron Leftwich RC	.60	1.50
476 Justin Gage RC	.50	1.25
477 Jason Witten RC	1.25	3.00
478 Lee Suggs RC	.40	1.00
479 Kareem Kelly RC	.30	.75
480 Rex Grossman RC	.50	1.25
481 Nate Burleson RC	.40	1.00
482 Chris Brown RC	.50	1.25
483 Julian Battle RC	.40	1.00
484 Carl Ford RC	.30	.75
485 Angelo Crowell RC	.40	1.00
486 Bennie Joppru RC	.30	.75
487 Aaron Walker RC	.40	1.00
488 Brandon Green RC	.30	.75
489 L.J. Smith RC	.50	1.25
490 Ken Dorsey RC	.40	1.00
491 Eugene Wilson RC	.50	1.25
492 Chaun Thompson RC	.30	.75
493 Kevin Curtis RC	.50	1.25
494 Marcus Trufant RC	.50	1.25
495 Andrew Williams RC	.30	.75
496 Visanthe Shiancoe RC	.50	1.25
497 Terrence Edwards RC	.30	.75
498 Rien Long RC	.30	.75
499 Nick Barnett RC	.50	1.25
500 Larry Johnson RC	.60	1.50
501 Ken Hamlin RC	.50	1.25
502 Johnathan Sullivan RC	.30	.75

Card	Low	High
❑ 503 Jeremi Johnson RC	.30	.75
❑ 504 William Joseph RC	.30	.75
❑ 505 Boss Bailey RC	.40	1.00
❑ 506 Anquan Boldin RC	1.25	3.00
❑ 507 Dave Ragone RC	.30	.75
❑ 508 DeJuan Groce RC	.50	1.25
❑ 509 Rashad Moore RC	.30	.75
❑ 510 Mike Doss RC	.50	1.25
❑ 511 Kenny Peterson RC	.40	1.00
❑ 512 Justin Griffith RC	.40	1.00
❑ 513 Jordan Gross RC	.30	.75
❑ 514 Terrence Holt RC	.40	1.00
❑ 515 Seneca Wallace RC	.50	1.25
❑ 516 Ovie Mughelli RC	.30	.75
❑ 517 Jerome McDougle RC	.30	.75
❑ 518 Kevin Williams RC	.50	1.25
❑ 519 Musa Smith RC	.40	1.00
❑ 520 Teyo Johnson RC	.40	1.00
❑ 521 Victor Hobson RC	.30	.75
❑ 522 Cory Redding RC	.40	1.00
❑ 523 Cecil Sapp RC	.30	.75
❑ 524 Brandon Lloyd RC	.50	1.25
❑ 525 Chris Simms RC	.50	1.25
❑ 526 Artose Pinner RC	.30	.75
❑ 527 DeWayne White RC	.30	.75
❑ 528 Doug Gabriel RC	.40	1.00
❑ 529 Calvin Pace RC	.40	1.00
❑ 530 Onterrio Smith RC	.40	1.00
❑ 531 Terrell Suggs RC	.60	1.50
❑ 532 Ronald Bellamy RC	.40	1.00
❑ 533 Jimmy Wilkerson RC	.40	1.00
❑ 534 Travis Anglin RC	.30	.75
❑ 535 Tyrone Calico RC	.40	1.00
❑ 536 Keenan Howry RC	.30	.75
❑ 537 Gibran Hamdan RC	.30	.75
❑ 538 Bryant Johnson RC	.50	1.25
❑ 539 Brad Banks RC	.40	1.00
❑ 540 Justin Fargas RC	.50	1.25
❑ 541 B.J. Askew RC	.40	1.00
❑ 542 J.R. Tolver RC	.40	1.00
❑ 543 Tully Banta-Cain RC	.50	1.25
❑ 544 Shaun McDonald RC	.50	1.25
❑ 545 Taylor Jacobs RC	.40	1.00
❑ 546 Ricky Manning RC	.40	1.00
❑ 547 Dallas Clark RC	1.00	2.50
❑ 548 Juston Wood RC	.30	.75
❑ 549 Andre Woolfolk RC	.40	1.00
❑ 550 Kyle Boller RC	.50	1.25
❑ CL1 Checklist Card 1	.02	.10
❑ CL2 Checklist Card 2	.02	.10
❑ CL3 Checklist Card 3	.02	.10
❑ CL4 Checklist Card 4	.02	.10

2004 Topps Total

Card	Low	High
❑ COMPLETE SET (440)	40.00	80.00
❑ 1 Donovan McNabb	.30	.75
❑ 2 Zach Thomas	.30	.75
❑ 3 Randy Moss	.30	.75
❑ 4 Kerry Collins	.25	.60
❑ 5 Hines Ward	.30	.75
❑ 6 Tyrone Calico	.25	.60
❑ 7 Patrick Ramsey	.25	.60
❑ 8 Jeff Garcia	.30	.75
❑ 9 Aveion Cason	.20	.50
❑ 10 Stephen Davis	.25	.60
❑ 11 Marcel Shipp	.30	.75
❑ 12 T.J. Duckett	.25	.60
❑ 13 Chris McAlister	.20	.50
❑ 14 Peter Warrick	.25	.60
❑ 15 Ahman Green	.30	.75
❑ 16 Deion Branch	.25	.60
❑ 17 David Boston	.20	.50
❑ 18 Wayne Chrebet	.25	.60
❑ 19 Michael Strahan	.25	.60
❑ 20 Amaz Battle	.25	.60
❑ 21 Darrell Jackson	.25	.60
❑ 22 Chris Chandler	.25	.60
❑ 23 Charlie Garner	.25	.60
❑ 24 James Thrash	.20	.50
❑ 25 LaDainian Tomlinson	.40	1.00
❑ 26 Jerry Porter	.25	.60
❑ 27 Jerome Pathon	.20	.50
❑ 28 Jerome Bettis	.30	.75
❑ 29 Eddie George	.25	.60
❑ 30 Jamal Lewis	.25	.60
❑ 31 Ricky Proehl	.25	.60
❑ 32 Josh Reed	.30	.75
❑ 33 David Terrell	.20	.50
❑ 34 Antonio Bryant	.30	.75
❑ 35 Domanick Davis	.25	.60
❑ 36 Artose Pinner	.20	.50
❑ 37 Jed Weaver	.20	.50
❑ 38 Johnnie Morton	.25	.60
❑ 39 Troy Edwards	.20	.50
❑ 40 Marvin Harrison	.30	.75
❑ 41 Chris Hovan	.20	.50
❑ 42 Boo Williams	.20	.50
❑ 43 Ike Hilliard	.25	.60
❑ 44 Sam Cowart	.20	.50
❑ 45 Shaun Alexander	.30	.75
❑ 46 Freddie Mitchell	.20	.50
❑ 47 Garrison Hearst	.25	.60
❑ 48 Joe Jurevicius	.20	.50
❑ 49 Freddie Jones	.20	.50
❑ 50 Michael Vick	.30	.75
❑ 51 Mike Rucker	.20	.50
❑ 52 Carson Palmer	.40	1.00
❑ 53 Az-Zahir Hakim	.20	.50
❑ 54 Billy Miller	.20	.50
❑ 55 Chad Pennington	.30	.75
❑ 56 Charles Woodson	.30	.75
❑ 57 Andre Carter	.20	.50
❑ 58 Maurice Morris	.25	.60
❑ 59 Leonard Little	.20	.50
❑ 60 Travis Henry	.25	.60
❑ 61 Thomas Jones	.25	.60
❑ 62 Dennis Northcutt	.20	.50
❑ 63 Quentin Griffin	.25	.60
❑ 64 Joey Harrington	.25	.60
❑ 65 Edgerrin James	.30	.75
❑ 66 Cortez Hankton	.20	.50
❑ 67 Jason Taylor	.30	.75
❑ 68 Eddie Kennison	.25	.60
❑ 69 Ty Law	.25	.60
❑ 70 Aaron Brooks	.25	.60
❑ 71 Antonio Gates	.30	.75
❑ 72 Antwaan Randle El	.25	.60
❑ 73 Kevan Barlow	.25	.60
❑ 74 Chris Brown	.25	.60
❑ 75 Clinton Portis	.30	.75
❑ 76 Rod Gardner	.20	.50
❑ 77 Isaac Bruce	.25	.60
❑ 78 Mike Alstott	.25	.60
❑ 79 Brian Westbrook	.30	.75
❑ 80 Amani Toomer	.25	.60
❑ 81 Justin Fargas	.25	.60
❑ 82 Michael Bennett	.25	.60
❑ 83 Dante Hall	.25	.60
❑ 84 Marcus Pollard	.20	.50
❑ 85 Fred Taylor	.25	.60
❑ 86 Tai Streets	.20	.50
❑ 87 Robert Ferguson	.20	.50
❑ 88 Roy Williams S	.25	.60
❑ 89 Lee Suggs	.30	.75
❑ 90 Chad Johnson	.25	.60
❑ 91 DeShaun Foster	.25	.60
❑ 92 Alge Crumpler	.25	.60
❑ 93 Travis Taylor	.20	.50
❑ 94 London Fletcher	.20	.50
❑ 95 Priest Holmes	.30	.75
❑ 96 A.J. Feeley	.25	.60
❑ 97 Kevin Faulk	.25	.60
❑ 98 Shaun Ellis	.20	.50
❑ 99 Tim Dwight	.25	.60
❑ 100 Peyton Manning	.60	1.50
❑ 101 Dane Looker	.25	.60
❑ 102 Mark Brunell	.25	.60
❑ 103 Bryant Johnson	.25	.60
❑ 104 Kelley Washington	.20	.50
❑ 105 Rex Grossman	.30	.75
❑ 106 William Green	.20	.50
❑ 107 Keyshawn Johnson	.25	.60
❑ 108 Trevor Pryce	.20	.50
❑ 109 Donald Driver	.30	.75
❑ 110 David Carr	.25	.60
❑ 111 Marcus Robinson	.25	.60
❑ 112 Justin McCareins	.20	.50
❑ 113 Tim Brown	.30	.75
❑ 114 James Farrior	.20	.50
❑ 115 Deuce McAllister	.30	.75
❑ 116 Simeon Rice	.25	.60
❑ 117 Koren Robinson	.30	.75
❑ 118 Kassim Osgood	.20	.50
❑ 119 Tim Rattay	.20	.50
❑ 120 Laveranues Coles	.25	.60
❑ 121 Brian Finneran	.20	.50
❑ 122 Todd Heap	.25	.60
❑ 123 Bobby Shaw	.20	.50
❑ 124 Anthony Thomas	.25	.60
❑ 125 Brett Favre	.75	2.00
❑ 126 Dwight Freeney	.30	.75
❑ 127 Randy McMichael	.20	.50
❑ 128 David Givens	.25	.60
❑ 129 Rich Gannon	.25	.60
❑ 130 Tiki Barber	.30	.75
❑ 131 Terrell Owens	.30	.75
❑ 132 Drew Bennett	.25	.60
❑ 133 Shawn Bryson	.20	.50
❑ 134 Jabar Gaffney	.25	.60
❑ 135 Jake Delhomme	.25	.60
❑ 136 Warrick Dunn	.25	.60
❑ 137 Brandon Lloyd	.20	.50
❑ 138 Brad Johnson	.25	.60
❑ 139 Jon Kitna	.25	.60
❑ 140 Marshall Faulk	.30	.75
❑ 141 Javon Walker	.25	.60
❑ 142 Nate Burleson	.25	.60
❑ 143 Jimmy Smith	.25	.60
❑ 144 Adewale Ogunleye	.25	.60
❑ 145 Trent Green	.25	.60
❑ 146 Richard Seymour	.20	.50
❑ 147 Donte' Stallworth	.25	.60
❑ 148 Curtis Martin	.30	.75
❑ 149 Todd Pinkston	.20	.50
❑ 150 Steve McNair	.30	.75
❑ 151 Josh McCown	.25	.60
❑ 152 Ray Lewis	.30	.75
❑ 153 Muhsin Muhammad	.25	.60
❑ 154 Quincy Morgan	.20	.50
❑ 155 Jake Plummer	.25	.60
❑ 156 Jason Witten	.30	.75
❑ 157 Dallas Clark	.30	.75
❑ 158 Onterrio Smith	.20	.50
❑ 159 Jeremy Shockey	.25	.60
❑ 160 Ricky Williams	.30	.75
❑ 161 Jevon Kearse	.25	.60
❑ 162 Plaxico Burress	.25	.60
❑ 163 Drew Brees	.30	.75
❑ 164 Bobby Engram	.25	.60
❑ 165 Torry Holt	.30	.75
❑ 166 Ladell Betts	.25	.60
❑ 167 Kelly Holcomb	.25	.60
❑ 168 Vinny Testaverde	.25	.60
❑ 169 Marty Booker	.25	.60
❑ 170 Rudi Johnson	.25	.60
❑ 171 Andra Davis	.20	.50
❑ 172 Kurt Warner	.30	.75
❑ 173 Troy Brown	.25	.60
❑ 174 Jerry Rice	.60	1.50
❑ 175 Daunte Culpepper	.30	.75
❑ 176 Darren Sharper	.25	.60
❑ 177 Charles Rogers	.25	.60
❑ 178 Ashley Lelie	.25	.60
❑ 179 Correll Buckhalter	.25	.60
❑ 180 Anquan Boldin	.30	.75
❑ 181 Terrell Suggs	.20	.50
❑ 182 Reggie Wayne	.25	.60
❑ 183 Duce Staley	.25	.60
❑ 184 Donnie Edwards	.25	.60
❑ 185 Joe Horn	.25	.60
❑ 186 LaVar Arrington	.25	.60
❑ 187 Keenan McCardell	.20	.50
❑ 188 Cedrick Wilson	.20	.50
❑ 189 Bubba Franks	.25	.60
❑ 190 Santana Moss	.25	.60
❑ 191 Peerless Price	.25	.60
❑ 192 Kyle Boller	.25	.60
❑ 193 Julius Peppers	.25	.60
❑ 194 Drew Bledsoe	.30	.75
❑ 195 Marc Bulger	.25	.60

	Card	Low	High
❑	196 Brian Urlacher	.30	.75
❑	197 Andre' Davis	.20	.50
❑	198 Terry Glenn	.25	.60
❑	199 Champ Bailey	.25	.60
❑	200 Tom Brady	.75	2.00
❑	201 Chris Chambers	.25	.60
❑	202 Tommy Maddox	.25	.60
❑	203 Derrick Brooks	.25	.60
❑	204 Corey Dillon	.25	.60
❑	205 Matt Hasselbeck	.30	.75
❑	206 Keith Brooking	.20	.50
❑	207 Steve Smith	.30	.75
❑	208 Tony Gonzalez	.30	.75
❑	209 Joey Galloway	.25	.60
❑	210 Derrick Mason	.25	.60
❑	211 Quincy Carter	.20	.50
❑	212 Rod Smith	.25	.60
❑	213 Andre Johnson	.30	.75
❑	214 Rod Woodson	.25	.60
❑	215 Byron Leftwich	.30	.75
❑	216 Kevin Dyson	.20	.50
❑	217 Keith Bulluck	.20	.50
❑	218 Eric Moulds	.25	.60
❑	219 Jamie Sharper	.20	.50
❑	220 Takeo Spikes	.20	.50
❑	221 C.Pace/F.Wakefield	.20	.50
❑	222 B.Smith/P.Kerney	.25	.60
❑	223 E.Reed/G.Baxter	.25	.60
❑	224 A.Schobel/J.Posey	.20	.50
❑	225 K.Jenkins/B.Buckner	.25	.60
❑	226 J.Smith/D.Clemons	.20	.50
❑	227 M.Haynes/B.Robinson	.20	.50
❑	228 C.Brown/G.Warren	.25	.60
❑	229 T.Newman/D.Woodson	.25	.60
❑	230 R.Johnson/M.Fatafehi	.20	.50
❑	231 R.Porcher/J.Hall RC	.25	.60
❑	232 K.Gbaja-Biamila/C.Hunt	.25	.60
❑	233 A.Glenn/M.Coleman	.25	.60
❑	234 N.Harper RC/J.Jefferson	.25	.60
❑	235 H.Douglas/T.Brackens	.20	.50
❑	236 V.Holliday/E.Hicks	.20	.50
❑	237 S.Knight/A.Freeman	.20	.50
❑	238 S.Martin/N.Rogers	.20	.50
❑	239 R.Colvin/W.McGinest	.25	.60
❑	240 O.Stoutmire/S.Williams	.20	.50
❑	241 E.Barton/V.Hobson	.20	.50
❑	242 W.Sapp/T.Washington	.25	.60
❑	243 C.Simon/D.Walker	.25	.60
❑	244 T.Polamalu/M.Logan	1.00	2.50
❑	245 J.Williams/A.Dingle RC	.20	.50
❑	246 B.Young/B.Whiting	.25	.60
❑	247 K.Hamlin/D.Robinson RC	.20	.50
❑	248 D.Lewis/R.Pickett	.20	.50
❑	249 A.McFarland/G.Spires	.20	.50
❑	250 A.Haynesworth/R.Long	.20	.50
❑	251 I.Ohalete/M.Bowen	.20	.50
❑	252 B.Berry/K.King	.25	.60
❑	253 E.Johnson/E.Jasper	.20	.50
❑	254 C.Tillman/J.Azumah	.25	.60
❑	255 M.Wiley/L.Glover	.25	.60
❑	256 S.Rogers/D.Wilkinson	.25	.60
❑	257 G.Walker/R.Smith	.20	.50
❑	258 M.Doss/I.Bashir	.25	.60
❑	259 M.Stroud/J.Henderson	.20	.50
❑	260 R.Sims/J.Browning	.25	.60
❑	261 J.Seau/M.Greenwood	.30	.75
❑	262 K.Williams/K.Mixon	.20	.50
❑	263 T.Warren/K.Traylor	.20	.50
❑	264 W.Allen/W.Peterson	.20	.50
❑	265 D.Barrett/R.Tongue	.20	.50
❑	266 P.Buchanon/D.Gibson	.25	.60
❑	267 L.Sheppard/S.Brown	.20	.50
❑	268 B.Taylor/M.Trufant	.25	.60
❑	269 M.Washington/M.Barrow	.20	.50
❑	270 C.Draft/M.Stewart	.20	.50
❑	271 M.Brown/M.Green	.25	.60
❑	272 E.Brown/M.McCree	.20	.50
❑	273 P.Surtain/S.Madison	.20	.50
❑	274 B.Dawkins/M.Lewis	.25	.60
❑	275 S.Springs/F.Smoot	.20	.50
❑	276 McKinnon/Fisher/Thompson	.20	.50
❑	277 Webster/McBride RC/Scott	.20	.50
❑	278 Boulware/Hartwell/Thomas	.25	.60
❑	279 Vincent/Milloy/Clements	.25	.60
❑	280 Witherspoon/Morgan/Fields	.25	.60
❑	281 Simmons/Hardy/Webster	.25	.60
❑	282 Odom RC/Brown/Briggs	1.00	2.50
❑	283 Holdman/Thompson/Lang	.20	.50
❑	284 Nguyen/Coakley/Singleton	.20	.50
❑	285 Wilson/Spragan RC/Holland	.20	.50
❑	286 Holmes/J.Davis RC/Bailey	.20	.50
❑	287 Barnett/Diggs/Navies	.25	.60
❑	288 Foreman/Peek/Wong	.20	.50
❑	289 Brock RC/Reagor/Tripplett	.25	.60
❑	290 Ayodele/Favors/Peterson	.20	.50
❑	291 Barber/Maslowsk/Fujita	.20	.50
❑	292 Claiborne/Henderson/Nattiel	.25	.60
❑	293 Bruschi/Phifer/Vrabel	.30	.75
❑	294 Grant/Howard/Sullivan	.20	.50
❑	295 Robbins/Joseph/Umenyiora	.20	.50
❑	296 Abra/Rober/Fergus.RC	.50	1.25
❑	297 Harris/Rudd/Brayton	.25	.60
❑	298 Simoneau/Wayne/Jones	.20	.50
❑	299 Porter/Bell/Haggans RC	.40	1.00
❑	300 Jammer/Davis/Florence	.20	.50
❑	301 Peterson/Ulbrich/Smith	.25	.60
❑	302 Simmons/Huff/Brown	.20	.50
❑	303 Tinoisamoa/Polley/Thomas	.20	.50
❑	304 Quarles/Wyms/Nece	.20	.50
❑	305 Carter/Hall/Simon	.25	.60
❑	306 Griffin/Daniels/Wynn	.20	.50
❑	307 Jackson/Wilson/Macklin	.20	.50
❑	308 Gregg/Douglas/Weaver	.20	.50
❑	309 Williams/Denney/Adams	.25	.60
❑	310 Hawkins/Minter/Manning	.20	.50
❑	311 James/Herring/Beckett	.20	.50
❑	312 Griffith/Little/Henry	.20	.50
❑	313 Lynch/Ferg.RC/Hern.RC	.25	.60
❑	314 Bly/Marion/Bryant	.20	.50
❑	315 Harris/Roman/McKenzie	.25	.60
❑	316 Thorn/Morris/Brackett RC	.30	.75
❑	317 Mathis/Darius/Bolden RC	.20	.50
❑	318 Warfield/Wesley/Woods	.20	.50
❑	319 Winfield/Russell RC/Chavous	.25	.60
❑	320 Harrison/Wilson/Poole	.25	.60
❑	321 Rodgers/Ruff/Hodge	.20	.50
❑	322 Green/Greisen/Emmons	.20	.50
❑	323 Von Oelhoffen/Smith/Hampton	.20	.50
❑	324 Godfrey/Foley/Leber	.20	.50
❑	325 Plummer/Parrish/Rumph	.20	.50
❑	326 Okeafor/Wistrom/Moore	.25	.60
❑	327 Archuleta/Williams/Butler	.20	.50
❑	328 Barber/Smith/Phillips	.25	.60
❑	329 Dyson/Schulters/Williams	.20	.50
❑	330 Thomas/Bellamy/Jones	.20	.50
❑	331 Philip Rivers RC	2.50	6.00
❑	332 Dwan Edwards RC	.40	1.00
❑	333 Ben Watson RC	.60	1.50
❑	334 Karlos Dansby RC	.60	1.50
❑	335 Cedric Cobbs RC	.50	1.25
❑	336 Chris Perry RC	.60	1.50
❑	337 Darius Watts RC	.50	1.25
❑	338 Ricardo Colclough RC	.60	1.50
❑	339 Derrick Hamilton RC	.40	1.00
❑	340 Devard Darling RC	.50	1.25
❑	341 Daryl Smith RC	.50	1.25
❑	342 Luke McCown RC	.60	1.50
❑	343 Dunta Robinson RC	.50	1.25
❑	344 Keith Smith RC	.40	1.00
❑	345 Ben Hartsock RC	.50	1.25
❑	346 J.P. Losman RC	.60	1.50
❑	347 Chris Cooley RC	.60	1.50
❑	348 Keary Colbert RC	.50	1.25
❑	349 Tommie Harris RC	.60	1.50
❑	350 Eli Manning RC	4.00	10.00
❑	351 Kevin Jones RC	.60	1.50
❑	352 Lee Evans RC	.75	2.00
❑	353 D.J. Williams RC	.60	1.50
❑	354 Ben Troupe RC	.50	1.25
❑	355 Mewelde Moore RC	.60	1.50
❑	356 Michael Clayton RC	.60	1.50
❑	357 Michael Jenkins RC	.60	1.50
❑	358 Adimchinobe Echemandu RC	.50	1.25
❑	359 Rashaun Woods RC	.40	1.00
❑	360 Bernard Berrian RC	.60	1.50
❑	361 Carlos Francis RC	.40	1.00
❑	362 Roy Williams RC	.75	2.00
❑	363 Sean Taylor RC	.60	1.50
❑	364 Steven Jackson RC	1.50	4.00
❑	365 Tatum Bell RC	.60	1.50
❑	366 Jonathan Vilma RC	.60	1.50
❑	367 Derrick Strait RC	.50	1.25
❑	368 Andy Hall RC	.50	1.25
❑	369 Jason Babin RC	.50	1.25
❑	370 Will Smith RC	.60	1.50
❑	371 Kenechi Udeze RC	.60	1.50
❑	372 Vince Wilfork RC	.60	1.50
❑	373 Ahmad Carroll RC	.60	1.50
❑	374 Marquise Hill RC	.40	1.00
❑	375 Ben Roethlisberger RC	5.00	12.00
❑	376 Chris Gamble RC	.50	1.25
❑	377 Junior Siavii RC	.40	1.00
❑	378 Teddy Lehman RC	.50	1.25
❑	379 Antwan Odom RC	.60	1.50
❑	380 DeAngelo Hall RC	.60	1.50
❑	381 Nathan Vasher RC	.60	1.50
❑	382 B.J. Symons RC	.40	1.00
❑	383 Reggie Williams RC	.60	1.50
❑	384 Michael Boulware RC	.60	1.50
❑	385 Matt Schaub RC	1.50	4.00
❑	386 Sean Jones RC	.50	1.25
❑	387 Courtney Watson RC	.50	1.25
❑	388 Nathaniel Adibi RC	.40	1.00
❑	389 Devery Henderson RC	.60	1.50
❑	390 Greg Jones RC	.60	1.50
❑	391 Joey Thomas RC	.40	1.00
❑	392 Drew Carter RC	.60	1.50
❑	393 Julius Jones RC	.75	2.00
❑	394 Keyaron Fox RC	.50	1.25
❑	395 Darrion Scott RC	.50	1.25
❑	396 Rich Gardner RC	.50	1.25
❑	397 Jeff Smoker RC	.50	1.25
❑	398 Will Poole RC	.60	1.50
❑	399 Samie Parker RC	.50	1.25
❑	400 Larry Fitzgerald RC	2.00	5.00
❑	401 Jerricho Cotchery RC	.60	1.50
❑	402 Ernest Wilford RC	.50	1.25
❑	403 Johnnie Morant RC	.50	1.25
❑	404 Craig Krenzel RC	.60	1.50
❑	405 Michael Turner RC	1.50	4.00
❑	406 D.J. Hackett RC	.60	1.50
❑	407 P.K. Sam RC	.40	1.00
❑	408 Triandos Luke RC	.40	1.00
❑	409 Josh Harris RC	.40	1.00
❑	410 Drew Henson RC	.40	1.00
❑	411 John Navarre RC	.50	1.25
❑	412 Cody Pickett RC	.50	1.25
❑	413 Clarence Moore RC	.50	1.25
❑	414 Michael Gaines RC	.40	1.00
❑	415 Derek Abney RC	.40	1.00
❑	416 Dontarrious Thomas RC	.50	1.25
❑	417 Reggie Torbor RC	.40	1.00
❑	418 Ryan Krause RC	.40	1.00
❑	419 Travis LaBoy RC	.50	1.25
❑	420 Kellen Winslow RC	.75	2.00
❑	421 Keiwan Ratliff RC	.40	1.00
❑	422 Gilbert Gardner RC	.40	1.00
❑	423 Jamaar Taylor RC	.40	1.00
❑	424 Matt Ware RC	.60	1.50
❑	425 Stuart Schweigert RC	.50	1.25
❑	426 Marcus Tubbs RC	.40	1.00
❑	427 Brandon Chillar RC	.50	1.25
❑	428 Shawntae Spencer RC	.40	1.00
❑	429 Marquis Cooper RC	.60	1.50
❑	430 Derrick Ward RC	.60	1.50
❑	431 Tim Euhus RC	.40	1.00
❑	432 Patrick Crayton RC	.75	2.00
❑	433 Caleb Miller RC	.40	1.00
❑	434 Donnell Washington RC	.50	1.25
❑	435 Thomas Tapeh RC	.50	1.25
❑	436 Randy Starks RC	.40	1.00
❑	437 Sloan Thomas RC	.50	1.25
❑	438 Maurice Mann RC	.40	1.00
❑	439 Jim Sorgi RC	.60	1.50
❑	440 Nate Lawrie RC	.40	1.00

2005 Topps Total

	Item	Low	High
❑	COMPLETE SET (550)	30.00	80.00
❑	COMP.PACKERS TIN (20)	10.00	20.00
❑	COMP.STEELERS TIN (20)	10.00	20.00

Card	Low	High
1 Michael Vick	.30	.75
2 O.Kreutz/Q.Mitchell RC	.25	.60
3 Re.Williams/Garrard/T.Edwards	.30	.75
4 Terence Newman	.20	.50
5 D.Jolley/C.Baker	.20	.50
6 D.Clark/S.Will.RC/B.Hamilton	.20	.50
7 Terrell Owens	.30	.75
8 I.Ohalete/A.Wilson	.20	.50
9 G.Walker/Payne/Rob.Smith	.20	.50
10 Quentin Jammer	.20	.50
11 Ke.Smith/D.Bly	.20	.50
12 C.Taylor/Ogden/B.Sams	.25	.60
13 Torry Holt	.25	.60
14 W.Henderson/N.Davenport	.25	.60
15 J.Siavii/Hicks/J.Allen	.30	.75
16 Keith Bulluck	.20	.50
17 K.Irvin/C.Chavous	.20	.50
18 F.Jackson/A.Bryant/A.Davis	.25	.60
19 Michael Pittman	.20	.50
20 Vanderjagt/H.Smith RC	.20	.50
21 J.Winborn/Ulbrich/D.Smith	.20	.50
22 Reggie Wayne	.25	.60
23 S.Lechler/Janikowski	.20	.50
24 K.Mathis RC/J.Webster/B.Scott	.20	.50
25 Daunte Culpepper	.30	.75
26 W.Peterson/W.Allen	.20	.50
27 T.Walter/F.Adams/L.Allen	.25	.60
28 Tauscher/M.Flanagan/Clifton RC	.20	.50
29 Jerome Bettis	.30	.75
30 M.Brown/R.McQuarters	.20	.50
31 Andre Johnson	.25	.60
32 Toefield/G.Jones/Fuamatu-Ma'Afala	.20	.50
33 G.Lewis/B.McMullen	.25	.60
34 Kyle Boller	.25	.60
35 Kacyvenski/T.White RC/Bates	.20	.50
36 Chris Brown	.25	.60
37 J.Phillips/B.Kelly	.20	.50
38 Saturday RC/Diem RC/Ta.Glenn	.30	.75
39 Clinton Portis	.30	.75
40 M.Scifres/N.Kaeding	.20	.50
41 Ke.Williams/Udeze/Johnstone	.20	.50
42 Tony Parrish	.20	.50
43 D.Armstrong/J.Gaffney	.20	.50
44 F.Bryant/C.Cash/Te.Holt	.20	.50
45 Kerry Collins	.25	.60
46 M.Strong/M.Morris	.20	.50
47 Robertson/J.Abraham/S.Ellis	.20	.50
48 Darrell Jackson	.25	.60
49 P.Price/A.Rossum	.20	.50
50 A.Henry/N.Jones RC/Frazier RC	.20	.50
51 Steven Jackson	.40	1.00
52 R.Sims/J.Browning	.20	.50
53 Robbins/Umenyiora/W.Joseph	.30	.75
54 Billy Volek	.25	.60
55 A.Ayodele/Da.Smith	.20	.50
56 I.Scott RC/Odom/T.Johnson	.20	.50
57 Onterrio Smith	.20	.50
58 M.Stover/D.Zastudil RC	.20	.50
59 Hunt/Gbaja-Biamila/Kampman RC	.30	.75
60 Dante Hall	.25	.60
61 J.Peterson/B.Young	.20	.50
62 Hardwick/Olivea RC/Oben	.20	.50
63 Chad Pennington	.30	.75
64 D.Clark/A.Moorehead	.25	.60
65 B.Taylor/K.Richard RC	.20	.50
66 K.Walker/J.Wade RC	.20	.50
67 Jeremy Shockey	.30	.75
68 Daylon McCutcheon	.20	.50
69 Coakley/Claiborne/Tinoisamoa	.20	.50
70 Roy Williams WR	.30	.75
71 L.Schulters/Ta.Williams	.20	.50
72 S.Brown/Hood RC/Wynn	.30	.75
73 Sean Taylor	.25	.60
74 L.Little/B.Chillar	.20	.50
75 Boiman/R.Starks/Clauss RC	.20	.50
76 Lee Suggs	.25	.60
77 P.Crayton/T.Glenn	.30	.75
78 Dansby/Darling/G.Hayes	.20	.50
79 Nick Barnett	.25	.60
80 R.Coleman/A.Lake RC	.20	.50
81 Berrian/J.Gage/D.Clark	.25	.60
82 Dominic Rhodes	.25	.60
83 C.Moore/R.Hymes	.20	.50
84 Fraley RC/Runyan/T.Thomas	.20	.50
85 Philip Rivers	.30	.75
86 A.Harris/A.Carroll	.20	.50
87 B.Sanders/Doss/J.Jefferson	.50	1.25
88 Cesaire RC/Ja.Will/Dingle	.20	.50
89 Eric Moulds	.25	.60
90 P.Zellner RC/R.Davis	.20	.50
91 K.Wong/Babin/A.Peek	.20	.50
92 Tony Richardson	.20	.50
93 G.Wesley/J.Woods	.20	.50
94 Fabini/Goodwin RC/K.Mawae	.20	.50
95 Tatum Bell	.25	.60
96 K.Lewis RC/C.Emmons	.20	.50
97 J.Galloway/W.Heller	.25	.60
98 Tom Brady	.60	1.50
99 R.Babers/B.Walker	.20	.50
100 Mickens/McGraw/Buckley	.20	.50
101 Zach Thomas	.30	.75
102 Co.Brown RC/A.Weaver	.20	.50
103 A.Will/J.Butler/K.Garrett	.20	.50
104 Troy Polamalu	.40	1.00
105 W.Sapp/T.Washington	.25	.60
106 T.Johnson/Crockett/Morant	.20	.50
107 Chris McAlister	.20	.50
108 C.Stanley RC/K.Brown	.20	.50
109 Drew Henson	.20	.50
110 James Hall	.20	.50
111 S.Player/N.Rackers	.20	.50
112 D.Watts/A.Lelie	.20	.50
113 J.David/N.Harper	.20	.50
114 R.Curry/D.Gabriel	.25	.60
115 R.Colclough/W.Williams	.25	.60
116 C.Tillman/J.Azumah	.20	.50
117 M.Kemoeatu RC/Ad.Thomas	.30	.75
118 M.Roman/J.Thomas	.20	.50
119 D.Henderson/M.Lewis	.20	.50
120 M.Furrey/Manumaleuna	.30	.75
121 R.Mahe/C.Buckhalter	.25	.60
122 E.Kinney/T.Fleming	.20	.50
123 W.Dunn/T.Duckett	.25	.60
124 T.Euhus/M.Campbell	.20	.50
125 P.Hunter/A.Glenn	.20	.50
126 R.Tongue/D.Barrett	.20	.50
127 S.Morris/L.Gordon	.20	.50
128 R.Clark RC/S.Springs	.60	1.50
129 J.Miller/A.Vinatieri	.30	.75
130 E.Warfield/W.Bartee	.20	.50
131 Me.Moore/M.Bennett	.25	.60
132 N.Goings/B.Hoover	.20	.50
133 Q.Harris/D.Macklin	.20	.50
134 E.Drummond/R.Swinton	.20	.50
135 J.Fargas/A.Whitted	.25	.60
136 N.Clements/T.McGee RC	.25	.60
137 T.Hollings/J.Wells	.20	.50
138 D.Cooper RC/K.Thomas RC	.20	.50
139 P.Dawson/D.Frost RC	.20	.50
140 J.McCown/J.Navarre	.25	.60
141 G.Ellis/K.Coleman	.20	.50
142 G.Wilson/B.Alexander	.20	.50
143 A.Woolfolk/L.Thompson	.20	.50
144 E.Conwell/B.Williams	.20	.50
145 D.Akers/Di.Johnson RC	.20	.50
146 Hillenmeyer RC/L.Briggs	.50	1.25
147 R.Mathis RC/G.Brackett	.50	1.25
148 J.Rice/R.Alexander	.60	1.50
149 E.Coleman/D.Strait	.20	.50
150 J.Hartwig RC/B.Troupe	.20	.50
151 S.Davis/D.Florence	.20	.50
152 P.Buchanon/M.Coleman	.20	.50
153 S.Heiden/A.Shea	.20	.50
154 T.Spikes/L.Fletcher	.20	.50
155 T.Laboy/A.Odom	.20	.50
156 A.Toomer/M.Cloud	.25	.60
157 L.Tynes/C.Horn	.25	.60
158 N.Diggs/P.Lenon RC	.20	.50
159 R.Long/A.Haynesworth	.20	.50
160 B.Askew/J.Sowell	.20	.50
161 John Carney Mitch Berger	.20	.50
162 K.Campbell/J.Wiggins	.25	.60
163 Jerramy Stevens	.25	.60
164 Willis McGahee	.30	.75
165 Ed Reed	.25	.60
166 Muhsin Muhammad	.25	.60
167 Donovin Darius	.20	.50
168 E.J. Henderson	.20	.50
169 Tony Banks	.20	.50
170 Fred Taylor	.30	.75
171 Jeremiah Trotter	.20	.50
172 Adam Archuleta	.20	.50
173 Marcus Trufant	.25	.60
174 Steve McNair	.30	.75
175 Ben Roethlisberger	.75	2.00
176 Derrick Blaylock	.20	.50
177 Michael Strahan	.25	.60
178 Robert Gallery	.20	.50
179 Drew Brees	.30	.75
180 David Kircus	.20	.50
181 Robert Ferguson	.25	.60
182 Jim Sorgi	.20	.50
183 Alge Crumpler	.25	.60
184 DeShaun Foster	.25	.60
185 Reuben Droughns	.20	.50
186 Charles Grant	.20	.50
187 Jason Taylor	.25	.60
188 James Thrash	.25	.60
189 LaDainian Tomlinson	.40	1.00
190 Tim Rattay	.20	.50
191 Jeff Garcia	.25	.60
192 Jerricho Cotchery	.25	.60
193 Chris Simms	.25	.60
194 Jevon Kearse	.25	.60
195 Kyle Brady	.20	.50
196 Trent Green	.25	.60
197 Antoine Winfield	.25	.60
198 Deion Branch	.25	.60
199 Rudi Johnson	.25	.60
200 Lee Evans	.25	.60
201 Stephen Davis	.25	.60
202 Darnell Dockett	.20	.50
203 Kurt Warner	.30	.75
204 Quincy Morgan	.20	.50
205 Daimon Shelton	.20	.50
206 Champ Bailey	.25	.60
207 Jamal Lewis	.25	.60
208 Brett Favre	.75	2.00
209 Charles Woodson	.25	.60
210 Koren Robinson	.25	.60
211 Chris Chambers	.25	.60
212 Dave Ragone	.20	.50
213 Travis Minor	.20	.50
214 Simeon Rice	.20	.50
215 Tommy Maddox	.25	.60
216 Aaron Stecker	.20	.50
217 Dwight Freeney	.25	.60
218 Thomas Jones	.25	.60
219 Patrick Ramsey	.25	.60
220 Travis Taylor	.20	.50
221 Chris Weinke	.20	.50
222 Marc Bulger	.25	.60
223 James Farrior	.20	.50
224 Billy Miller	.20	.50
225 Mike Peterson	.20	.50
226 Eddie Kennison	.20	.50
227 Aaron Brooks	.20	.50
228 Plaxico Burress	.25	.60
229 Jerry Porter	.25	.60
230 Joey Harrington	.30	.75
231 Bubba Franks	.25	.60
232 Michael Jenkins	.25	.60
233 Larry Fitzgerald	.30	.75
234 Troy Vincent	.25	.60
235 Chad Johnson	.25	.60
236 Roy Williams S	.25	.60
237 Corey Dillon	.25	.60
238 Donovan McNabb	.30	.75
239 Marcus Robinson	.25	.60
240 Derrick Brooks	.25	.60
241 David Bowens RC	.20	.50
242 Renaldo Wynn	.20	.50
243 Kevan Barlow	.20	.50
244 Antonio Gates	.30	.75
245 Duce Staley	.25	.60
246 Ernest Wilford	.25	.60
247 Kevin Jones	.25	.60
248 Julius Peppers	.25	.60
249 Terrell Suggs	.25	.60
250 Bertrand Berry	.20	.50
251 Brian Simmons	.20	.50
252 Jake Plummer	.25	.60
253 Brian Urlacher	.30	.75
254 Justin McCareins	.20	.50
255 L.J. Smith	.25	.60
256 Matt Hasselbeck	.25	.60
257 Rashaun Woods	.20	.50
258 Rodney Harrison	.25	.60
259 Brandon Stokley	.20	.50
260 Tony Gonzalez	.25	.60
261 J.P. Losman	.25	.60
262 DeAngelo Hall	.25	.60
263 Jake Delhomme	.30	.75

❑ 264 Shaun Rogers .20 .50
❑ 265 Donald Driver .30 .75
❑ 266 Will Smith .20 .50
❑ 267 Brian Westbrook .30 .75
❑ 268 A.J. Feeley .20 .50
❑ 269 Marshall Faulk .30 .75
❑ 270 Marques Tuiasosopo .20 .50
❑ 271 Curtis Martin .30 .75
❑ 272 Jason Witten .30 .75
❑ 273 Kellen Winslow .30 .75
❑ 274 Corey Bradford .25 .60
❑ 275 Samari Rolle .20 .50
❑ 276 Anquan Boldin .25 .60
❑ 277 Adrian Peterson .25 .60
❑ 278 Javon Walker .25 .60
❑ 279 Fred Smoot .20 .50
❑ 280 Mike Alstott .25 .60
❑ 281 Randy McMichael .20 .50
❑ 282 Jay Fiedler .20 .50
❑ 283 Jamie Sharper .20 .50
❑ 284 Eli Manning .60 1.50
❑ 285 Todd Pinkston .20 .50
❑ 286 La'Roi Glover .25 .60
❑ 287 Chris Perry .20 .50
❑ 288 David Carr .25 .60
❑ 289 Bryant Johnson .25 .60
❑ 290 Ray Lewis .30 .75
❑ 291 Tommie Harris .20 .50
❑ 292 Joe Horn .25 .60
❑ 293 Rod Smith .25 .60
❑ 294 Michael Clayton .25 .60
❑ 295 Tyrone Calico .25 .60
❑ 296 Santana Moss .25 .60
❑ 297 Hines Ward .30 .75
❑ 298 Jonathan Vilma .25 .60
❑ 299 Randy Moss .30 .75
❑ 300 Donte Stallworth .25 .60
❑ 301 Isaac Bruce .25 .60
❑ 302 Brian Griese .25 .60
❑ 303 Dennis Northcutt .20 .50
❑ 304 Michael Green .20 .50
❑ 305 Marvin Harrison .30 .75
❑ 306 Jimmy Smith .25 .60
❑ 307 Patrick Kerney .25 .60
❑ 308 Todd Heap .25 .60
❑ 309 Dan Morgan .20 .50
❑ 310 Charles Rogers .20 .50
❑ 311 Dunta Robinson .20 .50
❑ 312 Deuce McAllister .30 .75
❑ 313 Ronde Barber .25 .60
❑ 314 Brandon Lloyd .20 .50
❑ 315 Tiki Barber .30 .75
❑ 316 LaMont Jordan .25 .60
❑ 317 Lito Sheppard .25 .60
❑ 318 Laveranues Coles .25 .60
❑ 319 Drew Bennett .25 .60
❑ 320 Julius Jones .30 .75
❑ 321 Ahman Green .30 .75
❑ 322 Domanick Davis .20 .50
❑ 323 Byron Leftwich .25 .60
❑ 324 Nate Burleson .25 .60
❑ 325 David Givens .25 .60
❑ 326 Trent Dilfer .25 .60
❑ 327 T.J. Houshmandzadeh .25 .60
❑ 328 Keith Brooking .20 .50
❑ 329 Derrick Mason .25 .60
❑ 330 Ken Lucas .20 .50
❑ 331 Rex Grossman .30 .75
❑ 332 Edgerrin James .25 .60
❑ 333 Priest Holmes .30 .75
❑ 334 Donnie Edwards .20 .50
❑ 335 Pierson Prioleau RC .20 .50
❑ 336 Shaun Alexander .30 .75
❑ 337 D.J. Williams .20 .50
❑ 338 Peyton Manning .50 1.25
❑ 339 Carson Palmer .30 .75
❑ 340 Keyshawn Johnson .25 .60
❑ 341 Tory James .20 .50
❑ 342 Drew Bledsoe .30 .75
❑ 343 Chris Gamble .20 .50
❑ 344 Mi.Lewis/B.Dawkins .25 .60
❑ 345 Forney/McClure RC/Weiner RC .20 .50
❑ 346 R.Smart/Kasay/J.Kyle .20 .50
❑ 347 J.Ferguson/Reeves/Nguyen .20 .50
❑ 348 Crocker/Lehan RC/M.Jameson .20 .50
❑ 349 Tyree/Ja.Taylor/T.Carter .20 .50
❑ 350 R.Thomas/D.Jones/Simoneau .20 .50
❑ 351 Royal/McCants/T.Jacobs .20 .50
❑ 352 Welker/D.Thompson/Gilmore .30 .75
❑ 353 D.Lewis/Pickett/Ty.Jackson .20 .50
❑ 354 F.Brown/F.Thomas/J.Bellamy .20 .50
❑ 355 Asomugha/M.Anderson/Schweigert .20 .50
❑ 356 M.Stroud/J.Hender/Favors .20 .50
❑ 357 W.Shields/Roaf/B.Waters RC .20 .50
❑ 358 Hamilton/Nalen/Lepsis .20 .50
❑ 359 J.Smith/Geathers/D.Clemons .20 .50
❑ 360 Wire/R.Baker/L.Milloy .25 .60
❑ 361 Ayanbadejo/J.Scobey/Hambrick .20 .50
❑ 362 St.Smith/Proehl/Colbert .30 .75
❑ 363 N.Harris/D.Thomas/Offord .20 .50
❑ 364 L.Neal/M.Turner/Pinnock .30 .75
❑ 365 Faneca/M.Smith RC/Hartings .50 1.25
❑ 366 E.Moore/Pope/Ayanbadejo RC .25 .60
❑ 367 A.Plummer/Jo.Hanson RC/Spencer .20 .50
❑ 368 L.Betts/Brunell/C.Morton .25 .60
❑ 369 Pace/Timmerman/McCollum .20 .50
❑ 370 B.Thomas/Barton/Hobson .20 .50
❑ 371 S.Barber/K.Fox/K.Mitchell .20 .50
❑ 372 K.Edwards/Wilkinson/Redding .20 .50
❑ 373 Co.Jackson RC/Lang/McKinley .20 .50
❑ 374 Bannan/R.Edwards/S.Adams .20 .50
❑ 375 M.Schaub/D.White/Finneran .30 .75
❑ 376 Short/A.Wallace RC/K.Jenkins .20 .50
❑ 377 Leach/Carswell/Putzier .20 .50
❑ 378 Vrabel/T.Johnson/Bruschi .30 .75
❑ 379 Kiel/Je.Wilson RC/Fletcher .20 .50
❑ 380 Engelber/To.Brown RC/A.Adams .20 .50
❑ 381 Quarles/Gooch/D.White .20 .50
❑ 382 Madison/W.Poole/R.Howard .20 .50
❑ 383 Schneck RC/Gardocki/J.Reed .20 .50
❑ 384 J.Mitchell RC/Gross/Brzezinski RC .20 .50
❑ 385 Greisen/B.Green/A.Pierce .20 .50
❑ 386 C.Simon/D.Walker/McDougle .20 .50
❑ 387 D.Graham/Fauria/B.Watson .25 .60
❑ 388 E.Johnson/R.John/M.Coleman .20 .50
❑ 389 June/D.Thornton/Hutchins .25 .60
❑ 390 Teague/R.Tucker/M.Will.T .20 .50
❑ 391 M.Haynes/A.Brown/Ogunleye .20 .50
❑ 392 Ulmer RC/Br.Smith/De.Williams .20 .50
❑ 393 K.Faulk/Pass/Be.Johnson .25 .60
❑ 394 Tobeck RC/W.Jones/S.Hutchin .20 .50
❑ 395 V.Holliday/Y.Bell RC/K.Carter .20 .50
❑ 396 L.Foote/J.Porter/Al.Jackson .20 .50
❑ 397 Looker/K.Curtis/S.McDonald .25 .60
❑ 398 L.Marshall RC/C.Griffin/D.Evans .25 .60
❑ 399 D.Klecko/Izzo/R.Colvin .20 .50
❑ 400 M.Holland/Bentley/Gandy .20 .50
❑ 401 Petitgout/McKenzie RC /J.Whittle RC .20 .50
❑ 402 Sykes RC/Fatafehi/A.Wilson .20 .50
❑ 403 Meester RC/Ma.Will/Manuwai RC .20 .50
❑ 404 M.Schobel/K.Washing/Warrick .20 .50
❑ 405 M.Minter/R.Manning/C.Branch .20 .50
❑ 406 Jo.Reed/Jo.Smith/Aiken .20 .50
❑ 407 Birk/Liwienski/McKinnie .20 .50
❑ 408 Godfrey/Foley/Leber .20 .50
❑ 409 McFarland/Wyms/G.Spires .20 .50
❑ 410 E.Perry/Do.Lee/Booker .20 .50
❑ 411 Von Oelhoffen/Hoke RC/Aa.Smith .25 .60
❑ 412 B.Mitchell/Wistrom/Ra.Moore .20 .50
❑ 413 J.Green/Wilfork/T.Warren .25 .60
❑ 414 Middlebrooks/Lynch/N.Ferguson .25 .60
❑ 415 Reagor/R.Brock/Jo.Williams .20 .50
❑ 416 J.Dunn/S.Parker/La.Johnson .30 .75
❑ 417 La.Johnson/M.Wilkins RC/C.Miller .20 .50
❑ 418 Buckner/Moorehead/M.Rucker .20 .50
❑ 419 Denney/Kelsay/A.Schobel .20 .50
❑ 420 Singleton/B.James/K.O'Neil RC .20 .50
❑ 421 C.Thompson/Boyer/An.Davis .20 .50
❑ 422 D.Grant/Richardson RC/R.Mathis .20 .50
❑ 423 Schlesinger/Bryson/Pinner .20 .50
❑ 424 S.Johnson RC/R.Davis/Ru.Jones .20 .50
❑ 425 Phifer/Banta-Cain/McGinest .25 .60
❑ 426 McCardell/Osgood/E.Parker .25 .60
❑ 427 C.Woodard/Bernard/A.Cochran .20 .50
❑ 428 A.Battle/A.Walker/E.Johnson .20 .50
❑ 429 Salave'a RC/M.Wash/L.Arrington .30 .75
❑ 430 L.Mays/C.Wilson/Randle El .25 .60
❑ 431 D.Starks/E.Wilson/R.Gay .20 .50
❑ 432 Q.Griffin/M.Anderson/C.Sapp .25 .60
❑ 433 J.Thornton/L.Moore RC/Powell .20 .50
❑ 434 M.Gaines/Hankton/Seidman .20 .50
❑ 435 M.Haggan RC/Posey/A.Crowell .20 .50
❑ 436 O'Neal/M.Williams/K.Ratliff .20 .50
❑ 437 M.Light/Koppen RC/S.Neal RC .20 .50
❑ 438 C.Watson/D.Rodgers/J.Allen .20 .50
❑ 439 M.Boulware/Hamlin/Bierria RC .20 .50
❑ 440 T.Rogers RC/Unck RC/Roye .20 .50
❑ 441 Frank Gore RC 1.25 3.00
❑ 442 Mike Patterson RC .50 1.25
❑ 443 DeMarcus Ware RC 1.00 2.50
❑ 444 Chris Henry RC .60 1.50
❑ 445 Thomas Davis RC .50 1.25
❑ 446 Justin Miller RC .50 1.25
❑ 447 Shaun Cody RC .50 1.25
❑ 448 Alex Barron RC .40 1.00
❑ 449 Brock Berlin RC .50 1.25
❑ 450 Travis Johnson RC .40 1.00
❑ 451 Jerome Mathis RC .60 1.50
❑ 452 Lance Mitchell RC .50 1.25
❑ 453 Marlin Jackson RC .50 1.25
❑ 454 Charlie Frye RC .60 1.50
❑ 455 Luis Castillo RC .60 1.50
❑ 456 Fred Gibson RC .50 1.25
❑ 457 Dustin Fox RC .60 1.50
❑ 458 Ryan Fitzpatrick RC .60 1.50
❑ 459 Dan Orlovsky RC .60 1.50
❑ 460 Justin Tuck RC .75 2.00
❑ 461 Corey Webster RC .60 1.50
❑ 462 Travis Daniels RC .50 1.25
❑ 463 J.J. Arrington RC .60 1.50
❑ 464 David Greene RC .50 1.25
❑ 465 Alvin Pearman RC .40 1.00
❑ 466 Manuel White RC .50 1.25
❑ 467 Paris Warren RC .50 1.25
❑ 468 Patrick Estes RC .40 1.00
❑ 469 Cedric Houston RC .60 1.50
❑ 470 David Pollack RC .50 1.25
❑ 471 Craig Bragg RC .40 1.00
❑ 472 Vincent Jackson RC .75 2.00
❑ 473 Adam Jones RC .50 1.25
❑ 474 Matt Jones RC .60 1.50
❑ 475 Stefan LeFors RC .50 1.25
❑ 476 Heath Miller RC 1.25 3.00
❑ 477 Ryan Moats RC .50 1.25
❑ 478 Vernand Morency RC .50 1.25
❑ 479 Terrence Murphy RC .40 1.00
❑ 480 Kyle Orton RC 1.00 2.50
❑ 481 Roscoe Parrish RC .50 1.25
❑ 482 Courtney Roby RC .50 1.25
❑ 483 Aaron Rodgers RC 2.00 5.00
❑ 484 Carlos Rogers RC .60 1.50
❑ 485 Antrel Rolle RC .60 1.50
❑ 486 Eric Shelton RC .50 1.25
❑ 487 Alex Smith QB RC .60 1.50
❑ 488 Andrew Walter RC .50 1.25
❑ 489 Roddy White RC .75 2.00
❑ 490 Cadillac Williams RC 1.00 2.50
❑ 491 Mike Williams .50 1.25
❑ 492 Troy Williamson RC .60 1.50
❑ 493 Kirk Morrison RC .60 1.50
❑ 494 Tab Perry RC .60 1.50
❑ 495 Chad Owens RC .60 1.50
❑ 496 Lofa Tatupu RC .60 1.50
❑ 497 Craphonso Thorpe RC .50 1.25
❑ 498 Ryan Riddle RC .40 1.00
❑ 499 Marcus Maxwell RC .40 1.00
❑ 500 Barrett Ruud RC .60 1.50
❑ 501 Stanley Wilson RC .50 1.25
❑ 502 Mike Nugent RC .50 1.25
❑ 503 Eric King RC .40 1.00
❑ 504 Darryl Blackstock RC .40 1.00
❑ 505 Attiyah Ellison RC .40 1.00
❑ 506 Donte Nicholson RC .50 1.25
❑ 507 Airese Currie RC .50 1.25
❑ 508 Larry Brackins RC .40 1.00
❑ 509 Joel Dreessen RC .50 1.25
❑ 510 Cedric Benson RC .60 1.50
❑ 511 Mark Bradley RC .50 1.25
❑ 512 Reggie Brown RC .50 1.25
❑ 513 Ronnie Brown RC 2.00 5.00
❑ 514 Jason Campbell RC 1.00 2.50
❑ 515 Maurice Clarett .50 1.25
❑ 516 Mark Clayton RC .60 1.50
❑ 517 Braylon Edwards RC 1.50 4.00
❑ 518 Ciatrick Fason RC .50 1.25
❑ 519 Dan Cody RC .60 1.50
❑ 520 Taylor Stubblefield RC .40 1.00
❑ 521 J.R. Russell RC .40 1.00
❑ 522 Rian Wallace RC .50 1.25
❑ 523 Anthony Davis RC .50 1.25
❑ 524 Derek Anderson RC .60 1.50
❑ 525 Boomer Grigsby RC .60 1.50
❑ 526 Rasheed Marshall RC .50 1.25

Card	Low	High
❑ 527 Adrian McPherson RC	.50	1.25
❑ 528 Noah Herron RC	.60	1.50
❑ 529 Bryant McFadden RC	.50	1.25
❑ 530 Lionel Gates RC	.40	1.00
❑ 531 Matt Roth RC	.60	1.50
❑ 532 Derrick Johnson RC	.60	1.50
❑ 533 Stanford Routt RC	.50	1.25
❑ 534 Brandon Jacobs RC	.75	2.00
❑ 535 Kevin Burnett RC	.50	1.25
❑ 536 Ryan Claridge RC	.40	1.00
❑ 537 James Kilian RC	.40	1.00
❑ 538 Oshiomogho Atogwe RC	.40	1.00
❑ 539 Fabian Washington RC	.60	1.50
❑ 540 Marion Barber RC	2.00	5.00
❑ 541 Anttaj Hawthorne RC	.50	1.25
❑ 542 Zach Tuiasosopo RC	.40	1.00
❑ 543 Ellis Hobbs RC	.60	1.50
❑ 544 Alex Smith TE RC	.60	1.50
❑ 545 Erasmus James RC	.50	1.25
❑ 546 Channing Crowder RC	.50	1.25
❑ 547 Kelvin Hayden RC	.50	1.25
❑ 548 Darren Sproles RC	.75	2.00
❑ 549 Marcus Spears RC	.60	1.50
❑ 550 Dante Ridgeway RC	.40	1.00
❑ CL1 Checklist 1	.02	.10
❑ CL2 Checklist 2	.02	.10
❑ CL3 Checklist 3	.02	.10
❑ CL4 Checklist 4	.02	.10
❑ BR1 Ben Roethlisberger Jumbo	3.00	6.00
❑ VL1 Vince Lombardi Jumbo	3.00	6.00

2006 Topps Total

Card	Low	High
❑ COMPLETE SET (550)	25.00	60.00
❑ 1 C.Webster/S.Madison	.20	.50
❑ 2 Randy Moss	.30	.75
❑ 3 Garcia/Parry/Detmer	.25	.60
❑ 4 Matt Jones	.25	.60
❑ 5 C.Brown/G.Earl	.20	.50
❑ 6 Anderson/Steinbach/Braham	.20	.50
❑ 7 DeAngelo Hall	.25	.60
❑ 8 J.P. Losman	.25	.60
❑ 9 Kevin Jones	.25	.60
❑ 10 K.Dorsey/F.Gore	.30	.75
❑ 11 Nichol/Pearson RC/Allen	.20	.50
❑ 12 Brandon Lloyd	.25	.60
❑ 13 Jeremiah Trotter	.20	.50
❑ 14 Stone/Grove/Sims	.20	.50
❑ 15 Drew Brees	.30	.75
❑ 16 Jason Taylor	.25	.60
❑ 17 Tony Gonzalez	.25	.60
❑ 18 Brandon Stokley	.25	.60
❑ 19 Jake Plummer	.25	.60
❑ 20 Braylon Edwards	.30	.75
❑ 21 Berrian/Maynard/Gould RC	.25	.60
❑ 22 B.Sams/M.Stover	.20	.50
❑ 23 Darling/Huff/Dansby	.20	.50
❑ 24 Julius Peppers	.25	.60
❑ 25 Ferguson/Spears/Ellis	.20	.50
❑ 26 D.Lee/D.Martin	.20	.50
❑ 27 B.Johnson/B.Johnson	.25	.60
❑ 28 Bethel Johnson	.20	.50
❑ 29 Ellis/Robertson/Thomas	.20	.50
❑ 30 Willie Parker	.40	1.00
❑ 31 E.Shepherd/I.Hilliard	.20	.50
❑ 32 Troupe/Scaife/Mauck	.20	.50
❑ 33 Marc Bulger	.25	.60
❑ 34 M.Trufant/M.Boulware	.20	.50
❑ 35 Hardwick/Oben/Olivea	.20	.50
❑ 36 Ray Lewis	.30	.75
❑ 37 S.Lefors/C.Weinke	.20	.50
❑ 38 Kaesviharn/Pollack/Ohalete	.20	.50
❑ 39 G.Jones/A.Pearman	.20	.50
❑ 40 Allen/Hicks/Sims	.30	.75
❑ 41 Tiki Barber	.30	.75
❑ 42 N.Asomugha/F.Washington	.20	.50
❑ 43 Lewis/Adams/Emanuel	.20	.50
❑ 44 Rodney Harrison	.20	.50
❑ 45 H.Smith/A.Vinatieri	.25	.60
❑ 46 Orlovsky/Kitna/Bryson	.25	.60
❑ 47 Bubba Franks	.20	.50
❑ 48 A.Wilson/I.Gold	.20	.50
❑ 49 Davis/Thompson/McGinest	.20	.50
❑ 50 Nathan Vasher	.20	.50
❑ 51 J.Greer/T.Vincent	.20	.50
❑ 52 Rossum/Ptrsn/Koenen RC	.20	.50
❑ 53 DeMarcus Ware	.25	.60
❑ 54 L.Diamond RC/Booker	.20	.50
❑ 55 McKinnie/Birk/Hutchinson	.20	.50
❑ 56 Cole/Kearse/Patterson	.25	.60
❑ 57 Tubbs/Wistrom/Fisher	.20	.50
❑ 58 Curtis Martin	.30	.75
❑ 59 D.Macklin/A.Rolle	.20	.50
❑ 60 Lejeune/Howard/Bell	.20	.50
❑ 61 Reggie Brown	.20	.50
❑ 62 M.McKenzie/F.Thomas	.20	.50
❑ 63 Fletcher/Hartsock/Sorgi	.20	.50
❑ 64 Larry Fitzgerald	.30	.75
❑ 65 E.Moulds/V.Morency	.25	.60
❑ 66 Williams/Barnes/Naeole	.20	.50
❑ 67 Trent Green	.25	.60
❑ 68 D.Sproles/M.Turner	.30	.75
❑ 69 Chillar/Glover/Tinoisamoa	.25	.60
❑ 70 Chris Gamble	.20	.50
❑ 71 A.Jones/M.Waddell	.20	.50
❑ 72 Marshall/Washington/Daniels	.20	.50
❑ 73 Hines Ward	.30	.75
❑ 74 S.Knight/P.Surtain	.20	.50
❑ 75 McKinney/Wade/Wiegert	.20	.50
❑ 76 Rod Smith	.25	.60
❑ 77 D.Henson/T.Romo	2.00	5.00
❑ 78 Franklin RC/Gregg/Pryce	.20	.50
❑ 79 David Garrard	.30	.75
❑ 80 D.Smith/M.Peterson	.20	.50
❑ 81 Bowens/Traylor/Roth	.20	.50
❑ 82 Simeon Rice	.20	.50
❑ 83 M.Douglas/B.Young	.20	.50
❑ 84 Thornton/Reynolds RC/Sirmon	.20	.50
❑ 85 T.J. Houshmandzadeh	.25	.60
❑ 86 L.Betts/J.Campbell	.25	.60
❑ 87 Smith/Hartings/Faneca	.25	.60
❑ 88 Antonio Pierce	.20	.50
❑ 89 C.Kluwe/R.Longwell	.20	.50
❑ 90 Thomas/Manning/Poppinga	.20	.50
❑ 91 Willis McGahee	.30	.75
❑ 92 K.Smith/T.Holt	.20	.50
❑ 93 Wilson/Samuel/Hobbs	.25	.60
❑ 94 Pace/Timmerman/Barron	.20	.50
❑ 95 Fred Taylor	.25	.60
❑ 96 M.Doss/B.Sanders	.25	.60
❑ 97 Joe/Briggs/Ayanbadejo	.25	.60
❑ 98 Daunte Culpepper	.30	.75
❑ 99 C.Perry/T.Perry	.25	.60
❑ 100 Whitted/Janikowski/Lechler	.20	.50
❑ 101 Julius Jones	.25	.60
❑ 102 C.Lavalais/R.Coleman	.20	.50
❑ 103 Rucker/Ciurciu RC/Wallace	.20	.50
❑ 104 Rex Grossman	.30	.75
❑ 105 Dunta Robinson	.20	.50
❑ 106 Bockwoldt/Craft/Gleason	.20	.50
❑ 107 Chad Pennington	.25	.60
❑ 108 Heath Miller	.25	.60
❑ 109 D.Hackett/N.Burleson	.25	.60
❑ 110 Drew Bennett	.25	.60
❑ 111 Williams/Godfrey/Castillo	.20	.50
❑ 112 Doug Gabriel	.20	.50
❑ 113 A.Toomer/B.Jacobs	.30	.75
❑ 114 Travis Taylor	.20	.50
❑ 115 Terrell Suggs	.25	.60
❑ 116 Todd Heap	.25	.60
❑ 117 Reese/Williams/Boley	.20	.50
❑ 118 Odell Thurman	.20	.50
❑ 119 D.Watts/S.Alexander	.20	.50
❑ 120 Scobee/Hanson RC/Toefield	.20	.50
❑ 121 Donovan McNabb	.30	.75
❑ 122 A.Smith TE/A.Becht	.20	.50
❑ 123 Adam Archuleta	.20	.50
❑ 124 J.J. Arrington	.20	.50
❑ 125 Johnson/Simmons/Miller	.20	.50
❑ 126 Andruzzi/Bentley/Tucker	.20	.50
❑ 127 Aaron Rodgers	.30	.75
❑ 128 Brown/Gardner/Hobson	.20	.50
❑ 129 Antonio Bryant	.25	.60
❑ 130 Isaac Bruce	.25	.60
❑ 131 Quarles/Nece/Ruud	.20	.50
❑ 132 Williams/Elam/Sauerbrun	.20	.50
❑ 133 B.Hoover/N.Goings	.20	.50
❑ 134 Ward/Carter/Rolle	.20	.50
❑ 135 Dante Hall	.25	.60
❑ 136 Tom Brady	.50	1.25
❑ 137 R.Moats/C.Buckhalter	.25	.60
❑ 138 Arnaz Battle	.20	.50
❑ 139 Bernard/Hill/Lewis RC	.20	.50
❑ 140 Kampman/Gbaja-Biamila /Jenkins	.25	.60
❑ 141 Fowler RC/James/Burnett	.20	.50
❑ 142 Warrick Dunn	.25	.60
❑ 143 Eli Manning	.40	1.00
❑ 144 Clark/Brayton/Morrison	.20	.50
❑ 145 Zach Thomas	.30	.75
❑ 146 Anderson/Babin/Greenwood	.20	.50
❑ 147 Ron Dayne	.25	.60
❑ 148 D.Zastudil/P.Dawson	.20	.50
❑ 149 Williams/Mosley/Johnson	.20	.50
❑ 150 Donte Stallworth	.25	.60
❑ 151 Shawne Merriman	.25	.60
❑ 152 Thompson/Hentrich/Bironas	.20	.50
❑ 153 Clinton Portis	.30	.75
❑ 154 R.Curry/J.Morant	.25	.60
❑ 155 Dwight Freeney	.25	.60
❑ 156 B.Russell/D.McCutcheon	.20	.50
❑ 157 Brown/Green/Tillman	.25	.60
❑ 158 Takeo Spikes	.20	.50
❑ 159 Kurt Warner	.30	.75
❑ 160 Jonathan Vilma	.25	.60
❑ 161 James Farrior	.20	.50
❑ 162 D.Florence/Q.Jammer	.20	.50
❑ 163 Kevan Barlow	.25	.60
❑ 164 Haggans/Hampton/Smith	.20	.50
❑ 165 Walter Jones	.20	.50
❑ 166 Mayberry/Jacox RC/Holland	.20	.50
❑ 167 Byron Leftwich	.25	.60
❑ 168 Mike Williams WR	.25	.60
❑ 169 Jason Witten	.30	.75
❑ 170 Dennis Northcutt	.20	.50
❑ 171 Baker/Clements/Wire	.20	.50
❑ 172 Ronnie Cruz	.20	.50
❑ 173 E.Henderson/E.James	.20	.50
❑ 174 LaMont Jordan	.25	.60
❑ 175 Tyrone Calico	.20	.50
❑ 176 Nalen/Foster/Hamilton	.20	.50
❑ 177 Sam Gado	.30	.75
❑ 178 Randy McMichael	.20	.50
❑ 179 Brown/Sheppard/Ware	.25	.60
❑ 180 L.Little/A.Hargrove	.20	.50
❑ 181 Cadillac Williams	.30	.75
❑ 182 Feely/Morton/Tyree	.25	.60
❑ 183 Dallas Clark	.25	.60
❑ 184 Faggins/Sanders/Coleman	.20	.50
❑ 185 V.Holliday/K.Carter	.20	.50
❑ 186 Smith/Ulbrich/Winborn	.20	.50
❑ 187 S.Player/N.Rackers	.20	.50
❑ 188 Steve Smith	.30	.75
❑ 189 Cassel/Graham/Watson	.30	.75
❑ 190 J.Porter/L.Foote	.20	.50
❑ 191 Jamal Lewis	.25	.60
❑ 192 Michael Jenkins	.25	.60
❑ 193 Michael Strahan	.25	.60
❑ 194 Kyle Vanden Bosch	.20	.50
❑ 195 Shields/Roaf/Waters	.20	.50
❑ 196 Terry Glenn	.25	.60
❑ 197 Griffith/Green/Wilson	.20	.50
❑ 198 Philip Rivers	.30	.75
❑ 199 Tuck/Joseph/Robbins	.25	.60
❑ 200 LaDainian Tomlinson	.40	1.00
❑ 201 J.David/N.Harper	.20	.50
❑ 202 Hall/Bailey/Rogers	.20	.50
❑ 203 Donald Driver	.30	.75
❑ 204 Reuben Droughns	.25	.60
❑ 205 Wahle/Gross/Wharton	.20	.50
❑ 206 Jonathan Ogden	.20	.50
❑ 207 J.Bullocks/D.Smith	.20	.50
❑ 208 Nugent/Miller/Graham RC	.20	.50
❑ 209 Matt Hasselbeck	.25	.60
❑ 210 Derrick Brooks	.25	.60
❑ 211 Foxworth/Lynch/Ferguson	.20	.50
❑ 212 Stewart/Unck/Fisk	.20	.50
❑ 213 M.Will.T/Anderson RC/Villarrial	.20	.50
❑ 214 Saturday/Glenn/Diem	.20	.50
❑ 215 Larry Johnson	.25	.60
❑ 216 Marcus Robinson	.25	.60

❑ 217 Aaron Brooks .25 .60
❑ 218 Smith/Bartrum/Spach .20 .50
❑ 219 Steven Jackson .30 .75
❑ 220 Roy Williams WR .30 .75
❑ 221 L.Polite/P.Crayton .20 .50
❑ 222 Carson Palmer .30 .75
❑ 223 Brown/Kreutz/Tait .20 .50
❑ 224 Charles Woodson .25 .60
❑ 225 J.Payton/T.Henry .25 .60
❑ 226 K.Rhodes/E.Coleman .20 .50
❑ 227 Ronnie Brown .30 .75
❑ 228 David Carr .20 .50
❑ 229 Terence Newman .20 .50
❑ 230 Grigsby/Bell/Mitchell .20 .50
❑ 231 M.Vrabel/R.Colvin .25 .60
❑ 232 Heitmann/Smiley/Harris .20 .50
❑ 233 Joey Galloway .25 .60
❑ 234 Keith Bulluck .20 .50
❑ 235 Hall/Frost/Brown .20 .50
❑ 236 Dockett/Smith/Okeafor .20 .50
❑ 237 Mike Anderson .25 .60
❑ 238 Kellen Winslow .30 .75
❑ 239 Tatum Bell .20 .50
❑ 240 A.Pinner/C.Schlesinger .20 .50
❑ 241 Roman/Underwood/Collins .25 .60
❑ 242 Reggie Wayne .25 .60
❑ 243 Reggie Williams .25 .60
❑ 244 Pope/Spragan/Crowder .20 .50
❑ 245 Courtney Watson .20 .50
❑ 246 G.Lewis/B.McMullen .20 .50
❑ 247 Troy Polamalu .40 1.00
❑ 248 Smoker/Faulk/Looker .25 .60
❑ 249 Keyshawn Johnson .25 .60
❑ 250 J.Babineaux/C.Davis .20 .50
❑ 251 Marcel Shipp .20 .50
❑ 252 Brian Urlacher .30 .75
❑ 253 Haynesworth/LaBoy/Starks .20 .50
❑ 254 Derrick Burgess .20 .50
❑ 255 Harris/Thomas/Leber .20 .50
❑ 256 Henderson/Stroud/Hayward .20 .50
❑ 257 Travis Minor .20 .50
❑ 258 Rivera/Petitti/Johnson .20 .50
❑ 259 D.J. Williams .20 .50
❑ 260 Terrell Owens .30 .75
❑ 261 C.Wilson/D.Kreider .20 .50
❑ 262 Antonio Gates .30 .75
❑ 263 Ronde Barber .25 .60
❑ 264 Bryant Johnson .20 .50
❑ 265 Brett Favre .60 1.50
❑ 266 C.Stanley/K.Brown .20 .50
❑ 267 McKenzie/Petitgout/O'Hara .40 1.00
❑ 268 Chris Cooley .25 .60
❑ 269 Steve McNair .25 .60
❑ 270 Smith/Thornton/Geathers .20 .50
❑ 271 McClure/Forney/Lehr RC .15 .40
❑ 272 B.Sapp RC/McCleon/Warf .15 .40
❑ 273 Jeremy Shockey .30 .75
❑ 274 Chad Johnson .25 .60
❑ 275 Vincent RC/Flynn RC/Mulitalo .20 .50
❑ 276 Deuce McAllister .25 .60
❑ 277 Sapp/Kelly/Hamilton .25 .60
❑ 278 B.Manumaleuna/R.Fitzpatrick .25 .60
❑ 279 Spires/White/Wyms .20 .50
❑ 280 Josh McCown .25 .60
❑ 281 Derrick Johnson LB .25 .60
❑ 282 T.Bryant/C.Grant .20 .50
❑ 283 C.Houston/D.Blaylock .20 .50
❑ 284 David Givens .25 .60
❑ 285 Lindell/McGee/Moorman .20 .50
❑ 286 Charlie Frye .25 .60
❑ 287 Ahman Green .25 .60
❑ 288 Darren Sharper .25 .60
❑ 289 Justin McCareins .20 .50
❑ 290 Lofa Tatupu .25 .60
❑ 291 Brock/Reagor/Thomas .20 .50
❑ 292 Muhsin Muhammad .25 .60
❑ 293 Derrick Mason .25 .60
❑ 294 Jones/Mare/Welker .30 .75
❑ 295 Stecker/Henderson/Conwell .20 .50
❑ 296 Mawae/Roos/Olson .20 .50
❑ 297 M.Bradley/A.Peterson .25 .60
❑ 298 John Abraham .20 .50
❑ 299 Dockery/Rabach/Samuels .20 .50
❑ 300 Peyton Manning .50 1.25
❑ 301 Alge Crumpler .25 .60
❑ 302 Mathis/Richardson/Grant .20 .50
❑ 303 Tedy Bruschi .30 .75
❑ 304 Snee/Diehl RC/Whittle .40 1.00
❑ 305 J.Stevens/P.Warrick .25 .60
❑ 306 Trent Dilfer .25 .60
❑ 307 Marion Barber .30 .75
❑ 308 Robert Ferguson .20 .50
❑ 309 Chester Taylor .25 .60
❑ 310 Jerry Porter .25 .60
❑ 311 Buenning/Walker/Wade .20 .50
❑ 312 DeShaun Foster .25 .60
❑ 313 R.Parrish/K.Holcomb .20 .50
❑ 314 Chris Brown .25 .60
❑ 315 Woody/Backus/Raiola .20 .50
❑ 316 Andre Johnson .25 .60
❑ 317 S.Graham/K.Larson .20 .50
❑ 318 Mangum/Gaines/Shelton .20 .50
❑ 319 Ben Roethlisberger .50 1.25
❑ 320 T.Devoe/C.Adams .30 .75
❑ 321 Jake Delhomme .25 .60
❑ 322 Chris Chambers .25 .60
❑ 323 Chris Simms .25 .60
❑ 324 Ed Reed .25 .60
❑ 325 Charles Rogers .25 .60
❑ 326 Eddie Kennison .20 .50
❑ 327 Seymour/Warren/Wilfork .20 .50
❑ 328 Lorenzo Neal .20 .50
❑ 329 Taylor Jacobs .20 .50
❑ 330 K.Mathis/L.Milloy .20 .50
❑ 331 Glenn/Henry/Reeves .20 .50
❑ 332 B.Dawkins/M.Lewis .25 .60
❑ 333 Edgerrin James .25 .60
❑ 334 Lee Evans .25 .60
❑ 335 Pat Williams .20 .50
❑ 336 Arrington/Torbor/Moore .30 .75
❑ 337 Roy Williams S .25 .60
❑ 338 Joe Horn .25 .60
❑ 339 Keenan McCardell .25 .60
❑ 340 Lee RC/Nedney/Hicks .20 .50
❑ 341 Mark Brunell .25 .60
❑ 342 Jimmy Smith .25 .60
❑ 343 Deltha O'Neal .20 .50
❑ 344 Chris McAlister .20 .50
❑ 345 T.Williamson/J.Kleinsasser .25 .60
❑ 346 N.Herron/A.Thurman .20 .50
❑ 347 A.Brown/A.Ogunleye .20 .50
❑ 348 Michael Vick .30 .75
❑ 349 Laveranues Coles .25 .60
❑ 350 Alex Smith QB .25 .60
❑ 351 Billy Volek .20 .50
❑ 352 Cato June .25 .60
❑ 353 J.Jurevicius/F.Jackson .20 .50
❑ 354 Keary Colbert .25 .60
❑ 355 Griffith/Schaub/White .25 .60
❑ 356 Smith/Payne/Walker .20 .50
❑ 357 Samie Parker .20 .50
❑ 358 Plaxico Burress .25 .60
❑ 359 R.Bartell/O.Atogwe .20 .50
❑ 360 C.Roby/R.Williams .20 .50
❑ 361 Springs/Harris/Prioleau .20 .50
❑ 362 A.Crowell/L.Fletcher .20 .50
❑ 363 Nick Barnett .25 .60
❑ 364 Antoine Winfield .20 .50
❑ 365 Will Smith .20 .50
❑ 366 J.Cotchery/B.Askew .20 .50
❑ 367 Brian Westbrook .25 .60
❑ 368 Jerome Mathis .20 .50
❑ 369 C.Moore/D.Darling .20 .50
❑ 370 Eric Parker .20 .50
❑ 371 Bly/Wilson/Kennedy .20 .50
❑ 372 Champ Bailey .25 .60
❑ 373 Cedric Benson .25 .60
❑ 374 Gray RC/Tobeck/Locklear .20 .50
❑ 375 L.Tynes/D.Colquitt .20 .50
❑ 376 Dan Morgan .20 .50
❑ 377 Posey/Schobel/Kelsay .20 .50
❑ 378 Ekuban/Brown/Myers .20 .50
❑ 379 Reed/Colclough/Gardocki .20 .50
❑ 380 M.Pollard/S.Vines .20 .50
❑ 381 McQuarters/Buller/Deloatch .20 .50
❑ 382 Fred Smoot .20 .50
❑ 383 Walter/Anderson/Crockett .25 .60
❑ 384 Dominic Rhodes .25 .60
❑ 385 T.Thompson/M.Vanderjagt .25 .60
❑ 386 Sullivan/Melton/Bryant .20 .50
❑ 387 M.Scifres/N.Kaeding .20 .50
❑ 388 Erron Kinney .20 .50
❑ 389 Bergen/Edwards/McCoy .20 .50
❑ 390 B.Jones/K.Brady .20 .50
❑ 391 McKinley/Pool/Baxter .20 .50
❑ 392 Jackson/Giordano/Hayden .20 .50
❑ 393 Keith Brooking .20 .50
❑ 394 Josh Reed .20 .50
❑ 395 Thomas Jones .25 .60
❑ 396 D.Johnson CB/S.Spencer .20 .50
❑ 397 Woolfolk/Clauss/Gardner .20 .50
❑ 398 Kyle Boller .25 .60
❑ 399 P.Pass/K.Faulk .25 .60
❑ 400 Routt/Schweigert/Riddle .20 .50
❑ 401 Donnie Edwards .20 .50
❑ 402 Michael Clayton .25 .60
❑ 403 Kasay/Kyle/Robertson .20 .50
❑ 404 A.Carroll/A.Harris .25 .60
❑ 405 Priest Holmes .25 .60
❑ 406 Jabar Gaffney .20 .50
❑ 407 Mewelde Moore .20 .50
❑ 408 Torry Holt .25 .60
❑ 409 Mark Clayton .25 .60
❑ 410 Shaun Alexander .25 .60
❑ 411 T.Tillman/T.Daniels .20 .50
❑ 412 Deion Branch .25 .60
❑ 413 Fraley/Andrews/Darilek RC .20 .50
❑ 414 Anquan Boldin .25 .60
❑ 415 T.James/K.Ratliff .20 .50
❑ 416 Ernest Wilford .20 .50
❑ 417 Moore/Jones/Kendall .20 .50
❑ 418 Brian Griese .25 .60
❑ 419 B.Kelly/J.Phillips .20 .50
❑ 420 Patrick Ramsey .25 .60
❑ 421 Corey Dillon .25 .60
❑ 422 Santana Moss .25 .60
❑ 423 Thomas/Edwards/Boulware .25 .60
❑ 424 Ashley Lelie .20 .50
❑ 425 G.Wilson/W.Demps .30 .75
❑ 426 Darrell Jackson .25 .60
❑ 427 Williams/Udeze/Scott .20 .50
❑ 428 K.Lucas/M.Minter .20 .50
❑ 429 Lee Suggs .25 .60
❑ 430 Kaczur/Mruczkowski/Gorin .20 .50
❑ 431 Robert Gallery .20 .50
❑ 432 Osgood/Feeley/Jackson .25 .60
❑ 433 Domanick Davis .25 .60
❑ 434 Osi Umenyiora .25 .60
❑ 435 Drew Bledsoe .30 .75
❑ 436 J.Gage/E.Berlin .20 .50
❑ 437 Rudi Johnson .25 .60
❑ 438 J.Fargas/M.Tuiasosopo .25 .60
❑ 439 Antwaan Randle El .25 .60
❑ 440 Marvin Harrison .30 .75
❑ 441 Brandon Marshall RC .60 1.50
❑ 442 Wali Lundy RC .60 1.50
❑ 443 Bruce Gradkowski RC .60 1.50
❑ 444 Leonard Pope RC .60 1.50
❑ 445 Omar Jacobs RC .40 1.00
❑ 446 Travis Wilson RC .40 1.00
❑ 447 Derek Hagan RC .50 1.25
❑ 448 Devin Hester RC 1.25 3.00
❑ 449 Willie Reid RC .50 1.25
❑ 450 A.J. Hawk RC 1.00 2.50
❑ 451 DeAngelo Williams RC 1.25 3.00
❑ 452 Ashton Youboty RC .50 1.25
❑ 453 Abdul Hodge RC .50 1.25
❑ 454 Leon Washington RC .75 2.00
❑ 455 D'Qwell Jackson RC .50 1.25
❑ 456 Johnathan Joseph RC .50 1.25
❑ 457 Antonio Cromartie RC .60 1.50
❑ 458 Michael Robinson RC .50 1.25
❑ 459 Tye Hill RC .50 1.25
❑ 460 Mathias Kiwanuka RC .75 2.00
❑ 461 Vince Young RC 1.50 4.00
❑ 462 DeMeco Ryans RC .75 2.00
❑ 463 Brodrick Bunkley RC .50 1.25
❑ 464 Jay Cutler RC 1.50 4.00
❑ 465 Brad Smith RC .60 1.50
❑ 466 Elvis Dumervil RC .60 1.50
❑ 467 Cory Rodgers RC .60 1.50
❑ 468 Davin Joseph RC .50 1.25
❑ 469 Rocky McIntosh RC .60 1.50
❑ 470 Jason Avant RC .60 1.50
❑ 471 Anthony Schlegel RC .50 1.25
❑ 472 Kamerion Wimbley RC .60 1.50
❑ 473 Joseph Addai RC .75 2.00
❑ 474 Ernie Sims RC .50 1.25
❑ 475 Jimmy Williams RC .60 1.50
❑ 476 LenDale White RC .75 2.00
❑ 477 Brandon Williams RC .50 1.25
❑ 478 Ko Simpson RC .50 1.25
❑ 479 Jerious Norwood RC .60 1.50
❑ 480 P.J. Daniels RC .40 1.00

Card	Low	High
❑ 481 Mario Williams RC	.75	2.00
❑ 482 Santonio Holmes RC	1.50	4.00
❑ 483 Joe Klopfenstein RC	.50	1.25
❑ 484 Matt Leinart RC	1.00	2.50
❑ 485 Danieal Manning RC	.60	1.50
❑ 486 Andre Hall RC	.50	1.25
❑ 487 Chad Greenway RC	.60	1.50
❑ 488 Chad Jackson RC	.50	1.25
❑ 489 Skyler Green RC	.40	1.00
❑ 490 Donte Whitner RC	.60	1.50
❑ 491 Bobby Carpenter RC	.50	1.25
❑ 492 Jovon Bouknight RC	.50	1.25
❑ 493 Vernon Davis RC	.60	1.50
❑ 494 Kevin McMahan RC	.50	1.25
❑ 495 D.J. Shockley RC	.50	1.25
❑ 496 A.J. Nicholson RC	.40	1.00
❑ 497 Brian Calhoun RC	.50	1.25
❑ 498 Tim Day RC	.50	1.25
❑ 499 Devin Aromashodu RC	.60	1.50
❑ 500 Charlie Whitehurst RC	.60	1.50
❑ 501 Sinorice Moss RC	.60	1.50
❑ 502 Maurice Stovall RC	.50	1.25
❑ 503 Laurence Maroney RC	.75	2.00
❑ 504 James Anderson RC	.40	1.00
❑ 505 Darnell Bing RC	.50	1.25
❑ 506 Jerome Harrison RC	.60	1.50
❑ 507 Daniel Bullocks RC	.60	1.50
❑ 508 Will Blackmon RC	.60	1.50
❑ 509 Marcedes Lewis RC	.60	1.50
❑ 510 Lawrence Vickers RC	.50	1.25
❑ 511 Marques Hagans RC	.50	1.25
❑ 512 Jeremy Bloom RC	.50	1.25
❑ 513 Dominique Byrd RC	.50	1.25
❑ 514 Tarvaris Jackson RC	.60	1.50
❑ 515 Dusty Dvoracek RC	.60	1.50
❑ 516 Brodie Croyle RC	.60	1.50
❑ 517 Demetrius Williams RC	.50	1.25
❑ 518 Jason Allen RC	.50	1.25
❑ 519 Mike Hass RC	.60	1.50
❑ 520 Nick Mangold RC	.50	1.25
❑ 521 Brett Basanez RC	.60	1.50
❑ 522 Ben Obomanu RC	.50	1.25
❑ 523 Tamba Hali RC	.60	1.50
❑ 524 Gabe Watson RC	.40	1.00
❑ 525 Kelly Jennings RC	.60	1.50
❑ 526 Reggie Bush RC	1.50	4.00
❑ 527 Bernard Pollard RC	.50	1.25
❑ 528 Reggie McNeal RC	.50	1.25
❑ 529 Jonathan Orr RC	.50	1.25
❑ 530 Haloti Ngata RC	.60	1.50
❑ 531 David Thomas RC	.60	1.50
❑ 532 Ingle Martin RC	.50	1.25
❑ 533 Anthony Fasano RC	.60	1.50
❑ 534 Winston Justice RC	.60	1.50
❑ 535 Manny Lawson RC	.60	1.50
❑ 536 Kellen Clemens RC	.60	1.50
❑ 537 Adam Jennings RC	.50	1.25
❑ 538 Thomas Howard RC	.50	1.25
❑ 539 Cedric Humes RC	.50	1.25
❑ 540 Garrett Mills RC	.50	1.25
❑ 541 Jeff Webb RC	.50	1.25
❑ 542 Michael Huff RC	.60	1.50
❑ 543 Gerris Wilkinson RC	.40	1.00
❑ 544 Maurice Drew RC	1.25	3.00
❑ 545 John McCargo RC	.50	1.25
❑ 546 Todd Watkins RC	.40	1.00
❑ 547 Marcus Vick RC	.40	1.00
❑ 548 Greg Jennings RC	1.00	2.50
❑ 549 P.J. Pope RC	.60	1.50
❑ 550 D'Brickashaw Ferguson RC	.60	1.50

2007 Topps Total

Card	Low	High
❑ COMPLETE SET (550)	35.00	60.00
❑ 1 Cadillac Williams	.25	.60
❑ 2 Marcel Shipp/Troy Walters	.20	.50
❑ 3 Kerry Collins/Brandon Jones	.20	.50
❑ 4 J.J. Arrington	.25	.60
❑ 5 Albert Haynesworth	.20	.50
❑ 6 DeAngelo Hall	.25	.60
❑ 7 Kyle Vanden Bosch/Travis LaBoy		
/Andre Woolfolk	.20	.50
❑ 8 Kyle Boller/Justin Green		
/Demetrius Williams	.20	.50
❑ 9 Anquan Boldin	.25	.60
❑ 10 Anthony Thomas	.20	.50
❑ 11 Orlando Huff/Leonard Pope		
/Darnell Dockett	.20	.50
❑ 12 Mike Rucker/Kris Jenkins	.20	.50
❑ 13 Musa Smith/Mike Anderson	.25	.60
❑ 14 DeShaun Foster	.25	.60
❑ 15 Mark Clayton	.25	.60
❑ 16 Mike Minter		
Ken Lucas		
Richard Marshall	.20	.50
❑ 17 Ed Reed	.25	.60
❑ 18 Devin Hester	.30	.75
❑ 19 Brian Moorman		
Craig Nall		
Rian Lindell	.20	.50
❑ 20 Jamal Lewis	.25	.60
❑ 21 Chris Gamble	.20	.50
❑ 22 Kenny Wright		
Leigh Bodden		
Tim Carter	.20	.50
❑ 23 Tommie Harris		
Tank Johnson	.20	.50
❑ 24 Ryan Tucker		
Kevin Shaffer RC		
Hank Fraley	.20	.50
❑ 25 Brad Maynard		
Robbie Gould		
Adrian Peterson Bears	.20	.50
❑ 26 Terence Newman		
Anthony Henry	.20	.50
❑ 27 T.J. Houshmandzadeh	.25	.60
❑ 28 Travis Henry	.25	.60
❑ 29 Julius Jones	.25	.60
❑ 30 Kyle Johnson		
Nick Ferguson		
Dre Bly	.20	.50
❑ 31 Leonard Davis		
Marco Rivera		
Andre Gurode	.20	.50
❑ 32 Aaron Kampman		
Kabeer Gbaja-Biamila	.25	.60
❑ 33 Demetrin Veal RC		
Gerard Warren	.20	.50
❑ 34 Brett Favre	.60	1.50
❑ 35 Mike Bell	.25	.60
❑ 36 Ron Dayne	.25	.60
❑ 37 Jon Kitna	.20	.50
❑ 38 Kris Brown		
Dexter Wynn		
Samkon Gado	.20	.50
❑ 39 Daniel Bullocks		
Fernando Bryant		
Kenoy Kennedy	.20	.50
❑ 40 Peyton Manning	.50	1.25
❑ 41 Matt Schaub	.25	.60
❑ 42 Matt Jones	.25	.60
❑ 43 Jim Sorgi		
Ben Utecht	.20	.50
❑ 44 Dennis Northcutt		
Josh Scobee		
Alvin Pearman	.20	.50
❑ 45 Dallas Clark	.20	.50
❑ 46 Kris Wilson		
Michael Bennett	.20	.50
❑ 47 Jeff Saturday		
Tarik Glenn		
Ryan Diem	.20	.50
❑ 48 Daunte Culpepper	.25	.60
❑ 49 Damon Huard	.25	.60
❑ 50 Bryant McKinnie		
Matt Birk		
Steve Hutchinson	.20	.50
❑ 51 Ty Law	.25	.60
❑ 52 Rosevelt Colvin		
Mike Vrabel	.25	.60
❑ 53 Brian Waters		
Casey Wiegmann		
Will Shields	.20	.50
❑ 54 Chad Jackson	.20	.50
❑ 55 Bobby Wade		
Tony Richardson	.20	.50
❑ 56 Tedy Bruschi	.30	.75
❑ 57 Antoine Winfield	.20	.50
❑ 58 Jammal Brown		
Jeff Faine		
Jon Stinchcomb	.20	.50
❑ 59 Matt Light		
Logan Mankins		
Dan Koppen	.20	.50
❑ 60 Michael Strahan	.25	.60
❑ 61 Marques Colston	.30	.75
❑ 62 Johnnie Morant		
Ronald Curry	.25	.60
❑ 63 Will Demps/Gibril Wilson	.20	.50
❑ 64 Warren Sapp	.25	.60
❑ 65 William Joseph		
Fred Robbins		
Barry Cofield	.20	.50
❑ 66 Chris Carr		
Sebastian Janikowski		
Shane Lechler	.20	.50
❑ 67 Cedric Houston	.20	.50
❑ 68 Nate Washington	.20	.50
❑ 69 Jonathan Vilma	.25	.60
❑ 70 Willie Parker	.25	.60
❑ 71 Sheldon Brown		
Lito Sheppard	.20	.50
❑ 72 Najeh Davenport		
Charlie Batch		
Dan Kreider	.20	.50
❑ 73 Jevon Kearse	.25	.60
❑ 74 Luis Castillo		
Jamal Williams	.20	.50
❑ 75 Darren Howard		
Jerome McDougle		
Trent Cole	.20	.50
❑ 76 Vernon Davis	.25	.60
❑ 77 Antonio Gates	.25	.60
❑ 78 Chris Gray		
Chris Spencer		
Walter Jones	.20	.50
❑ 79 Terrence Kiel		
Drayton Florence		
Marlon McCree	.20	.50
❑ 80 V. Adeyanju/L.Glover	.20	.50
❑ 81 Ashley Lelie	.25	.60
❑ 82 Torry Holt	.25	.60
❑ 83 Maurice Morris		
Mack Strong	.20	.50
❑ 84 Jermaine Phillips		
Will Allen		
Shelton Quarles	.20	.50
❑ 85 Shaun Alexander	.25	.60
❑ 86 Vince Young	.30	.75
❑ 87 Orlando Pace		
Alex Barron		
Andy McCollum	.20	.50
❑ 88 Brandon Lloyd	.25	.60
❑ 89 Joey Galloway	.25	.60
❑ 90 Neil Rackers		
Scott Player	.20	.50
❑ 91 Peter Sirmon		
David Thornton	.20	.50
❑ 92 Bryant Johnson	.20	.50
❑ 93 Bo Scaife		
Cortland Finnegan		
Reynaldo Hill	.20	.50
❑ 94 John Abraham	.20	.50
❑ 95 Jason Campbell	.25	.60
❑ 96 Kelly Gregg		
Bart Scott		
Haloti Ngata	.25	.60
❑ 97 Adrian Wilson	.20	.50
❑ 98 Drew Carter		
Keary Colbert	.20	.50
❑ 99 Michael Jenkins		
D.J. Shockley		
Roddy White	.25	.60
❑ 100 Jake Delhomme	.25	.60
❑ 101 Terrell Suggs		
Trevor Pryce	.20	.50
❑ 102 Thomas Davis		
James Anderson		
Dan Morgan	.20	.50
❑ 103 Todd Heap	.20	.50
❑ 104 Bernard Berrian	.20	.50

❑ 105 Peerless Price .20 .50
❑ 106 Chris Henry .20 .50
❑ 107 Daimon Shelton
Robert Royal
Ryan Neufeld .20 .50
❑ 108 Kellen Winslow .25 .60
❑ 109 Rex Grossman .25 .60
❑ 110 Kamerion Wimbley
D'Qwell Jackson
Andra Davis .20 .50
❑ 111 Levi Jones
Willie Anderson .20 .50
❑ 112 Bradie James
Akin Ayodele .20 .50
❑ 113 Deltha O'Neal .20 .50
❑ 114 Javon Walker .25 .60
❑ 115 Jeremi Johnson
Doug Johnson
Reggie Kelly .20 .50
❑ 116 Quincy Morgan
Jason Elam
Paul Ernster .20 .50
❑ 117 Roy Williams S .25 .60
❑ 118 Donald Driver .30 .75
❑ 119 Miles Austin
Mat McBriar
Sam Hurd .30 .75
❑ 120 Dunta Robinson
Dexter McCleon .20 .50
❑ 121 Devale Ellis RC
Shaun McDonald .20 .50
❑ 122 Wali Lundy .20 .50
❑ 123 Tatum Bell .20 .50
❑ 124 Owen Daniels
Mark Bruener
Jeb Putzier .20 .50
❑ 125 Marquand Manuel
Nick Collins
Al Harris .20 .50
❑ 126 Morlon Greenwood
Shawn Barber
Shantee Orr .20 .50
❑ 127 Ahman Green .25 .60
❑ 128 Marvin Harrison .30 .75
❑ 129 Josh Thomas
Corey Simon
Raheem Brock .20 .50
❑ 130 Chris Naeole
Brad Meester
Maurice Williams .20 .50
❑ 131 Marcus Stroud
John Henderson .20 .50
❑ 132 Kendrell Bell
Derrick Johnson .20 .50
❑ 133 Byron Leftwich .25 .60
❑ 134 Trent Green .25 .60
❑ 135 Samie Parker .20 .50
❑ 136 Mewelde Moore .20 .50
❑ 137 Chris Chambers .25 .60
❑ 138 Chris Kluwe/Artose Pinner
/Ryan Longwell .20 .50
❑ 139 Travis Daniels/Michael Lehan
/Keith Adams .20 .50
❑ 140 Richard Seymour .20 .50
❑ 141 Jim Kleinsasser
/Brooks Bollinger .20 .50
❑ 142 Fred Thomas/Mike McKenzie .20 .50
❑ 143 Darren Sharper .25 .60
❑ 144 Will Smith .20 .50
❑ 145 Ellis Hobbs/Asante Samuel
/Chad Scott .20 .50
❑ 146 Simns/Shanle RC/Fujita .20 .50
❑ 147 Devery Henderson .20 .50
❑ 148 Jeremy Shockey .25 .60
❑ 149 Antonio Pierce/Reggie Torbor .20 .50
❑ 150 Zack Crockett/Justin Fargas .20 .50
❑ 151 Jerricho Cotchery .20 .50
❑ 152 Dominic Rhodes .25 .60
❑ 153 D'Brickashaw Ferguson
/Nick Mangold/Pete Kendall .20 .50
❑ 154 Nnamdi Asomugha/Fabian
Washington/Stuart Schweigert .20 .50
❑ 155 Andrew Walter .20 .50
❑ 156 Cedrick Wilson .20 .50
❑ 157 Dirk Johnson/David Akers
/Reno Mahe .20 .50
❑ 158 Troy Polamalu .30 .75
❑ 159 Casey Hampton/Aaron Smith .20 .50
❑ 160 Alan Faneca/Max Starks
/Marvel Smith .20 .50
❑ 161 Shawne Merriman .25 .60
❑ 162 Shaun Phillips/Randall Godfrey .20 .50
❑ 163 Jonas Jennings/Larry Allen
/Kwame Harris .20 .50
❑ 164 Nate Clements .20 .50
❑ 165 Marcus Pollard/Seneca Wallace .20 .50
❑ 166 Marcus Trufant/Jordan Babineaux
/Kelly Jennings .20 .50
❑ 167 Nate Burleson .20 .50
❑ 168 Isaac Bruce .25 .60
❑ 169 Deion Branch .25 .60
❑ 170 Alex Smith TE/Anthony Becht .20 .50
❑ 171 Brandon Chillar/Pisa Tinoisamoa
/Will Witherspoon .20 .50
❑ 172 Mark Jones/Matt Bryant
/Josh Bidwell .20 .50
❑ 173 Michael Clayton .25 .60
❑ 174 LenDale White .25 .60
❑ 175 Lamont Thompson/Chris Hope .20 .50
❑ 176 Chris Cooley .25 .60
❑ 177 Santana Moss .25 .60
❑ 178 Chike Okeafor/Bertrand Berry .20 .50
❑ 179 Chris Samuels/Jon Jansen
/Randy Thomas .20 .50
❑ 180 Matt Leinart .30 .75
❑ 181 Michael Vick .30 .75
❑ 182 Antrel Rolle/Roderick Hood
/Terrence Holt .20 .50
❑ 183 Michael Koenen/Morten Andersen
/Allen Rossum .20 .50
❑ 184 Joe Horn .25 .60
❑ 185 Chris McAlister/Samari Rolle .20 .50
❑ 186 Steve McNair .25 .60
❑ 187 Roscoe Parrish .20 .50
❑ 188 Sam Koch/Jonathan Ogden
/Matt Stover .20 .50
❑ 189 J.P. Losman .20 .50
❑ 190 John Kasay/Jason Baker .20 .50
❑ 191 Kiwaukee Thomas/Ko Simpson
/Donte Whitner .20 .50
❑ 192 Steve Smith .25 .60
❑ 193 Cedric Benson .25 .60
❑ 194 Rashied Davis .20 .50
❑ 195 Bryan Robinson/Justin Smith .20 .50
❑ 196 Mark Bradley/Brian Griese
/Desmond Clark .25 .60
❑ 197 Dexter Jackson/Keiwan Ratliff
/Johnathan Joseph .20 .50
❑ 198 Carson Palmer .30 .75
❑ 199 Joe Jurevicius .20 .50
❑ 200 Willie McGinest .20 .50
❑ 201 Terry Glenn .25 .60
❑ 202 Joshua Cribbs/Phil Dawson
/Dave Zastudil .30 .75
❑ 203 DeMarcus Ware/Greg Ellis
/Marcus Spears .25 .60
❑ 204 Bobby Carpenter/Aaron Glenn .20 .50
❑ 205 Cory Redding/Shaun Rogers .20 .50
❑ 206 Champ Bailey .25 .60
❑ 207 T.J. Duckett .20 .50
❑ 208 Damien Woody/Dominic Raiola
/Jeff Backus .20 .50
❑ 209 Kevin Jones .20 .50
❑ 210 Greg Jennings .25 .60
❑ 211 Cullen Jenkins/Corey Williams
/Ryan Pickett .20 .50
❑ 212 Anthony Weaver/Jason Babin .20 .50
❑ 213 Andre Johnson .25 .60
❑ 214 Kevin Walter/Jameel Cook
/Derrick Lewis .25 .60
❑ 215 Hunter Smith/Terrence Wilkins
/Adam Vinatieri .25 .60
❑ 216 Bob Sanders .25 .60
❑ 217 Greg Jones/David Garrard .25 .60
❑ 218 Reggie Wayne .25 .60
❑ 219 Fred Taylor .25 .60
❑ 220 Eddie Kennison .20 .50
❑ 221 Marty Booker .20 .50
❑ 222 Jeff Webb/Rod Gardner
/Dustin Colquitt .20 .50
❑ 223 Ronnie Brown .25 .60
❑ 224 Channing Crowder/Joey Porter .20 .50
❑ 225 Jason Allen/Renaldo Hill
/Yeremiah Bell .20 .50
❑ 226 Tarvaris Jackson .25 .60
❑ 227 Kevin Williams/Pat Williams .20 .50
❑ 228 Kenechi Udeze/Darrion Scott
/Dwight Smith .20 .50
❑ 229 Tom Brady .60 1.50
❑ 230 Roman Harper/Josh Bullocks .20 .50
❑ 231 James Sanders/Rodney
Harrison/Stephen Gostkowski .20 .50
❑ 232 Terrance Copper .25 .60
❑ 233 Brandon Jacobs .25 .60
❑ 234 Drew Brees .30 .75
❑ 235 Bryan Thomas/Shaun Ellis .20 .50
❑ 236 Amani Toomer .25 .60
❑ 237 Justin Miller .20 .50
❑ 238 Jared Lorenzen/David Tyree
/Sinorice Moss .25 .60
❑ 239 Brad Smith/Chris Baker .20 .50
❑ 240 Derrick Burgess/Tyler Brayton .20 .50
❑ 241 Jerry Porter .25 .60
❑ 242 Michael Huff .25 .60
❑ 243 Jeremiah Trotter .20 .50
❑ 244 Kirk Morrison/Sam Williams
/Thomas Howard .20 .50
❑ 245 Shawn Andrews/William Thomas
/Jon Runyan .20 .50
❑ 246 Santonio Holmes .25 .60
❑ 247 Jerame Tuman/Heath Miller .20 .50
❑ 248 Eric Parker .20 .50
❑ 249 Quentin Jammer .20 .50
❑ 250 Marcus McNeill/Nick Hardwick
/Mike Goff .20 .50
❑ 251 Mark Roman/Jeff Ulbrich
/Shawntae Spencer .20 .50
❑ 252 Walt Harris/Michael Lewis .20 .50
❑ 253 LeRoy Hill/Lofa Tatupu .25 .60
❑ 254 Bryant Young .20 .50
❑ 255 Darrell Jackson .25 .60
❑ 256 Deon Grant/Brian Russell
/Michael Boulware .20 .50
❑ 257 Drew Bennett .20 .50
❑ 258 Steven Jackson .30 .75
❑ 259 Dane Looker/Gus Frerotte
/Corey Chavous .20 .50
❑ 260 Ike Hilliard/Michael Pittman .20 .50
❑ 261 Simeon Rice .20 .50
❑ 262 Roydell Williams .20 .50
❑ 263 Mark Brunell/James Thrash .25 .60
❑ 264 Ben Troupe/Kevin Mawae
/Erron Kinney .20 .50
❑ 265 Clinton Portis .25 .60
❑ 266 Larry Fitzgerald .30 .75
❑ 267 Carlos Rogers/Fred Smoot/
Shawn Springs .20 .50
❑ 268 Gerald Hayes/Calvin Pace
/Karlos Dansby .20 .50
❑ 269 Warrick Dunn .25 .60
❑ 270 Keith Brooking/Brian Finneran .20 .50
❑ 271 Kynan Forney/Wayne Gandy
/Todd McClure .20 .50
❑ 272 Jerious Norwood .25 .60
❑ 273 Josh Reed/Shaud Williams .20 .50
❑ 274 Willis McGahee .25 .60
❑ 275 Terrence McGee .20 .50
❑ 276 Ronnie Prude/Jarret Johnson
/Dawan Landry .20 .50
❑ 277 Lee Evans .25 .60
❑ 278 Keyshawn Johnson .25 .60
❑ 279 Jordan Gross/Mike Wahle
/Will Montgomery .20 .50
❑ 280 Alex Brown/Adewale Ogunleye .20 .50
❑ 281 Muhsin Muhammad .25 .60
❑ 282 Olin Kreutz/John Tait
/Fred Miller .20 .50
❑ 283 Glenn Holt RC/Kyle Larson
/Shayne Graham .25 .60
❑ 284 Chris Perry .20 .50
❑ 285 Derek Anderson/Ken Dorsey .25 .60
❑ 286 Chad Johnson .25 .60
❑ 287 Charlie Frye .25 .60
❑ 288 Orpheus Roye/Ted Washington
/Robaire Smith .20 .50
❑ 289 Jason Witten .30 .75
❑ 290 Tony Romo .50 1.25
❑ 291 D.J. Williams/Ian Gold
/Al Wilson .20 .50
❑ 292 Ebenezer Ekuban/Kenard Lang .20 .50
❑ 293 Paris Lenon/Boss Bailey .20 .50
❑ 294 Rod Smith .25 .60
❑ 295 Mike Furrey .25 .60
❑ 296 Nick Harris/Jason Hanson

/Eddie Drummond .20 .50
❑ 297 Robert Ferguson .20 .50
❑ 298 Charles Woodson .25 .60
❑ 299 Chad Clifton/Mark Tauscher
/Rob Davis .20 .50
❑ 300 Travis Johnson/C.C. Brown
/Glenn Earl .20 .50
❑ 301 Mario Williams .25 .60
❑ 302 Anthony McFarland
/Robert Mathis .20 .50
❑ 303 George Wrighster
/Marcedes Lewis .20 .50
❑ 304 Joseph Addai .30 .75
❑ 305 Maurice Jones-Drew .30 .75
❑ 306 Ernest Wilford .20 .50
❑ 307 Donovin Darius/Nick Greisen
/Mike Peterson .20 .50
❑ 308 Larry Johnson .25 .60
❑ 309 Derek Hagan .20 .50
❑ 310 Ron Edwards/James Reed
/Jimmy Wilkerson .20 .50
❑ 311 Zach Thomas .25 .60
❑ 312 Vonnie Holliday/Keith Traylor .20 .50
❑ 313 Jason Rader/L.J. Shelton
/Cleo Lemon .20 .50
❑ 314 Chester Taylor .20 .50
❑ 315 Jabar Gaffney/Reche Caldwell .20 .50
❑ 316 E.J. Henderson/Dontarrious Thomas
/Ben Leber .20 .50
❑ 317 Donte Stallworth .25 .60
❑ 318 Jamie Martin/Mike Karney .20 .50
❑ 319 Hollis Thomas/Brian Young
/Charles Grant .20 .50
❑ 320 Reuben Droughns .25 .60
❑ 321 Eli Manning .30 .75
❑ 322 Corey Webster/R.W. McQuarters
/Sam Madison .20 .50
❑ 323 Erik Coleman/Kerry Rhodes .20 .50
❑ 324 Chad Pennington .25 .60
❑ 325 DeWayne Robertson
/Kimo Von Oelhoffen/Andre Dyson .20 .50
❑ 326 Courtney Anderson
/Robert Gallery/Randal Williams .20 .50
❑ 327 Randy Moss .30 .75
❑ 328 Brodrick Bunkley
/Mike Patterson .20 .50
❑ 329 Correll Buckhalter .25 .60
❑ 330 Donovan McNabb .30 .75
❑ 331 Chris Gardocki/Jeff Reed .20 .50
❑ 332 Vincent Jackson .20 .50
❑ 333 Ben Roethlisberger .40 1.00
❑ 334 Philip Rivers .30 .75
❑ 335 Larry Foote/Clark Haggans
/James Farrior .20 .50
❑ 336 Billy Volek/Brandon Manumaleuna
/Nate Kaeding .20 .50
❑ 337 Alex Smith QB .30 .75
❑ 338 Marques Douglas/
Manny Lawson .20 .50
❑ 339 Maurice Hicks/Joe Nedney
/Andy Lee .20 .50
❑ 340 D.J. Hackett .20 .50
❑ 341 Julian Peterson .20 .50
❑ 342 Patrick Kerney/Bryce Fisher
/Rocky Bernard .20 .50
❑ 343 Randy McMichael
/Joe Klopfenstein .20 .50
❑ 344 Leonard Little .20 .50
❑ 345 Jeff Garcia .25 .60
❑ 346 Cato June/Derrick Brooks .25 .60
❑ 347 Mike Alstott .25 .60
❑ 348 Keith Bulluck .20 .50
❑ 349 Kevin Carter/Greg Spires
/Chris Hovan .20 .50
❑ 350 Courtney Roby/Craig Hentrich
/Rob Bironas .20 .50
❑ 351 London Fletcher
/Marcus Washington .20 .50
❑ 352 Edgerrin James .25 .60
❑ 353 Antwaan Randle El .20 .50
❑ 354 Obafemi Ayanbadejo/Kurt Warner
/Sean Morey .25 .60
❑ 355 Renaldo Wynn/Phillip Daniels
/Andre Carter .20 .50
❑ 356 Roy Williams WR .25 .60
❑ 357 Alge Crumpler .25 .60
❑ 358 Brian Dawkins .25 .60
❑ 359 Chris Crocker/Lawyer Milloy
/Jimmy Williams .20 .50
❑ 360 Reggie Bush .40 1.00
❑ 361 Chris Kelsay/Angelo Crowell .20 .50
❑ 362 Sean Taylor .20 .50
❑ 363 Aaron Schobel .20 .50
❑ 364 Rock Cartwright/Ladell Betts
/Mike Sellers .20 .50
❑ 365 DeAngelo Williams .30 .75
❑ 366 Grady Jackson/Rod Coleman .20 .50
❑ 367 David Carr/Brad Hoover
/Michael Gaines .25 .60
❑ 368 Derrick Mason .20 .50
❑ 369 Brian Urlacher .30 .75
❑ 370 Ray Lewis .30 .75
❑ 371 Robert Geathers
/Madieu Williams/Landon Johnson .20 .50
❑ 372 Langston Walker/Jason Peters
/Derrick Dockery .20 .50
❑ 373 Jason Wright/Jerome Harrison .20 .50
❑ 374 Julius Peppers .25 .60
❑ 375 Braylon Edwards .25 .60
❑ 376 Lance Briggs/Mark Anderson .25 .60
❑ 377 Jay Cutler .30 .75
❑ 378 Nathan Vasher/Charles Tillman
/Ricky Manning Jr .20 .50
❑ 379 Brandon Marshall/Daniel Graham
/Patrick Ramsey .25 .60
❑ 380 Rudi Johnson .25 .60
❑ 381 Ernie Sims .20 .50
❑ 382 Marion Barber .30 .75
❑ 383 Bubba Franks/Aaron Rodgers .30 .75
❑ 384 Terrell Owens .30 .75
❑ 385 Vernand Morency .25 .60
❑ 386 Brad Johnson/Anthony Fasano
/Patrick Crayton .25 .60
❑ 387 Nick Barnett/Will Blackmon
/Abdul Hodge .20 .50
❑ 388 John Engelberger
/Elvis Dumervil .20 .50
❑ 389 DeMeco Ryans .25 .60
❑ 390 John Lynch .25 .60
❑ 391 Rashean Mathis .20 .50
❑ 392 Shawn Bryson/Brian Calhoun
/Dan Campbell .20 .50
❑ 393 Brian Williams/Paul Spicer
/Reggie Hayward .20 .50
❑ 394 A.J. Hawk .30 .75
❑ 395 Tamba Hali/Jared Allen .30 .75
❑ 396 Gary Brackett/Rob Morris .20 .50
❑ 397 Jason Taylor .20 .50
❑ 398 Dwight Freeney .25 .60
❑ 399 Donnie Spragan/Matt Roth
/Travares Tillman .20 .50
❑ 400 Marlin Jackson/Matt Giordano
/Antoine Bethea .20 .50
❑ 401 Ty Warren/Vince Wilfork .20 .50
❑ 402 Reggie Williams .25 .60
❑ 403 Wes Welker .30 .75
❑ 404 Tony Gonzalez .25 .60
❑ 405 Laurence Maroney .30 .75
❑ 406 Patrick Surtain/Greg Wesley
/Sammy Knight .20 .50
❑ 407 Steve Weatherford/Michael Lewis
/John Carney .20 .50
❑ 408 Will Allen/Andre Goodman .20 .50
❑ 409 Plaxico Burress .25 .60
❑ 410 Troy Williamson .20 .50
❑ 411 Victor Hobson/Eric Barton .20 .50
❑ 412 Ben Watson/Matt Cassel
/Kevin Faulk .30 .75
❑ 413 Justin McCareins/Mike Nugent
/Ben Graham .20 .50
❑ 414 Deuce McAllister .25 .60
❑ 415 LaMont Jordan .25 .60
❑ 416 Osi Umenyiora/Mathias Kiwanuka .20 .50
❑ 417 Reggie Brown .20 .50
❑ 418 Shaun O'Hara/Kareem McKenzie
/Chris Snee .20 .50
❑ 419 Hines Ward .30 .75
❑ 420 Leon Washington .25 .60
❑ 421 Ike Taylor/Deshea Townsend
/Bryant McFadden .20 .50
❑ 422 Laveranues Coles .25 .60
❑ 423 Lorenzo Neal/Michael Turner .30 .75
❑ 424 Dhani Jones/Takeo Spikes .20 .50
❑ 425 Frank Gore .30 .75
❑ 426 Brian Westbrook .25 .60
❑ 427 Michael Robinson/Moran Norris
/Trent Dilfer .25 .60
❑ 428 Kevin Curtis/Hank Baskett
/Greg Lewis .25 .60
❑ 429 Fakhir Brown/Tye Hill .20 .50
❑ 430 LaDainian Tomlinson .40 1.00
❑ 431 Marc Bulger .25 .60
❑ 432 Matt Wilhelm/Igor Olshansky
/Antonio Cromartie .20 .50
❑ 433 Chris Simms .20 .50
❑ 434 Derek Smith LB/Tully Banta-Cain .20 .50
❑ 435 Ronde Barber/Brian Kelly
/Phillip Buchanon .20 .50
❑ 436 Arnaz Battle .20 .50
❑ 437 David Givens .20 .50
❑ 438 Matt Hasselbeck .25 .60
❑ 439 Cornelius Griffin
/Rocky McIntosh .20 .50
❑ 440 Dominique Byrd/Jeff Wilkins
/Aaron Walker .20 .50
❑ 441 JaMarcus Russell RC .75 2.00
❑ 442 Brady Quinn RC 1.25 3.00
❑ 443 Drew Stanton RC .50 1.25
❑ 444 Troy Smith RC .75 2.00
❑ 445 Kevin Kolb RC 1.00 2.50
❑ 446 Trent Edwards RC 1.00 2.50
❑ 447 John Beck RC .60 1.50
❑ 448 Jordan Palmer RC .60 1.50
❑ 449 Chris Leak RC .50 1.25
❑ 450 Isiah Stanback RC .60 1.50
❑ 451 Tyler Palko RC .50 1.25
❑ 452 Jared Zabransky RC .60 1.50
❑ 453 Jeff Rowe RC .50 1.25
❑ 454 Zac Taylor RC .60 1.50
❑ 455 Lester Ricard RC .60 1.50
❑ 456 Adrian Peterson RC 5.00 12.00
❑ 457 Marshawn Lynch RC 1.00 2.50
❑ 458 Brandon Jackson RC .60 1.50
❑ 459 Michael Bush RC .60 1.50
❑ 460 Kenny Irons RC .60 1.50
❑ 461 Antonio Pittman RC .60 1.50
❑ 462 Tony Hunt RC .60 1.50
❑ 463 Darius Walker RC .50 1.25
❑ 464 Dwayne Wright RC .50 1.25
❑ 465 Lorenzo Booker RC .60 1.50
❑ 466 Kenneth Darby RC .60 1.50
❑ 467 Chris Henry RC .50 1.25
❑ 468 Selvin Young RC .60 1.50
❑ 469 Brian Leonard RC .50 1.25
❑ 470 Ahmad Bradshaw RC .75 2.00
❑ 471 Gary Russell RC .50 1.25
❑ 472 Kolby Smith RC .60 1.50
❑ 473 Thomas Clayton RC .50 1.25
❑ 474 Garrett Wolfe RC .60 1.50
❑ 475 Calvin Johnson RC 1.50 4.00
❑ 476 Ted Ginn Jr. RC 1.00 2.50
❑ 477 Dwayne Jarrett RC .60 1.50
❑ 478 Dwayne Bowe RC 1.00 2.50
❑ 479 Sidney Rice RC 1.25 3.00
❑ 480 Robert Meachem RC .60 1.50
❑ 481 Anthony Gonzalez RC .75 2.00
❑ 482 Craig Buster Davis RC .60 1.50
❑ 483 Aundrae Allison RC .50 1.25
❑ 484 Chansi Stuckey RC .60 1.50
❑ 485 David Clowney RC .60 1.50
❑ 486 Steve Smith RC 1.00 2.50
❑ 487 Courtney Taylor RC .50 1.25
❑ 488 Paul Williams RC .50 1.25
❑ 489 Johnnie Lee Higgins RC .60 1.50
❑ 490 Rhema McKnight RC .50 1.25
❑ 491 Jason Hill RC .60 1.50
❑ 492 Dallas Baker RC .50 1.25
❑ 493 Greg Olsen RC .75 2.00
❑ 494 Yamon Figurs RC .40 1.00
❑ 495 Scott Chandler RC .50 1.25
❑ 496 Matt Spaeth RC .60 1.50
❑ 497 Ben Patrick RC .50 1.25
❑ 498 Clark Harris RC .60 1.50
❑ 499 Martrez Milner RC .50 1.25
❑ 500 Joe Newton RC .50 1.25
❑ 501 Alan Branch RC .50 1.25
❑ 502 Amobi Okoye RC .60 1.50
❑ 503 DeMarcus Tank Tyler RC .50 1.25
❑ 504 Justin Harrell RC .60 1.50
❑ 505 Brandon Mebane RC .50 1.25
❑ 506 Gaines Adams RC .60 1.50
❑ 507 Jamaal Anderson RC .50 1.25
❑ 508 Adam Carriker RC .50 1.25
❑ 509 Jarvis Moss RC .60 1.50

- ❑ 510 Charles Johnson RC .40 1.00
- ❑ 511 Anthony Spencer RC .60 1.50
- ❑ 512 Quentin Moses RC .50 1.25
- ❑ 513 LaMarr Woodley RC .60 1.50
- ❑ 514 Victor Abiamiri RC .60 1.50
- ❑ 515 Ray McDonald RC .50 1.25
- ❑ 516 Tim Crowder RC .60 1.50
- ❑ 517 Patrick Willis RC 1.00 2.50
- ❑ 518 Brandon Siler RC .50 1.25
- ❑ 519 David Harris RC .50 1.25
- ❑ 520 Buster Davis RC .50 1.25
- ❑ 521 Lawrence Timmons RC .60 1.50
- ❑ 522 Paul Posluszny RC .75 2.00
- ❑ 523 Jon Beason RC .60 1.50
- ❑ 524 Rufus Alexander RC .60 1.50
- ❑ 525 Earl Everett RC .50 1.25
- ❑ 526 Stewart Bradley RC .60 1.50
- ❑ 527 Prescott Burgess RC .50 1.25
- ❑ 528 Leon Hall RC .60 1.50
- ❑ 529 Darrelle Revis RC .75 2.00
- ❑ 530 Aaron Ross RC .60 1.50
- ❑ 531 Daymeion Hughes RC .50 1.25
- ❑ 532 Marcus McCauley RC .50 1.25
- ❑ 533 Chris Houston RC .50 1.25
- ❑ 534 Tanard Jackson RC .40 1.00
- ❑ 535 Jonathan Wade RC .50 1.25
- ❑ 536 Josh Wilson RC .50 1.25
- ❑ 537 Eric Wright RC .60 1.50
- ❑ 538 A.J. Davis RC .40 1.00
- ❑ 539 David Irons RC .40 1.00
- ❑ 540 LaRon Landry RC .75 2.00
- ❑ 541 Reggie Nelson RC .50 1.25
- ❑ 542 Michael Griffin RC .60 1.50
- ❑ 543 Brandon Meriweather RC .60 1.50
- ❑ 544 Eric Weddle RC .50 1.25
- ❑ 545 Aaron Rouse RC .60 1.50
- ❑ 546 Josh Gattis RC .40 1.00
- ❑ 547 Joe Thomas RC .60 1.50
- ❑ 548 Levi Brown RC .60 1.50
- ❑ 549 Tony Ugoh RC .50 1.25
- ❑ 550 Ryan Kalil RC .50 1.25

2005 Topps Turkey Red

- ❑ COMPLETE SET (200) 125.00 250.00
- ❑ COMP.SET w/o SP's (249) 25.00 60.00
- ❑ 1A Eli Manning .75 2.00
- ❑ 1B Eli Manning Ad Back 4.00 10.00
- ❑ 2 Clinton Portis .40 1.00
- ❑ 3 Charles Woodson .30 .75
- ❑ 4A Ray Lewis .40 1.00
- ❑ 4B Ray Lewis Ad Back 2.00 5.00
- ❑ 5 Michael Clayton .30 .75
- ❑ 6 Eric Moulds .30 .75
- ❑ 7 Derrick Blaylock .25 .60
- ❑ 8 Carson Palmer .40 1.00
- ❑ 9 Zach Thomas .40 1.00
- ❑ 10 Dallas Clark .30 .75
- ❑ 11 DeAngelo Hall .30 .75
- ❑ 12 Terrell Owens .40 1.00
- ❑ 13 Brian Griese .30 .75
- ❑ 14 Dunta Robinson .25 .60
- ❑ 15 Kevan Barlow .25 .60
- ❑ 16 Jake Plummer .30 .75
- ❑ 17 James Farrior .25 .60
- ❑ 18A Peyton Manning .60 1.50
- ❑ 18B Peyton Manning Ad Back 3.00 8.00
- ❑ 19 Michael Bennett .30 .75
- ❑ 20 Brian Urlacher .40 1.00
- ❑ 21 Dante Hall .30 .75
- ❑ 22 Deion Branch .30 .75
- ❑ 23 Billy Volek .30 .75
- ❑ 24 Donald Driver .40 1.00
- ❑ 25 LaDainian Tomlinson CL .40 1.00
- ❑ 26 Donte Stallworth CL .25 .60
- ❑ 27 Joey Galloway .30 .75
- ❑ 28 Joey Harrington .40 1.00
- ❑ 29 T.J. Houshmandzadeh .30 .75
- ❑ 30 LaDainian Tomlinson .50 1.25
- ❑ 31 Darius Watts .25 .60
- ❑ 32 Chris Gamble .25 .60
- ❑ 33 Javon Walker .30 .75
- ❑ 34 Kevin Curtis .30 .75
- ❑ 35 Steven Jackson .50 1.25
- ❑ 36 J.P. Losman .30 .75
- ❑ 37A Champ Bailey .30 .75
- ❑ 37B Champ Bailey Ad Back 1.50 4.00
- ❑ 38 Tiki Barber .40 1.00
- ❑ 39 LaVar Arrington .40 1.00
- ❑ 40 Byron Leftwich .30 .75
- ❑ 41 Edgerrin James .30 .75
- ❑ 42 DeShaun Foster .30 .75
- ❑ 43 Darrell Jackson .30 .75
- ❑ 44 Julius Peppers .30 .75
- ❑ 45 David Carr .30 .75
- ❑ 46 Drew Bennett .30 .75
- ❑ 47 Antonio Gates .40 1.00
- ❑ 48A Deuce McAllister .40 1.00
- ❑ 48B Deuce McAllister Ad Back 2.00 5.00
- ❑ 49 Patrick Ramsey .30 .75
- ❑ 50 Antonio Bryant .30 .75
- ❑ 51 Quentin Jammer .25 .60
- ❑ 52 Chris Brown .30 .75
- ❑ 53 Eddie Kennison .25 .60
- ❑ 54 Steve McNair .40 1.00
- ❑ 55 Corey Bradford .30 .75
- ❑ 56 Chris Perry .25 .60
- ❑ 57 Curtis Martin .40 1.00
- ❑ 58 Mewelde Moore .25 .60
- ❑ 59 Travis Taylor .25 .60
- ❑ 60 Chad Pennington .40 1.00
- ❑ 61 Chad Johnson .30 .75
- ❑ 62 Kyle Boller .30 .75
- ❑ 63 Tyrone Calico .30 .75
- ❑ 64 Michael Pittman .25 .60
- ❑ 65 Kerry Collins .30 .75
- ❑ 66 Keary Colbert .25 .60
- ❑ 67 LaMont Jordan CL .25 .60
- ❑ 68 Robert Gallery .25 .60
- ❑ 69 Derrick Mason .30 .75
- ❑ 70 Brian Dawkins .30 .75
- ❑ 71 Chris Simms .30 .75
- ❑ 72 Marc Bulger .30 .75
- ❑ 73 Stephen Davis .30 .75
- ❑ 74 Kurt Warner .40 1.00
- ❑ 75 Todd Heap .30 .75
- ❑ 76 Domanick Davis CL .20 .50
- ❑ 77 Shaun Alexander .40 1.00
- ❑ 78 Jerry Porter .30 .75
- ❑ 79 Chester Taylor .30 .75
- ❑ 80A Michael Vick .40 1.00
- ❑ 80B Michael Vick Ad Back 2.00 5.00
- ❑ 81 Justin McCareins .25 .60
- ❑ 82 Fred Taylor .40 1.00
- ❑ 83 Laveranues Coles .30 .75
- ❑ 84 Steve Smith .40 1.00
- ❑ 85 Sean Taylor .30 .75
- ❑ 86 Marvin Harrison .40 1.00
- ❑ 87 Ashley Lelie .25 .60
- ❑ 88 Willis McGahee .40 1.00
- ❑ 89 Terence Newman .25 .60
- ❑ 90 Joe Horn .30 .75
- ❑ 91 Lee Suggs .30 .75
- ❑ 92 Keyshawn Johnson .30 .75
- ❑ 93 Desmond Clark .25 .60
- ❑ 94 T.J. Duckett .25 .60
- ❑ 95 Reggie Wayne .30 .75
- ❑ 96 Donte Stallworth .30 .75
- ❑ 97 Clarence Moore .25 .60
- ❑ 98 Jason Witten .40 1.00
- ❑ 99 Jake Delhomme .40 1.00
- ❑ 100 Julius Jones .40 1.00
- ❑ 101 Ben Troupe .25 .60
- ❑ 102 Hines Ward .40 1.00
- ❑ 103 Domanick Davis .25 .60
- ❑ 104 B.J. Sams .25 .60
- ❑ 105 Marcus Robinson .30 .75
- ❑ 106 Devery Henderson .25 .60
- ❑ 107 Matt Hasselbeck .30 .75
- ❑ 108 Antonio Pierce .25 .60
- ❑ 109 Santana Moss .30 .75
- ❑ 110 Adam Vinatieri .40 1.00
- ❑ 111 Michael Strahan .30 .75
- ❑ 112 Greg Jones .25 .60
- ❑ 113 Drew Brees .40 1.00
- ❑ 114 Marcus Robinson .30 .75
- ❑ 115 Michael Jenkins .30 .75
- ❑ 116 Randy McMichael .25 .60
- ❑ 117 Jonathan Vilma .30 .75
- ❑ 118 Greg Lewis .30 .75
- ❑ 119 Ernest Wilford .30 .75
- ❑ 120 Warrick Dunn .30 .75
- ❑ 121 Shaun Alexander CL .30 .75
- ❑ 122 Donnie Edwards .25 .60
- ❑ 123 Antwaan Randle El .30 .75
- ❑ 124 Rod Smith .30 .75
- ❑ 125 Ed Reed .30 .75
- ❑ 126 Muhsin Muhammad .30 .75
- ❑ 127 L.J. Smith .30 .75
- ❑ 128 Chris Chambers .30 .75
- ❑ 129 Matt Schaub .40 1.00
- ❑ 130 Andre Johnson .30 .75
- ❑ 131 Thomas Jones .30 .75
- ❑ 132 Robert Ferguson .30 .75
- ❑ 133 Jeremy Shockey .40 1.00
- ❑ 134 William Green .25 .60
- ❑ 135A Ben Roethlisberger 1.00 2.50
- ❑ 135B Ben Roethlisberger Ad Back 5.00 12.00
- ❑ 136A Donovan McNabb .40 1.00
- ❑ 136B Donovan McNabb Ad Back 2.00 5.00
- ❑ 137 Duce Staley .30 .75
- ❑ 138 Larry Fitzgerald .40 1.00
- ❑ 139 Charles Rogers .25 .60
- ❑ 140 Mark Brunell .30 .75
- ❑ 141 Kevin Jones .30 .75
- ❑ 142 LaMont Jordan .30 .75
- ❑ 143 Aaron Brooks .25 .60
- ❑ 144 Brian Westbrook .40 1.00
- ❑ 145 Larry Johnson .40 1.00
- ❑ 146 Tommy Maddox .30 .75
- ❑ 147 Corey Dillon .30 .75
- ❑ 148 William Henderson .30 .75
- ❑ 149 Tony Hollings .25 .60
- ❑ 150 Lee Evans .30 .75
- ❑ 151 Kelly Holcomb .25 .60
- ❑ 152 Reuben Droughns .25 .60
- ❑ 153 Keenan McCardell .30 .75
- ❑ 154 Ricky Williams .30 .75
- ❑ 155 Rashaun Woods .25 .60
- ❑ 156 D.J. Williams .25 .60
- ❑ 157 Tom Brady .75 2.00
- ❑ 158 Eric Parker .25 .60
- ❑ 159 Mike Anderson .25 .60
- ❑ 160 Roy Williams WR .40 1.00
- ❑ 161 Mike Vanderjagt .25 .60
- ❑ 162 Ronald Curry .30 .75
- ❑ 163 Priest Holmes .40 1.00
- ❑ 164 Bernard Berrian .30 .75
- ❑ 165 Brian Finneran .25 .60
- ❑ 166 Tony Gonzalez .30 .75
- ❑ 167 Chris McAlister .25 .60
- ❑ 168 Gus Frerotte .25 .60
- ❑ 169 Bryant Johnson .30 .75
- ❑ 170 Jay Fiedler .25 .60
- ❑ 171 Bubba Franks .30 .75
- ❑ 172 Tony Romo 5.00 10.00
- ❑ 173 Jamal Lewis .30 .75
- ❑ 174 Torry Holt .30 .75
- ❑ 175 Ladell Betts .30 .75
- ❑ 176 Bertrand Berry .25 .60
- ❑ 177 Josh McCown .30 .75
- ❑ 178 Jonathan Wells .25 .60
- ❑ 179 Plaxico Burress .30 .75
- ❑ 180 Rudi Johnson .30 .75
- ❑ 181 Cedric Benson RC .75 2.00
- ❑ 182 Carlos Rogers RC .75 2.00
- ❑ 183 Terrence Murphy RC .50 1.25
- ❑ 184 Frank Gore RC 1.50 4.00
- ❑ 185 Vincent Jackson RC 1.00 2.50
- ❑ 186 Ciatrick Fason RC .60 1.50
- ❑ 187 Alex Smith QB RC .75 2.00
- ❑ 188 Mike Williams .60 1.50
- ❑ 189 Kyle Orton RC 1.25 3.00
- ❑ 190A Ronnie Brown RC 2.50 6.00
- ❑ 190B Ronnie Brown 4.00 10.00
- ❑ 191 Charlie Frye RC .75 2.00
- ❑ 192 Mark Bradley RC .60 1.50
- ❑ 193 Antrel Rolle RC .75 2.00
- ❑ 194 Roscoe Parrish RC .60 1.50
- ❑ 195 Ryan Moats RC .60 1.50
- ❑ 196 Andrew Walter RC .60 1.50

Card	Low	High
❑ 197 Troy Williamson RC	.75	2.00
❑ 198 Cadillac Williams RC	1.25	3.00
❑ 199 Adam Jones RC	.60	1.50
❑ 200 Braylon Edwards RC	2.00	5.00
❑ 201 Vernand Morency RC	.60	1.50
❑ 202 Ryan Fitzpatrick RC	.75	2.00
❑ 203 Heath Miller RC	1.50	4.00
❑ 204 Eric Shelton RC	.60	1.50
❑ 205 Jason Campbell RC	1.00	2.50
❑ 206 David Pollack RC	.60	1.50
❑ 207 Stefan LeFors RC	.60	1.50
❑ 208 DeMarcus Ware RC	1.25	3.00
❑ 209 J.J. Arrington RC	.75	2.00
❑ 210 Marion Barber RC	2.50	6.00
❑ 211 Samkon Gado RC	.75	2.00
❑ 212 Roddy White RC	1.00	2.50
❑ 213 Brandon Jacobs RC	1.00	2.50
❑ 214 Mark Clayton RC	.75	2.00
❑ 215 Alex Smith TE RC	.75	2.00
❑ 216 Darren Sproles RC	1.00	2.50
❑ 217 Fabian Washington RC	.75	2.00
❑ 218 Brandon Jones RC	.75	2.00
❑ 219 Derrick Johnson RC	.75	2.00
❑ 220 Dan Orlovsky RC	.75	2.00
❑ 221 Aaron Rodgers RC	2.50	6.00
❑ 222 Cedric Houston RC	.75	2.00
❑ 223 Reggie Brown RC	.60	1.50
❑ 224 Scottie Vines RC	.75	2.00
❑ 225 Willie Parker	3.00	8.00
❑ 226 Matt Jones RC	.75	2.00
❑ 227 Odell Thurman RC	.75	2.00
❑ 228 Alvin Pearman RC	.50	1.25
❑ 229 Chris Henry RC	.75	2.00
❑ 230 Courtney Roby RC	.60	1.50
❑ 231 Isaac Bruce	.30	.75
❑ 232 Warrick Dunn CL	.25	.60
❑ 233 Willis McGahee CL	.30	.75
❑ 234 Marcus Pollard	.25	.60
❑ 235 Jason Taylor	.30	.75
❑ 236 Joe Namath	2.50	6.00
❑ 237 Joe Montana	4.00	10.00
❑ 238 Barry Sanders	2.50	6.00
❑ 239 Jim Brown	2.00	5.00
❑ 240 Terry Bradshaw	2.50	6.00
❑ 241 Ahman Green	.40	1.00
❑ 242 Tiki Barber CL	.30	.75
❑ 243 Julius Jones CL	.30	.75
❑ 244 Daunte Culpepper	.40	1.00
❑ 245 Edgerrin James CL	.25	.60
❑ 246 Trent Green	2.50	6.00
❑ 247 Dwight Freeney	2.50	6.00
❑ 248A Brett Favre	5.00	12.00
❑ 248B Brett Favre Ad Back	6.00	15.00
❑ 249 Marshall Faulk	3.00	8.00
❑ 250 Jerome Bettis	3.00	8.00
❑ 251 Nate Burleson	2.50	6.00
❑ 252 Brandon Lloyd	2.00	5.00
❑ 253 Randy Moss	3.00	8.00
❑ 254 Drew Bledsoe	3.00	8.00
❑ 255 Brandon Stokley	2.00	5.00
❑ 256 Takeo Spikes	2.00	5.00
❑ 257 Philip Rivers	3.00	8.00
❑ 258 Lito Sheppard	2.50	6.00
❑ 259 Jimmy Smith	2.50	6.00
❑ 260 Tatum Bell	2.50	6.00
❑ 261 Allen Rossum	2.00	5.00
❑ 262 Amani Toomer	2.50	6.00
❑ 263 Jabar Gaffney	2.00	5.00
❑ 264 Jonathan Ogden	2.00	5.00
❑ 265 John Abraham	2.00	5.00
❑ 266 Aaron Stecker	2.00	5.00
❑ 267 Jason Elam	2.00	5.00
❑ 268 Najeh Davenport	2.50	6.00
❑ 269 Alge Crumpler	2.50	6.00
❑ 270 Roy Williams S	2.50	6.00
❑ 271 Trent Dilfer	2.50	6.00
❑ 272 Anquan Boldin	2.50	6.00
❑ 273 Artose Pinner	2.00	5.00
❑ 274 David Garrard	3.00	8.00
❑ 275 Terry Glenn	2.00	5.00
❑ 276 Adam Archuleta	2.00	5.00
❑ 277 Jeremiah Trotter	2.00	5.00
❑ 278 Travis Henry	2.50	6.00
❑ 279 Rex Grossman	3.00	8.00
❑ 280 Maurice Morris	2.00	5.00
❑ 281 Mike Alstott	2.50	6.00
❑ 282 Justin Gage	2.50	6.00
❑ 283 Dennis Northcutt	2.00	5.00
❑ 284 David Givens	2.50	6.00
❑ 285 Dominic Rhodes	2.50	6.00
❑ 286 Gerald Ford	2.00	5.00
❑ 287 Ronald Reagan	2.00	5.00
❑ 288 John F. Kennedy	2.00	5.00
❑ 289 Ulysses S. Grant	2.00	5.00
❑ CL1 Jumbo Checklist 1	.40	1.00
❑ CL2 Jumbo Checklist 2	.40	1.00

2006 Topps Turkey Red

Card	Low	High
❑ COMPLETE SET (328)	100.00	200.00
❑ COMP.SET w/o SP's (274)	20.00	50.00
❑ 1 LaVar Arrington	.30	.75
❑ 2 Heath Miller	.25	.60
❑ 3 Antwaan Randle El	.25	.60
❑ 4 Derrick Mason	.25	.60
❑ 5 Deshaun Foster	.25	.60
❑ 6 Andre Johnson	.25	.60
❑ 7 Jonathan Vilma	.25	.60
❑ 8 Trent Dilfer	.25	.60
❑ 9 Tatum Bell	.20	.50
❑ 10 Bubba Franks	.20	.50
❑ 11 T.J. Houshmandzadeh	.25	.60
❑ 12 Adam Vinatieri	.25	.60
❑ 13 Quentin Jammer	.20	.50
❑ 14 Jim Kleinsasser	.20	.50
❑ 15 Priest Holmes	.25	.60
❑ 16 Courtney Roby	.20	.50
❑ 17 Chris Simms	.25	.60
❑ 18 Terry Glenn	.25	.60
❑ 19 Jonathan Ogden	.20	.50
❑ 20 Andrew Walter	.25	.60
❑ 21 Lito Sheppard	.25	.60
❑ 22 Kevan Barlow	.25	.60
❑ 23 Santana Moss	.25	.60
❑ 24 Kelly Holcomb	.20	.50
❑ 25 Thomas Jones	.25	.60
❑ 26 Dennis Northcutt	.20	.50
❑ 27 Najeh Davenport	.25	.60
❑ 28 Edgerrin James	.25	.60
❑ 29 Kevin Curtis	.25	.60
❑ 30 Brian Griese	.25	.60
❑ 31 Jason Taylor	.25	.60
❑ 32 T.J. Duckett	.20	.50
❑ 33 Antonio Bryant	.25	.60
❑ 34 Donald Driver	.30	.75
❑ 35 Brian Westbrook	.25	.60
❑ 36 Lofa Tatupu	.25	.60
❑ 37 Ben Troupe	.20	.50
❑ 38 Chris Cooley	.25	.60
❑ 39 Josh McCown	.25	.60
❑ 40 Chris Perry	.25	.60
❑ 41 Joe Horn	.25	.60
❑ 42 Kyle Boller	.25	.60
❑ 43 Keyshawn Johnson	.25	.60
❑ 44 Frank Gore	.30	.75
❑ 45 Terence Newman	.20	.50
❑ 46 Devery Henderson	.20	.50
❑ 47 Michael Strahan	.25	.60
❑ 48 Ladell Betts	.25	.60
❑ 49 Patrick Ramsey	.25	.60
❑ 50 Anquan Boldin	.25	.60
❑ 51 Nathan Vasher	.20	.50
❑ 52 Dominic Rhodes	.25	.60
❑ 53 Travis Minor	.20	.50
❑ 54 Torry Holt	.25	.60
❑ 55 Sam Gado	.30	.75
❑ 56 Fred Taylor	.25	.60
❑ 57 Braylon Edwards	.30	.75
❑ 58 Tyrone Calico	.20	.50
❑ 59 Derrick Burgess	.20	.50
❑ 60 Chester Taylor	.25	.60
❑ 61 Julius Peppers	.25	.60
❑ 62 L.J. Smith	.20	.50
❑ 63 Keenan McCardell	.25	.60
❑ 64 Lee Evans	.25	.60
❑ 65 Champ Bailey	.25	.60
❑ 66 Alex Smith QB	.25	.60
❑ 67 Tedy Bruschi	.30	.75
❑ 68 Roddy White	.25	.60
❑ 69 Marty Booker	.20	.50
❑ 70 Fred Smoot	.20	.50
❑ 71 A.J. Feeley	.20	.50
❑ 72 Kellen Winslow	.30	.75
❑ 73 Curtis Martin	.30	.75
❑ 74 Ronald Curry	.25	.60
❑ 75 Sam Madison	.20	.50
❑ 76 Keary Colbert	.25	.60
❑ 77 Marcus Pollard	.20	.50
❑ 78 James Farrior	.20	.50
❑ 79 Travis Henry	.25	.60
❑ 80 Samari Rolle	.20	.50
❑ 81 Rodney Harrison	.20	.50
❑ 82 Matt Schaub	.25	.60
❑ 83 Philip Rivers	.30	.75
❑ 84 DeMarcus Ware	.25	.60
❑ 85 Reggie Wayne	.25	.60
❑ 86 Derrick Johnson	.25	.60
❑ 87 Travis Taylor	.20	.50
❑ 88 Antonio Pierce	.20	.50
❑ 89 Jamal Lewis	.25	.60
❑ 90 Aaron Brooks	.25	.60
❑ 91 Michael Pittman	.20	.50
❑ 92 Jerricho Cotchery	.20	.50
❑ 93 Shayne Graham	.20	.50
❑ 94 Dante Hall	.25	.60
❑ 95 Warrick Dunn	.25	.60
❑ 96 Mewelde Moore	.20	.50
❑ 97 Brandon Lloyd	.25	.60
❑ 98 Chris Gamble	.20	.50
❑ 99 Odell Thurman	.20	.50
❑ 100 Osi Umenyiora	.25	.60
❑ 101 Jerry Porter	.25	.60
❑ 102 Brandon Stokley	.25	.60
❑ 103 Clinton Portis	.30	.75
❑ 104 Quentin Jammer	.20	.50
❑ 105 Reuben Droughns	.25	.60
❑ 106 Jason Campbell	.25	.60
❑ 107 LaBrandon Toefield	.20	.50
❑ 108 Nate Burleson	.25	.60
❑ 109 Antrel Rolle	.20	.50
❑ 110A Steve McNair PS	.25	.60
❑ 110B Steve McNair YS	.25	.60
❑ 111A Chad Johnson PBB	.25	.60
❑ 111B Chad Johnson No PBB	.25	.60
❑ 112 Steven Jackson	.30	.75
❑ 113 Ron Dayne	.25	.60
❑ 114 Deion Branch	.25	.60
❑ 115 Ed Reed	.25	.60
❑ 116 Ty Law	.20	.50
❑ 117 Drew Bledsoe	.30	.75
❑ 118 Chris McAlister	.20	.50
❑ 119 Plaxico Burress	.25	.60
❑ 120 Aaron Rodgers	.30	.75
❑ 121 Tony Gonzalez	.25	.60
❑ 122 David Givens	.25	.60
❑ 123 Michael Vick	.30	.75
❑ 124 Antonio Gates	.30	.75
❑ 125 Darrell Jackson	.25	.60
❑ 126 Adam Jones	.20	.50
❑ 127 LaDainian Tomlinson CL	.30	.75
❑ 128 Chad Pennington	.25	.60
❑ 129 Kevin Faulk	.25	.60
❑ 130 Isaac Bruce	.25	.60
❑ 131 Tom Brady CL	.40	1.00
❑ 132 Deuce McAllister	.25	.60
❑ 133 Laveranues Coles	.25	.60
❑ 134 Donnie Edwards	.20	.50
❑ 135 Brian Urlacher CL	.25	.60
❑ 136 Dallas Clark	.25	.60
❑ 137 Drew Bennett	.25	.60
❑ 138 Domanick Davis	.25	.60
❑ 139 Cadillac Williams CL	.25	.60
❑ 140 David Garrard	.30	.75
❑ 141 Shaun Alexander CL	.20	.50
❑ 142 Troy Williamson	.25	.60
❑ 143 Steve Smith CL	.25	.60
❑ 144 Jake Plummer	.25	.60
❑ 145 Carson Palmer CL	.25	.60
❑ 146 DeAngelo Hall	.25	.60
❑ 147 Michael Vick CL	.25	.60
❑ 148 Kyle Vanden Bosch	.20	.50

❑ 149 Larry Johnson CL .20 .50
❑ 150 LaDainian Tomlinson .40 1.00
❑ 151 Dunta Robinson .20 .50
❑ 152 Muhsin Muhammad .25 .60
❑ 153 Steven Jackson CL .25 .60
❑ 154 David Pollack .20 .50
❑ 155 Mark Brunell .25 .60
❑ 156 Donovan McNabb .30 .75
❑ 157 Jeremy Shockey .30 .75
❑ 158 Corey Dillon .25 .60
❑ 159 Mark Clayton .25 .60
❑ 160 Vincent Jackson .25 .60
❑ 161 Kurt Warner .30 .75
❑ 162 Marcus Robinson .25 .60
❑ 163 Takeo Spikes .20 .50
❑ 164 Charles Rogers .25 .60
❑ 165 J.P. Losman .25 .60
❑ 166 Matt Jones .25 .60
❑ 167 Rod Smith .25 .60
❑ 168 Steve Smith .30 .75
❑ 169 Michael Vick .30 .75
❑ 170 Mike Vanderjagt .20 .50
❑ 171 Amani Toomer .25 .60
❑ 172 Deltha O'Neal .20 .50
❑ 173 Michael Jenkins .25 .60
❑ 174 David Carr .20 .50
❑ 175 Chris Brown .25 .60
❑ 176 Kevin Jones .25 .60
❑ 177 Roy Williams S .25 .60
❑ 178 Marvin Harrison .30 .75
❑ 179 Drew Brees .30 .75
❑ 180 John Abraham .20 .50
❑ 181 Joseph Addai RC SP 2.50 6.00
❑ 182 Sinorice Moss RC SP 2.00 5.00
❑ 183A Vince Young PS RC 2.00 5.00
❑ 183B Vince Young OS SP 5.00 12.00
❑ 184 Vernon Davis RC SP 2.00 5.00
❑ 185 Brandon Williams RC SP 1.50 4.00
❑ 186 Derek Hagan RC SP 1.50 4.00
❑ 187 Brian Calhoun RC SP 1.50 4.00
❑ 188 Mario Williams RC SP 2.50 6.00
❑ 189 DeAngelo Williams RC SP 4.00 10.00
❑ 190 Jay Cutler RC SP 5.00 12.00
❑ 191 A.J. Hawk RC SP 3.00 8.00
❑ 192 Reggie Bush RC 2.00 5.00
❑ 193 Laurence Maroney RC SP 2.50 6.00
❑ 194 D'Brickashaw Ferguson RC SP 2.00 5.00
❑ 195 Jason Avant RC SP 2.00 5.00
❑ 196 Brodie Croyle RC SP 2.00 5.00
❑ 197 Michael Huff RC SP 2.00 5.00
❑ 198 LenDale White RC SP 2.50 6.00
❑ 199 Marcedes Lewis RC SP 2.00 5.00
❑ 200 Travis Wilson RC SP 1.25 3.00
❑ 201 Haloti Ngata RC SP 2.00 5.00
❑ 202 Greg Jennings RC SP 3.00 8.00
❑ 203 Leon Washington RC SP 2.50 6.00
❑ 204 Tamba Hali RC SP 2.00 5.00
❑ 205 Santonio Holmes RC SP 5.00 12.00
❑ 206 Jerome Harrison RC SP 2.00 5.00
❑ 207 Tarvaris Jackson RC SP 2.00 5.00
❑ 208 Mathias Kiwanuka RC SP 2.50 6.00
❑ 209 Omar Jacobs RC SP 1.25 3.00
❑ 210 Alan Zemaitis RC SP 2.00 5.00
❑ 211 Demetrius Williams RC SP 1.50 4.00
❑ 212 Bobby Carpenter RC SP 1.50 4.00
❑ 213 Tye Hill RC SP 1.50 4.00
❑ 214 Chad Jackson RC SP 1.50 4.00
❑ 215 Joe Klopfenstein RC SP 1.50 4.00
❑ 216 Kamerion Wimbley RC SP 2.00 5.00
❑ 217 Michael Robinson RC SP 1.50 4.00
❑ 218 David Thomas RC SP 2.00 5.00
❑ 219 Charlie Whitehurst RC SP 2.00 5.00
❑ 220 Jerious Norwood RC SP 2.00 5.00
❑ 221 Bruce Gradkowski RC SP 2.00 5.00
❑ 222 Kellen Clemens RC SP 2.00 5.00
❑ 223 Thomas Howard RC SP 1.50 4.00
❑ 224 Anthony Fasano RC SP 2.00 5.00
❑ 225 Maurice Drew RC SP 4.00 10.00
❑ 226 Antonio Cromartie RC SP 2.00 5.00
❑ 227 Mike Bell RC SP 2.00 5.00
❑ 228 D'Qwell Jackson RC SP 1.50 4.00
❑ 229A Matt Leinart TIB RC 1.25 3.00
❑ 229B Matt Leinart SIB SP 3.00 8.00
❑ 230 Maurice Stovall RC SP 1.50 4.00
❑ 231A Carson Palmer BJ .30 .75
❑ 231A Carson Palmer WJ .30 .75
❑ 232 Courtney Anderson .20 .50
❑ 233 D.J. Williams .20 .50
❑ 234 Chris Chambers .25 .60
❑ 235 Zach Thomas .30 .75
❑ 236 Reggie Brown .20 .50
❑ 237 Cadillac Williams .30 .75
❑ 238 Randy McMichael .20 .50
❑ 239 Brian Urlacher .30 .75
❑ 240 Cedric Houston .20 .50
❑ 241 Marc Bulger .25 .60
❑ 242 Mike Anderson .25 .60
❑ 243 Allen Rossum .20 .50
❑ 244 William Henderson .20 .50
❑ 245 Eddie Kennison .20 .50
❑ 246 Adam Archuleta .20 .50
❑ 247 Ryan Moats .25 .60
❑ 248 D.J. Hackett .25 .60
❑ 249 Marion Barber .30 .75
❑ 250 Mike Alstott .20 .50
❑ 251 Shawne Merriman .25 .60
❑ 252 Byron Leftwich .25 .60
❑ 253 Dan Morgan .20 .50
❑ 254 Ronnie Brown .30 .75
❑ 255 Mark Bradley .20 .50
❑ 256 Mike Williams .25 .60
❑ 257 Ronde Barber .25 .60
❑ 258 Bernard Berrian .25 .60
❑ 259 Gibril Wilson .20 .50
❑ 260 Scottie Vines .20 .50
❑ 261 Rex Grossman .30 .75
❑ 262 Daniel Graham .20 .50
❑ 263 Ernest Wilford .20 .50
❑ 264 Javon Walker .25 .60
❑ 265 Corey Webster .20 .50
❑ 266 Jon Kitna .25 .60
❑ 267 Arnaz Battle .20 .50
❑ 268 Robert Ferguson SP 1.50 4.00
❑ 269 Cedric Benson .25 .60
❑ 270 Michael Clayton .25 .60
❑ 271 Brandon Jacobs .30 .75
❑ 272 Jason Witten SP 2.50 6.00
❑ 273A Randy Moss BS .30 .75
❑ 273B Randy Moss PS .30 .75
❑ 274 Daunte Culpepper SP 2.50 6.00
❑ 275 Ronnie Brown .30 .75
❑ 276 Dwight Freeney .25 .60
❑ 277 LaMont Jordan .25 .60
❑ 278 Jeremiah Trotter .20 .50
❑ 279A Hines Ward PO sky .30 .75
❑ 279B Hines Ward BY sky .30 .75
❑ 280A Tom Brady PBB .50 1.25
❑ 280B Tom Brady No PBB .50 1.25
❑ 281 Charles Woodson .25 .60
❑ 282A Shaun Alexander GJ .25 .60
❑ 282B Shaun Alexander WJ .25 .60
❑ 283 Eric Moulds .25 .60
❑ 284A Ben Roethlisberger BS .50 1.25
❑ 284B Ben Roethlisberger PS .50 1.25
❑ 285 Matt Hasselbeck .25 .60
❑ 286 Willis McGahee .30 .75
❑ 287 Carlos Rogers .20 .50
❑ 288 Brett Favre .60 1.50
❑ 289 Larry Fitzgerald .30 .75
❑ 290 Billy Volek .20 .50
❑ 291 Julius Jones .25 .60
❑ 292 Trent Green .25 .60
❑ 293 Ashley Lelie .20 .50
❑ 294 Eli Manning .40 1.00
❑ 295 Alge Crumpler .25 .60
❑ 296 Rudi Johnson .25 .60
❑ 297 Troy Polamalu .40 1.00
❑ 298 Roy Williams WR .30 .75
❑ 299 Willie Parker .40 1.00
❑ 300 Jake Delhomme .25 .60
❑ 301 Champ Bailey .25 .60
❑ 302 Ahman Green .25 .60
❑ 303 Robert Gallery .20 .50
❑ 304 Todd Heap .25 .60
❑ 305 Joey Harrington .20 .50
❑ 306 Terrell Owens .30 .75
❑ 307 Joey Galloway .25 .60
❑ 308A Larry Johnson OS .25 .60
❑ 308A Larry Johnson PS .25 .60
❑ 309 Brian Dawkins .25 .60
❑ 310 Ray Lewis .30 .75
❑ 311A Tiki Barber OS .30 .75
❑ 311B Tiki Barber BS SP 2.50 6.00
❑ 312 Donte Stallworth .25 .60
❑ 313 Eric Parker .20 .50
❑ 314 Charlie Frye .25 .60
❑ 315A Peyton Manning BYS .50 1.25
❑ 315B Peyton Manning OS SP 15.00 40.00

2008 UD Masterpieces

❑ COMPLETE SET (105) 75.00 135.00
❑ COMP.SET w/o SP's (86) 15.00 40.00
❑ 1 Donnie Avery RC 1.00 2.50
❑ 2 Adrian Peterson 1.00 2.50
❑ 3 D.Tyree/E.Manning .50 1.25
❑ 4 Alan Ameche .30 .75
❑ 5 Barry Sanders .75 2.00
❑ 6 Bart Starr .75 2.00
❑ 7 Ben Roethlisberger .75 2.00
❑ 8 Brett Favre 1.25 3.00
❑ 9 Bob Sanders .40 1.00
❑ 10 Brett Favre 1.25 3.00
❑ 11 Brian Urlacher .50 1.25
❑ 12 Earl Bennett RC .75 2.00
❑ 13 Champ Bailey .30 .75
❑ 14 Chuck Bednarik .40 1.00
❑ 15 Dan Marino 1.00 2.50
❑ 16 Brian Bosworth .50 1.25
❑ 17 Devin Thomas RC .75 2.00
❑ 18 Andre Caldwell RC .75 2.00
❑ 19 Desmond Howard .30 .75
❑ 20 Devin Hester .50 1.25
❑ 21 Dick Butkus .60 1.50
❑ 22 Harry Douglas RC .60 1.50
❑ 23 Don Shula .30 .75
❑ 24 Donovan McNabb .50 1.25
❑ 25 Kevin O'Connell RC .75 2.00
❑ 26 Doug Flutie .40 1.00
❑ 27 Drew Pearson .40 1.00
❑ 28 Dwight Clark .40 1.00
❑ 29 Early Doucet RC .75 2.00
❑ 30 Ed Podolak .30 .75
❑ 31 Eli Manning .50 1.25
❑ 32 Joe Flacco RC 2.50 6.00
❑ 33 James Hardy RC .60 1.50
❑ 34 Franco Harris .50 1.25
❑ 35 Frank Reich .30 .75
❑ 36 Dexter Jackson RC .75 2.00
❑ 37 Gale Sayers .60 1.50
❑ 38 Chris Johnson RC 2.50 6.00
❑ 39 Herm Edwards .30 .75
❑ 40 Howard Cosell .40 1.00
❑ 41 Dustin Keller RC .75 2.00
❑ 42 Jamaal Charles RC 1.25 3.00
❑ 43 Jim Brown .60 1.50
❑ 44 Jim Thorpe .60 1.50
❑ 46 Joe Montana 1.00 2.50
❑ 47 Joe Namath .60 1.50
❑ 48 John David Booty RC .75 2.00
❑ 49 John Elway .75 2.00
❑ 50 Johnny Unitas .75 2.00
❑ 51 Jordy Nelson RC 1.00 2.50
❑ 52 Kellen Winslow Sr. .40 1.00
❑ 53 Eddie Royal RC 1.25 3.00
❑ 54 Kevin Dyson .30 .75
❑ 55 Kevin Dyson .30 .75
❑ 56 Kevin Smith RC 1.50 4.00
❑ 57 LaDainian Tomlinson .60 1.50
❑ 58 Limas Sweed RC .75 2.00
❑ 60 Malcolm Kelly RC .75 2.00
❑ 61 Mario Manningham RC .75 2.00
❑ 62 Marvin Harrison .50 1.25
❑ 63 Jerome Simpson RC .60 1.50
❑ 64 Matt Forte RC 1.50 4.00
❑ 66 Chris Long RC .75 2.00
❑ 67 Paul Hornung .50 1.25
❑ 68 Peyton Manning .75 2.00
❑ 69 Randy Moss .50 1.25
❑ 71 Ray Rice RC 1.00 2.50
❑ 72 Red Grange .60 1.50

Card		
❑ 73 Lester Hayes	.40	1.00
❑ 74 Sammy Baugh	.50	1.25
❑ 75 Adrian Peterson	1.00	2.50
❑ 76 Steve Slaton RC	1.00	2.50
❑ 77 Billy Sims	.40	1.00
❑ 78 Jack Lambert	.50	1.25
❑ 79 Scott Norwood	.30	.75
❑ 80 Snow Plow Game	.30	.75
❑ 81 Terrell Owens	.50	1.25
❑ 82 Terry Bradshaw	.75	2.00
❑ 83 Tom Brady	.75	2.00
❑ 84 Tom Brady	.75	2.00
❑ 85 Tony Romo	.75	2.00
❑ 86 Vince Lombardi	.75	2.00
❑ 87 Vince Young	.40	1.00
❑ 88 Walter Payton	1.00	2.50
❑ 89 Wes Welker	.50	1.25
❑ 90 Y.A. Tittle	.50	1.25
❑ 91 Peterson/Butkus TW	4.00	10.00
❑ 92 Unitas/P.Mann TW	5.00	12.00
❑ 93 Favre/Hornung TW	4.00	10.00
❑ 94 R.Moss/M.Blount TW	3.00	8.00
❑ 95 Horn/Mont/Theis/Quinn TW	5.00	12.00
❑ 96 B.Sanders/Swann TW	4.00	10.00
❑ 97 Hornung/Favre TW	4.00	10.00
❑ 98 Tarkenton/Peterson TW	4.00	10.00
❑ 99 E.ManningTittle TW	4.00	10.00
❑ 101 Rashard Mendenhall SP RC	2.50	6.00
❑ 102 Brian Brohm SP RC	1.25	3.00
❑ 103 Chad Henne SP RC	2.00	5.00
❑ 104 Jake Long SP RC	1.25	3.00
❑ 105 Felix Jones SP RC	2.50	6.00
❑ 106 Darren McFadden SP RC	2.50	6.00
❑ 107 DeSean Jackson SP RC	2.50	6.00
❑ 108 Glenn Dorsey SP RC	1.25	3.00
❑ 109 Jonathan Stewart SP RC	2.50	6.00
❑ 110 Matt Ryan SP RC	5.00	12.00

1991 Ultra

Card		
❑ COMPLETE SET (300)	7.50	20.00
❑ 1 Don Beebe	.01	.05
❑ 2 Shane Conlan	.01	.05
❑ 3 Pete Metzelaars	.01	.05
❑ 4 Jamie Mueller	.01	.05
❑ 5 Scott Norwood	.01	.05
❑ 6 Andre Reed	.02	.10
❑ 7 Leon Seals	.01	.05
❑ 8 Bruce Smith	.08	.25
❑ 9 Leonard Smith	.01	.05
❑ 10 Thurman Thomas	.08	.25
❑ 11 Lewis Billups	.01	.05
❑ 12 Jim Breech	.01	.05
❑ 13 James Brooks	.02	.10
❑ 14 Eddie Brown	.01	.05
❑ 15 Boomer Esiason	.02	.10
❑ 16 David Fulcher	.01	.05
❑ 17 Rodney Holman	.01	.05
❑ 18 Bruce Kozerski	.01	.05
❑ 19 Tim Krumrie	.01	.05
❑ 20 Tim McGee	.01	.05
❑ 21 Anthony Munoz	.02	.10
❑ 22 Leon White	.01	.05
❑ 23 Ickey Woods	.01	.05
❑ 24 Carl Zander	.01	.05
❑ 25 Brian Brennan	.01	.05
❑ 26 Thane Gash	.01	.05
❑ 27 Leroy Hoard	.02	.10
❑ 28 Mike Johnson	.01	.05
❑ 29 Reggie Langhorne	.01	.05
❑ 30 Kevin Mack	.01	.05
❑ 31 Clay Matthews	.02	.10
❑ 32 Eric Metcalf	.02	.10
❑ 33 Steve Atwater	.01	.05
❑ 34 Melvin Bratton	.01	.05
❑ 35 John Elway	.50	1.25
❑ 36 Bobby Humphrey	.01	.05
❑ 37 Mark Jackson	.01	.05
❑ 38 Vance Johnson	.01	.05
❑ 39 Ricky Nattiel	.01	.05
❑ 40 Steve Sewell	.01	.05
❑ 41 Dennis Smith	.01	.05
❑ 42 David Treadwell	.01	.05
❑ 43 Michael Young	.01	.05
❑ 44 Ray Childress	.01	.05
❑ 45 Cris Dishman RC	.01	.05
❑ 46 William Fuller	.02	.10
❑ 47 Ernest Givins	.02	.10
❑ 48 John Grimsley UER	.01	.05
❑ 49 Drew Hill	.01	.05
❑ 50 Haywood Jeffires	.02	.10
❑ 51 Sean Jones	.02	.10
❑ 52 Johnny Meads	.01	.05
❑ 53 Warren Moon	.08	.25
❑ 54 Al Smith	.01	.05
❑ 55 Lorenzo White	.01	.05
❑ 56 Albert Bentley	.01	.05
❑ 57 Duane Bickett	.01	.05
❑ 58 Bill Brooks	.01	.05
❑ 59 Jeff George	.08	.25
❑ 60 Mike Prior	.01	.05
❑ 61 Rohn Stark	.01	.05
❑ 62 Jack Trudeau	.01	.05
❑ 63 Clarence Verdin	.01	.05
❑ 64 Steve DeBerg	.01	.05
❑ 65 Emile Harry	.01	.05
❑ 66 Albert Lewis	.01	.05
❑ 67 Nick Lowery UER	.01	.05
❑ 68 Todd McNair	.01	.05
❑ 69 Christian Okoye	.01	.05
❑ 70 Stephone Paige	.01	.05
❑ 71 Kevin Porter UER	.01	.05
❑ 72 Derrick Thomas	.08	.25
❑ 73 Robb Thomas	.01	.05
❑ 74 Barry Word	.01	.05
❑ 75 Marcus Allen	.08	.25
❑ 76 Eddie Anderson	.01	.05
❑ 77 Tim Brown	.08	.25
❑ 78 Mervyn Fernandez	.01	.05
❑ 79 Willie Gault	.02	.10
❑ 80 Ethan Horton	.01	.05
❑ 81 Howie Long	.08	.25
❑ 82 Vance Mueller	.01	.05
❑ 83 Jay Schroeder	.01	.05
❑ 84 Steve Smith	.01	.05
❑ 85 Greg Townsend	.01	.05
❑ 86 Mark Clayton	.02	.10
❑ 87 Jim C. Jensen	.01	.05
❑ 88 Dan Marino	.50	1.25
❑ 89 Tim McKyer UER	.01	.05
❑ 90 John Offerdahl	.01	.05
❑ 91 Louis Oliver	.01	.05
❑ 92 Reggie Roby	.01	.05
❑ 93 Sammie Smith	.01	.05
❑ 94 Hart Lee Dykes	.01	.05
❑ 95 Irving Fryar	.02	.10
❑ 96 Tommy Hodson	.01	.05
❑ 97 Maurice Hurst	.01	.05
❑ 98 John Stephens	.01	.05
❑ 99 Andre Tippett	.01	.05
❑ 100 Mark Boyer	.01	.05
❑ 101 Kyle Clifton	.01	.05
❑ 102 James Hasty	.01	.05
❑ 103 Erik McMillan	.01	.05
❑ 104 Rob Moore	.08	.25
❑ 105 Joe Mott	.01	.05
❑ 106 Ken O'Brien	.01	.05
❑ 107 Ron Stallworth UER	.01	.05
❑ 108 Al Toon	.02	.10
❑ 109 Gary Anderson K	.01	.05
❑ 110 Bubby Brister	.01	.05
❑ 111 Thomas Everett	.01	.05
❑ 112 Merril Hoge	.01	.05
❑ 113 Louis Lipps	.01	.05
❑ 114 Greg Lloyd	.08	.25
❑ 115 Hardy Nickerson	.02	.10
❑ 116 Dwight Stone	.01	.05
❑ 117 Rod Woodson	.08	.25
❑ 118 Tim Worley	.01	.05
❑ 119 Rod Bernstine	.01	.05
❑ 120 Marion Butts	.02	.10
❑ 121 Gill Byrd	.01	.05
❑ 122 Arthur Cox	.01	.05
❑ 123 Burt Grossman	.01	.05
❑ 124 Ronnie Harmon	.01	.05
❑ 125 Anthony Miller	.02	.10
❑ 126 Leslie O'Neal	.02	.10
❑ 127 Gary Plummer	.01	.05
❑ 128 Sam Seale	.01	.05
❑ 129 Junior Seau	.08	.25
❑ 130 Broderick Thompson	.01	.05
❑ 131 Billy Joe Tolliver	.01	.05
❑ 132 Brian Blades	.02	.10
❑ 133 Jeff Bryant	.01	.05
❑ 134 Derrick Fenner	.01	.05
❑ 135 Jacob Green	.01	.05
❑ 136 Andy Heck	.01	.05
❑ 137 Patrick Hunter UER RC	.01	.05
❑ 138 Norm Johnson	.01	.05
❑ 139 Tommy Kane	.01	.05
❑ 140 Dave Krieg	.02	.10
❑ 141 John L. Williams	.01	.05
❑ 142 Terry Wooden	.01	.05
❑ 143 Steve Broussard	.01	.05
❑ 144 Keith Jones	.01	.05
❑ 145 Brian Jordan	.02	.10
❑ 146 Chris Miller	.02	.10
❑ 147 John Rade	.01	.05
❑ 148 Andre Rison	.02	.10
❑ 149 Mike Rozier	.01	.05
❑ 150 Deion Sanders	.15	.40
❑ 151 Neal Anderson	.02	.10
❑ 152 Trace Armstrong	.01	.05
❑ 153 Kevin Butler	.01	.05
❑ 154 Mark Carrier DB	.02	.10
❑ 155 Richard Dent	.02	.10
❑ 156 Dennis Gentry	.01	.05
❑ 157 Jim Harbaugh	.08	.25
❑ 158 Brad Muster	.01	.05
❑ 159 William Perry	.02	.10
❑ 160 Mike Singletary	.02	.10
❑ 161 Lemuel Stinson	.01	.05
❑ 162 Troy Aikman	.30	.75
❑ 163 Michael Irvin	.08	.25
❑ 164 Mike Saxon	.01	.05
❑ 165 Emmitt Smith	1.00	2.50
❑ 166 Jerry Ball	.01	.05
❑ 167 Michael Cofer	.01	.05
❑ 168 Rodney Peete	.02	.10
❑ 169 Barry Sanders	.50	1.25
❑ 170 Robert Brown	.01	.05
❑ 171 Anthony Dilweg	.01	.05
❑ 172 Tim Harris	.01	.05
❑ 173 Johnny Holland	.01	.05
❑ 174 Perry Kemp	.01	.05
❑ 175 Don Majkowski	.01	.05
❑ 176 Brian Noble	.01	.05
❑ 177 Jeff Query	.01	.05
❑ 178 Sterling Sharpe	.08	.25
❑ 179 Charles Wilson	.01	.05
❑ 180 Keith Woodside	.01	.05
❑ 181 Flipper Anderson UER	.01	.05
❑ 182 Bern Brostek	.01	.05
❑ 183 Pat Carter RC	.01	.05
❑ 184 Aaron Cox	.01	.05
❑ 185 Henry Ellard	.02	.10
❑ 186 Jim Everett	.02	.10
❑ 187 Cleveland Gary	.01	.05
❑ 188 Jerry Gray	.01	.05
❑ 189 Kevin Greene	.02	.10
❑ 190 Mike Wilcher	.01	.05
❑ 191 Alfred Anderson	.01	.05
❑ 192 Joey Browner	.01	.05
❑ 193 Anthony Carter	.02	.10
❑ 194 Chris Doleman	.01	.05
❑ 195 Rick Fenney	.01	.05
❑ 196 Darrell Fullington	.01	.05
❑ 197 Rich Gannon	.08	.25
❑ 198 Hassan Jones	.01	.05
❑ 199 Steve Jordan	.01	.05
❑ 200 Mike Merriweather	.01	.05
❑ 201 Al Noga	.01	.05
❑ 202 Herschel Walker	.02	.10
❑ 203 Wade Wilson	.02	.10
❑ 204 Morten Andersen	.01	.05
❑ 205 Gene Atkins	.01	.05
❑ 206 Toi Cook RC	.01	.05
❑ 207 Craig Heyward	.02	.10
❑ 208 Dalton Hilliard	.01	.05
❑ 209 Vaughan Johnson	.01	.05
❑ 210 Eric Martin	.01	.05

❑ 211 Brett Perriman .08 .25
❑ 212 Pat Swilling .02 .10
❑ 213 Steve Walsh .01 .05
❑ 214 Ottis Anderson .02 .10
❑ 215 Carl Banks .01 .05
❑ 216 Maurice Carthon .01 .05
❑ 217 Mark Collins .01 .05
❑ 218 Rodney Hampton .08 .25
❑ 219 Erik Howard .01 .05
❑ 220 Mark Ingram .02 .10
❑ 221 Pepper Johnson .01 .05
❑ 222 Dave Meggett .02 .10
❑ 223 Phil Simms .02 .10
❑ 224 Lawrence Taylor .08 .25
❑ 225 Lewis Tillman .01 .05
❑ 226 Everson Walls .01 .05
❑ 227 Fred Barnett .08 .25
❑ 228 Jerome Brown .01 .05
❑ 229 Keith Byars .01 .05
❑ 230 Randall Cunningham .08 .25
❑ 231 Byron Evans .01 .05
❑ 232 Wes Hopkins .01 .05
❑ 233 Keith Jackson .02 .10
❑ 234 Heath Sherman .01 .05
❑ 235 Anthony Toney .01 .05
❑ 236 Reggie White .08 .25
❑ 237 Rich Camarillo .01 .05
❑ 238 Ken Harvey .02 .10
❑ 239 Eric Hill .01 .05
❑ 240 Johnny Johnson .01 .05
❑ 241 Ernie Jones .01 .05
❑ 242 Tim McDonald .01 .05
❑ 243 Timm Rosenbach .01 .05
❑ 244 Jay Taylor .01 .05
❑ 245 Dexter Carter .01 .05
❑ 246 Mike Cofer .01 .05
❑ 247 Kevin Fagan .01 .05
❑ 248 Don Griffin .01 .05
❑ 249 Charles Haley .02 .10
❑ 250 Brent Jones .08 .25
❑ 251 Joe Montana UER .50 1.25
❑ 252 Darryl Pollard .01 .05
❑ 253 Tom Rathman .01 .05
❑ 254 Jerry Rice .30 .75
❑ 255 John Taylor .02 .10
❑ 256 Steve Young .30 .75
❑ 257 Gary Anderson RB .01 .05
❑ 258 Mark Carrier WR .08 .25
❑ 259 Chris Chandler .08 .25
❑ 260 Reggie Cobb .01 .05
❑ 261 Reuben Davis .01 .05
❑ 262 Willie Drewrey .01 .05
❑ 263 Ron Hall .01 .05
❑ 264 Eugene Marve .01 .05
❑ 265 Winston Moss UER .01 .05
❑ 266 Vinny Testaverde .02 .10
❑ 267 Broderick Thomas .01 .05
❑ 268 Jeff Bostic .01 .05
❑ 269 Earnest Byner .01 .05
❑ 270 Gary Clark .08 .25
❑ 271 Darrell Green .01 .05
❑ 272 Jim Lachey .01 .05
❑ 273 Wilber Marshall .01 .05
❑ 274 Art Monk .02 .10
❑ 275 Gerald Riggs .01 .05
❑ 276 Mark Rypien .02 .10
❑ 277 Ricky Sanders .01 .05
❑ 278 Alvin Walton .01 .05
❑ 279 Nick Bell RC .01 .05
❑ 280 Eric Bieniemy RC .01 .05
❑ 281 Jarrod Bunch RC .01 .05
❑ 282 Mike Croel RC .01 .05
❑ 283 Brett Favre RC 5.00 10.00
❑ 284 Moe Gardner RC .01 .05
❑ 285 Pat Harlow RC .01 .05
❑ 286 Randal Hill RC .02 .10
❑ 287 Todd Marinovich RC .01 .05
❑ 288 Russell Maryland RC .08 .25
❑ 289 Dan McGwire RC .01 .05
❑ 290 Ernie Mills UER RC .02 .10
❑ 291 Herman Moore RC .08 .25
❑ 292 Godfrey Myles RC .01 .05
❑ 293 Browning Nagle RC .01 .05
❑ 294 Mike Pritchard RC .08 .25
❑ 295 Esera Tuaolo RC .01 .05
❑ 296 Mark Vander Poel RC .01 .05
❑ 297 Ricky Watters RC .60 1.50
❑ 298 Chris Zorich RC .08 .25
❑ 299 Checklist Card .02 .10
❑ 300 Checklist Card .02 .10

1991 Ultra Update

❑ COMP.FACT.SET (100) 10.00 25.00
❑ U1 Brett Favre 7.50 15.00
❑ U2 Moe Gardner .02 .10
❑ U3 Tim McKyer .02 .10
❑ U4 Bruce Pickens RC .02 .10
❑ U5 Mike Pritchard .15 .40
❑ U6 Cornelius Bennett .07 .20
❑ U7 Phil Hansen RC .02 .10
❑ U8 Henry Jones RC .07 .20
❑ U9 Mark Kelso .02 .10
❑ U10 James Lofton .07 .20
❑ U11 Anthony Morgan RC .02 .10
❑ U12 Stan Thomas .02 .10
❑ U13 Chris Zorich .07 .20
❑ U14 Reggie Rembert .02 .10
❑ U15 Alfred Williams RC .02 .10
❑ U16 Michael Jackson WR RC .15 .40
❑ U17 Ed King RC .02 .10
❑ U18 Joe Morris .02 .10
❑ U19 Vince Newsome .02 .10
❑ U20 Tony Casillas .02 .10
❑ U21 Russell Maryland .15 .40
❑ U22 Jay Novacek .15 .40
❑ U23 Mike Croel .02 .10
❑ U24 Gaston Green .02 .10
❑ U25 Kenny Walker RC .02 .10
❑ U26 Melvin Jenkins RC .02 .10
❑ U27 Herman Moore .15 .40
❑ U28 Kelvin Pritchett RC .07 .20
❑ U29 Chris Spielman .07 .20
❑ U30 Vinnie Clark RC .02 .10
❑ U31 Allen Rice .02 .10
❑ U32 Vai Sikahema .02 .10
❑ U33 Esera Tuaolo .02 .10
❑ U34 Mike Dumas RC .02 .10
❑ U35 John Flannery RC .02 .10
❑ U36 Allen Pinkett .02 .10
❑ U37 Tim Barnett RC .02 .10
❑ U38 Dan Saleaumua .02 .10
❑ U39 Harvey Williams RC .15 .40
❑ U40 Nick Bell .02 .10
❑ U41 Roger Craig .07 .20
❑ U42 Ronnie Lott .07 .20
❑ U43 Todd Marinovich .02 .10
❑ U44 Robert Delpino .02 .10
❑ U45 Todd Lyght RC .02 .10
❑ U46 Robert Young RC .07 .20
❑ U47 Aaron Craver RC .02 .10
❑ U48 Mark Higgs RC .02 .10
❑ U49 Vestee Jackson .02 .10
❑ U50 Carl Lee .02 .10
❑ U51 Felix Wright .02 .10
❑ U52 Darrell Fullington .02 .10
❑ U53 Pat Harlow .02 .10
❑ U54 Eugene Lockhart .02 .10
❑ U55 Hugh Millen RC .02 .10
❑ U56 Leonard Russell RC .15 .40
❑ U57 Jon Vaughn RC .02 .10
❑ U58 Quinn Early .07 .20
❑ U59 Bobby Hebert .02 .10
❑ U60 Rickey Jackson .02 .10
❑ U61 Sam Mills .07 .20
❑ U62 Jarrod Bunch .02 .10
❑ U63 John Elliott .02 .10
❑ U64 Jeff Hostetler .07 .20
❑ U65 Ed McCaffrey RC 2.50 6.00
❑ U66 Kanavis McGhee RC .02 .10
❑ U67 Mo Lewis RC .07 .20
❑ U68 Browning Nagle .02 .10
❑ U69 Blair Thomas .02 .10
❑ U70 Antone Davis RC .02 .10
❑ U71 Brad Goebel RC .02 .10
❑ U72 Jim McMahon .07 .20
❑ U73 Clyde Simmons .02 .10
❑ U74 Randal Hill UER U71 .07 .20
❑ U75 Eric Swann RC .15 .40
❑ U76 Tom Tupa .02 .10
❑ U77 Jeff Graham RC .15 .40
❑ U78 Eric Green .02 .10
❑ U79 Neil O'Donnell RC .15 .40
❑ U80 Huey Richardson RC .02 .10
❑ U81 Eric Bioniemy .02 .10
❑ U82 John Friesz .15 .40
❑ U83 Eric Moten RC .02 .10
❑ U84 Stanley Richard RC .02 .10
❑ U85 Todd Bowles .02 .10
❑ U86 Merton Hanks RC .15 .40
❑ U87 Tim Harris .02 .10
❑ U88 Pierce Holt .02 .10
❑ U89 Ted Washington RC .02 .10
❑ U90 John Kasay RC .07 .20
❑ U91 Dan McGwire .02 .10
❑ U92 Lawrence Dawsey RC .07 .20
❑ U93 Charles McRae RC .02 .10
❑ U94 Jesse Solomon .02 .10
❑ U95 Robert Wilson RC .02 .10
❑ U96 Ricky Ervins RC .07 .20
❑ U97 Charles Mann .02 .10
❑ U98 Bobby Wilson RC .02 .10
❑ U99 Jerry Rice PV .60 1.50
❑ U100 Nick Bell/J.McMahon CL .02 .10

1992 Ultra

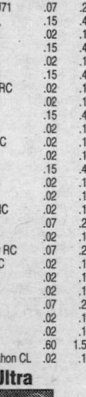

❑ COMPLETE SET (450) 6.00 15.00
❑ 1 Steve Broussard .02 .10
❑ 2 Rick Bryan .02 .10
❑ 3 Scott Case .02 .10
❑ 4 Darion Conner .02 .10
❑ 5 Bill Fralic .02 .10
❑ 6 Moe Gardner .02 .10
❑ 7 Tim Green .02 .10
❑ 8 Michael Haynes .07 .20
❑ 9 Chris Hinton .02 .10
❑ 10 Mike Kenn .02 .10
❑ 11 Tim McKyer .02 .10
❑ 12 Chris Miller .07 .20
❑ 13 Erric Pegram .07 .20
❑ 14 Mike Pritchard .07 .20
❑ 15 Andre Rison .07 .20
❑ 16 Jessie Tuggle .02 .10
❑ 17 Carlton Bailey RC .02 .10
❑ 18 Howard Ballard .02 .10
❑ 19 Cornelius Bennett .07 .20
❑ 20 Shane Conlan .02 .10
❑ 21 Kenneth Davis .02 .10
❑ 22 Kent Hull .02 .10
❑ 23 Mark Kelso .02 .10
❑ 24 James Lofton .07 .20
❑ 25 Keith McKeller .02 .10
❑ 26 Nate Odomes .02 .10
❑ 27 Jim Ritcher .02 .10
❑ 28 Leon Seals .02 .10
❑ 29 Darryl Talley .02 .10
❑ 30 Steve Tasker .07 .20
❑ 31 Thurman Thomas .15 .40
❑ 32 Will Wolford .02 .10
❑ 33 Jeff Wright .02 .10
❑ 34 Neal Anderson .02 .10
❑ 35 Trace Armstrong .02 .10
❑ 36 Mark Carrier DB .02 .10
❑ 37 Wendell Davis .02 .10
❑ 38 Richard Dent .07 .20
❑ 39 Shaun Gayle .02 .10
❑ 40 Jim Harbaugh .15 .40

Card	Low	High
❑ 41 Jay Hilgenberg	.02	.10
❑ 42 Darren Lewis	.02	.10
❑ 43 Steve McMichael	.07	.20
❑ 44 Anthony Morgan	.02	.10
❑ 45 Brad Muster	.02	.10
❑ 46 William Perry	.07	.20
❑ 47 John Roper	.02	.10
❑ 48 Lemuel Stinson	.02	.10
❑ 49 Tom Waddle	.02	.10
❑ 50 Donnell Woolford	.02	.10
❑ 51 Leo Barker RC	.02	.10
❑ 52 Eddie Brown	.02	.10
❑ 53 James Francis	.02	.10
❑ 54 David Fulcher UER	.02	.10
❑ 55 David Grant	.02	.10
❑ 56 Harold Green	.02	.10
❑ 57 Rodney Holman	.02	.10
❑ 58 Lee Johnson	.02	.10
❑ 59 Tim Krumrie	.02	.10
❑ 60 Tim McGee	.02	.10
❑ 61 Alonzo Mitz RC	.02	.10
❑ 62 Anthony Munoz	.07	.20
❑ 63 Alfred Williams	.02	.10
❑ 64 Stephen Braggs	.02	.10
❑ 65 Richard Brown RC	.02	.10
❑ 66 Randy Hilliard RC	.02	.10
❑ 67 Leroy Hoard	.07	.20
❑ 68 Michael Jackson	.07	.20
❑ 69 Mike Johnson	.02	.10
❑ 70 James Jones DT	.02	.10
❑ 71 Tony Jones T	.02	.10
❑ 72 Ed King	.02	.10
❑ 73 Kevin Mack	.02	.10
❑ 74 Clay Matthews	.07	.20
❑ 75 Eric Metcalf	.07	.20
❑ 76 Vince Newsome	.02	.10
❑ 77 Steve Beuerlein	.07	.20
❑ 78 Larry Brown DB	.02	.10
❑ 79 Tony Casillas	.02	.10
❑ 80 Alvin Harper	.07	.20
❑ 81 Issiac Holt	.02	.10
❑ 82 Ray Horton	.02	.10
❑ 83 Michael Irvin	.15	.40
❑ 84 Daryl Johnston	.15	.40
❑ 85 Kelvin Martin	.02	.10
❑ 86 Ken Norton	.07	.20
❑ 87 Jay Novacek	.07	.20
❑ 88 Emmitt Smith	1.50	3.00
❑ 89 Vinson Smith RC	.02	.10
❑ 90 Mark Stepnoski	.07	.20
❑ 91 Tony Tolbert	.02	.10
❑ 92 Alexander Wright	.02	.10
❑ 93 Steve Atwater	.02	.10
❑ 94 Tyrone Braxton	.02	.10
❑ 95 Michael Brooks	.02	.10
❑ 96 Mike Croel	.02	.10
❑ 97 John Elway	1.00	2.50
❑ 98 Simon Fletcher	.02	.10
❑ 99 Gaston Green	.02	.10
❑ 100 Mark Jackson	.02	.10
❑ 101 Keith Kartz	.02	.10
❑ 102 Greg Kragen	.02	.10
❑ 103 Greg Lewis	.02	.10
❑ 104 Karl Mecklenburg	.02	.10
❑ 105 Derek Russell	.02	.10
❑ 106 Steve Sewell	.02	.10
❑ 107 Dennis Smith	.02	.10
❑ 108 David Treadwell	.02	.10
❑ 109 Kenny Walker	.02	.10
❑ 110 Michael Young	.02	.10
❑ 111 Jerry Ball	.02	.10
❑ 112 Bennie Blades	.02	.10
❑ 113 Lomas Brown	.02	.10
❑ 114 Scott Conover RC	.02	.10
❑ 115 Ray Crockett	.02	.10
❑ 116 Mel Gray	.07	.20
❑ 117 Willie Green	.02	.10
❑ 118 Erik Kramer	.07	.20
❑ 119 Dan Owens	.02	.10
❑ 120 Rodney Peete	.07	.20
❑ 121 Brett Perriman	.15	.40
❑ 122 Barry Sanders	1.00	2.50
❑ 123 Chris Spielman	.07	.20
❑ 124 Marc Spindler	.02	.10
❑ 125 William White	.02	.10
❑ 126 Tony Bennett	.02	.10
❑ 127 Matt Brock	.02	.10
❑ 128 LeRoy Butler	.02	.10
❑ 129 Chuck Cecil	.02	.10
❑ 130 Johnny Holland	.02	.10
❑ 131 Perry Kemp	.02	.10
❑ 132 Don Majkowski	.02	.10
❑ 133 Tony Mandarich	.02	.10
❑ 134 Brian Noble	.02	.10
❑ 135 Bryce Paup	.15	.40
❑ 136 Sterling Sharpe	.15	.40
❑ 137 Darrell Thompson	.02	.10
❑ 138 Mike Tomczak	.02	.10
❑ 139 Vince Workman	.02	.10
❑ 140 Ray Childress	.02	.10
❑ 141 Cris Dishman	.02	.10
❑ 142 Curtis Duncan	.02	.10
❑ 143 William Fuller	.02	.10
❑ 144 Ernest Givins	.07	.20
❑ 145 Haywood Jeffires	.07	.20
❑ 146 Sean Jones	.02	.10
❑ 147 Lamar Lathon	.02	.10
❑ 148 Bruce Matthews	.02	.10
❑ 149 Bubba McDowell	.02	.10
❑ 150 Johnny Meads	.02	.10
❑ 151 Warren Moon	.15	.40
❑ 152 Mike Munchak	.07	.20
❑ 153 Bo Orlando RC	.02	.10
❑ 154 Al Smith	.02	.10
❑ 155 Doug Smith	.02	.10
❑ 156 Lorenzo White	.02	.10
❑ 157 Chip Banks	.02	.10
❑ 158 Duane Bickett	.02	.10
❑ 159 Bill Brooks	.02	.10
❑ 160 Eugene Daniel	.02	.10
❑ 161 Jon Hand	.02	.10
❑ 162 Jeff Herrod	.02	.10
❑ 163 Jessie Hester	.02	.10
❑ 164 Scott Radecic	.02	.10
❑ 165 Rohn Stark	.02	.10
❑ 166 Clarence Verdin	.02	.10
❑ 167 John Alt	.02	.10
❑ 168 Tim Barnett	.02	.10
❑ 169 Tim Grunhard	.02	.10
❑ 170 Dino Hackett	.02	.10
❑ 171 Jonathan Hayes	.02	.10
❑ 172 Bill Maas	.02	.10
❑ 173 Chris Martin	.02	.10
❑ 174 Christian Okoye	.02	.10
❑ 175 Stephone Paige	.02	.10
❑ 176 Jayice Pearson RC	.02	.10
❑ 177 Kevin Porter	.02	.10
❑ 178 Kevin Ross	.02	.10
❑ 179 Dan Saleaumua	.02	.10
❑ 180 Tracy Simien RC	.02	.10
❑ 181 Neil Smith	.15	.40
❑ 182 Derrick Thomas	.15	.40
❑ 183 Robb Thomas	.02	.10
❑ 184 Barry Word	.02	.10
❑ 185 Marcus Allen	.15	.40
❑ 186 Eddie Anderson	.02	.10
❑ 187 Nick Bell	.02	.10
❑ 188 Tim Brown	.15	.40
❑ 189 Mervyn Fernandez	.02	.10
❑ 190 Willie Gault	.07	.20
❑ 191 Jeff Gossett	.02	.10
❑ 192 Ethan Horton	.02	.10
❑ 193 Jeff Jaeger	.02	.10
❑ 194 Howie Long	.15	.40
❑ 195 Ronnie Lott	.07	.20
❑ 196 Todd Marinovich	.02	.10
❑ 197 Don Mosebar	.02	.10
❑ 198 Jay Schroeder	.02	.10
❑ 199 Anthony Smith	.02	.10
❑ 200 Greg Townsend	.02	.10
❑ 201 Lionel Washington	.02	.10
❑ 202 Steve Wisniewski	.02	.10
❑ 203 Flipper Anderson	.02	.10
❑ 204 Robert Delpino	.02	.10
❑ 205 Henry Ellard	.07	.20
❑ 206 Jim Everett	.07	.20
❑ 207 Kevin Greene	.07	.20
❑ 208 Darryl Henley	.02	.10
❑ 209 Damone Johnson	.02	.10
❑ 210 Larry Kelm	.02	.10
❑ 211 Todd Lyght	.02	.10
❑ 212 Jackie Slater	.02	.10
❑ 213 Michael Stewart	.02	.10
❑ 214 Pat Terrell	.02	.10
❑ 215 Robert Young	.02	.10
❑ 216 Mark Clayton	.07	.20
❑ 217 Bryan Cox	.07	.20
❑ 218 Jeff Cross	.02	.10
❑ 219 Mark Duper	.02	.10
❑ 220 Harry Galbreath	.02	.10
❑ 221 David Griggs	.02	.10
❑ 222 Mark Higgs	.02	.10
❑ 223 Vestee Jackson	.02	.10
❑ 224 John Offerdahl	.02	.10
❑ 225 Louis Oliver	.02	.10
❑ 226 Tony Paige	.02	.10
❑ 227 Reggie Roby	.02	.10
❑ 228 Pete Stoyanovich	.02	.10
❑ 229 Richmond Webb	.02	.10
❑ 230 Terry Allen	.15	.40
❑ 231 Ray Berry	.02	.10
❑ 232 Anthony Carter	.07	.20
❑ 233 Cris Carter	.30	.75
❑ 234 Chris Doleman	.02	.10
❑ 235 Rich Gannon	.15	.40
❑ 236 Steve Jordan	.02	.10
❑ 237 Carl Lee	.02	.10
❑ 238 Randall McDaniel	.05	.15
❑ 239 Mike Merriweather	.02	.10
❑ 240 Harry Newsome	.02	.10
❑ 241 John Randle	.07	.20
❑ 242 Henry Thomas	.02	.10
❑ 243 Bruce Armstrong	.02	.10
❑ 244 Vincent Brown	.02	.10
❑ 245 Marv Cook	.02	.10
❑ 246 Irving Fryar	.07	.20
❑ 247 Pat Harlow	.02	.10
❑ 248 Maurice Hurst	.02	.10
❑ 249 Eugene Lockhart	.02	.10
❑ 250 Greg McMurtry	.02	.10
❑ 251 Hugh Millen	.02	.10
❑ 252 Leonard Russell	.07	.20
❑ 253 Chris Singleton	.02	.10
❑ 254 Andre Tippett	.02	.10
❑ 255 Jon Vaughn	.02	.10
❑ 256 Morten Andersen	.02	.10
❑ 257 Gene Atkins	.02	.10
❑ 258 Wesley Carroll	.02	.10
❑ 259 Jim Dombrowski	.02	.10
❑ 260 Quinn Early	.07	.20
❑ 261 Bobby Hebert	.02	.10
❑ 262 Joel Hilgenberg	.02	.10
❑ 263 Rickey Jackson	.02	.10
❑ 264 Vaughan Johnson	.02	.10
❑ 265 Eric Martin	.02	.10
❑ 266 Brett Maxie	.02	.10
❑ 267 Fred McAfee RC	.02	.10
❑ 268 Sam Mills	.02	.10
❑ 269 Pat Swilling	.02	.10
❑ 270 Floyd Turner	.02	.10
❑ 271 Steve Walsh	.02	.10
❑ 272 Stephen Baker	.02	.10
❑ 273 Jarrod Bunch	.02	.10
❑ 274 Mark Collins	.02	.10
❑ 275 John Elliott	.02	.10
❑ 276 Myron Guyton	.02	.10
❑ 277 Rodney Hampton	.07	.20
❑ 278 Jeff Hostetler	.07	.20
❑ 279 Mark Ingram	.02	.10
❑ 280 Pepper Johnson	.02	.10
❑ 281 Sean Landeta	.02	.10
❑ 282 Leonard Marshall	.02	.10
❑ 283 Kanavis McGhee	.02	.10
❑ 284 Dave Meggett	.07	.20
❑ 285 Bart Oates	.02	.10
❑ 286 Phil Simms	.07	.20
❑ 287 Reyna Thompson	.02	.10
❑ 288 Lewis Tillman	.02	.10
❑ 289 Brad Baxter	.02	.10
❑ 290 Mike Brim RC	.02	.10
❑ 291 Chris Burkett	.02	.10
❑ 292 Kyle Clifton	.02	.10
❑ 293 James Hasty	.02	.10
❑ 294 Joe Kelly	.02	.10
❑ 295 Jeff Lageman	.02	.10
❑ 296 Mo Lewis	.02	.10
❑ 297 Erik McMillan	.02	.10
❑ 298 Scott Mersereau	.02	.10
❑ 299 Rob Moore	.07	.20
❑ 300 Tony Stargell	.02	.10
❑ 301 Jim Sweeney	.02	.10
❑ 302 Marvin Washington	.02	.10
❑ 303 Lonnie Young	.02	.10
❑ 304 Eric Allen	.02	.10

❑ 305 Fred Barnett	.15	.40
❑ 306 Keith Byars	.02	.10
❑ 307 Byron Evans	.02	.10
❑ 308 Wes Hopkins	.02	.10
❑ 309 Keith Jackson	.07	.20
❑ 310 James Joseph	.02	.10
❑ 311 Seth Joyner	.02	.10
❑ 312 Roger Ruzek	.02	.10
❑ 313 Clyde Simmons	.02	.10
❑ 314 William Thomas	.02	.10
❑ 315 Reggie White	.15	.40
❑ 316 Calvin Williams	.07	.20
❑ 317 Rich Camarillo	.02	.10
❑ 318 Jeff Faulkner	.02	.10
❑ 319 Ken Harvey	.02	.10
❑ 320 Eric Hill	.02	.10
❑ 321 Johnny Johnson	.02	.10
❑ 322 Ernie Jones	.02	.10
❑ 323 Tim McDonald	.02	.10
❑ 324 Freddie Joe Nunn	.02	.10
❑ 325 Luis Sharpe	.02	.10
❑ 326 Eric Swann	.07	.20
❑ 327 Aeneas Williams	.07	.20
❑ 328 Michael Zordich RC	.02	.10
❑ 329 Gary Anderson K	.02	.10
❑ 330 Bubby Brister	.02	.10
❑ 331 Barry Foster	.07	.20
❑ 332 Eric Green	.02	.10
❑ 333 Bryan Hinkle	.02	.10
❑ 334 Tunch Ilkin	.02	.10
❑ 335 Carnell Lake	.02	.10
❑ 336 Louis Lipps	.02	.10
❑ 337 David Little	.02	.10
❑ 338 Greg Lloyd	.07	.20
❑ 339 Neil O'Donnell	.07	.20
❑ 340 Rod Woodson	.15	.40
❑ 341 Rod Bernstine	.02	.10
❑ 342 Marion Butts	.02	.10
❑ 343 Gill Byrd	.02	.10
❑ 344 John Friesz	.07	.20
❑ 345 Burt Grossman	.02	.10
❑ 346 Courtney Hall	.02	.10
❑ 347 Ronnie Harmon	.02	.10
❑ 348 Shawn Jefferson	.02	.10
❑ 349 Nate Lewis	.02	.10
❑ 350 Craig McEwen RC	.02	.10
❑ 351 Eric Moten	.02	.10
❑ 352 Gary Plummer	.02	.10
❑ 353 Henry Rolling	.02	.10
❑ 354 Broderick Thompson	.02	.10
❑ 355 Derrick Walker	.02	.10
❑ 356 Harris Barton	.02	.10
❑ 357 Steve Bono RC	.15	.40
❑ 358 Todd Bowles	.02	.10
❑ 359 Dexter Carter	.02	.10
❑ 360 Michael Carter	.02	.10
❑ 361 Keith DeLong	.02	.10
❑ 362 Charles Haley	.07	.20
❑ 363 Merton Hanks	.07	.20
❑ 364 Tim Harris	.02	.10
❑ 365 Brent Jones	.07	.20
❑ 366 Guy McIntyre	.02	.10
❑ 367 Tom Rathman	.02	.10
❑ 368 Bill Romanowski	.02	.10
❑ 369 Jesse Sapolu	.02	.10
❑ 370 John Taylor	.07	.20
❑ 371 Steve Young	.60	1.50
❑ 372 Robert Blackmon	.02	.10
❑ 373 Brian Blades	.07	.20
❑ 374 Jacob Green	.02	.10
❑ 375 Dwayne Harper	.02	.10
❑ 376 Andy Heck	.02	.10
❑ 377 Tommy Kane	.02	.10
❑ 378 John Kasay	.02	.10
❑ 379 Cortez Kennedy	.07	.20
❑ 380 Bryan Millard	.02	.10
❑ 381 Rufus Porter	.02	.10
❑ 382 Eugene Robinson	.02	.10
❑ 383 John L. Williams	.02	.10
❑ 384 Terry Wooden	.02	.10
❑ 385 Gary Anderson RB	.02	.10
❑ 386 Ian Beckles	.02	.10
❑ 387 Mark Carrier WR	.07	.20
❑ 388 Reggie Cobb	.02	.10
❑ 389 Tony Covington	.02	.10
❑ 390 Lawrence Dawsey	.07	.20
❑ 391 Dan Hall	.02	.10
❑ 392 Keith McCants	.02	.10
❑ 393 Charles McRae	.02	.10
❑ 394 Tim Newton	.02	.10
❑ 395 Jesse Solomon	.02	.10
❑ 396 Vinny Testaverde	.07	.20
❑ 397 Broderick Thomas	.02	.10
❑ 398 Robert Wilson	.02	.10
❑ 399 Earnest Byner	.02	.10
❑ 400 Gary Clark	.15	.40
❑ 401 Andre Collins	.02	.10
❑ 402 Brad Edwards	.02	.10
❑ 403 Kurt Gouveia	.02	.10
❑ 404 Darrell Green	.02	.10
❑ 405 Joe Jacoby	.02	.10
❑ 406 Jim Lachey	.02	.10
❑ 407 Chip Lohmiller	.02	.10
❑ 408 Charles Mann	.02	.10
❑ 409 Wilber Marshall	.02	.10
❑ 410 Brian Mitchell	.07	.20
❑ 411 Art Monk	.07	.20
❑ 412 Mark Rypien	.02	.10
❑ 413 Ricky Sanders	.02	.10
❑ 414 Mark Schlereth RC	.02	.10
❑ 415 Fred Stokes	.02	.10
❑ 416 Bobby Wilson	.02	.10
❑ 417 Corey Barlow RC	.02	.10
❑ 418 Edgar Bennett RC	.15	.40
❑ 419 Eddie Blake RC	.02	.10
❑ 420 Terrell Buckley RC	.02	.10
❑ 421 Willie Clay RC	.02	.10
❑ 422 Rodney Culver RC	.02	.10
❑ 423 Ed Cunningham RC	.02	.10
❑ 424 Mark D'Onofrio RC	.02	.10
❑ 425 Matt Darby RC	.02	.10
❑ 426 Charles Davenport RC	.02	.10
❑ 427 Will Furrer RC	.02	.10
❑ 428 Keith Goganious RC	.02	.10
❑ 429 Mario Bailey RC	.02	.10
❑ 430 Chris Hakel RC	.02	.10
❑ 431 Keith Hamilton RC	.07	.20
❑ 432 Aaron Pierce RC	.02	.10
❑ 433 Amp Lee RC	.02	.10
❑ 434 Scott Lockwood RC	.02	.10
❑ 435 Ricardo McDonald RC	.02	.10
❑ 436 Dexter McNabb RC	.02	.10
❑ 437 Chris Mims RC	.02	.10
❑ 438 Mike Mooney RC	.02	.10
❑ 439 Ray Roberts RC	.02	.10
❑ 440 Patrick Rowe RC	.02	.10
❑ 441 Leon Searcy RC	.02	.10
❑ 442 Siran Stacy RC	.02	.10
❑ 443 Kevin Turner RC	.02	.10
❑ 444 Tommy Vardell RC	.02	.10
❑ 445 Bob Whitfield RC	.02	.10
❑ 446 Darryl Williams RC	.02	.10
❑ 447 Checklist 1-110	.02	.10
❑ 448 Checklist 111-224	.02	.10
❑ 449 Checklist 230-340 UER	.02	.10
❑ 450 Checklist 341-450	.02	.10
❑ AD Super Bowl XXVII Strip	.75	2.00

1993 Ultra

❑ COMPLETE SET (500)	7.50	20.00
❑ 1 Vinnie Clark	.02	.10
❑ 2 Darion Conner	.02	.10
❑ 3 Eric Dickerson	.07	.20
❑ 4 Moe Gardner	.02	.10
❑ 5 Tim Green	.02	.10
❑ 6 Roger Harper RC	.02	.10
❑ 7 Michael Haynes	.07	.20
❑ 8 Bobby Hebert	.02	.10
❑ 9 Chris Hinton	.02	.10
❑ 10 Pierce Holt	.02	.10
❑ 11 Mike Kenn	.02	.10
❑ 12 Lincoln Kennedy RC	.02	.10
❑ 13 Chris Miller	.07	.20
❑ 14 Mike Pritchard	.07	.20
❑ 15 Andre Rison	.07	.20
❑ 16 Deion Sanders	.30	.75
❑ 17 Tony Smith RB	.02	.10
❑ 18 Jessie Tuggle	.02	.10
❑ 19 Howard Ballard	.02	.10
❑ 20 Don Beebe	.02	.10
❑ 21 Cornelius Bennett	.07	.20
❑ 22 Bill Brooks	.02	.10
❑ 23 Kenneth Davis	.02	.10
❑ 24 Phil Hansen	.02	.10
❑ 25 Henry Jones	.02	.10
❑ 26 Jim Kelly	.15	.40
❑ 27 Nate Odomes	.02	.10
❑ 28 John Parrella RC	.02	.10
❑ 29 Andre Reed	.07	.20
❑ 30 Frank Reich	.07	.20
❑ 31 Jim Ritcher	.02	.10
❑ 32 Bruce Smith	.15	.40
❑ 33 Thomas Smith RC	.07	.20
❑ 34 Darryl Talley	.02	.10
❑ 35 Steve Tasker	.07	.20
❑ 36 Thurman Thomas	.15	.40
❑ 37 Jeff Wright	.02	.10
❑ 38 Neal Anderson	.02	.10
❑ 39 Trace Armstrong	.02	.10
❑ 40 Mark Carrier DB	.02	.10
❑ 41 Curtis Conway RC	.30	.75
❑ 42 Wendell Davis	.02	.10
❑ 43 Richard Dent	.07	.20
❑ 44 Shaun Gayle	.02	.10
❑ 45 Jim Harbaugh	.15	.40
❑ 46 Craig Heyward	.07	.20
❑ 47 Darren Lewis	.02	.10
❑ 48 Steve McMichael	.07	.20
❑ 49 William Perry	.07	.20
❑ 50 Carl Simpson RC	.02	.10
❑ 51 Alonzo Spellman	.02	.10
❑ 52 Keith Van Horne	.02	.10
❑ 53 Tom Waddle	.02	.10
❑ 54 Donnell Woolford	.02	.10
❑ 55 John Copeland RC	.07	.20
❑ 56 Derrick Fenner	.02	.10
❑ 57 James Francis	.02	.10
❑ 58 Harold Green	.02	.10
❑ 59 David Klingler	.02	.10
❑ 60 Tim Krumrie	.02	.10
❑ 61 Ricardo McDonald	.02	.10
❑ 62 Tony McGee RC	.07	.20
❑ 63 Carl Pickens	.07	.20
❑ 64 Lamar Rogers	.02	.10
❑ 65 Jay Schroeder	.02	.10
❑ 66 Daniel Stubbs	.02	.10
❑ 67 Steve Tovar RC	.02	.10
❑ 68 Alfred Williams	.02	.10
❑ 69 Darryl Williams	.02	.10
❑ 70 Jerry Ball	.02	.10
❑ 71 David Brandon	.02	.10
❑ 72 Rob Burnett	.02	.10
❑ 73 Mark Carrier WR	.07	.20
❑ 74 Steve Everitt RC	.02	.10
❑ 75 Dan Footman RC	.02	.10
❑ 76 Leroy Hoard	.07	.20
❑ 77 Michael Jackson	.07	.20
❑ 78 Mike Johnson	.02	.10
❑ 79 Bernie Kosar	.07	.20
❑ 80 Clay Matthews	.07	.20
❑ 81 Eric Metcalf	.07	.20
❑ 82 Michael Dean Perry	.07	.20
❑ 83 Vinny Testaverde	.07	.20
❑ 84 Tommy Vardell	.02	.10
❑ 85 Troy Aikman	.60	1.50
❑ 86 Larry Brown DB	.02	.10
❑ 87 Tony Casillas	.02	.10
❑ 88 Thomas Everett	.02	.10
❑ 89 Charles Haley	.07	.20
❑ 90 Alvin Harper	.07	.20
❑ 91 Michael Irvin	.15	.40
❑ 92 Jim Jeffcoat	.02	.10
❑ 93 Daryl Johnston	.15	.40
❑ 94 Robert Jones	.02	.10
❑ 95 Leon Lett RC	.07	.20
❑ 96 Russell Maryland	.02	.10
❑ 97 Nate Newton	.07	.20
❑ 98 Ken Norton	.07	.20
❑ 99 Jay Novacek	.07	.20
❑ 100 Darrin Smith RC	.07	.20

Card	Low	High
❑ 101 Emmitt Smith	1.25	3.00
❑ 102 Kevin Smith	.07	.20
❑ 103 Mark Stepnoski	.02	.10
❑ 104 Tony Tolbert	.02	.10
❑ 105 Kevin Williams RC WR	.15	.40
❑ 106 Steve Atwater	.02	.10
❑ 107 Rod Bernstine	.02	.10
❑ 108 Mike Croel	.02	.10
❑ 109 Robert Delpino	.02	.10
❑ 110 Shane Dronett	.02	.10
❑ 111 John Elway	1.25	3.00
❑ 112 Simon Fletcher	.02	.10
❑ 113 Greg Kragen	.02	.10
❑ 114 Tommy Maddox	.15	.40
❑ 115 Arthur Marshall RC	.02	.10
❑ 116 Karl Mecklenburg	.02	.10
❑ 117 Glyn Milburn RC	.15	.40
❑ 118 Reggie Rivers RC	.02	.10
❑ 119 Shannon Sharpe	.15	.40
❑ 120 Dennis Smith	.02	.10
❑ 121 Kenny Walker	.02	.10
❑ 122 Dan Williams RC	.02	.10
❑ 123 Bennie Blades	.02	.10
❑ 124 Lomas Brown	.02	.10
❑ 125 Bill Fralic	.02	.10
❑ 126 Mel Gray	.07	.20
❑ 127 Willie Green	.02	.10
❑ 128 Jason Hanson	.02	.10
❑ 129 Antonio London RC	.02	.10
❑ 130 Ryan McNeil RC	.15	.40
❑ 131 Herman Moore	.15	.40
❑ 132 Rodney Peete	.02	.10
❑ 133 Brett Perriman	.15	.40
❑ 134 Kelvin Pritchett	.02	.10
❑ 135 Barry Sanders	1.00	2.50
❑ 136 Tracy Scroggins	.02	.10
❑ 137 Chris Spielman	.07	.20
❑ 138 Pat Swilling	.02	.10
❑ 139 Andre Ware	.02	.10
❑ 140 Edgar Bennett	.15	.40
❑ 141 Tony Bennett	.02	.10
❑ 142 Matt Brock	.02	.10
❑ 143 Terrell Buckley	.02	.10
❑ 144 LeRoy Butler	.02	.10
❑ 145 Mark Clayton	.02	.10
❑ 146 Brett Favre	1.50	4.00
❑ 147 Jackie Harris	.02	.10
❑ 148 Johnny Holland	.02	.10
❑ 149 Bill Maas	.02	.10
❑ 150 Brian Noble	.02	.10
❑ 151 Bryce Paup	.07	.20
❑ 152 Ken Ruettgers	.02	.10
❑ 153 Sterling Sharpe	.15	.40
❑ 154 Wayne Simmons RC	.02	.10
❑ 155 John Stephens	.02	.10
❑ 156 George Teague RC	.07	.20
❑ 157 Reggie White	.15	.40
❑ 158 Micheal Barrow RC	.15	.40
❑ 159 Cody Carlson	.02	.10
❑ 160 Ray Childress	.02	.10
❑ 161 Cris Dishman	.02	.10
❑ 162 Curtis Duncan	.02	.10
❑ 163 William Fuller	.02	.10
❑ 164 Ernest Givins	.07	.20
❑ 165 Brad Hopkins RC	.02	.10
❑ 166 Haywood Jeffires	.07	.20
❑ 167 Lamar Lathon	.02	.10
❑ 168 Wilber Marshall	.02	.10
❑ 169 Bruce Matthews	.02	.10
❑ 170 Bubba McDowell	.02	.10
❑ 171 Warren Moon	.15	.40
❑ 172 Mike Munchak	.07	.20
❑ 173 Eddie Robinson	.02	.10
❑ 174 Al Smith	.02	.10
❑ 175 Lorenzo White	.02	.10
❑ 176 Lee Williams	.02	.10
❑ 177 Chip Banks	.02	.10
❑ 178 John Baylor	.02	.10
❑ 179 Duane Bickett	.02	.10
❑ 180 Kerry Cash	.02	.10
❑ 181 Quentin Coryatt	.07	.20
❑ 182 Rodney Culver	.02	.10
❑ 183 Steve Emtman	.02	.10
❑ 184 Jeff George	.15	.40
❑ 185 Jeff Herrod	.02	.10
❑ 186 Jessie Hester	.02	.10
❑ 187 Anthony Johnson	.07	.20
❑ 188 Reggie Langhorne	.02	.10
❑ 189 Roosevelt Potts RC	.02	.10
❑ 190 Rohn Stark	.02	.10
❑ 191 Clarence Verdin	.02	.10
❑ 192 Will Wolford	.02	.10
❑ 193 Marcus Allen	.15	.40
❑ 194 John Alt	.02	.10
❑ 195 Tim Barnett	.02	.10
❑ 196 J.J.Birden	.02	.10
❑ 197 Dale Carter	.02	.10
❑ 198 Willie Davis	.15	.40
❑ 199 Jaime Fields RC	.02	.10
❑ 200 Dave Krieg	.07	.20
❑ 201 Nick Lowery	.02	.10
❑ 202 Charles Mincy RC	.02	.10
❑ 203 Joe Montana	1.25	3.00
❑ 204 Christian Okoye	.02	.10
❑ 205 Dan Saleaumua	.02	.10
❑ 206 Will Shields RC	.15	.40
❑ 207 Tracy Simien	.02	.10
❑ 208 Neil Smith	.15	.40
❑ 209 Derrick Thomas	.15	.40
❑ 210 Harvey Williams	.07	.20
❑ 211 Barry Word	.02	.10
❑ 212 Eddie Anderson	.02	.10
❑ 213 Patrick Bates RC	.02	.10
❑ 214 Nick Bell	.02	.10
❑ 215 Tim Brown	.15	.40
❑ 216 Willie Gault	.02	.10
❑ 217 Gaston Green	.02	.10
❑ 218 Billy Joe Hobert RC	.15	.40
❑ 219 Ethan Horton	.02	.10
❑ 220 Jeff Hostetler	.07	.20
❑ 221 James Lofton	.07	.20
❑ 222 Howie Long	.15	.40
❑ 223 Todd Marinovich	.02	.10
❑ 224 Terry McDaniel	.02	.10
❑ 225 Winston Moss	.02	.10
❑ 226 Anthony Smith	.02	.10
❑ 227 Greg Townsend	.02	.10
❑ 228 Aaron Wallace	.02	.10
❑ 229 Lionel Washington	.02	.10
❑ 230 Steve Wisniewski	.02	.10
❑ 231 Flipper Anderson	.02	.10
❑ 232 Jerome Bettis RC	4.00	8.00
❑ 233 Marc Boutte	.02	.10
❑ 234 Shane Conlan	.02	.10
❑ 235 Troy Drayton RC	.07	.20
❑ 236 Henry Ellard	.07	.20
❑ 237 Jim Everett	.07	.20
❑ 238 Cleveland Gary	.02	.10
❑ 239 Sean Gilbert	.07	.20
❑ 240 Darryl Henley	.02	.10
❑ 241 David Lang	.02	.10
❑ 242 Todd Lyght	.02	.10
❑ 243 Anthony Newman	.02	.10
❑ 244 Roman Phifer	.02	.10
❑ 245 Gerald Robinson	.02	.10
❑ 246 Henry Rolling	.02	.10
❑ 247 Jackie Slater	.02	.10
❑ 248 Keith Byars	.02	.10
❑ 249 Marco Coleman	.02	.10
❑ 250 Bryan Cox	.02	.10
❑ 251 Jeff Cross	.02	.10
❑ 252 Irving Fryar	.07	.20
❑ 253 Mark Higgs	.02	.10
❑ 254 Dwight Hollier RC	.02	.10
❑ 255 Mark Ingram	.02	.10
❑ 256 Keith Jackson	.07	.20
❑ 257 Terry Kirby RC	.15	.40
❑ 258 Dan Marino	1.25	3.00
❑ 259 O.J. McDuffie RC	.15	.40
❑ 260 John Offerdahl	.02	.10
❑ 261 Louis Oliver	.02	.10
❑ 262 Pete Stoyanovich	.02	.10
❑ 263 Troy Vincent	.02	.10
❑ 264 Richmond Webb	.02	.10
❑ 265 Jarvis Williams	.02	.10
❑ 266 Terry Allen	.15	.40
❑ 267 Anthony Carter	.07	.20
❑ 268 Cris Carter	.15	.40
❑ 269 Roger Craig	.07	.20
❑ 270 Jack Del Rio	.02	.10
❑ 271 Chris Doleman	.02	.10
❑ 272 Qadry Ismail RC	.15	.40
❑ 273 Steve Jordan	.02	.10
❑ 274 Randall McDaniel	.05	.15
❑ 275 Audray McMillian	.02	.10
❑ 276 John Randle	.07	.20
❑ 277 Sean Salisbury	.02	.10
❑ 278 Todd Scott	.02	.10
❑ 279 Robert Smith RC	1.00	2.50
❑ 280 Henry Thomas	.02	.10
❑ 281 Ray Agnew	.02	.10
❑ 282 Bruce Armstrong	.02	.10
❑ 283 Drew Bledsoe RC	2.00	5.00
❑ 284 Vincent Brisby RC	.15	.40
❑ 285 Vincent Brown	.02	.10
❑ 286 Eugene Chung	.02	.10
❑ 287 Marv Cook	.02	.10
❑ 288 Pat Harlow	.02	.10
❑ 289 Jerome Henderson	.02	.10
❑ 290 Greg McMurtry	.02	.10
❑ 291 Leonard Russell	.07	.20
❑ 292 Chris Singleton	.02	.10
❑ 293 Chris Slade RC	.07	.20
❑ 294 Andre Tippett	.02	.10
❑ 295 Brent Williams	.02	.10
❑ 296 Scott Zolak	.02	.10
❑ 297 Morten Andersen	.02	.10
❑ 298 Gene Atkins	.02	.10
❑ 299 Mike Buck	.02	.10
❑ 300 Toi Cook	.02	.10
❑ 301 Jim Dombrowski	.02	.10
❑ 302 Vaughn Dunbar	.02	.10
❑ 303 Quinn Early	.07	.20
❑ 304 Joel Hilgenberg	.02	.10
❑ 305 Dalton Hilliard	.02	.10
❑ 306 Rickey Jackson	.02	.10
❑ 307 Vaughan Johnson	.02	.10
❑ 308 Reginald Jones	.02	.10
❑ 309 Eric Martin	.02	.10
❑ 310 Wayne Martin	.02	.10
❑ 311 Sam Mills	.02	.10
❑ 312 Brad Muster	.02	.10
❑ 313 Willie Roaf RC	.07	.20
❑ 314 Irv Smith RC	.02	.10
❑ 315 Wade Wilson	.02	.10
❑ 316 Carlton Bailey	.02	.10
❑ 317 Michael Brooks	.02	.10
❑ 318 Derek Brown TE	.02	.10
❑ 319 Marcus Buckley RC	.02	.10
❑ 320 Jarrod Bunch	.02	.10
❑ 321 Mark Collins	.02	.10
❑ 322 Eric Dorsey	.02	.10
❑ 323 Rodney Hampton	.07	.20
❑ 324 Mark Jackson	.02	.10
❑ 325 Pepper Johnson	.02	.10
❑ 326 Ed McCaffrey	.15	.40
❑ 327 Dave Meggett	.02	.10
❑ 328 Bart Oates	.02	.10
❑ 329 Mike Sherrard	.02	.10
❑ 330 Phil Simms	.07	.20
❑ 331 Michael Strahan RC	1.25	3.00
❑ 332 Lawrence Taylor	.15	.40
❑ 333 Brad Baxter	.02	.10
❑ 334 Chris Burkett	.02	.10
❑ 335 Kyle Clifton	.02	.10
❑ 336 Boomer Esiason	.07	.20
❑ 337 James Hasty	.02	.10
❑ 338 Johnny Johnson	.02	.10
❑ 339 Marvin Jones RC	.02	.10
❑ 340 Jeff Lageman	.02	.10
❑ 341 Mo Lewis	.02	.10
❑ 342 Ronnie Lott	.07	.20
❑ 343 Leonard Marshall	.02	.10
❑ 344 Johnny Mitchell	.02	.10
❑ 345 Rob Moore	.07	.20
❑ 346 Browning Nagle	.02	.10
❑ 347 Coleman Rudolph RC	.02	.10
❑ 348 Blair Thomas	.02	.10
❑ 349 Eric Thomas	.02	.10
❑ 350 Brian Washington	.02	.10
❑ 351 Marvin Washington	.02	.10
❑ 352 Eric Allen	.02	.10
❑ 353 Victor Bailey RC	.02	.10
❑ 354 Fred Barnett	.07	.20
❑ 355 Mark Bavaro	.02	.10
❑ 356 Randall Cunningham	.15	.40
❑ 357 Byron Evans	.02	.10
❑ 358 Andy Harmon RC	.07	.20
❑ 359 Tim Harris	.02	.10
❑ 360 Lester Holmes	.02	.10
❑ 361 Seth Joyner	.02	.10
❑ 362 Keith Millard	.02	.10
❑ 363 Leonard Renfro RC	.02	.10
❑ 364 Heath Sherman	.02	.10

❑ 365 Vai Sikahema .02 .10
❑ 366 Clyde Simmons .02 .10
❑ 367 William Thomas .02 .10
❑ 368 Herschel Walker .07 .20
❑ 369 Andre Waters .02 .10
❑ 370 Calvin Williams .07 .20
❑ 371 Johnny Bailey .02 .10
❑ 372 Steve Beuerlein .07 .20
❑ 373 Rich Camarillo .02 .10
❑ 374 Chuck Cecil .02 .10
❑ 375 Chris Chandler .07 .20
❑ 376 Gary Clark .07 .20
❑ 377 Ben Coleman RC .02 .10
❑ 378 Ernest Dye RC .02 .10
❑ 379 Ken Harvey .02 .10
❑ 380 Garrison Hearst RC .60 1.50
❑ 381 Randal Hill .02 .10
❑ 382 Robert Massey .02 .10
❑ 383 Freddie Joe Nunn .02 .10
❑ 384 Ricky Proehl .02 .10
❑ 385 Luis Sharpe .02 .10
❑ 386 Tyronne Stowe .02 .10
❑ 387 Eric Swann .07 .20
❑ 388 Aeneas Williams .02 .10
❑ 389 Chad Brown RC LB .07 .20
❑ 390 Dermontti Dawson .02 .10
❑ 391 Donald Evans .02 .10
❑ 392 Deon Figures RC .02 .10
❑ 393 Barry Foster .07 .20
❑ 394 Jeff Graham .07 .20
❑ 395 Eric Green .02 .10
❑ 396 Kevin Greene .07 .20
❑ 397 Carlton Haselrig .02 .10
❑ 398 Andre Hastings RC .07 .20
❑ 399 D.J. Johnson .02 .10
❑ 400 Carnell Lake .02 .10
❑ 401 Greg Lloyd .07 .20
❑ 402 Neil O'Donnell .15 .40
❑ 403 Darren Perry .02 .10
❑ 404 Mike Tomczak .02 .10
❑ 405 Rod Woodson .15 .40
❑ 406 Eric Bieniemy .02 .10
❑ 407 Marion Butts .02 .10
❑ 408 Gill Byrd .02 .10
❑ 409 Darren Carrington RC .02 .10
❑ 410 Darrien Gordon RC .02 .10
❑ 411 Burt Grossman .02 .10
❑ 412 Courtney Hall .02 .10
❑ 413 Ronnie Harmon .02 .10
❑ 414 Stan Humphries .07 .20
❑ 415 Nate Lewis .02 .10
❑ 416 Natrone Means RC .15 .40
❑ 417 Anthony Miller .07 .20
❑ 418 Chris Mims .02 .10
❑ 419 Leslie O'Neal .07 .20
❑ 420 Gary Plummer .02 .10
❑ 421 Stanley Richard .02 .10
❑ 422 Junior Seau .15 .40
❑ 423 Harry Swayne .02 .10
❑ 424 Jerrol Williams .02 .10
❑ 425 Harris Barton .02 .10
❑ 426 Steve Bono .07 .20
❑ 427 Kevin Fagan .02 .10
❑ 428 Don Griffin .02 .10
❑ 429 Dana Hall .02 .10
❑ 430 Adrian Hardy .02 .10
❑ 431 Brent Jones .07 .20
❑ 432 Todd Kelly RC .02 .10
❑ 433 Amp Lee .02 .10
❑ 434 Tim McDonald .02 .10
❑ 435 Guy McIntyre .02 .10
❑ 436 Tom Rathman .02 .10
❑ 437 Jerry Rice .75 2.00
❑ 438 Bill Romanowski .02 .10
❑ 439 Dana Stubblefield RC .15 .40
❑ 440 John Taylor .07 .20
❑ 441 Steve Wallace .02 .10
❑ 442 Michael Walter .02 .10
❑ 443 Ricky Watters .15 .40
❑ 444 Steve Young .60 1.50
❑ 445 Robert Blackmon .02 .10
❑ 446 Brian Blades .07 .20
❑ 447 Jeff Bryant .02 .10
❑ 448 Ferrell Edmunds .02 .10
❑ 449 Carlton Gray RC .02 .10
❑ 450 Dwayne Harper .02 .10
❑ 451 Andy Heck .02 .10
❑ 452 Tommy Kane .02 .10
❑ 453 Cortez Kennedy .07 .20
❑ 454 Kelvin Martin .02 .10
❑ 455 Dan McGwire .02 .10
❑ 456 Rick Mirer RC .15 .40
❑ 457 Rufus Porter .02 .10
❑ 458 Ray Roberts .02 .10
❑ 459 Eugene Robinson .02 .10
❑ 460 Chris Warren .07 .20
❑ 461 John L. Williams .02 .10
❑ 462 Gary Anderson RB .02 .10
❑ 463 Tyji Armstrong .02 .10
❑ 464 Reggie Cobb .02 .10
❑ 465 Eric Curry RC .02 .10
❑ 466 Lawrence Dawsey .02 .10
❑ 467 Steve DeBerg .02 .10
❑ 468 Santana Dotson .07 .20
❑ 469 Demetrius DuBose RC .02 .10
❑ 470 Paul Gruber .02 .10
❑ 471 Ron Hall .02 .10
❑ 472 Courtney Hawkins .02 .10
❑ 473 Hardy Nickerson .07 .20
❑ 474 Ricky Reynolds .02 .10
❑ 475 Broderick Thomas .02 .10
❑ 476 Mark Wheeler .02 .10
❑ 477 Jimmy Williams .02 .10
❑ 478 Carl Banks .02 .10
❑ 479 Reggie Brooks RC .07 .20
❑ 480 Earnest Byner .02 .10
❑ 481 Tom Carter RC .07 .20
❑ 482 Andre Collins .02 .10
❑ 483 Brad Edwards .02 .10
❑ 484 Ricky Ervins .02 .10
❑ 485 Kurt Gouveia .02 .10
❑ 486 Darrell Green .02 .10
❑ 487 Desmond Howard .07 .20
❑ 488 Jim Lachey .02 .10
❑ 489 Chip Lohmiller .02 .10
❑ 490 Charles Mann .02 .10
❑ 491 Tim McGee .02 .10
❑ 492 Brian Mitchell .07 .20
❑ 493 Art Monk .07 .20
❑ 494 Mark Rypien .02 .10
❑ 495 Ricky Sanders .02 .10
❑ 496 Checklist 1-126 .02 .10
❑ 497 Checklist 127-254 .02 .10
❑ 498 Checklist 255-382 .02 .10
❑ 499 Checklist 383-500 .02 .10
❑ 500 Inserts Checklist .02 .10

1994 Ultra

❑ COMPLETE SET (525) 10.00 25.00
❑ COMP.SERIES 1 (325) 5.00 12.00
❑ COMP.SERIES 2 (200) 5.00 12.00
❑ 1 Steve Beuerlein .07 .20
❑ 2 Gary Clark .07 .20
❑ 3 Randal Hill .02 .10
❑ 4 Seth Joyner .02 .10
❑ 5 Jamir Miller RC .07 .20
❑ 6 Ronald Moore .02 .10
❑ 7 Luis Sharpe .02 .10
❑ 8 Clyde Simmons .02 .10
❑ 9 Eric Swann .07 .20
❑ 10 Aeneas Williams .02 .10
❑ 11 Chris Doleman .02 .10
❑ 12 Bert Emanuel RC .15 .40
❑ 13 Moe Gardner .02 .10
❑ 14 Jeff George .15 .40
❑ 15 Roger Harper .02 .10
❑ 16 Pierce Holt .02 .10
❑ 17 Lincoln Kennedy .02 .10
❑ 18 Erric Pegram .02 .10
❑ 19 Andre Rison .07 .20
❑ 20 Deion Sanders .30 .75
❑ 21 Jessie Tuggle .02 .10
❑ 22 Cornelius Bennett .07 .20
❑ 23 Bill Brooks .02 .10
❑ 24 Jeff Burris RC .07 .20
❑ 25 Kent Hull .02 .10
❑ 26 Henry Jones .02 .10
❑ 27 Jim Kelly .15 .40
❑ 28 Marvcus Patton .02 .10
❑ 29 Andre Reed .07 .20
❑ 30 Bruce Smith .15 .40
❑ 31 Thomas Smith .02 .10
❑ 32 Thurman Thomas .15 .40
❑ 33 Jeff Wright .02 .10
❑ 34 Trace Armstrong .02 .10
❑ 35 Mark Carrier DB .02 .10
❑ 36 Dante Jones .02 .10
❑ 37 Erik Kramer .07 .20
❑ 38 Terry Obee .02 .10
❑ 39 Alonzo Spellman .02 .10
❑ 40 John Thierry RC .02 .10
❑ 41 Tom Waddle .02 .10
❑ 42 Donnell Woolford .02 .10
❑ 43 Tim Worley .02 .10
❑ 44 Chris Zorich .02 .10
❑ 45 John Copeland .02 .10
❑ 46 Harold Green .02 .10
❑ 47 David Klingler .02 .10
❑ 48 Ricardo McDonald .02 .10
❑ 49 Tony McGee .02 .10
❑ 50 Louis Oliver .02 .10
❑ 51 Carl Pickens .07 .20
❑ 52 Darnay Scott RC .30 .75
❑ 53 Steve Tovar .02 .10
❑ 54 Dan Wilkinson RC .07 .20
❑ 55 Darryl Williams .02 .10
❑ 56 Derrick Alexander WR RC .15 .40
❑ 57 Michael Jackson .07 .20
❑ 58 Tony Jones T .02 .10
❑ 59 Antonio Langham RC .07 .20
❑ 60 Eric Metcalf .07 .20
❑ 61 Stevon Moore .02 .10
❑ 62 Michael Dean Perry .07 .20
❑ 63 Anthony Pleasant .02 .10
❑ 64 Vinny Testaverde .07 .20
❑ 65 Eric Turner .02 .10
❑ 66 Tommy Vardell .02 .10
❑ 67 Troy Aikman .60 1.50
❑ 68 Larry Brown DB .02 .10
❑ 69 Shante Carver RC .02 .10
❑ 70 Charles Haley .07 .20
❑ 71 Michael Irvin .15 .40
❑ 72 Leon Lett .02 .10
❑ 73 Nate Newton .02 .10
❑ 74 Jay Novacek .07 .20
❑ 75 Darrin Smith .02 .10
❑ 76 Emmitt Smith 1.00 2.50
❑ 77 Tony Tolbert .02 .10
❑ 78 Erik Williams .02 .10
❑ 79 Kevin Williams WR .07 .20
❑ 80 Steve Atwater .02 .10
❑ 81 Rod Bernstine .02 .10
❑ 82 Ray Crockett .02 .10
❑ 83 Mike Croel .02 .10
❑ 84 Shane Dronett .02 .10
❑ 85 Jason Elam .07 .20
❑ 86 John Elway 1.25 3.00
❑ 87 Simon Fletcher .02 .10
❑ 88 Glyn Milburn .07 .20
❑ 89 Anthony Miller .07 .20
❑ 90 Shannon Sharpe .07 .20
❑ 91 Gary Zimmerman .02 .10
❑ 92 Bennie Blades .02 .10
❑ 93 Lomas Brown .02 .10
❑ 94 Mel Gray .02 .10
❑ 95 Jason Hanson .02 .10
❑ 96 Ryan McNeil .02 .10
❑ 97 Scott Mitchell .07 .20
❑ 98 Herman Moore .15 .40
❑ 99 Johnnie Morton RC .60 1.50
❑ 100 Robert Porcher .02 .10
❑ 101 Barry Sanders 1.00 2.50
❑ 102 Chris Spielman .07 .20
❑ 103 Pat Swilling .02 .10
❑ 104 Edgar Bennett .15 .40
❑ 105 Terrell Buckley .02 .10
❑ 106 Reggie Cobb .02 .10
❑ 107 Brett Favre 1.25 3.00
❑ 108 Sean Jones .02 .10
❑ 109 Ken Ruettgers .02 .10

Card		
❑ 110 Sterling Sharpe	.07	.20
❑ 111 Wayne Simmons	.02	.10
❑ 112 Aaron Taylor RC	.02	.10
❑ 113 George Teague	.02	.10
❑ 114 Reggie White	.15	.40
❑ 115 Micheal Barrow	.02	.10
❑ 116 Gary Brown	.02	.10
❑ 117 Cody Carlson	.02	.10
❑ 118 Ray Childress	.02	.10
❑ 119 Cris Dishman	.02	.10
❑ 120 Henry Ford RC	.02	.10
❑ 121 Haywood Jeffires	.07	.20
❑ 122 Bruce Matthews	.02	.10
❑ 123 Bubba McDowell	.02	.10
❑ 124 Marcus Robertson	.02	.10
❑ 125 Eddie Robinson	.02	.10
❑ 126 Webster Slaughter	.02	.10
❑ 127 Trev Alberts RC	.07	.20
❑ 128 Tony Bennett	.02	.10
❑ 129 Ray Buchanan	.02	.10
❑ 130 Quentin Coryatt	.02	.10
❑ 131 Eugene Daniel	.02	.10
❑ 132 Steve Emtman	.02	.10
❑ 133 Marshall Faulk RC	2.50	6.00
❑ 134 Jim Harbaugh	.15	.40
❑ 135 Roosevelt Potts	.02	.10
❑ 136 Rohn Stark	.02	.10
❑ 137 Marcus Allen	.15	.40
❑ 138 Donnell Bennett RC	.15	.40
❑ 139 Dale Carter	.02	.10
❑ 140 Tony Casillas	.02	.10
❑ 141 Mark Collins	.02	.10
❑ 142 Willie Davis	.07	.20
❑ 143 Tim Grunhard	.02	.10
❑ 144 Greg Hill RC	.15	.40
❑ 145 Joe Montana	1.25	3.00
❑ 146 Tracy Simien	.02	.10
❑ 147 Neil Smith	.07	.20
❑ 148 Derrick Thomas	.15	.40
❑ 149 Tim Brown	.15	.40
❑ 150 James Folston RC	.02	.10
❑ 151 Rob Fredrickson RC	.07	.20
❑ 152 Jeff Hostetler	.07	.20
❑ 153 Rocket Ismail	.07	.20
❑ 154 James Jett	.02	.10
❑ 155 Terry McDaniel	.02	.10
❑ 156 Winston Moss	.02	.10
❑ 157 Greg Robinson	.02	.10
❑ 158 Anthony Smith	.02	.10
❑ 159 Steve Wisniewski	.02	.10
❑ 160 Flipper Anderson	.02	.10
❑ 161 Jerome Bettis	.25	.60
❑ 162 Isaac Bruce RC	2.00	4.00
❑ 163 Shane Conlan	.02	.10
❑ 164 Wayne Gandy RC	.02	.10
❑ 165 Sean Gilbert	.02	.10
❑ 166 Todd Lyght	.02	.10
❑ 167 Chris Miller	.02	.10
❑ 168 Anthony Newman	.02	.10
❑ 169 Roman Phifer	.02	.10
❑ 170 Jackie Slater	.02	.10
❑ 171 Gene Atkins	.02	.10
❑ 172 Aubrey Beavers RC	.02	.10
❑ 173 Tim Bowens RC	.07	.20
❑ 174 J.B. Brown	.02	.10
❑ 175 Marco Coleman	.02	.10
❑ 176 Bryan Cox	.02	.10
❑ 177 Irving Fryar	.07	.20
❑ 178 Terry Kirby	.15	.40
❑ 179 Dan Marino	1.25	3.00
❑ 180 Troy Vincent	.02	.10
❑ 181 Richmond Webb	.02	.10
❑ 182 Terry Allen	.07	.20
❑ 183 Cris Carter	.30	.75
❑ 184 Jack Del Rio	.02	.10
❑ 185 Vencie Glenn	.02	.10
❑ 186 Randall McDaniel	.05	.15
❑ 187 Warren Moon	.15	.40
❑ 188 David Palmer RC	.15	.40
❑ 189 John Randle	.07	.20
❑ 190 Todd Scott	.02	.10
❑ 191 Todd Steussie RC	.07	.20
❑ 192 Henry Thomas	.02	.10
❑ 193 Dewayne Washington RC	.07	.20
❑ 194 Bruce Armstrong	.02	.10
❑ 195 Harlon Barnett	.02	.10
❑ 196 Drew Bledsoe	.40	1.00
❑ 197 Vincent Brisby	.07	.20
❑ 198 Vincent Brown	.02	.10
❑ 199 Marion Butts	.02	.10
❑ 200 Ben Coates	.07	.20
❑ 201 Todd Collins	.02	.10
❑ 202 Maurice Hurst	.02	.10
❑ 203 Willie McGinest RC	.15	.40
❑ 204 Ricky Reynolds	.02	.10
❑ 205 Chris Slade	.02	.10
❑ 206 Mario Bates RC	.15	.40
❑ 207 Derek Brown RBK	.02	.10
❑ 208 Vince Buck	.02	.10
❑ 209 Quinn Early	.07	.20
❑ 210 Jim Everett	.07	.20
❑ 211 Michael Haynes	.07	.20
❑ 212 Tyrone Hughes	.07	.20
❑ 213 Joe Johnson RC	.02	.10
❑ 214 Vaughan Johnson	.02	.10
❑ 215 Willie Roaf	.02	.10
❑ 216 Renaldo Turnbull	.02	.10
❑ 217 Michael Brooks	.02	.10
❑ 218 Dave Brown	.07	.20
❑ 219 Howard Cross	.02	.10
❑ 220 Stacey Dillard	.02	.10
❑ 221 Jumbo Elliott	.02	.10
❑ 222 Keith Hamilton	.02	.10
❑ 223 Rodney Hampton	.07	.20
❑ 224 Thomas Lewis RC	.07	.20
❑ 225 Dave Meggett	.02	.10
❑ 226 Corey Miller	.02	.10
❑ 227 Thomas Randolph RC	.02	.10
❑ 228 Mike Sherrard	.02	.10
❑ 229 Kyle Clifton	.02	.10
❑ 230 Boomer Esiason	.07	.20
❑ 231 Aaron Glenn RC	.15	.40
❑ 232 James Hasty	.02	.10
❑ 233 Bobby Houston	.02	.10
❑ 234 Johnny Johnson	.02	.10
❑ 235 Mo Lewis	.02	.10
❑ 236 Ronnie Lott	.07	.20
❑ 237 Rob Moore	.07	.20
❑ 238 Marvin Washington	.02	.10
❑ 239 Ryan Yarborough RC	.02	.10
❑ 240 Eric Allen	.02	.10
❑ 241 Victor Bailey	.02	.10
❑ 242 Fred Barnett	.07	.20
❑ 243 Mark Bavaro	.02	.10
❑ 244 Randall Cunningham	.15	.40
❑ 245 Byron Evans	.02	.10
❑ 246 William Fuller	.02	.10
❑ 247 Andy Harmon	.02	.10
❑ 248 William Perry	.07	.20
❑ 249 Herschel Walker	.07	.20
❑ 250 Bernard Williams RC	.02	.10
❑ 251 Dermontti Dawson	.02	.10
❑ 252 Deon Figures	.02	.10
❑ 253 Barry Foster	.02	.10
❑ 254 Kevin Greene	.07	.20
❑ 255 Charles Johnson RC	.15	.40
❑ 256 Levon Kirkland	.02	.10
❑ 257 Greg Lloyd	.07	.20
❑ 258 Neil O'Donnell	.15	.40
❑ 259 Darren Perry	.02	.10
❑ 260 Dwight Stone	.02	.10
❑ 261 Rod Woodson	.07	.20
❑ 262 John Carney	.02	.10
❑ 263 Isaac Davis RC	.02	.10
❑ 264 Courtney Hall	.02	.10
❑ 265 Ronnie Harmon	.02	.10
❑ 266 Stan Humphries	.07	.20
❑ 267 Vance Johnson	.02	.10
❑ 268 Natrone Means	.15	.40
❑ 269 Chris Mims	.02	.10
❑ 270 Leslie O'Neal	.02	.10
❑ 271 Stanley Richard	.02	.10
❑ 272 Junior Seau	.15	.40
❑ 273 Harris Barton	.02	.10
❑ 274 Dennis Brown	.02	.10
❑ 275 Eric Davis	.02	.10
❑ 276 William Floyd RC	.15	.40
❑ 277 John Johnson	.02	.10
❑ 278 Tim McDonald	.02	.10
❑ 279 Ken Norton Jr.	.07	.20
❑ 280 Jerry Rice	.60	1.50
❑ 281 Jesse Sapolu	.02	.10
❑ 282 Dana Stubblefield	.07	.20
❑ 283 Ricky Watters	.07	.20
❑ 284 Bryant Young RC	.25	.60
❑ 285 Steve Young	.40	1.00
❑ 286 Sam Adams RC	.07	.20
❑ 287 Brian Blades	.07	.20
❑ 288 Ferrell Edmunds	.02	.10
❑ 289 Patrick Hunter	.02	.10
❑ 290 Cortez Kennedy	.07	.20
❑ 291 Rick Mirer	.15	.40
❑ 292 Nate Odomes	.02	.10
❑ 293 Ray Roberts	.02	.10
❑ 294 Eugene Robinson	.02	.10
❑ 295 Rod Stephens	.02	.10
❑ 296 Chris Warren	.07	.20
❑ 297 Marty Carter	.02	.10
❑ 298 Horace Copeland	.02	.10
❑ 299 Eric Curry	.02	.10
❑ 300 Santana Dotson	.07	.20
❑ 301 Craig Erickson	.02	.10
❑ 302 Paul Gruber	.02	.10
❑ 303 Courtney Hawkins	.02	.10
❑ 304 Martin Mayhew	.02	.10
❑ 305 Hardy Nickerson	.07	.20
❑ 306 Errict Rhett RC	.15	.40
❑ 307 Vince Workman	.02	.10
❑ 308 Reggie Brooks	.07	.20
❑ 309 Tom Carter	.02	.10
❑ 310 Andre Collins	.02	.10
❑ 311 Brad Edwards	.02	.10
❑ 312 Kurt Gouveia	.02	.10
❑ 313 Darrell Green	.02	.10
❑ 314 Ethan Horton	.02	.10
❑ 315 Desmond Howard	.07	.20
❑ 316 Tre Johnson RC	.02	.10
❑ 317 Sterling Palmer RC	.02	.10
❑ 318 Heath Shuler RC	.15	.40
❑ 319 Tyronne Stowe	.02	.10
❑ 320 NFL 75th Anniversary	.02	.10
❑ 321 Checklist	.02	.10
❑ 322 Checklist	.02	.10
❑ 323 Checklist	.02	.10
❑ 324 Checklist	.02	.10
❑ 325 Checklist	.02	.10
❑ 326 Garrison Hearst	.15	.40
❑ 327 Eric Hill	.02	.10
❑ 328 Seth Joyner	.02	.10
❑ 329 Jim McMahon	.07	.20
❑ 330 Jamir Miller	.02	.10
❑ 331 Ricky Proehl	.02	.10
❑ 332 Clyde Simmons	.02	.10
❑ 333 Chris Doleman	.02	.10
❑ 334 Bert Emanuel	.15	.40
❑ 335 Jeff George	.15	.40
❑ 336 D.J. Johnson	.02	.10
❑ 337 Terance Mathis	.07	.20
❑ 338 Clay Matthews	.02	.10
❑ 339 Tony Smith RB	.02	.10
❑ 340 Don Beebe	.02	.10
❑ 341 Bucky Brooks RC	.02	.10
❑ 342 Jeff Burris	.07	.20
❑ 343 Kenneth Davis	.02	.10
❑ 344 Phil Hansen	.02	.10
❑ 345 Pete Metzelaars	.02	.10
❑ 346 Darryl Talley	.02	.10
❑ 347 Joe Cain	.02	.10
❑ 348 Curtis Conway	.15	.40
❑ 349 Shaun Gayle	.02	.10
❑ 350 Chris Gedney	.02	.10
❑ 351 Erik Kramer	.07	.20
❑ 352 Vinson Smith	.02	.10
❑ 353 John Thierry	.02	.10
❑ 354 Lewis Tillman	.02	.10
❑ 355 Mike Brim	.02	.10
❑ 356 Derrick Fenner	.02	.10
❑ 357 James Francis	.02	.10
❑ 358 Louis Oliver	.02	.10
❑ 359 Darnay Scott	.15	.40
❑ 360 Dan Wilkinson	.07	.20
❑ 361 Alfred Williams	.02	.10
❑ 362 Derrick Alexander WR	.15	.40
❑ 363 Rob Burnett	.02	.10
❑ 364 Mark Carrier WR	.07	.20
❑ 365 Steve Everitt	.02	.10
❑ 366 Leroy Hoard	.02	.10
❑ 367 Pepper Johnson	.02	.10
❑ 368 Antonio Langham	.07	.20
❑ 369 Shante Carver	.02	.10
❑ 370 Alvin Harper	.07	.20
❑ 371 Daryl Johnston	.07	.20
❑ 372 Russell Maryland	.02	.10
❑ 373 Kevin Smith	.02	.10

Card	Low	High
❑ 374 Mark Stepnoski	.02	.10
❑ 375 Darren Woodson	.07	.20
❑ 376 Allen Aldridge RC	.02	.10
❑ 377 Ray Crockett	.02	.10
❑ 378 Karl Mecklenburg	.02	.10
❑ 379 Anthony Miller	.07	.20
❑ 380 Mike Pritchard	.02	.10
❑ 381 Leonard Russell	.02	.10
❑ 382 Dennis Smith	.02	.10
❑ 383 Anthony Carter	.07	.20
❑ 384 Van Malone RC	.02	.10
❑ 385 Robert Massey	.02	.10
❑ 386 Scott Mitchell	.07	.20
❑ 387 Johnnie Morton	.25	.60
❑ 388 Brett Perriman	.07	.20
❑ 389 Tracy Scroggins	.02	.10
❑ 390 Robert Brooks	.15	.40
❑ 391 LeRoy Butler	.02	.10
❑ 392 Reggie Cobb	.02	.10
❑ 393 Sean Jones	.02	.10
❑ 394 George Koonce	.02	.10
❑ 395 Steve McMichael	.07	.20
❑ 396 Bryce Paup	.07	.20
❑ 397 Aaron Taylor	.02	.10
❑ 398 Henry Ford	.02	.10
❑ 399 Ernest Givins	.07	.20
❑ 400 Jeremy Nunley RC	.02	.10
❑ 401 Bo Orlando	.02	.10
❑ 402 Al Smith	.02	.10
❑ 403 Barron Wortham RC	.02	.10
❑ 404 Trev Alberts	.07	.20
❑ 405 Tony Bennett	.02	.10
❑ 406 Kerry Cash	.02	.10
❑ 407 Sean Dawkins RC	.15	.40
❑ 408 Marshall Faulk	.75	2.00
❑ 409 Jim Harbaugh	.15	.40
❑ 410 Jeff Herrod	.02	.10
❑ 411 Kimble Anders	.07	.20
❑ 412 Donnell Bennett	.07	.20
❑ 413 J.J. Birden	.02	.10
❑ 414 Mark Collins	.02	.10
❑ 415 Lake Dawson RC	.07	.20
❑ 416 Greg Hill	.15	.40
❑ 417 Charles Mincy	.02	.10
❑ 418 Greg Biekert	.02	.10
❑ 419 Rob Fredrickson	.07	.20
❑ 420 Nolan Harrison	.02	.10
❑ 421 Jeff Jaeger	.02	.10
❑ 422 Albert Lewis	.02	.10
❑ 423 Chester McGlockton	.02	.10
❑ 424 Tom Rathman	.02	.10
❑ 425 Harvey Williams	.07	.20
❑ 426 Isaac Bruce	.60	1.50
❑ 427 Troy Drayton	.02	.10
❑ 428 Wayne Gandy	.02	.10
❑ 429 Fred Stokes	.02	.10
❑ 430 Robert Young	.02	.10
❑ 431 Gene Atkins	.02	.10
❑ 432 Aubrey Beavers	.02	.10
❑ 433 Tim Bowens	.07	.20
❑ 434 Keith Byars	.02	.10
❑ 435 Jeff Cross	.02	.10
❑ 436 Mark Ingram	.02	.10
❑ 437 Keith Jackson	.02	.10
❑ 438 Michael Stewart	.02	.10
❑ 439 Chris Hinton	.02	.10
❑ 440 Qadry Ismail	.15	.40
❑ 441 Carlos Jenkins	.02	.10
❑ 442 Warren Moon	.15	.40
❑ 443 David Palmer	.07	.20
❑ 444 Jake Reed	.07	.20
❑ 445 Robert Smith	.15	.40
❑ 446 Todd Steussie	.07	.20
❑ 447 Dewayne Washington	.07	.20
❑ 448 Marion Butts	.02	.10
❑ 449 Tim Goad	.02	.10
❑ 450 Myron Guyton	.02	.10
❑ 451 Kevin Lee RC	.02	.10
❑ 452 Willie McGinest	.15	.40
❑ 453 Ricky Reynolds	.02	.10
❑ 454 Michael Timpson	.02	.10
❑ 455 Morten Andersen	.02	.10
❑ 456 Jim Everett	.07	.20
❑ 457 Michael Haynes	.07	.20
❑ 458 Joe Johnson	.02	.10
❑ 459 Wayne Martin	.02	.10
❑ 460 Sam Mills	.02	.10
❑ 461 Irv Smith	.02	.10
❑ 462 Carlton Bailey	.02	.10
❑ 463 Chris Calloway	.02	.10
❑ 464 Mark Jackson	.02	.10
❑ 465 Thomas Lewis	.07	.20
❑ 466 Thomas Randolph	.02	.10
❑ 467 Stevie Anderson RC	.02	.10
❑ 468 Brad Baxter	.02	.10
❑ 469 Aaron Glenn	.07	.20
❑ 470 Jeff Lageman	.02	.10
❑ 471 Johnny Mitchell	.02	.10
❑ 472 Art Monk	.07	.20
❑ 473 William Fuller	.02	.10
❑ 474 Charlie Garner RC	.50	1.25
❑ 475 Vaughn Hebron	.02	.10
❑ 476 Bill Romanowski	.02	.10
❑ 477 William Thomas	.02	.10
❑ 478 Greg Townsend	.02	.10
❑ 479 Bernard Williams	.02	.10
❑ 480 Calvin Williams	.07	.20
❑ 481 Eric Green	.02	.10
❑ 482 Charles Johnson	.15	.40
❑ 483 Carnell Lake	.02	.10
❑ 484 Byron Bam Morris RC	.07	.20
❑ 485 John L. Williams	.02	.10
❑ 486 Darren Carrington	.02	.10
❑ 487 Andre Coleman RC	.02	.10
❑ 488 Isaac Davis	.02	.10
❑ 489 Dwayne Harper	.02	.10
❑ 490 Tony Martin	.15	.40
❑ 491 Mark Seay RC	.15	.40
❑ 492 Richard Dent	.07	.20
❑ 493 William Floyd	.15	.40
❑ 494 Rickey Jackson	.02	.10
❑ 495 Brent Jones	.07	.20
❑ 496 Ken Norton Jr.	.07	.20
❑ 497 Gary Plummer	.02	.10
❑ 498 Deion Sanders	.30	.75
❑ 499 John Taylor	.07	.20
❑ 500 Lee Woodall RC	.02	.10
❑ 501 Bryant Young	.25	.60
❑ 502 Sam Adams	.07	.20
❑ 503 Howard Ballard	.02	.10
❑ 504 Michael Bates	.02	.10
❑ 505 Robert Blackmon	.02	.10
❑ 506 John Kasay	.02	.10
❑ 507 Kelvin Martin	.02	.10
❑ 508 Kevin Mawae RC	.15	.40
❑ 509 Rufus Porter	.02	.10
❑ 510 Lawrence Dawsey	.02	.10
❑ 511 Trent Dilfer RC	.50	1.25
❑ 512 Thomas Everett	.02	.10
❑ 513 Jackie Harris	.02	.10
❑ 514 Errict Rhett	.07	.20
❑ 515 Henry Ellard	.07	.20
❑ 516 John Friesz	.07	.20
❑ 517 Ken Harvey	.02	.10
❑ 518 Ethan Horton	.02	.10
❑ 519 Tre Johnson	.02	.10
❑ 520 Jim Lachey	.02	.10
❑ 521 Heath Shuler	.15	.40
❑ 522 Tony Woods	.02	.10
❑ 523 Checklist	.02	.10
❑ 524 Checklist	.02	.10
❑ 525 Checklist	.02	.10

1995 Ultra

Card	Low	High
❑ COMPLETE SET (550)	20.00	50.00
❑ COMP.SERIES 1 (350)	10.00	25.00
❑ COMP.SERIES 2 (200)	10.00	25.00
❑ 1 Michael Bankston	.02	.10
❑ 2 Larry Centers	.07	.20
❑ 3 Garrison Hearst	.15	.40
❑ 4 Eric Hill	.02	.10
❑ 5 Seth Joyner	.02	.10
❑ 6 Lorenzo Lynch	.02	.10
❑ 7 Jamir Miller	.02	.10
❑ 8 Clyde Simmons	.02	.10
❑ 9 Eric Swann	.07	.20
❑ 10 Aeneas Williams	.02	.10
❑ 11 Devin Bush RC	.02	.10
❑ 12 Ron Davis RC	.02	.10
❑ 13 Chris Doleman	.02	.10
❑ 14 Bert Emanuel	.15	.40
❑ 15 Jeff George	.07	.20
❑ 16 Roger Harper	.02	.10
❑ 17 Craig Heyward	.07	.20
❑ 18 Pierce Holt	.02	.10
❑ 19 D.J. Johnson	.02	.10
❑ 20 Terance Mathis	.07	.20
❑ 21 Chuck Smith	.02	.10
❑ 22 Jessie Tuggle	.02	.10
❑ 23 Cornelius Bennett	.07	.20
❑ 24 Ruben Brown RC	.15	.40
❑ 25 Jeff Burris	.02	.10
❑ 26 Matt Darby	.02	.10
❑ 27 Phil Hansen	.02	.10
❑ 28 Henry Jones	.02	.10
❑ 29 Jim Kelly	.15	.40
❑ 30 Mark Maddox RC	.02	.10
❑ 31 Andre Reed	.07	.20
❑ 32 Bruce Smith	.15	.40
❑ 33 Don Beebe	.02	.10
❑ 34 Kerry Collins RC	.75	2.00
❑ 35 Darion Conner	.02	.10
❑ 36 Pete Metzelaars	.02	.10
❑ 37 Sam Mills	.07	.20
❑ 38 Tyrone Poole RC	.15	.40
❑ 39 Joe Cain	.02	.10
❑ 40 Mark Carrier DB	.02	.10
❑ 41 Curtis Conway	.15	.40
❑ 42 Jeff Graham	.02	.10
❑ 43 Raymont Harris	.02	.10
❑ 44 Erik Kramer	.02	.10
❑ 45 Rashaan Salaam RC	.07	.20
❑ 46 Lewis Tillman	.02	.10
❑ 47 Donnell Woolford	.02	.10
❑ 48 Chris Zorich	.02	.10
❑ 49 Jeff Blake RC	.30	.75
❑ 50 Mike Brim	.02	.10
❑ 51 Ki-Jana Carter RC	.15	.40
❑ 52 James Francis	.02	.10
❑ 53 Carl Pickens	.07	.20
❑ 54 Darnay Scott	.07	.20
❑ 55 Steve Tovar	.02	.10
❑ 56 Dan Wilkinson	.07	.20
❑ 57 Alfred Williams	.02	.10
❑ 58 Darryl Williams	.02	.10
❑ 59 Derrick Alexander WR	.15	.40
❑ 60 Rob Burnett	.02	.10
❑ 61 Steve Everitt	.02	.10
❑ 62 Leroy Hoard	.02	.10
❑ 63 Michael Jackson	.07	.20
❑ 64 Pepper Johnson	.02	.10
❑ 65 Tony Jones T	.02	.10
❑ 66 Antonio Langham	.02	.10
❑ 67 Anthony Pleasant	.02	.10
❑ 68 Craig Powell RC	.02	.10
❑ 69 Vinny Testaverde	.07	.20
❑ 70 Eric Turner	.02	.10
❑ 71 Troy Aikman	.60	1.50
❑ 72 Charles Haley	.07	.20
❑ 73 Michael Irvin	.15	.40
❑ 74 Daryl Johnston	.07	.20
❑ 75 Robert Jones	.02	.10
❑ 76 Leon Lett	.02	.10
❑ 77 Russell Maryland	.02	.10
❑ 78 Jay Novacek	.07	.20
❑ 79 Darrin Smith	.02	.10
❑ 80 Emmitt Smith	1.25	2.50
❑ 81 Kevin Smith	.02	.10
❑ 82 Erik Williams	.02	.10
❑ 83 Kevin Williams WR	.07	.20
❑ 84 Sherman Williams RC	.02	.10
❑ 85 Darren Woodson	.07	.20
❑ 86 Elijah Alexander RC	.02	.10
❑ 87 Steve Atwater	.02	.10
❑ 88 Ray Crockett	.02	.10
❑ 89 Shane Dronett	.02	.10
❑ 90 Jason Elam	.07	.20
❑ 91 John Elway	1.25	3.00
❑ 92 Simon Fletcher	.02	.10
❑ 93 Glyn Milburn	.02	.10

❑ 94 Anthony Miller .07 .20
❑ 95 Leonard Russell .02 .10
❑ 96 Shannon Sharpe .07 .20
❑ 97 Bennie Blades .02 .10
❑ 98 Lomas Brown .02 .10
❑ 99 Willie Clay .02 .10
❑ 100 Luther Elliss RC .02 .10
❑ 101 Mike Johnson .02 .10
❑ 102 Robert Massey .02 .10
❑ 103 Scott Mitchell .07 .20
❑ 104 Herman Moore .15 .40
❑ 105 Brett Perriman .07 .20
❑ 106 Robert Porcher .02 .10
❑ 107 Barry Sanders 1.00 2.50
❑ 108 Chris Spielman .07 .20
❑ 109 Edgar Bennett .07 .20
❑ 110 Robert Brooks .15 .40
❑ 111 LeRoy Butler .02 .10
❑ 112 Brett Favre 1.50 3.00
❑ 113 Sean Jones .02 .10
❑ 114 John Jurkovic .02 .10
❑ 115 George Koonce .02 .10
❑ 116 Wayne Simmons .02 .10
❑ 117 George Teague .02 .10
❑ 118 Reggie White .15 .40
❑ 119 Micheal Barrow .02 .10
❑ 120 Gary Brown .02 .10
❑ 121 Cody Carlson .02 .10
❑ 122 Ray Childress .02 .10
❑ 123 Cris Dishman .02 .10
❑ 124 Bruce Matthews .02 .10
❑ 125 Steve McNair RC 1.25 3.00
❑ 126 Marcus Robertson .02 .10
❑ 127 Webster Slaughter .02 .10
❑ 128 Al Smith .02 .10
❑ 129 Tony Bennett .02 .10
❑ 130 Ray Buchanan .02 .10
❑ 131 Quentin Coryatt .07 .20
❑ 132 Sean Dawkins .07 .20
❑ 133 Marshall Faulk .75 2.00
❑ 134 Stephen Grant RC .02 .10
❑ 135 Jim Harbaugh .07 .20
❑ 136 Jeff Herrod .02 .10
❑ 137 Ellis Johnson RC .02 .10
❑ 138 Tony Siragusa .02 .10
❑ 139 Steve Beuerlein .07 .20
❑ 140 Tony Boselli RC .15 .40
❑ 141 Darren Carrington .02 .10
❑ 142 Reggie Cobb .02 .10
❑ 143 Kelvin Martin .02 .10
❑ 144 Kelvin Pritchett .02 .10
❑ 145 Joel Smeenge .02 .10
❑ 146 James O. Stewart RC .50 1.25
❑ 147 Marcus Allen .15 .40
❑ 148 Kimble Anders .07 .20
❑ 149 Dale Carter .07 .20
❑ 150 Mark Collins .02 .10
❑ 151 Willie Davis .07 .20
❑ 152 Lake Dawson .07 .20
❑ 153 Greg Hill .07 .20
❑ 154 Trezelle Jenkins RC .02 .10
❑ 155 Darren Mickell .02 .10
❑ 156 Tracy Simien .02 .10
❑ 157 Neil Smith .07 .20
❑ 158 William White .02 .10
❑ 159 Joe Aska RC .02 .10
❑ 160 Greg Biekert .02 .10
❑ 161 Tim Brown .15 .40
❑ 162 Rob Fredrickson .02 .10
❑ 163 Andrew Glover RC .02 .10
❑ 164 Jeff Hostetler .07 .20
❑ 165 Rocket Ismail .07 .20
❑ 166 Napoleon Kaufman RC .50 1.25
❑ 167 Terry McDaniel .02 .10
❑ 168 Chester McGlockton .07 .20
❑ 169 Anthony Smith .02 .10
❑ 170 Harvey Williams .02 .10
❑ 171 Steve Wisniewski .02 .10
❑ 172 Gene Atkins .02 .10
❑ 173 Aubrey Beavers .02 .10
❑ 174 Tim Bowens .02 .10
❑ 175 Bryan Cox .02 .10
❑ 176 Jeff Cross .02 .10
❑ 177 Irving Fryar .07 .20
❑ 178 Dan Marino 1.25 3.00
❑ 179 O.J. McDuffie .15 .40
❑ 180 Billy Milner RC .02 .10
❑ 181 Bernie Parmalee .07 .20
❑ 182 Troy Vincent .02 .10
❑ 183 Richmond Webb .02 .10
❑ 184 Derrick Alexander DE RC .02 .10
❑ 185 Cris Carter .15 .40
❑ 186 Jack Del Rio .02 .10
❑ 187 Qadry Ismail .07 .20
❑ 188 Ed McDaniel .02 .10
❑ 189 Randall McDaniel .05 .15
❑ 190 Warren Moon .07 .20
❑ 191 John Randle .07 .20
❑ 192 Jake Reed .07 .20
❑ 193 Fuad Reveiz .02 .10
❑ 194 Korey Stringer RC .10 .30
❑ 195 Dewayne Washington .07 .20
❑ 196 Bruce Armstrong .02 .10
❑ 197 Drew Bledsoe .40 1.00
❑ 198 Vincent Brisby .02 .10
❑ 199 Vincent Brown .02 .10
❑ 200 Marion Butts .02 .10
❑ 201 Ben Coates .07 .20
❑ 202 Myron Guyton .02 .10
❑ 203 Maurice Hurst .02 .10
❑ 204 Mike Jones .02 .10
❑ 205 Ty Law RC .60 1.50
❑ 206 Willie McGinest .07 .20
❑ 207 Chris Slade .02 .10
❑ 208 Mario Bates .07 .20
❑ 209 Quinn Early .07 .20
❑ 210 Jim Everett .02 .10
❑ 211 Mark Fields RC .15 .40
❑ 212 Michael Haynes .07 .20
❑ 213 Tyrone Hughes .07 .20
❑ 214 Joe Johnson .02 .10
❑ 215 Wayne Martin .02 .10
❑ 216 Willie Roaf .02 .10
❑ 217 Irv Smith .02 .10
❑ 218 Jimmy Spencer .02 .10
❑ 219 Winfred Tubbs .02 .10
❑ 220 Renaldo Turnbull .02 .10
❑ 221 Michael Brooks .02 .10
❑ 222 Dave Brown .07 .20
❑ 223 Chris Calloway .02 .10
❑ 224 Howard Cross .02 .10
❑ 225 John Elliott .02 .10
❑ 226 Keith Hamilton .02 .10
❑ 227 Rodney Hampton .07 .20
❑ 228 Thomas Lewis .07 .20
❑ 229 Thomas Randolph .02 .10
❑ 230 Mike Sherrard .02 .10
❑ 231 Michael Strahan .15 .40
❑ 232 Tyrone Wheatley RC .50 1.25
❑ 233 Brad Baxter .02 .10
❑ 234 Kyle Brady RC .15 .40
❑ 235 Kyle Clifton .02 .10
❑ 236 Hugh Douglas RC .15 .40
❑ 237 Boomer Esiason .07 .20
❑ 238 Aaron Glenn .02 .10
❑ 239 Bobby Houston .02 .10
❑ 240 Johnny Johnson .02 .10
❑ 241 Mo Lewis .02 .10
❑ 242 Johnny Mitchell .02 .10
❑ 243 Marvin Washington .02 .10
❑ 244 Fred Barnett .07 .20
❑ 245 Randall Cunningham .15 .40
❑ 246 William Fuller .02 .10
❑ 247 Charlie Garner .15 .40
❑ 248 Andy Harmon .02 .10
❑ 249 Greg Jackson .02 .10
❑ 250 Mike Mamula RC .02 .10
❑ 251 Bill Romanowski .02 .10
❑ 252 Bobby Taylor RC .15 .40
❑ 253 William Thomas .02 .10
❑ 254 Calvin Williams .07 .20
❑ 255 Michael Zordich .02 .10
❑ 256 Chad Brown .07 .20
❑ 257 Mark Bruener RC .07 .20
❑ 258 Dermontti Dawson .07 .20
❑ 259 Barry Foster .07 .20
❑ 260 Kevin Greene .07 .20
❑ 261 Charles Johnson .07 .20
❑ 262 Carnell Lake .02 .10
❑ 263 Greg Lloyd .07 .20
❑ 264 Byron Bam Morris .02 .10
❑ 265 Neil O'Donnell .07 .20
❑ 266 Darren Perry .02 .10
❑ 267 Ray Seals .02 .10
❑ 268 Kordell Stewart RC .60 1.50
❑ 269 John L. Williams .02 .10
❑ 270 Rod Woodson .07 .20
❑ 271 Jerome Bettis .15 .40
❑ 272 Isaac Bruce .30 .75
❑ 273 Kevin Carter RC .15 .40
❑ 274 Shane Conlan .02 .10
❑ 275 Troy Drayton .02 .10
❑ 276 Sean Gilbert .07 .20
❑ 277 Todd Lyght .02 .10
❑ 278 Chris Miller .02 .10
❑ 279 Anthony Newman .02 .10
❑ 280 Roman Phifer .02 .10
❑ 281 Robert Young .02 .10
❑ 282 John Carney .02 .10
❑ 283 Andre Coleman .02 .10
❑ 284 Courtney Hall .02 .10
❑ 285 Ronnie Harmon .02 .10
❑ 286 Dwayne Harper .02 .10
❑ 287 Stan Humphries .07 .20
❑ 288 Shawn Jefferson .02 .10
❑ 289 Tony Martin .07 .20
❑ 290 Natrone Means .07 .20
❑ 291 Chris Mims .02 .10
❑ 292 Leslie O'Neal .07 .20
❑ 293 Junior Seau .15 .40
❑ 294 Mark Seay .07 .20
❑ 295 Eric Davis .02 .10
❑ 296 William Floyd .07 .20
❑ 297 Merton Hanks .02 .10
❑ 298 Brent Jones .02 .10
❑ 299 Ken Norton Jr. .07 .20
❑ 300 Gary Plummer .02 .10
❑ 301 Jerry Rice .60 1.50
❑ 302 Deion Sanders .40 1.00
❑ 303 Jesse Sapolu .02 .10
❑ 304 J.J. Stokes RC .15 .40
❑ 305 Dana Stubblefield .07 .20
❑ 306 John Taylor .02 .10
❑ 307 Steve Wallace .02 .10
❑ 308 Lee Woodall .02 .10
❑ 309 Bryant Young .07 .20
❑ 310 Steve Young .50 1.25
❑ 311 Sam Adams .02 .10
❑ 312 Howard Ballard .02 .10
❑ 313 Robert Blackmon .02 .10
❑ 314 Brian Blades .07 .20
❑ 315 Joey Galloway RC .60 1.50
❑ 316 Carlton Gray .02 .10
❑ 317 Cortez Kennedy .07 .20
❑ 318 Rick Mirer .07 .20
❑ 319 Eugene Robinson .02 .10
❑ 320 Chris Warren .07 .20
❑ 321 Terry Wooden .02 .10
❑ 322 Derrick Brooks RC .60 1.50
❑ 323 Lawrence Dawsey .02 .10
❑ 324 Trent Dilfer .15 .40
❑ 325 Santana Dotson .02 .10
❑ 326 Thomas Everett .02 .10
❑ 327 Paul Gruber .02 .10
❑ 328 Jackie Harris .02 .10
❑ 329 Courtney Hawkins .02 .10
❑ 330 Martin Mayhew .02 .10
❑ 331 Hardy Nickerson .02 .10
❑ 332 Errict Rhett .07 .20
❑ 333 Warren Sapp RC .60 1.50
❑ 334 Charles Wilson .02 .10
❑ 335 Reggie Brooks .07 .20
❑ 336 Tom Carter .02 .10
❑ 337 Henry Ellard .07 .20
❑ 338 Ricky Ervins .02 .10
❑ 339 Darrell Green .02 .10
❑ 340 Ken Harvey .02 .10
❑ 341 Brian Mitchell .02 .10
❑ 342 Cory Raymer RC .02 .10
❑ 343 Heath Shuler .07 .20
❑ 344 Michael Westbrook RC .15 .40
❑ 345 Tony Woods .02 .10
❑ 346 Checklist .02 .10
❑ 347 Checklist .02 .10
❑ 348 Checklist .02 .10
❑ 349 Checklist .02 .10
❑ 350 Checklist .02 .10
❑ 351 Checklist .02 .10
❑ 352 Checklist .02 .10
❑ 353 Dave Krieg .02 .10
❑ 354 Rob Moore .07 .20
❑ 355 J.J. Birden .02 .10
❑ 356 Eric Metcalf .07 .20
❑ 357 Bryce Paup .07 .20

Card		
❑ 358 Willie Green	.07	.20
❑ 359 Derrick Moore	.02	.10
❑ 360 Michael Timpson	.02	.10
❑ 361 Eric Bieniemy	.02	.10
❑ 362 Keenan McCardell	.15	.40
❑ 363 Andre Rison	.07	.20
❑ 364 Lorenzo White	.02	.10
❑ 365 Deion Sanders	.40	1.00
❑ 366 Wade Wilson	.02	.10
❑ 367 Aaron Craver	.02	.10
❑ 368 Michael Dean Perry	.02	.10
❑ 369 Rod Smith WR RC	5.00	12.00
❑ 370 Henry Thomas	.02	.10
❑ 371 Mark Ingram	.02	.10
❑ 372 Chris Chandler	.07	.20
❑ 373 Mel Gray	.02	.10
❑ 374 Flipper Anderson	.02	.10
❑ 375 Craig Erickson	.02	.10
❑ 376 Mark Brunell	.40	1.00
❑ 377 Ernest Givins	.02	.10
❑ 378 Randy Jordan	.02	.10
❑ 379 Webster Slaughter	.02	.10
❑ 380 Tamarick Vanover RC	.15	.40
❑ 381 Gary Clark	.02	.10
❑ 382 Steve Emtman	.02	.10
❑ 383 Eric Green	.02	.10
❑ 384 Louis Oliver	.02	.10
❑ 385 Robert Smith	.15	.40
❑ 386 Dave Meggett	.02	.10
❑ 387 Eric Allen	.02	.10
❑ 388 Wesley Walls	.07	.20
❑ 389 Herschel Walker	.07	.20
❑ 390 Ronald Moore	.02	.10
❑ 391 Adrian Murrell	.07	.20
❑ 392 Charles Wilson	.02	.10
❑ 393 Derrick Fenner	.02	.10
❑ 394 Pat Swilling	.02	.10
❑ 395 Kelvin Martin	.02	.10
❑ 396 Rodney Peete	.02	.10
❑ 397 Ricky Watters	.07	.20
❑ 398 Erric Pegram	.07	.20
❑ 399 Leonard Russell	.02	.10
❑ 400 Alexander Wright	.02	.10
❑ 401 Darrien Gordon	.02	.10
❑ 402 Alfred Pupunu	.02	.10
❑ 403 Elvis Grbac	.15	.40
❑ 404 Derek Loville	.02	.10
❑ 405 Steve Broussard	.02	.10
❑ 406 Ricky Proehl	.02	.10
❑ 407 Bobby Joe Edmonds	.02	.10
❑ 408 Alvin Harper	.02	.10
❑ 409 Dave Moore RC	.02	.10
❑ 410 Terry Allen	.07	.20
❑ 411 Gus Frerotte	.07	.20
❑ 412 Leslie Shepherd RC	.07	.20
❑ 413 Stoney Case RC	.02	.10
❑ 414 Frank Sanders RC	.15	.40
❑ 415 Roell Preston RC	.07	.20
❑ 416 Lorenzo Styles RC	.02	.10
❑ 417 Justin Armour RC	.02	.10
❑ 418 Todd Collins RC	.50	1.25
❑ 419 Darick Holmes RC	.07	.20
❑ 420 Kerry Collins	.30	.75
❑ 421 Tyrone Poole	.07	.20
❑ 422 Rashaan Salaam	.07	.20
❑ 423 Todd Sauerbrun RC	.02	.10
❑ 424 Ki-Jana Carter	.15	.40
❑ 425 David Dunn RC	.02	.10
❑ 426 Ernest Hunter RC	.02	.10
❑ 427 Eric Zeier RC	.15	.40
❑ 428 Eric Bjornson RC	.02	.10
❑ 429 Sherman Williams	.02	.10
❑ 430 Terrell Davis RC	1.00	2.50
❑ 431 Luther Elliss	.02	.10
❑ 432 Kez McCorvey RC	.02	.10
❑ 433 Antonio Freeman RC	.50	1.25
❑ 434 Craig Newsome RC	.02	.10
❑ 435 Steve McNair	.60	1.50
❑ 436 Chris Sanders RC	.07	.20
❑ 437 Zack Crockett RC	.07	.20
❑ 438 Ellis Johnson	.02	.10
❑ 439 Tony Boselli	.15	.40
❑ 440 James O. Stewart	.15	.40
❑ 441 Trezelle Jenkins	.02	.10
❑ 442 Tamarick Vanover	.15	.40
❑ 443 Derrick Alexander DE	.02	.10
❑ 444 Chad May RC	.02	.10
❑ 445 James A.Stewart RC	.02	.10

Card		
❑ 446 Ty Law	.15	.40
❑ 447 Curtis Martin RC	1.25	3.00
❑ 448 Will Moore RC	.02	.10
❑ 449 Mark Fields	.07	.20
❑ 450 Ray Zellars RC	.07	.20
❑ 451 Charles Way RC	.02	.10
❑ 452 Tyrone Wheatley	.15	.40
❑ 453 Kyle Brady	.15	.40
❑ 454 Wayne Chrebet RC	1.00	2.50
❑ 455 Hugh Douglas	.07	.20
❑ 456 Chris T.Jones RC	.02	.10
❑ 457 Mike Mamula	.02	.10
❑ 458 Fred McCrary RC	.02	.10
❑ 459 Bobby Taylor	.15	.40
❑ 460 Mark Bruener	.07	.20
❑ 461 Kordell Stewart	.25	.60
❑ 462 Kevin Carter	.07	.20
❑ 463 Lovell Pinkney RC	.02	.10
❑ 464 Johnny Thomas WR RC	.02	.10
❑ 465 Terrell Fletcher RC	.02	.10
❑ 466 Jimmy Oliver RC	.02	.10
❑ 467 J.J. Stokes	.15	.40
❑ 468 Christian Fauria RC	.07	.20
❑ 469 Joey Galloway	.25	.60
❑ 470 Derrick Brooks	.25	.60
❑ 471 Warren Sapp	.15	.40
❑ 472 Michael Westbrook	.15	.40
❑ 473 Garrison Hearst ES	.15	.40
❑ 474 Jeff George ES	.07	.20
❑ 475 Terance Mathis ES	.07	.20
❑ 476 Andre Reed ES	.07	.20
❑ 477 Bruce Smith ES	.15	.40
❑ 478 Lamar Lathon ES	.02	.10
❑ 479 Curtis Conway ES	.15	.40
❑ 480 Jeff Blake ES	.15	.40
❑ 481 Carl Pickens ES	.07	.20
❑ 482 Eric Turner ES	.02	.10
❑ 483 Troy Aikman ES	.30	.75
❑ 484 Michael Irvin ES	.15	.40
❑ 485 Emmitt Smith ES	.50	1.25
❑ 486 John Elway ES	.60	1.50
❑ 487 Shannon Sharpe ES	.07	.20
❑ 488 Herman Moore ES	.15	.40
❑ 489 Barry Sanders ES	.50	1.25
❑ 490 Brett Favre ES	.60	1.50
❑ 491 Reggie White ES	.15	.40
❑ 492 Haywood Jeffires ES	.02	.10
❑ 493 Sean Dawkins ES	.02	.10
❑ 494 Marshall Faulk ES	.40	1.00
❑ 495 Desmond Howard ES	.07	.20
❑ 496 Steve Bono ES	.07	.20
❑ 497 Derrick Thomas ES	.15	.40
❑ 498 Irving Fryar ES	.07	.20
❑ 499 Terry Kirby ES	.07	.20
❑ 500 Dan Marino ES	.60	1.50
❑ 501 O.J. McDuffie ES	.15	.40
❑ 502 Cris Carter ES	.15	.40
❑ 503 Warren Moon ES	.07	.20
❑ 504 Jake Reed ES	.07	.20
❑ 505 Drew Bledsoe ES	.15	.40
❑ 506 Ben Coates ES	.07	.20
❑ 507 Jim Everett ES	.02	.10
❑ 508 Rodney Hampton ES	.07	.20
❑ 509 Mo Lewis ES	.02	.10
❑ 510 Tim Brown ES	.15	.40
❑ 511 Jeff Hostetler ES	.07	.20
❑ 512 Rocket Ismail ES	.07	.20
❑ 513 Chester McGlockton ES	.07	.20
❑ 514 Fred Barnett ES	.07	.20
❑ 515 Greg Lloyd ES	.07	.20
❑ 516 Byron Bam Morris ES	.02	.10
❑ 517 Rod Woodson ES	.07	.20
❑ 518 Jerome Bettis ES	.15	.40
❑ 519 Isaac Bruce ES	.15	.40
❑ 520 Stan Humphries ES	.07	.20
❑ 521 Natrone Means ES	.07	.20
❑ 522 Junior Seau ES	.15	.40
❑ 523 William Floyd ES	.07	.20
❑ 524 Jerry Rice ES	.30	.75
❑ 525 Steve Young ES	.25	.60
❑ 526 Cortez Kennedy ES	.07	.20
❑ 527 Rick Mirer ES	.07	.20
❑ 528 Chris Warren ES	.07	.20
❑ 529 Trent Dilfer ES	.15	.40
❑ 530 Errict Rhett ES	.07	.20
❑ 531 Darrell Green ES	.02	.10
❑ 532 Heath Shuler ES	.07	.20
❑ 533 Stoney Case RO	.02	.10

Card		
❑ 534 Eric Zeier RO	.07	.20
❑ 535 Kerry Collins RO	.15	.40
❑ 536 Steve McNair RO	.50	1.25
❑ 537 Kordell Stewart RO	.25	.60
❑ 538 Rob Johnson RO RC	.40	1.00
❑ 539 Eric Ball EE	.02	.10
❑ 540 Darrick Brownlow EE	.02	.10
❑ 541 Paul Butcher EE	.02	.10
❑ 542 Carlester Crumpler EE	.02	.10
❑ 543 Maurice Douglas EE	.02	.10
❑ 544 Keith Elias EE RC	.02	.10
❑ 545 Kenneth Gant EE	.02	.10
❑ 546 Corey Harris EE	.02	.10
❑ 547 Andre Hastings EE	.07	.20
❑ 548 Thomas Homco EE	.02	.10
❑ 549 Lenny McGill EE	.02	.10
❑ 550 Mark Pike EE	.02	.10
❑ P1 Promo Sheet	.75	2.00
❑ P264 Byron Bam Morris Prototype	.40	1.00

1996 Ultra

Card		
❑ COMPLETE SET (200)	10.00	25.00
❑ 1 Larry Centers	.08	.25
❑ 2 Garrison Hearst	.08	.25
❑ 3 Rob Moore	.08	.25
❑ 4 Eric Swann	.02	.10
❑ 5 Aeneas Williams	.02	.10
❑ 6 Bert Emanuel	.08	.25
❑ 7 Jeff George	.08	.25
❑ 8 Craig Heyward	.02	.10
❑ 9 Terance Mathis	.02	.10
❑ 10 Eric Metcalf	.02	.10
❑ 11 Cornelius Bennett	.02	.10
❑ 12 Darick Holmes	.02	.10
❑ 13 Jim Kelly	.20	.50
❑ 14 Bryce Paup	.02	.10
❑ 15 Bruce Smith	.08	.25
❑ 16 Mark Carrier WR	.02	.10
❑ 17 Kerry Collins	.20	.50
❑ 18 Lamar Lathon	.02	.10
❑ 19 Derrick Moore	.02	.10
❑ 20 Tyrone Poole	.02	.10
❑ 21 Curtis Conway	.20	.50
❑ 22 Jeff Graham	.02	.10
❑ 23 Raymont Harris	.08	.25
❑ 24 Erik Kramer	.02	.10
❑ 25 Rashaan Salaam	.08	.25
❑ 26 Jeff Blake	.20	.50
❑ 27 Ki-Jana Carter	.08	.25
❑ 28 Carl Pickens	.08	.25
❑ 29 Darnay Scott	.08	.25
❑ 30 Dan Wilkinson	.02	.10
❑ 31 Leroy Hoard	.02	.10
❑ 32 Michael Jackson	.08	.25
❑ 33 Andre Rison	.08	.25
❑ 34 Vinny Testaverde	.08	.25
❑ 35 Eric Turner	.02	.10
❑ 36 Troy Aikman	.50	1.25
❑ 37 Charles Haley	.08	.25
❑ 38 Michael Irvin	.20	.50
❑ 39 Daryl Johnston	.08	.25
❑ 40 Jay Novacek	.02	.10
❑ 41 Deion Sanders	.30	.75
❑ 42 Emmitt Smith	.75	2.00
❑ 43 Steve Atwater	.02	.10
❑ 44 Terrell Davis	.40	1.00
❑ 45 John Elway	1.00	2.50
❑ 46 Anthony Miller	.08	.25
❑ 47 Shannon Sharpe	.08	.25
❑ 48 Scott Mitchell	.08	.25
❑ 49 Herman Moore	.08	.25
❑ 50 Johnnie Morton	.08	.25
❑ 51 Brett Perriman	.02	.10
❑ 52 Barry Sanders	.75	2.00

❑ 53 Chris Spielman	.02	.10
❑ 54 Edgar Bennett	.08	.25
❑ 55 Robert Brooks	.20	.50
❑ 56 Mark Chmura	.08	.25
❑ 57 Brett Favre	1.00	2.50
❑ 58 Reggie White	.20	.50
❑ 59 Mel Gray	.02	.10
❑ 60 Haywood Jeffires	.02	.10
❑ 61 Steve McNair	.40	1.00
❑ 62 Chris Sanders	.08	.25
❑ 63 Rodney Thomas	.02	.10
❑ 64 Quentin Coryatt	.02	.10
❑ 65 Sean Dawkins	.02	.10
❑ 66 Ken Dilger	.08	.25
❑ 67 Marshall Faulk	.25	.60
❑ 68 Jim Harbaugh	.08	.25
❑ 69 Tony Boselli	.02	.10
❑ 70 Mark Brunell	.30	.75
❑ 71 Desmond Howard	.08	.25
❑ 72 Jimmy Smith	.20	.50
❑ 73 James O. Stewart	.08	.25
❑ 74 Marcus Allen	.20	.50
❑ 75 Steve Bono	.02	.10
❑ 76 Lake Dawson	.02	.10
❑ 77 Neil Smith	.08	.25
❑ 78 Derrick Thomas	.20	.50
❑ 79 Tamarick Vanover	.08	.25
❑ 80 Bryan Cox	.02	.10
❑ 81 Irving Fryar	.08	.25
❑ 82 Eric Green	.02	.10
❑ 83 Dan Marino	1.00	2.50
❑ 84 O.J. McDuffie	.08	.25
❑ 85 Bernie Parmalee	.02	.10
❑ 86 Cris Carter	.20	.50
❑ 87 Qadry Ismail	.08	.25
❑ 88 Warren Moon	.08	.25
❑ 89 Jake Reed	.08	.25
❑ 90 Robert Smith	.08	.25
❑ 91 Drew Bledsoe	.30	.75
❑ 92 Vincent Brisby	.02	.10
❑ 93 Ben Coates	.08	.25
❑ 94 Curtis Martin	.40	1.00
❑ 95 Willie McGinest	.02	.10
❑ 96 Dave Meggett	.02	.10
❑ 97 Mario Bates	.08	.25
❑ 98 Quinn Early	.02	.10
❑ 99 Jim Everett	.02	.10
❑ 100 Michael Haynes	.02	.10
❑ 101 Renaldo Turnbull	.02	.10
❑ 102 Dave Brown	.02	.10
❑ 103 Rodney Hampton	.08	.25
❑ 104 Mike Sherrard	.02	.10
❑ 105 Phillippi Sparks	.02	.10
❑ 106 Tyrone Wheatley	.08	.25
❑ 107 Hugh Douglas	.08	.25
❑ 108 Boomer Esiason	.08	.25
❑ 109 Aaron Glenn	.02	.10
❑ 110 Mo Lewis	.02	.10
❑ 111 Johnny Mitchell	.02	.10
❑ 112 Tim Brown	.20	.50
❑ 113 Jeff Hostetler	.02	.10
❑ 114 Rocket Ismail	.02	.10
❑ 115 Chester McGlockton	.02	.10
❑ 116 Harvey Williams	.02	.10
❑ 117 Fred Barnett	.02	.10
❑ 118 William Fuller	.02	.10
❑ 119 Charlie Garner	.08	.25
❑ 120 Ricky Watters	.08	.25
❑ 121 Calvin Williams	.02	.10
❑ 122 Kevin Greene	.08	.25
❑ 123 Greg Lloyd	.08	.25
❑ 124 Byron Bam Morris	.02	.10
❑ 125 Neil O'Donnell	.08	.25
❑ 126 Erric Pegram	.02	.10
❑ 127 Kordell Stewart	.20	.50
❑ 128 Yancey Thigpen	.08	.25
❑ 129 Rod Woodson	.08	.25
❑ 130 Jerome Bettis	.20	.50
❑ 131 Isaac Bruce	.20	.50
❑ 132 Troy Drayton	.02	.10
❑ 133 Sean Gilbert	.02	.10
❑ 134 Chris Miller	.02	.10
❑ 135 Andre Coleman	.02	.10
❑ 136 Ronnie Harmon	.02	.10
❑ 137 Aaron Hayden RC	.02	.10
❑ 138 Stan Humphries	.08	.25
❑ 139 Natrone Means	.08	.25
❑ 140 Junior Seau	.20	.50

❑ 141 William Floyd	.08	.25
❑ 142 Merton Hanks	.02	.10
❑ 143 Brent Jones	.02	.10
❑ 144 Derek Loville	.02	.10
❑ 145 Jerry Rice	.50	1.25
❑ 146 J.J. Stokes	.20	.50
❑ 147 Steve Young	.40	1.00
❑ 148 Brian Blades	.02	.10
❑ 149 Joey Galloway	.20	.50
❑ 150 Cortez Kennedy	.02	.10
❑ 151 Rick Mirer	.08	.25
❑ 152 Chris Warren	.08	.25
❑ 153 Derrick Brooks	.20	.50
❑ 154 Trent Dilfer	.20	.50
❑ 155 Alvin Harper	.02	.10
❑ 156 Jackie Harris	.02	.10
❑ 157 Hardy Nickerson	.02	.10
❑ 158 Errict Rhett	.08	.25
❑ 159 Terry Allen	.08	.25
❑ 160 Henry Ellard	.02	.10
❑ 161 Brian Mitchell	.02	.10
❑ 162 Heath Shuler	.08	.25
❑ 163 Michael Westbrook	.20	.50
❑ 164 Tim Biakabutuka RC	.20	.50
❑ 165 Tony Brackens RC	.20	.50
❑ 166 Rickey Dudley RC	.20	.50
❑ 167 Bobby Engram RC	.20	.50
❑ 168 Daryl Gardener RC	.02	.10
❑ 169 Eddie George RC	.60	1.50
❑ 170 Terry Glenn RC	.50	1.25
❑ 171 Kevin Hardy RC	.20	.50
❑ 172 Keyshawn Johnson RC	.50	1.25
❑ 173 Cedric Jones RC	.02	.10
❑ 174 Leeland McElroy RC	.08	.25
❑ 175 Jonathan Ogden RC	.20	.50
❑ 176 Lawrence Phillips RC	.20	.50
❑ 177 Simeon Rice RC	.50	1.25
❑ 178 Regan Upshaw RC	.02	.10
❑ 179 Justin Armour FI	.02	.10
❑ 180 Kyle Brady FI	.02	.10
❑ 181 Devin Bush FI	.02	.10
❑ 182 Kevin Carter FI	.02	.10
❑ 183 Wayne Chrebet FI	.30	.75
❑ 184 Napoleon Kaufman FI	.20	.50
❑ 185 Frank Sanders FI	.08	.25
❑ 186 Warren Sapp FI	.02	.10
❑ 187 Eric Zeier FI	.02	.10
❑ 188 Ray Zellars FI	.02	.10
❑ 189 Bill Brooks SW	.02	.10
❑ 190 Chris Calloway SW	.02	.10
❑ 191 Zack Crockett SW	.02	.10
❑ 192 Antonio Freeman SW	.20	.50
❑ 193 Tyrone Hughes SW	.02	.10
❑ 194 Daryl Johnston SW	.08	.25
❑ 195 Tony Martin SW	.02	.10
❑ 196 Keenan McCardell SW	.20	.50
❑ 197 Glyn Milburn SW	.02	.10
❑ 198 David Palmer SW	.02	.10
❑ 199 Checklist	.02	.10
❑ 200 Checklist	.02	.10
❑ P1 Promo Sheet	.75	2.00

1997 Ultra

❑ COMPLETE SET (350)	40.00	80.00
❑ COMP.SERIES 1 (200)	15.00	30.00
❑ COMP.SERIES 2 (150)	25.00	50.00
❑ 1 Brett Favre	1.25	2.50
❑ 2 Ricky Watters	.15	.40
❑ 3 Dan Marino	1.00	2.50
❑ 4 Bryan Still	.08	.25
❑ 5 Chester McGlockton	.08	.25
❑ 6 Tim Biakabutuka	.15	.40
❑ 7 Dave Brown	.08	.25
❑ 8 Mike Alstott	.25	.60
❑ 9 O.J. McDuffie	.15	.40
❑ 10 Mark Brunell	.30	.75
❑ 11 Michael Bates	.08	.25
❑ 12 Tyrone Wheatley	.15	.40
❑ 13 Eddie George	.25	.60
❑ 14 Kevin Greene	.15	.40
❑ 15 Jerris McPhail	.08	.25
❑ 16 Harvey Williams	.08	.25
❑ 17 Eric Swann	.08	.25
❑ 18 Carl Pickens	.15	.40
❑ 19 Terrell Davis	.30	.75
❑ 20 Charles Way	.08	.25
❑ 21 Jamie Asher	.08	.25
❑ 22 Qadry Ismail	.15	.40
❑ 23 Lawrence Phillips	.08	.25
❑ 24 John Friesz	.08	.25
❑ 25 Dorsey Levens	.25	.60
❑ 26 Willie McGinest	.08	.25
❑ 27 Chris T. Jones	.08	.25
❑ 28 Cortez Kennedy	.08	.25
❑ 29 Raymont Harris	.08	.25
❑ 30 William Roaf	.08	.25
❑ 31 Ted Johnson	.08	.25
❑ 32 Tony Martin	.15	.40
❑ 33 Jim Everett	.08	.25
❑ 34 Ray Zellars	.08	.25
❑ 35 Derrick Alexander WR	.15	.40
❑ 36 Leonard Russell	.08	.25
❑ 37 William Thomas	.08	.25
❑ 38 Karim Abdul-Jabbar	.15	.40
❑ 39 Kevin Turner	.08	.25
❑ 40 Robert Brooks	.15	.40
❑ 41 Kent Graham	.08	.25
❑ 42 Tony Brackens	.08	.25
❑ 43 Rodney Hampton	.15	.40
❑ 44 Drew Bledsoe	.30	.75
❑ 45 Barry Sanders	.75	2.00
❑ 46 Tim Brown	.25	.60
❑ 47 Reggie White	.25	.60
❑ 48 Terry Allen	.25	.60
❑ 49 Jim Harbaugh	.15	.40
❑ 50 John Elway	1.00	2.50
❑ 51 William Floyd	.15	.40
❑ 52 Michael Jackson	.15	.40
❑ 53 Larry Centers	.15	.40
❑ 54 Emmitt Smith	.75	2.00
❑ 55 Bruce Smith	.15	.40
❑ 56 Terrell Owens	.30	.75
❑ 57 Deion Sanders	.25	.60
❑ 58 Neil O'Donnell	.15	.40
❑ 59 Kordell Stewart	.25	.60
❑ 60 Bobby Engram	.15	.40
❑ 61 Keenan McCardell	.15	.40
❑ 62 Ben Coates	.15	.40
❑ 63 Curtis Martin	.30	.75
❑ 64 Hugh Douglas	.08	.25
❑ 65 Eric Moulds	.25	.60
❑ 66 Derrick Thomas	.25	.60
❑ 67 Byron Bam Morris	.08	.25
❑ 68 Bryan Cox	.08	.25
❑ 69 Rob Moore	.15	.40
❑ 70 Michael Haynes	.08	.25
❑ 71 Brian Mitchell	.08	.25
❑ 72 Alex Molden	.08	.25
❑ 73 Steve Young	.30	.75
❑ 74 Andre Reed	.15	.40
❑ 75 Michael Westbrook	.15	.40
❑ 76 Eric Metcalf	.15	.40
❑ 77 Tony Banks	.15	.40
❑ 78 Ken Dilger	.08	.25
❑ 79 John Henry Mills RC	.08	.25
❑ 80 Ashley Ambrose	.08	.25
❑ 81 Jason Dunn	.08	.25
❑ 82 Trent Dilfer	.25	.60
❑ 83 Wayne Chrebet	.25	.60
❑ 84 Ty Detmer	.15	.40
❑ 85 Aeneas Williams	.08	.25
❑ 86 Frank Wycheck	.08	.25
❑ 87 Jessie Tuggle	.08	.25
❑ 88 Steve McNair	.30	.75
❑ 89 Chris Slade	.08	.25
❑ 90 Anthony Johnson	.08	.25
❑ 91 Simeon Rice	.15	.40
❑ 92 Mike Tomczak	.08	.25
❑ 93 Sean Jones	.08	.25
❑ 94 Wesley Walls	.15	.40
❑ 95 Thurman Thomas	.25	.60
❑ 96 Scott Mitchell	.15	.40

Card		
❑ 97 Desmond Howard	.15	.40
❑ 98 Chris Warren	.15	.40
❑ 99 Glyn Milburn	.08	.25
❑ 100 Vinny Testaverde	.15	.40
❑ 101 James O.Stewart	.15	.40
❑ 102 Iheanyi Uwaezuoke	.08	.25
❑ 103 Stan Humphries	.15	.40
❑ 104 Terance Mathis	.15	.40
❑ 105 Thomas Lewis	.08	.25
❑ 106 Eddie Kennison	.15	.40
❑ 107 Rashaan Salaam	.08	.25
❑ 108 Curtis Conway	.15	.40
❑ 109 Chris Sanders	.08	.25
❑ 110 Marcus Allen	.25	.60
❑ 111 Gilbert Brown	.15	.40
❑ 112 Jason Sehorn	.15	.40
❑ 113 Zach Thomas	.25	.60
❑ 114 Bobby Hebert	.08	.25
❑ 115 Herman Moore	.15	.40
❑ 116 Ray Lewis	.40	1.00
❑ 117 Darnay Scott	.15	.40
❑ 118 Jamal Anderson	.25	.60
❑ 119 Keyshawn Johnson	.25	.60
❑ 120 Adrian Murrell	.15	.40
❑ 121 Sam Mills	.08	.25
❑ 122 Irving Fryar	.15	.40
❑ 123 Ki-Jana Carter	.08	.25
❑ 124 Gus Frerotte	.08	.25
❑ 125 Terry Glenn	.25	.60
❑ 126 Quentin Coryatt	.08	.25
❑ 127 Robert Smith	.15	.40
❑ 128 Jeff Blake	.15	.40
❑ 129 Natrone Means	.15	.40
❑ 130 Isaac Bruce	.25	.60
❑ 131 Lamar Lathon	.08	.25
❑ 132 Johnnie Morton	.15	.40
❑ 133 Jerry Rice	.50	1.25
❑ 134 Errict Rhett	.08	.25
❑ 135 Junior Seau	.25	.60
❑ 136 Joey Galloway	.15	.40
❑ 137 Napoleon Kaufman	.25	.60
❑ 138 Troy Aikman	.50	1.25
❑ 139 Kevin Hardy	.08	.25
❑ 140 Jimmy Smith	.15	.40
❑ 141 Edgar Bennett	.15	.40
❑ 142 Hardy Nickerson	.08	.25
❑ 143 Greg Lloyd	.08	.25
❑ 144 Dale Carter	.08	.25
❑ 145 Jake Reed	.15	.40
❑ 146 Cris Carter	.25	.60
❑ 147 Todd Collins	.08	.25
❑ 148 Mel Gray	.08	.25
❑ 149 Lawyer Milloy	.15	.40
❑ 150 Kimble Anders	.15	.40
❑ 151 Darick Holmes	.08	.25
❑ 152 Bert Emanuel	.15	.40
❑ 153 Marshall Faulk	.30	.75
❑ 154 Frank Sanders	.15	.40
❑ 155 Leeland McElroy	.08	.25
❑ 156 Rickey Dudley	.15	.40
❑ 157 Tamarick Vanover	.15	.40
❑ 158 Kerry Collins	.25	.60
❑ 159 Jeff Graham	.08	.25
❑ 160 Jerome Bettis	.25	.60
❑ 161 Greg Hill	.08	.25
❑ 162 John Mobley	.08	.25
❑ 163 Michael Irvin	.25	.60
❑ 164 Marvin Harrison	.25	.60
❑ 165 Jim Schwantz RC	.08	.25
❑ 166 Jermaine Lewis	.25	.60
❑ 167 Levon Kirkland	.08	.25
❑ 168 Nilo Silvan	.08	.25
❑ 169 Ken Norton	.08	.25
❑ 170 Yancey Thigpen	.15	.40
❑ 171 Antonio Freeman	.25	.60
❑ 172 Terry Kirby	.15	.40
❑ 173 Brad Johnson	.25	.60
❑ 174 Reidel Anthony RC	.25	.60
❑ 175 Tiki Barber RC	2.00	5.00
❑ 176 Pat Barnes RC	.25	.60
❑ 177 Michael Booker RC	.08	.25
❑ 178 Peter Boulware RC	.25	.60
❑ 179 Rae Carruth RC	.08	.25
❑ 180 Troy Davis RC	.15	.40
❑ 181 Corey Dillon RC	2.00	5.00
❑ 182 Jim Druckenmiller RC	.15	.40
❑ 183 Warrick Dunn RC	1.00	2.50
❑ 184 James Farrior RC	.25	.60
❑ 185 Yatil Green RC	.15	.40
❑ 186 Walter Jones RC	.25	.60
❑ 187 Tom Knight RC	.08	.25
❑ 188 Sam Madison RC	.25	.60
❑ 189 Tyrus McCloud RC	.08	.25
❑ 190 Orlando Pace RC	.25	.60
❑ 191 Jake Plummer RC	1.50	4.00
❑ 192 Dwayne Rudd RC	.25	.60
❑ 193 Darrell Russell RC	.08	.25
❑ 194 Sedrick Shaw RC	.15	.40
❑ 195 Shawn Springs RC	.15	.40
❑ 196 Bryant Westbrook RC	.08	.25
❑ 197 Danny Wuerffel RC	.25	.60
❑ 198 Reinard Wilson RC	.15	.40
❑ 199 Checklist	.08	.25
❑ 200 Checklist	.25	.60
❑ 201 Rick Mirer	.08	.25
❑ 202 Torrance Small	.08	.25
❑ 203 Ricky Proehl	.08	.25
❑ 204 Will Blackwell RC	.15	.40
❑ 205 Warrick Dunn	.50	1.25
❑ 206 Rob Johnson	.25	.60
❑ 207 Jim Schwantz	.08	.25
❑ 208 Ike Hilliard RC	.50	1.25
❑ 209 Chris Canty RC	.08	.25
❑ 210 Chris Boniol	.08	.25
❑ 211 Jim Druckenmiller	.08	.25
❑ 212 Tony Gonzalez RC	1.00	2.50
❑ 213 Scottie Graham	.08	.25
❑ 214 Byron Hanspard RC	.15	.40
❑ 215 Gary Brown	.08	.25
❑ 216 Darrell Russell	.08	.25
❑ 217 Sedrick Shaw	.15	.40
❑ 218 Boomer Esiason	.15	.40
❑ 219 Peter Boulware	.15	.40
❑ 220 Willie Green	.08	.25
❑ 221 Dietrich Jells	.08	.25
❑ 222 Freddie Jones RC	.15	.40
❑ 223 Eric Metcalf	.15	.40
❑ 224 John Henry Mills	.08	.25
❑ 225 Michael Timpson	.08	.25
❑ 226 Danny Wuerffel	.25	.60
❑ 227 Daimon Shelton RC	.08	.25
❑ 228 Henry Ellard	.08	.25
❑ 229 Flipper Anderson	.08	.25
❑ 230 Hunter Goodwin RC	.08	.25
❑ 231 Jay Graham RC	.15	.40
❑ 232 Duce Staley RC	2.50	6.00
❑ 233 Lamar Thomas	.08	.25
❑ 234 Rod Woodson	.15	.40
❑ 235 Zack Crockett	.08	.25
❑ 236 Ernie Mills	.08	.25
❑ 237 Kyle Brady	.08	.25
❑ 238 Jesse Campbell	.08	.25
❑ 239 Anthony Miller	.08	.25
❑ 240 Michael Haynes	.08	.25
❑ 241 Qadry Ismail	.15	.40
❑ 242 Tom Knight	.08	.25
❑ 243 Brian Manning RC	.08	.25
❑ 244 Derrick Mayes	.15	.40
❑ 245 Jamie Sharper RC	.15	.40
❑ 246 Sherman Williams	.08	.25
❑ 247 Yatil Green	.15	.40
❑ 248 Howard Griffith	.08	.25
❑ 249 Brian Blades	.08	.25
❑ 250 Mark Chmura	.15	.40
❑ 251 Chris Darkins	.08	.25
❑ 252 Willie Davis	.08	.25
❑ 253 Quinn Early	.08	.25
❑ 254 Marc Edwards RC	.08	.25
❑ 255 Charlie Jones	.08	.25
❑ 256 Jake Plummer	.60	1.50
❑ 257 Heath Shuler	.08	.25
❑ 258 Fred Barnett	.08	.25
❑ 259 William Henderson	.15	.40
❑ 260 Michael Booker	.08	.25
❑ 261 Chad Brown	.08	.25
❑ 262 Garrison Hearst	.15	.40
❑ 263 Leon Johnson RC	.15	.40
❑ 264 Antowain Smith RC	.75	2.00
❑ 265 Darnell Autry RC	.15	.40
❑ 266 Craig Heyward	.08	.25
❑ 267 Walter Jones	.08	.25
❑ 268 Dexter Coakley RC	.25	.60
❑ 269 Mercury Hayes	.08	.25
❑ 270 Brett Perriman	.08	.25
❑ 271 Chris Spielman	.08	.25
❑ 272 Kevin Greene	.15	.40
❑ 273 Kevin Lockett RC	.15	.40
❑ 274 Troy Davis	.15	.40
❑ 275 Brent Jones	.08	.25
❑ 276 Chris Chandler	.15	.40
❑ 277 Bryant Westbrook	.08	.25
❑ 278 Desmond Howard	.15	.40
❑ 279 Tyrone Hughes	.08	.25
❑ 280 Kez McCorvey	.08	.25
❑ 281 Stephen Davis	.25	.60
❑ 282 Steve Everitt	.08	.25
❑ 283 Andre Hastings	.08	.25
❑ 284 Marcus Robinson RC	2.00	5.00
❑ 285 Donnell Woolford	.08	.25
❑ 286 Mario Bates	.08	.25
❑ 287 Corey Dillon	.75	2.00
❑ 288 Jackie Harris	.08	.25
❑ 289 Lorenzo Neal	.08	.25
❑ 290 Anthony Pleasant	.08	.25
❑ 291 Andre Rison	.15	.40
❑ 292 Amani Toomer	.15	.40
❑ 293 Eric Turner	.08	.25
❑ 294 Elvis Grbac	.15	.40
❑ 295 Cris Dishman	.08	.25
❑ 296 Tom Carter	.08	.25
❑ 297 Mark Carrier DB	.08	.25
❑ 298 Orlando Pace	.15	.40
❑ 299 Jay Riemersma RC	.08	.25
❑ 300 Daryl Johnston	.15	.40
❑ 301 Joey Kent RC	.25	.60
❑ 302 Ronnie Harmon	.08	.25
❑ 303 Rocket Ismail	.15	.40
❑ 304 Terrell Davis	.30	.75
❑ 305 Sean Dawkins	.08	.25
❑ 306 Jeff George	.15	.40
❑ 307 David Palmer	.08	.25
❑ 308 Dwayne Rudd	.08	.25
❑ 309 J.J. Stokes	.15	.40
❑ 310 James Farrior	.15	.40
❑ 311 William Fuller	.08	.25
❑ 312 George Jones RC	.15	.40
❑ 313 John Allred RC	.08	.25
❑ 314 Tony Graziani RC	.25	.60
❑ 315 Jeff Hostetler	.08	.25
❑ 316 Keith Poole RC	.25	.60
❑ 317 Neil Smith	.15	.40
❑ 318 Steve Tasker	.08	.25
❑ 319 Mike Vrabel RC	6.00	15.00
❑ 320 Pat Barnes	.25	.60
❑ 321 James Hundon RC	.25	.60
❑ 322 O.J. Santiago RC	.15	.40
❑ 323 Billy Davis RC	.08	.25
❑ 324 Shawn Springs	.15	.40
❑ 325 Reinard Wilson	.08	.25
❑ 326 Charles Johnson	.15	.40
❑ 327 Micheal Barrow	.08	.25
❑ 328 Derrick Mason RC	1.25	3.00
❑ 329 Muhsin Muhammad	.15	.40
❑ 330 David LaFleur RC	.08	.25
❑ 331 Reidel Anthony	.15	.40
❑ 332 Tiki Barber	.75	2.00
❑ 333 Ray Buchanan	.08	.25
❑ 334 John Elway	1.00	2.50
❑ 335 Alvin Harper	.08	.25
❑ 336 Damon Jones RC	.08	.25
❑ 337 Dedric Ward RC	.15	.40
❑ 338 Jim Everett	.08	.25
❑ 339 Jon Harris	.08	.25
❑ 340 Warren Moon	.25	.60
❑ 341 Rae Carruth	.08	.25
❑ 342 John Mobley	.08	.25
❑ 343 Tyrone Poole	.08	.25
❑ 344 Mike Cherry RC	.08	.25
❑ 345 Horace Copeland	.08	.25
❑ 346 Deon Figures	.08	.25
❑ 347 Antwuan Wyatt RC	.08	.25
❑ 348 Tommy Vardell	.08	.25
❑ 349 Checklist (201-324)	.08	.25
❑ 350 Checklist (325-350/inserts)	.08	.25
❑ S1A T.Davis Sample AU	40.00	80.00
❑ AU3 Dan Marino AU	40.00	100.00
❑ S1 Terrell Davis Sample	1.25	3.00

1998 Ultra

❑ COMPLETE SET (425)	50.00	120.00
❑ COMP.SERIES 1 (225)	30.00	80.00
❑ COMP.SERIES 2 (200)	25.00	50.00
❑ 1 Barry Sanders	1.00	2.50
❑ 2 Brett Favre	1.50	3.00
❑ 3 Napoleon Kaufman	.30	.75
❑ 4 Robert Smith	.30	.75
❑ 5 Terry Allen	.30	.75
❑ 6 Vinny Testaverde	.20	.50
❑ 7 William Floyd	.10	.30
❑ 8 Carl Pickens	.20	.50
❑ 9 Antonio Freeman	.30	.75
❑ 10 Ben Coates	.20	.50
❑ 11 Elvis Grbac	.20	.50
❑ 12 Kerry Collins	.20	.50
❑ 13 Orlando Pace	.10	.30
❑ 14 Steve Broussard	.10	.30
❑ 15 Terance Mathis	.20	.50
❑ 16 Tiki Barber	.30	.75
❑ 17 Cris Carter	.30	.75
❑ 18 Eric Green	.10	.30
❑ 19 Eric Metcalf	.10	.30
❑ 20 Jeff George	.20	.50
❑ 21 Leslie Shepherd	.10	.30
❑ 22 Natrone Means	.20	.50
❑ 23 Scott Mitchell	.20	.50
❑ 24 Adrian Murrell	.20	.50
❑ 25 Gilbert Brown	.10	.30
❑ 26 Jimmy Smith	.20	.50
❑ 27 Mark Bruener	.10	.30
❑ 28 Troy Aikman	.60	1.50
❑ 29 Warrick Dunn	.30	.75
❑ 30 Jay Graham	.10	.30
❑ 31 Craig Whelihan RC	.10	.30
❑ 32 Ed McCaffrey	.20	.50
❑ 33 Jamie Asher	.10	.30
❑ 34 John Randle	.20	.50
❑ 35 Michael Jackson	.10	.30
❑ 36 Rickey Dudley	.10	.30
❑ 37 Sean Dawkins	.10	.30
❑ 38 Andre Rison	.20	.50
❑ 39 Bert Emanuel	.20	.50
❑ 40 Jeff Blake	.20	.50
❑ 41 Curtis Conway	.20	.50
❑ 42 Eddie Kennison	.20	.50
❑ 43 James McKnight	.30	.75
❑ 44 Rae Carruth	.10	.30
❑ 45 Tito Wooten RC	.10	.30
❑ 46 Cris Dishman	.10	.30
❑ 47 Ernie Conwell	.10	.30
❑ 48 Fred Lane	.10	.30
❑ 49 Jamal Anderson	.30	.75
❑ 50 Lake Dawson	.10	.30
❑ 51 Michael Strahan	.20	.50
❑ 52 Reggie White	.30	.75
❑ 53 Trent Dilfer	.30	.75
❑ 54 Troy Brown	.20	.50
❑ 55 Wesley Walls	.20	.50
❑ 56 Chidi Ahanotu	.10	.30
❑ 57 Dwayne Rudd	.10	.30
❑ 58 Jerry Rice	.60	1.50
❑ 59 Johnnie Morton	.20	.50
❑ 60 Sherman Williams	.10	.30
❑ 61 Steve McNair	.30	.75
❑ 62 Will Blackwell	.10	.30
❑ 63 Chris Chandler	.20	.50
❑ 64 Dexter Coakley	.10	.30
❑ 65 Horace Copeland	.10	.30
❑ 66 Jerald Moore	.10	.30
❑ 67 Leon Johnson	.10	.30
❑ 68 Mark Chmura	.20	.50
❑ 69 Micheal Barrow	.10	.30
❑ 70 Muhsin Muhammad	.20	.50
❑ 71 Terry Glenn	.30	.75
❑ 72 Tony Brackens	.10	.30
❑ 73 Chad Scott	.10	.30
❑ 74 Glenn Foley	.20	.50
❑ 75 Keenan McCardell	.20	.50
❑ 76 Peter Boulware	.10	.30
❑ 77 Reidel Anthony	.20	.50
❑ 78 William Henderson	.20	.50
❑ 79 Tony Martin	.20	.50
❑ 80 Tony Gonzalez	.30	.75
❑ 81 Charlie Jones	.10	.30
❑ 82 Chris Gedney	.10	.30
❑ 83 Chris Calloway	.10	.30
❑ 84 Dale Carter	.10	.30
❑ 85 Ki-Jana Carter	.10	.30
❑ 86 Shawn Springs	.10	.30
❑ 87 Antowain Smith	.30	.75
❑ 88 Eric Turner	.10	.30
❑ 89 John Mobley	.10	.30
❑ 90 Ken Dilger	.10	.30
❑ 91 Bobby Hoying	.20	.50
❑ 92 Curtis Martin	.30	.75
❑ 93 Drew Bledsoe	.50	1.25
❑ 94 Gary Brown	.10	.30
❑ 95 Marvin Harrison	.30	.75
❑ 96 Todd Collins	.10	.30
❑ 97 Chris Warren	.20	.50
❑ 98 Danny Kanell	.20	.50
❑ 99 Tony McGee	.10	.30
❑ 100 Rod Smith	.20	.50
❑ 101 Frank Sanders	.20	.50
❑ 102 Irving Fryar	.20	.50
❑ 103 Marcus Allen	.30	.75
❑ 104 Marshall Faulk	.40	1.00
❑ 105 Bruce Smith	.20	.50
❑ 106 Charlie Garner	.20	.50
❑ 107 Paul Justin	.10	.30
❑ 108 Randal Hill	.10	.30
❑ 109 Erik Kramer	.10	.30
❑ 110 Rob Moore	.20	.50
❑ 111 Shannon Sharpe	.20	.50
❑ 112 Warren Moon	.30	.75
❑ 113 Zach Thomas	.30	.75
❑ 114 Dan Marino	1.50	3.00
❑ 115 Duce Staley	.40	1.00
❑ 116 Eric Swann	.10	.30
❑ 117 Kenny Holmes	.10	.30
❑ 118 Merton Hanks	.10	.30
❑ 119 Raymont Harris	.10	.30
❑ 120 Terrell Davis	.30	.75
❑ 121 Thurman Thomas	.30	.75
❑ 122 Wayne Martin	.10	.30
❑ 123 Charles Way	.10	.30
❑ 124 Chuck Smith	.10	.30
❑ 125 Corey Dillon	.30	.75
❑ 126 Darnell Autry	.10	.30
❑ 127 Isaac Bruce	.30	.75
❑ 128 Joey Galloway	.20	.50
❑ 129 Kimble Anders	.20	.50
❑ 130 Aeneas Williams	.10	.30
❑ 131 Andre Hastings	.10	.30
❑ 132 Chad Lewis	.20	.50
❑ 133 J.J. Stokes	.20	.50
❑ 134 John Elway	1.25	3.00
❑ 135 Karim Abdul-Jabbar	.30	.75
❑ 136 Ken Harvey	.10	.30
❑ 137 Robert Brooks	.20	.50
❑ 138 Rodney Thomas	.10	.30
❑ 139 James Stewart	.20	.50
❑ 140 Billy Joe Hobert	.10	.30
❑ 141 Frank Wycheck	.10	.30
❑ 142 Jake Plummer	.30	.75
❑ 143 Jerris McPhail	.10	.30
❑ 144 Kordell Stewart	.30	.75
❑ 145 Terrell Owens	.30	.75
❑ 146 Willie Green	.10	.30
❑ 147 Anthony Miller	.10	.30
❑ 148 Courtney Hawkins	.10	.30
❑ 149 Larry Centers	.10	.30
❑ 150 Gus Frerotte	.10	.30
❑ 151 O.J. McDuffie	.20	.50
❑ 152 Ray Zellars	.10	.30
❑ 153 Terry Kirby	.10	.30
❑ 154 Tommy Vardell	.10	.30
❑ 155 Willie Davis	.10	.30
❑ 156 Chris Canty	.10	.30
❑ 157 Byron Hanspard	.10	.30
❑ 158 Chris Penn	.10	.30
❑ 159 Damon Jones	.10	.30
❑ 160 Derrick Mayes	.20	.50
❑ 161 Emmitt Smith	1.25	2.50
❑ 162 Keyshawn Johnson	.30	.75
❑ 163 Mike Alstott	.30	.75
❑ 164 Tom Carter	.10	.30
❑ 165 Tony Banks	.20	.50
❑ 166 Bryant Westbrook	.10	.30
❑ 167 Chris Sanders	.10	.30
❑ 168 Deion Sanders	.30	.75
❑ 169 Garrison Hearst	.30	.75
❑ 170 Jason Taylor	.20	.50
❑ 171 Jerome Bettis	.30	.75
❑ 172 John Lynch	.20	.50
❑ 173 Troy Davis	.10	.30
❑ 174 Freddie Jones	.10	.30
❑ 175 Herman Moore	.20	.50
❑ 176 Jake Reed	.20	.50
❑ 177 Mark Brunell	.30	.75
❑ 178 Ray Lewis	.30	.75
❑ 179 Stephen Davis	.10	.30
❑ 180 Tim Brown	.30	.75
❑ 181 Willie McGinest	.10	.30
❑ 182 Andre Reed	.20	.50
❑ 183 Darrien Gordon	.10	.30
❑ 184 David Palmer	.10	.30
❑ 185 James Jett	.20	.50
❑ 186 Junior Seau	.30	.75
❑ 187 Zack Crockett	.10	.30
❑ 188 Brad Johnson	.30	.75
❑ 189 Charles Johnson	.10	.30
❑ 190 Eddie George	.30	.75
❑ 191 Jermaine Lewis	.20	.50
❑ 192 Michael Irvin	.30	.75
❑ 193 Reggie Brown LB	.10	.30
❑ 194 Steve Young	.40	1.00
❑ 195 Warren Sapp	.20	.50
❑ 196 Wayne Chrebet	.30	.75
❑ 197 David Dunn	.10	.30
❑ 198 Dorsey Levens CL	.20	.50
❑ 199 Troy Aikman CL	.30	.75
❑ 200 John Elway CL	.30	.75
❑ 201 Peyton Manning RC	15.00	30.00
❑ 202 Ryan Leaf RC	1.25	3.00
❑ 203 Charles Woodson RC	1.50	4.00
❑ 204 Andre Wadsworth RC	1.00	2.50
❑ 205 Brian Simmons RC	1.00	2.50
❑ 206 Curtis Enis RC	.60	1.50
❑ 207 Randy Moss RC	8.00	20.00
❑ 208 Germane Crowell RC	1.00	2.50
❑ 209 Greg Ellis RC	.60	1.50
❑ 210 Kevin Dyson RC	1.25	3.00
❑ 211 Skip Hicks RC	1.00	2.50
❑ 212 Alonzo Mayes RC	.60	1.50
❑ 213 Robert Edwards RC	1.00	2.50
❑ 214 Fred Taylor RC	2.00	5.00
❑ 215 Robert Holcombe RC	1.00	2.50
❑ 216 John Dutton RC	.60	1.50
❑ 217 Vonnie Holliday RC	1.00	2.50
❑ 218 Tim Dwight RC	1.25	3.00
❑ 219 Tavian Banks RC	1.00	2.50
❑ 220 Marcus Nash RC	.60	1.50
❑ 221 Jason Peter RC	.60	1.50
❑ 222 Michael Myers RC	.60	1.50
❑ 223 Takeo Spikes RC	1.25	3.00
❑ 224 Kivuusama Mays RC	.60	1.50
❑ 225 Jacquez Green RC	1.00	2.50
❑ 226 Doug Flutie	.30	.75
❑ 227 Ike Hilliard	.20	.50
❑ 228 Craig Heyward	.10	.30
❑ 229 Kevin Hardy	.10	.30
❑ 230 Jason Dunn	.10	.30
❑ 231 Billy Davis	.10	.30
❑ 232 Chester McGlockton	.10	.30
❑ 233 Sean Gilbert	.10	.30
❑ 234 Bert Emanuel	.20	.50
❑ 235 Keith Byars	.10	.30
❑ 236 Tyrone Wheatley	.20	.50
❑ 237 Ricky Proehl	.10	.30
❑ 238 Michael Bates	.10	.30
❑ 239 Derrick Alexander	.20	.50
❑ 240 Harvey Williams	.10	.30
❑ 241 Mike Pritchard	.10	.30
❑ 242 Paul Justin	.10	.30
❑ 243 Jeff Hostetler	.10	.30
❑ 244 Eric Moulds	.30	.75
❑ 245 Jeff Burris	.10	.30

❑ 246 Gary Brown	.10	.30
❑ 247 Anthony Johnson	.10	.30
❑ 248 Dan Wilkinson	.10	.30
❑ 249 Chris Warren	.20	.50
❑ 250 Chris Darkins	.10	.30
❑ 251 Eric Metcalf	.10	.30
❑ 252 Pat Swilling	.10	.30
❑ 253 Lamar Smith	.20	.50
❑ 254 Quinn Early	.10	.30
❑ 255 Carlester Crumpler	.10	.30
❑ 256 Eric Bieniemy	.10	.30
❑ 257 Aaron Bailey	.10	.30
❑ 258 Neil O'Donnell	.20	.50
❑ 259 Rod Woodson	.20	.50
❑ 260 Ricky Whittle	.10	.30
❑ 261 Iheanyi Uwaezuoke	.10	.30
❑ 262 Heath Shuler	.10	.30
❑ 263 Darren Sharper	.30	.75
❑ 264 John Henry Mills	.10	.30
❑ 265 Marco Battaglia	.10	.30
❑ 266 Yancey Thigpen	.10	.30
❑ 267 Irv Smith	.10	.30
❑ 268 Jamie Sharper	.10	.30
❑ 269 Marcus Robinson	2.00	5.00
❑ 270 Dorsey Levens	.30	.75
❑ 271 Qadry Ismail	.20	.50
❑ 272 Desmond Howard	.20	.50
❑ 273 Webster Slaughter	.10	.30
❑ 274 Eugene Robinson	.10	.30
❑ 275 Bill Romanowski	.10	.30
❑ 276 Vincent Brisby	.10	.30
❑ 277 Errict Rhett	.20	.50
❑ 278 Albert Connell	.10	.30
❑ 279 Thomas Lewis	.10	.30
❑ 280 John Farquhar RC	.10	.30
❑ 281 Marc Edwards	.10	.30
❑ 282 Tyrone Davis	.10	.30
❑ 283 Eric Allen	.10	.30
❑ 284 Aaron Glenn	.10	.30
❑ 285 Roosevelt Potts	.10	.30
❑ 286 Kez McCorvey	.10	.30
❑ 287 Joey Kent	.20	.50
❑ 288 Jim Druckenmiller	.10	.30
❑ 289 Sean Dawkins	.10	.30
❑ 290 Edgar Bennett	.10	.30
❑ 291 Vinny Testaverde	.20	.50
❑ 292 Chris Slade	.10	.30
❑ 293 Lamar Lathon	.10	.30
❑ 294 Jackie Harris	.10	.30
❑ 295 Jim Harbaugh	.20	.50
❑ 296 Rob Fredrickson	.10	.30
❑ 297 Ty Detmer	.20	.50
❑ 298 Karl Williams	.10	.30
❑ 299 Troy Drayton	.10	.30
❑ 300 Curtis Martin	.30	.75
❑ 301 Tamarick Vanover	.10	.30
❑ 302 Lorenzo Neal	.10	.30
❑ 303 John Hall	.10	.30
❑ 304 Kevin Greene	.20	.50
❑ 305 Bryan Still	.10	.30
❑ 306 Neil Smith	.20	.50
❑ 307 Greg Lloyd	.10	.30
❑ 308 Shawn Jefferson	.10	.30
❑ 309 Aaron Taylor	.10	.30
❑ 310 Sedrick Shaw	.10	.30
❑ 311 O.J. Santiago	.10	.30
❑ 312 Kevin Abrams	.10	.30
❑ 313 Dana Stubblefield	.10	.30
❑ 314 Daryl Johnston	.20	.50
❑ 315 Bryan Cox	.10	.30
❑ 316 Jeff Graham	.10	.30
❑ 317 Mario Bates	.20	.50
❑ 318 Adrian Murrell	.20	.50
❑ 319 Greg Hill	.10	.30
❑ 320 Jahine Arnold	.10	.30
❑ 321 Justin Armour	.10	.30
❑ 322 Ricky Watters	.20	.50
❑ 323 Lamont Warren	.10	.30
❑ 324 Mack Strong	.30	.75
❑ 325 Damay Scott	.20	.50
❑ 326 Brian Mitchell	.10	.30
❑ 327 Rob Johnson	.20	.50
❑ 328 Kent Graham	.10	.30
❑ 329 Hugh Douglas	.10	.30
❑ 330 Simeon Rice	.20	.50
❑ 331 Rick Mirer	.10	.00
❑ 332 Randall Cunningham	.30	.75
❑ 333 Steve Atwater	.10	.30

❑ 334 Latario Rachal	.10	.30
❑ 335 Tony Martin	.20	.50
❑ 336 Leroy Hoard	.10	.30
❑ 337 Howard Griffith	.10	.30
❑ 338 Kevin Lockett	.10	.30
❑ 339 William Floyd	.10	.30
❑ 340 Jerry Ellison	.10	.30
❑ 341 Kyle Brady	.10	.30
❑ 342 Michael Westbrook	.20	.50
❑ 343 Kevin Turner	.10	.30
❑ 344 David LaFleur	.10	.30
❑ 345 Robert Jones	.10	.30
❑ 346 Dave Brown	.10	.30
❑ 347 Kevin Williams	.10	.30
❑ 348 Amani Toomer	.20	.50
❑ 349 Amp Lee	.10	.30
❑ 350 Bryce Paup	.10	.30
❑ 351 Dewayne Washington	.10	.30
❑ 352 Mercury Hayes	.10	.30
❑ 353 Tim Biakabutuka	.20	.50
❑ 354 Ray Crockett	.10	.30
❑ 355 Ted Washington	.10	.30
❑ 356 Pete Mitchell	.10	.30
❑ 357 Billy Jenkins RC	.10	.30
❑ 358 Troy Aikman CL	.30	.75
❑ 359 Drew Bledsoe CL	.30	.75
❑ 360 Steve Young CL	.30	.75
❑ 361 Antonio Freeman NG	.20	.50
❑ 362 Antowain Smith NG	.20	.50
❑ 363 Barry Sanders NG	.60	1.50
❑ 364 Bobby Hoying NG	.10	.30
❑ 365 Brett Favre NG	.75	2.00
❑ 366 Corey Dillon NG	.20	.50
❑ 367 Dan Marino NG	.75	2.00
❑ 368 Drew Bledsoe NG	.30	.75
❑ 369 Eddie George NG	.20	.50
❑ 370 Emmitt Smith NG	.60	1.50
❑ 371 Herman Moore NG	.20	.50
❑ 372 Jake Plummer NG	.20	.50
❑ 373 Jerome Bettis NG	.20	.50
❑ 374 Jerry Rice NG	.40	1.00
❑ 375 Joey Galloway NG	.20	.50
❑ 376 John Elway NG	.75	2.00
❑ 377 Kordell Stewart NG	.20	.50
❑ 378 Mark Brunell NG	.30	.75
❑ 379 Keyshawn Johnson NG	.20	.50
❑ 380 Steve Young NG	.30	.75
❑ 381 Steve McNair NG	.20	.50
❑ 382 Terrell Davis NG	.30	.75
❑ 383 Tim Brown NG	.20	.50
❑ 384 Troy Aikman NG	.40	1.00
❑ 385 Warrick Dunn NG	.30	.75
❑ 386 Ryan Leaf	1.25	3.00
❑ 387 Tony Simmons RC	.75	2.00
❑ 388 Rodney Williams RC	.50	1.25
❑ 389 John Avery RC	.75	2.00
❑ 390 Shaun Williams RC	.75	2.00
❑ 391 Anthony Simmons RC	.75	2.00
❑ 392 Rashaan Shehee RC	.75	2.00
❑ 393 Robert Holcombe	.75	2.00
❑ 394 Larry Shannon RC	.50	1.25
❑ 395 Skip Hicks	.75	2.00
❑ 396 Rod Rutledge RC	.50	1.25
❑ 397 Donald Hayes RC	.75	2.00
❑ 398 Curtis Enis	.50	1.25
❑ 399 Mikhael Ricks RC	.75	2.00
❑ 400 Brian Griese RC	2.50	6.00
❑ 401 Michael Pittman RC	1.50	4.00
❑ 402 Jacquez Green	.75	2.00
❑ 403 Jerome Pathon RC	1.25	3.00
❑ 404 Ahman Green RC	3.00	8.00
❑ 405 Marcus Nash	.50	1.25
❑ 406 Randy Moss	6.00	15.00
❑ 407 Terry Fair RC	.75	2.00
❑ 408 Jammi German RC	.50	1.25
❑ 409 Stephen Alexander RC	.75	2.00
❑ 410 Grant Wistrom RC	.75	2.00
❑ 411 Charlie Batch RC	1.25	3.00
❑ 412 Fred Taylor	1.50	4.00
❑ 413 Pat Johnson RC	.75	2.00
❑ 414 Robert Edwards	.75	2.00
❑ 415 Keith Brooking RC	1.25	3.00
❑ 416 Peyton Manning	12.50	25.00
❑ 417 Duane Starks RC	.50	1.25
❑ 418 Andre Wadsworth	.75	2.00
❑ 419 Brian Alford RC	.50	1.25
❑ 420 Brian Kelly RC	.75	2.00
❑ 421 Joe Jurevicius RC	1.25	3.00

❑ 422 Tebucky Jones RC	.50	1.25
❑ 423 R.W. McQuarters RC	.75	2.00
❑ 424 Kevin Dyson	1.00	2.50
❑ 425 Charles Woodson	1.25	3.00
❑ R1 Reggie White COMM	.25	.60
❑ P20 Jeff George Promo	.30	.75

1999 Ultra

❑ COMPLETE SET (300)	30.00	80.00
❑ COMP.SET w/o SP's (250)	8.00	20.00
❑ 1 Terrell Davis	.30	.75
❑ 2 Courtney Hawkins	.10	.30
❑ 3 Cris Carter	.30	.75
❑ 4 Darnay Scott	.10	.30
❑ 5 Darrell Green	.20	.50
❑ 6 Jimmy Smith	.20	.50
❑ 7 Doug Flutie	.30	.75
❑ 8 Michael Jackson	.10	.30
❑ 9 Warren Sapp	.20	.50
❑ 10 Greg Hill	.10	.30
❑ 11 Karim Abdul-Jabbar	.20	.50
❑ 12 Greg Ellis	.10	.30
❑ 13 Dan Marino	1.00	2.50
❑ 14 Napoleon Kaufman	.30	.75
❑ 15 Peyton Manning	1.00	2.50
❑ 16 Simeon Rice	.20	.50
❑ 17 Tony Simmons	.10	.30
❑ 18 Carlester Crumpler	.10	.30
❑ 19 Charles Johnson	.10	.30
❑ 20 Derrick Alexander	.10	.30
❑ 21 Kent Graham	.10	.30
❑ 22 Randall Cunningham	.30	.75
❑ 23 Trent Green	.30	.75
❑ 24 Chris Spielman	.10	.30
❑ 25 Carl Pickens	.20	.50
❑ 26 Bill Romanowski	.10	.30
❑ 27 Jermaine Lewis	.20	.50
❑ 28 Ahman Green	.30	.75
❑ 29 Bryan Still	.10	.30
❑ 30 Dorsey Levens	.30	.75
❑ 31 Frank Wycheck	.10	.30
❑ 32 Jerome Bettis	.30	.75
❑ 33 Reidel Anthony	.20	.50
❑ 34 Robert Jones	.10	.30
❑ 35 Terry Glenn	.30	.75
❑ 36 Tim Brown	.30	.75
❑ 37 Eric Metcalf	.10	.30
❑ 38 Kevin Greene	.20	.50
❑ 39 Takeo Spikes	.10	.30
❑ 40 Brian Mitchell	.10	.30
❑ 41 Duane Starks	.10	.30
❑ 42 Eddie George	.30	.75
❑ 43 Joe Jurevicius	.20	.50
❑ 44 Kimble Anders	.20	.50
❑ 45 Kordell Stewart	.20	.50
❑ 46 Leroy Hoard	.10	.30
❑ 47 Rod Smith	.20	.50
❑ 48 Terrell Owens	.30	.75
❑ 49 Ty Detmer	.20	.50
❑ 50 Charles Woodson	.30	.75
❑ 51 Andre Rison	.20	.50
❑ 52 Chris Slade	.10	.30
❑ 53 Frank Sanders	.20	.50
❑ 54 Michael Irvin	.20	.50
❑ 55 Jerome Pathon	.10	.30
❑ 56 Desmond Howard	.20	.50
❑ 57 Billy Davis	.10	.30
❑ 58 Anthony Simmons	.10	.30
❑ 59 James Jett	.20	.50
❑ 60 Jake Plummer	.20	.50
❑ 61 John Avery	.10	.30
❑ 62 Marvin Harrison	.30	.75
❑ 63 Merton Hanks	.10	.00
❑ 64 Ricky Proehl	.10	.30

Card	Low	High
❑ 65 Steve Beuerlein	.10	.30
❑ 66 Willie McGinest	.10	.30
❑ 67 Bryce Paup	.10	.30
❑ 68 Brett Favre	1.00	2.50
❑ 69 Brian Griese	.30	.75
❑ 70 Curtis Martin	.30	.75
❑ 71 Drew Bledsoe	.40	1.00
❑ 72 Jim Harbaugh	.20	.50
❑ 73 Joey Galloway	.20	.50
❑ 74 Natrone Means	.20	.50
❑ 75 O.J. McDuffie	.20	.50
❑ 76 Tiki Barber	.30	.75
❑ 77 Wesley Walls	.20	.50
❑ 78 Will Blackwell	.10	.30
❑ 79 Bert Emanuel	.20	.50
❑ 80 J.J. Stokes	.20	.50
❑ 81 Steve McNair	.30	.75
❑ 82 Adrian Murrell	.20	.50
❑ 83 Dexter Coakley	.10	.30
❑ 84 Jeff George	.20	.50
❑ 85 Marshall Faulk	.40	1.00
❑ 86 Tim Biakabutuka	.20	.50
❑ 87 Troy Drayton	.10	.30
❑ 88 Ty Law	.20	.50
❑ 89 Brian Simmons	.10	.30
❑ 90 Eric Allen	.10	.30
❑ 91 Jon Kitna	.30	.75
❑ 92 Junior Seau	.30	.75
❑ 93 Kevin Turner	.10	.30
❑ 94 Larry Centers	.10	.30
❑ 95 Robert Edwards	.10	.30
❑ 96 Rocket Ismail	.20	.50
❑ 97 Sam Madison	.10	.30
❑ 98 Stephen Alexander	.10	.30
❑ 99 Trent Dilfer	.20	.50
❑ 100 Vonnie Holliday	.10	.30
❑ 101 Charlie Garner	.20	.50
❑ 102 Deion Sanders	.30	.75
❑ 103 Jamal Anderson	.30	.75
❑ 104 Mike Vanderjagt	.10	.30
❑ 105 Aeneas Williams	.10	.30
❑ 106 Daryl Johnston	.20	.50
❑ 107 Hugh Douglas	.10	.30
❑ 108 Torrance Small	.10	.30
❑ 109 Amani Toomer	.10	.30
❑ 110 Amp Lee	.10	.30
❑ 111 Germane Crowell	.10	.30
❑ 112 Marco Battaglia	.10	.30
❑ 113 Michael Westbrook	.20	.50
❑ 114 Randy Moss	.75	2.00
❑ 115 Ricky Watters	.20	.50
❑ 116 Rob Johnson	.20	.50
❑ 117 Tony Gonzalez	.30	.75
❑ 118 Charles Way	.10	.30
❑ 119 Chris Penn	.10	.30
❑ 120 Eddie Kennison	.20	.50
❑ 121 Elvis Grbac	.20	.50
❑ 122 Eric Moulds	.30	.75
❑ 123 Terry Fair	.10	.30
❑ 124 Tony Banks	.20	.50
❑ 125 Chris Chandler	.20	.50
❑ 126 Emmitt Smith	.60	1.50
❑ 127 Herman Moore	.20	.50
❑ 128 Irv Smith	.10	.30
❑ 129 Kyle Brady	.10	.30
❑ 130 Lamont Warren	.10	.30
❑ 131 Troy Davis	.10	.30
❑ 132 Andre Reed	.20	.50
❑ 133 Justin Armour	.10	.30
❑ 134 James Hasty	.10	.30
❑ 135 Johnnie Morton	.20	.50
❑ 136 Reggie Barlow	.10	.30
❑ 137 Robert Holcombe	.10	.30
❑ 138 Sean Dawkins	.10	.30
❑ 139 Steve Atwater	.10	.30
❑ 140 Tim Dwight	.30	.75
❑ 141 Wayne Chrebet	.20	.50
❑ 142 Alonzo Mayes	.10	.30
❑ 143 Mark Brunell	.30	.75
❑ 144 Antowain Smith	.30	.75
❑ 145 Byron Bam Morris	.10	.30
❑ 146 Isaac Bruce	.30	.75
❑ 147 Bryan Cox	.10	.30
❑ 148 Bryant Westbrook	.10	.30
❑ 149 Duce Staley	.30	.75
❑ 150 Barry Sanders	1.00	2.50
❑ 151 La'Roi Glover RC	.30	.75
❑ 152 Ray Crockett	.10	.30

Card	Low	High
❑ 153 Tony Brackens	.10	.30
❑ 154 Roy Barker	.10	.30
❑ 155 Kerry Collins	.20	.50
❑ 156 Andre Wadsworth	.10	.30
❑ 157 Cameron Cleeland	.10	.30
❑ 158 Koy Detmer	.10	.30
❑ 159 Marcus Pollard	.10	.30
❑ 160 Patrick Jeffers RC	2.50	6.00
❑ 161 Aaron Glenn	.10	.30
❑ 162 Andre Hastings	.10	.30
❑ 163 Bruce Smith	.20	.50
❑ 164 David Palmer	.10	.30
❑ 165 Erik Kramer	.20	.50
❑ 166 Orlando Pace	.10	.30
❑ 167 Robert Brooks	.20	.50
❑ 168 Shawn Springs	.10	.30
❑ 169 Terance Mathis	.20	.50
❑ 170 Chris Calloway	.10	.30
❑ 171 Gilbert Brown	.10	.30
❑ 172 Charlie Jones	.10	.30
❑ 173 Curtis Enis	.10	.30
❑ 174 Eugene Robinson	.10	.30
❑ 175 Garrison Hearst	.20	.50
❑ 176 Jason Elam	.10	.30
❑ 177 John Randle	.20	.50
❑ 178 Keith Poole	.10	.30
❑ 179 Kevin Hardy	.10	.30
❑ 180 Keyshawn Johnson	.30	.75
❑ 181 O.J. Santiago	.10	.30
❑ 182 Jacquez Green	.10	.30
❑ 183 Bobby Engram	.20	.50
❑ 184 Damon Jones	.10	.30
❑ 185 Freddie Jones	.10	.30
❑ 186 Jake Reed	.20	.50
❑ 187 Jerry Rice	.60	1.50
❑ 188 Joey Kent	.10	.30
❑ 189 Lamar Smith	.20	.50
❑ 190 John Elway	1.00	2.50
❑ 191 Leon Johnson	.10	.30
❑ 192 Mark Chmura	.20	.50
❑ 193 Peter Boulware	.10	.30
❑ 194 Zach Thomas	.30	.75
❑ 195 Marc Edwards	.10	.30
❑ 196 Mike Alstott	.30	.75
❑ 197 Yancey Thigpen	.10	.30
❑ 198 Oronde Gadsden	.20	.50
❑ 199 Rae Carruth	.10	.30
❑ 200 Troy Aikman	.60	1.50
❑ 201 Shawn Jefferson	.10	.30
❑ 202 Rob Moore	.20	.50
❑ 203 Rickey Dudley	.10	.30
❑ 204 Jason Taylor	.10	.30
❑ 205 Curtis Conway	.20	.50
❑ 206 Darrien Gordon	.10	.30
❑ 207 Eric Green	.10	.30
❑ 208 Jessie Armstead	.10	.30
❑ 209 Keenan McCardell	.20	.50
❑ 210 Robert Smith	.30	.75
❑ 211 Mo Lewis	.10	.30
❑ 212 Ryan Leaf	.30	.75
❑ 213 Steve Young	.40	1.00
❑ 214 Tyrone Davis	.10	.30
❑ 215 Chad Brown	.10	.30
❑ 216 Ike Hilliard	.10	.30
❑ 217 Jimmy Hitchcock	.10	.30
❑ 218 Kevin Dyson	.20	.50
❑ 219 Levon Kirkland	.10	.30
❑ 220 Neil O'Donnell	.20	.50
❑ 221 Ray Lewis	.30	.75
❑ 222 Shannon Sharpe	.20	.50
❑ 223 Skip Hicks	.10	.30
❑ 224 Brad Johnson	.30	.75
❑ 225 Charlie Batch	.30	.75
❑ 226 Corey Dillon	.30	.75
❑ 227 Dale Carter	.10	.30
❑ 228 John Mobley	.10	.30
❑ 229 Hines Ward	.30	.75
❑ 230 Leslie Shepherd	.10	.30
❑ 231 Michael Strahan	.20	.50
❑ 232 R.W. McQuarters	.10	.30
❑ 233 Mike Pritchard	.10	.30
❑ 234 Antonio Freeman	.30	.75
❑ 235 Ben Coates	.20	.50
❑ 236 Michael Bates	.10	.30
❑ 237 Ed McCaffrey	.20	.50
❑ 238 Gary Brown	.10	.30
❑ 239 Mark Bruener	.10	.30
❑ 240 Mikhael Ricks	.10	.30

Card	Low	High
❑ 241 Muhsin Muhammad	.20	.50
❑ 242 Priest Holmes	.50	1.25
❑ 243 Stephen Davis	.30	.75
❑ 244 Vinny Testaverde	.20	.50
❑ 245 Warrick Dunn	.30	.75
❑ 246 Derrick Mayes	.10	.30
❑ 247 Fred Taylor	.30	.75
❑ 248 Drew Bledsoe CL	.20	.50
❑ 249 Eddie George CL	.20	.50
❑ 250 Steve Young CL	.20	.50
❑ 251 Jamal Anderson BB	.25	.60
❑ 252 D.Gordon/Romanowski BB	.10	.30
❑ 253 Shannon Sharpe BB	.10	.30
❑ 254 Terrell Davis BB	.40	1.00
❑ 255 Rod Smith BB	.10	.30
❑ 256 Rod Smith BB	.10	.30
❑ 257 John Elway BB	2.00	5.00
❑ 258 Tim Dwight BB	.25	.60
❑ 259 Elway/McC/Griff/Dav.BB	1.25	3.00
❑ 260 John Elway BB	2.00	5.00
❑ 261 Ricky Williams RC	2.50	6.00
❑ 262 Tim Couch RC	1.25	3.00
❑ 263 Chris Claiborne RC	.60	1.50
❑ 264 Champ Bailey RC	2.00	5.00
❑ 265 Torry Holt RC	3.00	8.00
❑ 266 Donovan McNabb RC	6.00	15.00
❑ 267 David Boston RC	1.25	3.00
❑ 268 Chris McAlister RC	1.00	2.50
❑ 269 Brock Huard RC	1.25	3.00
❑ 270 Daunte Culpepper RC	5.00	12.00
❑ 271 Matt Stinchcomb RC	.60	1.50
❑ 272 Edgerrin James RC	5.00	12.00
❑ 273 Jevon Kearse RC	2.50	6.00
❑ 274 Ebenezer Ekuban RC	1.00	2.50
❑ 275 Kris Farris RC	.60	1.50
❑ 276 Chris Terry RC	.60	1.50
❑ 277 Jerame Tuman RC	1.25	3.00
❑ 278 Akili Smith RC	1.00	2.50
❑ 279 Aaron Gibson RC	.60	1.50
❑ 280 Rahim Abdullah RC	1.00	2.50
❑ 281 Peerless Price RC	1.25	3.00
❑ 282 Antoine Winfield RC	1.00	2.50
❑ 283 Antuan Edwards RC	.60	1.50
❑ 284 Rob Konrad RC	1.25	3.00
❑ 285 Troy Edwards RC	1.00	2.50
❑ 286 John Thornton RC	.60	1.50
❑ 287 James Johnson RC	1.00	2.50
❑ 288 Gary Stills RC	.60	1.50
❑ 289 Mike Peterson RC	1.00	2.50
❑ 290 Kevin Faulk RC	1.25	3.00
❑ 291 Jared DeVries RC	.60	1.50
❑ 292 Martin Gramatica RC	.60	1.50
❑ 293 Montae Reagor RC	.60	1.50
❑ 294 Andy Katzenmoyer RC	1.00	2.50
❑ 295 Sedrick Irvin RC	.60	1.50
❑ 296 D'Wayne Bates RC	1.00	2.50
❑ 297 Amos Zereoue RC	1.25	3.00
❑ 298 Dre' Bly RC	1.25	3.00
❑ 299 Kevin Johnson RC	1.25	3.00
❑ 300 Cade McNown RC	1.00	2.50
❑ P247 Fred Taylor Promo	.75	2.00

2000 Ultra

Card	Low	High
❑ COMPLETE SET (249)	40.00	100.00
❑ COMP.SET w/o SP's (220)	7.50	20.00
❑ 1 Kurt Warner	.60	1.50
❑ 2 Derrick Alexander	.20	.50
❑ 3 Aaron Craver	.10	.30
❑ 4 Kevin Faulk	.20	.50
❑ 5 Marcus Robinson	.30	.75
❑ 6 Tony Banks	.20	.50
❑ 7 Jon Ritchie	.10	.30
❑ 8 Torry Holt	.30	.75
❑ 9 Joe Horn	.20	.50

Card	Low	High
❑ 10 Eddie George	.30	.75
❑ 11 Michael Westbrook	.20	.50
❑ 12 Gus Frerotte	.10	.30
❑ 13 Tim Brown	.30	.75
❑ 14 Tamarick Vanover	.10	.30
❑ 15 David Sloan	.10	.30
❑ 16 Darnay Scott	.10	.30
❑ 17 Junior Seau	.30	.75
❑ 18 Warren Sapp	.20	.50
❑ 19 Priest Holmes	.40	1.00
❑ 20 Jerry Rice	.60	1.50
❑ 21 Cade McNown	.10	.30
❑ 22 Johnnie Morton	.20	.50
❑ 23 Vinny Testaverde	.20	.50
❑ 24 James Jett	.10	.30
❑ 25 Tony Gonzalez	.20	.50
❑ 26 Charlie Batch	.30	.75
❑ 27 Tony Simmons	.10	.30
❑ 28 James Stewart	.20	.50
❑ 29 Corey Dillon	.30	.75
❑ 30 Ricky Williams	.30	.75
❑ 31 Ryan Leaf	.20	.50
❑ 32 Terry Allen	.20	.50
❑ 33 Freddie Jones	.10	.30
❑ 34 Terry Kirby	.10	.30
❑ 35 Charles Johnson	.20	.50
❑ 36 William Henderson	.20	.50
❑ 37 Stephen Alexander	.10	.30
❑ 38 Moe Williams	.20	.50
❑ 39 David Boston	.30	.75
❑ 40 Emmitt Smith	.60	1.50
❑ 41 Ken Oxendine	.10	.30
❑ 42 Byron Hanspard	.10	.30
❑ 43 Dwight Stone	.10	.30
❑ 44 Jim Harbaugh	.20	.50
❑ 45 Curtis Enis	.10	.30
❑ 46 Peerless Price	.20	.50
❑ 47 Terance Mathis	.20	.50
❑ 48 Mike Alstott	.30	.75
❑ 49 Rod Smith	.20	.50
❑ 50 Marshall Faulk	.40	1.00
❑ 51 Derrick Mayes	.20	.50
❑ 52 Keenan McCardell	.20	.50
❑ 53 Curtis Martin	.30	.75
❑ 54 Bobby Engram	.10	.30
❑ 55 Carl Pickens	.20	.50
❑ 56 Robert Smith	.30	.75
❑ 57 Ike Hilliard	.20	.50
❑ 58 Reidel Anthony	.20	.50
❑ 59 Jeff Graham	.10	.30
❑ 60 Mark Brunell	.30	.75
❑ 61 Joe Montgomery	.10	.30
❑ 62 Ed McCaffrey	.30	.75
❑ 63 Kenny Bynum	.10	.30
❑ 64 Curtis Conway	.20	.50
❑ 65 Trent Dilfer	.20	.50
❑ 66 Jake Reed	.20	.50
❑ 67 Jake Plummer	.20	.50
❑ 68 Tony Martin	.20	.50
❑ 69 Yatil Green	.10	.30
❑ 70 Keyshawn Johnson	.30	.75
❑ 71 Leroy Hoard	.10	.30
❑ 72 Skip Hicks	.10	.30
❑ 73 Marvin Harrison	.30	.75
❑ 74 Steve Beuerlein	.20	.50
❑ 75 Will Blackwell	.10	.30
❑ 76 Derek Loville	.10	.30
❑ 77 Warrick Dunn	.30	.75
❑ 78 Amos Zereoue	.30	.75
❑ 79 Ray Lucas	.20	.50
❑ 80 Randy Moss	.60	1.50
❑ 81 Wesley Walls	.10	.30
❑ 82 Jimmy Smith	.20	.50
❑ 83 Kordell Stewart	.20	.50
❑ 84 Brian Griese	.30	.75
❑ 85 Martin Gramatica	.10	.30
❑ 86 Chris Chandler	.20	.50
❑ 87 Reggie Barlow	.10	.30
❑ 88 Jeff George	.20	.50
❑ 89 Tavian Banks	.10	.30
❑ 90 Mushin Muhammad	.20	.50
❑ 91 Steve McNair	.30	.75
❑ 92 Hines Ward	.30	.75
❑ 93 Brian Mitchell	.10	.30
❑ 94 Daunte Culpepper	.40	1.00
❑ 95 Tim Dwight	.30	.75
❑ 96 Terrence Wilkins	.10	.30
❑ 97 Fred Lane	.10	.30
❑ 98 Brett Favre	1.00	2.50
❑ 99 Richie Anderson	.20	.50
❑ 100 Jamal Anderson	.30	.75
❑ 101 Doug Flutie	.30	.75
❑ 102 Charles Woodson	.20	.50
❑ 103 Jacquez Green	.10	.30
❑ 104 Olandis Gary	.30	.75
❑ 105 Steve Young	.40	1.00
❑ 106 Wayne Chrebet	.20	.50
❑ 107 Karim Abdul-Jabbar	.20	.50
❑ 108 Andre Rison	.20	.50
❑ 109 Eddie Kennison	.10	.30
❑ 110 Jevon Kearse	.30	.75
❑ 111 Tony Richardson RC	.20	.50
❑ 112 Jake Delhomme RC	1.25	3.00
❑ 113 Errict Rhett	.20	.50
❑ 114 Akili Smith	.10	.30
❑ 115 Tyrone Wheatley	.20	.50
❑ 116 Corey Bradford	.20	.50
❑ 117 J.J. Stokes	.20	.50
❑ 118 Simeon Rice	.20	.50
❑ 119 Brad Johnson	.30	.75
❑ 120 Edgerrin James	.50	1.25
❑ 121 Amani Toomer	.10	.30
❑ 122 O.J. McDuffie	.20	.50
❑ 123 Az-Zahir Hakim	.20	.50
❑ 124 Troy Edwards	.10	.30
❑ 125 Tim Biakabutuka	.20	.50
❑ 126 Jason Tucker	.10	.30
❑ 127 Charles Way	.10	.30
❑ 128 Terrell Davis	.30	.75
❑ 129 Garrison Hearst	.20	.50
❑ 130 Fred Taylor	.30	.75
❑ 131 Robert Holcombe	.10	.30
❑ 132 Frank Sanders	.20	.50
❑ 133 Morten Andersen	.10	.30
❑ 134 Cris Carter	.30	.75
❑ 135 Patrick Jeffers	.30	.75
❑ 136 Antonio Freeman	.30	.75
❑ 137 Jonathan Linton	.10	.30
❑ 138 Rashaan Shehee	.10	.30
❑ 139 Luther Broughton RC	.20	.50
❑ 140 Tim Couch	.20	.50
❑ 141 Keith Poole	.10	.30
❑ 142 Champ Bailey	.20	.50
❑ 143 Yancey Thigpen	.10	.30
❑ 144 Joey Galloway	.20	.50
❑ 145 Mac Cody	.10	.30
❑ 146 Damon Huard	.30	.75
❑ 147 Dorsey Levens	.20	.50
❑ 148 Donovan McNabb	.50	1.25
❑ 149 Jamie Asher	.10	.30
❑ 150 Peyton Manning	.75	2.00
❑ 151 Leslie Shepherd	.10	.30
❑ 152 Charlie Rogers	.10	.30
❑ 153 Tony Horne	.10	.30
❑ 154 Jim Miller	.10	.30
❑ 155 Richard Huntley	.10	.30
❑ 156 Germane Crowell	.10	.30
❑ 157 Natrone Means	.10	.30
❑ 158 Justin Armour	.10	.30
❑ 159 Drew Bledsoe	.40	1.00
❑ 160 Dedric Ward	.10	.30
❑ 161 Allen Rossum	.10	.30
❑ 162 Ricky Watters	.20	.50
❑ 163 Kerry Collins	.20	.50
❑ 164 James Johnson	.10	.30
❑ 165 Elvis Grbac	.20	.50
❑ 166 Larry Centers	.10	.30
❑ 167 Rob Moore	.20	.50
❑ 168 Jay Riemersma	.10	.30
❑ 169 Bill Schroeder	.20	.50
❑ 170 Deion Sanders	.30	.75
❑ 171 Jerome Bettis	.30	.75
❑ 172 Dan Marino	1.00	2.50
❑ 173 Terrell Owens	.30	.75
❑ 174 Kevin Carter	.10	.30
❑ 175 Lamar Smith	.20	.50
❑ 176 Ken Dilger	.10	.30
❑ 177 Napoleon Kaufman	.20	.50
❑ 178 Kevin Williams	.10	.30
❑ 179 Tremain Mack	.10	.30
❑ 180 Troy Aikman	.60	1.50
❑ 181 Glyn Milburn	.10	.30
❑ 182 Pete Mitchell	.10	.30
❑ 183 Cameron Cleeland	.10	.30
❑ 184 Qadry Ismail	.20	.50
❑ 185 Michael Pittman	.10	.30
❑ 186 Kevin Dyson	.20	.50
❑ 187 Matt Hasselbeck	.20	.50
❑ 188 Kevin Johnson	.30	.75
❑ 189 Rich Gannon	.30	.75
❑ 190 Stephen Davis	.30	.75
❑ 191 Frank Wycheck	.10	.30
❑ 192 Eric Moulds	.30	.75
❑ 193 Jon Kitna	.30	.75
❑ 194 Mario Bates	.10	.30
❑ 195 Na Brown	.10	.30
❑ 196 Jeff Blake	.20	.50
❑ 197 Charles Evans	.10	.30
❑ 198 Oronde Gadsden	.20	.50
❑ 199 Donnell Bennett	.10	.30
❑ 200 Isaac Bruce	.30	.75
❑ 201 Olindo Mare	.10	.30
❑ 202 Darnell McDonald	.10	.30
❑ 203 Charlie Garner	.20	.50
❑ 204 Shawn Jefferson	.10	.30
❑ 205 Adrian Murrell	.20	.50
❑ 206 Peter Boulware	.10	.30
❑ 207 LeShon Johnson	.10	.30
❑ 208 Herman Moore	.20	.50
❑ 209 Duce Staley	.30	.75
❑ 210 Sean Dawkins	.10	.30
❑ 211 Antowain Smith	.20	.50
❑ 212 Albert Connell	.10	.30
❑ 213 Jeff Garcia	.30	.75
❑ 214 Kimble Anders	.10	.30
❑ 215 Shaun King	.10	.30
❑ 216 Rocket Ismail	.20	.50
❑ 217 Andrew Glover	.10	.30
❑ 218 Rickey Dudley	.10	.30
❑ 219 Michael Basnight	.10	.30
❑ 220 Terry Glenn	.20	.50
❑ 221 Peter Warrick RC	1.25	3.00
❑ 222 Ron Dayne RC	1.25	3.00
❑ 223 Thomas Jones RC	2.00	5.00
❑ 224 Joe Hamilton RC	1.00	2.50
❑ 225 Tim Rattay RC	1.25	3.00
❑ 226 Chad Pennington RC	3.00	8.00
❑ 227 Dennis Northcutt RC	1.25	3.00
❑ 228 Troy Walters RC	1.25	3.00
❑ 229 Travis Prentice RC	1.00	2.50
❑ 230 Shaun Alexander RC	4.00	10.00
❑ 231 J.R. Redmond RC	1.00	2.50
❑ 232 Chris Redman RC	1.00	2.50
❑ 233 Tee Martin RC	1.25	3.00
❑ 234 Tom Brady RC	15.00	40.00
❑ 235 Travis Taylor RC	1.25	3.00
❑ 236 R.Jay Soward RC	1.00	2.50
❑ 237 Jamal Lewis RC	3.00	8.00
❑ 238 Giovanni Carmazzi RC	.75	2.00
❑ 239 Dez White RC	1.25	3.00
❑ 240 LaVar Arrington RC SP	20.00	50.00
❑ 241 Laveranues Coles RC	1.50	4.00
❑ 242 Sherrod Gideon RC	.75	2.00
❑ 243 Trung Canidate RC	1.00	2.50
❑ 244 Michael Wiley RC	1.00	2.50
❑ 245 Anthony Lucas RC	.75	2.00
❑ 246 Darrell Jackson RC	2.50	6.00
❑ 247 Plaxico Burress RC	2.50	6.00
❑ 248 Reuben Droughns RC	1.50	4.00
❑ 249 Marc Bulger RC	2.50	6.00
❑ 250 Danny Farmer RC	1.00	2.50

2001 Ultra

Card	Low	High
❑ COMP.SET w/o SP's (250)	10.00	25.00
❑ 1 Daunte Culpepper	.30	.75
❑ 2 Kurt Warner	.60	1.50
❑ 3 Emmitt Smith	.60	1.50
❑ 4 Eddie George	.30	.75
❑ 5 Ron Dayne	.30	.75
❑ 6 Zach Thomas	.30	.75

❑ 7 Itula Mili	.10	.30
❑ 8 Jake Reed	.20	.50
❑ 9 James Stewart	.20	.50
❑ 10 Terrence Wilkins	.10	.30
❑ 11 Jeff Blake	.20	.50
❑ 12 Kerry Collins	.20	.50
❑ 13 Christian Fauria	.10	.30
❑ 14 Jackie Harris	.10	.30
❑ 15 Kevin Johnson	.20	.50
❑ 16 Tony Martin	.10	.30
❑ 17 Joey Galloway	.20	.50
❑ 18 Junior Seau	.30	.75
❑ 19 Jason Tucker	.10	.30
❑ 20 Steve Beuerlein	.10	.30
❑ 21 Mike Cloud	.10	.30
❑ 22 Kevin Faulk	.20	.50
❑ 23 Az-Zahir Hakim	.10	.30
❑ 24 Charles Johnson	.10	.30
❑ 25 Curtis Martin	.30	.75
❑ 26 Eric Moulds	.20	.50
❑ 27 Bill Schroeder	.20	.50
❑ 28 Amani Toomer	.10	.30
❑ 29 Obafemi Ayanbadejo	.10	.30
❑ 30 Aaron Shea	.10	.30
❑ 31 Ken Dilger	.10	.30
❑ 32 Terry Glenn	.10	.30
❑ 33 Rocket Ismail	.20	.50
❑ 34 Dorsey Levens	.10	.30
❑ 35 Brian Mitchell	.10	.30
❑ 36 Tony Richardson	.10	.30
❑ 37 Sam Madison	.10	.30
❑ 38 Darren Sharper	.10	.30
❑ 39 Derrick Alexander	.20	.50
❑ 40 Aaron Brooks	.30	.75
❑ 41 Casey Crawford	.10	.30
❑ 42 Terrell Fletcher	.10	.30
❑ 43 William Henderson	.10	.30
❑ 44 Thomas Jones	.20	.50
❑ 45 Keenan McCardell	.10	.30
❑ 46 Chad Pennington	.50	1.25
❑ 47 Akili Smith	.10	.30
❑ 48 Hines Ward	.30	.75
❑ 49 Champ Bailey	.20	.50
❑ 50 Cris Carter	.30	.75
❑ 51 Corey Dillon	.30	.75
❑ 52 Tony Gonzalez	.20	.50
❑ 53 Darrell Jackson	.30	.75
❑ 54 Chad Lewis	.10	.30
❑ 55 Dave Moore	.10	.30
❑ 56 Jay Riemersma	.10	.30
❑ 57 J.J. Stokes	.20	.50
❑ 58 Frank Wycheck	.10	.30
❑ 59 Tiki Barber	.30	.75
❑ 60 Tony Carter	.10	.30
❑ 61 Rickey Dudley	.10	.30
❑ 62 John Lynch	.20	.50
❑ 63 Larry Foster	.10	.30
❑ 64 Willie Jackson	.10	.30
❑ 65 Jamal Lewis	.50	1.25
❑ 66 Herman Moore	.20	.50
❑ 67 Andre Rison	.20	.50
❑ 68 Michael Strahan	.20	.50
❑ 69 Charlie Batch	.30	.75
❑ 70 Larry Centers	.10	.30
❑ 71 Ron Dugans	.10	.30
❑ 72 Jeff Graham	.10	.30
❑ 73 Edgerrin James	.40	1.00
❑ 74 Jermaine Lewis	.10	.30
❑ 75 Charles Woodson	.20	.50
❑ 76 Chris Redman	.10	.30
❑ 77 Jon Ritchie	.10	.30
❑ 78 Fred Taylor	.30	.75
❑ 79 Jamal Anderson	.30	.75
❑ 80 Isaac Bruce	.30	.75
❑ 81 Terrell Davis	.30	.75
❑ 82 Rich Gannon	.30	.75
❑ 83 Joe Horn	.20	.50
❑ 84 Eddie Kennison	.20	.50
❑ 85 Steve McNair	.30	.75
❑ 86 Travis Prentice	.10	.30
❑ 87 Rod Smith	.20	.50
❑ 88 Ricky Watters	.20	.50
❑ 89 Michael Bates	.10	.30
❑ 90 Byron Chamberlain	.10	.30
❑ 91 Warrick Dunn	.30	.75
❑ 92 Elvis Grbac	.20	.50
❑ 93 Patrick Jeffers	.20	.50
❑ 94 Ray Lewis	.30	.75
❑ 95 Sammy Morris	.10	.30
❑ 96 Marcus Robinson	.30	.75
❑ 97 Travis Taylor	.20	.50
❑ 98 Fred Beasley	.10	.30
❑ 99 Chris Chandler	.20	.50
❑ 100 Tim Dwight	.30	.75
❑ 101 Ahman Green	.30	.75
❑ 102 Shawn Jefferson	.10	.30
❑ 103 Jeremy McDaniel	.10	.30
❑ 104 Sylvester Morris	.10	.30
❑ 105 John Randle	.10	.30
❑ 106 Vinny Testaverde	.20	.50
❑ 107 Anthony Becht	.10	.30
❑ 108 Wayne Chrebet	.20	.50
❑ 109 Stephen Boyd	.10	.30
❑ 110 Jacquez Green	.10	.30
❑ 111 MarTay Jenkins	.10	.30
❑ 112 Jason Gildon	.10	.30
❑ 113 Chad Morton	.10	.30
❑ 114 Deion Sanders	.30	.75
❑ 115 Yancey Thigpen	.10	.30
❑ 116 Marty Booker	.10	.30
❑ 117 Curtis Conway	.20	.50
❑ 118 Jermaine Fazande	.10	.30
❑ 119 Matthew Hatchette	.10	.30
❑ 120 Pat Johnson	.10	.30
❑ 121 Terance Mathis	.20	.50
❑ 122 Terrell Owens	.30	.75
❑ 123 Corey Simon	.20	.50
❑ 124 Darrick Vaughn	.10	.30
❑ 125 Drew Bledsoe	.40	1.00
❑ 126 Albert Connell	.10	.30
❑ 127 Brett Favre	1.00	2.50
❑ 128 Marvin Harrison	.30	.75
❑ 129 Keyshawn Johnson	.30	.75
❑ 130 Derrick Mason	.20	.50
❑ 131 Dennis Northcutt	.20	.50
❑ 132 Shannon Sharpe	.20	.50
❑ 133 Brian Urlacher	.50	1.25
❑ 134 Mike Anderson	.30	.75
❑ 135 Mark Bruener	.10	.30
❑ 136 Sean Dawkins	.10	.30
❑ 137 Jeff Garcia	.30	.75
❑ 138 Tony Horne	.10	.30
❑ 139 Shaun King	.10	.30
❑ 140 Cade McNown	.10	.30
❑ 141 Peerless Price	.20	.50
❑ 142 R.Jay Soward	.10	.30
❑ 143 Tyrone Wheatley	.20	.50
❑ 144 Richie Anderson	.10	.30
❑ 145 Mark Brunell	.30	.75
❑ 146 JaJuan Dawson	.10	.30
❑ 147 Charlie Garner	.20	.50
❑ 148 Desmond Howard	.10	.30
❑ 149 Jon Kitna	.20	.50
❑ 150 Duane Starks	.10	.30
❑ 151 J.R. Redmond	.10	.30
❑ 152 Duce Staley	.30	.75
❑ 153 Dez White	.10	.30
❑ 154 David Boston	.30	.75
❑ 155 Tim Couch	.20	.50
❑ 156 Jay Fiedler	.30	.75
❑ 157 Jessie Armstead	.10	.30
❑ 158 Rob Johnson	.20	.50
❑ 159 Brad Johnson	.30	.75
❑ 160 Derrick Mayes	.10	.30
❑ 161 Jerome Pathon	.20	.50
❑ 162 David Sloan	.10	.30
❑ 163 Wesley Walls	.10	.30
❑ 164 Shaun Alexander	.40	1.00
❑ 165 Derrick Brooks	.30	.75
❑ 166 Germane Crowell	.10	.30
❑ 167 Doug Flutie	.30	.75
❑ 168 Ike Hilliard	.20	.50
❑ 169 Hugh Douglas	.10	.30
❑ 170 Wane McGarity	.10	.30
❑ 171 Michael Pittman	.10	.30
❑ 172 Shawn Bryson	.10	.30
❑ 173 Richard Huntley	.10	.30
❑ 174 Darnell Autry	.10	.30
❑ 175 Plaxico Burress	.30	.75
❑ 176 Trent Dilfer	.20	.50
❑ 177 Jeff George	.20	.50
❑ 178 Qadry Ismail	.20	.50
❑ 179 Ryan Leaf	.20	.50
❑ 180 Jim Miller	.10	.30
❑ 181 Jerry Rice	.60	1.50
❑ 182 Kordell Stewart	.20	.50
❑ 183 Ricky Williams	.30	.75
❑ 184 James Allen	.20	.50
❑ 185 Courtney Brown	.20	.50
❑ 186 Reidel Anthony	.10	.30
❑ 187 Bubba Franks	.20	.50
❑ 188 Priest Holmes	.40	1.00
❑ 189 Napoleon Kaufman	.10	.30
❑ 190 Trevor Pryce	.10	.30
❑ 191 Jake Plummer	.20	.50
❑ 192 Jimmy Smith	.20	.50
❑ 193 Michael Wiley	.10	.30
❑ 194 Brock Huard	.10	.30
❑ 195 Troy Brown	.20	.50
❑ 196 Stephen Davis	.30	.75
❑ 197 Oronde Gadsden	.20	.50
❑ 198 Brad Hoover	.10	.30
❑ 199 La'Roi Glover	.10	.30
❑ 200 Donovan McNabb	.40	1.00
❑ 201 Jerry Porter	.20	.50
❑ 202 Robert Smith	.20	.50
❑ 203 Justin Watson	.10	.30
❑ 204 Tim Biakabutuka	.20	.50
❑ 205 Laveranues Coles	.30	.75
❑ 206 Marshall Faulk	.40	1.00
❑ 207 Jim Harbaugh	.20	.50
❑ 208 Doug Johnson	.10	.30
❑ 209 Tee Martin	.20	.50
❑ 210 Muhsin Muhammad	.20	.50
❑ 211 Darnay Scott	.10	.30
❑ 212 Jeremiah Trotter	.20	.50
❑ 213 Troy Aikman	.50	1.25
❑ 214 Kyle Brady	.10	.30
❑ 215 Sam Cowart	.10	.30
❑ 216 Darren Howard	.10	.30
❑ 217 Donald Hayes	.10	.30
❑ 218 Freddie Jones	.10	.30
❑ 219 Ed McCaffrey	.30	.75
❑ 220 David Patten	.10	.30
❑ 221 Brian Griese	.30	.75
❑ 222 Dedric Ward	.10	.30
❑ 223 Jerome Bettis	.30	.75
❑ 224 Greg Clark	.10	.30
❑ 225 Bobby Engram	.10	.30
❑ 226 Matt Hasselbeck	.20	.50
❑ 227 James Jett	.10	.30
❑ 228 Peyton Manning	.75	2.00
❑ 229 Randy Moss	.60	1.50
❑ 230 Warren Sapp	.20	.50
❑ 231 James Thrash	.20	.50
❑ 232 Mike Alstott	.30	.75
❑ 233 Tim Brown	.30	.75
❑ 234 Randall Cunningham	.30	.75
❑ 235 Antonio Freeman	.30	.75
❑ 236 Torry Holt	.30	.75
❑ 237 Jevon Kearse	.20	.50
❑ 238 James McKnight	.20	.50
❑ 239 Marcus Pollard	.10	.30
❑ 240 Lamar Smith	.20	.50
❑ 241 Peter Warrick	.30	.75
❑ 242 Donnell Bennett	.10	.30
❑ 243 Joe Johnson	.10	.30
❑ 244 Troy Edwards	.10	.30
❑ 245 Trent Green	.30	.75
❑ 246 Jason Taylor	.10	.30
❑ 247 Aeneas Williams	.10	.30
❑ 248 Johnnie Morton	.20	.50
❑ 249 Frank Sanders	.10	.30
❑ 250 Jason Sehorn	.10	.30
❑ 251 Chris Weinke RC	2.50	6.00
❑ 252 Bobby Newcombe RC	1.50	4.00
❑ 253 LaDainian Tomlinson RC	20.00	40.00
❑ 254 Chad Johnson RC	6.00	15.00
❑ 255 Derrick Gibson RC	1.50	4.00
❑ 256 Sage Rosenfels RC	2.50	6.00
❑ 257 LaMont Jordan RC	5.00	12.00
❑ 258 Mike McMahon RC	2.50	6.00
❑ 259 Vinny Sutherland RC	1.50	4.00
❑ 260 Drew Brees RC	10.00	20.00
❑ 261 Deuce McAllister RC	4.00	10.00
❑ 262 Kevan Barlow RC	2.50	6.00
❑ 263 Jamar Fletcher RC	1.50	4.00
❑ 264 Gerard Warren RC	2.50	6.00
❑ 265 Todd Heap RC	2.50	6.00
❑ 266 Travis Henry RC	2.50	6.00
❑ 267 Quincy Morgan RC	2.50	6.00
❑ 268 Anthony Thomas RC	2.50	6.00
❑ 269 Andre Carter RC	2.50	6.00
❑ 270 Freddie Mitchell RC	2.50	6.00

Card		
❑ 271 Richard Seymour RC	2.50	6.00
❑ 272 Josh Booty RC	2.50	6.00
❑ 273 Robert Ferguson RC	2.50	6.00
❑ 274 Marques Tuiasosopo RC	2.50	6.00
❑ 275 Reggie Wayne RC	5.00	12.00
❑ 276 Jabari Holloway RC	1.50	4.00
❑ 277 Rudi Johnson RC	5.00	12.00
❑ 278 Michael Bennett RC	2.50	6.00
❑ 279 Snoop Minnis RC	1.50	4.00
❑ 280 Dan Morgan RC	2.50	6.00
❑ 281 Rod Gardner RC	2.50	6.00
❑ 282 Jesse Palmer RC	2.50	6.00
❑ 283 Michael Vick RC	5.00	12.00
❑ 284 Chris Chambers RC	4.00	10.00
❑ 285 James Jackson RC	2.50	6.00
❑ 286 David Terrell RC	2.50	6.00
❑ 287 Koren Robinson RC	2.50	6.00
❑ 288 Travis Minor RC	1.50	4.00
❑ 289 Santana Moss RC	4.00	10.00
❑ 290 Josh Heupel RC	2.50	6.00
❑ 291 Jamal Reynolds RC	2.50	6.00
❑ 292 Ken-Yon Rambo RC	1.50	4.00
❑ 293 Cedrick Wilson RC	2.50	6.00
❑ 294 Alge Crumpler RC	3.00	8.00
❑ 295 Fred Smoot RC	2.50	6.00
❑ 296 Dan Alexander RC	2.50	6.00
❑ 297 Tim Hasselbeck RC	2.50	6.00
❑ 298 Will Allen RC	1.50	4.00
❑ 299 Keith Adams RC	1.50	4.00
❑ 300 Heath Evans RC	1.50	4.00
❑ U301 Quincy Carter RC	2.50	6.00
❑ U302 Derrick Blaylock RC	2.50	6.00
❑ U303 Correll Buckhalter RC	2.50	6.00
❑ U304 A.J. Feeley RC	2.50	6.00
❑ U305 Milton Wynn RC	1.50	4.00
❑ U306 Kevin Kasper RC	2.50	6.00
❑ U307 Justin McCareins RC	2.50	6.00
❑ U308 Dave Dickenson RC	1.50	4.00
❑ U309 Steve Smith RC	7.50	15.00
❑ U310 Moran Norris RC	1.00	2.50

2002 Ultra

Card		
❑ COMP.SET w/o SP's (200)	10.00	25.00
❑ 1 Donovan McNabb	.40	1.00
❑ 2 Chad Pennington	.30	.75
❑ 3 Shaun Alexander	.30	.75
❑ 4 Corey Dillon	.25	.60
❑ 5 Kurt Warner	.30	.75
❑ 6 Ed McCaffrey	.25	.60
❑ 7 Hugh Douglas	.20	.50
❑ 8 Tony Gonzalez	.25	.60
❑ 9 Travis Taylor	.20	.50
❑ 10 Tony Boselli	.25	.60
❑ 11 Chad Scott	.20	.50
❑ 12 Ernie Conwell	.20	.50
❑ 13 Brad Johnson	.25	.60
❑ 14 Donald Hayes	.20	.50
❑ 15 Emmitt Smith	.75	2.00
❑ 16 Jimmy Smith	.25	.60
❑ 17 Anthony Becht	.20	.50
❑ 18 Rod Gardner	.20	.50
❑ 19 Muhsin Muhammad	.25	.60
❑ 20 Troy Hambrick	.20	.50
❑ 21 Keenan McCardell	.25	.60
❑ 22 Laveranues Coles	.30	.75
❑ 23 Kevin Dyson	.25	.60
❑ 24 Grant Wistrom	.25	.60
❑ 25 Eric Moulds	.25	.60
❑ 26 Nate Clements	.20	.50
❑ 27 Terrell Davis	.30	.75
❑ 28 Aaron Glenn	.20	.50
❑ 29 Eric Hicks	.20	.50
❑ 30 Tiki Barber	.30	.75
❑ 31 Jake Plummer	.25	.60
❑ 32 Junior Seau	.30	.75
❑ 33 Marshall Faulk	.30	.75
❑ 34 Warrick Dunn	.25	.60
❑ 35 Bill Gramatica	.20	.50
❑ 36 Tim Couch	.20	.50
❑ 37 Kabeer Gbaja-Biamila	.25	.60
❑ 38 Kailee Wong	.20	.50
❑ 39 David Patten	.20	.50
❑ 40 Correll Buckhalter	.25	.60
❑ 41 Troy Brown	.25	.60
❑ 42 Drew Bledsoe	.30	.75
❑ 43 Travis Henry	.25	.60
❑ 44 Jim Miller	.25	.60
❑ 45 Rod Smith	.25	.60
❑ 46 Tai Streets	.20	.50
❑ 47 Snoop Minnis	.20	.50
❑ 48 Ron Dayne	.25	.60
❑ 49 Tyrone Wheatley	.25	.60
❑ 50 LaDainian Tomlinson	.50	1.25
❑ 51 Akili Smith	.25	.60
❑ 52 Warren Sapp	.25	.60
❑ 53 Adam Archuleta	.20	.50
❑ 54 Chris Fuamatu-Ma'afala	.20	.50
❑ 55 Marty Booker	.25	.60
❑ 56 Trevor Pryce	.20	.50
❑ 57 Peyton Manning	.60	1.50
❑ 58 Lamar Smith	.25	.60
❑ 59 Amani Toomer	.25	.60
❑ 60 Greg Biekert	.20	.50
❑ 61 Marcellus Wiley	.20	.50
❑ 62 Ahmed Plummer	.20	.50
❑ 63 Mike Alstott	.25	.60
❑ 64 Gary Walker	.20	.50
❑ 65 Champ Bailey	.30	.75
❑ 66 Chris Redman	.20	.50
❑ 67 David Terrell	.20	.50
❑ 68 Mike McMahon	.20	.50
❑ 69 Marvin Harrison	.30	.75
❑ 70 Jay Fiedler	.25	.60
❑ 71 JaJuan Dawson	.20	.50
❑ 72 Charlie Garner	.25	.60
❑ 73 Curtis Conway	.25	.60
❑ 74 J.J. Stokes	.20	.50
❑ 75 Ronde Barber	.25	.60
❑ 76 Alge Crumpler	.25	.60
❑ 77 Jamir Miller	.20	.50
❑ 78 Brett Favre	.75	2.00
❑ 79 Randy Moss	.30	.75
❑ 80 Joe Horn	.25	.60
❑ 81 Hines Ward	.30	.75
❑ 82 Lawyer Milloy	.25	.60
❑ 83 Aeneas Williams	.25	.60
❑ 84 Chris McAlister	.20	.50
❑ 85 Anthony Thomas	.25	.60
❑ 86 Johnnie Morton	.25	.60
❑ 87 Edgerrin James	.30	.75
❑ 88 Chris Chambers	.30	.75
❑ 89 Michael Strahan	.30	.75
❑ 90 Charles Woodson	.30	.75
❑ 91 Tim Dwight	.25	.60
❑ 92 Kevan Barlow	.20	.50
❑ 93 Donnie Abraham	.20	.50
❑ 94 Peter Boulware	.25	.60
❑ 95 Marcus Robinson	.25	.60
❑ 96 Shaun Rogers	.20	.50
❑ 97 Dominic Rhodes	.25	.60
❑ 98 Zach Thomas	.30	.75
❑ 99 Kerry Collins	.25	.60
❑ 100 Tim Brown	.30	.75
❑ 101 Garrison Hearst	.25	.60
❑ 102 Steve McNair	.30	.75
❑ 103 Fred Smoot	.25	.60
❑ 104 Isaac Bruce	.30	.75
❑ 105 Jamal Lewis	.25	.60
❑ 106 Brian Urlacher	.40	1.00
❑ 107 Takeo Spikes	.20	.50
❑ 108 Marcus Pollard	.20	.50
❑ 109 Jason Taylor	.30	.75
❑ 110 Deuce McAllister	.30	.75
❑ 111 Jerry Rice	.60	1.50
❑ 112 Terrell Owens	.30	.75
❑ 113 Eddie George	.25	.60
❑ 114 Rob Morris	.20	.50
❑ 115 Mike Brown	.25	.60
❑ 116 Joey Galloway	.25	.60
❑ 117 Fred Taylor	.30	.75
❑ 118 Rich Gannon	.25	.60
❑ 119 Chris Chandler	.25	.60
❑ 120 Koren Robinson	.20	.50
❑ 121 Dan Morgan	.20	.50
❑ 122 Rocket Ismail	.25	.60
❑ 123 Mark Brunell	.25	.60
❑ 124 John Abraham	.25	.60
❑ 125 Stephen Davis	.25	.60
❑ 126 Patrick Kerney	.20	.50
❑ 127 Anthony Henry	.20	.50
❑ 128 Scotty Anderson	.20	.50
❑ 129 Oronde Gadsden	.20	.50
❑ 130 Willie Jackson	.20	.50
❑ 131 Kendrell Bell	.20	.50
❑ 132 Ray Lewis	.30	.75
❑ 133 Quincy Carter	.20	.50
❑ 134 James Stewart	.20	.50
❑ 135 Travis Minor	.25	.60
❑ 136 Kyle Turley	.20	.50
❑ 137 Jason Gildon	.25	.60
❑ 138 David Boston	.20	.50
❑ 139 Justin Smith	.20	.50
❑ 140 Jamie Sharper	.25	.60
❑ 141 Antowain Smith	.25	.60
❑ 142 Freddie Mitchell	.20	.50
❑ 143 Frank Sanders	.20	.50
❑ 144 Kevin Johnson	.20	.50
❑ 145 Darren Sharper	.25	.60
❑ 146 Eric Johnson	.20	.50
❑ 147 Ty Law	.25	.60
❑ 148 James Thrash	.25	.60
❑ 149 Matt Hasselbeck	.30	.75
❑ 150 Peerless Price	.20	.50
❑ 151 T.J. Houshmandzadeh	.30	.75
❑ 152 Mike Anderson	.25	.60
❑ 153 Jermaine Lewis	.20	.50
❑ 154 Trent Green	.25	.60
❑ 155 Ron Dixon	.20	.50
❑ 156 Duce Staley	.25	.60
❑ 157 Drew Brees	.50	1.25
❑ 158 Torry Holt	.30	.75
❑ 159 Keyshawn Johnson	.25	.60
❑ 160 Michael Vick	.30	.75
❑ 161 Benjamin Gay	.20	.50
❑ 162 Bill Schroeder	.25	.60
❑ 163 Byron Chamberlain	.20	.50
❑ 164 Tedy Bruschi	.30	.75
❑ 165 Kordell Stewart	.25	.60
❑ 166 Deltha O'Neal	.20	.50
❑ 167 Quincy Morgan	.20	.50
❑ 168 Bubba Franks	.25	.60
❑ 169 Daunte Culpepper	.25	.60
❑ 170 Ricky Williams	.30	.75
❑ 171 Plaxico Burress	.25	.60
❑ 172 Trent Dilfer	.25	.60
❑ 173 Steve Smith	.30	.75
❑ 174 Greg Ellis	.20	.50
❑ 175 Tony Brackens	.20	.50
❑ 176 Santana Moss	.25	.60
❑ 177 Frank Wycheck	.20	.50
❑ 178 Michael Pittman	.25	.60
❑ 179 Peter Warrick	.25	.60
❑ 180 Antonio Freeman	.30	.75
❑ 181 Tom Brady	.75	2.00
❑ 182 Bobby Taylor	.25	.60
❑ 183 Jeff Garcia	.25	.60
❑ 184 Darrell Jackson	.25	.60
❑ 185 Chris Weinke	.20	.50
❑ 186 Darren Woodson	.25	.60
❑ 187 Hardy Nickerson	.20	.50
❑ 188 Wayne Chrebet	.25	.60
❑ 189 Samari Rolle	.20	.50
❑ 190 Jamal Anderson	.25	.60
❑ 191 James Jackson	.20	.50
❑ 192 Ahman Green	.30	.75
❑ 193 Michael Bennett	.25	.60
❑ 194 Aaron Brooks	.25	.60
❑ 195 Jerome Bettis	.30	.75
❑ 196 Jay Riemersma	.20	.50
❑ 197 Brian Griese	.25	.60
❑ 198 Priest Holmes	.30	.75
❑ 199 Curtis Martin	.30	.75
❑ 200 Derrick Mason	.25	.60
❑ 201 Antonio Bryant RC	2.00	5.00
❑ 202 David Carr RC	1.50	4.00
❑ 203 Eric Crouch RC	1.50	4.00
❑ 204 Freddie Milons RC	1.00	2.50
❑ 205 Najeh Davenport RC	1.50	4.00
❑ 206 Rohan Davey RC	1.50	4.00
❑ 207 T.J. Duckett RC	1.50	4.00

- ❑ 208 DeShaun Foster RC 1.50 4.00
- ❑ 209 Jabar Gaffney RC 1.50 4.00
- ❑ 210 William Green RC 1.25 3.00
- ❑ 211 Joey Harrington RC 1.50 4.00
- ❑ 212 Travis Stephens RC 1.00 2.50
- ❑ 213 Julius Peppers RC 2.50 6.00
- ❑ 214 Adrian Peterson RC 1.50 4.00
- ❑ 215 Josh Reed RC 1.25 3.00
- ❑ 216 Mike Williams RC 1.00 2.50
- ❑ 217 Javon Walker RC 1.50 4.00
- ❑ 218 Marquise Walker RC 1.00 2.50
- ❑ 219 Patrick Ramsey RC 1.50 4.00
- ❑ 220 Lamar Gordon RC 1.50 4.00
- ❑ 221 David Garrard RC 2.50 6.00
- ❑ 222 Major Applewhite RC 1.50 4.00
- ❑ 223 Andre Davis RC 1.25 3.00
- ❑ 224 Roy Williams RC 2.00 5.00
- ❑ 225 Tim Carter RC 1.25 3.00
- ❑ 226 Ron Johnson RC 1.25 3.00
- ❑ 227 Randy Fasani RC 1.25 3.00
- ❑ 228 Ashley Lelie RC 1.50 4.00
- ❑ 229 Ladell Betts RC 1.50 4.00
- ❑ 230 Antwaan Randle El RC 1.50 4.00
- ❑ 231 Jonathan Wells RC 1.50 4.00
- ❑ 232 Brian Westbrook RC 5.00 12.00
- ❑ 233 Clinton Portis RC 4.00 10.00
- ❑ 234 Luke Staley RC 1.00 2.50
- ❑ 235 Cliff Russell RC 1.00 2.50
- ❑ 236 Jeremy Shockey RC 2.50 6.00
- ❑ 237 Donte Stallworth RC 1.50 4.00
- ❑ 238 Daniel Graham RC 1.25 3.00
- ❑ 239 Reche Caldwell RC 1.50 4.00
- ❑ 240 Ryan Sims RC 1.50 4.00

2003 Ultra

- ❑ COMP.SET w/o SP's (160) 12.50 30.00
- ❑ 1 Rich Gannon .25 .60
- ❑ 2 Warren Sapp .25 .60
- ❑ 3 Steve McNair .30 .75
- ❑ 4 Donovan McNabb .30 .75
- ❑ 5 Chad Pennington .30 .75
- ❑ 6 Michael Vick .30 .75
- ❑ 7 Hines Ward .30 .75
- ❑ 8 Terrell Owens .30 .75
- ❑ 9 Brett Favre .75 2.00
- ❑ 10 Jeremy Shockey .30 .75
- ❑ 11 William Green .20 .50
- ❑ 12 Marvin Harrison .30 .75
- ❑ 13 Mark Brunell .25 .60
- ❑ 14 Todd Heap .25 .60
- ❑ 15 Tim Couch .20 .50
- ❑ 16 Javon Walker .25 .60
- ❑ 17 Zach Thomas .30 .75
- ❑ 18 Brian Westbrook .30 .75
- ❑ 19 Matt Hasselbeck .25 .60
- ❑ 20 Jevon Kearse .25 .60
- ❑ 21 David Boston .20 .50
- ❑ 22 Michael Bennett .25 .60
- ❑ 23 James Mungro .20 .50
- ❑ 24 Antowain Smith .25 .60
- ❑ 25 Laveranues Coles .25 .60
- ❑ 26 Curtis Conway .20 .50
- ❑ 27 Peerless Price .20 .50
- ❑ 28 Michael Strahan .25 .60
- ❑ 29 Tommy Maddox .25 .60
- ❑ 30 Dennis Northcutt .20 .50
- ❑ 31 Rod Gardner .20 .50
- ❑ 32 Marcel Shipp .20 .50
- ❑ 33 Quincy Morgan .20 .50
- ❑ 34 Reggie Wayne .25 .60
- ❑ 35 Troy Brown .25 .60
- ❑ 36 John Abraham .25 .60
- ❑ 37 Tim Dwight .20 .50
- ❑ 38 Jamal Lewis .30 .75
- ❑ 39 Chad Hutchinson .20 .50
- ❑ 40 Jerramy Stevens .25 .60
- ❑ 41 Deion Branch .25 .60
- ❑ 42 Jake Plummer .25 .60
- ❑ 43 Junior Seau .30 .75
- ❑ 44 T.J. Duckett .25 .60
- ❑ 45 Emmitt Smith .75 2.00
- ❑ 46 Edgerrin James .30 .75
- ❑ 47 David Patten .20 .50
- ❑ 48 Charlie Garner .25 .60
- ❑ 49 Quentin Jammer .20 .50
- ❑ 50 Corey Dillon .25 .60
- ❑ 51 Rod Smith .25 .60
- ❑ 52 Marc Boerigter .20 .50
- ❑ 53 Michael Lewis .20 .50
- ❑ 54 Kendrell Bell .20 .50
- ❑ 55 Isaac Bruce .30 .75
- ❑ 56 Warrick Dunn .25 .60
- ❑ 57 Antonio Bryant .30 .75
- ❑ 58 Peyton Manning .60 1.50
- ❑ 59 Ty Law .25 .60
- ❑ 60 Jerry Rice .60 1.50
- ❑ 61 Jeff Garcia .30 .75
- ❑ 62 Joey Galloway .25 .60
- ❑ 63 Aaron Glenn .20 .50
- ❑ 64 Aaron Brooks .25 .60
- ❑ 65 Tim Brown .30 .75
- ❑ 66 David Terrell .20 .50
- ❑ 67 Fred Smoot .20 .50
- ❑ 68 Brian Finneran .20 .50
- ❑ 69 Roy Williams .30 .75
- ❑ 70 Corey Bradford .20 .50
- ❑ 71 Deuce McAllister .30 .75
- ❑ 72 Jerry Porter .25 .60
- ❑ 73 Kevan Barlow .20 .50
- ❑ 74 Keith Brooking .25 .60
- ❑ 75 Brian Urlacher .50 1.25
- ❑ 76 Jabar Gaffney .20 .50
- ❑ 77 Randy Moss .30 .75
- ❑ 78 Charles Woodson .25 .60
- ❑ 79 Darrell Jackson .25 .60
- ❑ 80 John Lynch .25 .60
- ❑ 81 Chester Taylor .25 .60
- ❑ 82 Anthony Thomas .25 .60
- ❑ 83 Jonathan Wells .20 .50
- ❑ 84 Daunte Culpepper .30 .75
- ❑ 85 Phillip Buchanon .20 .50
- ❑ 86 Koren Robinson .25 .60
- ❑ 87 Ronde Barber .25 .60
- ❑ 88 Julius Peppers .30 .75
- ❑ 89 Clinton Portis .40 1.00
- ❑ 90 Jay Fiedler .25 .60
- ❑ 91 Donte Stallworth .25 .60
- ❑ 92 Marc Bulger .30 .75
- ❑ 93 Joe Jurevicius .25 .60
- ❑ 94 Jon Kitna .25 .60
- ❑ 95 Ricky Williams .25 .60
- ❑ 96 Joe Horn .25 .60
- ❑ 97 Jerome Bettis .30 .75
- ❑ 98 Kurt Warner .30 .75
- ❑ 99 Travis Henry .25 .60
- ❑ 100 Ahman Green .30 .75
- ❑ 101 Jimmy Smith .25 .60
- ❑ 102 Curtis Martin .30 .75
- ❑ 103 Simeon Rice .25 .60
- ❑ 104 Patrick Ramsey .25 .60
- ❑ 105 Josh Reed .20 .50
- ❑ 106 James Stewart .25 .60
- ❑ 107 Trent Green .25 .60
- ❑ 108 Randy McMichael .20 .50
- ❑ 109 Amos Zereoue .20 .50
- ❑ 110 Keyshawn Johnson .30 .75
- ❑ 111 DeShaun Foster .25 .60
- ❑ 112 Kevin Johnson .20 .50
- ❑ 113 Dwight Freeney .25 .60
- ❑ 114 Tom Brady .75 2.00
- ❑ 115 Santana Moss .25 .60
- ❑ 116 LaDainian Tomlinson .40 1.00
- ❑ 117 Joey Harrington .25 .60
- ❑ 118 Priest Holmes .30 .75
- ❑ 119 Amani Toomer .25 .60
- ❑ 120 Plaxico Burress .30 .75
- ❑ 121 Brad Johnson .25 .60
- ❑ 122 Champ Bailey .25 .60
- ❑ 123 Muhsin Muhammad .25 .60
- ❑ 124 Ashley Lelie .20 .50
- ❑ 125 Tony Gonzalez .25 .60
- ❑ 126 Kerry Collins .25 .60
- ❑ 127 Antwaan Randle El .25 .60
- ❑ 128 Torry Holt .30 .75
- ❑ 129 Ladell Betts .25 .60
- ❑ 130 Travis Taylor .20 .50
- ❑ 131 Marty Booker .25 .60
- ❑ 132 Patrick Surtain .20 .50
- ❑ 133 Duce Staley .25 .60
- ❑ 134 Shaun Alexander .30 .75
- ❑ 135 Eddie George .25 .60
- ❑ 136 Eric Moulds .25 .60
- ❑ 137 David Carr .30 .75
- ❑ 138 Fred Taylor .30 .75
- ❑ 139 Wayne Chrebet .25 .60
- ❑ 140 Bobby Taylor .25 .60
- ❑ 141 Derrick Brooks .25 .60
- ❑ 142 Stephen Davis .25 .60
- ❑ 143 Ray Lewis .30 .75
- ❑ 144 Kelly Holcomb .20 .50
- ❑ 145 Terry Glenn .25 .60
- ❑ 146 Jason Taylor .25 .60
- ❑ 147 Todd Pinkston .20 .50
- ❑ 148 Derrick Mason .25 .60
- ❑ 149 Chad Johnson .30 .75
- ❑ 150 Ed McCaffrey .25 .60
- ❑ 151 Tiki Barber .30 .75
- ❑ 152 Drew Brees .30 .75
- ❑ 153 Marshall Faulk .30 .75
- ❑ 154 Drew Bledsoe .30 .75
- ❑ 155 Andre Davis .20 .50
- ❑ 156 Donald Driver .30 .75
- ❑ 157 Chris Chambers .25 .60
- ❑ 158 Brian Dawkins .25 .60
- ❑ 159 Garrison Hearst .25 .60
- ❑ 160 Frank Wycheck .20 .50
- ❑ 161 Carson Palmer RC 6.00 15.00
- ❑ 162 Byron Leftwich RC 2.00 5.00
- ❑ 163 Charles Rogers RC 1.25 3.00
- ❑ 164 Andre Johnson RC 3.00 8.00
- ❑ 165 Chris Simms RC 1.50 4.00
- ❑ 166 Rex Grossman RC 1.50 4.00
- ❑ 167 Brandon Lloyd RC 1.50 4.00
- ❑ 168 Lee Suggs RC 1.25 3.00
- ❑ 169 Larry Johnson RC 2.00 5.00
- ❑ 170 Onterrio Smith RC 1.25 3.00
- ❑ 171 Dave Ragone RC 1.00 2.50
- ❑ 172 Taylor Jacobs RC 1.25 3.00
- ❑ 173 Kelley Washington RC 1.25 3.00
- ❑ 174 Bryant Johnson RC 1.50 4.00
- ❑ 175 Kyle Boller RC 1.50 4.00
- ❑ 176 Ken Dorsey RC 1.25 3.00
- ❑ 177 Kliff Kingsbury RC 1.25 3.00
- ❑ 178 Jason Gesser RC 1.25 3.00
- ❑ 179 Brian St.Pierre RC 1.50 4.00
- ❑ 180 Brad Banks RC 1.25 3.00
- ❑ 181 Seneca Wallace RC 1.50 4.00
- ❑ 182 Tony Romo RC 12.50 25.00
- ❑ 183 Terrell Suggs RC 2.00 5.00
- ❑ 184 Terence Newman RC 1.50 4.00
- ❑ 185 Willis McGahee RC 3.00 8.00
- ❑ 186 Justin Fargas RC 1.50 4.00
- ❑ 187 Musa Smith RC 1.25 3.00
- ❑ 188 Earnest Graham RC 1.50 4.00
- ❑ 189 Chris Brown RC 1.50 4.00
- ❑ 190 LaBrandon Toefield RC 1.25 3.00
- ❑ 191 Bennie Joppru RC 1.00 2.50
- ❑ 192 Jason Witten RC 4.00 10.00
- ❑ 193 Anquan Boldin RC 4.00 10.00
- ❑ 194 Talman Gardner RC 1.00 2.50
- ❑ 195 Justin Gage RC 1.50 4.00
- ❑ 196 Sam Aiken RC 1.50 4.00
- ❑ 197 Kevin Curtis RC 1.50 4.00
- ❑ 198 Terrence Edwards RC 1.00 2.50
- ❑ U199 DeWayne Robertson RC 1.25 3.00
- ❑ U200 Kevin Williams RC 1.50 4.00
- ❑ U201 Marcus Trufant RC 1.50 4.00
- ❑ U202 Jimmy Kennedy RC 1.25 3.00
- ❑ U203 Ty Warren RC 1.50 4.00
- ❑ U204 Michael Haynes RC 1.00 2.50
- ❑ U205 Jerome McDougle RC 1.00 2.50
- ❑ U206 Dallas Clark RC 3.00 8.00
- ❑ U207 William Joseph RC 1.00 2.50
- ❑ U208 Andre Woolfolk RC 1.25 3.00
- ❑ U209 Bethel Johnson RC 1.25 3.00
- ❑ U210 Teyo Johnson RC 1.25 3.00
- ❑ U211 Tyrone Calico RC 1.25 3.00
- ❑ U212 L.J. Smith RC 1.50 4.00
- ❑ U213 Nate Burleson RC 1.25 3.00
- ❑ U214 B.J. Askew RC 1.25 3.00

❑ U215 Billy McMullen RC	1.00	2.50
❑ U216 Domanick Davis RC	1.50	4.00
❑ U217 Doug Gabriel RC	1.25	3.00
❑ U218 Quentin Griffin RC	1.25	3.00

2004 Ultra

❑ COMP.SET w/o L13's (218)	25.00	60.00
❑ COMP.SET w/o SP's (200)	12.50	30.00
❑ COMP.UPDATE SET (21)	15.00	40.00
❑ 1 Michael Vick	.30	.75
❑ 2 Kelley Washington	.20	.50
❑ 3 Rex Grossman	.30	.75
❑ 4 Boss Bailey	.20	.50
❑ 5 Johnnie Morton	.25	.60
❑ 6 Michael Strahan	.25	.60
❑ 7 Joey Porter	.25	.60
❑ 8 Keenan McCardell	.20	.50
❑ 9 Quincy Carter	.20	.50
❑ 10 Travis Henry	.25	.60
❑ 11 Bertrand Berry	.25	.60
❑ 12 Marvin Harrison	.30	.75
❑ 13 Ty Law	.25	.60
❑ 14 Phillip Buchanon	.25	.60
❑ 15 Kevan Barlow	.25	.60
❑ 16 Eddie George	.25	.60
❑ 17 Drew Bledsoe	.30	.75
❑ 18 Antonio Bryant	.30	.75
❑ 19 Marcus Pollard	.20	.50
❑ 20 Brian Russell RC	.20	.50
❑ 21 Santana Moss	.25	.60
❑ 22 Julian Peterson	.25	.60
❑ 23 Justin McCareins	.20	.50
❑ 24 Ed Reed	.25	.60
❑ 25 Charles Tillman	.25	.60
❑ 26 Dat Nguyen	.20	.50
❑ 27 Ricky Manning	.20	.50
❑ 28 Dwight Freeney	.30	.75
❑ 29 Zach Thomas	.30	.75
❑ 30 Tiki Barber	.30	.75
❑ 31 Jay Riemersma	.20	.50
❑ 32 Joe Jurevicius	.20	.50
❑ 33 Marcel Shipp	.30	.75
❑ 34 Justin Gage	.25	.60
❑ 35 Charles Rogers	.25	.00
❑ 36 Eddie Kennison	.25	.60
❑ 37 Deion Branch	.25	.60
❑ 38 Matt Hasselbeck	.30	.75
❑ 39 L.J. Smith	.25	.60
❑ 40 Jamal Lewis	.25	.60
❑ 41 Muhsin Muhammad	.25	.60
❑ 42 Terence Newman	.25	.60
❑ 43 Jabar Gaffney	.25	.60
❑ 44 Junior Seau	.30	.75
❑ 45 Jeremy Shockey	.25	.60
❑ 46 Hines Ward	.30	.75
❑ 47 Brad Johnson	.25	.60
❑ 48 Kyle Boller	.25	.60
❑ 49 Steve Smith	.30	.75
❑ 50 Quincy Morgan	.20	.50
❑ 51 Corey Bradford	.25	.60
❑ 52 Ricky Williams	.30	.75
❑ 53 Amani Toomer	.25	.60
❑ 54 Plaxico Burress	.25	.60
❑ 55 Derrick Brooks	.25	.60
❑ 56 Dre Bly	.20	.50
❑ 57 Terrell Suggs	.20	.50
❑ 58 DeShaun Foster	.25	.60
❑ 59 Andre Davis	.20	.50
❑ 60 Rod Smith	.25	.60
❑ 61 Andre Johnson	.30	.75
❑ 62 Randy McMichael	.20	.50
❑ 63 Ike Hilliard	.25	.60
❑ 64 Antwaan Randle El	.25	.60
❑ 65 Warren Sapp	.25	.60

❑ 66 LaBrandon Toefield	.20	.50
❑ 67 Chad Johnson	.25	.60
❑ 68 Javon Walker	.25	.60
❑ 69 Jimmy Smith	.25	.60
❑ 70 Donte Stallworth	.25	.60
❑ 71 Brian Dawkins	.25	.60
❑ 72 Leonard Little	.20	.50
❑ 73 Ladell Betts	.25	.60
❑ 74 Ray Lewis	.30	.75
❑ 75 Stephen Davis	.25	.60
❑ 76 Dennis Northcutt	.20	.50
❑ 77 Ashley Lelie	.25	.60
❑ 78 Billy Miller	.20	.50
❑ 79 Chris Chambers	.25	.60
❑ 80 John Abraham	.20	.50
❑ 81 Quentin Jammer	.20	.50
❑ 82 Isaac Bruce	.25	.60
❑ 83 Peerless Price	.25	.60
❑ 84 Jake Delhomme	.25	.60
❑ 85 Lee Suggs	.30	.75
❑ 86 Shannon Sharpe	.25	.60
❑ 87 Domanick Davis	.25	.60
❑ 88 Daunte Culpepper	.30	.75
❑ 89 Shaun Ellis	.20	.50
❑ 90 Drew Brees	.30	.75
❑ 91 Torry Holt	.30	.75
❑ 92 Alge Crumpler	.25	.60
❑ 93 Mike Rucker	.20	.50
❑ 94 Tim Couch	.25	.60
❑ 95 Quentin Griffin	.25	.60
❑ 96 David Carr	.25	.60
❑ 97 Moe Williams	.20	.50
❑ 98 Chad Pennington	.30	.75
❑ 99 LaDainian Tomlinson	.40	1.00
❑ 100 Adam Archuleta	.20	.50
❑ 101 Julius Peppers	.25	.60
❑ 102 Clinton Portis	.30	.75
❑ 103 Marcus Stroud	.20	.50
❑ 104 Tom Brady	.75	2.00
❑ 105 Teyo Johnson	.25	.60
❑ 106 Terrell Owens	.30	.75
❑ 107 Keith Bulluck	.20	.50
❑ 108 Eric Moulds	.25	.60
❑ 109 Jake Plummer	.25	.60
❑ 110 Reggie Wayne	.25	.60
❑ 111 Tedy Bruschi	.30	.75
❑ 112 Rich Gannon	.25	.60
❑ 113 Tony Parrish	.20	.50
❑ 114 Steve McNair	.30	.75
❑ 115 T.J. Duckett	.25	.60
❑ 116 Peter Warrick	.25	.60
❑ 117 Donald Driver	.30	.75
❑ 118 Fred Taylor	.25	.60
❑ 119 Joe Horn	.25	.60
❑ 120 Jerry Porter	.25	.60
❑ 121 Marc Bulger	.25	.60
❑ 122 Trung Canidate	.20	.50
❑ 123 Warrick Dunn	.25	.60
❑ 124 Kelly Holcomb	.25	.60
❑ 125 Robert Ferguson	.20	.50
❑ 126 Byron Leftwich	.30	.75
❑ 127 Michael Lewis	.25	.60
❑ 128 Jerry Rice	.60	1.50
❑ 129 Marshall Faulk	.30	.75
❑ 130 Patrick Ramsey	.25	.60
❑ 131 Josh McCown	.25	.60
❑ 132 Anthony Thomas	.25	.60
❑ 133 Joey Harrington	.25	.60
❑ 134 Dante Hall	.25	.60
❑ 135 Daniel Graham	.20	.50
❑ 136 Richard Seymour	.20	.50
❑ 137 Brandon Lloyd	.20	.50
❑ 138 Anquan Boldin	.30	.75
❑ 139 Jon Kitna	.25	.60
❑ 140 Nick Barnett	.25	.60
❑ 141 Priest Holmes	.30	.75
❑ 142 Bethel Johnson	.20	.50
❑ 143 Shaun Alexander	.30	.75
❑ 144 Todd Heap	.25	.60
❑ 145 Brian Urlacher	.30	.75
❑ 146 Peyton Manning	.60	1.50
❑ 147 Jason Taylor	.30	.75
❑ 148 Kerry Collins	.25	.60
❑ 149 Tommy Maddox	.25	.60
❑ 150 Charles Lee	.20	.50
❑ 151 Tim Rattay	.20	.50
❑ 152 Carson Palmer	.40	1.00
❑ 153 Brett Favre	.75	2.00

❑ 154 Trent Green	.25	.60
❑ 155 Aaron Brooks	.25	.60
❑ 156 Brian Westbrook	.30	.75
❑ 157 Itula Mili	.20	.50
❑ 158 Keith Brooking	.20	.50
❑ 159 Rudi Johnson	.25	.60
❑ 160 Najeh Davenport	.25	.60
❑ 161 Kevin Johnson	.20	.50
❑ 162 Boo Williams	.20	.50
❑ 163 Corey Simon	.25	.60
❑ 164 Darrell Jackson	.25	.60
❑ 165 Damerien McCants	.20	.50
❑ 166 Willis McGahee	.30	.75
❑ 167 Terry Glenn	.25	.60
❑ 168 Dallas Clark	.30	.75
❑ 169 Randy Moss	.30	.75
❑ 170 Charles Woodson	.30	.75
❑ 171 Jeff Garcia	.30	.75
❑ 172 Chris Brown	.25	.60
❑ 173 Emmitt Smith	.75	2.00
❑ 174 Marty Booker	.25	.60
❑ 175 Artose Pinner	.20	.50
❑ 176 Tony Gonzalez	.30	.75
❑ 177 Troy Brown	.25	.60
❑ 178 Freddie Mitchell	.20	.50
❑ 179 Marcus Trufant	.20	.50
❑ 180 London Fletcher	.20	.50
❑ 181 Roy Williams S	.25	.60
❑ 182 Edgerrin James	.30	.75
❑ 183 Michael Bennett	.25	.60
❑ 184 Jerald Sowell	.20	.50
❑ 185 David Boston	.20	.50
❑ 186 Derrick Mason	.25	.60
❑ 187 Bryant Johnson	.25	.60
❑ 188 Corey Dillon	.25	.60
❑ 189 Ahman Green	.30	.75
❑ 190 Vonnie Holliday	.20	.50
❑ 191 Deuce McAllister	.30	.75
❑ 192 Donovan McNabb	.30	.75
❑ 193 Koren Robinson	.30	.75
❑ 194 Laveranues Coles	.25	.60
❑ 195 Takeo Spikes	.20	.50
❑ 196 Richie Anderson	.20	.50
❑ 197 Onterrio Smith	.20	.50
❑ 198 Curtis Martin	.30	.75
❑ 199 Antonio Gates	.30	.75
❑ 200 Champ Bailey	.25	.60
❑ 201 Eli Manning L13 RC	25.00	60.00
❑ 202 Philip Rivers L13 RC	20.00	50.00
❑ 203 Roy Williams L13 RC	6.00	15.00
❑ 204 Drew Henson L13 RC	3.00	8.00
❑ 205 Chris Perry L13 RC	5.00	12.00
❑ 206 Larry Fitzgerald L13 RC	15.00	40.00
❑ 207 Rashaun Woods L13 RC	3.00	8.00
❑ 208 Reggie Williams L13 RC	5.00	12.00
❑ 209 Mike Williams L13 RC	4.00	10.00
❑ 210 Kellen Winslow L13 RC	6.00	15.00
❑ 211 Steven Jackson L13 RC	12.00	30.00
❑ 212 Kevin Jones L13 RC	5.00	12.00
❑ 213 Ben Roethlisberger L13 RC	30.00	80.00
❑ 214 Michael Turner RC	3.00	8.00
❑ 215 Tatum Bell RC	1.25	3.00
❑ 216 Quincy Wilson RC	1.00	2.50
❑ 217 Devery Henderson RC	1.25	3.00
❑ 218 Ernest Wilford RC	1.00	2.50
❑ 219 Cody Pickett RC	1.00	2.50
❑ 220 Ryan Dinwiddie RC	.75	2.00
❑ 221 J.P. Losman RC	1.25	3.00
❑ 222 Derrick Knight RC	.75	2.00
❑ 223 Michael Jenkins RC	1.25	3.00
❑ 224 Greg Jones RC	1.25	3.00
❑ 225 Cedric Cobbs RC	1.00	2.50
❑ 226 Will Poole RC	1.25	3.00
❑ 227 Michael Clayton RC	1.25	3.00
❑ 228 Sean Taylor RC	1.25	3.00
❑ 229 Will Smith RC	1.25	3.00
❑ 230 Jonathan Vilma RC	1.25	3.00
❑ 231 Lee Evans RC	1.50	4.00
❑ 232 Julius Jones RC	1.50	4.00
❑ U234 D.J. Williams RC	1.25	3.00
❑ U235 Mewelde Moore RC	1.25	3.00
❑ U236 Ben Watson RC	1.25	3.00
❑ U237 Robert Gallery RC	1.25	3.00
❑ U238 DeAngelo Hall RC	1.25	3.00
❑ U239 Luke McCown RC	1.25	3.00
❑ U240 Ben Troupe RC	1.00	2.50
❑ U241 Keary Colbert RC	1.00	2.50
❑ U242 Matt Schaub RC	3.00	8.00

Card	Low	High
❑ U243 Kenechi Udeze RC	1.25	3.00
❑ U244 Jeff Smoker RC	1.00	2.50
❑ U245 Derrick Hamilton RC	.75	2.00
❑ U246 Bernard Berrian RC	1.25	3.00
❑ U247 Devard Darling RC	1.00	2.50
❑ U248 Johnnie Morant RC	1.00	2.50
❑ U249 Vince Wilfork RC	1.25	3.00
❑ U250 Jerricho Cotchery RC	1.25	3.00
❑ U251 Darius Watts RC	1.00	2.50
❑ U252 Carlos Francis RC	.75	2.00
❑ U253 P.K. Sam RC	.75	2.00

2005 Ultra

Card	Low	High
❑ COMP.SET w/o RC's (200)	12.50	30.00
❑ 201-213 L13 PRINT RUN 599 SER.#'d SETS		
❑ OVERALL ROOKIE ODDS 1:4 HOB, 1:5 RET		
❑ 1 Peyton Manning	.50	1.25
❑ 2 Brian Westbrook	.30	.75
❑ 3 Daunte Culpepper	.30	.75
❑ 4 Marvin Harrison	.30	.75
❑ 5 Edgerrin James	.25	.60
❑ 6 Reggie Wayne	.25	.60
❑ 7 Michael Vick	.30	.75
❑ 8 Donte Stallworth	.25	.60
❑ 9 Brian Urlacher	.30	.75
❑ 10 Hines Ward	.30	.75
❑ 11 Charles Rogers	.20	.50
❑ 12 Roy Williams WR	.30	.75
❑ 13 Julius Peppers	.25	.60
❑ 14 Eric Moulds	.25	.60
❑ 15 Ray Lewis	.30	.75
❑ 16 Byron Leftwich	.25	.60
❑ 17 Fred Taylor	.30	.75
❑ 18 Andre Johnson	.25	.60
❑ 19 Travis Henry	.25	.60
❑ 20 Tom Brady	.60	1.50
❑ 21 Drew Bledsoe	.30	.75
❑ 22 Tiki Barber	.30	.75
❑ 23 Larry Fitzgerald	.30	.75
❑ 24 Jeff Garcia	.25	.60
❑ 25 Rex Grossman	.30	.75
❑ 26 Larry Johnson	.30	.75
❑ 27 Curtis Martin	.30	.75
❑ 28 Chad Pennington	.30	.75
❑ 29 Dwight Freeney	.25	.60
❑ 30 Peerless Price	.20	.50
❑ 31 Rich Gannon	.25	.60
❑ 32 Matt Hasselbeck	.25	.60
❑ 33 Clinton Portis	.30	.75
❑ 34 Jerry Rice	.60	1.50
❑ 35 Jeremy Shockey	.30	.75
❑ 36 Tony Gonzalez	.25	.60
❑ 37 Deuce McAllister	.30	.75
❑ 38 Shaun Alexander	.30	.75
❑ 39 Peter Warrick	.20	.50
❑ 40 Isaac Bruce	.25	.60
❑ 41 Antonio Bryant	.25	.60
❑ 42 Mike Alstott	.25	.60
❑ 43 Domanick Davis	.20	.50
❑ 44 Jake Delhomme	.30	.75
❑ 45 Santana Moss	.25	.60
❑ 46 Ahman Green	.30	.75
❑ 47 David Carr	.25	.60
❑ 48 Kyle Boller	.25	.60
❑ 49 Chris Chambers	.25	.60
❑ 50 Quentin Griffin	.25	.60
❑ 51 Donovan McNabb	.30	.75
❑ 52 Eli Manning	.60	1.50
❑ 53 Julius Jones	.30	.75
❑ 54 Sean Taylor	.25	.60
❑ 55 Javon Walker	.25	.60
❑ 56 Randy Moss	.30	.75
❑ 57 Thomas Jones	.25	.60
❑ 58 Joey Harrington	.30	.75
❑ 59 Michael Boulware	.20	.50
❑ 60 Marshall Faulk	.30	.75
❑ 61 Tony Parrish	.20	.50
❑ 62 Bertrand Berry	.20	.50
❑ 63 Alge Crumpler	.25	.60
❑ 64 Aaron Brooks	.20	.50
❑ 65 Muhsin Muhammad	.25	.60
❑ 66 Simeon Rice	.20	.50
❑ 67 Corey Dillon	.25	.60
❑ 68 Willis McGahee	.30	.75
❑ 69 Ben Roethlisberger	.75	2.00
❑ 70 Chad Johnson	.25	.60
❑ 71 Jamal Lewis	.25	.60
❑ 72 Drew Brees	.30	.75
❑ 73 LaDainian Tomlinson	.40	1.00
❑ 74 Reuben Droughns	.20	.50
❑ 75 Priest Holmes	.30	.75
❑ 76 Jerry Porter	.25	.60
❑ 77 Chris Brown	.25	.60
❑ 78 Steve McNair	.30	.75
❑ 79 Troy Brown	.20	.50
❑ 80 Jerome Bettis	.30	.75
❑ 81 Patrick Kerney	.25	.60
❑ 82 Terrell Owens	.30	.75
❑ 83 Brett Favre	.75	2.00
❑ 84 Carson Palmer	.30	.75
❑ 85 Jake Plummer	.25	.60
❑ 86 Tedy Bruschi	.30	.75
❑ 87 Plaxico Burress	.25	.60
❑ 88 Jonathan Vilma	.25	.60
❑ 89 Ed Reed	.25	.60
❑ 90 Brian Dawkins	.25	.60
❑ 91 Anquan Boldin	.25	.60
❑ 92 Vinny Testaverde	.25	.60
❑ 93 David Givens	.25	.60
❑ 94 Rudi Johnson	.25	.60
❑ 95 Philip Rivers	.30	.75
❑ 96 Jimmy Smith	.25	.60
❑ 97 Emmitt Smith	.60	1.50
❑ 98 Eric Johnson	.20	.50
❑ 99 Jeremiah Trotter	.20	.50
❑ 100 Duce Staley	.25	.60
❑ 101 Warrick Dunn	.25	.60
❑ 102 Nate Burleson	.25	.60
❑ 103 Marc Bulger	.25	.60
❑ 104 Joe Horn	.25	.60
❑ 105 Rodney Harrison	.25	.60
❑ 106 Zach Thomas	.30	.75
❑ 107 Michael Clayton	.25	.60
❑ 108 Derrick Brooks	.25	.60
❑ 109 Michael Lewis	.20	.50
❑ 110 Kurt Warner	.30	.75
❑ 111 Jason Witten	.30	.75
❑ 112 Roy Williams S	.25	.60
❑ 113 Kabeer Gbaja-Biamila	.30	.75
❑ 114 Torry Holt	.25	.60
❑ 115 Tim Rattay	.20	.50
❑ 116 Josh McCown	.25	.60
❑ 117 Brian Griese	.25	.60
❑ 118 Patrick Ramsey	.25	.60
❑ 119 A.J. Feeley	.20	.50
❑ 120 Kerry Collins	.25	.60
❑ 121 Trent Green	.25	.60
❑ 122 Billy Volek	.25	.60
❑ 123 Travis Taylor	.20	.50
❑ 124 T.J. Houshmandzadeh	.25	.60
❑ 125 James Farrior	.20	.50
❑ 126 Bryan Scott	.20	.50
❑ 127 Lito Sheppard	.25	.60
❑ 128 David Patten	.20	.50
❑ 129 Antwaan Randle El	.25	.60
❑ 130 Antonio Gates	.30	.75
❑ 131 Brandon Stokley	.20	.50
❑ 132 Keyshawn Johnson	.25	.60
❑ 133 Amani Toomer	.25	.60
❑ 134 Shawn Springs	.20	.50
❑ 135 Eddie George	.20	.50
❑ 136 Kevin Jones	.25	.60
❑ 137 Darrell Jackson	.25	.60
❑ 138 Ricky Manning	.20	.50
❑ 139 Laveranues Coles	.25	.60
❑ 140 Champ Bailey	.25	.60
❑ 141 Rod Smith	.25	.60
❑ 142 Ashley Lelie	.20	.50
❑ 143 Charles Woodson	.25	.60
❑ 144 Drew Bennett	.25	.60
❑ 145 Derrick Mason	.25	.60
❑ 146 Donovin Darius	.20	.50
❑ 147 Dennis Northcutt	.20	.50
❑ 148 Jamie Sharper	.20	.50
❑ 149 Steven Jackson	.40	1.00
❑ 150 David Terrell	.20	.50
❑ 151 Onterrio Smith	.20	.50
❑ 152 Donald Driver	.30	.75
❑ 153 Antoine Winfield	.25	.60
❑ 154 Michael Pittman	.20	.50
❑ 155 Dan Morgan	.20	.50
❑ 156 Troy Polamalu	.40	1.00
❑ 157 Willie McGinest	.25	.60
❑ 158 Justin McCareins	.20	.50
❑ 159 Allen Rossum	.20	.50
❑ 160 Deion Branch	.25	.60
❑ 161 Deion Sanders	.40	1.00
❑ 162 Josh Reed	.20	.50
❑ 163 Lee Evans	.25	.60
❑ 164 Lee Suggs	.25	.60
❑ 165 Dante Hall	.25	.60
❑ 166 Eddie Kennison	.20	.50
❑ 167 Ken Dorsey	.20	.50
❑ 168 Andre Dyson	.20	.50
❑ 169 Keith Bulluck	.20	.50
❑ 170 Todd Pinkston	.20	.50
❑ 171 Jevon Kearse	.25	.60
❑ 172 Dunta Robinson	.20	.50
❑ 173 Steve Smith	.30	.75
❑ 174 Koren Robinson	.25	.60
❑ 175 Freddie Mitchell	.20	.50
❑ 176 L.J. Smith	.25	.60
❑ 177 Kevin Curtis	.25	.60
❑ 178 Marcus Robinson	.25	.60
❑ 179 Kellen Winslow	.30	.75
❑ 180 Reggie Williams	.25	.60
❑ 181 Bubba Franks	.25	.60
❑ 182 J.P. Losman	.25	.60
❑ 183 Chris Perry	.20	.50
❑ 184 Michael Jenkins	.25	.60
❑ 185 T.J. Duckett	.20	.50
❑ 186 Rashaun Woods	.20	.50
❑ 187 Ben Watson	.25	.60
❑ 188 Bryant Johnson	.25	.60
❑ 189 Dallas Clark	.25	.60
❑ 190 William Green	.20	.50
❑ 191 Daniel Graham	.25	.60
❑ 192 Jerramy Stevens	.25	.60
❑ 193 DeShaun Foster	.25	.60
❑ 194 Nick Goings	.20	.50
❑ 195 Ronald Curry	.25	.60
❑ 196 Kevan Barlow	.20	.50
❑ 197 Kevin Faulk	.25	.60
❑ 198 Eric Parker	.20	.50
❑ 199 Keenan McCardell	.25	.60
❑ 200 LaMont Jordan	.25	.60
❑ 201 Alex Smith QB L13 RC	15.00	40.00
❑ 202 Aaron Rodgers L13 RC	25.00	60.00
❑ 203 Cedric Benson L13 RC	7.50	20.00
❑ 204 Braylon Edwards L13 RC	20.00	40.00
❑ 205 Ronnie Brown L13 RC	30.00	60.00
❑ 206 Cadillac Williams L13 RC	15.00	40.00
❑ 207 Troy Williamson L13 RC	7.50	20.00
❑ 208 Mark Clayton L13 RC	7.50	20.00
❑ 209 Charlie Frye L13 RC	6.00	15.00
❑ 210 Mike Williams L13	6.00	15.00
❑ 211 Marion Barber L13 RC	15.00	40.00
❑ 212 Eric Shelton L13 RC	6.00	15.00
❑ 213 Antrel Rolle L13 RC	6.00	15.00
❑ 214 Heath Miller RC	4.00	10.00
❑ 215 Dan Cody RC	2.00	5.00
❑ 216 Adam Jones RC	1.50	4.00
❑ 217 Derrick Johnson RC	2.00	5.00
❑ 218 Alex Smith TE RC	2.00	5.00
❑ 219 Kyle Orton RC	3.00	8.00
❑ 220 David Pollack RC	1.50	4.00
❑ 221 Erasmus James RC	1.50	4.00
❑ 222 Justin Tuck RC	2.50	6.00
❑ 223 Jason Campbell RC	3.00	8.00
❑ 224 Dan Orlovsky RC	2.00	5.00
❑ 225 Thomas Davis RC	1.50	4.00
❑ 226 J.J. Arrington RC	2.00	5.00
❑ 227 Roddy White RC	2.50	6.00
❑ 228 David Greene RC	1.50	4.00
❑ 229 Ciatrick Fason RC	1.50	4.00
❑ 230 Chris Henry RC	2.00	5.00
❑ 231 Reggie Brown RC	1.50	4.00
❑ 232 Vernand Morency RC	1.50	4.00
❑ 233 Carlos Rogers RC	2.00	5.00
❑ 234 Ryan Moats RC	1.50	4.00

❑ 235 Roscoe Parrish RC 1.50 4.00
❑ 236 Terrence Murphy RC 1.25 3.00
❑ 237 Shawne Merriman RC 2.00 5.00
❑ 238 Courtney Roby RC 1.50 4.00
❑ 239 Mark Bradley RC 1.50 4.00
❑ 240 Marcus Spears RC 2.00 5.00
❑ 241 Justin Miller RC 1.50 4.00
❑ 242 Matt Jones RC 2.00 5.00
❑ 243 DeMarcus Ware RC 3.00 8.00
❑ 244 Fabian Washington RC 2.00 5.00
❑ 245 Marlin Jackson RC 1.50 4.00
❑ 246 Corey Webster RC 2.00 5.00
❑ 247 Brandon Jacobs RC 2.50 6.00
❑ 248 Frank Gore RC 4.00 10.00

2006 Ultra

❑ COMP.SET w/o RC's (200) 12.50 30.00
❑ 1 Larry Fitzgerald .30 .75
❑ 2 Anquan Boldin .25 .60
❑ 3 Kurt Warner .30 .75
❑ 4 Bryant Johnson .20 .50
❑ 5 Marcel Shipp .20 .50
❑ 6 J.J. Arrington .20 .50
❑ 7 Michael Vick .30 .75
❑ 8 Warrick Dunn .25 .60
❑ 9 T.J. Duckett .20 .50
❑ 10 Alge Crumpler .25 .60
❑ 11 Michael Jenkins .25 .60
❑ 12 DeAngelo Hall .25 .60
❑ 13 Kyle Boller .25 .60
❑ 14 Jamal Lewis .25 .60
❑ 15 Todd Heap .25 .60
❑ 16 Derrick Mason .25 .60
❑ 17 Ray Lewis .30 .75
❑ 18 Terrell Suggs .25 .60
❑ 19 J.P. Losman .25 .60
❑ 20 Willis McGahee .30 .75
❑ 21 Eric Moulds .25 .60
❑ 22 Lee Evans .25 .60
❑ 23 Roscoe Parrish .20 .50
❑ 24 Kelly Holcomb .20 .50
❑ 25 Jake Delhomme .25 .60
❑ 26 Steve Smith .30 .75
❑ 27 Stephen Davis .25 .60
❑ 28 Julius Peppers .25 .60
❑ 29 DeShaun Foster .25 .60
❑ 30 Keary Colbert .25 .60
❑ 31 Chris Gamble .20 .50
❑ 32 Kyle Orton .25 .60
❑ 33 Thomas Jones .25 .60
❑ 34 Rex Grossman .30 .75
❑ 35 Muhsin Muhammad .25 .60
❑ 36 Brian Urlacher .30 .75
❑ 37 Adrian Peterson .25 .60
❑ 38 Carson Palmer .30 .75
❑ 39 Chad Johnson .25 .60
❑ 40 Rudi Johnson .25 .60
❑ 41 Chris Perry .25 .60
❑ 42 T.J. Houshmandzadeh .25 .60
❑ 43 Chris Henry .20 .50
❑ 44 Deltha O'Neal .20 .50
❑ 45 Trent Dilfer .25 .60
❑ 46 Reuben Droughns .25 .60
❑ 47 Antonio Bryant .25 .60
❑ 48 Braylon Edwards .30 .75
❑ 49 Charlie Frye .25 .60
❑ 50 Dennis Northcutt .20 .50
❑ 51 Drew Bledsoe .30 .75
❑ 52 Julius Jones .25 .60
❑ 53 Keyshawn Johnson .25 .60
❑ 54 Jason Witten .30 .75
❑ 55 Roy Williams S .25 .60
❑ 56 Marion Barber .30 .75
❑ 57 Terry Glenn .25 .60
❑ 58 Jake Plummer .25 .60
❑ 59 Mike Anderson .25 .60
❑ 60 Champ Bailey .25 .60
❑ 61 Tatum Bell .20 .50
❑ 62 Rod Smith .25 .60
❑ 63 Ashley Lelie .20 .50
❑ 64 Joey Harrington .20 .50
❑ 65 Kevin Jones .25 .60
❑ 66 Roy Williams WR .30 .75
❑ 67 Mike Williams .25 .60
❑ 68 Marcus Pollard .20 .50
❑ 69 Jeff Garcia .25 .60
❑ 70 Brett Favre .60 1.50
❑ 71 Javon Walker .25 .60
❑ 72 Donald Driver .30 .75
❑ 73 Samkon Gado .30 .75
❑ 74 Najeh Davenport .25 .60
❑ 75 Robert Ferguson .20 .50
❑ 76 David Carr .20 .50
❑ 77 Domanick Davis .25 .60
❑ 78 Andre Johnson .25 .60
❑ 79 Jabar Gaffney .20 .50
❑ 80 Corey Bradford .20 .50
❑ 81 Dunta Robinson .20 .50
❑ 82 Peyton Manning .50 1.25
❑ 83 Edgerrin James .25 .60
❑ 84 Marvin Harrison .30 .75
❑ 85 Reggie Wayne .25 .60
❑ 86 Dallas Clark .25 .60
❑ 87 Dwight Freeney .25 .60
❑ 88 Cato June .25 .60
❑ 89 Byron Leftwich .25 .60
❑ 90 Fred Taylor .25 .60
❑ 91 Jimmy Smith .25 .60
❑ 92 Matt Jones .25 .60
❑ 93 Ernest Wilford .20 .50
❑ 94 Greg Jones .20 .50
❑ 95 Trent Green .25 .60
❑ 96 Priest Holmes .25 .60
❑ 97 Larry Johnson .25 .60
❑ 98 Tony Gonzalez .25 .60
❑ 99 Dante Hall .25 .60
❑ 100 Eddie Kennison .20 .50
❑ 101 Gus Frerotte .20 .50
❑ 102 Chris Chambers .25 .60
❑ 103 Ronnie Brown .30 .75
❑ 104 Ricky Williams .20 .50
❑ 105 Randy McMichael .20 .50
❑ 106 Zach Thomas .30 .75
❑ 107 Daunte Culpepper .30 .75
❑ 108 Nate Burleson .25 .60
❑ 109 Michael Bennett .20 .50
❑ 110 Mewelde Moore .20 .50
❑ 111 Troy Williamson .25 .60
❑ 112 Travis Taylor .20 .50
❑ 113 Jermaine Wiggins .20 .50
❑ 114 Tom Brady .50 1.25
❑ 115 Corey Dillon .25 .60
❑ 116 Deion Branch .25 .60
❑ 117 Tedy Bruschi .30 .75
❑ 118 David Givens .25 .60
❑ 119 Patrick Pass .20 .50
❑ 120 Aaron Brooks .25 .60
❑ 121 Deuce McAllister .25 .60
❑ 122 Joe Horn .25 .60
❑ 123 Donte Stallworth .25 .60
❑ 124 Antowain Smith .20 .50
❑ 125 Devery Henderson .20 .50
❑ 126 Eli Manning .40 1.00
❑ 127 Tiki Barber .30 .75
❑ 128 Jeremy Shockey .30 .75
❑ 129 Plaxico Burress .25 .60
❑ 130 Amani Toomer .25 .60
❑ 131 Michael Strahan .25 .60
❑ 132 Chad Pennington .25 .60
❑ 133 Curtis Martin .30 .75
❑ 134 Jonathan Vilma .25 .60
❑ 135 Laveranues Coles .25 .60
❑ 136 Justin McCareins .20 .50
❑ 137 Ty Law .20 .50
❑ 138 Kerry Collins .25 .60
❑ 139 LaMont Jordan .25 .60
❑ 140 Randy Moss .30 .75
❑ 141 Jerry Porter .25 .60
❑ 142 Doug Gabriel .20 .50
❑ 143 Zack Crockett .20 .50
❑ 144 Donovan McNabb .30 .75
❑ 145 Brian Westbrook .25 .60
❑ 146 Terrell Owens .30 .75
❑ 147 Jevon Kearse .25 .60
❑ 148 L.J. Smith .20 .50
❑ 149 Greg Lewis .20 .50
❑ 150 Ben Roethlisberger .50 1.25
❑ 151 Willie Parker .40 1.00
❑ 152 Hines Ward .30 .75
❑ 153 Jerome Bettis .30 .75
❑ 154 Antwaan Randle El .25 .60
❑ 155 Heath Miller .25 .60
❑ 156 Joey Porter .20 .50
❑ 157 Drew Brees .30 .75
❑ 158 LaDainian Tomlinson .40 1.00
❑ 159 Antonio Gates .30 .75
❑ 160 Keenan McCardell .25 .60
❑ 161 Donnie Edwards .20 .50
❑ 162 Shawne Merriman .25 .60
❑ 163 Eric Parker .20 .50
❑ 164 Alex Smith .25 .60
❑ 165 Kevan Barlow .25 .60
❑ 166 Frank Gore .30 .75
❑ 167 Brandon Lloyd .25 .60
❑ 168 Eric Johnson .20 .50
❑ 169 Julian Peterson .20 .50
❑ 170 Matt Hasselbeck .25 .60
❑ 171 Shaun Alexander .25 .60
❑ 172 Darrell Jackson .25 .60
❑ 173 Joe Jurevicius .20 .50
❑ 174 Jerramy Stevens .25 .60
❑ 175 D.J. Hackett .25 .60
❑ 176 Marc Bulger .25 .60
❑ 177 Steven Jackson .30 .75
❑ 178 Torry Holt .25 .60
❑ 179 Isaac Bruce .25 .60
❑ 180 Kevin Curtis .25 .60
❑ 181 Marshall Faulk .25 .60
❑ 182 Chris Simms .25 .60
❑ 183 Cadillac Williams .30 .75
❑ 184 Michael Pittman .20 .50
❑ 185 Michael Clayton .25 .60
❑ 186 Joey Galloway .25 .60
❑ 187 Brian Griese .25 .60
❑ 188 Steve McNair .25 .60
❑ 189 Chris Brown .25 .60
❑ 190 Drew Bennett .25 .60
❑ 191 Travis Henry .25 .60
❑ 192 Ben Troupe .20 .50
❑ 193 Billy Volek .20 .50
❑ 194 Erron Kinney .20 .50
❑ 195 Mark Brunell .25 .60
❑ 196 Santana Moss .25 .60
❑ 197 Clinton Portis .30 .75
❑ 198 Chris Cooley .25 .60
❑ 199 Ladell Betts .25 .60
❑ 200 Sean Taylor .30 .75
❑ 201 Matt Leinart L13 RC 15.00 40.00
❑ 202 Vince Young L13 RC 15.00 40.00
❑ 203 Reggie Bush L13 RC 40.00 80.00
❑ 204 D'Brick Ferguson L13 RC 8.00 20.00
❑ 205 DeAngelo Williams L13 RC 15.00 30.00
❑ 206 Jay Cutler L13 RC 25.00 60.00
❑ 207 A.J. Hawk L13 RC 15.00 30.00
❑ 208 Mario Williams L13 RC 10.00 25.00
❑ 209 Santonio Holmes L13 RC 12.00 30.00
❑ 210 Chad Greenway L13 RC 8.00 20.00
❑ 211 Laurence Maroney L13 RC 12.00 30.00
❑ 212 LenDale White L13 RC 15.00 30.00
❑ 213 Sinorice Moss L13 RC 10.00 25.00
❑ 214 A.J. Nicholson RC 1.25 3.00
❑ 215 Abdul Hodge RC 1.50 4.00
❑ 216 Jeremy Bloom RC 1.50 4.00
❑ 217 Anthony Fasano RC 2.00 5.00
❑ 218 Bobby Carpenter RC 1.50 4.00
❑ 219 Brian Calhoun RC 1.50 4.00
❑ 220 Brodie Croyle RC 2.00 5.00
❑ 221 Chad Jackson RC 1.50 4.00
❑ 222 Charlie Whitehurst RC 2.00 5.00
❑ 223 Claude Wroten RC 1.25 3.00
❑ 224 Darnell Bing RC 1.50 4.00
❑ 225 Darrell Hackney RC 1.50 4.00
❑ 226 David Thomas RC 2.00 5.00
❑ 227 Demetrius Williams RC 1.50 4.00
❑ 228 Derek Hagan RC 1.50 4.00
❑ 229 Devin Hester RC 4.00 10.00
❑ 230 Dominique Byrd RC 1.50 4.00
❑ 231 D'Qwell Jackson RC 1.50 4.00
❑ 232 Elvis Dumervil RC 2.00 5.00
❑ 233 Haloti Ngata RC 2.00 5.00

Card		
❑ 234 Hank Baskett RC	2.00	5.00
❑ 235 Jason Avant RC	2.00	5.00
❑ 236 Jerome Harrison RC	2.00	5.00
❑ 237 Jimmy Williams RC	2.00	5.00
❑ 238 Joe Klopfenstein RC	1.50	4.00
❑ 239 Joseph Addai RC	2.50	6.00
❑ 240 Kellen Clemens RC	2.00	5.00
❑ 241 Cory Rodgers RC	2.00	5.00
❑ 242 Leon Washington RC	2.50	6.00
❑ 243 Leonard Pope RC	2.00	5.00
❑ 244 Marcedes Lewis RC	2.00	5.00
❑ 245 Martin Nance RC	1.50	4.00
❑ 246 Mathias Kiwanuka RC	2.50	6.00
❑ 247 Maurice Drew RC	4.00	10.00
❑ 248 Maurice Stovall RC	1.50	4.00
❑ 249 Michael Huff RC	2.00	5.00
❑ 250 Mike Hass RC	2.00	5.00
❑ 251 Omar Jacobs RC	1.25	3.00
❑ 252 Orien Harris RC	1.50	4.00
❑ 253 Owen Daniels RC	2.00	5.00
❑ 254 Reggie McNeal RC	1.50	4.00
❑ 255 DeMeco Ryans RC	2.50	6.00
❑ 256 Tamba Hali RC	2.00	5.00
❑ 257 Ernie Sims RC	1.50	4.00
❑ 258 Thomas Howard RC	1.50	4.00
❑ 259 Todd Watkins RC	1.25	3.00
❑ 260 Travis Wilson RC	1.25	3.00
❑ 261 Greg Lee RC	1.25	3.00
❑ 262 Tye Hill RC	1.50	4.00
❑ 263 Vernon Davis RC	2.00	5.00

2007 Ultra

Card		
❑ COMP.SET w/o RCs (200)	15.00	40.00
❑ HOBBY PRODUCED WITH SILVER HOLOFOIL		
❑ 1 Bryant Johnson	.30	.75
❑ 2 Matt Leinart	.50	1.25
❑ 3 Edgerrin James	.40	1.00
❑ 4 Larry Fitzgerald	.50	1.25
❑ 5 Anquan Boldin	.40	1.00
❑ 6 Jerious Norwood	.40	1.00
❑ 7 Roddy White	.40	1.00
❑ 8 Keith Brooking	.30	.75
❑ 9 DeAngelo Hall	.40	1.00
❑ 10 Michael Vick	.50	1.25
❑ 11 Warrick Dunn	.40	1.00
❑ 12 Alge Crumpler	.40	1.00
❑ 13 Terrell Suggs	.30	.75
❑ 14 Derrick Mason	.30	.75
❑ 15 Todd Heap	.30	.75
❑ 16 Ray Lewis	.50	1.25
❑ 17 Steve McNair	.40	1.00
❑ 18 Willis McGahee	.40	1.00
❑ 19 Mark Clayton	.40	1.00
❑ 20 Aaron Schobel	.30	.75
❑ 21 Terrence McGee	.30	.75
❑ 22 J.P. Losman	.30	.75
❑ 23 Anthony Thomas	.30	.75
❑ 24 Lee Evans	.40	1.00
❑ 25 Keyshawn Johnson	.40	1.00
❑ 26 DeAngelo Williams	.50	1.25
❑ 27 Julius Peppers	.40	1.00
❑ 28 Jake Delhomme	.40	1.00
❑ 29 DeShaun Foster	.40	1.00
❑ 30 Steve Smith	.40	1.00
❑ 31 Mark Anderson	.40	1.00
❑ 32 Devin Hester	.50	1.25
❑ 33 Bernard Berrian	.30	.75
❑ 34 Muhsin Muhammad	.40	1.00
❑ 35 Rex Grossman	.40	1.00
❑ 36 Cedric Benson	.40	1.00
❑ 37 Brian Urlacher	.50	1.25
❑ 38 Reggie Kelly	.30	.75
❑ 39 Carson Palmer	.50	1.25
❑ 40 Rudi Johnson	.40	1.00
❑ 41 Chad Johnson	.40	1.00
❑ 42 T.J. Houshmandzadeh	.40	1.00
❑ 43 Jamal Lewis	.40	1.00
❑ 44 Charlie Frye	.40	1.00
❑ 45 Braylon Edwards	.40	1.00
❑ 46 Kellen Winslow	.40	1.00
❑ 47 DeMarcus Ware	.40	1.00
❑ 48 Roy Williams S	.40	1.00
❑ 49 Jason Witten	.50	1.25
❑ 50 Marion Barber	.50	1.25
❑ 51 Tony Romo	.75	2.00
❑ 52 Julius Jones	.40	1.00
❑ 53 Terrell Owens	.50	1.25
❑ 54 Terry Glenn	.40	1.00
❑ 55 Rod Smith	.40	1.00
❑ 56 Mike Bell	.40	1.00
❑ 57 Jason Elam	.30	.75
❑ 58 Jay Cutler	.50	1.25
❑ 59 Champ Bailey	.40	1.00
❑ 60 Javon Walker	.40	1.00
❑ 61 Tatum Bell	.30	.75
❑ 62 Jason Hanson	.30	.75
❑ 63 Jon Kitna	.30	.75
❑ 64 Kevin Jones	.30	.75
❑ 65 Roy Williams WR	.40	1.00
❑ 66 Mike Furrey	.40	1.00
❑ 67 Charles Woodson	.40	1.00
❑ 68 Aaron Kampman	.40	1.00
❑ 69 Bubba Franks	.30	.75
❑ 70 Brett Favre	1.00	2.50
❑ 71 Greg Jennings	.40	1.00
❑ 72 Donald Driver	.50	1.25
❑ 73 Ron Dayne	.40	1.00
❑ 74 DeMeco Ryans	.40	1.00
❑ 75 Jeb Putzier	.30	.75
❑ 76 Matt Schaub	.40	1.00
❑ 77 Ahman Green	.40	1.00
❑ 78 Andre Johnson	.40	1.00
❑ 79 Terrence Wilkins	.30	.75
❑ 80 Bob Sanders	.40	1.00
❑ 81 Dwight Freeney	.40	1.00
❑ 82 Dallas Clark	.30	.75
❑ 83 Adam Vinatieri	.40	1.00
❑ 84 Peyton Manning	.75	2.00
❑ 85 Joseph Addai	.50	1.25
❑ 86 Marvin Harrison	.50	1.25
❑ 87 Reggie Wayne	.40	1.00
❑ 88 Rashean Mathis	.30	.75
❑ 89 Matt Jones	.40	1.00
❑ 90 Fred Taylor	.40	1.00
❑ 91 Byron Leftwich	.40	1.00
❑ 92 David Garrard	.40	1.00
❑ 93 Reggie Williams	.40	1.00
❑ 94 Maurice Jones-Drew	.50	1.25
❑ 95 Damon Huard	.40	1.00
❑ 96 Dante Hall	.40	1.00
❑ 97 Eddie Kennison	.30	.75
❑ 98 Trent Green	.40	1.00
❑ 99 Larry Johnson	.40	1.00
❑ 100 Tony Gonzalez	.40	1.00
❑ 101 Jason Taylor	.30	.75
❑ 102 Randy McMichael	.30	.75
❑ 103 Zach Thomas	.40	1.00
❑ 104 Daunte Culpepper	.40	1.00
❑ 105 Ronnie Brown	.40	1.00
❑ 106 Chris Chambers	.40	1.00
❑ 107 Troy Williamson	.30	.75
❑ 108 Tony Richardson	.30	.75
❑ 109 Tarvaris Jackson	.40	1.00
❑ 110 Chester Taylor	.30	.75
❑ 111 Travis Taylor	.30	.75
❑ 112 Richard Seymour	.30	.75
❑ 113 Reche Caldwell	.30	.75
❑ 114 Tedy Bruschi	.50	1.25
❑ 115 Ben Watson	.30	.75
❑ 116 Tom Brady	1.00	2.50
❑ 117 Laurence Maroney	.50	1.25
❑ 118 Asante Samuel	.30	.75
❑ 119 Michael Lewis	.30	.75
❑ 120 Devery Henderson	.30	.75
❑ 121 Mike Karney	.30	.75
❑ 122 Will Smith	.30	.75
❑ 123 Drew Brees	.50	1.25
❑ 124 Deuce McAllister	.40	1.00
❑ 125 Reggie Bush	.60	1.50
❑ 126 Marques Colston	.50	1.25
❑ 127 Michael Strahan	.40	1.00
❑ 128 Reuben Droughns	.40	1.00
❑ 129 Jeremy Shockey	.40	1.00
❑ 130 Eli Manning	.50	1.25
❑ 131 Brandon Jacobs	.40	1.00
❑ 132 Plaxico Burress	.40	1.00
❑ 133 Jonathan Vilma	.40	1.00
❑ 134 Jerricho Cotchery	.30	.75
❑ 135 Thomas Jones	.40	1.00
❑ 136 Chad Pennington	.40	1.00
❑ 137 Leon Washington	.40	1.00
❑ 138 Laveranues Coles	.40	1.00
❑ 139 Dominic Rhodes	.40	1.00
❑ 140 Andrew Walter	.30	.75
❑ 141 Randy Moss	.50	1.25
❑ 142 Ronald Curry	.40	1.00
❑ 143 LaMont Jordan	.40	1.00
❑ 144 Justin Fargas	.30	.75
❑ 145 David Akers	.30	.75
❑ 146 Correll Buckhalter	.40	1.00
❑ 147 Brian Dawkins	.40	1.00
❑ 148 L.J. Smith	.30	.75
❑ 149 Donovan McNabb	.50	1.25
❑ 150 Brian Westbrook	.40	1.00
❑ 151 Reggie Brown	.30	.75
❑ 152 Cedrick Wilson	.30	.75
❑ 153 Aaron Smith	.30	.75
❑ 154 Troy Polamalu	.50	1.25
❑ 155 Ben Roethlisberger	.60	1.50
❑ 156 Willie Parker	.40	1.00
❑ 157 Hines Ward	.50	1.25
❑ 158 Santonio Holmes	.40	1.00
❑ 159 Eric Parker	.30	.75
❑ 160 Leslie O'Neal	.30	.75
❑ 161 Shawne Merriman	.40	1.00
❑ 162 Philip Rivers	.50	1.25
❑ 163 LaDainian Tomlinson	.60	1.50
❑ 164 Antonio Gates	.40	1.00
❑ 165 Walt Harris	.30	.75
❑ 166 Vernon Davis	.40	1.00
❑ 167 Alex Smith QB	.50	1.25
❑ 168 Frank Gore	.50	1.25
❑ 169 Arnaz Battle	.30	.75
❑ 170 Maurice Morris	.30	.75
❑ 171 Julian Peterson	.30	.75
❑ 172 D.J. Hackett	.30	.75
❑ 173 Lofa Tatupu	.40	1.00
❑ 174 Darrell Jackson	.40	1.00
❑ 175 Matt Hasselbeck	.40	1.00
❑ 176 Shaun Alexander	.40	1.00
❑ 177 Deion Branch	.40	1.00
❑ 178 Tye Hill	.30	.75
❑ 179 Isaac Bruce	.40	1.00
❑ 180 Marc Bulger	.40	1.00
❑ 181 Steven Jackson	.50	1.25
❑ 182 Torry Holt	.40	1.00
❑ 183 Drew Bennett	.30	.75
❑ 184 Jeff Garcia	.40	1.00
❑ 185 Michael Clayton	.40	1.00
❑ 186 Derrick Brooks	.40	1.00
❑ 187 Cadillac Williams	.40	1.00
❑ 188 Joey Galloway	.40	1.00
❑ 189 Ronde Barber	.30	.75
❑ 190 Chris Simms	.30	.75
❑ 191 Keith Bulluck	.30	.75
❑ 192 LenDale White	.40	1.00
❑ 193 David Givens	.30	.75
❑ 194 Vince Young	.50	1.25
❑ 195 Ladell Betts	.30	.75
❑ 196 Chris Cooley	.40	1.00
❑ 197 Antwaan Randle El	.30	.75
❑ 198 Jason Campbell	.40	1.00
❑ 199 Clinton Portis	.40	1.00
❑ 200 Santana Moss	.40	1.00
❑ 201 JaMarcus Russell L13 RC	5.00	12.00
❑ 202 Brady Quinn L13 RC	8.00	20.00
❑ 203 Calvin Johnson L13 RC	10.00	25.00
❑ 204 Joe Thomas L13 RC	4.00	10.00
❑ 205 Adrian Peterson L13 RC	30.00	80.00
❑ 206 Marshawn Lynch L13 RC	6.00	15.00
❑ 207 Ted Ginn Jr. L13 RC	6.00	15.00
❑ 208 Leon Hall L13 RC	4.00	10.00
❑ 209 Dwayne Bowe L13 RC	6.00	15.00
❑ 210 Steve Smith USC L13 RC	6.00	15.00
❑ 211 Robert Meachem L13 RC	4.00	10.00
❑ 212 LaRon Landry L13 RC	5.00	12.00
❑ 213 Dwayne Jarrett L13 RC	4.00	10.00
❑ 214 Darius Walker RC	2.00	5.00
❑ 215 Chris Leak RC	2.00	5.00
❑ 216 Darrelle Revis RC	3.00	8.00

❑ 217 Paul Posluszny RC	3.00	8.00
❑ 218 Daymeion Hughes RC	2.00	5.00
❑ 219 LaMarr Woodley RC	2.50	6.00
❑ 220 Garrett Wolfe RC	2.50	6.00
❑ 221 DeShawn Wynn RC	2.50	6.00
❑ 222 Alan Branch RC	2.00	5.00
❑ 223 Greg Olsen RC	3.00	8.00
❑ 224 Tyler Palko RC	2.00	5.00
❑ 225 Jordan Palmer RC	2.50	6.00
❑ 226 Drew Stanton RC	2.00	5.00
❑ 227 Jamaal Anderson RC	2.00	5.00
❑ 228 Eric Wright RC	2.50	6.00
❑ 229 Quentin Moses RC	2.00	5.00
❑ 230 Patrick Willis RC	4.00	10.00
❑ 231 Troy Smith RC	3.00	8.00
❑ 232 Amobi Okoye RC	2.50	6.00
❑ 233 Lawrence Timmons RC	2.50	6.00
❑ 234 H.B. Blades RC	2.00	5.00
❑ 235 Jared Zabransky RC	2.50	6.00
❑ 236 John Beck RC	2.50	6.00
❑ 237 Kevin Kolb RC	4.00	10.00
❑ 238 Matt Moore RC	3.00	8.00
❑ 239 Trent Edwards RC	4.00	10.00
❑ 240 Antonio Pittman RC	2.50	6.00
❑ 241 Brandon Jackson RC	2.50	6.00
❑ 242 Chris Henry RC	2.00	5.00
❑ 243 Dwayne Wright RC	2.00	5.00
❑ 244 Brian Leonard RC	2.00	5.00
❑ 245 Kenneth Darby RC	2.50	6.00
❑ 246 Kenny Irons RC	2.50	6.00
❑ 247 Kolby Smith RC	2.50	6.00
❑ 248 Lorenzo Booker RC	2.50	6.00
❑ 249 Drew Tate RC	2.00	5.00
❑ 250 Tanard Jackson RC	1.50	4.00
❑ 251 Michael Bush RC	2.50	6.00
❑ 252 Selvin Young RC	2.50	6.00
❑ 253 Tony Hunt RC	2.50	6.00
❑ 254 Tyrone Moss RC	1.50	4.00
❑ 255 Reggie Nelson RC	2.00	5.00
❑ 256 Zach Miller RC	2.50	6.00
❑ 257 Anthony Gonzalez RC	3.00	8.00
❑ 258 Adam Carriker RC	2.00	5.00
❑ 259 Sidney Rice RC	5.00	12.00
❑ 260 Aundrae Allison RC	2.00	5.00
❑ 261 Chansi Stuckey RC	2.50	6.00
❑ 262 Courtney Taylor RC	2.00	5.00
❑ 263 Craig Buster Davis RC	2.50	6.00
❑ 264 Dallas Baker RC	2.00	5.00
❑ 265 David Clowney RC	2.50	6.00
❑ 266 David Ball RC	1.50	4.00
❑ 267 Jason Hill RC	2.50	6.00
❑ 268 Johnnie Lee Higgins RC	2.50	6.00
❑ 269 Rhema McKnight RC	2.00	5.00
❑ 270 Gaines Adams RC	2.50	6.00
❑ 271 Mike Walker RC	2.50	6.00
❑ 272 Steve Breaston RC	2.50	6.00
❑ 273 Gary Russell RC	2.00	5.00
❑ 274 Marcus McCauley RC	2.00	5.00
❑ 275 Jarvis Moss RC	2.50	6.00
❑ 276 Syvelle Newton RC	2.00	5.00
❑ 277 DeMarcus Tank Tyler RC	2.00	5.00
❑ 278 Alvin Banks RC	2.00	5.00
❑ 279 Joel Filani RC	2.00	5.00
❑ 280 Chris Davis RC	2.00	5.00
❑ 281 Matt Trannon RC	2.00	5.00
❑ 282 Ryan Kalil RC	2.00	5.00
❑ 283 Lovi Brown RC	2.50	6.00
❑ 284 Anthony Spencer RC	2.50	6.00
❑ 285 Brandon Meriweather RC	2.50	6.00
❑ 286 Chris Houston RC	2.00	5.00
❑ 287 Michael Griffin RC	2.50	6.00
❑ 288 Jon Beason RC	2.50	6.00
❑ 289 Legedu Naanee RC	2.50	6.00
❑ 290 Eric Weddle RC	2.00	5.00
❑ 291 Isaiah Stanback RC	2.50	6.00
❑ 292 Aaron Ross RC	2.50	6.00
❑ 293 Sabby Piscitelli RC	2.50	6.00
❑ 294 Charles Johnson RC	1.50	4.00
❑ 295 Buster Davis RC	2.00	5.00
❑ 296 Justin Harrell RC	2.50	6.00
❑ 297 Stewart Bradley RC	2.50	6.00
❑ 298 A.J. Davis RC	1.50	4.00
❑ 299 David Irons RC	1.50	4.00
❑ 300 Scott Chandler RC	2.00	5.00

2007 Ultra Retail

❑ COMPLETE SET (300)	25.00	50.00

1991 Upper Deck

❑ COMPLETE SET (700)	6.00	15.00
❑ COMP.FACT.SET (700)	10.00	25.00
❑ COMP.SERIES 1 SET (500)	4.00	10.00
❑ COMP.SERIES 2 SET (200)	2.00	5.00
❑ COMP.FACT.SERIES 2 (200)	2.50	6.00
❑ 1 Dan McGwire CL	.01	.05
❑ 2 Eric Bieniemy RC	.01	.05
❑ 3 Mike Dumas RC	.01	.05
❑ 4 Mike Croel RC	.01	.05
❑ 5 Russell Maryland RC	.08	.25
❑ 6 Charles McRae RC	.01	.05
❑ 7 Dan McGwire RC	.01	.05
❑ 8 Mike Pritchard RC	.08	.25
❑ 9 Ricky Watters RC	.60	1.50
❑ 10 Chris Zorich RC	.08	.25
❑ 11 Browning Nagle RC	.01	.05
❑ 12 Wesley Carroll RC	.01	.05
❑ 13 Brett Favre RC	5.00	10.00
❑ 14 Rob Carpenter RC	.01	.05
❑ 15 Eric Swann RC	.08	.25
❑ 16 Stanley Richard RC	.01	.05
❑ 17 Herman Moore RC	.08	.25
❑ 18 Todd Marinovich RC	.01	.05
❑ 19 Aaron Craver RC	.01	.05
❑ 20 Chuck Webb RC	.01	.05
❑ 21 Todd Lyght RC	.01	.05
❑ 22 Greg Lewis RC	.01	.05
❑ 23 Eric Turner RC	.02	.10
❑ 24 Alvin Harper RC	.08	.25
❑ 25 Jarrod Bunch RC	.01	.05
❑ 26 Bruce Pickens RC	.01	.05
❑ 27 Harvey Williams RC	.08	.25
❑ 28 Randal Hill RC	.02	.10
❑ 29 Nick Bell RC	.01	.05
❑ 30 Jim Everett AT	.02	.10
❑ 31 R.Cunningham/Jackson AT	.01	.05
❑ 32 Steve DeBerg AT	.01	.05
❑ 33 Warren Moon/D.Hill AT	.02	.10
❑ 34 D.Marino/M.Clayton AT	.20	.50
❑ 35 J.Montana/J.Rice AT	.20	.50
❑ 36 Percy Snow	.01	.05
❑ 37 Kelvin Martin	.01	.05
❑ 38 Scott Case	.01	.05
❑ 39 John Gesek RC	.01	.05
❑ 40 Barry Word	.01	.05
❑ 41 Cornelius Bennett	.02	.10
❑ 42 Mike Kenn	.01	.05
❑ 43 Andre Reed	.02	.10
❑ 44 Bobby Hebert	.01	.05
❑ 45 William Perry	.02	.10
❑ 46 Dennis Byrd	.01	.05
❑ 47 Martin Mayhew	.01	.05
❑ 48 Issiac Holt	.01	.05
❑ 49 William White	.01	.05
❑ 50 JoJo Townsell	.01	.05
❑ 51 Jarvis Williams	.01	.05
❑ 52 Joey Browner	.01	.05
❑ 53 Pat Terrell	.01	.05
❑ 54 Joe Montana 3X UER	.50	1.25
❑ 55 Jeff Herrod	.01	.05
❑ 56 Cris Carter	.20	.50
❑ 57 Jerry Rice	.30	.75
❑ 58 Brett Perriman	.08	.25
❑ 59 Kevin Fagan	.01	.05
❑ 60 Wayne Haddix	.01	.05
❑ 61 Tommy Kane	.01	.05
❑ 62 Pat Beach	.01	.05
❑ 63 Jeff Lageman	.01	.05
❑ 64 Hassan Jones	.01	.05
❑ 65 Bennie Blades	.01	.05
❑ 66 Tim McGee	.01	.05
❑ 67 Robert Blackmon	.01	.05
❑ 68 Fred Stokes RC	.01	.05
❑ 69 Barney Bussey RC	.01	.05
❑ 70 Eric Metcalf	.02	.10
❑ 71 Mark Kelso	.01	.05
❑ 72 Neal Anderson TC	.01	.05
❑ 73 Boomer Esiason TC	.01	.05
❑ 74 Thurman Thomas TC	.08	.25
❑ 75 John Elway TC	.20	.50
❑ 76 Eric Metcalf TC	.02	.10
❑ 77 Vinny Testaverde TC	.02	.10
❑ 78 Johnny Johnson TC	.01	.05
❑ 79 Anthony Miller TC	.02	.10
❑ 80 Derrick Thomas TC	.02	.10
❑ 81 Jeff George TC	.02	.10
❑ 82 Troy Aikman TC	.15	.40
❑ 83 Dan Marino TC	.20	.50
❑ 84 Randall Cunningham TC	.02	.10
❑ 85 Deion Sanders TC	.01	.05
❑ 86 Jerry Rice TC	.15	.40
❑ 87 Lawrence Taylor TC	.02	.10
❑ 88 Al Toon TC	.01	.05
❑ 89 Barry Sanders TC	.20	.50
❑ 90 Warren Moon TC	.02	.10
❑ 91 Don Majkowski TC	.01	.05
❑ 92 Andre Tippett TC	.01	.05
❑ 93 Bo Jackson TC	.10	.30
❑ 94 Jim Everett TC	.02	.10
❑ 95 Art Monk TC	.02	.10
❑ 96 Morten Andersen TC	.01	.05
❑ 97 John L. Williams TC	.01	.05
❑ 98 Rod Woodson TC	.02	.10
❑ 99 Herschel Walker TC	.02	.10
❑ 100 Checklist 1-100	.01	.05
❑ 101 Steve Young	.30	.75
❑ 102 Jim Lachey	.01	.05
❑ 103 Tom Rathman	.01	.05
❑ 104 Earnest Byner	.01	.05
❑ 105 Karl Mecklenburg	.01	.05
❑ 106 Wes Hopkins	.01	.05
❑ 107 Michael Irvin	.08	.25
❑ 108 Burt Grossman	.01	.05
❑ 109 Jay Novacek UER	.08	.25
❑ 110 Ben Smith	.01	.05
❑ 111 Rod Woodson	.08	.25
❑ 112 Ernie Jones	.01	.05
❑ 113 Bryan Hinkle	.01	.05
❑ 114 Vai Sikahema	.01	.05
❑ 115 Bubby Brister	.01	.05
❑ 116 Brian Blades	.02	.10
❑ 117 Don Majkowski	.01	.05
❑ 118 Rod Bernstine	.01	.05
❑ 119 Brian Noble	.01	.05
❑ 120 Eugene Robinson	.01	.05
❑ 121 John Taylor	.02	.10
❑ 122 Vance Johnson	.01	.05
❑ 123 Art Monk	.02	.10
❑ 124 John Elway	.50	1.25
❑ 125 Dexter Carter	.01	.05
❑ 126 Anthony Miller	.02	.10
❑ 127 Keith Jackson	.02	.10
❑ 128 Albert Lewis	.01	.05
❑ 129 Billy Ray Smith	.01	.05
❑ 130 Clyde Simmons	.01	.05
❑ 131 Merril Hoge	.01	.05
❑ 132 Ricky Proehl	.01	.05
❑ 133 Tim McDonald	.01	.05
❑ 134 Louis Lipps	.01	.05
❑ 135 Ken Harvey	.02	.10
❑ 136 Sterling Sharpe	.02	.10
❑ 137 Gill Byrd	.01	.05
❑ 138 Tim Harris	.01	.05
❑ 139 Derrick Fenner	.01	.05

Card		
❑ 140 Johnny Holland	.01	.05
❑ 141 Ricky Sanders	.01	.05
❑ 142 Bobby Humphrey	.01	.05
❑ 143 Roger Craig	.02	.10
❑ 144 Steve Atwater	.01	.05
❑ 145 Ickey Woods	.01	.05
❑ 146 Randall Cunningham	.08	.25
❑ 147 Marion Butts	.02	.10
❑ 148 Reggie White	.08	.25
❑ 149 Ronnie Harmon	.01	.05
❑ 150 Mike Saxon	.01	.05
❑ 151 Greg Townsend	.01	.05
❑ 152 Troy Aikman	.30	.75
❑ 153 Shane Conlan	.01	.05
❑ 154 Deion Sanders	.15	.40
❑ 155 Bo Jackson	.10	.30
❑ 156 Jeff Hostetler	.02	.10
❑ 157 Albert Bentley	.01	.05
❑ 158 James Williams	.01	.05
❑ 159 Bill Brooks	.01	.05
❑ 160 Nick Lowery	.01	.05
❑ 161 Ottis Anderson	.02	.10
❑ 162 Kevin Greene	.02	.10
❑ 163 Neil Smith	.08	.25
❑ 164 Jim Everett	.02	.10
❑ 165 Derrick Thomas	.08	.25
❑ 166 John L. Williams	.01	.05
❑ 167 Timm Rosenbach	.01	.05
❑ 168 Leslie O'Neal	.02	.10
❑ 169 Clarence Verdin	.01	.05
❑ 170 Dave Krieg	.02	.10
❑ 171 Steve Broussard	.01	.05
❑ 172 Emmitt Smith	1.00	2.50
❑ 173 Andre Rison	.02	.10
❑ 174 Bruce Smith	.08	.25
❑ 175 Mark Clayton	.02	.10
❑ 176 Christian Okoye	.01	.05
❑ 177 Duane Bickett	.01	.05
❑ 178 Stephone Paige	.01	.05
❑ 179 Fredd Young	.01	.05
❑ 180 Mervyn Fernandez	.01	.05
❑ 181 Phil Simms	.02	.10
❑ 182 Pete Holohan	.01	.05
❑ 183 Pepper Johnson	.01	.05
❑ 184 Jackie Slater	.01	.05
❑ 185 Stephen Baker	.01	.05
❑ 186 Frank Cornish	.01	.05
❑ 187 Dave Waymer	.01	.05
❑ 188 Terance Mathis	.02	.10
❑ 189 Darryl Talley	.01	.05
❑ 190 James Hasty	.01	.05
❑ 191 Jay Schroeder	.01	.05
❑ 192 Kenneth Davis	.01	.05
❑ 193 Chris Miller	.02	.10
❑ 194 Scott Davis	.01	.05
❑ 195 Tim Green	.01	.05
❑ 196 Dan Saleaumua	.01	.05
❑ 197 Rohn Stark	.01	.05
❑ 198 John Alt	.01	.05
❑ 199 Steve Tasker	.02	.10
❑ 200 Checklist 101-200	.01	.05
❑ 201 Freddie Joe Nunn	.01	.05
❑ 202 Jim Breech	.01	.05
❑ 203 Roy Green	.01	.05
❑ 204 Gary Anderson RB	.01	.05
❑ 205 Rich Camarillo	.01	.05
❑ 206 Mark Bortz	.01	.05
❑ 207 Eddie Brown	.01	.05
❑ 208 Brad Muster	.01	.05
❑ 209 Anthony Munoz	.02	.10
❑ 210 Dalton Hilliard	.01	.05
❑ 211 Erik McMillan	.01	.05
❑ 212 Perry Kemp	.01	.05
❑ 213 Jim Thornton	.01	.05
❑ 214 Anthony Dilweg	.01	.05
❑ 215 Cleveland Gary	.01	.05
❑ 216 Leo Goeas	.01	.05
❑ 217 Mike Merriweather	.01	.05
❑ 218 Courtney Hall	.01	.05
❑ 219 Wade Wilson	.02	.10
❑ 220 Billy Joe Tolliver	.01	.05
❑ 221 Harold Green	.02	.10
❑ 222 Al(Bubba) Baker	.02	.10
❑ 223 Carl Zander	.01	.05
❑ 224 Thane Gash	.01	.05
❑ 225 Kevin Mack	.01	.05
❑ 226 Morten Andersen	.01	.05
❑ 227 Dennis Gentry	.01	.05
❑ 228 Vince Buck	.01	.05
❑ 229 Mike Singletary	.02	.10
❑ 230 Rueben Mayes	.01	.05
❑ 231 Mark Carrier WR	.08	.25
❑ 232 Tony Mandarich	.01	.05
❑ 233 Al Toon	.02	.10
❑ 234 Renaldo Turnbull	.01	.05
❑ 235 Broderick Thomas	.01	.05
❑ 236 Anthony Carter	.02	.10
❑ 237 Flipper Anderson	.01	.05
❑ 238 Jerry Robinson	.01	.05
❑ 239 Vince Newsome	.01	.05
❑ 240 Keith Millard	.01	.05
❑ 241 Reggie Langhorne	.01	.05
❑ 242 James Francis	.01	.05
❑ 243 Felix Wright	.01	.05
❑ 244 Neal Anderson	.02	.10
❑ 245 Boomer Esiason	.02	.10
❑ 246 Pat Swilling	.02	.10
❑ 247 Richard Dent	.02	.10
❑ 248 Craig Heyward	.02	.10
❑ 249 Ron Morris	.01	.05
❑ 250 Eric Martin	.01	.05
❑ 251 Jim C. Jensen	.01	.05
❑ 252 Anthony Toney	.01	.05
❑ 253 Sammie Smith	.01	.05
❑ 254 Calvin Williams	.02	.10
❑ 255 Dan Marino	.50	1.25
❑ 256 Warren Moon	.08	.25
❑ 257 Tommie Agee	.01	.05
❑ 258 Haywood Jeffires	.02	.10
❑ 259 Eugene Lockhart	.01	.05
❑ 260 Drew Hill	.01	.05
❑ 261 Vinny Testaverde	.02	.10
❑ 262 Jim Arnold	.01	.05
❑ 263 Steve Christie	.01	.05
❑ 264 Chris Spielman	.02	.10
❑ 265 Reggie Cobb	.01	.05
❑ 266 John Stephens	.01	.05
❑ 267 Jay Hilgenberg	.01	.05
❑ 268 Brent Williams	.01	.05
❑ 269 Rodney Hampton	.08	.25
❑ 270 Irving Fryar	.02	.10
❑ 271 Terry McDaniel	.01	.05
❑ 272 Reggie Roby	.01	.05
❑ 273 Allen Pinkett	.01	.05
❑ 274 Tim McKyer	.01	.05
❑ 275 Bob Golic	.01	.05
❑ 276 Wilber Marshall	.01	.05
❑ 277 Ray Childress	.01	.05
❑ 278 Charles Mann	.01	.05
❑ 279 Cris Dishman RC	.01	.05
❑ 280 Mark Rypien	.02	.10
❑ 281 Michael Cofer	.01	.05
❑ 282 Keith Byars	.01	.05
❑ 283 Mike Rozier	.01	.05
❑ 284 Seth Joyner	.02	.10
❑ 285 Jessie Tuggle	.01	.05
❑ 286 Mark Bavaro	.01	.05
❑ 287 Eddie Anderson	.01	.05
❑ 288 Sean Landeta	.01	.05
❑ 289 Howie Long/George Brett	.08	.25
❑ 290 Reyna Thompson	.01	.05
❑ 291 Ferrell Edmunds	.01	.05
❑ 292 Willie Gault	.02	.10
❑ 293 John Offerdahl	.01	.05
❑ 294 Tim Brown	.08	.25
❑ 295 Bruce Matthews	.02	.10
❑ 296 Kevin Ross	.01	.05
❑ 297 Lorenzo White	.01	.05
❑ 298 Dino Hackett	.01	.05
❑ 299 Curtis Duncan	.01	.05
❑ 300 Checklist 201-300	.01	.05
❑ 301 Andre Ware	.02	.10
❑ 302 David Little	.01	.05
❑ 303 Jerry Ball	.01	.05
❑ 304 Dwight Stone UER	.01	.05
❑ 305 Rodney Peete	.02	.10
❑ 306 Mike Baab	.01	.05
❑ 307 Tim Worley	.01	.05
❑ 308 Paul Farren	.01	.05
❑ 309 Carnell Lake	.01	.05
❑ 310 Clay Matthews	.02	.10
❑ 311 Alton Montgomery	.01	.05
❑ 312 Ernest Givins	.02	.10
❑ 313 Mike Horan	.01	.05
❑ 314 Sean Jones	.02	.10
❑ 315 Leonard Smith	.01	.05
❑ 316 Carl Banks	.01	.05
❑ 317 Jerome Brown	.01	.05
❑ 318 Everson Walls	.01	.05
❑ 319 Ron Heller	.01	.05
❑ 320 Mark Collins	.01	.05
❑ 321 Eddie Murray	.01	.05
❑ 322 Jim Harbaugh	.08	.25
❑ 323 Mel Gray	.02	.10
❑ 324 Keith Van Horne	.01	.05
❑ 325 Lomas Brown	.01	.05
❑ 326 Carl Lee	.01	.05
❑ 327 Ken O'Brien	.01	.05
❑ 328 Dermontti Dawson	.01	.05
❑ 329 Brad Baxter	.01	.05
❑ 330 Chris Doleman	.01	.05
❑ 331 Louis Oliver	.01	.05
❑ 332 Frank Stams	.01	.05
❑ 333 Mike Munchak	.02	.10
❑ 334 Fred Strickland	.01	.05
❑ 335 Mark Duper	.02	.10
❑ 336 Jacob Green	.01	.05
❑ 337 Tony Paige	.01	.05
❑ 338 Jeff Bryant	.01	.05
❑ 339 Lemuel Stinson	.01	.05
❑ 340 David Wyman	.01	.05
❑ 341 Lee Williams	.01	.05
❑ 342 Trace Armstrong	.01	.05
❑ 343 Junior Seau	.08	.25
❑ 344 John Roper	.01	.05
❑ 345 Jeff George	.08	.25
❑ 346 Herschel Walker	.02	.10
❑ 347 Sam Clancy	.01	.05
❑ 348 Steve Jordan	.01	.05
❑ 349 Nate Odomes	.01	.05
❑ 350 Martin Bayless	.01	.05
❑ 351 Brent Jones	.08	.25
❑ 352 Ray Agnew	.01	.05
❑ 353 Charles Haley	.02	.10
❑ 354 Andre Tippett	.01	.05
❑ 355 Ronnie Lott	.02	.10
❑ 356 Thurman Thomas	.08	.25
❑ 357 Fred Barnett	.08	.25
❑ 358 James Lofton	.02	.10
❑ 359 William Frizzell RC	.01	.05
❑ 360 Keith McKeller	.01	.05
❑ 361 Rodney Holman	.01	.05
❑ 362 Henry Ellard	.02	.10
❑ 363 David Fulcher	.01	.05
❑ 364 Jerry Gray	.01	.05
❑ 365 James Brooks	.02	.10
❑ 366 Tony Stargell	.01	.05
❑ 367 Keith McCants	.01	.05
❑ 368 Lewis Billups	.01	.05
❑ 369 Ervin Randle	.01	.05
❑ 370 Pat Leahy	.01	.05
❑ 371 Bruce Armstrong	.01	.05
❑ 372 Steve DeBerg	.01	.05
❑ 373 Guy McIntyre	.01	.05
❑ 374 Deron Cherry	.01	.05
❑ 375 Fred Marion	.01	.05
❑ 376 Michael Haddix	.01	.05
❑ 377 Kent Hull	.01	.05
❑ 378 Jerry Holmes	.01	.05
❑ 379 Jim Ritcher	.01	.05
❑ 380 Ed West	.01	.05
❑ 381 Richmond Webb	.01	.05
❑ 382 Mark Jackson	.01	.05
❑ 383 Tom Newberry	.01	.05
❑ 384 Ricky Nattiel	.01	.05
❑ 385 Keith Sims	.01	.05
❑ 386 Ron Hall	.01	.05
❑ 387 Ken Norton	.02	.10
❑ 388 Paul Gruber	.01	.05
❑ 389 Daniel Stubbs	.01	.05
❑ 390 Ian Beckles	.01	.05
❑ 391 Hoby Brenner	.01	.05
❑ 392 Tory Epps	.01	.05
❑ 393 Sam Mills	.01	.05
❑ 394 Chris Hinton	.01	.05
❑ 395 Steve Walsh	.01	.05
❑ 396 Simon Fletcher	.01	.05
❑ 397 Tony Bennett	.02	.10
❑ 398 Aundray Bruce	.01	.05
❑ 399 Mark Murphy	.01	.05
❑ 400 Checklist 301-400	.01	.05
❑ 401 Barry Sanders SL	.20	.50
❑ 402 Jerry Rice SL	.15	.40
❑ 403 Warren Moon SL	.02	.10

❑ 404 Derrick Thomas SL .02 .10
❑ 405 Nick Lowery LL .01 .05
❑ 406 Mark Carrier DB LL .02 .10
❑ 407 Michael Carter .01 .05
❑ 408 Chris Singleton .01 .05
❑ 409 Matt Millen .02 .10
❑ 410 Ronnie Lippett .01 .05
❑ 411 E.J. Junior .01 .05
❑ 412 Ray Donaldson .01 .05
❑ 413 Keith Willis .01 .05
❑ 414 Jessie Hester .01 .05
❑ 415 Jeff Cross .01 .05
❑ 416 Greg Jackson RC .01 .05
❑ 417 Alvin Walton .01 .05
❑ 418 Bart Oates .01 .05
❑ 419 Chip Lohmiller .01 .05
❑ 420 John Elliott .01 .05
❑ 421 Randall McDaniel .02 .10
❑ 422 Richard Johnson CB RC .01 .05
❑ 423 Al Noga .01 .05
❑ 424 Lamar Lathon .01 .05
❑ 425 Rick Fenney .01 .05
❑ 426 Jack Del Rio .02 .10
❑ 427 Don Mosebar .01 .05
❑ 428 Luis Sharpe .01 .05
❑ 429 Steve Wisniewski .01 .05
❑ 430 Jimmie Jones .01 .05
❑ 431 Freeman McNeil .01 .05
❑ 432 Ron Rivera .01 .05
❑ 433 Hart Lee Dykes .01 .05
❑ 434 Mark Carrier DB .02 .10
❑ 435 Rob Moore .08 .25
❑ 436 Gary Clark .08 .25
❑ 437 Heath Sherman .01 .05
❑ 438 Darrell Green .01 .05
❑ 439 Jessie Small .01 .05
❑ 440 Monte Coleman .01 .05
❑ 441 Leonard Marshall .01 .05
❑ 442 Richard Johnson .01 .05
❑ 443 Dave Meggett .02 .10
❑ 444 Barry Sanders .50 1.25
❑ 445 Lawrence Taylor .08 .25
❑ 446 Marcus Allen .08 .25
❑ 447 Johnny Johnson .01 .05
❑ 448 Aaron Wallace .01 .05
❑ 449 Anthony Thompson .01 .05
❑ 450 D.Marino/S.DeBerg CL .15 .40
❑ 451 Andre Rison TM .02 .10
❑ 452 Thurman Thomas TM .02 .10
❑ 453 Neal Anderson MVP .01 .05
❑ 454 Boomer Esiason MVP .01 .05
❑ 455 Eric Metcalf MVP .02 .10
❑ 456 Emmitt Smith TM .50 1.25
❑ 457 Bobby Humphrey MVP .01 .05
❑ 458 Barry Sanders TM .20 .50
❑ 459 Sterling Sharpe TM .02 .10
❑ 460 Warren Moon TM .02 .10
❑ 461 Albert Bentley MVP .01 .05
❑ 462 Steve DeBerg MVP .01 .05
❑ 463 Greg Townsend MVP .01 .05
❑ 464 Henry Ellard MVP .02 .10
❑ 465 Dan Marino TM .20 .50
❑ 466 Anthony Carter MVP .02 .10
❑ 467 John Stephens MVP .01 .05
❑ 468 Pat Swilling MVP .01 .05
❑ 469 Ottis Anderson MVP .02 .10
❑ 470 Dennis Byrd MVP .01 .05
❑ 471 Randall Cunningham TM .02 .10
❑ 472 Johnny Johnson TM .01 .05
❑ 473 Rod Woodson TM .02 .10
❑ 474 Anthony Miller MVP .02 .10
❑ 475 Jerry Rice TM .15 .40
❑ 476 John L.Williams MVP .01 .05
❑ 477 Wayne Haddix MVP .01 .05
❑ 478 Earnest Byner MVP .01 .05
❑ 479 Doug Widell .01 .05
❑ 480 Tommy Hodson .01 .05
❑ 481 Shawn Collins .01 .05
❑ 482 Rickey Jackson .01 .05
❑ 483 Tony Casillas .01 .05
❑ 484 Vaughan Johnson .01 .05
❑ 485 Floyd Dixon .01 .05
❑ 486 Eric Green .01 .05
❑ 487 Harry Hamilton .01 .05
❑ 488 Gary Anderson K .01 .05
❑ 489 Bruce Hill .01 .05
❑ 490 Gerald Williams .01 .05
❑ 491 Cortez Kennedy .08 .25
❑ 492 Chet Brooks .01 .05
❑ 493 Dwayne Harper RC .01 .05
❑ 494 Don Griffin .01 .05
❑ 495 Andy Heck .01 .05
❑ 496 David Treadwell .01 .05
❑ 497 Irv Pankey .01 .05
❑ 498 Dennis Smith .01 .05
❑ 499 Marcus Dupree .01 .05
❑ 500 Checklist 401-500 .01 .05
❑ 501 Wendell Davis .01 .05
❑ 502 Matt Bahr .01 .05
❑ 503 Rob Burnett RC .02 .10
❑ 504 Maurice Carthon .01 .05
❑ 505 Donnell Woolford .01 .05
❑ 506 Howard Ballard .01 .05
❑ 507 Mark Boyer .01 .05
❑ 508 Eugene Marve .01 .05
❑ 509 Joe Kelly .01 .05
❑ 510 Will Wolford .01 .05
❑ 511 Robert Clark .01 .05
❑ 512 Matt Brock RC .01 .05
❑ 513 Chris Warren .08 .25
❑ 514 Ken Willis .01 .05
❑ 515 George Jamison RC .01 .05
❑ 516 Rufus Porter .01 .05
❑ 517 Mark Higgs RC .01 .05
❑ 518 Thomas Everett .01 .05
❑ 519 Robert Brown .01 .05
❑ 520 Gene Atkins .01 .05
❑ 521 Hardy Nickerson .02 .10
❑ 522 Johnny Bailey .01 .05
❑ 523 William Frizzell .01 .05
❑ 524 Steve McMichael .02 .10
❑ 525 Kevin Porter .01 .05
❑ 526 Carwell Gardner .01 .05
❑ 527 Eugene Daniel .01 .05
❑ 528 Vestee Jackson .01 .05
❑ 529 Chris Goode .01 .05
❑ 530 Leon Seals .01 .05
❑ 531 Darion Conner .01 .05
❑ 532 Stan Brock .01 .05
❑ 533 Kirby Jackson RC .01 .05
❑ 534 Marv Cook .01 .05
❑ 535 Bill Fralic .01 .05
❑ 536 Keith Woodside .01 .05
❑ 537 Hugh Green .01 .05
❑ 538 Grant Feasel .01 .05
❑ 539 Bubba McDowell .01 .05
❑ 540 Vai Sikahema .01 .05
❑ 541 Aaron Cox .01 .05
❑ 542 Roger Craig .02 .10
❑ 543 Robb Thomas .01 .05
❑ 544 Ronnie Lott .02 .10
❑ 545 Robert Delpino .01 .05
❑ 546 Greg McMurtry .01 .05
❑ 547 Jim Morrissey RC .01 .05
❑ 548 Johnny Rembert .01 .05
❑ 549 Markus Paul RC .01 .05
❑ 550 Karl Wilson RC .01 .05
❑ 551 Gaston Green .01 .05
❑ 552 Willie Drewrey .01 .05
❑ 553 Michael Young .01 .05
❑ 554 Tom Tupa .01 .05
❑ 555 John Friesz .08 .25
❑ 556 Cody Carlson RC .01 .05
❑ 557 Eric Allen .01 .05
❑ 558 Thomas Benson .01 .05
❑ 559 Scott Mersereau RC .01 .05
❑ 560 Lionel Washington .01 .05
❑ 561 Brian Brennan .01 .05
❑ 562 Jim Jeffcoat .01 .05
❑ 563 Jeff Jaeger .01 .05
❑ 564 D.J. Johnson .01 .05
❑ 565 Danny Villa .01 .05
❑ 566 Don Beebe .01 .05
❑ 567 Michael Haynes .08 .25
❑ 568 Brett Faryniarz RC .01 .05
❑ 569 Mike Prior .01 .05
❑ 570 John Davis RC .01 .05
❑ 571 Vernon Turner RC .01 .05
❑ 572 Michael Brooks .01 .05
❑ 573 Mike Gann .01 .05
❑ 574 Ron Holmes .01 .05
❑ 575 Gary Plummer .01 .05
❑ 576 Bill Romanowski .01 .05
❑ 577 Chris Jacke .01 .05
❑ 578 Gary Reasons .01 .05
❑ 579 Tim Jorden RC .01 .05
❑ 580 Tim McKyer .01 .05
❑ 581 Johnnie Jackson RC .01 .05
❑ 582 Ethan Horton .01 .05
❑ 583 Pete Stoyanovich .01 .05
❑ 584 Jeff Query .01 .05
❑ 585 Frank Reich .02 .10
❑ 586 Riki Ellison .01 .05
❑ 587 Eric Hill .01 .05
❑ 588 Anthony Shelton RC .01 .05
❑ 589 Steve Smith .01 .05
❑ 590 Garth Jax RC .01 .05
❑ 591 Greg Davis RC .01 .05
❑ 592 Bill Maas .01 .05
❑ 593 Henry Rolling RC .01 .05
❑ 594 Keith Jones .01 .05
❑ 595 Tootie Robbins .01 .05
❑ 596 Brian Jordan .02 .10
❑ 597 Derrick Walker RC .01 .05
❑ 598 Jonathan Hayes .01 .05
❑ 599 Nate Lewis RC .01 .05
❑ 600 Checklist 501-600 .01 .05
❑ 601 Croel/Lewis/Tray/Walk CL .01 .05
❑ 602 James Jones RC .01 .05
❑ 603 Tim Barnett RC .01 .05
❑ 604 Ed King RC .01 .05
❑ 605 Shane Curry RF .01 .05
❑ 606 Mike Croel .01 .05
❑ 607 Bryan Cox RC .08 .25
❑ 608 Shawn Jefferson RC .02 .10
❑ 609 Kenny Walker RC .01 .05
❑ 610 Michael Jackson WR RC .08 .25
❑ 611 Jon Vaughn RC .01 .05
❑ 612 Greg Lewis .01 .05
❑ 613 Joe Valerio RF .01 .05
❑ 614 Pat Harlow RC .01 .05
❑ 615 Henry Jones RC .02 .10
❑ 616 Jeff Graham RC .08 .25
❑ 617 Darryll Lewis RC .02 .10
❑ 618 Keith Traylor RC .01 .05
❑ 619 Scott Miller RF .01 .05
❑ 620 Nick Bell .01 .05
❑ 621 John Flannery RC .01 .05
❑ 622 Leonard Russell RC .02 .10
❑ 623 Alfred Williams RC .01 .05
❑ 624 Browning Nagle .01 .05
❑ 625 Harvey Williams .02 .10
❑ 626 Dan McGwire .01 .05
❑ 627 Favre/Pritchard/Pegram CL .20 .50
❑ 628 William Thomas RC .01 .05
❑ 629 Lawrence Dawsey RC .02 .10
❑ 630 Aeneas Williams RC .08 .25
❑ 631 Stan Thomas RF .01 .05
❑ 632 Randal Hill .01 .05
❑ 633 Moe Gardner RC .01 .05
❑ 634 Alvin Harper .02 .10
❑ 635 Esera Tuaolo RC .01 .05
❑ 636 Russell Maryland .02 .10
❑ 637 Anthony Morgan RC .01 .05
❑ 638 Erric Pegram RC .08 .25
❑ 639 Herman Moore .08 .25
❑ 640 Ricky Ervins RC .02 .10
❑ 641 Kelvin Pritchett RC .02 .10
❑ 642 Roman Phifer RC .01 .05
❑ 643 Antone Davis RC .01 .05
❑ 644 Mike Pritchard .02 .10
❑ 645 Vinnie Clark RC .01 .05
❑ 646 Jake Reed RC .20 .50
❑ 647 Brett Favre 1.50 4.00
❑ 648 Todd Lyght .01 .05
❑ 649 Bruce Pickens .01 .05
❑ 650 Darren Lewis RC .01 .05
❑ 651 Wesley Carroll .01 .05
❑ 652 James Joseph RC .02 .10
❑ 653 Robert Delpino AR .01 .05
❑ 654 Deion Sanders/V.Glenn AR .01 .05
❑ 655 J.Rice/T.McDaniels AR .10 .30
❑ 656 B.Sanders/D.Thomas AR .20 .50
❑ 657 Ken Tippins AR .01 .05
❑ 658 Christian Okoye AR .01 .05
❑ 659 Rich Gannon .08 .25
❑ 660 Johnny Meads .01 .05
❑ 661 J.J.Birden RC .02 .10
❑ 662 Bruce Kozerski .01 .05
❑ 663 Felix Wright .01 .05
❑ 664 Al Smith .01 .05
❑ 665 Stan Humphries .08 .25
❑ 666 Alfred Anderson .01 .05
❑ 667 Nate Newton .02 .10

Card		
668 Vince Workman RC	.02	.10
669 Ricky Reynolds	.01	.05
670 Bryce Paup RC	.08	.25
671 Gill Fenerty	.01	.05
672 Darrell Thompson	.01	.05
673 Anthony Smith	.01	.05
674 Darryl Henley RC	.01	.05
675 Brett Maxie	.01	.05
676 Craig Taylor RC	.01	.05
677 Steve Wallace	.02	.10
678 Jeff Feagles RC	.01	.05
679 James Washington RC	.01	.05
680 Tim Harris	.01	.05
681 Dennis Gibson	.01	.05
682 Toi Cook RC	.01	.05
683 Lorenzo Lynch	.01	.05
684 Brad Edwards RC	.01	.05
685 Ray Crockett RC	.01	.05
686 Harris Barton	.01	.05
687 Byron Evans	.01	.05
688 Eric Thomas	.01	.05
689 Jeff Criswell	.01	.05
690 Eric Ball	.01	.05
691 Brian Mitchell	.02	.10
692 Quinn Early	.02	.10
693 Aaron Jones	.01	.05
694 Jim Dombrowski	.01	.05
695 Jeff Bostic	.01	.05
696 Tony Casillas	.01	.05
697 Ken Lanier	.01	.05
698 Henry Thomas	.01	.05
699 Steve Beuerlein	.02	.10
700 Checklist 601-700	.01	.05
1P Joe Montana Promo	1.00	2.50
500P Barry Sanders Promo	.75	2.00
SP1 Darrell Green Fastest	.20	.50
SP2 Don Shula 300th Win	.75	2.00

1992 Upper Deck

Card		
COMPLETE SET (620)	6.00	15.00
COMP.SERIES 1 (400)	4.00	10.00
COMP.SERIES 2 (220)	2.50	5.00
1 Bennett/Buckley/McNabb C	.02	.10
2 Edgar Bennett RC	.08	.25
3 Eddie Blake RC	.01	.05
4 Brian Bollinger RC	.01	.05
5 Joe Bowden RC	.01	.05
6 Terrell Buckley RC	.01	.05
7 Willie Clay RC	.01	.05
8 Ed Cunningham RC	.01	.05
9 Matt Darby RC	.01	.05
10 Will Furrer RC	.01	.05
11 Chris Hakel RC	.01	.05
12 Carlos Huerta	.01	.05
13 Amp Lee RC	.01	.05
14 Ricardo McDonald RC	.01	.05
15 Dexter McNabb RC	.01	.05
16 Chris Mims RC	.01	.05
17 Derrick Moore RC	.02	.10
18 Mark D'Onofrio RC	.01	.05
19 Patrick Rowe RC	.01	.05
20 Leon Searcy RC	.01	.05
21 Torrance Small RC	.02	.10
22 Jimmy Smith RC	1.25	3.00
23 Tony Smith WR RC	.01	.05
24 Siran Stacy RC	.01	.05
25 Kevin Turner RC	.01	.05
26 Tommy Vardell RC	.01	.05
27 Bob Whitfield RC	.01	.05
28 Darryl Williams RC	.01	.05
29 Jeff Sydner RC	.01	.05
30 Mike Croel/L.Russell CL	.01	.05
31 Todd Marinovich ART	.01	.05
32 Leonard Russell ART	.01	.05
33 Nick Bell ART	.01	.05
34 Alvin Harper ART	.01	.05
35 Mike Pritchard ART	.01	.05
36 Lawrence Dawsey AR	.01	.05
37 Tim Barnett AR	.01	.05
38 John Flannery AR	.01	.05
39 Stan Thomas AR	.01	.05
40 Ed King AR	.01	.05
41 Charles McRae AR	.01	.05
42 Eric Moten AR	.01	.05
43 Moe Gardner AR	.01	.05
44 Kenny Walker AR	.01	.05
45 Esera Tuaolo AR	.01	.05
46 Alfred Williams AR	.01	.05
47 Bryan Cox AR	.01	.05
48 Mo Lewis AR	.01	.05
49 Mike Croel ART	.01	.05
50 Stanley Richard AR	.01	.05
51 Tony Covington AR	.01	.05
52 Larry Brown DB AR	.01	.05
53 Aeneas Williams AR	.01	.05
54 John Kasay AR	.01	.05
55 Jon Vaughn ART	.01	.05
56 David Fulcher	.01	.05
57 Barry Foster	.02	.10
58 Terry Wooden	.01	.05
59 Gary Anderson K	.01	.05
60 Alfred Williams	.01	.05
61 Robert Blackmon	.01	.05
62 Brian Noble	.01	.05
63 Terry Allen	.08	.25
64 Darrell Green	.01	.05
65 Darren Comeaux	.01	.05
66 Rob Burnett	.01	.05
67 Jarrod Bunch	.01	.05
68 Michael Jackson	.02	.10
69 Greg Lloyd	.02	.10
70 Richard Brown RC	.01	.05
71 Harold Green	.01	.05
72 William Fuller	.01	.05
73 Mark Carrier DB TC	.01	.05
74 David Fulcher TC	.01	.05
75 Cornelius Bennett TC	.01	.05
76 Steve Atwater TC	.01	.05
77 Kevin Mack TC	.01	.05
78 Mark Carrier WR TC	.01	.05
79 Tim McDonald TC	.01	.05
80 Marion Butts TC	.01	.05
81 Christian Okoye TC	.01	.05
82 Jeff Herrod TC	.01	.05
83 Emmitt Smith TC	.25	.60
84 Mark Duper TC	.01	.05
85 Keith Jackson TC	.01	.05
86 Andre Rison TC	.02	.10
87 John Taylor TC	.01	.05
88 Rodney Hampton TC	.02	.10
89 Rob Moore TC	.01	.05
90 Chris Spielman TC	.01	.05
91 Haywood Jeffires TC	.01	.05
92 Sterling Sharpe TC	.02	.10
93 Irving Fryar TC	.01	.05
94 Marcus Allen TC	.02	.10
95 Henry Ellard TC	.01	.05
96 Mark Rypien TC	.01	.05
97 Pat Swilling TC	.01	.05
98 Brian Blades TC	.01	.05
99 Eric Green TC	.01	.05
100 Anthony Carter TC	.01	.05
101 Burt Grossman	.01	.05
102 Gary Anderson RB	.01	.05
103 Neil Smith	.08	.25
104 Jeff Feagles	.01	.05
105 Shane Conlan	.01	.05
106 Jay Novacek	.02	.10
107 Bill Brooks	.01	.05
108 Mark Ingram	.01	.05
109 Anthony Munoz	.02	.10
110 Wendell Davis	.01	.05
111 Jim Everett	.02	.10
112 Bruce Matthews	.01	.05
113 Mark Higgs	.01	.05
114 Chris Warren	.02	.10
115 Brad Baxter	.01	.05
116 Greg Townsend	.01	.05
117 Al Smith	.01	.05
118 Jeff Cross	.01	.05
119 Terry McDaniel	.01	.05
120 Ernest Givins	.02	.10
121 Fred Barnett	.02	.10
122 Flipper Anderson	.01	.05
123 Floyd Turner	.01	.05
124 Stephen Baker	.01	.05
125 Tim Johnson	.01	.05
126 Brent Jones	.02	.10
127 Leonard Marshall	.01	.05
128 Jim Price	.01	.05
129 Jessie Hester	.01	.05
130 Mark Carrier WR	.02	.10
131 Bubba McDowell	.01	.05
132 Andre Tippett	.01	.05
133 James Hasty	.01	.05
134 Mel Gray	.02	.10
135 Christian Okoye	.01	.05
136 Earnest Byner	.01	.05
137 Ferrell Edmunds	.01	.05
138 Henry Ellard	.02	.10
139 Rob Moore	.02	.10
140 Brian Jordan	.02	.10
141 Clarence Verdin	.01	.05
142 Cornelius Bennett	.02	.10
143 John Taylor	.02	.10
144 Derrick Thomas	.08	.25
145 Thurman Thomas	.08	.25
146 Warren Moon	.08	.25
147 Vinny Testaverde	.02	.10
148 Steve Bono RC	.08	.25
149 Robb Thomas	.01	.05
150 John Friesz	.02	.10
151 Richard Dent	.02	.10
152 Eddie Anderson	.01	.05
153 Kevin Greene	.02	.10
154 Marion Butts	.01	.05
155 Barry Sanders	.50	1.25
156 Andre Rison	.02	.10
157 Ronnie Lott	.02	.10
158 Eric Allen	.01	.05
159 Mark Clayton	.02	.10
160 Terance Mathis	.02	.10
161 Darryl Talley	.01	.05
162 Eric Metcalf	.02	.10
163 Reggie Cobb	.01	.05
164 Ernie Jones	.01	.05
165 David Griggs	.01	.05
166 Tom Rathman	.01	.05
167 Bubby Brister	.02	.10
168 Broderick Thomas	.01	.05
169 Chris Doleman	.01	.05
170 Charles Haley	.02	.10
171 Michael Haynes	.02	.10
172 Rodney Hampton	.02	.10
173 Nick Bell	.01	.05
174 Gene Atkins	.01	.05
175 Mike Merriweather	.01	.05
176 Reggie Roby	.01	.05
177 Bennie Blades	.01	.05
178 John L. Williams	.01	.05
179 Rodney Peete	.02	.10
180 Greg Montgomery	.01	.05
181 Vince Newsome	.01	.05
182 Andre Collins	.01	.05
183 Erik Kramer	.02	.10
184 Bryan Hinkle	.01	.05
185 Reggie White	.08	.25
186 Bruce Armstrong	.01	.05
187 Anthony Carter	.02	.10
188 Pat Swilling	.01	.05
189 Robert Delpino	.01	.05
190 Brent Williams	.01	.05
191 Johnny Johnson	.01	.05
192 Aaron Craver	.01	.05
193 Vincent Brown	.01	.05
194 Herschel Walker	.02	.10
195 Tim McDonald	.01	.05
196 Gaston Green	.01	.05
197 Brian Blades	.02	.10
198 Rod Bernstine	.01	.05
199 Brett Perriman	.02	.10
200 John Elway	.50	1.25
201 Michael Carter	.01	.05
202 Mark Carrier DB	.01	.05
203 Cris Carter	.20	.50
204 Kyle Clifton	.01	.05
205 Alvin Wright	.01	.05
206 Andre Ware	.01	.05
207 Dave Waymer	.01	.05
208 Darren Lewis	.01	.05

Card		
❑ 209 Joey Browner	.01	.05
❑ 210 Rich Miano	.01	.05
❑ 211 Marcus Allen	.08	.25
❑ 212 Steve Broussard	.01	.05
❑ 213 Joel Hilgenberg	.01	.05
❑ 214 Bo Orlando RC	.01	.05
❑ 215 Clay Matthews	.02	.10
❑ 216 Chris Hinton	.01	.05
❑ 217 Al Edwards	.01	.05
❑ 218 Tim Brown	.08	.25
❑ 219 Sam Mills	.01	.05
❑ 220 Don Majkowski	.01	.05
❑ 221 James Francis	.01	.05
❑ 222 Steve Hendrickson RC	.01	.05
❑ 223 James Thornton	.01	.05
❑ 224 Byron Evans	.01	.05
❑ 225 Pepper Johnson	.01	.05
❑ 226 Darryl Henley	.01	.05
❑ 227 Simon Fletcher	.01	.05
❑ 228 Hugh Millen	.01	.05
❑ 229 Tim McGee	.01	.05
❑ 230 Richmond Webb	.01	.05
❑ 231 Tony Bennett	.01	.05
❑ 232 Nate Odomes	.01	.05
❑ 233 Scott Case	.01	.05
❑ 234 Dalton Hilliard	.01	.05
❑ 235 Paul Gruber	.01	.05
❑ 236 Jeff Lageman	.01	.05
❑ 237 Tony Mandarich	.01	.05
❑ 238 Cris Dishman	.01	.05
❑ 239 Steve Walsh	.01	.05
❑ 240 Moe Gardner	.01	.05
❑ 241 Bill Romanowski	.01	.05
❑ 242 Chris Zorich	.02	.10
❑ 243 Stephone Paige	.01	.05
❑ 244 Mike Croel	.01	.05
❑ 245 Leonard Russell	.02	.10
❑ 246 Mark Rypien	.01	.05
❑ 247 Aeneas Williams	.02	.10
❑ 248 Steve Atwater	.01	.05
❑ 249 Michael Stewart	.01	.05
❑ 250 Pierce Holt	.01	.05
❑ 251 Kevin Mack	.01	.05
❑ 252 Sterling Sharpe	.08	.25
❑ 253 Lawrence Dawsey	.02	.10
❑ 254 Emmitt Smith	.60	1.50
❑ 255 Todd Marinovich	.01	.05
❑ 256 Neal Anderson	.01	.05
❑ 257 Mo Lewis	.01	.05
❑ 258 Vance Johnson	.01	.05
❑ 259 Rickey Jackson	.01	.05
❑ 260 Esera Tuaolo	.01	.05
❑ 261 Wilber Marshall	.01	.05
❑ 262 Keith Henderson	.01	.05
❑ 263 William Thomas	.01	.05
❑ 264 Rickey Dixon	.01	.05
❑ 265 Dave Meggett	.02	.10
❑ 266 Gerald Riggs	.01	.05
❑ 267 Tim Harris	.01	.05
❑ 268 Ken Harvey	.01	.05
❑ 269 Clyde Simmons	.01	.05
❑ 270 Irving Fryar	.02	.10
❑ 271 Darion Conner	.01	.05
❑ 272 Vince Workman	.01	.05
❑ 273 Jim Harbaugh	.08	.25
❑ 274 Lorenzo White	.01	.05
❑ 275 Bobby Hebert	.01	.05
❑ 276 Duane Bickett	.01	.05
❑ 277 Jeff Bryant	.01	.05
❑ 278 Scott Stephen	.01	.05
❑ 279 Bob Golic	.01	.05
❑ 280 Steve McMichael	.02	.10
❑ 281 Jeff Graham	.08	.25
❑ 282 Keith Jackson	.02	.10
❑ 283 Howard Ballard	.01	.05
❑ 284 Michael Brooks	.01	.05
❑ 285 Freeman McNeil	.02	.10
❑ 286 Rodney Holman	.01	.05
❑ 287 Eric Bieniemy	.01	.05
❑ 288 Seth Joyner	.01	.05
❑ 289 Carwell Gardner	.01	.05
❑ 290 Brian Mitchell	.02	.10
❑ 291 Chris Miller	.02	.10
❑ 292 Ray Berry	.01	.05
❑ 293 Matt Brock	.01	.05
❑ 294 Eric Thomas	.01	.05
❑ 295 John Kasay	.01	.05
❑ 296 Jay Hilgenberg	.01	.05
❑ 297 Darrell Thompson	.01	.05
❑ 298 Rich Gannon	.08	.25
❑ 299 Steve Young	.25	.60
❑ 300 Mike Kenn	.01	.05
❑ 301 Emmitt Smith SL	.25	.60
❑ 302 Haywood Jeffires SL	.01	.05
❑ 303 Michael Irvin SL	.08	.25
❑ 304 Warren Moon SL	.02	.10
❑ 305 Chip Lohmiller SL	.01	.05
❑ 306 Barry Sanders SL	.20	.50
❑ 307 Ronnie Lott SL	.02	.10
❑ 308 Pat Swilling SL	.01	.05
❑ 309 Thurman Thomas SL	.02	.10
❑ 310 Reggie Roby SL	.01	.05
❑ 311 Moon/Irvin/T.Thomas CL	.02	.10
❑ 312 Jacob Green	.01	.05
❑ 313 Stephen Braggs	.01	.05
❑ 314 Haywood Jeffires	.02	.10
❑ 315 Freddie Joe Nunn	.01	.05
❑ 316 Gary Clark	.02	.10
❑ 317 Tim Barnett	.01	.05
❑ 318 Mark Duper	.01	.05
❑ 319 Eric Green	.01	.05
❑ 320 Robert Wilson	.01	.05
❑ 321 Michael Ball	.01	.05
❑ 322 Eric Martin	.01	.05
❑ 323 Alexander Wright	.01	.05
❑ 324 Jessie Tuggle	.01	.05
❑ 325 Ronnie Harmon	.01	.05
❑ 326 Jeff Hostetler	.02	.10
❑ 327 Eugene Daniel	.01	.05
❑ 328 Ken Norton Jr.	.02	.10
❑ 329 Reyna Thompson	.01	.05
❑ 330 Jerry Ball	.01	.05
❑ 331 Leroy Hoard	.02	.10
❑ 332 Chris Martin	.01	.05
❑ 333 Keith McKeller	.01	.05
❑ 334 Brian Washington	.01	.05
❑ 335 Eugene Robinson	.01	.05
❑ 336 Maurice Hurst	.01	.05
❑ 337 Dan Saleaumua	.01	.05
❑ 338 Neil O'Donnell	.02	.10
❑ 339 Dexter Davis	.01	.05
❑ 340 Keith McCants	.01	.05
❑ 341 Steve Beuerlein	.02	.10
❑ 342 Roman Phifer	.01	.05
❑ 343 Bryan Cox	.02	.10
❑ 344 Art Monk	.02	.10
❑ 345 Michael Irvin	.08	.25
❑ 346 Vaughan Johnson	.01	.05
❑ 347 Jeff Herrod	.01	.05
❑ 348 Stanley Richard	.01	.05
❑ 349 Michael Young	.01	.05
❑ 350 Rod.Hampton/R.Cobb CL	.02	.10
❑ 351 Jim Harbaugh MVP	.02	.10
❑ 352 David Fulcher MVP	.01	.05
❑ 353 Thurman Thomas MVP	.02	.10
❑ 354 Gaston Green MVP	.01	.05
❑ 355 Leroy Hoard MVP	.01	.05
❑ 356 Reggie Cobb MVP	.01	.05
❑ 357 Tim McDonald MVP	.01	.05
❑ 358 Ronnie Harmon MVP UER	.01	.05
❑ 359 Derrick Thomas MVP	.02	.10
❑ 360 Jeff Herrod MVP	.01	.05
❑ 361 Michael Irvin MVP	.08	.25
❑ 362 Mark Higgs MVP	.01	.05
❑ 363 Reggie White MVP	.02	.10
❑ 364 Chris Miller MVP	.01	.05
❑ 365 Steve Young MVP	.10	.30
❑ 366 Rodney Hampton MVP	.02	.10
❑ 367 Jeff Lageman MVP	.01	.05
❑ 368 Barry Sanders MVP	.20	.50
❑ 369 Haywood Jeffires MVP	.01	.05
❑ 370 Tony Bennett MVP	.01	.05
❑ 371 Leonard Russell MVP	.01	.05
❑ 372 Jeff Jaeger MVP	.01	.05
❑ 373 Robert Delpino MVP	.01	.05
❑ 374 Mark Rypien MVP	.01	.05
❑ 375 Pat Swilling MVP	.01	.05
❑ 376 Cortez Kennedy MVP	.02	.10
❑ 377 Eric Green MVP	.01	.05
❑ 378 Cris Carter MVP	.02	.10
❑ 379 John Roper	.01	.05
❑ 380 Barry Word	.01	.05
❑ 381 Shawn Jefferson	.01	.05
❑ 382 Tony Casillas	.01	.05
❑ 383 John Baylor RC	.01	.05
❑ 384 Al Noga	.01	.05
❑ 385 Charles Mann	.01	.05
❑ 386 Gill Byrd	.01	.05
❑ 387 Chris Singleton	.01	.05
❑ 388 James Joseph	.01	.05
❑ 389 Larry Brown DB	.01	.05
❑ 390 Chris Spielman	.02	.10
❑ 391 Anthony Thompson	.01	.05
❑ 392 Karl Mecklenburg	.01	.05
❑ 393 Joe Kelly	.01	.05
❑ 394 Kanavis McGhee	.01	.05
❑ 395 Bill Maas	.01	.05
❑ 396 Marv Cook	.01	.05
❑ 397 Louis Lipps	.01	.05
❑ 398 Marty Carter RC	.01	.05
❑ 399 Louis Oliver	.01	.05
❑ 400 Eric Swann	.02	.10
❑ 401 Troy Auzenne RC	.01	.05
❑ 402 Kurt Barber	.01	.05
❑ 403 Marc Boutte RC	.01	.05
❑ 404 Dale Carter	.02	.10
❑ 405 Marco Coleman	.01	.05
❑ 406 Quentin Coryatt	.01	.05
❑ 407 Shane Dronett RC	.01	.05
❑ 408 Vaughn Dunbar	.01	.05
❑ 409 Steve Emtman	.01	.05
❑ 410 Dana Hall RC	.01	.05
❑ 411 Jason Hanson RC	.02	.10
❑ 412 Courtney Hawkins RC	.02	.10
❑ 413 Terrell Buckley	.01	.05
❑ 414 Robert Jones RC	.01	.05
❑ 415 David Klingler	.01	.05
❑ 416 Tommy Maddox	.60	1.50
❑ 417 Johnny Mitchell RC	.01	.05
❑ 418 Carl Pickens	.02	.10
❑ 419 Tracy Scroggins	.01	.05
❑ 420 Tony Sacca RC	.01	.05
❑ 421 Kevin Smith DB	.01	.05
❑ 422 Alonzo Spellman	.02	.10
❑ 423 Troy Vincent RC	.01	.05
❑ 424 Sean Gilbert RC	.02	.10
❑ 425 Larry Webster RC	.01	.05
❑ 426 Carl Pickens/Klingler CL	.02	.10
❑ 427 Bill Fralic	.01	.05
❑ 428 Kevin Murphy	.01	.05
❑ 429 Lemuel Stinson	.01	.05
❑ 430 Harris Barton	.01	.05
❑ 431 Dino Hackett	.01	.05
❑ 432 John Stephens	.01	.05
❑ 433 Keith Jennings RC	.01	.05
❑ 434 Derrick Fenner	.01	.05
❑ 435 Kenneth Gant RC	.01	.05
❑ 436 Willie Gault	.02	.10
❑ 437 Steve Jordan	.01	.05
❑ 438 Charles Haley	.02	.10
❑ 439 Keith Kartz	.01	.05
❑ 440 Nate Lewis	.01	.05
❑ 441 Doug Widell	.01	.05
❑ 442 William White	.01	.05
❑ 443 Eric Hill	.01	.05
❑ 444 Melvin Jenkins	.01	.05
❑ 445 David Wyman	.01	.05
❑ 446 Ed West	.01	.05
❑ 447 Brad Muster	.01	.05
❑ 448 Ray Childress	.01	.05
❑ 449 Kevin Ross	.01	.05
❑ 450 Johnnie Jackson S	.01	.05
❑ 451 Tracy Simien RC	.01	.05
❑ 452 Don Mosebar	.01	.05
❑ 453 Jay Hilgenberg	.01	.05
❑ 454 Wes Hopkins	.01	.05
❑ 455 Jay Schroeder	.01	.05
❑ 456 Jeff Bostic	.01	.05
❑ 457 Bryce Paup	.08	.25
❑ 458 Dave Waymer	.01	.05
❑ 459 Toi Cook	.01	.05
❑ 460 Anthony Smith	.01	.05
❑ 461 Don Griffin	.01	.05
❑ 462 Bill Hawkins	.01	.05
❑ 463 Courtney Hall	.01	.05
❑ 464 Jeff Uhlenhake	.01	.05
❑ 465 Mike Sherrard	.01	.05
❑ 466 James Jones DT	.01	.05
❑ 467 Jerrol Williams	.01	.05
❑ 468 Eric Ball	.01	.05
❑ 469 Randall McDaniel	.02	.10
❑ 470 Alvin Harper	.02	.10
❑ 471 Tom Waddle	.01	.05
❑ 472 Tony Woods	.01	.05

Card		
❑ 473 Kelvin Martin	.01	.05
❑ 474 Jon Vaughn	.01	.05
❑ 475 Gill Fenerty	.01	.05
❑ 476 Aundray Bruce	.01	.05
❑ 477 Morten Andersen	.01	.05
❑ 478 Lamar Lathon	.01	.05
❑ 479 Steve DeOssie	.01	.05
❑ 480 Marvin Washington	.01	.05
❑ 481 Herschel Walker	.02	.10
❑ 482 Howie Long	.08	.25
❑ 483 Calvin Williams	.02	.10
❑ 484 Brett Favre	1.25	2.50
❑ 485 Johnny Bailey	.01	.05
❑ 486 Jeff Gossett	.01	.05
❑ 487 Carnell Lake	.01	.05
❑ 488 Michael Zordich RC	.01	.05
❑ 489 Henry Rolling	.01	.05
❑ 490 Steve Smith	.01	.05
❑ 491 Vestee Jackson	.01	.05
❑ 492 Ray Crockett	.01	.05
❑ 493 Dexter Carter	.01	.05
❑ 494 Nick Lowery	.01	.05
❑ 495 Cortez Kennedy	.02	.10
❑ 496 Cleveland Gary	.01	.05
❑ 497 Kelly Stouffer	.01	.05
❑ 498 Carl Carter	.01	.05
❑ 499 Shannon Sharpe	.08	.25
❑ 500 Roger Craig	.02	.10
❑ 501 Willie Drewrey	.01	.05
❑ 502 Mark Schlereth RC	.01	.05
❑ 503 Tony Martin	.02	.10
❑ 504 Tom Newberry	.01	.05
❑ 505 Ron Hall	.01	.05
❑ 506 Scott Miller	.01	.05
❑ 507 Donnell Woolford	.01	.05
❑ 508 Dave Krieg	.02	.10
❑ 509 Erric Pegram	.02	.10
❑ 510 Checklist 401-510	.01	.05
❑ 511 Barry Sanders SBK	.25	.60
❑ 512 Thurman Thomas SBK	.02	.10
❑ 513 Warren Moon SBK	.02	.10
❑ 514 John Elway SBK	.20	.50
❑ 515 Ronnie Lott SBK	.02	.10
❑ 516 Emmitt Smith SBK	.25	.60
❑ 517 Andre Rison SBK	.02	.10
❑ 518 Steve Atwater SBK	.01	.05
❑ 519 Steve Young SBK	.10	.30
❑ 520 Mark Rypien SBK	.01	.05
❑ 521 Rich Camarillo	.01	.05
❑ 522 Mark Bavaro	.01	.05
❑ 523 Brad Edwards	.01	.05
❑ 524 Chad Hennings RC	.02	.10
❑ 525 Tony Paige	.01	.05
❑ 526 Shawn Moore	.01	.05
❑ 527 Sidney Johnson RC	.01	.05
❑ 528 Sanjay Beach RC	.01	.05
❑ 529 Kelvin Pritchett	.01	.05
❑ 530 Jerry Holmes	.01	.05
❑ 531 Al Del Greco	.01	.05
❑ 532 Bob Gagliano	.01	.05
❑ 533 Drew Hill	.01	.05
❑ 534 Donald Frank RC	.01	.05
❑ 535 Pio Sagapolutele RC	.01	.05
❑ 536 Jackie Slater	.01	.05
❑ 537 Vernon Turner	.01	.05
❑ 538 Bobby Humphrey	.01	.05
❑ 539 Audray McMillian	.01	.05
❑ 540 Gary Brown RC	.08	.25
❑ 541 Wesley Carroll	.01	.05
❑ 542 Nate Newton	.01	.05
❑ 543 Vai Sikahema	.01	.05
❑ 544 Chris Chandler	.08	.25
❑ 545 Nolan Harrison RC	.01	.05
❑ 546 Mark Green	.01	.05
❑ 547 Ricky Watters	.08	.25
❑ 548 J.J. Birden	.01	.05
❑ 549 Cody Carlson	.01	.05
❑ 550 Tim Green	.01	.05
❑ 551 Mark Jackson	.01	.05
❑ 552 Vince Buck	.01	.05
❑ 553 George Jamison	.01	.05
❑ 554 Anthony Pleasant	.01	.05
❑ 555 Reggie Johnson	.01	.05
❑ 556 John Jackson WR	.01	.05
❑ 557 Ian Beckles	.01	.05
❑ 558 Buford McGee	.01	.05
❑ 559 Fuad Reveiz UER	.01	.05
❑ 560 Joe Montana	.50	1.25
❑ 561 Phil Simms	.02	.10
❑ 562 Greg McMurtry	.01	.05
❑ 563 Gerald Williams	.01	.05
❑ 564 Dave Cadigan	.01	.05
❑ 565 Rufus Porter	.01	.05
❑ 566 Jim Kelly	.08	.25
❑ 567 Deion Sanders	.20	.50
❑ 568 Mike Singletary	.02	.10
❑ 569 Boomer Esiason	.02	.10
❑ 570 Andre Reed	.02	.10
❑ 571 James Washington	.01	.05
❑ 572 Jack Del Rio	.01	.05
❑ 573 Gerald Perry	.01	.05
❑ 574 Vinnie Clark	.01	.05
❑ 575 Mike Piel	.01	.05
❑ 576 Michael Dean Perry	.02	.10
❑ 577 Ricky Proehl	.01	.05
❑ 578 Leslie O'Neal	.02	.10
❑ 579 Russell Maryland	.01	.05
❑ 580 Eric Dickerson	.02	.10
❑ 581 Fred Strickland	.01	.05
❑ 582 Nick Lowery	.01	.05
❑ 583 Joe Milinichik RC	.01	.05
❑ 584 Mark Vlasic	.01	.05
❑ 585 James Lofton	.02	.10
❑ 586 Bruce Smith	.08	.25
❑ 587 Harvey Williams	.02	.10
❑ 588 Bernie Kosar	.02	.10
❑ 589 Carl Banks	.01	.05
❑ 590 Jeff George	.08	.25
❑ 591 Fred Jones RC	.01	.05
❑ 592 Todd Scott	.01	.05
❑ 593 Keith Jones	.01	.05
❑ 594A Tootie Robbins ERR	.01	.05
❑ 594B Tootie Robbins COR	.01	.05
❑ 595 Todd Philcox RC	.01	.05
❑ 596 Browning Nagle	.01	.05
❑ 597 Troy Aikman	.30	.75
❑ 598 Dan Marino	.50	1.25
❑ 599 Lawrence Taylor	.08	.25
❑ 600 Webster Slaughter	.01	.05
❑ 601 Aaron Cox	.01	.05
❑ 602 Matt Stover	.01	.05
❑ 603 Keith Sims	.01	.05
❑ 604 Dennis Smith	.01	.05
❑ 605 Kevin Porter	.01	.05
❑ 606 Anthony Miller	.02	.10
❑ 607 Ken O'Brien	.01	.05
❑ 608 Randall Cunningham	.08	.25
❑ 609 Timm Rosenbach	.01	.05
❑ 610 Junior Seau	.08	.25
❑ 611 Johnny Rembert	.01	.05
❑ 612 Rick Tuten	.01	.05
❑ 613 Willie Green	.01	.05
❑ 614 Sean Salisbury RC	.01	.05
❑ 615 Martin Bayless	.01	.05
❑ 616 Jerry Rice	.30	.75
❑ 617 Randal Hill	.01	.05
❑ 618 Dan McGwire	.01	.05
❑ 619 Merril Hoge	.01	.05
❑ 620 Checklist 571-620	.01	.05
❑ A560 Joe Montana Blowup UDA	6.00	15.00
❑ A598 Dan Marino Blowup UDA	6.00	15.00
❑ SP3 James Lofton Yardage	.30	.75
❑ SP4 Art Monk Catches	.20	.50

1992 Upper Deck Gold

Card		
❑ COMPLETE SET (50)	5.00	12.00
❑ G1 Steve Emtman RC	.02	.10
❑ G2 Carl Pickens RC	.10	.30
❑ G3 Dale Carter RC	.10	.30
❑ G4 Greg Skrepenak RC	.02	.10
❑ G5 Kevin Smith RC	.05	.15
❑ G6 Marco Coleman RC	.05	.15
❑ G7 David Klingler RC	.05	.15
❑ G8 Phillippi Sparks RC	.02	.10
❑ G9 Tommy Maddox RC	.60	1.50
❑ G10 Quentin Coryatt RC	.05	.15
❑ G11 Ty Detmer	.10	.30
❑ G12 Vaughn Dunbar RC	.02	.10
❑ G13 Ashley Ambrose RC	.10	.30
❑ G14 Kurt Barber RC	.02	.10
❑ G15 Chester McGlockton RC	.10	.30
❑ G16 Todd Collins RC	.02	.10
❑ G17 Steve Israel RC	.02	.10
❑ G18 Marquez Pope RC	.02	.10
❑ G19 Alonzo Spellman RC	.05	.15
❑ G20 Tracy Scroggins RC	.02	.10
❑ G21 Jim Kelly QC	.10	.30
❑ G22 Troy Aikman QC	.25	.60
❑ G23 Randall Cunningham QC	.10	.30
❑ G24 Bernie Kosar QC	.05	.15
❑ G25 Dan Marino QC	.40	1.00
❑ G26 Andre Reed	.05	.15
❑ G27 Deion Sanders	.20	.50
❑ G28 Randal Hill	.02	.10
❑ G29 Eric Dickerson	.05	.15
❑ G30 Jim Kelly	.10	.30
❑ G31 Bernie Kosar	.05	.15
❑ G32 Mike Singletary	.05	.15
❑ G33 Anthony Miller	.05	.15
❑ G34 Harvey Williams	.10	.30
❑ G35 Randall Cunningham	.10	.30
❑ G36 Joe Montana	.50	1.25
❑ G37 Dan McGwire	.02	.10
❑ G38 Al Toon	.05	.15
❑ G39 Carl Banks	.02	.10
❑ G40 Troy Aikman	.30	.75
❑ G41 Junior Seau	.10	.30
❑ G42 Jeff George	.10	.30
❑ G43 Michael Dean Perry	.05	.15
❑ G44 Lawrence Taylor	.10	.30
❑ G45 Dan Marino	.50	1.25
❑ G46 Jerry Rice	.30	.75
❑ G47 Boomer Esiason	.05	.15
❑ G48 Bruce Smith	.10	.30
❑ G49 Leslie O'Neal	.05	.15
❑ G50 Checklist Card	.02	.10

1993 Upper Deck

Card		
❑ COMPLETE SET (530)	10.00	25.00
❑ 1 Mirer/Hearst/Con/Ken CL	.08	.25
❑ 2 Eric Curry RC	.01	.05
❑ 3 Rick Mirer RC	.08	.25
❑ 4 Dan Williams RC	.01	.05
❑ 5 Marvin Jones RC	.01	.05
❑ 6 Willie Roaf RC	.02	.10
❑ 7 Reggie Brooks RC	.02	.10
❑ 8 Horace Copeland RC	.02	.10
❑ 9 Lincoln Kennedy RC	.01	.05
❑ 10 Curtis Conway RC	.15	.40
❑ 11 Drew Bledsoe RC	1.00	2.50
❑ 12 Patrick Bates RC	.01	.05
❑ 13 Wayne Simmons RC	.01	.05
❑ 14 Irv Smith RC	.01	.05
❑ 15 Robert Smith RC	.50	1.25
❑ 16 O.J.McDuffie RC	.08	.25
❑ 17 Darrien Gordon RC	.01	.05
❑ 18 John Copeland RC	.02	.10
❑ 19 Derek Brown RBK RC	.01	.05
❑ 20 Jerome Bettis RC	2.50	5.00
❑ 21 Deon Figures RC	.01	.05
❑ 22 Glyn Milburn RC	.08	.25
❑ 23 Garrison Hearst RC	.30	.75
❑ 24 Qadry Ismail RC	.08	.25
❑ 25 Terry Kirby RC	.08	.25
❑ 26 Lamar Thomas RC	.01	.05
❑ 27 Tom Carter RC	.02	.10

Card		
❑ 28 Andre Hastings RC	.02	.10
❑ 29 George Teague RC	.02	.10
❑ 30 Tommy Maddox CL	.02	.10
❑ 31 David Klingler ART	.01	.05
❑ 32 Tommy Maddox ART	.02	.10
❑ 33 Vaughn Dunbar ART	.01	.05
❑ 34 Rodney Culver ART	.01	.05
❑ 35 Carl Pickens ART	.02	.10
❑ 36 Courtney Hawkins ART	.01	.05
❑ 37 Tyji Armstrong ART	.01	.05
❑ 38 Ray Roberts ART	.01	.05
❑ 39 Troy Auzenne ART	.01	.05
❑ 40 Shane Dronett ART	.01	.05
❑ 41 Chris Mims ART	.01	.05
❑ 42 Sean Gilbert ART	.01	.05
❑ 43 Steve Emtman ART	.01	.05
❑ 44 Robert Jones ART	.01	.05
❑ 45 Marco Coleman ART	.01	.05
❑ 46 Ricardo McDonald ART	.01	.05
❑ 47 Quentin Coryatt ART	.02	.10
❑ 48 Dana Hall ART	.01	.05
❑ 49 Darren Perry ART	.01	.05
❑ 50 Darryl Williams ART	.01	.05
❑ 51 Kevin Smith ART	.01	.05
❑ 52 Terrell Buckley ART	.01	.05
❑ 53 Troy Vincent ART	.01	.05
❑ 54 Lin Elliott ART	.01	.05
❑ 55 Dale Carter ART	.01	.05
❑ 56 Steve Atwater HIT	.01	.05
❑ 57 Junior Seau HIT	.02	.10
❑ 58 Ronnie Lott HIT	.01	.05
❑ 59 Louis Oliver HIT	.01	.05
❑ 60 Cortez Kennedy HIT	.01	.05
❑ 61 Pat Swilling HIT	.01	.05
❑ 62 Hitmen Checklist	.01	.05
❑ 63 Curtis Conway TC	.08	.25
❑ 64 Alfred Williams TC	.01	.05
❑ 65 Jim Kelly TC	.02	.10
❑ 66 Simon Fletcher TC	.01	.05
❑ 67 Eric Metcalf TC	.01	.05
❑ 68 Lawrence Dawsey TC	.01	.05
❑ 69 Garrison Hearst TC	.08	.25
❑ 70 Anthony Miller TC	.01	.05
❑ 71 Neil Smith TC	.01	.05
❑ 72 Jeff George TC	.02	.10
❑ 73 Emmitt Smith TC	.30	.75
❑ 74 Dan Marino TC	.30	.75
❑ 75 Clyde Simmons TC	.01	.05
❑ 76 Deion Sanders TC	.08	.25
❑ 77 Ricky Watters TC	.02	.10
❑ 78 Rodney Hampton TC	.02	.10
❑ 79 Brad Baxter TC	.01	.05
❑ 80 Barry Sanders TC	.25	.60
❑ 81 Warren Moon TC	.02	.10
❑ 82 Brett Favre TC	.40	1.00
❑ 83 Drew Bledsoe TC	.50	1.25
❑ 84 Tim Brown TC	.02	.10
❑ 85 Cleveland Gary TC	.01	.05
❑ 86 Earnest Byner TC	.01	.05
❑ 87 Wayne Martin TC	.01	.05
❑ 88 Rick Mirer TC	.08	.25
❑ 89 Barry Foster TC	.01	.05
❑ 90 Terry Allen TC	.02	.10
❑ 91 Vinnie Clark	.01	.05
❑ 92 Howard Ballard	.01	.05
❑ 93 Eric Ball	.01	.05
❑ 94 Marc Boutte	.01	.05
❑ 95 Larry Centers RC	.08	.25
❑ 96 Gary Brown	.01	.05
❑ 97 Hugh Millen	.01	.05
❑ 98 Anthony Newman RC	.01	.05
❑ 99 Darrell Thompson	.01	.05
❑ 100 George Jamison	.01	.05
❑ 101 James Francis	.01	.05
❑ 102 Leonard Harris	.01	.05
❑ 103 Lomas Brown	.01	.05
❑ 104 James Lofton	.02	.10
❑ 105 Jamie Dukes	.01	.05
❑ 106 Quinn Early	.02	.10
❑ 107 Ernie Jones	.01	.05
❑ 108 Torrance Small	.01	.05
❑ 109 Michael Carter	.01	.05
❑ 110 Aeneas Williams	.01	.05
❑ 111 Renaldo Turnbull	.01	.05
❑ 112 Al Smith	.01	.05
❑ 113 Troy Auzenne	.01	.05
❑ 114 Stephen Baker	.01	.05
❑ 115 Daniel Stubbs	.01	.05

Card		
❑ 116 Dana Hall	.01	.05
❑ 117 Lawrence Taylor	.08	.25
❑ 118 Ron Hall	.01	.05
❑ 119 Derrick Fenner	.01	.05
❑ 120 Martin Mayhew	.01	.05
❑ 121 Jay Schroeder	.01	.05
❑ 122 Michael Zordich	.01	.05
❑ 123 Ed McCaffrey	.08	.25
❑ 124 John Stephens	.01	.05
❑ 125 Brad Edwards	.01	.05
❑ 126 Don Griffin	.01	.05
❑ 127 Broderick Thomas	.01	.05
❑ 128 Ted Washington	.01	.05
❑ 129 Haywood Jeffires	.02	.10
❑ 130 Gary Plummer	.01	.05
❑ 131 Mark Wheeler	.01	.05
❑ 132 Ty Detmer	.08	.25
❑ 133 Derrick Walker	.01	.05
❑ 134 Henry Ellard	.02	.10
❑ 135 Neal Anderson	.01	.05
❑ 136 Bruce Smith	.08	.25
❑ 137 Cris Carter	.08	.25
❑ 138 Vaughn Dunbar	.01	.05
❑ 139 Dan Marino	.60	1.50
❑ 140 Troy Aikman	.30	.75
❑ 141 Randall Cunningham	.08	.25
❑ 142 Daryl Johnston	.08	.25
❑ 143 Mark Clayton	.01	.05
❑ 144 Rich Gannon	.08	.25
❑ 145 Nate Newton	.02	.10
❑ 146 Willie Gault	.01	.05
❑ 147 Brian Washington	.01	.05
❑ 148 Fred Barnett	.02	.10
❑ 149 Gill Byrd	.01	.05
❑ 150 Art Monk	.02	.10
❑ 151 Stan Humphries	.02	.10
❑ 152 Charles Mann	.01	.05
❑ 153 Greg Lloyd	.02	.10
❑ 154 Marvin Washington	.01	.05
❑ 155 Bernie Kosar	.02	.10
❑ 156 Pete Metzelaars	.01	.05
❑ 157 Chris Hinton	.01	.05
❑ 158 Jim Harbaugh	.08	.25
❑ 159 Willie Davis	.08	.25
❑ 160 Leroy Thompson	.01	.05
❑ 161 Scott Miller	.01	.05
❑ 162 Eugene Robinson	.01	.05
❑ 163 David Little	.01	.05
❑ 164 Pierce Holt	.01	.05
❑ 165 James Hasty	.01	.05
❑ 166 Dave Krieg	.02	.10
❑ 167 Gerald Williams	.01	.05
❑ 168 Kyle Clifton	.01	.05
❑ 169 Bill Brooks	.01	.05
❑ 170 Vance Johnson	.01	.05
❑ 171 Greg Townsend	.01	.05
❑ 172 Jason Belser	.01	.05
❑ 173 Brett Perriman	.08	.25
❑ 174 Steve Jordan	.01	.05
❑ 175 Kelvin Martin	.01	.05
❑ 176 Greg Kragen	.01	.05
❑ 177 Kerry Cash	.01	.05
❑ 178 Chester McGlockton	.02	.10
❑ 179 Jim Kelly	.08	.25
❑ 180 Todd McNair	.01	.05
❑ 181 Leroy Hoard	.02	.10
❑ 182 Seth Joyner	.01	.05
❑ 183 Sam Gash RC	.08	.25
❑ 184 Joe Nash	.01	.05
❑ 185 Lin Elliott RC	.01	.05
❑ 186 Robert Porcher	.01	.05
❑ 187 Tommy Hodson	.01	.05
❑ 188 Greg Lewis	.01	.05
❑ 189 Dan Saleaumua	.01	.05
❑ 190 Chris Goode	.01	.05
❑ 191 Henry Thomas	.01	.05
❑ 192 Bobby Hebert	.01	.05
❑ 193 Clay Matthews	.02	.10
❑ 194 Mark Carrier WR	.02	.10
❑ 195 Anthony Pleasant	.01	.05
❑ 196 Eric Dorsey	.01	.05
❑ 197 Clarence Verdin	.01	.05
❑ 198 Marc Spindler	.01	.05
❑ 199 Tommy Maddox	.08	.25
❑ 200 Wendell Davis	.01	.05
❑ 201 John Fina	.01	.05
❑ 202 Alonzo Spellman	.01	.05
❑ 203 Darryl Williams	.01	.05

Card		
❑ 204 Mike Croel	.01	.05
❑ 205 Ken Norton Jr.	.02	.10
❑ 206 Mel Gray	.02	.10
❑ 207 Chuck Cecil	.01	.05
❑ 208 John Flannery	.01	.05
❑ 209 Chip Banks	.01	.05
❑ 210 Chris Martin	.01	.05
❑ 211 Dennis Brown	.01	.05
❑ 212 Vinny Testaverde	.02	.10
❑ 213 Nick Bell	.01	.05
❑ 214 Robert Delpino	.01	.05
❑ 215 Mark Higgs	.01	.05
❑ 216 Al Noga	.01	.05
❑ 217 Andre Tippett	.01	.05
❑ 218 Pat Swilling	.01	.05
❑ 219 Phil Simms	.02	.10
❑ 220 Ricky Proehl	.01	.05
❑ 221 William Thomas	.01	.05
❑ 222 Jeff Graham	.02	.10
❑ 223 Darion Conner	.01	.05
❑ 224 Mark Carrier DB	.01	.05
❑ 225 Willie Green	.01	.05
❑ 226 Reggie Rivers RC	.01	.05
❑ 227 Andre Reed	.02	.10
❑ 228 Deion Sanders	.20	.50
❑ 229 Chris Doleman	.01	.05
❑ 230 Jerry Ball	.01	.05
❑ 231 Eric Dickerson	.02	.10
❑ 232 Carlos Jenkins	.01	.05
❑ 233 Mike Johnson	.01	.05
❑ 234 Marco Coleman	.01	.05
❑ 235 Leslie O'Neal	.02	.10
❑ 236 Browning Nagle	.01	.05
❑ 237 Carl Pickens	.02	.10
❑ 238 Steve Emtman	.01	.05
❑ 239 Alvin Harper	.02	.10
❑ 240 Keith Jackson	.02	.10
❑ 241 Jerry Rice	.40	1.00
❑ 242 Cortez Kennedy	.02	.10
❑ 243 Tyji Armstrong	.01	.05
❑ 244 Troy Vincent	.01	.05
❑ 245 Randal Hill	.01	.05
❑ 246 Robert Blackmon	.01	.05
❑ 247 Junior Seau	.08	.25
❑ 248 Sterling Sharpe	.08	.25
❑ 249 Thurman Thomas	.08	.25
❑ 250 David Klingler	.01	.05
❑ 251 Jeff George	.08	.25
❑ 252 Anthony Miller	.02	.10
❑ 253 Earnest Byner	.01	.05
❑ 254 Eric Swann	.02	.10
❑ 255 Jeff Herrod	.01	.05
❑ 256 Eddie Robinson	.01	.05
❑ 257 Eric Allen	.01	.05
❑ 258 John Taylor	.02	.10
❑ 259 Sean Gilbert	.02	.10
❑ 260 Ray Childress	.01	.05
❑ 261 Michael Haynes	.02	.10
❑ 262 Greg McMurtry	.01	.05
❑ 263 Bill Romanowski	.01	.05
❑ 264 Todd Lyght	.01	.05
❑ 265 Clyde Simmons	.01	.05
❑ 266 Webster Slaughter	.01	.05
❑ 267 J.J. Birden	.01	.05
❑ 268 Aaron Wallace	.01	.05
❑ 269 Carl Banks	.01	.05
❑ 270 Ricardo McDonald	.01	.05
❑ 271 Michael Brooks	.01	.05
❑ 272 Dale Carter	.01	.05
❑ 273 Mike Pritchard	.02	.10
❑ 274 Derek Brown TE	.01	.05
❑ 275 Burt Grossman	.01	.05
❑ 276 Mark Schlereth	.01	.05
❑ 277 Karl Mecklenburg	.01	.05
❑ 278 Rickey Jackson	.01	.05
❑ 279 Ricky Ervins	.01	.05
❑ 280 Jeff Bryant	.01	.05
❑ 281 Eric Martin	.01	.05
❑ 282 Carlton Haselrig	.01	.05
❑ 283 Kevin Mack	.01	.05
❑ 284 Brad Muster	.01	.05
❑ 285 Kelvin Pritchett	.01	.05
❑ 286 Courtney Hawkins	.01	.05
❑ 287 Levon Kirkland	.01	.05
❑ 288 Steve DeBerg	.01	.05
❑ 289 Edgar Bennett	.08	.25
❑ 290 Michael Dean Perry	.02	.10
❑ 291 Richard Dent	.02	.10

Card	Low	High
❑ 292 Howie Long	.08	.25
❑ 293 Chris Mims	.01	.05
❑ 294 Kurt Barber	.01	.05
❑ 295 Wilber Marshall	.01	.05
❑ 296 Ethan Horton	.01	.05
❑ 297 Tony Bennett	.01	.05
❑ 298 Johnny Johnson	.01	.05
❑ 299 Craig Heyward	.02	.10
❑ 300 Steve Israel	.01	.05
❑ 301 Kenneth Gant	.01	.05
❑ 302 Eugene Chung	.01	.05
❑ 303 Harvey Williams	.02	.10
❑ 304 Jarrod Bunch	.01	.05
❑ 305 Darren Perry	.01	.05
❑ 306 Steve Christie	.01	.05
❑ 307 John Randle	.02	.10
❑ 308 Warren Moon	.08	.25
❑ 309 Charles Haley	.02	.10
❑ 310 Tony Smith RB	.01	.05
❑ 311 Steve Broussard	.01	.05
❑ 312 Alfred Williams	.01	.05
❑ 313 Terrell Buckley	.01	.05
❑ 314 Trace Armstrong	.01	.05
❑ 315 Brian Mitchell	.02	.10
❑ 316 Steve Atwater	.01	.05
❑ 317 Nate Lewis	.01	.05
❑ 318 Richard Brown	.01	.05
❑ 319 Rufus Porter	.01	.05
❑ 320 Pat Harlow	.01	.05
❑ 321 Anthony Smith	.01	.05
❑ 322 Jack Del Rio	.01	.05
❑ 323 Darryl Talley	.01	.05
❑ 324 Sam Mills	.01	.05
❑ 325 Chris Miller	.02	.10
❑ 326 Ken Harvey	.01	.05
❑ 327 Rod Woodson	.08	.25
❑ 328 Tony Tolbert	.01	.05
❑ 329 Todd Kinchen	.01	.05
❑ 330 Brian Noble	.01	.05
❑ 331 Dave Meggett	.01	.05
❑ 332 Chris Spielman	.02	.10
❑ 333 Barry Word	.01	.05
❑ 334 Jessie Hester	.01	.05
❑ 335 Michael Jackson	.02	.10
❑ 336 Mitchell Price	.01	.05
❑ 337 Michael Irvin	.08	.25
❑ 338 Simon Fletcher	.01	.05
❑ 339 Keith Jennings	.01	.05
❑ 340 Vai Sikahema	.01	.05
❑ 341 Roger Craig	.02	.10
❑ 342 Ricky Watters	.08	.25
❑ 343 Reggie Cobb	.01	.05
❑ 344 Kanavis McGhee	.01	.05
❑ 345 Barry Foster	.02	.10
❑ 346 Marion Butts	.01	.05
❑ 347 Bryan Cox	.01	.05
❑ 348 Wayne Martin	.01	.05
❑ 349 Jim Everett	.02	.10
❑ 350 Nate Odomes	.01	.05
❑ 351 Anthony Johnson	.02	.10
❑ 352 Rodney Hampton	.02	.10
❑ 353 Terry Allen	.08	.25
❑ 354 Derrick Thomas	.08	.25
❑ 355 Calvin Williams	.02	.10
❑ 356 Pepper Johnson	.01	.05
❑ 357 John Elway	.60	1.50
❑ 358 Steve Young	.30	.75
❑ 359 Emmitt Smith	.60	1.50
❑ 360 Brett Favre	.75	2.00
❑ 361 Cody Carlson	.01	.05
❑ 362 Vincent Brown	.01	.05
❑ 363 Gary Anderson RB	.01	.05
❑ 364 Jon Vaughn	.01	.05
❑ 365 Todd Marinovich	.01	.05
❑ 366 Carnell Lake	.01	.05
❑ 367 Kurt Gouveia	.01	.05
❑ 368 Lawrence Dawsey	.01	.05
❑ 369 Neil O'Donnell	.08	.25
❑ 370 Duane Bickett	.01	.05
❑ 371 Ronnie Harmon	.01	.05
❑ 372 Rodney Peete	.01	.05
❑ 373 Cornelius Bennett	.02	.10
❑ 374 Brad Baxter	.01	.05
❑ 375 Ernest Givins	.02	.10
❑ 376 Keith Byars	.01	.05
❑ 377 Eric Bieniemy	.01	.05
❑ 378 Mike Brim	.01	.05
❑ 379 Darren Lewis	.01	.05
❑ 380 Heath Sherman	.01	.05
❑ 381 Leonard Russell	.02	.10
❑ 382 Brent Jones	.02	.10
❑ 383 David Whitmore	.01	.05
❑ 384 Ray Roberts	.01	.05
❑ 385 John Offerdahl	.01	.05
❑ 386 Keith McCants	.01	.05
❑ 387 John Baylor	.01	.05
❑ 388 Amp Lee	.01	.05
❑ 389 Chris Warren	.02	.10
❑ 390 Herman Moore	.08	.25
❑ 391 Johnny Bailey	.01	.05
❑ 392 Tim Johnson	.01	.05
❑ 393 Eric Metcalf	.02	.10
❑ 394 Chris Chandler	.02	.10
❑ 395 Mark Rypien	.01	.05
❑ 396 Christian Okoye	.01	.05
❑ 397 Shannon Sharpe	.08	.25
❑ 398 Eric Hill	.01	.05
❑ 399 David Lang	.01	.05
❑ 400 Bruce Matthews	.01	.05
❑ 401 Harold Green	.01	.05
❑ 402 Mo Lewis	.01	.05
❑ 403 Terry McDaniel	.01	.05
❑ 404 Wesley Carroll	.01	.05
❑ 405 Richmond Webb	.01	.05
❑ 406 Andre Rison	.02	.10
❑ 407 Lonnie Young	.01	.05
❑ 408 Tommy Vardell	.01	.05
❑ 409 Gene Atkins	.01	.05
❑ 410 Sean Salisbury	.01	.05
❑ 411 Kenneth Davis	.01	.05
❑ 412 John L. Williams	.01	.05
❑ 413 Roman Phifer	.01	.05
❑ 414 Bennie Blades	.01	.05
❑ 415 Tim Brown	.08	.25
❑ 416 Lorenzo White	.01	.05
❑ 417 Tony Casillas	.01	.05
❑ 418 Tom Waddle	.01	.05
❑ 419 David Fulcher	.01	.05
❑ 420 Jessie Tuggle	.01	.05
❑ 421 Emmitt Smith SL	.30	.75
❑ 422 Clyde Simmons SL	.01	.05
❑ 423 Sterling Sharpe SL	.02	.10
❑ 424 Sterling Sharpe SL	.02	.10
❑ 425 Emmitt Smith SL	.30	.75
❑ 426 Dan Marino SL	.30	.75
❑ 427 Henry Jones SL	.01	.05
❑ 428 Thurman Thomas SL	.02	.10
❑ 429 Greg Montgomery SL	.01	.05
❑ 430 Pete Stoyanovich SL	.01	.05
❑ 431 Emmitt Smith CL	.15	.40
❑ 432 Steve Young BB	.15	.40
❑ 433 Jerry Rice BB	.20	.50
❑ 434 Ricky Watters BB	.02	.10
❑ 435 Barry Foster BB	.01	.05
❑ 436 Cortez Kennedy BB	.01	.05
❑ 437 Warren Moon BB	.02	.10
❑ 438 Thurman Thomas BB	.02	.10
❑ 439 Brett Favre BB	.40	1.00
❑ 440 Andre Rison BB	.02	.10
❑ 441 Barry Sanders BB	.25	.60
❑ 442 Chris Berman CL	.01	.05
❑ 443 Moe Gardner	.01	.05
❑ 444 Robert Jones	.01	.05
❑ 445 Reggie Langhorne	.01	.05
❑ 446 Flipper Anderson	.01	.05
❑ 447 James Washington	.01	.05
❑ 448 Aaron Craver	.01	.05
❑ 449 Jack Trudeau	.01	.05
❑ 450 Neil Smith	.08	.25
❑ 451 Chris Burkett	.01	.05
❑ 452 Russell Maryland	.01	.05
❑ 453 Drew Hill	.01	.05
❑ 454 Barry Sanders	.50	1.25
❑ 455 Jeff Cross	.01	.05
❑ 456 Bennie Thompson	.01	.05
❑ 457 Marcus Allen	.08	.25
❑ 458 Tracy Scroggins	.01	.05
❑ 459 LeRoy Butler	.01	.05
❑ 460 Joe Montana	.60	1.50
❑ 461 Eddie Anderson	.01	.05
❑ 462 Tim McDonald	.01	.05
❑ 463 Ronnie Lott	.02	.10
❑ 464 Gaston Green	.01	.05
❑ 465 Shane Conlan	.01	.05
❑ 466 Leonard Marshall	.01	.05
❑ 467 Melvin Jenkins	.01	.05
❑ 468 Don Beebe	.01	.05
❑ 469 Johnny Mitchell	.01	.05
❑ 470 Darryl Henley	.01	.05
❑ 471 Boomer Esiason	.02	.10
❑ 472 Mark Kelso	.01	.05
❑ 473 John Booty	.01	.05
❑ 474 Pete Stoyanovich	.01	.05
❑ 475 Thomas Smith RC	.02	.10
❑ 476 Carlton Gray RC	.01	.05
❑ 477 Dana Stubblefield RC	.08	.25
❑ 478 Ryan McNeil RC	.08	.25
❑ 479 Natrone Means RC	.08	.25
❑ 480 Carl Simpson RC	.01	.05
❑ 481 Robert O'Neal RC	.01	.05
❑ 482 Demetrius DuBose RC	.01	.05
❑ 483 Darrin Smith RC	.02	.10
❑ 484 Micheal Barrow RC	.08	.25
❑ 485 Chris Slade RC	.02	.10
❑ 486 Steve Tovar RC	.01	.05
❑ 487 Ron George RC	.01	.05
❑ 488 Steve Tasker	.02	.10
❑ 489 Will Furrer	.01	.05
❑ 490 Reggie White	.08	.25
❑ 491 Sean Jones	.01	.05
❑ 492 Gary Clark	.02	.10
❑ 493 Donnell Woolford	.01	.05
❑ 494 Steve Beuerlein	.02	.10
❑ 495 Anthony Carter	.02	.10
❑ 496 Louis Oliver	.01	.05
❑ 497 Chris Zorich	.01	.05
❑ 498 David Brandon	.01	.05
❑ 499 Bubba McDowell	.01	.05
❑ 500 Adrian Cooper	.01	.05
❑ 501 Bill Johnson	.01	.05
❑ 502 Shawn Jefferson	.01	.05
❑ 503 Siran Stacy	.01	.05
❑ 504 James Jones DT	.01	.05
❑ 505 Tom Rathman	.01	.05
❑ 506 Vince Buck	.01	.05
❑ 507 Kent Graham RC	.08	.25
❑ 508 Darren Carrington RC	.01	.05
❑ 509 Rickey Dixon	.01	.05
❑ 510 Toi Cook	.01	.05
❑ 511 Steve Smith	.01	.05
❑ 512 Eric Green	.01	.05
❑ 513 Phillippi Sparks	.01	.05
❑ 514 Lee Williams	.01	.05
❑ 515 Gary Reasons	.01	.05
❑ 516 Shane Dronett	.01	.05
❑ 517 Jay Novacek	.02	.10
❑ 518 Kevin Greene	.02	.10
❑ 519 Derek Russell	.01	.05
❑ 520 Quentin Coryatt	.02	.10
❑ 521 Santana Dotson	.02	.10
❑ 522 Donald Frank	.01	.05
❑ 523 Mike Prior	.01	.05
❑ 524 Dwight Hollier RC	.01	.05
❑ 525 Eric Davis	.01	.05
❑ 526 Dalton Hilliard	.01	.05
❑ 527 Rodney Culver	.01	.05
❑ 528 Jeff Hostetler	.02	.10
❑ 529 Ernie Mills	.01	.05
❑ 530 Craig Erickson	.02	.10
❑ P231 Eric Dickerson Promo	.50	1.25

1994 Upper Deck

Card	Low	High
❑ COMPLETE SET (330)	12.50	25.00
❑ 1 Dan Wilkinson RC	.07	.20
❑ 2 Antonio Langham RC	.07	.20
❑ 3 Derrick Alexander WR RC	.15	.40
❑ 4 Charles Johnson RC	.15	.40
❑ 5 Bucky Brooks RC	.02	.10
❑ 6 Trev Alberts RC	.07	.20
❑ 7 Marshall Faulk RC	2.50	6.00

Card		
❑ 8 Willie McGinest RC	.15	.40
❑ 9 Aaron Glenn RC	.15	.40
❑ 10 Ryan Yarborough RC	.02	.10
❑ 11 Greg Hill RC	.15	.40
❑ 12 Sam Adams RC	.07	.20
❑ 13 John Thierry RC	.02	.10
❑ 14 Johnnie Morton RC	.30	.75
❑ 15 LeShon Johnson RC	.07	.20
❑ 16 David Palmer RC	.15	.40
❑ 17 Trent Dilfer RC	.50	1.25
❑ 18 Jamir Miller RC	.07	.20
❑ 19 Thomas Lewis RC	.07	.20
❑ 20 Heath Shuler RC	.15	.40
❑ 21 Wayne Gandy	.02	.10
❑ 22 Isaac Bruce RC	2.00	4.00
❑ 23 Joe Johnson RC	.02	.10
❑ 24 Mario Bates RC	.15	.40
❑ 25 Bryant Young RC	.25	.60
❑ 26 William Floyd RC	.15	.40
❑ 27 Errict Rhett RC	.15	.40
❑ 28 Chuck Levy RC	.02	.10
❑ 29 Darnay Scott RC	.30	.75
❑ 30 Rob Fredrickson RC	.07	.20
❑ 31 Jamir Miller HW	.02	.10
❑ 32 Thomas Lewis HW	.02	.10
❑ 33 John Thierry HW	.02	.10
❑ 34 Sam Adams HW	.02	.10
❑ 35 Joe Johnson HW	.02	.10
❑ 36 Bryant Young HW	.10	.30
❑ 37 Wayne Gandy HW	.02	.10
❑ 38 LeShon Johnson HW	.02	.10
❑ 39 Mario Bates HW	.07	.20
❑ 40 Greg Hill HW	.07	.20
❑ 41 Andy Heck	.02	.10
❑ 42 Warren Moon	.15	.40
❑ 43 Jim Everett	.07	.20
❑ 44 Bill Romanowski	.02	.10
❑ 45 Michael Haynes	.07	.20
❑ 46 Chris Doleman	.02	.10
❑ 47 Merril Hoge	.02	.10
❑ 48 Chris Miller	.02	.10
❑ 49 Clyde Simmons	.02	.10
❑ 50 Jeff George	.15	.40
❑ 51 Jeff Burris RC	.07	.20
❑ 52 Ethan Horton	.02	.10
❑ 53 Scott Mitchell	.07	.20
❑ 54 Howard Ballard	.02	.10
❑ 55 Lewis Tillman	.02	.10
❑ 56 Marion Butts	.02	.10
❑ 57 Erik Kramer	.07	.20
❑ 58 Ken Norton Jr.	.07	.20
❑ 59 Anthony Miller	.07	.20
❑ 60 Chris Hinton	.02	.10
❑ 61 Ricky Proehl	.02	.10
❑ 62 Craig Heyward	.07	.20
❑ 63 Darryl Talley	.02	.10
❑ 64 Tim Worley	.02	.10
❑ 65 Derrick Fenner	.02	.10
❑ 66 Jerry Ball	.02	.10
❑ 67 Darrin Smith	.02	.10
❑ 68 Mike Croel	.02	.10
❑ 69 Ray Crockett	.02	.10
❑ 70 Tony Bennett	.02	.10
❑ 71 Webster Slaughter	.02	.10
❑ 72 Anthony Johnson	.07	.20
❑ 73 Charles Mincy	.02	.10
❑ 74 Calvin Jones RC	.02	.10
❑ 75 Henry Ellard	.07	.20
❑ 76 Troy Vincent	.02	.10
❑ 77 Sean Salisbury	.02	.10
❑ 78 Pat Harlow	.02	.10
❑ 79 James Williams RC	.02	.10
❑ 80 Dave Brown	.07	.20
❑ 81 Kent Graham	.07	.20
❑ 82 Seth Joyner	.02	.10
❑ 83 Deon Figures	.02	.10
❑ 84 Stanley Richard	.02	.10
❑ 85 Tom Rathman	.02	.10
❑ 86 Rod Stephens	.02	.10
❑ 87 Ray Seals	.02	.10
❑ 88 Andre Collins	.02	.10
❑ 89 Cornelius Bennett	.07	.20
❑ 90 Richard Dent	.07	.20
❑ 91 Louis Oliver	.02	.10
❑ 92 Rodney Peete	.02	.10
❑ 93 Jackie Harris	.02	.10
❑ 94 Tracy Simien	.02	.10
❑ 95 Greg Townsend	.02	.10
❑ 96 Michael Stewart	.02	.10
❑ 97 Irving Fryar	.07	.20
❑ 98 Todd Collins	.02	.10
❑ 99 Irv Smith	.02	.10
❑ 100 Chris Calloway	.02	.10
❑ 101 Kevin Greene	.07	.20
❑ 102 John Friesz	.07	.20
❑ 103 Steve Bono	.07	.20
❑ 104 Brian Blades	.07	.20
❑ 105 Reggie Cobb	.02	.10
❑ 106 Eric Swann	.07	.20
❑ 107 Mike Pritchard	.02	.10
❑ 108 Bill Brooks	.02	.10
❑ 109 Jim Harbaugh	.15	.40
❑ 110 David Whitmore	.02	.10
❑ 111 Eddie Anderson	.02	.10
❑ 112 Ray Crittenden RC	.02	.10
❑ 113 Mark Collins	.02	.10
❑ 114 Brian Washington	.02	.10
❑ 115 Barry Foster	.02	.10
❑ 116 Gary Plummer	.02	.10
❑ 117 Marc Logan	.02	.10
❑ 118 John L. Williams	.02	.10
❑ 119 Marty Carter	.02	.10
❑ 120 Kurt Gouveia	.02	.10
❑ 121 Ronald Moore	.02	.10
❑ 122 Pierce Holt	.02	.10
❑ 123 Henry Jones	.02	.10
❑ 124 Donnell Woolford	.02	.10
❑ 125 Steve Tovar	.02	.10
❑ 126 Anthony Pleasant	.02	.10
❑ 127 Jay Novacek	.07	.20
❑ 128 Dan Williams	.02	.10
❑ 129 Barry Sanders	1.00	2.50
❑ 130 Robert Brooks	.15	.40
❑ 131 Lorenzo White	.02	.10
❑ 132 Kerry Cash	.02	.10
❑ 133 Joe Montana	1.25	3.00
❑ 134 Jeff Hostetler	.07	.20
❑ 135 Jerome Bettis	.25	.60
❑ 136 Dan Marino	1.25	3.00
❑ 137 Vencie Glenn	.02	.10
❑ 138 Vincent Brown	.02	.10
❑ 139 Rickey Jackson	.02	.10
❑ 140 Carlton Bailey	.02	.10
❑ 141 Jeff Lageman	.02	.10
❑ 142 William Thomas	.02	.10
❑ 143 Neil O'Donnell	.15	.40
❑ 144 Shawn Jefferson	.02	.10
❑ 145 Steve Young	.40	1.00
❑ 146 Chris Warren	.07	.20
❑ 147 Courtney Hawkins	.02	.10
❑ 148 Brad Edwards	.02	.10
❑ 149 O.J.McDuffie	.15	.40
❑ 150 David Lang	.02	.10
❑ 151 Chuck Cecil	.02	.10
❑ 152 Norm Johnson	.02	.10
❑ 153 Pete Metzelaars	.02	.10
❑ 154 Shaun Gayle	.02	.10
❑ 155 Alfred Williams	.02	.10
❑ 156 Eric Turner	.02	.10
❑ 157A Emmitt Smith ERR 1900	1.00	2.50
❑ 157B Emmitt Smith COR	1.00	2.50
❑ 158 Steve Atwater	.02	.10
❑ 159 Robert Porcher	.02	.10
❑ 160 Edgar Bennett	.15	.40
❑ 161 Bubba McDowell	.02	.10
❑ 162 Jeff Herrod	.02	.10
❑ 163 Keith Cash	.02	.10
❑ 164 Patrick Bates	.02	.10
❑ 165 Todd Lyght	.02	.10
❑ 166 Mark Higgs	.02	.10
❑ 167 Carlos Jenkins	.02	.10
❑ 168 Drew Bledsoe	.40	1.00
❑ 169 Wayne Martin	.02	.10
❑ 170 Mike Sherrard	.02	.10
❑ 171 Ronnie Lott	.07	.20
❑ 172 Fred Barnett	.07	.20
❑ 173 Eric Green	.02	.10
❑ 174 Leslie O'Neal	.02	.10
❑ 175 Brent Jones	.07	.20
❑ 176 Jon Vaughn	.02	.10
❑ 177 Vince Workman	.02	.10
❑ 178 Ron Middleton	.02	.10
❑ 179 Terry McDaniel	.02	.10
❑ 180 Willie Davis	.07	.20
❑ 181 Gary Clark	.07	.20
❑ 182 Bobby Hebert	.02	.10
❑ 183 Russell Copeland	.02	.10
❑ 184 Chris Gedney	.02	.10
❑ 185 Tony McGee	.02	.10
❑ 186 Rob Burnett	.02	.10
❑ 187 Charles Haley	.07	.20
❑ 188 Shannon Sharpe	.07	.20
❑ 189 Mel Gray	.02	.10
❑ 190 George Teague	.02	.10
❑ 191 Ernest Givins	.07	.20
❑ 192 Ray Buchanan	.02	.10
❑ 193 J.J. Birden	.02	.10
❑ 194 Tim Brown	.15	.40
❑ 195 Tim Lester	.02	.10
❑ 196 Marco Coleman	.02	.10
❑ 197 Randall McDaniel	.05	.15
❑ 198 Bruce Armstrong	.02	.10
❑ 199 Willie Roaf	.02	.10
❑ 200 Greg Jackson	.02	.10
❑ 201 Johnny Mitchell	.02	.10
❑ 202 Calvin Williams	.07	.20
❑ 203 Jeff Graham	.02	.10
❑ 204 Darren Carrington	.02	.10
❑ 205 Jerry Rice	.60	1.50
❑ 206 Cortez Kennedy	.07	.20
❑ 207 Charles Wilson	.02	.10
❑ 208 James Jenkins RC	.02	.10
❑ 209 Ray Childress	.02	.10
❑ 210 LeRoy Butler	.02	.10
❑ 211 Randal Hill	.02	.10
❑ 212 Lincoln Kennedy	.02	.10
❑ 213 Kenneth Davis	.02	.10
❑ 214 Terry Obee	.02	.10
❑ 215 Ricardo McDonald	.02	.10
❑ 216 Pepper Johnson	.02	.10
❑ 217 Alvin Harper	.07	.20
❑ 218 John Elway	1.25	3.00
❑ 219 Derrick Moore	.02	.10
❑ 220 Terrell Buckley	.02	.10
❑ 221 Haywood Jeffires	.07	.20
❑ 222 Jessie Hester	.02	.10
❑ 223 Kimble Anders	.07	.20
❑ 224 Rocket Ismail	.07	.20
❑ 225 Roman Phifer	.02	.10
❑ 226 Bryan Cox	.02	.10
❑ 227 Cris Carter	.30	.75
❑ 228 Sam Gash	.02	.10
❑ 229 Renaldo Turnbull	.02	.10
❑ 230 Rodney Hampton	.07	.20
❑ 231 Johnny Johnson	.02	.10
❑ 232 Tim Harris	.02	.10
❑ 233 Leroy Thompson	.02	.10
❑ 234 Junior Seau	.15	.40
❑ 235 Tim McDonald	.02	.10
❑ 236 Eugene Robinson	.02	.10
❑ 237 Lawrence Dawsey	.02	.10
❑ 238 Tim Johnson	.02	.10
❑ 239 Jason Elam	.07	.20
❑ 240 Willie Green	.02	.10
❑ 241 Larry Centers	.15	.40
❑ 242 Erric Pegram	.02	.10
❑ 243 Bruce Smith	.15	.40
❑ 244 Alonzo Spellman	.02	.10
❑ 245 Carl Pickens	.07	.20
❑ 246 Michael Jackson	.07	.20
❑ 247 Kevin Williams WR	.07	.20
❑ 248 Glyn Milburn	.07	.20
❑ 249 Herman Moore	.15	.40
❑ 250 Brett Favre	1.25	3.00
❑ 251 Al Smith	.02	.10
❑ 252 Roosevelt Potts	.02	.10
❑ 253 Marcus Allen	.15	.40
❑ 254 Anthony Smith	.02	.10
❑ 255 Sean Gilbert	.02	.10
❑ 256 Keith Byars	.02	.10
❑ 257 Scottie Graham RC	.07	.20
❑ 258 Leonard Russell	.02	.10
❑ 259 Eric Martin	.02	.10
❑ 260 Jarrod Bunch	.02	.10
❑ 261 Rob Moore	.07	.20
❑ 262 Herschel Walker	.07	.20
❑ 263 Levon Kirkland	.02	.10
❑ 264 Chris Mims	.02	.10
❑ 265 Ricky Watters	.07	.20
❑ 266 Rick Mirer	.15	.40
❑ 267 Santana Dotson	.07	.20
❑ 268 Reggie Brooks	.07	.20
❑ 269 Garrison Hearst	.15	.40
❑ 270 Thurman Thomas	.15	.40

Card		
❑ 271 Johnny Bailey	.02	.10
❑ 272 Andre Rison	.07	.20
❑ 273 Jim Kelly	.15	.40
❑ 274 Mark Carrier DB	.02	.10
❑ 275 David Klingler	.02	.10
❑ 276 Eric Metcalf	.07	.20
❑ 277 Troy Aikman UER	.60	1.50
❑ 278 Simon Fletcher	.02	.10
❑ 279 Pat Swilling	.02	.10
❑ 280 Sterling Sharpe	.07	.20
❑ 281 Cody Carlson	.02	.10
❑ 282 Steve Emtman	.02	.10
❑ 283 Neil Smith	.07	.20
❑ 284 James Jett	.02	.10
❑ 285 Shane Conlan	.02	.10
❑ 286 Keith Jackson	.02	.10
❑ 287 Qadry Ismail	.15	.40
❑ 288 Chris Slade	.02	.10
❑ 289 Derek Brown RBK	.02	.10
❑ 290 Phil Simms	.07	.20
❑ 291 Boomer Esiason	.07	.20
❑ 292 Eric Allen	.02	.10
❑ 293 Rod Woodson	.07	.20
❑ 294 Ronnie Harmon	.02	.10
❑ 295 John Taylor	.07	.20
❑ 296 Ferrell Edmunds	.02	.10
❑ 297 Craig Erickson	.02	.10
❑ 298 Brian Mitchell	.02	.10
❑ 299 Dante Jones	.02	.10
❑ 300 John Copeland	.02	.10
❑ 301 Steve Beuerlein	.07	.20
❑ 302 Deion Sanders	.30	.75
❑ 303 Andre Reed	.07	.20
❑ 304 Curtis Conway	.15	.40
❑ 305 Harold Green	.02	.10
❑ 306 Vinny Testaverde	.07	.20
❑ 307 Michael Irvin	.15	.40
❑ 308 Rod Bernstine	.02	.10
❑ 309 Chris Spielman	.07	.20
❑ 310 Reggie White	.15	.40
❑ 311 Gary Brown	.02	.10
❑ 312 Quentin Coryatt	.02	.10
❑ 313 Derrick Thomas	.15	.40
❑ 314 Greg Robinson	.02	.10
❑ 315 Troy Drayton	.02	.10
❑ 316 Terry Kirby	.15	.40
❑ 317 John Randle	.07	.20
❑ 318 Ben Coates	.07	.20
❑ 319 Tyrone Hughes	.07	.20
❑ 320 Corey Miller	.02	.10
❑ 321 Brad Baxter	.02	.10
❑ 322 Randall Cunningham	.15	.40
❑ 323 Greg Lloyd	.07	.20
❑ 324 Stan Humphries	.07	.20
❑ 325 Dana Stubblefield	.07	.20
❑ 326 Kelvin Martin	.02	.10
❑ 327 Hardy Nickerson	.07	.20
❑ 328 Desmond Howard	.07	.20
❑ 329 Mark Carrier WR	.07	.20
❑ 330 Daryl Johnston	.07	.20
❑ P19 Joe Montana Promo	1.00	2.50

1995 Upper Deck

Card		
❑ COMPLETE SET (300)	12.50	30.00
❑ 1 Ki-Jana Carter RC	.15	.40
❑ 2 Tony Boselli RC	.15	.40
❑ 3 Steve McNair RC	1.50	4.00
❑ 4 Michael Westbrook RC	.15	.40
❑ 5 Kerry Collins RC	.75	2.00
❑ 6 Kevin Carter RC	.15	.40
❑ 7 James A.Stewart RC	.02	.10
❑ 8 Joey Galloway RC	.75	2.00
❑ 9 Kyle Brady RC	.15	.40
❑ 10 J.J. Stokes RC	.15	.40
❑ 11 Derrick Alexander DE RC	.02	.10
❑ 12 Warren Sapp RC	.75	2.00
❑ 13 Mark Fields RC	.15	.40
❑ 14 Tyrone Wheatley RC	.60	1.50
❑ 15 Napoleon Kaufman RC	.60	1.50
❑ 16 James O. Stewart RC	.60	1.50
❑ 17 Luther Elliss RC	.02	.10
❑ 18 Rashaan Salaam RC	.07	.20
❑ 19 Jimmy Oliver RC	.02	.10
❑ 20 Mark Bruener RC	.07	.20
❑ 21 Derrick Brooks RC	.75	2.00
❑ 22 Christian Fauria RC	.07	.20
❑ 23 Ray Zellars RC	.07	.20
❑ 24 Todd Collins RC	.50	1.25
❑ 25 Sherman Williams RC	.02	.10
❑ 26 Frank Sanders RC	.15	.40
❑ 27 Rodney Thomas RC	.07	.20
❑ 28 Rob Johnson RC	.50	1.25
❑ 29 Steve Stenstrom RC	.02	.10
❑ 30 Curtis Martin RC	1.50	4.00
❑ 31 Gary Clark	.02	.10
❑ 32 Troy Aikman	.60	1.50
❑ 33 Mike Sherrard	.02	.10
❑ 34 Fred Barnett	.07	.20
❑ 35 Henry Ellard	.07	.20
❑ 36 Terry Allen	.07	.20
❑ 37 Jeff Graham	.02	.10
❑ 38 Herman Moore	.15	.40
❑ 39 Brett Favre	1.25	3.00
❑ 40 Trent Dilfer	.15	.40
❑ 41 Derek Brown RBK	.02	.10
❑ 42 Andre Rison	.07	.20
❑ 43 Flipper Anderson	.02	.10
❑ 44 Jerry Rice	.60	1.50
❑ 45 Andre Reed	.07	.20
❑ 46 Sean Dawkins	.07	.20
❑ 47 Irving Fryar	.07	.20
❑ 48 Vincent Brisby	.02	.10
❑ 49 Rob Moore	.07	.20
❑ 50 Carl Pickens	.07	.20
❑ 51 Vinny Testaverde	.07	.20
❑ 52 Ray Childress	.02	.10
❑ 53 Eric Green	.02	.10
❑ 54 Anthony Miller	.07	.20
❑ 55 Lake Dawson	.07	.20
❑ 56 Tim Brown	.15	.40
❑ 57 Stan Humphries	.07	.20
❑ 58 Rick Mirer	.07	.20
❑ 59 Randal Hill	.02	.10
❑ 60 Charles Haley	.07	.20
❑ 61 Chris Calloway	.02	.10
❑ 62 Calvin Williams	.07	.20
❑ 63 Ethan Horton	.02	.10
❑ 64 Cris Carter	.15	.40
❑ 65 Curtis Conway	.15	.40
❑ 66 Scott Mitchell	.07	.20
❑ 67 Edgar Bennett	.07	.20
❑ 68 Craig Erickson	.02	.10
❑ 69 Jim Everett	.02	.10
❑ 70 Terance Mathis	.07	.20
❑ 71 Robert Young	.02	.10
❑ 72 Brent Jones	.02	.10
❑ 73 Bill Brooks	.07	.20
❑ 74 Marshall Faulk	.75	2.00
❑ 75 O.J. McDuffie	.15	.40
❑ 76 Ben Coates	.07	.20
❑ 77 Johnny Mitchell	.02	.10
❑ 78 Darnay Scott	.07	.20
❑ 79 Derrick Alexander WR	.15	.40
❑ 80 Lorenzo White	.02	.10
❑ 81 Charles Johnson	.07	.20
❑ 82 John Elway	1.25	3.00
❑ 83 Willie Davis	.07	.20
❑ 84 James Jett	.07	.20
❑ 85 Mark Seay	.07	.20
❑ 86 Brian Blades	.07	.20
❑ 87 Ronald Moore	.02	.10
❑ 88 Alvin Harper	.02	.10
❑ 89 Dave Brown	.07	.20
❑ 90 Randall Cunningham	.15	.40
❑ 91 Heath Shuler	.07	.20
❑ 92 Jake Reed	.07	.20
❑ 93 Donnell Woolford	.02	.10
❑ 94 Barry Sanders	1.00	2.50
❑ 95 Reggie White	.15	.40
❑ 96 Lawrence Dawsey	.02	.10
❑ 97 Michael Haynes	.07	.20
❑ 98 Bert Emanuel	.15	.40
❑ 99 Troy Drayton	.02	.10
❑ 100 Steve Young	.50	1.25
❑ 101 Bruce Smith	.15	.40
❑ 102 Roosevelt Potts	.02	.10
❑ 103 Dan Marino	1.25	3.00
❑ 104 Michael Timpson	.02	.10
❑ 105 Boomer Esiason	.07	.20
❑ 106 David Klingler	.07	.20
❑ 107 Eric Metcalf	.07	.20
❑ 108 Gary Brown	.02	.10
❑ 109 Neil O'Donnell	.07	.20
❑ 110 Shannon Sharpe	.07	.20
❑ 111 Joe Montana	1.25	3.00
❑ 112 Jeff Hostetler	.07	.20
❑ 113 Ronnie Harmon	.02	.10
❑ 114 Chris Warren	.07	.20
❑ 115 Larry Centers	.07	.20
❑ 116 Michael Irvin	.15	.40
❑ 117 Rodney Hampton	.07	.20
❑ 118 Herschel Walker	.07	.20
❑ 119 Reggie Brooks	.07	.20
❑ 120 Qadry Ismail	.07	.20
❑ 121 Chris Zorich	.02	.10
❑ 122 Chris Spielman	.07	.20
❑ 123 Sean Jones	.02	.10
❑ 124 Errict Rhett	.07	.20
❑ 125 Tyrone Hughes	.07	.20
❑ 126 Jeff George	.07	.20
❑ 127 Chris Miller	.02	.10
❑ 128 Ricky Watters	.07	.20
❑ 129 Jim Kelly	.15	.40
❑ 130 Tony Bennett	.02	.10
❑ 131 Terry Kirby	.07	.20
❑ 132 Drew Bledsoe	.40	1.00
❑ 133 Johnny Johnson	.02	.10
❑ 134 Dan Wilkinson	.07	.20
❑ 135 Leroy Hoard	.02	.10
❑ 136 Darryll Lewis	.02	.10
❑ 137 Barry Foster	.07	.20
❑ 138 Shane Dronett	.02	.10
❑ 139 Marcus Allen	.15	.40
❑ 140 Harvey Williams	.02	.10
❑ 141 Tony Martin	.07	.20
❑ 142 Rod Stephens	.02	.10
❑ 143 Eric Swann	.07	.20
❑ 144 Daryl Johnston	.07	.20
❑ 145 Dave Meggett	.02	.10
❑ 146 Charlie Garner	.15	.40
❑ 147 Ken Harvey	.02	.10
❑ 148 Warren Moon	.07	.20
❑ 149 Steve Walsh	.02	.10
❑ 150 Pat Swilling	.02	.10
❑ 151 Terrell Buckley	.02	.10
❑ 152 Courtney Hawkins	.02	.10
❑ 153 Willie Roaf	.02	.10
❑ 154 Chris Doleman	.02	.10
❑ 155 Jerome Bettis	.15	.40
❑ 156 Dana Stubblefield	.07	.20
❑ 157 Cornelius Bennett	.07	.20
❑ 158 Quentin Coryatt	.07	.20
❑ 159 Bryan Cox	.02	.10
❑ 160 Marion Butts	.02	.10
❑ 161 Aaron Glenn	.02	.10
❑ 162 Louis Oliver	.02	.10
❑ 163 Eric Turner	.02	.10
❑ 164 Cris Dishman	.02	.10
❑ 165 John L. Williams	.02	.10
❑ 166 Simon Fletcher	.02	.10
❑ 167 Neil Smith	.07	.20
❑ 168 Chester McGlockton	.07	.20
❑ 169 Natrone Means	.07	.20
❑ 170 Sam Adams	.02	.10
❑ 171 Clyde Simmons	.02	.10
❑ 172 Jay Novacek	.07	.20
❑ 173 Keith Hamilton	.02	.10
❑ 174 William Fuller	.02	.10
❑ 175 Tom Carter	.02	.10
❑ 176 John Randle	.07	.20
❑ 177 Lewis Tillman	.02	.10
❑ 178 Mel Gray	.02	.10
❑ 179 George Teague	.02	.10
❑ 180 Hardy Nickerson	.02	.10
❑ 181 Mario Bates	.07	.20
❑ 182 D.J. Johnson	.02	.10
❑ 183 Sean Gilbert	.07	.20
❑ 184 Bryant Young	.07	.20
❑ 185 Jeff Burris	.02	.10
❑ 186 Floyd Turner	.02	.10

Card	Low	High
187 Troy Vincent	.02	.10
188 Willie McGinest	.07	.20
189 James Hasty	.02	.10
190 Jeff Blake RC	.40	1.00
191 Stevon Moore	.02	.10
192 Ernest Givins	.02	.10
193 Byron Bam Morris	.02	.10
194 Ray Crockett	.02	.10
195 Dale Carter	.07	.20
196 Terry McDaniel	.02	.10
197 Leslie O'Neal	.07	.20
198 Cortez Kennedy	.07	.20
199 Seth Joyner	.02	.10
200 Emmitt Smith	1.00	2.50
201 Thomas Lewis	.07	.20
202 Andy Harmon	.02	.10
203 Ricky Ervins	.02	.10
204 Fuad Reveiz	.02	.10
205 John Thierry	.02	.10
206 Bennie Blades	.02	.10
207 LeShon Johnson	.07	.20
208 Charles Wilson	.02	.10
209 Joe Johnson	.02	.10
210 Chuck Smith	.02	.10
211 Roman Phifer	.02	.10
212 Ken Norton Jr.	.07	.20
213 Bucky Brooks	.02	.10
214 Ray Buchanan	.02	.10
215 Tim Bowens	.02	.10
216 Vincent Brown	.02	.10
217 Marcus Turner	.02	.10
218 Derrick Fenner	.02	.10
219 Antonio Langham	.02	.10
220 Cody Carlson	.02	.10
221 Greg Lloyd	.07	.20
222 Steve Atwater	.02	.10
223 Donnell Bennett	.07	.20
224 Rocket Ismail	.07	.20
225 John Carney	.02	.10
226 Eugene Robinson	.02	.10
227 Aeneas Williams	.02	.10
228 Darrin Smith	.02	.10
229 Phillippi Sparks	.02	.10
230 Eric Allen	.02	.10
231 Brian Mitchell	.02	.10
232 David Palmer	.07	.20
233 Mark Carrier DB	.02	.10
234 Dave Krieg	.02	.10
235 Robert Brooks	.15	.40
236 Eric Curry	.02	.10
237 Wayne Martin	.02	.10
238 Craig Heyward	.07	.20
239 Isaac Bruce	.30	.75
240 Deion Sanders	.40	1.00
241 Steve Tasker	.07	.20
242 Jim Harbaugh	.07	.20
243 Aubrey Beavers	.02	.10
244 Chris Slade	.02	.10
245 Mo Lewis	.02	.10
246 Alfred Williams	.02	.10
247 Michael Dean Perry	.02	.10
248 Marcus Robertson	.02	.10
249 Kevin Greene	.07	.20
250 Leonard Russell	.02	.10
251 Greg Hill	.07	.20
252 Rob Fredrickson	.02	.10
253 Junior Seau	.15	.40
254 Rick Tuten	.02	.10
255 Garrison Hearst	.15	.40
256 Russell Maryland	.02	.10
257 Michael Brooks	.02	.10
258 Bernard Williams	.02	.10
259 Reggie Roby	.02	.10
260 Dewayne Washington	.07	.20
261 Raymont Harris	.02	.10
262 Brett Perriman	.07	.20
263 LeRoy Butler	.02	.10
264 Santana Dotson	.02	.10
265 Irv Smith	.02	.10
266 Ron George	.02	.10
267 Marquez Pope	.02	.10
268 William Floyd	.07	.20
269 Matt Darby	.02	.10
270 Jeff Herrod	.02	.10
271 Bernie Parmalee	.07	.20
272 Leroy Thompson	.02	.10
273 Ronnie Lott	.07	.20
274 Steve Tovar	.02	.10
275 Michael Jackson	.07	.20
276 Al Smith	.02	.10
277 Rod Woodson	.07	.20
278 Glyn Milburn	.02	.10
279 Kimble Anders	.07	.20
280 Anthony Smith	.02	.10
281 Andre Coleman	.02	.10
282 Terry Wooden	.02	.10
283 Mickey Washington	.02	.10
284 Steve Beuerlein	.07	.20
285 Mark Brunell	.40	1.00
286 Keith Goganious	.02	.10
287 Desmond Howard	.07	.20
288 Darren Carrington	.02	.10
289 Derek Brown TE	.02	.10
290 Reggie Cobb	.02	.10
291 Jeff Lageman	.02	.10
292 Lamar Lathon	.02	.10
293 Sam Mills	.07	.20
294 Carlton Bailey	.02	.10
295 Mark Carrier WR	.07	.20
296 Willie Green	.07	.20
297 Frank Reich	.02	.10
298 Don Beebe	.02	.10
299 Tim McKyer	.02	.10
300 Pete Metzelaars	.02	.10
A19 Joe Montana	6.00	15.00
A103 Dan Marino	6.00	15.00
P1 Joe Montana Promo	.75	2.00
P2 Joe Montana Promo Numbered 19	.75	2.00
P3 Marshall Faulk Promo	.40	1.00

1996 Upper Deck

Card	Low	High
COMPLETE SET (300)	12.50	30.00
1 Keyshawn Johnson RC	.50	1.25
2 Kevin Hardy RC	.20	.50
3 Simeon Rice RC	.50	1.25
4 Jonathan Ogden RC	.20	.50
5 Cedric Jones RC	.02	.10
6 Lawrence Phillips RC	.20	.50
7 Tim Biakabutuka RC	.20	.50
8 Terry Glenn RC	.50	1.25
9 Rickey Dudley RC	.20	.50
10 Willie Anderson RC	.02	.10
11 Alex Molden RC	.02	.10
12 Regan Upshaw RC	.02	.10
13 Walt Harris RC	.02	.10
14 Eddie George RC	.60	1.50
15 John Mobley RC	.02	.10
16 Duane Clemons RC	.02	.10
17 Eddie Kennison RC	.20	.50
18 Marvin Harrison RC	1.25	3.00
19 Daryl Gardener RC	.02	.10
20 Leeland McElroy RC	.08	.25
21 Eric Moulds RC	.60	1.50
22 Alex Van Dyke RC	.08	.25
23 Mike Alstott RC	.50	1.25
24 Jeff Lewis RC	.08	.25
25 Bobby Engram RC	.20	.50
26 Derrick Mayes RC	.20	.50
27 Karim Abdul-Jabbar RC	.20	.50
28 Bobby Hoying RC	.20	.50
29 Stepfret Williams RC	.08	.25
30 Chris Darkins RC	.02	.10
31 Stephen Davis RC	.75	2.00
32 Danny Kanell RC	.20	.50
33 Tony Brackens RC	.20	.50
34 Leslie O'Neal	.02	.10
35 Chris Doleman	.02	.10
36 Larry Brown	.02	.10
37 Ronnie Harmon	.02	.10
38 Chris Spielman	.02	.10
39 John Jurkovic	.02	.10
40 Shawn Jefferson	.02	.10
41 William Floyd	.08	.25
42 Eric Davis	.02	.10
43 Willie Clay	.02	.10
44 Marco Coleman	.02	.10
45 Lorenzo White	.02	.10
46 Neil O'Donnell	.08	.25
47 Natrone Means	.08	.25
48 Cornelius Bennett	.02	.10
49 Steve Walsh	.02	.10
50 Jerome Bettis	.20	.50
51 Boomer Esiason	.08	.25
52 Glyn Milburn	.02	.10
53 Kevin Greene	.08	.25
54 Seth Joyner	.02	.10
55 Jeff Graham	.02	.10
56 Darren Woodson	.08	.25
57 Dale Carter	.02	.10
58 Lorenzo Lynch	.02	.10
59 Tim Brown	.20	.50
60 Jerry Rice	.50	1.25
61 Garrison Hearst	.08	.25
62 Eric Metcalf	.02	.10
63 Leroy Hoard	.02	.10
64 Thurman Thomas	.20	.50
65 Sam Mills	.02	.10
66 Curtis Conway	.20	.50
67 Carl Pickens	.08	.25
68 Deion Sanders	.30	.75
69 Shannon Sharpe	.08	.25
70 Herman Moore	.08	.25
71 Robert Brooks	.20	.50
72 Rodney Thomas	.02	.10
73 Ken Dilger	.08	.25
74 Mark Brunell	.30	.75
75 Marcus Allen	.20	.50
76 Dan Marino	1.00	2.50
77 Robert Smith	.08	.25
78 Drew Bledsoe	.30	.75
79 Jim Everett	.02	.10
80 Rodney Hampton	.08	.25
81 Adrian Murrell	.08	.25
82 Daryl Hobbs RC	.02	.10
83 Ricky Watters	.08	.25
84 Yancey Thigpen	.08	.25
85 Roman Phifer	.02	.10
86 Tony Martin	.08	.25
87 Dana Stubblefield	.08	.25
88 Joey Galloway	.20	.50
89 Errict Rhett	.08	.25
90 Terry Allen	.08	.25
91 Aeneas Williams	.02	.10
92 Craig Heyward	.02	.10
93 Vinny Testaverde	.08	.25
94 Bryce Paup	.02	.10
95 Kerry Collins	.20	.50
96 Rashaan Salaam	.08	.25
97 Dan Wilkinson	.02	.10
98 Jay Novacek	.02	.10
99 John Elway	1.00	2.50
100 Bennie Blades	.02	.10
101 Edgar Bennett	.08	.25
102 Darryll Lewis	.02	.10
103 Marshall Faulk	.25	.60
104 Bryan Schwartz	.02	.10
105 Tamarick Vanover	.08	.25
106 Terry Kirby	.08	.25
107 John Randle	.08	.25
108 Ted Johnson RC	.20	.50
109 Mario Bates	.08	.25
110 Phillippi Sparks	.02	.10
111 Marvin Washington	.02	.10
112 Terry McDaniel	.02	.10
113 Bobby Taylor	.02	.10
114 Carnell Lake	.02	.10
115 Troy Drayton	.02	.10
116 Darren Bennett	.02	.10
117 J.J. Stokes	.20	.50
118 Rick Mirer	.08	.25
119 Jackie Harris	.02	.10
120 Ken Harvey	.02	.10
121 Rob Moore	.08	.25
122 Jeff George	.08	.25
123 Andre Rison	.08	.25
124 Darick Holmes	.02	.10
125 Tim McKyer	.02	.10
126 Alonzo Spellman	.02	.10
127 Jeff Blake	.20	.50

❑ 128 Kevin Williams .02 .10
❑ 129 Anthony Miller .08 .25
❑ 130 Barry Sanders .75 2.00
❑ 131 Brett Favre 1.25 2.50
❑ 132 Steve McNair .40 1.00
❑ 133 Jim Harbaugh .08 .25
❑ 134 Desmond Howard .08 .25
❑ 135 Steve Bono .02 .10
❑ 136 Bernie Parmalee .02 .10
❑ 137 Warren Moon .08 .25
❑ 138 Curtis Martin .40 1.00
❑ 139 Irv Smith .02 .10
❑ 140 Thomas Lewis .02 .10
❑ 141 Kyle Brady .02 .10
❑ 142 Napoleon Kaufman .20 .50
❑ 143 Mike Mamula .02 .10
❑ 144 Erric Pegram .02 .10
❑ 145 Isaac Bruce .20 .50
❑ 146 Andre Coleman .02 .10
❑ 147 Merton Hanks .02 .10
❑ 148 Brian Blades .02 .10
❑ 149 Hardy Nickerson .02 .10
❑ 150 Michael Westbrook .20 .50
❑ 151 Larry Centers .08 .25
❑ 152 Morten Andersen .02 .10
❑ 153 Michael Jackson .08 .25
❑ 154 Bruce Smith .08 .25
❑ 155 Derrick Moore .02 .10
❑ 156 Mark Carrier DB .02 .10
❑ 157 John Copeland .02 .10
❑ 158 Emmitt Smith .75 2.00
❑ 159 Jason Elam .08 .25
❑ 160 Scott Mitchell .08 .25
❑ 161 Mark Chmura .08 .25
❑ 162 Blaine Bishop .02 .10
❑ 163 Tony Bennett .02 .10
❑ 164 Pete Mitchell .08 .25
❑ 165 Dan Saleaumua .02 .10
❑ 166 Pete Stoyanovich .02 .10
❑ 167 Cris Carter .20 .50
❑ 168 Vince Brisby .02 .10
❑ 169 Wayne Martin .02 .10
❑ 170 Tyrone Wheatley .08 .25
❑ 171 Mo Lewis .02 .10
❑ 172 Harvey Williams .02 .10
❑ 173 Calvin Williams .02 .10
❑ 174 Norm Johnson .02 .10
❑ 175 Mark Rypien .02 .10
❑ 176 Stan Humphries .08 .25
❑ 177 Derek Loville .02 .10
❑ 178 Christian Fauria .02 .10
❑ 179 Warren Sapp .02 .10
❑ 180 Henry Ellard .02 .10
❑ 181 Jamir Miller .02 .10
❑ 182 Jessie Tuggle .02 .10
❑ 183 Stevon Moore .02 .10
❑ 184 Jim Kelly .20 .50
❑ 185 Mark Carrier .02 .10
❑ 186 Chris Zorich .02 .10
❑ 187 Harold Green .02 .10
❑ 188 Chris Boniol .02 .10
❑ 189 Allen Aldridge .02 .10
❑ 190 Brett Perriman .02 .10
❑ 191 Chris Jacke .02 .10
❑ 192 Todd McNair .02 .10
❑ 193 Floyd Turner .02 .10
❑ 194 Jeff Lageman .02 .10
❑ 195 Derrick Thomas .20 .50
❑ 196 Eric Green .02 .10
❑ 197 Orlando Thomas .02 .10
❑ 198 Ben Coates .08 .25
❑ 199 Tyrone Hughes .02 .10
❑ 200 Dave Brown .02 .10
❑ 201 Brad Baxter .02 .10
❑ 202 Chester McGlockton .02 .10
❑ 203 Rodney Peete .02 .10
❑ 204 Willie Williams .02 .10
❑ 205 Kevin Carter .02 .10
❑ 206 Aaron Hayden RC .02 .10
❑ 207 Steve Young .40 1.00
❑ 208 Chris Warren .08 .25
❑ 209 Eric Curry .02 .10
❑ 210 Brian Mitchell .02 .10
❑ 211 Frank Sanders .08 .25
❑ 212 Terance Mathis UER .02 .10
❑ 213 Eric Turner .02 .10
❑ 214 Bill Brooks .02 .10
❑ 215 John Kasay .02 .10
❑ 216 Erik Kramer .02 .10
❑ 217 Darnay Scott .08 .25
❑ 218 Charles Haley .08 .25
❑ 219 Steve Atwater .02 .10
❑ 220 Jason Hanson .02 .10
❑ 221 LeRoy Butler .02 .10
❑ 222 Cris Dishman .02 .10
❑ 223 Sean Dawkins .02 .10
❑ 224 James O. Stewart .08 .25
❑ 225 Greg Hill .08 .25
❑ 226 Jeff Cross .02 .10
❑ 227 Qadry Ismail .08 .25
❑ 228 Dave Meggett .02 .10
❑ 229 Eric Allen .02 .10
❑ 230 Chris Calloway .02 .10
❑ 231 Wayne Chrebet .30 .75
❑ 232 Jeff Hostetler .02 .10
❑ 233 Andy Harmon .02 .10
❑ 234 Greg Lloyd .08 .25
❑ 235 Toby Wright .02 .10
❑ 236 Junior Seau .20 .50
❑ 237 Bryant Young .08 .25
❑ 238 Robert Blackmon .02 .10
❑ 239 Trent Dilfer .20 .50
❑ 240 Leslie Shepherd .02 .10
❑ 241 Eric Swann .02 .10
❑ 242 Bert Emanuel .08 .25
❑ 243 Antonio Langham .02 .10
❑ 244 Steve Christie .02 .10
❑ 245 Tyrone Poole .02 .10
❑ 246 Jim Flanigan .02 .10
❑ 247 Tony McGee .02 .10
❑ 248 Michael Irvin .20 .50
❑ 249 Byron Bam Morris .02 .10
❑ 250 Terrell Davis .40 1.00
❑ 251 Johnnie Morton .08 .25
❑ 252 Sean Jones .02 .10
❑ 253 Chris Sanders .08 .25
❑ 254 Quentin Coryatt .02 .10
❑ 255 Willie Jackson .08 .25
❑ 256 Mark Collins .02 .10
❑ 257 Randal Hill .02 .10
❑ 258 David Palmer .02 .10
❑ 259 Will Moore .02 .10
❑ 260 Michael Haynes .02 .10
❑ 261 Mike Sherrard .02 .10
❑ 262 William Thomas .02 .10
❑ 263 Kordell Stewart .20 .50
❑ 264 D'Marco Farr .02 .10
❑ 265 Terrell Fletcher .02 .10
❑ 266 Lee Woodall .02 .10
❑ 267 Eugene Robinson .02 .10
❑ 268 Alvin Harper .02 .10
❑ 269 Gus Frerotte .08 .25
❑ 270 Antonio Freeman .20 .50
❑ 271 Clyde Simmons .02 .10
❑ 272 Chuck Smith .02 .10
❑ 273 Steve Tasker .02 .10
❑ 274 Kevin Butler .02 .10
❑ 275 Steve Tovar .02 .10
❑ 276 Troy Aikman .50 1.25
❑ 277 Aaron Craver .02 .10
❑ 278 Henry Thomas .02 .10
❑ 279 Craig Newsome .02 .10
❑ 280 Brent Jones .02 .10
❑ 281 Micheal Barrow .02 .10
❑ 282 Ray Buchanan .02 .10
❑ 283 Jimmy Smith .20 .50
❑ 284 Neil Smith .08 .25
❑ 285 O.J. McDuffie .08 .25
❑ 286 Jake Reed .08 .25
❑ 287 Ty Law .20 .50
❑ 288 Torrance Small .02 .10
❑ 289 Hugh Douglas .08 .25
❑ 290 Pat Swilling .02 .10
❑ 291 Charlie Garner .08 .25
❑ 292 Ernie Mills .02 .10
❑ 293 John Carney .02 .10
❑ 294 Ken Norton .02 .10
❑ 295 Cortez Kennedy .02 .10
❑ 296 Derrick Brooks .20 .50
❑ 297 Heath Shuler .08 .25
❑ 298 Reggie White .20 .50
❑ 299 Kimble Anders .08 .25
❑ 300 Willie McGinest .02 .10
❑ P96 Dan Marino Promo .75 2.00
❑ MS1 Dan Marino 2.00 5.00
❑ MS2 Dan Marino 2.00 5.00
❑ P13 Dan Marino Promo 1.00 2.50

1997 Upper Deck

❑ COMPLETE SET (300) 20.00 40.00
❑ 1 Orlando Pace RC .25 .60
❑ 2 Darrell Russell RC .08 .25
❑ 3 Shawn Springs RC .15 .40
❑ 4 Bryant Westbrook RC .08 .25
❑ 5 Ike Hilliard RC .50 1.25
❑ 6 Peter Boulware RC .25 .60
❑ 7 Tom Knight RC .08 .25
❑ 8 Yatil Green RC .15 .40
❑ 9 Tony Gonzalez RC 1.00 2.50
❑ 10 Reidel Anthony RC .25 .60
❑ 11 Warrick Dunn RC 1.00 2.50
❑ 12 Kenny Holmes RC .25 .60
❑ 13 Jim Druckenmiller RC .15 .40
❑ 14 James Farrior RC .25 .60
❑ 15 David LaFleur RC .08 .25
❑ 16 Antowain Smith RC .75 2.00
❑ 17 Rae Carruth RC .08 .25
❑ 18 Dwayne Rudd RC .25 .60
❑ 19 Jake Plummer RC 1.50 4.00
❑ 20 Reinard Wilson RC .15 .40
❑ 21 Byron Hanspard RC .15 .40
❑ 22 Will Blackwell RC .15 .40
❑ 23 Troy Davis RC .15 .40
❑ 24 Corey Dillon RC 2.00 5.00
❑ 25 Joey Kent RC .25 .60
❑ 26 Renaldo Wynn RC .08 .25
❑ 27 Pat Barnes RC .25 .60
❑ 28 Kevin Lockett RC .15 .40
❑ 29 Darnell Autry RC .15 .40
❑ 30 Walter Jones RC .25 .60
❑ 31 Trevor Pryce RC .25 .60
❑ 32 Dan Marino SRF .50 1.25
❑ 33 Steve Young SRF .08 .25
❑ 34 John Elway SRF .50 1.25
❑ 35 Jerry Rice SRF .25 .60
❑ 36 Tim Brown SRF .25 .60
❑ 37 Deion Sanders SRF .25 .60
❑ 38 Troy Aikman SRF .25 .60
❑ 39 Barry Sanders SRF .40 1.00
❑ 40 Emmitt Smith SRF .40 1.00
❑ 41 Junior Seau SRF .25 .60
❑ 42 Neil Smith .15 .40
❑ 43 Brett Perriman .08 .25
❑ 44 Jim Everett .08 .25
❑ 45 Qadry Ismail .15 .40
❑ 46 Dana Stubblefield .08 .25
❑ 47 Bryant Young .08 .25
❑ 48 Ken Norton Jr. .08 .25
❑ 49 Terrell Owens .30 .75
❑ 50 Jerry Rice .50 1.25
❑ 51 Steve Young .30 .75
❑ 52 Terry Kirby .15 .40
❑ 53 Chris Doleman .08 .25
❑ 54 Lee Woodall .08 .25
❑ 55 Merton Hanks .08 .25
❑ 56 Garrison Hearst .15 .40
❑ 57 Rashaan Salaam .08 .25
❑ 58 Raymont Harris .08 .25
❑ 59 Curtis Conway .15 .40
❑ 60 Bobby Engram .15 .40
❑ 61 Bryan Cox .08 .25
❑ 62 Walt Harris .08 .25
❑ 63 Tyrone Hughes .08 .25
❑ 64 Rick Mirer .08 .25
❑ 65 Jeff Blake .15 .40
❑ 66 Carl Pickens .15 .40
❑ 67 Darnay Scott .15 .40
❑ 68 Tony McGee .08 .25
❑ 69 Ki-Jana Carter .08 .25

❑ 70 Ashley Ambrose	.08	.25
❑ 71 Dan Wilkinson	.08	.25
❑ 72 Chris Spielman	.08	.25
❑ 73 Todd Collins	.08	.25
❑ 74 Andre Reed	.15	.40
❑ 75 Quinn Early	.08	.25
❑ 76 Eric Moulds	.25	.60
❑ 77 Darick Holmes	.08	.25
❑ 78 Thurman Thomas	.25	.60
❑ 79 Bruce Smith	.15	.40
❑ 80 Bryce Paup	.08	.25
❑ 81 John Elway	1.00	2.50
❑ 82 Terrell Davis	.30	.75
❑ 83 Anthony Miller	.08	.25
❑ 84 Shannon Sharpe	.15	.40
❑ 85 Alfred Williams	.08	.25
❑ 86 John Mobley	.08	.25
❑ 87 Tory James	.08	.25
❑ 88 Steve Atwater	.08	.25
❑ 89 Darrien Gordon	.08	.25
❑ 90 Mike Alstott	.25	.60
❑ 91 Errict Rhett	.08	.25
❑ 92 Trent Dilfer	.25	.60
❑ 93 Courtney Hawkins	.08	.25
❑ 94 Warren Sapp	.15	.40
❑ 95 Regan Upshaw	.08	.25
❑ 96 Hardy Nickerson	.08	.25
❑ 97 Donnie Abraham RC	.25	.60
❑ 98 Larry Centers	.15	.40
❑ 99 Aeneas Williams	.08	.25
❑ 100 Kent Graham UER	.08	.25
❑ 101 Rob Moore	.15	.40
❑ 102 Frank Sanders	.15	.40
❑ 103 Leeland McElroy	.08	.25
❑ 104 Eric Swann	.08	.25
❑ 105 Simeon Rice	.15	.40
❑ 106 Seth Joyner	.08	.25
❑ 107 Stan Humphries	.15	.40
❑ 108 Tony Martin	.15	.40
❑ 109 Charlie Jones	.08	.25
❑ 110 Andre Coleman UER 103	.08	.25
❑ 111 Terrell Fletcher	.08	.25
❑ 112 Junior Seau	.25	.60
❑ 113 Eric Metcalf	.15	.40
❑ 114 Chris Penn	.08	.25
❑ 115 Marcus Allen	.25	.60
❑ 116 Greg Hill	.08	.25
❑ 117 Tamarick Vanover	.15	.40
❑ 118 Lake Dawson	.08	.25
❑ 119 Derrick Thomas	.25	.60
❑ 120 Dale Carter	.08	.25
❑ 121 Elvis Grbac	.15	.40
❑ 122 Aaron Bailey	.08	.25
❑ 123 Jim Harbaugh	.15	.40
❑ 124 Marshall Faulk	.30	.75
❑ 125 Sean Dawkins	.08	.25
❑ 126 Marvin Harrison	.25	.60
❑ 127 Ken Dilger	.08	.25
❑ 128 Tony Bennett	.08	.25
❑ 129 Jeff Herrod	.08	.25
❑ 130 Chris Gardocki	.08	.25
❑ 131 Cary Blanchard	.08	.25
❑ 132 Troy Aikman	.50	1.25
❑ 133 Emmitt Smith	.75	2.00
❑ 134 Sherman Williams	.08	.25
❑ 135 Michael Irvin	.25	.60
❑ 136 Eric Bjornson	.08	.25
❑ 137 Herschel Walker	.15	.40
❑ 138 Tony Tolbert	.08	.25
❑ 139 Deion Sanders	.25	.60
❑ 140 Daryl Johnston	.15	.40
❑ 141 Dan Marino	1.00	2.50
❑ 142 O.J. McDuffie	.15	.40
❑ 143 Troy Drayton	.08	.25
❑ 144 Karim Abdul-Jabbar	.15	.40
❑ 145 Stanley Pritchett	.08	.25
❑ 146 Fred Barnett	.08	.25
❑ 147 Zach Thomas	.25	.60
❑ 148 Shawn Wooden RC	.08	.25
❑ 149 Ty Detmer	.15	.40
❑ 150 Derrick Witherspoon	.08	.25
❑ 151 Ricky Watters	.15	.40
❑ 152 Charlie Garner	.15	.40
❑ 153 Chris T. Jones	.08	.25
❑ 154 Irving Fryar	.15	.40
❑ 155 Mike Mamula	.08	.25
❑ 156 Troy Vincent	.08	.25
❑ 157 Bobby Taylor	.08	.25
❑ 158 Chris Boniol	.08	.25
❑ 159 Devin Bush	.08	.25
❑ 160 Bert Emanuel	.15	.40
❑ 161 Jamal Anderson	.25	.60
❑ 162 Terance Mathis	.15	.40
❑ 163 Cornelius Bennett	.08	.25
❑ 164 Ray Buchanan	.08	.25
❑ 165 Chris Chandler	.15	.40
❑ 166 Dave Brown	.08	.25
❑ 167 Danny Kanell	.08	.25
❑ 168 Rodney Hampton	.15	.40
❑ 169 Tyrone Wheatley	.15	.40
❑ 170 Amani Toomer	.15	.40
❑ 171 Chris Calloway	.08	.25
❑ 172 Thomas Lewis	.08	.25
❑ 173 Phillippi Sparks	.08	.25
❑ 174 Mark Brunell	.30	.75
❑ 175 Keenan McCardell	.15	.40
❑ 176 Willie Jackson	.08	.25
❑ 177 Jimmy Smith	.15	.40
❑ 178 Pete Mitchell	.08	.25
❑ 179 Natrone Means	.15	.40
❑ 180 Kevin Hardy	.08	.25
❑ 181 Tony Brackens	.08	.25
❑ 182 James O. Stewart	.15	.40
❑ 183 Wayne Chrebet	.25	.60
❑ 184 Keyshawn Johnson	.25	.60
❑ 185 Adrian Murrell	.15	.40
❑ 186 Neil O'Donnell	.15	.40
❑ 187 Hugh Douglas	.08	.25
❑ 188 Mo Lewis	.08	.25
❑ 189 Marvin Washington	.08	.25
❑ 190 Aaron Glenn	.08	.25
❑ 191 Barry Sanders	.75	2.00
❑ 192 Scott Mitchell	.15	.40
❑ 193 Herman Moore	.15	.40
❑ 194 Johnnie Morton	.15	.40
❑ 195 Glyn Milburn	.08	.25
❑ 196 Reggie Brown LB	.15	.40
❑ 197 Jason Hanson	.08	.25
❑ 198 Steve McNair	.30	.75
❑ 199 Eddie George	.25	.60
❑ 200 Ronnie Harmon	.08	.25
❑ 201 Chris Sanders	.08	.25
❑ 202 Willie Davis	.08	.25
❑ 203 Frank Wycheck	.08	.25
❑ 204 Darryll Lewis	.08	.25
❑ 205 Blaine Bishop	.08	.25
❑ 206 Robert Brooks	.15	.40
❑ 207 Brett Favre	1.25	2.50
❑ 208 Edgar Bennett	.15	.40
❑ 209 Dorsey Levens	.25	.60
❑ 210 Derrick Mayes	.15	.40
❑ 211 Antonio Freeman	.25	.60
❑ 212 Mark Chmura	.15	.40
❑ 213 Reggie White	.25	.60
❑ 214 Gilbert Brown	.15	.40
❑ 215 LeRoy Butler	.08	.25
❑ 216 Craig Newsome	.08	.25
❑ 217 Kerry Collins	.25	.60
❑ 218 Wesley Walls	.15	.40
❑ 219 Muhsin Muhammad	.15	.40
❑ 220 Anthony Johnson	.08	.25
❑ 221 Tim Biakabutuka	.15	.40
❑ 222 Kevin Greene	.15	.40
❑ 223 Sam Mills	.08	.25
❑ 224 John Kasay	.08	.25
❑ 225 Micheal Barrow	.08	.25
❑ 226 Drew Bledsoe	.30	.75
❑ 227 Curtis Martin	.30	.75
❑ 228 Terry Glenn	.25	.60
❑ 229 Ben Coates	.15	.40
❑ 230 Shawn Jefferson	.08	.25
❑ 231 Willie McGinest	.08	.25
❑ 232 Ted Johnson	.08	.25
❑ 233 Lawyer Milloy	.15	.40
❑ 234 Ty Law	.15	.40
❑ 235 Willie Clay	.08	.25
❑ 236 Tim Brown	.25	.60
❑ 237 Rickey Dudley	.15	.40
❑ 238 Napoleon Kaufman	.25	.60
❑ 239 Chester McGlockton	.08	.25
❑ 240 Rob Fredrickson	.08	.25
❑ 241 Terry McDaniel	.08	.25
❑ 242 Desmond Howard	.15	.40
❑ 243 Jeff George	.15	.40
❑ 244 Isaac Bruce	.25	.60
❑ 245 Tony Banks	.15	.40
❑ 246 Lawrence Phillips UER 247	.08	.25
❑ 247 Kevin Carter	.08	.25
❑ 248 Roman Phifer	.08	.25
❑ 249 Keith Lyle	.08	.25
❑ 250 Eddie Kennison	.15	.40
❑ 251 Craig Heyward	.08	.25
❑ 252 Vinny Testaverde	.15	.40
❑ 253 Derrick Alexander WR	.15	.40
❑ 254 Michael Jackson	.15	.40
❑ 255 Byron Bam Morris	.08	.25
❑ 256 Eric Green	.08	.25
❑ 257 Ray Lewis	.40	1.00
❑ 258 Antonio Langham	.08	.25
❑ 259 Michael McCrary	.08	.25
❑ 260 Gus Frerotte	.08	.25
❑ 261 Terry Allen	.25	.60
❑ 262 Brian Mitchell	.08	.25
❑ 263 Michael Westbrook	.15	.40
❑ 264 Sean Gilbert	.08	.25
❑ 265 Rich Owens	.08	.25
❑ 266 Ken Harvey	.08	.25
❑ 267 Jeff Hostetler	.08	.25
❑ 268 Michael Haynes	.08	.25
❑ 269 Mario Bates	.08	.25
❑ 270 Renaldo Turnbull UER 273	.08	.25
❑ 271 Ray Zellars	.08	.25
❑ 272 Joe Johnson	.08	.25
❑ 273 Eric Allen	.08	.25
❑ 274 Heath Shuler	.08	.25
❑ 275 Daryl Hobbs	.08	.25
❑ 276 John Friesz	.08	.25
❑ 277 Brian Blades	.08	.25
❑ 278 Joey Galloway	.15	.40
❑ 279 Chris Warren	.15	.40
❑ 280 Lamar Smith	.25	.60
❑ 281 Cortez Kennedy	.08	.25
❑ 282 Chad Brown	.08	.25
❑ 283 Warren Moon	.25	.60
❑ 284 Jerome Bettis	.25	.60
❑ 285 Charles Johnson	.15	.40
❑ 286 Kordell Stewart	.25	.60
❑ 287 Erric Pegram	.08	.25
❑ 288 Norm Johnson	.08	.25
❑ 289 Levon Kirkland	.08	.25
❑ 290 Greg Lloyd	.08	.25
❑ 291 Carnell Lake	.08	.25
❑ 292 Brad Johnson	.25	.60
❑ 293 Cris Carter	.25	.60
❑ 294 Jake Reed	.15	.40
❑ 295 Robert Smith	.15	.40
❑ 296 Derrick Alexander DE	.08	.25
❑ 297 John Randle	.15	.40
❑ 298 Dixon Edwards	.08	.25
❑ 299 Orlando Thomas	.08	.25
❑ 300 Dewayne Washington	.08	.25

1998 Upper Deck

❑ COMPLETE SET (255)	75.00	150.00
❑ COMP.SET w/o SP's (213)	12.50	25.00
❑ 1 Peyton Manning RC	25.00	50.00
❑ 2 Ryan Leaf RC	2.00	5.00
❑ 3 Andre Wadsworth RC	1.25	3.00
❑ 4 Charles Woodson RC	3.00	8.00
❑ 5 Curtis Enis RC	1.00	2.50
❑ 6 Grant Wistrom RC	1.25	3.00
❑ 7 Greg Ellis RC	1.00	2.50
❑ 8 Fred Taylor RC	3.00	8.00
❑ 9 Duane Starks RC	1.00	2.50
❑ 10 Keith Brooking RC	2.00	5.00
❑ 11 Takeo Spikes RC	2.00	5.00
❑ 12 Jason Peter RC	1.00	2.50
❑ 13 Anthony Simmons RC	1.25	3.00
❑ 14 Kevin Dyson RC	2.00	5.00
❑ 15 Brian Simmons RC	1.25	3.00

Card	Low	High
❑ 16 Robert Edwards RC	1.25	3.00
❑ 17 Randy Moss RC	10.00	25.00
❑ 18 John Avery RC	1.25	3.00
❑ 19 Marcus Nash RC	1.00	2.50
❑ 20 Jerome Pathon RC	2.00	5.00
❑ 21 Jacquez Green RC	1.25	3.00
❑ 22 Robert Holcombe RC	1.25	3.00
❑ 23 Pat Johnson RC	1.25	3.00
❑ 24 Germane Crowell RC	1.25	3.00
❑ 25 Joe Jurevicius RC	2.00	5.00
❑ 26 Skip Hicks RC	1.25	3.00
❑ 27 Ahman Green RC	5.00	12.00
❑ 28 Brian Griese RC	4.00	10.00
❑ 29 Hines Ward RC	10.00	20.00
❑ 30 Tavian Banks RC	1.25	3.00
❑ 31 Tony Simmons RC	1.25	3.00
❑ 32 Victor Riley RC	1.00	2.50
❑ 33 Rashaan Shehee RC	1.25	3.00
❑ 34 R.W. McQuarters RC	1.25	3.00
❑ 35 Flozell Adams RC	1.00	2.50
❑ 36 Tra Thomas RC	1.00	2.50
❑ 37 Greg Favors RC	1.25	3.00
❑ 38 Jon Ritchie RC	1.25	3.00
❑ 39 Jesse Haynes RC	1.00	2.50
❑ 40 Ryan Sutter RC	1.00	2.50
❑ 41 Mo Collins RC	1.00	2.50
❑ 42 Tim Dwight RC	2.00	5.00
❑ 43 Chris Chandler	.15	.40
❑ 44 Byron Hanspard	.08	.25
❑ 45 Jessie Tuggle	.08	.25
❑ 46 Jamal Anderson	.25	.60
❑ 47 Terance Mathis	.15	.40
❑ 48 Morten Andersen	.08	.25
❑ 49 Jake Plummer	.25	.60
❑ 50 Mario Bates	.15	.40
❑ 51 Frank Sanders	.15	.40
❑ 52 Adrian Murrell	.15	.40
❑ 53 Simeon Rice	.15	.40
❑ 54 Aeneas Williams	.08	.25
❑ 55 Eric Swann UER	.08	.25
❑ 56 Jim Harbaugh	.15	.40
❑ 57 Michael Jackson	.08	.25
❑ 58 Peter Boulware	.08	.25
❑ 59 Errict Rhett	.15	.40
❑ 60 Jermaine Lewis	.15	.40
❑ 61 Eric Zeier	.15	.40
❑ 62 Rod Woodson	.15	.40
❑ 63 Rob Johnson	.25	.60
❑ 64 Antowain Smith	.25	.60
❑ 65 Bruce Smith	.15	.40
❑ 66 Eric Moulds	.25	.60
❑ 67 Andre Reed	.15	.40
❑ 68 Thurman Thomas	.25	.60
❑ 69 Lonnie Johnson	.08	.25
❑ 70 Kerry Collins	.15	.40
❑ 71 Kevin Greene	.15	.40
❑ 72 Fred Lane	.08	.25
❑ 73 Rae Carruth	.08	.25
❑ 74 Michael Bates	.08	.25
❑ 75 William Floyd	.08	.25
❑ 76 Sean Gilbert	.08	.25
❑ 77 Erik Kramer	.08	.25
❑ 78 Edgar Bennett	.08	.25
❑ 79 Curtis Conway	.15	.40
❑ 80 Darnell Autry	.08	.25
❑ 81 Ryan Wetnight RC	.08	.25
❑ 82 Walt Harris	.08	.25
❑ 83 Bobby Engram	.15	.40
❑ 84 Jeff Blake	.15	.40
❑ 85 Carl Pickens	.15	.40
❑ 86 Darnay Scott	.15	.40
❑ 87 Corey Dillon	.25	.60
❑ 88 Reinard Wilson	.08	.25
❑ 89 Ashley Ambrose	.08	.25
❑ 90 Troy Aikman	.50	1.25
❑ 91 Michael Irvin	.25	.60
❑ 92 Emmitt Smith	.75	2.00
❑ 93 Deion Sanders	.25	.60
❑ 94 David LaFleur	.08	.25
❑ 95 Chris Warren	.15	.40
❑ 96 Darren Woodson	.08	.25
❑ 97 John Elway	1.00	2.50
❑ 98 Terrell Davis	.25	.60
❑ 99 Rod Smith	.15	.40
❑ 100 Shannon Sharpe	.15	.40
❑ 101 Ed McCaffrey	.15	.40
❑ 102 Steve Atwater	.08	.25
❑ 103 John Mobley	.08	.25
❑ 104 Darrien Gordon	.08	.25
❑ 105 Barry Sanders	.75	2.00
❑ 106 Scott Mitchell	.15	.40
❑ 107 Herman Moore	.15	.40
❑ 108 Johnnie Morton	.15	.40
❑ 109 Robert Porcher	.08	.25
❑ 110 Bryant Westbrook	.08	.25
❑ 111 Tommy Vardell	.08	.25
❑ 112 Brett Favre	1.00	2.50
❑ 113 Dorsey Levens	.25	.60
❑ 114 Reggie White	.25	.60
❑ 115 Antonio Freeman	.25	.60
❑ 116 Robert Brooks	.15	.40
❑ 117 Mark Chmura	.15	.40
❑ 118 Derrick Mayes	.15	.40
❑ 119 Gilbert Brown	.08	.25
❑ 120 Marshall Faulk	.30	.75
❑ 121 Jeff Burris	.08	.25
❑ 122 Marvin Harrison	.25	.60
❑ 123 Quentin Coryatt	.08	.25
❑ 124 Ken Dilger	.08	.25
❑ 125 Zack Crockett	.08	.25
❑ 126 Mark Brunell	.25	.60
❑ 127 Bryce Paup	.08	.25
❑ 128 Tony Brackens	.08	.25
❑ 129 Renaldo Wynn	.08	.25
❑ 130 Keenan McCardell	.15	.40
❑ 131 Jimmy Smith	.15	.40
❑ 132 Kevin Hardy	.08	.25
❑ 133 Elvis Grbac	.15	.40
❑ 134 Tamarick Vanover	.08	.25
❑ 135 Chester McGlockton	.08	.25
❑ 136 Andre Rison	.15	.40
❑ 137 Derrick Alexander	.15	.40
❑ 138 Tony Gonzalez	.25	.60
❑ 139 Derrick Thomas	.25	.60
❑ 140 Dan Marino	1.00	2.50
❑ 141 Karim Abdul-Jabbar	.25	.60
❑ 142 O.J. McDuffie	.15	.40
❑ 143 Yatil Green	.08	.25
❑ 144 Charles Jordan	.08	.25
❑ 145 Brock Marion	.08	.25
❑ 146 Zach Thomas	.25	.60
❑ 147 Brad Johnson	.25	.60
❑ 148 Cris Carter	.25	.60
❑ 149 Jake Reed	.15	.40
❑ 150 Robert Smith	.25	.60
❑ 151 John Randle	.15	.40
❑ 152 Dwayne Rudd	.08	.25
❑ 153 Randall Cunningham	.25	.60
❑ 154 Drew Bledsoe	.40	1.00
❑ 155 Terry Glenn	.25	.60
❑ 156 Ben Coates	.15	.40
❑ 157 Willie Clay	.08	.25
❑ 158 Chris Slade	.08	.25
❑ 159 Derrick Cullors RC	.08	.25
❑ 160 Ty Law	.15	.40
❑ 161 Danny Wuerffel	.15	.40
❑ 162 Andre Hastings	.08	.25
❑ 163 Troy Davis	.08	.25
❑ 164 Billy Joe Hobert	.08	.25
❑ 165 Eric Guliford	.08	.25
❑ 166 Mark Fields	.08	.25
❑ 167 Alex Molden	.08	.25
❑ 168 Danny Kanell	.15	.40
❑ 169 Tiki Barber	.25	.60
❑ 170 Charles Way	.08	.25
❑ 171 Amani Toomer	.15	.40
❑ 172 Michael Strahan	.15	.40
❑ 173 Jessie Armstead	.08	.25
❑ 174 Jason Sehorn	.15	.40
❑ 175 Glenn Foley	.15	.40
❑ 176 Curtis Martin	.25	.60
❑ 177 Aaron Glenn	.08	.25
❑ 178 Keyshawn Johnson	.25	.60
❑ 179 James Farrior	.08	.25
❑ 180 Wayne Chrebet	.25	.60
❑ 181 Keith Byars	.08	.25
❑ 182 Jeff George	.15	.40
❑ 183 Napoleon Kaufman	.25	.60
❑ 184 Tim Brown	.25	.60
❑ 185 Darrell Russell	.08	.25
❑ 186 Rickey Dudley	.08	.25
❑ 187 James Jett	.15	.40
❑ 188 Desmond Howard	.15	.40
❑ 189 Bobby Hoying	.15	.40
❑ 190 Charlie Garner	.15	.40
❑ 191 Irving Fryar	.15	.40
❑ 192 Chris T. Jones	.08	.25
❑ 193 Mike Mamula	.08	.25
❑ 194 Troy Vincent	.08	.25
❑ 195 Kordell Stewart	.25	.60
❑ 196 Jerome Bettis	.25	.60
❑ 197 Will Blackwell	.08	.25
❑ 198 Levon Kirkland	.08	.25
❑ 199 Carnell Lake	.08	.25
❑ 200 Charles Johnson	.08	.25
❑ 201 Greg Lloyd	.08	.25
❑ 202 Donnell Woolford	.08	.25
❑ 203 Tony Banks	.15	.40
❑ 204 Amp Lee	.08	.25
❑ 205 Isaac Bruce	.25	.60
❑ 206 Eddie Kennison	.15	.40
❑ 207 Ryan McNeil	.08	.25
❑ 208 Mike Jones	.08	.25
❑ 209 Ernie Conwell	.08	.25
❑ 210 Natrone Means	.15	.40
❑ 211 Junior Seau	.25	.60
❑ 212 Tony Martin	.15	.40
❑ 213 Freddie Jones	.08	.25
❑ 214 Bryan Still	.08	.25
❑ 215 Rodney Harrison	.15	.40
❑ 216 Steve Young	.30	.75
❑ 217 Jerry Rice	.50	1.25
❑ 218 Garrison Hearst	.25	.60
❑ 219 J.J. Stokes	.15	.40
❑ 220 Ken Norton	.08	.25
❑ 221 Greg Clark	.08	.25
❑ 222 Terrell Owens	.25	.60
❑ 223 Bryant Young	.08	.25
❑ 224 Warren Moon	.25	.60
❑ 225 Jon Kitna	.25	.60
❑ 226 Ricky Watters	.15	.40
❑ 227 Chad Brown	.08	.25
❑ 228 Joey Galloway	.15	.40
❑ 229 Shawn Springs	.08	.25
❑ 230 Cortez Kennedy	.08	.25
❑ 231 Trent Dilfer	.25	.60
❑ 232 Warrick Dunn	.25	.60
❑ 233 Mike Alstott	.25	.60
❑ 234 Warren Sapp	.15	.40
❑ 235 Bert Emanuel	.15	.40
❑ 236 Reidel Anthony	.15	.40
❑ 237 Hardy Nickerson	.08	.25
❑ 238 Derrick Brooks	.25	.60
❑ 239 Steve McNair	.25	.60
❑ 240 Yancey Thigpen	.08	.25
❑ 241 Anthony Dorsett	.08	.25
❑ 242 Blaine Bishop	.08	.25
❑ 243 Kenny Holmes	.08	.25
❑ 244 Eddie George	.25	.60
❑ 245 Chris Sanders	.08	.25
❑ 246 Gus Frerotte	.08	.25
❑ 247 Terry Allen	.25	.60
❑ 248 Dana Stubblefield	.08	.25
❑ 249 Michael Westbrook	.15	.40
❑ 250 Darrell Green	.15	.40
❑ 251 Brian Mitchell	.08	.25
❑ 252 Ken Harvey	.08	.25
❑ CL1 Troy Aikman CL	.25	.60
❑ CL2 Dan Marino CL	.30	.75
❑ CL3 Herman Moore CL	.15	.40

1999 Upper Deck

Card	Low	High
❑ COMPLETE SET (270)	50.00	100.00
❑ COMP.SET w/o SP's (225)	12.50	25.00
❑ 1 Jake Plummer	.20	.50
❑ 2 Adrian Murrell	.20	.50
❑ 3 Rob Moore	.20	.50
❑ 4 Larry Centers	.10	.30
❑ 5 Simeon Rice	.20	.50
❑ 6 Andre Wadsworth	.10	.30

❑ 7 Frank Sanders	.20	.50
❑ 8 Tim Dwight	.30	.75
❑ 9 Ray Buchanan	.10	.30
❑ 10 Chris Chandler	.20	.50
❑ 11 Jamal Anderson	.30	.75
❑ 12 O.J. Santiago	.10	.30
❑ 13 Danny Kanell	.10	.30
❑ 14 Terance Mathis	.20	.50
❑ 15 Priest Holmes	.50	1.25
❑ 16 Tony Banks	.20	.50
❑ 17 Ray Lewis	.30	.75
❑ 18 Patrick Johnson	.10	.30
❑ 19 Michael Jackson	.10	.30
❑ 20 Michael McCrary	.10	.30
❑ 21 Jermaine Lewis	.20	.50
❑ 22 Eric Moulds	.30	.75
❑ 23 Doug Flutie	.30	.75
❑ 24 Antowain Smith	.30	.75
❑ 25 Rob Johnson	.20	.50
❑ 26 Bruce Smith	.20	.50
❑ 27 Andre Reed	.20	.50
❑ 28 Thurman Thomas	.20	.50
❑ 29 Fred Lane	.10	.30
❑ 30 Wesley Walls	.20	.50
❑ 31 Tim Biakabutuka	.20	.50
❑ 32 Kevin Greene	.10	.30
❑ 33 Steve Beuerlein	.10	.30
❑ 34 Muhsin Muhammad	.20	.50
❑ 35 Rae Carruth	.10	.30
❑ 36 Bobby Engram	.20	.50
❑ 37 Curtis Enis	.10	.30
❑ 38 Edgar Bennett	.10	.30
❑ 39 Erik Kramer	.10	.30
❑ 40 Steve Stenstrom	.10	.30
❑ 41 Alonzo Mayes	.10	.30
❑ 42 Curtis Conway	.20	.50
❑ 43 Tony McGee	.10	.30
❑ 44 Darnay Scott	.10	.30
❑ 45 Jeff Blake	.20	.50
❑ 46 Corey Dillon	.30	.75
❑ 47 Ki-Jana Carter	.10	.30
❑ 48 Takeo Spikes	.10	.30
❑ 49 Carl Pickens	.20	.50
❑ 50 Ty Detmer	.20	.50
❑ 51 Leslie Shepherd	.10	.30
❑ 52 Terry Kirby	.10	.30
❑ 53 Marquez Pope	.10	.30
❑ 54 Antonio Langham	.10	.30
❑ 55 Jamir Miller	.10	.30
❑ 56 Derrick Alexander DT	.10	.30
❑ 57 Troy Aikman	.60	1.50
❑ 58 Rocket Ismail	.20	.50
❑ 59 Emmitt Smith	.60	1.50
❑ 60 Michael Irvin	.20	.50
❑ 61 David LaFleur	.10	.30
❑ 62 Chris Warren	.10	.30
❑ 63 Deion Sanders	.30	.75
❑ 64 Greg Ellis	.10	.30
❑ 65 John Elway	1.00	2.50
❑ 66 Bubby Brister	.10	.30
❑ 67 Terrell Davis	.30	.75
❑ 68 Ed McCaffrey	.20	.50
❑ 69 John Mobley	.10	.30
❑ 70 Bill Romanowski	.10	.30
❑ 71 Rod Smith	.20	.50
❑ 72 Shannon Sharpe	.20	.50
❑ 73 Charlie Batch	.30	.75
❑ 74 Germane Crowell	.10	.30
❑ 75 Johnnie Morton	.10	.30
❑ 76 Barry Sanders	1.00	2.50
❑ 77 Robert Porcher	.10	.30
❑ 78 Stephen Boyd	.10	.30
❑ 79 Herman Moore	.20	.50
❑ 80 Brett Favre	1.00	2.50
❑ 81 Mark Chmura	.10	.30
❑ 82 Antonio Freeman	.30	.75
❑ 83 Robert Brooks	.20	.50
❑ 84 Vonnie Holliday	.10	.30
❑ 85 Bill Schroeder	.30	.75
❑ 86 Dorsey Levens	.30	.75
❑ 87 Santana Dotson	.10	.30
❑ 88 Peyton Manning	1.00	2.50
❑ 89 Jerome Pathon	.10	.30
❑ 90 Marvin Harrison	.30	.75
❑ 91 Ellis Johnson	.10	.30
❑ 92 Ken Dilger	.10	.30
❑ 93 E.G. Green	.10	.30
❑ 94 Jeff Burris	.10	.30
❑ 95 Mark Brunell	.30	.75
❑ 96 Fred Taylor	.30	.75
❑ 97 Jimmy Smith	.20	.50
❑ 98 James Stewart	.20	.50
❑ 99 Kyle Brady	.10	.30
❑ 100 Dave Thomas RC	.10	.30
❑ 101 Keenan McCardell	.20	.50
❑ 102 Elvis Grbac	.20	.50
❑ 103 Tony Gonzalez	.30	.75
❑ 104 Andre Rison	.20	.50
❑ 105 Donnell Bennett	.10	.30
❑ 106 Derrick Thomas	.30	.75
❑ 107 Warren Moon	.30	.75
❑ 108 Derrick Alexander WR	.20	.50
❑ 109 Dan Marino	1.00	2.50
❑ 110 O.J. McDuffie	.20	.50
❑ 111 Karim Abdul-Jabbar	.20	.50
❑ 112 John Avery	.10	.30
❑ 113 Sam Madison	.10	.30
❑ 114 Jason Taylor	.10	.30
❑ 115 Zach Thomas	.30	.75
❑ 116 Randall Cunningham	.30	.75
❑ 117 Randy Moss	.75	2.00
❑ 118 Cris Carter	.30	.75
❑ 119 Jake Reed	.20	.50
❑ 120 Matthew Hatchette	.10	.30
❑ 121 John Randle	.20	.50
❑ 122 Robert Smith	.30	.75
❑ 123 Drew Bledsoe	.40	1.00
❑ 124 Ben Coates	.20	.50
❑ 125 Terry Glenn	.30	.75
❑ 126 Ty Law	.20	.50
❑ 127 Tony Simmons	.10	.30
❑ 128 Ted Johnson	.10	.30
❑ 129 Tony Carter	.10	.30
❑ 130 Willie McGinest	.10	.30
❑ 131 Danny Wuerffel	.10	.30
❑ 132 Cameron Cleeland	.10	.30
❑ 133 Eddie Kennison	.20	.50
❑ 134 Joe Johnson	.10	.30
❑ 135 Andre Hastings	.10	.30
❑ 136 La'Roi Glover RC	.30	.75
❑ 137 Kent Graham	.10	.30
❑ 138 Tiki Barber	.30	.75
❑ 139 Gary Brown	.10	.30
❑ 140 Ike Hilliard	.10	.30
❑ 141 Jason Sehorn	.10	.30
❑ 142 Michael Strahan	.20	.50
❑ 143 Amani Toomer	.10	.30
❑ 144 Kerry Collins	.20	.50
❑ 145 Vinny Testaverde	.20	.50
❑ 146 Wayne Chrebet	.20	.50
❑ 147 Curtis Martin	.30	.75
❑ 148 Mo Lewis	.10	.30
❑ 149 Aaron Glenn	.10	.30
❑ 150 Steve Atwater	.10	.30
❑ 151 Keyshawn Johnson	.30	.75
❑ 152 James Farrior	.10	.30
❑ 153 Rich Gannon	.30	.75
❑ 154 Tim Brown	.30	.75
❑ 155 Darrell Russell	.10	.30
❑ 156 Rickey Dudley	.10	.30
❑ 157 Charles Woodson	.30	.75
❑ 158 James Jett	.20	.50
❑ 159 Napoleon Kaufman	.30	.75
❑ 160 Duce Staley	.30	.75
❑ 161 Doug Pederson	.10	.30
❑ 162 Bobby Hoying	.20	.50
❑ 163 Koy Detmer	.10	.30
❑ 164 Kevin Turner	.10	.30
❑ 165 Charles Johnson	.10	.30
❑ 166 Mike Mamula	.10	.30
❑ 167 Jerome Bettis	.30	.75
❑ 168 Courtney Hawkins	.10	.30
❑ 169 Will Blackwell	.10	.30
❑ 170 Kordell Stewart	.20	.50
❑ 171 Richard Huntley	.20	.50
❑ 172 Levon Kirkland	.10	.30
❑ 173 Hines Ward	.30	.75
❑ 174 Trent Green	.30	.75
❑ 175 Marshall Faulk	.40	1.00
❑ 176 Az-Zahir Hakim	.10	.30
❑ 177 Amp Lee	.10	.30
❑ 178 Robert Holcombe	.10	.30
❑ 179 Isaac Bruce	.30	.75
❑ 180 Kevin Carter	.10	.30
❑ 181 Jim Harbaugh	.20	.50
❑ 182 Junior Seau	.30	.75
❑ 183 Natrone Means	.20	.50
❑ 184 Ryan Leaf	.30	.75
❑ 185 Charlie Jones	.10	.30
❑ 186 Rodney Harrison	.10	.30
❑ 187 Mikhael Ricks	.10	.30
❑ 188 Steve Young	.40	1.00
❑ 189 Terrell Owens	.30	.75
❑ 190 Jerry Rice	.60	1.50
❑ 191 J.J. Stokes	.20	.50
❑ 192 Irv Smith	.10	.30
❑ 193 Bryant Young	.10	.30
❑ 194 Garrison Hearst	.20	.50
❑ 195 Jon Kitna	.30	.75
❑ 196 Ahman Green	.30	.75
❑ 197 Joey Galloway	.20	.50
❑ 198 Ricky Watters	.20	.50
❑ 199 Chad Brown	.10	.30
❑ 200 Shawn Springs	.10	.30
❑ 201 Mike Pritchard	.10	.30
❑ 202 Trent Dilfer	.20	.50
❑ 203 Reidel Anthony	.20	.50
❑ 204 Bert Emanuel	.20	.50
❑ 205 Warrick Dunn	.30	.75
❑ 206 Jacquez Green	.10	.30
❑ 207 Hardy Nickerson	.10	.30
❑ 208 Mike Alstott	.30	.75
❑ 209 Eddie George	.30	.75
❑ 210 Steve McNair	.30	.75
❑ 211 Kevin Dyson	.20	.50
❑ 212 Frank Wycheck	.10	.30
❑ 213 Jackie Harris	.10	.30
❑ 214 Blaine Bishop	.10	.30
❑ 215 Yancey Thigpen	.10	.30
❑ 216 Brad Johnson	.30	.75
❑ 217 Rodney Peete	.10	.30
❑ 218 Michael Westbrook	.20	.50
❑ 219 Skip Hicks	.10	.30
❑ 220 Brian Mitchell	.10	.30
❑ 221 Dan Wilkinson	.10	.30
❑ 222 Dana Stubblefield	.10	.30
❑ 223 Kordell Stewart CL	.20	.50
❑ 224 Fred Taylor CL	.30	.75
❑ 225 Warrick Dunn CL	.20	.50
❑ 226 Champ Bailey RC	1.25	3.00
❑ 227 Chris McAlister RC	.60	1.50
❑ 228 Jevon Kearse RC	1.50	4.00
❑ 229 Ebenezer Ekuban RC	.60	1.50
❑ 230 Chris Claiborne RC	.40	1.00
❑ 231 Andy Katzenmoyer RC	.60	1.50
❑ 232 Tim Couch RC	.75	2.00
❑ 233 Daunte Culpepper RC	4.00	10.00
❑ 234 Akili Smith RC	.60	1.50
❑ 235 Donovan McNabb RC	5.00	12.00
❑ 236 Sean Bennett RC	.40	1.00
❑ 237 Brock Huard RC	.75	2.00
❑ 238 Cade McNown RC	.60	1.50
❑ 239 Shaun King RC	.60	1.50
❑ 240 Joe Germaine RC	.60	1.50
❑ 241 Ricky Williams RC	2.00	5.00
❑ 242 Edgerrin James RC	4.00	10.00
❑ 243 Sedrick Irvin RC	.40	1.00
❑ 244 Kevin Faulk RC	.75	2.00
❑ 245 Rob Konrad RC	.75	2.00
❑ 246 James Johnson RC	.60	1.50
❑ 247 Amos Zereoue RC	.75	2.00
❑ 248 Torry Holt RC	2.50	6.00
❑ 249 D'Wayne Bates RC	.60	1.50
❑ 250 David Boston RC	.75	2.00
❑ 251 Dameane Douglas RC	.75	2.00
❑ 252 Troy Edwards RC	.60	1.50
❑ 253 Kevin Johnson RC	.75	2.00
❑ 254 Peerless Price RC	.75	2.00
❑ 255 Antoine Winfield RC	.60	1.50
❑ 256 Mike Cloud RC	.60	1.50
❑ 257 Joe Montgomery RC	.60	1.50
❑ 258 Jermaine Fazande RC	.60	1.50
❑ 259 Scott Covington RC	.75	2.00
❑ 260 Aaron Brooks RC	2.00	5.00
❑ 261 Patrick Kerney RC	.75	2.00
❑ 262 Cecil Collins RC	.40	1.00
❑ 263 Chris Greisen RC	.60	1.50
❑ 264 Craig Yeast RC	.60	1.50
❑ 265 Karsten Bailey RC	.60	1.50
❑ 266 Reginald Kelly RC	.40	1.00
❑ 267 Al Wilson RC	.60	1.50
❑ 268 Jeff Paulk RC	.40	1.00
❑ 269 Jim Kleinsasser RC	.75	2.00
❑ 270 Darrin Chiaverini RC	.60	1.50

2000 Upper Deck

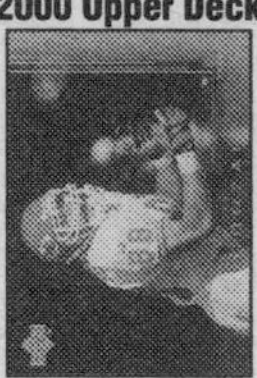

Card		
COMPLETE SET (1-270)	60.00	120.00
COMP.SET w/o SPs (222)	12.50	30.00
1 Jake Plummer	.20	.50
2 Michael Pittman	.10	.30
3 Rob Moore	.20	.50
4 David Boston	.30	.75
5 Frank Sanders	.20	.50
6 Aeneas Williams	.10	.30
7 Kwamie Lassiter	.10	.30
8 Rob Fredrickson	.10	.30
9 Tim Dwight	.30	.75
10 Chris Chandler	.20	.50
11 Jamal Anderson	.30	.75
12 Shawn Jefferson	.10	.30
13 Ken Oxendine	.10	.30
14 Terance Mathis	.20	.50
15 Bob Christian	.10	.30
16 Qadry Ismail	.20	.50
17 Jermaine Lewis	.20	.50
18 Rod Woodson	.20	.50
19 Michael McCrary	.10	.30
20 Tony Banks	.20	.50
21 Peter Boulware	.10	.30
22 Shannon Sharpe	.20	.50
23 Peerless Price	.20	.50
24 Rob Johnson	.20	.50
25 Eric Moulds	.30	.75
26 Doug Flutie	.30	.75
27 Jay Riemersma	.10	.30
28 Antowain Smith	.20	.50
29 Jonathan Linton	.10	.30
30 Muhsin Muhammad	.20	.50
31 Patrick Jeffers	.30	.75
32 Steve Beuerlein	.20	.50
33 Natrone Means	.10	.30
34 Tim Biakabutuka	.20	.50
35 Michael Bates	.10	.30
36 Chuck Smith	.10	.30
37 Wesley Walls	.10	.30
38 Cade McNown	.10	.30
39 Curtis Enis	.10	.30
40 Marcus Robinson	.30	.75
41 Eddie Kennison	.20	.50
42 Bobby Engram	.20	.50
43 Glyn Milburn	.10	.30
44 Marty Booker	.20	.50
45 Akili Smith	.10	.30
46 Corey Dillon	.30	.75
47 Darnay Scott	.20	.50
48 Tremain Mack	.10	.30
49 Damon Griffin	.10	.30
50 Takeo Spikes	.10	.30
51 Tony McGee	.10	.30
52 Tim Couch	.20	.50
53 Kevin Johnson	.30	.75
54 Darrin Chiaverini	.10	.30
55 Jamir Miller	.10	.30
56 Errict Rhett	.20	.50
57 Terry Kirby	.10	.30
58 Marc Edwards	.10	.30
59 Troy Aikman	.60	1.50
60 Emmitt Smith	.60	1.50
61 Rocket Ismail	.20	.50
62 Jason Tucker	.10	.30
63 Dexter Coakley	.10	.30
64 Joey Galloway	.20	.50
65 Wane McGarity	.10	.30
66 Terrell Davis	.30	.75
67 Olandis Gary	.30	.75
68 Brian Griese	.30	.75
69 Gus Frerotte	.10	.30
70 Byron Chamberlain	.10	.30
71 Ed McCaffrey	.30	.75
72 Rod Smith	.20	.50
73 Al Wilson	.10	.30
74 Charlie Batch	.30	.75
75 Germane Crowell	.10	.30
76 Sedrick Irvin	.10	.30
77 Johnnie Morton	.20	.50
78 Robert Porcher	.10	.30
79 Herman Moore	.20	.50
80 James Stewart	.20	.50
81 Brett Favre	1.00	2.50
82 Antonio Freeman	.30	.75
83 Bill Schroeder	.20	.50
84 Dorsey Levens	.20	.50
85 Corey Bradford	.20	.50
86 De'Mond Parker	.10	.30
87 Vonnie Holliday	.10	.30
88 Peyton Manning	.75	2.00
89 Edgerrin James	.50	1.25
90 Marvin Harrison	.30	.75
91 Ken Dilger	.10	.30
92 Terrence Wilkins	.10	.30
93 Marcus Pollard	.10	.30
94 Fred Lane	.10	.30
95 Mark Brunell	.30	.75
96 Fred Taylor	.30	.75
97 Jimmy Smith	.20	.50
98 Keenan McCardell	.20	.50
99 Carnell Lake	.10	.30
100 Tavian Banks	.10	.30
101 Kyle Brady	.10	.30
102 Hardy Nickerson	.10	.30
103 Elvis Grbac	.20	.50
104 Tony Gonzalez	.20	.50
105 Derrick Alexander WR	.20	.50
106 Donnell Bennett	.10	.30
107 Mike Cloud	.10	.30
108 Donnie Edwards	.10	.30
109 Jay Fiedler	.30	.75
110 James Johnson	.10	.30
111 Tony Martin	.20	.50
112 Damon Huard	.30	.75
113 O.J. McDuffie	.20	.50
114 Thurman Thomas	.20	.50
115 Zach Thomas	.30	.75
116 Oronde Gadsden	.20	.50
117 Randy Moss	.60	1.50
118 Robert Smith	.30	.75
119 Cris Carter	.30	.75
120 Matthew Hatchette	.10	.30
121 Daunte Culpepper	.40	1.00
122 Leroy Hoard	.10	.30
123 Drew Bledsoe	.40	1.00
124 Terry Glenn	.20	.50
125 Troy Brown	.20	.50
126 Kevin Faulk	.10	.30
127 Lawyer Milloy	.20	.50
128 Ricky Williams	.30	.75
129 Keith Poole	.10	.30
130 Jake Reed	.20	.50
131 Cam Cleeland	.10	.30
132 Jeff Blake	.20	.50
133 Andrew Glover	.10	.30
134 Kerry Collins	.20	.50
135 Amani Toomer	.20	.50
136 Joe Montgomery	.10	.30
137 Ike Hilliard	.20	.50
138 Tiki Barber	.30	.75
139 Pete Mitchell	.10	.30
140 Ray Lucas	.20	.50
141 Mo Lewis	.10	.30
142 Curtis Martin	.30	.75
143 Vinny Testaverde	.20	.50
144 Wayne Chrebet	.20	.50
145 Dedric Ward	.10	.30
146 Tim Brown	.30	.75
147 Rich Gannon	.30	.75
148 Tyrone Wheatley	.20	.50
149 Napoleon Kaufman	.20	.50
150 Charles Woodson	.20	.50
151 Darrell Russell	.10	.30
152 James Jett	.10	.30
153 Rickey Dudley	.10	.30
154 Jon Ritchie	.10	.30
155 Duce Staley	.30	.75
156 Donovan McNabb	.50	1.25
157 Torrance Small	.10	.30
158 Allen Rossum	.10	.30
159 Mike Mamula	.10	.30
160 Na Brown	.10	.30
161 Charles Johnson	.20	.50
162 Kent Graham	.10	.30
163 Troy Edwards	.10	.30
164 Jerome Bettis	.30	.75
165 Hines Ward	.30	.75
166 Kordell Stewart	.20	.50
167 Levon Kirkland	.10	.30
168 Richard Huntley	.10	.30
169 Marshall Faulk	.40	1.00
170 Kurt Warner	.60	1.50
171 Torry Holt	.30	.75
172 Isaac Bruce	.30	.75
173 Kevin Carter	.10	.30
174 Az-Zahir Hakim	.20	.50
175 Ricky Proehl	.10	.30
176 Jermaine Fazande	.10	.30
177 Curtis Conway	.20	.50
178 Freddie Jones	.10	.30
179 Junior Seau	.30	.75
180 Jeff Graham	.10	.30
181 Jim Harbaugh	.20	.50
182 Rodney Harrison	.10	.30
183 Steve Young	.40	1.00
184 Jerry Rice	.60	1.50
185 Charlie Garner	.20	.50
186 Terrell Owens	.30	.75
187 Jeff Garcia	.30	.75
188 Fred Beasley	.10	.30
189 J.J. Stokes	.20	.50
190 Ricky Watters	.20	.50
191 Jon Kitna	.30	.75
192 Derrick Mayes	.20	.50
193 Sean Dawkins	.10	.30
194 Charlie Rogers	.10	.30
195 Mike Pritchard	.10	.30
196 Cortez Kennedy	.10	.30
197 Christian Fauria	.10	.30
198 Warrick Dunn	.30	.75
199 Shaun King	.10	.30
200 Mike Alstott	.30	.75
201 Warren Sapp	.20	.50
202 Jacquez Green	.10	.30
203 Reidel Anthony	.10	.30
204 Dave Moore	.10	.30
205 Keyshawn Johnson	.30	.75
206 Eddie George	.30	.75
207 Steve McNair	.30	.75
208 Kevin Dyson	.20	.50
209 Jevon Kearse	.30	.75
210 Yancey Thigpen	.10	.30
211 Frank Wycheck	.10	.30
212 Isaac Byrd	.10	.30
213 Neil O'Donnell	.10	.30
214 Brad Johnson	.30	.75
215 Stephen Davis	.30	.75
216 Michael Westbrook	.20	.50
217 Albert Connell	.10	.30
218 Brian Mitchell	.10	.30
219 Bruce Smith	.20	.50
220 Stephen Alexander	.10	.30
221 Jeff George	.20	.50
222 Adrian Murrell	.10	.30
223 Courtney Brown RC	1.50	4.00
224 John Engelberger RC	1.00	2.50
225 Deltha O'Neal RC	1.50	4.00
226 Corey Simon RC	1.50	4.00
227 R.Jay Soward RC	1.00	2.50
228 Marc Bulger RC	3.00	8.00
229 Raynoch Thompson RC	1.00	2.50
230 Deon Grant RC	1.00	2.50
231 Darrell Jackson RC	3.00	8.00
232 Chris Cole RC	1.00	2.50
233 Trevor Gaylor RC	1.00	2.50
234 John Abraham RC	1.50	4.00
235 Chris Redman RC	1.00	2.50
236 Joe Hamilton RC	1.00	2.50
237 Chad Pennington RC	4.00	10.00
238 Tee Martin RC	1.50	4.00
239 Giovanni Carmazzi RC	.75	2.00
240 Tim Rattay RC	1.50	4.00
241 Ron Dayne RC	1.50	4.00
242 Shaun Alexander RC	5.00	12.00
243 Thomas Jones RC	2.50	6.00
244 Reuben Droughns RC	1.50	4.00
245 Jamal Lewis RC	4.00	10.00
246 Michael Wiley RC	1.00	2.50

Card	Low	High
❑ 247 J.R. Redmond RC	1.00	2.50
❑ 248 Travis Prentice RC	1.00	2.50
❑ 249 Todd Husak RC	1.50	4.00
❑ 250 Trung Canidate RC	1.00	2.50
❑ 251 Brian Urlacher RC	6.00	15.00
❑ 252 Anthony Becht RC	1.50	4.00
❑ 253 Bubba Franks RC	1.50	4.00
❑ 254 Tom Brady RC	20.00	50.00
❑ 255 Peter Warrick RC	1.50	4.00
❑ 256 Plaxico Burress RC	3.00	8.00
❑ 257 Sylvester Morris RC	1.00	2.50
❑ 258 Dez White RC	1.50	4.00
❑ 259 Travis Taylor RC	1.50	4.00
❑ 260 Todd Pinkston RC	1.50	4.00
❑ 261 Dennis Northcutt RC	1.50	4.00
❑ 262 Jerry Porter RC	2.00	5.00
❑ 263 Laveranues Coles RC	2.00	5.00
❑ 264 Danny Farmer RC	1.00	2.50
❑ 265 Curtis Keaton RC	1.00	2.50
❑ 266 Sherrod Gideon RC	.75	2.00
❑ 267 Ron Dugans RC	.75	2.00
❑ 268 Steve McNair CL	.20	.50
❑ 269 Jake Plummer CL	.20	.50
❑ 270 Antonio Freeman CL	.20	.50

2001 Upper Deck

Card	Low	High
❑ COMPLETE SET (280)	150.00	300.00
❑ COMP.SET w/o SP's (180)	10.00	25.00
❑ 1 Jake Plummer	.25	.60
❑ 2 David Boston	.20	.50
❑ 3 Thomas Jones	.25	.60
❑ 4 Frank Sanders	.20	.50
❑ 5 Eric Zeier	.20	.50
❑ 6 Jamal Anderson	.25	.60
❑ 7 Chris Chandler	.25	.60
❑ 8 Shawn Jefferson	.20	.50
❑ 9 Darrick Vaughn	.20	.50
❑ 10 Terance Mathis	.20	.50
❑ 11 Jamal Lewis	.30	.75
❑ 12 Shannon Sharpe	.30	.75
❑ 13 Elvis Grbac	.25	.60
❑ 14 Ray Lewis	.30	.75
❑ 15 Qadry Ismail	.25	.60
❑ 16 Chris Redman	.30	.75
❑ 17 Rob Johnson	.25	.60
❑ 18 Eric Moulds	.25	.60
❑ 19 Sammy Morris	.25	.60
❑ 20 Shawn Bryson	.20	.50
❑ 21 Jeremy McDaniel	.20	.50
❑ 22 Muhsin Muhammad	.25	.60
❑ 23 Brad Hoover	.25	.60
❑ 24 Tim Biakabutuka	.20	.50
❑ 25 Steve Beuerlein	.25	.60
❑ 26 Jeff Lewis	.20	.50
❑ 27 Wesley Walls	.20	.50
❑ 28 Cade McNown	.25	.60
❑ 29 James Allen	.20	.50
❑ 30 Marcus Robinson	.25	.60
❑ 31 Brian Urlacher	.40	1.00
❑ 32 Bobby Engram	.25	.60
❑ 33 Peter Warrick	.25	.60
❑ 34 Corey Dillon	.25	.60
❑ 35 Akili Smith	.20	.50
❑ 36 Danny Farmer	.20	.50
❑ 37 Ron Dugans	.20	.50
❑ 38 Jon Kitna	.25	.60
❑ 39 Tim Couch	.20	.50
❑ 40 Kevin Johnson	.20	.50
❑ 41 Travis Prentice	.20	.50
❑ 42 Spergon Wynn	.20	.50
❑ 43 Errict Rhett	.25	.60
❑ 44 Dennis Northcutt	.20	.50
❑ 45 Courtney Brown	.20	.50
❑ 46 Tony Banks	.20	.50
❑ 47 Emmitt Smith	.75	2.00
❑ 48 Joey Galloway	.25	.60
❑ 49 Rocket Ismail	.25	.60
❑ 50 Randall Cunningham	.30	.75
❑ 51 James McKnight	.20	.50
❑ 52 Terrell Davis	.30	.75
❑ 53 Mike Anderson	.25	.60
❑ 54 Brian Griese	.25	.60
❑ 55 Rod Smith	.25	.60
❑ 56 Ed McCaffrey	.25	.60
❑ 57 Eddie Kennison	.25	.60
❑ 58 Olandis Gary	.20	.50
❑ 59 Charlie Batch	.25	.60
❑ 60 Germane Crowell	.20	.50
❑ 61 James O. Stewart	.20	.50
❑ 62 Johnnie Morton	.25	.60
❑ 63 Brett Favre	1.00	2.50
❑ 64 Antonio Freeman	.30	.75
❑ 65 Dorsey Levens	.25	.60
❑ 66 Ahman Green	.30	.75
❑ 67 Bill Schroeder	.25	.60
❑ 68 Peyton Manning	.75	2.00
❑ 69 Edgerrin James	.30	.75
❑ 70 Marvin Harrison	.30	.75
❑ 71 Jerome Pathon	.20	.50
❑ 72 Ken Dilger	.20	.50
❑ 73 Mark Brunell	.30	.75
❑ 74 Fred Taylor	.30	.75
❑ 75 Jimmy Smith	.25	.60
❑ 76 Keenan McCardell	.25	.60
❑ 77 R.Jay Soward	.20	.50
❑ 78 Todd Collins	.20	.50
❑ 79 Tony Gonzalez	.25	.60
❑ 80 Derrick Alexander	.20	.50
❑ 81 Tony Richardson	.20	.50
❑ 82 Sylvester Morris	.20	.50
❑ 83 Oronde Gadsden	.20	.50
❑ 84 Lamar Smith	.25	.60
❑ 85 Jay Fiedler	.25	.60
❑ 86 Jason Taylor	.30	.75
❑ 87 Ray Lucas	.20	.50
❑ 88 O.J. McDuffie	.20	.50
❑ 89 Randy Moss	.40	1.00
❑ 90 Cris Carter	.30	.75
❑ 91 Daunte Culpepper	.30	.75
❑ 92 Moe Williams	.20	.50
❑ 93 Troy Walters	.20	.50
❑ 94 Drew Bledsoe	.30	.75
❑ 95 Terry Glenn	.25	.60
❑ 96 Kevin Faulk	.25	.60
❑ 97 J.R. Redmond	.20	.50
❑ 98 Troy Brown	.25	.60
❑ 99 Ricky Williams	.30	.75
❑ 100 Jeff Blake	.25	.60
❑ 101 Joe Horn	.25	.60
❑ 102 Albert Connell	.20	.50
❑ 103 Aaron Brooks	.25	.60
❑ 104 Chad Morton	.20	.50
❑ 105 Kerry Collins	.25	.60
❑ 106 Amani Toomer	.25	.60
❑ 107 Ron Dayne	.25	.60
❑ 108 Tiki Barber	.30	.75
❑ 109 Ike Hilliard	.25	.60
❑ 110 Ron Dixon	.20	.50
❑ 111 Jason Sehorn	.25	.60
❑ 112 Vinny Testaverde	.25	.60
❑ 113 Wayne Chrebet	.25	.60
❑ 114 Curtis Martin	.30	.75
❑ 115 Dedric Ward	.20	.50
❑ 116 Laveranues Coles	.30	.75
❑ 117 Windrell Hayes	.20	.50
❑ 118 Tim Brown	.30	.75
❑ 119 Rich Gannon	.25	.60
❑ 120 Tyrone Wheatley	.25	.60
❑ 121 Charlie Garner	.25	.60
❑ 122 Andre Rison	.25	.60
❑ 123 Charles Woodson	.30	.75
❑ 124 Trace Armstrong	.20	.50
❑ 125 Duce Staley	.25	.60
❑ 126 Donovan McNabb	.40	1.00
❑ 127 Darnell Autry	.20	.50
❑ 128 Charles Johnson	.20	.50
❑ 129 Torrance Small	.20	.50
❑ 130 Kordell Stewart	.25	.60
❑ 131 Jerome Bettis	.30	.75
❑ 132 Plaxico Burress	.25	.60
❑ 133 Bobby Shaw	.20	.50
❑ 134 Troy Edwards	.20	.50
❑ 135 Marshall Faulk	.30	.75
❑ 136 Kurt Warner	.40	1.00
❑ 137 Isaac Bruce	.30	.75
❑ 138 Torry Holt	.25	.60
❑ 139 Trent Green	.30	.75
❑ 140 Az-Zahir Hakim	.20	.50
❑ 141 Junior Seau	.30	.75
❑ 142 Curtis Conway	.25	.60
❑ 143 Doug Flutie	.30	.75
❑ 144 Jeff Graham	.20	.50
❑ 145 Freddie Jones	.20	.50
❑ 146 Marcellus Wiley	.20	.50
❑ 147 Jeff Garcia	.25	.60
❑ 148 Jerry Rice	.60	1.50
❑ 149 Fred Beasley	.20	.50
❑ 150 Terrell Owens	.30	.75
❑ 151 J.J. Stokes	.20	.50
❑ 152 Garrison Hearst	.25	.60
❑ 153 Ricky Watters	.25	.60
❑ 154 Shaun Alexander	.30	.75
❑ 155 Matt Hasselbeck	.30	.75
❑ 156 Brock Huard	.20	.50
❑ 157 Darrell Jackson	.25	.60
❑ 158 John Randle	.25	.60
❑ 159 Warrick Dunn	.30	.75
❑ 160 Shaun King	.20	.50
❑ 161 Ryan Leaf	.20	.50
❑ 162 Mike Alstott	.25	.60
❑ 163 Jacquez Green	.20	.50
❑ 164 Brad Johnson	.25	.60
❑ 165 Keyshawn Johnson	.25	.60
❑ 166 Eddie George	.30	.75
❑ 167 Steve McNair	.30	.75
❑ 168 Neil O'Donnell	.25	.60
❑ 169 Derrick Mason	.25	.60
❑ 170 Frank Wycheck	.20	.50
❑ 171 Kevin Dyson	.25	.60
❑ 172 Jevon Kearse	.25	.60
❑ 173 Jeff George	.25	.60
❑ 174 Stephen Davis	.25	.60
❑ 175 Larry Centers	.25	.60
❑ 176 Michael Westbrook	.20	.50
❑ 177 Stephen Alexander	.20	.50
❑ 178 Ron Dayne	.25	.60
❑ 179 Donovan McNabb	.40	1.00
❑ 180 Jimmy Smith	.25	.60
❑ 181 Adam Archuleta RC	1.25	3.00
❑ 182 A.J. Feeley RC	1.25	3.00
❑ 183 Alex Bannister RC	1.00	2.50
❑ 184 Alge Crumpler RC	1.50	4.00
❑ 185 Andre Carter RC	1.50	4.00
❑ 186 Andre Dyson RC	1.00	2.50
❑ 187 Anthony Thomas RC	1.50	4.00
❑ 188 Arther Love RC	1.00	2.50
❑ 189 Bobby Newcombe RC	1.25	3.00
❑ 190 Brandon Spoon RC	1.25	3.00
❑ 191 Carlos Polk RC	1.00	2.50
❑ 192 Casey Hampton RC	1.25	3.00
❑ 193 Cedrick Wilson RC	1.50	4.00
❑ 194 Chad Johnson RC	4.00	10.00
❑ 195 Chris Chambers RC	2.50	6.00
❑ 196 Chris Taylor RC	1.00	2.50
❑ 197 Chris Weinke RC	1.25	3.00
❑ 198 Correll Buckhalter RC	1.50	4.00
❑ 199 Damione Lewis RC	1.25	3.00
❑ 200 Dan Alexander RC	1.25	3.00
❑ 201 Dan Morgan RC	1.50	4.00
❑ 202 Willie Middlebrooks RC	1.25	3.00
❑ 203 David Terrell RC	1.25	3.00
❑ 204 Derrick Gibson RC	1.00	2.50
❑ 205 Deuce McAllister RC	2.00	5.00
❑ 206 Drew Brees RC	12.50	25.00
❑ 207 Edgerton Hartwell RC	1.00	2.50
❑ 208 Fred Smoot RC	1.50	4.00
❑ 209 Freddie Mitchell RC	1.00	2.50
❑ 210 Gary Baxter RC	1.25	3.00
❑ 211 Gerard Warren RC	1.25	3.00
❑ 212 Hakim Akbar RC	1.00	2.50
❑ 213 Heath Evans RC	1.25	3.00
❑ 214 Jabari Holloway RC	1.25	3.00
❑ 215 Jamal Reynolds RC	1.25	3.00
❑ 216 Jamar Fletcher RC	1.00	2.50
❑ 217 James Jackson RC	1.25	3.00
❑ 218 Jamie Winborn RC	1.25	3.00
❑ 219 Jesse Palmer RC	1.50	4.00
❑ 220 Josh Booty RC	1.25	3.00
❑ 221 Josh Heupel RC	1.50	4.00
❑ 222 Justin Smith RC	1.50	4.00

❑ 223 Karon Riley RC	1.00	2.50
❑ 224 Ken Lucas RC	1.25	3.00
❑ 225 Kenyatta Walker RC	1.00	2.50
❑ 226 Ken-Yon Rambo RC	1.00	2.50
❑ 227 Kevan Barlow RC	1.25	3.00
❑ 228 Kevin Kasper RC	1.25	3.00
❑ 229 Koren Robinson RC	1.50	4.00
❑ 230 LaDainian Tomlinson RC	12.00	30.00
❑ 231 LaMont Jordan RC	1.50	4.00
❑ 232 Leonard Davis RC	1.25	3.00
❑ 233 Marcus Stroud RC	1.25	3.00
❑ 234 Marques Tuiasosopo RC	1.25	3.00
❑ 235 Snoop Minnis RC	1.25	3.00
❑ 236 Michael Bennett RC	1.50	4.00
❑ 237 Michael Stone RC	1.00	2.50
❑ 238 Mike McMahon RC	1.25	3.00
❑ 239 Michael Vick RC	3.00	8.00
❑ 240 Moran Norris RC	1.00	2.50
❑ 241 Morlon Greenwood RC	1.00	2.50
❑ 242 Nate Clements RC	1.50	4.00
❑ 243 Orlando Huff RC	1.00	2.50
❑ 244 Quincy Morgan RC	1.25	3.00
❑ 245 Reggie Wayne RC	4.00	10.00
❑ 246 Richard Seymour RC	1.50	4.00
❑ 247 Robert Ferguson RC	1.50	4.00
❑ 248 Rod Gardner RC	1.25	3.00
❑ 249 Rudi Johnson RC	1.50	4.00
❑ 250 Sage Rosenfels RC	1.50	4.00
❑ 251 Santana Moss RC	2.50	6.00
❑ 252 Scotty Anderson RC	1.25	3.00
❑ 253 Sedrick Hodge RC	1.00	2.50
❑ 254 Shaun Rogers RC	1.50	4.00
❑ 255 Steve Hutchinson RC	1.25	3.00
❑ 256 T.J. Houshmandzadeh RC	2.50	6.00
❑ 257 Tay Cody RC	1.00	2.50
❑ 258 George Layne RC	1.00	2.50
❑ 259 Todd Heap RC	1.50	4.00
❑ 260 Tommy Polley RC	1.25	3.00
❑ 261 Tony Dixon RC	1.25	3.00
❑ 262 Brian Allen RC	1.00	2.50
❑ 263 Torrance Marshall RC	1.25	3.00
❑ 264 Travis Henry RC	1.50	4.00
❑ 265 Travis Minor RC	1.25	3.00
❑ 266 Vinny Sutherland RC	1.00	2.50
❑ 267 Will Allen RC	1.50	4.00
❑ 268 Derrick Blaylock RC	1.25	3.00
❑ 269 Zeke Moreno RC	1.25	3.00
❑ 270 Chris Barnes RC	1.00	2.50
❑ 271 Dee Brown RC	1.00	2.50
❑ 272 Reggie White RC	1.00	2.50
❑ 273 Derek Combs RC	1.00	2.50
❑ 274 Steve Smith RC	4.00	10.00
❑ 275 John Capel RC	1.00	2.50
❑ 276 Justin McCareins RC	1.25	3.00
❑ 277 Darnerien McCants RC	1.25	3.00
❑ 278 Eddie Berlin RC	1.00	2.50
❑ 279 Francis St. Paul RC	1.00	2.50
❑ 280 Quincy Carter RC	1.25	3.00

2002 Upper Deck

❑ COMP.SET w/o SP's (180)	10.00	25.00
❑ 1 Jake Plummer	.25	.60
❑ 2 Marcel Shipp	.20	.50
❑ 3 David Boston	.20	.50
❑ 4 Arnold Jackson	.20	.50
❑ 5 Frank Sanders	.20	.50
❑ 6 Freddie Jones	.20	.50
❑ 7 Michael Vick	.30	.75
❑ 8 Jamal Anderson	.25	.60
❑ 9 Warrick Dunn	.25	.60
❑ 10 Maurice Smith	.20	.50
❑ 11 Shawn Jefferson	.20	.50
❑ 12 Chris Redman	.20	.50
❑ 13 Jeff Blake	.25	.60
❑ 14 Jamal Lewis	.25	.60
❑ 15 Travis Taylor	.20	.50
❑ 16 Ray Lewis	.30	.75
❑ 17 Chris McAlister	.20	.50
❑ 18 Drew Bledsoe	.30	.75
❑ 19 Travis Henry	.25	.60
❑ 20 Larry Centers	.25	.60
❑ 21 Eric Moulds	.25	.60
❑ 22 Reggie Germany	.20	.50
❑ 23 Peerless Price	.20	.50
❑ 24 Chris Weinke	.20	.50
❑ 25 Lamar Smith	.25	.60
❑ 26 Nick Goings	.20	.50
❑ 27 Muhsin Muhammad	.25	.60
❑ 28 Isaac Byrd	.20	.50
❑ 29 Wesley Walls	.25	.60
❑ 30 Jim Miller	.25	.60
❑ 31 Anthony Thomas	.25	.60
❑ 32 Dez White	.20	.50
❑ 33 David Terrell	.20	.50
❑ 34 Marty Booker	.25	.60
❑ 35 Brian Urlacher	.40	1.00
❑ 36 Jon Kitna	.25	.60
❑ 37 Corey Dillon	.25	.60
❑ 38 Peter Warrick	.25	.60
❑ 39 Darnay Scott	.25	.60
❑ 40 Chad Johnson	.30	.75
❑ 41 Tim Couch	.20	.50
❑ 42 James Jackson	.20	.50
❑ 43 JaJuan Dawson	.20	.50
❑ 44 Kevin Johnson	.20	.50
❑ 45 Quincy Morgan	.20	.50
❑ 46 Courtney Brown	.20	.50
❑ 47 Quincy Carter	.20	.50
❑ 48 Emmitt Smith	.75	2.00
❑ 49 Joey Galloway	.25	.60
❑ 50 Rocket Ismail	.25	.60
❑ 51 Ken-Yon Rambo	.20	.50
❑ 52 Brian Griese	.25	.60
❑ 53 Terrell Davis	.30	.75
❑ 54 Mike Anderson	.25	.60
❑ 55 Shannon Sharpe	.30	.75
❑ 56 Ed McCaffrey	.25	.60
❑ 57 Rod Smith	.25	.60
❑ 58 Mike McMahon	.20	.50
❑ 59 James Stewart	.20	.50
❑ 60 Az-Zahir Hakim	.20	.50
❑ 61 Desmond Howard	.25	.60
❑ 62 Germane Crowell	.20	.50
❑ 63 Brett Favre	.75	2.00
❑ 64 Ahman Green	.25	.60
❑ 65 Antonio Freeman	.30	.75
❑ 66 Terry Glenn	.25	.60
❑ 67 Kabeer Gbaja-Biamila	.25	.60
❑ 68 Kent Graham	.20	.50
❑ 69 James Allen	.20	.50
❑ 70 Corey Bradford	.20	.50
❑ 71 Jermaine Lewis	.20	.50
❑ 72 Jamie Sharper	.25	.60
❑ 73 Peyton Manning	.60	1.50
❑ 74 Edgerrin James	.30	.75
❑ 75 Dominic Rhodes	.25	.60
❑ 76 Marvin Harrison	.30	.75
❑ 77 Qadry Ismail	.25	.60
❑ 78 Mark Brunell	.25	.60
❑ 79 Fred Taylor	.30	.75
❑ 80 Stacey Mack	.20	.50
❑ 81 Jimmy Smith	.25	.60
❑ 82 Keenan McCardell	.25	.60
❑ 83 Trent Green	.25	.60
❑ 84 Priest Holmes	.30	.75
❑ 85 Derrick Alexander	.25	.60
❑ 86 Johnnie Morton	.25	.60
❑ 87 Snoop Minnis	.20	.50
❑ 88 Tony Gonzalez	.25	.60
❑ 89 Jay Fiedler	.25	.60
❑ 90 Ricky Williams	.30	.75
❑ 91 Chris Chambers	.30	.75
❑ 92 Oronde Gadsden	.20	.50
❑ 93 Zach Thomas	.30	.75
❑ 94 Daunte Culpepper	.25	.60
❑ 95 Michael Bennett	.25	.60
❑ 96 Randy Moss	.30	.75
❑ 97 Sean Dawkins	.25	.60
❑ 98 Tom Brady	.75	2.00
❑ 99 Antowain Smith	.25	.60
❑ 100 David Patten	.20	.50
❑ 101 Troy Brown	.25	.60
❑ 102 Adam Vinatieri	.30	.75
❑ 103 Aaron Brooks	.25	.60
❑ 104 Deuce McAllister	.30	.75
❑ 105 Jake Reed	.25	.60
❑ 106 Jerome Pathon	.20	.50
❑ 107 Joe Horn	.25	.60
❑ 108 Kyle Turley	.20	.50
❑ 109 Kerry Collins	.25	.60
❑ 110 Ron Dayne	.25	.60
❑ 111 Tiki Barber	.30	.75
❑ 112 Amani Toomer	.25	.60
❑ 113 Ike Hilliard	.25	.60
❑ 114 Michael Strahan	.30	.75
❑ 115 Vinny Testaverde	.25	.60
❑ 116 Chad Pennington	.30	.75
❑ 117 Curtis Martin	.30	.75
❑ 118 Santana Moss	.25	.60
❑ 119 Laveranues Coles	.30	.75
❑ 120 Wayne Chrebet	.25	.60
❑ 121 Rich Gannon	.25	.60
❑ 122 Charlie Garner	.25	.60
❑ 123 Jerry Rice	.60	1.50
❑ 124 Tim Brown	.30	.75
❑ 125 Charles Woodson	.30	.75
❑ 126 Donovan McNabb	.40	1.00
❑ 127 Duce Staley	.25	.60
❑ 128 Correll Buckhalter	.25	.60
❑ 129 Freddie Mitchell	.20	.50
❑ 130 James Thrash	.25	.60
❑ 131 Todd Pinkston	.20	.50
❑ 132 Kordell Stewart	.25	.60
❑ 133 Jerome Bettis	.30	.75
❑ 134 Chris Fuamatu-Ma'afala	.20	.50
❑ 135 Hines Ward	.30	.75
❑ 136 Plaxico Burress	.25	.60
❑ 137 Kendrell Bell	.20	.50
❑ 138 Doug Flutie	.30	.75
❑ 139 Drew Brees	.50	1.25
❑ 140 LaDainian Tomlinson	.50	1.25
❑ 141 Curtis Conway	.25	.60
❑ 142 Tim Dwight	.25	.60
❑ 143 Junior Seau	.30	.75
❑ 144 Jeff Garcia	.25	.60
❑ 145 Garrison Hearst	.25	.60
❑ 146 Kevan Barlow	.20	.50
❑ 147 Terrell Owens	.30	.75
❑ 148 J.J. Stokes	.20	.50
❑ 149 Trent Dilfer	.25	.60
❑ 150 Shaun Alexander	.30	.75
❑ 151 Ricky Watters	.25	.60
❑ 152 Bobby Engram	.25	.60
❑ 153 Koren Robinson	.20	.50
❑ 154 Kurt Warner	.30	.75
❑ 155 Marshall Faulk	.30	.75
❑ 156 Isaac Bruce	.30	.75
❑ 157 Ricky Proehl	.25	.60
❑ 158 Terrence Wilkins	.20	.50
❑ 159 Torry Holt	.30	.75
❑ 160 Brad Johnson	.25	.60
❑ 161 Shaun King	.20	.50
❑ 162 Rob Johnson	.25	.60
❑ 163 Mike Alstott	.25	.60
❑ 164 Michael Pittman	.25	.60
❑ 165 Keyshawn Johnson	.25	.60
❑ 166 Steve McNair	.30	.75
❑ 167 Eddie George	.25	.60
❑ 168 Derrick Mason	.25	.60
❑ 169 Kevin Dyson	.25	.60
❑ 170 Frank Wycheck	.20	.50
❑ 171 Jevon Kearse	.25	.60
❑ 172 Danny Wuerffel	.25	.60
❑ 173 Stephen Davis	.25	.60
❑ 174 Michael Westbrook	.20	.50
❑ 175 Rod Gardner	.20	.50
❑ 176 Champ Bailey	.30	.75
❑ 177 Darrell Green	.30	.75
❑ 178 Kurt Warner CL	.25	.60
❑ 179 Brett Favre CL	.60	1.50
❑ 180 Randy Moss CL	.25	.60
❑ 181 David Boston SS	.75	2.00
❑ 182 Jake Plummer SS	1.00	2.50
❑ 183 Michael Vick SS	1.25	3.00
❑ 184 Drew Bledsoe SS	1.25	3.00
❑ 185 Anthony Thomas SS	1.00	2.50
❑ 186 Tim Couch SS	.75	2.00
❑ 187 Emmitt Smith SS	3.00	8.00
❑ 188 Ahman Green SS	1.00	2.50
❑ 189 Brett Favre SS	3.00	8.00

Card		
❑ 190 Edgerrin James SS	1.25	3.00
❑ 191 Peyton Manning SS	2.50	6.00
❑ 192 Mark Brunell SS	1.00	2.50
❑ 193 Daunte Culpepper SS	1.00	2.50
❑ 194 Randy Moss SS	1.25	3.00
❑ 195 Tom Brady SS	3.00	8.00
❑ 196 Aaron Brooks SS	1.00	2.50
❑ 197 Ricky Williams SS	1.25	3.00
❑ 198 Curtis Martin SS	1.25	3.00
❑ 199 Jerry Rice SS	2.50	6.00
❑ 200 Donovan McNabb SS	1.50	4.00
❑ 201 Jerome Bettis SS	1.25	3.00
❑ 202 Kordell Stewart SS	1.00	2.50
❑ 203 LaDainian Tomlinson SS	2.00	5.00
❑ 204 Jeff Garcia SS	1.00	2.50
❑ 205 Terrell Owens SS	1.25	3.00
❑ 206 Shaun Alexander SS	1.25	3.00
❑ 207 Kurt Warner SS	1.25	3.00
❑ 208 Marshall Faulk SS	1.25	3.00
❑ 209 Keyshawn Johnson SS	1.00	2.50
❑ 210 Steve McNair SS	1.25	3.00
❑ 211 Damien Anderson RC	1.50	4.00
❑ 212 Jason McAddley RC	1.50	4.00
❑ 213 Josh McCown RC	2.00	5.00
❑ 214 Josh Scobey RC	1.50	4.00
❑ 215 Preston Parsons RC	1.25	3.00
❑ 216 Dusty Bonner RC	1.25	3.00
❑ 217 Kahlil Hill RC	1.25	3.00
❑ 218 Kurt Kittner RC	1.25	3.00
❑ 219 T.J. Duckett RC	2.00	5.00
❑ 220 Chester Taylor RC	3.00	8.00
❑ 221 Kalimba Edwards RC	1.50	4.00
❑ 223 Ron Johnson RC	1.50	4.00
❑ 224 Tellis Redmon RC	1.25	3.00
❑ 225 Wes Pate RC	1.25	3.00
❑ 226 David Priestley RC	1.25	3.00
❑ 227 Josh Reed RC	1.50	4.00
❑ 228 Mike Williams RC	1.25	3.00
❑ 229 Ryan Denney RC	1.25	3.00
❑ 230 DeShaun Foster RC	2.00	5.00
❑ 231 Julius Peppers RC	3.00	8.00
❑ 232 Randy Fasani RC	1.50	4.00
❑ 233 Adrian Peterson RC	2.00	5.00
❑ 234 Alex Brown RC	2.00	5.00
❑ 235 Gavin Hoffman RC	1.25	3.00
❑ 236 Levi Jones RC	1.25	3.00
❑ 237 Andra Davis RC	1.25	3.00
❑ 238 Andre Davis RC	1.50	4.00
❑ 239 William Green RC	1.50	4.00
❑ 240 Antonio Bryant RC	2.50	6.00
❑ 241 Chad Hutchinson RC	1.25	3.00
❑ 242 Roy Williams RC	2.50	6.00
❑ 243 Woody Dantzler RC	1.50	4.00
❑ 244 Ashley Lelie RC	2.00	5.00
❑ 245 Clinton Portis RC	5.00	12.00
❑ 246 Lamont Thompson RC	1.50	4.00
❑ 247 James Mungro RC	2.00	5.00
❑ 248 Joey Harrington RC	2.00	5.00
❑ 249 Luke Staley RC	1.25	3.00
❑ 250 Craig Nall RC	1.50	4.00
❑ 251 Javon Walker RC	2.00	5.00
❑ 252 Najeh Davenport RC	2.00	5.00
❑ 253 David Carr RC	2.00	5.00
❑ 254 Saleem Rasheed RC	1.25	3.00
❑ 255 Mike Rumph RC	1.25	3.00
❑ 256 Jabar Gaffney RC	2.00	5.00
❑ 257 Jonathan Wells RC	2.00	5.00
❑ 258 Dwight Freeney RC	3.00	8.00
❑ 259 Larry Tripplett RC	1.25	3.00
❑ 260 David Garrard RC	3.00	8.00
❑ 261 John Henderson RC	2.00	5.00
❑ 262 Ryan Sims RC	2.00	5.00
❑ 263 Leonard Henry RC	1.25	3.00
❑ 264 Brian Allen RC	1.50	4.00
❑ 265 Atrews Bell RC	1.25	3.00
❑ 266 Bryant McKinnie RC	1.25	3.00
❑ 267 Kelly Campbell RC	1.50	4.00
❑ 268 Raonall Smith RC	1.25	3.00
❑ 269 Antwoine Womack RC	1.25	3.00
❑ 270 Daniel Graham RC	1.50	4.00
❑ 271 Deion Branch RC	2.00	5.00
❑ 272 Sam Simmons RC	1.25	3.00
❑ 273 Rohan Davey RC	2.00	5.00
❑ 274 Charles Grant RC	2.00	5.00
❑ 275 Derrick Lewis RC	1.25	3.00
❑ 276 Donte Stallworth RC	2.00	5.00
❑ 277 J.T. O'Sullivan RC	2.00	5.00
❑ 278 Keyuo Craver RC	1.25	3.00
❑ 279 Ricky Williams RC	1.50	4.00
❑ 280 Bryan Thomas RC	1.25	3.00
❑ 281 Jeremy Shockey RC	3.00	8.00
❑ 282 Tim Carter RC	1.50	4.00
❑ 283 Larry Ned RC	1.25	3.00
❑ 284 Napoleon Harris RC	1.50	4.00
❑ 285 Phillip Buchanon RC	2.00	5.00
❑ 286 Ronald Curry RC	2.00	5.00
❑ 287 Brian Westbrook RC	6.00	15.00
❑ 288 Freddie Milons RC	1.25	3.00
❑ 289 Lito Sheppard RC	2.00	5.00
❑ 290 Antwaan Randle El RC	2.00	5.00
❑ 291 Lee Mays RC	1.25	3.00
❑ 292 Daryl Jones RC	1.25	3.00
❑ 293 Justin Peelle RC	1.25	3.00
❑ 294 Quentin Jammer RC	2.00	5.00
❑ 295 Reche Caldwell RC	2.00	5.00
❑ 296 Seth Burford RC	1.25	3.00
❑ 297 Terry Charles RC	1.25	3.00
❑ 298 Brandon Doman RC	1.25	3.00
❑ 299 Maurice Morris RC	2.00	5.00
❑ 300 Eric Crouch RC	2.00	5.00
❑ 301 Lamar Gordon RC	2.00	5.00
❑ 302 Marquise Walker RC	1.25	3.00
❑ 303 Tracey Wistrom RC	1.50	4.00
❑ 304 Travis Stephens RC	1.25	3.00
❑ 305 Herb Haygood RC	1.25	3.00
❑ 306 Albert Haynesworth RC	2.00	5.00
❑ 307 Rocky Calmus RC	1.50	4.00
❑ 308 Cliff Russell RC	1.25	3.00
❑ 309 Ladell Betts RC	2.00	5.00
❑ 310A Patrick Ramsey RC	2.00	5.00
❑ 310B Ed Reed RC	6.00	15.00

2003 Upper Deck

Card		
❑ COMP.SET w/o SP's (180)	10.00	25.00
❑ 1 Brad Johnson	.25	.60
❑ 2 Derrick Brooks	.25	.60
❑ 3 Simeon Rice	.25	.60
❑ 4 Warren Sapp	.25	.60
❑ 5 Thomas Jones	.25	.60
❑ 6 Mike Alstott	.30	.75
❑ 7 Michael Pittman	.20	.50
❑ 8 Tim Brown	.30	.75
❑ 9 Rich Gannon	.25	.60
❑ 10 Charlie Garner	.25	.60
❑ 11 Jerry Porter	.25	.60
❑ 12 Phillip Buchanon	.20	.50
❑ 13 Charles Woodson	.25	.60
❑ 14 James Thrash	.20	.50
❑ 15 Duce Staley	.25	.60
❑ 16 Brian Westbrook	.30	.75
❑ 17 Correll Buckhalter	.25	.60
❑ 18 Koy Detmer	.20	.50
❑ 19 Brian Dawkins	.25	.60
❑ 20 Jon Ritchie	.20	.50
❑ 21 Ahman Green	.30	.75
❑ 22 Donald Driver	.30	.75
❑ 23 Bubba Franks	.25	.60
❑ 24 Javon Walker	.25	.60
❑ 25 Kabeer Gbaja-Biamila	.25	.60
❑ 26 Robert Ferguson	.20	.50
❑ 27 Eddie George	.25	.60
❑ 28 Jevon Kearse	.25	.60
❑ 29 Billy Volek	.25	.60
❑ 30 Frank Wycheck	.20	.50
❑ 31 Derrick Mason	.25	.60
❑ 32 Tommy Maddox	.25	.60
❑ 33 Jerome Bettis	.30	.75
❑ 34 Antwaan Randle El	.25	.60
❑ 35 Amos Zereoue	.20	.50
❑ 36 Hines Ward	.30	.75
❑ 37 Jeff Garcia	.30	.75
❑ 38 Terrell Owens	.30	.75
❑ 39 Tim Rattay	.20	.50
❑ 40 Brandon Doman	.20	.50
❑ 41 Tai Streets	.20	.50
❑ 42 Garrison Hearst	.25	.60
❑ 43 Kerry Collins	.25	.60
❑ 44 Tiki Barber	.30	.75
❑ 45 Amani Toomer	.25	.60
❑ 46 Jesse Palmer	.20	.50
❑ 47 Tim Carter	.20	.50
❑ 48 Michael Strahan	.25	.60
❑ 49 Ike Hilliard	.25	.60
❑ 50 Marvin Harrison	.30	.75
❑ 51 Peyton Manning	.60	1.50
❑ 52 Marcus Pollard	.20	.50
❑ 53 James Mungro	.20	.50
❑ 54 Reggie Wayne	.25	.60
❑ 55 Peerless Price	.20	.50
❑ 56 Warrick Dunn	.25	.60
❑ 57 T.J. Duckett	.25	.60
❑ 58 Keith Brooking	.25	.60
❑ 59 Doug Johnson	.20	.50
❑ 60 Brian Finneran	.20	.50
❑ 61 Chad Pennington	.30	.75
❑ 62 Curtis Martin	.30	.75
❑ 63 Marvin Jones	.20	.50
❑ 64 Wayne Chrebet	.25	.60
❑ 65 LaMont Jordan	.25	.60
❑ 66 Curtis Conway	.20	.50
❑ 67 Vinny Testaverde	.25	.60
❑ 68 Tim Couch	.20	.50
❑ 69 William Green	.20	.50
❑ 70 Andre Davis	.20	.50
❑ 71 Quincy Morgan	.20	.50
❑ 72 Dennis Northcutt	.20	.50
❑ 73 Kelly Holcomb	.20	.50
❑ 74 Jake Plummer	.25	.60
❑ 75 Mike Anderson	.25	.60
❑ 76 Ashley Lelie	.20	.50
❑ 77 Ed McCaffrey	.25	.60
❑ 78 Shannon Sharpe	.25	.60
❑ 79 Rod Smith	.25	.60
❑ 80 Terrell Davis	.30	.75
❑ 81 Antowain Smith	.25	.60
❑ 82 Kevin Faulk	.25	.60
❑ 83 David Patten	.20	.50
❑ 84 Deion Branch	.25	.60
❑ 85 Troy Brown	.25	.60
❑ 86 Rohan Davey	.20	.50
❑ 87 Jay Fiedler	.25	.60
❑ 88 Randy McMichael	.20	.50
❑ 89 Derrius Thompson	.20	.50
❑ 90 Jason Taylor	.25	.60
❑ 91 Zach Thomas	.30	.75
❑ 92 Ricky Williams	.25	.60
❑ 93 Deuce McAllister	.30	.75
❑ 94 Donte Stallworth	.25	.60
❑ 95 Jerome Pathon	.20	.50
❑ 96 Michael Lewis	.20	.50
❑ 97 Joe Horn	.25	.60
❑ 98 Priest Holmes	.30	.75
❑ 99 Johnnie Morton	.25	.60
❑ 100 Eddie Kennison	.20	.50
❑ 101 Dante Hall	.25	.60
❑ 102 Tony Gonzalez	.25	.60
❑ 103 Marc Boerigter	.20	.50
❑ 104 Drew Brees	.30	.75
❑ 105 David Boston	.20	.50
❑ 106 Reche Caldwell	.20	.50
❑ 107 Tim Dwight	.20	.50
❑ 108 Doug Flutie	.30	.75
❑ 109 Drew Bledsoe	.30	.75
❑ 110 Eric Moulds	.25	.60
❑ 111 Alex Van Pelt	.20	.50
❑ 112 Charles Johnson	.20	.50
❑ 113 Takeo Spikes	.20	.50
❑ 114 Josh Reed	.20	.50
❑ 115 Ladell Betts	.25	.60
❑ 116 Laveranues Coles	.25	.60
❑ 117 Champ Bailey	.25	.60
❑ 118 Trung Canidate	.20	.50
❑ 119 Kenny Watson	.20	.50
❑ 120 Rod Gardner	.20	.50
❑ 121 Kurt Warner	.30	.75
❑ 122 Lamar Gordon	.20	.50
❑ 123 Shaun McDonald RC	.40	1.00
❑ 124 Marc Bulger	.30	.75
❑ 125 Isaac Bruce	.30	.75
❑ 126 Torry Holt	.30	.75

Card	Low	High
127 Matt Hasselbeck	.25	.60
128 Maurice Morris	.20	.50
129 Bobby Engram	.20	.50
130 Darrell Jackson	.25	.60
131 Koren Robinson	.25	.60
132 Chris Redman	.20	.50
133 Todd Heap	.25	.60
134 Travis Taylor	.20	.50
135 Ron Johnson	.20	.50
136 Ray Lewis	.30	.75
137 Jake Delhomme	.30	.75
138 Muhsin Muhammad	.25	.60
139 Stephen Davis	.25	.60
140 Julius Peppers	.30	.75
141 Rodney Peete	.20	.50
142 Mark Brunell	.25	.60
143 Jimmy Smith	.25	.60
144 Kyle Brady	.20	.50
145 Kevin Lockett	.20	.50
146 David Garrard	.30	.75
147 Fred Taylor	.30	.75
148 Michael Bennett	.25	.60
149 Ronald Bellamy RC	.30	.75
150 Randy Moss	.30	.75
151 D'Wayne Bates	.20	.50
152 Josh McCown	.25	.60
153 Marquise Walker	.20	.50
154 Jeff Blake	.25	.60
155 Freddie Jones	.20	.50
156 Marcel Shipp	.20	.50
157 Troy Hambrick	.20	.50
158 Joey Galloway	.25	.60
159 Terry Glenn	.25	.60
160 Roy Williams	.30	.75
161 Antonio Bryant	.30	.75
162 Quincy Carter	.20	.50
163 Anthony Thomas	.25	.60
164 Marty Booker	.25	.60
165 Dez White	.20	.50
166 Adrian Peterson	.20	.50
167 Kordell Stewart	.25	.60
168 David Terrell	.20	.50
169 Jabar Gaffney	.20	.50
170 Bennie Joppru RC	.25	.60
171 Corey Bradford	.20	.50
172 David Carr	.30	.75
173 James Stewart	.25	.60
174 Ty Detmer	.20	.50
175 Az-Zahir Hakim	.20	.50
176 Bill Schroeder	.20	.50
177 Jon Kitna	.25	.60
178 Chad Johnson	.30	.75
179 Ron Dugans	.20	.50
180 Peter Warrick	.25	.60
181 Brett Favre SS	3.00	8.00
182 Emmitt Smith SS	3.00	8.00
183 LaDainian Tomlinson SS	1.50	4.00
184 Joey Harrington SS	1.00	2.50
185 Brian Urlacher SS	2.00	5.00
186 Daunte Culpepper SS	1.25	3.00
187 Jamal Lewis SS	1.25	3.00
188 Shaun Alexander SS	1.25	3.00
189 Marshall Faulk SS	1.25	3.00
190 Travis Henry SS	1.00	2.50
191 Trent Green SS	1.00	2.50
192 Aaron Brooks SS	1.00	2.50
193 Chris Chambers SS	1.00	2.50
194 Tom Brady SS	3.00	8.00
195 Clinton Portis SS	1.50	4.00
196 Kevin Johnson SS	.75	2.00
197 Santana Moss SS	1.00	2.50
198 Michael Vick SS	1.25	3.00
199 Edgerrin James SS	1.25	3.00
200 Jeremy Shockey SS	1.25	3.00
201 Kevan Barlow SS	.75	2.00
202 Plaxico Burress SS	1.25	3.00
203 Steve McNair SS	1.25	3.00
204 Donovan McNabb SS	1.25	3.00
205 Jerry Rice SS	2.50	6.00
206 Keyshawn Johnson SS	1.25	3.00
207 Patrick Ramsey SS	1.00	2.50
208 Stephen Davis SS	1.00	2.50
209 Corey Dillon SS	1.00	2.50
210 Chad Hutchinson SS	.75	2.00
211 Brad Banks RC	1.50	4.00
212 Kliff Kingsbury RC	1.50	4.00
213 Jason Gesser RC	1.50	4.00
214 Jason Johnson RC	1.25	3.00
215 Brian St.Pierre RC	2.00	5.00
216 Ken Dorsey RC	1.50	4.00
217 Seneca Wallace RC	2.00	5.00
218 Brooks Bollinger RC	2.00	5.00
219 Chris Brown RC	2.00	5.00
220 B.J Askew RC	1.50	4.00
221 Earnest Graham RC	2.00	5.00
222 Quentin Griffin RC	1.50	4.00
223 Musa Smith RC	1.50	4.00
224 Artose Pinner RC	1.25	3.00
225 Domanick Davis RC	2.00	5.00
226 Anquan Boldin RC	5.00	12.00
227 Talman Gardner RC	1.25	3.00
228 Brandon Lloyd RC	2.00	5.00
229 Bryant Johnson RC	2.00	5.00
230 Kareem Kelly RC	1.25	3.00
231 Arnaz Battle RC	2.00	5.00
232 Keenan Howry RC	1.25	3.00
233 Justin Gage RC	2.00	5.00
234 Tyrone Calico RC	1.50	4.00
235 Teyo Johnson RC	1.50	4.00
236 Malaefou MacKenzie RC	1.25	3.00
237 Terence Newman RC	2.00	5.00
238 Marcus Trufant RC	2.00	5.00
239 Mike Doss RC	2.00	5.00
240 Terrell Suggs RC	2.50	6.00
241 Carson Palmer RC	12.00	30.00
242 Byron Leftwich RC	4.00	10.00
243 Rex Grossman RC	3.00	8.00
244 Kyle Boller RC	3.00	8.00
245 Dave Ragone RC	2.00	5.00
246 Chris Simms RC	3.00	8.00
247 Larry Johnson RC	4.00	10.00
248 Lee Suggs RC	2.50	6.00
249 Justin Fargas RC	3.00	8.00
250 Onterrio Smith RC	2.50	6.00
251 Willis McGahee RC	6.00	15.00
252 Charles Rogers RC	2.50	6.00
253 Andre Johnson RC	6.00	15.00
254 Taylor Jacobs RC	2.50	6.00
255 Kelley Washington RC	2.50	6.00
256 Tony Romo RC	15.00	30.00
257 Jerel Myers RC	1.50	4.00
258 Kirk Farmer RC	2.00	5.00
259 Kevin Walter RC	2.50	6.00
260 Gibran Hamdan RC	1.50	4.00
261 Juston Wood RC	1.50	4.00
262 Travis Anglin RC	1.50	4.00
263 Marquel Blackwell RC	1.50	4.00
264 Jason Thomas RC	1.50	4.00
265 Carl Ford RC	1.50	4.00
266 Walter Young RC	1.50	4.00
267 Sultan McCullough RC	1.50	4.00
268 Dahrran Diedrick RC	1.50	4.00
269 Cecil Sapp RC	1.50	4.00
270 Doug Gabriel RC	2.00	5.00
271 LaBrandon Toefield RC	2.00	5.00
272 Adrian Madise RC	1.50	4.00
273 J.R. Tolver RC	2.00	5.00
274 Kevin Curtis RC	2.50	6.00
275 Bobby Wade RC	2.00	5.00
276 Sam Aiken RC	2.50	6.00
277 Mike Bush RC	1.50	4.00
278 Billy McMullen RC	1.50	4.00
279 Bethel Johnson RC	2.00	5.00
280 David Kircus RC	2.50	6.00
281 Zuriel Smith RC	1.50	4.00
282 LaTarence Dunbar RC	1.50	4.00
283 Nate Burleson RC	2.00	5.00
284 Antwone Savage RC	1.50	4.00
285 Terrence Edwards RC	1.50	4.00

2004 Upper Deck

Card	Low	High
COMPLETE SET (275)	75.00	135.00
COMP.SET w/o SP's (250)	30.00	60.00
COMP.SET w/o RC's (200)	10.00	25.00
201-225 ROOKIE STATED ODDS 1:8		
226-275 ROOKIE STATED ODDS 1:1		
UNPRICED PRINT PLATE PRINT RUN 1 SET		
1 Anquan Boldin	.30	.75
2 Josh McCown	.25	.60
3 Emmitt Smith	.75	2.00
4 Freddie Jones	.20	.50
5 Marcel Shipp	.30	.75
6 Shaun King	.20	.50
7 Michael Vick	.30	.75
8 T.J. Duckett	.25	.60
9 Peerless Price	.25	.60
10 Warrick Dunn	.25	.60
11 Keith Brooking	.20	.50
12 Brian Finneran	.20	.50
13 Anthony Wright	.25	.60
14 Kyle Boller	.25	.60
15 Jamal Lewis	.25	.60
16 Todd Heap	.25	.60
17 Ray Lewis	.30	.75
18 Terrell Suggs	.20	.50
19 Travis Taylor	.20	.50
20 Drew Bledsoe	.30	.75
21 Willis McGahee	.30	.75
22 Eric Moulds	.25	.60
23 Travis Henry	.25	.60
24 Takeo Spikes	.20	.50
25 Josh Reed	.30	.75
26 Lawyer Milloy	.20	.50
27 Stephen Davis	.25	.60
28 Jake Delhomme	.25	.60
29 Steve Smith	.30	.75
30 DeShaun Foster	.25	.60
31 Dan Morgan	.25	.60
32 Julius Peppers	.25	.60
33 Rod Smart	.25	.60
34 Rex Grossman	.30	.75
35 Thomas Jones	.25	.60
36 Marty Booker	.25	.60
37 Anthony Thomas	.25	.60
38 Brian Urlacher	.30	.75
39 Justin Gage	.25	.60
40 Chad Johnson	.25	.60
41 Carson Palmer	.40	1.00
42 Peter Warrick	.25	.60
43 Jon Kitna	.25	.60
44 Kelley Washington	.20	.50
45 Rudi Johnson	.25	.60
46 Jeff Garcia	.30	.75
47 Dennis Northcutt	.20	.50
48 Lee Suggs	.30	.75
49 Andre Davis	.20	.50
50 Quincy Morgan	.20	.50
51 Kelly Holcomb	.25	.60
52 Keyshawn Johnson	.25	.60
53 Quincy Carter	.20	.50
54 Antonio Bryant	.30	.75
55 Terry Glenn	.25	.60
56 Terence Newman	.25	.60
57 Roy Williams S	.25	.60
58 Champ Bailey	.25	.60
59 Jake Plummer	.25	.60
60 Quentin Griffin	.25	.60
61 John Lynch	.25	.60
62 Rod Smith	.25	.60
63 Ashley Lelie	.25	.60
64 Joey Harrington	.25	.60
65 Az-Zahir Hakim	.20	.50
66 Charles Rogers	.25	.60
67 Tai Streets	.20	.50
68 Shawn Bryson	.20	.50
69 Artose Pinner	.20	.50
70 Brett Favre	.75	2.00
71 Nick Barnett	.25	.60
72 Ahman Green	.30	.75
73 Kabeer Gbaja-Biamila	.25	.60
74 Javon Walker	.25	.60
75 Donald Driver	.30	.75
76 Tim Couch	.25	.60
77 David Carr	.25	.60
78 Corey Bradford	.25	.60
79 J.J. Moses	.20	.50
80 Domanick Davis	.25	.60
81 Jabar Gaffney	.25	.60
82 Andre Johnson	.30	.75

❑ 83 Marvin Harrison .30 .75
❑ 84 Peyton Manning .60 1.50
❑ 85 Dallas Clark .30 .75
❑ 86 Edgerrin James .30 .75
❑ 87 Reggie Wayne .25 .60
❑ 88 Dwight Freeney .30 .75
❑ 89 Byron Leftwich .30 .75
❑ 90 LaBrandon Toefield .20 .50
❑ 91 Fred Taylor .25 .60
❑ 92 Troy Edwards .20 .50
❑ 93 Jimmy Smith .25 .60
❑ 94 Kyle Brady .25 .60
❑ 95 Trent Green .25 .60
❑ 96 Tony Gonzalez .30 .75
❑ 97 Dante Hall .25 .60
❑ 98 Priest Holmes .30 .75
❑ 99 Eddie Kennison .25 .60
❑ 100 Johnnie Morton .25 .60
❑ 101 Jay Fiedler .20 .50
❑ 102 Junior Seau .30 .75
❑ 103 Ricky Williams .30 .75
❑ 104 Chris Chambers .25 .60
❑ 105 Zach Thomas .30 .75
❑ 106 David Boston .20 .50
❑ 107 A.J. Feeley .25 .60
❑ 108 Daunte Culpepper .30 .75
❑ 109 Onterrio Smith .20 .50
❑ 110 Randy Moss .30 .75
❑ 111 Moe Williams .20 .50
❑ 112 Michael Bennett .25 .60
❑ 113 Jim Kleinsasser .20 .50
❑ 114 Tom Brady .75 2.00
❑ 115 Kevin Faulk .25 .60
❑ 116 Deion Branch .25 .60
❑ 117 Corey Dillon .25 .60
❑ 118 Troy Brown .25 .60
❑ 119 Adam Vinatieri .30 .75
❑ 120 Tedy Bruschi .30 .75
❑ 121 Aaron Brooks .25 .60
❑ 122 Deuce McAllister .30 .75
❑ 123 Donte' Stallworth .25 .60
❑ 124 Joe Horn .25 .60
❑ 125 Jerome Pathon .20 .50
❑ 126 Boo Williams .20 .50
❑ 127 Jeremy Shockey .25 .60
❑ 128 Kurt Warner .30 .75
❑ 129 Amani Toomer .25 .60
❑ 130 Tiki Barber .30 .75
❑ 131 Ike Hilliard .25 .60
❑ 132 Michael Strahan .25 .60
❑ 133 Chad Pennington .30 .75
❑ 134 Santana Moss .25 .60
❑ 135 Wayne Chrebet .25 .60
❑ 136 Curtis Martin .30 .75
❑ 137 LaMont Jordan .30 .75
❑ 138 Justin McCareins .20 .50
❑ 139 Jerry Rice .60 1.50
❑ 140 Rich Gannon .25 .60
❑ 141 Tim Brown .30 .75
❑ 142 Jerry Porter .25 .60
❑ 143 Warren Sapp .25 .60
❑ 144 Charles Woodson .30 .75
❑ 145 Donovan McNabb .30 .75
❑ 146 Brian Westbrook .30 .75
❑ 147 Todd Pinkston .20 .50
❑ 148 Jevon Kearse .25 .60
❑ 149 Freddie Mitchell .20 .50
❑ 150 Correll Buckhalter .25 .60
❑ 151 Terrell Owens .30 .75
❑ 152 Tommy Maddox .25 .60
❑ 153 Duce Staley .25 .60
❑ 154 Plaxico Burress .25 .60
❑ 155 Hines Ward .30 .75
❑ 156 Antwaan Randle El .25 .60
❑ 157 Jerome Bettis .30 .75
❑ 158 Kendrell Bell .20 .50
❑ 159 LaDainian Tomlinson .40 1.00
❑ 160 Doug Flutie .30 .75
❑ 161 Quentin Jammer .20 .50
❑ 162 Drew Brees .30 .75
❑ 163 Reche Caldwell .25 .60
❑ 164 Tim Dwight .25 .60
❑ 165 Tim Rattay .20 .50
❑ 166 Kevan Barlow .25 .60
❑ 167 Brandon Lloyd .20 .50
❑ 168 Cedrick Wilson .20 .50
❑ 169 Julian Peterson .25 .60
❑ 170 Ahmed Plummer .20 .50
❑ 171 Matt Hasselbeck .30 .75
❑ 172 Koren Robinson .30 .75
❑ 173 Shaun Alexander .30 .75
❑ 174 Darrell Jackson .25 .60
❑ 175 Marcus Trufant .20 .50
❑ 176 Bobby Engram .25 .60
❑ 177 Marc Bulger .25 .60
❑ 178 Torry Holt .30 .75
❑ 179 Marshall Faulk .30 .75
❑ 180 Orlando Pace .25 .60
❑ 181 Isaac Bruce .25 .60
❑ 182 Kyle Turley .20 .50
❑ 183 Brad Johnson .25 .60
❑ 184 Charlie Garner .25 .60
❑ 185 Keenan McCardell .20 .50
❑ 186 Mike Alstott .25 .60
❑ 187 Derrick Brooks .25 .60
❑ 188 Brian Griese .25 .60
❑ 189 Steve McNair .30 .75
❑ 190 Chris Brown .25 .60
❑ 191 Eddie George .25 .60
❑ 192 Tyrone Calico .25 .60
❑ 193 Derrick Mason .25 .60
❑ 194 Drew Bennett .25 .60
❑ 195 Mark Brunell .25 .60
❑ 196 LaVar Arrington .25 .60
❑ 197 Clinton Portis .30 .75
❑ 198 Laveranues Coles .25 .60
❑ 199 Patrick Ramsey .25 .60
❑ 200 Rod Gardner .20 .50
❑ 201 Eli Manning RC 12.00 30.00
❑ 202 Larry Fitzgerald RC 6.00 15.00
❑ 203 Michael Jenkins RC 2.00 5.00
❑ 204 Ben Roethlisberger RC 15.00 40.00
❑ 205 Philip Rivers RC 8.00 20.00
❑ 206 Kellen Winslow RC 2.50 6.00
❑ 207 Kevin Jones RC 2.00 5.00
❑ 208 Steven Jackson RC 5.00 12.00
❑ 209 Reggie Williams RC 2.00 5.00
❑ 210 Chris Perry RC 2.00 5.00
❑ 211 Roy Williams RC 2.50 6.00
❑ 212 Rashaun Woods RC 1.25 3.00
❑ 213 Chris Gamble RC 1.50 4.00
❑ 214 Sean Taylor RC 2.00 5.00
❑ 215 Robert Gallery RC 2.00 5.00
❑ 216 Ben Troupe RC 1.50 4.00
❑ 217 Lee Evans RC 2.50 6.00
❑ 218 Michael Clayton RC 2.00 5.00
❑ 219 J.P. Losman RC 2.00 5.00
❑ 220 Devery Henderson RC 2.00 5.00
❑ 221 Drew Henson RC 1.25 3.00
❑ 222 DeAngelo Hall RC 2.00 5.00
❑ 223 Julius Jones RC 2.50 6.00
❑ 224 Ben Watson RC 2.00 5.00
❑ 225 Greg Jones RC 2.00 5.00
❑ 226 D.J. Williams RC .60 1.50
❑ 227 Tommie Harris RC .60 1.50
❑ 228 Shawn Andrews RC .50 1.25
❑ 229 Vince Wilfork RC .60 1.50
❑ 230 Dunta Robinson RC .50 1.25
❑ 231 Will Smith RC .60 1.50
❑ 232 Jonathan Vilma RC .60 1.50
❑ 233 Ricardo Colclough RC .60 1.50
❑ 234 Ahmad Carroll RC .60 1.50
❑ 235 Karlos Dansby RC .60 1.50
❑ 236 Matt Ware RC .60 1.50
❑ 237 Jim Sorgi RC .60 1.50
❑ 238 Will Poole RC .60 1.50
❑ 239 Derrick Strait RC .50 1.25
❑ 240 Andy Hall RC .50 1.25
❑ 241 Nathan Vasher RC .60 1.50
❑ 242 D.J. Hackett RC .60 1.50
❑ 243 Jason Babin RC .50 1.25
❑ 244 Derrick Hamilton RC .40 1.00
❑ 245 Michael Boulware RC .60 1.50
❑ 246 Michael Turner RC 1.50 4.00
❑ 247 Sean Jones RC .50 1.25
❑ 248 Ernest Wilford RC .50 1.25
❑ 249 Cedric Cobbs RC .50 1.25
❑ 250 Tatum Bell RC .60 1.50
❑ 251 Bernard Berrian RC .60 1.50
❑ 252 Vernon Carey RC .40 1.00
❑ 253 Kenechi Udeze RC .60 1.50
❑ 254 P.K. Sam RC .40 1.00
❑ 255 Ben Hartsock RC .50 1.25
❑ 256 Chris Cooley RC .60 1.50
❑ 257 Josh Harris RC .40 1.00
❑ 258 Cody Pickett RC .50 1.25
❑ 259 Carlos Francis RC .40 1.00
❑ 260 Devard Darling RC .50 1.25
❑ 261 Johnnie Morant RC .50 1.25
❑ 262 John Navarre RC .50 1.25
❑ 263 Kris Wilson RC .50 1.25
❑ 264 Jerricho Cotchery RC .60 1.50
❑ 265 Darius Watts RC .50 1.25
❑ 266 Quincy Wilson RC .50 1.25
❑ 267 Maurice Mann RC .40 1.00
❑ 268 Samie Parker RC .50 1.25
❑ 269 B.J. Symons RC .40 1.00
❑ 270 Matt Schaub RC 1.50 4.00
❑ 271 Jeff Smoker RC .50 1.25
❑ 272 Craig Krenzel RC .60 1.50
❑ 273 Luke McCown RC .60 1.50
❑ 274 Mewelde Moore RC .60 1.50
❑ 275 Keary Colbert RC .50 1.25

2005 Upper Deck

❑ COMPLETE SET (275) 125.00 250.00
❑ COMP.SET w/o SP's (250) 30.00 60.00
❑ COMP.SET w/o RC's (200) 12.50 30.00
❑ 201-225 ROOKIE STATED ODDS 1:8
❑ 226-275 ROOKIE STATED ODDS 1:1
❑ 1 Larry Fitzgerald .30 .75
❑ 2 Anquan Boldin .25 .60
❑ 3 Kurt Warner .30 .75
❑ 4 Josh McCown .25 .60
❑ 5 Bryant Johnson .25 .60
❑ 6 Duane Starks .20 .50
❑ 7 Michael Vick .30 .75
❑ 8 Warrick Dunn .25 .60
❑ 9 T.J. Duckett .20 .50
❑ 10 Peerless Price .20 .50
❑ 11 Alge Crumpler .25 .60
❑ 12 Patrick Kerney .25 .60
❑ 13 Ed Reed .25 .60
❑ 14 Ray Lewis .30 .75
❑ 15 Kyle Boller .25 .60
❑ 16 Ma'Ake Kemoeatu RC .20 .50
❑ 17 Jamal Lewis .25 .60
❑ 18 Derrick Mason .25 .60
❑ 19 J.P. Losman .25 .60
❑ 20 Willis McGahee .30 .75
❑ 21 Lawyer Milloy .25 .60
❑ 22 Lee Evans .25 .60
❑ 23 Eric Moulds .25 .60
❑ 24 Takeo Spikes .20 .50
❑ 25 Jake Delhomme .30 .75
❑ 26 DeShaun Foster .25 .60
❑ 27 Keary Colbert .20 .50
❑ 28 Stephen Davis .25 .60
❑ 29 Nick Goings .20 .50
❑ 30 Julius Peppers .25 .60
❑ 31 Rex Grossman .30 .75
❑ 32 Brian Urlacher .30 .75
❑ 33 Thomas Jones .25 .60
❑ 34 Muhsin Muhammad .25 .60
❑ 35 Anthony Thomas .20 .50
❑ 36 Bernard Berrian .25 .60
❑ 37 Carson Palmer .30 .75
❑ 38 Chad Johnson .25 .60
❑ 39 Peter Warrick .20 .50
❑ 40 T.J. Houshmandzadeh .25 .60
❑ 41 Rudi Johnson .25 .60
❑ 42 Justin Smith .20 .50
❑ 43 Jeff Garcia .25 .60
❑ 44 Lee Suggs .25 .60
❑ 45 William Green .20 .50
❑ 46 Kellen Winslow .30 .75
❑ 47 Dennis Northcutt .20 .50
❑ 48 Antonio Bryant .25 .60
❑ 49 Julius Jones .30 .75
❑ 50 Drew Bledsoe .30 .75

Card	Low	High
❑ 51 Keyshawn Johnson	.25	.60
❑ 52 Al Johnson	.20	.50
❑ 53 Jason Witten	.30	.75
❑ 54 Roy Williams S	.25	.60
❑ 55 Jake Plummer	.25	.60
❑ 56 Champ Bailey	.25	.60
❑ 57 Tatum Bell	.25	.60
❑ 58 Reuben Droughns	.20	.50
❑ 59 Ashley Lelie	.20	.50
❑ 60 Rod Smith	.25	.60
❑ 61 Kevin Jones	.25	.60
❑ 62 Roy Williams WR	.30	.75
❑ 63 Charles Rogers	.20	.50
❑ 64 Joey Harrington	.30	.75
❑ 65 Az-Zahir Hakim	.20	.50
❑ 66 Dre Bly	.20	.50
❑ 67 Brett Favre	.75	2.00
❑ 68 Javon Walker	.25	.60
❑ 69 Ahman Green	.30	.75
❑ 70 Donald Driver	.30	.75
❑ 71 Robert Ferguson	.25	.60
❑ 72 Nick Barnett	.25	.60
❑ 73 David Carr	.25	.60
❑ 74 Domanick Davis	.20	.50
❑ 75 Andre Johnson	.25	.60
❑ 76 Jabar Gaffney	.20	.50
❑ 77 Dunta Robinson	.20	.50
❑ 78 Jamie Sharper	.20	.50
❑ 79 Peyton Manning	.50	1.25
❑ 80 Edgerrin James	.25	.60
❑ 81 Marvin Harrison	.30	.75
❑ 82 Reggie Wayne	.25	.60
❑ 83 Brandon Stokley	.20	.50
❑ 84 Dwight Freeney	.25	.60
❑ 85 Byron Leftwich	.25	.60
❑ 86 Fred Taylor	.30	.75
❑ 87 Jimmy Smith	.25	.60
❑ 88 Greg Jones	.20	.50
❑ 89 Donovin Darius	.20	.50
❑ 90 Reggie Williams	.25	.60
❑ 91 Priest Holmes	.30	.75
❑ 92 Larry Johnson	.30	.75
❑ 93 Tony Gonzalez	.25	.60
❑ 94 Trent Green	.25	.60
❑ 95 Eddie Kennison	.20	.50
❑ 96 Johnnie Morton	.25	.60
❑ 97 Jason Taylor	.25	.60
❑ 98 A.J. Feeley	.20	.50
❑ 99 Sammy Morris	.20	.50
❑ 100 Chris Chambers	.25	.60
❑ 101 Randy McMichael	.20	.50
❑ 102 Zach Thomas	.30	.75
❑ 103 Antoine Winfield	.25	.60
❑ 104 Daunte Culpepper	.30	.75
❑ 105 Michael Bennett	.25	.60
❑ 106 Nate Burleson	.25	.60
❑ 107 Onterrio Smith	.20	.50
❑ 108 Marcus Robinson	.25	.60
❑ 109 Tom Brady	.60	1.50
❑ 110 Corey Dillon	.25	.60
❑ 111 David Givens	.25	.60
❑ 112 David Patten	.20	.50
❑ 113 Adam Vinatieri	.30	.75
❑ 114 Troy Brown	.20	.50
❑ 115 Aaron Brooks	.20	.50
❑ 116 Deuce McAllister	.30	.75
❑ 117 Joe Horn	.25	.60
❑ 118 Donte Stallworth	.25	.60
❑ 119 Charles Grant	.20	.50
❑ 120 Jerome Pathon	.20	.50
❑ 121 Eli Manning	.60	1.50
❑ 122 Tiki Barber	.30	.75
❑ 123 Amani Toomer	.25	.60
❑ 124 Jeremy Shockey	.30	.75
❑ 125 Michael Strahan	.25	.60
❑ 126 Plaxico Burress	.25	.60
❑ 127 Chad Pennington	.30	.75
❑ 128 Curtis Martin	.30	.75
❑ 129 Laveranues Coles	.25	.60
❑ 130 Wayne Chrebet	.25	.60
❑ 131 Jonathan Vilma	.25	.60
❑ 132 Justin McCareins	.20	.50
❑ 133 Kerry Collins	.25	.60
❑ 134 Jerry Porter	.25	.60
❑ 135 LaMont Jordan	.25	.60
❑ 136 Randy Moss	.30	.75
❑ 137 Barry Sims	.20	.50
❑ 138 Warren Sapp	.25	.60
❑ 139 Donovan McNabb	.30	.75
❑ 140 Brian Westbrook	.30	.75
❑ 141 Terrell Owens	.30	.75
❑ 142 Jevon Kearse	.25	.60
❑ 143 Brian Dawkins	.25	.60
❑ 144 Ben Roethlisberger	.75	2.00
❑ 145 Jerome Bettis	.30	.75
❑ 146 Duce Staley	.25	.60
❑ 147 Cedrick Wilson	.20	.50
❑ 148 Hines Ward	.30	.75
❑ 149 Antwaan Randle El	.25	.60
❑ 150 Troy Polamalu	.40	1.00
❑ 151 Philip Rivers	.30	.75
❑ 152 Drew Brees	.30	.75
❑ 153 LaDainian Tomlinson	.40	1.00
❑ 154 Antonio Gates	.30	.75
❑ 155 Reche Caldwell	.20	.50
❑ 156 Eric Parker	.20	.50
❑ 157 Kevan Barlow	.20	.50
❑ 158 Tim Rattay	.20	.50
❑ 159 Eric Johnson	.20	.50
❑ 160 Rashaun Woods	.20	.50
❑ 161 Brandon Lloyd	.20	.50
❑ 162 Julian Peterson	.20	.50
❑ 163 Matt Hasselbeck	.25	.60
❑ 164 Shaun Alexander	.30	.75
❑ 165 Michael Boulware	.20	.50
❑ 166 Darrell Jackson	.25	.60
❑ 167 Koren Robinson	.25	.60
❑ 168 Marcus Trufant	.25	.60
❑ 169 Marc Bulger	.25	.60
❑ 170 Steven Jackson	.40	1.00
❑ 171 Marshall Faulk	.30	.75
❑ 172 Issac Bruce	.25	.60
❑ 173 Torry Holt	.25	.60
❑ 174 Michael Clayton	.25	.60
❑ 175 Michael Pittman	.20	.50
❑ 176 Brian Griese	.25	.60
❑ 177 Joey Galloway	.25	.60
❑ 178 Derrick Brooks	.25	.60
❑ 179 Josh Savage RC	.20	.50
❑ 180 Steve McNair	.30	.75
❑ 181 Chris Brown	.25	.60
❑ 182 Billy Volek	.25	.60
❑ 183 Ben Troupe	.20	.50
❑ 184 Drew Bennett	.25	.60
❑ 185 Clinton Portis	.30	.75
❑ 186 Mark Brunell	.25	.60
❑ 187 Patrick Ramsey	.25	.60
❑ 188 Sean Taylor	.25	.60
❑ 189 LaVar Arrington	.30	.75
❑ 190 Santana Moss	.25	.60
❑ 191 David Terrell	.20	.50
❑ 192 Deion Branch	.25	.60
❑ 193 Chester Taylor	.25	.60
❑ 194 Derrick Blaylock	.20	.50
❑ 195 Shaun Ellis	.20	.50
❑ 196 Terrell Suggs	.25	.60
❑ 197 Charles Woodson	.25	.60
❑ 198 Jason Elam	.20	.50
❑ 199 Lawrence Tynes RC	.25	.60
❑ 200 David Akers	.20	.50
❑ 201 Alex Smith QB RC	2.50	6.00
❑ 202 Aaron Rodgers RC	8.00	20.00
❑ 203 Ronnie Brown RC	8.00	20.00
❑ 204 Cadillac Williams RC	4.00	10.00
❑ 205 Braylon Edwards RC	6.00	15.00
❑ 206 Antrel Rolle RC	2.50	6.00
❑ 207 Cedric Benson RC	2.50	6.00
❑ 208 Troy Williamson RC	2.50	6.00
❑ 209 Mark Clayton RC	2.50	6.00
❑ 210 Matt Jones RC	2.50	6.00
❑ 211 Reggie Brown RC	2.00	5.00
❑ 212 Charlie Frye RC	2.50	6.00
❑ 213 Heath Miller RC	5.00	12.00
❑ 214 Vincent Jackson RC	3.00	8.00
❑ 215 Andrew Walter RC	2.00	5.00
❑ 216 Roddy White RC	3.00	8.00
❑ 217 Adam Jones RC	2.00	5.00
❑ 218 J.J. Arrington RC	2.50	6.00
❑ 219 Eric Shelton RC	2.00	5.00
❑ 220 Terrence Murphy RC	1.50	4.00
❑ 221 Frank Gore RC	5.00	12.00
❑ 222 Roscoe Parrish RC	2.00	5.00
❑ 223 Jason Campbell RC	4.00	10.00
❑ 224 Carlos Rogers RC	2.50	6.00
❑ 225 Mike Williams	2.00	5.00
❑ 226 Erasmus James RC	.60	1.50
❑ 227 Travis Johnson RC	.50	1.25
❑ 228 Dan Cody RC	.75	2.00
❑ 229 Thomas Davis RC	.60	1.50
❑ 230 David Pollack RC	.60	1.50
❑ 231 David Greene RC	.60	1.50
❑ 232 Alex Smith TE RC	.75	2.00
❑ 233 Ryan Moats RC	.60	1.50
❑ 234 Ciatrick Fason RC	.60	1.50
❑ 235 Vernand Morency RC	.60	1.50
❑ 236 Fred Gibson RC	.60	1.50
❑ 237 Craphonso Thorpe RC	.60	1.50
❑ 238 Kevin Everett RC	.75	2.00
❑ 239 Kyle Orton RC	1.25	3.00
❑ 240 Derek Anderson RC	.75	2.00
❑ 241 Derrick Johnson RC	.75	2.00
❑ 242 Mark Bradley RC	.60	1.50
❑ 243 Chris Henry RC	.75	2.00
❑ 244 DeMarcus Ware RC	1.25	3.00
❑ 245 Luis Castillo RC	.75	2.00
❑ 246 Mike Patterson RC	.60	1.50
❑ 247 Brodney Pool RC	.60	1.50
❑ 248 Barrett Ruud RC	.75	2.00
❑ 249 Darren Sproles RC	1.00	2.50
❑ 250 Stefan LeFors RC	.60	1.50
❑ 251 Josh Bullocks RC	.75	2.00
❑ 252 Kevin Burnett RC	.60	1.50
❑ 253 Lofa Tatupu RC	.75	2.00
❑ 254 Matt Roth RC	.75	2.00
❑ 255 Shaun Cody RC	.60	1.50
❑ 256 Shawne Merriman RC	.75	2.00
❑ 257 Corey Webster RC	.75	2.00
❑ 258 Channing Crowder RC	.60	1.50
❑ 259 Justin Miller RC	.60	1.50
❑ 260 Eric Green RC	.50	1.25
❑ 261 Marcus Spears RC	.75	2.00
❑ 262 Marlin Jackson RC	.60	1.50
❑ 263 Odell Thurman RC	.75	2.00
❑ 264 Mike Nugent RC	.60	1.50
❑ 265 Marion Barber RC	2.50	6.00
❑ 266 Anttaj Hawthorne RC	.60	1.50
❑ 267 Dan Orlovsky RC	.75	2.00
❑ 268 Fabian Washington RC	.75	2.00
❑ 269 Justin Tuck RC	1.00	2.50
❑ 270 Jerome Mathis RC	.75	2.00
❑ 271 Ronald Bartell RC	.60	1.50
❑ 272 Kirk Morrison RC	.75	2.00
❑ 273 Adrian McPherson RC	.60	1.50
❑ 274 Matt Cassel RC	2.50	6.00
❑ 275 Maurice Clarett	.60	1.50

2006 Upper Deck

Card	Low	High
❑ COMPLETE SET (275)	150.00	300.00
❑ COMP.SET w/o SP's (250)	30.00	60.00
❑ COMP.SET w/o RC's (200)	12.00	30.00
❑ 1 Larry Fitzgerald	.30	.75
❑ 2 Anquan Boldin	.25	.60
❑ 3 J.J. Arrington	.20	.50
❑ 4 Kurt Warner	.30	.75
❑ 5 Neil Rackers	.20	.50
❑ 6 Edgerrin James	.25	.60
❑ 7 Michael Vick	.30	.75
❑ 8 Alge Crumpler	.25	.60
❑ 9 Warrick Dunn	.25	.60
❑ 10 Michael Jenkins	.25	.60
❑ 11 Roddy White	.25	.60
❑ 12 DeAngelo Hall	.25	.60
❑ 13 Jamal Lewis	.25	.60
❑ 14 Derrick Mason	.25	.60
❑ 15 Todd Heap	.25	.60
❑ 16 Kyle Boller	.25	.60
❑ 17 Ray Lewis	.30	.75
❑ 18 Ed Reed	.25	.60
❑ 19 Willis McGahee	.30	.75
❑ 20 Lee Evans	.25	.60

- ❑ 21 J.P. Losman .25 .60
- ❑ 22 Rashad Baker .20 .50
- ❑ 23 Takeo Spikes .20 .50
- ❑ 24 Aaron Schobel .20 .50
- ❑ 25 Steve Smith .30 .75
- ❑ 26 Jake Delhomme .25 .60
- ❑ 27 DeShaun Foster .25 .60
- ❑ 28 Keary Colbert .25 .60
- ❑ 29 Julius Peppers .25 .60
- ❑ 30 Ma'Ake Kemoeatu .20 .50
- ❑ 31 Rex Grossman .30 .75
- ❑ 32 Muhsin Muhammad .25 .60
- ❑ 33 Brian Urlacher .30 .75
- ❑ 34 Thomas Jones .25 .60
- ❑ 35 Cedric Benson .25 .60
- ❑ 36 Nathan Vasher .20 .50
- ❑ 37 Rudi Johnson .25 .60
- ❑ 38 Chad Johnson .25 .60
- ❑ 39 T.J. Houshmandzadeh .25 .60
- ❑ 40 Chris Henry .20 .50
- ❑ 41 Deltha O'Neal .20 .50
- ❑ 42 Odell Thurman .20 .50
- ❑ 43 Carson Palmer .30 .75
- ❑ 44 Charlie Frye .25 .60
- ❑ 45 Reuben Droughns .25 .60
- ❑ 46 Braylon Edwards .30 .75
- ❑ 47 Kellen Winslow Jr. .30 .75
- ❑ 48 Steve Heiden .20 .50
- ❑ 49 Joe Jurevicius .20 .50
- ❑ 50 Drew Bledsoe .30 .75
- ❑ 51 Julius Jones .25 .60
- ❑ 52 Terrell Owens .30 .75
- ❑ 53 Terry Glenn .25 .60
- ❑ 54 Jason Witten .30 .75
- ❑ 55 DeMarcus Ware .25 .60
- ❑ 56 Roy Williams S .25 .60
- ❑ 57 Jake Plummer .25 .60
- ❑ 58 Tatum Bell .20 .50
- ❑ 59 Al Wilson .20 .50
- ❑ 60 Rod Smith .25 .60
- ❑ 61 Ashley Lelie .20 .50
- ❑ 62 Champ Bailey .25 .60
- ❑ 63 Javon Walker .25 .60
- ❑ 64 Jon Kitna .25 .60
- ❑ 65 Kevin Jones .25 .60
- ❑ 66 Roy Williams WR .30 .75
- ❑ 67 Mike Williams .25 .60
- ❑ 68 Marcus Pollard .20 .50
- ❑ 69 Dre Bly .20 .50
- ❑ 70 Brett Favre .60 1.50
- ❑ 71 Ahman Green .25 .60
- ❑ 72 Donald Driver .30 .75
- ❑ 73 Robert Ferguson .20 .50
- ❑ 74 Bubba Franks .20 .50
- ❑ 75 Kabeer Gbaja-Biamila .25 .60
- ❑ 76 David Carr .20 .50
- ❑ 77 Domanick Davis .25 .60
- ❑ 78 Andre Johnson .25 .60
- ❑ 79 Eric Moulds .25 .60
- ❑ 80 Jeb Putzier .20 .50
- ❑ 81 Dunta Robinson .20 .50
- ❑ 82 Peyton Manning .50 1.25
- ❑ 83 Dominic Rhodes .25 .60
- ❑ 84 Reggie Wayne .25 .60
- ❑ 85 Marvin Harrison .30 .75
- ❑ 86 Dallas Clark .25 .60
- ❑ 87 Dwight Freeney .25 .60
- ❑ 88 Bob Sanders .25 .60
- ❑ 89 Byron Leftwich .25 .60
- ❑ 90 Fred Taylor .25 .60
- ❑ 91 Greg Jones .20 .50
- ❑ 92 Ernest Wilford .20 .50
- ❑ 93 John Henderson .20 .50
- ❑ 94 Matt Jones .25 .60
- ❑ 95 Trent Green .25 .60
- ❑ 96 Larry Johnson .25 .60
- ❑ 97 Priest Holmes .25 .60
- ❑ 98 Eddie Kennison .20 .50
- ❑ 99 Tony Gonzalez .25 .60
- ❑ 100 Dante Hall .25 .60
- ❑ 101 Daunte Culpepper .30 .75
- ❑ 102 Ronnie Brown .30 .75
- ❑ 103 Marty Booker .20 .50
- ❑ 104 Chris Chambers .25 .60
- ❑ 105 Randy McMichael .20 .50
- ❑ 106 Zach Thomas .30 .75
- ❑ 107 Brad Johnson .25 .60
- ❑ 108 Chester Taylor .25 .60
- ❑ 109 Antoine Winfield .20 .50
- ❑ 110 Koren Robinson .20 .50
- ❑ 111 Travis Taylor .20 .50
- ❑ 112 Darren Sharper .25 .60
- ❑ 113 Tom Brady .50 1.25
- ❑ 114 Corey Dillon .25 .60
- ❑ 115 Deion Branch .25 .60
- ❑ 116 Reche Caldwell .20 .50
- ❑ 117 Ben Watson .20 .50
- ❑ 118 Tedy Bruschi .30 .75
- ❑ 119 Rodney Harrison .20 .50
- ❑ 120 Drew Brees .30 .75
- ❑ 121 Deuce McAllister .25 .60
- ❑ 122 Joe Horn .25 .60
- ❑ 123 Donte Stallworth .25 .60
- ❑ 124 Devery Henderson .20 .50
- ❑ 125 Will Smith .20 .50
- ❑ 126 Eli Manning .40 1.00
- ❑ 127 Tiki Barber .30 .75
- ❑ 128 Plaxico Burress .25 .60
- ❑ 129 Amani Toomer .25 .60
- ❑ 130 Jeremy Shockey .30 .75
- ❑ 131 Michael Strahan .25 .60
- ❑ 132 Osi Umenyiora .25 .60
- ❑ 133 Chad Pennington .25 .60
- ❑ 134 Curtis Martin .30 .75
- ❑ 135 Justin McCareins .20 .50
- ❑ 136 Laveranues Coles .25 .60
- ❑ 137 Jonathan Vilma .25 .60
- ❑ 138 Shaun Ellis .20 .50
- ❑ 139 Aaron Brooks .25 .60
- ❑ 140 LaMont Jordan .25 .60
- ❑ 141 Randy Moss .30 .75
- ❑ 142 Jerry Porter .25 .60
- ❑ 143 Doug Gabriel .20 .50
- ❑ 144 Derrick Burgess .20 .50
- ❑ 145 Donovan McNabb .30 .75
- ❑ 146 Brian Westbrook .25 .60
- ❑ 147 Jevon Kearse .25 .60
- ❑ 148 Reggie Brown .20 .50
- ❑ 149 L.J. Smith .20 .50
- ❑ 150 Brian Dawkins .25 .60
- ❑ 151 Ben Roethlisberger .50 1.25
- ❑ 152 Willie Parker .40 1.00
- ❑ 153 Hines Ward .30 .75
- ❑ 154 Cedrick Wilson .20 .50
- ❑ 155 Heath Miller .25 .60
- ❑ 156 Joey Porter .20 .50
- ❑ 157 Troy Polamalu .40 1.00
- ❑ 158 Philip Rivers .30 .75
- ❑ 159 LaDainian Tomlinson .40 1.00
- ❑ 160 Keenan McCardell .25 .60
- ❑ 161 Eric Parker .20 .50
- ❑ 162 Antonio Gates .30 .75
- ❑ 163 Shawne Merriman .25 .60
- ❑ 164 Donnie Edwards .20 .50
- ❑ 165 Alex Smith QB .25 .60
- ❑ 166 Frank Gore .30 .75
- ❑ 167 Antonio Bryant .25 .60
- ❑ 168 Eric Johnson .20 .50
- ❑ 169 Arnaz Battle .20 .50
- ❑ 170 Bryant Young .20 .50
- ❑ 171 Matt Hasselbeck .25 .60
- ❑ 172 Shaun Alexander .25 .60
- ❑ 173 Darrell Jackson .25 .60
- ❑ 174 Etric Pruitt .20 .50
- ❑ 175 Julian Peterson .20 .50
- ❑ 176 Lofa Tatupu .25 .60
- ❑ 177 Marc Bulger .25 .60
- ❑ 178 Steven Jackson .30 .75
- ❑ 179 Torry Holt .25 .60
- ❑ 180 Kevin Curtis .25 .60
- ❑ 181 Isaac Bruce .25 .60
- ❑ 182 Leonard Little .20 .50
- ❑ 183 Chris Simms .25 .60
- ❑ 184 Cadillac Williams .30 .75
- ❑ 185 Joey Galloway .25 .60
- ❑ 186 Michael Clayton .25 .60
- ❑ 187 Derrick Brooks .25 .60
- ❑ 188 Ronde Barber .25 .60
- ❑ 189 Billy Volek .20 .50
- ❑ 190 Chris Brown .25 .60
- ❑ 191 Drew Bennett .25 .60
- ❑ 192 Ben Troupe .20 .50
- ❑ 193 David Givens .25 .60
- ❑ 194 Adam Jones .20 .50
- ❑ 195 Mark Brunell [illegible] [illegible]
- ❑ 196 Clinton Portis .30 .75
- ❑ 197 Santana Moss .25 .60
- ❑ 198 Chris Cooley .25 .60
- ❑ 199 Antwaan Randle El .25 .60
- ❑ 200 Sean Taylor .30 .75
- ❑ 201 A.J. Hawk RC 4.00 10.00
- ❑ 202 Anthony Fasano RC 2.50 6.00
- ❑ 203 Brian Calhoun RC 2.00 5.00
- ❑ 204 Chad Greenway RC 2.50 6.00
- ❑ 205 Chad Jackson RC 2.00 5.00
- ❑ 206 DeAngelo Williams RC 5.00 12.00
- ❑ 207 D'Brickashaw Ferguson RC 2.50 6.00
- ❑ 208 Brodie Croyle RC 2.50 6.00
- ❑ 209 Haloti Ngata RC 2.50 6.00
- ❑ 210 Jay Cutler RC 6.00 15.00
- ❑ 211 Joseph Addai RC 3.00 8.00
- ❑ 212 Laurence Maroney RC 3.00 8.00
- ❑ 213 LenDale White RC 3.00 8.00
- ❑ 214 Maurice Drew RC 5.00 12.00
- ❑ 215 Mario Williams RC 3.00 8.00
- ❑ 216 Matt Leinart RC 4.00 10.00
- ❑ 217 Maurice Stovall RC 2.00 5.00
- ❑ 218 Michael Huff RC 2.50 6.00
- ❑ 219 Reggie Bush RC 6.00 15.00
- ❑ 220 Santonio Holmes RC 6.00 15.00
- ❑ 221 Sinorice Moss RC 2.50 6.00
- ❑ 222 Kellen Clemens RC 2.50 6.00
- ❑ 223 Tarvaris Jackson RC 2.50 6.00
- ❑ 224 Vernon Davis RC 2.50 6.00
- ❑ 225 Vince Young RC 6.00 15.00
- ❑ 226 Donte Whitner RC 1.00 2.50
- ❑ 227 Antonio Cromartie RC 1.00 2.50
- ❑ 228 Ashton Youboty RC .75 2.00
- ❑ 229 Bobby Carpenter RC .75 2.00
- ❑ 230 Brad Smith RC 1.00 2.50
- ❑ 231 Brandon Williams RC .75 2.00
- ❑ 232 Dominique Byrd RC .75 2.00
- ❑ 233 Brodrick Bunkley RC .75 2.00
- ❑ 234 Charlie Whitehurst RC 1.00 2.50
- ❑ 235 Demetrius Williams RC .75 2.00
- ❑ 236 Cory Rodgers RC 1.00 2.50
- ❑ 237 Daniel Bullocks RC 1.00 2.50
- ❑ 238 Manny Lawson RC 1.00 2.50
- ❑ 239 Darrell Hackney RC .75 2.00
- ❑ 240 Darryl Tapp RC .75 2.00
- ❑ 241 David Thomas RC 1.00 2.50
- ❑ 242 DeMeco Ryans RC 1.25 3.00
- ❑ 243 Derek Hagan RC .75 2.00
- ❑ 244 Devin Hester RC 2.00 5.00
- ❑ 245 D'Qwell Jackson RC .75 2.00
- ❑ 246 Brandon Marshall RC 1.00 2.50
- ❑ 247 Ernie Sims RC .75 2.00
- ❑ 248 Gabe Watson RC .60 1.50
- ❑ 249 Jason Allen RC .75 2.00
- ❑ 250 Greg Jennings RC 1.50 4.00
- ❑ 251 Marcus Vick RC .60 1.50
- ❑ 252 Jason Avant RC 1.00 2.50
- ❑ 253 Jeremy Bloom RC .75 2.00
- ❑ 254 Jerome Harrison RC 1.00 2.50
- ❑ 255 Joe Klopfenstein RC .75 2.00
- ❑ 256 Johnathan Joseph RC .75 2.00
- ❑ 257 Jimmy Williams RC 1.00 2.50
- ❑ 258 Kamerion Wimbley RC 1.00 2.50
- ❑ 259 Leon Washington RC 1.25 3.00
- ❑ 260 Marcedes Lewis RC 1.00 2.50
- ❑ 261 Marcus McNeill RC .75 2.00
- ❑ 262 Mathias Kiwanuka RC 1.25 3.00
- ❑ 263 Leonard Pope RC 1.00 2.50
- ❑ 264 Tamba Hali RC 1.00 2.50
- ❑ 265 Mike Hass RC 1.00 2.50
- ❑ 266 Omar Jacobs RC .60 1.50
- ❑ 267 Jerious Norwood RC 1.00 2.50
- ❑ 268 Owen Daniels RC 1.00 2.50
- ❑ 269 P.J. Daniels RC .60 1.50
- ❑ 270 Ray Edwards RC 1.00 2.50
- ❑ 271 Michael Robinson RC .75 2.00
- ❑ 272 Rocky McIntosh RC 1.00 2.50
- ❑ 273 Travis Wilson RC .60 1.50
- ❑ 274 Tye Hill RC .75 2.00
- ❑ 275 Thomas Howard RC .75 2.00

2007 Upper Deck

Card		
COMPLETE SET (300)	150.00	250.00
COMP.SET w/o RC's (200)	12.50	30.00
1 Karlos Dansby	.20	.50
2 Edgerrin James	.25	.60
3 Matt Leinart	.30	.75
4 Larry Fitzgerald	.30	.75
5 Anquan Boldin	.25	.60
6 Joe Horn	.25	.60
7 Michael Jenkins	.25	.60
8 Michael Vick	.30	.75
9 Warrick Dunn	.25	.60
10 Alge Crumpler	.25	.60
11 Derrick Mason	.20	.50
12 Ed Reed	.25	.60
13 Willis McGahee	.25	.60
14 Steve McNair	.25	.60
15 Mark Clayton	.25	.60
16 Todd Heap	.20	.50
17 Ray Lewis	.30	.75
18 J.P. Losman	.20	.50
19 Peerless Price	.20	.50
20 Lee Evans	.25	.60
21 Anthony Thomas	.20	.50
22 David Carr	.25	.60
23 DeAngelo Williams	.30	.75
24 Julius Peppers	.25	.60
25 Jake Delhomme	.25	.60
26 DeShaun Foster	.25	.60
27 Steve Smith	.25	.60
28 Muhsin Muhammad	.25	.60
29 Rex Grossman	.25	.60
30 Desmond Clark	.20	.50
31 Devin Hester	.30	.75
32 Cedric Benson	.25	.60
33 Bernard Berrian	.20	.50
34 Brian Urlacher	.30	.75
35 Justin Smith	.20	.50
36 T.J. Houshmandzadeh	.25	.60
37 Carson Palmer	.30	.75
38 Rudi Johnson	.25	.60
39 Chad Johnson	.25	.60
40 Kamerion Wimbley	.20	.50
41 Charlie Frye	.25	.60
42 Tim Carter	.20	.50
43 Jamal Lewis	.25	.60
44 Kellen Winslow	.25	.60
45 Braylon Edwards	.25	.60
46 Roy Williams S	.25	.60
47 Marion Barber	.30	.75
48 Jason Witten	.30	.75
49 Terry Glenn	.25	.60
50 Demarcus Ware	.25	.60
51 Tony Romo	.50	1.25
52 Julius Jones	.25	.60
53 Terrell Owens	.30	.75
54 Mike Bell	.25	.60
55 John Lynch	.25	.60
56 Rod Smith	.25	.60
57 Travis Henry	.25	.60
58 Jay Cutler	.30	.75
59 Javon Walker	.25	.60
60 Champ Bailey	.25	.60
61 Tatum Bell	.20	.50
62 Mike Furrey	.25	.60
63 Jon Kitna	.20	.50
64 Kevin Jones	.20	.50
65 Roy Williams WR	.25	.60
66 Bubba Franks	.20	.50
67 Charles Woodson	.25	.60
68 Brett Favre	.60	1.50
69 Donald Driver	.30	.75
70 A.J. Hawk	.30	.75
71 Ahman Green	.25	.60
72 DeMeco Ryans	.25	.60
73 Matt Schaub	.25	.60
74 Andre Johnson	.25	.60
75 Mario Williams	.25	.60
76 Ron Dayne	.25	.60
77 Dwight Freeney	.25	.60
78 Dallas Clark	.20	.50
79 Peyton Manning	.50	1.25
80 Marvin Harrison	.30	.75
81 Reggie Wayne	.25	.60
82 Joseph Addai	.30	.75
83 Matt Jones	.25	.60
84 David Garrard	.25	.60
85 Ernest Wilford	.20	.50
86 Reggie Williams	.25	.60
87 Maurice Jones-Drew	.30	.75
88 Fred Taylor	.25	.60
89 Byron Leftwich	.25	.60
90 Eddie Kennison	.20	.50
91 Samie Parker	.20	.50
92 Derrick Johnson	.20	.50
93 Trent Green	.25	.60
94 Larry Johnson	.25	.60
95 Tony Gonzalez	.25	.60
96 Damon Huard	.25	.60
97 Zach Thomas	.25	.60
98 Daunte Culpepper	.25	.60
99 Ronnie Brown	.25	.60
100 Jason Taylor	.20	.50
101 Chris Chambers	.25	.60
102 Antoine Winfield	.20	.50
103 Ryan Longwell	.20	.50
104 Chester Taylor	.20	.50
105 Tarvaris Jackson	.25	.60
106 Troy Williamson	.20	.50
107 Rodney Harrison	.20	.50
108 Randy Moss	.30	.75
109 Stephen Gostkowski	.20	.50
110 Donte Stallworth	.25	.60
111 Tom Brady	.60	1.50
112 Laurence Maroney	.30	.75
113 Ben Watson	.20	.50
114 Tedy Bruschi	.30	.75
115 Charles Grant	.20	.50
116 Michael Lewis	.20	.50
117 Drew Brees	.30	.75
118 Marques Colston	.30	.75
119 Reggie Bush	.40	1.00
120 Deuce McAllister	.25	.60
121 Amani Toomer	.25	.60
122 Reuben Droughns	.25	.60
123 Michael Strahan	.25	.60
124 Plaxico Burress	.25	.60
125 Osi Umenyiora	.20	.50
126 Eli Manning	.30	.75
127 Jeremy Shockey	.25	.60
128 Brandon Jacobs	.25	.60
129 Jonathan Vilma	.25	.60
130 Jerricho Cotchery	.20	.50
131 Chris Baker	.20	.50
132 Chad Pennington	.25	.60
133 Leon Washington	.25	.60
134 Laveranues Coles	.25	.60
135 Nnamdi Asomugha	.20	.50
136 Dominic Rhodes	.25	.60
137 Warren Sapp	.25	.60
138 Justin Fargas	.20	.50
139 Ronald Curry	.25	.60
140 Brian Dawkins	.25	.60
141 L.J. Smith	.20	.50
142 Mike Patterson	.20	.50
143 Brian Westbrook	.25	.60
144 Reggie Brown	.20	.50
145 Donovan McNabb	.30	.75
146 Hines Ward	.30	.75
147 James Farrior	.20	.50
148 Ike Taylor	.20	.50
149 Santonio Holmes	.25	.60
150 Ben Roethlisberger	.50	1.25
151 Willie Parker	.25	.60
152 Troy Polamalu	.30	.75
153 Michael Turner	.30	.75
154 Vincent Jackson	.20	.50
155 Nate Kaeding	.20	.50
156 Philip Rivers	.30	.75
157 Antonio Gates	.25	.60
158 Shawne Merriman	.25	.60
159 LaDainian Tomlinson	.40	1.00
160 Arnaz Battle	.20	.50
161 Nate Clements	.20	.50
162 Ashley Lelie	.25	.60
163 Alex Smith QB	.30	.75
164 Frank Gore	.30	.75
165 Vernon Davis	.25	.60
166 Mack Strong	.20	.50
167 Lofa Tatupu	.25	.60
168 Maurice Morris	.20	.50
169 Bobby Engram	.20	.50
170 Matt Hasselbeck	.25	.60
171 Shaun Alexander	.25	.60
172 Deion Branch	.25	.60
173 Leonard Little	.20	.50
174 Pisa Tinoisamoa	.20	.50
175 Drew Bennett	.20	.50
176 Steven Jackson	.30	.75
177 Marc Bulger	.25	.60
178 Torry Holt	.25	.60
179 Isaac Bruce	.25	.60
180 Ronde Barber	.20	.50
181 Chris Simms	.20	.50
182 Mike Alstott	.25	.60
183 Derrick Brooks	.25	.60
184 Cadillac Williams	.25	.60
185 Michael Clayton	.25	.60
186 Joey Galloway	.25	.60
187 Brandon Jones	.20	.50
188 Keith Bulluck	.20	.50
189 Nick Harper	.20	.50
190 David Givens	.20	.50
191 Vince Young	.30	.75
192 LenDale White	.25	.60
193 Mark Brunell	.25	.60
194 Sean Taylor	.20	.50
195 Chris Cooley	.25	.60
196 Brandon Lloyd	.25	.60
197 Jason Campbell	.25	.60
198 Clinton Portis	.25	.60
199 Santana Moss	.25	.60
200 Antwaan Randle El	.20	.50
201 Levi Brown RC	1.50	4.00
202 Alan Branch RC	1.25	3.00
203 Buster Davis RC	1.25	3.00
204 Steve Breaston RC	1.50	4.00
205 Justin Blalock RC	1.00	2.50
206 Chris Houston RC	1.25	3.00
207 Laurent Robinson RC	1.50	4.00
208 Ben Grubbs RC	1.25	3.00
209 Troy Smith RC	2.00	5.00
210 Yamon Figurs RC	1.00	2.50
211 Le'Ron McClain RC	1.50	4.00
212 Trent Edwards RC	2.50	6.00
213 Dwayne Wright RC	1.25	3.00
214 Jon Beason RC	1.50	4.00
215 Ryan Kalil RC	1.25	3.00
216 Dan Bazuin RC	1.25	3.00
217 Garrett Wolfe RC	1.50	4.00
218 Michael Okwo RC	1.25	3.00
219 Chris Leak RC	1.25	3.00
220 Leon Hall RC	1.50	4.00
221 Jeff Rowe RC	1.25	3.00
222 Eric Wright RC	1.50	4.00
223 Isaiah Stanback RC	1.50	4.00
224 Anthony Spencer RC	1.50	4.00
225 Jarvis Moss RC	1.50	4.00
226 Tim Crowder RC	1.50	4.00
227 Ikaika Alama-Francis RC	1.50	4.00
228 Justin Harrell RC	1.50	4.00
229 Brandon Jackson RC	1.50	4.00
230 James Jones RC	1.50	4.00
231 Jacoby Jones RC	1.50	4.00
232 Tony Ugoh RC	1.25	3.00
233 Daymeion Hughes RC	1.25	3.00
234 Reggie Nelson RC	1.25	3.00
235 Justin Durant RC	1.25	3.00
236 Turk McBride RC	1.25	3.00
237 DeMarcus Tank Tyler RC	1.25	3.00
238 Kolby Smith RC	1.50	4.00
239 Lorenzo Booker RC	1.50	4.00
240 Marcus McCauley RC	1.25	3.00
241 Brandon Meriweather RC	1.50	4.00
242 Antonio Pittman RC	1.50	4.00
243 Usama Young RC	1.25	3.00
244 Aaron Ross RC	1.50	4.00
245 Zak DeOssie RC	1.25	3.00
246 Darrelle Revis RC	2.00	5.00

❑ 247 David Harris RC 1.25 3.00
❑ 248 Zach Miller RC 1.50 4.00
❑ 249 Johnnie Lee Higgins RC 1.50 4.00
❑ 250 Michael Bush RC 1.50 4.00
❑ 251 Quentin Moses RC 1.25 3.00
❑ 252 Victor Abiamiri RC 1.50 4.00
❑ 253 Tony Hunt RC 1.50 4.00
❑ 254 Stewart Bradley RC 1.50 4.00
❑ 255 Lawrence Timmons RC 1.50 4.00
❑ 256 LaMarr Woodley RC 1.50 4.00
❑ 257 Matt Spaeth RC 1.50 4.00
❑ 258 Eric Woddle RC 1.25 3.00
❑ 259 Scott Chandler RC 1.25 3.00
❑ 260 Anthony Waters RC 1.25 3.00
❑ 261 Joe Staley RC 1.25 3.00
❑ 262 Jason Hill RC 1.50 4.00
❑ 263 Josh Wilson RC 1.25 3.00
❑ 264 Brandon Mebane RC 1.25 3.00
❑ 265 Adam Carriker RC 1.25 3.00
❑ 266 Jonathan Wade RC 1.25 3.00
❑ 267 Arron Sears RC 1.25 3.00
❑ 268 Sabby Piscitelli RC 1.50 4.00
❑ 269 Quincy Black RC 1.50 4.00
❑ 270 Michael Griffin RC 1.50 4.00
❑ 271 Chris Henry RB RC 1.25 3.00
❑ 272 Paul Williams RC 1.25 3.00
❑ 273 Chris Davis RC 1.25 3.00
❑ 274 H.B. Blades RC 1.25 3.00
❑ 275 Jordan Palmer RC 1.50 4.00
❑ 276 JaMarcus Russell RC 2.00 5.00
❑ 277 Calvin Johnson RC 4.00 10.00
❑ 278 Brady Quinn RC 3.00 8.00
❑ 279 Adrian Peterson RC 12.00 30.00
❑ 280 Marshawn Lynch RC 2.50 6.00
❑ 281 Ted Ginn Jr. RC 2.50 6.00
❑ 282 LaRon Landry RC 2.00 5.00
❑ 283 Jamaal Anderson RC 1.25 3.00
❑ 284 Amobi Okoye RC 1.50 4.00
❑ 285 Dwayne Bowe RC 2.50 6.00
❑ 286 Greg Olsen RC 2.00 5.00
❑ 287 Gaines Adams RC 1.50 4.00
❑ 288 Patrick Willis RC 2.50 6.00
❑ 289 Drew Stanton RC 1.25 3.00
❑ 290 Kevin Kolb RC 2.50 6.00
❑ 291 John Beck RC 1.50 4.00
❑ 292 Anthony Gonzalez RC 2.00 5.00
❑ 293 Sidney Rice RC 3.00 8.00
❑ 294 Robert Meachem RC 1.50 4.00
❑ 295 Joe Thomas RC 1.50 4.00
❑ 296 Dwayne Jarrett RC 1.50 4.00
❑ 297 Kenny Irons RC 1.50 4.00
❑ 298 Brian Leonard RC 1.25 3.00
❑ 299 Craig Buster Davis RC 1.50 4.00
❑ 300 Steve Smith USC RC 2.50 6.00

2008 Upper Deck

❑ COMPLETE SET (325) 125.00 250.00
❑ COMP.SET w/o SP's (300) 25.00 50.00
❑ COMP.SET w/o RC's (200) 10.00 25.00
❑ 1 Edgerrin James .20 .50
❑ 2 Matt Leinart .25 .60
❑ 3 Larry Fitzgerald .25 .60
❑ 4 Anquan Boldin .20 .50
❑ 5 Antrel Rolle .15 .40
❑ 6 Joe Horn .20 .50
❑ 7 Warrick Dunn .20 .50
❑ 8 Alge Crumpler .20 .50
❑ 9 Jerious Norwood .20 .50
❑ 10 Michael Jenkins .15 .40
❑ 11 Derrick Mason .15 .40
❑ 12 Ed Reed .20 .50
❑ 13 Willis McGahee .20 .50
❑ 14 Steve McNair .20 .50
❑ 15 Todd Heap .15 .40
❑ 16 Ray Lewis .25 .60
❑ 17 Terrell Suggs .15 .40
❑ 18 Trent Edwards .25 .60
❑ 19 Lee Evans .20 .50
❑ 20 Roscoe Parrish .15 .40
❑ 21 Marshawn Lynch .25 .60
❑ 22 Stacy Andrews .15 .40
❑ 23 DeAngelo Williams .20 .50
❑ 24 Julius Peppers .20 .50
❑ 25 Steve Smith .20 .50
❑ 26 Jake Delhomme .20 .50
❑ 27 Lance Briggs .15 .40
❑ 28 Rex Grossman .20 .50
❑ 29 Devin Hester .25 .60
❑ 30 Bernard Berrian .20 .50
❑ 31 Brian Urlacher .25 .60
❑ 32 Cedric Benson .20 .50
❑ 33 Greg Olsen .20 .50
❑ 34 T.J. Houshmandzadeh .20 .50
❑ 35 Carson Palmer .25 .60
❑ 36 Rudi Johnson .20 .50
❑ 37 Chad Johnson .20 .50
❑ 38 Kurt Warner .25 .60
❑ 39 Kamerion Wimbley .15 .40
❑ 40 Josh Cribbs .25 .60
❑ 41 Jamal Lewis .20 .50
❑ 42 Kellen Winslow .20 .50
❑ 43 Braylon Edwards .20 .50
❑ 44 Eric Wright .15 .40
❑ 45 Anthony Henry .15 .40
❑ 46 Roy Williams S .20 .50
❑ 47 Marion Barber .25 .60
❑ 48 Jason Witten .25 .60
❑ 49 DeMarcus Ware .20 .50
❑ 50 Tony Romo .40 1.00
❑ 51 Julius Jones .20 .50
❑ 52 Terrell Owens .25 .60
❑ 53 Greg Ellis .15 .40
❑ 54 Patrick Crayton .20 .50
❑ 55 John Lynch .20 .50
❑ 56 Brandon Marshall .20 .50
❑ 57 Travis Henry .20 .50
❑ 58 Jay Cutler .25 .60
❑ 59 Dre Bly .15 .40
❑ 60 Javon Walker .20 .50
❑ 61 Champ Bailey .15 .40
❑ 62 Tatum Bell .15 .40
❑ 63 Calvin Johnson .25 .60
❑ 64 Jon Kitna .20 .50
❑ 65 Roy Williams WR .20 .50
❑ 66 Ernie Sims .15 .40
❑ 67 Aaron Kampman .20 .50
❑ 68 Bubba Franks .15 .40
❑ 69 Charles Woodson .20 .50
❑ 70 Brett Favre .60 1.50
❑ 71 Donald Driver .20 .50
❑ 72 A.J. Hawk .20 .50
❑ 73 Ahman Green .20 .50
❑ 74 DeMeco Ryans .20 .50
❑ 75 Andre Johnson .20 .50
❑ 76 Mario Williams .20 .50
❑ 77 Ron Dayne .20 .50
❑ 78 Dwight Freeney .20 .50
❑ 79 Dallas Clark .20 .50
❑ 80 Peyton Manning .40 1.00
❑ 81 Marvin Harrison .25 .60
❑ 82 Reggie Wayne .20 .50
❑ 83 Joseph Addai .25 .60
❑ 84 Matt Jones .20 .50
❑ 85 David Garrard .20 .50
❑ 86 Ernest Wilford .15 .40
❑ 87 Reggie Williams .20 .50
❑ 88 Maurice Jones-Drew .20 .50
❑ 89 Fred Taylor .20 .50
❑ 90 Reggie Nelson .15 .40
❑ 91 Dwayne Bowe .20 .50
❑ 92 Samie Parker .15 .40
❑ 93 Derrick Johnson .15 .40
❑ 94 Larry Johnson .20 .50
❑ 95 Brodie Croyle .20 .50
❑ 96 Tony Gonzalez .20 .50
❑ 97 Jared Allen .25 .60
❑ 98 Zach Thomas .20 .50
❑ 99 Ronnie Brown .20 .50
❑ 100 Jason Taylor .20 .50
❑ 101 Ted Ginn Jr. .20 .50
❑ 102 John Beck .15 .40
❑ 103 Antoine Winfield .15 .40
❑ 104 Adrian Peterson .50 1.25
❑ 105 Bob Sanders .20 .50
❑ 106 Sidney Rice .25 .60
❑ 107 Chester Taylor .15 .40
❑ 108 Wes Welker .25 .60
❑ 109 Rodney Harrison .15 .40
❑ 110 Randy Moss .25 .60
❑ 111 Donte Stallworth .20 .50
❑ 112 Tom Brady .40 1.00
❑ 113 Laurence Maroney .20 .50
❑ 114 Ben Watson .15 .40
❑ 115 Tedy Bruschi .25 .60
❑ 116 Mike Vrabel .15 .40
❑ 117 Charles Grant .15 .40
❑ 118 Drew Brees .25 .60
❑ 119 Marques Colston .20 .50
❑ 120 Reggie Bush .25 .60
❑ 121 Deuce McAllister .20 .50
❑ 122 Mike McKenzie .15 .40
❑ 123 Amani Toomer .20 .50
❑ 124 Michael Strahan .20 .50
❑ 125 Plaxico Burress .20 .50
❑ 126 Osi Umenyiora .15 .40
❑ 127 Eli Manning .25 .60
❑ 128 Jeremy Shockey .20 .50
❑ 129 Brandon Jacobs .20 .50
❑ 130 Antonio Pierce .15 .40
❑ 131 Jonathan Vilma .20 .50
❑ 132 Jerricho Cotchery .15 .40
❑ 133 Kellen Clemens .20 .50
❑ 134 Leon Washington .20 .50
❑ 135 Thomas Jones .20 .50
❑ 136 Kirk Morrison .15 .40
❑ 137 Nnamdi Asomugha .15 .40
❑ 138 Derrick Burgess .15 .40
❑ 139 Justin Fargas .15 .40
❑ 140 Ronald Curry .20 .50
❑ 141 JaMarcus Russell .25 .60
❑ 142 Brian Dawkins .20 .50
❑ 143 Brian Westbrook .20 .50
❑ 144 Reggie Brown .15 .40
❑ 145 Donovan McNabb .25 .60
❑ 146 Hines Ward .20 .50
❑ 147 Santonio Holmes .20 .50
❑ 148 Ben Roethlisberger .40 1.00
❑ 149 Willie Parker .20 .50
❑ 150 Troy Polamalu .25 .60
❑ 151 James Farrior .15 .40
❑ 152 Heath Miller .15 .40
❑ 153 Chris Chambers .20 .50
❑ 154 Philip Rivers .25 .60
❑ 155 Antonio Gates .20 .50
❑ 156 Shawne Merriman .20 .50
❑ 157 LaDainian Tomlinson .30 .75
❑ 158 Antonio Cromartie .15 .40
❑ 159 Shaun Phillips .15 .40
❑ 160 Jamal Williams .15 .40
❑ 161 Arnaz Battle .15 .40
❑ 162 Nate Clements .15 .40
❑ 163 Alex Smith QB .20 .50
❑ 164 Frank Gore .20 .50
❑ 165 Vernon Davis .15 .40
❑ 166 Patrick Willis .20 .50
❑ 167 Lofa Tatupu .20 .50
❑ 168 Patrick Kerney .15 .40
❑ 169 Bobby Engram .15 .40
❑ 170 Matt Hasselbeck .20 .50
❑ 171 Shawn Andrews .15 .40
❑ 172 Deion Branch .20 .50
❑ 173 D.J. Hackett .15 .40
❑ 174 Leonard Little .15 .40
❑ 175 Pisa Tinoisamoa .15 .40
❑ 176 Steven Jackson .25 .60
❑ 177 Marc Bulger .20 .50
❑ 178 Torry Holt .20 .50
❑ 179 Isaac Bruce .20 .50
❑ 180 Randy McMichael .15 .40
❑ 181 Ronde Barber .15 .40
❑ 182 Cadillac Williams .20 .50
❑ 183 Derrick Brooks .20 .50
❑ 184 Michael Clayton .20 .50
❑ 185 Jeff Garcia .20 .50
❑ 186 Joey Galloway .20 .50
❑ 187 Gaines Adams .15 .40
❑ 188 Keith Bulluck .15 .40
❑ 189 Nick Harper .15 .40
❑ 190 David Givens .15 .40
❑ 191 Vince Young .20 .50
❑ 192 LenDale White .20 .50

Card	Low	High
193 Eric Moulds	.20	.50
194 Jason Campbell	.20	.50
195 Randall Godfrey	.15	.40
196 Chris Cooley	.20	.50
197 Brandon Lloyd	.15	.40
198 Clinton Portis	.20	.50
199 Santana Moss	.15	.40
200 London Fletcher	.15	.40
201 Will Franklin RC	.60	1.50
202 Jerome Felton RC	.50	1.25
203 Adrian Arrington RC	.60	1.50
204 Alex Brink RC	.75	2.00
205 Allen Patrick RC	.60	1.50
206 Andre Caldwell RC	.75	2.00
207 Anthony Morelli RC	.75	2.00
208 Antoine Cason RC	.75	2.00
209 Aqib Talib RC	.75	2.00
210 Ben Moffitt RC	.50	1.25
211 Caleb Campbell RC	.75	2.00
212 T.C. Ostrander RC	.60	1.50
213 Bruce Davis RC	.75	2.00
214 Calais Campbell RC	.60	1.50
215 Chris Williams RC	.60	1.50
216 Chad Henne RC	1.25	3.00
217 Chevis Jackson RC	.60	1.50
218 Chris Ellis RC	.60	1.50
219 Chris Johnson RC	2.50	6.00
220 Cory Boyd RC	.60	1.50
221 Craig Steltz RC	.60	1.50
222 DJ Hall RC	.60	1.50
223 Chauncey Washington RC	.60	1.50
224 Darius Reynaud RC	.60	1.50
225 Davone Bess RC	1.00	2.50
226 DeJuan Tribble RC	.50	1.25
227 DeMario Pressley RC	.60	1.50
228 Dennis Keyes RC	.50	1.25
229 Derrick Harvey RC	.60	1.50
230 Donnie Avery RC	1.00	2.50
231 Xavier Omon RC	.75	2.00
232 Dre Moore RC	.60	1.50
233 Dustin Keller RC	.75	2.00
234 Earl Bennett RC	.75	2.00
235 Erik Ainge RC	.75	2.00
236 Erin Henderson RC	.60	1.50
237 Curtis Lofton RC	.75	2.00
238 Felix Jones RC	1.50	4.00
239 Josh Barrett RC	.50	1.25
240 Gosder Cherilus RC	.60	1.50
241 Harry Douglas RC	.60	1.50
242 Colt Brennan RC	1.25	3.00
243 J Leman RC	.60	1.50
244 Jack Ikegwuonu RC	.60	1.50
245 Jacob Hester RC	.75	2.00
246 Jacob Tamme RC	.75	2.00
247 Jamaal Charles RC	1.25	3.00
248 James Hardy RC	.60	1.50
249 Jermichael Finley RC	.75	2.00
250 Jerod Mayo RC	1.00	2.50
251 Joe Flacco RC	2.50	6.00
252 John Carlson RC	.75	2.00
253 John David Booty RC	.75	2.00
254 Jonathan Goff RC	.60	1.50
255 Jonathan Hefney RC	.60	1.50
256 Jordon Dizon RC	.75	2.00
257 Jordy Nelson RC	1.00	2.50
258 Josh Johnson RC	.75	2.00
259 Justin Forsett RC	.75	2.00
260 Kalvin McRae RC	.60	1.50
261 Keenan Burton RC	.60	1.50
262 Kellen Davis RC	.50	1.25
263 Kentwan Balmer RC	.60	1.50
264 Keon Lattimore RC	.60	1.50
265 Kevin O'Connell RC	.75	2.00
266 Kevin Smith RC	1.25	3.00
267 Thomas DeCoud RC	.50	1.25
268 Malcolm Kelly RC	.75	2.00
269 Marcus Monk RC	.75	2.00
270 Mario Manningham RC	.75	2.00
271 Mario Urrutia RC	.60	1.50
272 Martellus Bennett RC	.75	2.00
273 Martin Rucker RC	.60	1.50
274 Matt Flynn RC	.75	2.00
275 Matt Forte RC	1.50	4.00
276 Owen Schmitt RC	.75	2.00
277 Paul Hubbard RC	.60	1.50
278 Paul Smith RC	.75	2.00
279 Philip Wheeler RC	.75	2.00
280 Quentin Groves RC	.60	1.50
281 Quintin Demps RC	.75	2.00
282 Rashard Mendenhall RC	1.50	4.00
283 Ray Rice RC	1.50	4.00
284 Ryan Clady RC	.75	2.00
285 Ryan Grice-Mullen RC	.75	2.00
286 Ryan Torain RC	.75	2.00
287 Spencer Larsen RC	.50	1.25
288 Marcus Thomas RC	.60	1.50
289 Shawn Crable RC	.75	2.00
290 Frank Okam RC	.50	1.25
291 Tashard Choice RC	.75	2.00
292 Terrell Thomas RC	.60	1.50
293 Thomas Brown RC	.75	2.00
294 Tom Zbikowski RC	.75	2.00
295 Simeon Castille RC	.60	1.50
296 Trevor Laws RC	.75	2.00
297 Vernon Gholston RC	.75	2.00
298 Vince Hall RC	.50	1.25
299 Xavier Adibi RC	.60	1.50
300 Yvenson Bernard RC	.75	2.00
301 Andre Woodson SP RC	2.50	6.00
302 Brian Brohm SP RC	2.50	6.00
303 Devin Thomas SP RC	2.50	6.00
304 Dennis Dixon SP RC	2.50	6.00
305 Matt Ryan SP RC	10.00	25.00
306 Darren McFadden SP RC	5.00	12.00
307 Jonathan Stewart SP RC	5.00	12.00
308 Mike Hart SP RC	2.50	6.00
309 DeSean Jackson SP RC	5.00	12.00
310 Early Doucet SP RC	2.50	6.00
311 Lavelle Hawkins SP RC	2.00	5.00
312 Limas Sweed SP RC	2.50	6.00
313 Jake Long SP RC	2.50	6.00
314 Sam Baker SP RC	1.50	4.00
315 Glenn Dorsey SP RC	2.50	6.00
316 Sedrick Ellis SP RC	2.50	6.00
317 Chris Long SP RC	2.50	6.00
318 Lawrence Jackson SP RC	2.00	5.00
319 Ali Highsmith SP RC	1.50	4.00
320 Dan Connor SP RC	2.50	6.00
321 Kenny Phillips SP RC	2.50	6.00
322 Keith Rivers SP RC	2.50	6.00
323 Justin King SP RC	2.00	5.00
324 Mike Jenkins SP RC	2.50	6.00
325 Fred Davis SP RC	2.50	6.00

2009 Upper Deck

Card	Low	High
COMPLETE SET (325)	90.00	150.00
COMP.SET w/o SP's (300)	25.00	50.00
COMP.SET w/o RC's (200)	10.00	25.00
1 Kurt Warner	.25	.60
2 Tim Hightower	.20	.50
3 Larry Fitzgerald	.25	.60
4 Anquan Boldin	.20	.50
5 Steve Breaston	.20	.50
6 Matt Leinart	.20	.50
7 Adrian Wilson	.15	.40
8 Michael Turner	.20	.50
9 Jerious Norwood	.20	.50
10 Roddy White	.20	.50
11 Michael Jenkins	.15	.40
12 Matt Ryan	.25	.60
13 John Abraham	.15	.40
14 Ed Reed	.20	.50
15 Willis McGahee	.20	.50
16 Ray Rice	.25	.60
17 Le'Ron McClain	.20	.50
18 Derrick Mason	.15	.40
19 Joe Flacco	.25	.60
20 Ray Lewis	.25	.60
21 Mark Clayton	.15	.40
22 Lee Evans	.20	.50
23 Marshawn Lynch	.20	.50
24 Leodis McKelvin	.15	.40
25 Trent Edwards	.20	.50
26 Terrell Owens	.25	.60
27 Roscoe Parrish	.15	.40
28 DeAngelo Williams	.25	.60
29 Jonathan Stewart	.20	.50
30 Steve Smith	.20	.50
31 Muhsin Muhammad	.20	.50
32 Jake Delhomme	.20	.50
33 Jon Beason	.15	.40
34 Julius Peppers	.20	.50
35 Brian Urlacher	.25	.60
37 Matt Forte	.25	.60
38 Tommie Harris	.15	.40
39 Lance Briggs	.20	.50
40 Devin Hester	.25	.60
41 Olin Kreutz	.15	.40
42 Leon Hall	.15	.40
43 Cedric Benson	.20	.50
44 Reggie Kelly	.15	.40
45 Carson Palmer	.25	.60
46 Chad Johnson	.20	.50
47 Laveranues Coles	.20	.50
48 Jamal Lewis	.20	.50
49 Braylon Edwards	.20	.50
50 Derek Anderson	.20	.50
51 Joe Thomas	.20	.50
52 Brady Quinn	.20	.50
53 Marion Barber	.25	.60
54 Jason Witten	.25	.60
55 Bradie James	.15	.40
56 Tony Romo	.40	1.00
57 DeMarcus Ware	.20	.50
58 Felix Jones	.25	.60
59 Roy Williams WR	.20	.50
60 Brandon Marshall	.20	.50
61 Eddie Royal	.20	.50
62 Michael Pittman	.15	.40
63A Jay Cutler	.25	.60
63B Kyle Orton	.20	.50
64 Champ Bailey	.20	.50
65 Daunte Culpepper	.20	.50
66 Kevin Smith	.20	.50
67 Calvin Johnson	.25	.60
68 Jason Hanson	.15	.40
69 Rudi Johnson	.15	.40
70 Ryan Grant	.20	.50
71 Greg Jennings	.25	.60
72 Donald Driver	.20	.50
73 Aaron Rodgers	.25	.60
74 Aaron Kampman	.20	.50
75 Charles Woodson	.20	.50
76 Will Blackmon	.15	.40
77 A.J. Hawk	.20	.50
78 Steve Slaton	.20	.50
79 Andre Johnson	.20	.50
80 Kevin Walter	.20	.50
81 Kris Brown	.15	.40
82 Matt Schaub	.20	.50
83 DeMeco Ryans	.20	.50
84 Mario Williams	.20	.50
85 Peyton Manning	.40	1.00
86 Joseph Addai	.25	.60
87 Reggie Wayne	.20	.50
88 Anthony Gonzalez	.20	.50
89 Dallas Clark	.20	.50
90 Adam Vinatieri	.20	.50
91 Dwight Freeney	.20	.50
92 Bob Sanders	.20	.50
93 Maurice Jones-Drew	.20	.50
94 Marcedes Lewis	.15	.40
95 Justin Durant	.15	.40
96 Rashean Mathis	.15	.40
97 David Garrard	.20	.50
98 Tony Gonzalez	.20	.50
99 Larry Johnson	.20	.50
100 Dwayne Bowe	.20	.50
101 Matt Cassel	.20	.50
102 Tyler Thigpen	.15	.40
103 Ronnie Brown	.20	.50
104 Ricky Williams	.20	.50
105 Greg Camarillo	.20	.50
106 Ted Ginn Jr.	.20	.50
107 Chad Pennington	.20	.50
108 Joey Porter	.20	.50
109 Adrian Peterson	.50	1.25
110 Visanthe Shiancoe	.15	.40
111 Bernard Berrian	.20	.50
112A Sage Rosenfels	.15	.40
112B Brett Favre	75.00	135.00
112C Brett Favre passing	30.00	60.00
113 Jared Allen	.25	.60
114 Chester Taylor	.15	.40

Card		
❑ 115 Tom Brady	.40	1.00
❑ 116 Wes Welker	.25	.60
❑ 117 Stephen Gostkowski	.15	.40
❑ 118 Randy Moss	.25	.60
❑ 119 Kevin Faulk	.15	.40
❑ 120 Sammy Morris	.15	.40
❑ 121 Reggie Bush	.25	.60
❑ 122 Drew Brees	.25	.60
❑ 123 Pierre Thomas	.20	.50
❑ 124 Lance Moore	.20	.50
❑ 125 Marques Colston	.20	.50
❑ 126 Jeremy Shockey	.15	.40
❑ 127 Eli Manning	.25	.60
❑ 128 Brandon Jacobs	.20	.50
❑ 129 Domenik Hixon	.15	.40
❑ 130 Ahmad Bradshaw	.20	.50
❑ 131 Steve Smith USC	.20	.50
❑ 132 Thomas Jones	.20	.50
❑ 133 Bart Scott	.15	.40
❑ 134 Dustin Keller	.15	.40
❑ 135 Kellen Clemens	.15	.40
❑ 136 Leon Washington	.20	.50
❑ 137 Jerricho Cotchery	.15	.40
❑ 138 Johnnie Lee Higgins	.15	.40
❑ 139 Justin Fargas	.15	.40
❑ 140 Darren McFadden	.25	.60
❑ 141 JaMarcus Russell	.20	.50
❑ 142 Kirk Morrison	.15	.40
❑ 143 Brian Westbrook	.20	.50
❑ 144 DeSean Jackson	.20	.50
❑ 145 Donovan McNabb	.25	.60
❑ 146 Shawn Andrews	.15	.40
❑ 147 Asante Samuel	.15	.40
❑ 148 Reggie Brown	.15	.40
❑ 149 Willie Parker	.20	.50
❑ 150 Hines Ward	.20	.50
❑ 151 Santonio Holmes	.20	.50
❑ 152 Ben Roethlisberger	.40	1.00
❑ 153 James Harrison	.25	.60
❑ 154 Troy Polamalu	.25	.60
❑ 155 Rashard Mendenhall	.20	.50
❑ 156 LaDainian Tomlinson	.25	.60
❑ 157 Vincent Jackson	.20	.50
❑ 158 Antonio Gates	.20	.50
❑ 159 Philip Rivers	.25	.60
❑ 160 Shawne Merriman	.20	.50
❑ 161 Antonio Cromartie	.15	.40
❑ 162 Chris Chambers	.20	.50
❑ 163 Darren Sproles	.20	.50
❑ 164 Frank Gore	.20	.50
❑ 165 Isaac Bruce	.20	.50
❑ 166 Alex Smith	.15	.40
❑ 167 Patrick Willis	.20	.50
❑ 168 Josh Morgan	.15	.40
❑ 169 Shaun Hill	.20	.50
❑ 170 Vernon Davis	.15	.40
❑ 171 Julius Jones	.20	.50
❑ 172 Matt Hasselbeck	.20	.50
❑ 173 Lofa Tatupu	.20	.50
❑ 174 Deion Branch	.20	.50
❑ 175 T.J. Houshmandzadeh	.20	.50
❑ 176 Steven Jackson	.20	.50
❑ 177 Antonio Pittman	.15	.40
❑ 178 Donnie Avery	.20	.50
❑ 179 Marc Bulger	.20	.50
❑ 180 Oshiomogho Atogwe	.15	.40
❑ 181 Warrick Dunn	.20	.50
❑ 182 Kellen Winslow	.20	.50
❑ 183 Barrett Ruud	.15	.40
❑ 184 Michael Clayton	.15	.40
❑ 185 Aqib Talib	.15	.40
❑ 186 Ronde Barber	.15	.40
❑ 187 Cadillac Williams	.20	.50
❑ 188 Chris Johnson	.25	.60
❑ 189 LenDale White	.20	.50
❑ 190 Bo Scaife	.15	.40
❑ 191 Kerry Collins	.20	.50
❑ 192 Cortland Finnegan	.15	.40
❑ 193 Vince Young	.20	.50
❑ 194 Clinton Portis	.20	.50
❑ 195 Santana Moss	.20	.50
❑ 196 Chris Cooley	.20	.50
❑ 197 Antwaan Randle El	.15	.40
❑ 198 Jason Campbell	.20	.50
❑ 199 London Fletcher	.15	.40
❑ 200 Albert Haynesworth	.15	.40
❑ 201 Morgan Trent RC	.60	1.50
❑ 202 Everette Brown RC	.75	2.00
❑ 203 Clay Matthews RC	1.25	3.00
❑ 204 Eben Britton RC	.60	1.50
❑ 205 Andre Brown RC	.60	1.50
❑ 206 DeAngelo Smith RC	.60	1.50
❑ 207 Glen Coffee RC	1.00	2.50
❑ 208 Jairus Byrd RC	1.00	2.50
❑ 209 Sherrod Martin RC	.60	1.50
❑ 210 Victor Harris RC	.75	2.00
❑ 211 Sen'Derrick Marks RC	.50	1.25
❑ 212 Shawn Nelson RC	.60	1.50
❑ 213 Captain Munnerlyn RC	.60	1.50
❑ 214 D.J. Moore RC	.60	1.50
❑ 215 Gerald McRath RC	.60	1.50
❑ 216 Alphonso Smith RC	.60	1.50
❑ 217 Darius Butler RC	.75	2.00
❑ 218 Chase Coffman RC	.60	1.50
❑ 219 Mike Goodson RC	.75	2.00
❑ 220 Ron Brace RC	.60	1.50
❑ 221 William Beatty RC	.50	1.25
❑ 222 Michael Hamlin RC	.60	1.50
❑ 223 Marcus Freeman RC	.75	2.00
❑ 224 Michael Oher RC	1.50	4.00
❑ 225 Patrick Chung RC	.75	2.00
❑ 226 Larry English RC	.75	2.00
❑ 227 Connor Barwin RC	.60	1.50
❑ 228 Eric Wood RC	.60	1.50
❑ 229 Peria Jerry RC	.60	1.50
❑ 230 Clint Sintim RC	.75	2.00
❑ 231 Fili Moala RC	.60	1.50
❑ 232 Keenan Lewis RC	.75	2.00
❑ 233 Derrick Williams RC	.75	2.00
❑ 234 Kaluka Maiava RC	.75	2.00
❑ 235 Rhett Bomar RC	.60	1.50
❑ 236 Sean Smith RC	.75	2.00
❑ 237 Antoine Caldwell RC	.50	1.25
❑ 238 Cody Brown RC	.60	1.50
❑ 239 Travis Beckum RC	.60	1.50
❑ 240 William Moore RC	.60	1.50
❑ 241 Brian Robiskie RC	.75	2.00
❑ 242 Curtis Painter RC	.75	2.00
❑ 243 Vontae Davis RC	.75	2.00
❑ 244 Richard Quinn RC	.60	1.50
❑ 245 Robert Ayers RC	.75	2.00
❑ 246 Brandon Gibson RC	.75	2.00
❑ 247 Alex Mack RC	.60	1.50
❑ 248 Asher Allen RC	.60	1.50
❑ 249 Max Unger RC	.60	1.50
❑ 250 Herman Johnson RC	.60	1.50
❑ 251 Jamon Meredith RC	.60	1.50
❑ 252 Jonathan Luigs RC	.50	1.25
❑ 253 Phil Loadholt RC	.60	1.50
❑ 254 Sebastian Vollmer RC	.50	1.25
❑ 255 Michael Mitchell RC	.75	2.00
❑ 256 Javon Ringer RC	.75	2.00
❑ 257 Nate Davis RC	.75	2.00
❑ 258 Rudy Carpenter RC	.60	1.50
❑ 259 Paul Kruger RC	.60	1.50
❑ 260 Stephen McGee RC	.75	2.00
❑ 261 Ian Johnson RC	.75	2.00
❑ 262 Mike Wallace RC	1.50	4.00
❑ 263 Brian Hartline RC	.75	2.00
❑ 264 Devin Moore RC	.60	1.50
❑ 265 Jared Cook RC	.60	1.50
❑ 266 Sammie Stroughter RC	.75	2.00
❑ 267 Quan Cosby RC	.60	1.50
❑ 268 Brooks Foster RC	.60	1.50
❑ 269 Anthony Hill RC	.50	1.25
❑ 270 Mike Thomas RC	.75	2.00
❑ 271 Eugene Monroe RC	.60	1.50
❑ 272 Rodney Ferguson RC	.60	1.50
❑ 273 Rey Maualuga RC	1.25	3.00
❑ 274 Tony Fiammetta RC	.60	1.50
❑ 275 Michael Johnson RC	.50	1.25
❑ 276 Evander Hood RC	1.25	3.00
❑ 277 Austin Collie RC	1.50	4.00
❑ 278 Jason Phillips RC	.60	1.50
❑ 279 Ramses Barden RC	.60	1.50
❑ 280 Louis Delmas RC	.75	2.00
❑ 281 James Davis RC	.75	2.00
❑ 282 Demetrius Byrd RC	.60	1.50
❑ 283 Frank Summers RC	.75	2.00
❑ 284 Juaquin Iglesias RC	.75	2.00
❑ 285 Jasper Brinkley RC	.60	1.50
❑ 286 Louis Murphy RC	.75	2.00
❑ 287 Kevin Barnes RC	.60	1.50
❑ 288 Gartrell Johnson RC	.60	1.50
❑ 289 Matt Shaughnessy RC	.60	1.50
❑ 290 Patrick Turner RC	.60	1.50
❑ 291 Cornelius Ingram RC	.50	1.25
❑ 292 Jarron Gilbert RC	.60	1.50
❑ 293 James Casey RC	.60	1.50
❑ 294 Rashad Jennings RC	.75	2.00
❑ 295 Deon Butler RC	.75	2.00
❑ 296 James Laurinaitis RC	1.00	2.50
❑ 297 Brandon Tate RC	.60	1.50
❑ 298 Nic Harris RC	.60	1.50
❑ 299 Brian Cushing RC	1.00	2.50
❑ 300 Alex Magee RC	.60	1.50
❑ 301 Andre Smith RC	2.00	5.00
❑ 302 Shonn Greene RC	4.00	10.00
❑ 303 Pat White RC	3.00	8.00
❑ 304 Malcolm Jenkins RC	2.00	5.00
❑ 305 Matthew Stafford RC	6.00	15.00
❑ 306 Michael Crabtree RC	5.00	12.00
❑ 307 Tyson Jackson RC	2.00	5.00
❑ 308 Brandon Pettigrew RC	2.50	6.00
❑ 309 Brian Orakpo RC	2.50	6.00
❑ 310 Jeremy Maclin RC	4.00	10.00
❑ 311 Jason Smith RC	1.50	4.00
❑ 312 Chris Wells RC	5.00	12.00
❑ 313 Aaron Curry RC	2.50	6.00
❑ 314 Mark Sanchez RC	8.00	20.00
❑ 315 Aaron Maybin RC	2.00	5.00
❑ 316 B.J. Raji RC	2.50	6.00
❑ 317 Kenny Britt RC	3.00	8.00
❑ 318 Mohamed Massaquoi RC	2.00	5.00
❑ 319 Knowshon Moreno RC	5.00	12.00
❑ 320 Percy Harvin RC	6.00	15.00
❑ 321 Hakeem Nicks RC	4.00	10.00
❑ 322 LeSean McCoy RC	4.00	10.00
❑ 323 Darrius Heyward-Bey RC	3.00	8.00
❑ 324 Josh Freeman RC	4.00	10.00
❑ 325 Donald Brown RC	4.00	10.00
❑ 0 Michael Vick	10.00	25.00

2008 Upper Deck Draft Edition

Card		
❑ COMPLETE SET (250)	25.00	60.00
❑ COMP.RC SET (100)	15.00	30.00
❑ 1 Anthony Morelli RC	.50	1.25
❑ 2 Adarius Bowman RC	.40	1.00
❑ 3 Ali Highsmith RC	.30	.75
❑ 4 Andre Woodson RC	.50	1.25
❑ 5 Allen Patrick RC	.40	1.00
❑ 6 Antoine Cason RC	.50	1.25
❑ 7 Aqib Talib RC	.50	1.25
❑ 8 Ben Moffitt RC	.30	.75
❑ 9 Gosder Cherilus RC	.40	1.00
❑ 10 Brian Brohm RC	.50	1.25
❑ 11 Calais Campbell RC	.40	1.00
❑ 12 Chad Henne RC	.75	2.00
❑ 13 Chevis Jackson RC	.40	1.00
❑ 14 Davone Bess RC	.60	1.50
❑ 15 Justin Forsett RC	.50	1.25
❑ 16 Chris Ellis RC	.40	1.00
❑ 17 Chris Long RC	.50	1.25
❑ 18 Colt Brennan RC	.75	2.00
❑ 19 Craig Steltz RC	.40	1.00
❑ 20 DJ Hall RC	.40	1.00
❑ 21 Dan Connor RC	.50	1.25
❑ 22 Darren McFadden RC	1.00	2.50
❑ 23 DeMario Pressley RC	.40	1.00
❑ 24 Dennis Dixon RC	.50	1.25
❑ 25 Derrick Harvey RC	.40	1.00
❑ 26 DeSean Jackson RC	1.00	2.50
❑ 27 D.Rodgers-Cromartie RC	.50	1.25
❑ 28 Donnie Avery RC	.60	1.50
❑ 29 Dorien Bryant RC	.40	1.00
❑ 30 Dre Moore RC	.40	1.00
❑ 31 Kellen Davis RC	.30	.75
❑ 32 DaJuan Morgan RC	.40	1.00
❑ 33 Earl Bennett RC	.50	1.25
❑ 34 Early Doucet RC	.50	1.25
❑ 35 Kentwan Balmer RC	.40	1.00
❑ 36 Erik Ainge RC	.50	1.25

Card		
❑ 37 Felix Jones RC	1.00	2.50
❑ 38 Frank Okam RC	.30	.75
❑ 39 Fred Davis RC	.50	1.25
❑ 40 Glenn Dorsey RC	.50	1.25
❑ 41 Harry Douglas RC	.40	1.00
❑ 42 Jack Ikegwuonu RC	.40	1.00
❑ 43 Bruce Davis RC	.50	1.25
❑ 44 Jacob Tamme RC	.50	1.25
❑ 45 Jake Long RC	.50	1.25
❑ 46 Jamaal Charles RC	.75	2.00
❑ 47 James Hardy RC	.40	1.00
❑ 48 Erin Henderson RC	.40	1.00
❑ 49 J Leman RC	.40	1.00
❑ 50 Joe Flacco RC	1.50	4.00
❑ 51 John Carlson RC	.50	1.25
❑ 52 John David Booty RC	.50	1.25
❑ 53 Jonathan Hefney RC	.40	1.00
❑ 54 Jonathan Stewart RC	1.00	2.50
❑ 55 Jordy Nelson RC	.60	1.50
❑ 56 Josh Johnson RC	.50	1.25
❑ 57 Jacob Hester RC	.50	1.25
❑ 58 Keenan Burton RC	.40	1.00
❑ 59 Keith Rivers RC	.50	1.25
❑ 60 Kenny Phillips RC	.50	1.25
❑ 61 Kevin Smith RC	.75	2.00
❑ 62 Lavelle Hawkins RC	.40	1.00
❑ 63 Lawrence Jackson RC	.40	1.00
❑ 64 Limas Sweed RC	.50	1.25
❑ 65 Adrian Arrington RC	.40	1.00
❑ 66 Malcolm Kelly RC	.50	1.25
❑ 67 Martellus Bennett RC	.50	1.25
❑ 68 Marcus Monk RC	.50	1.25
❑ 69 Mario Manningham RC	.50	1.25
❑ 70 Mario Urrutia RC	.40	1.00
❑ 71 Martin Rucker RC	.40	1.00
❑ 72 Matt Flynn RC	.50	1.25
❑ 73 Matt Forte RC	1.00	2.50
❑ 74 Matt Ryan RC	2.00	5.00
❑ 75 Mike Hart RC	.50	1.25
❑ 76 Mike Jenkins RC	.50	1.25
❑ 77 Vernon Gholston RC	.50	1.25
❑ 78 Owen Schmitt RC	.50	1.25
❑ 79 Jonathan Goff RC	.40	1.00
❑ 80 Shawn Crable RC	.50	1.25
❑ 81 Justin King RC	.40	1.00
❑ 82 Philip Wheeler RC	.50	1.25
❑ 83 Paul Smith RC	.50	1.25
❑ 84 Rashard Mendenhall RC	1.00	2.50
❑ 85 Ray Rice RC	1.00	2.50
❑ 86 Ryan Clady RC	.50	1.25
❑ 87 Ryan Torain RC	.50	1.25
❑ 88 Sam Baker RC	.30	.75
❑ 89 Quintin Demps RC	.50	1.25
❑ 90 Sam Keller RC	.50	1.25
❑ 91 Phillip Merling RC	.40	1.00
❑ 92 Steve Slaton RC	.60	1.50
❑ 93 Tashard Choice RC	.50	1.25
❑ 94 Terrell Thomas RC	.40	1.00
❑ 95 Thomas Brown RC	.50	1.25
❑ 96 Tom Zbikowski RC	.50	1.25
❑ 97 DeJuan Tribble RC	.30	.75
❑ 98 Trevor Laws RC	.50	1.25
❑ 99 Vince Hall RC	.30	.75
❑ 100 Xavier Adibi RC	.40	1.00
❑ 101 Edgerrin James	.25	.60
❑ 102 Matt Leinart	.30	.75
❑ 103 Larry Fitzgerald	.30	.75
❑ 104 Joe Horn	.25	.60
❑ 105 Warrick Dunn	.25	.60
❑ 106 Jerious Norwood	.25	.60
❑ 107 Ed Reed	.25	.60
❑ 108 Willis McGahee	.25	.60
❑ 109 Steve McNair	.25	.60
❑ 110 Ray Lewis	.30	.75
❑ 111 J.P. Losman	.20	.50
❑ 112 Lee Evans	.25	.60
❑ 113 Marshawn Lynch	.30	.75
❑ 114 Eric Moulds	.25	.60
❑ 115 Julius Peppers	.25	.60
❑ 116 Steve Smith	.25	.60
❑ 117 DeShaun Foster	.25	.60
❑ 118 Devin Hester	.30	.75
❑ 119 Bernard Berrian	.25	.60
❑ 120 Cedric Benson	.25	.60
❑ 121 Thomas Jones	.25	.60
❑ 122 T.J. Houshmandzadeh	.25	.60
❑ 123 Carson Palmer	.30	.75
❑ 124 Chad Johnson	.25	.60
❑ 125 Derek Anderson	.25	.60
❑ 126 Kellen Winslow	.25	.60
❑ 127 Braylon Edwards	.25	.60
❑ 128 Anthony Henry	.20	.50
❑ 129 Marion Barber	.30	.75
❑ 130 DeMarcus Ware	.25	.60
❑ 131 Tony Romo	.50	1.25
❑ 132 Brandon Marshall	.25	.60
❑ 133 Jay Cutler	.30	.75
❑ 134 Champ Bailey	.20	.50
❑ 135 Tatum Bell	.20	.50
❑ 136 Calvin Johnson	.30	.75
❑ 137 Jon Kitna	.25	.60
❑ 138 Ernie Sims	.20	.50
❑ 139 Aaron Kampman	.25	.60
❑ 140 Charles Woodson	.25	.60
❑ 141 A.J. Hawk	.25	.60
❑ 142 DeMeco Ryans	.25	.60
❑ 143 Andre Johnson	.25	.60
❑ 144 Mario Williams	.25	.60
❑ 145 Dwight Freeney	.25	.60
❑ 146 Dallas Clark	.25	.60
❑ 147 Joseph Addai	.30	.75
❑ 148 David Garrard	.25	.60
❑ 149 Reggie Nelson	.20	.50
❑ 150 Maurice Jones-Drew	.25	.60
❑ 151 Dwayne Bowe	.25	.60
❑ 152 Derrick Johnson	.20	.50
❑ 153 Brodie Croyle	.25	.60
❑ 154 Ronnie Brown	.25	.60
❑ 155 Ted Ginn Jr.	.25	.60
❑ 156 Channing Crowder	.20	.50
❑ 157 Antoine Winfield	.20	.50
❑ 158 Adrian Peterson	.60	1.50
❑ 159 Sidney Rice	.30	.75
❑ 160 Wes Welker	.30	.75
❑ 161 Laurence Maroney	.25	.60
❑ 162 Ben Watson	.20	.50
❑ 163 Drew Brees	.30	.75
❑ 164 Reggie Bush	.30	.75
❑ 165 Marques Colston	.25	.60
❑ 166 Amani Toomer	.25	.60
❑ 167 Osi Umenyiora	.20	.50
❑ 168 Eli Manning	.30	.75
❑ 169 Jonathan Vilma	.25	.60
❑ 170 Kellen Clemens	.25	.60
❑ 171 Kirk Morrison	.20	.50
❑ 172 Nnamdi Asomugha	.20	.50
❑ 173 JaMarcus Russell	.30	.75
❑ 174 Brian Westbrook	.25	.60
❑ 175 Reggie Brown	.20	.50
❑ 176 Brian Dawkins	.25	.60
❑ 177 Hines Ward	.25	.60
❑ 178 Santonio Holmes	.25	.60
❑ 179 Ben Roethlisberger	.40	1.00
❑ 180 Shawne Merriman	.25	.60
❑ 181 LaDainian Tomlinson	.40	1.00
❑ 182 Antonio Cromartie	.20	.50
❑ 183 Shaun Phillips	.20	.50
❑ 184 Patrick Willis	.25	.60
❑ 185 Alex Smith QB	.25	.60
❑ 186 Frank Gore	.25	.60
❑ 187 Lofa Tatupu	.25	.60
❑ 188 Bobby Engram	.20	.50
❑ 189 Deion Branch	.25	.60
❑ 190 Steven Jackson	.30	.75
❑ 191 Pisa Tinoisamoa	.20	.50
❑ 192 Torry Holt	.25	.60
❑ 193 Cadillac Williams	.25	.60
❑ 194 Michael Clayton	.25	.60
❑ 195 Gaines Adams	.20	.50
❑ 196 Vince Young	.25	.60
❑ 197 LenDale White	.25	.60
❑ 198 Chris Cooley	.25	.60
❑ 199 Clinton Portis	.25	.60
❑ 200 Santana Moss	.20	.50
❑ 201 B.Brohm/M.Urrutia	.60	1.50
❑ 202 D.McFadden/F.Jones	1.25	3.00
❑ 203 D.Tribble/M.Ryan	2.50	6.00
❑ 204 E.Doucet/G.Dorsey	.60	1.50
❑ 205 J.Long/M.Hart	.60	1.50
❑ 206 C.Brennan/D.Bess	1.00	2.50
❑ 207 J.Booty/F.Davis	.60	1.50
❑ 208 D.Anderson/S.Jackson	.75	2.00
❑ 209 T.Brady/B.Edwards	1.25	3.00
❑ 210 R.Bush/M.Leinart	.75	2.00
❑ 211 A.Highsmith/J.Leman	.50	1.25
❑ 212 A.Cason/D.Tribble	.60	1.50
❑ 213 C.Brennan/D.Dixon	1.00	2.50
❑ 214 D.McFadden/M.Hart	1.25	3.00
❑ 215 F.Davis/M.Rucker	.60	1.50
❑ 216 J.Hefney/C.Steltz	.50	1.25
❑ 217 L.Sweed/M.Manningham	.60	1.50
❑ 218 S.Baker/J.Long	.60	1.50
❑ 219 K.Balmer/G.Dorsey	.60	1.50
❑ 220 S.Slaton/R.Rice	1.25	3.00
❑ 221 A.Highsmith/D.Connor	.60	1.50
❑ 222 A.Cason/T.Thomas	.60	1.50
❑ 223 B.Brohm/A.Woodson	.60	1.50
❑ 224 C.Long/Q.Groves	.60	1.50
❑ 225 C.Steltz/K.Phillips	.60	1.50
❑ 226 F.Davis/J.Carlson	.60	1.50
❑ 227 G.Dorsey/S.Ellis	.60	1.50
❑ 228 J.Long/S.Baker	.60	1.50
❑ 229 L.Sweed/E.Doucet	.60	1.50
❑ 230 T.Choice/D.McFadden	1.25	3.00
❑ 231 A.Highsmith/C.Jackson	.50	1.25
❑ 232 C.Henne/M.Manningham	1.00	2.50
❑ 233 L.Hawkins/D.Jackson	1.25	3.00
❑ 234 E.Henderson/D.Moore	.50	1.25
❑ 235 M.Kelly/A.Patrick	.60	1.50
❑ 236 M.Urrutia/H.Douglas	.50	1.25
❑ 237 M.Rucker/A.Spieker	.50	1.25
❑ 238 F.Jones/P.Hillis	1.25	3.00
❑ 239 J.Hefney/E.Ainge	.60	1.50
❑ 240 V.Hall/X.Adibi	.50	1.25
❑ 241 C.Brennan/D.Lowery	1.00	2.50
❑ 242 D.Dixon/K.Rivers	.60	1.50
❑ 243 H.Douglas/M.Jenkins	.60	1.50
❑ 244 J.Hester/K.Phillips	.60	1.50
❑ 245 J.Hefney/D.Hall	.50	1.25
❑ 246 M.Kelly/F.Okam	.60	1.50
❑ 247 J.Leman/M.Manningham	.60	1.50
❑ 248 M.Ryan/C.Long	2.50	6.00
❑ 249 J.Booty/A.Cason	.60	1.50
❑ 250 S.Keller/A.Patrick	.60	1.50

2009 Upper Deck Draft Edition

Card		
❑ COMPLETE SET (295)	50.00	100.00
❑ COMP.SET w/o SP's (200)	25.00	50.00
❑ 1 Curtis Painter RC	.40	1.00
❑ 2 DeAngelo Smith RC	.30	.75
❑ 3 Matthew Stafford RC	2.00	5.00
❑ 4 Chris Wells RC	1.00	2.50
❑ 5 Michael Johnson RC	.25	.60
❑ 6 Percy Harvin RC	1.25	3.00
❑ 7 Michael Crabtree RC	1.00	2.50
❑ 8 Knowshon Moreno RC	1.00	2.50
❑ 9 Jason Smith RC	.30	.75
❑ 10 James Laurinaitis RC	.50	1.25
❑ 11 Rey Maualuga RC	.60	1.50
❑ 12 Hunter Cantwell RC	.40	1.00
❑ 13 Chase Daniel RC	.50	1.25
❑ 14 Alphonso Smith RC	.30	.75
❑ 15 Jason Phillips RC	.30	.75
❑ 16 Pat White RC	.60	1.50
❑ 17 Peria Jerry RC	.30	.75
❑ 18 Graham Harrell RC	.40	1.00
❑ 19 Sammie Stroughter RC	.40	1.00
❑ 20 James Davis RC	.40	1.00
❑ 21 Javon Ringer RC	.40	1.00
❑ 22 D.J. Moore RC	.30	.75
❑ 23 Nate Davis RC	.40	1.00
❑ 24 P.J. Hill RC	.30	.75
❑ 25 Kevin Barnes RC	.30	.75
❑ 26 Darrius Heyward-Bey RC	.60	1.50
❑ 28 Glen Coffee RC	.50	1.25
❑ 29 Jaison Williams RC	.30	.75
❑ 30 Brian Robiskie RC	.40	1.00
❑ 31 Derrick Williams RC	.40	1.00
❑ 32 Darius Passmore RC	.30	.75
❑ 33 Chase Coffman RC	.30	.75
❑ 34 Cornelius Ingram RC	.25	.60
❑ 35 Travis Beckum RC	.30	.75

❑ 36 Brandon Pettigrew RC .50 1.25
❑ 37 Louis Delmas RC .40 1.00
❑ 38 Alex Mack RC .30 .75
❑ 39 Duke Robinson RC .25 .60
❑ 40 Jarett Dillard RC .40 1.00
❑ 41 Kraig Urbik RC .30 .75
❑ 42 Herman Johnson RC .30 .75
❑ 43 Otis Wiley RC .25 .60
❑ 44 Michael Oher RC .75 2.00
❑ 45 Phil Loadholt RC .30 .75
❑ 46 Alex Boone RC .40 1.00
❑ 47 Max Unger RC .30 .75
❑ 48 Andre Smith RC .40 1.00
❑ 49 Fili Moala RC .30 .75
❑ 52 Terrance Taylor RC .40 1.00
❑ 53 Sen'Derrick Marks RC .25 .60
❑ 54 Tyson Jackson RC .40 1.00
❑ 55 Captain Munnerlyn RC .30 .75
❑ 56 Ian Campbell RC .30 .75
❑ 57 Asher Allen RC .30 .75
❑ 58 Brandon Tate RC .30 .75
❑ 59 Darry Beckwith RC .30 .75
❑ 60 Jasper Brinkley RC .30 .75
❑ 61 Brian Cushing RC .50 1.25
❑ 62 Dannell Ellerbe RC .30 .75
❑ 63 Marcus Freeman RC .40 1.00
❑ 64 Maurice Crum RC .30 .75
❑ 65 Anthony Heygood RC .25 .60
❑ 66 Patrick Chung RC .40 1.00
❑ 67 Jeremy Maclin RC .75 2.00
❑ 68 Troy Kropog RC .25 .60
❑ 69 William Moore RC .30 .75
❑ 70 Kevin Ellison RC .30 .75
❑ 71 Malcolm Jenkins RC .40 1.00
❑ 72 Victor Harris RC .40 1.00
❑ 73 Vontae Davis RC .40 1.00
❑ 74 Matt Shaughnessy RC .25 .60
❑ 75 Mike Mickens RC .30 .75
❑ 76 LeSean McCoy RC .75 2.00
❑ 77 Rudy Carpenter RC .30 .75
❑ 78 Arian Foster RC .40 1.00
❑ 79 Devin Moore RC .30 .75
❑ 80 Tyrell Sutton RC .30 .75
❑ 81 Ian Johnson RC .40 1.00
❑ 82 James Casey RC .30 .75
❑ 83 Paul Kruger RC .30 .75
❑ 84 Kenny Britt RC .60 1.50
❑ 85 Josh Freeman RC .75 2.00
❑ 86 Louis Murphy RC .40 1.00
❑ 87 Demetrius Byrd RC .30 .75
❑ 88 Brandon Gibson RC .40 1.00
❑ 89 Aaron Kelly RC .30 .75
❑ 90 Keenan Lewis RC .40 1.00
❑ 91 Nathan Brown RC .30 .75
❑ 92 Connor Barwin RC .30 .75
❑ 93 B.J. Raji RC .50 1.25
❑ 94 Tom Brandstater RC .40 1.00
❑ 95 Shonn Greene RC .75 2.00
❑ 96 Brannan Southerland RC .30 .75
❑ 97 Eben Britton RC .30 .75
❑ 98 Jairus Byrd RC .50 1.25
❑ 99 Nic Harris RC .30 .75
❑ 100 Ryan Purvis RC .30 .75
❑ 101 Clay Matthews RC .60 1.50
❑ 102 Mark Sanchez RC 1.50 4.00
❑ 103 Brian Orakpo RC .50 1.25
❑ 104 Tim Jamison RC .30 .75
❑ 105 Jonathan Luigs RC .25 .60
❑ 106 Darius Butler RC .40 1.00
❑ 107 Eugene Monroe RC .30 .75
❑ 108 Xavier Fulton RC .25 .60
❑ 109 Andrew Gardner RC .25 .60
❑ 110 Jamon Meredith RC .30 .75
❑ 111 Jason Watkins RC .30 .75
❑ 112 Fenuki Tupou RC .25 .60
❑ 113 Juaquin Iglesias RC .40 1.00
❑ 114 Marko Mitchell RC .30 .75
❑ 115 Kenny McKinley RC .40 1.00
❑ 116 Ramses Barden RC .30 .75
❑ 117 Jeremy Childs RC .30 .75
❑ 119 Tiquan Underwood RC .30 .75
❑ 120 Quan Cosby RC .30 .75
❑ 121 David Veikune RC .30 .75
❑ 122 Brennan Marion RC .30 .75
❑ 123 Morgan Trent RC .30 .75
❑ 124 Larry English RC .40 1.00
❑ 125 Mohamed Massaquoi RC .40 1.00
❑ 126 Aaron Curry RC .50 1.25
❑ 127 Rashad Jennings RC .40 1.00
❑ 128 Jeremiah Johnson RC .40 1.00
❑ 129 Michael Hamlin RC .30 .75
❑ 130 Andre Brown RC .30 .75
❑ 132 Keegan Herring RC .30 .75
❑ 133 Willie Tuitama RC .30 .75
❑ 134 Cedric Peerman RC .30 .75
❑ 135 Gerald McRath RC .30 .75
❑ 136 Jared Cook RC .30 .75
❑ 137 Austin Collie RC .75 2.00
❑ 138 Garrett Reynolds RC .30 .75
❑ 139 Cullen Harper RC .40 1.00
❑ 140 Donald Brown RC .75 2.00
❑ 141 John Parker Wilson RC .40 1.00
❑ 142 Derek Pegues RC .25 .60
❑ 143 Rhett Bomar RC .30 .75
❑ 144 Mike Reilly RC .30 .75
❑ 145 Clint Sintim RC .40 1.00
❑ 146 Courtney Greene RC .25 .60
❑ 147 Sean Smith RC .40 1.00
❑ 148 Shawn Nelson RC .30 .75
❑ 149 Hakeem Nicks RC .75 2.00
❑ 150 Bear Pascoe RC .40 1.00
❑ 151 Clinton Portis .25 .60
❑ 152 Brett Favre .75 2.00
❑ 153 Drew Brees .30 .75
❑ 154 Peyton Manning .50 1.25
❑ 155 Eli Manning .30 .75
❑ 156 Tony Romo .50 1.25
❑ 157 Jay Cutler .30 .75
❑ 158 Brandon Marshall .25 .60
❑ 159 LaDainian Tomlinson .30 .75
❑ 160 Michael Turner .25 .60
❑ 161 Darren McFadden .30 .75
❑ 162 Devin Hester .30 .75
❑ 163 Marion Barber .30 .75
❑ 164 Troy Polamalu .30 .75
❑ 165 Ben Roethlisberger .50 1.25
❑ 166 Chris Johnson .30 .75
❑ 167 Matt Forte .30 .75
❑ 168 Matt Ryan .30 .75
❑ 169 Aaron Rodgers .30 .75
❑ 170 Greg Jennings .30 .75
❑ 171 Brian Westbrook .25 .60
❑ 172 Adrian Peterson .60 1.50
❑ 173 Larry Fitzgerald .30 .75
❑ 174 Reggie Wayne .25 .60
❑ 175 Trent Edwards .25 .60
❑ 176 Marshawn Lynch .25 .60
❑ 177 Brian Urlacher .30 .75
❑ 178 Jason Campbell .25 .60
❑ 179 Ronnie Brown .25 .60
❑ 180 Anquan Boldin .25 .60
❑ 181 Brady Quinn .25 .60
❑ 182 Roddy White .25 .60
❑ 183 Felix Jones .30 .75
❑ 184 Jason Witten .30 .75
❑ 185 Andre Johnson .25 .60
❑ 186 Calvin Johnson .30 .75
❑ 187 Tom Brady .50 1.25
❑ 188 A.J. Hawk .25 .60
❑ 189 Patrick Willis .25 .60
❑ 190 Philip Rivers .30 .75
❑ 191 Chris Cooley .20 .50
❑ 192 Dwayne Bowe .25 .60
❑ 193 Mario Williams .25 .60
❑ 194 DeMarcus Ware .25 .60
❑ 195 Joey Porter .25 .60
❑ 196 Hines Ward .25 .60
❑ 197 Lance Briggs .25 .60
❑ 198 Frank Gore .25 .60
❑ 199 Nnamdi Asomugha .20 .50
❑ 200 Donovan McNabb .30 .75
❑ 201 Chris Wells SR 1.00 2.50
❑ 202 Mark Sanchez SR 1.50 4.00
❑ 203 Curtis Painter SR .40 1.00
❑ 204 Michael Crabtree SR 1.00 2.50
❑ 205 Knowshon Moreno SR 1.00 2.50
❑ 206 LeSean McCoy SR .75 2.00
❑ 207 Shonn Greene SR .75 2.00
❑ 208 Matthew Stafford SR 1.25 3.00
❑ 209 Josh Freeman SR .75 2.00
❑ 210 Pat White SR .60 1.50
❑ 211 Aaron Curry SR .50 1.25
❑ 212 Alphonso Smith SR .30 .75
❑ 213 Darrius Heyward-Bey SR .60 1.50
❑ 214 Percy Harvin SR 1.25 3.00
❑ 215 James Laurinaitis SR .50 1.25
❑ 216 Brian Robiskie SR .40 1.00
❑ 217 Jeremy Maclin SR .75 2.00
❑ 218 William Moore SR .30 .75
❑ 219 Chase Coffman SR .30 .75
❑ 220 Brandon Pettigrew SR .50 1.25
❑ 221 Hakeem Nicks SR .75 2.00
❑ 222 Michael Johnson SR .25 .60
❑ 223 Fili Moala SR .30 .75
❑ 224 Rey Maualuga SR .60 1.50
❑ 225 Brian Cushing SR .50 1.25
❑ 226 Donald Brown SR .75 2.00
❑ 227 Malcolm Jenkins SR .40 1.00
❑ 228 Vontae Davis SR .40 1.00
❑ 229 Patrick Chung SR .40 1.00
❑ 230 Sen'Derrick Marks SR .25 .60
❑ 231 T.Polamalu/R.Maualuga AA .60 1.50
❑ 232 J.Wilson/An.Smith AA .40 1.00
❑ 233 M.Crabtree/W.Welker AA 1.00 2.50
❑ 234 H.Ward/M.Stafford AA 1.25 3.00
❑ 235 M.Stafford/K.Moreno AA 1.25 3.00
❑ 236 J.Laurinaitis/A.Hawk AA .50 1.25
❑ 237 C.Harper/J.Davis AA .40 1.00
❑ 238 A.Peterson/J.Iglesias AA .75 2.00
❑ 239 D.Brees/C.Painter AA .40 1.00
❑ 240 G.Harrell/M.Crabtree AA 1.00 2.50
❑ 241 P.Jerry/P.Willis AA .30 .75
❑ 242 C.Johnson/M.Johnson AA .25 .60
❑ 243 M.Sanchez/A.Munoz AA 1.50 4.00
❑ 244 E.Brown/A.Boldin AA .40 1.00
❑ 245 R.Maualuga/B.Cushing AA .60 1.50
❑ 246 C.Sintim/E.Monroe AA .40 1.00
❑ 247 P.Harvin/L.Murphy AA 1.25 3.00
❑ 248 L.McCoy/L.Fitzgerald AA .75 2.00
❑ 249 J.Campbell/S.Marks AA .30 .75
❑ 250 Massaquoi/K.Moreno AA 1.00 2.50
❑ 251 J.Wilson/M.Stafford CC 1.25 3.00
❑ 252 M.Johnson/E.Brown CC .25 .60
❑ 253 W.Moore/G.Harrell CC .40 1.00
❑ 254 J.Ringer/C.Wells CC .40 1.00
❑ 255 B.Robiskie/D.Williams CC .40 1.00
❑ 256 Heyward-Bey/A.Kelly CC .60 1.50
❑ 257 D.Byrd/P.Harvin CC 1.25 3.00
❑ 258 S.Marks/K.Moreno CC 1.00 2.50
❑ 259 M.Jenkins/V.Davis CC .40 1.00
❑ 260 B.Pettigrew/C.Coffman CC .50 1.25
❑ 261 B.Orakpo/G.Harrell CC .50 1.25
❑ 262 A.Smith/M.Oher CC .75 2.00
❑ 263 Laurinaitis/S.Greene CC .75 2.00
❑ 264 T.Jackson/A.Smith CC .40 1.00
❑ 265 B.Gibson/R.Maualuga CC .40 1.00
❑ 266 C.Wells/S.Greene CC 1.00 2.50
❑ 267 M.Crabtree/J.Maclin CC .75 2.00
❑ 268 M.Sanchez/R.Carpenter CC 1.50 4.00
❑ 269 Q.Cosby/M.Crabtree CC 1.00 2.50
❑ 270 P.Hill/J.Ringer CC .30 .75
❑ 271 Knowshon Moreno AA 1.00 2.50
❑ 272 Michael Crabtree AA 1.00 2.50
❑ 273 Herman Johnson AA .30 .75
❑ 274 Fili Moala AA .30 .75
❑ 275 James Laurinaitis AA .50 1.25
❑ 276 Jeremy Maclin AA .75 2.00
❑ 277 Chase Coffman AA .30 .75
❑ 278 Jarett Dillard AA .40 1.00
❑ 279 Michael Oher AA .75 2.00
❑ 280 Javon Ringer AA .40 1.00
❑ 281 Aaron Maybin AA .40 1.00
❑ 282 Andre Smith AA .40 1.00
❑ 283 Rey Maualuga AA .60 1.50
❑ 284 Malcolm Jenkins AA .40 1.00
❑ 285 Shonn Greene AA .75 2.00
❑ 286 Adrian Peterson AA 1.00 2.50
❑ 287 Peyton Manning AA .75 2.00
❑ 288 Calvin Johnson AA .50 1.25
❑ 289 Darren McFadden AA .50 1.25
❑ 290 A.J. Hawk AA .40 1.00
❑ 291 Roeth/Rivers/Eli DC .75 2.00
❑ 292 Forte/McFdd/C.Jhnsn DC .50 1.25
❑ 293 Tomlin/Brees/Wayne DC .50 1.25
❑ 294 J.Kelly/Craig/D.Green DC .40 1.00
❑ 295 M.Willi/V.Young/Bush DC .40 1.00
❑ 296 J.Cmpbll/Rodgrs/Barbr DC .50 1.25
❑ 297 Ryan/McFadd/Flacco DC .50 1.25
❑ 298 C.Wdson/Ward/P.Mann DC .75 2.00
❑ 299 D.Hester/Hawk/Cutler DC .50 1.25
❑ 300 Cooley/Fitzg/Roeth DC .75 2.00

2007 Upper Deck First Edition

Card		
❑ COMPLETE SET (200)	20.00	40.00
❑ COMP.SET w/o RCs (100)	8.00	20.00
❑ 1 Matt Leinart	.15	.40
❑ 2 Larry Fitzgerald	.15	.40
❑ 3 Anquan Boldin	.12	.30
❑ 4 Michael Vick	.15	.40
❑ 5 Warrick Dunn	.12	.30
❑ 6 Alge Crumpler	.12	.30
❑ 7 Steve McNair	.12	.30
❑ 8 Mark Clayton	.12	.30
❑ 9 Todd Heap	.10	.25
❑ 10 Ray Lewis	.15	.40
❑ 11 J.P. Losman	.10	.25
❑ 12 Lee Evans	.12	.30
❑ 13 Anthony Thomas	.10	.25
❑ 14 Jake Delhomme	.12	.30
❑ 15 DeShaun Foster	.12	.30
❑ 16 Steve Smith	.12	.30
❑ 17 Cedric Benson	.12	.30
❑ 18 Bernard Berrian	.10	.25
❑ 19 Brian Urlacher	.15	.40
❑ 20 Carson Palmer	.15	.40
❑ 21 Rudi Johnson	.12	.30
❑ 22 Chad Johnson	.12	.30
❑ 23 Kellen Winslow	.12	.30
❑ 24 Braylon Edwards	.12	.30
❑ 25 Tony Romo	.25	.60
❑ 26 Julius Jones	.12	.30
❑ 27 Terrell Owens	.15	.40
❑ 28 Jay Cutler	.15	.40
❑ 29 Javon Walker	.12	.30
❑ 30 Champ Bailey	.12	.30
❑ 31 Jon Kitna	.10	.25
❑ 32 Kevin Jones	.10	.25
❑ 33 Roy Williams WR	.12	.30
❑ 34 Brett Favre	.30	.75
❑ 35 Donald Driver	.15	.40
❑ 36 A.J. Hawk	.15	.40
❑ 37 Andre Johnson	.12	.30
❑ 38 Mario Williams	.12	.30
❑ 39 Ron Dayne	.12	.30
❑ 40 Peyton Manning	.25	.60
❑ 41 Marvin Harrison	.15	.40
❑ 42 Reggie Wayne	.12	.30
❑ 43 Joseph Addai	.15	.40
❑ 44 Maurice Jones-Drew	.15	.40
❑ 45 Fred Taylor	.12	.30
❑ 46 Byron Leftwich	.12	.30
❑ 47 Larry Johnson	.12	.30
❑ 48 Tony Gonzalez	.12	.30
❑ 49 Damon Huard	.12	.30
❑ 50 Ronnie Brown	.12	.30
❑ 51 Jason Taylor	.10	.25
❑ 52 Chris Chambers	.12	.30
❑ 53 Chester Taylor	.10	.25
❑ 54 Tarvaris Jackson	.12	.30
❑ 55 Troy Williamson	.10	.25
❑ 56 Tom Brady	.30	.75
❑ 57 Laurence Maroney	.15	.40
❑ 58 Ben Watson	.10	.25
❑ 59 Asante Samuel	.10	.25
❑ 60 Chad Pennington	.12	.30
❑ 61 Leon Washington	.12	.30
❑ 62 Laveranues Coles	.12	.30
❑ 63 Eli Manning	.15	.40
❑ 64 Jeremy Shockey	.12	.30
❑ 65 Brandon Jacobs	.12	.30
❑ 66 Drew Brees	.15	.40
❑ 67 Marques Colston	.15	.40
❑ 68 Reggie Bush	.20	.50
❑ 69 Deuce McAllister	.12	.30
❑ 70 Jerry Porter	.12	.30
❑ 71 Justin Fargas	.10	.25
❑ 72 Randy Moss	.15	.40
❑ 73 Brian Westbrook	.12	.30
❑ 74 Reggie Brown	.10	.25
❑ 75 Donovan McNabb	.15	.40
❑ 76 Ben Roethlisberger	.20	.50
❑ 77 Willie Parker	.12	.30
❑ 78 Troy Polamalu	.15	.40
❑ 79 Antonio Gates	.12	.30
❑ 80 Shawne Merriman	.12	.30
❑ 81 LaDainian Tomlinson	.20	.50
❑ 82 Alex Smith QB	.15	.40
❑ 83 Frank Gore	.15	.40
❑ 84 Vernon Davis	.12	.30
❑ 85 Steven Jackson	.15	.40
❑ 86 Marc Bulger	.12	.30
❑ 87 Torry Holt	.12	.30
❑ 88 Isaac Bruce	.12	.30
❑ 89 Matt Hasselbeck	.12	.30
❑ 90 Shaun Alexander	.12	.30
❑ 91 Deion Branch	.12	.30
❑ 92 Cadillac Williams	.12	.30
❑ 93 Michael Clayton	.12	.30
❑ 94 Joey Galloway	.12	.30
❑ 95 Vince Young	.15	.40
❑ 96 LenDale White	.12	.30
❑ 97 Jason Campbell	.12	.30
❑ 98 Clinton Portis	.12	.30
❑ 99 Santana Moss	.12	.30
❑ 100 Antwaan Randle El	.10	.25
❑ 101 JaMarcus Russell RC	.75	2.00
❑ 102 Brady Quinn RC	1.25	3.00
❑ 103 Calvin Johnson RC	1.50	4.00
❑ 104 Adrian Peterson RC	5.00	12.00
❑ 105 Joe Thomas RC	.60	1.50
❑ 106 Levi Brown RC	.60	1.50
❑ 107 Gaines Adams RC	.60	1.50
❑ 108 Adam Carriker RC	.50	1.25
❑ 109 Ted Ginn Jr. RC	1.00	2.50
❑ 110 Anthony Gonzalez RC	.75	2.00
❑ 111 Troy Smith RC	.75	2.00
❑ 112 Leon Hall RC	.60	1.50
❑ 113 LaMarr Woodley RC	.60	1.50
❑ 114 Alan Branch RC	.50	1.25
❑ 115 Patrick Willis RC	1.00	2.50
❑ 116 Reggie Nelson RC	.50	1.25
❑ 117 Paul Posluszny RC	.75	2.00
❑ 118 Dwayne Bowe RC	1.00	2.50
❑ 119 Steve Smith RC	1.00	2.50
❑ 120 Dwayne Jarrett RC	.60	1.50
❑ 121 Marshawn Lynch RC	1.00	2.50
❑ 122 Darius Walker RC	.50	1.25
❑ 123 Daymeion Hughes RC	.50	1.25
❑ 124 LaRon Landry RC	.75	2.00
❑ 125 Jon Beason RC	.60	1.50
❑ 126 Lawrence Timmons RC	.60	1.50
❑ 127 Drew Stanton RC	.50	1.25
❑ 128 Trent Edwards RC	1.00	2.50
❑ 129 John Beck RC	.60	1.50
❑ 130 Kevin Kolb RC	1.00	2.50
❑ 131 Amobi Okoye RC	.60	1.50
❑ 132 Michael Bush RC	.60	1.50
❑ 133 Darrelle Revis RC	.75	2.00
❑ 134 H.B. Blades RC	.50	1.25
❑ 135 Jamaal Anderson RC	.50	1.25
❑ 136 Robert Meachem RC	.60	1.50
❑ 137 Sidney Rice RC	1.25	3.00
❑ 138 Craig Davis RC	.60	1.50
❑ 139 Paul Williams RC	.50	1.25
❑ 140 Greg Olsen RC	.75	2.00
❑ 141 Jarvis Moss RC	.60	1.50
❑ 142 Justin Harrell RC	.60	1.50
❑ 143 DeMarcus Tank Tyler RC	.50	1.25
❑ 144 Aaron Ross RC	.60	1.50
❑ 145 Chris Houston RC	.50	1.25
❑ 146 Brandon Meriweather RC	.60	1.50
❑ 147 Eric Weddle RC	.50	1.25
❑ 148 Lorenzo Booker RC	.60	1.50
❑ 149 Buster Davis RC	.50	1.25
❑ 150 Antonio Pittman RC	.60	1.50
❑ 151 Chris Henry RC	.50	1.25
❑ 152 Kenny Irons RC	.60	1.50
❑ 153 Brandon Jackson RC	.60	1.50
❑ 154 Tony Hunt RC	.60	1.50
❑ 155 Brian Leonard RC	.50	1.25
❑ 156 Garrett Wolfe RC	.60	1.50
❑ 157 Yamon Figurs RC	.40	1.00
❑ 158 Johnnie Lee Higgins RC	.60	1.50
❑ 159 Jordan Palmer RC	.60	1.50
❑ 160 Chris Leak RC	.50	1.25
❑ 161 Rhema McKnight RC	.50	1.25
❑ 162 Dwayne Wright RC	.50	1.25
❑ 163 Matt Moore RC	.75	2.00
❑ 164 Jeff Rowe RC	.50	1.25
❑ 165 Zach Miller RC	.60	1.50
❑ 166 Ben Patrick RC	.50	1.25
❑ 167 Joe Staley RC	.50	1.25
❑ 168 Eric Wright RC	.60	1.50
❑ 169 Aundrae Allison RC	.50	1.25
❑ 170 Steve Breaston RC	.60	1.50
❑ 171 David Harris RC	.50	1.25
❑ 172 Brandon Siler RC	.50	1.25
❑ 173 Tim Shaw RC	.50	1.25
❑ 174 Selvin Young RC	.60	1.50
❑ 175 Michael Griffin RC	.60	1.50
❑ 176 Kenneth Darby RC	.60	1.50
❑ 177 Anthony Spencer RC	.60	1.50
❑ 178 Charles Johnson RC	.40	1.00
❑ 179 Quentin Moses RC	.50	1.25
❑ 180 DeShawn Wynn RC	.60	1.50
❑ 181 Scott Chandler RC	.50	1.25
❑ 182 Stewart Bradley RC	.60	1.50
❑ 183 Ahmad Bradshaw RC	.75	2.00
❑ 184 Matt Spaeth RC	.60	1.50
❑ 185 Ray McDonald RC	.50	1.25
❑ 186 Ben Grubbs RC	.50	1.25
❑ 187 Jon Abbate RC	.40	1.00
❑ 188 Victor Abiamiri RC	.60	1.50
❑ 189 Courtney Taylor RC	.50	1.25
❑ 190 A.J. Davis RC	.40	1.00
❑ 191 Nate Harris RC	.50	1.25
❑ 192 Jonathan Wade RC	.50	1.25
❑ 193 Tim Crowder RC	.60	1.50
❑ 194 Legedu Naanee RC	.60	1.50
❑ 195 Quinn Pitcock RC	.50	1.25
❑ 196 Marcus McCauley RC	.50	1.25
❑ 197 Sabby Piscitelli RC	.60	1.50
❑ 198 Tanard Jackson RC	.40	1.00
❑ 199 Josh Gattis RC	.40	1.00
❑ 200 Rufus Alexander RC	.60	1.50

2008 Upper Deck First Edition

Card		
❑ COMPLETE SET (225)	20.00	40.00
❑ COMP.FACT.SET (226)	25.00	40.00
❑ 1 Edgerrin James	.12	.30
❑ 2 Matt Leinart	.15	.40
❑ 3 Larry Fitzgerald	.15	.40
❑ 4 Anquan Boldin	.12	.30
❑ 5 Antrel Rolle	.10	.25
❑ 6 Joe Horn	.12	.30
❑ 7 Warrick Dunn	.12	.30
❑ 8 Jerious Norwood	.12	.30
❑ 9 Michael Jenkins	.10	.25
❑ 10 Ed Reed	.12	.30
❑ 11 Willis McGahee	.12	.30
❑ 12 Steve McNair	.12	.30
❑ 13 Todd Heap	.10	.25
❑ 14 Ray Lewis	.15	.40
❑ 15 Terrell Suggs	.10	.25
❑ 16 Trent Edwards	.15	.40
❑ 17 Lee Evans	.12	.30
❑ 18 Roscoe Parrish	.10	.25
❑ 19 Marshawn Lynch	.15	.40
❑ 20 DeAngelo Williams	.12	.30
❑ 21 Julius Peppers	.12	.30
❑ 22 Steve Smith	.12	.30
❑ 23 Cedric Benson	.12	.30
❑ 24 Greg Olsen	.12	.30
❑ 25 Lance Briggs	.10	.25
❑ 26 Rex Grossman	.12	.30
❑ 27 Devin Hester	.15	.40
❑ 28 Brian Urlacher	.15	.40
❑ 29 T.J. Houshmandzadeh	.12	.30

Card	Low	High
❑ 30 Carson Palmer	.15	.40
❑ 31 Rudi Johnson	.12	.30
❑ 32 Chad Johnson	.12	.30
❑ 33 Chris Henry	.10	.25
❑ 34 Kamerion Wimbley	.10	.25
❑ 35 Joshua Cribbs	.15	.40
❑ 36 Jamal Lewis	.12	.30
❑ 37 Kellen Winslow	.12	.30
❑ 38 Braylon Edwards	.12	.30
❑ 39 Marion Barber	.15	.40
❑ 40 Jason Witten	.15	.40
❑ 41 DeMarcus Ware	.12	.30
❑ 42 Tony Romo	.25	.60
❑ 43 Terrell Owens	.15	.40
❑ 44 John Lynch	.12	.30
❑ 45 Brandon Marshall	.12	.30
❑ 46 Jay Cutler	.15	.40
❑ 47 Dre Bly	.10	.25
❑ 48 Champ Bailey	.10	.25
❑ 49 Tatum Bell	.10	.25
❑ 50 Calvin Johnson	.15	.40
❑ 51 Jon Kitna	.12	.30
❑ 52 Roy Williams WR	.12	.30
❑ 53 Ernie Sims	.10	.25
❑ 54 Aaron Kampman	.12	.30
❑ 55 Charles Woodson	.12	.30
❑ 56 Brett Favre	.40	1.00
❑ 57 Donald Driver	.12	.30
❑ 58 A.J. Hawk	.12	.30
❑ 59 DeMeco Ryans	.12	.30
❑ 60 Andre Johnson	.12	.30
❑ 61 Mario Williams	.12	.30
❑ 62 Ron Dayne	.12	.30
❑ 63 Dwight Freeney	.12	.30
❑ 64 Dallas Clark	.12	.30
❑ 65 Peyton Manning	.25	.60
❑ 66 Marvin Harrison	.15	.40
❑ 67 Reggie Wayne	.12	.30
❑ 68 Matt Jones	.12	.30
❑ 69 David Garrard	.12	.30
❑ 70 Reggie Williams	.12	.30
❑ 71 Maurice Jones-Drew	.12	.30
❑ 72 Fred Taylor	.12	.30
❑ 73 Dwayne Bowe	.12	.30
❑ 74 Derrick Johnson	.10	.25
❑ 75 Larry Johnson	.12	.30
❑ 76 Tony Gonzalez	.12	.30
❑ 77 Ronnie Brown	.12	.30
❑ 78 Jason Taylor	.12	.30
❑ 79 Ted Ginn Jr.	.12	.30
❑ 80 John Beck	.10	.25
❑ 81 Adrian Peterson	.30	.75
❑ 82 Sidney Rice	.15	.40
❑ 83 Chester Taylor	.10	.25
❑ 84 Bernard Berrian	.12	.30
❑ 85 Wes Welker	.15	.40
❑ 86 Randy Moss	.15	.40
❑ 87 Tom Brady	.25	.60
❑ 88 Laurence Maroney	.12	.30
❑ 89 Mike Vrabel	.10	.25
❑ 90 Drew Brees	.15	.40
❑ 91 Marques Colston	.12	.30
❑ 92 Reggie Bush	.15	.40
❑ 93 Mike McKenzie	.10	.25
❑ 94 Michael Strahan	.12	.30
❑ 95 Plaxico Burress	.12	.30
❑ 96 Eli Manning	.15	.40
❑ 97 Jeremy Shockey	.12	.30
❑ 98 Brandon Jacobs	.12	.30
❑ 99 Jerricho Cotchery	.10	.25
❑ 100 Kellen Clemens	.12	.30
❑ 101 Leon Washington	.12	.30
❑ 102 Thomas Jones	.12	.30
❑ 103 Kirk Morrison	.10	.25
❑ 104 Nnamdi Asomugha	.10	.25
❑ 105 Derrick Burgess	.10	.25
❑ 106 Ronald Curry	.12	.30
❑ 107 JaMarcus Russell	.15	.40
❑ 108 Brian Dawkins	.12	.30
❑ 109 Brian Westbrook	.12	.30
❑ 110 Reggie Brown	.10	.25
❑ 111 Donovan McNabb	.15	.40
❑ 112 Hines Ward	.12	.30
❑ 113 Santonio Holmes	.12	.30
❑ 114 Ben Roethlisberger	.20	.50
❑ 115 Willie Parker	.12	.30
❑ 116 Troy Polamalu	.15	.40
❑ 117 Philip Rivers	.15	.40
❑ 118 Antonio Gates	.12	.30
❑ 119 Shawne Merriman	.12	.30
❑ 120 LaDainian Tomlinson	.20	.50
❑ 121 Antonio Cromartie	.10	.25
❑ 122 Alex Smith QB	.12	.30
❑ 123 Frank Gore	.12	.30
❑ 124 Vernon Davis	.10	.25
❑ 125 Patrick Willis	.12	.30
❑ 126 Lofa Tatupu	.12	.30
❑ 127 Patrick Kerney	.10	.25
❑ 128 Bobby Engram	.10	.25
❑ 129 Matt Hasselbeck	.12	.30
❑ 130 Deion Branch	.12	.30
❑ 131 Pisa Tinoisamoa	.10	.25
❑ 132 Steven Jackson	.15	.40
❑ 133 Marc Bulger	.12	.30
❑ 134 Torry Holt	.12	.30
❑ 135 Randy McMichael	.10	.25
❑ 136 Ronde Barber	.10	.25
❑ 137 Cadillac Williams	.12	.30
❑ 138 Joey Galloway	.12	.30
❑ 139 Jeff Garcia	.12	.30
❑ 140 Gaines Adams	.10	.25
❑ 141 Keith Bulluck	.10	.25
❑ 142 Nick Harper	.10	.25
❑ 143 Vince Young	.12	.30
❑ 144 LenDale White	.12	.30
❑ 145 Alge Crumpler	.12	.30
❑ 146 Jason Campbell	.12	.30
❑ 147 Chris Cooley	.12	.30
❑ 148 Brandon Lloyd	.10	.25
❑ 149 Clinton Portis	.12	.30
❑ 150 Santana Moss	.10	.25
❑ 151 Alex Brink RC	.60	1.50
❑ 152 Anthony Morelli RC	.60	1.50
❑ 153 Antoine Cason RC	.60	1.50
❑ 154 Aqib Talib RC	.60	1.50
❑ 155 Calais Campbell RC	.50	1.25
❑ 156 Erin Henderson RC	.50	1.25
❑ 157 Chris Johnson RC	2.00	5.00
❑ 158 DJ Hall RC	.50	1.25
❑ 159 DeJuan Tribble RC	.40	1.00
❑ 160 Derrick Harvey RC	.50	1.25
❑ 161 Mike Jenkins RC	.60	1.50
❑ 162 Dustin Keller RC	.60	1.50
❑ 163 Erik Ainge RC	.60	1.50
❑ 164 Felix Jones RC	1.25	3.00
❑ 165 Gosder Cherilus RC	.50	1.25
❑ 166 Jack Ikegwuonu RC	.50	1.25
❑ 167 Jacob Hester RC	.60	1.50
❑ 168 Chauncey Washington RC	.50	1.25
❑ 169 J Leman RC	.50	1.25
❑ 170 Joe Flacco RC	2.00	5.00
❑ 171 John David Booty RC	.60	1.50
❑ 172 Jordy Nelson RC	.75	2.00
❑ 173 Josh Johnson RC	.60	1.50
❑ 174 Kenny Phillips RC	.60	1.50
❑ 175 Malcolm Kelly RC	.60	1.50
❑ 176 Marcus Monk RC	.60	1.50
❑ 177 Mario Manningham RC	.60	1.50
❑ 178 Mario Urrutia RC	.50	1.25
❑ 179 Martin Rucker RC	.50	1.25
❑ 180 Matt Flynn RC	.60	1.50
❑ 181 Matt Forte RC	1.25	3.00
❑ 182 Jerome Felton RC	.40	1.00
❑ 183 Owen Schmitt RC	.60	1.50
❑ 184 Ryan Grice-Mullen RC	.60	1.50
❑ 185 Paul Hubbard RC	.50	1.25
❑ 186 Quentin Groves RC	.50	1.25
❑ 187 Ray Rice RC	1.25	3.00
❑ 188 Ryan Clady RC	.60	1.50
❑ 189 Ryan Torain RC	.60	1.50
❑ 190 Adrian Arrington RC	.50	1.25
❑ 191 Shawn Crable RC	.60	1.50
❑ 192 Allen Patrick RC	.50	1.25
❑ 193 Tashard Choice RC	.60	1.50
❑ 194 Terrell Thomas RC	.50	1.25
❑ 195 Thomas Brown RC	.60	1.50
❑ 196 Tom Zbikowski RC	.60	1.50
❑ 197 Jermichael Finley RC	.60	1.50
❑ 198 Trevor Laws RC	.60	1.50
❑ 199 Vince Hall RC	.40	1.00
❑ 200 Xavier Adibi RC	.50	1.25
❑ 201 Ali Highsmith RC	.40	1.00
❑ 202 Andre Woodson RC	.60	1.50
❑ 203 Brian Brohm RC	.60	1.50
❑ 204 Chad Henne RC	1.00	2.50
❑ 205 Chris Long RC	.60	1.50
❑ 206 Colt Brennan RC	1.00	2.50
❑ 207 Dan Connor RC	.60	1.50
❑ 208 Darren McFadden RC	1.25	3.00
❑ 209 Dennis Dixon RC	.60	1.50
❑ 210 DeSean Jackson RC	1.25	3.00
❑ 211 Early Doucet RC	.60	1.50
❑ 212 Fred Davis RC	.60	1.50
❑ 213 Glenn Dorsey RC	.60	1.50
❑ 214 Jake Long RC	.60	1.50
❑ 215 Jonathan Stewart RC	1.25	3.00
❑ 216 Justin King RC	.50	1.25
❑ 217 Keith Rivers RC	.60	1.50
❑ 218 Lavelle Hawkins RC	.50	1.25
❑ 219 Lawrence Jackson RC	.50	1.25
❑ 220 Limas Sweed RC	.60	1.50
❑ 221 Matt Ryan RC	2.50	6.00
❑ 222 Mike Hart RC	.60	1.50
❑ 223 Earl Bennett RC	.60	1.50
❑ 224 Sam Baker RC	.40	1.00
❑ 225 Sedrick Ellis RC	.60	1.50

2009 Upper Deck First Edition

Card	Low	High
❑ COMPLETE SET (200)		
❑ 1 Kurt Warner	.15	.40
❑ 2 Tim Hightower	.12	.30
❑ 3 Larry Fitzgerald	.15	.40
❑ 4 Anquan Boldin	.12	.30
❑ 5 Steve Breaston	.12	.30
❑ 6 Matt Ryan	.15	.40
❑ 7 Michael Jenkins	.10	.25
❑ 8 Jerious Norwood	.12	.30
❑ 9 Roddy White	.12	.30
❑ 10 Michael Turner	.12	.30
❑ 11 Ed Reed	.12	.30
❑ 12 Willis McGahee	.12	.30
❑ 13 Joe Flacco	.15	.40
❑ 14 Ray Lewis	.15	.40
❑ 15 Derrick Mason	.10	.25
❑ 16 Lee Evans	.12	.30
❑ 17 Marshawn Lynch	.12	.30
❑ 18 Trent Edwards	.12	.30
❑ 19 Leodis McKelvin	.10	.25
❑ 20 Terrell Owens	.15	.40
❑ 21 DeAngelo Williams	.15	.40
❑ 22 Steve Smith	.12	.30
❑ 23 Muhsin Muhammad	.12	.30
❑ 24 Jonathan Stewart	.12	.30
❑ 25 Jake Delhomme	.12	.30
❑ 26 Devin Hester	.15	.40
❑ 27 Matt Forte	.15	.40
❑ 28 Lance Briggs	.12	.30
❑ 29 Jay Cutler	.15	.40
❑ 30 Brian Urlacher	.15	.40
❑ 31 Carson Palmer	.15	.40
❑ 32 Chad Johnson	.12	.30
❑ 33 Laveranues Coles	.12	.30
❑ 34 Cedric Benson	.12	.30
❑ 35 Jamal Lewis	.12	.30
❑ 36 Derek Anderson	.12	.30
❑ 37 Brady Quinn	.12	.30
❑ 38 Braylon Edwards	.12	.30
❑ 39 Felix Jones	.15	.40
❑ 40 Jason Witten	.15	.40
❑ 41 Roy Williams WR	.12	.30
❑ 42 DeMarcus Ware	.12	.30
❑ 43 Tony Romo	.25	.60
❑ 44 Marion Barber	.15	.40
❑ 45 Kyle Orton	.12	.30
❑ 46 Eddie Royal	.12	.30
❑ 47 Champ Bailey	.12	.30
❑ 48 Brandon Marshall	.12	.30
❑ 49 Jason Hanson	.10	.25
❑ 50 Calvin Johnson	.15	.40
❑ 51 Kevin Smith	.12	.30
❑ 52 Daunte Culpepper	.12	.30
❑ 53 A.J. Hawk	.12	.30
❑ 54 Aaron Rodgers	.15	.40
❑ 55 Donald Driver	.12	.30
❑ 56 Greg Jennings	.15	.40
❑ 57 Ryan Grant	.12	.30
❑ 58 Matt Schaub	.12	.30
❑ 59 Andre Johnson	.12	.30
❑ 60 Steve Slaton	.12	.30
❑ 61 Mario Williams	.12	.30
❑ 62 DeMeco Ryans	.12	.30
❑ 63 Peyton Manning	.25	.60
❑ 64 Joseph Addai	.15	.40
❑ 65 Reggie Wayne	.12	.30
❑ 66 Anthony Gonzalez	.10	[illegible]
❑ 67 Dallas Clark	.12	.30

Card	Low	High
❑ 68 Bob Sanders	.12	.30
❑ 69 Maurice Jones-Drew	.12	.30
❑ 70 David Garrard	.12	.30
❑ 71 Marcedes Lewis	.10	.25
❑ 72 Rashean Mathis	.10	.25
❑ 73 Justin Durant	.10	.25
❑ 74 Larry Johnson	.12	.30
❑ 75 Matt Cassel	.12	.30
❑ 76 Tyler Thigpen	.10	.25
❑ 77 Dwayne Bowe	.12	.30
❑ 78 Ronnie Brown	.12	.30
❑ 79 Greg Camarillo	.12	.30
❑ 80 Ted Ginn Jr.	.12	.30
❑ 81 Chad Pennington	.12	.30
❑ 82 Joey Porter	.12	.30
❑ 83 Adrian Peterson	.30	.75
❑ 84 Bernard Berrian	.12	.30
❑ 85 Jared Allen	.15	.40
❑ 86 Chester Taylor	.10	.25
❑ 87 Visanthe Shiancoe	.10	.25
❑ 88 Tom Brady	.25	.60
❑ 89 Wes Welker	.15	.40
❑ 90 Randy Moss	.15	.40
❑ 91 Kevin Faulk	.10	.25
❑ 92 Sammy Morris	.10	.25
❑ 93 Reggie Bush	.15	.40
❑ 94 Drew Brees	.15	.40
❑ 95 Lance Moore	.12	.30
❑ 96 Pierre Thomas	.12	.30
❑ 97 Marques Colston	.12	.30
❑ 98 Brandon Jacobs	.12	.30
❑ 99 Ahmad Bradshaw	.12	.30
❑ 100 Steve Smith USC	.12	.30
❑ 101 Eli Manning	.15	.40
❑ 102 Domenik Hixon	.10	.25
❑ 103 Thomas Jones	.12	.30
❑ 104 Jerricho Cotchery	.10	.25
❑ 105 Kellen Clemens	.10	.25
❑ 106 Dustin Keller	.10	.25
❑ 107 Leon Washington	.12	.30
❑ 108 Darren McFadden	.15	.40
❑ 109 JaMarcus Russell	.12	.30
❑ 110 Johnnie Lee Higgins	.10	.25
❑ 111 Justin Fargas	.10	.25
❑ 112 Asante Samuel	.10	.25
❑ 113 Brian Westbrook	.12	.30
❑ 114 DeSean Jackson	.12	.30
❑ 115 Donovan McNabb	.15	.40
❑ 116 Shawn Andrews	.10	.25
❑ 117 Troy Polamalu	.15	.40
❑ 118 Willie Parker	.12	.30
❑ 119 Ben Roethlisberger	.25	.60
❑ 120 Santonio Holmes	.12	.30
❑ 121 Hines Ward	.12	.30
❑ 122 James Harrison	.15	.40
❑ 123 Darren Sproles	.12	.30
❑ 124 LaDainian Tomlinson	.15	.40
❑ 125 Philip Rivers	.15	.40
❑ 126 Antonio Gates	.12	.30
❑ 127 Vincent Jackson	.12	.30
❑ 128 Patrick Willis	.12	.30
❑ 129 Frank Gore	.12	.30
❑ 130 Vernon Davis	.10	.25
❑ 131 Julius Jones	.12	.30
❑ 132 Matt Hasselbeck	.12	.30
❑ 133 Deion Branch	.12	.30
❑ 134 Lofa Tatupu	.12	.30
❑ 135 Marc Bulger	.12	.30
❑ 136 Donnie Avery	.12	.30
❑ 137 Steven Jackson	.12	.30
❑ 138 Kellen Winslow	.12	.30
❑ 139 Cadillac Williams	.12	.30
❑ 140 Michael Clayton	.10	.25
❑ 141 Ronde Barber	.10	.25
❑ 142 Kerry Collins	.12	.30
❑ 143 Chris Johnson	.15	.40
❑ 144 LenDale White	.12	.30
❑ 145 Bo Scaife	.10	.25
❑ 146 Clinton Portis	.12	.30
❑ 147 Jason Campbell	.12	.30
❑ 148 Santana Moss	.12	.30
❑ 149 Antwaan Randle El	.10	.25
❑ 150 Albert Haynesworth	.10	.25
❑ 151 Ramses Barden RC	.40	1.00
❑ 152 Andre Brown RC	.40	1.00
❑ 153 Patrick Turner RC	.40	1.00
❑ 154 Mike Wallace RC	1.00	2.50
❑ 155 Derrick Williams RC	.50	1.25
❑ 156 Deon Butler RC	.50	1.25
❑ 157 Juaquin Iglesias RC	.50	1.25
❑ 158 Stephen McGee RC	.50	1.25
❑ 159 Patrick Chung RC	.50	1.25
❑ 160 Darius Butler RC	.50	1.25
❑ 161 Alex Mack RC	.40	1.00
❑ 162 Glen Coffee RC	.60	1.50
❑ 163 Nate Davis RC	.50	1.25
❑ 164 Chase Coffman RC	.40	1.00
❑ 165 Evander Hood RC	.75	2.00
❑ 166 James Laurinaitis RC	.60	1.50
❑ 167 Vontae Davis RC	.50	1.25
❑ 168 Brian Robiskie RC	.50	1.25
❑ 169 Eugene Monroe RC	.40	1.00
❑ 170 Javon Ringer RC	.50	1.25
❑ 171 Clay Matthews RC	.75	2.00
❑ 172 Rey Maualuga RC	.75	2.00
❑ 173 Brian Cushing RC	.60	1.50
❑ 174 Michael Oher RC	1.00	2.50
❑ 175 Brandon Tate RC	.40	1.00
❑ 176 Andre Smith RC	.50	1.25
❑ 177 Shonn Greene RC	1.00	2.50
❑ 178 Pat White RC	.75	2.00
❑ 179 Malcolm Jenkins RC	.50	1.25
❑ 180 Matthew Stafford RC	2.00	5.00
❑ 181 Michael Crabtree RC	1.25	3.00
❑ 182 Tyson Jackson RC	.50	1.25
❑ 183 Brandon Pettigrew RC	.60	1.50
❑ 184 Brian Orakpo RC	.60	1.50
❑ 185 Jeremy Maclin RC	1.00	2.50
❑ 186 Jason Smith RC	.40	1.00
❑ 187 Chris Wells RC	1.25	3.00
❑ 188 Aaron Curry RC	.60	1.50
❑ 189 Mark Sanchez RC	2.00	5.00
❑ 190 Aaron Maybin RC	.50	1.25
❑ 191 B.J. Raji RC	.60	1.50
❑ 192 Kenny Britt RC	.75	2.00
❑ 193 Mohamed Massaquoi RC	.50	1.25
❑ 194 Knowshon Moreno RC	1.25	3.00
❑ 195 Percy Harvin RC	1.50	4.00
❑ 196 Hakeem Nicks RC	1.00	2.50
❑ 197 LeSean McCoy RC	1.00	2.50
❑ 198 Darrius Heyward-Bey RC	.75	2.00
❑ 199 Josh Freeman RC	1.00	2.50
❑ 200 Donald Brown RC	1.00	2.50

2009 Upper Deck Heroes

Card	Low	High
❑ 1 Brett Favre	.75	2.00
❑ 2 Brett Favre	.75	2.00
❑ 3 LaDainian Tomlinson	.30	.75
❑ 4 LaDainian Tomlinson	.30	.75
❑ 5 LaDainian Tomlinson	.30	.75
❑ 6 LaDainian Tomlinson	.30	.75
❑ 7 Jay Cutler	.30	.75
❑ 8 Jay Cutler	.30	.75
❑ 9 Jay Cutler	.30	.75
❑ 10 Jay Cutler	.30	.75
❑ 11 Drew Brees	.30	.75
❑ 12 Drew Brees	.30	.75
❑ 13 Drew Brees	.30	.75
❑ 14 Drew Brees	.30	.75
❑ 15 Matt Forte	.30	.75
❑ 16 Matt Forte	.30	.75
❑ 17 Matt Forte	.30	.75
❑ 18 Matt Forte	.30	.75
❑ 19 Darren McFadden	.30	.75
❑ 20 Darren McFadden	.30	.75
❑ 21 Darren McFadden	.30	.75
❑ 22 Darren McFadden	.30	.75
❑ 23 Ben Roethlisberger	.50	1.25
❑ 24 Ben Roethlisberger	.50	1.25
❑ 25 Ben Roethlisberger	.50	1.25
❑ 26 Ben Roethlisberger	.50	1.25
❑ 27 Brett Favre	.75	2.00
❑ 28 Brett Favre	.75	2.00
❑ 29 Peyton Manning	.50	1.25
❑ 30 Peyton Manning	.50	1.25
❑ 31 Peyton Manning	.50	1.25
❑ 32 Peyton Manning	.50	1.25
❑ 33 Tony Romo	.50	1.25
❑ 34 Tony Romo	.50	1.25
❑ 35 Tony Romo	.50	1.25
❑ 36 Tony Romo	.50	1.25
❑ 37 Devin Hester	.30	.75
❑ 38 Devin Hester	.30	.75
❑ 39 Devin Hester	.30	.75
❑ 40 Devin Hester	.30	.75
❑ 41 Eli Manning	.30	.75
❑ 42 Eli Manning	.30	.75
❑ 43 Eli Manning	.30	.75
❑ 44 Eli Manning	.30	.75
❑ 45 A.J. Hawk	.25	.60
❑ 46 A.J. Hawk	.25	.60
❑ 47 A.J. Hawk	.25	.60
❑ 48 A.J. Hawk	.25	.60
❑ 49 Adrian Peterson	.60	1.50
❑ 50 Adrian Peterson	.60	1.50
❑ 51 Adrian Peterson	.60	1.50
❑ 52 Adrian Peterson	.60	1.50
❑ 53 Dallas Clark	.25	.60
❑ 54 Dallas Clark	.25	.60
❑ 55 Dallas Clark	.25	.60
❑ 56 Dallas Clark	.25	.60
❑ 57 Larry Fitzgerald	.30	.75
❑ 58 Larry Fitzgerald	.30	.75
❑ 59 Larry Fitzgerald	.30	.75
❑ 60 Larry Fitzgerald	.30	.75
❑ 61 Philip Rivers	.30	.75
❑ 62 Philip Rivers	.30	.75
❑ 63 Philip Rivers	.30	.75
❑ 64 Philip Rivers	.30	.75
❑ 65 Brian Westbrook	.25	.60
❑ 66 Brian Westbrook	.25	.60
❑ 67 Brian Westbrook	.25	.60
❑ 68 Brian Westbrook	.25	.60
❑ 69 Tom Brady	.50	1.25
❑ 70 Tom Brady	.50	1.25
❑ 71 Tom Brady	.50	1.25
❑ 72 Tom Brady	.50	1.25
❑ 73 Clinton Portis	.25	.60
❑ 74 Clinton Portis	.25	.60
❑ 75 Clinton Portis	.25	.60
❑ 76 Clinton Portis	.25	.60
❑ 77 Marvin Harrison	.30	.75
❑ 78 Marvin Harrison	.30	.75
❑ 79 Marvin Harrison	.30	.75
❑ 80 Marvin Harrison	.30	.75
❑ 81 Aaron Rodgers	.30	.75
❑ 82 Aaron Rodgers	.30	.75
❑ 83 Aaron Rodgers	.30	.75
❑ 84 Aaron Rodgers	.30	.75
❑ 85 Kurt Warner	.30	.75
❑ 86 Kurt Warner	.30	.75
❑ 87 Kurt Warner	.30	.75
❑ 88 Kurt Warner	.30	.75
❑ 89 Steven Jackson	.25	.60
❑ 90 Steven Jackson	.25	.60
❑ 91 Steven Jackson	.25	.60
❑ 92 Steven Jackson	.25	.60
❑ 93 Reggie Wayne	.25	.60
❑ 94 Reggie Wayne	.25	.60
❑ 95 Reggie Wayne	.25	.60
❑ 96 Reggie Wayne	.25	.60
❑ 97 Calvin Johnson	.30	.75
❑ 98 Calvin Johnson	.30	.75
❑ 99 Calvin Johnson	.30	.75
❑ 100 Calvin Johnson	.30	.75
❑ 101 LeSean McCoy RC	1.00	2.50
❑ 102 LeSean McCoy RC	1.00	2.50
❑ 103 Michael Crabtree RC	1.25	3.00
❑ 104 Michael Crabtree RC	1.25	3.00
❑ 105 Jeremy Maclin RC	1.00	2.50
❑ 106 Jeremy Maclin RC	1.00	2.50
❑ 107 Chris Wells RC	1.25	3.00
❑ 108 Chris Wells RC	1.25	3.00
❑ 109 Nate Davis RC	.50	1.25
❑ 110 Nate Davis RC	.50	1.25
❑ 111 Percy Harvin RC	1.50	4.00
❑ 112 Percy Harvin RC	1.50	4.00
❑ 113 Knowshon Moreno RC	1.25	3.00
❑ 114 Knowshon Moreno RC	1.25	3.00
❑ 115 Curtis Painter RC	.50	1.25
❑ 116 Curtis Painter RC	.50	1.25
❑ 117 Matthew Stafford RC	1.50	4.00
❑ 118 Matthew Stafford RC	1.50	4.00
❑ 119 Chase Coffman RC	.40	1.00

Card		
❑ 120 Chase Coffman RC	.40	1.00
❑ 121 Shonn Greene RC	1.00	2.50
❑ 122 Shonn Greene RC	1.00	2.50
❑ 123 Marcus Freeman RC	.50	1.25
❑ 124 Marcus Freeman RC	.50	1.25
❑ 125 Brian Robiskie RC	.50	1.25
❑ 126 Brian Robiskie RC	.50	1.25
❑ 127 James Laurinaitis RC	.60	1.50
❑ 128 James Laurinaitis RC	.60	1.50
❑ 129 Pat White RC	.75	2.00
❑ 130 Pat White RC	.75	2.00
❑ 131 James Davis RC	.50	1.25
❑ 132 James Davis RC	.50	1.25
❑ 133 Darrius Heyward-Bey RC	.75	2.00
❑ 134 Darrius Heyward-Bey RC	.75	2.00
❑ 135 Everette Brown RC	.50	1.25
❑ 136 Everette Brown RC	.50	1.25
❑ 137 Sean Smith RC	.50	1.25
❑ 138 Sean Smith RC	.50	1.25
❑ 139 Fili Moala RC	.40	1.00
❑ 140 Fili Moala RC	.40	1.00
❑ 141 Juaquin Iglesias RC	.50	1.25
❑ 142 Juaquin Iglesias RC	.50	1.25
❑ 143 Mark Sanchez RC	2.00	5.00
❑ 144 Mark Sanchez RC	2.00	5.00
❑ 145 Derrick Williams RC	.50	1.25
❑ 146 Derrick Williams RC	.50	1.25
❑ 147 Brandon Gibson RC	.50	1.25
❑ 148 Brandon Gibson RC	.50	1.25
❑ 149 Brandon Pettigrew RC	.60	1.50
❑ 150 Brandon Pettigrew RC	.60	1.50
❑ 151 Donald Brown RC	1.00	2.50
❑ 152 Donald Brown RC	1.00	2.50
❑ 153 Josh Freeman RC	1.00	2.50
❑ 154 Josh Freeman RC	1.00	2.50
❑ 155 Andre Smith RC	.50	1.25
❑ 156 Andre Smith RC	.50	1.25
❑ 157 Hakeem Nicks RC	1.00	2.50
❑ 158 Hakeem Nicks RC	1.00	2.50
❑ 161 Keenan Lewis RC	.50	1.25
❑ 162 Keenan Lewis RC	.50	1.25
❑ 163 Louis Murphy RC	.50	1.25
❑ 164 Louis Murphy RC	.50	1.25
❑ 165 Demetrius Byrd RC	.40	1.00
❑ 166 Demetrius Byrd RC	.40	1.00
❑ 167 Malcolm Jenkins RC	.50	1.25
❑ 168 Malcolm Jenkins RC	.50	1.25
❑ 169 Brian Cushing RC	.60	1.50
❑ 170 Brian Cushing RC	.60	1.50
❑ 171 Vontae Davis RC	.50	1.25
❑ 172 Vontae Davis RC	.50	1.25
❑ 173 Rey Maualuga RC	.75	2.00
❑ 174 Rey Maualuga RC	.75	2.00
❑ 175 Michael Johnson RC	.30	.75
❑ 176 Michael Johnson RC	.30	.75
❑ 177 Jonathan Luigs RC	.30	.75
❑ 178 Jonathan Luigs RC	.30	.75
❑ 179 D.J. Moore RC	.40	1.00
❑ 180 D.J. Moore RC	.40	1.00
❑ 181 William Moore RC	.40	1.00
❑ 182 William Moore RC	.40	1.00
❑ 183 Brian Orakpo RC	.60	1.50
❑ 184 Brian Orakpo RC	.60	1.50
❑ 185 Aaron Curry RC	.60	1.50
❑ 186 Aaron Curry RC	.60	1.50
❑ 187 Michael Oher RC	1.00	2.50
❑ 188 Michael Oher RC	1.00	2.50
❑ 189 Darius Butler RC	.50	1.25
❑ 190 Darius Butler RC	.50	1.25
❑ 191 Sen'Derrick Marks RC	.30	.75
❑ 192 Sen'Derrick Marks RC	.30	.75
❑ 193 Javon Ringer RC	.50	1.25
❑ 194 Javon Ringer RC	.50	1.25
❑ 195 Tyson Jackson RC	.50	1.25
❑ 196 Tyson Jackson RC	.50	1.25
❑ 197 Graham Harrell RC	.50	1.25
❑ 198 Graham Harrell RC	.50	1.25
❑ 201 Paul Hornung	.50	1.25
❑ 202 Paul Hornung	.50	1.25
❑ 203 Paul Hornung	.50	1.25
❑ 204 Paul Hornung	.50	1.25
❑ 205 Paul Hornung	.50	1.25
❑ 206 Bob Griese	.50	1.25
❑ 207 Bob Griese	.50	1.25
❑ 208 Bob Griese	.50	1.25
❑ 209 Bob Griese	.50	1.25
❑ 210 Bob Griese	.50	1.25
❑ 211 Jerry Kramer	.40	1.00
❑ 212 Jerry Kramer	.40	1.00
❑ 213 Jerry Kramer	.40	1.00
❑ 214 Jerry Kramer	.40	1.00
❑ 215 Jerry Kramer	.40	1.00
❑ 216 Merlin Olsen	.40	1.00
❑ 217 Merlin Olsen	.40	1.00
❑ 218 Merlin Olsen	.40	1.00
❑ 219 Merlin Olsen	.40	1.00
❑ 220 Mike Singletary	.50	1.25
❑ 221 Mike Singletary	.50	1.25
❑ 222 Mike Singletary	.50	1.25
❑ 223 Mike Singletary	.50	1.25
❑ 224 Don Maynard	.40	1.00
❑ 225 Don Maynard	.40	1.00
❑ 226 Don Maynard	.40	1.00
❑ 227 Don Maynard	.40	1.00
❑ 232 Terry Bradshaw	.75	2.00
❑ 233 Terry Bradshaw	.75	2.00
❑ 234 Emmitt Smith	.75	2.00
❑ 235 Emmitt Smith	.75	2.00
❑ 236 Bob Lilly	.40	1.00
❑ 237 Bob Lilly	.40	1.00
❑ 238 Bob Lilly	.40	1.00
❑ 239 Bob Lilly	.40	1.00
❑ 240 Thurman Thomas	.50	1.25
❑ 241 Thurman Thomas	.50	1.25
❑ 242 Thurman Thomas	.50	1.25
❑ 243 Thurman Thomas	.50	1.25
❑ 247 Jack Ham	.40	1.00
❑ 248 Jack Ham	.40	1.00
❑ 249 Jack Ham	.40	1.00
❑ 250 Mike Ditka	.40	1.00
❑ 251 Mike Ditka	.40	1.00
❑ 252 Troy Aikman	.60	1.50
❑ 253 Troy Aikman	.60	1.50
❑ 254 Roger Staubach	.60	1.50
❑ 255 Roger Staubach	.60	1.50
❑ 261 Bart Starr	.75	2.00
❑ 262 Bart Starr	.75	2.00
❑ 266 Steve Young	.60	1.50
❑ 267 Steve Young	.60	1.50
❑ 268 Steve Young	.60	1.50
❑ 269 Darrell Green	.40	1.00
❑ 270 Darrell Green	.40	1.00
❑ 271 Darrell Green	.40	1.00
❑ 272 Earl Campbell	.50	1.25
❑ 273 Earl Campbell	.50	1.25
❑ 274 Earl Campbell	.50	1.25
❑ 275 Fred Biletnikoff	.50	1.25
❑ 276 Fred Biletnikoff	.50	1.25
❑ 277 Fred Biletnikoff	.50	1.25
❑ 278 Fred Biletnikoff	.50	1.25
❑ 279 Alex Karras	.40	1.00
❑ 280 Alex Karras	.40	1.00
❑ 281 Alex Karras	.40	1.00
❑ 282 Alex Karras	.40	1.00
❑ 283 Lawrence Taylor	.50	1.25
❑ 284 Lawrence Taylor	.50	1.25
❑ 285 Lawrence Taylor	.50	1.25
❑ 286 Jim Kelly	.50	1.25
❑ 287 Jim Kelly	.50	1.25
❑ 288 Jim Kelly	.50	1.25
❑ 289 Phil Simms	.40	1.00
❑ 290 Phil Simms	.40	1.00
❑ 291 Phil Simms	.40	1.00
❑ 292 Phil Simms	.40	1.00
❑ 297 Alan Page	.40	1.00
❑ 298 Alan Page	.40	1.00
❑ 299 Alan Page	.40	1.00
❑ 300 Alan Page	.40	1.00
❑ 301 Kristi Yamaguchi	.40	1.00
❑ 302 Kristi Yamaguchi	.40	1.00
❑ 303 Kristi Yamaguchi	.40	1.00
❑ 304 Kristi Yamaguchi	.40	1.00
❑ 305 Peggy Fleming	.40	1.00
❑ 306 Peggy Fleming	.40	1.00
❑ 307 Peggy Fleming	.40	1.00
❑ 308 Peggy Fleming	.40	1.00
❑ 325 Michael Johnson Track	.50	1.25
❑ 326 Michael Johnson Track	.50	1.25
❑ 327 Michael Johnson Track	.50	1.25
❑ 328 Michael Johnson Track	.50	1.25
❑ 329 Laird Hamilton	.40	1.00
❑ 330 Laird Hamilton	.40	1.00
❑ 331 Laird Hamilton	.40	1.00
❑ 332 Laird Hamilton	.40	1.00
❑ 333 Lindsay Davenport	.40	1.00
❑ 334 Lindsay Davenport	.40	1.00
❑ 335 Lindsay Davenport	.40	1.00
❑ 336 Lindsay Davenport	.40	1.00
❑ 337 Phil Dalhausser	.40	1.00
❑ 338 Phil Dalhausser	.40	1.00
❑ 339 Phil Dalhausser	.40	1.00
❑ 340 Phil Dalhausser	.40	1.00
❑ 341 Pablo Picasso	.40	1.00
❑ 342 Vincent Van Gogh	.40	1.00
❑ 343 Thomas Edison	.40	1.00
❑ 344 George Washington	.40	1.00
❑ 345 Mount Rushmore	.40	1.00
❑ 346 Paul Revere	.40	1.00
❑ 347 Sitting Bull	.40	1.00
❑ 348 Sir Isaac Newton	.40	1.00
❑ 349 Wolfgang Mozart	.40	1.00
❑ 350 Ludwig Beethoven	.40	1.00
❑ 351 Woodstock Anniv.	.40	1.00
❑ 352 Wyatt Earp	.40	1.00
❑ 353 Benjamin Franklin	.40	1.00
❑ 354 Christopher Columbus	.40	1.00
❑ 355 Florence Nightingale	.40	1.00
❑ 356 Johnny Appleseed	.40	1.00
❑ 357 William Wallace	.40	1.00
❑ 358 Frederick Douglass	.40	1.00
❑ 359 Davy Crockett	.40	1.00
❑ 360 Daniel Boone	.40	1.00
❑ 361 Pete Best	.50	1.25
❑ 362 Pete Best	.50	1.25
❑ 363 Pete Best	.50	1.25
❑ 364 Pete Best	.50	1.25
❑ 373 Justin Hayward	.50	1.25
❑ 374 Justin Hayward	.50	1.25
❑ 375 Justin Hayward	.50	1.25
❑ 376 Steve Vai	.50	1.25
❑ 377 Steve Vai	.50	1.25
❑ 378 Steve Vai	.50	1.25
❑ 379 Tony Iommi	.50	1.25
❑ 380 Tony Iommi	.50	1.25
❑ 381 Tony Iommi	.50	1.25
❑ 382 Tom Morello	.50	1.25
❑ 383 Tom Morello	.50	1.25
❑ 384 Tom Morello	.50	1.25
❑ 401 Brett Favre ART	2.00	5.00
❑ 402 Peyton Manning ART	1.25	3.00
❑ 403 Tony Romo ART	1.25	3.00
❑ 404 Devin Hester ART	.75	2.00
❑ 405 Eli Manning ART	.75	2.00
❑ 406 Ben Roethlisberger ART	1.25	3.00
❑ 407 Calvin Johnson ART	.75	2.00
❑ 408 LaDainian Tomlinson ART	.75	2.00
❑ 409 Larry Fitzgerald ART	.75	2.00
❑ 410 Philip Rivers ART	.75	2.00
❑ 411 Brian Westbrook ART	.60	1.50
❑ 412 Tom Brady ART	1.25	3.00
❑ 413 Plaxico Burress ART	.60	1.50
❑ 414 Marvin Harrison ART	.75	2.00
❑ 415 Aaron Rodgers ART	.75	2.00
❑ 416 Carson Palmer ART	.75	2.00
❑ 417 Jay Cutler ART	.75	2.00
❑ 418 Drew Brees ART	.75	2.00
❑ 419 Darren McFadden ART	.75	2.00
❑ 420 Matt Forte ART	.75	2.00
❑ 421 Paul Hornung ART	.75	2.00
❑ 422 Bob Griese ART	.75	2.00
❑ 423 Jerry Kramer ART	.60	1.50
❑ 425 Mike Singletary ART	.75	2.00
❑ 426 Don Maynard ART	.60	1.50
❑ 427 Randall Cunningham ART	.75	2.00
❑ 429 Emmitt Smith ART	1.25	3.00
❑ 430 Bob Lilly ART	.60	1.50
❑ 431 Thurman Thomas ART	.75	2.00
❑ 432 Tony Dorsett ART	.75	2.00
❑ 433 Jack Ham ART	.60	1.50
❑ 434 Mike Ditka ART	.60	1.50
❑ 436 Alex Karras ART	.60	1.50
❑ 437 Troy Aikman ART	1.00	2.50
❑ 438 Alan Page ART	.60	1.50
❑ 439 Fred Biletnikoff ART	.75	2.00
❑ 440 Earl Campbell ART	.75	2.00
❑ 441 Kristi Yamaguchi ART	.60	1.50
❑ 442 Peggy Fleming ART	.60	1.50
❑ 447 Laird Hamilton ART	.60	1.50
❑ 448 Lindsay Davenport ART	.60	1.50
❑ 449 Michael Johnson Trck ART	.60	1.50
❑ 450 Phil Dalhausser ART	.60	1.50
❑ 451 Pablo Picasso ART	.60	1.50
❑ 452 Vincent Van Gogh ART	.60	1.50
❑ 453 Thomas Edison ART	.60	1.50
❑ 454 George Washington ART	.60	1.50
❑ 455 Mount Rushmore ART	.60	1.50
❑ 456 Paul Revere ART	.60	1.50

❑ 457 Sitting Bull ART .60 1.50
❑ 458 Wolfgang Mozart ART .60 1.50
❑ 459 Ludwig Beethoven ART .60 1.50
❑ 460 Woodstock Anniv. ART .60 1.50
❑ 461 Wyatt Earp ART .60 1.50
❑ 462 Benjamin Franklin ART .60 1.50
❑ 463 Christopher Columbus ART .60 1.50
❑ 464 Florence Nightingale ART .60 1.50
❑ 465 Johnny Appleseed ART .60 1.50
❑ 466 William Wallace ART .60 1.50
❑ 467 Frederick Douglass ART .60 1.50
❑ 468 Davy Crockett ART .60 1.50
❑ 469 Daniel Boone ART .60 1.50
❑ 470 Sir Isaac Newton ART .60 1.50
❑ 471 B.Favre/J.Namath 2.00 5.00
❑ 472 E.Manning/Manning 1.50 4.00
❑ 473 Maynard/Biletnikoff .75 2.00
❑ 474 E.Manning/T.Brady 1.50 4.00
❑ 475 M.Harrison/R.Wayne 1.00 2.50
❑ 476 T.Romo/T.Aikman 1.50 4.00
❑ 478 Roethlis/C.Palmer 1.50 4.00
❑ 479 E.Manning/T.Romo 1.50 4.00
❑ 480 L.Tomlinson/P.Rivers 1.00 2.50
❑ 481 B.Sanders/G.Howe HH 1.50 4.00
❑ 483 R.Bourque/T.Brady HH 1.50 4.00
❑ 484 E.Manning/M.Messier HH 1.00 2.50
❑ 485 Roethlis/E.Malkin HH 1.50 4.00
❑ 486 Lemieux/Bradshaw HH 1.50 4.00
❑ 488 M.Modano/T.Romo HH 1.50 4.00
❑ 489 B.Hull/M.Ditka HH .75 2.00

2008 Upper Deck Icons

❑ COMP.SET w/o RC's (100) 8.00 20.00
❑ 1 Edgerrin James .25 .60
❑ 2 Larry Fitzgerald .30 .75
❑ 3 Matt Leinart .30 .75
❑ 4 Jamal Lewis .25 .60
❑ 5 Aaron Rodgers .30 .75
❑ 6 Steve McNair .25 .60
❑ 7 Ray Lewis .30 .75
❑ 8 Todd Heap .20 .50
❑ 9 Willis McGahee .25 .60
❑ 10 Marshawn Lynch .30 .75
❑ 11 Roscoe Parrish .20 .50
❑ 12 Trent Edwards .30 .75
❑ 13 DeShaun Foster .25 .60
❑ 14 Julius Peppers .25 .60
❑ 15 Thomas Jones .25 .60
❑ 16 Brian Urlacher .30 .75
❑ 17 Devin Hester .30 .75
❑ 18 Rex Grossman .25 .60
❑ 19 Carson Palmer .30 .75
❑ 20 T.J. Houshmandzadeh .25 .60
❑ 21 Rudi Johnson .25 .60
❑ 22 Derek Anderson .25 .60
❑ 23 Kellen Winslow .25 .60
❑ 24 Braylon Edwards .25 .60
❑ 25 Tony Romo .50 1.25
❑ 26 Terrell Owens .30 .75
❑ 27 Marion Barber .30 .75
❑ 28 Brandon Marshall .25 .60
❑ 29 Travis Henry .25 .60
❑ 30 Champ Bailey .20 .50
❑ 31 Calvin Johnson .30 .75
❑ 32 Joseph Addai .30 .75
❑ 33 Jon Kitna .25 .60
❑ 34 Brett Favre .75 2.00
❑ 35 Donald Driver .25 .60
❑ 36 Ryan Grant .30 .75
❑ 37 Greg Jennings .25 .60
❑ 38 DeMeco Ryans .25 .60
❑ 39 Andre Johnson .25 .60
❑ 40 Matt Schaub .25 .60
❑ 41 Peyton Manning .50 1.25
❑ 42 Reggie Wayne .25 .60
❑ 43 Bob Sanders .25 .60
❑ 44 David Garrard .25 .60
❑ 45 Maurice Jones-Drew .25 .60
❑ 46 Matt Jones .25 .60
❑ 47 Fred Taylor .25 .60
❑ 48 Tony Gonzalez .25 .60
❑ 49 Derrick Johnson .20 .50
❑ 50 Dwayne Bowe .25 .60
❑ 51 Larry Johnson .25 .60
❑ 52 Ronnie Brown .25 .60
❑ 53 Ted Ginn Jr. .25 .60
❑ 54 Jason Taylor .25 .60
❑ 55 Tarvaris Jackson .25 .60
❑ 56 Adrian Peterson .60 1.50
❑ 57 Ben Roethlisberger .40 1.00
❑ 58 Tom Brady .50 1.25
❑ 59 Randy Moss .30 .75
❑ 60 Laurence Maroney .25 .60
❑ 61 Wes Welker .30 .75
❑ 62 Drew Brees .30 .75
❑ 63 Marques Colston .25 .60
❑ 64 Reggie Bush .30 .75
❑ 65 Eli Manning .30 .75
❑ 66 Antonio Pierce .20 .50
❑ 67 Plaxico Burress .25 .60
❑ 68 Jeremy Shockey .25 .60
❑ 69 Jonathan Vilma .25 .60
❑ 70 JaMarcus Russell .30 .75
❑ 71 Kirk Morrison .20 .50
❑ 72 Ronald Curry .25 .60
❑ 73 Brian Westbrook .25 .60
❑ 74 Brian Dawkins .25 .60
❑ 75 Donovan McNabb .30 .75
❑ 76 Santonio Holmes .25 .60
❑ 77 Willie Parker .25 .60
❑ 78 Troy Polamalu .30 .75
❑ 79 LaDainian Tomlinson .40 1.00
❑ 80 Shawne Merriman .25 .60
❑ 81 Antonio Cromartie .20 .50
❑ 82 Antonio Gates .25 .60
❑ 83 Alex Smith QB .25 .60
❑ 84 Frank Gore .25 .60
❑ 85 Patrick Willis .25 .60
❑ 86 Matt Hasselbeck .25 .60
❑ 87 Shaun Alexander .25 .60
❑ 88 Deion Branch .25 .60
❑ 89 Steven Jackson .30 .75
❑ 90 Torry Holt .25 .60
❑ 91 Marc Bulger .25 .60
❑ 92 Jeff Garcia .25 .60
❑ 93 Cadillac Williams .25 .60
❑ 94 Joey Galloway .25 .60
❑ 95 Vince Young .25 .60
❑ 96 LenDale White .25 .60
❑ 97 Albert Haynesworth .20 .50
❑ 98 Jason Campbell .25 .60
❑ 99 Chris Cooley .25 .60
❑ 100 Clinton Portis .25 .60
❑ 101 Earl Bennett RC 1.25 3.00
❑ 102 Adrian Arrington RC 1.00 2.50
❑ 103 Ali Highsmith RC .75 2.00
❑ 104 Allen Patrick RC 1.00 2.50
❑ 105 Andre Caldwell RC 1.25 3.00
❑ 106 Andre Woodson RC 1.25 3.00
❑ 107 Antoine Cason RC 1.25 3.00
❑ 108 Aqib Talib RC 1.25 3.00
❑ 109 Ben Moffitt RC .75 2.00
❑ 110 Brian Brohm RC 1.25 3.00
❑ 111 Bruce Davis RC 1.25 3.00
❑ 112 Calais Campbell RC 1.00 2.50
❑ 113 Chad Henne RC 2.00 5.00
❑ 114 Chevis Jackson RC 1.00 2.50
❑ 115 Chris Ellis RC 1.00 2.50
❑ 116 Chris Johnson RC 4.00 10.00
❑ 117 Chris Long RC 1.25 3.00
❑ 118 Colt Brennan RC 2.00 5.00
❑ 119 Craig Steltz RC 1.00 2.50
❑ 120 DJ Hall RC 1.00 2.50
❑ 121 Dan Connor RC 1.25 3.00
❑ 122 Darren McFadden RC 2.50 6.00
❑ 123 Davone Bess RC 1.50 4.00
❑ 124 DeMario Pressley RC 1.00 2.50
❑ 125 Dennis Dixon RC 1.25 3.00
❑ 126 DeSean Jackson RC 2.50 6.00
❑ 127 Donnie Avery RC 1.50 4.00
❑ 128 Jerome Simpson RC 1.00 2.50
❑ 129 Dre Moore RC 1.00 2.50
❑ 130 Dwight Lowery RC 1.00 2.50
❑ 131 Early Doucet RC 1.25 3.00
❑ 132 Erik Ainge RC 1.25 3.00
❑ 133 Felix Jones RC 2.50 6.00
❑ 134 Fred Davis RC 1.25 3.00
❑ 135 Glenn Dorsey RC 1.25 3.00
❑ 136 Harry Douglas RC 1.00 2.50
❑ 137 Eddie Royal RC 2.00 5.00
❑ 138 Jack Ikegwuonu RC 1.00 2.50
❑ 139 Jacob Hester RC 1.25 3.00
❑ 140 Jacob Tamme RC 1.25 3.00
❑ 141 Jake Long RC 1.25 3.00
❑ 142 Jamaal Charles RC 2.00 5.00
❑ 143 James Hardy RC 1.00 2.50
❑ 144 J Leman RC 1.00 2.50
❑ 145 Joe Flacco RC 4.00 10.00
❑ 146 John Carlson RC 1.25 3.00
❑ 147 John David Booty RC 1.25 3.00
❑ 148 Jonathan Goff RC 1.00 2.50
❑ 149 Jonathan Hefney RC 1.00 2.50
❑ 150 Jonathan Stewart RC 2.50 6.00
❑ 151 Jordy Nelson RC 1.50 4.00
❑ 152 Josh Johnson RC 1.25 3.00
❑ 153 Justin Forsett RC 1.25 3.00
❑ 154 Justin King RC 1.00 2.50
❑ 155 Keenan Burton RC 1.00 2.50
❑ 156 Keith Rivers RC 1.25 3.00
❑ 157 Kenny Phillips RC 1.25 3.00
❑ 158 Kentwan Balmer RC 1.00 2.50
❑ 159 Kevin O'Connell RC 1.25 3.00
❑ 160 Kevin Smith RC 2.00 5.00
❑ 161 Alex Brink RC 1.25 3.00
❑ 162 Lavelle Hawkins RC 1.00 2.50
❑ 163 Lawrence Jackson RC 1.00 2.50
❑ 164 Limas Sweed RC 1.25 3.00
❑ 165 Malcolm Kelly RC 1.25 3.00
❑ 166 Marcus Monk RC 1.25 3.00
❑ 167 Mario Manningham RC 1.25 3.00
❑ 168 Mario Urrutia RC 1.00 2.50
❑ 169 Martellus Bennett RC 1.25 3.00
❑ 170 Martin Rucker RC 1.00 2.50
❑ 171 Matt Flynn RC 1.25 3.00
❑ 172 Matt Forte RC 2.50 6.00
❑ 173 Matt Ryan RC 5.00 12.00
❑ 174 Mike Hart RC 1.25 3.00
❑ 175 Mike Jenkins RC 1.25 3.00
❑ 176 Owen Schmitt RC 1.25 3.00
❑ 177 Paul Smith RC 1.25 3.00
❑ 178 Philip Wheeler RC 1.25 3.00
❑ 179 Quentin Groves RC 1.00 2.50
❑ 180 Quintin Demps RC 1.25 3.00
❑ 181 Rashard Mendenhall RC 2.50 6.00
❑ 182 Ray Rice RC 2.50 6.00
❑ 183 Ryan Clady RC 1.25 3.00
❑ 184 Ryan Torain RC 1.25 3.00
❑ 185 Sam Baker RC .75 2.00
❑ 186 Anthony Morelli RC 1.25 3.00
❑ 187 Sedrick Ellis RC 1.25 3.00
❑ 188 Dexter Jackson RC 1.25 3.00
❑ 189 Shawn Crable RC 1.25 3.00
❑ 190 Steve Slaton RC 1.50 4.00
❑ 191 Tashard Choice RC 1.25 3.00
❑ 192 Terrell Thomas RC 1.00 2.50
❑ 193 Thomas Brown RC 1.25 3.00
❑ 194 Tom Zbikowski RC 1.25 3.00
❑ 195 Gosder Cherilus RC 1.00 2.50
❑ 196 Trevor Laws RC 1.25 3.00
❑ 197 Vernon Gholston RC 1.25 3.00
❑ 198 Vince Hall RC .75 2.00
❑ 199 Xavier Adibi RC 1.00 2.50
❑ 200 Yvenson Bernard RC 1.25 3.00
❑ 201 Jerome Felton RC .75 2.00
❑ 202 Simeon Castille RC 1.00 2.50
❑ 203 Craig Stevens RC 1.00 2.50
❑ 204 Barry Richardson RC .75 2.00
❑ 205 Beau Bell RC 1.00 2.50
❑ 206 Caleb Campbell RC 1.25 3.00
❑ 207 T.C. Ostrander RC 1.00 2.50
❑ 208 Brad Cottam RC 1.25 3.00
❑ 209 Brandon Flowers RC 1.25 3.00
❑ 211 Chauncey Washington RC 1.00 2.50
❑ 212 Chris Williams RC 1.00 2.50
❑ 213 Cory Boyd RC 1.00 2.50
❑ 214 Will Franklin RC 1.00 2.50
❑ 215 Jo-Lonn Dunbar RC 1.00 2.50
❑ 216 Xavier Omon RC 1.25 3.00
❑ 217 Darius Reynaud RC 1.00 2.50
❑ 218 Dantrell Savage RC 1.25 3.00
❑ 219 DeJuan Tribble RC .75 2.00
❑ 220 Dennis Keyes RC .75 2.00
❑ 221 Devin Thomas RC 1.25 3.00
❑ 222 Marcus Griffin RC .75 2.00

Card	Low	High
❑ 223 Drew Radovich RC	1.00	2.50
❑ 224 Marcus Thomas RC	1.00	2.50
❑ 225 Frank Okam RC	.75	2.00
❑ 226 Brian Bonner RC	.75	2.00
❑ 227 Jamie Silva RC	1.00	2.50
❑ 228 Jehuu Caulcrick RC	1.00	2.50
❑ 229 Jermichael Finley RC	1.25	3.00
❑ 230 Jerod Mayo RC	1.50	4.00
❑ 231 Brandon McAnderson RC	1.00	2.50
❑ 232 Jordon Dizon RC	1.25	3.00
❑ 233 Josh Barrett RC	.75	2.00
❑ 234 Kalvin McRae RC	1.00	2.50
❑ 235 Kellen Davis RC	.75	2.00
❑ 236 Keon Lattimore RC	1.00	2.50
❑ 237 Leodis McKelvin RC	1.25	3.00
❑ 239 Curtis Lofton RC	1.25	3.00
❑ 240 Paul Hubbard RC	1.00	2.50
❑ 241 Titus Brown RC	.75	2.00
❑ 242 Ryan Grice-Mullen RC	1.25	3.00
❑ 243 Spencer Larsen RC	.75	2.00
❑ 244 Thomas DeCoud RC	.75	2.00
❑ 245 Erin Henderson RC	1.00	2.50
❑ 246 Tracy Porter RC	1.50	4.00
❑ 247 Trae Williams RC	.75	2.00
❑ 248 Trevor Scott RC	1.00	2.50
❑ 249 Wesley Woodyard RC	1.00	2.50
❑ 250 Xavier Lee RC	1.00	2.50

2009 Upper Deck Icons

Card	Low	High
❑ COMP.SET w/o SP's (100)	8.00	20.00
❑ 101-170 ROOKIE PRINT RUN 599		
❑ 171-200 LEGEND PRINT RUN 599		
❑ 1 Tony Romo	.50	1.25
❑ 2 Marion Barber	.30	.75
❑ 3 Terrell Owens	.30	.75
❑ 4 Jason Witten	.30	.75
❑ 5 DeMarcus Ware	.25	.60
❑ 6 Eli Manning	.30	.75
❑ 7 Brandon Jacobs	.25	.60
❑ 8 Antonio Pierce	.20	.50
❑ 9 Donovan McNabb	.30	.75
❑ 10 Brian Westbrook	.25	.60
❑ 11 DeSean Jackson	.25	.60
❑ 12 Chris Cooley	.20	.50
❑ 13 Jason Campbell	.25	.60
❑ 14 Clinton Portis	.25	.60
❑ 15 Santana Moss	.25	.60
❑ 16 Tim Hightower	.25	.60
❑ 17 Larry Fitzgerald	.30	.75
❑ 18 Anquan Boldin	.25	.60
❑ 19 Kurt Warner	.30	.75
❑ 20 Frank Gore	.25	.60
❑ 21 Patrick Willis	.25	.60
❑ 22 Isaac Bruce	.25	.60
❑ 23 Julius Jones	.25	.60
❑ 24 Steven Jackson	.25	.60
❑ 25 Matt Forte	.30	.75
❑ 26 Brian Urlacher	.30	.75
❑ 27 Kyle Orton	.25	.60
❑ 28 Calvin Johnson	.30	.75
❑ 29 Aaron Rodgers	.30	.75
❑ 30 Ryan Grant	.25	.60
❑ 31 Greg Jennings	.30	.75
❑ 32 A.J. Hawk	.25	.60
❑ 33 Aaron Kampman	.25	.60
❑ 34 Adrian Peterson	.60	1.50
❑ 35 Matt Ryan	.30	.75
❑ 36 Michael Turner	.25	.60
❑ 37 Jake Delhomme	.25	.60
❑ 38 Steve Smith	.25	.60
❑ 39 DeAngelo Williams	.30	.75
❑ 40 Drew Brees	.30	.75
❑ 41 Reggie Bush	.30	.75
❑ 42 Marques Colston	.25	.60
❑ 43 Jonathan Vilma	.20	.50
❑ 44 Earnest Graham	.20	.50
❑ 45 Jeff Garcia	.25	.60
❑ 46 Trent Edwards	.25	.60
❑ 47 Marshawn Lynch	.25	.60
❑ 48 Lee Evans	.25	.60
❑ 49 Chad Pennington	.25	.60
❑ 50 Ronnie Brown	.25	.60
❑ 51 Joey Porter	.25	.60
❑ 52 Tom Brady	.50	1.25
❑ 53 Randy Moss	.30	.75
❑ 54 Wes Welker	.30	.75
❑ 55 Bart Scott	.20	.50
❑ 56 Thomas Jones	.25	.60
❑ 57 Laveranues Coles	.25	.60
❑ 58 Jerricho Cotchery	.20	.50
❑ 59 Jay Cutler	.30	.75
❑ 60 Brandon Marshall	.25	.60
❑ 61 Eddie Royal	.25	.60
❑ 62 Tyler Thigpen	.20	.50
❑ 63 Larry Johnson	.25	.60
❑ 64 Dwayne Bowe	.25	.60
❑ 65 Tony Gonzalez	.25	.60
❑ 66 JaMarcus Russell	.25	.60
❑ 67 Darren McFadden	.30	.75
❑ 68 Philip Rivers	.30	.75
❑ 69 LaDainian Tomlinson	.30	.75
❑ 70 Antonio Gates	.25	.60
❑ 71 Vincent Jackson	.25	.60
❑ 72 Derrick Mason	.20	.50
❑ 73 Ray Lewis	.30	.75
❑ 74 Joe Flacco	.30	.75
❑ 75 Carson Palmer	.30	.75
❑ 76 Chad Johnson	.25	.60
❑ 77 T.J. Houshmandzadeh	.25	.60
❑ 78 Keith Rivers	.20	.50
❑ 79 Jamal Lewis	.25	.60
❑ 80 Brady Quinn	.25	.60
❑ 81 Braylon Edwards	.25	.60
❑ 82 Ben Roethlisberger	.50	1.25
❑ 83 Willie Parker	.25	.60
❑ 84 Hines Ward	.25	.60
❑ 85 Troy Polamalu	.30	.75
❑ 86 James Harrison	.30	.75
❑ 87 Steve Slaton	.25	.60
❑ 88 Matt Schaub	.25	.60
❑ 89 Andre Johnson	.25	.60
❑ 90 Peyton Manning	.50	1.25
❑ 91 Joseph Addai	.30	.75
❑ 92 Reggie Wayne	.25	.60
❑ 93 Bob Sanders	.25	.60
❑ 94 David Garrard	.25	.60
❑ 95 John Henderson	.20	.50
❑ 96 Maurice Jones-Drew	.25	.60
❑ 97 LenDale White	.25	.60
❑ 98 Chris Johnson	.30	.75
❑ 99 Albert Haynesworth	.20	.50
❑ 100 Roddy White	.25	.60
❑ 101 Matthew Stafford RC	5.00	12.00
❑ 102 Mark Sanchez RC	6.00	15.00
❑ 103 Eben Britton RC	1.25	3.00
❑ 104 Josh Freeman RC	3.00	8.00
❑ 105 Chris Wells RC	4.00	10.00
❑ 106 Javon Ringer RC	1.50	4.00
❑ 107 Knowshon Moreno RC	4.00	10.00
❑ 108 James Davis RC	1.50	4.00
❑ 109 Victor Harris RC	1.50	4.00
❑ 110 P.J. Hill RC	1.25	3.00
❑ 111 Michael Crabtree RC	4.00	10.00
❑ 112 Darrius Heyward-Bey RC	2.50	6.00
❑ 113 Jeremy Maclin RC	3.00	8.00
❑ 114 Percy Harvin RC	5.00	12.00
❑ 115 Brian Robiskie RC	1.50	4.00
❑ 116 Aaron Kelly RC	1.25	3.00
❑ 117 Kenny Britt RC	2.50	6.00
❑ 118 Ramses Barden RC	1.25	3.00
❑ 119 Alphonso Smith RC	1.25	3.00
❑ 120 Demetrius Byrd RC	1.25	3.00
❑ 121 Chase Coffman RC	1.25	3.00
❑ 122 Brandon Pettigrew RC	2.00	5.00
❑ 123 Clay Matthews RC	2.50	6.00
❑ 124 Fili Moala RC	1.25	3.00
❑ 125 Michael Oher RC	3.00	8.00
❑ 126 Andre Smith RC	1.50	4.00
❑ 127 Derek Pegues RC	1.00	2.50
❑ 128 Jason Smith RC	1.25	3.00
❑ 129 Duke Robinson RC	1.00	2.50
❑ 130 Max Unger RC	1.25	3.00
❑ 131 Hakeem Nicks RC	3.00	8.00
❑ 132 Alex Mack RC	1.25	3.00
❑ 133 Nate Davis RC	1.50	4.00
❑ 134 Andre Brown RC	1.25	3.00
❑ 135 Eugene Monroe RC	1.25	3.00
❑ 136 Alex Boone RC	1.50	4.00
❑ 137 Graham Harrell RC	1.50	4.00
❑ 138 Jonathan Luigs RC	1.00	2.50
❑ 139 Brian Orakpo RC	2.00	5.00
❑ 140 Patrick Chung RC	1.50	4.00
❑ 141 Austin Collie RC	3.00	8.00
❑ 142 Tyson Jackson RC	1.50	4.00
❑ 143 Michael Johnson RC	1.00	2.50
❑ 144 Devin Moore RC	1.25	3.00
❑ 145 Juaquin Iglesias RC	1.50	4.00
❑ 146 Quan Cosby RC	1.25	3.00
❑ 147 D.J. Moore RC	1.25	3.00
❑ 148 LeSean McCoy RC	3.00	8.00
❑ 149 Sean Smith RC	1.50	4.00
❑ 150 B.J. Raji RC	2.00	5.00
❑ 151 Jared Cook RC	1.25	3.00
❑ 152 Everette Brown RC	1.50	4.00
❑ 153 Cedric Peerman RC	1.25	3.00
❑ 154 James Laurinaitis RC	2.00	5.00
❑ 155 Rey Maualuga RC	2.50	6.00
❑ 156 Brandon Tate RC	1.25	3.00
❑ 157 Aaron Curry RC	2.00	5.00
❑ 158 Brian Cushing RC	2.00	5.00
❑ 159 Rashad Jennings RC	1.50	4.00
❑ 160 Marcus Freeman RC	1.50	4.00
❑ 161 Malcolm Jenkins RC	1.50	4.00
❑ 162 Vontae Davis RC	1.50	4.00
❑ 163 Mike Mickens RC	1.25	3.00
❑ 164 Derrick Williams RC	1.50	4.00
❑ 165 William Moore RC	1.25	3.00
❑ 166 Shonn Greene RC	3.00	8.00
❑ 167 Mohamed Massaquoi RC	1.50	4.00
❑ 168 Aaron Maybin RC	1.50	4.00
❑ 169 Donald Brown RC	3.00	8.00
❑ 170 Darius Butler RC	1.50	4.00
❑ 171 Bob Griese	2.00	5.00
❑ 172 Jack Youngblood	1.25	3.00
❑ 173 Thurman Thomas	2.00	5.00
❑ 174 Rocky Bleier	1.50	4.00
❑ 175 Jack Ham	1.50	4.00
❑ 176 Darrell Green	1.50	4.00
❑ 177 Paul Hornung	2.00	5.00
❑ 178 Ken Anderson	1.50	4.00
❑ 179 Joe Theismann	2.00	5.00
❑ 180 Barry Sanders	3.00	8.00
❑ 181 Bob Lilly	1.50	4.00
❑ 182 Merlin Olsen UER	1.50	4.00
❑ 183 Fred Biletnikoff	2.00	5.00
❑ 184 Earl Campbell	2.00	5.00
❑ 185 Jim Kelly	2.00	5.00
❑ 186 Daryl Johnston	2.00	5.00
❑ 187 Mike Ditka	1.50	4.00
❑ 188 Lem Barney	1.25	3.00
❑ 189 Mike Singletary	2.00	5.00
❑ 190 Don Maynard	1.50	4.00
❑ 191 Anthony Munoz	1.50	4.00
❑ 192 Ron Yary	1.25	3.00
❑ 193 John Elway	3.00	8.00
❑ 194 Terry Bradshaw	3.00	8.00
❑ 195 Billy Sims	1.50	4.00
❑ 196 Bubba Smith	1.25	3.00
❑ 197 Jerry Kramer	1.50	4.00
❑ 198 Alan Page	1.50	4.00
❑ 199 Tom Rathman	1.25	3.00
❑ 200 Alex Karras	1.50	4.00

2006 Upper Deck Rookie Premiere

Card	Low	High
❑ COMPLETE SET (30)	10.00	20.00

2006 Aspire

❑ COMPLETE SET (36)	10.00	25.00
❑ 1 Reggie Bush	1.00	2.50
❑ 2 Matt Leinart	.60	1.50
❑ 3 Vince Young	1.00	2.50
❑ 4 Mario Williams	.50	1.25
❑ 5 Michael Huff	.40	1.00
❑ 6 Vernon Davis	.40	1.00
❑ 7 LenDale White	.50	1.25
❑ 8 Brodie Croyle	.40	1.00
❑ 9 Drew Olson	.25	.60
❑ 10 Maurice Drew	.75	2.00
❑ 11 Tye Hill	.30	.75
❑ 12 Michael Robinson	.30	.75
❑ 13 Joseph Addai	.50	1.25
❑ 14 Paul Pinegar	.25	.60
❑ 15 Jimmy Williams	.40	1.00
❑ 16 D.J. Shockley	.30	.75
❑ 17 Mike Hass	.40	1.00
❑ 18 Demetrius Williams	.30	.75
❑ 19 Reggie McNeal	.30	.75
❑ 20 Charlie Whitehurst	.40	1.00
❑ 21 Maurice Stovall	.30	.75
❑ 22 Sinorice Moss	.40	1.00
❑ 23 Jason Avant	.40	1.00
❑ 24 Omar Jacobs	.25	.60
❑ 25 Laurence Maroney	.50	1.25
❑ 26 Martin Nance	.30	.75
❑ 27 Leonard Pope	.40	1.00
❑ 28 Rodrique Wright	.25	.60
❑ 29 David Thomas	.40	1.00
❑ 30 Will Blackmon	.40	1.00
❑ 31 Dominique Byrd	.30	.75
❑ 32 D'Brickashaw Ferguson	.40	1.00
❑ 33 Reggie Bush	1.00	2.50
❑ 34 Matt Leinart	.60	1.50
❑ 35 Vince Young	1.00	2.50
❑ 36 Jay Cutler	1.00	2.50

2007 Aspire

❑ COMPLETE SET (33)	8.00	20.00
❑ 1 JaMarcus Russell	.50	1.25
❑ 2 Brady Quinn	.75	2.00
❑ 3 Drew Stanton	.30	.75
❑ 4 John Beck	.40	1.00
❑ 5 Trent Edwards	.60	1.50
❑ 6 Troy Smith	.50	1.25
❑ 7 Kevin Kolb	.60	1.50
❑ 8 Jared Zabransky	.40	1.00
❑ 9 Jordan Palmer	.40	1.00
❑ 10 Chris Leak	.30	.75
❑ 11 Adrian Peterson	3.00	8.00
❑ 12 Marshawn Lynch	.60	1.50
❑ 13 Brian Leonard	.30	.75
❑ 14 Antonio Pittman	.40	1.00
❑ 15 Kenny Irons	.40	1.00
❑ 16 Michael Bush	.40	1.00
❑ 17 Darius Walker	.30	.75
❑ 18 Calvin Johnson	1.00	2.50
❑ 19 Robert Meachem	.40	1.00
❑ 20 Dwayne Bowe	.60	1.50
❑ 21 Sidney Rice	.75	2.00
❑ 22 Craig Buster Davis	.40	1.00
❑ 23 Steve Smith USC	.60	1.50
❑ 24 Anthony Gonzalez	.50	1.25
❑ 25 Greg Olsen	.50	1.25
❑ 26 Zach Miller	.25	.60
❑ 27 Levi Brown	.40	1.00
❑ 28 Gaines Adams	.40	1.00
❑ 29 Leon Hall	.40	1.00
❑ 30 Ted Ginn Jr.	.60	1.50
❑ 31 Patrick Willis	.60	1.50
❑ 32 Adam Carriker	.30	.75
❑ 33 Aaron Ross	.40	1.00

2008 Aspire

❑ COMPLETE SET (33)	8.00	20.00
❑ 1 Matt Ryan	1.50	4.00
❑ 2 Brian Brohm	.40	1.00
❑ 3 Chad Henne	.60	1.50
❑ 4 Joe Flacco	1.25	3.00
❑ 5 John David Booty	.40	1.00
❑ 6 Josh Johnson	.40	1.00
❑ 7 Erik Ainge	.40	1.00
❑ 8 Dennis Dixon	.40	1.00
❑ 9 Darren McFadden	.75	2.00
❑ 10 Rashard Mendenhall	.75	2.00
❑ 11 Jonathan Stewart	.75	2.00
❑ 12 Jamaal Charles	.60	1.50
❑ 13 Felix Jones	.75	2.00
❑ 14 Ray Rice	.75	2.00
❑ 15 Kevin Smith	.60	1.50
❑ 16 Steve Slaton	.50	1.25
❑ 17 Mike Hart	.40	1.00
❑ 18 Malcolm Kelly	.40	1.00
❑ 19 DeSean Jackson	.75	2.00
❑ 20 Limas Sweed	.40	1.00
❑ 21 Early Doucet	.40	1.00
❑ 22 Andre Caldwell	.40	1.00
❑ 23 Devin Thomas	.40	1.00
❑ 24 James Hardy	.30	.75
❑ 25 Fred Davis	.40	1.00
❑ 26 Jake Long	.40	1.00
❑ 27 Sedrick Ellis	.40	1.00
❑ 28 Vernon Gholston	.40	1.00
❑ 29 Keith Rivers	.40	1.00
❑ 30 Mike Jenkins	.40	1.00
❑ 31 Derrick Harvey	.30	.75
❑ 32 Dan Connor	.40	1.00
❑ 33 Leodis McKelvin	.40	1.00

1996 Press Pass

❑ COMPLETE SET (55)	7.50	20.00
❑ 1 Keyshawn Johnson	.60	1.50
❑ 2 Jonathan Ogden	.25	.60
❑ 3 Duane Clemons	.07	.20
❑ 4 Kevin Hardy	.07	.20
❑ 5 Eddie George	1.00	2.50
❑ 6 Karim Abdul-Jabbar	.25	.60
❑ 7 Terry Glenn	.25	.60
❑ 8 Leeland McElroy	.15	.40
❑ 9 Simeon Rice	.30	.75
❑ 10 Roman Oben	.07	.20
❑ 11 Daryl Gardener	.07	.20
❑ 12 Marcus Coleman	.07	.20
❑ 13 Christian Peter	.07	.20
❑ 14 Tim Biakabutuka	.25	.60
❑ 15 Eric Moulds	.60	1.50
❑ 16 Chris Darkins	.07	.20
❑ 17 Andre Johnson	.07	.20
❑ 18 Lawyer Milloy	.25	.60
❑ 19 Jon Runyan	.07	.20
❑ 20 Mike Alstott	.60	1.50
❑ 21 Jeff Hartings	.25	.60
❑ 22 Amani Toomer	.50	1.25
❑ 23 Danny Kanell	.25	.60
❑ 24 Marco Battaglia	.07	.20
❑ 25 Stephen Davis	.60	1.50
❑ 26 Johnny McWilliams	.07	.20
❑ 27 Israel Ifeanyi	.07	.20
❑ 28 Scott Slutzker	.07	.20
❑ 29 Bryant Mix	.07	.20
❑ 30 Brian Roche	.07	.20
❑ 31 Stanley Pritchett	.07	.20
❑ 32 Jerome Woods	.07	.20
❑ 33 Tommie Frazier	.15	.40
❑ 34 Stepfret Williams	.07	.20
❑ 35 Ray Mickens	.07	.20
❑ 36 Alex Van Dyke	.07	.20
❑ 37 Bobby Hoying	.25	.60
❑ 38 Tony Brackens	.25	.60
❑ 39 Dietrich Jells	.07	.20
❑ 40 Jason Odom	.07	.20
❑ 41 Randall Godfrey	.07	.20
❑ 42 Willie Anderson	.07	.20
❑ 43 Tony Banks	.25	.60
❑ 44 Michael Cheever	.07	.20
❑ 45 Je'Rod Cherry	.07	.20
❑ 46 Chris Doering	.07	.20
❑ 47 Steve Taneyhill	.07	.20
❑ 48 Kyle Wachholtz	.07	.20
❑ 49 Dusty Zeigler	.07	.20
❑ 50 Derrick Mayes	.15	.40
❑ 51 Orpheus Roye	.07	.20
❑ 52 Sedric Clark	.07	.20
❑ 53 Richard Huntley	.15	.40
❑ 54 Donnie Edwards	.25	.60
❑ 55 Zach Thomas CL	.25	.60
❑ RED Lawrence Phillips	2.50	6.00
❑ P1 Tim Biakabutuka Promo	.40	1.00

1997 Press Pass

❑ COMPLETE SET (49)	7.50	20.00
❑ 1 Orlando Pace	.20	.50
❑ 2 Warrick Dunn	.50	1.25
❑ 3 Danny Wuerffel	.20	.50
❑ 4 Darnell Autry	.07	.20
❑ 5 Troy Davis	.07	.20
❑ 6 Jake Plummer	.75	2.00
❑ 7 Corey Dillon	1.00	2.50
❑ 8 Reidel Anthony	.20	.50
❑ 9 Byron Hanspard	.10	.30
❑ 10 Tiki Barber	1.00	2.50
❑ 11 Ike Hilliard	.20	.50
❑ 12 Rae Carruth	.07	.20
❑ 13 Yatil Green	.10	.30
❑ 14 Peter Boulware	.20	.50
❑ 15 Jim Druckenmiller	.10	.30
❑ 16 Pat Barnes	.07	.20
❑ 17 Trevor Pryce	.20	.50
❑ 18 Kevin Lockett	.07	.20
❑ 19 Koy Detmer	.20	.50
❑ 20 Bryant Westbrook	.07	.20
❑ 21 Darrell Russell	.07	.20
❑ 22 Tony Gonzalez	.50	1.25
❑ 23 Shawn Springs	.10	.30
❑ 24 Chris Canty	.07	.20
❑ 25 David LaFleur	.07	.20

- 26 Dwayne Rudd .07 .20
- 27 Bob Sapp .20 .50
- 28 Mike Vrabel .75 2.00
- 29 Antowain Smith .40 1.00
- 30 Keith Poole .07 .20
- 31 Sedrick Shaw .10 .30
- 32 Tremain Mack .07 .20
- 33 Matt Russell .07 .20
- 34 Reinard Wilson .10 .30
- 35 Marc Edwards .10 .30
- 36 Greg Jones .07 .20
- 37 Michael Booker .07 .20
- 38 James Farrior .20 .50
- 39 Danny Wuerffel HL .10 .30
- 40 Troy Davis HL .07 .20
- 41 Corey Dillon HL .40 1.00
- 42 Jake Plummer HL .30 .75
- 43 Peter Boulware HL .10 .30
- 44 Eddie Robinson CO .20 .50
- 45 Bobby Bowden CO .30 .75
- 46 Steve Spurrier CO .50 1.25
- 47 Gary Barnett CO .07 .20
- 48 Joe Paterno CO SP 20.00 50.00
- 49 Tom Osborne CO .50 1.25
- 50 Jarrett Irons CL .07 .20

1998 Press Pass

- COMPLETE SET (50) 7.50 20.00
- 1 Peyton Manning 3.00 8.00
- 2 Ryan Leaf .20 .50
- 3 Charles Woodson .30 .75
- 4 Andre Wadsworth .10 .30
- 5 Randy Moss 2.00 5.00
- 6 Curtis Enis .08 .25
- 7 Tra Thomas .08 .25
- 8 Flozell Adams .08 .25
- 9 Jason Peter .08 .25
- 10 Brian Simmons .10 .30
- 11 Takeo Spikes .20 .50
- 12 Michael Myers .08 .25
- 13 Kevin Dyson .20 .50
- 14 Grant Wistrom .10 .30
- 15 Fred Taylor .50 1.25
- 16 Germane Crowell .10 .30
- 17 Sam Cowart .10 .30
- 18 Anthony Simmons LB .10 .30
- 19 Robert Edwards .10 .30
- 20 Shaun Williams .10 .30
- 21 Phil Savoy .08 .25
- 22 Leonard Little .20 .50
- 23 Saladin McCullough .08 .25
- 24 Duane Starks .08 .25
- 25 John Avery .10 .30
- 26 Vonnie Holliday .20 .50
- 27 Tim Dwight .20 .50
- 28 Donovin Darius .10 .30
- 29 Alonzo Mayes .08 .25
- 30 Jerome Pathon .20 .50
- 31 Brian Kelly .10 .30
- 32 Hines Ward 1.25 2.50
- 33 Jacquez Green .10 .30
- 34 Marcus Nash .08 .25
- 35 Ahman Green .60 1.50
- 36 Joe Jurevicius .20 .50
- 37 Tavian Banks .10 .30
- 38 Donald Hayes .10 .30
- 39 Robert Holcombe .10 .30
- 40 E.G. Green .10 .30
- 41 John Dutton .08 .25
- 42 Skip Hicks .10 .30
- 43 Pat Johnson .10 .30
- 44 Keith Brooking .20 .50
- 45 Alan Faneca .40 1.00
- 46 Steve Spurrier CO .40 1.00
- 47 Mike Price CO .08 .25
- 48 Bobby Bowden CO .10 .30
- 49 Tom Osborne CO .40 1.00
- 50 Peyton Manning CL .60 1.50
- P1 Randy Moss Promo 1.50 4.00

1999 Press Pass

- COMPLETE SET (45) 7.50 20.00
- 1 Ricky Williams .50 1.25
- 2 Tim Couch .25 .60
- 3 Champ Bailey .40 1.00
- 4 Chris Claiborne .10 .30
- 5 Donovan McNabb 1.25 3.00
- 6 Edgerrin James 1.00 2.50
- 7 Akili Smith .40 1.00
- 8 John Tait .10 .30
- 9 Jevon Kearse .60 1.50
- 10 Torry Holt .60 1.50
- 11 Troy Edwards .15 .40
- 12 Chris McAlister .15 .40
- 13 Daunte Culpepper 1.00 2.50
- 14 Andy Katzenmoyer .15 .40
- 15 David Boston .25 .60
- 16 Ebenezer Ekuban .15 .40
- 17 Peerless Price .25 .60
- 18 Shaun King .15 .40
- 19 Joe Germaine .15 .40
- 20 Brock Huard .25 .60
- 21 Michael Bishop .25 .60
- 22 Amos Zereoue .25 .60
- 23 Sedrick Irvin .10 .30
- 24 Autry Denson .15 .40
- 25 Kevin Faulk .25 .60
- 26 James Johnson .15 .40
- 27 D'Wayne Bates .15 .40
- 28 Kevin Johnson .40 1.00
- 29 Tai Streets .25 .60
- 30 Craig Yeast .15 .40
- 31 Dre' Bly .25 .60
- 32 Anthony Poindexter .10 .30
- 33 Jared DeVries .10 .30
- 34 Rob Konrad .25 .60
- 35 Dat Nguyen .25 .60
- 36 Cade McNown .15 .40
- 37 Scott Covington .25 .60
- 38 Jon Jansen .10 .30
- 39 Rufus French .10 .30
- 40 Mike Rucker .25 .60
- 41 Aaron Gibson .10 .30
- 42 Kris Farris .10 .30
- 43 Anthony McFarland .10 .30
- 44 Matt Stinchcomb .15 .40
- 45 Dee Miller CL .10 .30

2000 Press Pass

- COMPLETE SET (45) 10.00 25.00
- 1 Peter Warrick .20 .50
- 2 Travis Claridge .08 .25
- 3 Courtney Brown .25 .60
- 4 Plaxico Burress .40 1.00
- 5 Chad Pennington .40 1.00
- 6 Thomas Jones .30 .75
- 7 Ron Dayne .20 .50
- 8 Brian Urlacher .75 2.00
- 9 Corey Simon .25 .60
- 10 Chris Samuels .15 .40
- 11 Stockar McDougle .08 .25
- 12 Deon Grant .15 .40
- 13 Cosey Coleman .08 .25
- 14 Sylvester Morris .15 .40
- 15 Shyrone Stith .15 .40
- 16 Shaun Alexander .60 1.50
- 17 Dez White .20 .50
- 18 John Engelberger .15 .40
- 19 Tim Rattay .20 .50
- 20 Todd Pinkston .20 .50
- 21 John Abraham .20 .50
- 22 R.Jay Soward .15 .40
- 23 Shaun Ellis .20 .50
- 24 Keith Bulluck .20 .50
- 25 Jerry Porter .25 .60
- 26 Darren Howard .15 .40
- 27 Joe Hamilton .15 .40
- 28 Deltha O'Neal .20 .50
- 29 Chris Redman .15 .40
- 30 Deon Dyer .15 .40
- 31 Jamal Lewis .40 1.00
- 32 Chris Hovan .15 .40
- 33 Raynoch Thompson .15 .40
- 34 Travis Taylor .20 .50
- 35 Sebastian Janikowski .20 .50
- 36 Travis Prentice .15 .40
- 37 Tom Brady 10.00 20.00
- 38 Tee Martin .20 .50
- 39 J.R. Redmond .15 .40
- 40 Dennis Northcutt .20 .50
- 41 Laveranues Coles .25 .60
- 42 Danny Farmer .15 .40
- 43 Darrell Jackson .40 1.00
- 44 Chris McIntosh .08 .25
- 45 Peter Warrick CL .15 .40
- P1 Peter Warrick Promo .75 2.00

2001 Press Pass

- COMPLETE SET (50) 10.00 25.00
- COMP.FACT.SET (46) 10.00 25.00
- COMP.SET w/o SP's (45) 7.50 20.00
- 1 Michael Vick CL .40 1.00
- 2 Drew Brees 1.50 4.00
- 3 Michael Vick .60 1.50
- 4 Chris Weinke .25 .60
- 5 Marques Tuiasosopo .25 .60
- 6 Josh Booty .25 .60
- 7 Josh Heupel .30 .75
- 8 Sage Rosenfels .30 .75
- 9 Mike McMahon .25 .60
- 10 Deuce McAllister .40 1.00
- 11 LaDainian Tomlinson 2.00 5.00
- 12 LaMont Jordan .30 .75
- 13 James Jackson .25 .60
- 14 Travis Henry .30 .75
- 15 Anthony Thomas .30 .75
- 16 Travis Minor .25 .60
- 17 Michael Bennett .30 .75
- 18 Kevan Barlow .25 .60
- 19 Rudi Johnson .30 .75
- 20 Santana Moss .50 1.25
- 21 Quincy Morgan .25 .60
- 22 Rod Gardner .25 .60
- 23 David Terrell .25 .60
- 24 Chris Chambers .50 1.25
- 25 Reggie Wayne .75 2.00
- 26 Ken-Yon Rambo .20 .50
- 27 Chad Johnson .75 2.00
- 28 Snoop Minnis .25 .60
- 29 Freddie Mitchell .20 .50
- 30 Koren Robinson .30 .75
- 31 Bobby Newcombe .25 .60
- 32 Robert Ferguson .30 .75
- 33 Todd Heap .30 .75

❑ 34 Steve Hutchinson .25 .60
❑ 35 Leonard Davis .25 .60
❑ 36 Kenyatta Walker .20 .50
❑ 37 Justin Smith .30 .75
❑ 38 Jamal Reynolds .25 .60
❑ 39 Richard Seymour .30 .75
❑ 40 Shaun Rogers .30 .75
❑ 41 Gerard Warren .25 .60
❑ 42 Jamar Fletcher .20 .50
❑ 43 Gary Baxter .25 .60
❑ 44 Nate Clements .30 .75
❑ 45 Derrick Gibson .20 .50
❑ 46 Drew Brees PP 3.00 8.00
❑ 47 Michael Vick PP 1.25 3.00
❑ 48 Deuce McAllister PP .75 2.00
❑ 49 LaDainian Tomlinson PP 4.00 10.00
❑ 50 David Terrell PP .50 1.25

2002 Press Pass

❑ COMPLETE SET (50) 15.00 40.00
❑ COMP.SET w/o SP's (45) 10.00 25.00
❑ 1 David Carr .40 1.00
❑ 2 Eric Crouch .40 1.00
❑ 3 Rohan Davey .40 1.00
❑ 4 David Garrard .60 1.50
❑ 5 Joey Harrington .40 1.00
❑ 6 Kurt Kittner .25 .60
❑ 7 David Neill .25 .60
❑ 8 Patrick Ramsey .40 1.00
❑ 9 Antwaan Randle El .40 1.00
❑ 10 Damien Anderson .30 .75
❑ 11 T.J. Duckett .40 1.00
❑ 12 DeShaun Foster .40 1.00
❑ 13 Lamar Gordon .40 1.00
❑ 14 William Green .30 .75
❑ 15 Leonard Henry .25 .60
❑ 16 Adrian Peterson .40 1.00
❑ 17 Clinton Portis 1.00 2.50
❑ 18 Jonathan Wells .40 1.00
❑ 19 Brian Westbrook 1.25 3.00
❑ 20 Antonio Bryant .50 1.25
❑ 21 Reche Caldwell .40 1.00
❑ 22 Kelly Campbell .30 .75
❑ 23 Andre Davis .30 .75
❑ 24 Jabar Gaffney .40 1.00
❑ 25 Ron Johnson .30 .75
❑ 26 Ashley Lelie .40 1.00
❑ 27 Josh Reed .30 .75
❑ 28 Cliff Russell .25 .60
❑ 29 Donte Stallworth .40 1.00
❑ 30 Javon Walker .40 1.00
❑ 31 Marquise Walker .25 .60
❑ 32 Daniel Graham .30 .75
❑ 33 Jeremy Shockey .60 1.50
❑ 34 Bryant McKinnie .25 .60
❑ 35 Mike Pearson .25 .60
❑ 36 Mike Williams .25 .60
❑ 37 Phillip Buchanon .40 1.00
❑ 38 Quentin Jammer .40 1.00
❑ 39 Kalimba Edwards .30 .75
❑ 40 Julius Peppers .60 1.50
❑ 41 Wendell Bryant .25 .60
❑ 42 John Henderson .40 1.00
❑ 43 Ryan Sims .40 1.00
❑ 44 Roy Williams .50 1.25
❑ 45 David Carr CL .30 .75
❑ 46 David Carr PP 1.25 3.00
❑ 47 Joey Harrington PP 1.25 3.00
❑ 48 T.J. Duckett PP 1.25 3.00
❑ 49 Donte Stallworth PP 1.25 3.00
❑ 50 William Green PP 1.00 2.50

2003 Press Pass

❑ COMPLETE SET (50) 20.00 50.00
❑ COMP.SET w/o SP's (45) 10.00 25.00
❑ 1 Brad Banks .30 .75
❑ 2 Kyle Boller .40 1.00
❑ 3 Ken Dorsey .30 .75
❑ 4 Jason Gesser .30 .75
❑ 5 Rex Grossman .40 1.00
❑ 6 Kliff Kingsbury .30 .75
❑ 7 Dyron Leftwich .50 1.25
❑ 8 Carson Palmer 1.50 4.00
❑ 9 Dave Ragone .25 .60
❑ 10 Chris Simms .40 1.00
❑ 11 Brian St.Pierre .40 1.00
❑ 12 Chris Brown .40 1.00
❑ 13 Avon Cobourne .25 .60
❑ 14 Dahrran Diedrick .25 .60
❑ 15 Justin Fargas .40 1.00
❑ 16 Earnest Graham .40 1.00
❑ 17 Larry Johnson .50 1.25
❑ 18 Willis McGahee .75 2.00
❑ 19 Musa Smith .30 .75
❑ 20 Onterrio Smith .30 .75
❑ 21 Lee Suggs .30 .75
❑ 22 Anquan Boldin 1.00 2.50
❑ 23 Talman Gardner .25 .60
❑ 24 Taylor Jacobs .30 .75
❑ 25 Andre Johnson .75 2.00
❑ 26 Bryant Johnson .40 1.00
❑ 27 Brandon Lloyd .40 1.00
❑ 28 Charles Rogers .30 .75
❑ 29 Kelley Washington .30 .75
❑ 30 Teyo Johnson .30 .75
❑ 31 Bennie Joppru .25 .60
❑ 32 Jason Witten 1.00 2.50
❑ 33 Andrew Pinnock .30 .75
❑ 34 Jordan Gross .25 .60
❑ 35 Kwame Harris .25 .60
❑ 36 Eric Steinbach .25 .60
❑ 37 Brett Williams .25 .60
❑ 38 Terence Newman .40 1.00
❑ 39 Marcus Trufant .40 1.00
❑ 40 Andre Woolfolk .30 .75
❑ 41 Terrell Suggs .50 1.25
❑ 42 Jimmy Kennedy .30 .75
❑ 43 Boss Bailey .30 .75
❑ 44 Mike Doss .40 1.00
❑ 45 Carson Palmer CL .60 1.50
❑ 46 Carson Palmer PP 3.00 8.00
❑ 47 Byron Leftwich PP 1.00 2.50
❑ 48 Charles Rogers PP .60 1.50
❑ 49 Kyle Boller PP .75 2.00
❑ 50 Andre Johnson PP 1.50 4.00

2004 Press Pass

❑ COMPLETE SET (50) 20.00 50.00
❑ COMP.SET w/o SP's (45) 12.50 30.00
❑ 1 Casey Clausen .30 .75
❑ 2 Craig Krenzel .40 1.00
❑ 3 J.P. Losman .40 1.00
❑ 4 Eli Manning 2.50 6.00
❑ 5 Luke McCown .40 1.00
❑ 6 John Navarre .30 .75
❑ 7 Cody Pickett .30 .75
❑ 8 Philip Rivers 1.50 4.00
❑ 9 Ben Roethlisberger 3.00 8.00
❑ 10 Matt Schaub 1.00 2.50
❑ 11 Cedric Cobbs .30 .75
❑ 12 Steven Jackson 1.00 2.50
❑ 13 Kevin Jones .40 1.00
❑ 14 Greg Jones .40 1.00
❑ 15 Julius Jones .50 1.25
❑ 16 Jarrett Payton .30 .75
❑ 17 Chris Perry .40 1.00
❑ 18 Michael Turner 1.00 2.50
❑ 19 Quincy Wilson .30 .75
❑ 20 Jason Wright .25 .60
❑ 21 Bernard Berrian .40 1.00
❑ 22 Michael Clayton .40 1.00
❑ 23 Devard Darling .30 .75
❑ 24 Lee Evans .50 1.25
❑ 25 Larry Fitzgerald 1.25 3.00
❑ 26 Devery Henderson .40 1.00
❑ 27 Michael Jenkins .40 1.00
❑ 28 Darius Watts .30 .75
❑ 29 Mike Williams .30 .75
❑ 30 Roy Williams WR .50 1.25
❑ 31 Rashaun Woods .25 .60
❑ 32 Ben Troupe .30 .75
❑ 33 Shawn Andrews .30 .75
❑ 34 Robert Gallery .40 1.00
❑ 35 Tommie Harris .40 1.00
❑ 36 Vince Wilfork .40 1.00
❑ 37 Will Smith .40 1.00
❑ 38 Teddy Lehman .30 .75
❑ 39 Jonathan Vilma .40 1.00
❑ 40 D.J. Williams .40 1.00
❑ 41 DeAngelo Hall .40 1.00
❑ 42 Dunta Robinson .30 .75
❑ 43 Derrick Strait .30 .75
❑ 44 Keith Smith .25 .60
❑ 45 Eli Manning CL 1.25 3.00
❑ 46 Eli Manning PP 4.00 10.00
❑ 47 Ben Roethlisberger PP 5.00 12.00
❑ 48 Larry Fitzgerald PP 2.00 5.00
❑ 49 Roy Williams PP .75 2.00
❑ 50 Philip Rivers PP 2.50 6.00

2005 Press Pass

❑ COMPLETE SET (50) 25.00 50.00
❑ COMP.SET w/o PP'S (45) 12.50 30.00
❑ POWER PICK STATED ODDS 1:14 H/R
❑ UNPRICED HOBBY SOLO PRINT RUN 1 SET
❑ 1 Derek Anderson .40 1.00
❑ 2 Brock Berlin .30 .75
❑ 3 Charlie Frye .40 1.00
❑ 4 Gino Guidugli .25 .60
❑ 5 David Greene .30 .75
❑ 6 Stefan LeFors .30 .75
❑ 7 Dan Orlovsky .40 1.00
❑ 8 Kyle Orton .60 1.50
❑ 9 Aaron Rodgers 1.25 3.00
❑ 10 Alex Smith QB .40 1.00
❑ 11 Andrew Walter .30 .75
❑ 12 Jason White .40 1.00
❑ 13 J.J. Arrington .40 1.00
❑ 14 Ronnie Brown 1.25 3.00
❑ 15 Anthony Davis .30 .75
❑ 16 Kay-Jay Harris .30 .75
❑ 17 T.A. McLendon .25 .60
❑ 18 Ryan Moats .30 .75
❑ 19 Vernand Morency .30 .75
❑ 20 Cadillac Williams .60 1.50
❑ 21 Mark Bradley .30 .75
❑ 22 Reggie Brown .30 .75
❑ 23 Mark Clayton .40 1.00
❑ 24 Braylon Edwards 1.00 2.50

❑ 25 Fred Gibson .30 .75
❑ 26 Terrence Murphy .25 .60
❑ 27 J.R. Russell .25 .60
❑ 28 Craphonso Thorpe .30 .75
❑ 29 Roddy White .50 1.25
❑ 30 Mike Williams .30 .75
❑ 31 Troy Williamson .40 1.00
❑ 32 Heath Miller .75 2.00
❑ 33 Alex Smith TE .40 1.00
❑ 34 Khalif Barnes .25 .60
❑ 35 Jammal Brown .40 1.00
❑ 36 Brandon Browner .25 .60
❑ 37 Marlin Jackson .30 .75
❑ 38 Carlos Rogers .40 1.00
❑ 39 Antrel Rolle .40 1.00
❑ 40 Dan Cody .40 1.00
❑ 41 Erasmus James .30 .75
❑ 42 David Pollack .30 .75
❑ 43 Anttaj Hawthorne .30 .75
❑ 44 Derrick Johnson .40 1.00
❑ 45 Ronnie Brown CL .60 1.50
❑ 46 Cadillac Williams PP 1.25 3.00
❑ 47 Aaron Rodgers PP 2.50 6.00
❑ 48 Alex Smith QB PP .75 2.00
❑ 49 Braylon Edwards PP 2.00 5.00
❑ 50 Mike Williams PP .60 1.50

2006 Press Pass

❑ COMPLETE SET (50) 20.00 50.00
❑ COMP.SET w/o SP's (45) 10.00 25.00
❑ POWER PICK ODDS 1:14
❑ UNPRICED SOLO SER.#'d TO 1
❑ 1 Brodie Croyle .40 1.00
❑ 2 Jay Cutler 1.00 2.50
❑ 3 Omar Jacobs .25 .60
❑ 4 Matt Leinart .60 1.50
❑ 5 Drew Olson .25 .60
❑ 6 Michael Robinson .30 .75
❑ 7 D.J. Shockley .30 .75
❑ 8 Brad Smith .40 1.00
❑ 9 Marcus Vick .25 .60
❑ 10 Charlie Whitehurst .40 1.00
❑ 11 Vince Young 1.00 2.50
❑ 12 Joseph Addai .50 1.25
❑ 13 Reggie Bush 1.00 2.50
❑ 14 Jerome Harrison .40 1.00
❑ 15 Laurence Maroney .50 1.25
❑ 16 Leon Washington .50 1.25
❑ 17 LenDale White .50 1.25
❑ 18 DeAngelo Williams .75 2.00
❑ 19 Jason Avant .40 1.00
❑ 20 Derek Hagan .30 .75
❑ 21 Chris Hannon .30 .75
❑ 22 Santonio Holmes 1.00 2.50
❑ 23 Chad Jackson .30 .75
❑ 24 Greg Lee .25 .60
❑ 25 Sinorice Moss .40 1.00
❑ 26 Martin Nance .30 .75
❑ 27 Maurice Stovall .30 .75
❑ 28 Travis Wilson .25 .60
❑ 29 Dominique Byrd .30 .75
❑ 30 Vernon Davis .40 1.00
❑ 31 Marcedes Lewis .40 1.00
❑ 32 Leonard Pope .40 1.00
❑ 33 Jimmy Williams .40 1.00
❑ 34 Darnell Bing .30 .75
❑ 35 Michael Huff .40 1.00
❑ 36 Mathias Kiwanuka .50 1.25
❑ 37 Mario Williams .50 1.25
❑ 38 Haloti Ngata .40 1.00
❑ 39 Gabe Watson .25 .60
❑ 40 Rodrique Wright .25 .60
❑ 41 D'Brickashaw Ferguson .40 1.00
❑ 42 Chad Greenway .40 1.00
❑ 43 A.J. Hawk .60 1.50
❑ 44 DeMeco Ryans .50 1.25
❑ 45 Reggie Bush CL .50 1.25
❑ 46 Reggie Bush PP 2.00 5.00
❑ 47 Matt Leinart PP 1.25 3.00
❑ 48 Vince Young PP 2.00 5.00
❑ 49 A.J. Hawk PP 1.25 3.00
❑ 50 DeAngelo Williams PP 1.50 4.00

2007 Press Pass

❑ COMPLETE SET (105) 25.00 60.00
❑ COMP.SET w/o SP's (100) 15.00 40.00
❑ 101-105 POWER PICK ODDS 1:14
❑ UNPRICED SOLO SER.#'d TO 1
❑ 1 Chris Leak .25 .60
❑ 2 Brady Quinn .60 1.50
❑ 3 JaMarcus Russell .40 1.00
❑ 4 Troy Smith .40 1.00
❑ 5 Drew Stanton .25 .60
❑ 6 Michael Bush .30 .75
❑ 7 Tony Hunt .30 .75
❑ 8 Kenny Irons .30 .75
❑ 9 Brandon Jackson .30 .75
❑ 10 Marshawn Lynch .50 1.25
❑ 11 Adrian Peterson 2.50 6.00
❑ 12 Antonio Pittman .30 .75
❑ 13 Brian Leonard .25 .60
❑ 14 Dwayne Bowe .50 1.25
❑ 15 Ted Ginn Jr. .50 1.25
❑ 16 Anthony Gonzalez .40 1.00
❑ 17 Dwayne Jarrett .30 .75
❑ 18 Calvin Johnson .75 2.00
❑ 19 Robert Meachem .30 .75
❑ 20 Sidney Rice .60 1.50
❑ 21 Garrett Wolfe .30 .75
❑ 22 Leon Hall .30 .75
❑ 23 Gaines Adams .30 .75
❑ 24 Jamaal Anderson .25 .60
❑ 25 Alan Branch .25 .60
❑ 26 Amobi Okoye .30 .75
❑ 27 Paul Posluszny .40 1.00
❑ 28 Lawrence Timmons .30 .75
❑ 29 LaRon Landry .40 1.00
❑ 30 Reggie Nelson .25 .60
❑ 31 John Beck .30 .75
❑ 32 Trent Edwards .50 1.25
❑ 33 Kevin Kolb .50 1.25
❑ 34 Jordan Palmer .30 .75
❑ 35 Lorenzo Booker .30 .75
❑ 36 Darius Walker .25 .60
❑ 37 Dwayne Wright .25 .60
❑ 38 DeShawn Wynn .30 .75
❑ 39 Zach Miller .30 .75
❑ 40 Greg Olsen .40 1.00
❑ 41 Aundrae Allison .25 .60
❑ 42 Dallas Baker .25 .60
❑ 43 Jason Hill .30 .75
❑ 44 Steve Smith USC .50 1.25
❑ 45 Darrelle Revis .40 1.00
❑ 46 Aaron Ross .30 .75
❑ 47 Adam Carriker .25 .60
❑ 48 Charles Johnson .20 .50
❑ 49 Jarvis Moss .30 .75
❑ 50 Patrick Willis .50 1.25
❑ 51 John Beck LDR .30 .75
❑ 52 JaMarcus Russell LDR .40 1.00
❑ 53 Troy Smith LDR .40 1.00
❑ 54 Jordan Palmer LDR .30 .75
❑ 55 Kevin Kolb LDR .50 1.25
❑ 56 Brady Quinn LDR .60 1.50
❑ 57 Garrett Wolfe LDR .30 .75
❑ 58 Dwayne Wright LDR .25 .60
❑ 59 Ahmad Bradshaw LDR .40 1.00
❑ 60 Johnnie Lee Higgins LDR .30 .75
❑ 61 Robert Meachem LDR .30 .75
❑ 62 Rhema McKnight LDR .25 .60
❑ 63 Calvin Johnson LDR .75 2.00
❑ 64 Joel Filani LDR .25 .60
❑ 65 Dwayne Bowe LDR .50 1.25
❑ 66 Daymeion Hughes LDR .25 .60
❑ 67 Reggie Nelson LDR .25 .60
❑ 68 LaMarr Woodley TC .30 .75
❑ 69 Troy Smith TC .40 1.00
❑ 70 Brady Quinn TC .60 1.50
❑ 71 Calvin Johnson TC .75 2.00
❑ 72 Paul Posluszny TC .40 1.00
❑ 73 Aaron Ross TC .30 .75
❑ 74 Patrick Willis TC .50 1.25
❑ 75 Troy Smith AA .40 1.00
❑ 76 Marshawn Lynch AA .50 1.25
❑ 77 Johnnie Lee Higgins AA .30 .75
❑ 78 Dwayne Jarrett AA .30 .75
❑ 79 Calvin Johnson AA .75 2.00
❑ 80 Robert Meachem AA .30 .75
❑ 81 Zach Miller AA .30 .75
❑ 82 Gaines Adams AA .30 .75
❑ 83 Paul Posluszny AA .40 1.00
❑ 84 Leon Hall AA .30 .75
❑ 85 LaRon Landry AA .40 1.00
❑ 86 Reggie Nelson AA .25 .60
❑ 87 Aaron Ross AA .30 .75
❑ 88 M.Lynch/D.Hughes TM .50 1.25
❑ 89 C.Leak/R.Nelson TM .25 .60
❑ 90 L.Booker/L.Thomas TM .30 .75
❑ 91 J.Russell/D.Bowe TM .40 1.00
❑ 92 B.Jackson/A.Carriker TM .30 .75
❑ 93 B.Quinn/D.Walker TM .60 1.50
❑ 94 T.Smith/A.Pittman TM .40 1.00
❑ 95 T.Ginn Jr./A.Gonzalez TM .40 1.00
❑ 96 T.Hunt/P.Posluszny TM .40 1.00
❑ 97 D.Jarrett/S.Smith TM .50 1.25
❑ 98 Joseph Addai SS .60 1.50
❑ 99 Reggie Bush SS .75 2.00
❑ 100 Vince Young SS .60 1.50
❑ 101 Brady Quinn PP 1.50 4.00
❑ 102 JaMarcus Russell PP 1.00 2.50
❑ 103 Adrian Peterson PP 6.00 15.00
❑ 104 Calvin Johnson PP 2.00 5.00
❑ 105 Ted Ginn Jr. PP 1.25 3.00

2008 Press Pass

❑ COMPLETE SET (105) 20.00 50.00
❑ COMP.SET w/o SP's (100) 12.00 30.00
❑ 101-105 POWER PICK ODDS 1:14
❑ 1 Glenn Dorsey .30 .75
❑ 2 Chris Long .30 .75
❑ 3 Dan Connor .30 .75
❑ 4 Aqib Talib .30 .75
❑ 5 Kenny Phillips .30 .75
❑ 6 Erik Ainge .30 .75
❑ 7 John David Booty .30 .75
❑ 8 Colt Brennan .50 1.25
❑ 9 Brian Brohm .30 .75
❑ 10 Joe Flacco 1.00 2.50
❑ 11 Chad Henne .50 1.25
❑ 12 Matt Ryan 1.25 3.00
❑ 13 Andre Woodson .30 .75
❑ 14 Jamaal Charles .50 1.25
❑ 15 Matt Forte .60 1.50
❑ 17 Jacob Hester .30 .75
❑ 18 Chris Johnson 1.00 2.50
❑ 19 Felix Jones .60 1.50
❑ 20 Darren McFadden .60 1.50
❑ 21 Rashard Mendenhall .60 1.50
❑ 22 Ray Rice .60 1.50
❑ 23 Steve Slaton .40 1.00
❑ 24 Kevin Smith .50 1.25
❑ 25 Jonathan Stewart .60 1.50
❑ 26 Fred Davis .30 .75
❑ 27 Adrian Arrington .25 .60
❑ 28 Earl Bennett .30 .75
❑ 29 Adarius Bowman .25 .60
❑ 30 Early Doucet .30 .75
❑ 31 James Hardy .25 .60

Card	Low	High
❑ 32 DJ Hall	.25	.60
❑ 33 DeSean Jackson	.60	1.50
❑ 34 Malcolm Kelly	.30	.75
❑ 35 Mario Manningham	.30	.75
❑ 36 Limas Sweed	.30	.75
❑ 37 Devin Thomas	.30	.75
❑ 38 Lavelle Hawkins	.25	.60
❑ 39 Andre Caldwell	.30	.75
❑ 40 Vernon Gholston	.30	.75
❑ 41 Derrick Harvey	.25	.60
❑ 42 Keith Rivers	.30	.75
❑ 43 Mike Jenkins	.30	.75
❑ 44 Leodis McKelvin	.30	.75
❑ 45 Dennis Dixon	.30	.75
❑ 46 Josh Johnson	.30	.75
❑ 47 Tashard Choice	.30	.75
❑ 48 Chauncey Washington	.25	.60
❑ 49 John Carlson	.30	.75
❑ 50 Donnie Avery	.40	1.00
❑ 51 Darren McFadden TC	.50	1.25
❑ 52 Matt Ryan TC	1.00	2.50
❑ 53 Glenn Dorsey TC	.25	.60
❑ 54 Dan Connor TC	.25	.60
❑ 55 Fred Davis TC	.25	.60
❑ 56 Chris Long TC	.25	.60
❑ 57 Dennis Dixon COL	.25	.60
❑ 58 Colt Brennan COL	.40	1.00
❑ 59 Matt Ryan COL	1.00	2.50
❑ 60 Brian Brohm COL	.25	.60
❑ 61 Andre Woodson COL	.25	.60
❑ 62 Erik Ainge COL	.25	.60
❑ 63 Kevin Smith COL	.40	1.00
❑ 64 Matt Forte COL	.50	1.25
❑ 65 Darren McFadden COL	.50	1.25
❑ 66 Jonathan Stewart COL	.50	1.25
❑ 67 Rashard Mendenhall COL	.50	1.25
❑ 68 Ray Rice COL	.50	1.25
❑ 69 Jamaal Charles COL	.40	1.00
❑ 70 Chris Johnson COL	.75	2.00
❑ 71 Jordy Nelson COL	.30	.75
❑ 72 Davone Bess COL	.30	.75
❑ 73 Donnie Avery COL	.30	.75
❑ 74 Devin Thomas COL	.25	.60
❑ 75 Mario Manningham COL	.25	.60
❑ 76 Dan Connor AA	.25	.60
❑ 77 Glenn Dorsey AA	.25	.60
❑ 78 Mike Jenkins AA	.25	.60
❑ 79 J Leman AA	.20	.50
❑ 80 Chris Long AA	.25	.60
❑ 81 Darren McFadden AA	.50	1.25
❑ 82 Jordy Nelson AA	.30	.75
❑ 83 Martin Rucker AA	.20	.50
❑ 84 Matt Ryan AA	1.00	2.50
❑ 85 Kevin Smith AA	.40	1.00
❑ 86 Aqib Talib AA	.25	.60
❑ 87 Steve Slaton AA	.30	.75
❑ 88 Jonathan Stewart AA	.50	1.25
❑ 89 DeSean Jackson AA	.50	1.25
❑ 90 Woodson/K.Burton TM	.20	.50
❑ 91 G.Dorsey/J.Hester TM	.20	.50
❑ 92 B.Brohm/H.Douglas TM	.15	.40
❑ 93 Henne/Manningham TM	.30	.75
❑ 94 J.Charles/L.Sweed TM	.30	.75
❑ 95 J.Booty/Washington TM	.20	.50
❑ 96 J.Forsett/D.Jackson TM	.40	1.00
❑ 97 M.Flynn/E.Doucet TM	.20	.50
❑ 99 D.Dixon/J.Stewart TM	.40	1.00
❑ 100 McFadden/Jones TM	.40	1.00
❑ 101 Darren McFadden PP	1.25	3.00
❑ 102 Matt Ryan PP	2.50	6.00
❑ 103 Brian Brohm PP	.60	1.50
❑ 104 Jonathan Stewart PP	1.25	3.00
❑ 105 Malcolm Kelly PP	.60	1.50

2009 Press Pass

Card	Low	High
❑ COMPLETE SET (105)	20.00	50.00
❑ COMP.SET w/o PP's (100)	12.00	30.00
❑ 1 Rhett Bomar	.25	.60
❑ 2 Chase Daniel	.40	1.00
❑ 3 Nate Davis	.30	.75
❑ 4 Josh Freeman	.60	1.50
❑ 5 Graham Harrell	.30	.75
❑ 6 Mark Sanchez	1.25	3.00
❑ 7 Matthew Stafford	1.00	2.50
❑ 8 Pat White	.50	1.25
❑ 9 Andre Brown	.25	.60
❑ 10 Donald Brown	.60	1.50
❑ 11 Glen Coffee	.40	1.00
❑ 12 James Davis	.30	.75
❑ 13 Mike Goodson	.30	.75
❑ 14 Shonn Greene	.60	1.50
❑ 15 P.J. Hill	.25	.60
❑ 16 Ian Johnson	.30	.75
❑ 17 Jeremiah Johnson	.30	.75
❑ 18 LeSean McCoy	.60	1.50
❑ 19 Knowshon Moreno	.75	2.00
❑ 20 Javon Ringer	.30	.75
❑ 21 Chris Wells	.75	2.00
❑ 22 Ramses Barden	.25	.60
❑ 23 Kenny Britt	.50	1.25
❑ 24 Michael Crabtree	.75	2.00
❑ 25 Percy Harvin	1.00	2.50
❑ 26 Darrius Heyward-Bey	.50	1.25
❑ 27 Juaquin Iglesias	.30	.75
❑ 28 Jeremy Maclin	.60	1.50
❑ 29 Mohamed Massaquoi	.30	.75
❑ 30 Louis Murphy	.30	.75
❑ 31 Hakeem Nicks	.60	1.50
❑ 32 Brian Robiskie	.30	.75
❑ 33 Brandon Tate	.25	.60
❑ 34 Derrick Williams	.30	.75
❑ 35 Chase Coffman	.25	.60
❑ 36 Brandon Pettigrew	.40	1.00
❑ 37 Everette Brown	.30	.75
❑ 38 Tyson Jackson	.30	.75
❑ 39 Kenny McKinley	.30	.75
❑ 40 Aaron Maybin	.30	.75
❑ 41 Brian Orakpo	.40	1.00
❑ 42 Aaron Curry	.40	1.00
❑ 43 Brian Cushing	.40	1.00
❑ 44 James Laurinaitis	.40	1.00
❑ 45 Rey Maualuga	.50	1.25
❑ 46 Vontae Davis	.30	.75
❑ 47 Victor Harris	.30	.75
❑ 48 Malcolm Jenkins	.30	.75
❑ 49 D.J. Moore	.25	.60
❑ 50 Alphonso Smith	.25	.60
❑ 51 Chase Coffman TC	.20	.50
❑ 52 Michael Crabtree TC	.60	1.50
❑ 53 Shonn Greene TC	.50	1.25
❑ 54 Graham Harrell TC	.25	.60
❑ 55 Malcolm Jenkins TC	.25	.60
❑ 56 James Laurinaitis TC	.30	.75
❑ 57 Rey Maualuga TC	.40	1.00
❑ 58 Brian Orakpo TC	.30	.75
❑ 59 Kenny Britt LL	.40	1.00
❑ 60 Donald Brown LL	.50	1.25
❑ 61 Glen Coffee LL	.30	.75
❑ 62 Quan Cosby LL	.20	.50
❑ 63 Michael Crabtree LL	.60	1.50
❑ 64 Chase Daniel LL	.30	.75
❑ 65 Nate Davis LL	.25	.60
❑ 66 Jarett Dillard LL	.25	.60
❑ 67 Shonn Greene LL	.50	1.25
❑ 68 Graham Harrell LL	.25	.60
❑ 69 Austin Collie LL	.50	1.25
❑ 70 Gartrell Johnson LL	.20	.50
❑ 71 Jeremy Maclin LL	.50	1.25
❑ 72 LeSean McCoy LL	.50	1.25
❑ 73 Knowshon Moreno LL	.60	1.50
❑ 74 Hakeem Nicks LL	.50	1.25
❑ 75 Javon Ringer LL	.25	.60
❑ 76 Mark Sanchez LL	1.00	2.50
❑ 77 Matthew Stafford LL	.75	2.00
❑ 78 Donald Brown AA	.50	1.25
❑ 79 Chase Coffman AA	.20	.50
❑ 80 Michael Crabtree AA	.60	1.50
❑ 81 Aaron Curry AA	.30	.75
❑ 82 Jarett Dillard AA	.25	.60
❑ 83 Shonn Greene AA	.50	1.25
❑ 84 Malcolm Jenkins AA	.25	.60
❑ 85 James Laurinaitis AA	.30	.75
❑ 86 Jeremy Maclin AA	.50	1.25
❑ 87 Rey Maualuga AA	.40	1.00
❑ 88 Brian Orakpo AA	.30	.75
❑ 89 Javon Ringer AA	.25	.60
❑ 90 Alphonso Smith AA	.20	.50
❑ 91 M.Stafford/K.Moreno TM	.60	1.50
❑ 92 M.Sanchez/R.Maualuga TM	.75	2.00
❑ 93 G.Harrell/M.Crabtree TM	.50	1.25
❑ 94 C.Daniel/J.Maclin TM	.40	1.00
❑ 95 C.Wells/B.Robiskie TM	.50	1.25
❑ 96 P.Harvin/L.Murphy TM	.60	1.50
❑ 97 H.Nicks/B.Tate TM	.15	.40
❑ 98 A.Maybin/D.Williams TM	.20	.50
❑ 99 M.Jenkins/J.Laurinaitis TM	.25	.60
❑ 100 J.Ringer/B.Hoyer TM	.20	.50
❑ 101 Matthew Stafford PP	2.00	5.00
❑ 102 Mark Sanchez PP	2.50	6.00
❑ 103 Michael Crabtree PP	1.50	4.00
❑ 104 Chris Wells PP	1.50	4.00
❑ 105 Jeremy Maclin PP	1.25	3.00

2002 Press Pass JE

Card	Low	High
❑ COMPLETE SET (45)	10.00	25.00
❑ 1 David Carr	.40	1.00
❑ 2 Julius Peppers	.60	1.50
❑ 3 Joey Harrington	.40	1.00
❑ 4 Mike Williams	.25	.60
❑ 5 Quentin Jammer	.40	1.00
❑ 6 Ryan Sims	.40	1.00
❑ 7 Bryant McKinnie	.25	.60
❑ 8 Roy Williams	.50	1.25
❑ 9 John Henderson	.40	1.00
❑ 10 Wendell Bryant	.25	.60
❑ 11 Donte Stallworth	.40	1.00
❑ 12 Jeremy Shockey	.60	1.50
❑ 13 William Green	.30	.75
❑ 14 Phillip Buchanon	.40	1.00
❑ 15 T.J. Duckett	.40	1.00
❑ 16 Ashley Lelie	.40	1.00
❑ 17 Javon Walker	.40	1.00
❑ 18 Daniel Graham	.30	.75
❑ 19 Jerramy Stevens	.40	1.00
❑ 20 Patrick Ramsey	.40	1.00
❑ 21 Jabar Gaffney	.40	1.00
❑ 22 DeShaun Foster	.40	1.00
❑ 23 Kalimba Edwards	.30	.75
❑ 24 Josh Reed	.30	.75
❑ 25 Mike Pearson	.25	.60
❑ 26 Andre Davis	.30	.75
❑ 27 Reche Caldwell	.40	1.00
❑ 28 Clinton Portis	1.00	2.50
❑ 29 Maurice Morris	.40	1.00
❑ 30 Ladell Betts	.40	1.00
❑ 31 Antwaan Randle El	.40	1.00
❑ 32 Antonio Bryant	.50	1.25
❑ 33 Josh McCown	.40	1.00
❑ 34 Lamar Gordon	.40	1.00
❑ 35 Marquise Walker	.25	.60
❑ 36 Cliff Russell	.25	.60
❑ 37 Brian Westbrook	1.25	3.00
❑ 38 Eric Crouch	.40	1.00
❑ 39 Jonathan Wells	.40	1.00
❑ 40 David Garrard	.60	1.50
❑ 41 Rohan Davey	.40	1.00
❑ 42 Ron Johnson	.30	.75
❑ 43 Kurt Kittner	.25	.60
❑ 44 Adrian Peterson	.40	1.00
❑ 45 David Carr CL	.30	.75

2003 Press Pass JE

Card	Low	High
❑ COMPLETE SET (45)	10.00	25.00
❑ 1 Boss Bailey	.30	.75
❑ 2 Brad Banks	.30	.75
❑ 3 Anquan Boldin	1.00	2.50
❑ 4 Kyle Boller	.40	1.00
❑ 5 Chris Brown	.40	1.00
❑ 6 Avon Cobourne	.25	.60
❑ 7 Ken Dorsey	.30	.75
❑ 8 Justin Fargas	.40	1.00
❑ 9 Talman Gardner	.25	.60
❑ 10 Jason Gesser	.30	.75
❑ 11 Earnest Graham	.40	1.00
❑ 12 Jordon Gross	.25	.60
❑ 13 Rex Grossman	.40	1.00
❑ 14 Kwame Harris	.25	.60
❑ 15 Taylor Jacobs	.30	.75
❑ 16 Larry Johnson	.50	1.25
❑ 17 Bryant Johnson	.40	1.00
❑ 18 Andre Johnson	.75	2.00
❑ 19 Teyo Johnson	.30	.75
❑ 20 William Joseph	.25	.60
❑ 21 Bennie Joppru	.25	.60
❑ 22 Jimmy Kennedy	.30	.75
❑ 23 Kliff Kingsbury	.30	.75
❑ 24 Byron Leftwich	.50	1.25
❑ 25 Brandon Lloyd	.40	1.00
❑ 26 Jerome McDougle	.25	.60
❑ 27 Willis McGahee	.75	2.00
❑ 28 Terence Newman	.40	1.00
❑ 29 Carson Palmer	1.50	4.00
❑ 30 Terry Pierce	.25	.60
❑ 31 Dave Ragone	.25	.60
❑ 32 DeWayne Robertson	.30	.75
❑ 33 Charles Rogers	.30	.75
❑ 34 Chris Simms	.40	1.00
❑ 35 Musa Smith	.30	.75
❑ 36 Onterrio Smith	.30	.75
❑ 37 Brian St.Pierre	.40	1.00
❑ 38 Lee Suggs	.30	.75
❑ 39 Terrell Suggs	.50	1.25
❑ 40 Marcus Trufant	.40	1.00
❑ 41 Seneca Wallace	.40	1.00
❑ 42 Kelley Washington	.30	.75
❑ 43 Jason Witten	1.00	2.50
❑ 44 Andre Woolfolk	.30	.75
❑ 45 Byron Leftwich CL	.20	.50

2006 Press Pass Legends

Card	Low	High
❑ COMP.SET w/o SP's (90)	20.00	40.00
❑ UNPRICED PLATINUM PRINT RUN 1		
❑ UNPRICED PRINT PLATES SER.#'d TO 1		
❑ UNPRICED RED PRINT RUN 5		
❑ 1 Brodie Croyle	.50	1.25
❑ 2 Tarvaris Jackson	.50	1.25
❑ 3 Derek Hagan	.40	1.00
❑ 4 Devin Aromashodu	.50	1.25
❑ 5 Mathias Kiwanuka	.60	1.50
❑ 6 Omar Jacobs	.30	.75
❑ 7 Tye Hill	.40	1.00
❑ 8 Charlie Whitehurst	.50	1.25
❑ 9 Joe Klopfenstein	.40	1.00
❑ 10 Chad Jackson	.40	1.00
❑ 11 Leon Washington	.60	1.50
❑ 12 Ernie Sims	.40	1.00
❑ 13 Leonard Pope	.50	1.25
❑ 14 D.J. Shockley	.40	1.00
❑ 15 Joseph Addai	.60	1.50
❑ 16 Vernon Davis	.50	1.25
❑ 17 DeAngelo Williams	1.00	2.50
❑ 18 Sinorice Moss	.50	1.25
❑ 19 Martin Nance	.40	1.00
❑ 20 Jason Avant	.50	1.25
❑ 21 Laurence Maroney	.60	1.50
❑ 22 Brad Smith	.50	1.25
❑ 23 Mario Williams	.60	1.50
❑ 24 Brett Basanez	.50	1.25
❑ 25 Anthony Fasano	.50	1.25
❑ 26 Maurice Stovall	.40	1.00
❑ 27 Bobby Carpenter	.40	1.00
❑ 28 A.J. Hawk	.75	2.00
❑ 29 Santonio Holmes	1.25	3.00
❑ 30 Ashton Youboty	.40	1.00
❑ 31 Travis Wilson	.30	.75
❑ 32 Haloti Ngata	.50	1.25
❑ 33 Demetrius Williams	.40	1.00
❑ 34 Mike Hass	.50	1.25
❑ 35 Michael Robinson	.40	1.00
❑ 36 Greg Lee	.30	.75
❑ 37 Cory Rodgers	.50	1.25
❑ 38 Michael Huff	.50	1.25
❑ 39A Vince Young Clr	1.25	3.00
❑ 39B Vince Young B&W	2.00	5.00
❑ 40 Reggie McNeal	.40	1.00
❑ 41 Bruce Gradkowski	.50	1.25
❑ 42 Darrell Hackney	.40	1.00
❑ 43 Maurice Drew	1.00	2.50
❑ 44 Marcedes Lewis	.50	1.25
❑ 45 Drew Olson	.30	.75
❑ 46 Darnell Bing	.40	1.00
❑ 47A Reggie Bush Clr	1.25	3.00
❑ 47B Reggie Bush B&W	2.00	5.00
❑ 48 Dominique Byrd	.40	1.00
❑ 49A Matt Leinart Clr	.75	2.00
❑ 49B Matt Leinart B&W	1.25	3.00
❑ 50 LenDale White	.60	1.50
❑ 51A Jay Cutler Clr	1.25	3.00
❑ 51B Jay Cutler B&W	2.00	5.00
❑ 52 D'Brickashaw Ferguson	.50	1.25
❑ 53 Marcus Vick	.30	.75
❑ 54 Jimmy Williams	.50	1.25
❑ 55 Jerome Harrison	.50	1.25
❑ 56 Ozzie Newsome	.50	1.25
❑ 57 Ken Stabler	.75	2.00
❑ 58A Bo Jackson B&W	.75	2.00
❑ 58B Bo Jackson Clr	1.25	3.00
❑ 59 Steve Spurrier	.75	2.00
❑ 60 Charlie Ward	.50	1.25
❑ 61 Fran Tarkenton	.75	2.00
❑ 62 Herschel Walker	.50	1.25
❑ 63 Billy Cannon	.50	1.25
❑ 64 Y.A. Tittle	.60	1.50
❑ 65 Roger Craig	.60	1.50
❑ 66 Tommie Frazier	.50	1.25
❑ 67 Rocky Bleier	.60	1.50
❑ 68A Tim Brown B&W	.60	1.50
❑ 68B Tim Brown Clr	1.00	2.50
❑ 69 Paul Hornung	.60	1.50
❑ 70 Joe Theismann	.60	1.50
❑ 71 Howard Cassady	.50	1.25
❑ 72 Archie Griffin	.40	1.00
❑ 73 Jack Tatum	.40	1.00
❑ 74 Paul Warfield	.50	1.25
❑ 75 Brian Bosworth	.60	1.50
❑ 76 Billy Sims	.50	1.25
❑ 77A Barry Sanders B&W	1.00	2.50
❑ 77B Barry Sanders Clr	1.50	4.00
❑ 78 Thurman Thomas	.50	1.25
❑ 79 Jack Ham	.50	1.25
❑ 80 Franco Harris	.60	1.50
❑ 81A Dan Marino B&W	1.25	3.00
❑ 81B Dan Marino Clr	2.00	5.00
❑ 82 Len Dawson	.60	1.50
❑ 83 Jim Plunkett	.50	1.25
❑ 84 Bob Lilly	.50	1.25
❑ 85 Steve Largent	.60	1.50
❑ 86 Ronnie Lott	.50	1.25
❑ 87 Bobby Bowden	.60	1.50
❑ 88 Bo Schembechler	.40	1.00
❑ 89 Darrell Royal	.50	1.25
❑ 90 Ara Parseghian	.50	1.25
❑ 91 Johnny Lattner SP	2.00	5.00
❑ 92 Desmond Howard SP	2.50	6.00

2007 Press Pass Legends

Card	Low	High
❑ COMPLETE SET (100)	20.00	40.00
❑ 1 Kenneth Darby	.50	1.25
❑ 2 Chris Henry	.40	1.00
❑ 3 Zach Miller	.30	.75
❑ 4 Jamaal Anderson	.40	1.00
❑ 5 Kenny Irons	.50	1.25
❑ 6 Courtney Taylor	.40	1.00
❑ 7 John Beck	.50	1.25
❑ 8 Daymeion Hughes	.40	1.00
❑ 9 Marshawn Lynch	.75	2.00
❑ 10 Gaines Adams	.50	1.25
❑ 11 Chansi Stuckey	.50	1.25
❑ 12 Aundrae Allison	.40	1.00
❑ 13 Dallas Baker	.40	1.00
❑ 14 Chris Leak	.40	1.00
❑ 15 Jarvis Moss	.50	1.25
❑ 16 Reggie Nelson	.40	1.00
❑ 17 DeShawn Wynn	.50	1.25
❑ 18 Paul Williams	.40	1.00
❑ 19 Dwayne Wright	.40	1.00
❑ 20 Lorenzo Booker	.50	1.25
❑ 21 Buster Davis	.40	1.00
❑ 22 Lawrence Timmons	.50	1.25
❑ 23 Quentin Moses	.40	1.00
❑ 24 Calvin Johnson	1.25	3.00
❑ 25 Kevin Kolb	.75	2.00
❑ 26 Michael Bush	.50	1.25
❑ 27 Amobi Okoye	.50	1.25
❑ 28 Kolby Smith	.50	1.25
❑ 29 Joseph Addai	.50	1.25
❑ 30 Dwayne Bowe	.75	2.00
❑ 31 Craig Buster Davis	.50	1.25
❑ 32 LaRon Landry	.60	1.50
❑ 33 JaMarcus Russell	.60	1.50
❑ 34 Greg Olsen	.60	1.50
❑ 35 Alan Branch	.40	1.00
❑ 36 Leon Hall	.50	1.25
❑ 37 Drew Stanton	.40	1.00
❑ 38 Adam Carriker	.40	1.00
❑ 39 Brandon Jackson	.50	1.25
❑ 40 Jeff Rowe	.40	1.00
❑ 41 Garrett Wolfe	.50	1.25
❑ 42 Brady Quinn	1.00	2.50
❑ 43 Ted Ginn Jr.	.75	2.00
❑ 44 Anthony Gonzalez	.60	1.50
❑ 45 Antonio Pittman	.50	1.25
❑ 46 Troy Smith	.60	1.50
❑ 47 Adrian Peterson	4.00	10.00
❑ 48 Patrick Willis	.75	2.00
❑ 49 Tony Hunt	.50	1.25
❑ 50 Paul Posluszny	.60	1.50
❑ 51 Darrelle Revis	.60	1.50
❑ 52 Brian Leonard	.40	1.00
❑ 53 Sidney Rice	1.00	2.50
❑ 54 Trent Edwards	.75	2.00
❑ 55 Robert Meachem	.50	1.25
❑ 56 Michael Griffin	.50	1.25
❑ 57 Aaron Ross	.50	1.25
❑ 58 Vince Young	.50	1.25
❑ 59 Joel Filani	.40	1.00
❑ 60 Dwayne Jarrett	.50	1.25
❑ 61 Steve Smith USC	.75	2.00
❑ 62 Johnnie Lee Higgins	.50	1.25
❑ 63 Jordan Palmer	.50	1.25
❑ 64 David Clowney	.50	1.25
❑ 65 Jason Hill	.50	1.25
❑ 66 Ozzie Newsome	.50	1.25
❑ 67 Ken Stabler	.75	2.00
❑ 68 Bart Starr	1.00	2.50
❑ 69 Pat Sullivan	.40	1.00
❑ 70 Doug Flutie	.60	1.50

Card	Low	High
71 Ty Detmer	.40	1.00
72 Danny Wuerffel	.40	1.00
73 Jack Youngblood	.50	1.25
74 Fred Biletnikoff	.60	1.50
75 Herschel Walker	.50	1.25
76 Dick Butkus	.75	2.00
77 Y.A. Tittle	.60	1.50
78 Randy White	.50	1.25
79 Jerry Rice	1.00	2.50
80 Joe Bellino	.40	1.00
81 Tommie Frazier	.50	1.25
82 Tom Osborne	.50	1.25
83 Tom Rathman	.40	1.00
84 Johnny Rodgers	.40	1.00
85 Mike Rozier	.40	1.00
86 Jerome Bettis	.60	1.50
87 Paul Hornung	.60	1.50
88 Alan Page	.40	1.00
89 Rudy Ruettiger	.60	1.50
90 Joe Theismann	.60	1.50
91 Archie Griffin	.40	1.00
92 Brian Bosworth	.60	1.50
93 Steve Owens	.40	1.00
94 Billy Sims	.50	1.25
95 Archie Manning	.60	1.50
96 Raymond Berry	.50	1.25
97 James Lofton	.40	1.00
98 Marcus Allen	.60	1.50
99 John Hannah	.40	1.00
100 Dick Butkus CL	.50	1.25

2008 Press Pass Legends Bowl Edition

Card	Low	High
COMPLETE SET (100)		
1 Troy Aikman	2.50	6.00
2 Tedy Bruschi	1.50	4.00
3 Earl Campbell	2.00	5.00
4 Cris Collinsworth	1.50	4.00
5 Bill Cowher	2.00	5.00
6 Eric Dickerson	1.50	4.00
7 Glenn Dorsey	1.00	2.50
8 Brett Favre	4.00	10.00
9 Joe Flacco	3.00	8.00
10 Matt Forte	2.00	5.00
11 Tommie Frazier	1.50	4.00
12 DeSean Jackson	2.00	5.00
13 Chris Johnson	3.00	8.00
14 Jimmy Johnson	1.50	4.00
15 Felix Jones	2.00	5.00
16 Lee Roy Jordan	1.50	4.00
17 Jim Kelly	2.00	5.00
18 Jack Lambert	2.00	5.00
19 Chris Long	1.00	2.50
20 Darren McFadden	2.00	5.00
21 Rashard Mendenhall	2.00	5.00
22 Joe Montana	5.00	12.00
23 Warren Moon	2.50	6.00
24 Ray Rice	2.00	5.00
25 Eddie Royal	1.50	4.00
26 Matt Ryan	4.00	10.00
27 Gale Sayers	2.50	6.00
28 Mike Singletary	2.00	5.00
29 Steve Slaton	1.25	3.00
30 Kevin Smith	1.50	4.00
31 Chris Spielman	1.50	4.00
32 Ken Stabler	2.00	5.00
33 Jonathan Stewart	2.00	5.00
34 Barry Switzer	2.00	5.00
35 Herschel Walker	1.50	4.00
36 Steve Young	2.50	6.00
37 Derrick Brooks	1.25	3.00
38 Joey Galloway	1.25	3.00
39 Frank Gore	1.25	3.00
40 Paul Hornung	2.00	5.00
41 Sonny Jurgensen	1.50	4.00
42 Ray Lewis	1.50	4.00
43 George Rogers	1.25	3.00
44 Dick Butkus	2.50	6.00
45 Cris Carter	2.00	5.00
46 Bob Griese	2.00	5.00
47 Bo Jackson	2.50	6.00
48 Billy Kilmer	1.50	4.00
49 Floyd Little	1.25	3.00
50 Tommy McDonald	1.50	4.00
51 Tom Rathman	1.50	4.00
52 Billy Sims	1.50	4.00
53 Steve Spurrier	2.00	5.00
54 Aaron Kampman	1.25	3.00
55 Mike Rozier	1.25	3.00
56 Y.A. Tittle	2.00	5.00
57 Craig Morton	1.25	3.00
58 Hugh McElhenny	1.25	3.00
59 Roger Craig	1.50	4.00
60 Ty Detmer	1.25	3.00
61 Craig James	1.50	4.00
62 Tommy Nobis	1.25	3.00
63 Pat Sullivan	1.25	3.00
64 Joe Theismann	2.00	5.00
65 Zach Thomas	1.25	3.00
66 Danny Wuerffel	1.25	3.00
67 Raymond Berry	1.50	4.00
68 Rocky Bleier	1.50	4.00
69 Billy Cannon	1.25	3.00
70 Anthony Carter	1.25	3.00
71 John Jefferson	1.25	3.00
72 Johnny Rodgers	1.25	3.00
73 Charles White	1.25	3.00
74 Sam Huff	1.50	4.00
75 Paul Warfield	1.50	4.00
76 Donnie Avery	1.25	3.00
77 Davone Bess	1.25	3.00
78 John David Booty	1.00	2.50
79 Colt Brennan	1.50	4.00
80 Jamaal Charles	1.50	4.00
81 Harry Douglas	.75	2.00
82 Chad Henne	1.50	4.00
83 Malcolm Kelly	1.00	2.50
84 Josh Morgan	1.00	2.50
85 Jordy Nelson	1.25	3.00
86 Limas Sweed	1.00	2.50
87 Devin Thomas	1.00	2.50
88 James Lofton	1.25	3.00
89 Donnie Avery	1.25	3.00
90 Joe Flacco	3.00	8.00
91 Matt Forte	2.00	5.00
92 DeSean Jackson	2.00	5.00
93 Chris Johnson	3.00	8.00
94 Felix Jones	2.00	5.00
95 Darren McFadden	2.00	5.00
96 Eddie Royal	1.50	4.00
97 Matt Ryan	4.00	10.00
98 Steve Slaton	1.25	3.00
99 Kevin Smith	1.50	4.00
100 Jonathan Stewart	2.00	5.00

2001 Press Pass SE

Card	Low	High
COMPLETE SET (45)	20.00	40.00
1 Michael Vick	.60	1.50
2 Drew Brees	1.50	4.00
3 Quincy Carter	.25	.60
4 Marques Tuiasosopo	.25	.60
5 Chris Weinke	.25	.60
6 Sage Rosenfels	.30	.75
7 Jesse Palmer	.30	.75
8 Mike McMahon	.25	.60
9 Josh Booty	.25	.60
10 Josh Heupel	.30	.75
11 LaDainian Tomlinson	2.00	5.00
12 Deuce McAllister	.40	1.00
13 Michael Bennett	.30	.75
14 Anthony Thomas	.30	.75
15 LaMont Jordan	.30	.75
16 Travis Henry	.30	.75
17 James Jackson	.25	.60
18 Kevan Barlow	.25	.60
19 Travis Minor	.25	.60
20 Rudi Johnson	.30	.75
21 David Terrell	.25	.60
22 Koren Robinson	.30	.75
23 Rod Gardner	.25	.60
24 Santana Moss	.50	1.25
25 Freddie Mitchell	.20	.50
26 Reggie Wayne	.75	2.00
27 Quincy Morgan	.25	.60
28 Chris Chambers	.50	1.25
29 Robert Ferguson	.30	.75
30 Chad Johnson	.75	2.00
31 Snoop Minnis	.25	.60
32 Todd Heap	.30	.75
33 Steve Hutchinson	.25	.60
34 Leonard Davis	.25	.60
35 Kenyatta Walker	.20	.50
36 Justin Smith	.30	.75
37 Andre Carter	.30	.75
38 Jamal Reynolds	.25	.60
39 Gerard Warren	.25	.60
40 Richard Seymour	.30	.75
41 Damione Lewis	.25	.60
42 Jamar Fletcher	.20	.50
43 Nate Clements	.30	.75
44 Derrick Gibson	.20	.50
45 David Terrell CL	.20	.50

2004 Press Pass SE

Card	Low	High
COMPLETE SET (40)	15.00	30.00
1 Shawn Andrews	.30	.75
2 Casey Clausen	.30	.75
3 Michael Clayton	.40	1.00
4 Cedric Cobbs	.30	.75

Card		
❑ 5 Devard Darling	.30	.75
❑ 6 Lee Evans	.50	1.25
❑ 7 Larry Fitzgerald	1.25	3.00
❑ 8 Robert Gallery	.40	1.00
❑ 9 DeAngelo Hall	.40	1.00
❑ 10 Tommie Harris	.40	1.00
❑ 11 Ben Hartsock	.30	.75
❑ 12 Devery Henderson	.40	1.00
❑ 13 Steven Jackson	1.00	2.50
❑ 14 Michael Jenkins	.40	1.00
❑ 15 Greg Jones	.40	1.00
❑ 16 Kevin Jones	.40	1.00
❑ 17 Teddy Lehman	.30	.75
❑ 18 J.P. Losman	.40	1.00
❑ 19 Eli Manning	2.50	6.00
❑ 20 Mewelde Moore	.40	1.00
❑ 21 John Navarre	.30	.75
❑ 22 Jarrett Payton	.30	.75
❑ 23 Chris Perry	.40	1.00
❑ 24 Cody Pickett	.30	.75
❑ 25 Philip Rivers	1.50	4.00
❑ 26 Ben Roethlisberger	3.00	8.00
❑ 27 Matt Schaub	1.00	2.50
❑ 28 Will Smith	.40	1.00
❑ 29 Ben Troupe	.30	.75
❑ 30 Michael Turner	1.00	2.50
❑ 31 Ben Watson	.40	1.00
❑ 32 Darius Watts	.30	.75
❑ 33 Vince Wilfork	.40	1.00
❑ 34 Mike Williams	.30	.75
❑ 35 Reggie Williams	.40	1.00
❑ 36 Roy Williams WR	.50	1.25
❑ 37 Quincy Wilson	.30	.75
❑ 38 Rashaun Woods	.25	.60
❑ 39 Jason Wright	.25	.60
❑ 40 Eli Manning CL	1.25	3.00
❑ NNO Eli Manning Mini Helmet	60.00	120.00

2005 Press Pass SE

Card		
❑ COMPLETE SET (40)	10.00	25.00
❑ 1 Charlie Frye	.40	1.00
❑ 2 David Greene	.30	.75
❑ 3 Gino Guidugli	.25	.60
❑ 4 Stefan LeFors	.30	.75
❑ 5 Dan Orlovsky	.40	1.00
❑ 6 Kyle Orton	.60	1.50
❑ 7 Aaron Rodgers	1.25	3.00
❑ 8 Alex Smith QB	.40	1.00
❑ 9 Andrew Walter	.30	.75
❑ 10 Jason White	.40	1.00
❑ 11 J.J. Arrington	.40	1.00
❑ 12 Marion Barber	1.25	3.00
❑ 13 Ronnie Brown	1.25	3.00
❑ 14 Anthony Davis	.30	.75
❑ 15 Ciatrick Fason	.30	.75
❑ 16 T.A. McLendon	.25	.60
❑ 17 Vernand Morency	.30	.75
❑ 18 Walter Reyes	.25	.60
❑ 19 Cadillac Williams	.60	1.50
❑ 20 Mark Bradley	.30	.75
❑ 21 Reggie Brown	.30	.75
❑ 22 Mark Clayton	.40	1.00
❑ 23 Braylon Edwards	1.00	2.50
❑ 24 Fred Gibson	.30	.75
❑ 25 Chris Henry	.40	1.00
❑ 26 Terrence Murphy	.25	.60
❑ 27 J.R. Russell	.25	.60
❑ 28 Craphonso Thorpe	.30	.75
❑ 29 Roddy White	.50	1.25
❑ 30 Mike Williams	.30	.75
❑ 31 Troy Williamson	.40	1.00
❑ 32 Heath Miller	.75	2.00
❑ 33 Alex Smith TE	.40	1.00
❑ 34 Jammal Brown	.40	1.00
❑ 35 Marlin Jackson	.30	.75
❑ 36 Antrel Rolle	.40	1.00
❑ 37 Dan Cody	.40	1.00
❑ 38 Derrick Johnson	.40	1.00
❑ 39 Thomas Davis	.30	.75
❑ 40 Aaron Rodgers CL	.60	1.50

2006 Press Pass SE

Card		
❑ COMPLETE SET (40)	12.50	30.00
❑ 1 Joseph Addai	.50	1.25
❑ 2 Jason Avant	.40	1.00
❑ 3 Reggie Bush	1.00	2.50
❑ 4 Dominique Byrd	.30	.75
❑ 5 Brodie Croyle	.40	1.00
❑ 6 Jay Cutler	1.00	2.50
❑ 7 Vernon Davis	.40	1.00
❑ 8 Maurice Drew	.75	2.00
❑ 9 Anthony Fasano	.40	1.00
❑ 10 D'Brickashaw Ferguson	.40	1.00
❑ 11 Bruce Gradkowski	.40	1.00
❑ 12 Darrell Hackney	.30	.75
❑ 13 Derek Hagan	.30	.75
❑ 14 Jerome Harrison	.40	1.00
❑ 15 A.J. Hawk	.60	1.50
❑ 16 Santonio Holmes	1.00	2.50
❑ 17 Michael Huff	.40	1.00
❑ 18 Chad Jackson	.30	.75
❑ 19 Omar Jacobs	.25	.60
❑ 20 Matt Leinart	.60	1.50
❑ 21 Marcedes Lewis	.40	1.00
❑ 22 Laurence Maroney	.50	1.25
❑ 23 Reggie McNeal	.30	.75
❑ 24 Sinorice Moss	.40	1.00
❑ 25 Martin Nance	.30	.75
❑ 26 Haloti Ngata	.40	1.00
❑ 27 Leonard Pope	.40	1.00
❑ 28 Michael Robinson	.30	.75
❑ 29 D.J. Shockley	.30	.75
❑ 30 Maurice Stovall	.30	.75
❑ 31 Marcus Vick	.25	.60
❑ 32 Leon Washington	.50	1.25
❑ 33 LenDale White	.50	1.25
❑ 34 Charlie Whitehurst	.40	1.00
❑ 35 Jimmy Williams	.40	1.00
❑ 36 Mario Williams	.50	1.25
❑ 37 DeAngelo Williams	.75	2.00
❑ 38 Demetrius Williams	.30	.75
❑ 39 Vince Young	1.00	2.50
❑ 40 Vince Young CL	.50	1.00

2007 Press Pass SE

Card		
❑ COMPLETE SET (50)	15.00	40.00
❑ 1 Reggie Nelson	.30	.75
❑ 2 Patrick Willis	.60	1.50
❑ 3 Brian Leonard	.30	.75
❑ 4 Sidney Rice	.75	2.00
❑ 5 Robert Meachem	.40	1.00
❑ 6 Chris Leak	.30	.75
❑ 7 Calvin Johnson	1.00	2.50
❑ 8 Charles Johnson	.25	.60
❑ 9 Kevin Kolb	.60	1.50
❑ 10 Drew Stanton	.30	.75
❑ 11 Antonio Pittman	.40	1.00
❑ 12 Troy Smith	.50	1.25
❑ 13 Steve Smith USC	.60	1.50
❑ 14 Leon Hall	.40	1.00
❑ 15 Brandon Jackson	.40	1.00
❑ 16 Ted Ginn Jr.	.60	1.50
❑ 17 Aundrae Allison	.30	.75
❑ 18 DeShawn Wynn	.40	1.00
❑ 19 Dwayne Wright	.30	.75
❑ 20 Michael Bush	.40	1.00
❑ 21 Dwayne Bowe	.60	1.50
❑ 22 Adam Carriker	.30	.75
❑ 23 Paul Posluszny	.50	1.25
❑ 24 Aaron Ross	.40	1.00
❑ 25 Lorenzo Booker	.40	1.00
❑ 26 Jamaal Anderson	.30	.75
❑ 27 Zach Miller	.40	1.00
❑ 28 Dallas Baker	.30	.75
❑ 29 Adrian Peterson	3.00	8.00
❑ 30 Dwayne Jarrett	.40	1.00
❑ 31 Greg Olsen	.50	1.25
❑ 32 Darius Walker	.30	.75
❑ 33 Alan Branch	.30	.75
❑ 34 Marshawn Lynch	.60	1.50
❑ 35 JaMarcus Russell	.50	1.25
❑ 36 Anthony Gonzalez	.50	1.25
❑ 37 Gaines Adams	.40	1.00
❑ 38 Craig Buster Davis	.40	1.00
❑ 39 Jason Hill	.40	1.00
❑ 40 Kenny Irons	.40	1.00
❑ 41 John Beck	.40	1.00
❑ 42 Lawrence Timmons	.40	1.00
❑ 43 Trent Edwards	.60	1.50
❑ 44 Tony Hunt	.40	1.00
❑ 45 Darrelle Revis	.50	1.25
❑ 46 Jarvis Moss	.40	1.00
❑ 47 LaRon Landry	.50	1.25
❑ 48 Brady Quinn	.75	2.00
❑ 49 Jordan Palmer	.40	1.00
❑ 50 Rhema McKnight	.30	.75

2009 Press Pass SE

Card	Low	High
COMPLETE SET (50)	12.50	30.00
1 Nate Davis	.40	1.00
2 Josh Freeman	.75	2.00
3 Graham Harrell	.40	1.00
4 Mark Sanchez	1.50	4.00
5 Matthew Stafford	1.25	3.00
6 Pat White	.60	1.50
7 Andre Brown	.30	.75
8 Donald Brown	.75	2.00
9 Glen Coffee	.50	1.25
10 Mike Goodson	.40	1.00
11 Shonn Greene	.75	2.00
12 Jeremiah Johnson	.40	1.00
13 LeSean McCoy	.75	2.00
14 Knowshon Moreno	1.00	2.50
15 Javon Ringer	.40	1.00
16 Chris Wells	1.00	2.50
17 Ramses Barden	.30	.75
18 Kenny Britt	.60	1.50
19 Michael Crabtree	1.00	2.50
20 Percy Harvin	1.25	3.00
21 Darrius Heyward Bey	.60	1.50
22 Juaquin Iglesias	.40	1.00
23 Jeremy Maclin	.75	2.00
24 Hakeem Nicks	.75	2.00
25 Brian Robiskie	.40	1.00
26 Brandon Tate	.30	.75
27 Derrick Williams	.40	1.00
28 Brandon Pettigrew	.50	1.25
29 Everette Brown	.40	1.00
30 Tyson Jackson	.40	1.00
31 Aaron Maybin	.40	1.00
32 Brian Orakpo	.50	1.25
33 Aaron Curry	.50	1.25
34 Brian Cushing	.50	1.25
35 James Laurinaitis	.50	1.25
36 Rey Maualuga	.60	1.50
37 Vontae Davis	.40	1.00
38 Malcolm Jenkins	.40	1.00
39 D.J. Moore	.30	.75
40 Victor Harris	.40	1.00
41 Alphonso Smith	.30	.75
42 B.J. Raji	.50	1.25
43 Rhett Bomar	.30	.75
44 Ian Johnson	.40	1.00
45 James Davis	.40	1.00
46 Cedric Peerman	.30	.75
47 Jarett Dillard	.40	1.00
48 Louis Murphy	.40	1.00
49 Mike Thomas	.40	1.00
50 Jared Cook	.30	.75

1999 SAGE

Card	Low	High
COMPLETE SET (50)	15.00	30.00
1 Rahim Abdullah	.25	.60
2 Jerry Azumah	.25	.60
3 Champ Bailey	.50	1.25
4 D'Wayne Bates	.25	.60
5 Michael Bishop	.40	1.00
6 David Boston	.40	1.00
7 Fernando Bryant	.25	.60
8 Tony Bryant	.25	.60
9 Chris Claiborne	.15	.40
10 Mike Cloud	.25	.60
11 Cecil Collins	.15	.40
12 Tim Couch	.40	1.00
13 Daunte Culpepper	1.50	4.00
14 Jared DeVries	.25	.60
15 Adrian Dingle	.25	.60
16 Antuan Edwards	.25	.60
17 Troy Edwards	.25	.60
18 Kevin Faulk	.40	1.00
19 Rufus French	.15	.40
20 Martin Gramatica	.15	.40
21 Torry Holt	1.00	2.50
22 Sedrick Irvin	.15	.40
23 Edgerrin James	1.50	4.00
24 Jon Jansen	.15	.40
25 Andy Katzenmoyer	.25	.60
26 Jevon Kearse	1.00	2.50
27 Patrick Kerney	.40	1.00
28 Lamar King	.25	.60
29 Shaun King	.25	.60
30 Jim Kleinsasser	.40	1.00
31 Rob Konrad	.40	1.00
32 Brian Kuklick	.25	.60
33 Chris McAlister	.25	.60
34 Darnell McDonald	.25	.60
35 Reggie McGrew	.25	.60
36 Donovan McNabb	2.00	5.00
37 Cade McNown	.25	.60
38 Dat Nguyen	.40	1.00
39 Solomon Page	.15	.40
40 Mike Peterson	.40	1.00
41 Anthony Poindexter	.25	.60
42 Peerless Price	.40	1.00
43 Mike Rucker	.40	1.00
44 L.J. Shelton	.15	.40
45 Akili Smith	.60	1.50
46 John Tait	.15	.40
47 Fred Vinson	.25	.60
48 Al Wilson	.40	1.00
49 Antoine Winfield	.25	.60
50 Damien Woody	.25	.60

2000 SAGE

Card	Low	High
COMPLETE SET (50)	6.00	15.00
1 John Abraham	.30	.75
2 Shaun Alexander	1.00	2.50
3 LaVar Arrington	.60	1.50
4 Courtney Brown	.40	1.00
5 Keith Bulluck	.30	.75
6 Plaxico Burress	.60	1.50
7 Giovanni Carmazzi	.15	.40
8 Kwame Cavil	.15	.40
9 Cosey Coleman	.15	.40
10 Laveranues Coles	.40	1.00
11 Tim Couch	.30	.75
12 Ron Dayne	.30	.75
13 Reuben Droughns	.40	1.00
14 Shaun Ellis	.30	.75
15 John Engelberger	.25	.60
16 Danny Farmer	.25	.60
17 Dwayne Goodrich	.30	.75
18 Deon Grant	.25	.60
19 Chris Hovan	.25	.60
20 Darren Howard	.25	.60
21 Todd Husak	.30	.75
22 Thomas Jones	.50	1.25
23 Curtis Keaton	.25	.60
24 Jamal Lewis	.60	1.50
25 Anthony Lucas	.15	.40
26 Tee Martin	.30	.75
27 Stockar McDougle	.15	.40
28 Corey Moore	.15	.40
29 Rob Morris	.25	.60
30 Sammy Morris	.30	.75
31 Sylvester Morris	.25	.60
32 Chad Pennington	.75	2.00
33 Todd Pinkston	.30	.75
34 Ahmed Plummer	.30	.75
35 Jerry Porter	.40	1.00
36 Travis Prentice	.25	.60
37 Tim Rattay	.30	.75
38 Chris Redman	.25	.60
39 J.R. Redmond	.25	.60
40 Chris Samuels	.25	.60
41 Brandon Short	.25	.60
42 Corey Simon	.40	1.00
43 R.Jay Soward	.25	.60
44 Shyrone Stith	.25	.60
45 Raynoch Thompson	.25	.60
46 Brian Urlacher	1.25	3.00
47 Todd Wade	.15	.40
48 Troy Walters	.30	.75
49 Dez White	.30	.75
50 Michael Wiley	.25	.60

2001 SAGE

Card	Low	High
COMPLETE SET (50)	7.50	20.00
1 Will Allen	.30	.75
2 Adam Archuleta	.25	.60
3 Jeff Backus	.20	.50
4 Alex Bannister	.20	.50
5 Gary Baxter	.25	.60
6 Michael Bennett	.30	.75
7 Josh Booty	.25	.60
8 Drew Brees	1.50	4.00
9 Correll Buckhalter	.30	.75
10 Quincy Carter	.25	.60
11 Chris Chambers	.50	1.25
12 Alge Crumpler	.30	.75
13 Andre Dyson	.20	.50
14 Robert Ferguson	.30	.75
15 Jamar Fletcher	.20	.50
16 Rod Gardner	.25	.60
17 Reggie Germany	.20	.50
18 Derrick Gibson	.20	.50
19 Casey Hampton	.25	.60
20 Tim Hasselbeck	.25	.60
21 Todd Heap	.30	.75
22 Travis Henry	.30	.75
23 Josh Heupel	.30	.75
24 Willie Howard	.20	.50
25 Steve Hutchinson	.25	.60
26 James Jackson	.25	.60
27 Rudi Johnson	.30	.75
28 LaMont Jordan	.30	.75
29 Torrance Marshall	.25	.60
30 Deuce McAllister	.40	1.00
31 Willie Middlebrooks	.25	.60
32 Quincy Morgan	.25	.60
33 Santana Moss	.50	1.25
34 Jesse Palmer	.30	.75
35 Carlos Polk	.20	.50
36 Ken-Yon Rambo	.20	.50
37 Jamal Reynolds	.25	.60
38 Koren Robinson	.30	.75
39 Richard Seymour	.30	.75
40 Justin Smith	.30	.75
41 Fred Smoot	.30	.75

Card	Low	High
❑ 42 Marcus Stroud	.25	.60
❑ 43 David Terrell	.25	.60
❑ 44 LaDainian Tomlinson	2.00	5.00
❑ 45 Ja'Mar Toombs	.20	.50
❑ 46 Michael Vick	.60	1.50
❑ 47 Kenyatta Walker	.20	.50
❑ 48 Gerard Warren	.25	.60
❑ 49 Reggie Wayne	.75	2.00
❑ 50 Jamie Winborn	.25	.60

2003 SAGE

Card	Low	High
❑ COMPLETE SET (45)	10.00	25.00
❑ 1 Sam Aiken	.50	1.25
❑ 2 Boss Bailey	.40	1.00
❑ 3 Brad Banks	.40	1.00
❑ 4 Tully Banta-Cain	.50	1.25
❑ 5 Arnaz Battle	.50	1.25
❑ 6 Ronald Bellamy	.40	1.00
❑ 7 Kyle Boller	.50	1.25
❑ 8 Chris Brown	.50	1.25
❑ 9 Tyrone Calico	.40	1.00
❑ 10 Dallas Clark	1.00	2.50
❑ 11 Kevin Curtis	.50	1.25
❑ 12 Sammy Davis	.40	1.00
❑ 13 Dahrran Diedrick	.30	.75
❑ 14 Ken Dorsey	.40	1.00
❑ 15 Justin Fargas	.50	1.25
❑ 16 Justin Gage	.50	1.25
❑ 17 Jason Gesser	.40	1.00
❑ 18 Cie Grant	.40	1.00
❑ 19 Rex Grossman	.50	1.25
❑ 20 E.J. Henderson	.40	1.00
❑ 21 Taylor Jacobs	.40	1.00
❑ 22 Bryant Johnson	.50	1.25
❑ 23 Larry Johnson	.00	1.50
❑ 24 Teyo Johnson	.40	1.00
❑ 25 Kliff Kingsbury	.40	1.00
❑ 26 Brandon Lloyd	.50	1.25
❑ 27 Rashean Mathis	.40	1.00
❑ 28 Jerome McDougle	.30	.75
❑ 29 Willis McGahee	1.00	2.50
❑ 30 Billy McMullen	.30	.75
❑ 31 Terence Newman	.50	1.25
❑ 32 Donnie Nickey	.30	.75
❑ 33 Terry Pierce	.30	.75
❑ 34 Dave Ragone	.30	.75
❑ 35 Charles Rogers	.40	1.00
❑ 36 Chris Simms	.50	1.25
❑ 37 Musa Smith	.40	1.00
❑ 38 Lee Suggs	.40	1.00
❑ 39 Terrell Suggs	.60	1.50
❑ 40 Marcus Trufant	.50	1.25
❑ 41 Seneca Wallace	.50	1.25
❑ 42 Kelley Washington	.40	1.00
❑ 43 Matt Wilhelm	.40	1.00
❑ 44 Jason Witten	1.25	3.00
❑ 45 George Wrighster	.30	.75

2004 SAGE

Card	Low	High
❑ COMPLETE SET (46)	12.50	30.00
❑ STATED PRINT RUN 3200 SETS		
❑ 1 Tatum Bell	.40	1.00
❑ 2 Bernard Berrian	.40	1.00
❑ 3 Michael Boulware	.40	1.00
❑ 4 Drew Carter	.40	1.00
❑ 5 Maurice Clarett	.30	.75
❑ 6 Casey Clausen	.30	.75
❑ 7 Michael Clayton	.40	1.00
❑ 8 Chris Collins	.25	.60
❑ 9 Karlos Dansby	.40	1.00
❑ 10 Devard Darling	.30	.75
❑ 11 Lee Evans	.50	1.25
❑ 12 Clarence Farmer	.25	.60
❑ 13 Chris Gamble	.30	.75
❑ 14 Jake Grove	.25	.60
❑ 15 DeAngelo Hall	.40	1.00
❑ 16 Josh Harris	.25	.60
❑ 17 Tommie Harris	.40	1.00
❑ 18 Devery Henderson	.40	1.00
❑ 19 Steven Jackson	1.00	2.50
❑ 20 Michael Jenkins	.40	1.00
❑ 21 Greg Jones	.40	1.00
❑ 22 Kevin Jones	.40	1.00
❑ 23 Sean Jones	.30	.75
❑ 24 Derrick Knight	.25	.60
❑ 25 Craig Krenzel	.40	1.00
❑ 26 Jared Lorenzen	.30	.75
❑ 27 Eli Manning	2.50	6.00
❑ 28 John Navarre	.30	.75
❑ 29 Chris Perry	.40	1.00
❑ 30 Cody Pickett	.30	.75
❑ 31 Will Poole	.40	1.00
❑ 32 Philip Rivers	1.50	4.00
❑ 33 Ell Roberson	.40	1.00
❑ 34 Dunta Robinson	.30	.75
❑ 35 Ben Roethlisberger	3.00	8.00
❑ 36 Rod Rutherford	.25	.60
❑ 37 P.K. Sam	.25	.60
❑ 38 Matt Schaub	1.00	2.50
❑ 39 Will Smith	.40	1.00
❑ 40 Jeff Smoker	.30	.75
❑ 41 Ben Troupe	.30	.75
❑ 42 Ernest Wilford	.30	.75
❑ 43 Reggie Williams	.40	1.00
❑ 44 Roy Williams WR	.50	1.25
❑ 45 Quincy Wilson	.30	.75
❑ 46 Rashaun Woods	.25	.60

2005 SAGE

Card	Low	High
❑ COMPLETE SET (54)	12.50	30.00
❑ 1 Derek Anderson	.50	1.25
❑ 2 J.J. Arrington	.50	1.25
❑ 3 Marion Barber	1.50	4.00
❑ 4 Brock Berlin	.40	1.00
❑ 5 Jammal Brown	.50	1.25
❑ 6 Reggie Brown	.40	1.00
❑ 7 Ronnie Brown	1.50	4.00
❑ 8 Jason Campbell	.75	2.00
❑ 9 Mark Clayton	.50	1.25
❑ 10 Channing Crowder	.40	1.00
❑ 11 Anthony Davis	.40	1.00
❑ 12 Josh Davis	.30	.75
❑ 13 Thomas Davis	.40	1.00
❑ 14 Clatrick Fason	.40	1.00
❑ 15 Ryan Fitzpatrick	.50	1.25
❑ 16 Charlie Frye	.50	1.25
❑ 17 Fred Gibson	.40	1.00
❑ 18 Johnathan Goddard	.40	1.00
❑ 19 Frank Gore	1.00	2.50
❑ 20 David Greene	.40	1.00
❑ 21 Kay-Jay Harris	.40	1.00
❑ 22 Marlin Jackson	.40	1.00
❑ 23 Brandon Jacobs	.60	1.50
❑ 24 Derrick Johnson	.50	1.25
❑ 25 Matt Jones	.50	1.25
❑ 26 T.A. McLendon	.30	.75
❑ 27 Adrian McPherson	.40	1.00
❑ 28 Justin Miller	.40	1.00
❑ 29 Vernand Morency	.40	1.00
❑ 30 Terrence Murphy	.30	.75
❑ 31 Dan Orlovsky	.50	1.25
❑ 32 Kyle Orton	.75	2.00
❑ 33 Roscoe Parrish	.40	1.00
❑ 34 Brodney Pool	.40	1.00
❑ 35 Dante Ridgeway	.30	.75
❑ 36 Chris Rix	.40	1.00
❑ 37 Aaron Rodgers	1.50	4.00
❑ 38 Carlos Rogers	.50	1.25
❑ 39 J.R. Russell	.30	.75
❑ 40 Alex Smith TE	.50	1.25
❑ 41 Alex Smith QB	.50	1.25
❑ 42 Taylor Stubblefield	.30	.75
❑ 43 Craphonso Thorpe	.40	1.00
❑ 44 Andrew Walter	.40	1.00
❑ 45 DeMarcus Ware	.75	2.00
❑ 46 Fabian Washington	.50	1.25
❑ 47 Corey Webster	.50	1.25
❑ 48 Jason White	.50	1.25
❑ 49 Roddy White	.60	1.50
❑ 50 Cadillac Williams	.75	2.00
❑ 51 Troy Williamson	.50	1.25
❑ 52 Maurice Clarett	.40	1.00
❑ 53 Ben Roethlisberger	1.25	3.00
❑ 54 Antrel Rolle	.50	1.25

2006 SAGE

Card	Low	High
❑ COMPLETE SET (60)	15.00	30.00
❑ 1 Joseph Addai	.60	1.50
❑ 2 Devin Aromashodu	.50	1.25
❑ 3 Jason Avant	.50	1.25
❑ 4 Hank Baskett	.50	1.25
❑ 5 Mike Bell	.50	1.25
❑ 6 Will Blackmon	.50	1.25
❑ 7 Daniel Bullocks	.50	1.25
❑ 8 Reggie Bush	1.25	3.00
❑ 9 Dominique Byrd	.40	1.00
❑ 10 Brian Calhoun	.40	1.00
❑ 11 Bobby Carpenter	.40	1.00
❑ 12 Antonio Cromartie	.50	1.25

Card	Low	High
❑ 13 Brodie Croyle	.50	1.25
❑ 14 Jay Cutler	1.25	3.00
❑ 15 Vernon Davis	.50	1.25
❑ 16 Anthony Fasano	.50	1.25
❑ 17 D'Brickashaw Ferguson	.50	1.25
❑ 18 Charles Gordon	.40	1.00
❑ 19 Bruce Gradkowski	.50	1.25
❑ 20 Skyler Green	.30	.75
❑ 21 Jerome Harrison	.50	1.25
❑ 22 Mike Hass	.50	1.25
❑ 23 Taurean Henderson	.50	1.25
❑ 24 Devin Hester	1.00	2.50
❑ 25 Tye Hill	.40	1.00
❑ 26 Michael Huff	.50	1.25
❑ 27 Tarvaris Jackson	.50	1.25
❑ 28 Omar Jacobs	.30	.75
❑ 29 Maurice Drew	1.00	2.50
❑ 30 Winston Justice	.50	1.25
❑ 31 Matt Leinart	.75	2.00
❑ 32 Laurence Maroney	.60	1.50
❑ 33 Reggie McNeal	.40	1.00
❑ 34 Marcus McNeill	.40	1.00
❑ 35 Erik Meyer	.40	1.00
❑ 36 Sinorice Moss	.50	1.25
❑ 37 Martin Nance	.40	1.00
❑ 38 Drew Olson	.30	.75
❑ 39 Jonathan Orr	.40	1.00
❑ 40 Paul Pinegar	.30	.75
❑ 41 Leonard Pope	.50	1.25
❑ 42 Gerald Riggs Jr.	.40	1.00
❑ 43 Michael Robinson	.40	1.00
❑ 44 DeMeco Ryans	.60	1.50
❑ 45 D.J. Shockley	.40	1.00
❑ 46 Ernie Sims	.40	1.00
❑ 47 Dwayne Slay	.40	1.00
❑ 48 Maurice Stovall	.40	1.00
❑ 49 David Thomas	.50	1.25
❑ 50 Leon Washington	.60	1.50
❑ 51 Pat Watkins	.50	1.25
❑ 52 LenDale White	.60	1.50
❑ 53 Charlie Whitehurst	.50	1.25
❑ 54 Demetrius Williams	.40	1.00
❑ 55 Jimmy Williams	.50	1.25
❑ 56 Mario Williams	.60	1.50
❑ 57 Rodrique Wright	.30	.75
❑ 58 Ashton Youboty	.40	1.00
❑ 59 Vince Young	1.25	3.00
❑ 60 Alan Zemaitis	.50	1.25

2007 SAGE

Card	Low	High
❑ COMPLETE SET (62)	15.00	30.00
❑ 1 Gaines Adams	.50	1.25
❑ 2 Aundrae Allison	.40	1.00
❑ 3 Dallas Baker	.40	1.00
❑ 4 David Ball	.30	.75
❑ 5 John Beck	.50	1.25
❑ 6 Dwayne Bowe	.75	2.00
❑ 7 Alan Branch	.40	1.00
❑ 8 Steve Breaston	.50	1.25
❑ 9 Levi Brown	.50	1.25
❑ 10 Michael Bush	.50	1.25
❑ 11 Adam Carriker	.40	1.00
❑ 12 David Clowney	.50	1.25
❑ 13 Ken Darby	.50	1.25
❑ 14 Craig Buster Davis	.50	1.25
❑ 15 Trent Edwards	.75	2.00
❑ 16 Earl Everett	.40	1.00
❑ 17 Yamon Figurs	.30	.75
❑ 18 Joel Filani	.40	1.00
❑ 19 Ted Ginn Jr.	.75	2.00
❑ 20 Anthony Gonzalez	.60	1.50
❑ 21 Michael Griffin	.50	1.25
❑ 22 Leon Hall	.50	1.25
❑ 23 Chris Henry	.40	1.00
❑ 24 Johnnie Lee Higgins	.50	1.25
❑ 25 Jason Hill	.50	1.25
❑ 26 David Irons	.30	.75
❑ 27 Kenny Irons	.50	1.25
❑ 28 Calvin Johnson	1.25	3.00
❑ 29 Ryan Kalil	.40	1.00
❑ 30 Kevin Kolb	.75	2.00
❑ 31 Chris Leak	.40	1.00
❑ 32 Brian Leonard	.40	1.00
❑ 33 Marshawn Lynch	.75	2.00
❑ 34 Robert Meachem	.50	1.25
❑ 35 Brandon Meriweather	.50	1.25
❑ 36 Zach Miller	.50	1.25
❑ 37 Jarvis Moss	.50	1.25
❑ 38 Greg Olsen	.60	1.50
❑ 39 Tyler Palko	.40	1.00
❑ 40 Jordan Palmer	.50	1.25
❑ 41 Adrian Peterson	4.00	10.00
❑ 42 Antonio Pittman	.50	1.25
❑ 43 Brady Quinn	1.00	2.50
❑ 44 Sidney Rice	1.00	2.50
❑ 45 Aaron Ross	.50	1.25
❑ 46 Jeff Rowe	.40	1.00
❑ 47 JaMarcus Russell	.60	1.50
❑ 48 Kolby Smith	.50	1.25
❑ 49 Steve Smith USC	.75	2.00
❑ 50 Troy Smith	.60	1.50
❑ 51 Jason Snelling	.40	1.00
❑ 52 Isaiah Stanback	.50	1.25
❑ 53 Drew Stanton	.40	1.00
❑ 54 Courtney Taylor	.40	1.00
❑ 55 Lawrence Timmons	.50	1.25
❑ 56 DeMarcus Tank Tyler	.40	1.00
❑ 57 Darius Walker	.40	1.00
❑ 58 Paul Williams	.40	1.00
❑ 59 Patrick Willis	.75	2.00
❑ 60 Garrett Wolfe	.50	1.25
❑ 61 LaMarr Woodley	.50	1.25
❑ 62 Jared Zabransky	.50	1.25

2008 SAGE

Card	Low	High
❑ COMPLETE SET (60)	20.00	40.00
❑ 1 Erik Ainge	.50	1.25
❑ 2 Adrian Arrington	.40	1.00
❑ 3 Donnie Avery	.60	1.50
❑ 4 Sam Baker	.30	.75
❑ 5 John David Booty	.50	1.25
❑ 6 Adarius Bowman	.40	1.00
❑ 7 Brian Brohm	.50	1.25
❑ 8 Keenan Burton	.40	1.00
❑ 9 Andre Caldwell	.50	1.25
❑ 10 John Carlson	.50	1.25
❑ 11 Antoine Cason	.50	1.25
❑ 12 Jamaal Charles	.75	2.00
❑ 13 Tashard Choice	.50	1.25
❑ 14 Ryan Clady	.50	1.25
❑ 15 Dan Connor	.50	1.25
❑ 16 Fred Davis	.50	1.25
❑ 17 Dennis Dixon	.50	1.25
❑ 18 Early Doucet	.50	1.25
❑ 19 Sedrick Ellis	.50	1.25
❑ 20 Joe Flacco	1.50	4.00
❑ 21 Brandon Flowers	.50	1.25
❑ 22 Matt Flynn	.50	1.25
❑ 23 Will Franklin	.40	1.00
❑ 24 Vernon Gholston	.50	1.25
❑ 25 James Hardy	.40	1.00
❑ 26 Mike Hart	.50	1.25
❑ 27 Derrick Harvey	.40	1.00
❑ 28 Lavelle Hawkins	.40	1.00
❑ 29 Chad Henne	.75	2.00
❑ 30 Jacob Hester	.50	1.25
❑ 31 DeSean Jackson	1.00	2.50
❑ 32 Lawrence Jackson	.40	1.00
❑ 33 Mike Jenkins	.50	1.25
❑ 34 Josh Johnson	.50	1.25
❑ 35 Felix Jones	1.00	2.50
❑ 36 Dustin Keller	.50	1.25
❑ 37 Sam Keller	.50	1.25
❑ 38 Malcolm Kelly	.50	1.25
❑ 39 Jake Long	.50	1.25
❑ 40 Darren McFadden	1.00	2.50
❑ 41 Leodis McKelvin	.50	1.25
❑ 42 Rashard Mendenhall	1.00	2.50
❑ 43 Jordy Nelson	.60	1.50
❑ 44 Kevin O'Connell	.50	1.25
❑ 45 Allen Patrick	.40	1.00
❑ 46 Kenny Phillips	.50	1.25
❑ 47 Darius Reynaud	.40	1.00
❑ 48 Ray Rice	1.00	2.50
❑ 49 Jason Rivers	.50	1.25
❑ 50 Keith Rivers	.50	1.25
❑ 51 Martin Rucker	.40	1.00
❑ 52 Matt Ryan	2.00	5.00
❑ 53 Owen Schmitt	.50	1.25
❑ 54 Steve Slaton	.60	1.50
❑ 55 Kevin Smith	.75	2.00
❑ 56 Paul Smith	.50	1.25
❑ 57 Jonathan Stewart	1.00	2.50
❑ 58 Limas Sweed	.50	1.25
❑ 59 Devin Thomas	.50	1.25
❑ 60 Tom Zbikowski	.50	1.25

2000 SAGE HIT

Card	Low	High
❑ COMPLETE SET (50)	10.00	25.00
❑ 1 Jerry Porter	.40	1.00
❑ 2 Tim Couch	.30	.75
❑ 3 Chris Samuels	.25	.60
❑ 4 Plaxico Burress	.60	1.50
❑ 5 Michael Wiley	.25	.60
❑ 6 Thomas Jones	.50	1.25
❑ 7 Chris Redman	.25	.60
❑ 8 Anthony Lucas	.15	.40
❑ 9 Kwame Cavil	.15	.40
❑ 10 Chad Pennington	.75	2.00
❑ 11 LaVar Arrington	.75	2.00
❑ 12 Giovanni Carmazzi	.15	.40
❑ 13 Tim Rattay	.30	.75
❑ 14 Laveranues Coles	.40	1.00
❑ 15 Mario Edwards	.25	.60
❑ 16 John Engelberger	.25	.60
❑ 17 Tee Martin	.30	.75
❑ 18 R.Jay Soward	.25	.60
❑ 19 Ahmed Plummer	.30	.75
❑ 20 Na'il Diggs	.25	.60
❑ 21 J.R. Redmond	.25	.60
❑ 22 Dez White	.30	.75

❑ 23 Reuben Droughns .40 1.00
❑ 24 Sylvester Morris .25 .60
❑ 25 Cosey Coleman .15 .40
❑ 26 Corey Moore .15 .40
❑ 27 Curtis Keaton .25 .60
❑ 28 Danny Farmer .25 .60
❑ 29 Travis Claridge .15 .40
❑ 30 Troy Walters .30 .75
❑ 31 Jamal Lewis .60 1.50
❑ 32 Shaun King .15 .40
❑ 33 Ron Dayne .30 .75
❑ 34 Keith Bulluck .30 .75
❑ 35 Corey Simon .40 1.00
❑ 36 Deon Dyer .25 .60
❑ 37 Shaun Alexander 1.00 2.50
❑ 38 Shyrone Stith .25 .60
❑ 39 Shaun Ellis .30 .75
❑ 40 Todd Pinkston .30 .75
❑ 41 Travis Prentice .25 .60
❑ 42 Chris Hovan .25 .60
❑ 43 Brandon Short .25 .60
❑ 44 Brian Urlacher 1.25 3.00
❑ 45 Rob Morris .30 .75
❑ 46 Raynoch Thompson .25 .60
❑ 47 Deon Grant .25 .60
❑ 48 Stockar McDougle .15 .40
❑ 49 Darren Howard .25 .60
❑ 50 Courtney Brown .40 1.00

2001 SAGE HIT

❑ COMPLETE SET (50) 10.00 25.00
❑ 1 David Terrell .25 .60
❑ 2 Jamar Fletcher .20 .50
❑ 3 Koren Robinson .30 .75
❑ 4 Ken-Yon Rambo .20 .50
❑ 5 LaDainian Tomlinson 2.00 5.00
❑ 6 Santana Moss .50 1.25
❑ 7 Michael Vick .60 1.50
❑ 8 Steve Hutchinson .25 .60
❑ 9 Robert Ferguson .30 .75
❑ 10 Torrance Marshall .25 .60
❑ 11 Scotty Anderson .25 .60
❑ 12 Derrick Gibson .20 .50
❑ 13 Marcus Stroud .25 .60
❑ 14 Josh Heupel .30 .75
❑ 15 Drew Brees 1.50 4.00
❑ 16 Gerard Warren .25 .60
❑ 17 Quincy Carter .25 .60
❑ 18 Gary Baxter .25 .60
❑ 19 Alex Bannister .20 .50
❑ 21 Andre Dyson .20 .50
❑ 22 Deuce McAllister .40 1.00
❑ 23 Rod Gardner .25 .60
❑ 24 Jamie Winborn .25 .60
❑ 26 Kenyatta Walker .20 .50
❑ 27 Tim Hasselbeck .25 .60
❑ 31 Jeff Backus .20 .50
❑ 33 Willie Howard .20 .50
❑ 34 Josh Booty .25 .60
❑ 37 Jesse Palmer .30 .75
❑ 38 Carlos Polk .20 .50
❑ 39 Richard Seymour .30 .75
❑ 40 Adam Archuleta .25 .60
❑ 41 James Jackson .25 .60
❑ 42 Willie Middlebrooks .25 .60
❑ 43 Ja'Mar Toombs .20 .50
❑ 44 Chris Chambers .50 1.25
❑ 45 Reggie Germany .20 .50
❑ 46 Casey Hampton .25 .60
❑ 47 Reggie Wayne .75 2.00
❑ 48 Jamal Reynolds .25 .60
❑ 49 Justin Smith .30 .75
❑ 50 Quincy Morgan .25 .60

2002 SAGE HIT

❑ COMPLETE SET (47) 10.00 25.00
❑ 1 John Henderson .40 1.00
❑ 2 Tim Carter .30 .75
❑ 3 Joey Harrington .40 1.00
❑ 4 Marquise Walker .25 .60
❑ 5 Quentin Jammer .40 1.00
❑ 6 Rohan Davey .40 1.00
❑ 7A Eric Crouch QB .40 1.00
❑ 7B Eric Crouch RB .40 1.00
❑ 8 David Carr .40 1.00
❑ 9 Maurice Morris .40 1.00
❑ 10 Jabar Gaffney .40 1.00
❑ 11 David Neill .25 .60
❑ 12 Randy Fasani .30 .75
❑ 13 Alex Brown .40 1.00
❑ 14 J.T. O'Sullivan .40 1.00
❑ 15 Kurt Kittner .25 .60
❑ 16 Ashley Lelie .40 1.00
❑ 17 Reche Caldwell .40 1.00
❑ 18 T.J. Duckett .40 1.00
❑ 19 Chester Taylor .60 1.50
❑ 20 Jonathan Wells .40 1.00
❑ 21 Kelly Campbell .30 .75
❑ 22 Bryant McKinnie .25 .60
❑ 23 Lito Sheppard .40 1.00
❑ 24 Donte Stallworth .40 1.00
❑ 25 Josh Reed .30 .75
❑ 26 DeShaun Foster .40 1.00
❑ 27 Patrick Ramsey .40 1.00
❑ 28 Clinton Portis 1.00 2.50
❑ 29 Albert Haynesworth .40 1.00
❑ 31 Cliff Russell .25 .60
❑ 32 Luke Staley .25 .60
❑ 33 Ron Johnson .30 .75
❑ 34 Travis Stephens .25 .60
❑ 35 Chad Hutchinson .25 .60
❑ 36 Lamar Gordon .40 1.00
❑ 37 Larry Tripplett .25 .60
❑ 38 Napoleon Harris .30 .75
❑ 39 Daniel Graham .30 .75
❑ 40 Antonio Bryant .50 1.25
❑ 41 Javon Walker .40 1.00
❑ 42 Brian Poli-Dixon .25 .60
❑ 43 Jeremy Shockey .60 1.50
❑ 44 Andre Davis .30 .75
❑ 45 Ladell Betts .40 1.00
❑ 46 Michael Vick .40 1.00
❑ NNO David Carr CL .30 .75

2003 SAGE HIT

❑ COMPLETE SET (48) 10.00 25.00
❑ 1 Charles Rogers .30 .75
❑ 2 Willis McGahee .75 2.00
❑ 3 Arnaz Battle .40 1.00
❑ 4 Terence Newman .40 1.00
❑ 5 Larry Johnson .50 1.25
❑ 6 Taylor Jacobs .30 .75
❑ 7 Kyle Boller .40 1.00
❑ 8 Rex Grossman .40 1.00
❑ 9 Jerome McDougle .25 .60
❑ 10 Jason Witten 1.00 2.50
❑ 11 Ken Dorsey .30 .75
❑ 12 Justin Gage .40 1.00
❑ 13 Andy Groom .25 .60
❑ 14 Seneca Wallace .40 1.00
❑ 15 Dave Ragone .25 .60
❑ 16 Kliff Kingsbury .30 .75
❑ 17 Jason Gesser .30 .75
❑ 18 George Wrighster .25 .60
❑ 19 Ronald Bellamy .30 .75
❑ 20 Donnie Nickey .25 .60
❑ 21 Billy McMullen .25 .60
❑ 22 Lee Suggs .30 .75
❑ 23 Chris Brown .40 1.00
❑ 24 Bryant Johnson .40 1.00
❑ 25 Justin Fargas .40 1.00
❑ 26 Brandon Lloyd .40 1.00
❑ 27 Tyrone Calico .30 .75
❑ 28 Sam Aiken .40 1.00
❑ 29 Cie Grant .30 .75
❑ 30 Dahrran Diedrick .25 .60
❑ 31 Kelley Washington .30 .75
❑ 32 Musa Smith .30 .75
❑ 33 Kevin Curtis .40 1.00
❑ 34 Terry Pierce .25 .60
❑ 35 Matt Wilhelm .30 .75
❑ 36 Rashean Mathis .30 .75
❑ 37 Brad Banks .30 .75
❑ 38 Tully Banta-Cain .40 1.00
❑ 39 Sammy Davis .30 .75
❑ 40 Teyo Johnson .30 .75
❑ 41 Chris Simms .40 1.00
❑ 42 E.J. Henderson .30 .75
❑ 43 Terrell Suggs .50 1.25
❑ 44 Dallas Clark .75 2.00
❑ 45 Marcus Trufant .40 1.00
❑ 46 Boss Bailey .30 .75
❑ 47 David Carr .40 1.00
❑ NNO Charles Rogers CL .25 .60

2004 SAGE HIT

❑ COMPLETE SET (46) 12.50 30.00
❑ 1 Reggie Williams .40 1.00

❑ 2 Bernard Berrian .40 1.00
❑ 3 Lee Evans .50 1.25
❑ 4 Roy Williams WR .50 1.25
❑ 5 Josh Harris .25 .60
❑ 6 Greg Jones .40 1.00
❑ 7 Ben Roethlisberger 3.00 8.00
❑ 8 Drew Carter .40 1.00
❑ 9 Devery Henderson .40 1.00
❑ 10 Eli Manning 2.50 6.00
❑ 11 Karlos Dansby .40 1.00
❑ 12 Michael Jenkins .40 1.00
❑ 13 Maurice Clarett .30 .75
❑ 14 Michael Clayton .40 1.00
❑ 15 Casey Clausen .30 .75
❑ 16 John Navarre .30 .75
❑ 17 Philip Rivers 1.50 4.00
❑ 18 Jeff Smoker .30 .75
❑ 19 Ernest Wilford .30 .75
❑ 20 Derrick Knight .25 .60
❑ 21 Chris Gamble .30 .75
❑ 22 Jared Lorenzen .30 .75
❑ 23 Chris Perry .40 1.00
❑ 24 Rod Rutherford .25 .60
❑ 25 Kevin Jones .40 1.00
❑ 26 Michael Boulware .40 1.00
❑ 27 Tatum Bell .40 1.00
❑ 28 Will Poole .40 1.00
❑ 29 Jake Grove .25 .60
❑ 30 Ell Roberson .40 1.00
❑ 31 Devard Darling .30 .75
❑ 32 Dunta Robinson .30 .75
❑ 33 Cody Pickett .30 .75
❑ 34 Steven Jackson 1.00 2.50
❑ 35 Matt Schaub 1.00 2.50
❑ 36 Sean Jones .30 .75
❑ 37 Tommie Harris .40 1.00
❑ 38 Chris Collins .25 .60
❑ 39 Will Smith .40 1.00
❑ 40 DeAngelo Hall .40 1.00
❑ 41 Rashaun Woods .25 .60
❑ 42 Ben Troupe .30 .75
❑ 43 Quincy Wilson .30 .75
❑ 44 P.K. Sam .25 .60
❑ 45 Clarence Farmer .25 .60
❑ NNO Eli Manning CL 1.25 3.00
❑ EM Eli Manning SEC/30 20.00 50.00

2005 SAGE HIT

❑ COMPLETE SET (50) 10.00 25.00
❑ 1 Craphonso Thorpe .30 .75
❑ 2 Derrick Johnson .40 1.00
❑ 3 Frank Gore SP 1.00 2.50
❑ 4 Ciatrick Fason .30 .75
❑ 5 Charlie Frye .40 1.00
❑ 6 Antrel Rolle .40 1.00
❑ 7 Dan Orlovsky .40 1.00
❑ 8 Aaron Rodgers 1.25 3.00
❑ 9 Mark Clayton .40 1.00
❑ 10 Thomas Davis .30 .75
❑ 11 Alex Smith QB .40 1.00
❑ 12 Fred Gibson SP .40 1.00
❑ 13 Maurice Clarett SP .40 1.00
❑ 14 David Greene .30 .75
❑ 15 Carlos Rogers .40 1.00
❑ 16 Andrew Walter .30 .75
❑ 17 Jason Campbell .60 1.50
❑ 18 Jason White .40 1.00
❑ 19 Matt Jones .40 1.00
❑ 20 Marion Barber SP 1.50 4.00
❑ 21 Taylor Stubblefield .25 .60
❑ 22 Jammal Brown SP .50 1.25
❑ 23 Ronnie Brown 1.25 3.00
❑ 24 Cadillac Williams .60 1.50
❑ 25 Kay-Jay Harris .30 .75
❑ 26 Reggie Brown .30 .75
❑ 27 Troy Williamson .40 1.00
❑ 28 Anthony Davis .30 .75
❑ 29 Josh Davis SP .30 .75
❑ 30 J.J. Arrington .40 1.00
❑ 31 Alex Smith TE .40 1.00
❑ 32 Corey Webster SP .50 1.25
❑ 33 Vernand Morency .30 .75
❑ 34 Derek Anderson .40 1.00
❑ 35 DeMarcus Ware SP .75 2.00
❑ 36 Kyle Orton .60 1.50
❑ 37 Brock Berlin .30 .75
❑ 38 Marlin Jackson .30 .75
❑ 39 Channing Crowder .30 .75
❑ 40 Roddy White .50 1.25
❑ 41 Roscoe Parrish .30 .75
❑ 42 Adrian McPherson .30 .75
❑ 43 Brodney Pool .30 .75
❑ 44 T.A. McLendon .25 .60
❑ 45 Terrence Murphy .25 .60
❑ 46 Chris Rix .30 .75
❑ 47 Ben Roethlisberger SP 1.25 3.00
❑ 48 Dante Ridgeway SP .30 .75
❑ 49 Justin Miller .30 .75
❑ 50 Johnathan Goddard SP .40 1.00
❑ ROY Roethlisberger ROY/100 7.50 20.00

2006 SAGE HIT

❑ COMPLETE SET (55) 10.00 25.00
❑ #56 ISSUED AT 2006 ANAHEIM NATIONAL
❑ 1 Reggie McNeal .30 .75
❑ 2 Jimmy Williams SP .40 1.00
❑ 3 D.J. Shockley SP .30 .75
❑ 4 Omar Jacobs .25 .60
❑ 5 Reggie Bush 1.00 2.50
❑ 6 Charlie Whitehurst .40 1.00
❑ 7 Michael Huff .40 1.00
❑ 8 Tye Hill .30 .75
❑ 9 Mario Williams .50 1.25
❑ 10 Vince Young 1.00 2.50
❑ 11 Matt Leinart UER .60 1.50
❑ 12 Brodie Croyle .40 1.00
❑ 13 Paul Pinegar .25 .60
❑ 14 Drew Olson .25 .60
❑ 15 Martin Nance .30 .75
❑ 16 David Thomas .40 1.00
❑ 17 Dwayne Slay SP .30 .75
❑ 18 Vernon Davis .40 1.00
❑ 19 Taurean Henderson SP .40 1.00
❑ 20 Maurice Drew .75 2.00
❑ 21 LenDale White .50 1.25
❑ 22 Laurence Maroney .50 1.25
❑ 23 Leon Washington .50 1.25
❑ 24 Erik Meyer SP .30 .75
❑ 25 Maurice Stovall .30 .75
❑ 26 Ashton Youboty .30 .75
❑ 27 Devin Aromashodu .40 1.00
❑ 28 Mike Hass .40 1.00
❑ 29 Jonathan Orr .30 .75
❑ 30 Joseph Addai .50 1.25
❑ 31 Leonard Pope .40 1.00
❑ 32 Michael Robinson .30 .75
❑ 33 Mike Bell .40 1.00
❑ 34 Ernie Sims SP .30 .75
❑ 35 Skyler Green .25 .60
❑ 36 Demetrius Williams .30 .75
❑ 37 Winston Justice .40 1.00
❑ 38 Sinorice Moss .40 1.00
❑ 39 Charles Gordon SP .30 .75
❑ 40 Gerald Riggs .30 .75
❑ 41 Jerome Harrison .40 1.00
❑ 42 Bobby Carpenter .30 .75
❑ 43 Dominique Byrd .30 .75
❑ 44 Bruce Gradkowski .40 1.00
❑ 45 Rodrique Wright .25 .60
❑ 46 D'Brickashaw Ferguson .40 1.00
❑ 47 Daniel Bullocks SP .40 1.00
❑ 48 Jason Avant .40 1.00
❑ 49 Will Blackmon .40 1.00
❑ 50 Devin Hester SP .75 2.00
❑ 51 Alan Zemaitis SP .40 1.00
❑ 52 Hank Baskett .40 1.00
❑ 53 Cadillac Williams ROY SP 1.25 3.00
❑ 54 Bush/Leinart CL SP .75 2.00
❑ 55 Vince Young CL SP .75 2.00
❑ 56 Jay Cutler 1.00 2.50

2007 SAGE HIT

❑ COMPLETE SET (64) 10.00 25.00
❑ 1 Paul Williams .30 .75
❑ 2 JaMarcus Russell .50 1.25
❑ 3 Robert Meachem .40 1.00
❑ 4 Sidney Rice .75 2.00
❑ 5 Drew Stanton .30 .75
❑ 6 Jeff Rowe .30 .75
❑ 7 Zach Miller .25 .60
❑ 8 Joel Filani .30 .75
❑ 9 Chris Henry .30 .75
❑ 10 Brady Quinn .75 2.00
❑ 11 Anthony Gonzalez .50 1.25
❑ 12 Chris Leak .30 .75
❑ 13 David Clowney .40 1.00
❑ 14 Isaiah Stanback .40 1.00
❑ 15 Steve Breaston .40 1.00
❑ 16 Yamon Figurs .25 .60
❑ 17 Lawrence Timmons .40 1.00
❑ 18 Greg Olsen .50 1.25
❑ 19 Michael Bush .40 1.00
❑ 20 Alan Branch .30 .75
❑ 21 Johnnie Lee Higgins .40 1.00
❑ 22 Aundrae Allison .30 .75
❑ 23 Kenny Irons .40 1.00
❑ 24 Marshawn Lynch .60 1.50
❑ 25 Earl Everett .30 .75
❑ 26 Courtney Taylor .30 .75
❑ 27 Michael Griffin .40 1.00
❑ 28 Adrian Peterson 3.00 8.00
❑ 29 Leon Hall .40 1.00
❑ 30 David Ball .25 .60
❑ 31 Aaron Ross .40 1.00
❑ 32 John Beck .40 1.00
❑ 33 Kolby Smith .40 1.00
❑ 34 Ken Darby .40 1.00
❑ 35 Trent Edwards .60 1.50
❑ 36 Craig Buster Davis .40 1.00
❑ 37 Ryan Kalil .30 .75
❑ 38 Jason Snelling .30 .75
❑ 39 Tyler Palko .30 .75
❑ 40 Dwayne Bowe .60 1.50
❑ 41 Dallas Baker .30 .75
❑ 42 Steve Smith USC .60 1.50
❑ 43 Jason Hill .40 1.00
❑ 44 Kevin Kolb .60 1.50
❑ 45 Jared Zabransky .40 1.00
❑ 46 Brian Leonard .30 .75
❑ 47 Darius Walker .30 .75
❑ 48 Adam Carriker .30 .75
❑ 49 Patrick Willis .60 1.50
❑ 50 Troy Smith .50 1.25

Card	Low	High
❑ 51 Brandon Meriweather	.40	1.00
❑ 52 Jarvis Moss	.40	1.00
❑ 53 Levi Brown	.40	1.00
❑ 54 David Irons	.25	.60
❑ 55 Garrett Wolfe	.40	1.00
❑ 56 LaMarr Woodley	.40	1.00
❑ 57 DeMarcus Tank Tyler	.30	.75
❑ 58 Jordan Palmer	.40	1.00
❑ 59 Antonio Pittman	.40	1.00
❑ 60 Gaines Adams	.40	1.00
❑ 61 Calvin Johnson	1.00	2.50
❑ ML Matt Leinart	.60	1.50
❑ RB Reggie Bush	.75	2.00
❑ VY Vince Young	.60	1.50

2008 SAGE HIT

Card	Low	High
❑ COMPLETE SET (100)	15.00	40.00
❑ COMP.LOW SERIES (50)	7.50	20.00
❑ COMP.HIGH SERIES (50)	7.50	20.00
❑ 1 John David Booty	.40	1.00
❑ 2 Will Franklin	.30	.75
❑ 3 Danny Woodhead	.60	1.50
❑ 5 Joe Flacco	1.25	3.00
❑ 6 Brian Brohm	.40	1.00
❑ 7 Chad Henne	.60	1.50
❑ 8 Marcus Thomas	.30	.75
❑ 9 Early Doucet	.40	1.00
❑ 10 Dennis Dixon	.40	1.00
❑ 11 Xavier Adibi	.30	.75
❑ 12 Matt Ryan	1.50	4.00
❑ 13 T.C. Ostrander	.30	.75
❑ 14 Bernard Morris	.30	.75
❑ 15 Sam Baker	.25	.60
❑ 16 Adrian Arrington	.30	.75
❑ 17 Kevin O'Connell	.40	1.00
❑ 18 Jacob Hester	.40	1.00
❑ 19 Keenan Burton	.30	.75
❑ 20 Darius Reynaud	.30	.75
❑ 21 Keon Lattimore	.30	.75
❑ 22 Tashard Choice	.40	1.00
❑ 24 Paul Smith	.40	1.00
❑ 25 Jamaal Charles	.60	1.50
❑ 26 Yvenson Bernard	.40	1.00
❑ 27 Alex Brink	.40	1.00
❑ 28 James Hardy	.30	.75
❑ 29 Martin Rucker	.30	.75
❑ 30 Steve Slaton	.50	1.25
❑ 31 Derrick Harvey	.30	.75
❑ 32 Andre Callender	.40	1.00
❑ 33 Jabari Arthur	.30	.75
❑ 34 Bruce Hocker	.40	1.00
❑ 35 Kalvin McRae	.30	.75
❑ 36 Lawrence Jackson	.30	.75
❑ 37 Tyrell Johnson	.40	1.00
❑ 38 Marcus Howard	.40	1.00
❑ 39 Sam Keller	.40	1.00
❑ 40 Keith Rivers	.40	1.00
❑ 41 Brandon Flowers	.40	1.00
❑ 42 Adarius Bowman	.30	.75
❑ 43 Ricky Santos	.40	1.00
❑ 44 Jordon Dizon	.40	1.00
❑ 45 Robert Jordan	.30	.75
❑ 46 Maurice Purify	.40	1.00
❑ 47 Lavelle Hawkins	.30	.75
❑ 48 Jason Rivers	.40	1.00
❑ 49 John Carlson	.40	1.00
❑ 50 Vernon Gholston	.40	1.00
❑ 51 D.McFadden/F.Jones	.50	1.25
❑ 52 M.Ryan/A.Callender	1.00	2.50
❑ 53 D.Jackson/M.Lynch	.50	1.25
❑ 55 B.Brohm/M.Bush	.25	.60
❑ 56 C.Henne/M.Hart	.25	.60
❑ 57 B.Quinn/J.Carlson	.50	1.25
❑ 58 J.Stewart/D.Dixon	.50	1.25
❑ 59 A.Peterson/M.Kelly	1.00	2.50
❑ 60 R.Rice/B.Leonard	.50	1.25
❑ 61 J.Booty/F.Davis	.25	.60
❑ 62 J.Charles/L.Sweed	.40	1.00
❑ 63 M.Ryan/B.Brohm	1.00	2.50
❑ 64 D.McFadden/R.Mendenhall	.50	1.25
❑ 65 M.Kelly/D.Jackson	.50	1.25
❑ 66 J.Flacco/J.Johnson	.75	2.00
❑ 67 A.Peterson/P.Willis	1.00	2.50
❑ 68 Devin Thomas	.40	1.00
❑ 69 Beau Bell	.30	.75
❑ 70 Owen Schmitt	.40	1.00
❑ 71 Paul Raymond	.30	.75
❑ 72 Jordy Nelson	.50	1.25
❑ 73 Ray Rice	.75	2.00
❑ 74 Darrell Strong	.30	.75
❑ 75 Felix Jones	.75	2.00
❑ 76 Kevin Smith	.60	1.50
❑ 77 Justin Forsett	.40	1.00
❑ 78 Antoine Cason	.40	1.00
❑ 79 Ryan Clady	.40	1.00
❑ 80 Mike Hart	.40	1.00
❑ 81 Kenny Phillips	.40	1.00
❑ 82 Jonathan Stewart	.75	2.00
❑ 83 Fred Davis	.40	1.00
❑ 84 Malcolm Kelly	.40	1.00
❑ 86 Allen Patrick	.30	.75
❑ 87 Brent Miller	.30	.75
❑ 88 Andre Caldwell	.40	1.00
❑ 89 Josh Johnson	.40	1.00
❑ 90 Erik Ainge	.40	1.00
❑ 92 Dan Connor	.40	1.00
❑ 93 Leodis McKelvin	.40	1.00
❑ 94 Sedrick Ellis	.40	1.00
❑ 95 Rashard Mendenhall	.75	2.00
❑ 96 Mike Jenkins	.40	1.00
❑ 97 Dustin Keller	.40	1.00
❑ 98 Donnie Avery	.50	1.25
❑ 99 DeSean Jackson	.75	2.00
❑ 100 Darren McFadden	.75	2.00

2009 SAGE HIT

Card	Low	High
❑ COMPLETE SET (100)	15.00	40.00
❑ COMP.LOW SERIES (50)	7.50	20.00
❑ COMP.HIGH SERIES (50)	10.00	25.00
❑ 1 Patrick Turner	.30	.75
❑ 2 Malcolm Jenkins	.40	1.00
❑ 3 Eugene Monroe	.30	.75
❑ 4 D.J. Boldin	.30	.75
❑ 5A Michael Crabtree ball at chest	1.00	2.50
❑ 5B Michael Crabtree ball in air	1.00	2.50
❑ 6A Mark Sanchez facing left	1.50	4.00
❑ 6B Mark Sanchez facing right	1.50	4.00
❑ 7 Cornelius Ingram	.25	.60
❑ 8A Darrius Heyward-Bey no ball	.60	1.50
❑ 8B Darrius Heyward-Bey with ball	.60	1.50
❑ 9A Jeremy Maclin no helmet visor	.75	2.00
❑ 9B Jeremy Maclin helmet visor	.75	2.00
❑ 10 Brian Cushing	.50	1.25
❑ 11A Josh Freeman hips hidden	.75	2.00
❑ 11B Josh Freeman hips in view	.75	2.00
❑ 12 Curtis Painter	.40	1.00
❑ 13A Nate Davis pointing	.40	1.00
❑ 13B Nate Davis holding ball	.40	1.00
❑ 14 Hunter Cantwell	.40	1.00
❑ 15A Pat White head shot	.60	1.50
❑ 15B Pat White running ball	.60	1.50
❑ 16 Mike Teel	.40	1.00
❑ 17 Tom Brandstater	.40	1.00
❑ 18 Jarett Dillard	.40	1.00
❑ 19 Sammie Stroughter	.40	1.00
❑ 20 Aaron Kelly	.30	.75
❑ 21 Darius Passmore	.30	.75
❑ 22 Alphonso Smith	.30	.75
❑ 23A Javon Ringer one hand on ball	.40	1.00
❑ 23B Javon Ringer two hands on ball	.40	1.00
❑ 24 Jeremiah Johnson	.40	1.00
❑ 25A LeSean McCoy blu jsy	.75	2.00
❑ 25B LeSean McCoy white jsy	.75	2.00
❑ 26 Tim Jamison	.30	.75
❑ 27 David Bruton	.30	.75
❑ 28 Worrell Williams	.30	.75
❑ 29 Matt Shaughnessy	.25	.60
❑ 30 Nathan Brown	.30	.75
❑ 31 Mike Reilly	.30	.75
❑ 32 Darrell Mack	.30	.75
❑ 33 James Laurinaitis	.50	1.25
❑ 34A Donald Brown two hands on ball	.75	2.00
❑ 34B Donald Brown one hand on ball	.75	2.00
❑ 35 Marlon Lucky	.30	.75
❑ 36 Roy Miller	.40	1.00
❑ 37 Eric Wood	.30	.75
❑ 38 Freddie Brown	.30	.75
❑ 39 Taurus Johnson	.30	.75
❑ 40 Ryan Purvis	.30	.75
❑ 41 Darius Butler	.40	1.00
❑ 42 Ricky Jean-Francois	.40	1.00
❑ 43 Kaluka Maiava	.40	1.00
❑ 44 Brandon Underwood	.40	1.00
❑ 45 Chase Coffman	.30	.75
❑ 46 Jamon Meredith	.30	.75
❑ 47 Clay Matthews	.60	1.50
❑ 48 Brian Orakpo	.50	1.25
❑ 49 Jeremy Childs	.30	.75
❑ 50 Devin Moore	.30	.75
❑ 51 M.Ryan/J.Flacco SO	.50	1.25
❑ 52 M.Stafford/M.Sanchez SO	.75	2.00
❑ 53 K.Moreno/C.Wells SO	.60	1.50
❑ 54 M.Crabtree/J.Maclin SO	.50	1.25
❑ 55 M.Crabtree/G.Harrell TM	.60	1.50
❑ 56 M.Stafford/K.Moreno TM	.75	2.00
❑ 57 Sanchez/Maualuga TM	1.00	2.50
❑ 58 C.Wells/J.Laurinaitis TM	.30	.75
❑ 59 Matthew Stafford	.75	2.00
❑ 60 Jason Boltus	.30	.75
❑ 61 Chase Clement	.40	1.00
❑ 62 Aaron Brown	.40	1.00
❑ 63 Kevin Ogletree	.40	1.00
❑ 64 Scott McKillop	.30	.75
❑ 65 Clint Sintim	.40	1.00
❑ 66 Andre Brown	.30	.75
❑ 67 John Parker Wilson	.40	1.00
❑ 68 Brian Hoyer	.40	1.00
❑ 69 B.J. Raji	.50	1.25
❑ 70 Stephen McGee	.40	1.00
❑ 71 Louis Murphy	.40	1.00
❑ 72 Jason Smith	.30	.75
❑ 73 Cullen Harper	.40	1.00
❑ 74 Johnny Knox	.60	1.50
❑ 75 Alex Boone	.40	1.00
❑ 76 Tyrell Fenroy	.30	.75
❑ 77 Eben Britton	.30	.75
❑ 78 Chris Wells	1.00	2.50
❑ 79 Mike Mickens	.30	.75
❑ 80 Brian Robiskie	.40	1.00
❑ 81 Brooks Foster	.30	.75
❑ 82 Jamarko Simmons	.30	.75
❑ 83 Brian Mandeville	.30	.75
❑ 84 Jared Cook	.30	.75
❑ 85 Brandon Williams	.40	1.00
❑ 86 Rashad Jennings	.40	1.00
❑ 87 James Casey	.30	.75
❑ 88 Hakeem Nicks	.75	2.00
❑ 89 Juaquin Iglesias	.40	1.00
❑ 90 Mike Thomas	.40	1.00
❑ 91 Jared Bronson	.30	.75
❑ 92 C.J. Spillman	.30	.75
❑ 93 Marcus Freeman	.40	1.00
❑ 94 David Veikune	.30	.75
❑ 95 Gartrell Johnson	.30	.75
❑ 96 Graham Harrell	.40	1.00
❑ 97 Ryan Palmer	.40	1.00
❑ 98 Demetrius Byrd	.30	.75
❑ 99 Rey Maualuga	.60	1.50
❑ 100 Knowshon Moreno	1.00	2.50

Acknowledgments

Every year we make active solicitations for expert input. We are particularly appreciative of the help (however extensive or cursory) provided for this volume. We receive many inquiries, comments, and questions regarding material within this book. In fact, each and every one is read and digested. Time constraints, however, prevent us from personally replying. But keep sharing your knowledge. Even though we cannot respond to each letter, you are making significant contributions to the hobby through your interest and comments.

The effort to continually refine and improve our books also involves a growing number of people and types of expertise on our home team. Our company boasts a substantial Sports Data Publishing team, which strengthens our ability to provide comprehensive analysis of the marketplace.

Our football analysts played a major part in compiling this year's book, traveling thousands of miles during the past year to attend sportscard shows and visit card shops around the United States and Canada. The Beckett Football specialists are Brian Fleischer and Dan Hitt (Senior Manager of SDP).

Dave Lee's input as Beckett Football editor this past year helped immeasurably; Rich Klein as research analyst and primary proofer also added many hours of painstaking work.

The effort was ably assisted by the rest of the SDP Team: Matt Brumley, Keith Hower, Grant Sandground (Senior Price Guide Editor), and Tim Trout.

The price-gathering and analytical talents of this fine group of hobbyists have helped make our Beckett team stronger, while making this guide and its companion monthly Price Guide more widely recognized as the hobby's most reliable and relied-upon source of pricing information.

In addition, Bill Sutherland and Soma Madhdhipitla contributed many programming improvements to make this process smoother. Also, this book could not be produced without the fine work of our prepress team. Under the leadership of Pete Adauto, Gean Paul Figari was responsible for the layout and general presentation of this book.

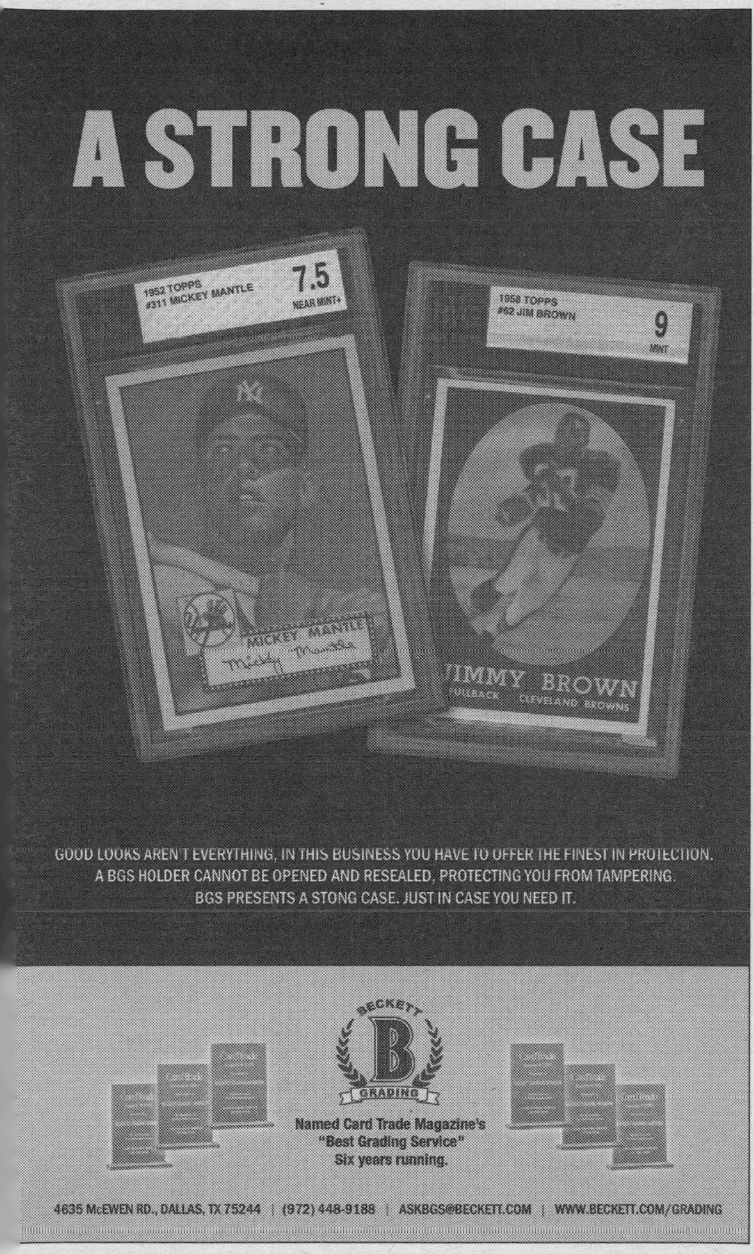